2022

Harris

Southern California

Business Directory and Buyers Guide

Exclusive Provider of
Dun & Bradstreet Library Solutions

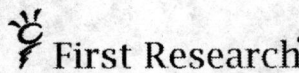

Published February 2022 next update February 2023

Publisher

Mergent Inc.
444 Madison Ave
New York, NY 10022

©Mergent Inc All Rights Reserved
2022 Mergent Business Press
ISSN 1080-2614
ISBN 978-1-64972-634-6

MERGENT
BUSINESS PRESS
by FTSE Russell

TABLE OF CONTENTS

SUMMARY OF CONTENTS

Number of Companies 23,545
Number of Decision Makers 69,619
Minimum Number of Employees .... 13 (Manufacturers)
Minimum Number of Employees .... 50 (Services)

EXPLANATORY NOTES

How to Cross-Reference in This Directory

Sequential Entry Numbers. Each establishment in the Geographic Section is numbered sequentially (G-0000). The number assigned to each establishment is referred to as its "entry number." To make cross-referencing easier, each listing in the Geographic, SIC, Alphabetic and Product Sections includes the establishment's entry number. To facilitate locating an entry in the Geographic Section, the entry numbers for the first listing on the left page and the last listing on the right page are printed at the top of the page next to the city name.

Source Suggestions Welcome

Although all known sources were used to compile this directory, it is possible that companies were inadvertently omitted. Your assistance in calling attention to such omissions would be greatly appreciated. A special form on the facing page will help you in the reporting process.

Analysis

Every effort has been made to contact all firms to verify their information. The one exception to this rule is the annual sales figure, which is considered by many companies to be confidential information. Therefore, estimated sales have been calculated by multiplying the nationwide average sales per employee for the firm's major SIC/NAICS code by the firm's number of employees. Nationwide averages for sales per employee by SIC/NAICS codes are provided by the U.S. Department of Commerce and are updated annually. All sales—sales (est)—have been estimated by this method. The exceptions are parent companies (PA), division headquarters (DH) and headquarter locations (HQ) which may include an actual corporate sales figure—sales (corporate-wide) if available.

Types of Companies

Descriptive and statistical data are included for companies in the entire state. These comprise manufacturers, machine shops, fabricators, assemblers and printers. Also identified are corporate offices in the state.

Employment Data

The employment figure shown in the Products & Services Section includes male and female employees and embraces all levels of the company. This directory includes manufacturing companies with 13 or more employees and service companies with 50 or more employees. This figure is for the facility listed and does not include other plants or offices. It should be recognized that these figures represent an approximate year-round average. These employment figures are broken into codes A through F and used in the Product and SIC Sections to further help you in qualifying a company. Be sure to check the footnotes on the bottom right hand pages for the code breakdowns.

Standard Industrial Classification (SIC)

The Standard Industrial Classification (SIC) system used in this directory was developed by the federal government for use in classifying establishments by the type of activity they are engaged in. The SIC classifications used in this directory are from the 1987 edition published by the U.S. Government's Office of Management and Budget. The SIC system separates all activities into broad industrial divisions (e.g., manufacturing, mining, retail trade). It further subdivides each division. The range of manufacturing industry classes extends from two-digit codes (major industry group) to four-digit codes (product).

For example:

Industry Breakdown	Code	Industry, Product, etc.
*Major industry group	20	Food and kindred products
Industry group	203	Canned and frozen foods
*Industry	2033	Fruits and vegetables, etc.

*Classifications used in this directory

Only two-digit and four-digit codes are used in this directory.

Arrangement

1. The **Products & Services Section** contains complete in-depth corporate data. This section lists companies under their primary SIC. SIC codes are in numerical order with companies listed alphabetically under each code. A numerical and alphabetical index precedes this section.

> IMPORTANT NOTICE: It is a violation of both federal and state law to transmit an unsolicited advertisement to a facsimile machine. Any user of this product that violates such laws may be subject to civil and criminal penalties, which may exceed $500 for each transmission of an unsolicited facsimile. Harris InfoSource provides fax numbers for lawful purposes only and expressly forbids the use of these numbers in any unlawful manner.

2. The **Alphabetic Section** lists all companies with their full physical or mailing addresses and telephone number.

3. The **Geographic Section** is sorted by cities listed in alphabetic order and companies listed alphabetically within each city.

USER'S GUIDE TO LISTINGS

PRODUCT & SERVICES SECTION

Standard Industrial Classification (SIC) description

Sequential entry number

Division

Physical address

Fax number

Decision-makers

Employment at this location

Foreign trade
▲ = Import ▼ = Export
◆ = Import/Export

Publicly or privately owned

Web address

Primary SIC code & secondary SIC codes

HQ = Headquarters
DH = Division headquarters
PA = Parent company

5199-Nondurable Goods, Wholesale, N.E.C.

(P-17231)
READY BOX CO (HQ) ✿
Storage Division
Also Called: RBC
853 Industrial Rd, Venice (90291-1482)
PO Box 1000 (90294-9050)
Phone 310 999-7777
Toll Free: 800 888-8800
Fax: 310 999-6666
George Carlsen, President
Leo Luxor, Purch Agent
◆ **EMP**: 1,400 **EST**: 1955
SQ FT: 190,000
Sales (est.) : 1MM-4.9MM
Sales (corporate-wide): 1.45B
Privately Owned
WEB: www.readymovers.com
SIC: **5199**, 4214 Wholesale wooden & corrugated boxes
HQ: Paperboard Box Co
   400 5th Ave
   New York, NY 10001
   212 555-3300

New business established in last 2 years

Designates this location as a headquarters

Mailing address

Business phone

Toll free number

Year established

Industry specific information square footage admissions (educational institutions)

Estimated annual sales K=Thousands; MM=Millions

Actual corporate wide sales M=Millions; B=Billions

Product description

ALPHABETIC SECTION

Address, city & ZIP

R & R Sealants (HQ) .... C 818 247-6319
   651 Tally Blvd, Burbank 91505 *(P-1710)*
Rake, J R Co .... D 310 542-3000
   21 45th, Malibu 90265 *(P-1715)*
Ready Box Co (HQ) .... A 310 999-4444
   704 Lawrence Rd 90291, Venice 90294 *(P-17231)*

Products & Services Section entry number where full company information appears

Designates this location as a headquarters

Business phone

Indicates approximate employment figure:
A = Over 500 employees
B = 251-500, C = 101-250,
D = 51-100, E = 20-50,
F = 10-19

GEOGRAPHIC SECTION

City, State & County

HQ = Headquarters
DH = Division headquarters
PA = Parent company

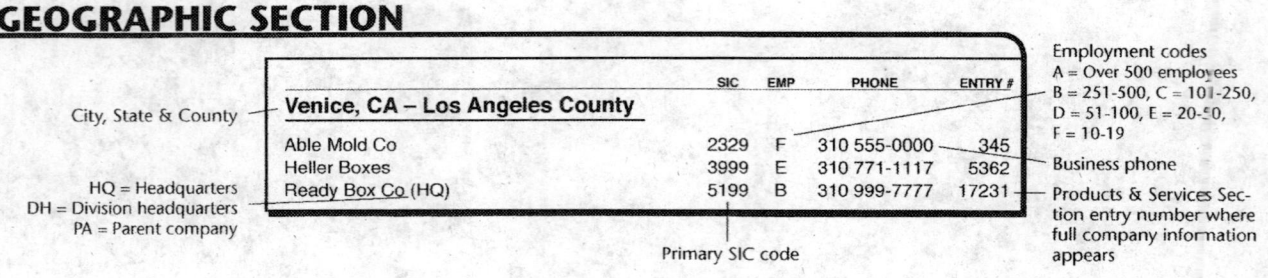

	SIC	EMP	PHONE	ENTRY #
Venice, CA – Los Angeles County				
Able Mold Co	2329	F	310 555-0000	345
Heller Boxes	3999	E	310 771-1117	5362
Ready Box Co (HQ)	5199	B	310 999-7777	17231

Employment codes
A = Over 500 employees
B = 251-500, C = 101-250,
D = 51-100, E = 20-50,
F = 10-19

Business phone

Products & Services Section entry number where full company information appears

Primary SIC code

NUMERICAL INDEX of SIC DESCRIPTIONS

ALPHABETICAL INDEX of SIC DESCRIPTIONS

PRODUCT & SERVICES SECTION
Companies listed alphabetically under their primary SIC
In-depth company data listed

ALPHABETIC SECTION
Company listings in alphabetical order

GEOGRAPHIC SECTION
Companies sorted by city in alphabetical order

SIC

PRDTS & SVCS

ALPHABETIC

GEOGRAPHIC

Southern California
County Map

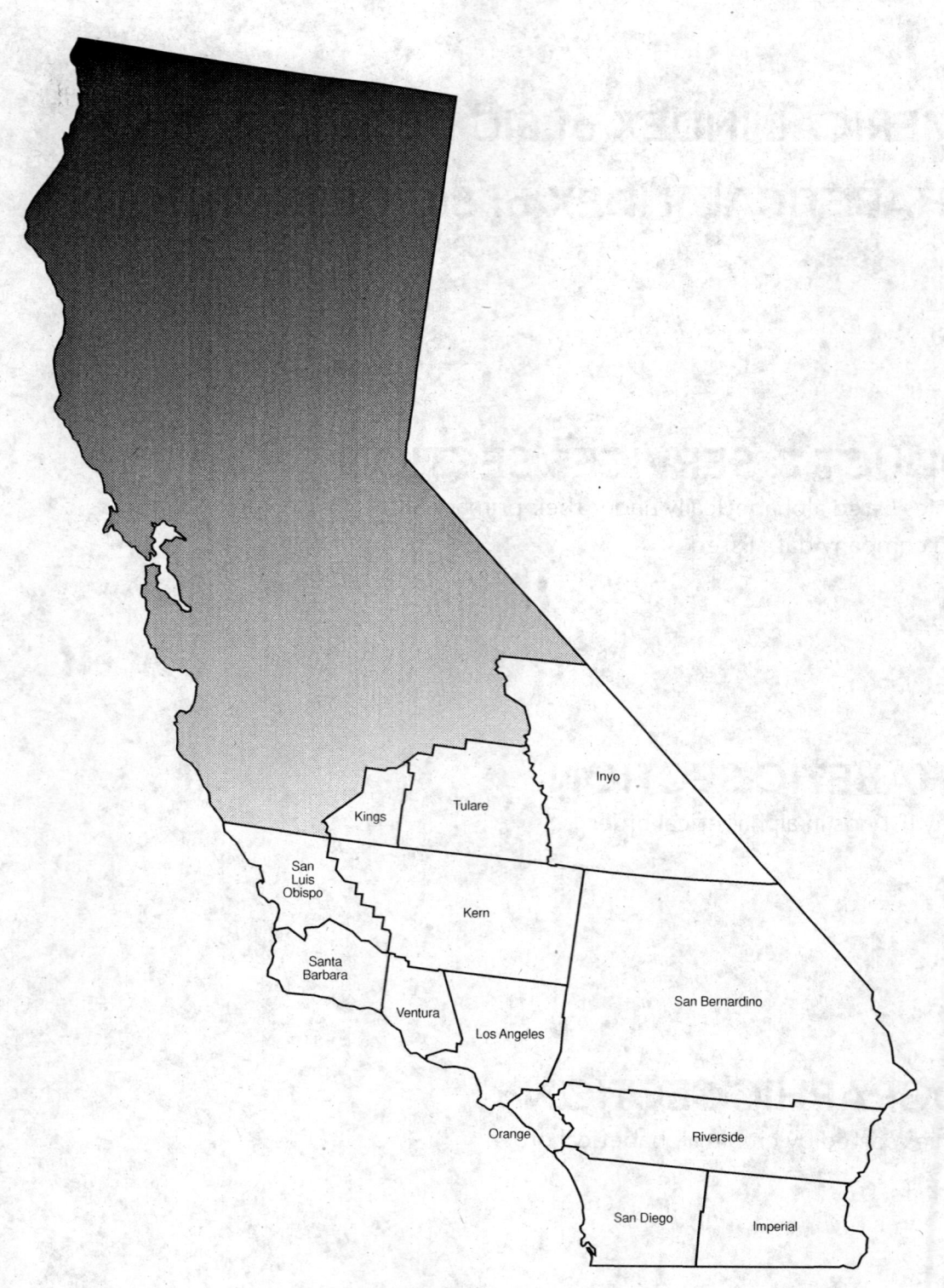

SIC INDEX

Standard Industrial Classification Numerical Index

SIC NO	PRODUCT

01 agricultural production-crops

0111 Wheat
0115 Corn
0119 Cash Grains, NEC
0131 Cotton
0133 Sugarcane & Sugar Beets
0134 Irish Potatoes
0139 Field Crops, Except Cash Grains, NEC
0161 Vegetables & Melons
0171 Berry Crops
0172 Grapes
0173 Tree Nuts
.0174 Citrus Fruits
0175 Deciduous Tree Fruits
0179 Fruits & Tree Nuts, NEC
0181 Ornamental Floriculture & Nursery Prdts
0182 Food Crops Grown Under Cover
0191 Crop Farming, Misc

02 agricultural production-livestock and animal specialties

0211 Beef Cattle Feedlots
0212 Beef Cattle, Except Feedlots
0214 Sheep & Goats
0241 Dairy Farms
0252 Chicken Egg Farms
0279 Animal Specialties, NEC
0291 Animal Production, NEC

07 agricultural services

0711 Soil Preparation Svcs
0721 Soil Preparation, Planting & Cultivating Svc
0722 Crop Harvesting By Machine
0723 Crop Preparation, Except Cotton Ginning
0724 Cotton Ginning
0742 Veterinary Animal Specialties
0751 Livestock Svcs, Except Veterinary
0752 Animal Specialty Svcs, Exc Veterinary
0761 Farm Labor Contractors & Crew Leaders
0762 Farm Management Svcs
0781 Landscape Counseling & Planning
0782 Lawn & Garden Svcs
0783 Ornamental Shrub & Tree Svc

08 forestry

0811 Timber Tracts
0851 Forestry Svcs

09 fishing, hunting, and trapping

0921 Finfish Farming & Fish Hatcheries
0971 Hunting & Trapping

10 metal mining

1041 Gold Ores
1081 Metal Mining Svcs
1099 Metal Ores, NEC

12 coal mining

1221 Bituminous Coal & Lignite: Surface Mining
1231 Anthracite Mining
1241 Coal Mining Svcs

13 oil and gas extraction

1311 Crude Petroleum & Natural Gas
1321 Natural Gas Liquids
1381 Drilling Oil & Gas Wells
1382 Oil & Gas Field Exploration Svcs
1389 Oil & Gas Field Svcs, NEC

14 mining and quarrying of nonmetallic minerals, except fuels

1411 Dimension Stone
1422 Crushed & Broken Limestone
1423 Crushed & Broken Granite
1429 Crushed & Broken Stone, NEC
1442 Construction Sand & Gravel
1446 Industrial Sand
1459 Clay, Ceramic & Refractory Minerals, NEC
1479 Chemical & Fertilizer Mining
1481 Nonmetallic Minerals Svcs, Except Fuels
1499 Miscellaneous Nonmetallic Mining

15 building construction-general contractors and operative builders

1521 General Contractors, Single Family Houses
1522 General Contractors, Residential Other Than Single Family
1531 Operative Builders
1541 General Contractors, Indl Bldgs & Warehouses
1542 General Contractors, Nonresidential & Non-indl Bldgs

16 heavy construction other than building construction-contractors

1611 Highway & Street Construction
1622 Bridge, Tunnel & Elevated Hwy Construction
1623 Water, Sewer & Utility Line Construction
1629 Heavy Construction, NEC

17 construction-special trade contractors

1711 Plumbing, Heating & Air Conditioning Contractors
1721 Painting & Paper Hanging Contractors
1731 Electrical Work
1741 Masonry & Other Stonework
1742 Plastering, Drywall, Acoustical & Insulation Work
1743 Terrazzo, Tile, Marble & Mosaic Work
1751 Carpentry Work
1752 Floor Laying & Other Floor Work, NEC
1761 Roofing, Siding & Sheet Metal Work
1771 Concrete Work
1781 Water Well Drilling
1791 Structural Steel Erection
1793 Glass & Glazing Work
1794 Excavating & Grading Work
1795 Wrecking & Demolition Work
1796 Installation Or Erection Of Bldg Eqpt & Machinery, NEC
1799 Special Trade Contractors, NEC

20 food and kindred products

2011 Meat Packing Plants
2013 Sausages & Meat Prdts
2015 Poultry Slaughtering, Dressing & Processing
2021 Butter
2022 Cheese
2023 Milk, Condensed & Evaporated
2024 Ice Cream
2026 Milk
2032 Canned Specialties
2033 Canned Fruits, Vegetables & Preserves
2034 Dried Fruits, Vegetables & Soup
2035 Pickled Fruits, Vegetables, Sauces & Dressings
2037 Frozen Fruits, Juices & Vegetables
2038 Frozen Specialties
2041 Flour, Grain Milling
2043 Cereal Breakfast Foods
2044 Rice Milling
2045 Flour, Blended & Prepared
2046 Wet Corn Milling
2047 Dog & Cat Food
2048 Prepared Feeds For Animals & Fowls
2051 Bread, Bakery Prdts Exc Cookies & Crackers
2052 Cookies & Crackers
2053 Frozen Bakery Prdts
2062 Sugar, Cane Refining
2063 Sugar, Beet
2064 Candy & Confectionery Prdts
2066 Chocolate & Cocoa Prdts
2067 Chewing Gum
2068 Salted & Roasted Nuts & Seeds
2075 Soybean Oil Mills
2076 Vegetable Oil Mills
2077 Animal, Marine Fats & Oils
2079 Shortening, Oils & Margarine
2082 Malt Beverages
2084 Wine & Brandy
2085 Liquors, Distilled, Rectified & Blended
2086 Soft Drinks
2087 Flavoring Extracts & Syrups
2091 Fish & Seafoods, Canned & Cured
2092 Fish & Seafoods, Fresh & Frozen
2095 Coffee
2096 Potato Chips & Similar Prdts
2097 Ice
2098 Macaroni, Spaghetti & Noodles
2099 Food Preparations, NEC

21 tobacco products

2111 Cigarettes
2121 Cigars
2131 Tobacco, Chewing & Snuff

22 textile mill products

2211 Cotton, Woven Fabric
2221 Silk & Man-Made Fiber
2231 Wool, Woven Fabric
2241 Fabric Mills, Cotton, Wool, Silk & Man-Made
2252 Hosiery, Except Women's
2253 Knit Outerwear Mills
2254 Knit Underwear Mills
2257 Circular Knit Fabric Mills
2258 Lace & Warp Knit Fabric Mills
2259 Knitting Mills, NEC
2261 Cotton Fabric Finishers
2262 Silk & Man-Made Fabric Finishers
2269 Textile Finishers, NEC
2273 Carpets & Rugs
2281 Yarn Spinning Mills
2282 Yarn Texturizing, Throwing, Twisting & Winding Mills
2284 Thread Mills
2295 Fabrics Coated Not Rubberized
2297 Fabrics, Nonwoven
2298 Cordage & Twine
2299 Textile Goods, NEC

23 apparel and other finished products made from fabrics and similar material

2311 Men's & Boys' Suits, Coats & Overcoats
2321 Men's & Boys' Shirts
2322 Men's & Boys' Underwear & Nightwear
2323 Men's & Boys' Neckwear
2325 Men's & Boys' Separate Trousers & Casual Slacks
2326 Men's & Boys' Work Clothing
2329 Men's & Boys' Clothing, NEC
2331 Women's & Misses' Blouses
2335 Women's & Misses' Dresses
2337 Women's & Misses' Suits, Coats & Skirts
2339 Women's & Misses' Outerwear, NEC
2341 Women's, Misses' & Children's Underwear & Nightwear
2342 Brassieres, Girdles & Garments
2353 Hats, Caps & Millinery
2361 Children's & Infants' Dresses & Blouses
2369 Girls' & Infants' Outerwear, NEC
2371 Fur Goods
2381 Dress & Work Gloves
2385 Waterproof Outerwear
2386 Leather & Sheep Lined Clothing
2387 Apparel Belts
2389 Apparel & Accessories, NEC
2391 Curtains & Draperies
2392 House furnishings: Textile
2393 Textile Bags
2394 Canvas Prdts
2395 Pleating & Stitching For The Trade
2396 Automotive Trimmings, Apparel Findings, Related Prdts
2397 Schiffli Machine Embroideries
2399 Fabricated Textile Prdts, NEC

24 lumber and wood products, except furniture

2411 Logging
2421 Saw & Planing Mills
2426 Hardwood Dimension & Flooring Mills
2431 Millwork
2434 Wood Kitchen Cabinets
2435 Hardwood Veneer & Plywood
2439 Structural Wood Members, NEC
2441 Wood Boxes
2448 Wood Pallets & Skids
2449 Wood Containers, NEC
2451 Mobile Homes
2452 Prefabricated Wood Buildings & Cmpnts
2491 Wood Preserving
2493 Reconstituted Wood Prdts
2499 Wood Prdts, NEC

25 furniture and fixtures

2511 Wood Household Furniture
2512 Wood Household Furniture, Upholstered
2514 Metal Household Furniture
2515 Mattresses & Bedsprings

SIC NO	PRODUCT
2517	Wood T V, Radio, Phono & Sewing Cabinets
2519	Household Furniture, NEC
2521	Wood Office Furniture
2522	Office Furniture, Except Wood
2531	Public Building & Related Furniture
2541	Wood, Office & Store Fixtures
2542	Partitions & Fixtures, Except Wood
2591	Drapery Hardware, Window Blinds & Shades
2599	Furniture & Fixtures, NEC

26 paper and allied products

SIC NO	PRODUCT
2611	Pulp Mills
2621	Paper Mills
2631	Paperboard Mills
2652	Set-Up Paperboard Boxes
2653	Corrugated & Solid Fiber Boxes
2655	Fiber Cans, Tubes & Drums
2656	Sanitary Food Containers
2657	Folding Paperboard Boxes
2671	Paper Coating & Laminating for Packaging
2672	Paper Coating & Laminating, Exc for Packaging
2673	Bags: Plastics, Laminated & Coated
2674	Bags: Uncoated Paper & Multiwall
2675	Die-Cut Paper & Board
2676	Sanitary Paper Prdts
2677	Envelopes
2678	Stationery Prdts
2679	Converted Paper Prdts, NEC

27 printing, publishing, and allied industries

SIC NO	PRODUCT
2711	Newspapers: Publishing & Printing
2721	Periodicals: Publishing & Printing
2731	Books: Publishing & Printing
2732	Book Printing, Not Publishing
2741	Misc Publishing
2752	Commercial Printing: Lithographic
2754	Commercial Printing: Gravure
2759	Commercial Printing
2761	Manifold Business Forms
2771	Greeting Card Publishing
2782	Blankbooks & Looseleaf Binders
2789	Bookbinding
2791	Typesetting
2796	Platemaking & Related Svcs

28 chemicals and allied products

SIC NO	PRODUCT
2812	Alkalies & Chlorine
2813	Industrial Gases
2816	Inorganic Pigments
2819	Indl Inorganic Chemicals, NEC
2821	Plastics, Mtrls & Nonvulcanizable Elastomers
2822	Synthetic Rubber (Vulcanizable Elastomers)
2823	Cellulosic Man-Made Fibers
2824	Synthetic Organic Fibers, Exc Cellulosic
2833	Medicinal Chemicals & Botanical Prdts
2834	Pharmaceuticals
2835	Diagnostic Substances
2836	Biological Prdts, Exc Diagnostic Substances
2841	Soap & Detergents
2842	Spec Cleaning, Polishing & Sanitation Preparations
2843	Surface Active & Finishing Agents, Sulfonated Oils
2844	Perfumes, Cosmetics & Toilet Preparations
2851	Paints, Varnishes, Lacquers, Enamels
2865	Cyclic-Crudes, Intermediates, Dyes & Org Pigments
2869	Industrial Organic Chemicals, NEC
2873	Nitrogenous Fertilizers
2875	Fertilizers, Mixing Only
2879	Pesticides & Agricultural Chemicals, NEC
2891	Adhesives & Sealants
2892	Explosives
2893	Printing Ink
2899	Chemical Preparations, NEC

29 petroleum refining and related industries

SIC NO	PRODUCT
2911	Petroleum Refining
2951	Paving Mixtures & Blocks
2952	Asphalt Felts & Coatings
2992	Lubricating Oils & Greases
2999	Products Of Petroleum & Coal, NEC

30 rubber and miscellaneous plastics products

SIC NO	PRODUCT
3011	Tires & Inner Tubes
3021	Rubber & Plastic Footwear
3052	Rubber & Plastic Hose & Belting
3053	Gaskets, Packing & Sealing Devices
3061	Molded, Extruded & Lathe-Cut Rubber Mechanical Goods
3069	Fabricated Rubber Prdts, NEC
3081	Plastic Unsupported Sheet & Film
3082	Plastic Unsupported Profile Shapes
3083	Plastic Laminated Plate & Sheet

SIC NO	PRODUCT
3084	Plastic Pipe
3085	Plastic Bottles
3086	Plastic Foam Prdts
3087	Custom Compounding Of Purchased Plastic Resins
3088	Plastic Plumbing Fixtures
3089	Plastic Prdts

31 leather and leather products

SIC NO	PRODUCT
3111	Leather Tanning & Finishing
3131	Boot & Shoe Cut Stock & Findings
3143	Men's Footwear, Exc Athletic
3144	Women's Footwear, Exc Athletic
3149	Footwear, NEC
3161	Luggage
3171	Handbags & Purses
3172	Personal Leather Goods
3199	Leather Goods, NEC

32 stone, clay, glass, and concrete products

SIC NO	PRODUCT
3211	Flat Glass
3221	Glass Containers
3229	Pressed & Blown Glassware, NEC
3231	Glass Prdts Made Of Purchased Glass
3241	Cement, Hydraulic
3251	Brick & Structural Clay Tile
3253	Ceramic Tile
3255	Clay Refractories
3259	Structural Clay Prdts, NEC
3261	China Plumbing Fixtures & Fittings
3262	China, Table & Kitchen Articles
3263	Earthenware, Whiteware, Table & Kitchen Articles
3264	Porcelain Electrical Splys
3269	Pottery Prdts, NEC
3271	Concrete Block & Brick
3272	Concrete Prdts
3273	Ready-Mixed Concrete
3275	Gypsum Prdts
3281	Cut Stone Prdts
3291	Abrasive Prdts
3292	Asbestos products
3295	Minerals & Earths: Ground Or Treated
3296	Mineral Wool
3297	Nonclay Refractories
3299	Nonmetallic Mineral Prdts, NEC

33 primary metal industries

SIC NO	PRODUCT
3312	Blast Furnaces, Coke Ovens, Steel & Rolling Mills
3313	Electrometallurgical Prdts
3315	Steel Wire Drawing & Nails & Spikes
3316	Cold Rolled Steel Sheet, Strip & Bars
3317	Steel Pipe & Tubes
3321	Gray Iron Foundries
3322	Malleable Iron Foundries
3324	Steel Investment Foundries
3325	Steel Foundries, NEC
3334	Primary Production Of Aluminum
3339	Primary Nonferrous Metals, NEC
3341	Secondary Smelting & Refining Of Nonferrous Metals
3351	Rolling, Drawing & Extruding Of Copper
3353	Aluminum Sheet, Plate & Foil
3354	Aluminum Extruded Prdts
3355	Aluminum Rolling & Drawing, NEC
3356	Rolling, Drawing-Extruding Of Nonferrous Metals
3357	Nonferrous Wire Drawing
3363	Aluminum Die Castings
3364	Nonferrous Die Castings, Exc Aluminum
3365	Aluminum Foundries
3366	Copper Foundries
3369	Nonferrous Foundries: Castings, NEC
3398	Metal Heat Treating
3399	Primary Metal Prdts, NEC

34 fabricated metal products, except machinery and transportation equipment

SIC NO	PRODUCT
3411	Metal Cans
3412	Metal Barrels, Drums, Kegs & Pails
3421	Cutlery
3423	Hand & Edge Tools
3425	Hand Saws & Saw Blades
3429	Hardware, NEC
3431	Enameled Iron & Metal Sanitary Ware
3432	Plumbing Fixture Fittings & Trim, Brass
3433	Heating Eqpt
3441	Fabricated Structural Steel
3442	Metal Doors, Sash, Frames, Molding & Trim
3443	Fabricated Plate Work
3444	Sheet Metal Work
3446	Architectural & Ornamental Metal Work
3448	Prefabricated Metal Buildings & Cmpnts
3449	Misc Structural Metal Work

SIC NO	PRODUCT
3451	Screw Machine Prdts
3452	Bolts, Nuts, Screws, Rivets & Washers
3462	Iron & Steel Forgings
3463	Nonferrous Forgings
3465	Automotive Stampings
3466	Crowns & Closures
3469	Metal Stampings, NEC
3471	Electroplating, Plating, Polishing, Anodizing & Coloring
3479	Coating & Engraving, NEC
3482	Small Arms Ammunition
3483	Ammunition, Large
3484	Small Arms
3489	Ordnance & Access, NEC
3491	Industrial Valves
3492	Fluid Power Valves & Hose Fittings
3493	Steel Springs, Except Wire
3494	Valves & Pipe Fittings, NEC
3495	Wire Springs
3496	Misc Fabricated Wire Prdts
3497	Metal Foil & Leaf
3498	Fabricated Pipe & Pipe Fittings
3499	Fabricated Metal Prdts, NEC

35 industrial and commercial machinery and computer equipment

SIC NO	PRODUCT
3511	Steam, Gas & Hydraulic Turbines & Engines
3519	Internal Combustion Engines, NEC
3523	Farm Machinery & Eqpt
3524	Garden, Lawn Tractors & Eqpt
3531	Construction Machinery & Eqpt
3532	Mining Machinery & Eqpt
3533	Oil Field Machinery & Eqpt
3534	Elevators & Moving Stairways
3535	Conveyors & Eqpt
3536	Hoists, Cranes & Monorails
3537	Indl Trucks, Tractors, Trailers & Stackers
3541	Machine Tools: Cutting
3542	Machine Tools: Forming
3543	Industrial Patterns
3544	Dies, Tools, Jigs, Fixtures & Indl Molds
3545	Machine Tool Access
3546	Power Hand Tools
3547	Rolling Mill Machinery & Eqpt
3548	Welding Apparatus
3549	Metalworking Machinery, NEC
3552	Textile Machinery
3553	Woodworking Machinery
3554	Paper Inds Machinery
3555	Printing Trades Machinery & Eqpt
3556	Food Prdts Machinery
3559	Special Ind Machinery, NEC
3561	Pumps & Pumping Eqpt
3562	Ball & Roller Bearings
3563	Air & Gas Compressors
3564	Blowers & Fans
3565	Packaging Machinery
3566	Speed Changers, Drives & Gears
3567	Indl Process Furnaces & Ovens
3568	Mechanical Power Transmission Eqpt, NEC
3569	Indl Machinery & Eqpt, NEC
3571	Electronic Computers
3572	Computer Storage Devices
3575	Computer Terminals
3577	Computer Peripheral Eqpt, NEC
3578	Calculating & Accounting Eqpt
3579	Office Machines, NEC
3581	Automatic Vending Machines
3582	Commercial Laundry, Dry Clean & Pressing Mchs
3585	Air Conditioning & Heating Eqpt
3589	Service Ind Machines, NEC
3592	Carburetors, Pistons, Rings & Valves
3593	Fluid Power Cylinders & Actuators
3594	Fluid Power Pumps & Motors
3596	Scales & Balances, Exc Laboratory
3599	Machinery & Eqpt, Indl & Commercial NEC

36 electronic and other electrical equipment and components, except computer

SIC NO	PRODUCT
3612	Power, Distribution & Specialty Transformers
3613	Switchgear & Switchboard Apparatus
3621	Motors & Generators
3624	Carbon & Graphite Prdts
3625	Relays & Indl Controls
3629	Electrical Indl Apparatus, NEC
3631	Household Cooking Eqpt
3632	Household Refrigerators & Freezers
3634	Electric Household Appliances
3639	Household Appliances, NEC
3641	Electric Lamps
3643	Current-Carrying Wiring Devices

SIC NO	PRODUCT

3644 Noncurrent-Carrying Wiring Devices
3645 Residential Lighting Fixtures
3646 Commercial, Indl & Institutional Lighting Fixtures
3647 Vehicular Lighting Eqpt
3648 Lighting Eqpt, NEC
3651 Household Audio & Video Eqpt
3652 Phonograph Records & Magnetic Tape
3661 Telephone & Telegraph Apparatus
3663 Radio & T V Communications, Systs & Eqpt, Broad-cast/Studio
3669 Communications Eqpt, NEC
3671 Radio & T V Receiving Electron Tubes
3672 Printed Circuit Boards
3674 Semiconductors
3675 Electronic Capacitors
3676 Electronic Resistors
3677 Electronic Coils & Transformers
3678 Electronic Connectors
3679 Electronic Components, NEC
3691 Storage Batteries
3692 Primary Batteries: Dry & Wet
3694 Electrical Eqpt For Internal Combustion Engines
3695 Recording Media
3699 Electrical Machinery, Eqpt & Splys, NEC

37 transportation equipment

3711 Motor Vehicles & Car Bodies
3713 Truck & Bus Bodies
3714 Motor Vehicle Parts & Access
3715 Truck Trailers
3716 Motor Homes
3721 Aircraft
3724 Aircraft Engines & Engine Parts
3728 Aircraft Parts & Eqpt, NEC
3731 Shipbuilding & Repairing
3732 Boat Building & Repairing
3743 Railroad Eqpt
3751 Motorcycles, Bicycles & Parts
3761 Guided Missiles & Space Vehicles
3764 Guided Missile/Space Vehicle Propulsion Units & parts
3769 Guided Missile/Space Vehicle Parts & Eqpt, NEC
3792 Travel Trailers & Campers
3795 Tanks & Tank Components
3799 Transportation Eqpt, NEC

38 measuring, analyzing and controlling instruments; photographic, medical an

3812 Search, Detection, Navigation & Guidance Systs & Instrs
3821 Laboratory Apparatus & Furniture
3822 Automatic Temperature Controls
3823 Indl Instruments For Meas, Display & Control
3824 Fluid Meters & Counters
3825 Instrs For Measuring & Testing Electricity
3826 Analytical Instruments
3827 Optical Instruments
3829 Measuring & Controlling Devices, NEC
3841 Surgical & Medical Instrs & Apparatus
3842 Orthopedic, Prosthetic & Surgical Appliances/Splys
3843 Dental Eqpt & Splys
3844 X-ray Apparatus & Tubes
3845 Electromedical & Electrotherapeutic Apparatus
3851 Ophthalmic Goods
3861 Photographic Eqpt & Splys
3873 Watch & Clock Devices & Parts

39 miscellaneous manufacturing industries

3911 Jewelry: Precious Metal
3914 Silverware, Plated & Stainless Steel Ware
3915 Jewelers Findings & Lapidary Work
3931 Musical Instruments
3942 Dolls & Stuffed Toys
3944 Games, Toys & Children's Vehicles
3949 Sporting & Athletic Goods, NEC
3951 Pens & Mechanical Pencils
3952 Lead Pencils, Crayons & Artist's Mtrls
3953 Marking Devices
3955 Carbon Paper & Inked Ribbons
3961 Costume Jewelry & Novelties
3965 Fasteners, Buttons, Needles & Pins
3991 Brooms & Brushes
3993 Signs & Advertising Displays
3996 Linoleum & Hard Surface Floor Coverings, NEC
3999 Manufacturing Industries, NEC

40 railroad transportation

4011 Railroads, Line-Hauling Operations
4013 Switching & Terminal Svcs

41 local and suburban transit and interurban highway passenger transportation

4111 Local & Suburban Transit
4119 Local Passenger Transportation: NEC
4121 Taxi Cabs
4131 Intercity & Rural Bus Transportation
4141 Local Bus Charter Svc
4142 Bus Charter Service, Except Local
4151 School Buses
4173 Bus Terminal & Svc Facilities

42 motor freight transportation and warehousing

4212 Local Trucking Without Storage
4213 Trucking, Except Local
4214 Local Trucking With Storage
4215 Courier Svcs, Except Air
4221 Farm Product Warehousing & Storage
4222 Refrigerated Warehousing & Storage
4225 General Warehousing & Storage
4226 Special Warehousing & Storage, NEC
4231 Terminal & Joint Terminal Maint Facilities

44 water transportation

4412 Deep Sea Foreign Transportation Of Freight
4424 Deep Sea Domestic Transportation Of Freight
4449 Water Transportation Of Freight, NEC
4481 Deep Sea Transportation Of Passengers
4489 Water Transport Of Passengers, NEC
4491 Marine Cargo Handling
4492 Towing & Tugboat Svcs
4493 Marinas
4499 Water Transportation Svcs, NEC

45 transportation by air

4512 Air Transportation, Scheduled
4513 Air Courier Svcs
4522 Air Transportation, Nonscheduled
4581 Airports, Flying Fields & Terminal Svcs

46 pipelines, except natural gas

4612 Crude Petroleum Pipelines
4613 Refined Petroleum Pipelines

47 transportation services

4724 Travel Agencies
4725 Tour Operators
4729 Passenger Transportation Arrangement, NEC
4731 Freight Forwarding & Arrangement
4741 Railroad Car Rental
4783 Packing & Crating Svcs
4785 Fixed Facilities, Inspection, Weighing Svcs Transptn
4789 Transportation Svcs, NEC

48 communications

4812 Radiotelephone Communications
4813 Telephone Communications, Except Radio
4822 Telegraph & Other Message Communications
4832 Radio Broadcasting Stations
4833 Television Broadcasting Stations
4841 Cable & Other Pay TV Svcs
4899 Communication Svcs, NEC

49 electric, gas, and sanitary services

4911 Electric Svcs
4922 Natural Gas Transmission
4924 Natural Gas Distribution
4931 Electric & Other Svcs Combined
4932 Gas & Other Svcs Combined
4939 Combination Utilities, NEC
4941 Water Sply
4952 Sewerage Systems
4953 Refuse Systems
4959 Sanitary Svcs, NEC
4961 Steam & Air Conditioning Sply
4971 Irrigation Systems

50 wholesale trade¨durable goods

5012 Automobiles & Other Motor Vehicles Wholesale
5013 Motor Vehicle Splys & New Parts Wholesale
5014 Tires & Tubes Wholesale
5015 Motor Vehicle Parts, Used Wholesale
5021 Furniture Wholesale
5023 Home Furnishings Wholesale
5031 Lumber, Plywood & Millwork Wholesale
5032 Brick, Stone & Related Construction Mtrls Wholesale
5033 Roofing, Siding & Insulation Mtrls Wholesale
5039 Construction Materials, NEC Wholesale
5043 Photographic Eqpt & Splys Wholesale
5044 Office Eqpt Wholesale
5045 Computers & Peripheral Eqpt & Software Wholesale
5046 Commercial Eqpt, NEC Wholesale

5047 Medical, Dental & Hospital Eqpt & Splys Wholesale
5048 Ophthalmic Goods Wholesale
5049 Professional Eqpt & Splys, NEC Wholesale
5051 Metals Service Centers
5063 Electrl Apparatus, Eqpt, Wiring Splys Wholesale
5064 Electrical Appliances, TV & Radios Wholesale
5065 Electronic Parts & Eqpt Wholesale
5072 Hardware Wholesale
5074 Plumbing & Heating Splys Wholesale
5075 Heating & Air Conditioning Eqpt & Splys Wholesale
5078 Refrigeration Eqpt & Splys Wholesale
5082 Construction & Mining Mach & Eqpt Wholesale
5083 Farm & Garden Mach & Eqpt Wholesale
5084 Industrial Mach & Eqpt Wholesale
5085 Industrial Splys Wholesale
5087 Service Establishment Eqpt & Splys Wholesale
5088 Transportation Eqpt & Splys, Except Motor Vehicles Wholesale
5091 Sporting & Recreational Goods & Splys Wholesale
5092 Toys & Hobby Goods & Splys Wholesale
5093 Scrap & Waste Materials Wholesale
5094 Jewelry, Watches, Precious Stones Wholesale
5099 Durable Goods: NEC Wholesale

51 wholesale trade¨nondurable goods

5111 Printing & Writing Paper Wholesale
5112 Stationery & Office Splys Wholesale
5113 Indl & Personal Svc Paper Wholesale
5122 Drugs, Drug Proprietaries & Sundries Wholesale
5131 Piece Goods, Notions & Dry Goods Wholesale
5136 Men's & Boys' Clothing & Furnishings Wholesale
5137 Women's, Children's & Infants Clothing Wholesale
5139 Footwear Wholesale
5141 Groceries, General Line Wholesale
5142 Packaged Frozen Foods Wholesale
5143 Dairy Prdts, Except Dried Or Canned Wholesale
5144 Poultry & Poultry Prdts Wholesale
5145 Confectionery Wholesale
5146 Fish & Seafood Wholesale
5147 Meats & Meat Prdts Wholesale
5148 Fresh Fruits & Vegetables Wholesale
5149 Groceries & Related Prdts, NEC Wholesale
5153 Grain & Field Beans Wholesale
5154 Livestock Wholesale
5159 Farm-Prdt Raw Mtrls, NEC Wholesale
5162 Plastics Materials & Basic Shapes Wholesale
5169 Chemicals & Allied Prdts, NEC Wholesale
5171 Petroleum Bulk Stations & Terminals
5172 Petroleum & Petroleum Prdts Wholesale
5181 Beer & Ale Wholesale
5182 Wine & Distilled Alcoholic Beverages Wholesale
5191 Farm Splys Wholesale
5192 Books, Periodicals & Newspapers Wholesale
5193 Flowers, Nursery Stock & Florists' Splys Wholesale
5194 Tobacco & Tobacco Prdts Wholesale
5198 Paints, Varnishes & Splys Wholesale
5199 Nondurable Goods, NEC Wholesale

60 depository institutions

6011 Federal Reserve Banks
6021 National Commercial Banks
6022 State Commercial Banks
6029 Commercial Banks, NEC
6035 Federal Savings Institutions
6036 Savings Institutions, Except Federal
6061 Federal Credit Unions
6062 State Credit Unions
6081 Foreign Banks, Branches & Agencies
6091 Nondeposit Trust Facilities
6099 Functions Related To Deposit Banking, NEC

61 nondepository credit institutions

6111 Federal Credit Agencies
6141 Personal Credit Institutions
6153 Credit Institutions, Short-Term Business
6159 Credit Institutions, Misc Business
6162 Mortgage Bankers & Loan Correspondents
6163 Loan Brokers

62 security and commodity brokers, dealers, exchanges, and services

6211 Security Brokers & Dealers
6221 Commodity Contracts Brokers & Dealers
6282 Investment Advice
6289 Security & Commodity Svcs, NEC

63 insurance carriers

6311 Life Insurance Carriers
6321 Accident & Health Insurance
6324 Hospital & Medical Svc Plans Carriers
6331 Fire, Marine & Casualty Insurance

SIC

SIC NO	PRODUCT
6351	Surety Insurance Carriers
6361	Title Insurance
6371	Pension, Health & Welfare Funds
6399	Insurance Carriers, NEC

64 insurance agents, brokers, and service

6411	Insurance Agents, Brokers & Svc

65 real estate

6512	Operators Of Nonresidential Bldgs
6513	Operators Of Apartment Buildings
6514	Operators Of Dwellings, Except Apartments
6515	Operators of Residential Mobile Home Sites
6519	Lessors Of Real Estate, NEC
6531	Real Estate Agents & Managers
6541	Title Abstract Offices
6552	Land Subdividers & Developers
6553	Cemetery Subdividers & Developers

67 holding and other investment offices

6712	Offices Of Bank Holding Co's
6719	Offices Of Holding Co's, NEC
6722	Management Investment Offices
6726	Unit Investment Trusts, Face-Amount Certificate Offices
6732	Education, Religious & Charitable Trusts
6733	Trusts Except Educational, Religious & Charitable
6794	Patent Owners & Lessors
6798	Real Estate Investment Trusts
6799	Investors, NEC

70 hotels, rooming houses, camps, and other lodging places

7011	Hotels, Motels & Tourist Courts
7021	Rooming & Boarding Houses
7032	Sporting & Recreational Camps
7033	Trailer Parks & Camp Sites
7041	Membership-Basis Hotels

72 personal services

7211	Power Laundries, Family & Commercial
7213	Linen Sply
7215	Coin Operated Laundries & Cleaning
7216	Dry Cleaning Plants, Except Rug Cleaning
7217	Carpet & Upholstery Cleaning
7218	Industrial Launderers
7219	Laundry & Garment Svcs, NEC
7221	Photographic Studios, Portrait
7231	Beauty Shops
7241	Barber Shops
7261	Funeral Svcs & Crematories
7291	Tax Return Preparation Svcs
7299	Miscellaneous Personal Svcs, NEC

73 business services

7311	Advertising Agencies
7312	Outdoor Advertising Svcs
7313	Radio, TV & Publishers Adv Reps
7319	Advertising, NEC
7322	Adjustment & Collection Svcs
7323	Credit Reporting Svcs
7331	Direct Mail Advertising Svcs
7334	Photocopying & Duplicating Svcs
7335	Commercial Photography
7336	Commercial Art & Graphic Design
7338	Secretarial & Court Reporting Svcs
7342	Disinfecting & Pest Control Svcs

SIC NO	PRODUCT
7349	Building Cleaning & Maintenance Svcs, NEC
7352	Medical Eqpt Rental & Leasing
7353	Heavy Construction Eqpt Rental & Leasing
7359	Equipment Rental & Leasing, NEC
7361	Employment Agencies
7363	Help Supply Svcs
7371	Custom Computer Programming Svcs
7372	Prepackaged Software
7373	Computer Integrated Systems Design
7374	Data & Computer Processing & Preparation
7375	Information Retrieval Svcs
7376	Computer Facilities Management Svcs
7377	Computer Rental & Leasing
7378	Computer Maintenance & Repair
7379	Computer Related Svcs, NEC
7381	Detective & Armored Car Svcs
7382	Security Systems Svcs
7383	News Syndicates
7384	Photofinishing Labs
7389	Business Svcs, NEC

75 automotive repair, services, and parking

7513	Truck Rental & Leasing, Without Drivers
7514	Passenger Car Rental
7515	Passenger Car Leasing
7519	Utility Trailers & Recreational Vehicle Rental
7521	Automobile Parking Lots & Garages
7532	Top, Body & Upholstery Repair & Paint Shops
7534	Tire Retreading & Repair Shops
7536	Automotive Glass Replacement Shops
7537	Automotive Transmission Repair Shops
7538	General Automotive Repair Shop
7539	Automotive Repair Shops, NEC
7542	Car Washes
7549	Automotive Svcs, Except Repair & Car Washes

76 miscellaneous repair services

7622	Radio & TV Repair Shops
7623	Refrigeration & Air Conditioning Svc & Repair Shop
7629	Electrical & Elex Repair Shop, NEC
7631	Watch, Clock & Jewelry Repair
7641	Reupholstery & Furniture Repair
7692	Welding Repair
7694	Armature Rewinding Shops
7699	Repair Shop & Related Svcs, NEC

78 motion pictures

7812	Motion Picture & Video Tape Production
7819	Services Allied To Motion Picture Prdtn
7822	Motion Picture & Video Tape Distribution
7829	Services Allied To Motion Picture Distribution
7832	Motion Picture Theaters, Except Drive-In
7833	Drive-In Motion Picture Theaters
7841	Video Tape Rental

79 amusement and recreation services

7911	Dance Studios, Schools & Halls
7922	Theatrical Producers & Misc Theatrical Svcs
7929	Bands, Orchestras, Actors & Entertainers
7933	Bowling Centers
7941	Professional Sports Clubs & Promoters
7948	Racing & Track Operations
7991	Physical Fitness Facilities
7992	Public Golf Courses
7993	Coin-Operated Amusement Devices & Arcades

SIC NO	PRODUCT
7996	Amusement Parks
7997	Membership Sports & Recreation Clubs
7999	Amusement & Recreation Svcs, NEC

80 health services

8011	Offices & Clinics Of Doctors Of Medicine
8021	Offices & Clinics Of Dentists
8031	Offices & Clinics Of Doctors Of Osteopathy
8042	Offices & Clinics Of Optometrists
8049	Offices & Clinics Of Health Practitioners, NEC
8051	Skilled Nursing Facilities
8052	Intermediate Care Facilities
8059	Nursing & Personal Care Facilities, NEC
8062	General Medical & Surgical Hospitals
8063	Psychiatric Hospitals
8069	Specialty Hospitals, Except Psychiatric
8071	Medical Laboratories
8072	Dental Laboratories
8082	Home Health Care Svcs
8092	Kidney Dialysis Centers
8093	Specialty Outpatient Facilities, NEC
8099	Health & Allied Svcs, NEC

81 legal services

8111	Legal Svcs

83 social services

8322	Individual & Family Social Svcs
8331	Job Training & Vocational Rehabilitation Svcs
8351	Child Day Care Svcs
8361	Residential Care
8399	Social Services, NEC

84 museums, art galleries, and botanical and zoological gardens

8412	Museums & Art Galleries
8422	Arboreta, Botanical & Zoological Gardens

86 membership organizations

8611	Business Associations
8621	Professional Membership Organizations
8631	Labor Unions & Similar Organizations
8641	Civic, Social & Fraternal Associations
8651	Political Organizations
8699	Membership Organizations, NEC

87 engineering, accounting, research, management, and related services

8711	Engineering Services
8712	Architectural Services
8713	Surveying Services
8721	Accounting, Auditing & Bookkeeping Svcs
8731	Commercial Physical & Biological Research
8732	Commercial Economic, Sociological & Educational Research
8733	Noncommercial Research Organizations
8734	Testing Laboratories
8741	Management Services
8742	Management Consulting Services
8743	Public Relations Svcs
8744	Facilities Support Mgmt Svcs
8748	Business Consulting Svcs, NEC

89 services, not elsewhere classified

8999	Services Not Elsewhere Classified

SIC INDEX

Standard Industrial Classification Alphabetical Index

SIC NO	PRODUCT
6162	Mortgage Bankers & Loan Correspondents
7822	Motion Picture & Video Tape Distribution
7812	Motion Picture & Video Tape Production
7832	Motion Picture Theaters, Except Drive-In
3716	Motor Homes
3714	Motor Vehicle Parts & Access
5015	Motor Vehicle Parts, Used Wholesale
5013	Motor Vehicle Splys & New Parts Wholesale
3711	Motor Vehicles & Car Bodies
3751	Motorcycles, Bicycles & Parts
3621	Motors & Generators
8412	Museums & Art Galleries
3931	Musical Instruments

N

SIC NO	PRODUCT
6021	National Commercial Banks
4924	Natural Gas Distribution
1321	Natural Gas Liquids
4922	Natural Gas Transmission
7383	News Syndicates
2711	Newspapers: Publishing & Printing
2873	Nitrogenous Fertilizers
3297	Nonclay Refractories
8733	Noncommercial Research Organizations
3644	Noncurrent-Carrying Wiring Devices
6091	Nondeposit Trust Facilities
5199	Nondurable Goods, NEC Wholesale
3364	Nonferrous Die Castings, Exc Aluminum
3463	Nonferrous Forgings
3369	Nonferrous Foundries: Castings, NEC
3357	Nonferrous Wire Drawing
3299	Nonmetallic Mineral Prdts, NEC
1481	Nonmetallic Minerals Svcs, Except Fuels
8059	Nursing & Personal Care Facilities, NEC

O

SIC NO	PRODUCT
5044	Office Eqpt Wholesale
2522	Office Furniture, Except Wood
3579	Office Machines, NEC
8021	Offices & Clinics Of Dentists
8011	Offices & Clinics Of Doctors Of Medicine
8031	Offices & Clinics Of Doctors Of Osteopathy
8049	Offices & Clinics Of Health Practitioners, NEC
8042	Offices & Clinics Of Optometrists
6712	Offices Of Bank Holding Co's
6719	Offices Of Holding Co's, NEC
1382	Oil & Gas Field Exploration Svcs
1389	Oil & Gas Field Svcs, NEC
3533	Oil Field Machinery & Eqpt
1531	Operative Builders
6513	Operators Of Apartment Buildings
6514	Operators Of Dwellings, Except Apartments
6512	Operators Of Nonresidential Bldgs
6515	Operators Of Residential Mobile Home Sites
3851	Ophthalmic Goods
5048	Ophthalmic Goods Wholesale
3827	Optical Instruments
3489	Ordnance & Access, NEC
0181	Ornamental Floriculture & Nursery Prdts
0783	Ornamental Shrub & Tree Svc
3842	Orthopedic, Prosthetic & Surgical Appliances/Splys
7312	Outdoor Advertising Svcs

P

SIC NO	PRODUCT
5142	Packaged Frozen Foods Wholesale
3565	Packaging Machinery
4783	Packing & Crating Svcs
1721	Painting & Paper Hanging Contractors
5198	Paints, Varnishes & Splys Wholesale
2851	Paints, Varnishes, Lacquers, Enamels
2671	Paper Coating & Laminating for Packaging
2672	Paper Coating & Laminating, Exc for Packaging
3554	Paper Inds Machinery
2621	Paper Mills
2631	Paperboard Mills
2542	Partitions & Fixtures, Except Wood
7515	Passenger Car Leasing
7514	Passenger Car Rental
4729	Passenger Transportation Arrangement, NEC
6794	Patent Owners & Lessors
2951	Paving Mixtures & Blocks
3951	Pens & Mechanical Pencils
6371	Pension, Health & Welfare Funds
2844	Perfumes, Cosmetics & Toilet Preparations
2721	Periodicals: Publishing & Printing
6141	Personal Credit Institutions
3172	Personal Leather Goods
2879	Pesticides & Agricultural Chemicals, NEC
5172	Petroleum & Petroleum Prdts Wholesale
5171	Petroleum Bulk Stations & Terminals

SIC NO	PRODUCT
2911	Petroleum Refining
2834	Pharmaceuticals
3652	Phonograph Records & Magnetic Tape
7334	Photocopying & Duplicating Svcs
7384	Photofinishing Labs
3861	Photographic Eqpt & Splys
5043	Photographic Eqpt & Splys Wholesale
7221	Photographic Studios, Portrait
7991	Physical Fitness Facilities
2035	Pickled Fruits, Vegetables, Sauces & Dressings
5131	Piece Goods, Notions & Dry Goods Wholesale
1742	Plastering, Drywall, Acoustical & Insulation Work
3085	Plastic Bottles
3086	Plastic Foam Prdts
3083	Plastic Laminated Plate & Sheet
3084	Plastic Pipe
3088	Plastic Plumbing Fixtures
3089	Plastic Prdts
3082	Plastic Unsupported Profile Shapes
3081	Plastic Unsupported Sheet & Film
5162	Plastics Materials & Basic Shapes Wholesale
2821	Plastics, Mtrls & Nonvulcanizable Elastomers
2796	Platemaking & Related Svcs
2395	Pleating & Stitching For The Trade
5074	Plumbing & Heating Splys Wholesale
3432	Plumbing Fixture Fittings & Trim, Brass
1711	Plumbing, Heating & Air Conditioning Contractors
8651	Political Organizations
3264	Porcelain Electrical Splys
2096	Potato Chips & Similar Prdts
3269	Pottery Prdts, NEC
5144	Poultry & Poultry Prdts Wholesale
2015	Poultry Slaughtering, Dressing & Processing
3546	Power Hand Tools
7211	Power Laundries, Family & Commercial
3612	Power, Distribution & Specialty Transformers
3448	Prefabricated Metal Buildings & Cmpnts
2452	Prefabricated Wood Buildings & Cmpnts
7372	Prepackaged Software
2048	Prepared Feeds For Animals & Fowls
3229	Pressed & Blown Glassware, NEC
3692	Primary Batteries: Dry & Wet
3399	Primary Metal Prdts, NEC
3339	Primary Nonferrous Metals, NEC
3334	Primary Production Of Aluminum
3672	Printed Circuit Boards
5111	Printing & Writing Paper Wholesale
2893	Printing Ink
3555	Printing Trades Machinery & Eqpt
2999	Products Of Petroleum & Coal, NEC
5049	Professional Eqpt & Splys, NEC Wholesale
8621	Professional Membership Organizations
7941	Professional Sports Clubs & Promoters
8063	Psychiatric Hospitals
2531	Public Building & Related Furniture
7992	Public Golf Courses
8743	Public Relations Svcs
2611	Pulp Mills
3561	Pumps & Pumping Eqpt

R

SIC NO	PRODUCT
7948	Racing & Track Operations
3663	Radio & T V Communications, Systs & Eqpt, Broadcast/Studio
3671	Radio & T V Receiving Electron Tubes
7622	Radio & TV Repair Shops
4832	Radio Broadcasting Stations
7313	Radio, TV & Publishers Adv Reps
4812	Radiotelephone Communications
4741	Railroad Car Rental
3743	Railroad Eqpt
4011	Railroads, Line-Hauling Operations
3273	Ready-Mixed Concrete
6531	Real Estate Agents & Managers
6798	Real Estate Investment Trusts
2493	Reconstituted Wood Prdts
3695	Recording Media
4613	Refined Petroleum Pipelines
4222	Refrigerated Warehousing & Storage
7623	Refrigeration & Air Conditioning Svc & Repair Shop
5078	Refrigeration Eqpt & Splys Wholesale
4953	Refuse Systems
3625	Relays & Indl Controls
7699	Repair Shop & Related Svcs, NEC
8361	Residential Care
3645	Residential Lighting Fixtures
7641	Reupholstery & Furniture Repair
2044	Rice Milling
3547	Rolling Mill Machinery & Eqpt
3351	Rolling, Drawing & Extruding Of Copper

SIC NO	PRODUCT
3356	Rolling, Drawing-Extruding Of Nonferrous Metals
5033	Roofing, Siding & Insulation Mtrls Wholesale
1761	Roofing, Siding & Sheet Metal Work
7021	Rooming & Boarding Houses
3021	Rubber & Plastic Footwear
3052	Rubber & Plastic Hose & Belting

S

SIC NO	PRODUCT
2068	Salted & Roasted Nuts & Seeds
2656	Sanitary Food Containers
2676	Sanitary Paper Prdts
4959	Sanitary Svcs, NEC
2013	Sausages & Meat Prdts
6036	Savings Institutions, Except Federal
2421	Saw & Planing Mills
3596	Scales & Balances, Exc Laboratory
2397	Schiffli Machine Embroideries
4151	School Buses
5093	Scrap & Waste Materials Wholesale
3451	Screw Machine Prdts
3812	Search, Detection, Navigation & Guidance Systs & Instrs
3341	Secondary Smelting & Refining Of Nonferrous Metals
7338	Secretarial & Court Reporting Svcs
6289	Security & Commodity Svcs, NEC
6211	Security Brokers & Dealers
7382	Security Systems Svcs
3674	Semiconductors
5087	Service Establishment Eqpt & Splys Wholesale
3589	Service Ind Machines, NEC
7829	Services Allied To Motion Picture Distribution
7819	Services Allied To Motion Picture Prdtn
8999	Services Not Elsewhere Classified
2652	Set-Up Paperboard Boxes
4952	Sewerage Systems
0214	Sheep & Goats
3444	Sheet Metal Work
3731	Shipbuilding & Repairing
2079	Shortening, Oils & Margarine
3993	Signs & Advertising Displays
2262	Silk & Man-Made Fabric Finishers
2221	Silk & Man-Made Fiber
3914	Silverware, Plated & Stainless Steel Ware
8051	Skilled Nursing Facilities
3484	Small Arms
3482	Small Arms Ammunition
2841	Soap & Detergents
8399	Social Services, NEC
2086	Soft Drinks
0711	Soil Preparation Svcs
0721	Soil Preparation, Planting & Cultivating Svc
2075	Soybean Oil Mills
2842	Spec Cleaning, Polishing & Sanitation Preparations
3559	Special Ind Machinery, NEC
1799	Special Trade Contractors, NEC
4226	Special Warehousing & Storage, NEC
8069	Specialty Hospitals, Except Psychiatric
8093	Specialty Outpatient Facilities, NEC
3566	Speed Changers, Drives & Gears
3949	Sporting & Athletic Goods, NEC
7032	Sporting & Recreational Camps
5091	Sporting & Recreational Goods & Splys Wholesale
6022	State Commercial Banks
6062	State Credit Unions
5112	Stationery & Office Splys Wholesale
2678	Stationery Prdts
4961	Steam & Air Conditioning Sply
3511	Steam, Gas & Hydraulic Turbines & Engines
3325	Steel Foundries, NEC
3324	Steel Investment Foundries
3317	Steel Pipe & Tubes
3493	Steel Springs, Except Wire
3315	Steel Wire Drawing & Nails & Spikes
3691	Storage Batteries
3259	Structural Clay Prdts, NEC
1791	Structural Steel Erection
2439	Structural Wood Members, NEC
2063	Sugar, Beet
2062	Sugar, Cane Refining
0133	Sugarcane & Sugar Beets
6351	Surety Insurance Carriers
2843	Surface Active & Finishing Agents, Sulfonated Oils
3841	Surgical & Medical Instrs & Apparatus
8713	Surveying Services
3613	Switchgear & Switchboard Apparatus
4013	Switching & Terminal Svcs
2824	Synthetic Organic Fibers, Exc Cellulosic
2822	Synthetic Rubber (Vulcanizable Elastomers)

T

SIC NO	PRODUCT
3795	Tanks & Tank Components

SIC

SIC NO	PRODUCT
7291	Tax Return Preparation Svcs
4121	Taxi Cabs
4822	Telegraph & Other Message Communications
3661	Telephone & Telegraph Apparatus
4813	Telephone Communications, Except Radio
4833	Television Broadcasting Stations
4231	Terminal & Joint Terminal Maint Facilities
1743	Terrazzo, Tile, Marble & Mosaic Work
8734	Testing Laboratories
2393	Textile Bags
2269	Textile Finishers, NEC
2299	Textile Goods, NEC
3552	Textile Machinery
7922	Theatrical Producers & Misc Theatrical Svcs
2284	Thread Mills
0811	Timber Tracts
7534	Tire Retreading & Repair Shops
3011	Tires & Inner Tubes
5014	Tires & Tubes Wholesale
6541	Title Abstract Offices
6361	Title Insurance
5194	Tobacco & Tobacco Prdts Wholesale
2131	Tobacco, Chewing & Snuff
7532	Top, Body & Upholstery Repair & Paint Shops
4725	Tour Operators
4492	Towing & Tugboat Svcs
5092	Toys & Hobby Goods & Splys Wholesale
7033	Trailer Parks & Camp Sites
5088	Transportation Eqpt & Splys, Except Motor Vehicles Wholesale
3799	Transportation Eqpt, NEC
4789	Transportation Svcs, NEC
4724	Travel Agencies
3792	Travel Trailers & Campers
0173	Tree Nuts
3713	Truck & Bus Bodies
7513	Truck Rental & Leasing, Without Drivers
3715	Truck Trailers
4213	Trucking, Except Local
6733	Trusts Except Educational, Religious & Charitable
2791	Typesetting

U

SIC NO	PRODUCT
6726	Unit Investment Trusts, Face-Amount Certificate Offices
7519	Utility Trailers & Recreational Vehicle Rental

V

SIC NO	PRODUCT
3494	Valves & Pipe Fittings, NEC
2076	Vegetable Oil Mills
0161	Vegetables & Melons
3647	Vehicular Lighting Eqpt
0742	Veterinary Animal Specialties
7841	Video Tape Rental

W

SIC NO	PRODUCT
3873	Watch & Clock Devices & Parts
7631	Watch, Clock & Jewelry Repair
4941	Water Sply
4489	Water Transport Of Passengers, NEC
4449	Water Transportation Of Freight, NEC
4499	Water Transportation Svcs, NEC
1781	Water Well Drilling
1623	Water, Sewer & Utility Line Construction
2385	Waterproof Outerwear
3548	Welding Apparatus
7692	Welding Repair
2046	Wet Corn Milling

SIC NO	PRODUCT
0111	Wheat
2084	Wine & Brandy
5182	Wine & Distilled Alcoholic Beverages Wholesale
3495	Wire Springs
2331	Women's & Misses' Blouses
2335	Women's & Misses' Dresses
2339	Women's & Misses' Outerwear, NEC
2337	Women's & Misses' Suits, Coats & Skirts
3144	Women's Footwear, Exc Athletic
5137	Women's, Children's & Infants Clothing Wholesale
2341	Women's, Misses' & Children's Underwear & Nightwear
2441	Wood Boxes
2449	Wood Containers, NEC
2511	Wood Household Furniture
2512	Wood Household Furniture, Upholstered
2434	Wood Kitchen Cabinets
2521	Wood Office Furniture
2448	Wood Pallets & Skids
2499	Wood Prdts, NEC
2491	Wood Preserving
2517	Wood T V, Radio, Phono & Sewing Cabinets
2541	Wood, Office & Store Fixtures
3553	Woodworking Machinery
2231	Wool, Woven Fabric
1795	Wrecking & Demolition Work

X

SIC NO	PRODUCT
3844	X-ray Apparatus & Tubes

Y

SIC NO	PRODUCT
2281	Yarn Spinning Mills
2282	Yarn Texturizing, Throwing, Twisting & Winding Mills

PRODUCTS & SERVICES SECTION

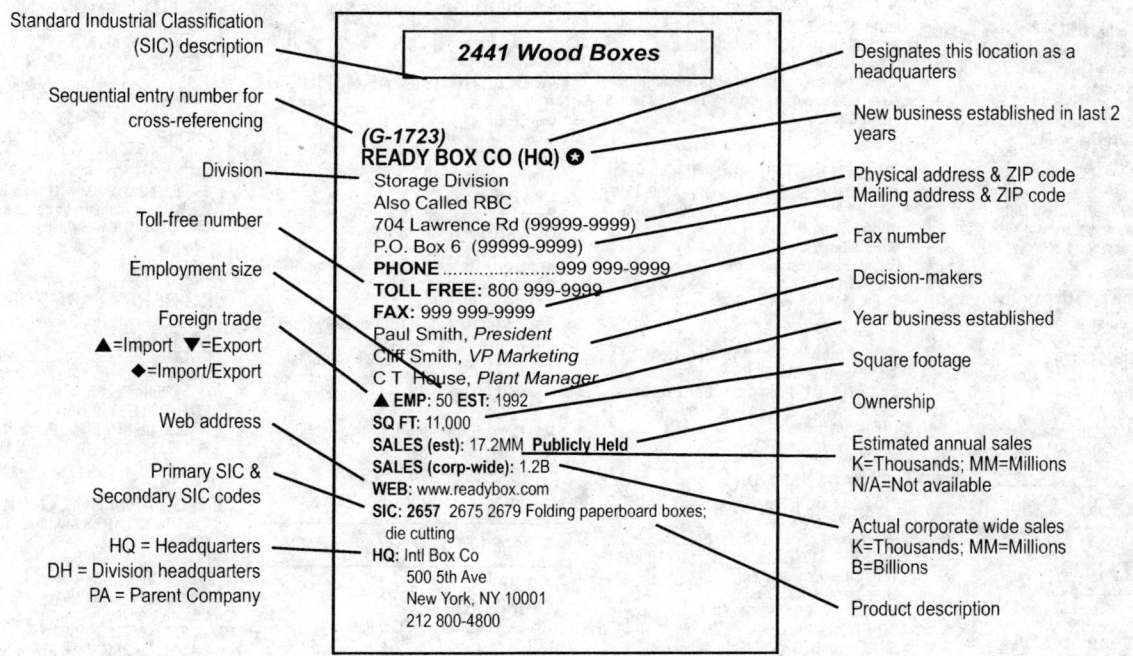

Standard Industrial Classification (SIC) description

Sequential entry number for cross-referencing

Division

Toll-free number

Employment size

Foreign trade
▲=Import ▼=Export
◆=Import/Export

Web address

Primary SIC & Secondary SIC codes

HQ = Headquarters
DH = Division headquarters
PA = Parent Company

2441 Wood Boxes

(G-1723)
READY BOX CO (HQ) ✪
Storage Division
Also Called RBC
704 Lawrence Rd (99999-9999)
P.O. Box 6 (99999-9999)
PHONE 999 999-9999
TOLL FREE: 800 999-9999
FAX: 999 999-9999
Paul Smith, *President*
Cliff Smith, *VP Marketing*
C T House, *Plant Manager*
▲ EMP: 50 EST: 1992
SQ FT: 11,000
SALES (est): 17.2MM Publicly Held
SALES (corp-wide): 1.2B
WEB: www.readybox.com
SIC: 2657 2675 2679 Folding paperboard boxes;
  die cutting
HQ: Intl Box Co
  500 5th Ave
  New York, NY 10001
  212 800-4800

Designates this location as a headquarters

New business established in last 2 years

Physical address & ZIP code
Mailing address & ZIP code

Fax number

Decision-makers

Year business established

Square footage

Ownership

Estimated annual sales
K=Thousands; MM=Millions
N/A=Not available

Actual corporate wide sales
K=Thousands; MM=Millions
B=Billions

Product description

- Companies in this section are listed numerically under their primary SIC Companies are in alphabetical order under each code.

- A numerical and alphabetcal index precedes this section.

- **Sequential Entry Numbers.** Each establishment in this section is numbered sequentially. The number assigned to each establishment's Entry Number. To make cross-referencing easier, each listing in the Product's & Services, Alphabetic and Geographical Section includes the establishment's entry number. To facilitate locating an entry in this section, the entry numbers for the first listing on the left page and the last listing on the right page are printed at the top of the page next to the Standard Industrial Classification (SIC) description.

- Further information can be found in the Explanatory Notes starting on page 5.

- See the footnotes for symbols and abbreviations.

IMPORTANT NOTICE: It is a violation of both federal and state law to transmit an unsolicited advertisement to a facsimile machine. Any user of this product that violates such laws may be subject to civil and criminal penalties which may exceed $500 for each transmission of an unsolicited facsimile. Harris InfoSource provides fax numbers for lawful purposes only and expressly forbids the use of these numbers in any unlawful manner.

0131 Cotton

(P-1)
C J RITCHIE FARMS
11878 Avenue 328, Visalia (93291-9238)
PHONE 559 625-1114
Clarence J Ritchie, *Partner*
Jeff Ritchie, *Partner*
Larry Ritchie, *Partner*
EMP: 57 EST: 1947
SQ FT: 3,600
SALES (est): 2.6MM Privately Held
SIC: 0131 0119 0115 0181 Cottonseed
  farm; barley farm; corn; ornamental nursery products

(P-2)
J G BOSWELL COMPANY
21101 Bear Mountain Blvd, Bakersfield
(93311-9412)
P.O. Box 9759 (93389-9759)
PHONE 661 327-7721
Dave Cosyns, *Manager*
Christina Ortiz, *Admin Asst*
EMP: 145
SALES (corp-wide): 370.2MM Privately
Held
WEB: www.eastlakeco.com
SIC: 0131 0111 0724 Cotton; wheat; cotton ginning

PA: J. G. Boswell Company
  101 W Walnut St
  Pasadena CA 91103
  626 583-3000

(P-3)
J G BOSWELL COMPANY
Also Called: Ranching Shop
28001 S Dairy Ave, Corcoran (93212)
P.O. Box 877 (93212-0877)
PHONE 559 992-5141
Paul Athorp, *Branch Mgr*
Vern Mullins, *Purch Agent*
EMP: 145
SALES (corp-wide): 370.2MM Privately
Held
WEB: www.eastlakecom.com
SIC: 0131 0724 0182 Cotton; cotton ginning; food crops grown under cover
PA: J. G. Boswell Company
  101 W Walnut St
  Pasadena CA 91103
  626 583-3000

(P-4)
STONE LAND COMPANY (PA)
Also Called: Stone Ranch
28521 Nevada Ave, Stratford (93266)
P.O. Box 146 (93266-0146)
PHONE 559 947-3185
Jack G Stone, *President*
Sally Moreno, *Corp Secy*
William Stone, *Vice Pres*

▲ EMP: 100 EST: 1948
SQ FT: 2,000 Privately Held
SIC: 0131 0191 0111 Cotton; general
  farms, primarily crop; wheat

(P-5)
VIGNOLO FARMS INC
33342 Dresser Ave, Bakersfield
(93308-9634)
P.O. Box 1270, Shafter (93263-1270)
PHONE 661 746-2148
Robert J Vignolo, *President*
EMP: 150 EST: 1938
SQ FT: 2,500
SALES (est): 9.3MM Privately Held
WEB: www.topbrassmarketing.com
SIC: 0131 0172 0134 Cotton; grapes;
  Irish potatoes

0139 Field Crops, Except Cash Grains, NEC

(P-6)
GARLIC COMPANY
18602 Zerker Rd, Shafter (93263-9101)
PHONE 661 393-4212
John Layous, *Managing Prtnr*
Joe Lane, *Partner*
Bill Lane, *Plant Mgr*
Scott Wilson, *Maintence Staff*

Dwight Plank, *Manager*
◆ EMP: 125 EST: 1980
SQ FT: 150,000
SALES (est): 46.3MM Privately Held
WEB: www.thegarliccompany.com
SIC: 0139 2099 0191 Herb or spice farm;
  food preparations; general farms, primarily crop

(P-7)
HAYDAY FARMS INC
15500 S Commercial St, Blythe
(92225-2750)
P.O. Box 1226 (92226-1226)
PHONE 760 922-4713
Atsuya Ichida, *President*
Dale Tyson, *Vice Pres*
◆ EMP: 75 EST: 1986
SQ FT: 2,160
SALES (est): 17.4MM Privately Held
WEB: www.darland.net
SIC: 0139 0722 0723 Hay farm; hay, machine harvesting services; field crops, except cash grains, market preparation
  services

(P-8)
HERB THYME FARM INC
7909 Crossway Dr, Pico Rivera
(90660-4449)
PHONE 603 542-3690
EMP: 70

SALES (est): 1.2MM **Privately Held**
SIC: 0139 Field Crop Farm

(P-9)
MEDTERRA CBD LLC
9805 Research Dr, Irvine (92618-4304)
PHONE....................800 971-1288
John Hartenbach, *CEO*
Sierra Hennen, *Partner*
John Preston Larsen, *President*
Matthew Taylor, *Chief Mktg Ofcr*
Natasha Cuda, *Officer*
EMP: 89 **EST:** 2017
SQ FT: 29,252
SALES (est): 12MM **Privately Held**
WEB: www.medterracbd.com
SIC: 0139 Herb or spice farm

(P-10)
SANDRIDGE PARTNERS LP
19087 Milan Rd, Buttonwillow
(93206-9777)
P.O. Box 605 (93206-0605)
PHONE....................408 738-4444
John Vidovich, *General Ptnr*
EMP: 66 **EST:** 2005
SALES (est): 3.4MM **Privately Held**
SIC: 0139 Peanut farm

0161 Vegetables & Melons

(P-11)
BOLTHOUSE FARMS
3200 E Brundage Ln, Bakersfield (93304)
PHONE....................661 366-7205
William Bolthouse, *Owner*
◆ **EMP:** 2300 **EST:** 1915
SALES (est): 95.6MM
SALES (corp-wide): 1B **Privately Held**
WEB: www.bolthouse.com
SIC: 0161 Carrot farm
HQ: Wm. Bolthouse Farms, Inc.
7200 E Brundage Ln
Bakersfield CA 93307
661 366-7209

(P-12)
BOLTHOUSE INVESTMENT COMPANY
7200 E Brundage Ln, Bakersfield (93307-3016)
PHONE....................661 366-7209
Fax: 661 366-2834
▲ **EMP:** 13
SALES (est): 5.9MM
SALES (corp-wide): 7.8B **Publicly Held**
SIC: 0161 2099 Holding Company For General Crop Farm
HQ: Campbell Investment Company
1 Campbell Pl
Camden NJ 08103

(P-13)
CALIFORNIA WATERCRESS INC (PA)
550 E Telegraph Rd, Fillmore (93015-9667)
P.O. Box 874 (93016-0874)
PHONE....................805 524-4808
Alfred C Beserra, *President*
Teresa Beserra, *Admin Sec*
EMP: 65 **EST:** 1966
SQ FT: 1,000
SALES (est): 5MM **Privately Held**
WEB: www.californiawatercress.com
SIC: 0161 Vegetables & melons

(P-14)
FRESH VENTURE FARMS LLC
1181 S Wolff Rd, Oxnard (93033-2105)
PHONE....................805 754-4449
Robert Boelts,
EMP: 80 **EST:** 2012
SQ FT: 4,000
SALES (est): 3.5MM **Privately Held**
SIC: 0161 0191 Vegetables & melons;
general farms, primarily crop

(P-15)
GENERIS HOLDINGS LP (PA)
7200 E Brundage Ln, Bakersfield (93307-3016)
PHONE....................661 366-7209
Jeffrey Dunn, *CEO*

Phil Kooy, *Officer*
Aj Bernstein, *Vice Pres*
Brian Dilley, *Vice Pres*
Donna Schmitz, *Admin Sec*
EMP: 47 **EST:** 2019
SALES (est): 1B **Privately Held**
SIC: 0161 2037 2033 2099 Carrot farm;
fruit juices; vegetable juices: packaged in cans, jars, etc.; sauces: gravy, dressing & dip mixes

(P-16)
GOLD COAST FARMS INC
123 N Depot St, Santa Maria (93458-3907)
PHONE....................805 928-2727
Ronald Burk, *President*
Sandra Espinola, *Treasurer*
Robert Espinola, *Vice Pres*
Mary Burk, *Admin Sec*
Cathy Manson, *Admin Asst*
EMP: 57 **EST:** 1978
SQ FT: 800
SALES (est): 7.9MM **Privately Held**
WEB: www.goldcoastpack.com
SIC: 0161 0171 Broccoli farm; cauliflower farm; pepper farm, sweet & hot (vegetables); strawberry farm

(P-17)
LUCKY FARMS INC
1194 E Brier Dr, San Bernardino (92408-2838)
P.O. Box 985, Loma Linda (92354-0985)
PHONE....................909 799-6688
Wen S Liaou, *President*
Gary Liaou, *Vice Pres*
▲ **EMP:** 60 **EST:** 1982
SQ FT: 28,000
SALES (est): 8.4MM **Privately Held**
WEB: www.luckyfarms.com
SIC: 0161 Corn farm, sweet

(P-18)
SAN MIGUEL PRODUCE INC
Also Called: Cut N Clean Greens
600 E Hueneme Rd, Oxnard (93033-8298)
PHONE....................805 488-0981
Roy I Nishimori, *CEO*
Jan Berk, *COO*
Jennifer Osborne, *Sales Staff*
Krystal Moraga, *Director*
Ed Alvarez, *Manager*
▲ **EMP:** 500 **EST:** 1979
SALES (est): 52MM **Privately Held**
WEB: www.sanmiguelproduce.com
SIC: 0161 0723 4212 Vegetables & melons; vegetable packing services; farm to market haulage, local

(P-19)
SANTA BARBARA FARMS LLC (PA)
1200 Union Sugar Ave, Lompoc (93436-9740)
PHONE....................805 736-9776
Robert M Witt, *CEO*
Charles Witt, *COO*
RC Gerber, *CFO*
▲ **EMP:** 248 **EST:** 1980
SQ FT: 2,800
SALES (est): 25.6MM **Privately Held**
SIC: 0161 0181 Vegetables & melons; florists' greens & flowers

(P-20)
TEIXEIRA FARMS DESERT INC
2600 Bonita Lateral Rd, Santa Maria (93458-9798)
PHONE....................805 928-3801
Allan Teixeira, *President*
Glenn Teixeira, *Treasurer*
Marvin Teixeira, *Vice Pres*
Pam Lind, *Office Mgr*
Dean Teixeira, *Admin Sec*
EMP: 87 **EST:** 1950
SALES (est): 3.8MM **Privately Held**
WEB: www.teixeirafarms.com
SIC: 0161 Broccoli farm

(P-21)
TRI-FANUCCHI FARMS INC
3728 David Rd, Arvin (93203-9610)
PHONE....................661 858-2264
Charles Fanucchi Sr, *President*
Frank M Fanucchi, *Admin Sec*
Gregory Bielli, *Director*

EMP: 67 **EST:** 1916
SQ FT: 2,000
SALES (est): 6.9MM **Privately Held**
SIC: 0161 0131 Vegetables & melons; cotton

(P-22)
WM BOLTHOUSE FARMS INC (HQ)
7200 E Brundage Ln, Bakersfield (93307-3016)
PHONE....................661 366-7209
Jeffrey Dunn, *CEO*
Mike Rosenthal, *CFO*
Brian Donnan, *Vice Pres*
Dave Schoonmaker, *Vice Pres*
Julie Ream, *Executive*
◆ **EMP:** 2848 **EST:** 1970
SQ FT: 700,000
SALES (est): 314.5MM
SALES (corp-wide): 1B **Privately Held**
WEB: www.bolthouse.com
SIC: 0161 2037 2033 2099 Carrot farm;
fruit juices; vegetable juices: packaged in cans, jars, etc.; sauces: gravy, dressing & dip mixes
PA: Generis Holdings, Lp
7200 E Brundage Ln
Bakersfield CA 93307
661 366-7209

0171 Berry Crops

(P-23)
AGRIFROST LLC
4324 E Vineyard Ave, Oxnard (93036-1056)
PHONE....................805 485-2519
Robert B Jones,
Annette Baietti, *Controller*
Richard Jones,
EMP: 50 **EST:** 2018
SALES (est): 2.1MM **Privately Held**
SIC: 0171 Berry crops; strawberry farm; blueberry farm

(P-24)
CJJ FARMING INC
125 W Mill St, Santa Maria (93458-4325)
PHONE....................805 739-1723
Juan Cisneros, *President*
Jesus Cisneros, *Admin Sec*
EMP: 50 **EST:** 1990
SALES (est): 6.8MM **Privately Held**
WEB: www.gogoldenstate.com
SIC: 0171 0161 Strawberry farm; squash farm

(P-25)
DARENSBERRIES LLC
Also Called: D B Specialty Farms
714 S Blosser Rd, Santa Maria (93458-4914)
P.O. Box 549 (93456-0549)
PHONE....................805 937-8000
Daren Gee,
EMP: 250 **EST:** 1994
SQ FT: 1,500
SALES (est): 9.6MM **Privately Held**
WEB: www.darensberries.com
SIC: 0171 Strawberry farm

(P-26)
ECLIPSE BERRY FARMS LLC
11812 San Vicente Blvd # 250, Los Angeles (90049-6632)
PHONE....................310 207-7879
Norman Gilfenbain, *Mng Member*
Ventura Strawberry,
Rudy Garza, *Mng Member*
Robert Wiviott, *Mng Member*
▼ **EMP:** 100 **EST:** 1999
SQ FT: 2,500
SALES (est): 10MM **Privately Held**
SIC: 0171 5148 Berry crops; fresh fruits & vegetables

(P-27)
ETCHANDY FARMS LLC
4324 E Vineyard Ave, Oxnard (93036-1056)
P.O. Box 5770 (93031-5770)
PHONE....................805 983-4700
Michael Etchandy,

EMP: 99 **EST:** 2014
SQ FT: 400
SALES (est): 8.5MM **Privately Held**
SIC: 0171 Strawberry farm

(P-28)
FRESHWAY FARMS LLC
2165 W Main St, Santa Maria (93458-9739)
P.O. Box 5369 (93456-5369)
PHONE....................805 349-7170
Paul M Allen, *Mng Member*
EMP: 150 **EST:** 2014
SALES (est): 8.8MM **Privately Held**
WEB: www.mainstreetproduce.com
SIC: 0171 0161 Strawberry farm; broccoli farm

(P-29)
J&G BERRY FARMS LLC
720 Rosemary Rd, Santa Maria (93454-8007)
PHONE....................831 750-9408
Jose Luis Rocha, *Mng Member*
Guadalupe Rocha,
EMP: 220 **EST:** 2016
SALES (est): 2.5MM **Privately Held**
SIC: 0171 7389 Strawberry farm;

(P-30)
L & G FARMING CO INC
1141 Tama Ln, Santa Maria (93455-1127)
PHONE....................805 928-1559
Luis Chavez, *President*
Daniel Chavez, *Vice Pres*
Consuello Chavez, *Admin Sec*
Lorena Chavez, *Controller*
▲ **EMP:** 50 **EST:** 1986
SALES (est): 2.1MM **Privately Held**
WEB: www.dlfarmmgmt.com
SIC: 0171 0161 Strawberry farm; squash farm; cauliflower farm; broccoli farm

(P-31)
LAS POSAS BERRY FARMS LLC
730 S A St, Oxnard (93030-7138)
PHONE....................805 483-1000
Manuel Magdaleno, *CEO*
EMP: 100 **EST:** 2013
SALES (est): 1.8MM **Privately Held**
SIC: 0171 Berry crops

(P-32)
ORANGE COUNTY PRODUCE LLC
11405 Jeffrey Rd, Irvine (92602-0503)
PHONE....................949 451-0880
Matthew K Kawamura, *Mng Member*
John Kubo, *Officer*
Blanca Lloyoza, *Executive*
Ana Lozoya, *Administration*
Blanca Lozoya, *MIS Mgr*
EMP: 100 **EST:** 1998
SQ FT: 1,000
SALES (est): 10.2MM **Privately Held**
WEB: www.ocproduce.com
SIC: 0171 Strawberry farm

(P-33)
RED BLOSSOM SALES INC
865 Black Rd, Santa Maria (93458-9701)
PHONE....................805 349-9404
Ruben Trevino, *Manager*
Rachelle Dietz, *Sales Staff*
Delia Galvan, *Sales Staff*
Carole Patterson, *Director*
EMP: 501 **Privately Held**
WEB: www.redblossom.com
SIC: 0171 Strawberry farm
PA: Red Blossom Sales, Inc.
400 W Ventura Blvd # 140
Camarillo CA 93010

(P-34)
REITER AFFL COMPANIES LLC (PA)
730 S A St, Oxnard (93030-7138)
PHONE....................805 483-1000
Garland Reiter, *CEO*
Jonathan Paris, *Vice Pres*
Jim Pingel, *Vice Pres*
Eric Reiter, *Vice Pres*
Brad Hileman, *Exec Dir*
EMP: 129 **EST:** 2006

SALES (est): 61.7MM **Privately Held**
WEB: www.berry.net
SIC: 0171 Raspberry farm

(P-35)
REITER BERRY FARMS INC (PA)
730 S A St, Oxnard (93030-7138)
PHONE..............................805 483-1000
Garland Reiter, *CEO*
EMP: 142 EST: 1980
SALES (est): 14.9MM **Privately Held**
WEB: www.berry.net
SIC: 0171 Raspberry farm; strawberry farm

(P-36)
RINCON PACIFIC LLC
1312 Del Norte Rd, Camarillo
(93010-8502)
PHONE..............................805 986-8806
Kenneth Hasegawa,
EMP: 100 EST: 2001
SALES (est): 8.3MM **Privately Held**
WEB: www.rinconfresh.com
SIC: 0171 Strawberry farm

(P-37)
SANTA ROSA BERRY FARMS LLC
3500 Camino Ave Ste 250, Oxnard
(93030-7999)
PHONE..............................805 981-3060
Bryan D Fiscalini,
EMP: 300 EST: 2010
SQ FT: 3,500
SALES (est): 11.6MM **Privately Held**
WEB: www.srbfarms.com
SIC: 0171 Berry crops

(P-38)
SUPERIOR FRUIT LLC
4324 E Vineyard Ave, Oxnard
(93036-1056)
PHONE..............................805 485-2519
Robert Jones,
Richard Jones,
EMP: 200
SQ FT: 6,000
SALES (est): 200MM **Privately Held**
SIC: 0171 Strawberry farm

0172 Grapes

(P-39)
7TH STANDARD RANCH COMPANY
Also Called: Sun Pacific Farming
33374 Lerdo Hwy, Bakersfield
(93308-9782)
PHONE..............................661 399-0416
Berne Evans, *Partner*
Robert Reniers, *Partner*
Howard Nager, *Vice Pres*
Kristen Tallman, *Technology*
Elwyn Pratt, *Analyst*
EMP: 500 EST: 1986
SQ FT: 140,000
SALES (est): 27.4MM **Privately Held**
WEB: www.sunpacific.com
SIC: 0172 4222 Grapes; refrigerated
    warehousing & storage

(P-40)
ANTHONY VINEYARDS INC
52 301 Enterprise Way, Coachella (92236)
PHONE..............................760 391-5488
Roberto Bianco, *Manager*
Scott Slater, *CEO*
EMP: 100
SALES (est): 10.9MM **Privately Held**
SIC: 0172 0174 Grapes; grapefruit grove
PA: Anthony Vineyards, Inc.
    5512 Valpredo Ave
    Bakersfield CA 93307
    661 858-6211

(P-41)
ANTHONY VINEYARDS INC (PA)
5512 Valpredo Ave, Bakersfield
(93307-9178)
P.O. Box 9578 (93389-9578)
PHONE..............................661 858-6211
Domenick T Bianco, *President*

Paul A Loeffel, *CFO*
Domenick Bianco, *Treasurer*
Robert O Bianco, *Senior VP*
James Dad, *Info Svcs Mgr*
◆ EMP: 50 EST: 1972
SQ FT: 125,000
SALES: 10.9MM **Privately Held**
WEB: www.anthonyvineyards.com
SIC: 0172 0174 Grapes; grapefruit grove;
    tangerine grove

(P-42)
BABCOCK ENTERPRISES INC
Also Called: Babcock Vineyards
5175 E Highway 246, Lompoc
(93436-9613)
P.O. Box 637 (93438-0637)
PHONE..............................805 736-1455
Bryan Babcock, *President*
Walter Babcock, *President*
Mona Babcock, *Corp Secy*
Terrie Marlin, *General Mgr*
Rebecca Cogswell, *Accounting Mgr*
EMP: 25 EST: 1979
SALES (est): 3.4MM **Privately Held**
WEB: www.babcockwinery.com
SIC: 0172 2084 8734 Grapes; wines;
    food testing service

(P-43)
BECKMEN VINEYARDS
2670 Ontiveros Rd, Los Olivos (93441)
P.O. Box 542 (93441-0542)
PHONE..............................805 688-8664
Thomas Beckmen, *Owner*
Neil Redmond, *Sales Staff*
▲ EMP: 30 EST: 1985
SQ FT: 3,000
SALES (est): 5.8MM **Privately Held**
WEB: www.beckmenvineyards.com
SIC: 0172 2084 Grapes; wine cellars;
    bonded: engaged in blending wines

(P-44)
DAN TUDOR & SONS (PA)
11081 Zachary Ave, Delano (93215-9596)
P.O. Box 1361 (93216-1361)
PHONE..............................661 792-2933
Anthony Buksa, *Partner*
John Buksa, *Partner*
Christian Tudor, *Partner*
John Tudor, *Partner*
EMP: 59 EST: 1937
SQ FT: 53,000
SALES (est): 2.8MM **Privately Held**
SIC: 0172 Grapes

(P-45)
DELMART FARMS INC
30988 Riverside Cntrl Vly, Shafter (93263)
PHONE..............................661 746-2148
EMP: 100
SQ FT: 1,000
SALES (est): 2.5MM **Privately Held**
SIC: 0172 0131 0134 0724 Grape Vine-
    yard Cotton Farm Irish Potato Farm Cot-
    ton Ginning Services

(P-46)
GIUMARRA VINEYARDS CORPORATION
Giumarra Winery
11220 Edison Hwy, Bakersfield
(93307-8431)
P.O. Box 1969 (93303-1969)
PHONE..............................661 395-7071
Barry Douglas, *Manager*
David Aquino, *Human Res Dir*
EMP: 189
SALES (corp-wide): 134.6MM **Privately Held**
WEB: www.giumarravineyards.com
SIC: 0172 Grapes
PA: Giumarra Vineyards Corporation
    11220 Edison Hwy
    Edison CA 93220
    661 395-7000

(P-47)
GIUMARRA VINEYARDS CORPORATION (PA)
11220 Edison Hwy, Edison (93220)
P.O. Box 1969, Bakersfield (93303-1969)
PHONE..............................661 395-7000
Wayne Childress, *CEO*
William Butler, *CFO*

Jeffrey Giumarra, *CFO*
Mimi Dorsey, *Vice Pres*
Mimi Corsaro-Dorsey, *Admin Sec*
▲ EMP: 500 EST: 1946
SQ FT: 10,000
SALES (est): 134.6MM **Privately Held**
WEB: www.giumarravineyards.com
SIC: 0172 2084 2086 Grapes; wines; fruit
    drinks (less than 100% juice): packaged
    in cans, etc.

(P-48)
J & L VINEYARDS
1850 Ramada Dr Ste 3, Paso Robles
(93446-3932)
PHONE..............................559 268-1627
Donald Laub, *Partner*
Raymond Jacobson, *Partner*
EMP: 100 EST: 1980
SALES (est): 4.6MM **Privately Held**
SIC: 0172 Grapes

(P-49)
M CARATAN DISC INC
Also Called: Caliente Farms
33787 Cecil Ave, Delano (93215-9597)
PHONE..............................661 725-2566
Martin Caratin, *CEO*
Keith Andrew, *COO*
John Carter, *Facilities Mgr*
▼ EMP: 150 EST: 1946
SQ FT: 6,000
SALES (est): 13.5MM **Privately Held**
WEB: www.columbinevineyards.com
SIC: 0172 0174 0723 Grapes; orange
    grove; almond hulling & shelling services

(P-50)
MT VIEW FARMING INC
23595 Road 140, Tulare (93274-9646)
PHONE..............................559 688-2906
Aram Kinosian, *President*
EMP: 57 EST: 1975
SQ FT: 30,000
SALES (est): 3.1MM **Privately Held**
SIC: 0172 0762 Grapes; vineyard man-
    agement & maintenance services

(P-51)
PANDOL & SONS
401 Road 192, Delano (93215-9598)
PHONE..............................661 725-3755
Cheri Diebel, *CEO*
Jack V Pandol, *Partner*
Lucy Pandol, *Partner*
Steve Pandol III, *Partner*
Sherry Dibdel, *CFO*
EMP: 98 EST: 1930
SQ FT: 10,000
SALES (est): 24.9MM **Privately Held**
WEB: www.pandol.com
SIC: 0172 0723 Grapes; fruit (fresh) pack-
    ing services

(P-52)
RENZONI VINEYARDS INC
Also Called: Robert Rnzoni Vineyards Winery
37350 De Portola Rd, Temecula
(92592-9024)
PHONE..............................951 302-8466
Robert Renzoni, *President*
Fred Renzoni, *Treasurer*
John Bayus, *Consultant*
▲ EMP: 37 EST: 2007
SALES (est): 2.7MM **Privately Held**
WEB: www.robertrenzonivineyards.com
SIC: 0172 2084 Grapes; wines

(P-53)
RICHARD BAGDASARIAN INC
65500 Lincoln St, Mecca (92254-6500)
P.O. Box 698 (92254-0698)
PHONE..............................760 396-2168
Nicholas L Bozick, *CEO*
Michael Bozick, *President*
Darrell Billings, *CFO*
Bobbie Bozick, *Exec VP*
John Nixon, *Technician*
▲ EMP: 60 EST: 1951
SQ FT: 40,000
SALES (est): 14.4MM **Privately Held**
WEB: www.bagdasarianinc.com
SIC: 0172 0174 Grapes; citrus fruits

(P-54)
RIVERBENCH LLC (PA)
Also Called: Riverbench Vineyard & Winery
6020 Foxen Canyon Rd, Santa Maria
(93454-9656)
PHONE..............................805 937-8340
Laura Booras, *General Mgr*
Danae Smith, *Director*
▲ EMP: 45 EST: 1994
SALES (est): 2.7MM **Privately Held**
WEB: www.riverbench.com
SIC: 0172 2084 Grapes; wines

(P-55)
VINCENT B ZANINOVICH SONS INC
Also Called: V B Z
20715 Ave 8, Richgrove (93261)
P.O. Box 1000 (93261-1000)
PHONE..............................661 720-9031
John V Zaninovich, *President*
Vincent Zaninovich, *President*
Andrew Zaninovich, *Vice Pres*
◆ EMP: 1000 EST: 1930
SQ FT: 15,450
SALES (est): 26.7MM **Privately Held**
SIC: 0172 Grapes

0173 Tree Nuts

(P-56)
KEENAN FARMS INC
31510 Plymouth Ave, Kettleman City
(93239-9721)
P.O. Box 99, Avenal (93204-0099)
PHONE..............................559 945-1400
Robert M Keenan, *CEO*
Teresa Keenan, *Chief Mktg Ofcr*
Manny Guerrero, *Vice Pres*
Charles J Keenan III, *Vice Pres*
Stephen Skaggs, *Engineer*
◆ EMP: 100 EST: 1972
SALES (est): 23.2MM **Privately Held**
WEB: www.keenanpistachio.com
SIC: 0173 2068 Pistachio grove; nuts:
    dried, dehydrated, salted or roasted

(P-57)
SUPREME ALMONDS CALIFORNIA INC
16897 Highway 43, Wasco (93280-9611)
PHONE..............................661 746-6475
Randy Loemhof, *President*
◆ EMP: 100 EST: 2008
SALES (est): 6MM **Privately Held**
WEB: www.supremealmonds.com
SIC: 0173 Almond grove

(P-58)
TEJON RANCH CO (PA)
4436 Lebec Rd, Lebec (93243-9705)
P.O. Box 1000 (93243-1000)
PHONE..............................661 248-3000
Gregory S Bielli, *President*
Norman J Metcalfe, *Ch of Bd*
Allen E Lyda, *CFO*
Robert Velasquez, *CFO*
Joe Rentfro, *Exec VP*
▼ EMP: 119 EST: 1936
SALES (est): 37.8MM **Publicly Held**
WEB: www.tejonranch.com
SIC: 0173 0172 6531 Almond grove; pis-
    tachio grove; walnut grove; grapes; real
    estate brokers & agents

(P-59)
WONDERFUL ORCHARDS LLC (HQ)
6801 E Lerdo Hwy, Shafter (93263-9610)
PHONE..............................661 399-4456
Stuart Resnick,
William Phillimore,
◆ EMP: 150 EST: 1998
SQ FT: 10,000
SALES: 157.6MM
SALES (corp-wide): 2B **Privately Held**
WEB: www.wonderfulorchards.com
SIC: 0173 0179 Almond grove; olive grove
PA: The Wonderful Company Llc
    11444 W Olympic Blvd # 210
    Los Angeles CA 90064
    310 966-5700

(P-60)
WONDERFUL ORCHARDS LLC
Also Called: Wonderfulpistachiosandalmonds
13646 Highway 33, Lost Hills (93249-9719)
P.O. Box 400 (93249-0400)
PHONE..............................661 797-6400
Dennis Elam, *Branch Mgr*
Jason Hester, *Software Dev*
Tom Hazelof, *Sales Staff*
Pedro Salinas, *Manager*
EMP: 147
SALES (corp-wide): 2B **Privately Held**
WEB: www.wonderfulorchards.com
SIC: 0173 0191 Almond grove; general
farms, primarily crop
HQ: Wonderful Orchards Llc
6801 E Lerdo Hwy
Shafter CA 93263
661 399-4456

(P-61)
WONDERFUL ORCHARDS LLC
21707 Lerdo Hwy, Mc Kittrick (93251-9758)
PHONE..............................661 797-2509
Robert Baker, *Manager*
EMP: 147
SALES (corp-wide): 2B **Privately Held**
WEB: www.wonderfulorchards.com
SIC: 0173 0191 Almond grove; general
farms, primarily crop
HQ: Wonderful Orchards Llc
6801 E Lerdo Hwy
Shafter CA 93263
661 399-4456

0174 Citrus Fruits

(P-62)
EXETER PACKERS INC
Also Called: Sun Pacific Shippers
1095 E Green St, Pasadena (91106-2503)
PHONE..............................626 993-6245
Bob Reniers, *General Mgr*
Celine Benedict, *Executive Asst*
Morgan Parker, *Technology*
Michael N Perez, *Safety Mgr*
Louis De Lapaz, *Sales Staff*
EMP: 82
SALES (corp-wide): 75.1MM **Privately Held**
WEB: www.sunpacific.com
SIC: 0174 0172 0161 0723 Orange
grove; grapes; tomato farm; fruit (fresh)
packing services; vegetable packing serv-
ices; packaging materials
PA: Exeter Packers, Inc.
1250 E Myer Ave
Exeter CA 93221
559 592-5168

(P-63)
**HRONIS INC A CALIFORNIA
CORP (PA)**
10443 Hronis Rd, Delano (93215-9556)
PHONE..............................661 725-2503
Kosta Hronis, *President*
Pete Hronis, *Vice Pres*
Nick Hronis, *Sales Staff*
Chris Fierros, *Warehouse Mgr*
Sonia Ponce, *Manager*
▼ **EMP:** 143 **EST:** 1945
SQ FT: 150,000
SALES (est): 30.3MM **Privately Held**
WEB: www.hronis.net
SIC: 0174 0172 Citrus fruits; grapes

(P-64)
**JOHNSTON FARMS FMLY LTD
PARTNR**
13031 E Packinghouse Rd, Edison (93220)
PHONE..............................661 366-3201
Tari Johnston, *Principal*
Terry Henderson, *Principal*
Dennis B Johnston, *Principal*
Gerald Johnston, *Principal*
Kevin Johnston, *Principal*
◆ **EMP:** 65 **EST:** 1953
SQ FT: 100,000
SALES (est): 9.4MM **Privately Held**
WEB: www.johnstonfarms.com
SIC: 0174 0134 0161 Orange grove; Irish
potatoes; pepper farm, sweet & hot (veg-
etables)

(P-65)
SATICOY LEMON ASSOCIATION
Also Called: Saticoy Fruit Exchange
7560 Bristol Rd, Ventura (93003-7027)
P.O. Box 46, Santa Paula (93061-0046)
PHONE..............................805 654-6500
John Elliott, *Branch Mgr*
Juan Martinez, *Supervisor*
EMP: 35
SALES (corp-wide): 26.6MM **Privately
Held**
WEB: www.saticoylemon.com
SIC: 0174 Lemon grove
PA: Saticoy Lemon Association
103 N Peck Rd
Santa Paula CA 93060
805 654-6500

(P-66)
WONDERFUL CITRUS LLC (HQ)
1701 S Lexington St, Delano (93215-9200)
PHONE..............................661 720-2400
Craig B Cooper, *Mng Member*
EMP: 187 **EST:** 2011
SALES (est): 81.9MM
SALES (corp-wide): 2B **Privately Held**
WEB: www.wonderfulcitrus.com
SIC: 0174 Citrus fruits
PA: The Wonderful Company Llc
11444 W Olympic Blvd # 210
Los Angeles CA 90064
310 966-5700

(P-67)
WONDERFUL COMPANY LLC
Also Called: Paramount Citrus
1901 S Lexington St, Delano (93215-9207)
PHONE..............................661 720-2400
Freddie Hernandez, *Manager*
Stacy Jaffa, *Senior Mgr*
Barbara Mock, *Director*
EMP: 273
SALES (corp-wide): 2B **Privately Held**
WEB: www.wonderful.com
SIC: 0174 3911 Citrus fruits; jewelry, pre-
cious metal
PA: The Wonderful Company Llc
11444 W Olympic Blvd # 210
Los Angeles CA 90064
310 966-5700

0179 Fruits & Tree Nuts, NEC

(P-68)
C C GRABER CO
Also Called: Graber Olive House
315 E 4th St, Ontario (91764-2709)
P.O. Box 511 (91762-8511)
PHONE..............................909 983-1761
Clifford C Graber II, *President*
Robert D Graber, *Ch of Bd*
Mary E Graber, *Vice Pres*
EMP: 27 **EST:** 1894
SQ FT: 10,000
SALES (est): 3.3MM **Privately Held**
WEB: www.graberolives.com
SIC: 0179 5947 2033 2032 Olive grove;
artcraft & carvings; canned fruits & spe-
cialties; canned specialties

(P-69)
**DOLE FOOD COMPANY INC
(HQ)**
1 Dole Dr, Westlake Village (91362-7300)
PHONE..............................818 874-4000
David Murdock, *Ch of Bd*
Johan Linden, *President*
Johan Malmqvist, *CFO*
Yoon Hugh, *Senior VP*
Charlene Mims, *Senior VP*
◆ **EMP:** 596 **EST:** 1851
SALES (est): 1B **Privately Held**
WEB: www.dole.com
SIC: 0179 0161 0175 0174 Pineapple
farm; banana grove; lettuce farm; celery
farm; cauliflower farm; broccoli farm; de-
ciduous tree fruits; citrus fruits; fruit juices:
fresh; fruit juices: packaged in cans, jars,
etc.; fruits; vegetables

(P-70)
DOLE HOLDING COMPANY LLC
1 Dole Dr, Westlake Village (91362-7300)
PHONE..............................818 879-6600

David H Murdock, *Ch of Bd*
EMP: 74999 **EST:** 2004
SALES (est): 57.6MM **Privately Held**
SIC: 0179 0174 0175 0161 Pineapple
farm; citrus fruits; deciduous tree fruits;
lettuce farm; fruits; fruit juices: fresh
PA: Dhm Holding Company, Inc.
1 Dole Dr
Westlake Village CA 91362

(P-71)
MUNGER BROS LLC
Also Called: Munger Farm
786 Road 188, Delano (93215-9508)
PHONE..............................661 721-0390
Baldev K Munger,
Kewel K Munger,
Rick Smith, *Director*
Matt Hoezee, *Manager*
Jose Saldana, *Manager*
▲ **EMP:** 600 **EST:** 1998
SQ FT: 50,000
SALES (est): 34.2MM **Privately Held**
SIC: 0179 2033 Avocado orchard; canned
fruits & specialties

0181 Ornamental Floriculture & Nursery Prdts

(P-72)
A-G SOD FARMS INC
Also Called: Addink Turf
2900 Adams St Ste C120, Riverside
(92504-8317)
PHONE..............................951 687-7581
Sonya Dawe, *Enginr/R&D Mgr*
EMP: 78
SALES (corp-wide): 16.8MM **Privately
Held**
WEB: www.agsod.com
SIC: 0181 Sod farms
PA: A-G Sod Farms, Inc.
2900 Adams St Ste C120
Riverside CA 92504
951 687-7581

(P-73)
BLX GROUP INC
71534 Sahara Rd, Rancho Mirage
(92270-4340)
PHONE..............................760 776-6622
EMP: 95
SALES (est): 2MM **Privately Held**
SIC: 0181 Ornamental Nursery

(P-74)
BROKAW NURSERY LLC
5501 Elizabeth Rd, Ventura (93004-1002)
P.O. Box 4818 (93007-0818)
PHONE..............................805 647-2262
Ellen Brokaw, *President*
Kay Mendel, *CFO*
Robert C Brokaw, *Vice Pres*
Marge Apodaca, *Principal*
Consuelo Fernandez, *Research*
EMP: 52 **EST:** 1956
SQ FT: 5,000
SALES (est): 7.9MM **Privately Held**
WEB: www.brokawnursery.com
SIC: 0181 0179 Nursery stock, growing of;
avocado orchard

(P-75)
DLT GROWERS INC
13131 S Bon View Ave, Ontario
(91761-8226)
PHONE..............................909 947-8198
Jaime Delatorre, *President*
Ricardo Delatorre, *Vice Pres*
EMP: 50 **EST:** 1988
SQ FT: 400
SALES (est): 4MM **Privately Held**
WEB: www.dltgrowers.com
SIC: 0181 5193 Nursery stock, growing of;
flowers & nursery stock

(P-76)
**FLORAL GIFT HM DECOR INTL
INC**
3200 Golf Course Dr Ste B, Ventura
(93003-7615)
P.O. Box 2673, Camarillo (93011-2673)
PHONE..............................818 849-8832

Dolly Ives, *CEO*
Edwin M Ives, *President*
▲ **EMP:** 25 **EST:** 1973
SALES (est): 2MM **Privately Held**
SIC: 0181 3999 Florists' greens cultivated:
growing of; foliage, artificial & preserved

(P-77)
GLAD-A-WAY GARDENS NC
2669 E Clark Ave, Santa Maria
(93455-5815)
P.O. Box 2550 (93457-2550)
PHONE..............................805 938-0569
Brian Caird, *President*
Lance Runels, *Vice Pres*
Erin Caird, *Admin Sec*
Lorena Nol, *Manager*
▲ **EMP:** 172 **EST:** 1964
SQ FT: 15,000
SALES (est): 16.3MM **Privately Held**
WEB: www.gladaway.com
SIC: 0181 Flowers: grown under cover
(e.g. greenhouse production)

(P-78)
**GRAND VIEW GERANIUM
GRDNS INC**
18307 Central Ave, Carson (90746-4017)
PHONE..............................310 217-0490
Fax: 310 217-0536
EMP: 60
SQ FT: 2,500
SALES (est): 3.2MM **Privately Held**
WEB: www.gvgeranium.com
SIC: 0181 Ornamental Nursery

(P-79)
HINES GROWERS INC
27368 Via Industria # 201, Temecula
(92590-4856)
PHONE..............................800 554-4065
▲ **EMP:** 430 **EST:** 2012
SALES (est): 711.7K
SALES (corp-wide): 229.5MM **Privately
Held**
SIC: 0181 5261 Ornamental nursery prod-
ucts; nurseries & garden centers
HQ: Csn Winddown, Inc.
27368 Via Industria # 201
Temecula CA 92590

(P-80)
JIMENEZ NURSERY INC
Also Called: Jimenez Nursery and Land-
scapes
3800 Via Real, Carpinteria (93013-3051)
P.O. Box 2460, Santa Barbara (93120-
2460)
PHONE..............................805 684-7955
Manuel Jimenez, *CEO*
Alicia Jimenez, *Treasurer*
Sela Jimenez, *Admin Asst*
Imelda Jimenez, *Human Resources*
Marta Reynoso, *Manager*
EMP: 100 **EST:** 1996
SALES (est): 6.8MM **Privately Held**
WEB: www.jimeneznursery.com
SIC: 0181 Nursery stock, growing of

(P-81)
L E COOKE CO
26333 Road 140, Visalia 93292-9452)
PHONE..............................559 732-9146
David Henry Cox, *CEO*
Ron Ludekens, *President*
Patti Agnew, *Department Mgr*
Phillip Cox, *Admin Mgr*
Rosie Frias, *Sales Mgr*
▲ **EMP:** 200 **EST:** 1944
SQ FT: 6,000
SALES (est): 10.3MM **Privately Held**
WEB: www.lecooke.com
SIC: 0181 Nursery stock, growing of

(P-82)
LA VERNE NURSERY INC
3653 Center St, Piru (93040-8051)
P.O. Box 410 (93040-0410)
PHONE..............................805 521-0111
Richard Wilson, *CEO*
EMP: 90 **EST:** 1980
SQ FT: 16,000

SALES (est): 4.8MM **Privately Held**
WEB: www.lavernenursery.com
SIC: 0181 Nursery stock, growing of; fruit stocks, growing of

(P-83)
LUMBER CITY CORP
Also Called: Do It Center
2695 Cochran St, Simi Valley (93065-2664)
PHONE.................................805 522-0533
Mike McKenzie, *Manager*
Lori Westhoff, *Merchandising*
EMP: 55
SALES (corp-wide): 72.8MM **Privately Held**
WEB: www.doitbest.com
SIC: 5251 5211 0181 Hardware; lumber & other building materials; ornamental nursery products
PA: Lumber City Corp.
20525 Nordhoff St Ste 210
Chatsworth CA 91311
818 407-3888

(P-84)
MARATHON LAND INC
2599 E Hueneme Rd, Oxnard (93033-8112)
P.O. Box 579, Port Hueneme (93044-0579)
PHONE.................................805 488-3585
Jurgen Gramckow, *President*
EMP: 130 **EST:** 1977
SQ FT: 3,000
SALES (est): 5.7MM **Privately Held**
WEB: www.sod.com
SIC: 0181 Sod farms

(P-85)
MONROVIA NURSERY COMPANY (PA)
Also Called: Monrovia Growes
817 E Monrovia Pl, Azusa (91702-6297)
P.O. Box 1385 (91702-1385)
PHONE.................................626 334-9321
Miles R Rosedale, *CEO*
William B Usrey, *President*
Richard Van Landinghan, *President*
Steve Thigpen, *COO*
Dennis Conner, *Vice Pres*
▲ **EMP:** 567
SQ FT: 50,000
SALES (est): 436.6MM **Privately Held**
WEB: www.monrovia.com
SIC: 0181 5193 5261 Nursery stock, growing of; flowers & florists' supplies; nurseries & garden centers

(P-86)
MULROSES USA INC
741 S San Pedro St, Los Angeles (90014-2417)
PHONE.................................213 489-1761
Patricio Nasser, *Manager*
EMP: 100 **EST:** 2010
SALES (est): 3.3MM **Privately Held**
SIC: 0181 Roses, growing of

(P-87)
NORMANS NURSERY INC
5770 Casitas Pass Rd, Carpinteria (93013-3061)
PHONE.................................805 684-1411
Martin Manzo, *Manager*
Barbara Hayes, *Opers Staff*
EMP: 210
SALES (corp-wide): 95.8MM **Privately Held**
WEB: www.normansnursery.com
SIC: 0181 Nursery stock, growing of
PA: Norman's Nursery, Inc.
8665 Duarte Rd
San Gabriel CA 91775
626 285-9795

(P-88)
OCEAN BREEZE INTERNATIONAL
Also Called: Mobis Wholesale
3910 Via Real, Carpinteria (93013-1266)
PHONE.................................805 684-1747
Rene Van Wingerden, *President*
June Van Wingerden, *Vice Pres*
▲ **EMP:** 60 **EST:** 1974
SQ FT: 900,000

SALES (est): 9.1MM **Privately Held**
SIC: 0181 Flowers: grown under cover (e.g. greenhouse production)

(P-89)
PACIFIC EARTH RESOURCES (PA)
Also Called: Pacific Sd/Pcfic Arbor Nrsries
305 Hueneme Rd, Camarillo (93012-8522)
PHONE.................................805 986-8277
Richard Rogers, *Owner*
Elizabeth Rogers, *Partner*
Irma Mullaley, *Director*
EMP: 80 **EST:** 1958
SQ FT: 8,000
SALES (est): 24.1MM **Privately Held**
SIC: 0181 Sod farms; nursery stock, growing of

(P-90)
PACIFIC ERTH RSRCES LTD A CAL
Also Called: Pacific Sod
315 Hueneme Rd, Camarillo (93012-8522)
PHONE.................................209 892-3000
Raymond Freitas, *Manager*
Rhoda Meyer, *Human Res Mgr*
EMP: 90
SALES (corp-wide): 24.1MM **Privately Held**
SIC: 0181 Sod farms
PA: Pacific Earth Resources, Ltd., A California Limited Partnership
305 Hueneme Rd
Camarillo CA 93012
805 986-8277

(P-91)
PLANTEL NURSERIES INC (PA)
Also Called: Plantel Tranplanting Services
2775 E Clark Ave, Santa Maria (93455-5813)
PHONE.................................805 349-8952
Scott Nicholson, *President*
Les Graulich, *Treasurer*
Craig Reade, *Vice Pres*
EMP: 20 **EST:** 1985
SQ FT: 1,300,000
SALES (est): 19.3MM **Privately Held**
WEB: www.plantelnurseries.com
SIC: 0181 5193 3523 Seeds, vegetable: growing of; nursery stock; transplanters

(P-92)
PLANTEL NURSERIES INC
3990 Foxen Canyon Rd, Santa Maria (93454-9666)
PHONE.................................805 934-4300
Gerald Tonascia, *Manager*
Shane Sanchez, *Maintence Staff*
Lynn Leube, *Manager*
Carmen Valencia, *Manager*
Pedro Sotelo, *Supervisor*
EMP: 172
SALES (corp-wide): 19.3MM **Privately Held**
WEB: www.plantelnurseries.com
SIC: 0181 5193 Seeds, vegetable: growing of; nursery stock
PA: Plantel Nurseries Inc
2775 E Clark Ave
Santa Maria CA 93455
805 349-8952

(P-93)
PYRAMID FLOWERS INC
3813 Doris Ave, Oxnard (93030-4706)
PHONE.................................805 382-8070
Fred Van Wingerden, *President*
Edith Van Wingerden, *Vice Pres*
Marcos Van Wingerden, *Prdtn Mgr*
▲ **EMP:** 120 **EST:** 1991
SQ FT: 900,000
SALES (est): 16MM **Privately Held**
WEB: www.pyramidflowers.com
SIC: 0181 Flowers grown in field nurseries

(P-94)
RICHARD WILSON WELLINGTON
Also Called: Colorama Wholesale Nursery
1025 N Todd Ave, Azusa (91702-1602)
P.O. Box 1328, Glendora (91740-1328)
PHONE.................................626 812-7881
Richard Wilson, *Owner*

Terry Wilson, *Financial Exec*
Phillip Sanchez, *Manager*
▲ **EMP:** 100 **EST:** 1984
SQ FT: 70,000
SALES (est): 9.6MM **Privately Held**
WEB: www.coloramanursery.com
SIC: 0181 5193 Nursery stock, growing of; nursery stock

(P-95)
RIVER RIDGE FARMS INC
3135 Los Angeles Ave, Oxnard (93036-1010)
PHONE.................................805 647-6880
Rieuwert Jan Vis, *President*
▲ **EMP:** 95 **EST:** 1992
SQ FT: 440
SALES (est): 13.8MM **Privately Held**
WEB: www.riverridgefarms.net
SIC: 0181 5193 Flowers grown in field nurseries; flowers: grown under cover (e.g. greenhouse production); plants, potted

(P-96)
SUPERIOR SOD I LP
17821 17th St Ste 165, Tustin (92780-2172)
P.O. Box 1911, Tehachapi (93581-5911)
PHONE.................................909 923-5068
Michael Considine, *Partner*
Richard H Considine, *Partner*
Trudy Considine, *Partner*
Peter Moore, *Partner*
EMP: 125 **EST:** 1988
SQ FT: 1,400
SALES (est): 7.9MM **Privately Held**
WEB: www.superiorsod.com
SIC: 0181 0782 Sod farms; lawn & garden services

(P-97)
WEST COAST TURF (PA)
42540 Melanie Pl, Palm Desert (92211-5127)
P.O. Box 4563 (92261-4563)
PHONE.................................760 340-7300
John M Foster, *President*
Joe Foster, *Vice Pres*
Natina Coloring, *Products*
EMP: 50 **EST:** 1990
SQ FT: 2,000
SALES (est): 19.2MM **Privately Held**
WEB: www.westcoastturf.com
SIC: 0181 Sod farms

(P-98)
WESTERLAY ORCHIDS LP
3504 Via Real, Carpinteria (93013-3048)
PHONE.................................805 684-5411
Antoine Overgaag, *President*
Darlene Gonzales, *Human Res Mgr*
Ray Rodarte, *Opers Mgr*
Tanner Allen, *Manager*
▲ **EMP:** 117 **EST:** 2003
SALES (est): 8.4MM **Privately Held**
WEB: www.westerlayorchids.com
SIC: 0181 Flowers grown in field nurseries

0182 Food Crops Grown Under Cover

(P-99)
CHANNEL ISLNDS VGTBLE FRMS INC (PA)
595 Victoria Ave, Oxnard (93030-4710)
PHONE.................................805 984-1910
Steve Nishimori, *President*
Karen Nishimori, *Vice Pres*
EMP: 60 **EST:** 1994
SQ FT: 2,000
SALES (est): 3.8MM **Privately Held**
SIC: 0182 Vegetable crops grown under cover

(P-100)
NORTH SHORE GREENHOUSES INC
Also Called: North Shore Living Herbs
82900 Johnson St, Thermal (92274-9319)
PHONE.................................760 397-0400
Leonardus Overgaag, *President*
Omar Felix, *President*

Suzette Overgaag, *Vice Pres*
Carli Buehler, *Technology*
▲ **EMP:** 105 **EST:** 1987
SALES (est): 15MM **Privately Held**
WEB: www.northshore.farm
SIC: 0182 Food crops grown under cover

0191 Crop Farming, Misc

(P-101)
BLACKJACK FRMS DE LA CSTA CNTL
Also Called: Black Jack Farms
2385 A St, Santa Maria (93455-1073)
PHONE.................................805 347-1333
Jose Garcia, *CEO*
Pat Iniguez, *Administration*
EMP: 140 **EST:** 2017
SALES (est): 3.8MM **Privately Held**
SIC: 0191 General farms, primarily crop

(P-102)
CENTRAL COAST AGRICULTURE INC (PA)
8701 Santa Rosa Rd, Buellton (93427-8406)
PHONE.................................805 694-8594
John De Friel, *CEO*
Shannon Izydorek, *Executive Asst*
Dawn Gabrielson, *Senior Buyer*
Matt Limon, *Mfg Staff*
Khalid Al-Naser, *Marketing Staff*
EMP: 69 **EST:** 2015
SALES (est): 18.3MM **Privately Held**
WEB: www.ccagriculture.com
SIC: 0191 2099 General farms, primarily crop; food preparations

(P-103)
CRYSTAL ORGANIC FARMS LLC
6900 Mountain View Rd, Bakersfield (93307-9627)
PHONE.................................661 845-5200
Jeff Meger, *President*
EMP: 1210 **EST:** 2003
SALES (est): 1.6MM
SALES (corp-wide): 1.8B **Privately Held**
WEB: www.grimmway.com
SIC: 0191 General farms, primarily crop
PA: Grimmway Enterprises, Inc.
14141 Di Giorgio Rd
Arvin CA 93203
800 301-3101

(P-104)
D M CAMP & SONS (PA)
4520 E Merced Ave, Bakersfield (93308-9747)
P.O. Box 80007 (93380-0007)
PHONE.................................661 399-5511
D M Camp Jr, *Partner*
Clayton P Camp, *Partner*
Edwin A Camp, *Partner*
EMP: 66 **EST:** 1961
SQ FT: 1,500
SALES (est): 14.1MM **Privately Held**
WEB: www.dmcamp.com
SIC: 0191 General farms, primarily crop

(P-105)
DV CUSTOM FARMING LLC
2101 Mettler Frontage E, Bakersfield (93307-9649)
PHONE.................................661 858-2888
Donald J Valpredo, *Owner*
EMP: 80 **EST:** 2004
SALES (est): 1.9MM **Privately Held**
SIC: 0191 General farms, primarily crop

(P-106)
EARTHRISE NUTRITIONALS LLC (HQ)
2151 Michelson Dr Ste 262, Irvine (92612-1374)
PHONE.................................949 623-0980
Amha Belay,
Rebecca Deal, *Human Res Mgr*
Antonio Flores, *Production*
Ichi Kato,
Lilia De La Cruz, *Manager*
▲ **EMP:** 25 **EST:** 1981

PRODUCTS & SVCS

SALES (est): 24MM **Privately Held**
WEB: www.earthrise.com
SIC: 0191 2099 2834 General farms, primarily crop; food preparations; pharmaceutical preparations

(P-107)
GREENHEART FARMS INC
902 Zenon Way, Arroyo Grande (93420-5807)
PHONE.............805 481-2234
Hoy Buell, *CEO*
Grace Duran, *CFO*
Leo Wolf, *Treasurer*
Henry Katzenstein, *Vice Pres*
Jeanie Haupt, *Business Dir*
▲ **EMP:** 350 **EST:** 1979
SQ FT: 225,000
SALES (est): 33.1MM **Privately Held**
WEB: www.greenheartfarms.com
SIC: 0191 General farms, primarily crop

(P-108)
GRIMMWAY ENTERPRISES INC
Also Called: Premiere Packing
6301 Zerker Rd, Shafter (93263-9628)
P.O. Box 81498, Bakersfield (93380-1498)
PHONE.............661 399-0844
Randy Mower, *Vice Pres*
EMP: 145
SALES (corp-wide): 1.8B **Privately Held**
WEB: www.grimmway.com
SIC: 0191 0174 General farms, primarily crop; citrus fruits
PA: Grimmway Enterprises, Inc.
14141 Di Giorgio Rd
Arvin CA 93203
800 301-3101

(P-109)
HANSEN RANCHES
7124 Whitley Ave, Corcoran (93212-9669)
P.O. Box 398 (93212-0398)
PHONE.............559 992-3111
James Hansen, *Partner*
Nis Hansen, *Director*
EMP: 60 **EST:** 1987
SQ FT: 4,000
SALES (est): 4.4MM **Privately Held**
WEB: www.hansenranches.com
SIC: 0191 General farms, primarily crop

(P-110)
HERITAGE FARMS LLC (PA)
2309 E Us Highway 98, Holtville (92250-9543)
PHONE.............442 283-5145
Jennifer Reynolds, *Principal*
EMP: 61 **EST:** 2015
SALES (est): 2.1MM **Privately Held**
WEB: www.heritagefarmsllc.com
SIC: 0191 General farms, primarily crop

(P-111)
INNOVATIVE PRODUCE INC
1615 W Main St, Santa Maria (93458-9737)
P.O. Box 1952 (93456-1952)
PHONE.............805 349-2714
George J Adam, *President*
Deborah Adam, *Vice Pres*
Chris Wallin, *General Mgr*
Jose Ruiz, *Opers Mgr*
Lacy Litten, *Opers Staff*
EMP: 50 **EST:** 2008
SQ FT: 10,000
SALES (est): 8.7MM **Privately Held**
WEB: www.innovativeproduce.com
SIC: 0191 General farms, primarily crop

(P-112)
JAKOV DULCICH AND SONS LLC
31956 Peterson Rd, Mc Farland (93250-9606)
PHONE.............661 792-6360
Jakov Dulcich, *Owner*
Jon Thomas, *CFO*
Delia Armstrong, *Executive*
Mayra Contreas, *Executive*
Nick Dulcich, *Executive*
▲ **EMP:** 250 **EST:** 1963
SALES (est): 14.6MM **Privately Held**
WEB: www.dulcich.com
SIC: 0191 General farms, primarily crop

(P-113)
JOE HEGER FARMS LLC
1625 Drew Rd, El Centro (92243-9584)
PHONE.............760 353-5111
Joe Heger,
EMP: 150 **EST:** 1999
SALES (est): 9.4MM **Privately Held**
SIC: 0191 General farms, primarily crop

(P-114)
KIRSCHENMAN ENTERPRISES INC
10100 Digiorgio Rd, Bakersfield (93307)
PHONE.............661 366-5736
Wayne Kirschenman, *CEO*
Norma Rapp, *Treasurer*
▼ **EMP:** 60 **EST:** 1963
SQ FT: 25,000
SALES (est): 10.7MM **Privately Held**
WEB: www.kirschenman.com
SIC: 0191 General farms, primarily crop

(P-115)
MURANAKA FARM
11018 W Los Angeles Ave, Moorpark (93021-9744)
P.O. Box 189 (93020-0189)
PHONE.............805 529-0201
Greg EMI, *President*
EMP: 237
SALES (corp-wide): 26.4MM **Privately Held**
WEB: www.muranakafarm.com
SIC: 0191 General farms, primarily crop
PA: Muranaka Farm
11018 E Los Angeles Ave
Moorpark CA 93021
805 529-0201

(P-116)
OLD TIME FARMING INC (PA)
1141 Tama Ln, Santa Maria (93455-1127)
PHONE.............805 349-3886
Juan Cardenas, *CEO*
Graciela Cardenas, *Vice Pres*
Maria Villapando, *Administration*
EMP: 108 **EST:** 2020
SALES (est): 3.3MM **Privately Held**
SIC: 0191 General farms, primarily crop

(P-117)
RANCHO LAGUNA FARMS LLC
2410 W Main St, Santa Maria (93458-9712)
P.O. Box 6617 (93456-6617)
PHONE.............805 925-7805
Larry Ferini, *Mng Member*
Tracy Ferini,
EMP: 100 **EST:** 1996
SALES (est): 10.4MM **Privately Held**
WEB: www.lagunaproduce.com
SIC: 0191 General farms, primarily crop

(P-118)
SCARBOROUGH FARMS INC
731 Pacific Ave, Oxnard (93030-7322)
P.O. Box 1267 (93032-1267)
PHONE.............805 483-9113
Ann Stein, *President*
Wayne G Jansen, *President*
Christina Gonzalez, *Sales Mgr*
Clay Barbosa, *Manager*
EMP: 150 **EST:** 1986
SALES (est): 13MM **Privately Held**
WEB: www.scarboroughfarms.com
SIC: 0191 General farms, primarily crop

(P-119)
SUN WORLD INTERNATIONAL LLC (HQ)
5701 Truxtun Ave Ste 200, Bakersfield (93309-0651)
P.O. Box 80298 (93380-0298)
PHONE.............661 392-5000
David Marguleas, *CEO*
David Hostetter, *CFO*
Keith Mitchell, *CFO*
Andrew Simpson, *Exec VP*
Michael J Aiton, *Senior VP*
▲ **EMP:** 449 **EST:** 2005
SALES (est): 34.2MM **Privately Held**
WEB: www.sun-world.com
SIC: 0191 General farms, primarily crop

(P-120)
THOMPSON FAMILY FARMS LLC
16478 Beach Blvd, Ste 391, Westminster (92683-7860)
PHONE.............714 848-7536
EMP: 50
SALES (est): 665.5K **Privately Held**
SIC: 0191 General Farms, Primarily Crop

(P-121)
THOMSON INTERNATIONAL INC
11220 S Vineland Rd, Bakersfield (93307-9489)
PHONE.............661 845-1111
Jack Thomson, *President*
EMP: 16
SALES (corp-wide): 4.5MM **Privately Held**
WEB: www.thomsoninternational.net
SIC: 0191 2099 0723 0172 General farms, primarily crop; food preparations; crop preparation services for market; grapes; vegetables & melons
PA: Thomson International, Incorporated
9852 Buena Vista Blvd
Bakersfield CA 93307
661 845-1166

(P-122)
TOOR FARMING LLC
27725 Road 92, Visalia (93277-9481)
PHONE.............559 500-1331
Arpinder Toor,
Bitta Toor, *Principal*
Santokh Toor, *Mng Member*
▲ **EMP:** 70 **EST:** 2001
SALES (est): 36.4MM **Privately Held**
SIC: 0191 General farms, primarily crop

0211 Beef Cattle Feedlots

(P-123)
BRANDT CO INC
Also Called: Brandt Cattle
7015 Brandt Rd, Calipatria (92233-9761)
PHONE.............760 348-2295
William Brent, *Manager*
EMP: 53
SALES (corp-wide): 11.7MM **Privately Held**
WEB: www.brandtbeef.com
SIC: 0211 0139 Beef cattle feedlots; alfalfa farm; grass seed farm
PA: Brandt Co., Inc.
299 W Main St
Brawley CA 92227
760 344-3430

(P-124)
MESQUITE CATTLE FEEDERS INC
1504 Us Highway 78, Brawley (92227-9429)
P.O. Box 1025 (92227-1025)
PHONE.............760 344-2944
Frank Irigoyen, *CEO*
Paul Cameron, *President*
Robert Presley, *Corp Secy*
Gregory Braun, *Vice Pres*
EMP: 50 **EST:** 1996
SALES (est): 6MM **Privately Held**
SIC: 0211 Beef cattle feedlots

(P-125)
MOIOLA BROS CTTLE FDERS LTD A
Also Called: Moiola Bros Cattle Feeders
1594 Gonder Rd, Brawley (92227-9533)
PHONE.............760 344-1919
James Moiola, *Managing Prtnr*
Tom Moiola, *Partner*
EMP: 59 **EST:** 1945
SALES (est): 3.1MM **Privately Held**
WEB: www.moiolabros.com
SIC: 0211 Beef cattle feedlots

(P-126)
SUPERIOR CATTLE FEEDERS LLC (PA)
551 S Industrial Ave, Calipatria (92233)
P.O. Box 1828 (92233-1828)
PHONE.............760 348-2218

Dmingue Antchagno,
Robert A Lofton,
EMP: 54 **EST:** 1996
SALES (est): 3.9MM **Privately Held**
SIC: 0211 Beef cattle feedlots

0212 Beef Cattle, Except Feedlots

(P-127)
BIDART BROS (PA)
Also Called: Bidart Bros Land & Development
4805 Centennial Plaza Way # 100, Bakersfield (93312-1925)
PHONE.............661 832-2447
Leonard A Bidart, *CEO*
John Bidart Jr, *Vice Pres*
Robert Sullivan, *Vice Pres*
Crystal Martin, *Clerk*
EMP: 147 **EST:** 1946
SQ FT: 20,000
SALES (est): 10.3MM **Privately Held**
WEB: www.bidartapplerecall.com
SIC: 0212 0191 Beef cattle except feedlots; general farms, primarily crop

(P-128)
J G BOSWELL COMPANY
26073 Santa Fe Ave, Corcoran (93212)
P.O. Box 877 (93212-0877)
PHONE.............559 992-5011
Mark Grewal, *Vice Pres*
Stacy Martin-Mcnabb, *Human Res Mgr*
EMP: 73
SALES (corp-wide): 370.2MM **Privately Held**
WEB: www.eastlakeco.com
SIC: 0212 Beef cattle except feedlots
PA: J. G. Boswell Company
101 W Walnut St
Pasadena CA 91103
626 583-3000

0214 Sheep & Goats

(P-129)
ETCHEGARAY FARMS LLC
32324 Famoso Rd, Mc Farland (93250)
P.O. Box 964, Visalia (93273-0964)
PHONE.............661 393-0920
Sam Etchegaray,
Sam Etcegaray, *General Mgr*
EMP: 50 **EST:** 1985
SQ FT: 8,000
SALES (est): 5.5MM **Privately Held**
SIC: 0214 0172 0179 0174 Lamb feedlot; grapes; avocado orchard; grapefruit grove

0241 Dairy Farms

(P-130)
ALTA-DENA CERTIFIED DAIRY LLC (DH)
17637 E Valley Blvd, City of Industry (91744-5731)
PHONE.............626 964-6401
John Keith,
Jack Tewers, *CFO*
Bob Pettigrew, *Vice Pres*
Steve Schaffer, *General Mgr*
Carl Reynolds, *Purch Mgr*
EMP: 370 **EST:** 1945
SQ FT: 100,000
SALES (est): 98MM **Publicly Held**
SIC: 0241 Dairy farms

(P-131)
BOSMAN DAIRY LLC
6802 Avenue 120 A, Tipton (93272-9525)
PHONE.............559 752-7018
Clarence Bosman, *Partner*
Frank Bosman, *Partner*
EMP: 130 **EST:** 1959
SALES (est): 17.9MM **Privately Held**
SIC: 0241 Dairy farms

(P-132)
FERN OAKS FRMS A CAL GEN PRTNR
17001 Avenue 160, Porterville (93257-9258)
PHONE.................................559 684-8220
Greg Fernandes, *Partner*
Gregory Fernandes, *Partner*
EMP: 50 EST: 2017
SQ FT: 3,000
SALES (est): 1.2MM **Privately Held**
SIC: 0241 Milk production

(P-133)
HIGH PLAINS RANCH LLC (PA)
2911 Hanford Armona Rd, Hanford (93230-9379)
PHONE.................................559 583-1277
Bernard Te Velde, *Mng Member*
EMP: 120 EST: 2014
SQ FT: 2,000
SALES (est): 8.4MM **Privately Held**
SIC: 0241 Dairy farms

(P-134)
MAPLE DAIRY LP
15857 Bear Mountain Blvd, Bakersfield (93311-9413)
PHONE.................................661 396-9600
John Bos, *Partner*
A J Bos, *Partner*
EMP: 75 EST: 1998
SALES (est): 15.5MM **Privately Held**
WEB: www.makinmilk.com
SIC: 0241 Dairy farms

(P-135)
NIELSENS CREAMERY (PA)
Also Called: Hoffman Farms
21346 Road 140, Tulare (93274-9363)
P.O. Box 579 (93275-0579)
PHONE.................................559 686-4744
Chase Hoffman, *Partner*
Marion N Hoffman, *Partner*
Jodi Chandler, *Office Mgr*
Dan Orozco, *Engineer*
EMP: 50 EST: 1968
SQ FT: 11,000
SALES (est): 2.2MM **Privately Held**
WEB: www.hoffmange.com
SIC: 0241 Milk production

(P-136)
ROBERT D VANDEREYK
Also Called: Robert Vander Eyk & Sons Dairy
9441 Avenue 104, Pixley (93256-9694)
PHONE.................................559 909-3195
Robert Vander Eyk, *Partner*
EMP: 65
SQ FT: 10,000
SALES (corp-wide): 844.4K **Privately Held**
SIC: 0241 Dairy farms
PA: Robert D Vandereyk
    9441 Avenue 104
    Pixley CA 93256
    559 909-3195

(P-137)
ROCKVIEW FARMS INC
Also Called: Pond Heifer Ranch
11695 Jumper Ave, Wasco (93280-9577)
PHONE.................................661 792-3583
Amos De Groot, *President*
Eric Goedhart, *Vice Pres*
EMP: 51 EST: 1986
SQ FT: 500
SALES (est): 5.7MM
SALES (corp-wide): 70.7MM **Privately Held**
WEB: www.rockviewfarms.com
SIC: 0241 0139 Dairy heifer replacement farm; alfalfa farm
PA: Rockview Dairies, Inc.
    7011 Stewart And Gray Rd
    Downey CA 90241
    562 927-5511

(P-138)
SUNRISE FOOD SERVICE INC
Also Called: Sunrise Dairy
2307 E 49th St, Vernon (90058-2820)
PHONE.................................323 264-8364
Istvan Kodo, *CEO*
EMP: 59 EST: 2004

SALES (est): 1.8MM **Privately Held**
WEB: www.sunrisefoodservice.com
SIC: 0241 Dairy farms

0252 Chicken Egg Farms

(P-139)
FOSTER FARMS LLC
770 N Plano St, Porterville (93257-6329)
PHONE.................................559 793-5501
Paul Bravinder, *Manager*
Tom Farrell, *Plant Mgr*
Dave Gilpin, *Manager*
Claudia Ramos, *Manager*
EMP: 30
SQ FT: 81,000 **Privately Held**
WEB: www.fosterfarms.com
SIC: 0252 2015 Chicken eggs; poultry slaughtering & processing
PA: Foster Farms, Llc
    1000 Davis St
    Livingston CA 95334

0279 Animal Specialties, NEC

(P-140)
HONEY ISABELLS INC
Also Called: Isabell's Honey Farm
539 N Glenoaks Blvd # 207, Burbank (91502-3201)
PHONE.................................800 708-8485
Oganes Kabakchuzyan, *CEO*
EMP: 46 EST: 2019
SALES (est): 2.5MM **Privately Held**
WEB: www.isabellshoneyfarm.com
SIC: 0279 2099 Apiary (bee & honey farm); honey, strained & bottled

---

0291 Animal Production, NEC

(P-141)
E & T FOODS INC
Also Called: Monrovia Ranch Market
14827 Seventh St, Victorville (92395-4023)
P.O. Box 661912, Arcadia (91066-1912)
PHONE.................................760 843-7730
Franco Duenas, *Branch Mgr*
EMP: 330 **Privately Held**
SIC: 0291 General farms, primarily animals
PA: E & T Foods, Inc.
    328 W Huntington Dr
    Monrovia CA 91016

(P-142)
ISLES RANCH PARTNERS (PA)
26 Corporate Plaza Dr # 200, Newport Beach (92660-7971)
PHONE.................................949 383-2354
Tom Orradre, *Partner*
Tom B Orradre, *Partner*
Christopher A Shiota, *Vice Pres*
Aimee Martin, *Managing Dir*
Robert Shiota, *Managing Dir*
EMP: 51 EST: 2013
SALES (est): 1.7MM **Privately Held**
SIC: 0291 General farms, primarily animals

(P-143)
LAGUNA BCH GOLF BNGLOW VLG LLC
Also Called: Ranch At Laguna Beach, The
31106 Coast Hwy, Laguna Beach (92651-8130)
PHONE.................................949 499-2271
Mark Christy, *Principal*
Kurt Bjorkman, *General Mgr*
Johnny Sanabria, *Asst Controller*
Lisa Rosecrans, *Human Resources*
Caitlin Curry, *Mktg Dir*
EMP: 50 EST: 2013
SALES (est): 5.8MM **Privately Held**
WEB: www.theranchlb.com
SIC: 0291 General farms, primarily animals

(P-144)
NORCO RANCH INC (DH)
12005 Cabernet Dr, Fontana (92337-7703)
P.O. Box 910, Norco (92860-0917)
PHONE.................................951 737-6735

Ric Sundal, *CEO*
EMP: 350 EST: 1951
SQ FT: 120,000
SALES (est): 30.6MM
SALES (corp-wide): 2.8B **Privately Held**
WEB: www.norcorancheggs.com
SIC: 0291 General farms, primarily animals
HQ: Moark, Llc
    28 Under The Mountain Rd
    North Franklin CT 06254
    951 332-3300

(P-145)
R RANCH MARKET
1112 Walnut Ave, Tustin (92780-5607)
PHONE.................................714 573-1182
Jubira Martinez, *Owner*
EMP: 95 EST: 2011
SALES (est): 446.7K
SALES (corp-wide): 56.6MM **Privately Held**
WEB: www.rranchmarkets.com
SIC: 0291 General farms, primarily animals
PA: R-Ranch Market, Incorporated
    13985 Live Oak Ave
    Irwindale CA 91706
    626 814-2900

(P-146)
SEAFOOD RANCH GRILL INC
2120 Grand Ave Ste A, Chino Hills (91709-4842)
PHONE.................................909 590-7232
Mimmie Rivera, *Branch Mgr*
EMP: 61
SALES (corp-wide): 87.2K **Privately Held**
SIC: 0291 General farms, primarily animals
PA: Seafood Ranch Grill, Inc.
    11338 Villanueva St
    Fontana CA

0711 Soil Preparation Svcs

(P-147)
QUALITY SPRAYERS INC
3020 E La Palma Ave, Anaheim (92806-2622)
PHONE.................................562 376-5177
Michael Farquhar, *President*
Justin Casey, *General Mgr*
EMP: 58 EST: 1960
SQ FT: 7,500
SALES (est): 1.2MM **Privately Held**
WEB: www.qualitysprayers.com
SIC: 0711 Weed control services before planting

0721 Soil Preparation, Planting & Cultivating Svc

(P-148)
OAKRIDGE LANDSCAPE INC (PA)
28064 Avenue Stanford K, Valencia (91355-1159)
PHONE.................................661 295-7228
Jeffrey E Myers, *CEO*
Victor Valle, *Partner*
Len Poloniato, *Vice Pres*
Gary Scott, *Branch Mgr*
Ken Aldrich, *General Mgr*
EMP: 132 EST: 2001
SALES (est): 27.1MM **Privately Held**
WEB: www.oakridgelandscape.net
SIC: 0721 0781 Irrigation system operation, not providing water; landscape services

(P-149)
SUNRIDGE NURSERIES INC
441 Vineland Rd, Bakersfield (93307-9556)
PHONE.................................661 363-8463
Craig Stoller, *CEO*
Glen Stoller, *President*
Terrie Stoller, *Corp Secy*
EMP: 70 EST: 1977
SQ FT: 60,000
SALES (est): 13.4MM **Privately Held**
WEB: www.sunridgenurseries.com
SIC: 0721 Vines, cultivation of

0722 Crop Harvesting By Machine

(P-150)
BOSWELL PROPERTIES INC
101 W Walnut St, Pasadena (91103-3636)
PHONE.................................626 583-3000
Curt Rowe, *President*
Melvin L Eltiste, *Treasurer*
Sherm Railsback, *Vice Pres*
Joseph A Morris, *Controller*
EMP: 1235 EST: 1982
SALES (est): 753.4K
SALES (corp-wide): 370.2MM **Privately Held**
WEB: www.tulago.com
SIC: 0722 6552 Cotton, machine harvesting services; subdividers & developers
PA: J. G. Boswell Company
    101 W Walnut St
    Pasadena CA 91103
    626 583-3000

(P-151)
BYRD HARVEST INC
Also Called: Byrd Produce
192 Guadalupe St, Guadalupe (93434-1514)
P.O. Box 60 (93434-0060)
PHONE.................................805 343-1608
Joe George, *President*
Barbara Stanley, *Treasurer*
Mary Jorge, *Human Res Dir*
EMP: 53 EST: 1964
SQ FT: 5,000
SALES (est): 1.1MM **Privately Held**
SIC: 0722 Field crops, except cash grains, machine harvesting services

(P-152)
CASTLE ROCK FARMING AND TRNSPT
Also Called: Castle Rock Vineyards
501 Richgrove Dr, Richgrove (93261)
P.O. Box 299 (93261-0299)
PHONE.................................661 721-1058
Albert L Good, *President*
Laura Berryessa, *Sales Staff*
Daniel Gomez, *Sales Staff*
Cidro Ochoa, *Manager*
◆ EMP: 67 EST: 1993
SALES (est): 3.2MM **Privately Held**
SIC: 0722 Grapes, machine harvesting services

(P-153)
DANELL BROS INC
Also Called: Hanford Truck Repair & Parts
8265 Hanford Armona Rd, Hanford (93230-9344)
PHONE.................................559 582-1251
Danny Danell, *President*
Marigail Danell, *Corp Secy*
Mike Danell, *Vice Pres*
Mary Kiely, *Finance*
Danny D Danell, *Manager*
▲ EMP: 80 EST: 1970
SQ FT: 3,000
SALES (est): 10.6MM **Privately Held**
WEB: www.danellcustomharvesting.com
SIC: 0722 0241 Crop harvesting; dairy heifer replacement farm

(P-154)
DANELL CUSTOM HARVESTING LLC
8265 Hanford Armona Rd, Hanford (93230-9344)
PHONE.................................559 582-1251
Rance Danell,
EMP: 150 EST: 2010
SALES (est): 13.1MM **Privately Held**
WEB: www.danellcustomharvesting.com
SIC: 0722 Crop harvesting

(P-155)
EVERYTABLE PBC (PA)
1101 W 23rd St, Los Angeles (90007-1890)
PHONE.................................917 319-6156
Samuel Polk, *CEO*
David Foster, *President*
Chad Massura, *Opers Staff*
Jorge Garcia, *Sales Associate*
Monica Grippo, *Marketing Staff*

PRODUCTS & SVCS

EMP: 75 **EST:** 2015
SALES (est): 10.3MM **Privately Held**
WEB: www.everytable.com
SIC: 0722 Crop harvesting

(P-156)
LOS DOS VALLES HARVSTG & PKG
2365 Westgate Rd, Santa Maria (93455-1045)
P.O. Box 1942 (93456-1942)
PHONE...........................805 739-1688
Felipe C Zepeda, *President*
EMP: 150 **EST:** 1985
SQ FT: 4,500
SALES (est): 6.8MM **Privately Held**
SIC: 0722 0723 Vegetables & melons, machine harvesting services; vegetable packing services

(P-157)
NEW HOPE HARVESTING LLC
918 Nita Ct, Santa Maria (93454-3122)
PHONE...........................805 478-4469
Guadalupe Gaspar, *Principal*
Eugenia Martinez, *Principal*
EMP: 60 **EST:** 2015
SALES (est): 4MM **Privately Held**
SIC: 0722 Crop harvesting

(P-158)
NOBLESSE OBLIGE INC
Also Called: Eight Star Equipment
2015 Silsbee Rd, El Centro (92243-9671)
PHONE...........................760 353-3336
Alex Abatti Jr, *President*
David Wells, *CFO*
Sid Swarthout, *Admin Sec*
EMP: 250 **EST:** 1985
SALES (est): 1.7MM **Privately Held**
SIC: 0722 Combining services; cotton, machine harvesting services; hay, machine harvesting services; vegetables & melons, machine harvesting services

(P-159)
SMITH PACKING INC (PA)
111 W Chapel St, Santa Maria (93458-4301)
P.O. Box 1338 (93456-1338)
PHONE...........................805 348-1818
Vernon Smith III, *President*
Liz Salavar, *Admin Sec*
David Baker, *Manager*
EMP: 119 **EST:** 1996
SALES (est): 9.1MM **Privately Held**
WEB: www.smithpackinginc.com
SIC: 0722 Crop harvesting

0723 Crop Preparation, Except Cotton Ginning

(P-160)
ALLIED AVOCADOS & CITRUS INC
1203 S Sespe St, Fillmore (93015-9767)
PHONE...........................805 625-7155
Brayen Guzman, *President*
Lupe Guzman, *COO*
EMP: 60 **EST:** 2015
SALES (est): 28MM **Privately Held**
WEB: www.alliedfruits.com
SIC: 0723 Fruit (farm-dried) packing services

(P-161)
BOSKOVICH FARMS INC (PA)
711 Diaz Ave, Oxnard (93030-7247)
P.O. Box 1352 (93032-1352)
PHONE...........................805 487-2299
George S Boskovich Jr, *CEO*
Philip J Boskovich Jr, *President*
Lisa A Perez, *Accounting Mgr*
Enrique Sandoval, *Accountant*
Marcos Gutierrez, *Prdtn Mgr*
▲ **EMP:** 205 **EST:** 1915
SQ FT: 7,000
SALES (est): 66.3MM **Privately Held**
WEB: www.boskovichfarms.com
SIC: 0723 5812 0161 Crop preparation services for market; eating places; rooted vegetable farms; lettuce & leaf vegetable farms

(P-162)
CENTRAL VALLEY ALMOND ASSN
12655 Garzoli Ave, Mc Farland (93250-9648)
P.O. Box 487 (93250-0487)
PHONE...........................661 792-2171
Ray Van Beek, *President*
Joost Demoes, *President*
Clinton Shick, *Admin Sec*
EMP: 51 **EST:** 1971
SALES (est): 2.7MM **Privately Held**
WEB: www.centralvalleyalmond.com
SIC: 0723 Almond hulling & shelling services

(P-163)
CORONA - CLLEGE HTS ORNGE LMON
8000 Lincoln Ave, Riverside (92504-4343)
PHONE...........................951 359-6451
John Demshki, *President*
Jennie Sistos, *Controller*
Keith French, *Export Mgr*
Betty Arreola, *Manager*
Mayren Bracamontes, *Manager*
▼ **EMP:** 300 **EST:** 1905
SQ FT: 180,000
SALES (est): 25.5MM **Privately Held**
WEB: www.cchcitrus.com
SIC: 0723 Fruit (fresh) packing services

(P-164)
CRISP WAREHOUSE INC
Also Called: Crisp California Walnuts
20500 Main St, Stratford (93266-9758)
P.O. Box 490, Lemoore (93245-0490)
PHONE...........................559 947-9221
James R Crisp, *President*
Stacie Annon, *CFO*
◆ **EMP:** 50 **EST:** 1976
SQ FT: 50,000
SALES (est): 1.3MM **Privately Held**
WEB: www.crispwarehouse.com
SIC: 0723 Walnut hulling & shelling services

(P-165)
DESERT VALLEY DATE INC
86740 Industrial Way, Coachella (92236-2718)
PHONE...........................760 398-0999
George Kirkjan, *President*
Tamara Kirkjan, *Vice Pres*
Alice Orduno, *Manager*
◆ **EMP:** 50
SQ FT: 42,000
SALES (est): 8.7MM **Privately Held**
WEB: www.desertvalleydate.com
SIC: 0723 Crop preparation services for market

(P-166)
EXETER ENGINEERING INC
Also Called: TTI Technologies
109 W Pine St, Exeter (93221-1612)
P.O. Box 457 (93221-0457)
PHONE...........................559 592-3161
Jeffrey Batchman, *CEO*
Jack Bedwell, *General Mgr*
Stephanie Reynoso, *Purchasing*
Steve Lyon, *Purch Agent*
Matt Lonczynski, *Sales Engr*
▲ **EMP:** 70 **EST:** 1978
SQ FT: 20,000
SALES (est): 10.5MM **Privately Held**
WEB: www.exeterengineering.com
SIC: 0723 Vegetable sorting services; fruit sorting services

(P-167)
EXETER PACKERS INC (PA)
Also Called: Sun Pacific Packers
1250 E Myer Ave, Exeter (93221-9345)
P.O. Box 217 (93221-0217)
PHONE...........................559 592-5168
Berne Evans III, *CEO*
Robert Reniers, *President*
Ernie Larsen, *CFO*
Jeanne Wilkinson, *Controller*
Heidi Hill, *Clerk*
◆ **EMP:** 230 **EST:** 1975
SQ FT: 70,000

SALES (est): 75.1MM **Privately Held**
WEB: www.sunpacific.com
SIC: 0723 Fruit (fresh) packing services

(P-168)
EXETER PACKERS INC
Also Called: Euclid Parking
23744 Avenue 181, Porterville (93257-9579)
PHONE...........................559 784-8820
Lenard Shelton, *General Mgr*
EMP: 137
SALES (corp-wide): 75.1MM **Privately Held**
WEB: www.sunpacific.com
SIC: 0723 Fruit (fresh) packing services
PA: Exeter Packers, Inc.
　1250 E Myer Ave
　Exeter CA 93221
　559 592-5168

(P-169)
EXETER-IVANHOE CITRUS ASSN
901 Rocky Hill Dr, Exeter (93221-1322)
PHONE...........................559 592-3141
Kevin Riddle, *President*
Terry Orr, *General Mgr*
Marick Rosario, *Office Mgr*
Mike Hulsey, *Controller*
Joey Martinez, *Supervisor*
EMP: 75 **EST:** 1925
SQ FT: 30,000
SALES (est): 10.6MM **Privately Held**
WEB: www.exetercitrus.com
SIC: 0723 Fruit (fresh) packing services

(P-170)
FISHER RANCH LLC
10610 Ice Plant Rd, Blythe (92225-2757)
PHONE...........................760 922-4151
Dana B Fisher, *President*
Meloni Carnes, *Manager*
Mike George, *Manager*
EMP: 99 **EST:** 1998 **Privately Held**
WEB: www.fisherranch.com
SIC: 0723 Field crops, except cash grains, market preparation services

(P-171)
GILLETTE CITRUS COMPANY
10175 S Anchor Ave, Dinuba (93618-9204)
PHONE...........................559 626-4236
Jay Gillette, *Partner*
Dean Gillette, *Partner*
Mark Gillette, *Partner*
EMP: 60 **EST:** 1983
SQ FT: 14,000
SALES (est): 4.1MM **Privately Held**
WEB: www.gillettecitrus.com
SIC: 0723 Fruit (fresh) packing services

(P-172)
GRIMMWAY ENTERPRISES INC
6101 Zerker Rd, Shafter (93263-9611)
P.O. Box 81498, Bakersfield (93380-1498)
PHONE...........................661 393-3320
Bob Grimm, *Principal*
Dulce Rueda, *Clerk*
EMP: 242
SALES (corp-wide): 1.8B **Privately Held**
WEB: www.grimmway.com
SIC: 0723 Vegetable packing services
PA: Grimmway Enterprises, Inc.
　14141 Di Giorgio Rd
　Arvin CA 93203
　800 301-3101

(P-173)
GRIMMWAY ENTERPRISES INC
Also Called: Grimmway Frozen Foods
830 Sycamore Rd, Arvin (93203-2132)
P.O. Box 81498, Bakersfield (93380-1498)
PHONE...........................661 854-6250
Brandon Grimm, *Manager*
EMP: 242
SALES (corp-wide): 1.8B **Privately Held**
WEB: www.grimmway.com
SIC: 0723 Vegetable packing services
PA: Grimmway Enterprises, Inc.
　14141 Di Giorgio Rd
　Arvin CA 93203
　800 301-3101

(P-174)
GRIMMWAY ENTERPRISES INC
Also Called: Grimmway Farms
11412 Malaga Rd, Arvin (93203-9641)
P.O. Box 81498, Bakersfield (93380-1498)
PHONE...........................661 854-6200
Brian Manson, *Programmer Anys*
Gerado Raya, *Purch Mgr*
Hector Pacheco, *Opers Mgr*
Gina Price, *QC Mgr*
Guerman Ibarra, *Production*
EMP: 242
SALES (corp-wide): 1.8B **Privately Held**
WEB: www.grimmway.com
SIC: 0723 4783 Vegetable packing services; containerization of goods for shipping
PA: Grimmway Enterprises, Inc
　14141 Di Giorgio Rd
　Arvin CA 93203
　800 301-3101

(P-175)
GRIMMWAY ENTERPRISES INC
Also Called: Grimmway Farms
6900 Mountain View Rd, Bakersfield (93307-9627)
P.O. Box 81498 (93380-1498)
PHONE...........................661 845-5200
Bob Grimm, *Owner*
Randy Furtner, *Officer*
Jeff Meger, *Vice Pres*
Joel Sherman, *Vice Pres*
Sue Beal, *Office Mgr*
EMP: 200
SALES (corp-wide): 1.8B **Privately Held**
WEB: www.grimmway.com
SIC: 0723 Vegetable packing services
PA: Grimmway Enterprises, Inc.
　14141 Di Giorgio Rd
　Arvin CA 93203
　800 301-3101

(P-176)
GUADALUPE COOLING COMPANY INC
2040 Guadalupe Rd, Guadalupe (93434)
PHONE...........................805 343-2331
Dan Vincent, *Manager*
EMP: 73
SALES (corp-wide): 14MM **Privately Held**
WEB: www.westernprecooling.com
SIC: 0723 Vacuum cooling
PA: Guadalupe Cooling Company Inc
　2040 Guadalupe Rd
　Nipomo CA 93444
　805 249-3110

(P-177)
J G BOSWELL COMPANY
Also Called: Processing Office
710 Bainum Ave, Corcoran (93212-9603)
P.O. Box 457 (93212-0457)
PHONE...........................559 992-2141
Janice Salgado, *General Mgr*
Cassandra Frey, *Admin Asst*
Daniel Hays, *Engineer*
Freddy Pinto, *Accountant*
Sabrina Singhapattanapo, *Accountant*
EMP: 100
SALES (corp-wide): 370.2MM **Privately Held**
WEB: www.eastlakeco.com
SIC: 0723 Crop preparation services for market
PA: J. G. Boswell Company
　101 W Walnut St
　Pasadena CA 91103
　626 583-3000

(P-178)
KERN RIDGE GROWERS LLC
25429 Barbara St, Arvin (93203-9748)
P.O. Box 455 (93203-0455)
PHONE...........................661 854-3141
Robert Giragosian,
▼ **EMP:** 500 **EST:** 1973
SQ FT: 53,000
SALES: 48.2MM **Privately Held**
WEB: www.kernridge.com
SIC: 0723 5148 Vegetable packing services; vegetables, fresh

(P-179)
KLINK CITRUS ASSOCIATION
Also Called: Klink Citrus Exchange
32921 Road 159, Ivanhoe (93235-1455)
P.O. Box 188 (93235-0188)
PHONE.................................559 798-1881
Eric Meling, *CEO*
EMP: 170
SQ FT: 50,000
SALES (est): 18.7MM **Privately Held**
WEB: www.growers.sunkist.com
SIC: 0723 Fruit (fresh) packing services

(P-180)
LIMONEIRA COMPANY (PA)
1141 Cummings Rd Ofc, Santa Paula
(93060-9783)
PHONE.................................805 525-5541
Harold S Edwards, *President*
Gordon E Kimball, *Ch of Bd*
Alex M Teague, *COO*
Mark Palamountain, *CFO*
Anthony Ecuyer, *Vice Pres*
◆ **EMP:** 272 **EST:** 1893
SALES (est): 164.5MM **Publicly Held**
WEB: www.limoneira.com
SIC: 0723 0174 0179 6531 Fruit (fresh)
packing services; citrus fruits; lemon
grove; orange grove; avocado orchard;
real estate agents & managers; real es-
tate leasing & rentals; commodity in-
vestors

(P-181)
LO BUE BROS INC
Also Called: Lo Bue Bros East
713 E Hermosa St, Lindsay (93247-2204)
PHONE.................................559 562-6367
EMP: 200
SALES (corp-wide): 40.7MM **Privately
Held**
SIC: 0723 5148 0174 Crop Preparation
For Market Whol Fruits/Vegetables Citrus
Fruit Grove
PA: Lo Bue Bros., Inc.
201 S Sweetbriar Ave
Lindsay CA 93247
559 562-2548

(P-182)
MONARCH NUT COMPANY LLC
Also Called: Munger Farms
786 Road 188, Delano (93215-9508)
PHONE.................................661 725-6458
Kamie Munger, *Mng Member*
Stephanie Thiessen, *Vice Pres*
David Munger,
Sylvia Pimentel, *Clerk*
◆ **EMP:** 250 **EST:** 1986
SQ FT: 20,000
SALES (est): 26.2MM **Privately Held**
SIC: 0723 7389 Tree nuts (general) hulling
& shelling services; packaging & labeling
services

(P-183)
RAMCO ENTERPRISES LP
Also Called: Ramco Employment Services
520 E 3rd St Ste B, Oxnard (93030-0182)
PHONE.................................805 486-9328
Jesse Espinoza, *Branch Mgr*
EMP: 558
SALES (corp-wide): 92.8MM **Privately
Held**
WEB: www.ramcoenterpriseslp.com
SIC: 0723 Crop preparation services for
market
PA: Ramco Enterprises, L.P.
710 La Guardia St
Salinas CA 93905
831 758-5272

(P-184)
REDLANDS FOOTHILL GROVES
304 9th St, Redlands (92374-3404)
PHONE.................................909 793-2164
Robert Knight, *Plant Mgr*
EMP: 50 **EST:** 1924
SQ FT: 48,000
SALES (est): 4.6MM **Privately Held**
WEB: www.redlandschamber.org
SIC: 0723 Fruit (fresh) packing services

(P-185)
**SATICOY LEMON ASSOCIATION
(PA)**
Also Called: Saticoy Fruit Exchange
103 N Peck Rd, Santa Paula (93060-3099)
P.O. Box 46 (93061-0046)
PHONE.................................805 654-6500
Glenn A Miller, *President*
Jerry Pogorzelski, *CFO*
Jima Garrett, *Admin Sec*
Marty Coert, *Opers Mgr*
Raul Arias, *Plant Mgr*
▲ **EMP:** 100 **EST:** 1933
SALES (est): 26.6MM **Privately Held**
WEB: www.saticoylemon.com
SIC: 0723 Fruit (fresh) packing services

(P-186)
SUN PACIFIC MARICOPA
Also Called: Maricopa Packers
31452 Old River Rd, Bakersfield
(93311-9621)
PHONE.................................661 847-1015
Bern Evans, *Managing Prtnr*
EMP: 87 **EST:** 2006
SQ FT: 450,000
SALES (est): 2.5MM **Privately Held**
WEB: www.sunpacific.com
SIC: 0723 Fruit (fresh) packing services

(P-187)
**SUN RICH FRESH FOODS USA
INC (PA)**
515 E Rincon St, Corona (92879-1391)
PHONE.................................951 735-3800
Brian Tieszen, *President*
Carl Svangtun, *President*
Neville Israel, *CFO*
▲ **EMP:** 197 **EST:** 1992
SQ FT: 33,000
SALES (est): 49.9MM **Privately Held**
WEB: www.freshfoodgroup.com
SIC: 0723 Fruit (fresh) packing services

(P-188)
SUN WORLD INC
5544 California Ave # 280, Bakersfield
(93309-1616)
PHONE.................................805 833-6460
Howard P Marguleas, *Ch of Bd*
John P Brincko, *President*
Paul W Knupp, *Corp Secy*
John F Knopf, *Acting CFO*
David O Marguleas, *Senior VP*
◆ **EMP:** 1500 **EST:** 1977
SQ FT: 17,441
SALES (est): 7.6MM **Privately Held**
SIC: 0723 Crop preparation services for
market

(P-189)
**SUN WORLD INTERNATIONAL
INC (PA)**
16351 Driver Rd, Bakersfield (93308-9733)
P.O. Box 80298 (93380-0298)
PHONE.................................661 392-5000
Keith Brackpool, *Ch of Bd*
Timothy J Shaheen, *CEO*
Keith Mitchell, *Exec VP*
Andrew Simpson, *Exec VP*
Terry Bacon, *Vice Pres*
◆ **EMP:** 1500 **EST:** 1976
SQ FT: 160,000
SALES (est): 355MM **Privately Held**
WEB: www.sun-world.com
SIC: 0723 0172 0174 0175 Vegetable
crops market preparation services; veg-
etable packing services; grapes; citrus
fruits; deciduous tree fruits; date orchard;
mango grove; melon farms; pepper farm,
sweet & hot (vegetables)

(P-190)
TALLEY FARMS
2900 Lopez Dr, Arroyo Grande
(93420-4999)
P.O. Box 360 (93421-0360)
PHONE.................................805 489-2508
Brian Talley, *President*
Todd Talley, *Treasurer*
Rayn Talley, *Vice Pres*
Lisa Loogman, *Office Admin*
Rosemary Talley, *Admin Sec*
EMP: 175 **EST:** 1954
SQ FT: 2,000

SALES (est): 21.2MM **Privately Held**
WEB: www.talleyfarmsfreshharvest.com
SIC: 0723 0161 Vegetable packing serv-
ices; vegetables & melons

(P-191)
**TANIMURA ANTLE FRESH
FOODS INC**
Also Called: Salad Time Farms
4401 Foxdale St, Baldwin Park
(91706-2161)
P.O. Box 4070, Salinas (93912-4070)
PHONE.................................831 424-6100
Randy Sipled, *Manager*
EMP: 281
SALES (corp-wide): 321.4MM **Privately
Held**
WEB: www.taproduce.com
SIC: 0723 Vegetable packing services
PA: Tanimura & Antle Fresh Foods, Inc.
1 Harris Rd
Salinas CA 93908
831 455-2950

(P-192)
**WONDERFUL CITRUS
COOPERATIVE (PA)**
1901 S Lexington St, Delano (93215-9207)
PHONE.................................661 720-2400
David Krause, *President*
▲ **EMP:** 538 **EST:** 2006
SQ FT: 50,000
SALES (est): 28.7MM **Privately Held**
SIC: 0723 Fruit (fresh) packing services

(P-193)
**WONDERFUL CITRUS PACKING
LLC (HQ)**
Also Called: Paramount Citrus Packing Co
1901 S Lexington St, Delano (93215-9207)
PHONE.................................661 720-2400
Craig B Cooper, *Mng Member*
◆ **EMP:** 273 **EST:** 1950
SQ FT: 400,000
SALES (est): 280.3MM
SALES (corp-wide): 2B **Privately Held**
WEB: www.wonderfulcitrus.com
SIC: 0723 0174 2033 Fruit (fresh) pack-
ing services; orange grove; fruit juices;
fresh
PA: The Wonderful Company Llc
11444 W Olympic Blvd # 210
Los Angeles CA 90064
310 966-5700

(P-194)
WONDERFUL COMPANY LLC
5001 California Ave, Bakersfield
(93309-1671)
PHONE.................................559 781-7438
EMP: 383
SALES (corp-wide): 2B **Privately Held**
WEB: www.wonderful.com
SIC: 0723 Fruit crops market preparation
services
PA: The Wonderful Company Llc
11444 W Olympic Blvd # 210
Los Angeles CA 90064
310 966-5700

(P-195)
WONDERFUL COMPANY LLC
11444 W Olympic Blvd # 210, Los Angeles
(90064-1559)
PHONE.................................661 720-2609
Craig B Cooper, *Manager*
EMP: 383
SALES (corp-wide): 2B **Privately Held**
WEB: www.wonderful.com
SIC: 0723 Fruit (fresh) packing services
PA: The Wonderful Company Llc
11444 W Olympic Blvd # 210
Los Angeles CA 90064
310 966-5700

(P-196)
WONDERFUL COMPANY LLC
6801 E Lerdo Hwy, Shafter (93263-9610)
PHONE.................................661 399-4456
EMP: 383
SALES (corp-wide): 2B **Privately Held**
WEB: www.wonderful.com
SIC: 0723 Fruit crops market preparation
services

PA: The Wonderful Company Llc
11444 W Olympic Blvd # 210
Los Angeles CA 90064
310 966-5700

0742 Veterinary Animal Specialties

(P-197)
ANIMAL SPECIALTY GROUP
Also Called: Kortz Gregg Dvm Dplomate
Acvim
4641 Colorado Blvd, Los Angeles
(90039-1105)
PHONE.................................818 244-7977
Kirk Wendelburg Dvm, *Owner*
Michael Huber,
Stacey A Sullivan, *Neurology*
Sarah Wait, *Supervisor*
EMP: 65 **EST:** 1990
SALES (est): 7.5MM **Privately Held**
WEB: www.asgvets.com
SIC: 0742 Veterinarian, animal specialties

(P-198)
DELPHIC ENTERPRISES INC
Also Called: Pinnacle Veterinary Center
23026 Soledad Canyon Rd, Santa Clarita
(91350-2634)
PHONE.................................661 254-2000
Nirip Shokar, *President*
EMP: 72 **EST:** 2016
SALES (est): 2.7MM
SALES (corp-wide): 32.1MM **Privately
Held**
WEB: www.peoplepetsandvets.com
SIC: 0742 Animal hospital services, pets &
other animal specialties
PA: People, Pets And Vets, Llc
6541 Sexton Dr Nw Ste G
Olympia WA 98502
360 515-0563

(P-199)
HEALTH TECH PROF PDTS INC
Also Called: Animal Health & Sanitary Sup
11614 Sterling Ave, Riverside
(92503-4994)
PHONE.................................800 424-7536
Chris Quinlan, *President*
Colin McAdam, *Sales Staff*
EMP: 14 **EST:** 2006
SALES (est): 1.7MM **Privately Held**
WEB: www.htproducts.net
SIC: 0742 5199 3999 Animal hospital
services, pets & other animal specialties;
pet supplies; pet supplies

(P-200)
**HUMPHREY GCPZZI VTRNARY
GROUP**
4774 Donlon Rd, Somis (93066-9766)
PHONE.................................805 386-4291
Michael Giacopuzzi, *President*
Richard Giacopuzzi, *Vice Pres*
Colleen Whiting, *Practice Mgr*
Valerie Wilson, *Receptionist*
EMP: 60 **EST:** 1945
SALES (est): 5.2MM **Privately Held**
WEB: www.humphreygiacopuzziandassoci-
ates.com
SIC: 0742 Animal hospital services, pets &
other animal specialties

(P-201)
**NATIONAL VETERINARY ASSOC
INC (HQ)**
29229 Canwood St Ste 100, Agoura Hills
(91301-1503)
PHONE.................................805 777-7722
Greg Hartmann, *CEO*
Thomas Sawicki, *COO*
R James Woloshyn, *CFO*
Carol Henry, *Chief Mktg Ofcr*
Kevin Schneider, *Vice Pres*
EMP: 770 **EST:** 1996
SQ FT: 5,000
SALES (est): 860MM **Privately Held**
WEB: www.nva.com
SIC: 0742 Animal hospital services, pets &
other animal specialties

PRODUCTS & SVCS

PA: Veterinary Specialists Of North America Llc
106 Apple St Ste 102
Tinton Falls NJ 07724
732 704-9222

(P-202)
SANTA MONICA PET MED CTR INC
1534 14th St, Santa Monica (90404-3303)
PHONE.....................310 393-8218
Kirstin Pirkl, *CEO*
EMP: 52 **EST:** 1962
SQ FT: 3,200
SALES (est): 8.9MM **Privately Held**
WEB: www.petmedical.com
SIC: 0742 Animal hospital services, pets & other animal specialties

(P-203)
V C A CENTRAL ANIMAL HOSPITAL
281 N Central Ave, Upland (91786-4215)
PHONE.....................909 981-2855
Dr Ronald L Beeley, *President*
Theresa Dieringer, *Treasurer*
Richard T Johnson, *Vice Pres*
Richard Johnson, *Vice Pres*
Marjorie Fong, *Principal*
EMP: 67 **EST:** 1973
SALES (est): 8.7MM
SALES (corp-wide): 42.8B **Privately Held**
WEB: www.vcacentral.com
SIC: 0742 Animal hospital services, pets & other animal specialties; veterinarian, animal specialties
HQ: Vca Inc.
12401 W Olympic Blvd
Los Angeles CA 90064
310 571-6500

(P-204)
VALLEY ANIMAL MEDICAL CENTER
46920 Jefferson St, Indio (92201-7920)
PHONE.....................760 342-4711
Gary Homec, *President*
EMP: 663 **EST:** 1979
SQ FT: 12,000
SALES (est): 1.5MM **Privately Held**
WEB: www.animalmedicalvets.com
SIC: 0742 Animal hospital services, pets & other animal specialties
PA: Pet Drx Veterinary Group, Inc.
560 S Winchester Blvd
San Jose CA

(P-205)
VCA ANIMAL HOSPITALS INC (DH)
Also Called: VCA TLC Animal Hospital
12401 W Olympic Blvd, Los Angeles (90064-1022)
PHONE.....................310 571-6500
Robert Antin, *President*
Tomas Fuller, *Treasurer*
Cindi Kazimir, *Executive*
Randall Popkin, *Principal*
John Zimmerman, *Exec Dir*
EMP: 245 **EST:** 2000
SQ FT: 3,200
SALES (est): 254.3MM
SALES (corp-wide): 42.8B **Privately Held**
WEB: www.vcaspecialtyvets.com
SIC: 0742 Animal hospital services, pets & other animal specialties
HQ: Vca Inc.
12401 W Olympic Blvd
Los Angeles CA 90064
310 571-6500

(P-206)
VCA PRFESSIONAL ANIMAL LAB INC
12401 W Olympic Blvd, Los Angeles (90064-1022)
PHONE.....................310 571-6500
Robert L Antin, *President*
EMP: 72 **EST:** 1986
SALES (est): 4.1MM
SALES (corp-wide): 42.8B **Privately Held**
WEB: www.vcahospitals.com
SIC: 0742 Animal hospital services, pets & other animal specialties

HQ: Vca Inc.
12401 W Olympic Blvd
Los Angeles CA 90064
310 571-6500

(P-207)
VETCO HOSPITALS INC (HQ)
4790 Irvine Blvd Ste 105, Irvine (92620-1998)
PHONE.....................858 483-4145
K Bryan Shobe, *CEO*
Gary L Brown, *President*
▲ **EMP:** 62 **EST:** 1996
SALES (est): 1MM
SALES (corp-wide): 1.9MM **Privately Held**
WEB: www.vippetcare.com
SIC: 0742 Veterinarian, animal specialties

(P-208)
VETERINARY CTRS OF AMRICA-TEXAS (DH)
Also Called: Sandy Lake Animal Hospital
12401 W Olympic Blvd, Los Angeles (90064-1022)
PHONE.....................310 571-6500
Robert L Antin, *President*
EMP: 62 **EST:** 1973
SQ FT: 5,500
SALES (est): 20.4MM
SALES (corp-wide): 42.8B **Privately Held**
WEB: www.vcahospitals.com
SIC: 0742 Animal hospital services, pets & other animal specialties; veterinarian, animal specialties
HQ: Vca Inc.
12401 W Olympic Blvd
Los Angeles CA 90064
310 571-6500

(P-209)
VICAR OPERATING INC (DH)
Also Called: Veterinary Centers America VCA
12401 W Olympic Blvd, Los Angeles (90064-1022)
PHONE.....................310 571-6500
Robert Antin, *President*
Butch Allen, *Vice Pres*
Juliet Bailey, *Vice Pres*
Maria Druse, *Vice Pres*
Betty Facey CPA, *Vice Pres*
EMP: 364 **EST:** 1985
SALES (est): 93.3MM
SALES (corp-wide): 42.8B **Privately Held**
WEB: www.vcahospitals.com
SIC: 0742 Animal hospital services, pets & other animal specialties
HQ: Vca Inc.
12401 W Olympic Blvd
Los Angeles CA 90064
310 571-6500

0751 Livestock Svcs, Except Veterinary

(P-210)
AMERICAN BEEF PACKERS INC
13677 Yorba Ave, Chino (91710-5059)
PHONE.....................909 628-4888
Lawrence Miller, *President*
Henry Wong, *Sales Mgr*
EMP: 250 **EST:** 2008
SALES (est): 25.4MM **Privately Held**
SIC: 0751 2011 5147 Slaughtering: custom livestock services; beef products from beef slaughtered on site; meats & meat products

0752 Animal Specialty Svcs, Exc Veterinary

(P-211)
AMERICAN BUILDING JANTR INC (PA)
5527 South St, Lakewood (90713-1301)
PHONE.....................562 986-4474
Mike Alvidrez, *President*
EMP: 64 **EST:** 2004

SALES (est): 3.2MM **Privately Held**
WEB: www.americanbuildingjanitorial.com
SIC: 0752 7349 Animal specialty services; janitorial service, contract basis

(P-212)
CITY OF LOS ANGELES
Also Called: Animal Services Dept
3201 Lacy St, Los Angeles (90031-1867)
PHONE.....................213 473-7511
EMP: 104 **Privately Held**
SIC: 9199 0752 General Government
PA: City Of Los Angeles
200 N Spring St Ste 303
Los Angeles CA 90012
213 978-0600

(P-213)
LOS ANGELES EQUESTRIAN CENTER
480 W Riverside Dr, Burbank (91506-3209)
PHONE.....................818 840-9063
Tim Behunin, *President*
Kenneth Mowry, *Admin Sec*
EMP: 52 **EST:** 1990
SALES (est): 4.1MM **Privately Held**
WEB: www.thelaec.com
SIC: 0752 7999 Boarding services, horses: racing & non-racing; horse shows

0761 Farm Labor Contractors & Crew Leaders

(P-214)
COASTAL HARVESTING INC
503 S Palm Ave, Santa Paula (93060-3364)
PHONE.....................805 525-6250
EMP: 300
SALES (est): 10.2MM **Privately Held**
SIC: 0761 Farm Labor Contractor

(P-215)
IRISH FARMS CO INC (PA)
8711 Goldfinch Dr, Bakersfield (93312-1914)
PHONE.....................661 746-4392
Jame Ryan, *CEO*
EMP: 50 **EST:** 1985
SQ FT: 1,500
SALES (est): 162.5K **Privately Held**
SIC: 0761 Farm labor contractors

(P-216)
J A CONTRACTING INC
2209 W Tulare Ave, Visalia (93277-2137)
P.O. Box 2109, Tulare (93275-2109)
PHONE.....................559 733-4865
EMP: 300
SQ FT: 1,500
SALES (est): 9MM **Privately Held**
WEB: www.jacontracting.net
SIC: 0761 Farm Labor Contractor

(P-217)
L&D FARM LABOR
53762 Sapphire Ln, Coachella (92236-7335)
PHONE.....................760 408-6311
Tania Alonzo, *President*
EMP: 50 **EST:** 2017
SALES (est): 1.5MM **Privately Held**
SIC: 0761 Farm labor contractors

(P-218)
PACIFIC SUN LABOR
350 G St, Brawley (92227-2413)
PHONE.....................760 556-5085
Alejandro Palacios, *President*
EMP: 52 **EST:** 2018
SALES (est): 626.1K **Privately Held**
SIC: 0761 Crew leaders, farm labor: contracting services

(P-219)
VENEGAS FARMING LLC
8002 Balcom Canyon Rd, Somis (93066-2107)
PHONE.....................805 529-5038
Guillermo Venegas,
EMP: 50 **EST:** 2009
SALES (est): 2.3MM **Privately Held**
SIC: 0761 Farm labor contractors

0762 Farm Management Svcs

(P-220)
AG-WISE ENTERPRISES INC (PA)
5100 California Ave # 209, Bakersfield (93309-0716)
P.O. Box 9729 (93389-9729)
PHONE.....................661 325-1567
Bruce Berreta, *President*
Ed Ray, *CFO*
EMP: 150 **EST:** 1983
SQ FT: 4,400
SALES (est): 17MM **Privately Held**
WEB: www.ag-wiseinc.com
SIC: 0762 Farm management services

(P-221)
ESPARZA ENTERPRISES INC
251 W Main St Ste G&F, Brawley (92227-2201)
PHONE.....................760 344-2031
Luis Esparza, *Branch Mgr*
EMP: 171
SALES (corp-wide): 135MM **Privately Held**
WEB: www.esparzainc.com
SIC: 0762 Farm management services
PA: Esparza Enterprises, Inc.
3851 Fruitvale Ave
Bakersfield CA 93308
661 831-0002

(P-222)
GLESS RANCH INC (PA)
18541 Van Buren Blvd, Riverside (92508-9261)
PHONE.....................951 780-8458
John J Gless, *CEO*
EMP: 50
SALES (est): 13.5MM **Privately Held**
WEB: www.glessranch.com
SIC: 0762 Apple orchard

(P-223)
HANSEN EQUIPMENT COMPANY LLC
7124 Whitley Ave, Corcoran (93212-9669)
P.O. Box 398 (93212-0398)
PHONE.....................559 992-3111
James B Hansen,
Betsy Hansen,
EMP: 50 **EST:** 2000
SALES (est): 12MM **Privately Held**
SIC: 0762 Farm management services

(P-224)
LARRY JACINTO FARMING INC
9555 N Wabash Ave, Redlands (92374-2714)
P.O. Box 275, Mentone (92359-0275)
PHONE.....................909 794-2276
Larry Jacinto, *President*
Dennis Drexler, *Corp Secy*
EMP: 100 **EST:** 1992
SQ FT: 3,000
SALES (est): 2.6MM **Privately Held**
WEB: www.jacintofarmstrees.com
SIC: 0762 Farm management services

(P-225)
MESA VINEYARD MANAGEMENT INC (PA)
110 Gibson Rd, Templeton (93465-9510)
P.O. Box 789 (93465-0789)
PHONE.....................805 434-4100
Dana Merrill, *President*
Matt Andrus, *CFO*
Bryan Wallingford, *Manager*
Carlos Guzman, *Asst Mgr*
Sarah Wilcoxson, *Receptionist*
EMP: 75 **EST:** 1988
SQ FT: 3,200
SALES (est): 15.6MM **Privately Held**
WEB: www.mesavineya d.com
SIC: 0762 Vineyard management & maintenance services

(P-226)
PEREZ CONTRACTING LLC
12620 Snow Rd, Bakersfield (93314-8021)
PHONE.....................661 399-2700
Fax: 805 239-8076
EMP: 150

▲ = Import ▼=Export
◆ =Import/Export

SALES (est): 4.6MM **Privately Held**
SIC: **0762** Farm Management Services

(P-227)
RICO FARM LABOR INC
735 E Pleasant St, Santa Paula
(93060-2027)
P.O. Box 750 (93061-0750)
PHONE...................................805 525-4523
Manuel Rico, *President*
Elena Garcia, *Admin Sec*
EMP: 50 EST: 2001
SALES (est): 2.1MM **Privately Held**
WEB: www.harveyshvac.com
SIC: **0762** Orchard management & maintenance services

(P-228)
SIERRA PACIFIC FARMS INC (PA)
Also Called: Somis Pacific AG Management
43406 Business Park Dr, Temecula
(92590-5526)
P.O. Box 1537 (92593-1537)
PHONE...................................951 699-9980
Scott A McIntyre, *CEO*
Debbie McIntyre, *CFO*
Scott McIntyre, *CFO*
Ryan Rochefort, *Vice Pres*
EMP: 68
SQ FT: 3,000
SALES (est): 16.3MM **Privately Held**
WEB: www.spfarminc.com
SIC: **0762** Farm management services

(P-229)
SUN PACIFIC FARMING COOP INC (PA)
Also Called: Allied Farming Company
1250 E Myer Ave, Exeter (93221-9345)
P.O. Box 1125 (93221-7125)
PHONE...................................559 592-7121
Berne H Evans III, *CEO*
Toby Maitland, *CFO*
Toby Maitland-Lewis, *CFO*
Bob Reniers, *Treasurer*
Sutton Hunter, *Technician*
EMP: 500 EST: 1973
SQ FT: 70,000
SALES (est): 73.7MM **Privately Held**
WEB: www.sunpacific.com
SIC: **0762** Citrus grove management & maintenance services

(P-230)
SUN PACIFIC FARMING COOP INC
Also Called: Sun Pacific Farms
33374 Lerdo Hwy, Bakersfield
(93308-9782)
PHONE...................................661 399-0376
Ernie Larson, *Manager*
EMP: 96
SALES (corp-wide): 73.7MM **Privately Held**
WEB: www.sunpacific.com
SIC: **0762** **5148** **0174** Citrus grove management & maintenance services; fresh fruits & vegetables; citrus fruits
PA: Sun Pacific Farming Cooperative, Inc.
1250 E Myer Ave
Exeter CA 93221
559 592-7121

0781 Landscape Counseling & Planning

(P-231)
A GROWING CONCERN LANDSCAPES
17382 Gothard St, Huntington Beach
(92647-6203)
PHONE...................................714 843-5137
Douglas Neal, *Owner*
EMP: 59 EST: 1982
SALES (est): 1.9MM **Privately Held**
WEB: www.growingconcern.com
SIC: **0781** Landscape services

(P-232)
AMERICAN LANDSCAPE INC
Also Called: American Golf Construction
7013 Owensmouth Ave, Canoga Park
(91303-2006)
PHONE...................................818 999-2041
Gary Peterson, *President*
Jamie Tsui, *Admin Sec*
David Gonzalez, *Project Engr*
Pam Edmiston, *Director*
Laurie Levavi, *Manager*
▲ EMP: 250 EST: 1973
SQ FT: 14,000
SALES (est): 29.5MM **Privately Held**
WEB: www.americanlandscape.com
SIC: **0781** Landscape services

(P-233)
AMERICAN LANDSCAPE MGT INC (PA)
Also Called: Custom Lawn Services
7013 Owensmouth Ave, Canoga Park
(91303-2006)
PHONE...................................818 999-2041
Mickey Strauss, *President*
Gary Peterson, *Vice Pres*
Jason Bryne, *Accountant*
Joe Pulliam, *Sales Staff*
EMP: 125 EST: 1975
SQ FT: 14,000
SALES (est): 21.8MM **Privately Held**
WEB: www.americanlandscape.com
SIC: **0781** Landscape services

(P-234)
BENNETT ENTPS A CAL LDSCP CNTG
Also Called: Bennett Landscape
25889 Belle Porte Ave, Harbor City
(90710-3393)
PHONE...................................310 534-3543
Sean Bennett, *President*
EMP: 90 EST: 1977
SQ FT: 10,500
SALES (est): 10.2MM **Privately Held**
WEB: www.bennett-landscape.com
SIC: **0781** Landscape services

(P-235)
BILL & DAVES LDSCP MAINT INC
32750 Keller Rd, Winchester (92596-9444)
PHONE...................................951 943-6455
David Leidenfrost, *Principal*
William Reimer, *Principal*
EMP: 50 EST: 1997
SALES (est): 250.1K **Privately Held**
WEB: www.billanddaves.com
SIC: **0781** Landscape services

(P-236)
BRIGHTVIEW GOLF MAINT INC
405 Glen Annie Rd, Santa Barbara
(93117-1427)
PHONE...................................805 968-6400
Richard Hasah, *Manager*
EMP: 103
SALES (corp-wide): 2.3B **Publicly Held**
SIC: **0781** Landscape services
HQ: Brightview Golf Maintenance, Inc.
27001 Agoura Rd Ste 350
Agoura Hills CA 91301
818 223-8500

(P-237)
BRIGHTVIEW GOLF MAINT INC (DH)
27001 Agoura Rd Ste 350, Agoura Hills
(91301-5112)
PHONE...................................818 223-8500
Burton Sperber, *Ch of Bd*
Richard A Sperber, *Ch of Bd*
Gregory Pieschala, *President*
Andrew Mandell, *CFO*
Michael L Dingman, *Chairman*
EMP: 100 EST: 1965
SALES (est): 51.1MM
SALES (corp-wide): 2.3B **Publicly Held**
WEB: www.brightview.com
SIC: **0781** Landscape services
HQ: Brightview Companies, Llc
27001 Agoura Rd Ste 350
Calabasas CA 91301
818 223-8500

(P-238)
BRIGHTVIEW LANDSCAPE DEV INC (DH)
27001 Agoura Rd Ste 350, Calabasas
(91301-5112)
PHONE...................................818 223-8500
Thomas Donnelly, *CEO*
Eric Johnson, *Partner*
Thomas C Donelly, *President*
Kenneth L Hutcheson, *President*
Andrew J Brennan, *COO*
◆ EMP: 50 EST: 1949
SQ FT: 25,000
SALES (est): 804.6MM
SALES (corp-wide): 2.3B **Publicly Held**
SIC: **0781** Landscape counseling & planning
HQ: Brightview Companies, Llc
27001 Agoura Rd Ste 350
Calabasas CA 91301
818 223-8500

(P-239)
BRIGHTVIEW LANDSCAPE SVCS INC
715 W La Cadena Dr, Riverside
(92501-1338)
PHONE...................................951 684-2730
EMP: 120
SALES (corp-wide): 2.3B **Publicly Held**
WEB: www.brightview.com
SIC: **0781** Landscape services
HQ: Brightview Landscape Services, Inc.
27001 Agoura Rd Ste 350
Agoura Hills CA 91301
818 223-8500

(P-240)
BRIGHTVIEW LANDSCAPE SVCS INC
1900 S Lewis St, Anaheim (92805-6718)
PHONE...................................714 215-7423
EMP: 120
SALES (corp-wide): 2.3B **Publicly Held**
WEB: www.brightview.com
SIC: **0781** Landscape services
HQ: Brightview Landscape Services, Inc.
27001 Agoura Rd Ste 350
Agoura Hills CA 91301
818 223-8500

(P-241)
BRIGHTVIEW LANDSCAPE SVCS INC
32202 Paseo Adelanto, San Juan Capistrano (92675-3601)
PHONE...................................714 546-7843
EMP: 120
SALES (corp-wide): 2.3B **Publicly Held**
WEB: www.brightview.com
SIC: **0781** Landscape services
HQ: Brightview Landscape Services, Inc.
27001 Agoura Rd Ste 350
Agoura Hills CA 91301
818 223-8500

(P-242)
BRIGHTVIEW LANDSCAPE SVCS INC
47 Plateau, Aliso Viejo (92656-8027)
PHONE...................................310 829-4707
Brett Park, *President*
EMP: 120
SALES (corp-wide): 2.3B **Publicly Held**
WEB: www.brightview.com
SIC: **0781** Landscape architects
HQ: Brightview Landscape Services, Inc.
27001 Agoura Rd Ste 350
Agoura Hills CA 91301
818 223-8500

(P-243)
BRIGHTVIEW LANDSCAPE SVCS INC
8726 Calabash Ave, Fontana (92335-3040)
PHONE...................................909 946-3196
Leon Vitort, *Branch Mgr*
Refugio Sainz, *Production*
EMP: 120
SALES (corp-wide): 2.3B **Publicly Held**
WEB: www.brightview.com
SIC: **0781** Landscape services

HQ: Brightview Landscape Services, Inc.
27001 Agoura Rd Ste 350
Agoura Hills CA 91301
818 223-8500

(P-244)
BRIGHTVIEW LANDSCAPE SVCS INC
1960 S Yale St, Santa Ana (92704-3929)
PHONE...................................714 546-7843
Dave Hanson, *Manager*
Felipe Aguilera, *Branch Mgr*
Brian Chesnut, *Branch Mgr*
Joaquin Velasquez, *Finance Mgr*
Howard Mees, *VP Opers*
EMP: 120
SALES (corp-wide): 2.3B **Publicly Held**
WEB: www.brightview.com
SIC: **0781** **0782** Landscape services; lawn & garden services
HQ: Brightview Landscape Services, Inc.
27001 Agoura Rd Ste 350
Agoura Hills CA 91301
818 223-8500

(P-245)
BRIGHTVIEW LANDSCAPE SVCS INC
17846 Van Buren Blvd, Riverside
(92508-9195)
PHONE...................................714 939-6600
EMP: 120
SALES (corp-wide): 2.3B **Publicly Held**
WEB: www.brightview.com
SIC: **0781** Landscape services
HQ: Brightview Landscape Services, Inc.
27001 Agoura Rd Ste 350
Agoura Hills CA 91301
818 223-8500

(P-246)
BRIGHTVIEW LANDSCAPE SVCS INC
2064 Eastman Ave Ste 104, Ventura
(93003-7787)
PHONE...................................805 642-9300
Frank Annino, *Manager*
EMP: 120
SALES (corp-wide): 2.3B **Publicly Held**
WEB: www.brightview.com
SIC: **0781** Landscape services
HQ: Brightview Landscape Services, Inc.
27001 Agoura Rd Ste 350
Agoura Hills CA 91301
818 223-8500

(P-247)
BRIGHTVIEW LANDSCAPE SVCS INC
1 University Dr, Aliso Viejo (92656-8081)
PHONE...................................949 480-4187
EMP: 120
SALES (corp-wide): 2.3B **Publicly Held**
WEB: www.brightview.com
SIC: **0781** Landscape services
HQ: Brightview Landscape Services, Inc.
27001 Agoura Rd Ste 350
Agoura Hills CA 91301
818 223-8500

(P-248)
BRIGHTVIEW LANDSCAPE SVCS INC
17813 S Main St Ste 105, Gardena
(90248-3542)
PHONE...................................310 327-8700
Andrea Musick, *Manager*
Gerrad Hill, *Branch Mgr*
Andrew Mori, *Branch Mgr*
Tom Cutrono, *Sales Staff*
Gilberto Rocha-Lugo, *Accounts Mgr*
EMP: 120
SQ FT: 1,530
SALES (corp-wide): 2.3B **Publicly Held**
WEB: www.brightview.com
SIC: **0781** **0782** Landscape services; landscape contractors
HQ: Brightview Landscape Services, Inc.
27001 Agoura Rd Ste 350
Agoura Hills CA 91301
818 223-8500

(P-249)
BRIGHTVIEW TREE COMPANY
P.O. Box 1611 (92307-0031)
PHONE..............................760 955-2560
EMP: 95 Privately Held
WEB: www.brightview.com
SIC: 0781 Landscape services
HQ: Brightview Tree Company
24151 Ventura Blvd # 108
Calabasas CA 91302
818 223-8500

(P-250)
CALIFORNIA SKATEPARKS
285 N Benson Ave, Upland (91786-5614)
PHONE..............................909 949-1601
Joseph M Ciaglia Jr, President
Zach Wormhoudt, Principal
Mario Rodriguez, Project Mgr
Bill Minadeo, Analyst
Ashley Ciaglia, Marketing Mgr
EMP: 150 EST: 1977
SALES (est): 12.7MM Privately Held
WEB: www.californiaskateparks.com
SIC: 0781 Landscape services

(P-251)
CICILEO LANDSCAPES INC
4565 Hollister Ave, Santa Barbara
(93110-1709)
P.O. Box 60912 (93160-0912)
PHONE..............................805 967-3939
Michael J Cicileo, President
EMP: 50 EST: 1978
SALES (est): 4.8MM Privately Held
WEB: www.cicileolandscapes.com
SIC: 0781 0782 Landscape planning serv-
ices; garden maintenance services

(P-252)
CRESTVIEW LANDSCAPE INC
13915 Saticoy St, Panorama City
(91402-6521)
PHONE..............................818 962-7771
Harold Young, CEO
Augustine Bucio, President
EMP: 100 EST: 2020
SALES (est): 1.3MM Privately Held
SIC: 0781 Landscape architects

(P-253)
DL LONG LANDSCAPING INC
5475 G St, Chino (91710-5233)
PHONE..............................909 628-5531
David L Long, President
EMP: 100 EST: 1974
SQ FT: 1,550
SALES (est): 12.5MM Privately Held
SIC: 0781 Landscape architects

(P-254)
EARTHSCAPES LANDSCAPE INC
1420 S Allec St, Anaheim (92805-6305)
PHONE..............................714 936-7810
Brian Olsen, CEO
EMP: 50 EST: 2017
SALES (est): 5.6MM Privately Held
SIC: 0781 0782 Landscape services; land-
scape contractors

(P-255)
ECOTECH SERVICES INC
2143 S Myrtle Ave, Monrovia (91016-4838)
PHONE..............................626 335-1500
Marcos Quezada, President
Joshua Rosa, Graphic Designe
Eddie Rodriguez, Supervisor
EMP: 50 EST: 2010
SALES (est): 2.6MM Privately Held
WEB: www.ecotechservices.net
SIC: 0781 Landscape services

(P-256)
FENDERSCAPE INC
Also Called: Proscape Landscape
1446 E Hill St, Signal Hill (90755-3527)
PHONE..............................562 988-2228
David Fender, President
Linda Fender, Treasurer
Jimmy Medina, Office Mgr
Jordan Fender, Opers Mgr
Colin Fender, Manager
EMP: 127 EST: 1984
SQ FT: 1,893

SALES (est): 7.3MM Privately Held
WEB: www.proscapelandscaping.com
SIC: 0781 Landscape services

(P-257)
FS COMMERCIAL LANDSCAPE INC (PA)
5151 Pedley Rd, Riverside (92509-3937)
PHONE..............................951 360-7070
G John Wood, President
Dirk Bennett, Accounts Mgr
EMP: 75 EST: 1993
SQ FT: 1,500
SALES (est): 12.1MM Privately Held
WEB: www.fslandscape.net
SIC: 0781 Landscape services

(P-258)
GARDEN VIEW INC
417 E Huntington Dr, Monrovia
(91016-3632)
PHONE..............................626 303-4043
Mark Meahl, President
Diana Showes, Manager
EMP: 50 EST: 2004
SQ FT: 1,500 Privately Held
WEB: www.garden-view.com
SIC: 0781 0782 Landscape architects;
garden services; landscape contractors

(P-259)
GOTHIC LANDSCAPING INC
Also Called: Gothic Grounds Mgmt
27413 Tourney Rd Ste 200, Valencia
(91355-5606)
PHONE..............................661 257-5085
Ron Georgio, President
Karen Klein, Business Dir
Nora Farag, Accountant
Mark Richards, Opers Mgr
Abigail Gouin, Accounts Mgr
EMP: 55
SALES (corp-wide): 51.6MM Privately
Held
WEB: www.gothiclandscape.com
SIC: 0781 0782 Landscape services; lawn
& garden services
PA: Gothic Landscaping, Inc.
27413 Tourney Rd
Santa Clarita CA 91355
661 678-1400

(P-260)
GREENSCREEN
Also Called: Atmospheric-Greenscreen
725 S Figueroa St # 1825, Los Angeles
(90017-2827)
PHONE..............................310 837-0526
Ruth Katzenstein, President
John Souza, CEO
Charlene Mortale, Division VP
Reuben Freed, Project Mgr
Ransom Mayfield, Project Mgr
EMP: 29 EST: 1995
SQ FT: 1,200
SALES (est): 1.3MM Privately Held
WEB: www.greenscreen.com
SIC: 0781 7363 3446 Landscape plan-
ning services; help supply services; archi-
tectural metalwork

(P-261)
HARVEST LANDSCAPE ENTPS INC (PA)
Also Called: Harvest Landscape Maintenance
2339 N Batavia St, Orange (92865-2001)
P.O. Box 3877 (92857-0877)
PHONE..............................714 693-8100
Stephen G Schinhofen, CEO
Bill Tolmasoff, CFO
Gabriel Anguiano, Division Pres
Robert Gavela,
Mariana Salgado, Administration
EMP: 145 EST: 2003
SALES (est): 15.1MM Privately Held
WEB: www.hlei.us
SIC: 0781 Landscape services

(P-262)
HYDRO-DIG INC
700 E Sycamore St, Anaheim
(92805-2831)
PHONE..............................714 772-9947
Martin C Rippens, President
Gary Tavan, Vice Pres
EMP: 70 EST: 1964

SQ FT: 5,000
SALES (est): 944.7K Privately Held
SIC: 0781 Landscape architects

(P-263)
KEVIN PERSONS INC
Also Called: Ground Maintenance Services
2977 Los Feliz Dr, Thousand Oaks
(91362-3411)
P.O. Box 4857, Westlake Village (91359-
1857)
PHONE..............................805 371-8746
Kevin Persons, President
EMP: 50 EST: 1981
SALES (est): 5.7MM Privately Held
SIC: 0781 Landscape services

(P-264)
LAND CONCERN LTD
1750 E Deere Ave Ste A, Santa Ana
(92705-5761)
PHONE..............................949 250-4822
Robert M Sawyer, President
Janet Sawyer, Treasurer
Michael T Imlay, Vice Pres
Andy Bowden, Principal
EMP: 55 EST: 1974
SQ FT: 12,000
SALES (est): 3.8MM Privately Held
WEB: www.landconcern.com
SIC: 0781 Landscape architects

(P-265)
LANDCARE USA LLC
Also Called: Trugreen
216 N Clara St, Santa Ana (92703-3518)
PHONE..............................949 559-7771
Kenny Stites, Branch Mgr
Don Cully, Vice Pres
EMP: 183
SALES (corp-wide): 181.5MM Privately
Held
WEB: www.landcare.com
SIC: 0781 Landscape services
PA: Landcare Usa L.L.C.
5295 Westview Dr Ste 100
Frederick MD 21703
301 874-3300

(P-266)
MARINA LANDSCAPE MAINT INC
1900 S Lewis St, Anaheim (92805-6718)
PHONE..............................714 939-6600
Robert B Cowan, CEO
EMP: 450 EST: 2014
SALES (est): 28.8MM
SALES (corp-wide): 2.3B Publicly Held
WEB: www.brightview.com
SIC: 0781 Landscape services
HQ: Brightview Landscape Services, Inc.
980 Jolly Rd Ste 300
Blue Bell PA 19422
484 567-7204

(P-267)
MERCHANTS LANDSCAPE SERVICES
8748 Industrial Ln 1, Rancho Cucamonga
(91730-4526)
PHONE..............................909 981-1022
Freddy Martinez, Manager
Martin Herrera, Branch Mgr
Edgar Valdovinos, Branch Mgr
EMP: 150
SALES (corp-wide): 79.3MM Privately
Held
WEB: www.merchantslandscape.com
SIC: 0781 Landscape planning services;
landscape services
HQ: Merchants Landscape Services, Inc
1639 E Edinger Ave Ste C
Santa Ana CA 92705
714 972-8200

(P-268)
MISSION LDSCP COMPANIES INC
536 E Dyer Rd, Santa Ana (92707-3737)
P.O. Box 15026 (92735-0026)
PHONE..............................714 545-9962
David Dubois, CEO
Kristen Parkins, President
Beth Du Boise, Treasurer
Cindy Clark, Admin Sec

EMP: 200 EST: 1973
SQ FT: 11,000
SALES (est): 20.3MM Privately Held
WEB: www.missionlandscape.com
SIC: 0781 Landscape services

(P-269)
MISSION LDSCP COMPANIES INC
16672 Millikan Ave, Irvine (92606-5008)
P.O. Box 15026, Santa Ana (92735-0026)
PHONE..............................800 545-9963
David Dubois, CEO
Bud Birch, Vice Pres
Jon Cernok, Vice Pres
Jesus Armenta, Regional Mgr
Ricardo Vargas, Regional Mgr
EMP: 127 EST: 1977
SALES (est): 18.2MM Privately Held
WEB: www.missionlandscape.com
SIC: 0781 Landscape counseling services

(P-270)
MORRISON LANDSCAPE
Also Called: Earthco
1225 E Wakeham Ave, Santa Ana
(92705-4145)
PHONE..............................714 571-0455
Robert Morrison, President
Denise Morrison, Vice Pres
Kyle Morrison, Opers Mgr
Lola Smith,
Dan Morrison, Manager
EMP: 50 EST: 2003
SALES (est): 9.7MM Privately Held
WEB: www.earthcompany.org
SIC: 0781 Landscape services

(P-271)
NATURES IMAGE INC
20361 Hermana Cir, Lake Forest
(92630-8701)
PHONE..............................949 680-4400
Michelle M Caruana, CEO
John Caruana, Vice Pres
CAM Pham, Administration
Jacqueline Morales, Empl Rel Mgr
Mitch Farr, Opers Mgr
EMP: 95 EST: 1996
SQ FT: 13,800
SALES (est): 9.8MM Privately Held
WEB: www.naturesimage.net
SIC: 0781 0782 Landscape services; land-
scape contractors

(P-272)
NIEVES LANDSCAPE INC
1629 E Edinger Ave, Santa Ana
(92705-5001)
PHONE..............................714 835-7332
Gregorio Nieves, President
Anne Cashman, Office Mgr
Patricia White, Admin Sec
Gloria Mora, Purch Mgr
EMP: 150 EST: 1985
SALES (est): 16.7MM Privately Held
WEB: www.nieveslandscape.com
SIC: 0781 Landscape services

(P-273)
OUTSIDE LINES INC
2150 S Twne Cntre Pl Ste, Anaheim
(92806)
PHONE..............................714 637-4747
John Wickham Zimmerman, CEO
Hugh F Hughes, President
Jack Larsen, Vice Pres
John S Cunningham, Regional Mgr
Andrea Schroeder, Office Mgr
EMP: 50 EST: 2007
SALES (est): 10.9MM Privately Held
WEB: www.otl-inc.com
SIC: 0781 Landscape counseling & plan-
ning

(P-274)
PACIFIC RESTORATION GROUP INC
325 E Ellis Ave, Perris (92570-8413)
P.O. Box 429 (92572-0429)
PHONE..............................951 940-6069
John Richards, President
Daniel Richards, CFO
Patricia Richards, Admin Sec
EMP: 50 EST: 1993
SQ FT: 10,000

SALES (est): 5.9MM **Privately Held**
SIC: 0781 Landscape services

(P-275)
PIERRE LANDSCAPE INC
5455 2nd St, Irwindale (91706-2072)
PHONE..................................626 587-2121
Harold Young, *CEO*
Joseph Lowden, *President*
Monty Khouri, *CFO*
Evelyn Diaz, *Executive*
Gabriel Cordero, *Project Mgr*
EMP: 200 EST: 1980
SQ FT: 9,425
SALES (est): 26.1MM **Privately Held**
WEB: www.pierrelandscape.com
SIC: 0781 Landscape architects

(P-276)
PLATINUM LANDSCAPE INC
42575 Melanie Pl Ste C, Palm Desert
(92211-5162)
PHONE..................................760 200-3673
Christopher Johnson, *President*
Cherie Johnson, *Vice Pres*
EMP: 150
SQ FT: 3,000
SALES (est): 18MM **Privately Held**
WEB: www.platinumlandscapeinc.com
SIC: 0781 Landscape services

(P-277)
PRECISION LANDSCAPE & TURF
940 S Leslie St, La Habra (90631-6854)
PHONE..................................714 525-2318
Kevin Whinery, *President*
Gina Whinery, *Vice Pres*
EMP: 50 EST: 1983
SQ FT: 7,000
SALES (est): 1.5MM **Privately Held**
WEB: www.pltco.com
SIC: 0781 Landscape services

(P-278)
SAN VAL CORP (PA)
Also Called: San Val Alarm System
72203 Adelaid St, Thousand Palms
(92276-2321)
P.O. Box 12860, Palm Desert (92255-2860)
PHONE..................................760 346-3999
Robert J Sandifer, *President*
Sharon L Sandifer, *Admin Sec*
EMP: 425 EST: 1975
SALES (est): 17.3MM **Privately Held**
SIC: 0781 7381 Landscape services; burglary protection service

(P-279)
SEQUOIA ENVIRONMENTAL SVCS INC
1 University Dr, Aliso Viejo (92656-8081)
PHONE..................................949 480-4742
Danny McNamara, *CEO*
Scott Collins, *Treasurer*
Wendy Chen, *Office Mgr*
Malcolm Thomas, *Admin Sec*
EMP: 64 EST: 2015
SALES (est): 2.8MM **Privately Held**
WEB: www.sequoiaes.com
SIC: 0781 7349 Landscape services; janitorial service, contract basis

(P-280)
SIERRA LANDSCAPE DEVELOPMENT
2209 1/2 Chico Ave, South El Monte
(91733-1608)
PHONE..................................626 447-5260
Kevin Watchler, *CEO*
Candace Cleeland, *Project Engr*
EMP: 50 EST: 1983
SQ FT: 8,500
SALES (est): 7.1MM **Privately Held**
WEB: www.sierralandscapedev.com
SIC: 0781 1629 0782 1711 Landscape services; irrigation system construction; landscape contractors; irrigation sprinkler system installation

(P-281)
SLADE INDUSTRIAL LANDSCAPE INC
8838 Zelzah Ave, Sherwood Forest
(91325-3139)
P.O. Box 571960, Tarzana (91357-1960)
PHONE..................................818 885-1916
David Slade, *President*
Sylvia Slade, *Corp Secy*
Jesse Slade, *Vice Pres*
EMP: 55 EST: 1962
SALES (est): 4.4MM **Privately Held**
WEB: www.sladeindlandscape.com
SIC: 0781 0782 Landscape planning services; landscape contractors; garden maintenance services; lawn services

(P-282)
SOUTHWEST LANDSCAPE INC
2205 S Standard Ave, Santa Ana
(92707-3036)
P.O. Box 15611 (92735-0611)
PHONE..................................714 545-1084
Dan Hansen, *President*
Robert Hansen, *Vice Pres*
Casey Silva, *Marketing Staff*
Todd Shaw, *Sr Project Mgr*
Angelia Beckstrom, *Director*
EMP: 80 EST: 1982
SQ FT: 7,800
SALES (est): 4.6MM **Privately Held**
WEB: www.southwestlandscape.org
SIC: 0781 Landscape services

(P-283)
SPECIALIZED LDSCP MGT SVCS INC
Also Called: SLM Services
4212 Past Los Angles Ave, Simi Valley
(93063)
PHONE..................................805 520-7590
Rene Emeterio, *President*
Wendy Emeterio, *COO*
Ramon Salgado, *Opers Spvr*
EMP: 77 EST: 2006
SALES (est): 3.1MM **Privately Held**
WEB: www.slmlandscape.net
SIC: 0781 Landscape services

(P-284)
SUNSET LANDSCAPE MAINTENANCE
27201 Burbank, El Toro (92610-2500)
PHONE..................................949 455-4636
James Roughan, *President*
Claudia Roughan, *Corp Secy*
Laurie Savolainen, *Office Mgr*
Freddy Gonzalez, *Supervisor*
EMP: 100 EST: 1976
SQ FT: 6,300
SALES (est): 10.9MM **Privately Held**
WEB: www.sunsetlandscapemaintenanceinc.com
SIC: 0781 Landscape services

(P-285)
SWINKS CREATIONS INC (PA)
2769 Wanda Ave, Simi Valley
(93065-1518)
PHONE..................................805 522-0412
Mark Alan Swink, *CEO*
EMP: 73 EST: 2003
SALES (est): 2.1MM **Privately Held**
WEB: www.swinkscreations.com
SIC: 0781 1521 1799 Landscape services; general remodeling, single-family houses; kitchen & bathroom remodeling

(P-286)
T D WHITTON CONSTRUCTION INC
4801 Wible Rd, Bakersfield (93313-2647)
PHONE..................................661 834-5894
Marty Whitton, *President*
Travis Whitton, *Ch of Bd*
Emogene Whitton, *Treasurer*
EMP: 20 EST: 1982
SQ FT: 2,000
SALES (est): 1MM **Privately Held**
SIC: 0781 2951 Landscape services; asphalt paving mixtures & blocks

(P-287)
TERRA PACIFIC LANDSCAPE (HQ)
12891 Nelson St, Garden Grove
(92840-5018)
PHONE..................................714 567-0177
Rich Wingard, *President*
EMP: 89 EST: 1988
SALES (est): 17.7MM
SALES (corp-wide): 51.6MM **Privately Held**
WEB: www.terrapac.com
SIC: 0781 Landscape services
PA: Gothic Landscaping, Inc.
27413 Tourney Rd
Santa Clarita CA 91355
661 678-1400

(P-288)
VILLA PARK LANDSCAPE (PA)
739 W Katella Ave Ste B, Orange
(92867-4634)
PHONE..................................714 538-3788
Gwynn Neelon, *President*
Javier Reyes, *Vice Pres*
EMP: 72 EST: 1986
SQ FT: 4,000
SALES (est): 8.6MM **Privately Held**
WEB: www.villaparklandscape.com
SIC: 0781 Landscape services

(P-289)
WESTERN SIERRA LANDSCAPES INC
2400 Eastman Ave, Oxnard (93030-5187)
PHONE..................................805 983-0070
William C B Burr, *President*
Peter Christl, *CFO*
Linda Burr, *Vice Pres*
EMP: 50 EST: 1997
SALES (est): 1.1MM
SALES (corp-wide): 12.5MM **Privately Held**
WEB: www.vencowestern.com
SIC: 0781 Landscape services
PA: Venco Western, Inc.
2400 Eastman Ave
Oxnard CA 93030
805 981-2400

0782 Lawn & Garden Svcs

(P-290)
AMERICAN LANDSCAPE MGT INC
Also Called: Custom Lawn Services
1607 Los Angeles Ave I, Ventura
(93004-3237)
PHONE..................................805 647-5077
Armondo Bello, *Manager*
Arturo Perez, *Manager*
EMP: 75 **Privately Held**
WEB: www.americanlandscape.com
SIC: 0782 0783 0781 Landscape contractors; ornamental shrub & tree services; landscape planning services
PA: American Landscape Management, Inc.
7013 Owensmouth Ave
Canoga Park CA 91303

(P-291)
ARTISTIC MAINTENANCE INC
16092 Construction Cir E, Irvine
(92606-4401)
PHONE..................................949 733-8690
Rudy Moracco, *Manager*
EMP: 59
SALES (corp-wide): 17.7MM **Privately Held**
WEB: www.artisticmaintenance.com
SIC: 0782 Landscape contractors; garden maintenance services
HQ: Artistic Maintenance, Inc.
15510 Rckfeld Blvd Ste C2
Irvine CA 92618
949 581-9817

(P-292)
AZTECA LANDSCAPE (PA)
1525 E Ontario Ave # 101, Corona
(92881-3794)
PHONE..................................909 673-0889
Aurora Farias, *President*
Rosa M Lopez, *President*
EMP: 112 EST: 1975
SALES: 7.1MM **Privately Held**
WEB: www.aztecalandscape.com
SIC: 0782 Landscape contractors

(P-293)
CACHO LANDSCAPE MAINT CO INC
711 Truman St, San Fernando
(91340-3314)
P.O. Box 922764, Sylmar (91392-2764)
PHONE..................................818 365-0773
Eddie Cacho, *President*
Diana Cacho, *CFO*
Genaro Gutierrez, *Vice Pres*
EMP: 50 EST: 1979
SQ FT: 3,184
SALES (est): 3.8MM **Privately Held**
WEB: www.cachomaintenance.com
SIC: 0782 Landscape contractors

(P-294)
CAL-WEST NURSERIES INC
138 North Dr, Norco (92860-1637)
PHONE..................................951 270-0667
Michael Whiting, *President*
Steve Sidwell, *Project Mgr*
Matt Whiting, *Purch Agent*
EMP: 150 EST: 1968
SQ FT: 1,700
SALES (est): 8.8MM **Privately Held**
WEB: www.calwestlandscape.com
SIC: 0782 0181 Landscape contractors; nursery stock, growing of

(P-295)
CALIFORNIA LDSCP & DESIGN INC
Also Called: CA Landscape and Design
273 N Benson Ave, Upland (91786-5614)
PHONE..................................909 949-1601
Joseph Ciaglia Jr, *CEO*
Margaret Mingura, *CFO*
EMP: 120 EST: 1988
SQ FT: 1,500
SALES (est): 15.3MM **Privately Held**
WEB: www.callandscape.com
SIC: 0782 Landscape contractors

(P-296)
CENTRESCAPES INC
165 Gentry St, Pomona (91767-2184)
PHONE..................................909 392-3303
Mark Marcus, *President*
Grace Loya, *Corp Secy*
EMP: 88 EST: 1992
SQ FT: 7,000
SALES (est): 7.2MM **Privately Held**
WEB: www.centrescapes.com
SIC: 0782 Landscape contractors

(P-297)
COMPLETE LANDSCAPE CARE INC
13316 Leffingwell Rd, Whittier
(90605-4136)
PHONE..................................562 946-4441
Tom Murray, *President*
EMP: 57 EST: 1998
SQ FT: 26,000
SALES (est): 3.1MM **Privately Held**
WEB: www.completelandscapecare.com
SIC: 0782 1711 Landscape contractors; irrigation sprinkler system installation

(P-298)
DAVID OLLIS LANDSCAPE DEV INC
450 Kansas St Ste 104, Redlands
(92373-1481)
PHONE..................................909 307-1911
David Ollis, *President*
EMP: 50 EST: 1990
SALES (est): 5.3MM **Privately Held**
WEB: www.davidollis.com
SIC: 0782 Landscape contractors

(P-299)
DE LA TORRE LDSCP & MAINT CORP
656 Paseo Grande, Corona (92882-2837)
P.O. Box 3018 (92878-3018)
PHONE..................................951 549-3525

PRODUCTS & SVCS

Robert De La Torre, *President*
Socorro De La Torre, *Vice Pres*
Veronica De La Torre, *Admin Sec*
Veronica Dela Torre, *Controller*
EMP: 53 **EST:** 1989
SQ FT: 1,108
SALES (est): 1.9MM **Privately Held**
WEB: www.delatorrelandscape.com
SIC: 0782 Landscape contractors

(P-300)
DESERT HAVEN ENTERPRISES INC
43437 Copeland Cir, Lancaster
(93535-4672)
P.O. Box 2110 (93539-2110)
PHONE...................661 948-8402
Jenni C Moran, *CEO*
Roberta Terry, *CFO*
Ramona Aloyo, *Human Res Dir*
EMP: 543 **EST:** 1954
SQ FT: 15,000
SALES (est): 8.2MM **Privately Held**
WEB: www.deserthaven.org
SIC: 0782 8331 Lawn & garden services; work experience center

(P-301)
DIVERSCAPE INC
Also Called: Diversified Landscape Co
21730 Bundy Canyon Rd, Wildomar
(92595-8780)
PHONE...................951 245-1686
Vicki Moralez, *President*
Paul Moralez, *Vice Pres*
James Angelosanto, *General Mgr*
EMP: 90 **EST:** 1989
SQ FT: 4,000
SALES (est): 12.5MM **Privately Held**
WEB: www.diversifiedlandscape.com
SIC: 0782 1611 Garden maintenance services; landscape contractors; general contractor, highway & street construction

(P-302)
DMA GREENCARE CONTRACTING INC
950 N Tustin Ave Ste 118, Anaheim
(92807-1759)
PHONE...................714 630-9470
Dennis Aldridge, *CEO*
Darin Doucette, *Officer*
Eddie Acosta, *Project Mgr*
Franco Hernandez, *Project Engr*
Octavio Valencia, *Purchasing*
EMP: 50 **EST:** 2001
SALES (est): 10MM **Privately Held**
WEB: www.dmacontracting.com
SIC: 0782 Landscape contractors

(P-303)
EMERALD LANDSCAPE SERVICES INC
26415 Summit Cir, Santa Clarita
(91350-2991)
PHONE...................714 844-2200
John C Croul, *President*
Pam Mc Entire, *Consultant*
EMP: 70 **EST:** 1986
SALES (est): 3.4MM
SALES (corp-wide): 27.4MM **Privately Held**
WEB: www.emeraldlandscapeservices.com
SIC: 0782 0781 Landscape contractors; landscape planning services
PA: Stay Green Inc.
26415 Summit Cir
Santa Clarita CA 91350
661 291-2800

(P-304)
EXCEL LANDSCAPE INC
710 Rimpau Ave Ste 108, Corona
(92879-5724)
P.O. Box 77995 (92877-0133)
PHONE...................951 735-9650
Jose Alfaro, *President*
Marty Fox, *Sales Executive*
▲ **EMP:** 120 **EST:** 1975
SQ FT: 1,200
SALES (est): 5.9MM **Privately Held**
WEB: www.excellandscape.com
SIC: 0782 Lawn care services; garden maintenance services

(P-305)
FAR EAST LANDSCAPE & MAINT INC
6201 1/2 Van Nuys Blvd, Van Nuys
(91401-2710)
P.O. Box 950351, Mission Hills (91395-0351)
PHONE...................800 887-3227
Tony Moon, *President*
EMP: 52 **EST:** 1983 **Privately Held**
WEB: www.fareastlandscape.com
SIC: 0782 Landscape contractors; lawn care services

(P-306)
G C LANDSCAPE INC
Also Called: Country Garden Ldscp & Maint
6465 Wayazpa Blvd 3110, Anaheim
(92805)
PHONE...................714 535-5640
Mike Sardo, *President*
Chiclet Velarma, *Accounts Mgr*
EMP: 50 **EST:** 1994
SQ FT: 41,000
SALES (est): 2.1MM **Privately Held**
SIC: 0782 Lawn & garden services

(P-307)
GOTHIC LANDSCAPING INC (PA)
Also Called: Gothic Ground Management
27413 Tourney Rd, Santa Clarita
(91355-5602)
PHONE...................661 678-1400
Jon S Georgio, *President*
Ronald Georgio, *Vice Pres*
Mike Georgio, *Principal*
Autumn Conover, *Regional Mgr*
Karen Klein, *Controller*
EMP: 200 **EST:** 1984
SQ FT: 5,000
SALES (est): 51.6MM **Privately Held**
WEB: www.gothiclandscape.com
SIC: 0782 Landscape contractors; lawn services

(P-308)
GS BROTHERS INC (PA)
20331 Main St, Carson (90745-1033)
PHONE...................310 833-1369
Alan M Gaudenti, *President*
Robert M Gaudenti, *Corp Secy*
Marge Gonzalez, *Manager*
EMP: 190 **EST:** 1963
SALES (est): 12.9MM **Privately Held**
WEB: www.gsbrothers.com
SIC: 0782 Landscape contractors

(P-309)
HE JULIEN & ASSOCIATES INC
Also Called: C&R Maintenance
2275 E Hueneme Rd, Oxnard
(93033-8112)
P.O. Box 817, Port Hueneme (93044-0817)
PHONE...................805 488-8342
EMP: 50
SQ FT: 3,568
SALES (est): 1.4MM **Privately Held**
SIC: 0782 Lawn/Garden Services

(P-310)
INTERNATIONAL ENVMTL CORP
Also Called: IEC
13432 Wentworth St, Arleta (91331-6347)
P.O. Box 4218, Panorama City (91412-4218)
PHONE...................818 892-9341
Henry Cespedes, *Owner*
Jan Cespedes, *Corp Secy*
Eric Cespedes, *Vice Pres*
EMP: 67 **EST:** 1968
SQ FT: 800
SALES (est): 7.5MM **Privately Held**
WEB: www.iectrees.com
SIC: 0782 0181 Lawn services; nursery stock, growing of

(P-311)
IRRISCAPE CONSTRUCTION INC
20182 Carancho Rd, Temecula
(92590-4348)
PHONE...................951 694-6936
Robert Smith, *President*
EMP: 100

SQ FT: 1,500
SALES (est): 8.5MM **Privately Held**
WEB: www.irriscapeconstruction.com
SIC: 0782 Landscape contractors

(P-312)
JAMES H COWAN & ASSOCIATES INC
5126 Clareton Dr Ste 200, Agoura Hills
(91301-4529)
PHONE...................310 457-2574
Clark J Cowan, *President*
Kendall Whitney, *Admin Sec*
EMP: 95
SQ FT: 3,500
SALES (est): 7MM **Privately Held**
SIC: 0782 Landscape contractors

(P-313)
KITSON LANDSCAPE MGT INC
5787 Thornwood Dr, Goleta (93117-3801)
PHONE...................805 681-9460
Sarah Kitson, *President*
Dave Fudurich, *CFO*
David Fudurich, *Treasurer*
Brent Kitson, *Vice Pres*
Susan Ellis, *Office Mgr*
EMP: 80 **EST:** 1969
SQ FT: 52,272
SALES (est): 4.7MM **Privately Held**
WEB: www.kitsonlandscape.com
SIC: 0782 Landscape contractors

(P-314)
L BARRIOS AND ASSOCIATES INC
302 E Fthill Blvd Ste 101, San Dimas
(91773)
P.O. Box 3948 (91773-7948)
PHONE...................909 592-5893
John Barrios, *President*
Jennifer Stock, *Admin Sec*
EMP: 50 **EST:** 1955
SALES (est): 6.8MM **Privately Held**
WEB: www.lbarrios.com
SIC: 0782 1711 Landscape contractors; lawn services; irrigation sprinkler system installation

(P-315)
LANDCARE USA LLC
Also Called: Trugreen
1196 Patricia Ave, Simi Valley
(93065-3149)
PHONE...................805 520-9394
Noe Alcaraz, *Branch Mgr*
EMP: 52
SALES (corp-wide): 181.5MM **Privately Held**
WEB: www.landcare.com
SIC: 0782 Lawn care services
PA: Landcare Usa L.L.C.
5295 Westview Dr Ste 100
Frederick MD 21703
301 874-3300

(P-316)
LANDCARE USA LLC
Also Called: Trugreen
1616 Marlborough Ave S, Riverside
(92507-2041)
PHONE...................951 320-1522
Martin McKenna, *Branch Mgr*
EMP: 52
SALES (corp-wide): 181.5MM **Privately Held**
WEB: www.landcare.com
SIC: 0782 Lawn care services
PA: Landcare Usa L.L.C.
5295 Westview Dr Ste 100
Frederick MD 21703
301 874-3300

(P-317)
LANDCARE USA LLC
Also Called: Trugreen Lndcare Michael Bogan
15606 Cornet St, Santa Fe Springs
(90670-5514)
PHONE...................714 936-9512
EMP: 52
SALES (corp-wide): 181.5MM **Privately Held**
WEB: www.landcare.com
SIC: 0782 Lawn care services

PA: Landcare Usa L.L.C.
5295 Westview Dr Ste 100
Frederick MD 21703
301 874-3300

(P-318)
LANDCARE USA LLC
1315 W 130th St, Gardena (90247-1503)
PHONE...................310 719-1008
Don Cully, *Branch Mgr*
Rodrigo De Mello Sangy, *Branch Mgr*
EMP: 52
SALES (corp-wide): 181.5MM **Privately Held**
WEB: www.landcare.com
SIC: 0782 Lawn care services; lawn services
PA: Landcare Usa L.L.C.
5295 Westview Dr Ste 100
Frederick MD 21703
301 874-3300

(P-319)
LANDCARE USA LLC
Also Called: Trugreen
7755 Deering Ave, Canoga Park
(91304-5653)
PHONE...................818 346-7552
Raul Sanchez, *Branch Mgr*
EMP: 52
SALES (corp-wide): 181.5MM **Privately Held**
WEB: www.landcare.com
SIC: 0782 Lawn care services; landscape contractors
PA: Landcare Usa L.L.C.
5295 Westview Dr Ste 100
Frederick MD 21703
301 874-3300

(P-320)
LANDSCAPE DEVELOPMENT INC
1290 Carbide Dr, Corona (92831-7268)
PHONE...................951 371-9370
Tom McDaniel, *President*
Richard Barnes, *COO*
Anne Cleveland, *Business Dir*
Melissa Diez, *Purch Agent*
Alicia Syverson, *Director*
EMP: 148
SALES (corp-wide): 89.8MM **Privately Held**
WEB: www.landscapedevelopment.com
SIC: 0782 Landscape contractors
PA: Landscape Development, Inc.
28447 Witherspoon Pkwy
Valencia CA 91355
661 295-1970

(P-321)
LANDSCAPE DEVELOPMENT INC (PA)
28447 Witherspoon Pkwy, Valencia
(91355-4174)
PHONE...................661 295-1970
Gary Horton, *CEO*
Mark Crutcher, *COO*
Tim Myers, *CFO*
Timothy Myers Sr, *CFO*
Casper Correll, *Vice Pres*
▲ **EMP:** 350 **EST:** 1983
SALES (est): 89.8MM **Privately Held**
WEB: www.landscapedevelopment.com
SIC: 0782 5039 Landscape contractors; soil erosion control fabrics

(P-322)
LANDSCAPE SUPPORT SERVICES
12610 Saticoy St S, North Hollywood
(91605-4313)
P.O. Box 55307, Sherman Oaks (91413-0307)
PHONE...................818 475-0680
Soheila Sturm, *President*
EMP: 52 **EST:** 2011
SQ FT: 2,500
SALES (est): 6.6MM **Privately Held**
WEB: www.landscapesupportservices.com
SIC: 0782 0781 1611 1629 Landscape contractors; landscape counseling & planning; grading; irrigation system construction

(P-323)
LIBERTY LANDSCAPING INC (PA)
5212 El Rivino Rd, Riverside (92509-1807)
PHONE......................................951 683-2999
Alejandro Casillas, *President*
EMP: 200 **EST:** 1997
SQ FT: 43,560
SALES: 11.5MM **Privately Held**
WEB: www.libertylandscaping.com
SIC: 0782 0783 Landscape contractors; tree trimming services for public utility lines

(P-324)
MARIPOSA LANDSCAPES INC (PA)
Also Called: Mariposa Horticultural Entps
6232 Santos Diaz St, Irwindale (91702-3267)
PHONE......................................626 960-0196
Terry Noriega, *President*
David Hall, *Vice Pres*
Antonio Valenzuela, *Vice Pres*
Antonio Karraa, *Area Mgr*
Jennifer Ting, *Office Mgr*
EMP: 236 **EST:** 1977
SQ FT: 2,000
SALES (est): 29.4MM **Privately Held**
WEB: www.mariposa-ca.com
SIC: 0782 Garden maintenance services; lawn care services; landscape contractors

(P-325)
MEDLIN DEVELOPMENT
320 Tropicana Ranch Rd, Colton (92324-3605)
PHONE......................................909 825-5296
EMP: 50
SQ FT: 1,800
SALES (est): 1.5MM **Privately Held**
SIC: 0782 Lawn/Garden Services

(P-326)
MONARCH LANDSCAPE HOLDINGS LLC (PA)
550 S Hope St Ste 1675, Los Angeles (90071-2692)
PHONE......................................213 816-1750
Tony W Lee, *Mng Member*
Michael Hope, *Manager*
EMP: 77 **EST:** 2015
SALES (est): 48MM **Privately Held**
SIC: 0782 Garden services

(P-327)
MPL ENTERPRISES INC
Also Called: Mike Parker Landscape
2302 S Susan St, Santa Ana (92704-4421)
PHONE......................................714 545-1717
Michael Parker, *President*
Jeff Williams, *Sales Executive*
Eric Anderson, *Manager*
EMP: 90
SQ FT: 2,000
SALES (est): 4.1MM **Privately Held**
WEB: www.mikeparkerlandscape.com
SIC: 0782 Landscape contractors

(P-328)
OAK RIDGE LANDWORKS
Also Called: Landscape Contractor
3106 Tanglewood Ct, Thousand Oaks (91360-2863)
PHONE......................................805 630-8377
Kevin Lydick, *CEO*
EMP: 57 **EST:** 2013
SALES (est): 2.5MM **Privately Held**
WEB: www.oakridgelandworks.com
SIC: 0782 Landscape contractors

(P-329)
OCONNELL LANDSCAPE MAINT INC
860 E Watson Center Rd, Carson (90745-4120)
PHONE......................................800 339-1106
Jack Rush, *Branch Mgr*
EMP: 430
SALES (corp-wide): 51.5MM **Privately Held**
WEB: www.oclm.com
SIC: 0782 Landscape contractors

PA: O'connell Landscape Maintenance Inc.
23091 Arroyo Vis
Rcho Sta Marg CA 92688
949 589-2007

(P-330)
PARK LANDSCAPE MAINTENANCE (PA)
Also Called: Park Landscape Maint 1-2-3-4
22421 Gilberto Ste A, Rcho STA Marg (92688-2104)
PHONE......................................949 546-8300
Robert Morrison, *President*
Tom Tracy, *Shareholder*
Mike Tracy, *CEO*
Tom England, *CFO*
EMP: 300 **EST:** 1986
SQ FT: 10,000
SALES (est): 6.4MM **Privately Held**
WEB: www.parkwestinc.com
SIC: 0782 Lawn care services

(P-331)
PARK LANDSCAPE MAINTENANCE
5140 E Airport Dr Ste B, Ontario (91761-7806)
PHONE......................................909 605-8878
Paul Esparza, *Division Mgr*
EMP: 50
SALES (corp-wide): 6.4MM **Privately Held**
WEB: www.parkwestinc.com
SIC: 0782 Landscape contractors
PA: Park Landscape Maintenance Inc
22421 Gilberto Ste A
Rcho Sta Marg CA 92688
949 546-8300

(P-332)
PARK WEST COMPANIES INC (PA)
Also Called: Tracy & Ryder
22421 Gilberto Ste A, Rcho STA Marg (92688-2104)
PHONE......................................949 546-8300
Michael S Tracy, *Director*
Tom Tracy, *CEO*
Jack Lantry, *COO*
Jim Tracy, *Corp Secy*
Bart Ryder, *Vice Pres*
EMP: 310 **EST:** 1997
SQ FT: 20,000
SALES (est): 85MM **Privately Held**
WEB: www.parkwestinc.com
SIC: 0782 1629 6719 Landscape contractors; golf course construction; personal holding companies, except banks

(P-333)
PARK WEST LANDSCAPE INC
13105 Crenshaw Blvd, Hawthorne (90250-5513)
PHONE......................................310 363-4100
Rose Vargas, *Branch Mgr*
EMP: 87
SALES (corp-wide): 85MM **Privately Held**
WEB: www.parkwestinc.com
SIC: 0782 Landscape contractors
HQ: Park West Landscape, Inc.
22421 Gilberto Ste A
Rcho Sta Marg CA 92688

(P-334)
PARK WEST RESCOM INC
22421 Gilberto, Rcho STA Marg (92688-2104)
PHONE......................................949 546-8300
Michael S Tracy, *CEO*
Bart Ryder, *President*
EMP: 53 **EST:** 2002
SQ FT: 10,000
SALES (est): 790.2K **Privately Held**
WEB: www.parkwestinc.com
SIC: 0782 Landscape contractors

(P-335)
PARKWOOD LANDSCAPE MAINT INC
16443 Hart St, Van Nuys (91406-4608)
PHONE......................................818 988-9677
David Melito, *President*
Laura Zierhut, *Controller*

EMP: 95 **EST:** 1988
SQ FT: 1,500
SALES (est): 9.5MM **Privately Held**
WEB: www.parkwoodlandscape.com
SIC: 0782 Landscape contractors

(P-336)
PENNEY LAWN SERVICE INC
Also Called: Penny Lawn Service
4000 Allen Rd, Bakersfield (93314-9091)
PHONE......................................661 587-4788
Dan Penny, *Owner*
Sandy Penny, *Owner*
EMP: 100 **EST:** 1989
SQ FT: 1,275
SALES (est): 4.7MM **Privately Held**
WEB: www.penneylawnservice.com
SIC: 0782 Landscape contractors

(P-337)
PLOWBOY LANDSCAPES INC
2190 N Ventura Ave, Ventura (93001-1343)
P.O. Box 1802 (93002-1802)
PHONE......................................805 643-4966
Douglas Wasson, *President*
Greg Dygert, *General Mgr*
Barry Petersen, *Maintence Staff*
John Barton, *Maint Spvr*
Manuel Vega, *Manager*
EMP: 55 **EST:** 1974
SQ FT: 3,500
SALES (est): 6MM **Privately Held**
WEB: www.plowboylandscapes.com
SIC: 0782 Landscape contractors

(P-338)
RANCHO CALIFORNIA LDSCPG INC
13801 S Western Ave, Gardena (90249-2517)
PHONE......................................310 768-1680
Sal Mora, *President*
Ramon Sandoval, *Opers-Prdtn-Mfg*
EMP: 50 **EST:** 1998
SQ FT: 33,610
SALES (est): 3.8MM **Privately Held**
WEB: www.ranchocalifornia.biz
SIC: 0782 Landscape contractors

(P-339)
RESIDENT GROUP SERVICES INC (PA)
Also Called: Rgs Services
1156 N Grove St, Anaheim (92806-2109)
PHONE......................................714 630-5300
James M Gilly, *President*
Michael K Hayde, *CEO*
Claudia Garcia, *Admin Asst*
Dee Castro, *Controller*
Paul Bird, *Maintence Staff*
EMP: 149 **EST:** 1983
SQ FT: 15,000
SALES (est): 19.8MM **Privately Held**
SIC: 0782 Landscape contractors

(P-340)
S G D ENTERPRISES
Also Called: Four Seasons Landscaping
14937 Delano St, Van Nuys (91411-2123)
PHONE......................................323 658-1047
Stephen G Darrison, *President*
EMP: 50 **EST:** 1988
SQ FT: 1,800
SALES (est): 5.9MM **Privately Held**
WEB: www.fourseasonslandscapin-gandtree.com
SIC: 0782 6512 6513 Landscape contractors; nonresidential building operators; apartment building operators

(P-341)
SENIOR WELLNESS INNOVATION GRP (PA)
7403 Adwen St, Downey (90241-4415)
PHONE......................................562 746-2182
Erick Ramirez, *Principal*
EMP: 63 **EST:** 2016
SALES (est): 416.9K **Privately Held**
SIC: 0782 7699 7349 1799 Lawn & garden services; cleaning services; building & office cleaning services; janitorial service, contract basis; construction site cleanup

(P-342)
SHINSUKE CLIFFORD YAMAMOTO INC
Also Called: S C Yamamoto
2031 Emery Ave, La Habra (90631-5777)
PHONE......................................714 992-5783
Shinsuke C Yamamoto, *President*
EMP: 51 **EST:** 1975
SQ FT: 7,660
SALES (est): 1.3MM **Privately Held**
WEB: www.scyamamoto.com
SIC: 0782 Garden maintenance services; landscape contractors

(P-343)
SILVERWOOD LANDSCAPE CNSTR INC
2209 S Lyon St, Santa Ana (92705-5305)
P.O. Box 15940 (92735-0940)
PHONE......................................714 427-6134
Steven Paul Lancaster, *President*
Matthew Diluzio, *CFO*
Megan Flanagan, *Project Mgr*
EMP: 50 **EST:** 1995
SALES (est): 6.6MM **Privately Held**
WEB: www.silverwoodlandscape.com
SIC: 0782 Landscape contractors

(P-344)
SOTO COMPANY INC
34275 Camino Capistrano A, Capistrano Beach (92624-1917)
PHONE......................................949 493-9403
Joe Soto, *President*
Carol Soto, *Corp Secy*
EMP: 75 **EST:** 1975
SQ FT: 4,000
SALES (est): 3.7MM **Privately Held**
WEB: www.sotocompany.com
SIC: 0782 Landscape contractors

(P-345)
TRACY & RYDER LANDSCAPE INC
22421 Gilberto Ste A, Rcho STA Marg (92688-2104)
PHONE......................................949 858-7017
Michael S Tracy, *Manager*
EMP: 70
SALES (corp-wide): 85MM **Privately Held**
SIC: 0782 Lawn & garden services
HQ: Tracy & Ryder Landscape, Inc
5375 Cameron St Ste G
Las Vegas NV 89118
702 248-6336

(P-346)
TROPICAL PLAZA NURSERY INC
9642 Santiago Blvd, Villa Park (92867-2521)
PHONE......................................714 998-4100
Leslie T Fields, *President*
Mike Feilds, *Vice Pres*
Lucas Fields, *Mktg Dir*
Victor Zamora, *Superintendent*
EMP: 100 **EST:** 1950
SQ FT: 5,000
SALES (est): 2.6MM **Privately Held**
WEB: www.tropicalplaza.com
SIC: 0782 Landscape contractors

(P-347)
ULTIMATE LANDSCAPING MGT
700 E Sycamore St, Anaheim (92805-2831)
PHONE......................................714 502-9711
James Berne, *President*
Marlyn Arcos, *Accounts Mgr*
Anayeli Espino, *Accounts Mgr*
Angelica Herrera, *Accounts Mgr*
EMP: 80 **EST:** 1984
SALES (est): 5MM **Privately Held**
SIC: 0782 Landscape contractors

(P-348)
VAUGHN WEEDMAN INC (PA)
Also Called: Northwest Landscape Services
550 S Hope St Ste 1675, Los Angeles (90071-2692)
PHONE......................................425 481-0919
Vaughn Weedman, *President*
Joel Olivares, *Branch Mgr*
Marcelino Alvarez, *Foreman/Supr*

(PA)=Parent Co (HQ)=Headquarters (DH)=Div Headquarters
✪ = New Business established in last 2 years

Raul Varela, *Foreman/Supr*
Michael Bernards, *Manager*
EMP: 125 **EST:** 1989
SALES (est): 13.9MM **Privately Held**
SIC: 0782 Landscape contractors

(P-349)
VENCO WESTERN INC (PA)
2400 Eastman Ave, Oxnard (93030-5187)
PHONE.................................805 981-2400
Linda Del Nagro Burr, *President*
Craig Owen, *Accounts Mgr*
EMP: 150 **EST:** 1977
SQ FT: 15,000
SALES (est): 12.5MM **Privately Held**
WEB: www.vencowestern.com
SIC: 0782 Landscape contractors

(P-350)
VINTAGE ASSOCIATES INC
Also Called: Vintage Nursery
78755 Darby Rd, Bermuda Dunes
(92203-9621)
P.O. Box 5250, La Quinta (92248-5250)
PHONE.................................760 772-3673
Gregory Gritters, *President*
Alan W Hollinger, *Opers Mgr*
Jesus Campos, *Manager*
Fernando Fregoso, *Manager*
Bruce Brown, *Superintendent*
EMP: 160 **EST:** 1989
SQ FT: 1,000
SALES (est): 12.8MM **Privately Held**
WEB: www.vintagelandscape.com
SIC: 0782 5193 5261 Landscape contractors; nursery stock; nurseries

(P-351)
W B STARR INC
20602 Canada Rd, Lake Forest
(92630-8100)
PHONE.................................949 770-8835
William B Starr, *President*
Martha L Starr, *Vice Pres*
EMP: 65 **EST:** 1975
SQ FT: 10,000
SALES (est): 4.7MM **Privately Held**
WEB: www.wbstarr.com
SIC: 0782 Garden maintenance services

(P-352)
WM VANDERGEEST LDSCP CARE INC
3342 W Castor St, Santa Ana
(92704-3908)
PHONE.................................714 545-8432
Allan M Curr, *President*
Sherry Curr, *Treasurer*
Chris Curr, *Vice Pres*
EMP: 51 **EST:** 1974
SQ FT: 10,000
SALES (est): 1.7MM **Privately Held**
WEB: www.vandergeestlandscapecare.com
SIC: 0782 Landscape contractors

0783 Ornamental Shrub & Tree Svc

(P-353)
BC TREE SERVICE INC
4288 Quatal Canyon Rd, Maricopa
(93252-9624)
P.O. Box 23303, Ventura (93002-3303)
PHONE.................................805 649-6875
Brett Cunningham, *CEO*
EMP: 60 **EST:** 1990
SALES (est): 4.8MM **Privately Held**
WEB: www.bigctree.com
SIC: 0783 1795 Planting, pruning & trimming services; demolition, buildings & other structures

(P-354)
BROOKER ASSOCIATES
16372 Cnstr Cir E 5, Irvine (92618)
PHONE.................................949 559-4877
EMP: 52
SALES (corp-wide): 5.4MM **Privately Held**
SIC: 0783 1721 1542 Contractor Of Landscaping & Maintenance Painting Tenant Renovation Improvement

PA: Brooker Associates
2331 E Lambert Rd
La Habra CA 90631
714 773-9490

(P-355)
CLS LANDSCAPE MANAGEMENT INC
4329 State St Ste B, Montclair
(91763-6082)
PHONE.................................909 628-3005
Kevin L Davis, *President*
Gloria Gonzalez, *Office Mgr*
Leslie Lodahl, *Office Mgr*
Kimberly Davis, *Admin Sec*
EMP: 325 **EST:** 1983
SQ FT: 2,500
SALES (est): 21MM **Privately Held**
WEB: www.clslandscape.com
SIC: 0783 0782 Ornamental shrub & tree services; lawn & garden services

(P-356)
FINCH TREE SURGERY INC
841 E Mission Rd, San Gabriel
(91776-2745)
PHONE.................................626 287-9838
Randal Finch, *President*
Fred C Finch, *Ch of Bd*
Karin Finch, *Corp Secy*
EMP: 56 **EST:** 1967
SALES (est): 845.3K **Privately Held**
WEB: www.bartlett.com
SIC: 0783 Planting, pruning & trimming services

(P-357)
GREAT SCOTT TREE SERVICE INC (PA)
10761 Court Ave, Stanton (90680-2435)
PHONE.................................714 826-1750
Scott Griffiths, *President*
Steve Guzowski, *Bd of Directors*
Jacob Griffiths, *Vice Pres*
Steve Guzonski, *Administration*
Jaime Meza, *Opers Staff*
EMP: 120
SQ FT: 28,675
SALES (est): 13.3MM **Privately Held**
WEB: www.greatscotttreecare.com
SIC: 0783 Pruning services, ornamental tree

(P-358)
LEONARD CHAIDEZ INC
Also Called: Leonard Chaidez Tree Service
2298 N Batavia St, Orange (92865-3106)
P.O. Box 29, Anaheim (92815-0029)
PHONE.................................714 279-8173
Leonard Chaidez, *President*
Deborah Foushee, *Admin Sec*
Jamie Lance, *Manager*
EMP: 60 **EST:** 1977
SQ FT: 2,000
SALES (est): 3.1MM **Privately Held**
SIC: 0783 0781 8748 0782 Planting, pruning & trimming services; landscape services; environmental consultant; lawn & garden services

(P-359)
ORIGINAL MOWBRAYS TREE SVC INC (PA)
686 E Mill St, San Bernardino
(92408-1610)
PHONE.................................909 383-7009
Dwight Anderson, *Principal*
Rick J Mowbray, *Project Mgr*
EMP: 196 **EST:** 1972
SQ FT: 1,000
SALES (est): 79.4MM **Privately Held**
WEB: www.mowbrays.com
SIC: 0783 Tree trimming services for public utility lines

(P-360)
PACIFIC COAST TREE EXPERTS
21525 Strathern St, Canoga Park
(91304-4137)
PHONE.................................805 506-1211
Nicolas Pinedo, *Principal*
Armando Valdez, *CEO*
Eymy Lopez, *Office Mgr*
Antonio Ramirez Bonilla, *Manager*
EMP: 150 **EST:** 2010

SALES (est): 12.6MM **Privately Held**
WEB: www.pacificcoasttreeexperts.com
SIC: 0783 Planting, pruning & trimming services

(P-361)
SENNA TREE COMPANY LLC
9255 Sunland Blvd, Sun Valley
(91352-2055)
PHONE.................................818 957-5755
John Mote, *President*
Mae Menier, *Marketing Staff*
EMP: 55 **EST:** 1997
SALES (est): 3.3MM **Privately Held**
WEB: www.sennatree.com
SIC: 0783 5193 Planting, pruning & trimming services; nursery stock

(P-362)
TREEPEOPLE INC
12601 Mulholland Dr, Beverly Hills
(90210-1332)
PHONE.................................818 753-4600
Walt Burkley, *Ch of Bd*
Andy Lipkis, *President*
Gwyn Quillen, *Treasurer*
Paul Bergman, *Admin Sec*
Laura Derby, *Administration*
EMP: 50 **EST:** 1970
SQ FT: 21,000
SALES: 8.5MM **Privately Held**
WEB: www.treepeople.org
SIC: 0783 8641 Planting, pruning & trimming services; environmental protection organization

(P-363)
WEST COAST ARBORISTS INC
11405 Nardo St, Ventura (93004-3201)
PHONE.................................805 671-5092
Lorenzo Perez, *Owner*
Andy Trotter, *Vice Pres*
EMP: 122
SALES (corp-wide): 44.5MM **Privately Held**
WEB: www.westcoastarborists.com
SIC: 0783 Planting, pruning & trimming services
PA: West Coast Arborists, Inc.
2200 E Via Burton
Anaheim CA 92806
714 991-1900

(P-364)
WEST COAST ARBORISTS INC
21718 Walnut Ave, Grand Terrace
(92313-4437)
PHONE.................................909 783-6544
Patrick Mahoney, *President*
EMP: 122
SALES (corp-wide): 44.5MM **Privately Held**
WEB: www.westcoastarborists.com
SIC: 0783 Planting, pruning & trimming services
PA: West Coast Arborists, Inc.
2200 E Via Burton
Anaheim CA 92806
714 991-1900

0811 Timber Tracts

(P-365)
BOETHING TREELAND FARMS INC (PA)
23475 Long Valley Rd, Woodland Hills
(91367-6006)
PHONE.................................818 883-1222
Bruce Edgar Pherson, *CEO*
Marjorie Boething Arnold, *Shareholder*
Sally Boething Hilton, *Shareholder*
Cathy Boething Pherson, *Shareholder*
Marji Boething, *CFO*
EMP: 60 **EST:** 1953
SQ FT: 1,500
SALES (est): 29.8MM **Privately Held**
WEB: www.boethingtreeland.com
SIC: 0811 5261 Tree farm; nurseries

(P-366)
BRIGHTVIEW TREE COMPANY
Also Called: Specimen Contracting
9500 Foothill Blvd, Sunland (91040-1857)
PHONE.................................818 951-5500

Tadd Russikoff, *Manager*
EMP: 81 **Privately Held**
WEB: www.brightview.com
SIC: 0811 Tree farm
HQ: Brightview Tree Company
24151 Ventura Blvd # 108
Calabasas CA 91302
818 223-8500

(P-367)
BRIGHTVIEW TREE COMPANY
Also Called: Environmental Industries
3200 W Telegraph Rd, Fillmore
(93015-9623)
PHONE.................................714 546-7975
Susan Flores, *Branch Mgr*
EMP: 81 **Privately Held**
WEB: www.brightview.com
SIC: 0811 0782 Tree farm; lawn services
HQ: Brightview Tree Company
24151 Ventura Blvd # 108
Calabasas CA 91302
818 223-8500

(P-368)
HOLIDAY TREE FARMS INC
329 Van Norman Rd, Montebello
(90640-5314)
P.O. Box 1688, West Covina (91793-1688)
PHONE.................................323 276-1900
Greg Rondeau, *Principal*
EMP: 126
SALES (corp-wide): 40.2MM **Privately Held**
WEB: www.holidaytreefarm.com
SIC: 0811 Tree farm
PA: Holiday Tree Farms, Inc.
800 Nw Cornell Ave
Corvallis OR 97330
541 753-3236

(P-369)
YEW BIO-PHARM GROUP INC (PA)
9460 Telstar Ave Ste 6, El Monte
(91731-2904)
PHONE.................................626 401-9588
Zhiguo Wang, *Ch of Bd*
Guifang Qi, *Treasurer*
EMP: 85 **EST:** 1996
SALES (est): 27.3MM **Publicly Held**
WEB: www.yewbiopharm.com
SIC: 0811 Tree farm

0851 Forestry Svcs

(P-370)
BRADCO INDUSTRIAL CORPORATION
Also Called: Bradco Environmental
1671 Sessums Dr, Redlands (92374-1906)
P.O. Box 390, Crestline (92325-0390)
PHONE.................................888 272-3261
Brad Bauder, *President*
Tracey Bauder, *CFO*
EMP: 17 **EST:** 2002
SQ FT: 900
SALES (est): 730.1K **Privately Held**
WEB: www.bracoenvironmental.com
SIC: 0851 241? Forestry services; wood chips, produced in the field

(P-371)
CALIFORNIA SILVER-AGRICULTURE
831 Ash Ave, Lindsay (93247-1449)
PHONE.................................559 562-3795
Raul L Acevedo, *Owner*
EMP: 50
SALES (est): 50K **Privately Held**
SIC: 0851 Forestry services

(P-372)
REDDING TREE GROWERS CORP
18985 Avenue 256 Apt A, Exeter
(93221-9558)
P.O. Box 845 (93221-0845)
PHONE.................................559 594-9299
Francisco Acevedo, *President*
Amelia Acevedo, *Vice Pres*
EMP: 100 **EST:** 1990 **Privately Held**
WEB: www.redding-tree-growers-corp.sbcontract.com

SIC: 0851 Reforestation services

0921 Finfish Farming & Fish Hatcheries

(P-373)
KENT SEATECH LLC
Also Called: Kent Seafarms
70775 Buchanan St, Mecca (92254)
P.O. Box 757 (92254-0757)
PHONE..............................760 396-2301
Wayne Steurd, *Manager*
Tom Tuterow, *Project Mgr*
Dour Davidson, *Sales Executive*
Brian Clagg, *Sales Mgr*
EMP: 50 **Privately Held**
WEB: www.kentseatech.com
SIC: 0921 Fish hatcheries & preserves
HQ: Kent Seatech Llc
11125 Flintkote Ave Ste J
San Diego CA 92121
858 452-5765

1041 Gold Ores

(P-374)
GOLDEN QUEEN MINING CO LLC
2818 Silver Queen Rd, Mojave
(93501-7021)
P.O. Box 1030 (93502-1030)
PHONE..............................661 824-4300
Thomas Clay, *Ch of Bd*
Robert Walish, *President*
Andree St-Germain, *CFO*
Brenda Dayton, *Admin Sec*
Cynthia Cain, *Admin Asst*
EMP: 180 EST: 2014
SQ FT: 2,500
SALES (est): 61.9MM
SALES (corp-wide): 58.4MM **Privately Held**
WEB: www.goldenqueen.com
SIC: 1041 Gold ores mining
PA: Golden Queen Mining Co. Ltd
580 Hornby St Suite 880
Vancouver BC V6C 3
604 417-7952

(P-375)
LOST DUTCHMANS MININGS ASSN (DH)
43445 Bus Pk Dr Ste 113, Temecula
(92590-3671)
P.O. Box 891509 (92589-1509)
PHONE..............................951 699-4749
Perry Massie, *President*
Tom Massie, *Admin Sec*
▲ EMP: 30 EST: 1995
SQ FT: 3,200
SALES (est): 7.3MM
SALES (corp-wide): 136.3MM **Privately Held**
WEB: www.outdoorchannelplus.com
SIC: 1041 Gold ores

(P-376)
STAVATTI INDUSTRIES LTD
3670 El Camino Dr, San Bernardino
(92404-2025)
P.O. Box 211258, Eagan MN (55121-2658)
PHONE..............................651 238-5369
Christopher R Beskar, *Branch Mgr*
Christopher Beskar, *CEO*
EMP: 50
SALES (corp-wide): 3.8MM **Privately Held**
SIC: 1041 1081 3511 3533 Gold ores mining; metal mining exploration & development services; turbines & turbine generator set units, complete; oil & gas field machinery; truck trailers
PA: Stavatti Industries Ltd
1061 Tiffany Dr
Eagan MN 55123
651 238-5369

1081 Metal Mining Svcs

(P-377)
NATIONAL EWP INC
Also Called: National Explrtion Wells Pumps
5566 Arrow Hwy, Montclair (91763-1606)
PHONE..............................909 931-4014
Tom Moreland, *Branch Mgr*
Vince Hardie, *Manager*
Justina Speas, *Manager*
Brandon Cobbs, *Assistant*
Sophie Rominger, *Commercial*
EMP: 15
SALES (corp-wide): 29.9MM **Privately Held**
WEB: www.nationalewp.com
SIC: 1081 Metal mining exploration & development services
PA: National Ewp, Inc.
3707 Manzanita Ln
Elko NV 89801
775 753-7355

(P-378)
PERERA CNSTR & DESIGN INC
2890 Inland Empire Blvd, Ontario
(91764-4649)
PHONE..............................909 484-6350
Henry Perera Jr, *CEO*
Gilbert J Moreno, *CFO*
Tony Bojorquez, *Director*
Fredy Mata, *Superintendent*
EMP: 35 EST: 1989
SQ FT: 20,000
SALES (est): 35.1MM **Privately Held**
WEB: www.pererainc.com
SIC: 1081 Metal mining exploration & development services

(P-379)
RYO RIO TINTO MINERALS
300 Falcon St, Wilmington (90744-6407)
PHONE..............................310 522-5322
Tedine Long, *Principal*
▼ EMP: 18 EST: 2008
SALES (est): 10.4MM **Privately Held**
SIC: 1081 Metal mining services

1221 Bituminous Coal & Lignite: Surface Mining

(P-380)
CHEVRON MINING INC
Moly
67750 Bailey Rd, Mountain Pass (92366)
PHONE..............................760 856-7625
Allen Randle, *Branch Mgr*
EMP: 238
SALES (corp-wide): 94.6B **Publicly Held**
SIC: 1221 Surface mining, bituminous
HQ: Chevron Mining Inc.
116 Invrneco Dr E Ste 207
Englewood CO 80112
303 930-3600

1231 Anthracite Mining

(P-381)
MIDSTREAM ENERGY PARTNERS USA
9224 Tupman Rd, Tupman (93276)
PHONE..............................661 765-4087
Stanley Owerko, *President*
Kari Lusk, *Managing Dir*
Robert Espinoza, *Supervisor*
Sharanya Shanbhogue, *Supervisor*
EMP: 28 EST: 2012
SALES (est): 23.9MM **Privately Held**
SIC: 1231 1382 1311 1321 Anthracite mining; oil & gas exploration services; crude petroleum & natural gas; natural gas liquids

1241 Coal Mining Svcs

(P-382)
GREKA INC
1791 Sinton Rd, Santa Maria (93458-9708)
P.O. Box 5489 (93456-5489)
PHONE..............................805 347-8700
Andy Devegvar, *President*
Randeep Grewal, *CEO*
EMP: 15 EST: 1997
SQ FT: 3,000
SALES (est): 2.2MM **Privately Held**
WEB: www.greka.com
SIC: 1241 1081 Coal mining services; metal mining services

(P-383)
RIO TINTO MINERALS INC
Also Called: Reno Tenco
14486 Borax Rd, Boron (93516-2017)
PHONE..............................760 762-7121
Xiaoling Liu, *CEO*
Preston Chiaro, *President*
Simon Trott, *Officer*
Simone Niven, *Executive*
Hugo Bague, *Principal*
◆ EMP: 150 EST: 2006
SALES (est): 154.1MM
SALES (corp-wide): 44.6B **Privately Held**
WEB: www.riotinto.com
SIC: 1241 Coal mining services
HQ: U.S. Borax Inc.
200 E Randolph St # 7100
Chicago IL 60601
773 270-6500

(P-384)
TAFT PRODUCTION COMPANY
950 Petroleum Club Rd, Taft (93268-9748)
P.O. Box 1277 (93268-1277)
PHONE..............................661 765-7194
Daniel S Jaffee, *President*
EMP: 95 EST: 2002
SALES (est): 28.4MM
SALES (corp-wide): 304.9MM **Publicly Held**
WEB: www.oildri.com
SIC: 1241 1081 Coal mining services; metal mining services
PA: Oil-Dri Corporation Of America
410 N Michigan Ave Fl 4
Chicago IL 60611
312 321-1515

1311 Crude Petroleum & Natural Gas

(P-385)
AERA ENERGY LLC
Also Called: Kernridge Division
19590 7th Standard Rd, Mc Kittrick
(93251-9709)
PHONE..............................661 334-3100
Marie Crosby, *Principal*
Johnny Stieg, *Production*
EMP: 81
SALES (corp-wide): 180.5B **Privately Held**
WEB: www.aeraenergy.com
SIC: 1311 Natural gas production; crude petroleum production
HQ: Aera Energy Services Company
10000 Ming Ave
Bakersfield CA 93311
661 665-5000

(P-386)
BENTLEY-SIMONSON INC
1746 S Victoria Ave Ste F, Ventura
(93003-6190)
PHONE..............................805 650-2794
James Bentley, *Ch of Bd*
Theodore Bentley, *Ch of Bd*
Clifton O Simonson, *President*
Petter Romming, *Vice Pres*
EMP: 20 EST: 1987
SQ FT: 1,000
SALES (est): 2.4MM **Privately Held**
SIC: 1311 Crude petroleum production

(P-387)
BEP (LP) I LLC
515 Suth Flwr St Ste 4800, Los Angeles
(90071)
PHONE..............................213 225-5900
John R Butler, *Director*
EMP: 15 EST: 2012
SALES (est): 314.3K **Privately Held**
SIC: 1311 Crude petroleum & natural gas

(P-388)
BERRY PETROLEUM COMPANY LLC
25121 Sierra Hwy, Newhall (91321-2007)
PHONE..............................661 255-6066
Eddie Azevedo, *Manager*
Kari Hochstatter, *Analyst*
Natasha Barber, *Manager*
Joseph Cobb, *Manager*
EMP: 13
SALES (corp-wide): 523.8MM **Publicly Held**
WEB: www.bry.com
SIC: 1311 Crude petroleum production; natural gas production
HQ: Berry Petroleum Company, Llc
11117 River Run Blvd
Bakersfield CA 93311
661 616-3900

(P-389)
BERRY PETROLEUM COMPANY LLC
28700 Hovey Hills Rd, Taft (93268)
P.O. Box 925 (93268-0925)
PHONE..............................661 769-8820
Tom Cruise, *Manager*
EMP: 13
SALES (corp-wide): 523.8MM **Publicly Held**
WEB: www.bry.com
SIC: 1311 Crude petroleum production
HQ: Berry Petroleum Company, Llc
11117 River Run Blvd
Bakersfield CA 93311
661 616-3900

(P-390)
BERRY PETROLEUM COMPANY LLC (HQ)
11117 River Run Blvd, Bakersfield
(93311-8957)
PHONE..............................661 616-3900
Trem Smith, *President*
Michael Helm, *Officer*
Kurt Neher, *Exec VP*
Kurt E Neher, *Exec VP*
Garrett Zola, *Engineer*
EMP: 225 EST: 1985
SALES (est): 97.6MM
SALES (corp-wide): 523.8MM **Publicly Held**
WEB: www.bry.com
SIC: 1311 Crude petroleum production; natural gas production
PA: Berry Corporation (Bry)
16000 Dallas Pkwy Ste 500
Dallas TX 75248
661 616-3900

(P-391)
BETA OPERATING COMPANY LLC
Also Called: Beta Offshore
111 W Ocean Blvd, Long Beach
(90802-4633)
PHONE..............................562 628-1526
Marielle Lomax, *Engineer*
Veronica Banuelos, *Accountant*
Kimberly Dreiske, *Personnel Assit*
Lorraine Lopez, *Purchasing*
EMP: 55
SALES (corp-wide): 202.1MM **Publicly Held**
WEB: www.betaoffshore.com
SIC: 1311 Crude petroleum production; natural gas production
HQ: Beta Operating Company, Llc
500 Dallas St Ste 1600
Houston TX 77002

PRODUCTS & SVCS

(P-392)
BEVERLY HILLCREST OIL CORP
27241 Burbank, El Toro (92610-2500)
PHONE.........................949 598-7300
Morris Hodges, *President*
Katherine Hodges, *Vice Pres*
EMP: 15 **EST:** 1979
SALES (est): 1.2MM **Privately Held**
SIC: 1311 1321 Crude petroleum production; natural gas liquids production

(P-393)
BREA CANON OIL CO INC
23903 Normandie Ave, Harbor City
(90710-1400)
PHONE.........................310 326-4002
Andrew Barkler, *President*
Ray Javier, *Vice Pres*
Rod Benny, *Manager*
EMP: 17 **EST:** 2004
SALES (est): 3.1MM **Privately Held**
SIC: 1311 Crude petroleum production

(P-394)
BREITBURN GP LLC
707 Wilshire Blvd # 4600, Los Angeles
(90017-3501)
PHONE.........................213 225-5900
Halbert S Washburn, *CEO*
EMP: 18 **EST:** 2006
SALES (est): 1MM **Privately Held**
WEB: www.mavresources.com
SIC: 1311 Crude petroleum & natural gas

(P-395)
CALIFORNIA RESOURCES CORP (PA)
27200 Tourney Rd Ste 200, Santa Clarita
(91355-4910)
PHONE.........................888 848-4754
Mark A McFarland, *Ch of Bd*
Francisco J Leon, *CFO*
Chris Gould, *Exec VP*
Shawn M Kerns, *Exec VP*
Michael L Preston, *Executive*
EMP: 245 **EST:** 2014
SALES (est): 2.2B **Publicly Held**
WEB: www.crc.com
SIC: 1311 Crude petroleum & natural gas

(P-396)
CALIFORNIA RESOURCES PROD CORP
3450 E 5th St, Oxnard (93033-2100)
PHONE.........................805 483-8017
EMP: 83
SALES (corp-wide): 2.4B **Publicly Held**
SIC: 1311 1382 Crude Petroleum/Natural Gas Production Oil/Gas Exploration Services
HQ: California Resources Production Corporation
11109 River Run Blvd
Bakersfield CA 91355
661 869-8000

(P-397)
CALIFORNIA RESOURCES PROD CORP
4900 W Lokern Rd, Mc Kittrick
(93251-9764)
PHONE.........................661 869-8000
EMP: 25
SALES (corp-wide): 2.2B **Publicly Held**
WEB: www.crc.com
SIC: 1311 1382 Crude petroleum production; oil & gas exploration services
HQ: California Resources Production Corporation
27200 Tourney Rd Ste 200
Santa Clarita CA 91355

(P-398)
CALIFORNIA RESOURCES PROD CORP (HQ)
Also Called: Vintage Production California
27200 Tourney Rd Ste 200, Santa Clarita
(91355-4910)
PHONE.........................661 869-8000
Richard Oringderff,
EMP: 125 **EST:** 2005

SALES (est): 192MM
SALES (corp-wide): 2.2B **Publicly Held**
WEB: www.crc.com
SIC: 1311 1382 Crude petroleum production; oil & gas exploration services
PA: California Resources Corporation
27200 Tourney Rd Ste 200
Santa Clarita CA 91355
888 848-4754

(P-399)
CARBON CALIFORNIA COMPANY LLC
270 Quail Ct Ste 201, Santa Paula
(93060-9206)
PHONE.........................805 933-1901
Patrick R McDonald, *CEO*
Mark D Pierce, *President*
Kevin D Struzeski, *CFO*
EMP: 19 **EST:** 2016
SALES (est): 6.7MM
SALES (corp-wide): 116.6MM **Publicly Held**
WEB: www.carbonenergycorp.com
SIC: 1311 Crude petroleum & natural gas
PA: Carbon Energy Corporation
1700 Broadway Ste 1170
Denver CO 80290
720 407-7043

(P-400)
CARNEROS ENERGY INC
4550 California Ave # 720, Bakersfield
(93309-7012)
PHONE.........................661 616-5600
John Rainwater, *President*
Mickey Wiesinger, *Manager*
EMP: 19 **EST:** 2001
SQ FT: 7,000
SALES (est): 1.9MM **Privately Held**
SIC: 1311 Crude petroleum & natural gas production

(P-401)
CHEVRON CORPORATION
324 W El Segundo Blvd, El Segundo
(90245-3635)
PHONE.........................310 615-5000
William Simok, *Exec Dir*
Henry Kusch, *General Mgr*
Maria E Bonifacio, *Admin Asst*
Craig Carter, *IT/INT Sup*
Nickolas Stephens, *Technology*
EMP: 812
SALES (corp-wide): 94.6B **Publicly Held**
WEB: www.chevron.com
SIC: 5541 1311 1382 1321 Filling stations, gasoline; crude petroleum production; oil & gas exploration services; natural gas liquids
PA: Chevron Corporation
6001 Bollinger Canyon Rd
San Ramon CA 94583
925 842-1000

(P-402)
COOPER & BRAIN INC
655 E D St, Wilmington (90744-6003)
P.O. Box 1177 (90748-1177)
PHONE.........................310 834-4411
Robert E Brain, *President*
Joel A Cooper, *Corp Secy*
EMP: 37 **EST:** 1948
SQ FT: 4,000
SALES (est): 7.5MM **Privately Held**
SIC: 1311 Crude petroleum production

(P-403)
GALILEO TECHNOLOGIES CORP
11800 Clark St, Arcadia (91006-6000)
PHONE.........................626 447-3100
Osvaldo Del Campo, *CEO*
Imed Joffe, *President*
Kristine Manukyan, *Office Mgr*
Carlos Griffouliere, *Controller*
◆ **EMP:** 77 **EST:** 2011
SALES (est): 15.4MM **Privately Held**
WEB: www.galileoar.com
SIC: 1311 Natural gas production

(P-404)
GREGG HAMMORK ENTERPRIZES INC
Also Called: Gregg's Mission Viejo Mobile
23002 Alicia Pkwy, Mission Viejo
(92692-1636)
PHONE.........................949 586-7902
Gregg Hammork, *President*
EMP: 28 **EST:** 1990
SQ FT: 3,000
SALES (est): 10.5MM **Privately Held**
SIC: 1311 Crude petroleum & natural gas production

(P-405)
HATHAWAY LLC
4205 Atlas Ct, Bakersfield (93308-4510)
P.O. Box 81385 (93380-1385)
PHONE.........................661 393-2004
Chad Hathaway,
Sandra Cook, *Vice Pres*
Joe Weiss, *Principal*
Chad Knight, *Controller*
Curtis Huge, *Opers Mgr*
EMP: 38 **EST:** 2000
SQ FT: 4,500
SALES (est): 15.2MM **Privately Held**
WEB: www.hathawayllc.com
SIC: 1311 Crude petroleum production

(P-406)
HELLMAN PROPERTIES LLC
711 First St, Seal Beach (90740)
P.O. Box 2398 (90740-1398)
PHONE.........................562 431-6022
Jerry Tone,
EMP: 28 **EST:** 1920
SQ FT: 200
SALES (est): 14.8MM **Privately Held**
SIC: 1311 Crude petroleum production

(P-407)
NAFTEX WESTSIDE PARTNERS LIMIT
1900 Avenue Of The Stars, Los Angeles
(90067-4301)
PHONE.........................310 277-9004
Hormoz Ameri, *General Ptnr*
EMP: 55 **EST:** 1988
SQ FT: 1,200
SALES (est): 3.6MM **Privately Held**
SIC: 1311 Crude petroleum production

(P-408)
PACIFIC ENERGY RESOURCES LTD (PA)
111 W Ocean Blvd Ste 1240, Long Beach
(90802-4645)
PHONE.........................562 628-1526
Richard Young, *Partner*
Gina Gillette, *Partner*
David Hoy, *Partner*
Elizabeth Young Weinstein, *Partner*
EMP: 16 **EST:** 1977
SQ FT: 4,000
SALES (est): 4.8MM **Privately Held**
WEB: www.pacenergy.com
SIC: 1311 Crude petroleum & natural gas

(P-409)
QUANTUM TECHNOLOGIES INC
25242 Arctic Ocean Dr, Lake Forest
(92630-8821)
PHONE.........................949 399-4500
Dean K Aoki, *CEO*
Alan Niedzwiecki, *President*
Bradley J Timon, *CFO*
Mark Arold, *Vice Pres*
Neel Sirosh, *Principal*
EMP: 18 **EST:** 2008
SALES (est): 3.3MM **Privately Held**
WEB: www.qtww.com
SIC: 1311 Crude petroleum & natural gas

(P-410)
SEQUOIA EXPLORATION INC
5913 Sundale Ave, Bakersfield
(93309-2829)
PHONE.........................661 303-0564
Timothy G Smale, *President*
EMP: 21 **EST:** 1991
SALES (est): 4.7MM **Privately Held**
SIC: 1311 Crude petroleum production

(P-411)
TRC OPERATING COMPANY INC
805 Blackgold Ct, Taft (93268-9736)
P.O. Box 227 (93268-0227)
PHONE.........................661 763-0081
Tracy Rogers, *CEO*
Charles Comfort, *Corp Secy*
Ronnie Rogers, *Vice Pres*
EMP: 14 **EST:** 1994
SALES (est): 6.2MM **Privately Held**
WEB: www.trcoperatingcompany.com
SIC: 1311 Crude petroleum production

(P-412)
UNIFIED FIELD SERVICES CORP
6906 Downing Ave, Bakersfield
(93308-5812)
PHONE.........................661 325-8962
Wesley R Furrh Jr, *President*
Joe Watkins, *President*
Sara Davisson, *Office Mgr*
EMP: 26 **EST:** 2015
SALES: 67.7MM **Privately Held**
WEB: www.unifiedfsc.com
SIC: 1311 Crude petroleum & natural gas

(P-413)
VAQUERO ENERGY INCORPORATED
15545 Hermosa Rd, Bakersfield
(93307-9477)
PHONE.........................661 363-7240
Ken Hunter, *President*
Melissa Layman, *Office Mgr*
Wyatt Shipley, *Opers Staff*
Hector Gonzalez, *Foreman Supr*
EMP: 50 **EST:** 2007
SALES (est): 5.1MM **Privately Held**
SIC: 1311 Crude petroleum production

(P-414)
VENOCO INC
4483 Mcgrath St Ste 101, Ventura
(93003-7737)
PHONE.........................805 644-1400
Fax: 805 644-1401
EMP: 24
SALES (corp-wide): 224.2MM **Privately Held**
SIC: 1311 Crude Petroleum/Natural Gas Production
HQ: Venoco, Inc.
370 17th St Ste 3900
Denver CO 80202
303 626-8300

(P-415)
VICTORY OIL COMPANY
461 W 6th St Ste 300, San Pedro
(90731-2678)
PHONE.........................310 519-9500
Eric Johnson, *President*
S L Hutchison, *Vice Pres*
EMP: 59 **EST:** 1934
SQ FT: 8,500
SALES (est): 4.7MM **Privately Held**
SIC: 1311 Crude petroleum production

(P-416)
WEST NEWPORT OIL COMPANY
1080 W 17th St, Costa Mesa (92627-4503)
P.O. Box 1487 Newport Beach (92659-0487)
PHONE.........................949 631-1100
Robert A Armstrong, *President*
Jay Stair, *Vice Pres*
Margaret Armstrong, *Admin Sec*
EMP: 24 **EST:** 1975
SQ FT: 3,000
SALES (est): 3.2MM
SALES (corp-wide): 3.5MM **Privately Held**
WEB: www.armstrongpetroleum.com
SIC: 1311 Crude petroleum production
PA: Armstrong Petroleum Corporation
1080 W 17th St
Costa Mesa CA 92627
949 650-4000

(P-417)
WORLD OIL CORP
9302 Garfield Ave, South Gate
(90280-3896)
P.O. Box 1 (90280-0001)
PHONE.........................562 928-0100
Robert S Roth, *CEO*

Jeff Baxter, *Exec VP*
Thomas Dileva, *General Mgr*
Lloyd Lomax, *Terminal Mgr*
Jim Dillon, *Manager*
EMP: 384 **EST:** 1973
SALES (est): 134.7MM **Privately Held**
WEB: www.worldoilcorp.com
SIC: 1311 Crude petroleum & natural gas

1321 Natural Gas Liquids

(P-418)
ATLANTIC RICHFIELD COMPANY (DH)
Also Called: A R C O
4 Centerpointe Dr Ste 200, La Palma
(90623-1074)
PHONE..........................800 333-3991
Robert A Malone, *President*
Ian Springett, *CFO*
▲ **EMP:** 2200 **EST:** 1870
SALES (est): 559.9MM
SALES (corp-wide): 180.3B **Privately Held**
WEB: www.arco.com
SIC: 5541 1321 2911 Filling stations, gasoline; natural gas liquids; petroleum refining
HQ: Bp America Inc
  4101 Winfield Rd Ste 200
  Warrenville IL 60555
  630 420-5111

(P-419)
BLYTHE ENERGY INC
385 N Buck Blvd, Blythe (92225-3301)
P.O. Box 1210 (92226-1210)
PHONE..........................760 922-9950
David M Harris, *CEO*
Paul Thessen, *President*
Mark Brennan, *Treasurer*
Scott Carver, *Admin Sec*
EMP: 15 **EST:** 1998
SALES (est): 28MM
SALES (corp-wide): 4.2MM **Privately Held**
WEB: www.altagas.ca
SIC: 1321 4939 Natural gas liquids production; combination utilities
HQ: Altagas Power Holdings (U.S.) Inc.
  1411 3rd St Ste A
  Port Huron MI 48060
  810 887-4105

(P-420)
HEXAGON AGILITY INC
3335 Susan St Ste 100, Costa Mesa
(92626-1647)
PHONE..........................949 236-5520
Seung Baik, *President*
Andrew Griffiths, *CFO*
EMP: 15 **EST:** 2016
SALES (est): 14.7MM **Privately Held**
WEB: www.hexagonagility.com
SIC: 1321 Natural gas liquids production

1381 Drilling Oil & Gas Wells

(P-421)
AERA ENERGY SERVICES COMPANY (HQ)
Also Called: Aera Energy LLC
10000 Ming Ave, Bakersfield (93311-1301)
P.O. Box 11164 (93389-1164)
PHONE..........................661 665-5000
Christina S Sistrunk, *President*
Bill Hanson, *Exec VP*
Robert C Alberstadt, *Senior VP*
Brent D Carnahan, *Senior VP*
Lynne J Carrithers, *Senior VP*
EMP: 800
SALES (est): 1.9B
SALES (corp-wide): 344.8B **Privately Held**
WEB: www.aeraenergy.com
SIC: 1381 Directional drilling oil & gas wells
PA: Royal Dutch Shell Plc
  Shell Centre
  London
  207 934-1234

(P-422)
AERA ENERGY SERVICES COMPANY
Also Called: Security Front Desk
59231 Main Camp Rd, Mc Kittrick
(93251-9740)
PHONE..........................661 665-4400
Mike Brown, *Principal*
EMP: 41
SALES (corp-wide): 180.5B **Privately Held**
WEB: www.aeraenergy.com
SIC: 1381 Directional drilling oil & gas wells
HQ: Aera Energy Services Company
  10000 Ming Ave
  Bakersfield CA 93311
  661 665-5000

(P-423)
AERA ENERGY SERVICES COMPANY
Also Called: Aera Energy South Midway
29235 Highway 33, Maricopa
(93252-9793)
PHONE..........................661 665-3200
Andy Anderson, *Manager*
Bob Alberstadt, *Senior VP*
Sergio De Castro, *Senior VP*
Thomas Fischer, *Exploration*
Pat Anderson, *Executive Asst*
EMP: 41
SALES (corp-wide): 180.5B **Privately Held**
WEB: www.aeraenergy.com
SIC: 1381 Directional drilling oil & gas wells
HQ: Aera Energy Services Company
  10000 Ming Ave
  Bakersfield CA 93311
  661 665-5000

(P-424)
BLE INC
Also Called: Beryl Lockhart Enterprises
11360 Goss St, Sun Valley (91352-3205)
PHONE..........................818 504-9577
Beryl P Lockhart, *CEO*
EMP: 46 **EST:** 1965
SQ FT: 2,200
SALES (est): 11.9MM **Privately Held**
SIC: 1381 Drilling oil & gas wells

(P-425)
CROWN DRILLING SERVICES INC
5300 Woodmere Dr Ste 101, Bakersfield
(93313-2797)
PHONE..........................661 479-0710
Alan E White, *CEO*
EMP: 16 **EST:** 2016
SALES (est): 3.4MM **Privately Held**
SIC: 1381 Service well drilling

(P-426)
DICK HOWELLS HOLE DRLG SVC INC
Also Called: Howell Drilling
2579 E 67th St, Long Beach (90805-1701)
PHONE..........................562 633-9898
Richard Howell Jr, *President*
Patty Howell, *Treasurer*
Paul Howell, *Vice Pres*
EMP: 23 **EST:** 1971
SALES (est): 7.1MM **Privately Held**
WEB: www.howelldrilling.com
SIC: 1381 1629 1741 Drilling oil & gas wells; blasting contractor, except building demolition; foundation building

(P-427)
ELYSIUM JENNINGS LLC
1600 Norris Rd, Bakersfield (93308-2234)
PHONE..........................661 679-1700
Steve Layton,
EMP: 140 **EST:** 2003
SALES (est): 10.1MM **Privately Held**
WEB: www.ebresources.com
SIC: 1381 Drilling oil & gas wells
PA: E & B Natural Resources Management Corporation
  1608 Norris Rd
  Bakersfield CA 93308

(P-428)
EXCALIBUR WELL SERVICES CORP
22034 Rosedale Hwy, Bakersfield
(93314-9704)
PHONE..........................661 589-5338
Stephen Layton, *President*
Frachsco Galesi, *President*
Gordon Isbel, *Vice Pres*
Mary Telupessy, *Business Mgr*
Cori Varner, *Accountant*
EMP: 120 **EST:** 2006
SALES (est): 20.1MM **Privately Held**
SIC: 1381 1389 Drilling oil & gas wells; fishing for tools, oil & gas field

(P-429)
GEO GUIDANCE DRILLING SVCS INC (PA)
200 Old Yard Dr, Bakersfield (93307-4268)
P.O. Box 42647 (93384-2647)
PHONE..........................661 833-9999
Joseph Williams, *CEO*
Charles B Peters, *Treasurer*
Matt Lemke, *Admin Sec*
EMP: 43 **EST:** 2011
SQ FT: 3,000
SALES (est): 13.8MM **Privately Held**
WEB: www.geoguidancedrilling.com
SIC: 1381 Drilling oil & gas wells

(P-430)
GOLDEN STATE DRILLING INC
3500 Fruitvale Ave, Bakersfield
(93308-5106)
PHONE..........................661 589-0730
Philip F Phelps, *President*
James Phelps, *Treasurer*
Velma Phelps, *Vice Pres*
Mike McCutcheon, *Manager*
EMP: 75
SALES (est): 11.4MM **Privately Held**
WEB: www.gsdrilling.com
SIC: 1381 Directional drilling oil & gas wells

(P-431)
J & H DRILLING CO INC
13124 Firestone Blvd, Santa Fe Springs
(90670-5517)
PHONE..........................714 994-0402
Brian Hoien, *President*
Stephen Jones, *Corp Secy*
William Jones, *Vice Pres*
EMP: 13 **EST:** 1989
SQ FT: 5,000
SALES (est): 4.3MM **Privately Held**
WEB: www.jhdrillco.com
SIC: 1381 8748 Directional drilling oil & gas wells; environmental consultant

(P-432)
KUSTER CO OIL WELL SERVICES
Also Called: Kuster Company
2900 E 29th St, Long Beach (90806-2398)
PHONE..........................562 595-0661
John Davidson, *CEO*
▲ **EMP:** 23 **EST:** 1996 **Privately Held**
WEB: www.probe1.com
SIC: 1381 Drilling oil & gas wells
PA: Probe Holdings, Inc.
  1132 Everman Pkwy Ste 100
  Fort Worth TX 76140

(P-433)
LEGEND PUMP & WELL SERVICE INC
1324 W Rialto Ave, San Bernardino
(92410-1611)
PHONE..........................909 384-1000
Keith Collier, *President*
EMP: 20 **EST:** 2010
SALES (est): 4.6MM **Privately Held**
WEB: www.legendpump.net
SIC: 1381 1781 Service well drilling; water well servicing

(P-434)
LEON KROUS DRILLING INC
9300 Borden Ave, Sun Valley (91352-2006)
PHONE..........................818 833-4654
Leon Krus, *President*
EMP: 25 **EST:** 1981

SQ FT: 1,000
SALES (est): 7.6MM **Privately Held**
WEB:
www.leonkrousdrilling.thebluebook.com
SIC: 1381 Directional drilling oil & gas wells

(P-435)
PACIFIC OPERATORS INC
205 E Carrillo St Ste 200, Santa Barbara
(93101-7181)
PHONE..........................805 899-3144
Richard L Carone, *President*
Robert P Carone, *Vice Pres*
EMP: 24 **EST:** 1984
SQ FT: 3,100
SALES (est): 1.5MM **Privately Held**
SIC: 1381 Drilling oil & gas wells

(P-436)
PETRO-LUD INC
12625 Jomani Dr Ste 104, Bakersfield
(93312-3445)
PHONE..........................661 747-4779
Clayton Ludington, *Principal*
EMP: 19 **EST:** 2012
SALES (est): 7.1MM **Privately Held**
WEB: www.petro-lud.com
SIC: 1381 Drilling oil & gas wells

(P-437)
PRIMEBORE DRCTONAL BORING CORP
10822 Vernon Ave, Ontario (91762-4041)
PHONE..........................909 821-4643
Jess B Basave, *CEO*
EMP: 13 **EST:** 2003
SALES (est): 1.6MM **Privately Held**
SIC: 1381 Directional drilling oil & gas wells

(P-438)
T & D SERVICES INC
Also Called: T&D Trenchless
42363 Guava St, Murrieta (92562-7271)
P.O. Box 609 (92564-0609)
PHONE..........................951 304-1190
Donald Van Dyke, *President*
Dawn Van Dyke, *Treasurer*
EMP: 13 **EST:** 2002
SQ FT: 1,200
SALES (est): 3.7MM **Privately Held**
WEB: www.trenchless.biz
SIC: 1381 Directional drilling oil & gas wells

(P-439)
WEST AMERICAN ENERGY CORP
4949 Buckley Way Ste 207, Bakersfield
(93309-4882)
P.O. Box 22016 (93390-2016)
PHONE..........................661 747-7732
Howard Caywood, *President*
EMP: 16 **EST:** 2000
SQ FT: 640
SALES (est): 1.1MM **Privately Held**
SIC: 1381 Drilling oil & gas wells

1382 Oil & Gas Field Exploration Svcs

(P-440)
ARGUELLO INC
17100 Clle Mariposa Reina, Goleta
(93117-9737)
PHONE..........................805 567-1632
James C Flores, *President*
Winston Taldert, *CFO*
Doss Dourgeois, *Exec VP*
John F Wombwell, *Exec VP*
EMP: 23 **EST:** 1999
SALES (est): 9.5MM
SALES (corp-wide): 14.2B **Publicly Held**
WEB: www.fcx.com
SIC: 1382 Oil & gas exploration services
HQ: Freeport-Mcmoran Oil & Gas Llc
  700 Milam St Ste 3100
  Houston TX 77002
  713 579-6000

PRODUCTS & SVCS

(P-441)
BNK PETROLEUM (US) INC
3623 Old Conejo Rd # 207, Newbury Park
(91320-0800)
PHONE..................805 484-3613
Wolf E Regener, *President*
Gary W Johnson, *Officer*
Ray W Payne, *Vice Pres*
Ray Payne, *Vice Pres*
Steven M Warshauer, *Executive*
EMP: 25 EST: 2006
SALES (est): 8MM Privately Held
WEB: www.bnkpetroleum.com
SIC: 1382 Oil & gas exploration services

(P-442)
**BREITBURN ENERGY
HOLDINGS LLC**
707 Wilshire Blvd # 4600, Los Angeles
(90017-3612)
PHONE..................213 225-5900
Eric Whitford, *IT/INT Sup*
Robert Nowak, *Technology*
Corey Gilchrist, *Engineer*
Harold Im, *Engineer*
Bridget Lisenbe, *Production*
EMP: 19 EST: 2009
SALES (est): 1.2MM Privately Held
WEB: www.mavresources.com
SIC: 1382 Oil & gas exploration services

(P-443)
**CALIFRNIA RSRCES ELK HILLS
LLC**
27200 Tourney Rd Ste 200, Santa Clarita
(91355-4910)
PHONE..................661 412-0000
Karen Plotts,
Michael L Preston,
Marshall D Smith,
EMP: 400 EST: 1997
SALES (est): 136.9MM
SALES (corp-wide): 2.2B Publicly Held
WEB: www.crc.com
SIC: 1382 Oil & gas exploration services
PA: California Resources Corporation
27200 Tourney Rd Ste 200
Santa Clarita CA 91355
888 848-4754

(P-444)
CRC SERVICES LLC
27200 Tourney Rd Ste 200, Santa Clarita
(91355-4910)
PHONE..................888 848-4754
James Kahrhoff Jr,
EMP: 18 EST: 2014
SALES (est): 6.4MM
SALES (corp-wide): 2.2B Publicly Held
WEB: www.crc.com
SIC: 1382 Oil & gas exploration services
PA: California Resources Corporation
27200 Tourney Rd Ste 200
Santa Clarita CA 91355
888 848-4754

(P-445)
DCOR LLC (PA)
1000 Town Center Dr Fl 6, Oxnard
(93036-1132)
P.O. Box 3401, Ventura (93006-3401)
PHONE..................805 535-2000
Bill Templeton,
Andrew Prestridge, *President*
Alan C Templeton, *CFO*
Greg Cavette, *Vice Pres*
Dennis Conley, *Vice Pres*
EMP: 199 EST: 2001
SALES (est): 62.9MM Privately Held
WEB: www.dcorllc.com
SIC: 1382 Oil & gas exploration services

(P-446)
DEMENNO KERDOON
2000 N Alameda St, Compton
(90222-2799)
PHONE..................310 537-7100
Shane Bamelin, *Principal*
Jim Ennis, *COO*
Jim Tice, *Principal*
Mike Patterson, *Director*
EMP: 20 EST: 2007
SQ FT: 11,614
SALES (est): 2.7MM Privately Held
SIC: 1382 Oil & gas exploration services

(P-447)
DRILLMEC INC (DH)
8140 Rosecrans Ave, Paramount
(90723-2754)
PHONE..................281 885-0777
Paulo Brando Ballerini, *President*
Massimo Tartagni, *CFO*
Eleazar Guillen, *Manager*
◆ EMP: 23 EST: 1998
SALES (est): 32.8MM
SALES (corp-wide): 16.4MM Privately
Held
WEB: www.drillmec.com
SIC: 1382 Oil & gas exploration services
HQ: Soilmec Spa
Via Dismano 5819
Cesena FC 47522
054 731-9111

(P-448)
**E & B NTRAL RESOURCES MGT
CORP**
1848 Perkins Rd, New Cuyama (93254)
P.O. Box 179 (93254-0179)
PHONE..................661 766-2501
Edward Fetterman, *Branch Mgr*
EMP: 18 Privately Held
WEB: www.ebresources.com
SIC: 1382 Oil & gas exploration services
PA: E & B Natural Resources Management
Corporation
1608 Norris Rd
Bakersfield CA 93308

(P-449)
**E & B NTRAL RESOURCES MGT
CORP (PA)**
1608 Norris Rd, Bakersfield (93308-2234)
PHONE..................661 679-1714
Steve Layton, *President*
Joyce Holtzclaw, *Partner*
Frank J Ronkese, *CFO*
Jeff Blesener, *Senior VP*
Jeff Jones, *Vice Pres*
EMP: 65 EST: 1972
SALES (est): 169.4MM Privately Held
WEB: www.ebresources.com
SIC: 1382 Oil & gas exploration services

(P-450)
E AND B NATURAL RESOURCES
1600 Norris Rd, Bakersfield (93308-2234)
PHONE..................661 679-1700
EMP: 52
SALES (est): 9.4MM Privately Held
WEB: www.ebresources.com
SIC: 1382 Oil And Gas Exploration Services

(P-451)
**EAGLE DOMINION ENERGY
CORP**
Also Called: Eagle Dominion Trust
200 N Hayes Ave, Oxnard (93030-5420)
P.O. Box 7004 (93031-7004)
PHONE..................805 272-9557
Roger H Shears, *President*
Nancy Davis, *Vice Pres*
EMP: 14 EST: 1997
SQ FT: 1,500
SALES (est): 320.8K Privately Held
SIC: 1382 Oil & gas exploration services

(P-452)
ELK HILLS POWER LLC
27200 Tourney Rd Ste 315, Santa Clarita
(91355-5389)
PHONE..................888 848-4754
EMP: 26 EST: 1999
SALES (est): 1.9MM Privately Held
WEB: www.crc.com
SIC: 1382 Oil & gas exploration services

(P-453)
GREKA INTEGRATED INC (PA)
1700 Sinton Rd, Santa Maria (93458-9708)
P.O. Box 5489 (93456-5489)
PHONE..................805 347-8700
Randeep S Grewal, *CEO*
Ken Miller, *CFO*
Susan Whalen, *Vice Pres*
▲ EMP: 129 EST: 2000

SALES (est): 24.3MM Privately Held
WEB: www.greka.com
SIC: 1382 Oil & gas exploration services

(P-454)
GRENFIELD CONSULTING
1801 Century Park E Fl 23, Los Angeles
(90067-2325)
PHONE..................310 286-0200
EMP: 26
SALES (est): 1MM Privately Held
SIC: 1382 8742 Oil/Gas Exploration Services Management Consulting Services

(P-455)
LINNCO LLC
5201 Truxtun Ave, Bakersfield
(93309-0421)
PHONE..................661 616-3900
Sam Cloud, *Analyst*
EMP: 239
SALES (corp-wide): 127.7MM Publicly
Held
SIC: 1382 Oil & gas exploration services
PA: Linnco, Llc
600 Travis St Ste 5100
Houston TX 77002
281 840-4000

(P-456)
**MACPHERSON OIL COMPANY
LLC**
24118 Round Mountain Rd, Bakersfield
(93308-9115)
P.O. Box 5368 (93388-5368)
PHONE..................661 556-6096
Wes Duncan, *Manager*
Zack Macpherson, *Technician*
Rommel Almanza, *Technology*
Geoffrey Butler, *Analyst*
Rubin Kim, *Controller*
EMP: 22
SALES (corp-wide): 28.2MM Privately
Held
WEB: www.macphersonenergy.com
SIC: 1382 1311 Oil & gas exploration services; crude petroleum & natural gas production
HQ: Macpherson Oil Company Llc
100 Wilshire Blvd Ste 800
Santa Monica CA 90401
310 452-3880

(P-457)
**MAGNETRON POWER
INVENTIONS INC**
2226 W 232nd St, Torrance (90501-5720)
PHONE..................310 462-6970
Ninan N Johnson, *CEO*
Joicey Johnson, *Software Engr*
Arun Jose, *Engineer*
Sujith Kumar, *Engineer*
EMP: 22 EST: 1999
SQ FT: 2,500
SALES (est): 5MM Privately Held
WEB: www.magnetronusa.com
SIC: 1382 Oil & gas exploration services

(P-458)
NATIONS PETROLEUM CAL LLC
9600 Ming Ave Ste 300, Bakersfield
(93311-1365)
PHONE..................661 387-6402
Phil Sorvet,
EMP: 56 EST: 2002
SALES (est): 5.4MM
SALES (corp-wide): 2.1MM Privately
Held
WEB: www.nationspetroleum.com
SIC: 1382 Oil & gas exploration services
PA: Nations Petroleum Company Ltd
255 5 Ave Sw Suite 750
Calgary AB T2P 3
403 206-1420

(P-459)
NEON ENERGY CORPORATION
1401 Coml Way Ste 200, Bakersfield
(93309)
P.O. Box 12110 (93389-2110)
PHONE..................661 829-2505
Kenneth Charsinsky, *CEO*
Donald G Nelson, *President*
EMP: 31 EST: 2006
SQ FT: 5,400

SALES (est): 2.6MM Privately Held
WEB: www.neoncapital.com.au
SIC: 1382 Oil & gas exploration services
PA: Neon Capital Ltd
33 Yilgarn St
Shenton Park WA

(P-460)
NEWPORT ENERGY
19200 Von Karman Ave # 4, Irvine
(92612-8553)
PHONE..................408 250-7545
Nyle Khan, *CEO*
Gordon Burk, *COO*
EMP: 25 EST: 1984
SQ FT: 5,000
SALES (est): 1.6MM Privately Held
SIC: 1382 Oil & gas exploration services

(P-461)
PEAK OPERATOR II LLC
300 E Esplanade Dr # 181, Oxnard
(93036-1238)
PHONE..................805 436-2555
Robert A Bell, *President*
Larry D Janssen, *Vice Pres*
Darin Holden, *Production*
EMP: 14 EST: 2012
SALES (est): 3.4MM Privately Held
SIC: 1382 Oil & gas exploration services

(P-462)
QRE OPERATING LLC
707 Wilshire Blvd # 4600, Los Angeles
(90017-3501)
PHONE..................213 225-5900
Alan L Smith, *Mng Member*
EMP: 90 EST: 2010
SALES (est): 1.4MM Privately Held
SIC: 1382 Oil & gas exploration services
PA: Qr Energy, Lp
707 Wilshire Blvd # 4600
Los Angeles CA 90017

(P-463)
SAMEDAN OIL CORPORATION
Also Called: Noble Energy
1360 Landing Ave, Sea Beach
(90740-6525)
PHONE..................661 319-5038
Holli Ladhani, *Director*
EMP: 69
SALES (corp-wide): 57.6MM Privately
Held
WEB: www.nblenergy.com
SIC: 1382 Oil & gas exploration services
PA: Samedan Oil Corporation
1001 Noble Energy Way
Houston TX 77070
580 223-4110

(P-464)
**SANTA MARIA ENRGY
HOLDINGS LLC**
2811 Airpark Dr, Santa Maria (93455-1417)
P.O. Box 7202 (93456-7202)
PHONE..................805 938-3320
David Pratt, *CEO*
EMP: 24 EST: 2008
SALES (est): 2.9MM Privately Held
WEB: www.santamariaenergy.com
SIC: 1382 Oil & gas exploration services

(P-465)
SEISMIC RESERVOIR 2020 INC
3 Pointe Dr Ste 212, Brea (92821-7624)
PHONE..................562 697-9711
EMP: 21
SALES: 4MM Privately Held
SIC: 1382 Oil/Gas Exploration Services

(P-466)
**SENECA RESOURCES
COMPANY LLC**
4800 Corporate Ct, Bakersfield
(93311-8706)
PHONE..................661 391-3540
EMP: 14
SALES (corp-wide): 1.5B Publicly Held
WEB: www.nationalfuel.com
SIC: 1382 Oil & gas exploration services

HQ: Seneca Resources Company, Llc
1201 La St Ste 2600
Houston TX 77002
713 654-2600

(P-467)
SENTINEL PEAK RSOURCES CAL LLC
1200 Discovery Dr Ste 100, Bakersfield
(93309-7033)
PHONE..................................661 395-5214
EMP: 79
SALES (corp-wide): 345MM **Privately Held**
WEB: www.sentinelpeakresources.com
SIC: 1382 Oil & gas exploration services
HQ: Sentinel Peak Resources California Llc
6501 E Belleview Ave # 400
Englewood CO 80111
720 749-1105

(P-468)
SENTINEL PEAK RSOURCES CAL LLC
5640 S Fairfax Ave, Los Angeles
(90056-1266)
PHONE..................................323 298-2200
Oscar Villagomez, *Administration*
Gregory Craley, *Technical Staff*
EMP: 79
SALES (corp-wide): 345MM **Privately Held**
WEB: www.sentinelpeakresources.com
SIC: 1382 Oil & gas exploration services
HQ: Sentinel Peak Resources California Llc
6501 E Belleview Ave # 400
Englewood CO 80111
720 749-1105

(P-469)
SIGNAL HILL PETROLEUM INC
2633 Cherry Ave, Signal Hill (90755-2008)
PHONE..................................562 595-6440
Jerrel Barto, *Ch of Bd*
Craig C Barto, *President*
Michael Kuzmits, *Vice Pres*
Richard Higley, *Exploration*
Jillmarie Robinson, *Office Admin*
EMP: 49 EST: 1984
SALES (est): 27.4MM **Privately Held**
WEB: www.shpi.net
SIC: 1382 Geological exploration, oil & gas field

(P-470)
TERMO COMPANY
3275 Cherry Ave, Long Beach
(90807-5213)
P.O. Box 2767 (90801-2767)
PHONE..................................562 595-7401
David E Combs, *President*
Norbert Buss, *Vice Pres*
Francis Roth, *Vice Pres*
Donna Sheaffer, *Admin Sec*
Christopher Cacek, *Technician*
EMP: 21 EST: 1933
SQ FT: 18,034
SALES (est): 14.6MM **Privately Held**
WEB: www.termoco.com
SIC: 1382 Oil & gas exploration services

(P-471)
U S WEATHERFORD L P
19608 Broken Ct, Shafter (93263-9583)
PHONE..................................661 746-3415
EMP: 27 **Privately Held**
SIC: 1382 Wireline/Oil Field Services
HQ: U S Weatherford L P
2000 Saint James Pl
Houston TX 70395
713 693-4000

(P-472)
UNIVERSAL DYNAMICS INC
5313 3rd St, Irwindale (91706-2085)
PHONE..................................626 480-0035
Issa Alasker, *President*
Sahak Sahakian, *Accounting Mgr*
John Scolaro, *Manager*
EMP: 21 EST: 2004
SQ FT: 15,000
SALES (est): 4.1MM **Privately Held**
WEB: www.udinc.net
SIC: 1382 7382 Oil & gas exploration services; security systems services

(P-473)
WARREN E&P INC
Also Called: Warren E & P
400 Oceangate Ste 200, Long Beach
(90802-4306)
PHONE..................................214 393-9688
James A Watt, *CEO*
EMP: 67 EST: 1973
SQ FT: 7,000
SALES (est): 17.8MM **Publicly Held**
WEB: www.warrenresources.com
SIC: 1382 Oil & gas exploration services
PA: Warren Resources, Inc.
5420 Lbj Fwy Ste 600
Dallas TX 75240

1389 Oil & Gas Field Svcs, NEC

(P-474)
AC PUMPING UNIT REPAIR INC
2625 Dawson Ave, Signal Hill
(90755-2019)
PHONE..................................562 492-1300
Michael Quike, *CEO*
Micheal Quirke, *President*
Alfonso Campas, *CEO*
EMP: 14 EST: 2006
SALES (est): 2.9MM **Privately Held**
WEB: www.acpumping.com
SIC: 1389 Oil & gas wells: building, repairing & dismantling

(P-475)
ALLY ENTERPRISES
5001 E Commercecenter Dr # 260, Bakersfield (93309-1663)
P.O. Box 20580 (93390-0580)
PHONE..................................661 412-9933
Rick Noland, *President*
EMP: 20 EST: 2016
SALES (est): 1.4MM **Privately Held**
SIC: 1389 Oil field services

(P-476)
ANATESCO INC
128 Bedford Way, Bakersfield
(93308-1702)
P.O. Box 5694 (93388-5694)
PHONE..................................661 399-6990
Douglas Paul Denesha, *President*
Jean Denesha, *Vice Pres*
Jeremy Denesha, *Technology*
Mike Rolin, *Manager*
EMP: 14 EST: 1978
SQ FT: 3,000
SALES (est): 4.1MM **Privately Held**
WEB: www.anatesco.com
SIC: 1389 Oil field services

(P-477)
B & B PIPE AND TOOL CO (PA)
3035 Walnut Ave, Long Beach
(90807-5221)
PHONE..................................562 424-0704
Craig Braly, *President*
Stephanie Braly, *Corp Secy*
▲ EMP: 23 EST: 1951
SQ FT: 2,000
SALES (est): 11.4MM **Privately Held**
WEB: www.bbpipe.com
SIC: 1389 Oil field services

(P-478)
B & L CASING SERVICE LLC
Also Called: United Wealth Control
21054 Kratzmeyer Rd, Bakersfield
(93314-9482)
P.O. Box 22260 (93390-2260)
PHONE..................................661 589-9080
Larry Jenkins, *Mng Member*
Brian Jenkins, *Vice Pres*
Stuart Feliz, *District Mgr*
Andrew Miles, *Sales Staff*
Robin Shipp, *Manager*
EMP: 13 EST: 1989
SALES (est): 2.5MM **Privately Held**
WEB: www.blservicesinc.com
SIC: 1389 Oil field services

(P-479)
BARTO SIGNAL PETROLEUM INC
1041 W 18th St Ste A101, Costa Mesa
(92627-4583)
PHONE..................................949 631-8066
Jerrel C Barto, *President*
Craig Barto, *President*
Eric Barto, *Admin Sec*
EMP: 15 EST: 1986
SQ FT: 4,800
SALES (est): 355.9K **Privately Held**
SIC: 1389 Servicing oil & gas wells

(P-480)
BASIC ENERGY SERVICES INC
6710 Stewart Way, Bakersfield (93308)
PHONE..................................661 588-3800
EMP: 34
SALES (corp-wide): 411.3MM **Publicly Held**
WEB: www.basices.com
SIC: 1389 Cementing oil & gas well casings
PA: Basic Energy Services, Inc.
801 Cherry St Ste 2100
Fort Worth TX 76102
817 334-4100

(P-481)
BLACK GOLD PUMP & SUPPLY INC
2459 Lewis Ave, Signal Hill (90755-3427)
PHONE..................................323 298-0077
Michael L Bair, *CEO*
James L Hurd, *President*
Steve Bollweg, *CFO*
Thomas E Casec, *Corp Secy*
Erin Meehan, *Executive Asst*
▲ EMP: 17 EST: 1982
SALES (est): 4.9MM **Privately Held**
WEB: www.blackgoldpump.com
SIC: 1389 Oil field services

(P-482)
C & H TESTING SERVICE INC (PA)
6224 Price Way, Bakersfield (93308-5117)
P.O. Box 9907 (93389-1907)
PHONE..................................661 589-4030
Donald T Hoover, *President*
Karen K Hoover, *Corp Secy*
Ken Dickinson, *General Mgr*
Cesar Chavez, *Accountant*
EMP: 30 EST: 1981
SQ FT: 1,500
SALES (est): 8.5MM **Privately Held**
WEB: www.candhtesting.com
SIC: 1389 Oil field services

(P-483)
C&J WELL SERVICES LLC ✪
3752 Allen Rd, Bakersfield (93314-9242)
PHONE..................................661 589-5220
Joana Lerma, *Principal*
Danielle Hunter, *Exec VP*
EMP: 900 EST: 2021
SALES (est): 15.7MM **Privately Held**
SIC: 1389 Servicing oil & gas wells

(P-484)
CAL COAST ACIDIZING CO
Also Called: Cal Coast Acidizing Service
6226 Dominion Rd, Santa Maria
(93454-9177)
P.O. Box 2050, Orcutt (93457-2050)
PHONE..................................805 934-2411
Bruce Edward Conway, *CEO*
EMP: 53 EST: 1966
SQ FT: 2,000
SALES (est): 25.2MM **Privately Held**
WEB: www.ccacidizing.com
SIC: 1389 Oil field services

(P-485)
CAL QUAKE CONSTRUCTION INC
636 N Formosa Ave, Los Angeles
(90036-1943)
PHONE..................................323 931-2969
Sheldon Perluss, *President*
John Taferner, *Vice Pres*
Isael Duarte, *Opers Staff*
EMP: 21 EST: 2000

SALES (est): 6.7MM **Privately Held**
WEB: www.cal-quake.com
SIC: 1389 Construction, repair & dismantling services

(P-486)
CALPI INC
7141 Downing Ave, Bakersfield
(93308-5815)
P.O. Box 81795 (93380-1795)
PHONE..................................661 589-5648
Robert Larkie Barnett, *President*
Jeff Barnett, *Vice Pres*
EMP: 47 EST: 1981
SQ FT: 5,032
SALES (est): 3.3MM **Privately Held**
WEB: www.calpiinc.com
SIC: 1389 4959 Cleaning wells; servicing oil & gas wells; toxic or hazardous waste cleanup

(P-487)
CAPSULE MANUFACTURING INC
Also Called: Capsule Mfg
1399 N Miller St, Anaheim (92806-1412)
PHONE..................................949 245-4151
Chad Bowker, *President*
EMP: 68 EST: 2015
SALES (est): 2.5MM **Privately Held**
SIC: 1389 Construction, repair & dismantling services

(P-488)
CASING SPECIALTIES INC
12454 Snow Rd, Bakersfield (93314-8015)
PHONE..................................661 399-5522
Russell C Davis, *Owner*
EMP: 25 EST: 2010 **Privately Held**
WEB: www.casingspecialties.com
SIC: 1389 Cementing oil & gas well casings; oil field services

(P-489)
CENTRAL CALIFORNIA CNSTR INC
7221 Downing Ave, Bakersfield
(93308-5817)
PHONE..................................661 978-8230
Dereke Gerecke, *Principal*
Tammie K Rankin-Gerecke, *Principal*
Urssula Sizemore, *Bookkeeper*
EMP: 23 EST: 2005
SALES (est): 6.2MM **Privately Held**
SIC: 1389 Construction, repair & dismantling services

(P-490)
CJ BERRY WELL SERVICES MGT LLC ✪
3752 Allen Rd, Bakersfield (93314-9242)
PHONE..................................661 589-5220
Joana Lerma, *Principal*
Danielle Hunter, *Exec VP*
Stacy Urbina, *Executive Asst*
EMP: 900 EST: 2021
SALES (est): 16MM **Privately Held**
SIC: 1389 Servicing oil & gas wells

(P-491)
CJD CONSTRUCTION SVCS INC
416 S Vermont Ave, Glendora
(91741-6256)
PHONE..................................626 335-1116
Diego A Debenedetto, *President*
Diego Dibenedetto, *President*
Richard Barnes, *CIO*
EMP: 40 EST: 2004
SALES (est): 2.7MM **Privately Held**
SIC: 1389 Construction, repair & dismantling services

(P-492)
CL KNOX INC
Also Called: Advanced Industrial Services
34933 Imperial Ave, Bakersfield
(93308-9579)
PHONE..................................661 837-0477
Leslie Knox, *President*
Chris Knox, *Corp Secy*
Eric Toy, *Project Mgr*
Stephanie Smith, *Manager*
EMP: 80 EST: 1992

SALES (est): 10MM **Privately Held**
WEB: www.aisleaders.com
SIC: 1389 8742 Oil field services; industrial consultant

(P-493)
CUMMINGS VACUUM SERVICE INC
Also Called: Cummings Transportation
19605 Broken Ct, Shafter (93263-9583)
PHONE....................................661 746-1786
Pam Cummings, *President*
Ted Cummings, *Vice Pres*
Tom Pruitt, *Manager*
EMP: 60 **EST:** 1980
SQ FT: 3,000
SALES (est): 8.4MM **Privately Held**
WEB: www.cummings2.com
SIC: 1389 Oil field services

(P-494)
DE VRIES INTERNATIONAL INC (PA)
17671 Armstrong Ave, Irvine (92614-5727)
PHONE....................................949 252-1212
Don Devries, *President*
David Kazmierski, *QC Mgr*
David Granados, *
Lori Bradley, *Accounts Mgr*
▲ **EMP:** 54 **EST:** 1984
SALES (est): 20.5MM **Privately Held**
WEB: www.devriesintl.com
SIC: 1389 Lease tanks, oil field: erecting, cleaning & repairing

(P-495)
DWAYNES ENGINEERING & CNSTR
3559 Addie Ave, Fellows (93224-9634)
PHONE....................................661 762-7261
Dwayne Emfinger, *President*
EMP: 17 **EST:** 1979
SALES (est): 2.2MM **Privately Held**
SIC: 1389 Construction, repair & dismantling services

(P-496)
ELYSIUM WEST LLC
1600 Norris Rd, Bakersfield (93308-2234)
PHONE....................................661 679-1700
Stephen Layton, *CEO*
EMP: 21 **EST:** 2003
SALES (est): 3.4MM **Privately Held**
WEB: www.ebresources.com
SIC: 1389 Oil & gas wells: building, repairing & dismantling

(P-497)
ENGEL & GRAY INC
745 W Betteravia Rd Ste A, Santa Maria (93455-1298)
P.O. Box 5020 (93456-5020)
PHONE....................................805 925-2771
Carl W Engel Jr, *President*
Robert Engel, *Vice Pres*
EMP: 35 **EST:** 1946
SQ FT: 3,000
SALES (est): 5.8MM **Privately Held**
WEB: www.engelandgray.com
SIC: 1389 1623 7389 2875 Construction, repair & dismantling services; haulage, oil field; pipeline construction; crane & aerial lift service; compost

(P-498)
ENGINEERED WELL SVC INTL INC
3120 Standard St, Bakersfield (93308-6241)
PHONE....................................866 913-6283
Paul Sturgeon, *CEO*
John E Powell Jr, *Principal*
EMP: 13 **EST:** 2009
SALES (est): 4MM **Privately Held**
SIC: 1389 Oil field services

(P-499)
ERDLE PERFORATING CO INC
7300 W Sunnyview Ave, Visalia (93291-9605)
PHONE....................................559 651-1889
EMP: 15 **EST:** 2014
SALES (est): 5.5MM **Privately Held**
WEB: www.diamondperf.com
SIC: 1389 Perforating well casings

(P-500)
ETHOSENERGY FIELD SERVICES LLC (DH)
10455 Slusher Dr Bldg 12, Santa Fe Springs (90670-3750)
PHONE....................................310 639-3523
Mark Jones, *President*
Patricia Lelito, *CFO*
Mike Fieldhouse, *Vice Pres*
EMP: 44 **EST:** 1970
SALES (est): 38.2MM
SALES (corp-wide): 7.5B **Privately Held**
WEB: www.ethosenergyfs.com
SIC: 1389 8711 3462 Oil consultants; industrial engineers; pump, compressor & turbine forgings

(P-501)
FIELD FOUNDATION
15306 Carmenita Rd, Santa Fe Springs (90670-5606)
P.O. Box 4236, Cerritos (90703-4236)
PHONE....................................562 921-3567
Irwin Field, *Owner*
EMP: 13 **EST:** 1948
SALES (est): 532.6K **Privately Held**
SIC: 1389 Oil sampling service for oil companies

(P-502)
FIRST ENERGY SERVICES INC
1031 Carrier Parkway Ave, Bakersfield (93308-9670)
P.O. Box 80844 (93380-0844)
PHONE....................................661 387-1972
Richard Chase, *President*
Charlotte Maddon, *Treasurer*
Jack Chase, *Vice Pres*
EMP: 20
SQ FT: 7,000
SALES (est): 3.2MM **Privately Held**
SIC: 1389 Oil field services

(P-503)
GENE WTSON CNSTR A CAL LTD PRT
10312 Skiles Dr, Bakersfield (93311-3066)
PHONE....................................661 763-5254
Gene Watson, *Ltd Ptnr*
Patricia Watson, *Ltd Ptnr*
EMP: 22 **EST:** 1993
SALES (est): 443.6K **Privately Held**
WEB: www.total-western.com
SIC: 1389 1382 Oil field services; oil & gas exploration services

(P-504)
GRAYSON SERVICE INC
1845 Greeley Rd, Bakersfield (93314-9547)
PHONE....................................661 589-5444
Carol A Grayson, *President*
Cheryl Grayson, *Vice Pres*
EMP: 22 **EST:** 1969
SALES (est): 5.7MM **Privately Held**
SIC: 1389 Servicing oil & gas wells

(P-505)
HAMO CONSTRACTION
3650 Altura Ave, La Crescenta (91214-2460)
PHONE....................................818 415-3334
Hamlet Karamyan, *Owner*
EMP: 47 **EST:** 2013
SALES (est): 525K **Privately Held**
SIC: 1389 Construction, repair & dismantling services

(P-506)
HANSAI INC
13012 Moore St, Cerritos (90703-2226)
PHONE....................................714 539-3311
Brian W Han, *President*
▲ **EMP:** 13 **EST:** 2006
SALES (est): 357.1K **Privately Held**
WEB: www.umeken.com
SIC: 1389 Construction, repair & dismantling services

(P-507)
HILLS WLDG & ENGRG CONTR INC
Also Called: Hwe Mechanical
22038 Stockdale Hwy, Bakersfield (93314-8889)
PHONE....................................661 746-5400
Debora M Hill, *Vice Pres*
Robert Hill, *Shareholder*
EMP: 92 **EST:** 1999
SALES (est): 9.6MM **Privately Held**
WEB: www.hillswelding.com
SIC: 1389 Testing, measuring, surveying & analysis services

(P-508)
HIRSH INC
Also Called: Better Mens Clothes
860 S Los Angeles St # 900, Los Angeles (90014-3311)
PHONE....................................213 622-9441
EMP: 50
SALES (est): 1MM **Privately Held**
SIC: 1389 Oil And Gas Field Services, Nec, Nsk

(P-509)
HORIZON WELL LOGGING INC
711 Saint Andrews Way, Lompoc (93436-1326)
PHONE....................................805 733-0972
Doug Milham, *President*
Bill Gilmour, *Managing Dir*
James Eastes, *Opers Staff*
Jim Eastes, *Opers Staff*
John Armstrong, *Director*
▲ **EMP:** 26 **EST:** 1992
SALES (est): 4.9MM **Privately Held**
WEB: www.horizon-well-logging.com
SIC: 1389 Oil field services

(P-510)
INSTRUMENT CONTROL SERVICES
Also Called: I C S
6085 King Dr Unit 100, Ventura (93003-7178)
PHONE....................................805 642-1999
Michael Leblanc, *Exec Dir*
Joseph Edward Locklear, *President*
Warren Hague, *Project Mgr*
Tim Rollins, *Foreman/Supr*
EMP: 45 **EST:** 1994
SQ FT: 6,100
SALES (est): 11.3MM **Privately Held**
WEB: www.instrumentcontrol.com
SIC: 1389 7699 7373 7299 Construction, repair & dismantling services; industrial equipment services; valve repair, industrial; systems integration services; banquet hall facilities

(P-511)
JAGUAR ENERGY LLC (PA)
2404 Colony Plz, Newport Beach (92660-6357)
PHONE....................................949 706-7060
Corbin Blume, *
EMP: 31 **EST:** 2016
SALES (est): 2.6MM **Privately Held**
WEB: www.jaguar-energy.com
SIC: 1389 Oil field services

(P-512)
JERRY MELTON & SONS CNSTR
Also Called: Jerry Melton & Sons Cnstr
100 Jamison Ln, Taft (93268-4329)
PHONE....................................661 765-5546
Jerry W Melton, *President*
Karen Melton, *Treasurer*
Judy Melton, *Vice Pres*
Steven Melton, *Admin Sec*
EMP: 85 **EST:** 1971
SALES (est): 11.6MM **Privately Held**
SIC: 1389 Oil & gas wells: building, repairing & dismantling; grading oil & gas well foundations

(P-513)
JOHN M PHILLIPS LLC
Also Called: John M Phillips Oil Field Eqp
2800 Gibson St, Bakersfield (93308-6106)
PHONE....................................661 327-3118
Melody Shamaker, *Office Mgr*
EMP: 35

SALES (corp-wide): 8.1MM **Privately Held**
WEB: www.johnmphillips.com
SIC: 1389 Oil field services
PA: John M. Phillips, Llc
2755 Dawson Ave
Signal Hill CA 90755
562 595-7363

(P-514)
K C RESTORATION CO INC
1514 W 130th St, Gardena (90249-2104)
PHONE....................................310 230-0597
Carolyn Lehne Macleod, *President*
Katherine Cecilia Lehne, *Principal*
Steve Lehne, *Principal*
EMP: 35 **EST:** 1991
SALES (est): 6.1MM **Privately Held**
WEB: www.kcrestorationinc.com
SIC: 1389 2431 1752 1741 Construction, repair & dismantling services; windows & window parts & trim, wood; wood floor installation & refinishing; masonry & other stonework; glass & glazing work; painting & paper hanging

(P-515)
M-I LLC
4400 Fanucchi Way, Shafter (93263-9552)
PHONE....................................561 321-5400
Forest Purpiance, *Branch Mgr*
EMP: 31 **Publicly Held**
WEB: www.slb.com
SIC: 1389 Mud service, oil field drilling; oil field services
HQ: M-I L.L.C.
5950 N Course Dr
Houston TX 77072
281 561-1300

(P-516)
MARK SHEFFIELD CONSTRUCTION
9105 Langley Rd, Bakersfield (93312-2156)
PHONE....................................661 589-8520
Mark Sheffield, *President*
Linda Sheffield, *Treasurer*
Steven Sheffield, *Vice Pres*
EMP: 23 **EST:** 1977
SALES (est): 6.1MM **Privately Held**
SIC: 1389 7389 Oil field services; crane & aerial lift service

(P-517)
MEC-CCC S ALL N ONE
13800 Prkcnter Ln Apt 304, Tustin (92782)
PHONE....................................909 529-0013
Emma Jones, *President*
EMP: 50 **EST:** 2016
SALES (est): 1MM **Privately Held**
WEB: www.mecccsallnone.com
SIC: 1389 1799 Construction, repair & dismantling services; welding on site

(P-518)
MMI SERVICES INC
4042 Patton Way Bakersfield (93308-5030)
PHONE....................................661 589-9366
Steve McGowan, *President*
Mel McGowan, *CEO*
Eric Olson, *Vice Pres*
Roxanne Campbell, *Info Tech Dir*
Luis Martinez, *Manager*
EMP: 250 **EST:** 1985
SQ FT: 4,500
SALES (est): 39.6MM **Privately Held**
WEB: www.mmi-services.com
SIC: 1389 Oil field services

(P-519)
MOLLER RETAIL INC
6591 Collins Dr Ste E11, Moorpark (93021-1493)
PHONE....................................805 299-8200
John Moller, *CEO*
EMP: 14 **EST:** 2012
SALES (est): 3.3MM **Privately Held**
SIC: 1389 Construction, repair & dismantling services

(P-520)
MR T TRANSPORT
15535 Garfield Ave, Paramount
(90723-4033)
P.O. Box 61 (90723-0061)
PHONE..................................562 602-5536
EMP: 17
SQ FT: 9,426
SALES (est): 1.9MM **Privately Held**
WEB: www.mrtspooling.com
SIC: **1389** 4212 7629 Oil And Gas Field
  Services, Nec, Nsk

(P-521)
MTS STIMULATION SERVICES
INC (PA)
Also Called: M T S
7131 Charity Ave, Bakersfield
(93308-5870)
PHONE..................................661 589-5804
Monda Dyrd, *President*
Polly Clark, *Shareholder*
Gary Starling, *Shareholder*
Craig Barto, *Ch of Bd*
Lorena Quintero, *Office Mgr*
EMP: 15 EST: 1983
SQ FT: 1,400
SALES (est): 8MM **Privately Held**
WEB: www.mts-stim.com
SIC: **1389** Oil field services

(P-522)
NABORS WELL SERVICES CO
2567 N Ventura Ave C, Ventura
(93001-1201)
PHONE..................................805 648-2731
Paul Smith, *Manager*
James Bentley, *Branch Mgr*
Justin Case, *Technology*
Kevin Harsy, *VP Finance*
Melanie Housey, *Controller*
EMP: 86 **Privately Held**
WEB: www.nabors.com
SIC: **1389** Oil field services
HQ: Nabors Well Services Co.
  515 W Greens Rd Ste 1000
  Houston TX 77067
  281 874-0035

(P-523)
NABORS WELL SERVICES CO
1025 Earthmover Ct, Bakersfield
(93314-9529)
PHONE..................................661 588-6140
Tom Jaquez, *Manager*
Greg Tremain, *Executive*
EMP: 86 **Privately Held**
WEB: www.nabors.com
SIC: **1389** Oil field services
HQ: Nabors Well Services Co.
  515 W Greens Rd Ste 1000
  Houston TX 77067
  281 874-0035

(P-524)
NABORS WELL SERVICES CO
19431 S Santa Fe Ave, Compton
(90221-5912)
PHONE..................................310 639-7074
Gary Kaufman, *Human Res Mgr*
Konai Tupou, *Supervisor*
EMP: 86 **Privately Held**
WEB: www.nabors.com
SIC: **1389** Oil field services
HQ: Nabors Well Services Co.
  515 W Greens Rd Ste 1000
  Houston TX 77067
  281 874-0035

(P-525)
NABORS WELL SERVICES CO
7515 Rosedale Hwy, Bakersfield
(93308-5727)
PHONE..................................661 589-3970
Alan Pounds, *Chief Mktg Ofcr*
Jerry Fernandez, *Area Mgr*
Melanie Mendoza, *Maintence Staff*
Ron C Cleveland, *Manager*
EMP: 86 **Privately Held**
WEB: www.nabors.com
SIC: **1389** 1382 Servicing oil & gas wells;
  oil & gas exploration services
HQ: Nabors Well Services Co.
  515 W Greens Rd Ste 1000
  Houston TX 77067
  281 874-0035

(P-526)
NABORS WELL SERVICES CO
19431 S Santa Fe Ave, Compton
(90221-5912)
PHONE..................................310 639-7074
Bernie Fish, *Manager*
Juan Landron, *IT/INT Sup*
Gary Kaufman, *Human Res Mgr*
Paul Harper, *Purch Agent*
EMP: 86 **Privately Held**
WEB: www.nabors.com
SIC: **1389** Oil field services
HQ: Nabors Well Services Co.
  515 W Greens Rd Ste 1000
  Houston TX 77067
  281 874-0035

(P-527)
NABORS WELL SERVICES CO
1954 James Rd, Bakersfield (93308-9749)
PHONE..................................661 392-7668
Dave Warner, *District Mgr*
EMP: 86 **Privately Held**
WEB: www.nabors.com
SIC: **1389** Oil field services
HQ: Nabors Well Services Co.
  515 W Greens Rd Ste 1000
  Houston TX 77067
  281 874-0035

(P-528)
NORMAN WIRELINE SERVICE
INC
1301 James Rd, Bakersfield (93308-9844)
PHONE..................................661 399-5697
James Norman, *President*
EMP: 13 EST: 1980
SALES (est): 600K **Privately Held**
WEB: www.norman-wireline-services-
  inc.hub.biz
SIC: **1389** Construction, repair & disman-
  tling services; oil field services

(P-529)
OIL WELL SERVICE COMPANY
(PA)
10840 Norwalk Blvd, Santa Fe Springs
(90670-3826)
PHONE..................................562 612-0600
Jack Frost, *President*
Connie Laws, *Treasurer*
Richard Laws, *Vice Pres*
Matt Hensley, *Admin Sec*
Rod Boller,
EMP: 105 EST: 1940
SQ FT: 9,000
SALES (est): 31.9MM **Privately Held**
WEB: www.ows1.com
SIC: **1389** Oil field services

(P-530)
OIL WELL SERVICE COMPANY
10255 Enos Ln, Shafter (93263-9572)
PHONE..................................661 746-4809
Rick Hobbs, *Office Mgr*
Scott Haynes, *Supervisor*
EMP: 60
SALES (corp-wide): 31.9MM **Privately
Held**
WEB: www.ows1.com
SIC: **1389** Swabbing wells
PA: Oil Well Service Company
  10840 Norwalk Blvd
  Santa Fe Springs CA 90670
  562 612-0600

(P-531)
OIL WELL SERVICE COMPANY
1015 Mission Rock Rd, Santa Paula
(93060-9730)
PHONE..................................805 525-2103
Harvey Himinell, *Manager*
EMP: 60
SALES (corp-wide): 31.9MM **Privately
Held**
WEB: www.ows1.com
SIC: **1389** Oil field services
PA: Oil Well Service Company
  10840 Norwalk Blvd
  Santa Fe Springs CA 90670
  562 612-0600

(P-532)
PACIFIC PERFORATING INC
25090 Highway 33, Fellows (93224-9777)
PHONE..................................661 768-9224
Troy Ducharme, *President*
Perry Parker, *Vice Pres*
▼ EMP: 25 EST: 1969
SQ FT: 4,000
SALES (est): 7.4MM **Privately Held**
WEB: www.variperm.com
SIC: **1389** Oil field services

(P-533)
PACIFIC PROCESS SYSTEMS
INC (PA)
7401 Rosedale Hwy, Bakersfield
(93308-5736)
PHONE..................................661 321-9681
Jerry Wise, *CEO*
Robert Peterson, *CFO*
Alan George, *Corp Secy*
Curt Avis, *Opers Mgr*
Eddie Grajeda, *Manager*
▼ EMP: 90 EST: 1995
SQ FT: 7,000
SALES (est): 35.1MM **Privately Held**
WEB: www.pps-equipment.com
SIC: **1389** 7353 5082 Testing, measuring,
  surveying & analysis services; oil field
  equipment, rental or leasing; oil field
  equipment

(P-534)
PACIFIC SURVEYS LLC
1785 W Arrow Rte, Upland (91786-7677)
PHONE..................................909 949-0850
Michael Ridder,
Joe Abreau, *Vice Pres*
Steve Watkins, *Manager*
EMP: 13
SALES (corp-wide): 3.2MM **Privately
Held**
SIC: **1389** Well logging
PA: Pacific Surveys, Llc
  4456 Via Saint Ambrose
  Claremont CA 91711
  909 625-6262

(P-535)
PACIFIC SURVEYS LLC (PA)
4456 Via Saint Ambrose, Claremont
(91711-8302)
PHONE..................................909 625-6262
Michael Ritter, *Mng Member*
Kim Ridder, *Info Tech Mgr*
Richard Laporte,
Mike Schumacher, *Manager*
EMP: 13 EST: 1998
SALES (est): 3.2MM **Privately Held**
WEB: www.pacificsurveys.com
SIC: **1389** Well logging

(P-536)
PALMER TANK &
CONSTRUCTION INC
2464 S Union Ave, Bakersfield
(93307-5007)
PHONE..................................661 834-1110
Jerry Palmer, *President*
EMP: 36 EST: 1971
SQ FT: 1,200
SALES (est): 8.6MM **Privately Held**
WEB: www.palmertank.com
SIC: **1389** 5731 Oil & gas wells: building,
  repairing & dismantling; antennas

(P-537)
PC MECHANICAL INC
2803 Industrial Pkwy, Santa Maria
(93455-1811)
PHONE..................................805 925-2888
Lew Parker, *President*
Brandon Burginger, *COO*
Mary Parker, *Exec VP*
Mitch Caron, *Vice Pres*
Anthony Caron, *Design Engr*
EMP: 50 EST: 1991
SQ FT: 67,000
SALES (est): 10MM **Privately Held**
WEB: www.pcmechanical.com
SIC: **1389** Oil field services

(P-538)
PRO-VAC INC
26857 Henry Rd, Fellows (93224-9794)
P.O. Box 153, Taft (93268-8153)
PHONE..................................661 765-7298
Dennis Hill, *Owner*
EMP: 28 EST: 1982
SALES (est): 5.1MM **Privately Held**
SIC: **1389** Oil field services

(P-539)
PRODUCTION DATA INC
1210 33rd St, Bakersfield (93301-2124)
P.O. Box 3266 (93385-3266)
PHONE..................................661 327-4776
Gerald Tonnelli, *President*
EMP: 22 EST: 1972
SQ FT: 1,800
SALES (est): 5.5MM **Privately Held**
WEB: www.productiondatainc.com
SIC: **1389** Oil field services

(P-540)
PROS INCORPORATED
3400 Patton Way, Bakersfield
(93308-5722)
P.O. Box 20996 (93390-0996)
PHONE..................................661 589-5400
Robert Lewis, *President*
Teresa Leal, *CFO*
Randy Dubois, *Exploration*
Jack Turner, *Sales Staff*
EMP: 58 EST: 2007
SALES (est): 17.8MM **Privately Held**
WEB: www.proswelltesting.com
SIC: **1389** Oil field services

(P-541)
PSC INDUSTRIAL
OUTSOURCING LP
Also Called: Hydrochempsc
200 Old Yard Dr, Bakersfield (93307-4268)
PHONE..................................661 833-9991
Peter Burger, *Principal*
EMP: 59
SALES (corp-wide): 468MM **Privately
Held**
WEB: www.hydrochempsc.com
SIC: **1389** Oil field services
PA: Psc Industrial Outsourcing, Lp
  900 Georgia Ave
  Deer Park TX 77536
  713 393-5600

(P-542)
REPIPE1 RESTORATION INC
19326 Ventura Blvd # 200, Tarzana
(91356-3016)
PHONE..................................626 252-0778
David Tashroudian, *President*
EMP: 35 EST: 2015
SALES (est): 3MM **Privately Held**
WEB: www.repipe1.com
SIC: **1389** Construction, repair & disman-
  tling services

(P-543)
RICHARD YARBROUGH
Also Called: R & R Pumping Unit Repr & Svc
2493 N Ventura Ave, Ventura (93001-1314)
PHONE..................................805 643-1021
Richard Yarbrough, *Owner*
EMP: 22 EST: 1980
SALES (est): 2MM **Privately Held**
SIC: **1389** Oil & gas wells: building, repair-
  ing & dismantling; pumping of oil & gas
  wells

(P-544)
ROBERT HEELY
CONSTRUCTION LP (PA)
Also Called: Robert Heely Construction
5401 Woodmere Dr, Bakersfield
(93313-2777)
PHONE..................................661 617-1400
Robert Heely, *Chairman*
Craig Bonna, *President*
Robert Hopkins, *Vice Pres*
Chrystal Abbott, *Human Res Mgr*
Juan Palos, *Foreman/Supr*
EMP: 20 EST: 1974
SQ FT: 7,000
SALES (est): 53MM **Privately Held**
WEB: www.rhcteam.com
SIC: **1389** Oil field services

(P-545)
SCHLUMBERGER TECHNOLOGY CORP
Also Called: Schlumberger Well Services
2841 Pegasus Dr, Bakersfield
(93308-6896)
PHONE.....................661 864-4750
Fax: 661 642-2065
EMP: 70 Privately Held
SIC: 1389 1382 Oil/Gas Field Services
Oil/Gas Exploration Services
HQ: Schlumberger Technology Corp
100 Gillingham Ln
Sugar Land TX 77478
281 285-8500

(P-546)
SMITH INTERNATIONAL INC
Also Called: Omni Seals, Inc.
11031 Jersey Blvd Ste A, Rancho Cuca-
monga (91730-5150)
PHONE.....................909 906-7900
Monte Russell, Managing Dir
EMP: 130 Publicly Held
WEB: www.smithcodevelopment.com
SIC: 1389 Oil field services
HQ: Smith International, Inc.
1310 Rankin Rd
Houston TX 77073
281 443-3370

(P-547)
STEELCLAD INC
2664 Saturn St Ste A, Brea (92821-6789)
PHONE.....................714 529-0277
Caren Hallam, President
EMP: 17 EST: 1995
SQ FT: 4,000
SALES (est): 5.5MM Privately Held
WEB: www.steelcladinc.com
SIC: 1389 0782 Oil field services; land-
scape contractors

(P-548)
THETA OILFIELD SERVICES INC
5201 California Ave # 370, Bakersfield
(93309-1674)
PHONE.....................661 633-2792
Dan A Newman, President
Patti Johnson, Manager
EMP: 48 EST: 2007
SALES (est): 30.4MM
SALES (corp-wide): 1.9B Publicly Held
WEB: www.thetaportal.com
SIC: 1389 Oil field services
PA: Championx Corporation
2445 Tech Frest Blvd Bldg
The Woodlands TX 77381
281 403-5772

(P-549)
TIGER CASED HOLE SERVICES INC
Also Called: Tiger Case Hole Services
2828 Junipero Ave, Signal Hill
(90755-2112)
PHONE.....................562 426-4044
Minnie P Baxter, Admin Sec
Joseph S Baxter, CFO
Jesus Hernandez, District Mgr
▲ EMP: 23 EST: 1994
SQ FT: 6,000
SALES (est): 2.6MM Privately Held
SIC: 1389 Oil field services

(P-550)
TITAN OILFIELD SERVICES INC
21535 Kratzmeyer Rd, Bakersfield
(93314-9482)
PHONE.....................661 861-1630
Terry Hibbitts, President
Tim Barman, Vice Pres
Tony Palacpac, Admin Sec
EMP: 34 EST: 2011
SALES (est): 19.2MM Privately Held
WEB: www.titan-ofs.com
SIC: 1389 Oil field services

(P-551)
TOTAL-WESTERN INC (HQ)
8049 Somerset Blvd, Paramount
(90723-4396)
PHONE.....................562 220-1450
Paul F Conrad, CEO
Payman Farrokhyar, President

Mary A Pool, CFO
Earl Grebing, Vice Pres
Jerry Balos, Director
EMP: 133 EST: 1972
SQ FT: 13,000
SALES (est): 220.1MM
SALES (corp-wide): 489.5MM Privately
Held
WEB: www.total-western.com
SIC: 1389 Oil field services; construction,
repair & dismantling services; excavating
slush pits & cellars; grading oil & gas well
foundations
PA: Bragg Investment Company, Inc.
6251 N Paramount Blvd
Long Beach CA 90805
562 984-2400

(P-552)
TRI-TECH RESTORATION CNSTR INC
3301 N San Fernando Blvd, Burbank
(91504-2531)
PHONE.....................800 900-8448
Michael Boyd, Principal
Joe Juarez, Technician
Alen Haghverdi, Manager
Shant Kavarian, Manager
EMP: 13 EST: 2009
SALES (est): 943.9K Privately Held
WEB: www.tritechrestoration.com
SIC: 1389 Construction, repair & disman-
tling services

(P-553)
TRUITT OILFIELD MAINT CORP
1051 James Rd, Bakersfield (93308-9753)
P.O. Box 5066 (93388-5066)
PHONE.....................661 871-4099
Kimberly Sue New, President
Steve New, Vice Pres
Adam Ocegueda, Manager
EMP: 300 EST: 1978
SQ FT: 3,000
SALES (est): 31.7MM Privately Held
WEB: www.truittcorp.com
SIC: 1389 Oil field services

(P-554)
TRYAD SERVICE CORPORATION
5900 E Lerdo Hwy, Shafter (93263-4023)
PHONE.....................661 391-1524
James Varner, President
Estate of Burl G Varner, Shareholder
Danny Seely, Vice Pres
▲ EMP: 90
SALES (est): 9.3MM Privately Held
WEB: www.jdrush.com
SIC: 1389 Oil & gas wells: building, repair-
ing & dismantling

(P-555)
U S WEATHERFORD L P
2815 Fruitvale Ave, Bakersfield
(93308-5907)
PHONE.....................661 589-9483
Rick Benton, Branch Mgr
EMP: 199 Privately Held
WEB: www.weatherford.com
SIC: 1389 Oil field services
HQ: U S Weatherford L P
179 Weatherford Dr
Schriever LA 70395
985 493-6100

(P-556)
ULTRAMAR INC
Also Called: Valero
961 S La Paloma Ave, Wilmington
(90744-6420)
PHONE.....................310 834-7254
Mark Phair, Manager
EMP: 22
SALES (corp-wide): 64.9B Publicly Held
SIC: 1389 Gas field services
HQ: Ultramar Inc.
1 Valero Way
San Antonio TX 78249
210 345-2000

(P-557)
VAQUERO ENERGY INC
4700 Stockdale Hwy # 120, Bakersfield
(93309-2654)
P.O. Box 13550 (93389-3550)
PHONE.....................661 616-0600

Kenneth H Hunter, CEO
Seth Hunter, Vice Pres
Cary Nikkel, Admin Sec
Kasey Todd, Technical Staff
Nikki Tramel, Controller
EMP: 21 EST: 2000
SALES (est): 9MM Privately Held
WEB: www.vaqueroenergy.com
SIC: 1389 Testing, measuring, surveying &
analysis services

(P-558)
WEATHERFORD COMPLETION SYSTEMS
Also Called: Peric Oil Tool
19468 Creek Rd, Bakersfield (93314-8451)
PHONE.....................661 746-1391
Dennis Church, District Mgr
▼ EMP: 13 EST: 2000
SALES (est): 7.6MM Privately Held
SIC: 1389 Oil field services

(P-559)
WEATHERFORD INTERNATIONAL LLC
250 W Stanley Ave, Ventura (93001-1305)
P.O. Box 1668 (93002-1668)
PHONE.....................805 643-1279
Scott Antosen, Branch Mgr
Michael Hambrick, Opers Staff
Jason Goldenbee, Supervisor
EMP: 14 Privately Held
WEB: www.weatherford.com
SIC: 1389 Oil field services
HQ: Weatherford International, Llc
2000 Saint James Pl
Houston TX 77056
713 693-4000

1411 Dimension Stone

(P-560)
ARCHWOOD MFG GROUP INC
15058 Delano St, Van Nuys (91411-2016)
PHONE.....................818 781-7673
Carlos E Subero, Principal
EMP: 15 EST: 2005
SALES (est): 1MM Privately Held
WEB: www.cabinetbydesign.com
SIC: 1411 Marble, dimension-quarrying

(P-561)
ARRIAGA USA INC
Also Called: Stoneland
7127 Radford Ave, North Hollywood
(91605-5746)
PHONE.....................818 764-1777
EMP: 55
SALES (corp-wide): 10MM Privately
Held
WEB: www.stonelandusa.com
SIC: 1411 Marble, dimension-quarrying
PA: Arriaga Usa, Inc.
12000 Sherman Way
North Hollywood CA 91605
818 982-9559

(P-562)
CHANDLER AGGREGATES INC (PA)
24867 Maitri Rd, Corona (92883-5136)
P.O. Box 78450 (92877-0148)
PHONE.....................951 277-1341
Larry Werner, President
Skip Begg, Sales Executive
EMP: 20 EST: 1994
SALES (est): 8.6MM Privately Held
WEB: www.wernercorp.net
SIC: 1411 1422 Dimension stone; crushed
& broken limestone

1422 Crushed & Broken Limestone

(P-563)
CALMAT CO
16101 Hwy 156, Maricopa (93252)
P.O. Box 22800, Bakersfield (93390-2800)
PHONE.....................661 858-2673
Angela Bailey, Manager
EMP: 24 Publicly Held
SIC: 1422 Crushed & broken limestone

HQ: Calmat Co.
500 N Brand Blvd Ste 500 # 500
Glendale CA 91203
818 553-8821

1423 Crushed & Broken Granite

(P-564)
JUNIPER ROCK CORPORATION
Also Called: ARB
26000 Commercentre Dr, Lake Forest
(92630-8816)
PHONE.....................949 500-1797
Eric Amlee, General Mgr
EMP: 28 EST: 2009
SALES (est): 8.9MM Publicly Held
WEB: www.primoriscorp.com
SIC: 1423 Crushed & broken granite
PA: Primoris Services Corporation
2300 N Field St Ste 1900
Dallas TX 75201

1429 Crushed & Broken Stone, NEC

(P-565)
PAUL HUBBS CONSTRUCTION INC (PA)
542 W C St, Colton (92324-2140)
PHONE.....................951 360-3990
Jay P Hubbs, President
Lucile M Hubbs, Treasurer
John L Hubbs, Vice Pres
Pat Hubbs, Admin Sec
Janet Piontkowski, Controller
EMP: 18 EST: 1961
SQ FT: 4,000
SALES (est): 2.6MM Privately Held
SIC: 1429 Riprap quarrying

(P-566)
TRIANGLE ROCK PRODUCTS LLC
500 N Brand Blvd Ste 500 # 500, Glendale
(91203-3319)
PHONE.....................818 553-8820
Stanley G Bass, President
Annie Hovanessian,
EMP: 425 EST: 1978
SQ FT: 20,000
SALES (est): 11.1MM Publicly Held
SIC: 1429 1442 2951 3273 Igneous rock,
crushed & broken-quarrying; construction
sand & gravel; asphalt paving mixtures &
blocks; ready-mixed concrete; nonresi-
dential building operators
HQ: Calmat Co.
500 N Brand Blvd Ste 500 # 500
Glendale CA 91203
818 553-8821

1442 Construction Sand & Gravel

(P-567)
ALAMEDA CONSTRUCTION SVCS INC
2528 E 125th St, Compton (90222-1502)
PHONE.....................310 635-3277
Kevin Ramsey, CEO
Tracey Watson, Vice Pres
Traci Watson, Vice Pres
Patrice Nails-Johnson, Office Mgr
April Hawley, Fellow
EMP: 20 EST: 1992
SQ FT: 8,000
SALES (est): 6MM Privately Held
WEB: www.alamedaconstruction.com
SIC: 1442 Construction sand & gravel

(P-568)
CALPORTLAND
2025 E Financial Way, Glendora
(91741-4692)
P.O. Box 567, Thousand Palms (92276-
0567)
PHONE.....................760 343-3403

Terri Stelter, *President*
Debra Rubenzer, *Corp Secy*
Diane Sarauer, *Vice Pres*
Yolanda Diaz, *Executive Asst*
Leslie Kearney, *Credit Staff*
EMP: 96 **EST:** 1973
SQ FT: 480
SALES (est): 1.5MM **Privately Held**
WEB: www.calportland.com
SIC: 1442 Gravel mining; construction sand mining

(P-569)
CHANDLERS PLOS VRDES SAND GRAV
26311 Palos Verdes Dr E, Rllng HLS Est (90274-4254)
P.O. Box 15450, Irvine (92623-5450)
PHONE...................................310 784-2900
John Roberston Sr, *President*
Linda Wood, *Treasurer*
▲ **EMP:** 13 **EST:** 1937
SQ FT: 4,000
SALES (est): 8.3MM **Privately Held**
WEB: www.chandlerscorp.com
SIC: 1442 Construction sand mining; gravel mining
PA: Chandler's Sand And Gravel, Llc
17392 Daimler St
Irvine CA 92614
310 784-2900

(P-570)
DAN COPP CRUSHING CORP
22765 Savi Ranch Pkwy E, Yorba Linda (92887-4620)
PHONE...................................714 777-6400
Karen Ayres, *Admin Sec*
Jason Ayres, *President*
Robert Virgil, *Vice Pres*
Kyle Stansbury, *Marketing Staff*
EMP: 15 **EST:** 1978
SALES (est): 2.6MM **Privately Held**
WEB: www.narecycle.com
SIC: 1442 Construction sand & gravel

(P-571)
GAIL MATERIALS INC
10060 Dawson Canyon Rd, Corona (92883-2112)
PHONE...................................951 667-6106
Nick Leinen, *CEO*
Mitch Leinen, *President*
Kurt Hutcheson, *Opers Mgr*
Kurth Hutcheson, *Opers Mgr*
John Ross, *Opers Mgr*
▲ **EMP:** 40 **EST:** 1987
SQ FT: 5,000
SALES (est): 17.1MM **Privately Held**
WEB: www.gailmaterials.net
SIC: 1442 Construction sand & gravel

(P-572)
NORTH COUNTY SAND AND GRAV INC
26227 Sherman Rd, Sun City (92585-9223)
PHONE...................................951 928-2881
M J La Paglia III, *President*
Michael J La Paglia III, *President*
Tracy Paglia, *CFO*
Kacey Cowan, *Sales Mgr*
EMP: 18 **EST:** 1985
SALES (est): 4.7MM **Privately Held**
WEB: www.northcountysandandgravel.com
SIC: 1442 5032 Construction sand & gravel; sand, construction; gravel

(P-573)
PECK ROAD GRAVEL PIT
128 Live Oak Ave, Monrovia (91016-5050)
P.O. Box 1286 (91017-1286)
PHONE...................................626 574-7570
Steve Bubalo, *President*
Louise Bubalo, *Treasurer*
Stephanie Bubalo Becerra, *Vice Pres*
EMP: 16 **EST:** 1995
SALES (est): 2.1MM **Privately Held**
SIC: 1442 Construction sand & gravel

(P-574)
SPECIALTY ROCK INC
5405 Alton Pkwy Irvine, Irvine (92604)
PHONE...................................909 334-2265
Richard Newman, *CEO*
Michael Holcomb, *CEO*

▼ **EMP:** 13 **EST:** 2009
SQ FT: 4,100
SALES (est): 676.4K **Privately Held**
SIC: 1442 Construction sand & gravel

(P-575)
WAYNE J SAND & GRAVEL INC
9455 Buena Vista St, Moorpark (93021)
PHONE...................................805 529-1323
Brett Jones, *President*
EMP: 28 **EST:** 1994
SALES (est): 2.4MM **Privately Held**
WEB: www.waynejsandandgravelinc.com
SIC: 1442 Construction sand mining; gravel mining

(P-576)
WEST COAST AGGREGATE SUPPLY
Also Called: Aggregate West Coast
92500 Airport Blvd, Thermal (92274)
P.O. Box 790 (92274-0790)
PHONE...................................760 342-7598
Marvin Struiksma, *President*
EMP: 14 **EST:** 1994
SALES (est): 6MM **Privately Held**
SIC: 1442 Common sand mining

1446 Industrial Sand

(P-577)
PIONEER SANDS LLC
9952 Enos Ln, Bakersfield (93314)
PHONE...................................661 746-5789
Donna Bartlett, *Branch Mgr*
EMP: 23
SALES (corp-wide): 6.6B **Publicly Held**
WEB: www.pwgillibrand.com
SIC: 1446 Silica mining
HQ: Pioneer Sands Llc
777 Hidden Rdg
Irving TX 75038
972 444-9001

(P-578)
PIONEER SANDS LLC
31302 Ortega Hwy, San Juan Capistrano (92675)
PHONE...................................949 728-0171
Mike Miclette, *Branch Mgr*
EMP: 23
SALES (corp-wide): 6.6B **Publicly Held**
SIC: 1446 Silica sand mining
HQ: Pioneer Sands Llc
777 Hidden Rdg
Irving TX 75038
972 444-9001

(P-579)
PW GILLIBRAND CO INC (PA)
4537 Ish Dr, Simi Valley (93063-7667)
P.O. Box 1019 (93062-1019)
PHONE...................................805 526-2195
Celine Gillibrand, *CEO*
Richard Valencia, *President*
Jim Costello, *Corp Secy*
EMP: 71 **EST:** 1957
SQ FT: 11,000
SALES (est): 25.2MM **Privately Held**
WEB: www.pwgillibrand.com
SIC: 1446 Grinding sand mining

1479 Chemical & Fertilizer Mining

(P-580)
SEARLES VALLEY MINERALS INC
80201 Trona Rd, Trona (93562)
PHONE...................................760 372-2259
Burnell Blanchard, *Vice Pres*
EMP: 39 **Privately Held**
WEB: www.svminerals.com
SIC: 1479 Salt & sulfur mining
HQ: Searles Valley Minerals Inc.
9401 Indian Creek Pkwy
Overland Park KS 66210

(P-581)
SEARLES VALLEY MINERALS INC
13068 Main St, Trona (93562-1911)
PHONE...................................760 672-2053
EMP: 39 **Privately Held**
WEB: www.svminerals.com
SIC: 1479 Salt & sulfur mining
HQ: Searles Valley Minerals Inc.
9401 Indian Creek Pkwy
Overland Park KS 66210

1481 Nonmetallic Minerals Svcs, Except Fuels

(P-582)
IMERYS MINERALS CALIFORNIA INC
Also Called: Imerys Filtration Minerals
2500 Miguelito Canyon Rd, Lompoc (93436)
PHONE...................................805 736-1221
Kenneth Schweibert, *Manager*
Jeff Taniguchi, *Manager*
Bob Froehlich, *Supervisor*
EMP: 536
SALES (corp-wide): 3.2MM **Privately Held**
WEB: www.imerys.com
SIC: 1481 3295 Nonmetallic mineral services; minerals, ground or treated
HQ: Imerys Minerals California, Inc.
2500 San Miguelito Rd
Lompoc CA 93436

(P-583)
MP MINE OPERATIONS LLC
67750 Bailey Rd, Mountain Pass (92366)
PHONE...................................702 277-0848
James H Litinsky, *CEO*
Michael Rosethal, *COO*
EMP: 108 **EST:** 2017
SALES (est): 35.8MM
SALES (corp-wide): 134.3MM **Publicly Held**
WEB: www.mpmaterials.com
SIC: 1481 1099 Mine exploration, nonmetallic minerals; rare-earth ores mining
PA: Mp Materials Corp.
6720 Via Austi Pkwy # 45
Las Vegas NV 89119
702 844-6111

1499 Miscellaneous Nonmetallic Mining

(P-584)
BRAZIL MINERALS INC
155 N Lake Ave Ste 800, Pasadena (91101-1857)
PHONE...................................213 590-2500
Marc Fogassa, *Ch of Bd*
Gisele Souza, *Vice Pres*
EMP: 15 **EST:** 2012
SALES (est): 1.1MM **Privately Held**
SIC: 1499 Diamond mining, industrial

(P-585)
DICAPERL CORPORATION (DH)
Also Called: Grefco Dicaperl
23705 Crenshaw Blvd # 10, Torrance (90505-5236)
PHONE...................................610 667-6640
Ray Perelman, *CEO*
Glenn Jones, *President*
Mike Cull, *Treasurer*
Barry Katz, *Senior VP*
▼ **EMP:** 90 **EST:** 1992
SQ FT: 5,000
SALES (est): 10.4MM **Privately Held**
WEB: www.dicalite.com
SIC: 1499 3677 Perlite mining; filtration devices, electronic
HQ: Grefco Minerals Inc.
1 Bala Ave Ste 310
Bala Cynwyd PA 19004
610 660-8820

(P-586)
FEATHEROCK INC (PA)
20219 Bahama St, Chatsworth (91311-6204)
PHONE...................................818 882-3888
Eric Anderson, *President*
Bob Campagna, *Controller*
Olivia Nicholson, *Sales Staff*
EMP: 15
SQ FT: 20,000
SALES (est): 1.7MM **Privately Held**
WEB: www.featherock.com
SIC: 1499 Pumice mining

(P-587)
IMERYS MINERALS CALIFORNIA INC (DH)
2500 San Miguelito Rd, Lompoc (93436-9743)
P.O. Box 519 (93438-0519)
PHONE...................................805 736-1221
Douglas A Smith, *President*
John Leichty, *CFO*
John Oskam, *Vice Pres*
Bruno Van Herpen, *Vice Pres*
Ken Rasmussen, *General Mgr*
◆ **EMP:** 70 **EST:** 1991
SQ FT: 11,600
SALES (est): 276.9MM
SALES (corp-wide): 3.2MM **Privately Held**
WEB: www.imerys.com
SIC: 1499 3295 Diatomaceous earth mining; minerals, ground or treated

---

1521 General Contractors, Single Family Houses

(P-588)
1ST CENTURY BUILDERS INC
5737 Kanan Rd, Agoura Hills (91301-1601)
PHONE...................................818 254-7183
Colin Pratt, *CEO*
EMP: 18 **EST:** 2017
SALES (est): 2.3MM **Privately Held**
SIC: 1521 1389 New construction, single-family houses; construction, repair & dismantling services

(P-589)
A M ORTEGA CONSTRUCTION INC
58 Kellogg St, Ventura (93001-1732)
PHONE...................................951 360-1352
Archie Maurice Ortega, *Branch Mgr*
Derek Sexton, *Superintendent*
EMP: 54
SALES (corp-wide): 55.5MM **Privately Held**
WEB: www.amortega.com
SIC: 1521 Single-family housing construction
PA: A. M. Ortega Construction, Inc.
10125 Channel Rd
Lakeside CA 92040
619 390-1988

(P-590)
ACE INDUSTRIAL SUPPLY INC (PA)
7535 N San Fernando Rd, Burbank (91505-1044)
PHONE...................................818 252-1981
Tim Stearns, *Principal*
Holden Stearns, *Executive Asst*
Angie Cortez, *Admin Asst*
Richard Benton, *CIO*
Larry Lawrence, *Data Proc Dir*
◆ **EMP:** 107 **EST:** 1983
SQ FT: 25,000
SALES (est): 33.9MM **Privately Held**
WEB: www.acetools.com
SIC: 1521 Single-family housing construction

(P-591)
ALLIED CONSTRUCTION SERVICES
4740 Green Rver Rd Ste 10, Corona (92878)
PHONE...................................951 405-3193
Dean Hoffman Jr, *Principal*
EMP: 50 **EST:** 2017

PRODUCTS & SVCS

SALES (est): 2.5MM **Privately Held**
SIC: **1521** Single-family housing construction

(P-592)
AMERICO BUILDERS LLC
1511 E Orangethorpe Ave, Fullerton (92831-5204)
PHONE............................714 430-7730
William L Butler, *Manager*
Christopher Kent, *Manager*
EMP: 50 EST: 2019
SALES (est): 6.2MM **Privately Held**
WEB: www.americo.builders
SIC: **1521** Single-family housing construction

(P-593)
ARYA GROUP INC
Also Called: Arya Design Group
10490 Santa Monica Blvd, Los Angeles (90025-5033)
PHONE............................310 446-7000
Ardie Tavangarian, *President*
EMP: 50 EST: 1978
SQ FT: 3,000
SALES (est): 14.3MM **Privately Held**
SIC: **1521 1542** New construction, single-family houses; commercial & office building, new construction

(P-594)
ASCENSION CONSTRUCTORS INC (PA)
7211 Haven Ave, Alta Loma (91701-6064)
PHONE............................909 242-3106
Anthony Mario Labriola, *Principal*
Anthony Labriola, *General Mgr*
EMP: 69 EST: 2015
SALES (est): 1.9MM **Privately Held**
SIC: **1521** Single-family housing construction

(P-595)
BROOKFELD STHLAND HOLDINGS LLC
Also Called: Brookfield Residential
3200 Park Center Dr # 1000, Costa Mesa (92626-7163)
PHONE............................714 427-6868
Edrian Soley,
Thiago Waechter, *Administration*
Suhi Siva, *Analyst*
Lui Thomas, *Controller*
Carleton Clark, *Purchasing*
EMP: 160 EST: 1996
SALES (est): 53.6MM
SALES (corp-wide): 47.9B **Publicly Held**
WEB: www.brookfieldresidential.com
SIC: **1521** Single-family housing construction
HQ: Brookfield Homes Corporation
3201 Jermantown Rd
Fairfax VA 22030
703 270-1400

(P-596)
BROWNCO CONSTRUCTION CO INC
1000 E Katella Ave, Anaheim (92805-6617)
PHONE............................714 935-9600
Scot Alah Brown, *President*
Jeff Radtke, *Vice Pres*
Carla Marquez, *IT/INT Sup*
Andrew Brown, *Project Mgr*
Michael Campbell, *Project Mgr*
EMP: 87
SQ FT: 15,000
SALES (est): 23.6MM **Privately Held**
WEB: www.browncoinc.com
SIC: **1521** Single-family housing construction

(P-597)
CALATLANTIC GROUP INC
13200 Fiji Way, Marina Del Rey (90292)
PHONE............................310 821-9843
EMP: 59
SALES (corp-wide): 2.4B **Publicly Held**
SIC: **1521** Single-Family House Construction
PA: Calatlantic Group, Inc.
15360 Barranca Pkwy
Irvine CA 22209
949 789-1600

(P-598)
COASTLINE CNSTR & AWNG CO INC
5742 Research Dr, Huntington Beach (92649-1617)
PHONE............................714 891-9798
John W Almquist, *President*
EMP: 100 EST: 1980
SQ FT: 1,600
SALES (est): 9.8MM **Privately Held**
WEB: www.coastlineconawn.com
SIC: **1521** Mobile home repair, on site

(P-599)
CROWN CONTRACTING INC
7311 Hopi Trl, Yucca Valley (92284-2512)
PHONE............................760 203-4613
Marvin Burton, *President*
Lacy Pinney, *Manager*
EMP: 50 EST: 1971
SALES (est): 8.1MM **Privately Held**
WEB: www.crowncontracting.com
SIC: **1521 1542** Single-family housing construction; commercial & office building contractors

(P-600)
DENNIS ALLEN ASSOCIATES (PA)
201 N Milpas St, Santa Barbara (93103-3201)
PHONE............................805 884-8777
Dennis W Allen, *President*
Ian Cronshaw, *Vice Pres*
Jessica Dias, *Executive Asst*
Jennifer Cushnie, *Admin Sec*
Nelson Bruce, *Project Mgr*
EMP: 95 EST: 1983
SALES (est): 33.8MM **Privately Held**
WEB: www.buildallen.com
SIC: **1521 1542** General remodeling, single-family houses; new construction, single-family houses; commercial & office buildings, renovation & repair; commercial & office building, new construction

(P-601)
DISASTER RSTRTION PRFSSNALS IN
Also Called: Service Master By ARS
1517 W 130th St, Gardena (90249-2103)
PHONE............................310 301-8030
Ahmad Elzarou, *CEO*
EMP: 80 EST: 2003
SALES (est): 4.4MM **Privately Held**
SIC: **1521 7299 1542** Repairing fire damage, single-family houses; home improvement & renovation contractor agency; commercial & office building contractors

(P-602)
EBC INC (PA)
Also Called: Ellis Building Contractors
219 Manhattan Beach Blvd # 3, Manhattan Beach (90266-5324)
PHONE............................310 753-6407
Brad Ellis, *President*
Patricia Ellis, *Admin Sec*
EMP: 95 EST: 1980
SALES (est): 922K **Privately Held**
SIC: **1521 1542** New construction, single-family houses; commercial & office building, new construction

(P-603)
EMERCON CONSTRUCTION INC (PA)
125 E Bristol Ln, Orange (92865-2749)
P.O. Box 1141, Murrieta (92564-1141)
PHONE............................714 630-9615
Richard Anderson, *President*
Joan Anderson, *COO*
Joan E Anderson, *Exec VP*
Frank Brady, *Exec VP*
Ron Chavez, *Branch Mgr*
EMP: 50 EST: 1987
SALES (est): 11.1MM **Privately Held**
WEB: www.emercon.com
SIC: **1521** Repairing fire damage, single-family houses

(P-604)
EXCEL CONTRACTORS INC
Also Called: Progression Drywall Corp
348 E Avenue K8 Ste B, Lancaster (93535-4514)
PHONE............................661 942-6944
John Rockey, *President*
Rose Rockey, *Vice Pres*
EMP: 100 EST: 1987
SALES (est): 18.6MM **Privately Held**
WEB: www.progressiondrywall.com
SIC: **1521 1742 1542** Single-family home remodeling, additions & repairs; drywall; commercial & office building, new construction

(P-605)
FORT HILL CONSTRUCTION (PA)
12711 Ventura Blvd # 390, Studio City (91604-2431)
PHONE............................323 656-7425
George Peper, *President*
Gordon Foote, *CFO*
James Kweskin, *Vice Pres*
Mike Mc Grail, *Vice Pres*
Joseph Goldfarb, *Admin Sec*
▲ EMP: 70 EST: 1971
SQ FT: 4,000
SALES (est): 10.2MM **Privately Held**
WEB: www.forthill.com
SIC: **1521** New construction, single-family houses

(P-606)
GENERATION CONSTRUCTION INC
15650 El Prado Rd, Chino (91710-9108)
P.O. Box 991 (91708-0991)
PHONE............................909 923-2077
Antwan De Paul, *President*
Karla Diaz, *Admin Asst*
Alicia Nash, *Administration*
EMP: 150
SALES (est): 30MM **Privately Held**
WEB: www.gconstruction.com
SIC: **1521** Single-family housing construction

(P-607)
GRANTS CUSTOM CABINETS
7310 Kingsbury Rd, Templeton (93465-8304)
PHONE............................805 466-9680
EMP: 185
SALES (est): 4.5MM **Privately Held**
SIC: **1521** Single-Family House Construction

(P-608)
HALE CORPORATION
513 S Myrtle Ave Ste A, Monrovia (91016-6154)
PHONE............................626 358-4523
Richard T Hale Jr, *President*
Susan Hale, *Corp Secy*
EMP: 98 EST: 1977
SQ FT: 3,000
SALES (est): 19.5MM **Privately Held**
WEB: www.thehalecorp.com
SIC: **1521 1542** New construction, single-family houses; commercial & office building, new construction

(P-609)
HAMBURGER HOME
3701 Wilshire Blvd # 900, Los Angeles (90010-2804)
PHONE............................213 637-5000
Sandra Cohen, *Principal*
EMP: 80
SALES (corp-wide): 16.6MM **Privately Held**
WEB: www.aviva.org
SIC: **1521** Single-family housing construction
PA: Hamburger Home
7120 Franklin Ave
Los Angeles CA 90046
323 876-0550

(P-610)
HANOVER BUILDERS INC
141 Duesenberg Dr Ste 6, Westlake Village (91362-3471)
PHONE............................818 706-2279
Donald Hanover, *President*

Mark Stief, *Project Mgr*
EMP: 50 EST: 1993
SALES (est): 7.6MM **Privately Held**
WEB: www.hanoverbuildersinc.com
SIC: **1521** New construction, single-family houses

(P-611)
HMM CONSTRUCTION INC
3541 Old Conejo Rd, Newbury Park (91320-2158)
PHONE............................805 377-1402
Hector Molina, *CEO*
EMP: 50 EST: 2018
SALES (est): 7.9MM **Privately Held**
WEB: www.hmmconstructioninc.com
SIC: **1521** Single-family housing construction

(P-612)
HOLLAND CONSTRUCTION
5000 E Spring St Ste 500, Long Beach (90815-5235)
PHONE............................562 285-5300
Jeffery Dickerson, *President*
Sanuel Giannini, *Vice Pres*
John Hendry, *Vice Pres*
Orville Hinerman, *Vice Pres*
Bert Levesque, *Vice Pres*
EMP: 73 EST: 2011
SALES (est): 5.4MM
SALES (corp-wide): 112MM **Privately Held**
WEB: www.hollandpartnergroup.com
SIC: **1521** Single-family housing construction
PA: Holland Partners Rock Creek Landing, Llc
1111 Main St Ste 700
Vancouver WA 98660
360 694-7888

(P-613)
HOWARD CDM
Also Called: Howard Construction
3750 Long Beach Blvd, Long Beach (90807-3310)
PHONE............................562 427-4124
Martin D Howard, *President*
William G Burkett, *CFO*
Steven C Phillips, *Exec VP*
John Buda, *Project Engr*
Parker Cole, *Project Engr*
◆ EMP: 50 EST: 1972
SQ FT: 7,000
SALES (est): 20.3MM **Privately Held**
WEB: www.howardcdm.com
SIC: **1521** Single-family housing construction

(P-614)
IN OAKWOOD CNSTR RSTRTION SVCS (DH)
4955 E Hunter Ave, Anaheim (92807-2058)
PHONE............................714 529-8300
Sheldon Yellen, *CEO*
Todd H Benson, *President*
Joseph Ciolino, *CFO*
Jyl Benson, *Vice Pres*
Jyl B Soriano, *Vice Pres*
EMP: 50 EST: 1988
SALES (est): 13.9MM **Privately Held**
WEB: www.oakwoodteam.com
SIC: **1521 1522 1542** Repairing fire damage, single-family houses; remodeling, multi-family dwellings; commercial & office buildings, renovation & repair
HQ: Belfor - Ocrs, Llc
4955 E Hunter Ave
Anaheim CA 9280?
714 529-8300

(P-615)
JPM INDUSTRIES INC
Also Called: Baldwin Construction
13326 Elliot Ave, Chino (91710-5254)
PHONE............................909 592-2292
John Petrov, *President*
EMP: 50 EST: 2015
SALES (est): 7.3MM **Privately Held**
SIC: **1521** Single-family housing construction

(P-616)
K HOVNANIAN COMPANIES CAL INC (HQ)
Also Called: K Hovnanian
400 Exchange Ste 200, Irvine
(92602-1340)
PHONE..........................714 368-4500
Nicholas Pappas, *President*
EMP: 65 EST: 1994
SALES (est): 207.1MM
SALES (corp-wide): 2.3B Publicly Held
WEB: www.khov.com
SIC: 1521 New construction, single-family houses
PA: Hovnanian Enterprises, Inc.
    90 Matawan Rd Ste 105
    Matawan NJ 07747
    732 747-7800

(P-617)
KAR CONSTRUCTION INC
1306 Brooks St, Ontario (91762-3611)
PHONE..........................909 988-5054
Kurt Alan Rothweiler, *Principal*
Margaret Rothweiler, *Admin Sec*
Tom Garrison, *Project Mgr*
Kyle Billings, *Engineer*
Roberta McCormick, *Finance*
EMP: 70 EST: 2010
SALES (est): 13.9MM Privately Held
WEB: www.karconstruction.com
SIC: 1521 Single-family housing construction

(P-618)
KB HOME GRATER LOS ANGELES INC (HQ)
10990 Wilshire Blvd # 700, Los Angeles
(90024-3913)
PHONE..........................310 231-4000
Bruce Karatz, *CEO*
EMP: 90 EST: 1957
SQ FT: 40,000
SALES (est): 64MM
SALES (corp-wide): 4.1B Publicly Held
WEB: www.kbhome.com
SIC: 1521 1522 Single-family home remodeling, additions & repairs; multi-family dwelling construction
PA: Kb Home
    10990 Wilshire Blvd Fl 7
    Los Angeles CA 90024
    310 231-4000

(P-619)
KB HOME GRATER LOS ANGELES INC
36310 Inland Valley Dr, Wildomar
(92595-7595)
PHONE..........................951 691-5300
George Brenner, *Manager*
John Carlson, *Production*
Les Mayeda, *Manager*
EMP: 164
SALES (corp-wide): 4.1B Publicly Held
SIC: 1521 1522 Single-family home remodeling, additions & repairs; multi-family dwelling construction
HQ: Kb Home Greater Los Angeles Inc.
    10990 Wilshire Blvd # 700
    Los Angeles CA 90024
    310 231-4000

(P-620)
KG CONSTRCTONS SLTIONS USA INC (PA)
7450 Greenbush Ave, North Hollywood
(91605-4005)
PHONE..........................800 295-9109
Eran Gurion, *President*
▲ EMP: 70 EST: 2008
SALES (est): 373.3K Privately Held
SIC: 1521 Single-family housing construction

(P-621)
LENNAR HOMES CALIFORNIA INC (DH)
Also Called: Lennar Builders
15131 Alton Pkwy Ste 190, Irvine
(92618-2386)
PHONE..........................949 349-8000
Bill Binder, *Project Mgr*
Kathy Dale, *Asst Controller*
Andrew Han, *Director*

EMP: 124 EST: 1996
SALES (est): 103.5MM
SALES (corp-wide): 22.4B Publicly Held
WEB: www.lennar.com
SIC: 1521 6552 New construction, single-family houses; subdividers & developers
HQ: Lennar Homes, Inc.
    700 Nw 107th Ave Ste 115
    Miami FL 33172
    305 559-4000

(P-622)
MATRIX GROUP INTERNATIONAL INC
1520 W Cameron Ave, West Covina
(91790-2713)
PHONE..........................626 960-6205
EMP: 70
SALES (est): 2.7MM Privately Held
SIC: 1521 Single-Family House Construction

(P-623)
MGB CONSTRUCTION INC
91 Commercial Ave, Riverside
(92507-1111)
PHONE..........................951 342-0303
Emily Beach, *President*
Emilly Beach, *President*
Tamara Jenkins, *Office Mgr*
Chris Maurer, *Sr Project Mgr*
EMP: 150 EST: 2001
SALES (est): 18.9MM Privately Held
WEB: www.mgbconstruction.net
SIC: 1521 Single-family housing construction

(P-624)
MILES CONSTRUCTION GROUP INC
41725 Elm St Ste 303, Murrieta
(92562-1401)
PHONE..........................951 260-2504
Adam Miles, *President*
S Parkinson, *Corp Secy*
G King, *Vice Pres*
Mike Stevens, *General Mgr*
White Colton, *Project Mgr*
EMP: 50 EST: 2012
SALES (est): 3.7MM Privately Held
WEB: www.milesconstructiongroup.com
SIC: 1521 Single-family housing construction

(P-625)
NHS WESTERN DIVISION INC
Also Called: Fixd Construction Co.
175 N Indian Hill Blvd # 203, Claremont
(91711-4665)
PHONE..........................909 947-9931
Damien Melle, *CEO*
Mia Melle, *President*
EMP: 89 EST: 2012
SALES (est): 5.1MM Privately Held
SIC: 1521 Single-family housing construction

(P-626)
NLMS ELITE CONSTRUCTION CO
1254 S Waterman Ave, San Bernardino
(92408-2855)
PHONE..........................626 205-8417
Nathan Murphy, *Owner*
EMP: 15 EST: 2008
SALES (est): 874.4K Privately Held
SIC: 1521 1389 1542 1531 Single-family housing construction; construction, repair & dismantling services; commercial & office building contractors; custom builders, non-residential; speculative builder, multi-family dwellings

(P-627)
PACIFIC BAY PROPERTIES (PA)
4041 Macarthur Blvd # 500, Newport Beach
(92660-2512)
PHONE..........................949 440-7200
Malcolm S McDonald, *President*
EMP: 50 EST: 1993
SALES (est): 9.5MM Privately Held
SIC: 1521 Single-family housing construction

(P-628)
PACIFIC COMMUNITIES BLDR INC (PA)
1000 Dove St Ste 300, Newport Beach
(92660-2850)
PHONE..........................949 660-8988
Nelson Chung, *President*
Christine Chung, *CFO*
Shiung Lin, *Admin Sec*
Rosan Mickey, *VP Sls/Mktg*
Tara Talvin, *Sales Staff*
EMP: 85 EST: 1991
SQ FT: 21,000
SALES (est): 31.2MM Privately Held
WEB: www.pacificcommunities.com
SIC: 1521 New construction, single-family houses

(P-629)
PACIFIC DESIGN DIRECTIONS INC
Also Called: Pacific Interior Design
8171 E Kaiser Blvd, Anaheim
(92808-2214)
PHONE..........................714 685-7766
Susan S Stoneburner, *President*
Kristen S Stolle, *Division Mgr*
Kristen Stolle, *Division Mgr*
Carlos Diez, *Sr Project Mgr*
EMP: 50 EST: 1979
SQ FT: 8,600
SALES: 15MM Privately Held
WEB: www.pacdesign.com
SIC: 1521 1731 7389 8712 Single-family housing construction; general electrical contractor; interior designer; architectural services

(P-630)
PACIFIC WEST CONSTRUCTION
1601 Pcf Cast Hwy Ste 160, Hermosa Beach (90254)
PHONE..........................310 997-2340
Adrian Hernandez, *CEO*
EMP: 50 EST: 2012
SQ FT: 1,000
SALES (est): 6MM Privately Held
WEB: www.pwconstructionservices.com
SIC: 1521 1542 1522 Single-family housing construction; commercial & office building contractors; commercial & office buildings, renovation & repair; apartment building construction; multi-family dwellings, new construction

(P-631)
PAPICH CONSTRUCTION CO INC (PA)
398 Sunrise Ter, Arroyo Grande
(93420-4419)
P.O. Box 2210, Pismo Beach (93448-2210)
PHONE..........................805 473-3016
Jason William Papich, *President*
April Papich, *Officer*
Jeffrey McGuire, *Vice Pres*
Craig Caballero, *Project Mgr*
Keith Oconnor, *Project Mgr*
EMP: 173 EST: 1997
SQ FT: 6,000
SALES (est): 63.6MM Privately Held
WEB: www.papichco.com
SIC: 1521 Single-family housing construction

(P-632)
PEVELERS CUSTOM INTERIORS INC
4203 Spencer St, Torrance (90503-2421)
PHONE..........................310 214-5049
Rodney Peveler, *President*
Clairese Peveler, *Corp Secy*
EMP: 13 EST: 1971
SQ FT: 4,000
SALES (est): 1.1MM Privately Held
WEB: www.pevelers.com
SIC: 1521 2434 2521 General remodeling, single-family houses; wood kitchen cabinets; wood office furniture

(P-633)
PGC CONSTRUCTION INC
Also Called: Architectural Shtmtl Contr
42309 Winchester Rd Ste C, Temecula
(92590-4859)
PHONE..........................760 549-4121

Philip G Chapman, *CEO*
EMP: 21 EST: 2008
SALES (est): 4MM Privately Held
SIC: 1521 3444 1761 Single-family housing construction; skylights, sheet metal; architectural sheet metal work

(P-634)
PRIMECARE QUALITY HM CARE INC
2372 Morse Ave, Irvine (92614-6234)
PHONE..........................949 681-3515
EMP: 99
SALES (est): 3.6MM Privately Held
SIC: 1521 Single-Family House Construction

(P-635)
REGIONAL CONNECTOR CONSTRS
1995 Agua Mansa Rd, Riverside
(92509-2405)
PHONE..........................951 368-6400
Patty Macias, *Office Mgr*
EMP: 50 EST: 2014
SALES (est): 4.2MM Privately Held
WEB: www.teamrcc.com
SIC: 1521 New construction, single-family houses

(P-636)
SEARS HOME IMPRV PDTS INC
730 S Orange Ave, West Covina
(91790-2613)
PHONE..........................626 671-1892
EMP: 139
SALES (corp-wide): 4.1B Privately Held
SIC: 1521 General remodeling, single-family houses
HQ: Sears Home Improvement Products, Inc.
    1024 Florida Central Pkwy
    Longwood FL 32750
    407 767-0990

(P-637)
SEARS HOME IMPRV PDTS INC
2900 N Bellflower Blvd, Long Beach
(90815-1149)
PHONE..........................562 485-4904
EMP: 139
SALES (corp-wide): 4.1B Privately Held
SIC: 1521 General remodeling, single-family houses
HQ: Sears Home Improvement Products, Inc.
    1024 Florida Central Pkwy
    Longwood FL 32750
    407 767-0990

(P-638)
SEARS HOME IMPRV PDTS INC
5665 Rosemead Blvd, Temple City
(91780-1804)
PHONE..........................626 988-9134
Larry Hotz, *Consultant*
EMP: 139
SALES (corp-wide): 4.1B Privately Held
SIC: 1521 General remodeling, single-family houses
HQ: Sears Home Improvement Products, Inc.
    1024 Florida Central Pkwy
    Longwood FL 32750
    407 767-0990

(P-639)
SEATTLE TNNEL PRTNERS A JINT V
555 Anton Blvd Ste 1000, Costa Mesa
(92626-7019)
PHONE..........................206 971-8701
Chris Dixon, *Project Executi*
▲ EMP: 300 EST: 2010
SALES (est): 15.4MM Privately Held
SIC: 1521 Single-family home remodeling, additions & repairs

(P-640)
SHEA HMES LTD PRTNR A CAL LTD (HQ)
655 Brea Canyon Rd, Walnut
(91789-3078)
PHONE..........................909 594-9500
Jim Shontere, *Partner*

PRODUCTS & SVCS

John F Shea LP, *Partner*
EMP: 50 **EST:** 1989
SQ FT: 29,000
SALES (est): 387.9MM
SALES (corp-wide): 2.1B **Privately Held**
WEB: www.jfshea.com
SIC: 1521 New construction, single-family
houses
PA: J. F. Shea Co., Inc.
655 Brea Canyon Rd
Walnut CA 91789
909 594-9500

(P-641)
SILVERADO FRAMING & CNSTR
3091 E La Cadena Dr, Riverside
(92507-2630)
PHONE..............................951 352-1100
Ed Solis, *President*
EMP: 100 **EST:** 2011
SQ FT: 2,500
SALES (est): 10.2MM **Privately Held**
WEB: www.silveradoframingandconstruc-
tioninc.com
SIC: 1521 Single-family housing construc-
tion

(P-642)
SMA BUILDERS INC
16134 Leadwell St, Van Nuys
(91406-3424)
PHONE..............................818 994-8306
Shawn Antin, *President*
Diana Antin, *Vice Pres*
EMP: 50 **EST:** 1985
SALES (est): 13.1MM **Privately Held**
WEB: www.smabuilders.net
SIC: 1521 New construction, single-family
houses

(P-643)
SUPERIOR CONSTRUCTION INC
265 N Joy St, Corona (92879-0600)
P.O. Box 1148 (92878-1148)
PHONE..............................951 808-8780
Kenneth Day, *President*
Arlene Pabrazinsky, *IT Executive*
Don Mc Lellan, *Sls & Mktg Exec*
EMP: 100 **EST:** 1976
SQ FT: 3,000
SALES (est): 16.1MM **Privately Held**
WEB: www.superiorconstruction.com
SIC: 1521 1542 New construction, single-
family houses; commercial & office build-
ing, new construction

(P-644)
TNHC REALTY AND CNSTR INC (PA)
15231 Laguna Canyon Rd # 25, Irvine
(92618-7714)
PHONE..............................949 382-7800
H Lawrence Webb, *CEO*
Stephen Jordan, *Vice Pres*
Roderick Villery, *Sales Staff*
Roger De Haro, *Representative*
Obrian Jennings, *Representative*
EMP: 106 **EST:** 2009
SALES (est): 4.3MM **Privately Held**
WEB: www.nwhm.com
SIC: 1521 New construction, single-family
houses

(P-645)
TRICON AMERICAN HOMES LLC
15771 Red Hill Ave, Tustin (92780-7303)
P.O. Box 15086, Santa Ana (92735-0086)
PHONE..............................844 874-2661
Kevin Baldridge, *Mng Member*
Alan O'Brien, *COO*
Bill Richard, *Exec VP*
Terry Chen, *Vice Pres*
Dawn Dalton, *Vice Pres*
EMP: 210 **EST:** 2012
SALES (est): 35.6MM
SALES (corp-wide): 478.1MM **Privately Held**
WEB: www.triconresidential.com
SIC: 1521 Single-family home remodeling,
additions & repairs
PA: Tricon Residential Inc
7 St Thomas St Suite 801
Toronto ON M5S 2
416 925-7228

(P-646)
ULTIMATE REMOVAL INC
Also Called: Ultimate Demo
2168 Pomona Blvd, Pomona (91768-3332)
P.O. Box 1220 (91769-1220)
PHONE..............................909 524-0800
John W Welch, *President*
Patrick Coleman, *CFO*
Eddie Somoza, *Project Mgr*
Aldo Castillo, *Foreman/Supr*
Rudy Trujillo, *Superintendent*
EMP: 124 **EST:** 1995
SQ FT: 9,900
SALES (est): 9.4MM **Privately Held**
WEB: www.ultimateremoval.com
SIC: 1521 Single-family housing construc-
tion

(P-647)
US BEST REPAIR SERVICE INC
Also Called: US Best Repairs
1652 Edinger Ave Ste E, Tustin
(92780-6530)
PHONE..............................888 750-2378
Mark Zaverl, *CEO*
Kyle Keller, *COO*
Brian Craycraft, *CFO*
Cino Wise, *Officer*
Jeff Bougher, *Vice Pres*
EMP: 101 **EST:** 2008
SALES (est): 12MM **Privately Held**
WEB: www.usbestrepairs.com
SIC: 1521 1522 1542 Single-family home
remodeling, additions & repairs; remodel-
ing, multi-family dwellings; commercial &
office buildings, renovation & repair

(P-648)
VORWALLER & BROOKS INC
72182 Corporate Way, Thousand Palms
(92276-3324)
PHONE..............................760 262-6300
Eugene Sheldon Vorwaller, *President*
Jason Brooks, *Vice Pres*
EMP: 55 **EST:** 2011
SALES (est): 9.2MM **Privately Held**
SIC: 1521 New construction, single-family
houses

(P-649)
WALTON ASSOCIATED COMPANIES
Also Called: Walton Company, The
2001 E Fincl Way Ste 200, Glendora
(91741)
PHONE..............................626 963-8505
William Raymond Sr, *Ch of Bd*
Richard Walker Sr, *President*
Richard Walker Jr, *CFO*
Charlene Thompson, *Treasurer*
Richard Moses, *Vice Pres*
EMP: 54 **EST:** 1947
SQ FT: 9,000
SALES (est): 7.1MM **Privately Held**
WEB: www.thewaltoncompanies.com
SIC: 1521 1542 6552 New construction,
single-family houses; commercial & office
buildings, prefabricated erection; subdi-
viders & developers

(P-650)
WARMINGTON RESIDENTIAL CAL INC
3090 Pullman St, Costa Mesa
(92626-5901)
PHONE..............................714 557-5511
James Warmington Jr, *President*
Mike Riddlesberger, *CFO*
Matt Tingler, *Vice Pres*
Maribel Maciel, *Manager*
EMP: 150 **EST:** 2003
SALES (est): 35MM **Privately Held**
WEB: www.homesbywarmington.com
SIC: 1521 New construction, single-family
houses

(P-651)
WILLIAM LYON HOMES (HQ)
4695 Macarthur Ct Ste 800, Newport Beach
(92660-1863)
PHONE..............................949 833-3600
Matthew Zaist, *President*
William Lyon, *Ch of Bd*
Brian Doyle, *COO*
Colin Severn, *CFO*

Jason Liljestrom, *Senior VP*
EMP: 363 **EST:** 1956
SALES (est): 2B
SALES (corp-wide): 6.1B **Publicly Held**
WEB: www.taylormorrison.com
SIC: 1521 New construction, single-family
houses
PA: Taylor Morrison Home Corporation
4900 N Scottsdale Rd # 2
Scottsdale AZ 85251
480 840-8100

(P-652)
WILLIAM LYON HOMES INC (DH)
4695 Macarthur Ct Ste 800, Newport Beach
(92660-1863)
P.O. Box 7520 (92658-7520)
PHONE..............................949 833-3600
William H Lyon, *Ch of Bd*
Colin Severn, *CFO*
Nicholas Stilwell, *Treasurer*
Doug Harris, *Senior VP*
Danny George, *Vice Pres*
EMP: 87 **EST:** 1992
SQ FT: 30,000
SALES (est): 337.8MM
SALES (corp-wide): 6.1B **Publicly Held**
WEB: www.taylormorrison.com
SIC: 1521 New construction, single-family
houses

(P-653)
WOOD CASTLE CONSTRUCTION INC
770 W Golden Grove Way, Covina
(91722-3255)
PHONE..............................626 966-8600
Daniel Toro, *President*
Victor Quintana, *Treasurer*
Julio Toro, *Vice Pres*
Steve Dominguez, *Purchasing*
EMP: 50
SALES (est): 5.9MM **Privately Held**
WEB: www.woodcastleconstruction.com
SIC: 1521 Single-family housing construc-
tion

1522 General Contractors, Residential Other Than Single Family

(P-654)
716 MANAGEMENT INC
Also Called: Brentwood Builders
3900 W Alameda Ave # 120, Burbank
(91505-4316)
PHONE..............................818 471-4956
Michael Pietrzak, *President*
EMP: 70 **EST:** 2016
SALES (est): 5.1MM **Privately Held**
WEB: www.brentwood.builders
SIC: 1522 1542 1531 1521 Residential
construction; multi-family dwelling construction; remodeling, multi-family
dwellings; restaurant construction; ; single-family home remodeling, additions &
repairs

(P-655)
BERNARDS BUILDERS INC
555 1st St, San Fernando (91340-3051)
PHONE..............................818 898-1521
Doug Bernards, *Chairman*
Greg Simons, *President*
Jeffrey G Bernards, *CEO*
Ken Menager, *CFO*
EMP: 270 **EST:** 2013
SALES (est): 64.6MM
SALES (corp-wide): 160.4MM **Privately Held**
WEB: www.bernards.com
SIC: 1522 Residential construction
PA: Bernards Bros. Inc.
555 1st St
San Fernando CA 91340
818 898-1521

(P-656)
BLH CONSTRUCTION COMPANY
20750 Ventura Blvd # 155, Woodland Hills
(91364-6202)
PHONE..............................818 905-3837
Charles Brumbaugh, *CEO*

Brian Holland, *COO*
EMP: 150 **EST:** 2001
SALES (est): 57.3MM **Privately Held**
WEB: www.blh-construction.com
SIC: 1522 Apartment building construction

(P-657)
COBALT CONSTRUCTION COMPANY
2259 Ward Ave Ste 200, Simi Valley
(93065-1880)
P.O. Box 802018, Santa Clarita (91380-
2018)
PHONE..............................805 577-6222
Darin Kruse, *CEO*
Dru Guillot, *Director*
Carolyn Kruse, *Manager*
▲ **EMP:** 70 **EST:** 1978
SQ FT: 43,000
SALES (est): 25.1MM **Privately Held**
WEB: www.cobaltcc.com
SIC: 1522 8711 1542 Multi-family
dwellings, new construction; construction
& civil engineering; commercial & office
building, new construction; specialized
public building contractors

(P-658)
HASSEN DEVELOPMENT CORPORATION
1932 E Garvey Ave S, West Covina
(91791-1910)
PHONE..............................626 967-7374
Ziad Alhassen, *President*
Tarek Alhassen, *Vice Pres*
EMP: 60 **EST:** 1978
SALES (est): 5.6MM **Privately Held**
WEB: www.hassen.com
SIC: 1522 1542 6552 Residential con-
struction; commercial & office building,
new construction; subdividers & develop-
ers

(P-659)
ISEC INCORPORATED
9381 Haven Ave Ste 101, Rancho Cuca-
monga (91730-5339)
PHONE..............................714 761-5151
Mark Loeffler, *Principal*
Wilson Zhong, *Project Engr*
Timothy Carter, *Opers Mgr*
Anthony Jiron, *Sr Project Mgr*
Colleen Atta, *Manager*
EMP: 60
SALES (corp-wide): 317.2MM **Privately Held**
WEB: www.isecinc.com
SIC: 1522 1542 Residential construction;
commercial & office building contractors
PA: Isec, Incorporated
6000 Greenwood Plaza Blvd # 200
Greenwood Village CO 80111
303 790-1444

(P-660)
KENNARD DEVELOPMENT GROUP
Also Called: Kdg Construction Consulting
1025 N Brand Blvd Ste 300, Glendale
(91202-3633)
PHONE..............................818 241-0800
Lydia Kennard, *CEO*
Bernie Duker, *Project Mgr*
Allen Holland, *Technical Staff*
Yuki Takasue, *Engineer*
Jeffrey Lilly, *Finance*
EMP: 98 **EST:** 1980
SQ FT: 2,500
SALES (est): 15.6MM **Privately Held**
WEB: www.kdgcc.com
SIC: 1522 1541 1623 1611 Residential
construction; industrial buildings & ware-
houses; water, sewer & utility lines; high-
way & street construction; bridge, tunnel
& elevated highway

(P-661)
LA STRADA CONTRACTING CO
26247 Enterprise Ct, Lake Forest
(92630-8412)
P.O. Box 7141, Orange (92863-7141)
PHONE..............................949 680-4237
Rudy Ruiz, *Presiden*
Robbie Lamb, *Asst Supt*
EMP: 14 **EST:** 2000
SQ FT: 2,300

SALES (est): 5MM **Privately Held**
WEB: www.lastradacontracting.com
SIC: **1522** 1623 1611 3271 Hotel/motel &
multi-family home construction; water &
sewer line construction; underground utilities contractor; highway & street construction; concrete construction: roads,
highways, sidewalks, etc.; paving blocks,
concrete

(P-662)
MUR-SOL BUILDERS INC
119 E Saint Joseph St, Arcadia
(91006-7221)
PHONE.............................626 447-0558
EMP: 50 EST: 1999
SALES (est): 6.3MM **Privately Held**
WEB: www.mur-solbuilders.com
SIC: **1522** Residential construction

(P-663)
NO HOLIDAYS CORPORATION ✪
1137 El Centro St Apt E, South Pasadena
(91030-3256)
PHONE.............................310 848-7351
Ronauji Durham, *CEO*
EMP: 50 EST: 2021
SALES (est): 125K **Privately Held**
SIC: **1522** 1521 7389 Remodeling, multi-
family dwellings; general remodeling, sin-
gle-family houses; business services

(P-664)
**OLEN RESIDENTIAL REALTY
CORP (HQ)**
Also Called: Olen Companies, The
7 Corporate Plaza Dr, Newport Beach
(92660-7904)
PHONE.............................949 644-6536
Igor M Olenicoff, *President*
Jan Bullington, *Manager*
EMP: 70 EST: 1992
SALES (est): 106.8MM **Privately Held**
WEB: www.olenproperties.com
SIC: **1522** Multi-family dwellings, new con-
struction

(P-665)
PNG BUILDERS
Also Called: GENERAL CONTRACTOR
2392 Bateman Ave, Duarte (91010-3312)
PHONE.............................626 256-9539
Steven Mathison, *CEO*
Valerie Quintero, *Executive*
Gina Bockhold, *Principal*
Michelle McNeal, *Principal*
Louie Garcia, *Admin Sec*
EMP: 70 EST: 1959
SQ FT: 33,000
SALES: 148.1MM **Privately Held**
WEB: www.png.builders
SIC: **1522** 1542 Residential construction;
commercial & office building contractors;
commercial & office building, new con-
struction

(P-666)
REGIS CONTRACTORS LP
18825 Bardeen Ave, Irvine (92612-1520)
PHONE.............................949 253-0455
Jackie McDade, *Partner*
EMP: 334 EST: 1995
SQ FT: 18,000
SALES (est): 2.3MM
SALES (corp-wide): 58.8MM **Privately
Held**
WEB: www.sares-regis.com
SIC: **1522** Apartment building construction
PA: Sares Regis Group Operating, Inc.
18802 Bardeen Ave
Irvine CA 92612
949 756-5959

(P-667)
RRM CONSTRUCTION INC
9135 Cord Ave, Downey (90240-2433)
PHONE.............................562 440-3539
Cesar Montano, *CEO*
EMP: 50 EST: 2017
SALES (est): 2MM **Privately Held**
SIC: **1522** Residential construction

(P-668)
RSI CONSTRUCTION INC
620 Newport Center Dr # 12, Newport
Beach (92660-6420)
PHONE.............................949 720-1116
Ronald Simon, *Ch of Bd*
Jonathan Robertson, *Senior VP*
Dale Ladouceur, *Vice Pres*
Brian Eid, *Finance Dir*
EMP: 55 EST: 2008
SQ FT: 13,000
SALES (est): 3MM **Privately Held**
WEB: www.rsihc.com
SIC: **1522** Residential construction
PA: Rsi Holding Llc
620 Nwport Ctr Dr Fl 12 Flr 12
Newport Beach CA 92660

(P-669)
SHEA HOMES VANTIS LLC
655 Brea Canyon Rd, Walnut
(91789-3078)
PHONE.............................909 594-9500
Keir Santos, *Admin Sec*
Melanie Maher, *Mktg Dir*
Jeffrey Spizser, *Superintendent*
EMP: 86 EST: 2011
SALES (est): 11.2MM
SALES (corp-wide): 2.1B **Privately Held**
SIC: **1522** Apartment building construction
HQ: Shea Homes Limited Partnership, A
California Limited Partnership
655 Brea Canyon Rd
Walnut CA 91789

(P-670)
TRI POINTE HOMES INC
57 Furlong, Irvine (92602-1812)
PHONE.............................714 389-5933
Paul Faubion, *Branch Mgr*
EMP: 158
SALES (corp-wide): 3.2B **Publicly Held**
WEB: www.tripointehomes.com
SIC: **1522** Residential construction
HQ: Tri Pointe Homes, Inc.
19540 Jamboree Rd Ste 300
Irvine CA 92612

(P-671)
TRI POINTE HOMES INC (HQ)
19540 Jamboree Rd Ste 300, Irvine
(92612-8452)
P.O. Box 57088 (92619-7088)
PHONE.............................949 438-1400
Douglas Bauer, *CEO*
Barry S Sternlicht, *Ch of Bd*
Darren Dupree, *President*
Thomas J Mitchell, *President*
Douglas F Bauer, *CEO*
EMP: 116 EST: 2009
SALES (est): 1.3B
SALES (corp-wide): 3.2B **Publicly Held**
WEB: www.tripointehomes.com
SIC: **1522** Residential construction
PA: Tri Pointe Homes, Inc.
940 Suthwood Blvd Ste 200
Incline Village NV 89451
775 413-1030

(P-672)
WALL TO WALL BUILDERS INC
35350 Twin Willow Rd, Murrieta
(92563-2405)
PHONE.............................909 246-7003
Michael Wall, *President*
Michael David Wsll, *President*
EMP: 50 EST: 2000
SALES (est): 2.9MM **Privately Held**
WEB: www.walltowallbuilders.co.uk
SIC: **1522** 1542 1521 Residential con-
struction; nonresidential construction; sin-
gle-family home remodeling, additions &
repairs

(P-673)
WALTON CONSTRUCTION INC
Also Called: Walton Construction Services
358 E Foothill Blvd # 100, San Dimas
(91773-1264)
PHONE.............................909 267-7777
Blake Jackson, *President*
E Lee Jackson, *CFO*
Rick Walker, *CFO*

David Jackson, *Admin Sec*
Kirk Green, *Project Mgr*
EMP: 80 EST: 2004
SQ FT: 8,000
SALES (est): 57MM **Privately Held**
SIC: **1522** 1542 Apartment building con-
struction; commercial & office building
contractors

(P-674)
**WESTERN NATIONAL PRPTS
LLC (PA)**
Also Called: Arkebauer Properties
8 Executive Cir, Irvine (92614-6746)
P.O. Box 19528 (92623-9528)
PHONE.............................949 862-6200
David Stone, *Ch of Bd*
Rex Delong, *President*
Michael K Hayde, *CEO*
Jeffrey R Scott, *CFO*
Debra Meute, *Vice Pres*
▲ EMP: 129 EST: 1981
SQ FT: 37,000
SALES (est): 60.6MM **Privately Held**
WEB: www.wng.com
SIC: **1522** 6513 6512 6531 Apartment
building construction; apartment building
operators; nonresidential building opera-
tors; real estate agents & managers

(P-675)
ZASTROW CONSTRUCTION INC
Also Called: Reliance Company
3267 Verdugo Rd, Los Angeles
(90065-2035)
PHONE.............................323 478-1956
Mark Zastrow, *President*
Patti Eldridge, *Treasurer*
Kai Wilson, *Vice Pres*
Karen Smith, *Info Tech Dir*
Pranab Maharana, *Engineer*
EMP: 84 EST: 1976
SQ FT: 2,000
SALES (est): 13MM **Privately Held**
WEB: www.leisdstudent.ws
SIC: **1522** Multi-family dwelling construc-
tion; multi-family dwellings, new construc-
tion

1531 Operative Builders

(P-676)
**FIELDSTONE COMMUNITIES
INC (PA)**
16 Technology Dr Ste 125, Irvine
(92618-2325)
PHONE.............................949 790-5400
William H McFarland, *CEO*
Peter Ochs, *Ch of Bd*
Frank Foster, *President*
David Langlois, *Exec VP*
Jim Hanson, *Senior VP*
EMP: 130 EST: 1986
SQ FT: 15,000
SALES (est): 23.3MM **Privately Held**
SIC: **1531** Speculative builder, single-fam-
ily houses

(P-677)
KAUFMAN AND BROAD LIMITED
Also Called: Kaufman & Broad
10990 Wilshire Blvd Fl 7, Los Angeles
(90024-3907)
PHONE.............................310 231-4000
EMP: 151
SALES (est): 7.6MM
SALES (corp-wide): 3.5B **Publicly Held**
WEB: www.kbhomesutah.com
SIC: **1531** Operative Builders
PA: Kb Home
10990 Wilshire Blvd Fl 5
Los Angeles CA 90024
310 231-4000

(P-678)
KB HOME (PA)
10990 Wilshire Blvd Fl 7, Los Angeles
(90024-3907)
PHONE.............................310 231-4000
Jeffrey T Mezger, *Ch of Bd*
Matthew W Mandino, *COO*
Jeff J Kaminski, *CFO*
Albert Z Praw, *Exec VP*
Brian J Woram, *Exec VP*

EMP: 100 EST: 1957
SALES (est): 4.1B **Publicly Held**
WEB: www.kbhome.com
SIC: **1531** Operative builders: speculative
builder, multi-family dwellings; speculative
builder, single-family houses

(P-679)
**LANDSEA HOMES
CORPORATION (HQ)**
660 Nwport Ctr Dr Ste 300, Newport Beach
(92660)
PHONE.............................949 345-8080
John Ho, *CEO*
Ming Tian, *Ch of Bd*
Michael Forsum, *President*
Franco Tenerelli,
Dave Felix, *Vice Pres*
EMP: 63 EST: 2017
SQ FT: 16,209
SALES (corp-wide): 136.5MM **Publicly
Held**
WEB: www.landseahomes.com
SIC: **1531** Operative builders; condo-
minium developers; speculative builder,
single-family houses
PA: Landsea Holdings Corporation
1500 Broadway Ste 1901
New York NY 10036
646 647-1161

(P-680)
LENNAR CORPORATION
15131 Alton Pkwy Ste 190, Irvine
(92618-2386)
PHONE.............................949 349-8000
Jonathan Jaffe, *COO*
David James, *Vice Pres*
Kari Neil, *Executive Asst*
Laura Brill, *Administration*
Marlon Taylor, *Project Mgr*
EMP: 100
SALES (corp-wide): 22.4B **Publicly Held**
WEB: www.lennar.com
SIC: **1531** Speculative builder, single-fam-
ily houses
PA: Lennar Corporation
700 Nw 107th Ave Ste 400
Miami FL 33172
305 559-4000

(P-681)
LEWIS COMPANIES (PA)
1156 N Mountain Ave, Upland
(91786-3633)
PHONE.............................909 985-0971
Richard A Lewis, *President*
Ted Erkan, *Vice Pres*
Goldy S Lewis, *Principal*
Randall W Lewis, *Principal*
Robert E Lewis, *Principal*
EMP: 200
SALES (est): 49.6MM **Privately Held**
WEB: www.lewisgroupofcompanies.com
SIC: **1531** Operative builders

(P-682)
**TRI POINTE CONTRACTORS LP
(HQ)**
5 Peters Canyon Rd # 100, Irvine
(92606-1791)
PHONE.............................949 478-8600
Doug Bauer, *Partner*
EMP: 99 EST: 2010
SALES (est): 24.3MM
SALES (corp-wide): 3.2B **Publicly Held**
WEB: www.tripointegroup.com
SIC: **1531** Speculative builder, single-fam-
ily houses
PA: Tri Pointe Homes, Inc.
940 Suthwood Blvd Ste 200
Incline Village NV 89451
775 413-1030

(P-683)
**VAN DAELE DEVELOPMENT
CORP**
Also Called: Van Daele Homes
2900 Adams St Ste C25, Riverside
(92504-8312)
PHONE.............................951 354-6800
Michael B Van Daele, *CEO*
Jeff Hack, *President*
Bryon Hopkins, *Regional Mgr*
Sherrell Schwartz, *Admin Asst*
Kellie Agard, *Info Tech Mgr*

EMP: 110 EST: 1987
SQ FT: 6,000
SALES (est): 35.4MM **Privately Held**
WEB: www.vandaele.com
SIC: **1531** Speculative builder, single-family houses

(P-684)
WARMINGTON HOMES (PA)
3090 Pullman St, Costa Mesa
(92626-7936)
PHONE..................................714 434-4435
Timothy P Hogan, *President*
James P Warmington, *Ch of Bd*
Michael McClellan, *President*
Greg Oberling, *President*
Jack Schwellenbach, *President*
▲ EMP: 120 EST: 1972
SQ FT: 40,000
SALES (est): 94.3MM **Privately Held**
WEB: www.homesbywarmington.com
SIC: **1531** Speculative builder, single-family houses

(P-685)
WARMINGTON HOMES
15615 Alton Pkwy Ste 150, Irvine
(92618-7302)
PHONE..................................949 679-3100
EMP: 128
SALES (corp-wide): 94.3MM **Privately Held**
WEB: www.homesbywarmington.com
SIC: **1531** Speculative builder, single-family house
PA: Warmington Homes
3090 Pullman St
Costa Mesa CA 92626
714 434-4435

1541 General Contractors, Indl Bldgs & Warehouses

(P-686)
AHTNA-CDM JV
3200 El Cmino Real Ste 24, Irvine (92602)
PHONE..................................714 824-3470
Craig O'Rourke, *Principal*
EMP: 50 EST: 2017
SQ FT: 5,000
SALES (est): 3.7MM **Privately Held**
SIC: **1541** Industrial buildings, new construction

(P-687)
AMERICAN DE ROSA LAMPARTS LLC
10650 4th St, Rancho Cucamonga
(91730-5918)
PHONE..................................800 777-4440
EMP: 53
SALES (corp-wide): 19.7MM **Privately Held**
WEB: www.luminancebrands.com
SIC: **1541** Industrial buildings & warehouses
PA: American De Rosa Lamparts, Llc
370 Falls Commerce Pkwy
Cuyahoga Falls OH 44224
800 777-4440

(P-688)
ANGELES CONTRACTOR INC (PA)
783 Phillips, Rowland Heights
(91748-1147)
PHONE..................................714 523-1021
Young W Kang, *President*
John Pak, *Vice Pres*
Alex Cho, *Project Mgr*
Peter Park, *Project Mgr*
Duane Trevino, *Project Mgr*
EMP: 75 EST: 1998
SQ FT: 30,000
SALES (est): 26MM **Privately Held**
WEB: www.angelescontractor.com
SIC: **1541** Industrial buildings, new construction

(P-689)
BAKELL LLC
Also Called: Jdi Distribution
24723 Redlands Blvd Ste F, Loma Linda
(92354-4021)
PHONE..................................800 292-2137
Private Information, *Mng Member*
Deborah Blevins,
Justin Jordan,
EMP: 65 EST: 2015
SALES (est): 6MM **Privately Held**
WEB: www.bakell.com
SIC: **1541** 5149 2051 3299 Food products manufacturing or packing plant construction; baking supplies; bakery: wholesale or wholesale/retail combined; mica products; mica, ground or otherwise treated; food colorings

(P-690)
BETHLEHEM CONSTRUCTION INC
425 J St, Wasco (93280-2335)
PHONE..................................661 758-1001
Michael J Addleman, *Branch Mgr*
EMP: 86
SALES (corp-wide): 74.7MM **Privately Held**
WEB: www.bethlehemconstruction.com
SIC: **1541** 1542 Warehouse construction; commercial & office building, new construction
PA: Bethlehem Construction Incorporated
5505 Titchenal Rd
Cashmere WA 98815
509 782-1001

(P-691)
CENTRIC BRANDS LLC
5900 Triumph St, Commerce (90040-1610)
PHONE..................................323 837-3700
Marc B Crossman, *President*
EMP: 70 **Privately Held**
WEB: www.centricbrands.com
SIC: **1541** Industrial buildings & warehouses
PA: Centric Brands Llc
350 5th Ave Fl 6
New York NY 10118

(P-692)
CHALMERS CORPORATION
Also Called: C.E.G. Construction
7901 Crossway Dr, Pico Rivera
(90660-4449)
PHONE..................................562 948-4850
Tracy John Chalmers, *CEO*
James N Devling, *CFO*
Frank Ramos, *Project Mgr*
EMP: 55 EST: 1992
SQ FT: 45,000
SALES (est): 36.6MM **Privately Held**
WEB: www.chalmersequity.com
SIC: **1541** 8742 Industrial buildings & warehouses; management consulting services

(P-693)
CLARK CNSTR GROUP - CAL INC
18201 Von Karman Ave # 800, Irvine
(92612-1092)
PHONE..................................714 754-0764
Richard M Heim, *President*
EMP: 450 EST: 2012
SALES (corp-wide): 1.6B **Privately Held**
WEB: www.s2ngroup.com
SIC: **1541** 1542 Industrial buildings & warehouses; nonresidential construction
HQ: Clark Construction Group, Llc
7500 Old Georgtwn Rd # 3
Bethesda MD 20814
301 272-8100

(P-694)
CMC REBAR WEST
10840 Norwalk Blvd, Santa Fe Springs
(90670-3826)
PHONE..................................714 692-7082
Lee Albright, *Branch Mgr*
EMP: 139 **Privately Held**
SIC: **1541** Industrial buildings & warehouses

HQ: Cmc Rebar West
3880 Murphy Canyon Rd # 100
San Diego CA 92123

(P-695)
CONEJO PACIFIC TECHNOLOGIES
1560 Newbury Rd Ste 1, Newbury Park
(91320-3448)
PHONE..................................805 498-5315
EMP: 65
SQ FT: 100
SALES (est): 4.3MM **Privately Held**
SIC: **1541** 0782 Industrial Building Construction Lawn/Garden Services

(P-696)
DENVER D DARLING INC
Also Called: Darco Construction
8402 Katella Ave, Stanton (90680-3215)
PHONE..................................714 761-8299
Denver D Darling, *President*
Wayne Darling, *Vice Pres*
Ron Neilsen, *Project Mgr*
EMP: 71 EST: 1978
SQ FT: 10,000
SALES (est): 5.6MM **Privately Held**
WEB: www.darcoconstruction.com
SIC: **1541** 1771 Industrial buildings, new construction; concrete work

(P-697)
EXCEL CONSTRUCTION SVCS INC (PA)
1950 Raymer Ave, Fullerton (92833-2513)
PHONE..................................714 680-9200
Karen Ratzlaff, *CEO*
Krista Alvarez, *Executive Asst*
Heather Camp, *Executive Asst*
Sonny Kim, *Controller*
EMP: 54 EST: 2004
SQ FT: 12,000
SALES (est): 54.8MM **Privately Held**
WEB: www.excelconstruction.biz
SIC: **1541** 1711 1731 1741 Industrial buildings & warehouses; plumbing, heating, air-conditioning contractors; electrical work; masonry & other stonework; plastering, drywall & insulation; commercial & office building contractors

(P-698)
FRIZE CORPORATION
16605 Gale Ave, City of Industry
(91745-1802)
PHONE..................................800 834-2127
James N Frize, *President*
Brad Daugherty, *Project Mgr*
Andy McGurn, *Project Mgr*
Jon Oleinick, *Project Mgr*
Jeff Barber, *Foreman/Supr*
EMP: 80 EST: 1981
SQ FT: 25,000
SALES (est): 36.6MM **Privately Held**
WEB: www.frizecorp.com
SIC: **1541** 1542 Industrial buildings & warehouses; commercial & office building contractors

(P-699)
FULLMER CONSTRUCTION
1725 S Grove Ave, Ontario (91761-4530)
PHONE..................................909 947-9467
Robert A Fullmer, *President*
Gered Yetter, *CFO*
James Fullmer, *Corp Secy*
Brad Anderson, *Vice Pres*
Bradley J Anderson, *Vice Pres*
◆ EMP: 120 EST: 1946
SQ FT: 20,000
SALES (est): 63.1MM **Privately Held**
WEB: www.fullmerco.com
SIC: **1541** Industrial buildings, new construction

(P-700)
GRIMMWAY ENTERPRISES INC
Grimmway Farm
12020 Malaga Rd, Arvin (93203-9527)
PHONE..................................661 854-6240
Mike Blakley, *Supervisor*
EMP: 484

SALES (corp-wide): 1.8B **Privately Held**
WEB: www.grimmway.com
SIC: **1541** 1542 Industrial buildings & warehouses; nonresidential construction
PA: Grimmway Enterprises, Inc.
14141 Di Giorgio Rd
Arvin CA 93203
800 301-3101

(P-701)
H C OLSEN CNSTR CO INC
710 Los Angeles Ave, Monrovia
(91016-4250)
PHONE..................................626 359-8900
Linda Jacqueline Pearson, *CEO*
Karl Pearson, *Corp Secy*
Brenda Gutierrez, *Administration*
Chris Leblanc, *CIO*
Paul Hudson, *Sr Project Mgr*
EMP: 75 EST: 1946
SQ FT: 12,800
SALES (est): 37.2MM **Privately Held**
WEB: www.hcolsen.com
SIC: **1541** Industrial buildings, new construction

(P-702)
HAL HAYS CONSTRUCTION INC (PA)
4181 Latham St, Riverside (92501-1729)
PHONE..................................951 788-0703
Hal Hays, *Exec Dir*
E Denise Hays, *CFO*
Karun Mani, *Program Mgr*
Lori McDaniel, *Technology*
Mazharuddin Mohammed, *Project Engr*
EMP: 113 EST: 1990
SQ FT: 28,400
SALES (est): 54.1MM **Privately Held**
WEB: www.halhays.com
SIC: **1541** 1542 1623 1629 Industrial buildings & warehouses; commercial & office buildings, renovation & repair; water, sewer & utility lines; dams, waterways, docks & other marine construction; highway & street paving contractor; concrete work

(P-703)
JH BRYANT JR INC (PA)
17217 S Broadway, Gardena (90248-3117)
PHONE..................................310 532-1840
Barbara Bryant, *CEO*
John Bryant III, *President*
David Bryant, *COO*
Joseph Perez, *Vice Pres*
Bobby Ricks, *Division Mgr*
EMP: 50
SQ FT: 6,500
SALES (est): 13MM **Privately Held**
WEB: www.jhbryant.com
SIC: **1541** Industrial buildings & warehouses

(P-704)
JULIUS STEVE CONSTRUCTION INC
Also Called: S R J
230 Calle Pintoresco, San Clemente
(92672-7503)
PHONE..................................949 369-7820
Leigh Thornburg Julius, *CEO*
Pete Ferrarini, *President*
Shane Hankins, *General Mgr*
Marcie Miller, *CIO*
Mike Heitzman, *Technology*
EMP: 50 EST: 1984
SQ FT: 6,700
SALES (est): 20.8MM **Privately Held**
WEB: www.stevejuliusconstruction.com
SIC: **1541** Industrial buildings, new construction

(P-705)
KCS WEST INC
250 E 1st St Ste 700, Los Angeles
(90012-3813)
PHONE..................................323 269-0020
Elmond Wan, *President*
Tracy Thomas, *Vice Pres*
John Schiller, *Executive*
Mike Vickery, *Executive*
Judith McMillon, *Admin Asst*
EMP: 68 EST: 2007

SALES (est): 28.8MM **Privately Held**
WEB: www.kcswest.com
SIC: **1541** Industrial buildings & warehouses
HQ: Kajima International Inc.
 3550 Lenox Rd Ne Ste 1850
 Atlanta GA 30326
 440 544-2600

(P-706)
KEMP BROS CONSTRUCTION INC
10135 Geary Ave, Santa Fe Springs (90670-3253)
PHONE.............................562 236-5000
Greg S Solaas, *President*
Steven Solaas, *President*
Steve Rosenfield, *COO*
Judy Anderson, *Office Mgr*
Luis Cevallos, *Project Mgr*
EMP: 50 EST: 1954
SQ FT: 15,500
SALES (est): 8.4K **Privately Held**
WEB: www.kempbros.com
SIC: **1541 1542** Industrial buildings, new construction; hospital construction

(P-707)
KUSTOM KANOPIES INC
210 Senior Cir, Lompoc (93436-1491)
PHONE.............................801 399-3400
Wesley R Robison, *President*
Sharee Robison, *Corp Secy*
Ronald E Schwartz, *Vice Pres*
EMP: 30
SQ FT: 56,000
SALES (est): 4MM **Privately Held**
SIC: **1541 5999 3444** Industrial buildings & warehouses; awnings; sheet metalwork

(P-708)
MILLIE AND SEVERSON INC
3601 Serpentine Dr, Los Alamitos (90720-2440)
PHONE.............................562 493-3611
Scott Feest, *President*
Robert E Wissmann, *Senior VP*
Robert Cavecche, *Vice Pres*
Brian Cresap, *Vice Pres*
John Grossman, *Vice Pres*
EMP: 75 EST: 1945
SQ FT: 15,000
SALES (est): 56.2MM **Privately Held**
WEB: www.mandsinc.com
SIC: **1541** Industrial buildings, new construction; renovation, remodeling & repairs: industrial buildings; steel building construction; warehouse construction
PA: Severson Group Incorporated
 3601 Serpentine Dr
 Los Alamitos CA 90720

(P-709)
MODERN BUILDING INC
29991 Cyn Hls Rd Ste 1709, Lake Elsinore (92532-2579)
P.O. Box 772, Chico (95927-0772)
PHONE.............................951 297-3311
L Gage Chrysler, *CEO*
Gary Fowler, *Corp Secy*
James Seegert, *Vice Pres*
Debbie Barnett, *Administration*
Phil Strawn, *Project Mgr*
EMP: 50 EST: 1973
SQ FT: 5,000
SALES (est): 31.8MM **Privately Held**
WEB: www.modernbuildinginc.com
SIC: **1541 1542** Industrial buildings, new construction; commercial & office building, new construction

(P-710)
OLTMANS CONSTRUCTION CO (PA)
10005 Mission Mill Rd, Whittier (90601-1739)
P.O. Box 985 (90608-0985)
PHONE.............................562 948-4242
Joseph O Oltmans II, *Ch of Bd*
John Gormly, *President*
Dan Schlothan, *CFO*
Tom Augustine, *Vice Pres*
Michael Englhard, *Vice Pres*
▼ EMP: 85 EST: 1932
SQ FT: 33,000

SALES (est): 259.2MM **Privately Held**
WEB: www.oltmans.com
SIC: **1541 1542** Industrial buildings, new construction; renovation, remodeling & repairs: industrial buildings; commercial & office building, new construction; commercial & office buildings, renovation & repair

(P-711)
OLTMANS CONSTRUCTION CO
270 Conejo Ridge Ave # 210, Thousand Oaks (91361-4957)
PHONE.............................805 495-9553
Robert Larson, *Manager*
Kristi Lopez, *Admin Asst*
Heith Bibby, *Project Mgr*
Christopher Gray, *Project Mgr*
Troy Griffin, *Project Mgr*
EMP: 438
SQ FT: 2,600
SALES (corp-wide): 259.2MM **Privately Held**
WEB: www.oltmans.com
SIC: **1541 1542** Industrial buildings & warehouses; nonresidential construction
PA: The Oltmans Construction Co
 10005 Mission Mill Rd
 Whittier CA 90601
 562 948-4242

(P-712)
ORANGE COAST BUILDING SVCS INC
2191 S Dupont Dr, Anaheim (92806-6102)
PHONE.............................714 453-6300
Kevin W Franklin, *President*
Kevin Erdkamp, *Exec VP*
Mindy Hislop, *Executive Asst*
Mike Mastropietro, *Director*
EMP: 123 EST: 1986
SQ FT: 6,000
SALES (est): 31.3MM **Privately Held**
WEB: www.ocbsonline.com
SIC: **1541 1542** Industrial buildings, new construction; commercial & office building contractors

(P-713)
PARSONS PROJECT SERVICES INC
100 W Walnut St, Pasadena (91124-0001)
PHONE.............................626 440-4000
Charles Harrington, *CEO*
Todd K Wager, *President*
EMP: 80 EST: 1995
SALES (est): 22.9MM
SALES (corp-wide): 3.9B **Publicly Held**
WEB: www.parsons.com
SIC: **1541** Industrial buildings & warehouses
PA: The Parsons Corporation
 5875 Trinity Pkwy Ste 300
 Centreville VA 20120
 703 988-8500

(P-714)
PERKINS DEVELOPMENT GROUP INC (PA)
8306 Wilshire Blvd, Beverly Hills (90211-2304)
PHONE.............................213 447-4464
Richard G Perkins Jr, *CEO*
Bonnie Corwin, *Opers Staff*
EMP: 71 EST: 2016
SALES (est): 8.5MM **Privately Held**
WEB: www.perkinsdevgroup.com
SIC: **1541 8712** Industrial buildings, new construction; architectural services

(P-715)
PROTECTIVE WTHER STRCTURES INC
Also Called: P W S
5290 Orcutt Rd, San Luis Obispo (93401-8336)
PHONE.............................805 547-8797
Timothy Perozzi, *President*
John Walker, *Treasurer*
John Hunter, *Vice Pres*
Ruby Tang, *Finance*
Debby Escalante, *Sales Associate*
EMP: 16 EST: 1994
SQ FT: 4,000

SALES (est): 4.4MM **Privately Held**
WEB: www.pwssteelbuildings.com
SIC: **1541 3792** Steel building construction; travel trailers & campers

(P-716)
SHIMS BARGAIN INC
Also Called: JC Sales
7030 E Slauson Ave, Commerce (90040-3621)
PHONE.............................323 726-8800
Andy Kim, *Manager*
Ben Cho, *Human Resources*
EMP: 92 **Privately Held**
WEB: www.jcsalesweb.com
SIC: **1541** Industrial buildings & warehouses
PA: Shims Bargain, Inc.
 2600 S Soto St
 Vernon CA 90058

(P-717)
SMITH MCHNCL-LCTRICAL-PLUMBING
Also Called: Smith Electric Service
1340 W Betteravia Rd, Santa Maria (93455-1030)
PHONE.............................805 621-5000
Michael Brannon, *President*
Sara Dalton, *Officer*
Larry Brannon, *Vice Pres*
Joyce Gardner, *General Mgr*
Donna Michaud, *Administration*
EMP: 150 EST: 1980
SQ FT: 10,000
SALES (est): 69.1MM **Privately Held**
WEB: www.smith-electric.com
SIC: **1541 1711 1731 1542** Industrial buildings, new construction; plumbing, heating, air-conditioning contractors; fire detection & burglar alarm systems specialization; nonresidential construction

(P-718)
SPECTRUM CNSTR GROUP INC
16 Goodyear Ste 140, Irvine (92618-3760)
PHONE.............................949 299-1400
Bisher Aljazzar, *CEO*
Melissa Dizon, *Asst Controller*
EMP: 99 EST: 2016
SALES (est): 23.5MM **Privately Held**
WEB: www.spectrumcgi.com
SIC: **1541 1622 1542 1611** Steel building construction; bridge, tunnel & elevated highway; commercial & office building, new construction; school building construction; institutional building construction; highway & street construction

(P-719)
SPH HOLDINGS INC (HQ)
4120 N Palm St, Fullerton (92835-1026)
PHONE.............................714 441-3900
Dan Stauber, *CEO*
Steve Graham, *CFO*
Emma Kruger, *Administration*
Karen Howland, *Accounting Mgr*
Brendan Meehan, *Production*
EMP: 130 EST: 2010
SALES (est): 25.3MM
SALES (corp-wide): 596.8MM **Publicly Held**
WEB: www.stauberusa.com
SIC: **1541** Pharmaceutical manufacturing plant construction
PA: Hawkins, Inc.
 2381 Rosegate
 Roseville MN 55113
 612 331-6910

(P-720)
STANTRU RESOURCES INC
Also Called: Stantru Reinforcing Steel
11175 Redwood Ave, Fontana (92337-7137)
P.O. Box 310189 (92331-0189)
PHONE.............................909 587-1441
Ida Ichen, *President*
William M Klorman, *Manager*
EMP: 83 EST: 1991

SALES (est): 12.6MM **Privately Held**
SIC: **1541 1542** Industrial buildings, new construction; pharmaceutical manufacturing plant construction; commercial & office building, new construction; school building construction; institutional building construction

(P-721)
SYNEAR FOODS USA LLC
9601 Canoga Ave, Chatsworth (91311-4115)
PHONE.............................818 341-3588
EMP: 31 EST: 2015
SALES (est): 10.3MM **Privately Held**
WEB: www.xn—6rt99bodw19r.com
SIC: **1541 2038** Food products manufacturing or packing plant construction; breakfasts, frozen & packaged
PA: Zhengzhou Synear Food Co., Ltd.
 No.15, Middle Part, Yingcai Street,
 Huiji District
 Zhengzhou 45004

(P-722)
TORRES CONSTRUCTION CORP (PA)
1370 N El Molino Ave, Pasadena (91104-5026)
PHONE.............................323 257-7460
Martha McGowin, *President*
Mael Torres, *Treasurer*
Esteban Torres, *Vice Pres*
Paul Gonzalez, *Safety Mgr*
EMP: 86 EST: 1993
SQ FT: 7,500
SALES (est): 22.4MM **Privately Held**
WEB: www.torresconstruction.com
SIC: **1541** Industrial buildings & warehouses

(P-723)
TRI-TECH RESTORATION CO INC
3301 N San Fernando Blvd, Burbank (91504-2531)
PHONE.............................818 565-3900
Armine Bakmazian, *President*
Ray Boykin, *Vice Pres*
Michael Boyd, *Admin Sec*
Shant Kavarian, *Info Tech Mgr*
Carlos Garcia, *Project Mgr*
EMP: 70 EST: 1995
SQ FT: 35,000 **Privately Held**
WEB: www.tritechrestoration.com
SIC: **1541** Industrial buildings & warehouses

(P-724)
UNIVERSAL DUST CLLCTR MFG SUP (PA)
Also Called: UDC
1041 N Kraemer Pl, Anaheim (92806-2611)
PHONE.............................714 630-8588
Theresa A Shaffer, *CEO*
Curt Schendel, *President*
Debbie Huerta, *CFO*
Deborah Huerta, *CFO*
Gary Foo, *Officer*
EMP: 89 EST: 1984
SQ FT: 30,000
SALES (est): 69.5MM **Privately Held**
SIC: **1541** Industrial buildings, new construction

(P-725)
UPRITE CONSTRUCTION CORP
Also Called: General Contractor
2211 Michelson Dr Ste 500, Irvine (92612-1391)
PHONE.............................949 877-8877
Robert Dellaringa, *CEO*
Joe Martino, *COO*
Brad Krouse, *Vice Pres*
Phil Tanghal, *Vice Pres*
Kristina Piraino, *Project Mgr*
EMP: 73 EST: 1991
SQ FT: 3,500
SALES (est): 61.7MM **Privately Held**
WEB: www.upriteco.com
SIC: **1541** Warehouse construction

PRODUCTS & SVCS

(P-726)
W N G CONSTRUCTION JV INC (PA)
4175 E La Palma Ave # 125, Anaheim (92807-1842)
PHONE..................714 524-7100
Wafik Bishai, *President*
Tommie Brozick, *CFO*
George Toro, *Vice Pres*
EMP: 71 EST: 2013
SQ FT: 1,200
SALES (est): 8MM Privately Held
SIC: 1541 1542 Industrial buildings & warehouses; commercial & office building contractors

(P-727)
WEST HILLS CONSTRUCTION INC
423 Jenks Cir Ste 101, Corona (92878-5040)
PHONE..................800 515-5270
Ross L Wood, *President*
Rusty Wood, *Vice Pres*
Vonnie Bash, *Office Mgr*
Glenn Cole, *Project Mgr*
Stephanie Wood, *Director*
EMP: 50 EST: 1989
SQ FT: 7,500
SALES (est): 10.2MM Privately Held
WEB: www.whc.us.com
SIC: 1541 Industrial buildings, new construction

1542 General Contractors, Nonresidential & Non-indl Bldgs

(P-728)
2H CONSTRUCTION INC
2653 Walnut Ave, Signal Hill (90755-1830)
PHONE..................562 424-5567
Sean Hitchcock, *President*
Ericka Hitchcock, *CFO*
Ronald Compton, *Vice Pres*
EMP: 70 EST: 1997
SQ FT: 8,000
SALES (est): 50MM Privately Held
WEB: www.2hconstruction.com
SIC: 1542 Commercial & office building, new construction

(P-729)
ACCESS PACIFIC INC
2835 Sierra Grande St, Pasadena (91107-3448)
PHONE..................626 792-0616
Tomas Torres, *President*
EMP: 50 EST: 2009
SALES (est): 15.3MM Privately Held
WEB: www.st-construction.com
SIC: 1542 Nonresidential construction

(P-730)
AIS CONSTRUCTION COMPANY
7015 Vista Rincon Dr, Ventura (93001)
P.O. Box 4209, San Luis Obispo (93403-4209)
PHONE..................805 928-9467
Andy Sheaffer, *President*
EMP: 85 EST: 1996
SQ FT: 4,000
SALES (est): 12.4MM Privately Held
WEB:
SIC: 1542 Commercial & office building contractors

(P-731)
AK CONSTRUCTORS INC
Also Called: AK Electrical Services
1751 Jenks Dr, Corona (92878-5016)
PHONE..................951 280-0269
Kenneth G Dougher, *President*
Kenneth Dougher, *Senior Partner*
Micheal Harrington, *Corp Secy*
Robert Griffin, *Principal*
Kurt Meyers, *Principal*
EMP: 65 EST: 2003
SALES (est): 25.4MM Privately Held
WEB: www.akconstructors.com
SIC: 1542 Commercial & office building, new construction

(P-732)
ALLIANCE PROTECTION SERVICE
Also Called: P C Services
45130 Golf Center Pkwy A, Indio (92201-7328)
PHONE..................760 347-3747
Daphne Ray, *Owner*
Ricardo Gallegos, *Project Mgr*
Dan Blum, *Manager*
Twila Crook, *Representative*
EMP: 50 EST: 1979
SQ FT: 3,000
SALES (est): 4.1MM Privately Held
WEB: www.allianceprotection.com
SIC: 5999 1542 1521 Alarm signal systems; commercial & office building contractors; single-family housing construction

(P-733)
AMERICAN INCORPORATED (PA)
Also Called: American Air
1345 N American St, Visalia (93291-9334)
PHONE..................559 651-1776
Corwyn Oldfield, *CEO*
Frank Saucedo, *CFO*
Michael Brandenburg, *Vice Pres*
Lois Oldfield, *Vice Pres*
Cassandra Frates, *Administration*
EMP: 422 EST: 1973
SQ FT: 115,000
SALES (est): 187.4MM Privately Held
WEB: www.aminc.com
SIC: 1542 1541 1731 1711 Commercial & office building contractors; industrial buildings & warehouses; electrical work; plumbing contractors; warm air heating & air conditioning contractor; refrigeration contractor; demolition, buildings & other structures

(P-734)
ANCHOR-41 CONSTRUCTION LLC
9301 W Airport Dr Ste A, Visalia (93277-9500)
PHONE..................559 740-7776
David Ruiz, *Mng Member*
Maribel Dorado, *Office Mgr*
EMP: 15 EST: 2017
SALES (est): 1.8MM Privately Held
WEB: www.anchor41.com
SIC: 1542 1389 Commercial & office building contractors; construction, repair & dismantling services

(P-735)
ANDERSON BURTON CNSTR INC (PA)
121 Nevada St, Arroyo Grande (93420-2609)
PHONE..................805 481-5096
Joann Anderson, *President*
Robert Hinshaw, *Vice Pres*
Deb Morrison, *Admin Asst*
Gerry Bacon, *Project Mgr*
Dan Carrisosa, *Project Mgr*
EMP: 99 EST: 1999
SQ FT: 5,000
SALES (est): 27.9MM Privately Held
WEB: www.andersonburton.com
SIC: 1542 1522 Commercial & office building, new construction; residential construction

(P-736)
ANDREW L YOUNGQUIST CNSTR INC
3187 Red Hill Ave Ste 200, Costa Mesa (92626-3454)
PHONE..................949 862-5611
Andrew L Youngquist, *Ch of Bd*
James Lefler, *President*
Richard Lee Youngquist, *Vice Pres*
EMP: 90 EST: 1996
SQ FT: 10,319
SALES (est): 13.2MM Privately Held
SIC: 1542 1522 8741 Commercial & office building contractors; residential construction; construction management

(P-737)
ARAGON CONSTRUCTION INC
5440 Arrow Hwy, Montclair (91763-1604)
PHONE..................909 621-2200
Joseph E Aragon, *President*
Regina Aragon, *General Mgr*
Gina Aragon, *Office Mgr*
Eduardo Velazquez, *Project Mgr*
John Diaz, *Finance*
EMP: 55 EST: 2001
SALES (est): 24MM Privately Held
WEB: www.aragonconstruction.com
SIC: 1542 Institutional building construction; commercial & office buildings, renovation & repair; shopping center construction; specialized public building contractors

(P-738)
ARNEL DEVELOPMENT COMPANY (PA)
949 S Coast Dr Ste 600, Costa Mesa (92626-7734)
PHONE..................714 481-5000
George L Argyros, *Ch of Bd*
Dave Ball, *President*
Charles E Packard, *Exec VP*
John Biggs, *Vice Pres*
EMP: 59 EST: 1968
SQ FT: 20,000
SALES (est): 18.2MM Privately Held
WEB: www.arneloffice.com
SIC: 1542 1531 Commercial & office building contractors; cooperative apartment developers

(P-739)
ART GAUTREAU INC
Also Called: Agi General Contracting
8210 Katella Ave Ste I, Stanton (90680-3271)
PHONE..................714 934-8066
Chris Gautreau, *President*
Andrew Gautreau, *Vice Pres*
Mark Bonnell, *Superintendent*
Bill Durini, *Superintendent*
EMP: 50 EST: 1978
SQ FT: 6,000
SALES (est): 35.6MM Privately Held
WEB: www.agigc.com
SIC: 1542 Commercial & office buildings, renovation & repair

(P-740)
AVENDREN BUILDING SYSTEMS INC
3660 Placentia Ln, Riverside (92501-1120)
PHONE..................909 806-0938
Nancy Jensen-Vahovick, *CEO*
Chuck Vahovick, *Treasurer*
EMP: 13
SQ FT: 80,000
SALES (corp-wide): 1.5MM Privately Held
WEB: www.avendren.com
SIC: 1542 3272 School building construction; areaways, basement window: concrete
PA: Avendren Building Systems Incorporated
3660 Placentia Ln B
Riverside CA 92501
909 946-3333

(P-741)
AXIS CONSTRUCTION INC
901 S Glendale Ave # 200, Glendale (91205-5614)
PHONE..................818 545-9292
Bahram Movassaghi, *President*
Ahmad Sharfizadeh, *Treasurer*
EMP: 73 EST: 1988
SQ FT: 1,200
SALES (est): 7MM Privately Held
SIC: 1542 Commercial & office building contractors; commercial & office buildings, renovation & repair

(P-742)
BEL ESPRIT BUILDERS INC
23112 Alcalde Dr Ste A, Laguna Hills (92653-1458)
PHONE..................949 709-3500
David K Jackson, *President*
Debra Jackson, *Admin Sec*
EMP: 50 EST: 1996
SALES (est): 10.5MM Privately Held
WEB: www.belespritbuilders.com
SIC: 1542 Nonresidential construction

(P-743)
BERGMAN KPRS LLC (PA)
2850 Saturn St Ste 100, Brea (92821-1701)
PHONE..................714 324-7000
Mark C Bergman,
John Buchanan, *CIO*
Vince Bakulich, *Project Mgr*
Salvatore Chirco, *Project Mgr*
Lori Hansen, *Project Mgr*
EMP: 125 EST: 1982
SQ FT: 7,500
SALES (est): 69.9MM Privately Held
WEB: www.bergmankprs.com
SIC: 1542 Restaurant construction

(P-744)
BOGART CONSTRUCTION INC
9980 Irvine Center Dr # 200, Irvine (92618-4365)
PHONE..................949 453-1400
Brad K Bogart, *President*
Noel Amand, *Project Mgr*
Jason Flores, *Project Mgr*
Dan Miller, *Project Mgr*
Megan Diblasi, *Project Engr*
EMP: 55 EST: 1990
SQ FT: 10,000
SALES (est): 38.7MM Privately Held
WEB: www.bogartconstruction.com
SIC: 1542 Commercial & office building, new construction

(P-745)
BOMEL CONSTRUCTION CO INC (PA)
96 Corporate Park Ste 100, Irvine (92606-3136)
PHONE..................714 921-1660
Kent Matranga, *CEO*
Derral McGinnis, *COO*
Lisa McGinnis, *CFO*
James Ure, *Exec VP*
Jim Ure, *Exec VP*
EMP: 51 EST: 1970
SQ FT: 8,000
SALES (est): 101MM Privately Held
WEB: www.bomelconstruction.com
SIC: 1542 Commercial & office building, new construction

(P-746)
BOMEL CONSTRUCTION CO INC
939 E Francis St, Ontario (91761-5631)
PHONE..................909 923-3319
Richard Laughlin, *Manager*
EMP: 80
SALES (corp-wide): 101MM Privately Held
WEB: www.bomelconstruction.com
SIC: 1542 Commercial & office building, new construction
PA: Bomel Construction Co., Inc.
96 Corporate Park Ste 100
Irvine CA 92606
714 921-1660

(P-747)
BR BUILDING RESOURCES CO
2247 Lindsay Way, Glendora (91740-5398)
P.O. Box 2090 (91740-2090)
PHONE..................626 963-4880
Gary Pellant, *President*
Juan Banos, *CEO*
Vanessa Banos, *COO*
Jose Banos, *CFO*
Ronald Moore, *Exec VP*
EMP: 120 EST: 2009
SQ FT: 9,000
SALES (est): 28MM Privately Held
WEB: www.brco.com
SIC: 1542 Commercial & office buildings, renovation & repair

(P-748)
C W DRIVER INCORPORATED (PA)
468 N Rosemead Blvd, Pasadena (91107-3010)
PHONE................................626 351-8800
Dana Roberts, *President*
Richard Freeark, *COO*
Bessie Kouvara, *CFO*
Carl Lowman, *CFO*
Robert Maxwell, *Senior VP*
EMP: 60 **EST:** 1919
SQ FT: 14,000
SALES (est): 186.9MM **Privately Held**
WEB: www.cwdriver.com
SIC: 1542 Commercial & office building, new construction

(P-749)
CAL SELECT BUILDERS INC
23253 La Palma Ave, Yorba Linda (92887-4768)
PHONE................................714 694-0203
Elden Johnson, *President*
Chris Kretz, *Project Mgr*
EMP: 61 **EST:** 1989
SQ FT: 5,000
SALES (est): 13.3MM **Privately Held**
WEB: www.calselect.com
SIC: 1542 Restaurant construction

(P-750)
CALIFORNIA STRL CONCEPTS INC
28358 Constellation Rd # 660, Valencia (91355-5010)
PHONE................................661 257-6903
Jeffrey Horne, *CEO*
Penny Horne, *Vice Pres*
EMP: 85 **EST:** 2006
SALES (est): 20.1MM **Privately Held**
WEB: www.cscbuilding.net
SIC: 1542 Commercial & office building, new construction

(P-751)
CHARLES E THOMAS COMPANY INC (PA)
Also Called: C E T
13701 Alma Ave, Gardena (90249-2523)
PHONE................................310 323-6730
Jerry Thomas, *President*
Brian Hurley, *Vice Pres*
Ann Thomas, *Vice Pres*
Greg Thomas, *Vice Pres*
Ha Trinh, *Accountant*
▼ **EMP:** 60 **EST:** 1949
SQ FT: 15,000
SALES (est): 58.1MM **Privately Held**
WEB: www.cethomas.net
SIC: 1542 7699 Design & erection, combined: non-residential; service station equipment repair

(P-752)
CHARLES PNKOW BLDRS LTD A CAL (PA)
199 S Los Robles Ave # 3, Pasadena (91101-2452)
PHONE................................626 304-1190
Scott Anderson, *CEO*
Dave Eichten, *President*
Dick Walterhouse, *Officer*
Maria Carlson, *Vice Pres*
Jack Mollenkopf, *Vice Pres*
EMP: 50 **EST:** 1986
SQ FT: 40,000
SALES (est): 161.8MM **Privately Held**
WEB: www.pankow.com
SIC: 1542 Commercial & office building, new construction

(P-753)
CHINA PACIFIC INC
Also Called: China Pac Sheet Metal Mfg
1777 N Main St, Los Angeles (90031-2516)
PHONE................................323 222-9580
Kenneth Tsan, *President*
Frank Ho, *Vice Pres*
EMP: 15 **EST:** 1984
SQ FT: 10,000
SALES (est): 2.9MM **Privately Held**
WEB: www.chinapacificcoinc.com
SIC: 1542 3444 3589 Restaurant construction; restaurant sheet metalwork; cooking equipment, commercial

(P-754)
CLARION CONSTRUCTION INC
21067 Commerce Point Dr, Walnut (91789-3052)
PHONE................................909 598-4060
Bradley Owen, *President*
Bruce Kidd, *Vice Pres*
Karen Snider, *Vice Pres*
Dana Spann, *Vice Pres*
Shelly Claisse, *Administration*
EMP: 50 **EST:** 1988
SQ FT: 10,000
SALES (est): 25.2MM **Privately Held**
WEB: www.clarionconst.com
SIC: 1542 Commercial & office building, new construction

(P-755)
CLARK CNSTR GROUP - CAL LP
18201 Von Karman Ave # 800, Irvine (92612-1092)
PHONE................................714 429-9779
Richard M Heim, *CEO*
EMP: 393 **EST:** 2004
SQ FT: 5,000
SALES (est): 97.5MM
SALES (corp-wide): 1.6B **Privately Held**
WEB: www.s2ngroup.com
SIC: 1542 Commercial & office building, new construction
HQ: Clark Construction Group, Llc
7500 Old Georgtwn Rd # 3
Bethesda MD 20814
301 272-8100

(P-756)
CLAY CORONA COMPANY (PA)
22079 Knabe Rd, Corona (92883-7111)
PHONE................................951 277-2667
Gerald K Deleo, *President*
Joyce Deleo, *Corp Secy*
Craig Deleo, *Vice Pres*
Rose Villasenor, *Office Mgr*
EMP: 23 **EST:** 1947
SALES (est): 9.4MM **Privately Held**
WEB: www.coronaclayco.com
SIC: 1542 3295 8711 1794 Commercial & office building contractors; minerals, ground or treated; construction & civil engineering; excavation work

(P-757)
CM CONSTRUCTION SERVICES INC (PA)
8300 W Doe Ave, Visalia (93291-9261)
P.O. Box 6237 (93290-6237)
PHONE................................559 735-9556
Monique Miron, *President*
Kari Rivera, *Project Mgr*
EMP: 24 **EST:** 2002 **Privately Held**
WEB: www.cmconstructionservices.com
SIC: 1542 1522 3999 8741 Nonresidential construction; institutional building construction; residential construction; carpet tackles; construction management; general contractor, highway & street construction

(P-758)
DAVID L MANWARREN CORP
9146 9th St, Rancho Cucamonga (91730-4405)
PHONE................................909 989-5883
David L Manwarren, *President*
Jean Manwarren, *Vice Pres*
▼ **EMP:** 27 **EST:** 1981
SQ FT: 44,000
SALES (est): 6.5MM **Privately Held**
WEB: www.agenceproscenium.com
SIC: 1542 3999 Design & erection, combined: non-residential; foliage, artificial & preserved

(P-759)
DEL AMO CONSTRUCTION
23840 Madison St, Torrance (90505-6009)
PHONE................................310 378-6203
Steve Donahue, *CEO*
Ed Hong, *CFO*
Susan Donahue, *Treasurer*
Jason Cave, *Vice Pres*
Harry Donahue, *Vice Pres*
EMP: 55 **EST:** 1998
SQ FT: 4,000
SALES (est): 52.1MM **Privately Held**
WEB: www.delamoconstruction.com
SIC: 1542 1771 Commercial & office building, new construction; concrete work

(P-760)
DIANI BUILDING CORP (PA)
351 N Blosser Rd, Santa Maria (93458-4219)
P.O. Box 5757 (93456-5757)
PHONE................................805 925-9533
Michael J Diani, *President*
Jeffrey Neal, *COO*
Lowell Ledgerwood, *Treasurer*
Peter Hemesath, *Vice Pres*
Jason Diani, *Admin Sec*
EMP: 98 **EST:** 2004
SQ FT: 11,000
SALES (est): 29.1MM **Privately Held**
WEB: www.diani.com
SIC: 1542 Commercial & office building, new construction

(P-761)
DPR CONSTRUCTION A GEN PARTNR
88 W Colo Blvd Ste 301, Pasadena (91105)
PHONE................................626 463-1265
Dal Swain, *Branch Mgr*
Alicia Loh Ortiz, *Project Mgr*
EMP: 141 **Privately Held**
WEB: www.dpr.com
SIC: 1542 Commercial & office building, new construction
HQ: Dpr Construction, A General Partnership
1450 Veterans Blvd
Redwood City CA 94063

(P-762)
ENVIRONMENTAL CONSTRUCTION INC
21550 Oxnard St Ste 1060, Woodland Hills (91367-7123)
PHONE................................818 449-8920
Farid Soroudi, *CEO*
Zia Abhari, *President*
EMP: 90 **EST:** 2004
SQ FT: 2,500
SALES (est): 22.6MM **Privately Held**
WEB:
www.environmentalconstructioninc.com
SIC: 1542 Commercial & office building contractors

(P-763)
FRANK SCHIPPER CONSTRUCTION CO
Also Called: Fscc
610 E Cota St, Santa Barbara (93103-3166)
P.O. Box 246 (93102-0246)
PHONE................................805 963-4359
Frank Schipper, *President*
Arlan Schipper, *Vice Pres*
Paul Wieckowski, *Vice Pres*
Kaitlin Barrett, *Project Mgr*
Matt Scranton, *Project Mgr*
EMP: 50
SQ FT: 2,200
SALES (est): 14.4MM **Privately Held**
WEB: www.schipperconstruction.com
SIC: 1542 8742 1611 Commercial & office buildings, renovation & repair; commercial & office building, new construction; business consultant; general contractor, highway & street construction

(P-764)
G W MURPHY CNSTR CO INC
15901 Olden St, Sylmar (91342-1051)
PHONE................................818 362-8391
Ronald Tutor, *President*
William Sparks, *Treasurer*
EMP: 102 **EST:** 1946
SQ FT: 42,000
SALES (est): 11MM
SALES (corp-wide): 5.3B **Publicly Held**
WEB: www.tutorperini.com
SIC: 1542 1541 1522 1521 Commercial & office building, new construction; industrial buildings & warehouses; condominium construction; townhouse construction
HQ: Tutor-Saliba Corporation
15901 Olden St
Sylmar CA 91342
818 362-8391

(P-765)
G3 GROUP LA INC (PA)
2500 Townsgate Rd, Thousand Oaks (91361-2630)
PHONE................................323 848-4186
Terry Robert Goebel, *Principal*
EMP: 56 **EST:** 2016
SALES (est): 1.6MM **Privately Held**
SIC: 1542 Nonresidential construction

(P-766)
GGG DEMOLITION INC (PA)
1130 W Trenton Ave, Orange (92867-3536)
PHONE................................714 699-9350
Gregg Miller, *Admin Sec*
Shane La Plante, *Project Mgr*
Everett Aoys, *Safety Dir*
Mario Garcia, *Foreman/Supr*
EMP: 98 **EST:** 2012
SALES (est): 16.4MM **Privately Held**
WEB: www.gggdemo.com
SIC: 1542 Specialized public building contractors

(P-767)
GRANI INSTALLATION INC (PA)
5411 Commercial Dr, Huntington Beach (92649-1231)
PHONE................................714 898-0441
Gregory A Grani, *CEO*
Henry Uranga, *Project Mgr*
EMP: 100 **EST:** 1973
SQ FT: 6,000
SALES (est): 28.1MM **Privately Held**
WEB: www.grani.biz
SIC: 1542 1742 Commercial & office buildings, renovation & repair; acoustical & ceiling work

(P-768)
HAREL GENERAL CONTRACTORS INC
6015 Washington Blvd, Culver City (90232-7425)
PHONE................................310 558-8304
Gill Harel, *President*
Ron Harel, *Vice Pres*
EMP: 50 **EST:** 1981
SALES (est): 6.6MM **Privately Held**
WEB: www.harelgc.com
SIC: 1542 Commercial & office building, new construction

(P-769)
HAYHOE CONSTRUCTION CORP
17821 17th St Ste 150, Tustin (92780-2153)
PHONE................................714 508-2400
John Hayhoe, *President*
Kyle Hayhoe, *Vice Pres*
Margaret Montenaro, *Executive*
Sharon Hayhoe, *Admin Sec*
▲ **EMP:** 55 **EST:** 1985
SQ FT: 5,400
SALES (est): 1.2MM **Privately Held**
WEB: www.hayhoeconstruction.com
SIC: 1542 Mausoleum construction; commercial & office building contractors

(P-770)
HHS CONSTRUCTION LLC (HQ)
2042 S Grove Ave, Ontario (91761-5617)
PHONE................................909 393-3322
John Navarrete, *Mng Member*
Tom Wilbert, *President*
Kevin Knoblock, *Vice Pres*
Marvin Garcia, *Purch Mgr*
Michael Schwing, *Manager*
EMP: 119 **EST:** 2003

PRODUCTS & SVCS

SALES (est): 58.7MM
SALES (corp-wide): 190.9MM **Privately Held**
WEB: www.congruex.com
SIC: **1542** 1731 Commercial & office building, new construction; fiber optic cable installation
PA: Congruex Llc
2615 13th St
Boulder CO 80304
720 749-2318

(P-771)
HITT CONTRACTING INC
3733 Motor Ave Ste 200, Los Angeles (90034-6403)
PHONE...................................424 326-1042
EMP: 279
SALES (corp-wide): 1.2B **Privately Held**
WEB: www.hitt.com
SIC: **1542** 1531 Nonresidential construction; operative builders
PA: Hitt Contracting, Inc.
2900 Fairview Park Dr
Falls Church VA 22042
703 846-9000

(P-772)
HOLBROOK CONSTRUCTION INC
9814 Norwalk Blvd Ste 200, Santa Fe Springs (90670-2992)
PHONE...................................714 523-1150
Laurence A Holbrook, *President*
Richard Holbrook, *CFO*
Lisa Garcia, *Controller*
Patty Granados, *Human Res Mgr*
EMP: 75 EST: 1985
SQ FT: 3,000
SALES (est): 18.8MM **Privately Held**
WEB: www.holbrookconstruction.net
SIC: **1542** Commercial & office building, new construction

(P-773)
HOUALLA ENTERPRISES LTD
Also Called: Metro Bldrs & Engineers Group
2610 Avon St, Newport Beach (92663-4706)
PHONE...................................949 515-4350
Fouad Houalla, *President*
Aref Mikati, *CTO*
Ronald Blanchard, *Engineer*
Elliott N Prescott, *Property Mgr*
Hossein Kashfi, *Sr Project Mgr*
▲ EMP: 85 EST: 1987
SQ FT: 1,200
SALES (est): 23.1MM **Privately Held**
WEB: www.metrobuilders.com
SIC: **1542** Commercial & office building, new construction; specialized public building contractors

(P-774)
J D DIFFENBAUGH INC
6865 Airport Dr, Riverside (92504-1903)
P.O. Box 4457 (92514-4457)
PHONE...................................951 351-6865
Jack Hawkins, *CEO*
Marvin J Hawkins Jr, *President*
EMP: 60 EST: 1959
SQ FT: 15,000
SALES (est): 12.3MM **Privately Held**
WEB: www.diffenbaugh.com
SIC: **1542** 1541 Commercial & office building, new construction; industrial buildings, new construction

(P-775)
JOCER ENTERPRISES INC
Also Called: Castlebrook Barns
14600 Whittram Ave, Fontana (92335-3112)
PHONE...................................909 822-0500
Spencer Graffam, *President*
Jodi Graffam, *Vice Pres*
EMP: 50 EST: 1999
SQ FT: 23,000
SALES (est): 11.3MM **Privately Held**
WEB: www.castlebrookbarns.com
SIC: **1542** Nonresidential construction

(P-776)
JOHN M FRANK CONSTRUCTION INC
Also Called: John M Frank Service Group
913 E 4th St, Santa Ana (92701-4748)
PHONE...................................714 210-3600
John M Frank, *CEO*
Myra Mageo, *Executive*
Laurie Dawson, *Admin Sec*
Tim Whelan, *Superintendent*
EMP: 80 EST: 1984
SALES (est): 24MM **Privately Held**
WEB: www.johnmfrankconstruction.com
SIC: **1542** 5411 5812 Commercial & office building, new construction; commercial & office buildings, renovation & repair; supermarkets; family restaurants; restaurant, lunch counter

(P-777)
JONES BROTHERS CNSTR CORP (PA)
Also Called: Peck Jones Construction
1601 Cloverfield Blvd, Santa Monica (90404-4082)
PHONE...................................310 470-1885
J Gregory Jones, *President*
Jerve M Jones, *Chm Emeritus*
EMP: 61 EST: 1923
SALES (est): 15MM **Privately Held**
SIC: **1542** Commercial & office building contractors

(P-778)
JUNE A GROTHE CONSTRUCTION INC
Also Called: J G Construction
15632 El Prado Rd, Chino (91710-9108)
PHONE...................................909 993-9393
Jack Grothe, *Principal*
June A Grothe, *CEO*
Wally Clark, *Vice Pres*
Kelly Stevens, *General Mgr*
Herschel Hulce, *Project Mgr*
EMP: 65 EST: 1993
SQ FT: 15,500
SALES (est): 32.9MM **Privately Held**
WEB: www.jgconstruction.com
SIC: **1542** Shopping center construction

(P-779)
KLASSEN CORPORATION (PA)
2021 Westwind Dr, Bakersfield (93301-3015)
PHONE...................................661 327-0875
Jerry D Klassen, *President*
Bob Klassen, *COO*
Troy Fringer, *CFO*
Ed Childres, *Vice Pres*
Mark Delmarter, *Vice Pres*
EMP: 68 EST: 1977
SQ FT: 7,981
SALES (est): 28.6MM **Privately Held**
WEB: www.klassencorp.com
SIC: **1542** Commercial & office building, new construction

(P-780)
KPRS CONSTRUCTION SERVICES INC (PA)
2850 Saturn St Ste 110, Brea (92821-1701)
PHONE...................................714 672-0800
Joel H Stensby, *President*
Lev Rabinovich, *Treasurer*
Corey Evans, *Vice Pres*
Keith Taylor, *Executive*
Norman Rabinovich, *Creative Dir*
EMP: 91 EST: 1995
SQ FT: 31,000
SALES (est): 546.9MM **Privately Held**
WEB: www.kprsinc.com
SIC: **1542** 8711 Commercial & office building, new construction; building construction consultant

(P-781)
LAURUS CONSTRUCTION CORP
3189 Red Hill Ave Ste D, Costa Mesa (92626-3426)
P.O. Box 1679 (92628-1679)
PHONE...................................714 641-0318
Eric Reyes, *President*
Sharon Chan, *Exec VP*
EMP: 50 EST: 2000

SQ FT: 2,000
SALES (est): 10.2MM **Privately Held**
WEB: www.laurusconstruction.com
SIC: **1542** 1522 Commercial & office buildings, renovation & repair; residential construction

(P-782)
LEDESMA & MEYER CNSTR CO INC
9441 Haven Ave, Rancho Cucamonga (91730-5845)
PHONE...................................909 297-1100
Kris Meyer, *President*
Joseph M Ledesma, *CEO*
Tom Smith, *Opers Staff*
Jeff Carter, *Superintendent*
Gary Ledbetter, *Superintendent*
EMP: 68 EST: 1997
SALES (est): 10.4MM **Privately Held**
WEB: www.lmcci.com
SIC: **1542** School building construction

(P-783)
LEWIS DEVELOPMENT CO (PA)
Also Called: Lewis Homes
1156 N Mountain Ave, Upland (91786-3633)
P.O. Box 670 (91785-0670)
PHONE...................................909 946-7506
Richard A Lewis, *President*
Western Supply Corp, *Partner*
Kimmel Enterprises, *Partner*
Leon C Swails, *COO*
David L Linden, *Vice Pres*
EMP: 121 EST: 1955
SQ FT: 18,300
SALES (est): 16.2MM **Privately Held**
WEB: www.lewisretailcenters.com
SIC: **1542** Commercial & office building, new construction

(P-784)
LMC HOLLYWOOD HIGHLAND
Also Called: Lennar Multi Family Community
95 Enterprise Ste 200, Aliso Viejo (92656-2611)
PHONE...................................949 448-1600
Todd Farrell, *CEO*
EMP: 500 EST: 2013
SALES (est): 69.2MM **Privately Held**
SIC: **1542** Commercial & office building contractors

(P-785)
MALLCRAFT INC
2225 Windsor Ave, Altadena (91001-5306)
P.O. Box 91983, Pasadena (91109-1983)
PHONE...................................626 765-9100
Gerald L Fishbein, *Ch of Bd*
Leslie E Hansen, *President*
Sheena E Pappas, *Vice Pres*
Sheena Pappas, *Vice Pres*
Jill Garber, *Admin Sec*
EMP: 68 EST: 1965
SQ FT: 5,000
SALES (est): 5.6MM **Privately Held**
SIC: **1542** Commercial & office building, new construction

(P-786)
MCCARTHY BLDG COMPANIES INC
20401 Sw Birch St Ste 200, Newport Beach (92660-1796)
PHONE...................................949 851-8383
Fermin Glasper, *Vice Pres*
Aaron Lich, *Vice Pres*
Mike Stapf, *Vice Pres*
Michael Benford, *Business Dir*
Jaren Murphy, *Business Dir*
EMP: 347
SALES (corp-wide): 4.7B **Privately Held**
WEB: www.mccarthybuildingcompanies.com
SIC: **1542** 1541 Institutional building construction; commercial & office building, new construction; industrial buildings, new construction
HQ: Mccarthy Building Companies, Inc.
12851 Manchester Rd
Saint Louis MO 63131
314 968-3300

(P-787)
MCCARTHY BLDG COMPANIES INC
Southern California Division
20401 Sw Birch St Ste 300, Newport Beach (92660-1798)
PHONE...................................949 351-8383
Randy Highland, *Branch Mgr*
EMP: 75
SALES (corp-wide): 4.7B **Privately Held**
WEB: www.mccarthybuildingcompanies.com
SIC: **1542** Commercial & office building, new construction
HQ: Mccarthy Building Companies, Inc.
12851 Manchester Rd
Saint Louis MO 63131
314 968-3300

(P-788)
MCCARTHY BLDG COMPANIES INC
1113 S Bush St, Orange (92868-4222)
PHONE...................................949 851-8383
Pat Peterson, *Branch Mgr*
EMP: 59
SALES (corp-wide): 4.7B **Privately Held**
WEB: www.mccarthybuildingcompanies.com
SIC: **1542** Commercial & office building, new construction
HQ: Mccarthy Building Companies, Inc.
12851 Manchester Rd
Saint Louis MO 63131
314 968-3300

(P-789)
MCCARTHY BLDG COMPANIES INC
6363 Regent St, Huntington Park (90255-3545)
PHONE...................................949 851-8383
EMP: 59
SALES (corp-wide): 4.7B **Privately Held**
WEB: www.mccarthybuildingcompanies.com
SIC: **1542** Commercial & office building, new construction
HQ: Mccarthy Building Companies, Inc.
12851 Manchester Rd
Saint Louis MO 63131
314 968-3300

(P-790)
MCCARTHY BLDG COMPANIES INC
18943 Airport Way, Santa Ana (92707-5211)
PHONE...................................949 851-8383
EMP: 59
SALES (corp-wide): 4.7B **Privately Held**
WEB: www.mccarthybuildingcompanies.com
SIC: **1542** Commercial & office building, new construction
HQ: Mccarthy Building Companies, Inc.
12851 Manchester Rd
Saint Louis MO 63131
314 968-3300

(P-791)
MCCARTHY FRAMING CNSTR INC
Also Called: McCarthy Construction
15133 Grevillea Ave, Lawndale (90260-2017)
PHONE...................................310 219-3038
Patrick McCarthy, *Owner*
▲ EMP: 60 EST: 1976
SALES (est): 5.2MM **Privately Held**
SIC: **1542** Commercial & office building, new construction

(P-792)
MERUELO ENTERPRISES INC (PA)
9550 Firestone Blvd # 105, Downey (90241-5560)
PHONE...................................562 745-2300
Alex Meruelo, *CEO*
Al Stoller, *CFO*
Joe Marchica, *Vice Pres*
Lexi Miech, *Sales Staff*
EMP: 501 EST: 1986

SALES (est): 663.7MM **Privately Held**
WEB: www.merueloenterprises.com
SIC: **1542** Nonresidential construction

(P-793)
MOOREFIELD CONSTRUCTION INC (PA)
600 N Tustin Ave Ste 210, Santa Ana (92705-3781)
PHONE....................714 972-0700
Ann Moorefield, *CEO*
Mike Moorefield, *President*
Teri Coffey, *Vice Pres*
Hal Moorefield, *Vice Pres*
Larry Moorefield, *Vice Pres*
EMP: 60 EST: 1957
SQ FT: 8,490
SALES: 234.5MM **Privately Held**
WEB: www.moorefieldconstruction.com
SIC: **1542** Shopping center construction

(P-794)
NATIONAL CONSTRUCTION & MAINT
Also Called: NCM
23846 Sunnymead Blvd # 10, Moreno Valley (92553-0535)
PHONE....................909 888-7042
John Omar Blanco, *CEO*
EMP: 50 EST: 2001
SQ FT: 600
SALES (est): 9.6MM **Privately Held**
WEB: www.ncmco.com
SIC: **1542** Commercial & office building contractors

(P-795)
NEAR-CAL CORP
512 Chaney St, Lake Elsinore (92530-2747)
PHONE....................951 245-5400
Carl J Johnson, *Ch of Bd*
John Jacobs, *Vice Pres*
Steve Sanderson, *Vice Pres*
Mary Saenz, *Admin Sec*
Richard Barnes, *CIO*
EMP: 50 EST: 1964
SQ FT: 10,000
SALES (est): 30MM **Privately Held**
WEB: www.nearcal.com
SIC: **1542** 1541 Commercial & office building, new construction; factory construction

(P-796)
NEVELL GROUP INC (PA)
Also Called: N G I
3001 Enterprise St # 200, Brea (92821-6210)
PHONE....................714 579-7501
Michael J Nevell, *President*
Bryan Bodine, *CFO*
Bruce Pasqua, *Senior VP*
Troy Chavez, *Project Mgr*
Eric Hartzheim, *Project Mgr*
EMP: 125 EST: 2002
SQ FT: 35,000
SALES (est): 137.1MM **Privately Held**
WEB: www.nevellgroup.com
SIC: **1542** Commercial & office building, new construction

(P-797)
NEXT VENTURE INC
Also Called: Sierra Group
560 Rverdale Drv Glendale, Glendale (91204)
PHONE....................818 637-2888
Carl Frommer, *President*
Scott Martin, *CFO*
Richard Freeman, *Exec VP*
David Garrison, *Division Mgr*
Warren Markar, *Admin Asst*
EMP: 55 EST: 1995
SQ FT: 7,000
SALES (est): 14MM **Privately Held**
WEB: www.callsierra.com
SIC: **1542** Commercial & office building, new construction

(P-798)
PAAT & KIMMEL DEVELOPMENT INC
600 N Mountain Ave, Upland (91786-4331)
PHONE....................909 315-8074
Victor Paat, *CEO*

Hortencia Cervantes, *Office Mgr*
EMP: 60 EST: 2014
SALES (est): 13.2MM **Privately Held**
SIC: **1542** Commercial & office building, new construction

(P-799)
PACE DEVELOPMENT CABINETRY INC
7642 Windfield Dr, Huntington Beach (92647-7139)
PHONE....................714 842-5336
Anthony Joseph Rini, *President*
Carol S Rini, *Corp Secy*
Jaclyn S Rini, *Vice Pres*
EMP: 20 EST: 1977
SALES (est): 1.7MM **Privately Held**
WEB: www.pacecabinetry.net
SIC: **1542** 5712 2434 Commercial & office building, new construction; customized furniture & cabinets; wood kitchen cabinets

(P-800)
PARKCO BUILDING COMPANY
24795 State Highway 74, Perris (92570-8759)
PHONE....................714 444-1441
W Adrian Hoyle, *President*
Joel Templeton, *Project Mgr*
Robert Galindo, *Project Engr*
EMP: 99 EST: 2013
SALES (est): 14MM **Privately Held**
WEB: www.parkcobuilding.com
SIC: **1542** 1771 1799 Commercial & office building, new construction; garage construction; foundation & footing contractor; erection & dismantling of forms for poured concrete

(P-801)
PARSONS GVRNMENT SVCS INTL INC
100 W Walnut St, Pasadena (91124-0001)
PHONE....................626 440-6000
Thomas L Roell, *President*
Curtis A Bower, *Exec VP*
Gary L Stone, *Senior VP*
EMP: 149 EST: 1969
SALES (est): 10.2MM
SALES (corp-wide): 3.9B **Publicly Held**
WEB: www.parsons.com
SIC: **1542** Commercial & office building, new construction
PA: The Parsons Corporation
   5875 Trinity Pkwy Ste 300
   Centreville VA 20120
   703 988-8500

(P-802)
PCL CONSTRUCTION SERVICES INC
655 N Central Ave # 1600, Glendale (91203-1438)
PHONE....................818 246-3481
Dale Kain, *Manager*
Ron Sitton, *Project Mgr*
Jacob Hagman, *Project Engr*
Tim Joyce, *Project Engr*
Alexa Rizeq, *Project Engr*
EMP: 191
SQ FT: 17,619
SALES (corp-wide): 5.9B **Privately Held**
SIC: **1542** Commercial & office building, new construction
HQ: Pcl Construction Services, Inc.
   2000 S Colo Blvd Ste 2-50
   Denver CO 80222
   303 365-6500

(P-803)
PCL CONSTRUCTION SERVICES INC
100 Universal City Plz, North Hollywood (91608-1002)
PHONE....................818 509-7816
EMP: 119
SALES (corp-wide): 5.9B **Privately Held**
SIC: **1542** Commercial & office building, new construction
HQ: Pcl Construction Services, Inc.
   2000 S Colo Blvd Ste 2-50
   Denver CO 80222
   303 365-6500

(P-804)
PCL INDUSTRIAL SERVICES INC
1500 S Union Ave, Bakersfield (93307-4144)
PHONE....................661 832-3995
Joe W Carrieri, *CEO*
Gary L Basher, *Corp Secy*
Kirby Evenson, *Administration*
Elias Ramirez, *Project Mgr*
Mark Schneider, *Project Engr*
EMP: 300 EST: 2002
SALES (est): 128.2MM **Privately Held**
SIC: **1542** Commercial & office building, new construction

(P-805)
PCN3 INC
11082 Winners Cir Ste B, Los Alamitos (90720-2893)
PHONE....................562 493-4124
Brian Abghari, *CEO*
Phyllis Martinez, *Bookkeeper*
EMP: 50 EST: 1999
SQ FT: 2,000
SALES (est): 10.8MM **Privately Held**
WEB: www.pcn3.com
SIC: **1542** Commercial & office building, new construction

(P-806)
PENWAL INDUSTRIES INC
10611 Acacia St, Rancho Cucamonga (91730-5410)
PHONE....................909 466-1555
Chris A Pennington, *Principal*
Rusty Lamberson, *Manager*
Paige Pennington, *Manager*
▲ EMP: 100 EST: 1981
SQ FT: 65,000
SALES (est): 26.1MM **Privately Held**
WEB: www.penwal.com
SIC: **1542** 3999 8742 3993 Shopping center construction; advertising display products; management consulting services; signs & advertising specialties

(P-807)
PERRY COAST CONSTRUCTION INC
Also Called: West Coast Construction
14130 Meridian Pkwy, Riverside (92518-3043)
PHONE....................951 774-0677
Robert Perry, *President*
Erin Perry, *Treasurer*
Britney Perry, *Admin Sec*
EMP: 105 EST: 2012
SALES (est): 21.3MM **Privately Held**
WEB: www.wcconcrete.com
SIC: **1542** Restaurant construction

(P-808)
PHILMONT MANAGEMENT INC
3450 Wilshire Blvd # 850, Los Angeles (90010-2211)
PHONE....................213 380-0159
Monica Nam, *President*
EMP: 99 EST: 1997
SQ FT: 6,000 **Privately Held**
WEB: www.philmontinc.com
SIC: **1542** Commercial & office building, new construction

(P-809)
PINNACLE CONTRACTING CORP
21800 Burbank Blvd # 210, Woodland Hills (91367-6470)
PHONE....................818 888-6548
Mark Tieman, *CEO*
Mark A Tieman, *President*
Michael Grossman, *Chairman*
Susan Berson, *Vice Pres*
Denise Grossman, *Admin Sec*
EMP: 50 EST: 1993
SQ FT: 3,500
SALES (est): 13.2MM **Privately Held**
WEB: www.pincon.com
SIC: **1542** Commercial & office building, new construction

(P-810)
PINNER CONSTRUCTION CO INC (PA)
Also Called: General Contractor
1255 S Lewis St, Anaheim (92805-6424)
PHONE....................714 490-4000
Dirk Griffin, *CEO*
Teresa Parks, *Office Mgr*
Stephanie Burdo, *Administration*
Roxanne Couture, *Administration*
Jeff Hauck, *Project Mgr*
▲ EMP: 85 EST: 1919
SQ FT: 6,700
SALES: 179.6MM **Privately Held**
WEB: www.pinnerconstruction.com
SIC: **1542** Commercial & office building, new construction; hospital construction; stadium construction

(P-811)
POVAC INVESTMENTS INC
388 Cordova St Ste 280, Pasadena (91101-5839)
PHONE....................626 405-0400
Patrick Chraghchian, *CEO*
Patrick Charghehian, *President*
Fred Hovsepian, *Admin Sec*
▲ EMP: 50 EST: 1994
SALES (est): 8MM **Privately Held**
SIC: **1542** Nonresidential construction

(P-812)
PRATS/COFFEE INC
4652 E 3rd St, Los Angeles (90022-1615)
PHONE....................323 780-4022
Leo Prats, *President*
Gary Ayala, *Project Engr*
Steve Pribyl, *Architect*
EMP: 56 EST: 1979
SQ FT: 6,000
SALES (est): 2.5MM **Privately Held**
WEB: www.pratsinc.com
SIC: **1542** 1541 1521 8712 Commercial & office building, new construction; commercial & office buildings, renovation & repair; industrial buildings & warehouses; new construction, single-family houses; architectural services

(P-813)
R & L BROSAMER INC
2916 W Main St, Visalia (93291-5731)
P.O. Box 238, Alamo (94507-0238)
PHONE....................559 739-8215
Larry Roeder, *Office Mgr*
EMP: 360
SALES (corp-wide): 3.5B **Privately Held**
WEB: www.brosamer.com
SIC: **1542** Commercial & office building, new construction
HQ: R & L Brosamer, Inc.
   1390 Willow Pass Rd # 95
   Concord CA 94520

(P-814)
RBA BUILDERS INC
17601 Sampson Ln, Huntington Beach (92647-6750)
PHONE....................714 895-9000
Robert Anderson, *CEO*
Gilbert Martinez, *Vice Pres*
Bryan Pavalko, *Vice Pres*
Jon Pedersen, *Project Mgr*
Mark Weeger, *Project Mgr*
EMP: 82 EST: 2007
SALES: 49.7MM **Privately Held**
WEB: www.rbabuildersinc.com
SIC: **1542** Commercial & office building, new construction

(P-815)
RESOURCE ENVIRONMENTAL INC
13100 Alondra Blvd # 108, Cerritos (90703-2262)
PHONE....................562 468-7000
Jared Sloan Cooper, *President*
Edgar Escarcega, *Manager*
Albert Sanchez, *Manager*
Chase Tinsley, *Manager*
Benjamin Serrano, *Superintendent*
EMP: 75 EST: 2005

PRODUCTS & SVCS

SALES (est): 10MM **Privately Held**
WEB: www.resourceenvironmental.com
SIC: **1542** Nonresidential construction

(P-816)
RICHARDSON GROUP
413 S Glassell St, Orange (92866-1905)
PHONE....................................714 997-3970
Kimm Richardson, *President*
Steve Richardson, *Treasurer*
Susanne Richardson, *Vice Pres*
EMP: 62 EST: 1972
SQ FT: 1,500
SALES (est): 4.7MM **Privately Held**
WEB: www.therichardsongroup.com
SIC: **1542** 1541 Commercial & office build-
ing, new construction; hospital construc-
tion; industrial buildings & warehouses

(P-817)
ROBERT CLAPPER CNSTR SVCS INC
Also Called: RC Construction Services
2223 N Locust Ave, Rialto (92377-4113)
PHONE....................................909 829-3688
Robert W Clapper, *Principal*
Rebecca Clapper, *Corp Secy*
Rich Negley, *Project Mgr*
Jonathan Wollam, *Project Mgr*
Gabriel Urioste, *Project Engr*
EMP: 100 EST: 1994
SALES (est): 35MM **Privately Held**
WEB: www.rcconstruction.com
SIC: **1542** 1771 Commercial & office build-
ing, new construction; school building
construction; institutional building con-
struction; concrete work; curb & sidewalk
contractors; foundation & footing contrac-
tor

(P-818)
S J AMOROSO CNSTR CO LLC
275 Baker St Ste B, Costa Mesa
(92626-4566)
PHONE....................................650 654-1900
Richard Armsworthy, *Branch Mgr*
Philip Tanghal, *Vice Pres*
Sam Chihabi, *Executive*
Melissa Perreault, *Admin Asst*
Eric Dorrell, *Project Mgr*
EMP: 64
SALES (corp-wide): 104.8MM **Privately
Held**
WEB: www.sjamoroso.com
SIC: **1542** Commercial & office building,
new construction
PA: S. J. Amoroso Construction Co., Llc
390 Bridge Pkwy
Redwood City CA 94065
650 654-1900

(P-819)
SAN-MAR CONSTRUCTION CO INC
4875 E La Palma Ave # 601, Anaheim
(92807-1955)
PHONE....................................714 693-5400
Sandra Drew, *CEO*
David Drew, *Vice Pres*
Darren Drew, *Project Mgr*
Tamara Kennedy, *Human Res Dir*
EMP: 200 EST: 1993
SQ FT: 3,000
SALES (est): 32.3MM **Privately Held**
WEB: www.san-mar.com
SIC: **1542** Commercial & office building,
new construction

(P-820)
SANDER LANGSTON LP
Also Called: Snyder Langston
17962 Cowan, Irvine (92614-6026)
PHONE....................................949 863-9200
Jason Rich, *President*
John Rochford, *CEO*
Gary Campanaro, *CFO*
Rick Cavecche, *Vice Pres*
Chip McCorkle, *Vice Pres*
EMP: 175 EST: 1986
SQ FT: 16,000
SALES (est): 413MM **Privately Held**
WEB: www.snyderlangston.com
SIC: **1542** 8742 1522 Commercial & of-
fice building, new construction; real estate
consultant; residential construction

(P-821)
SAVANT CONSTRUCTION INC
13830 Mountain Ave, Chino (91710-9014)
P.O. Box 636 (91708-0636)
PHONE....................................909 614-4300
John L Aldridge, *President*
Brad Hastings, *Corp Secy*
Darren Nowicki, *Vice Pres*
Penny Rodela, *Admin Asst*
Gerard Mahoney, *Sr Project Mgr*
EMP: 52 EST: 1990
SQ FT: 36,000
SALES (est): 29.3MM **Privately Held**
WEB: www.savantconstruction.com
SIC: **1542** Commercial & office building,
new construction

(P-822)
SEA PAC ENGINEERING INC
625 S Nh Ave Fl 2 Flr 2, Los Angeles
(90005)
PHONE....................................213 487-6130
John Lee, *President*
Sarah Lee, *Admin Sec*
George Clouse, *Sr Project Mgr*
◆ EMP: 71 EST: 1993
SQ FT: 1,700
SALES (est): 16.9MM **Privately Held**
WEB: www.seapaceng.com
SIC: **1542** Nonresidential construction

(P-823)
SERVICE FIRST CONTRACTORS
2510 N Grand Ave Ste 110, Santa Ana
(92705-8754)
PHONE....................................714 573-2200
Mark Bucher, *CEO*
Frank Vanderberg, *President*
Stan Hatch, *Treasurer*
Gary Bucher, *Admin Sec*
EMP: 50 EST: 1982
SQ FT: 6,500
SALES (est): 15.5MM **Privately Held**
SIC: **1542** 1522 6512 Commercial & of-
fice building contractors; residential con-
struction; nonresidential building
operators

(P-824)
SEVERSON GROUP INCORPORATED (PA)
3601 Serpentine Dr, Los Alamitos
(90720-2440)
PHONE....................................562 493-3611
Jonathan Edward Severson, *President*
Brian Cresap, *Treasurer*
Scott Feest, *Vice Pres*
Ben Severson, *Vice Pres*
Robert Severson, *Vice Pres*
EMP: 60 EST: 1990
SQ FT: 15,000
SALES (est): 56.8MM **Privately Held**
WEB: www.theseversongroup.com
SIC: **1542** 1541 Commercial & office build-
ing, new construction; hospital construc-
tion; institutional building construction;
industrial buildings, new construction

(P-825)
SHAWMUT WOODWORKING & SUP INC
Also Called: Shawmut Design and Cnstr
11390 W Olympic Blvd Fl 2, Los Angeles
(90064-1607)
PHONE....................................323 602-1000
Leonard Porzio, *Principal*
Reza Amirkhalili, *COO*
Roger Tougas, *CFO*
Marianne Monte, *Officer*
Dave Benson, *Vice Pres*
EMP: 145
SALES (corp-wide): 1.1B **Privately Held**
WEB: www.shawmut.com
SIC: **1542** Commercial & office building,
new construction
PA: Shawmut Woodworking & Supply, Inc.
560 Harrison Ave Ste 200
Boston MA 02118
617 622-7000

(P-826)
SIERRA PACIFIC CONSTRS INC
22212 Ventura Blvd # 300, Woodland Hills
(91364-1530)
PHONE....................................747 888-5000

Ken Laspada, *Vice Pres*
Andrew Witham, *Vice Pres*
Mary Capistrano, *Project Engr*
Deonna McDonald, *Project Engr*
Ken Mkrtchian, *Project Engr*
EMP: 99 EST: 1983
SQ FT: 13,500
SALES (est): 46.3MM **Privately Held**
WEB: www.spcinc.com
SIC: **1542** Commercial & office buildings,
renovation & repair

(P-827)
SIGMA SERVICES INC (PA)
2140 Eastman Ave Ste 110, Ventura
(93003-7786)
P.O. Box 368, Goleta (93116-0368)
PHONE....................................805 642-8377
Vivian Solodkin, *President*
Louie Valenzuela, *CFO*
Louie Valenzuela, *CFO*
Benjamin Valenzuela Jr, *Vice Pres*
EMP: 59 EST: 1999
SQ FT: 4,200
SALES (est): 12.1MM **Privately Held**
WEB: www.sigmaservices.net
SIC: **1542** 6531 7349 1731 Commercial
& office building contractors; real estate
managers; janitorial service, contract
basis; electrical work; facilities support
services

(P-828)
SILVER CREEK INDUSTRIES LLC
2830 Barrett Ave, Perris (92571-3258)
PHONE....................................951 943-5393
Brett D Bashaw, *CEO*
Micheal Rhodes, *Corp Secy*
EMP: 175 EST: 2005
SQ FT: 25,000
SALES (est): 92MM **Privately Held**
WEB: www.silver-creek.net
SIC: **1542** 2452 Commercial & office build-
ing contractors; prefabricated wood build-
ings

(P-829)
SILVERLINE CONSTRUCTION INC (PA)
1421 W 132nd St, Gardena (90249-2105)
PHONE....................................310 327-4970
Michael Murphy, *President*
Darrin Nutter, *VP Bus Dvlpt*
Michele McGrath, *Controller*
Adrian Villasenor, *Manager*
EMP: 203 EST: 1999
SALES (est): 114.6MM **Privately Held**
WEB: www.silverlineconstructioninc.com
SIC: **1542** Commercial & office building,
new construction

(P-830)
SIMMONS CONSTRUCTION INC
19252 Flightpath Way, Bakersfield
(93308-1615)
PHONE....................................661 636-1321
Charles J Simmons, *President*
Evalee Simmons, *Vice Pres*
EMP: 50 EST: 1988
SALES (est): 23.7MM **Privately Held**
SIC: **1542** Commercial & office building,
new construction

(P-831)
SINANIAN DEVELOPMENT INC
18980 Ventura Blvd # 200, Tarzana
(91356-3228)
PHONE....................................818 996-9666
Antranik Sinanian, *CEO*
Harry Sinanian, *Shareholder*
Sinan Sinanian, *President*
Andy Sinanian, *Co-President*
EMP: 70 EST: 1981
SQ FT: 4,000
SALES (est): 33.7MM **Privately Held**
WEB: www.sinanian.com
SIC: **1542** 1522 6552 Commercial & of-
fice building, new construction; residential
construction; subdividers & developers

(P-832)
SOUTH COAST PIERING INC
Also Called: Saber
43300 Bus Pk Dr Ste 204, Temecula
(92590-5524)
PHONE....................................800 922-2488
Franz M Froehlich, *CEO*
EMP: 70 EST: 2003
SALES (est): 8.5MM **Privately Held**
SIC: **1542** Commercial & office buildings,
renovation & repair

(P-833)
STREAMLINE FINISHES INC
26429 Rancho Pkwy S # 140, Lake Forest
(92630-8330)
PHONE....................................949 600-8964
William Seidel, *President*
Elijah Goldtrap, *VP Bus Dvlpt*
Kaitlin Pentico, *Project Engr*
Miguel Garcia, *Engineer*
Mario Rico, *Superintendent*
EMP: 80 EST: 2004
SQ FT: 6,000
SALES (est): 20.6MM **Privately Held**
WEB: www.streamlinefinishes.com
SIC: **1542** Commercial & office building
contractors

(P-834)
STRONGHOLD ENGINEERING INC (PA)
150 W Walnut Ave, Perris (92571-3262)
PHONE....................................951 684-9303
Beverly A Bailey, *President*
Quintous Crews, *Officer*
Cory Vaughan, *Exec VP*
Scott Bailey, *Vice Pres*
Timothy Buchanan, *Project Mgr*
EMP: 58 EST: 1993
SQ FT: 21,000
SALES (est): 109.1MM **Privately Held**
WEB: www.strongholdengineering.com
SIC: **1542** Commercial & office building,
new construction

(P-835)
SUMMER SYSTEMS INC
28942 Hancock Pkwy, Valencia
(91355-1069)
PHONE....................................661 257-4419
Don London, *President*
Connie London, *Admin Sec*
Bob Burson, *Opers Staff*
EMP: 80 EST: 1988
SQ FT: 20,000
SALES (est): 29.2MM **Privately Held**
WEB: www.summersystems.net
SIC: **1542** Nonresidential construction

(P-836)
TASLIMI CONSTRUCTION CO INC
1805 Colorado Ave, Santa Monica
(90404-3411)
PHONE....................................310 447-3000
Shidan Taslimi, *Principal*
Mehran Taslimi, *Vice Pres*
Jonathan Fanelli, *Executive*
Susanne Taslimi, *Admin Sec*
Houshang Banani, *Information Mgr*
EMP: 66 EST: 1985
SQ FT: 8,500
SALES (est): 24.4MM **Privately Held**
WEB: www.taslimi.com
SIC: **1542** Commercial & office building,
new construction; commercial & office
buildings, renovation & repair

(P-837)
TECHNO COATINGS INC
785 E Debra Ln, Anaheim (92805-6334)
PHONE....................................714 774-4671
Michael Birney, *Branch Mgr*
EMP: 75
SALES (corp-wide): 41MM **Privately
Held**
WEB: www.technocoatings.com
SIC: **1542** Commercial & office buildings,
renovation & repair
PA: Techno Coatings, Inc.
1391 S Allec St
Anaheim CA 92305
714 635-1130

(P-838)

TECHNO COATINGS INC
795 Debra St, Anaheim (92805)
PHONE..........................714 774-4671
Michael Birney, *President*
Cameron Simmons, *Manager*
EMP: 75
SALES (corp-wide): 41MM **Privately Held**
WEB: www.technocoatings.com
SIC: **1542** 1629 1721 1799 Commercial & office buildings, renovation & repair; blasting contractor, except building demolition; painting & paper hanging; wallcovering contractors; coating of concrete structures with plastic; coating of metal structures at construction site; waterproofing
PA: Techno Coatings, Inc.
1391 S Allec St
Anaheim CA 92805
714 635-1130

(P-839)

TEMALPAKH INC
Also Called: Works Floor & Wall, The
73750 Spyder Cir, Palm Desert (92211-6023)
PHONE..........................760 770-5778
Gerald A Flowers, *CEO*
Michael Collins, *Vice Pres*
Rusty Harling, *Admin Sec*
Steve Isen, *Sales Staff*
EMP: 65 EST: 1998
SQ FT: 13,000
SALES (est): 15MM **Privately Held**
SIC: **1542** 5713 5211 Commercial & office buildings, renovation & repair; floor covering stores; tile, ceramic

(P-840)

TILLER CONSTRUCTORS PARTNR INC
306 W Katella Ave Ste A, Orange (92867-4755)
PHONE..........................714 771-5600
Lin Lindstedt, *President*
Kerry Evert, *Vice Pres*
Patty Baker, *Administration*
Amanda Stern, *Accountant*
Brian Cheney, *Sales Staff*
EMP: 64 EST: 1988
SQ FT: 4,000
SALES (est): 24.1MM **Privately Held**
WEB: www.tillerconstructors.com
SIC: **1542** Institutional building construction

(P-841)

TURNER CONSTRUCTION COMPANY
1900 S State College Blvd # 200, Anaheim (92806-6197)
PHONE..........................714 940-9000
Bernie Morrissey, *Vice Pres*
Kathleen Swarat, *Admin Asst*
Stephanie Mattson, *Administration*
Homero Morales, *Project Engr*
Daisy Pate, *Project Engr*
EMP: 300
SALES (corp-wide): 1B **Privately Held**
WEB: www.turnerconstruction.com
SIC: **1542** Commercial & office building, new construction
HQ: Turner Construction Company Inc
375 Hudson St Fl 6
New York NY 10014
212 229-6000

(P-842)

TUTOR PERINI CORPORATION (PA)
15901 Olden St, Sylmar (91342-1051)
PHONE..........................818 362-8391
Ronald N Tutor, *Ch of Bd*
James A Frost, *President*
Leonard J Rejcek, *President*
Gary G Smalley, *CFO*
Michael R Klein, *Vice Ch Bd*
▲ EMP: 160 EST: 1894

SALES (est): 5.3B **Publicly Held**
WEB: www.tutorperini.com
SIC: **1542** 8741 1611 1791 Commercial & office building contractors; construction management; concrete construction: roads, highways, sidewalks, etc.; structural steel erection; concrete reinforcement, placing of; construction & civil engineering

(P-843)

TUTOR-SALIBA CORPORATION (HQ)
15901 Olden St, Sylmar (91342-1051)
PHONE..........................818 362-8391
Ronald N Tutor, *CEO*
Jack Frost, *COO*
John D Barrett, *Senior VP*
David L Randall, *Senior VP*
William B Sparks, *Senior VP*
▲ EMP: 100 EST: 2003
SQ FT: 20,000
SALES (est): 30MM
SALES (corp-wide): 5.3B **Publicly Held**
WEB: www.tutorperini.com
SIC: **1542** 1629 7353 1799 Commercial & office building, new construction; subway construction; cranes & aerial lift equipment, rental or leasing; rigging & scaffolding; subdividers & developers
PA: Tutor Perini Corporation
15901 Olden St
Sylmar CA 91342
818 362-8391

(P-844)

UNITED SEAL COATING SLURRYSEAL
3463 State St Ste 522, Santa Barbara (93105-2662)
PHONE..........................805 563-4922
Luis Rodriguez, *President*
Justin Rodriguez, *Treasurer*
Al Rodriguez, *Vice Pres*
Michelle Rodriguez, *Admin Sec*
EMP: 14 EST: 2000
SQ FT: 2,500
SALES (est): 1.6MM **Privately Held**
SIC: **1542** 1522 7363 2951 Commercial & office building, new construction; residential construction; truck driver services; asphalt paving mixtures & blocks

(P-845)

USS CAL BUILDERS INC
8031 Main St, Stanton (90680-2452)
PHONE..........................714 828-4882
Allen Othman, *CEO*
Jennifer Hotrum, *President*
Rabih El Zein, *Vice Pres*
Eric Othman, *Admin Sec*
Omar Abutaleb, *Project Mgr*
EMP: 135 EST: 1992
SALES (est): 57.5MM **Privately Held**
WEB: www.usscalbuilders.com
SIC: **1542** Specialized public building contractors

(P-846)

VANCREST CONSTRUCTION CORP
7171 N Figueroa St, Los Angeles (90042-1279)
PHONE..........................323 256-0011
John T Van Dyke, *President*
Jim Van Dyke, *Vice Pres*
Thomas Stefek, *Project Mgr*
Jeffrey Van Dyke, *Project Mgr*
EMP: 50 EST: 1988
SQ FT: 2,000
SALES (est): 11MM **Privately Held**
WEB: www.vancrestconstruction.com
SIC: **1542** Commercial & office buildings, renovation & repair

(P-847)

WE ONEIL CONSTRUCTION CO CAL
Also Called: W E O'Neil Construction
9485 Haven Ave Ste 101, Rancho Cucamonga (91730-5877)
PHONE..........................909 466-5300
John Finn, *Branch Mgr*
Timothy Addis, *Vice Pres*
Saundra Price, *Associate Dir*

Monica Martin, *Office Mgr*
Jennifer Worstell, *Executive Asst*
EMP: 87
SALES (corp-wide): 605.3MM **Privately Held**
SIC: **1542** 1541 1522 1521 Commercial & office building, new construction; industrial buildings & warehouses; residential construction; single-family houses
HQ: W.E. O'neil Construction Co Of California
909 N Pacific Coast Hwy # 400
El Segundo CA 90245
310 643-7900

(P-848)

WEBCOR CONSTRUCTION LP
Also Called: Webcor Builders
550 S Hope St Ste 2100, Los Angeles (90071-2625)
PHONE..........................213 239-2800
Leo Bandini, *Vice Pres*
Matt Reece, *CFO*
Kamran Azarbal, *Treasurer*
Rob Volpentest, *Vice Pres*
Hetty Chung, *Executive Asst*
EMP: 656 **Privately Held**
WEB: www.webcor.com
SIC: **1542** Commercial & office building, new construction
HQ: Webcor Construction L.P.
207 King St Ste 300
San Francisco CA 94107

(P-849)

WHITING-TURNER CONTRACTING CO
29209 Canwood St Ste 100, Agoura Hills (91301-1592)
PHONE..........................818 879-8100
Tavio Darchangelo, *Vice Pres*
Steven Gurske, *Project Mgr*
Jimmy Wooten, *Engineer*
Thomas Salazar, *Manager*
EMP: 106
SALES (corp-wide): 8.7B **Privately Held**
WEB: www.whiting-turner.com
SIC: **1542** Nonresidential construction
PA: The Whiting-Turner Contracting Company
300 E Joppa Rd Ste 800
Baltimore MD 21286
410 821-1100

(P-850)

WHITING-TURNER CONTRACTING CO
250 Commerce Ste 150, Irvine (92602-1345)
PHONE..........................949 863-0800
Len Cannatelli Jr, *Exec VP*
Sean Kaford, *Project Engr*
Frida Lohmann, *Project Engr*
James Byers, *Accountant*
Ben Franco, *Sr Project Mgr*
EMP: 106
SALES (corp-wide): 8.7B **Privately Held**
WEB: www.whiting-turner.com
SIC: **1542** 1541 Commercial & office building, new construction; industrial buildings & warehouses
PA: The Whiting-Turner Contracting Company
300 E Joppa Rd Ste 800
Baltimore MD 21286
410 821-1100

(P-851)

WM KLORMAN CONSTRUCTION CORP
23047 Ventura Blvd Fl 2, Woodland Hills (91364-1146)
PHONE..........................818 591-5969
William M Klorman, *President*
Doug Fowler, *Vice Pres*
Ida Chen, *VP Finance*
Alla Sandler, *Accountant*
Brett Thumm, *Foreman/Supr*
EMP: 65 EST: 1981
SQ FT: 4,000

SALES (est): 25.2MM **Privately Held**
WEB: www.klorman.com
SIC: **1542** 1521 Commercial & office building, new construction; new construction; single-family houses

1611 Highway & Street Construction

(P-852)

ADOPT-A-HIGHWAY MAINTENANCE
Also Called: Adopt-A-Beach
3158 Red Hill Ave Ste 200, Costa Mesa (92626-3416)
PHONE..........................800 200-0003
Peter Morin, *CEO*
Patricia Nelson, *President*
Dan Day, *CFO*
Dennis Day, *Admin Sec*
EMP: 104
SQ FT: 6,000
SALES (est): 21.1MM **Privately Held**
WEB: www.adoptahighway.com
SIC: **1611** 4959 Highway & street maintenance; sanitary services

(P-853)

ALL AMERICAN ASPHALT (PA)
Also Called: All American Agrigate
400 E 6th St, Corona (92879-1521)
P.O. Box 2229 (92878-2229)
PHONE..........................951 736-7600
Mark Albert Luer, *President*
Mark Luer, *President*
Thomas Toscas, *CFO*
Rudy Pitscheneder, *Principal*
Marissa Herrera, *Office Mgr*
EMP: 60 EST: 1969
SALES (est): 121.9MM **Privately Held**
WEB: www.allamericanasphalt.com
SIC: **1611** 5032 Highway & street paving contractor; brick, stone & related material

(P-854)

ALL AMERICAN ASPHALT
All American Service and Sup
1776 All American Way, Corona (92879-2070)
P.O. Box 2229 (92878-2229)
PHONE..........................951 736-7617
Kim McGuire, *Manager*
EMP: 72
SALES (corp-wide): 121.9MM **Privately Held**
WEB: www.allamericanasphalt.com
SIC: **1611** Highway & street paving contractor
PA: All American Asphalt
400 E 6th St
Corona CA 92879
951 736-7600

(P-855)

ALL AMERICAN ASPHALT
11549 Bradley Ave, San Fernando (91340-2519)
PHONE..........................818 361-6141
Judy Branaman, *Branch Mgr*
EMP: 72
SALES (corp-wide): 121.9MM **Privately Held**
WEB: www.allamericanasphalt.com
SIC: **1611** Highway & street paving contractor
PA: All American Asphalt
400 E 6th St
Corona CA 92879
951 736-7600

(P-856)

ALL AMERICAN ASPHALT
Camco Construction Supply
1776 All American Way, Corona (92879-2070)
PHONE..........................951 736-7617
Kim McGuire, *Branch Mgr*
EMP: 72
SALES (corp-wide): 121.9MM **Privately Held**
WEB: www.allamericanasphalt.com
SIC: **1611** Highway & street paving contractor

PRODUCTS & SVCS

PA: All American Asphalt
400 E 6th St
Corona CA 92879
951 736-7600

(P-857)
AMERICAN ASPHALT SOUTH INC
19792 El Rivino Rd, Riverside (92509-1851)
P.O. Box 310036, Fontana (92331-0036)
PHONE.....................909 427-8276
Alan Henderson, *President*
Jeff Petty, *Vice Pres*
Lyle Stone, *Admin Sec*
EMP: 76 **EST:** 2000
SALES (est): 19.9MM **Privately Held**
WEB: www.americanasphalt.com
SIC: 1611 Highway & street maintenance

(P-858)
AMG CONSTRUCTION GROUP
1103 W Gardena Blvd # 201, Gardena (90248-5239)
PHONE.....................800 310-2609
Calvin Jackson, *CEO*
EMP: 69 **EST:** 2016
SQ FT: 1,600
SALES (est): 3.8MM **Privately Held**
SIC: 1611 General contractor, highway & street construction

(P-859)
ASSOCIATED READY MIX CON INC
392 S Del Norte Blvd, Oxnard (93030-7914)
PHONE.....................805 485-4155
D Ruffin, *Branch Mgr*
EMP: 101 **Privately Held**
WEB: www.aareadymix.com
SIC: 5211 1611 Concrete & cinder block; concrete construction: roads, highways, sidewalks, etc.
PA: Associated Ready Mix Concrete, Inc.
4621 Teller Ave Ste 130
Newport Beach CA 92660

(P-860)
ATKINSON CONSTRUCTION INC
18201 Von Karman Ave # 800, Irvine (92612-1092)
PHONE.....................303 410-2540
John O'Keefe, *President*
Brandon Dully, *Vice Pres*
Gilbert Lizan, *Executive*
Megan Dunn, *Project Engr*
Brianne Canino, *Business Mgr*
EMP: 450 **EST:** 2004
SALES (est): 82.1MM
SALES (corp-wide): 1.6B **Privately Held**
WEB: www.atkn.com
SIC: 1611 1622 Highway & street construction; bridge, tunnel & elevated highway
HQ: Clark Construction Group, Llc
7500 Old Georgtwn Rd # 3
Bethesda MD 20814
301 272-8100

(P-861)
BEADOR CONSTRUCTION CO INC
26320 Lester Cir, Corona (92883-6399)
PHONE.....................951 674-7352
David A Beador, *President*
EMP: 80 **EST:** 1996
SQ FT: 1,415
SALES (est): 22.2MM **Privately Held**
SIC: 1611 General contractor, highway & street construction

(P-862)
BECHO INC
15901 Olden St, Sylmar (91342-1051)
PHONE.....................818 362-8391
Tim Smith, *President*
Louis Lucido, *President*
William B Sparks, *Treasurer*
Steve Pavoggi, *Vice Pres*
Jim Tripp, *Vice Pres*
▲ **EMP:** 60 **EST:** 1979
SQ FT: 8,000

SALES (est): 30.9MM
SALES (corp-wide): 5.3B **Publicly Held**
WEB: www.bechoinc.com
SIC: 1611 1622 1799 Highway & street paving contractor; bridge construction; shoring & underpinning work
PA: Tutor Perini Corporation
15901 Olden St
Sylmar CA 91342
818 362-8391

(P-863)
BENS ASPHALT & MAINT CO INC
Also Called: Medina Construction
2537 Rubidoux Blvd, Riverside (92509-2142)
PHONE.....................951 248-1103
EMP: 90 **Privately Held**
WEB: www.bensasphalt.com
SIC: 1611 Surfacing & paving
PA: Ben's Asphalt & Maintenance Company, Inc.
2200 S Yale St Ste A
Santa Ana CA 92704

(P-864)
BURTCH TRUCKING INC
Also Called: Burtch Construction
18815 Highway 65, Bakersfield (93308-9794)
P.O. Box 80546 (93380-0546)
PHONE.....................661 399-1736
Brenn Burtch McGowan, *President*
Linda Kay Burtch, *Principal*
Josh Rhoden, *Superintendent*
Marian Arandel, *Clerk*
EMP: 53 **EST:** 1979
SQ FT: 4,000
SALES (est): 11.4MM **Privately Held**
SIC: 1611 Highway & street paving contractor

(P-865)
CALIFORNIA DEPARTMENT TRNSP
Also Called: Caltrans Eastern Reg Rd Maint
1940 Workman Mill Rd, Whittier (90601-1414)
PHONE.....................562 692-0823
Edward Toledo, *Manager*
Alfonso Sanchez, *Manager*
EMP: 75 **Privately Held**
WEB: www.dot.ca.gov
SIC: 1611 9621 Highway & street maintenance; regulation, administration of transportation;
HQ: California, Department Of Transportation
1120 N St
Sacramento CA 95814

(P-866)
CALIFORNIA DEPARTMENT TRNSP
Also Called: Caltrans
2201 S Thornburg St, Santa Maria (93455-1241)
PHONE.....................805 922-1987
Brad Warren, *Manager*
EMP: 75 **Privately Held**
WEB: www.dot.ca.gov
SIC: 1611 9621 Highway & street maintenance; regulation, administration of transportation;
HQ: California, Department Of Transportation
1120 N St
Sacramento CA 95814

(P-867)
CALIFORNIA DEPARTMENT TRNSP
Also Called: Caltrans
640 N Main St, Templeton (93465-9010)
PHONE.....................805 434-1812
Tim Griffin, *Branch Mgr*
EMP: 75 **Privately Held**
WEB: www.dot.ca.gov
SIC: 1611 9621 Highway & street construction; regulation, administration of transportation;

HQ: California, Department Of Transportation
1120 N St
Sacramento CA 95814

(P-868)
CALIFORNIA DEPARTMENT TRNSP
1607 Adams Ave, El Centro (92243-1903)
PHONE.....................760 352-1129
Sal Gonzalez, *Manager*
EMP: 75 **Privately Held**
WEB: www.dot.ca.gov
SIC: 1611 9621 Highway & street maintenance; regulation, administration of transportation;
HQ: California, Department Of Transportation
1120 N St
Sacramento CA 95814

(P-869)
CALIFORNIA PAV GRADING CO INC
3253 Verdugo Rd, Los Angeles (90065-2035)
P.O. Box 65966 (90065-0966)
PHONE.....................323 372-5920
Foster Dennis, *President*
Lee Sepielli, *Corp Secy*
Jeff Macduffie, *Manager*
Kent Dennis, *Contractor*
EMP: 58
SQ FT: 1,600
SALES (est): 14.9MM **Privately Held**
WEB: www.calpave.com
SIC: 1611 Highway & street paving contractor

(P-870)
CHAPARRAL CONSTRUCTION CORP
2101 Ventura Blvd, Oxnard (93036-8951)
P.O. Box 4786, Ventura (93007-0786)
PHONE.....................805 647-8606
Jesse J Castillo, *President*
EMP: 51 **EST:** 1975
SALES (est): 2MM **Privately Held**
WEB: www.chaparralconst.com
SIC: 1611 General contractor, highway & street construction

(P-871)
CHARLES C REGAN INC
Also Called: Regan Paving
216 N Smith Ave, Corona (92878-3240)
PHONE.....................951 735-8100
Timothy G Regan, *CEO*
Marcie Melendez, *Office Mgr*
EMP: 68 **EST:** 1969
SQ FT: 4,000
SALES (est): 14MM **Privately Held**
WEB: www.reganpaving.com
SIC: 1611 Highway & street paving contractor

(P-872)
CHIEF TRNSP & ENGRG CONTRS INC
Also Called: Chief Engineering Co
4056 Tamarind Rdg, Lake Elsinore (92530-2041)
P.O. Box 677 (92531-0677)
PHONE.....................951 258-6607
Jose Aceituno Jr, *CEO*
EMP: 78 **EST:** 2002
SALES (est): 8MM **Privately Held**
SIC: 1611 Highway & street construction

(P-873)
CITY SERVICE CONTRACTING INC (PA)
Also Called: City Service Paving
920 Lawrence St, Placentia (92870-7031)
PHONE.....................714 632-6610
Mike Garvin, *CEO*
Jon Beach, *CFO*
George Puente, *Vice Pres*
EMP: 72 **EST:** 1975
SALES (est): 23MM **Privately Held**
WEB: www.asphaltandconcrete.com
SIC: 1611 Surfacing & paving

(P-874)
COMMERCIAL COATING COMPANY INC
Also Called: Commercial Paving
2809 W Avenue 37, Los Angeles (90065-3620)
P.O. Box 65557 (90065-0557)
PHONE.....................323 256-1331
Andrian Loera, *President*
William Emerson, *Treasurer*
EMP: 52 **EST:** 1983
SQ FT: 10,000
SALES (est): 13.2MM **Privately Held**
WEB: www.compav.com
SIC: 1611 Resurfacing contractor

(P-875)
DENNIS M MCCOY & SONS INC
32107 Lindero Canyon Rd # 212 Westlake Village (91361-4255)
PHONE.....................818 874-3872
Dennis McCoy, *CEO*
Morgan McCoy, *President*
Greg Abercrombie, *Controller*
EMP: 75 **EST:** 1994
SQ FT: 3,000
SALES (est): 12.9MM **Privately Held**
WEB: www.mccoyandsons.com
SIC: 1611 Grading

(P-876)
EBS GENERAL ENGINEERING INC
1345 Quarry St Ste 101, Corona (92879-1734)
PHONE.....................951 279-6869
Joseph Nanci, *President*
Tom Nanci, *Controller*
EMP: 90 **EST:** 1994
SQ FT: 4,000
SALES (est): 11.6MM **Privately Held**
WEB: www.mail.ebs-inc.us
SIC: 1611 Highway & street construction

(P-877)
EMERALD ACQUISITION LLC
Also Called: Emerald Paving Company
6381 Industry Way, Westminster (92683-3693)
PHONE.....................714 891-8752
Derek M Davis, *President*
Erinn Steingold, *CFO*
Mike Clarke, *Exec VP*
Marc Mone, *Project Mgr*
EMP: 92 **EST:** 2006
SQ FT: 20,000
SALES (est): 12.7MM **Privately Held**
WEB: www.empave.com
SIC: 1611 Surfacing & paving
PA: M A C Contracting Corp.
6301 W Sunrise Blvd
Plantation FL 33313

(P-878)
FEC FTURE CONTRS ENGINEERS INC
184 Technology Dr Ste 205, Irvine (92618-2435)
PHONE.....................949 328-9758
Sam Katbi, *CEO*
EMP: 60 **EST:** 2010
SALES (est): 8.5MM **Privately Held**
SIC: 1611 1531 1542 1522 General contractor, highway & street construction; ; commercial & office building, new construction; residential construction

(P-879)
FOOTHILL / ESTRN TRNSP CRRDOR
125 Pacifica Ste 100, Irvine (92618-3324)
PHONE.....................949 754-3400
Michael Kraman, *CEO*
Amy Potter, *CFO*
EMP: 70 **EST:** 1986
SQ FT: 10,000
SALES: 209.3MM **Privately Held**
WEB: www.thetollroads.com
SIC: 1611 General contractor, highway & street construction

▲ = Import ▼=Export
◆ =Import/Export

(P-880)
GCI CONSTRUCTION INC
1031 Calle Recodo Ste D, San Clemente (92673-6269)
PHONE....................................714 957-0233
Terry Gillespie, *President*
Floyd Bennett, *Treasurer*
Richard Tirrell, *Vice Pres*
EMP: 50 EST: 1984
SQ FT: 3,000
SALES (est): 8.9MM **Privately Held**
WEB: www.gciconstructioninc.com
SIC: 1611 Highway & street construction

(P-881)
GRANITE CONSTRUCTION COMPANY
Also Called: Southern California Regional
38000 Monroe St, Indio (92203-9500)
PHONE....................................760 775-7500
Jay McQuillen, *Manager*
EMP: 393 **Publicly Held**
WEB: www.graniteconstruction.com
SIC: 1611 1771 General contractor, high-way & street construction; concrete work
HQ: Granite Construction Company
  585 W Beach St
  Watsonville CA 95076
  831 724-1011

(P-882)
GRANITE CONSTRUCTION COMPANY
5335 Debbie Rd, Santa Barbara (93111-2001)
P.O. Box 6744 (93160-6744)
PHONE....................................805 964-9951
Bruce McGowan, *Manager*
Jacob Kockrow, *Project Engr*
Brian Larninan, *Human Res Dir*
Quan-Handley Patty, *Manager*
EMP: 169
SQ FT: 65,396 **Publicly Held**
WEB: www.graniteconstruction.com
SIC: 1611 General contractor, highway & street construction
HQ: Granite Construction Company
  585 W Beach St
  Watsonville CA 95076
  831 724-1011

(P-883)
GRIFFITH COMPANY (PA)
3050 E Birch St, Brea (92821-6248)
PHONE....................................714 984-5500
Jamie Angus, *President*
Thomas L Foss, *Ch of Bd*
Jim Waltze, *Ch of Bd*
Jaimie Angus, *President*
Steve Ruelas, *Officer*
EMP: 60 EST: 1922
SQ FT: 100,000
SALES (est): 129.7MM **Privately Held**
WEB: www.griffithcompany.net
SIC: 1611 General contractor, highway & street construction
PA: Griffith Company
  3050 E Birch St
  Brea CA 92821
  714 984-5500

(P-884)
GRIFFITH COMPANY
1128 Carrier Parkway Ave, Bakersfield (93308-9666)
P.O. Box 70157 (93387-0157)
PHONE....................................661 392-6640
Rus Grigg, *Manager*
Walter Weishaar, *Vice Pres*
Barbara Newton, *Accountant*
Joe Archuleta, *Superintendent*
Mandy Smith, *Clerk*
EMP: 317
SALES (corp-wide): 129.7MM **Privately Held**
WEB: www.griffithcompany.net
SIC: 1611 General contractor, highway & street construction
PA: Griffith Company
  3050 E Birch St
  Brea CA 92821
  714 984-5500

(P-885)
GRIFFITH COMPANY
12200 Bloomfield Ave, Santa Fe Springs (90670-4742)
PHONE....................................562 929-1128
Dan Magrew, *Manager*

Luke Walker, *Vice Pres*
Dan McGrew, *VP Bus Dvlpt*
Mark Davenport, *Division Mgr*
Tracey Novak, *Administration*
EMP: 60
SQ FT: 4,036
SALES (corp-wide): 129.7MM **Privately Held**
WEB: www.griffithcompany.net
SIC: 1611 1622 General contractor, high-way & street construction; bridge con-struction; tunnel construction
PA: Griffith Company
  3050 E Birch St
  Brea CA 92821
  714 984-5500

(P-886)
HARDY & HARPER INC
32 Rancho Cir, Lake Forest (92630-8325)
PHONE....................................714 444-1851
Daniel Thomas Maas, *CEO*
Fred T Maas Sr, *Director*
EMP: 50 EST: 1946
SALES (est): 14MM **Privately Held**
WEB: www.hardyandharper.com
SIC: 1611 2951 Surfacing & paving; as-phalt paving mixtures & blocks

(P-887)
HILLCREST CONTRACTING INC
1467 Circle City Dr, Corona (92879-1668)
P.O. Box 1898 (92878-1898)
PHONE....................................951 273-9600
Glenn J Salsbury, *President*
E G Lindholm, *Vice Pres*
James Wong, *Vice Pres*
Darcy Searle, *Project Mgr*
Theresa Stout, *Human Res Dir*
EMP: 75 EST: 1984
SQ FT: 11,600
SALES (est): 20.5MM **Privately Held**
WEB: www.hillcrestcontracting.com
SIC: 1611 General contractor, highway & street construction

(P-888)
INTERNATIONAL PAVING SVCS INC
Also Called: I P S
1199 Opal Ave, Mentone (92359-1284)
P.O. Box 10458, San Bernardino (92423-0458)
PHONE....................................909 794-2101
Brent Rieger, *President*
EMP: 80 EST: 2007
SALES (est): 11.5MM **Privately Held**
WEB: www.ipspaving.com
SIC: 1611 Surfacing & paving

(P-889)
INTERNTNAL PVMENT SLUTIONS INC
1209 Van Buren St Ste 3, Thermal (92274-8800)
P.O. Box 10458, San Bernardino (92423-0458)
PHONE....................................909 794-2101
Brent Rieger, *President*
Dennis Rieger, *Treasurer*
EMP: 50 EST: 1996
SQ FT: 3,000
SALES (est): 12.6MM **Privately Held**
WEB: www.ipspaving.com
SIC: 1611 Surfacing & paving

(P-890)
JACOBSSON ENGRG CNSTR INC
72310 Varner Rd, Thousand Palms (92276-3362)
P.O. Box 14430, Palm Desert (92255-4430)
PHONE....................................760 345-8700
Dan Jacobsson, *President*
Ingeborg Jacobsson, *Treasurer*
EMP: 75 EST: 1991
SQ FT: 9,000
SALES (est): 12.7MM **Privately Held**
WEB: www.jacobssoninc.com
SIC: 1611 Highway & street construction

(P-891)
JAMES MCMINN INC
21834 Cactus Ave, Riverside (92518-3005)
PHONE....................................909 514-1231
Jim McMinn, *President*
Rick Monge, *Vice Pres*
Keith Archibek, *Project Mgr*
Michelle Spence, *Controller*
Trevor Norton, *Foreman/Supr*
EMP: 50 EST: 2005
SALES (est): 8.1MM **Privately Held**
WEB: www.jamesmcminninc.com
SIC: 1611 Grading

(P-892)
JB BOSTICK COMPANY INC (PA)
2870 E La Cresta Ave, Anaheim (92806-1816)
PHONE....................................714 238-2121
James B Bostick, *President*
Jerry Hamlin, *Vice Pres*
EMP: 75 EST: 1964
SQ FT: 2,870
SALES (est): 27.6MM **Privately Held**
WEB: www.jbbostick.com
SIC: 1611 1771 Grading; concrete work

(P-893)
JJ FISHER CONSTRUCTION INC
261 W Dana St Ste 100, Nipomo (93444-9151)
P.O. Box 2219 (93444-2219)
PHONE....................................805 723-5220
Jayson Fisher, *CEO*
Mark Sczbecki, *CFO*
EMP: 65 EST: 2010
SALES (est): 12MM **Privately Held**
SIC: 1611 1771 1794 1761 Gravel or dirt road construction; concrete work; curb construction; blacktop (asphalt) work; ex-cavation work; gutter & downspout con-tractor

(P-894)
KEC ENGINEERING
200 N Sherman Ave, Corona (92882-7162)
P.O. Box 909 (92878-0909)
PHONE....................................951 734-3010
James Elfring, *President*
Les Card, *Vice Pres*
Jim Burton, *Exec Dir*
Brandon Card, *Project Engr*
Jon White, *Project Engr*
EMP: 110 EST: 1953
SQ FT: 9,600
SALES (est): 16.9MM **Privately Held**
WEB: www.kecengineering.com
SIC: 1611 General contractor, highway & street construction

(P-895)
KIEWIT INFRASTRUCTURE WEST CO
10704 Shoemaker Ave, Santa Fe Springs (90670-4040)
PHONE....................................562 946-1816
Ken Riley, *Manager*
David Linderman, *Project Mgr*
EMP: 125
SQ FT: 12,514
SALES (corp-wide): 10.2B **Privately Held**
WEB: www.kiewit.com
SIC: 1611 1542 1541 General contractor, highway & street construction; nonresi-dential construction; industrial buildings & warehouses
HQ: Kiewit Infrastructure West Co.
  3555 Farnam St
  Omaha NE 68131
  402 342-2052

(P-896)
LAIRD CONSTRUCTION CO INC
9460 Lucas Ranch Rd, Rancho Cuca-monga (91730-5743)
PHONE....................................909 989-5595
James R Laird, *President*
Ben Schonseld, *CFO*
Sarah B Laird, *Treasurer*
Ralph J Laird, *Vice Pres*
Jerold B Laird, *Admin Sec*
EMP: 65 EST: 1946
SQ FT: 5,000

SALES (est): 5.8MM **Privately Held**
WEB: www.lairdconstruction.com
SIC: 1611 1794 Highway & street paving contractor; excavation work

(P-897)
LARRY JACINTO CONSTRUCTION INC
9555 N Wabash Ave, Redlands (92374-2714)
P.O. Box 615, Mentone (92359-0615)
PHONE....................................909 794-2151
Larry Frankland Jacinto, *CEO*
Eric Nixon, *Exec VP*
Gerry Punongbayan, *Assistant*
Scott Smith, *Superintendent*
Doug Straw, *Superintendent*
EMP: 80 EST: 1971
SQ FT: 8,500
SALES (est): 22.2MM **Privately Held**
WEB: www.larryjacintoconstruction.com
SIC: 1611 Grading; highway & street paving contractor; sidewalk construction

(P-898)
MACRO-Z-TECHNOLOGY COMPANY (PA)
Also Called: M Z T
841 E Washington Ave, Santa Ana (92701-3878)
PHONE....................................714 564-1130
Bryan J Zatica, *CEO*
Jackie Bach, *Marketing Staff*
Ben Smith, *Superintendent*
EMP: 97 EST: 1989
SQ FT: 3,000
SALES (est): 31.3MM **Privately Held**
WEB: www.mztco.com
SIC: 1611 1542 8711 Concrete construc-tion: roads, highways, sidewalks, etc.; commercial & office building contractors; engineering services

(P-899)
MAMCO INC (PA)
Also Called: Alabbasi
764 Ramona Expy Ste C, Perris (92571-9716)
PHONE....................................951 776-9300
Marwan Alabbasi, *CEO*
Elizabeth Alabbasi, *President*
Rumzi Alabbasi, *Vice Pres*
EMP: 117 EST: 2002
SQ FT: 2,200
SALES (est): 33.6MM **Privately Held**
SIC: 1611 General contractor, highway & street construction

(P-900)
MANHOLE ADJUSTING INC
9500 Beverly Rd, Pico Rivera (90660-2135)
PHONE....................................323 725-1387
John Corcoran, *President*
Maria E Corcoran, *Vice Pres*
Aung Win, *General Mgr*
Abel Ruiz-Gonzalez, *Sales Executive*
EMP: 50 EST: 1978
SALES (est): 10.8MM **Privately Held**
WEB: www.manholeadjusting.com
SIC: 1611 General contractor, highway & street construction; highway & street paving contractor

(P-901)
MATICH CORPORATION (PA)
1596 E Harry Shepard Blvd, San Bernardino (92408-0197)
P.O. Box 10, Highland (92346-1010)
PHONE....................................909 382-7400
Stephen A Matich, *CEO*
Martin A Matich, *Chairman*
Randall Valadez, *Treasurer*
Patrick A Matich, *Exec VP*
Robert M Matich, *Exec VP*
EMP: 60 EST: 1918
SQ FT: 10,000
SALES (est): 42MM **Privately Held**
WEB: www.matichcorp.com
SIC: 1611 2951 General contractor, high-way & street construction; asphalt paving mixtures & blocks

PRODUCTS & SVCS

(P-902)
MC LAUGHLIN ENGRG & MIN INC (PA)
27636 Ynez Rd Ste L7, Temecula (92591-4645)
PHONE..................951 699-7957
Jerry Dalrymple, *President*
EMP: 54 **EST:** 1992
SQ FT: 3,500
SALES (est): 7MM **Privately Held**
SIC: **1611** 8711 Grading; mining engineer

(P-903)
NATIONAL PAVING COMPANY INC
4361 Fort Dr, Riverside (92509-6784)
P.O. Box 3649 (92519-3649)
PHONE..................951 369-1332
Richard J Lindholm, *President*
Lawrence Spicher, *CFO*
Allen Warthan, *Manager*
EMP: 78 **EST:** 1986
SQ FT: 4,000
SALES (est): 15.5MM **Privately Held**
WEB: www.nationalpaving.com
SIC: **1611** Highway & street paving contractor; surfacing & paving

(P-904)
ORTIZ ENTERPRISES INCORPORATED (PA)
6 Cushing Ste 200, Irvine (92618-4230)
PHONE..................949 753-1414
Patrick Ortiz, *President*
Jill Ortiz, *Vice Pres*
Cary B Purves, *Vice Pres*
Dave Byrnes, *CPA*
Eddie Hurtado, *Purchasing*
EMP: 79 **EST:** 1984
SQ FT: 12,000
SALES (est): 31.5MM **Privately Held**
WEB: www.ortizent.com
SIC: **1611** General contractor, highway & street construction

(P-905)
PALP INC
Also Called: Excel Paving Co
2230 Lemon Ave, Long Beach (90806-5124)
P.O. Box 16405 (90806-0995)
PHONE..................562 599-5841
Curtis P Brown, *CEO*
George McRae, *Senior VP*
Bruce Flatt, *Vice Pres*
Michelle Drakulich, *Admin Sec*
Ken Corry, *Project Mgr*
EMP: 225 **EST:** 1976
SQ FT: 11,000
SALES (est): 105.1MM **Privately Held**
WEB: www.excelpavingcompany.com
SIC: **1611** 8711 Highway & street paving contractor; grading; engineering services

(P-906)
PAVEMENT COATINGS CO (PA)
10240 San Sevaine Way, Jurupa Valley (91752-1100)
PHONE..................714 826-3011
Douglas Max Ford, *CEO*
Van Duncan, *CFO*
Marco Estrada, *Director*
Van Paul Duncan, *Manager*
Barry Short, *Superintendent*
EMP: 145 **EST:** 1974
SALES (est): 17.2MM **Privately Held**
WEB: www.pavementrecycling.com
SIC: **1611** Highway & street paving contractor

(P-907)
PENA GRADING & DEMOLITION INC
Also Called: Pena Trucking
11253 Vinedale St, Sun Valley (91352-3217)
PHONE..................818 768-5202
Orestes Pena, *President*
Irma Pena, *Vice Pres*
Fernando Fuentes, *Manager*
Walter Marucci, *Manager*
Dagmara Pawelczyk, *Manager*
EMP: 50 **EST:** 1974
SQ FT: 8,000

SALES (est): 9.3MM **Privately Held**
WEB: www.penaweb.com
SIC: **1611** 4953 1795 1794 Grading; recycling; waste materials; wrecking & demolition work; demolition, buildings & other structures; excavation work; excavation & grading, building construction

(P-908)
POWERTEC COMPANY INC
5150 E La Palma Ave # 209, Anaheim (92807-2095)
P.O. Box 7296, Riverside (92513-7296)
PHONE..................951 332-1198
Jesus Murguia Adame, *President*
Hector Hernandez, *CFO*
Michael Castillo, *Vice Pres*
Camerino Lauriano, *Admin Sec*
EMP: 65 **EST:** 2017
SALES (est): 12MM **Privately Held**
SIC: **1611** 8748 8741 General contractor, highway & street construction; telecommunications consultant; office management

(P-909)
RICK HAMM CONSTRUCTION INC
201 W Carleton Ave, Orange (92867-3607)
PHONE..................714 532-0815
Rick Hamm, *President*
Llana Hamm, *Corp Secy*
EMP: 90 **EST:** 1977
SQ FT: 25,000
SALES (est): 19.4MM **Privately Held**
WEB: www.rickhamm.com
SIC: **1611** 1771 1791 1741 General contractor, highway & street construction; patio construction, concrete; precast concrete structural framing or panels, placing of; masonry & other stonework; erection & dismantling of forms for poured concrete

(P-910)
RJ NOBLE COMPANY (PA)
15505 E Lincoln Ave, Orange (92865-1015)
P.O. Box 620 (92856-9020)
PHONE..................714 637-1550
Michael J Carver, *President*
James N Ducote, *CFO*
James Ducote, *CFO*
Brenda Carver, *Vice Pres*
Craig Porter, *Vice Pres*
EMP: 144 **EST:** 1950
SQ FT: 5,500
SALES (est): 60.7MM **Privately Held**
WEB: www.rjnoblecompany.com
SIC: **1611** Highway & street paving contractor

(P-911)
S & S PAVING INC
23875 Ventura Blvd # 202, Calabasas (91302-1491)
PHONE..................818 591-0668
Jose Hurtado, *President*
Jan Pick, *Treasurer*
James Varga, *Vice Pres*
Virginia Martinez, *Admin Sec*
Luke Weiss, *Director*
EMP: 72 **EST:** 1971
SQ FT: 1,600
SALES (est): 13.6MM **Privately Held**
WEB: www.sspavinginc.com
SIC: **1611** 2951 1629 Grading; asphalt paving mixtures & blocks; land leveling

(P-912)
SAN JQUIN HLLS TRNSP CRRDOR AG (PA)
Also Called: JOINT POWERS AGENCY
125 Pacifica Ste 100, Irvine (92618-3324)
P.O. Box 53770 (92619-3770)
PHONE..................949 754-3400
Michael Kraman, *CEO*
EMP: 70 **EST:** 1986
SQ FT: 17,000
SALES (est): 198.9MM **Privately Held**
WEB: www.thetollroads.com
SIC: **1611** General contractor, highway & street construction

(P-913)
SECURITY PAVING COMPANY INC (PA)
Also Called: Valley Base Materials
3075 Townsgate Rd Ste 210, Westlake Village (91361-3223)
PHONE..................818 362-9200
Mike Mattivi, *CEO*
Albert Mattivi, *President*
Brian Algren, *Vice Pres*
Joseph Ferndino, *Vice Pres*
Thomas J Mattivi, *Vice Pres*
EMP: 99 **EST:** 1947
SALES (est): 61.4MM **Privately Held**
WEB: www.securitypaving.com
SIC: **1611** Highway & street paving contractor

(P-914)
SEQUEL CONTRACTORS INC
13546 Imperial Hwy, Santa Fe Springs (90670-4821)
PHONE..................562 802-7227
Thomas S Pack, *CEO*
Abel Magellanes, *Vice Pres*
EMP: 50 **EST:** 1990
SQ FT: 80,000
SALES (est): 14.3MM **Privately Held**
SIC: **1611** Highway & street construction

(P-915)
SIALIC CONTRACTORS CORPORATION
Also Called: Shawnan
12240 Woodruff Ave, Downey (90241-5608)
PHONE..................562 803-9977
Shawn Smith, *President*
John Smith, *Admin Sec*
EMP: 68 **EST:** 1993
SQ FT: 24,000
SALES (est): 7.4MM **Privately Held**
SIC: **1611** General contractor, highway & street construction

(P-916)
SKANSKA USA CVIL W CAL DST INC (DH)
1995 Agua Mansa Rd, Riverside (92509-2405)
PHONE..................951 684-5360
Richard Cavallero, *CEO*
Michael Cobelli, *COO*
Joseph Nogues, *CFO*
Michael Aparicio, *Exec VP*
Lisa Picard, *Exec VP*
EMP: 700 **EST:** 1919
SQ FT: 15,000
SALES (est): 457.9MM
SALES (corp-wide): 18.5B **Privately Held**
SIC: **1611** 1622 1629 8711 General contractor, highway & street construction; bridge construction; highway construction, elevated; dam construction; engineering services; asphalt paving mixtures & blocks
HQ: Skanska Usa Civil Inc.
    7520 Astoria Blvd Ste 200
    East Elmhurst NY 11370
    718 340-0777

(P-917)
SOUTHWEST CON STRUCTURES INC
124 River Rd, Corona (92878-5834)
PHONE..................951 278-0377
James Hill, *President*
Holly Yowell, *Officer*
EMP: 55 **EST:** 2009
SQ FT: 3,000
SALES (est): 5.2MM **Privately Held**
WEB: www.southwestconcrete.net
SIC: **1611** Concrete construction: roads, highways, sidewalks, etc.

(P-918)
SULLY-MILLER CONTRACTING CO (DH)
Also Called: Blue Diamond Materials
135 S State College Blvd # 400, Brea (92821-5819)
PHONE..................714 578-9600
John Harrington, *President*
Christian Ransinangue, *CFO*
Jon Layne, *Chief Mktg Ofcr*

Matt Mallory, *Officer*
Michael Oremen, *Officer*
EMP: 399 **EST:** 1997
SALES (est): 210.3MM
SALES (corp-wide): 271.8MM **Privately Held**
WEB: www.sully-miller.com
SIC: **1611** Highway & street paving contractor

(P-919)
SULLY-MILLER HOLDING CORP
135 S State College Blvd # 400, Brea (92821-5819)
PHONE..................714 578-9600
George W Sully, *Principal*
Jeremiah Brooks, *Project Mgr*
Ken Barker, *Manager*
Anthony Lino, *Manager*
Andy Probert, *Superintendent*
EMP: 63
SALES (est): 3.7MM
SALES (corp-wide): 271.8MM **Privately Held**
WEB: www.sully-miller.com
SIC: **1611** Highway & street paving contractor
HQ: Colas Inc.
    73 Headquarters Plz 10t
    Morristown NJ 07960

(P-920)
SUPERIOR PAVING COMPANY INC
Also Called: United Paving Company
1880 N Delilah St, Corona (92879-1892)
PHONE..................951 739-9200
Sabas Trujillo, *CEO*
Steven Fitzpatrick, *Vice Pres*
Alejandra Garcia, *Admin Asst*
Biridiana Arevalo, *Hum Res Coord*
Analue Barcenas, *Production*
EMP: 85 **EST:** 2008
SQ FT: 3,000
SALES (est): 22.7MM **Privately Held**
WEB: www.united-paving.com
SIC: **1611** Highway & street paving contractor

(P-921)
SYSTEMS PAVING INC (PA)
1570 Brookhollow Dr, Santa Ana (92705-5438)
PHONE..................949 263-8301
Larry Green, *CEO*
Douglas Lueck, *President*
Syed Zaidi, *COO*
Scott Neamand, *CFO*
Joshua Erlich, *Vice Pres*
EMP: 61 **EST:** 1992
SQ FT: 13,000
SALES (est): 40.8MM **Privately Held**
WEB: www.systempavers.com
SIC: **1611** Surfacing & paving

(P-922)
TBS CONTRACTING INC
13602 Milton Ave, Westminster (92683-2914)
P.O. Box 1284 (92684-1284)
PHONE..................714 894-2206
Thomas Bruce Schaefer, *President*
EMP: 57 **EST:** 1974
SQ FT: 1,000
SALES (est): 5.6MM **Privately Held**
SIC: **1611** Highway & street paving contractor

(P-923)
TORO ENTERPRISES INC
2101 Ventura Blvd, Oxnard (93036-8951)
P.O. Box 6285 (93031-6285)
PHONE..................805 483-4515
Sean Castillo, *President*
Buffy Castillo, *Shareholder*
Teresa Ortega, *Shareholder*
Reuben Ortega, *Vice Pres*
Monica Ramirez, *Accountant*
EMP: 67 **EST:** 1994
SALES (est): 28.7MM **Privately Held**
WEB: www.toroenterprises.com
SIC: **1611** Concrete construction: roads, highways, sidewalks, etc.

(P-924)
TURMAN CONSTRUCTION CO INC
4301 Park Circle Dr, Bakersfield (93309-4004)
PHONE..................................661 831-0905
Jeff S Turman, *President*
Jo Ann Turman, *Admin Sec*
EMP: 58 EST: 1964
SQ FT: 3,000
SALES (est): 7.2MM **Privately Held**
WEB: www.turmanconstruction.com
SIC: 1611 1629 Grading; earthmoving contractor

(P-925)
UNIVERSAL ASPHALT CO INC
10610 Painter Ave, Santa Fe Springs (90670-4091)
P.O. Box 2548 (90670-0548)
PHONE..................................562 941-0201
Daniel M Houck, *President*
Richard Houck, *Project Mgr*
EMP: 50 EST: 1965
SQ FT: 22,000
SALES (est): 10.2MM **Privately Held**
WEB: www.universalasphalt.com
SIC: 1611 Highway & street paving contractor

(P-926)
VANCE CORPORATION
Also Called: General Engineering Contractor
17761 Slover Ave, Bloomington (92316-2330)
PHONE..................................909 355-4333
Derek Ritarita, *CEO*
Robert Erautt, *CFO*
Christian Peacock, *Admin Sec*
EMP: 50 EST: 1981
SQ FT: 10,000
SALES (est): 10.5MM **Privately Held**
WEB: www.vancecorp.net
SIC: 1611 General contractor, highway & street construction

1622 Bridge, Tunnel & Elevated Hwy Construction

(P-927)
FLATIRON WEST INC
16341 Chino Corona Rd, Chino (91708-9233)
PHONE..................................909 597-8413
Thomas J Rademacher, *Ch of Bd*
EMP: 160
SALES (corp-wide): 1B **Privately Held**
WEB: www.flatironcorp.com
SIC: 1622 1611 Bridge construction; highway & street construction
HQ: Flatiron West, Inc.
16470 W Bernardo Dr 120
San Diego CA 92127
-

(P-928)
FLUOR DANIEL CONSTRUCTION CO (DH)
3 Polaris Way, Aliso Viejo (92656-5338)
PHONE..................................949 349-2000
Paul Buckham, *President*
EMP: 500 EST: 1953
SALES: 129.9MM
SALES (corp-wide): 15.6B **Publicly Held**
WEB: www.fluor.com
SIC: 1622 Bridge, tunnel & elevated highway
HQ: Fluor Enterprises, Inc.
6700 Las Colinas Blvd
Irving TX 75039
469 398-7000

(P-929)
MCM CONSTRUCTION INC
19010 Slover Ave, Bloomington (92316-2459)
PHONE..................................909 875-0533
Nella Flores, *Branch Mgr*
Vernon Paine, *Project Mgr*
EMP: 121

SALES (corp-wide): 75.6MM **Privately Held**
WEB: www.mcmconstructioninc.com
SIC: 1622 Bridge construction
PA: M.C.M. Construction, Inc.
6413 32nd St
North Highlands CA 95660
916 334-1221

(P-930)
OC 405 PARTNERS JOINT VENTURE
3100 W Lake Center Dr # 200, Santa Ana (92704-6917)
PHONE..................................858 251-2200
Ashok Patel,
EMP: 75 EST: 2016
SQ FT: 69,000
SALES (est): 35.8MM
SALES (corp-wide): 711.8MM **Privately Held**
WEB: www.oc405partners.com
HQ: Ohla Usa, Inc.
2615 Ulmer St
Flushing NY 11354
-

1623 Water, Sewer & Utility Line Construction

(P-931)
A & H COMMUNICATIONS INC
15 Chrysler, Irvine (92618-2009)
PHONE..................................949 250-4555
Brian Elliott, *President*
Brett Howard, *Vice Pres*
Kevin Okumura, *Division Mgr*
Ryan Benda, *Project Mgr*
Jack Banuelos, *Purch Mgr*
EMP: 250 EST: 2000
SALES (est): 43.9MM **Privately Held**
WEB: www.aandh.com
SIC: 1623 Cable laying construction

(P-932)
ADVANCED CABLE TECHNOLOGIES
13400 Saticoy St Ste 30, North Hollywood (91605-7615)
PHONE..................................818 262-6484
Yader V Gomez, *President*
Josh Neaf, *Vice Pres*
EMP: 50 EST: 2006
SALES (est): 3.9MM **Privately Held**
WEB: www.advancedcabletechnologies.com
SIC: 1623 Cable laying construction

(P-933)
ARB INC (HQ)
26000 Commercentre Dr, Lake Forest (92630-8816)
PHONE..................................949 598-9242
Tom McCormick, *CEO*
Scott Summers, *President*
John P Schauerman, *Treasurer*
Greg Dahl, *Vice Pres*
Timothy Healy, *Vice Pres*
▲ EMP: 140 EST: 1960
SALES (est): 743.4MM **Publicly Held**
WEB: www.primoriscorp.com
SIC: 1623 1629 Oil & gas line & compressor station construction; industrial plant construction; waste disposal plant construction; waste water & sewage treatment plant construction

(P-934)
ARIZONA PIPELINE COMPANY (PA)
17372 Lilac St, Hesperia (92345-5162)
P.O. Box 401865 (92340-1865)
PHONE..................................760 244-8212
Lowell Duane Moyers, *Chairman*
Nina Moyers, *CEO*
Steve Lords, *CFO*
Tom Seals, *Corp Secy*
Steven Lords, *Officer*
EMP: 400 EST: 1979
SQ FT: 5,000

SALES: 173.7MM **Privately Held**
WEB: www.arizonapipeline.com
SIC: 1623 Pipeline construction

(P-935)
ARIZONA PIPELINE COMPANY
1745 Sampson Ave, Corona (92879-1864)
PHONE..................................951 270-3100
John Guzlow, *Vice Pres*
Bill Burris, *Division Mgr*
Ken Hertel, *Maintence Staff*
Steve Dilday, *Manager*
Shane Fox, *Superintendent*
EMP: 200
SALES (corp-wide): 173.7MM **Privately Held**
WEB: www.arizonapipeline.com
SIC: 1623 8711 Underground utilities contractor; engineering services
PA: Arizona Pipeline Company
17372 Lilac St
Hesperia CA 92345
760 244-8212

(P-936)
BALI CONSTRUCTION INC
9852 Joe Vargas Way, South El Monte (91733-3108)
PHONE..................................626 442-8003
Ted Polich, *President*
Michael E Brooks, *CEO*
Tom Bensfield, *Division Mgr*
Chris Fowler, *Project Mgr*
Laven Lee, *Purchasing*
EMP: 100 EST: 1987
SQ FT: 7,000
SALES (est): 34MM **Privately Held**
WEB: www.baliconstruction.com
SIC: 1623 Underground utilities contractor

(P-937)
BLOIS CONSTRUCTION INC
3201 Sturgis Rd, Oxnard (93030-8931)
P.O. Box 672 (93032-0672)
PHONE..................................805 485-0011
James B Blois, *President*
Dan Moore, *COO*
Steve Woodworth, *CFO*
Dan Schultz, *Vice Pres*
Cesar Hernandez, *Project Mgr*
EMP: 150
SQ FT: 10,000
SALES (est): 19.8MM **Privately Held**
WEB: www.bloisconstruction.com
SIC: 1623 Underground utilities contractor

(P-938)
BOUDREAU PIPELINE CORPORATION
463 N Smith Ave, Corona (92878-4305)
PHONE..................................951 493-6780
Alan J Boudreau, *CEO*
Ron Jacobson, *CFO*
Christie Boudreau, *Vice Pres*
Jonathan Hoang, *Admin Asst*
Juana Velasquez, *Administration*
EMP: 300 EST: 2000
SQ FT: 14,000
SALES (est): 66.8MM **Privately Held**
WEB: www.boudreaupipeline.com
SIC: 1623 Pipeline construction

(P-939)
C P CONSTRUCTION CO INC
105 N Loma Pl, Upland (91786-5620)
P.O. Box 1206, Ontario (91762-0206)
PHONE..................................909 981-1091
Charles Pfister Jr, *President*
Charles Michael Pfister, *Corp Secy*
Mark E Pfister, *Vice Pres*
Russel Pfister, *Vice Pres*
EMP: 50 EST: 1965
SQ FT: 4,000
SALES (est): 13MM **Privately Held**
WEB: www.cpconst.com
SIC: 1623 Sewer line construction; pipeline construction

(P-940)
CA STATION MANAGEMENT INC
3200 E Guasti Rd Ste 100, Ontario (91761-8661)
PHONE..................................909 245-6251
Taqi Chaudry, *CEO*
EMP: 250 EST: 2016

SALES (est): 32.7MM **Privately Held**
SIC: 1623 7389 8082 Underground utilities contractor; telephone answering service; home health care services

(P-941)
CITY HANFORD PUBLIC IMPRV CORP
900 S 10th Ave, Hanford (93230-5234)
PHONE..................................559 585-2550
Gary Misenhimer, *Branch Mgr*
EMP: 58
SALES (corp-wide): 17.2MM **Privately Held**
WEB: www.ci.hanford.ca.us
SIC: 1623 9199 Water, sewer & utility lines;
PA: City Of Hanford
315 N Douty St 321
Hanford CA 93230
559 585-2515

(P-942)
CITY OF FOUNTAIN VALLEY
10200 Slater Ave, Fountain Valley (92708-4736)
PHONE..................................714 593-4441
Mark Lewis, *Director*
EMP: 50
SALES (corp-wide): 67MM **Privately Held**
WEB: www.fountainvalley.org
SIC: 1623 Water, sewer & utility lines
PA: City Of Fountain Valley
10200 Slater Ave
Fountain Valley CA 92708
714 593-4410

(P-943)
CMAC CONSTRUCTION COMPANY
Also Called: Cmac Cnstr Refinery & Pipeline
1450 Santa Fe Ave, Long Beach (90813-1248)
PHONE..................................562 435-5611
Michael L Mc Fadden, *CEO*
EMP: 55
SQ FT: 3,000
SALES: 9.3MM **Privately Held**
WEB: www.cmac.us
SIC: 1623 Pipeline construction

(P-944)
COLICH SONS
Also Called: Colich & Sons
547 W 140th St, Gardena (90248-1589)
PHONE..................................323 770-2920
Tom Colich, *Partner*
John Colich, *Partner*
EMP: 58 EST: 1976
SQ FT: 4,500
SALES (est): 9.9MM **Privately Held**
SIC: 1623 8711 Sewer line construction; engineering services

(P-945)
CONSTRUCTION SPECIALTY SVC INC
Also Called: C S S
4550 Buck Owens Blvd, Bakersfield (93308-4948)
P.O. Box 9429 (93389-9429)
PHONE..................................661 864-7573
Daniel I George, *President*
Denise George, *CFO*
Charlie Williams, *Controller*
EMP: 53 EST: 2008
SQ FT: 1,000
SALES (est): 14.2MM **Privately Held**
WEB: www.cssincorp.biz
SIC: 1623 3271 Pipeline construction; concrete block & brick

(P-946)
DIVERSIFIED UTILITY SVCS INC
3105 Unicorn Rd, Bakersfield (93308-6858)
P.O. Box 80417 (93380-0417)
PHONE..................................661 325-3212
Leigh Ann Anderson, *CEO*
Cody Anderson, *Shareholder*
William Mitchell, *Shareholder*
Steven S Anderson, *CFO*
Vanessa Cromwell, *Officer*
EMP: 272

SALES (est): 63.7MM **Privately Held**
WEB: www.diversifiedutilityservices.com
SIC: **1623** Underground utilities contractor

(P-947)
E A SHIELDS INC
Also Called: Shield E A Sewer Construction
6613 Olympia Dr, Bakersfield
(93309-5445)
PHONE...................................661 325-5969
Greg Shields, *President*
Chantal Rogers-Keene, *Treasurer*
Pier Munagay, *Vice Pres*
Yinnela Shields, *Admin Sec*
EMP: 14 EST: 1949
SQ FT: 400
SALES (est): 1MM **Privately Held**
WEB: www.eashields.com
SIC: **1623** 3273 3272 Sewer line con-
struction; ready-mixed concrete; septic
tanks, concrete

(P-948)
FISHEL COMPANY
647 Young St, Santa Ana (92705-5633)
PHONE...................................714 668-9268
Jeong Jeon, *Branch Mgr*
EMP: 104
SALES (corp-wide): 540MM **Privately
Held**
WEB: www.teamfishel.com
SIC: **1623** Underground utilities contractor
PA: The Fishel Company
1366 Dublin Rd
Columbus OH 43215
614 274-8100

(P-949)
GENERAL PRODUCTION SVC CAL INC
Also Called: G P S
1333 Kern St, Taft (93268-9700)
P.O. Box 344 (93268-0344)
PHONE...................................661 765-5330
Charles Beard, *CEO*
Oreste Risi, *President*
Darin Jeffries, *Officer*
Rusty Risi, *Executive*
Terry Heinz, *Area Mgr*
EMP: 180
SALES (est): 54.6MM **Privately Held**
WEB: www.genprod.com
SIC: **1623** Oil & gas pipeline construction

(P-950)
GRFCO INC
4517 Wade Ave, Perris (92571-7492)
P.O. Box 1747, Brea (92822-1747)
PHONE...................................951 657-8887
George Frost, *CEO*
EMP: 59 EST: 1974
SALES (est): 8MM **Privately Held**
SIC: **1623** Water & sewer line construction

(P-951)
HCI INC (HQ)
Also Called: H C I
6830 Airport Dr, Riverside (92504-1904)
P.O. Box 5389, Norco (92860-8097)
PHONE...................................951 520-4200
Steven G Silagi, *President*
Robert Johns, *Area Spvr*
Kelly Denbaugh, *General Mgr*
Annette Carranza, *Administration*
Bryan Bray, *Project Mgr*
◆ EMP: 300 EST: 1981
SALES (est): 157.5MM
SALES (corp-wide): 180.1MM **Privately
Held**
WEB: www.hci-inc.com
SIC: **1623** Telephone & communication line
construction
PA: Lombardy Holdings, Inc.
151 Kalmus Dr Ste F6
Costa Mesa CA 92626
951 808-4550

(P-952)
HENKELS & MCCOY INC
2840 Ficus St, Pomona (91766-6501)
PHONE...................................909 517-3011
Michael Giarratano, *Senior VP*
Pierre Adam, *Vice Pres*
Amber Russell, *Executive Asst*
Melinda Reitmayer, *Administration*
Dean Adams, *CIO*

EMP: 300
SALES (corp-wide): 1.1B **Privately Held**
WEB: www.henkels.com
SIC: **1623** Electric power line construction;
transmitting tower (telecommunication)
construction; oil & gas pipeline construction
HQ: Henkels & Mccoy, Inc
985 Jolly Rd
Blue Bell PA 19422
215 283-7600

(P-953)
HERMAN WEISSKER INC (HQ)
1645 Brown Ave, Riverside (92509-1859)
PHONE...................................951 826-8800
Luis Alberto Armona, *CEO*
Ron Politte, *President*
Marty Mayeda, *CFO*
Brandi Green, *Admin Asst*
Katrina Suman, *Admin Asst*
EMP: 497 EST: 1959
SQ FT: 12,000
SALES (est): 101.2MM
SALES (corp-wide): 663.7MM **Privately
Held**
WEB: www.hermanweissker.com
SIC: **1623** 1731 Underground utilities con-
tractor; electrical work
PA: Meruelo Enterprises, Inc.
9550 Firestone Blvd # 105
Downey CA 90241
562 745-2300

(P-954)
HJ CONSTRUCTION INC
2320 Clark Valley Rd, San Luis Obispo
(93402-4606)
P.O. Box 3325 (93403-3325)
PHONE...................................805 534-1617
Dominic Judge, *President*
EMP: 20 EST: 2004
SALES (est): 1.3MM **Privately Held**
WEB: www.hjconstruct.com
SIC: **1623** 1794 3295 Water, sewer & util-
ity lines; excavation & grading, building
construction; minerals, ground or treated

(P-955)
HP COMMUNICATIONS INC (PA)
13341 Temescal Canyon Rd, Corona
(92883-4980)
PHONE...................................951 572-1200
Nicholas Goldman, *President*
Ahmad Olomi, *Exec VP*
Chris Price, *Vice Pres*
Dale Barnhart, *Area Mgr*
Tim Mottram, *Area Mgr*
EMP: 238 EST: 1998
SQ FT: 130,680
SALES (est): 101.5MM **Privately Held**
WEB: www.hpcomminc.com
SIC: **1623** Communication line & transmis-
sion tower construction

(P-956)
IRISH COMMUNICATION COMPANY (DH)
2649 Stingle Ave, Rosemead (91770-3326)
P.O. Box 457 (91770-0457)
PHONE...................................626 288-6170
Gregory C Warde, *CEO*
Dan Mitchell, *President*
Pat D Furnare, *Chairman*
Dennis Brackney, *Vice Pres*
Larry Manke, *Vice Pres*
EMP: 100 EST: 1985
SQ FT: 9,000
SALES (est): 54.8MM
SALES (corp-wide): 64MM **Privately
Held**
WEB: www.irishteam.com
SIC: **1623** 8748 1731 Telephone & com-
munication line construction; telecommu-
nications consultant; communications
specialization
HQ: Irish Construction
2641 River Ave
Rosemead CA 91770
626 288-8530

(P-957)
IRISH CONSTRUCTION (HQ)
2641 River Ave, Rosemead (91770-3392)
P.O. Box 579 (91770-0579)
PHONE...................................626 288-8530

Gregory C Warde, *Ch of Bd*
Ken West, *President*
William E Wilbanks, *President*
Randall W Dale, *Corp Secy*
Randy Billingsly, *Vice Pres*
EMP: 150 EST: 1947
SQ FT: 15,000
SALES (est): 64MM **Privately Held**
WEB: www.irishteam.com
SIC: **1623** Telephone & communication line
construction
PA: Manhattan Capital Corporation
2641 River Ave
Rosemead CA 91770
626 288-8530

(P-958)
K S FABRICATION & MACHINE INC
Also Called: KS Fabrication & Machine
6205 District Blvd, Bakersfield
(93313-2141)
P.O. Box 41630 (93384-1630)
PHONE...................................661 617-1700
Kevin S Small, *CEO*
Becky Scott, *CFO*
Alan Skalaski, *Vice Pres*
EMP: 150 EST: 1999
SALES (est): 30.4MM **Privately Held**
WEB: www.ksilp.com
SIC: **1623** Water, sewer & utility lines

(P-959)
KANA PIPELINE INC
12620 Magnolia Ave, Riverside
(92503-4636)
PHONE...................................714 986-1400
Dan Locke, *President*
Patrick Burns, *CFO*
Rizwan Rana, *Project Mgr*
Kaycee Fink, *Human Res Dir*
EMP: 100 EST: 1984
SQ FT: 55,000
SALES (est): 31.6MM **Privately Held**
WEB: www.kanapipeline.com
SIC: **1623** 1629 Water main construction;
sewer line construction; drainage system
construction

(P-960)
KS INDUSTRIES LP (PA)
Also Called: K S I
6205 District Blvd, Bakersfield
(93313-2141)
P.O. Box 41630 (93384-1630)
PHONE...................................661 617-1700
Kevin Small, *Partner*
Scott Becky, *CFO*
Bret Kingsbury, *CFO*
Allan Faughn, *Vice Pres*
Michael Lackey, *Vice Pres*
EMP: 2000
SQ FT: 20,000
SALES (est): 403.9MM **Privately Held**
WEB: www.ksilp.com
SIC: **1623** Water, sewer & utility lines

(P-961)
LOMBARDY HOLDINGS INC (PA)
151 Kalmus Dr Ste F6, Costa Mesa
(92626-5965)
P.O. Box 6019, Norco (92860-8034)
PHONE...................................951 808-4550
Marc Laulhere, *CEO*
Michael Johanns, *Bd of Directors*
Dmitri L Stockton, *Bd of Directors*
Pam Laulhere, *Admin Sec*
EMP: 200 EST: 1940
SQ FT: 80,000
SALES (est): 180.1MM **Privately Held**
WEB: www.deere.com
SIC: **1623** 5211 Telephone & communica-
tion line construction; cable television line
construction; electrical construction mate-
rials

(P-962)
M C C EQUIPMENT RENTALS INC
Also Called: McC Pipeline
32389 Dunlap Blvd, Yucaipa (92399-1724)
P.O. Box 1730 (92399-1439)
PHONE...................................909 795-9300
Kenneth Paul Munoz, *President*
Danielle Gatlin, *Admin Sec*
EMP: 82 EST: 2003

SQ FT: 1,300
SALES (est): 9.9MM **Privately Held**
WEB: www.mccpipeline.com
SIC: **1623** Pipeline construction

(P-963)
MLADEN BUNTICH CNSTR CO INC
1500 W 9th St, Upland (91786-5636)
PHONE...................................909 920-9977
Mladen Buntich Jr, *Ch of Bd*
Lee Roesner, *Vice Pres*
Scott Peterson, *Admin Sec*
Marcia Cogan, *Asst Controller*
Brandon Sjulin, *Director*
▲ EMP: 60 EST: 1975
SQ FT: 4,000
SALES (est): 20MM **Privately Held**
WEB: www.buntich.com
SIC: **1623** 8711 8322 Sewer line con-
struction; pipeline construction; engineer-
ing services; individual & family services

(P-964)
PACIFIC W SPACE CMMNCTIONS INC
Also Called: P W C
900 W Gladstone St, San Dimas
(91773-1734)
PHONE...................................909 592-4321
Sheryl F Patton, *CEO*
Joanna Patton, *CFO*
John Tarango, *Treasurer*
Betty Fonteno, *Corp Secy*
Rich Patton, *Vice Pres*
EMP: 69 EST: 1981
SQ FT: 2,000
SALES (est): 19.9MM **Privately Held**
WEB: www.pwcinc.com
SIC: **1623** Communication line & transmis-
sion tower construction

(P-965)
PAULUS ENGINEERING INC
2871 E Coronado St, Anaheim
(92806-2504)
PHONE...................................714 632-3322
Ronald Paulus, *President*
Jason Paulus, *Vice Pres*
Cyndi Valencia, *Administration*
Michelle June, *CTO*
Roger Betten, *Project Mgr*
EMP: 60
SQ FT: 40,000
SALES (est): 11.5MM **Privately Held**
WEB: www.paulusengineering.com
SIC: **1623** Sewer line construction; pipeline
construction

(P-966)
PRECISION PIPELINE LLC
10400 Trademark St, Rancho Cucamonga
(91730-5826)
PHONE...................................909 229-6858
EMP: 441
SALES (corp-wide): 6.3B **Publicly Held**
WEB: www.precisionpipellc.com
SIC: **1623** Pipeline construction
HQ: Precision Pipeline Llc
3314 56th St
Eau Claire WI 54703
715 874-4510

(P-967)
S E C C CORPORATION
16224 Koala Rd, Adelanto (92301-3915)
PHONE...................................760 246-6218
Manuel Armenta, *Manager*
EMP: 100 **Privately Held**
WEB: www.secc-corp.com
SIC: **1623** Transmitting tower (telecommu-
nication) construction
PA: S E C C Corporation
14945 La Palma Dr
Chino CA 91710

(P-968)
S E PIPE LINE CONSTRUCTION CO
11832 Bloomfield Ave, Santa Fe Springs
(90670-4693)
PHONE...................................562 868-9771
Charles Rikel, *President*
James Doulames, *Vice Pres*

Thomas Tustin, *Admin Sec*
Shannon Hearn, *Project Mgr*
Daniel Ibarra, *Manager*
EMP: 100 **EST:** 1946
SQ FT: 5,000
SALES (est): 22.3MM **Privately Held**
WEB: www.sepipeline.com
SIC: 1623 Gas main construction; electric power line construction; oil & gas pipeline construction

(P-969)

SAM HILL & SONS INC

Also Called: WMS Transportation
2627 Beene Rd, Ventura (93003-7203)
P.O. Box 5670 (93005-0670)
PHONE....................................805 620-0828
Ronald Hill, *President*
Brett Franklin, *Foreman/Supr*
EMP: 50 **EST:** 1980
SQ FT: 1,000
SALES (est): 8.2MM **Privately Held**
WEB: www.samhillandsons.com
SIC: 1623 Underground utilities contractor

(P-970)

SHOFFEITT PIPELINE INC

15801 Rockfield Blvd L, Irvine
(92618-2869)
PHONE....................................949 581-1600
Kathy Shoffeitt, *President*
John Shoffeitt, *Vice Pres*
Laura Hudson, *Office Mgr*
EMP: 80 **EST:** 2013
SQ FT: 3,200
SALES (est): 10.6MM **Privately Held**
WEB: www.shoffeittpipeline.com
SIC: 1623 Underground utilities contractor

(P-971)

SOLEX CONTRACTING INC

42146 Remington Ave, Temecula
(92590-2547)
PHONE....................................951 308-1706
Jerry Allen, *President*
Keith Schultz, *Vice Pres*
Tony Granados, *Project Mgr*
Mike Saavedra, *Project Mgr*
Andrea Clements, *Controller*
EMP: 110 **EST:** 2004
SQ FT: 12,000
SALES (est): 40.3MM **Privately Held**
WEB: www.solexcontracting.com
SIC: 1623 1542 1541 Communication line & transmission tower construction; commercial & office building, new construction; renovation, remodeling & repairs: industrial buildings

(P-972)

SOUTHWEST CONTRACTORS (PA)

Also Called: Bowman Pipeline Contractors
136 Allen Rd 100, Bakersfield
(93314-3710)
PHONE....................................661 588-0484
Floyd E Bowman Jr, *CEO*
Kathy Bowman, *Vice Pres*
Amanda Diaz, *Controller*
Gabe Perez, *Safety Dir*
Frank Charolla, *Opers Mgr*
EMP: 25 **EST:** 1981
SALES (est): 49MM **Privately Held**
WEB: www.southwestcontractors.net
SIC: 1623 3443 Oil & gas pipeline construction; industrial vessels, tanks & containers

(P-973)

SPIESS CONSTRUCTION CO INC

Also Called: Scci
201 S Broadway St Ste 140, Orcutt
(93455-4611)
P.O. Box 2849, Santa Maria (93457-2849)
PHONE....................................805 937-5859
Scott A Coleman, *President*
Barry L Matchett, *Vice Pres*
Frank L Forthun, *Assistant VP*
EMP: 60 **EST:** 1977
SALES (est): 21.9MM **Privately Held**
WEB: www.weldedsteeltanks.com
SIC: 1623 Sewer line construction

(P-974)

SPINIELLO COMPANIES

2650 Pomona Blvd, Pomona (91768-3220)
PHONE....................................909 629-1000
Priscilla Moyer, *Manager*
James Dang, *Project Mgr*
EMP: 152
SALES (corp-wide): 90MM **Privately Held**
WEB: www.spiniello.com
SIC: 1623 Water, sewer & utility lines
PA: Spiniello Companies
354 Eisenhower Pkwy # 1200
Livingston NJ 07039
973 808-8383

(P-975)

SRD ENGINEERING INC

5300 Highland Ct, Yorba Linda
(92886-4000)
P.O. Box 517, Nye MT (59061-0517)
PHONE....................................714 630-2480
Deborah Denton, *CEO*
Sheri Halsey, *Accounting Mgr*
EMP: 65 **EST:** 1991
SALES (est): 9.4MM **Privately Held**
SIC: 1623 Water & sewer line construction

(P-976)

SUKUT CONSTRUCTION LLC

4010 W Chandler Ave, Santa Ana
(92704-5202)
PHONE....................................714 540-5351
Michael Crawford, *Principal*
Paul Kuliev, *CFO*
Gade Mobley, *Executive*
Joe Philbin, *Principal*
Mike Zanaboni, *Principal*
EMP: 99 **EST:** 2014
SALES (est): 27.3MM **Privately Held**
WEB: www.sukut.com
SIC: 1623 1629 1611 Water, sewer & utility lines; pipe laying construction; earthmoving contractor; grading

(P-977)

T A RIVARD INC

8884 Jurupa Rd, Riverside (92509-3162)
P.O. Box 33190 (92519-0190)
PHONE....................................951 360-8596
Timothy A Rivard, *President*
Janet Rivard, *Corp Secy*
EMP: 61 **EST:** 1979
SQ FT: 3,400
SALES (est): 5MM **Privately Held**
SIC: 1623 Water main construction; sewer line construction

(P-978)

THERMAL ENERGY SOLUTIONS INC

100 Quantico Ave, Bakersfield
(93307-2839)
PHONE...................:............661 489-4100
Gabriela Lopez De Ayala, *CEO*
Nelson Ayala, *Vice Pres*
EMP: 14 **EST:** 2008
SALES (est): 2.7MM **Privately Held**
WEB: www.thermalenergyinc.com
SIC: 1623 1711 3494 7699 Oil & gas line & compressor station construction; process piping contractor; line strainers, for use in piping systems; tank & boiler cleaning service; insulation of pipes & boilers

(P-979)

TURN AROUND COMMUNICATIONS INC

100 N Barranca St Ste 260, West Covina
(91791-1637)
P.O. Box 6121, El Monte (91734-2121)
PHONE....................................626 443-2400
Sayeid Kouhkan, *President*
Nick Fernandez, *Senior Mgr*
EMP: 170 **EST:** 2002
SALES (est): 31.6MM **Privately Held**
WEB: www.turnaroundcommunications.net
SIC: 1623 Telephone & communication line construction

(P-980)

UTAH PACIFIC CONSTRUCTION CO

40940 Eleanora Way, Murrieta
(92562-5946)
PHONE.........................,.......951 677-9876
Craig R Young, *President*
Brian Keeline, *Vice Pres*
Jason Bent, *Safety Mgr*
Chris Medellin, *Manager*
Ann Young, *Manager*
EMP: 55 **EST:** 1987
SQ FT: 5,000
SALES (est): 3.5MM **Privately Held**
WEB: www.utah-pacific.com
SIC: 1623 Sewer line construction; water main construction; pipeline construction

(P-981)

VADNAIS TRENCHLESS SVCS INC

26000 Commercentre Dr, Lake Forest
(92630-8816)
P.O. Box 5166 (92609-8666)
PHONE....................................858 550-1460
Paul Vadnais, *CEO*
EMP: 106 **EST:** 2014
SALES (est): 39.5MM **Publicly Held**
WEB: www.primoriscorp.com
SIC: 1623 1622 Pipeline construction; tunnel construction
PA: Primoris Services Corporation
2300 N Field St Ste 1900
Dallas TX 75201

(P-982)

VALVERDE CONSTRUCTION INC

10936 Shoemaker Ave, Santa Fe Springs
(90670-4533)
P.O. Box 3223 (90670-0223)
PHONE....................................562 906-1826
Joe A Valverde, *President*
Rose Valverde, *Treasurer*
Edward Valverde, *Vice Pres*
Christopher Valverde, *Admin Sec*
EMP: 75 **EST:** 1972
SQ FT: 9,000
SALES (est): 21.6MM **Privately Held**
WEB: www.valverde.webflow.io
SIC: 1623 Water main construction; sewer line construction; telephone & communication line construction; cable laying construction

(P-983)

VCI CONSTRUCTION LLC (HQ)

1921 W 11th St Ste A, Upland
(91786-3508)
PHONE....................................909 946-0905
John Xanthos, *President*
Vic Marovish, *CFO*
Edgar Escobar, *Vice Pres*
Logan Teal, *Vice Pres*
Gary Sharp, *Division Mgr*
EMP: 100 **EST:** 1998
SQ FT: 29,500
SALES (est): 91.1MM
SALES (corp-wide): 3.2B **Publicly Held**
WEB: www.dycomind.com
SIC: 1623 Underground utilities contractor; transmitting tower (telecommunication) construction
PA: Dycom Industries, Inc.
11780 Us Highway 1 # 600
Palm Beach Gardens FL 33408
561 627-7171

(P-984)

W A RASIC CNSTR CO INC (PA)

4150 Long Beach Blvd, Long Beach
(90807-2650)
PHONE....................................562 928-6111
Peter L Rasic, *CEO*
Tim Cloud, *Division Mgr*
Randall Yoo, *CTO*
Ryan Plunk, *Project Mgr*
Jack Quick, *Project Mgr*
EMP: 382 **EST:** 1978
SQ FT: 8,500
SALES (est): 121.5MM **Privately Held**
WEB: www.warasic.com
SIC: 1623 Sewer line construction

(P-985)

WATKINS CONSTRUCTION CO INC

Also Called: Johnston Vacuum Tank Service
112 E Cedar St, Taft (93268-9708)
P.O. Box 243 (93268-0243)
PHONE....................................661 763-5395
Eddie Watkins Sr, *President*
Mary King, *Manager*
EMP: 60 **EST:** 1967
SQ FT: 4,800
SALES (est): 10.8MM **Privately Held**
WEB: www.wci-jvt.com
SIC: 1623 Oil & gas pipeline construction

(P-986)

WEST STATES SKANSKA INC

1995 Agua Mansa Rd, Riverside
(92509-2405)
PHONE....................................970 565-4903
Curtis Brotten, *President*
Denise Rozporka, *Project Engr*
EMP: 163 **EST:** 1982
SQ FT: 800
SALES (est): 90.8K
SALES (corp-wide): 18.5B **Privately Held**
SIC: 1623 1541 Water, sewer & utility lines; industrial buildings & warehouses
HQ: Skanska Usa Civil West Rocky Mountain District Inc.
1995 Agua Mansa Rd
Riverside CA 92509
970 565-8000

(P-987)

WINTER PARK UTILITY SVCS LLC (PA)

8141 E Kaiser Blvd # 212, Anaheim
(92808-2227)
PHONE....................................714 283-6080
Dennis Eastman, *President*
Srm-Enco LLC.
EMP: 63 **EST:** 2005
SQ FT: 2,000
SALES (est): 8.7MM **Privately Held**
SIC: 1623 Electric power line construction

1629 Heavy Construction, NEC

(P-988)

BEMUS LANDSCAPE INC

1225 Puerta Del Sol # 500, San Clemente
(92673-6312)
P.O. Box 74268 (92673-0143)
PHONE....................................714 557-7910
William Howard Bemus, *President*
Jonathon Parry, *Corp Secy*
Bill Bemus, *Vice Pres*
Martine Bemus, *Vice Pres*
Jay Orona, *Branch Mgr*
EMP: 300 **EST:** 1973
SQ FT: 7,000
SALES (est): 36.8MM **Privately Held**
WEB: www.bemus.com
SIC: 1629 0782 Drainage system construction; landscape contractors

(P-989)

BRIGHTVIEW COMPANIES LLC (DH)

27001 Agoura Rd Ste 350, Calabasas
(91301-5112)
PHONE....................................818 223-8500
John Feenan, *CEO*
Eric Johnson, *Partner*
Thomas C Donnelly, *President*
Jeff Herold, *President*
Brian Chesnut, *Vice Pres*
◆ **EMP:** 175 **EST:** 2006
SALES (est): 2.2B
SALES (corp-wide): 2.3B **Publicly Held**
WEB: www.brightview.com
SIC: 1629 0782 0781 Golf course construction; lawn & garden services; landscape services
HQ: Brightview Landscape Services, Inc.
980 Jolly Rd Ste 300
Blue Bell PA 19422
484 567-7204

PRODUCTS & SVCS

(P-990)
C A RASMUSSEN INC (PA)
28548 Livingston Ave, Valencia
(91355-4171)
PHONE....................661 367-9040
Charles A Rasmussen, *President*
D I C K Greenburg, *CFO*
Doug Misley, *Exec VP*
Tim Macdonald, *Vice Pres*
Mike Medema, *Vice Pres*
EMP: 50 **EST:** 1964
SQ FT: 20,000
SALES (est): 57.5MM **Privately Held**
WEB: www.carasmussen.com
SIC: 1629 1611 Earthmoving contractor;
grading

(P-991)
CAL WEST UNDERGROUND INC
951 6th St, Norco (92860-1442)
PHONE....................951 371-6775
Jeffrey M Abernathy, *President*
EMP: 63 **EST:** 1999
SQ FT: 1,200
SALES (est): 14.8MM **Privately Held**
SIC: 1629 Trenching contractor

(P-992)
CATTRAC CONSTRUCTION INC
15030 Slover Ave, Fontana (92337-7237)
PHONE....................909 355-1146
Stephanie A Jacinto, *CEO*
Greg Dineen, *Vice Pres*
Danny Saldivar, *Project Mgr*
Rita Stark, *Controller*
Bruce McBride, *Manager*
EMP: 60 **EST:** 1971
SQ FT: 5,000
SALES (est): 32.9MM **Privately Held**
WEB: www.cattrac.com
SIC: 1629 7353 4213 Earthmoving con-
tractor; earth moving equipment, rental or
leasing; trucking, except local

(P-993)
CE ALLENCOMPANY INC
2109 Gundry Ave, Long Beach
(90755-3517)
PHONE....................562 989-6100
C E Peter Allen, *President*
EMP: 50 **EST:** 1995
SQ FT: 1,277
SALES (est): 10.2MM **Privately Held**
WEB: www.allenco-oilwellservice.com
SIC: 1629 7353 Industrial plant construc-
tion; oil equipment rental services

(P-994)
E E BLACK LIMITED (HQ)
15901 Olden St, Sylmar (91342-1051)
PHONE....................671 646-4861
Ronald Tutor, *President*
John Barrett, *Vice Pres*
Leonard Kaae, *General Mgr*
EMP: 996 **EST:** 1926
SALES (est): 25MM
SALES (corp-wide): 5.3B **Publicly Held**
WEB: www.eeblackphilippines.com
SIC: 1629 1611 Land preparation con-
struction; highway & street paving con-
tractor; airport runway construction
PA: Tutor Perini Corporation
15901 Olden St
Sylmar CA 91342
818 362-8391

(P-995)
ENVIROGENICS SYSTEMS COMPANY
9255 Telstar Ave, El Monte (91731-2845)
PHONE....................818 573-9220
Dr Fadi Abbash, *President*
R Kadaj, *Vice Pres*
EMP: 100 **EST:** 1967
SQ FT: 91,000
SALES (est): 6.4MM **Privately Held**
SIC: 1629 Industrial plant construction

(P-996)
ESOLAR INC (DH)
900 Glenneyre St, Laguna Beach
(92651-2707)
PHONE....................818 303-9500
▲ **EMP:** 78

SALES (est): 11.2MM
SALES (corp-wide): 142.9MM **Privately
Held**
WEB: www.esolar.com
SIC: 1629 Heavy Construction

(P-997)
FOUNDATION PILE INC
8375 Almeria Ave, Fontana (92335-3283)
PHONE....................909 350-1584
Derek Halecky, *CEO*
Peter Brandl, *President*
Nikki Sjoblom, *CFO*
Dermot Fallon, *Vice Pres*
Don Hilton, *Vice Pres*
EMP: 97 **EST:** 1978
SALES (est): 53.1MM
SALES (corp-wide): 55.4MM **Privately
Held**
WEB: www.foundationpiledriving.com
SIC: 1629 1794 Pile driving contractor; ex-
cavation & grading, building construction
PA: Foundation Constructors, Inc.
81 Big Break Rd
Oakley CA 94561
925 754-6633

(P-998)
GTM MANAGEMENT COMPANY INC
Also Called: M I M
3930b Cherry Ave, Long Beach
(90807-3727)
P.O. Box 22624 (90801-5624)
PHONE....................562 988-0449
Robert Griffin, *President*
Dennis Schlarbaum, *Admin Sec*
Margaret Panting, *Manager*
EMP: 50 **EST:** 1993
SQ FT: 5,000
SALES (est): 1.1MM **Privately Held**
WEB: www.graywolfindustrial.com
SIC: 1629 Industrial plant construction

(P-999)
HERZOG CONTRACTING CORP
3760 Kilroy Arprt Way # 120, Long Beach
(90806-2455)
P.O. Box 1089, Saint Joseph MO (64502-
1089)
PHONE....................562 595-7414
Jennifer Lord, *Branch Mgr*
Greg Dunn, *Project Mgr*
Chris Comer, *Safety Mgr*
EMP: 119
SALES (corp-wide): 269MM **Privately
Held**
WEB: www.herzog.com
SIC: 1629 1611 4953 Railroad & railway
roadbed construction; highway & street
paving contractor; sanitary landfill opera-
tion
PA: Herzog Contracting Corp.
600 S Riverside Rd
Saint Joseph MO 64507
816 233-9001

(P-1000)
JILK HEAVY CONSTRUCTION INC
500 S Kraemer Blvd # 380, Brea
(92821-6779)
PHONE....................310 830-6323
James Jilk, *President*
John S Meek, *President*
Lisa Paila, *Office Mgr*
Chad Goodwin, *Project Mgr*
Ken Allred, *Manager*
EMP: 60 **EST:** 1995
SALES (est): 12.5MM **Privately Held**
WEB: www.jilkhc.com
SIC: 1629 Marine construction

(P-1001)
MANSON CONSTRUCTION CO
340 Golden Shore Ste 310, Long Beach
(90802-4229)
PHONE....................562 983-2340
Tim Henson, *Branch Mgr*
Dave Vanwagner, *Engineer*
Roberto Davila, *Chief Engr*
Johnny Gregory, *Foreman/Supr*
Jennifer Stuessy, *Receptionist*
EMP: 70

SALES (corp-wide): 391.8MM **Privately
Held**
WEB: www.mansonconstruction.com
SIC: 1629 Marine construction
HQ: Manson Construction Co.
5209 E Marginal Way S
Seattle WA 98134
206 762-0850

(P-1002)
PSI MANAGEMENT TEAM INC
Partition Specialties
12342 Mccann Dr, Santa Fe Springs
(90670-3333)
PHONE....................562 236-3860
Kevin Bogle, *Branch Mgr*
Robert Kaminski, *Sales Mgr*
EMP: 80
SQ FT: 10,000
SALES (corp-wide): 19.2MM **Privately
Held**
WEB: www.psi3g.com
SIC: 1629 Dams, waterways, docks &
other marine construction; land prepara-
tion construction
PA: Psi Management Team, Inc.
7428 Redwood Blvd Ste 101
Novato CA 94945
415 193-3859

(P-1003)
RAIN BIRD DISTRIBUTION CORP
1000 W Sierra Madre Ave, Azusa
(91702-1700)
P.O. Box 37 (91702-0037)
PHONE....................626 963-9311
Anthony Lafetra, *CEO*
Anthony W Lafetra, *CEO*
Arthur Ludwick, *Corp Secy*
Anthony Dabruzzi, *Regl Sales Mgr*
EMP: 47 **EST:** 1946
SQ FT: 20,000
SALES (est): 2.9MM **Privately Held**
SIC: 1629 3523 Irrigation system con-
struction; fertilizing, spraying, dusting & ir-
rigation machinery

(P-1004)
SKANSKA USA CVIL W RCKY MTN DS (DH)
Also Called: SKANSKA ROCKY MOUNTAIN
DISTRICT
1995 Agua Mansa Rd, Riverside
(92509-2405)
PHONE....................970 565-8000
Curtis Broughton, *Senior VP*
David Sitton, *Vice Pres*
Tammy Hampton, *General Mgr*
Gary Moss, *Project Mgr*
Dylan Thompson, *Project Mgr*
EMP: 70 **EST:** 1950
SQ FT: 22,500
SALES: 139.4K
SALES (corp-wide): 18.5B **Privately Held**
SIC: 1629 1611 1711 Dam construction;
general contractor, highway & street con-
struction; mechanical contractor
HQ: Skanska Usa Civil Inc.
7520 Astoria Blvd Ste 200
East Elmhurst NY 11370
718 340-0777

(P-1005)
SLATER INC
11045 Rose Ave, Fontana (92337-7051)
P.O. Box 759 (92334-0759)
PHONE....................909 822-6800
Phillip S Slater, *CEO*
Edward Johnson, *CFO*
Steve David, *Vice Pres*
Karim Rizk, *Controller*
EMP: 97 **EST:** 1981
SQ FT: 6,000
SALES (est): 20.5MM **Privately Held**
WEB: www.slaterinc.com
SIC: 1629 8711 Drainage system con-
struction; engineering services

(P-1006)
TIMEC COMPANIES INC
2997 E Maria St, E Rncho Dmngz
(90221-5801)
PHONE....................310 885-4710
Craig Crowder, *CEO*
Brian Hafer, *Vice Pres*
Mark Herzfeld, *Vice Pres*

EMP: 140 **Privately Held**
SIC: 1629 Industrial plant construction;
chemical plant & refinery construction; oil
refinery construction
HQ: Timec Companies Inc
155 Corporate Pl
Vallejo CA 94590
707 642-2222

(P-1007)
VISTA STEEL CO INC
331 W Lewis St, Ventura (93001-1394)
PHONE....................805 653-1189
John Swaffar, *Branch Mgr*
EMP: 24
SALES (corp-wide): 6.8MM **Privately
Held**
WEB: www.vistasteelcompany.com
SIC: 1629 3449 Dams, waterways, docks
& other marine construction; miscella-
neous metalwork
PA: Vista Steel Co Inc
6100 Francis Botello Rd
Goleta CA 93117
805 964-4732

(P-1008)
WARREN COLLINS AND ASSOC INC (PA)
Also Called: Collins Company
5470 Daniels St, Chino (91710-9012)
PHONE....................909 548-6708
Larry W Collins, *President*
Nancy Collins, *Treasurer*
Natalie Mamola, *Office Mgr*
Scott Fritz, *Sales Executive*
Parker Collins, *Manager*
▲ **EMP:** 23 **EST:** 1975
SQ FT: 8,000
SALES (est): 6.4MM **Privately Held**
WEB: www.collinscompany.com
SIC: 1629 3949 1799 3446 Athletic &
recreation facilities construction; sporting
& athletic goods; scaffolding construction;
scaffolds, mobile or stationary: metal

(P-1009)
WOOD BROS INC
14147 18th Ave, Lemoore (93245-9741)
P.O. Box 216 (93245-0216)
PHONE....................559 924-7715
William S Wood, *CEO*
Donald T Wood, *Corp Secy*
Jerry Ghiglia, *Executive*
Brianna Hill, *General Mgr*
Tim Smith, *General Mgr*
EMP: 100 **EST:** 1984
SQ FT: 30,000
SALES (est): 27.7MM **Privately Held**
WEB: www.woodbrosinc.com
SIC: 1629 Dredging contractor

(P-1010)
WORLEY FIELD SERVICES INC
2600 Michelson Dr Ste 500, Irvine
(92612-6506)
P.O. Box 6025, Cypress (90630-0025)
PHONE....................949 224-7585
Brandy Marquez, *Branch Mgr*
Deiandra Lawson-Simms, *Admin Asst*
EMP: 77 **Privately Held**
SIC: 1629 Earthmoving contractor
HQ: Worley Field Services, Inc.
5995 Rogerdale Rd
Houston TX 77072
832 351-6000

1711 Plumbing, Heating & Air Conditioning Contractors

(P-1011)
20/20 PLUMBING & HEATING INC (PA)
Also Called: Honeywell Authorized Dealer
7343 Orangewood Dr Ste B, Riverside
(92504-1053)
PHONE....................951 396-2020
Thomas Lew Baker, *CEC*
Mallory Watson, *Administration*
Daniel Smith, *Design Engr*
Grant Kiely, *Project Mgr*
Kimani Upshur, *Project Mgr*
EMP: 197 **EST:** 2014

SALES (est): 33.7MM **Privately Held**
WEB: www.2020ph.com
SIC: **1711** Plumbing contractors

(P-1012)
A-AVIS HM SVCS PLBG HTG AC INC
600 E Valley Blvd, Colton (92324-3122)
PHONE..................................909 825-3600
James Ed Ballard, *President*
Sheila Brook, *Admin Sec*
EMP: 52 **EST:** 1964
SQ FT: 1,700
SALES (est): 3.2MM **Privately Held**
WEB: www.avisac.com
SIC: **1711** Plumbing contractors; warm air heating & air conditioning contractor

(P-1013)
ACCUTHERM REFRIGERATON INC
Also Called: Accutherm Air Heating & Coolg
11264 Monarch St Ste A, Garden Grove (92841-1449)
PHONE..................................714 766-7800
Jeff Recker, *President*
Jeffrey Recker, *Vice Pres*
Jonathan Recker, *Maintence Staff*
Rick Tran, *Manager*
EMP: 53 **EST:** 2000
SQ FT: 6,800
SALES (est): 6.9MM **Privately Held**
WEB: www.accuthermrefrigeration.com
SIC: **1711** Refrigeration contractor

(P-1014)
ACH MECHANICAL CONTRACTORS INC
411 Business Center Ct, Redlands (92373-8084)
PHONE..................................909 307-2850
Hector Vargas, *President*
Jeff Russell, *Project Mgr*
Conrad Talens, *Project Mgr*
Sergio Vargas, *Project Mgr*
Robert Candelario, *Manager*
EMP: 80
SQ FT: 14,450
SALES (est): 35MM **Privately Held**
WEB: www.achmechanical.com
SIC: **1711** Mechanical contractor

(P-1015)
ACOSOLAR INC
4120 Valley Blvd Ste A, Walnut (91789-1404)
PHONE..................................626 575-8822
Yong Wang, *CEO*
Longhua Tang, *President*
Haijuan Fu, *CFO*
Kyle Wong, *Sales Mgr*
EMP: 14 **EST:** 2011
SQ FT: 2,200
SALES (est): 4MM **Privately Held**
WEB: www.acosolar.com
SIC: **5211 1711 3629 7389** Solar heating equipment; energy conservation products; solar energy contractor; inverters, nonrotating: electrical;
PA: Nanjing Hongyuan Renewable Energy Technology Co.,Ltd
5012, Qianren Building, Jiangning Development Zone
Nanjing 21003

(P-1016)
AD RECEIVABLES CORP (PA)
5457 Crenshaw Blvd, Los Angeles (90043-2407)
P.O. Box 431490 (90043-9490)
PHONE..................................323 296-8787
Jack Stephan Sr, *President*
Jack Stephan Jr, *Vice Pres*
Russell Stephan, *Admin Sec*
EMP: 64 **EST:** 1946
SQ FT: 18,000
SALES (est): 7.3MM **Privately Held**
WEB: www.adeedo.com
SIC: **1711** Plumbing contractors; warm air heating & air conditioning contractor

(P-1017)
ADVANTAGE PLUMBING GROUP INC
3331 Orangewood Ave, Los Alamitos (90720-3813)
P.O. Box 733 (90720-0733)
PHONE..................................714 898-6020
EMP: 67
SALES (est): 4.6MM **Privately Held**
SIC: **1711 5074** Plumbing/Heating/Air Cond Contractor Whol Plumbing Equipment/Supplies

(P-1018)
AERO AUTOMATIC SPRINKLER CO
170 N Maple St, Corona (92878-3203)
PHONE..................................951 273-1889
Gary Beyschau, *Principal*
EMP: 50
SALES (corp-wide): 10.2B **Privately Held**
WEB: www.aerofire.com
SIC: **1711** Fire sprinkler system installation
HQ: Aero Automatic Sprinkler Company
21605 N Central Ave
Phoenix AZ 85024
623 580-7800

(P-1019)
AG AIR CONDITIONING & HTG INC
Also Called: AG Heating and AC
14620 Keswick St, Van Nuys (91405-1203)
PHONE..................................818 988-5388
Yuval Giron, *CEO*
Yitchak Giron, *President*
EMP: 50 **EST:** 2007 **Privately Held**
WEB: www.agair.com
SIC: **1711** Warm air heating & air conditioning contractor

(P-1020)
AIR CONTROL SYSTEMS INC
1940 S Grove Ave, Ontario (91761-5615)
PHONE..................................909 786-4230
Robert Leotaud, *CEO*
Travis Blaylock, *Project Mgr*
Marty Boley, *Project Mgr*
Chad Williams, *Director*
Byron Alejandrino, *Manager*
EMP: 50 **EST:** 1991
SQ FT: 17,995
SALES (est): 18.6MM **Privately Held**
WEB: www.aircontrolsystems.net
SIC: **1711** Warm air heating & air conditioning contractor; ventilation & duct work contractor

(P-1021)
AIRE-RITE AC & RFRGN INC
15122 Bolsa Chica St, Huntington Beach (92649-1025)
P.O. Box 3419 (92605-3419)
PHONE..................................714 895-2338
Donald Langston, *CEO*
Carol Langston, *Corp Secy*
David Langston, *Vice Pres*
Thaer Mustafa, *Technician*
Don Langston,
EMP: 97 **EST:** 1972
SQ FT: 22,000
SALES (est): 16.6MM **Privately Held**
WEB: www.airenite.com
SIC: **1711** Warm air heating & air conditioning contractor

(P-1022)
ALDOC INC
910 E Orangefair Ln, Anaheim (92801-1103)
PHONE..................................714 836-8477
P S Meckley, *President*
Philip Shurman Meckley, *President*
EMP: 60 **EST:** 2005
SALES (est): 2.8MM **Privately Held**
SIC: **1711** Plumbing contractors

(P-1023)
ALL TMPERATURES CONTROLLED INC
Also Called: Honeywell Authorized Dealer
9720 Topanga Canyon Pl, Chatsworth (91311-4134)
PHONE..................................818 882-1478
George Mego, *President*

Nancy Miller, *CFO*
Cheryl Piper, *Treasurer*
Kathy Gomes, *Executive*
Nick Mego, *General Mgr*
EMP: 72 **EST:** 1978
SQ FT: 13,481
SALES (est): 11.6MM **Privately Held**
WEB: www.alltemperaturescontrolled.com
SIC: **1711** Warm air heating & air conditioning contractor; heating & air conditioning contractors

(P-1024)
AMERICAN CONTRACTORS INC
404 W Blueridge Ave, Orange (92865-4204)
PHONE..................................714 282-5700
Gilbert L Wiggam, *CEO*
Christopher Wiggam, *Vice Pres*
EMP: 65 **EST:** 1974
SQ FT: 11,000 **Privately Held**
WEB: www.aciplumbing.com
SIC: **1711 1623** Plumbing contractors; sewer line construction

(P-1025)
AMERICAN INCORPORATED
3450 Sacramento Dr, San Luis Obispo (93401-7199)
PHONE..................................805 597-6545
EMP: 274
SALES (corp-wide): 75MM **Privately Held**
WEB: www.aminc.com
SIC: **1711** Plumbing/Heating/Air Cond Contractor
PA: American Incorporated
1345 N American St
Visalia CA 93291
559 651-1776

(P-1026)
AMGREEN SOLAR & ELECTRIC INC
1367 Venice Blvd, Los Angeles (90006-5519)
PHONE..................................213 388-5647
Minseon Ko, *CEO*
Eunice Ko, *Principal*
▲ EMP: 50 **EST:** 2013
SALES (est): 5.5MM **Privately Held**
SIC: **1711 1731** Solar energy contractor; lighting contractor

(P-1027)
AMPAM PARKS MECHANICAL INC
17036 Avalon Blvd, Carson (90746-1206)
PHONE..................................310 835-1532
Charles E Parks III, *CEO*
James C Wright, *CFO*
Roland Kazandjian, *Vice Pres*
Jason Parks, *Vice Pres*
John D Parks, *Vice Pres*
▲ EMP: 800
SQ FT: 16,000
SALES (est): 156.9MM **Privately Held**
WEB: www.ampam.com
SIC: **1711** Plumbing contractors

(P-1028)
AMS AMERICAN MECH SVCS MD INC
2116 E Walnut Ave, Fullerton (92831-4845)
PHONE..................................714 888-6820
Charles S Knight, *General Mgr*
EMP: 170
SALES (corp-wide): 1.5B **Privately Held**
WEB: www.amsofusa.com
SIC: **1711** Mechanical contractor
HQ: Ams American Mechanical Services Of Maryland, Inc.
13300 Mid Atlantic Blvd
Laurel MD 20708
301 206-5070

(P-1029)
ANDERSON AIR CONDITIONING LP
2100 E Walnut Ave, Fullerton (92831-4845)
PHONE..................................714 998-6850
Edward Dunn, *General Ptnr*
Mitchell J Haynam, *Partner*
EMP: 60 **EST:** 1969

SALES (est): 10.3MM **Privately Held**
WEB: www.aac-ams.com
SIC: **1711** Warm air heating & air conditioning contractor; heating & air conditioning contractors
PA: American Mechanical Services Of Maryland, L.L.C.
13300 Mid Atlantic Blvd
Laurel MD 20708

(P-1030)
ARROWHEAD BRASS & PLUMBING LLC
4900 Valley Blvd, Los Angeles (90032-3317)
PHONE..................................323 221-9137
Fred Schneider, *CEO*
Jim Kapparos, *Marketing Staff*
Joe Rella, *Sales Staff*
Jose Berumen, *Maint Spvr*
Rosie Figueroa, *Cust Mgr*
▲ EMP: 80 **EST:** 1936
SQ FT: 35,000
SALES (est): 8.3MM **Privately Held**
WEB: www.champion-arrowhead.com
SIC: **1711** Plumbing contractors

(P-1031)
ARTIC MECHANICAL INC (PA)
10440 Trademark St, Rancho Cucamonga (91730-5826)
PHONE..................................909 980-2539
Daniel Hallisey, *President*
John Hadley, *CFO*
Valerie Terrill, *Office Mgr*
Arthur Cano, *Technician*
Ray Freeman, *Technician*
EMP: 77 **EST:** 1999
SQ FT: 15,500
SALES (est): 24.5MM **Privately Held**
WEB: www.articmechanical.com
SIC: **1711** Warm air heating & air conditioning contractor

(P-1032)
BARR ENGINEERING INC
12612 Clark St, Santa Fe Springs (90670-3950)
PHONE..................................562 944-1722
Peter Buongiorno, *President*
Ken Rogers, *COO*
Pamela Price-Recchia, *Corp Secy*
Mike Buongiorno, *Vice Pres*
Frank Pe, *Vice Pres*
EMP: 82 **EST:** 1958
SQ FT: 12,200
SALES (est): 13.3MM **Privately Held**
WEB: www.barrengineering.com
SIC: **1711** Warm air heating & air conditioning contractor

(P-1033)
BERNEL INC
Also Called: Vfs Fire Protection Services
501 W Southern Ave, Orange (92865-3217)
PHONE..................................714 778-6070
Randy Roland Nelson, *CEO*
Kevin Berthoud, *Vice Pres*
Mario Lopez, *Vice Pres*
Jonathan Thomas, *Executive*
Aaron Esparza, *Accounts Exec*
EMP: 140 **EST:** 1994
SQ FT: 7,800
SALES (est): 29.3MM **Privately Held**
WEB: www.vfsfire.com
SIC: **1711 7382** Fire sprinkler system installation; security systems services; fire alarm maintenance & monitoring

(P-1034)
BONANZA PLUMBING INC (PA)
2259 Hamner Ave, Norco (92860-2608)
PHONE..................................951 360-8262
James Dean Potts, *President*
Ray Goldsboro, *Superintendent*
EMP: 79 **EST:** 1996
SALES (est): 7.9MM **Privately Held**
WEB: www.bonanzaplumbing.com
SIC: **1711** Plumbing contractors

PRODUCTS & SVCS

(P-1035)
BONESO BROTHERS CNSTR INC
2758 Concrete Ct, Paso Robles (93446-5936)
PHONE..................805 227-4450
Steve Boneso, *President*
Rob Boneso, *Vice Pres*
EMP: 80 EST: 1999
SQ FT: 4,000
SALES (est): 40MM Privately Held
WEB: www.bonesobrothersconstruction.com
SIC: 1711 1542 Mechanical contractor; nonresidential construction

(P-1036)
BREEZE AIR CONDITIONING LLC
75145 Saint Charles Pl A, Palm Desert (92211-9048)
PHONE..................760 346-0855
Joe Coker, *Mng Member*
EMP: 59 EST: 1980
SQ FT: 33,000
SALES (est): 10MM Privately Held
WEB: www.breezeac.com
SIC: 1711 3444 5075 3433 Warm air heating & air conditioning contractor; sheet metalwork; warm air heating & air conditioning; logs, gas fireplace

(P-1037)
BRIGHTVIEW LANDSCAPE DEV INC
13691 Vaughn St, San Fernando (91340-3072)
PHONE..................818 838-4700
Greg Motschenbacher, *Branch Mgr*
EMP: 75
SALES (corp-wide): 2.3B Publicly Held
WEB: www.brightview.com
SIC: 1711 0781 Irrigation sprinkler system installation; landscape services
HQ: Brightview Landscape Development, Inc.
27001 Agoura Rd Ste 350
Calabasas CA 91301
818 223-8500

(P-1038)
BRIGHTVIEW LANDSCAPE DEV INC
8 Hughes Ste 125, Irvine (92618-2079)
PHONE..................714 546-7975
Gins Garmann, *Manager*
Greg Barker, *VP Opers*
Jeff Mutch, *Marketing Mgr*
EMP: 75
SALES (corp-wide): 2.3B Publicly Held
WEB: www.brightview.com
SIC: 1711 0781 Irrigation sprinkler system installation; heating & air conditioning contractors; landscape services
HQ: Brightview Landscape Development, Inc.
27001 Agoura Rd Ste 350
Calabasas CA 91301
818 223-8500

(P-1039)
BROADSTREET SOLAR INC
Also Called: Broadstreet Power
16112 Hart St, Van Nuys (91406-3903)
PHONE..................818 206-1464
Ahmad M Yakub, *CEO*
EMP: 50
SQ FT: 2,400
SALES (est): 6.9MM Privately Held
WEB: www.broadstreetsolar.com
SIC: 1711 Solar energy contractor

(P-1040)
BRYMAX CONSTRUCTION SVCS INC
7436 Lorge Cir, Huntington Beach (92647-3619)
PHONE..................949 200-9619
Brooke Willems, *CEO*
Michael Willems, *President*
Tony Teriitehau, *COO*
Steve Sylvester, *CFO*
Robin Feldman, *Office Mgr*
EMP: 79 EST: 2015
SALES (est): 7.3MM Privately Held
WEB: www.brymaxservices.com
SIC: 1711 5075 5065 4225 Plumbing, heating, air-conditioning contractors; warm air heating & air conditioning; electronic parts & equipment; general warehousing & storage

(P-1041)
C & L REFRIGERATION CORP
Also Called: Honeywell Authorized Dealer
4111 N Palm St, Fullerton (92835-1025)
P.O. Box 2319, Brea (92822-2319)
PHONE..................800 901-4822
Ronald J Cassell Jr, *CEO*
Larry Jaslove, *Vice Pres*
Scott Tredo, *Vice Pres*
Chelsea Henry, *Administration*
Joe Knotts, *Info Tech Mgr*
EMP: 150 EST: 1978
SQ FT: 18,000
SALES (est): 40.2MM Privately Held
WEB: www.clrefrigeration.com
SIC: 1711 Refrigeration contractor; warm air heating & air conditioning contractor

(P-1042)
CASPIAN COMMERCIAL PLBG INC
711 Ivy St, Glendale (91204-1003)
PHONE..................818 649-2500
Anahit Alexandrian, *President*
Santos Cabrera, *Foreman/Supr*
Unice Liu, *
EMP: 65 EST: 2011
SALES (est): 10.6MM Privately Held
WEB: www.ftpccp.com
SIC: 1711 Plumbing contractors

(P-1043)
CFP DESIGNS INC
Also Called: Dlb Fire Protection
3001 Petrol Rd, Bakersfield (93308-9739)
PHONE..................661 903-8940
Celina Jaramillo, *Admin Asst*
Mike Boyance, *Senior Mgr*
Brandon Strange, *Superintendent*
EMP: 51 EST: 2016
SALES (est): 4.7MM Privately Held
WEB: www.dlbfire.com
SIC: 1711 Fire sprinkler system installation

(P-1044)
CFP FIRE PROTECTION INC
153 Technology Dr Ste 200, Irvine (92618-2461)
PHONE..................949 727-3277
Matt Krofcheck, *President*
Josh Hobgood, *Corp Secy*
Richard Hellewell, *Controller*
EMP: 100 EST: 2002
SQ FT: 21,960
SALES (est): 13.2MM Privately Held
WEB: www.cfpfire.com
SIC: 1711 Fire sprinkler system installation
PA: Mx Holdings Us, Inc.
153 Technology Dr Ste 200
Irvine CA 92618

(P-1045)
CIRCULATING AIR INC (PA)
Also Called: Honeywell Authorized Dealer
7337 Varna Ave, North Hollywood (91605-4009)
PHONE..................818 764-0530
Joseph Gallagher, *CEO*
Susan Gallagher, *President*
Marcy Ahlstrom, *Treasurer*
Joe Gallagher, *Exec VP*
David Rowan, *General Mgr*
EMP: 100 EST: 1965
SQ FT: 13,000
SALES (est): 27.9MM Privately Held
WEB: www.circulatingair.com
SIC: 1711 Mechanical contractor

(P-1046)
CLAY DUNN ENTERPRISES INC
Also Called: Air-TEC
1606 E Carson St, Carson (90745-2504)
P.O. Box 5444 (90749-5444)
PHONE..................310 549-1698
Clayton N Dunn, *President*
Hayley Amberg, *Admin Sec*
Drew Mallad, *Info Tech Mgr*
Reiner Caraballo, *Project Mgr*
Mike Conkey, *Controller*
EMP: 175
SQ FT: 18,000
SALES (est): 76MM Privately Held
WEB: www.airtecperforms.com
SIC: 1711 Warm air heating & air conditioning contractor

(P-1047)
CONTROL AC SVC CORP
5200 E La Palma Ave, Anaheim (92807-2019)
PHONE..................714 777-8600
Kendrick Ellis, *President*
Greg Rummler, *CFO*
Stanley Ellis, *Vice Pres*
Ben Herrin, *CIO*
Marcus Terry, *Info Tech Mgr*
EMP: 51 EST: 1990
SALES (est): 11.6MM Privately Held
WEB: www.controlac.com
SIC: 1711 Warm air heating & air conditioning contractor

(P-1048)
COOLSYS COML INDUS SLTIONS INC (DH)
145 S State College Blvd, Brea (92821-5818)
PHONE..................714 510-9609
Bradley Norman Howard, *Ch of Bd*
Andrew Mandell, *COO*
Scott Rosner, *CFO*
Beth Goldstein, *Exec VP*
John Manzanares, *Exec VP*
EMP: 582 EST: 1995
SALES (est): 523.1MM
SALES (corp-wide): 1.7B Publicly Held
WEB: www.sourcerefrigeration.com
SIC: 1711 Refrigeration contractor
HQ: Coolsys, Inc.
145 S State College Blvd
Brea CA 92821
714 510-9577

(P-1049)
CORONAL LOST HILLS LLC (PA)
301 N Lake Ave Ste 202, Pasadena (91101-5127)
PHONE..................855 267-6625
Jonathan D Jaffrey, *CEO*
EMP: 53 EST: 2013
SALES (est): 2.1MM Privately Held
WEB: www.coronalenergy.com
SIC: 1711 Solar energy contractor

(P-1050)
CRITCHFELD MECH INC STHERN CAL
15391 Springdale St, Huntington Beach (92649-1100)
PHONE..................949 390-2900
Mike Pearlman, *CEO*
EMP: 100 EST: 2004
SALES (est): 10.4MM Privately Held
SIC: 1711 Warm air heating & air conditioning contractor

(P-1051)
D/K MECHANICAL CONTRACTORS INC
3870 E Eagle Dr, Anaheim (92807-1706)
PHONE..................714 970-0180
Gary Brubaker, *President*
Don Giarratano, *Vice Pres*
EMP: 58 EST: 1981
SALES (est): 1.3MM Privately Held
SIC: 1711 Plumbing contractors; warm air heating & air conditioning contractor

(P-1052)
DAART ENGINEERING COMPANY INC
4100 Garner Rd, Riverside (92501-1004)
PHONE..................909 888-8696
Timothy C Cantwell, *President*
James D Dunn, *Corp Secy*
Robert Pfeifer, *Admin Sec*
EMP: 70
SALES: 9MM Privately Held
SIC: 1711 Fire sprinkler system installation

(P-1053)
DAVE WILLIAMS PLBG & ELEC INC
75140 Saint Charles Pl C, Palm Desert (92211-9044)
PHONE..................730 296-1397
Daniel Williams, *President*
Dave Williams, *Vice Pres*
Mike Perezchica, *Purch Agent*
EMP: 110 EST: 2008
SALES (est): 10MM Privately Held
WEB: www.dwpeinc.com
SIC: 1711 Plumbing contractors; fire sprinkler system installation

(P-1054)
DAVIDSONS AC & HTG INC
Also Called: Davidsons AC Htg & Sh
495 S Sierra Way, San Bernardino (92408-1444)
PHONE..................909 885-2703
Richard S Davidson, *Presiden*
EMP: 22 EST: 1985
SQ FT: 2,500
SALES (est): 2.4MM Privately Held
WEB: www.davidsonsairandheat.com
SIC: 1711 3444 Warm air heating & air conditioning contractor; sheet metal specialties, not stamped

(P-1055)
DESERT MECHANICAL INC
Also Called: Dmi
15870 Olden St, Sylmar (91342-1241)
PHONE..................702 873-7333
Casey M Condron, *President*
Joseph Guglielmo, *Senior VP*
Andre Burnthon, *Vice Pres*
Alex L Hodson, *Vice Pres*
Dan Naylor, *Vice Pres*
EMP: 1100 EST: 1977
SQ FT: 25,000
SALES (est): 103.4MM
SALES (corp-wide): 5.3B Publicly Held
WEB: www.lvdmi.com
SIC: 1711 Plumbing contractors
PA: Tutor Perini Corporation
15901 Olden St
Sylmar CA 91342
818 362-8391

(P-1056)
DON BRANDEL PLUMBING INC
15100 Texaco Ave, Paramount (90723-3916)
PHONE..................562 408-0400
Greg Brandel, *President*
Dennis Castaldo, *Exec VP*
Jim Brandel, *Vice Pres*
Charron Castaldo, *Admin Sec*
Pam Evans, *Manager*
EMP: 50 EST: 1948
SQ FT: 20,000
SALES (est): 11.5MM Privately Held
WEB: www.brandelplumbing.com
SIC: 1711 Plumbing contractors

(P-1057)
DUTTON HOME SERVICES LLC
Also Called: Dutton Plumbing
997 Flower Glen St, Simi Valley (93065-1926)
PHONE..................702 625-9104
Kim Miramontes, *CFO*
EMP: 50 EST: 2010
SALES (est): 4MM
SALES (corp-wide): 125MM Privately Held
WEB: www.duttonplumbing.com
SIC: 1711 Plumbing contractors
PA: Goettl Home Services, Llc
8311 W Sunset Rd Ste 200
Las Vegas NV 89113
702 830-7740

(P-1058)
ECB CORP (PA)
Also Called: Omniduct
6400 Artesia Blvd, Buena Park (90620-1006)
PHONE..................714 385-8900
Robert Brumleu, *Presiden*
Steve Philp, *CFO*
Steven G Philp, *CFO*
Sam Luk, *Project Leader*
Ian Castellanos, *IT/INT Sup*

▲ **EMP:** 100 **EST:** 1980
SQ FT: 56,000
SALES (est): 39.4MM **Privately Held**
WEB: www.omniduct.com
SIC: 1711 3444 Ventilation & duct work
contractor; ducts, sheet metal

(P-1059)
ECOTECH RFRGN & HVAC INC
630 S Sunkist St Ste R, Anaheim
(92806-4529)
PHONE..............................888 833-8100
Erich Christopher Munzner, *CEO*
Mark Bartolo, *Director*
EMP: 60 **EST:** 2014
SALES (est): 4.7MM **Privately Held**
WEB: www.ecotech-hvacr.com
SIC: 1711 Refrigeration contractor

(P-1060)
ELECNOR INC (DH)
4331 Schaefer Ave, Chino (91710-5451)
PHONE..............................909 993-5470
Jose Castellanos, *CEO*
Ivan Guillermo Ballesteros, *Principal*
Alberto Garcia, *VP Engrg*
Tom Gebelin, *Project Mgr*
Elisa Lim, *Project Mgr*
▲ **EMP:** 192 **EST:** 2003
SQ FT: 5,000
SALES (est): 245MM
SALES (corp-wide): 16.1MM **Privately Held**
WEB: www.elecnorbelco.com
SIC: 1711 Solar energy contractor
HQ: Elecnor Sa
Calle Marques De Mondejar 33
Madrid 28028
914 179-900

(P-1061)
ELECTRIC ON TARGET INC
17691 Mitchell N Ste A, Irvine
(92614-6828)
PHONE..............................949 247-3842
Heberto Dominguez II, *Vice Pres*
Brian Watts, *Principal*
EMP: 67 **EST:** 2008
SALES (est): 11.6MM **Privately Held**
WEB: www.ontargetelectric.com
SIC: 1711 Solar energy contractor

(P-1062)
ENERGY ENTERPRISES USA INC (PA)
Also Called: Canopy Energy
6842 Van Nuys Blvd # 800, Van Nuys
(91405-4660)
PHONE..............................424 339-0005
Lior Agam, *CEO*
Jordan Cohen, *COO*
Heather Pollock, *Project Mgr*
Frank Schwartz, *Controller*
Jennifer Martin, *Sales Mgr*
EMP: 100 **EST:** 2011
SQ FT: 11,000
SALES (est): 16MM **Privately Held**
WEB: www.canopyenergy.com
SIC: 1711 Solar energy contractor

(P-1063)
ENVISE (HQ)
12131 Western Ave, Garden Grove
(92841-2914)
PHONE..............................800 613-6240
Chris Lofaso, *CEO*
Ryan Nagle, *Vice Pres*
Travis Fletcher, *Branch Mgr*
Tim Potter, *Branch Mgr*
Sherry McMillan, *Admin Asst*
EMP: 68 **EST:** 2015
SALES: 88.8MM
SALES (corp-wide): 940.1MM **Privately Held**
WEB: www.enviseco.com
SIC: 1711 Plumbing, heating, air-condition-
ing contractors
PA: Southland Industries
12131 Western Ave
Garden Grove CA 92841
800 613-6240

(P-1064)
ENVISE
12131 Western Ave, Garden Grove
(92841-2914)
PHONE..............................714 901-5800
Travis Feltcher, *Branch Mgr*
Jason Gladney, *Vice Pres*
Jody Baldwin, *Branch Mgr*
Annabelle Caberte, *Office Mgr*
Craig Gonzalez, *Opers Mgr*
EMP: 63
SALES (corp-wide): 940.1MM **Privately Held**
WEB: www.enviseco.com
SIC: 1711 Plumbing, heating, air-condition-
ing contractors
HQ: Envise
12131 Western Ave
Garden Grove CA 92841
800 613-6240

(P-1065)
ESS LLC
Also Called: Evergreen Solar Services
5227 Dantes View Dr, Agoura Hills
(91301-2313)
PHONE..............................888 303-6424
Jacob Stephens, *President*
Surayya Nayya, *Engineer*
Abu Al-Sous, *Sales Staff*
EMP: 100 **EST:** 2011
SALES (est): 30.8MM **Privately Held**
SIC: 1711 Solar energy contractor

(P-1066)
FERREIRA SERVICE INC (PA)
1811 Tortuga St, Acton (93510-1898)
P.O. Box 3142, San Ramon (94583-8142)
PHONE..............................925 831-9330
Susan Ferreira, *CEO*
Albert Ferreira, *President*
Raymond Ferreira, *COO*
Susan Town, *Data Proc Exec*
EMP: 65 **EST:** 1978
SQ FT: 10,000
SALES (est): 6.2MM **Privately Held**
WEB: www.ferreira.com
SIC: 1711 Mechanical contractor

(P-1067)
FIRE SAFE SYSTEMS INC
1312 Kingsdale Ave, Redondo Beach
(90278-3926)
PHONE..............................310 542-0585
Michael Moller, *CEO*
Joyce Moller, *President*
Sandra Marquez, *Office Mgr*
Nora Llamas, *Admin Asst*
Mark Brancato, *Project Mgr*
EMP: 60 **EST:** 1993
SQ FT: 3,000
SALES (est): 11.4MM **Privately Held**
WEB: www.firesafesystems.com
SIC: 1711 Fire sprinkler system installation

(P-1068)
FIRE SPRINKLER SYSTEMS INC (PA)
705 E Harrison St Ste 200, Corona
(92879-1398)
P.O. Box 2378 (92878-2378)
PHONE..............................800 915-3473
Harold Roger, *President*
Michael Kerby, *CFO*
Ralph Tolomei, *Officer*
Amy Descoteaux, *Engineer*
Lilia Castro, *Human Res Mgr*
EMP: 99 **EST:** 1993
SALES (est): 14.8MM **Privately Held**
WEB: www.fireinc.net
SIC: 1711 Fire sprinkler system installation

(P-1069)
FISCHER INC
1372 W 26th St, San Bernardino
(92405-3029)
PHONE..............................909 881-2910
Michael G Fischer, *President*
EMP: 55 **EST:** 1984
SQ FT: 1,600
SALES (est): 4.5MM **Privately Held**
SIC: 1711 Plumbing contractors

(P-1070)
FREEDOM FOREVER LLC
43445 Bus Pk Dr Ste 104, Temecula
(92590-3670)
PHONE..............................888 557-6431
Brett Bouchy,
Danny Rubin, *Vice Pres*
James Pastula, *Regional Mgr*
Barry Stovall, *Software Engr*
Greg Vasilion, *Project Mgr*
EMP: 212 **EST:** 2016
SALES (est): 31.2MM **Privately Held**
WEB: www.freedomforever.com
SIC: 1711 Solar energy contractor

(P-1071)
FREEDOM SOLAR SERVICES
Also Called: Freedom Forever
43445 Bus Pk Dr Ste 110, Temecula
(92590-3671)
PHONE..............................888 557-6431
Brett Leon Bouchy, *CEO*
EMP: 150 **EST:** 2012
SALES (est): 13.1MM **Privately Held**
WEB: www.freedomsolarco.com
SIC: 1711 Solar energy contractor

(P-1072)
FRONTIER MECHANICAL INC
Also Called: Frontier Plumbing
6309 Seven Seas Ave, Bakersfield
(93308-5133)
PHONE..............................661 589-6203
Rick Palmer, *President*
Brenda Palmer, *Shareholder*
EMP: 93 **EST:** 1987
SQ FT: 120,000
SALES (est): 13.9MM **Privately Held**
WEB: www.frontier-plumbing.com
SIC: 1711 1521 Plumbing contractors;
new construction, single-family houses

(P-1073)
GAR BENNETT LLC
955 S Commerce Way, Lemoore
(93245-9001)
PHONE..............................559 582-9336
Greg Musson, *Branch Mgr*
EMP: 50
SALES (corp-wide): 154.2MM **Privately Held**
WEB: www.garbennett.com
SIC: 1711 3272 Irrigation sprinkler system
installation; pipe, concrete or lined with
concrete
PA: Gar Bennett, Llc
8246 Crawford Ave
Reedley CA 93654
559 638-6311

(P-1074)
GENERAL ENGINEERING WSTN INC (PA)
Also Called: Thermal Air
1140 N Red Gum St, Anaheim
(92806-2516)
PHONE..............................714 630-3200
Stephen Weiss, *CEO*
Joseph Urban, *President*
EMP: 60 **EST:** 1973
SQ FT: 10,000 **Privately Held**
WEB: www.thermalair.com
SIC: 1711 Mechanical contractor

(P-1075)
GENERAL UNDERGROUND
701 W Grove Ave, Orange (92865-3213)
P.O. Box 29830, Anaheim (92809-0194)
PHONE..............................714 632-8646
Robert Anderson, *CEO*
Terry Householder, *President*
Karla Distrola, *Vice Pres*
Susie Ziegler, *Office Mgr*
Danny Martinez, *Superintendent*
EMP: 110 **EST:** 1985
SQ FT: 8,000
SALES (est): 23.6MM **Privately Held**
WEB: www.gufpinc.com
SIC: 1711 Fire sprinkler system installation

(P-1076)
GRAYCON INC
232 S 8th Ave, City of Industry
(91746-3200)
PHONE..............................626 961-9640
Joseph F Klein, *CEO*

Wayne Lyons, *COO*
Jim Smith, *Regional Mgr*
Mike Yackee, *Project Mgr*
Roger Vargas, *Controller*
EMP: 50 **EST:** 1968
SQ FT: 12,000
SALES (est): 12.5MM **Privately Held**
WEB: www.graycon.net
SIC: 1711 Mechanical contractor; warm air
heating & air conditioning contractor

(P-1077)
GREERS BNNER A BAKERSFIELD INC
Also Called: Honeywell Authorized Dealer
4115 Buck Owens Blvd, Bakersfield
(93308-4963)
PHONE..............................661 322-5858
Kent Matthew Greer, *CEO*
Lyn Kalar, *Admin Sec*
EMP: 52 **EST:** 1952
SQ FT: 4,500
SALES (est): 2.7MM **Privately Held**
WEB: www.bannerair.com
SIC: 1711 Warm air heating & air condi-
tioning contractor

(P-1078)
GUARDIAN FIRE SERVICE INC
Also Called: Guardian Fire & Safety
8248 W Doe Ave, Visalia (93291-9263)
PHONE..............................559 651-0919
John Maly, *President*
EMP: 21 **EST:** 2010
SALES (est): 2.5MM **Privately Held**
WEB: www.guardiansafety.com
SIC: 5999 1711 3842 Fire extinguishers;
fire sprinkler system installation; personal
safety equipment

(P-1079)
GUNDLACH PLBG & SHTMTL CO LTD
Also Called: Gundlach Plumbing AC & Htg
4415 Foster Ave, Bakersfield (93308-4576)
P.O. Box 1738 (93302-1738)
PHONE..............................661 327-3052
Shelly Lynne Wonderly, *CEO*
Ken Wonderly, *Vice Pres*
EMP: 51 **EST:** 1900
SQ FT: 4,800
SALES (est): 1.3MM **Privately Held**
WEB: www.gundlachsservice.com
SIC: 1711 Plumbing contractors; heating &
air conditioning contractors

(P-1080)
H L MOE CO INC (PA)
Also Called: Keefe Plumbing Services
526 Commercial St, Glendale
(91203-2861)
PHONE..............................818 572-2100
Martha Tennyson, *CEO*
Michael C Davis, *President*
Robert Francis, *Vice Pres*
Jeff Hachey, *Vice Pres*
Richard Herrea, *Vice Pres*
EMP: 130 **EST:** 1927
SALES (est): 25.5MM **Privately Held**
WEB: www.moeplumbing.com
SIC: 1711 Plumbing contractors

(P-1081)
HALDEMAN INC
2937 Tanager Ave, Commerce
(90040-2761)
PHONE..............................323 726-7011
Tom Haldeman, *Ch of Bd*
Mark O Donnell, *President*
Jeff Dandridge, *CFO*
Sue Haldeman, *Treasurer*
Holt Dandridge, *Vice Pres*
EMP: 50 **EST:** 1933
SQ FT: 45,000
SALES (est): 10.9MM **Privately Held**
WEB: www.haldemaninc.com
SIC: 1711 Mechanical contractor

(P-1082)
HPS MECHANICAL INC (PA)
3100 E Belle Ter, Bakersfield (93307-6830)
PHONE..............................661 397-2121
Les Denherder, *President*
Scott Denherder, *Vice Pres*
Roger Lane, *Project Mgr*
Jun Angeles, *Project Engr*

Jamie Ramos, *Human Res Mgr*
EMP: 127 **EST:** 1959
SALES (est): 50.9MM **Privately Held**
WEB: www.hpsmechanical.com
SIC: 1711 Plumbing contractors

(P-1083)
INFINITY PLUMBING DESIGNS INC
9182 Stellar Ct, Corona (92883-4923)
PHONE..................................951 737-4436
Andrew D Carlson, *President*
John M Raya, *Exec VP*
Joe Beckworth, *Vice Pres*
Carlos Garza, *Vice Pres*
Darrik Carlson, *Office Mgr*
EMP: 300 **EST:** 2006
SQ FT: 5,925
SALES (est): 27.1MM **Privately Held**
WEB: www.infinityplumbingdesigns.com
SIC: 1711 Plumbing contractors

(P-1084)
INFINITY SVC GROUP INC A CAL C
Also Called: Allstar Home Services
9155 Archibald Ave # 302, Rancho Cucamonga (91730-5238)
P.O. Box 4229 (91729-4229)
PHONE..................................909 466-6237
Justin Speelman, *President*
Jason Carroll, *CFO*
Leighton Jenner, *Vice Pres*
James McNeeley, *Admin Sec*
EMP: 54 **EST:** 2004
SQ FT: 3,200
SALES (est): 7.1MM **Privately Held**
WEB: www.sheriffplumbing.com
SIC: 1711 Plumbing contractors

(P-1085)
J M CARDEN SPRINKLER CO INC
2909 Fletcher Dr, Los Angeles (90065-1479)
PHONE..................................323 258-8300
Michael Carden, *President*
Allison Jacobson, *Treasurer*
Carroll B Carden, *Corp Secy*
Dick Wallace Pe, *Vice Pres*
Richard Wallace, *Vice Pres*
EMP: 60 **EST:** 1953
SQ FT: 48,000
SALES (est): 11.7MM **Privately Held**
WEB: www.jmcfire.com
SIC: 1711 Fire sprinkler system installation

(P-1086)
JCT COMPANY LLC
Also Called: Aliso Air Conditioning & Htg
29736 Avnida De Las Bnder, Rancho Santa Margari (92688)
PHONE..................................949 589-2021
Jeffrey Loftus,
Monika Hall, *Department Mgr*
Lauren Barbarino, *Administration*
Debbie Covarrubias, *Administration*
Shawn Cooney, *Sales Staff*
EMP: 50 **EST:** 1998
SALES (est): 5.3MM **Privately Held**
SIC: 1711 Warm air heating & air conditioning contractor

(P-1087)
JPI DEVELOPMENT GROUP INC
41205 Golden Gate Cir, Murrieta (92562-6991)
PHONE..................................951 973-7680
Brad Janikowski, *President*
Dan Janikowski, *Vice Pres*
EMP: 60 **EST:** 2000
SQ FT: 6,000
SALES (est): 10MM **Privately Held**
SIC: 1711 Plumbing contractors

(P-1088)
K & S AIR CONDITIONING INC
Also Called: K&S
143 E Meats Ave, Orange (92865-3309)
PHONE..................................714 685-0077
Steven Patz, *President*
Renee Patz, *Vice Pres*
Dave Guido, *General Mgr*
Jeff Tureck, *Manager*
Allan Lemelin, *Asst Mgr*

EMP: 140 **EST:** 1952
SQ FT: 18,000
SALES (est): 27.5MM **Privately Held**
WEB: www.kandsair.com
SIC: 1711 Warm air heating & air conditioning contractor

(P-1089)
KEN STARR INC
Also Called: Home Comfort USA
1120 N Tustin Ave, Anaheim (92807-1712)
PHONE..................................714 632-8789
Ken Starr, *President*
Paul Buono, *Vice Pres*
EMP: 80 **EST:** 2011
SQ FT: 9,000
SALES (est): 14MM **Privately Held**
WEB: www.homecomfortusa.com
SIC: 1711 Warm air heating & air conditioning contractor; heating & air conditioning contractors

(P-1090)
KEY AIR CNDITIONING CONTRS INC
10905 Laurel Ave, Santa Fe Springs (90670-4513)
PHONE..................................562 941-2233
Richard Rivera, *President*
Robert Donat, *Vice Pres*
Larry Stikeleather, *Vice Pres*
Matt Walters, *Manager*
Whitney Kidwell, *Receptionist*
EMP: 87 **EST:** 1993
SQ FT: 35,000
SALES (est): 26.5MM **Privately Held**
WEB: www.keyairconditioning.net
SIC: 1711 Warm air heating & air conditioning contractor

(P-1091)
KINCAID INDUSTRIES INC
31065 Plantation Dr, Thousand Palms (92276-6623)
PHONE..................................760 343-5457
Scott Kincaid, *CEO*
Dave Seipel, *Project Mgr*
Tim Berg, *Sr Project Mgr*
EMP: 116 **EST:** 1995
SQ FT: 7,000
SALES (est): 65.4MM **Privately Held**
WEB: www.kincaidindustries.com
SIC: 1711 Plumbing contractors

(P-1092)
LAND FORMS LANSCAPE CNSTR INC
Also Called: Land Forms Landscape Cnstr
1901 Carnegie Ave Ste 1e, Santa Ana (92705-5504)
PHONE..................................949 582-0877
Luke Alvarado, *CEO*
Jon Gilmer, *President*
Brian Olsen, *President*
Sandy Wallace, *CFO*
Claudia Lopez, *Admin Asst*
EMP: 50 **EST:** 1989
SALES (est): 9.6MM **Privately Held**
WEB: www.landformslandscaping.com
SIC: 1711 0782 Irrigation sprinkler system installation; landscape contractors

(P-1093)
LDI MECHANICAL INC (PA)
Also Called: Honeywell Authorized Dealer
1587 E Bentley Dr, Corona (92879-1738)
PHONE..................................951 340-9685
Lloyd Smith, *President*
Mike Smith, *Senior VP*
Robert Smith, *Senior VP*
Steve Buren, *Vice Pres*
Jeff Minarik, *Vice Pres*
EMP: 353 **EST:** 1985
SQ FT: 38,000
SALES (est): 87.5MM **Privately Held**
WEB: www.ldimechanical.com
SIC: 1711 Mechanical contractor

(P-1094)
LIMBACH COMPANY LP
Also Called: Western Air & Refrigeration
1709 Apollo Ct, Seal Beach (90740-5617)
PHONE..................................714 653-7000
Charlie Bacon, *CEO*
John T Jordan Jr, *CFO*
Robert C Morgan, *Vice Pres*

Olivia Gonzalez, *Office Mgr*
George Scholten, *Sales Mgr*
EMP: 167 **EST:** 2002
SALES (est): 97.4MM **Privately Held**
WEB: www.limbachinc.com
SIC: 1711 Mechanical contractor
HQ: Limbach Company Llc
　　1251 Waterfront Pl # 201
　　Pittsburgh PA 15222
　　412 359-2173

(P-1095)
LINC WESTERN AIR LP
152 Technology Dr, Irvine (92618-2401)
PHONE..................................949 330-1535
David A Whaley, *CEO*
Scott Giacobbe, *President*
Leslie C Cunningham, *Vice Pres*
EMP: 71 **EST:** 2003
SALES (est): 704K **Privately Held**
SIC: 1711 Heating & air conditioning contractors

(P-1096)
LOZANO PLUMBING SERVICES INC
Also Called: Plumbing Master
3615 Presley Ave, Riverside (92507-4448)
P.O. Box 53137 (92517-4137)
PHONE..................................951 683-4840
Andrew Lozano, *President*
Felipe Lozano, *CEO*
Rebecca Lynn Pearson, *Controller*
Monica Villaquiran, *Controller*
Emma Contreras, *Accounts Mgr*
EMP: 130 **EST:** 2004
SALES (est): 13.5MM **Privately Held**
WEB: www.plumbingmaster.com
SIC: 1711 Plumbing contractors

(P-1097)
LPSH HOLDINGS INC (PA)
Also Called: Horizon Solar Power
7100 W Florida Ave, Hemet (92545-3410)
PHONE..................................855 647-5061
Frank Kneller, *CEO*
Leroy Polvoorde, *President*
Xochilt Lopez, *Office Mgr*
Gail Polvoorde, *Admin Sec*
Caleb Quinto, *Manager*
EMP: 437 **EST:** 2013
SALES (est): 32.8MM **Privately Held**
SIC: 1711 Solar energy contractor

(P-1098)
LPSH HOLDINGS INC
Also Called: Horizon Solar Power
3570 W Florida Ave # 168, Hemet (92545-3518)
PHONE..................................951 926-1176
Zachary Allman, *Accounts Mgr*
EMP: 88
SALES (corp-wide): 32.8MM **Privately Held**
SIC: 1711 Solar energy contractor
PA: Lpsh Holdings, Inc.
　　7100 W Florida Ave
　　Hemet CA 92545
　　855 647-5061

(P-1099)
M & M PLUMBING INC
6782 Columbus St, Riverside (92504-1118)
PHONE..................................951 354-5388
Robert Malcom, *President*
Glenn Malcolm, *Principal*
EMP: 80 **EST:** 2002
SALES (est): 5.9MM **Privately Held**
WEB: www.mmplumbing.net
SIC: 1711 Plumbing contractors

(P-1100)
MDDR INC
Also Called: Econo Air
555 Vanguard Way, Brea (92821-3933)
PHONE..................................714 792-1993
Michael Richards, *President*
Rhonda Richards, *Admin Sec*
Scott Sunblad, *Sales Staff*
EMP: 110 **EST:** 1991
SALES (est): 26.8MM **Privately Held**
WEB: www.myeconoair.com
SIC: 1711 1731 Warm air heating & air conditioning contractor; electrical work

(P-1101)
MEMEGED TEVUOT SHEMESH (PA)
Also Called: Titan Solar
5550 Topanga Canyon Blvd # 280, Woodland Hills (91367-7471)
PHONE..................................866 575-1211
Ofir Haimoff, *Owner*
EMP: 152 **EST:** 2011
SQ FT: 20,000
SALES (est): 16.9MM **Privately Held**
SIC: 1711 5074 Solar energy contractor; heating equipment & panels, solar

(P-1102)
MESA ENERGY SYSTEMS INC (HQ)
Also Called: Emcor Services Mesa Energy
2 Cromwell, Irvine (92618-1816)
PHONE..................................949 460-0460
Robert A Lake, *President*
Steve Hunt, *CFO*
Kip Bagley, *Vice Pres*
Michael Ecshner, *Vice Pres*
Charles G Fletcher Jr, *Vice Pres*
EMP: 210 **EST:** 1984
SQ FT: 55,000
SALES (est): 114MM
SALES (corp-wide): 8.8B **Publicly Held**
WEB: www.mesaenergy.com
SIC: 1711 7623 Warm air heating & air conditioning contractor; refrigeration service & repair
PA: Emcor Group, Inc.
　　301 Merritt 7 Fl 6
　　Norwalk CT 06851
　　203 849-7800

(P-1103)
MORRIS LEVIN AND SON
Also Called: Morris Levin Rent & Parts Ctr
1816 S K St, Tulare (93274-6842)
PHONE..................................559 686-8665
Paul Atlas, *President*
Tom Colesberry, *CFO*
David Atlas, *Vice Pres*
Marilyn Atlas, *Vice Pres*
Lesa Zack, *Credit Mgr*
EMP: 125 **EST:** 1934
SQ FT: 40,000
SALES (est): 22.4MM **Privately Held**
WEB: www.morrislevin.com
SIC: 5251 1711 7359 Hardware; plumbing, heating, air-conditioning contractors; rental store, general

(P-1104)
MUIR-CHASE PLUMBING CO INC
Also Called: M C
4530 Brazil St Ste 1, Los Angeles (90039-1000)
PHONE..................................818 500-1940
Don Chase, *President*
Jay Chase, *Vice Pres*
Gail Comstock, *Vice Pres*
Grant Muir, *Vice Pres*
James M Muir, *Vice Pres*
EMP: 90 **EST:** 1975
SQ FT: 5,000
SALES (est): 23.7MM **Privately Held**
WEB: www.muirchase.com
SIC: 1711 7699 Plumbing contractors; sewer cleaning & rodding

(P-1105)
MULTI MECHANICAL INC
Also Called: Honeywell Authorized Dealer
469 Blaine St, Corona (92879-1304)
PHONE..................................714 632-7404
Brandon Abblitt, *CEO*
Thomas Alvey, *Purch Mgr*
Jeremy Towers, *Superintendent*
EMP: 75 **EST:** 2003
SALES (est): 25.9MM **Privately Held**
WEB: www.multimechanical.com
SIC: 1711 Mechanical contractor

(P-1106)
MURRAY PLUMBING AND HTG CORP (PA)
Also Called: Murray Company
18414 S Santa Fe Ave E Rncho Dmngz (90221-5612)
PHONE..................................310 637-1500

Kevan Steffey, *Chairman*
James De Flavio, *CEO*
Richard Murray, *Vice Pres*
Don Odom, *Vice Pres*
James Patton, *Vice Pres*
EMP: 980 **EST:** 1913
SQ FT: 26,000
SALES: 310.6MM **Privately Held**
WEB: www.murraycompany.com
SIC: 1711 Plumbing contractors

(P-1107)
NEW POWER INC
887 Marlborough Ave, Riverside (92507-2133)
PHONE....................800 980-9825
Thomas Shaffer, *President*
Matt Collins, *CFO*
EMP: 83 **EST:** 2009
SALES (est): 7.7MM **Privately Held**
WEB: www.newpower.company
SIC: 1711 Solar energy contractor

(P-1108)
NEXGEN AIR LOS ANGELES (PA)
Also Called: Nexgen Air Heating and Plbg
700 N Valley St Ste Jk, Anaheim (92801-3824)
PHONE....................714 331-9633
Ismael Valdez, *President*
EMP: 52 **EST:** 2015
SALES (est): 6.6MM **Privately Held**
WEB: www.nexgenairandplumbing.com
SIC: 1711 Warm air heating & air conditioning contractor

(P-1109)
NP MECHANICAL INC
9129 Stellar Ct, Corona (92883-4924)
P.O. Box 309 (92878-0309)
PHONE....................951 667-4220
Cecil J Hallinan, *CEO*
Richard Hallinan, *COO*
EMP: 400 **EST:** 2005
SALES: 60.3MM **Privately Held**
WEB: www.npmechanicalinc.net
SIC: 1711 Mechanical contractor; fire sprinkler system installation

(P-1110)
ONE CALL PLUMBER SANTA BARBARA
1016 Cliff Dr Apt 309, Santa Barbara (93109-1784)
PHONE....................805 364-6337
EMP: 100 **EST:** 2017
SALES (est): 2.4MM **Privately Held**
WEB: www.plumbersinsantabarbara.com
SIC: 1711 Plumbing contractors

(P-1111)
ONTARIO REFRIGERATION SVC INC (PA)
635 S Mountain Ave, Ontario (91762-4114)
PHONE....................909 984-2771
Phillip C Talleur, *President*
Mike Gould, *Principal*
Mark Gambetti, *General Mgr*
Phil Talleur, *General Mgr*
Tammy Aragon, *Admin Sec*
EMP: 54 **EST:** 1971
SQ FT: 5,300
SALES (est): 52.3MM **Privately Held**
WEB: www.ontariorefrigeration.com
SIC: 1711 Warm air heating & air conditioning contractor

(P-1112)
ORANGE COUNTY SERVICES INC (PA)
Also Called: George Brazil Plbg Htg & AC
3801 Lenawee Ave, Culver City (90232-3008)
PHONE....................310 515-1001
Michael N Diamond, *President*
Goldyne Diamond, *Admin Sec*
EMP: 71 **EST:** 1993
SALES (est): 1MM **Privately Held**
WEB: www.georgebrazil.net
SIC: 1711 1731 Plumbing contractors; electrical work

(P-1113)
ORIGINAL SID BLACKMAN PLBG INC
1160 S 2nd St, El Centro (92243-3446)
P.O. Box 3487 (92244-3487)
PHONE....................760 352-3632
Thomas Blackman, *President*
Sid Blackman, *Officer*
Michael Wickline, *Admin Sec*
EMP: 68 **EST:** 1992
SALES (est): 9MM **Privately Held**
WEB: www.blackmanplumbing.net
SIC: 1711 Plumbing contractors

(P-1114)
PACIFIC RIM MECH CONTRS INC
1701 E Edinger Ave Ste F2, Santa Ana (92705-5028)
PHONE....................714 285-2600
John Heusner, *Manager*
Mark Treseder, *Engineer*
Valerie McGuire, *Controller*
EMP: 250
SALES (corp-wide): 131.9MM **Privately Held**
WEB: www.prmech.com
SIC: 1711 Mechanical contractor
PA: Pacific Rim Mechanical Contractors, Inc.
  9125 Rehco Rd
  San Diego CA 92121
  858 974-6500

(P-1115)
PAN-PACIFIC MECHANICAL LLC (PA)
18250 Euclid St, Fountain Valley (92708-6112)
PHONE....................949 474-9170
Cindy Lanette McMackin, *President*
Ronald G McMackin, *CEO*
Steve Sylvester, *CFO*
Ryan Cavanaugh, *Vice Pres*
Michael S Clair, *Vice Pres*
▲ **EMP:** 150
SQ FT: 60,000
SALES (est): 373.5MM **Privately Held**
WEB: www.ppmechanical.com
SIC: 1711 Plumbing contractors

(P-1116)
PAR ENGINEERING INC
Also Called: Commercial Cooling
17855 Arenth Ave, City of Industry (91748-1129)
PHONE....................626 964-8700
Hassan John Milani, *President*
Jim Conner, *Manager*
Jeannine Lugo, *Supervisor*
EMP: 50 **EST:** 1965
SQ FT: 70,000
SALES (est): 14MM **Privately Held**
WEB: www.commercialcooling.com
SIC: 1711 Refrigeration contractor

(P-1117)
PIPE RESTORATION INC
Also Called: Ace Duraflo Pipe Restoration
3122 W Alpine St, Santa Ana (92704-6912)
PHONE....................714 564-7600
Larry Gillanders, *CEO*
Mike Carper, *Exec VP*
Jason Houck, *Director*
EMP: 50 **EST:** 2001
SQ FT: 6,000
SALES (est): 8.4MM **Privately Held**
WEB: www.restoremypipes.com
SIC: 1711 Plumbing contractors

(P-1118)
PIPELINE RESTORATION PLBG INC
2700 S Main St, Santa Ana (92707-3431)
PHONE....................949 510-2281
EMP: 50 **EST:** 2015
SALES (est): 3.5MM **Privately Held**
WEB: www.slableakfix.com
SIC: 1711 Plumbing contractors

(P-1119)
PLUMBING PIPING & CNSTR INC
5950 Lakeshore Dr, Cypress (90630-3371)
PHONE....................714 821-0490
Bruce Cook Jr, *President*
Bill Collins, *Vice Pres*

Craig Zimmerman, *Vice Pres*
Brian Buchanan, *Controller*
Sheryl Spark, *Instructor*
EMP: 100 **EST:** 1960
SQ FT: 12,600
SALES (est): 24.7MM **Privately Held**
WEB: www.1ppc.com
SIC: 1711 Plumbing, heating, air-conditioning contractors

(P-1120)
PLUMBING SYSTEMS WEST INC
31491 Outer Highway 10, Redlands (92373-7568)
PHONE....................909 794-3823
Bob Grable, *President*
EMP: 68 **EST:** 2013
SALES (est): 7.4MM **Privately Held**
WEB: www.plumbingsystems.net
SIC: 1711 Plumbing contractors

(P-1121)
PPC ENTERPRISES INC
Also Called: Premier Plumbing Company
5920 Rickenbacker Ave, Riverside (92504-1042)
PHONE....................951 354-5402
Jeffrey Geiger, *President*
Dawn Geiger, *CFO*
EMP: 125 **EST:** 1982
SQ FT: 10,000
SALES (est): 12.1MM **Privately Held**
WEB: www.premierplumbingcompany.com
SIC: 1711 Plumbing contractors

(P-1122)
PRECISE AIR SYSTEMS INC
Also Called: Hvac Installation and Repair
5467 W San Fernando Rd, Los Angeles (90039-1014)
P.O. Box 39609 (90039-0609)
PHONE....................818 646-9757
Toll Free:....................877 -
Fred Khachekian, *President*
Dzila Dornian, *Office Mgr*
Sevan Parsekhian, *Engineer*
Shakeh Petrosian, *Controller*
Samuel Yadegar, *Sales Staff*
EMP: 91 **EST:** 1975
SQ FT: 3,200
SALES (est): 18.5MM **Privately Held**
WEB: www.preciseairsystems.com
SIC: 1711 Warm air heating & air conditioning contractor; heating & air conditioning contractors

(P-1123)
PRO-CRAFT CONSTRUCTION INC
500 Iowa St Ste 100, Redlands (92373-8070)
PHONE....................909 790-5222
Timothy McFayden, *President*
Susan Mc Fayden, *CFO*
Chris McFayden, *Vice Pres*
Nina Fajardo, *Office Mgr*
Anthony Avila, *Project Mgr*
EMP: 142 **EST:** 2006
SALES (est): 27MM **Privately Held**
WEB: www.procraftci.com
SIC: 1711 Plumbing contractors

(P-1124)
PROGRESSIVE POWER GROUP INC
12552 Western Ave, Garden Grove (92841-4013)
PHONE....................714 899-2300
Ross A Butcher, *CEO*
Chris Hammerstone, *Principal*
Chris Staskewicz, *Principal*
Sandra Griffin, *Project Mgr*
Scott Kessinger, *Sales Staff*
EMP: 50
SQ FT: 12,000
SALES (est): 11.1MM **Privately Held**
WEB: www.propowergroup.com
SIC: 1711 5211 Solar energy contractor; solar heating equipment

(P-1125)
QUICK SYSTEMS INC
5042 Wilshire Blvd # 28533, Los Angeles (90036-4305)
PHONE....................702 335-3574
Alma Roundy, *CEO*

Stewart Knudson, *CEO*
EMP: 50
SQ FT: 6,000
SALES: 6.4MM **Privately Held**
SIC: 1711 Solar energy contractor

(P-1126)
RAWLINGS MECHANICAL CORP (PA)
11615 Pendleton St, Sun Valley (91352-2502)
P.O. Box 703 (91353-0703)
PHONE....................323 875-2040
Robert S Bratton, *President*
Rex Horney, *Vice Pres*
Patricia Wood, *Admin Sec*
Ken Burton, *Project Mgr*
Brian Foster, *Project Mgr*
EMP: 74 **EST:** 1953
SQ FT: 22,000
SALES (est): 29.8MM **Privately Held**
WEB: www.rawlingsmechanical.com
SIC: 1711 Mechanical contractor

(P-1127)
REC SOLAR COMMERCIAL CORP
3450 Broad St Ste 105, San Luis Obispo (93401-7214)
PHONE....................844 732-7652
Matt Walz, *CEO*
Gary Morris, *CFO*
EMP: 120 **EST:** 2013
SQ FT: 15,000
SALES (est): 1.1MM
SALES (corp-wide): 23.8B **Publicly Held**
WEB: www.sustainablesolutions.duke-energy.com
SIC: 1711 Solar energy contractor
PA: Duke Energy Corporation
  550 S Tryon St
  Charlotte NC 28202
  704 382-3853

(P-1128)
RELIABLE ENERGY MANAGEMENT INC
Also Called: Honeywell Authorized Dealer
6829 Walthall Way, Paramount (90723-2028)
PHONE....................562 984-5511
George R Garcia, *President*
Judy Garcia, *Treasurer*
David Reyes, *Vice Pres*
Sal Salazar, *Program Mgr*
Isabel Garibay, *Office Mgr*
EMP: 80 **EST:** 1995
SALES (est): 18.9MM **Privately Held**
WEB: www.relenergy.com
SIC: 1711 Heating & air conditioning contractors

(P-1129)
RENOVA ENERGY CORP
75181 Mediterranean, Palm Desert (92211-9094)
PHONE....................760 568-3413
Vincent Battaglia, *Ch of Bd*
Marvin Roman, *President*
Dixie Faber, *CFO*
Nate Lewis, *Officer*
Lea Goodsell, *Exec VP*
EMP: 50 **EST:** 2007
SQ FT: 5,200
SALES (est): 15.4MM **Privately Held**
WEB: www.renovaenergy.com
SIC: 1711 Solar energy contractor

(P-1130)
RESIDENTIAL FIRE SYSTEMS INC
8085 E Crystal Dr, Anaheim (92807-2523)
PHONE....................714 666-8450
Ty Maley, *President*
Ruben Hernandez, *Treasurer*
Cesar Anchondo, *Vice Pres*
Jack Maley, *Admin Sec*
Gabe Velasco, *Engineer*
EMP: 75 **EST:** 2000
SQ FT: 6,200
SALES (est): 19.5MM **Privately Held**
WEB: www.resfire.com
SIC: 1711 5063 Fire sprinkler system installation; signaling equipment, electrical

(P-1131)
RLH FIRE PROTECTION INC (PA)
4300 Stine Rd Ste 800, Bakersfield (93313-2354)
P.O. Box 42470 (93384-2470)
PHONE..............................661 322-9344
Terrence J Olson, *CEO*
Michael Hardcastle, *Ch of Bd*
Jason Norton, *President*
Margaret McCarty, *Treasurer*
Clifford Arthurs, *Vice Pres*
EMP: 75
SQ FT: 8,000
SALES (est): 27.9MM **Privately Held**
WEB: www.rlhfp.com
SIC: **1711** 1542 Fire sprinkler system installation; nonresidential construction

(P-1132)
RUSSELL SIGLER INC
2641 E Lindsey Privado Dr, Ontario (91761-3454)
PHONE..............................909 390-7838
Paul Setter, *Branch Mgr*
EMP: 68
SALES (corp-wide): 174.2MM **Privately Held**
WEB: www.siglers.com
SIC: **1711** Heating & air conditioning contractors
PA: Russell Sigler, Inc.
9702 W Tonto St
Tolleson AZ 85353
623 388-5100

(P-1133)
S S W MECHANICAL CNSTR INC
Also Called: Ssw
670 S Oleander Rd, Palm Springs (92264-1502)
P.O. Box 3160 (92263-3160)
PHONE..............................760 327-1481
Sean Wood, *President*
W T Hayes, *Vice Pres*
EMP: 140 EST: 1996
SQ FT: 7,000
SALES (est): 26.6MM **Privately Held**
WEB: www.sswmechanical.com
SIC: **1711** Plumbing contractors

(P-1134)
SCORPIO ENTERPRISES
Also Called: Airemasters Air Conditioning
12556 Mccann Dr, Santa Fe Springs (90670-3337)
PHONE..............................562 946-9464
Charles Everett Thompson, *CEO*
Linda Thompson, *Vice Pres*
Stephanie Terrell-Haney, *Office Mgr*
Taylor Dean, *Manager*
Jeff Thompson, *Manager*
▼ EMP: 55 EST: 1974
SQ FT: 14,800
SALES (est): 10.5MM **Privately Held**
WEB: www.airemasters-ac.com
SIC: **1711** Warm air heating & air conditioning contractor; heating & air conditioning contractors

(P-1135)
SDG ENTERPRISES
Also Called: Century West Plumbing
822 Hampshire Rd Ste H, Westlake Village (91361-2850)
PHONE..............................805 777-7978
Nick Simili, *President*
Vincent Simili, *CFO*
Vincent Dipinto, *Vice Pres*
Robert Garcia, *Vice Pres*
EMP: 100 EST: 1999
SQ FT: 3,000
SALES (est): 14.1MM **Privately Held**
SIC: **1711** Plumbing contractors

(P-1136)
SEEMS PLUMBING CO INC
5400 W Rosecrans Ave Lower, Hawthorne (90250-6686)
PHONE..............................310 297-4969
Ed Hutcherson, *President*
Jonathan Sevel, *Administration*
Mark Hutcherson, *Sales Staff*
EMP: 50 EST: 1995
SALES (est): 3.9MM **Privately Held**
SIC: **1711** Plumbing contractors

(P-1137)
SERVICE GENIUS LOS ANGELES INC
9761 Variel Ave, Chatsworth (91311-4315)
PHONE..............................818 200-3379
William Monk, *President*
EMP: 100 EST: 2018
SALES (est): 10MM **Privately Held**
WEB: www.servicegenius.com
SIC: **1711** Heating & air conditioning contractors

(P-1138)
SHELDON MECHANICAL CORPORATION
26015 Avenue Hall, Santa Clarita (91355-1241)
PHONE..............................661 286-1361
Dan Boute, *President*
Beverly Nisenson, *Treasurer*
Stanley Nisenson, *Vice Pres*
Chrystal Bout'e, *Admin Sec*
Benjamin Webster, *Project Engr*
EMP: 80 EST: 1984
SQ FT: 45,000
SALES (est): 24MM **Privately Held**
WEB: www.sheldonmech.com
SIC: **1711** Mechanical contractor

(P-1139)
SKYPOWER HOLDINGS LLC
4700 Wilshire Blvd, Los Angeles (90010-3853)
PHONE..............................323 860-4900
Kerry Adler, *CEO*
AVI Shemesh, *President*
Brittany Hurley, *Managing Dir*
EMP: 101 EST: 2010
SALES (est): 4.3MM **Privately Held**
WEB: www.cimgroup.com
SIC: **1711** Solar energy contractor

(P-1140)
SMART ENERGY SOLAR INC
Also Called: Smart Energy USA
1641 Comm St, Corona (92880)
PHONE..............................800 405-1978
Leo Joaquin Bautista, *Principal*
EMP: 120 EST: 2013
SALES (est): 20MM **Privately Held**
WEB: www.smartenergyusa.com
SIC: **1711** Solar energy contractor

(P-1141)
SOLAR ENERGY LLC
21600 Oxnard St Ste 1200, Woodland Hills (91367-4949)
PHONE..............................818 449-5816
EMP: 80 EST: 2009
SALES (est): 7.2MM **Privately Held**
SIC: **1711** Plumbing/Heating/Air Cond Contractor

(P-1142)
SOLAR SPECTRUM LLC
Also Called: Sungevity
27368 Via Industria # 101, Temecula (92590-4852)
PHONE..............................844 777-6527
Patrick McGivern, *CEO*
William Nettles, *President*
David White, *CFO*
Sloane Morgan, *Officer*
Anne Goodrich, *General Mgr*
EMP: 266 EST: 2017
SALES (est): 51.1MM **Privately Held**
SIC: **1711** 8713 Solar energy contractor; surveying services

(P-1143)
SOLCIUS LLC
12155 Magnolia Ave 12b, Riverside (92503-4967)
PHONE..............................951 772-0030
Bryan Jackson, *Branch Mgr*
Britton Nilsen, *Vice Pres*
Shauna Mertz, *Executive Asst*
Brennan Campbell, *IT/INT Sup*
Michael Paris, *Engineer*
EMP: 69
SALES (corp-wide): 45MM **Privately Held**
WEB: www.solcius.com
SIC: **1711** Solar energy contractor

PA: Solcius, Llc
1555 N Freedom Blvd
Provo UT 84604
800 960-4150

(P-1144)
SOUTH CHINA SHEET METAL INC
Also Called: General Restaurant Equipment
1740 Albion St, Los Angeles (90031-2520)
PHONE..............................323 225-1522
Kam C Law, *CEO*
T K Yeung, *Vice Pres*
◆ EMP: 34 EST: 1982
SQ FT: 24,000
SALES (est): 1.6MM **Privately Held**
SIC: **1711** 3589 3444 Ventilation & duct work contractor; refrigeration contractor; commercial cooking & foodwarming equipment; sheet metalwork

(P-1145)
SOUTH COAST MECHANICAL INC
800 E Orangethorpe Ave, Anaheim (92801-1123)
PHONE..............................714 738-6644
James Reynolds, *CEO*
Zoltan Bulgozdi, *President*
Aaron Germain, *Vice Pres*
Oscar Ramirez, *General Mgr*
Tomas Bernal, *Project Mgr*
EMP: 75 EST: 2004
SALES (est): 25.5MM **Privately Held**
WEB: www.scfacilityservices.com
SIC: **1711** 7699 Mechanical contractor; industrial machinery & equipment repair

(P-1146)
SOUTH WEST SUN SOLAR INC
13752 Harbor Blvd, Garden Grove (92843-4009)
PHONE..............................714 582-3909
Hieu Nguyen, *CEO*
Mimi Ngo, *President*
Kay Heap, *Regional Mgr*
Thai Nguyen, *Regional Mgr*
EMP: 50 EST: 2014
SALES (est): 5.7MM **Privately Held**
WEB: www.southwestsunsolar.com
SIC: **1711** Solar energy contractor

(P-1147)
SOUTHLAND INDUSTRIES (PA)
12131 Western Ave, Garden Grove (92841-2914)
PHONE..............................800 613-6240
Theodore D Lynch, *Ch of Bd*
Charles M Allen, *COO*
Kevin J Coghlan, *CFO*
Kevin Coghlan, *CFO*
Tony SF Wang, *Treasurer*
EMP: 50 EST: 1949
SALES: 940.1MM **Privately Held**
WEB: www.southlandind.com
SIC: **1711** Plumbing, heating, air-conditioning contractors

(P-1148)
STERLING PLUMBING INC
3111 W Central Ave, Santa Ana (92704-5302)
PHONE..............................714 641-5480
Rodney Robbins, *President*
Leslie Schaefer, *CFO*
Lesley Levinson, *Human Resources*
Alo Bazan, *Purch Agent*
EMP: 100 EST: 2003
SALES (est): 13.1MM **Privately Held**
WEB: www.sterlingplumbinginc.com
SIC: **1711** Plumbing contractors

(P-1149)
SUMMIT FIRE PROTECTION
520 Texas St, Redlands (92374-3036)
PHONE..............................909 793-0676
Wayne Johnson, *Owner*
Keith Monson, *Technician*
EMP: 52 EST: 1978
SQ FT: 5,000
SALES (est): 7.8MM **Privately Held**
WEB: www.summitfire.com
SIC: **1711** Fire sprinkler system installation

(P-1150)
SUNPRO SOLAR INC
34859 Frederick St # 101, Wildomar (92595-7007)
PHONE..............................951 678-7733
Adam Evans, *President*
Adam Joshua Evans, *President*
Shannon Jackson, *Admin Asst*
Kari Daum, *Consultant*
Lawrence Goda, *Consultant*
EMP: 64 EST: 2008
SQ FT: 2,300
SALES (est): 9.5MM **Privately Held**
WEB: www.gosunpro.com
SIC: **1711** Solar energy contractor

(P-1151)
SUNRUN INSTALLATION SVCS INC (HQ)
775 Fiero Ln Ste 200, San Luis Obispo (93401-7904)
PHONE..............................415 580-6900
Lynn Jurich, *CEO*
Cyndi Adcock, *Partner*
Ryan Stepp, *Partner*
Robert Komin Jr, *CFO*
Dan Alcombright, *Vice Pres*
▲ EMP: 68 EST: 1997
SQ FT: 26,000
SALES (est): 179.1MM **Publicly Held**
WEB: www.sunrun.com
SIC: **1711** Solar energy contractor

(P-1152)
SUNRUN INSTALLATION SVCS INC
5777 Olivas Park Dr O, Ventura (93003-7925)
PHONE..............................805 658-1236
Tim Folk, *Manager*
EMP: 270 **Publicly Held**
SIC: **1711** Solar energy contractor
HQ: Sunrun Installation Services Inc.
775 Fiero Ln Ste 200
San Luis Obispo CA 93401
415 580-6900

(P-1153)
SUTTLES PLUMBING & MECH CORP
2267 Agate Ct, Simi Valley (93065-1843)
PHONE..............................818 718-9779
Stephanie Aguilar, *President*
Bryan Suttles, *Vice Pres*
Stephen Suttles, *Vice Pres*
Sheralyn Suttles, *Admin Sec*
Shy Suttles, *Human Res Dir*
EMP: 75 EST: 1970
SQ FT: 6,000
SALES (est): 10.8MM **Privately Held**
SIC: **1711** Plumbing contractors; warm air heating & air conditioning contractor

(P-1154)
THERMA HOLDINGS LLC
2390 Bateman Ave, Duarte (91010-3312)
PHONE..............................626 446-1854
Kevin Stiver, *Director*
EMP: 50
SALES (corp-wide): 402.3MM **Privately Held**
WEB: www.therma.com
SIC: **1711** Mechanical contractor
PA: Therma Holdings Llc
1601 Las Plumas Ave
San Jose CA 95133
408 347-3400

(P-1155)
THERMALAIR INC (HQ)
1140 N Red Gum St, Anaheim (92806-2516)
PHONE..............................714 630-3200
Stephen C Weiss, *CEO*
William Reece, *President*
Rich Perez, *Exec VP*
Cindy Hatch, *Regional Mgr*
Theresa Bransky, *Admin Asst*
EMP: 67 EST: 1948
SQ FT: 8,500
SALES (est): 10.6MM **Privately Held**
WEB: www.thermalair.com
SIC: **1711** Mechanical contractor; ventilation & duct work contractor; refrigeration contractor

PA: General Engineering Western, Inc.
1140 N Red Gum St
Anaheim CA 92806
714 630-3200

(P-1156)
TONOPAH SOLAR ENERGY LLC
520 Broadway Fl 6, Santa Monica
(90401-2420)
PHONE.............................310 315-2200
Kevin Smith, *Mng Member*
Rosie Sandoval, *General Mgr*
Cindy Sopko, *Controller*
▲ **EMP:** 60 **EST:** 2011
SALES (est): 3.5MM **Privately Held**
SIC: 1711 Solar energy contractor

(P-1157)
TRILOGY PLUMBING INC
1525 S Sinclair St, Anaheim (92806-5934)
PHONE.............................714 441-2952
Dennis Burk, *President*
Linda Burk, *Vice Pres*
Tom Price, *Vice Pres*
Mike McManus, *Director*
EMP: 250 **EST:** 2003
SQ FT: 18,000
SALES (est): 35.7MM **Privately Held**
WEB: www.trilogyplumbing.com
SIC: 1711 Septic system construction

(P-1158)
TRUE AIR MECHANICAL INC
Also Called: True Home Heating and AC
4 Faraday, Irvine (92618-2714)
PHONE.............................888 316-0642
Scott Flora, *CEO*
Mont Flora, *COO*
Jeff Flora, *Principal*
Cheryl Atkins, *Administration*
Glen Nichols, *Project Mgr*
EMP: 180
SALES (est): 21.8MM **Privately Held**
WEB: www.trueairinc.com
SIC: 1711 Warm air heating & air conditioning contractor

(P-1159)
UNIVERSITY MARELICH MECH INC
1000 N Kraemer Pl, Anaheim
(92806-2610)
PHONE.............................714 632-2600
Scott Baker, *Senior VP*
Walter S Baker, *CEO*
John R Wycoff, *CFO*
John Ellis, *Vice Pres*
EMP: 53 **EST:** 2005
SQ FT: 24,384
SALES (est): 5.8MM
SALES (corp-wide): 8.8B **Publicly Held**
WEB: www.marelich.com
SIC: 1711 Mechanical contractor
PA: Emcor Group, Inc.
301 Merritt 7 Fl 6
Norwalk CT 06851
203 849-7800

(P-1160)
VALLEY CLARK PLBG & HTG CO INC (PA)
Also Called: Clark Plumbing Co
7640 Gloria Ave Ste L, Van Nuys
(91406-1800)
PHONE.............................818 782-1047
Robert J Brunald, *President*
Traci Brunald, *Vice Pres*
EMP: 50 **EST:** 1945
SQ FT: 8,000
SALES (est): 11MM **Privately Held**
WEB: www.clarkplumbing.com
SIC: 1711 Plumbing contractors

(P-1161)
WEST-TECH MECHANICAL INC
5589 Brooks St Ste A, Montclair
(91763-4519)
PHONE.............................909 635-1170
Gus Wahid, *President*
Samir Wahid, *Vice Pres*
Kelly Blanchard, *Office Admin*
Hassan Mirza, *Project Mgr*
Vic Sebastian, *Project Mgr*
EMP: 15 **EST:** 1989
SQ FT: 3,500

SALES (est): 3.9MM **Privately Held**
WEB: www.westtechmechanical.com
SIC: 1711 Mechanical contractor;
awnings & canopies

(P-1162)
WESTERN ALLIED CORPORATION
Also Called: Honeywell Authorized Dealer
12046 Florence Ave, Santa Fe Springs
(90670-4406)
P.O. Box 3628 (90670-1628)
PHONE.............................562 944-6341
Howell L Poe, *CEO*
Rick Collier, *Vice Pres*
Tani Poe, *Vice Pres*
Mike Sanderson, *Vice Pres*
Alan Slabodkin, *Vice Pres*
EMP: 45 **EST:** 1960
SQ FT: 15,000
SALES (est): 24.8MM **Privately Held**
WEB: www.wasocal.com
SIC: 1711 3433 3432 Warm air heating & air conditioning contractor; heating equipment, except electric; plumbing fixture fittings & trim

(P-1163)
XCEL MECHANICAL SYSTEMS INC
1710 W 130th St, Gardena (90249-2004)
PHONE.............................310 660-0090
Kevin Michel, *President*
Steve Prisk, *Safety Dir*
Brandon Miller, *Foreman/Supr*
Phil Bonney, *Marketing Staff*
Eric Dela Torre, *Manager*
EMP: 175 **EST:** 1996
SQ FT: 10,000
SALES (est): 49.5MM **Privately Held**
WEB: www.xcelmech.com
SIC: 1711 Mechanical contractor

(P-1164)
ZERO ENERGY CONTRACTING LLC
13850 Cerritos Corprt Dr, Cerritos
(90703-2467)
PHONE.............................626 701-3180
Michael Murphy,
EMP: 93 **EST:** 2009
SALES (est): 9.9MM **Privately Held**
SIC: 1711 Solar energy contractor

1721 Painting & Paper Hanging Contractors

(P-1165)
ADVANCED INDUSTRIAL SVCS INC
Also Called: Advanced Industrial Svcs Cal
7831 Alondra Blvd, Paramount
(90723-5005)
PHONE.............................562 940-8305
Rex Johnston, *President*
EMP: 85 **EST:** 2007
SALES (est): 12MM **Privately Held**
WEB: www.adinservices.com
SIC: 1721 Industrial painting

(P-1166)
ADVANTAGE PNTG SOLUTIONS INC
14734 Yorba Ct, Chino (91710-9210)
PHONE.............................951 739-9204
Anthony Trujillo, *CEO*
Shevon Gonzales, *CFO*
Daniel Lang, *Manager*
EMP: 60 **EST:** 2014
SALES (est): 3MM **Privately Held**
WEB:
www.advantagepaintingsolutions.com
SIC: 1721 Residential painting

(P-1167)
ANNA CORPORATION
Also Called: Jfp Company
2078 2nd St, Norco (92860-2804)
PHONE.............................951 736-6037
Anna L Degiacomo, *President*
Jaime Flores, *Vice Pres*
Mia Fikse, *Admin Sec*
Luis Tull, *Manager*

EMP: 50 **EST:** 1990
SQ FT: 6,500
SALES (est): 5.2MM **Privately Held**
WEB: www.jfpco.com
SIC: 1721 Commercial painting

(P-1168)
ARCHITECTURAL COATINGS INC
1565 E Edinger Ave, Santa Ana
(92705-4907)
PHONE.............................714 701-1360
Sally K Rimmer, *President*
EMP: 50 **EST:** 1995
SALES (est): 4.7MM **Privately Held**
SIC: 1721 Residential painting; commercial painting

(P-1169)
ARENA PAINTING CONTRACTORS INC
525 E Alondra Blvd, Gardena
(90248-2903)
PHONE.............................310 316-2446
Wilson Grant, *CEO*
Guy Grant II, *President*
Peter Gulliver, *Manager*
EMP: 100
SQ FT: 10,000
SALES (est): 11.5MM **Privately Held**
WEB: www.arenapainting.biz
SIC: 1721 Commercial painting

(P-1170)
BLASTCO TEXAS INC
11905 Regentview Ave, Downey
(90241-5515)
PHONE.............................562 869-0200
Dale Kulczyk, *Manager*
Jay Soper, *General Mgr*
Jeremi Day, *QC Mgr*
EMP: 90
SALES (corp-wide): 15.8MM **Privately Held**
WEB: www.tfwarren.com
SIC: 1721 Commercial painting
PA: Blastco Texas Inc.
16201 Wood Dr
Channelview TX 77530
281 590-3200

(P-1171)
BORBON INCORPORATED
2560 W Woodland Dr, Anaheim
(92801-2636)
PHONE.............................714 994-0170
David Morales, *President*
Jacquelyn Fiorentino, *Admin Asst*
Nicole Fiorentino, *Manager*
Kyle Kipper, *Manager*
EMP: 120 **EST:** 1974
SALES (est): 11.4MM **Privately Held**
WEB: www.borbon.net
SIC: 1721 Exterior residential painting contractor; wallcovering contractors

(P-1172)
CAL/PAC PNTNGS CTNGS ACQSTION
608 N Eckhoff St, Orange (92868-1004)
PHONE.............................714 628-1514
Dave Bedillion, *President*
Mike Stevenson, *CFO*
Lee Ann Green, *Controller*
EMP: 60 **EST:** 2001
SQ FT: 2,000
SALES (est): 7.1MM **Privately Held**
SIC: 1721 Residential painting

(P-1173)
CAMPBELL PAINTING INC
Also Called: Campbell Construction
14175 Telephone Ave Ste M, Chino
(91710-5761)
PHONE.............................919 591-4300
Gerry Campbell, *CEO*
EMP: 60 **EST:** 2005
SALES (est): 5.9MM **Privately Held**
SIC: 1721 Painting & paper hanging

(P-1174)
CRAMER PAINTING INC
4080 Mission Blvd, Montclair (91763-6011)
PHONE.............................909 397-5770
Steven L Cramer, *President*

Anne McWeeney, *Admin Sec*
EMP: 50 **EST:** 1978
SQ FT: 6,800
SALES (est): 6.9MM **Privately Held**
WEB: www.cramerpainting.com
SIC: 1721 Commercial painting

(P-1175)
CWPNC INC
Also Called: College Works Painting
1682 Langley Ave, Irvine (92614-5620)
PHONE.............................714 564-7904
Matthew K Stewart, *President*
Taylor Duncan, *Exec VP*
Kyle Lindsey, *Exec VP*
Seth Bailey, *Vice Pres*
Jon Carrasquillo, *Vice Pres*
EMP: 96 **EST:** 1998
SQ FT: 3,000
SALES (est): 10.2MM **Privately Held**
WEB: www.collegeworks.com
SIC: 1721 Residential painting
PA: National Services Group, Inc.
1682 Langley Ave
Irvine CA 92614

(P-1176)
D P S INC
Also Called: Empire Community Painting
1682 Langley Ave, Irvine (92614-5620)
PHONE.............................714 564-7900
Jason Reid, *President*
Tracy Meneses, *CFO*
Jeff Gunhus, *Vice Pres*
Matt Stewart, *Vice Pres*
Spencer Pepe, *Admin Sec*
EMP: 117 **EST:** 1993
SQ FT: 1,000
SALES (est): 6.2MM **Privately Held**
WEB: www.empireworks.com
SIC: 1721 Painting & paper hanging
PA: National Services Group, Inc.
1682 Langley Ave
Irvine CA 92614

(P-1177)
DUGGAN & ASSOCIATES INC
1442 W 135th St, Gardena (90249-2218)
PHONE.............................323 965-1502
Chris M Duggan, *President*
Nelson Cullum, *Project Mgr*
Kate Workman, *Accountant*
◆ **EMP:** 65 **EST:** 1989
SQ FT: 10,000
SALES (est): 11.9MM **Privately Held**
WEB: www.dugganandassociates.net
SIC: 1721 Residential painting; commercial wallcovering contractor

(P-1178)
EMPCC INC
Also Called: Empire Community Painting
1682 Langley Ave Fl 2, Irvine (92614-5620)
PHONE.............................714 564-7900
Jason Reid, *President*
Tracy Meneses, *CFO*
Jeff Gunhus, *Vice Pres*
Matt Stewart, *Vice Pres*
Spencer Pepe, *Admin Sec*
EMP: 172 **EST:** 2003
SQ FT: 1,000
SALES (est): 1.1MM **Privately Held**
SIC: 1721 Painting & paper hanging
PA: Mip Empire, Inc.
1682 Langley Ave Fl 2
Irvine CA 92614

(P-1179)
FREEDOM PAINTING INC
8822 Calmada Ave, Whittier (90605-2006)
PHONE.............................562 696-0785
Gerald Lundgren, *President*
Roselina Lundgren, *Treasurer*
Beverly Lundgren, *Vice Pres*
Deanna Lundgren, *Vice Pres*
EMP: 50 **EST:** 1970
SQ FT: 8,000 **Privately Held**
SIC: 1721 Residential painting

(P-1180)
GENERAL COATINGS CORPORATION
9349 Feron Blvd, Rancho Cucamonga (91730-4516)
PHONE...............909 204-4150
Craig Kinsman, *Owner*
Richard Roberts, *Controller*
Hector Cueva, *Manager*
Peter McDevitt, *Manager*
EMP: 83
SALES (corp-wide): 35.9MM **Privately Held**
WEB: www.gencoat.com
SIC: 1721 Painting & paper hanging
PA: General Coatings Corporation
6711 Nancy Ridge Dr
San Diego CA 92121
858 587-1277

(P-1181)
GENERAL COATINGS CORPORATION
600 W Freedom Ave, Orange (92865-2537)
PHONE...............858 587-1277
Craig Kinsman, *Branch Mgr*
EMP: 83
SQ FT: 7,047
SALES (corp-wide): 35.9MM **Privately Held**
WEB: www.gencoat.com
SIC: 1721 Painting & paper hanging
PA: General Coatings Corporation
6711 Nancy Ridge Dr
San Diego CA 92121
858 587-1277

(P-1182)
GPS PAINTING WALLCOVERING INC
1307 E Saint Gertrude Pl C, Santa Ana (92705-5228)
PHONE...............714 730-8904
Eliot Schneider, *President*
Sergio Gutierrez, *Project Mgr*
Ed Lares, *Project Mgr*
Shayn Sowers, *Manager*
EMP: 110 **EST:** 2001
SALES (est): 18.8MM **Privately Held**
WEB:
www.gpspaintingandwallcovering.com
SIC: 1721 Painting & paper hanging

(P-1183)
HARRIS & RUTH PAINTING CONTG (PA)
28408 Lorna Ave, West Covina (91790)
PHONE...............626 960-4004
Terry Cairy, *President*
Mark Heydorff, *COO*
Bruce Boyer, *Vice Pres*
Chanel Salazar-Perez, *Assistant*
EMP: 70 **EST:** 1970
SQ FT: 1,000
SALES (est): 10.4MM **Privately Held**
WEB: www.harris-ruthpainting.com
SIC: 1721 Exterior commercial painting contractor; industrial painting

(P-1184)
J M V B INC
Also Called: Spc Building Services
12118 Severn Way, Riverside (92503-4804)
P.O. Box 614, Orange (92856-6614)
PHONE...............714 288-9797
Benjamin J Rodriguez, *President*
Benjamin Rodriguez, *Marketing Staff*
EMP: 80 **EST:** 1993
SALES (est): 5.2MM **Privately Held**
WEB: www.spcbs.com
SIC: 1721 Painting & paper hanging

(P-1185)
JFP PAINTING
2078 2nd St, Norco (92860-2804)
PHONE...............951 736-6037
Anna Floris, *Principal*
Chris Pennington, *Project Mgr*
Wilmer Zermeno, *Warehouse Mgr*
EMP: 60 **EST:** 1996
SALES (est): 2.4MM **Privately Held**
WEB: www.jfpco.com
SIC: 1721 Painting & paper hanging

(P-1186)
JOHNSON & TURNER PAINTING CO
8241 Electric Ave, Stanton (90680-2640)
PHONE...............714 828-8282
Dale Bodwell, *President*
Michelle Bodwell, *Office Mgr*
▲ **EMP:** 50
SQ FT: 6,000
SALES (est): 4.1MM **Privately Held**
WEB: www.jtpaint.com
SIC: 1721 Residential painting

(P-1187)
LA WEB INC
Also Called: Chinese La Daily News
9639 Telstar Ave, El Monte (91731-3003)
PHONE...............626 453-8800
Walter Chang, *President*
Frank Du, *Account Dir*
▲ **EMP:** 25 **EST:** 1989
SALES (est): 2.4MM **Privately Held**
WEB: www.chinesedaily.com
SIC: 1721 2711 Painting & paper hanging; newspapers, publishing & printing

(P-1188)
LIVING COLORS INC
16026 Rayen St, North Hills (91343-4814)
PHONE...............818 893-5068
Raymond Sponsler, *President*
Paula Sponsler, *Treasurer*
EMP: 60 **EST:** 1973
SALES (est): 3.5MM **Privately Held**
WEB: www.lcipaint.com
SIC: 1721 Residential painting

(P-1189)
MEYER COATINGS INC
Also Called: Meyer Construction Services
1927 N Glassell St, Orange (92865-4313)
PHONE...............714 467-4600
Diana Meyer, *CEO*
Scott Meyer, *President*
Scott D Meyer, *CFO*
Kylie Suica, *Admin Asst*
John Beltran, *Project Mgr*
EMP: 50 **EST:** 2002
SQ FT: 4,800
SALES (est): 13.1MM **Privately Held**
WEB: www.tpx.com
SIC: 1721 Commercial painting

(P-1190)
MJP EMPIRE INC (PA)
1682 Langley Ave Fl 2, Irvine (92614-5620)
PHONE...............714 564-7900
Jason Reid, *President*
Tracy Meneses, *CFO*
Jeff Gunhus, *Vice Pres*
Matt Stewart, *Vice Pres*
Spencer Pepe, *Admin Sec*
EMP: 128 **EST:** 2004
SALES (est): 13.6MM **Privately Held**
SIC: 1721 Painting & paper hanging

(P-1191)
NORTH ORANGE COAST PNTG INC
3969 Sierra Ave, Norco (92860-1390)
P.O. Box 520 (92860-0520)
PHONE...............951 279-2694
Fax: 951 279-9510
EMP: 100
SALES (est): 5MM **Privately Held**
SIC: 1721 Painting/Paper Hanging Contractor

(P-1192)
PBC PAVERS INC
Also Called: Peterson Bros Construction
1560 W Lambert Rd, Brea (92821-2826)
PHONE...............714 278-0488
Robert Peterson, *President*
Valerie Payne, *CFO*
Tim Angelo, *Vice Pres*
Eldin Peterson, *Vice Pres*
Jill Allers, *Administration*
▲ **EMP:** 80 **EST:** 1995
SALES (est): 9MM **Privately Held**
WEB: www.pbccompanies.com
SIC: 1721 Pavement marking contractor

(P-1193)
POWER MAINTENANCE SERVICES INC
Also Called: Pilot Painting & Construction
5555 Corporate Ave, Cypress (90630-4708)
P.O. Box 6377, Anaheim (92816-0377)
PHONE...............714 229-5900
Steve Gilkey, *President*
EMP: 60 **EST:** 2017
SQ FT: 7,856
SALES (est): 5.8MM **Privately Held**
WEB: www.pilotpainting.com
SIC: 1721 Residential painting

(P-1194)
PS2 (PA)
17903 S Hobart Blvd, Gardena (90248-3613)
PHONE...............310 243-2980
Peter Schmit, *President*
Peter Short, *Admin Sec*
Ryan Webb, *Project Mgr*
EMP: 68 **EST:** 1997
SQ FT: 2,000
SALES (est): 10.3MM **Privately Held**
WEB: www.ps2-inc.com
SIC: 1721 Residential painting

(P-1195)
RANDALL - MCANANY COMPANY
1528 W 178th St, Gardena (90248-3204)
PHONE...............310 822-3344
Timothy Mc Anany, *President*
Nancy Mc Anany, *Corp Secy*
Don Murray, *Project Mgr*
Shawn Missaghi, *Controller*
Steve Forsythe, *Purch Mgr*
EMP: 60 **EST:** 1978 **Privately Held**
WEB: www.rmcompany.com
SIC: 1721 Commercial painting; commercial wallcovering contractor

(P-1196)
RC WENDT PAINTING INC
21612 Surveyor Cir, Huntington Beach (92646-7068)
PHONE...............714 960-2700
Robert C Wendt, *President*
Jeri Wendt, *Corp Secy*
Scott Wendt, *Vice Pres*
EMP: 110 **EST:** 1980
SALES (est): 9.6MM **Privately Held**
WEB: www.wendtcompanies.com
SIC: 1721 Residential painting; commercial painting

(P-1197)
RTE ENTERPRISES INC
Also Called: Color Concepts
21530 Roscoe Blvd, Canoga Park (91304-4144)
PHONE...............818 999-5300
Ron Evenhaim, *President*
EMP: 100 **EST:** 1987
SQ FT: 2,000
SALES (est): 5.6MM **Privately Held**
WEB: www.ceocolorcon1.com
SIC: 1721 1742 Painting & paper hanging; plastering, drywall & insulation

(P-1198)
SANDERS & WOHRMAN CORPORATION
709 N Poplar St, Orange (92868-1013)
PHONE...............714 919-0446
John Thomas Wohrman, *Principal*
Todd Wohrman, *Treasurer*
Raymond Wohrman, *Admin Mgr*
Joe Hatchell, *Project Mgr*
Stephen Stewart, *Manager*
EMP: 150 **EST:** 1979
SQ FT: 12,000
SALES (est): 23.3MM **Privately Held**
WEB: www.swpainting.com
SIC: 1721 Residential painting

(P-1199)
STERNDAHL ENTERPRISES INC
11861 Branford St, Sun Valley (91352-1032)
PHONE...............818 834-8199
Dennis S Sterndahl, *President*
Myra Rico, *Treasurer*
Troy Hill, *Vice Pres*
Ron Holder, *Vice Pres*
Deborah A Sterndahl, *Vice Pres*
EMP: 50 **EST:** 1980
SQ FT: 16,366
SALES (est): 21MM **Privately Held**
WEB: www.sterndahl.com
SIC: 1721 Pavement marking contractor

(P-1200)
VERTEX COATINGS INC
1291 W State St, Ontario (91752-4015)
PHONE...............909 923-5795
Russ Phillips, *President*
Stacy Phillips, *Executive*
Veronica Ibarra, *Office Mgr*
April Denny, *Admin Asst*
Genesiz Martinez-Perez, *Project Engr*
EMP: 74 **EST:** 1990
SQ FT: 11,000
SALES (est): 8.8MM **Privately Held**
WEB: www.vertexcoatings.com
SIC: 1721 Commercial painting

(P-1201)
WEST COAST INTERIORS INC
Also Called: West Coast Painting
1610 W Linden St, Riverside (92507-6810)
PHONE...............951 778-3592
Mark Herbert, *CEO*
Dan Slavin, *President*
Santos Garcia, *COO*
Matt Gormley, *Project Mgr*
Keith Caneva, *Controller*
EMP: 600 **EST:** 1968
SQ FT: 8,000
SALES (est): 59.4MM **Privately Held**
WEB: www.wcdp.com
SIC: 1721 Wallcovering contractors

(P-1202)
WILSON & HAMPTON PNTG CONTRS
1524 W Mable St, Anaheim (92802-1097)
P.O. Box 9949 (92812-7943)
PHONE...............714 772-5091
Doug Hampton, *President*
Douglas J Hampton, *President*
Cliff Hampton, *COO*
Scott Hallie, *Officer*
Clifford C Hampton, *Vice Pres*
EMP: 60 **EST:** 1923
SQ FT: 44,000
SALES (est): 9.8MM **Privately Held**
WEB: www.wilsonhampton.com
SIC: 1721 7641 Residential painting; furniture repair & maintenance; office furniture repair & maintenance

---

1731 Electrical Work

(P-1203)
A M ORTEGA CONSTRUCTION INC
Also Called: A.M. Ortega Construction
224 N Sherman Ave, Corona (92882-1843)
PHONE...............951 360-1352
Archie Ortega, *President*
EMP: 76
SALES (corp-wide): 55.5MM **Privately Held**
WEB: www.amortega.com
SIC: 1731 Electrical work
PA: A. M. Ortega Construction, Inc.
10125 Channel Rd
Lakeside CA 92040
619 390-1988

(P-1204)
A-1 ELECTRIC SERVICE CO INC
4204 Sepulveda Blvd, Culver City (90230-4709)
P.O. Box 6453, Malibu (90264-6453)
PHONE...............310 204-1077
Linda Pieper, *CEO*
Scott Pieper, *Vice Pres*
Eric Cashman, *Technology*
EMP: 50 **EST:** 1998
SQ FT: 5,000
SALES (est): 9MM **Privately Held**
WEB: www.a-1electric.com
SIC: 1731 General electrical contractor

(P-1205)
A-C ELECTRIC COMPANY (PA)
Also Called: Autometd Cntrls Technical Svcs
2921 Harger Way, Bakersfield
(93308-1543)
P.O. Box 31977 (93380-1977)
PHONE..................661 410-0000
Thomas L Alexander, *Ch of Bd*
Daren T Alexander, *President*
Thomas P Zauder, *CFO*
David M Morton, *Exec VP*
David Morton, *Vice Pres*
EMP: 50
SQ FT: 10,000
SALES: 66.6MM **Privately Held**
WEB: www.a-celectric.com
SIC: 1731 General electrical contractor

(P-1206)
A-C ELECTRIC COMPANY
Visalia Division
1035 W Murray Ave, Visalia (93291-4721)
P.O. Box 328 (93279-0328)
PHONE..................559 732-4733
Larry J Dietz, *Manager*
Jeff Runyon, *Project Mgr*
Corky Barcone, *Prdtn Mgr*
EMP: 73
SALES (corp-wide): 66.6MM **Privately Held**
WEB: www.a-celectric.com
SIC: 1731 General electrical contractor
PA: A-C Electric Company
2921 Harger Way
Bakersfield CA 93308
661 410-0000

(P-1207)
AAA ELCTRCAL CMMUNICATIONS INC (PA)
Also Called: AAA Property Services
25007 Anza Dr, Valencia (91355-3414)
PHONE..................800 892-4784
Joann Katinos, *CEO*
Brian Higgins, *President*
Steve Chrisopulos, *Regional Mgr*
Angela Polen, *Division Mgr*
Polen Timothy, *Division Mgr*
EMP: 133 EST: 1995
SQ FT: 6,000
SALES (est): 31.4MM **Privately Held**
WEB: www.aaafacilityservices.com
SIC: 1731 1711 7349 1721 General electrical contractor; plumbing, heating, air-conditioning contractors; building maintenance services; commercial painting; commercial & office buildings, renovation & repair

(P-1208)
AAA NETWORK SOLUTIONS INC
8401 Page St, Buena Park (90621-3821)
PHONE..................714 484-2711
John A McKenna Jr, *CEO*
Jeffrey E Nashbor, *CFO*
Keith Hippard, *Vice Pres*
Daniel Rey, *Superintendent*
EMP: 60 EST: 2009
SALES (est): 24.3MM
SALES (corp-wide): 1.8B **Privately Held**
WEB: www.convergeone.com
SIC: 1731 General electrical contractor
HQ: Convergeone, Inc.
10900 Nesbitt Ave S
Minneapolis MN 55437

(P-1209)
ACS COMMUNICATIONS INC
Also Called: Fiber Optic Technologies
680 Knox St Ste 150, Torrance
(90502-1325)
PHONE..................310 767-2145
Robby Sawyer, *President*
EMP: 69
SALES (corp-wide): 573.9MM **Privately Held**
SIC: 1731 Communications specialization
HQ: Acs Communications, Inc.
2535 Brockton Dr Ste 400
Austin TX 78758
512 837-4400

(P-1210)
AJ KIRKWOOD & ASSOCIATES INC
4300 N Harbor Blvd, Fullerton
(92835-1091)
PHONE..................714 505-1977
Arch Kirkwood, *Chairman*
James Klassen, *President*
Michael Hewson, *CFO*
Eric Fiorino, *Exec VP*
Aidan Culligan, *Senior VP*
EMP: 500 EST: 1996
SALES (est): 110MM **Privately Held**
WEB: www.ajk-a.com
SIC: 1731 8748 7389 General electrical contractor; communications consulting; design services

(P-1211)
ALBD ELECTRIC AND CABLE
Also Called: A Lighting By Design
995 E Discovery Ln, Anaheim
(92801-1147)
PHONE..................949 440-1216
Chad Lambert, *CEO*
James Black, *President*
Sherry Tatreau, *Executive Asst*
John Laszlo, *Project Mgr*
Isaias Serna, *Project Mgr*
EMP: 100 EST: 2002
SQ FT: 12,000
SALES (est): 20MM **Privately Held**
WEB: www.albdinc.com
SIC: 1731 3651 General electrical contractor; household audio & video equipment

(P-1212)
ALLTECH INDUSTRIES INC
301 E Pomona Blvd, Monterey Park
(91755-7300)
PHONE..................323 450-2168
Hilda Perez, *President*
EMP: 30 EST: 2010
SQ FT: 2,000
SALES (est): 3MM **Privately Held**
WEB: www.needalarm.wixsite.com
SIC: 1731 7381 3669 7382 Fire detection & burglar alarm systems specialization; security guard service; burglar alarm apparatus, electric; fire alarm maintenance & monitoring

(P-1213)
ANDERSON & HOWARD ELECTRIC INC
Also Called: Anderson Howard
15 Chrysler, Irvine (92618-2009)
PHONE..................949 250-4555
Brian E Elliott, *President*
Brett Howard, *COO*
Charles B Howard, *Vice Pres*
Tom Howard, *Admin Sec*
Michael Cruz, *Director*
EMP: 210 EST: 1967
SALES (est): 63MM **Privately Held**
WEB: www.aandh.com
SIC: 1731 General electrical contractor

(P-1214)
APOLLO ELECTRIC
330 N Basse Ln, Brea (92821-3906)
PHONE..................714 256-8414
Leroy H Holt, *CEO*
Gregg L Holt, *Treasurer*
Brent Holt, *Vice Pres*
Kelly Shay, *Vice Pres*
Anita Hunter, *Office Mgr*
EMP: 60 EST: 1966
SQ FT: 18,000
SALES (est): 14.8MM **Privately Held**
WEB: www.apolloelect.com
SIC: 1731 General electrical contractor

(P-1215)
ARDENT COMPANIES INC
4842 Airport Dr, Bakersfield (93308-9786)
PHONE..................661 633-1465
Glenn Dubuc, *Manager*
EMP: 75
SALES (corp-wide): 8.8B **Publicly Held**
WEB: www.ardent.us
SIC: 1731 General electrical contractor

HQ: Ardent Companies, Inc.
4824 Rosedale Ln
Bakersfield CA 93314
661 633-1465

(P-1216)
ASSI SECURITY (PA)
1370 Reynolds Ave Ste 201, Irvine
(92614-5547)
PHONE..................949 955-0244
William Dominic Vuono, *President*
Michael Willey, *Vice Pres*
Diego Herrera, *Technician*
Dan Gonzalez, *Project Mgr*
Ismael Mercado, *Project Mgr*
EMP: 67 EST: 1993
SQ FT: 10,000
SALES (est): 15.6MM **Privately Held**
WEB: www.assisecurity.com
SIC: 1731 7382 Voice, data & video wiring contractor; security systems services

(P-1217)
ATK AUDIOTEK
Also Called: Atk Services
28238 Avenue Crocker, Valencia
(91355-1248)
PHONE..................661 705-3700
Michael Murray Macdonald, *President*
James Harmala, *CFO*
J Scott Harmala, *Vice Pres*
John M Stewart, *Admin Sec*
Bronwen Grebe, *Admin Asst*
EMP: 85 EST: 1983
SQ FT: 25,000
SALES (est): 26MM **Privately Held**
WEB: www.atkaudiotek.com
SIC: 1731 7359 Voice, data & video wiring contractor; sound & lighting equipment rental

(P-1218)
ATMC INCORPORATED (PA)
Also Called: Atm Consultants
725 W Baseline Rd, Claremont
(91711-1615)
PHONE..................909 390-0470
Toshio Hashioka, *President*
Kim Edwards, *Vice Pres*
Joseph Kardos, *Vice Pres*
EMP: 60 EST: 1982
SQ FT: 12,000
SALES (est): 4.2MM **Privately Held**
WEB: www.atmc.com
SIC: 1731 5044 Banking machine installation & service; bank automatic teller machines

(P-1219)
BERGELECTRIC CORP
13375 Estelle St, Corona (92879-1881)
PHONE..................951 520-0851
EMP: 84
SALES (corp-wide): 483.1MM **Privately Held**
WEB: www.bergelectric.com
SIC: 1731 General electrical contractor
PA: Bergelectric Corp.
3182 Lionshead Ave
Carlsbad CA 92010
760 638-2374

(P-1220)
BERGELECTRIC CORP
5142 Clareton Dr Ste 140, Agoura Hills
(91301-4528)
PHONE..................818 991-8600
Jacob Wood, *Manager*
EMP: 84
SALES (corp-wide): 483.1MM **Privately Held**
WEB: www.bergelectric.com
SIC: 1731 General electrical contractor
PA: Bergelectric Corp.
3182 Lionshead Ave
Carlsbad CA 92010
760 638-2374

(P-1221)
BERGELECTRIC CORP
15776 Gateway Cir, Tustin (92780-6469)
PHONE..................949 250-7005
Mark Bauer, *Manager*
Charles Anderson, *Project Mgr*
James Bartlett, *Project Mgr*
Eddie Soula, *Opers Mgr*

Jared Harris, *Foreman/Supr*
EMP: 84
SALES (corp-wide): 483.1MM **Privately Held**
WEB: www.bergelectric.com
SIC: 1731 General electrical contractor
PA: Bergelectric Corp.
3182 Lionshead Ave
Carlsbad CA 92010
760 638-2374

(P-1222)
BLUEWAVE TECHNOLOGIES
Also Called: Genesys Solutions
2901 W Coast Hwy Ste 200, Newport Beach (92663-4045)
PHONE..................949 500-4652
Juan Hurtado, *CEO*
EMP: 20 EST: 2016
SQ FT: 2,000
SALES (est): 980.9K **Privately Held**
SIC: 1731 3825 4813 Communications specialization; voice, data & video wiring contractor; network analyzers; data telephone communications

(P-1223)
BRAUN ELECTRIC COMPANY INC (HQ)
3000 E Belle Ter, Bakersfield (93307-7093)
PHONE..................661 633-1451
John A Braun, *President*
Kevin Blankenship, *Vice Pres*
Kevin B Coghlin, *Vice Pres*
William Despain, *Area Mgr*
Jeff Coghlin, *IT/INT Sup*
EMP: 50 EST: 1945
SQ FT: 11,000
SALES (est): 56.1MM **Privately Held**
WEB: www.braunelec.com
SIC: 1731 General electrical contractor
PA: C&B Holding Co., Inc.
3000 Belle Terrace
Bakersfield CA 93304
661 633-1451

(P-1224)
BRIGGS ELECTRIC INC (PA)
14381 Franklin Ave, Tustin (92780-7010)
PHONE..................714 544-2500
Jeff Perry, *President*
Thomas J Perry, *President*
Todd Perry, *CFO*
Brad Weaver, *Officer*
Arlo Hanski, *Manager*
▲ EMP: 100 EST: 1946
SQ FT: 5,500
SALES (est): 51MM **Privately Held**
WEB: www.briggselectric.com
SIC: 1731 General electrical contractor

(P-1225)
BUDGET ELECTRICAL CONTRS INC
25051 5th St, San Bernardino
(92410-5119)
PHONE..................909 381-2646
Danny E Guy, *CEO*
William Morris Diesel, *President*
EMP: 150 EST: 1984
SQ FT: 5,000
SALES (est): 17.1MM **Privately Held**
SIC: 1731 General electrical contractor

(P-1226)
BUILDING ELCTRONIC CONTRLS INC (PA)
2246 Lindsay Way, Glendora (91740-5398)
PHONE..................909 305-1600
Richard Taylor, *President*
Shelley Taylor, *Vice Pres*
EMP: 48 EST: 1996
SQ FT: 13,000
SALES (est): 17.2MM **Privately Held**
WEB: www.becinc.net
SIC: 1731 3699 General electrical contractor; security control equipment & systems; security devices

(P-1227)
C&R SYSTEMS INC (PA)
1835 Capital St, Corona (92878-3227)
PHONE..................951 270-0255
Pam Mosbaugh, *President*
Robert V Cross, *Principal*

Linda Van Meter, *Sales Staff*
Robbie Sorensen, *Warehouse Mgr*
Tim Potts, *Manager*
EMP: 50 **EST:** 1983
SQ FT: 8,000
SALES (est): 8.2MM **Privately Held**
WEB: www.crsys.net
SIC: 1731 Telephone & telephone equipment installation

(P-1228)
C-G SYSTEMS INC
Also Called: California Gate Entry Systems
1470 N Hundley St, Anaheim (92806-1322)
PHONE..................714 632-8882
Kevin Squire, *CEO*
Jonathan Groome, *Department Mgr*
EMP: 27 **EST:** 1982
SALES (est): 8.4MM **Privately Held**
WEB: www.californiagate.com
SIC: 1731 3699 3315 5731 Fire detection & burglar alarm systems specialization; security devices; fence gates posts & fittings: steel; video cameras, recorders & accessories; dealers, security

(P-1229)
CALENERGY LLC
7030 Gentry Rd, Calipatria (92233-9720)
PHONE..................402 231-1527
Bill Fehrman, *President*
Brian C Smith, *Manager*
EMP: 350 **EST:** 2013
SALES (est): 30.3MM **Privately Held**
SIC: 1731 Electric power systems contractors

(P-1230)
CAROL ELECTRIC COMPANY INC
3822 Cerritos Ave, Los Alamitos (90720-2420)
PHONE..................562 431-1870
John R Fuqua, *Ch of Bd*
Allen Moffitt, *President*
Brian Moffitt, *Exec VP*
Erik Anderson, *Project Mgr*
Jeff Fetters, *Project Mgr*
EMP: 90 **EST:** 1979
SQ FT: 10,000
SALES (est): 17.4MM **Privately Held**
WEB: www.carolelectric.com
SIC: 1731 General electrical contractor

(P-1231)
CBR ELECTRIC INC
22 Rancho Cir, Lake Forest (92630-8325)
PHONE..................949 455-0331
Cary Raffety, *President*
Shawn Cotter, *Vice Pres*
Alysia Wagner, *Manager*
EMP: 150 **EST:** 1989
SQ FT: 4,000
SALES (est): 9.7MM **Privately Held**
WEB: www.cbrelectric.com
SIC: 1731 Electrical work

(P-1232)
CHAMPION ELECTRIC INC
3950 Garner Rd, Riverside (92501-1005)
PHONE..................951 276-9619
Glenn Rowden, *President*
Cynthia D Rowden, *CFO*
Tom Rowden, *Vice Pres*
Bryce Willis, *Admin Asst*
Liset Galv N, *Accountant*
EMP: 65 **EST:** 1991
SQ FT: 12,000
SALES (est): 10.8MM **Privately Held**
WEB: www.championelec.com
SIC: 1731 General electrical contractor

(P-1233)
CLEANTEK ELECTRIC INC
403 W 21st St, San Pedro (90731-5509)
PHONE..................424 400-3315
Carl Pancutt, *CEO*
Carl James Mark Pancutt, *CEO*
EMP: 20 **EST:** 2019
SALES (est): 2MM **Privately Held**
WEB: www.cleantek.co
SIC: 1731 3621 3694 General electrical contractor; generators for gas-electric or oil-electric vehicles; battery charging generators, automobile & aircraft

(P-1234)
COMET ELECTRIC INC
21625 Prairie St, Chatsworth (91311-5833)
PHONE..................818 340-0965
Adam Saitman, *Principal*
Jason Pennington, *CFO*
Keith Berson, *Exec VP*
Steve Goad, *Vice Pres*
Ryan Fera, *Project Mgr*
EMP: 150
SQ FT: 12,000
SALES (est): 37MM **Privately Held**
WEB: www.cometelectric.com
SIC: 1731 General electrical contractor

(P-1235)
COMMUNICATION TECH SVCS LLC
1590 S Milliken Ave Ste H, Ontario (91761-2326)
PHONE..................508 382-2700
Chris Ungson, *Manager*
Patrice McCloskey, *Officer*
Shane Rubin, *Vice Pres*
Karen Knueven, *Administration*
Jason Jaconetta, *Technician*
EMP: 266 **Privately Held**
WEB: www.cts1.com
SIC: 1731 8748 Voice, data & video wiring contractor; fiber optic cable installation; telephone & telephone equipment installation; communications consulting
PA: Communication Technology Services, Llc
33 Locke Dr Ste 201
Marlborough MA 01752

(P-1236)
CONTRA COSTA ELECTRIC INC
3208 Landco Dr, Bakersfield (93308-6156)
PHONE..................661 322-4036
Richard Trainer, *Manager*
Paul White, *Division Mgr*
Josh Thorndike, *Manager*
Gerald Lockett, *Superintendent*
EMP: 104
SALES (corp-wide): 8.8B **Publicly Held**
WEB: www.ccelectric.com
SIC: 1731 General electrical contractor
HQ: Contra Costa Electric, Inc.
825 Howe Rd
Martinez CA 94553
925 229-4250

(P-1237)
COVE ELECTRIC INC
77971 Wildcat Dr Ste F, Palm Desert (92211-4133)
PHONE..................760 568-9924
Charles Bojkovsky, *President*
Michele Bojkovsky, *Shareholder*
Jeannie Stewart, *CFO*
Steve Tavares, *Vice Pres*
EMP: 70
SQ FT: 4,500
SALES (est): 8.7MM **Privately Held**
WEB: www.coveelectric.com
SIC: 1731 General electrical contractor

(P-1238)
CROSSTOWN ELEC & DATA INC
5454 Diaz St, Baldwin Park (91706-2026)
PHONE..................626 813-6693
Dave Heermance, *CEO*
Cortney Gomez, *Office Mgr*
Victor Contreras, *Network Enginr*
Jim Degner, *Network Enginr*
Sam Nasser, *Network Enginr*
EMP: 100 **EST:** 1998
SQ FT: 2,500
SALES (est): 31.4MM **Privately Held**
WEB: www.crosstowndata.com
SIC: 1731 General electrical contractor

(P-1239)
CSI ELECTRICAL CONTRACTORS INC
41769 11th St W Ste B, Palmdale (93551-1418)
PHONE..................661 723-0869
Roland Tamayo, *Branch Mgr*
Mike Shea, *Executive*
Kevin Tamayo, *Regional Mgr*
Carl Reza, *Technician*

Jake McGinley, *Project Mgr*
EMP: 278
SALES (corp-wide): 2.2B **Publicly Held**
WEB: www.csielectric.com
SIC: 1731 General electrical contractor
HQ: Csi Electrical Contractors, Inc.
10623 Fulton Wells Ave
Santa Fe Springs CA 90670

(P-1240)
CSI ELECTRICAL CONTRACTORS INC (HQ)
Also Called: C S I
10623 Fulton Wells Ave, Santa Fe Springs (90670-3741)
P.O. Box 2887 (90670-0887)
PHONE..................562 946-0700
Steven M Watts, *CEO*
Andy Klein, *President*
Paul Pica, *President*
Rick Yauney, *CFO*
Andrew Soffa, *Exec VP*
EMP: 150 **EST:** 1990
SQ FT: 49,044
SALES (est): 146.3MM
SALES (corp-wide): 2.2B **Publicly Held**
WEB: www.csielectric.com
SIC: 1731 General electrical contractor
PA: Myr Group Inc.
12150 E 112th Ave
Henderson CO 80640
303 286-8000

(P-1241)
DAN FREITAS ELECTRIC
983 E Levin Ave, Tulare (93274-6525)
PHONE..................559 686-9572
Daniel Freitas, *President*
Jeanette Freitas, *Executive*
EMP: 60 **EST:** 1984
SQ FT: 14,460
SALES (est): 10.4MM **Privately Held**
WEB: www.danfreitaselectric.com
SIC: 1731 General electrical contractor

(P-1242)
DEGENERATE SOUND INC (PA)
16000 Ventura Blvd, Encino (91436-2744)
PHONE..................818 385-1933
David Weise, *Administration*
EMP: 77 **EST:** 2017
SALES (est): 554.5K **Privately Held**
SIC: 1731 Sound equipment specialization

(P-1243)
DIENERS ELECTRIC INC
Also Called: Channel Electric Supply
167 Lambert St, Oxnard (93036-1044)
P.O. Box 946 (93032-0946)
PHONE..................805 988-1515
Robert R Diener, *President*
David Romero, *Shareholder*
Ann G Diener, *Treasurer*
EMP: 66 **EST:** 1946
SQ FT: 7,000
SALES (est): 1.7MM **Privately Held**
WEB: www.dienerselectric.com
SIC: 1731 General electrical contractor

(P-1244)
DONCO & SONS INC
Also Called: Donco Associates & Sons
2871 E Blue Star St, Anaheim (92806-2508)
PHONE..................714 779-0099
Donavon W Fink, *President*
Diane Fink, *Treasurer*
Dave Fink, *Vice Pres*
Mark Fink, *Vice Pres*
EMP: 43 **EST:** 1980
SALES (est): 3.9MM **Privately Held**
WEB: www.donco.com
SIC: 1731 3993 Electrical work; electric signs

(P-1245)
EDWARDS TECHNOLOGIES INC
139 Maryland St, El Segundo (90245-4116)
PHONE..................310 536-7070
Brian Edwards, *President*
▲ **EMP:** 108 **EST:** 1984
SQ FT: 10,000
SALES (est): 14.9MM **Privately Held**
WEB: www.edwardstechnologies.com
SIC: 1731 Sound equipment specialization

(P-1246)
ELECTRIC SVC & SUP CO PASADENA
Also Called: Essco
2668 E Foothill Blvd, Pasadena (91107-3409)
PHONE..................626 795-8641
Stanley R Lazarian, *President*
Nancy Rose, *Treasurer*
Iris Lazarian, *Vice Pres*
EMP: 66 **EST:** 1946
SALES (est): 2.6MM **Privately Held**
WEB: www.esscoelectric.com
SIC: 1731 General electrical contractor

(P-1247)
ELITE ELECTRIC
9415 Bellegrave Ave, Riverside (92509-2741)
PHONE..................951 681-5811
Carl Eric Dawson, *President*
Carl Dawson, *Executive*
Krista Olson, *Division Mgr*
Tara Fogliasso, *Office Mgr*
Marshall Hockersmith, *Project Mgr*
EMP: 80 **EST:** 1978
SQ FT: 1,720
SALES (est): 12.6MM **Privately Held**
WEB: www.elite-electricinc.com
SIC: 1731 General electrical contractor

(P-1248)
ENERPATH SERVICES INC
1758 Orange Tree Ln, Redlands (92374-2856)
PHONE..................909 335-1699
Stephen Guthrie, *President*
Janina Guthrie, *Treasurer*
Jonathan Baty, *Admin Sec*
EMP: 72 **EST:** 1989
SQ FT: 4,500
SALES (est): 3.2MM **Privately Held**
SIC: 1731 8748 Lighting contractor; lighting consultant

(P-1249)
ESYS ENERGY CONTROL COMPANY
4520 Stine Rd Ste 7, Bakersfield (93313-2372)
PHONE..................661 833-1902
Fabio Russoniello, *President*
Andrea Prise, *Auditor*
Andrew Landwehr, *Manager*
EMP: 60 **EST:** 1985
SQ FT: 12,000
SALES (est): 12.5MM **Privately Held**
WEB: www.esys.us
SIC: 1731 5084 Electronic controls installation; controlling instruments & accessories

(P-1250)
EV CONNECT INC
615 N Nash St Ste 203, El Segundo (90245-2851)
PHONE..................310 751-7997
Jordan Ramer, *President*
Patrick Macdonald-King, *COO*
David Hughes, *CFO*
John Karambelas, *Officer*
Rose Devries, *Vice Pres*
EMP: 59 **EST:** 2010
SALES (est): 9.6MM **Privately Held**
WEB: www.evconnect.com
SIC: 1731 5072 8748 Electrical work; hardware; business consulting

(P-1251)
EV INFRASTRUCTURE LLC
1690 Scenic Ave, Costa Mesa (92626-1410)
PHONE..................714 908-5266
Ilan Tordjman, *President*
EMP: 50 **EST:** 2020
SALES (est): 5.4MM
SALES (corp-wide): 91.3MM **Privately Held**
WEB: www.whitedeerenergy.com
SIC: 1731 Electric power systems contractors
PA: White Deer Energy Lp
700 Louisiana St Ste 4770
Houston TX 77002
713 581-6900

(P-1252)

FAITH ELECTRIC LLC
1980 Orange Tree Ln # 106, Redlands
(92374-2803)
PHONE..................................909 767-2682
Elijah Adams, *CEO*
EMP: 135 **EST:** 2014
SQ FT: 5,000
SALES (est): 11.1MM **Privately Held**
WEB: www.faithelectricllc.com
SIC: 1731 General electrical contractor

(P-1253)

FEI ENTERPRISES INC
633 S La Brea Ave, Los Angeles
(90036-3521)
PHONE..................................323 937-0856
Gabriel Fedida, *CEO*
▲ **EMP:** 50 **EST:** 1988
SALES (est): 7.2MM **Privately Held**
WEB: www.feienterprises.com
SIC: 1731 5063 General electrical contractor; burglar alarm systems

(P-1254)

FIRST FIRE SYSTEMS INC (PA)
5947 Burchard Ave, Los Angeles
(90034-1701)
PHONE..................................310 559-0900
Juda Roshanzamir, *President*
Elias Farah, *CFO*
Robbie Kashani, *Executive*
Richard Velasco, *Technician*
Vahe Aboolian, *Project Mgr*
EMP: 99 **EST:** 1980
SQ FT: 9,400
SALES (est): 11.8MM **Privately Held**
WEB: www.ffstech.com
SIC: 1731 Fire detection & burglar alarm systems specialization

(P-1255)

FISK ELECTRIC COMPANY
15870 Olden St, Sylmar (91342-1241)
PHONE..................................818 884-1166
Orvil Anthony, *Senior VP*
Clay Collins, *Vice Pres*
John Hogan, *Project Mgr*
David Allenbrand, *Senior Mgr*
EMP: 165
SALES (corp-wide): 5.3B **Publicly Held**
WEB: www.fiskcorp.com
SIC: 1731 General electrical contractor
HQ: Fisk Electric Company
10855 Westview Dr
Houston TX 77043
713 868-6111

(P-1256)

FLATIRON ELECTRIC GROUP INC
15335 Fairfield Ranch Rd # 200, Chino Hills
(91709-8833)
PHONE..................................714 228-9631
Kurt Welter, *President*
John Diciurcio, *CEO*
Javier Sevilla, *COO*
Lars Leitner, *CFO*
EMP: 50 **EST:** 2005
SALES (est): 11.3MM
SALES (corp-wide): 1B **Privately Held**
WEB: www.flatironcorp.com
SIC: 1731 General electrical contractor
HQ: Flatiron West, Inc.
16470 W Bernardo Dr 120
San Diego CA 92127

(P-1257)

FOLEY OK ELECTRIC INC
5459 Diaz St, Irwindale (91706-2027)
P.O. Box 2337 (91706-1183)
PHONE..................................818 962-8555
Lila Foley, *President*
Keri Foley, *Treasurer*
O K Foley, *Vice Pres*
Erin Eggertsen, *Admin Sec*
EMP: 75 **EST:** 1959
SQ FT: 1,000
SALES (est): 3.3MM **Privately Held**
SIC: 1731 General electrical contractor

(P-1258)

GAMMILL ELECTRIC INC
Also Called: Gammil Services
16224 Arrow Hwy, Baldwin Park
(91706-2015)
PHONE..................................626 812-4515
John R Oldham, *President*
Jackie Oldham, *Treasurer*
Paul Rasmussen, *Vice Pres*
EMP: 13
SQ FT: 5,000
SALES (est): 3.3MM **Privately Held**
WEB: www.gammillelectric.com
SIC: 1731 7629 3613 General electrical contractor; generator repair; control panels, electric

(P-1259)

GEMCON INC
Also Called: Gemini Construction and SEC Co
7660 San Fernando Rd, Sun Valley
(91352-4349)
PHONE..................................818 767-0892
Joseph Annese, *President*
EMP: 14 **EST:** 1984
SQ FT: 7,000
SALES (est): 376.2K **Privately Held**
SIC: 1731 1542 3699 Safety & security specialization; commercial & office buildings, renovation & repair; security devices

(P-1260)

GREGG ELECTRIC INC
608 W Emporia St, Ontario (91762-3709)
PHONE..................................909 983-1794
Randall F Fehlman, *President*
Victoria Mensen, *CFO*
James Fehlman, *Vice Pres*
EMP: 150 **EST:** 1961
SQ FT: 15,000
SALES (est): 28.1MM **Privately Held**
WEB: www.greggelectric.com
SIC: 1731 General electrical contractor

(P-1261)

HACKNEY ELECTRIC INC (PA)
23286 Arroyo Vis, Rcho STA Marg
(92688-2610)
PHONE..................................949 264-4000
David J Hackney, *President*
Rebecca Hackney, *Vice Pres*
EMP: 58 **EST:** 1993
SQ FT: 6,200
SALES (est): 15.5MM **Privately Held**
WEB: www.hackneyelectric.com
SIC: 1731 General electrical contractor

(P-1262)

HARRIS L WOODS ELEC CONTR
Also Called: Woods Electric Company
9214 Norwalk Blvd, Santa Fe Springs
(90670-2924)
P.O. Box 2367 (90670-0367)
PHONE..................................562 945-8751
Sandra Woods, *President*
Ralph L Woods, *Admin Sec*
EMP: 55 **EST:** 1975
SQ FT: 5,000
SALES (est): 10.2MM **Privately Held**
SIC: 1731 General electrical contractor

(P-1263)

HELIX ELECTRIC INC
13100 Alondra Blvd # 108, Cerritos
(90703-2262)
P.O. Box 85298, San Diego (92186-5298)
PHONE..................................562 941-7200
Acey Long, *Vice Pres*
Cheryl Brookshier, *Administration*
Robert Barrera, *Project Mgr*
Nancy Gutierrez, *Project Mgr*
Aj Protteau, *Analyst*
EMP: 179
SALES (corp-wide): 408.8MM **Privately Held**
WEB: www.helixelectric.com
SIC: 1731 General electrical contractor
PA: Helix Electric, Inc.
6795 Flanders Dr
San Diego CA 92121
858 535-0505

(P-1264)

HHS COMMUNICATIONS INC
2042 S Grove Ave, Ontario (91761-5617)
PHONE..................................909 230-5170
Royce S Jaime, *President*
Cynthia Martinez, *Info Tech Mgr*
EMP: 60 **EST:** 2007
SALES (est): 13.9MM
SALES (corp-wide): 190.9MM **Privately Held**
WEB: www.congruex.com
SIC: 1731 Fiber optic cable installation
PA: Congruex Llc
2615 13th St
Boulder CO 80304
720 749-2318

(P-1265)

HIGH-LIGHT ELECTRIC INC
1460 E Cooley Dr Ste 100, Colton
(92324-3933)
P.O. Box 1248 (92324-0822)
PHONE..................................951 352-9646
Erwin Mendoza, *President*
Josue Zavala, *Executive*
Alfredo Limon, *Foreman/Supr*
EMP: 60 **EST:** 1996
SALES (est): 17.6MM **Privately Held**
WEB: www.hleincusa.com
SIC: 1731 General electrical contractor

(P-1266)

HIMCO NATIONAL INC
Also Called: Himco Security Products
120 E 33rd St, Los Angeles (90011-2313)
PHONE..................................323 231-9104
Markos Cerna, *Manager*
Alondra Soto, *Controller*
EMP: 17
SALES (corp-wide): 7.5MM **Privately Held**
WEB: www.himcosecurity.com
SIC: 1731 3496 3442 Electrical work; miscellaneous fabricated wire products; metal doors, sash & trim
PA: Himco National, Incorporated
3326 S Main St
Los Angeles CA
323 232-2222

(P-1267)

IES COMMERCIAL INC
1633 Maria St, Burbank (91504-3420)
PHONE..................................713 860-1500
Steve Tucker, *Owner*
EMP: 84 **Publicly Held**
WEB: www.iescomm.com
SIC: 1731 General electrical contractor
HQ: Ies Commercial, Inc.
2801 S Fair Ln Ste 101
Tempe AZ 85282
480 379-6200

(P-1268)

INTERIOR ELECTRIC INCORPORATED
747 N Main St, Orange (92868-1105)
PHONE..................................714 771-9098
Mark Beverly, *President*
Gus Baquerizo, *Vice Pres*
Mark Maskevich, *Vice Pres*
Glen Nielsen, *Vice Pres*
Chad Stewart, *Vice Pres*
EMP: 75
SQ FT: 10,000
SALES (est): 13.2MM **Privately Held**
WEB: www.ie-systems.net
SIC: 1731 General electrical contractor

(P-1269)

JEEVA CORP
Also Called: Satellite Pros
750 E E St Unit B, Ontario (91764-3821)
PHONE..................................909 238-4073
Orlando Uranga, *CEO*
Rita Uranga, *CFO*
EMP: 70
SQ FT: 1,800
SALES (est): 2.5MM **Privately Held**
SIC: 1731 Cable television installation

(P-1270)

JMG SECURITY SYSTEMS INC
17150 Newhope St Ste 109, Fountain Valley (92708-4273)
PHONE..................................714 545-8882

Ken Jacobs, *CEO*
Mike Brayard, *COO*
Mike Christensen, *COO*
Michael Christensen, *Exec VP*
Gil Ledesma, *Vice Pres*
EMP: 70 **EST:** 1987
SQ FT: 14,000
SALES (est): 14.2MM **Privately Held**
WEB: www.jmgsecurity.com
SIC: 1731 5063 Safety & security specialization; burglar alarm systems

(P-1271)

KDC INC (HQ)
Also Called: Kdc Systems
4462 Corporate Center Dr, Los Alamitos
(90720-2539)
PHONE..................................714 828-7000
Earnest Lee Brown, *President*
Ben Martin, *CFO*
Ryan Lee, *Executive*
Terree Rola, *Administration*
Rick Duncan, *Project Mgr*
EMP: 347 **EST:** 1976
SQ FT: 57,000
SALES (est): 57.6MM
SALES (corp-wide): 8.8B **Publicly Held**
WEB: www.kdc-systems.com
SIC: 1731 1611 3823 General electrical contractor; general contractor, highway & street construction; industrial instrmnts msrmnt display/control process variable
PA: Emcor Group, Inc.
301 Merritt 7 Fl 6
Norwalk CT 06851
203 849-7800

(P-1272)

KITE ELECTRIC INC
Also Called: K E
2 Thomas, Irvine (92618-2512)
PHONE..................................949 380-7471
Tracy Adams, *President*
EMP: 120 **EST:** 2000
SALES (est): 13.5MM **Privately Held**
WEB: www.kiteelectric.com
SIC: 1731 Electrical work

(P-1273)

L TECH NETWORK SERVICES INC
3424 Garfield Ave A, Commerce
(90040-3104)
PHONE..................................562 222-1121
Robert O Lopez, *President*
EMP: 65 **EST:** 1990
SALES (est): 5MM **Privately Held**
WEB: www.ltechnet.com
SIC: 1731 Communications specialization

(P-1274)

LA SIGNAL
155 N Eucla Ave, La Puente (91744)
P.O. Box 610, San Dimas (91773-0610)
PHONE..................................909 599-2201
Ray Morales, *Principal*
Lorenzo Lopez, *Manager*
EMP: 15 **EST:** 2011
SALES (est): 1.3MM **Privately Held**
WEB: www.lasignal.com
SIC: 1731 3648 3669 Electrical work; street lighting fixtures; traffic signals, electric

(P-1275)

LEED ELECTRIC INC
13138 Arctic Cir, Santa Fe Springs
(90670-5508)
PHONE..................................562 270-9500
Seth Jamali Dinan, *President*
Tien Bui, *Foreman/Supr*
EMP: 135 **EST:** 1979
SQ FT: 8,480
SALES (est): 21.3MM **Privately Held**
WEB: www.leedelectric.com
SIC: 1731 General electrical contractor

(P-1276)

LITTLEJOHN-REULAND CORPORATION
4575 Pacific Blvd, Vernon (90058-2207)
P.O. Box 58487, Los Angeles (90058-0487)
PHONE..................................323 587-5255
Richard Pena, *President*
Barry Mileski, *Vice Pres*
Dolores Robinson, *Admin Sec*

Sean Sampson, *Plant Mgr*
Marco Vasquez, *Foreman/Supr*
EMP: 45 **EST:** 1926
SQ FT: 50,000
SALES: 7.2MM **Privately Held**
WEB: www.littlejohn-reuland.com
SIC: 1731 7694 5063 5511 General electrical contractor; armature rewinding shops; electrical supplies; new & used car dealers; general automotive repair shops

(P-1277)
M & R JOINT VENTURE ELECTRICAL
Also Called: Marrow Meadows
231 Benton Ct, Walnut (91789-5213)
PHONE.....................909 598-7700
Robert E Meadows, *Vice Pres*
Morrow-Meadows Corporation, *Co-Venturer*
Gary Deadmon, *Vice Pres*
David Hill, *Vice Pres*
Robert Atkinson, *Project Mgr*
EMP: 60 **EST:** 1994
SALES (est): 13.4MM **Privately Held**
SIC: 1731 General electrical contractor

(P-1278)
M L SERVICES INC
Also Called: Sunset Lighting Services
5 Peters Canyon Rd # 140, Irvine (92606-1791)
PHONE.....................800 272-2179
Michael Landig, *President*
Jane Landig, *Corp Secy*
EMP: 59 **EST:** 1990
SQ FT: 3,000
SALES (est): 5.4MM **Privately Held**
SIC: 1731 General electrical contractor; lighting contractor

(P-1279)
MARK LAND ELECTRIC INC
7876 Deering Ave, Canoga Park (91304-5005)
PHONE.....................818 883-5110
Lloyd Saitman, *CEO*
John Bennet, *CFO*
Don Dewhurst, *Vice Pres*
Stewart Franklin, *Vice Pres*
Dean Olson, *Vice Pres*
EMP: 329 **EST:** 1981
SQ FT: 10,000
SALES (est): 26.3MM **Privately Held**
WEB: www.lmela.com
SIC: 1731 General electrical contractor

(P-1280)
MB HERZOG ELECTRIC INC
15709 Illinois Ave, Paramount (90723-4112)
PHONE.....................562 531-2002
Ryan M Herzog, *CEO*
Kevin Ryan, *Vice Pres*
Gail Acosta, *Executive*
Brent Macdonald, *Division Mgr*
Greg Stumpf, *Foreman/Supr*
EMP: 200 **EST:** 1974
SQ FT: 6,200
SALES: 45.1MM **Privately Held**
WEB: www.herzogelectric.com
SIC: 1731 General electrical contractor

(P-1281)
MEDLEY COMMUNICATIONS INC (PA)
43015 Black Deer Loop, Temecula (92590-3564)
PHONE.....................951 245-5200
Darrin Medley, *President*
Cindy Carreon, *Director*
Jesus Medina, *Director*
EMP: 175 **EST:** 1985
SALES (est): 16.6MM **Privately Held**
WEB: www.medleycom.net
SIC: 1731 8748 Cable television installation; communications consulting

(P-1282)
METCALFE SECURITY INC
3161 Bostonian Dr, Los Alamitos (90720-4237)
PHONE.....................213 605-2785
Michael Metcalfe, *President*
EMP: 61 **EST:** 2015
SALES (est): 2.7MM **Privately Held**
SIC: 1731 Safety & security specialization

(P-1283)
MORROW-MEADOWS CORPORATION (PA)
Also Called: Cherry City Electric
231 Benton Ct, City of Industry (91789-5213)
PHONE.....................858 974-3650
Robert E Meadows, *Vice Pres*
Craig Earley, *Exec VP*
Robert Meadows, *Exec VP*
Bob Atkinson, *Vice Pres*
David Hill, *Vice Pres*
EMP: 850
SQ FT: 55,000
SALES (est): 302.6MM **Privately Held**
WEB: www.morrow-meadows.com
SIC: 1731 General electrical contractor

(P-1284)
MSL ELECTRIC INC
2918 E La Jolla St, Anaheim (92806-1305)
PHONE.....................714 693-4837
Warren L Moore, *President*
Sally Moore, *Admin Sec*
EMP: 60
SALES (est): 12.1MM **Privately Held**
WEB: www.mslelectric.com
SIC: 1731 General electrical contractor

(P-1285)
NATIONAL FAIL SAFE INC
Also Called: National Fail-Safe SEC Systems
6442 Industry Way, Westminster (92683-3600)
PHONE.....................562 493-5447
Al Puskas, *President*
Kathy Puskas, *Vice Pres*
Bill Bennett, *Sales Associate*
Cristyn Van Fossen, *Sales Staff*
Nick Woodside, *Manager*
EMP: 50 **EST:** 1972
SQ FT: 10,000
SALES (est): 11MM **Privately Held**
WEB: www.nationalfailsafe.us
SIC: 1731 7382 Fire detection & burglar alarm systems specialization; fire alarm maintenance & monitoring

(P-1286)
NAZZARENO ELECTRIC CO INC
1250 E Gene Autry Way, Anaheim (92805-6716)
PHONE.....................714 712-4744
Paul Rick Nazzareno, *President*
EMP: 75 **EST:** 1993
SQ FT: 10,000
SALES (est): 9.9MM **Privately Held**
WEB: www.nazzareno.com
SIC: 1731 General electrical contractor

(P-1287)
NRG POWER INC
3011 S Shannon St, Santa Ana (92704-6320)
PHONE.....................714 424-6484
Than V Nguyen, *President*
John Toan Nguyen, *Vice Pres*
Elaine Diep, *Office Mgr*
EMP: 57 **EST:** 1997
SQ FT: 5,700
SALES (est): 6.9MM **Privately Held**
WEB: www.nrgpower.net
SIC: 1731 General electrical contractor

(P-1288)
OBRYANT ELECTRIC INC
9314 Eton Ave, Chatsworth (91311-5809)
PHONE.....................818 407-1986
Cathy O'Bryant, *President*
Steve O'Bryant, *Admin Sec*
Peter Anselmo, *Project Mgr*
Farid Portillo, *Foreman/Supr*
EMP: 200 **EST:** 1978
SQ FT: 25,000
SALES (est): 52.6MM **Privately Held**
WEB: www.obryantelectric.com
SIC: 1731 General electrical contractor

(P-1289)
OILFIELD ELECTRIC COMPANY
Also Called: Oilfield Electric & Motor
1801 N Ventura Ave, Ventura (93001-1597)
PHONE.....................805 648-3131
Alan Dale Fletcher, *CEO*
Jana Fletcher, *President*
Mark E Dilley, *Info Tech Dir*

EMP: 60
SQ FT: 10,000
SALES (est): 11.9MM **Privately Held**
WEB: www.oilfld.com
SIC: 1731 7629 General electrical contractor; electrical repair shops

(P-1290)
PACIFIC INTL ELC CO INC
Also Called: Pacific Industrial Electric
230 N Orange Ave, Brea (92821-4072)
P.O. Box 9788 (92822-9788)
PHONE.....................714 990-9280
Roxanne Medina, *CEO*
Frederick Lewis Pradels, *CEO*
John Tietz, *Treasurer*
Garry White, *Vice Pres*
EMP: 63 **EST:** 1971
SQ FT: 14,500
SALES (est): 26.2MM **Privately Held**
WEB: www.wordpress.pacificindustrialelectric.com
SIC: 1731 8711 General electrical contractor; electrical or electronic engineering

(P-1291)
PACIFIC UTLITY INSTLLATION INC
510 Malloy Ct, Corona (92878-4045)
PHONE.....................714 970-6430
William B Pfeifer, *CEO*
Daniel Mole, *President*
▲ **EMP:** 65 **EST:** 1997
SALES (est): 13.3MM **Privately Held**
WEB: www.pacificutility.com
SIC: 1731 1623 General electrical contractor; water, sewer & utility lines

(P-1292)
PATRIC COMMUNICATIONS INC (PA)
Also Called: Advanced Electronic Solutions
15215 Alton Pkwy Ste 200, Irvine (92618-2613)
PHONE.....................619 579-2898
Sean P McDermott, *President*
Colleen Emick, *CFO*
Richard P Apgar, *Vice Pres*
Katherine Alford, *Admin Sec*
Kathy Alford, *Admin Sec*
EMP: 70 **EST:** 1981
SALES (est): 9.7MM **Privately Held**
SIC: 1731 1751 3699 Fire detection & burglar alarm systems specialization; carpentry work; security devices

(P-1293)
PAVLETICH ELC CMMNICATIONS INC (PA)
6308 Seven Seas Ave, Bakersfield (93308-5132)
PHONE.....................661 589-9473
John Pavletich, *CEO*
Scott Pavletich, *President*
Erin Cockrell, *Office Mgr*
Annette Pavletich, *Administration*
Melissa Arceo, *Receptionist*
EMP: 89 **EST:** 1994
SQ FT: 15,000
SALES (est): 15.1MM **Privately Held**
WEB: www.pavelectric.com
SIC: 1731 General electrical contractor

(P-1294)
PETRELLI ELECTRIC INC
11615 Davenport Rd, Agua Dulce (91390-4690)
P.O. Box 801148, Santa Clarita (91380-1148)
PHONE.....................661 268-7312
Cindy Petrelli, *CEO*
Bill Murray, *Vice Pres*
Salvatore Petrelli, *Vice Pres*
Katelyn Petrelli, *Admin Asst*
Chad Altom, *Technician*
EMP: 66 **EST:** 1983
SALES (est): 13MM **Privately Held**
WEB: www.petrellielectr.wpengine.com
SIC: 1731 7629 General electrical contractor; electrical equipment repair, high voltage

(P-1295)
PINNACLE NETWORKING SVCS INC
Also Called: Pinnacle Communication Svcs
730 Fairmont Ave, Glendale (91203-1078)
PHONE.....................818 241-6009
Avo Amirian, *CEO*
Joe Licursi, *President*
Shawn Wilson, *Info Tech Dir*
Joseph Carlin, *Project Mgr*
Ashley Pipkins, *Project Mgr*
EMP: 75 **EST:** 1994
SQ FT: 10,000
SALES (est): 19.9MM **Privately Held**
WEB: www.pinnacleinc.com
SIC: 1731 Communications specialization

(P-1296)
PIVOT INTERIORS INC
Pivot Interiors-Receiving Only
3200 Park Center Dr # 100, Costa Mesa (92626-7104)
PHONE.....................949 988-5400
Ken Baugh, *CEO*
Mike Vandenberg, *Sr Project Mgr*
EMP: 92
SALES (corp-wide): 91.3MM **Privately Held**
WEB: www.pivotinteriors.com
SIC: 1731 Electrical work
PA: Pivot Interiors, Inc.
    3355 Scott Blvd Ste 110
    Santa Clara CA 95054
    408 432-5600

(P-1297)
PMD INDUSTRIES INC
Also Called: Eie Electric
703 Randolph Ave, Costa Mesa (92626-5917)
PHONE.....................949 222-0999
Phillip M Davis, *President*
Howard C Waters, *CFO*
EMP: 50 **EST:** 1992
SQ FT: 2,500
SALES (est): 7.7MM **Privately Held**
SIC: 1731 7373 Electrical work; computer integrated systems design

(P-1298)
PONDEROSA ELECTRIC INC
3911 E La Palma Ave Ste D, Anaheim (92807-1719)
PHONE.....................949 253-3100
Dale Arnold, *President*
EMP: 60 **EST:** 1986
SALES (est): 5.9MM **Privately Held**
WEB: www.ponderosaelectric.com
SIC: 1731 General electrical contractor

(P-1299)
PORTERMATT ELECTRIC INC
5431 Production Dr, Huntington Beach (92649-1524)
PHONE.....................714 596-8788
Tim Matthews, *President*
John F Porter III, *Vice Pres*
EMP: 90 **EST:** 1998
SQ FT: 5,300
SALES (est): 19.3MM **Privately Held**
WEB: www.portermatt.com
SIC: 1731 1799 General electrical contractor; athletic & recreation facilities construction

(P-1300)
POWERFULL SYSTEMS INC
Also Called: Shading Solutions
5222 Venice Blvd, Los Angeles (90019-5236)
PHONE.....................310 836-9333
Shalom Illouz, *President*
Eric Myers, *COO*
Ofer Abutbul, *Vice Pres*
Carlos Fawcett, *Human Resources*
EMP: 50 **EST:** 2004
SQ FT: 7,500
SALES (est): 6.1MM **Privately Held**
WEB: www.powerfullsystems.com
SIC: 1731 5999 Electronic controls installation; general electrical contractor; audiovisual equipment & supplies

(P-1301)
PREMIER SIGNS SERVICE INC
2985 Durahart St, Riverside (92507-3420)
PHONE..........................951 204-7693
Jessica Arriaga, *CEO*
Diane Arriaga, *CFO*
Matthew Arriaga, *Admin Sec*
Brett McKeehan, *Marketing Mgr*
EMP: 14 EST: 2012
SQ FT: 6,000
SALES (est): 2.3MM **Privately Held**
WEB: www.premiersignservice.com
SIC: 1731 1799 3993 1741 Electrical
work; sign installation & maintenance;
welding on site; signs & advertising spe-
cialties; foundation building

(P-1302)
PROFESSNAL ELEC CNSTR SVCS INC
Also Called: Pecs
9112 Santa Anita Ave, Rancho Cucamonga
(91730-6143)
PHONE..........................909 373-4100
Diane Casey, *CEO*
Robert W Casey, *CFO*
Jose Ramirez, *Project Mgr*
EMP: 102 EST: 2007
SQ FT: 15,000
SALES (est): 14.8MM **Privately Held**
WEB: www.pecs.biz
SIC: 1731 General electrical contractor

(P-1303)
PYRO-COMM SYSTEMS INC (PA)
15531 Container Ln, Huntington Beach
(92649-1530)
PHONE..........................714 902-8000
Michael Donahue, *President*
Ronald Cummings, *Vice Pres*
Nanci Donahue, *Vice Pres*
Kevin Green, *Regional Mgr*
Melissa Tadlock, *Administration*
EMP: 150 EST: 1980
SQ FT: 10,000
SALES (est): 38.4MM **Privately Held**
WEB: www.pyrocomm.com
SIC: 1731 5063 Fire detection & burglar
alarm systems specialization; fire alarm
systems

(P-1304)
R & R ELECTRIC
2029 Century Park E A4, Los Angeles
(90067-2901)
PHONE..........................310 785-0288
Ricardo Ramos, *Owner*
Brenda Mitchell, *Office Admin*
Mario Mata, *CIO*
Rick Alcantar, *Project Mgr*
Randy Chiasson, *Project Mgr*
EMP: 50 EST: 1986
SQ FT: 5,000
SALES (est): 9.8MM **Privately Held**
WEB: www.rr-electric.com
SIC: 1731 General electrical contractor

(P-1305)
RANCHO PACIFIC ELECTRIC INC
9063 Santa Anita Ave, Rancho Cucamonga
(91730-6142)
PHONE..........................909 476-1022
Steve Robinson, *President*
Dave Robinson, *Corp Secy*
Jason Lindley, *Project Engr*
Albert Cisneros, *Foreman/Supr*
Robert Greathouse, *Manager*
EMP: 50 EST: 1983
SQ FT: 4,500
SALES (est): 10.8MM **Privately Held**
WEB: www.ranchopacificelectric.com
SIC: 1731 General electrical contractor

(P-1306)
RDM ELECTRIC CO INC (PA)
4260 E Brickell St, Ontario (91761-1511)
PHONE..........................909 591-0990
Robert McDonnell, *President*
Diane McDonnell, *Officer*
Anthony Gerdes, *Vice Pres*
Rob McDonnell, *Vice Pres*
Robert D McDonnell Jr, *Vice Pres*
EMP: 71 EST: 1987

SALES (est): 17.7MM **Privately Held**
WEB: www.rdmcompanies.com
SIC: 1731 General electrical contractor

(P-1307)
RED HAWK FIRE & SEC CA INC (DH)
7605 N San Fernando Rd, Los Angeles
(90065)
PHONE..........................818 683-1500
Sean Flint, *CEO*
EMP: 99 EST: 1995
SQ FT: 15,500
SALES (est): 10MM
SALES (corp-wide): 5.3B **Publicly Held**
WEB: www.adt.com
SIC: 1731 Fire detection & burglar alarm
systems specialization
HQ: Adt Commercial Llc
1501 W Yamato Rd
Boca Raton FL 33431
877 387-0188

(P-1308)
RGA ELECTRIC INC
Also Called: Anthony Electric
10207 Freeman Ave, Santa Fe Springs
(90670-3409)
PHONE..........................562 941-6380
Dorothy M Pantleo, *President*
Geno J Pantleo, *Vice Pres*
Geno Pantleo, *Vice Pres*
Russell Pantleo, *Vice Pres*
EMP: 62 EST: 1959
SQ FT: 23,000
SALES (est): 15MM **Privately Held**
WEB: www.anthonyelectric.com
SIC: 1731 General electrical contractor

(P-1309)
RICARDO RAMOS
Also Called: R&R Electric
2803 Carlsbad St, Redondo Beach
(90278-1716)
PHONE..........................310 785-0288
R Ramos, *Owner*
Richard Ramos, *Owner*
EMP: 50 EST: 1998
SALES (est): 2.1MM **Privately Held**
WEB: www.rr-electric.com
SIC: 1731 General electrical contractor

(P-1310)
RJB ENTERPRISES INC
Also Called: Ultimate Communication Sys-
tems
2579 W Woodland Dr, Anaheim
(92801-2608)
PHONE..........................714 484-3101
Robert Bohan, *President*
Donald Ramirez, *Manager*
EMP: 50 EST: 1987
SQ FT: 3,500
SALES (est): 9MM **Privately Held**
SIC: 1731 Voice, data & video wiring con-
tractor

(P-1311)
ROSENDIN ELECTRIC INC
1730 S Anaheim Way, Anaheim
(92805-6537)
PHONE..........................714 739-1334
Cliff Thompson, *Branch Mgr*
Rick Gonzales, *Sr Project Mgr*
Dustin Earhart, *Manager*
Quinn Wholean, *Manager*
EMP: 668
SALES (corp-wide): 1.8B **Privately Held**
WEB: www.rosendin.com
SIC: 1731 General electrical contractor
PA: Rosendin Electric, Inc.
880 Mabury Rd
San Jose CA 95133
408 286-2800

(P-1312)
ROSENDIN HOLDINGS INC (PA)
400 S Hope St, Los Angeles (90071-2801)
PHONE..........................213 891-9619
Tom Sorley, *CEO*
EMP: 1204 EST: 2010
SALES (est): 175.1MM **Privately Held**
SIC: 1731 General electrical contractor

(P-1313)
SBE CONTRACTING
17256 Red Hill Ave, Irvine (92614-5628)
PHONE..........................714 544-5066
Jeff Wilson, *President*
Erica Rodriguez, *Manager*
EMP: 50 EST: 2004
SALES (est): 10.4MM **Privately Held**
WEB: www.sbeoc.com
SIC: 1731 General electrical contractor

(P-1314)
SBE ELECTRICAL CONTRACTING INC
2817 Mcgaw Ave, Irvine (92614-5835)
PHONE..........................714 544-5066
Jeffery S Wilson, *CEO*
EMP: 105 EST: 2016
SALES (est): 9.4MM **Privately Held**
WEB: www.sbeoc.com
SIC: 1731 General electrical contractor

(P-1315)
SERVICE 1ST ELECTRICAL SVCS
1092 N Armando St, Anaheim
(92806-2605)
PHONE..........................714 630-9699
James Graham, *President*
EMP: 50 EST: 1988
SALES (est): 3.1MM **Privately Held**
SIC: 1731 Electrical work

(P-1316)
SFADIA INC
Also Called: Green Energy Innovations
8485 Artesia Blvd Ste A, Buena Park
(90621-4194)
PHONE..........................323 622-1930
Pilje Park, *President*
Pil Soon Um, *Vice Pres*
Jay Lee, *Research*
▲ **EMP: 86 EST:** 2010
SALES (est): 12.2MM **Privately Held**
WEB: www.geinnovationsinc.com
SIC: 1731 Energy management controls

(P-1317)
SPECIALTY CONSTRUCTION INC
645 Clarion Ct, San Luis Obispo
(93401-8177)
PHONE..........................805 543-1706
Rudolph Bachmann, *President*
Chris Teaford, *CFO*
Jeffrey Martin, *Senior VP*
Doug Clay, *Vice Pres*
Douglas Clay, *Vice Pres*
EMP: 80 EST: 1992
SQ FT: 8,000
SALES (est): 27.3MM **Privately Held**
WEB: www.specialtyconstruction.com
SIC: 1731 Telephone & telephone equip-
ment installation

(P-1318)
SPECTRA I CALIFORNIA
Also Called: Spectra Industrial Electric
21818 S Wilmington Ave # 402, Carson
(90810-1642)
PHONE..........................310 835-0808
Michael J Merrill, *President*
Richard Mangan, *Vice Pres*
Roger Theroux, *Division Mgr*
Ed Curtis, *Project Mgr*
Laura Carr, *Accountant*
EMP: 70 EST: 1989
SQ FT: 20,000
SALES (est): 13.7MM **Privately Held**
WEB: www.spectrainc.com
SIC: 1731 Access control systems special-
ization

(P-1319)
SRBRAY LLC (PA)
Also Called: Power Plus
5500 E La Palma Ave, Anaheim
(92807-2108)
PHONE..........................714 765-7551
Steven R Bray, *President*
Sam Cerny, *Vice Pres*
Brian Schultz, *Vice Pres*
Philip Mayer, *Executive*
Aaron Haney, *General Mgr*
EMP: 50 EST: 2009

SALES (est): 112.9MM **Privately Held**
WEB: www.powerplus.com
SIC: 1731 7359 Standby or emergency
power specialization; equipment rental &
leasing

(P-1320)
STC NETCOM INC (PA)
11611 Industry Ave, Fontana (92337-6931)
PHONE..........................951 685-8181
Giuseppe Floro, *President*
Shawnda Letourneau, *Treasurer*
Jeffry Kinne, *Admin Sec*
Ramon Estrada, *Project Mgr*
Brian Klepacki, *Project Mgr*
EMP: 70 EST: 1990
SQ FT: 6,000
SALES (est): 13.5MM **Privately Held**
WEB: www.stcnetcom.com
SIC: 1731 Fiber optic cable installation;
telephone & telephone equipment instal-
lation

(P-1321)
SUNWEST ELECTRIC INC
3064 E Miraloma Ave, Anaheim
(92806-1810)
PHONE..........................714 630-8700
Brien Pariseau, *President*
Doug Lyvers, *CFO*
Chris Montante, *Division Mgr*
Barry Walters, *Project Mgr*
John Richards, *Foreman/Supr*
EMP: 175 EST: 1985
SQ FT: 20,000
SALES (est): 25.2MM **Privately Held**
WEB: www.sunwestelectric.net
SIC: 1731 Electrical work

(P-1322)
SUPERIOR ELEC MECH & PLBG INC
8613 Helms Ave, Rancho Cucamonga
(91730-4521)
PHONE..........................909 357-9400
David A Stone Jr, *CEO*
Walt Schobel, *President*
Pam Metzer, *CFO*
Lou Juarez, *Manager*
EMP: 291 EST: 2001
SQ FT: 50,000
SALES (est): 29.7MM **Privately Held**
WEB: www.superioremp.com
SIC: 1731 1711 General electrical contrac-
tor; mechanical contractor

(P-1323)
SURGENER ELECTRIC INC
Also Called: McKee Electric
732 Angus Ln, Bakersfield (93308-4404)
PHONE..........................661 399-3321
Lester C Surgener II, *CEO*
R L Surgener, *President*
Diane Dansby, *Corp Secy*
Richard Barnes, *CIO*
Richard Young, *Technician*
EMP: 64 EST: 1947
SALES (est): 5.1MM **Privately Held**
SIC: 1731 General electrical contractor

(P-1324)
SWINFORD ELECTRIC INC
Also Called: A & R Electric
1150 E Elm Ave, Fullerton (92831-5024)
PHONE..........................714 578-8888
Sharon Swinford, *President*
Michael Swinford, *Corp Secy*
Rick Swinford, *Vice Pres*
Jayzell Johnson, *Admin Asst*
Robert Price, *Project Mgr*
EMP: 50 EST: 1979
SQ FT: 5,400
SALES (est): 11.3MM **Privately Held**
SIC: 1731 General electrical contractor

(P-1325)
T BOYER COMPANY
1656 Babcock St, Costa Mesa
(92627-4330)
PHONE..........................949 642-2431
Thomas Boyer, *President*
EMP: 50 EST: 1988
SQ FT: 1,600
SALES (est): 7.4MM **Privately Held**
WEB: www.boyerco.com
SIC: 1731 General electrical contractor

PRODUCTS & SVCS

(P-1326)
T MCGEE ELECTRIC INC
2390 S Reservoir St, Pomona
(91766-6410)
P.O. Box 1111,.Chino (91708-1111)
PHONE..................................909 591-6461
Trent L Mc Gee, *President*
EMP: 100 EST: 1986
SALES (est): 8.2MM **Privately Held**
WEB: www.tmcgeeelectric.com
SIC: 1731 General electrical contractor

(P-1327)
TAFT ELECTRIC COMPANY (PA)
1694 Eastman Ave, Ventura (93003-5782)
P.O. Box 3416 (93006-3416)
PHONE..................................805 642-0121
James Marsh, *President*
David Calvert, *CFO*
Aaron Gregory, *Division Mgr*
Carol A Smith, *Admin Sec*
Alfredo Diaz, *Project Mgr*
EMP: 282 EST: 1942
SQ FT: 40,000
SALES (est): 55.3MM **Privately Held**
WEB: www.taftelectric.com
SIC: 1731 1629 General electrical con-
tractor; waste water & sewage treatment
plant construction

(P-1328)
THOMA ELECTRIC INC
Also Called: Thoma Electric Co
3562 Empleo St Ste C, San Luis Obispo
(93401-7367)
P.O. Box 1167 (93406-1167)
PHONE..................................805 543-3850
William A Thoma, *President*
Bill Thoma, *COO*
Ed Thoma, *Vice Pres*
Edward C Thoma, *Vice Pres*
Jeffrey Thoma, *Vice Pres*
EMP: 55 EST: 1962
SQ FT: 7,500
SALES (est): 10.9MM **Privately Held**
WEB: www.thomaelectric.com
SIC: 1731 8711 General electrical contrac-
tor; electrical or electronic engineering

(P-1329)
**TIME AND ALARM SYSTEMS
(PA)**
3828 Wacker Dr, Jurupa Valley
(91752-1147)
PHONE..................................951 685-1761
Keith A Senn, *CEO*
Jolene McKay, *Administration*
Sam Salazar, *Project Mgr*
Timothy McGuire, *Engineer*
Dan Rogers, *Opers Mgr*
EMP: 58 EST: 1978
SQ FT: 12,000
SALES (est): 11.5MM **Privately Held**
WEB: www.timeandalarm.com
SIC: 1731 Fire detection & burglar alarm
systems specialization

(P-1330)
**TRI-SIGNAL INTEGRATION INC
(PA)**
Also Called: Honeywell Authorized Dealer
28110 Avenue Stanford D, Santa Clarita
(91355-1161)
PHONE..................................818 566-8558
Robert McKibben, *President*
Michael Swisher, *COO*
Dennis Furden, *CFO*
Tom Kommer, *Senior VP*
Rett Hicks, *Vice Pres*
EMP: 100 EST: 1998
SQ FT: 16,000
SALES (est): 50.9MM **Privately Held**
WEB: www.tri-signal.com
SIC: 1731 Fire detection & burglar alarm
systems specialization

(P-1331)
TRL SYSTEMS INCORPORATED
Also Called: T R L
9531 Milliken Ave, Rancho Cucamonga
(91730-6006)
PHONE..................................909 390-8392
Lynn Purdy, *Chairman*
Mark L Purdy, *President*
Patrick Lewis, *Vice Pres*

Sy Granillo, *Executive*
Peter Javryd, *Executive*
EMP: 100 EST: 1980
SQ FT: 14,000
SALES (est): 50.7MM **Privately Held**
WEB: www.trlsystems.com
SIC: 1731 General electrical contractor

(P-1332)
**TURNUPSEED ELECTRIC
SERVICE**
1580 S K St, Tulare (93274-6400)
P.O. Box 26 (93275-0026)
PHONE..................................559 686-1541
Wallace J Nelson, *President*
Terri Grant, *Corp Secy*
David Turnupseed, *Vice Pres*
Bryan Siebuhr, *Sales Executive*
Stephen Powell, *Manager*
EMP: 55 EST: 1949
SQ FT: 8,000
SALES (est): 10.3MM **Privately Held**
WEB: www.turnupseed.com
SIC: 1731 7694 5063 General electrical
contractor; rewinding stators; electric
motor repair; motors, electric

(P-1333)
TWIN POWER USA LLC
Also Called: Twin Power Indus Solutions
40424 Jacob Way, Murrieta (92563-4916)
PHONE..................................714 609-6014
Michael Darwish, *CEO*
David Darwish, *Vice Pres*
David Darwich, *General Mgr*
Darwish Michael, *General Mgr*
EMP: 20 EST: 2014
SALES (est): 2.1MM **Privately Held**
WEB: www.twinpowerusa.com
SIC: 1731 8748 8711 8742 General elec-
trical contractor; systems analysis & engi-
neering consulting services; systems
engineering consultant, ex. computer or
professional; consulting engineer; energy
conservation engineering; management
engineering; inspection & testing services; annunciators, relay & solid state
types

(P-1334)
UNISON ELECTRIC
16652 Gemini Ln, Huntington Beach
(92647-4429)
PHONE..................................714 375-5915
Lance E Charlesworth, *President*
Kristi Kirkenslager, *Corp Secy*
Gary Charlesworth, *Exec VP*
Ron Moralli, *Project Mgr*
Adam Olguin, *Foreman/Supr*
EMP: 50
SQ FT: 6,000
SALES (est): 10.3MM **Privately Held**
WEB: www.unisonelectric.com
SIC: 1731 General electrical contractor

(P-1335)
UNITED CONTRACTORS INC
8032 Chester Ave, Stanton (90680-3201)
PHONE..................................714 828-6275
Jack H Gebelin, *President*
James Gebelin, *Corp Secy*
Thomas F Gebelin, *Vice Pres*
EMP: 55 EST: 1960
SQ FT: 4,800
SALES (est): 5.6MM **Privately Held**
SIC: 1731 General electrical contractor

(P-1336)
VECTOR RESOURCES INC (PA)
Also Called: Vectorusa
20917 Higgins Ct, Torrance (90501-1723)
PHONE..................................310 436-1000
David Zukerman, *President*
Robert Messinger, *Exec VP*
Jeff Zukerman, *Exec VP*
Jeffrey Zukerman, *Exec VP*
Robert Ray, *Vice Pres*
EMP: 275 EST: 1988

SALES (est): 56.6MM **Privately Held**
WEB: www.vectorusa.com
SIC: 1731 3651 7373 Communications
specialization; computer installation; clock
radio & telephone combinations; video
camera-audio recorders, household use;
systems engineering, computer related;
turnkey vendors, computer systems;
value-added resellers, computer systems

(P-1337)
WEST COAST LTG & ENRGY INC
18550 Minthorn St, Lake Elsinore
(92530-2784)
PHONE..................................951 296-0680
Johnny Odell Leach, *President*
Tammy Leach, *Corp Secy*
Thomas Hazen, *Officer*
EMP: 90 EST: 1994
SQ FT: 2,646
SALES (est): 13.3MM **Privately Held**
WEB:
www.westcoastlightingandenergy.com
SIC: 1731 General electrical contractor

(P-1338)
**WORLD WIND ELECTRICAL
SVCS INC**
Also Called: World Wind & Solar
228 W Tehachapi Blvd, Tehachapi
(93561-1634)
PHONE..................................661 822-4877
Edward Cummings, *President*
Harvey Stephens, *Vice Pres*
Brian Schmidt, *Branch Mgr*
Joaquin Mallorquin, *Project Mgr*
Joe Candelaria, *Opers Staff*
EMP: 563 EST: 2009
SALES (est): 12.1MM
SALES (corp-wide): 488.1MM **Privately
Held**
WEB: www.worldwindsolar.com
SIC: 1731 3621 8742 Electrical work;
windmills, electric generating; mainte-
nance management consultant
HQ: Pearce Services, Llc
1222 Vine St Ste 301
Paso Robles CA 93446
805 467-2528

(P-1339)
WORLDWIND SERVICES LLC
Also Called: World Wind & Solar
1222 Vine St Ste 301, Paso Robles
(93446-2333)
PHONE..................................661 822-4877
Mark McLanahan, *CEO*
Kristin Osborn, *CFO*
Matthew Gillette, *Admin Sec*
EMP: 700 EST: 2007
SALES (est): 67.2MM
SALES (corp-wide): 488.1MM **Privately
Held**
WEB: www.worldwindsolar.com
SIC: 1731 1389 8742 Electrical work;
construction, repair & dismantling serv-
ices; maintenance management consult-
ant
HQ: Pearce Services, Llc
1222 Vine St Ste 301
Paso Robles CA 93446
805 467-2528

(P-1340)
**WP ELECTRIC
COMMUNICATIONS INC**
14198 Albers Way, Chino (91710-6938)
PHONE..................................909 606-3510
Debra Rooney, *President*
Jim Roche, *Vice Pres*
Roseann Briggs, *Office Mgr*
Ryan Marshall, *Manager*
EMP: 50
SQ FT: 8,100
SALES (est): 6MM **Privately Held**
WEB: www.wpelectric.com
SIC: 1731 General electrical contractor

1741 Masonry & Other Stonework

(P-1341)
**B&B INDUSTRIAL SERVICES
INC (PA)**
14549 Manzanita Dr, Fontana
(92335-5378)
PHONE..................................909 428-3167
Lyndon Brewer, *President*
Ted Brewer, *Vice Pres*
Tim Brewer, *Admin Sec*
Frank Bibian, *Warehouse Mgr*
EMP: 262 EST: 1993
SQ FT: 12,000
SALES (est): 24.9MM **Privately Held**
WEB: www.midphase.com
SIC: 1741 Refractory or acid brick masonry

(P-1342)
DESIGN MASONRY INC
20703 Santa Clara St, Canyon Country
(91351-2424)
PHONE..................................661 252-2784
Scott Floyd, *President*
Randall Carpenter, *Vice Pres*
Randy Carpenter, *Vice Pres*
EMP: 70 EST: 2009
SALES (est): 12MM **Privately Held**
WEB: www.designmasonry.com
SIC: 1741 Stone masonry

(P-1343)
FRANK S SMITH MASONRY INC
2830 Pomona Blvd, Pomona (91768-3224)
PHONE..................................909 468-0525
Frank E Smith, *President*
Kevin J Smith, *CFO*
Brian E Smith, *Vice Pres*
EMP: 100 EST: 1938
SQ FT: 54,000
SALES (est): 10.9MM **Privately Held**
WEB: www.franksmithmasonry.com
SIC: 1741 Bricklaying; concrete block ma-
sonry laying

(P-1344)
**GBC CONCRETE MASNRY
CNSTR INC**
561 Birch St, Lake Elsinore (92530-2732)
PHONE..................................951 245-2355
Tom Daniel, *President*
EMP: 170 EST: 1985
SQ FT: 8,000
SALES (est): 24.8MM **Privately Held**
WEB: www.gbcconstruction.com
SIC: 1741 1771 Foundation building; con-
crete work

(P-1345)
HARDROCK TILE & MARBLE INC
23151 Verdugo Dr Ste 11', Laguna Hills
(92653-1340)
PHONE..................................714 282-1766
Fax: 714 282-0501
EMP: 52
SQ FT: 1,400
SALES (est): 4.9MM **Privately Held**
WEB: www.hardrocktilemarble.com
SIC: 1741 Masonry/Stone Contractor

(P-1346)
HBA INCORPORATED
512 E Vermont Ave, Anaheim
(92805-5603)
P.O. Box 25861 (92825-5861)
PHONE..................................714 635-8602
Gerald G Pyle, *President*
Joe Alessandrini, *CFO*
EMP: 100 EST: 2006
SALES (est): 11MM **Privately Held**
WEB: www.hbabuild.com
SIC: 1741 Masonry & other stonework

(P-1347)
J GINGER MASONRY LP (PA)
8188 Lincoln Ave Ste 100, Riverside
(92504-4329)
PHONE..................................951 688-5050
John L Ginger, *Partner*
Brad Fogg, *President*
Stephanie Casillas, *Project Engr*
EMP: 265 EST: 1978

74   2022 Southern California Business
Directory and Buyers Guide   ▲ = Import ▼=Export
◆ =Import/Export

SALES (est): 55MM **Privately Held**
WEB: www.jgingermasonry.com
SIC: **1741** Masonry & other stonework

(P-1348)
JAMES FEDOR MASONRY INC
54859 Bodine Dr, Thermal (92274-8911)
P.O. Box 1397, La Quinta (92247-1397)
PHONE.................................760 772-3036
EMP: 70
SALES: 2MM **Privately Held**
WEB: www.jamesfedormasonryinc.com
SIC: **1741** Masonry/Stone Contractor

(P-1349)
MASONRY CONCEPTS INC
15408 Cornet St, Santa Fe Springs
(90670-5534)
PHONE.................................562 802-3700
Ronald O Udall, *President*
Peter Sturdivant, *Corp Secy*
Russell Knight, *Vice Pres*
EMP: 100 EST: 1983
SQ FT: 10,000
SALES (est): 9.7MM **Privately Held**
WEB: www.masonry-concepts.com
SIC: **1741** Masonry & other stonework

(P-1350)
NIBBELINK MASONRY CNSTR CORP
2010 W Avenue K, Lancaster (93536-5229)
PHONE.................................661 948-7859
Troy Nibbelink, *President*
Gerald J Nibbelink, *Vice Pres*
EMP: 60 EST: 1976
SQ FT: 2,000
SALES (est): 19MM **Privately Held**
WEB: www.nibbelinkmasonryconst.com
SIC: **1741 1771** Masonry & other stonework; exterior concrete stucco contractor

(P-1351)
PRO STRUCTURAL INC
29190 Riverside Dr, Lake Elsinore
(92530-2610)
PHONE.................................951 526-2010
Robert A Yowell, *President*
Holly Yowell, *CFO*
Russell T Frazier, *Vice Pres*
EMP: 60 EST: 2015
SALES: 5.1MM **Privately Held**
WEB: www.prostructuralinc.com
SIC: **1741** Masonry & other stonework

(P-1352)
SMG STONE COMPANY INC
8460 San Fernando Rd, Sun Valley
(91352-3227)
PHONE.................................818 767-0000
Solomon Aryeh, *President*
Carina Moreno, *Admin Sec*
Reggie Chua, *Project Engr*
Luis Perez, *Project Engr*
▲ EMP: 80 EST: 1995
SQ FT: 12,000
SALES (est): 12.3MM **Privately Held**
WEB: www.smgstone.com
SIC: **1741 8711 5032** Masonry & other stonework; engineering services; marble building stone

(P-1353)
SPECTRA COMPANY
2510 Supply St, Pomona (91767-2113)
PHONE.................................909 599-0760
Ray Adamyk, *CEO*
Tim Harris, *COO*
Ann Dresselhaus, *Admin Sec*
Paul Chambers, *Admin Asst*
Ean Frank, *Project Mgr*
▲ EMP: 125 EST: 1985
SQ FT: 7,000
SALES (est): 16MM **Privately Held**
WEB: www.spectracompany.com
SIC: **1741 1771 1743 1721** Masonry & other stonework; concrete work; terrazzo; tile, marble, mosaic work; painting & paper hanging; carpentry work

(P-1354)
SUPERIOR MASONRY WALLS LTD
300 W Olive St Ste A, Colton (92324-1765)
PHONE.................................909 370-1800

Daniel Lee, *President*
Jeremiah Curtis, *CFO*
EMP: 75 EST: 2011 **Privately Held**
WEB: www.superiormasonrywalls.com
SIC: **1741** Masonry & other stonework

(P-1355)
VARIATIONS IN STONE INC
360 La Perle Pl, Costa Mesa (92627-7749)
PHONE.................................949 438-8337
Joseph Dorando, *CFO*
James Joseph Dorando, *President*
EMP: 75 EST: 2015
SALES (est): 2MM **Privately Held**
SIC: **1741** Masonry & other stonework

(P-1356)
VINCENT CONTRACTORS INC
4501 E La Palma Ave # 200, Anaheim
(92807-1904)
PHONE.................................714 693-1726
Justin Erdtsieck, *President*
Kenny Vo, *Accounts Mgr*
EMP: 430 EST: 2016
SQ FT: 5,538
SALES (est): 19.9MM **Privately Held**
SIC: **1741 1742** Masonry & other stonework; plastering, drywall & insulation

(P-1357)
WINEGARDNER MASONRY INC
32147 Dunlap Blvd Ste A, Yucaipa
(92399-1757)
PHONE.................................909 795-9711
Carolyn Winegardner, *CEO*
Julie Salazar, *President*
Tucker Silliman, *Project Engr*
EMP: 50 EST: 1977
SQ FT: 7,500
SALES (est): 14.1MM **Privately Held**
WEB: www.winegardnermasonry.com
SIC: **1741** Bricklaying; concrete block masonry laying

1742 Plastering, Drywall, Acoustical & Insulation Work

(P-1358)
A A GONZALEZ INC
13264 Ralston Ave, Sylmar (91342-7607)
P.O. Box 408, San Fernando (91341-0408)
PHONE.................................818 367-2242
Albert Gonzales, *President*
Aida Lepe, *Treasurer*
EMP: 100 EST: 1992
SALES (est): 8.8MM **Privately Held**
SIC: **1742** Plastering, drywall & insulation

(P-1359)
ADS CONSTRUCTION INC
2321 Eastbury Way, Santa Maria
(93455-1212)
PHONE.................................805 310-6788
Danny Amburgey, *President*
EMP: 85 EST: 2008
SALES (est): 3MM **Privately Held**
SIC: **1742** Drywall

(P-1360)
ALAN SMITH POOL PLASTERING INC
227 W Carleton Ave, Orange (92867-3607)
PHONE.................................714 628-9494
Stephen Scherer, *President*
Teresa Smith, *CFO*
Alan Smith, *Executive*
Mike Mayernick, *Division Mgr*
Michael Sickels, *Sales Staff*
▲ EMP: 78
SQ FT: 5,000
SALES (est): 8.1MM **Privately Held**
WEB: www.alansmithpools.com
SIC: **1742** Plastering, plain or ornamental

(P-1361)
ALERT INSULATION COMPANY INC
15913 Old Valley Blvd A, La Puente
(91744-5439)
PHONE.................................626 961-9113
Donald W Kent, *President*
Charles Klinakis, *Vice Pres*
Joe Rodriguez, *General Mgr*

Jeff Chaffin, *Manager*
EMP: 66 EST: 1989
SQ FT: 4,500
SALES (est): 12.7MM
SALES (corp-wide): 1.6B **Publicly Held**
WEB: www.alertinsulation.com
SIC: **1742** Insulation, buildings
PA: Installed Building Products, Inc.
495 S High St Ste 50
Columbus OH 43215
614 221-3399

(P-1362)
ALL WALL INC
46150 Commerce St Ste 102, Indio
(92201-3418)
PHONE.................................760 600-5108
Saul M Gonzalez, *President*
Yvette Ambriz, *President*
Saul Miranda, *Vice Pres*
EMP: 89 EST: 2012
SALES (est): 6.3MM **Privately Held**
WEB: www.allwalldi.com
SIC: **1742 1721 7389** Drywall; exterior residential painting contractor; interior residential painting contractor; exterior commercial painting contractor; interior commercial painting contractor;

(P-1363)
ANCCA CORPORATION
Also Called: N-U Enterprise
7 Goddard, Irvine (92618-4600)
PHONE.................................949 553-0084
Nicole Hunt, *Corp Secy*
EMP: 99 EST: 2008 **Privately Held**
SIC: **1742** Plastering, drywall & insulation

(P-1364)
ANNING-JOHNSON COMPANY
13250 Temple Ave, City of Industry
(91746-1583)
PHONE.................................626 369-7131
Larry Domino, *Vice Pres*
Rick Kent, *Project Mgr*
EMP: 50
SALES (corp-wide): 461.9MM **Privately Held**
WEB: www.anningjohnson.com
SIC: **1742 1761 1799** Acoustical & ceiling work; roofing, siding & sheet metal work; building site preparation
HQ: Anning-Johnson Company
1959 Anson Dr
Melrose Park IL 60160
708 681-1300

(P-1365)
ANSCHUTZ FILM GROUP
1888 Century Park E # 1400, Los Angeles
(90067-1718)
PHONE.................................310 887-1000
EMP: 5002
SALES (est): 4.9MM
SALES (corp-wide): 110.5MM **Privately Held**
SIC: **1742** Plastering, Drywall, And Insulation, Nsk
PA: The Anschutz Corporation
555 17th St Ste 2400
Denver CO 80202
303 298-1000

(P-1366)
ARGUS CONTRACTING LLC (DH)
11807 Smith Ave, Santa Fe Springs
(90670-3226)
PHONE.................................562 422-7370
Craig Skeie, *President*
Luann E Irwin, *,*
EMP: 68 EST: 2001
SQ FT: 3,300
SALES (est): 7.3MM **Privately Held**
WEB: www.irexcontracting.com
SIC: **1742** Insulation, buildings
HQ: Irex Corporation
120 N Lime St
Lancaster PA 17602
717 397-3633

(P-1367)
BEST INTERIORS INC (PA)
2100 E Via Burton, Anaheim (92806-1219)
PHONE.................................714 490-7999
Dennis Ayres, *President*

Michael Herrig, *CFO*
Mike Herrig, *CFO*
Prudencia Rios, *Office Mgr*
Elise Wright, *Administration*
EMP: 150 EST: 1986
SQ FT: 20,000
SALES (est): 50.5MM **Privately Held**
WEB: www.bestinteriors.net
SIC: **1742** Drywall

(P-1368)
C D R ENTERPRISES INC
42302 8th St E, Lancaster (93535-5440)
P.O. Box 507, Friant (93626-0507)
PHONE.................................661 940-0344
EMP: 70
SALES (est): 2.6MM **Privately Held**
SIC: **1742** Plastering Contractor

(P-1369)
CAPITAL DRYWALL LP
333 S Grand Ave Ste 4070, Los Angeles
(90071-1544)
PHONE.................................909 599-6818
Frank Scardino, *President*
Art Toscano, *Vice Pres*
Angela Gates, *Admin Sec*
EMP: 249 EST: 1980
SQ FT: 8,000
SALES (est): 3.1MM **Privately Held**
SIC: **1742** Drywall
PA: U.S. Builder Services, Llc
272 E Deerpath Ste 308
Lake Forest IL 60045

(P-1370)
CASTON INC
354 S Allen St, San Bernardino
(92408-1508)
PHONE.................................909 381-1619
James I Malachowski Jr, *President*
Mark Landon, *Project Mgr*
EMP: 100 EST: 2010
SALES (est): 18.1MM **Privately Held**
WEB: www.castoninc.com
SIC: **1742** Drywall

(P-1371)
CHURCH & LARSEN INC
16103 Avenida Padilla, Irwindale
(91702-3223)
PHONE.................................626 303-8741
Raymond W Larsen, *President*
Kenneth R Larsen, *Vice Pres*
Kenneth P Larsen, *Vice Pres*
EMP: 250 EST: 1980
SQ FT: 10,800
SALES (est): 13.2MM **Privately Held**
WEB: www.churchandlarsen.com
SIC: **1742** Drywall

(P-1372)
DIAZ PLASTERING INC
4900 California Ave 210b, Bakersfield
(93309-7024)
P.O. Box 11014 (93389-1014)
PHONE.................................661 244-8228
Jovani Diaz, *President*
EMP: 60 EST: 2010
SALES (est): 8MM **Privately Held**
WEB: www.diazplastering.com
SIC: **1742** Plastering, plain or ornamental

(P-1373)
DMS-BKL DRYWALL & INTR SYSTEMS
2900 E Belle Ter Unit A, Bakersfield
(93307-6925)
PHONE.................................415 508-4968
David Schmitt, *CEO*
EMP: 50 EST: 2019
SALES (est): 3MM **Privately Held**
SIC: **1742** Plastering, drywall & insulation

(P-1374)
ELLJAY ACOUSTICS INC
511 Cameron St, Placentia (92870-6425)
PHONE.................................714 961-1173
Ronald B Bishop, *President*
Matt Paul, *Project Mgr*
EMP: 70
SQ FT: 6,900
SALES (est): 8.2MM **Privately Held**
WEB: www.elljay.com
SIC: **1742** Acoustical & ceiling work

(P-1375)

FIVE STAR PLASTERING INC
23022 La Cadena Dr # 200, Laguna Hills
(92653-1362)
PHONE................949 683-5091
Thomas Blythe, *President*
EMP: 100 **EST:** 2010
SALES (est): 4.3MM **Privately Held**
WEB: www.fivestarplastering.com
SIC: 1742 Drywall

(P-1376)

G BROTHERS CONSTRUCTION INC
7070 Patterson Dr, Garden Grove
(92841-1438)
PHONE................714 590-3070
Rick Gutierrez, *President*
Mike Gutierrez, *Vice Pres*
EMP: 50 **EST:** 1993
SQ FT: 6,500
SALES (est): 6.1MM **Privately Held**
WEB: www.gbrothers.net
SIC: 1742 Drywall

(P-1377)

HI-TEMP INSULATION INC
4700 Calle Alto, Camarillo (93012-8489)
PHONE................805 484-2774
Sieg Borck, *CEO*
Diane Humphrey, *Vice Pres*
David Blake, *CIO*
Ted Heys, *Engineer*
Fecialita Allen, *Controller*
▲ **EMP:** 410 **EST:** 1964
SQ FT: 100,000
SALES (est): 56.6MM **Privately Held**
WEB: www.hi-tempinsulation.com
SIC: 1742 Insulation, buildings

(P-1378)

HUTCHISON CORPORATION
Also Called: Inner Space Constructors Div
6107 Obispo Ave, Long Beach
(90805-3799)
PHONE................310 763-7991
Robert J Hutchison, *Ch of Bd*
Linda Mc Dannold, *Corp Secy*
Stephen Mc Dannold, *Vice Pres*
EMP: 50 **EST:** 1971
SQ FT: 50,000
SALES (est): 2.6MM **Privately Held**
SIC: 1742 1521 1542 Acoustical & ceiling work; single-family housing construction; commercial & office building, new construction

(P-1379)

IL COLORE INC (PA)
2082 Se Bristol St Ste 4, Newport Beach
(92660-1739)
PHONE................949 975-1325
Patrick Jackson, *President*
EMP: 51 **EST:** 1998
SALES (est): 1.7MM **Privately Held**
WEB: www.ilcolore.com
SIC: 1742 5032 Plastering, plain or ornamental; cement

(P-1380)

INFINITY DRYWALL CONTG INC
225 S Loara St, Anaheim (92802-1019)
PHONE................714 634-2255
Dennis Lafreniere, *President*
James Darling, *Vice Pres*
Liza Lafreniere, *Vice Pres*
Mariah Craig, *Administration*
Paul Hilo, *Project Mgr*
EMP: 60 **EST:** 2006
SALES (est): 5.1MM **Privately Held**
WEB: www.infinitydw.com
SIC: 1742 1751 Drywall; framing contractor

(P-1381)

INTERIOR EXPERTS GEN BLDRS INC
4534 Carter Ct, Chino (91710-5060)
PHONE................909 203-4922
Adam Lopez, *President*
Luis Martinez, *Project Mgr*
Christian Escalera, *Project Engr*
Anthony Lopez, *Controller*
Ron Lopez, *Marketing Staff*
EMP: 80 **EST:** 1992

SQ FT: 9,000
SALES (est): 11MM **Privately Held**
WEB: www.interiorexperts.com
SIC: 1742 Drywall

(P-1382)

JADE INC
11126 Sepulveda Blvd B, Mission Hills
(91345-1130)
PHONE................818 365-7137
Steven Arteaga, *CEO*
Jay Arteaga, *President*
Cheryl Taylor, *Treasurer*
Michelle Vojtech, *Vice Pres*
Gail De Ande, *Admin Sec*
EMP: 75 **EST:** 1974
SQ FT: 5,000
SALES (est): 8.1MM **Privately Held**
WEB: www.jadedrywall.com
SIC: 1742 Drywall

(P-1383)

JOHN JORY CORPORATION (PA)
2180 N Glassell St, Orange (92865-3308)
PHONE................714 279-7901
Kenneth Johnson, *CEO*
Mohammad Maghazeh, *Vice Pres*
Jack Jory, *Admin Sec*
John Jory, *Admin Sec*
EMP: 385 **EST:** 1965
SALES (est): 28.2MM **Privately Held**
WEB: www.johnjorycorp.com
SIC: 1742 Drywall

(P-1384)

KEENAN HPKINS SDER STWELL CNTR (PA)
Also Called: Khs & S Contractors
5109 E La Palma Ave Ste A, Anaheim
(92807-2066)
PHONE................714 695-3670
David Suder, *President*
Philip Cherne, *COO*
Dennis Norman, *Officer*
Robert Luker, *Senior VP*
John Platon, *Senior VP*
▲ **EMP:** 65 **EST:** 1996
SALES (est): 108.8MM **Privately Held**
WEB: www.khss.com
SIC: 1742 1751 1743 1741 Plastering, plain or ornamental; carpentry work; terrazzo, tile, marble, mosaic work; masonry & other stonework; painting & paper hanging

(P-1385)

MARTIN BROS/MARCOWALL INC (PA)
17104 S Figueroa St, Gardena
(90248-3097)
P.O. Box 2089 (90247-0089)
PHONE................310 532-5335
Mohammad Chahine, *CEO*
David Aguilera, *Exec VP*
Damon Hoover, *Vice Pres*
Greg Hutson, *Vice Pres*
Ana Tinajero, *Office Mgr*
EMP: 110 **EST:** 1966
SQ FT: 6,000
SALES (est): 25.1MM **Privately Held**
WEB: www.martinbros.net
SIC: 1742 Drywall

(P-1386)

MARTIN INTEGRATED SYSTEMS
1525 W Orange Grove Ave D, Orange
(92868-1109)
PHONE................714 998-9100
Marshall Hovivian, *President*
Anne Reizer, *Corp Secy*
Jeff Anderson, *Project Mgr*
Wayne Davis, *Superintendent*
EMP: 55 **EST:** 1989
SALES (est): 10.5MM **Privately Held**
WEB: www.martinintegrated.com
SIC: 1742 Drywall

(P-1387)

MOWERY THOMASON INC
1225 N Red Gum St, Anaheim
(92806-1821)
PHONE................714 666-1717
Robert J Heimerl, *President*
Toni Heimerl, *Corp Secy*
Todd Heimerl, *Vice Pres*
EMP: 175 **EST:** 1957

SQ FT: 8,000
SALES (est): 16.1MM **Privately Held**
WEB: www.mowerythomason.com
SIC: 1742 Drywall; plastering, plain or ornamental

(P-1388)

OJ INSULATION LP (PA)
Also Called: Abco Insulation
600 S Vincent Ave, Azusa (91702-5145)
PHONE................800 707-9278
Pamela A Henson, *Partner*
Todd Riffey, *Vice Pres*
Mark Newman, *Division Mgr*
Christina Cortez, *Administration*
Michelle Skeldon, *Business Mgr*
EMP: 148 **EST:** 2006
SQ FT: 12,000
SALES (est): 16.5MM **Privately Held**
WEB: www.ojinc.com
SIC: 1742 1751 1741 Insulation, buildings; carpentry work; masonry & other stonework

(P-1389)

ORANGE COUNTY PLST CO INC
3191 Arprt Loop Dr Ste B1, Costa Mesa
(92626)
PHONE................714 957-1971
Robert G Smith, *President*
EMP: 128 **EST:** 1995
SALES (est): 11.8MM **Privately Held**
SIC: 1742 Plastering, plain or ornamental; drywall

(P-1390)

ORANGE COUNTY THERMAL INDS INC
1350 N Hundley St, Anaheim (92806-1301)
PHONE................714 279-9416
Eduardo Olivares, *President*
Gabi Olivares, *Executive*
Laura Langford, *General Mgr*
Jeremy Williams, *General Mgr*
Hiede Boysen, *Admin Asst*
EMP: 51 **EST:** 2010
SQ FT: 10,000
SALES (est): 12.3MM **Privately Held**
WEB: www.teamocti.com
SIC: 1742 3296 Insulation, buildings; acoustical board & tile, mineral wool

(P-1391)

PACIFIC RIM CONTRACTORS INC
1315 E Saint Andrew Pl B, Santa Ana
(92705-4919)
PHONE................714 641-7380
Jerry Tyner, *President*
Aaron Tyner, *Vice Pres*
Justin Tyner, *Opers Mgr*
Tina Feraco, *Manager*
Beatriz Briseno, *Asst Office Mgr*
EMP: 57 **EST:** 1986
SQ FT: 3,000
SALES (est): 5.1MM **Privately Held**
WEB: www.pacificrimcontractors.com
SIC: 1742 1721 Drywall; painting & paper hanging

(P-1392)

PACIFIC SYSTEMS INTERIORS INC
190 E Arrow Hwy Ste D, San Dimas
(91773-3314)
PHONE................310 436-6820
Michelle Orr McNeal, *Director*
EMP: 150 **EST:** 1987
SQ FT: 30,000
SALES (est): 38.6MM **Privately Held**
WEB: www.pacsysinteriors.com
SIC: 1742 1542 Drywall; nonresidential construction

(P-1393)

PADILLA CONSTRUCTION COMPANY
Also Called: Garris Plastering
1620 N Brian St, Orange (92867-3422)
PHONE................714 685-8500
Ralph Padilla, *Principal*
Tom Mattera, *Vice Pres*
Harold Norton, *Executive*
Dennis Davies, *VP Opers*
EMP: 250 **EST:** 1963

SALES (est): 26.5MM **Privately Held**
WEB: www.padillaconstruction.com
SIC: 1742 Plastering, drywall & insulation

(P-1394)

PETROCHEM INSULATION INC
19010 S Alameda St, Compton
(90221-6201)
PHONE................310 638-6663
Erich Freudenthaler, *Manager*
EMP: 64
SALES (corp-wide): 2.7B **Privately Held**
WEB: www.petrocheminc.com
SIC: 1742 3531 Insulation, buildings; construction machinery
HQ: Petrochem Insulation, Inc.
1501 W Ftnhead Pkwy # 550
Tempe AZ 85282
707 644-7455

(P-1395)

QUALITY PRODUCTION SVCS INC
18711 S Broadwick St, Compton
(90220-6427)
PHONE................310 406-3350
Arshak George Kotoyantz, *President*
Jonathan Escalante, *Project Mgr*
Jesus Garcia, *Manager*
Shana Monllor, *Manager*
EMP: 100 **EST:** 1995
SALES (est): 11.6MM **Privately Held**
WEB: www.qpscompany.com
SIC: 1742 Drywall

(P-1396)

RICE DRYWALL INC
919 E 6th St, Santa Ana (92701-4725)
PHONE................714 543-5400
John H Laing, *President*
Keith Barakat, *Vice Pres*
Kim Riker, *Admin Sec*
Ryan Penne, *Project Mgr*
EMP: 56 **EST:** 1973
SQ FT: 8,000
SALES (est): 5.4MM **Privately Held**
WEB: www.ricedw.com
SIC: 1742 Drywall

(P-1397)

RICHMOND PLASTERING INC
12102 Centralia Rd Ste B, Hawaiian Gardens (90716-1003)
PHONE................562 924-4202
Tim Richmond, *President*
Debbie Richmond, *Corp Secy*
Claude Curtis, *Opers Staff*
▲ **EMP:** 50 **EST:** 1979
SQ FT: 1,375
SALES (est): 5MM **Privately Held**
WEB: www.richmondplastering.com
SIC: 1742 Plastering, plain or ornamental

(P-1398)

ROYAL WEST DRYWALL INC
2008 2nd St, Norco (92860-2804)
PHONE................951 271-4600
Paul Diguiseppe, *CEO*
EMP: 100 **EST:** 1988
SQ FT: 20,473
SALES (est): 13.7MM **Privately Held**
WEB: www.royalwestdrywall.com
SIC: 1742 Drywall

(P-1399)

RUTHERFORD CO INC (PA)
2107 Crystal St, Los Angeles (90039-2901)
PHONE................323 666-5284
Paul Rutherford, *President*
James Rutherford, *Treasurer*
Brad Rutherford, *Vice Pres*
Sheila Rutherford, *Admin Sec*
EMP: 100 **EST:** 1970
SQ FT: 15,000
SALES (est): 11.4MM **Privately Held**
WEB: www.rutherfordco.net
SIC: 1742 Plastering, plain or ornamental

(P-1400)

SAN MARINO PLASTERING INC
4501 E La Palma Ave # 200, Anaheim
(92807-1950)
PHONE................714 693-7840
Fred Erdtsieck, *President*
Edward Birn, *CFO*
EMP: 54 **EST:** 1994

SALES (est): 1MM **Privately Held**
SIC: 1742 Plastering, plain or ornamental

(P-1401)
SIERRA LATHING COMPANY INC
1189 Leiske Dr, Rialto (92376-8633)
PHONE..................................909 421-0211
Gary K Waldron, *CEO*
Connie Waldron, *Treasurer*
Dianna Authier, *Controller*
EMP: 200 **EST:** 1958
SQ FT: 10,000
SALES (est): 18.5MM **Privately Held**
SIC: 1742 1751 Drywall; framing contractor

(P-1402)
SPECIALTY TEAM PLASTERING INC
4652 Vintage Ranch Ln, Santa Barbara (93110-2079)
PHONE..................................805 966-3858
Jaime Melgosa, *President*
Robin Melgosa, *Vice Pres*
EMP: 130 **EST:** 1993
SQ FT: 1,000 **Privately Held**
WEB: www.specialtyteamplastering.com
SIC: 1742 Plastering, plain or ornamental

(P-1403)
SUNSHINE METAL CLAD INC
7201 Edison Hwy, Bakersfield (93307-9011)
PHONE..................................661 366-0575
James R Eudy, *President*
Linda Payne, *CFO*
▲ **EMP:** 100 **EST:** 1979
SQ FT: 50,000
SALES (est): 12.2MM **Privately Held**
WEB: www.smcinsulation.com
SIC: 1742 Insulation, buildings

(P-1404)
SUPERIOR WALL SYSTEMS INC
Also Called: Sws
1232 E Orangethorpe Ave, Fullerton (92831-5224)
PHONE..................................714 278-0000
Ronald Lee Hudson, *CEO*
EMP: 500
SQ FT: 40,000
SALES (est): 48.9MM **Privately Held**
WEB: www.superiorwallsystems.com
SIC: 1742 Drywall

(P-1405)
TEMECULA VALLEY DRYWALL INC
Also Called: Timberlake Painting
41228 Raintree Ct, Murrieta (92562-7089)
PHONE..................................951 600-1742
Doug A Misemer, *CEO*
Sandy Villella, *Corp Secy*
Lorry Hales, *Vice Pres*
Jim Morton, *Manager*
EMP: 75 **EST:** 1990
SQ FT: 8,000
SALES (est): 11MM **Privately Held**
WEB: www.tvdrywall.com
SIC: 1742 1721 Drywall; painting & paper hanging

(P-1406)
THERMO POWER INDUSTRIES
10570 Humbolt St, Los Alamitos (90720-2439)
PHONE..................................562 799-0087
Edward Lydic, *CEO*
John G Carroll, *CFO*
John Carroll, *CFO*
Blanca Munoz, *Office Mgr*
Carlos Diaz, *Superintendent*
EMP: 50 **EST:** 1986
SQ FT: 5,500
SALES (est): 7.9MM **Privately Held**
WEB: www.thermopowerindustries.com
SIC: 1742 1721 3479 Insulation, buildings; commercial painting; coating, rust preventive

(P-1407)
TOMMY GUN PLASTERING INC
944 4th St, Calimesa (92320-1205)
PHONE..................................909 795-9966

Tommy Lucero, *CEO*
EMP: 60 **EST:** 2002
SQ FT: 1,800
SALES (est): 6.2MM **Privately Held**
WEB: www.tommygunplastering.com
SIC: 1742 Drywall

(P-1408)
TRUTEAM OF CALIFORNIA INC
2389 A St, Santa Maria (93455-1073)
PHONE..................................805 345-3239
Craig Bricker, *Branch Mgr*
EMP: 51
SALES (corp-wide): 2.7B **Publicly Held**
WEB: www.truteam.com
SIC: 1742 Insulation, buildings
HQ: Truteam Of California, Inc.
260 Jimmy Ann Dr
Daytona Beach FL 32114

(P-1409)
WEST COAST DRYWALL & CO INC
1610 W Linden St, Riverside (92507-6810)
PHONE..................................951 778-3592
Mark Herbert, *CEO*
Dan Slavin, *President*
Santos Garcia, *Vice Pres*
Colleen Butler, *Human Resources*
Humberto Gonzalez, *Safety Mgr*
EMP: 400 **EST:** 2002
SQ FT: 18,962
SALES (est): 36.8MM **Privately Held**
WEB: www.wcdp.com
SIC: 1742 Drywall

1743 Terrazzo, Tile, Marble & Mosaic Work

(P-1410)
ALEXS TILE WORKS INC
208b N Calle Cesar Chavez, Santa Barbara (93103-3231)
P.O. Box 810 (93102-0810)
PHONE..................................805 967-5308
EMP: 25
SALES (est): 1.3MM **Privately Held**
SIC: 1743 3272 Tile/Marble Contractor Mfg Concrete Products

(P-1411)
ARRIAGA USA INC (PA)
Also Called: Stoneland
12000 Sherman Way, North Hollywood (91605-3727)
PHONE..................................818 982-9559
Shalom Rubin, *President*
◆ **EMP:** 60 **EST:** 2002
SALES (est): 10MM **Privately Held**
WEB: www.stonelandusa.com
SIC: 1743 Tile installation, ceramic

(P-1412)
CERAMIC TILE ART INC
11601 Pendleton St, Sun Valley (91352-2502)
PHONE..................................818 767-9088
Itamar Levy, *President*
Bobbie Kmet, *Office Mgr*
▲ **EMP:** 75 **EST:** 1993
SALES (est): 6.5MM **Privately Held**
WEB: www.ceramictileart.us
SIC: 1743 Tile installation, ceramic

(P-1413)
CITY TILE & STONE TILE INC
14720 Keswick St, Van Nuys (91405-1205)
PHONE..................................818 994-0100
Chagay Tzur, *President*
Avishay Erlich, *CFO*
Anat Tzur, *Administration*
Bob Becerra, *Engineer*
Omar Alias, *Manager*
EMP: 62 **EST:** 1993
SQ FT: 4,000
SALES (est): 12.6MM **Privately Held**
WEB: www.citytileandstone.com
SIC: 1743 Tile installation, ceramic

(P-1414)
COASTAL TILE INC
Also Called: Coastal The
13226 Moorpark St Apt 104, Sherman Oaks (91423-5177)
PHONE..................................818 988-6134
Ronig Yemini, *President*
Eyal Reguev, *Vice Pres*
▲ **EMP:** 100 **EST:** 1993
SALES (est): 9MM **Privately Held**
SIC: 1743 Tile installation, ceramic

(P-1415)
ELEGANZA TILES INC (PA)
3125 E Coronado St, Anaheim (92806-1915)
PHONE..................................714 224-1700
Mike Darmawan, *CEO*
Vonny Purnama, *Vice Pres*
Lidy Henny, *Branch Mgr*
Kevin Kuhner, *Branch Mgr*
Mark Nielsen, *Branch Mgr*
◆ **EMP:** 70
SALES (est): 21.9MM **Privately Held**
WEB: www.eleganzatiles.com
SIC: 1743 Tile installation, ceramic

(P-1416)
EMSER TILE LLC
5300 Shea Center Dr, Ontario (91761-7883)
PHONE..................................909 974-1600
Gabriel Castro, *Branch Mgr*
Stephanie Robinson, *Project Mgr*
Scott Charlesworth, *Manager*
EMP: 60
SALES (corp-wide): 273.9MM **Privately Held**
WEB: www.emser.com
SIC: 1743 Tile installation, ceramic
PA: Emser Tile, Llc
8431 Santa Monica Blvd
Los Angeles CA 90069
323 650-2000

(P-1417)
KDI ELEMENTS
79431 Country Club Dr, Bermuda Dunes (92203-1200)
P.O. Box 14150, Palm Desert (92255-4150)
PHONE..................................760 345-9933
Paul Klein, *CEO*
Jeanette Nichols, *Project Mgr*
EMP: 57 **EST:** 1990
SALES (est): 3.8MM **Privately Held**
WEB: www.kdielements.com
SIC: 1743 5999 1741 Tile installation, ceramic; monuments & tombstones; masonry & other stonework

(P-1418)
KIRBY INDUSTRIES INC
2109 S Lyon St, Santa Ana (92705-5303)
PHONE..................................714 437-0789
Scott Kirby, *President*
Jerald Kirby, *CFO*
Thomas Jackson, *Vice Pres*
EMP: 17 **EST:** 1988
SALES (est): 1.1MM **Privately Held**
WEB: www.kirby-industries.hub.biz
SIC: 1743 3281 Tile installation, ceramic; marble, building: cut & shaped

(P-1419)
LEGACY TILE AND STONE INC
26825 Jefferson Ave Ste D, Murrieta (92562-8964)
PHONE..................................951 296-1096
Robert Blackmore Jr, *President*
EMP: 50 **EST:** 2014
SALES (est): 3.7MM **Privately Held**
WEB: www.legacytilestone.com
SIC: 1743 Tile installation, ceramic

(P-1420)
MATRIX SURFACES INC
5449 E La Palma Ave, Anaheim (92807-2022)
PHONE..................................714 696-5449
Jerry Eugene Jones, *CEO*
Laura J Jones, *Vice Pres*
Karl Watkins, *Controller*
Matej Balun,
▲ **EMP:** 60 **EST:** 2001
SQ FT: 5,000

SALES (est): 10.2MM **Privately Held**
WEB: www.matrixsurfaces.com
SIC: 1743 Tile installation, ceramic

(P-1421)
PREMIER TILE & MARBLE
15000 S Main St, Gardena (90248-1945)
PHONE..................................310 516-1712
Greg Games, *President*
Chris Samp, *Office Mgr*
Lilian Games, *Admin Sec*
EMP: 55
SALES (est): 15MM **Privately Held**
SIC: 1743 5032 Tile installation, ceramic; ceramic wall & floor tile

(P-1422)
REINHARDT BROTHERS MBL & TILE
1450 W 228th St Ste 17, Torrance (90501-5086)
PHONE..................................310 325-0174
Laszlo Reindhardt, *President*
▲ **EMP:** 16 **EST:** 1998
SALES (est): 761.8K **Privately Held**
WEB: www.rbro.net
SIC: 1743 3499 Tile installation, ceramic; fire- or burglary-resistive products

(P-1423)
TILE & MARBLE DESIGN CO INC
Also Called: Marbleworks
7421 Vincent Cir, Huntington Beach (92648-1246)
PHONE..................................714 847-6472
David Blataric, *CEO*
EMP: 32 **EST:** 2005
SALES (est): 3.2MM **Privately Held**
SIC: 1743 3281 Tile installation, ceramic; marble, building: cut & shaped

---

1751 Carpentry Work

(P-1424)
ALEKSANDAR INC
1542 W 130th St, Gardena (90249-2104)
PHONE..................................310 516-7700
Aleksandar Radovanovic, *CEO*
Victor Addotta, *Vice Pres*
EMP: 15 **EST:** 1993
SALES (est): 2.5MM **Privately Held**
WEB: www.cncthecity.com
SIC: 1751 2431 1721 Cabinet & finish carpentry; millwork; wallcovering contractors

(P-1425)
ALL SEASONS FRAMING CORP
1022 Fuller St, Santa Ana (92701-4213)
PHONE..................................714 634-2324
Dave Karos, *President*
Gerado Rodarte, *Admin Sec*
EMP: 50 **EST:** 1996 **Privately Held**
WEB: www.allseasonsframing.com
SIC: 1751 Framing contractor

(P-1426)
ALTA FINISH & STAIR INC
12625 Frederick St l529, Moreno Valley (92553-5216)
PHONE..................................951 496-0117
Felix Millan, *CEO*
Victor Martinez, *CFO*
EMP: 52 **EST:** 2015
SALES (est): 3.9MM **Privately Held**
SIC: 1751 Carpentry work

(P-1427)
AMES CONSTRUCTION INC
391 N Main St Ste 302, Corona (92878-4006)
PHONE..................................951 356-1275
Mark Biloki, *Project Mgr*
Tony Spinetti, *Project Mgr*
EMP: 121
SALES (corp-wide): 1.3B **Privately Held**
WEB: www.amesconstruction.com
SIC: 5712 1751 1522 1521 Customized furniture & cabinets; cabinet building & installation; residential construction; single-family housing construction

PA: Ames Construction, Inc.
2500 County Road 42 W
Burnsville MN 55337
952 435-7106

(P-1428)
BRODIE HOLDINGS INC
Also Called: Brodie Construction & Recycl
83256 Indio Blvd, Indio (92201-4718)
PHONE..................................760 775-3744
EMP: 30
SQ FT: 11,000
SALES (est): 1.7MM **Privately Held**
WEB: www.brodiecabinets.com
SIC: 1751 1542 1522 2611 Carpentry
Contractor Nonresidential Cnstn Residential Construction Pulp Mill Whol
Scrap/Waste Mat

(P-1429)
CHI DOORS HOLDINGS INC
Also Called: CHI Overhead Doors
4495 E Wall St Ste 103, Ontario
(91761-8186)
PHONE..................................909 605-1508
EMP: 124 **Publicly Held**
WEB: www.chiohd.com
SIC: 1751 Garage door, installation or
erection
HQ: C.H.I Doors Holdings, Inc.
1485 Sunrise Dr
Arthur IL 61911
217 543-2135

(P-1430)
CLOSET WORLD INC
14438 Don Julian Rd, City of Industry
(91746-3101)
PHONE..................................626 855-0846
EMP: 91 **Privately Held**
WEB: www.closetworld.com
SIC: 1751 5211 Cabinet building & installation; closets, interiors & accessories
PA: Closet World, Inc.
3860 Capitol Ave
City Of Industry CA 90601
-

(P-1431)
COMMERCIAL DOOR COMPANY INC
1374 E 9th St, Pomona (91766-3831)
PHONE..................................714 529-2179
David O Holmes, *CEO*
Carol Holmes, *Corp Secy*
Sandra Garcia, *Admin Asst*
Karla Norman, *Administration*
Steven Holmes, *Manager*
EMP: 60
SQ FT: 10,000
SALES (est): 9.6MM **Privately Held**
WEB: www.commercialdoorcompany.com
SIC: 1751 Garage door, installation or
erection

(P-1432)
CRAFTSMAN LATH AND PLASTER INC
8325 63rd St, Riverside (92509-6004)
PHONE..................................951 685-9922
Kevin Tunstill, *President*
EMP: 350 **EST:** 2015
SALES (est): 12.5MM **Privately Held**
WEB: www.craftsmanlp.com
SIC: 1751 Carpentry work

(P-1433)
CWP CABINETS INC
10007 Yucca Rd, Adelanto (92301-2242)
PHONE..................................760 246-4530
Michael Rodriguez, *CEO*
EMP: 115 **EST:** 2011
SALES (est): 9.8MM **Privately Held**
SIC: 1751 2434 2541 5712 Cabinet
building & installation; wood kitchen cabinets; wood partitions & fixtures; cabinet
work, custom

(P-1434)
EMPIRE LEASING INC
Also Called: Alliance Construction
2045 Placentia Ave Ste A, Costa Mesa
(92627-6239)
PHONE..................................949 646-7400
Fax: 949 645-3461
EMP: 75

SALES (est): 3.1MM **Privately Held**
WEB: www.empireleasinginc.com
SIC: 1751 1795 Carpentry Contractor
Wrecking/Demolition Contractor

(P-1435)
EPPINK OF CALIFORNIA INC
11900 Center St, South Gate (90280-7834)
PHONE..................................562 633-1275
Erik Eppink, *CEO*
Michael Hunter, *Vice Pres*
▲ **EMP:** 50 **EST:** 1986
SQ FT: 20,000
SALES (est): 5.5MM **Privately Held**
WEB: www.eppink.com
SIC: 1751 Carpentry work

(P-1436)
FENNEL INC
Also Called: Thompson Cnstr Sup Door
Frame
1169 Sherborn St, Corona (92879-5005)
P.O. Box 78300 (92877-0143)
PHONE..................................951 284-2020
Kenneth R Thompson, *CEO*
Robert Leos, *Vice Pres*
EMP: 65 **EST:** 2012
SALES (est): 2.9MM **Privately Held**
SIC: 1751 5251 5999 Garage door, installation or erection; door locks & lock sets;
art, picture frames & decorations

(P-1437)
GATEHOUSE MSI LLC
Also Called: McMurray Stern
15511 Carmenita Rd, Santa Fe Springs
(90670-5609)
PHONE..................................562 623-3000
Kenneth De Angelis, *Principal*
Donise Jackson, *CFO*
Michael Crespo, *Vice Pres*
Tom O'Neill, *Vice Pres*
Dale Bennett, *Plan/Corp Dev D*
EMP: 50 **EST:** 1980
SQ FT: 30,000
SALES (est): 15MM **Privately Held**
WEB: www.mcmurraystern.com
SIC: 1751 1771 Cabinet & finish carpentry; stucco, gunite & grouting contractors

(P-1438)
GRANT CONSTRUCTION INC
7702 Meany Ave Ste 103, Bakersfield
(93308-5199)
PHONE..................................661 588-4586
Grant Fraysier, *President*
Barbara Palmer, *Executive Asst*
Lee Bell, *IT/INT Sup*
Lillian TSE, *Analyst*
Martin Schumacher, *Director*
EMP: 159 **EST:** 1994
SQ FT: 1,000
SALES (est): 31MM **Privately Held**
WEB: www.graniteconstruction.com
SIC: 1751 1771 Framing contractor; concrete work

(P-1439)
HAKES SASH & DOOR INC
31945 Corydon St, Lake Elsinore
(92530-8524)
PHONE..................................951 674-2414
Allen J Hakes, *President*
Dan Farnum, *Vice Pres*
Teo Villasenor, *Vice Pres*
Peter Shetland, *Department Mgr*
Glenn Hakes, *Division Mgr*
EMP: 190 **EST:** 2005
SQ FT: 2,000
SALES (est): 19.4MM **Privately Held**
WEB: www.hakesdoor.net
SIC: 1751 3442 5211 Window & door installation & erection; window & door
frames; sash, wood or metal

(P-1440)
HOME ORGANIZERS INC
Also Called: Closet World, The
3860 Capitol Ave, City of Industry
(90601-1733)
PHONE..................................562 699-9945
Frank Melkonian, *President*
EMP: 660 **EST:** 2001

SALES (est): 52.5MM **Privately Held**
WEB: www.closetworld.com
SIC: 1751 2541 Cabinet building & installation; cabinets, lockers & shelving

(P-1441)
ISEC INCORPORATED
Also Called: Laboratory Specialist
20 Centerpoint Dr # 140, La Palma
(90623-2563)
PHONE..................................714 761-5151
Greg Timmerman, *Manager*
EMP: 75
SALES (corp-wide): 317.2MM **Privately
Held**
WEB: www.isecinc.com
SIC: 1751 Cabinet & finish carpentry
PA: Isec, Incorporated
6000 Greenwood Plaza Blvd # 200
Greenwood Village CO 80111
303 790-1444

(P-1442)
ISEC INCORPORATED
2363 Teller Rd Ste 106, Newbury Park
(91320-6058)
PHONE..................................805 375-6957
Kevin Zimmerman, *Branch Mgr*
EMP: 75
SALES (corp-wide): 317.2MM **Privately
Held**
WEB: www.isecinc.com
SIC: 1751 Cabinet & finish carpentry
PA: Isec, Incorporated
6000 Greenwood Plaza Blvd # 200
Greenwood Village CO 80111
303 790-1444

(P-1443)
ISEC INCORPORATED
Also Called: Intermountain Specialty Eqp
20 Centerpointe Dr # 140, La Palma
(90623-2563)
PHONE..................................714 761-5151
Greg Timmerman, *Vice Pres*
Mike Cahoon, *Business Mgr*
Patrick Caulder, *Opers Staff*
Morton John, *Manager*
EMP: 75
SQ FT: 5,000
SALES (corp-wide): 317.2MM **Privately
Held**
WEB: www.isecinc.com
SIC: 1751 Cabinet & finish carpentry
PA: Isec, Incorporated
6000 Greenwood Plaza Blvd # 200
Greenwood Village CO 80111
303 790-1444

(P-1444)
JT WINDOWS INC
9261 Independence Ave, Chatsworth
(91311-5905)
P.O. Box 4317, Westlake Village (91359-
1317)
PHONE..................................818 709-7950
Tom Burns, *President*
Janet Burns, *Vice Pres*
Eric Czarske, *Sales Staff*
EMP: 40 **EST:** 1978
SQ FT: 34,000
SALES (est): 3.4MM **Privately Held**
WEB: www.jtwindows.com
SIC: 1751 2431 Window & door installation & erection; millwork

(P-1445)
LAURENCE-HOVENIER INC
179 N Maple St, Corona (92878-3260)
PHONE..................................951 736-2990
Ronald Laurence, *President*
Fred Hovenier, *Vice Pres*
Fred E Hovenier, *Vice Pres*
Karen Diercksmeier, *Administration*
EMP: 190 **EST:** 1979
SQ FT: 6,000
SALES (est): 25.3MM **Privately Held**
WEB: www.framingcontractors.com
SIC: 1751 Framing contractor

(P-1446)
LEXINGTON SCENERY & PROPS INC
12800 Raragoon St, Arleta (91331-4321)
PHONE..................................818 768-5768
EMP: 120

SALES (est): 4.9MM **Privately Held**
SIC: 1751 2542 3993 Carpentry Contractor Mfg Partitions/Fixtures-Nonwood Mfg
Signs/Advertising Specialties

(P-1447)
NORCAL INC
Also Called: Seeley Brothers
1400 Moonstone, Brea (92821-2801)
PHONE..................................714 224-3949
Michael Seeley, *Partner*
Joe Calvillo, *Partner*
Phil Norys, *Partner*
Matthew Lencsak, *Underwriter*
EMP: 175 **EST:** 1987
SQ FT: 62,000
SALES (est): 26.7MM **Privately Held**
WEB: www.seeleybros.com
SIC: 1751 Finish & trim carpentry

(P-1448)
NORCAL INC
Also Called: Seeley Brothers
1400 Moonstone, Brea (92821-2801)
PHONE..................................714 224-3949
EMP: 105
SQ FT: 60,000
SALES (est): 4.5MM **Privately Held**
WEB: www.seeleybros.com
SIC: 1751 Carpentry Contractor

(P-1449)
PRE CON INDUSTRIES INC
950 Riata Ln, Nipomo (93444-9484)
P.O. Box 5728, Santa Maria (93456-5728)
PHONE..................................805 481-7305
John Amburgey, *President*
EMP: 50 **Privately Held**
WEB: www.preconindustries.com
SIC: 1751 1742 1542 Carpentry work;
drywall; commercial & office building contractors
PA: Pre Con Industries, Inc.
725 Oak St
Santa Maria CA 93454

(P-1450)
PRE CON INDUSTRIES INC (PA)
Also Called: Premier Drywall
725 Oak St, Santa Maria (93454-6215)
P.O. Box 5728 (93456-5728)
PHONE..................................805 345-3147
John Amburgey, *President*
James Amburgey, *Vice Pres*
Jose Rosas, *Vice Pres*
Iris Gutierrez, *Administration*
Joe Fuhring, *Controller*
EMP: 68 **EST:** 1990
SQ FT: 3,200
SALES (est): 10.6MM **Privately Held**
WEB: www.preconindustries.com
SIC: 1751 1742 1542 Lightweight steel
framing (metal stud) installation; drywall;
commercial & office building contractors

(P-1451)
PRIME TECH CABINETS INC
2215 S Standard Ave, Santa Ana
(92707-3036)
PHONE..................................949 757-4900
Hassan Farjamrad, *President*
Zahra Farjamrad, *Vice Pres*
Zora Farjamrad, *Vice Pres*
Eddie Aldave, *Human Res Mgr*
David Bondy, *Purch Agent*
EMP: 110 **EST:** 1988
SALES (est): 9.2MM **Privately Held**
WEB: www.ptcabinets.com
SIC: 1751 Cabinet building & installation

(P-1452)
RANCH HOUSE DOORS INC
Also Called: R H D
1527 Pomona Rd, Corona (92878-4359)
PHONE..................................951 278-2884
Michael James Neal, *CEO*
Sandra Neal, *President*
Cristian Neal, *CFO*
Ralph Tan, *Principal*
Cristi Tan, *Controller*
EMP: 70 **EST:** 1997
SQ FT: 33,000

SALES (est): 11MM Privately Held
WEB: www.ranchhousedoors.com
SIC: 1751 Garage door, installation or
erection

(P-1453)
RESCOM OVERHEAD DOORS INC
1430 Richardson St, San Bernardino
(92408-2962)
PHONE..................................909 799-8555
A B Siemer, President
EMP: 18 EST: 1985
SALES (est): 646.6K Privately Held
WEB: www.ontracdoors.com
SIC: 1751 7699 5211 3429 Garage door,
installation or erection; door & window re-
pair; door & window products; door locks,
bolts & checks

(P-1454)
ROY E WHITEHEAD INC
Also Called: Rew
2245 Via Cerro, Riverside (92509-2412)
PHONE..................................951 682-1490
David Whitehead, CEO
Chris Bagley, President
Dennis Whitehead, Treasurer
Dan Gilley, Vice Pres
Daniel Gilley, Vice Pres
EMP: 75 EST: 1955
SQ FT: 36,000
SALES (est): 11.8MM Privately Held
WEB: www.royewhitehead.com
SIC: 1751 Cabinet building & installation

(P-1455)
SI INC
Also Called: Sather Installation
26035 Jefferson Ave, Murrieta
(92562-6983)
PHONE..................................951 304-9444
EMP: 50
SQ FT: 8,000
SALES (est): 4.7MM Privately Held
WEB: www.sicorp.us
SIC: 1751 Contractor - Carpentry Work

(P-1456)
SILVER STRAND
8945 Fullbright Ave, Chatsworth
(91311-6124)
PHONE..................................818 701-9707
David Meador, Principal
Greg Diez, General Mgr
Shayne Ramirez, Controller
Robert Lamkie, Manager
EMP: 50 EST: 1984
SQ FT: 7,500
SALES (est): 7.1MM Privately Held
WEB: www.silverstrandinc.com
SIC: 1751 Cabinet & finish carpentry

(P-1457)
SMITH BROS INC (PA)
Also Called: Smith Bros Finished Carpentry
2301 Townsgate Rd Ste A, Westlake Village
(91361-2502)
PHONE..................................805 449-2841
Dan Smith, President
Shirley Letizia, Admin Asst
Ani Reihs, Administration
Marc Dean, Project Mgr
Matt Reeves, Project Engr
EMP: 59 EST: 1980
SQ FT: 9,000
SALES (est): 6.7MM Privately Held
WEB: www.smith-bros.net
SIC: 1751 Finish & trim carpentry

(P-1458)
STOREFRONT REPAIR INC
Also Called: Storefront Door Repair
17032 Palmdale Ln Ste B, Huntington
Beach (92647-8450)
PHONE..................................714 842-1337
Mary Travato, President
Pete Travato, Vice Pres
Sam Travato, Vice Pres
EMP: 16 EST: 1985
SQ FT: 2,400

SALES (est): 1.7MM Privately Held
WEB: www.sdoorinc.com
SIC: 1751 7699 5211 3429 Window &
door (prefabricated) installation; door &
window repair; door & window products;
door locks, bolts & checks

(P-1459)
TRUFORM CONSTRUCTION CORP
1041 N Shepard St, Anaheim
(92806-2817)
PHONE..................................714 630-7447
Dan Ruppe, President
EMP: 50 EST: 1987
SQ FT: 1,400
SALES (est): 2.8MM Privately Held
SIC: 1751 1742 Lightweight steel framing
(metal stud) installation; drywall

(P-1460)
TWR ENTERPRISES INC
1661 Railroad St, Corona (92878-5003)
PHONE..................................951 279-2000
Thomas W Rhodes, President
George Dawald, Vice Pres
Amy Strommer, Vice Pres
Debbie Diter, Controller
Roy Loaisiga, Opers Staff
EMP: 200 EST: 1985
SQ FT: 20,000
SALES (est): 19.9MM Privately Held
WEB: www.twrframing.com
SIC: 1751 Framing contractor

(P-1461)
VERSATILE BUILDING PDTS LLC
Also Called: Garagecoatings.com
245 W Carl Karcher Way, Anaheim
(92801-2499)
PHONE..................................714 829-2600
Mike Meursing, President
Vicki Hooites, Vice Pres
Justin Buchanan, Opers Staff
EMP: 15 EST: 1999
SALES (est): 6.9MM Privately Held
WEB: www.garagecoatings.com
SIC: 1751 3272 2851 6794 Cabinet
building & installation; concrete products;
epoxy coatings; franchises, selling or li-
censing

(P-1462)
VORTEX INDUSTRIES INC (PA)
Also Called: Vortex Doors
20 Odyssey, Irvine (92618-3144)
PHONE..................................714 434-8000
Elizabeth Turner Everett, CEO
Brian Bailey, COO
Deirdre Palladino, Human Resources
Brian Newberry, Manager
Steve Wickens, Manager
▲ EMP: 25 EST: 1937
SQ FT: 10,000
SALES (est): 127.1MM Privately Held
WEB: www.vortexdoors.com
SIC: 1751 3441 7699 Garage door, instal-
lation or erection; fabricated structural
metal; door & window repair

(P-1463)
WESLAR INC
28310 Constellation Rd, Valencia
(91355-5078)
PHONE..................................661 702-1362
Larry Kern, President
Wes Toy, Vice Pres
EMP: 100 EST: 1981
SQ FT: 5,500
SALES (est): 10MM Privately Held
WEB: www.weslarinc.com
SIC: 1751 Framing contractor

(P-1464)
WIN-DOR INC (PA)
450 Delta Ave, Brea (92821-2935)
PHONE..................................714 576-2030
Gary Templin, CEO
Wolfgang Wirthgen, President
David May, General Mgr
May David, Info Tech Dir
McClusky Preston, Purch Mgr
EMP: 170 EST: 1994
SQ FT: 73,000

SALES (est): 52.9MM Privately Held
WEB: www.windoronline.com
SIC: 1751 3446 Window & door (prefabricated) installation; guards, made from
pipe

(P-1465)
X-ACT FINISH & TRIM INC
248 Glider Cir, Corona (92878-5033)
PHONE..................................951 582-9229
Jessie A Moreno, President
EMP: 60 EST: 2003
SALES (est): 9.1MM Privately Held
WEB: www.xactfinish.com
SIC: 1751 Finish & trim carpentry

1752 Floor Laying & Other Floor Work, NEC

(P-1466)
DFS FLOORING INC (PA)
15651 Saticoy St, Van Nuys (91406-3234)
PHONE..................................818 374-5200
Richard Friedman, CEO
Greg Keyes, Vice Pres
Dean Roth, Vice Pres
Scott Sidlow, Vice Pres
Howard Hoffman, Executive
EMP: 65
SQ FT: 19,865
SALES (est): 30.3MM Privately Held
WEB: www.dfsflooring.com
SIC: 1752 Wood floor installation & refin-
ishing

(P-1467)
HY-TECH TILE INC
1355 Palmyrita Ave, Riverside
(92507-1601)
PHONE..................................951 788-0550
Tom Shoemaker, President
Narcis Postolache, CEO
Cristina Olteanu, CFO
Mario Factor, Vice Pres
Bryan Shoemaker, Project Mgr
EMP: 110 EST: 1994
SQ FT: 12,000
SALES (est): 16.3MM Privately Held
WEB: www.hytechtile.com
SIC: 1752 1743 Ceramic floor tile installa-
tion; terrazzo, tile, marble, mosaic work

(P-1468)
KYA SERVICES LLC
1800 E Mcfadden Ave, Santa Ana
(92705-4708)
PHONE..................................714 659-6476
John Leyds, Mng Member
Daniel Arambula, Project Mgr
Ed Perez, Project Mgr
Terri Bell, Controller
Derrick B Mendoza,
EMP: 50 EST: 2013
SALES (est): 12.8MM Privately Held
WEB: www.thekyagroup.com
SIC: 1752 Carpet laying

(P-1469)
RM PARTNERS INC
Also Called: Sterling Carpets & Flooring
1439 S State College Blvd, Anaheim
(92806-5718)
PHONE..................................714 765-5725
Richard Mandel, President
John Ernst, Treasurer
EMP: 40 EST: 1962
SQ FT: 16,000
SALES (est): 6.3MM Privately Held
WEB: www.sterlingflooring.com
SIC: 5713 1752 2273 Carpets; carpet lay-
ing; dyeing & finishing of tufted rugs &
carpets

(P-1470)
VINTAGE DESIGN LLC (HQ)
25200 Commercentre Dr, Lake Forest
(92630-8810)
PHONE..................................949 900-5400
Timothy Patrick Buckley, CEO
Jennifer Buckley, Admin Sec
Melanie Monroe, Admin Asst
Doug McGaugh, Info Tech Mgr
Connor Mawson, Purch Agent
EMP: 60 EST: 1986

SQ FT: 16,000
SALES (est): 27.2MM
SALES (corp-wide): 272.3MM Privately
Held
WEB: www.vintagedesigninc.com
SIC: 1752 Carpet laying; vinyl floor tile &
sheet installation; asphalt tile installation
PA: Artisan Design Group, Llc
3401 Olympus Blvd Ste 450
Coppell TX 75019
817 424-3076

(P-1471)
WEST COAST SURFACES INC
27620 Commerce Center Dr # 107, Temec-
ula (92590-2539)
PHONE..................................951 699-0600
Thomas Lahood, President
Kristi Lewis, Office Mgr
EMP: 20 EST: 2011
SQ FT: 2,400
SALES (est): 1.4MM Privately Held
SIC: 1752 1743 3281 3253 Ceramic floor
tile installation; terrazzo, tile, marble, mo-
saic work; tile installation, ceramic; gran-
ite, cut & shaped; ceramic wall & floor tile;
floor tile, ceramic

1761 Roofing, Siding & Sheet Metal Work

(P-1472)
A PLUS CUSTOM METAL SUPPLY INC
Also Called: A Plus Custom Shtmtl & Sup
1891 1st St, Norco (92860-3139)
P.O. Box 178 (92860-0178)
PHONE..................................951 736-7900
David Maizland, Owner
EMP: 16 EST: 1984
SQ FT: 6,700
SALES (est): 1.3MM Privately Held
SIC: 1761 3444 5074 1799 Sheet metal-
work; gutter & downspout contractor;
metal roofing & roof drainage equipment;
ventilators, sheet metal; fireplaces, pre-
fabricated; closet organizers, installation
& design

(P-1473)
ALL YEAR ROOFING INC
16828 S Broadway, Gardena (90248-3110)
PHONE..................................310 851-9440
Timothy H P Adams, President
Julie Adams, Shareholder
Julie Jentges-Adams, Shareholder
EMP: 99 EST: 1996
SALES (est): 1.1MM Privately Held
WEB: www.allyearroofing.com
SIC: 1761 1799 Roofing contractor; water-
proofing

(P-1474)
BISHOP INC (PA)
Also Called: Mike's Business Card
1928 W Business Center Dr, Orange
(92867-7906)
PHONE..................................714 628-1208
Michael R Pinedo, CEO
Holly Pinedo, President
Jake Pinedo, Manager
Cliff Welch, Manager
Marlene Strickland, Assistant
▲ EMP: 69 EST: 1998
SQ FT: 10,000
SALES (est): 12.3MM Privately Held
WEB: www.bishopinc.net
SIC: 1761 1771 1799 1611 Roofing con-
tractor; parking lot construction; water-
proofing; fence construction; highway &
street paving contractor; access flooring
system installation; commercial painting

(P-1475)
BORAL ROOFING LLC (DH)
Also Called: Boral Building Products
7575 Irvine Center Dr # 100, Irvine
(92618-3092)
PHONE..................................949 756-1605
Al Born, Mng Member
Hugh Laurie, Vice Pres
Christi Schnell, Business Anlyst
Kristin Mains, Technology
Ann Iten, Marketing Staff

◆ **EMP:** 30 **EST:** 1997
SQ FT: 10,000
SALES (est): 394.6MM **Privately Held**
WEB: www.boralroof.com
SIC: 1761 3272 3259 Roofing contractor;
roofing tile & slabs, concrete; architectural
clay products
HQ: Boral Industries Inc.
200 Mansell Ct E Ste 310
Roswell GA 30076
770 645-4500

(P-1476)
CANNON FABRICATION INC
Also Called: Canfab
182 Granite St Ste 101, Corona
(92879-1288)
PHONE.............................951 278-1830
Donald J Prosser, *CEO*
Mary D Prosser, *President*
William Prosser Jr, *Vice Pres*
Juan Fuentes, *Design Engr*
EMP: 61 **EST:** 1988
SQ FT: 43,000
SALES (est): 11.1MM **Privately Held**
WEB: www.canfab.com
SIC: 1761 Sheet metalwork

(P-1477)
CAT EXTERIORS INC
1290 N Hancock St Ste 102, Anaheim
(92807-1986)
PHONE.............................714 985-6906
Ryan Connet, *Vice Pres*
EMP: 50 **EST:** 2016
SALES (est): 5.3MM **Privately Held**
WEB: www.catexteriors.pro
SIC: 1761 Roofing contractor

(P-1478)
CLAUD TOWNSLEY INC
Also Called: Central Roofing Company
555 W 182nd St, Gardena (90248-3400)
PHONE.............................310 527-6770
William E Knapp, *President*
Jonathan Townsley, *CEO*
Janet Townsley, *Exec VP*
Marcia Kumashita, *Office Mgr*
Andres Lopez, *Administration*
EMP: 60 **EST:** 1992
SQ FT: 12,000
SALES (est): 10.3MM **Privately Held**
WEB: www.centralroof.com
SIC: 1761 Roofing contractor

(P-1479)
CMF INC
Also Called: Custom Metal Fabricators
1317 W Grove Ave, Orange (92865-4137)
PHONE.............................714 637-2409
David Duclett, *CEO*
Vic Maynez, *President*
Chris Demott, *CFO*
Darren Sagert, *CFO*
Mark Allen, *Vice Pres*
EMP: 100 **EST:** 1956
SQ FT: 11,000
SALES (est): 26.1MM **Privately Held**
WEB: www.cmfinc.com
SIC: 1761 Sheet metalwork

(P-1480)
COMMERCIAL ROOFING SYSTEMS INC
11735 Goldring Rd, Arcadia (91006-5894)
PHONE.............................626 359-5354
Glenn Hiller, *President*
Allan Londo, *Superintendent*
EMP: 55 **EST:** 1989
SQ FT: 9,800
SALES (est): 7.5MM **Privately Held**
SIC: 1761 Roofing contractor

(P-1481)
CROWNER SHEET METAL PDTS INC
14346 Arrow Hwy, Baldwin Park
(91706-1335)
PHONE.............................626 960-4971
Kim M Baier, *CEO*
Dennis Curran, *Vice Pres*
Russell Dunegan, *Admin Sec*
EMP: 50 **EST:** 1945
SQ FT: 9,000
SALES (est): 9MM **Privately Held**
SIC: 1761 Sheet metalwork

(P-1482)
DESERT AIR CONDITIONING INC
Also Called: Honeywell Authorized Dealer
590 S Williams Rd, Palm Springs
(92264-1551)
PHONE.............................760 323-3383
Jeffrey Shaw, *CEO*
Todd Shaw, *Vice Pres*
Michael Trefun, *Office Mgr*
Valerie Botts, *Executive Asst*
Aurora Garcia,
EMP: 50 **EST:** 1954
SQ FT: 1,500
SALES (est): 11.3MM **Privately Held**
WEB: www.desertairps.com
SIC: 1761 1711 Sheet metalwork; warm
air heating & air conditioning contractor

(P-1483)
DUKE PACIFIC INC
13950 Monte Vista Ave, Chino
(91710-5535)
P.O. Box 1800 (91708-1800)
PHONE.............................909 591-0191
Gregory C Severson, *President*
Judith E Braaten, *Corp Secy*
James J Enright IV, *Vice Pres*
Karen Rowlands, *Human Res Dir*
Merv Chantland, *Opers Mgr*
EMP: 100
SQ FT: 10,000
SALES (est): 16.3MM **Privately Held**
WEB: www.dukepacific.com
SIC: 1761 Roofing contractor

(P-1484)
EDJE-ENTERPRISES
520 Crane St Ste B, Lake Elsinore
(92530-2777)
PHONE.............................951 245-7070
Edward Joseph Jennen, *President*
Maryjane Jennen, *Admin Sec*
EMP: 82 **EST:** 2006
SQ FT: 8,000
SALES (est): 7.9MM **Privately Held**
WEB: www.edje-enterprises.com
SIC: 1761 Architectural sheet metal work

(P-1485)
FIRST AVENUE INC
5105 Heintz St, Baldwin Park
(91706-1820)
PHONE.............................626 856-2076
Brett Maurer, *President*
EMP: 60 **EST:** 1991
SALES (est): 6.3MM **Privately Held**
SIC: 1761 Roofing, siding & sheet metal
work

(P-1486)
GARCIA ROOFING INC
201 Mount Vernon Ave, Bakersfield
(93307-2741)
P.O. Box 70250 (93387-0250)
PHONE.............................661 325-5736
Mike Garcia, *President*
Denise Roberts, *Corp Secy*
▲ **EMP:** 50 **EST:** 1975
SQ FT: 5,000
SALES (est): 7MM **Privately Held**
WEB: www.garciaroofing.com
SIC: 1761 Roofing contractor

(P-1487)
HERBERT MALARKEY ROOFING CO
9301 Garfield Ave, South Gate
(90280-3804)
PHONE.............................562 806-8000
John Stromme, *Manager*
Dale Rushing, *COO*
Michael Chambers-Purcel, *Project Mgr*
Jennifer Dai, *Accounting Mgr*
EMP: 83
SALES (corp-wide): 90.9MM **Privately Held**
WEB: www.malarkeyroofing.com
SIC: 1761 Roofing contractor
PA: Herbert Malarkey Roofing Company
3131 N Columbia Blvd
Portland OR 97217
503 283-1191

(P-1488)
HOWARD ROOFING COMPANY INC
245 N Mountain View Ave, Pomona
(91767-5629)
PHONE.............................909 622-5598
Larry K Malekow, *President*
Mitch T Caldwell, *Vice Pres*
Ron A Malekow, *Vice Pres*
EMP: 70 **EST:** 1977
SQ FT: 27,000
SALES (est): 19.4MM **Privately Held**
WEB: www.howardroofing.com
SIC: 1761 Roofing contractor

(P-1489)
HOYT ROOFS INC
1809 N Orangethorpe Park, Anaheim
(92801-1141)
PHONE.............................714 773-1820
Brian Hoyt, *CEO*
EMP: 50 **EST:** 2017
SALES (est): 7MM **Privately Held**
WEB: www.hoytroofs.com
SIC: 1761 Roofing contractor

(P-1490)
JAMES A QUAGLINO INC
Also Called: Quaglino Roofing
815 Fiero Ln, San Luis Obispo
(93401-8700)
PHONE.............................805 543-0560
Matt Quaglino, *President*
Daniela Medrano, *Officer*
Steve Quaglino, *Vice Pres*
David Sutcliffe, *Vice Pres*
Susan Miles, *Property Mgr*
EMP: 55 **EST:** 1922
SQ FT: 12,000
SALES (est): 13.2MM **Privately Held**
WEB: www.quaglino.com
SIC: 5251 1761 Hardware; roofing con-
tractor

(P-1491)
JM ROOFING COMPANY INC
Also Called: Action Roofing
534 E Ortega St, Santa Barbara
(93103-3016)
PHONE.............................805 966-3696
John J Martin Jr, *President*
Sharon Fritz, *Corp Secy*
Kumar Atterbury, *Vice Pres*
Peggy Martin, *Vice Pres*
Steve Martin, *Vice Pres*
EMP: 70 **EST:** 1985
SQ FT: 5,000
SALES (est): 10.5MM **Privately Held**
SIC: 1761 Roofing contractor

(P-1492)
KINGSPAN LIGHT & AIR LLC
401 Goetz Ave, Santa Ana (92707-3709)
PHONE.............................714 540-8950
Gene Murtagh,
Rudy Pavlik, *Engineer*
Ronald Caudill, *Director*
EMP: 150 **EST:** 2016
SALES (est): 36.7MM **Privately Held**
WEB: www.kingspan.com
SIC: 1761 Skylight installation

(P-1493)
KPU ROOFING
1497 Freesia Way, Beaumont
(92223-7806)
PHONE.............................909 586-2531
Juan Gomez, *President*
EMP: 50 **EST:** 2018
SALES (est): 1.3MM **Privately Held**
SIC: 1761 Roofing contractor

(P-1494)
LA ROCQUE BETTER ROOFS INC
9077 Arrow Rte Ste 100, Rancho Cuca-
monga (91730-4430)
PHONE.............................909 476-2699
Guy D Larocque, *President*
Linda Robinson, *Vice Pres*
Dennis Grant, *General Mgr*
Gemma Magbulos, *Executive Asst*
Jillian La Rocque, *Receptionist*
EMP: 75 **EST:** 1984

SALES (est): 10MM **Privately Held**
WEB: www.larocquebetterroofs.com
SIC: 1761 Roofing contractor

(P-1495)
LEONARD ROOFING INC
43280 Bus Pk Dr Ste 107, Temecula
(92590-3676)
PHONE.............................951 506-3811
Bruce S Leonard, *President*
Adrianna Resendiz, *Accounting Mgr*
Perez Felix, *Production*
Julio Lopez, *Production*
Albert Heredia, *Manager*
▲ **EMP:** 137 **EST:** 2004
SALES (est): 15.8MM **Privately Held**
WEB: www.leonardroofing.com
SIC: 1761 Roofing contractor

(P-1496)
MARANATHA SHEET METAL INC
411 N Sullivan St, Santa Ana (92703-3419)
PHONE.............................714 602-7764
Kelly June Melendes, *President*
John Melendes, *Vice Pres*
Melissa Melendes, *Vice Pres*
Raul Mendoza, *Project Engr*
Robert Melendes, *Purch Mgr*
EMP: 59 **EST:** 2007 **Privately Held**
WEB: www.maranathasheetmetal.com
SIC: 1761 Architectural sheet metal work

(P-1497)
MCGARRY MECHANICAL INC
1370 N Mccan St, Anaheim (92806-1316)
PHONE.............................714 630-4600
Stephen Mc Garry, *President*
James Donald Mc Garry, *Treasurer*
EMP: 13 **EST:** 1978
SQ FT: 8,000
SALES (est): 268.4K **Privately Held**
WEB: www.ceolangerbiomechanics.com
SIC: 1761 3444 1711 Roofing, siding &
sheet metal work; sheet metalwork;
plumbing, heating, air-conditioning con-
tractors

(P-1498)
MS INDUSTRIAL SHTMTL INC
Also Called: Baghouse and Indus Shtmtl Svcs
1731 Pomona Rd, Corona (92878-4363)
PHONE.............................951 272-6610
Nancy Nicola, *Ch of Bd*
Dan Suffel, *Vice Pres*
Warren Lampkin, *Principal*
Mary Serna, *Info Tech Mgr*
Michael Magan, *Sales Engr*
EMP: 130
SQ FT: 35,000
SALES (est): 46.6MM **Privately Held**
WEB: www.1888baghouse.com
SIC: 1761 Sheet metalwork

(P-1499)
PACIFIC STRUCFRAME LLC
1600 Chicago Ave Ste R11, Riverside
(92507-2040)
PHONE.............................951 405-8536
John B Hanna, *President*
EMP: 91 **EST:** 2017
SQ FT: 2,000
SALES (est): 5.9MM **Privately Held**
WEB: www.pacificstrucframe.com
SIC: 1761 Roofing, siding & sheet metal
work

(P-1500)
PERFORMANCE SHEETS LLC
440 Baldwin Park Blvd, City of Industry
(91746-1407)
PHONE.............................626 333-0195
Mike Crosson, *President*
Forest Felvey,
Michael Feterik, *Mng Member*
Greg Hall, *Mng Member*
▲ **EMP:** 125 **EST:** 2006
SALES (est): 26.4MM **Privately Held**
WEB: www.performancesheets.net
SIC: 1761 Sheet metalwork
HQ: Smurfit Kappa North America Llc
125 E John Carpenter Fwy # 925
Irving TX 75062
800 306-8326

(P-1501)
PETERSEN-DEAN INC
Also Called: Petersendean
21616 Golden Triangle Rd # 101, Santa
Clarita (91350-3993)
PHONE....................661 254-3322
EMP: 100
SALES (corp-wide): 335.8MM **Privately
Held**
WEB: www.needaroof.com
SIC: **1761** Roofing/Siding Contractor
PA: Petersen-Dean, Inc.
39300 Civic Center Dr # 300
Fremont CA 94551
707 469-7470

(P-1502)
PLATINUM ROOFING INC
11500 W Olympic Blvd # 530, Los Angeles
(90064-1676)
PHONE....................408 280-5028
Bill Shevlin, *CEO*
Sean Marzola, *COO*
Rafael Lapizco, *Vice Pres*
Juan Orosco, *Opers Mgr*
EMP: 80
SALES (est): 13.5MM **Privately Held**
WEB: www.platinumroofinginc.com
SIC: **1761** Roofing contractor

(P-1503)
RED POINTE ROOFING LP (PA)
1814 N Neville St, Orange (92865-4216)
PHONE....................714 685-0010
Aaron Martin, *Partner*
Sean Brophy, *Partner*
John Patterson, *Partner*
Erika Munoz, *Office Admin*
Larry Burks, *Sr Project Mgr*
EMP: 83 EST: 2013
SALES: 24.9MM **Privately Held**
WEB: www.redpointeroofing.com
SIC: **1761** Roofing contractor

(P-1504)
RSS INC (PA)
3939 E Guasti Rd Ste A, Ontario
(91761-1574)
PHONE....................909 321-5958
Derek P Robertson, *Principal*
EMP: 73 EST: 2016
SALES (est): 149.7K **Privately Held**
SIC: **1761** Roofing contractor

(P-1505)
SBB ROOFING INC (PA)
Also Called: Bilt-Well Roofing & Mtl Co
3310 Verdugo Rd, Los Angeles
(90065-2845)
P.O. Box 65827 (90065-0827)
PHONE....................323 254-2888
Bruce Radenbaugh, *President*
Steven Radenbaugh, *Vice Pres*
Jodi Burks, *Executive*
Lupe Diaz, *Executive*
EMP: 180 EST: 1984
SQ FT: 5,000
SALES (est): 10.3MM **Privately Held**
WEB: www.biltwellroofing.com
SIC: **1761** Roofing contractor

(P-1506)
TECTA AMERICA SOUTHERN CAL INC
1217 E Wakeham Ave, Santa Ana
(92705-4145)
PHONE....................714 973-6233
Daniel L Klein, *CEO*
Wanda Koehl, *Office Mgr*
Frank Downing, *Opers Mgr*
Jason Pence, *Production*
Javier Sarabia, *Foreman/Supr*
EMP: 60 EST: 2002
SALES (est): 19MM
SALES (corp-wide): 811MM **Privately
Held**
WEB: www.tectaamerica.com
SIC: **1761** Roofing contractor
PA: Tecta America Corp.
9450 Bryn Mawr Ave
Rosemont IL 60018
847 581-3888

(P-1507)
TINCO SHEET METAL INC
958 N Eastern Ave, Los Angeles
(90063-1308)
PHONE....................323 263-0511
Brian Powell, *President*
Jim Stock, *CFO*
Michael Nevarez, *Chairman*
Laura Nevarez, *Admin Sec*
▲ EMP: 250 EST: 2003
SQ FT: 18,000
SALES (est): 38MM **Privately Held**
WEB: www.tincosheetmetal.com
SIC: **1761** Roofing contractor

(P-1508)
TOM BYER ROOFING SERVICE INC
17712 Metzler Ln, Huntington Beach
(92647-6245)
P.O. Box 771 (92648-0771)
PHONE....................714 847-9332
Tom Byer, *President*
Brian Wolsky, *Vice Pres*
EMP: 22 EST: 1987
SALES (est): 1.5MM **Privately Held**
WEB: www.tombyerroofingservice.com
SIC: **1761** **2439** Roofing contractor;
trusses, wooden roof

(P-1509)
WEISS SHEET METAL COMPANY
Also Called: Metcoe Skylight Specialties
1715 W 135th St, Gardena (90249-2507)
PHONE....................310 354-2700
Andre Sarai, *President*
Steve Linder, *Vice Pres*
Morris Saraie, *Vice Pres*
▼ EMP: 45 EST: 1937
SQ FT: 33,000
SALES: 25.4MM **Privately Held**
WEB: www.metcoe.com
SIC: **1761** **3211** Skylight installation; archi-
tectural sheet metal work; skylight glass

(P-1510)
WESTERN PACIFIC ROOFING CORP
3462 E La Campana Way, Palm Springs
(92262-5416)
PHONE....................661 273-1336
Sig Hall, *Manager*
EMP: 110
SALES (corp-wide): 11.2MM **Privately
Held**
WEB: www.westpacroof.com
SIC: **1761** **1799** Roofing contractor; water-
proofing
PA: Western Pacific Roofing Corp.
2229 E Avenue Q
Palmdale CA 93550
661 273-1336

(P-1511)
WESTERN SINGLE PLY INC
8535 Sultana Ave Ste B, Fontana
(92335-3395)
PHONE....................909 574-9735
Phill Bueller, *Principal*
Phil Bueller, *Principal*
EMP: 50 EST: 2004
SALES (est): 2MM **Privately Held**
SIC: **1761** Roofing, siding & sheet metal
work

1771 Concrete Work

(P-1512)
ASPHALT MANAGEMENT INC
7243 Somerset Blvd, Paramount
(90723-3998)
PHONE....................562 630-6811
Fax: 562 529-5899
EMP: 50
SQ FT: 5,000
SALES (est): 2.7MM **Privately Held**
SIC: **1771** Concrete Contractor

(P-1513)
B & M CONTRACTORS INC
4473 Cochran St, Simi Valley (93063-3065)
PHONE....................805 581-5480
Dave Moore, *President*
Randall Bilsland, *Vice Pres*

Lady Hobbs, *Admin Asst*
EMP: 70
SALES (est): 9.5MM **Privately Held**
WEB: www.bamconcrete.com
SIC: **1771** Concrete work

(P-1514)
BALTAZAR CONSTRUCTION INC
236 E Arrow Hwy, Covina (91722-1817)
PHONE....................626 339-8620
Baltazar Jimenez Siqueiros, *CEO*
EMP: 50 EST: 2002
SALES (est): 8.7MM **Privately Held**
WEB: www.hrsteelinc.com
SIC: **1771** Blacktop (asphalt) work

(P-1515)
BAYMARR CONSTRUCTORS INC
6950 Mcdivitt Dr, Bakersfield (93313-2046)
PHONE....................661 395-1676
Eric Recktenwald, *CEO*
Jack Whitney, *President*
Pat Howes, *Corp Secy*
EMP: 111
SQ FT: 10,000
SALES (est): 14.8MM **Privately Held**
WEB: www.baymarrconstructors.com
SIC: **1771** Concrete work

(P-1516)
BEACH PAVING INC
749 N Poplar St, Orange (92868-1013)
P.O. Box 10442, Costa Mesa (92627-0162)
PHONE....................714 978-2414
Curtis Rummel, *President*
EMP: 39 EST: 1979
SQ FT: 1,000
SALES (est): 2.3MM **Privately Held**
WEB: www.beachpavinginc.com
SIC: **1771** **2951** Blacktop (asphalt) work;
asphalt paving mixtures & blocks

(P-1517)
BEDROCK COMPANY
2970 Myers St, Riverside (92503-5524)
PHONE....................951 273-1931
Glenn E Jackson Jr, *CEO*
Joe Meza, *Vice Pres*
Jackie O Connell, *Office Mgr*
Jackie Connell, *Office Mgr*
Carlene Jackson, *Admin Sec*
EMP: 70 EST: 1993
SQ FT: 5,000
SALES (est): 18.2MM **Privately Held**
WEB: www.thebedrockco.com
SIC: **1771** Concrete work

(P-1518)
BOGH ENGINEERING INC
401 W Fourth St, Beaumont (92223-2613)
PHONE....................951 845-5130
Mark A Bogh, *President*
EMP: 56 EST: 2000
SALES (est): 6.2MM **Privately Held**
WEB: www.boghengineering.com
SIC: **1771** Concrete work

(P-1519)
CALMEX ENGINEERING INC
2764 S Vista Ave, Bloomington
(92316-3270)
PHONE....................909 546-1311
Robert Stone, *President*
Rosie Lopez, *Director*
EMP: 51
SQ FT: 11,000
SALES (est): 36.2MM **Privately Held**
WEB: www.calmex-engineering-inc.hub.biz
SIC: **1771** Blacktop (asphalt) work

(P-1520)
CRAWFORD ASSOCIATES
2635 E Chanslor Way, Blythe
(92225-9805)
P.O. Box 807 (92226-0807)
PHONE....................760 922-6804
Bill Crawford, *Partner*
Cody Crawford, *Partner*
Tommy Crawford, *Partner*
Laura Loyd, *Admin Sec*
EMP: 27 EST: 1975
SQ FT: 1,500

SALES (est): 6.6MM **Privately Held**
WEB: www.crawfordconcrete.com
SIC: **1771** **3273** Concrete work; ready-
mixed concrete

(P-1521)
DAKOTA DRILLING & CONCRETE INC
2235 Statham Blvd, Oxnard (93033-3913)
PHONE....................818 833-4654
Leon M Krous, *President*
EMP: 50 EST: 2003
SQ FT: 2,000
SALES (est): 5MM **Privately Held**
WEB: www.dakotadrilling.us
SIC: **1771** Concrete work

(P-1522)
DIVERSIFIED COATINGS LININGS
4810 Cheyenne Way, Chino (91710-5509)
P.O. Box 741, Walnut (91788-0741)
PHONE....................909 591-6366
Charlotte Smullen, *President*
EMP: 24 EST: 1984
SQ FT: 7,000
SALES (est): 1.8MM **Privately Held**
SIC: **1771** **2851** Flooring contractor; epoxy
coatings; polyurethane coatings

(P-1523)
EKEDAL CONCRETE INC
19600 Fairchild Ste 123, Irvine
(92612-2509)
PHONE....................949 729-8082
Dave Ekedal, *President*
Ryan Ekedal, *Vice Pres*
Jim Lock, *Superintendent*
Mark Arcaris, *Supervisor*
EMP: 100 EST: 1974
SALES (est): 8.1MM **Privately Held**
WEB: www.ekedalconcrete.com
SIC: **1771** Concrete work

(P-1524)
GOLDEN EMPIRE CON PDTS INC
Also Called: Structure Cast
8261 Mccutchen Rd, Bakersfield
(93311-9407)
PHONE....................661 833-4490
Brent Dezember, *CEO*
Anna Dezember, *Admin Sec*
Anthony Morales, *Administration*
EMP: 60 EST: 2011
SALES (est): 9.1MM **Privately Held**
WEB: www.structurecast.com
SIC: **1771** Concrete work

(P-1525)
GOLDSMITH CONSTRUCTION CO INC
2683 Lime Ave, Signal Hill (90755-2709)
PHONE....................562 595-5975
William Goldsmith, *President*
Susan Goldsmith, *Treasurer*
Kelly Goldsmith, *Vice Pres*
Kelly Mogg, *Vice Pres*
Andrew Musquiz, *Project Mgr*
EMP: 50 EST: 1983
SQ FT: 6,000
SALES (est): 12.2MM **Privately Held**
WEB: www.dot-testing.com
SIC: **1771** **1629** **5082** Concrete work; oil
refinery construction; construction & min-
ing machinery

(P-1526)
GONSALVES & SANTUCCI INC
Also Called: Conco Cement Co
13052 Dahlia St, Fontana (92337-6926)
PHONE....................909 350-0474
Steve Gonzales, *President*
EMP: 475
SALES (corp-wide): 164.7MM **Privately
Held**
WEB: www.conconow.com
SIC: **1771** Concrete pumping
PA: Gonsalves & Santucci, Inc.
5141 Commercial Cir
Concord CA 94520
925 685-6799

(P-1527)
GUY YOCOM CONSTRUCTION INC (PA)
3299 Horseless Carriage R, Norco
(92860-3604)
PHONE..................951 284-3456
Guy W Yocom, *Principal*
Greg Wilson, *CFO*
Richard Majestic, *Exec VP*
Chris Armstrong, *Vice Pres*
John Hamilton, *Vice Pres*
EMP: 578 EST: 1978
SQ FT: 41,000
SALES (est): 122.8MM **Privately Held**
WEB: www.yocominc.com
SIC: **1771** Concrete work

(P-1528)
HB PARKCO CONSTRUCTION INC (PA)
24795 State Highway 74, Perris
(92570-8759)
PHONE..................714 567-4752
Brett D Behrns, *CEO*
W Adrian Hoyle, *President*
Micheal Barry, *CFO*
EMP: 394 EST: 2002
SALES (est): 2.5K **Privately Held**
WEB: www.hbparkco.com
SIC: **1771** Parking lot construction

(P-1529)
HEIDI CORPORATION
Also Called: Donald J Schefflers Cnstr
727 N Vernon Ave, Azusa (91702-2232)
PHONE..................626 333-6317
Donald J Scheffler, *President*
Denton Sua, *General Mgr*
▲ EMP: 75 EST: 1990
SQ FT: 15,000
SALES (est): 10.6MM **Privately Held**
WEB:
www.donaldschefflerconstruction.com
SIC: **1771** Concrete work

(P-1530)
HOME FRANCHISE CONCEPTS LLC (PA)
Also Called: All American Decorative Con
19000 Macarthur Blvd # 100, Irvine
(92612-1416)
PHONE..................949 404-1100
Chad Hallock, *President*
Todd Jackson, *COO*
Shirin Behzadi, *CFO*
Tom Hillebrandt, *CFO*
Tony Forbes, *Exec VP*
EMP: 90 EST: 2014
SALES (est): 43.6MM **Privately Held**
WEB: www.homefranchiseconcepts.com
SIC: **1771** 6794 Concrete work; franchises, selling or licensing

(P-1531)
INLAND CC INC
Also Called: ICC
13820 Slover Ave, Fontana (92337-7037)
PHONE..................909 355-1318
Marvin Hawkins, *CEO*
Karen Hawkins, *President*
Pat Walsh, *Project Mgr*
EMP: 150 EST: 1995
SALES (est): 39.5MM **Privately Held**
SIC: **1771** Foundation & footing contractor

(P-1532)
JEZOWSKI & MARKEL CONTRS INC
749 N Poplar St, Orange (92868-1013)
PHONE..................714 978-2222
Leonard Michael Barth, *Principal*
Joseph Dean, *Vice Pres*
Dorothy Destefano, *Admin Sec*
Yesenia Martinez, *Purchasing*
EMP: 145 EST: 1953
SQ FT: 4,500
SALES (est): 22.2MM **Privately Held**
WEB: www.jmcontractors.com
SIC: **1771** Foundation & footing contractor

(P-1533)
JKB CORPORATION
561 S Walnut St, La Habra (90631-6035)
PHONE..................562 905-3477
John D Brown, *President*

Kathy Brown, *Vice Pres*
John Brown, *Sales Executive*
EMP: 50
SQ FT: 4,000
SALES (est): 6.4MM **Privately Held**
WEB: www.jkbconcrete.com
SIC: **1771** Concrete work

(P-1534)
JOHN KENNEY CONSTRUCTION INC
619 E Montecito St, Santa Barbara
(93103-3217)
P.O. Box 40929 (93140-0929)
PHONE..................805 884-1579
Jonathan Kenney, *President*
Jordan Kenney, *Vice Pres*
Tricia Ford, *Bookkeeper*
Chris Talerico, *Opers Staff*
EMP: 52 EST: 1984
SQ FT: 5,000
SALES (est): 8.9MM **Privately Held**
WEB: www.kenneyconstruction.com
SIC: **1771** Concrete work

(P-1535)
JT WIMSATT CONTG CO INC (PA)
28064 Avenue Stanford B, Valencia
(91355-1159)
PHONE..................661 775-8090
John E Wimsatt III, *President*
Tricia Wimsatt, *Vice Pres*
Shant Azaian, *Project Mgr*
Bryce Reps, *Human Res Dir*
Maria Dela Cruz, *Director*
EMP: 259 EST: 1992
SALES (est): 30.2MM **Privately Held**
WEB: www.jtwimsatt.com
SIC: **1771** Concrete work

(P-1536)
KP CONCRETE & STEEL INC
3835 E 9th St, Pomona (91766-3916)
PHONE..................909 461-4163
Jose Rojas, *CEO*
Roberto Perez, *Treasurer*
EMP: 15 EST: 2014
SALES (est): 2.6MM **Privately Held**
SIC: **1771** 3312 Concrete work; stainless steel

(P-1537)
LARGO CONCRETE INC
1690 W Foothill Blvd B, Upland
(91786-8433)
PHONE..................909 981-7844
Paul Burkel, *Principal*
Cheryl Stapleton, *Manager*
EMP: 356 **Privately Held**
WEB: www.largoconcrete.com
SIC: **1771** Concrete work
PA: Largo Concrete, Inc.
2741 Walnut Ave Ste 110
Tustin CA 92780

(P-1538)
MARNE CONSTRUCTION INC
Also Called: Newval Chemical
749 N Poplar St, Orange (92868-1013)
PHONE..................714 935-0995
Charles Randolph, *President*
Dara Kargari, *CFO*
L Michael Barth, *Vice Pres*
Tony Naranjo, *Vice Pres*
Gustavo Vega, *Project Mgr*
EMP: 80 EST: 1993
SQ FT: 10,000
SALES (est): 12.3MM **Privately Held**
WEB: www.marneconstruction.com
SIC: **1771** Concrete work

(P-1539)
MCGUIRE CONTRACTING INC
16579 Slover Ave, Fontana (92337-7508)
P.O. Box 310361 (92331-0361)
PHONE..................909 357-1200
David McGuire, *President*
Kathie Vilas, *CEO*
Sandy McGuire, *Admin Sec*
Manny Wilson, *Project Mgr*
George Doan, *Controller*
EMP: 51 EST: 2002
SQ FT: 1,800

SALES (est): 6.4MM **Privately Held**
WEB: www.mcguirecontracting.com
SIC: **1771** Concrete work

(P-1540)
MEDINA CONCRETE CONSTRUCTION
Also Called: Alejandro Medina
2368 W 1st Ave, San Bernardino
(92407-6134)
P.O. Box 1341, Azusa (91702-1341)
PHONE..................909 474-9640
EMP: 50
SALES (est): 4.2MM **Privately Held**
WEB:
www.medinaconcreteconstruction.com
SIC: **1771** Concrete Contractor

(P-1541)
MORLEY CONSTRUCTION COMPANY (HQ)
3330 Ocean Park Blvd # 101, Santa Monica
(90405-3202)
PHONE..................310 399-1600
Mark Benjamin, *Ch of Bd*
Tod Paris, *CFO*
Bert Lewitt, *Exec VP*
Arun Asher, *Vice Pres*
Reginald Jackson, *Vice Pres*
▲ EMP: 80 EST: 1947
SQ FT: 20,000
SALES (est): 30.2MM
SALES (corp-wide): 87MM **Privately Held**
WEB: www.morleyconcrete.com
SIC: **1771** 1522 1542 Concrete work; condominium construction; commercial & office building, new construction
PA: Morley Builders, Inc.
3330 Ocean Park Blvd # 101
Santa Monica CA 90405
310 399-1600

(P-1542)
MORRISON CONCRETE INC
14114 Rosecrans Ave Ste C, Santa Fe Springs (90670-5214)
PHONE..................562 802-1450
Bradley Morrison, *President*
EMP: 50 EST: 1979
SALES (est): 7.2MM **Privately Held**
WEB: www.morrisonconcreteinc.com
SIC: **1771** Concrete work

(P-1543)
NED L WEBSTER CONCRETE CNSTR
8800 Grimes Canyon Rd, Moorpark
(93021-9768)
PHONE..................805 529-4900
Ned Webster, *Principal*
EMP: 75 EST: 2000
SALES (est): 6.9MM **Privately Held**
SIC: **1771** Concrete work

(P-1544)
OPTIMUM CON FUNDATIONS USA INC
6258 Rustic Ln, Jurupa Valley
(92509-7228)
PHONE..................877 212-7994
Mario Garcia, *CEO*
Scott Cable, *President*
EMP: 55 EST: 2016
SALES (est): 20MM **Privately Held**
SIC: **1771** Concrete work

(P-1545)
PACIFIC PAVINGSTONE INC
Also Called: Pacific Outdoor Living
8309 Tujunga Ave Unit 201, Sun Valley
(91352-3216)
PHONE..................818 244-4000
Terry Morrill, *President*
Trent Morrill, *Vice Pres*
Chad Morrill, *Admin Sec*
Sean Douglas, *Consultant*
Nick Padilla, *Consultant*
EMP: 115
SALES (est): 13MM **Privately Held**
WEB: www.pacificpavingstone.com
SIC: **1771** Driveway contractor

(P-1546)
PENHALL HOLDING COMPANY
1801 W Penhall Way, Anaheim
(92801-6700)
PHONE..................714 772-6450
Kathy Wall, *Admin Sec*
Lee Barnett, *CFO*
Terry Cooley, *Vice Pres*
Roger Raney, *Vice Pres*
Bruno Rodriguez, *Branch Mgr*
EMP: 67 EST: 2010
SALES (est): 5MM **Privately Held**
WEB: www.penhall.com
SIC: **1771** Concrete work

(P-1547)
PETERSON BROS CONTRUCTION INC
Also Called: Pbc Companies
1560 W Lambert Rd, Brea (92821-2826)
PHONE..................714 278-0488
Elden Peterson, *CEO*
Robert K Peterson, *Ch of Bd*
Patrick Burns, *CFO*
Mike Hoefnagels, *Vice Pres*
Jack Saldate, *Vice Pres*
▲ EMP: 600 EST: 1983
SQ FT: 24,000
SALES (est): 73.7MM **Privately Held**
WEB: www.pbccompanies.com
SIC: **1771** 3531 1741 Concrete work; pavers; concrete block masonry laying

(P-1548)
SANTA CLARITA CONCRETE
16164 Sierra Hwy, Santa Clarita
(91390-4733)
PHONE..................661 252-2012
Wayne Crawford, *President*
Keith Crawford, *Vice Pres*
Eric Stoh, *Vice Pres*
EMP: 50 EST: 1988
SQ FT: 5,000
SALES (est): 11.9MM **Privately Held**
WEB: www.santaclaritaconcrete.com
SIC: **1771** Foundation & footing contractor

(P-1549)
SCI INC
18501 Collier Ave B106, Lake Elsinore
(92530-2764)
PHONE..................951 245-7511
Mark A Dix, *President*
Richard Hallihan, *Controller*
Mark Dix, *Manager*
Mike Hepinger, *Manager*
EMP: 65 EST: 1999
SQ FT: 3,000
SALES (est): 13MM **Privately Held**
WEB: www.tiltupsbysci.com
SIC: **1771** Concrete work

(P-1550)
SERVICON SYSTEMS INC
3329 Jack Northrop Ave, Hawthorne
(90250-4426)
PHONE..................310 970-0700
Julio E Ramirez, *Branch Mgr*
Tate Rick, *Vice Pres*
Juan Campos, *Opers Spvr*
Edwin Stephenson, *Opers Staff*
Elena Goncharova, *Marketing Mgr*
EMP: 1472
SALES (corp-wide): 83.3MM **Privately Held**
WEB: www.servicon.com
SIC: **1771** Flooring contractor
PA: Servicon Systems, Inc.
3965 Landmark St
Culver City CA 90232
310 204-5040

(P-1551)
STEFAN MERLI PLASTERING CO INC (PA)
Also Called: Merli Concrete Pumping
1230 W 130th St, Gardena (90247-1502)
PHONE..................310 323-0404
Stefan R Merli, *President*
Adele Merli, *Treasurer*
Gunther Merli, *Admin Sec*
Robert Shultz, *VP Sales*
Kurt Merli, *Sales Staff*
EMP: 63 EST: 1958
SQ FT: 5,000

▲ = Import ▼=Export
◆ =Import/Export

SALES (est): 18.2MM **Privately Held**
SIC: 1771 Concrete pumping

(P-1552)
STRUCTURAL CONCRETE GROUP INC
11038 Washington Blvd, Whittier (90606-3006)
PHONE...................818 923-0984
Ismael Gutierrez, *CEO*
EMP: 50 EST: 2017
SALES (est): 4.8MM **Privately Held**
SIC: 1771 Concrete work

(P-1553)
SUPERIOR GUNITE (HQ)
12306 Van Nuys Blvd, Sylmar (91342-6086)
PHONE...................818 896-9199
Anthony L Federico, *President*
Steve Crawford, *Vice Pres*
Nick Hacopian, *Vice Pres*
Brian Popp, *Division Mgr*
Gene McKay, *General Mgr*
EMP: 145 EST: 1964
SQ FT: 5,000
SALES (est): 31.4MM
SALES (corp-wide): 5.3B **Publicly Held**
WEB: www.shotcrete.com
SIC: 1771 Gunite contractor
PA: Tutor Perini Corporation
15901 Olden St
Sylmar CA 91342
818 362-8391

(P-1554)
SURE FORMING SYSTEMS INC
10602 Humbolt St, Los Alamitos (90720-2448)
PHONE...................562 598-6348
Samuel F Shon, *President*
Wanda L Shon, *Corp Secy*
EMP: 50 EST: 1972
SQ FT: 6,200
SALES (est): 9.9MM **Privately Held**
SIC: 1771 Concrete work

(P-1555)
TEAM FINISH INC
155 Arovista Cir Ste A, Brea (92821-3842)
PHONE...................714 671-9190
Thomas M Stangl, *President*
Mary Stangl, *CFO*
EMP: 80 EST: 1996
SQ FT: 1,200
SALES (est): 8.7MM **Privately Held**
SIC: 1771 Concrete work

(P-1556)
UNITED BROTHERS CONCRETE INC
41905 Boardwalk Ste K, Palm Desert (92211-9091)
PHONE...................760 346-1013
Lauro Barcenas, *President*
Oscar Barcenas, *Treasurer*
Luis Barcenas, *Vice Pres*
EMP: 150 EST: 1999
SQ FT: 2,000
SALES (est): 16.9MM **Privately Held**
SIC: 1771 Concrete work

(P-1557)
VALENCIA BROS INC
Also Called: Valencia Brothers Concrete
257 Maple Ave, El Centro (92243-3311)
PHONE...................760 353-2168
EMP: 80 EST: 2000
SQ FT: 1,700
SALES (est): 4.4MM **Privately Held**
SIC: 1771 Concrete Contractor

(P-1558)
Z-BEST CONCRETE INC
2575 Main St, Riverside (92501-2238)
PHONE...................951 774-1870
Roger Crott, *President*
Jerry Faust, *Vice Pres*
EMP: 80 EST: 1989
SQ FT: 2,400
SALES (est): 12.4MM **Privately Held**
SIC: 1771 1741 Concrete work; masonry & other stonework

1781 Water Well Drilling

(P-1559)
BEKS ACQUISITION INC
Also Called: Bc2 Environmental
1150 W Trenton Ave, Orange (92867-3536)
PHONE...................714 744-2990
Kurt Samuelson, *President*
EMP: 50 EST: 2008
SALES (est): 4.1MM **Privately Held**
WEB: www.bc2env.com
SIC: 1781 Water well drilling

(P-1560)
GREGG DRILLING LLC
2726 Walnut Ave, Signal Hill (90755-1832)
PHONE...................562 427-6899
John Gregg, *President*
Chris Christensen, *Vice Pres*
Patrick Keating, *Vice Pres*
Sonja De Keyser-Meurs, *Admin Sec*
Stacey Fuller, *Admin Asst*
EMP: 160 EST: 2018
SQ FT: 17,000
SALES (est): 8MM **Privately Held**
WEB: www.greggdrilling.com
SIC: 1781 Water well drilling

(P-1561)
KENAI DRILLING LIMITED
2651 Patton Way, Bakersfield (93308-5745)
PHONE...................661 587-0117
Gene Kramer, *Branch Mgr*
Jennifer Phoutrides, *Administration*
Tyler Loudon, *Engineer*
Gina De Venuta, *Manager*
Heath Loper, *Superintendent*
EMP: 132 Privately Held
WEB: www.kenaidrilling.com
SIC: 1781 Water well servicing
PA: Kenai Drilling Limited
6430 Cat Canyon Rd
Santa Maria CA 93454

(P-1562)
MAGCO DRILLING INC
1391 Manchester Rd, San Dimas (91773-3715)
PHONE...................626 969-1000
Holly A Maggio, *President*
John Klein, *Vice Pres*
Bob Rodriguez, *Branch Mgr*
Ida Lengson, *Controller*
Silvia Macias, *Human Res Mgr*
▲ **EMP: 131 EST:** 2005
SQ FT: 8,550
SALES (est): 13MM
SALES (corp-wide): 417.2MM **Privately Held**
WEB: www.magcodrilling.com
SIC: 1781 Water well drilling
HQ: Aldridge Construction Inc.
10625 N County Rd Ste 200
Frisco TX 75033
855 486-1100

(P-1563)
ZIM INDUSTRIES INC
Bakersfield Well & Pump Co
7212 Fruitvale Ave, Bakersfield (93308-9529)
PHONE...................661 393-9661
John Zimmerer, *Manager*
Bob Zimmerer, *General Mgr*
Aaron Hanna, *Manager*
EMP: 140
SALES (corp-wide): 40.4MM **Privately Held**
WEB: www.zimindustries.com
SIC: 1781 7699 Water well servicing; pumps & pumping equipment repair
PA: Zim Industries, Inc.
4532 E Jefferson Ave
Fresno CA 93725
559 834-1551

1791 Structural Steel Erection

(P-1564)
ALLIED STEEL CO INC
1027 Palmyrita Ave, Riverside (92507-1701)
PHONE...................951 241-7000
Brian P Chapman, *President*
Nicky Chapman, *Treasurer*
Jeff Chapman, *Vice Pres*
Mike Chapman, *Vice Pres*
Perry K Chapman, *Vice Pres*
EMP: 60 EST: 1944
SQ FT: 48,000
SALES (est): 16.3MM **Privately Held**
WEB: www.alliedsteelco.com
SIC: 1791 3441 Structural steel erection; fabricated structural metal

(P-1565)
ANAS IRON SUPPLY INC
1322 Santa Anita Ave, South El Monte (91733-3837)
PHONE...................626 401-0483
Ana L Meza, *Principal*
EMP: 13 EST: 2014
SALES (est): 1MM **Privately Held**
WEB: www.anasironsupply.com
SIC: 1791 1799 3441 Iron work, structural; ornamental metal work; fabricated structural metal

(P-1566)
ANVIL STEEL CORPORATION
Also Called: Anvil Iron
134 W 168th St, Gardena (90248-2729)
PHONE...................310 329-5811
Gerry Bustrum, *CEO*
Paul Schifino, *President*
Mike Norton, *Vice Pres*
Janet Alvarez, *Administration*
Flores Jazmin, *Administration*
▲ **EMP: 90 EST:** 1973
SQ FT: 4,000
SALES (est): 27.2MM **Privately Held**
WEB: www.anvilsteel.com
SIC: 1791 Iron work, structural

(P-1567)
BAPKO METAL INC
180 S Anita Dr, Orange (92868-3304)
PHONE...................714 639-9380
Fred Bagatourian, *President*
Tim Black, *CFO*
Clint Rieber, *CFO*
Heather Wiliams, *Admin Sec*
Adam Cherry, *Project Mgr*
EMP: 80
SQ FT: 4,000
SALES (est): 23.4MM **Privately Held**
WEB: www.bapko.com
SIC: 1791 3441 Structural steel erection; fabricated structural metal

(P-1568)
BELLIS STEEL COMPANY INC (PA)
8740 Vanalden Ave, Northridge (91324-3691)
PHONE...................818 886-5601
Theron Arthur Ghrist, *CEO*
Gail R Ghrist, *Vice Pres*
Alan Miley, *General Mgr*
Anna Longoria, *Controller*
Andrea Cervantes, *HR Admin*
EMP: 50 EST: 1961
SQ FT: 2,500
SALES (est): 16.1MM **Privately Held**
WEB: www.bellissteel.com
SIC: 1791 5051 Concrete reinforcement, placing of; iron & steel (ferrous) products

(P-1569)
CECAL ENTERPRISES INC
26081 Merit Cir Ste 106, Laguna Hills (92653-7017)
PHONE...................949 380-7100
Robert Caronna, *President*
Bobby Caronna, *Business Mgr*
Sherrina Thurman, *Controller*
EMP: 50 EST: 2001
SQ FT: 2,500

SALES (est): 3MM **Privately Held**
WEB: www.cecalent.com
SIC: 1791 Precast concrete structural framing or panels, placing of

(P-1570)
COAST IRON & STEEL CO
12300 Lakeland Rd, Santa Fe Springs (90670-3869)
P.O. Box 2846 (90670-0846)
PHONE...................562 946-4421
Greg White, *President*
Cyndi White Cramer, *Shareholder*
Carrie White, *Shareholder*
Jared White, *Shareholder*
Ronald G White, *CEO*
▲ **EMP: 50 EST:** 1953
SQ FT: 360,000
SALES (est): 13.6MM **Privately Held**
SIC: 1791 3441 Structural steel erection; fabricated structural metal

(P-1571)
INTEGRITY REBAR PLACERS
1345 Nandina Ave, Perris (92571-9402)
PHONE...................951 696-6843
Kenneth Negrete, *President*
Richard Rabay, *Vice Pres*
Jay Ferguson, *Technology*
Emily Webster, *Accounting Mgr*
Adam Garcia, *Superintendent*
▲ **EMP: 200 EST:** 2005
SALES (est): 24MM **Privately Held**
WEB: www.integrityrebarplacers.com
SIC: 1791 Structural steel erection

(P-1572)
KCB TOWERS INC
27260 Meines St, Highland (92346-4223)
P.O. Box 100 (92346-0100)
PHONE...................909 862-0322
S Lynn Bogh, *CEO*
Sharon Bogh, *Corp Secy*
Miles Bogh, *Vice Pres*
Garth Bogh, *Safety Mgr*
EMP: 100
SQ FT: 12,000
SALES (est): 18.1MM **Privately Held**
WEB: www.kcbtowers.com
SIC: 1791 3441 Concrete reinforcement, placing of; fabricated structural metal

(P-1573)
LA STEEL SERVICES INC
1180 Olympic Dr Ste 108, Corona (92881-3393)
PHONE...................951 393-2013
Pamela L Albright, *CEO*
Lee Albright, *President*
Richard Rabay, *Vice Pres*
Pamela Albright, *General Mgr*
EMP: 50 EST: 2015
SALES (est): 4.2MM **Privately Held**
WEB: www.lasteelservices.com
SIC: 1791 Concrete reinforcement, placing of

(P-1574)
MARTINEZ STEEL CORPORATION
1500 S Haven Ave Ste 150, Ontario (91761-2971)
PHONE...................909 946-0686
Harry Williams, *CEO*
Pete Morales, *Vice Pres*
Jose Sanchez, *Executive*
Andy Pachucki, *Project Mgr*
Eddie Alamo, *Controller*
EMP: 200 EST: 1994
SALES (est): 25.8MM **Privately Held**
WEB: www.martinezsteel.com
SIC: 1791 Structural steel erection

(P-1575)
MARTINEZ STEEL INC
8920 Vernon Ave Ste 128, Montclair (91763-1663)
PHONE...................909 946-0686
Joe Martinez, *President*
Debbie Martinez, *Admin Sec*
EMP: 60 EST: 1994
SQ FT: 852 **Privately Held**
WEB: www.martinezsteel.com
SIC: 1791 Concrete reinforcement, placing of

PRODUCTS & SVCS

(P-1576)
MCINTYRE COMPANY (PA)
2817 E Cedar St Ste 200, Ontario
(91761-8568)
PHONE....................909 962-6322
Roger Mc Intyre, *President*
Scott Mc Intyre, *Vice Pres*
EMP: 59 EST: 1959
SQ FT: 10,000
SALES (est): 10.3MM Privately Held
SIC: 1791 Structural steel erection

(P-1577)
MECHANICAL INDUSTRIES INC
Also Called: M I I
314 Yampa St, Bakersfield (93307-2722)
PHONE....................661 634-9477
Jerry L Nordine, *President*
Jerry Miranda, *Vice Pres*
Nicole Hernandez, *Project Admn*
Scott Nordine, *Purch Agent*
Rick Martin, *Production*
EMP: 50 EST: 1993
SQ FT: 43,000
SALES (est): 11.7MM Privately Held
WEB: www.mii-us.com
SIC: 1791 Structural steel erection

(P-1578)
R & B REINFORCING STEEL CORP
13581 5th St, Chino (91710-5166)
PHONE....................909 591-1726
David McDaniel, *CEO*
Robert Bessette, *President*
Dave McDaniel, *CFO*
Nancy Bessette, *Admin Sec*
EMP: 80 EST: 1983
SQ FT: 30,000
SALES (est): 9.3MM Privately Held
WEB: www.rbsteel.net
SIC: 1791 Iron work, structural

(P-1579)
REBAR ENGINEERING INC
10706 Painter Ave, Santa Fe Springs
(90670-4581)
P.O. Box 3986 (90670-1986)
PHONE....................562 946-2461
Charles L Krebs, *President*
Jack Garroutte, *Exec VP*
EMP: 250 EST: 1963
SQ FT: 6,500
SALES (est): 34.5MM Privately Held
WEB: www.changsteelinc.com
SIC: 1791 Concrete reinforcement, placing of

(P-1580)
RICHWELL STEEL CO INC
134 W 168th St, Gardena (90248-2729)
PHONE....................310 324-4455
Stephen William Pronchow, *President*
Nick Prochnow, *Corp Secy*
Chris Prochnow, *Vice Pres*
Mindy Salinas, *Assistant*
EMP: 51 EST: 1947
SALES (est): 8MM Privately Held
WEB: www.i-am-not-government-property.com
SIC: 1791 3441 Iron work, structural; fabricated structural metal

(P-1581)
RIKA CORPORATION
Also Called: Diversified Metal Works
332 W Brenna Ln, Orange (92867-5637)
PHONE....................949 830-9050
John E Ferguson, *CEO*
Justin Ferguson, *Vice Pres*
Juan Cervantes, *Project Mgr*
▲ EMP: 100 EST: 1977
SQ FT: 8,000
SALES (est): 15MM Privately Held
WEB: www.dmwk.com
SIC: 1791 Structural steel erection

(P-1582)
RIVERTON STEEL CONSTRUCTION
10130 Adella Ave, South Gate
(90280-5314)
P.O. Box 4063 (90280-8463)
PHONE....................323 564-1881
Claude Ritchot, *CEO*

James Hanson, *President*
EMP: 18 EST: 1984
SQ FT: 100,000
SALES (est): 1MM Privately Held
SIC: 1791 3449 3441 Structural steel erection; miscellaneous metalwork; fabricated structural metal

(P-1583)
SO-CAL STRL STL FBRICATION INC
130 S Spruce Ave, Rialto (92376-9005)
PHONE....................909 877-1299
Craig B Yates, *CEO*
Kim Yates, *Vice Pres*
EMP: 50 EST: 1995
SQ FT: 40,000
SALES (est): 13.2MM Privately Held
SIC: 1791 Structural steel erection

(P-1584)
WHITES STEEL INC (PA)
45524 Towne St, Indio (92201-4446)
P.O. Box 846, Thermal (92274-0846)
PHONE....................760 347-3401
Edwin Neumeyer, *CEO*
EMP: 17 EST: 1995
SALES (est): 14.6MM Privately Held
WEB: www.whitessteel.com
SIC: 1791 3446 3599 Structural steel erection; architectural metalwork; machine shop, jobbing & repair

(P-1585)
YOUNGS IRON WORKS INC
9133 De Garmo Ave, Sun Valley
(91352-2695)
PHONE....................818 768-3877
Claudia Mae Tucker, *Principal*
Claudia Tucker, *Corp Secy*
EMP: 14 EST: 1947
SQ FT: 10,000
SALES (est): 3.5MM Privately Held
WEB: www.yiw.biz
SIC: 1791 3441 Structural steel erection; fabricated structural metal

1793 Glass & Glazing Work

(P-1586)
GIROUX GLASS INC (PA)
850 W Wash Blvd Ste 200, Los Angeles
(90015-3359)
PHONE....................213 747-7406
Nataline Lomedico, *CEO*
Blane Midkiff, *Partner*
Anne-Merelie Murrell, *Ch of Bd*
Stephanie Lamb, *COO*
Robert Burkhammer, *Exec VP*
▲ EMP: 120 EST: 1946
SALES (est): 49.6MM Privately Held
WEB: www.girouxglass.com
SIC: 1793 Glass & glazing work

(P-1587)
PERFECTION GLASS INC
554 3rd St, Lake Elsinore (92530-2729)
PHONE....................951 674-0240
Richard L Warren, *President*
Dane Warren, *Treasurer*
Chris Bonnet, *Admin Sec*
EMP: 50 EST: 2003
SQ FT: 4,200
SALES (est): 12.5MM Privately Held
SIC: 1793 Glass & glazing work

(P-1588)
RYNOCLAD TECHNOLOGIES INC
780 E Francis St Ste M, Ontario
(91761-5553)
PHONE....................951 264-3441
Victor Wright, *CEO*
Troy Thomas, *CFO*
Joe Barnes, *Vice Pres*
EMP: 200 EST: 2011
SALES (est): 25MM Privately Held
WEB: www.rynoclad.com
SIC: 1793 Glass & glazing work

(P-1589)
SWARTZ GLASS COMPANY INC (PA)
821 Lincoln Blvd, Venice (90291-2846)
PHONE....................310 392-0001
Raphael Swartz, *CEO*
Ray Swartz, *Owner*
Michael Swartz, *Treasurer*
Mark Swartz, *Vice Pres*
EMP: 18 EST: 1933
SQ FT: 2,500
SALES (est): 4.3MM Privately Held
WEB: www.swartzglassvenice.com
SIC: 5231 1793 7536 3231 Glass, leaded or stained; glass & glazing work; automotive glass replacement shops; products of purchased glass

(P-1590)
WOODBRIDGE GLASS INC
14321 Myford Rd, Tustin (92780-7022)
PHONE....................714 838-4444
Virginia Siciliani, *President*
Jim Siciliani, *Corp Secy*
John Siciliani, *Vice Pres*
Jose Saldivar, *Administration*
Trent Zinn, *Info Tech Mgr*
▲ EMP: 205
SQ FT: 8,500
SALES (est): 81MM Privately Held
WEB: www.woodbridgeglass.com
SIC: 1793 5231 Glass & glazing work; glass, leaded or stained

1794 Excavating & Grading Work

(P-1591)
ARNETT CONSTRUCTION INC
Also Called: A A Construction
626 W 1st St, Rialto (92376-5715)
P.O. Box 488 (92377-0488)
PHONE....................909 421-7960
Albert Arnett, *President*
Wayne Arnett, *Treasurer*
Shirley Arnett, *Vice Pres*
Lea Ann Hibbetts, *Admin Sec*
EMP: 20 EST: 1983
SQ FT: 1,200
SALES (est): 3.5MM Privately Held
SIC: 1794 1611 1542 3531 Excavation & grading, building construction; concrete construction: roads, highways, sidewalks, etc.; nonresidential construction; plows: construction, excavating & grading

(P-1592)
CALEX ENGINEERING INC
Also Called: Calex Engineering Co.
23651 Pine St, Newhall (91321-3106)
PHONE....................661 254-1866
Ryan Seitz, *President*
Mike Neilson, *CEO*
Roy Williams, *Technology*
EMP: 70 EST: 1975
SQ FT: 1,800
SALES (est): 20.3MM Privately Held
WEB: www.calex.net
SIC: 1794 Excavation work

(P-1593)
COASTAL GRADING AND EXCAVATING
756 Calle Plano, Camarillo (93012-8555)
P.O. Box 2459, Moorpark (93020-2459)
PHONE....................805 445-6433
Thomas Staben Jr, *President*
EMP: 50 EST: 2004
SALES (est): 5.6MM Privately Held
SIC: 1794 Excavation work

(P-1594)
CREW INC
19618 S Susana Rd, Compton
(90221-5716)
PHONE....................310 608-6860
David M Lalonde, *President*
Darrin Lalonde, *Vice Pres*
Andrew Kerr, *Human Res Mgr*
Warren Duke, *Purch Mgr*
EMP: 60 EST: 1994
SQ FT: 5,000

SALES (est): 15.4MM Privately Held
WEB: www.crewgrading.com
SIC: 1794 Excavation & grading, building construction

(P-1595)
GILLIAM & SONS INC
Also Called: Valco Construction
9831 Rosedale Hwy, Bakersfield
(93312-2604)
P.O. Box 9955 (93389-1955)
PHONE....................561 589-0913
Bill W Gilliam, *CEO*
Scott Gilliam, *Vice Pres*
Nancy Northern, *Controller*
EMP: 50 EST: 1969
SQ FT: 2,500
SALES (est): 11.6MM Privately Held
WEB: www.gilliamandsons.com
SIC: 1794 Excavation & grading, building construction

(P-1596)
GUINN CORPORATION
6533 Rosedale Hwy, Bakersfield
(93308-5903)
P.O. Box 1339 (93302-1339)
PHONE....................661 325-6109
Gary Guinn, *CEO*
Jeff Affonso, *Corp Secy*
Tim Guinn, *Vice Pres*
EMP: 75 EST: 1952
SQ FT: 3,600
SALES (est): 16.2MM Privately Held
WEB: www.guinnconstruction.com
SIC: 1794 Excavation & grading, building construction

(P-1597)
HOWARD CONTRACTING INC
12354 Carson St, Hawaiian Gardens
(90716-1604)
PHONE....................562 596-2969
Frederick Stanley Howard, *CEO*
Viki R Howard, *Corp Secy*
Stanley L Howard, *Vice Pres*
Stanley Howard, *Vice Pres*
EMP: 50 EST: 1984
SQ FT: 3,500
SALES (est): 9.7MM Privately Held
WEB: www.howardcontracting.com
SIC: 1794 Excavation & grading, building construction

(P-1598)
INLAND EROSION CTRL SVCS INC
42181 Avnida Alvrado Ste, Temecula
(92590)
P.O. Box 728, Murrieta (92564-0728)
PHONE....................951 301-8334
Todd Close, *President*
Carlos Garcia, *Vice Pres*
EMP: 59 EST: 2001
SQ FT: 1,000
SALES (est): 8.1MM Privately Held
WEB: www.inlanderosion.com
SIC: 1794 Excavation & grading, building construction

(P-1599)
JEFF CARPENTER INC
1380 W Oleander Ave, Perris (92571-7863)
PHONE....................951 657-5115
Jeff Carpenter, *President*
EMP: 60 EST: 1985
SQ FT: 1,300
SALES (est): 8.8MM Privately Held
WEB: www.jeffcarpenterinc.com
SIC: 1794 Excavation work

(P-1600)
LOVCO CONSTRUCTION INC
1300 E Burnett St, Signa Hill (90755-3512)
P.O. Box 90335, Long Beach (90809-0335)
PHONE....................562 595-1601
Terry C Lovingier, *President*
Katie Lovingier, *Treasurer*
Steve Barnett, *Vice Pres*
Matt Lovinger, *Vice Pres*
Mike McGougan, *Vice Pres*
EMP: 125 EST: 1988
SQ FT: 2,500

SALES (est): 22.1MM **Privately Held**
WEB: www.lovcoconstruction.com
SIC: 1794 1771 1611 Excavation & grading, building construction; concrete work; highway & street construction; general contractor, highway & street construction

(P-1601)
MGE UNDERGROUND INC
2501 Golden Hill Rd, Paso Robles (93446-6391)
P.O. Box 4189 (93447-4189)
PHONE................................805 238-3510
Michael Joe Goldstein, *President*
Summer Goldstein, *CFO*
Summer Golstein, *Admin Sec*
Kelly Morrison, *Admin Sec*
Jeremy Dyck, *Project Mgr*
EMP: 85 **EST:** 1997
SALES (est): 31.5MM **Privately Held**
WEB: www.mgeunderground.com
SIC: 1794 Excavation work

(P-1602)
NEGRANTI CONSTRUCTION
Also Called: Negranti Construciton
1424 Old Creek Rd, Cayucos (93430-1561)
P.O. Box 198 (93430-0198)
PHONE................................805 995-3357
Jon Negranti, *President*
EMP: 21 **EST:** 1965
SQ FT: 600
SALES (est): 2.1MM **Privately Held**
WEB: www.negranti-higgins.com
SIC: 1794 1442 1623 1795 Excavation & grading, building construction; construction sand mining; gravel mining; underground utilities contractor; demolition, buildings & other structures

(P-1603)
REED THOMAS COMPANY INC
1025 N Santiago St, Santa Ana (92701-3800)
PHONE................................714 558-7691
Harvey T Biegle, *President*
Omar Hernandez, *Manager*
Darryll Radatz, *Manager*
EMP: 90 **EST:** 1981
SQ FT: 8,800
SALES (est): 13.4MM **Privately Held**
WEB: www.reedthomas.com
SIC: 1794 Excavation & grading, building construction

(P-1604)
STURGEON SERVICES INTL INC (PA)
Also Called: Sturgeon & Son
3511 Gilmore Ave, Bakersfield (93308-6205)
P.O. Box 2840 (93303-2840)
PHONE................................661 322-4408
Paul H Sturgeon, *President*
Oliver Sturgeon, *Ch of Bd*
Joe D'Angelo, *CFO*
Gina Blankenship, *Vice Pres*
Corina Lopez, *Administration*
EMP: 50 **EST:** 1972
SQ FT: 5,000
SALES (est): 67.5MM **Privately Held**
WEB: www.sturgeonservices.com
SIC: 1794 Excavation work

(P-1605)
STURGEON SON GRADING & PAV INC (PA)
3511 Gilmore Ave, Bakersfield (93308-6205)
P.O. Box 2840 (93303-2840)
PHONE................................661 322-4408
John E Powell, *CEO*
Paul Sturgeon, *President*
Oliver Sturgeon, *Principal*
EMP: 180 **EST:** 1927
SQ FT: 3,500
SALES (est): 58.9MM **Privately Held**
WEB: www.sturgeonservices.com
SIC: 1794 8711 Excavation work; engineering services

(P-1606)
SUB-ZERO EXCAVATING INC
1916 Duncan St, Simi Valley (93065-3414)
PHONE................................805 522-5043

Lisa Fletcher, *President*
EMP: 53 **EST:** 1998
SALES (est): 3.1MM **Privately Held**
WEB: www.subzeroexcavating.com
SIC: 1794 Excavation & grading, building construction

(P-1607)
SUKUT CONSTRUCTION INC
4010 W Chandler Ave, Santa Ana (92704-5202)
PHONE................................714 540-5351
Michael Crawford, *President*
Paul Kuliev, *CFO*
Myron Sukut, *Chairman*
Eddie Juarez, *Vice Pres*
Greg Leblanc, *Vice Pres*
▲ **EMP:** 200 **EST:** 1968
SQ FT: 12,000
SALES (est): 137.7MM **Privately Held**
WEB: www.sukut.com
SIC: 1794 1611 1623 1629 Excavation & grading, building construction; general contractor, highway & street construction; water & sewer line construction; dams, waterways, docks & other marine construction

(P-1608)
TIDWELL EXCAV ACQUISITION INC
1691 Los Angeles Ave, Ventura (93004-3213)
PHONE................................805 647-4707
Alex Miruello, *President*
Louis Armona, *Treasurer*
Timothy Wayne Goodwin, *Vice Pres*
EMP: 90 **EST:** 1956
SALES (est): 12.4MM
SALES (corp-wide): 663.7MM **Privately Held**
WEB: www.tidwell-inc.com
SIC: 1794 Excavation & grading, building construction
PA: Meruelo Enterprises, Inc.
9550 Firestone Blvd # 105
Downey CA 90241
562 745-2300

1795 Wrecking & Demolition Work

(P-1609)
AMERICAN WRECKING INC
2459 Lee Ave, South El Monte (91733-1407)
PHONE................................626 350-8303
Jose Luis Galaviz, *President*
Jay Gonzalez, *COO*
Juan Galaviz, *Vice Pres*
Warne Galaviz, *Vice Pres*
Robert Hall, *Vice Pres*
EMP: 100 **EST:** 1989
SQ FT: 1,000
SALES (est): 23.3MM **Privately Held**
WEB: www.americanwreckinginc.com
SIC: 1795 Demolition, buildings & other structures

(P-1610)
CAL EMPIRE ENGINEERING INC
628 E Edna Pl, Covina (91723-1312)
P.O. Box 1995, Corona (92878-1995)
PHONE................................626 915-8030
Greg Miller, *President*
Kevin Milllar, *General Mgr*
Sheree Kaplan, *Administration*
Adrian Barba, *Superintendent*
Billy Bugarin, *Superintendent*
EMP: 50 **EST:** 2016
SALES (est): 8.4MM **Privately Held**
WEB: www.calempire.com
SIC: 1795 1794 1623 Concrete breaking for streets & highways; excavation work; underground utilities contractor

(P-1611)
CLEVELAND WRECKING COMPANY (DH)
Also Called: CWC Acquisition
999 W Town And Country Rd, Orange (92868-4713)
PHONE................................626 967-4287
James Sheridan, *President*

Andrew Varga, *President*
EMP: 68 **EST:** 1910
SQ FT: 60,000
SALES (est): 6.2MM
SALES (corp-wide): 13.2B **Publicly Held**
WEB: www.aecom.com
SIC: 1795 1796 1799 Demolition, buildings & other structures; machinery dismantling; asbestos removal & encapsulation
HQ: Urs Group, Inc.
300 S Grand Ave Ste 900
Los Angeles CA 90071
213 593-8000

(P-1612)
DANNY RYAN PRECISION CONTG INC
1818 N Orangethorpe Park, Anaheim (92801-1140)
PHONE................................949 642-6664
Danny Ryan, *President*
EMP: 90 **EST:** 1991
SQ FT: 10,000
SALES (est): 19MM **Privately Held**
SIC: 1795 1799 Demolition, buildings & other structures; asbestos removal & encapsulation

(P-1613)
EMPIRE DEMOLITION INC
1623 Leeson Ln, Corona (92879-2061)
PHONE................................909 393-8300
Kris Huff, *CEO*
Collin Cumbee, *CFO*
EMP: 100 **EST:** 1997
SQ FT: 8,000
SALES (est): 11.1MM **Privately Held**
WEB: www.empiredemolition.com
SIC: 1795 Demolition, buildings & other structures

(P-1614)
GD HEIL INC
1031 Segovia Cir, Placentia (92870-7137)
PHONE................................714 687-9100
James A Langford, *CEO*
Gary Heil, *President*
Steve Mc Clain, *Vice Pres*
Laura Heil, *Admin Sec*
EMP: 160 **EST:** 1992
SQ FT: 20,770
SALES (est): 25.1MM **Privately Held**
WEB: www.gdheil.com
SIC: 1795 Demolition, buildings & other structures

(P-1615)
HULK CONSTRUCTION
4352 Lakeview Ave, Yorba Linda (92886-2422)
PHONE................................714 701-9458
EMP: 80
SALES (est): 3.2MM **Privately Held**
SIC: 1795 Wrecking/Demolition Contractor

(P-1616)
INTERIOR RMOVAL SPECIALIST INC
8990 Atlantic Ave, South Gate (90280-3505)
PHONE................................323 357-6900
Carlos Herrera, *CEO*
Isabel Herrera, *Vice Pres*
EMP: 150 **EST:** 1994
SALES (est): 0 **Privately Held**
WEB: www.irsdemo.com
SIC: 1795 Demolition, buildings & other structures

(P-1617)
MILLER ENVIRONMENTAL INC
1130 W Trenton Ave, Orange (92867-3536)
PHONE................................714 385-0099
Gregg Miller, *President*
Deborah Holland, *Vice Pres*
Rob Schaefer, *Vice Pres*
Nicole Lesage, *Office Mgr*
Dennis Parker, *Opers Staff*
EMP: 150 **EST:** 1999
SQ FT: 3,000
SALES (est): 33MM **Privately Held**
WEB: www.millerenvironmental.com
SIC: 1795 4953 Demolition, buildings & other structures; hazardous waste collection & disposal

(P-1618)
NORTHERN HOLDINGS
Also Called: New Frnters Ntral Mrktplace 10
1531 Froom Ranch Way, San Luis Obispo (93405-7211)
PHONE................................805 785-0194
Steve Dominguez, *Branch Mgr*
Kim James, *Manager*
EMP: 69 **Privately Held**
WEB: www.newfrontiersmarket.com
SIC: 5411 1795 1794 0161 Grocery stores, chain; demolition, buildings & other structures; excavation & grading, building construction; vegetables & melons
PA: Northern Holdings
1984 Old Mission Dr
Solvang CA 93463

(P-1619)
NORTHSTAR CONTG GROUP INC
13320 Cambridge St, Santa Fe Springs (90670-4904)
PHONE................................714 639-7600
John Leonard, *Vice Pres*
EMP: 60
SALES (corp-wide): 640.1MM **Privately Held**
WEB: www.northstar.com
SIC: 1795 1799 Wrecking & demolition work; asbestos removal & encapsulation
HQ: Northstar Contracting Group, Inc.
2614-20 Barrington Ct
Hayward CA 94545

(P-1620)
NORTHSTAR DEM & REMEDIATION LP (DH)
404 N Berry St, Brea (92821-3104)
PHONE................................714 672-3500
Jose Alonso, *Vice Pres*
Jeffrey P Adix, *Treasurer*
Gregory G Dicarlo, *Vice Pres*
Andy Hixson, *Vice Pres*
Kamal Sookram, *Vice Pres*
EMP: 174 **EST:** 2007
SQ FT: 19,000
SALES (est): 100.8MM
SALES (corp-wide): 640.1MM **Privately Held**
SIC: 1795 1799 8744 Demolition, buildings & other structures; decontamination services;
HQ: Northstar Group Services, Inc.
370 7th Ave Ste 1803
New York NY 10001
212 951-3660

(P-1621)
VICTORIOUS RED
4260 Artesia Ave Unit B, Fullerton (92833-2518)
PHONE................................657 529-8911
Adalberto Escutia, *CEO*
Gustavo Escutia, *Principal*
Jasmin Escutia, *Opers Mgr*
EMP: 50 **EST:** 2017
SALES (est): 6MM **Privately Held**
WEB: www.victoriousred.com
SIC: 1795 1542 Wrecking & demolition work; nonresidential construction

1796 Installation Or Erection Of Bldg Eqpt & Machinery, NEC

(P-1622)
CALIFORNIA AIR CONVEYING CORP
16260 Minnesota Ave, Paramount (90723-4916)
PHONE................................562 531-4570
John De Long Jr, *President*
Leslie De Long, *Admin Sec*
Nathan Black, *Project Mgr*
EMP: 15 **EST:** 1978
SQ FT: 5,000

SALES (est): 3.3MM **Privately Held**
WEB: www.calaircon.com
SIC: **1796** 3444 Pollution control equipment installation; machine guards, sheet metal

(P-1623)
CLASSIC INSTALLS INC
22475 Baxter Rd, Wildomar (92595-9040)
PHONE................................951 678-9906
Dirk Steffen, *CEO*
Elizabeth Burch, *Project Mgr*
Tony Evans, *Technology*
Kathy Hilderbrand, *Opers Staff*
Nicole Steen, *Opers Staff*
EMP: 70 EST: 2007
SALES (est): 75.5K **Privately Held**
WEB:
SIC: **1796** Installing building equipment

(P-1624)
MAINTECH RESOURCES INC
9112 Rose St, Bellflower (90706-6420)
PHONE................................562 804-0664
John Ellen, *President*
Kurt Williams, *Project Mgr*
Brian Day, *Foreman/Supr*
Dave Ellis, *Manager*
EMP: 36 EST: 1984
SQ FT: 1,200
SALES (est): 5.1MM **Privately Held**
WEB: www.maintech-hq.com
SIC: **1796** 1731 8711 3498 Installing building equipment; general electrical contractor; structural engineering; coils, pipe; fabricated from purchased pipe

(P-1625)
MITSUBISHI ELECTRIC US INC (DH)
Also Called: Meus
5900 Katella Ave Ste C, Cypress (90630-5065)
P.O. Box 6007 (90630-0007)
PHONE................................714 220-2500
Mike Corbo, *President*
Masahiro Oya, *Ch of Bd*
Koichi Kawabata, *Treasurer*
Perry Pappous, *Exec VP*
Jared Baker, *Senior VP*
◆ EMP: 200 EST: 2000
SQ FT: 10,400
SALES (est): 931.5MM **Privately Held**
WEB: www.us.mitsubishielectric.com
SIC: **1796** 3534 5065 3669 Elevator installation & conversion; escalators, passenger & freight; electronic parts; semiconductor devices; visual communication systems
HQ: Mitsubishi Electric Us Holdings, Inc.
5900 Katella Ave Ste A
Cypress CA 90630
714 220-2500

(P-1626)
PERFORMANCE CONTRACTING INC
4955 E Landon Dr, Anaheim (92807-1972)
PHONE................................913 310-7120
William Massey, *Manager*
EMP: 99
SALES (corp-wide): 2.4B **Privately Held**
WEB: www.performancecontracting.com
SIC: **1796** Installing building equipment
HQ: Performance Contracting, Inc.
11145 Thompson Ave
Lenexa KS 66219
913 888-8600

(P-1627)
UNITED RIGGERS & ERECTORS INC (PA)
4188 Valley Blvd, Walnut (91789-1446)
P.O. Box 728 (91788-0728)
PHONE................................909 978-0400
Brian D Kelley, *CEO*
Thomas J Kruss, *COO*
Merary Argueta, *Administration*
Tom Larsen, *Project Mgr*
Frank Cangey, *Engineer*
EMP: 100
SQ FT: 58,000
SALES: 20.5MM **Privately Held**
WEB: www.urenet.com
SIC: **1796** Machinery installation

(P-1628)
VERENGO INC (DH)
Also Called: Verengo Solar
20285 S Wstn Ave Ste 200, Torrance (90501)
PHONE................................310 803-9053
Dan Squiller, *CEO*
Manel Sweetmore, *CFO*
EMP: 539 EST: 2009
SALES (est): 179.5MM
SALES (corp-wide): 11.4B **Publicly Held**
SIC: **5211** 1796 Solar heating equipment; power generating equipment installation
HQ: Crius Solar Fulfillment, Llc
535 Connecticut Ave # 100
Norwalk CT 06854
203 663-5089

1799 Special Trade Contractors, NEC

(P-1629)
911 RESTORATION ENTPS INC (PA)
Also Called: I P Global
7721 Densmore Ave, Van Nuys (91406-1920)
PHONE................................818 373-4880
Peleg Lindenberg, *President*
Diane Noonan, *CFO*
Miri Offir, *Chief Mktg Ofcr*
Tomer Feldman, *Principal*
Sagiv Winer, *Principal*
EMP: 199 EST: 2003
SALES (est): 6MM **Privately Held**
WEB: www.911restorationlosangeles.com
SIC: **1799** Fireproofing buildings

(P-1630)
A-1 BUILDING & FENCE MTLS INC
Also Called: A-1 Steel Fence Company
2210 Chico Ave, South El Monte (91733-1609)
PHONE................................562 693-4853
Teodoro Moreno, *President*
Frank Moreno, *Vice Pres*
Carmelita Moreno, *Admin Sec*
EMP: 26 EST: 1940
SALES (est): 2.3MM **Privately Held**
WEB: www.a1steelfence.com
SIC: **1799** 3699 3496 Fence construction; electrical equipment & supplies; miscellaneous fabricated wire products

(P-1631)
A-1 ENTERPRISES INC
Also Called: A-1 Fence
2831 E La Cresta Ave, Anaheim (92806-1817)
PHONE................................714 630-3390
Norman Shepherd, *President*
James Sypitkowski, *Vice Pres*
Abe Montoya, *General Mgr*
EMP: 45 EST: 1953
SQ FT: 39,000
SALES (est): 9.3MM **Privately Held**
WEB: www.a1fence.com
SIC: **1799** 3446 Fence construction; acoustical suspension systems, metal

(P-1632)
AAA RESTORATION INC
29850 2nd St, Lake Elsinore (92532-2420)
PHONE................................951 471-5828
Kirk Munio, *President*
Allison Burns, *Office Mgr*
EMP: 50 EST: 2003
SQ FT: 1,400
SALES (est): 10.5MM **Privately Held**
WEB: www.aaa-restoration.com
SIC: **1799** Home/office interiors finishing, furnishing & remodeling

(P-1633)
ALCORN FENCE COMPANY (PA)
9901 Glenoaks Blvd, Sun Valley (91352-1089)
P.O. Box 1249 (91353-1249)
PHONE................................818 983-0650
Thomas Joseph Stack, *CEO*
Greg Erickson, *President*
Oscar Mancialla, *CFO*

Douglas Sorgani, *Division Mgr*
Michael Rider, *Project Mgr*
EMP: 60 EST: 1942
SQ FT: 18,000
SALES (est): 24.3MM **Privately Held**
WEB: www.alcorn-fence.com
SIC: **1799** Fence construction

(P-1634)
ANCON MARINE
6496 Brandt Rd, Calipatria (92233-9762)
PHONE................................760 348-9606
Tom Baker, *Branch Mgr*
EMP: 64
SALES (corp-wide): 183.5MM **Privately Held**
WEB: www.anconservices.com
SIC: **1799** Athletic & recreation facilities construction
PA: Ancon Marine, Llc
22707 Wilmington Ave
Carson CA 90745
310 522-5110

(P-1635)
ANTIS ROOFG WATERPROOFING LLC
2649 Campus Dr, Irvine (92612-1601)
PHONE................................949 461-9222
Charles G Antis, *President*
Drew Smith, *Executive*
Susan Degrassi, *VP Admin*
Morgan White, *Business Mgr*
Ernie Basulto, *Human Res Dir*
EMP: 95 EST: 1988
SALES (est): 18.8MM **Privately Held**
WEB: www.antisroofing.com
SIC: **1799** 1761 Waterproofing; roofing contractor

(P-1636)
ARTISAN GLASS AND DESIGN INC
Also Called: Glazier
2665 W Woodland Dr, Anaheim (92801-2629)
PHONE................................714 542-0507
Robert King, *CEO*
Tim Groff, *Officer*
Ben Gouvion, *Engineer*
Jayme Giesick, *Human Resources*
EMP: 67 EST: 2007
SALES (est): 7.2MM **Privately Held**
WEB: www.artisanglassdesign.com
SIC: **1799** 1793 Glass tinting, architectural or automotive; fiberglass work; glass & glazing work

(P-1637)
ASBESTOS INSTANT RESPONSE INC
3517 W Washington Blvd, Los Angeles (90018-1122)
PHONE................................323 733-0508
Eric Chevasson, *President*
Steven Liedernan, *COO*
Robert Samson, *Project Mgr*
Joy Keaton, *Controller*
Yuri Ubeda, *Manager*
EMP: 65 EST: 2000
SQ FT: 1,500
SALES (est): 7.8MM **Privately Held**
WEB: www.airinc.ws
SIC: **1799** Asbestos removal & encapsulation

(P-1638)
ATI RESTORATION LLC (PA)
3360 E La Palma Ave, Anaheim (92806-2814)
PHONE................................714 283-9990
Gary Moore, *CEO*
Yun Kim, *CFO*
Jeff Moore, *Co-President*
Ryan Moore, *Co-President*
Scott Moore, *Exec VP*
▲ EMP: 128 EST: 1989
SQ FT: 57,000
SALES (est): 287.1MM **Privately Held**
WEB: www.atirestoration.com
SIC: **1799** 1541 1742 1731 Antenna installation; industrial buildings & warehouses; plastering, drywall & insulation; electrical work; painting & paper hanging; plumbing, heating, air-conditioning contractors

(P-1639)
BIG BEAR BOWLING BARN INC
Also Called: Fun Flex
40625 Big Bear Blvd, Big Bear Lake (92315)
P.O. Box 1152 (92315-1152)
PHONE................................909 878-2695
William Douglas Ross, *President*
EMP: 20 EST: 2010
SALES (est): 1MM **Privately Held**
WEB: www.bowlingbarn.com
SIC: **1799** 3949 Bowling alley installation; bowling alleys & accessories

(P-1640)
BIGGE GROUP
14511 Industry Cir, La Mirada (90638-5814)
PHONE................................714 523-4092
EMP: 121 **Privately Held**
WEB: www.bigge.com
SIC: **1799** Rigging & scaffolding
PA: Bigge Group
10700 Bigge St
San Leandro CA 94577

(P-1641)
BKM OFFICE ENVIRONMENTS INC (PA)
816 Via Alondra, Camarillo (93012-8045)
PHONE................................805 339-6388
Peter Sloan, *CEO*
Brenda Sloan, *President*
Angie Bell, *General Mgr*
Lisa Hollander, *Project Mgr*
James Edwards, *Accounts Mgr*
EMP: 19 EST: 2003
SQ FT: 10,000
SALES (est): 12.4MM **Privately Held**
WEB: www.bkmoe.com
SIC: **5712** 1799 1761 2522 Office furniture; office furniture installation; roofing, siding & sheet metal work; office furniture, except wood

(P-1642)
BRAVO SIGN & DESIGN INC
520 S Central Park Ave E, Anaheim (92802-1472)
PHONE................................714 284-0500
Frank Fiore, *President*
Debbie Fiore, *Engineer*
Connie Chaffins, *Bookkeeper*
EMP: 18 EST: 1990
SQ FT: 12,000
SALES (est): 1.9MM **Privately Held**
WEB: www.bravosign.com
SIC: **1799** 3993 Sign installation & maintenance; signs & advertising specialties

(P-1643)
BRICKLEY CONSTRUCTION CO INC
Also Called: Brickley Enviromental
957 Reece St, San Bernardino (92411-2356)
PHONE................................909 888-2010
James L Brickley, *CEO*
Thomas Brickley, *President*
Annorr Gowdy, *CFO*
Shane Brickley, *Vice Pres*
Tim Brickley, *Vice Pres*
EMP: 50 EST: 1980
SQ FT: 10,000
SALES (est): 13.3MM **Privately Held**
WEB: www.brickleyenv.com
SIC: **1799** 4959 Asbestos removal & encapsulation; environmental cleanup services

(P-1644)
CALDERON DRYWALL CONTRS INC (PA)
2085 N Nordic St, Orange (92865-3953)
PHONE................................714 900-1863
Juan Calderon, *Presiden*
EMP: 100 EST: 2017
SALES (est): 6.2MM **Privately Held**
WEB: www.calderondrywall.net
SIC: **1799** Special trade contractors

(P-1645)
CALIFORNIA ACCESS SCAFFOLD LLC
331 Vineland Ave, City of Industry (91746-2321)
PHONE.................310 324-3388
Daniel Johnson, *CEO*
Daniel Styles, *CFO*
James Johnson, *Vice Pres*
Kevin Johnson, *Project Mgr*
Aldo Lopez, *Project Mgr*
EMP: 56 **EST:** 2012 **Privately Held**
WEB: www.cascaffold.com
SIC: 1799 Scaffolding construction

(P-1646)
CALIFORNIA CLOSET CO O (PA)
5921 Skylab Rd, Huntington Beach (92647-2062)
PHONE.................714 899-4905
Bill Barton, *President*
Scott Seigel, *President*
Rob Donaldson, *Vice Pres*
Davyd Funk, *Vice Pres*
Mike Cassidy, *General Mgr*
▲ **EMP:** 102 **EST:** 1982
SQ FT: 3,200
SALES (est): 16MM **Privately Held**
WEB: www.californiaclosets.com
SIC: 1799 Closet organizers, installation & design

(P-1647)
CLEAN HRBORS ES INDUS SVCS INC
118 Pier S Ave, Long Beach (90802-1039)
PHONE.................562 436-0636
EMP: 50
SALES (corp-wide): 3.1B **Publicly Held**
SIC: 1799 Steam cleaning of building exteriors
HQ: Clean Harbors Es Industrial Services, Inc.
4760 World Hstn Pkwy
Houston TX 77032
713 672-8004

(P-1648)
CLOSET FACTORY INC (PA)
12800 S Broadway, Los Angeles (90061-1160)
PHONE.................310 516-7000
John La Barbera, *CEO*
Greg Stein, *President*
Kathryn La Barbera, *Exec VP*
Paris Bernhardt, *Vice Pres*
Joan Focht, *Vice Pres*
EMP: 94 **EST:** 1983
SQ FT: 40,000
SALES (est): 28.1MM **Privately Held**
WEB: www.closetfactory.com
SIC: 1799 Closet organizers, installation & design

(P-1649)
CLOSET WORLD INC
320 S 6th Ave, City of Industry (91746-3126)
PHONE.................800 576-7717
EMP: 110 **Privately Held**
WEB: www.closetworld.com
SIC: 1799 Closet organizers, installation & design
PA: Closet World, Inc.
3860 Capitol Ave
City Of Industry CA 90601

(P-1650)
CLOSET WORLD INC
13272 Garden Grove Blvd, Garden Grove (92843-2205)
PHONE.................714 890-5860
Jerry Egner, *Branch Mgr*
EMP: 110 **Privately Held**
WEB: www.closetworld.com
SIC: 1799 6794 Closet organizers, installation & design; franchises, selling or licensing
PA: Closet World, Inc.
3860 Capitol Ave
City Of Industry CA 90601

(P-1651)
COURTNEY INC (PA)
16781 Millikan Ave, Irvine (92606-5009)
PHONE.................949 222-2050
George Courtney, *CEO*
John Ferguson, *Vice Pres*
Mildred Courtney, *Admin Sec*
Alex Tokunaga, *Controller*
Samantha Cugini, *Manager*
EMP: 80 **EST:** 1994
SALES (est): 34.8MM **Privately Held**
WEB: www.courtneyinc.com
SIC: 1799 Waterproofing

(P-1652)
CROWN FENCE CO
12118 Bloomfield Ave, Santa Fe Springs (90670-4703)
PHONE.................562 864-5177
Eric Fiedler, *Executive*
Eric W Fiedler, *Vice Pres*
Steve Long, *Controller*
Rulie Casique, *Opers Staff*
Paul Eifert, *Sales Mgr*
▲ **EMP:** 96 **EST:** 1923
SQ FT: 36,000
SALES (est): 24.2MM **Privately Held**
WEB: www.crownfence.com
SIC: 1799 5039 Fence construction; wire fence, gates & accessories

(P-1653)
D&A ENDEAVORS INC
Also Called: SERVPRO of Beverly Hills
8484 Wilshire Blvd # 605, Beverly Hills (90211-3227)
PHONE.................310 390-7540
Arezo Jeffries, *CEO*
Daniel Jeffries, *President*
Elliot Jeffries, *Bookkeeper*
EMP: 80 **EST:** 2014
SALES (est): 5.3MM **Privately Held**
WEB: www.servpro.com
SIC: 1799 8744 7349 1741 Construction site cleanup; asbestos removal & encapsulation; ; building maintenance services; tuckpointing or restoration

(P-1654)
DAVIDSON ENTERPRISES INC
3223 Brittan St, Bakersfield (93308-4902)
PHONE.................661 325-2145
Robert Davidson, *Ch of Bd*
Philip R Davidson, *President*
Margaret Davidson, *Treasurer*
Donna Davidson, *Admin Sec*
▲ **EMP:** 20 **EST:** 1959
SALES (est): 6.5MM **Privately Held**
WEB: www.davidsontank.com
SIC: 1799 3531 7699 Petroleum storage tanks, pumping & draining; trucks, off-highway; industrial equipment services; industrial machinery & equipment repair

(P-1655)
FARWEST CORROSION CONTROL CO (PA)
12029 Regentview Ave, Downey (90241-5517)
PHONE.................310 532-9524
Troy Gordon Rankin Jr, *CEO*
Roy Rankin Jr, *President*
Marnie Rankin, *COO*
Marian Rankin, *Treasurer*
Steve Sosa, *Principal*
◆ **EMP:** 65 **EST:** 1956
SQ FT: 42,000
SALES (est): 40.7MM **Privately Held**
WEB: www.farwestcorrosion.com
SIC: 1799 Corrosion control installation

(P-1656)
FENCECORP INC (HQ)
18440 Van Buren Blvd, Riverside (92508-9258)
PHONE.................951 686-3170
T Perrry Massie, *CEO*
Dale Marriott, *President*
Gary Hansen, *Vice Pres*
Rhonda Marks, *Office Mgr*
Jessi Cobb, *Office Admin*
EMP: 170 **EST:** 2006
SQ FT: 5,000

SALES (est): 31.6MM
SALES (corp-wide): 69.2MM **Privately Held**
WEB: www.fencecorp.us
SIC: 1799 Fence construction
PA: Fenceworks, Inc.
870 Main St
Riverside CA 92501
951 788-5620

(P-1657)
FENCEWORKS INC (PA)
Also Called: Golden State Fence Co.
870 Main St, Riverside (92501-1016)
PHONE.................951 788-5620
Jason Ostrander, *CEO*
Mel Kay, *President*
Rene Tavares, *CFO*
John Wilmore, *Exec VP*
Jenna Kornmann, *Administration*
▲ **EMP:** 250 **EST:** 1998
SQ FT: 20,000
SALES (est): 69.2MM **Privately Held**
WEB: www.fenceworks.us
SIC: 1799 Fence construction

(P-1658)
FLIGHT LINE PRODUCTS LLC
28732 Witherspoon Pkwy, Valencia (91355-5425)
PHONE.................661 775-8366
Eric Jensen, *President*
Alex Chavez, *Engineer*
Sean Herndon, *Engineer*
EMP: 59 **EST:** 2014
SQ FT: 86,000
SALES (est): 21MM
SALES (corp-wide): 363.7MM **Privately Held**
WEB: www.wencor.com
SIC: 1799 2399 Renovation of aircraft interiors; seat belts, automobile & aircraft
PA: Wencor Group, Llc
416 Dividend Dr
Peachtree City GA 30269
678 490-0140

(P-1659)
FRESH AIR ENVIRONMENTAL SVCS
10675 Rush St, South El Monte (91733-3439)
PHONE.................323 913-1965
Kevan Stark, *President*
David Delgado, *Project Mgr*
EMP: 60 **EST:** 1993
SQ FT: 7,000
SALES (est): 6.4MM **Privately Held**
WEB: www.freshair.biz
SIC: 1799 Asbestos removal & encapsulation

(P-1660)
G W SURFACES (PA)
Also Called: Showershapes
2432 Palma Dr, Ventura (93003-5732)
PHONE.................805 642-5004
James A Garver, *President*
Georgann Garver, *Corp Secy*
Tidus Gutierrez, *Vice Pres*
Eric Beck, *Director*
EMP: 100
SQ FT: 30,000
SALES (est): 18.6MM **Privately Held**
WEB: www.gwsurfaces.com
SIC: 1799 Counter top installation

(P-1661)
GLOBAL ENTERTAINMENT INDS INC
2948 N Ontario St, Burbank (91504-2016)
PHONE.................818 567-0000
Christopher Hyde, *President*
Teresa Harris, *Executive*
▲ **EMP:** 55 **EST:** 1987
SQ FT: 65,000
SALES (est): 5.4MM **Privately Held**
WEB: www.globalentind.com
SIC: 1799 Prop, set or scenery construction, theatrical

(P-1662)
GOOD FELLAS INDUSTRIES INC
Also Called: G F I
4400 Bandini Blvd, Vernon (90058-4310)
P.O. Box 861657, Los Angeles (90086-1657)
PHONE.................323 924-9495
Judd A Shipper, *CEO*
Ronald Shipper, *Vice Pres*
Yara Garcia, *Project Mgr*
Arlene Peralta, *Project Mgr*
Janet Gregory,
◆ **EMP:** 85
SQ FT: 40,000
SALES (est): 15MM **Privately Held**
WEB: www.gfi-inc.net
SIC: 5719 1799 2591 Bedding (sheets, blankets, spreads & pillows); drapery track installation; shade, curtain & drapery hardware

(P-1663)
GREGG DRILLING & TESTING INC (PA)
2726 Walnut Ave, Signal Hill (90755-1832)
PHONE.................562 427-6899
John M Gregg, *President*
Ronald Boggess, *COO*
Daniel Meyer, *CFO*
Chris Christensen, *Vice Pres*
Patrick Keating, *Vice Pres*
▲ **EMP:** 71 **EST:** 1985
SQ FT: 17,000
SALES (est): 27.1MM **Privately Held**
WEB: www.greggdrilling.com
SIC: 1799 1781 Core drilling & cutting; water well drilling

(P-1664)
HARTMARK CAB DESIGN & MFG INC
3575 Grapevine St, Jurupa Valley (91752-3505)
PHONE.................909 591-9153
Gary Allen Hartmark, *President*
Marnell Hartmark, *Treasurer*
Mikael Hartmark, *Engineer*
EMP: 45 **EST:** 1986
SQ FT: 44,000
SALES (est): 11.9MM **Privately Held**
WEB: www.hartmark.com
SIC: 1799 2434 1751 Kitchen cabinet installation; wood kitchen cabinets; cabinet & finish carpentry

(P-1665)
HEINAMAN CONTRACT GLAZING INC (PA)
26981 Vista Ter Ste E, Lake Forest (92630-8127)
PHONE.................949 587-0266
John L Heinaman, *President*
Gaye Howhannesian, *Treasurer*
Angela Heinaman, *Exec VP*
Mark Heinaman, *Vice Pres*
◆ **EMP:** 50 **EST:** 1988
SQ FT: 4,950
SALES (est): 21.1MM **Privately Held**
WEB: www.heinaman.net
SIC: 1799 1793 Window treatment installation; glass & glazing work

(P-1666)
J PEREZ ASSOCIATES INC (PA)
Also Called: J. Perez & Associates
10833 Valley View St # 200, Cypress (90630-5049)
PHONE.................562 801-5397
Joe Perez, *CEO*
Craig Hammond, *CFO*
Tony Perez, *Vice Pres*
Jesse Hernandez, *Accounting Mgr*
Crystal Vigil, *Accounting Mgr*
EMP: 55 **EST:** 1992
SQ FT: 15,000
SALES (est): 16.5MM **Privately Held**
WEB: www.jperez.com
SIC: 1799 Sign installation & maintenance

(P-1667)
JEFFRIES GLOBAL INC
Also Called: SERVPRO Jeffries Global
8484 Wilshire Blvd # 605, Beverly Hills (90211-3227)
PHONE.................888 255-3488

Daniel Jeffries, *Principal*
EMP: 85 **EST:** 2020
SALES (est): 7.2MM **Privately Held**
SIC: 1799 Asbestos removal & encapsulation

(P-1668)
JOHN S CARTER INC
1102 Highland Rd, Santa Ynez
(93460-9603)
PHONE..................805 962-5889
Mark J Sauter, *President*
Mark Sauter, *President*
Tracy Sauter, *Corp Secy*
EMP: 14 **EST:** 1957
SQ FT: 200
SALES (est): 1.7MM **Privately Held**
WEB: www.jscarterinc.com
SIC: 1799 1389 Shoring & underpinning work; boring for building construction; oil field services

(P-1669)
JONES/COVEY GROUP INCORPORATED
Also Called: Jones Covey Group
9595 Lucas Ranch Rd # 100, Rancho Cucamonga (91730-5725)
PHONE..................888 972-7581
Bret Christopher Covey, *CEO*
James Chamberlain, *CFO*
Robert Christie, *Executive*
Ellen Collins, *Administration*
Sue Hulse, *Administration*
EMP: 63 **EST:** 2001
SQ FT: 2,400
SALES (est): 27.8MM **Privately Held**
WEB: www.jonescovey.com
SIC: 1799 Service station equipment installation & maintenance

(P-1670)
KARCHER ENVIRONMENTAL INC (PA)
2300 E Orangewood Ave, Anaheim
(92806-6112)
P.O. Box 7385, Orange (92863-7385)
PHONE..................714 385-1490
Benjamin R Karcher, *President*
Jeff Spellman, *Project Mgr*
Earl Maijala, *Opers Staff*
Mark Kavanaugh, *Sales Staff*
EMP: 50 **EST:** 1985
SQ FT: 26,400
SALES (est): 10.5MM **Privately Held**
WEB: www.karcherenv.com
SIC: 1799 1742 Asbestos removal & encapsulation; insulation, buildings

(P-1671)
KING SUPPLY COMPANY LLC
6340 Valley View St, Buena Park
(90620-1032)
PHONE..................714 670-8980
Michelle McCloud, *Branch Mgr*
Peter Jimenez, *Sales Staff*
EMP: 91 **Privately Held**
WEB: www.kingmetals.com
SIC: 1799 Ornamental metal work
PA: King Supply Company, Llc
9611 E R L Thornton Fwy
Dallas TX 75228

(P-1672)
M GAW INC
Also Called: Jet Sets
6910 Farmdale Ave, North Hollywood
(91605-6210)
PHONE..................818 503-7997
Michael Gaw, *President*
Jenny Brinkman, *Research*
EMP: 90 **EST:** 1991
SQ FT: 15,000
SALES (est): 10.1MM **Privately Held**
WEB: www.jetsets.com
SIC: 1799 Prop, set or scenery construction, theatrical

(P-1673)
MATRIX ENVIRONMENTAL INC
2330 Cherry Indus Cir, Long Beach
(90805-4417)
PHONE..................562 236-2704
Jason McKeever, *President*
Chris Dickinson, *Project Mgr*

Rhonda Puckett, *Controller*
Patty Martinez, *Manager*
EMP: 60 **EST:** 2003
SQ FT: 9,000
SALES: 21.9MM **Privately Held**
WEB: www.matrixla.net
SIC: 1799 Athletic & recreation facilities construction

(P-1674)
MATRIX INDUSTRIES INC
2330 E Cherry Indus Cir, Long Beach
(90805-4417)
PHONE..................562 236-2700
EMP: 260
SQ FT: 10,000
SALES (est): 15.5MM **Privately Held**
SIC: 1799 Trade Contractor

(P-1675)
MISSION POOLS OF ESCONDIDO
Also Called: Mission Pools of Lake Forest
22600 Lambert St Ste 1104, Lake Forest
(92630-1627)
PHONE..................949 588-0100
Don Ogden, *Manager*
Jessica Wiggins, *Office Mgr*
Humphrey Casey, *Sales Staff*
Gregg Gearhart, *Superintendent*
EMP: 105
SALES (corp-wide): 21.5MM **Privately Held**
WEB: www.missionpools.com
SIC: 1799 Swimming pool construction
PA: Mission Pools Of Escondido
755 W Grand Ave
Escondido CA 92025
760 743-2605

(P-1676)
MOVER SERVICES INC
Also Called: Atlas Mover Services
721 E Compton Blvd, Rancho Dominguez
(90220-1103)
PHONE..................310 868-5143
John Moses, *President*
Michelle Moses, *Vice Pres*
EMP: 50 **EST:** 1996
SQ FT: 33,000
SALES (est): 6.6MM **Privately Held**
WEB: www.msirelocation.com
SIC: 1799 4214 5712 Office furniture installation; household goods moving & storage, local; office furniture

(P-1677)
MP AERO LLC
7701 Woodley Ave, Van Nuys
(91406-1732)
PHONE..................818 901-9828
Christine Paschal, *CFO*
Ryan Hogan, *Vice Pres*
EMP: 85
SQ FT: 165,000
SALES (est): 10.6MM **Privately Held**
WEB: www.mpaero.com
SIC: 1799 3721 Renovation of aircraft interiors; research & development on aircraft by the manufacturer

(P-1678)
NITE-LITE SIGNS INC
25583 Avenue Stanford, Valencia
(91355-1101)
PHONE..................818 341-0987
John Due, *CEO*
Warren Due, *Vice Pres*
EMP: 28 **EST:** 1975
SQ FT: 4,500
SALES (est): 1.4MM **Privately Held**
WEB: www.nlsign.com
SIC: 1799 3993 Sign installation & maintenance; signs & advertising specialties

(P-1679)
PACIFIC AQUASCAPE INC
17520 Newhope St Ste 120, Fountain Valley (92708-8203)
PHONE..................714 843-5734
Johan Perslow, *Chairman*
Cory M Severson, *President*
Kevin Curran, *Vice Pres*
Michael Krebs, *Vice Pres*
Bob Lobo, *Vice Pres*
EMP: 75 **EST:** 1994

SQ FT: 21,000
SALES (est): 16.7MM **Privately Held**
WEB: www.pacificaquascapeintl.com
SIC: 1799 Swimming pool construction

(P-1680)
PARKING NETWORK INC
1625 W Olympic Blvd # 1010, Los Angeles
(90015-3809)
PHONE..................213 613-1500
Frank Zelaya, *CEO*
Rose Zelaya, *President*
Ron Parto, *Vice Pres*
Robert Neer, *Marketing Staff*
Les Quast, *Manager*
EMP: 120 **EST:** 2001
SALES (est): 9.8MM **Privately Held**
WEB: www.parkingnetwork.net
SIC: 1799 8748 Parking lot maintenance; business consulting

(P-1681)
PRECISION PERFORMANCE PRODUCTS (PA)
Also Called: TNT Welding
7747 Edison Ave, Fontana (92336-3633)
PHONE..................909 356-4868
Troy Tinnes, *President*
Steven Huerth, *Vice Pres*
EMP: 16
SALES (est): 1.7MM **Privately Held**
WEB: www.precisionperformance.com
SIC: 1799 7692 Welding on site; welding repair

(P-1682)
PW STEPHENS ENVMTL INC (PA)
15201 Pipeline Ln Ste B, Huntington Beach
(92649-5704)
PHONE..................714 892-2028
Scott Johnson, *President*
Monica Coey, *CEO*
Steve McFarlane, *Vice Pres*
James Brown, *Project Mgr*
Paco Mendez, *Purchasing*
EMP: 234 **EST:** 2008
SALES (est): 32.6MM **Privately Held**
WEB: www.pwsei.com
SIC: 1799 Athletic & recreation facilities construction; asbestos removal & encapsulation

(P-1683)
R-CON GENERAL BUILDING INC (PA)
18017 Chtswrth St Ste 665, Granada Hills
(91344-5608)
PHONE..................818 235-6465
EMP: 55 **EST:** 2012
SALES (est): 565.5K **Privately Held**
SIC: 1799 Special trade contractors

(P-1684)
REGENT AEROSPACE CORPORATION (PA)
28110 Harrison Pkwy, Valencia
(91355-4109)
PHONE..................661 257-3000
Reza Soltanianzadeh, *CEO*
Reza Soltanian, *President*
Everardo Guereca, *COO*
Louie David, *CFO*
Fariba Bolourchi, *Treasurer*
▲ **EMP:** 200 **EST:** 1993
SQ FT: 90,000
SALES (est): 100.2MM **Privately Held**
WEB: www.regentaerospace.com
SIC: 1799 5088 Athletic & recreation facilities construction; aircraft & parts

(P-1685)
REPUBLIC FENCE CO INC (PA)
11309 Danube Ave, Granada Hills
(91344-4323)
PHONE..................818 341-5323
David Woolf, *President*
Bonnie Woolf, *Treasurer*
EMP: 26 **EST:** 1973
SQ FT: 11,000
SALES (est): 4.5MM **Privately Held**
WEB: www.republicfenceco.com
SIC: 1799 3312 5085 Fence construction; structural shapes & pilings, steel; fasteners & fastening equipment

(P-1686)
REY-CREST ROOFG WATERPROOFING
Also Called: Rey-Crest Roofg Waterproofing
3065 Verdugo Rd, Los Angeles
(90065-2014)
PHONE..................323 257-9329
George Reyes, *President*
Georgia Reyes, *Corp Secy*
Michael Reyes, *Project Mgr*
EMP: 80 **EST:** 1969
SQ FT: 10,000
SALES (est): 14.2MM **Privately Held**
WEB: www.rey-crestroofing.com
SIC: 1799 1761 Waterproofing; roofing contractor

(P-1687)
SCENARIO COCKRAM USA INC (DH)
605 8th St, San Fernando (91340-1400)
PHONE..................818 650-0999
Malcolm Batten, *President*
Robert Sirgiovanni, *Vice Pres*
Tom Stapleton, *Vice Pres*
Ryan Trinidad, *General Mgr*
Don Scott, *Prdtn Dir*
EMP: 188 **EST:** 2015
SALES (est): 16.6MM **Privately Held**
WEB: www.cockramscenario.com
SIC: 1799 Prop, set or scenery construction, theatrical

(P-1688)
SCENIC EXPRESS INC
9380 San Fernando Rd, Sun Valley
(91352-1419)
PHONE..................323 254-4351
Kevin Gadd, *President*
Ty Rossiter, *Technician*
EMP: 20 **EST:** 1978
SQ FT: 25,000
SALES (est): 3.6MM **Privately Held**
WEB: www.cmflores72.wixsite.com
SIC: 1799 2541 Prop, set or scenery construction, theatrical; wood partitions & fixtures

(P-1689)
SCENIC ROUTE INC
13516 Desmond St, Pacoima
(91331-2315)
PHONE..................818 896-6006
Ulf Henriksson, *President*
Sean Culhane, *Vice Pres*
Micheal Goglia, *Vice Pres*
Tim Healy, *Technical Staff*
Jordan Woods-Wahl, *Technical Staff*
▲ **EMP:** 50 **EST:** 1987
SQ FT: 25,000
SALES (est): 12.4MM **Privately Held**
WEB: www.thescenicroute.com
SIC: 1799 Prop, set or scenery construction, theatrical

(P-1690)
SHORING ENGINEERS
Also Called: Shoring & Excavating
12645 Clark St, Santa Fe Springs
(90670-3951)
PHONE..................562 944-9331
George A Woodley Sr, *Vice Pres*
George A Woodleysr, *President*
Ren Contreras, *Vice Pres*
Jason E Weinstein, *Vice Pres*
George A Woodley Jr, *Vice Pres*
▲ **EMP:** 60 **EST:** 1966
SALES (est): 12.9MM **Privately Held**
WEB: www.shoringengineers.com
SIC: 1799 8711 Shore cleaning & maintenance; engineering services

(P-1691)
SUNLAND SCAFFOLD
24885 Whitewood Rd # 106, Murrieta
(92563-2014)
PHONE..................951 595-9402
Arnulfo Wiedensohler, *President*
EMP: 60 **EST:** 2019
SALES (est): 1.4MM **Privately Held**
SIC: 1799 Scaffolding construction

(P-1692)
TAIT ENVIRONMENTAL SVCS INC (PA)
701 Parkcenter Dr, Santa Ana (92705-3541)
P.O. Box 11118 (92711-1118)
PHONE..................................714 560-8200
Thomas F Tait, *CEO*
Richard Tait, *President*
Jason Jones, *CFO*
Alex Hoime, *Vice Pres*
Stan Iverson, *Vice Pres*
▲ EMP: 55 EST: 1964
SQ FT: 8,900
SALES (est): 13.6MM **Privately Held**
WEB: www.tait.com
SIC: **1799** 8748 Gas leakage detection; environmental consultant

(P-1693)
TEAM WEST CONTRACTING CORP
2733 S Vista Ave, Bloomington (92316-3269)
PHONE..................................951 340-3426
Dawn Lilly, *Office Mgr*
Jerry R Pacheco, *President*
Stephen Knehans, *Treasurer*
Michael Ellefson, *Officer*
Bryan Girard, *Officer*
EMP: 92 EST: 2009
SQ FT: 7,200
SALES (est): 8.5MM **Privately Held**
WEB: www.twc-corp.com
SIC: **1799** Fence construction

(P-1694)
TESERRA (PA)
Also Called: California Pools
86100 Avenue 54, Coachella (92236-3813)
P.O. Box 1280 (92236-1280)
PHONE..................................760 340-9000
Bob Smith, *President*
James Harebottle, *CFO*
Adrian Herrera, *Human Resources*
EMP: 379 EST: 1985
SQ FT: 10,000
SALES (est): 39.7MM **Privately Held**
WEB: www.teserraoutdoors.com
SIC: **1799** Swimming pool construction

(P-1695)
THE TEECOR GROUP INC
Also Called: Key Environmental Services
1450 S Burlington Ave, Los Angeles (90006-5409)
PHONE..................................213 632-2350
Kalani Childs, *President*
Eric Youssef, *Executive*
EMP: 60 EST: 1999
SQ FT: 5,000
SALES (est): 6MM **Privately Held**
WEB: www.teecor.com
SIC: **1799** Asbestos removal & encapsulation

(P-1696)
TROYER CONTRACTING COMPANY INC
10122 Freeman Ave, Santa Fe Springs (90670-3408)
PHONE..................................562 944-6452
Mark Troyer, *CEO*
▲ EMP: 55 EST: 1995
SQ FT: 15,208
SALES (est): 13.6MM **Privately Held**
WEB: www.troyercontracting.co
SIC: **1799** 1761 Waterproofing; roofing contractor

(P-1697)
VALLEY SUN MECH CNSTR INC
4205 Atlas Ct, Bakersfield (93308-4510)
P.O. Box 515, Oxford IN (47971-0515)
PHONE..................................661 321-9070
EMP: 64
SQ FT: 5,200
SALES (est): 4.3MM **Privately Held**
SIC: **1799** Special Trade Contractors, Nec, Nsk

(P-1698)
WASHINGTON ORNA IR WORKS INC (PA)
Also Called: Washington Iron Works
17926 S Broadway, Gardena (90248-3540)
P.O. Box 460 (90247-0846)
PHONE..................................310 327-8660
Daniel Welsh, *CEO*
Chris Powell, *CFO*
Tom Pederson, *Treasurer*
Luke Welsh, *Vice Pres*
Herb Walker, *Project Mgr*
EMP: 117 EST: 1966
SQ FT: 141,240
SALES (est): 37.6MM **Privately Held**
WEB: www.washingtoniron.com
SIC: **1799** 3446 Ornamental metal work; architectural metalwork

(P-1699)
WATERPRFING ROFG SOLUTIONS INC
11041 Santa Monica Blvd, Los Angeles (90025-3523)
PHONE..................................310 571-0892
Homayoun Kazemi, *CEO*
Mauricio Barahona, *Principal*
EMP: 72 EST: 2001
SALES (est): 11MM **Privately Held**
WEB: www.wandrsolutions.com
SIC: **1799** Waterproofing

(P-1700)
WAYNE PERRY INC (PA)
8281 Commonwealth Ave, Buena Park (90621-2537)
PHONE..................................714 826-0352
Wayne Perry, *President*
Adam Leiter, *Treasurer*
Ed Smith, *Assoc VP*
Daniel McGill, *Vice Pres*
Greg Nicholson, *Vice Pres*
EMP: 185
SQ FT: 4,000
SALES (est): 33.3MM **Privately Held**
WEB: www.wpinc.com
SIC: **1799** 8711 Decontamination services; petroleum storage tank installation, underground; engineering services

(P-1701)
WCC INC
20717 Centre Pointe Pkwy, Santa Clarita (91350-2967)
PHONE..................................661 251-3865
John Woodward, *President*
Lisa Woodward, *CFO*
Guy Woodward, *Admin Sec*
EMP: 14 EST: 1982
SQ FT: 7,000
SALES (est): 2.9MM **Privately Held**
WEB: www.woodwardkb.com
SIC: **1799** 2434 Kitchen & bathroom remodeling; wood kitchen cabinets

(P-1702)
WEST COAST FIRESTOPPING INC
1130 W Trenton Ave, Orange (92867-3536)
PHONE..................................714 935-1104
Karl Stoll, *President*
Brian Collard, *Project Engr*
Joe Riordan, *Marketing Staff*
Angel Andrade, *Manager*
Jarrod Laugenour, *Manager*
EMP: 80 EST: 2007
SALES (est): 6.9MM **Privately Held**
WEB: www.westcoastfirestop.com
SIC: **1799** Fireproofing buildings

(P-1703)
WESTAR MANUFACTURING INC
Also Called: Quik-Shor
13217 Laureldale Ave, Downey (90242-5140)
PHONE..................................562 633-0581
Bill Fick, *Vice Pres*
Chris Musser, *Chief Mktg Ofcr*
Ryan Roth, *Opers Staff*
EMP: 31 EST: 1985
SALES (est): 1.8MM **Privately Held**
SIC: **1799** 3531 Shoring & underpinning work; construction machinery

(P-1704)
WOODS MAINTENANCE SERVICES INC
Also Called: Hydro-Pressure Systems
7250 Coldwater Canyon Ave, North Hollywood (91605-4203)
PHONE..................................818 764-2515
Barry Woods, *President*
Diane Woods, *Principal*
Jeff Woods, *General Mgr*
Josh Woods, *Opers Staff*
EMP: 135 EST: 1975
SALES (est): 17.2MM **Privately Held**
WEB: www.graffiticontrol.com
SIC: **1799** Cleaning building exteriors

2011 Meat Packing Plants

(P-1705)
ASIA FOOD INC
566 Monterey Pass Rd, Monterey Park (91754-2417)
PHONE..................................626 284-1328
Bingham Lee, *CEO*
Chui Lee, *President*
▲ EMP: 43 EST: 1993
SQ FT: 15,000
SALES (est): 4.5MM **Privately Held**
WEB: www.asianfoods.com
SIC: **2011** 2032 2092 2037 Meat packing plants; Chinese foods: packaged in cans, jars, etc.; fresh or frozen packaged fish; frozen fruits & vegetables; frozen specialties; fruit (fresh) packing services; vegetable packing services

(P-1706)
BURNETT & SON MEAT CO INC
Also Called: Burnett Fine Foods
1420 S Myrtle Ave, Monrovia (91016-4153)
PHONE..................................626 357-2165
Donald L Burnett, *President*
Chris Glosson, *VP Bus Dvlpt*
Marissa Casella, *Sales Staff*
▲ EMP: 80 EST: 1978
SQ FT: 20,000
SALES (est): 26.3MM **Privately Held**
WEB: www.burnettandson.com
SIC: **2011** Meat by-products from meat slaughtered on site; beef products from beef slaughtered on site

(P-1707)
CARGILL MEAT SOLUTIONS CORP
13034 Excelsior Dr, Norwalk (90650-6867)
PHONE..................................562 345-5240
EMP: 391
SALES (corp-wide): 113.4B **Privately Held**
WEB: www.cargill.com
SIC: **2011** Meat packing plants
HQ: Cargill Meat Solutions Corp
151 N Main St Ste 900
Wichita KS 67202
316 291-2500

(P-1708)
CARGILL MEAT SOLUTIONS CORP
Cargill Food Distribution
10602 N Trademark Pkwy # 500, Rancho Cucamonga (91730-5937)
PHONE..................................909 476-3120
Guy Milam, *General Mgr*
EMP: 391
SALES (corp-wide): 113.4B **Privately Held**
WEB: www.cargill.com
SIC: **2011** Meat by-products from meat slaughtered on site
HQ: Cargill Meat Solutions Corp
151 N Main St Ste 900
Wichita KS 67202
316 291-2500

(P-1709)
CENTRAL VALLEY MEAT CO INC (PA)
10431 8 3/4 Ave, Hanford (93230-9248)
PHONE..................................559 583-9624
Brian Coelho, *CEO*
Lawrence Coelho, *President*

Bruce Hunt, *CFO*
Steve Coelho, *Vice Pres*
Brain Cohen, *Vice Pres*
▲ EMP: 200 EST: 1990
SQ FT: 30,000
SALES (est): 168.8MM **Privately Held**
WEB: www.centralvalleymeat.com
SIC: **2011** Meat packing plants

(P-1710)
CLOUGHERTY PACKING LLC (DH)
Also Called: Smithfield Foods
3049 E Vernon Ave, Vernon (90058-1800)
P.O. Box 58870, Los Angeles (90058-0870)
PHONE..................................323 583-4621
Kenneth J Baptist, *President*
Lidwina Van Kooten, *Vice Pres*
Donna Harkema, *Executive*
Marcos Ortega, *Planning Mgr*
Keith Lee, *Planning*
EMP: 300
SQ FT: 1,000,000
SALES (est): 242.1MM **Privately Held**
WEB: www.farmerjohn.com
SIC: **2011** 2013 Meat packing plants; sausages & other prepared meats
HQ: Smithfield Foods, Inc.
200 Commerce St
Smithfield VA 23430
757 365-3000

(P-1711)
FIRSTCLASS FOODS - TROJAN INC
Also Called: First Class Foods
12500 Inglewood Ave, Hawthorne (90250-4217)
P.O. Box 2397 (90251-2397)
PHONE..................................310 676-2500
Salomon Benzimra, *President*
Lucy Benzimra, *CFO*
Albert Benzimra, *Corp Secy*
Felix Benzimra, *VP Sales*
EMP: 135 EST: 1963
SQ FT: 45,000
SALES (est): 22MM **Publicly Held**
WEB: www.firstclassfoods.com
SIC: **2011** 5147 Meat packing plants; meats & meat products
HQ: Us Foods, Inc.
9399 W Higgins Rd # 100
Rosemont IL 60018

(P-1712)
GAYLORDS HRI MEATS
Also Called: Gaylord's Meat Co
1100 E Ash Ave Ste C, Fullerton (92831-5004)
PHONE..................................714 526-2278
Michael Smith, *Ch of Bd*
Vance Dixon, *President*
EMP: 18 EST: 1975
SQ FT: 10,000
SALES (est): 1.9MM **Privately Held**
WEB: www.gaylordsmeatcompany.com
SIC: **2011** 5147 5144 Meat packing plants; meats & meat products; poultry & poultry products

(P-1713)
GOLDEN WEST FOOD GROUP INC (PA)
4401 S Downey Rd, Vernon (90058-2518)
PHONE..................................888 807-3663
Erik Litmanovich, *CEO*
Michael Bean, *Vice Pres*
Ernie Ruiz, *Warehouse Mgr*
Pano Fragoulis, *Senior Mgr*
Steven Kwun, *Manager*
EMP: 34 EST: 1985
SALES (est): 256.8MM **Privately Held**
WEB: www.gwfg.com
SIC: **2011** 2013 2015 Meat packing plants; sausages & other prepared meats; poultry, slaughtered & dressed

(P-1714)
K & M PACKING CO INC
Also Called: K & M Meat Co
2443 E 27th St, Vernon (90058-1219)
PHONE..................................323 585-5318
Felix Goldberg, *President*
Roz White, *Executive*
EMP: 45 EST: 1977

SQ FT: 30,000
SALES (est): 7.5MM **Privately Held**
WEB: www.kmfoodservice.com
SIC: 2011 Meat packing plants

(P-1716)
MATTERN SAUSAGES INC
1003 N Parker St, Orange (92867-5519)
PHONE..................714 628-9630
William Matter, *Manager*
EMP: 14
SQ FT: 6,123
SALES (corp-wide): 1.2MM **Privately Held**
SIC: 2011 Meat packing plants
PA: Mattern Sausages, Inc.
4327 E Chapman Ave
Orange CA 92869
714 639-3550

(P-1716)
NAGLES VEAL INC
1411 E Base Line St, San Bernardino (92410-4113)
PHONE..................909 383-7075
Michael Lemler, *President*
Timothy Haggard, *General Mgr*
Cathy Martin,
▲ **EMP:** 50 **EST:** 1983
SQ FT: 12,500
SALES (est): 12.7MM **Privately Held**
WEB: www.nagleveal.com
SIC: 2011 Veal from meat slaughtered on site; beef products from beef slaughtered on site; lamb products from lamb slaughtered on site

(P-1717)
OWB PACKERS LLC
57 Shank Rd, Brawley (92227-9616)
PHONE..................760 351-2700
Eric W Brandt, *Mng Member*
Patrick Towle, *Finance*
EMP: 36 **EST:** 2016
SALES (est): 7.4MM **Privately Held**
WEB: www.oneworldbeef.com
SIC: 2011 Meat packing plants

(P-1718)
R B R MEAT COMPANY INC
Also Called: Rightway
5151 Alcoa Ave, Vernon (90058-3715)
P.O. Box 58225, Los Angeles (90058-0225)
PHONE..................323 973-4868
Irwin Miller, *President*
Larry Vanden Bos, *Vice Pres*
James Craig, *Vice Pres*
EMP: 87 **EST:** 1951
SQ FT: 65,000
SALES (est): 7.1MM **Privately Held**
SIC: 2011 Meat packing plants

(P-1719)
SERV-RITE MEAT COMPANY INC
Also Called: Packers Bar M
2515 N San Fernando Rd, Los Angeles (90065-1325)
P.O. Box 65026 (90065-0026)
PHONE..................323 227-1911
Gary Marks, *CEO*
Norman Marks, *Vice Pres*
Norma Marks, *Admin Sec*
Nora Hizon, *Human Res Dir*
Al Hamichart, *Manager*
EMP: 55 **EST:** 1976
SQ FT: 55,000
SALES (est): 14.7MM **Privately Held**
WEB: www.bar-m.com
SIC: 2011 Meat packing plants

(P-1720)
SSRE HOLDINGS LLC
Also Called: Signature Fresh
18901 Railroad St, City of Industry (91748-1322)
PHONE..................800 314-2098
Stanley Joseph Wetch, *Mng Member*
EMP: 100 **EST:** 2014
SALES (est): 18.2MM **Privately Held**
SIC: 2011 Meat by-products from meat slaughtered on site

(P-1721)
UNITED FOOD GROUP LLC
3425 E Vernon Ave, Vernon (90058-1811)
PHONE..................323 588-5286

Dayle Kanemaki, *Director*
EMP: 17 **EST:** 1995
SALES (est): 400.5K **Privately Held**
SIC: 2011 Meat packing plants

(P-1722)
V J PROVISION INC
Also Called: Jacobellis
410 S Varney St, Burbank (91502-2124)
PHONE..................818 843-3945
Sam Jacobellis, *President*
George Jacobellis, *Treasurer*
Vito Jacobellis, *Vice Pres*
Tony Jacobellis, *Admin Sec*
EMP: 17 **EST:** 1974
SQ FT: 11,300
SALES (est): 257.4K **Privately Held**
SIC: 2011 Meat packing plants

(P-1723)
VENUS FOODS INC
770 S Stimson Ave, City of Industry (91745-1638)
PHONE..................626 369-5188
Gin Shen Wu, *Ch of Bd*
Robert Y Tsai, *President*
Shih-Ai Meng, *Treasurer*
T K Chow, *Vice Pres*
▲ **EMP:** 20 **EST:** 1980
SQ FT: 20,000
SALES (est): 2.4MM **Privately Held**
WEB: www.venusfoods.com
SIC: 2011 2099 Meat packing plants; food preparations

(P-1724)
VIZ CATTLE CORPORATION
Also Called: Sukarne
17890 Castleton St # 350, City of Industry (91748-5793)
PHONE..................310 884-5260
Edwin Botero, *President*
Juan Castro, *Sales Staff*
▲ **EMP:** 24 **EST:** 1992
SALES (est): 8MM **Privately Held**
WEB: www.sukarne.com
SIC: 2011 5154 Meat packing plants; cattle
PA: Grupo Viz, S.A. De C.V.
Av. Diana Tang No. 59-A
Culiacan SIN. 80300

(P-1725)
WEST LAKE FOOD CORPORATION
Also Called: Tay Ho
301 N Sullivan St, Santa Ana (92703-3417)
PHONE..................714 973-2286
Chieu Nguyen, *CEO*
Chuong Nguyen, *Vice Pres*
Jayce Yenson, *Admin Sec*
◆ **EMP:** 75 **EST:** 1986
SALES (est): 13.8MM **Privately Held**
SIC: 2011 Meat packing plants

2013 Sausages & Meat Prdts

(P-1726)
ALPENA SAUSAGE INC
5329 Craner Ave, North Hollywood (91601-3313)
PHONE..................818 505-9482
Frederick Thaller, *President*
EMP: 17 **EST:** 1969
SQ FT: 6,000
SALES (est): 211.2K **Privately Held**
SIC: 2013 Sausages from purchased meat

(P-1727)
BAR-S FOODS CO
Also Called: Bar-S Foods Co. Los Angeles
4919 Alcoa Ave, Vernon (90058-3022)
PHONE..................323 589-3600
EMP: 92 **Privately Held**
WEB: www.bar-s.com
SIC: 2013 Sausages & other prepared meats
HQ: Bar-S Foods Co.
5090 N 40th St Ste 300
Phoenix AZ 85018
602 264-7272

(P-1728)
BOYD SPECIALTIES LLC
1016 E Cooley Dr Ste N, Colton (92324-3962)
PHONE..................909 219-5120
Jae Boyd, *CEO*
Sue Boyd, *Officer*
▲ **EMP:** 52 **EST:** 2008
SQ FT: 10,000
SALES (est): 6MM **Privately Held**
SIC: 2013 Snack sticks, including jerky: from purchased meat

(P-1729)
C R W DISTRIBUTORS INC
1223 Wilshire Blvd # 153, Santa Monica (90403-5406)
PHONE..................310 463-4577
Brian Wrye, *President*
EMP: 13 **EST:** 1989
SQ FT: 7,000
SALES (est): 162.8K **Privately Held**
SIC: 2013 Prepared beef products from purchased beef

(P-1730)
CATTANEO BROS INC
769 Caudill St, San Luis Obispo (93401-5729)
PHONE..................805 543-7188
Mike Kaney, *President*
Jayne Kaney, *Corp Secy*
William Cattaneo Sr, *Founder*
Ken Castro, *Production*
Katelyn Kaney, *Marketing Staff*
EMP: 20 **EST:** 1946
SQ FT: 5,500
SALES (est): 2.8MM **Privately Held**
WEB: www.cattaneobros.com
SIC: 2013 5961 Beef, dried: from purchased meat; sausages from purchased meat; food, mail order

(P-1731)
DEREK AND CONSTANCE LEE CORP (PA)
Also Called: Great River Food
19355 San Jose Ave, City of Industry (91748-1420)
PHONE..................909 595-8831
Derek E Lee, *President*
▲ **EMP:** 95 **EST:** 1985
SQ FT: 50,000
SALES (est): 16.4MM **Privately Held**
WEB: www.greatriverfood.com
SIC: 2013 1541 Sausages & other prepared meats; food products manufacturing or packing plant construction

(P-1732)
FORMOSA MEAT COMPANY INC
Also Called: Universal Meat Company
10646 Fulton Ct, Rancho Cucamonga (91730-4848)
PHONE..................909 987-0470
Cheng-Ting Shih, *Vice Pres*
Hsiu-O Kan, *Treasurer*
▲ **EMP:** 40 **EST:** 1995
SQ FT: 23,000
SALES (est): 6.6MM **Privately Held**
WEB: www.formosa.com
SIC: 2013 Snack sticks, including jerky: from purchased meat

(P-1733)
GOLDEN ISLAND JERKY CO INC (DH)
10646 Fulton Ct, Rancho Cucamonga (91730-4848)
PHONE..................844 362-3222
Cheng Shih, *President*
▲ **EMP:** 23 **EST:** 2012
SALES (est): 21.1MM
SALES (corp-wide): 47B **Publicly Held**
WEB: www.goldenislandjerky.com
SIC: 2013 Snack sticks, including jerky: from purchased meat
HQ: The Hillshire Brands Company
400 S Jefferson St Ste 1n
Chicago IL 60607
312 614-6000

(P-1734)
HAWA CORPORATION (PA)
Also Called: Beef Jerky Factory
125 E Laurel St, Colton (92324-2462)
PHONE..................909 825-8882
Waleed Saab, *Vice Pres*
EMP: 18 **EST:** 2009
SQ FT: 34,500
SALES (est): 4.9MM **Privately Held**
WEB: www.enjoybeefjerky.com
SIC: 2013 Beef, dried: from purchased meat

(P-1735)
HORMEL FOODS CORP SVCS LLC
2 Venture Ste 250, Irvine (92618-7408)
PHONE..................949 753-5350
Randy Kemmipz, *Manager*
Judy Alcala, *Manager*
EMP: 20
SALES (corp-wide): 9.6B **Publicly Held**
WEB: www.hormelfoods.com
SIC: 2013 Canned meats (except baby food) from purchased meat: beef stew from purchased meat; corned beef from purchased meat; spreads, sandwich: meat from purchased meat
HQ: Hormel Foods Corporate Services, Llc
1 Hormel Pl
Austin MN 55912

(P-1736)
KITCHEN CUTS LLC
6045 District Blvd, Maywood (90270-3560)
PHONE..................323 560-7415
Raul Tapia Sr, *CEO*
EMP: 77 **EST:** 2011
SALES (est): 3.5MM
SALES (corp-wide): 95.1MM **Privately Held**
WEB: www.kitchen-cuts.com
SIC: 2013 Beef stew from purchased meat
PA: Tapia Enterprises, Inc.
6067 District Blvd
Maywood CA 90270
323 560-7415

(P-1737)
KMB FOODS INC (PA)
1010 S Sierra Way, San Bernardino (92408-2124)
PHONE..................626 447-0545
Scott Biedermann, *President*
Sam Mangiaterra, *COO*
Becky Benham, *Administration*
▲ **EMP:** 20 **EST:** 1998
SQ FT: 6,000
SALES (est): 3.5MM **Privately Held**
SIC: 2013 2099 Prepared beef products from purchased beef; food preparations

(P-1738)
KRUSE AND SON INC
235 Kruse Ave, Monrovia (91016-4899)
P.O. Box 945 (91017-0945)
PHONE..................626 358-4536
David R Kruse, *CEO*
EMP: 25 **EST:** 1949
SQ FT: 20,000
SALES (est): 8.3MM **Privately Held**
WEB: www.kruseandson.com
SIC: 2013 Ham, smoked: from purchased meat

(P-1739)
LA ESPANOLA MEATS INC
25020 Doble Ave, Harbor City (90710-3155)
PHONE..................310 539-0455
Alex Motamedi, *CEO*
Juana Faraone, *President*
Frank Faraone, *Treasurer*
◆ **EMP:** 25 **EST:** 1975
SQ FT: 8,800
SALES (est): 3.8MM **Privately Held**
WEB: www.laespanolameats.com
SIC: 2013 5421 Sausages & related products, from purchased meat; meat markets, including freezer provisioners

(P-1740)
MARISA FOODS LLC
1401 Santa Fe Ave, Long Beach
(90813-1236)
PHONE...................................562 437-7775
Vincent Passanisi,
Liana Passanisi,
EMP: 13 **EST:** 2007
SALES (est): 1.7MM **Privately Held**
WEB: www.marisafoods.com
SIC: 2013 Sausages & other prepared
meats

(P-1741)
**ONE WORLD MEAT COMPANY
LLC**
6363 Knott Ave, Buena Park (90620-1021)
PHONE...................................800 782-1670
Eric Brandt, *CEO*
EMP: 15 **EST:** 2019
SALES (est): 1.7MM **Privately Held**
SIC: 2013 Prepared beef products from
purchased beef

(P-1742)
**PAMPANGA FOODS COMPANY
INC**
1835 N Orngthrp Park A, Anaheim
(92801-1143)
PHONE...................................714 773-0537
Ray Reyes, *President*
Coni Reyes, *Vice Pres*
EMP: 69 **EST:** 1984
SQ FT: 11,000
SALES (est): 13.5MM **Privately Held**
WEB: www.pampangafood.com
SIC: 2013 5812 8742 2011 Sausages &
other prepared meats; eating places; food
& beverage consultant; sausages from
meat slaughtered on site; ethnic foods,
frozen; food preparations

(P-1743)
**PAPA CANTELLAS
INCORPORATED**
Also Called: Papa Cantella's Sausage Plant
3341 E 50th St, Vernon (90058-3003)
PHONE...................................323 584-7272
Thomas P Cantella, *CEO*
Chris Stafford, *Vice Pres*
Roche Sanchez, *Purch Mgr*
Tracy Perry, *Sales Staff*
Gladys Betancourt, *Manager*
EMP: 60 **EST:** 1981
SQ FT: 13,000
SALES (est): 13.3MM **Privately Held**
WEB: www.papacantella.com
SIC: 2013 Sausages from purchased meat

(P-1744)
PEOPLES SAUSAGE COMPANY
1132 E Pico Blvd, Los Angeles
(90021-2224)
PHONE...................................213 627-8633
Mark Bianchetti, *President*
EMP: 16 **EST:** 1929
SQ FT: 5,500
SALES (est): 2.4MM **Privately Held**
WEB: www.peopleschoicebeefjerky.com
SIC: 2013 5147 Beef, dried: from pur-
chased meat; meats, fresh

(P-1745)
POCINO FOODS COMPANY
14250 Lomitas Ave, City of Industry
(91746-3014)
P.O. Box 2219, La Puente (91746-0219)
PHONE...................................626 968-8000
Frank J Pocino, *President*
Ravi Sheshadri, *CFO*
Jim Pierson, *Vice Pres*
Frank G Pocino, *Vice Pres*
Connie Rivas, *Technician*
▲ **EMP:** 100 **EST:** 1933
SQ FT: 70,000
SALES (est): 24.7MM **Privately Held**
WEB: www.pocinofoods.com
SIC: 2013 Sausages from purchased meat

(P-1746)
PROVENA FOODS INC (HQ)
5010 Eucalyptus Ave, Chino (91710-9216)
PHONE...................................909 627-1082
Theodore L Arena, *President*
Thomas J Mulroney, *CFO*

Santo Zito, *Vice Pres*
Ronald A Provera, *Admin Sec*
▲ **EMP:** 60 **EST:** 1960
SALES (est): 19.7MM
SALES (corp-wide): 9.6B **Publicly Held**
WEB: www.hormelfoods.com
SIC: 2013 2032 2098 Sausages & other
prepared meats; canned specialties; Ital-
ian foods: packaged in cans, jars, etc.;
macaroni: packaged in cans, jars, etc.;
macaroni & spaghetti
PA: Hormel Foods Corporation
1 Hormel Pl
Austin MN 55912
507 437-5611

(P-1747)
RAEMICA INC
Also Called: Far West Meats
7759 Victoria Ave, Highland (92346-5637)
P.O. Box 248 (92346-0248)
PHONE...................................909 864-1990
Thomas R Serrato, *CEO*
Michael Serrato, *Corp Secy*
Wade Snyder, *Vice Pres*
EMP: 41 **EST:** 1978
SQ FT: 35,000
SALES (est): 7.4MM **Privately Held**
WEB: www.farwestmeat.com
SIC: 2013 5421 Cured meats from pur-
chased meat; meat markets, including
freezer provisioners

(P-1748)
RICE FIELD CORPORATION
14500 Valley Blvd, City of Industry
(91746-2918)
PHONE...................................626 968-6917
Derek Lee, *Principal*
▲ **EMP:** 120
SQ FT: 100,000
SALES (est): 18.9MM **Privately Held**
WEB: www.ricefieldcorporation.com
SIC: 2013 Sausages & other prepared
meats

(P-1749)
S & S FOODS LLC
1120 W Foothill Blvd, Azusa (91702-2818)
PHONE...................................626 633-1609
Kirk Smith,
Randy Shuman, *President*
Robert Horowitz, *CEO*
Horst Sieben, *CFO*
Richard Shiraishi, *Vice Pres*
▲ **EMP:** 220 **EST:** 1998
SQ FT: 115,000
SALES (est): 46.9MM
SALES (corp-wide): 972MM **Privately
Held**
WEB: www.ctifoods.com
SIC: 2013 Cooked meats from purchased
meat
HQ: Cti Foods Holding Co., Llc
2106 E State Highway 114 # 400
Southlake TX 76092

(P-1750)
SAAB ENTERPRISES INC
Also Called: Enjoy Food
1433 Miller Dr, Colton (92324-2456)
PHONE...................................909 823-2228
Waleed Saab, *President*
Walleb Saab, *President*
Saadi Kabab, *Vice Pres*
EMP: 14 **EST:** 2001
SQ FT: 38,000
SALES (est): 685.7K **Privately Held**
SIC: 2013 Beef, dried: from purchased
meat

(P-1751)
SETTLERS JERKY INC
307 Paseo Sonrisa, Walnut (91789-2721)
PHONE...................................909 444-3999
Cherron L Hart, *CEO*
Aaron J Anderson, *CEO*
EMP: 27 **EST:** 2011
SQ FT: 20,000
SALES (est): 5MM **Privately Held**
WEB: www.settlersjerky.com
SIC: 2013 Snack sticks, including jerky:
from purchased meat

(P-1752)
SQUARE H BRANDS INC
Also Called: Hoffy
2731 S Soto St, Vernon (90058-8026)
PHONE...................................323 267-4600
Henry Haskell, *CEO*
William Hannigan, *CFO*
Steven Hobin, *Research*
◆ **EMP:** 150 **EST:** 1995
SQ FT: 100,000
SALES (est): 54.9MM **Privately Held**
WEB: www.squarehbrands.com
SIC: 2013 Sausages from purchased meat

(P-1753)
SWIFT BEEF COMPANY
Also Called: Jbs Case Ready
15555 Meridian Pkwy, Riverside
(92518-3046)
PHONE...................................951 571-2237
Andre Nogueira, *CEO*
EMP: 200 **EST:** 2015
SALES (est): 93.2MM **Publicly Held**
WEB: www.jbsfoodsgroup.com
SIC: 2013 Beef, dried: from purchased
meat
HQ: Jbs Usa Food Company
1770 Promontory Cir
Greeley CO 80634
970 506-8000

(P-1754)
T&J SAUSAGE KITCHEN INC
Also Called: T & J Sausage Kitchen
2831 E Miraloma Ave, Anaheim
(92806-1804)
PHONE...................................714 632-8350
Tom Drozdowski, *CEO*
David Armendariz, *Vice Pres*
Mike Aranda, *Production*
EMP: 45
SQ FT: 20,000
SALES (est): 9.2MM **Privately Held**
WEB: www.tandjsausage.com
SIC: 2013 Sausages & other prepared
meats

(P-1755)
YONEKYU USA INC
611 N 20th St, Montebello (90640-3135)
PHONE...................................323 581-4194
Osamu Saito, *President*
Kenji Ikeda, *CEO*
Arihito Tanaka, *CFO*
Don Ferris, *Exec VP*
Hiroyuki Tashiro, *Prdtn Mgr*
▼ **EMP:** 52 **EST:** 1992
SALES (est): 21.3MM **Privately Held**
WEB: www.yqusa.com
SIC: 2013 Sausages from purchased meat
HQ: Yonekyu Corp. Inc.
1259, Terabayashi, Okanomiya
Numazu SZO 410-0

2015 Poultry Slaughtering, Dressing & Processing

(P-1756)
COMMODITY SALES CO
517 S Clarence St, Los Angeles
(90033-4225)
PHONE...................................323 980-5463
William T Zant, *President*
Sal Paramo, *Safety Mgr*
EMP: 120 **EST:** 1967
SQ FT: 14,522
SALES (est): 6.5MM **Privately Held**
SIC: 2015 5144 5142 Poultry slaughtering
& processing; poultry & poultry products;
packaged frozen goods

(P-1757)
FOSTER POULTRY FARMS
770 N Plano St, Porterville (93257-6329)
PHONE...................................559 793-5501
Paul Bravinder, *Manager*
EMP: 464
SALES (corp-wide): 1.2B **Privately Held**
WEB: www.fosterfarms.com
SIC: 2015 5421 Chicken, processed:
fresh; meat & fish markets

PA: Foster Poultry Farms
1000 Davis St
Livingston CA 95334
209 394-7901

(P-1758)
FOSTER POULTRY FARMS
1805 N Santa Fe Ave, Compton
(90221-1009)
PHONE...................................310 223-1499
Ronald Altman, *Branch Mgr*
Arselia Guerrero, *Human Res Mgr*
Norma Bustamante, *Director*
Guadalupe Davila-Rueda, *Supervisor*
EMP: 464
SALES (corp-wide): 1.2B **Privately Held**
WEB: www.fosterfarms.com
SIC: 2015 Poultry slaughtering & process-
ing
PA: Foster Poultry Farms
1000 Davis St
Livingston CA 95334
209 394-7901

(P-1759)
GLENOAKS FOOD INC
11030 Randall St, Sun Valley (91352-2621)
PHONE...................................818 768-9091
John J Fallon III, *CEO*
Marvin Caeser, *Shareholder*
Katty Majailovic, *Shareholder*
Amy Hackett, *Purchasing*
EMP: 40 **EST:** 1996
SQ FT: 30,000
SALES (est): 3.2MM **Privately Held**
WEB: www.jcrivers.com
SIC: 2015 2013 3999 2091 Poultry
slaughtering & processing; beef, dried:
from purchased meat; pet supplies; fish,
dried

(P-1760)
INGENUE INC
Also Called: Q C Poultry
6114 Scott Way, Commerce (90040-3518)
P.O. Box 17238, Anaheim (92817-7238)
PHONE...................................323 726-8084
Nick Macis, *President*
Michelle Macis, *Admin Sec*
Angelique Macis, *Assistant*
EMP: 100 **EST:** 1998
SQ FT: 10,000
SALES (est): 15.4MM **Privately Held**
SIC: 2015 Poultry slaughtering & process-
ing

(P-1761)
KIFUKI USA CO INC (HQ)
15547 1st St, Irwindale (91706-6201)
PHONE...................................626 334-8090
Kuniaki Ishikaiwa, *President*
▲ **EMP:** 90 **EST:** 1989
SQ FT: 52,000
SALES (est): 57.6MM **Privately Held**
WEB: www.kifukiusa.openfos.com
SIC: 2015 2013 2035 Eggs, processed:
dehydrated; poultry, processed; beef,
dried: from purchased meat; seasonings
& sauces, except tomato & dry; dress-
ings, salad: raw & cooked (except dry
mixes); mayonnaise

(P-1762)
**LOS ANGELES POULTRY CO
INC**
4816 Long Beach Ave, Los Angeles
(90058-1915)
P.O. Box 58328 (90058-0328)
PHONE...................................323 232-1619
David Dahan, *President*
Dror Dahan, *Vice Pres*
Dave Popiela, *General Mgr*
EMP: 88 **EST:** 1988
SQ FT: 32,000
SALES (est): 8.3MM **Privately Held**
WEB: www.lapoultry.com
SIC: 2015 Poultry slaughtering & process-
ing

(P-1763)
RICH CHICKS LLC
13771 Gramercy Pl, Gardena
(90249-2470)
PHONE...................................209 879-4104
Charlie Brust, *Vice Pres*
EMP: 20 **Privately Held**

PRODUCTS & SVCS

WEB: www.richchicks.com
SIC: 2015 Chicken, processed: frozen
PA: Rich Chicks, Llc
　　4276 N Tracy Blvd
　　Tracy CA 95304

(P-1764)
WESTERN SUPREME INC
Also Called: California Poultry
846 Produce Ct, Los Angeles
(90021-1832)
P.O. Box 21441 (90021-0441)
PHONE................................213 627-3861
Frank Fogarty, *President*
Marlene Fogarty, *Corp Secy*
EMP: 125 **EST:** 1991
SQ FT: 10,000
SALES (est): 11.1MM **Privately Held**
SIC: 2015 Chicken slaughtering & process-
ing

(P-1765)
WIN FAT FOOD LLC
700 Monterey Pass Rd A, Monterey Park
(91754-3618)
PHONE................................323 261-1869
MEI Lan Liang,
Jun Yuan Liang,
EMP: 15 **EST:** 2005
SALES (est): 3.2MM **Privately Held**
WEB: www.winfatfood.com
SIC: 2015 Poultry slaughtering & process-
ing

2021 Butter

(P-1766)
VENTURA FOODS LLC
Also Called: Saffola Quality Foods
2900 Jurupa St, Ontario (91761-2915)
PHONE................................323 262-9157
Tom Bospic, *Manager*
Kari Cox, *Marketing Staff*
EMP: 20 **Privately Held**
WEB: www.venturafoods.com
SIC: 2021 2035 5199 2079 Creamery
butter; dressings, salad: raw & cooked
(except dry mixes); oils, animal or veg-
etable; edible fats & oils
PA: Ventura Foods, Llc
　　40 Pointe Dr
　　Brea CA 92821

2022 Cheese

(P-1767)
ARIZA CHEESE CO INC
7602 Jackson St, Paramount (90723-4912)
PHONE................................562 630-4144
Fatima Cristina Ariza, *CEO*
Ausencio Ariza, *President*
EMP: 40 **EST:** 1970
SQ FT: 8,000
SALES (est): 3.9MM **Privately Held**
WEB: www.arizacheeseco.com
SIC: 2022 Natural cheese

(P-1768)
CACIQUE FOODS LLC (PA)
Also Called: Cacique Cheese
800 Royal Oaks Dr Ste 200, Monrovia
(91016-6364)
P.O. Box 1047 (91017-1047)
PHONE................................626 961-3399
Ana De Cardenas-Raptis, *CEO*
Francoise Mattice, *CFO*
Jennie De Cardenas, *Exec VP*
Gilbert B De Cardenas, *Vice Pres*
Peter Stavropoulos, *Risk Mgmt Dir*
EMP: 230 **EST:** 1976
SQ FT: 82,000
SALES (est): 129MM **Privately Held**
WEB: www.caciqueinc.com
SIC: 2022 Natural cheese

(P-1769)
CASTLE IMPORTING INC
14550 Miller Ave, Fontana (92336-1696)
PHONE................................909 428-9200
Vito Borruso, *President*
Giancomo Borruso, *CFO*

Josephine Borruso, *Admin Sec*
Rogelio Mendez, *QC Mgr*
▲ **EMP:** 17 **EST:** 1989
SQ FT: 68,000
SALES (est): 4.1MM **Privately Held**
WEB: www.castleimporting.com
SIC: 2022 5812 Processed cheese; eating
places

(P-1770)
EINSTEIN NOAH REST GROUP INC
Also Called: Noah's New York Bagels
16304 Beach Blvd, Westminster
(92683-7857)
PHONE................................714 847-4609
Fransico Valdez, *Manager*
EMP: 180 **Privately Held**
WEB: www.bagelbrands.com
SIC: 2022 5812 Spreads, cheese; cafe
PA: Einstein Noah Restaurant Group, Inc.
　　555 Zang St Ste 300
　　Lakewood CO 80228

(P-1771)
EXCELPRO INC (PA)
1630 Amapola Ave, Torrance (90501-3101)
PHONE................................323 415-8544
Peter Ernster, *President*
Gregg Rowland, *CFO*
John H Ernster Jr, *Admin Sec*
EMP: 21 **EST:** 1973
SQ FT: 36,000
SALES (est): 2.7MM **Privately Held**
SIC: 2022 2023 Processed cheese; di-
etary supplements, dairy & non-dairy
based

(P-1772)
GOLDEN VALLEY DAIRY PRODUCTS
1025 E Bardsley Ave, Tulare (93274-5752)
PHONE................................559 687-1188
John Prince, *CEO*
EMP: 103 **EST:** 1996
SALES (est): 9MM
SALES (corp-wide): 2.8B **Privately Held**
WEB: www.landolakesinc.com
SIC: 2022 Cheese, natural & processed
PA: Land O'lakes, Inc.
　　4001 Lexington Ave N
　　Arden Hills MN 55126
　　651 375-2222

(P-1773)
GREEN VALLEY FOODS PRODUCT
25684 Community Blvd, Barstow
(92311-9671)
PHONE................................760 964-1105
Hector Huerta, *President*
EMP: 15 **EST:** 1996
SQ FT: 10,000
SALES (est): 2MM **Privately Held**
SIC: 2022 Cheese, natural & processed

(P-1774)
IDB HOLDINGS INC (DH)
601 S Rockefeller Ave, Ontario
(91761-7871)
PHONE................................909 390-5624
Jim Dekeyser, *CEO*
Peter Dolan, *Corp Secy*
Daniel O'Connell, *Asst Sec*
◆ **EMP:** 15
SQ FT: 4,000
SALES (est): 106.2MM
SALES (corp-wide): 2.5B **Privately Held**
WEB: www.ornuafoods.co.uk
SIC: 2022 5143 Processed cheese;
cheese
HQ: Ornua Foods Uk Limited
　　Sunnyhills Road Barnfields Industrial
　　Estate
　　Leek STAFFS ST13
　　153 839-9111

(P-1775)
KAROUN DAIRIES INC (PA)
Also Called: Karoun Cheese
13023 Arroyo St, San Fernando
(91340-1540)
PHONE................................818 767-7000
Anto Baghdassarian, *President*

Rostom Baghdassarian, *COO*
Tsolak Khatcherian, *CFO*
Ohan Baghdassarian, *Vice Pres*
Seta Baghdassarian, *Admin Sec*
▲ **EMP:** 40 **EST:** 1991
SQ FT: 70,000
SALES (est): 53.5MM **Privately Held**
WEB: www.karouncheese.com
SIC: 2022 5143 Natural cheese; cheese

(P-1776)
LAND OLAKES INC
400 S M St, Tulare (93274-5431)
PHONE................................559 687-8287
Jack Gherty, *CEO*
Ernest Ornelas, *Branch Mgr*
Ted Salmon, *Safety Mgr*
Evan Magana, *Foreman/Supr*
Dion Silva, *Manager*
EMP: 96
SALES (corp-wide): 2.8B **Privately Held**
WEB: www.landolakesinc.com
SIC: 2022 Cheese, natural & processed
PA: Land O'lakes, Inc.
　　4001 Lexington Ave N
　　Arden Hills MN 55126
　　651 375-2222

(P-1777)
LEPRINO FOODS COMPANY
490 F St, Lemoore (93245-2661)
PHONE................................559 924-7722
Dave Direking, *Branch Mgr*
Greg Hyslop, *Maintence Staff*
Tony Rodriguez, *Manager*
John Smith, *Manager*
EMP: 253
SALES (corp-wide): 1.9B **Privately Held**
WEB: www.leprinofoods.com
SIC: 2022 Natural cheese; whey, raw or
liquid
PA: Leprino Foods Company
　　1830 W 38th Ave
　　Denver CO 80211
　　303 480-2600

(P-1778)
LEPRINO FOODS COMPANY
351 Belle Haven Dr, Lemoore
(93245-9247)
PHONE................................559 924-7939
James Leprino, *President*
Kris Gholson, *Project Mgr*
Kevin Lewis, *Project Mgr*
Deana Lawrence, *Enginr/R&D Asst*
David Avila, *HR Admin*
EMP: 200
SALES (corp-wide): 1.9B **Privately Held**
WEB: www.leprinofoods.com
SIC: 2022 Natural cheese
PA: Leprino Foods Company
　　1830 W 38th Ave
　　Denver CO 80211
　　303 480-2600

(P-1779)
LIFE IS LIFE LLC
Also Called: Parmela Creamery
7888 Cherry Ave Ste C, Fontana
(92336-4273)
PHONE................................310 584-7541
Ryan Hayes Salomone, *Mng Member*
EMP: 17 **EST:** 2012
SALES (est): 3MM **Privately Held**
SIC: 2022 Imitation cheese

(P-1780)
SAPUTO CHEESE USA INC
800 E Paige Ave, Tulare (93274-6863)
PHONE................................559 687-8411
Derek Pollak, *Prdtn Mgr*
Bridget Freitas, *Supervisor*
EMP: 300 **Privately Held**
WEB: www.saputousafoodservice.com
SIC: 2022 Cheese spreads, dips, pastes &
other cheese products
HQ: Saputo Cheese Usa Inc.
　　1 Overlook Pt Ste 300
　　Lincolnshire IL 60069

(P-1781)
SCHREIBER FOODS INC
1901 Via Burton, Fullerton (92831-5341)
PHONE................................714 490-7360
Terri McKenna-Rose, *Regl Sales Mgr*

EMP: 29
SALES (corp-wide): 1.6B **Privately Held**
WEB: www.schreiberfoods.com
SIC: 2022 Processed cheese; natural
cheese
PA: Schreiber Foods, Inc.
　　400 N Washington St
　　Green Bay WI 54301
　　920 437-7601

2023 Milk, Condensed & Evaporated

(P-1782)
BETTER BAR MANUFACTURING LLC
6975 Arlington Ave, Riverside
(92503-1537)
PHONE................................951 525-3111
Tariq Kelker,
EMP: 20 **EST:** 2018
SALES (est): 1.3MM **Privately Held**
SIC: 2023 Dietary supplements, dairy &
non-dairy based

(P-1783)
BETTER NUTRITIONALS LLC (PA)
3390 Hrseless Carriage Dr, Norco
(92860-3635)
PHONE................................310 356-9019
Sharon Hoffman, *CEO*
Rosario Bosco, *Vice Pres*
Donel Melendez, *Manager*
▼ **EMP:** 959 **EST:** 2015
SQ FT: 100,000
SALES (est): 400MM **Privately Held**
WEB: www.betternutritionals.com
SIC: 2023 Dietary supplements, dairy &
non-dairy based

(P-1784)
BETTER NUTRITIONALS LLC
17120 S Figueroa St Ste B, Gardena
(90248-3024)
PHONE................................310 356-9019
Sharon Hoffman, *Manager*
EMP: 50
SALES (corp-wide): 400MM **Privately Held**
WEB: www.betternutritionals.com
SIC: 2023 Dietary supplements, dairy &
non-dairy based
PA: Better Nutritionals, Llc
　　3390 Hrseless Carriage Dr
　　Norco CA 92860
　　310 356-9019

(P-1785)
BIO-NUTRITIONAL RES GROUP INC (PA)
Also Called: Bnrg
6 Morgan Ste 100, Irvine (92618-1920)
P.O. Box 3669, Torrance (90510-3669)
PHONE................................714 427-6990
Kevin Lawrence, *CEO*
Curtis Steinhaus, *COO*
Karen L Stensby, *Treasurer*
Jack Thomas, *Vice Pres*
Jennifer Pera, *Controller*
EMP: 184 **EST:** 1991
SQ FT: 3,000
SALES (est): 44.5MM **Privately Held**
WEB: www.powercrunch.com
SIC: 2023 Dietary supplements, dairy &
non-dairy based

(P-1786)
BIORAY INC
10 Mason Ste B, Irvine (92618-2773)
PHONE................................949 305-7454
Stephanie Ray, *President*
Tim Ray, *President*
Teri Woods, *Officer*
EMP: 15 **EST:** 1990
SALES (est): 2.3MM **Privately Held**
WEB: www.bioray.com
SIC: 2023 Dietary supplements, dairy &
non-dairy based

▲ = Import ▼=Export
◆ =Import/Export

(P-1787)
BIORIGINAL FOOD & SCIENCE
1851 Kaiser Ave, Irvine (92614-5707)
PHONE..................................949 622-9030
EMP: 20
SALES (corp-wide): 268.6MM **Privately Held**
WEB: www.bioriginal.com
SIC: 2023 Dietary supplements, dairy & non-dairy based
HQ: Bioriginal Food & Science Corp
102 Melville St
Saskatoon SK S7J 0
306 975-1166

(P-1788)
CAMPER PACKAGING LLC
Also Called: Phoenix Custom Packaging
13208 Arctic Cir, Santa Fe Springs (90670-5510)
PHONE..................................562 239-6167
Jason Camper,
Sophary Ly,
Jamie Sanchez,
EMP: 19 EST: 2019
SALES (est): 1.5MM **Privately Held**
SIC: 2023 Dry, condensed, evaporated dairy products

(P-1789)
CAPTEK HOLDINGS LLC
16218 Arthur St, Cerritos (90703-2131)
PHONE..................................562 921-9511
David Wood,
EMP: 21 EST: 2011
SALES (est): 564.1K **Privately Held**
WEB: www.capteksoftgel.com
SIC: 2023 Dietary supplements, dairy & non-dairy based

(P-1790)
ESPERER WEBSTORES LLC
Also Called: Diatomaceous Earth.com
3820 State St Ste B, Santa Barbara (93105-3182)
PHONE..................................805 880-1900
David Stephen Sorensen, *Mng Member*
EMP: 19 EST: 2016
SALES (est): 1.6MM **Privately Held**
SIC: 2023 5499 Dietary supplements, dairy & non-dairy based; vitamin food stores

(P-1791)
FEIHE INTERNATIONAL INC (PA)
2275 Huntington Dr # 278, San Marino (91108-2640)
PHONE..................................626 757-8885
You B Leng, *President*
Vincent Mariani, *Chief Mktg Ofcr*
Hua Liu, *Vice Pres*
Patricia Calderon, *District Mgr*
Aldo Fernandez, *District Mgr*
EMP: 1932 EST: 1985
SALES (est): 362.9MM **Privately Held**
SIC: 2023 Dry, condensed, evaporated dairy products

(P-1792)
FENCHEM INC (HQ)
15308 El Prado Rd Bldg 8, Chino (91710-7659)
PHONE..................................909 597-8880
Shufeng Fan, *CEO*
Alvin Zhang, *General Mgr*
Liang Chunyi, *Sales Mgr*
Mariana Mengwj, *Sales Staff*
Ryan Fortner, *Accounts Mgr*
▲ EMP: 22 EST: 2007
SALES (est): 14MM **Privately Held**
WEB: www.fenchem.com
SIC: 2023 Dietary supplements, dairy & non-dairy based

(P-1793)
GSL TECH INC
3134 Maxson Rd, El Monte (91732-3102)
PHONE..................................877 572-9617
Weihua Zhang, *President*
Shu Zhang, *Vice Pres*
▲ EMP: 16 EST: 1997
SALES (est): 2.2MM **Privately Held**
WEB: www.gslsupplements.com
SIC: 2023 5499 2834 Dietary supplements, dairy & non-dairy based; vitamin food stores; pharmaceutical preparations

(P-1794)
HEALTH AND HAPPINESS H&H INC
10000 Wash Blvd Fl 6, Culver City (90232-2781)
PHONE..................................619 330-6030
Charles Ravel, *President*
EMP: 19 EST: 2009
SALES (est): 1.5MM **Privately Held**
SIC: 2023 Dietary supplements, dairy & non-dairy based

(P-1795)
HERITAGE DISTRIBUTING COMPANY
Also Called: Ninth Avenue Foods
425 S 9th Ave, City of Industry (91746-3314)
PHONE..................................626 333-9526
Ted De Groot, *Branch Mgr*
Jennifer Aguiar, *Controller*
Peter Ulloa, *Maintence Staff*
EMP: 22 **Privately Held**
SIC: 2023 2026 Dry, condensed, evaporated dairy products; fluid milk
PA: Heritage Distributing Company
5743 Smithway St Ste 105
Commerce CA 90040

(P-1796)
K-MAX HEALTH PRODUCTS INTERNAT
1468 E Mission Blvd, Pomona (91766-2229)
PHONE..................................909 455-0158
Angela Ye, *CEO*
▲ EMP: 13 EST: 2005
SALES (est): 186.5K **Privately Held**
SIC: 2023 Dietary supplements, dairy & non-dairy based

(P-1797)
KADENWOOD PER & PET CARE LLC
450 Nwport Ctr Dr Ste 550, Newport Beach (92660)
PHONE..................................949 287-6789
Erick Dickens,
EMP: 25 EST: 2019
SALES (est): 1.3MM **Privately Held**
SIC: 2023 Dietary supplements, dairy & non-dairy based

(P-1798)
KERRY INC
64405 Lincoln St, Mecca (92254-6501)
P.O. Box 398 (92254-0398)
PHONE..................................760 396-2116
Darren Worden, *President*
EMP: 20 **Privately Held**
WEB: www.kerry.com
SIC: 2023 Dry, condensed, evaporated dairy products
HQ: Kerry Inc.
3400 Millington Rd
Beloit WI 53511
608 363-1200

(P-1799)
LONIX PHARMACEUTICAL INC
5001 Earle Ave, Rosemead (91770-1169)
PHONE..................................626 287-4700
Chak Yeung Chan, *President*
Wendy Cheung, *Office Mgr*
EMP: 18 EST: 2013
SQ FT: 5,000
SALES (est): 500K **Privately Held**
SIC: 2023 Dietary supplements, dairy & non-dairy based

(P-1800)
MEGANUTRA INC
17332 Irvine Blvd Ste 101, Tustin (92780-3021)
PHONE..................................949 835-2591
Hai Ou, *Branch Mgr*
EMP: 13
SALES (corp-wide): 884.6K **Privately Held**
WEB: www.naturesnutra.com
SIC: 2023 Dietary supplements, dairy & non-dairy based

PA: Meganutra, Inc.
128 Carnegie Row Ste 107
Norwood MA 02062
781 762-9600

(P-1801)
MUSCLEPHARM CORPORATION (PA)
4500 Park Granada Ste 2, Calabasas (91302-1663)
PHONE..................................800 292-3909
Ryan Drexler, *Ch of Bd*
Sabina Rizvi, *President*
Troy Bolotnick, *COO*
Brian Casutto, *Exec VP*
Christopher Harrelson, *Creative Dir*
EMP: 54 EST: 2006
SQ FT: 30,302
SALES (est): 64.4MM **Publicly Held**
WEB: www.musclepharm.com
SIC: 2023 Dietary supplements, dairy & non-dairy based

(P-1802)
NATURALIFE ECO VITE LABS
Also Called: Paragon Laboratories
20433 Earl St, Torrance (90503-2414)
PHONE..................................310 370-1563
Jay Kaufman, *CEO*
Steven Billis, *CFO*
Richard Kaufman, *Exec VP*
Claire Kaufman, *Admin Sec*
Vicky Hembree, *Purchasing*
▲ EMP: 100 EST: 1971
SQ FT: 25,000
SALES (est): 21.6MM **Privately Held**
WEB: www.paragonlabsusa.com
SIC: 2023 2844 2834 5122 Dietary supplements, dairy & non-dairy based; toilet preparations; suppositories; vitamins & minerals

(P-1803)
NESTLE USA INC
7301 District Blvd, Bakersfield (93313-2042)
PHONE..................................661 398-3536
Andrew Mullins, *Controller*
EMP: 208
SALES (corp-wide): 92.3B **Privately Held**
WEB: www.nestleusa.com
SIC: 2023 Evaporated milk
HQ: Nestle Usa, Inc.
1812 N Moore St Ste 118
Rosslyn VA 22209
440 264-7249

(P-1804)
PHARMATECH MANUFACTURING INC
4480 Shopping Ln, Simi Valley (93063-3451)
PHONE..................................805 404-7169
Aditya Sharma Shrey, *Administration*
EMP: 20 EST: 2013
SALES (est): 1.7MM **Privately Held**
WEB: www.pharmatechmfg.com
SIC: 2023 Dietary supplements, dairy & non-dairy based

(P-1805)
PROLACTA BIOSCIENCE INC
1800 Highland Ave, Duarte (91010-2837)
PHONE..................................626 599-9260
Scott A Elster, *CEO*
Karen Poulos, *Program Mgr*
Matthew Harbowy, *Software Dev*
EMP: 304
SALES (corp-wide): 130.3MM **Privately Held**
WEB: www.prolacta.com
SIC: 2023 Dried & powdered milk & milk products
PA: Prolacta Bioscience, Inc.
757 Baldwin Park Blvd
City Of Industry CA 91746
626 599-9260

(P-1806)
TROPICAL FUNCTIONAL LABS LLC
Also Called: Tahiti Trading Company
7111 Arlington Ave Ste F, Riverside (92503-1522)
PHONE..................................951 688-2619

Lawrence Logsdon, *President*
Jan Obirek, *Vice Pres*
▲ EMP: 15 EST: 1999
SALES (est): 1.8MM **Privately Held**
SIC: 2023 Dietary supplements, dairy & non-dairy based

(P-1807)
VITAWEST NUTRACEUTICALS INC
Also Called: Chocolates and Health
10880 Mulberry Ave, Fontana (92337-7027)
PHONE..................................888 557-8012
Iraiz Gomez, *CEO*
EMP: 13 EST: 2016
SALES (est): 2.5MM **Privately Held**
WEB: www.vitawestnutra.com
SIC: 2023 Dietary supplements, dairy & non-dairy based

(P-1808)
YBCC INC
17800 Castleton St # 386, City of Industry (91748-1791)
PHONE..................................626 213-3945
Xiuhua Song, *President*
EMP: 38
SALES: 2.2MM **Privately Held**
SIC: 2023 Dietary supplements, dairy & non-dairy based

2024 Ice Cream

(P-1809)
ARDENSEL & CO INTL INC
Also Called: Ice Cream Way, The
30131 Town Center Dr # 298, Laguna Niguel (92677-2034)
PHONE..................................949 365-6943
Coskun Suermeli, *President*
EMP: 13 EST: 2014
SALES (est): 797.7K **Privately Held**
SIC: 2024 3677 5065 7389 Dairy based frozen desserts; non-dairy based frozen desserts; inductors; electronic; intercommunication equipment, electronic; styling of fashions, apparel, furniture, textiles, etc.; medical & hospital equipment

(P-1810)
BIG CHILL
10850 W Olympic Blvd, Los Angeles (90064-2014)
PHONE..................................310 441-0643
Diane Dinow, *Owner*
Carrie Russell, *Systems Mgr*
EMP: 16 EST: 1991
SALES (est): 199.6K **Privately Held**
WEB: www.thebiggchill.com
SIC: 5812 2024 Frozen yogurt stand; yogurt desserts, frozen

(P-1811)
BROTHERS INTL DESSERTS (PA)
Also Called: Brothers Desserts
3400 W Segerstrom Ave, Santa Ana (92704-6405)
PHONE..................................949 655-0080
Gary M Winkler, *CEO*
▲ EMP: 119 EST: 1974
SALES (est): 30.6MM **Privately Held**
WEB: www.brothersdesserts.com
SIC: 2024 Ice cream, bulk

(P-1812)
DAIRY QUEEN
1407 E Washington St, Colton (92324-4611)
PHONE..................................909 422-1501
Michelle Kapunski, *Owner*
EMP: 21 EST: 2008
SALES (est): 295.7K **Privately Held**
WEB: www.dairyqueen.com
SIC: 5812 2024 Ice cream stands or dairy bars; ice cream & frozen desserts

(P-1813)
DANONE US LLC
3500 Barranca Pkwy # 240, Irvine (92606-8226)
PHONE..................................949 474-9670
John Mastrotaolo, *Director*

PRODUCTS & SVCS

EMP: 131
SALES (corp-wide): 735.6MM **Privately Held**
WEB: www.danonenorthamerica.com
SIC: 2024 Ice cream & frozen desserts
HQ: Danone Us, Llc
1 Maple Ave
White Plains NY 10605
914 872-8400

(P-1814)
DOLCE DOLCI LLC
Also Called: Villa Dolce Gelato
16745 Saticoy St Ste 112, Van Nuys (91406-2710)
PHONE..............................818 343-8400
Wes Schertz,
Wesley Schertz, *Managing Prtnr*
EMP: 19
SALES (corp-wide): 16MM **Privately Held**
SIC: 2024 Ice cream & ice milk
PA: Dolce Dolci, Llc
23055 Sherman Way
West Hills CA 91307
818 343-8400

(P-1815)
DON WHITTEMORE CORP
Also Called: Dandy Don's Gourmet Ice Cream
501 Library St, San Fernando (91340-2523)
PHONE..............................818 994-0111
Linda Whittemore, *President*
Don Whittemore, *Vice Pres*
EMP: 19 **EST:** 1975
SALES (est): 613.1K **Privately Held**
SIC: 5812 2024 8743 5947 Caterers; ice cream & ice milk; public relations services; gifts & novelties; ice cream (packaged)

(P-1816)
DREYERS GRAND ICE CREAM INC
351 Cheryl Ln, City of Industry (91789-3003)
PHONE..............................909 444-2253
EMP: 131
SALES (corp-wide): 177.9K **Privately Held**
SIC: 5812 2024 Ice cream stands or dairy bars; ice cream & frozen desserts
HQ: Dreyer's Grand Ice Cream, Inc.
5929 College Ave
Oakland CA 94618
510 594-9466

(P-1817)
FARCHITECTURE BB LLC
Also Called: Coolhaus
8588 Washington Blvd, Culver City (90232-7463)
PHONE..............................917 701-2777
Natasha Case, *Mng Member*
Daniel Fishman, *President*
Ryan Bennett, *CFO*
Dan Fishman, *Vice Pres*
Teena Nguyen, *General Mgr*
EMP: 30 **EST:** 2009
SALES (est): 4.9MM **Privately Held**
SIC: 2024 Ice cream, packaged: molded, on sticks, etc.

(P-1818)
HARRISON BEVERAGE INC
Also Called: Harrison Group
726 Arabian Ln, Walnut (91789-1297)
PHONE..............................626 757-1159
Diana Tsai, *President*
▲ **EMP:** 17 **EST:** 2000
SQ FT: 72,000
SALES (est): 1.1MM **Privately Held**
WEB: www.harrisonbeverage.com
SIC: 2024 Ices, flavored (frozen dessert)

(P-1819)
K-CAL GROUP INC (PA)
7171 Talasi Dr Corona, Eastvale (92880)
PHONE..............................626 922-1103
Zhuqi Zhang, *CEO*
Kevin Zhang, *Marketing Mgr*
EMP: 18 **EST:** 2012
SALES (est): 1.8MM **Privately Held**
WEB: www.kcalgroupinc.com
SIC: 2024 Ice cream & ice milk

(P-1820)
MACKIE INTERNATIONAL INC (PA)
Also Called: Sun Ice USA
4193 Flat Rock Dr Ste 200, Riverside (92505-7113)
PHONE..............................951 346-0530
Ernesto U Dacay Jr, *President*
Cruz Coronado, *Clerk*
◆ **EMP:** 40 **EST:** 1983
SALES (est): 3MM **Privately Held**
WEB: www.mackieinternational.net
SIC: 2024 2086 5199 Ices, flavored (frozen dessert); fruit pops, frozen; gelatin pops, frozen; fruit drinks (less than 100% juice): packaged in cans, etc.; baskets

(P-1821)
PARADIS
2323 Honolulu Ave, Montrose (91020-1821)
PHONE..............................818 248-1004
Mark Pedersen, *Principal*
Rory Moser, *Marketing Staff*
Albert Thomas, *Director*
Jesus Hernandez, *Manager*
▲ **EMP:** 16 **EST:** 2011
SALES (est): 423.1K **Privately Held**
WEB: www.paradis-icecream.com
SIC: 5812 2024 5143 Ice cream stands or dairy bars; ice cream & frozen desserts; ice cream & ices

(P-1822)
ROSA BROTHERS MILK CO INC (PA)
10090 2nd Ave, Hanford (93230-9370)
PHONE..............................559 582-8825
Noel M Rosa, *President*
Rolland Rosa, *Vice Pres*
Lance Heath, *Prdtn Mgr*
Kathleen Johnson, *Sales Staff*
Nicole Schott, *Sales Staff*
EMP: 35 **EST:** 2011
SALES (est): 3.5MM **Privately Held**
WEB: www.rosabrothers.com
SIC: 2024 2026 Ice cream & frozen desserts; half & half

(P-1823)
SUPERIOR DAIRY PRODUCTS CO
325 N Douty St, Hanford (93230-3993)
PHONE..............................559 582-0481
Susan Wing, *President*
Tim Jones, *Vice Pres*
EMP: 18 **EST:** 1929
SQ FT: 7,500
SALES (est): 825K **Privately Held**
SIC: 2024 Ice cream & ice milk

(P-1824)
SWEETY NOVELTY INC
633 Monterey Pass Rd, Monterey Park (91754-2418)
PHONE..............................310 533-6010
Traci Lee, *President*
Stephen Lee, *Vice Pres*
Patty Lee, *Manager*
▲ **EMP:** 13 **EST:** 1985
SQ FT: 11,680
SALES (est): 1.4MM **Privately Held**
SIC: 2024 Ice cream & frozen desserts

(P-1825)
THRIFTY PAYLESS INC
Thrifty Ice Cream
9200 Telstar Ave, El Monte (91731-2814)
PHONE..............................626 571-0122
EMP: 32297
SALES (corp-wide): 24B **Publicly Held**
SIC: 2024 Ice cream & frozen desserts
HQ: Thrifty Payless, Inc.
30 Hunter Ln
Camp Hill PA 17011

(P-1826)
TROPICALE FOODS INC
1237 W State St, Ontario (91762-4015)
P.O. Box 2224, Chino (91708-2224)
PHONE..............................909 635-0390
Ruben Gutierrez, *President*
John Hagen, *CFO*
Guadalupe Gutierrez, *Vice Pres*

Yemeni Mesa, *Office Mgr*
Lupe Gutierrez, *Admin Sec*
▲ **EMP:** 49 **EST:** 1999
SALES (est): 27MM **Privately Held**
WEB: www.heladosmexico.com
SIC: 2024 Ice milk, packaged: molded, on sticks, etc.

(P-1827)
WE THE PIE PEOPLE LLC
Also Called: Jc's Pie Pops
9909 Topanga Canyon Blvd # 159, Chatsworth (91311-3602)
PHONE..............................818 349-1880
Jennifer Constantine, *Mng Member*
Thomas Spler,
▲ **EMP:** 50 **EST:** 2012
SALES (est): 2.9MM **Privately Held**
WEB: www.piepops.com
SIC: 2024 Non-dairy based frozen desserts

(P-1828)
ZIEGENFELDER COMPANY
12290 Colony Ave, Chino (91710-2095)
PHONE..............................909 590-0493
Allan Hawthorne, *Branch Mgr*
EMP: 23
SALES (corp-wide): 18MM **Privately Held**
WEB: www.twinpops.com
SIC: 2024 Ice cream, packaged: molded, on sticks, etc.
PA: The Ziegenfelder Company
87 18th St
Wheeling WV 26003
304 232-6360

2026 Milk

(P-1829)
AFP ADVANCED FOOD PRODUCTS LLC
900 N Plaza Dr, Visalia (93291-8826)
PHONE..............................559 651-1737
Corky Fortin, *Branch Mgr*
EMP: 119
SALES (corp-wide): 6.6B **Privately Held**
WEB: www.afpllc.com
SIC: 2026 Fluid milk
HQ: Afp Advanced Food Products Llc
402 S Custer Ave
New Holland PA 17557
717 355-8667

(P-1830)
ALTA-DENA CERTIFIED DAIRY LLC
123 Aero Camino, Goleta (93117-3177)
PHONE..............................805 685-8328
EMP: 134 **Publicly Held**
SIC: 2026 Mfg Fluid Milk
HQ: Alta-Dena Certified Dairy, Llc
17637 E Valley Blvd
City Of Industry CA 91744
626 964-6401

(P-1831)
AYO FOODS LLC
927 Main St, Delano (93215-1729)
P.O. Box 1987 (93216-1987)
PHONE..............................661 345-5457
Matt Billings, *Mng Member*
EMP: 50 **EST:** 2018
SALES (est): 100K **Privately Held**
WEB: www.ayoyogurt.com
SIC: 2026 Yogurt

(P-1832)
CALIFORNIA DAIRIES INC (PA)
2000 N Plaza Dr, Visalia (93291-9358)
PHONE..............................559 625-2200
Brad Anderson, *CEO*
Michael Burdeny, *President*
Peter Enster, *President*
Michael Johnson, *President*
Mark Larson, *President*
◆ **EMP:** 80 **EST:** 1938
SQ FT: 7,878,400
SALES: 3.3B **Privately Held**
WEB: www.californiadairies.com
SIC: 2026 2021 2023 Fluid milk; creamery butter; dry, condensed, evaporated dairy products

(P-1833)
DAIRY FARMERS AMERICA INC
4375 N Ventura Ave, Ventura (93001-1124)
PHONE..............................805 653-0042
Kevin Clark, *Manager*
Steven Hatten, *Plant Mgr*
David Chaparro, *Maintence Staff*
Ricardo Chavez, *Manager*
EMP: 109
SALES (corp-wide): 17.8B **Privately Held**
WEB: www.dfamilk.com
SIC: 2026 2022 2021 2023 Milk processing (pasteurizing, homogenizing, bottling); natural cheese; creamery butter; condensed milk; ice cream & ice milk; roasted coffee
PA: Dairy Farmers Of America, Inc.
1405 N 98th St
Kansas City KS 66111
816 801-6455

(P-1834)
FARMDALE CREAMERY INC
1049 W Base Line St, San Bernardino (92411-2310)
PHONE..............................909 888-4938
Norman R Shotts III, *CEO*
Michael Shotts, *President*
Scott Hofferber, *CFO*
Nicholas Sibilio, *Vice Pres*
Nicholas Sibilio, *Vice Pres*
▲ **EMP:** 100
SQ FT: 110,000
SALES (est): 21.8MM **Privately Held**
WEB: www.farmdale.net
SIC: 2026 2022 Buttermilk, cultured; natural cheese

(P-1835)
GENERAL MILLS INC
1055 Sandhill Ave, Carson (90746-1312)
P.O. Box 4589 (90749-4589)
PHONE..............................310 605-6108
Jeff Crandle, *Manager*
EMP: 25
SQ FT: 62,497
SALES (corp-wide): 18.1B **Publicly Held**
WEB: www.generalmills.com
SIC: 2026 2041 Yogurt; flour mixes
PA: General Mills, Inc.
1 General Mills Blvd
Minneapolis MN 55426
763 764-7600

(P-1836)
GOOD CULTURE LLC
1621 Alton Pkwy Ste 250, Irvine (92606-4876)
PHONE..............................949 545-9945
Jesse Merrill, *Mng Member*
Amanda Beatty, *Research*
Wayne Olson, *VP Opers*
Danielle Sternlicht, *Marketing Staff*
Kinaya Pettiford, *Sales Staff*
EMP: 25 **EST:** 2014
SALES (est): 2MM **Privately Held**
WEB: www.goodculture.com
SIC: 2026 2023 Fluid milk; dry, condensed, evaporated dairy products

(P-1837)
HERITAGE DISTRIBUTING COMPANY (PA)
Also Called: Rex Creamery
5743 Smithway St Ste 105, Commerce (90040-1548)
P.O. Box 668, Downey (90241-0668)
PHONE..............................323 838-1225
Ted S Degroot, *President*
Gary Ericks, *Purchasing*
EMP: 24 **EST:** 1998
SALES (est): 14.4MM **Privately Held**
SIC: 2026 Milk processing (pasteurizing, homogenizing, bottling)

(P-1838)
PAC FILL INC
Also Called: Sun Dairy Co
5471 W San Fernando Rd, Los Angeles (90039-1014)
PHONE..............................818 409-0117
Vahik Sarkissian, *CEO*
Edward Sarkissian, *Vice Pres*
Jerry Nicoghosian, *Admin Sec*
Ed Sarkissian, *Director*
EMP: 25 **EST:** 1977

SQ FT: 22,000
SALES (est): 4.9MM **Privately Held**
WEB: www.sundairy.com
SIC: **2026** 2086 Yogurt; carbonated soft drinks, bottled & canned

(P-1839)
PARAMOUNT DAIRY INC
15255 Texaco Ave, Paramount (90723-3917)
PHONE.....................562 361-1800
Phillip C Chang, *Branch Mgr*
EMP: 135
SALES (corp-wide): 6.5MM **Privately Held**
WEB: www.paramountdairy.com
SIC: **2026** Yogurt
PA: Paramount Dairy, Inc.
    17801 Cartwright Rd
    Irvine CA 92614
    949 265-8077

(P-1840)
STREMICKS HERITAGE FOODS LLC (HQ)
4002 Westminster Ave, Santa Ana (92703-1310)
PHONE.....................714 775-5000
Louis J Stremick, *Mng Member*
Rob Ball, *Vice Pres*
Jin Jo, *Vice Pres*
Robin Rogers, *Executive*
Lou Stremick, *CTO*
▼ EMP: 300 EST: 1916
SALES (est): 448.9MM
SALES (corp-wide): 17.8B **Privately Held**
WEB: www.heritage-foods.com
SIC: **2026** Cream, sour
PA: Dairy Farmers Of America, Inc.
    1405 N 98th St
    Kansas City KS 66111
    816 801-6455

(P-1841)
WIN SOON INC
Also Called: Epoca Yocool
4569 Firestone Blvd, South Gate (90280-3343)
PHONE.....................323 564-5070
Jun Sang Lee, *President*
Byung K Yoo, *Vice Pres*
Brian Ju, *General Mgr*
Justin Lee, *Accountant*
Kris Son, *Marketing Staff*
▲ EMP: 25 EST: 1993
SQ FT: 7,000
SALES (est): 6.5MM **Privately Held**
WEB: www.winsoonepoca.com
SIC: **2026** 5149 Yogurt; soft drinks

(P-1842)
WWF OPERATING COMPANY LLC
Also Called: White Wave Foods
18275 Arenth Ave Bldg 1, City of Industry (91748-1225)
PHONE.....................626 810-1775
Bob King, *Manager*
EMP: 25
SALES (corp-wide): 735.6MM **Privately Held**
WEB: www.danonenorthamerica.com
SIC: **2026** Milk processing (pasteurizing, homogenizing, bottling)
HQ: Wwf Operating Company, Llc
    12002 Airport Way
    Broomfield CO 80021

(P-1843)
YOPLAIT U S A INC
1055 Sandhill Ave, Carson (90746-1332)
PHONE.....................310 632-9502
Terry Lennon, *Principal*
EMP: 13 EST: 2009
SALES (est): 1.1MM **Privately Held**
SIC: **2026** Yogurt

2032 Canned Specialties

(P-1844)
ADESA INTERNATIONAL LLC
1440 S Vineyard Ave, Ontario (91761-8042)
PHONE.....................909 321-8240
Alberto Santiago,
EMP: 24 EST: 2013
SQ FT: 1,500
SALES (est): 3.2MM **Privately Held**
SIC: **2032** Mexican foods: packaged in cans, jars, etc.

(P-1845)
AFP ADVANCED FOOD PRODUCTS LLC
1211 E Noble Ave, Visalia (93292-3040)
PHONE.....................559 627-2070
Barry Ritchard, *Branch Mgr*
EMP: 33
SALES (corp-wide): 6.6B **Privately Held**
WEB: www.afpllc.com
SIC: **2032** 2022 2026 Puddings, except meat: packaged in cans, jars, etc.; soups, except seafood: packaged in cans, jars, etc.; cheese spreads, dips, pastes & other cheese products; spreads, cheese; pastes, cheese; fluid milk
HQ: Afp Advanced Food Products Llc
    402 S Custer Ave
    New Holland PA 17557
    717 355-8667

(P-1846)
CAER INC
Also Called: Yumi
8070 Melrose Ave, Los Angeles (90046-7015)
PHONE.....................415 879-9864
Angela Sutherland, *CEO*
Evelyn Rusli, *President*
▲ EMP: 27 EST: 2015
SALES (est): 3.4MM **Privately Held**
WEB: www.helloyumi.com
SIC: **2032** 7389 Baby foods, including meats: packaged in cans, jars, etc.;

(P-1847)
CALI FOOD COMPANY INC
Cali Noodles
8258 Saigon Pl, Garden Grove (92844-1087)
PHONE.....................714 821-8630
EMP: 23
SALES (corp-wide): 508.8K **Privately Held**
WEB: www.califoodco.com
SIC: **2032** Italian foods: packaged in cans, jars, etc.
PA: Cali Food Company, Inc.
    45401 Research Ave
    Fremont CA 94539
    408 515-3178

(P-1848)
CORN MAIDEN FOODS INC
24201 Frampton Ave, Harbor City (90710-2105)
PHONE.....................310 784-0400
Pascal Dropsy, *President*
EMP: 65 EST: 1995
SQ FT: 40,000
SALES (est): 7.8MM **Privately Held**
WEB: www.cornmaidenfoods.com
SIC: **2032** Canned specialties

(P-1849)
DOLORES CANNING CO INC
1020 N Eastern Ave, Los Angeles (90063-3214)
P.O. Box 63187 (90063-0187)
PHONE.....................323 263-9155
David Munoz, *President*
Frank T Munoz, *President*
Steve A Munoz, *CEO*
EMP: 25 EST: 1956
SQ FT: 5,000
SALES (est): 5MM **Privately Held**
WEB: www.dolorescanning.com
SIC: **2032** 2011 Mexican foods: packaged in cans, jars, etc.; meat packing plants

(P-1850)
FRESH PACKING CORPORATION
4333 S Maywood Ave, Vernon (90058-2521)
P.O. Box 3009, Alhambra (91803-0009)
PHONE.....................213 612-0136
Monica Zambada Lopez, *CEO*
EMP: 20 EST: 2009
SALES (est): 4MM **Privately Held**
WEB: www.freshpackingcorp.com
SIC: **2032** Chili with or without meat: packaged in cans, jars, etc.

(P-1851)
JIMENEZ MEXICAN FOODS INC
11010 Wells Ave, Riverside (92505-2751)
PHONE.....................951 351-0102
Roberto Jimenez, *CEO*
Veronica Jimenez, *CFO*
EMP: 20 EST: 2001
SALES (est): 2.1MM **Privately Held**
WEB: www.jimenezfoods.com
SIC: **2032** Mexican foods: packaged in cans, jars, etc.

(P-1852)
JUANITAS FOODS
Also Called: Pico Pica Foods
645 N Eubank Ave, Wilmington (90744)
P.O. Box 847 (90748-0847)
PHONE.....................310 834-5339
Aaron De La Torre, *CEO*
James Steveson, *CFO*
Mark De La Torre, *Chairman*
Jim Stephenson, *CIO*
Margarito Rodriguez, *VP Finance*
EMP: 125 EST: 1946
SQ FT: 85,000
SALES (est): 50.2MM **Privately Held**
WEB: www.juanitas.com
SIC: **2032** Mexican foods: packaged in cans, jars, etc.

(P-1853)
LA INDIANA TAMALES INC
1142 S Indiana St, Los Angeles (90023-3215)
PHONE.....................323 262-4682
Raul Ramos, *President*
EMP: 15 EST: 1999
SQ FT: 8,000
SALES (est): 1.5MM **Privately Held**
WEB: www.laindianatamales.com
SIC: **2032** Tamales: packaged in cans, jars, etc.

(P-1854)
MEDITERRANEOTASTE INC (PA)
3400 Irvine Ave, Newport Beach (92660-3116)
PHONE.....................714 395-6755
Mary Hidalgo, *President*
Cory Baehr, *Vice Pres*
EMP: 46 EST: 2013
SALES (est): 202.2K **Privately Held**
SIC: **2032** Ethnic foods: canned, jarred, etc.

(P-1855)
SHINE FOOD INC (PA)
19216 Normandie Ave, Torrance (90502-1011)
PHONE.....................310 329-3829
Stephen Y S Lee, *CEO*
Tracy Lee, *Vice Pres*
▲ EMP: 50
SQ FT: 30,000
SALES (est): 13.3MM **Privately Held**
WEB: www.shinefoods.com
SIC: **2032** Canned specialties

(P-1856)
T & T FOODS INC
Also Called: Colonel Lee's Enterprises
3080 E 50th St, Vernon (90058-2918)
PHONE.....................323 588-2158
Michelle MA, *CEO*
David MA, *Vice Pres*
EMP: 50 EST: 1967
SQ FT: 19,000
SALES (est): 9.2MM **Privately Held**
WEB: www.tandtfoods.net
SIC: **2032** 2099 Ethnic foods: canned, jarred, etc.; food preparations

(P-1857)
TAY HO FOOD CORPORATION
2430 Cape Cod Way, Santa Ana (92703-3540)
PHONE.....................714 973-2286
Jayce Yenson, *CEO*
Chuong Nguyen, *Vice Pres*
MAI Nguyen, *Admin Sec*
EMP: 17 EST: 2002
SQ FT: 27,000
SALES (est): 723.1K **Privately Held**
WEB: www.tayho.com
SIC: **2032** Ethnic foods: canned, jarred, etc.

2033 Canned Fruits, Vegetables & Preserves

(P-1858)
ASEPTIC TECHNOLOGY LLC
24855 Corbit Pl, Yorba Linda (92887-5543)
PHONE.....................714 694-0168
Joshua Cua,
Julie Hodson, *President*
Clay White, *CEO*
Noel Calma, *CFO*
Lan Pham, *CFO*
EMP: 117 EST: 2013
SQ FT: 59,300
SALES (est): 7.5MM **Privately Held**
WEB: www.asepticllc.com
SIC: **2033** Canned fruits & specialties

(P-1859)
BEAUMONT JUICE INC
Also Called: Perricone Juices
550 B St, Beaumont (92223-2672)
PHONE.....................951 769-7171
Robert Paul Rovzar, *CEO*
Joe Percone, *CFO*
Joe Perricone, *CFO*
Paul Golub, *Treasurer*
Will Martin, *Executive*
▲ EMP: 98 EST: 1994
SQ FT: 30,000
SALES (est): 24MM **Privately Held**
WEB: www.perriconefarms.com
SIC: **2033** Fruit juices: fresh
PA: G B & P Citrus Co Inc
    1601 E Olympic Blvd Ste 1
    Los Angeles CA 90021
    213 312-1380

(P-1860)
BIG HEART PET BRANDS
Also Called: Star-Kist
24700 Main St, Carson (90745-6321)
PHONE.....................310 519-3791
EMP: 190
SALES (corp-wide): 5.6B **Publicly Held**
SIC: **2033** Mfg Canned Fruits/Vegetables
HQ: Big Heart Pet Brands
    1 Maritime Plz Fl 2
    San Francisco CA 94111
    415 247-3000

(P-1861)
DICKEYS BARBECUE REST INC
Also Called: Dickeys Barbecue Pit
17245 17th St, Tustin (92780-1974)
PHONE.....................714 602-3874
Roland Dickey, *Branch Mgr*
EMP: 25
SALES (corp-wide): 103.9MM **Privately Held**
WEB: www.dickeys.com
SIC: **5812** 2033 Barbecue restaurant; tomato products: packaged in cans, jars, etc.
HQ: Dickey's Barbecue Restaurants, Inc.
    18583 Dallas Pkwy
    Dallas TX 75287
    972 248-9899

(P-1862)
HEALTH-ADE LLC (HQ)
24325 Crenshaw Blvd, Torrance (90505-5349)
PHONE.....................844 337-6368
Jack Belsito, *CEO*
Justin Trout, *COO*
Gary Cooperman, *CFO*
Deborah Moroz, *Officer*
Daina Slekys Trout, *Officer*

EMP: 13 EST: 2012
SQ FT: 38,500
SALES (est): 6.6MM
SALES (corp-wide): 20.9MM **Privately Held**
WEB: www.health-ade.com
SIC: 2033 2037 5149 Fruit juices: packaged in cans, jars, etc.; fruit juices; juices
PA: First Beverage Capital, Llc
1800 Avenue Of The Stars # 1425
Los Angeles CA 90067
310 481-5100

(P-1863)
HK CANNING INC (PA)
130 N Garden St, Ventura (93001-2529)
PHONE....................805 652-1392
Henry Knaust, *President*
Carol Knaust, *Vice Pres*
EMP: 37 **EST:** 1996
SQ FT: 91,552 **Privately Held**
SIC: 2033 Vegetables: packaged in cans, jars, etc.

(P-1864)
HUY FONG FOODS INC
4800 Azusa Canyon Rd, Irwindale (91706-1938)
PHONE....................626 286-8328
David Tran, *President*
Ada Tran, *CFO*
Donna Lam, *Admin Sec*
Christina Martinez, *Representative*
◆ **EMP:** 20 **EST:** 1980
SQ FT: 68,000
SALES (est): 8.6MM **Privately Held**
WEB: www.huyfong.com
SIC: 2033 Chili sauce, tomato: packaged in cans, jars, etc.

(P-1865)
JG BOSWELL TOMATO - KERN LLC
36889 Hwy 58, Buttonwillow (93206)
PHONE....................661 764-9000
Sherm Railsback, *Principal*
James W Boswell, *Principal*
Joel Molina, *Accounting Mgr*
◆ **EMP:** 40 **EST:** 1998
SQ FT: 1,080
SALES (est): 9.2MM **Privately Held**
SIC: 2033 Tomato products: packaged in cans, jars, etc.

(P-1866)
LOS OLIVOS PACKAGING INC (PA)
929 Ridgecrest St, Monterey Park (91754-4622)
PHONE....................323 261-2218
Fax: 323 261-1026
▲ **EMP:** 105 **EST:** 1925
SQ FT: 22,000
SALES (est): 9.3MM **Privately Held**
SIC: 2033 Mfg Canned Fruits/Vegetables

(P-1867)
MONTEREY BAY BEVERAGE CO INC
14535 Benefit St Unit 4, Sherman Oaks (91403-3741)
PHONE....................818 784-4885
EMP: 25
SQ FT: 5,500
SALES (est): 2.1MM **Privately Held**
SIC: 2033 5921 Mfg Canned Fruits/Vegetables Ret Alcoholic Beverages

(P-1868)
NAKED JUICE CO GLENDORA INC
1333 S Mayflower Ave # 100, Monrovia (91016-5265)
PHONE....................626 873-2600
Monty Sharma, *CEO*
Tom Hicks, *President*
Paul Travis, *Vice Pres*
EMP: 400 **EST:** 1976
SALES (est): 19.2MM
SALES (corp-wide): 70.3B **Publicly Held**
WEB: www.nakedjuice.com
SIC: 5499 2033 Juices, fruit or vegetable; fruit juices: fresh

PA: Pepsico, Inc.
700 Anderson Hill Rd
Purchase NY 10577
914 253-2000

(P-1869)
NASCO GOURMET FOODS INC
Also Called: Platinum Distribution
22720 Savi Ranch Pkwy, Yorba Linda (92887-4608)
PHONE....................714 279-2100
Burhan Nasser, *President*
Mary Beth Nasser, *Corp Secy*
Jerry Pascoe, *Vice Pres*
EMP: 90 **EST:** 1990
SQ FT: 42,000
SALES (est): 1.9MM
SALES (corp-wide): 44.5MM **Privately Held**
WEB: www.nasserco.com
SIC: 2033 Seasonings, tomato: packaged in cans, jars, etc.
PA: Nasser Company, Inc.
22720 Savi Ranch Pkwy
Yorba Linda CA 92887
714 279-2100

(P-1870)
NU-HEALTH CALIFORNIA LLC
16910 Cherie Pl, Carson (90746-1305)
P.O. Box 12376, Marina Del Rey (90295-3376)
PHONE....................800 806-0519
Dmitriy Sharin,
Sabrina Jaramillo, *Executive*
Karina Trinidad, *Admin Mgr*
Evan Foster, *General Mgr*
Abel Estrada, *Manager*
EMP: 15 **EST:** 2015
SALES (est): 800K **Privately Held**
WEB: www.nuhealthfruit.com
SIC: 2033 Canned fruits & specialties

(P-1871)
ODWALLA INC
700 Isis Ave, Inglewood (90301-2913)
PHONE....................310 342-3920
Doug Kinsey, *Manager*
EMP: 53
SALES (corp-wide): 33B **Publicly Held**
WEB: www.coca-cola.com
SIC: 2033 Fruit juices: packaged in cans, jars, etc.
HQ: Odwalla, Inc.
1 Coca Cola Plz Nw
Atlanta GA 30313
479 721-6260

(P-1872)
OLAM TOMATO PROCESSORS INC
1175 S 19th Ave, Lemoore (93245-9747)
PHONE....................559 447-1390
EMP: 23 **Privately Held**
WEB: www.olamus.com
SIC: 2033 Tomato sauce: packaged in cans, jars, etc.
HQ: Olam Tomato Processors, Inc.
205 E River Park Cir # 310
Fresno CA 93720

(P-1873)
PRESSED JUICERY INC
2348 Park Ave, Tustin (92782-2702)
PHONE....................714 258-7266
EMP: 14
SALES (corp-wide): 124.2MM **Privately Held**
WEB: www.pressed.com
SIC: 5499 2033 Juices, fruit or vegetable; barbecue sauce: packaged in cans, jars, etc.
PA: Pressed Juicery, Inc.
4016 Wilshire Blvd
Los Angeles CA 90010
310 477-7171

(P-1874)
REFRESCO BEVERAGES US INC
Also Called: Crosby Fruit Products
11751 Pacific Ave, Fontana (92337-6961)
PHONE....................951 685-0481
Kirk Karassa, *Branch Mgr*
Salvador Juarez, *Opers Staff*
EMP: 150

SQ FT: 99,500
SALES (corp-wide): 1.3B **Privately Held**
WEB: www.refresco-na.com
SIC: 2033 Fruit juices: packaged in cans, jars, etc.
HQ: Refresco Beverages Us Inc.
8112 Woodland Center Blvd
Tampa FL 33614

(P-1875)
SUNDOWN FOODS USA INC
10891 Business Dr, Fontana (92337-8235)
PHONE....................909 606-6797
Jeff Wartell, *President*
▲ **EMP:** 30 **EST:** 1998
SALES (est): 4.3MM **Privately Held**
WEB: www.sundownfoods.com
SIC: 2033 Vegetables & vegetable products in cans, jars, etc.

(P-1876)
SUNNYGEM LLC
500 N F St, Wasco (93280-1435)
PHONE....................661 758-0491
John Vidovich, *Mng Member*
Susan Huseman, *Controller*
Buck Moore, *Plant Mgr*
Lisa Lamborn, *QC Mgr*
Andrew Murray, *Sales Staff*
◆ **EMP:** 300 **EST:** 2005
SQ FT: 270,000
SALES (est): 60.4MM **Privately Held**
WEB: www.sunnygem.com
SIC: 2033 3556 Fruit juices: fresh; juice extractors, fruit & vegetable: commercial type

(P-1877)
TAPATIO FOODS LLC
Also Called: Tapatio Hot Sauce
4685 District Blvd, Vernon (90058-2731)
PHONE....................323 587-8933
Jose L Saavedra, *Mng Member*
Dolores McCoy,
EMP: 16 **EST:** 1971
SQ FT: 30,000
SALES (est): 4.1MM **Privately Held**
WEB: www.tapatiohotsauce.com
SIC: 2033 Canned fruits & specialties

(P-1878)
TROPICAL PRESERVING CO INC
1711 E 15th St, Los Angeles (90021-2715)
PHONE....................213 748-5108
Ronald Randall, *President*
Joe Davis, *Consultant*
EMP: 23 **EST:** 1928
SQ FT: 25,000
SALES (est): 4MM **Privately Held**
WEB: www.tropicalpreserving.com
SIC: 2033 Jams, jellies & preserves: packaged in cans, jars, etc.

(P-1879)
VITA-PAKT CITRUS PRODUCTS CO (PA)
4825 Calloway Dr Ste 102, Bakersfield (93312-9707)
P.O. Box 309, Covina (91723-0309)
PHONE....................626 332-1101
James R Boyles, *CEO*
Lloyd Shimizu, *CFO*
Linda Bernal, *Controller*
Lily Hernandez, *HR Admin*
Nick Cook, *Sales Staff*
◆ **EMP:** 50 **EST:** 1957
SALES (est): 32.5MM **Privately Held**
WEB: www.vita-pakt.com
SIC: 2033 2037 Apple sauce: packaged in cans, jars, etc.; fruit juices, frozen

(P-1880)
WALKER FOODS INC
Also Called: La Flora Del Sur
237 N Mission Rd, Los Angeles (90033-2103)
PHONE....................323 268-5191
Robert L Walker Jr, *President*
Denise Walker, *Admin Sec*
EMP: 65 **EST:** 1914
SQ FT: 150,000

SALES (est): 15MM **Privately Held**
WEB: www.walkerfoods.net
SIC: 2033 2032 2099 Canned fruits & specialties; canned specialties; ready-to-eat meals, salads & sandwiches

(P-1881)
WONDERFUL CITRUS PACKING LLC
1701 S Lexington St, Delano 93215-9200)
PHONE....................561 720-2400
EMP: 14
SALES (corp-wide): 2B **Privately Held**
WEB: www.wonderfulcitrus.com
SIC: 2033 Fruit juices: fresh
HQ: Wonderful Citrus Packing Llc
1901 S Lexington St
Delano CA 93215

2034 Dried Fruits, Vegetables & Soup

(P-1882)
HADLEY FRUIT ORCHARDS INC (PA)
48980 Seminole Dr, Cabazon (92230-2112)
P.O. Box 495 (92230-0495)
PHONE....................951 849-5255
Gerald Bench, *President*
James Taylor, *Ch of Bd*
Fred Bond, *CFO*
Dennis Flint, *Treasurer*
John Taylor, *Admin Sec*
EMP: 35 **EST:** 1931
SALES (est): 4.6MM **Privately Held**
WEB: www.hadleyfruitorchards.com
SIC: 5961 2034 5499 5441 Food, mail order; fruit, mail order; fruits, mail order or de-hydrated, except freeze-dried; dried fruit; nuts

(P-1883)
INLAND EMPIRE FOODS INC (PA)
5425 Wilson St, Riverside (92509-2434)
PHONE....................951 682-8222
Mark H Sterner, *President*
Paul Stiritz, *Vice Pres*
▼ **EMP:** 35 **EST:** 1985
SQ FT: 85,000
SALES (est): 9MM **Privately Held**
WEB: www.inlandempirefoods.com
SIC: 2034 Vegetables, dried or dehydrated (except freeze-dried)

(P-1884)
STUTZ PACKING COMPANY
82689 Avenue 45, Indio (92201-2386)
PHONE....................760 342-1666
Jack Stutz, *President*
Patty Stutz, *Admin Sec*
EMP: 13 **EST:** 2013
SALES (est): 4.8MM **Privately Held**
WEB: www.stutzpacking.com
SIC: 2034 Dehydrated fruits, vegetables, soups

2035 Pickled Fruits, Vegetables, Sauces & Dressings

(P-1885)
A-1 ESTRN-HOME-MADE PICKLE INC
1832 Johnston St, Los Angeles (90031-3447)
PHONE....................323 223-1141
Martin Morhar, *President*
Murray Berger, *Vice Pres*
EMP: 16 **EST:** 1972
SQ FT: 40,000
SALES (est): 2.3MM **Privately Held**
SIC: 2035 Pickled fruits & vegetables

(P-1886)
COUSINS FOODS LLC
Also Called: Jericho Foods
2021 1st St, San Fernando (91340-2611)
PHONE..................................818 767-3842
Zadi Janah, *CEO*
Ziad Janah, *COO*
Oana Rosu, *Office Mgr*
Moshe Sarid, *Mng Member*
EMP: 20 EST: 2011
SALES: 2.6MM **Privately Held**
SIC: **5411** 2035 1541 Grocery stores, independent; dressings, salad: raw & cooked (except dry mixes); food products manufacturing or packing plant construction

(P-1887)
GEDNEY FOODS COMPANY
12243 Branford St, Sun Valley
(91352-1010)
P.O. Box 8, Chaska MN (55318-0008)
PHONE..................................952 448-2612
Charles Weil, *CEO*
Barry Stecter, *President*
James R Cook, *Vice Pres*
Carl Tuttle, *Vice Pres*
▲ EMP: 125
SALES (est): 19.3MM **Privately Held**
WEB: www.gedneyfoods.com
SIC: **2035** Pickles, vinegar

(P-1888)
GFF INC
Also Called: Girard Food Service
145 Willow Ave, City of Industry
(91746-2047)
PHONE..................................323 232-6255
Jack Tucey, *Chairman*
Bill Perry, *President*
William Perry, *President*
Farrell Hirsch, *CEO*
Vince Hungerford, *Vice Pres*
▲ EMP: 89
SQ FT: 92,000
SALES (est): 34.7MM
SALES (corp-wide): 455.1MM **Privately Held**
WEB: www.girardsdressings.com
SIC: **2035** Pickles, sauces & salad dressings
PA: Haco Holding Ag
     Worbstrasse 262
     GUmligen BE 3073
     319 501-111

(P-1889)
GINGER GOLDEN PRODUCTS INC
5860 Bandini Blvd, Commerce
(90040-2925)
PHONE..................................323 838-1070
Koichi Takeuchi, *President*
Yoshiji Kono, *Vice Pres*
▲ EMP: 14 EST: 2000
SQ FT: 15,000
SALES (est): 863.2K **Privately Held**
WEB: www.g-ginger.com
SIC: **2035** 2099 Pickled fruits & vegetables; food preparations

(P-1890)
LOS ANGELES SALAD INTL INC
623 W La Habra Blvd, La Habra
(90631-5310)
PHONE..................................626 322-9000
Robert E Hana II, *President*
▲ EMP: 39 EST: 2005
SALES (est): 1.1MM **Privately Held**
WEB: www.lasalad.com
SIC: **2035** Pickles, sauces & salad dressings

(P-1891)
MAJESTIC GARLIC INC
2222 Foothill Blvd Ste E, La Canada
(91011-1485)
PHONE..................................951 677-0555
Lucie Sabounjian, *Owner*
EMP: 15 EST: 2006
SALES (est): 500K **Privately Held**
WEB: www.majesticgarlic.com
SIC: **2035** Spreads, garlic

(P-1892)
MOREHOUSE FOODS INC
760 Epperson Dr, City of Industry
(91748-1336)
PHONE..................................626 854-1655
David L Latter Sr, *Chairman*
David L Latter Jr, *President*
Paul Latter, *Vice Pres*
Mike Paulus, *Vice Pres*
William Marroquin, *Warehouse Mgr*
◆ EMP: 50 EST: 1898
SQ FT: 65,000
SALES (est): 16.5MM **Privately Held**
WEB: www.morehousefoods.com
SIC: **2035** 5149 Mustard, prepared (wet); horseradish, prepared; seasonings, sauces & extracts

(P-1893)
Q & B FOODS INC (DH)
15547 1st St, Irwindale (91706-6201)
PHONE..................................626 334-8090
Kuniaki Ishikaiwa, *President*
Akio Okumura, *CEO*
Jerry Shepherd, *Exec VP*
Norman Ives, *Vice Pres*
Maximilian Bastianelli, *Sales Mgr*
◆ EMP: 69 EST: 1982
SQ FT: 52,000
SALES (est): 48.5MM **Privately Held**
WEB: www.qbfoods.com
SIC: **2035** Dressings, salad: raw & cooked (except dry mixes)

(P-1894)
SLAPFISH HUNTINGTON BEACH LLC
10661 Ellis Ave Ste F, Fountain Valley
(92708-6914)
PHONE..................................714 963-3900
Jethro Naude, *Manager*
EMP: 25 EST: 2011
SALES (est): 396.4K **Privately Held**
WEB: www.slapfishrestaurant.com
SIC: **5812** 2035 Seafood restaurants; seasonings, seafood sauces (except tomato & dry)

2037 Frozen Fruits, Juices & Vegetables

(P-1895)
CALIFRNIA CITRUS PRODUCERS INC
525 E Lindmore St, Lindsay (93247-2559)
P.O. Box 6940, Visalia (93290-6940)
PHONE..................................559 562-5169
Frank T Elliott IV, *President*
EMP: 63 EST: 1983
SQ FT: 40,000
SALES (est): 2.2MM
SALES (corp-wide): 37.4MM **Privately Held**
WEB: www.mr-sunshine.net
SIC: **2037** Fruit juice concentrates, frozen
PA: Wileman Bros. & Elliott, Inc.
     40232 Road 128
     Cutler CA 93615
     559 651-8378

(P-1896)
CANADAS FINEST FOODS INC
Also Called: Reliant Foodservice
26090 Ynez Rd, Temecula (92591-6000)
PHONE..................................951 296-1040
David Canada, *President*
Jamie Zinn, *Officer*
Kathy Bellare, *Purch Mgr*
Joe Demeter, *Opers Mgr*
Sandie Mullins, *Sales Staff*
▲ EMP: 70 EST: 1996
SQ FT: 102,000
SALES (est): 520MM **Privately Held**
WEB: www.reliantfoods.com
SIC: **2037** 2024 Fruit juices; dairy based frozen desserts

(P-1897)
CROWN CITRUS COMPANY INC
551 W Main St, Brawley (92227-2262)
PHONE..................................760 344-1930
Mark McBroom, *President*
EMP: 17 EST: 2007

SALES (est): 1.2MM **Privately Held**
WEB: www.fivecrowns.com
SIC: **2037** Citrus pulp, dried

(P-1898)
DOLE PACKAGED FOODS LLC (HQ)
Also Called: Glacier Foods Division
3059 Townsgate Rd, Westlake Village
(91361-5861)
P.O. Box 5132 (91359-5132)
PHONE..................................805 601-5500
David A Delorenzo, *Mng Member*
Bob Barnhouse, *Vice Pres*
Jasmine Arias, *Admin Sec*
Denise Henslee, *Admin Asst*
Michael Laverty, *IT/INT Sup*
◆ EMP: 550 EST: 1967
SQ FT: 81,000
SALES (est): 256.9MM **Privately Held**
WEB: www.dolesunshine.com
SIC: **2037** Fruits, quick frozen & cold pack (frozen); vegetables, quick frozen & cold pack, excl. potato products

(P-1899)
EXETER SPECIALTIES
301 N G St, Exeter (93221-1123)
P.O. Box 10180, Terra Bella (93270-0180)
PHONE..................................559 592-5999
Sukhmander Smara, *Principal*
EMP: 13 EST: 2003
SALES (est): 619.1K **Privately Held**
WEB: www.cityofexeter.com
SIC: **2037** Fruits, quick frozen & cold pack (frozen)

(P-1900)
IMPERIAL VALLEY FOODS INC
1961 Buchanan Ave, Calexico
(92231-4306)
P.O. Box 233 Paulin Ave (92231)
PHONE..................................760 203-1896
Gustavo Cabellero Jr, *President*
Edna Cabellero, *Treasurer*
Frank Brewer, *Vice Pres*
Fernando Cabellero, *Vice Pres*
▲ EMP: 300 EST: 2006
SALES (est): 25.1MM **Privately Held**
SIC: **2037** Frozen fruits & vegetables

(P-1901)
J HELLMAN FROZEN FOODS INC (PA)
1601 E Olympic Blvd # 200, Los Angeles
(90021-1941)
P.O. Box 86267 (90086-0267)
PHONE..................................213 243-9105
Tracy Hellman, *CEO*
Bryce Hellman, *President*
EMP: 50 EST: 1990
SQ FT: 21,000
SALES (est): 4.8MM **Privately Held**
WEB: www.jhellmanfrozenfoods.com
SIC: **2037** Frozen fruits & vegetables

(P-1902)
JUMP START JUICE BAR
Also Called: Jumpstart Juice
8001 Irvine Center Dr # 40, Irvine
(92618-2938)
PHONE..................................949 754-3120
EMP: 15
SALES (est): 630K **Privately Held**
SIC: **2037** Health And Wellness Spec In Nutritional Juice Bar

(P-1903)
KOR SHOTS INC
29160 Heathercliff Rd # 4273, Malibu
(90264-1083)
PHONE..................................805 351-0700
Jordan Retamar, *CEO*
Rachel Forillere, *Officer*
Michelle Perez, *Opers Staff*
Erskine Smith, *Sales Dir*
EMP: 20 EST: 2017
SALES (est): 2.9MM **Privately Held**
WEB: www.korshots.com
SIC: **2037** 2033 Fruit juices; fruit juices: fresh; vegetable juices: fresh

(P-1904)
LA ALOE LLC
2301 E 7th St Ste A152, Los Angeles
(90023-1044)
PHONE..................................888 968-2563
Dino Sarti,
Manuel Campos,
Daniel Stepper,
▲ EMP: 21
SQ FT: 47,000
SALES (est): 4MM **Privately Held**
SIC: **2037** Fruit juices

(P-1905)
LANGERS JUICE COMPANY INC
129 Stephen St, City of Industry (91744)
PHONE..................................626 336-3100
Richard Barnes, *CIO*
Marcos Bouret, *Production*
Roland Gomez, *Manager*
Humberto Gerdts, *Transportation*
EMP: 300 EST: 2016
SALES (est): 11.5MM **Privately Held**
WEB: www.langers.com
SIC: **2037** Fruit juices

(P-1906)
OXNARD LEMON COMPANY
2001 Sunkist Cir, Oxnard (93033-3902)
P.O. Box 2240 (93034-2240)
PHONE..................................805 483-1173
Sam Mayhew, *General Mgr*
Nancy Low, *Office Mgr*
Peter Vela, *Manager*
Tom Mayhew, *Superintendent*
EMP: 35 EST: 1996
SALES (est): 3.1MM **Privately Held**
WEB: www.limoneira.com
SIC: **2037** 0723 5148 Frozen fruits & vegetables; crop preparation services for market; fresh fruits & vegetables

(P-1907)
PACKERS FOOD PRODUCTS INC
Also Called: Gems of Fruit Co
701 W Kimberly Ave # 210, Placentia
(92870-6342)
PHONE..................................913 262-6200
Ed Haft, *President*
Ivan Veselic, *Vice Pres*
Robert Marks, *QC Mgr*
Jerri Ayala, *Manager*
▲ EMP: 49 EST: 1984
SQ FT: 2,500
SALES (est): 5.2MM **Privately Held**
SIC: **2037** Fruits, quick frozen & cold pack (frozen); fruit juice concentrates, frozen

(P-1908)
QUALITY PRODUCED LLC (PA)
Also Called: Pulp Story
11693 San Vicente Blvd, Los Angeles
(90049-5105)
PHONE..................................310 592-8834
Mitchel Dreier, *Mng Member*
EMP: 34 EST: 2012
SALES (est): 992.8K **Privately Held**
SIC: **2037** Fruit juices

(P-1909)
RAW JUICERY INC
915 Mateo St Ste 207, Los Angeles
(90021-1786)
PHONE..................................213 221-6081
Ryan Davidson, *CEO*
EMP: 15 EST: 2017
SALES (est): 528.5K **Privately Held**
WEB: www.rawjuicery.com
SIC: **2037** Fruit juices

(P-1910)
SMOOTHIE INC
Also Called: Barfresh
3600 Wilshire Blvd # 172, Los Angeles
(90010-2603)
PHONE..................................310 598-7113
Riccardo Delle Coste, *CEO*
Arnold Tinter, *CFO*
EMP: 15 EST: 2014
SALES (est): 1MM **Privately Held**
WEB: www.barfresh.com
SIC: **2037** Frozen fruits & vegetables

PRODUCTS & SVCS

(P-1911)
SUNSATION INC
100 S Cambridge Ave, Claremont
(91711-4842)
PHONE..................909 542-0280
Perry Eichor, *CEO*
David Bryant, *CFO*
EMP: 48 EST: 2003
SQ FT: 30,000
SALES (est): 5.2MM **Privately Held**
SIC: 2037 Fruit juices

(P-1912)
VENTURA COASTAL LLC (PA)
2325 Vista Del Mar Dr, Ventura
(93001-3751)
P.O. Box 69 (93002-0069)
PHONE...................805 653-7000
William M Borgers,
Bill Borgers, *CEO*
Will Borgers, *Financial Analy*
Mike Stuebing, *VP Opers*
Donald Dames,
◆ EMP: 56 EST: 1951
SQ FT: 25,000
SALES: 31.9K **Privately Held**
WEB: www.venturacoastal.com
SIC: 2037 Fruit juice concentrates, frozen

2038 Frozen Specialties

(P-1913)
AJ SONS INC
Also Called: Langlois
2975 Laguna Canyon Rd, Laguna Beach
(92651-1148)
PHONE...................949 497-1741
Robert J Cavanan, *President*
Michael Cavanagh, *Plant Mgr*
EMP: 13 EST: 2012
SALES (est): 722.4K **Privately Held**
WEB: www.langloisfoods.com
SIC: 2038 Frozen specialties

(P-1914)
AJINOMOTO FOODS NORTH AMER INC
Also Called: Windsor Foods
4200 Concours Ste 100, Ontario
(91764-4982)
PHONE...................909 477-4700
Steve Charles, *Manager*
EMP: 244 **Privately Held**
WEB: www.ajinomotofoods.com
SIC: 2038 5142 Frozen specialties; packaged frozen goods
HQ: Ajinomoto Foods North America, Inc.
4200 Concours Ste 100
Ontario CA 91764

(P-1915)
AJINOMOTO FOODS NORTH AMER INC (DH)
4200 Concours Ste 100, Ontario
(91764-4982)
PHONE...................909 477-4700
Sumio Maeda, *President*
Taro Komura, *COO*
James Caltabiano, *CFO*
Daniel O'Brien, *CIO*
Gayatri Dhekane, *Business Anlyst*
▲ EMP: 100 EST: 2015
SQ FT: 56,000
SALES (est): 1B **Privately Held**
WEB: www.ajinomotofoods.com
SIC: 2038 2037 Frozen specialties; frozen fruits & vegetables
HQ: Ajinomoto North America Holdings, Inc.
7124 N Marine Dr
Portland OR 97203
503 505-5783

(P-1916)
ASTROCHEF LLC
Also Called: Pegasus Foods
1111 Mateo St, Los Angeles (90021-1717)
P.O. Box 86404 (90086-0404)
PHONE...................213 627-9860
Jim Zaferis, *CEO*
Evangelos Ambatielos, *President*
Vanessa Thanos, *Vice Pres*
Barry Street, *Managing Dir*

Stephen Castanedo, *General Mgr*
EMP: 55 EST: 1998
SQ FT: 60,000
SALES (est): 15.4MM **Privately Held**
WEB: www.astrochef.com
SIC: 2038 Frozen specialties

(P-1917)
BEYOND MEAT INC (PA)
119 Standard St, El Segundo (90245-3833)
PHONE...................866 756-4112
Ethan Brown, *President*
Seth Goldman, *Ch of Bd*
Sanjay Shah, *COO*
Sanjay C Shah, *COO*
Mark J Nelson, *CFO*
▲ EMP: 20 EST: 2009
SALES (est): 406.7MM **Publicly Held**
WEB: www.beyondmeat.com
SIC: 2038 2013 Frozen specialties; frozen meats from purchased meat

(P-1918)
BEYOND MEAT INC
1325 E El Segundo Blvd, El Segundo
(90245-4303)
PHONE...................310 567-3323
Aaron Hicks, *Branch Mgr*
Mark Nelson, *CFO*
Chuck Muth, *Officer*
Dan Caswell, *CIO*
Melinda Cope, *Engineer*
EMP: 26
SALES (corp-wide): 406.7MM **Publicly Held**
WEB: www.beyondmeat.com
SIC: 2038 Frozen specialties
PA: Beyond Meat, Inc.
119 Standard St
El Segundo CA 90245
866 756-4112

(P-1919)
CARDENAS MARKETS LLC
2929 S Vineyard Ave, Ontario
(91761-6484)
PHONE...................909 947-4824
Alfredo Contreras, *Manager*
EMP: 166
SALES (corp-wide): 1.1B **Privately Held**
WEB: www.cardenasmarkets.com
SIC: 2038 5411 Frozen specialties; grocery stores
PA: Cardenas Markets Llc
2501 E Guasti Rd
Ontario CA 91761
909 923-7426

(P-1920)
CARDENAS MARKETS LLC
1621 E Francis St, Ontario (91761-8324)
PHONE...................909 923-7426
Javier Ramirez, *COO*
EMP: 166
SALES (corp-wide): 1.1B **Privately Held**
WEB: www.cardenasmarkets.com
SIC: 2038 5411 Frozen specialties; grocery stores
PA: Cardenas Markets Llc
2501 E Guasti Rd
Ontario CA 91761
909 923-7426

(P-1921)
CAULIPOWER LLC
16200 Ventura Blvd # 400, Encino
(91436-4918)
PHONE...................844 422-8544
Gail Becker, *CEO*
Katie Lefkowitz, *COO*
Cassie Abrams, *CFO*
JP Mackey, *Officer*
Julie Lim, *Exec VP*
EMP: 49
SQ FT: 500
SALES (est): 45MM **Privately Held**
WEB: www.eatcaulipower.com
SIC: 2038 Pizza, frozen

(P-1922)
CEDARLANE NATURAL FOODS INC
717 E Artesia Blvd, Carson (90746-1200)
PHONE...................310 527-7833
EMP: 617

SALES (corp-wide): 124MM **Privately Held**
WEB: www.cedarlanefoods.com
SIC: 2038 Dinners, frozen & packaged
PA: Cedarlane Natural Foods, Inc.
1135 E Artesia Blvd
Carson CA 90746
310 886-7720

(P-1923)
CULINARY BRANDS INC (PA)
3280 E 44th St, Vernon (90058-2426)
PHONE...................626 289-3000
Frank Calma, *President*
Mohsen Ganeian, *Principal*
EMP: 149 EST: 2011
SQ FT: 2,000
SALES (est): 15.7MM **Privately Held**
WEB: www.culinaryinternational.com
SIC: 2038 Frozen specialties

(P-1924)
DEL REAL LLC (PA)
Also Called: Del Real Foods
11041 Inland Ave, Jurupa Valley
(91752-1155)
PHONE...................951 681-0395
Michael Axelrod, *CEO*
Viviano Del Villar Jr, *COO*
Manuel Martinez, *CFO*
Herb Bowden, *Treasurer*
Viviano Villar, *Vice Pres*
EMP: 117 EST: 2003
SQ FT: 175,000
SALES (est): 68.6MM **Privately Held**
WEB: www.delrealfoods.com
SIC: 2038 Ethnic foods, frozen

(P-1925)
DON MIGUEL MEXICAN FOODS INC (HQ)
Also Called: Don Miguel Foods
333 S Anita Dr Ste 1000, Orange
(92868-3318)
PHONE...................714 385-4500
Jeff Frank, *CEO*
Saralyn Brown, *Vice Pres*
Betty Jimenez, *Research*
Michael Chaignot, *VP Finance*
Donald Goglia, *VP Mfg*
▲ EMP: 45 EST: 1908
SQ FT: 80,000
SALES (est): 128.8MM **Privately Held**
WEB: www.megamexfoods.com
SIC: 2038 Frozen specialties

(P-1926)
EXCELLINE FOOD PRODUCTS LLC
833 N Hollywood Way, Burbank
(91505-2814)
PHONE...................818 701-7710
Carlos Angulo, *CEO*
EMP: 25 EST: 1979
SQ FT: 23,000
SALES (est): 3.2MM **Privately Held**
WEB: www.excellinefoods.com
SIC: 2038 Ethnic foods, frozen

(P-1927)
FIVE STAR GOURMET FOODS INC
3880 Ebony St, Ontario (91761-1500)
PHONE...................909 390-0032
Tal Shoshan, *CEO*
Michael Solomon, *President*
Masha Simonian, *CFO*
Michelle Eoff, *Exec VP*
Phil Abreo, *Vice Pres*
EMP: 750 EST: 1999
SQ FT: 130,000
SALES (est): 124.8MM **Privately Held**
WEB: www.fivestargourmetfoods.com
SIC: 2038 2099 Frozen specialties; ready-to-eat meals, salads & sandwiches

(P-1928)
GOLDEN STATE FOODS CORP
640 S 6th Ave, City of Industry
(91746-3086)
PHONE...................626 465-7500
Chad Buechel, *Branch Mgr*
Frank Listi, *President*
John Polley, *Vice Pres*
Danny V Constantino, *Opers Mgr*

EMP: 350
SALES (corp-wide): 821K **Privately Held**
WEB: www.goldenstatefoods.com
SIC: 2038 2087 2026 2051 Frozen specialties; flavoring extracts & syrups; fluid milk; bread, cake & related products
PA: Golden State Foods Corp
18301 Von Karman Ave # 1
Irvine CA 92612
949 247-8000

(P-1929)
HARVEST FARMS INC
45000 Yucca Ave, Lancaster (93534-2526)
PHONE...................661 945-3636
Craig Shugert, *CEO*
Eric Shiring, *CFO*
Joe Hughes, *General Mgr*
Jean Flowers, *Accounting Mgr*
Mark Duarte, *Opers Staff*
▲ EMP: 100 EST: 1947
SQ FT: 18,000
SALES (est): 23.3MM
SALES (corp-wide): 519.5MM **Privately Held**
WEB: www.harvestfarms.com
SIC: 2038 5144 Lunches, frozen & packaged; poultry & poultry products
HQ: Good Source Solutions Inc.
3115 Melrose Dr Ste 160
Carlsbad CA 92010
858 455-4800

(P-1930)
ITALIAS PIZZA KITCHEN LTD (PA)
15554 Producer Ln, Huntington Beach
(92649-1308)
PHONE...................714 861-8178
Michael O'Brien, *President*
Douglas Archibald, *Partner*
Michael O'Brein, *Partner*
EMP: 14 EST: 2019
SALES (est): 1MM **Privately Held**
WEB: www.italiaspk.com
SIC: 2038 2045 Pizza, frozen; pizza doughs, prepared: from purchased flour

(P-1931)
LA MEXICANA LLC
10615 Ruchti Rd, South Gate
(90280-7427)
PHONE...................323 277-3660
Angelo Fraggos, *CEO*
EMP: 40 EST: 2006
SQ FT: 45,000
SALES (est): 4.1MM
SALES (corp-wide): 665.7MM **Privately Held**
WEB: www.lamexicanasalsa.com
SIC: 2038 Ethnic foods, frozen
PA: Blue Point Capital Partners Llc
127 Public Sq Ste 5100
Cleveland OH 44114
216 535-4700

(P-1932)
LA MOUSSE DESSERTS INC
18211 S Broadway, Gardena (90248-3535)
PHONE...................310 478-6051
Leah Noble, *President*
EMP: 23 EST: 2017
SQ FT: 11,000
SALES (est): 2.1MM **Privately Held**
WEB: www.lamoussedesserts.com
SIC: 2038 Frozen specialties

(P-1933)
NESTLE USA INC
Also Called: Nestle Dist Ctr & Logistics
3450 Dulles Dr, Jurupa Valley
(91752-3242)
PHONE...................951 360-7200
Dean Ingram, *Branch Mgr*
Angela Davis, *Manager*
EMP: 73
SALES (corp-wide): 92.3B **Privately Held**
WEB: www.nestleusa.com
SIC: 2038 Frozen specialties
HQ: Nestle Usa, Inc.
1812 N Moore St Ste 118
Rosslyn VA 22209
440 264-7249

(P-1934)
PASCO CORPORATION OF AMERICA
19191 S Vt Ave Ste 420, Torrance (90502-1051)
PHONE.....................................503 289-6500
Hiroyuki Horie, *CEO*
◆ EMP: 37 EST: 1979
SALES (est): 1MM **Privately Held**
WEB: www.pascoamerica.com
SIC: 2038 Ethnic foods, frozen
PA: Pasco Shikishima Corporation
5-3, Shirakabe, Higashi-Ku
Nagoya AIC 461-0

(P-1935)
PICTSWEET COMPANY
732 Hanson Way, Santa Maria (93458-9710)
P.O. Box 5878 (93456-5878)
PHONE.....................................805 928-4414
Thomas Kerulas, *Branch Mgr*
William Curde, *Manager*
EMP: 300
SALES (corp-wide): 403.3MM **Privately Held**
WEB: www.pictsweetfarms.com
SIC: 2038 2099 Frozen specialties; food preparations
PA: The Pictsweet Company
10 Pictsweet Dr
Bells TN 38006
731 663-7600

(P-1936)
REAL VISION FOODS LLC
8707 Utica Ave, Rancho Cucamonga (91730-5100)
PHONE.....................................253 228-5050
Joseph Ertman, *President*
EMP: 50 EST: 2019
SALES (est): 4MM **Privately Held**
WEB: www.realvisionfoods.com
SIC: 2038 Snacks, including onion rings, cheese sticks, etc.

(P-1937)
RIGHTIME ENTERPRISE (PA)
2716 E Florence Ave, Huntington Park (90255-5747)
PHONE.....................................323 574-0310
Mikhail Cheban, *President*
EMP: 39 EST: 1995
SQ FT: 6,600
SALES (est): 4.9MM **Privately Held**
SIC: 5932 2038 Pawnshop; ethnic foods, frozen

(P-1938)
RUIZ FOOD PRODUCTS INC (PA)
501 S Alta Ave, Dinuba (93618-2100)
P.O. Box 37 (93618-0037)
PHONE.....................................559 591-5510
Rachel Cullen, *President*
Kim R Beck, *Ch of Bd*
Forrest Chandler, *CFO*
Wayne Partin, *Bd of Directors*
Olga Balderama, *Vice Pres*
EMP: 1884 EST: 1965
SQ FT: 200,000
SALES (est): 476.6MM **Privately Held**
WEB: www.ruizfoodservice.com
SIC: 2038 2099 Ethnic foods, frozen; food preparations

(P-1939)
SHINE FOOD INC
Jesse Lord
21100 S Western Ave, Torrance (90501-1700)
PHONE.....................................310 533-6010
John Freschi, *Manager*
EMP: 90
SALES (corp-wide): 13.3MM **Privately Held**
WEB: www.shinefoods.com
SIC: 2038 2053 2052 2051 Frozen specialties; frozen bakery products, except bread; cookies & crackers; bread, cake & related products

PA: Shine Food, Inc.
19216 Normandie Ave
Torrance CA 90502
310 329-3829

(P-1940)
TAWA SUPERMARKET INC (PA)
Also Called: 99 Ranch Market
6281 Regio Ave, Buena Park (90620-1023)
PHONE.....................................714 521-8899
Chang Hua K Chen, *CEO*
Jonson Chen, *Vice Chairman*
Yong You, *COO*
Alice Chen, *CFO*
Daniel Au, *Vice Pres*
▲ EMP: 65 EST: 1985
SQ FT: 117,000
SALES (est): 309.3MM **Privately Held**
SIC: 5411 2038 Supermarkets, chain; breakfasts, frozen & packaged

2041 Flour, Grain Milling

(P-1941)
ANDREW LLC
Also Called: Sanluisina
17058 Lagos Dr, Chino Hills (91709-3998)
PHONE.....................................909 270-9356
Miriam Navarro, *Mng Member*
EMP: 18 EST: 2012
SALES (est): 1.5MM **Privately Held**
SIC: 2041 Corn meal

(P-1942)
ARDENT MILLS LLC
2020 E Steel Rd, Colton (92324-4008)
PHONE.....................................951 201-1170
Brad Beckwith, *Branch Mgr*
Keshav Nair, *Manager*
Adam Piccolo, *Associate*
EMP: 16
SALES (corp-wide): 571.3MM **Privately Held**
WEB: www.ardentmills.com
PA: Ardent Mills, Llc
1875 Lawrence St Ste 1400
Denver CO 80202
800 851-9618

(P-1943)
ARDENT MILLS LLC
Also Called: Cargill Flour Milling Division
19684 Cajon Blvd, San Bernardino (92407-1813)
PHONE.....................................909 887-3407
Nelson Selmer, *Branch Mgr*
Gabe Lopez, *Safety Mgr*
Kevin Donnelly, *Maintence Staff*
EMP: 16
SQ FT: 26,180
SALES (corp-wide): 571.3MM **Privately Held**
WEB: www.ardentmills.com
SIC: 2041 Flour mills, cereal (except rice)
PA: Ardent Mills, Llc
1875 Lawrence St Ste 1400
Denver CO 80202
800 851-9618

(P-1944)
HONEYVILLE GRAIN INC
9175 Milliken Ave, Rancho Cucamonga (91730-5509)
PHONE.....................................909 243-1050
Ed Hemphill, *Principal*
Doug Stoker, *Division Mgr*
Carlos Trujillo, *Credit Mgr*
Kyle Watson, *Sales Staff*
Gonzalo Cachu, *Maintence Staff*
EMP: 28 EST: 1951
SALES (est): 1.6MM **Privately Held**
WEB: www.honeyville.com
SIC: 2041 Flour & other grain mill products

(P-1945)
LACEY MILLING COMPANY
217 W 5th St Ste 231, Hanford (93230-5034)
P.O. Box 1193 (93232-1193)
PHONE.....................................559 584-6634
Charles Lendrum, *President*
Karen Lacey, *Shareholder*
Tim Lacey, *Shareholder*
Scott Lendrum, *Treasurer*

Holly Caldera, *Admin Sec*
EMP: 19 EST: 1887
SQ FT: 40,000
SALES (est): 1.4MM **Privately Held**
SIC: 2041 Flour

(P-1946)
LT FOODS AMERICAS INC (HQ)
11130 Warland Dr, Cypress (90630-5032)
PHONE.....................................562 340-4040
Abhinav Arora, *CEO*
Mukesh Agrawal, *CFO*
Andrew Cops, *Vice Pres*
Marci Gerlach, *Vice Pres*
SAI Krishnan, *Vice Pres*
◆ EMP: 90 EST: 1992
SQ FT: 30,000
SALES: 153MM **Privately Held**
WEB: www.ltfoodsglobal.com
SIC: 2041 5149 Flour & other grain mill products; pasta & rice

2043 Cereal Breakfast Foods

(P-1947)
CARIBBEAN COFFEE COMPANY INC
495 Pine Ave Ste A, Goleta (93117-3709)
PHONE.....................................805 692-2200
John O Goerke, *CEO*
EMP: 20 EST: 1991
SALES (est): 1.5MM **Privately Held**
WEB: www.caribbeancoffee.com
SIC: 2043 2095 Coffee substitutes, made from grain; roasted coffee; freeze-dried coffee

(P-1948)
EAST WEST TEA COMPANY LLC
Also Called: Golden Temple
1616 Preuss Rd, Los Angeles (90035-4212)
PHONE.....................................310 275-9891
Gurudhan S Khalsa, *Manager*
K Khalsa, *Vice Pres*
EMP: 226
SALES (corp-wide): 56.3MM **Privately Held**
WEB: www.eastwesttea.com
SIC: 2043 2099 2064 8721 Cereal breakfast foods; tea blending; candy & other confectionery products; billing & bookkeeping service
PA: East West Tea Company, Llc
1325 Westec Dr
Eugene OR 97402
541 461-2160

(P-1949)
ORGANIC MILLING INC
505 W Allen Ave, San Dimas (91773-1487)
PHONE.....................................800 638-8686
Wolfgang Buehler, *Principal*
Lupe Martinez, *Vice Pres*
EMP: 89 EST: 2009
SALES (est): 11MM **Privately Held**
WEB: www.organicmilling.com
SIC: 2043 Cereal breakfast foods

2045 Flour, Blended & Prepared

(P-1950)
BAKEMARK USA LLC (PA)
7351 Crider Ave, Pico Rivera (90660-3705)
PHONE.....................................562 949-1054
Jim Parker, *Mng Member*
John Kupniewski, *Vice Pres*
Steve Scales, *Vice Pres*
Carlos Recinos, *Technician*
Chad Ostrom, *Project Mgr*
◆ EMP: 574 EST: 1928
SQ FT: 275,000
SALES (est): 582.3MM **Privately Held**
WEB: www.bakemark.com
SIC: 2045 5149 3556 2099 Flours & flour mixes, from purchased flour; bakery products; food products machinery; food preparations

(P-1951)
BRIDGFORD FOODS CORPORATION (HQ)
1308 N Patt St, Anaheim (92801-2551)
P.O. Box 3773 (92803-3773)
PHONE.....................................714 526-5533
William L Bridgford, *Ch of Bd*
John V Simmons, *President*
Ray Lancy, *CFO*
Raymond F Lancy, *CFO*
Allan L Bridgford Sr, *Vice Pres*
EMP: 384 EST: 1932
SALES: 197.9MM **Publicly Held**
WEB: www.bridgford.com
SIC: 2045 2099 2015 2013 Biscuit dough, prepared: from purchased flour; doughs, frozen or refrigerated: from purchased flour; sandwiches, assembled & packaged: for wholesale market; salads, fresh or refrigerated; poultry sausage, luncheon meats & other poultry products; snack sticks, including jerky: from purchased meat; cheese, natural & processed; dips, cheese-based; frozen specialties
PA: Bridgford Industries Incorporated
1601 S Good Latimer Expy
Dallas TX 75226
214 428-1535

(P-1952)
LANGLOIS COMPANY
Also Called: Langlois Flour Company
10810 San Sevaine Way, Jurupa Valley (91752-1116)
PHONE.....................................951 360-3900
Richard W Langlois, *President*
Lynn Langlois Nye, *Treasurer*
Jeff Langlois, *Vice Pres*
Sally Langlois, *Vice Pres*
Teresa Cisneros, *Admin Asst*
▼ EMP: 50 EST: 1950
SQ FT: 48,000
SALES (est): 8.8MM **Privately Held**
WEB: www.langloiscompany.com
SIC: 2045 2035 2079 2099 Blended flour: from purchased flour; mayonnaise; vegetable refined oils (except corn oil); gelatin dessert preparations; flavoring extracts & syrups

(P-1953)
POPLA INTERNATIONAL INC
1740 S Sacramento Ave, Ontario (91761-7744)
PHONE.....................................909 923-6899
Mike Shinozaki, *President*
Ashley Shinozaki, *Admin Sec*
◆ EMP: 41
SQ FT: 8,000
SALES (est): 4.1MM **Privately Held**
WEB: www.popla.com
SIC: 2045 Prepared flour mixes & doughs

2046 Wet Corn Milling

(P-1954)
SMART FOODS LLC
3398 Leonis Blvd Vernon, Vernon (90058)
PHONE.....................................818 660-2238
Keyvan Khalifian,
◆ EMP: 25 EST: 2015
SALES (est): 1.3MM **Privately Held**
WEB: www.avocadooilusa.com
SIC: 2046 2076 Corn oil, refined; vegetable oil mills; coconut oil

2047 Dog & Cat Food

(P-1955)
ARTHUR DOGSWELL LLC (PA)
11301 W Olympic Blvd, Los Angeles (90064-1653)
PHONE.....................................888 559-8833
Brad Casper, *Mng Member*
Berenice Officer, *Vice Pres*
Elizabeth Eyraud, *Planning*
Anabel Jordan, *Accounting Mgr*
Raidas Korsakas, *Analyst*
▲ EMP: 33 EST: 2003
SQ FT: 2,000

SALES (est): 26.3MM **Privately Held**
WEB: www.dogswell.com
SIC: 2047 5149 Dog food; pet foods

(P-1956)
CANINE CAVIAR PET FOODS DE INC
4131 Tigris Way, Riverside (92503-4844)
PHONE.....................714 223-1800
Jeff A Baker, *Principal*
EMP: 18 EST: 2019
SALES (est): 1.6MM **Privately Held**
WEB: www.caninecaviar.com
SIC: 2047 Dog & cat food

(P-1957)
GRANDMA LUCYS LLC
30432 Esperanza, Rcho STA Marg (92688-2144)
PHONE.....................949 206-8547
Eric Shook, *Partner*
Breann Lee Shook,
EMP: 19 EST: 1999
SALES (est): 2.2MM **Privately Held**
WEB: www.grandmalucys.com
SIC: 5999 2047 Pets & pet supplies; dog & cat food

(P-1958)
J&R TAYLOR BROTHERS ASSOC INC
Also Called: Premium Pet Foods
16321 Arrow Hwy, Irwindale (91706-2018)
PHONE.....................626 334-9301
Rick Taylor, *President*
◆ EMP: 58 EST: 1967
SALES (est): 23.8MM
SALES (corp-wide): 2.7B **Publicly Held**
WEB: www.central.com
SIC: 2047 2048 Dog food; prepared feeds
PA: Central Garden & Pet Company
1340 Treat Blvd Ste 600
Walnut Creek CA 94597
925 948-4000

(P-1959)
MARS PETCARE US INC
2765 Lexington Way, San Bernardino (92407-1842)
PHONE.....................909 887-8131
Ed Skokan, *Manager*
EMP: 50
SQ FT: 76,000
SALES (corp-wide): 42.8B **Privately Held**
WEB: www.williamsonchamber.com
SIC: 2047 2048 Dog food; prepared feeds
HQ: Mars Petcare Us, Inc.
2013 Ovation Pkwy
Franklin TN 37067
615 807-4626

(P-1960)
MARS PETCARE US INC
13243 Nutro Way, Victorville (92395-7789)
PHONE.....................760 261-7900
EMP: 32
SALES (corp-wide): 42.8B **Privately Held**
WEB: www.williamsonchamber.com
SIC: 2047 Cat food
HQ: Mars Petcare Us, Inc.
2013 Ovation Pkwy
Franklin TN 37067
615 807-4626

(P-1961)
PERFECTION PET FOODS LLC (DH)
Also Called: Perfection Pet Brands
1111 N Miller Park Ct, Visalia (93291-9454)
PHONE.....................559 302-4880
Kevin Kruse, *CEO*
Jeremy Wilhelm, *President*
Brian Ubegin, *CFO*
Mike Gagene, *Vice Pres*
Rob Haynes, *Vice Pres*
EMP: 47 EST: 2011
SALES (est): 11.2MM
SALES (corp-wide): 587.3MM **Privately Held**
WEB: www.perfectionpetfoods.com
SIC: 2047 Dog food
HQ: Western Milling, Llc
31120 W St
Goshen CA 93227
559 302-1000

2048 Prepared Feeds For Animals & Fowls

(P-1962)
A SHOC BEVERAGE LLC
844 Production Pl, Newport Beach (92663-2810)
PHONE.....................949 490-1612
Lance Collins, *Mng Member*
Kyle Ostrowsky, *Controller*
EMP: 50 EST: 2018
SALES (est): 5.8MM **Privately Held**
SIC: 2048 Mineral feed supplements

(P-1963)
CANINE CAVIAR PET FOODS INC
4131 Tigris Way, Riverside (92503-4844)
P.O. Box 5872, Norco (92860-8029)
PHONE.....................714 223-1800
Jeff Baker, *President*
Gary Ward, *Vice Pres*
Jamie Carper, *Marketing Staff*
◆ EMP: 30 EST: 1996
SQ FT: 6,000
SALES (est): 5.4MM **Privately Held**
WEB: www.caninecaviar.com
SIC: 2048 Canned pet food (except dog & cat)

(P-1964)
DEXT COMPANY OF MARYLAND (DH)
Also Called: Reconserve of Maryland
2811 Wilshire Blvd # 410, Santa Monica (90403-4803)
P.O. Box 2211 (90407-2211)
PHONE.....................310 458-1574
Meyer Luskin, *Ch of Bd*
Robert McMullen, *President*
Rida Hamed, *Vice Pres*
Gerald Truelove, *Vice Pres*
EMP: 20 EST: 1985
SQ FT: 4,000
SALES (est): 8.5MM
SALES (corp-wide): 297.6MM **Privately Held**
WEB: www.reconserve.com
SIC: 2048 Prepared feeds
HQ: Reconserve, Inc.
2811 Wilshire Blvd # 410
Santa Monica CA 90403
310 458-1574

(P-1965)
GEORGE VERHOEVEN GRAIN INC (PA)
5355 E Airport Dr, Ontario (91761-8604)
PHONE.....................909 605-1531
Randall Verhoeven, *President*
Robert Verhoeven, *Vice Pres*
EMP: 15 EST: 1988
SQ FT: 2,100
SALES (est): 6.4MM **Privately Held**
WEB: www.verhoevengraininc.com
SIC: 2048 5153 Livestock feeds; grain elevators

(P-1966)
HARBOR GREEN GRAIN LP
13181 Crssroads Pkwy N, City of Industry (91746)
PHONE.....................310 991-8089
Shing Lo, *President*
Zach Xu, *CEO*
Kevin Yoon, *COO*
◆ EMP: 45 EST: 2014
SALES (est): 4.2MM **Privately Held**
SIC: 2048 Alfalfa, cubed

(P-1967)
HERBERT RIZZARDINI
Also Called: Gateway Hardware
6259 Highway 178, Inyokern (93527)
P.O. Box 1180 (93527-1180)
PHONE.....................760 377-4571
Herbert Rizzardini, *Owner*
EMP: 18 EST: 1987
SQ FT: 7,000
SALES (est): 3.8MM **Privately Held**
WEB: www.gatewayhardware.com
SIC: 5251 2048 Hardware; livestock feeds

(P-1968)
HRK PET FOOD PRODUCTS INC
12924 Pierce St, Pacoima (91331-2526)
PHONE.....................818 897-2521
Joey Herrick, *President*
Lynnda Herrick, *Vice Pres*
▲ EMP: 20 EST: 1999
SQ FT: 30,000
SALES (est): 628.7K **Privately Held**
SIC: 2048 Canned pet food (except dog & cat)

(P-1969)
IMPERIAL PREMIX LLC (PA)
Also Called: Imperial Pre Mix Company
422 E Barioni Blvd, Imperial (92251-1775)
P.O. Box 278 (92251-0278)
PHONE.....................760 355-7997
Ray Pedersen,
Ronald Pedersen,
EMP: 14 EST: 1960
SALES (est): 1.2MM **Privately Held**
WEB: www.premixit.com
SIC: 2048 Prepared feeds

(P-1970)
INTERNATIONAL PROCESSING CORP (DH)
233 Wilshire Blvd Ste 310, Santa Monica (90401-1206)
P.O. Box 2211 (90407-2211)
PHONE.....................310 458-1574
Bob McMullen, *President*
EMP: 25 EST: 1953
SALES (est): 41.3MM
SALES (corp-wide): 297.6MM **Privately Held**
WEB: www.reconserve.com
SIC: 2048 Prepared feeds
HQ: Reconserve, Inc.
2811 Wilshire Blvd # 410
Santa Monica CA 90403
310 458-1574

(P-1971)
LEGACY EPOCH LLC (HQ)
Also Called: Feedonomics LLC
21011 Warner Center Ln A, Woodland Hills (91367-6509)
PHONE.....................844 673-7305
Shawn Lipman, *CEO*
Gary Putterman, *CFO*
Gary Putterman, *Officer*
Jason Nichol, *Vice Pres*
Justin Junio, *Executive*
EMP: 82 EST: 2015
SALES (est): 11.2MM
SALES (corp-wide): 152.3MM **Publicly Held**
WEB: www.feedonomics.com
SIC: 2048 Chicken feeds, prepared
PA: Bigcommerce Holdings, Inc.
11305 Four Points Dr I
Austin TX 78726
512 865-4500

(P-1972)
NATURAL BALANCE PET FOODS INC (DH)
100 N First St Ste 200, Burbank (91502-1845)
P.O. Box 397, Upland (91785-0397)
PHONE.....................800 829-4493
Joseph Herrick, *President*
David J West, *CEO*
Lynnda Herrick, *Corp Secy*
Lee Kunkler, *District Mgr*
Leslie Hancock, *Research*
▲ EMP: 49 EST: 1989
SQ FT: 55,000
SALES (est): 20.9MM
SALES (corp-wide): 8B **Publicly Held**
WEB: www.naturalbalanceinc.com
SIC: 2048 5199 Prepared feeds; pet supplies

(P-1973)
PITMAN FAMILY FARMS
10365 Iona Ave, Hanford (93230-9553)
PHONE.....................559 585-3330
Al Ward, *Plant Mgr*
Julian Chase, *Officer*
Joe Stone, *Officer*
Pres Salcido, *Prdtn Supt*
Anna Richo, *General Counsel*

EMP: 55
SALES (corp-wide): 207.5MM **Privately Held**
WEB: www.pitmanfarms.com
SIC: 2048 Livestock feeds
PA: Pitman Farms
1075 North Ave
Sanger CA 93657
559 875-9300

(P-1974)
RECONSERVE INC (HQ)
Also Called: Dext Company
2811 Wilshire Blvd # 410, Santa Monica (90403-4803)
P.O. Box 2211 (90407-2211)
PHONE.....................310 458-1574
Meyer Luskin, *CEO*
David Luskin, *COO*
Rudy Alvarez, *Vice Pres*
Bryan Bergquist, *Vice Pres*
Joe Douglas, *Vice Pres*
EMP: 25 EST: 1966
SQ FT: 5,000
SALES (est): 184.9MM
SALES (corp-wide): 297.6MM **Privately Held**
WEB: www.reconserve.com
SIC: 2048 Livestock feeds
PA: Scope Industries
2811 Wilshire Blvd # 410
Santa Monica CA 90403
310 458-1574

(P-1975)
STAR MILLING CO
24067 Water Ave, Perris (92570-7395)
P.O. Box 1987 (92572-1987)
PHONE.....................951 657-3143
William R Cramer Jr, *President*
Keith Williams, *General Mgr*
Jane Anderson, *Admin Sec*
Chuck Grable, *Opers Mgr*
Stacy Kuhns, *Sales Staff*
◆ EMP: 229 EST: 1970
SQ FT: 25,000
SALES (est): 30.5MM **Privately Held**
WEB: www.starmilling.com
SIC: 2048 Poultry feeds

(P-1976)
SUN-GRO COMMODITIES INC (PA)
34575 Famoso Rd, Bakersfield (93308-9769)
PHONE.....................661 393-2612
Donald G Smith, *CEO*
Lori Melendez, *Treasurer*
Scott Smith, *Vice Pres*
Wendy Smith, *Admin Sec*
EMP: 25 EST: 1974
SQ FT: 1,400
SALES (est): 4.7MM **Privately Held**
WEB: www.sun-gro.com
SIC: 2048 4212 Livestock feeds; local trucking, without storage

(P-1977)
VIVOTEIN LLC
231 S Pleasant Ave, Ontario (91761-1730)
PHONE.....................918 344-8742
Harout Ajaryan, *Mng Member*
EMP: 16 EST: 2016
SALES (est): 2.4MM **Privately Held**
WEB: www.vivotein.com
SIC: 2048 Prepared feeds

2051 Bread, Bakery Prdts Exc Cookies & Crackers

(P-1978)
ALBERTSONS LLC
Also Called: Albertsons 6514
8938 Trautwein Rd Ste A, Riverside (92508-9191)
PHONE.....................951 656-6603
Bill Brown, *Manager*
EMP: 190
SALES (corp-wide): 69.6B **Publicly Held**
WEB: www.albertsons.com
SIC: 5411 2051 Supermarkets, chain; bread, cake & related products

HQ: Albertson's Llc
250 E Parkcenter Blvd
Boise ID 83706
208 395-4722

(P-1979)
ALBERTSONS LLC
Also Called: Albertsons 6376
1301 N Norma St, Ridgecrest
(93555-2508)
PHONE..............................760 446-2544
Manny Harow, *Manager*
Randy Morgan, *Executive*
EMP: 190
SALES (corp-wide): 69.6B **Publicly Held**
WEB: www.albertsons.com
SIC: 5411 2051 Supermarkets, chain;
bread, cake & related products
HQ: Albertson's Llc
250 E Parkcenter Blvd
Boise ID 83706
208 395-4722

(P-1980)
BAKE R US INC
Also Called: Dave's Donuts & Baking Co
13400 S Western Ave, Gardena
(90249-1928)
P.O. Box 3160, Santa Monica (90408-
3160)
PHONE..............................310 630-5873
Fairy Aframian, *CEO*
Mike Aframian, *President*
EMP: 28 **EST:** 1960
SALES (est): 3.2MM **Privately Held**
WEB: www.davesbaking.com
SIC: 2051 Doughnuts, except frozen

(P-1981)
BAKERS KNEADED LLC
148 W 132nd St Ste D, Los Angeles
(90061-1649)
PHONE..............................213 321-9952
Carlos Enriquez, *Mng Member*
Paul Cox,
EMP: 20 **EST:** 2017
SALES (est): 2MM **Privately Held**
SIC: 2051 Bread, all types (white, wheat,
rye, etc): fresh or frozen

(P-1982)
BAKERY DEPOT INC
4489 Bandini Blvd, Vernon (90058-4309)
PHONE..............................323 261-8388
Wilton Thinh Thai, *CEO*
◆ **EMP:** 15 **EST:** 2005
SALES (est): 2.6MM **Privately Held**
WEB: www.bakerydepotinc.com
SIC: 2051 Bakery: wholesale or whole-
sale/retail combined

(P-1983)
**BAY CITIES ITALIAN BAKERY
INC**
1120 W Mahalo Pl, Compton (90220-5443)
PHONE..............................310 608-1881
Linda Ferrera, *President*
Mario Ferrera, *CEO*
EMP: 16 **EST:** 1983
SQ FT: 7,200
SALES (est): 522.8K **Privately Held**
WEB: www.bay-cities-italian-bakery-
inc.hub.biz
SIC: 2051 5461 Bakery: wholesale or
wholesale/retail combined; bakeries

(P-1984)
**BESTWAY SANDWICHES INC
(PA)**
1530 1st St, San Fernando (91340-2708)
PHONE..............................818 361-1800
Khachatur Budagyan, *CEO*
EMP: 226 **EST:** 2008
SALES (est): 15.9MM **Privately Held**
SIC: 2051 Bread, all types (white, wheat,
rye, etc): fresh or frozen

(P-1985)
BIMBO BAKERIES USA INC
480 S Vail Ave, Montebello (90640-4947)
PHONE..............................323 720-6099
Edgar Jaramillo, *Branch Mgr*
EMP: 18 **Privately Held**
WEB: www.arnoldbread.com
SIC: 2051 Bakery: wholesale or whole-
sale/retail combined

HQ: Bimbo Bakeries Usa, Inc
255 Business Center Dr # 200
Horsham PA 19044
215 347-5500

(P-1986)
BT BAKING
8702 Valley Blvd, Rosemead (91770-1712)
PHONE..............................213 880-9828
Bryant Tang, *President*
◆ **EMP:** 14 **EST:** 2010
SALES (est): 304.5K **Privately Held**
SIC: 2051 Bread, cake & related products

(P-1987)
**CALIFORNIA CHURROS
CORPORATION**
751 Via Lata, Colton (92324-3930)
PHONE..............................909 370-4777
Jorge D Martinez, *CEO*
Jorge D Martinez Sr, *President*
Frank Ruvalcaba, *Vice Pres*
Eva A Martinez, *Admin Sec*
EMP: 151 **EST:** 1980
SQ FT: 54,800
SALES (est): 2.4MM
SALES (corp-wide): 1B **Publicly Held**
WEB: www.churros.com
SIC: 2051 Pastries, e.g. danish: except
frozen
HQ: J & J Snack Foods Corp. Of California
5353 S Downey Rd
Vernon CA 90058
323 581-0171

(P-1988)
CALIMEX DELI
711 1/2 S Kern Ave, Los Angeles
(90022-2574)
PHONE..............................323 261-7271
Manuel Cortez, *Ch of Bd*
Juan Cortez, *Principal*
Belen Medrano, *Principal*
EMP: 20 **EST:** 1994
SQ FT: 50,000
SALES (est): 1.3MM **Privately Held**
WEB: www.ordercalimexdeli.com
SIC: 5812 2051 Delicatessen (eating
places); bakery: wholesale or
wholesale/retail combined

(P-1989)
CCF CHINA OPERATING CORP
26901 Malibu Hills Rd, Calabasas Hills
(91301-5354)
PHONE..............................818 871-3000
David Overton, *CEO*
EMP: 26 **EST:** 2014
SALES (est): 1MM **Publicly Held**
WEB: www.thecheesecakefactory.com
SIC: 5812 2051 American restaurant;
cakes, bakery: except frozen
PA: The Cheesecake Factory Incorporated
26901 Malibu Hills Rd
Calabasas Hills CA 91301

(P-1990)
CCF INTERNATIONAL LLC
26901 Malibu Hills Rd, Calabasas
(91301-5354)
PHONE..............................818 871-3000
EMP: 17 **EST:** 2017
SALES (est): 611K **Publicly Held**
WEB: www.thecheesecakefactory.com
SIC: 5812 2051 American restaurant;
cakes, bakery: except frozen
PA: The Cheesecake Factory Incorporated
26901 Malibu Hills Rd
Calabasas Hills CA 91301

(P-1991)
**CENTRAL CALIFORNIA BAKING
CO**
701 Industrial Dr Ca, Exeter (93221-2102)
PHONE..............................559 592-2270
Ken Hall, *Administration*
Diana Philips, *Accounting Mgr*
EMP: 178 **EST:** 2019
SALES (est): 171K
SALES (corp-wide): 536.1MM **Privately
Held**
WEB: www.franzbakery.com
SIC: 2051 Bakery: wholesale or whole-
sale/retail combined

PA: United States Bakery
315 Ne 10th Ave
Portland OR 97232
503 232-2191

(P-1992)
**CHEESECAKE FACTORY INC
(PA)**
Also Called: CHEESECAKE FACTORY, THE
26901 Malibu Hills Rd, Calabasas Hills
(91301-5354)
PHONE..............................818 871-3000
David Overton, *Ch of Bd*
David M Gordon, *President*
Matthew E Clark, *CFO*
Edie Garritano-Ames, *Bd of Directors*
Scarlett May, *Exec VP*
▲ **EMP:** 17863 **EST:** 1972
SQ FT: 88,000
SALES (est): 1.9B **Publicly Held**
WEB: www.thecheesecakefactory.com
SIC: 5812 2051 American restaurant;
cakes, bakery: except frozen

(P-1993)
CORBIN-HILL INC
Also Called: Corbin Foods
2961 W Macarthur Blvd # 1, Santa Ana
(92704-6913)
P.O. Box 28139 (92799-8139)
PHONE..............................714 966-6695
Ji Corbin, *Ch of Bd*
A Moreno, *President*
R W Carlyle, *CFO*
Karen Kelley, *Admin Sec*
EMP: 18 **EST:** 1982
SQ FT: 20,000
SALES (est): 864.7K **Privately Held**
SIC: 2051 Bread, cake & related products

(P-1994)
DAWN FOOD PRODUCTS INC
15601 Mosher Ave, Tustin (92780-6426)
PHONE..............................714 258-1223
Joe Barsoppi, *General Mgr*
Mela Martinez, *Executive*
Carol Shokraee, *Business Mgr*
Michael Gallenstien, *Finance*
Terry McDaniel, *Production*
EMP: 150
SALES (corp-wide): 1.7B **Privately Held**
WEB: www.dawnfoods.com
SIC: 2051 Pastries, e.g. danish: except
frozen; breads, rolls & buns
HQ: Dawn Food Products, Inc.
3333 Sargent Rd
Jackson MI 49201

(P-1995)
DILLON COMPANIES INC
Also Called: Food 4 Less
4250 Van Buren Blvd, Riverside
(92503-2602)
PHONE..............................951 352-8353
Rocky Scmit, *Manager*
EMP: 135
SALES (corp-wide): 132.5B **Publicly
Held**
WEB: www.dillons.com
SIC: 5411 2051 Supermarkets, chain;
bread, cake & related products
HQ: Dillon Companies, Inc.
2700 E 4th Ave
Hutchinson KS 67501
620 665-5511

(P-1996)
DISTINCT INDULGENCE INC
Also Called: Mrs Appletree's Bakery
5018 Lante St, Baldwin Park (91706-1839)
PHONE..............................818 546-1700
Robert W Gray, *President*
Suzanne Gray, *Corp Secy*
Carlos Castro, *Sales Executive*
▲ **EMP:** 38 **EST:** 1985
SQ FT: 10,000
SALES (est): 7.8MM **Privately Held**
WEB: www.mrsappletree.com
SIC: 2051 5499 Bakery: wholesale or
wholesale/retail combined; health & di-
etetic food stores

(P-1997)
EL METATE INC
Also Called: El Metate Market
817 W 19th St, Costa Mesa (92627-3518)
PHONE..............................949 646-9362
Jason Murrieta, *General Mgr*
Claudia Del Val, *Manager*
EMP: 190
SALES (corp-wide): 25MM **Privately
Held**
WEB: www.elmetate.com
SIC: 2051 2052 2099 5812 Breads, rolls
& buns; cakes, pies & pastries; cookies;
tortillas, fresh or refrigerated; Mexican
restaurant
PA: El Metate, Inc.
838 E 1st St
Santa Ana CA 92701
714 542-3913

(P-1998)
EL SEGUNDO BREAD BAR LLC
701 E El Segundo Blvd, El Segundo
(90245-4108)
PHONE..............................310 615-9898
Myrna Al-Midani, *CEO*
Ali Chalabi, *President*
▲ **EMP:** 32 **EST:** 2004
SQ FT: 8,000
SALES (est): 3.5MM **Privately Held**
WEB: www.breadbar.la
SIC: 2051 5149 Bread, all types (white,
wheat, rye, etc): fresh or frozen; bakery
products

(P-1999)
FEEMSTER CO INC
Also Called: Some Crust Bakery
119 Yale Ave, Claremont (91711-4723)
PHONE..............................909 621-9772
Larry Feemster, *President*
Sandra Feemster, *Officer*
Tasha Cockrell, *Vice Pres*
Scott Feemster, *Manager*
Katrina Murillo, *Manager*
EMP: 19 **EST:** 1997
SQ FT: 3,000
SALES (est): 3.6MM **Privately Held**
WEB: www.somecrust.com
SIC: 2051 5461 Bread, cake & related
products; bakeries

(P-2000)
FIESTA MEXICAN FOODS INC
979 G St, Brawley (92227-2615)
PHONE..............................760 344-3580
Raymond Armenta, *President*
EMP: 30 **EST:** 1956
SQ FT: 4,000
SALES (est): 2.5MM **Privately Held**
SIC: 2051 2099 Pastries, e.g. danish: ex-
cept frozen; tortillas, fresh or refrigerated

(P-2001)
**FOOD FOR LIFE BAKING CO
INC (PA)**
Also Called: Natural Food Mill
2991 Doherty St, Corona (92879-5811)
P.O. Box 1434 (92878-1434)
PHONE..............................951 273-3031
R James Torres, *President*
Scott Kraus, *CFO*
Charles Torres, *Vice Pres*
Linda Biro, *Purch Mgr*
Luis Rocha, *Plant Mgr*
▲ **EMP:** 100 **EST:** 1970
SQ FT: 170,000
SALES (est): 25.3MM **Privately Held**
WEB: www.foodforlife.com
SIC: 2051 Bakery: wholesale or whole-
sale/retail combined

(P-2002)
FRISCO BAKING COMPANY INC
621 W Avenue 26, Los Angeles
(90065-1095)
PHONE..............................323 225-6111
Aldo Pricco Jr, *CEO*
James Pricco, *President*
Ronald Perata, *Treasurer*
Mary Anne Fetter, *Vice Pres*
John Pricco, *Vice Pres*
EMP: 115 **EST:** 1938
SQ FT: 18,000

PRODUCTS & SVCS

SALES (est): 16.4MM **Privately Held**
WEB: www.friscobakingcompany.com
SIC: 2051 Bread, all types (white, wheat, rye, etc): fresh or frozen

(P-2003)
GELSONS MARKETS
13455 Maxella Ave, Marina Del Rey (90292-5682)
PHONE..............................310 306-3192
Romel Montero, *General Mgr*
EMP: 87
SALES (corp-wide): 384.7MM **Privately Held**
WEB: www.gelsons.com
SIC: 5411 2051 5461 Supermarkets, chain; bread, cake & related products; bakeries
HQ: Gelson's Markets
    13833 Freeway Dr
    Santa Fe Springs CA 90670
    310 638-2842

(P-2004)
GIULIANO-PAGANO CORPORATION
Also Called: Giuliano's Bakery
1264 E Walnut St, Carson (90746-1319)
PHONE..............................310 537-7700
Nancy Ritmire Giuliano, *Ch of Bd*
Gregory Ritmire, *President*
EMP: 100 EST: 1952
SQ FT: 40,000
SALES (est): 24.2MM **Privately Held**
SIC: 2051 Bakery: wholesale or wholesale/retail combined

(P-2005)
GOLD COAST BAKING COMPANY INC (PA)
Also Called: Gold Coast Bakeries
1590 E Saint Gertrude Pl, Santa Ana (92705-5310)
PHONE..............................714 545-2253
Rick Anderson, *CEO*
Mark Press, *President*
Dan Cuellar, *Vice Pres*
Bill Dozier, *Executive*
Tony Lucas, *Opers Staff*
EMP: 206 EST: 2003
SQ FT: 60,000
SALES (est): 46.2MM **Privately Held**
WEB: www.goldcoastbakery.com
SIC: 2051 Bakery: wholesale or wholesale/retail combined

(P-2006)
GRAND CASINO ON MAIN INC
3826 Main St, Culver City (90232-2620)
PHONE..............................310 253-9066
Linda Boyle, *President*
Frank Lamanna, *Vice Pres*
▲ EMP: 13 EST: 2001
SALES (est): 426.7K **Privately Held**
WEB: www.grandcasinobakery.com
SIC: 2051 Bread, cake & related products

(P-2007)
HOUSTON CHEESECAKE FCTRY CORP
26901 Malibu Hills Rd, Calabasas Hills (91301-5354)
PHONE..............................818 871-3000
Michael Alan Rivero, *President*
EMP: 43 EST: 1995
SALES (est): 1.9MM **Publicly Held**
WEB: www.thecheesecakefactory.com
SIC: 5812 2051 American restaurant; cakes, bakery: except frozen
PA: The Cheesecake Factory Incorporated
    26901 Malibu Hills Rd
    Calabasas Hills CA 91301

(P-2008)
ITS ALL ABOUT CAKE INC
24921 Dana Pt Hbr D Ste B, Dana Point (92629-2933)
PHONE..............................949 240-7100
Dianne Richey, *Mng Member*
Jordan Richey, *Vice Pres*
David Richey,
EMP: 14 EST: 1993
SQ FT: 3,000

SALES (est): 1.3MM **Privately Held**
WEB: www.itsallaboutthecake.com
SIC: 5461 5812 2051 Cakes; Italian restaurant; cafe; cakes, bakery: except frozen

(P-2009)
JEANNINES BKG CO SANTA BARBARA (PA)
Also Called: Jeannine's Bakery
15 E Figueroa St, Santa Barbara (93101-2781)
P.O. Box 8929, Goleta (93118-8929)
PHONE..............................805 966-1717
Gordon W Hardey, *CEO*
Eleanor Hardey, *President*
EMP: 17 EST: 1991
SQ FT: 1,800
SALES (est): 1.5MM **Privately Held**
WEB: www.jeannines.com
SIC: 2051 5812 Bread, cake & related products; American restaurant

(P-2010)
JEREMYS ELECTRIC
3009 Honolulu Ave, La Crescenta (91214-3714)
PHONE..............................818 249-5656
Jeremy Tomas Jover, *Principal*
EMP: 16 EST: 2001
SALES (est): 186K **Privately Held**
SIC: 5812 2051 Eating places; doughnuts, except frozen

(P-2011)
KDS DONUT CHINESE FOODS
Also Called: Rising Sun Chinese Food
26761 Portola Pkwy Ste 2g, Foothill Ranch (92610-1759)
PHONE..............................949 588-1688
Ien Ji, *Principal*
Lezly Elm, *Manager*
EMP: 13 EST: 1995
SALES (est): 186.4K **Privately Held**
WEB: www.risingsunfoothillranch.com
SIC: 5812 2051 Chinese restaurant; doughnuts, except frozen

(P-2012)
KING EXPRESS INC
Also Called: King Ex Chinese Fd & Donut
12053 Vanowen St, North Hollywood (91605-5962)
PHONE..............................818 503-2772
Joel Lim, *Manager*
EMP: 16 EST: 1993
SALES (est): 220.8K **Privately Held**
SIC: 5812 2051 Chinese restaurant; doughnuts, except frozen

(P-2013)
LAURAS FRENCH BAKING CO INC
722 S Oxford Ave Apt 107, Los Angeles (90005-2996)
PHONE..............................323 585-5144
Laura Kim, *President*
Mike Ji, *Vice Pres*
Sterling Kim, *Vice Pres*
EMP: 18 EST: 1997
SQ FT: 18,600
SALES (est): 1MM **Privately Held**
WEB: www.labakery.com
SIC: 2051 Bakery: wholesale or wholesale/retail combined

(P-2014)
LAVASH CORPORATION OF AMERICA
Also Called: Old Fashion Lavash
2835 Newell St, Los Angeles (90039-3817)
PHONE..............................323 663-5249
Edmond Hartounin, *President*
EMP: 25 EST: 1980
SQ FT: 10,000
SALES (est): 2.3MM **Privately Held**
SIC: 2051 Bakery: wholesale or wholesale/retail combined

(P-2015)
LEY GRAND FOODS CORPORATION
287 S 6th Ave, La Puente (91746-2916)
PHONE..............................626 336-2244
Frank Chen, *President*

Chien Chen, *Vice Pres*
J J Chen, *Admin Sec*
▲ EMP: 23 EST: 1989
SQ FT: 4,000
SALES (est): 2MM **Privately Held**
WEB: www.leygrandfoods.com
SIC: 2051 Bread, cake & related products

(P-2016)
LITTLE BROTHERS BAKERY LLC
320 W Alondra Blvd, Gardena (90248-2423)
PHONE..............................310 225-3790
Paul C Giuliano,
Anthony S Giuliano,
Joann Giuliano,
Paul G Giuliano Jr,
▲ EMP: 65 EST: 1999
SQ FT: 15,000
SALES (est): 9.8MM **Privately Held**
WEB: www.littlebrothersbakery.com
SIC: 2051 5149 Bakery: wholesale or wholesale/retail combined; bakery products

(P-2017)
LUPITAS BAKERY INC (PA)
1848 W Florence Ave, Los Angeles (90047-2123)
PHONE..............................323 752-2391
Able Diaz, *President*
Martha Diaz, *Admin Sec*
EMP: 18 EST: 1985
SQ FT: 8,000
SALES (est): 1.7MM **Privately Held**
WEB: www.mylupitasbakery.com
SIC: 2051 5461 Bread, all types (white, wheat, rye, etc): fresh or frozen; bread

(P-2018)
MARIE CALLENDER PIE SHOPS INC
Also Called: Marie Callender's Pie Shops
18889 Brookhurst St, Fountain Valley (92708-7303)
PHONE..............................714 963-6791
EMP: 60
SALES (corp-wide): 239MM **Privately Held**
SIC: 5812 2051 Eating Places
HQ: Marie Callender Pie Shops, Inc.
    6075 Poplar Ave Ste 800
    Memphis TN 38119
    901 766-6400

(P-2019)
MILKY MAMA LLC
10722 Arrow Rte Ste 104, Rancho Cucamonga (91730-4809)
PHONE..............................877 886-4559
Krystal Duhaney, *Mng Member*
EMP: 14 EST: 2016
SALES (est): 1.8MM **Privately Held**
WEB: www.milky-mama.com
SIC: 2051 Bakery products, partially cooked (except frozen)

(P-2020)
MOCHI ICE CREAM COMPANY LLC (PA)
Also Called: Mikawaya
5563 Alcoa Ave, Vernon (90058-3730)
PHONE..............................323 587-5504
Jerry Bucan, *CEO*
Craig Berger, *CFO*
Tom Bulowski, *Vice Pres*
Michael Cheng, *Info Tech Dir*
Sondra Sonnenberg, *Sales Staff*
◆ EMP: 30 EST: 1910
SQ FT: 10,000
SALES (est): 19.6MM **Privately Held**
WEB: www.mymochi.com
SIC: 2051 2024 5451 Cakes, pies & pastries; ice cream & frozen desserts; ice cream (packaged)

(P-2021)
MODAAN INC (PA)
Also Called: Layer Cake Bakery
4250 Barranca Pkwy Ste I, Irvine (92604-1731)
PHONE..............................949 786-0223
Jin Yang, *President*
EMP: 16 EST: 2007

SQ FT: 1,600
SALES (est): 272.5K **Privately Held**
WEB: www.layercakebakery.com
SIC: 5461 2051 5149 Cakes; cakes, bakery: except frozen; coffee & tea

(P-2022)
MRS REDDS PIE CO INC
150 S La Cadena Dr, Colton (92324-3416)
P.O. Box 555 (92324-0555)
PHONE..............................909 825-4800
Tom P Telliard, *President*
Nick Telliard, *Vice Pres*
EMP: 20 EST: 1956
SQ FT: 76,030
SALES (est): 3.6MM **Privately Held**
SIC: 2051 Cakes, bakery: except frozen; pies, bakery: except frozen; yeast goods, sweet: except frozen

(P-2023)
NEW YORK FROZEN FOODS INC
Mamma Bella Foods
5100 Rivergrade Rd, Baldwin Park (91706-1406)
PHONE..............................626 338-3000
Bob Willist, *Branch Mgr*
EMP: 50
SALES (corp-wide): 1.4B **Publicly Held**
SIC: 2051 Buns, bread type: fresh or frozen
HQ: New York Frozen Foods, Inc.
    25900 Fargo Ave
    Bedford OH 44146
    216 292-5655

(P-2024)
NORMANDIE COUNTRY BAKERY INC (PA)
3022 S Cochran Ave, Los Angeles (90016-3706)
PHONE..............................323 939-5528
Josette Leblond, *President*
▲ EMP: 14 EST: 1996
SQ FT: 12,000
SALES (est): 1.4MM **Privately Held**
WEB: www.chefjosette.com
SIC: 2051 2011 Bakery: wholesale or wholesale/retail combined; sausages from meat slaughtered on site

(P-2025)
NOUSHIG INC
Also Called: Amoretti
451 Lombard St, Oxnard (93030-5143)
PHONE..............................805 983-2903
Jack Barsoumian, *CEO*
Hayop L Barsoumian, *President*
Maral Barsoumian, *Corp Secy*
Larry Meagher, *Vice Pres*
Levon Barsoumian, *Office Mgr*
◆ EMP: 50 EST: 1998
SQ FT: 10,000
SALES (est): 10.8MM **Privately Held**
WEB: www.amoretti.com
SIC: 2051 5149 Bread, cake & related products; soft drinks

(P-2026)
OAKHURST INDUSTRIES INC (PA)
Also Called: Freund Baking
2050 S Tubeway Ave, Commerce (90040-1624)
P.O. Box 911457, Los Angeles (90091-1238)
PHONE..............................323 724-3000
James Freund, *President*
Jonathan Freund, *Vice Pres*
Ronald Martin, *Vice Pres*
Linda F Freund, *Admin Sec*
Will Gallardo, *Safety Mgr*
EMP: 140 EST: 1981
SQ FT: 81,000
SALES (est): 64.7MM **Privately Held**
SIC: 2051 5149 Buns, bread type: fresh or frozen; rolls, bread type: fresh or frozen; groceries & related products

(P-2027)
OLD NEW YORK BAGEL DELI CO INC (PA)
Also Called: Old New York Deli & Bagel Co
4972 Verdugo Way, Camarillo (93012-8632)
P.O. Box 1288, Somis (93066-1288)
PHONE..................................805 484-3354
Michael J Raimondo, *President*
Julie Raimondo, *Vice Pres*
EMP: 34 EST: 1994
SQ FT: 2,400
SALES (est): 2.8MM Privately Held
WEB: www.oldnewyork.com
SIC: 2051 5812 Bakery: wholesale or wholesale/retail combined; coffee shop

(P-2028)
ORANGE BAKERY INC (HQ)
17751 Cowan, Irvine (92614-6064)
PHONE..................................949 863-1377
Yukinobu Saito, *CEO*
Yokinobu Saito, *CEO*
Yoshiaki Okazaki, *COO*
Kota Ueki, *CFO*
Mikio Kobayashi, *Chairman*
▲ EMP: 102 EST: 1978
SQ FT: 45,000
SALES (est): 48.6MM Privately Held
WEB: www.orangebakery.com
SIC: 2051 Bread, cake & related products

(P-2029)
PIE RISE LTD
Also Called: Marie Callender's Pie Shops
29051 S Western Ave, Rancho Palos Verdes (90275-0806)
PHONE..................................310 832-4559
Jim Louder, *Partner*
John Turner, *Partner*
EMP: 50 EST: 1971
SQ FT: 5,000
SALES (est): 1.2MM Privately Held
WEB: www.mariecallenders.com
SIC: 5812 2051 5461 Restaurant, family: chain; pies, bakery: except frozen; bakeries

(P-2030)
PORTOS FOOD PRODUCT INC
2085 Garfield Ave, Commerce (90040-1803)
PHONE..................................323 480-8400
Raul Porto, *Owner*
Margarita Navarro, *Vice Pres*
Ofelia Celestino, *Asst Controller*
Victor Lim, *Purch Mgr*
Robert Segura, *Prdtn Mgr*
▲ EMP: 92 EST: 2007
SALES (est): 7.3MM Privately Held
SIC: 2051 Bakery: wholesale or wholesale/retail combined

(P-2031)
PYRENEES FRENCH BAKERY INC
717 E 21st St, Bakersfield (93305-5240)
P.O. Box 3626 (93385-3626)
PHONE..................................661 322-7159
Marianne Laxague, *President*
Juanita Laxague, *Corp Secy*
Cheri Laxague, *Asst Mgr*
EMP: 23 EST: 1945
SQ FT: 33,750
SALES (est): 1.5MM Privately Held
WEB: www.pyreneesfrenchbakery.com
SIC: 2051 5461 Bakery: wholesale or wholesale/retail combined; bread, all types (white, wheat, rye, etc): fresh or frozen; bakeries

(P-2032)
RENAUDS BAKERY AND BISTRO INC (PA)
Also Called: Renaud's Patisserie & Bistro
3315 State St, Santa Barbara (93105-2623)
PHONE..................................805 569-2400
Nicole Black Gonthier, *CEO*
Michael Harte, *CEO*
Renaud Gonthier, *Principal*
EMP: 91 EST: 2007

SALES (est): 1.8MM Privately Held
SIC: 5812 2051 French restaurant; bakery: wholesale or wholesale/retail combined

(P-2033)
SGB BETTER BAKING CO LLC
14528 Blythe St, Van Nuys (91402-6006)
PHONE..................................818 787-9992
Chris Botticella, *CEO*
Ash Aghasi, *COO*
EMP: 57 EST: 2019
SALES (est): 4.6MM
SALES (corp-wide): 22.6MM Privately Held
WEB: www.thebetterbakingcompany.com
SIC: 2051 5149 Bakery: wholesale or wholesale/retail combined; bakery products
PA: Surge Global Bakeries Holdings Llc
13336 Paxton St
Pacoima CA 91331
818 896-0525

(P-2034)
SGB BUBBLES BAKING CO LLC
15215 Keswick St, Van Nuys (91405-1014)
PHONE..................................818 786-1700
Tom Beauchamp,
Blanca Izaguirre, *Accountant*
Lewis Sharp,
EMP: 100 EST: 2019
SQ FT: 50,000
SALES (est): 100K Privately Held
WEB: www.bubblesbakingco.com
SIC: 2051 5461 Bread, cake & related products; biscuits, baked: baking powder & raised; bakeries

(P-2035)
SONORA BAKERY INC
4484 Whittier Blvd, Los Angeles (90022-1534)
PHONE..................................323 269-2253
Hector Oratowski, *President*
Dennis Oratowski, *Treasurer*
Theresa Oratowski, *Vice Pres*
EMP: 30 EST: 1986
SQ FT: 6,000
SALES (est): 1.5MM Privately Held
WEB: www.sonorabakery.com
SIC: 5461 2051 1812 Bakeries; bread, cake & related products; caterers

(P-2036)
STATER BROS MARKETS
1131 N State College Blvd, Anaheim (92806-2704)
PHONE..................................714 991-5310
Scott Jefferson, *Manager*
EMP: 35 Privately Held
WEB: www.staterbros.com
SIC: 5411 5912 5992 2051 Supermarkets, chain; drug stores; florists; bread, cake & related products
HQ: Stater Bros. Markets
301 S Tippecanoe Ave
San Bernardino CA 92408
909 733-5000

(P-2037)
SUGAR FOODS CORPORATION
6190 E Slauson Ave, Commerce (90040-3010)
PHONE..................................323 727-8290
Harland Gray, *Manager*
Sherry De Keyser, *Human Resources*
EMP: 100
SALES (corp-wide): 286.3MM Privately Held
WEB: www.sugarfoods.com
SIC: 2051 2052 2099 Bread, cake & related products; cookies & crackers; food preparations
PA: Sugar Foods Corporation
950 3rd Ave Fl 21
New York NY 10022
212 753-6900

(P-2038)
SUPER CENTER CONCEPTS INC
Also Called: Superior Warehouse
10211 Avalon Blvd, Los Angeles (90003-4819)
PHONE..................................323 241-6789

Mat Kovacs, *Branch Mgr*
EMP: 112 Privately Held
WEB: www.superiorgrocers.com
SIC: 5411 2051 5812 5461 Supermarkets, independent; bread, cake & related products; carry-out only (except pizza) restaurant; bakeries
PA: Super Center Concepts, Inc.
15510 Carmenita Rd
Santa Fe Springs CA 90670

(P-2039)
UNITED STATES BAKERY
Also Called: Franz Family Bakeries
457 E Martin Luthr Kng Jr, Los Angeles (90011-5650)
PHONE..................................323 232-6124
EMP: 48
SALES (corp-wide): 536.1MM Privately Held
WEB: www.franzbakery.com
SIC: 2051 Bread & related products
PA: United States Bakery
315 Ne 10th Ave
Portland OR 97232
503 232-2191

(P-2040)
US DONUTS & YOGURT
11719 Whittier Blvd, Whittier (90601-3939)
PHONE..................................562 695-8867
Chhay NY, *Owner*
EMP: 20 EST: 1996
SALES (est): 559K Privately Held
SIC: 5812 2051 Ice cream stands or dairy bars; doughnuts, except frozen

(P-2041)
VENICE BAKING CO
134 Main St, El Segundo (90245-3801)
PHONE..................................310 322-7357
James N Desisto, *CEO*
Larry De Sisto, *President*
Miguel Gomez, *Planning*
Phil Alva, *Purch Mgr*
Joseph Fong,
EMP: 40 EST: 1959
SQ FT: 35,000
SALES (est): 5.2MM Privately Held
WEB: www.venicebakery.com
SIC: 2051 5149 Bread, all types (white, wheat, rye, etc): fresh or frozen; baking supplies; pizza supplies

(P-2042)
VIE DE FRANCE YAMAZAKI INC
Also Called: Vie De France 108
3046 E 50th St, Vernon (90058-2918)
PHONE..................................323 582-1241
Driss Goulhiane, *Branch Mgr*
Ken Bertke, *Engineer*
Laura Ramirez, *Human Res Mgr*
Gemal Michael, *QC Mgr*
Ann Cox, *Sales Mgr*
EMP: 808 Privately Held
WEB: www.viedefrance.com
SIC: 5812 2051 Restaurant, family: chain; breads, rolls & buns
HQ: Vie De France Yamazaki, Inc.
2070 Chain Bridge Rd # 500
Vienna VA 22182

(P-2043)
VONS COMPANIES INC
Also Called: Vons 2030
25850 The Old Rd, Stevenson Ranch (91381-1710)
PHONE..................................661 254-3570
Brian Flaherty, *Manager*
EMP: 91
SALES (corp-wide): 69.6B Publicly Held
SIC: 5411 5912 2051 5461 Supermarkets, chain; drug stores; bread, cake & related products; bakeries
HQ: The Vons Companies Inc
5918 Stoneridge Mall Rd
Pleasanton CA 94588
925 467-3000

(P-2044)
VONS COMPANIES INC
Also Called: Vons 2139
1390 N Allen Ave, Pasadena (91104-1617)
PHONE..................................626 798-7603

Tim Saller, *Branch Mgr*
Stephanie Pham, *Pharmacist*
EMP: 91
SALES (corp-wide): 69.6B Publicly Held
SIC: 5411 5912 5992 2051 Supermarkets, chain; drug stores; florists; bread, cake & related products
HQ: The Vons Companies Inc
5918 Stoneridge Mall Rd
Pleasanton CA 94588
925 467-3000

(P-2045)
VONS COMPANIES INC
Also Called: Vons 2407
475 W Main St, Brawley (92227-2244)
PHONE..................................760 351-3002
Frank Huerta, *Manager*
EMP: 91
SALES (corp-wide): 69.6B Publicly Held
SIC: 5411 5912 2051 7384 Supermarkets, chain; drug stores; bread, cake & related products; photofinish laboratories; florists; bakeries
HQ: The Vons Companies Inc
5918 Stoneridge Mall Rd
Pleasanton CA 94588
925 467-3000

(P-2046)
VONS COMPANIES INC
Also Called: Vons 2124
7789 Foothill Blvd, Tujunga (91042-2195)
PHONE..................................818 353-4917
Kevin Micalles, *Manager*
EMP: 91
SQ FT: 39,200
SALES (corp-wide): 69.6B Publicly Held
SIC: 5411 5912 5992 2051 Supermarkets, chain; drug stores; florists; bread, cake & related products
HQ: The Vons Companies Inc
5918 Stoneridge Mall Rd
Pleasanton CA 94588
925 467-3000

(P-2047)
VONS COMPANIES INC
Also Called: Vons 2381
535 N Mckinley St, Corona (92879-1297)
PHONE..................................951 278-8284
Rick Williams, *Manager*
EMP: 91
SALES (corp-wide): 69.6B Publicly Held
SIC: 5411 5912 2051 5461 Supermarkets, chain; drug stores; bread, cake & related products; bakeries
HQ: The Vons Companies Inc
5918 Stoneridge Mall Rd
Pleasanton CA 94588
925 467-3000

(P-2048)
VONS COMPANIES INC
Also Called: Vons 2111
24160 Lyons Ave, Newhall (91321-2442)
PHONE..................................661 259-9214
Phil Nakamura, *Manager*
EMP: 91
SALES (corp-wide): 69.6B Publicly Held
SIC: 5411 5912 2051 Supermarkets, chain; drug stores; bread, cake & related products
HQ: The Vons Companies Inc
5918 Stoneridge Mall Rd
Pleasanton CA 94588
925 467-3000

(P-2049)
WESTERN BAGEL BAKING CORP (PA)
7814 Sepulveda Blvd, Van Nuys (91405-1062)
PHONE..................................818 786-5847
Corie Ustin, *Chief Mktg Ofcr*
Jeff Ustin, *Executive*
Debbie Simon, *Office Mgr*
Chuck Jones, *Human Res Dir*
Erik Dahl, *VP Opers*
▼ EMP: 225
SQ FT: 23,500
SALES: 60.9MM Privately Held
WEB: www.westernbagel.com
SIC: 2051 5461 Bagels, fresh or frozen; bagels

PRODUCTS & SVCS

(P-2050)
WESTERN BAGEL BAKING CORP
21749 Ventura Blvd, Woodland Hills (91364-1835)
PHONE...............818 887-5451
Tim Brennen, *Principal*
EMP: 18
SALES (corp-wide): 60.9MM **Privately Held**
WEB: www.westernbagel.com
SIC: **2051** 5461 Bagels, fresh or frozen; bagels
PA: Western Bagel Baking Corp
   7814 Sepulveda Blvd
   Van Nuys CA 91405
   818 786-5847

(P-2051)
WESTERN BAGEL BAKING CORP
Also Called: Western Bagel Too
11628 Santa Monica Blvd # 12, Los Angeles (90025-2950)
PHONE...............310 479-4823
Fax: 310 826-2383
EMP: 20
SALES (corp-wide): 39.6MM **Privately Held**
SIC: **2051** Mfg Bread/Related Products
PA: Western Bagel Baking Corp
   7814 Sepulveda Blvd
   Van Nuys CA 91405
   818 786-5847

(P-2052)
WINCHELLS FRANCHISING LLC
Also Called: Winchell's Donut House
1695 W Pacific Coast Hwy, Long Beach (90810-4028)
PHONE...............562 437-8463
EMP: 22
SQ FT: 1,397 **Privately Held**
WEB: www.yumyumdonuts.com
SIC: **5461** 2051 Retail Bakeries
HQ: Winchell's Franchising, Llc
   18830 San Jose Ave
   City Of Industry CA 91748
   626 964-1478

(P-2053)
WINCHELLS FRANCHISING LLC
Also Called: Winchell's Donut House
14530 Brand Blvd, San Fernando (91340-4328)
PHONE...............818 361-9017
EMP: 22 **Privately Held**
WEB: www.yumyumdonuts.com
SIC: **5461** 2051 Retail Bakeries
HQ: Winchell's Franchising, Llc
   18830 San Jose Ave
   City Of Industry CA 91748
   626 964-1478

(P-2054)
YAMAZAKI CALIFORNIA INC
123 Japanese Vlg Plz Mall, Los Angeles (90012-3908)
PHONE...............213 624-2773
Kazumasa Tsugita, *President*
Shinichi Suzuki, *Vice Pres*
▲ **EMP:** 16 **EST:** 1977
SQ FT: 6,600
SALES (est): 1.1MM **Privately Held**
WEB: www.yamazakipan.co.jp
SIC: **5461** 2051 Cakes; bakery: wholesale or wholesale/retail combined
PA: Yamazaki Baking Co., Ltd.
   3-10-1, Iwamotocho
   Chiyoda-Ku TKY 101-0

2052 Cookies & Crackers

(P-2055)
ALBERTSONS LLC
Also Called: Albertsons 6798
30901 Riverside Dr, Lake Elsinore (92530-4934)
PHONE...............951 245-4461
Brad Sharp, *Manager*
EMP: 190

SALES (corp-wide): 69.6B **Publicly Held**
WEB: www.albertsons.com
SIC: **5411** 5992 2052 2051 Supermarkets, chain; florists; cookies & crackers; bread, cake & related products
HQ: Albertson's Llc
   250 E Parkcenter Blvd
   Boise ID 83706
   208 395-4722

(P-2056)
AMAYS BAKERY & NOODLE CO INC (PA)
837 E Commercial St, Los Angeles (90012-3413)
PHONE...............213 626-2713
Kee Hom, *CEO*
▲ **EMP:** 63
SQ FT: 20,000
SALES (est): 9.3MM **Privately Held**
WEB: www.amaysbakery.com
SIC: **2052** 2098 Cookies; noodles (e.g. egg, plain & water), dry

(P-2057)
ASPIRE BAKERIES LLC
15963 Strathern St, Van Nuys (91406-1313)
PHONE...............818 904-8230
Marcus Garcia, *Branch Mgr*
EMP: 91
SALES (corp-wide): 1.7B **Privately Held**
WEB: www.aryzta.com
SIC: **2052** Cookies
HQ: Aspire Bakeries Llc
   350 N Orleans St 3001n
   Chicago IL 60654
   855 427-9982

(P-2058)
BISCOMERICA CORP
565 W Slover Ave, Rialto (92377)
P.O. Box 1070 (92377-1070)
PHONE...............909 877-5997
Nadi Soltan, *Ch of Bd*
Ayad Fargo, *President*
Gordon Cramer, *Vice Pres*
Rob Gallitto, *CIO*
Kevin Abraham, *Asst Controller*
◆ **EMP:** 252 **EST:** 1979
SQ FT: 250,000
SALES (est): 71.6MM **Privately Held**
WEB: www.biscomericacorp.com
SIC: **2052** 2064 Cookies; candy & other confectionery products

(P-2059)
BLOOMFIELD BAKERS
10711 Bloomfield St, Los Alamitos (90720-2503)
PHONE...............626 610-2253
William R Ross, *General Ptnr*
Maggie Acquisition Corp, *General Ptnr*
Aiko Acquisition Corp, *Partner*
Gary Marx, *Branch Mgr*
▼ **EMP:** 600 **EST:** 1992
SQ FT: 75,000
SALES (est): 105.9MM
SALES (corp-wide): 4.3B **Publicly Held**
WEB: www.barbakers.com
SIC: **2052** 2064 Cookies; candy & other confectionery products
HQ: Treehouse Private Brands, Inc.
   2021 Spring Rd Ste 600
   Oak Brook IL 60523

(P-2060)
BREAD LOS ANGELES
1527 Beach St, Montebello (90640-5431)
PHONE...............323 201-3953
Vachik M Elchibegian,
Melecio Espain, *Opers Mgr*
Beatrice M Elchibegian,
▲ **EMP:** 16 **EST:** 2003
SALES (est): 2.3MM **Privately Held**
WEB: www.breadlosangeles.com
SIC: **2052** 2051 Cookies & crackers; bread, cake & related products

(P-2061)
CRUMBL COOKIES ❂
23702 El Toro Rd Ste B, Lake Forest (92630-8905)
PHONE...............949 519-0791
Spencer Hanks, *Owner*

EMP: 70 **EST:** 2021
SALES (est): 2.9MM **Privately Held**
SIC: **2052** Cookies

(P-2062)
D F STAUFFER BISCUIT CO INC
Laguna Cookie Company
4041 W Garry Ave, Santa Ana (92704-6315)
PHONE...............714 546-6855
Albert Ovalle, *Manager*
EMP: 50 **Privately Held**
WEB: www.stauffers.com
SIC: **2052** Cookies
HQ: D F Stauffer Biscuit Co Inc
   360 S Belmont St
   York PA 17403
   717 815-4600

(P-2063)
ELEMENTS FOOD GROUP INC
5560 Brooks St, Montclair (91763-4522)
P.O. Box 4020, Newport Beach (92661-4020)
PHONE...............909 983-2011
Wayne Sorensen, *President*
EMP: 60 **EST:** 2004
SQ FT: 23,000
SALES (est): 7.2MM **Privately Held**
WEB: www.elementsfoods.com
SIC: **2052** 2038 Bakery products, dry; breakfasts, frozen & packaged; dinners, frozen & packaged; lunches, frozen & packaged

(P-2064)
FOWLIE ENTERPRISES INC
Also Called: Pretzelmaker
1143 Fern Oaks Dr, Santa Paula (93060-1203)
PHONE...............805 583-2800
EMP: 25
SALES (est): 1.6MM **Privately Held**
SIC: **2052** 2096 Mfg Cookies/Crackers Mfg Potato Chips/Snacks

(P-2065)
J & J SNACK FOODS CORP CAL (HQ)
5353 S Downey Rd, Vernon (90058-3725)
PHONE...............323 581-0171
Dennis Moore, *Vice Pres*
Robyn Shreiber, *Vice Pres*
Leong Tan, *Executive*
Jerry Lockridge, *Purch Dir*
Mark Self, *QC Mgr*
▲ **EMP:** 212 **EST:** 1978
SQ FT: 132,000
SALES (est): 103.4MM
SALES (corp-wide): 1B **Publicly Held**
WEB: www.jjsnack.com
SIC: **2052** 5149 Pretzels; cookies
PA: J & J Snack Foods Corp.
   6000 Central Hwy
   Pennsauken NJ 08109
   856 665-9533

(P-2066)
JUST OFF MELROSE INC
1196 Montalvo Way, Palm Springs (92262-5441)
PHONE...............714 533-4566
Brandon Tesmer, *President*
David Parker, *Executive*
EMP: 24 **EST:** 1986
SQ FT: 12,000
SALES (est): 1.6MM **Privately Held**
WEB: www.justoffmelrose.com
SIC: **2052** 2051 Crackers, dry; cookies; bakery products, dry; bread, cake & related products

(P-2067)
KEEBLER COMPANY
14000 183rd St, La Palma (90623-1010)
PHONE...............714 228-1555
EMP: 60
SALES (corp-wide): 12.9B **Publicly Held**
SIC: **2052** 2051 Mfg Cookies/Crackers Mfg Bread/Related Products
HQ: Keebler Company
   1 Kellogg Sq
   Battle Creek MI 49017
   269 961-2000

(P-2068)
LAGUNA COOKIE COMPANY INC
4041 W Garry Ave, Santa Ana (92704-6315)
PHONE...............714 546-6855
Takeshi Izumi, *CEO*
Rod Sanchez, *Manager*
EMP: 100 **EST:** 1981
SQ FT: 55,000
SALES (est): 28.3MM **Privately Held**
WEB: www.stauffers.com
SIC: **2052** Cookies
HQ: D F Stauffer Biscuit Co Inc
   360 S Belmont St
   York PA 17403
   717 815-4600

(P-2069)
NEW HRZNS SRVING INDVDALS WITH (PA)
Also Called: New Horizons Center & Workshop
15725 Parthenia St, North Hills (91343-4913)
PHONE...............818 894-9301
Cynthia Kawa, *CEO*
Leilani Downer, *Comms Mgr*
SRI RAO, *Controller*
Sharoll Jackson, *Hum Res Coord*
Jesse Funes, *Director*
▲ **EMP:** 100 **EST:** 1954
SQ FT: 60,000
SALES (est): 15.9MM **Privately Held**
WEB: www.newhorizons-sf.org
SIC: **8243** 2052 Software training, computer; cookies

(P-2070)
PADERIA LLC
18279 Brookhurst St Ste 1, Fountain Valley (92708-6750)
PHONE...............949 478-5273
Nathan Vuong,
Ngoc Tran, *Manager*
EMP: 14 **EST:** 2016
SALES (est): 984K **Privately Held**
SIC: **2052** Cookies & crackers

(P-2071)
PAK GROUP LLC
Also Called: Dellarise
236 N Chester Ave Ste 200, Pasadena (91106-5166)
PHONE...............626 316-6555
Walter Postelwait, *President*
Ken Chase, *CFO*
Khosrow Pakravan,
▲ **EMP:** 38 **EST:** 2012
SQ FT: 6,200
SALES (est): 2.3MM **Privately Held**
WEB: www.bellarise.com
SIC: **2052** 2099 5149 Bakery products, dry; food preparations; yeast
PA: Tech Us Corp
   236 N Chester Ave Ste 200
   Pasadena CA 91106
   626 316-6555

(P-2072)
SOUTH COAST BAKING LLC (PA)
Also Called: South Coast Baking Co.
1722 Kettering, Irvine (92614-5616)
PHONE...............949 851-9654
Kent Hayden, *CEO*
James Bergeson, *Partner*
Rick Ptak, *COO*
Paul Trujillo, *VP Bus Dvlp*
Carole Ann Sushkoff, *Controller*
◆ **EMP:** 55 **EST:** 2011
SQ FT: 22,500
SALES (est): 102.9MM **Privately Held**
WEB: www.risebakingcompany.com
SIC: **2052** 5149 Cookies; cookies

(P-2073)
STATER BROS MARKETS
10114 Adams Ave, Huntington Beach (92646-4907)
PHONE...............714 963-0949
Kevin Wagner, *Manager*
EMP: 35 **Privately Held**
WEB: www.staterbros.com

SIC: **5411** 5912 5992 2052 Supermarkets, chain; drug stores; florists; cookies & crackers; bread, cake & related products
HQ: Stater Bros. Markets
301 S Tippecanoe Ave
San Bernardino CA 92408
909 733-5000

(P-2074)
SUPER CENTER CONCEPTS INC
Also Called: Superior Super Warehouse
7300 Atlantic Ave, Cudahy (90201-4305)
PHONE..................................323 562-8980
Peter Buyn, *Branch Mgr*
EMP: 112 **Privately Held**
WEB: www.superiorgrocers.com
SIC: **5411** 5421 2052 2051 Grocery stores, independent; meat & fish markets; cookies & crackers; bread, cake & related products; miniwarehouse, warehousing, bakeries
PA: Super Center Concepts, Inc.
15510 Carmenita Rd
Santa Fe Springs CA 90670

(P-2075)
UMEYA INC
Also Called: Umeya Rice Cake Co
414 Crocker St, Los Angeles (90013-2115)
P.O. Box 1071, Glendale (91209-1071)
PHONE..................................213 626-8341
Tak Hamano, *President*
Bunji Hayata, *Corp Secy*
▲ EMP: 24 EST: 1938
SQ FT: 16,000
SALES (est): 826.2K **Privately Held**
WEB: www.umeya.co
SIC: **2052** Cookies; crackers, dry

(P-2076)
UTBBB INC
10711 Bloomfield St, Los Alamitos (90720-2503)
PHONE..................................562 594-4411
Gary Marks, *CEO*
William R Ross, *President*
Gene Kester, *Principal*
◆ EMP: 94 EST: 1985
SQ FT: 1,000
SALES (est): 4.6MM
SALES (corp-wide): 4.3B **Publicly Held**
WEB: www.treehousefoods.com
SIC: **2052** 5141 Cookies & crackers; food brokers
HQ: Treehouse Private Brands, Inc.
2021 Spring Rd Ste 600
Oak Brook IL 60523

2053 Frozen Bakery Prdts

(P-2077)
HC BRILL
Also Called: Telco Food
2111 W Valley Blvd, Colton (92324-1814)
PHONE..................................909 825-7343
Michelle Stirling, *Principal*
EMP: 26
SALES (corp-wide): 5.4MM **Privately Held**
SIC: **2053** 2051 Pies, bakery: frozen; bread, cake & related products
PA: H.C. Brill
2003 S Bibb Dr
Tucker GA
770 723-3449

(P-2078)
LINNS FRUIT BIN INC (PA)
Also Called: Linn's Main Bin
2535 Village Ln Ste A, Cambria (93428-3428)
PHONE..................................805 927-1499
Maureen Linn, *President*
Renee Linn, *President*
John Linn, *Vice Pres*
Aaron Linn, *General Mgr*
Phil Purdin, *Admin Asst*
EMP: 35 EST: 1995
SQ FT: 16,000

SALES (est): 11.4MM **Privately Held**
WEB: www.linnsfruitbin.com
SIC: **5431** 2053 5812 Fruit & vegetable markets; frozen bakery products, except bread; cakes, bakery: frozen; eating places

(P-2079)
MARYS COUNTRY KITCHEN
Also Called: Malibu Kitchen
3900 Cross Creek Rd Ste 3, Malibu (90265-4962)
PHONE..................................310 456-7845
William Miller, *Owner*
EMP: 15 EST: 2000
SALES (est): 970.7K **Privately Held**
WEB: www.malibucountrymart.com
SIC: **2053** Pies, bakery: frozen

2063 Sugar, Beet

(P-2080)
SPRECKELS SUGAR COMPANY INC
395 W Keystone Rd, Brawley (92227-9739)
P.O. Box 581 (92227-0581)
PHONE..................................760 344-3110
John Richmond, *President*
Neil Rudeen, *Ch of Bd*
Jeff Plathe, *CEO*
Jay Creiglow, *Engineer*
Robert Ruiz, *Controller*
▲ EMP: 260 EST: 1905
SALES (est): 50.5MM
SALES (corp-wide): 376.8MM **Privately Held**
WEB: www.smbsc.com
SIC: **2063** Beet sugar from beet sugar refinery
PA: Southern Minnesota Beet Sugar Cooperative
83550 County Road 21
Renville MN 56284
320 329-8305

2064 Candy & Confectionery Prdts

(P-2081)
ADAMS AND BROOKS INC
4345 Hallmark Pkwy, San Bernardino (92407-1829)
PHONE..................................213 392-8700
EMP: 90
SALES (corp-wide): 23MM **Privately Held**
SIC: **2064** Mfg Candy/Confectionery
PA: Adams And Brooks, Inc.
4345 Hallmark Pkwy
San Bernardino CA 92407
909 880-2305

(P-2082)
CALIFORNIA SNACK FOODS INC
Also Called: California Candy
2131 Tyler Ave, South El Monte (91733-2754)
PHONE..................................626 444-4508
Murl W Nelson, *CEO*
Steve Nelson, *President*
Paul Mullen, *Vice Pres*
Mary Nelson, *Admin Sec*
EMP: 45 EST: 1961
SQ FT: 30,000
SALES (est): 7.1MM **Privately Held**
WEB: www.californiasnackfoods.com
SIC: **2064** 2024 2099 2051 Fruits: candied, crystallized, or glazed; juice pops, frozen; popcorn, packaged: except already popped; cakes, pies & pastries; dried & dehydrated soup mixes; novelties & specialties, metal

(P-2083)
COUNTRY HOUSE
Also Called: Seloah Gourmet Food
2852 Walnut Ave Ste C1, Tustin (92780-7033)
PHONE..................................714 505-8988
Monica Ching, *Owner*

▲ EMP: 26 EST: 1994
SQ FT: 9,400
SALES (est): 4.5MM **Privately Held**
WEB: www.countryhousenatural.com
SIC: **2064** Candy & other confectionery products

(P-2084)
DIVINE FOODS INC
Also Called: Rise Bar
16752 Millikan Ave, Irvine (92606-5010)
PHONE..................................800 440-6476
Peter Spenuzza, *President*
▲ EMP: 20 EST: 1999
SQ FT: 15,000
SALES (est): 4MM **Privately Held**
WEB: www.risebar.com
SIC: **2064** Breakfast bars

(P-2085)
EZAKI GLICO USA CORPORATION
18022 Cowan Ste 110, Irvine (92614-6805)
PHONE..................................949 251-0144
Akitoshi Oku, *President*
George Iwashita, *Marketing Staff*
Delron Dozier, *Sales Staff*
Glico Kudoh, *Manager*
▲ EMP: 19 EST: 1996
SALES (est): 9MM **Privately Held**
WEB: www.glico.com
SIC: **2064** 8111 Candy & other confectionery products; general practice attorney, lawyer
PA: Ezaki Glico Co.,Ltd.
4-6-5, Utajima, Nishiyodogawa-Ku
Osaka OSK 555-0

(P-2086)
FOOD TECHNOLOGY AND DESIGN LLC
Also Called: Food Pharma
10012 Painter Ave, Santa Fe Springs (90670-3016)
PHONE..................................562 944-7821
Glen Marinelli, *Mng Member*
Gary Cleaveland, *Executive*
Claudia Villanueva, *Technician*
Regina Medina, *Safety Mgr*
Vicki Cortese, *Sales Mgr*
EMP: 40 EST: 2001
SQ FT: 20,000
SALES (est): 9.4MM **Privately Held**
SIC: **2064** Candy & other confectionery products

(P-2087)
HGC HOLDINGS INC
3303 Mrtin Lther King Jr, Lynwood (90262-1905)
PHONE..................................323 567-2226
Robert I Hadgraft, *CEO*
David Worth, *CEO*
Robert Worth, *Admin Sec*
▲ EMP: 19 EST: 1944
SQ FT: 90,000
SALES (est): 693.5K **Privately Held**
SIC: **2064** 5441 Chocolate candy, except solid chocolate; candy

(P-2088)
HOTLIX (PA)
Also Called: Hotlix Candy
966 Griffin St, Grover Beach (93433-3019)
P.O. Box 447 (93483-0447)
PHONE..................................805 473-0596
Larry Peterman, *President*
Richard Lara, *Data Proc Staff*
Kathy Mitchell, *VP Sls/Mktg*
▼ EMP: 25 EST: 1983
SQ FT: 1,500
SALES (est): 6.5MM **Privately Held**
WEB: www.hotlix.com
SIC: **2064** Lollipops & other hard candy

(P-2089)
ISLAND SNACKS INC
Also Called: Island Products
7650 Stage Rd, Buena Park (90621-1226)
PHONE..................................714 994-1228
Alin Barak, *President*
◆ EMP: 20 EST: 1980
SQ FT: 6,600

SALES (est): 5.7MM **Privately Held**
WEB: www.islandsnack.com
SIC: **2064** Candy & other confectionery products

(P-2090)
JEWEL DATE COMPANY INC
48440 Prairie Dr, Palm Desert (92260-6546)
PHONE..................................760 399-4474
Gregory Raumin, *President*
◆ EMP: 20 EST: 1995
SALES (est): 5.2MM **Privately Held**
SIC: **2064** Sugared dates

(P-2091)
LB BEADELS LLC
70 Atlantic Ave, Long Beach (90802-5202)
PHONE..................................562 726-1700
Joshua Beadel, *Principal*
EMP: 14 EST: 2013
SALES (est): 1.9MM **Privately Held**
WEB: www.the-breakfast-bar.com
SIC: **2064** Breakfast bars

(P-2092)
LDVC INC
Also Called: Lasdos Victorias Candy Company
9606 Valley Blvd, Rosemead (91770-1510)
PHONE..................................626 448-4611
Jenny Lee, *President*
David Lee, *CFO*
EMP: 17 EST: 1991
SQ FT: 8,000
SALES (est): 509.9K **Privately Held**
WEB: www.ldvc.net
SIC: **2064** Candy & other confectionery products

(P-2093)
LOGANS CANDIES
125 W B St, Ontario (91762-3502)
PHONE..................................909 984-5410
Jerry Rowley, *Owner*
EMP: 16 EST: 1953
SQ FT: 2,800
SALES (est): 500K **Privately Held**
WEB: www.loganscandies.com
SIC: **5441** 2064 Candy; candy & other confectionery products

(P-2094)
MAGIC GUMBALL INTERNATIONAL
9310 Mason Ave, Chatsworth (91311-5201)
PHONE..................................818 716-1888
Don Hart, *President*
Guy Hart, *Vice Pres*
◆ EMP: 14 EST: 1995
SALES (est): 399K **Privately Held**
WEB: www.magicgumballs.com
SIC: **2064** 3581 2067 Candy & other confectionery products; automatic vending machines; chewing gum

(P-2095)
MANHATTAN CONFECTIONERS INC
Also Called: Jo's Candies
2530 W 237th St, Torrance (90505-5217)
PHONE..................................310 257-0260
Thomas King, *President*
▲ EMP: 16 EST: 1946
SQ FT: 20,000
SALES (est): 1.3MM **Privately Held**
SIC: **2064** 5145 Candy & other confectionery products; candy

(P-2096)
MAVE ENTERPRISES INC
Also Called: It's Delish
11555 Cantara St Ste B-E, North Hollywood (91605-1652)
P.O. Box 480620, Los Angeles (90048-1620)
PHONE..................................818 767-4533
Amy Grawitzky, *CEO*
Moshe Grawitzky, *Vice Pres*
Rochell Legarreta, *Admin Sec*
Roberto Munoz, *Manager*
▲ EMP: 35 EST: 1992
SQ FT: 35,000

PRODUCTS & SVCS

SALES (est): 5MM **Privately Held**
SIC: 2064 2099 2033 2068 Candy & other confectionery products; seasonings & spices; canned fruits & specialties; salted & roasted nuts & seeds

(P-2097)
MCKEEVER DANLEE CONFECTIONARY
760 N Mckeever Ave, Azusa (91702-2349)
PHONE.....................626 334-8964
Gerald Morris, *President*
David A Pistole, *CFO*
Brian Halpert, *Corp Secy*
EMP: 122 **EST:** 1994
SQ FT: 10,000
SALES (est): 2.6MM
SALES (corp-wide): 179.1MM **Privately Held**
WEB: www.morrisnational.com
SIC: 2064 Candy & other confectionery products
HQ: Morris National, Inc.
760 N Mckeever Ave
Azusa CA 91702
626 385-2000

(P-2098)
MORINAGA AMERICA INC (HQ)
4 Park Plz Ste 750, Irvine (92614-5211)
PHONE.....................949 732-1155
Masanori Yasunaga, *CEO*
Hideki Uehara, *President*
Yoshiyuki Ishiguro, *CFO*
Ivan Elizalde, *Regl Sales Mgr*
Jacob Heller, *Marketing Staff*
◆ **EMP:** 32 **EST:** 2007
SQ FT: 170
SALES (est): 5.3MM **Privately Held**
WEB: www.morinaga-america.com
SIC: 2064 Candy & other confectionery products

(P-2099)
MY FAVORITE COMPANY INC (PA)
8322 Beverly Blvd Ste 302, Los Angeles (90048-2665)
P.O. Box 69977 (90069-0977)
PHONE.....................310 659-3611
Mark Eisenberg, *President*
Neil Wright, *Vice Pres*
▲ **EMP:** 13 **EST:** 1984
SALES (est): 2.2MM **Privately Held**
SIC: 2064 5092 3942 7389 Candy & other confectionery products; toys & hobby goods & supplies; dolls & stuffed toys; balloons, novelty & toy; toys & games

(P-2100)
NELLSON NUTRACEUTICAL INC
5115 E La Palma Ave, Anaheim (92807-2018)
PHONE.....................844 635-5766
Scott Greenwood, *CEO*
Ben Muhlenkamp, *President*
Jeff Moran, *CEO*
Paul Hanson, *Senior VP*
Bart Child, *Vice Pres*
▲ **EMP:** 297 **EST:** 1961
SQ FT: 100,000
SALES (est): 26.3MM **Privately Held**
SIC: 2064 Candy bars, including chocolate covered bars

(P-2101)
NO NUTS LLC
750 Calle Plano, Camarillo (93012-8555)
PHONE.....................805 309-2420
Spencer Thompson, *Mng Member*
EMP: 15 **EST:** 2020
SALES (est): 664.5K **Privately Held**
WEB: www.gononuts.com
SIC: 2064 Granola & muesli, bars & clusters

(P-2102)
RAMISONS INC
Pizza Press, The
1534 S Harbor Blvd, Anaheim (92802-2312)
PHONE.....................714 323-7134
Kiana Beuler, *Branch Mgr*

Robert Stidham, *COO*
Jennifer Moore, *Marketing Staff*
Mark Miller, *Manager*
EMP: 15
SALES (corp-wide): 13.9MM **Privately Held**
WEB: www.thepizzapress.com
SIC: 5812 2064 Pizzeria, independent; breakfast bars
PA: Ramisons, Inc.
1734 S Harbor Blvd
Anaheim CA 92802
714 774-8111

(P-2103)
SANDERS CANDY FACTORY INC
5051 Calmview Ave, Baldwin Park (91706-1802)
PHONE.....................626 814-2038
Timothy Sanders, *CEO*
Steven L Peralez, *Corp Secy*
Mark Sanders, *Vice Pres*
EMP: 20 **EST:** 1989
SQ FT: 40,000
SALES (est): 10.4MM **Privately Held**
SIC: 2064 Candy & other confectionery products

(P-2104)
SEES CANDIES INC (DH)
20600 S Alameda St, Carson (90810-1105)
PHONE.....................800 347-7337
Patrick Egan, *CEO*
Ken Scott, *CFO*
Bernie Bishop, *Vice Pres*
Eileen Duag, *Vice Pres*
Alison Godin, *CIO*
▲ **EMP:** 500 **EST:** 1935
SQ FT: 250,000
SALES (est): 584.9MM
SALES (corp-wide): 245.5B **Publicly Held**
WEB: www.sees.com
SIC: 2064 5441 Candy & other confectionery products; candy
HQ: See's Candy Shops, Incorporated
210 El Camino Real
South San Francisco CA 94080
650 761-2490

(P-2105)
SENCHA NATURALS INC
1101 Monterey Pass Rd A, Monterey Park (91754-3629)
PHONE.....................213 353-9908
David Kerdoon, *President*
▲ **EMP:** 15 **EST:** 2008
SALES (est): 2.2MM **Privately Held**
WEB: www.senchanaturals.com
SIC: 2064 Candy & other confectionery products

(P-2106)
SENOR SNACKS MANUFACTURING LTD
2325 Raymer Ave, Fullerton (92833-2514)
PHONE.....................714 739-1073
Jose V Mazon, *Partner*
EMP: 16 **EST:** 1984
SALES (est): 480K **Privately Held**
SIC: 2064 Candy & other confectionery products

(P-2107)
SUGARFINA USA LLC
1700 E Walnut Ave Ste 500, El Segundo (90245-2609)
PHONE.....................855 784-2734
Scott Laporta, *CEO*
Steven Borse, *Mng Member*
EMP: 200 **EST:** 2019
SALES (est): 13.6MM **Privately Held**
WEB: www.sugarfina.com
SIC: 2064 Candy & other confectionery products

2066 Chocolate & Cocoa Prdts

(P-2108)
VERY SPECIAL CHOCOLATS INC
760 N Mckeever Ave, Azusa (91702-2349)
PHONE.....................626 334-7838
Gerry Morris Zubatoff, *CEO*
Gerald Morris, *President*
David Pistole, *CFO*
Bram Morris, *Admin Sec*
▲ **EMP:** 152 **EST:** 1986
SQ FT: 40,000
SALES (est): 2.7MM
SALES (corp-wide): 179.1MM **Privately Held**
WEB: www.morrisnational.com
SIC: 2066 Chocolate & cocoa products
HQ: Morris National, Inc.
760 N Mckeever Ave
Azusa CA 91702
626 385-2000

2068 Salted & Roasted Nuts & Seeds

(P-2109)
180 SNACKS INC
Also Called: MAREBLU NATURALS
1151 N Armando St, Anaheim (92806-2609)
PHONE.....................714 238-1192
Michael Kim, *President*
Katherine Kim, *Vice Pres*
Eugene Kim, *QA Dir*
Michael Runion, *VP Sales*
▲ **EMP:** 47 **EST:** 2004
SQ FT: 10,000
SALES (est): 104.2K **Privately Held**
WEB: www. 180snacks.com
SIC: 2068 2034 Salted & roasted nuts & seeds; dried & dehydrated fruits

(P-2110)
BRIGHT FOODS LLC
777 S Alameda St Ste 220, Los Angeles (90021-1657)
PHONE.....................708 263-7771
Brenden Schaefer, *Mng Member*
EMP: 13 **EST:** 2019
SALES (est): 1.5MM **Privately Held**
WEB: www.brightfoods.com
SIC: 2068 2034 Nuts: dried, dehydrated, salted or roasted; dried & dehydrated fruits

(P-2111)
CAL TREEHOUSE ALMONDS LLC (PA)
6914 Road 160, Earlimart (93219-9627)
P.O. Box 12150 (93219-2150)
PHONE.....................559 757-5020
Jonathan Meyer,
Tim Hoyt, *CFO*
Joe Gardiner, *Sales Staff*
Brian Tormey, *Sales Staff*
Keith B Gardiner, *Sales Staff*
◆ **EMP:** 124 **EST:** 2002
SALES (est): 18.6MM **Privately Held**
WEB: www.treehousealmonds.com
SIC: 2068 2041 0173 Nuts: dried, dehydrated, salted or roasted; flour; almond grove

(P-2112)
G & P GROUP INC
Also Called: Mr. Nature
13842 Bettencourt St, Cerritos (90703-1010)
PHONE.....................323 268-2686
George Barraza, *Managing Dir*
Philip Borup, *Managing Dir*
▼ **EMP:** 13 **EST:** 2011
SALES (est): 2.3MM **Privately Held**
WEB: www.mrnature.com
SIC: 2068 0723 Salted & roasted nuts & seeds; fruit (farm-dried) packing services

(P-2113)
MIXED NUTS INC
7909 Crossway Dr, Pico Rivera (90660-4449)
PHONE.....................323 587-6887
Vanik Hartounian, *President*
◆ **EMP:** 25 **EST:** 1986
SALES (est): 7.6MM **Privately Held**
WEB: www.mixednutsinc.com
SIC: 2068 5145 Nuts: dried, dehydrated, salted or roasted; nuts, salted or roasted

(P-2114)
NICHOLS PISTACHIO
Also Called: Nichols Farms
13762 1st Ave, Hanford (93230-9316)
PHONE.....................559 584-6811
Chuck Nichols, *CEO*
Susan Nichols, *Treasurer*
Adam Kistler, *Engineer*
Jennifer Dunlap, *Manager*
April McDaniel, *Manager*
◆ **EMP:** 200 **EST:** 1990
SQ FT: 110,000
SALES (est): 62MM **Privately Held**
WEB: www.nicholsfarms.com
SIC: 2068 Salted & roasted nuts & seeds

(P-2115)
PRIMEX FARMS LLC (PA)
16070 Wildwood Rd, Wasco (93280-9210)
PHONE.....................661 758-7790
Ali Amin, *President*
Brad Gleason, *CFO*
Ignasius Handoko, *Principal*
Janet Llenos, *Accounting Mgr*
Ebi Hajizadeh, *Accountant*
EMP: 30
SQ FT: 136,837
SALES (est): 116.5MM **Privately Held**
WEB: www.primexfarms.com
SIC: 2068 Nuts: dried, dehydrated, salted or roasted

(P-2116)
SNAK CLUB LLC
Also Called: New Century Snacks
5560 E Slauson Ave, Commerce (90040-2921)
PHONE.....................323 278-9578
Farhad Morshed, *President*
Kyle Ragsdale, *Exec VP*
Nader Morovati, *Vice Pres*
Bob Riley, *Sales Staff*
Michael Halsey, *Manager*
EMP: 70
SALES (corp-wide): 177.6MM **Privately Held**
WEB: www.centurysnacks.com
SIC: 2068 2099 Salted & roasted nuts & seeds; food preparations
HQ: Snak Club, Llc
607 N Nash St
El Segundo CA 90245
310 322-4400

(P-2117)
WONDERFUL ALMOND COOPERATIVE
11444 W Olympic Blvd 10th, Los Angeles (90064-1549)
PHONE.....................310 966-5800
EMP: 23 **EST:** 2014
SALES (est): 289.5K **Privately Held**
WEB: www.wonderful.com
SIC: 2068 Salted & roasted nuts & seeds

(P-2118)
WONDERFUL PSTCHIOS ALMONDS LLC (HQ)
Also Called: Paramount Farms
11444 W Olympic Blvd, Los Angeles (90064-1549)
P.O. Box 200937, Dallas TX (75320-0937)
PHONE.....................310 966-4650
Stewart Resnick, *President*
Michael Hohmann, *CFO*
Bill Phillimore, *Exec VP*
Craig B Cooper, *Senior VP*
James Kfouri, *Admin Sec*
◆ **EMP:** 25 **EST:** 1989
SQ FT: 15,000

SALES (est): 915.3MM
SALES (corp-wide): 2B Privately Held
WEB: www.wonderfulpistachiosandal-
monds.com
SIC: 2068 Salted & roasted nuts & seeds
PA: The Wonderful Company Llc
11444 W Olympic Blvd # 210
Los Angeles CA 90064
310 966-5700

2075 Soybean Oil Mills

(P-2119)
MIYAKO ORIENTAL FOODS INC
Also Called: Yamajirushi Miso
4287 Puente Ave, Baldwin Park
(91706-3420)
PHONE....................626 962-9633
Noritoshi Kanai, President
Teruo Shimizu, Vice Pres
▲ EMP: 14 EST: 1976
SQ FT: 18,000
SALES (est): 8.5MM Privately Held
WEB: www.coldmountainmiso.com
SIC: 2075 Soybean oil, cake or meal
HQ: Mutual Trading Co., Inc.
4200 Shirley Ave
El Monte CA 91731
213 626-9458

(P-2120)
SOYFOODS OF AMERICA
1091 Hamilton Rd, Duarte (91010-2743)
PHONE....................626 358-3836
Ka Nin Lee, President
EMP: 27 EST: 1981
SQ FT: 15,000
SALES (est): 4.4MM Privately Held
WEB: www.soyfoodsusa.com
SIC: 2075 Soybean oil mills

2076 Vegetable Oil Mills

(P-2121)
GLOBAL AGRI-TRADE
15500 S Avalon Blvd, Rancho Dominguez
(90220-3205)
PHONE....................562 320-8550
Haresh Kumar Bhatt, CEO
Jignesh Bhatt, Vice Pres
Jurgen Godau, Vice Pres
Ravin Banta, Office Mgr
Lynn Willis, Controller
▲ EMP: 36 EST: 2006
SQ FT: 2,500
SALES (est): 6.8MM Privately Held
WEB: www.globalagritrade.com
SIC: 2076 5199 Palm kernel oil; oils, ani-
mal or vegetable

2077 Animal, Marine Fats & Oils

(P-2122)
BAKER COMMODITIES INC (PA)
4020 Bandini Blvd, Vernon (90058-4274)
PHONE....................323 268-2801
James M Andreoli, President
Denis Luckey, Exec VP
Jason Andreoli, Vice Pres
Mitchell Ebright, Vice Pres
Jeff Schnobrich, Branch Mgr
▼ EMP: 150
SQ FT: 12,000
SALES (est): 153.6MM Privately Held
WEB: www.bakercommodities.com
SIC: 2077 2048 Tallow rendering, inedible;
poultry feeds

(P-2123)
BAKER COMMODITIES INC
7480 Hanford Armona Rd, Hanford
(93230-9343)
P.O. Box 1286 (93232-1286)
PHONE....................559 686-4797
Doug Fletcher, Manager
EMP: 32

SALES (corp-wide): 153.6MM Privately
Held
WEB: www.bakercommodities.com
SIC: 2077 2048 Tallow rendering, inedible;
prepared feeds
PA: Baker Commodities, Inc.
4020 Bandini Blvd
Vernon CA 90058
323 268-2801

(P-2124)
BAKER COMMODITIES INC
3001 Sierra Pine Ave, Vernon
(90058-4120)
PHONE....................323 318-8260
EMP: 32
SALES (corp-wide): 153.6MM Privately
Held
WEB: www.bakercommodities.com
SIC: 2077 Animal & marine fats & oils
PA: Baker Commodities, Inc.
4020 Bandini Blvd
Vernon CA 90058
323 268-2801

(P-2125)
CAPTEK MIDCO INC (HQ)
16218 Arthur St, Cerritos (90703-2131)
PHONE....................562 921-9511
David Wood, CEO
Theresa Johnson, Vice Pres
EMP: 200 EST: 2015
SALES (est): 203.2MM Privately Held
WEB: www.capteksoftgel.com
SIC: 2077 Animal & marine fats & oils
PA: Captek Holdings Inc.
16218 Arthur St
Cerritos CA 90703
562 921-9511

(P-2126)
D & D SERVICES INC
Also Called: D & D Cremations Service
4105 Bandini Blvd, Vernon (90058-4208)
P.O. Box 55338, Valencia (91385-0338)
PHONE....................323 261-4176
William M Gorman, President
Roseanne Gorman, Treasurer
Vincent Gorman, Vice Pres
Bill Gorman, Executive
EMP: 41 EST: 1967
SQ FT: 100,000
SALES (est): 6MM Privately Held
SIC: 2077 Animal & marine fats & oils

(P-2127)
PARK WEST ENTERPRISES INC
Also Called: Co-West Commodities
2586 Shenandoah Way, San Bernardino
(92407-1845)
PHONE....................909 383-8341
Sergio Perez, CEO
Freddie Peterson, CFO
EMP: 26 EST: 1996
SALES (est): 5.6MM Privately Held
WEB: www.co-west.com
SIC: 2077 Animal & marine fats & oils

2079 Shortening, Oils & Margarine

(P-2128)
CARGILL INCORPORATED
566 N Gilbert St, Fullerton (92833-2549)
PHONE....................323 588-2274
EMP: 50
SQ FT: 28,410
SALES (corp-wide): 134.8B Privately
Held
SIC: 2079 2046 2013 2011 Mfg Edible
Fats/Oils Wet Corn Milling Mfg Prepared
Meats Meat Packing Plant Mfg Animal
Fats/Oils
PA: Cargill, Incorporated
15407 Mcginty Rd W
Wayzata MN 55391
952 742-7575

(P-2129)
CIUTI INTERNATIONAL INC
Also Called: Cuiti International
8790 Rochester Ave Ste A, Rancho Cucamonga (91730-4925)
PHONE....................909 484-1414

Marcello Trincale, CEO
Eric Trincale, President
Tona Lutz, Controller
Watkins Jason, Sales Dir
Jason Watkins, Sales Dir
▲ EMP: 15 EST: 2004
SQ FT: 20,000
SALES (est): 6.6MM Privately Held
WEB: www.ciuti.com
SIC: 2079 5149 Olive oil; groceries & re-
lated products

(P-2130)
GEMSA ENTERPRISES LLC
Also Called: Gemsa Oils
14370 Gannet St, La Mirada (90638-5221)
P.O. Box 1447 (90637-1447)
PHONE....................714 521-1736
Emilio Viscomi,
Angela Verrico Viscomi,
▲ EMP: 20 EST: 1996
SQ FT: 60,000
SALES (est): 10.1MM Privately Held
WEB: www.gemsaoils.com
SIC: 2079 Olive oil

(P-2131)
LIBERTY VEGETABLE OIL COMPANY
15306 Carmenita Rd, Santa Fe Springs
(90670-5606)
P.O. Box 4207, Cerritos (90703-4207)
PHONE....................562 921-3567
Irwin Field, President
Ronald Field, Admin Sec
◆ EMP: 40
SQ FT: 30,000
SALES (est): 9MM Privately Held
WEB: www.libertyvegetableoil.com
SIC: 2079 Olive oil

(P-2132)
VENTURA FOODS LLC
2900 Jurupa St, Ontario (91761-2915)
PHONE....................714 257-3700
Wayne Kess, Manager
EMP: 68 Privately Held
WEB: www.venturafoods.com
SIC: 2079 2035 Vegetable shortenings
(except corn oil); cooking oils, except
corn: vegetable refined; pickles, sauces &
salad dressings
PA: Ventura Foods, Llc
40 Pointe Dr
Brea CA 92821

(P-2133)
VENTURA FOODS LLC (PA)
Also Called: Lou Ana Foods
40 Pointe Dr, Brea (92821-3652)
PHONE....................714 257-3700
Christopher Furman, President
Erika Noonburg-Morgan, CFO
Andy Euser, Officer
Luis Andrade, Exec VP
Tom Metelmann, Exec VP
◆ EMP: 200 EST: 1996
SALES (est): 2B Privately Held
WEB: www.venturafoods.com
SIC: 2079 2035 Vegetable shortenings
(except corn oil); cooking oils, except
corn: vegetable refined; pickles, sauces &
salad dressings

(P-2134)
WILSEY FOODS INC
40 Pointe Dr, Brea (92821-3652)
PHONE....................714 257-3700
Takashi Fukunaga, CEO
Steve Takagi, President
Hiro Matsumura, Vice Pres
◆ EMP: 1000 EST: 1919
SQ FT: 103,378
SALES (est): 53MM Privately Held
WEB: www.venturafoods.com
SIC: 2079 5149 Cooking oils, except corn:
vegetable refined; vegetable shortenings
(except corn oil); shortening, vegetable
HQ: Mbk Usa Holdings, Inc.
200 Park Ave Fl 36
New York NY 10166
212 878-6773

2082 Malt Beverages

(P-2135)
14 CANNONS BREWING COMPANY INC
31125 Via Colinas Ste 907, Westlake Vil-
lage (91362-3974)
PHONE....................818 652-6971
Marshall Haraden, CEO
EMP: 13 EST: 2017
SALES (est): 2.1MM Privately Held
WEB: www.14cannons.com
SIC: 2082 Beer (alcoholic beverage)

(P-2136)
32 NORTH BREWING CO LLC (PA)
2238 N Glassell St Ste E, Orange
(92865-2742)
PHONE....................619 363-2622
Steve Peterson, Principal
Michael Peterson, Principal
EMP: 15 EST: 2016
SALES (est): 1.3MM Privately Held
WEB: www.32northbrew.com
SIC: 2082 5813 Ale (alcoholic beverage);
bars & lounges

(P-2137)
ASSOCIATED MICROBREWERIES INC
901 S Coast Dr Ste A, Costa Mesa
(92626-7790)
PHONE....................714 546-2739
David Sadeler, Manager
Daren Lindsey, Sales Staff
EMP: 75
SALES (corp-wide): 39.1MM Privately
Held
WEB: www.karlstrauss.com
SIC: 2082 Beer (alcoholic beverage)
PA: Associated Microbreweries, Inc.
5985 Santa Fe St
San Diego CA 92109
858 273-2739

(P-2138)
BELMONT BREWING COMPANY INC
Also Called: B B C
25 39th Pl, Long Beach (90803-2806)
PHONE....................562 433-3891
David Hansen, President
David Lott, Vice Pres
Jessica Bellows, Regional Mgr
EMP: 44 EST: 1989
SQ FT: 7,000
SALES (est): 3.1MM Privately Held
WEB: www.belmontbrewing.com
SIC: 5812 2082 American restaurant; malt
beverages

(P-2139)
BOAVENTURE BREWING CO
Also Called: Bonaventure Brewing Co
404 S Figueroa St 418a, Los Angeles
(90071-1710)
PHONE....................213 236-0802
Loren Zimmerman, Partner
Melissa Hutchins, Vice Pres
David Hansen,
David Lott,
EMP: 33 EST: 1997
SQ FT: 10,000
SALES (est): 612.4K Privately Held
WEB: www.bonaventurebrewing.com
SIC: 5813 5812 2082 Chicken restaurant;
bars & lounges; beer (alcoholic beverage)

(P-2140)
BROUWERIJ WEST
110 E 22nd St, San Pedro (90731-7202)
PHONE....................908 391-2599
Brian Garrido, Comms Dir
Eric Silva, Sales Staff
EMP: 13 EST: 2017
SALES (est): 1MM Privately Held
WEB: www.brouwerijwest.com
SIC: 2082 Malt beverages

(P-2141)
BU LLC
9073 Pulsar Ct Ste A, Corona
(92883-7357)
PHONE....................951 277-7470
Ryan Mason, *Mng Member*
Andres Kummen, *Officer*
EMP: 15 **EST:** 2018
SQ FT: 1,500
SALES (est): 2MM **Privately Held**
SIC: 2082 Malt beverages

(P-2142)
DUDES BREWING COMPANY
1840 W 208th St, Somis (93066)
P.O. Box 276 (93066-0276)
PHONE....................424 271-2915
Toby Humes, *Owner*
EMP: 20 **EST:** 2013
SALES (est): 2.4MM **Privately Held**
WEB: www.thedudesbrew.com
SIC: 2082 5921 Beer (alcoholic beverage); beer (packaged)

(P-2143)
FERMENTED SCIENCES INC
3200 Golf Course Dr, Ventura
(93003-7696)
PHONE....................818 427-8442
William Moses, *CEO*
Chelsea Brewders, *CFO*
William Castagna, *Admin Sec*
Robert Adams, *Director*
Brad Barnhorn, *Director*
EMP: 26 **EST:** 2016
SALES (est): 4.8MM **Privately Held**
SIC: 2082 Beer (alcoholic beverage)

(P-2144)
FIRESTONE WALKER INC (PA)
Also Called: Firestone Walker Brewing Co
1400 Ramada Dr, Paso Robles
(93446-3993)
PHONE....................805 225-5911
David Walker, *CEO*
Austin Connolly, *CFO*
Evan Partridge, *Officer*
Andy Wickstrom, *Creative Dir*
Adam Firestone, *Principal*
▲ **EMP:** 468 **EST:** 1997
SALES (est): 155.5MM **Privately Held**
WEB: www.firestonebeer.com
SIC: 2082 Beer (alcoholic beverage)

(P-2145)
GLACIER DESIGN SYSTEMS INC (PA)
5405 Production Dr, Huntington Beach
(92649-1524)
PHONE....................714 897-2337
Robert Asahi, *VP Opers*
William Schilling, *Vice Pres*
Nick Smith, *Manager*
▲ **EMP:** 15
SQ FT: 8,500
SALES (est): 3MM **Privately Held**
WEB: www.glacier-design.com
SIC: 2082 5078 Beer (alcoholic beverage); refrigerated beverage dispensers

(P-2146)
GRAMIC ENTERPRISES INC
21770 Deveron Cv, Yorba Linda
(92887-2662)
PHONE....................714 329-8627
Michael Sy, *President*
▲ **EMP:** 14 **EST:** 2005
SALES (est): 1.1MM **Privately Held**
SIC: 2082 Malt beverages

(P-2147)
INDIAN WELLS COMPANIES
Also Called: Indian Wells Brewery
2565 State Highway 14, Inyokern
(93527-2700)
PHONE....................760 377-4290
Greg Antonaros, *Partner*
Rick Lovett, *Partner*
Lafawn Antonaros, *General Mgr*
Jeanne Bingham, *Broker*
Pete Mitchell, *VP Mktg*
▲ **EMP:** 14 **EST:** 1993

SALES (est): 1.8MM **Privately Held**
WEB: www.mojavered.com
SIC: 2082 2086 Beer (alcoholic beverage); pasteurized & mineral waters, bottled & canned

(P-2148)
ISLAND BREWING CO
5049 6th St, Carpinteria (93013-2001)
PHONE....................805 745-8272
Paul Wright, *President*
EMP: 15 **EST:** 2004
SALES (est): 2.1MM **Privately Held**
WEB: www.islandbrewingcompany.com
SIC: 2082 Beer (alcoholic beverage)

(P-2149)
LEFT COAST BREWING COMPANY
1245 Puerta Del Sol, San Clemente
(92673-6310)
PHONE....................949 218-3961
George Hadjis, *President*
Dora Hadjis, *CFO*
Pete Lacava, *General Mgr*
Tracy Turbeville, *Executive Asst*
Erica Carbajal, *Sales Staff*
EMP: 15 **EST:** 2004
SQ FT: 7,500 **Privately Held**
WEB: www.leftcoastbrewing.com
SIC: 2082 Beer (alcoholic beverage)

(P-2150)
MILLER BREWING CO
15801 1st St, Irwindale (91706-2069)
PHONE....................626 353-1604
EMP: 18 **EST:** 2016
SALES (est): 3.8MM **Privately Held**
SIC: 2082 Beer (alcoholic beverage)

(P-2151)
OTTANO INC
11555 Los Osos Valley Rd, San Luis Obispo (93405-6472)
PHONE....................805 547-2088
Nipool Patel, *President*
EMP: 26 **EST:** 2007
SALES (est): 823.5K **Privately Held**
WEB: www.ottano.com
SIC: 2082 Beer (alcoholic beverage)

(P-2152)
PABST BREWING COMPANY LLC (PA)
10635 Santa Monica Blvd, Los Angeles
(90025-8300)
PHONE....................310 470-0962
Eugene Kashper,
Daniel McHugh, *Chief Mktg Ofcr*
Brian Smith, *Officer*
Rob Urband, *Officer*
Edward Gustenhoven, *Vice Pres*
▼ **EMP:** 240 **EST:** 1844
SQ FT: 12,500
SALES (est): 146.7MM **Privately Held**
WEB: www.pabst.com
SIC: 2082 Beer (alcoholic beverage)

(P-2153)
POWER BRANDS CONSULTING LLC
5805 Sepulveda Blvd # 501, Van Nuys
(91411-2546)
PHONE....................818 989-9646
Darin Ezra,
Martin Molina, *COO*
Charles Quinn, *Vice Pres*
Saul Hirschhorn, *VP Business*
Alex Gillis, *Graphic Designe*
EMP: 40 **EST:** 2006
SQ FT: 5,000
SALES (est): 12.3MM **Privately Held**
WEB: www.powerbrands.us
SIC: 2082 8742 Malt beverage products; food & beverage consultant

(P-2154)
REDONDO BEACH BREWING CO INC
1814 S Catalina Ave, Redondo Beach
(90277-5505)
PHONE....................310 316-8477
John Waters, *CFO*
David Zislis, *President*
EMP: 22 **EST:** 1993

SQ FT: 4,500
SALES (est): 373.9K **Privately Held**
WEB: www.redondobeachbrewco.com
SIC: 5812 2082 5813 Chicken restaurant; beer (alcoholic beverage); drinking places

(P-2155)
RT ROGERS BREWING CO LLC
38 E Montecito Ave Ste 1, Sierra Madre
(91024-2958)
PHONE....................818 371-0838
Kelly Rogers,
Daniel Zhou,
EMP: 13 **EST:** 2016
SALES (est): 312.6K **Privately Held**
SIC: 5813 2082 Bars & lounges; ale (alcoholic beverage)

(P-2156)
TAVISTOCK RESTAURANTS LLC
Also Called: Alcatraz Brewing Company
20 City Blvd W Ste R1, Orange
(92868-3116)
PHONE....................714 939-8686
Jarred Creagan, *Manager*
Amy Poscman, *Executive*
EMP: 150
SALES (corp-wide): 195MM **Privately Held**
WEB:
www.tavistockrestaurantcollection.com
SIC: 5813 5812 2082 Bars & lounges; American restaurant; malt beverages
PA: Tavistock Restaurants Llc
4705 S Apk Vnlnd Rd # 210
Orlando FL 32819
407 909-7101

(P-2157)
TEMBLOR BREWING LLC
3200 Buck Owens Blvd, Bakersfield
(93308-6318)
PHONE....................661 489-4855
Donald Bynum, *CEO*
EMP: 49 **EST:** 2014
SQ FT: 19,000
SALES (est): 5.4MM **Privately Held**
WEB: www.temblorbrewing.com
SIC: 2082 5813 Ale (alcoholic beverage); bars & lounges

(P-2158)
TOPA TOPA BREWING
120 Santa Barbara St, Santa Barbara
(93101-1934)
PHONE....................805 324-4150
EMP: 13 **EST:** 2017
SALES (est): 214.7K **Privately Held**
WEB: www.topatopa.beer
SIC: 5813 2082 Saloon; malt beverages

(P-2159)
TOWNE PARK BREW INC
1566 W Lincoln Ave, Anaheim
(92801-5850)
PHONE....................714 844-2492
Brett Lawrence, *President*
EMP: 25 **EST:** 2014
SQ FT: 20,000
SALES (est): 250K **Privately Held**
WEB: www.towneparkbrew.com
SIC: 2082 5149 Beer (alcoholic beverage); beverages, except coffee & tea

(P-2160)
USMILK NUTRITION INC
28381 Vincent Moraga Dr, Temecula
(92590-3653)
PHONE....................951 888-2228
Thiet Dinh Nguyen, *CEO*
Arnel Ryan, *Vice Pres*
EMP: 14 **EST:** 2015
SALES (est): 1.6MM **Privately Held**
WEB: www.usmilknutrition.com
SIC: 2082 Malt beverages

(P-2161)
W CELLARS INC
927 N La Cienega Blvd, Los Angeles
(90069-4709)
PHONE....................714 655-2025
Maria Thomas, *Principal*
EMP: 15 **EST:** 2018
SALES (est): 1.2MM **Privately Held**
SIC: 2082 Beer (alcoholic beverage)

(P-2162)
WOOBO DISTRIBUTION
16261 Phoebe Ave, La Mirada
(90638-5611)
PHONE....................714 522-5505
Charles A Lee, *CEO*
EMP: 14 **EST:** 2012
SALES (est): 1.5MM **Privately Held**
SIC: 2082 5182 2084 Beer (alcoholic beverage); neutral spirits; wines, brandy & brandy spirits

2084 Wine & Brandy

(P-2163)
21SEEDS INC
8605 Santa Monica Blvd, West Hollywood
(90069-4109)
PHONE....................310 415-8605
Nicole Emanuel, *CFO*
EMP: 15 **EST:** 2018
SALES (est): 1.2MM **Privately Held**
WEB: www.21seeds.com
SIC: 2084 Wines, brandy & brandy spirits

(P-2164)
AGUA DULCE VINEYARDS LLC
9640 Sierra Hwy, Agua Dulce
(91390-4622)
PHONE....................661 268-7402
Raymond A Watt,
Steve Wizan, *General Mgr*
EMP: 20 **EST:** 2001
SALES (est): 1.7MM **Privately Held**
WEB: www.aguadulcewinery.com
SIC: 2084 5921 Wines; wine

(P-2165)
ALFRED DOMAINE
7525 Orcutt Rd, San Luis Obispo
(93401-8341)
PHONE....................805 541-9463
Terry Speizer, *President*
▲ **EMP:** 15 **EST:** 1997
SQ FT: 3,000
SALES (est): 348.7K **Privately Held**
WEB: www.chamisalvineyards.com
SIC: 2084 Wines

(P-2166)
ASV WINES INC (PA)
1998 Road 152, Delano (93215-9437)
PHONE....................661 792-3159
Marko B Zaninovich, *President*
Kent Stephens, *CFO*
Christophe Legrandjacques, *Director*
Andrew Beckwith, *Manager*
Melinda Leung, *Manager*
◆ **EMP:** 15 **EST:** 1981
SQ FT: 4,000
SALES (est): 6.8MM **Privately Held**
WEB: www.asvwines.com
SIC: 2084 Wines

(P-2167)
BEL VINO LLC
33515 Rancho Cal Rd, Temecula
(92591-4929)
PHONE....................951 676-6414
David M Wilcox, *Principal*
Erika Batiz, *General Mgr*
EMP: 14 **EST:** 2015
SALES (est): 1.5MM **Privately Held**
WEB: www.belvinowinery.com
SIC: 2084 Wines

(P-2168)
BRIDLEWOOD WINERY LLC
Also Called: E and J Gallo
3555 Roblar Ave, Santa Ynez
(93460-9724)
PHONE....................805 688-9000
Ej Gallo, *President*
EMP: 20 **EST:** 1997
SQ FT: 28,000
SALES (est): 4.1MM **Privately Held**
WEB: www.bridlewoodestatewinery.com
SIC: 2084 5182 Wines; wine

(P-2169)

BUTTONWOOD FARM WINERY INC
1500 Alamo Pintado Rd, Solvang (93463-9756)
P.O. Box 1007 (93464-1007)
PHONE..........................805 688-3032
Bret C Davenport, *President*
Elizabeth Williams, *Treasurer*
Seyburn Zorthian, *Vice Pres*
EMP: 18 EST: 1988
SALES (est): 1.8MM Privately Held
WEB: www.buttonwoodwinery.com
SIC: 2084 Wines

(P-2170)

CALCAREOUS VINEYARD LLC
3430 Peachy Canyon Rd, Paso Robles (93446-7685)
PHONE..........................805 239-0289
Dana Brown,
Daneen Eaton, *Buyer*
Jacqui Pailing, *Teacher*
Bob Duffy, *Manager*
Leslee Falkenberg, *Manager*
▲ **EMP: 15 EST: 2000**
SALES (est): 1.3MM Privately Held
WEB: www.calcareous.com
SIC: 2084 Wines

(P-2171)

CALIPASO WINERY LLC
4230 Buena Vista Dr, Paso Robles (93446-9533)
PHONE..........................805 226-9296
Alan Kinne, *Mng Member*
Trevor Iba, *Finance*
EMP: 13 EST: 2012
SALES (est): 3.5MM Privately Held
WEB: www.calipasowinery.com
SIC: 2084 Wines

(P-2172)

CALLAWAY VINEYARD & WINERY
32720 Rancho Cal Rd, Temecula (92591-4925)
P.O. Box 9014 (92589-9014)
PHONE..........................951 676-4001
Mike Jellison, *President*
Donna Craig, *Sales Staff*
▲ **EMP: 70 EST: 1969**
SALES (est): 8.1MM Privately Held
WEB: www.callawaywinery.com
SIC: 2084 Wine cellars, bonded: engaged in blending wines; wines

(P-2173)

CASTLEROCK FARMS LLC
Also Called: Castle Rock Vineyards
501 Richgrove Dr, Delano (93215-9461)
PHONE..........................661 721-1933
Albert L Good, *Mng Member*
EMP: 24 EST: 2004
SALES (est): 724.8K Privately Held
SIC: 2084 Wines

(P-2174)

CASTORO CELLARS (PA)
1315 N Bethel Rd, Templeton (93465-9403)
P.O. Box 954 (93465-0954)
PHONE..........................805 467-2002
Neils Udsen, *President*
Berit Udsen, *Vice Pres*
Luke Udsen, *Marketing Staff*
Carrie Searl, *Manager*
▼ **EMP: 16 EST: 1983**
SALES (est): 5.5MM Privately Held
WEB: www.castorocellars.com
SIC: 2084 Wines

(P-2175)

CENTRAL COAST WINE WAREHOUSE (PA)
Also Called: Central Coast Wine Services
2717 Aviation Way Ste 101, Santa Maria (93455-1506)
PHONE..........................805 928-9210
Jim Lunt, *Ltd Ptnr*
Jeff Maiken, *Ltd Ptnr*
▲ **EMP: 29 EST: 1988**
SQ FT: 35,000

SALES (est): 4.8MM Privately Held
SIC: 2084 5182 7389 Wines; bottling wines & liquors; field warehousing

(P-2176)

CHAMBERS & CHAMBERS INC
Also Called: Chambers Chmbers Wine Mrchants
14011 Ventura Blvd 210e, Sherman Oaks (91423-5215)
PHONE..........................818 995-6961
Glen Grisham, *Director*
EMP: 13
SALES (corp-wide): 27.5MM Privately Held
WEB: www.chamberswines.com
SIC: 2084 5182 Wines; wine
PA: Chambers & Chambers, Inc.
511 Alexis Ct
Napa CA 94558
415 642-5500

(P-2177)

CHAMISAL VINEYARDS LLC
7525 Orcutt Rd, San Luis Obispo (93401-8341)
PHONE..........................866 808-9463
Andrea De Palo, *Principal*
Norman L Goss, *Principal*
Andrea Palo, *Sales Staff*
▲ **EMP: 15 EST: 1972**
SALES (est): 3.1MM
SALES (corp-wide): 64.1MM Publicly Held
WEB: www.chamisalvineyards.com
SIC: 2084 0172 Wines; grapes
PA: Crimson Wine Group, Ltd.
5901 Silverado Trl
Napa CA 94558
800 486-0503

(P-2178)

CORBETT CANYON VINEYARDS
2195 Corbett Canyon Rd, Arroyo Grande (93420-4974)
P.O. Box 3159, San Luis Obispo (93403-3159)
PHONE..........................805 782-9463
Arthur Ciocca, *President*
Paul Flowers, *Vice Pres*
EMP: 13 EST: 1979
SALES (est): 1.8MM Privately Held
WEB: www.vinarium-usa.com
SIC: 2084 Wines
HQ: The Wine Group Inc
17000 E State Highway 120
Ripon CA 95366
209 599-4111

(P-2179)

COURTSIDE CELLARS LLC
2425 Mission St, San Miguel (93451-9556)
PHONE..........................805 467-2882
David McHenry, *General Mgr*
Amy Spain, *Regional Mgr*
Chelsea Cameron, *Finance*
Mike Otto, *Sales Staff*
Tisha Lasley, *Director*
EMP: 17
SALES (corp-wide): 10.2MM Privately Held
WEB: www.tolosawine.com
SIC: 2084 Wine cellars, bonded: engaged in blending wines; wines
PA: Courtside Cellars, Llc
4910 Edna Rd
San Luis Obispo CA 93401
805 782-0500

(P-2180)

COURTSIDE CELLARS LLC (PA)
Also Called: Tolosa Winery
4910 Edna Rd, San Luis Obispo (93401-7938)
PHONE..........................805 782-0500
Bob Schiebelhut,
Carla Wiley, *Officer*
Josh Baker, *General Mgr*
June Mclvor, *General Mgr*
Darren Worley, *Marketing Staff*
▲ **EMP: 30 EST: 1998**
SQ FT: 70,000
SALES (est): 10.2MM Privately Held
WEB: www.tolosawinery.com
SIC: 2084 Wines

(P-2181)

DANZA DEL SOL WINERY INC
39050 De Portola Rd, Temecula (92592-8833)
P.O. Box 892889 (92589-2889)
PHONE..........................951 302-6363
Robert Olson, *President*
Patricia O 'brien, *Vice Pres*
Georgiana Wong, *Vice Pres*
Georgie Wong, *Vice Pres*
Loradel Garcia, *Accountant*
EMP: 21 EST: 2015
SALES (est): 4.9MM Privately Held
WEB: www.danzadelsolwinery.com
SIC: 2084 Wines

(P-2182)

EOS ESTATE WINERY
2300 Airport Rd, Paso Robles (93446-8549)
P.O. Box 1287 (93447-1287)
PHONE..........................805 239-2562
Frank Arciero, *Partner*
Phil Arciero, *Partner*
Fern Underwood, *Partner*
Sandy Throop, *Opers Staff*
▲ **EMP: 47 EST: 1986**
SALES (est): 4.7MM Privately Held
WEB: www.eosvintage.com
SIC: 2084 0172 3172 Wines; grapes; personal leather goods

(P-2183)

FALKNER WINERY INC
40620 Calle Contento, Temecula (92591-5041)
PHONE..........................951 676-6741
Ray Falkner, *CEO*
Loretta Falkner, *Principal*
EMP: 65 EST: 1993
SALES (est): 8.3MM Privately Held
WEB: www.falknerwinery.com
SIC: 2084 7299 Wines; banquet hall facilities

(P-2184)

FIRESTONE VINEYARD LP
Also Called: Curtis Winery
5000 Zaca Station Rd, Los Olivos (93441-4566)
P.O. Box 244 (93441-0244)
PHONE..........................805 688-3940
Michael L Gravelle, *Partner*
Adam Firestone, *Partner*
Olga Peddie, *Officer*
David Crory, *Vice Pres*
Chuck Dalton, *Vice Pres*
▲ **EMP: 85 EST: 1976**
SQ FT: 45,000
SALES (est): 12.5MM
SALES (corp-wide): 81.2MM Privately Held
WEB: www.firestonewine.com
SIC: 2084 0172 Wines; grapes
HQ: Foley Family Wines, Inc.
200 Concourse Blvd
Santa Rosa CA 95403

(P-2185)

FLOOD RANCH COMPANY
Also Called: Rancho Sisquoc Winery
6600 Foxen Canyon Rd, Santa Maria (93454-9656)
PHONE..........................805 937-3616
Ed A Holt, *Manager*
Peter Mateus, *Manager*
EMP: 33
SALES (corp-wide): 6.6MM Privately Held
WEB: www.ranchosisquoc.com
SIC: 2084 Wines
PA: Flood Ranch Company
870 Market St Ste 1100
San Francisco CA 94102
415 982-5645

(P-2186)

FOXEN VINEYARD INC
7600 Foxen Canyon Rd, Santa Maria (93454-9170)
PHONE..........................805 937-4251
Richard Dore, *President*
William Wathen, *Corp Secy*
EMP: 35 EST: 1987
SQ FT: 4,000

SALES (est): 4.3MM Privately Held
WEB: www.foxenvineyard.com
SIC: 2084 Wines

(P-2187)

GAINEY VINEYARD
3950 E Highway 246, Santa Ynez (93460)
P.O. Box 910 (93460-0910)
PHONE..........................805 688-0558
Daniel H Gainey, *President*
Sunny Ramirez, *Manager*
▲ **EMP: 39 EST: 1983**
SQ FT: 20,000
SALES (est): 7.3MM Privately Held
WEB: www.gaineyvineyard.com
SIC: 2084 Wines

(P-2188)

GROWEST INC (PA)
Also Called: Growest Development
1660 Chicago Ave Ste M11, Riverside (92507-2033)
PHONE..........................951 638-1000
John Bremer, *President*
EMP: 15 EST: 1998
SALES (est): 17MM Privately Held
WEB: www.growest.com
SIC: 2084 5193 Wines; nursery stock

(P-2189)

HALTER PROPERTIES LLC
Also Called: Halter Ranch Vineyard
8910 Adelaida Rd, Paso Robles (93446-8798)
PHONE..........................805 226-9455
Hanjorg Wyss,
Helsa Hasikin, *Bookkeeper*
Gracie Nino, *Marketing Mgr*
Tessa Eberle, *Mktg Coord*
Mitch Wyss,
▲ **EMP: 30 EST: 2000**
SALES (est): 6.7MM Privately Held
WEB: www.halterranch.com
SIC: 2084 Wines

(P-2190)

HALTER WINERY LLC
8910 Adelaida Rd, Paso Robles (93446-8798)
PHONE..........................805 226-9455
Mitchell S Wyss,
Bryce Mullins, *General Mgr*
Machelle Cerbo, *Admin Asst*
Brett Reichard, *Technician*
Nicholas May, *Production*
EMP: 32 EST: 2002
SALES (est): 6.1MM Privately Held
WEB: www.halterranch.com
SIC: 2084 Wines

(P-2191)

HARMONY CELLARS
3255 Harmony Valley Rd, Harmony (93435-5000)
PHONE..........................805 927-1625
Kimberly Mulligan, *Partner*
Charles Mulligan, *Partner*
EMP: 13 EST: 1989
SALES (est): 1.8MM Privately Held
WEB: www.harmonycellars.com
SIC: 2084 5813 5921 Wine cellars, bonded: engaged in blending wines; wine bar; wine

(P-2192)

HILLIARD BRUCE VINEYARDS LLC (PA)
2097 Vineyard View Ln, Lompoc (93436-2628)
PHONE..........................805 736-5366
John C Hilliard, *Mng Member*
Christine Bruce,
EMP: 19 EST: 2006
SALES (est): 1.1MM Privately Held
WEB: www.hilliardbruce.com
SIC: 2084 Wines

(P-2193)

HILLSIDE WINES & SPIRITS LLC
15751 Tapia St, Irwindale (91706-2177)
P.O. Box 5903, Santa Monica (90409-5903)
PHONE..........................424 268-5168
Caroline Laclotte, *Mng Member*
▲ **EMP: 14 EST: 2005**

PRODUCTS & SVCS

SALES (est): 526K Privately Held
WEB: www.hillsidewinesspirits.com
SIC: 2084 Wines

(P-2194)
HOPE FAMILY WINES (PA)
1585 Live Oak Rd, Paso Robles
(93446-9637)
P.O. Box 3260 (93447-3260)
PHONE.................................805 238-4112
Austin Hope, *President*
Stasi Seay, *Records Dir*
Shane Guerrier, *Manager*
Rachael Rosenbloom, *Retailers*
EMP: 49 EST: 2011
SALES (est): 5.9MM Privately Held
WEB: www.hopefamilywines.com
SIC: 2084 Wines

(P-2195)
J FILIPPI VINTAGE CO (PA)
12467 Baseline Rd, Rancho Cucamonga
(91739-9522)
PHONE.................................909 899-5755
Joseph P Filippi, *President*
James Filippi, *Shareholder*
Gino L Filippi, *Vice Pres*
▲ EMP: 16 EST: 1922
SQ FT: 50,000
SALES (est): 3MM Privately Held
SIC: 5921 2084 Wine; wines

(P-2196)
J LOHR WINERY CORPORATION
6169 Airport Rd, Paso Robles
(93446-9547)
PHONE.................................805 239-8900
J Lohr, *Owner*
Rita Di, *Vice Pres*
Ray Wetzel, *Regional Mgr*
Angeleena Parra, *Admin Asst*
Yoanna Ucan, *Administration*
EMP: 47
SALES (corp-wide): 42MM Privately
Held
WEB: www.jlohr.com
SIC: 2084 Wines
PA: J. Lohr Winery Corporation
1000 Lenzen Ave
San Jose CA 95126
408 288-5057

(P-2197)
JACKSON FAMILY WINES INC
Also Called: Cambria Winery
5475 Chardonnay Ln, Santa Maria
(93454-9600)
PHONE.................................805 938-7300
Bill Hammond, *Branch Mgr*
Cameron Gunlock, *Maintence Staff*
Katy Rogers, *Director*
Tara Machin, *Manager*
Matt Mahoney, *Manager*
EMP: 30 Privately Held
WEB: www.kj.com
SIC: 2084 Wines
PA: Jackson Family Wines, Inc.
421 And 425 Aviation Blvd
Santa Rosa CA 95403

(P-2198)
JAMES TOBIN CELLARS INC
8950 Union Rd, Paso Robles (93446-9356)
PHONE.................................805 239-2204
Tobin J Shumrick, *President*
Claire Silver, *Shareholder*
Ben Lunt, *Manager*
EMP: 32 EST: 1987
SQ FT: 10,000
SALES (est): 5.5MM Privately Held
WEB: www.tobinjames.com
SIC: 2084 Wine cellars, bonded: engaged
in blending wines

(P-2199)
JUSTIN VINEYARDS & WINERY LLC (DH)
11680 Chimney Rock Rd, Paso Robles
(93446-9792)
PHONE.................................805 238-6932
Stewart A Resnick, *President*
Deborah Baldwin, *Vice Pres*
Craig B Cooper, *Manager*
Nina Leschinsky, *Director*
Timothy Argie, *Manager*

◆ EMP: 39 EST: 2010
SQ FT: 60,000
SALES (est): 10.6MM
SALES (corp-wide): 2B Privately Held
WEB: www.justinwine.com
SIC: 2084 Wines

(P-2200)
LAETITIA VINEYARD & WINERY INC
Also Called: Laetitia Winery
453 Laetitia Vineyard Dr, Arroyo Grande
(93420-9701)
PHONE.................................805 481-1772
Selim K Zilkha, *President*
Lino Bozzano, *Bd of Directors*
Dave Hickey, *Production*
Robert Chetwood, *Manager*
Wnedell Cottle, *Manager*
▲ EMP: 65 EST: 1994
SALES (est): 9MM Privately Held
WEB: www.laetitiawine.com
SIC: 2084 Wines

(P-2201)
LAFOND VINEYARD INC
Also Called: Santa Ynez Winery
114 E Haley St Ste M, Santa Barbara
(93101-5323)
PHONE.................................805 962-9303
Pierre Lafond, *President*
Marty Poole, *CFO*
EMP: 14 EST: 1996
SQ FT: 1,400
SALES (est): 611.1K Privately Held
WEB: www.lafondwinery.com
SIC: 2084 Wines

(P-2202)
LEONESSE CELLARS LLC
38311 De Portola Rd, Temecula
(92592-8923)
P.O. Box 1371 (92593-1371)
PHONE.................................951 302-7601
Gary Winder, *Mng Member*
Rebaux Stey, *General Mgr*
Kelly Newcom, *Buyer*
Kelly Newcomb, *Buyer*
Diana Bogg, *Opers Staff*
▲ EMP: 25 EST: 2003
SQ FT: 6,000
SALES (est): 3.2MM Privately Held
WEB: www.leonesscellars.com
SIC: 2084 Wines

(P-2203)
LEVECKE LLC
10810 Inland Ave, Jurupa Valley
(91752-3235)
PHONE.................................951 681-8600
Tim Levecke, *Mng Member*
Brad Gilreath, *Vice Pres*
Michael Olsker, *Vice Pres*
Lauren Elmes, *Accountant*
Richard Sarenana, *Opers Mgr*
▲ EMP: 31 EST: 1949
SQ FT: 150,000
SALES (est): 2.9MM Privately Held
WEB: www.levecke.com
SIC: 2084 Wines, brandy & brandy spirits

(P-2204)
LOUIDAR LLC
Also Called: Mount Palomar Winery
33820 Rancho Cal Rd, Temecula
(92591-4930)
P.O. Box 891510 (92589-1510)
PHONE.................................951 676-5047
Peter Poole, *Principal*
Louis Darwish, *Mng Member*
Shellie Milne, *Director*
Sean Cole, *Manager*
Kimberly Dargel, *Manager*
EMP: 30 EST: 1997
SQ FT: 4,000
SALES (est): 3.6MM Privately Held
SIC: 2084 Wines

(P-2205)
MARGARITA VINEYARDS LLC
679 Calf Canyon Hwy, Creston
(93432-9700)
PHONE.................................805 226-8600
Liz Holtzclaw, *Manager*
EMP: 13 Privately Held
WEB: www.margarita-adventures.com

SIC: 2084 Wines
PA: Margarita Vineyards Llc
22720 El Camino Real
Santa Margarita CA 93453

(P-2206)
MAURICE CARRIE WINERY
34225 Rancho Cal Rd, Temecula
(92591-5054)
PHONE.................................951 676-1711
Buddy Linn, *President*
Cheri Linn, *Vice Pres*
Jana Prias, *Sales Mgr*
Cindi Van Roekel, *Clerk*
EMP: 17 EST: 1958
SQ FT: 14,000
SALES (est): 1MM Privately Held
WEB: www.ultimatevineyards.com
SIC: 2084 5921 0172 Wines; wine;
grapes

(P-2207)
MELVILLE WINERY LLC
5185 E Highway 246, Lompoc
(93436-9613)
PHONE.................................805 735-7030
Ronald Melville, *President*
Kurt Ammann, *General Mgr*
Cindy Eoff, *Sales Staff*
Brent Melville,
Chad Melville,
EMP: 14 EST: 1996
SALES (est): 2MM Privately Held
WEB: www.melvillewinery.com
SIC: 2084 Wines

(P-2208)
MIDNIGHT CELLARS INC
Also Called: Midnight Cellars Winery
2925 Anderson Rd, Paso Robles
(93446-6610)
PHONE.................................805 239-8904
Richard Hartenberger, *President*
Robert Hartenberger, *President*
Demetra Kaperonis, *General Mgr*
Mary Hartenberger, *Admin Sec*
Karen Jones, *Manager*
EMP: 13 EST: 1995
SALES (est): 1.6MM Privately Held
WEB: www.midnightcellars.com
SIC: 2084 Wines

(P-2209)
MONTE DE ORO WINERY
35820 Rancho Cal Rd, Temecula
(92591-5126)
PHONE.................................951 491-6551
Kenneth Zignorski, *Principal*
Ken Zignorski, *Managing Prtnr*
Kelley O'Neill, *Admin Asst*
Betty Muro, *Controller*
Jordan Laliotis, *Opers Mgr*
EMP: 13 EST: 2010
SALES (est): 5.8MM Privately Held
WEB: www.montedeoro.com
SIC: 2084 Wines

(P-2210)
NINER WINE ESTATES LLC
2400 W Highway 46, Paso Robles
(93446-8602)
PHONE.................................805 239-2233
Richard T Niner,
Rebecca Ogrady, *CFO*
Sue Underwood, *Vice Pres*
Jordyn Tindell, *Marketing Staff*
Tucker Spear, *Sales Staff*
▲ EMP: 25 EST: 2004
SALES (est): 7.7MM Privately Held
WEB: www.ninerwine.com
SIC: 2084 Wines

(P-2211)
OPOLO VINEYARDS INC
2801 Townsgate Rd Ste 123, Westlake Village (91361-3033)
P.O. Box 277, Paso Robles (93447-0277)
PHONE.................................805 238-9593
EMP: 79
SALES (corp-wide): 9.7MM Privately
Held
WEB: www.opolo.com
SIC: 2084 Wines

PA: Opolo Vineyards, Inc.
7110 Vineyard Dr
Paso Robles CA 93446
805 238-9593

(P-2212)
PHASE 2 CELLARS LLC
4910 Edna Rd, San Luis Obispo
(93401-7938)
PHONE.................................805 782-0300
Kenneth Robin Baggett, *Mng Member*
EMP: 26 EST: 2015
SALES (est): 1.9MM Privately Held
WEB: www.phase2cellars.com
SIC: 2084 Wines

(P-2213)
PONTE WINERY
35053 Rancho Cal Rd, Temecula
(92591-4008)
PHONE.................................951 694-8855
James Hochgesang, *Manager*
Laura Slattery, *Manager*
EMP: 16 EST: 2016
SALES (est): 4MM Privately Held
WEB: www.pontewinery.com
SIC: 2084 Wines

(P-2214)
POURING WITH HEART LLC
515 W 7th St, Los Angeles (90014-2500)
PHONE.................................213 817-5321
EMP: 16 EST: 2019
SALES (est): 3.2MM Privately Held
WEB: www.pouringwithheart.com
SIC: 2084 Wines

(P-2215)
RABBIT RIDGE WINE SALES INC (PA)
Also Called: RABBIT RIDGE VINEYARDS
1172 San Marcos Rd, Paso Robles
(93446-7343)
P.O. Box 456, Healdsburg (95448-0456)
PHONE.................................661 877-7525
Leroy Codding, *CEO*
Steven Jones, *CFO*
Erich Russell, *Founder*
EMP: 18 EST: 1980
SALES (est): 1.9MM Privately Held
WEB: www.rabbitridgewinery.com
SIC: 2084 0172 Wine cellars, bonded: engaged in blending wines; grapes

(P-2216)
RBZ VINEYARDS LLC
Also Called: Sextant Wines
2324 W Highway 46, Paso Robles
(93446-8602)
P.O. Box 391 (93447-0391)
PHONE.................................805 542-0133
Craig Stoller, *Principal*
Carly Douglas, *Marketing Staff*
Amy Griffith, *Director*
EMP: 30 EST: 2006
SALES (est): 5.3MM Privately Held
WEB: www.sextantwines.com
SIC: 2084 Wines

(P-2217)
ROLLING HILLS VINEYARD INC
4213 Pascal Pl, Pls Vrds Prsl
(90274-3943)
PHONE.................................310 541-5098
EMP: 24
SALES (corp-wide): 94.4K Privately Held
SIC: 2084 Wines, brandy & brandy spirits
PA: Rolling Hills Vineyard, Inc.
6200 E Canyon Rim Rd # 201
Anaheim CA

(P-2218)
ROYAL WINE CORPORATION
Also Called: Herzog Wine Cellars
3201 Camino Del Sol, Oxnard
(93030-8915)
PHONE.................................805 983-1560
Joseph Herzog, *Vice Pres*
Karen Hultmark, *Executive Asst*
Jacy Basile, *Controller*
Jeremy Dewey, *Foreman/Supr*
Jenny Guy, *Marketing Staff*
EMP: 23

SALES (corp-wide): 87.3MM **Privately Held**
WEB: www.royalwine.com
SIC: 2084 5182 Wines; wine; liquor
PA: Royal Wine Corporation
63 Lefante Dr
Bayonne NJ 07002
718 384-2400

(P-2219)
SAINT FRNCIS WINERY TASTING RM (PA)
100 Pythian Rd, Camarillo (93012)
PHONE.....................707 833-4668
Christopher Silva, *President*
Jake Terrell, *Manager*
EMP: 26 EST: 2010
SALES (est): 437K **Privately Held**
WEB: www.stfranciswinery.com
SIC: 2084 Wines

(P-2220)
SAN ANTONIO WINERY INC (PA)
Also Called: San Antonio Gift Shop
737 Lamar St, Los Angeles (90031-2591)
PHONE.....................323 223-1401
Santo Riboli, *CEO*
Maddelena Riboli, *Corp Secy*
Steve Riboli, *Vice Pres*
Elise Keeling, *Store Mgr*
Nicole Storin, *Project Mgr*
◆ EMP: 101 EST: 1917
SQ FT: 310,000
SALES (est): 50.7MM **Privately Held**
WEB: www.sanantoniowinery.com
SIC: 2084 5182 5812 Wines; wine; eating places

(P-2221)
SANS WINE & SPIRITS CO
17885 Sky Park Cir Ste J, Irvine (92614-6307)
PHONE.....................714 423-3883
Louis J Sansevero, *CEO*
EMP: 17 EST: 2018
SALES (est): 556.5K **Privately Held**
WEB: www.sansws.com
SIC: 2084 Wines, brandy & brandy spirits

(P-2222)
SOUTH COAST WINERY INC
Also Called: South Coast Winery Resort Spa
34843 Rancho Cal Rd, Temecula (92591-4006)
PHONE.....................951 587-9463
James A Carter, *President*
Krystal Aponte, *Op Rm Dir*
Hollie Horning, *Controller*
Millay Dimond, *Director*
Danny Vouaux, *Director*
▲ EMP: 32 EST: 2001
SALES (est): 10.4MM
SALES (corp-wide): 40.5MM **Privately Held**
WEB: www.southcoastwinery.com
SIC: 2084 7011 7991 Wines; resort hotel; spas
PA: Grove Spruce Inc
3719 S Plaza Dr
Santa Ana CA 92704
714 546-4255

(P-2223)
STOLPMAN VINEYARDS LLC
1700 Industrial Way B, Lompoc (93436-4947)
P.O. Box B, Los Olivos (93441)
PHONE.....................805 736-5000
Tom Stolpman, *Branch Mgr*
EMP: 21
SALES (corp-wide): 3.4MM **Privately Held**
WEB: www.stolpmanvineyards.com
SIC: 2084 Wines
PA: Stolpman Vineyards Llc
2434 Alamo Pintado Rd
Los Olivos CA 93441
805 736-5000

(P-2224)
STUART CELLARS LLC
41006 Simi Ct, Temecula (92591-4988)
PHONE.....................951 676-6414
Marshall Stuart,
▲ EMP: 14 EST: 1996
SQ FT: 2,240

SALES (est): 764.6K **Privately Held**
WEB: www.stuartcellars.com
SIC: 2084 Wines

(P-2225)
SYLVESTER WINERY INC
5115 Buena Vista Dr, Paso Robles (93446-8558)
PHONE.....................805 227-4000
Syliva Phillini, *President*
Scott Keller, *CFO*
Meghan Askin, *Sales Staff*
EMP: 19 EST: 1995
SALES (est): 2.4MM **Privately Held**
WEB: www.levignewinery.com
SIC: 2084 Wines

(P-2226)
TABLAS CREEK VINEYARD LLC
9339 Adelaida Rd, Paso Robles (93446-9785)
PHONE.....................805 237-1231
Bob Haas, *Partner*
Jason Haas, *Partner*
Thurman Randy, *IT/INT Sup*
Jennifer McDermott, *Asst Controller*
Darren Delmore, *Natl Sales Mgr*
▲ EMP: 18 EST: 1990
SQ FT: 40,000
SALES (est): 3.6MM **Privately Held**
WEB: www.tablascreek.com
SIC: 2084 Wines

(P-2227)
TALLEY VINEYARDS
3031 Lopez Dr, Arroyo Grande (93420-4999)
P.O. Box 360 (93421-0360)
PHONE.....................805 489-0446
Brian Talley, *President*
Carrie Isbell, *Administration*
David Block, *Natl Sales Mgr*
Evan Jones, *Natl Sales Mgr*
Lindsey Bateman, *Marketing Staff*
▲ EMP: 15 EST: 1989
SQ FT: 2,000
SALES (est): 3MM **Privately Held**
WEB: www.talleyvineyards.com
SIC: 2084 Wines

(P-2228)
TEMECULA VALLEY WINERY MGT LLC
Also Called: Leonesse Cellars
27495 Diaz Rd, Temecula (92590-3414)
PHONE.....................951 699-8896
Willem Rebaux Steyn,
Marina Souther, *Project Mgr*
Ashleigh Prose, *Human Res Mgr*
Kelly Newcomb, *Merchandise Mgr*
Jasmine Reyes, *Marketing Mgr*
EMP: 56 EST: 2008
SQ FT: 40,000
SALES (est): 10.2MM **Privately Held**
WEB: www.tvwinerymanagement.com
SIC: 2084 Wines

(P-2229)
TERRAVANT WINE COMPANY LLC (PA)
70 Industrial Way, Buellton (93427-9567)
PHONE.....................805 688-4245
Lew Eisaguirre, *President*
Mike Jackson, *Officer*
Eric J Guerra, *Senior VP*
Joe Padilla, *Senior VP*
Jeffrey Monteleone, *Vice Pres*
▲ EMP: 107 EST: 2006
SQ FT: 25,000
SALES (est): 25.4MM **Privately Held**
WEB: www.summerlandwinebrands.com
SIC: 2084 Wines

(P-2230)
THORNTON WINERY
Also Called: Cafe Champagne
32575 Rancho Cal Rd, Temecula (92591-4935)
P.O. Box 9008 (92589-9008)
PHONE.....................951 699-0099
John M Thornton, *Ch of Bd*
Steve Thornton, *President*
Danila Eusebi,
Cheryl Rolph, *Manager*
EMP: 98 EST: 1975
SQ FT: 41,000

SALES (est): 7.7MM **Privately Held**
WEB: www.thorntonwine.com
SIC: 2084 5812 5947 Wine cellars, bonded; engaged in blending wines; eating places; gift shop

(P-2231)
TOOTH AND NAIL WINERY
3090 Anderson Rd, Paso Robles (93446-9616)
PHONE.....................805 369-6100
Kim Walker, *President*
Judi Timmons, *Accounting Mgr*
Ted Gibson, *Regional*
EMP: 14 EST: 2014
SALES (est): 2.7MM **Privately Held**
WEB: www.toothandnailwine.com
SIC: 2084 Wines

(P-2232)
TREANA WINERY LLC
Also Called: Liberty School
4280 Second Wind Way, Paso Robles (93446-6309)
P.O. Box 3260 (93447-3260)
PHONE.....................805 237-2932
Charles Hope,
Charles Wagner,
Abigail Rapp, *Manager*
▲ EMP: 30 EST: 1996
SALES (est): 4.5MM **Privately Held**
WEB: www.hopefamilywines.com
SIC: 2084 Wines

(P-2233)
TURLEY WINE CELLARS
2900 Vineyard Dr, Templeton (93465-9417)
PHONE.....................805 434-1030
Larry Turley, *President*
Lynn Stiefeling, *Controller*
Malanie Anderson, *Opers Mgr*
EMP: 16 EST: 1928
SQ FT: 3,500
SALES (est): 2MM **Privately Held**
WEB: www.turleywinecellars.com
SIC: 2084 Wines

(P-2234)
WATERS EDGE WINERIES INC
Also Called: Waters Edge Winery
8560 Vineyard Ave Ste 408, Rancho Cucamonga (91730-4351)
PHONE.....................909 468-9463
Ken Lineberger, *Principal*
Adriana Serrano, *Admin Asst*
EMP: 17 EST: 2012
SALES (est): 2.4MM **Privately Held**
WEB: www.watersedgewineries.com
SIC: 2084 6794 Wines; franchises; selling or licensing

(P-2235)
WEST BAY COMPANY LLC
132 E Carrillo St, Santa Barbara (93101-2111)
PHONE.....................805 969-5803
Stephen T B Miller, *Administration*
Rand Posin, *CFO*
EMP: 22 EST: 2010
SALES (est): 621.1K **Privately Held**
WEB: www.thornhillcompanies.com
SIC: 2084 Wines

(P-2236)
WIENS CELLARS LLC
35055 Via Del Ponte, Temecula (92592-8022)
PHONE.....................951 694-9892
George M Wiens,
Jeff Wiens, *General Mgr*
Doug Wiens, *Opers Staff*
Jaime Purinton, *Sales Staff*
Sandy Ballard, *Manager*
EMP: 31 EST: 2001
SALES (est): 8.9MM **Privately Held**
WEB: www.wienscellars.com
SIC: 2084 Wines

(P-2237)
WILLIAM JAMES CELLARS (PA)
613 Woodgreen Way, Nipomo (93444-9599)
PHONE.....................805 478-9412
Robin Bogue, *Principal*
EMP: 23 EST: 2010

SALES (est): 91.4K **Privately Held**
WEB: www.williamjamescellars.com
SIC: 2084 Wines

(P-2238)
WILSON CREEK WNERY VNYARDS INC
35960 Rancho Cal Rd, Temecula (92591-5088)
PHONE.....................951 699-9463
Gerald R Wilson, *CEO*
William J Wilson, *CEO*
Chuck Spiegel, *Vice Pres*
Rosemary Wilson, *Vice Pres*
Michelle Glover, *Regional Mgr*
EMP: 110 EST: 2000
SQ FT: 6,000
SALES (est): 26.6MM **Privately Held**
WEB: www.wilsoncreekwinery.com
SIC: 2084 8999 Wines; personal services

(P-2239)
WINC INC
5340 Alla Rd Ste 105, Los Angeles (90066-7049)
PHONE.....................855 282-5829
Alexander Oxman, *CEO*
Geoff McFarlane, *Founder*
Mickey Deehan, *Vice Pres*
Alex Goodwin, *Vice Pres*
Matt Thelen, *Vice Pres*
EMP: 146 EST: 2007
SALES (est): 30.7MM **Privately Held**
WEB: www.winc.com
SIC: 2084 Wines

(P-2240)
WINE WRANGLER INC
2985 Theatre Dr Ste 7, Paso Robles (93446-4531)
P.O. Box 696, Templeton (93465-0696)
PHONE.....................805 238-5700
Coy Barnes, *President*
Sarah Barnes, *Vice Pres*
EMP: 14 EST: 2005
SALES (est): 1MM **Privately Held**
WEB: www.thewinewrangler.com
SIC: 2084 Wines

2085 Liquors, Distilled, Rectified & Blended

(P-2241)
BAR NONE INC
1302 Santa Fe Dr, Tustin (92780-6495)
PHONE.....................714 259-8450
John Underwood, *President*
Elizabeth Underwood, *Corp Secy*
EMP: 18 EST: 1963
SQ FT: 20,000
SALES (est): 5.1MM
SALES (corp-wide): 366.6MM **Publicly Held**
WEB: www.barnoneinc.com
SIC: 2085 2087 3565 Cocktails, alcoholic; beverage bases, concentrates, syrups, powders & mixes; bottling machinery: filling, capping, labeling
PA: First Advantage Corporation
1 Concrse Pkwy Ne Ste 200
Atlanta GA 30328
888 314-9761

(P-2242)
HEMILANE INC
909 E El Segundo Blvd, El Segundo (90245-4110)
PHONE.....................424 277-1134
EMP: 15 EST: 2015
SALES (est): 1MM **Privately Held**
SIC: 2085 Distilled & blended liquors

(P-2243)
J RILEY DISTILLERY INC
11855 Beverly Ct, Loma Linda (92354-3933)
PHONE.....................909 792-0510
Jason Riley, *CEO*
Douglas Kidd, *Co-Owner*
EMP: 13 EST: 2016
SALES (est): 320K **Privately Held**
SIC: 2085 Distilled & blended liquors

PRODUCTS & SVCS

(P-2244)
ROK DRINKS LLC
17383 W Sunset Blvd # 300, Pacific Palisades (90272-4191)
PHONE...................................323 654-2740
Jonathan Kendrick, CEO
Graham Higgins, COO
EMP: 20 EST: 2014
SALES (est): 3.8MM
SALES (corp-wide): 14.3MM **Privately Held**
WEB: www.rokitdrinks.com
SIC: 2085 Rum (alcoholic beverage); vodka (alcoholic beverage); gin (alcoholic beverage)
PA: Rok Stars Limited
    Rok House
    Wolverhampton W MIDLANDS
    190 237-4896

(P-2245)
SAZERAC COMPANY INC
2202 E Del Amo Blvd, Carson (90749)
P.O. Box 6263 (90749-6263)
PHONE...................................310 604-8717
Michael Dominick, Manager
EMP: 15
SALES (corp-wide): 1.2B **Privately Held**
WEB: www.sazerac.com
SIC: 2085 Distilled & blended liquors
PA: Sazerac Company, Inc.
    101 Magazine St Fl 5
    New Orleans LA 70130
    866 729-3722

(P-2246)
STILLHOUSE LLC
8201 Beverly Blvd Ste 300, Los Angeles (90048-4542)
PHONE...................................323 498-1111
Brad Beckerman, CEO
Paul Sheppard, COO
Brad Gietter, Vice Pres
Alex Blough, Executive
Nils Berglund, Office Mgr
EMP: 32 EST: 2009
SALES (est): 4.2MM **Privately Held**
WEB: www.stillhouse.com
SIC: 2085 Corn whiskey
PA: Bacardi Limited
    65 Pitts Bay Road
    Hamilton

(P-2247)
SURF CITY STILL WORKS LLC
16561 Gemini Ln, Huntington Beach (92647-4464)
PHONE...................................714 253-7606
EMP: 13 EST: 2018
SALES (est): 2.7MM **Privately Held**
WEB: www.surfcitystillworks.com
SIC: 2085 Distilled & blended liquors

2086 Soft Drinks

(P-2248)
ADVANCED REFRESHMENT LLC (HQ)
Also Called: Advanced H2o
2560 E Philadelphia St, Ontario (91761-7768)
PHONE...................................425 746-8100
Robert Abramowitz,
EMP: 200 EST: 1998
SQ FT: 270,000
SALES (est): 4.6MM
SALES (corp-wide): 151.5MM **Privately Held**
WEB: www.niagarawater.com
SIC: 2086 Mineral water, carbonated: packaged in cans, bottles, etc.
PA: Niagara Bottling, Llc
    1440 Bridgegate Dr
    Diamond Bar CA 91765
    909 230-5000

(P-2249)
AMERICAN BOTTLING COMPANY
Also Called: Dr Pepper Snapple Group
1188 Mt Vernon Ave, Riverside (92507-1829)
PHONE...................................951 341-7500

Vince Spurgeon, Sales/Mktg Mgr
EMP: 14 **Publicly Held**
WEB: www.drpepper.com
SIC: 2086 5149 Soft drinks: packaged in cans, bottles, etc.; soft drinks
HQ: The American Bottling Company
    6425 Hall Of Fame Ln
    Frisco TX 75034

(P-2250)
AMERICAN BOTTLING COMPANY
230 E 18th St, Bakersfield (93305-5609)
PHONE...................................661 323-7921
Brian Sutton, Manager
EMP: 14 **Publicly Held**
WEB: www.keurigdrpepper.com
SIC: 2086 5149 Soft drinks: packaged in cans, bottles, etc.; soft drinks
HQ: The American Bottling Company
    6425 Hall Of Fame Ln
    Frisco TX 75034

(P-2251)
AMERICAN BOTTLING COMPANY
1166 Arroyo St, San Fernando (91340-1824)
PHONE...................................818 898-1471
Ed Nemecek, Branch Mgr
EMP: 14 **Publicly Held**
WEB: www.keurigdrpepper.com
SIC: 2086 5149 Soft drinks: packaged in cans, bottles, etc.; soft drinks
HQ: The American Bottling Company
    6425 Hall Of Fame Ln
    Frisco TX 75034

(P-2252)
AMERICAN BOTTLING COMPANY
618 Hanson Way, Santa Maria (93458-9734)
PHONE...................................805 928-1001
Richard Roese, Branch Mgr
EMP: 14 **Publicly Held**
WEB: www.keurigdrpepper.com
SIC: 2086 Soft drinks: packaged in cans, bottles, etc.
HQ: The American Bottling Company
    6425 Hall Of Fame Ln
    Frisco TX 75034

(P-2253)
AMERICAN BOTTLING COMPANY
Also Called: 7 Up / R C Bottling Co
3220 E 26th St, Vernon (90058-8008)
PHONE...................................323 268-7779
Russ Wolfe, Controller
EMP: 14 **Publicly Held**
WEB: www.keurigdrpepper.com
SIC: 2086 5149 Soft drinks: packaged in cans, bottles, etc.; groceries & related products
HQ: The American Bottling Company
    6425 Hall Of Fame Ln
    Frisco TX 75034

(P-2254)
AMERIPEC INC
6965 Aragon Cir, Buena Park (90620-1118)
PHONE...................................714 690-9191
Ping C Wu, CEO
Ed Muratori, General Mgr
Mathew Bamberger, Purchasing
Hue Ngo, QC Mgr
David Delacruz, Opers Staff
EMP: 150 EST: 1988
SQ FT: 215,000
SALES (est): 27.2MM **Privately Held**
WEB: www.ameripec.com
SIC: 2086 Carbonated soft drinks, bottled & canned
HQ: President Global Corporation
    6965 Aragon Cir
    Buena Park CA 90620

(P-2255)
AQUAHYDRATE INC
5870 W Jefferson Blvd D, Los Angeles (90016-3159)
P.O. Box 69798, West Hollywood (90069-0798)
PHONE...................................310 559-5058
John Cochran, CEO
Joe Gleason, President
Mark Loeffler, Corp Secy
Ericka Pittman, Chief Mktg Ofcr
Al Hermsen, Vice Pres
◆ EMP: 81 EST: 2003
SALES (est): 10.3MM **Privately Held**
WEB: www.aquahydrate.com
SIC: 2086 Mineral water, carbonated: packaged in cans, bottles, etc.

(P-2256)
ASEPTIC SLTONS USA VNTURES LLC
Also Called: Aseptic Solutions USA-Corona
484 Alcoa Cir, Corona (92878-9323)
PHONE...................................951 736-9230
Alan Morris,
Bob Danko, Vice Pres
Aaron Harris, Vice Pres
Tyrone Wills, Technician
Andrey Campos, Engineer
◆ EMP: 117 EST: 2004
SQ FT: 67,000
SALES (est): 26.5MM **Privately Held**
WEB: www.asepticusa.com
SIC: 2086 Carbonated beverages, nonalcoholic: bottled & canned
PA: Glanbia Public Limited Company
    Glanbia House
    Kilkenny R95 E

(P-2257)
BARFRESH CORPORATION INC
3600 Wilshire Blvd # 1720, Los Angeles (90010-2621)
PHONE...................................303 502-5233
Riccardo Delle Coste, President
Arnold Tinter, Ch of Bd
David Jordan, President
EMP: 15 EST: 2012
SALES (est): 3.9MM **Privately Held**
WEB: www.barfresh.com
SIC: 2086 Bottled & canned soft drinks

(P-2258)
BLK INTERNATIONAL LLC
26565 Agoura Rd Ste 205, Calabasas (91302-3595)
PHONE...................................424 282-3443
Sara Bergstein, CEO
John Kim, COO
Boho Brands, Mng Member
Jacqueline Wilkie, Manager
Louise Wilkie, Manager
EMP: 21 EST: 2016
SQ FT: 5,500
SALES (est): 3MM **Privately Held**
WEB: www.shop.getblk.com
SIC: 2086 Water, pasteurized: packaged in cans, bottles, etc.

(P-2259)
BLUE SKY NATURAL BEVERAGE CO
1 Monster Way, Corona (92879-7101)
PHONE...................................800 426-7367
EMP: 13 EST: 2019
SALES (est): 2.6MM
SALES (corp-wide): 4.6B **Publicly Held**
WEB: www.monsterbevcorp.com
SIC: 2086 Carbonated beverages, nonalcoholic: bottled & canned
PA: Monster Beverage Corporation
    1 Monster Way
    Corona CA 92879
    951 739-6200

(P-2260)
BOTTLING GROUP LLC
Also Called: Pepsico
6659 Sycamore Canyon Blvd, Riverside (92507-0733)
PHONE...................................951 697-3200
Jon Hess, Principal
Dave Alhadeff, Safety Mgr
Becky Banda, QC Mgr

Anthony Garcia, Opers Staff
Nick Scimia, Marketing Staff
EMP: 54 EST: 2011
SALES (est): 19.6MM **Privately Held**
WEB: www.pepsico.com
SIC: 2086 Carbonated soft drinks, bottled & canned

(P-2261)
CHAMELEON BEVERAGE COMPANY INC (PA)
6444 E 26th St, Commerce (90040-3214)
PHONE...................................323 724-8223
Derek Reineman, President
Erin Zheo, CFO
Stuart Rosen, Vice Pres
Morgan Reed, General Mgr
Lok Man Chiu, Technology
◆ EMP: 60 EST: 1995
SQ FT: 100,000
SALES (est): 12.4MM **Privately Held**
WEB: www.chameleonbeverage.com
SIC: 2086 5149 Water, pasteurized: packaged in cans, bottles, etc.; soft drinks

(P-2262)
COASTAL COCKTAILS INC
Also Called: Modern Gourmet Foods
18011 Mitchell S Ste B, Irvine (92614-6863)
PHONE...................................949 250-3129
Boaz Shonfeld, CEO
Mark Greenhall, President
Nadeem Mumal, CEO
Ofer Amram, CFO
Jason Hoffman, Vice Pres
▲ EMP: 50 EST: 2009
SALES (est): 13.7MM **Privately Held**
WEB: www.bd-software.com
SIC: 2086 5149 Bottled & canned soft drinks; food gift baskets

(P-2263)
CRYSTAL GEYSER WATER COMPANY
1233 E California Ave, Bakersfield (93307-1205)
PHONE...................................661 323-6296
Gerhard Gaugel, Branch Mgr
Jon Ellis, Vice Pres
Carmen Maib, Plant Mgr
EMP: 44 **Privately Held**
WEB: www.crystalgeyser.com
SIC: 2086 5141 2099 2033 Mineral water, carbonated: packaged in cans, bottles, etc.; carbonated beverages, nonalcoholic: bottled & canned; groceries, general line; food preparations; canned fruits & specialties; bottled water delivery
HQ: Crystal Geyser Water Company
    501 Washington St
    Calistoga CA 94515
    707 265-3900

(P-2264)
CRYSTAL GEYSER WATER COMPANY
2351 E Brundage Ln Ste A, Bakersfield (93307-3063)
PHONE...................................661 321-0896
Robert Hofferd, Manager
Kevin Moloughney, Vice Pres
EMP: 44 **Privately Held**
WEB: www.crystalgeyser.com
SIC: 2086 Mineral water, carbonated: packaged in cans, bottles, etc.
HQ: Crystal Geyser Water Company
    501 Washington St
    Calistoga CA 94515
    707 265-3900

(P-2265)
GENIUS PRODUCTS MT INC
556 N Dmnd Bar Blvd Ste 1, Diamond Bar (91765-1000)
PHONE...................................510 671-0219
Chris Clifford, CEO
EMP: 110 EST: 2019
SALES (est): 9.9MM **Privately Held**
SIC: 2086 Carbonated beverages, nonalcoholic: bottled & canned

(P-2266)
GREEN SPOT PACKAGING INC
100 S Cambridge Ave, Claremont
(91711-4842)
PHONE..........................909 625-8771
John Tsu, *CEO*
Dana Staal, *COO*
Terry Hughes, *Vice Pres*
Eddie Sanchez, *Technical Mgr*
EMP: 20 **EST:** 1934
SQ FT: 100,000
SALES (est): 11.3MM **Privately Held**
WEB: www.greenspotusa.com
SIC: 2086 Fruit drinks (less than 100% juice): packaged in cans, etc.
PA: Green Spot International
C/O Grand Pavilion Main Entrance
West Bay GR CAYMAN

(P-2267)
GTS LIVING FOODS LLC
Also Called: Synergy Beverages
4415 Bandini Blvd, Vernon (90058-4309)
P.O. Box 2352, Beverly Hills (90213-2352)
PHONE..........................323 581-7787
George Thomas Dave,
EMP: 700 **EST:** 1994
SALES (est): 172.1MM **Privately Held**
WEB: www.gtslivingfoods.com
SIC: 2086 Bottled & canned soft drinks

(P-2268)
HAPPY CELLS INC
Also Called: Teaonic
15911 Arminta St, Van Nuys (91406-1807)
PHONE..........................818 528-5080
Desiree Chesler, *Mng Member*
Fleur Chesler, *CEO*
Nicole Ackerman, *Regl Sales Mgr*
Michael Levine, *Marketing Staff*
EMP: 14 **EST:** 2015
SALES (est): 1.4MM **Privately Held**
WEB: www.teaonic.com
SIC: 2086 Tea, iced: packaged in cans, bottles, etc.

(P-2269)
KEVITA INC (HQ)
2220 Celsius Ave Ste A, Oxnard (93030-5181)
PHONE..........................805 200-2250
Andrea Theodore, *CEO*
Ada Cheng, *CFO*
Cynthia Nastanski, *Admin Sec*
EMP: 58 **EST:** 2009
SQ FT: 17,000
SALES (est): 60MM
SALES (corp-wide): 70.3B **Publicly Held**
WEB: www.kevita.com
SIC: 2086 Bottled & canned soft drinks
PA: Pepsico, Inc.
700 Anderson Hill Rd
Purchase NY 10577
914 253-2000

(P-2270)
LA BOTTLEWORKS INC
1605 Beach St, Montebello (90640-5432)
PHONE..........................323 724-4076
Ryan Marsh, *CEO*
Matthew Marsh, *Vice Pres*
Linda Valenzuela, *General Mgr*
Jennifer Harlin, *Accountant*
EMP: 20 **EST:** 2013
SALES (est): 1.1MM **Privately Held**
WEB: www.labottleworks.com
SIC: 2086 Bottled & canned soft drinks

(P-2271)
MONSTER BEVERAGE COMPANY
1990 Pomona Rd, Corona (92878-4355)
PHONE..........................866 322-4466
Mark Hall, *Principal*
Tami Fox, *Vice Pres*
Sam Pontrelli, *Vice Pres*
Keith Riley, *Vice Pres*
Kate Webb, *Business Dir*
EMP: 39 **EST:** 2010
SALES (est): 4.3MM
SALES (corp-wide): 4.6B **Publicly Held**
WEB: www.monsterbevcorp.com
SIC: 2086 Soft drinks: packaged in cans, bottles, etc.

PA: Monster Beverage Corporation
1 Monster Way
Corona CA 92879
951 739-6200

(P-2272)
MONSTER BEVERAGE CORPORATION (PA)
1 Monster Way, Corona (92879-7101)
PHONE..........................951 739-6200
Rodney C Sacks, *Ch of Bd*
Guy P Carling, *President*
Emelie C Tirre, *President*
Thomas J Kelly, *CFO*
Hilton H Schlosberg, *Vice Ch Bd*
EMP: 984 **EST:** 1985
SQ FT: 141,000
SALES (est): 4.6B **Publicly Held**
WEB: www.monsterbevcorp.com
SIC: 2086 Carbonated beverages, nonalcoholic: bottled & canned

(P-2273)
NIAGARA BOTTLING INTL LLC
2560 E Philadelphia St, Ontario (91761-7768)
PHONE..........................909 230-5000
Andrew Peykoff, *President*
EMP: 19 **EST:** 2014
SALES (est): 911.8K **Privately Held**
WEB: www.niagarawater.com
SIC: 2086 Water, pasteurized: packaged in cans, bottles, etc.

(P-2274)
ORANGE BANG INC
13115 Telfair Ave, Sylmar (91342-3574)
PHONE..........................818 833-1000
David Fox, *President*
EMP: 40 **EST:** 1971
SQ FT: 33,000
SALES (est): 4.2MM **Privately Held**
WEB: www.orangebang.com
SIC: 2086 Soft drinks: packaged in cans, bottles, etc.

(P-2275)
OXIGEN BEVERAGES (USA) INC
12130 Millennium, Los Angeles (90094-2945)
PHONE..........................424 284-2177
Blair Bentham, *President*
Jeff Seavey, *Officer*
EMP: 19
SALES (est): 3.8MM **Privately Held**
WEB: www.drinkoxigen.com
SIC: 2086 Carbonated beverages, nonalcoholic: bottled & canned

(P-2276)
OXIGENESIS INC
2917 Union Rd Ste B, Paso Robles (93446-7313)
PHONE..........................805 549-0275
Stephen R Krauss, *President*
EMP: 14 **EST:** 2013
SALES (est): 1.3MM **Privately Held**
WEB: www.poweredbyoxygen.com
SIC: 2086 Bottled & canned soft drinks

(P-2277)
PEPSI BOTTLING GROUP
Also Called: Pepsico
6230 Descanso Ave, Buena Park (90620-1013)
PHONE..........................714 522-9742
EMP: 16 **EST:** 2017
SALES (est): 2.1MM **Privately Held**
WEB: www.pepsico.com
SIC: 2086 Carbonated soft drinks, bottled & canned

(P-2278)
PEPSI COLA BTLG OF BKERSFIELD
215 E 21st St, Bakersfield (93305-5186)
PHONE..........................661 327-9992
James B Lindsey Jr, *President*
Fay W Penney, *Corp Secy*
Marjorie Lindsey, *Vice Pres*
EMP: 25 **EST:** 1953
SQ FT: 30,000
SALES (est): 1.7MM **Privately Held**
WEB: www.pepsico.com
SIC: 2086 Soft drinks: packaged in cans, bottles, etc.

(P-2279)
PEPSICO
1650 E Central Ave, San Bernardino (92408-2611)
PHONE..........................562 818-9429
EMP: 17 **EST:** 2015
SALES (est): 1MM **Privately Held**
WEB: www.pepsico.com
SIC: 2086 Carbonated soft drinks, bottled & canned

(P-2280)
PEPSICO INC
8530 Wilshire Blvd # 300, Beverly Hills (90211-3122)
PHONE..........................323 785-2820
Taylor Liptak, *Marketing Mgr*
Peter Hess, *Engineer*
EMP: 18
SALES (corp-wide): 70.3B **Publicly Held**
WEB: www.pepsico.com
SIC: 2086 Carbonated soft drinks, bottled & canned
PA: Pepsico, Inc.
700 Anderson Hill Rd
Purchase NY 10577
914 253-2000

(P-2281)
RED BULL MEDIA HSE N AMER INC
1630 Stewart St Ste A, Santa Monica (90404-4020)
PHONE..........................310 393-4647
Jennifer Barney, *Branch Mgr*
Erica Mack, *Marketing Staff*
EMP: 54
SALES (corp-wide): 6.7B **Privately Held**
SIC: 2086 Carbonated beverages, nonalcoholic: bottled & canned
HQ: Red Bull Media House North America, Inc.
1740 Stewart St
Santa Monica CA 90404
310 393-4647

(P-2282)
REFRESCO BEVERAGES US INC
631 S Waterman Ave, San Bernardino (92408-2329)
PHONE..........................909 915-1400
Armando Martinez, *Branch Mgr*
Tamara Kizer, *Maintence Staff*
EMP: 49
SALES (corp-wide): 1.3B **Privately Held**
WEB: www.refresco-na.com
SIC: 2086 Carbonated beverages, nonalcoholic: bottled & canned
HQ: Refresco Beverages Us Inc.
8112 Woodland Center Blvd
Tampa FL 33614

(P-2283)
REFRESCO BEVERAGES US INC
Also Called: San Bernardino Canning Co.
499 E Mill St, San Bernardino (92408-1523)
PHONE..........................909 915-1430
Ed Williams, *Manager*
John Rushing, *Controller*
Rhonda Mata, *Human Res Mgr*
EMP: 49
SQ FT: 76,180
SALES (corp-wide): 1.3B **Privately Held**
WEB: www.refresco-na.com
SIC: 2086 5149 Carbonated beverages, nonalcoholic: bottled & canned; soft drinks
HQ: Refresco Beverages Us Inc.
8112 Woodland Center Blvd
Tampa FL 33614

(P-2284)
REYES COCA-COLA BOTTLING LLC (PA)
3 Park Plz Ste 600, Irvine (92614-2575)
PHONE..........................213 744-8616
James Quincy, *CEO*
Nehal Desai, *CFO*
Nancy Kung, *Finance*
Anne Mao, *Manager*
◆ **EMP:** 300 **EST:** 1902
SQ FT: 80,000

SALES (est): 850.1MM **Privately Held**
WEB: www.coca-cola.com
SIC: 2086 Bottled & canned soft drinks

(P-2285)
REYES COCA-COLA BOTTLING LLC
4320 Ride St, Bakersfield (93313-4831)
PHONE..........................661 324-6531
Ed Shell, *Manager*
EMP: 57
SALES (corp-wide): 850.1MM **Privately Held**
WEB: www.coca-cola.com
SIC: 2086 Bottled & canned soft drinks
PA: Reyes Coca-Cola Bottling, L.L.C.
3 Park Plz Ste 600
Irvine CA 92614
213 744-8616

(P-2286)
REYES COCA-COLA BOTTLING LLC
8729 Cleta St, Downey (90241-5202)
PHONE..........................562 803-8100
Kim Curtis, *Manager*
EMP: 90
SQ FT: 76,395
SALES (corp-wide): 850.1MM **Privately Held**
WEB: www.coca-cola.com
SIC: 2086 5149 Bottled & canned soft drinks; groceries & related products
PA: Reyes Coca-Cola Bottling, L.L.C.
3 Park Plz Ste 600
Irvine CA 92614
213 744-8616

(P-2287)
REYES COCA-COLA BOTTLING LLC
5335 Walker St, Ventura (93003-7406)
PHONE..........................805 644-2211
Jim Donelson, *Manager*
EMP: 57
SALES (corp-wide): 850.1MM **Privately Held**
WEB: www.coca-cola.com
SIC: 2086 5149 Bottled & canned soft drinks; groceries & related products
PA: Reyes Coca-Cola Bottling, L.L.C.
3 Park Plz Ste 600
Irvine CA 92614
213 744-8616

(P-2288)
REYES COCA-COLA BOTTLING LLC
86375 Industrial Way, Coachella (92236-2729)
PHONE..........................760 396-4500
Andrell Gritley, *General Mgr*
EMP: 57
SALES (corp-wide): 850.1MM **Privately Held**
WEB: www.coca-cola.com
SIC: 2086 Bottled & canned soft drinks
PA: Reyes Coca-Cola Bottling, L.L.C.
3 Park Plz Ste 600
Irvine CA 92614
213 744-8616

(P-2289)
REYES COCA-COLA BOTTLING LLC
120 E Jones St, Santa Maria (93454-5101)
PHONE..........................805 925-2629
Dan Suchecki, *Manager*
EMP: 57
SQ FT: 50
SALES (corp-wide): 850.1MM **Privately Held**
WEB: www.coca-cola.com
SIC: 2086 Bottled & canned soft drinks
PA: Reyes Coca-Cola Bottling, L.L.C.
3 Park Plz Ste 600
Irvine CA 92614
213 744-8616

(P-2290)
REYES COCA-COLA BOTTLING LLC
10670 6th St, Rancho Cucamonga (91730-5912)
PHONE..........................909 980-3121

PRODUCTS & SVCS

Sid Campa, *Manager*
EMP: 57
SALES (corp-wide): 850.1MM **Privately Held**
WEB: www.coca-cola.com
SIC: 2086 5149 Bottled & canned soft drinks; groceries & related products
PA: Reyes Coca-Cola Bottling, L.L.C.
3 Park Plz Ste 600
Irvine CA 92614
213 744-8616

(P-2291)
REYES COCA-COLA BOTTLING LLC
1000 Fairway Dr, Santa Maria (93455-1512)
PHONE................................805 614-3702
Dan Suchecki, *Manager*
EMP: 57
SALES (corp-wide): 850.1MM **Privately Held**
WEB: www.coca-cola.com
SIC: 2086 Bottled & canned soft drinks
PA: Reyes Coca-Cola Bottling, L.L.C.
3 Park Plz Ste 600
Irvine CA 92614
213 744-8616

(P-2292)
REYES COCA-COLA BOTTLING LLC
11634 Patton Rd, Downey (90241-5212)
PHONE................................562 536-8847
Larry Loeffler, *Branch Mgr*
EMP: 57
SALES (corp-wide): 850.1MM **Privately Held**
WEB: www.coca-cola.com
SIC: 2086 Bottled & canned soft drinks
PA: Reyes Coca-Cola Bottling, L.L.C.
3 Park Plz Ste 600
Irvine CA 92614
213 744-8616

(P-2293)
REYES COCA-COLA BOTTLING LLC
666 Union St, Montebello (90640-6624)
PHONE................................323 278-2600
Gary Drees, *Manager*
EMP: 57
SQ FT: 127,556
SALES (corp-wide): 850.1MM **Privately Held**
WEB: www.coca-cola.com
SIC: 2086 Bottled & canned soft drinks
PA: Reyes Coca-Cola Bottling, L.L.C.
3 Park Plz Ste 600
Irvine CA 92614
213 744-8616

(P-2294)
REYES COCA-COLA BOTTLING LLC
700 W Grove Ave, Orange (92865-3214)
PHONE................................714 974-1901
Thomas Murphy, *Branch Mgr*
EMP: 57
SQ FT: 7,043
SALES (corp-wide): 850.1MM **Privately Held**
WEB: www.coca-cola.com
SIC: 2086 Bottled & canned soft drinks
PA: Reyes Coca-Cola Bottling, L.L.C.
3 Park Plz Ste 600
Irvine CA 92614
213 744-8616

(P-2295)
REYES COCA-COLA BOTTLING LLC
1338 E 14th St, Los Angeles (90021-2344)
PHONE................................213 744-8659
Perry Fitch, *General Mgr*
EMP: 57
SALES (corp-wide): 850.1MM **Privately Held**
WEB: www.coca-cola.com
SIC: 2086 Bottled & canned soft drinks
PA: Reyes Coca-Cola Bottling, L.L.C.
3 Park Plz Ste 600
Irvine CA 92614
213 744-8616

(P-2296)
REYES COCA-COLA BOTTLING LLC
15346 Anacapa Rd, Victorville (92392-2448)
PHONE................................760 241-2653
Rose Wols, *Manager*
EMP: 57
SALES (corp-wide): 850.1MM **Privately Held**
WEB: www.coca-cola.com
SIC: 2086 Bottled & canned soft drinks
PA: Reyes Coca-Cola Bottling, L.L.C.
3 Park Plz Ste 600
Irvine CA 92614
213 744-8616

(P-2297)
REYES COCA-COLA BOTTLING LLC
126 S 3rd St, El Centro (92243-2542)
PHONE................................760 352-1561
Jose Chaira, *Manager*
EMP: 57
SALES (corp-wide): 850.1MM **Privately Held**
WEB: www.coca-cola.com
SIC: 2086 Bottled & canned soft drinks
PA: Reyes Coca-Cola Bottling, L.L.C.
3 Park Plz Ste 600
Irvine CA 92614
213 744-8616

(P-2298)
SEQUOIA PURE WATER INC
1640 W 134th St, Compton (90222-1624)
PHONE................................310 637-8500
Dae Young Lee, *President*
EMP: 14 **EST:** 1999
SQ FT: 80,000
SALES (est): 215K **Privately Held**
SIC: 2086 Pasteurized & mineral waters, bottled & canned

(P-2299)
SHASTA BEVERAGES INC
14405 Artesia Blvd, La Mirada (90638-5886)
PHONE................................714 523-2280
Bruce McDowell, *Opers-Prdtn-Mfg*
Karl Baer, *Vice Pres*
Brent Bott, *Exec Dir*
Gerald Smith, *Branch Mgr*
Israel Lumbi, *Planning*
EMP: 70
SALES (corp-wide): 1B **Publicly Held**
WEB: www.shastapop.com
SIC: 2086 5149 Soft drinks: packaged in cans, bottles, etc.; soft drinks
HQ: Shasta Beverages, Inc.
26901 Indl Blvd
Hayward CA 94545
954 581-0922

(P-2300)
STRATUS GROUP DUO LLC
4401 S Downey Rd, Vernon (90058-2518)
PHONE................................323 581-3663
Dara Killilea, *Mng Member*
EMP: 30
SALES (est): 30K **Privately Held**
SIC: 2086 Bottled & canned soft drinks

(P-2301)
TOGNAZZINI BEVERAGE SERVICE
Also Called: Coca-Cola
241 Roemer Way, Santa Maria (93454-1129)
PHONE................................805 928-1144
Jim Tognazzini, *Owner*
Meck Tognazzini, *Co-Owner*
EMP: 28 **EST:** 1965
SQ FT: 18,000
SALES (est): 3MM **Privately Held**
WEB: www.togbev.com
SIC: 2086 7699 Bottled & canned soft drinks; fountain repair

(P-2302)
UNIX PACKAGING LLC
Also Called: Mammoth Water
9 Minson Way, Montebello (90640-6744)
PHONE................................213 627-5050
Bobby Melamed, *CEO*

Kourosh Melamed, *CFO*
Shawn Arianpour, *Vice Pres*
Trisha Tan, *Vice Pres*
Nazy Danesh, *General Counsel*
▲ **EMP:** 120 **EST:** 2010
SQ FT: 125,000
SALES (est): 65.3MM **Privately Held**
WEB: www.unixpackaging.com
SIC: 2086 Pasteurized & mineral waters, bottled & canned

(P-2303)
WANU WATER INC
12424 Wilshire Blvd # 1115, Los Angeles (90025-1071)
PHONE................................310 401-1733
Greg Rayburn, *CEO*
Todd Ogara, *President*
Danelle Larsen, *CFO*
Saban Poudyal, *Controller*
Crystal Blount, *Manager*
EMP: 13 **EST:** 2012
SALES (est): 3.8MM **Privately Held**
WEB: www.wanuwater.com
SIC: 2086 Soft drinks: packaged in cans, bottles, etc.

(P-2304)
ZEVIA LLC
15821 Ventura Blvd # 145, Encino (91436-5201)
PHONE................................310 202-7000
Padraic Spence, *Mng Member*
Robert Gay Sr, *Officer*
Bill Beech, *Vice Pres*
Keith Carlson, *Vice Pres*
Jeff Dean, *Vice Pres*
EMP: 75 **EST:** 2007
SALES: 110MM **Publicly Held**
WEB: www.zevia.com
SIC: 2086 Bottled & canned soft drinks
PA: Zevia Pbc
15821 Ventura Blvd # 145
Encino CA 91436
310 202-7000

(P-2305)
ZICO BEVERAGES LLC (HQ)
2101 E El Segundo Blvd # 40, El Segundo (90245-4518)
P.O. Box 1734, Atlanta GA (30301-1734)
PHONE................................866 729-9426
Ronald J Lewis, *Mng Member*
Marie D Quintero-Johnson, *Mng Member*
▲ **EMP:** 64 **EST:** 2009
SQ FT: 10,000
SALES (est): 17.1MM
SALES (corp-wide): 33B **Publicly Held**
WEB: www.zico.com
SIC: 2086 Bottled & canned soft drinks
PA: The Coca-Cola Company
1 Coca Cola Plz Nw
Atlanta GA 30313
404 676-2121

2087 Flavoring Extracts & Syrups

(P-2306)
AMERICAN FRUITS & FLAVORS LLC (HQ)
Also Called: Juice Division
10725 Sutter Ave, Pacoima (91331-2553)
P.O. Box 331060 (91333-1060)
PHONE................................818 899-9574
William Haddad, *President*
Sara Tapia, *CFO*
Hilton Schlosberg, *Officer*
Bill Haddad, *Vice Pres*
Jack Haddad, *Vice Pres*
◆ **EMP:** 125 **EST:** 1975
SQ FT: 10,000
SALES (est): 97.3MM
SALES (corp-wide): 4.6B **Publicly Held**
WEB: www.americanfruits-flavors.com
SIC: 2087 Concentrates, drink; powders, drink; syrups, drink
PA: Monster Beverage Corporation
1 Monster Way
Corona CA 92879
951 739-6200

(P-2307)
AMERICAN FRUITS & FLAVORS LLC
12950 Pierce St, Pacoima (91331-2526)
PHONE................................818 899-9574
EMP: 33
SALES (corp-wide): 4.6B **Publicly Held**
WEB: www.americanfruits-flavors.com
SIC: 2087 Concentrates, drink
HQ: American Fruits And Flavors, Llc
10725 Sutter Ave
Pacoima CA 91331
818 899-9574

(P-2308)
AMERICAN FRUITS & FLAVORS LLC
Also Called: Flavors Division
1547 Knowles Ave, Los Angeles (90063-1606)
PHONE................................323 264-7791
Stacy West, *Branch Mgr*
Stacey West, *Opers Mgr*
Ken Jennings, *Production*
Frank Alvarado, *Manager*
Luis Avalos, *Manager*
EMP: 33
SALES (corp-wide): 4.6B **Publicly Held**
WEB: www.americanfruits-flavors.com
SIC: 2087 Extracts, flavoring
HQ: American Fruits And Flavors, Llc
10725 Sutter Ave
Pacoima CA 91331
818 899-9574

(P-2309)
BERRI PRO INC
929 Colorado Ave, Santa Monica (90401-2716)
PHONE................................781 929-8288
Jerome Joseph TSE, *CEO*
Kelly Reddell, *Vice Pres*
EMP: 19 **EST:** 2015
SALES (est): 3.2MM **Privately Held**
WEB: www.berrifit.com
SIC: 2087 Concentrates, drink

(P-2310)
BETTER BEVERAGES INC (PA)
Also Called: Chem-Mark of Orange County
10624 Midway Ave, Cerritos (90703-1581)
P.O. Box 1399, Bellflower (90707-1399)
PHONE................................562 924-8321
H Ronald Harris, *CEO*
Tricia Harris, *Corp Secy*
Patrick Dickson, *Vice Pres*
Mike Harris, *Vice Pres*
William Kendig, *Vice Pres*
▲ **EMP:** 80
SQ FT: 15,000
SALES (est): 12.9MM **Privately Held**
WEB: www.betbev.com
SIC: 2087 7359 5169 Beverage bases; syrups, drink; equipment rental & leasing; industrial gases

(P-2311)
BLUE PACIFIC FLAVORS INC
1354 Marion Ct, City of Industry (91745-2418)
PHONE................................626 934-0099
Donald F Wilkes, *President*
Donna Stratford, *Purch Agent*
Thuy Huynh, *Director*
▲ **EMP:** 35 **EST:** 1993
SQ FT: 40,000
SALES (est): 10.2MM **Privately Held**
WEB: www.bluepacificflavors.com
SIC: 2087 2869 Extracts, flavoring; perfumes, flavorings & food additives

(P-2312)
BYRNES & KIEFER CO
501 Airpark Dr, Fullerton (92833-2501)
PHONE................................714 554-4000
EMP: 55 **EST:** 2012
SALES (est): 3.8MM **Privately Held**
WEB: www.bkcompany.com
SIC: 2087 Colorings, confectioners'

(P-2313)
CALIFRNIA CSTM FRITS FLVORS IN (PA)
Also Called: California Cstm Frt & Flavors
15800 Tapia St, Irwindale (91706-2178)
PHONE..........................626 736-4130
Mike Mulhausen, *President*
Nicole Banuelos, *President*
Daniel Birshan, *Research*
Phyllis Ferguson, *Purch Dir*
Kim Alcala, *Purchasing*
◆ EMP: 35 EST: 1984
SALES (est): 33.8MM **Privately Held**
WEB: www.ccff.com
SIC: 2087 2033 2099 5083 Extracts, flavoring; fruits: packaged in cans, jars, etc.; food preparations; dairy machinery & equipment

(P-2314)
CARMI FLVR & FRAGRANCE CO INC (PA)
Also Called: Carmi Flavors
6030 Scott Way, Commerce (90040-3516)
PHONE..........................323 888-9240
Eliot Carmi, *President*
Lucie Nicholls, *General Mgr*
Sarah Foster, *Office Mgr*
Serhan Rende, *Engineer*
Roger Speakman, *Plant Mgr*
▲ EMP: 40 EST: 1980
SQ FT: 35,000
SALES (est): 16MM **Privately Held**
WEB: www.carmiflavors.com
SIC: 2087 2844 Extracts, flavoring; toilet preparations

(P-2315)
COCA-COLA COMPANY
1650 S Vintage Ave, Ontario (91761-3656)
PHONE..........................909 975-5200
EMP: 100
SALES (corp-wide): 44.2B **Publicly Held**
SIC: 2087 5149 Mfg Flavor Extracts/Syrup Whol Groceries
PA: The Coca-Cola Company
1 Coca Cola Plz Nw
Atlanta GA 30313
404 676-2121

(P-2316)
COMMON COLLABS LLC
1820 E Walnut Ave, Fullerton (92831-4844)
PHONE..........................714 519-3245
Freddy Lopez, *Mng Member*
Patrick Curtis,
EMP: 35 EST: 2019
SALES (est): 2.7MM **Privately Held**
WEB: www.commoncollabs.com
SIC: 2087 Beverage bases

(P-2317)
CREATIVE ESSENCES INC
15320 Cornet St, Santa Fe Springs (90670-5532)
PHONE..........................310 638-9277
Elvie Daliva, *Principal*
Victor Zhang, *VP Bus Dvlpt*
Leila Holodnak, *Principal*
Elvira Dagsaan, *General Mgr*
EMP: 22 EST: 2013
SALES (est): 3.5MM **Privately Held**
WEB: www.creativeessences.com
SIC: 2087 Flavoring extracts & syrups

(P-2318)
CUSTOM INGREDIENTS INC (PA)
160 Calle Iglesia Ste 102, San Clemente (92672-7551)
PHONE..........................949 276-7994
Alex Wendling, *President*
Michael L Wendling, *CEO*
Steven Bishop, *CFO*
Steve Bishop, *Exec VP*
Alexander Wendling, *Admin Sec*
EMP: 45 EST: 2000
SALES (est): 13.3MM **Privately Held**
WEB: www.customflavors.com
SIC: 2087 Beverage bases, concentrates, syrups, powders & mixes

(P-2319)
DELANO GROWERS GRAPE PRODUCTS
32351 Bassett Ave, Delano (93215-9699)
PHONE..........................661 725-3255
Jim Cesare, *President*
Daniel Lord, *Plant Mgr*
▲ EMP: 55 EST: 1940
SQ FT: 40,000
SALES (est): 11.8MM **Privately Held**
WEB: www.delanogrowersgrapeproducts.com
SIC: 2087 Concentrates, drink

(P-2320)
DISTRIBUTORS PROCESSING INC
Also Called: D P I
17656 Avenue 168, Porterville (93257-9263)
PHONE..........................559 781-0297
Randy Walker, *President*
Gary Jacinto, *Ch of Bd*
William Blatnick, *Corp Secy*
Marcia Pierce, *Admin Sec*
Mike Rincker, *Research*
▼ EMP: 17 EST: 1965
SQ FT: 23,050
SALES (est): 3.2MM **Privately Held**
SIC: 2087 Extracts, flavoring

(P-2321)
DR SMOOTHIE BRANDS INC
1730 Raymer Ave, Fullerton (92833-2530)
PHONE..........................714 449-9787
Sam Lteif, *CEO*
Cara Anderson, *Human Resources*
Wes Lanier, *Plant Engr*
Susy Sandoval, *Sales Staff*
▼ EMP: 18 EST: 2006
SQ FT: 30,000
SALES (est): 9.2MM
SALES (corp-wide): 2MM **Privately Held**
WEB: www.drsmoothie.com
SIC: 2087 Beverage bases, concentrates, syrups, powders & mixes
HQ: Juice Tyme, Inc.
4401 S Oakley Ave
Chicago IL 60609
773 579-1291

(P-2322)
DR SMOOTHIE ENTERPRISES
1730 Raymer Ave, Fullerton (92833-2530)
PHONE..........................714 449-9787
Bill Haugh, *President*
William P Haugh, *Principal*
Mike Finch, *Marketing Staff*
Shawn Davis, *Sales Staff*
Alex Bustamante, *Warehouse Mgr*
▼ EMP: 21 EST: 1998
SQ FT: 30,000
SALES (est): 4.4MM **Privately Held**
WEB: www.drsmoothie.com
SIC: 2087 Beverage bases, concentrates, syrups, powders & mixes

(P-2323)
FELBRO FOOD PRODUCTS INC
5700 W Adams Blvd, Los Angeles (90016-2402)
PHONE..........................323 936-5266
Michael Feldman, *CEO*
Barton Feldmar, *President*
Barton J Feldmar, *CEO*
Diana Price, *CEO*
Yvette Bores, *Research*
EMP: 49 EST: 1946
SQ FT: 35,000
SALES (est): 10.3MM **Privately Held**
WEB: www.felbro.com
SIC: 2087 Syrups, drink

(P-2324)
FLAVOR FACTORY INC
2058 2nd St, Norco (92860-2804)
PHONE..........................951 273-9877
Daniel S Wixted, *President*
Mary J Wixted, *Admin Sec*
EMP: 15 EST: 2005
SQ FT: 13,750
SALES (est): 2MM **Privately Held**
WEB: www.flavorfactory.net
SIC: 2087 Concentrates, flavoring (except drink)

(P-2325)
FLAVOR HOUSE INC
16378 Koala Rd, Adelanto (92301-3916)
PHONE..........................760 246-9131
Richard Staley, *President*
▲ EMP: 40
SQ FT: 23,600
SALES (est): 7.2MM **Privately Held**
WEB: www.flavorhouseinc.com
SIC: 2087 Flavoring extracts & syrups

(P-2326)
FPG OC INC
24855 Corbit Pl Ste B, Yorba Linda (92887-5543)
PHONE..........................714 692-2950
Joshua Cua, *CEO*
Priscilla Latter, *President*
Julie Hodson, *Vice Pres*
◆ EMP: 29 EST: 2003
SQ FT: 74,300
SALES (est): 1.3MM **Privately Held**
SIC: 2087 Extracts, flavoring

(P-2327)
FROZEN BEAN INC
9238 Bally Ct, Rancho Cucamonga (91730-5313)
PHONE..........................855 837-6936
John Bae, *CEO*
Thuy Dang, *Principal*
Alma Gasporra, *Natl Sales Mgr*
Andrea Ramos, *Marketing Staff*
Kenneth Ro, *Sales Staff*
▼ EMP: 30 EST: 2011
SALES (est): 4.8MM **Privately Held**
WEB: www.thefrozenbean.com
SIC: 2087 Beverage bases, concentrates, syrups, powders & mixes

(P-2328)
GOLDEN STATE FOODS CORP (PA)
18301 Von Karman Ave # 1, Irvine (92612-1009)
PHONE..........................949 247-8000
Mark Wetterau, *Ch of Bd*
Mike Waitukaitis, *Vice Chairman*
Chad Buechel, *President*
Campbell Cooper, *President*
Ryan Hammer, *President*
◆ EMP: 35 EST: 1969
SALES (est): 821K **Privately Held**
WEB: www.goldenstatefoods.com
SIC: 2087 5142 5148 5149 Syrups, drink; packaged frozen goods; vegetables; vegetables, fresh; condiments; meats, cured or smoked

(P-2329)
HERBALIFE MANUFACTURING LLC
20481 Crescent Bay Dr, Lake Forest (92630-8817)
PHONE..........................949 457-0951
Gerry Holly, *Senior VP*
Richard Grinnals, *Manager*
◆ EMP: 75 EST: 2009
SQ FT: 145,000
SALES (est): 32.2MM **Privately Held**
WEB: www.herbalife.com
SIC: 2087 2023 Beverage bases, concentrates, syrups, powders & mixes; dietary supplements, dairy & non-dairy based
HQ: Herbalife International, Inc.
800 W Olympic Blvd # 406
Los Angeles CA 90015
310 410-9600

(P-2330)
J & J PROCESSING INC
Also Called: Custom Foods
14715 Anson Ave, Santa Fe Springs (90670-5305)
PHONE..........................562 926-2333
James B Nelson, *CEO*
Paul Nelson, *Exec VP*
Lisa Goldstein, *Research*
▲ EMP: 50 EST: 1972
SQ FT: 44,000
SALES (est): 8.6MM **Privately Held**
WEB: www.custom-foods.com
SIC: 2087 2041 2099 Beverage bases; flour & other grain mill products; seasonings: dry mixes; spices, including grinding

(P-2331)
LA PAZ PRODUCTS INC
345 Oak Pl, Brea (92821-4122)
P.O. Box 459 (92822-0459)
PHONE..........................714 990-0982
Suanne Casey, *CEO*
Roy Farhi, *Sales Dir*
Laura Collins, *Manager*
▼ EMP: 18
SQ FT: 18,000
SALES (est): 3.4MM **Privately Held**
WEB: www.lapazproducts.com
SIC: 2087 Cocktail mixes, nonalcoholic

(P-2332)
MARTIN BAUER INC
20710 S Alameda St, Long Beach (90810-1107)
PHONE..........................310 669-2100
Peter Hafermann, *Manager*
EMP: 17
SALES (corp-wide): 710.2MM **Privately Held**
WEB: www.botanicals.com
SIC: 2087 2099 Flavoring extracts & syrups; spices, including grinding
HQ: Martin Bauer Inc.
400 Plaza Dr Ste 303
Secaucus NJ 07094
201 659-3100

(P-2333)
MISSION FLAVORS FRAGRANCES INC
25882 Wright, El Toro (92610-3503)
PHONE..........................949 461-3344
Patrick S Imburgia, *CEO*
Rich Flanagan, *Vice Pres*
Brenda Hannon, *Administration*
Kirsten McCraw, *Administration*
Paul Loskutoff, *Marketing Mgr*
EMP: 15 EST: 1987
SALES (est): 4.8MM **Privately Held**
WEB: www.thasegawa.com
SIC: 2087 Extracts, flavoring; syrups, flavoring (except drink)
HQ: T. Hasegawa U.S.A. Inc.
14017 183rd St
Cerritos CA 90703
714 522-1900

(P-2334)
NEWPORT FLAVORS & FRAGRANCES
Also Called: Nature's Flavors
833 N Elm St, Orange (92867-7909)
PHONE..........................714 771-2200
William R Sabo, *CEO*
James Thelen, *CFO*
Jeanne A Rossman, *Admin Sec*
Jeanne Grossman, *Buyer*
Lane Melland, *Director*
▲ EMP: 30 EST: 1984
SALES (est): 5.5MM **Privately Held**
WEB: www.naturesflavors.com
SIC: 2087 Extracts, flavoring

(P-2335)
PBF & E LLC
Also Called: Guelaguetza
3014 W Olympic Blvd, Los Angeles (90006-2516)
PHONE..........................213 427-0340
Bricia Lopez, *Mng Member*
Paulina Lopez,
EMP: 50 EST: 2000
SALES (est): 4.9MM **Privately Held**
WEB: www.ilovemole.com
SIC: 5812 2087 Mexican restaurant; cocktail mixes, nonalcoholic

(P-2336)
SCISOREK & SON FLAVORS INC
Also Called: S&S Flavours
2951 Enterprise St, Brea (92821-6212)
PHONE..........................714 524-0550
Mark Tuerffs, *President*
Dan Hart, *Vice Pres*
Curtis Krystek, *Plant Mgr*
Robert Olson, *Director*
EMP: 50 EST: 1928
SQ FT: 33,000

SALES (est): 5MM **Privately Held**
WEB: www.ssflavors.com
SIC: 2087 Extracts, flavoring

(P-2337)
SYMRISE INC
332 Forest Ave, Laguna Beach
(92651-2117)
PHONE................................949 276-4600
Steve Koehr, *Branch Mgr*
EMP: 37 **Privately Held**
WEB: www.symrise.com
SIC: 2087 Syrups, drink
HQ: Symrise Inc.
300 North St
Teterboro NJ 07608
201 288-3200

(P-2338)
T HASEGAWA USA INC (HQ)
14017 183rd St, Cerritos (90703-7000)
PHONE................................714 522-1900
Tom Damiano, *CEO*
Tokujiro Hasegawa, *President*
Dan Freimuth, *Exec VP*
Kim Burnett, *Vice Pres*
Mark Webster, *Vice Pres*
▲ **EMP:** 50 **EST:** 1978
SQ FT: 56,000
SALES (est): 50MM **Privately Held**
WEB: www.thasegawa.com
SIC: 2087 Extracts, flavoring

(P-2339)
WEIDER HEALTH AND FITNESS
21100 Erwin St, Woodland Hills
(91367-3772)
PHONE................................818 884-6800
Eric Weider, *President*
Tonja Fuller, *Treasurer*
Lian Katz, *Treasurer*
George Lengvari, *Vice Ch Bd*
Peggy Sukawaty, *Executive Asst*
EMP: 466 **EST:** 1940
SQ FT: 6,000
SALES (est): 30.5MM **Privately Held**
SIC: 2087 7991 7999 Beverage bases, concentrates, syrups, powders & mixes; physical fitness facilities; physical fitness instruction

2091 Fish & Seafoods, Canned & Cured

(P-2340)
AQUAMAR INC
10888 7th St, Rancho Cucamonga
(91730-5421)
PHONE................................909 481-4700
Hugo Yamakawa, *Principal*
Dennis Tortora, *CFO*
Taka Iwasaki, *Vice Pres*
Saemi Cheon, *Opers Staff*
Andrew Davidoff, *Sales Dir*
◆ **EMP:** 150 **EST:** 1991
SQ FT: 42,000
SALES (est): 25.8MM **Privately Held**
WEB: www.aquamarseafood.com
SIC: 2091 2092 Shellfish, canned & cured; fresh or frozen packaged fish

(P-2341)
GLADSTONES INC
330 S Pine Ave, Long Beach (90802-4531)
PHONE................................562 432-8588
Gladstone J Jones, *CEO*
EMP: 15 **EST:** 1985
SALES (est): 434K **Privately Held**
WEB: www.gladstoneslongbeach.com
SIC: 2091 Seafood products: packaged in cans, jars, etc.

(P-2342)
THAI UNION NORTH AMERICA INC (HQ)
2150 E Grand Ave, El Segundo
(90245-5024)
PHONE................................424 397-8556
Bryan Rosenberg, *President*
Rungtiwa Snider, *Vice Pres*
Jose Abbad, *Business Dir*
Andreia Meyers, *Administration*
Apiradee Triampo, *Controller*
◆ **EMP:** 39 **EST:** 1996

SALES (est): 101.3MM **Privately Held**
WEB: www.thaiunion.com
SIC: 2091 Tuna fish: packaged in cans, jars, etc.; salmon: packaged in cans, jars, etc.

(P-2343)
YAMASA ENTERPRISES
Also Called: Yamasa Fish Cake
515 Stanford Ave, Los Angeles
(90013-2189)
PHONE................................213 626-2211
Frank Kawana, *President*
Yuji Kawana, *Vice Pres*
Sachie Kawana, *Admin Sec*
▲ **EMP:** 27 **EST:** 1939
SQ FT: 20,000
SALES (est): 5.7MM **Privately Held**
WEB: www.yamasafishcake.com
SIC: 2091 Fish & seafood cakes: packaged in cans, jars, etc.

2092 Fish & Seafoods, Fresh & Frozen

(P-2344)
ADVANCED FRESH CNCPTS FRNCHISE
Also Called: Afcfc
19205 S Laurel Park Rd, Rancho
Dominguez (90220-6032)
PHONE................................310 604-3200
Jeffrey Seiler, *CEO*
Dave Chou, *Regional Mgr*
Jeffrey Asido, *Research*
Lennie Chea, *Analyst*
Julie Vanta, *Analyst*
▲ **EMP:** 24 **EST:** 2002
SALES (est): 5.6MM
SALES (corp-wide): 28.2MM **Privately Held**
WEB: www.afcsushi.com
SIC: 2092 6794 Fresh or frozen packaged fish; franchises, selling or licensing
PA: Advanced Fresh Concepts Corp.
19205 S Laurel Park Rd
Rancho Dominguez CA 90220
310 604-3630

(P-2345)
FISHERMANS PRIDE PRCESSORS INC
Also Called: Neptune Foods
4510 S Alameda St, Vernon (90058-2011)
PHONE................................323 232-1980
Howard Choi, *CEO*
Hector Poon, *COO*
Martin Tsai, *Executive*
Thomas Han, *CIO*
Carmen Aguila, *Human Res Mgr*
◆ **EMP:** 300 **EST:** 1954
SQ FT: 125,000
SALES (est): 47.8MM **Privately Held**
SIC: 2092 Fresh or frozen packaged fish

(P-2346)
LONG BEACH SEAFOODS CO
4643 Hackett Ave, Lakewood (90713-2632)
PHONE................................562 432-7300
Tony Delucia, *President*
Star Delucia, *Vice Pres*
EMP: 29 **EST:** 1921
SQ FT: 50,000
SALES (est): 1.6MM **Privately Held**
SIC: 2092 5146 Fresh or frozen packaged fish; fish & seafoods

(P-2347)
NIKKO ENTERPRISE CORPORATION
Also Called: Hanna Fuji Sushi
13168 Sandoval St, Santa Fe Springs
(90670-6600)
PHONE................................562 941-6080
Tlang T Mawii, *CEO*
Sein Myint, *Shareholder*
Robby Sharma, *Vice Pres*
EMP: 23 **EST:** 1995
SQ FT: 5,000
SALES (est): 4.4MM **Privately Held**
WEB: www.necsushi.com
SIC: 2092 Fresh or frozen fish or seafood chowders, soups & stews

(P-2348)
OCEAN DIRECT LLC (HQ)
Also Called: Boardwalk Solutions
13771 Gramercy Pl, Gardena
(90249-2470)
PHONE................................424 266-9300
Neil Kinney,
Richard Barnes, *CIO*
Matthew Hamel, *Info Tech Mgr*
John Bagley, *Controller*
Stacy Smullen, *Opers Mgr*
▼ **EMP:** 184 **EST:** 2003
SQ FT: 20,000
SALES (est): 39.1MM
SALES (corp-wide): 56.3MM **Privately Held**
WEB: www.oceandirect.com
SIC: 2092 2022 2037 2033 Fresh or frozen fish or seafood chowders, soups & stews; prepared fish or other seafood cakes & sticks; natural cheese; frozen fruits & vegetables; vegetables & vegetable products in cans, jars, etc.; groceries, general line
PA: Richmond Wholesale Meat, Llc
2920 Regatta Blvd
Richmond CA 94804
510 233-5111

(P-2349)
SANTA MONICA SEAFOOD COMPANY (PA)
18531 S Broadwick St, Rancho Dominguez
(90220-6440)
PHONE................................310 886-7900
Toll Free:................................888 -
Roger O'Brien, *CEO*
Michael Cigliano II, *Vice Pres*
Cindy Duncan, *Vice Pres*
John Mathews, *Vice Pres*
Nancy E Osorio, *Vice Pres*
▲ **EMP:** 100 **EST:** 1939
SQ FT: 65,000
SALES (est): 121.9MM **Privately Held**
WEB: www.santamonicaseafood.com
SIC: 2092 5146 Seafoods, frozen: prepared; seafoods

(P-2350)
SIMPLY FRESH LLC
Also Called: Rojo's
11215 Knott Ave Ste A, Cypress
(90630-5495)
PHONE................................714 562-5000
Dale Jabour, *CEO*
Evelyn Reher, *QA Dir*
Hector Madrid, *Opers Mgr*
▼ **EMP:** 160 **EST:** 1987
SQ FT: 20,000
SALES (est): 44.2MM
SALES (corp-wide): 113.5MM **Privately Held**
WEB: www.simplyff.com
SIC: 2092 Fresh or frozen packaged fish
PA: Lakeview Farms, Llc
1600 Gressel Dr
Delphos OH 45833
419 695-9925

2095 Coffee

(P-2351)
APFFELS COFFEE INC
12115 Pacific St, Santa Fe Springs
(90670-2989)
P.O. Box 2506 (90670-0506)
PHONE................................562 309-0400
Darryl Blunk, *CEO*
Alvin Apffel, *President*
Mike Rogers, *Exec VP*
Edward Apffel, *Vice Pres*
Louie Romero, *Accountant*
◆ **EMP:** 95 **EST:** 1914
SQ FT: 100,000
SALES (est): 7.3MM **Privately Held**
WEB: www.apffels.com
SIC: 2095 5149 Coffee roasting (except by wholesale grocers); coffee, green or roasted

(P-2352)
BLACK DROP COFFEE INC
225 W Fairview Ave, San Gabriel
(91776-2942)
PHONE................................323 742-5666
Mark Stiles, *CEO*
EMP: 13 **EST:** 2015
SALES (est): 537.1K **Privately Held**
WEB: www.blackdropcoffee.com
SIC: 2095 Coffee roasting (except by wholesale grocers)

(P-2353)
F GAVINA & SONS INC
Also Called: Gavia
2700 Fruitland Ave, Vernon (90058-2893)
PHONE................................323 582-0671
Pedro Gavina, *President*
Jose Gavina, *Treasurer*
Leonor Gavi A-Valls, *Vice Pres*
Francisco M Gavina, *Vice Pres*
Leonora Gavina, *Vice Pres*
▲ **EMP:** 295
SQ FT: 239,000
SALES (est): 77.4MM **Privately Held**
WEB: www.gavina.com
SIC: 2095 Coffee roasting (except by wholesale grocers)

(P-2354)
GOURMET COFFEE WAREHOUSE INC (PA)
Also Called: Groundwork Coffee Company
920 N Formosa Ave, Los Angeles
(90046-6702)
PHONE................................323 871-8930
Richard Karno, *President*
EMP: 20 **EST:** 1991
SQ FT: 10,000
SALES (est): 8.9MM **Privately Held**
SIC: 2095 5149 5499 Coffee roasting (except by wholesale grocers; coffee & tea; coffee

(P-2355)
GROUNDWORK COFFEE ROASTERS LLC
5457 Cleon Ave, North Hollywood
(91601-2834)
PHONE................................818 506-6020
Steven Levan,
Samantha Mitchell, *Project Mgr*
Kim Schultz, *Human Resources*
Evan Dohrmann, *VP Opers*
Drew Pawlan, *Marketing Staff*
EMP: 160 **EST:** 2011
SQ FT: 4,650
SALES (est): 16.6MM **Privately Held**
WEB: www.groundworkcoffee.com
SIC: 2095 5812 5149 Roasted coffee; contract food services; coffee, green or roasted

(P-2356)
KAV AMERICA AG INC
422 Commercial Rd, San Bernardino
(92408-3706)
PHONE................................855 528-8721
Tak Lam, *CEO*
▲ **EMP:** 19 **EST:** 2011
SALES (est): 1.7MM **Privately Held**
WEB: www.kavamerica.com
SIC: 2095 Coffee extracts

(P-2357)
SANTA BARBARA COFFEE LLC
Also Called: Red Star Coffee
6489 Calle Real Ste G, Goleta
(93117-1538)
PHONE................................805 683-2555
Daniel M Randall, *Mng Member*
Werner Diaz,
Kevin C Donnelly,
EMP: 17 **EST:** 2004
SQ FT: 1,645
SALES (est): 1.1MM **Privately Held**
SIC: 2095 5499 Coffee roasting (except by wholesale grocers); coffee

(P-2358)
SANTA BARBARA COFFEE & TEA INC
Also Called: Santa Barbarba Roasting
321 Motor Way, Santa Barbara
(93101-3436)
PHONE.....................805 898-3700
Corey Russell, *CEO*
Brolin Russell, *Opers Staff*
EMP: 70 **EST:** 1988
SQ FT: 4,700
SALES (est): 1.2MM **Privately Held**
WEB: www.sbcoffee.com
SIC: 5812 2095 Coffee shop; coffee roasting (except by wholesale grocers)

2096 Potato Chips & Similar Prdts

(P-2359)
ANITAS MEXICAN FOODS CORP (PA)
3454 N Mike Daley Dr, San Bernardino
(92407-1890)
PHONE.....................909 884-8706
Ricardo Alvarez, *President*
Ricardo Robles, *CEO*
Rene Robles, *COO*
Paul Omness, *Vice Pres*
Jacqueline Robles, *Admin Sec*
▲ **EMP:** 319 **EST:** 1936
SQ FT: 330,000
SALES (est): 50MM **Privately Held**
WEB: www.anitasmfc.com
SIC: 2096 Potato chips & similar snacks

(P-2360)
CHICK N SKIN LLC
913 S Charlotte Ave, San Gabriel
(91776-2701)
PHONE.....................626 759-2925
Edward Chien, *President*
EMP: 15
SALES (est): 750K **Privately Held**
WEB: www.chicknskin.com
SIC: 2096 Pork rinds

(P-2361)
CJ FOODS USA INC
5700 Wilshire Blvd # 550, Los Angeles
(90036-3659)
PHONE.....................213 427-5566
Geon IL Lee, *CEO*
EMP: 155 **EST:** 2020
SALES (est): 13.3MM **Privately Held**
WEB: www.cjfoods.com
SIC: 2096 Potato chips & similar snacks

(P-2362)
KING HENRYS INC
Also Called: Manufacturing
29124 Hancock Pkwy 1, Valencia
(91355-1066)
PHONE.....................818 536-3692
Trina Davidian, *CEO*
◆ **EMP:** 45 **EST:** 1989
SQ FT: 44,000
SALES (est): 12.3MM **Privately Held**
WEB: www.kinghenrys.com
SIC: 2096 2064 Cheese curls & puffs; breakfast bars

(P-2363)
MARQUEZ MARQUEZ INC
Also Called: Marquez & Marquez Food PR
11821 Industrial Ave, South Gate
(90280-7914)
PHONE.....................562 408-0960
Elias Marquez, *President*
EMP: 29 **EST:** 1993
SALES (est): 2.7MM **Privately Held**
WEB: www.marquezmarquez.com
SIC: 2096 2041 Corn chips & other corn-based snacks; flour

(P-2364)
POPSALOT LLC
Also Called: Popsalot Gourmet Popcorn
7723 Somerset Blvd, Paramount
(90723-4104)
P.O. Box 7040, Beverly Hills (90212-7040)
PHONE.....................213 761-0156
Noah Sheray,

Jason Conn, *Sales Mgr*
▼ **EMP:** 20 **EST:** 2005
SQ FT: 8,400
SALES (est): 2.6MM **Privately Held**
WEB: www.popsalot.com
SIC: 2096 Popcorn, already popped (except candy covered)

(P-2365)
SENOR SNACKS INC
Also Called: Senor Snacks Holdings
2325 Raymer Ave, Fullerton (92833-2514)
PHONE.....................714 739-1073
EMP: 15
SQ FT: 16,264
SALES (est): 2.4MM **Privately Held**
WEB: www.senorsnacks.com
SIC: 2096 Mfg Potato Chips/Snacks

(P-2366)
SNACK IT FORWARD LLC
Also Called: World Peas Brand
6080 Center Dr Ste 600, Los Angeles
(90045-1540)
PHONE.....................310 242-5517
Nick Desai, *CEO*
Bryan Cameron, *COO*
Tom McCraw, *COO*
Daniel Cady, *Creative Dir*
Daisy Sandoval, *Finance*
EMP: 23 **EST:** 2011
SQ FT: 500
SALES (est): 5.4MM **Privately Held**
WEB: www.peatos.com
SIC: 2096 Cheese curls & puffs

(P-2367)
TACO WORKS INC
3424 Sacramento Dr, San Luis Obispo
(93401-7128)
PHONE.....................805 541-1556
Roy D Bayly, *President*
Theresa Bayly, *Admin Sec*
Doug Morrison, *Regl Sales Mgr*
EMP: 20 **EST:** 1976
SQ FT: 9,900
SALES (est): 2.5MM **Privately Held**
WEB: www.tacoworks.net
SIC: 2096 5145 Tortilla chips; snack foods

2097 Ice

(P-2368)
ARCTIC GLACIER USA INC
17011 Central Ave, Carson (90746-1303)
PHONE.....................310 638-0321
Sharon Cooper, *Manager*
EMP: 200
SALES (corp-wide): 628.1MM **Privately Held**
WEB: www.arcticglacier.com
SIC: 2097 Manufactured ice
HQ: Arctic Glacier U.S.A., Inc.
1654 Marthaler Ln
Saint Paul MN 55118
204 784-5873

(P-2369)
CHINO ICE SERVICE
3640 Francis Ave, Chino (91710-1512)
PHONE.....................909 628-2105
Gerald Ades, *Owner*
EMP: 18 **EST:** 1951
SQ FT: 6,000
SALES (est): 2.2MM **Privately Held**
WEB: www.coldstarice.com
SIC: 2097 Block ice

(P-2370)
FRESH INNOVATIONS LLC
Also Called: Terminal Freezers
908 E 3rd St, Oxnard (93030-6119)
P.O. Box 472 (93032-0472)
PHONE.....................805 483-2265
John Brashear, *Manager*
EMP: 33
SALES (corp-wide): 8.9MM **Privately Held**
WEB: www.fresh-innovations.com
SIC: 2097 4222 Manufactured ice; refrigerated warehousing & storage
PA: Fresh Innovations, Llc
1135 Mountain View Ave
Oxnard CA 93030
805 201-2331

(P-2371)
ICE MAN INC
8710 Park St, Bellflower (90706-5527)
PHONE.....................562 633-4423
Jim Mueller, *President*
Jeff Hendershot, *Corp Secy*
Diane Mueller, *Vice Pres*
EMP: 21 **EST:** 1974
SQ FT: 5,000
SALES (est): 2.3MM **Privately Held**
WEB: www.theicemaninc.com
SIC: 2097 Block ice; ice cubes

(P-2372)
KAR ICE SERVICE INC (PA)
2521 Solar Way, Barstow (92311-3616)
P.O. Box 1197 (92312-1197)
PHONE.....................760 256-2648
Tom Lewis, *President*
Micheal Lewis, *CFO*
Carol Lewis, *Corp Secy*
EMP: 18 **EST:** 1980
SQ FT: 14,400
SALES (est): 1.2MM **Privately Held**
SIC: 2097 Ice cubes

(P-2373)
PARTY TIME ICE
983 N Pacific Ave, San Pedro
(90731-1633)
PHONE.....................310 833-0187
Ambrose Marchant III, *Ch of Bd*
Marea Marchant, *CFO*
Douglas N Marchant, *
EMP: 16 **EST:** 1978
SQ FT: 5,000
SALES (est): 1MM **Privately Held**
WEB: www.partytimeice.com
SIC: 2097 Manufactured ice

(P-2374)
SOUTHERN CALIFORNIA ICE CO
Also Called: Arrowhead Ice
22921 Lockness Ave, Torrance
(90501-5118)
PHONE.....................310 325-1040
Sharon Corbin, *President*
EMP: 13 **EST:** 1935
SQ FT: 11,000
SALES (est): 2.4MM **Privately Held**
WEB: www.southerncaliforniaice.com
SIC: 2097 Ice cubes

2098 Macaroni, Spaghetti & Noodles

(P-2375)
FLORENCE MACARONI COMPANY
1312 W 2nd St, San Pedro (90732-3210)
PHONE.....................310 548-5942
Beatrice Esposito, *President*
Pat Peterson, *Treasurer*
Joseph Esposito, *Vice Pres*
EMP: 19 **EST:** 1968
SQ FT: 8,000
SALES (est): 223.7K **Privately Held**
SIC: 2098 Macaroni products (e.g. alphabets, rings & shells), dry; spaghetti, dry

(P-2376)
FUNGS VILLAGE INC
5339 E Washington Blvd, Commerce
(90040-2111)
PHONE.....................323 881-1600
Albert Lee, *President*
▲ **EMP:** 20 **EST:** 1984
SQ FT: 18,000
SALES (est): 2.1MM **Privately Held**
WEB: www.fungsvillage.com
SIC: 2098 Noodles (e.g. egg, plain & water), dry

(P-2377)
MYOJO USA INC
6220 Prescott Ct, Chino (91710-7111)
PHONE.....................909 464-1411
Yoshie Nakamura, *President*
Takuro Okada, *CFO*
▲ **EMP:** 16 **EST:** 1991
SQ FT: 20,759

SALES (est): 6.7MM **Privately Held**
WEB: www.myojo.com
SIC: 2098 Noodles (e.g. egg, plain & water), dry
PA: Nissin Foods Holdings Co.,Ltd.
6-28-1, Shinjuku
Shinjuku-Ku TKY 160-0

(P-2378)
NANKA SEIMEN CO
3030 Leonis Blvd, Vernon (90058-2914)
PHONE.....................323 585-9967
Shoichi Sayano, *President*
Kanji Sayano, *Shareholder*
Reigo Sayano, *Shareholder*
Fusako Yoshida, *Treasurer*
Toshiaki Yoshida, *Vice Pres*
▲ **EMP:** 18 **EST:** 1905
SQ FT: 20,000
SALES (est): 2.3MM **Privately Held**
WEB: www.nankaseimen.com
SIC: 2098 Noodles (e.g. egg, plain & water), dry

(P-2379)
NESTLE REFRIGERATED FOOD CO
800 N Brand Blvd Fl 5, Glendale
(91203-4281)
PHONE.....................818 549-6000
Fax: 818 549-6399
EMP: 500
SALES (est): 63.7MM
SALES (corp-wide): 94.6B **Privately Held**
SIC: 2098 2033 Mfg Macaroni/Spaghetti Mfg Canned Fruits/Vegetables
HQ: Nestle Usa, Inc.
800 N Brand Blvd
Glendale CA 22209
818 549-6000

(P-2380)
NISSIN FOODS USA COMPANY INC (HQ)
2001 W Rosecrans Ave, Gardena
(90249-2994)
PHONE.....................310 327-8478
Hiroyuki Yoshida, *CEO*
Evelyn Jareno, *President*
Takahiro Enomoto, *Vice Pres*
Khin Leong, *Vice Pres*
Richard Turk, *Vice Pres*
◆ **EMP:** 200
SQ FT: 200,000
SALES (est): 123.5MM **Privately Held**
WEB: www.nissinfoods.com
SIC: 2098 2038 Noodles (e.g. egg, plain & water), dry; ethnic foods, frozen

(P-2381)
PEKING NOODLE CO INC
1514 N San Fernando Rd, Los Angeles
(90065-1282)
PHONE.....................323 223-0897
Frank Tong, *President*
Stephen Tong, *President*
Donna Tong, *Corp Secy*
Shandy Wong, *Clerk*
▲ **EMP:** 40 **EST:** 1928
SQ FT: 40,000
SALES (est): 7MM **Privately Held**
WEB: www.pekingnoodle.com
SIC: 2098 2052 Noodles (e.g. egg, plain & water), dry; cookies & crackers

(P-2382)
SAKURA NOODLE INC
620 E 7th St, Los Angeles (90021-1461)
PHONE.....................213 623-2396
Shohachi Suzuki, *President*
Taketoshi Inagaki, *Admin Sec*
▲ **EMP:** 13 **EST:** 1978
SQ FT: 9,000
SALES (est): 682.6K **Privately Held**
WEB: www.sakuranoodleinc.com
SIC: 2098 2099 Noodles (e.g. egg, plain & water), dry; food preparations

PRODUCTS & SVCS

(P-2383)
SANYO FOODS CORP AMERICA (DH)
Also Called: Yorba Linda Country Club
11955 Monarch St, Garden Grove
(92841-2194)
PHONE..................................714 891-3671
Junichiro Ida, *CEO*
Hiroaki Obuchi, *Admin Sec*
Tae Jones, *Accounting Mgr*
◆ **EMP:** 30 **EST:** 1978
SQ FT: 130,000
SALES (est): 20MM **Privately Held**
WEB: www.sanyofoodsamerica.com
SIC: 2098 7997 Noodles (e.g. egg, plain & water), dry; golf club, membership

---

2099 Food Preparations, NEC

(P-2384)
AB MAURI FOOD INC
Also Called: Fleis Chmanns Vinegar
12604 Hiddencreek Way A, Cerritos
(90703-2137)
PHONE..................................562 483-4619
Dave Billings, *President*
EMP: 27
SALES (corp-wide): 18.2B **Privately Held**
WEB: www.abmna.com
SIC: 2099 2087 Vinegar; flavoring extracts & syrups
HQ: Ab Mauri Food Inc.
4240 Duncan Ave Ste 150
Saint Louis MO 63110
314 392-0800

(P-2385)
ADELANTO ELEMENTARY SCHOOL DST
Also Called: Desert Trils Prpratory Academy
14350 Bellflower St, Adelanto
(92301-4246)
P.O. Box 400880, Hesperia (92340-0880)
PHONE..................................760 530-7680
Mandy Plantz, *Principal*
Hardy Black, *Bd of Directors*
Holly Eckes, *Bd of Directors*
Marnella Mayberry, *Bd of Directors*
Natalie Granados, *CIO*
EMP: 24
SALES (corp-wide): 115.4MM **Privately Held**
WEB: www.aesd.net
SIC: 2099 Food preparations
PA: Adelanto Elementary School District
11824 Air Expy
Adelanto CA 92301
760 246-8691

(P-2386)
AGUSA
1055 S 19th Ave, Lemoore (93245-9747)
PHONE..................................559 924-4785
Joel Delira, *CEO*
Inigo Martinez, *COO*
Danny Serrano, *CFO*
Javier Souchard, *CFO*
Joel De Lira, *General Mgr*
◆ **EMP:** 36
SQ FT: 28,000
SALES (est): 8.2MM **Privately Held**
WEB: www.agusa.biz
SIC: 2099 Food preparations

(P-2387)
AIR FAYRE USA INC
1720 W 135th St, Gardena (90249-2508)
PHONE..................................310 808-1061
Stephen Yapp, *CEO*
Joe Golio, *President*
M Clegg, *General Mgr*
Francis Frago, *General Mgr*
Lacei Aguilar, *Hum Res Coord*
EMP: 200 **EST:** 2008
SALES (est): 14.7MM **Privately Held**
WEB: www.airfayre.com
SIC: 5812 2099 Caterers; box lunches, for sale off premises
HQ: Journey Group Limited
One Bartholomew Close
London EC1A

(P-2388)
ALFRED LOUIE INCORPORATED
4501 Shepard St, Bakersfield
(93313-2310)
PHONE..................................661 831-2520
Victor Louie, *President*
Maryann Louie, *Shareholder*
Samuel Louie, *Shareholder*
Gordon Louie, *Corp Secy*
EMP: 18 **EST:** 1979
SQ FT: 28,000
SALES (est): 1.7MM **Privately Held**
SIC: 2099 0182 Noodles, fried (Chinese); bean sprouts grown under cover

(P-2389)
AMERICAN NATURALS COMPANY LLC
3737 Longridge Ave, Sherman Oaks
(91423-4919)
PHONE..................................323 201-6891
Carlo Brandon, *CEO*
EMP: 22 **EST:** 2014
SALES (est): 1.5MM **Privately Held**
WEB: www.americannaturalscompany.com
SIC: 2099 Bouillon cubes

(P-2390)
AREVALO TORTILLERIA INC
3033 Supply Ave, Commerce (90040-2709)
P.O. Box 788, Los Angeles (90078-0788)
PHONE..................................323 888-1711
Edward Arello, *Manager*
Jennie Rodriguez, *Human Resources*
EMP: 30
SALES (corp-wide): 18.8MM **Privately Held**
WEB: www.arevalos.com
SIC: 2099 Tortillas, fresh or refrigerated
PA: Arevalo Tortilleria, Inc.
1537 W Mines Ave
Montebello CA 90640
323 888-1711

(P-2391)
AREVALO TORTILLERIA INC (PA)
1537 W Mines Ave, Montebello
(90640-5414)
P.O. Box 788 (90640-0788)
PHONE..................................323 888-1711
Jose Luis Arevalo, *CEO*
Emilia Arevalo, *Admin Sec*
Daniel Arevalo, *Info Tech Mgr*
Norma Sanchez, *Human Res Mgr*
Hector Marrero, *Maintence Staff*
▲ **EMP:** 82 **EST:** 1985
SQ FT: 20,000
SALES (est): 18.8MM **Privately Held**
WEB: www.arevalos.com
SIC: 2099 Food preparations

(P-2392)
ARRIETTA INCORPORATED
Also Called: La Tolteca Mexican Foods
429 N Azusa Ave, Azusa (91702-3442)
PHONE..................................626 334-0302
Benjamin E Arrietta, *President*
Ben D Arrietta, *CFO*
Tim Arrietta, *Vice Pres*
Jean Arrietta, *Admin Sec*
EMP: 33 **EST:** 1948
SQ FT: 19,000
SALES (est): 5MM **Privately Held**
SIC: 5411 2099 5812 Delicatessens; tortillas, fresh or refrigerated; Mexican restaurant

(P-2393)
ASIANA CUISINE ENTERPRISES INC
Also Called: Ace Sushi
22771 S Wstn Ave Ste 100, Torrance
(90501)
PHONE..................................310 327-2223
Harlan Chin, *President*
Gary Chin, *CFO*
▲ **EMP:** 560 **EST:** 1990
SQ FT: 6,000
SALES (est): 25.2MM **Privately Held**
SIC: 2099 5812 8741 Ready-to-eat meals, salads & sandwiches; fast food restaurants & stands; management services

(P-2394)
BANZAI FOODS LLC
10937 El Coco Cir, Fountain Valley
(92708-5316)
PHONE..................................714 200-9933
Jeff Aoki, *Principal*
EMP: 15 **EST:** 2012
SALES (est): 293.6K **Privately Held**
SIC: 2099 Food preparations

(P-2395)
BCD FOOD INC
13507 S Normandie Ave, Gardena
(90249-2605)
PHONE..................................310 323-1200
Tae Ro Lee, *President*
▲ **EMP:** 18 **EST:** 2006
SALES (est): 1.3MM **Privately Held**
SIC: 2099 Box lunches, for sale off premises

(P-2396)
BDS NATURAL PRODUCTS INC (PA)
Also Called: Npms Natural Products Mil Svcs
14824 S Main St, Gardena (90248-1919)
PHONE..................................310 518-2227
Steven Brenneis, *CEO*
David Solomon, *Vice Pres*
Brandy Guedea, *Purchasing*
Edgar Sandoval, *Supervisor*
▲ **EMP:** 50 **EST:** 1999
SQ FT: 80,000
SALES (est): 12.7MM **Privately Held**
WEB: www.bdsnatural.com
SIC: 2099 5149 Seasonings & spices; tea blending; natural & organic foods

(P-2397)
BENEVOLENCE FOOD PRODUCTS LLC
2761 Saturn St Ste D, Brea (92821-6707)
PHONE..................................888 832-3738
Jacob Ryan, *Exec Dir*
EMP: 24 **EST:** 2010
SALES (est): 678K **Privately Held**
SIC: 2099 Food preparations

(P-2398)
BEST FORMULATIONS INC
17758 Rowland St, City of Industry
(91748-1148)
PHONE..................................626 912-9998
Charles Ung, *Chairman*
Jeffrey Goh, *President*
Eugene Ung, *CEO*
Robin C Koon, *Exec VP*
Nighat Ansari, *Vice Pres*
◆ **EMP:** 200
SQ FT: 50,000
SALES (est): 78.3MM **Privately Held**
WEB: www.bestformulations.com
SIC: 2099 8748 5149 2834 Food preparations; business consulting; health foods; pharmaceutical preparations

(P-2399)
BOTANAS MEXICO INC
11122 Rush St, South El Monte
(91733-3549)
PHONE..................................626 279-1512
Carlos Aleman, *President*
Miriam Aleman, *Vice Pres*
◆ **EMP:** 16 **EST:** 2008
SALES (est): 2.3MM **Privately Held**
SIC: 2099 5499 Seasonings & spices; spices, including grinding; spices & herbs

(P-2400)
BRISTOL FARMS (HQ)
915 E 230th St, Carson (90745-5005)
PHONE..................................310 233-4700
Adam Caldecott, *CEO*
Chris Roles, *Store Dir*
Catherine Pries, *Advt Staff*
Amy Kafkaloff,
EMP: 100
SQ FT: 73,667
SALES (est): 95.3MM **Privately Held**
WEB: www.bristolfarms.com
SIC: 2099 5411 Ready-to-eat meals, salads & sandwiches; grocery stores, chain

(P-2401)
C & F FOODS INC
12400 Wilshire Blvd # 1180, Los Angeles
(90025-1058)
PHONE..................................626 723-1000
◆ **EMP:** 400
SALES (est): 181.6MM **Privately Held**
WEB: www.cnf-foods.com
SIC: 2099 Food Preparations, Nec, Nsk

(P-2402)
CADENCE GOURMET LLC
Also Called: Cadence Gourmet Involve Foods
155 Klug Cir, Corona (92878-5424)
PHONE..................................951 444-9269
Brian J Wynn, *CEO*
David Wells, *President*
Jason Triail, *Vice Pres*
Patricia Cabello, *Technician*
John Malcuit, *Controller*
▲ **EMP:** 30 **EST:** 2004
SQ FT: 12,000
SALES (est): 8.4MM **Privately Held**
WEB: www.cadencekitchen.com
SIC: 2099 Food preparations

(P-2403)
CALAVO GROWERS INC (PA)
1141 Cummings Rd Ste A, Santa Paula
(93060-9118)
PHONE..................................805 525-1245
Steven Hollister, *CEO*
J Link Leavens, *Ch of Bd*
Eyvonne Ortega, *President*
Mark Lodge, *COO*
Kevin Manion, *CFO*
EMP: 904 **EST:** 1924
SALES (est): 1B **Publicly Held**
WEB: www.calavo.com
SIC: 2099 5148 Salads, fresh or refrigerated; fruits; fruits, fresh

(P-2404)
CAMINO REAL FOODS INC (PA)
Also Called: Camino Real Kitchens
2638 E Vernon Ave, Vernon (90058-1825)
P.O. Box 30729, Los Angeles (90030-0729)
PHONE..................................323 585-6599
Rob Cross, *President*
Richard Lunsford, *CFO*
Chris Perry, *CFO*
Yessica Carrillo, *Admin Asst*
Yuhan Wang, *Planning*
EMP: 150 **EST:** 1980
SALES (est): 100.1MM **Privately Held**
WEB: www.caminorealkitchens.com
SIC: 2099 Food preparations

(P-2405)
CARRILLOS TORTILLERIA INC (PA)
1242 Pico St, San Fernando (91340-3503)
PHONE..................................818 365-1636
Amelia Luna, *President*
William Luna, *Treasurer*
Steven Luna, *Admin Sec*
EMP: 13 **EST:** 1966
SQ FT: 5,066
SALES (est): 1MM **Privately Held**
WEB: www.carrillostortilleria.com
SIC: 5812 2099 Mexican restaurant; tortillas, fresh or refrigerated

(P-2406)
CEDARLANE NATURAL FOODS INC (PA)
1135 E Artesia Blvd, Carson (90746-1602)
PHONE..................................310 886-7720
Robert Atallah, *CEO*
Neil Holmes, *CFO*
Kristin Harper, *Vice Pres*
Maly Sea, *Research*
Celia Gonzalez, *Human Res Mgr*
▲ **EMP:** 100 **EST:** 1981
SQ FT: 270,000
SALES (est): 124MM **Privately Held**
WEB: www.cedarlanefoods.com
SIC: 2099 Food preparations

(P-2407)
CHEF MERITO INC (PA)
Also Called: Merito.com
7915 Sepulveda Blvd, Van Nuys
(91405-1032)
PHONE..................................818 787-0100

Jose J Corugedo, *CEO*
Plinio J Garcia Sr, *Shareholder*
Jose Corugedo, *CFO*
Natt Hasson, *Admin Sec*
Nathaly Aquino, *Administration*
▲ **EMP:** 81 **EST:** 1985
SQ FT: 30,000
SALES (est): 15.6MM **Privately Held**
WEB: www.chefmerito.com
SIC: 2099 2033 2032 2044 Spices, including grinding; jellies, edible, including imitation: in cans, jars, etc.; soups, except seafood: packaged in cans, jars, etc.; enriched rice (vitamin & mineral fortified); sausages & other prepared meats

(P-2408)
CHEFMASTER
501 Airpark Dr, Fullerton (92833-2501)
PHONE......................714 554-4000
Aaron G Byrnes, *President*
Taygun Basaran, *Vice Pres*
▲ **EMP:** 35 **EST:** 1939
SALES (est): 1.3MM **Privately Held**
WEB: www.chefmaster.com
SIC: 2099 Sugar powdered from purchased ingredients

(P-2409)
CJ FOODS INC (HQ)
Also Called: CJ America
4 Centerpointe Dr Ste 100, La Palma (90623-1074)
PHONE......................714 367-7200
Pious Jung, *CEO*
Tori Bodenhamer, *Regional Mgr*
Nicole Koenig, *Manager*
EMP: 25 **EST:** 1995
SALES (est): 41.9MM **Privately Held**
WEB: www.cjfoods.com
SIC: 2099 Food preparations

(P-2410)
CJ FOODS MANUFACTURING CORP
500 S State College Blvd, Fullerton (92831-5114)
PHONE......................714 888-3500
Joo Hong Shin, *President*
▲ **EMP:** 41 **EST:** 2012
SALES (est): 8.7MM **Privately Held**
SIC: 2099 Seasonings & spices

(P-2411)
CLW FOODS LLC
3425 E Vernon Ave, Vernon (90058-1811)
PHONE......................323 432-4600
Jeff Sterling, *Exec VP*
EMP: 17
SALES (corp-wide): 6MM **Privately Held**
WEB: www.clwfoods.com
SIC: 2099 Dessert mixes & fillings
PA: Clw Foods, Llc
8765 E 3rd St
Hanford CA 93230
559 639-6661

(P-2412)
COSMOS FOOD CO INC
16015 Phoenix Dr, City of Industry (91745-1624)
PHONE......................323 221-9142
David Kim, *President*
EMP: 45 **EST:** 1971
SQ FT: 85,000
SALES (est): 7.2MM **Privately Held**
WEB: www.cosmosfood.com
SIC: 2099 5149 Tortillas, fresh or refrigerated; groceries & related products

(P-2413)
CRAVE FOODS INC
2043 Imperial St, Los Angeles (90021-3203)
PHONE......................562 900-7272
Shaheda Sayed, *President*
Riaz A Surti, *Senior VP*
▲ **EMP:** 40 **EST:** 1992
SQ FT: 20,000
SALES (est): 3.5MM **Privately Held**
WEB: www.hearthyfoods.com
SIC: 2099 Food preparations

(P-2414)
CULINARY INTERNATIONAL LLC (PA)
3280 E 44th St, Vernon (90058-2426)
PHONE......................626 289-3000
Cesar Rodarte,
EMP: 201 **EST:** 2017
SALES (est): 22.8MM **Privately Held**
WEB: www.culinaryinternational.com
SIC: 2099 2038 5149 Food preparations; ethnic foods, frozen; natural & organic foods; specialty food items

(P-2415)
CURATION FOODS INC (HQ)
2811 Airpark Dr, Santa Maria (93455-1417)
P.O. Box 727, Guadalupe (93434-0727)
PHONE......................800 454-1355
Bill Richardville, *CEO*
Tim Nykoluk, *President*
Debra Vanhorsen, *President*
Glenn Wells, *Senior VP*
Ann Baker, *Vice Pres*
◆ **EMP:** 80 **EST:** 1979
SQ FT: 200,000
SALES: 470.5MM
SALES (corp-wide): 544.1MM **Publicly Held**
WEB: www.ooliveoil.com
SIC: 2099 0723 Food preparations; vegetable packing services
PA: Landec Corporation
5201 Great America Pkwy # 232
Santa Clara CA 95054
650 306-1650

(P-2416)
DAD INVESTMENTS
Also Called: Cater Tots Too
2929 Halladay St, Santa Ana (92705-5622)
PHONE......................714 751-8500
Nadia Tayob, *President*
EMP: 22 **EST:** 2016
SALES (est): 1.7MM **Privately Held**
SIC: 5812 2099 Caterers; food preparations

(P-2417)
DAD INVESTMENTS
16 Medlar, Irvine (92618-3947)
PHONE......................310 627-6316
Nadia Tayob, *CEO*
EMP: 32 **EST:** 2016
SALES (est): 1.1MM **Privately Held**
SIC: 2099 5812 Food preparations; caterers

(P-2418)
DEAN DISTRIBUTORS INC
5015 Hallmark Pkwy, San Bernardino (92407-1871)
PHONE......................323 587-8147
John D Garinger, *Branch Mgr*
Jay Brown, *General Mgr*
David Mojarro, *Purchasing*
EMP: 21
SALES (corp-wide): 5.3MM **Privately Held**
WEB: www.deandistributors.com
SIC: 2099 2087 2834 Sauces: dry mixes; syrups, flavoring (except drink); pharmaceutical preparations
PA: Dean Distributors, Inc.
800 Airport Blvd Ste 312
Burlingame CA 94010
800 792-0816

(P-2419)
DELIVERY ZONE LLC
120 S Anderson St, Los Angeles (90033-3220)
PHONE......................323 780-0888
Carl Ferro,
John Stewart,
EMP: 15 **EST:** 1997
SQ FT: 4,700
SALES (est): 768K **Privately Held**
WEB: www.sunfare.com
SIC: 2099 4215 Ready-to-eat meals, salads & sandwiches; courier services, except by air

(P-2420)
DELORI-NUTIFOOD PRODUCTS INC
Also Called: Delori Foods
17043 Green Dr, City of Industry (91745-1812)
P.O. Box 92668 (91715-2668)
PHONE......................626 965-3006
Jaime Brown, *CEO*
Blanca Brown, *Treasurer*
▲ **EMP:** 32 **EST:** 1991
SALES (est): 6.5MM **Privately Held**
WEB: www.deloriproducts.com
SIC: 2099 Jelly, corncob (gelatin)

(P-2421)
DIAMOND CRYSTAL BRANDS INC
Also Called: Diamond Crystal Brands-Hormel
8700 W Doe Ave, Visalia (93291-8900)
PHONE......................559 651-7782
Robert Elderdice, *Branch Mgr*
Terry Seifert, *Plant Mgr*
Michael Carter, *QC Mgr*
EMP: 40
SALES (corp-wide): 155.9MM **Privately Held**
WEB: www.dcbrands.com
SIC: 2099 Food preparations
PA: Diamond Crystal Brands, Inc
2000 Riveredge Pkwy # 950
Atlanta GA 30328
912 651-5112

(P-2422)
DIANAS MEXICAN FOOD PDTS INC (PA)
Also Called: La Bonita
16330 Pioneer Blvd, Norwalk (90650-7042)
P.O. Box 369 (90651-0369)
PHONE......................562 926-5802
Samuel Magana, *CEO*
Alma Meza, *CFO*
Hortensia Magana, *Vice Pres*
Rosario Zavanero, *Executive*
Alma Messa, *Info Tech Dir*
EMP: 50 **EST:** 1975
SQ FT: 4,068
SALES (est): 26MM **Privately Held**
WEB: www.dianas.net
SIC: 2099 5812 Tortillas, fresh or refrigerated; ethnic food restaurants

(P-2423)
DIANAS MEXICAN FOOD PDTS INC
Also Called: Labonita Diana's Mexican Food
300 E Sepulveda Blvd, Carson (90745-5923)
PHONE......................310 834-4886
Carlos Andres, *Manager*
EMP: 73
SQ FT: 1,660
SALES (corp-wide): 26MM **Privately Held**
WEB: www.dianas.net
SIC: 5411 2099 5812 Delicatessens; food preparations; Mexican restaurant
PA: Diana's Mexican Food Products, Inc.
16330 Pioneer Blvd
Norwalk CA 90650
562 926-5802

(P-2424)
DIANAS MEXICAN FOOD PDTS INC
2905 Durfee Ave, El Monte (91732-3517)
PHONE......................626 444-0555
Samuel Magana, *Owner*
EMP: 32
SQ FT: 13,530
SALES (corp-wide): 26MM **Privately Held**
WEB: www.dianas.net
SIC: 2099 5812 Tortillas, fresh or refrigerated; Mexican restaurant
PA: Diana's Mexican Food Products, Inc.
16330 Pioneer Blvd
Norwalk CA 90650
562 926-5802

(P-2425)
DIVINE PASTA COMPANY
550 Ceres Ave, Los Angeles (90013-1717)
PHONE......................818 559-7440

Alexander Palermo, *President*
EMP: 16 **EST:** 2018
SALES (est): 1.5MM **Privately Held**
WEB: www.divinepasta.com
SIC: 2099 Pasta, uncooked: packaged with other ingredients

(P-2426)
DRIFTWOOD DAIRY HOLDING CORP
10724 Lower Azusa Rd, El Monte (91731-1390)
PHONE......................626 444-9591
EMP: 15 **EST:** 1946
SALES (est): 380.4K **Privately Held**
WEB: www.driftwooddairy.net
SIC: 2099 Food preparations

(P-2427)
EARTHRISE NUTRITIONALS LLC
113 E Hoober Rd, Calipatria (92233-9703)
P.O. Box 270 (92233-0270)
PHONE......................760 348-5027
Jose Perez, *Manager*
EMP: 29 **Privately Held**
WEB: www.earthrise.com
SIC: 2099 Chicory root, dried
HQ: Earthrise Nutritionals Llc
2151 Michelson Dr Ste 262
Irvine CA 92612
949 623-0980

(P-2428)
EL GALLITO MARKET INC
12242 Valley Blvd, El Monte (91732-3108)
PHONE......................626 442-1190
Sandra Veisaga, *President*
Mario Rodriguez, *Treasurer*
EMP: 35 **EST:** 1974
SQ FT: 1,200
SALES (est): 2.3MM **Privately Held**
WEB: www.elgallitomkt.com
SIC: 2099 5421 5411 Tortillas, fresh or refrigerated; meat & fish markets; grocery stores

(P-2429)
EL INDIO TORTILLERIA
Also Called: El Indio Tortillas Fctry
1502 W 5th St, Santa Ana (92703-2902)
PHONE......................714 542-3114
Humberto Sanchez, *President*
Graciela Sanchez, *Treasurer*
EMP: 13 **EST:** 1948
SQ FT: 4,500
SALES (est): 850K **Privately Held**
WEB: www.elindiotortilleria.co
SIC: 2099 Tortillas, fresh or refrigerated

(P-2430)
EVERSON SPICE COMPANY INC
2667 Gundry Ave, Long Beach (90755-1808)
PHONE......................562 595-4785
Kim Everson, *CEO*
Ken Hopkins, *President*
Thomas Everson, *Admin Sec*
Robyn Eckardt, *IT/INT Sup*
Juan Medina, *Technology*
▲ **EMP:** 35 **EST:** 1987
SQ FT: 35,000
SALES (est): 5.6MM **Privately Held**
WEB: www.eversonspice.com
SIC: 2099 Spices, including grinding

(P-2431)
F I O IMPORTS INC
Also Called: Contessa Premium Foods
5980 Alcoa Ave, Vernon (90058-3925)
PHONE......................323 263-5100
Dirk Leuenberger, *President*
Bob Nielsen, *CFO*
Tom Jedrzejewicz, *Info Tech Mgr*
Robert Santich, *Info Tech Mgr*
Rosslyn Banayat, *Human Res Dir*
EMP: 180 **EST:** 2002
SALES (est): 41.7MM **Privately Held**
WEB: www.aquastar.com
SIC: 2099 Food preparations
HQ: Aqua Star (Usa), Corp.
2025 1st Ave Ste 200
Seattle WA 98121
800 232-6280

P R O D U C T S & S V C S

(P-2432)
FAYES FOODS INC
Also Called: Fay's Foods
10650 Burbank Blvd, North Hollywood
(91601-2511)
PHONE...................818 508-8392
EMP: 37
SQ FT: 15,000
SALES: 5MM **Privately Held**
SIC: 2099 5812 5149 5141 Mfg Food
　Preparations Eating Place Whol Gro-
　ceries Whol General Groceries

(P-2433)
FLORES BROTHERS INC
Also Called: Durango Foods
7777 Scout Ave, Bell (90201-4941)
PHONE...................562 806-9128
David Flores, *President*
Armando Flores, *Vice Pres*
EMP: 15 EST: 2005
SALES (est): 1.2MM **Privately Held**
SIC: 2099 Emulsifiers, food

(P-2434)
FOOD-O-MEX CORPORATION
Also Called: El Dorado Mexican Food Pdts
2928 N Main St, Los Angeles (90031-3325)
PHONE...................323 225-1737
Eleanor Lopez, *President*
Elenore Lopez, *President*
Philip Manly, *Vice Pres*
EMP: 15 EST: 1957
SQ FT: 18,000
SALES (est): 645.5K **Privately Held**
SIC: 2099 Tortillas, fresh or refrigerated

(P-2435)
FOODOLOGY LLC
Also Called: Sproutime
8920 Norris Ave, Sun Valley (91352-2740)
PHONE...................818 252-1888
Leslie Starus,
John Ybarra, *Plant Mgr*
Mike Payton,
Robert Wong, *Manager*
EMP: 75 EST: 1980
SQ FT: 20,000
SALES (est): 7.7MM **Privately Held**
SIC: 2099 Ready-to-eat meals, salads &
　sandwiches

(P-2436)
FOUR SEASONS HUMMUS INC
11030 Randall St, Sun Valley (91352-2621)
PHONE...................305 409-0449
Francisco Mejia, *Director*
Omar Mejia, *CEO*
EMP: 17 EST: 2019
SALES (est): 1.1MM **Privately Held**
WEB: www.fourseasonshummus.com
SIC: 2099 Sauces: gravy, dressing & dip
　mixes

(P-2437)
FRESH & READY FOODS LLC
(PA)
1145 Arroyo St Ste B, San Fernando
(91340-1842)
PHONE...................818 837-7600
Art Sezgin, *President*
Julio Martinez, *Vice Pres*
John Saladino, *Vice Pres*
Bradley Deyoung, *Director*
EMP: 99 EST: 2015
SALES (est): 20.5MM **Privately Held**
WEB: www.freshandreadyfoods.com
SIC: 2099 Salads, fresh or refrigerated

(P-2438)
FRESHREALM LLC (PA)
34 N Palm St Ste 100, Ventura
(93001-2610)
P.O. Box 2770 (93002-2770)
PHONE...................800 264-1297
Michael R Lippold, *CEO*
Peter Hajas, *Officer*
Ajay Mallina, *Manager*
Robert Paulis, *Manager*
Tracey Lepore, *Associate*
EMP: 15 EST: 2013
SQ FT: 5,000
SALES (est): 29.1MM **Privately Held**
WEB: www.freshrealm.com
SIC: 2099 Food preparations

(P-2439)
FUJI FOOD PRODUCTS INC (PA)
14420 Bloomfield Ave, Santa Fe Springs
(90670-5410)
PHONE...................562 404-2590
Farrell Hirsch, *CEO*
Javier Aceves, *CFO*
Philip Schoen, *Regional Mgr*
Jonathan Masamori, *District Mgr*
Diana Alonso, *Admin Asst*
▲ EMP: 100 EST: 2010
SQ FT: 90,000
SALES (est): 203.2MM **Privately Held**
WEB: www.fujisansushi.com
SIC: 2099 Food preparations

(P-2440)
FUJI NATURAL FOODS INC (HQ)
13500 S Hamner Ave, Ontario
(91761-2605)
P.O. Box 3728 (91761-0973)
PHONE...................909 947-1008
Katsushiro Nakagawa, *CEO*
Ikuzo Sugiyama, *President*
◆ EMP: 72 EST: 1979
SQ FT: 65,000
SALES (est): 13.8MM **Privately Held**
WEB: www.fujinf.com
SIC: 2099 Food preparations

(P-2441)
GLOBAL VISION HOLDINGS INC
19200 Von Karman Ave 6, Irvine
(92612-8553)
PHONE...................949 281-6438
Glen Carnes, *CEO*
Kaylee Duff, *COO*
Prasangi Munindradasa, *Vice Pres*
EMP: 13 EST: 2010
SALES (est): 439.9K **Privately Held**
WEB: www.versantinternational.com
SIC: 2099 Food preparations

(P-2442)
GLUTEN FREE FOODS MFG LLC
(PA)
5010 Eucalyptus Ave, Chino (91710-9216)
PHONE...................909 823-8230
Luis Faura, *Mng Member*
EMP: 51 EST: 2015
SALES (est): 1.1MM **Privately Held**
WEB: www.glutenfreefoodsmfg.com
SIC: 2099 Pasta, uncooked: packaged with
　other ingredients

(P-2443)
GOLD COAST INGREDIENTS INC
2429 Yates Ave, Commerce (90040-1917)
PHONE...................323 724-8935
Clarence H Brasher, *CEO*
James A Sgro, *President*
Kenneth Chu, *Vice Pres*
Laurie Goddard, *Vice Pres*
Jon Wellwood, *General Mgr*
◆ EMP: 53
SQ FT: 50,000
SALES (est): 21.8MM **Privately Held**
WEB: www.goldcoastinc.com
SIC: 2099 Almond pastes

(P-2444)
GOLD STAR FOODS INC (HQ)
3781 E Airport Dr, Ontario (91761-1558)
P.O. Box 4328 (91761-8828)
PHONE...................909 843-9600
Sean Leer, *President*
Les Wong, *COO*
Greg Johnson, *CFO*
Mahvash Howell, *Vice Pres*
C Scott Salmon, *Vice Pres*
▲ EMP: 216 EST: 2007
SQ FT: 38,000
SALES: 329.2MM
SALES (corp-wide): 519.5MM **Privately
Held**
WEB: www.goldstarfoods.com
SIC: 2099 Ready-to-eat meals, salads &
　sandwiches
PA: Highview Capital, Llc
　11755 Wilshire Blvd # 14
　Los Angeles CA 90025
　310 806-9780

(P-2445)
GOLDEN SPECIALTY FOODS
LLC
14605 Best Ave, Norwalk (90650-5258)
PHONE...................562 802-2537
Philip Pisciotta, *CEO*
Jeff Chan, *President*
Deryk Howard, *CFO*
◆ EMP: 25 EST: 1979
SQ FT: 31,000
SALES (est): 5.1MM **Privately Held**
WEB: www.goldenspecialtyfoods.com
SIC: 2099 2032 Food preparations;
　canned specialties

(P-2446)
GOODMAN FOOD PRODUCTS
INC (PA)
Also Called: Don Lee Farms
200 E Beach Ave Fl 1, Inglewood
(90302-3404)
PHONE...................310 674-3180
Donald Goodman, *CEO*
Delores Rose, *CIO*
Danny Goodman, *Software Dev*
Norma Lagunas, *Research*
Jameela Sanchez, *Purch Mgr*
▲ EMP: 250 EST: 1982
SQ FT: 55,000
SALES (est): 71.6MM **Privately Held**
WEB: www.donleefarms.com
SIC: 2099 Food preparations

(P-2447)
GPDE SLVA SPCES
INCRPORATION (PA)
Also Called: Peterson's Spices
8531 Loch Lomond Dr, Pico Rivera
(90660-2509)
PHONE...................562 407-2643
Ravi De Silva, *President*
Nalin Kulasooriya, *CFO*
Rupa De Silva, *Vice Pres*
Binuka De Silva, *Sales Mgr*
◆ EMP: 30 EST: 2008
SQ FT: 60,000
SALES (est): 13.2MM **Privately Held**
WEB: www.cinnamononline.com
SIC: 2099 5149 Chili pepper or powder;
　spices, including grinding; spices & sea-
　sonings

(P-2448)
HARRIS SPICE COMPANY INC
3110 E Miraloma Ave, Anaheim
(92806-1906)
PHONE...................714 507-1919
Prashant Shah, *CEO*
▼ EMP: 29 EST: 2010
SALES (est): 9.2MM
SALES (corp-wide): 236.6MM **Privately
Held**
WEB: www.harrisspice.com
SIC: 5499 2099 Tea; food preparations
PA: Harris Freeman & Co., Inc.
　3110 E Miraloma Ave
　Anaheim CA 92806
　714 765-7525

(P-2449)
HESPERIA UNIFIED SCHOOL
DST
Also Called: Hesperia Usd Food Service
11176 G Ave, Hesperia (92345-8315)
PHONE...................760 948-1051
Janet Clesceri, *Branch Mgr*
Ella Rogers, *Bd of Directors*
Marcy Kittinger, *Clerk*
EMP: 36
SALES (corp-wide): 299.5MM **Privately
Held**
WEB: www.cottonwoodelementary.org
SIC: 2099 8322 8299 Box lunches, for
　sale off premises; geriatric social service;
　arts & crafts schools
PA: Hesperia Unified School District
　15576 Main St
　Hesperia CA 92345
　760 244-4411

(P-2450)
HONEY BENNETTS FARM INC
(PA)
Also Called: Bennett's Honey Farm
3176 Honey Ln, Fillmore (93015-2026)
PHONE...................805 521-1375
Gilebert Vannoy, *President*
Ann Lindsay Bennett, *Principal*
Karen Grammer, *Opers Staff*
EMP: 24 EST: 1978
SQ FT: 20,000
SALES (est): 4MM **Privately Held**
WEB: www.bennetthoney.com
SIC: 2099 5191 0279 Honey, strained &
　bottled; farm supplies; apiary (bee &
　honey farm)

(P-2451)
HOUSE FOODS AMERICA CORP
(HQ)
Also Called: Hinoichi Tofu
7351 Orangewood Ave, Garden Grove
(92841-1411)
PHONE...................714 901-4350
Tsuyoshi Kido, *President*
Tadashi Okamoto, *CFO*
Vinaykumar Patel, *Supervisor*
▲ EMP: 311 EST: 1947
SQ FT: 30,000
SALES (est): 74.4MM **Privately Held**
WEB: www.house-foods.com
SIC: 2099 Food preparations

(P-2452)
INGREDIENTS BY NATURE LLC
5555 Brooks St, Montclair (91763-4547)
PHONE...................909 230-6200
Matt Outz, *President*
Bo Zhu, *Executive*
Allie Mello, *Development*
Xanh T Phan, *QC Mgr*
EMP: 26 EST: 2010
SALES (est): 5.3MM **Privately Held**
WEB: www.ingredientsbynature.com
SIC: 2099 Molasses, mixed or blended:
　from purchased ingredients

(P-2453)
INTERNTIONAL TEA
IMPORTERS INC (PA)
Also Called: India Tea Importers
2140 Davie Ave, Commerce (90040-1706)
PHONE...................562 801-9600
Brendan Shah, *CEO*
Bianca Shah, *CEO*
Bhavin Shah, *CFO*
Reena Shah, *Vice Pres*
◆ EMP: 53 EST: 1992
SQ FT: 21,500
SALES (est): 9.4MM **Privately Held**
WEB: www.teavendor.com
SIC: 2099 5149 Tea blending; coffee &
　tea; tea; tea bagging

(P-2454)
JAYONE FOODS INC
7212 Alondra Blvd, Paramount
(90723-3902)
PHONE...................562 633-7400
Seung Hoon Lee, *President*
Chil Park, *Vice Pres*
Jung Yoon, *General Mgr*
Elizabeth Yoo, *IT/INT Sup*
Ik T Kim, *Opers Staff*
◆ EMP: 50 EST: 1999
SQ FT: 28,000
SALES (est): 50MM **Privately Held**
WEB: www.jayonefoods.com
SIC: 2099 Food preparations

(P-2455)
JIMENES FOOD INC
7046 Jackson St, Paramount (90723-4835)
PHONE...................562 602-2505
Reyna Jimenez, *President*
Juan Jimenez, *Vice Pres*
EMP: 30 EST: 1998
SQ FT: 11,000
SALES (est): 6.1MM **Privately Held**
WEB: www.juanjs.com
SIC: 2099 Tortillas, fresh or refrigerated

(P-2456)
JOY PROCESSED FOODS INC
1330 Seabright Ave, Long Beach
(90813-1189)
PHONE................................562 435-1106
Alvin Clawson, *President*
EMP: 14 **EST:** 1966
SQ FT: 5,000
SALES (est): 1.1MM **Privately Held**
SIC: 2099 Vegetables, peeled for the trade

(P-2457)
JSL FOODS INC (PA)
3550 Pasadena Ave, Los Angeles
(90031-1946)
PHONE................................323 223-2484
Teiji Kawana, *President*
Koji Kawana, *Exec VP*
Darren Tristano, *Exec VP*
Edwardo Rivas, *Info Tech Mgr*
Jonathan Gonzalez, *Research*
◆ **EMP:** 114 **EST:** 1990
SALES (est): 26.4MM **Privately Held**
WEB: www.jslfoods.com
SIC: 2099 5142 2052 Pasta, uncooked:
packaged with other ingredients; pack-
aged frozen goods; cookies

(P-2458)
KATE FARMS INC
101 Innovation Pl, Santa Barbara
(93108-2268)
P.O. Box 50840 (93150-0840)
PHONE................................805 845-2446
Richard Laver, *President*
Tom Beecher, *CFO*
Michelle Laver, *Vice Pres*
Sharon Machon, *Sales Staff*
Anne Brettschneider, *Director*
EMP: 123 **EST:** 2015
SALES (est): 1.8MM **Privately Held**
WEB: www.katefarms.com
SIC: 2099 Ready-to-eat meals, salads &
sandwiches

(P-2459)
KERRY INGREDIENTS
1916 S Tubeway Ave, Commerce
(90040-1612)
PHONE................................323 430-9718
Edgardo Camacaro, *Maintence Staff*
EMP: 13 **EST:** 2020
SALES (est): 669.7K **Privately Held**
WEB: www.kerry.com
SIC: 2099 Food preparations

(P-2460)
KHYBER FOODS
INCORPORATED
Also Called: Sun Glo Foods
500 S Acacia Ave, Fullerton (92831-5102)
P.O. Box 4324 (92834-4324)
PHONE................................714 879-0900
A R Ghafoori, *President*
Larry Ballard, *Corp Secy*
▲ **EMP:** 13 **EST:** 1964
SQ FT: 55,000
SALES (est): 471.1K **Privately Held**
SIC: 2099 Food preparations

(P-2461)
KTS KITCHENS INC
1065 E Walnut St Ste C, Carson
(90746-1384)
PHONE................................310 764-0850
Kathleen D Taggares, *CEO*
Joan Paris, *Corp Secy*
EMP: 250 **EST:** 1987
SALES (est): 51.1MM **Privately Held**
WEB: www.ktskitchens.com
SIC: 2099 2035 Pizza, refrigerated: except
frozen; dressings, salad: raw & cooked
(except dry mixes)

(P-2462)
LA BARCA TORTILLERIA INC
3047 Whittier Blvd, Los Angeles
(90023-1651)
P.O. Box 23548 (90023-0548)
PHONE................................323 268-1744
Jose Luis Arevalo, *CEO*
Antonio Arevalo, *President*
Alexander Arevalo, *Corp Secy*
EMP: 50 **EST:** 1988
SQ FT: 6,000

SALES (est): 5.1MM **Privately Held**
SIC: 2099 Tortillas, fresh or refrigerated

(P-2463)
LA CHAPALITA INC (PA)
1724 Chico Ave, El Monte (91733-2942)
PHONE................................626 443-8556
Luis E Moya Jr, *President*
Claudia Moya, *Officer*
EMP: 20 **EST:** 1981
SQ FT: 15,000
SALES (est): 4.3MM **Privately Held**
WEB: www.lachapalita.com
SIC: 2099 Tortillas, fresh or refrigerated

(P-2464)
LA COLONIAL TORTILLA PDTS INC
Also Called: La Colonial Mexican Foods
543 Monterey Pass Rd, Monterey Park
(91754-2416)
PHONE................................626 289-3647
Daniel Robles, *President*
Adrian Robles, *Vice Pres*
EMP: 185 **EST:** 1950
SQ FT: 27,000
SALES (est): 15.6MM **Privately Held**
WEB: www.lacolonial-la.com
SIC: 2099 Tortillas, fresh or refrigerated

(P-2465)
LA FORTALEZA INC
525 N Ford Blvd, Los Angeles
(90022-1104)
PHONE................................323 261-1211
Hermila Josefina Ortiz, *CEO*
David Ortiz, *Vice Pres*
Ramiro Ortiz Jr, *Vice Pres*
Tony Cassillia, *General Mgr*
EMP: 98 **EST:** 1990
SQ FT: 40,000
SALES (est): 9.5MM **Privately Held**
WEB: www.lafortalezaproducts.net
SIC: 2099 2096 Tortillas, fresh or refriger-
ated; potato chips & similar snacks

(P-2466)
LA GLORIA FOODS CORP (PA)
Also Called: La Gloria Tortilleria
3455 E 1st St, Los Angeles (90063-2945)
PHONE................................323 262-0410
Maria De La Luz Vera, *CEO*
Luz V De La, *Agent*
▼ **EMP:** 80 **EST:** 1954
SQ FT: 8,000
SALES (est): 7MM **Privately Held**
WEB: www.lagloriafoods.com
SIC: 2099 5461 5812 Tortillas, fresh or re-
frigerated; bread; Mexican restaurant

(P-2467)
LA GLORIA FOODS CORP
Also Called: La Gloria Flour Tortillas
3285 E Cesar E Chavez Ave, Los Angeles
(90063-2853)
PHONE................................323 263-6755
Daniel Torrez, *Manager*
EMP: 20
SALES (corp-wide): 7MM **Privately Held**
WEB: www.lagloriafoods.com
SIC: 2099 5461 Tortillas, fresh or refriger-
ated; bakeries
PA: La Gloria Foods Corp.
3455 E 1st St
Los Angeles CA 90063
323 262-0410

(P-2468)
LA PRINCESITA TORTILLERIA INC (PA)
Also Called: Abalquiga
3432 E Cesar E Chavez Ave, Los Angeles
(90063-4146)
PHONE................................323 267-0673
Francisco Ramirez, *President*
EMP: 19 **EST:** 1974
SQ FT: 2,195
SALES (est): 2.8MM **Privately Held**
WEB: www.laprincesitayablanquita.com
SIC: 2099 Tortillas, fresh or refrigerated

(P-2469)
LABRUCHERIE PRODUCE LLC
1407 S La Brucherie Rd, El Centro
(92243-9677)
PHONE................................760 352-2170

Jean Labrucherie, *Mng Member*
Steph Weldon, *CFO*
Tim Labrucherie, *Principal*
Ricardo Canchola, *Director*
Rick Magallanes, *Manager*
EMP: 42 **EST:** 2011
SALES (est): 6.7MM
SALES (corp-wide): 9.3MM **Privately
Held**
WEB: www.lbproduce.com
SIC: 2099 0191 Vegetables, peeled for the
trade; general farms, primarily crop
PA: Tjl Capital, Inc.
1407 S La Brucherie Rd
El Centro CA 92243
760 352-2170

(P-2470)
LANTY INC
9660 Flair Dr, El Monte (91731-3017)
PHONE................................626 582-8001
Dongmei LI, *CEO*
EMP: 181
SALES (est): 7.5MM **Privately Held**
SIC: 2099 Vegetables, peeled for the trade

(P-2471)
LAS GLONDRINAS MEXICAN FD PDTS (PA)
27124 Paseo Espada # 803, San Juan
Capistrano (92675-6787)
PHONE................................949 240-3440
Arturo Galindo Jr, *President*
Maria Galindo, *Corp Secy*
EMP: 18 **EST:** 1984
SQ FT: 3,000
SALES (est): 3.8MM **Privately Held**
WEB: www.lasgolondrinas.biz
SIC: 5812 2099 Mexican restaurant; tor-
tillas, fresh or refrigerated

(P-2472)
LASSONDE PAPPAS AND CO INC
1755 E Acacia St, Ontario (91761-7702)
PHONE................................909 923-4041
Rick Jochums, *Manager*
Juan Carrillo, *General Mgr*
EMP: 27
SALES (corp-wide): 402MM **Privately
Held**
WEB: www.lassondepappas.com
SIC: 2099 Food preparations
HQ: Lassonde Pappas And Company, Inc.
1 Collins Dr Ste 200
Carneys Point NJ 08069
856 455-1000

(P-2473)
LEE KUM KEE (USA) FOODS INC
14455 Don Julian Rd, City of Industry
(91746-3102)
PHONE................................626 709-1888
Simon Wu, *President*
Alan Lui, *CFO*
Dickson Chan, *Treasurer*
Ken Low, *Info Tech Mgr*
Carina Ching, *Purch Agent*
EMP: 99
SQ FT: 54,000
SALES (est): 3.6MM **Privately Held**
WEB: www.usa.lkk.com
SIC: 2099 Sauces: gravy, dressing & dip
mixes

(P-2474)
LEHMAN FOODS INC
Also Called: Fresh & Ready
1145 Arroyo St Ste B, San Fernando
(91340-1842)
PHONE................................818 837-7600
Charles Lehman, *CEO*
Art Sezgin, *President*
Harry Iknadosian, *Vice Pres*
Michael Morse, *VP Sales*
Cameron Childs, *Sales Staff*
EMP: 25 **EST:** 1990
SQ FT: 15,000
SALES (est): 5MM **Privately Held**
SIC: 2099 Salads, fresh or refrigerated;
sandwiches, assembled & packaged: for
wholesale market

(P-2475)
LETS DO LUNCH
Also Called: Integrated Food Service
310 W Alondra Blvd, Gardena
(90248-2423)
PHONE................................310 523-3664
Paul G Giuliano, *President*
Jon Sugimoto, *Vice Pres*
Richard Wood, *Regl Sales Mgr*
David Watzke, *Director*
Jean-Yves Courbin, *Manager*
▲ **EMP:** 80 **EST:** 1991
SQ FT: 57,000
SALES (est): 20.2MM **Privately Held**
WEB: www.ldlcatering.com
SIC: 2099 Sandwiches, assembled &
packaged: for wholesale market

(P-2476)
LOS PERICOS FOOD PRODUCTS LLC
2301 Valley Blvd, Pomona (91768-1105)
PHONE................................909 623-5625
Marcelino Ortega, *Partner*
Guadalupe Ortega, *Partner*
Luis Ortega, *Partner*
EMP: 46 **EST:** 1962
SQ FT: 20,000
SALES (est): 4.2MM **Privately Held**
WEB: www.lospericosfood.com
SIC: 2099 Tortillas, fresh or refrigerated

(P-2477)
MAPLEGROVE GLUTEN FREE FOODS
5010 Eucalyptus Ave, Chino (91710-9216)
PHONE................................909 334-7828
Raj Sukul, *President*
EMP: 14 **EST:** 2006
SALES (est): 1.2MM **Privately Held**
WEB: www.pastarisofoods.com
SIC: 2099 Food preparations

(P-2478)
MARS FOOD US LLC (HQ)
2001 E Cashdan St Ste 201, Rancho
Dominguez (90220-6438)
PHONE................................310 933-0670
Vincent Howell, *Mng Member*
Stephanie Oliver, *Manager*
◆ **EMP:** 500 **EST:** 1936
SALES (est): 220.5MM
SALES (corp-wide): 42.8B **Privately Held**
WEB: www.mars.com
SIC: 2099 Food preparations
PA: Mars, Incorporated
6885 Elm St Ste 1
Mc Lean VA 22101
703 821-4900

(P-2479)
MARUCHAN INC (HQ)
15800 Laguna Canyon Rd, Irvine
(92618-3103)
PHONE................................949 789-2300
Noritaka Sumimoto, *CEO*
Sarah Otaki, *Administration*
Natalie Plumb, *Human Resources*
Masaaki Miyashita, *Purch Mgr*
Hideyuki Nozawa, *Purch Mgr*
◆ **EMP:** 450
SQ FT: 300,000
SALES (est): 243MM **Privately Held**
WEB: www.maruchan.com
SIC: 2099 Food preparations

(P-2480)
MARUKAN VINEGAR U S A INC (HQ)
16203 Vermont Ave, Paramount
(90723-5042)
PHONE................................562 630-6060
Yasuo Sasada, *Ch of Bd*
Toshio Takeuchi, *President*
Denzaemon Sasada, *CEO*
Junichi Oyama, *Exec VP*
Shugi Yamada, *Vice Pres*
◆ **EMP:** 20 **EST:** 1649
SQ FT: 20,000
SALES (est): 10.8MM **Privately Held**
WEB: www.marukan-usa.com
SIC: 2099 Vinegar

(P-2481)
MARUKOME USA INC
17132 Pullman St, Irvine (92614-5524)
PHONE..................................949 863-0110
Shigeru Shirasaka, *President*
Toshio Abe, *Corp Secy*
Takeshi Azuma, *Prdtn Mgr*
Kazuhiko Fushimi, *Marketing Staff*
▲ **EMP:** 17 **EST:** 2004
SQ FT: 134,172
SALES (est): 7.5MM **Privately Held**
WEB: www.marukomeusa.com
SIC: 2099 Seasonings & spices
PA: Marukome Co.,Ltd.
883, Amori
Nagano NAG 380-0

(P-2482)
MCCORMICK FRESH HERBS LLC
1575 W Walnut Pkwy, Compton (90220-5022)
PHONE..................................323 278-9750
EMP: 75
SALES (est): 5.8MM
SALES (corp-wide): 4.2B **Publicly Held**
SIC: 2099 Mfg Food Preparations
PA: Mccormick & Company Incorporated
18 Loveton Cir
Sparks MD 21031
410 771-7301

(P-2483)
MCI FOODS INC
Also Called: Los Cabos Mexican Foods
13013 Molette St, Santa Fe Springs (90670-5521)
PHONE..................................562 977-4000
Alberta Southard, *Ch of Bd*
Daniel Southard, *President*
Chris Hakmiller, *Vice Pres*
John M Southard, *Vice Pres*
John Southard, *Vice Pres*
EMP: 140 **EST:** 1970
SQ FT: 15,000
SALES (est): 23.2MM **Privately Held**
WEB: www.mcifoods.com
SIC: 2099 Food preparations

(P-2484)
MCK ENTERPRISES INC
Also Called: Valley Spuds
910 Commercial Ave, Oxnard (93030-7232)
PHONE..................................805 483-5292
Evelyn Gardiner, *President*
Al Melino, *President*
Travis Dergan, *Manager*
EMP: 87 **EST:** 2004
SQ FT: 60,000
SALES (est): 5.1MM **Privately Held**
WEB: www.mck-enterprises.com
SIC: 2099 Food preparations

(P-2485)
MILLERS AMERICAN HONEY INC
Also Called: Superior Honey Company
1455 Riverview Dr, San Bernardino (92408-2931)
P.O. Box 500, Colton (92324-0500)
PHONE..................................909 825-1722
George T Murdock, *CEO*
Steve Smith, *Vice Pres*
◆ **EMP:** 22 **EST:** 1894
SQ FT: 33,000
SALES (est): 930.2K **Privately Held**
WEB: www.millershoney.com
SIC: 2099 Honey, strained & bottled

(P-2486)
MINSLEY INC
989 S Monterey Ave, Ontario (91761-3463)
PHONE..................................909 458-1100
Song Tae Jin, *CEO*
Christina Gomez, *Manager*
Brian Jung, *Manager*
▲ **EMP:** 40 **EST:** 2002
SQ FT: 42,000
SALES (est): 8MM **Privately Held**
WEB: www.minsley.com
SIC: 2099 Packaged combination products: pasta, rice & potato

(P-2487)
MIZKAN AMERICA INC
Also Called: Indian Summer
10037 8th St, Rancho Cucamonga (91730-5210)
PHONE..................................909 484-8743
Pete Marsing, *Branch Mgr*
Rich Kellison, *Representative*
EMP: 51
SQ FT: 58,500 **Privately Held**
WEB: www.mizkan.com
SIC: 2099 Vinegar
HQ: Mizkan America, Inc.
1661 Feehanville Dr 100a
Mount Prospect IL 60056
847 590-0059

(P-2488)
MOJAVE FOODS CORPORATION
6200 E Slauson Ave, Commerce (90040-3012)
PHONE..................................323 890-8900
Richard D Lipka, *CEO*
Craig M Berger, *CFO*
◆ **EMP:** 200 **EST:** 1953
SQ FT: 110,000
SALES (est): 51MM
SALES (corp-wide): 5.6B **Publicly Held**
WEB: www.mojavefoods.com
SIC: 2099 Butter, renovated & processed
PA: Mccormick & Company Incorporated
24 Schilling Rd Ste 1
Hunt Valley MD 21031
410 771-7301

(P-2489)
MOORE FARMS INC
916 S Derby St, Arvin (93203-2312)
P.O. Box 698 (93203-0698)
PHONE..................................661 854-5588
John Moore, *President*
EMP: 38 **EST:** 1955
SQ FT: 2,000
SALES (est): 2.5MM **Privately Held**
WEB: www.moorefarmsca.com
SIC: 2099 0134 Potatoes, peeled for the trade; Irish potatoes

(P-2490)
MORINAGA NUTRITIONAL FOODS INC
3838 Del Amo Blvd Ste 201, Torrance (90503-7709)
P.O. Box 7969 (90504-9369)
PHONE..................................310 787-0200
Hiroyuki Imanishi, *President*
Tetsuhisa Tato, *Vice Pres*
Susan Buch R, *Mktg Dir*
Thinh Tran, *Sales Mgr*
Robert Concepcion, *Manager*
▼ **EMP:** 19 **EST:** 1985
SQ FT: 2,782
SALES (est): 9.1MM **Privately Held**
WEB: www.morinaga-usa.com
SIC: 2099 Food preparations
PA: Morinaga Milk Industry Co., Ltd.
5-33-1, Shiba
Minato-Ku TKY 108-0

(P-2491)
MR TORTILLA INC
1112 Arroyo St, San Fernando (91340-1850)
PHONE..................................818 307-7414
Anthony Alcazar, *President*
Tony Alcazar, *CEO*
Edgar Rodriguez, *Plant Mgr*
Ronald Alcazar, *Opers Staff*
EMP: 30 **EST:** 2012
SALES (est): 3.1MM **Privately Held**
WEB: www.mrtortilla.com
SIC: 2099 Tortillas, fresh or refrigerated

(P-2492)
MRS FOODS INCORPORATED (PA)
Also Called: La Rancherita Tortilleria Deli
4406 W 5th St, Santa Ana (92703-3224)
PHONE..................................714 554-2791
Laura Perez, *President*
Roxana Perez, *Treasurer*
Shirley Serna, *Admin Sec*
▲ **EMP:** 40 **EST:** 1981
SQ FT: 4,000

SALES (est): 3.9MM **Privately Held**
SIC: 2099 5812 Tortillas, fresh or refrigerated; fast-food restaurant, independent

(P-2493)
NATREN INC
3105 Willow Ln, Thousand Oaks (91361-4919)
PHONE..................................805 371-4737
Yordan Trenev, *CEO*
Natasha Trenev, *President*
Odessa Braza, *Admin Sec*
Michael Chapovsky, *Info Tech Dir*
Tim Malone, *IT/INT Sup*
EMP: 60 **EST:** 1983
SQ FT: 22,000
SALES (est): 11.6MM **Privately Held**
WEB: www.natren.com
SIC: 2099 8011 Food preparations; offices & clinics of medical doctors

(P-2494)
NECTAVE INC
6700 Caballero Blvd, Buena Park (90620-1134)
PHONE..................................714 736-9811
Robert Chavez, *CEO*
Richard Ellinghausen, *President*
EMP: 15 **EST:** 2011
SQ FT: 30,000
SALES (est): 693.4K **Privately Held**
WEB: www.nectave.com
SIC: 2099 Sorghum syrups; for sweetening

(P-2495)
NINA MIA INC
Also Called: Pasta Mia
826 Enterprise Way, Fullerton (92831-5015)
PHONE..................................714 773-5588
Diego Mazza, *President*
Jessica Mazza, *Vice Pres*
Janet Vandergrift, *Human Resources*
Kevin Gruezo, *Purch Mgr*
▲ **EMP:** 80 **EST:** 1984
SQ FT: 32,000
SALES (est): 14.9MM **Privately Held**
WEB: www.pastamia.com
SIC: 2099 Pasta, uncooked: packaged with other ingredients

(P-2496)
NINAS MEXICAN FOODS INC
20631 Valley Blvd Ste A, Walnut (91789-2751)
PHONE..................................909 468-5888
Ruben Vasquez, *President*
▲ **EMP:** 40 **EST:** 1989
SQ FT: 14,000
SALES (est): 4.6MM **Privately Held**
SIC: 2099 Tortillas, fresh or refrigerated

(P-2497)
OASIS DATE GARDEN INC
59111 Grapefruit Blvd, Thermal (92274-8813)
P.O. Box 757 (92274-0757)
PHONE..................................760 399-5665
James Freimuth, *President*
Chris Nelsen, *Vice Pres*
Darrell Billings, *Controller*
Maribel Aguilar, *Personnel*
▲ **EMP:** 21 **EST:** 1918
SQ FT: 14,000
SALES (est): 3.8MM **Privately Held**
WEB: www.oasisdate.com
SIC: 2099 5431 5148 0179 Food preparations; fruit stands or markets; fruits; date orchard

(P-2498)
OLD PUEBLO RANCH INC
Also Called: La Reina
316 N Ford Blvd, Los Angeles (90022-1121)
PHONE..................................800 367-7522
Ricardo Robles, *CEO*
EMP: 30 **EST:** 2011
SALES (est): 644.3K **Privately Held**
SIC: 2099 Food preparations

(P-2499)
ORGANIC MILLING CORPORATION (PA)
505 W Allen Ave, San Dimas (91773-1487)
PHONE..................................909 599-0961

Bruce Olsen, *President*
Norm Bowers, *Vice Pres*
John Duenas, *Principal*
Chris Wadden, *General Mgr*
Michael Lopez, *IT/INT Sup*
◆ **EMP:** 108 **EST:** 2001
SQ FT: 43,000
SALES (est): 25.1MM **Privately Held**
WEB: www.organicmilling.com
SIC: 2099 Food preparations

(P-2500)
ORGANIC MILLING CORPORATION
305 S Acacia St Ste A, San Dimas (91773-2928)
PHONE..................................909 305-0185
Lupe Martinez, *Branch Mgr*
Connie Monk, *Controller*
Robert Miller, *Maintence Staff*
EMP: 32
SALES (corp-wide): 25.1MM **Privately Held**
WEB: www.organicmilling.com
SIC: 2099 Food preparations
PA: Organic Milling Corporation
505 W Allen Ave
San Dimas CA 91773
909 599-0961

(P-2501)
ORIGEN FOOD INC (PA)
230 W Avenue 26 Ste 239, Los Angeles (90031-1812)
PHONE..................................800 420-4927
Shad Loh, *CEO*
EMP: 23 **EST:** 2013
SALES (est): 265.9K **Privately Held**
SIC: 2099 7371 Food preparations; computer software development & applications

(P-2502)
OTAFUKU FOODS INC
13117 Molette St, Santa Fe Springs (90670-5523)
PHONE..................................562 404-4700
Naoyoshi Saki, *Chairman*
Takamitsu Ozawa, *President*
▲ **EMP:** 22 **EST:** 1998
SQ FT: 2,000
SALES (est): 5MM **Privately Held**
WEB: www.otafukufoods.com
SIC: 2099 Food preparations
PA: Otafuku Holdings Co., Ltd.
7-4-27, Shoko-Center, Nishi-Ku
Hiroshima HIR 733-0

(P-2503)
OUT OF SHELL LLC
Also Called: Ling's
9658 Remer St, South El Monte (91733-3033)
PHONE..................................626 401-1923
Alice Liu,
Bing Yang,
EMP: 200 **EST:** 1999
SALES (est): 19.1MM **Privately Held**
WEB: www.outoftheshell.com
SIC: 2099 Food preparations

(P-2504)
OVERHILL FARMS INC (DH)
Also Called: Chicago Brothers
2727 E Vernon Ave, Vernon (90058-1822)
P.O. Box 58806 (90058-0806)
PHONE..................................323 582-9977
James Rudis, *President*
Rick Alvarez, *President*
Denise Ouellette, *President*
Robert C Bruning, *CFO*
Francisco Andrade, *General Mgr*
EMP: 200 **EST:** 1995
SQ FT: 170,000
SALES (est): 12.9MM **Privately Held**
WEB: www.overhillfarms.com
SIC: 2099 Food preparations

(P-2505)
PACIFIC CULINARY GROUP INC
566 Monterey Pass Rd, Monterey Park (91754-2417)
PHONE..................................626 284-1328
Bingham Lee, *CEO*
Lin MA, *President*

EMP: 20 EST: 2013
SALES (est): 1MM Privately Held
WEB: www.pacificdentalgroup.com
SIC: 2099 Food preparations

(P-2506)
PACIFIC SPICE COMPANY INC
Also Called: Pacific Natural Spices
6430 E Slauson Ave, Commerce
(90040-3108)
PHONE...............................323 726-9190
Gershon D Schlussel, CEO
Akiba E Schlussel, President
Sharon Schlussel, Admin Sec
Katherine Semaan, Admin Asst
Jason Yasumi, Technical Mgr
◆ EMP: 82 EST: 1966
SQ FT: 150,000
SALES (est): 21.2MM Privately Held
WEB: www.pacspice.com
SIC: 2099 5149 Spices, including grinding;
spices & seasonings

(P-2507)
PALERMO FAMILY LP
Also Called: Divine Pasta Company
140 W Providencia Ave, Burbank
(91502-2121)
PHONE...............................213 542-3300
Alexander Palermo, Principal
Todd Ramsey, Opers Mgr
Tigran Keshishyan, Manager
EMP: 49 EST: 1991
SQ FT: 30,000
SALES (est): 7.6MM Privately Held
WEB: www.divinepasta.com
SIC: 2099 Packaged combination prod-
ucts: pasta, rice & potato

(P-2508)
PASSPORT FOODS (SVC) LLC
2539 E Philadelphia St, Ontario
(91761-7774)
PHONE...............................909 627-7312
Mark Thomson, CEO
EMP: 150 EST: 2019
SALES (est): 29.5MM Privately Held
WEB: www.passportglobalfoods.com
SIC: 2099 Packaged combination prod-
ucts: pasta, rice & potato

(P-2509)
PLANT RANCH LLC
242 N Avenue 25 Ste 114, Los Angeles
(90031-1881)
PHONE...............................818 384-9727
Gary Robert Huerta, Mng Member
EMP: 17 EST: 2016
SALES (est): 935.4K Privately Held
WEB: www.plantranchfoods.com
SIC: 2099 Food preparations

(P-2510)
PROPORTION FOODS LLC
3501 E Vernon Ave, Vernon (90058-1813)
PHONE...............................515 735-9800
EMP: 50
SALES (corp-wide): 113.4B Privately
Held
SIC: 2099 Food Preparations, Nec, Nsk
HQ: Proportion Foods, Llc
101 Chisholm Trail Rd
Round Rock TX 78681
512 735-9800

(P-2511)
PSW INC
Also Called: Taste Nirvana International
281 Corporate Terrace St, Corona
(92879-6000)
PHONE...............................951 371-7100
Jack Wattanaporn, President
Christian Villanueva, Sales Staff
▲ EMP: 15 EST: 1989
SALES (est): 2.4MM Privately Held
WEB: www.tastenirvana.com
SIC: 2099 2095 5141 Tea blending;
roasted coffee; groceries, general line

(P-2512)
**QST INGREDIENTS AND PACKG
INC**
9734-40 6th St Rch, Rancho Cucamonga
(91730)
PHONE...............................909 989-4343
Chris Topps, President

Anthony Castillo, Opers Staff
Ramon Castillo, Director
▲ EMP: 15 EST: 2005
SALES (est): 4MM Privately Held
WEB: www.qsting.com
SIC: 2099 5046 Seasonings & spices;
commercial cooking & food service equip-
ment

(P-2513)
QUEST NUTRITION LLC
2221 Park Pl, El Segundo (90245-4909)
PHONE...............................562 446-3321
EMP: 28
SALES (est): 10MM Privately Held
SIC: 2099 Mfg Food Preparations

(P-2514)
**RAMA FOOD MANUFACTURE
CORP (PA)**
1486 E Cedar St, Ontario (91761-8300)
P.O. Box 4045 (91761-1002)
PHONE...............................909 923-5305
Karen Trang Ving, CEO
▲ EMP: 29 EST: 1984
SQ FT: 25,000
SALES (est): 6MM Privately Held
WEB: www.ramafood.com
SIC: 2099 Noodles, fried (Chinese)

(P-2515)
READY PAC FOODS INC (HQ)
4401 Foxdale St, Irwindale (91706-2161)
PHONE...............................626 856-8686
Mary Thompson, CEO
Dan Redfern, CFO
Jason Bellan, Vice Pres
Scott Wilkerson, Vice Pres
Joseph Poynter, Technician
◆ EMP: 2000 EST: 2000
SQ FT: 135,000
SALES (est): 973.1MM
SALES (corp-wide): 2.6MM Privately
Held
WEB: www.readypac.com
SIC: 2099 5148 Salads, fresh or refriger-
ated; vegetables, fresh
PA: Bonduelle
Rue De La Woestyne
Renescure
328 498-280

(P-2516)
**REYNALDOS MEXICAN FOOD
CO INC**
11929 Woodruff Ave, Downey
(90241-5601)
P.O. Box 1033, Northbrook IL (60065-
1033)
PHONE...............................562 803-3188
Joe Garcia, President
EMP: 18 EST: 2011
SALES (est): 530.6K Privately Held
SIC: 2099 Food preparations

(P-2517)
**REYNALDOS MEXICAN FOOD
CO LLC (PA)**
3301 E Vernon Ave, Vernon (90058-1809)
PHONE...............................562 803-3188
Douglas Reed, CFO
Gilbert D Cardenas, Principal
Drew Carothers, Plant Mgr
Miguel Aguilar, Sales Staff
Marisol Scrugham,
EMP: 160 EST: 2006
SALES (est): 34MM Privately Held
WEB: www.sabrosurafoods.com
SIC: 2099 Food preparations

(P-2518)
RISVOLDS INC
1234 W El Segundo Blvd, Gardena
(90247-1593)
PHONE...............................323 770-2674
Tim Brandon, CEO
Ed Scoullar, President
Wendy O 'neill, Vice Pres
Jenifer Peterson, Purch Mgr
EMP: 65
SQ FT: 30,000
SALES (est): 12MM Privately Held
WEB: www.risvolds.com
SIC: 2099 Salads, fresh or refrigerated

(P-2519)
**ROMEROS FOOD PRODUCTS
INC (PA)**
15155 Valley View Ave, Santa Fe Springs
(90670-5323)
PHONE...............................562 802-1858
Richard Scandalito, CEO
Leon Romero Sr, President
Leon S Romero, CEO
Raul Romero Sr, Vice Pres
EMP: 100 EST: 1971
SQ FT: 20,000 Privately Held
WEB: www.romerosfood.com
SIC: 2099 2096 5461 Tortillas, fresh or re-
frigerated; tortilla chips; bakeries

(P-2520)
RUIZ MEXICAN FOODS INC (PA)
Also Called: Ruiz Flour Tortillas
1200 Marlborough Ave A, Riverside
(92507-2158)
PHONE...............................909 947-7811
Dolores C Ruiz, CEO
Jonathan Elguea, Info Tech Mgr
Dana Warren, Accountant
Steve Hernandez, Controller
Ana Loza, Human Res Mgr
▼ EMP: 139 EST: 1976
SQ FT: 38,000
SALES (est): 21MM Privately Held
WEB: www.ruizflourtortillas.com
SIC: 2099 3556 Tortillas, fresh or refriger-
ated; food products machinery

(P-2521)
SALADISH INC
12 W Colorado Blvd, Pasadena
(91105-1923)
PHONE...............................626 304-3100
Seung Hee Lee, Principal
EMP: 13
SALES (corp-wide): 327.9K Privately
Held
SIC: 2099 Ready-to-eat meals, salads &
sandwiches
PA: Saladish, Inc.
28901 S Wstn Ave Ste 123
Rancho Palos Verdes CA 90275
310 521-0300

(P-2522)
SAUER BRANDS INC
184 Suburban Rd, San Luis Obispo
(93401-7502)
PHONE...............................805 597-8900
William W Lovette, CEO
EMP: 65
SALES (corp-wide): 111.6MM Privately
Held
WEB: www.sauerbrands.com
SIC: 2099 Seasonings & spices
PA: Sauer Brands, Inc.
2000 W Broad St
Richmond VA 23220
804 359-5786

(P-2523)
SHORE FRONT LLC
Also Called: Subway
3973 Trolley Ct, Brea (92823-1054)
PHONE...............................714 612-3751
Ajay Maini,
Anil Kumar, President
EMP: 40 EST: 2009
SALES (est): 3.7MM Privately Held
WEB: www.subway.com
SIC: 2099 5812 Ready-to-eat meals, sal-
ads & sandwiches; eating places; sand-
wiches & submarines shop; cafe

(P-2524)
SILAO TORTILLERIA INC
250 N California Ave, City of Industry
(91744-4323)
PHONE...............................626 961-0761
Leandro Espinosa Sr, President
Leandro Espinosa Jr, Vice Pres
EMP: 44 EST: 1955
SALES (est): 4.2MM Privately Held
WEB: www.silaotortilleria.com
SIC: 2099 Tortillas, fresh or refrigerated

(P-2525)
**SINCERE ORIENT COMMERCIAL
CORP**
Also Called: Sincere Orient Food Company
15222 Valley Blvd, City of Industry
(91746-3323)
PHONE...............................626 333-8882
Andy Khun, President
▲ EMP: 70 EST: 1984
SQ FT: 12,000
SALES (est): 9.3MM Privately Held
WEB: www.sincereorient.com
SIC: 2099 Packaged combination prod-
ucts: pasta, rice & potato

(P-2526)
**SONORA MILLS FOODS INC
(PA)**
Also Called: Pop Chips
3064 E Maria St, E Rncho Dmngz
(90221-5804)
PHONE...............................310 639-5333
Patrick Turpin, CEO
Martin Basch, Vice Pres
Kay Ko, VP Finance
Ryan Raish, Sales Mgr
▲ EMP: 145 EST: 1991
SQ FT: 80,000
SALES (est): 32.4MM Privately Held
SIC: 2099 Food preparations

(P-2527)
SOUP BASES LOADED INC
2355 E Francis St, Ontario (91761-7727)
PHONE...............................909 230-6890
Alan Portney, President
Minh Dao, Research
Laura Harlow, Technical Staff
Elizabeth Trujillo, Buyer
EMP: 45 EST: 1997
SQ FT: 27,000
SALES (est): 9.9MM Privately Held
WEB: www.soupbasesloaded.com
SIC: 2099 2034 Seasonings: dry mixes;
dried & dehydrated soup mixes

(P-2528)
STANESS JONEKOS ENTPS INC
Also Called: Eat Like A Woman
4000 W Magnolia Blvd D, Burbank
(91505-2827)
PHONE...............................818 606-2710
Staness Jonekos, Owner
EMP: 27 EST: 1988
SALES (est): 1.3MM Privately Held
WEB: www.eatlikeawoman.com
SIC: 2099 Food preparations

(P-2529)
SUN RICH FOODS INTL CORP
1240 N Barsten Way, Anaheim
(92806-1822)
PHONE...............................714 632-7577
Walid A Barakat, President
Shirley Barakat, CFO
Alex Barakat, Vice Pres
EMP: 22 EST: 1981
SQ FT: 6,500
SALES (est): 1.2MM Privately Held
WEB: www.sunrichfoods.com
SIC: 2099 Food preparations

(P-2530)
SUNRISE GROWERS INC
Also Called: Oxnard 2 Warehouse
2640 Sturgis Rd, Oxnard (93030-7931)
PHONE...............................612 619-9545
Jill Barnett, President
EMP: 138 EST: 2011
SALES (est): 11.1MM
SALES (corp-wide): 789.2MM Privately
Held
WEB: www.sunopta.com
SIC: 2099 Food preparations
HQ: Sunopta Foods Inc.
7301 Ohms Ln Ste 600
Edina MN 55439

(P-2531)
T HASEGAWA USA INC
2026 Cecilia Cir, Corona (92881-3389)
PHONE...............................951 264-1121
Alberto Guerrero, Engineer
EMP: 60 Privately Held

(PA)=Parent Co (HQ)=Headquarters (DH)=Div Headquarters
✪ = New Business established in last 2 years

2022 Southern California Business
Directory and Buyers Guide

123

PRODUCTS & SVCS

WEB: www.thasegawa.com
SIC: 2099 Food preparations
HQ: T. Hasegawa U.S.A. Inc.
14017 183rd St
Cerritos CA 90703
714 522-1900

(P-2532)
TAMPICO SPICE CO INCORPORATED
Also Called: Tampico Spice Company
5901 S Central Ave 5941, Los Angeles (90001-1128)
P.O. Box 1229 (90001-0229)
PHONE..................323 235-3154
George Martinez, CEO
Baudelia Martinez, Treasurer
Delia Navarro, Treasurer
Gabriel Martinez, Vice Pres
Icela Sanchez, Admin Sec
▲ EMP: 40 EST: 1946
SQ FT: 150,000
SALES (est): 9.3MM Privately Held
WEB: www.tampicospice.com
SIC: 2099 Spices, including grinding; seasonings: dry mixes

(P-2533)
TARAZI SPECIALTY FOODS LLC
13727 Seminole Dr, Chino (91710-5515)
PHONE..................909 628-3601
Alexandra Vorbeck, Mng Member
▲ EMP: 13 EST: 2013
SALES (est): 1.8MM Privately Held
WEB: www.tarazifoods.com
SIC: 2099 Seasonings: dry mixes

(P-2534)
TATTOOED CHEF INC (PA)
6305 Alondra Blvd, Paramount (90723-3750)
PHONE..................562 602-0822
Salvatore Galletti, President
Stephanie Dieckmann, COO
Charles Cargile, CFO
Sarah Galletti, Creative Dir
EMP: 90 EST: 2018
SALES (est): 148.4MM Publicly Held
SIC: 2099 Food preparations

(P-2535)
TEALOVE INC
9810 Sierra Ave Ste A, Fontana (92335-6779)
PHONE..................714 408-8245
Elli Nguyen, CFO
EMP: 20 EST: 2018
SALES (est): 250K Privately Held
SIC: 5499 2099 2086 5812 Tea: tea blending; tea, iced: packaged in cans, bottles, etc.; coffee shop

(P-2536)
TEVA FOODS INC
4401 S Downey Rd, Vernon (90058-2518)
P.O. Box 58128, Los Angeles (90058-0128)
PHONE..................323 267-8110
Erik Litmanovich, President
EMP: 28 EST: 2008
SALES (est): 1.3MM Privately Held
WEB: www.gwfg.com
SIC: 2099 Salads, fresh or refrigerated

(P-2537)
THG BRANDS INC
Also Called: Hummus Guy, The
1810 Abalone Ave, Torrance (90501-3703)
P.O. Box 1039, Redondo Beach (90278-0039)
PHONE..................844 694-8327
Noel D Bonn, CEO
Chris Krunnell, Partner
Mohamed Cherif, COO
John Molino, CFO
EMP: 20 EST: 2014
SALES (est): 3.4MM Privately Held
WEB: www.thehummusguy.com
SIC: 2099 Food preparations

(P-2538)
TOM HARRIS INC
Also Called: Uncle Bum's Gourmet Sauces
5821 Wilderness Ave, Riverside (92504-1004)
PHONE..................951 352-5700

Tom Harris, President
Richard Harris, Vice Pres
EMP: 13 EST: 1990
SQ FT: 140,000
SALES (est): 279.7K Privately Held
WEB: www.triplehfoods.com
SIC: 2099 2035 Food preparations; pickles, sauces & salad dressings

(P-2539)
TONE IT UP INC
1110 Manhattan Ave, Manhattan Beach (90266-5313)
PHONE..................310 376-7645
Russell Sternlicht, CEO
Christine Sana, CFO
Brian Leckrone, Opers Staff
Keith Lundstrom, Sales Staff
Bari Lieberman, Director
▲ EMP: 31 EST: 2009
SQ FT: 3,000
SALES (est): 19.8MM Privately Held
WEB: www.toneitup.com
SIC: 5499 2099 5149 Health & dietetic food stores; food preparations; groceries & related products

(P-2540)
TORTILLERIA LA CALIFORNIA INC
2241 Cypress Ave, Los Angeles (90065-1214)
PHONE..................323 221-8940
Sergio Sanchez, President
EMP: 13 EST: 1972
SQ FT: 20,000
SALES (est): 1.1MM Privately Held
SIC: 2099 Tortillas, fresh or refrigerated

(P-2541)
TORTILLERIA LA MEJOR
Also Called: La Mejor Restaurant
684 S Farmersville Blvd, Farmersville (93223-2042)
P.O. Box 657 (93223-0657)
PHONE..................559 747-0739
Rafael Vasquez, Owner
Octaviana Vasquez, Co-Owner
EMP: 55 EST: 1970
SALES (est): 5.9MM Privately Held
WEB: www.lamejorfarmersville.com
SIC: 2099 5411 Tortillas, fresh or refrigerated; grocery stores, independent

(P-2542)
TORTILLERIA SAN MARCOS
Also Called: San Marco's Tortilla & Market
1927 E 1st St, Los Angeles (90033-3412)
PHONE..................323 263-0208
Gregorio Garcia, President
Amparo Garcia, Vice Pres
EMP: 14 EST: 1987
SQ FT: 8,750
SALES (est): 825K Privately Held
SIC: 2099 Tortillas, fresh or refrigerated

(P-2543)
TRIPLE H FOOD PROCESSORS LLC
5821 Wilderness Ave, Riverside (92504-1004)
PHONE..................951 352-5700
Tom Harris,
Raquel Bozek, Executive
Richard J Harris,
▲ EMP: 60 EST: 1976
SQ FT: 120,000
SALES (est): 17.1MM Privately Held
WEB: www.triplehfoods.com
SIC: 2099 2035 2033 Food preparations; pickles, sauces & salad dressings; jams, jellies & preserves: packaged in cans, jars, etc.

(P-2544)
UNIFIED NUTRIMEALS
5469 Ferguson Dr, Commerce (90022-5118)
PHONE..................323 923-9335
Shabir Kashyap, President
Phil Chavez, CFO
Hugo Meza, Vice Pres
EMP: 85 EST: 2005 Privately Held
WEB: www.unifiednutrimeals.com

SIC: 5812 2099 Contract food services; caterers; ready-to-eat meals, salads & sandwiches

(P-2545)
UPPER CRUST ENTERPRISES INC
411 Center St, Los Angeles (90012-3435)
PHONE..................213 625-0038
Gary Kawaguchi, CEO
Ed Shelley, CFO
Edward Shelley, CFO
Ken Kawaguchi, Vice Pres
Tom Shea, Vice Pres
◆ EMP: 87 EST: 2006
SQ FT: 45,000
SALES (est): 10.3MM Privately Held
WEB: www.uppercrustent.com
SIC: 2099 Bread crumbs, not made in bakeries

(P-2546)
VIRGINIA PARK LLC
Also Called: Virginia Park Foods
2225 Via Cerro Ste A, Riverside (92509-2440)
P.O. Box 1567, New York NY (10159-1567)
PHONE..................816 592-0776
Manoj Venugopal, Mng Member
Brian Rudolf,
Scott Rudolph,
EMP: 15 EST: 2015
SQ FT: 35,000
SALES (est): 1MM
SALES (corp-wide): 8.8MM Privately Held
WEB: www.virginiaparkfoods.com
SIC: 2099 Pasta, uncooked: packaged with other ingredients
PA: Banza Llc
1570 Woodward Ave Fl 3
Detroit MI 48226
914 338-8009

(P-2547)
WELLINGTON FOODS INC
1930 California Ave, Corona (92881-6491)
PHONE..................562 989-0111
Anthony E Harnack Sr, Chairman
Jim Melvani, CEO
Amy Nguyen, Research
Kim Butler, Purch Mgr
Tony Mosca, VP Sales
▲ EMP: 50 EST: 1974
SQ FT: 50,000
SALES (est): 13MM Privately Held
WEB: www.wellingtonfoods.com
SIC: 2099 Food preparations

(P-2548)
WORLDWIDE SPECIALTIES INC
Also Called: California Specialty Farms
2420 Modoc St, Los Angeles (90021-2916)
PHONE..................323 587-2200
Mady Joes, Manager
Bruce Hoffman, General Mgr
Lizandro Cisneros, Purchasing
EMP: 120 Privately Held
WEB: www.californiaspecialtyfarms.com
SIC: 2099 Almond pastes
PA: Worldwide Specialties, Inc.
2421 E 16th St 1
Los Angeles CA 90021

2111 Cigarettes

(P-2549)
HOOK IT UP
1513 S Grand Ave, Santa Ana (92705-4410)
PHONE..................714 600-0100
Zack Zakari, CEO
EMP: 18 EST: 2014
SQ FT: 5,000
SALES (est): 770.1K Privately Held
SIC: 2111 Cigarettes

(P-2550)
PHILIP MORRIS USA INC
185 Technology Dr, Irvine (92618-2412)
PHONE..................949 453-3500
EMP: 69

SALES (corp-wide): 25.4B Publicly Held
SIC: 2111 Mfg Cigarettes
HQ: Philip Morris Usa Inc.
6601 W Brd St
Richmond VA 23230
804 274-2000

(P-2551)
RECELL USA INC
Also Called: Tobacco Crush
10321 Magnolia Ave, Riverside (92505-1809)
PHONE..................951 353-1600
EMP: 14 EST: 2014
SALES (est): 4.9MM Privately Held
SIC: 2111 Cigarettes

(P-2552)
SMOKELESS SELECTS LLC (PA)
27576 Commerce Center Dr # 114, Temecula (92590-2537)
PHONE..................619 564-8250
Eddie Quiroz, Managing Prtnr
EMP: 14 EST: 2010
SALES (est): 1.1MM Privately Held
WEB: www.smokefreemail.com
SIC: 2111 Cigarettes

(P-2553)
USA SALES INC
Also Called: Statewide Distributors
1560 S Archibald Ave, Ontario (91761-7629)
PHONE..................909 390-9606
Kabiruddin Ali, CEO
EMP: 20 EST: 2005
SALES (est): 4.4MM Privately Held
WEB: www.usasalesinc.net
SIC: 2111 2121 Cigarettes; cigars

(P-2554)
VITACIG INC
433 N Camden Dr Fl 6, Beverly Hills (90210-4416)
PHONE..................310 402-6937
Paul Rosenberg, CEO
Mike Hawkins, CFO
EMP: 24 EST: 2016
SALES (est): 1MM Publicly Held
WEB: www.bots.bz
SIC: 2111 Cigarettes
PA: Bots, Inc.
2901 S Highland Dr 3b
Las Vegas NV 89109
570 778-6459

2131 Tobacco, Chewing & Snuff

(P-2555)
FANTASIA DISTRIBUTION INC
Also Called: Fantasia Hookah Tobacco
1566 W Embassy St, Anaheim (92802-1016)
PHONE..................714 817-8300
Randy Jacob Bahbah, CEO
Issa Bahbah, CFO
◆ EMP: 13 EST: 2007
SALES (est): 2.2MM Privately Held
WEB: www.fantasiadistribution.com
SIC: 2131 Smoking tobacco

2211 Cotton, Woven Fabric

(P-2556)
ALSTYLE APPAREL LLC
1501 E Cerritos Ave, Anaheim (92805-6400)
PHONE..................714 765-0400
EMP: 2835 EST: 2014
SALES (est): 583K
SALES (corp-wide): 1.3B Privately Held
SIC: 2211 Apparel & outerwear fabrics, cotton
HQ: Alstyle Apparel & Activewear Management Co.
1501 E Cerritos Ave
Anaheim CA 92805
714 765-0400

(P-2557)
AMERICAN APPAREL RETAIL INC (DH)
747 Warehouse St, Los Angeles (90021-1106)
P.O. Box 5129, Brandon MS (39047-5129)
PHONE..................213 488-0226
Paula Schneider, *CEO*
Son Nguyen, *Planning*
Jerome Reynolds, *Credit Mgr*
Miguel Elizarraraz, *Analyst*
Kaitlyn Estaba, *Sales Associate*
◆ **EMP:** 100 **EST:** 2004
SALES (est): 27.1MM
SALES (corp-wide): 1.9B **Privately Held**
WEB: www.americanapparel.com
SIC: 2211 Apparel & outerwear fabrics, cotton
HQ: App Winddown, Llc
747 Warehouse St
Los Angeles CA 90021
213 488-0226

(P-2558)
APTAN CORP
2000 S Main St, Los Angeles (90007-1420)
PHONE..................213 748-5271
Ronald Tanzman, *President*
EMP: 33 **EST:** 1972
SQ FT: 10,000
SALES (est): 1.6MM **Privately Held**
WEB: www.aptan-corp.com
SIC: 2211 2396 Linings & interlinings, cotton; elastic fabrics, cotton; pads, shoulder: for coats, suits, etc.

(P-2559)
BELAGIO ENTERPRISES INC
3737 Ross St, Vernon (90058-1635)
PHONE..................323 731-6934
Ruben Melamed, *CEO*
Danny Elyassi, *Vice Pres*
Debi Schmitz, *Sales Staff*
▲ **EMP:** 20 **EST:** 2002
SALES (est): 9MM **Privately Held**
WEB: www.belagioenterprises.com
SIC: 2211 2269 Decorative trim & specialty fabrics, including twist weave; decorative finishing of narrow fabrics

(P-2560)
BONDED FIBERLOFT INC
2748 Tanager Ave, Commerce (90040-2721)
PHONE..................323 726-7820
Mark Bidner, *CEO*
Mike Wood, *CFO*
EMP: 299 **EST:** 1998
SQ FT: 96,000
SALES (est): 1MM **Privately Held**
WEB: www.relianceproducts.mb.ca
SIC: 2211 2823 2299 Broadwoven fabric mills, cotton; cellulosic manmade fibers; batts & batting: cotton mill waste & related material
PA: Western Synthetic Fiber Inc
2 Atlantic Ave Fl 4
Boston MA

(P-2561)
CALA ACTION INC
2440 Troy Ave, South El Monte (91733-1432)
PHONE..................213 272-9759
Hongfang LI, *CEO*
EMP: 20 **EST:** 2017
SALES (est): 1.2MM **Privately Held**
SIC: 2211 Apparel & outerwear fabrics, cotton

(P-2562)
CENTRIC BRANDS INC
Also Called: Joe's Dsert Hlls Prmium Otlets
48650 Seminole Dr Ste 170, Cabazon (92230-2118)
PHONE..................951 797-5077
EMP: 49 **Privately Held**
WEB: www.centricbrands.com
SIC: 2211 Denims
PA: Centric Brands Llc
350 5th Ave Fl 6
New York NY 10118

(P-2563)
CENTRIC BRANDS INC
Also Called: Joe's Jeans
1500 Cotner Ave Ste 1, Los Angeles (90025-3303)
PHONE..................323 837-3700
Chris Muller, *Exec VP*
Rico Robles, *Opers Staff*
EMP: 49 **Privately Held**
WEB: www.centricbrands.com
SIC: 2211 Denims
PA: Centric Brands Llc
350 5th Ave Fl 6
New York NY 10118

(P-2564)
COLORMAX INDUSTRIES INC (PA)
1627 Paloma St, Los Angeles (90021-3013)
PHONE..................213 748-6600
Gholamreza Amighi, *President*
Goodarz Haydarzadeh, *CEO*
REA Neri, *Controller*
EMP: 25 **EST:** 1988
SQ FT: 64,000
SALES (est): 3.6MM **Privately Held**
WEB: www.colormax.us
SIC: 2211 2269 2261 2254 Broadwoven fabric mills, cotton; finishing plants; finishing plants, cotton; dyeing & finishing knit underwear

(P-2565)
COTTYON INC
Also Called: Cotty On
2202 E Anderson St, Vernon (90058-3451)
PHONE..................323 589-1563
EMP: 20
SALES (est): 1.9MM **Privately Held**
SIC: 2211 Cotton Broadwoven Fabric Mill

(P-2566)
CREATIVE COSTUMING DESIGNS INC
15402 Electronic Ln, Huntington Beach (92649-1334)
PHONE..................714 895-0982
Noreen Roberts, *President*
Kevin Roberts, *CFO*
Marva Aylouche, *Assistant*
Ashley Porter, *Associate*
EMP: 35 **EST:** 2009
SQ FT: 5,300
SALES (est): 2.7MM **Privately Held**
WEB: www.creative-costuming.com
SIC: 2211 Apparel & outerwear fabrics, cotton

(P-2567)
DEAR JOHN DENIM INC
Also Called: Dear John American Classic
12318 Lower Azusa Rd, Arcadia (91006-5872)
PHONE..................626 350-5100
Chiu Yeung, *CEO*
▲ **EMP:** 15 **EST:** 2013
SALES (est): 2MM **Privately Held**
WEB: www.dearjohndenim.com
SIC: 2211 Denims

(P-2568)
DYNAMIC DENIM CORPORATION
5609 Mckinley Ave, Los Angeles (90011-5225)
PHONE..................323 232-2524
Martin Barrack, *CEO*
EMP: 13 **EST:** 2014
SALES (est): 1.1MM **Privately Held**
WEB: www.dynamicdenim.com
SIC: 2211 Denims

(P-2569)
EAST SHORE GARMENT COMPANY LLC
2015 E 48th St, Vernon (90058-2021)
PHONE..................323 923-4454
Michael Don Hutchinson,
EMP: 20 **EST:** 2017

SALES (est): 3.2MM
SALES (corp-wide): 58MM **Privately Held**
WEB: www.eastshoregarment.com
SIC: 2211 Broadwoven fabric mills, cotton
PA: Lakeshirts Llc
750 Randolph Rd
Detroit Lakes MN 56501
218 847-2171

(P-2570)
FACTORY ONE STUDIO INC
6700 Avalon Blvd Ste 101, Los Angeles (90003-1920)
PHONE..................323 752-1670
Steve C Rhee, *CEO*
EMP: 52 **EST:** 2017
SALES (est): 10MM **Privately Held**
WEB: www.factoryonestudio.com
SIC: 2211 Denims

(P-2571)
FIRST FINISH INC
11126 Wright Rd, Lynwood (90262-3122)
PHONE..................310 631-6717
Keyomars Fard, *President*
▲ **EMP:** 25 **EST:** 2003
SQ FT: 10,000
SALES (est): 2.6MM **Privately Held**
WEB: www.thefirstfinish.com
SIC: 2211 Jean fabrics

(P-2572)
G KAGAN AND SONS INC (PA)
Also Called: Kagan Trim Center
3957 S Hill St, Los Angeles (90037-1313)
PHONE..................323 583-1400
Jed Kagan, *President*
Maria Juarez, *Executive*
Rod Kagan, *Admin Sec*
Catharine Wassom, *Sales Staff*
◆ **EMP:** 25 **EST:** 1946
SQ FT: 50,000
SALES (est): 5MM **Privately Held**
WEB: www.kagantrim.com
SIC: 2211 Apparel & outerwear fabrics, cotton

(P-2573)
GREY STUDIO INC
629 S Clarence St, Los Angeles (90023-1107)
PHONE..................323 780-8111
Kendrick D Kim, *President*
EMP: 13 **EST:** 2005
SALES (est): 361.2K **Privately Held**
SIC: 2211 Denims

(P-2574)
HIDDEN JEANS INC
Also Called: Cello Jeans
7210 Dominion Cir, Commerce (90040-3647)
PHONE..................213 746-4223
Kenny Park, *CEO*
Adam Lee, *Vice Pres*
◆ **EMP:** 30 **EST:** 2007
SQ FT: 4,000
SALES (est): 4.8MM **Privately Held**
SIC: 2211 2339 Denims; jeans: women's, misses' & juniors'

(P-2575)
IMAJEAN NATION INC
3600 E Olympic Blvd, Los Angeles (90023-3121)
PHONE..................323 980-9000
Chung Hee Bae, *President*
EMP: 50 **EST:** 2004
SALES (est): 2.3MM **Privately Held**
SIC: 2211 Denims

(P-2576)
INTEGRATED MARKETING GROUP LLC
528 W Briardale Ave, Orange (92865-4208)
PHONE..................714 771-2401
Gregory Dahlstrom, *Mng Member*
Greg Dahlstrom, *Mng Member*
Lisa Nava, *Manager*
▲ **EMP:** 19 **EST:** 2004
SALES (est): 2.7MM **Privately Held**
WEB: www.integratedmarketing-group.com
SIC: 2211 Apparel & outerwear fabrics, cotton

(P-2577)
JML TEXTILE INC
Also Called: W & M Textile
5801 S 2nd St, Vernon (90058-3403)
PHONE..................323 584-2323
Seung Choon Lim, *CEO*
Seung Hoon Lim, *President*
▲ **EMP:** 23 **EST:** 2005
SQ FT: 350,000
SALES (est): 1.6MM **Privately Held**
SIC: 2211 Apparel & outerwear fabrics, cotton

(P-2578)
KATHRYN M IRELAND INC (PA)
1750 W Adams Blvd, Los Angeles (90018-2704)
PHONE..................323 965-9888
Kathryn Ireland, *President*
Kathryn Landreth, *Consultant*
▲ **EMP:** 125 **EST:** 1998
SQ FT: 1,500
SALES (est): 2MM **Privately Held**
WEB: www.kathrynireland.com
SIC: 2211 7389 Broadwoven fabric mills, cotton; interior design services

(P-2579)
KNIT GENERATION GROUP INC
3818 S Broadway, Los Angeles (90037-1412)
PHONE..................213 221-5081
Joseph Dania, *CEO*
EMP: 25 **EST:** 2013
SALES (est): 2.8MM **Privately Held**
WEB: www.knitgeneration.net
SIC: 2211 Broadwoven fabric mills, cotton

(P-2580)
LOS ANGELES MILLS INC
2331 E 8th St, Los Angeles (90021-1732)
PHONE..................213 622-8031
William G Meyer, *President*
▲ **EMP:** 19 **EST:** 1963
SALES (est): 509.4K **Privately Held**
WEB: www.lamills.net
SIC: 2211 2299 2281 2221 Cotton broad woven goods; yarns, specialty & novelty; yarn spinning mills; broadwoven fabric mills, manmade; throwing & winding mills

(P-2581)
MSP GROUP INC
206 W 140th St, Los Angeles (90061-1006)
PHONE..................310 660-0022
Jong H Lim, *President*
▲ **EMP:** 28 **EST:** 1996
SQ FT: 1,000
SALES (est): 4.8MM **Privately Held**
WEB: www.mspdesigngroup.com
SIC: 2211 Apparel & outerwear fabrics, cotton

(P-2582)
NOT ONLY JEANS INC
3004 S Main St, Los Angeles (90007-3825)
PHONE..................213 765-9725
EMP: 20
SALES (est): 2.2MM **Privately Held**
SIC: 2211 Denim Pants

(P-2583)
NUTRADE INC
Also Called: Dreamworks Knitting
2808 Willis St, Santa Ana (92705-5714)
PHONE..................949 477-2300
Alan Hashemian, *CEO*
▼ **EMP:** 14 **EST:** 1998
SALES (est): 564.1K **Privately Held**
WEB: www.dreamworksknitting.com
SIC: 2211 Apparel & outerwear fabrics, cotton

(P-2584)
NUX GROUP INC
5164 Alcoa Ave, Vernon (90058-3716)
P.O. Box 58102 (90058-0102)
PHONE..................323 780-4700
Malek S Neman, *President*
Christina Jones, *Sales Staff*
Rick Ramseier, *Sales Staff*
EMP: 17 **EST:** 2010
SALES (est): 2.3MM **Privately Held**
WEB: www.nuxactive.com
SIC: 2211 Apparel & outerwear fabrics, cotton

P R O D U C T S & S V C S

(P-2585)
PJY INC
Also Called: Intimo Industry
3251 Leonis Blvd, Vernon (90058-3018)
PHONE................................323 583-7737
Paul Yang, *President*
Jorge Vigil, *Production*
▲ **EMP:** 40 **EST:** 2004
SALES (est): 5.3MM **Privately Held**
WEB: www.intimoindustry.com
SIC: 2211 Long cloth, cotton

(P-2586)
SAITEX (USA) LLC
6074 Malburg Way, Vernon (90058-3946)
PHONE................................323 391-6116
Sanjeev Bahl, *CEO*
EMP: 14 **EST:** 2019
SALES (est): 1.1MM **Privately Held**
SIC: 2211 Denims

(P-2587)
SKY JEANS INC
6600 Avalon Blvd Ste 102, Los Angeles
(90003-1960)
PHONE................................323 778-2065
EMP: 20
SALES (est): 1.1MM **Privately Held**
SIC: 2211 Mfg Denim Clothing

(P-2588)
SLEEPOW LTD
11706 Darlington Ave, Los Angeles
(90049-5517)
PHONE................................646 688-0808
EMP: 40
SQ FT: 600
SALES (est): 2.9MM **Privately Held**
SIC: 2211 Cotton Broadwoven Fabric Mill

(P-2589)
STANZINO INC
17937 Santa Rita St, Encino (91316-3602)
PHONE................................818 602-5171
David Ghods, *Branch Mgr*
EMP: 88
SALES (corp-wide): 4MM **Privately Held**
SIC: 2211 Apparel & outerwear fabrics,
cotton
PA: Stanzino, Inc.
16325 S Avalon Blvd
Gardena CA 90248
213 746-8822

(P-2590)
STANZINO INC (PA)
Also Called: Apparel House USA
16325 S Avalon Blvd, Gardena
(90248-2909)
PHONE................................213 746-8822
David Ghods, *CEO*
EMP: 57 **EST:** 2011
SALES (est): 4MM **Privately Held**
SIC: 2211 Apparel & outerwear fabrics,
cotton

(P-2591)
SUGAR LIPS INC
Also Called: Sugarlips Clothing
2250 Maple Ave, Los Angeles
(90011-1190)
PHONE................................213 742-9001
Charles Park, *Principal*
EMP: 18 **EST:** 2004
SALES (est): 344.9K **Privately Held**
WEB: www.sugarlips.com
SIC: 2211 Apparel & outerwear fabrics,
cotton

(P-2592)
TUA FASHION INC (PA)
Also Called: Tua USA
8936 Appian Way, Los Angeles
(90046-7737)
PHONE................................213 422-2384
Yum Cho, *President*
Mark Cho, *COO*
Andrew Cho, *Principal*
Duck J Cho, *Principal*
EMP: 17 **EST:** 1999
SQ FT: 22,000
SALES (est): 1.7MM **Privately Held**
WEB: www.tuausa.com
SIC: 2211 Apparel & outerwear fabrics,
cotton

(P-2593)
VETERAN ENTERPRISE INC
Also Called: Veteran Company
620 Gladys Ave, Los Angeles
(90021-1004)
PHONE................................323 937-2233
Abraham Tashdjian, *CEO*
Harry Tashdjian, *Manager*
▲ **EMP:** 14 **EST:** 2010
SALES (est): 8.5MM **Privately Held**
WEB: www.veteranco.com
SIC: 2211 2221 Upholstery, tapestry &
wall coverings: cotton; upholstery, tapes-
try & wall covering fabrics

(P-2594)
XCVI LLC (PA)
2311 S Santa Fe Ave, Los Angeles
(90058-1154)
PHONE................................213 749-2661
Alon Zeltzer,
Mordechia Zelter,
Gita Zeltzer,
Tabitha Romero, *Manager*
▲ **EMP:** 120
SQ FT: 60,000
SALES (est): 20.8MM **Privately Held**
WEB: www.xcvi.com
SIC: 2211 Apparel & outerwear fabrics,
cotton; sheets, bedding & table cloths:
cotton

2221 Silk & Man-Made Fiber

(P-2595)
DAE SHIN USA INC
610 N Gilbert St, Fullerton (92833-2555)
PHONE................................714 578-8900
Jae Weon Lee, *CEO*
▲ **EMP:** 100 **EST:** 1999
SQ FT: 10,000
SALES (est): 11MM **Privately Held**
WEB: www.daeshintextile.co.kr
SIC: 2221 Textile mills, broadwoven: silk &
manmade, also glass
PA: Daeshin Textile Co.,Ltd.
16 Haean-Ro 397beon-Gil, Danwon-
Gu
Ansan 15614

(P-2596)
DOOL FNA INC
Also Called: Grand Textile
16624 Edwards Rd, Cerritos (90703-2438)
PHONE................................562 483-4100
Jae Weon Lee, *CEO*
▲ **EMP:** 120
SALES (est): 16.3MM **Privately Held**
SIC: 2221 Textile mills, broadwoven: silk &
manmade, also glass

(P-2597)
FABRICMATE SYSTEMS INC
2781 Golf Course Dr A, Ventura
(93003-7941)
PHONE................................805 642-7470
Craig Lanuza, *President*
Manoj Pradhan, *CFO*
Mike Pradhan, *Officer*
Colleen Burns, *Administration*
Jeff Gompert, *Manager*
▲ **EMP:** 27 **EST:** 1995
SQ FT: 16,116
SALES (est): 5.3MM **Privately Held**
WEB: www.fabricmate.com
SIC: 2221 Upholstery, tapestry & wall cov-
ering fabrics

(P-2598)
FABRITEX INC
2301 E 7th Ste D102, Los Angeles
(90023-1041)
PHONE................................213 747-1417
Kourosh Dayan, *President*
Norick Minisians, *CFO*
▲ **EMP:** 14 **EST:** 1987
SQ FT: 30,000 **Privately Held**
SIC: 2221 5131 Linings, rayon or silk;
piece goods & other fabrics

(P-2599)
FABTEX INC
Also Called: Ft Textiles
1202 W Struck Ave, Orange (92867-3532)
PHONE................................714 538-0877
William P Friese, *Systems Staff*
Glenn Halterman, *Treasurer*
Dave Francis, *Administration*
Matthew Wagner, *Administration*
Lou Newman, *Sales Staff*
EMP: 105
SALES (corp-wide): 49.5MM **Privately
Held**
WEB: www.fabtex.com
SIC: 2221 2515 2392 2391 Draperies &
drapery fabrics, manmade fiber & silk;
bedding, manmade or silk fabric; mat-
tresses & bedsprings; household furnish-
ings; curtains & draperies
PA: Fabtex, Inc.
111 Woodbine Ln
Danville PA 17821
800 778-2791

(P-2600)
JUICY COUTURE INC
1580 Jesse St, Los Angeles (90021-1317)
PHONE................................888 824-8826
Pamela Levy, *CEO*
Ellen Rodriguez, *Senior VP*
Lisa Rodericks, *Admin Sec*
▲ **EMP:** 160 **EST:** 1990
SALES (est): 23.6MM **Publicly Held**
WEB: www.juicycouture.com
SIC: 2221 Broadwoven fabric mills, man-
made
HQ: Kate Spade Holdings Llc
5822 Haverford Ave 2
Philadelphia PA 19131
212 354-4900

(P-2601)
NEXT AUTO TECH CENTER
6821 Crenshaw Blvd, Los Angeles
(90043-4666)
PHONE................................323 483-6767
Jay Park, *Administration*
EMP: 25 **EST:** 2018
SALES (est): 1MM **Privately Held**
WEB: www.next-auto-tech-center.busi-
ness.site
SIC: 2221 Automotive fabrics, manmade
fiber

(P-2602)
POP 82 INC
8211 Orangethorpe Ave, Buena Park
(90621-3811)
PHONE................................714 523-8500
Steven North, *CEO*
Bill Blandin, *Vice Pres*
Marisela Ramos, *Admin Sec*
EMP: 15 **EST:** 2013
SQ FT: 15,000
SALES (est): 1.2MM **Privately Held**
WEB: www.pop82.com
SIC: 2221 7389 Acrylic broadwoven fab-
rics; printing broker

(P-2603)
**S&B DEVELOPMENT GROUP
LLC**
1901 Avenue Of The Stars # 200, Los An-
geles (90067-6001)
PHONE................................213 446-2818
Nathalio Ortez, *CEO*
Bijan Israel, *Mng Member*
EMP: 48 **EST:** 2008
SQ FT: 50,000
SALES (est): 4.1MM **Privately Held**
SIC: 2221 5023 Broadwoven fabric mills,
manmade; sheets, textile

(P-2604)
SPD MANUFACTURING INC
1101 E Truslow Ave, Fullerton
(92831-4625)
PHONE................................985 302-1902
Debra Macaluso, *CEO*
EMP: 19 **EST:** 2018
SALES (est): 1.2MM **Privately Held**
SIC: 2221 Apparel & outerwear fabric,
manmade fiber or silk

(P-2605)
TEXTILE PRODUCTS INC
2512-2520 W Woodland Dr, Anaheim
(92801)
PHONE................................714 761-0401
Piyush A Shah, *CEO*
Kevin Gearin, *Vice Pres*
Susan Canales, *Accountant*
Allyson Baligad, *QC Mgr*
▲ **EMP:** 26 **EST:** 1976
SQ FT: 16,000
SALES (est): 13.8MM **Privately Held**
WEB: www.textileproducts.com
SIC: 2221 Manmade & synthetic broadwo-
ven fabrics
HQ: Kordsa Teknik Tekstil Anonim Sirketi
No:90 Alikahya Fatih Manalelsi
Kocaeli 41100

(P-2606)
TOMASINI INC
1001 E 60th St, Los Angeles (90001-1018)
PHONE................................323 231-2349
Angela Brown, *President*
EMP: 14 **EST:** 1988
SQ FT: 5,500
SALES (est): 389.7K **Privately Held**
WEB: www.tomasinibedding.com
SIC: 2221 5719 Bedding, manmade or silk
fabric; comforters & quilts, manmade fiber
& silk; bedding (sheets, blankets, spreads
& pillows)

(P-2607)
U-SUN TEXTILES INC
3104 E Ana St, Compton (90221-5607)
PHONE................................310 609-1155
EMP: 13 **EST:** 2005
SALES (est): 358.8K **Privately Held**
SIC: 2221 Textile mills, broadwoven: silk &
manmade, also glass

(P-2608)
ZELOUF WEST LTD (PA)
110 E 9th St Ste B743, Los Angeles
(90079-3743)
PHONE................................213 417-1346
Danny Zelouf, *CEO*
▲ **EMP:** 44 **EST:** 2008
SALES (est): 193.3K **Privately Held**
SIC: 2221 2299 Textile mills, broadwoven:
silk & manmade, also glass; fibers, textile:
recovery from textile mill waste & rags

2231 Wool, Woven Fabric

(P-2609)
511 INC (DH)
Also Called: 5.11 Tactical Series
1360 Reynolds Ave Ste 101, Irvine
(92614-5535)
PHONE................................949 800-1511
Thomas Edward Davin, *CEO*
Dan Costa, *President*
Jeff Hamilton, *CFO*
Thomas Ashbrook, *Vice Pres*
Francisco Morales, *Vice Pres*
◆ **EMP:** 269 **EST:** 2003
SQ FT: 93,000
SALES (est): 151.2MM **Publicly Held**
WEB: www.511tactical.com
SIC: 5699 2231 2393 Uniforms; ap-
parel & outerwear broadwoven fabrics;
boots; canvas bags
HQ: 5.11 Ta, Inc.
4300 Spyres Way
Modesto CA 95356
209 527-4511

(P-2610)
**AMERICAN AP DYG & FINSHG
INC**
747 Warehouse St, Los Angeles
(90021-1106)
P.O. Box 5129, Brandon MS (39047-5129)
PHONE................................310 644-4001
Sang Ho Lim, *President*
Joe Yi, *Office Mgr*
▲ **EMP:** 46 **EST:** 2004
SALES (est): 7.3MM
SALES (corp-wide): 1.9B **Privately Held**
SIC: 2231 Dyeing & finishing: wool or simi-
lar fibers

HQ: App Winddown, Llc
747 Warehouse St
Los Angeles CA 90021
213 488-0226

(P-2611)
COMFORT INDUSTRIES INC
12266 Rooks Rd, Whittier (90601-1613)
PHONE....................................562 692-8288
Kevin Do, *CEO*
Ken Quach, *Vice Pres*
Kevin Deal, *Admin Sec*
Michael Tang, *Sales Staff*
◆ EMP: 35 EST: 1998
SQ FT: 18,000
SALES (est): 4.5MM **Privately Held**
WEB: www.comfortind.com
SIC: 2231 Upholstery fabrics, wool

(P-2612)
FAM LLC (PA)
Also Called: Fam Brands
5553-B Bandini Blvd, Bell (90201)
PHONE....................................323 888-7755
Frank Zarabi, *President*
Carrie Henley, *President*
Etienne Capgras, *Vice Pres*
Norah Emamjomeh, *Vice Pres*
Jennifer Reier, *Surgery Dir*
▲ EMP: 152 EST: 1985
SQ FT: 75,000
SALES (est): 102.3MM **Privately Held**
WEB: www.fambrands.com
SIC: 2231 Apparel & outerwear broadwoven fabrics

(P-2613)
LEKOS DYE & FINISHING INC
3131 E Harcourt St, Compton
(90221-5505)
PHONE....................................310 763-0900
Ilgun Lee, *President*
Daniel Lee, *CFO*
▲ EMP: 65 EST: 2003
SQ FT: 72,000
SALES (est): 6.5MM **Privately Held**
SIC: 2231 Dyeing & finishing: wool or similar fibers

(P-2614)
TRI-STAR DYEING & FINSHG INC
15125 Marquardt Ave, Santa Fe Springs
(90670-5705)
PHONE....................................562 483-0123
Jang You, *Principal*
▲ EMP: 63 EST: 2006
SQ FT: 60,000
SALES (est): 8.1MM **Privately Held**
WEB: www.tristar-df.com
SIC: 2231 Dyeing & finishing: wool or similar fibers

2241 Fabric Mills, Cotton, Wool, Silk & Man-Made

(P-2615)
AX II INC
Also Called: Gin'l Fabrics
13921 S Figueroa St, Los Angeles
(90061-1027)
PHONE....................................310 292-6523
Anthony Xepolis, *President*
Ginny Xepolis, *Vice Pres*
EMP: 18 EST: 1981
SALES (est): 518.3K **Privately Held**
SIC: 2241 2396 Narrow fabric mills; automotive & apparel trimmings

(P-2616)
CHUA & SONS CO INC
Also Called: Reliable Tape Products
3300 E 50th St, Vernon (90058-3004)
P.O. Box 58261, Los Angeles (90058-0261)
PHONE....................................323 588-8044
Shirley Chua, *President*
▲ EMP: 23 EST: 1984
SQ FT: 67,000
SALES (est): 3.1MM **Privately Held**
SIC: 2241 Fabric tapes

(P-2617)
MAKO INC
736 Monterey Pass Rd, Monterey Park
(91754-3607)
PHONE....................................323 262-2168
John Chaing, *President*
Jenney Tsung, *Vice Pres*
◆ EMP: 13 EST: 1989
SALES (est): 1.2MM **Privately Held**
WEB: www.makoinc.com
SIC: 2241 Trimmings, textile

(P-2618)
SANTA FE TEXTILES INC
17370 Mount Herrmann St, Fountain Valley
(92708-4104)
PHONE....................................949 251-1960
Fax: 949 251-9006
EMP: 18
SQ FT: 25,000
SALES (est): 1.4MM **Privately Held**
SIC: 2241 3496 Mfg Textile & Wire Braiding

(P-2619)
**WEST COAST TRIMMINGS CORP
(PA)**
7100 Wilson Ave, Los Angeles
(90001-2249)
PHONE....................................323 587-0701
Arnold F Pretz Jr, *President*
Robert D Clarke, *Treasurer*
James R McBride, *Vice Pres*
▲ EMP: 18 EST: 1922
SQ FT: 12,000 **Privately Held**
WEB: www.westcoasttrimming.com
SIC: 2241 5131 Trimmings, textile; drapery material, woven

2252 Hosiery, Except Women's

(P-2620)
GILDAN USA INC
28200 Highway 189, Lake Arrowhead
(92352-9700)
PHONE....................................909 485-1475
EMP: 45
SALES (corp-wide): 1.9B **Privately Held**
WEB: www.gildancorp.com
SIC: 2252 Hosiery
HQ: Gildan Usa Inc.
1980 Clements Ferry Rd
Charleston SC 29492

(P-2621)
GOLDEN GATE HOSIERY INC
14095 Laurelwood Pl, Chino (91710-5495)
PHONE....................................909 464-0805
Sang Hoon Moon, *President*
SAE Yang Chang, *Corp Secy*
▲ EMP: 13 EST: 1997
SQ FT: 13,000
SALES (est): 393.7K **Privately Held**
WEB: www.ggsocks.com
SIC: 2252 Socks

(P-2622)
SAY IT WITH A SOCK LLC
11111 Santa Monica Blvd, Los Angeles
(90025-3333)
PHONE....................................800 208-0879
EMP: 14
SALES (corp-wide): 614.4K **Privately
Held**
WEB: www.sayitwithasock.com
SIC: 2252 Socks
PA: Say It With A Sock Llc
10200 Venice Blvd Ste 108
Culver City CA 90232
424 284-8416

(P-2623)
SAY IT WITH A SOCK LLC (PA)
10200 Venice Blvd Ste 108, Culver City
(90232-3347)
PHONE....................................424 284-8416
Daniel Elan Seeff, *Principal*
EMP: 27 EST: 2016
SALES (est): 614.4K **Privately Held**
WEB: www.sayitwithasock.com
SIC: 2252 Socks

(P-2624)
UNIVERSAL HOSIERY INC
28337 Constellation Rd, Valencia
(91355-5048)
PHONE....................................661 702-8444
Johnathan Ekizian, *President*
▲ EMP: 75 EST: 1994
SQ FT: 44,000
SALES (est): 4.8MM **Privately Held**
WEB: www.universalhosiery.com
SIC: 2252 Socks

(P-2625)
US HOSIERY INC
1415 S Main St, Los Angeles (90015-2501)
PHONE....................................213 742-0101
Chong S Won, *CEO*
▲ EMP: 18 EST: 2000
SALES (est): 1.3MM **Privately Held**
WEB: www.ushosieryshop.com
SIC: 2252 Socks

2253 Knit Outerwear Mills

(P-2626)
BALL OF COTTON INC
6400 E Wash Blvd Unit 10, Commerce
(90040-1820)
PHONE....................................323 888-9448
Eddy Park, *President*
Elizabeth Park, *Vice Pres*
EMP: 13 EST: 1991
SQ FT: 7,000
SALES (est): 1MM **Privately Held**
WEB: www.ballofcottonusa.com
SIC: 2253 Sweaters & sweater coats, knit

(P-2627)
BYER CALIFORNIA
Alfred Paquette Division
1201 Rio Vista Ave, Los Angeles
(90023-2609)
PHONE....................................323 780-7615
Jan Shostak, *Manager*
Dan Shostak, *Prdtn Mgr*
EMP: 56
SQ FT: 10,000
SALES (corp-wide): 289MM **Privately
Held**
WEB: www.byerca.com
SIC: 2253 2339 2335 Dresses, knit;
women's & misses' outerwear; women's,
juniors' & misses' dresses
PA: Byer California
66 Potrero Ave
San Francisco CA 94103
415 626-7844

(P-2628)
COMPLETE GARMENT INC
2101 E 38th St, Vernon (90058-1616)
PHONE....................................323 846-3731
Steven Shaul, *CEO*
EMP: 21 EST: 2000
SQ FT: 40,000
SALES (est): 1.5MM **Privately Held**
SIC: 2253 Dyeing & finishing knit outerwear, excl. hosiery & glove

(P-2629)
**DELTA PACIFIC ACTIVEWEAR
INC**
331 S Hale Ave, Fullerton (92831-4805)
PHONE....................................714 871-9281
Imran Parekh, *President*
▲ EMP: 80 EST: 1998
SALES (est): 8MM **Privately Held**
WEB: www.delpacific.com
SIC: 2253 2331 2321 T-shirts & tops, knit;
women's & misses' blouses & shirts;
men's & boys' furnishings

(P-2630)
DM COLLECTIVE INC
4536 District Blvd, Vernon (90058-2712)
PHONE....................................323 923-2400
Daniel S Lee, *CEO*
Monica Lee, *CFO*
▲ EMP: 18 EST: 1997
SALES (est): 1.2MM **Privately Held**
SIC: 2253 5131 Warm weather knit outerwear, including beachwear; knit fabrics

(P-2631)
**FANTASY ACTIVEWEAR INC
(PA)**
Also Called: Fantasy Manufacturing
5383 Alcoa Ave, Vernon (90058-3734)
PHONE....................................213 705-4111
Anwar Gajiani, *President*
Yassmin Gajiani, *Vice Pres*
▲ EMP: 144 EST: 1991
SQ FT: 20,000
SALES (est): 21.8MM **Privately Held**
SIC: 2253 2331 2321 T-shirts & tops, knit;
women's & misses' blouses & shirts;
men's & boys' furnishings

(P-2632)
**FANTASY DYEING & FINISHING
INC**
5383 Alcoa Ave, Vernon (90058-3734)
PHONE....................................323 983-9988
Anwar M Gajiani, *CEO*
EMP: 36 EST: 2003
SALES (est): 4.1MM **Privately Held**
SIC: 2253 Dyeing & finishing knit outerwear, excl. hosiery & glove

(P-2633)
FORTUNE SWIMWEAR LLC (HQ)
Also Called: CHARLIE JADE
2340 E Olympic Blvd Ste A, Los Angeles
(90021-2544)
PHONE....................................310 733-2130
Fred Kayne, *Mng Member*
Ann Kennedy, *CFO*
Alan Shamma, *Engineer*
Adeline Kevorkian, *Controller*
Delia Chang, *Production*
◆ EMP: 30 EST: 2002
SQ FT: 10,000
SALES: 163.4K **Privately Held**
WEB: www.coaststylegroupbrands.com
SIC: 2253 2335 Bathing suits & swimwear,
knit; women's, juniors' & misses' dresses

(P-2634)
FUTURESTITCH INC
144 Avenida Serra, San Clemente
(92672-4759)
PHONE....................................760 707-2003
Taylor Shupe, *CEO*
EMP: 15 EST: 2018
SALES (est): 23.5MM **Privately Held**
WEB: www.futurestitch.com
SIC: 2253 Knit outerwear mills

(P-2635)
GARDENA TEXTILE INC
245 W 135th St, Los Angeles (90061-1625)
PHONE....................................310 327-5060
EMP: 18
SQ FT: 22,000
SALES (est): 106K **Privately Held**
SIC: 2253 Knitting Mill And Whol Fabric

(P-2636)
HIGH-END KNITWEAR INC
Also Called: T Q M Apparel Group
1100 S Hope St Ph 202, Los Angeles
(90015-2197)
PHONE....................................323 582-6061
EMP: 35
SQ FT: 30,000
SALES (est): 3.9MM **Privately Held**
SIC: 2253 Knit Outerwear Mill

(P-2637)
ISIQALO LLC
Also Called: Spectra USA
5610 Daniels St, Chino (91710-9024)
PHONE....................................714 683-2820
Thomas Fenchel,
Nick Agakanian,
▼ EMP: 350 EST: 2012
SALES (est): 75MM **Privately Held**
WEB: www.spectrausa.net
SIC: 2253 5136 5137 2321 T-shirts &
tops, knit; jackets, knit; men's & boys'
clothing; women's & children's clothing;
sport shirts, men's & boys': from purchased materials; T-shirts & tops,
women's: made from purchased materials

(P-2638)
JBS PRIVATE LABEL INC
Also Called: J B'S Private Label
4383 Irvine Ave, Studio City (91604-2705)
P.O. Box 1898 (91614-0898)
PHONE..................................818 762-3736
EMP: 28
SQ FT: 2,500
SALES (est): 700K **Privately Held**
SIC: 2253 5199 2339 2337 Knit Outer-
wear Mill Whol Nondurable Goods Mfg
Women/Miss Outerwear

(P-2639)
MJCK CORPORATION
Also Called: Xzavier
3222 E Washington Blvd, Vernon
(90058-8022)
PHONE..................................888 992-8437
Tae Y Choi, *President*
EMP: 17 EST: 2010
SALES (est): 726.7K **Privately Held**
SIC: 2253 2361 T-shirts & tops, knit; t-
shirts & tops: girls', children's & infants'

(P-2640)
PATTERN KNITTING MILLS INC
7963 Paramount Blvd, Pico Rivera
(90660-4809)
PHONE..................................310 801-1126
Amir Asgarynejad, *President*
Ray Mariano, *Bookkeeper*
EMP: 25 EST: 1988
SQ FT: 60,000
SALES (est): 1.5MM **Privately Held**
SIC: 2253 Knit outerwear mills

(P-2641)
STUDIO9D8 INC
9743 Alesia St, South El Monte
(91733-3008)
PHONE..................................626 350-0832
Ann Lem, *CEO*
EMP: 30 EST: 2011
SALES (est): 5.5MM **Privately Held**
WEB: www.studio9d8.com
SIC: 2253 2515 T-shirts & tops, knit; stu-
dio couches

(P-2642)
STYLE KNITS INC
1745 Chapin Rd, Montebello (90640-6609)
PHONE..................................323 890-9080
Patrick Quinn, *President*
EMP: 15 EST: 1987
SALES (est): 575.4K **Privately Held**
SIC: 2253 Knit outerwear mills

(P-2643)
THIENES APPAREL INC
1811 Floradale Ave, South El Monte
(91733-3605)
PHONE..................................626 575-2818
Chao Wen Chang, *Principal*
▲ EMP: 31 EST: 1997
SQ FT: 17,500
SALES (est): 3MM **Privately Held**
WEB: www.thienes.com
SIC: 2253 Blouses, knit

(P-2644)
YOUNG KNITTING MILLS
3499 E 15th St, Los Angeles (90023-3833)
PHONE..................................323 980-8677
Fax: 323 980-5198
EMP: 21
SQ FT: 25,000
SALES (est): 961.3K **Privately Held**
SIC: 2253 Operates A Knit Outerwear Mill

2254 Knit Underwear Mills

(P-2645)
MEUNDIES INC
3650 Holdrege Ave, Los Angeles
(90016-4304)
PHONE..................................888 552-6775
Jonathan Shokrian, *CEO*
Ashley Smith, *Officer*
Noah Taubman, *Vice Pres*
Andrew Teague, *Creative Dir*
Adrienne Steele, *Executive Asst*
EMP: 40 EST: 2011
SQ FT: 2,500

SALES (est): 4.8MM **Privately Held**
WEB: www.meundies.com
SIC: 5611 5621 2254 Men's & boys' clothing stores; women's clothing stores; nightwear (nightgowns, negligees, pajamas),
knit

2257 Circular Knit Fabric Mills

(P-2646)
MATCHMASTER DYG & FINSHG INC
Antex Knitting Mills
3750 Broadway Pl, Los Angeles
(90007-4400)
PHONE..................................323 232-2061
EMP: 65
SALES (corp-wide): 123.1MM **Privately
Held**
SIC: 2257 5199 Weft Knit Fabric Mill Whol
Nondurable Goods
PA: Matchmaster Dyeing & Finishing, Inc.
3750 S Broadway
Los Angeles CA 90007
323 232-2061

(P-2647)
SHARA-TEX INC
3338 E Slauson Ave, Vernon (90058-3915)
PHONE..................................323 587-7200
Shahram Fahimian, *Ch of Bd*
S Tony Souferian, *President*
▲ EMP: 45
SQ FT: 55,000
SALES (est): 8.6MM **Privately Held**
WEB: www.shara-tex.com
SIC: 2257 Weft knit fabric mills

(P-2648)
TENENBLATT CORPORATION
Also Called: Antex Knitting Mills
3750 Broadway Pl, Los Angeles
(90007-4400)
PHONE..................................323 232-2061
William Tenenblatt, *President*
Anna Tenenblatt, *Vice Pres*
◆ EMP: 96 EST: 1973
SQ FT: 60,000
SALES (est): 3MM
SALES (corp-wide): 66.3MM **Privately
Held**
WEB: www.antexknitting.com
SIC: 2257 Dyeing & finishing circular knit
fabrics
PA: Matchmaster Dyeing & Finishing, Inc.
3750 S Broadway
Los Angeles CA 90007
323 232-2061

2258 Lace & Warp Knit Fabric Mills

(P-2649)
COSMO TEXTILES INC
13984 Orange Ave, Paramount
(90723-2029)
PHONE..................................562 220-1177
Chul Kang, *President*
Andrew Kim, *Shareholder*
Joseph Myung, *Corp Secy*
Jun Lee, *MIS Dir*
Hyung Choi, *Controller*
EMP: 60 EST: 1995
SQ FT: 45,000
SALES (est): 6.1MM **Privately Held**
SIC: 2258 2257 Cloth, warp knit; weft knit
fabric mills

(P-2650)
PRIME ALLIANCE LLC
360 W Victoria St, Compton (90220-6061)
PHONE..................................310 764-1000
EMP: 50
SQ FT: 60,000
SALES: 7.2MM **Privately Held**
SIC: 2258 Fabric Dyeing

2259 Knitting Mills, NEC

(P-2651)
AZITEX TRADING CORP
Also Called: Azitex Knitting Mills
1850 E 15th St, Los Angeles (90021-2820)
PHONE..................................213 745-7072
Michael Azizi, *President*
Andrew Azizi, *Corp Secy*
Mozie Azizi, *Vice Pres*
▲ EMP: 60 EST: 1986
SQ FT: 50,000
SALES (est): 9.7MM **Privately Held**
WEB: www.azitex-trading-co-knitting-
mills.business.site
SIC: 2259 2253 Convertors, knit goods;
knit outerwear mills

(P-2652)
COTTON KNITS TRADING
3097 E Ana St, Compton (90221-5604)
PHONE..................................310 884-9600
Ali Farid, *President*
Hadi E Farid, *Vice Pres*
▲ EMP: 23 EST: 1988
SQ FT: 110,000
SALES (est): 1MM **Privately Held**
SIC: 2259 Bags & bagging, knit

(P-2653)
MIDTHRUST IMPORTS INC
830 E 14th Pl, Los Angeles (90021-2120)
PHONE..................................213 749-6651
Kamran Noman, *CEO*
Farschad Abolfathi, *Prdtn Mgr*
▲ EMP: 20 EST: 1983
SALES (est): 3.3MM **Privately Held**
WEB: www.kiosk.midthrust.com
SIC: 2259 Convertors, knit goods

(P-2654)
SAS TEXTILES INC
3100 E 44th St, Vernon (90058-2406)
PHONE..................................323 277-5555
Sohrab Sassounian, *President*
Albert Sassounian, *Treasurer*
Soheil Sassounian, *Vice Pres*
Miriam Galeon, *Asst Controller*
▲ EMP: 70 EST: 1991
SQ FT: 40,000
SALES (est): 15.5MM **Privately Held**
WEB: www.sastextile.com
SIC: 2259 2257 7389 Convertors, knit
goods; weft knit fabric mills; textile & ap-
parel services

2261 Cotton Fabric Finishers

(P-2655)
AS MATCH DYEING CO INC
Also Called: National Dyeing
2522 E 37th St, Vernon (90058-1725)
PHONE..................................323 277-0470
Geun Jo Cha, *President*
Young C Kim, *Admin Sec*
▲ EMP: 109 EST: 1995
SQ FT: 60,000
SALES (est): 5.3MM **Privately Held**
WEB: www.hitexdyeing.com
SIC: 2261 2262 2269 Finishing plants,
cotton; finishing plants, manmade fiber &
silk fabrics; finishing plants

(P-2656)
BIG STUDIO INC
1247 E Hill St, Long Beach (90755-3523)
PHONE..................................562 989-2444
Mitchell Kron, *President*
EMP: 14 EST: 1993
SQ FT: 11,424
SALES (est): 1.2MM **Privately Held**
WEB: www.bigstudio.com
SIC: 2261 Screen printing of cotton broad-
woven fabrics

(P-2657)
CAITAC GARMENT PROCESSING INC
14725 S Broadway, Gardena (90248-1813)
PHONE..................................310 217-9888
Muneyuki Ishii, *CEO*
Azusa Sahara, *CFO*
Daisy Rodriguez, *Admin Asst*

Hiroyuki Shigenai, *CIO*
Griselda Contreras, *Personnel Assit*
▲ EMP: 270 EST: 1991
SQ FT: 200,000
SALES (est): 40.7MM **Privately Held**
WEB: www.caitacgarment.com
SIC: 2261 2339 2325 5651 Screen print-
ing of cotton broadwoven fabrics;
women's & misses' outerwear; men's &
boys' trousers & slacks; jeans stores; em-
broidery kits
PA: Caitac Holdings Corp.
3-12, Showacho, Kita-Ku
Okayama OKA 700-0

(P-2658)
HARRYS DYE AND WASH INC
1015 E Orangethorpe Ave, Anaheim
(92801-1135)
PHONE..................................714 446-0300
Harry Choung, *President*
Kang Ho Lee, *Vice Pres*
EMP: 30 EST: 1994
SQ FT: 20,000
SALES (est): 3.3MM **Privately Held**
SIC: 2261 2269 Finishing plants, cotton;
finishing plants

(P-2659)
LORBER INDUSTRIES CALIFORNIA
Also Called: Lorber Industries of Claif
823 N Roxbury Dr, Beverly Hills
(90210-3017)
PHONE..................................310 275-1568
Tom Lorber, *President*
John Robertson, *CFO*
Michael Gruener, *Vice Pres*
Greg Lorber, *Vice Pres*
Michael Painter, *Vice Pres*
EMP: 24 EST: 1969
SALES (est): 2.2MM **Privately Held**
SIC: 2261 2262 2253 2257 Screen printing of cotton broadwoven fabrics; bleach-
ing cotton broadwoven fabrics; shrinking
cotton cloth; napping of cotton broadwoven fabrics; screen printing: manmade
fiber & silk broadwoven fabrics; bleach-
ing: manmade fiber & silk broadwoven
fabrics; shrinking: manmade fiber & silk
cloth; napping: manmade fiber & silk
broadwoven fabrics; knit outerwear mills;
weft knit fabric mills

(P-2660)
TFCF INC
11718 Burke St, Santa Fe Springs
(90670-2504)
PHONE..................................562 469-3444
Justin Cho, *CEO*
EMP: 15 EST: 2018
SALES (est): 1.8MM **Privately Held**
WEB: www.tfcfcorp.com
SIC: 2261 2253 2211 2221 Screen printing of cotton broadwoven fabrics; dyeing
& finishing knit outerwear, excl. hosiery &
glove; apparel & outerwear fabrics, cotton; apparel & outerwear fabric, manmade fiber or silk

(P-2661)
TOMORROWS LOOK INC
Also Called: Dimensions In Screen Printing
17462 Von Karman Ave, Irvine
(92614-6206)
PHONE..................................949 596-8400
Steven E Mellgren, *CEO*
Torrey Mellgren, *Admin Sec*
EMP: 70 EST: 1986
SQ FT: 36,000
SALES (est): 6MM **Privately Held**
SIC: 2261 Screen printing of cotton broad-
woven fabrics

(P-2662)
WASHINGTON GRMENT DYG FNSHG IN
1332 E 18th St, Los Angeles (90021-3027)
PHONE..................................213 747-1111
Pradip Shah, *Manager*
EMP: 35

128   2022 Southern California Business
Directory and Buyers Guide   ▲ = Import ▼=Export
◆ =Import/Export

SALES (corp-wide): 3.8MM Privately Held
WEB: www.washingtongarment.com
SIC: 2261 2262 Finishing plants, cotton; finishing plants, manmade fiber & silk fabrics
PA: Washington Garment Dyeing & Finishing, Inc.
1341 E Washington Blvd
Los Angeles CA 90021
213 747-1111

2262 Silk & Man-Made Fabric Finishers

(P-2663)
FINAL FINISH INC
10910 Norwalk Blvd, Santa Fe Springs (90670-3828)
PHONE..........................562 777-7774
Luis Ibarria, President
EMP: 19 EST: 1987
SQ FT: 20,000
SALES (est): 1.3MM Privately Held
SIC: 2262 Preshrinking: manmade fiber & silk broadwoven fabrics; dyeing: manmade fiber & silk broadwoven fabrics

(P-2664)
INX PRINTS INC
1802 Kettering, Irvine (92614-5618)
PHONE..........................949 660-9190
Harold A Haase Jr, CEO
David Van Steenhuyse, Owner
▼ EMP: 100 EST: 2004
SQ FT: 26,000
SALES (est): 16.8MM Privately Held
WEB: www.inx-prints-inc.hub.biz
SIC: 2262 Screen printing: manmade fiber & silk broadwoven fabrics

(P-2665)
SPREADCO INC
803 Us Highway 78, Brawley (92227-9514)
P.O. Box 1400 (92227-1320)
PHONE..........................760 351-0747
Mario Valenzuela, President
Roque Valenzuela, Admin Sec
EMP: 20 EST: 2007
SALES (est): 1.9MM Privately Held
WEB: www.spreadco.net
SIC: 2262 Chemical coating or treating: manmade broadwoven fabrics

(P-2666)
UNIVERSAL DYEING AND PRTG INC
2303 E 11th St, Los Angeles (90021-2846)
PHONE..........................213 746-0818
Kee Sung Hwang, President
Betty Hwang, Admin Sec
▲ EMP: 22 EST: 1990
SQ FT: 95,000
SALES (est): 3.6MM Privately Held
WEB: www.udptextile.com
SIC: 2262 Printing: manmade fiber & silk broadwoven fabrics

(P-2667)
WASHINGTON GARMENT DYEING (PA)
1341 E Washington Blvd, Los Angeles (90021-3037)
PHONE..........................213 747-1111
Vijay Shah, President
Pradip Shah, Vice Pres
EMP: 25 EST: 1988
SQ FT: 20,000
SALES (est): 3.8MM Privately Held
WEB: www.washingtongarment.com
SIC: 2262 2261 2269 Dyeing: manmade fiber & silk broadwoven fabrics; dyeing cotton broadwoven fabrics; finishing plants

2269 Textile Finishers, NEC

(P-2668)
ALMORE DYE HOUSE INC
6850 Tujunga Ave, North Hollywood (91605-6324)
PHONE..........................818 506-5444

Jeffery Teichner, President
Donald Teichner, Vice Pres
Stuart Teichner, Admin Sec
EMP: 32 EST: 1919
SQ FT: 20,000
SALES (est): 2.4MM Privately Held
WEB: www.almoredyehouse.com
SIC: 2269 Dyeing: raw stock yarn & narrow fabrics

(P-2669)
CAL PACIFIC DYEING & FINISHING
233 E Gardena Blvd, Gardena (90248-2800)
PHONE..........................310 327-3792
Russell C Shoemaker, President
Price Shoemaker, CFO
Brian Vieweg, Program Mgr
EMP: 19 EST: 1966
SQ FT: 100,000
SALES (est): 342.4K Privately Held
SIC: 2269 Dyeing: raw stock yarn & narrow fabrics; finishing: raw stock, yarn & narrow fabrics

(P-2670)
EXPO DYEING & FINISHING INC
1365 N Knollwood Cir, Anaheim (92801-1312)
PHONE..........................714 220-9583
Eduardo J Kim, President
▲ EMP: 170 EST: 1987
SQ FT: 86,000
SALES (est): 23.8MM Privately Held
WEB: www.expodye.com
SIC: 2269 Dyeing: raw stock yarn & narrow fabrics

(P-2671)
FREEDOM WOOD FINISHING INC
Also Called: Freedom Finishing
600 Wilshire Blvd # 1200, Los Angeles (90017-3212)
PHONE..........................213 534-6620
Dean Schlaufman, CFO
Richard Pack, Partner
Maya Jackson, Vice Pres
EMP: 16 EST: 1995
SQ FT: 10,000
SALES (est): 722.5K Privately Held
SIC: 2269 Finishing plants

(P-2672)
GEARMENT INC
14801 Able Ln Ste 102, Huntington Beach (92647-2059)
PHONE..........................323 822-9999
Ton Le, President
Tom Le, President
EMP: 100 EST: 2016
SALES (est): 13MM Privately Held
WEB: www.gearment.com
SIC: 2269 Printing of narrow fabrics

(P-2673)
J MICHELLE OF CALIFORNIA
Also Called: Edie Lee
6409 Gayhart St, Commerce (90040-2505)
PHONE..........................323 585-8500
Paul Bogner, President
EMP: 14 EST: 1985
SALES (est): 633K Privately Held
SIC: 2269 Finishing plants

(P-2674)
LINEN SALVAGE ET CIE LLC
1073 Stearns Dr, Los Angeles (90035-2638)
PHONE..........................323 904-3100
Andrea Bernstein, Principal
EMP: 36 EST: 2018
SALES (est): 1.2MM Privately Held
WEB: www.linensalvageetcie.com
SIC: 5719 2269 Linens: linen fabrics: dyeing, finishing & printing

(P-2675)
MATCHMASTER DYG & FINSHG INC
3700 S Broadway, Los Angeles (90007-4434)
PHONE..........................323 233-4281
William Tenenblatt, CEO

EMP: 18
SALES (corp-wide): 66.3MM Privately Held
WEB: www.antexknitting.com
SIC: 2269 Finishing plants
PA: Matchmaster Dyeing & Finishing, Inc.
3750 S Broadway
Los Angeles CA 90007
323 232-2061

(P-2676)
MATCHMASTER DYG & FINSHG INC (PA)
Also Called: Antex Knitting Mills
3750 S Broadway, Los Angeles (90007-4436)
PHONE..........................323 232-2061
William Tenenblatt, President
◆ EMP: 250 EST: 1977
SQ FT: 66,000
SALES (est): 66.3MM Privately Held
WEB: www.antexknitting.com
SIC: 2269 Dyeing: raw stock yarn & narrow fabrics

(P-2677)
PACIFIC COAST BACH LABEL INC
3015 S Grand Ave, Los Angeles (90007-3814)
PHONE..........................213 612-0314
Dan Finnegan, President
Shelly Rojas, Sales Staff
▲ EMP: 23 EST: 1989
SALES (est): 2.1MM Privately Held
WEB: www.pcblabel.com
SIC: 2269 2679 Labels, cotton: printed; labels, paper: made from purchased material

(P-2678)
PACIFIC CONTNTL TEXTILES INC (HQ)
Also Called: Pct
2880 E Ana St, Compton (90221-5602)
PHONE..........................310 604-1100
Edmund Kim, CEO
John Yi, Opers Staff
Matt Nasab, Director
Xochitl Nunez, Manager
◆ EMP: 199 EST: 1983
SALES (est): 29.4MM
SALES (corp-wide): 30.4MM Privately Held
WEB: www.ekii.com
SIC: 2269 2329 Finishing plants; men's & boys' sportswear & athletic clothing
PA: Edmund Kim International, Inc.
2880 E Ana St
Compton CA 90221
310 604-1100

(P-2679)
REZEX CORPORATION
Also Called: Geltman Industries
1930 E 51st St, Vernon (90058-2804)
PHONE..........................213 622-2015
Shari Rezai, President
Amir R Rezai, Vice Pres
Mary Bejines, Finance Mgr
Ron Cueto, Manager
EMP: 25 EST: 1981
SALES (est): 4.1MM Privately Held
WEB: www.geltman.com
SIC: 2269 Finishing plants

(P-2680)
TAG-IT PACIFIC INC
21900 Burbank Blvd # 270, Woodland Hills (91367-7461)
PHONE..........................818 444-4100
Colin Dyne, CEO
Steven Forte, CEO
Cornelia Boylston, Info Tech Dir
◆ EMP: 53 EST: 1991
SALES (est): 7.2MM Privately Held
WEB: www.taloninternational.com
SIC: 2269 Labels, cotton: printed
PA: Talon International, Inc.
21900 Burbank Blvd # 101
Woodland Hills CA 91367

2273 Carpets & Rugs

(P-2681)
AMERICAN COVER DESIGN 26 INC
2131 E 52nd St, Vernon (90058-3498)
PHONE..........................323 582-8666
Daniel Mahgerefteh, CEO
EMP: 19 EST: 2001
SALES (est): 1.3MM Privately Held
WEB: www.americancoverdesign.com
SIC: 2273 Rugs, machine woven

(P-2682)
ATLAS CARPET MILLS INC
3201 S Susan St, Santa Ana (92704-6838)
P.O. Box 11467, Mobile AL (36671-0467)
PHONE..........................323 724-7930
James Horwich, President
Ada Horwich, Vice Pres
Markos Varpas, Vice Pres
Stan Dunford, Executive
Mark Hesther, Executive
▲ EMP: 229 EST: 1969
SALES (est): 42.1MM
SALES (corp-wide): 315.9MM Publicly Held
WEB: www.manningtoncommercial.com
SIC: 2273 Rugs, tufted
HQ: Tdg Operations, Llc
716 Bill Myles Dr
Saraland AL 36571
251 679-3512

(P-2683)
BENTLEY MILLS INC (PA)
14641 Don Julian Rd, City of Industry (91746-3106)
PHONE..........................626 333-4585
Ralph Grogan, President
Jim Harley, COO
Eric Petty, CFO
Aimee Alfonso, Vice Pres
Tom Mee, Vice Pres
◆ EMP: 250
SQ FT: 390,000
SALES (est): 184.7MM Privately Held
WEB: www.bentleymills.com
SIC: 2273 2299 Carpets, textile fiber; batting, wadding, padding & fillings

(P-2684)
CATALINA CARPET MILLS INC (PA)
Also Called: Catalina Home
14418 Best Ave, Santa Fe Springs (90670-5133)
PHONE..........................562 926-5811
Duane Jensen, President
Jack Heinrich, Vice Pres
Jamie Cawelti, Administration
Catherine Vivo, Marketing Staff
Kyle Burnette, Manager
▲ EMP: 57 EST: 1975
SQ FT: 60,000
SALES (est): 11.1MM Privately Held
WEB: www.catalinahome.com
SIC: 2273 5023 Finishers of tufted carpets & rugs; floor coverings

(P-2685)
CREATIVE ACCENTS
6294 Curtis Pl, California City (93505-6006)
P.O. Box 2510, Tehachapi (93581-2510)
PHONE..........................760 373-1222
Mike Hensler, President
Jesse Davis, Manager
▲ EMP: 20 EST: 1967
SQ FT: 22,000
SALES (est): 1.8MM Privately Held
SIC: 2273 Carpets & rugs

(P-2686)
CRITERION SUPPLY INC
6985 Arlington Ave Ste P, Riverside (92503-1524)
PHONE..........................562 222-2382
Jim Voss, Manager
EMP: 19
SALES (corp-wide): 117.7MM Privately Held
WEB: www.interiorlogicgroup.com
SIC: 2273 Carpets & rugs

HQ: Criterion Supply, Inc.
4500 Se Criterion Ct # 100
Portland OR 97222
503 654-0206

(P-2687)
CRITERION SUPPLY INC
13006 Saticoy St Ste 4, North Hollywood
(91605-3512)
PHONE...................................562 222-2382
James Voss, *Manager*
EMP: 19
SALES (corp-wide): 117.7MM **Privately
Held**
WEB: www.interiorlogicgroup.com
SIC: 2273 Carpets & rugs
HQ: Criterion Supply, Inc.
4500 Se Criterion Ct # 100
Portland OR 97222
503 654-0206

(P-2688)
**DECORATORS RUG
WAREHOUSE INC (PA)**
1810 Loma Vista Dr, Beverly Hills
(90210-1929)
PHONE...................................310 638-8300
Saleh Shalomi, *President*
EMP: 60 **EST:** 2005
SALES (est): 118.5K **Privately Held**
SIC: 2273 Rugs: twisted paper, grass,
reed, coir, sisal, jute, etc.

(P-2689)
**DURKAN PATTERNED CARPETS
INC**
3633 Lenawee Ave 120, Los Angeles
(90016-4319)
PHONE...................................310 838-2898
Kathy Stein, *Manager*
EMP: 248 **Publicly Held**
SIC: 2273 Carpets, hand & machine made
HQ: Durkan Patterned Carpets, Inc.
121 Goodwill Dr
Dalton GA 30721
706 278-7037

(P-2690)
FABRICA INTERNATIONAL INC
Also Called: Fabrica Fine Carpet
3201 S Susan St, Santa Ana (92704-6838)
P.O. Box 2007, Dalton GA (30722-2007)
PHONE...................................949 261-7181
Greg Uttecht, *President*
Jon A Faulkner, *CEO*
Santa Mendoza, *Accountant*
Christine Boccard, *Sales Staff*
Jackie Bardin, *Manager*
▲ **EMP:** 167 **EST:** 1974
SQ FT: 107,000
SALES (est): 36.3MM
SALES (corp-wide): 315.9MM **Publicly
Held**
WEB: www.fabrica.com
SIC: 2273 Carpets, hand & machine made;
rugs, braided & hooked
PA: The Dixie Group Inc
475 Reed Rd
Dalton GA 30720
706 876-5800

(P-2691)
INTERFACEFLOR LLC
1111 S Grand Ave Ste 103, Los Angeles
(90015-2164)
PHONE...................................213 741-2139
EMP: 82
SALES (corp-wide): 1.1B **Publicly Held**
WEB: www.interface.com
SIC: 2273 Finishers of tufted carpets &
rugs
HQ: Interfaceflor, Llc
1503 Orchard Hill Rd
Lagrange GA 30240

(P-2692)
**MARSPRING CORPORATION
(PA)**
Also Called: Marflex
4920 S Boyle Ave, Vernon (90058-3017)
P.O. Box 58643 (90058-0643)
PHONE...................................323 589-5637
Ronald J Greitzer, *President*
Stan Greitzer, *Vice Pres*

Stanley Greitzer, *Vice Pres*
▲ **EMP:** 34 **EST:** 1950
SQ FT: 54,008
SALES (est): 4.8MM **Privately Held**
SIC: 2273 Carpets, textile fiber

(P-2693)
MAT CACTUS MFG CO
930 W 10th St, Azusa (91702-1936)
PHONE...................................626 969-0444
Debra Hartranft-Dering, *President*
Cailey Dering, *Treasurer*
Micheal Armstrong, *Info Tech Mgr*
George Roberts, *Technician*
Robert Dering, *Regl Sales Mgr*
▲ **EMP:** 20 **EST:** 1934
SQ FT: 35,000
SALES (est): 4.2MM **Privately Held**
WEB: www.cactusmat.com
SIC: 2273 5023 3069 Carpets & rugs;
floor coverings; mats or matting, rubber

(P-2694)
OHNO AMERICA INC
Also Called: Soho Carpet & Rugs
18781 Winnwood Ln, Santa Ana
(92705-1215)
PHONE...................................770 773-3820
▲ **EMP:** 20
SQ FT: 36,000
SALES (est): 1.6MM
SALES (corp-wide): 47.9MM **Privately
Held**
SIC: 2273 Mfg Carpets/Rugs
PA: Ohno Inc.
5-15-1, Harayamadai, Minami-Ku
Sakai OSK 590-0
722 970-566

(P-2695)
RUGGABLE LLC (PA)
18005 Savarona Way, Carson
(90746-1409)
PHONE...................................310 295-0098
Jeneva Bell,
EMP: 49 **EST:** 2017
SALES (est): 24.1MM **Privately Held**
WEB: www.ruggable.com
SIC: 5961 2273 ; rugs, hand & machine
made

(P-2696)
STANTON CARPET CORP
Also Called: Hibernia Woolen Mills
2209 Pine Ave, Manhattan Beach
(90266-2832)
PHONE...................................562 945-8711
Debbie Dearo, *Manager*
EMP: 44
SALES (corp-wide): 52.8MM **Privately
Held**
WEB: www.stantoncarpet.com
SIC: 2273 Carpets & rugs
PA: Stanton Carpet Corp.
100 Sunnyside Blvd # 100
Woodbury NY 11797
516 822-5878

(P-2697)
STUDENT SPORTS LLC
23954 Madison St, Torrance (90505-6011)
PHONE...................................310 791-1142
Andy Bark, *Principal*
Laura Tamilin, *CFO*
Michael Fletcher, *Personnel*
Patrick Bark, *Director*
Zack Greer, *Director*
EMP: 13 **EST:** 2008
SALES (est): 2.7MM **Privately Held**
WEB: www.areacodebaseball.com
SIC: 2273 Carpets & rugs

(P-2698)
TDG OPERATIONS LLC
340 S Avenue 17, Los Angeles
(90031-2505)
PHONE...................................323 724-9000
Charles Jones, *Manager*
EMP: 29
SALES (corp-wide): 315.9MM **Publicly
Held**
WEB: www.dixie-home.com
SIC: 2273 Rugs, tufted

HQ: Tdg Operations, Llc
716 Bill Myles Dr
Saraland AL 36571
251 679-3512

(P-2699)
TDG OPERATIONS LLC
6433 Gayhart St, Commerce (90040-2505)
PHONE...................................323 724-9000
Pancha Vega, *Manager*
EMP: 29
SALES (corp-wide): 315.9MM **Publicly
Held**
WEB: www.dixie-home.com
SIC: 2273 Rugs, tufted
HQ: Tdg Operations, Llc
716 Bill Myles Dr
Saraland AL 36571
251 679-3512

2281 Yarn Spinning Mills

(P-2700)
KUK RIM USA INC
Also Called: Encore Tex Inc
7507 Roseberry Ave, Huntington Park
(90255)
PHONE...................................323 277-9256
Sang Yoon Lee, *President*
Karen Sung, *Accounting Mgr*
EMP: 200
SALES (est): 9MM **Privately Held**
SIC: 2281 Yarn spinning mills

(P-2701)
PHARR-PALOMAR INC
6781 8th St, Buena Park (90620-1097)
P.O. Box 1939, Mc Adenville NC (28101-
1939)
PHONE...................................714 522-4811
H W Gosney, *Principal*
Jim Howard, *Corp Secy*
Walt Davenport, *Vice Pres*
Bill Carstarphen,
EMP: 1380 **EST:** 1972
SQ FT: 52,000
SALES (est): 4.7MM
SALES (corp-wide): 329.7MM **Privately
Held**
WEB: www.pharrusa.com
SIC: 2281 2282 Yarn spinning mills; carpet
yarn: twisting, winding or spooling
HQ: Pharr Yarns, Llc
100 Main St
Mc Adenville NC 28101
704 824-3551

(P-2702)
TDG OPERATIONS LLC
Also Called: Candlewick-Porterville
600 S E St, Porterville (93257-5318)
PHONE...................................559 781-4116
Dennis Johnson, *Branch Mgr*
Darryl Tamashiro, *Technology*
Harry Gloth, *Marketing Staff*
EMP: 60
SQ FT: 144,964
SALES (corp-wide): 315.9MM **Publicly
Held**
SIC: 2281 2221 Yarn spinning mills;
broadwoven fabric mills, manmade
HQ: Tdg Operations, Llc
475 Reed Rd
Dalton GA 30720
706 876-5851

2284 Thread Mills

(P-2703)
MEDRANO RAYMUNDO
Also Called: Best Ink and Thread
1752 S Bon View Ave, Ontario
(91761-4411)
PHONE...................................909 947-5507
Raymundo Medrano, *Owner*
EMP: 16 **EST:** 2010
SALES (est): 1MM **Privately Held**
WEB: www.bestinkandthread.com
SIC: 2284 2759 Embroidery thread;
screen printing

(P-2704)
**POLYTEX MANUFACTURING
INC (PA)**
1140 S Hope St, Los Angeles (90015-2119)
PHONE...................................323 726-0140
Men Tao, *President*
▲ **EMP:** 15 **EST:** 1989
SQ FT: 8,000
SALES (est): 1.8MM **Privately Held**
SIC: 2284 Thread mills

2295 Fabrics Coated Not Rubberized

(P-2705)
AOC LLC
Also Called: AOC California Plant
19991 Seaton Ave, Perris (92570-8724)
PHONE...................................951 657-5161
John Mulrine, *Manager*
George Farrington, *Technical Mgr*
Cliff Jones, *Technical Mgr*
Irwin Morfe, *Engineer*
Philip Hale, *Manager*
EMP: 100
SALES (corp-wide): 166.7K **Privately
Held**
WEB: www.aocresins.com
SIC: 2295 2821 5169 Resin or plastic
coated fabrics; plastics materials & resins;
synthetic resins, rubber & plastic materi-
als
HQ: Aoc, Llc
955 Highway 57
Piperton TN 38017

(P-2706)
CALIFORNIA COMBINING CORP
5607 S Santa Fe Ave, Vernon
(90058-3525)
P.O. Box 509, South Gate (90280-0509)
PHONE...................................323 589-5727
Charlette Heller, *CEO*
Vincent Rosato, *President*
Kathy Diaz, *Corp Secy*
▲ **EMP:** 37 **EST:** 1947
SQ FT: 68,000
SALES (est): 5.4MM **Privately Held**
WEB: www.flamelaminatingcorp.com
SIC: 2295 Coated fabrics, not rubberized

(P-2707)
**CYTEC AEROSPACE MTLS CA
INC**
Also Called: Cytec Engineered Materials
851 W 18th St, Costa Mesa (92627-4410)
PHONE...................................714 899-0400
David Drillock, *CEO*
Hisham Alameddine, *President*
Chris Jouppi, *President*
Jim Davis, *CEO*
Guillaume Gignac, *Vice Pres*
▲ **EMP:** 140 **EST:** 1984
SQ FT: 51,300
SALES (est): 37.4MM
SALES (corp-wide): 13MM **Privately
Held**
WEB: www.solvay.com
SIC: 2295 2891 Coated fabrics, not rub-
berized; adhesives & sealants
HQ: Cytec Industries Inc.
4500 Mcginnis Ferry Rd
Alpharetta GA 30005

(P-2708)
FLEXFIRM HOLDINGS LLC
2300 Chico Ave, El Monte 91733-1611)
PHONE...................................323 283-1173
Barry Eichorn, *President*
EMP: 15 **EST:** 1968
SQ FT: 10,000
SALES (est): 2.1MM **Privately Held**
WEB: www.flexfirmproducts.com
SIC: 2295 Resin or plastic coated fabrics

(P-2709)
KASLEN TEXTILES LLC
2140 E 51st St, Vernon (90058-2817)
PHONE...................................323 588-7700
David Raminfard, *CEO*
Belkis Del Campo, *Officer*

Daniel Zaretsky, *CTO*
Matt Karnofel, *Info Tech Mgr*
Margarette Cladis, *Contract Mgr*
▲ **EMP:** 16 **EST:** 2010
SQ FT: 36,000
SALES (est): 3.4MM **Privately Held**
WEB: www.kaslentextiles.com
SIC: 2295 Coated fabrics, not rubberized

2297 Fabrics, Nonwoven

(P-2710)
TEXOLLINI INC
2575 E El Presidio St, Long Beach
(90810-1114)
PHONE.................................310 537-3400
Daniel Kadisha, *President*
◆ **EMP:** 250 **EST:** 1989
SQ FT: 200,000
SALES (est): 59.6MM **Privately Held**
WEB: www.texollini.com
SIC: 2297 2262 2269 2221 Nonwoven
fabrics; dyeing: manmade fiber & silk
broadwoven fabrics; finishing plants;
broadwoven fabric mills, manmade

2298 Cordage & Twine

(P-2711)
**ASSOCTED WIRE ROPE
RIGGING INC**
910 Mahar Ave, Wilmington (90744-3829)
PHONE.................................310 448-5444
Scott Fishfader, *President*
▲ **EMP:** 24 **EST:** 1995
SALES (est): 1MM **Privately Held**
WEB: www.associatedwirerope.com
SIC: 2298 3315 5051 3536 Wire rope
centers; wire, steel: insulated or armored;
rope, wire (not insulated); hoists, cranes
& monorails; miscellaneous fabricated
wire products; industrial machinery &
equipment

(P-2712)
CABLECO
13100 Firestone Blvd, Santa Fe Springs
(90670-5517)
PHONE.................................562 942-8076
Greg Bailey, *Principal*
JP Pezina, *Sales Staff*
▲ **EMP:** 28 **EST:** 2002
SALES (est): 2.5MM **Privately Held**
WEB: www.carpenterrigging.com
SIC: 2298 Cable, fiber

(P-2713)
**COORDNTED WIRE ROPE
RGGING INC (HQ)**
Also Called: Coordinated Companies
1707 E Anaheim St, Wilmington
(90744-4706)
PHONE.................................310 834-8535
Phiip T Gibson, *CEO*
Christen Burgett, *Vice Pres*
Kristin Burgett, *Vice Pres*
Bo Kentner, *Opers Mgr*
Bo Kentar, *Marketing Staff*
▲ **EMP:** 20 **EST:** 1962
SQ FT: 8,640
SALES (est): 12.1MM
SALES (corp-wide): 19.2MM **Privately
Held**
WEB: www.coordinatedcompanies.com
SIC: 5251 2298 Hardware; wire rope cen-
ters
PA: Coordinated Equipment Co.
1707 E Anaheim St
Wilmington CA 90744
310 834-8535

(P-2714)
DYNAMEX CORPORATION
155 E Albertoni St, Carson (90746-1405)
PHONE.................................310 329-0399
Ben Bravin, *President*
◆ **EMP:** 56 **EST:** 1975
SALES (est): 3.3MM **Privately Held**
SIC: 2298 Cable, fiber

(P-2715)
KANEX PRO INC
500 S Brea Blvd Unit B, Brea (92821-5383)
PHONE.................................714 332-1681
Kelvin Yan, *President*
▲ **EMP:** 18 **EST:** 2015
SALES (est): 758.1K **Privately Held**
WEB: www.kanexpro.com
SIC: 2298 3679 3613 3299 Cable, fiber;
static power supply converters for elec-
tronic applications; power switching
equipment; mica, splitting

(P-2716)
PACIFIC FIBRE & ROPE CO INC
903 Flint Ave 927, Wilmington
(90744-3740)
P.O. Box 187 (90748-0187)
PHONE.................................310 834-4567
Mark Goldman, *President*
Allen Goldman, *President*
Michael Goldman, *Treasurer*
Ronald Goldman, *Vice Pres*
▲ **EMP:** 15 **EST:** 1930
SQ FT: 45,000 **Privately Held**
WEB: www.pacificfibre.com
SIC: 2298 5085 Cordage: abaca, sisal,
henequen, hemp, jute or other fiber; rope,
except wire rope

(P-2717)
PELICAN ROPE WORKS
1600 E Mcfadden Ave, Santa Ana
(92705-4310)
PHONE.................................714 545-0116
Gaylord C Whipple, *President*
Paul Ottone, *Opers Staff*
Roderick Woods, *VP Sls/Mktg*
◆ **EMP:** 15 **EST:** 1981
SQ FT: 20,000
SALES (est): 4.9MM **Privately Held**
WEB: www.pelicanrope.com
SIC: 2298 Ropes & fiber cables

2299 Textile Goods, NEC

(P-2718)
AMERICAN DAWN INC (PA)
Also Called: ADI
401 W Artesia Blvd, Compton
(90220-5518)
PHONE.................................800 821-2221
Adnan Rawjee, *President*
Mahmud G Rawjee, *Ch of Bd*
Lillian Huang, *CFO*
Kenny Cohen, *Vice Pres*
Timothy Phippen, *Vice Pres*
◆ **EMP:** 60 **EST:** 1980
SQ FT: 212,000
SALES (est): 25MM **Privately Held**
WEB: www.americandawninc.com
SIC: 2299 5023 5131 2393 Linen fabrics;
linens & towels; textiles, woven; cushions,
except spring & carpet: purchased materi-
als; pillows, bed: made from purchased
materials

(P-2719)
**AMERICAN FOAM FIBER &
SUPS INC (PA)**
Also Called: Foam Depot
255 S 7th Ave Ste A, City of Industry
(91746-3256)
PHONE.................................626 969-7268
Jack Hung, *President*
Irene Hung, *Vice Pres*
▲ **EMP:** 71 **EST:** 2006
SALES (est): 4.3MM **Privately Held**
WEB: www.affsinc.com
SIC: 2299 Hair, curled: for upholstery, pil-
low & quilt filling

(P-2720)
**AMPM MAINTENANCE
CORPORATION**
1010 E 14th St, Los Angeles (90021-2212)
PHONE.................................424 230-1300
Mohammad Saderi, *President*
EMP: 48 **EST:** 2020
SALES (est): 1.5MM **Privately Held**
SIC: 2299 Textile goods

(P-2721)
**AMRAPUR OVERSEAS
INCORPORATED (PA)**
Also Called: Colonial Home Textiles
1560 E 6th St Ste 101, Corona
(92879-1712)
PHONE.................................714 893-8808
Chandru H Wadhwani, *CEO*
Neil Mandell, *Officer*
Jennifer Azran, *Vice Pres*
Dawn Fields, *Vice Pres*
Laxmi Wadhwani, *Admin Sec*
◆ **EMP:** 25 **EST:** 1983
SQ FT: 130,000
SALES (est): 8.4MM **Privately Held**
WEB: www.amrapur.com
SIC: 2299 2269 5023 Linen fabrics; linen
fabrics: dyeing, finishing & printing; linens
& towels

(P-2722)
BRK GROUP LLC
6415 Bandini Blvd, Commerce
(90040-3117)
PHONE.................................562 949-4394
Vy Nguyen, *Mng Member*
Carter Bucklin, *Sales Staff*
Jeff Miller, *Mng Member*
Tobe Kramer, *Manager*
▲ **EMP:** 24 **EST:** 2004
SALES (est): 1.7MM **Privately Held**
WEB: www.brk-group.com
SIC: 2299 Textile mill waste & remnant pro-
cessing

(P-2723)
DECCOFELT CORPORATION
555 S Vermont Ave, Glendora
(91741-6206)
P.O. Box 156 (91740-0156)
PHONE.................................626 963-8511
Gerald L Heinrich, *CEO*
Kathy Smith, *Executive*
Ashley Strader, *Purchasing*
Petrzilek Eric, *Sales Staff*
Sherrie Sifontes,
▲ **EMP:** 24
SQ FT: 33,000
SALES (est): 4.7MM **Privately Held**
WEB: www.deccofelt.com
SIC: 2299 Felts & felt products

(P-2724)
ETRADE 24 INC
20524 Ventura Blvd # 102, Woodland Hills
(91364-6217)
PHONE.................................818 712-0574
Ana Maria Padilla, *CEO*
EMP: 25 **EST:** 2018
SALES (est): 2.8MM **Privately Held**
WEB: www.us.etrade24.com
SIC: 2299 2326 7389 Batting, wadding,
padding & fillings; medical & hospital uni-
forms, men's; brokers' services

(P-2725)
EVEREST GROUP USA INC
2030 S Carlos Ave, Ontario (91761-8032)
PHONE.................................909 923-1818
Peter Ho, *CEO*
Niko Peng, *President*
◆ **EMP:** 20 **EST:** 2008
SALES (est): 4.8MM **Privately Held**
SIC: 2299 Broadwoven fabrics: linen, jute,
hemp & ramie

(P-2726)
J H TEXTILES INC
2301 E 55th St, Vernon (90058-3435)
PHONE.................................323 585-4124
Jong Soon Hur, *CEO*
▲ **EMP:** 25 **EST:** 2003
SQ FT: 80,000 **Privately Held**
WEB: www.jhtextilesinc.com
SIC: 2299 Textile mill waste & remnant pro-
cessing

(P-2727)
L A SANI-FELT CO
830 E 59th St, Los Angeles (90001-1086)
PHONE.................................323 233-5278
Melvyn Goodman, *President*
Lynn Goodman, *Corp Secy*
John Cioffi, *Vice Pres*
EMP: 15 **EST:** 1969
SQ FT: 55,000

SALES (est): 1.4MM **Privately Held**
SIC: 2299 2282 Batts & batting: cotton mill
waste & related material; polypropylene
filament yarn: twisting, winding, etc.

(P-2728)
LAYNE LABORATORIES INC
Also Called: Patina Products
4303 Huasna Rd, Arroyo Grande
(93420-6175)
P.O. Box 1259 (93421-1259)
PHONE.................................805 242-7918
John Waterman, *CEO*
Patricia Moffitt, *President*
Krys Wood, *Prdtn Mgr*
◆ **EMP:** 20 **EST:** 1990
SQ FT: 40,000
SALES (est): 1.6MM **Privately Held**
WEB: www.laynelabs.com
SIC: 2299 Batting, wadding, padding & fill-
ings

(P-2729)
LF VISUALS INC
Also Called: Little Folk Visuals
39620 Entrepreneur Ln, Palm Desert
(92211-0400)
P.O. Box 14243 (92255-4243)
PHONE.................................760 345-5571
Michael Firman, *CEO*
▲ **EMP:** 15 **EST:** 1982
SQ FT: 7,300
SALES (est): 1.7MM **Privately Held**
WEB: www.littlefolkvisuals.com
SIC: 2299 Felts & felt products

(P-2730)
MFB WORLDWIDE INC (PA)
4901 Patata St 201-204, Cudahy
(90201-5942)
PHONE.................................323 562-2339
Daniel Holmes, *CEO*
Pedro Garcia, *COO*
Robert Harrison, *Chief Mktg Ofcr*
EMP: 15
SQ FT: 20,000
SALES (est): 2.9MM **Privately Held**
SIC: 2299 Fabrics: linen, jute, hemp, ramie

(P-2731)
NEW ICON INC (PA)
15136 Valley Blvd, City of Industry
(91746-3356)
PHONE.................................626 620-4387
Heping Li, *CEO*
EMP: 14 **EST:** 2016
SALES (est): 97.5K **Privately Held**
SIC: 2299 Fabrics: linen, jute, hemp, ramie

(P-2732)
NEXTRADE INC (PA)
Also Called: Nextex International
12411 Industrial Ave, South Gate
(90280-8221)
PHONE.................................562 944-9950
Jang R Cho, *President*
◆ **EMP:** 22 **EST:** 1998
SQ FT: 40,000
SALES (est): 10.2MM **Privately Held**
SIC: 2299 Batting, wadding, padding & fill-
ings

(P-2733)
OTT TEXTILE INC (PA)
10507 Valley Blvd Ste 858, El Monte
(91731-2411)
PHONE.................................626 566-5858
Allen GE Jun Wang, *Principal*
▲ **EMP:** 29 **EST:** 2011
SALES (est): 215.3K **Privately Held**
SIC: 2299 Fabrics: linen, jute, hemp, ramie

(P-2734)
**PACESETTER FABRICS LLC
(HQ)**
11450 Sheldon St, Sun Valley
(91352-1121)
PHONE.................................213 741-9999
Ramin Namvar,
Sean Namvar,
◆ **EMP:** 17 **EST:** 1997
SQ FT: 36,000
SALES (est): 7.7MM **Privately Held**
SIC: 2299 Tops & top processing, man-
made or other fiber

(PA)=Parent Co (HQ)=Headquarters (DH)=Div Headquarters
✿ = New Business established in last 2 years

2022 Southern California Business
Directory and Buyers Guide

131

P R O D U C T S & S V C S

(P-2735)
PD PRODUCTS LLC
Also Called: Pipe Dream Products
21350 Lassen St, Chatsworth
(91311-4254)
PHONE.................................818 772-0100
Olga Kalinina, *Controller*
Marion Demello, *CFO*
Chris Armstrong, *Sales Executive*
Mona Madrigal, *Sales Staff*
Christine Lawrence, *Director*
EMP: 21 **EST:** 2013
SALES (est): 2.4MM
SALES (corp-wide): 63.6MM **Privately Held**
WEB: www.diamondproductsllc.com
SIC: 2299 5092 Yarns, specialty & novelty; toys
PA: Diamond Products, Llc
8501 Fllbrook Ave Ste 370
West Hills CA 91304
818 772-0100

(P-2736)
PROGRESSIVE PRODUCTS INC
8804 Windmill Pl, Riverside (92508-6617)
PHONE.................................951 784-9930
Todd Schmidt, *President*
Jacqueline Schmidt, *Vice Pres*
Todd M Schmidt, *Admin Sec*
Umut Cetinkol, *Controller*
Jenny Beckett, *Purch Mgr*
◆ **EMP:** 13 **EST:** 1999
SALES (est): 6.8MM
SALES (corp-wide): 3.6B **Privately Held**
WEB: www.bekaertdeslee.com
SIC: 2299 Fabrics: linen, jute, hemp, ramie
HQ: Bekaertdeslee Usa Inc.
200 St Business Park Dr
Winston Salem NC 27107
336 747-4900

(P-2737)
REDWOOD WELLNESS LLC
11814 Jefferson Blvd, Culver City
(90230-6310)
PHONE.................................323 843-2676
Robert Rosenheck, *CEO*
EMP: 38 **EST:** 2017
SALES (est): 1.7MM **Privately Held**
SIC: 2299 Hemp yarn, thread, roving & textiles

(P-2738)
STONE HARBOR INC
5015 District Blvd, Vernon (90058-2719)
PHONE.................................323 277-2777
▲ **EMP:** 18
SQ FT: 60,000
SALES (est): 5MM **Privately Held**
SIC: 2299 Textile Goods, Nec, Nsk

(P-2739)
TEXTILES & SON LLC (PA)
Also Called: Otis Textile
1750 W Adams Blvd, Los Angeles
(90018-2704)
PHONE.................................323 965-9888
Otis Weis, *Manager*
EMP: 50 **EST:** 2018
SALES (est): 556.4K **Privately Held**
SIC: 2299 Broadwoven fabrics: linen, jute, hemp & ramie

2311 Men's & Boys' Suits, Coats & Overcoats

(P-2740)
AMWEAR USA INC
Also Called: Tactsquad
250 Benjamin Dr, Corona (92879-6508)
PHONE.................................800 858-6755
Hong LI Hawkins, *CEO*
Hang Guo, *Principal*
EMP: 32 **EST:** 2017
SALES (est): 4.5MM **Privately Held**
WEB: www.tactsquad.com
SIC: 2311 5699 Men's & boys' uniforms; uniforms

(P-2741)
BARCO UNIFORMS INC
350 W Rosecrans Ave, Gardena
(90248-1728)
PHONE.................................310 323-7315
David Murphy, *CEO*
Danny Robertson, *President*
David Aquino, *COO*
David Ayers, *CFO*
Michaela Griggs, *Senior VP*
◆ **EMP:** 246 **EST:** 1929
SQ FT: 74,000
SALES (est): 56.8MM **Privately Held**
WEB: www.barcouniforms.com
SIC: 2311 2326 2337 Men's & boys' uniforms; men's & boys' work clothing; uniforms, except athletic: women's, misses' & juniors'

(P-2742)
BERNARDI FINANCIAL INC
Also Called: Bernardi of California
459 S Peck Dr, Beverly Hills (90212-4115)
PHONE.................................323 581-1900
Bernard Rein, *President*
Jane Su, *Accounts Mgr*
◆ **EMP:** 39 **EST:** 1977
SALES (est): 4MM **Privately Held**
SIC: 2311 Suits, men's & boys': made from purchased materials; coats, tailored, men's & boys': from purchased materials

(P-2743)
BLUE SPHERE INC
Also Called: Lucky-13 Apparel
10869 Portal Dr, Los Alamitos
(90720-2508)
PHONE.................................714 953-7555
Robert Kloetzly, *President*
Nancy Perez, *Representative*
▲ **EMP:** 35 **EST:** 1989
SALES (est): 3MM **Privately Held**
WEB: www.bluespheremfg.com
SIC: 2311 2331 2369 Men's & boys' suits & coats; women's & misses' blouses & shirts; girls' & children's outerwear

(P-2744)
CROSSPORT MOCEAN
1611 Babcock St, Newport Beach
(92663-2805)
PHONE.................................949 646-1701
Bill Levitt, *President*
Pamela Green, *Treasurer*
Tim Hindman, *Admin Sec*
▲ **EMP:** 18 **EST:** 1991
SQ FT: 3,000
SALES (est): 2.5MM **Privately Held**
WEB: www.mocean.net
SIC: 2311 Policemen's uniforms: made from purchased materials

(P-2745)
LITO CHILDRENS WEAR INC
3730 Union Pacific Ave, Los Angeles
(90023-3773)
PHONE.................................323 260-4692
Tom Lee, *Ch of Bd*
Garven LI, *Manager*
▼ **EMP:** 16 **EST:** 1974
SQ FT: 13,000
SALES (est): 1.4MM **Privately Held**
WEB:
www.litochildrensweaj.mfgpages.com
SIC: 2311 2361 2369 Suits, men's & boys': made from purchased materials; dresses: girls', children's & infants'; girls' & children's outerwear

(P-2746)
NEW CHEF FASHION INC
3223 E 46th St, Vernon (90058-2407)
PHONE.................................323 581-0300
G Lucien Salama, *President*
Brian Comeno, *Exec VP*
Chantal Salama, *Vice Pres*
Gabriella Salama, *Marketing Staff*
Stan Spigelman, *Sales Staff*
▲ **EMP:** 89 **EST:** 1989
SALES (est): 21MM **Privately Held**
WEB: www.newchef.com
SIC: 2311 2339 2326 5137 Men's & boys' uniforms; women's & misses' outerwear; men's & boys' work clothing; uniforms, women's & children's

(P-2747)
RDD ENTERPRISES INC
Also Called: Americawear
4638 E Washinton Blvd, Commerce
(90040)
PHONE.................................213 746-0020
Tony Lomeli, *Branch Mgr*
EMP: 14 **Privately Held**
WEB: www.rddusa.com
SIC: 2311 Military uniforms, men's & youths': purchased materials
PA: R.D.D. Enterprises, Inc.
4638 E Washington Blvd
Commerce CA
213 742-0666

(P-2748)
ROBINSON TEXTILES INC
24532 Woodward Ave, Lomita
(90717-1110)
PHONE.................................310 527-8110
Gary Lovemark, *President*
◆ **EMP:** 13 **EST:** 1979
SALES (est): 606.9K **Privately Held**
SIC: 2311 Men's & boys' uniforms

(P-2749)
SAMPAV INC
Also Called: Valley Department Store
15802 Ellington Way, Chino Hills
(91709-7963)
PHONE.................................909 984-8646
Kamal Hassamal, *President*
Pavan Hassamal, *Vice Pres*
▲ **EMP:** 18 **EST:** 1996
SALES (est): 2.3MM **Privately Held**
SIC: 2311 5136 5699 Men's & boys' uniforms; uniforms, men's & boys'; uniforms

(P-2750)
SANTANA FORMAL ACCESSORIES INC
707 Arroyo St Ste B, San Fernando
(91340-1855)
P.O. Box 2248, Agoura Hills (91376-2248)
PHONE.................................818 898-3677
Delores Tennant, *President*
Doug Freed, *CFO*
EMP: 15 **EST:** 1970
SQ FT: 18,000
SALES (est): 439.9K **Privately Held**
WEB: www.santanaapparel.com
SIC: 2311 2339 2323 2389 Vests: made from purchased materials; women's & misses' outerwear; bow ties, men's & boys': made from purchased materials; cummerbunds

(P-2751)
TYLER TRAFFICANTE INC (PA)
Also Called: Richard Tyler
700 S Palm Ave, Alhambra (91803-1528)
PHONE.................................323 869-9299
Lisa Trafficante, *President*
Richard Tyler, *Vice Pres*
EMP: 51 **EST:** 1986
SQ FT: 30,000
SALES (est): 3.8MM **Privately Held**
WEB: www.hbpta.org
SIC: 2311 2335 5611 5621 Tailored suits & formal jackets; gowns, formal; suits, men's; dress shops; women's & misses' outerwear

(P-2752)
UNIVERSAL MERCHANDISE INC
Also Called: Mds
5422 Aura Ave, Tarzana (91356-3004)
P.O. Box 572152 (91357-2152)
PHONE.................................818 344-2044
Itender Singh, *President*
Jasbir Singh, *Vice Pres*
▲ **EMP:** 14 **EST:** 1994
SQ FT: 4,000
SALES (est): 522K **Privately Held**
SIC: 2311 5049 2339 5136 Men's & boys' uniforms; religious supplies; uniforms, athletic: women's, misses' & juniors'; uniforms, men's & boys'; uniforms, women's & children's

(P-2753)
WARRENS DEPARTMENT STORE INC
Also Called: House of Uniforms
9800 De Soto Ave, Chatsworth
(91311-4411)
PHONE.................................888 577-2735
Warren F Ackerman, *Chairman*
Cheryl Clough, *President*
Fred Kemmerling, *Vice Pres*
EMP: 14 **EST:** 1951
SALES (est): 351.4K **Privately Held**
SIC: 2311 2337 Men's & boys' uniforms; uniforms, except athletic: women's, misses' & juniors'

2321 Men's & Boys' Shirts

(P-2754)
101 APPAREL INC
1802 N Glassell St, Orange (92865-4312)
PHONE.................................714 454-8988
Eric Crandell, *Owner*
EMP: 13 **EST:** 2005
SALES (est): 1.9MM **Privately Held**
WEB: www.101apparel.com
SIC: 2321 2353 Sport shirts, men's & boys': from purchased materials; hats & caps

(P-2755)
BPS TACTICAL INC
2165 E Colton Ave, Mentone (92359-9657)
P.O. Box 868 (92359-0868)
PHONE.................................909 794-2435
William F Blankenship Jr, *President*
EMP: 13 **EST:** 1975
SQ FT: 1,800
SALES (est): 1.3MM **Privately Held**
WEB: www.bpstacticalgear.com
SIC: 2321 5699 Uniform shirts: made from purchased materials; uniforms

(P-2756)
GINO CORPORATION
Also Called: Shaka Wear
555 E Jefferson Blvd, Los Angeles
(90011-2430)
PHONE.................................323 234-7979
Sung Uk Park, *CEO*
◆ **EMP:** 28 **EST:** 2004
SALES (est): 2MM **Privately Held**
WEB: www.shakawear.com
SIC: 2321 5136 Men's & boys' dress shirts; shirts, men's & boys'

(P-2757)
JL DESIGN ENTERPRISES INC
Also Called: Jl Racing.com
1451 Edinger Ave Ste C, Tustin
(92780-6250)
PHONE.................................714 479-0240
Jolene Sparza, *President*
Kenneth Mills, *Vice Pres*
Kathryn Mills, *Merchandise Mgr*
Brian Delong, *Sales Staff*
Robert Frichtel, *Manager*
▲ **EMP:** 63 **EST:** 1983
SALES (est): 4.9MM **Privately Held**
WEB: www.jlpaddling.com
SIC: 2321 Sport shirts, men's & boys': from purchased materials

(P-2758)
JUST FOR FUN INC
Also Called: Jff Uniforms
557 Van Ness Ave, Torrance (90501-1424)
PHONE.................................310 320-1327
Corinne Stolz, *President*
Gary Stolz, *Vice Pres*
▲ **EMP:** 24 **EST:** 1975
SQ FT: 11,000
SALES (est): 1.9MM **Privately Held**
WEB: www.jffuniforms.com
SIC: 2321 2337 2339 2326 Uniform shirts: made from purchased materials; uniforms, except athletic: women's, misses' & juniors'; women's & misses' outerwear; men's & boys' work clothing

(P-2759)
OTIMO INC
2937 S Alameda St, Vernon (90058-1326)
PHONE.................................323 233-8894

EMP: 25
SALES (est): 114.8K **Privately Held**
SIC: 2321 2325 2329 2331 Garment
Manufacturer

(P-2760)
ROMAR GROUP INC (PA)
Also Called: Ameru
837 Traction Ave Unit 406, Los Angeles
(90013-1868)
PHONE.................................213 621-4403
Don Polk, *President*
Melpo Mantzavinos, *Senior VP*
EMP: 56 EST: 1997
SQ FT: 5,000
SALES (est): 183.8K **Privately Held**
SIC: 2321 2325 2329 2331 Men's &
boys' sports & polo shirts; men's &
boys' trousers & slacks; men's & boys' sports-
wear & athletic clothing; women's &
misses' blouses & shirts; embroidering of
advertising on shirts, etc.

(P-2761)
STARLION INC
Also Called: Star Lion
706 E 32nd St, Los Angeles (90011-2406)
PHONE.................................323 233-8823
Mike Lim, *President*
Moon Lim, *Principal*
EMP: 20 EST: 1984
SQ FT: 11,000
SALES (est): 1.4MM **Privately Held**
WEB: www.fashionface.com
SIC: 2321 2331 Men's & boys' dress
shirts; women's & misses' blouses &
shirts

(P-2762)
TEXTILE UNLIMITED
CORPORATION (PA)
20917 Higgins Ct, Torrance (90501-1723)
PHONE.................................310 263-7400
James Y Kim, *CEO*
Stanley Kim, *President*
Sam Lee, *President*
Yumi Park, *Admin Sec*
◆ EMP: 440 EST: 1994
SALES (est): 37.6MM **Privately Held**
WEB: www.tuc.net
SIC: 2321 2325 2329 2331 Men's &
boys' furnishings; women's & misses' ath-
letic clothing & sportswear; men's & boys'
athletic uniforms; women's & misses'
blouses & shirts

(P-2763)
TOP HEAVY CLOTHING
COMPANY INC (PA)
28381 Vincent Moraga Dr, Temecula
(92590-3653)
PHONE.................................951 442-8839
Tadd D Chilcott, *President*
Douglas Lo, *Vice Pres*
▲ EMP: 65 EST: 1995
SQ FT: 40,000
SALES (est): 8.9MM **Privately Held**
WEB: www.topheavyclothing.com
SIC: 2321 Men's & boys' dress shirts;
men's & boys' sports & polo shirts

2322 Men's & Boys'
Underwear & Nightwear

(P-2764)
STATESIDE MERCHANTS LLC
Also Called: Pair of Thieves
5813 Washington Blvd, Culver City
(90232-7330)
PHONE.................................424 251-5190
David Ehrenberg, *Mng Member*
Alan Stuart,
Cash Warren,
◆ EMP: 25 EST: 2012
SQ FT: 3,000
SALES (est): 2.9MM **Privately Held**
WEB: www.pairofthieves.com
SIC: 2322 2341 Men's & boys' underwear
& nightwear; women's & children's under-
garments

2323 Men's & Boys' Neckwear

(P-2765)
MUTT COUTURE INC (PA)
973 E Fthill Blvd Ste 105, San Luis Obispo
(93405)
PHONE.................................805 469-6888
EMP: 22 EST: 2015
SALES (est): 53.5K **Privately Held**
WEB: www.muttcoutureinc.com
SIC: 2323 Men's & boys' neckwear

(P-2766)
UNDERCURRENT
EDUCATIONAL
Also Called: Ueis
3350 E 7th St Ste 343, Long Beach
(90804-5003)
PHONE.................................800 430-1183
EMP: 80
SALES (est): 3.7MM **Privately Held**
WEB: www.ueiscorp.com
SIC: 2323 5999 8299 Mfg Men's/Boy's
Neckwear Ret Misc Merchandise
School/Educational Services

2325 Men's & Boys' Separate
Trousers & Casual Slacks

(P-2767)
AG ADRIANO GOLDSCHMIED
INC (PA)
Also Called: AG Jeans
2741 Seminole Ave, South Gate
(90280-5550)
PHONE.................................323 357-1111
U Yul Ku, *President*
Adriano Suarez, *Vice Pres*
Jennifer Grosso, *Executive*
Mark Aguilar, *Store Mgr*
Jordyn Coty, *Store Mgr*
▲ EMP: 73 EST: 2000
SQ FT: 150,000
SALES (est): 27.5MM **Privately Held**
WEB: www.agjeans.com
SIC: 2325 2339 5136 5137 Men's &
boys' trousers & slacks; women's &
misses' outerwear; men's & boys' cloth-
ing; women's & children's clothing; family
clothing stores

(P-2768)
CORDOVAN & GREY LTD
4826 Gregg Rd, Pico Rivera (90660-2107)
PHONE.................................562 699-8300
Fax: 213 699-9910
EMP: 22
SALES (est): 1.3MM **Privately Held**
SIC: 2325 Mfg Men's/Boy's Trousers

(P-2769)
GRACING INC
Also Called: Grace In La
17003 Evergreen Pl, City of Industry
(91745-1819)
PHONE.................................626 269-6818
Jane Liu, *Principal*
EMP: 25 EST: 2012
SALES (est): 2.5MM **Privately Held**
SIC: 5621 2325 5651 Women's clothing
stores; jeans: men's, youths' & boys';
jeans stores

(P-2770)
J&C APPAREL
757 Towne Ave Unit B, Los Angeles
(90021-1419)
PHONE.................................323 490-8260
Cipriano Serrano, *President*
EMP: 40 EST: 2017
SALES (est): 1.3MM **Privately Held**
SIC: 2325 Men's & boys' trousers & slacks

(P-2771)
KI-P C USA JEANS INC
6738 Los Verdes Dr Apt 2, Rancho Palos
Verdes (90275-7603)
PHONE.................................310 234-8185
Chong Chu Kim, *President*
EMP: 80 EST: 1996

SALES (est): 4MM **Privately Held**
SIC: 2325 2339 Jeans: men's, youths' &
boys'; jeans: women's, misses' & juniors'

(P-2772)
LEVI STRAUSS & CO
316 N Beverly Dr, Beverly Hills
(90210-4701)
PHONE.................................310 246-9044
EMP: 13
SALES (corp-wide): 4.4B **Privately Held**
SIC: 2325 Jeans Men's Youths' And Boys'
PA: Levi Strauss & Co.
1155 Battery St
San Francisco CA 94111
415 501-6000

(P-2773)
ROB INC
Also Called: Robin's Jeans
6760 Foster Bridge Blvd, Bell Gardens
(90201-2030)
PHONE.................................562 806-5589
Robert Chretien, *CEO*
Gilberto Jimenez, *Vice Pres*
Nancy Seye, *General Mgr*
Laura Banda, *Controller*
Rose Contreras, *Prdtn Mgr*
◆ EMP: 90 EST: 2005
SQ FT: 26,000
SALES (est): 20.1MM **Privately Held**
SIC: 2325 2339 2369 Jeans: men's,
youths' & boys'; men's & boys' dress
slacks & shorts; trousers, dress (sepa-
rate): men's, youths' & boys'; women's &
misses' culottes, knickers & shorts; knickers: women's, misses' & juniors'; jeans:
women's, misses' & juniors'; shorts (outerwear): girls' & children's; jackets: girls',
children's & infants'; jeans: girls', children's & infants'

(P-2774)
SEMORE INC
Also Called: Nubile
1437 Santee St Ste 201, Los Angeles
(90015-2590)
PHONE.................................213 746-4122
Fax: 213 746-2426
▲ EMP: 18
SQ FT: 10,000
SALES (est): 1.6MM **Privately Held**
WEB: www.solosemore.com
SIC: 2325 2321 2331 Mfg Men's/Boy's
Trousers Mfg Men's/Boy's Furnishings
Mfg Women's/Misses' Blouses

(P-2775)
TRUE RELIGION APPAREL INC
(HQ)
Also Called: True Religion Brand Jeans
500 W 190th St Ste 300, Gardena
(90248-4269)
PHONE.................................323 266-3072
Michael Buckley, *CEO*
Lynne Koplin, *President*
Eric Bauer, *CFO*
Peter F Collins, *CFO*
David Chiovetti, *Senior VP*
▲ EMP: 300 EST: 2001
SALES (est): 270MM
SALES (corp-wide): 350MM **Privately
Held**
WEB: www.truereligion.com
SIC: 2325 2339 2369 Men's & boys'
trousers & slacks; jeans: men's, youths' &
boys'; women's & misses' outerwear;
jeans: women's, misses' & juniors'; jeans:
girls', children's & infants'
PA: Trlg Intermediate Holdings, Llc
1888 Rosecrans Ave
Manhattan Beach CA 90266
323 266-3072

2326 Men's & Boys' Work
Clothing

(P-2776)
BUNKERHILL INDUS GROUP INC
Also Called: Big Front Uniforms
4535 Huntington Dr S, Los Angeles
(90032-1940)
PHONE.................................323 227-4222
EMP: 15

SALES (est): 950K **Privately Held**
SIC: 2326 Mfg Men's/Boy's Work Clothing

(P-2777)
BUY INSTA SLIM INC
Also Called: Instantfigure
17831 Sky Park Cir Ste C, Irvine
(92614-6105)
PHONE.................................949 263-2301
Eeman Jalili, *CEO*
Monir Jalili, *President*
Ehsan Jalili, *Vice Pres*
Houshang Jalili, *Vice Pres*
▲ EMP: 14 EST: 2010
SALES (est): 5MM **Privately Held**
WEB: www.instaslim.com
SIC: 2326 5961 7389 Men's & boys' work
clothing; women's apparel, mail order;

(P-2778)
FIGS INC
2834 Colorado Ave Ste 100, Santa Monica
(90404-3644)
PHONE.................................424 300-8330
Heather Hasson, *Ch of Bd*
Andrea Wasienko, *CEO*
Jeffrey D Lawrence, *CFO*
Trina Spear, *Co-CEO*
Alex Tshering, *Senior VP*
▲ EMP: 202 EST: 2013
SQ FT: 27,000
SALES (est): 263.1MM **Privately Held**
WEB: www.wearfigs.com
SIC: 2326 5699 Work apparel, except uni-
forms; work clothing

(P-2779)
HOT TOPIC INC (DH)
Also Called: Shockhound
18305 San Jose Ave, City of Industry
(91748-1237)
PHONE.................................626 839-4681
Steve Vranes, *CEO*
Emily Rence, *Partner*
George Wehlitz, *CFO*
Nisaa Abdur-Rahim, *Officer*
William Fowler, *Exec VP*
◆ EMP: 800 EST: 1988
SQ FT: 250,000
SALES (est): 770.2MM **Privately Held**
WEB: www.hottopic.com
SIC: 2326 5699 5632 Men's & boys' work
clothing; designers, apparel; apparel ac-
cessories

(P-2780)
IMAGE APPAREL FOR
BUSINESS INC
1618 E Edinger Ave, Santa Ana
(92705-5019)
PHONE.................................714 541-5247
Keith Knerr, *CEO*
Robert Duffield, *Controller*
Mike Gilber, *Manager*
EMP: 25 EST: 2009
SALES (est): 2.5MM **Privately Held**
WEB: www.ia4b.com
SIC: 2326 2339 2353 7213 Men's &
boys' work clothing; uniforms, athletic:
women's, misses' & juniors'; uniform hats
& caps; linen supply

(P-2781)
IMAGE SOLUTIONS APPAREL
INC
19571 Magellan Dr, Torrance (90502-1136)
PHONE.................................310 464-8991
Christopher Kelley, *President*
Rachel Acker, *Executive Asst*
Gendron Katie, *Technology*
Paula Fox, *Controller*
Alana Owens, *Opers Staff*
▲ EMP: 95 EST: 1997
SQ FT: 4,500
SALES (est): 30.8MM **Privately Held**
WEB: www.imageinc.com
SIC: 2326 Work uniforms

(P-2782)
INDIE SOURCE
1933 S Broadway, Los Angeles
(90007-4501)
PHONE.................................424 200-2027
Jesse Dombrowiak, *President*
Moshe Vhanunu, *Director*
EMP: 20 EST: 2014

SALES (est): 750K **Privately Held**
WEB: www.indiesource.com
SIC: 2326 7336 Men's & boys' work clothing; graphic arts & related design

(P-2783)
KNK APPAREL INC
223 W Rosecrans Ave, Gardena
(90248-1831)
PHONE..............................310 768-3333
John Kang, *President*
EMP: 13 EST: 1993
SQ FT: 90,000
SALES (est): 373.9K **Privately Held**
SIC: 2326 2339 Men's & boys' work clothing; women's & misses' outerwear

(P-2784)
LA TRIUMPH INC
Also Called: Medgear
13336 Alondra Blvd, Cerritos (90703-2205)
PHONE..............................562 404-7657
Hasina Lakhani, *CEO*
Amin Lakhani, *President*
▲ EMP: 24 EST: 2003
SQ FT: 40,000
SALES (est): 2.8MM **Privately Held**
WEB: www.pacuniforms.com
SIC: 2326 Medical & hospital uniforms, men's; work uniforms

(P-2785)
MEXAPPAREL INC (PA)
2344 E 38th St, Vernon (90058-1627)
PHONE..............................323 364-8600
Maria Maniatis, *President*
Fred Kalmar, *CFO*
Hubert Guez, *Vice Pres*
Nomaan Yousef, *Controller*
EMP: 34 EST: 1991
SQ FT: 277,000
SALES (est): 2.6MM **Privately Held**
SIC: 2326 Service apparel (baker, barber, lab, etc.), washable: men's

(P-2786)
PAIGE LLC (HQ)
Also Called: Paige Premium Denim
10119 Jefferson Blvd, Culver City
(90232-3519)
PHONE..............................310 733-2100
Michael Geller, *President*
Michael Henschel, *COO*
Walter Lacher, *CFO*
Paige Adams-Geller, *Officer*
Andrew Gerberi, *Vice Pres*
◆ EMP: 150 EST: 2004
SQ FT: 40,000
SALES (est): 51.5MM **Privately Held**
WEB: www.paigeusa.net
SIC: 2326 2331 Men's & boys' work clothing; women's & misses' blouses & shirts
PA: Ppd Holding, Llc
    10119 Jefferson Blvd
    Culver City CA 90232
    310 733-2100

(P-2787)
PROVIDENCE INDUSTRIES LLC
Also Called: Mydyer.
18191 Von Karman Ave # 100, Irvine
(92612-7103)
PHONE..............................562 420-9091
Daniel S Kang, *President*
Dan Kang, *President*
James Lee, *CFO*
Kim Lilly, *Exec VP*
Jennifer Gim, *Vice Pres*
◆ EMP: 60 EST: 1997
SALES (est): 16.2MM **Privately Held**
WEB: www.mydyer.com
SIC: 2326 2331 Men's & boys' work clothing; blouses, women's & juniors': made from purchased material

(P-2788)
ROF LLC
Also Called: Ring of Fire
7800 Arprt Bus Pkwy Stdio, Van Nuys
(91406)
PHONE..............................818 933-4000
Isaac Bitton,
Eran Bitton,
▲ EMP: 45 EST: 2008
SQ FT: 60,000

SALES (est): 6.8MM **Privately Held**
WEB: www.ringoffireclothing.com
SIC: 2326 Men's & boys' work clothing

(P-2789)
SEOLLEM CORPORATION
2856 E Pico Blvd, Los Angeles
(90023-3610)
PHONE..............................323 265-3266
Bong Ja Yoo, *CEO*
EMP: 15 EST: 2004
SALES (est): 542.6K **Privately Held**
WEB: www.seollemcorp.com
SIC: 2326 Men's & boys' work clothing

(P-2790)
SPEKTRUM MANUFACTURING INC
1939 S Susan St, Santa Ana (92704-3901)
PHONE..............................949 702-2807
Robby Khalek, *President*
EMP: 14 EST: 1990
SALES (est): 544.8K **Privately Held**
SIC: 2326 Men's & boys' work clothing

(P-2791)
STRATEGIC DISTRIBUTION L P
Also Called: Cherokee Uniforms
9800 De Soto Ave, Chatsworth
(91311-4411)
PHONE..............................818 671-2100
Michael Singer, *Partner*
▲ EMP: 240 EST: 2003
SALES (est): 97.7MM **Privately Held**
WEB: www.careismatic.com
SIC: 2326 2337 3143 3144 Work uniforms; medical & hospital uniforms, men's; uniforms, except athletic: women's, misses' & juniors'; men's footwear, except athletic; women's footwear, except athletic; uniforms & work clothing; shoes
PA: Careismatic Brands, Inc.
    9800 De Soto Ave
    Chatsworth CA 91311

(P-2792)
WAY OUT WEST INC
21800 Oxnard St Ste 770, Woodland Hills
(91367-3675)
PHONE..............................310 769-6937
Michael C Goldberg, *President*
Mark J Goldberg, *President*
Michael Goldberg, *CEO*
▲ EMP: 31 EST: 1979
SALES (est): 2.7MM **Privately Held**
WEB: www.wayoutwestinc.com
SIC: 2326 2385 Industrial garments, men's & boys'; waterproof outerwear

---

2329 Men's & Boys' Clothing, NEC

(P-2793)
3 POINT DISTRIBUTION LLC
Also Called: Ezekiel
170 Technology Dr, Irvine (92618-2401)
P.O. Box 2568, Newport Beach (92659-1668)
PHONE..............................949 266-2700
Steven A Kurtzman,
Sara Christian, *Software Dev*
Marisela Garcia, *Production*
Mike Martin, *Natl Sales Mgr*
Daniel Kurtzman,
◆ EMP: 20 EST: 2000
SQ FT: 42,000
SALES (est): 5.8MM **Privately Held**
WEB: www.3pointdistribution.com
SIC: 2329 Men's & boys' sportswear & athletic clothing

(P-2794)
4 WHAT ITS WORTH INC (PA)
Also Called: Tyte Jeans
5815 Smithway St, Commerce
(90040-1605)
PHONE..............................323 728-4503
Alden Halpern, *CEO*
Kyle Soladay, *CFO*
◆ EMP: 51 EST: 1993
SQ FT: 38,000

SALES (est): 13.5MM **Privately Held**
WEB: www.rewash.com
SIC: 2329 5961 5651 5699 Knickers, dress (separate): men's & boys'; ; jeans stores; designers; apparel

(P-2795)
A AND G INC (HQ)
Also Called: Alstyle Apparel
11296 Harrel St, Jurupa Valley
(91752-3715)
PHONE..............................714 765-0400
Keith S Walters, *President*
Kevin Potter, *Vice Pres*
Gloria Del Mundo, *Administration*
Aziz Kazi, *Purch Agent*
Jim Henry, *Sales Staff*
◆ EMP: 627 EST: 1978
SALES (est): 103MM
SALES (corp-wide): 1.9B **Privately Held**
WEB: www.gildanbrands.com
SIC: 2329 2253 Athletic (warmup, sweat & jogging) suits: men's & boys'; T-shirts & tops, knit
PA: Les Vetements De Sport Gildan Inc
    600 Boul De Maisonneuve O 33eme
    etage
    Montreal QC H3A 3
    514 735-2023

(P-2796)
ACTIVEAPPAREL INC (PA)
11076 Venture Dr, Jurupa Valley
(91752-3234)
PHONE..............................951 361-0060
Wasif M Siddique, *President*
Khan Baloch, *Admin Sec*
Alex Vedder, *Sales Staff*
Angela Zaragoza, *Director*
▲ EMP: 19 EST: 1993
SQ FT: 30,000
SALES (est): 9.7MM **Privately Held**
WEB: www.activeapparel.net
SIC: 2329 2339 7389 Men's & boys' sportswear & athletic clothing; women's & misses' athletic clothing & sportswear; sewing contractor

(P-2797)
AMERICAN SOCCER COMPANY INC (PA)
Also Called: Score Sports
726 E Anaheim St, Wilmington
(90744-3635)
P.O. Box 1219 (90748-1219)
PHONE..............................310 830-6161
Maria G Menzel, *CEO*
Rosa Cursage, *President*
Anne Hernandez, *Officer*
Alexander Menzel, *Vice Pres*
Dan Kulavil, *Info Tech Mgr*
◆ EMP: 297 EST: 1975
SQ FT: 30,000
SALES (est): 35.8MM **Privately Held**
WEB: www.scoresports.com
SIC: 5699 2329 2339 3949 Uniforms; men's & boys' athletic uniforms; uniforms, athletic: women's, misses' & juniors'; sporting & athletic goods

(P-2798)
ANDARI FASHION INC
9626 Telstar Ave, El Monte (91731-3004)
PHONE..............................626 575-2759
WEI Chen Wang, *President*
Lillian Wang, *President*
Charles Chang, *Vice Pres*
Lydia Yang, *Prgrmr*
Judy Liu, *Production*
◆ EMP: 120 EST: 1991
SQ FT: 50,000
SALES (est): 12.5MM **Privately Held**
WEB: www.andari.com
SIC: 2329 2339 2253 5199 Sweaters & sweater jackets: men's & boys'; women's & misses' accessories; sweaters & sweater coats, knit; art goods & supplies; knit goods

(P-2799)
ANGELS GARMENTS
Also Called: Angel Manufacturing
525 E 12th St Ste 107, Los Angeles
(90015-2645)
PHONE..............................213 748-0581
Jae R Kim, *Owner*

EMP: 15 EST: 1983
SALES (est): 556.3K **Privately Held**
WEB: www.angelsgarment.com
SIC: 2329 2339 2361 Men's & boys' sportswear & athletic clothing; women's & misses' outerwear; girls' & children's dresses, blouses & shirts

(P-2800)
ANTAEUS FASHIONS GROUP INC
2400 Chico Ave, South El Monte
(91733-1613)
PHONE..............................626 452-0797
Yungchieh Lin, *CEO*
Peter Lin, *CFO*
Michael Lin, *Executive*
Shangwen Lin, *Admin Sec*
Silvia Shih, *Accounts Mgr*
▲ EMP: 24 EST: 1991
SQ FT: 10,000
SALES (est): 1.4MM **Privately Held**
WEB: www.atfusa.com
SIC: 2329 2339 Men's & boys' sportswear & athletic clothing; women's & misses' athletic clothing & sportswear

(P-2801)
ARIES 33 LLC
3400 S Main St, Los Angeles (90007-4412)
PHONE..............................310 355-8330
Daniel Guez, *CEO*
Robin Saeks, *CFO*
EMP: 20
SQ FT: 28,000
SALES (est): 15MM **Privately Held**
SIC: 2329 7389 2339 Men's & boys' sportswear & athletic clothing; apparel designers, commercial; women's & misses' outerwear

(P-2802)
B O A INC
580 W Lambert Rd Ste L, Brea
(92821-3913)
PHONE..............................714 256-8960
David Fleming, *President*
Pamela Fleming, *Vice Pres*
▲ EMP: 34 EST: 1992
SQ FT: 6,000
SALES (est): 3.1MM **Privately Held**
SIC: 2329 2337 2339 Men's & boys' sportswear & athletic clothing; women's & misses' suits & coats; women's & misses' outerwear

(P-2803)
BOARDRIDERS INC (HQ)
Also Called: Billabong
5600 Argosy Ave Ste 100, Huntington Beach (92649-1063)
PHONE..............................714 889-5404
Arne Arens, *CEO*
Thomas Chambolle, *President*
Greg Healy, *President*
Shannan North, *President*
Nate Smith, *President*
▼ EMP: 599 EST: 1986
SALES (est): 494.9MM **Privately Held**
WEB: www.boardriders.com
SIC: 2329 2339 3949 5136 Men's & boys' sportswear & athletic clothing; women's & misses' athletic clothing & sportswear; sporting & athletic goods; winter sports equipment; skateboards; windsurfing boards (sailboards) & equipment; sportswear, men's & boys'; sportswear, women's & children's

(P-2804)
BODY GLOVE INTERNATIONAL LLC
6255 W Sunset Blvd # 550, Hollywood
(90028-7403)
PHONE..............................310 374-3441
Michael Devirgilio, *President*
Cory M Baker, *COO*
Warren Clamen, *CFO*
◆ EMP: 17 EST: 1997

134   2022 Southern California Business
Directory and Buyers Guide   ▲ = Import ▼=Export
◆ =Import/Export

SALES (est): 592.3K **Privately Held**
WEB: www.bodyglove.com
SIC: 2329 3949 3069 Bathing suits & swimwear: men's & boys'; bathing suits: women's, misses' & juniors'; bathing suits & swimwear: girls', children's & infants'; wet suits, rubber; shorts (outerwear): men's, youths' & boys'; men's & boys' clothing; apparel belts, men's & boys'; men's & boys' outerwear; shirts, men's & boys'

(P-2805)
DC SHOES INC (DH)
5600 Argosy Ave Ste 100, Huntington Beach (92649-1063)
PHONE....................................714 889-4206
Charles Exon, *CEO*
Brad Holman, *CFO*
Scott Fullerton, *Vice Pres*
Jeff Shine, *Vice Pres*
Sean Pence, *Principal*
◆ EMP: 132 EST: 1993
SQ FT: 100,000
SALES (est): 62.3MM **Privately Held**
WEB: www.dcshoes.com
SIC: 2329 5136 5137 5139 Men's & boys' sportswear & athletic clothing; men's & boys' clothing; women's & children's clothing; footwear
HQ: Boardriders, Inc.
    5600 Argosy Ave Ste 100
    Huntington Beach CA 92649
    714 889-5404

(P-2806)
EDMUND KIM INTERNATIONAL INC (PA)
2880 E Ana St, Compton (90221-5602)
PHONE....................................310 604-1100
Edmund K Kim, *President*
Reza Farmehr, *CFO*
Leonard Aclan, *Credit Staff*
Lynn Sunjara, *Manager*
◆ EMP: 20 EST: 1997
SALES (est): 30.4MM **Privately Held**
WEB: www.ekii.com
SIC: 2329 2261 7218 2253 Athletic (warmup, sweat & jogging) suits: men's & boys'; dyeing cotton broadwoven fabrics; industrial launderers; dresses & skirts; commercial printing, lithographic

(P-2807)
FEAR OF GOD LLC (PA)
3940 Lrl Cyn Blvd Ste 42, Studio City (91604-3709)
PHONE....................................213 235-7985
Jerry Manuel, *Mng Member*
Glenn Milus, *CFO*
Lao Lee, *Manager*
EMP: 39 EST: 2011
SALES (est): 5.9MM **Privately Held**
WEB: www.fearofgod.com
SIC: 2329 Sweaters & sweater jackets: men's & boys'

(P-2808)
FETISH GROUP INC (PA)
Also Called: Tag Rag
1013 S Los Angeles St # 700, Los Angeles (90015-1782)
PHONE....................................323 587-7873
Raphael Sabbah, *CEO*
Orly Dahan, *Vice Pres*
▲ EMP: 39 EST: 1986
SQ FT: 28,000
SALES (est): 5.1MM **Privately Held**
SIC: 2329 2339 2369 Men's & boys' sportswear & athletic clothing; women's & misses' athletic clothing & sportswear; girls' & children's outerwear

(P-2809)
FOURBRO INC
13772 A Better Way, Garden Grove (92843-3906)
PHONE....................................714 277-3858
Rasheed Hussain, *President*
Mohamed Abuthahir, *Corp Secy*
▲ EMP: 15 EST: 1997
SQ FT: 34,000

SALES (est): 677.6K **Privately Held**
SIC: 2329 2331 2321 Men's & boys' sportswear & athletic clothing; women's & misses' blouses & shirts; men's & boys' furnishings

(P-2810)
FUNNY-BUNNY INC (PA)
Also Called: Cachcach
1513b E Saint Gertrude Pl, Santa Ana (92705-5309)
PHONE....................................714 957-1114
Paul Kohne, *President*
▲ EMP: 95 EST: 1983
SQ FT: 25,000
SALES (est): 8MM **Privately Held**
SIC: 2329 2369 Men's & boys' sportswear & athletic clothing; slacks: girls' & children's

(P-2811)
GLOBAL CASUALS INC
18505 S Broadway, Gardena (90248-4632)
PHONE....................................310 817-2828
Jack Tsao, *General Mgr*
▲ EMP: 55 EST: 1995
SQ FT: 2,000
SALES (est): 855.9K
SALES (corp-wide): 75.2MM **Privately Held**
WEB: www.unionbay.com
SIC: 2329 Men's & boys' sportswear & athletic clothing
PA: Seattle Pacific Industries, Inc.
    1633 W Lake Ave N Ste 30
    Seattle WA 98109
    253 872-8822

(P-2812)
HOT SHOPPE DESIGNS INC
1323 Calle Avanzado, San Clemente (92673-6351)
PHONE....................................949 487-2828
David Marietti, *CEO*
Max Frost, *Opers Staff*
▲ EMP: 15 EST: 1982
SQ FT: 6,500
SALES (est): 1.5MM **Privately Held**
WEB: www.hotshoppedesigns.com
SIC: 2329 5136 7336 7389 Riding clothes:, men's, youths' & boys'; shirts, men's & boys'; package design; lettering & sign painting services

(P-2813)
HURLEY INTERNATIONAL LLC (PA)
3080 Bristol St, Costa Mesa (92626-3093)
PHONE....................................949 548-9375
John Schweitzer,
Marlene Groscup, *CFO*
Benjamin Edwards, *Vice Pres*
Alex Hawkins, *Vice Pres*
Ryan Mangan, *Vice Pres*
◆ EMP: 200 EST: 2001
SALES (est): 108.1MM **Privately Held**
WEB: www.hurley.com
SIC: 2329 5137 Knickers, dress (separate): men's & boys'; women's & children's clothing

(P-2814)
J K STAR CORP
1123 N Stanford Ave, Los Angeles (90059-3516)
PHONE....................................310 538-0185
▲ EMP: 80
SQ FT: 50,000
SALES: 3.7MM **Privately Held**
SIC: 2329 2339 Mfg Sports Apparel

(P-2815)
JS APPAREL INC
1751 E Del Amo Blvd, Carson (90746-2938)
PHONE....................................310 631-6333
Ki S Kim, *CEO*
▲ EMP: 99 EST: 2004
SALES (est): 10.8MM **Privately Held**
WEB: www.jsapparel.net
SIC: 2329 Men's & boys' sportswear & athletic clothing; women's & misses' outerwear

(P-2816)
KORAL LLC
Also Called: Koral Activewear
5124 Pacific Blvd, Vernon (90058-2218)
PHONE....................................323 391-1060
Marcelo Kugel, *Mng Member*
Liz Hampshire,
Peter Koral,
Ilana Kugel,
EMP: 36 EST: 2002
SALES (est): 3.5MM **Privately Held**
WEB: www.koral.com
SIC: 2329 2339 Men's & boys' sportswear & athletic clothing; women's & misses' athletic clothing & sportswear

(P-2817)
KRISSY OP SHINS USA INC
Also Called: International Baggyz
2408 S Broadway, Los Angeles (90007-2716)
PHONE....................................213 747-2591
Hae Shin, *President*
Donna Shin, *Vice Pres*
EMP: 14 EST: 1984
SALES (est): 243.3K **Privately Held**
SIC: 2329 Men's & boys' sportswear & athletic clothing

(P-2818)
L A CSTM AP & PROMOTIONS INC (PA)
2680 Temple Ave, Long Beach (90806-2209)
PHONE....................................562 595-1770
Chris Roybal, *President*
Luis Hernandez, *General Mgr*
Peter Calderon, *Purch Mgr*
EMP: 55 EST: 1984
SQ FT: 10,000
SALES (est): 5.1MM **Privately Held**
WEB: www.lacustomapparel.com
SIC: 2329 5136 Athletic (warmup, sweat & jogging) suits: men's & boys'; men's & boys' clothing

(P-2819)
LEATHERUPCOM (PA)
955 Venice Blvd, Los Angeles (90015-3235)
PHONE....................................213 763-6185
Aaron Goshen, *Manager*
Frank Flores, *General Mgr*
EMP: 18 EST: 2011
SALES (est): 262.2K **Privately Held**
WEB: www.leatherup.com
SIC: 2329 Jackets (suede, leatherette, etc.), sport: men's & boys'

(P-2820)
LIQUID GRAPHICS INC
2701 S Harbor Blvd Unit A, Santa Ana (92704-5839)
PHONE....................................949 486-3588
Josh Merrell, *President*
Mark Hyman, *CFO*
Matt Rosenthal, *Sales Staff*
◆ EMP: 130 EST: 1997
SQ FT: 100,000
SALES (est): 25MM **Privately Held**
WEB: www.liquidgraphicsmfg.com
SIC: 2329 Men's & boys' sportswear & athletic clothing

(P-2821)
LOST INTERNATIONAL LLC
170 Technology Dr, Irvine (92618-2401)
PHONE....................................949 600-6950
Mike Reola, *Mng Member*
Matt Biolos,
Joel Cooper,
▲ EMP: 13 EST: 1999
SALES (est): 576.9K **Privately Held**
SIC: 2329 Athletic (warmup, sweat & jogging) suits: men's & boys'

(P-2822)
QUANTUM CONCEPT INC
5701 S Eastrn Ave Ste 220, Commerce (90040)
PHONE....................................323 888-8601
Sung Tack Cho, *CEO*
◆ EMP: 13 EST: 2000
SQ FT: 12,000

SALES (est): 1.4MM **Privately Held**
SIC: 2329 5136 Athletic (warmup, sweat & jogging) suits: men's & boys'; men's & boys' clothing

(P-2823)
SPEEDO USA INC
6251 Katella Ave, Cypress (90630-5234)
PHONE....................................657 465-3800
Linda J Wachner, *Ch of Bd*
Jim Gerson, *President*
Kathy Van Ness, *President*
Antonio Alvarez, *CEO*
Stanley S Lerstein, *CEO*
◆ EMP: 400 EST: 1990
SQ FT: 10,000
SALES (est): 122.9MM
SALES (corp-wide): 7.1B **Publicly Held**
WEB: www.us.speedo.com
SIC: 2329 2339 2321 3949 Athletic (warmup, sweat & jogging) suits: men's & boys'; baseball uniforms: men's, youths' & boys'; ski & snow clothing: men's & boys'; bathing suits & swimwear: men's & boys'; bathing suits: women's, misses' & juniors'; ski jackets & pants: women's, misses' & juniors'; athletic clothing: women's, misses' & juniors'; men's & boys' sports & polo shirts; water sports equipment; sports apparel; military goods & regalia; bathing suits
HQ: Warnaco Inc.
    501 Fashion Ave Fl 14
    New York NY 10018
    212 287-8000

(P-2824)
SPORTSROBE INC
8654 Hayden Pl, Culver City (90232-2902)
PHONE....................................310 559-3999
Allen Ruegsegger, *President*
Mary Ann Ruegsegger, *Vice Pres*
EMP: 49 EST: 1979
SQ FT: 14,000
SALES (est): 4.2MM **Privately Held**
WEB: www.sportsstudio.net
SIC: 2329 Baseball uniforms: men's, youths' & boys'; football uniforms: men's, youths' & boys'

(P-2825)
STEADY CLOTHING INC
2851 E White Star Ave A, Anaheim (92806-2550)
PHONE....................................714 444-2058
Eric Anthony, *President*
Joshua Brownfield, *Vice Pres*
Johnny Baldaray, *Webmaster*
▲ EMP: 17 EST: 1994
SALES (est): 4MM **Privately Held**
WEB: www.steadyclothing.com
SIC: 2329 2339 Men's & boys' sportswear & athletic clothing; sportswear, women's

(P-2826)
STRAIGHT DOWN ENTERPRISES (PA)
Also Called: Straight Down Clothing Company
625 Clarion Ct, San Luis Obispo (93401-8177)
PHONE....................................805 543-3086
Michael Rowley, *CEO*
Brian Cotta, *Software Dev*
Judith Dsouza, *Project Mgr*
Robert Ogden, *Sales Mgr*
Tiffany Sloan, *Sales Staff*
▲ EMP: 20 EST: 1989
SQ FT: 21,000
SALES (est): 4.8MM **Privately Held**
WEB: www.straightdown.com
SIC: 2329 2339 Men's & boys' sportswear & athletic clothing; women's & misses' outerwear

(P-2827)
STREAMLINE DSIGN SLKSCREEN INC (PA)
Also Called: Old Guys Rule
1299 S Wells Rd, Ventura (93004-1901)
PHONE....................................805 884-1025
Thom Hill, *CEO*
Leo Tosh, *General Mgr*
▲ EMP: 67 EST: 1995
SQ FT: 33,000

SALES (est): 10MM Privately Held
WEB: www.oldguysrule.com
SIC: 2329 5136 5611 Men's & boys' sportswear & athletic clothing; men's & boys' clothing; men's & boys' clothing stores

(P-2828)
TARTAN FASHION INC
4357 Rowland Ave, El Monte (91731-1119)
PHONE..........................626 575-2828
Joann Sun, *President*
◆ **EMP: 20 EST:** 2002
SQ FT: 20,363
SALES (est): 1.8MM **Privately Held**
SIC: 2329 Men's & boys' sportswear & athletic clothing

(P-2829)
TRAVISMATHEW LLC (HQ)
15202 Graham St, Huntington Beach (92649-1109)
PHONE..........................562 799-6900
Travis Brasher,
Justin Schnieder, *Store Mgr*
Caylee Scott, *Store Mgr*
Samantha Delapa, *Project Mgr*
Erin Ficker, *Research*
▲ **EMP: 16 EST:** 2007
SALES (est): 6.4MM
SALES (corp-wide): 1.5B **Publicly Held**
WEB: www.travismathew.com
SIC: 2329 5699 Athletic (warmup, sweat & jogging) suits: men's & boys'; sports apparel
PA: Callaway Golf Company
2180 Rutherford Rd
Carlsbad CA 92008
760 931-1771

(P-2830)
TRUWEST INC
5592 Engineer Dr, Huntington Beach (92649-1122)
P.O. Box 1855 (92647-1855)
PHONE..........................714 895-2444
EMP: 28
SQ FT: 13,000
SALES (est): 2.8MM **Privately Held**
WEB: www.truwest.com
SIC: 2329 2339 Mfg Men's/Boy's Clothing Mfg Women's/Misses' Outerwear

(P-2831)
WATERFRONT DESIGN GROUP LLC
122 E Washington Blvd, Los Angeles (90015-3601)
PHONE..........................213 746-5800
Steven Goldman,
EMP: 23 **EST:** 2001
SALES (est): 1.6MM **Privately Held**
SIC: 2329 Men's & boys' sportswear & athletic clothing

(P-2832)
WATT ENTERPRISE INC
Also Called: Pacific Coast Sportswear
10575 Bechler River Ave, Fountain Valley (92708-6908)
PHONE..........................714 963-0781
Al Watt Jr, *President*
Lisa Hahn, *Manager*
EMP: 16 **EST:** 1996
SALES (est): 827.1K **Privately Held**
WEB: www.pcsportswear.com
SIC: 2329 2339 5091 Men's & boys' sportswear & athletic clothing; women's & misses' athletic clothing & sportswear; athletic goods

(P-2833)
ZK ENTERPRISES INC
Also Called: Unique Sales
4368 District Blvd, Vernon (90058-3124)
PHONE..........................213 622-7012
Ron Kelfer, *President*
Kathy Kelfer, *Vice Pres*
EMP: 40 **EST:** 1985
SQ FT: 13,000
SALES (est): 3.7MM **Privately Held**
WEB: www.uniquesalesco.com
SIC: 2329 2339 Athletic (warmup, sweat & jogging) suits: men's & boys'; jogging & warmup suits: women's, misses & juniors'

2331 Women's & Misses' Blouses

(P-2834)
ALLIANCE APPAREL INC
Also Called: Blu Heaven
3422 Garfield Ave, Commerce (90040-3104)
PHONE..........................323 888-8900
Tae Hoo Shin, *President*
Michael Park, *Vice Pres*
▲ **EMP: 40 EST:** 1999
SQ FT: 17,500
SALES (est): 3.3MM **Privately Held**
WEB: www.imagenationapparel.com
SIC: 2331 Blouses, women's & juniors': made from purchased material

(P-2835)
ALPINESTARS USA
2780 W 237th St, Torrance (90505-5270)
PHONE..........................310 891-0222
Giovanni Mazzarolo, *CEO*
Josh Bevan, *Director*
▲ **EMP: 70 EST:** 1986
SQ FT: 28,380
SALES (est): 23.5MM
SALES (corp-wide): 1.5MM **Privately Held**
WEB: www.alpinestar.com
SIC: 2331 2326 Women's & misses' blouses & shirts; men's & boys' work clothing
HQ: Alpinestars Spa
Viale Enrico Fermi 5
Asolo TV 31011
042 352-86

(P-2836)
BAILEY 44 LLC
Also Called: Ali & Jay
4700 S Boyle Ave, Vernon (90058-3000)
PHONE..........................213 228-1930
Shelli Segal, *Mng Member*
Melissa Dench, *Vice Pres*
Elizabeth O'Malley, *Technical Staff*
Kristine To, *Nurse*
Lizette Galdamez, *Assistant*
EMP: 35 **EST:** 2012
SALES (est): 11.3MM **Privately Held**
WEB: www.bailey44.com
SIC: 2331 5621 Blouses, women's & juniors': made from purchased material; boutiques

(P-2837)
BLTEE LLC
7101 Telegraph Rd, Montebello (90640-6511)
P.O. Box 2762, Santa Fe Springs (90670-0762)
PHONE..........................213 802-1736
Elano Miguel Elias, *Mng Member*
EMP: 45 **EST:** 2013
SQ FT: 4,900
SALES (est): 10MM **Privately Held**
SIC: 2331 5136 Women's & misses' blouses & shirts; shirts, men's & boys'

(P-2838)
BLUPRINT CLOTHING CORP
6013 Randolph St, Commerce (90040-3417)
PHONE..........................323 780-4347
Ju Hyun Kim, *CEO*
Liz Lee, *Vice Pres*
Jake Lee, *Technology*
Gina Balag, *Controller*
Ginalyn Balag, *Controller*
▲ **EMP: 75 EST:** 2005
SALES (est): 30MM **Privately Held**
WEB: www.bluprintcorp.com
SIC: 2331 Women's & misses' blouses & shirts; blouses, women's & juniors': made from purchased material; shirts, women's & juniors': made from purchased materials

(P-2839)
C-QUEST INC
Also Called: Ava James
1439 S Herbert Ave, Los Angeles (90023-4047)
PHONE..........................323 980-1400

Nam Ho Paik, *CEO*
Nam H Paik, *CEO*
Nam Paik, *Officer*
◆ **EMP: 22 EST:** 2003
SQ FT: 100,000
SALES (est): 4.6MM **Privately Held**
SIC: 2331 Women's & misses' blouses & shirts

(P-2840)
COLON MANUFACTURING INC (PA)
Also Called: Coc Inc
1100 S San Pedro St, Los Angeles (90015-2328)
PHONE..........................213 749-6149
Thomas T Byun, *President*
Julia Anna Byun, *Admin Sec*
EMP: 19 **EST:** 1991
SALES (est): 2.5MM **Privately Held**
SIC: 2331 2335 2337 Women's & misses' blouses & shirts; women's, juniors' & misses' dresses; women's & misses' suits & coats

(P-2841)
CURE APPAREL LLC
Also Called: Liberty Love
3338 S Malt Ave, Commerce (90040-3126)
PHONE..........................562 927-7460
Amir Seilabi, *Vice Pres*
▲ **EMP: 15 EST:** 2008
SQ FT: 5,000
SALES (est): 1.9MM **Privately Held**
WEB: www.cureapparel.com
SIC: 2331 Blouses, women's & juniors': made from purchased material

(P-2842)
EASTWEST CLOTHING INC (PA)
Also Called: Language Los Angeles
40 E Verdugo Ave, Burbank (91502-1931)
PHONE..........................323 980-1177
Michael Schreier, *CEO*
Arvril Ozen, *COO*
Avril Ozen, *COO*
▲ **EMP: 39 EST:** 1995
SQ FT: 10,000
SALES (est): 4.6MM **Privately Held**
WEB: www.languagelosangeles.com
SIC: 2331 Women's & misses' blouses & shirts

(P-2843)
FORTUNE CASUALS LLC (PA)
Also Called: Judy Ann
10119 Jefferson Blvd, Culver City (90232-3519)
PHONE..........................310 733-2100
Fred Kayne, *Mng Member*
Michael Geller,
Walt Lacher,
◆ **EMP: 100 EST:** 1999
SQ FT: 40,000
SALES (est): 8.1MM **Privately Held**
SIC: 2331 2339 2321 T-shirts & tops, women's: made from purchased materials; slacks: women's, misses' & juniors'; men's & boys' furnishings

(P-2844)
GLORIA LANCE INC (PA)
Also Called: Electric Designs
15616 S Broadway, Gardena (90248-2211)
PHONE..........................310 767-4400
Robert Hempling, *President*
Gloria Lopez, *Treasurer*
Zvia Hempling, *Vice Pres*
Miguel Lopez, *Admin Sec*
◆ **EMP: 90**
SQ FT: 25,000
SALES (est): 16.4MM **Privately Held**
SIC: 2331 2339 2335 Blouses, women's & juniors': made from purchased material; sportswear, women's; bridal & formal gowns

(P-2845)
GURU KNITS INC
Also Called: Antex Knitting Mills
225 W 38th St, Los Angeles (90037-1405)
PHONE..........................323 235-9424
Kevin Port, *CEO*
William Tenenblatt, *President*
◆ **EMP: 60 EST:** 2007

SALES (est): 6.5MM **Privately Held**
WEB: www.aceross.com
SIC: 2331 2361 Women's & misses' blouses & shirts; blouses: girls', children's & infants'

(P-2846)
HARKHAM INDUSTRIES INC (PA)
Also Called: Jonathan Martin
857 S San Pedro St # 300, Los Angeles (90014-2432)
PHONE..........................323 586-4600
Uri Harkham, *President*
◆ **EMP: 50 EST:** 1974
SQ FT: 140,000
SALES (est): 5.5MM **Privately Held**
WEB: www.jonathanmartin.com
SIC: 2331 2335 2337 2339 Blouses, women's & juniors': made from purchased material; women's & misses' dresses; skirts, separate: women's, misses' & juniors'; women's & misses' outerwear

(P-2847)
IHEARTRAVES LLC
250 S Glendora Ave, West Covina (91790-3039)
PHONE..........................626 628-6482
Brian Lim, *CEO*
Scott Elliott, *President*
Alie McCaskill, *Merchandise Mgr*
Christine Lim, *Director*
Kellie Burch, *Manager*
EMP: 19 **EST:** 2012
SALES (est): 1.9MM **Privately Held**
WEB: www.iheartraves.com
SIC: 5632 2331 Apparel accessories; women's & misses' blouses & shirts

(P-2848)
J HEYRI INC
Also Called: Everleigh
6900 S Alameda St, Huntington Park (90255-3619)
PHONE..........................323 588-1234
Tiffany Lin, *President*
Sunny Choi, *CEO*
Alexis Kwak, *Vice Pres*
◆ **EMP: 20 EST:** 2010
SQ FT: 3,000
SALES (est): 2.2MM **Privately Held**
SIC: 2331 Women's & misses' blouses & shirts

(P-2849)
JUNTEE OF CALIFORNIA INC
1031 S Broadway Rm 327, Los Angeles (90015-4006)
PHONE..........................213 742-0246
Jamshid Younesi, *President*
Azam Shirzeh, *Treasurer*
EMP: 35 **EST:** 1987
SQ FT: 3,000
SALES (est): 1.9MM **Privately Held**
SIC: 2331 Women's & misses' blouses & shirts

(P-2850)
K TOO
Also Called: K-Too
800 E 12th St Ste 117, Los Angeles (90021-2199)
PHONE..........................213 747-7766
Jae Hee Kim, *CEO*
Erik Kim, *Vice Pres*
Kelley Kim, *Principal*
Audrey Kim, *Manager*
◆ **EMP: 41 EST:** 2007
SALES (est): 2.9MM **Privately Held**
WEB: www.ktoousa.com
SIC: 2331 Women's & misses' blouses & shirts

(P-2851)
KAMIRAN INC
Also Called: Mesmerize
1415 Maple Ave Ste 220, Los Angeles (90015-3103)
PHONE..........................213 746-9161
Kamram Hakimi, *President*
Kambi Hakimi, *Vice Pres*
Rebecca Cuje, *Sales Staff*
▲ **EMP: 13 EST:** 1987
SQ FT: 6,000

SALES (est): 1.6MM **Privately Held**
WEB: www.mesmerrice.net
SIC: 2331 Women's & misses' blouses & shirts

(P-2852)
KATHY IRELAND WORLDWIDE LLC
39 Princeton Dr, Rancho Mirage (92270-3115)
P.O. Box 1410 (92270-1052)
PHONE....................310 557-2700
Kathy Ireland, *CEO*
Stephen Roseberry, *President*
Erik Sterling, *CFO*
Steve Glick, *Exec VP*
Bialik Benjamin, *Vice Pres*
EMP: 25 **EST:** 1997
SALES (est): 4.8MM **Privately Held**
WEB: www.kathyireland.com
SIC: 2331 2335 2337 5023 Women's & misses' blouses & shirts; women's, juniors' & misses' dresses; women's & misses' suits & coats; rugs

(P-2853)
KUREIJI INC
Also Called: Retail
1442 Chico Ave, South El Monte (91733-2936)
PHONE....................626 788-2657
Philippe Lee, *CEO*
EMP: 16 **EST:** 2014
SALES (est): 1.7MM **Privately Held**
WEB: www.kureiji.com
SIC: 2331 Shirts, women's & juniors': made from purchased materials

(P-2854)
LA MAMBA LLC
150 N Myers St, Los Angeles (90033-2109)
PHONE....................323 526-3526
Vera Campbell,
Stephen Brown,
Denni Kopelan,
▲ **EMP:** 31 **EST:** 2008
SALES (est): 3.3MM **Privately Held**
SIC: 2331 Blouses, women's & juniors': made from purchased material

(P-2855)
LF SPORTSWEAR INC (PA)
Also Called: Furst
5333 Mcconnell Ave, Los Angeles (90066-7025)
PHONE....................310 437-4100
Phillip L Furst, *CEO*
Marsha Furst, *Vice Pres*
Steve Katz, *Vice Pres*
Anura Jayawardena, *Info Tech Mgr*
Stephanie Ocon, *Human Res Dir*
◆ **EMP:** 30 **EST:** 1980
SQ FT: 35,000
SALES (est): 9.1MM **Privately Held**
WEB: www.lfstores.com
SIC: 2331 5137 2211 Women's & misses' blouses & shirts; women's & children's dresses, suits, skirts & blouses; denims

(P-2856)
LOVEMARKS INC
Also Called: Paper Crane
1100 S San Pedro St C01, Los Angeles (90015-2328)
PHONE....................213 514-5888
Samuel Paik, *President*
Monica Ramos, *Software Dev*
▲ **EMP:** 35 **EST:** 2010
SALES (est): 2MM **Privately Held**
SIC: 2331 Women's & misses' blouses & shirts

(P-2857)
LSPACE AMERICA LLC
Also Called: L Space
3500 Hyland Ave Ste 100, Costa Mesa (92626-1459)
PHONE....................949 596-8726
Paul Carr, *Mng Member*
Lauren Kula, *CFO*
Ben Brown, *Technology*
Corrin Meyers, *Credit Mgr*
Natalie Derse, *Cust Mgr*
◆ **EMP:** 20 **EST:** 2008

SALES (est): 3.2MM **Privately Held**
WEB: www.lspace.com
SIC: 2331 Women's & misses' blouses & shirts; bathing suits & swimwear, knit

(P-2858)
MF INC
Also Called: Welovefine
2010 E 15th St, Los Angeles (90021-2823)
PHONE....................213 627-2498
Danish Gajiani, *CEO*
Faizan Bakali, *President*
Bill Bussiere, *CFO*
Dean Allen, *Chief Mktg Ofcr*
Melody Yu, *Technical Staff*
◆ **EMP:** 120 **EST:** 1999
SQ FT: 700,000
SALES (est): 24.6MM
SALES (corp-wide): 195.4MM **Privately Held**
WEB: www.madengine.com
SIC: 2331 2253 T-shirts & tops, women's: made from purchased materials; shirts, women's & juniors': made from purchased materials; T-shirts & tops, knit
PA: Mad Engine, Llc
6740 Cobra Way Ste 100
San Diego CA 92121
858 558-5270

(P-2859)
MONROW INC
1404 S Main St Ste C, Los Angeles (90015-2566)
PHONE....................213 741-6007
Megan George, *President*
Alba Castillo, *Production*
Rebecca Gallegos, *Production*
EMP: 29 **EST:** 2007
SALES (est): 12.1MM **Privately Held**
WEB: www.monrow.com
SIC: 2331 T-shirts & tops, women's: made from purchased material

(P-2860)
MOONSTAR MFG INC
5101 Pacific Blvd, Vernon (90058-2217)
PHONE....................323 581-1656
Francis Membreno, *CEO*
EMP: 13 **EST:** 2008
SALES (est): 1.4MM **Privately Held**
SIC: 2331 Blouses, women's & juniors': made from purchased material

(P-2861)
MXF DESIGNS INC
Also Called: Nally & Millie
5327 Valley Blvd, Los Angeles (90032-3930)
PHONE....................323 266-1451
James Park, *President*
Nally Park, *Shareholder*
▼ **EMP:** 95 **EST:** 1994
SALES (est): 5.2MM **Privately Held**
WEB: www.nallyandmillie.com
SIC: 2331 Blouses, women's & juniors': made from purchased material; T-shirts & tops, women's: made from purchased materials

(P-2862)
MYMICHELLE COMPANY LLC (HQ)
Also Called: My Michelle
13077 Temple Ave, La Puente (91746-1418)
PHONE....................626 934-4166
Arthur Gordon, *President*
Caren Belair, *President*
Perri Cohen, *President*
Susan Stokes, *President*
Roger D Joseph, *Treasurer*
◆ **EMP:** 300 **EST:** 1948
SQ FT: 600,000

SALES (est): 44.5MM
SALES (corp-wide): 535.6MM **Privately Held**
WEB: www.kellwood.com
SIC: 2331 2337 2335 2361 Blouses, women's & juniors': made from purchased material; shirts, women's & juniors': made from purchased materials; skirts, separate: women's, misses' & juniors'; dresses, paper: cut & sewn; blouses: girls', children's & infants'; shirts: girls', children's & infants'; girls' & children's outerwear; women's & misses' athletic clothing & sportswear
PA: Kellwood Company, Llc
13071 Temple Ave
City Of Industry CA 91746
626 934-4122

(P-2863)
NOTHING TO WEAR INC (PA)
Also Called: Figure 8
630 Maple Ave, Torrance (90503-5001)
PHONE....................310 328-0408
Cindy Nunes Freeman, *President*
Darrin Freeman, *CFO*
◆ **EMP:** 35 **EST:** 1991
SQ FT: 18,000
SALES (est): 5.9MM **Privately Held**
SIC: 2331 2335 2339 Women's & misses' blouses & shirts; women's, juniors' & misses' dresses; women's & misses' accessories

(P-2864)
PROJECT SOCIAL T LLC
615 S Clarence St, Los Angeles (90023-1107)
PHONE....................323 266-4500
Mike Chodler, *Mng Member*
Tom Scorer, *Vice Pres*
Olivia Coflin, *Marketing Staff*
EMP: 30 **EST:** 2011
SALES (est): 15MM **Privately Held**
WEB: www.projectsocialt.com
SIC: 2331 5137 5621 Women's & misses' blouses & shirts; women's & children's clothing; women's clothing stores

(P-2865)
SADIE & SAGE LLC (PA)
Also Called: Sage The Label
673 Monterey Pass Rd, Monterey Park (91754-2418)
PHONE....................213 234-2188
Sinae Kim, *CEO*
Steven Kim, *Admin Sec*
Ryan Shelton, *Media Spec*
Shannon Barnes, *Education*
▲ **EMP:** 14 **EST:** 2015
SALES (est): 2.4MM **Privately Held**
WEB: www.sadieandsage.com
SIC: 2331 5137 Women's & misses' blouses & shirts; women's & children's clothing

(P-2866)
SENSE FASHION CORPORATION
Also Called: Sense Fashions
2415 Merced Ave, South El Monte (91733-1921)
PHONE....................626 454-3381
June Ho, *President*
Charles Loh, *Vice Pres*
◆ **EMP:** 16 **EST:** 1993
SQ FT: 14,000
SALES (est): 2.1MM **Privately Held**
SIC: 2331 2335 2339 2329 Blouses, women's & juniors': made from purchased material; shirts, women's & juniors': made from purchased materials; sportswear, women's; men's & boys' sportswear & athletic clothing

(P-2867)
T2C INC
1348 S Flower St, Los Angeles (90015-2908)
PHONE....................213 741-5232
Shawn Janet, *President*
Arlene Mungcal, *Manager*
EMP: 18 **EST:** 2002
SQ FT: 3,500
SALES (est): 1.9MM **Privately Held**
SIC: 2331 Women's & misses' blouses & shirts

(P-2868)
TAAD GROUP INC (HQ)
Also Called: Nicola
1601 Perrino Pl Ste B, Los Angeles (90023-2663)
PHONE....................213 545-0009
SE Jong Yoon, *CEO*
▲ **EMP:** 13 **EST:** 1972
SALES (est): 4.8MM **Privately Held**
SIC: 2331 Women's & misses' blouses & shirts
PA: K Saymee Inc
6409 Gayhart St
Commerce CA 90040
323 832-9323

(P-2869)
TEAM FASHION
2303 E 55th St, Vernon (90058-3435)
PHONE....................323 589-3388
EMP: 15
SQ FT: 80,000
SALES (est): 1.6MM **Privately Held**
SIC: 2331 Mfg Women's/Misses' Blouses

(P-2870)
THREE DOTS LLC
7340 Lampson Ave, Garden Grove (92841-2902)
PHONE....................714 799-6333
Sharon Lebon,
Bruno Lenon,
▲ **EMP:** 72 **EST:** 1995
SALES (est): 14.6MM
SALES (corp-wide): 15.8MM **Privately Held**
WEB: www.threedots.com
SIC: 2331 T-shirts & tops, women's: made from purchased materials
PA: Three Dots, Inc.
11791 Monarch St
Garden Grove CA 92841
714 799-6333

(P-2871)
THREE PLUS ONE INC
Also Called: Audrey 3plus1
3007 Fruitland Ave, Vernon (90058-3626)
PHONE....................213 623-3070
Kim Yon MI, *President*
Durey Kim,
EMP: 14 **EST:** 2007
SALES (est): 1.2MM **Privately Held**
WEB: www.moneygram.com
SIC: 2331 Women's & misses' blouses & shirts

(P-2872)
TIANELLO INC
Also Called: Tianello By Steve Barraza
138 W 38th St, Los Angeles (90037-1404)
PHONE....................323 231-0599
Steven Barraza, *President*
Barraza Steve, *Vice Pres*
Paul Farnacio, *Manager*
Rachel Mendez, *Manager*
▲ **EMP:** 185 **EST:** 1992
SQ FT: 25,000
SALES (est): 19MM **Privately Held**
WEB: www.tianello.com
SIC: 2331 5621 2339 Women's & misses' blouses & shirts; women's clothing stores; women's & misses' outerwear

(P-2873)
UMGEE USA INC
1565 E 23rd St, Los Angeles (90011-1801)
PHONE....................323 526-9138
Boyng Ki GI, *President*
Kevin Cho, *Director*
Miranda Miriam, *Manager*
◆ **EMP:** 18 **EST:** 2001
SALES (est): 1.1MM **Privately Held**
WEB: www.umgeeusa.com
SIC: 2331 2335 Women's & misses' blouses & shirts; women's, juniors' & misses' dresses

(P-2874)
UNGER FABRIK LLC (PA)
18525 Railroad St, City of Industry (91748-1316)
PHONE....................626 469-8080
Yongbin Luo, *CEO*
Celso Ong, *Controller*
◆ **EMP:** 110 **EST:** 1998

PRODUCTS & SVCS

SQ FT: 300,000
SALES (est): 20.3MM Privately Held
SIC: 2331 Women's & misses' blouses & shirts

(P-2875)
W5 CONCEPTS INC
2049 E 38th St, Vernon (90058-1614)
PHONE............................323 231-2415
Kyung Eun Kim, *CEO*
Nancy Ramirez, *Manager*
EMP: 20 EST: 2014
SQ FT: 3,800
SALES (est): 2.8MM Privately Held
WEB: www.w5concepts.com
SIC: 2331 Women's & misses' blouses & shirts

2335 Women's & Misses' Dresses

(P-2876)
ALMACK LINERS INC
9541 Cozycroft Ave, Chatsworth (91311-5102)
PHONE............................818 718-5878
Susana Almack, *President*
EMP: 25 EST: 1985
SQ FT: 3,000
SALES (est): 3.4MM Privately Held
WEB: www.almackliners.com
SIC: 2335 2329 Women's, juniors' & misses' dresses; men's & boys' sportswear & athletic clothing

(P-2877)
AQUARIUS RAGS LLC (PA)
Also Called: ABS By Allen Schwartz
15821 Ventura Blvd # 270, Encino (91436-2915)
PHONE............................213 895-4400
Allen Schwartz, *Mng Member*
Kirk Foster,
Armand Marciano,
▲ **EMP: 34 EST: 2003**
SALES (est): 13.1MM Privately Held
SIC: 2335 Women's, juniors' & misses' dresses

(P-2878)
AVALON APPAREL LLC (PA)
Also Called: Disorderly Kids
2520 W 6th St, Los Angeles (90057-3174)
PHONE............................323 581-3511
Elliot Schutzer, *Mng Member*
Elisabeth Zdunczyk, *Technical Staff*
Tiffany O 'brien, *Prdtn Mgr*
Kelly Geib, *Sales Staff*
Terri Cohen,
EMP: 165 EST: 2004
SQ FT: 5,000
SALES (est): 26.9MM Privately Held
WEB: www.dkidsgroup.com
SIC: 2335 Ensemble dresses: women's, misses' & juniors'

(P-2879)
AWAKE INC
Also Called: Jem Sportswear
10711 Walker St, Cypress (90630-4720)
PHONE............................818 365-9361
Jeffrey A Marine, *CEO*
Orna Stark, *President*
▲ **EMP: 34 EST: 2001**
SQ FT: 65,000
SALES (est): 3.7MM Privately Held
SIC: 2335 Women's, juniors' & misses' dresses

(P-2880)
BEE DARLIN INC (PA)
Also Called: Bee Darlin and Be Smart
1875 E 22nd St, Los Angeles (90058-1033)
PHONE............................213 749-2116
Steve Namm, *President*
Jill Namm, *Treasurer*
Edwina Von Bjorn, *Principal*
▲ **EMP: 90 EST: 1977**
SQ FT: 30,000
SALES (est): 11.5MM Privately Held
WEB: www.beedarlin.com
SIC: 2335 Dresses, paper: cut & sewn

(P-2881)
CAROL ANDERSON INC (PA)
Also Called: Carol Anderson By Invitation
18700 S Laurel Park Rd, Rancho Dominguez (90220-6003)
PHONE............................310 638-3333
Jan Janura, *President*
Carol M Anderson, *President*
Jan A Janura, *President*
Carol Andersen, *Software Dev*
Marlo Natwick, *Consultant*
◆ **EMP: 25 EST: 1977**
SQ FT: 50,000
SALES (est): 8.7MM Privately Held
WEB: www.cabionline.com
SIC: 2335 2339 Women's, juniors' & misses' dresses; shorts (outerwear): women's, misses' & juniors'

(P-2882)
CHOON INC (PA)
Also Called: Pezeme
1443 E 4th St, Los Angeles (90033-4214)
PHONE............................213 225-2500
Choon S Nakamura, *President*
Daniel Nakamura, *Vice Pres*
Manopan Prajimnork, *Production*
◆ **EMP: 31**
SALES (est): 5.4MM Privately Held
WEB: www.choon.com
SIC: 2335 Women's, juniors' & misses' dresses

(P-2883)
COMPLETE CLOTHING COMPANY (PA)
Also Called: Willow
4950 E 49th St, Vernon (90058-2736)
PHONE............................323 277-1470
Eleanor M Sanchez, *President*
Fil Torres, *Controller*
▲ **EMP: 28 EST: 1995**
SQ FT: 30,000
SALES (est): 9.7MM Privately Held
WEB: www.shopwillow.com
SIC: 2335 2339 2337 2331 Women's, juniors' & misses' dresses; sportswear, women's; women's & misses' suits & coats; women's & misses' blouses & shirts

(P-2884)
GAZE USA INC
1665 Mateo St, Los Angeles (90021-2854)
PHONE............................213 622-0022
EMP: 18
SALES (est): 12MM Privately Held
SIC: 2335 Nonclassifiable Establishments

(P-2885)
GINZA COLLECTION DESIGN INC
6015 Obispo Ave, Long Beach (90805-3756)
PHONE............................562 531-1116
Ty Yeh, *President*
WEI Chen Yeh, *Admin Sec*
EMP: 44 EST: 1986
SALES (est): 464.1K
SALES (corp-wide): 4.4MM Privately Held
WEB: www.kennethwinston.com
SIC: 2335 Wedding gowns & dresses
PA: Private Label By G Inc.
6015 Obispo Ave
Long Beach CA 90805
562 531-1116

(P-2886)
HUANG QI
4700 Miller Dr Ste H, Temple City (91780-3757)
PHONE............................626 442-6808
EMP: 15
SALES (est): 640.5K Privately Held
SIC: 2335 Mfg Bridal Gowns

(P-2887)
J C TRIMMING COMPANY INC
Also Called: JC Industries
3800 S Hill St, Los Angeles (90037-1416)
PHONE............................323 235-4458
Eric Shin, *CEO*
Hyunjin Wang, *Accountant*
◆ **EMP: 65 EST: 1993**

SALES (est): 8.7MM Privately Held
WEB: www.jcila.com
SIC: 2335 2326 Women's, juniors' & misses' dresses; men's & boys' work clothing

(P-2888)
JAY-CEE BLOUSE CO INC
Also Called: La Rose of California
823 Maple Ave Ste 200, Los Angeles (90014-2232)
PHONE............................213 622-0116
Stephen Roseman, *President*
Edith Roseman, *Vice Pres*
Richard Roseman, *Vice Pres*
EMP: 18 EST: 1959
SALES (est): 646K Privately Held
SIC: 2335 2331 Women's, juniors' & misses' dresses; blouses, women's & juniors': made from purchased material

(P-2889)
JODI KRISTOPHER LLC (PA)
Also Called: City Triangles
1950 Naomi Ave, Los Angeles (90011-1342)
PHONE............................323 890-8000
Ira Rosenberg, *President*
Ellen Delosh-Bacher, *Shareholder*
Jan Smith, *Shareholder*
Ira Fogelman, *CFO*
Alice Rosenberg, *Admin Sec*
▲ **EMP: 180 EST: 1990**
SQ FT: 100,000
SALES (est): 26.8MM Privately Held
WEB: www.hottempered.com
SIC: 2335 Women's, juniors' & misses' dresses

(P-2890)
JWC STUDIO INC (PA)
Also Called: Johnny Was Showroom
2423 E 23rd St, Los Angeles (90058-1201)
PHONE............................323 231-8222
Eli Levite, *President*
▼ **EMP: 26 EST: 1994**
SQ FT: 30,000
SALES (est): 5.7MM Privately Held
WEB: www.johnnywas.com
SIC: 2335 Women's, juniors' & misses' dresses

(P-2891)
LCI LAUNDRY INC
Also Called: Laundry By Shelli Segal
5835 S Eastrn Ave Ste 100, Commerce (90040)
PHONE............................323 767-1900
Paul Sharron, *Ch of Bd*
Paula Schneider, *President*
▲ **EMP: 125 EST: 1976**
SQ FT: 58,000
SALES (est): 19.6MM Publicly Held
WEB: www.laundrybyshellisegal.com
SIC: 2335 2339 2331 Dresses, paper: cut & sewn; women's & misses' athletic clothing & sportswear; women's & misses' blouses & shirts
HQ: Kate Spade Holdings Llc
5822 Haverford Ave 2
Philadelphia PA 19131
212 354-4900

(P-2892)
LOTUS ORIENT CORP (PA)
Also Called: Venus Bridal Gowns
411 S California St, San Gabriel (91776-2527)
P.O. Box 280 (91778-0280)
PHONE............................626 285-5796
Eugene Wu, *President*
▲ **EMP: 34 EST: 1985**
SQ FT: 6,400
SALES (est): 2.6MM Privately Held
WEB: www.lotusorient.com
SIC: 2335 5621 Wedding gowns & dresses; bridal shops

(P-2893)
MISS KIM INC
Also Called: Miss Cristina
911 New Depot St Apt 9, Los Angeles (90012-1139)
PHONE............................213 741-0888
Leticia Alvarez, *CEO*
Sung H Kim, *CFO*

EMP: 16 EST: 2012
SALES (est): 2.5MM Privately Held
SIC: 2335 5137 Ensemble dresses: women's, misses' & juniors' dresses

(P-2894)
OLA NATION LLC
Also Called: Go Sales.us
915 W Barbara Ave, West Covina (91790-4135)
PHONE............................310 256-0638
Oscar Linares, *President*
EMP: 20 EST: 2007
SALES (est): 757.8K Privately Held
SIC: 2335 Bridal & formal gowns

(P-2895)
PRIVATE BRAND MDSG CORP
Also Called: Jody of California
214 W Olympic Blvd, Los Angeles (90015-1605)
PHONE............................213 749-0191
William Berman, *President*
John Berman, *COO*
Rochelle Berman, *Corp Secy*
Marc Schwartz, *Vice Pres*
EMP: 23 EST: 1954
SQ FT: 6,000
SALES (est): 3.1MM Privately Held
WEB: www.jodyca.com
SIC: 2335 2339 Women's, juniors' & misses' dresses; sportswear, women's

(P-2896)
PROMISES PROMISES INC
3121 S Grand Ave, Los Angeles (90007-3816)
PHONE............................213 749-7725
Eugene Hardy, *President*
▲ **EMP: 29 EST: 1978**
SALES (est): 3.8MM Privately Held
SIC: 2335 Women's, juniors' & misses' dresses

(P-2897)
SUSANNAS INC
Also Called: Susanna Beverly Hills
9647 Santa Monica Blvd, Beverly Hills (90210-4401)
PHONE............................310 276-7510
Susanna Chung-Forest, *President*
Pierre Forest, *Vice Pres*
Matthew Forest, *Mktg Dir*
EMP: 13 EST: 1975
SQ FT: 8,000
SALES (est): 1.2MM Privately Held
WEB: www.susannabh.com
SIC: 5699 2335 Customized clothing & apparel; women's, juniors' & misses' dresses

(P-2898)
TRIXXI CLOTHING COMPANY INC (PA)
6817 E Acco St, Commerce (90040-1901)
PHONE............................323 585-4200
Annette Soufrine, *CEO*
Leslie Flores, *President*
Janet Edwards, *Controller*
▲ **EMP: 113 EST: 2001**
SQ FT: 35,000
SALES (est): 33.1MM Privately Held
WEB: www.trixxi.com
SIC: 2335 2331 Women's, juniors' & misses' dresses; blouses, women's & juniors': made from purchased material

(P-2899)
VALMAS INC
Also Called: Sam & Lavi
1233 S Boyle Ave, Los Angeles (90023-2601)
PHONE............................323 677-2211
Sam Arasteh, *President*
Emily Chen, *Manager*
▲ **EMP: 13 EST: 2009**
SALES (est): 560.9K Privately Held
SIC: 2335 Women's, juniors' & misses' dresses

(P-2900)
WILLIAMSON GRANADOS
Also Called: La Rosa De Mexico
15004 Paramount Blvd, Paramount (90723-3411)
PHONE............................424 296-5494

Williamson Granados, *Owner*
EMP: 13 **EST:** 2013
SALES (est): 552.3K **Privately Held**
WEB: www.quinceaneras.ws
SIC: 2335 Wedding gowns & dresses

(P-2901)
YMI JEANSWEAR INC (PA)
Also Called: Ymi Jeanswear
1155 S Boyle Ave, Los Angeles
(90023-2109)
PHONE..................................323 581-7700
Moshe Moshezaga, *CEO*
David Vered, *President*
Michael Silvestri, *Vice Pres*
Dania Guterrez, *Administration*
Yessica Lopez, *Production*
◆ **EMP:** 15 **EST:** 2000
SALES (est): 16.4MM **Privately Held**
WEB: www.ymijeans.com
SIC: 2335 5621 Women's, juniors' &
misses' dresses; women's clothing stores

2337 Women's & Misses' Suits, Coats & Skirts

(P-2902)
EVA FRANCO INC
1704 Hooper Ave, Los Angeles
(90021-3112)
PHONE..................................213 746-4776
Eva Franco,
Robert Arbogast, *CFO*
Ben Kotler, *Sales Staff*
▲ **EMP:** 15 **EST:** 2004
SALES (est): 1.5MM **Privately Held**
WEB: www.evafranco.com
SIC: 2337 2331 2335 Skirts, separate:
women's, misses' & juniors'; women's &
misses' blouses & shirts; women's, jun-
iors' & misses' dresses

(P-2903)
KAYO OF CALIFORNIA (PA)
Also Called: Kayo Clothing Company
11854 Alameda St, Lynwood (90262-4019)
PHONE..................................323 233-6107
Jack Ostrovsky, *Ch of Bd*
Jeffrey Michaels, *CEO*
Annabelle Wall, *CFO*
Jonathan Kaye, *Vice Pres*
Mireya Morales, *CIO*
▲ **EMP:** 45 **EST:** 1968
SALES (est): 14.5MM **Privately Held**
WEB: www.kayoclothingco.com
SIC: 2337 2339 Skirts, separate:
women's, misses' & juniors'; sportswear,
women's; shorts (outerwear): women's,
misses' & juniors'; slacks: women's,
misses' & juniors'

(P-2904)
KELLER CLASSICS INC (PA)
Also Called: Nannette Keller
19628 Country Oaks St, Tehachapi
(93561-8490)
PHONE..................................805 524-1322
Nannette Keller, *President*
Roger Keller, *CFO*
Richard Scott, *Admin Sec*
EMP: 35 **EST:** 1993
SQ FT: 12,000
SALES (est): 3.6MM **Privately Held**
SIC: 2337 5621 Women's & misses' suits
& skirts; women's clothing stores

(P-2905)
KOMAROV ENTERPRISES INC
Also Called: Kisca
10939 Venice Blvd, Los Angeles
(90034-7015)
PHONE..................................213 244-7000
Dimitri Komarov, *President*
Dimitri Leiberman, *Vice Pres*
Dimitry Liberman, *Vice Pres*
Ashley Segal, *Vice Pres*
Shelley Komarov, *Creative Dir*
▲ **EMP:** 75 **EST:** 1997
SALES (est): 9.1MM **Privately Held**
WEB: www.komarov.com
SIC: 2337 2331 Women's & misses' suits
& coats; women's & misses' blouses &
shirts

(P-2906)
POETRY CORPORATION (PA)
2111 Long Beach Ave, Los Angeles
(90058-1023)
PHONE..................................213 765-8957
▲ **EMP:** 24
SQ FT: 50,000
SALES (est): 3.7MM **Privately Held**
SIC: 2337 Mfg Women's/Misses'
Suits/Coats

(P-2907)
S STUDIO INC
Also Called: Sue Wong
3030 W 6th St, Los Angeles (90020-1506)
PHONE..................................213 388-7400
Dieter Raabe, *President*
Sue Wong, *Ch of Bd*
Josh Homann, *Sales Executive*
▲ **EMP:** 16 **EST:** 1995
SQ FT: 28,000
SALES (est): 2.9MM **Privately Held**
WEB: www.suewong.com
SIC: 2337 Women's & misses' suits &
skirts

(P-2908)
TOPSON DOWNS CALIFORNIA INC
3545 Motor Ave, Los Angeles
(90034-4806)
PHONE..................................310 558-0300
Kris Scott, *Branch Mgr*
Camille Bergher, *Creative Dir*
Alex Perez, *Info Tech Mgr*
Alyssa Stratiff, *Business Anlyst*
Molly Gibson, *Technical Staff*
EMP: 250
SALES (corp-wide): 450.1MM **Privately Held**
WEB: www.topsondowns.com
SIC: 2337 5621 Women's & misses' suits
& coats; ready-to-wear apparel, women's
PA: Topson Downs Of California, Inc.
3840 Watseka Ave
Culver City CA 90232
310 558-0300

2339 Women's & Misses' Outerwear, NEC

(P-2909)
AAKAA INC (PA)
1100 S San Pedro St C08, Los Angeles
(90015-2385)
PHONE..................................213 221-7086
Jeong Hee Kim, *Administration*
EMP: 13 **EST:** 2015
SALES (est): 550.2K **Privately Held**
WEB: www.aakaafashion.com
SIC: 2339 Women's & misses' athletic
clothing & sportswear

(P-2910)
AARON CORPORATION
Also Called: J P Sportswear
2645 Industry Way, Lynwood (90262-4007)
PHONE..................................323 235-5959
Paul Shechet, *President*
Francisco Balleste, *Vice Pres*
Ana Almeida, *Plant Mgr*
Eli Shechet, *Marketing Staff*
▲ **EMP:** 170
SALES (est): 17.8MM **Privately Held**
WEB: www.jpsportswear.us
SIC: 2339 Women's & misses' athletic
clothing & sportswear

(P-2911)
AB&R INC
Also Called: Billy Blues
5849 Smithway St, Commerce
(90040-1605)
PHONE..................................323 727-0007
Rene Allison Thomas, *President*
William Scott Curtis, *Vice Pres*
Billy Curtis, *Sales Staff*
▲ **EMP:** 23 **EST:** 1997
SQ FT: 10,500
SALES (est): 535.3K **Privately Held**
WEB: www.mybillyblues.com
SIC: 2339 Women's & misses' outerwear

(P-2912)
ABS BY ALLEN SCHWARTZ LLC (HQ)
15821 Ventura Blvd # 270, Encino
(91436-4775)
PHONE..................................213 895-4400
Allen Schwartz, *Mng Member*
Kirk Foster, *CFO*
Hope Lee, *Planning*
Camelia Torre, *IT/INT Sup*
Johnny Schwartz, *Mktg Dir*
▲ **EMP:** 108 **EST:** 2004
SALES (est): 11MM
SALES (corp-wide): 13.1MM **Privately Held**
WEB: www.allenschwartz.com
SIC: 2339 5621 Women's & misses' outer-
wear; women's clothing stores
PA: Aquarius Rags, Llc
15821 Ventura Blvd # 270
Encino CA 91436
213 895-4400

(P-2913)
ABS CLOTHING COLLECTION INC
Also Called: A.B.S. By Allen Schwartz
15821 Ventura Blvd # 270, Encino
(91436-2915)
PHONE..................................213 895-4400
Allen Schwartz, *President*
EMP: 14 **EST:** 1982
SALES (est): 409.9K **Privately Held**
SIC: 2339 5621 Women's & misses' outer-
wear; women's clothing stores

(P-2914)
ALBION KNITTING MILLS INC
2152 Sacramento St, Los Angeles
(90021-1722)
PHONE..................................213 624-7740
George Ainslie, *President*
Albion Mill, *Assistant*
EMP: 14 **EST:** 1923
SQ FT: 15,000
SALES (est): 394.8K **Privately Held**
WEB: www.broadwayalbion.com
SIC: 2339 2329 2253 Uniforms, athletic:
women's, misses' & juniors'; jackets
(suede, leatherette, etc.), sport: men's &
boys'; knit outerwear mills

(P-2915)
AMBIANCE USA INC
Also Called: Wax Jean By Ambiance
930 Towne Ave, Los Angeles (90021-2022)
PHONE..................................213 765-9600
EMP: 35
SALES (corp-wide): 25MM **Privately Held**
WEB: www.waxjean.com
SIC: 2339 Jeans: women's, misses' & jun-
iors'
PA: Ambiance U.S.A., Inc.
930 Towne Ave
Los Angeles CA 90021
323 587-0007

(P-2916)
AMBIANCE USA INC
2465 E 23rd St, Los Angeles (90058-1201)
PHONE..................................323 587-0007
EMP: 35
SALES (corp-wide): 25MM **Privately Held**
WEB: www.waxjean.com
SIC: 2339 Women's & misses' outerwear
PA: Ambiance U.S.A., Inc.
930 Towne Ave
Los Angeles CA 90021
323 587-0007

(P-2917)
AMBIANCE USA INC (PA)
Also Called: Ambiance Apparel
930 Towne Ave, Los Angeles (90021-2022)
PHONE..................................323 587-0007
Sang Noh, *CEO*
Christine Chung, *Council Mbr*
◆ **EMP:** 100 **EST:** 1999
SALES (est): 25MM **Privately Held**
WEB: www.ambianceapparel.us
SIC: 2339 5137 Women's & misses' outer-
wear; women's & children's clothing

(P-2918)
APPAREL PROD SVCS GLOBL LLC
Also Called: APS Global
8954 Lurline Ave, Chatsworth
(91311-6103)
P.O. Box 5011, Woodland Hills (91365-
5011)
PHONE..................................818 700-3700
Clayton Medley,
Roxana Dragan, *Opers Staff*
Eric Billings, *Production*
Richard Cohen,
Paul Stanley,
◆ **EMP:** 42 **EST:** 2013
SQ FT: 15,000
SALES (est): 8.4MM **Privately Held**
SIC: 2339 2329 Women's & misses' ath-
letic clothing & sportswear; men's & boys'
sportswear & athletic clothing

(P-2919)
ASSOLUTO INC
Also Called: Molly Max
215 S Santa Fe Ave Apt 5, Los Angeles
(90012-4350)
PHONE..................................213 748-1116
Ugo Capasso, *CEO*
◆ **EMP:** 13 **EST:** 1986
SQ FT: 2,600
SALES (est): 624.7K **Privately Held**
SIC: 2339 Women's & misses' athletic
clothing & sportswear

(P-2920)
AZTECA JEANS INC
6600 Avalon Blvd, Los Angeles
(90003-1959)
PHONE..................................323 758-7721
EMP: 50
SALES (est): 3.4MM **Privately Held**
SIC: 2339 Mfg Women's/Misses' Outer-
wear

(P-2921)
BARE NOTHINGS INC (PA)
17705 Sampson Ln, Huntington Beach
(92647-6790)
PHONE..................................714 848-8532
Ann Mase, *President*
Ronald Mase, *Vice Pres*
EMP: 22 **EST:** 1977 **Privately Held**
WEB: www.barenothings.com
SIC: 2339 Bathing suits: women's, misses'
& juniors'

(P-2922)
BB CO INC
Also Called: Wild Lizard
1753 E 21st St, Los Angeles (90058-1006)
PHONE..................................213 550-1158
Kyoung K Frazier, *President*
▲ **EMP:** 30 **EST:** 1998
SQ FT: 22,000
SALES (est): 7.5MM **Privately Held**
SIC: 2339 Women's & misses' athletic
clothing & sportswear

(P-2923)
BE BOP CLOTHING
Also Called: Rebel Jeans
5833 Avalon Blvd, Los Angeles
(90003-1307)
PHONE..................................323 846-0121
Guillermo Granados, *President*
Marcus Sphatt, *Vice Pres*
Michael Harb, *Admin Sec*
Cristy Song, *Accounting Mgr*
EMP: 350 **EST:** 1987
SQ FT: 100,000
SALES (est): 19.8MM **Privately Held**
SIC: 2339 Sportswear, women's

(P-2924)
BEBE STUDIO INC
Also Called: B E B E
10250 Santa Monica Blvd # 6, Los Angeles
(90067-6404)
PHONE..................................213 362-2323
Manny Mashouf, *President*
Marc So, *CFO*
Gary Bosch, *Admin Sec*
▲ **EMP:** 150 **EST:** 2002
SQ FT: 46,685

PRODUCTS & SVCS

SALES (est): 26MM **Publicly Held**
WEB: www.bebe.com
SIC: 5719 5621 5661 2339 Linens;
women's clothing stores; women's shoes;
women's & misses' accessories
PA: Bebe Stores, Inc.
400 Valley Dr
Brisbane CA 94005
415 715-3900

(P-2925)
BLUE BLUSH CLOTHING INC
(PA)
2021 E 49th St, Vernon (90058-2801)
PHONE..................................323 923-2895
Jay Cho, *CEO*
Jason Cho, *Vice Pres*
EMP: 14 EST: 2014
SQ FT: 30,000
SALES (est): 3.1MM **Privately Held**
WEB: www.blueblushclothing.com
SIC: 2339 Athletic clothing: women's,
misses' & juniors'

(P-2926)
BU RU LLC
Also Called: Shop Buru
826 E 3rd St, Los Angeles (90013-1820)
PHONE..................................424 316-2878
Morgan Hutchinson, *Mng Member*
Brutt Hutchinson, *Mng Member*
EMP: 17 EST: 2013
SALES (est): 1.4MM **Privately Held**
SIC: 5961 5621 2339 ; women's clothing
stores; women's & misses' athletic cloth-
ing & sportswear

(P-2927)
BURNING TORCH INC
1738 Cordova St, Los Angeles
(90007-1129)
PHONE..................................323 733-7700
Karyn Craven, *President*
Rose Marron, *Prdtn Mgr*
▲ EMP: 20 EST: 1999
SQ FT: 5,000
SALES (est): 3MM **Privately Held**
WEB: www.burningtorchinc.com
SIC: 2339 Sportswear, women's

(P-2928)
C M G INC
Also Called: Tarrant Apparel Group
801 S Figueroa St, Los Angeles
(90017-5504)
PHONE..................................323 780-8250
Charles Ghailian, *President*
Julie Ghailian, *Treasurer*
EMP: 25 EST: 1988
SALES (est): 2.7MM **Privately Held**
SIC: 2339 Women's & misses' athletic
clothing & sportswear

(P-2929)
CAMP SMIDGEMORE INC (DH)
Also Called: Renee Claire Inc
3641 10th Ave, Los Angeles (90018-4114)
PHONE..................................323 634-0333
Wendy Luttrel, *CEO*
Renee Bertrand, *President*
▲ EMP: 22 EST: 2001
SQ FT: 13,000
SALES (est): 7.7MM
SALES (corp-wide): 283.3MM **Privately
Held**
WEB: www.komarbrands.com
SIC: 2339 2341 Women's & misses' outer-
wear; pajamas & bedjackets: women's &
children's
HQ: Komar Intimates, Llc
90 Hudson St
Jersey City NJ 07302
212 725-1500

(P-2930)
CAROL WIOR INC
Also Called: Slimsuit
7533 Garfield Ave, Bell (90201-4817)
PHONE..................................562 927-0052
Carol Wior, *President*
Troy Berg, *CEO*
Lucy Weddell, *Treasurer*
Niki Wior, *Vice Pres*
Kathy Means, *Executive*
▲ EMP: 44 EST: 1991
SQ FT: 77,000

SALES (est): 3.7MM **Privately Held**
WEB: www.carolwiorinc.com
SIC: 2339 5621 5699 Bathing suits: women's,
misses' & juniors'; sportswear, women's;
beachwear: women's, misses' & juniors';
bathing suits

(P-2931)
CEE SPORTSWEAR
6409 Gayhart St, Commerce (90040-2505)
PHONE..................................323 726-8158
Paul Bogner, *President*
▲ EMP: 19 EST: 1958
SQ FT: 57,000
SALES (est): 1.1MM **Privately Held**
WEB: www.ceesportswear.com
SIC: 2339 Maternity clothing

(P-2932)
CITIZENS OF HUMANITY LLC
(PA)
Also Called: Goldsign
5715 Bickett St, Huntington Park
(90255-2624)
PHONE..................................323 923-1240
Jerome Dahan, *CEO*
Amy Williams, *President*
Robert Hermanns, *CFO*
Shelley Barham, *Vice Pres*
Kevin Swett, *Vice Pres*
◆ EMP: 171 EST: 2005
SQ FT: 70,000
SALES (est): 40.9MM **Privately Held**
WEB: www.citizensofhumanity.com
SIC: 2339 Jeans: women's, misses' & jun-
iors'

(P-2933)
CLASSIC TEES INC
4915 Walnut Grove Ave, San Gabriel
(91776-2021)
PHONE..................................626 607-0255
Paul Chauderson, *President*
Connie Lam, *Vice Pres*
EMP: 14 EST: 1995
SQ FT: 15,000
SALES (est): 631.3K **Privately Held**
WEB: www.classictees.com
SIC: 2339 Women's & misses' athletic
clothing & sportswear

(P-2934)
CLOTHING ILLUSTRATED INC
(PA)
Also Called: Love Stitch
2030 E 15th St, Los Angeles (90021-2823)
PHONE..................................213 403-9950
Danny Forouzesh, *President*
Cyrous Forouzesh, *CFO*
▲ EMP: 35 EST: 2002
SALES (est): 8.9MM **Privately Held**
WEB: www.shoplovestitch.com
SIC: 2339 Women's & misses' outerwear

(P-2935)
CREW KNITWEAR LLC (PA)
Also Called: Hiatus
660 S Myers St, Los Angeles (90023-1015)
PHONE..................................323 526-3888
Peter Jung, *CEO*
Chris Y Jung, *President*
Dawn Williams, *Vice Pres*
Julie Stevens, *Sales Staff*
Quinn Rees, *Mktg Coord*
▲ EMP: 122 EST: 2001
SQ FT: 39,000
SALES (est): 13.6MM **Privately Held**
WEB: www.crewknitwear.com
SIC: 2339 Women's & misses' outerwear

(P-2936)
DARBO MANUFACTURING
COMPANY
363 Glenoaks St, Brea (92821-2117)
PHONE..................................714 529-7693
EMP: 25
SQ FT: 7,500
SALES (est): 1.2MM **Privately Held**
WEB: www.dancewearforyou.com
SIC: 2339 2369 2389 Mfg Athletic Sports-
wear Including Leotards And Leggings
And Costumes

(P-2937)
DAVID GRMENT CTNG FSING
SVC IN
Also Called: Clothng/Pparel/Uniform/ppe Mfg
5008 S Boyle Ave, Vernon (90058-3904)
PHONE..................................323 216-1574
Mario Alvarado, *CEO*
David Alvarado, *President*
▲ EMP: 45 EST: 1987
SQ FT: 15,000
SALES (est): 3.3MM **Privately Held**
SIC: 2339 2326 2329 Women's & misses'
athletic clothing & sportswear; men's &
boys' work clothing; men's & boys' sports-
wear & athletic clothing

(P-2938)
DDA HOLDINGS INC
Also Called: A Commom Thread
834 S Broadway Ste 600, Los Angeles
(90014-3217)
PHONE..................................213 624-5200
Anthony Graham, *CEO*
Sandra Balestier, *President*
▲ EMP: 25 EST: 2007
SQ FT: 15,000
SALES (est): 4.8MM **Privately Held**
WEB: www.ddaholdings.com
SIC: 2339 Women's & misses' athletic
clothing & sportswear

(P-2939)
DESIGN TODAYS INC (PA)
11707 Cetona Way, Porter Ranch
(91326-4604)
PHONE..................................213 745-3091
Sung OK Hong, *President*
EMP: 26 EST: 1987
SALES (est): 3.7MM **Privately Held**
SIC: 2339 Women's & misses' outerwear

(P-2940)
DHM INTERNATIONAL CORP
Also Called: Sunshine Enterprises
901 Monterey Pass Rd, Monterey Park
(91754-3610)
PHONE..................................323 263-3888
Scott Yuen, *President*
Joe Yuen, *Vice Pres*
Ross Yuen, *Vice Pres*
▲ EMP: 16 EST: 2003
SQ FT: 28,000
SALES (est): 938.8K **Privately Held**
SIC: 2339 2326 Women's & misses' outer-
wear; men's & boys' work clothing

(P-2941)
DNAM APPAREL INDUSTRIES
LLC
Also Called: Ed Hardy
4938 Triggs St, Commerce (90022-4832)
PHONE..................................323 859-0114
Henri Levy,
Michael Cohen, *CFO*
▲ EMP: 32 EST: 2004
SALES (est): 2.7MM **Privately Held**
SIC: 2339 5137 Service apparel, wash-
able: women's; women's & children's
clothing

(P-2942)
DOSA INC
850 S Broadway Ste 700, Los Angeles
(90014-3238)
PHONE..................................213 627-3672
Christina Kim, *President*
▲ EMP: 30 EST: 1983
SQ FT: 15,000
SALES (est): 2MM **Privately Held**
WEB: www.dosainc.com
SIC: 2339 Sportswear, women's

(P-2943)
ETHICALLY MADE GOODS INC
1613 Santee St, Los Angeles (90015-3627)
PHONE..................................213 683-1123
Agustin Ramirez, *CEO*
EMP: 13 EST: 2018
SALES (est): 775.3K **Privately Held**
SIC: 2339 Women's & misses' athletic
clothing & sportswear

(P-2944)
FAST SPORTSWEAR INC
6400 E Washington Blvd, Commerce
(90040-1820)
PHONE..................................323 720-1078
Young Kuen Kim, *President*
Sook In Kim, *Vice Pres*
EMP: 17 EST: 1990
SQ FT: 200,000
SALES (est): 1.2MM **Privately Held**
SIC: 2339 Sportswear, women's

(P-2945)
GAZE USA INC
1665 Mateo St, Los Angeles (90021-2854)
PHONE..................................213 622-0022
Ji S Hong, *CEO*
Stephen S Whang, *President*
EMP: 25 EST: 2010
SALES (est): 2.9MM **Privately Held**
SIC: 2339 5651 3999 Women's & misses'
athletic clothing & sportswear; unisex
clothing stores; bristles, dressing of

(P-2946)
GOLF APPAREL BRANDS INC
Also Called: La Mode
404 Fordyce Rd, Los Angeles
(90049-2011)
PHONE..................................310 327-5188
Edward J Kahn, *President*
W Barry Kahn, *Vice Pres*
◆ EMP: 20 EST: 1977
SALES (est): 1.1MM **Privately Held**
WEB: www.lamode.com
SIC: 2339 Women's & misses' outerwear

(P-2947)
GOOD AMERICAN LLC (PA)
3125 S La Cienega Blvd, Los Angeles
(90016-3110)
PHONE..................................213 357-5100
Emma Grede, *CEO*
Ryan Slyper, *Officer*
Rocco Vienhage, *Exec VP*
Kelly Lockhart, *Vice Pres*
Kara Blitstein, *Executive*
EMP: 33 EST: 2016
SALES (est): 2.9MM **Privately Held**
WEB: www.goodamerican.com
SIC: 2339 5137 5621 Jeans: women's,
misses' & juniors'; women's & children's
clothing; women's clothing stores;
women's specialty clothing stores

(P-2948)
GYPSY 05 INC
3200 Union Pacific Ave, Los Angeles
(90023-4203)
PHONE..................................323 265-2700
Dotan Shoham, *President*
Catalina Doto, *Manager*
Tracee Rhodes, *Manager*
▲ EMP: 25 EST: 2005
SALES (est): 2.2MM **Privately Held**
WEB: www.gypsy05.com
SIC: 2339 Women's & misses' athletic
clothing & sportswear

(P-2949)
HEARTS DELIGHT
4035 N Ventura Ave, Ventura (93001-1163)
PHONE..................................805 648-7123
Deborah Mesker, *Owner*
EMP: 27 EST: 1986
SQ FT: 2,000
SALES (est): 1.7MM **Privately Held**
WEB: www.shop.heartsdelightclothiers.com
SIC: 2339 5621 Women's & misses' outer-
wear; boutiques

(P-2950)
HEATHER BY BORDEAUX INC
5983 Malburg Way, Vernon (90058-3945)
PHONE..................................213 622-0555
Afshin Raminfar, *CEO*
Anna Dood, *Production*
Justine Pregler, *Producer*
Ardy Raminfar, *Marketing Staff*
▲ EMP: 39 EST: 2003
SALES (est): 4.1MM **Privately Held**
WEB: www.heatherfashion.com
SIC: 2339 Service apparel, washable:
women's

(P-2951)
HONEY PUNCH INC (PA)
1535 Rio Vista Ave, Los Angeles
(90023-2619)
PHONE....................................323 800-3812
Tae Sung Kang, *President*
Huyon Kang, *Vice Pres*
Angel Rodriguez, *E-Commerce*
Gabriel Cisneros, *Warehouse Mgr*
▲ **EMP:** 13 **EST:** 2002
SALES (est): 2.2MM **Privately Held**
WEB: www.myhoneypunch.com
SIC: 2339 5621 Women's & misses' ath-
letic clothing & sportswear; women's
clothing stores

(P-2952)
I AM BEYOND LLC
Also Called: Beyond Yoga
11248 Playa Ct, Culver City (90230-6127)
PHONE....................................310 882-6476
Jodi Guber,
Michelle Wahler,
▲ **EMP:** 14 **EST:** 2005
SALES (est): 6.1MM **Privately Held**
WEB: www.beyondyoga.com
SIC: 2339 5137 5621 Sportswear,
women's; women's & children's clothing;
women's clothing stores

(P-2953)
J & F DESIGN INC
Also Called: Next Generation
2042 Garfield Ave, Commerce
(90040-1804)
PHONE....................................323 526-4444
Jack Farshi, *President*
Abraham Safarian, *Buyer*
◆ **EMP:** 67 **EST:** 1991
SQ FT: 100,000
SALES (est): 9.2MM **Privately Held**
WEB: www.bobbyjackbrand.com
SIC: 2339 Sportswear, women's

(P-2954)
JANIN
10031 Hunt Ave, South Gate (90280-6310)
PHONE....................................323 564-0995
Jose Estevez, *Owner*
EMP: 210 **EST:** 1987
SQ FT: 10,000
SALES (est): 5.4MM **Privately Held**
SIC: 2339 Neckwear & ties: women's,
misses' & juniors'

(P-2955)
JAYA APPAREL GROUP LLC
2760 Fruitland Ave, Vernon (90058-3608)
PHONE....................................714 904-9051
Sam Hinning, *Manager*
EMP: 21
SALES (corp-wide): 43.8MM **Privately
Held**
WEB: www.jayaapparelgroup.com
SIC: 2339 Women's & misses' athletic
clothing & sportswear
PA: Jaya Apparel Llc
5175 S Soto St
Vernon CA 90058
323 584-3500

(P-2956)
JAYA APPAREL GROUP LLC
Likely
5175 S Soto St, Vernon (90058-3620)
PHONE....................................323 584-3500
EMP: 21
SALES (corp-wide): 43.8MM **Privately
Held**
WEB: www.jayaapparelgroup.com
SIC: 2339 Women's & misses' jackets &
coats, except sportswear
PA: Jaya Apparel Group Llc
5175 S Soto St
Vernon CA 90058
323 584-3500

(P-2957)
JAYA APPAREL GROUP LLC (PA)
5175 S Soto St, Vernon (90058-3620)
PHONE....................................323 584-3500
Jane Siskin, *CEO*
Don Lewis, *Officer*
Salvador Lopez, *Graphic Designe*
Maila Santos, *Finance Mgr*
Victor Balderas, *Analyst*

◆ **EMP:** 80 **EST:** 2005
SQ FT: 170,000
SALES (est): 43.8MM **Privately Held**
WEB: www.jayaapparelgroup.com
SIC: 2339 2337 Women's & misses' jack-
ets & coats, except sportswear; shorts
(outerwear): women's, misses' & juniors';
women's & misses' suits & skirts

(P-2958)
JD/CMC INC
Also Called: Color ME Cotton
2834 E 11th St, Los Angeles (90023-3406)
PHONE....................................818 767-2260
Mari Tatevosian, *President*
Anait Grigorian, *Admin Sec*
◆ **EMP:** 35 **EST:** 1991
SQ FT: 12,000
SALES (est): 3.2MM **Privately Held**
WEB: www.cmcclick.com
SIC: 2339 Women's & misses' outerwear

(P-2959)
**JOLYN CLOTHING COMPANY
LLC**
150 5th St Ste 100, Huntington Beach
(92648-5139)
PHONE....................................714 794-2149
Warren Lief Pedersen, *President*
Brandon Molina, *COO*
Ann Dawson, *Vice Pres*
Mallyce Miller, *Creative Dir*
Kelsea Smith, *Sales Dir*
EMP: 30 **EST:** 2007
SALES (est): 3MM **Privately Held**
WEB: www.jolyn.com
SIC: 2339 5621 Women's & misses' ath-
letic clothing & sportswear; women's
sportswear

(P-2960)
JT DESIGN STUDIO INC (PA)
Also Called: 860, Shameless, Hot Wire
860 S Los Angeles St # 912, Los Angeles
(90014-3319)
PHONE....................................213 891-1500
Ted Cooper, *President*
Robert Grossman, *Vice Pres*
▲ **EMP:** 24 **EST:** 1998
SALES (est): 2.2MM **Privately Held**
WEB: www.jtdesignstudio.com
SIC: 2339 Women's & misses' athletic
clothing & sportswear

(P-2961)
JUST FOR WRAPS INC (PA)
Also Called: A-List
4871 S Santa Fe Ave, Vernon
(90058-2103)
PHONE....................................213 239-0503
Vrajesh Lal, *CEO*
Rakesh Lal, *Vice Pres*
Edna Asuncion, *Accounting Mgr*
Bukul Chawla, *Manager*
▲ **EMP:** 130 **EST:** 1980
SALES (est): 25.3MM **Privately Held**
WEB: www.wrapper.com
SIC: 2339 2335 2337 Sportswear,
women's; women's, juniors' & misses'
dresses; women's & misses' suits & coats

(P-2962)
KIM & CAMI PRODUCTIONS INC
2950 Leonis Blvd, Vernon (90058-2916)
PHONE....................................323 584-1300
Kimberly A Hiatt, *President*
Cami Gasmer, *CFO*
▲ **EMP:** 40 **EST:** 1999
SQ FT: 1,000
SALES (est): 5.2MM **Privately Held**
SIC: 2339 Sportswear, women's

(P-2963)
KLK FORTE INDUSTRY INC (PA)
Also Called: Honey Punch
1535 Rio Vista Ave, Los Angeles
(90023-2619)
PHONE....................................323 415-9181
Katherine Kim, *CEO*
◆ **EMP:** 45 **EST:** 2012
SQ FT: 30,000
SALES (est): 6MM **Privately Held**
SIC: 2339 Women's & misses' outerwear

(P-2964)
KORAL INDUSTRIES LLC (PA)
Also Called: Koral Los Angeles
5124 Pacific Blvd, Vernon (90058-2218)
PHONE....................................323 585-5343
David Koral,
Danmar Gonzalez, *Prdtn Mgr*
Peter Koral,
▲ **EMP:** 51 **EST:** 2012
SQ FT: 60,000
SALES (est): 6.5MM **Privately Held**
WEB: www.koral.com
SIC: 2339 Service apparel, washable:
women's

(P-2965)
KYMSTA CORP
1506 W 12th St, Los Angeles (90015-2013)
PHONE....................................213 380-8118
Roxanne Heptner, *President*
Arthur Pereira, *CFO*
EMP: 15 **EST:** 1990
SQ FT: 25,000
SALES (est): 661K **Privately Held**
SIC: 2339 Women's & misses' athletic
clothing & sportswear

(P-2966)
L Y A GROUP INC
1317 S Grand Ave, Los Angeles
(90015-3008)
PHONE....................................213 683-1123
Claudia L Blanco, *CEO*
Augustin Ramirez, *President*
▲ **EMP:** 30 **EST:** 2003
SALES (est): 4.2MM **Privately Held**
SIC: 2339 Jeans: women's, misses' & jun-
iors'

(P-2967)
LAT LLC
Also Called: G Girl Clothing
2618 Fruitland Ave, Vernon (90058-2220)
PHONE....................................323 233-3017
Simon Cho, *Mng Member*
Robert Baker, *CTO*
Sung H Cho,
▲ **EMP:** 40 **EST:** 1999
SALES (est): 4.3MM **Privately Held**
SIC: 2339 Women's & misses' outerwear

(P-2968)
LEE THOMAS INC (PA)
13800 S Figueroa St, Los Angeles
(90061-1026)
PHONE....................................310 532-7560
Lee Opolinsky, *President*
Thomas Mahoney, *Vice Pres*
EMP: 30 **EST:** 1981
SQ FT: 45,000
SALES (est): 4.2MM **Privately Held**
SIC: 2339 Women's & misses' athletic
clothing & sportswear

(P-2969)
MANHATTAN BEACHWEAR INC
10700 Valley View St, Cypress
(90630-4835)
PHONE....................................714 892-7354
EMP: 100
SALES (corp-wide): 229.8MM **Privately
Held**
SIC: 2339 Mfg Women's/Misses' Outer-
wear
PA: Manhattan Beachwear, Inc.
10700 Valley View St
Cypress CA 90630
714 892-7354

(P-2970)
MARCEA INC
1742 Crenshaw Blvd, Torrance
(90501-3311)
P.O. Box 48317, Los Angeles (90048-0317)
PHONE....................................213 746-5191
Marcia D Lane, *President*
EMP: 17 **EST:** 1988
SQ FT: 2,500
SALES (est): 703.4K **Privately Held**
SIC: 2339 Sportswear, women's

(P-2971)
MARIKA LLC
5553-B Bandini Blvd, Bell (90201)
PHONE....................................323 888-7755
Frank M Zarabi, *Mng Member*

Patrick Shaowl,
▲ **EMP:** 100 **EST:** 2011
SQ FT: 160,000
SALES (est): 9.4MM **Privately Held**
WEB: www.marika.com
SIC: 2339 Athletic clothing: women's,
misses' & juniors'; women's & misses'
athletic clothing & sportswear

(P-2972)
MAX LEON INC (PA)
Also Called: Max Studio.com
3100 New York Dr, Pasadena
(91107-1524)
P.O. Box 70879 (91117-7879)
PHONE....................................626 797-6886
Leon Max, *President*
Jacqueline Paasman, *Executive Asst*
Spencer Benda, *Administration*
Jesse Munoz, *Manager*
▲ **EMP:** 100 **EST:** 1979
SQ FT: 65,000
SALES (est): 53.2MM **Privately Held**
WEB: www.maxstudio.com
SIC: 2339 5632 Sportswear, women's; ap-
parel accessories

(P-2973)
MGT INDUSTRIES INC (PA)
Also Called: CALIFORNIA DYNASTY
13889 S Figueroa St, Los Angeles
(90061-1025)
PHONE....................................310 516-5900
Jeffrey P Mirvis, *CEO*
Alessandra Strahl, *President*
Phil Nathanson, *CFO*
Michael Brooks, *Exec VP*
Mike Brooks, *Vice Pres*
▲ **EMP:** 113 **EST:** 1983
SQ FT: 82,000
SALES: 4.1K **Privately Held**
WEB: www.mgtind.com
SIC: 2339 Women's & misses' outerwear

(P-2974)
MIMI CHICA (PA)
Also Called: Mimi Chica Design
161 W 33rd St, Los Angeles (90007-4106)
PHONE....................................323 264-9278
Paul Spoleti, *President*
EMP: 17 **EST:** 2009
SALES (est): 1.5MM **Privately Held**
WEB: www.mimichica.com
SIC: 2339 Women's & misses' culottes,
knickers & shorts: women's; jeans: women's,
misses' & juniors'; slacks: women's,
misses' & juniors'

(P-2975)
MONTEREY CANYON LLC (PA)
1515 E 15th St, Los Angeles (90021-2711)
PHONE....................................213 741-0209
Fabian Oberfeld,
Richard Sneider,
▲ **EMP:** 70 **EST:** 1977
SALES (est): 7.1MM **Privately Held**
SIC: 2339 Sportswear, women's

(P-2976)
NEXXEN APPAREL INC (PA)
Also Called: Check It Out
1555 Los Palos St, Los Angeles
(90023-3218)
PHONE....................................323 267-9900
Jai Sim, *President*
Carol Chang, *Vice Pres*
Billy Sim, *Vice Pres*
EMP: 18 **EST:** 1998
SQ FT: 10,000
SALES (est): 3.1MM **Privately Held**
SIC: 2339 Women's & misses' outerwear

(P-2977)
NILS INC (PA)
Also Called: Nils Skiwear
3151 Airway Ave Ste V, Costa Mesa
(92626-4627)
PHONE....................................714 755-1600
Nils Andersson, *CEO*
Richard Leffler, *President*
Lisa Batson, *Credit Mgr*
Jordan Batha, *Marketing Mgr*
▲ **EMP:** 15 **EST:** 1953

SALES (est): 2.5MM **Privately Held**
WEB: www.nils.us
SIC: 2339 Women's & misses' athletic clothing & sportswear; ski jackets & pants: women's, misses' & juniors'; snow suits: women's, misses' & juniors'

(P-2978)
PACE SPORTSWEAR INC
12781 Monarch St, Garden Grove (92841-3920)
PHONE......................714 891-8716
Leonor Saavedra, *CEO*
Maria Marsh, *President*
▲ **EMP:** 18 **EST:** 1978
SQ FT: 6,500
SALES (est): 1.1MM **Privately Held**
WEB: www.pacesportswear.com
SIC: 2339 2329 Athletic clothing: women's, misses' & juniors'; athletic (warmup, sweat & jogging) suits: men's & boys'

(P-2979)
PACIFIC ATHLETIC WEAR INC
7340 Lampson Ave, Garden Grove (92841-2902)
PHONE......................714 751-8006
John Hillenbrand, *President*
Gabriela Hillenbrand, *Vice Pres*
Alex Hillenbrand, *Project Mgr*
▲ **EMP:** 70 **EST:** 1994
SALES (est): 6.4MM **Privately Held**
WEB: www.pacificathleticwear.com
SIC: 2339 Uniforms, athletic: women's, misses' & juniors'

(P-2980)
PATTERSON KINCAID LLC
5175 S Soto St, Vernon (90058-3620)
PHONE......................323 584-3559
Jane Siskin, *Mng Member*
Jilali Elbasri,
◆ **EMP:** 56 **EST:** 2010
SQ FT: 35,000
SALES (est): 1.1MM
SALES (corp-wide): 43.8MM **Privately Held**
WEB: www.jayaapparelgroup.com
SIC: 2339 Women's & misses' outerwear
PA: Jaya Apparel Group Llc
    5175 S Soto St
    Vernon CA 90058
    323 584-3500

(P-2981)
PEEP INC
Also Called: Peep Studio
720 Towne Ave, Los Angeles (90021-1418)
PHONE......................213 748-5500
Kamran Samooha, *President*
▲ **EMP:** 13 **EST:** 1990
SQ FT: 2,000
SALES (est): 1.1MM **Privately Held**
SIC: 2339 Sportswear, women's

(P-2982)
PETER K INC (PA)
Also Called: Next ERA
5175 S Soto St, Vernon (90058-3620)
PHONE......................323 585-5343
Peter Koral, *President*
▲ **EMP:** 142 **EST:** 1982
SALES (est): 9.2MM **Privately Held**
SIC: 2339 2369 Sportswear, women's; girls' & children's outerwear

(P-2983)
PIERRE MITRI (PA)
Also Called: Watch L.A.
1138 Wall St, Los Angeles (90015-2320)
PHONE......................213 747-1838
Pierre D Mitri, *Owner*
▲ **EMP:** 17 **EST:** 1989
SQ FT: 6,000
SALES (est): 1.9MM **Privately Held**
WEB: www.watchla.com
SIC: 2339 Jeans: women's, misses' & juniors'; women's & misses' athletic clothing & sportswear

(P-2984)
PIET RETIEF INC
Also Called: Peter Cohen Companies
1914 6th Ave, Los Angeles (90018-1124)
PHONE......................323 732-8312

Peter Cohen, *President*
Anna Cohen, *Treasurer*
Lee Stuart Cox, *Vice Pres*
EMP: 34 **EST:** 1983
SQ FT: 4,800
SALES (est): 1.6MM **Privately Held**
SIC: 2339 Sportswear, women's

(P-2985)
POINT CONCEPTION INC
Also Called: Kechika
23121 Arroyo Vis Ste A, Rcho STA Marg (92688-2633)
PHONE......................949 589-6890
Jeff Jung, *CEO*
Jamie Jung, *President*
Victoria Jung, *Corp Secy*
◆ **EMP:** 35 **EST:** 1979
SQ FT: 20,000
SALES (est): 3.8MM **Privately Held**
WEB: www.kechika.com
SIC: 2339 Bathing suits: women's, misses' & juniors'; sportswear, women's

(P-2986)
PUTNAM ACCESSORY GROUP INC
4455 Fruitland Ave, Vernon (90058-3222)
PHONE......................323 306-1330
John Putnam, *President*
▲ **EMP:** 20 **EST:** 2012
SALES (est): 965.9K **Privately Held**
WEB: www.putnamaccessorygroup.com
SIC: 2339 2389 Women's & misses' accessories; men's miscellaneous accessories

(P-2987)
Q&A7 LLC
Also Called: Q&A Clothing
2155 E 7th St Ste 150, Los Angeles (90023-1032)
PHONE......................323 364-4250
Aaron Voref,
Nicholas Rozansky,
◆ **EMP:** 19 **EST:** 2016
SQ FT: 10,000
SALES (est): 1.7MM **Privately Held**
SIC: 2339 5137 Women's & misses' athletic clothing & sportswear; athletic clothing: women's, misses' & juniors'; women's & children's clothing

(P-2988)
RAJ MANUFACTURING LLC
2692 Dow Ave, Tustin (92780-7208)
PHONE......................714 838-3110
Joseph Binotto,
EMP: 35 **EST:** 2006
SALES (est): 926.5K **Privately Held**
WEB: www.rajswim.com
SIC: 2339 Bathing suits: women's, misses' & juniors'

(P-2989)
RHAPSODY CLOTHING INC
Also Called: Epilogue and Arrested
810 E Pico Blvd Ste 24, Los Angeles (90021-2375)
PHONE......................213 614-8887
Bryan Kang, *CEO*
Yoon MI Kang, *Vice Pres*
Joi Dela Rama, *Manager*
▲ **EMP:** 65 **EST:** 1994
SALES (est): 8.2MM **Privately Held**
WEB: www.rhapsodyclothing.com
SIC: 2339 Shorts (outerwear): women's, misses' & juniors'; jeans: women's, misses' & juniors'

(P-2990)
ROTAX INCORPORATED
Also Called: Gamma
2940 Leonis Blvd, Vernon (90058-2916)
P.O. Box 58071, Los Angeles (90058-0071)
PHONE......................323 589-5999
Arthur Torssien, *President*
Ripsick Kepenekian, *Vice Pres*
▲ **EMP:** 40 **EST:** 1993
SALES (est): 2.5MM **Privately Held**
WEB: www.rotax1.com
SIC: 2339 2329 Women's & misses' outerwear; men's & boys' sportswear & athletic clothing

(P-2991)
ROYAL APPAREL INC
4331 Baldwin Ave, El Monte (91731-1103)
PHONE......................626 579-5168
Kung-Shih Yang, *President*
Sheena Yang, *Corp Secy*
Michael Hsu, *Vice Pres*
▲ **EMP:** 21 **EST:** 1987
SQ FT: 24,000
SALES (est): 739.2K **Privately Held**
WEB: www.royalapparel.net
SIC: 2339 Leotards: women's, misses' & juniors'; women's & misses' athletic clothing & sportswear

(P-2992)
SECOND GENERATION INC
Also Called: Fish Bowl
1950 Naomi Ave, Los Angeles (90011-1342)
PHONE......................213 743-8700
Michael Weisberg, *CEO*
Dale Kaufman, *CFO*
▲ **EMP:** 68 **EST:** 1996
SQ FT: 11,000
SALES (est): 9.8MM **Privately Held**
WEB: www.bebopclothing.com
SIC: 2339 5621 Women's & misses' athletic clothing & sportswear; women's clothing stores

(P-2993)
SLL INC
5401 S Soto St, Vernon (90058-3618)
PHONE......................323 581-9040
Lisa Rudes, *Principal*
EMP: 14 **EST:** 2002
SALES (est): 271.1K **Privately Held**
SIC: 2339 Sportswear, women's

(P-2994)
SOLE SURVIVOR CORPORATION
Also Called: Gramicci Comfort Engineered
28632 Roadside Dr Ste 200, Agoura Hills (91301-6088)
PHONE......................818 338-3760
Donald N Love, *CEO*
▲ **EMP:** 14 **EST:** 1982
SQ FT: 46,000
SALES (est): 358.8K **Privately Held**
SIC: 2339 2329 5137 5136 Sportswear, women's; men's & boys' sportswear & athletic clothing; women's & children's clothing; men's & boys' clothing

(P-2995)
SPIRIT CLOTHING COMPANY
Also Called: Spirit Active Wear
2211 E 37th St, Vernon (90058-1427)
PHONE......................213 784-0251
Jake Pitaszink, *President*
Christi Carano, *Executive*
▼ **EMP:** 25 **EST:** 1983
SQ FT: 19,000
SALES (est): 4.1MM **Privately Held**
WEB: www.spiritjersey.com
SIC: 2339 2329 Athletic clothing: women's, misses' & juniors'; men's & boys' sportswear & athletic clothing

(P-2996)
SSC APPAREL INC
Also Called: Soprano
2025 Long Beach Ave, Los Angeles (90058-1021)
P.O. Box 1358, Lomita (90717-5358)
PHONE......................213 748-5511
Julie Kim, *CEO*
Alexis Kim, *President*
Jamie Yoon, *Consultant*
▲ **EMP:** 14 **EST:** 2000
SQ FT: 20,000
SALES (est): 732.9K **Privately Held**
SIC: 2339 Women's & misses' athletic clothing & sportswear

(P-2997)
ST JOHN KNITS INC (DH)
17522 Armstrong Ave, Irvine (92614-5876)
PHONE......................949 225-8857
Eran Cohen, *CEO*
Louise Baker, *Vice Pres*
David Muniz, *Store Dir*
Gail Zizzo, *Regional Mgr*
Debra Fox, *Store Mgr*

EMP: 1012 **EST:** 1962
SALES (est): 107.7MM
SALES (corp-wide): 571.3MM **Privately Held**
WEB: www.stjohnknits.com
SIC: 2339 2253 2389 Women's & misses' accessories; knit outerwear mills; men's miscellaneous accessories
HQ: St. John Knits International, Incorporated
    17522 Armstrong Ave
    Irvine CA 92614
    949 863-1171

(P-2998)
ST JOHN KNITS INTL INC (HQ)
Also Called: St John Knits
17522 Armstrong Ave, Irvine (92614-5876)
PHONE......................949 863-1171
Geoffroy Van Raemdonck, *CEO*
James Kelley, *Partner*
Bernd Beetz, *Ch of Bd*
Glenn McMahon, *CEO*
Bruce Fetter, *COO*
◆ **EMP:** 150 **EST:** 1962
SQ FT: 71,100
SALES (est): 355.4MM
SALES (corp-wide): 571.3MM **Privately Held**
WEB: www.stjohnknits.com
SIC: 2339 Sportswear, women's
PA: Gray Vestar Investors Llc
    17622 Armstrong Ave
    Irvine CA 92614
    949 863-1171

(P-2999)
STONY APPAREL CORP (PA)
Also Called: Eyeshadow
1500 S Evergreen Ave, Los Angeles (90023-3618)
PHONE......................323 981-9080
Lu Kong, *CEO*
Dean Wiener, *COO*
Anthony Millar, *CFO*
Elyse Copeland, *Vice Pres*
Stephen B Maiman, *Admin Sec*
▲ **EMP:** 79 **EST:** 1996
SQ FT: 200,000
SALES (est): 21MM **Privately Held**
WEB: www.stonyapparel.com
SIC: 2339 Women's & misses' athletic clothing & sportswear

(P-3000)
TCJ MANUFACTURING LLC
Also Called: Velvet Heart
2744 E 11th St, Los Angeles (90023-3404)
PHONE......................213 488-8400
Gabrielle Tsabag, *Mng Member*
Jordan Tsabag, *Vice Pres*
Moshe Tsabag,
▲ **EMP:** 22 **EST:** 2008
SALES (est): 3.2MM **Privately Held**
SIC: 2339 Athletic clothing: women's, misses' & juniors'

(P-3001)
TCW TRENDS INC
2886 Columbia St, Torrance (90503-3808)
PHONE......................310 533-5177
Charanjiv S Mansingh, *President*
Prerana Sachdev Khanna, *Vice Pres*
Gurvinder Singh Sandhu, *Vice Pres*
Rohaidah Chehassan, *Finance Dir*
Yamini Patel, *Production*
▲ **EMP:** 24 **EST:** 2001
SQ FT: 10,000
SALES (est): 4.6MM **Privately Held**
WEB: www.tcwusa.com
SIC: 2339 2326 5137 Aprons, except rubber or plastic: women's, misses', juniors'; men's & boys' work clothing; coordinate sets: women's, children's & infants'

(P-3002)
TEMPTED APPAREL CORP
4516 Loma Vista Ave, Vernon (90058-2602)
PHONE......................323 859-2480
Steven Schoenholz, *President*
Moy Valentine, *CFO*
Heide Buchholz, *Vice Pres*
Steve Scholods, *Administration*
Moy Valentin, *Controller*
▲ **EMP:** 50 **EST:** 1996

SALES (est): 5.9MM **Privately Held**
WEB: www.temptedapparel.com
SIC: 2339 Women's & misses' outerwear

(P-3003)
TOAD & CO INTERNATIONAL INC (PA)
2020 Alameda Padre Serra, Santa Barbara (93103-1756)
P.O. Box 21508 (93121-1508)
PHONE..................805 957-1474
Gordon Seabury, *President*
Kyle Boettcher, *Vice Pres*
Katie Hodgdon, *Admin Sec*
Ponch Membreno, *Opers Staff*
Kelly Milazzo, *Opers Staff*
▲ **EMP:** 35 **EST:** 1991
SQ FT: 7,000
SALES (est): 17.7MM **Privately Held**
WEB: www.toadandco.com
SIC: 2339 2329 Women's & misses' athletic clothing & sportswear; men's & boys' sportswear & athletic clothing

(P-3004)
TOSKA INC
Also Called: Tz
1100 S San Pedro St I06, Los Angeles (90015-2387)
PHONE..................213 746-0088
Nancy Choi, *President*
▲ **EMP:** 15 **EST:** 1998
SALES (est): 1.4MM **Privately Held**
WEB: www.toska4u.com
SIC: 2339 5137 Women's & misses' outerwear; women's & children's clothing

(P-3005)
TOUCH ME FASHION INC (PA)
Also Called: Teen Bell
906 E 60th St, Los Angeles (90001-1017)
PHONE..................323 234-9200
Hyun Soon Chung, *President*
▲ **EMP:** 45 **EST:** 2006
SALES (est): 737.4K **Privately Held**
SIC: 2339 Women's & misses' outerwear

(P-3006)
TREIVUSH INDUSTRIES
Also Called: B B Blu
940 W Washington Blvd, Los Angeles (90015-3312)
PHONE..................213 745-7774
Menachem Treivush, *President*
EMP: 100 **EST:** 1983
SQ FT: 125,000
SALES (est): 9.1MM **Privately Held**
WEB: www.treivush.com
SIC: 2339 5137 Sportswear, women's; sportswear, women's & children's

(P-3007)
VICTORY PROFESSIONAL PDTS INC
Also Called: Victory Koredrry
5601 Engineer Dr, Huntington Beach (92649-1123)
PHONE..................714 887-0621
Marc Spitaleri, *President*
Victor Talmadge, *Director*
▲ **EMP:** 28 **EST:** 1979
SQ FT: 8,500
SALES (est): 3MM **Privately Held**
WEB: www.victorykoredry.com
SIC: 2339 2329 2393 Women's & misses' athletic clothing & sportswear; men's & boys' sportswear & athletic clothing; textile bags

(P-3008)
VXB & ORFWID INC
Also Called: Lost & Wander
5041 S Santa Fe Ave B, Vernon (90058-2123)
PHONE..................213 222-0030
Jillian J Yoo, *CEO*
EMP: 20 **EST:** 2014
SALES (est): 1.8MM **Privately Held**
WEB: www.lostandwander.com
SIC: 2339 Sportswear, women's

(P-3009)
W & W CONCEPT INC
Also Called: Perseption
4890 S Alameda St, Vernon (90058-2806)
PHONE..................323 233-9202

Wonsook Chong, *President*
Jay Joo, *CFO*
▲ **EMP:** 55 **EST:** 1996
SQ FT: 45,000
SALES (est): 8.7MM **Privately Held**
SIC: 2339 Sportswear, women's

(P-3010)
YMI JEANSWEAR INC
1015 Wall St Ste 115, Los Angeles (90015-2392)
PHONE..................213 746-6681
Colin Smyth, *VP Opers*
Marcus Kim, *Manager*
EMP: 54
SALES (corp-wide): 16.4MM **Privately Held**
WEB: www.ymijeans.com
SIC: 2339 2325 Jeans: women's, misses' & juniors'; men's & boys' jeans & dungarees
PA: Y.M.I Jeanswear, Inc.
1155 S Boyle Ave
Los Angeles CA 90023
323 581-7700

(P-3011)
ZOOEY APPAREL INC
1526 Cloverfield Blvd C, Santa Monica (90404-3772)
PHONE..................310 315-2880
Alice Heller, *President*
EMP: 24 **EST:** 2003
SQ FT: 5,000
SALES (est): 2.4MM **Privately Held**
SIC: 2339 Women's & misses' outerwear

2341 Women's, Misses' & Children's Underwear & Nightwear

(P-3012)
AFR APPAREL INTERNATIONAL INC
Also Called: Parisa Lingerie & Swim Wear
19401 Business Center Dr, Northridge (91324-3506)
PHONE..................818 773-5000
Amir Moghadam, *President*
Brenda J Moghadam, *Exec VP*
Olga Yaromenka, *Associate*
▲ **EMP:** 60 **EST:** 1992
SQ FT: 46,000
SALES (est): 25MM **Privately Held**
WEB: www.parisausa.com
SIC: 2341 2342 2369 5137 Women's & children's nightwear; bras, girdles & allied garments; bathing suits & swimwear: girls', children's & infants'; lingerie

(P-3013)
CALOR APPAREL GROUP INTL CORP
Also Called: True Grit
884 W 16th St, Newport Beach (92663-2802)
PHONE..................949 548-9095
Bruce W Bennett III, *CEO*
John R Provine, *Treasurer*
▲ **EMP:** 20 **EST:** 1990
SQ FT: 7,000
SALES (est): 1.1MM **Privately Held**
SIC: 2341 2329 2342 5961 Women's & children's underwear; men's & boys' sportswear & athletic clothing; bras, girdles & allied garments; mail order house; women's apparel, mail order

(P-3014)
CHARLES KOMAR & SONS INC
Also Called: Komar Distribution Services
11850 Riverside Dr, Jurupa Valley (91752-1001)
PHONE..................951 934-1377
Lisa Casillas, *Branch Mgr*
EMP: 307
SALES (corp-wide): 283.3MM **Privately Held**
WEB: www.komarbrands.com
SIC: 2341 Women's & children's underwear

PA: Charles Komar & Sons, Inc.
90 Hudson St Fl 9
Jersey City NJ 07302
212 725-1500

(P-3015)
GUESS INC (PA)
1444 S Alameda St, Los Angeles (90021-2433)
PHONE..................213 765-3100
Carlos Alberini, *CEO*
Alex Yemenidjian, *Ch of Bd*
Kathryn Anderson, *CFO*
Paul Marciano, *Ch Credit Ofcr*
◆ **EMP:** 700 **EST:** 1981
SQ FT: 341,700
SALES (est): 1.8B **Publicly Held**
WEB: www.guess.com
SIC: 2341 2325 2369 6794 Women's & children's underwear; women's & children's nightwear; nightgowns & negligees: women's & children's; men's & boys' trousers & slacks; shorts (outerwear): men's, youths' & boys'; men's & boys' jeans & dungarees; girls' & children's outerwear; children's culottes & shorts; shorts (outerwear): girls' & children's; children's snowsuits, coats & jackets; copyright buying & licensing

(P-3016)
HONEST COMPANY INC (PA)
12130 Millennium Ste 500, Los Angeles (90094-2946)
PHONE..................310 917-9199
Nikolaos Vlahos, *CEO*
Jessica Alba, *Ch of Bd*
Kelly Kennedy, *CFO*
Donald Frey, *Officer*
Jasmin Manner, *Officer*
▲ **EMP:** 188 **EST:** 2011
SQ FT: 46,518
SALES (est): 300.5MM **Publicly Held**
WEB: www.honest.com
SIC: 2341 2833 5961 Panties: women's, misses', children's & infants'; vitamins, natural or synthetic: bulk, uncompounded; catalog & mail-order houses

(P-3017)
MAIDENFORM LLC
100 Citadel Dr Ste 323, Commerce (90040-1592)
PHONE..................323 724-9558
EMP: 178
SALES (corp-wide): 5.7B **Publicly Held**
SIC: 2341 Mfg Women/Miss Underwear
HQ: Maidenform Llc
1000 E Hanes Mill Rd
Winston Salem NC 27105
336 519-8080

(P-3018)
NATIONAL CORSET SUPPLY HOUSE (PA)
Also Called: Louden Madelon
3240 E 26th St, Vernon (90058-8008)
PHONE..................323 261-0265
Roy Schlobohm, *CEO*
Kirk Schlobohm, *COO*
Ron Schlobohm, *Purchasing*
Al Saenz, *Plant Mgr*
Jesse Ocegueda, *Sales Associate*
◆ **EMP:** 65 **EST:** 1948
SQ FT: 25,000
SALES (est): 15.6MM **Privately Held**
WEB: www.shirleyofhollywood.com
SIC: 2341 5137 Women's & children's undergarments; corsets

(P-3019)
SELECTRA INDUSTRIES CORP
5166 Alcoa Ave, Vernon (90058-3716)
PHONE..................323 581-8500
John Neman, *President*
Malek Neman, *CFO*
Mark Neman, *Admin Sec*
Leslie Valle, *Manager*
▲ **EMP:** 85 **EST:** 2000
SQ FT: 30,000
SALES (est): 12.4MM **Privately Held**
WEB: www.selectraindustries.com
SIC: 2341 2339 Women's & children's underwear; sportswear, women's

2342 Brassieres, Girdles & Garments

(P-3020)
BRAGEL INTERNATIONAL INC
Also Called: Brava
3383 Pomona Blvd, Pomona (91768-3297)
PHONE..................909 598-8808
Clotilde Chen, *CEO*
Kenny Chen, *Shareholder*
Alice Chen, *Treasurer*
Daren Peng, *Vice Pres*
Lena Huang, *Accounts Mgr*
▲ **EMP:** 45 **EST:** 1989
SQ FT: 30,000
SALES (est): 7.3MM **Privately Held**
WEB: www.bragel.com
SIC: 2342 Brassieres

(P-3021)
METRIC PRODUCTS INC (PA)
4630 Leahy St, Culver City (90232-3515)
PHONE..................310 815-9000
Shirley Magidson, *President*
Rita Haft, *Vice Pres*
Debra Magidson, *Admin Sec*
▲ **EMP:** 27 **EST:** 1948
SQ FT: 25,000
SALES (est): 7.9MM **Privately Held**
WEB: www.metric-products.com
SIC: 2342 3496 Brassieres; fabrics, woven wire

(P-3022)
OFFLINE INC (PA)
2250 Maple Ave, Los Angeles (90011-1190)
PHONE..................213 742-9001
Charles Park, *President*
Karen Park, *CFO*
▲ **EMP:** 45 **EST:** 2002
SQ FT: 50,000
SALES (est): 8.8MM **Privately Held**
WEB: www.offlineinc.com
SIC: 2342 2326 Foundation garments, women's; industrial garments, men's & boys'

2353 Hats, Caps & Millinery

(P-3023)
AGRON INC
2440 S Sepulveda Blvd # 201, Los Angeles (90064-1748)
PHONE..................310 473-7223
Wade Siegel, *President*
Anton Schiff, *CFO*
Julie Taylor, *Information Mgr*
Jason Schoenberger, *Business Mgr*
Renee Rozenberg, *Finance*
◆ **EMP:** 60 **EST:** 1989
SQ FT: 10,000
SALES (est): 18.6MM **Privately Held**
SIC: 2353 2393 3949 3171 Hats, caps & millinery; canvas bags; sporting & athletic goods; women's handbags & purses

(P-3024)
AUGUST HAT COMPANY INC (PA)
Also Called: August Accessories
2021 Calle Yucca, Thousand Oaks (91360-2257)
PHONE..................805 983-4651
Roque Valladares, *President*
Ann Valladares, *Corp Secy*
▲ **EMP:** 23 **EST:** 1990
SALES (est): 3.3MM **Privately Held**
SIC: 2353 2381 Hats, caps & millinery; fabric dress & work gloves; scarves, hoods, headbands, etc.: women's

(P-3025)
CALI-FAME LOS ANGELES INC
Also Called: Kennedy Athletics
20934 S Santa Fe Ave, Carson (90810-1131)
PHONE..................310 747-5263
Michael G Kennedy, *CEO*
Brian Kennedy, *President*
Linelle Kennedy, *Corp Secy*

Timothy Kennedy, *Vice Pres*
Jesse Khat, *Webmaster*
▲ **EMP:** 92 **EST:** 1925
SQ FT: 30,000
SALES (est): 8.9MM **Privately Held**
WEB: www.califame.com
SIC: 2353 Uniform hats & caps

(P-3026)
HEADMASTER INC (PA)
3000 S Croddy Way, Santa Ana
(92704-6305)
PHONE....................714 556-5244
Dong J Park, *President*
Jimmy J Park, *Vice Pres*
▲ **EMP:** 27 **EST:** 1985
SQ FT: 35,000
SALES (est): 2.1MM **Privately Held**
WEB: www.headmaster.com
SIC: 2353 Hats: cloth, straw & felt

2361 Children's & Infants' Dresses & Blouses

(P-3027)
ALL ACCESS APPAREL INC (PA)
Also Called: Self Esteem
1515 Gage Rd, Montebello (90640-6613)
PHONE....................323 889-4300
Richard Clareman, *CEO*
Michael Conway, *CFO*
Andrea Rankin, *Exec VP*
Bobette Stott, *Senior VP*
Maria Peralta, *Vice Pres*
◆ **EMP:** 130 **EST:** 1997
SQ FT: 122,000
SALES (est): 18.2MM **Privately Held**
WEB: www.selfesteemclothing.com
SIC: 2361 2335 2331 Girls' & children's
dresses, blouses & shirts; women's, jun-
iors' & misses' dresses; women's &
misses' blouses & shirts

(P-3028)
AST SPORTSWEAR INC (PA)
2701 E Imperial Hwy, Brea (92821-6713)
P.O. Box 17219, Anaheim (92817-7219)
PHONE....................714 223-2030
Shoaib Dadabhoy, *CEO*
Abdul Rashid, *COO*
Taher Dadabhoy, *Admin Sec*
▲ **EMP:** 479 **EST:** 1995
SQ FT: 42,000
SALES (est): 50.8MM **Privately Held**
WEB: www.astsportswear.com
SIC: 2361 5131 5699 T-shirts & tops:
girls', children's & infants'; T-shirts & tops,
women's: made from purchased materi-
als; sports apparel

(P-3029)
COLOR IMAGE APPAREL INC (PA)
Also Called: Bellacanvas
6670 Flotilla St, Commerce (90040-1816)
PHONE....................855 793-3100
Daniel Harris, *CEO*
Chris Blakeslee, *Exec VP*
Summer Barry, *Vice Pres*
Marco Degeorge, *Vice Pres*
Mark Stanczyk, *Vice Pres*
◆ **EMP:** 45 **EST:** 1992
SQ FT: 105,000
SALES (est): 147.5MM **Privately Held**
WEB: www.bellacanvas.com
SIC: 2361 5136 5137 Girls' & children's
dresses, blouses & shirts; men's & boys'
clothing; women's & children's clothing

(P-3030)
COTTON GENERATION INC
Also Called: Trouble At The Mill
6051 Maywood Ave, Huntington Park
(90255-3211)
PHONE....................323 581-8555
Mohamad Toluee, *President*
Masoud Parvinjah, *Vice Pres*
Shadi Toloueenia, *Technology*
EMP: 15 **EST:** 1994
SQ FT: 45,000

SALES (est): 1.2MM **Privately Held**
WEB: www.troubleatthemill.com
SIC: 2361 2339 7389 T-shirts & tops:
girls', children's & infants'; sportswear,
women's; textile & apparel services

(P-3031)
CRESTONE LLC
Also Called: Hazel Clothes
2511 S Alameda St, Vernon (90058-1309)
PHONE....................323 588-8857
Robert Cho, *Mng Member*
Maria Madriz, *Production*
Ruben Romero, *Sales Mgr*
Janet Cho, *Mng Member*
▲ **EMP:** 16 **EST:** 2005
SQ FT: 10,000
SALES (est): 6.2MM **Privately Held**
WEB: www.hazelclothes.com
SIC: 2361 2331 Girls' & children's
dresses, blouses & shirts; women's &
misses' blouses & shirts

(P-3032)
KWDZ MANUFACTURING LLC (PA)
337 S Anderson St, Los Angeles
(90033-3742)
PHONE....................323 526-3526
Vera Campbell,
Gene Bonilla,
◆ **EMP:** 75 **EST:** 1999
SQ FT: 45,000
SALES (est): 9.5MM **Privately Held**
WEB: www.beautees.us
SIC: 2361 T-shirts & tops: girls', children's
& infants'

(P-3033)
L A S A M INC
Also Called: Natural Elements
3844 S Santa Fe Ave, Vernon
(90058-1713)
PHONE....................323 586-8717
Sandy Maroney, *President*
Dennis Maroney, *Admin Sec*
EMP: 16 **EST:** 1981
SQ FT: 5,000
SALES (est): 387.8K **Privately Held**
SIC: 2361 Girls' & children's dresses,
blouses & shirts

(P-3034)
LIDA CHILDRENS WEAR INC
3113 E California Blvd, Pasadena
(91107-5352)
PHONE....................626 967-8868
◆ **EMP:** 50
SALES (est): 3.7MM **Privately Held**
WEB: www.lidachildren.com
SIC: 2361 2311 2369 2335 Mfg Girls
Dresses/Blouse Mfg Mens/Boys
Suit/Coats Mfg Girl/Child Outerwear Mfg
Women/Misses Dresses

(P-3035)
MISYD CORP (PA)
Also Called: Ruby Rox
30 Fremont Pl, Los Angeles (90005-3858)
PHONE....................213 742-1800
Robert Borman, *President*
Joseph Hanasab, *CFO*
▲ **EMP:** 79 **EST:** 1993
SQ FT: 35,000
SALES (est): 7.8MM **Privately Held**
WEB: www.misyd.com
SIC: 2361 Shirts: girls', children's & infants'

(P-3036)
ROSE GENUINE INC
Also Called: Jinelle
834 S Broadway Ste 1100, Los Angeles
(90014-3510)
P.O. Box 555970 (90055-0970)
PHONE....................213 747-4120
John Golshan, *President*
Mike Golshan, *Admin Sec*
Sel Gonzalez, *Bookkeeper*
◆ **EMP:** 13 **EST:** 1982
SQ FT: 15,000
SALES (est): 1.7MM **Privately Held**
WEB: www.genuinerose.com
SIC: 2361 Dresses: girls', children's & in-
fants'

(P-3037)
RSDG INTERNATIONAL INC
2127 Aralia St, Newport Beach
(92660-4131)
P.O. Box 4032, Diamond Bar (91765-0032)
PHONE....................626 256-4190
Ralph Silva, *President*
▲ **EMP:** 13 **EST:** 1994
SQ FT: 9,000
SALES (est): 255.9K **Privately Held**
WEB: www.rsdgintl.com
SIC: 2361 Girls' & children's dresses,
blouses & shirts

(P-3038)
WINSTAR TEXTILE INC
16815 E Johnson Dr, City of Industry
(91745-2417)
PHONE....................626 357-1133
Der Yeu Lu, *CEO*
Davis Lu, *President*
Huimin Dou, *Principal*
Alan KAO, *Manager*
▲ **EMP:** 25 **EST:** 1999
SQ FT: 3,400
SALES (est): 1.5MM **Privately Held**
SIC: 2361 2325 Blouses: girls', children's
& infants'; men's & boys' trousers &
slacks

2369 Girls' & Infants' Outerwear, NEC

(P-3039)
BABY GUESS INC
1444 S Alameda St, Los Angeles
(90021-2433)
PHONE....................213 765-3100
Maurice Marciano, *Ch of Bd*
EMP: 66 **EST:** 1999
SALES (est): 5.9MM
SALES (corp-wide): 1.8B **Publicly Held**
WEB: www.guess.com
SIC: 2369 Jackets: girls', children's & in-
fants'; skirts: girls', children's & infants';
slacks: girls' & children's
PA: Guess , Inc.
1444 S Alameda St
Los Angeles CA 90021
213 765-3100

(P-3040)
FLAP HAPPY INC
2857 E 11th St, Los Angeles (90023-3405)
PHONE....................310 453-3527
Laurie Snyder, *President*
Walter Snyder, *Vice Pres*
EMP: 19 **EST:** 1988
SQ FT: 12,000
SALES (est): 590.9K **Privately Held**
WEB: www.flaphappy.com
SIC: 2369 2353 Girls' & children's outer-
wear; hats & caps

(P-3041)
FRANKIES BIKINIS LLC
4030 Del Rey Ave, Venice (90292-5602)
PHONE....................323 354-4133
Francheska Aiello, *CEO*
Miriam Aiello, *President*
Frank Messmann, *COO*
EMP: 36 **EST:** 2013
SALES (est): 3.4MM **Privately Held**
WEB: www.frankiesbikinis.com
SIC: 2369 Bathing suits & swimwear: girls',
children's & infants'

(P-3042)
GRACING BRAND MANAGEMENT INC
Also Called: Gbm
1108 W Vly Blvd Ste 660, Alhambra
(91803)
PHONE....................626 297-2472
Sabrina Yam, *CEO*
Vico Yam, *President*
EMP: 492 **EST:** 2017
SALES (est): 417MM **Privately Held**
SIC: 2369 5137 5131 2211 Bathing suits
& swimwear: girls', children's & infants';
swimsuits: women's, children's & infants';
trimmings, apparel; apparel & outerwear
fabrics, cotton

(P-3043)
MANHATTAN BEACHWEAR LLC (PA)
10855 Bus Ctr Dr Ste C, Cypress (90630)
PHONE....................657 384-2110
Allan Colvin,
Joshua Adidjaja,
EMP: 65 **EST:** 2020
SALES (est): 10MM **Privately Held**
SIC: 2369 2329 Bathing suits &
swimwear: girls', children's & infants';
bathing suits & swimwear: men's & boys'

(P-3044)
RMLA INC
Also Called: La Chic
1972 E 20th St, Vernon (90058-1005)
PHONE....................213 749-4333
Ralph Maya, *CEO*
Jan Adamcyk, *Bd of Directors*
Jack Maya, *Vice Pres*
▲ **EMP:** 16 **EST:** 1991
SALES (est): 4MM **Privately Held**
WEB: www.rmla.com
SIC: 2369 Girls' & children's outerwear

(P-3045)
TRLG INTERMEDIATE HOLDINGS LLC (PA)
1888 Rosecrans Ave, Manhattan Beach
(90266-3712)
PHONE....................323 266-3072
Dalli Snyder,
Dalibor Snyder, *CFO*
Alan Weiss, *Vice Pres*
Denise Feher, *General Mgr*
Melissa McCarthy, *Store Mgr*
◆ **EMP:** 52 **EST:** 2017
SQ FT: 119,000
SALES (est): 350MM **Privately Held**
WEB: www.moneygram.com
SIC: 2369 2325 2339 Girls' & children's
outerwear; men's & boys' trousers &
slacks; women's & misses' outerwear

(P-3046)
UN DEUX TROIS INC (PA)
2301 E 7th St, Los Angeles (90023-1035)
PHONE....................323 588-1067
Colin Shorkend, *President*
Beverly Shorkend, *CFO*
Cydney Shorkend, *Admin Sec*
Frank Perez, *Controller*
Erin Shorkend, *Director*
▲ **EMP:** 24 **EST:** 1988
SALES (est): 2.7MM **Privately Held**
SIC: 2369 5137 Girls' & children's outer-
wear; fur clothing, women's & children's

(P-3047)
VESTURE GROUP INCORPORATED
Also Called: Pinky Los Angeles
3405 W Pacific Ave, Burbank (91505-1555)
PHONE....................818 842-0200
Robert Galishoff, *CEO*
Gail Lupacchini, *Vice Pres*
Annette Rodriguez, *Controller*
Kathy Fortner, *Production*
Suzanne Monroe, *Sales Executive*
▲ **EMP:** 48 **EST:** 2007
SQ FT: 3,500
SALES (est): 6MM **Privately Held**
WEB: www.vesturegroupinc.com
SIC: 2369 2335 Skirts: girls', children's &
infants'; women's, juniors' & misses'
dresses

2371 Fur Goods

(P-3048)
FUR ACCENTS LLC
349 W Grove Ave, Orange (92865-3205)
PHONE....................714 403-5286
Steven Goodyear, *Mng Member*
EMP: 15 **EST:** 2016
SALES (est): 2MM **Privately Held**
WEB: www.furaccents.com
SIC: 2371 5632 Fur goods; fur apparel

2381 Dress & Work Gloves

(P-3049)
MECHANIX WEAR LLC (PA)
28525 Witherspoon Pkwy, Valencia
(91355-5417)
PHONE...................800 222-4296
Michael Hale, *CEO*
Jordan Dull, *Partner*
Jesse Spungin, *President*
Bari Waalk, *COO*
Kevin Reynolds, *CFO*
▲ **EMP:** 137 **EST:** 1984
SQ FT: 24,000
SALES (est): 67.6MM **Privately Held**
WEB: www.mechanix.com
SIC: 2381 Fabric dress & work gloves

(P-3050)
ORBITA CORP (PA)
Also Called: Estam
1136 Crocker St, Los Angeles
(90021-2014)
PHONE...................213 746-4783
Dae Seung Park, *President*
▲ **EMP:** 15 **EST:** 1997
SALES (est): 1.3MM **Privately Held**
SIC: 2381 Fabric dress & work gloves

(P-3051)
SVO ENTERPRISE
9854 Baldwin Pl, El Monte (91731-2202)
PHONE...................626 406-4770
Scott Streitfld CPA, *Administration*
EMP: 25 **EST:** 2013
SALES (est): 1.2MM **Privately Held**
SIC: 2381 Fabric dress & work gloves

2385 Waterproof Outerwear

(P-3052)
**TWENTY FOUR 7 GLOBL
SLTONS INC**
1460 Beachey Pl, Carson (90746-4002)
PHONE...................323 319-2724
Barry Woon, *President*
▲ **EMP:** 20 **EST:** 2012
SALES (est): 3.3MM **Privately Held**
WEB: www.twentyfour7-global.com
SIC: 2385 3421 3085 2393 Aprons, waterproof: made from purchased materials; cutlery; plastics bottles; textile bags; work uniforms; restaurant furniture, wood or metal

2386 Leather & Sheep Lined Clothing

(P-3053)
AJG INC
Also Called: Astrologie California
7220 E Slauson Ave, Commerce
(90040-3625)
PHONE...................323 346-0171
Angelo Ghailian, *CEO*
Kenny Doo, *Manager*
▲ **EMP:** 20 **EST:** 2003
SALES (est): 4.7MM **Privately Held**
WEB: www.astrologieca.com
SIC: 2386 5131 5199 Leather & sheep-lined clothing; knit fabrics; fabrics, yarns & knit goods

(P-3054)
CHROME HEARTS LLC (PA)
921 N Mansfield Ave, Los Angeles
(90038-2311)
PHONE...................323 957-7544
Richard Stark, *Mng Member*
Dalibor Snyder, *CFO*
Teresita Diaz, *Principal*
Peter Struthers, *Office Mgr*
Ish Mustafa, *Project Mgr*
▲ **EMP:** 50 **EST:** 2005
SQ FT: 50,000
SALES (est): 24.8MM **Privately Held**
WEB: www.chromehearts.com
SIC: 2386 3911 2511 2371 Leather & sheep-lined clothing; jewelry, precious metal; wood household furniture; fur goods

(P-3055)
DISTINCTIVE INDS TEXAS INC
9419 Ann St, Santa Fe Springs
(90670-2613)
PHONE...................323 889-5766
Dwight Forrester, *Branch Mgr*
EMP: 26 **Privately Held**
SIC: 2386 Coats & jackets, leather & sheep-lined
PA: Distinctive Industries Of Texas, Inc.
4516 Seton Center Pkwy # 13
Austin TX 78759

(P-3056)
DISTINCTIVE INDS TEXAS INC
Also Called: Roadwire Distinctive Inds
10618 Shoemaker Ave, Santa Fe Springs
(90670-4038)
PHONE...................512 491-3500
Dwight Forrester, *Principal*
EMP: 26 **Privately Held**
SIC: 2386 Leather & sheep-lined clothing
PA: Distinctive Industries Of Texas, Inc.
4516 Seton Center Pkwy # 13
Austin TX 78759

(P-3057)
EURO BELLO USA
10660 Wilshire Blvd, Los Angeles
(90024-4522)
PHONE...................213 446-2818
Bijan Israel, *President*
Natalio Oscar, *Manager*
EMP: 46 **EST:** 2014
SQ FT: 20,000
SALES (est): 18MM **Privately Held**
SIC: 2386 2211 Garments, leather; apparel & outerwear fabrics, cotton

(P-3058)
JEJOMI DESIGNS INC
Also Called: Long Pine Leathers
2626 Fruitland Ave, Vernon (90058-2220)
PHONE...................323 584-4211
Jorge Castellon, *President*
Cecilia Polanco, *Treasurer*
Susan Castellon, *Vice Pres*
▲ **EMP:** 14 **EST:** 1985
SQ FT: 9,200
SALES (est): 1.2MM **Privately Held**
SIC: 2386 Coats & jackets, leather & sheep-lined

(P-3059)
OHECK LLC
5830 Bickett St, Huntington Park
(90255-2627)
PHONE...................323 923-2700
Eric Jweon, *Mng Member*
EMP: 38 **EST:** 2012
SQ FT: 52,000
SALES (est): 1.5MM **Privately Held**
SIC: 2386 Garments, leather

(P-3060)
SCULLY SPORTSWEAR INC
Also Called: Scully Leather Wear
1701 Pacific Ave, Oxnard (93033-2745)
PHONE...................805 483-6339
Daniel Scully, *CEO*
Robert Swink, *Vice Pres*
Sommer Herbert, *Info Tech Mgr*
Charlane Gage, *Sales Staff*
Yadira Gonzalez, *Sales Staff*
▲ **EMP:** 60 **EST:** 1906
SQ FT: 80,000
SALES (est): 13.2MM **Privately Held**
WEB: www.scullyleather.com
SIC: 2386 5099 Coats & jackets, leather & sheep-lined; garments, leather; luggage; cases, carrying

2387 Apparel Belts

(P-3061)
LEJON OF CALIFORNIA INC
Also Called: Lejon Tulliani
1229 Railroad St, Corona (92882-1838)
PHONE...................951 736-1229
John W Shirinian, *President*
Mara Rivera, *Office Mgr*
Jack Shirinian, *Admin Sec*

▲ **EMP:** 40 **EST:** 1968
SQ FT: 33,000
SALES (est): 5.9MM **Privately Held**
WEB: www.lejon.com
SIC: 2387 3172 Apparel belts; personal leather goods

(P-3062)
STREETS AHEAD INC
Also Called: Hyde
5510 S Soto St Unit B, Vernon
(90058-3623)
PHONE...................323 277-0860
David Sack, *CEO*
Michael Fructuoso, *Controller*
▲ **EMP:** 20 **EST:** 1982
SQ FT: 28,000
SALES (est): 2.6MM **Privately Held**
WEB: www.streetsaheadinc.com
SIC: 2387 Apparel belts

(P-3063)
WESTSIDE ACCESSORIES INC (PA)
8920 Vernon Ave Ste 128, Montclair
(91763-1663)
PHONE...................626 858-5452
Carol Cantagallo, *President*
▲ **EMP:** 20 **EST:** 1991
SALES (est): 1.1MM **Privately Held**
WEB: www.belts-etc.com
SIC: 2387 Apparel belts

2389 Apparel & Accessories, NEC

(P-3064)
**ACADEMIC CH CHOIR GWNS
MFG INC**
Also Called: Academic Cap & Gown
20644 Superior St, Chatsworth
(91311-4414)
PHONE...................818 886-8697
Mike Cronan, *President*
Evelyn Cronan, *Vice Pres*
Mark Cronan, *Vice Pres*
Lois Montoya, *Regl Sales Mgr*
Mary Gonzalez, *Sales Staff*
◆ **EMP:** 30 **EST:** 1947
SQ FT: 13,000
SALES (est): 24.3MM **Privately Held**
WEB: www.academicapparel.com
SIC: 2389 2353 Clergymen's vestments; academic vestments (caps & gowns); uniforms & vestments; hats, caps & millinery

(P-3065)
**ANAYA BROTHERS CUTTING
LLC**
3130 Leonis Blvd, Vernon (90058-3012)
PHONE...................323 582-5758
Martin Anaya Jr, *Owner*
EMP: 90
SALES (est): 5MM **Privately Held**
SIC: 2389 Apparel & accessories

(P-3066)
APP WINDDOWN LLC (HQ)
Also Called: American Apparel
747 Warehouse St, Los Angeles
(90021-1106)
P.O. Box 5129, Brandon MS (39047-5129)
PHONE...................213 488-0226
Chelsea Grayson, *CEO*
Alma Amaya, *President*
Mike Manalac, *Director*
◆ **EMP:** 19 **EST:** 2005
SALES (est): 61.7MM
SALES (corp-wide): 1.9B **Privately Held**
WEB: www.mygildan.com
SIC: 2389 2311 2331 Men's miscellaneous accessories; men's & boys' suits & coats; women's & misses' blouses & shirts
PA: Les Vetements De Sport Gildan Inc
600 Boul De Maisonneuve O 33eme etage
Montreal QC H3A 3
514 735-2023

(P-3067)
ARTICA & ARBOX LLC
9355 Wilshire Blvd # 300, Beverly Hills
(90210-5439)
PHONE...................213 446-6272
Irene Roth, *Branch Mgr*
EMP: 16
SALES (corp-wide): 330.2K **Privately Held**
SIC: 2389 Men's miscellaneous accessories
PA: Artica & Arbox, Llc
10880 Wilshire Blvd # 2100
Los Angeles CA 90024
310 315-6200

(P-3068)
CALIFRNIA CSTUME CLLCTIONS INC (PA)
Also Called: California Costume Int'l
210 S Anderson St, Los Angeles
(90033-3205)
PHONE...................323 262-8383
Tak Kwan Woo, *CEO*
Peter Woo, *President*
Charles Woo, *Treasurer*
Quinton Young, *Info Tech Mgr*
Melvin Hui, *Graphic Designe*
◆ **EMP:** 299 **EST:** 1992
SQ FT: 300,000
SALES (est): 37MM **Privately Held**
WEB: www.californiacostumes.com
SIC: 2389 5092 Costumes; toys

(P-3069)
CHARADES LLC (PA)
20579 Valley Blvd, Walnut (91789-2730)
PHONE...................626 435-0077
Jerry B Beck,
Howard Beige,
Mark Beige,
▲ **EMP:** 239 **EST:** 2000
SALES (est): 9.2MM **Privately Held**
WEB: www.charadescostumes.com
SIC: 2389 Costumes

(P-3070)
CINEMA SECRETS INC
6639 Odessa Ave, Van Nuys (91406-5746)
PHONE...................818 846-0579
Barbara Stein, *President*
Michael Stein, *CEO*
Daniel Stein, *CFO*
Danny Stein, *CFO*
Maurice Stein, *Vice Pres*
▲ **EMP:** 60 **EST:** 1985
SALES (est): 11MM **Privately Held**
WEB: www.cinemasecrets.com
SIC: 5999 5699 2389 5122 Cosmetics; costumes, masquerade or theatrical; costumes; cosmetics

(P-3071)
CONQUER NATION INC
5525 S Soto St, Vernon (90058-3622)
PHONE...................310 562-8000
Jerry Saeedian, *CEO*
EMP: 142
SALES (est): 15MM **Privately Held**
WEB: www.conquernation.com
SIC: 2389 Hospital gowns

(P-3072)
CUSTOM CHARACTERS INC
621 Thompson Ave, Glendale
(91201-2032)
PHONE...................818 507-5940
Ryan Rhodes, *President*
Drew Herron, *Treasurer*
Victoria Arcenale, *Accounting Mgr*
EMP: 18 **EST:** 1985
SQ FT: 5,200
SALES (est): 1.8MM **Privately Held**
WEB: www.customcharacters.com
SIC: 2389 3999 Costumes; stage hardware & equipment, except lighting

(P-3073)
**DECKERS OUTDOOR
CORPORATION (PA)**
Also Called: DECKERS BRANDS
250 Coromar Dr, Goleta (93117-3697)
PHONE...................805 967-7611
David Powers, *President*
Michael F Devine III, *Ch of Bd*

David E Lafitte, *COO*
Steven J Fasching, *CFO*
Lauri Shanahan, *Bd of Directors*
▲ EMP: 2222 EST: 1975
SQ FT: 185,000
SALES (est): 2.5B **Publicly Held**
WEB: www.deckers.com
SIC: 2389 2339 3021 Men's miscella-
neous accessories; women's & misses'
accessories; sandals, rubber

(P-3074)
DIAMOND COLLECTION LLC
Also Called: Charades
20579 Valley Blvd, Walnut (91789-2730)
PHONE.................................626 435-0077
Marc Lavich,
EMP: 30 EST: 2016
SALES (est): 1.5MM **Privately Held**
SIC: 2389 5137 Costumes; dresses

(P-3075)
DIANA DID-IT DESIGNS INC
Also Called: Princess Paradise
20579 Valley Blvd, Walnut (91789-2730)
PHONE.................................970 226-5062
Diana Clements, *President*
Brad Clements, *Treasurer*
◆ EMP: 26 EST: 1980
SALES (est): 2MM **Privately Held**
WEB: www.princessparadisestore.com
SIC: 2389 7299 Costumes; costume rental

(P-3076)
LETS GO APPAREL INC (PA)
Also Called: Uptown
1729 E Washington Blvd, Los Angeles
(90021-3124)
PHONE.................................213 863-1767
Chang Wha Yoon, *President*
▼ EMP: 22 EST: 2013
SQ FT: 30,000
SALES (est): 4.1MM **Privately Held**
SIC: 2389 5661 5632 Academic vest-
ments (caps & gowns); shoes, custom;
apparel accessories

(P-3077)
LLC MARSH PERKINS
80080 Via Pessaro, La Quinta
(92253-7581)
PHONE.................................760 880-4558
Diane Lohman,
EMP: 15 EST: 2016
SALES (est): 314.1K **Privately Held**
SIC: 2389 Apparel & accessories

(P-3078)
LOS ANGELES APPAREL INC
Also Called: La Apparel
647 E 59th St, Los Angeles (90001-1001)
PHONE.................................323 745-4986
Dov Charney, *CEO*
Morris Charney, *Director*
David Nisenbaum, *Director*
Bonnie Guo, *Supervisor*
EMP: 450 EST: 2016
SALES (est): 32.2MM **Privately Held**
WEB: www.losangelesapparel.net
SIC: 2389 Uniforms & vestments

(P-3079)
**MDC INTERIOR SOLUTIONS
LLC**
Also Called: Komar Apparel Supply
6900 E Washington Blvd, Los Angeles
(90040-1908)
PHONE.................................800 621-4006
Gary Rothschild, *Manager*
EMP: 22
SALES (corp-wide): 75.2MM **Privately
Held**
WEB: www.mdcwall.com
SIC: 2389 Men's miscellaneous acces-
sories
PA: Mdc Interior Solutions, Llc
400 High Grove Blvd
Glendale Heights IL 60139
847 437-4000

(P-3080)
ML KISHIGO MFG CO LLC
11250 Slater Ave, Fountain Valley
(92708-5421)
PHONE.................................949 852-1963
Loren H Wall, *CEO*

John Ambrosio, *Vice Pres*
Karen Wall, *Vice Pres*
Thomas Tran, *Purch Mgr*
Carly Gibson, *Merchandising*
▲ EMP: 86 EST: 1971
SALES (est): 14MM
SALES (corp-wide): 13.4B **Privately Held**
WEB: www.kishigo.com
SIC: 2389 5099 Men's miscellaneous ac-
cessories; safety equipment & supplies
PA: Bunzl Public Limited Company
York House
London W1H 7
208 560-1244

(P-3081)
PATAGONIA INC
47 N Fair Oaks Ave, Pasadena
(91103-3608)
PHONE.................................626 795-0319
Alan Burt, *Branch Mgr*
EMP: 14
SALES (corp-wide): 408.6MM **Privately
Held**
WEB: www.patagoniaprovisions.com
SIC: 2389 5137 Men's miscellaneous ac-
cessories; women's & children's clothing
HQ: Patagonia, Inc.
259 W Santa Clara St
Ventura CA 93001
805 643-8616

(P-3082)
R & R INDUSTRIES INC
204 Avenida Fabricante, San Clemente
(92672-7538)
PHONE.................................800 234-5611
Robert Pare, *President*
Roger Poulin, *Treasurer*
Neil Samuels, *Vice Pres*
▲ EMP: 30 EST: 1978
SQ FT: 8,150
SALES (est): 3.6MM **Privately Held**
WEB: www.rrind.com
SIC: 2389 2759 Uniforms & vestments;
promotional printing

(P-3083)
**RG COSTUMES &
ACCESSORIES INC**
726 Arrow Grand Cir, Covina (91722-2147)
PHONE.................................626 858-9559
Roger Lee, *President*
Michael Lee, *Vice Pres*
◆ EMP: 30 EST: 1982
SQ FT: 21,000 **Privately Held**
WEB: www.rgcostume.com
SIC: 2389 7299 Costumes; costume rental

(P-3084)
SHAFTON INC
4427 Sancola Ave, Toluca Lake
(91602-2519)
PHONE.................................818 985-5025
David Janzow, *President*
Becky Allen, *Corp Secy*
Linda Putnam, *Supervisor*
EMP: 16 EST: 1975
SALES (est): 633.6K **Privately Held**
WEB: www.shaftoninc.com
SIC: 2389 Theatrical costumes

(P-3085)
SHANE HUNTER LLC
Also Called: Aqua Blues
1013 S Los Angeles St # 1000, Los Angeles
(90015-1789)
PHONE.................................415 627-7730
Michael Thaler, *Manager*
Michael H Thaler,
▲ EMP: 43 EST: 1989
SALES (est): 88MM **Privately Held**
SIC: 2389 2326 3841 Disposable gar-
ments & accessories; medical & hospital
uniforms, men's; surgical & medical in-
struments

(P-3086)
STRINGKING INC (PA)
19100 S Vermont Ave, Gardena
(90248-4413)
PHONE.................................310 503-8901
Jake McCampbell, *CEO*
EMP: 184 EST: 2020

SALES (est): 50MM **Privately Held**
SIC: 5699 2389 Customized clothing &
apparel; disposable garments & accessories

(P-3087)
TRUE WARRIOR LLC
21226 Lone Star Way, Santa Clarita
(91390-4226)
PHONE.................................661 237-6588
Edward Luster,
EMP: 20
SALES (est): 508.6K **Privately Held**
SIC: 2389 3069 Apparel & accessories;
boot or shoe products, rubber

(P-3088)
**UNDERWRAPS COSTUME
CORPORATION**
Also Called: Underwraps Costumes
9600 Irondale Ave, Chatsworth
(91311-5008)
P.O. Box 9603, Canoga Park (91309-0603)
PHONE.................................818 349-5300
Payman Shaffa, *CEO*
Irene Shaffa, *Vice Pres*
Veronica McCoy, *Accounting Mgr*
▲ EMP: 16 EST: 2004
SQ FT: 45,000
SALES (est): 2.2MM **Privately Held**
WEB: www.underwraps.net
SIC: 2389 Costumes

(P-3089)
VOLER SOFTGOODS (PA)
21 Saratoga Ave, Grover Beach
(93433-1538)
PHONE.................................805 473-7808
Jacques Deyo, *Owner*
Michelle Costanzo, *General Mgr*
Roman Gaslan, *Opers Staff*
Ed Fonda, *Accounts Mgr*
EMP: 56 EST: 2001
SALES (est): 544.9K **Privately Held**
WEB: www.voler.com
SIC: 2389 Apparel & accessories

(P-3090)
**WALT DSNEY IMGNRING RES
DEV IN**
1200 N Miller St Unit D, Anaheim
(92806-1954)
PHONE.................................714 781-3152
Dawn Paily, *Programmer Anys*
Troy Cadwallader, *Manager*
Tony Maddox, *Manager*
EMP: 99
SALES (corp-wide): 65.3B **Publicly Held**
WEB: www.disneyimaginations.com
SIC: 2389 Masquerade costumes
HQ: Walt Disney Imagineering Research &
Development, Inc.
1401 Flower St
Glendale CA 91201
818 544-6500

2391 Curtains & Draperies

(P-3091)
AMTEX CALIFORNIA INC
Also Called: Ameritex International
113 S Utah St, Los Angeles (90033-3213)
PHONE.................................323 859-2200
Saq Hafeez, *President*
Alia Hafeez, *Vice Pres*
◆ EMP: 45
SQ FT: 40,000
SALES (est): 5.2MM **Privately Held**
WEB: www.ameritexinternational.ameri-
commerce.com
SIC: 2391 2392 5023 Draperies, plastic &
textile: from purchased materials; bed-
spreads & bed sets: made from pur-
chased materials; curtains; bedspreads

(P-3092)
BLUE RIBBON DRAPERIES INC
Also Called: Drapery Affair
5109 Walker St, Ventura (93003-7370)
PHONE.................................805 983-4848
Roy Donald, *CEO*
Gene Donald, *President*
Delrose Donald, *Corp Secy*
EMP: 37 EST: 1982

SQ FT: 9,000
SALES (est): 9.2MM **Privately Held**
WEB: www.draperyaffair.com
SIC: 5713 2391 Floor covering stores; cot-
tage sets (curtains): made from pur-
chased materials

(P-3093)
S & K THEATRICAL DRAP INC
Also Called: Sk Drapes
7313 Varna Ave, North Hollywood
(91605-4009)
PHONE.................................818 503-0596
Carmela Skogman, *President*
Damian Schmidt, *Vice Pres*
Kevin Skogman, *Marketing Staff*
EMP: 16 EST: 1965
SALES (est): 2.2MM **Privately Held**
WEB: www.sktheatricaldraperies.com
SIC: 2391 Draperies, plastic & textile: from
purchased materials

(P-3094)
SEW WHAT INC
Also Called: Rent What
1978 E Gladwick St, Compton
(90220-6201)
PHONE.................................310 639-6000
Megan Duckett, *President*
Adam Duckett, *Vice Pres*
Rick Garcia, *Manager*
Marilyn Moss, *Accounts Mgr*
◆ EMP: 35 EST: 1997
SQ FT: 15,000
SALES (est): 5.4MM **Privately Held**
WEB: www.sewwhatinc.com
SIC: 2391 5049 Curtains & draperies; the-
atrical equipment & supplies

(P-3095)
**SUPERIOR WINDOW
COVERINGS INC**
7683 N San Fernando Rd, Burbank
(91505-1073)
PHONE.................................818 762-6685
Marco Bonilla, *President*
Mario Murillo, *Info Tech Dir*
Diana Castillo, *Sales Staff*
▲ EMP: 35 EST: 1979
SQ FT: 4,000
SALES (est): 3.1MM **Privately Held**
WEB: www.superiorwindowcoverings.com
SIC: 2391 2591 Draperies, plastic & tex-
tile: from purchased materials; blinds ver-
tical

2392 House furnishings: Textile

(P-3096)
BOJER INC
177 S Peckham Rd, Azusa (91702-3237)
PHONE.................................626 334-1711
Doris Gabai, *President*
Joey Gabai, *Vice Pres*
Shelly Gabai, *Sales Mgr*
EMP: 20 EST: 1991
SQ FT: 12,974
SALES (est): 2.5MM **Privately Held**
WEB: www.bojeroutdoor.com
SIC: 2392 Cushions & pillows

(P-3097)
**BRENTWOOD ORIGINALS INC
(PA)**
20639 S Fordyce Ave, Carson
(90810-1019)
PHONE.................................925 202-9290
Loren H Sweet, *President*
Joel Fierberg, *CFO*
Bill Bronstein, *Senior VP*
Tom Rose, *Senior VP*
Craig Torrey, *Senior VP*
◆ EMP: 215 EST: 1958
SQ FT: 1,200,000
SALES (est): 92MM **Privately Held**
WEB: www.brentwoodoriginals.com
SIC: 2392 Cushions & pillows

(P-3098)
CLASSIC SLIPCOVER INC
4300 District Blvd, Vernon (90058-3110)
PHONE.................................323 583-0804

David Illulian, *CEO*
Chris Wroolie, *President*
▲ **EMP:** 17 **EST:** 1993
SQ FT: 15,000
SALES (est): 2.3MM **Privately Held**
SIC: 2392 5714 Slipcovers: made of fabric, plastic etc.; slip covers

(P-3099)
COMFORT BEDDING MFG INC
11680 Wright Rd, Lynwood (90262-3945)
PHONE..............................310 667-7720
Igal Rosenberg, *CEO*
EMP: 13 **EST:** 2013
SALES (est): 849.3K **Privately Held**
WEB: www.comfortbedding.com
SIC: 2392 Mattress pads

(P-3100)
COTTON TALE DESIGNS INC
16291 Sierra Ridge Way, Hacienda Heights (91745-5545)
PHONE..............................714 435-9558
Larry D Aspegren, *President*
Nina Selby, *President*
Larry Aspegren, *Vice Pres*
▲ **EMP:** 14 **EST:** 1991
SQ FT: 16,500
SALES (est): 368.9K **Privately Held**
WEB: www.cottontaledesigns.com
SIC: 2392 2361 2211 Household furnishings; girls' & children's dresses, blouses & shirts; bed sheeting, cotton

(P-3101)
CUSTOM QUILTING INC
2832 Walnut Ave Ste D, Tustin (92780-7002)
PHONE..............................714 731-7271
Alfredo Zermeno, *Owner*
Elda Zermeno, *Vice Pres*
EMP: 28 **EST:** 1983
SALES (est): 1.6MM **Privately Held**
WEB: www.customquiltinginc.com
SIC: 2392 5719 Bedspreads & bed sets: made from purchased materials; bedding (sheets, blankets, spreads & pillows)

(P-3102)
H2 HOME COLLECTION INC
505 21st St, Huntington Beach (92648-3304)
PHONE..............................714 916-9513
Deanna Hodges, *Principal*
Taylor Gibbons, *Asst Mgr*
EMP: 22 **EST:** 2017
SALES (est): 1MM **Privately Held**
SIC: 2392 5023 Household furnishings; home furnishings

(P-3103)
INSTANT TUCK INC
9663 Santa Monica Blvd, Beverly Hills (90210-4303)
PHONE..............................310 955-8824
Adrian Gluck, *CEO*
EMP: 30 **EST:** 2019
SALES (est): 1.1MM **Privately Held**
SIC: 2392 Mattress pads

(P-3104)
KLEEN MAID INC
11450 Sheldon St, Sun Valley (91352-1121)
PHONE..............................323 581-3000
Sean Solouki, *CEO*
Kamyar Solouki, *President*
Hamid Moghaven, *Vice Pres*
◆ **EMP:** 13 **EST:** 2000
SALES (est): 600.1K **Privately Held**
SIC: 2392 3991 Mops, floor & dust; brushes, household or industrial

(P-3105)
LA LINEN INC
1760 E 15th St, Los Angeles (90021-2716)
PHONE..............................213 745-4004
Danny Levy, *CEO*
Shahrzad Mahdavi, *Mktg Dir*
EMP: 30 **EST:** 2010
SQ FT: 16,500

SALES (est): 2.5MM **Privately Held**
WEB: www.lalinen.com
SIC: 5719 2392 2391 Linens; tablecloths & table settings; napkins, fabric & nonwoven: made from purchased materials; tablecloths: made from purchased materials; curtains & draperies

(P-3106)
LAMBS & IVY INC
Also Called: Bed Time Originals
2042 E Maple Ave, El Segundo (90245-5008)
PHONE..............................310 322-3800
Barbara Laiken, *President*
Dan Simone, *CFO*
Cathy Ravdin, *Vice Pres*
Karin Kerylow, *Sales Staff*
Lilian Heu, *Cust Mgr*
◆ **EMP:** 60
SQ FT: 30,000
SALES (est): 6.9MM **Privately Held**
WEB: www.lambsivy.com
SIC: 2392 Blankets, comforters & beddings

(P-3107)
MATTEO LLC
1000 E Cesar E Chavez Ave, Los Angeles (90033-1204)
PHONE..............................213 617-2813
Matthew Lenoci, *Mng Member*
▲ **EMP:** 50 **EST:** 1996
SQ FT: 25,000
SALES (est): 10.3MM **Privately Held**
WEB: www.matteola.com
SIC: 2392 Blankets, comforters & beddings

(P-3108)
MICRONOVA MANUFACTURING INC
3431 Lomita Blvd, Torrance (90505-5010)
PHONE..............................310 784-6990
Audrey J Reynolds Lowman, *CEO*
Oliver Nicio, *Info Tech Mgr*
Debra Southard, *Finance*
Heidi Garlick, *Purch Mgr*
Phillip Lecompte, *Mfg Spvr*
▲ **EMP:** 30 **EST:** 1984
SQ FT: 28,310
SALES (est): 7.3MM **Privately Held**
WEB: www.micronova-mfg.com
SIC: 2392 Mops, floor & dust

(P-3109)
NORTHWESTERN CONVERTING CO
Also Called: Premier Mop & Broom
2395 Railroad St, Corona (92878-5411)
PHONE..............................800 959-3402
Tom Buckles, *President*
Thomas M Buckles, *President*
▲ **EMP:** 100 **EST:** 1935
SALES (est): 16.3MM **Privately Held**
WEB: www.northwesternc.openfos.com
SIC: 2392 Household furnishings

(P-3110)
OMNIA LEATHER MOTION INC
Also Called: Cathy Ireland Home
4950 Edison Ave, Chino (91710-5713)
PHONE..............................909 393-4400
Peter Zolferino, *President*
Luie Nastri, *Vice Pres*
Katherine Skinner, *Merchandising*
▲ **EMP:** 200 **EST:** 1989
SALES (est): 9.8MM **Privately Held**
WEB: www.omnialeather.com
SIC: 2392 Household furnishings

(P-3111)
PACIFIC CAST FTHER CUSHION LLC (HQ)
7600 Industry Ave, Pico Rivera (90660-4302)
PHONE..............................562 801-9995
Neil Puro, *President*
Eric Moen, *Treasurer*
Cristina Kopecky, *Vice Pres*
Joseph Crawford, *Admin Sec*
Marc Pfefferle,
◆ **EMP:** 110 **EST:** 1986
SQ FT: 100,000

SALES (est): 12.8MM
SALES (corp-wide): 257MM **Privately Held**
WEB: www.pcfcushion.com
SIC: 2392 Cushions & pillows
PA: Pacific Coast Feather, Llc
901 W Yamato Rd Ste 250
Boca Raton FL 33431
206 624-1057

(P-3112)
PACIFIC COAST HOME FURN INC (PA)
Also Called: Sherry Kline
2424 Saybrook Ave, Commerce (90040-2510)
PHONE..............................323 838-7808
Parviz Banafshe, *President*
Shahrokh Samani, *CFO*
▲ **EMP:** 19 **EST:** 1988
SQ FT: 35,000
SALES (est): 5MM **Privately Held**
WEB:
www.pacificcoasthomefurnishings.com
SIC: 2392 3261 Cushions & pillows; bathroom accessories/fittings, vitreous china or earthenware

(P-3113)
PACIFIC URETHANES LLC
1671 Champagne Ave Ste A, Ontario (91761-3660)
PHONE..............................909 390-8400
Darrell Nance, *Mng Member*
Neil Silverman,
▲ **EMP:** 200 **EST:** 2010
SQ FT: 250,000
SALES (est): 41.7MM
SALES (corp-wide): 4.2B **Publicly Held**
WEB: www.elitecomfortsolutions.com
SIC: 2392 5021 Blankets, comforters & beddings; beds & bedding
PA: Leggett & Platt, Incorporated
1 Leggett Rd
Carthage MO 64836
417 358-8131

(P-3114)
PARACHUTE HOME INC
3525 Eastham Dr, Culver City (90232-2440)
PHONE..............................310 903-0353
Ariel Kaye, *CEO*
Amy Hoban, *Creative Dir*
Noelle Berry, *CIO*
Jacob Thornton, *Controller*
Justine Kumamoto, *Merchandising*
EMP: 138 **EST:** 2013
SQ FT: 13,000
SALES (est): 10MM **Privately Held**
WEB: www.parachutehome.com
SIC: 2392 5719 Sheets, fabric: made from purchased materials; bedding (sheets, blankets, spreads & pillows)

(P-3115)
PRO-MART INDUSTRIES INC (PA)
Also Called: Promart Dazz
17421 Von Karman Ave, Irvine (92614-6205)
PHONE..............................949 428-7700
Azad Sabounjian, *CEO*
Arnold Shecter, *Sales Staff*
Heather Huett-Barger, *Director*
Marcina Deharo, *Manager*
▲ **EMP:** 39 **EST:** 1970
SQ FT: 120,000
SALES (est): 10.5MM **Privately Held**
WEB: www.shopsmartdesign.com
SIC: 2392 1799 5085 Bags, laundry: made from purchased materials; closet organizers, installation & design; bins & containers, storage

(P-3116)
QUILTING HOUSE
16872 Millikan Ave, Irvine (92606-5012)
PHONE..............................949 476-7090
Richard Shields, *Owner*
Sheri Shields, *Co-Owner*
EMP: 19
SQ FT: 16,000

SALES (est): 922.1K **Privately Held**
WEB: www.quiltinghouse.com
SIC: 2392 2391 Cushions & pillows; bedspreads & bed sets: made from purchased materials; pillows, bed: made from purchased materials; curtains & draperies

(P-3117)
RELIANCE UPHOLSTERY SUP CO INC
Also Called: Reliance Carpet Cushion
4920 S Boyle Ave, Huntington Park (90255)
P.O. Box 58584, Vernon (90058-0584)
PHONE..............................323 321-2300
Ronald J Greitzer, *CEO*
Stanley Grietzer, *President*
Sheldon P Wallach, *CFO*
Doug Williams, *Vice Pres*
EMP: 95 **EST:** 1931
SQ FT: 360,000
SALES (est): 5.2MM **Privately Held**
WEB: www.reliancecarpetcushion.com
SIC: 2392 Linings, carpet: textile, except felt; cushions & pillows

(P-3118)
ROYAL BLUE INC
9025 Wilshire Blvd # 301, Beverly Hills (90211-1831)
PHONE..............................310 888-0156
Diana Moinian, *President*
Sami Kahen, *Admin Sec*
▲ **EMP:** 21 **EST:** 2005 **Privately Held**
WEB: www.royalblueintl.com
SIC: 2392 2299 Household furnishings; towels & towelings, linen & linen-and-cotton mixtures

(P-3119)
SIBYL SHEPARD INC
Also Called: Sarris Interiors
8225 Alondra Blvd, Paramount (90723-4401)
PHONE..............................562 531-8612
C Nicholas Sarris, *President*
Chris Andrew Sarris, *Treasurer*
Byron Sarris, *Director*
EMP: 23 **EST:** 1957
SQ FT: 15,000
SALES (est): 1.4MM **Privately Held**
WEB: www.sibyl-shepard-inc.hub.biz
SIC: 2392 Bedspreads & bed sets: made from purchased materials; towels, fabric & nonwoven: made from purchased materials; washcloths & bath mitts: made from purchased materials; shower curtains: made from purchased materials

(P-3120)
SPENCER N ENTERPRISES LLC
Also Called: Spencer Home Decor
425 S Lemon Ave, City of Industry (91789-2911)
PHONE..............................626 448-0374
Jeffrey Werner, *President*
Charles F Kuehne, *CFO*
Steve Rausch, *Technology*
▲ **EMP:** 100 **EST:** 2003
SQ FT: 100,000
SALES (est): 13.2MM **Privately Held**
WEB: www.spencerhomedecor.com
SIC: 2392 Cushions & pillows
HQ: Spencer Intermediate, Llc
60 E 42nd St Ste 1250
New York NY

(P-3121)
SUNRISE PILLOW CO INC
2215 Merced Ave, El Monte (91733-2622)
PHONE..............................626 401-9283
Adnan K Hermas, *President*
EMP: 14 **EST:** 1985
SQ FT: 11,500
SALES (est): 1MM **Privately Held**
SIC: 2392 5719 Pillows, bed: made from purchased materials; bedding (sheets, blankets, spreads & pillows)

P R O D U C T S   &   S V C S

(P-3122)
UNIVERSAL CUSHION COMPANY INC (PA)
Also Called: Cloud Nine Comforts
1610 Mandeville Canyon Rd, Los Angeles (90049-2524)
PHONE..............................323 887-8000
Sharyl G Bloom, *President*
Sharyl Bloom, *President*
Betty Bluml, *Purch Mgr*
▲ EMP: 34 EST: 1989
SALES (est): 4MM **Privately Held**
WEB: www.cloudninecomforts.com
SIC: 2392 2221 2211 Cushions & pillows; comforters & quilts: made from purchased materials; pillowcases: made from purchased materials; comforters & quilts, manmade fiber & silk; sheets & sheetings, cotton; pillowcases; piques, cotton

(P-3123)
VFT INC
Also Called: Vertical Fiber Technologies
1040 S Vail Ave, Montebello (90640-6020)
PHONE..............................323 728-2280
John Chang, *President*
Jesus Holguin, *Sales Staff*
▲ EMP: 40 EST: 1998
SQ FT: 70,000
SALES (est): 3.3MM **Privately Held**
WEB: www.bedtimelinens.com
SIC: 2392 Household furnishings

2393 Textile Bags

(P-3124)
ACTION BAG & COVER INC
18401 Mount Langley St, Fountain Valley (92708-6904)
PHONE..............................714 965-7777
Byung Ki Lee, *President*
▲ EMP: 80 EST: 1978
SQ FT: 15,000
SALES (est): 5.2MM **Privately Held**
WEB: www.actionbaginc.com
SIC: 2393 Canvas bags

(P-3125)
CONTINENTAL MARKETING SVC INC
15381 Proctor Ave, City of Industry (91745-1022)
PHONE..............................626 626-8888
Dawn Du, *President*
Lam Du, *Office Mgr*
EMP: 17 EST: 1986
SALES (est): 2MM **Privately Held**
SIC: 2393 Bags & containers, except sleeping bags: textile

(P-3126)
CTA MANUFACTURING INC
Also Called: Bagmasters
1160 California Ave, Corona (92881-3324)
PHONE..............................951 280-2400
Richard Whittier, *President*
Alexander Borghard, *Vice Pres*
Gayne Whittier, *Vice Pres*
Michael Webb, *Social Dir*
Scott Conk, *Controller*
▲ EMP: 40 EST: 1922
SQ FT: 23,000
SALES (est): 8.4MM **Privately Held**
WEB: www.ctamfg.com
SIC: 2393 Textile bags

(P-3127)
GOLD CREST INDUSTRIES INC
1018 E Acacia St, Ontario (91761-4553)
P.O. Box 3280 (91761-0928)
PHONE..............................909 930-9069
Jose Garcia, *President*
Jenaro Garcia, *Vice Pres*
EMP: 40 EST: 1963
SQ FT: 14,000
SALES (est): 3.6MM **Privately Held**
WEB: www.goldcrestind.com
SIC: 2393 3999 2392 Cushions, except spring & carpet: purchased materials; garden umbrellas; household furnishings

(P-3128)
JU-JU-BE INTL LLC
Also Called: Jujube
35 Argonaut Ste B2, Aliso Viejo (92656-4151)
PHONE..............................877 258-5823
Joseph Croft, *President*
Rob Hagen, *COO*
Rachelle Croft, *Vice Pres*
Robert Hanson, *Vice Pres*
Pamela Young, *Controller*
▲ EMP: 23 EST: 2007
SALES (est): 3.2MM **Privately Held**
WEB: www.jujube.com
SIC: 2393 Bags & containers, except sleeping bags: textile

(P-3129)
OUTDOOR RECREATION GROUP (PA)
Also Called: Outdoor Products
3450 Mount Vernon Dr, View Park (90008-4936)
PHONE..............................323 226-0830
Joel Altshule, *Ch of Bd*
Andrew Altshule, *CEO*
Robert Guzman, *Vice Pres*
Annie Kure, *Vice Pres*
Mario Espinoza, *Mktg Dir*
◆ EMP: 37 EST: 1946
SQ FT: 90,000
SALES (est): 14MM **Privately Held**
WEB: www.torgusa.com
SIC: 2393 3949 Textile bags; camping equipment & supplies

(P-3130)
RIVERSIDE TENT AND AWNG CO INC
231 E Alcandro Blvd Ste A, Riverside (92508)
PHONE..............................951 683-1925
Chilton E Burt, *President*
Betty Burt, *Vice Pres*
▲ EMP: 13 EST: 1919
SQ FT: 20,000
SALES (est): 353K **Privately Held**
WEB: www.riversideawning.com
SIC: 2393 2394 Canvas bags; canvas & related products

(P-3131)
WESSCO INTL LTD A CAL LTD PRTN (PA)
11400 W Olympic Blvd, Los Angeles (90064-1550)
PHONE..............................310 477-4272
Robert Bregman, *President*
Nick Bregman, *COO*
Tyler Shepodd, *CFO*
Alex Silva, *Creative Dir*
Jenna Peskin, *Opers Staff*
◆ EMP: 28 EST: 1979
SQ FT: 7,000
SALES (est): 10.1MM **Privately Held**
WEB: www.wessco.net
SIC: 2393 Textile bags

2394 Canvas Prdts

(P-3132)
A&R TARPAULINS INC
Also Called: AR Tech Aerospace
16246 Valley Blvd, Fontana (92335-7831)
P.O. Box 1400 (92334-1400)
PHONE..............................909 829-4444
Carmen Weisbart, *President*
Charles Rosselet, *Corp Secy*
Bud Weisbart, *Vice Pres*
Jessica Gunawan, *General Mgr*
Albert Greggen, *Info Tech Mgr*
EMP: 34 EST: 1977
SQ FT: 15,000
SALES (est): 6.5MM **Privately Held**
WEB: www.artarpaulins.com
SIC: 2394 Awnings, fabric: made from purchased materials

(P-3133)
A-AZTEC RENTS & SELLS INC (PA)
Also Called: Aztec Tents
2665 Columbia St, Torrance (90503-3801)
PHONE..............................310 347-3010
Chuck Miller, *CEO*
Eric Lee, *COO*
Alex Kouzmanoff, *Vice Pres*
Eric Vanderploeg, *Executive*
David Bradley, *General Mgr*
◆ EMP: 125
SQ FT: 70,000
SALES (est): 18.6MM **Privately Held**
WEB: www.aztectent.com
SIC: 2394 Canvas & related products

(P-3134)
ABC SUN CONTROL LLC
7241 Ethel Ave, North Hollywood (91605-4215)
PHONE..............................818 982-6989
Donald B Smallwood,
Martina H Smallwood,
▲ EMP: 16 EST: 1979
SQ FT: 30,000
SALES (est): 2.3MM **Privately Held**
WEB: www.abcsuncontrolsystems.com
SIC: 2394 Awnings, fabric: made from purchased materials

(P-3135)
CARAVAN CANOPY INTL INC
17512 Studebaker Rd, Cerritos (90703-2637)
PHONE..............................714 367-3000
Lindy Jung Park, *CEO*
David Hudrlik, *President*
Steve Ragland, *Sales Mgr*
◆ EMP: 50 EST: 1999
SQ FT: 50,000
SALES (est): 14.6MM **Privately Held**
WEB: www.caravancanopy.com
SIC: 2394 3444 2392 Canvas & related products; awnings & canopies; chair covers & pads: made from purchased materials

(P-3136)
CASTILLO MARITESS
Also Called: American Supply
1490 S Vineyard Ave Ste G, Ontario (91761-8043)
P.O. Box 2322, Chino (91708-2322)
PHONE..............................949 216-0468
Maritess Castillo, *Owner*
Von Castillo, *Co-Owner*
EMP: 16 EST: 2013
SQ FT: 1,600
SALES (est): 400K **Privately Held**
SIC: 2394 Liners & covers, fabric: made from purchased materials

(P-3137)
E-Z UP DIRECTCOM
Also Called: EZ Up Factory Store
1900 2nd St, Colton (92324)
PHONE..............................909 426-0060
Rose Kilstrom,
Gregg Lee, *COO*
Hope Dennis, *Sales Staff*
Maky Melsh, *Sales Staff*
Lisa Tsapatolis, *Sales Staff*
EMP: 22 EST: 2007
SALES (est): 339.5K **Privately Held**
SIC: 2394 Shades, canvas: made from purchased materials

(P-3138)
EIDE INDUSTRIES INC
16215 Piuma Ave, Cerritos (90703-1528)
PHONE..............................562 402-8335
Don Araiza, *President*
Jesus Borrego, *Vice Pres*
Dan Neill, *Vice Pres*
Joe Belli, *Admin Sec*
Rafael Cobian, *Human Resources*
◆ EMP: 80 EST: 1938
SQ FT: 41,000
SALES (est): 20.6MM **Privately Held**
WEB: www.eideindustries.com
SIC: 2394 Tents: made from purchased materials; awnings, fabric: made from purchased materials

(P-3139)
FRAMETENT INC
Also Called: Central Tent
26480 Summit Cir, Santa Clarita (91350-2991)
PHONE..............................661 290-3375
Nattha Chunapongse, *President*
Hendrawan Setioadi, *Engineer*
◆ EMP: 30 EST: 1994
SALES (est): 4.9MM **Privately Held**
SIC: 2394 5999 Tents: made from purchased materials; tents

(P-3140)
GOLDEN FLEECE DESIGNS
441 S Victory Blvd, Burbank (91502-2353)
PHONE..............................323 849-1901
Antoinette Argyropoulos, *President*
Symeon Argyropoulos, *Chairman*
Maria Argyropoulos, *Vice Pres*
EMP: 13 EST: 1970
SQ FT: 16,000
SALES (est): 1.1MM **Privately Held**
WEB: www.goldenfleecedesigns.com
SIC: 2394 5199 Canvas & related products; advertising specialties

(P-3141)
INTERNATIONAL E-Z UP INC (PA)
1900 2nd St, Norco (92860-2803)
PHONE..............................800 457-4233
William Bradford Smith, *CEO*
Mark Carter, *Ch of Bd*
Brad Smith, *President*
Jason Miller, *Software Dev*
Jonathan Bader, *Technician*
◆ EMP: 93 EST: 1983
SQ FT: 115,000
SALES (est): 32.9MM **Privately Held**
WEB: www.ezup.com
SIC: 2394 Shades, canvas: made from purchased materials

(P-3142)
PACIFIC PLAY TENTS INC
2801 E 12th St, Los Angeles (90023-3621)
PHONE..............................323 269-0431
Victor Preisler, *CEO*
Brian Jablan, *Vice Pres*
Andrea Alexanian, *Graphic Designe*
◆ EMP: 21 EST: 1993
SQ FT: 75,000
SALES (est): 1.1MM **Privately Held**
WEB: www.pacificplaytents.com
SIC: 2394 5941 5092 Tents: made from purchased materials; sporting goods & bicycle shops; toys; games, toys & children's vehicles

(P-3143)
PARADISE MANUFACTURING CO INC
Also Called: Arden/Paradise Manufacturing
13364 Aerospace Dr 100 Victorville (92394-7902)
PHONE..............................909 477-3460
Robert Sachs, *President*
Michael Sachs, *Vice Pres*
EMP: 35 EST: 1934
SALES (est): 1MM **Privately Held**
SIC: 2394 Air cushions & mattresses, canvas; canvas awnings & canopies

(P-3144)
RDD ENTERPRISES INC
Also Called: R D D USA Division
4638 E Washington Blvd, Commerce (90040-1026)
PHONE..............................213 742-0666
Tony Lomeli, *Principal*
EMP: 24 **Privately Held**
WEB: www.rddusa.com
SIC: 5699 2394 Military goods & regalia; tents: made from purchased materials
PA: R.D.D. Enterprises, Inc.
4638 E Washington Blvd
Commerce CA
213 742-0666

(P-3145)
SCHULZ LEATHER COMPANY INC
Also Called: Schulz Industries
16247 Minnesota Ave, Paramount
(90723-4915)
PHONE....................562 633-1081
Robert Schulz, *President*
Lillian Schulz, *Treasurer*
Charles Schulz, *Vice Pres*
EMP: 13 **EST:** 1950
SQ FT: 12,000
SALES (est): 1.1MM **Privately Held**
WEB: www.schulzindustries.com
SIC: 2394 2393 3161 2273 Liners & covers, fabric: made from purchased materials; bags & containers, except sleeping bags; textile; luggage; carpets & rugs; narrow fabric mills; broadwoven fabric mills, manmade

(P-3146)
SUPERIOR AWNING INC
14555 Titus St, Panorama City
(91402-4920)
PHONE....................818 780-7200
Brian Hotchkiss, *President*
Julie Hotchkiss, *Vice Pres*
Regina Calderon, *Opers Staff*
EMP: 40 **EST:** 1984
SQ FT: 11,776
SALES (est): 4.8MM **Privately Held**
WEB: www.superiorawning.com
SIC: 2394 5999 3444 Awnings, fabric: made from purchased materials; awnings; sheet metalwork

(P-3147)
ULLMAN SAILS INC (PA)
2710 S Croddy Way, Santa Ana
(92704-5206)
PHONE....................714 432-1860
Bruce Cooper, *President*
Chuck Skewes, *Manager*
EMP: 15 **EST:** 1967
SQ FT: 10,900
SALES (est): 2.8MM **Privately Held**
WEB: www.ullmansails.com
SIC: 2394 Sails: made from purchased materials

(P-3148)
VAE INDUSTRIES CORPORATION
Also Called: Vitabri Canopies
5402 Research Dr, Huntington Beach
(92649-1542)
PHONE....................714 842-7500
Damien Vieille, *CEO*
Mathieu Hayaud, *Vice Pres*
Sheila Myers, *General Mgr*
Kristen Kaake, *Project Mgr*
Preston Treadwell, *Graphic Designe*
◆ **EMP:** 22 **EST:** 2010
SQ FT: 7,500
SALES (est): 3.1MM **Privately Held**
WEB: www.instent.com
SIC: 2394 5999 Canopies, fabric: made from purchased materials; tents: made from purchased materials; banners

---

2395 Pleating & Stitching For The Trade

(P-3149)
ACADEMY AWNING INC
1501 Beach St, Montebello (90640-5431)
PHONE....................800 422-9646
James D Richman, *President*
Maury Rice, *Corp Secy*
Tom Shapiro, *Vice Pres*
Allice Miranda, *Manager*
EMP: 25 **EST:** 1992
SALES (est): 5.8MM **Privately Held**
WEB: www.academyinc.com
SIC: 2395 5999 Quilted fabrics or cloth; awnings

(P-3150)
AMERICAN QUILTING COMPANY INC
Also Called: Antaky Quilting Company
1540 Calzona St, Los Angeles
(90023-3254)
PHONE....................323 233-2500
Derek Antaky, *CEO*
Elias Antaky Jr, *Vice Pres*
▲ **EMP:** 30 **EST:** 1917
SALES (est): 2.4MM **Privately Held**
WEB: www.antakyquilting.com
SIC: 2395 Quilting, for the trade

(P-3151)
BEST- IN- WEST
Also Called: Best-In-West Emblem Co
2279 Eagle Glen Pkwy # 1, Corona
(92883-0790)
PHONE....................909 947-6507
Eric Roberts, *President*
Heriberto Perez, *Treasurer*
Beatriz Roberts, *Admin Sec*
EMP: 34 **EST:** 1980
SQ FT: 15,000
SALES (est): 820.1K **Privately Held**
SIC: 2395 2759 Embroidery products, except schiffli machine; commercial printing

(P-3152)
CHRISTINE ALEXANDER INC
110 E 9th St Ste B336, Los Angeles
(90079-3336)
PHONE....................213 488-1114
EMP: 24 **Privately Held**
SIC: 2395 Pleating/Stitching Services

(P-3153)
EMBROIDERTEX WEST LTD (PA)
435 E 16th St, Los Angeles (90015-3726)
PHONE....................213 749-4319
Leonard Kleiderman, *President*
EMP: 15 **EST:** 1977
SQ FT: 13,000
SALES (est): 4.4MM **Privately Held**
SIC: 2395 2397 Embroidery products, except schiffli machine; schiffli machine embroideries

(P-3154)
EMBROIDERY ONE CORP
1359 Channing St, Los Angeles
(90021-2410)
PHONE....................213 572-0280
Danny Yektafar, *President*
Sassan Yektafar, *Bd of Directors*
John Mora, *Manager*
Danny Yekta, *Manager*
EMP: 19 **EST:** 1978
SQ FT: 4,600
SALES (est): 516.7K **Privately Held**
WEB: www.embroidery-one.com
SIC: 2395 Embroidery products, except schiffli machine; embroidery & art needlework

(P-3155)
EQUIPMENT DE SPORT USA INC
Also Called: Elan Blanc
39301 Badger St Ste 500, Palm Desert
(92211-1162)
PHONE....................760 772-5544
Sharon Elaine Burr, *President*
Brian Burr, *Vice Pres*
▼ **EMP:** 13 **EST:** 1982
SQ FT: 2,500
SALES (est): 718.9K **Privately Held**
SIC: 2395 Embroidery & art needlework

(P-3156)
LA PALM FURNITURES & ACC INC (PA)
Also Called: Royal Plasticware
1650 W Artesia Blvd, Gardena
(90248-3217)
PHONE....................310 217-2700
Dorra Ngan, *CEO*
Donna Sada, *Vice Pres*
Monica Lee, *Sales Executive*
Jessica Rodriguez, *Sales Mgr*
Shawn Morse, *Sales Staff*
▲ **EMP:** 52 **EST:** 1996
SQ FT: 30,000

SALES (est): 10.6MM **Privately Held**
WEB: www.royal-ware.com
SIC: 2395 Embroidery products, except schiffli machine

(P-3157)
LAKESHIRTS LLC
Also Called: Yesterdays Sportswear
1400 Railroad St Ste 104, Paso Robles
(93446-1771)
PHONE....................805 239-1290
Mark Fritz, *Branch Mgr*
EMP: 45
SALES (corp-wide): 58MM **Privately Held**
WEB: www.blue84.com
SIC: 2395 Embroidery & art needlework
PA: Lakeshirts Llc
750 Randolph Rd
Detroit Lakes MN 56501
218 847-2171

(P-3158)
MANHATTAN STITCHING CO INC
8362 Artesia Blvd Ste E, Buena Park
(90621-4179)
PHONE....................714 521-9479
Maxine Jossel, *President*
Cory Miller, *President*
Lynne Miller, *Vice Pres*
Katie Berkhimer, *Opers Staff*
Shane Art, *Director*
EMP: 37 **EST:** 2005
SQ FT: 750
SALES (est): 2.5MM **Privately Held**
WEB: www.manhattanstitching.com
SIC: 2395 2759 7389 Embroidery products, except schiffli machine; promotional printing; screen printing; advertising, promotional & trade show services

(P-3159)
MELMARC PRODUCTS INC
752 S Campus Ave, Ontario (91761-1728)
PHONE....................714 549-2170
Brian Hirth, *President*
Leila Drager, *COO*
Harish Naran, *CFO*
Rommel Mendoza, *Officer*
Christine Tomongin, *Executive*
▲ **EMP:** 160 **EST:** 1987
SQ FT: 85,000
SALES (est): 24MM **Privately Held**
WEB: www.melmarc.com
SIC: 2395 2396 Pleating & stitching; screen printing on fabric articles

(P-3160)
N STITCHES PRINTS INC
16009 S Broadway, Gardena (90248-2417)
PHONE....................310 366-7537
Ali Amir, *President*
Nanji Farwah, *Manager*
EMP: 17 **EST:** 1999
SQ FT: 3,800
SALES (est): 800K **Privately Held**
WEB: www.snpink.com
SIC: 2395 Embroidery products, except schiffli machine

(P-3161)
NATIONAL EMBLEM INC (PA)
3925 E Vernon St, Long Beach
(90815-1727)
P.O. Box 15680 (90815-0680)
PHONE....................310 515-5055
Milton H Lubin Sr, *President*
Milton H Lubin Jr, *Vice Pres*
Rose Atkinson, *Office Mgr*
Letty Lubin, *Purchasing*
Shannon Van, *Sales Staff*
▲ **EMP:** 250 **EST:** 1972
SQ FT: 60,000
SALES (est): 25.3MM **Privately Held**
WEB: www.nationalemblem.com
SIC: 2395 2396 Emblems, embroidered; automotive & apparel trimmings

(P-3162)
OUTLOOK RESOURCES INC
Also Called: Leftbank Art
14930 Alondra Blvd, La Mirada
(90638-5752)
PHONE....................714 522-2452
Chris Hyun, *President*
Janell Jernigan, *Administration*

Cecilia Popescu, *Manager*
◆ **EMP:** 100 **EST:** 2008
SALES (est): 9.8MM **Privately Held**
WEB: www.leftbankart.com
SIC: 2395 5999 Pleating & stitching; art dealers

(P-3163)
REBECCA INTERNATIONAL INC
4587 E 48th St, Vernon (90058-3201)
PHONE....................323 973-2602
Eli Kahen, *Owner*
EMP: 25 **EST:** 2015
SQ FT: 1,500 **Privately Held**
WEB: www.rebeccainternational.com
SIC: 2395 2759 7299 Embroidery products, except schiffli machine; screen printing; stitching services

(P-3164)
SOUTHLAND HOME FABRICS INC
Also Called: F & Sfabrics
10629 W Pico Blvd, Los Angeles
(90064-2213)
PHONE....................310 475-1637
Richard Snyder, *President*
EMP: 15 **EST:** 1998
SALES (est): 124.5K **Privately Held**
WEB: www.fsfabricslosangeles.com
SIC: 5949 2395 Fabric stores piece goods; quilted fabrics or cloth

(P-3165)
WINNING TEAM INC
24922 Anza Dr Ste E, Valencia
(91355-1228)
P.O. Box 802197 (91380-2197)
PHONE....................661 295-1428
Harris G Birken, *President*
EMP: 15 **EST:** 1993
SQ FT: 6,000
SALES (est): 1MM **Privately Held**
WEB: www.thewinningteam.com
SIC: 2395 2253 Embroidery products, except schiffli machine; jackets, knit

---

2396 Automotive Trimmings, Apparel Findings, Related Prdts

(P-3166)
ABSOLUTE SCREENPRINT INC
333 Cliffwood Park St, Brea (92821-4104)
P.O. Box 9069 (92822-9069)
PHONE....................714 529-2120
Steven Restivo, *CEO*
Andrea Restivo, *CFO*
▲ **EMP:** 250 **EST:** 1991
SQ FT: 65,000
SALES (est): 23.8MM **Privately Held**
WEB: www.absolutescreenprint.com
SIC: 2396 3993 2759 Screen printing on fabric articles; signs & advertising specialties; screen printing

(P-3167)
ACCURATE SCREEN PROCESSING
3538 Foothill Blvd, La Crescenta
(91214-1828)
PHONE....................818 957-3965
Fax: 818 957-6445
EMP: 15
SQ FT: 2,320
SALES (est): 1.1MM
SALES (corp-wide): 2.8MM **Privately Held**
SIC: 2396 Mfg Auto/Apparel Trimming
PA: Accurate Dial & Nameplate Inc
329 Mira Loma Ave
Glendale CA 91204
323 245-9181

(P-3168)
ATELIER LUXURY GROUP LLC
Also Called: Amiri
1330 Channing St, Los Angeles
(90021-2411)
PHONE....................310 751-2444
Michael Amiri, *Mng Member*
EMP: 45 **EST:** 2019
SQ FT: 30,000

SALES (est): 2.6MM **Privately Held**
SIC: 2396 2311 2321 2331 Apparel &
other linings, except millinery; men's &
boys' suits & coats; men's & boys' furnishings; women's & misses' blouses & shirts;
men's miscellaneous accessories

(P-3169)
C S DASH COVER INC
14020 Paramount Blvd, Paramount
(90723-2606)
PHONE.....................................562 790-8300
Cameron Zada, *President*
Diana Berg, *General Mgr*
Karsten Berg, *General Mgr*
▲ EMP: 16 EST: 1992
SQ FT: 3,200
SALES (est): 1.9MM **Privately Held**
WEB: www.csdashcovers.com
SIC: 2396 5521 Automotive trimmings,
fabric; used car dealers

(P-3170)
CKCC INC
Also Called: Nissi Trim
1017 San Julian St, Los Angeles
(90015-2311)
PHONE.....................................213 629-0939
Thuong T Nguyen, *CEO*
EMP: 20 EST: 2014
SALES (est): 175.1K **Privately Held**
SIC: 2396 Trimming, fabric

(P-3171)
D AND J MARKETING INC
Also Called: DJM Suspension
580 W 184th St, Gardena (90248-4202)
PHONE.....................................310 538-1583
Jeffery J Ullmann, *President*
Mark Dunham, *Vice Pres*
▲ EMP: 32 EST: 1985
SQ FT: 18,000
SALES (est): 3.4MM **Privately Held**
SIC: 2396 2531 3714 Automotive trim-
mings, fabric; public building & related fur-
niture; motor vehicle parts & accessories

(P-3172)
DISTINCTIVE INDUSTRIES
Also Called: Specialty Division
10618 Shoemaker Ave, Santa Fe Springs
(90670-4038)
PHONE.....................................800 421-9777
Dwight Forrister, *CEO*
Aaron Forrister, *Vice Pres*
▲ EMP: 410 EST: 1969
SQ FT: 110,000
SALES (est): 48.2MM **Privately Held**
WEB: www.distinctiveindustries.com
SIC: 2396 3086 Automotive trimmings,
fabric; plastics foam products
PA: Distinctive Industries Of Texas, Inc.
4516 Seton Center Pkwy # 13
Austin TX 78759

(P-3173)
G&A APPAREL GROUP
Also Called: G&A Bias Les
3610 S Broadway, Los Angeles
(90007-4430)
PHONE.....................................323 234-1746
EMP: 30
SQ FT: 4,000
SALES (est): 2.4MM **Privately Held**
SIC: 2396 Mfg Apparel Trimmings

(P-3174)
GRAPHIC PRINTS INC
Also Called: Pipeline
904 Silver Spur Rd # 415, Rllng HLS Est
(90274-3800)
P.O. Box 459, Gardena (90248-0459)
PHONE.....................................310 870-1239
Alan Greenberg, *CEO*
Tamotsu Inouye, *COO*
Richard Greenberg, *Corp Secy*
EMP: 45 EST: 1971
SQ FT: 22,000
SALES (est): 5MM **Privately Held**
WEB: www.pipelinegear.com
SIC: 2396 2339 2329 Screen printing on
fabric articles; women's & misses' athletic
clothing & sportswear; men's & boys'
sportswear & athletic clothing

(P-3175)
I D BRAND LLC
3185 Airway Ave Ste A, Costa Mesa
(92626-4601)
PHONE.....................................949 422-7057
Colin Cormac,
Trishia Keenan, *Software Dev*
Keely Bryant, *Sales Staff*
Andrew Hockaday,
Melissa Nakashima, *Manager*
▲ EMP: 23 EST: 1995
SQ FT: 6,400
SALES (est): 4.6MM **Privately Held**
WEB: www.brandid.com
SIC: 2396 Apparel findings & trimmings

(P-3176)
J & H PRODUCTION
4481 S Santa Fe Ave, Vernon
(90058-2101)
PHONE.....................................323 261-6600
Joseph Hendifar, *Partner*
Sassan Kohan, *Partner*
EMP: 20 EST: 1988
SQ FT: 8,000
SALES (est): 790.5K **Privately Held**
SIC: 2396 Pads, shoulder: for coats, suits,
etc.

(P-3177)
KAMM INDUSTRIES INC
Also Called: Prp Seats
43352 Business Park Dr, Temecula
(92590-3665)
PHONE.....................................800 317-6253
Aaron Wedeking, *CEO*
Mike Doherty, *Co-Owner*
Justin Constant, *Marketing Staff*
Jason Dearmond, *Marketing Staff*
▲ EMP: 43 EST: 2009
SALES (est): 5MM **Privately Held**
WEB: www.prpseats.com
SIC: 2396 Automotive trimmings, fabric

(P-3178)
NORTH AMERICAN TEXTILE CO LLC (PA)
Also Called: N A T C O
346 W Cerritos Ave, Glendale
(91204-2704)
PHONE.....................................818 409-0019
Esteban E Arslanian Sr,
Armine Madanyan, *Graphic Designe*
Ta Cipriano, *Accountant*
Danielle Perdue, *Sales Staff*
Armando Arslanian,
◆ EMP: 49 EST: 1991
SQ FT: 18,000
SALES (est): 11MM **Privately Held**
SIC: 2396 7389 Apparel findings & trim-
mings; textile & apparel services

(P-3179)
ORBO MANUFACTURING INC ✪
12740 Lakeland Rd, Santa Fe Springs
(90670-4633)
PHONE.....................................562 222-4535
Roberto Galvez, *CEO*
EMP: 25 EST: 2021
SALES (est): 1.4MM **Privately Held**
SIC: 2396 Furniture trimmings, fabric

(P-3180)
ROYAL TRIM
2529 Chambers St, Vernon (90058-2107)
PHONE.....................................323 583-2121
Farzad Pakravan, *President*
▲ EMP: 14 EST: 1986
SQ FT: 30,000
SALES (est): 657.8K **Privately Held**
SIC: 2396 2395 Apparel findings & trim-
mings; pleating & stitching

(P-3181)
SECURITY TEXTILE CORPORATION
1457 E Washington Blvd, Los Angeles
(90021-3039)
PHONE.....................................213 747-2673
Doug Weitman, *CEO*
Brian Weitman, *President*
Mary Larimore, *Human Res Mgr*
Jeff Waldman, *Sales Dir*
▲ EMP: 33 EST: 1972
SQ FT: 85,000

SALES (est): 625.6K **Privately Held**
WEB: www.stc-qst.com
SIC: 2396 5131 Automotive & apparel
trimmings; sewing supplies & notions

(P-3182)
SIMSO TEX SUBLIMATION (PA)
3028 E Las Hermanas St, Compton
(90221-5511)
PHONE.....................................310 885-9717
Joe Simsoly, *CEO*
Eli Simsollo, *President*
Kaden Simsollo, *Admin Sec*
▲ EMP: 78 EST: 2001
SQ FT: 38,000
SALES (est): 6.3MM **Privately Held**
SIC: 2396 Fabric printing & stamping

(P-3183)
SJ&L BIAS BINDING & TEX CO INC
Also Called: Superior Bias Trims
1950 E 20th St, Vernon (90058-1005)
PHONE.....................................213 747-5271
Lynn Menichiwi, *CEO*
Joseph Menichini, *Vice Pres*
▲ EMP: 44 EST: 1950
SQ FT: 11,000
SALES (est): 1.1MM **Privately Held**
SIC: 2396 Pads, shoulder: for coats, suits,
etc.

(P-3184)
WESTIN AUTOMOTIVE PRODUCTS INC (PA)
320 W Covina Blvd, San Dimas
(91773-2907)
PHONE.....................................626 960-6762
Robert West, *President*
Deborah Quiroz, *Vice Pres*
Marcela Mata, *Controller*
Jeff West, *Sales Mgr*
David Crockett, *Sales Staff*
▲ EMP: 35 EST: 1994
SQ FT: 10,000
SALES (est): 60MM **Privately Held**
WEB: www.westinautomotive.com
SIC: 2396 Automotive & apparel trimmings

(P-3185)
WORLD UPHOLSTERY & TRIM INC
1320 E Main St, Santa Paula (93060-2926)
PHONE.....................................805 921-0100
Michael May, *President*
Fran Adler, *Vice Pres*
EMP: 14 EST: 1974
SALES (est): 2.1MM **Privately Held**
WEB: www.worlduph.com
SIC: 2396 Automotive trimmings, fabric

2399 Fabricated Textile Prdts, NEC

(P-3186)
A LOT TO SAY INC
1541 S Vineyard Ave, Ontario
(91761-7717)
PHONE.....................................877 366-8448
Jennifer Spannich Danmiller, *CEO*
Alisson Spannich Powers, *COO*
EMP: 20 EST: 2008
SALES (est): 978.7K **Privately Held**
SIC: 2399 Banners, made from fabric

(P-3187)
AAA FLAG & BANNER MFG CO INC (PA)
8937 National Blvd, Los Angeles
(90034-3307)
PHONE.....................................310 836-3200
Howard S Furst, *President*
Luis Mora, *President*
David Esqueda, *Exec VP*
Lm Rosenfeld, *Exec VP*
Lm Rosenfeld-Jobso, *Exec VP*
▲ EMP: 150 EST: 1971
SQ FT: 4,000
SALES (est): 52.9MM **Privately Held**
WEB: www.aaaflag.com
SIC: 5999 2399 Flags; banners, pennants
& flags

(P-3188)
ACTION EMBROIDERY CORP (PA)
1315 Brooks St, Ontario (91762-3612)
PHONE.....................................909 983-1359
Ira Newman, *President*
Steven Mendelow, *Treasurer*
▲ EMP: 120
SQ FT: 12,000
SALES (est): 22.7MM **Privately Held**
WEB: www.actionembroiderycorp.com
SIC: 2399 2395 Emblems, badges & in-
signia: from purchased materials; pleating
& stitching

(P-3189)
ADVANTAGE PRODUCTS GROUP LLC
Also Called: Advantage Bridal
15620 S Figueroa St, Gardena
(90248-2127)
PHONE.....................................310 371-2060
Toll Free:....................................877 -
Sandra J Keller, *Owner*
▲ EMP: 24 EST: 1991
SALES (est): 1.2MM **Privately Held**
WEB: www.advantagebridal.com
SIC: 5621 2399 7389 5699 Bridal shops;
ready-to-wear apparel, women's; teenage
apparel; hand woven apparel; styling of
fashions, apparel, furniture, textiles, etc.;
customized clothing & apparel

(P-3190)
AIRBORNE SYSTEMS N AMER CA INC
3100 W Segerstrom Ave, Santa Ana
(92704-5812)
PHONE.....................................714 662-1400
Bryce Wiedeman, *President*
Sean P Maroney, *Treasurer*
Terrance M Paradie, *Principal*
Halle F Terrion, *Admin Sec*
▼ EMP: 200 EST: 1919
SQ FT: 160,000
SALES (est): 52.4MM
SALES (corp-wide): 4.8B **Publicly Held**
WEB: www.airborne-sys.com
SIC: 2399 Parachutes
HQ: Airborne Systems North America Inc.
5800 Magnolia Ave
Pennsauken NJ 08109
856 663-1275

(P-3191)
BEVERLY BAY INC (PA)
P.O. Box 8078 (91327-8078)
PHONE.....................................818 852-2408
Morgan Ein, *President*
EMP: 16 EST: 2007
SALES (est): 111K **Privately Held**
SIC: 2399 Automotive covers, except seat
& tire covers

(P-3192)
CAL TRENDS ACCESSORIES LLC
Also Called: Cal Trend Automotive Products
2121 S Anne St, Santa Ana (92704-4408)
P.O. Box 5007 (92704-0007)
PHONE.....................................714 708-5115
Roger Loomis,
Cesar Hernandez, *Buyer*
EMP: 28 EST: 1982
SALES (est): 2.3MM **Privately Held**
WEB: www.caltrend.com
SIC: 2399 3751 3714 Automotive covers,
except seat & tire covers; motorcycle ac-
cessories; motor vehicle parts & acces-
sories

(P-3193)
DISPLAY FABRICATION GROUP INC
1231 N Miller St Ste 100, Anaheim
(92806-1950)
PHONE.....................................714 373-2100
Luis Ocampo, *President*
Robert Valles, *Engineer*
Nina Liddi, *Controller*
Craig Moloney, *VP Opers*
Leslie McCarter, *Director*
◆ EMP: 50 EST: 2002
SQ FT: 100,000

▲ = Import ▼=Export
◆ =Import/Export

SALES (est): 3.5MM **Privately Held**
WEB: www.displayfg.com
SIC: 2399 Belting, fabric: made from purchased materials

(P-3194)
DSY EDUCATIONAL CORPORATION
Also Called: Main Street Banner
525 Maple St, Carpinteria (93013-2070)
P.O. Box 41829, Santa Barbara (93140-1829)
PHONE..................................805 684-8111
David Yothers, *President*
Sharon Yothers, *Corp Secy*
EMP: 27 EST: 1960
SQ FT: 15,000
SALES (est): 1MM **Privately Held**
SIC: 2399 7336 Banners, made from fabric; flags, fabric; commercial art & graphic design

(P-3195)
EXXEL OUTDOORS INC
343 Baldwin Park Blvd, City of Industry (91746-1406)
PHONE..................................626 369-7278
Armen Kouleyan, *General Mgr*
Laura Sutcliffe, *Analyst*
Lori Ash, *Human Resources*
Nikki Weishel, *Buyer*
Nils Davis, *Sales Dir*
EMP: 146
SALES (corp-wide): 123.4MM **Privately Held**
WEB: www.exxel.com
SIC: 2399 Sleeping bags
PA: Exxel Outdoors, Inc.
300 American Blvd
Haleyville AL 35565
205 486-5258

(P-3196)
FALCON AUTOMOTIVE INC
1305 E Wakeham Ave, Santa Ana (92705-4145)
PHONE..................................714 569-1085
Peter Eberhardt, *President*
▲ EMP: 16 EST: 1988
SQ FT: 16,000
SALES (est): 178.5K **Privately Held**
WEB: www.falconauto.com
SIC: 2399 2273 3714 Automotive covers, except seat & tire covers; seat covers, automobile; automobile floor coverings, except rubber or plastic; motor vehicle parts & accessories

(P-3197)
FXC CORPORATION
Guardian Parachute Division
3050 Red Hill Ave, Costa Mesa (92626-4524)
PHONE..................................714 557-8032
Frank X Chevrier, *Manager*
Stephanie Pinnell, *Administration*
Frank Velazquez, *Technology*
Scott Lund, *Engineer*
Kelly Densmore, *Manager*
EMP: 64
SALES (corp-wide): 12.4MM **Privately Held**
WEB: www.fxcguardian.com
SIC: 2399 3429 Parachutes; parachute hardware
PA: Fxc Corporation
3050 Red Hill Ave
Costa Mesa CA 92626
714 556-7400

(P-3198)
GOLD METROPOLITAN MEDIA (PA)
16000 Blythe St, Van Nuys (91406-1812)
PHONE..................................818 348-1913
Andrew Gold, *President*
Mike Vizvary, *COO*
Ken Gold, *Vice Pres*
Shelly Silveri, *Finance Dir*
Lecia Rdzak, *Production*
EMP: 30 EST: 2016
SALES (est): 2.6MM **Privately Held**
WEB: www.goldmetropolitan.com
SIC: 2399 7312 Banners, pennants & flags; poster advertising, outdoor

(P-3199)
HITEX DYEING & FINISHING INC
355 Vineland Ave, City of Industry (91746-2321)
PHONE..................................626 363-0160
Young C Kim, *President*
▲ EMP: 36 EST: 2010
SALES (est): 555.2K **Privately Held**
WEB: www.hitexdye.com
SIC: 2399 2257 Nets, launderers & dyers; dyeing & finishing circular knit fabrics

(P-3200)
SCOTTEX INC
12828 S Broadway, Los Angeles (90061-1116)
PHONE..................................310 516-1411
Stanley Jung, *President*
▲ EMP: 28 EST: 1995
SQ FT: 19,000
SALES (est): 1.2MM **Privately Held**
WEB: www.scottex.com
SIC: 2399 Hand woven & crocheted products

(P-3201)
SEABORN CANVAS
435 N Harbor Blvd Ste B1, San Pedro (90731-2271)
PHONE..................................310 519-1208
Juanita Wade, *Owner*
▼ EMP: 25 EST: 1987
SQ FT: 5,000
SALES (est): 1.1MM **Privately Held**
WEB: www.seabornflags.com
SIC: 2399 2394 Banners, pennants & flags; flags, fabric; canvas & related products

(P-3202)
YOUNG SUNG (USA) INC
1122 S Alvarado St, Los Angeles (90006-4110)
PHONE..................................213 427-2580
Pyung Kwon, *President*
▲ EMP: 15 EST: 1985
SQ FT: 15,600
SALES (est): 1.6MM **Privately Held**
SIC: 2399 Seat covers, automobile

2411 Logging

(P-3203)
US DOOR AND FENCE LLC
3880 Garner Rd, Riverside (92501-1066)
PHONE..................................951 300-0010
Gang Wu, *Mng Member*
Nick Anis, *Vice Pres*
Aizhen Chen, *Mng Member*
Chunjie Sun, *Mng Member*
Yicheng Sun, *Mng Member*
▲ EMP: 22 EST: 2012
SQ FT: 30,000
SALES (est): 2.8MM **Privately Held**
WEB: www.usdoorfence.com
SIC: 2411 3089 3315 3442 Rails, fence: round or split; fences, gates & accessories: plastic; fence gates posts & fittings: steel; screen & storm doors & windows; screen doors, metal; storm doors or windows, metal; metal doors; fences, gates, posts & flagpoles; metal doors, sash & trim
HQ: Ningbo Win Success Machinery Co.,Ltd
Area B, Zhenhai Economic Development Zone, Zhenhai District
Ningbo 31502

(P-3204)
WASHBURN GROVE MANAGEMENT INC
27781 Fairview Ave, Hemet (92544-8521)
PHONE..................................909 322-4690
Dennis Washburn, *President*
David Washburn, *Vice Pres*
EMP: 24 EST: 1991
SALES (est): 2.6MM **Privately Held**
SIC: 2411 0783 Logging; ornamental shrub & tree services

(P-3205)
WELL ANALYSIS CORPORATION INC (PA)
Also Called: Welaco
5500 Woodmere Dr, Bakersfield (93313-2776)
P.O. Box 20008 (93390-0008)
PHONE..................................661 283-9510
Judy L Bebout, *CEO*
Dan Bebout, *CFO*
Brenda Muniozguren, *Vice Pres*
Robert Muniozguren, *Admin Sec*
Chuck Obrien, *Safety Mgr*
▲ EMP: 27 EST: 1989
SQ FT: 1,400
SALES (est): 9.2MM **Privately Held**
WEB: www.welacogroup.com
SIC: 2411 1389 Logging; oil field services

(P-3206)
WEST COAST TIMBER CORP
6221 Apache Rd, Westminster (92683-1919)
PHONE..................................714 893-4374
EMP: 15
SALES: 700K **Privately Held**
SIC: 2411 Logging

2421 Saw & Planing Mills

(P-3207)
ARTESIA SAWDUST PRODUCTS INC
13434 S Ontario Ave, Ontario (91761-7956)
PHONE..................................909 947-5983
Brigitte De Laura-Espinoza, *President*
Anthony Espinoza, *Vice Pres*
EMP: 35 EST: 1960
SQ FT: 2,700
SALES (est): 9.6MM **Privately Held**
WEB: www.artesiasawdust.com
SIC: 2421 Sawdust & shavings; wood chips, produced at mill

(P-3208)
B P JOHN RECYCLE INC
Also Called: B P John Hauling
38875 Avenida La Cresta, Murrieta (92562-9155)
PHONE..................................951 696-1144
Edward F Metzler, *President*
Lynda Metzler, *Admin Sec*
EMP: 15 EST: 1980
SALES (est): 1MM **Privately Held**
SIC: 2421 4212 Fuelwood, from mill waste; light haulage & cartage, local

(P-3209)
CHAPMAN DESIGNS INC
11203 Shoemaker Ave, Santa Fe Springs (90670-4644)
PHONE..................................562 698-4600
Michael Chapman, *President*
John Chapman, *Vice Pres*
EMP: 20 EST: 1986
SALES (est): 1.9MM **Privately Held**
WEB: www.chapmandesignsinc.com
SIC: 2421 Specialty sawmill products

(P-3210)
FULGHUM FIBRES INC (HQ)
333 S Grand Ave Ste 4100, Los Angeles (90071-1571)
PHONE..................................706 651-1000
O T Fulghum Jr, *President*
H Heyward Wells, *President*
Anthony M Hauff, *CFO*
King Judy A, *Corp Secy*
Anthony Hauff, *Exec VP*
EMP: 16 EST: 1956
SALES (est): 43.4MM
SALES (corp-wide): 150.7MM **Privately Held**
WEB: www.thepricecompanies.com
SIC: 2421 Chipper mill
PA: Rentech, Inc.
10880 Wilshire Blvd # 1101
Los Angeles CA 90024
310 571-9800

(P-3211)
HMR BUILDING SYSTEMS LLC
620 Newport Center Dr # 12, Newport Beach (92660-6420)
PHONE..................................951 749-4700
Ronald Simon,
RSI Holding LLC,
▲ EMP: 80 EST: 2008
SQ FT: 90,000
SALES (est): 688.3K **Privately Held**
WEB: www.rsihc.com
SIC: 2421 Building & structural materials, wood
PA: Rsi Holding Llc
620 Nwport Ctr Dr Fl 12 Flr 12
Newport Beach CA 92660

(P-3212)
PLUM CREEK TIMBERLANDS LP
615 N Benson Ave, Upland (91786-5076)
PHONE..................................909 949-2255
EMP: 117
SALES (corp-wide): 7.2B **Publicly Held**
SIC: 2421 Sawmill/Planing Mill
HQ: Plum Creek Timberlands, L.P.
601 Union St Ste 3100
Seattle WA 98101
206 467-3600

(P-3213)
STRATA FOREST PRODUCTS INC (PA)
Also Called: Profile Planing Mill
2600 S Susan St, Santa Ana (92704-5816)
PHONE..................................714 751-0800
Richard W Hormuth, *President*
John Hormuth, *President*
Michelle Grohnke, *Opers Staff*
▲ EMP: 50 EST: 1991
SQ FT: 38,000
SALES (est): 10.9MM **Privately Held**
WEB: www.strataforest.com
SIC: 2421 Planing mills

2426 Hardwood Dimension & Flooring Mills

(P-3214)
BAXSTRA INC
Also Called: Martin Erattrud Co
1224 W 132nd St, Gardena (90247-1506)
PHONE..................................323 770-4171
Patrick Baxter, *Vice Pres*
Allan Stratford, *Owner*
EMP: 26 EST: 1997
SALES (est): 5.2MM **Privately Held**
WEB: www.martinbrattrud.com
SIC: 2426 Frames for upholstered furniture, wood

(P-3215)
BMW OF PALM SPRINGS
3737 E Palm Canyon Dr, Palm Springs (92264-5205)
PHONE..................................760 324-7071
Frank Hickinbotham, *Principal*
Bob Hogan, *General Mgr*
Joe Foster, *Foreman/Supr*
Nick Alexander, *Sales Staff*
David Ball, *Sales Staff*
EMP: 16 EST: 2015
SALES (est): 4.4MM **Privately Held**
WEB: www.bmwpalmsprings.com
SIC: 2426 3545 Vehicle stock, hardwood; thread cutting dies

(P-3216)
COLEPRO INC
7351 Heil Ave Ste B, Huntington Beach (92647-4534)
PHONE..................................714 488-0996
Katherine Coleman, *CEO*
Matt Coleman, *Principal*
EMP: 13 EST: 2010
SALES (est): 1.3MM **Privately Held**
WEB: www.coleproinc.com
SIC: 2426 Furniture stock & parts, hardwood

(P-3217)
ELITE SLIDES INC
11220 Wright Rd, Santa Ana (92706)
PHONE..................................310 537-4210
EMP: 80
SQ FT: 40,000
SALES (est): 957.3K **Privately Held**
SIC: 2426 Hardwood Dimension/Floor Mill

(P-3218)
EXCAVO LLC
13428 Maxella Ave Ste 409, Marina Del
Rey (90292-5620)
PHONE..................................310 823-7670
EMP: 15
SQ FT: 2,250
SALES (est): 1.4MM **Privately Held**
WEB: www.excavofurniture.com
SIC: 2426 Manufacture Wood Furniture

(P-3219)
FURNITURE TECHNOLOGIES INC
17227 Columbus St, Adelanto (92301)
P.O. Box 1076 (92301-1076)
PHONE..................................760 246-9180
Kenneth Drum, CEO
Carlos Caballero, Manager
EMP: 24 EST: 1998
SQ FT: 31,000
SALES (est): 4.9MM **Privately Held**
WEB: www.ftical.com
SIC: 2426 Furniture stock & parts, hard-
wood

(P-3220)
LA HARDWOOD FLOORING INC (PA)
Also Called: Eternity Floors
9880 San Fernando Rd, Pacoima
(91331-2603)
PHONE..................................818 361-0099
Doron Gal, President
Eliyahu Shuat, Principal
Isaac Lee, Regional Mgr
▲ EMP: 17 EST: 2005
SQ FT: 12,000
SALES (est): 9.3MM **Privately Held**
WEB: www.eternityflooring.com
SIC: 2426 5211 Flooring, hardwood; floor-
ing, wood

(P-3221)
MCMURTRIE & MCMURTRIE INC
Also Called: Tru-Wood Products
915 W 5th St, Azusa (91702-3311)
P.O. Box 1940, Monrovia (91017-5940)
PHONE..................................626 815-0177
Richard McMurtrie, CEO
Bill Cherry, Corp Secy
▲ EMP: 46 EST: 1990
SQ FT: 97,000
SALES (est): 2.7MM **Privately Held**
SIC: 2426 2431 5031 Frames for uphol-
stered furniture, wood; trim, wood; lum-
ber, plywood & millwork

(P-3222)
MONTCLAIR WOOD CORPORATION
545 N Mountain Ave, Upland (91786-5073)
PHONE..................................909 985-0302
John Slavek Grey, President
Louis Jimenez, Vice Pres
EMP: 17 EST: 1990
SQ FT: 70,000
SALES (est): 850K **Privately Held**
SIC: 2426 5031 Furniture stock & parts,
hardwood; lumber: rough, dressed & fin-
ished

(P-3223)
O INDUSTRIES CORPORATION
1930 W 139th St, Gardena (90249-2408)
P.O. Box 779, Dana Point (92629-0779)
PHONE..................................310 719-2289
Rhonda Oerding, CEO
William Oerding, COO
Anders Oerding, Vice Pres
▼ EMP: 15 EST: 2010
SQ FT: 40,000
SALES (est): 3MM **Privately Held**
WEB: www.oindcorp.com
SIC: 2426 Flooring, hardwood

(P-3224)
PARQUET BY DIAN INC
16601 S Main St, Gardena (90248-2722)
PHONE..................................310 527-3779
Anatoli Efros, CEO
Dima Efros, President
EMP: 92 EST: 1993
SALES (est): 3.8MM **Privately Held**
WEB: www.parquet.com
SIC: 2426 Parquet flooring, hardwood

(P-3225)
SUNLAND WOODWORKS
7253 Lankershim Blvd, North Hollywood
(91605-3804)
PHONE..................................818 982-3110
Jeffrey Bastedo, CEO
EMP: 14 EST: 2010
SALES (est): 374.2K **Privately Held**
WEB: www.sunlandwood.com
SIC: 2426 Frames for upholstered furni-
ture, wood

(P-3226)
WEST COAST FURN FRAMERS INC
17402 Eucalyptus St, Hesperia
(92345-5118)
PHONE..................................760 669-5275
Katelynn Galiana-Baca, President
Katelynn Baca, CEO
Javier Galiana, Admin Sec
EMP: 27 EST: 2017
SALES (est): 2.2MM **Privately Held**
SIC: 2426 Frames for upholstered furni-
ture, wood

2431 Millwork

(P-3227)
ABC CUSTOM WOOD SHUTTERS INC
Also Called: Golden West Shutters
20561 Pascal Way, Lake Forest
(92630-8119)
PHONE..................................949 595-0300
David Harris, Vice Pres
John Stahman, Vice Pres
EMP: 35 EST: 1991
SALES (est): 3.6MM **Privately Held**
WEB: www.gwshutters.com
SIC: 2431 Door shutters, wood; window
shutters, wood

(P-3228)
AMERICAN CABINET WORKS
13518 S Normandie Ave, Gardena
(90249-2606)
PHONE..................................310 715-6815
Alex Medrano, Owner
Erick Garcia, Project Mgr
EMP: 22 EST: 1999
SQ FT: 5,000
SALES (est): 3.7MM **Privately Held**
WEB: www.americancabinetworks.com
SIC: 2431 Millwork

(P-3229)
ANDERCO INC
540 Airpark Dr, Fullerton (92833-2503)
PHONE..................................714 446-9508
Peter Johnson, President
Ralph Johnson, Vice Pres
Aaron Olson, CPA
Judy Arreguin, Sales Executive
▲ EMP: 50 EST: 1983
SQ FT: 70,000
SALES (est): 8.1MM **Privately Held**
SIC: 2431 5031 Door frames, wood; doors
& windows

(P-3230)
ARCH-RITE INC
1062 N Armando St, Anaheim
(92806-2605)
P.O. Box 6207, Fullerton (92834-6207)
PHONE..................................714 630-9305
Michael Barry, President
George Goodwin, Vice Pres
EMP: 28 EST: 1988
SQ FT: 15,000
SALES (est): 540.5K **Privately Held**
SIC: 2431 Windows & window parts & trim,
wood

(P-3231)
ARCHITCTRAL MLLWK SNTA BARBARA
Also Called: Manufacturers of Wood Products
8 N Nopal St, Santa Barbara (93103-3317)
P.O. Box 4699 (93140-4699)
PHONE..................................805 965-7011
Thomas G Mathews, President
Ronald Mathews, Shareholder
Glenice Mathews, CEO
Joseph J Mathews, Vice Pres
Mike Hendrick, Engineer
EMP: 40 EST: 1968
SQ FT: 10,000
SALES (est): 4.2MM **Privately Held**
WEB: www.archmill.com
SIC: 2431 Millwork

(P-3232)
ART GLASS ETC INC
Also Called: AG Millworks
3111 Golf Course Dr, Ventura
(93003-7604)
PHONE..................................805 644-4494
Rachid El Etel, President
Aida El Etel, CFO
Maria Burden, Marketing Staff
Laura Graybill, Sales Staff
Christian Perry, Sales Staff
▲ EMP: 50 EST: 1986
SALES (est): 7.4MM **Privately Held**
WEB: www.agmillworks.com
SIC: 2431 Doors & door parts & trim,
wood; windows & window parts & trim,
wood

(P-3233)
AVALON SHUTTERS INC
3407 N Perris Blvd, Perris (92571-3100)
PHONE..................................909 937-4900
Douglas Noel Serbin, CEO
Joe Martinez, Regional Mgr
Dawn Baron, District Mgr
Richard Lozano, Recruiter
Jody Strickland, Safety Mgr
▲ EMP: 215 EST: 1989
SQ FT: 85,000
SALES (est): 20MM **Privately Held**
WEB: www.avalonshutters.com
SIC: 2431 Window shutters, wood; door
shutters, wood; blinds (shutters), wood

(P-3234)
B & G MILLWORKS
12522 Lakeland Rd, Santa Fe Springs
(90670-3940)
PHONE..................................562 944-4599
Gene Harden, Partner
Brad Simons, Partner
Catalina Montezuma, Office Mgr
Tom Borba, Project Mgr
EMP: 14 EST: 1991
SALES (est): 2.1MM **Privately Held**
WEB: www.bgmillworks.com
SIC: 2431 1751 5084 Millwork; carpentry
work; woodworking machinery

(P-3235)
CALIFORNIA DECOR
Also Called: Salon Brandy
541 E Pine St, Compton (90222-2817)
PHONE..................................310 603-9944
James Lee Jenkins, President
Richard Mars, Corp Secy
EMP: 16 EST: 1974
SQ FT: 36,000
SALES (est): 520.2K **Privately Held**
SIC: 2431 7359 2522 2512 Woodwork,
interior & ornamental; equipment rental &
leasing; office furniture, except wood; up-
holstered household furniture; wood
household furniture

(P-3236)
CALIFORNIA MILLWORKS CORP
Also Called: California Classics
27772 Avenue Scott, Santa Clarita
(91355-3417)
PHONE..................................661 294-2345
Steven Gadol, President
Lay Cho, President
Steven Godol, Vice Pres
Edmond Cho, Vice Pres
EMP: 22 EST: 1981
SQ FT: 149,000
SALES (est): 3.5MM
SALES (corp-wide): 5.1MM **Privately Held**
WEB: www.california-classics.com
SIC: 2431 Doors, wood
PA: Old English Milling & Woodworks, Inc.
27772 Avenue Scott
Santa Clarita CA 91355
661 294-9171

(P-3237)
CALIFRNIA DLUXE WNDOWS INDS IN (PA)
20735 Superior St, Chatsworth
(91311-4416)
PHONE..................................818 349-5566
Aaron Adirim, President
Patricia Kerins, CFO
Cory Fletcher, Info Tech Mgr
Anthony Mariani, Project Mgr
Leoni Paez, Controller
EMP: 47 EST: 1999
SQ FT: 60,000
SALES (est): 12.3MM **Privately Held**
WEB: www.cdwindows.com
SIC: 2431 2824 Windows & window parts
& trim, wood; vinyl fibers

(P-3238)
CHARLES GEMEINER CABINETS
3225 Exposition Pl, Los Angeles
(90018-4032)
PHONE..................................323 299-8696
Charles Gemeiner, Owner
EMP: 13 EST: 1984
SQ FT: 20,000
SALES (est): 800K **Privately Held**
SIC: 2431 1751 Millwork; cabinet building
& installation

(P-3239)
CUSTOM QUALITY DOOR & TRIM INC
1116 Bradford Cir, Corona (92882-1874)
PHONE..................................951 278-0066
Michael Leroy Hughes, CEO
Shawn Hughes, President
Karen Berger, Controller
Leah Ortiz, Controller
EMP: 20 EST: 2008
SALES (est): 3.2MM **Privately Held**
WEB: www.cqdoorandtrim.com
SIC: 2431 Doors & door parts & trim, wood

(P-3240)
DAN LUNA INC
23400 Peralta Dr Ste I, Laguna Hills
(92653-1731)
PHONE..................................949 859-3631
Dan Luna, Principal
EMP: 13 EST: 2011
SALES (est): 1.7MM **Privately Held**
WEB: www.danlunawoodworking.com
SIC: 2431 Millwork

(P-3241)
DAY STAR INDUSTRIES
13727 Excelsior Dr, Santa Fe Springs
(90670-5104)
PHONE..................................562 926-8800
Dan R Prigmore, President
Anne Prigmore, Treasurer
Christine Robertson, Vice Pres
EMP: 19 EST: 1985
SALES (est): 3.1MM **Privately Held**
WEB: www.daystarindustries.com
SIC: 2431 Millwork

(P-3242)
DE LARSHE CABINETRY LLC
Also Called: L-G Wood Products
2000 S Reservoir St, Pomona
(91766-5545)
PHONE..................................909 627-2757
Scott League, Mng Member
Jeff Cregger,
EMP: 20 EST: 1987
SQ FT: 19,500
SALES (est): 684.7K **Privately Held**
WEB: www.lgwoodproducts.com
SIC: 2431 2448 Staircases & stairs, wood;
wood pallets & skids

(P-3243)

DECORE-ATIVE SPC NC LLC (PA)

2772 Peck Rd, Monrovia (91016-5005)
PHONE..................................626 254-9191
Jack Lansford Sr, *CEO*
Jack Lansford Jr, *President*
Billie Lansford, *Treasurer*
Eric Lansford, *Senior VP*
Marcos Arroyo, *Regional Mgr*
▲ **EMP:** 650
SALES (est): 202.6MM **Privately Held**
WEB: www.decore.com
SIC: 2431 Millwork

(P-3244)

DECORE-ATIVE SPC NC LLC

4414 Azusa Canyon Rd, Irwindale (91706-2740)
PHONE..................................626 960-7731
David Thompson, *Branch Mgr*
Enrique Fuentes, *Maint Spvr*
EMP: 111
SALES (corp-wide): 202.6MM **Privately Held**
WEB: www.decore.com
SIC: 2431 Millwork
PA: Decore-Ative Specialties Nc Llc
2772 Peck Rd
Monrovia CA 91016
626 254-9191

(P-3245)

DOOR & HARDWARE INSTALLERS INC

Also Called: Cabinet & Millwork Installers
14300 Davenport Rd Ste 1a, Agua Dulce (91390-5004)
PHONE..................................661 298-9383
Arthur Benson, *President*
Ardith Swanger, *Info Tech Mgr*
EMP: 20 **EST:** 1995
SQ FT: 15,000
SALES (est): 1MM **Privately Held**
SIC: 2431 Doors, wood

(P-3246)

DREES WOOD PRODUCTS INC

14020 Orange Ave, Paramount (90723-2018)
PHONE..................................562 633-7337
Ed Drees, *Manager*
EMP: 50
SALES (corp-wide): 12.1MM **Privately Held**
WEB: www.dreeswoodproducts.com
SIC: 2431 Doors, wood
PA: Drees Wood Products, Inc.
14003 Orange Ave
Paramount CA 90723
562 633-7337

(P-3247)

DYNAMIC WOODWORKS INC

Also Called: K & D Contracting
3509 Crooked Creek Dr, Diamond Bar (91765-3722)
PHONE..................................562 483-8400
Gloria C Vigil, *President*
EMP: 15
SALES (est): 1.7MM **Privately Held**
WEB: www.dynamicwoodworks.com
SIC: 2431 Millwork

(P-3248)

EL & EL WOOD PRODUCTS CORP (PA)

6011 Schaefer Ave, Chino (91710-7043)
P.O. Box 5105 (91708-5105)
PHONE..................................909 591-0339
Cathy Vidas, *President*
Paul Conley, *Vice Pres*
Jeremy Brainard, *Info Tech Mgr*
Martha Valadez, *Human Resources*
Ezequiel Loza, *Opers Mgr*
◆ **EMP:** 137 **EST:** 1963
SQ FT: 72,000
SALES (est): 27.7MM **Privately Held**
WEB: www.elandelwoodproducts.com
SIC: 2431 Millwork

(P-3249)

FINELINE WOODWORKING INC

Also Called: Fineline Architectural Mllwk
1139 Baker St, Costa Mesa (92626-4114)
PHONE..................................714 540-5468
Marc Butman, *CEO*
Jon Muller, *COO*
Tom Crone, *CFO*
Stephen Chiang, *IT/INT Sup*
Jesse Meinke, *Project Mgr*
EMP: 60
SQ FT: 20,000
SALES (est): 6.4MM **Privately Held**
WEB: www.finelinewood.com
SIC: 2431 Millwork

(P-3250)

GANAHL LUMBER COMPANY

Also Called: Benjamin Moore Authorized Ret
150 W Blaine St, Corona (92878-4047)
P.O. Box 1326 (92878-1326)
PHONE..................................951 278-4000
Mark Ganahl, *Principal*
Kate Shaddow, *Credit Mgr*
Dave Temple, *Sales Staff*
Robert Reeves, *Manager*
Angi Guerrero, *Assistant*
EMP: 81
SALES (corp-wide): 502.3MM **Privately Held**
WEB: www.ganahllumber.com
SIC: 5211 2431 5031 1751 Millwork & lumber; millwork; lumber: rough, dressed & finished; window & door (prefabricated) installation; hardware; structural wood members
PA: Ganahl Lumber Company
1220 E Ball Rd
Anaheim CA 92805
714 772-5444

(P-3251)

GM WINDOWS & DOORS INC

4303 Santa Ana St, Huntington Park (90255-6810)
PHONE..................................323 771-0348
William A Cisneros Munoz, *CEO*
EMP: 15 **EST:** 2019
SALES (est): 1.6MM **Privately Held**
WEB: www.gmwindowsdoors.com
SIC: 2431 Doors, wood

(P-3252)

GONZALEZ FELICIANO

Also Called: Paradise Kitchen Doors
1583 E Grand Ave, Pomona (91766-3808)
PHONE..................................909 236-1372
Feliciano Gonzalez, *Owner*
EMP: 15 **EST:** 2015
SALES (est): 674.3K **Privately Held**
SIC: 2431 Doors, wood

(P-3253)

HALEY BROS INC (HQ)

6291 Orangethorpe Ave, Buena Park (90620-1339)
PHONE..................................714 670-2112
Thomas J Cobb, *CEO*
George Hulbert, *CFO*
Thomas Cobb, *Admin Sec*
Ingrid Bradford, *Human Resources*
Brad Lamoutian, *Purchasing*
▲ **EMP:** 196 **EST:** 1987
SQ FT: 24,000
SALES (est): 31MM
SALES (corp-wide): 111.9MM **Privately Held**
WEB: www.haleybros.com
SIC: 2431 Doors, wood
PA: T. M. Cobb Company
500 Palmyrita Ave
Riverside CA 92507
951 248-2400

(P-3254)

HIS LIFE WOODWORKS

15107 S Main St, Gardena (90248-1923)
PHONE..................................310 756-0170
John Johnson Jr, *President*
Garrett Brim, *Vice Pres*
David Sulser, *Project Mgr*
Anne Schmidt, *Controller*
EMP: 40
SQ FT: 15,000

SALES: 2.8MM **Privately Held**
WEB: www.hislifewoodworks.com
SIC: 2431 Millwork

(P-3255)

HOSPITALITY WOOD PRODUCTS INC

7206 E Gage Ave, Commerce (90040-3813)
PHONE..................................562 806-5564
Michael Romero, *President*
Carlos Escalante, *Treasurer*
Victor Garcia, *Vice Pres*
EMP: 17 **EST:** 2001
SALES (est): 2.4MM **Privately Held**
SIC: 2431 Interior & ornamental woodwork & trim

(P-3256)

ICI ARCHITECTURAL MILLWORK INC

14059 Garfield Ave, Paramount (90723-2143)
PHONE..................................323 759-4993
Izhak Korin, *CEO*
Robert A Babayan, *President*
EMP: 15 **EST:** 2007
SALES (est): 2.4MM **Privately Held**
WEB: www.icimillwork.com
SIC: 2431 Millwork

(P-3257)

KARLS CUSTOM SASH & DOORS LLC

Also Called: Karl's Sash & Doors
18292 Gothard St, Huntington Beach (92648-1225)
PHONE..................................714 842-7877
Anton Seitz, *Managing Prtnr*
EMP: 15 **EST:** 1980
SQ FT: 9,900
SALES (est): 1MM **Privately Held**
SIC: 2431 Door sashes, wood; doors, wood

(P-3258)

KASTLE STAIR INC (PA)

7422 Mountjoy Dr, Huntington Beach (92648-1231)
PHONE..................................714 596-2600
Rose Phillips, *President*
EMP: 20 **EST:** 1983
SALES (est): 5.7MM **Privately Held**
SIC: 2431 Staircases & stairs, wood

(P-3259)

KLS DOORS LLC (PA)

Also Called: Chaparral
501 Kettering Dr, Ontario (91761-8150)
PHONE..................................909 605-6468
Varry Methvin,
Kent Snyder,
EMP: 27 **EST:** 2008
SALES (est): 503.2K **Privately Held**
WEB: www.klsdoors.com
SIC: 2431 Doors & door parts & trim, wood

(P-3260)

L & L CUSTOM SHUTTERS INC

3133 Yukon Ave, Costa Mesa (92626-2921)
PHONE..................................714 996-9539
Larry Allen, *President*
Lillian Allen, *Treasurer*
Ralph Gerardo, *Vice Pres*
EMP: 16 **EST:** 1980
SQ FT: 9,000
SALES (est): 588.6K **Privately Held**
WEB: www.llshutters.com
SIC: 2431 Window shutters, wood

(P-3261)

L&F WOOD LLC

Also Called: Boardhouse
416 E Alondra Blvd, Gardena (90248-2902)
PHONE..................................310 400-5569
Russell Walker, *Mng Member*
Anna Roque, *Executive Asst*
Michael Dutko,
Christine A Meyer,
▲ **EMP:** 13 **EST:** 2012
SQ FT: 20,000

SALES (est): 1MM **Privately Held**
SIC: 2431 5211 5031 Millwork; millwork & lumber; millwork

(P-3262)

LEEPERS WOOD TURNING CO INC (PA)

Also Called: Leeper's Stair Products
341 Bonnie Cir Ste 104, Corona (92876-5195)
P.O. Box 17098, Long Beach (90807-7098)
PHONE..................................562 422-6525
Michael Skinner, *President*
Barbara Skinner, *Ch of Bd*
Molly Rubio, *Treasurer*
◆ **EMP:** 38 **EST:** 1946
SQ FT: 29,000
SALES (est): 5.9MM **Privately Held**
WEB: www.ljsmith.com
SIC: 2431 Staircases & stairs, wood; staircases, stairs & railings

(P-3263)

LRB MILLWORK & CASEWORK INC

2760 S Iowa Ave, Colton (92324-5801)
PHONE..................................951 328-0105
Rene Alberto Bernhardt, *President*
Edward Jauregui, *Project Mgr*
Mike Moreno, *Manager*
EMP: 15 **EST:** 2005
SQ FT: 34,979
SALES (est): 1.3MM **Privately Held**
WEB: www.lrbmillwork.com
SIC: 2431 Millwork

(P-3264)

LUXOR INDUSTRIES INTERNATIONAL

1250 E Franklin Ave, Pomona (91766-5449)
PHONE..................................909 469-4757
Randy Rodriguez, *President*
EMP: 21 **EST:** 1993
SQ FT: 36,000
SALES (est): 398.5K **Privately Held**
SIC: 2431 Millwork

(P-3265)

MASONITE ENTRY DOOR CORP

25100 Globe St, Moreno Valley (92551-9528)
PHONE..................................951 243-2261
Lawrence Repar, *President*
▲ **EMP:** 13 **EST:** 2006
SALES (est): 599K **Privately Held**
SIC: 2431 Doors, wood

(P-3266)

METAL TEK ENGINEERING INC

7426 Cherry Ave Ste 210, Fontana (92336-4263)
PHONE..................................909 821-4158
Moises Lopez, *President*
EMP: 14 **EST:** 2004
SQ FT: 2,000
SALES (est): 532.1K **Privately Held**
SIC: 2431 Staircases, stairs & railings

(P-3267)

MILLCRAFT INC

2850 E White Star Ave, Anaheim (92806-2517)
PHONE..................................714 632-9621
Lars Eppick, *President*
Philip De Marco, *Treasurer*
Reginald Skipcott, *Vice Pres*
David McNatt, *General Mgr*
Ray Pfeifer, *Admin Sec*
EMP: 70 **EST:** 1983
SQ FT: 34,000
SALES (est): 9.4MM **Privately Held**
WEB: www.millcraftinc.com
SIC: 2431 2434 Doors, wood; wood kitchen cabinets

(P-3268)

MILLER WOODWORKING INC

1429 259th St, Harbor City (90710-3326)
PHONE..................................310 257-6806
Steve Miller, *President*
Steve Barratt, *Sales Staff*
EMP: 20 **EST:** 1986
SQ FT: 17,000

SALES (est): 6MM **Privately Held**
WEB: www.millerwoodworking.com
SIC: 2431 Millwork

(P-3269)
MILLWORKS BY DESIGN INC
4525 Runway St, Simi Valley (93063-3479)
PHONE..................818 597-1326
Daniel S Parish, *CEO*
Zachary D Eglit, *President*
Brian Peterson, *Executive*
Adam Henninger, *Project Mgr*
Aaron Telian, *Project Mgr*
▲ **EMP:** 37 **EST:** 2007
SALES (est): 4.9MM **Privately Held**
WEB: www.millworksbydesign.com
SIC: 2431 Millwork

(P-3270)
MOLDINGS PLUS INC
1856 S Grove Ave, Ontario (91761-5613)
PHONE..................909 947-3310
Robert Bryant, *President*
Steve Totri, *Vice Pres*
Roy Harrod, *Sales Mgr*
▲ **EMP:** 20 **EST:** 1972
SQ FT: 13,500
SALES (est): 4.2MM **Privately Held**
WEB: www.moldingsplus.com
SIC: 2431 Moldings, wood: unfinished &
prefinished; doors & door parts & trim,
wood; moldings & baseboards, ornamen-
tal & trim

(P-3271)
MONTY VENTSAM INC
Also Called: Ventsam Sash & Door Mfg Co
9495 San Fernando Rd, Sun Valley
(91352-1421)
PHONE..................818 768-6424
Monty Ventsam, *President*
EMP: 15 **EST:** 1978
SQ FT: 8,000
SALES (est): 644.5K **Privately Held**
SIC: 2431 5211 Door sashes, wood; door
trim, wood; door & window products

(P-3272)
MTD KITCHEN INC
13213 Sherman Way, North Hollywood
(91605-4649)
PHONE..................818 764-2254
Gil Alkoby, *CEO*
Nenita Marasigan, *Project Mgr*
EMP: 85 **EST:** 2012
SALES (est): 7.2MM **Privately Held**
WEB: www.mtdkitchen.com
SIC: 2431 2441 1799 2434 Millwork;
cases, wood; kitchen cabinet installation;
vanities, bathroom: wood

(P-3273)
NEVADA WINDOW SUPPLY INC
Also Called: ATI Windows
1455 Columbia Ave, Riverside
(92507-2013)
PHONE..................951 300-0100
Stephan Schwartz, *CEO*
Daniel Schwartz, *President*
Stephen Schwartz, *CEO*
EMP: 20 **EST:** 2005
SALES (est): 551K **Privately Held**
WEB: www.vinylwindows.co
SIC: 2431 Window frames, wood

(P-3274)
NEWMAN BROS CALIFORNIA INC (PA)
Also Called: A-1 Grit Co
1901 Massachusetts Ave, Riverside
(92507-2618)
P.O. Box 5675 (92517-5675)
PHONE..................951 782-0102
Harold Newman, *CEO*
EMP: 19 **EST:** 1973
SALES (est): 2.7MM **Privately Held**
WEB: www.a1grit.com
SIC: 2431 3291 5199 8711 Millwork; grit,
steel; architects' supplies (non-durable);
consulting engineer

(P-3275)
NICKS DOORS INC
Also Called: Nick's Cabinet Doors
1052 W Kirkwall Rd, Azusa (91702-5126)
PHONE..................626 812-6491

Nicolas Huizar, *President*
Anna Huizar, *Treasurer*
Sal Huizar, *Vice Pres*
Socorro Huizar, *Admin Sec*
EMP: 15 **EST:** 1984
SQ FT: 32,000
SALES (est): 2MM **Privately Held**
SIC: 2431 5211 Doors, wood; door & win-
dow products

(P-3276)
OAK-IT INC
143 Business Center Dr, Corona
(92878-3257)
PHONE..................951 735-5973
Lori Barrett, *President*
EMP: 17 **EST:** 2003
SALES (est): 1.8MM **Privately Held**
WEB: www.oakitinc.com
SIC: 2431 Millwork

(P-3277)
OLD ENGLISH MIL WOODWORKS INC (PA)
Also Called: Old English Mil & Woodworks
27772 Avenue Scott, Santa Clarita
(91355-3417)
PHONE..................661 294-9171
Lay Cho, *President*
Edmond Cho, *Vice Pres*
EMP: 30 **EST:** 1977
SQ FT: 30,000
SALES (est): 5.1MM **Privately Held**
WEB: www.oldenglishmilling.com
SIC: 2431 2439 1751 Staircases & stairs,
wood; window frames, wood; door
frames, wood; structural wood members;
carpentry work

(P-3278)
ORANGE WOODWORKS INC
1215 N Parker St, Orange (92867-4613)
PHONE..................714 997-2600
Jeff McMillian, *President*
Amanda Marchant, *Manager*
EMP: 45 **EST:** 1984
SQ FT: 120,000
SALES (est): 7.2MM **Privately Held**
WEB: www.orangewoodworks.com
SIC: 2431 Millwork

(P-3279)
PACIFIC ARCHTECTURAL MLLWK INC (PA)
Also Called: Reveal Windows & Doors
1031 S Leslie St, La Habra (90631-6843)
PHONE..................562 905-3200
John Higman, *CEO*
Roy Gustin, *President*
Alice Vanberpool, *Vice Pres*
Guy Stadig, *General Mgr*
Randy Bradley, *Network Mgr*
◆ **EMP:** 99 **EST:** 2007
SQ FT: 31,000
SALES (est): 13.3MM **Privately Held**
WEB: www.pacmillwork.com
SIC: 2431 Planing mill, millwork

(P-3280)
PARAMOUNT WINDOWS & DOORS
Also Called: Paramount Window & Doors
723 W Mill St, San Bernardino
(92410-3347)
PHONE..................909 888-4688
Don Mc Farland, *CEO*
EMP: 17 **EST:** 1999
SQ FT: 10,000
SALES (est): 1.7MM **Privately Held**
WEB:
www.paramountwindowsanddoors.com
SIC: 2431 5211 Windows & window parts
& trim, wood; doors & door parts & trim,
wood; door & window products

(P-3281)
PINECRAFT CUSTOM SHUTTERS INC
Also Called: Sterling Shutters
946 W 17th St, Costa Mesa (92627-4403)
P.O. Box 2417, Newport Beach (92659-
1417)
PHONE..................949 642-9317
Frank L Gerardo Sr, *President*
Anthony Gerardo, *Vice Pres*

EMP: 13 **EST:** 1964
SQ FT: 12,000
SALES (est): 361.2K **Privately Held**
WEB:
www.daniabeachgaragedoorrepair.com
SIC: 2431 Door shutters, wood

(P-3282)
PRECISION COMPANIES INC
Also Called: Precision Doors & Millwork
15088 La Palma Dr, Chino (91710-9669)
PHONE..................909 548-2700
Joseph J Felix, *President*
Marcia Felix, *Treasurer*
Melodee Kroll, *Sales Staff*
EMP: 15 **EST:** 1994
SQ FT: 5,000
SALES (est): 5MM **Privately Held**
SIC: 2431 3441 3442 Millwork; fabricated
structural metal; metal doors, sash & trim

(P-3283)
PRECISION MILLWORK LLC
14300 Davenport Rd Ste 4a, Agua Dulce
(91390-5000)
PHONE..................661 402-5021
Ardith Swanger, *Mng Member*
Kelly Tebbitt, *Accountant*
Jim Elbe, *Sales Staff*
Miguel Pena,
Michelle St John,
EMP: 15 **EST:** 2012
SQ FT: 5,000
SALES (est): 2.5MM **Privately Held**
WEB: www.precisionmillworkllc.com
SIC: 2431 Millwork

(P-3284)
Q RAILING USA INC
14321 Franklin Ave Ste A, Tustin
(92780-7016)
PHONE..................714 259-1372
Andre V Uitert, *President*
Jan Hulin, *General Mgr*
Elizabeth Brown, *Administration*
Patrick Nguyen, *Project Mgr*
Elizabeth Thomason, *Opers Staff*
◆ **EMP:** 13 **EST:** 2008
SQ FT: 7,000
SALES (est): 2.7MM **Privately Held**
WEB: www.q-railing.com
SIC: 2431 Staircases, stairs & railings

(P-3285)
QUALITY SHUTTERS INC
3359 Chicago Ave Ste A, Riverside
(92507-6820)
PHONE..................951 683-4939
Agustin Flores, *Owner*
EMP: 49 **EST:** 2002
SALES (est): 3.4MM **Privately Held**
SIC: 2431 Window frames, wood

(P-3286)
RENAISSNCE FRNCH DORS SASH INC (PA)
Also Called: Renaissance Doors & Windows
38 Segada, Rcho STA Marg (92688-2744)
PHONE..................714 578-0090
Michael Jenkins, *President*
James Jenkins, *Corp Secy*
Thomas Jenkins, *Vice Pres*
EMP: 129 **EST:** 1982
SQ FT: 75,000
SALES (est): 10.1MM **Privately Held**
SIC: 2431 Doors, wood

(P-3287)
SADDLEBACK STAIR & MILLWORK
23291 Peralta Dr Ste B4, Laguna Hills
(92653-1426)
PHONE..................949 460-0384
Miles Densmore, *President*
Irene Densmore, *Vice Pres*
EMP: 14 **EST:** 1982
SALES (est): 741.3K **Privately Held**
SIC: 2431 Staircases & stairs, wood

(P-3288)
SIERRA WOODWORKING INC
960 6th St Ste 101a, Norco (92860-1440)
PHONE..................949 493-4528
Maurice Kendall, *President*
EMP: 13 **EST:** 1985
SQ FT: 10,000

SALES (est): 591.8K **Privately Held**
WEB: www.sierrawoodworking.com
SIC: 2431 2541 2521 2439 Millwork;
cabinets, except refrigerated: show, display, etc.: wood; wood office furniture;
structural wood members; wood kitchen
cabinets; decorative wood & woodwork

(P-3289)
SKYCO SHADING SYSTEMS INC
3411 W Fordham Ave, Santa Ana
(92704-4422)
PHONE..................714 708-3038
Sandra Young, *President*
▲ **EMP:** 28 **EST:** 1994
SQ FT: 16,000
SALES (est): 5.8MM **Privately Held**
WEB: www.skycoshade.com
SIC: 5719 2431 Window furnishings; mill-
work

(P-3290)
SMI ARCHITECTURAL MILLWORK INC
Also Called: SMI Millwork
2116 W Chestnut Ave, Santa Ana
(92703-4306)
PHONE..................714 567-0112
Robert Stolo, *President*
Timothy J Stolo, *Vice Pres*
Iris Santos, *Office Mgr*
Karen Kawasaki, *Admin Sec*
Berniece Ricker, *Purchasing*
EMP: 35 **EST:** 1997
SQ FT: 1,500
SALES (est): 5.4MM **Privately Held**
WEB: www.smimillwork.com
SIC: 5211 2431 Millwork & lumber; mill-
work

(P-3291)
SOUTH COAST STAIRS INC
30251 Tomas, Rcho STA Marg
(92688-2123)
PHONE..................949 858-1685
Chris Galloway, *President*
Mary Galloway, *Vice Pres*
Tamera Selchau, *Admin Sec*
EMP: 40 **EST:** 1980
SQ FT: 2,000
SALES (est): 2.7MM **Privately Held**
WEB: www.scstairs.com
SIC: 2431 2439 5211 Staircases & stairs,
wood; structural wood members; millwork
& lumber

(P-3292)
STEINER & MATEER INC
Also Called: Shuttercraft of California
8333 Secura Way, Santa Fe Springs
(90670-2299)
PHONE..................562 464-9082
Richard K Oliver, *President*
EMP: 13 **EST:** 1935
SQ FT: 20,000
SALES (est): 725.2K **Privately Held**
SIC: 2431 Louver doors, wood

(P-3293)
T M COBB COMPANY (PA)
Also Called: Haley Bros
500 Palmyrita Ave, Riverside (92507-1196)
PHONE..................951 248-2400
Jeffrey Cobb, *President*
Thomas J Cobb, *Vice Pres*
Thomas Cobb, *Vice Pres*
Elaine Ascencio, *Administration*
Peter Bonilla, *Administration*
▲ **EMP:** 23 **EST:** 1947
SALES (est): 111.9MM **Privately Held**
WEB: www.tmcobb.com
SIC: 2431 3442 Door frames, wood; win-
dow & door frames

(P-3294)
TABER COMPANY INC
1442 Ritchey St, Santa Ana (92705-4717)
PHONE..................714 543-7100
Brian Taber, *President*
Mackenzie Flood, *Administration*
Edvin Babakhani, *Project Mgr*
Steven Dunn, *Project Mgr*
Miguel Franco, *Project Mgr*
EMP: 65 **EST:** 2002
SQ FT: 11,000

SALES (est): 15.4MM **Privately Held**
WEB: www.taberco.net
SIC: **2431** Millwork

(P-3295)
TRAVIS-AMERICAN GROUP LLC
Also Called: Travis Industries
11450 Sheldon St, Sun Valley
(91352-1121)
PHONE.....................................714 258-1200
Thomas D Bell, *President*
Martin Vargas, *Project Mgr*
Stephen Saponaro, *VP Finance*
Gina Holley, *Controller*
Lyle Zastrow, *VP Opers*
EMP: 17 EST: 1978
SQ FT: 5,300
SALES (est): 747.8K **Privately Held**
SIC: **2431** 2499 2426 2591 Moldings, wood: unfinished & prefinished; veneer work, inlaid; furniture stock & parts, hardwood; venetian blinds; paints, varnishes & supplies

(P-3296)
W B POWELL INC
630 Parkridge Ave, Norco (92860-3124)
PHONE.....................................951 270-0095
Charles G Mayhew, *CEO*
Chuck Mayhew, *President*
Doug Westra, *CFO*
Steve Wimberly, *Senior VP*
Steven Wimberly, *Vice Pres*
EMP: 57 EST: 1993
SALES (est): 12.7MM
SALES (corp-wide): 86.8MM **Privately Held**
WEB: www.wbpowell.com
SIC: **2431** 2439 Millwork; structural wood members
PA: Foldcraft Co.
7300 147th St W Ste 500
Saint Paul MN 55124
507 789-5111

(P-3297)
WESTERN INTEGRATED MTLS INC (PA)
3310 E 59th St, Long Beach (90805-4504)
PHONE.....................................562 634-2823
Larry Farrah, *President*
Edward G Farrah, *Vice Pres*
Jim Halbrook, *Principal*
Debra Price, *Principal*
Alex Rojas, *Principal*
▲ EMP: 30 EST: 1975
SQ FT: 20,000
SALES (est): 5.3MM **Privately Held**
WEB: www.aluminumdoorframes.com
SIC: **2431** 3442 Millwork; window & door frames

(P-3298)
WHOLESALE SHUTTER COMPANY INC
411 Olive Ave, Beaumont (92223-2640)
PHONE.....................................951 845-8786
Sabiha Patel, *CEO*
Sabiha Simjee, *Executive*
▲ EMP: 14 EST: 1992
SQ FT: 10,000
SALES (est): 1.3MM **Privately Held**
WEB: www.wholesaleshutter.com
SIC: **2431** Door shutters, wood; blinds (shutters), wood

(P-3299)
WILCO BUILDING CORPORATION
2005 Palma Dr Ste A, Ventura
(93003-5750)
PHONE.....................................805 765-4188
Benjamin Wilson, *CEO*
EMP: 13 EST: 2015
SQ FT: 9,000
SALES (est): 439.3K **Privately Held**
SIC: **2431** 8741 1542 Millwork; construction management; restaurant construction

(P-3300)
WINDOW PRODUCTS MANAGEMENT INC
Also Called: Arjay's Window Fashions
5917 Olivas Park Dr Ste F, Ventura
(93003-7613)
PHONE.....................................805 677-6800
John Norman Edwards, *President*
Larry Mesa, *Administration*
EMP: 18 EST: 2004
SALES (est): 5.3MM **Privately Held**
WEB:
www.windowproductsmanagement.com
SIC: **2431** 2591 Windows & window parts & trim, wood; window shades

(P-3301)
WOODMILL SEATING INC
1250 E Franklin Ave, Pomona
(91766-5449)
PHONE.....................................909 622-1615
Stephen C Rodriguez, *Principal*
EMP: 16 EST: 2008
SALES (est): 526.9K **Privately Held**
SIC: **2431** Millwork

(P-3302)
WOODWORK PIONEERS CORP
1757 S Claudina Way, Anaheim
(92805-6544)
PHONE.....................................714 991-1017
Karina Avalos, *President*
EMP: 50 EST: 2016
SALES (est): 2.4MM **Privately Held**
WEB: www.woodworkpioneers.com
SIC: **2431** Millwork

2434 Wood Kitchen Cabinets

(P-3303)
A PLUS CABINETS INC
83930 Dr Carreon Blvd, Indio
(92201-7177)
PHONE.....................................760 322-5262
Rhett Ferrell, *President*
EMP: 13 EST: 1993
SQ FT: 2,500
SALES (est): 1.6MM **Privately Held**
WEB: www.apluscabinetsinc.net
SIC: **2434** Wood kitchen cabinets

(P-3304)
ARANDAS WOODCRAFT INC
137 W 157th St, Gardena (90248-2225)
P.O. Box 3954 (90247-7507)
PHONE.....................................310 538-9945
EMP: 40
SQ FT: 19,000
SALES (est): 4.7MM **Privately Held**
WEB: www.arandaswoodcraft.com
SIC: **2434** 2541 Mfg Wood Kitchen Cabinets Mfg Wood Partitions/Fixtures

(P-3305)
ARCADIA CABINETRY LLC
5467 Brooks St, Montclair (91763-4563)
PHONE.....................................909 550-0074
Kathy Massey, *Principal*
Chris Wagstaff, *Regional Mgr*
Richard Barnes, *CIO*
EMP: 13 EST: 2018
SALES (est): 3.2MM **Privately Held**
WEB: www.arcadiacabinetry.com
SIC: **2434** Wood kitchen cabinets

(P-3306)
ARTCRAFTERS CABINETS
5446 Cleon Ave, North Hollywood
(91601-2897)
PHONE.....................................818 752-8960
Jack R Walter, *President*
Steve Counter, *Vice Pres*
Bob Schindler, *Vice Pres*
Sharon E Walter, *Vice Pres*
Dawn Kunihiro, *Office Mgr*
EMP: 50 EST: 1949
SQ FT: 20,000
SALES (est): 5.4MM **Privately Held**
WEB: www.artcrafter.com
SIC: **2434** 2521 2431 Wood kitchen cabinets; wood office furniture; millwork

(P-3307)
BESTONLINECABINETS
5100 Walnut Grove Ave, San Gabriel
(91776-2026)
PHONE.....................................626 589-6827
Cheng Josh Qian, *CEO*
EMP: 21 EST: 2011
SALES (est): 2.1MM **Privately Held**
WEB: www.bestonlinecabinets.com
SIC: **2434** Wood kitchen cabinets

(P-3308)
CABINET FACTORY OUTLET
1141 W Katella Ave, Orange (92867-3519)
PHONE.....................................714 635-9080
EMP: 16
SALES (est): 1.2MM **Privately Held**
WEB: www.cabinetoutlet.com
SIC: **5211** 2434 Lumber And Other Building Materials, Nsk

(P-3309)
CABINET MASTER & SON INC (PA)
5429 Via Corona St, Los Angeles
(90022-2201)
PHONE.....................................323 727-9717
Bladimiro W Malaszczuk, *President*
EMP: 18 EST: 2004
SALES (est): 206.6K **Privately Held**
WEB: www.thecabinetmasterandson.com
SIC: **2434** Wood kitchen cabinets

(P-3310)
CABINETS 2000 LLC
11100 Firestone Blvd, Norwalk
(90650-2269)
PHONE.....................................562 868-0909
Frank Hamadani, *Chairman*
Nematollah Abdollahi, *President*
Sherwood Prusso, *President*
Azam Abdollahi, *CFO*
Sue Abdollahi, *CFO*
EMP: 180 EST: 1988
SQ FT: 103,000
SALES (est): 46.8MM
SALES (corp-wide): 1.9B **Privately Held**
WEB: www.cabinets2000.com
SIC: **2434** 1751 Wood kitchen cabinets; cabinet & finish carpentry
PA: Acproducts, Inc.
3551 Plano Pkwy Ste 200
The Colony TX 75056
214 469-3000

(P-3311)
CABINETS R US
1240 N Fee Ana St, Anaheim (92807-1817)
PHONE.....................................562 483-6886
Stephanie Chang, *Administration*
◆ EMP: 20 EST: 2013
SALES (est): 1.5MM **Privately Held**
WEB: www.cabinetsrus.us
SIC: **2434** Wood kitchen cabinets

(P-3312)
CALIFORNIA WOODWORKING INC
1726 Ives Ave, Oxnard (93033-4072)
PHONE.....................................805 982-9090
Edward Vickery, *President*
Lucas Vickery, *Vice Pres*
Susan Vickery, *Admin Sec*
Maria G Reyes, *Project Mgr*
Maria Reyes, *Project Mgr*
EMP: 30 EST: 1990
SQ FT: 8,000
SALES (est): 3.8MM **Privately Held**
WEB: www.calwoodinc.com
SIC: **2434** Wood kitchen cabinets

(P-3313)
CALIFRNIA DSGNERS CHICE CSTM C
547 Constitution Ave F, Camarillo
(93012-8572)
PHONE.....................................805 987-5820
Mark Mulchay, *President*
Russell Leavitt, *Admin Sec*
Michelle Cekov, *Bookkeeper*
EMP: 38 EST: 1989
SALES (est): 5MM **Privately Held**
WEB: www.cdcc-inc.com
SIC: **2434** Wood kitchen cabinets

(P-3314)
CARPET WAGON-GLENDALE INC (PA)
Also Called: Payless Kitchen Cabinets
3614 San Fernando Rd, Glendale
(91204-2944)
PHONE.....................................818 937-9545
Avedis Barsoumian, *President*
EMP: 15 EST: 2004
SALES (est): 2.7MM **Privately Held**
WEB: www.paylesskitchencabinets.com
SIC: **2434** Wood kitchen cabinets

(P-3315)
CLASSIC BATH DESIGNS INC
11544 Sheldon St, Sun Valley
(91352-1124)
PHONE.....................................818 767-1144
Phillip J Bogna, *President*
Tom Bogna, *President*
Nancy Bogna, *Treasurer*
Remy Bogna, *Consultant*
EMP: 29 EST: 1984
SQ FT: 7,500
SALES (est): 2.4MM **Privately Held**
WEB: www.cbdcabinets.com
SIC: **2434** Wood kitchen cabinets

(P-3316)
CORONA MILLWORKS COMPANY (PA)
5572 Edison Ave, Chino (91710-6936)
PHONE.....................................909 606-3288
Jose Corona, *CEO*
Cindy Struck, *Administration*
Frances Young, *Human Resources*
Kevin Judd, *Opers Mgr*
Armando Aguilar, *Plant Mgr*
▲ EMP: 142 EST: 1995
SQ FT: 8,700
SALES (est): 25.6MM **Privately Held**
WEB: www.coronamillworks.com
SIC: **2434** Wood kitchen cabinets

(P-3317)
DREES WOOD PRODUCTS INC (PA)
14003 Orange Ave, Paramount
(90723-2017)
PHONE.....................................562 633-7337
Ed Drees, *CEO*
Eric Schultz, *Sales Executive*
EMP: 50 EST: 1982
SALES (est): 12.1MM **Privately Held**
WEB: www.dreeswoodproducts.com
SIC: **2434** Wood kitchen cabinets

(P-3318)
ELITE STONE & CABINET INC
1655 E Mission Blvd, Pomona
(91766-2321)
PHONE.....................................909 629-6988
EMP: 16 EST: 2015
SALES (est): 432.7K **Privately Held**
WEB: www.elitestonegroup.com
SIC: **2434** 5032 1741 Wood kitchen cabinets; building stone; stone masonry

(P-3319)
EXCEL CABINETS INC
225 Jason Ct, Corona (92879-6199)
PHONE.....................................951 279-4545
Charles W Ketzel, *CEO*
Carl Nielsen, *CFO*
Sandra Ketzel, *Corp Secy*
Keith Ketzel, *Vice Pres*
Kevin Ketzel, *Vice Pres*
▲ EMP: 35 EST: 1990
SALES (est): 5.5MM **Privately Held**
WEB: www.excelcabinetsinc.com
SIC: **2434** Wood kitchen cabinets

(P-3320)
I AND E CABINETS INC
14660 Raymer St, Van Nuys (91405-1217)
PHONE.....................................818 933-6480
Israel Chlomovitz, *CEO*
Ettie Chlomovitz, *Treasurer*
EMP: 34 EST: 1981
SQ FT: 9,000 **Privately Held**
WEB: www.iecabinets.com
SIC: **2434** Wood kitchen cabinets

PRODUCTS & SVCS

(P-3321)
K & Z CABINET CO INC
1450 S Grove Ave, Ontario (91761-4523)
PHONE..................................909 947-3567
Dennis Chan, *President*
Hugo Cervera, *Project Mgr*
Troy Zerillo, *Sr Project Mgr*
EMP: 60 EST: 1975
SQ FT: 59,000
SALES (est): 12.2MM **Privately Held**
WEB: www.kzcabt.com
SIC: 2434 2431 Wood kitchen cabinets; millwork

(P-3322)
KAISER FOUNDATION HOSPITALS
Also Called: Kaiser Prmnnte Nat Fclties Svc
3355 E 26th St, Vernon (90058-4169)
PHONE..................................323 264-4310
Jose Montero, *Principal*
Yolanda Parra, *Manager*
EMP: 78
SALES (corp-wide): 30.5B **Privately Held**
WEB: www.kaisercenter.com
SIC: 5712 2434 Cabinet work, custom; vanities, bathroom: wood
HQ: Kaiser Foundation Hospitals Inc
    1 Kaiser Plz
    Oakland CA 94612
    510 271-6611

(P-3323)
KITCHEN POST INC
8617 Baseline Rd, Rancho Cucamonga
(91730-1111)
PHONE..................................909 948-6768
Randy Ludwig, *President*
EMP: 13 EST: 2005
SALES (est): 1.4MM **Privately Held**
WEB: www.kitchenpost.com
SIC: 2434 Wood kitchen cabinets

(P-3324)
KOBIS WINDOWS & DOORS MFG INC
7326 Laurel Canyon Blvd, North Hollywood
(91605-3710)
PHONE..................................818 764-6400
Kobi Louria, *CEO*
▲ EMP: 25 EST: 1999
SALES (est): 4MM **Privately Held**
WEB: www.kobiwindows.net
SIC: 2434 2431 1522 Vanities, bathroom: wood; millwork; residential construction

(P-3325)
LA BATH VANITY INC (PA)
1071 W 9th St, Upland (91786-5702)
PHONE..................................909 303-3323
Lingcong Luo, *CEO*
EMP: 18 EST: 2018
SALES (est): 20K **Privately Held**
WEB: www.morenobath.com
SIC: 2434 Vanities, bathroom: wood

(P-3326)
MILLBROOK KITCHENS INC
15960 Downey Ave, Paramount
(90723-5116)
PHONE..................................310 684-3366
▲ EMP: 15
SQ FT: 450,000
SALES: 450K **Privately Held**
SIC: 2434 1799 Mfg Wood Kitchen Cabinets Trade Contractor Trade Contractor

(P-3327)
MILLWOOD CABINET CO INC
2321 Virginia Ave, Bakersfield
(93307-2545)
PHONE..................................661 327-0371
David T Millwood Jr, *President*
Sandra Millwood, *Treasurer*
Diana Shackelford, *Admin Sec*
EMP: 17 EST: 1973
SQ FT: 18,000
SALES (est): 2.3MM **Privately Held**
WEB: www.millwoodcabinet.com
SIC: 2434 2541 Wood kitchen cabinets; wood partitions & fixtures

(P-3328)
NORM TESSIER CABINETS INC
11989 6th St, Rancho Cucamonga
(91730-6133)
PHONE..................................909 987-8955
David L Beavers, *President*
Denise Beavers, *Vice Pres*
Jennifer Beavers, *Office Mgr*
EMP: 16 EST: 1978
SQ FT: 20,000
SALES (est): 2MM **Privately Held**
WEB: www.normtessiercabinets.com
SIC: 2434 Wood kitchen cabinets

(P-3329)
PATRICKS CABINETS
10160 Redwood Ave, Fontana
(92335-6237)
P.O. Box 787, Yucaipa (92399-0787)
PHONE..................................909 823-2524
Chris Dyer, *Owner*
EMP: 16 EST: 1974
SQ FT: 10,000
SALES (est): 488.8K **Privately Held**
SIC: 2434 Vanities, bathroom: wood

(P-3330)
PROFESSIONAL CABINET SOLUTIONS
2111 Eastridge Ave, Riverside
(92507-0778)
PHONE..................................909 614-2900
EMP: 891 EST: 2018
SALES (est): 851.8K **Privately Held**
WEB: www.americanwoodmark.com
SIC: 2434 Wood kitchen cabinets

(P-3331)
PROFESSIONAL CABINET SOLUTIONS
2111 Eastridge Ave, Riverside
(92507-0778)
PHONE..................................909 614-2900
S Cary Dunston, *CEO*
Tim Carr, *Regional Mgr*
Brittney Flynn, *Personnel Assit*
Michael Young, *Materials Mgr*
Roger Glaser, *Opers Staff*
EMP: 250 EST: 1996
SALES (est): 46.7MM
SALES (corp-wide): 1.7B **Publicly Held**
WEB: www.americanwoodmark.com
SIC: 2434 Wood kitchen cabinets
HQ: Rsi Home Products, Inc.
    400 E Orangethorpe Ave
    Anaheim CA 92801
    714 449-2200

(P-3332)
REGAL KITCHENS LLC
3480 Sunset Ln, Oxnard (93035-4129)
PHONE..................................786 953-6578
Tony Pace, *President*
George Flack, *CFO*
Robert Sweeney,
◆ EMP: 15 EST: 1957
SQ FT: 168,000
SALES (est): 1.4MM **Privately Held**
SIC: 2434 Wood kitchen cabinets

(P-3333)
ROYAL CABINETS INC
1299 E Phillips Blvd, Pomona
(91766-5429)
PHONE..................................909 629-8565
Clay Smith, *President*
Bill Roan, *COO*
Marlene Ulsh, *General Mgr*
Kris Wengel, *Buyer*
Marcus Barackman, *Opers Staff*
▲ EMP: 600 EST: 1984
SQ FT: 70,000
SALES (est): 57.4MM **Privately Held**
WEB: www.royalcabinets.com
SIC: 2434 2511 Wood kitchen cabinets; wood household furniture

(P-3334)
ROYAL INDUSTRIES INC
Also Called: Royal Cabinets
1299 E Phillips Blvd, Pomona
(91766-5429)
PHONE..................................909 629-8565
Clay R Smith, *CEO*
Dan McGinn, *President*

Gus Danjoi, *CFO*
Kathy Goodrow, *Admin Sec*
EMP: 130
SALES (est): 19.1MM **Privately Held**
WEB: www.royalcabinets.com
SIC: 2434 Vanities, bathroom: wood

(P-3335)
SANTA MONICA MILLWORKS
2568 Channel Dr Ste C, Ventura
(93003-4563)
PHONE..................................805 643-0010
William Lunche, *President*
EMP: 20 EST: 1996
SALES (est): 1.2MM **Privately Held**
SIC: 2434 Wood kitchen cabinets

(P-3336)
SE INDUSTRIES INC
300 W Collins Ave, Orange (92867-5506)
PHONE..................................714 744-3200
Jan Schaffer, *President*
EMP: 15 EST: 1997
SQ FT: 27,000
SALES (est): 300.9K **Privately Held**
WEB: www.seindustries.com
SIC: 2434 Wood kitchen cabinets

(P-3337)
SOUTHCOAST CABINET INC (PA)
755 Pinefalls Ave, Walnut (91789-3027)
PHONE..................................909 594-3089
Dante M Senese, *CEO*
John Lopez, *President*
Danny Mendoza, *Info Tech Dir*
Ron St Jean, *Safety Mgr*
Scott Fibrow, *Opers Staff*
EMP: 42 EST: 1983
SQ FT: 108,000
SALES (est): 8.5MM **Privately Held**
WEB: www.southcoastcabinet.com
SIC: 2434 Wood kitchen cabinets

(P-3338)
SUPERIOR MILLWORK OF SB INC
7330 Hollister Ave Ste B, Goleta
(93117-2868)
PHONE..................................805 685-1744
Joseph Morin, *President*
Diana Morin, *CFO*
EMP: 16 EST: 1972
SQ FT: 10,000
SALES (est): 2MM **Privately Held**
SIC: 2434 2431 Wood kitchen cabinets; millwork

(P-3339)
SWISS CABINET
12430 Montague St Ste 212, Pacoima
(91331-2149)
PHONE..................................818 571-9917
Vardan Nazaryan, *Owner*
EMP: 13 EST: 2002
SALES (est): 356.6K **Privately Held**
WEB: www.swisscabinets.com
SIC: 2434 5084 1751 Wood kitchen cabinets; woodworking machinery; cabinet & finish carpentry

(P-3340)
TARA ENTERPRISES INC
27023 Mack Bean Pkwy, Valencia (91355)
PHONE..................................661 510-2206
EMP: 15
SALES (est): 1.2MM **Privately Held**
SIC: 2434 Wood Kitchen Cabinets

(P-3341)
TESSA MIA CORP
9565 Vassar Ave, Chatsworth
(91311-4141)
PHONE..................................877 740-5757
Zack Karni, *CEO*
Yom Tov Yohanan, *CFO*
EMP: 27 EST: 2019
SALES (est): 5.5MM **Privately Held**
SIC: 2434 Wood kitchen cabinets

(P-3342)
TONUSA LLC
Also Called: Contemporary Bath.com
16770 E Johnson Dr, City of Industry
(91745-2414)
PHONE..................................626 961-8700
Yin M Ng,
Christine Hsu, *Office Mgr*
Raymond Kovacs, *Opers Staff*
Cody Legler, *Products*
James Ng,
▲ EMP: 15 EST: 2006
SQ FT: 4,000
SALES (est): 2.3MM **Privately Held**
WEB: www.tonusa.com
SIC: 2434 Vanities, bathroom: wood

(P-3343)
TRUE DESIGN INC
9427 Norwalk Blvd, Santa Fe Springs
(90670-2943)
PHONE..................................562 699-2001
Hani ABI Naked, *CEO*
Thomas Cavelti, *CFO*
EMP: 15
SQ FT: 17,000
SALES: 3MM **Privately Held**
SIC: 2434 Wood kitchen cabinets

(P-3344)
ULTRA BUILT KITCHENS INC
1814 E 43rd St, Los Angeles (90058-1517)
PHONE..................................323 232-3362
Iris Yanes, *President*
Eduardo Yanes, *Treasurer*
Daisy Blanco, *Vice Pres*
EMP: 28 EST: 1993
SQ FT: 18,000
SALES (est): 3.7MM **Privately Held**
WEB: www.ultrabuiltkitchens.net
SIC: 2434 Vanities, bathroom: wood

(P-3345)
UNITED CABINET COMPANY INC
1510 S Mountain View Ave, San Bernardino
(92408-3134)
PHONE..................................909 796-3015
Dennis Rice, *President*
Gayle L Rice, *Shareholder*
Doris Rice, *Corp Secy*
Jeffery Westrom, *Vice Pres*
EMP: 20 EST: 1963
SQ FT: 10,000
SALES (est): 1.8MM **Privately Held**
SIC: 2434 Wood kitchen cabinets

(P-3346)
W L RUBOTTOM CO
320 W Lewis St, Ventura (93001-1335)
PHONE..................................805 648-6943
Gary McCoy, *President*
Lawrence Rubottom, *Vice Pres*
Mark Rubottom, *VP Opers*
Tom Speer, *Sales Staff*
EMP: 55
SQ FT: 40,000
SALES (est): 7.6MM **Privately Held**
WEB: www.wlrubottom.com
SIC: 2434 Wood kitchen cabinets

(P-3347)
WOODIE WOODPECKERS WOODWORKS
21268 Deering Ct, Canoga Park
(91304-5015)
PHONE..................................818 999-2090
Darlene Somers, *CFO*
Darlene M Somers, *General Mgr*
EMP: 13 EST: 1974
SQ FT: 15,000
SALES (est): 1.1MM **Privately Held**
WEB: www.woodiewww.com
SIC: 2434 Wood kitchen cabinets

(P-3348)
WOODPECKER CABINET INC
21512 Nordhoff St, Chatsworth
(91311-5822)
PHONE..................................310 404-4805
Izaac Sananes, *CEO*
River Cook, *Manager*
EMP: 20 EST: 2005

SALES (est): 1.2MM **Privately Held**
WEB: www.woodpecker-cabinets.com
SIC: **2434** 1799 Wood kitchen cabinets; kitchen cabinet installation

(P-3349)
WYNDHAM COLLECTION LLC
1175 Aviation Pl, San Fernando (91340-1460)
PHONE...................................888 522-8476
Martin Symes, *Mng Member*
Christophe Blondeau, *Vice Pres*
Mark Sweeney, *Marketing Staff*
Harry Parsamyan,
Sammy Parsamyan,
EMP: 26 EST: 2011
SQ FT: 100,000
SALES (est): 3.7MM **Privately Held**
WEB: www.wyndhamcollection.com
SIC: **2434** Vanities, bathroom: wood

2435 Hardwood Veneer & Plywood

(P-3350)
GENERAL VENEER MFG CO
8652 Otis St, South Gate (90280-3292)
P.O. Box 1607 (90280-1607)
PHONE...................................323 564-2661
William Dewitt, *President*
Ed Bewitt, *Treasurer*
Ed Witt, *Treasurer*
Douglas Bradley, *Vice Pres*
Gil Stewart, *Purch Mgr*
EMP: 50 EST: 1942
SQ FT: 200,000
SALES (est): 8.7MM **Privately Held**
WEB: www.generalveneer.com
SIC: **2435** 3365 Hardwood veneer & plywood; aerospace castings, aluminum

(P-3351)
JC HANSCOM INC
Also Called: Panel Works
11830 Wakeman St, Santa Fe Springs (90670-2129)
PHONE...................................562 789-9955
John C Hanscom, *President*
Marsha Hanscom, *Vice Pres*
EMP: 26 EST: 1999
SQ FT: 23,000
SALES (est): 3.1MM **Privately Held**
WEB: www.panelworksveneer.com
SIC: **2435** Panels, hardwood plywood

(P-3352)
MALAKAN INC (PA)
412 1/2 S Central Ave, Glendale (91204-1602)
PHONE...................................310 910-9270
Radik Khachatryan, *President*
▲ EMP: 36 EST: 2014
SQ FT: 8,000
SALES (est): 2.8MM **Privately Held**
WEB: www.malakaninc.com
SIC: **2435** Hardwood veneer & plywood

(P-3353)
PLYCRAFT INDUSTRIES INC
Also Called: Concepts & Wood
2100 E Slauson Ave, Huntington Park (90255-2727)
PHONE...................................323 587-8101
Ashley Joffe, *President*
Nathan Joffe, *CFO*
Donald R Greenberg, *Exec VP*
George Samoya, *CIO*
▲ EMP: 180 EST: 1979
SQ FT: 71,187
SALES (est): 56MM **Privately Held**
WEB: www.plycraft.com
SIC: **2435** Plywood, hardwood or hardwood faced; veneer stock, hardwood

(P-3354)
SONORA FACE CO
5233 Randolph St, Maywood (90270-3448)
PHONE...................................323 560-8188
Ossiel Calvillo, *President*
▲ EMP: 25 EST: 1984
SQ FT: 20,000
SALES (est): 2.5MM **Privately Held**
WEB: www.sonora-face-co.hub.biz
SIC: **2435** Veneer stock, hardwood

(P-3355)
SWANER HARDWOOD CO INC (PA)
5 W Magnolia Blvd, Burbank (91502-1776)
PHONE...................................818 953-5350
Keith M Swaner, *CEO*
Gary Swaner, *President*
Stephen Haag, *Treasurer*
Steve Haag, *Vice Pres*
Beverly Swaner, *Admin Sec*
▲ EMP: 70 EST: 1967
SQ FT: 4,500
SALES (est): 52MM **Privately Held**
WEB: www.swanerhardwood.com
SIC: **2435** 5031 Hardwood veneer & plywood; lumber: rough, dressed & finished; plywood

---

2439 Structural Wood Members, NEC

(P-3356)
BROWN HNYCUTT TRUSS SYSTEMS IN
16775 Smoke Tree St, Hesperia (92345-6165)
P.O. Box 401804 (92340-1804)
PHONE...................................760 244-8887
Michael Hough, *President*
EMP: 29 EST: 1968
SQ FT: 1,800
SALES (est): 6.7MM **Privately Held**
SIC: **2439** Trusses, wooden roof

(P-3357)
CAL SOUTHERN COMPONENTS INC
9927 C Ave, Hesperia (92345-6048)
P.O. Box 401550 (92340-1550)
PHONE...................................760 949-5144
James Mc Cabe, *President*
EMP: 17 EST: 1978
SQ FT: 2,000
SALES (est): 217.1K **Privately Held**
SIC: **2439** Trusses, wooden roof

(P-3358)
CALIFORNIA TRUSFRAME LLC (HQ)
Also Called: Ctf
25220 Hancock Ave Ste 350, Murrieta (92562-0903)
PHONE...................................951 350-4880
Shawn Overholtzer, *President*
Steve Hawkins, *General Mgr*
Jim Swan, *CTO*
Chae Kim, *Chief Engr*
Jason Ward, *VP Human Res*
EMP: 681 EST: 2011
SQ FT: 5,000
SALES (est): 41.8MM
SALES (corp-wide): 8.5B **Publicly Held**
WEB: www.caltrusframe.com
PA: Builders Firstsource, Inc.
2001 Bryan St Ste 1600
Dallas TX 75201
214 880-3500

(P-3359)
CALIFORNIA TRUSS COMPANY (PA)
23665 Cajalco Rd, Perris (92570-8181)
PHONE...................................951 657-7491
Kenneth M Cloyd, *President*
Jim Butler, *CFO*
Mike Ruede, *Vice Pres*
EMP: 244 EST: 1970
SQ FT: 5,000
SALES (est): 19.3MM **Privately Held**
WEB: www.caltrusframe.com
SIC: **2439** Trusses, wooden roof

(P-3360)
DIXIELINE LUMBER COMPANY LLC
2625 Durahart St, Riverside (92507-2654)
PHONE...................................951 224-8491
EMP: 1256

(P-3361)
GOLDENWOOD TRUSS CORPORATION
11032 Nardo St, Ventura (93004-3210)
PHONE...................................805 659-2520
Kevin Tollefson, *President*
Darin Ranson, *Vice Pres*
Myron Hodgson, *Admin Sec*
Frank Delgado, *Design Engr*
Molly Calderon, *Controller*
EMP: 80 EST: 1998
SALES (est): 9.7MM **Privately Held**
WEB: www.goldenwoodtruss.com
SIC: **2439** Trusses, wooden roof

(P-3362)
HANSON TRUSS INC
13950 Yorba Ave, Chino (91710-5520)
PHONE...................................909 591-9256
Donald R Hanson, *President*
Tom Hanson, *Corp Secy*
Rick Patterson, *Manager*
EMP: 300 EST: 1985
SQ FT: 4,000
SALES (est): 27.6MM **Privately Held**
SIC: **2439** Trusses, wooden roof

(P-3363)
HESPERIA HOLDING INC
9780 E Ave, Hesperia (92345-6174)
PHONE...................................760 244-8787
William Nalls, *President*
Mark Presgraves, *Vice Pres*
Don Shimp, *Principal*
EMP: 74 EST: 2000
SALES (est): 4.8MM **Privately Held**
WEB: www.capitalholdingsinc.com
SIC: **2439** Structural wood members

(P-3364)
HIGH SIERRA TRUSS COMPANY INC
1201 S K St, Tulare (93274-6424)
PHONE...................................559 688-6611
Oral E Micham, *President*
EMP: 18 EST: 2005
SQ FT: 800
SALES (est): 671.4K **Privately Held**
SIC: **2439** Arches, laminated lumber

(P-3365)
IMPERIAL ROOF TRUSS INC
701 E 2nd St, Imperial (92251-1724)
P.O. Box 1004 (92251-1004)
PHONE...................................760 355-1809
Raul Parra, *President*
EMP: 23 EST: 1986
SQ FT: 280
SALES (est): 1.9MM **Privately Held**
SIC: **2439** Trusses, wooden roof

(P-3366)
INLAND TRUSS INC (PA)
275 W Rider St, Perris (92571-3225)
PHONE...................................951 300-1758
Dan Irwin, *President*
Ernie Castro, *Treasurer*
Debbie Meier, *Office Mgr*
Adam Stocker, *Consultant*
EMP: 66 EST: 1991
SQ FT: 1,200
SALES (est): 7MM **Privately Held**
WEB: www.inlandempiretruss.com
SIC: **2439** Trusses, wooden roof

(P-3367)
SIMPSON STRONG-TIE COMPANY INC
12246 Holly St, Riverside (92509-2314)
PHONE...................................714 871-8373
Dave Bastian, *Branch Mgr*
Jonathan Freeman, *Plant Supt*
EMP: 250
SQ FT: 40,845

SALES (corp-wide): 8.5B **Publicly Held**
WEB: www.dixieline.com
SIC: **5211** 5251 2439 5072 Lumber & other building materials; builders' hardware; trusses, wooden roof; hardware
HQ: Dixieline Lumber Company Llc
3250 Sports Arena Blvd
San Diego CA 92110
619 224-4120

SALES (corp-wide): 1.2B **Publicly Held**
WEB: www.strongtie.com
SIC: **2439** 3429 Structural wood members; manufactured hardware (general)
HQ: Simpson Strong-Tie Company Inc.
5956 W Las Positas Blvd
Pleasanton CA 94588
925 560-9000

(P-3368)
SPATES FABRICATORS INC
85435 Middleton St, Thermal (92274-9619)
PHONE...................................760 397-4122
Tom Spates, *President*
David Spates, *Vice Pres*
Frankie Spates, *Admin Sec*
Patricia Spates, *Dept Chairman*
Marilyn Clardie, *Project Mgr*
EMP: 51 EST: 1976
SQ FT: 40,000
SALES (est): 10.5MM **Privately Held**
WEB: www.spates.com
SIC: **2439** Trusses, except roof: laminated lumber; trusses, wooden roof

(P-3369)
SPS INC
3000 E Miraloma Ave, Anaheim (92806-1808)
PHONE...................................714 632-8333
Dan Shiner, *Vice Pres*
Teresa Denker, *Prgrmr*
Jeff Hall, *Opers Staff*
EMP: 17 EST: 2015
SALES (est): 4.7MM **Privately Held**
WEB: www.spsconstruction.com
SIC: **2439** Trusses, wooden roof

(P-3370)
T L TIMMERMAN CONSTRUCTION
Also Called: Timco
9845 Santa Fe Ave E, Hesperia (92345-6216)
P.O. Box 402563 (92340-2563)
PHONE...................................760 244-2532
Timothy L Timmerman, *President*
Anita Timmerman, *Vice Pres*
EMP: 30 EST: 1976
SQ FT: 7,700
SALES (est): 2.5MM **Privately Held**
SIC: **2439** Trusses, wooden roof

(P-3371)
TRI STATE TRUSS CORPORATION
600 River Rd, Needles (92363)
P.O. Box 628 (92363-0628)
PHONE...................................760 326-3868
Richard C Huebner, *CEO*
Mike Terry, *President*
EMP: 23 EST: 1978
SQ FT: 1,500
SALES (est): 1.2MM **Privately Held**
SIC: **2439** Trusses, wooden roof; trusses, except roof: laminated lumber

(P-3372)
TRI-CO BUILDING SUPPLY INC
Also Called: Truspro
695 Obispo St, Guadalupe (93434-1631)
P.O. Box 850 (93434-0850)
PHONE...................................805 343-2555
Patrick A Herring Sr, *President*
Memory Herring, *Corp Secy*
Frank Sparks, *Officer*
Steve Herring, *Vice Pres*
EMP: 36 EST: 1975
SQ FT: 2,500
SALES (est): 3.9MM **Privately Held**
WEB: www.truspro.com
SIC: **2439** Trusses, wooden roof

2441 Wood Boxes

(P-3373)
A & J INDUSTRIES INC
Also Called: A & J Manufacturing
1430 240th St, Harbor City (90710-1307)
P.O. Box 90596, Los Angeles (90009-0596)
PHONE...................................310 216-2170
Patrick Doucette, *CEO*
Keith Bell, *Admin Sec*
◆ EMP: 18 EST: 1945

SQ FT: 40,000
SALES (est): 3MM **Privately Held**
WEB: www.ajcases.com
SIC: 2441 Chests & trunks, wood

(P-3374)
ARBO BOX INC
2900 Supply Ave, Commerce (90040-2708)
PHONE..................................562 404-2726
Robert Wharton, *CEO*
EMP: 15 **EST:** 1975
SQ FT: 14,200
SALES (est): 718.5K **Privately Held**
WEB: www.arbobox.com
SIC: 2441 Nailed wood boxes & shook

(P-3375)
ARMORED GROUP INC
Also Called: Innerspace Cases
11555 Cantara St, North Hollywood
(91605-1652)
PHONE..................................818 767-3030
Louis Kaye, *President*
Loretta Kaye, *Treasurer*
Joshua Kaye, *Info Tech Mgr*
EMP: 34 **EST:** 1986
SQ FT: 15,000
SALES (est): 3MM **Privately Held**
WEB: www.innerspacecases.com
SIC: 2441 Cases, wood

(P-3376)
BASAW MANUFACTURING INC
(PA)
11323 Hartland St, North Hollywood
(91605-6310)
PHONE..................................818 765-6650
Robert Allen, *President*
Hugh Mullen, *Treasurer*
Eleazar Padilla, *Vice Pres*
Jorge Cea,
Martha Rivera,
▲ **EMP:** 32 **EST:** 1990
SALES (est): 9.4MM **Privately Held**
WEB: www.basaw.com
SIC: 2441 7389 Shipping cases, wood:
nailed or lock corner; packaging & label-
ing services

(P-3377)
CAL-COAST PKG & CRATING
INC
2040 E 220th St, Carson (90810-1603)
PHONE..................................310 518-7215
Dale Loughry, *President*
Amy Lopez, *Project Mgr*
Joe Rangel, *Sales Mgr*
Valerie L Dahlk, *Manager*
▲ **EMP:** 35 **EST:** 1957
SQ FT: 58,000
SALES (est): 4.9MM **Privately Held**
WEB: www.calcoastpacking.com
SIC: 2441 2449 Shipping cases, wood:
nailed or lock corner; wood containers

(P-3378)
NELSON CASE CORPORATION
650 S Jefferson St Ste A, Placentia
(92870-6640)
PHONE..................................714 528-2215
Edward Bobadilla, *CEO*
John Bovadilla Jr, *CEO*
Virginia Sandburg, *CFO*
Scott Mana, *Sales Associate*
EMP: 19 **EST:** 1995
SALES (est): 3.1MM **Privately Held**
WEB: www.nelsoncasecorp.com
SIC: 2441 5199 5099 2449 Packing
cases, wood: nailed or lock corner; ship-
ping cases, wood: nailed or lock corner;
bags, baskets & cases; cases, carrying;
shipping cases, wood: wirebound

(P-3379)
PROCASES INC
Also Called: Az-Iz Case Co
8205 Industry Ave, Pico Rivera
(90660-4827)
PHONE..................................323 585-4447
Afshin Zakhor, *CEO*
▲ **EMP:** 13 **EST:** 1993
SALES (est): 2.6MM **Privately Held**
WEB: www.procases.com
SIC: 2441 Shipping cases, wood: nailed or
lock corner

2448 Wood Pallets & Skids

(P-3380)
AAA PALLET RECYCLING &
MFG INC
23120 Oleander Ave, Perris (92570-5662)
PHONE..................................951 681-7748
Tyson Paulis, *CEO*
EMP: 22 **EST:** 1994
SQ FT: 152,460
SALES (est): 5MM **Privately Held**
SIC: 2448 Pallets, wood

(P-3381)
ARNIES SUPPLY SERVICE LTD
(PA)
1541 N Ditman Ave, Los Angeles
(90063-2501)
P.O. Box 26, Monterey Park (91754-0026)
PHONE..................................323 263-1696
Arnold Espino, *President*
Madeline Espino, *Treasurer*
Maria Espino, *Admin Sec*
EMP: 25 **EST:** 1975
SALES (est): 4.1MM **Privately Held**
WEB: www.arniessupplyservice.net
SIC: 2448 Pallets, wood

(P-3382)
BRUCE IVERSEN
Also Called: B&B Pallet Company
11734 Grande Vista Dr, Whittier
(90601-2319)
PHONE..................................310 537-4168
Bruce Iversen, *Owner*
EMP: 14 **EST:** 1965
SALES (est): 5MM **Privately Held**
SIC: 2448 2421 Pallets, wood; sawdust &
shavings

(P-3383)
COMMERCIAL LBR & PALLET
CO INC (PA)
135 Long Ln, City of Industry (91746-2633)
PHONE..................................626 968-0631
Raymond Gutierrez II, *President*
Mary Gutierrez, *Treasurer*
Carlos Casas, *Opers Mgr*
Jason Gutierrez, *Sales Executive*
EMP: 150 **EST:** 1941
SQ FT: 10,000
SALES (est): 30.4MM **Privately Held**
WEB: www.clcpallets.com
SIC: 2448 5031 Pallets, wood; lumber:
rough, dressed & finished

(P-3384)
CORREA PALLET INC (PA)
Also Called: National Wholesale Lumber
13036 Avenue 76, Pixley (93256-9458)
PHONE..................................559 757-1790
Martin Correa, *President*
EMP: 48 **EST:** 2002
SALES (est): 10.3MM **Privately Held**
WEB: www.correapallets.com
SIC: 2448 Pallets, wood

(P-3385)
CORTEZ PALLETS SERVICE INC
(PA)
14739 Proctor Ave, La Puente
(91746-3203)
P.O. Box 2552 (91746-0552)
PHONE..................................626 961-9891
Salvadore Cortez, *President*
Julia Cortez, *Vice Pres*
Salvadore Cortez Jr, *Admin Sec*
EMP: 18 **EST:** 1976
SQ FT: 2,000
SALES (est): 3.9MM **Privately Held**
WEB: www.industrypallets.com
SIC: 2448 Pallets, wood

(P-3386)
CROWN PALLET COMPANY INC
15151 Salt Lake Ave, La Puente
(91746-3316)
PHONE..................................626 937-6565
Robert Miller, *President*
▲ **EMP:** 17 **EST:** 1978
SQ FT: 400

SALES (est): 334.9K **Privately Held**
WEB: www.pacificcoastpallets.com
SIC: 2448 2441 Pallets, wood; nailed
wood boxes & shook

(P-3387)
D L B PALLETS (PA)
4510 Rutile St, Riverside (92509-2649)
P.O. Box 10513, San Bernardino (92423-
0513)
PHONE..................................951 360-9896
Daniel Bodbyl, *President*
Anna Bodbyl, *Treasurer*
EMP: 15 **EST:** 1986
SALES (est): 1.8MM **Privately Held**
WEB: www.dlbpallets.com
SIC: 2448 5031 Pallets, wood; pallets,
wood

(P-3388)
E VASQUEZ DISTRIBUTORS INC
Also Called: Oxnard Pallet Company
4524 E Pleasant Valley Rd, Oxnard
(93033-2309)
P.O. Box 1748 (93032-1748)
PHONE..................................805 487-8458
Elias Vasquez Jr, *President*
Beatrice Vasquez, *CFO*
Vannessa Vasquez, *Vice Pres*
EMP: 30 **EST:** 1989
SQ FT: 480
SALES (est): 5MM **Privately Held**
WEB: www.oxnardpalletco.com
SIC: 2448 4214 Pallets, wood; local truck-
ing with storage

(P-3389)
G C PALLETS INC
5490 26th St, Riverside (92509-2212)
PHONE..................................909 357-8515
Mayra Gaona, *CEO*
Sebastian Gaona, *CEO*
EMP: 30 **EST:** 2001
SALES (est): 2.9MM **Privately Held**
WEB: www.gcpalletsusa.com
SIC: 2448 Pallets, wood

(P-3390)
G O PALLETS INC
15642 Slover Ave, Fontana (92337-7362)
PHONE..................................909 823-4663
Guatalupe Ojeda, *President*
Lina Montes, *Office Mgr*
EMP: 17 **EST:** 1983
SALES (est): 1.1MM **Privately Held**
WEB: www.gopalletsinc.com
SIC: 2448 Pallets, wood

(P-3391)
HARDING CONTAINERS INTL
INC
4000 Santa Fe Ave, Long Beach
(90810-1832)
PHONE..................................310 549-7272
Victor Hsing, *President*
Keith R Mayer, *Vice Pres*
▲ **EMP:** 38 **EST:** 1992
SQ FT: 1,000
SALES (est): 1.6MM **Privately Held**
SIC: 2448 Cargo containers, wood & wood
with metal

(P-3392)
IDEAL PALLET SYSTEM INC
7422 Cedar Dr, Huntington Beach
(92647-5498)
P.O. Box 2300 (92647-0300)
PHONE..................................714 847-9657
Toll Free:..................................877
Melvin Mermelstein, *President*
Edie Mermelstein, *CFO*
EMP: 16 **EST:** 1965
SQ FT: 3,500
SALES (est): 457.4K **Privately Held**
WEB: www.idealpallet.com
SIC: 2448 Pallets, wood

(P-3393)
IFCO SYSTEMS NORTH
AMERICA INC
14750 Miller Ave, Fontana (92336-1685)
PHONE..................................909 356-0697
EMP: 46 **Privately Held**
SIC: 2448 Mfg Wood Pallets/Skids

HQ: Ifco Systems North America, Inc.
13100 Nw Fwy Ste 625
Houston TX 77040

(P-3394)
IFCO SYSTEMS US LLC
8950 Rochester Ave # 150, Rancho Cuca-
monga (91730-5541)
PHONE..................................909 484-4332
Mike Ellis, *Principal*
Marcus Blood, *General Mgr*
Eric Smith, *General Mgr*
Jeff Widrig, *General Mgr*
Cindy Sanchez, *Office Mgr*
EMP: 53 **Privately Held**
WEB: www.ifco.com
SIC: 2448 Pallets, wood
PA: Ifco Systems Us, Llc
3030 N Rocky Point Dr W # 300
Tampa FL 33607

(P-3395)
INCA PALLETS SUPPLY INC
1349 S East End Ave, Pomona
(91766-5412)
PHONE..................................909 622-1414
Zuleica Quimones, *President*
EMP: 30 **EST:** 2003
SALES (est): 847.7K **Privately Held**
SIC: 2448 7699 Pallets, wood; pallet re-
pair

(P-3396)
INDUSTRIAL WOOD PRODUCTS
INC
5123 Brooks St, Montclair (91763-4806)
P.O. Box 3121 (91763-922?)
PHONE..................................909 625-1247
Jaime Ramirez, *President*
Lydia Ramirez, *Vice Pres*
EMP: 18 **EST:** 1984
SALES (est): 2.5MM **Privately Held**
SIC: 5211 2448 2449 2441 Millwork &
lumber; pallets, wood; cargo containers,
wood; rectangular boxes & crates, wood;
nailed wood boxes & shook

(P-3397)
LONG BEACH WOODWORKS
LLC
Also Called: Pacific Pallet Co
1261 Highland Ave, Glendale (91202-2055)
PHONE..................................562 437-2293
Steven P Amato,
Sam Amato,
EMP: 16 **EST:** 1969
SQ FT: 2,000
SALES (est): 2.4MM **Privately Held**
SIC: 2448 Pallets, wood

(P-3398)
LOPEZ PALLETS INC
11080 Redwood Ave, Fontana
(92337-7130)
P.O. Box 847, Rancho Cucamonga (91729-
0847)
PHONE..................................909 823-0865
Jesus M Lopez, *President*
EMP: 16 **EST:** 1995
SQ FT: 700
SALES (est): 1.7MM **Privately Held**
WEB: www.lopezpallets.com
SIC: 2448 7699 Pallets, wood; skids,
wood; pallet repair

(P-3399)
MEZA PALLET INC
14619 Merrill Ave, Fontana (92335-4219)
PHONE..................................909 829-0223
Leodegario G Meza, *President*
Michael Meza, *President*
EMP: 15 **EST:** 1988
SALES (est): 1.6MM **Privately Held**
WEB: www.mezapalletsinc.com
SIC: 2448 Pallets, wood

(P-3400)
NARANJO PALLETS
6653 Loveland St, Bell Gardens
(90201-1942)
PHONE..................................323 637-8019
Luis Naranjo, *Principal*
EMP: 15 **EST:** 2016

SALES (est): 131.9K **Privately Held**
SIC: 2448 Pallets, wood & wood with metal

(P-3401)
PACIFIC COAST PALLETS INC
15151 Salt Lake Ave, La Puente
(91746-3316)
PHONE....................626 937-6565
Richard Reeves, *President*
EMP: 14 EST: 1979
SQ FT: 600
SALES (est): 1MM **Privately Held**
WEB: www.pacificcoastpallets.com
SIC: 2448 7699 Pallets, wood; pallet repair

(P-3402)
PALLET DEPOT INC
19049 Avenue 242, Lindsay (93247-9698)
PHONE....................916 645-0490
Jamie Anderson, *President*
Mike Anderson, *Vice Pres*
Sharon Anderson, *Director*
EMP: 70 EST: 1994
SALES (est): 3.2MM **Privately Held**
SIC: 2448 Pallets, wood & wood with metal

(P-3403)
PALLET MASTERS INC
655 E Florence Ave, Los Angeles
(90001-2319)
PHONE....................323 758-1713
Stephen H Anderson, *President*
Tim Hwang, *Controller*
Bridgette Latham, *Manager*
EMP: 55 EST: 1991
SQ FT: 105,000
SALES (est): 9MM **Privately Held**
WEB: www.palletmasters.com
SIC: 2448 2441 2439 Pallets, wood; skids, wood; boxes, wood; structural wood members

(P-3404)
PRIORITY PALLET INC
1060 E Third St, Beaumont (92223-3020)
PHONE....................951 769-9399
Raymond Guiterrez, *President*
Christina Cedeno, *Human Resources*
EMP: 20 EST: 1999
SALES (est): 2.1MM **Privately Held**
WEB: www.clcpallets.com
SIC: 2448 Pallets, wood

(P-3405)
RAMIREZ PALLETS INC
8431 Sultana Ave, Fontana (92335-3298)
PHONE....................909 822-2066
Cresencio Ramirez, *President*
EMP: 35 EST: 1977
SALES (est): 3.8MM **Privately Held**
WEB: www.ramirezpallets.com
SIC: 2448 Pallets, wood

(P-3406)
ROGER R CARUSO ENTERPRISES INC
Also Called: Century Pallets
2911 Norton Ave, Lynwood (90262-1810)
PHONE....................714 778-6006
Roger R Caruso, *President*
Rose Caruso, *Admin Sec*
▲ EMP: 20 EST: 1973
SQ FT: 92,000
SALES (est): 2.2MM **Privately Held**
WEB: www.centurypallets.com
SIC: 2448 Pallets, wood

(P-3407)
SAN FERNANDO VLY PALLET CO INC (PA)
21540 Nordhoff St, Chatsworth
(91311-5822)
PHONE....................818 341-1200
Susana Eroza, *President*
George Eroza, *Vice Pres*
EMP: 14 EST: 1996
SALES (est): 1.3MM **Privately Held**
WEB: www.sfvpallet.com
SIC: 2448 Pallets, wood

(P-3408)
SATCO INC (PA)
1601 E El Segundo Blvd, El Segundo
(90245-4334)
PHONE....................310 322-4719
Mike Proctor, *CEO*
Micheal Proctor, *President*
Vincent Voong, *COO*
Richard Weis, *CFO*
Peter Looker, *Exec VP*
▲ EMP: 125 EST: 1968
SQ FT: 27,000
SALES (est): 71.2MM **Privately Held**
WEB: www.satco-inc.com
SIC: 2448 3537 Pallets, wood & metal combination; containers (metal), air cargo

(P-3409)
STANDARD LUMBER COMPANY INC (HQ)
Also Called: United Wholesale Lumber Co
27770 Entertainment Dr, Valencia
(91355-1092)
PHONE....................559 651-2037
Thomas J Thayer, *CEO*
Tory Fithian, *Sales Staff*
John Garcia, *Manager*
EMP: 35 EST: 1950
SQ FT: 10,000
SALES (est): 10.8MM
SALES (corp-wide): 222.6MM **Privately Held**
WEB: www.fruitgrowerssupply.com
SIC: 2448 2441 Pallets, wood; nailed wood boxes & shook
PA: Fruit Growers Supply Company Inc
27770 N Entrmt Dr Fl 3 Flr 3
Valencia CA 91355
888 997-4855

(P-3410)
SUN PAC STORAGE CONTAINERS INC
23222 Olive Ave Ste A, Lake Forest
(92630-5301)
P.O. Box 339 (92609-0339)
PHONE....................949 458-2347
Tom Harris, *Owner*
Jay Bester, *Sales Associate*
Larry Spears, *Sales Staff*
EMP: 15 EST: 2004
SALES (est): 2MM **Privately Held**
WEB: www.sunpaccontainers.com
SIC: 2448 4225 Cargo containers, wood & wood with metal; warehousing, self-storage

(P-3411)
VISALIA PALLET LLC
5932 W Elowin Dr, Visalia (93291-9222)
PHONE....................559 627-4829
Scott Boyajian, *Principal*
EMP: 20 EST: 2001
SALES (est): 392K **Privately Held**
WEB: www.teampsc.com
SIC: 2448 Pallets, wood

(P-3412)
WILMINGTON WOODWORKS INC
318 E C St, Wilmington (90744-6614)
P.O. Box 581 (90748-0581)
PHONE....................310 834-1015
Ronald Young, *President*
Pat Mace, *Shareholder*
EMP: 21 EST: 1960
SALES (est): 679.8K **Privately Held**
WEB: www.wilmwoodworks.com
SIC: 2448 Pallets, wood

2449 Wood Containers, NEC

(P-3413)
APEX DRUM COMPANY INC
Also Called: Apex Container Services
6226 Ferguson Dr, Commerce
(90022-5399)
PHONE....................323 721-8994
Abe Michlin, *CEO*
Sybil Flom, *Admin Sec*
Noah Flom, *Sales Mgr*
EMP: 19 EST: 1946
SQ FT: 40,000

SALES (est): 6.2MM **Privately Held**
WEB: www.apexdrum.com
SIC: 2449 5085 Containers, plywood & veneer wood; shipping cases & drums, wood: wirebound & plywood; cooperage stock; drums, new or reconditioned

(P-3414)
FRANK KAMS & ASSOCIATES INC
Also Called: California Redwood Products
242 W Hanna St, Colton (92324-2772)
PHONE....................909 382-0047
Frank L Kams, *CEO*
Eleanor Kams, *Corp Secy*
▲ EMP: 15 EST: 1976
SQ FT: 44,700
SALES (est): 486.9K **Privately Held**
SIC: 2449 5083 Rectangular boxes & crates, wood; lawn & garden machinery & equipment

(P-3415)
JDC DEVELOPMENT GROUP INC
Also Called: Dggr Packaging Crating & Foam
1321 N Blue Gum St, Anaheim
(92806-1750)
PHONE....................714 575-1108
Joseph Dibenedetto Jr, *President*
Joseph Di Benedetto Jr, *President*
EMP: 16 EST: 2003
SALES (est): 402K **Privately Held**
SIC: 2449 2631 Rectangular boxes & crates, wood; container, packaging & boxboard

(P-3416)
OMEGA CASE COMPANY INC
2231 N Hollywood Way, Burbank
(91505-1113)
PHONE....................818 238-9263
Omar Gonzales, *Owner*
Cris Vargas, *Opers Mgr*
EMP: 18 EST: 2005
SALES (est): 626.2K **Privately Held**
WEB: www.omegacase.com
SIC: 2449 Shipping cases & drums, wood: wirebound & plywood

(P-3417)
PICNIC AT ASCOT INC
3237 W 131st St, Hawthorne (90250-5514)
PHONE....................310 674-3098
Paul Whitlock, *President*
Jill Brown, *Vice Pres*
Karen Burke, *Natl Sales Mgr*
Elsa Laguna, *Marketing Staff*
◆ EMP: 30 EST: 1992
SQ FT: 20,000
SALES (est): 3.7MM **Privately Held**
WEB: www.picnicatascot.com
SIC: 2449 5947 Baskets: fruit & vegetable, round stave, till, etc.; gift, novelty & souvenir shop

2451 Mobile Homes

(P-3418)
CASTAIC LAKE RV PARK INC
Also Called: Castaic R V Park
31540 Ridge Route Rd, Castaic
(91384-3358)
PHONE....................661 257-3340
Arthur Staudigel, *President*
C Dan Foote, *Treasurer*
Clyde Widrig, *Vice Pres*
Robert C Tallent, *Admin Sec*
EMP: 19 EST: 1978
SALES (est): 637.5K **Privately Held**
WEB: www.castaiclakervpark.com
SIC: 2451 5411 7011 5921 Mobile homes; grocery stores, independent; hotels & motels; liquor stores

(P-3419)
D-MAC INC
1105 E Discovery Ln, Anaheim
(92801-1121)
PHONE....................714 808-3918
David A Wade, *Principal*
Leo Hernandez, *Accounting Mgr*
EMP: 26 EST: 1998

SALES (est): 4.4MM **Privately Held**
WEB: www.d-macinc.com
SIC: 2451 5039 5032 Mobile home frames; structural assemblies, prefabricated: non-wood; paving materials; plastering materials

(P-3420)
DVELE INC
25525 Redlands Blvd, Loma Linda
(92354-2009)
P.O. Box 1710 (92354-0150)
PHONE....................909 796-2561
Luca Brammer, *COO*
Lucas Forte, *Project Mgr*
Mike Beckwith, *Engineer*
Ian Garrity, *Director*
EMP: 45
SALES (corp-wide): 5.3MM **Privately Held**
WEB: www.dvele.com
SIC: 2451 2452 Mobile homes, except recreational; prefabricated buildings, wood
PA: Dvele, Inc.
2201 Market St
San Francisco CA

(P-3421)
DVELE OMEGA CORPORATION
Also Called: Hallmark Southwest
25525 Redlands Blvd, Loma Linda
(92354-2009)
P.O. Box 1710 (92354-0150)
PHONE....................909 796-2561
Luca Brammer, *President*
EMP: 100 EST: 2018
SQ FT: 5,000
SALES (est): 12MM **Privately Held**
WEB: www.dvele.com
SIC: 2451 2452 Mobile homes, personal or private use; mobile homes, industrial or commercial use; prefabricated wood buildings; modular homes, prefabricated, wood; panels & sections, prefabricated, wood

(P-3422)
FLEETWOOD HOMES CALIFORNIA INC (DH)
7007 Jurupa Ave, Riverside (92504-1015)
P.O. Box 7638 (92513-7638)
PHONE....................951 351-2494
Elvin Smith, *President*
Lyle N Larkin, *Treasurer*
Boyd R Plowman, *Exec VP*
Roger L Howsmon, *Senior VP*
Forrest D Theobald, *Senior VP*
▲ EMP: 280 EST: 1963
SQ FT: 262,900
SALES (est): 65.4MM **Privately Held**
WEB: www.fleetwoodhomes.com
SIC: 2451 Mobile homes
HQ: Fleetwood Enterprises, Inc.
1351 Pomona Rd Ste 230
Corona CA 92882
951 354-3000

(P-3423)
FLEETWOOD HOMES OF FLORIDA (DH)
3125 Myers St, Riverside (92503-5527)
P.O. Box 7638 (92513-7638)
PHONE....................909 261-4274
Edward B Caudill, *President*
Boyd R Plowman, *CFO*
Lyle N Larkin, *Treasurer*
Forrest D Theobald, *Senior VP*
▲ EMP: 447 EST: 1970
SQ FT: 262,900
SALES (est): 8.8MM **Privately Held**
SIC: 2451 Mobile homes, except recreational
HQ: Fleetwood Enterprises, Inc.
1351 Pomona Rd Ste 230
Corona CA 92882
951 354-3000

(P-3424)
FLEETWOOD HOMES OF KENTUCKY (DH)
1351 Pomona Rd Ste 230, Corona
(92882-7165)
PHONE....................800 688-1745
Elden L Smith, *Principal*

PRODUCTS & SVCS

Boyd R Plowman, *CFO*
Roger L Howsmon, *Treasurer*
Forrest D Theobald, *Senior VP*
Lyle N Larkin, *Vice Pres*
EMP: 80 **EST:** 1998
SALES (est): 4MM **Privately Held**
SIC: 2451 Mobile homes
HQ: Fleetwood Enterprises, Inc.
　1351 Pomona Rd Ste 230
　Corona CA 92882
　951 354-3000

(P-3425)
**FLEETWOOD HOMES OF PA
(DH)**
1351 Pomona Rd Ste 230, Corona
(92882-7165)
PHONE......................717 367-8222
Elden L Smith, *Principal*
Edward B Caudill, *President*
Boyd R Plowman, *CFO*
Lyle N Larkin, *Treasurer*
Christopher J Braun, *Senior VP*
EMP: 80 **EST:** 1995
SQ FT: 262,900
SALES (est): 2.5MM **Privately Held**
SIC: 2451 Mobile homes, except recreational
HQ: Fleetwood Enterprises, Inc.
　1351 Pomona Rd Ste 230
　Corona CA 92882
　951 354-3000

**2452 Prefabricated Wood
Buildings & Cmpnts**

(P-3426)
ADAPTIVE SHELTERS LLC
427 E 17th St Ste F268, Costa Mesa
(92627-3201)
PHONE......................949 923-5444
Matthew Bays, *Mng Member*
Dave Arfin, *Mng Member*
EMP: 50 **EST:** 2017
SALES (est): 1.6MM **Privately Held**
WEB: www.adaptivedesigns.com
SIC: 2452 Modular homes, prefabricated, wood

(P-3427)
ALAN PRE-FAB BUILDING CORP
17817 Evelyn Ave, Gardena (90248-3735)
PHONE......................310 538-0333
Toll Free:......................888 -
John W Andrus, *President*
Bill Andrus, *Vice Pres*
Bret Andrus, *Vice Pres*
Ann Andrus, *Admin Sec*
EMP: 16 **EST:** 1971
SQ FT: 49,000
SALES (est): 1.9MM **Privately Held**
WEB: www.alanprefab.com
SIC: 2452 7359 Prefabricated wood buildings; equipment rental & leasing

(P-3428)
**APPLIED POLYTECH SYSTEMS
INC**
Also Called: A P S
26000 Springbrook Ave # 102, Santa Clarita
(91350-2590)
PHONE......................818 504-9261
Christine Wagner, *President*
Chris Wagner, *Data Proc Staff*
EMP: 30 **EST:** 1988
SQ FT: 6,000
SALES (est): 2.2MM **Privately Held**
WEB: www.apsincprecast.com
SIC: 2452 Prefabricated wood buildings

(P-3429)
PLH PRODUCTS INC
10541 Calle Lee Ste 119, Los Alamitos
(90720-6782)
PHONE......................714 739-6622
Seung Woo Lee, *Ch of Bd*
Kyung Min Park, *President*
Won Yong Lee, *CFO*
◆ **EMP:** 405 **EST:** 1992
SALES (est): 38.5MM **Privately Held**
WEB: www.plhproducts.com
SIC: 2452 2449 5999 Sauna rooms, prefabricated, wood; hot tubs, wood; sauna equipment & supplies

(P-3430)
WALDEN STRUCTURES INC
1000 Bristol St N 126, Newport Beach
(92660-8916)
PHONE......................909 389-9100
Charlie Walden, *Owner*
Curtis H Claire, *President*
Michael J Dominici, *CFO*
EMP: 400 **EST:** 1996
SQ FT: 150,000
SALES (est): 41.1MM **Privately Held**
WEB: www.silver-creek.net
SIC: 2452 Modular homes, prefabricated, wood

2491 Wood Preserving

(P-3431)
COUNTERTOP FACTORY (PA)
2740 E Coronado St, Anaheim
(92806-2401)
PHONE......................562 903-4080
Bruce D Smith, *CEO*
Karen Smith, *CFO*
Victor Andalon, *Manager*
▲ **EMP:** 19 **EST:** 2003
SALES (est): 2.5MM **Privately Held**
WEB: www.thecountertopfactory.net
SIC: 2491 Structural lumber & timber, treated wood

(P-3432)
**FONTANA WOOD TREATING
INC**
Also Called: California Cascade Fontana
8395 Sultana Ave, Fontana (92335-3238)
PHONE......................909 357-2136
Allie Kimes, *Principal*
Fred Garcia, *Traffic Mgr*
Michelle Prieto, *Production*
Cheryl Meyer, *Sales Staff*
EMP: 18 **EST:** 2015
SALES (est): 2.9MM **Privately Held**
SIC: 2491 Wood preserving

(P-3433)
**HOOVER TREATED WOOD PDTS
INC**
Also Called: Hoover Treated Wood Pdts Plant
5601 District Blvd, Bakersfield
(93313-2129)
PHONE......................661 833-0429
EMP: 18
SALES (corp-wide): 2.8B **Publicly Held**
WEB: www.frtw.com
SIC: 2491 Structural lumber & timber, treated wood
HQ: Hoover Treated Wood Products, Inc.
　154 Wire Rd
　Thomson GA 30824
　706 595-5058

**2493 Reconstituted Wood
Prdts**

(P-3434)
REGARDS ENTERPRISES INC
Also Called: Quality Marble & Granite
731 S Taylor Ave, Ontario (91761-1847)
PHONE......................909 983-0655
Evan Cohen, *CEO*
▲ **EMP:** 19 **EST:** 2013
SQ FT: 95,000
SALES (est): 2.5MM **Privately Held**
SIC: 2493 3281 Marbleboard (stone face hard board); granite, cut & shaped

---

2499 Wood Prdts, NEC

(P-3435)
AETCO INC
2825 Metropolitan Pl, Pomona
(91767-1853)
P.O. Box 458, San Dimas (91773-0458)
PHONE......................909 593-2521
Anthony Taylor, *President*
Jeanne Shinogle, *Vice Pres*
Barbara Taylor, *Admin Sec*
EMP: 14 **EST:** 1979
SQ FT: 12,500

SALES (est): 548.2K **Privately Held**
WEB: www.aetcoinc.com
SIC: 2499 3429 3842 2326 Policemen's clubs, wood; handcuffs & leg irons; surgical appliances & supplies; men's & boys' work clothing

(P-3436)
ALACO LADDER COMPANY
5167 G St, Chino (91710-5143)
PHONE......................909 591-7561
Gil Jacobs, *President*
Mario Garcia, *Vice Pres*
▼ **EMP:** 25 **EST:** 1946
SQ FT: 26,000
SALES (est): 5.7MM **Privately Held**
WEB: www.alacoladder.com
SIC: 2499 3354 3499 Ladders, wood; aluminum extruded products; metal ladders
PA: B, E & P Enterprises, Llc
　5167 G St
　Chino CA 91710
　909 591-7561

(P-3437)
APOLLO WOOD RECOVERY INC
7225 Edison Ave, Ontario (91762-7507)
P.O. Box 1927, Chino (91708-1927)
PHONE......................909 371-9510
Shawn Nutter, *President*
Adam Demichele, *CFO*
Philip Reiker,
EMP: 13 **EST:** 1995
SALES (est): 2MM **Privately Held**
WEB: www.apollowoodproducts.com
SIC: 2499 Insulating material, cork

(P-3438)
ART FOR KIDS INC
Also Called: Afk Furniture
23191 Arroyo Vis, Rcho STA Marg
(92688-2616)
PHONE......................949 459-2800
Gale Sedigh, *President*
Bijan Sedigh, *Vice Pres*
▲ **EMP:** 24 **EST:** 1982
SQ FT: 10,000
SALES (est): 5.9MM **Privately Held**
WEB: www.afkfurniture.com
SIC: 5712 2499 Juvenile furniture; applicators, wood

(P-3439)
B E & P ENTERPRISES LLC (PA)
Also Called: Alaco Ladder Company
5167 G St, Chino (91710-5143)
PHONE......................909 591-7561
Mario Garcia,
Martha Villar, *Office Mgr*
Pedro Jimenez, *Plant Mgr*
Sue Ritchey, *Sales Executive*
Stephen Bernstein,
EMP: 24 **EST:** 1946
SALES (est): 5.7MM **Privately Held**
WEB: www.alacoladder.com
SIC: 2499 3499 3354 Ladders, wood; ladders, portable; metal; aluminum extruded products

(P-3440)
BK SEMS USA INC
4 Executive Park Ste 270, Irvine (92614)
PHONE......................949 390-7120
EMP: 19 **EST:** 2002
SALES (est): 3MM **Privately Held**
SIC: 2499 Mfg Wood Products

(P-3441)
BRENT-WOOD PRODUCTS INC
777 E Rosecrans Ave, Los Angeles
(90059-3563)
P.O. Box 59178 (90059-0178)
PHONE......................800 400-7335
Lawrence D Hobbs, *CEO*
Birgitta Olin, *President*
Anna Pinili, *Corp Secy*
Roberto Mercado, *Prdtn Mgr*
Jordan Hobbs, *Consultant*
▼ **EMP:** 30 **EST:** 1963
SQ FT: 26,000
SALES (est): 4.6MM **Privately Held**
WEB: www.brent-wood.com
SIC: 2499 Reels, plywood

(P-3442)
DELGADO BROTHERS LLC
647 E 59th St, Los Angeles (90001-1001)
PHONE......................323 233-9793
Felipe Delgado, *Partner*
Antonio Delgado, *Partner*
Rafael Delgado Jr, *Partner*
Ramiro Delgado, *Partner*
Carlos Espinoza, *Office Mgr*
▲ **EMP:** 21 **EST:** 2006
SQ FT: 105,000
SALES (est): 1.5MM **Privately Held**
WEB: www.delgadobrospictureframes.com
SIC: 2499 Picture frame molding, finished

(P-3443)
FORMSOLVER INC
Also Called: Framatic Company
3041 N North Coolidge Ave, Los Angeles
(90039-3413)
PHONE......................323 664-7888
David Dedlow, *President*
Edwina Dedlow, *Vice Pres*
Dwayne Johnson, *Software Engr*
Donna Ruckman, *Controller*
▲ **EMP:** 13 **EST:** 1976
SQ FT: 12,500
SALES (est): 1MM **Privately Held**
WEB: www.chickenbabycell.com
SIC: 2499 Picture frame molding, finished

(P-3444)
FOSTER PLANING MILL CO
1258 W 58th St, Los Angeles (90037-3917)
PHONE......................323 759-9156
Robert Stanley, *President*
EMP: 13 **EST:** 1937
SQ FT: 15,000
SALES (est): 618.2K **Privately Held**
WEB: www.fosterplaningmill.com
SIC: 2499 2431 Picture & mirror frames, wood; venetian blind slats, wood

(P-3445)
GL WOODWORKING INC
Also Called: Millers Woodworking
14341 Franklin Ave, Tustin (92780-7010)
PHONE......................949 515-2192
Grant Miller, *Owner*
EMP: 63 **EST:** 2004
SALES (est): 7MM **Privately Held**
SIC: 2499 Decorative wood & woodwork

(P-3446)
MODERN WOODWORKS INC
7949 Deering Ave, Canoga Park
(91304-5009)
PHONE......................800 575-3475
George Mekhtarian, *CEO*
Allen Mekhtarian, *Vice Pres*
Debra Schweitzer, *Admin Asst*
▲ **EMP:** 35 **EST:** 1996
SQ FT: 10,000
SALES (est): 4.6MM **Privately Held**
WEB: www.californialightworks.com
SIC: 2499 3648 Carved & turned wood; lighting equipment

(P-3447)
NATIONAL MILLWORKS LLC
32020 Allen Ave, Hemet (92545-9523)
PHONE......................619 823-0395
Ashlee Craig, *Principal*
EMP: 13 **EST:** 2015
SALES (est): 564.3K **Privately Held**
SIC: 2499 Wood products

(P-3448)
OUTDOOR DIMENSIONS LLC
5325 E Hunter Ave, Anaheim (92807-2054)
PHONE......................714 578-9555
Donald Pickler, *President*
Denise Mills, *CFO*
Valerie Hardman, *Vice Pres*
Brian Pickler, *Vice Pres*
Christy Whittaker, *Vice Pres*
EMP: 160 **EST:** 1974
SQ FT: 80,000
SALES (est): 39.2MM **Privately Held**
WEB: www.outdoordimensions.com
SIC: 2499 3993 3281 Signboards, wood; signs & advertising specialties; cut stone & stone products

(P-3449)
PACIFIC PANEL PRODUCTS CORP
15601 Arrow Hwy, Irwindale (91706-2004)
P.O. Box 2204 (91706-1126)
PHONE..........................626 851-0444
Jon R Dickey, *CEO*
Cory Dickey, *Plant Mgr*
Jeff Elliot, *Sales Staff*
Renee Valencia,
Fabian Hurtado, *Manager*
▲ **EMP:** 39 **EST:** 1994
SQ FT: 79,800
SALES (est): 7.7MM **Privately Held**
WEB: www.pacificpanel.com
SIC: 2499 Decorative wood & woodwork

(P-3450)
PICTURE THIS FRAMING INC
631 S State College Blvd, Fullerton (92831-5115)
PHONE..........................714 447-8749
Neil Oleary, *President*
Neil O'Leary, *President*
Ginger Greenleaf, *Vice Pres*
EMP: 16 **EST:** 1985
SQ FT: 8,000
SALES (est): 1.5MM **Privately Held**
WEB: www.signatureframe.com
SIC: 2499 Picture & mirror frames, wood

(P-3451)
PRO TOUR MEMORABILIA LLC
Also Called: Ptm Images
700 N San Vicente Blvd G696, West Hollywood (90069-5073)
P.O. Box 15084, Beverly Hills (90209-1084)
PHONE..........................424 303-7200
Jonathan Bass,
Devin Dickey, *Sales Staff*
▲ **EMP:** 25 **EST:** 1995
SQ FT: 8,000
SALES (est): 3MM **Privately Held**
WEB: www.protourmemorabilia.com
SIC: 2499 Picture & mirror frames, wood

(P-3452)
QUALITY FIRST WOODWORKS INC
1264 N Lakeview Ave, Anaheim (92807-1831)
PHONE..........................714 632-0480
Mark Nappy, *President*
Chad Nappy, *Corp Secy*
Randy Dell, *Vice Pres*
Enio Dominguez, *Project Mgr*
EMP: 115 **EST:** 1989
SQ FT: 30,000
SALES (est): 14MM **Privately Held**
WEB: www.qfwinc.com
SIC: 2499 Decorative wood & woodwork; cabinet building & installation

(P-3453)
REDWORKS INDUSTRIES LLC
23986 Aliso Creek Rd, Laguna Niguel (92677-3908)
PHONE..........................949 334-7081
Melissa Soto,
Juan C Soto,
EMP: 35 **EST:** 2015
SQ FT: 15,000
SALES (est): 950K **Privately Held**
SIC: 2499 Applicators, wood

(P-3454)
ROSS FABRICATION & WELDING INC
1154 Basta Ave, Bakersfield (93308-4477)
PHONE..........................661 393-1242
Jeffrey Ross, *President*
Julie Ross, *CFO*
EMP: 13 **EST:** 2008
SALES (est): 791.1K **Privately Held**
SIC: 2499 Food handling & processing products, wood

(P-3455)
SURVEY STAKE AND MARKER INC
Also Called: Nichols Lumber
13470 Dalewood St, Baldwin Park (91706-5834)
PHONE..........................626 960-4802

Judith A Nichols, *President*
Evelyn M Rumsey, *Vice Pres*
Charles F Nichols, *Admin Sec*
Charles Nichols, *Admin Sec*
EMP: 42 **EST:** 1956
SQ FT: 3,000
SALES (est): 1.5MM **Privately Held**
WEB: www.nicholslumber.com
SIC: 2499 Surveyors' stakes, wood

(P-3456)
TIMMONS WOOD PRODUCTS INC
4675 Wade Ave, Perris (92571-7494)
PHONE..........................951 940-4700
Eddie Timmons, *President*
Shaine Timmons, *Vice Pres*
EMP: 24 **EST:** 1948
SQ FT: 45,000
SALES (est): 3.1MM **Privately Held**
SIC: 2499 Handles, poles, dowels & stakes: wood

(P-3457)
UNIVERSITY FRAMES INC
3060 E Miraloma Ave, Anaheim (92806-1810)
PHONE..........................714 575-5100
John G Winn, *CEO*
Diane Winn, *Vice Pres*
Liz Smith, *Executive*
Danny Winn, *Opers Mgr*
John Winn, *Director*
▲ **EMP:** 50 **EST:** 1996
SQ FT: 20,000
SALES (est): 10.3MM **Privately Held**
WEB: www.universityframes.com
SIC: 2499 5999 Picture frame molding, finished; picture frames, ready made

(P-3458)
WALTON COMPANY INC
17900 Sampson Ln, Huntington Beach (92647-7149)
PHONE..........................714 847-8800
Don Walton, *President*
◆ **EMP:** 26 **EST:** 1960
SQ FT: 12,000
SALES (est): 2.8MM **Privately Held**
WEB: www.thewaltoncompany.com
SIC: 2499 Cork & cork products

(P-3459)
YTI ENTERPRISES INC
Also Called: Laminating Technologies
1260 S State College Pkwy, Anaheim (92806-5240)
PHONE..........................714 632-8696
Judith Rochverger, *President*
Jair N Rochverger, *CFO*
EMP: 15 **EST:** 1996
SQ FT: 16,500
SALES (est): 4.6MM **Privately Held**
SIC: 2499 Seats, toilet

2511 Wood Household Furniture

(P-3460)
ALDER & CO LLC
412 Wallace St, Bakersfield (93307-1447)
PHONE..........................661 326-0320
Bryan Shimp, *Mng Member*
Adriana Caceres, *Partner*
Jose Luis Garcia,
Adan Perez,
Humberto Cobian, *Mng Member*
EMP: 14 **EST:** 2004
SQ FT: 10,000
SALES (est): 1.1MM **Privately Held**
WEB: www.alderandco.com
SIC: 2511 Wood household furniture

(P-3461)
ARTS CUSTOM CABINETS INC
897 E Tulare Rd, Lindsay (93247-2244)
P.O. Box 218 (93247-0218)
PHONE..........................559 562-2766
Art Serna, *President*
Leonor Dela Fuente Serna, *Admin Sec*
EMP: 23 **EST:** 1976
SQ FT: 45,000

SALES (est): 2.2MM **Privately Held**
WEB: www.artscabinets.com
SIC: 2511 2434 Kitchen & dining room furniture; vanities; bathroom: wood

(P-3462)
ASPEN BRANDS CORPORATION
2959 Fairview Rd, Costa Mesa (92626-4117)
PHONE..........................702 946-9430
Michael Rocha, *CEO*
▲ **EMP:** 14 **EST:** 2016
SALES (est): 772.9K **Privately Held**
WEB: www.aspenbrands.com
SIC: 2511 3231 3641 5021 Chairs, household, except upholstered: wood; tables, household: wood; products of purchased glass; electric light bulbs, complete; tables, occasional; chairs; glassware; lighting fixtures

(P-3463)
AW INDUSTRIES INC
Also Called: Skog Furniture
1810 S Reservoir St, Pomona (91766-5541)
PHONE..........................909 629-1500
Ted Wong, *President*
Beatrice Wong, *Admin Sec*
▲ **EMP:** 13 **EST:** 1985
SQ FT: 46,000
SALES (est): 578.5K **Privately Held**
SIC: 2511 Wood household furniture

(P-3464)
BAU FURNITURE MFG INC (PA)
21 Kelly Ln, Ladera Ranch (92694-1463)
PHONE..........................949 643-2729
Thomas Bau, *President*
Linda Bau, *President*
EMP: 40 **EST:** 1978
SALES (est): 3.4MM **Privately Held**
SIC: 2511 2512 2521 Tables, household: wood; chairs, household, except upholstered: wood; upholstered household furniture; tables, office: wood; chairs, office: padded, upholstered or plain: wood

(P-3465)
BIG TREE FURNITURE & INDS INC (PA)
760 S Vail Ave, Montebello (90640-4954)
PHONE..........................310 894-7500
Joe Ho, *CEO*
Leticia Melendez, *Supervisor*
◆ **EMP:** 49 **EST:** 1985
SALES (est): 8.5MM **Privately Held**
SIC: 2511 Wood household furniture

(P-3466)
BROWNWOOD FURNITURE INC
9805 6th St Ste 104, Rancho Cucamonga (91730-5751)
PHONE..........................909 945-5613
Rick Vartanian, *President*
Pat Eberly, *Vice Pres*
Jose Navarro, *Vice Pres*
◆ **EMP:** 150 **EST:** 1979
SQ FT: 107,000
SALES (est): 5.3MM **Privately Held**
WEB: www.brownwoodfurniture.com
SIC: 2511 Wood bedroom furniture

(P-3467)
DOREL HOME FURNISHINGS INC
5400 Shea Center Dr, Ontario (91761-7892)
PHONE..........................909 390-5705
EMP: 157
SALES (corp-wide): 2.7B **Privately Held**
WEB: www.ameriwoodhome.com
SIC: 2511 Console tables: wood; coffee tables: wood; tea wagons: wood
HQ: Dorel Home Furnishings, Inc.
410 E 1st St S
Wright City MO 63390
636 745-3351

(P-3468)
DOUG MOCKETT & COMPANY INC
1915 Abalone Ave, Torrance (90501-3706)
P.O. Box 3333, Manhattan Beach (90266-1333)
PHONE..........................310 318-2491
Susan Darby Gordon, *CEO*
Tyra Cunningham, *President*
Edwin Deacruz, *Executive*
Sonia Marie H Mockett, *Admin Sec*
Diego Wuethrich, *IT Executive*
◆ **EMP:** 40 **EST:** 1984
SALES (est): 11.5MM **Privately Held**
WEB: www.mockett.com
SIC: 2511 Unassembled or unfinished furniture, household: wood

(P-3469)
DROPSHIP VENDOR GROUP LLC
Also Called: Vifah
9469 Opal Ave Ste 6, Mentone (92359-9901)
PHONE..........................424 391-6943
▲ **EMP:** 50
SALES (est): 10MM **Privately Held**
WEB: www.vifahwholesale.com
SIC: 5712 2511 2514 Furniture Stores

(P-3470)
EMANUEL MOREZ INC
Also Called: Amos Art Studio
8754 Yolanda Ave, Northridge (91324-3831)
PHONE..........................818 780-2787
Amos Stockfish, *President*
▲ **EMP:** 16 **EST:** 1987
SQ FT: 26,000
SALES (est): 1MM **Privately Held**
WEB: www.emanuelmorez.com
SIC: 2511 2499 1751 Wood household furniture; decorative wood & woodwork; carved & turned wood; cabinet & finish carpentry

(P-3471)
FREMARC INDUSTRIES INC (PA)
Also Called: Fremarc Designs
18810 San Jose Ave, City of Industry (91748-1325)
PHONE..........................626 965-0802
Maurice M Donenfeld, *President*
Harriette Donenfeld, *Corp Secy*
▲ **EMP:** 78
SQ FT: 45,000
SALES (est): 7.6MM **Privately Held**
WEB: www.fremarc.com
SIC: 2511 Wood household furniture

(P-3472)
FRENCH TRADITION (PA)
2413 Moreton St, Torrance (90505-5310)
PHONE..........................310 719-9977
Franck Valles, *President*
Julie Valles, *Vice Pres*
EMP: 15 **EST:** 1984
SALES (est): 2.9MM **Privately Held**
WEB: www.thefrenchtradition.com
SIC: 2511 Wood household furniture

(P-3473)
FURNITURE TECHNICS INC
Also Called: Furniture Techniques
2900 Supply Ave, Commerce (90040-2708)
PHONE..........................562 802-0261
Cesar Rousseau, *President*
Ricardo Flores, *Admin Sec*
EMP: 25 **EST:** 1988
SALES (est): 266.4K **Privately Held**
SIC: 2511 2426 Wood household furniture; furniture stock & parts, hardwood

(P-3474)
JP PRODUCTS LLC
2054 Davie Ave, Commerce (90040-1705)
PHONE..........................310 237-6237
Patrick Mooney, *Mng Member*
Arthur Felix, *Sales Staff*
Jacqueline Mooney, *Mng Member*
EMP: 46 **EST:** 2010
SQ FT: 35,000
SALES (est): 3.5MM **Privately Held**
SIC: 2511 Wood household furniture

(P-3475)
LANPAR INC
Also Called: Oakwood Interiors
1333 S Bon View Ave, Ontario
(91761-4404)
PHONE.....................541 484-1962
Nick Lanphier, *Ch of Bd*
▲ **EMP:** 16 **EST:** 1982
SQ FT: 180,000
SALES (est): 565K **Privately Held**
WEB: www.fineoak.com
SIC: 2511 Wood bedroom furniture

(P-3476)
LEGACY COMMERCIAL HOLDINGS INC
Also Called: Armen Living
28939 Avenue Williams, Valencia
(91355-4183)
PHONE.....................818 767-6626
Kevin Kevonian, *President*
Kevon Kevonian, *President*
Jim Sperrazza, *Exec VP*
Honigsfeld Lee, *Vice Pres*
Lily Mendoza, *Purchasing*
▲ **EMP:** 25 **EST:** 2007
SALES (est): 23.3MM **Privately Held**
WEB: www.armenliving.com
SIC: 2511 2514 2531 2521 Kitchen & dining room furniture; metal lawn & garden furniture; public building & related furniture; wood office furniture

(P-3477)
M F G EUROTEC INC
Also Called: BV Wilms
84464 Cabazon Center Dr, Indio
(92201-6200)
PHONE.....................760 863-0033
Jody R Williams, *President*
A R Williams, *Treasurer*
William Vinton Williams, *Principal*
Jason Williams, *Admin Sec*
EMP: 13 **EST:** 1993
SQ FT: 18,500
SALES (est): 1.2MM **Privately Held**
SIC: 2511 5211 1751 Wood household furniture; cabinets, kitchen; cabinet & finish carpentry

(P-3478)
MIKHAIL DARAFEEV INC (PA)
5075 Edison Ave, Chino (91710-5716)
PHONE.....................909 613-1818
Antonina Darafeev, *President*
Paul Darafeev, *Treasurer*
George Darafeev, *Admin Sec*
▲ **EMP:** 50 **EST:** 1957
SALES (est): 11.5MM **Privately Held**
WEB: www.darafeev.com
SIC: 2511 Stools, household: wood

(P-3479)
MINTON-SPIDELL INC (PA)
8467 Steller Dr, Culver City (90232-2424)
PHONE.....................310 836-0403
Maurice N Spidell, *President*
Rick A Nelson, *Agent*
EMP: 17 **EST:** 1959
SQ FT: 9,000
SALES (est): 1.5MM **Privately Held**
WEB: www.minton-spidell.com
SIC: 2511 Wood household furniture

(P-3480)
MORETTIS DESIGN COLLECTION
16926 Keegan Ave Ste C, Carson
(90746-1322)
PHONE.....................310 638-5555
Mori Afshar, *President*
Gwen Rawlins, *Office Mgr*
▲ **EMP:** 30 **EST:** 1992
SALES (est): 1.9MM **Privately Held**
WEB: www.morettisdesign.com
SIC: 2511 Wood household furniture; kitchen & dining room furniture

(P-3481)
NEWCO INTERNATIONAL INC
Also Called: Harmony Kids
13600 Vaughn St, San Fernando
(91340-3017)
PHONE.....................818 834-7100
Howard Napolske, *President*

Ernest Johnston, *Vice Pres*
▲ **EMP:** 19 **EST:** 2004
SQ FT: 20,000
SALES (est): 1.3MM **Privately Held**
WEB: www.newcointernational.com
SIC: 2511 Children's wood furniture

(P-3482)
NOVA LIFESTYLE INC (PA)
6565 E Washington Blvd, Commerce
(90040-1821)
PHONE.....................323 888-9999
Thanh H Lam, *Ch of Bd*
Jeffery Chuang, *CFO*
Charlie La, *Bd of Directors*
Huy La, *Bd of Directors*
Steven Qiang Liu, *Vice Pres*
EMP: 22 **EST:** 2011
SALES (est): 11.3MM **Publicly Held**
WEB: www.novalifestyle.com
SIC: 2511 2512 Wood household furniture; upholstered household furniture; chairs: upholstered on wood frames

(P-3483)
OAK TREE FURNITURE INC
13681 Newport Ave Ste 8, Tustin
(92780-7815)
PHONE.....................562 944-0754
Tim Sopp, *President*
Elaine Sopp, *Vice Pres*
▲ **EMP:** 14 **EST:** 1977
SALES (est): 640K **Privately Held**
WEB: www.oaktreefurnitureredding.com
SIC: 2511 Wood household furniture

(P-3484)
P J MILLIGAN COMPANY LLC (PA)
Also Called: P J Milligan & Associates
436 E Gutierrez St, Santa Barbara
(93101-1709)
PHONE.....................805 963-4038
Patrick Milligan, *CEO*
▲ **EMP:** 13 **EST:** 1989
SQ FT: 18,000 **Privately Held**
SIC: 2511 5712 Wood household furniture; furniture stores

(P-3485)
PLUSH HOME INC
6507 Lindenhurst Ave, Los Angeles
(90048-4733)
PHONE.....................323 852-1912
Steven Ho, *President*
EMP: 14 **EST:** 2003
SALES (est): 1MM **Privately Held**
WEB: www.plushhome.com
SIC: 2511 7389 Wood household furniture; interior designer

(P-3486)
RADFORD CABINETS INC
216 E Avenue K8, Lancaster (93535-4527)
PHONE.....................661 729-8931
Steven Radford, *President*
Katie Radford, *CFO*
Robert Mendoza, *Vice Pres*
Sue Allen, *Executive*
Sharon Radford, *Admin Sec*
EMP: 70 **EST:** 1992
SQ FT: 20,000
SALES (est): 9.2MM **Privately Held**
WEB: www.radfordcabinetsinc.com
SIC: 2511 2434 2521 Kitchen & dining room furniture; wood kitchen cabinets; cabinets, office: wood

(P-3487)
RUSS BASSETT CORP
Also Called: Group Five
8189 Byron Rd, Whittier (90606-2615)
PHONE.....................562 945-2445
Mike Dressendorfer, *CEO*
Peter Fink, *President*
Sasha Johnson, *President*
Marie Gomez, *Human Resources*
▲ **EMP:** 115 **EST:** 1959
SQ FT: 112,000
SALES (est): 24.1MM **Privately Held**
WEB: www.russbassett.com
SIC: 2511 Wood household furniture

(P-3488)
SANDBERG FURNITURE MFG CO INC (PA)
5705 Alcoa Ave, Vernon (90058-3794)
P.O. Box 58291, Los Angeles (90058-0291)
PHONE.....................323 582-0711
John Sandberg, *CEO*
Linda Hart, *COO*
Mark Nixon, *Senior VP*
Thomas Bass, *VP Finance*
Scott Sandberg, *Marketing Staff*
▲ **EMP:** 225 **EST:** 1918
SALES (est): 35.3MM **Privately Held**
WEB: www.sandbergfurniture.com
SIC: 2511 Wood bedroom furniture

(P-3489)
TEXTURED DESIGN FURNITURE INC
Also Called: Texture Design
1303 S Claudina St, Anaheim
(92805-6235)
PHONE.....................714 502-9121
J Luis Gonzales, *President*
▲ **EMP:** 34 **EST:** 1985
SQ FT: 34,000
SALES (est): 761.1K **Privately Held**
SIC: 2511 Wood household furniture

(P-3490)
TREND MANOR FURN MFG CO INC
17047 Gale Ave, City of Industry
(91745-1808)
PHONE.....................626 964-6493
Theodore Vecchione, *President*
▲ **EMP:** 42 **EST:** 1946
SQ FT: 63,000
SALES (est): 4.6MM **Privately Held**
WEB: www.trendmanor.com
SIC: 2511 Wood household furniture

(P-3491)
WEST COAST CATRG TRCKS MFG INC
1217 Goodrich Blvd, Commerce
(90022-5124)
PHONE.....................323 278-1279
Juan Gomez, *President*
Jesus Gomez, *Director*
EMP: 14 **EST:** 2004
SQ FT: 18,000
SALES (est): 1.1MM **Privately Held**
WEB: www.westcoastcateringtrucks.com
SIC: 2511 Stands, household, wood

(P-3492)
WOODLAND BEDROOMS INC
3423 Merced St, Los Angeles
(90065-1660)
PHONE.....................562 408-1558
Gustavo Loza, *President*
Delia Loza, *Vice Pres*
▲ **EMP:** 15 **EST:** 1981
SQ FT: 60,000
SALES (est): 1.1MM **Privately Held**
WEB: www.woodlandbed.com
SIC: 2511 Wood household furniture

(P-3493)
WOODVILLE INC
11680 Wright Rd, Lynwood (90262-3945)
PHONE.....................323 636-0223
George Graff, *President*
Bill Gray, *Treasurer*
Terry Hendrickson, *Vice Pres*
Shirley Graff, *Admin Sec*
EMP: 13 **EST:** 1979
SQ FT: 50,000
SALES (est): 146.5K **Privately Held**
SIC: 2511 Bed frames, except water bed frames: wood

2512 Wood Household Furniture, Upholstered

(P-3494)
A RUDIN INC (PA)
Also Called: A Rudin Designs
6062 Alcoa Ave, Vernon (90058-3902)
PHONE.....................323 589-5547
Arnold Rudin, *President*

Ralph Rudin, *Vice Pres*
Louis Dechristopher, *Sales Staff*
◆ **EMP:** 92 **EST:** 1918
SQ FT: 117,000
SALES (est): 8MM **Privately Held**
WEB: www.arudin.com
SIC: 2512 5021 Upholstered household furniture; household furniture

(P-3495)
AMERASIA FURN CMPNNTS MFG IMPR
2772 Norton Ave, Lynwood (90262-1835)
PHONE.....................310 638-0570
Khue Van Cao, *CEO*
Alfred Varela Jr, *President*
▲ **EMP:** 22 **EST:** 2006
SQ FT: 55,000
SALES (est): 476.6K **Privately Held**
SIC: 2512 Upholstered household furniture

(P-3496)
BURTON JAMES INC
428 Turnbull Canyon Rd, City of Industry
(91745-1011)
PHONE.....................626 961-7221
Raymond Zoref, *CEO*
Harry Robbins, *CFO*
Brandy Wong, *Director*
EMP: 80 **EST:** 1983
SQ FT: 28,000
SALES (est): 9.7MM **Privately Held**
WEB: www.burtonjames.com
SIC: 2512 Upholstered household furniture

(P-3497)
CHROMCRAFT RVNGTON DOUGLAS IND (PA)
Also Called: Douglas Casual Living
1011 S Grove Ave, Ontario (91761-3437)
PHONE.....................909 930-9891
Willa LI, *CEO*
▲ **EMP:** 31 **EST:** 2008
SQ FT: 45,000
SALES (est): 10MM **Privately Held**
SIC: 2512 5021 Upholstered household furniture; household furniture

(P-3498)
CISCO BROS CORP (PA)
Also Called: Cisco & Brothers Designs
5340 Harbor St, Commerce (90040-3927)
PHONE.....................323 778-8612
Francisco Pinedo, *CEO*
Alba E Pinedo, *Exec VP*
Tyson Radtke, *Site Mgr*
◆ **EMP:** 145 **EST:** 1993
SALES (est): 25.8MM **Privately Held**
WEB: www.ciscohome.net
SIC: 2512 Upholstered household furniture

(P-3499)
COMMERCIAL INTR RESOURCES INC
Also Called: Contract Resources
6077 Rickenbacker Rd, Commerce
(90040-3031)
PHONE.....................562 926-5885
Roberta Tuchman, *CEO*
Stanley Rice, *President*
Barbara Rice, *Corp Secy*
Stephanie Lesko, *Vice Pres*
EMP: 65
SQ FT: 28,000
SALES (est): 7.6MM **Privately Held**
WEB: www.villahallmark.com
SIC: 2512 Upholstered household furniture

(P-3500)
CUSTOM UPHOLSTERED FURN INC
Also Called: Upholstery Workroom
5000 W Jefferson Blvd, Los Angeles
(90016-3925)
PHONE.....................323 731-3033
EMP: 14
SALES (est): 982.6K **Privately Held**
SIC: 2512 Mfg Upholstered Household Furniture

(P-3501)
DELLAROBBIA INC (PA)
119 Waterworks Way, Irvine (92618-3110)
PHONE.....................949 251-9532
David Soonlan, *President*

▲ = Import ▼=Export
◆ =Import/Export

Sunee Soonlan, *Admin Sec*
▲ **EMP:** 48 **EST:** 1979
SQ FT: 27,000
SALES (est): 1.9MM **Privately Held**
SIC: 2512 Upholstered household furniture

(P-3502)
E J LAUREN LLC
Also Called: Ejl
9400 Hall Rd, Downey (90241-5365)
PHONE..................................562 803-1113
Antonio Ocampo, *Mng Member*
◆ **EMP:** 50 **EST:** 2009
SQ FT: 20,000
SALES (est): 5.8MM **Privately Held**
WEB: www.ejlauren.com
SIC: 2512 Upholstered household furniture

(P-3503)
GENESIS TC INC
Also Called: Genesis 2000
524 Hofgaarden St, La Puente
(91744-5529)
PHONE..................................626 968-4455
Anthony Moreno, *President*
EMP: 17 **EST:** 2003
SALES (est): 864K **Privately Held**
SIC: 2512 Wood upholstered chairs &
couches

(P-3504)
GOMEN FURNITURE MFG INC
11612 Wright Rd, Lynwood (90262-3945)
PHONE..................................310 635-4894
Leonardo Gonzalez, *President*
▲ **EMP:** 30 **EST:** 1990
SALES (est): 3MM **Privately Held**
WEB: www.gomenfurnmfg.com
SIC: 2512 7641 Upholstered household
furniture; upholstery work

(P-3505)
HAMMER COLLECTION INC
14427 S Main St, Gardena (90248-1913)
P.O. Box 2458, Manhattan Beach (90267-
2458)
PHONE..................................310 515-0276
Frank Hammer, *President*
Eva Hammer, *Vice Pres*
▲ **EMP:** 23 **EST:** 1989
SQ FT: 30,000
SALES (est): 615.8K **Privately Held**
WEB: www.hammerfinefurniture.com
SIC: 2512 2511 Upholstered household
furniture; wood household furniture

(P-3506)
HARBOR FURNITURE MFG INC
(PA)
Also Called: Harbor House
12508 Center St, South Gate (90280-8079)
PHONE..................................323 636-1201
Malcolm Tuttleton Jr, *President*
Brent Tuttleton, *Vice Pres*
▲ **EMP:** 25 **EST:** 1929
SQ FT: 40,000
SALES (est): 2.6MM **Privately Held**
SIC: 2512 2511 6514 2521 Upholstered
household furniture; wood household fur-
niture; dwelling operators, except apart-
ments; wood office furniture

(P-3507)
LITTLE CASTLE FURNITURE CO
INC
301 Todd Ct, Oxnard (93030-5192)
P.O. Box 4254, Westlake Village (91359-
1254)
PHONE..................................805 278-4646
Kayvan Torabian, *President*
▲ **EMP:** 24 **EST:** 1998
SQ FT: 9,000
SALES (est): 4.4MM **Privately Held**
WEB: www.littlecastleinc.com
SIC: 2512 Upholstered household furniture

(P-3508)
MARGE CARSON INC (PA)
13300 Crssrads Pkwy N Ste, City of Indus-
try (91746)
P.O. Box 1283, Pomona (91769-1283)
PHONE..................................626 571-1111
James Labarge, *CEO*
Dominic Ching, *CFO*
Laura Lady, *Executive*
Braulio Ornelas, *Plant Mgr*

Laura Labarge, *Mktg Dir*
▲ **EMP:** 82 **EST:** 1951
SQ FT: 88,000
SALES (est): 17.6MM **Privately Held**
WEB: www.margecarson.com
SIC: 2512 2511 Living room furniture: up-
holstered on wood frames; wood house-
hold furniture

(P-3509)
MARLIN DESIGNS LLC
1900 E Warner Ave Ste J, Santa Ana
(92705-5549)
PHONE..................................949 637-7257
Ronald Whitlock, *Mng Member*
EMP: 150 **EST:** 1995
SALES (est): 13MM **Privately Held**
WEB: www.marlin-designs.com
SIC: 2512 Upholstered household furniture

(P-3510)
MARTIN/BRATTRUD INC
1224 W 132nd St, Gardena (90247-1566)
PHONE..................................323 770-4171
Allan G Stratford, *President*
Patrick Baxter, *Vice Pres*
Martin Brattrud, *Vice Pres*
EMP: 95
SQ FT: 38,000
SALES (est): 14.3MM **Privately Held**
WEB: www.martinbrattrud.com
SIC: 2512 2511 Upholstered household
furniture; tables, household: wood

(P-3511)
MIKE CIMS INC
2300 E Curry St, Long Beach (90805-3211)
PHONE..................................562 428-8390
Lucia Angela Cimarusti, *CEO*
◆ **EMP:** 39 **EST:** 1980
SQ FT: 100,000
SALES (est): 1.5MM **Privately Held**
WEB: www.mikecims.com
SIC: 2512 Living room furniture: uphol-
stered on wood frames

(P-3512)
MPB FURNITURE
CORPORATION
Also Called: Ashley Furniture
414 W Ridgecrest Blvd, Ridgecrest
(93555-4015)
PHONE..................................760 375-4800
Mike McGee, *President*
Bill Farris, *General Mgr*
EMP: 33 **EST:** 2005
SQ FT: 18,000
SALES (est): 1MM **Privately Held**
WEB: www.ashleyfurniture.com
SIC: 2512 Upholstered household furniture

(P-3513)
RC FURNITURE INC
1111 Jellick Ave, City of Industry
(91748-1212)
PHONE..................................626 964-4100
Rene Cazares, *President*
▲ **EMP:** 81 **EST:** 1986
SQ FT: 25,000
SALES (est): 17MM **Privately Held**
WEB: www.renecazares.com
SIC: 2512 5021 Upholstered household
furniture; furniture

(P-3514)
REPUBLIC FURNITURE MFG
INC
2241 E 49th St, Vernon (90058-2822)
PHONE..................................323 235-2144
Karen Rosen-Hirsch, *President*
Judy Rosen, *Vice Pres*
EMP: 22 **EST:** 1963
SQ FT: 38,000
SALES (est): 1MM **Privately Held**
WEB: www.republicfurniture.net
SIC: 2512 2515 Living room furniture: up-
holstered on wood frames; mattresses &
bedsprings

(P-3515)
ROMAN UPHOLSTERY MFG INC
2008 Cotner Ave, Los Angeles
(90025-5604)
PHONE..................................310 479-3252
Steven Hipsman, *President*
Arthur J Hipsman, *Treasurer*

EMP: 14 **EST:** 1963
SQ FT: 5,000
SALES (est): 900K **Privately Held**
SIC: 2512 7641 Upholstered household
furniture; reupholstery

(P-3516)
ROYAL CUSTOM DESIGNS LLC
13951 Monte Vista Ave, Chino
(91710-5536)
PHONE..................................909 591-8990
Raya Trietsch, *President*
Darius Panah, *CEO*
George Trietsch, *Treasurer*
Jack Sissoyev, *CIO*
Martha Clark, *Project Dir*
▲ **EMP:** 120
SQ FT: 35,000
SALES (est): 17.4MM **Privately Held**
WEB: www.royalcustomdesigns.com
SIC: 2512 Upholstered household furniture

(P-3517)
SOFA U LOVE LLC (PA)
Also Called: Factory Showroom Exchange
1207 N Western Ave, Los Angeles
(90029-1018)
PHONE..................................323 464-3397
Varougan Karapetian, *President*
EMP: 22 **EST:** 1976
SQ FT: 22,000
SALES (est): 3.7MM **Privately Held**
WEB: www.sofaulove.com
SIC: 2512 5712 Upholstered household
furniture; furniture stores

(P-3518)
SOLE DESIGNS INC
11685 Mcbean Dr, El Monte (91732-1104)
PHONE..................................626 452-8642
Linda Le, *CEO*
Lam Tran, *President*
▲ **EMP:** 17 **EST:** 1996
SQ FT: 8,000
SALES (est): 2.5MM **Privately Held**
WEB: www.soledesigns.com
SIC: 2512 Upholstered household furniture

(P-3519)
STITCH INDUSTRIES INC
Also Called: Joybird
6055 E Wash Blvd Ste 900, Commerce
(90040-2453)
PHONE..................................888 282-0842
Kurt L Darrow, *CEO*
Chris Stormer, *Shareholder*
EMP: 50 **EST:** 2013
SALES (est): 28.3MM
SALES (corp-wide): 1.7B **Publicly Held**
WEB: www.joybird.com
SIC: 2512 5961 5712 Upholstered house-
hold furniture; catalog & mail-order
houses; furniture stores
PA: La-Z-Boy Incorporated
1 Lazboy Dr
Monroe MI 48162
734 242-1444

(P-3520)
SUPERB CHAIR CORPORATION
Also Called: Patricia Edwards
6861 Watcher St, Commerce (90040-3715)
PHONE..................................562 776-1771
Audrey Smith, *President*
James E Smith, *Vice Pres*
Julie Smith, *Vice Pres*
EMP: 27 **EST:** 1971
SQ FT: 36,000
SALES (est): 1.6MM **Privately Held**
WEB: www.patriciaedwards.com
SIC: 2512 Living room furniture: uphol-
stered on wood frames; chairs: uphol-
stered on wood frames; couches, sofas &
davenports: upholstered on wood frames

(P-3521)
VIOSKI INC
1625 S Magnolia Ave, Monrovia
(91016-4509)
PHONE..................................626 359-4571
Douglas Desantis, *CEO*
EMP: 17 **EST:** 2015
SALES (est): 441K **Privately Held**
WEB: www.vioski.com
SIC: 2512 Couches, sofas & davenports:
upholstered on wood frames

(P-3522)
YEN-NHAI INC
Also Called: Nathan Anthony Furniture
4940 District Blvd, Vernon (90058-2718)
PHONE..................................323 584-1315
Khai MAI, *President*
Norman Mojica, *Manager*
EMP: 40 **EST:** 1995
SALES (est): 3.6MM **Privately Held**
WEB: www.nafurniture.com
SIC: 2512 Upholstered household furniture

2514 Metal Household
Furniture

(P-3523)
A A CATER TRUCK MFG CO INC
Also Called: Hizco Truck Body
750 E Slauson Ave, Los Angeles
(90011-5236)
PHONE..................................323 233-2343
Vahe Karapetian, *President*
Richard Gomez, *Engineer*
Clarence Stokes, *Asst Controller*
EMP: 35 **EST:** 1971
SQ FT: 60,000
SALES (est): 1.6MM **Privately Held**
WEB: www.aacatertruck.com
SIC: 2514 7538 Metal household furniture;
general truck repair

(P-3524)
ALL AMERICAN FRAME & BEDG
CORP
4641 Ardine St, Cudahy (90201-5801)
PHONE..................................323 773-7415
Don Diep, *President*
Suzuyo Diep, *Admin Sec*
▲ **EMP:** 18 **EST:** 1989
SQ FT: 10,600
SALES (est): 1.4MM **Privately Held**
WEB: www.allamericanframe.com
SIC: 2514 Beds, including folding & cabi-
net, household: metal; frames for box
springs or bedsprings: metal

(P-3525)
ATLANTIC REPRESENTATIONS
INC
Also Called: Snowsound USA
10018 Santa Fe Springs Rd, Santa Fe
Springs (90670-2922)
P.O. Box 2399 (90670-0399)
PHONE..................................562 903-9550
Leo Dardashti, *President*
Shahriar Dardashti, *President*
Michael Dardashti, *Exec VP*
Farnaz Dardashti, *Vice Pres*
Matt Penalber, *Project Dir*
▲ **EMP:** 30 **EST:** 1984
SQ FT: 150,000
SALES (est): 7.3MM **Privately Held**
WEB: www.atlantic-inc.com
SIC: 2514 2511 Metal household furniture;
wood household furniture

(P-3526)
ATLAS SURVIVAL SHELTERS
LLC
7407 Telegraph Rd, Montebello
(90640-6515)
PHONE..................................323 727-7084
Ronal D Hubbard, *Mng Member*
EMP: 25 **EST:** 2011
SQ FT: 30,000 **Privately Held**
WEB: www.atlassurvivalshelters.com
SIC: 2514 Beds, including folding & cabi-
net, household: metal

(P-3527)
CASUALWAY USA LLC
Also Called: Casualway Home & Garden
1623 Lola Way, Oxnard (93030-5080)
PHONE..................................805 660-7408
Guoxiang Wu,
Jian He, *Co-Owner*
Ralph Ybarra, *Vice Pres*
EMP: 99
SALES (est): 2.4MM **Privately Held**
SIC: 2514 Garden furniture, metal

(P-3528)
GRACO CHILDRENS PRODUCTS INC
17182 Nevada St, Victorville (92394-7806)
PHONE.....................770 418-7200
EMP: 195
SALES (corp-wide): 9.3B Publicly Held
SIC: 2514 Juvenile furniture, household: metal
HQ: Graco Children's Products Inc.
6655 Pachtree Dunwoody Rd
Atlanta GA 30328
770 418-7200

(P-3529)
JBI LLC
Also Called: Buchbinder, Jay Industries
18521 S Santa Fe Ave, Compton
(90221-5624)
PHONE.....................310 537-2910
Claudio Luna, Manager
EMP: 49
SALES (corp-wide): 63.1MM Privately Held
WEB: www.jbi-interiors.com
SIC: 2514 2221 2511 Tables, household: metal; fiberglass fabrics; wood household furniture
PA: Jbi, Llc
2650 E El Presidio St
Long Beach CA 90810
310 886-8034

(P-3530)
JONATHAN LOUIS INTERNATIONAL
12919 S Figueroa St, Los Angeles
(90061-1134)
PHONE.....................323 770-3330
Juan Valle, President
EMP: 70 EST: 1985
SALES (est): 2MM Privately Held
WEB: www.jonathanlouis.net
SIC: 2514 Metal kitchen & dining room furniture

(P-3531)
PACIFIC CASUAL LLC
1060 Avenida Acaso, Camarillo
(93012-8712)
PHONE.....................805 445-8310
Rick Stephens, Mng Member
Dale C Boles, CEO
Peter Schultz, Vice Pres
Shaun Sweeney, Vice Pres
Jay Weber, Vice Pres
▲ EMP: 35 EST: 2002
SQ FT: 29,000
SALES (est): 5.5MM Privately Held
WEB: www.pacificcasual.com
SIC: 2514 Metal lawn & garden furniture

(P-3532)
RSI HOME PRODUCTS INC (HQ)
400 E Orangethorpe Ave, Anaheim
(92801-1046)
PHONE.....................714 449-2200
Alex Calabrese, CEO
David Lowrie, CFO
Dwayne Medlin, Chief Mktg Ofcr
Jeff Hoeft, Exec VP
Jonathan Keefe, Vice Pres
▲ EMP: 700 EST: 1994
SQ FT: 675,000
SALES (est): 1B
SALES (corp-wide): 1.7B Publicly Held
WEB: www.americanwoodmark.com
SIC: 2514 2541 3281 2434 Kitchen cabinets: metal; counter & sink tops; cut stone & stone products; wood kitchen cabinets
PA: American Woodmark Corporation
561 Shady Elm Rd
Winchester VA 22602
540 665-9100

(P-3533)
RSI HOME PRODUCTS MFG INC
400 E Orangethorpe Ave, Anaheim
(92801-1046)
P.O. Box 4120 (92803-4120)
PHONE.....................714 449-2200
Thomas Chieffe, CEO
Jeff Hoeft, President
▲ EMP: 100 EST: 2000

SALES (est): 70.9MM
SALES (corp-wide): 1.7B Publicly Held
WEB: www.americanwoodmark.com
SIC: 2514 2541 3281 2434 Kitchen cabinets: metal; counter & sink tops; cut stone & stone products; wood kitchen cabinets
HQ: Rsi Home Products, Inc.
400 E Orangethorpe Ave
Anaheim CA 92801
714 449-2200

(P-3534)
SURROUNDING ELEMENTS LLC
33051 Calle Aviador Ste A, San Juan Capistrano (92675-4780)
PHONE.....................949 582-9000
Moss Shacter, Mng Member
Anthony C Geach,
EMP: 20 EST: 2001
SQ FT: 15,000
SALES (est): 2.4MM Privately Held
WEB: www.surroundingelements.com
SIC: 2514 Lawn furniture: metal

(P-3535)
TREASURE GARDEN INC (PA)
13401 Brooks Dr, Baldwin Park
(91706-2294)
PHONE.....................626 814-0168
Oliver MA, President
Margaret Chang, COO
Benjamin MA, Vice Pres
Traci Lyons, Marketing Staff
Jennifer Dorr, Sales Staff
◆ EMP: 50 EST: 1984
SQ FT: 45,000
SALES (est): 27.7MM Privately Held
WEB: www.treasuregarden.com
SIC: 5261 2514 Nurseries & garden centers; lawn furniture: metal

(P-3536)
TROPITONE FURNITURE CO INC (HQ)
5 Marconi, Irvine (92618-2594)
PHONE.....................949 595-2010
Randy Danielson, Exec VP
Randall Danielson, CFO
Iris Barrios, Engineer
Jacqueline Yang, Accountant
Teri Hatzenbuhler, Sales Staff
◆ EMP: 300 EST: 1954
SQ FT: 100,000
SALES (est): 100MM Privately Held
WEB: www.tropitone.com
SIC: 2514 2522 Garden furniture, metal; camp furniture: metal; office furniture, except wood

(P-3537)
VICTOR MARTIN INC
Also Called: Corsican Furniture
1640 W 132nd St, Gardena (90249-2039)
PHONE.....................323 587-3101
Martin Perfit, President
Marvin Alperin, General Ptnr
EMP: 25 EST: 1972
SQ FT: 100,000
SALES (est): 378.4K Privately Held
SIC: 2514 Beds, including folding & cabinet, household: metal

(P-3538)
WESLEY ALLEN INC (PA)
Also Called: Iron Beds of America
1001 E 60th St, Los Angeles (90001-1098)
PHONE.....................323 231-4275
Victor Sawan, CEO
Reyes Meza, Prdtn Mgr
▲ EMP: 140 EST: 1976
SQ FT: 100,000
SALES (est): 19MM Privately Held
WEB: www.wesleyallen.com
SIC: 2514 Metal household furniture

2515 Mattresses & Bedsprings

(P-3539)
ADVANCED INNVTIVE RCVERY TECH (PA)
Also Called: Smart Foam Pads
23615 El Toro Rd Ste 207, Lake Forest
(92630-4707)
PHONE.....................949 273-8100
Robert Doherty, CEO
Timothy G Woodward, COO
Michael Seffer, CFO
Michael Poston, Opers Staff
EMP: 15 EST: 2011
SQ FT: 4,000
SALES (est): 9MM Publicly Held
WEB: www.airtechinnovation.com
SIC: 2515 Mattresses, containing felt, foam rubber, urethane, etc.

(P-3540)
ADVANCED INNVTIVE RCVERY TECH
3401 Space Center Ct # 811, Jurupa Valley
(91752-1128)
PHONE.....................949 273-8100
Brad Bannister, Manager
EMP: 30
SALES (corp-wide): 9MM Publicly Held
WEB: www.airtechinnovation.com
SIC: 2515 Mattresses, containing felt, foam rubber, urethane, etc.
PA: Advanced Innovative Recovery Technologies, Inc.
23615 El Toro Rd Ste 207
Lake Forest CA 92630
949 273-8100

(P-3541)
AMERICAN NATIONAL MFG INC
252 Mariah Cir, Corona (92879-1751)
PHONE.....................951 273-7888
Eve Miller, President
Craig Miller, Vice Pres
Chad Miller, Director
◆ EMP: 110 EST: 1993
SQ FT: 75,000
SALES (est): 16.7MM Privately Held
WEB: www.americannationalmfg.com
SIC: 2515 5712 Mattresses & bedsprings; furniture stores

(P-3542)
AMF SUPPORT SURFACES INC (DH)
1691 N Delilah St, Corona (92879-1885)
PHONE.....................951 549-6800
Fredrick Kohnke, CEO
Carole A Wyatt, President
Charles C Wyatt, President
Curt Wyatt, CEO
Kara Johan, COO
▲ EMP: 162 EST: 1932
SQ FT: 40,000
SALES (est): 26MM
SALES (corp-wide): 3B Publicly Held
SIC: 2515 Mattresses, containing felt, foam rubber, urethane, etc.

(P-3543)
BOYD FLOTATION INC
Also Called: Boyd Specialty Sleep
7551 Cherry Ave, Fontana (92336-4276)
PHONE.....................314 997-5222
Alfred Mayen, Manager
EMP: 33 Privately Held
WEB: www.boydsleep.com
SIC: 5712 2515 Mattresses; mattresses & bedsprings
PA: Boyd Flotation, Inc.
2440 Adie Rd
Maryland Heights MO 63043

(P-3544)
BRENTWOOD HOME LLC (PA)
Also Called: Silverrest
701 Burning Tree Rd Ste A, Fullerton
(92833-1451)
PHONE.....................562 949-3759
Vy Nguyen, CEO
EMP: 128 EST: 2015

SQ FT: 80,000
SALES (est): 33.6MM Privately Held
SIC: 2515 5021 5712 Mattresses, containing felt, foam rubber, urethane, etc.; mattresses; mattresses

(P-3545)
CUEVAS MATTRESS INC
Also Called: Springpudic
3504 E Olympic Blvd, Los Angeles
(90023-3924)
PHONE.....................310 631-8382
Isabel Cuevas, President
EMP: 14
SALES (corp-wide): 1.1MM Privately Held
SIC: 2515 Mattresses & bedsprings
PA: Cuevas Mattress Inc.
5843 S Broadway
Los Angeles CA 90003
310 631-8382

(P-3546)
DELLA ROBBIA INC
796 E Harrison St, Corona (92879-1348)
PHONE.....................951 372-9199
David Soonlan, President
▲ EMP: 20 EST: 1980
SQ FT: 72,000
SALES (est): 5MM Privately Held
WEB: www.dellarobbia.com
SIC: 2515 Sofa beds (convertible sofas)

(P-3547)
DIAMOND MATTRESS COMPANY INC (PA)
Also Called: Diamond Mattress Nf
3112 E Las Hermanas St, Compton
(90221-5578)
PHONE.....................310 638-0363
Shaun Pennington, President
Breana Pennington, Vice Pres
Carlos Santana, Controller
Leilani Akiona, Human Resources
Tony Ribali, Purch Mgr
▲ EMP: 78 EST: 1955
SQ FT: 31,000
SALES (est): 33.4MM Privately Held
WEB: www.diamondmattress.com
SIC: 5712 2515 Mattresses; bedsprings, assembled

(P-3548)
ES KLUFT & COMPANY INC (PA)
11096 Jersey Blvd Ste 101, Rancho Cucamonga (91730-5158)
PHONE.....................909 373-4211
David Binke, CEO
Ron Bruneau, COO
Alan Docherty, CFO
Alwyna Luceno, Office Mgr
Celia Correa, Accounting Mgr
◆ EMP: 217 EST: 2004
SALES (est): 53.1MM Privately Held
WEB: www.aireloom.com
SIC: 2515 Mattresses, innerspring or box spring

(P-3549)
GOLDEN MATTRESS CO INC
11680 Wright Rd, Lynwood (90262-3945)
PHONE.....................323 887-1888
San Dang, CEO
Phuc Nguyen, Vice Pres
◆ EMP: 52 EST: 1980
SALES (est): 4.2MM Privately Held
WEB: www.goldenmattressinc.com
SIC: 2515 5021 Mattresses & foundations; mattresses

(P-3550)
HOSPITALITY SLEEP SYSTEMS INC
107 E Rialto Ave, San Bernardino
(92408-1128)
PHONE.....................909 387-9779
Cristiana Solorio, CEO
EMP: 14 EST: 2011
SALES (est): 1.3MM Privately Held
WEB: www.hotelmattresses.com
SIC: 2515 Mattresses & foundations; mattresses, innerspring or box spring

(P-3551)
KINGDOM MATTRESS CO INC
Also Called: Kingdom Matress Company
2425 S Malt Ave, Commerce (90040-3201)
PHONE.................................562 630-5531
Jose Flores, *President*
EMP: 47 **EST:** 1999
SALES (est): 4.3MM **Privately Held**
SIC: 2515 Mattresses & bedsprings

(P-3552)
LEGGETT & PLATT INCORPORATED
Also Called: Lpcc 6008
1050 S Dupont Ave, Ontario (91761-1578)
PHONE.................................909 937-1010
Barry Kubasak, *Manager*
EMP: 96
SALES (corp-wide): 4.2B **Publicly Held**
WEB: www.leggett.com
SIC: 2515 Mattresses, innerspring or box
spring
PA: Leggett & Platt, Incorporated
1 Leggett Rd
Carthage MO 64836
417 358-8131

(P-3553)
MARSPRING CORPORATION
4920 S Boyle Ave, Vernon (90058-3017)
PHONE.................................800 522-5252
Ronald Greitzer, *Manager*
EMP: 28
SALES (corp-wide): 4.8MM **Privately Held**
SIC: 2515 Spring cushions
PA: Marspring Corporation
4920 S Boyle Ave
Vernon CA 90058
323 589-5637

(P-3554)
MARSPRING CORPORATION
Also Called: Los Angeles Fiber Co
5190 S Santa Fe Ave, Vernon
(90058-3532)
P.O. Box 58643, Los Angeles (90058-0643)
PHONE.................................310 484-6849
Ronald Greitzer, *President*
EMP: 28
SALES (corp-wide): 4.8MM **Privately Held**
SIC: 2515 Spring cushions
PA: Marspring Corporation
4920 S Boyle Ave
Vernon CA 90058
323 589-5637

(P-3555)
MIRACLE BEDDING CORPORATION
3700 Capitol Ave, City of Industry
(90601-1731)
PHONE.................................562 908-2370
CAM Hua, *President*
CAM Tu Hua, *President*
Quyen Lieu, *Treasurer*
▲ **EMP:** 28 **EST:** 1991
SQ FT: 100,000
SALES (est): 1.2MM **Privately Held**
SIC: 2515 5719 5712 Mattresses, containing felt, foam rubber, urethane, etc.; mattresses, innerspring or box spring; bedding (sheets, blankets, spreads & pillows); mattresses

(P-3556)
PURA NATURALS INC
3401 Space Center Ct # 811, Jurupa Valley
(91752-1128)
PHONE.................................949 273-8100
Brad Bannister, *Manager*
EMP: 30
SALES (corp-wide): 9MM **Publicly Held**
WEB: www.puranaturalsproducts.com
SIC: 2515 Mattresses, containing felt, foam rubber, urethane, etc.
HQ: Pura Naturals, Inc.
23615 El Toro Rd Ste X300
Lake Forest CA 92630
949 273-8100

(P-3557)
RELIEF-MART INC
Also Called: Selectabed
28505 Canwood St Ste C, Agoura Hills
(91301-3207)
PHONE.................................805 379-4300
Rick T Swartzburg, *CEO*
Jim Swartzburg, *President*
Ryan Worsham, *Human Res Mgr*
Doug Konzen, *Production*
▲ **EMP:** 42
SQ FT: 36,000
SALES (est): 500K **Privately Held**
WEB: www.reliefmart.com
SIC: 5999 2515 2392 Medical apparatus & supplies; mattresses & foundations; cushions & pillows

(P-3558)
ROYAL-PEDIC MATTRESS MFG LLC (PA)
341 N Robertson Blvd, Beverly Hills
(90211-1705)
PHONE.................................310 278-9594
Martin E Kelemen, *Mng Member*
Georgette Cota, *Production*
Tom Sarkela, *Natl Sales Mgr*
Gary Knutson, *Manager*
▲ **EMP:** 22 **EST:** 1946
SQ FT: 3,200
SALES (est): 3.4MM **Privately Held**
WEB: www.royalpedic.com
SIC: 5712 2515 Mattresses; mattresses & bedsprings

(P-3559)
SKY RIDER EQUIPMENT CO INC
1180 N Blue Gum St, Anaheim
(92806-2409)
PHONE.................................714 632-6890
Martin Villegas, *CEO*
Carl Gray, *President*
Dev Donnelley, *Vice Pres*
Karl Keranen, *Vice Pres*
Michael Eaton, *General Mgr*
▲ **EMP:** 30 **EST:** 1984
SQ FT: 12,000
SALES (est): 7.2MM **Privately Held**
WEB: www.sky-rider.com
SIC: 2515 7349 5719 Foundations & platforms; window cleaning; window shades

(P-3560)
SOUTH BAY INTERNATIONAL INC
8570 Hickory Ave, Rancho Cucamonga
(91739-9632)
PHONE.................................909 718-5000
Guohai Tang, *President*
Daniella Serven, *CEO*
Wendiao Hou, *CFO*
Dani Serven, *Vice Pres*
Weijun She, *Admin Sec*
▲ **EMP:** 25 **EST:** 1993
SALES (est): 50MM **Privately Held**
WEB: www.southbayinternational.com
SIC: 2515 Mattresses & bedsprings

(P-3561)
VISIONARY SLEEP LLC
2060 S Wineville Ave A, Ontario
(91761-3633)
PHONE.................................909 605-2010
Carter Gronbach, *VP Opers*
EMP: 58
SALES (corp-wide): 4.6MM **Privately Held**
SIC: 2515 Mattresses, innerspring or box spring
PA: Visionary Sleep, Llc
1721 Moon Lake Blvd
Hoffman Estates IL 60169
812 945-4155

2517 Wood T V, Radio, Phono & Sewing Cabinets

(P-3562)
SPARTAK ENTERPRISES INC
11186 Venture Dr, Jurupa Valley
(91752-1194)
PHONE.................................951 360-0610
Armen Babayan, *President*

EMP: 14 **EST:** 1993
SQ FT: 40,000
SALES (est): 358.4K **Privately Held**
SIC: 2517 2522 Wood television & radio cabinets; office furniture, except wood

(P-3563)
WEBB MASSEY CO INC
201 W Carleton Ave, Orange (92867-3678)
P.O. Box 4969 (92863-4969)
PHONE.................................714 639-6012
EMP: 32
SALES (est): 1.7MM **Privately Held**
SIC: 2517 Mfg Stereo Speaker Cabinets

2519 Household Furniture, NEC

(P-3564)
ACRYLIC DISTRIBUTION CORP
8501 Lankershim Blvd, Sun Valley
(91352-3127)
PHONE.................................818 767-8448
Shlomi Haziza, *Principal*
Soli Amor, *Treasurer*
Nick Enriques, *General Mgr*
▲ **EMP:** 22 **EST:** 1992
SALES (est): 3.2MM **Privately Held**
WEB: www.hstudio.com
SIC: 2519 Furniture, household: glass, fiberglass & plastic

(P-3565)
ARKTURA LLC (HQ)
18225 S Figueroa St, Gardena
(90248-4216)
PHONE.................................310 532-1050
Chris Kabatsi, *CEO*
Kelli Larkin, *Office Mgr*
Brenda Davis, *Office Admin*
Omar Ramirez, *Marketing Staff*
Patricia Hoffman, *Sales Staff*
▲ **EMP:** 30 **EST:** 2008
SALES (est): 10.3MM
SALES (corp-wide): 936.9MM **Publicly Held**
WEB: www.arktura.com
SIC: 2519 Furniture, household: glass, fiberglass & plastic
PA: Armstrong World Industries, Inc.
2500 Columbia Ave
Lancaster PA 17603
717 397-0611

(P-3566)
DON ALDERSON ASSOCIATES INC
3327 La Cienega Pl, Los Angeles
(90016-3116)
PHONE.................................310 837-5141
Juan Guardado, *Principal*
EMP: 40 **EST:** 1979
SALES (est): 1.4MM **Privately Held**
SIC: 2519 Household furniture, except wood or metal: upholstered

(P-3567)
MEADOW DECOR INC
1477 E Cedar St Ste F, Ontario
(91761-8330)
PHONE.................................909 923-2558
Jun Chen, *CEO*
David Mok, *Ch of Bd*
John Chen, *President*
Jiali Zhang, *Principal*
Robyn Ferrell, *Project Mgr*
▲ **EMP:** 13 **EST:** 2000
SALES (est): 2.9MM **Privately Held**
WEB: www.meadowdecor.com
SIC: 2519 2392 Lawn & garden furniture, except wood & metal; cushions & pillows

(P-3568)
NEXT DAY FRAME INC
11560 Wright Rd, Lynwood (90262-3944)
PHONE.................................310 886-0851
Nancy Abelar, *CEO*
EMP: 65 **EST:** 2012
SALES (est): 5.3MM **Privately Held**
SIC: 2519 Household furniture, except wood or metal: upholstered

(P-3569)
NICHOLAS MICHAEL DESIGNS INC
2330 Raymer Ave, Fullerton (92833-2515)
PHONE.................................714 562-8101
Michael A Cimarusti, *CEO*
Bruce Triolo, *Vice Pres*
Alison Diaz, *Account Dir*
▲ **EMP:** 120 **EST:** 2003
SALES (est): 21.7MM **Privately Held**
WEB: www.mndca.com
SIC: 2519 Household furniture, except wood or metal: upholstered

(P-3570)
P F PLASTICS INC
Also Called: Crystal Craft
2044 Wright Ave, La Verne (91750-5821)
PHONE.................................909 392-4488
Arash Youssefy, *CEO*
Parviz Youssefy, *President*
EMP: 13 **EST:** 1982
SQ FT: 10,300
SALES (est): 1.9MM **Privately Held**
WEB: www.crystalcraft.com
SIC: 2519 2541 Household furniture, except wood or metal: upholstered; display fixtures, wood; store fixtures, wood

(P-3571)
PATIO & DOOR OUTLET INC (PA)
Also Called: Patio Outlet
410 W Fletcher Ave, Orange (92865-2612)
PHONE.................................714 974-9900
Christopher Lyons, *President*
▲ **EMP:** 29 **EST:** 1993
SQ FT: 200,000
SALES (est): 3.1MM **Privately Held**
WEB: www.patiomfg.com
SIC: 2519 5712 2514 5031 Garden furniture, except wood, stone or concrete; outdoor & garden furniture; garden furniture, metal; lumber, plywood & millwork; furniture

(P-3572)
SEATING COMPONENT MFG INC
3951 E Miraloma Ave, Anaheim
(92806-6201)
PHONE.................................714 693-3376
Daryl Fossier, *President*
EMP: 17 **EST:** 1991
SQ FT: 12,000
SALES (est): 1.8MM **Privately Held**
WEB: www.scmmfg.com
SIC: 2519 Fiberglass furniture, household: padded or plain

(P-3573)
VINOTEMP INTERNATIONAL CORP
700 W 16th St, Long Beach (90813-1411)
PHONE.................................310 886-3332
Ramone Almejo, *Branch Mgr*
EMP: 28 **Privately Held**
WEB: www.vinotemp.com
SIC: 2519 Household furniture, except wood or metal: upholstered
PA: Vinotemp International Corporation
732 S Racetrack Rd
Henderson NV 89015

(P-3574)
WISE LIVING INC
2001 W 60th St, Los Angeles (90047-1037)
PHONE.................................323 541-0410
Jose A Pinedo, *CEO*
Jeff Fitch, *Representative*
EMP: 35 **EST:** 2009
SALES (est): 3.5MM **Privately Held**
WEB: www.wiselivinginc.com
SIC: 2519 Household furniture, except wood or metal: upholstered

2521 Wood Office Furniture

(P-3575)
A M CABINETS INC (PA)
239 E Gardena Blvd, Gardena
(90248-2813)
PHONE.................................310 532-1919

PRODUCTS & SVCS

Alex H Mc Kay Jr, *CEO*
Alex H McKay, *COO*
Dane McKay, *Vice Pres*
Travis McKay, *General Mgr*
Nancy Wolfinger, *Admin Sec*
EMP: 88 **EST:** 1975
SQ FT: 35,000
SALES (est): 14.8MM **Privately Held**
WEB: www.amcabinets.com
SIC: 2521 2434 2541 Wood office furniture; wood kitchen cabinets; counters or counter display cases, wood

(P-3576)
AMERICON
900 Flynn Rd, Camarillo (93012-8703)
PHONE..................................805 987-0412
Bill Farrah, *President*
Dan Moro, *Sales Staff*
EMP: 17 **EST:** 1982
SQ FT: 30,000
SALES (est): 4MM **Privately Held**
WEB: www.visionmaster-usa.com
SIC: 2521 3663 Wood office furniture; radio & TV communications equipment

(P-3577)
ANTIQUE DESIGNS LTD INC
916 W Hyde Park Blvd, Inglewood (90302-3308)
PHONE..................................310 671-5400
▲ **EMP:** 31
SQ FT: 6,000
SALES: 120K **Privately Held**
WEB: www.antiquedesigns.net
SIC: 2521 2426 2511 Mfg Wood Household Furn Mfg Wood Office Furn

(P-3578)
ARCADIA CONTRACTORS INC
5692 Fresca Dr, La Palma (90623-1048)
PHONE..................................714 562-8200
Joe Sweeney, *CEO*
Hans Domingo, *Mfg Staff*
EMP: 52 **EST:** 1988
SALES (est): 3.1MM **Privately Held**
WEB: www.arcadiacontract.com
SIC: 2521 Wood office furniture

(P-3579)
BAUSMAN AND COMPANY INC (PA)
1500 Crafton Ave Bldg 124, Mentone (92359-1304)
PHONE..................................909 947-0139
Craig L Johnson, *CEO*
Craig Johnson, *CEO*
Robert Williams, *Vice Pres*
EMP: 249
SALES (est): 34.7MM **Privately Held**
WEB: www.bausman.net
SIC: 2521 2511 Wood office furniture; wood household furniture

(P-3580)
CASEWORX INC
1130 Research Dr, Redlands (92374-4562)
PHONE..................................909 799-8550
Bruce Humphrey, *President*
Gregg Schneider, *Admin Sec*
▲ **EMP:** 37 **EST:** 1992
SQ FT: 28,000
SALES (est): 6.1MM **Privately Held**
WEB: www.caseworx.com
SIC: 2521 Cabinets, office: wood

(P-3581)
CRI SUB 1 (DH)
Also Called: E O C
1715 S Anderson Ave, Compton (90220-5005)
PHONE..................................310 537-1657
Ken Bodger, *CEO*
Richard L Sinclair Jr, *President*
Charles Hess, *Vice Pres*
▲ **EMP:** 31 **EST:** 1969
SQ FT: 120,000
SALES (est): 9.9MM
SALES (corp-wide): 58.5MM **Privately Held**
SIC: 2521 Cabinets, office: wood; chairs, office: padded, upholstered or plain: wood; panel systems & partitions (freestanding), office: wood

(P-3582)
CYGAL ART DECO INC
8687 Melrose Ave Ste B300, West Hollywood (90069-5758)
PHONE..................................424 288-4011
Catrine Karl, *Owner*
EMP: 14 **EST:** 2014
SALES (est): 368.1K **Privately Held**
WEB: www.cygal.com
SIC: 2521 Wood office furniture

(P-3583)
DESKMAKERS INC
6525 Flotilla St, Commerce (90040-1713)
PHONE..................................323 264-2260
Philip Polishook, *CEO*
Daniel Boiles, *Vice Pres*
John Bornstein, *Vice Pres*
John Whichard, *Vice Pres*
April Simental, *Finance*
◆ **EMP:** 50 **EST:** 1982
SQ FT: 105,000
SALES (est): 12.8MM **Privately Held**
WEB: www.deskmakers.com
SIC: 2521 Desks, office: wood

(P-3584)
FORTRESS INC
Also Called: Off Broadway
1721 Wright Ave, La Verne (91750-5841)
PHONE..................................909 593-8600
Donald I Wolper, *President*
Nancy Ancheta, *Controller*
Carol Wolper, *Marketing Staff*
▲ **EMP:** 35 **EST:** 1959
SQ FT: 100
SALES (est): 5.3MM **Privately Held**
WEB: www.fortresseating.com
SIC: 2521 2522 Chairs, office: padded, upholstered or plain: wood; chairs, office: padded or plain, except wood

(P-3585)
FURNITURE SOLUTIONS INC
1347 N Blue Gum St, Anaheim (92806-1750)
P.O. Box 3578, Fullerton (92834-3578)
PHONE..................................714 666-0424
Karen Valverde, *Exec VP*
Daniel Nolazco, *President*
EMP: 22 **EST:** 1993
SQ FT: 25,000
SALES (est): 579.5K **Privately Held**
WEB: www.furnituresolutions.com
SIC: 2521 2511 Wood office furniture; wood household furniture

(P-3586)
GALTECH COMPUTER CORPORATION
Also Called: Galtech International
501 Flynn Rd, Camarillo (93012-8756)
P.O. Box 305, Newbury Park (91319-0305)
PHONE..................................805 376-1060
Fei Lin Ko, *CEO*
Jim Lai, *Shareholder*
Robert Ko, *President*
▲ **EMP:** 20 **EST:** 1991
SQ FT: 32,000
SALES (est): 11.9MM **Privately Held**
WEB: www.galtechcorp.com
SIC: 2521 Benches, office: wood

(P-3587)
GRAHAM LEE ASSOCIATES INC
8674 Atlantic Ave, South Gate (90280-3502)
PHONE..................................323 581-8203
Charles Graham, *President*
Michael Chu, *Shareholder*
Brian Krueger, *Shareholder*
Ywart Lee, *Vice Pres*
EMP: 18 **EST:** 1981
SQ FT: 11,000
SALES (est): 2.1MM **Privately Held**
WEB: www.grahamlee.com
SIC: 2521 Cabinets, office: wood

(P-3588)
KINGS CABINET SYSTEMS
426 Park Ave, Hanford (93230-4440)
PHONE..................................559 584-9662
Fax: 559 584-9670
EMP: 13 **EST:** 1977
SQ FT: 12,500

SALES (est): 1.2MM **Privately Held**
SIC: 2521 Mfg Laminated Cabinets & Countertops

(P-3589)
KUSHWOOD CHAIR INC
1290 E Elm St, Ontario (91761-4025)
PHONE..................................909 930-2100
Daniel Kusvhinikov, *President*
Roger Douglas, *Vice Pres*
EMP: 30 **EST:** 1979
SQ FT: 450,000
SALES (est): 1MM **Privately Held**
SIC: 2521 2511 Wood office furniture; unassembled or unfinished furniture, household: wood

(P-3590)
N S HAAS INC
649 Beachport Dr, Port Hueneme (93041-3066)
PHONE..................................805 874-1155
Nahid Jaffee, *Principal*
EMP: 13 **EST:** 2015
SALES (est): 748.5K **Privately Held**
SIC: 2521 Wood office furniture

(P-3591)
NAKAMURA-BEEMAN INC
8520 Wellsford Pl, Santa Fe Springs (90670-2226)
PHONE..................................562 696-1400
Mike Beeman, *President*
Alex Arriola, *Purch Agent*
Jack Loudermill, *Opers Mgr*
EMP: 40 **EST:** 1978
SQ FT: 20,000
SALES (est): 6.1MM **Privately Held**
WEB: www.nbifixtures.com
SIC: 2521 3429 2541 Wood office furniture; cabinet hardware; display fixtures, wood

(P-3592)
NEW MAVERICK DESK INC
15100 S Figueroa St, Gardena (90248-1724)
PHONE..................................310 217-1554
John Long, *CEO*
Rich Mealey, *President*
Ted Jaroszewicz, *CEO*
Donald Clark, *Purchasing*
Tony Catson, *Sales Mgr*
▲ **EMP:** 150 **EST:** 1997
SQ FT: 1,000
SALES (est): 25.8MM **Privately Held**
WEB: www.maverickdesk.com
SIC: 2521 Wood office furniture
HQ: Workstream Inc.
  3158 Production Dr
  Fairfield OH 45014

(P-3593)
NORSTAR OFFICE PRODUCTS INC (PA)
Also Called: Boss
5353 Jillson St, Commerce (90040-2115)
PHONE..................................323 262-1919
William W Huang, *President*
Howard Fineman, *VP Sales*
Sophie Chu, *Manager*
◆ **EMP:** 40 **EST:** 1991
SQ FT: 150,000
SALES (est): 110.9MM **Privately Held**
WEB: www.boss-chair.com
SIC: 2521 2522 Chairs, office: padded, upholstered or plain: wood; chairs, office: padded or plain, except wood

(P-3594)
OAK DESIGN CORPORATION
13272 6th St, Chino (91710-4108)
PHONE..................................909 628-9597
Ismaell Castellanos, *President*
Julio Salas, *President*
EMP: 17 **EST:** 1991
SALES (est): 6.1MM **Privately Held**
WEB: www.odcproducts.com
SIC: 2521 2434 2511 Wood office furniture; wood kitchen cabinets; wood bedroom furniture

(P-3595)
OFFICE CHAIRS INC
Also Called: Oci
14815 Radburn Ave, Santa Fe Springs (90670-5319)
PHONE..................................562 802-0464
Sharon Klapper, *President*
Joseph J Klapper Jr, *Corp Secy*
Donald J Simek, *Exec VP*
Jay Klapper, *Technology*
▲ **EMP:** 60 **EST:** 1974
SQ FT: 60,000
SALES (est): 9.3MM **Privately Held**
WEB: www.ocisitwell.com
SIC: 2521 2512 Wood office furniture; chairs: upholstered on wood frames

(P-3596)
OFS BRANDS HOLDINGS INC
5559 Mcfadden Ave, Huntington Beach (92649-1317)
PHONE..................................714 903-2257
Craig Baker, *President*
EMP: 525 **EST:** 2018
SALES (est): 5.9MM
SALES (corp-wide): 228.8MM **Privately Held**
WEB: www.ofs.com
SIC: 2521 Wood office furniture
PA: Ofs Brands Holdings Inc.
  1204 E 6th St
  Huntingburg IN 47542
  800 521-5381

(P-3597)
PARKINSON ENTERPRISES INC
Also Called: Salman
135 S State College Blvd # 625, Brea (92821-5823)
PHONE..................................714 626-0275
Michael Parkinson, *CEO*
Carolyn Parkinson, *Admin Sec*
EMP: 70 **EST:** 1993
SQ FT: 75,000
SALES (est): 9.1MM **Privately Held**
SIC: 2521 Wood office furniture

(P-3598)
RBF GROUP INTERNATIONAL
Also Called: Rbf Lifestyle Holdings
1441 W 2nd St, Pomona (91766-1202)
PHONE..................................626 333-5700
Robert Brown, *CEO*
▲ **EMP:** 16 **EST:** 2007
SALES (est): 2.1MM **Privately Held**
SIC: 2521 Chairs, office: padded, upholstered or plain: wood

(P-3599)
S & H CABINETS AND MFG INC
10860 Mulberry Ave, Fontana (92337-7027)
PHONE..................................909 357-0551
Michael Hansen, *CEO*
Richard Hansen, *Vice Pres*
Jessica Resendez, *Office Mgr*
Jacob Dowell, *Engineer*
EMP: 40 **EST:** 1954
SQ FT: 22,000
SALES (est): 6.2MM **Privately Held**
WEB: www.shcabinets.com
SIC: 2521 2541 2431 Cabinets, office: wood; table or counter tops, plastic laminated; millwork

(P-3600)
SPACESTOR INC
5450 W 83rd St, Los Angeles (90045-3204)
PHONE..................................310 410-0220
Charles Hubert Kingston, *CEO*
Wilson Russ, *Project Mgr*
Alex Harvey, *Sales Dir*
▲ **EMP:** 14 **EST:** 2013
SALES (est): 16.6MM **Privately Held**
WEB: www.spacestor.us.com
SIC: 2521 2522 5712 Wood office furniture; office furniture, except wood; office furniture

(P-3601)
STOLO CABINETS INC (PA)
Also Called: Stolo Custom Cabinets
860 Challenger St, Brea (92821-2946)
PHONE..................................714 529-7303
Gary Stolo, *Vice Pres*

Robert F Stolo, *Corp Secy*
Breanna Myhre, *Vice Pres*
Justin Stolo, *Vice Pres*
Jo Nagel, *Admin Asst*
EMP: 45 **EST:** 1953
SQ FT: 15,000
SALES (est): 9.8MM **Privately Held**
WEB: www.stolocabinets.com
SIC: 2521 Cabinets, office: wood

(P-3602)
TRINITY OFFICE FURNITURE INC
1050 W Rialto Ave, San Bernardino (92410-2376)
P.O. Box 1526, Wildomar (92595-1526)
PHONE....................909 888-5551
James B Kesterson, *President*
Marci Kesterson, *Admin Sec*
▲ **EMP:** 17 **EST:** 1987
SQ FT: 135,000
SALES (est): 1.1MM **Privately Held**
SIC: 2521 2511 5021 Wood office furniture; wood household furniture; office furniture

(P-3603)
VALLEY OAKS INDUSTRIES
Also Called: Valley Oak Cabinets
3550 E Highway 246 Ste Ae, Santa Ynez (93460-9480)
P.O. Box 1097 (93460-1097)
PHONE....................805 688-2754
Tom Carlson, *President*
Kim Carlson, *Vice Pres*
EMP: 17 **EST:** 1982
SALES (est): 2.5MM **Privately Held**
WEB: www.valleyoakindustries.com
SIC: 2521 2511 Wood office furniture; wood household furniture

---

2522 Office Furniture, Except Wood

(P-3604)
AMERICAN FURNITURE SYSTEMS INC
Also Called: Advantage Custom Fixtures
14105 Avalon Blvd, Los Angeles (90061-2637)
P.O. Box 1235, San Gabriel (91778-1235)
PHONE....................626 457-9900
Allen Sterris, *President*
EMP: 24 **EST:** 1930
SQ FT: 50,000
SALES (est): 2.5MM **Privately Held**
WEB: www.americanfurnituresys.com
SIC: 2522 5411 Office furniture, except wood; convenience stores

(P-3605)
ANGELL & GIROUX INC
2727 Alcazar St, Los Angeles (90033-1106)
P.O. Box 33156 (90033-0156)
PHONE....................323 269-8596
Richard M Hart, *CEO*
Carol A Hart, *Vice Pres*
Kenneth Hart, *Vice Pres*
EMP: 52 **EST:** 1956
SQ FT: 13,000
SALES (est): 8.9MM **Privately Held**
WEB: www.angellandgiroux.com
SIC: 2522 3479 Cabinets, office: except wood; painting, coating & hot dipping; enameling, including porcelain, of metal products

(P-3606)
ARTE DE MEXICO INC (PA)
1000 Chestnut St, Burbank (91506-1623)
PHONE....................818 753-4559
Gerald J Stoffers, *CEO*
Thea Stoffers, *Controller*
▲ **EMP:** 90
SQ FT: 103,000
SALES (est): 22.5MM **Privately Held**
WEB: www.artedemexico.com
SIC: 2522 3645 Office furniture, except wood; residential lighting fixtures

(P-3607)
ELITE MFG CORP
Also Called: Elite Modern
12143 Altamar Pl, Santa Fe Springs (90670-2501)
PHONE....................888 354-8356
Peter Luong, *CEO*
Michael Luong, *CFO*
Robinson Ho, *Vice Pres*
Carl Muller, *Design Engr Mgr*
Catherine Chan, *Controller*
▲ **EMP:** 102 **EST:** 1988
SQ FT: 62,000
SALES (est): 16.1MM **Privately Held**
WEB: www.elitemodern.com
SIC: 2522 2514 Office furniture, except wood; metal household furniture

(P-3608)
ERGONONMIC COMFORT DESIGN INC
9140 Stellar Ct Ste B, Corona (92883-4902)
P.O. Box 79018 (92877-0167)
PHONE....................951 277-1558
Aldolfo Agramonte, *President*
Patricia Agramonte, *Vice Pres*
Scott Slaughter, *VP Sales*
▲ **EMP:** 18 **EST:** 1994
SQ FT: 22,000
SALES (est): 3.6MM **Privately Held**
SIC: 2522 Office chairs, benches & stools, except wood

(P-3609)
EXEMPLIS LLC
Also Called: Sit On It
6280 Artesia Blvd, Buena Park (90620-1004)
PHONE....................714 995-4800
Paul Devries, *Manager*
Marlon Sese, *Administration*
EMP: 43 **Privately Held**
WEB: www.sitonit.net
SIC: 2522 2521 2512 Chairs, office: padded or plain, except wood; wood office furniture; upholstered household furniture
PA: Exemplis Llc
6415 Katella Ave
Cypress CA 90630

(P-3610)
EXEMPLIS LLC
Also Called: Ideon
6280 Artesia Blvd, Buena Park (90620-1004)
PHONE....................714 898-5500
Craig Dumity, *Director*
Graham Wilkinson, *Officer*
Layne Morton, *Vice Pres*
Marlon Sese, *Administration*
Bobby Smith, *Planning*
EMP: 43 **Privately Held**
WEB: www.sitonit.net
SIC: 2522 5021 Chairs, office: padded or plain, except wood; furniture
PA: Exemplis Llc
6415 Katella Ave
Cypress CA 90630

(P-3611)
EXEMPLIS LLC (PA)
Also Called: Sitonit
6415 Katella Ave, Cypress (90630-5245)
PHONE....................714 995-4800
Paul Devries, *CEO*
Mike Mekjian, *President*
Mike Phelan, *CFO*
Graham Wilkinson, *Officer*
Patrick Sommerfield, *Exec VP*
◆ **EMP:** 40 **EST:** 1996
SQ FT: 20,000
SALES (est): 157.5MM **Privately Held**
WEB: www.sitonit.net
SIC: 2522 Chairs, office: padded or plain, except wood

(P-3612)
HAWORTH INC
144 N Robertson Blvd # 202, West Hollywood (90048-3109)
PHONE....................310 854-7633
EMP: 17

SALES (corp-wide): 1.2B **Privately Held**
SIC: 2522 5021 Mfg Office Furniture-Nonwood Whol Furniture
HQ: Haworth, Inc.
1 Haworth Ctr
Holland MI 49423
616 393-3000

(P-3613)
KORDEN INC
611 S Palmetto Ave, Ontario (91762-4124)
PHONE....................909 988-8979
Barjona S Meek, *Principal*
Thomas Mc Cormick, *President*
Jim Ethridge, *Exec VP*
EMP: 59 **EST:** 1949
SQ FT: 75,000
SALES (est): 2.5MM **Privately Held**
WEB: www.korden.com
SIC: 2522 Stools, office: except wood

(P-3614)
MCDOWELL CRAIG OFF SYSTEMS INC
Also Called: McDowell-Craig Office Furn
13146 Firestone Blvd, Norwalk (90650)
P.O. Box 349 (90651-0349)
PHONE....................562 921-4441
Brent G McDowell, *President*
Jeffrey C McDowell, *Admin Sec*
EMP: 70 **EST:** 1995
SQ FT: 117,000
SALES (est): 8MM **Privately Held**
WEB: www.mcdowellcraig.com
SIC: 2522 Office furniture, except wood

(P-3615)
MODULAR OFFICE SOLUTIONS INC
11701 6th St, Rancho Cucamonga (91730-6030)
PHONE....................909 476-4200
Daniel G Coelho, *CEO*
Jorge E Robles, *President*
▲ **EMP:** 32 **EST:** 1999
SQ FT: 173,000
SALES (est): 1.2MM **Privately Held**
WEB: www.chicagoofficefurniture.com
SIC: 2522 2521 Office furniture, except wood; wood office furniture

(P-3616)
SISNEROS INC
Also Called: Sisneros Office Furntiure
12717 Los Nietos Rd, Santa Fe Springs (90670-3007)
PHONE....................562 777-9797
Luis Sisneros, *President*
Margarita Sisneros, *Vice Pres*
EMP: 21 **EST:** 1994
SQ FT: 20,000
SALES (est): 2.6MM **Privately Held**
SIC: 2522 Office furniture, except wood

(P-3617)
VERSA PRODUCTS INC (PA)
Also Called: Versatables.com
14105 Avalon Blvd, Los Angeles (90061-2637)
PHONE....................310 353-7100
Christopher Laudadio, *CEO*
Chris Stormer, *General Mgr*
Han Sun, *Engineer*
Thomas Tanaka, *Engineer*
Brad Stevens, *Senior Engr*
▲ **EMP:** 108 **EST:** 2000
SQ FT: 35,000
SALES (est): 21.6MM **Privately Held**
WEB: www.versatables.com
SIC: 2522 Office desks & tables: except wood

2531 Public Building & Related Furniture

(P-3618)
AEROFOAM INDUSTRIES INC
Also Called: QUALITY FOAM PACKAGING
31855 Corydon St, Lake Elsinore (92530-8501)
PHONE....................951 245-4429
Noel Castellon Jr, *President*
Ruth Castellon, *Treasurer*

James Barrett, *Vice Pres*
Jim Barrett, *Vice Pres*
Castellon Noel, *Vice Pres*
▲ **EMP:** 80
SQ FT: 150,000
SALES (est): 9.8MM **Privately Held**
WEB: www.aerofoams.com
SIC: 2531 Seats, aircraft

(P-3619)
AIRO INDUSTRIES COMPANY
429 Jessie St, San Fernando (91340-2541)
PHONE....................818 838-1008
Bahram Salem, *President*
Mike Salem, *Vice Pres*
Kasunthika Ilippuli, *Marketing Staff*
Ryan Ranjbar, *Sales Staff*
Sean Aby, *Director*
▲ **EMP:** 25 **EST:** 1989
SQ FT: 20,000
SALES (est): 4.2MM **Privately Held**
WEB: www.airoindustries.com
SIC: 2531 4581 Seats, aircraft; aircraft upholstery repair

(P-3620)
COD USA INC
Also Called: Creative Outdoor Distrs USA
25954 Commercentre Dr, Lake Forest (92630-8815)
PHONE....................949 381-7367
Heather Smulson, *President*
Brian Horowitz, *CEO*
Barbara Tolbert, *COO*
◆ **EMP:** 23 **EST:** 2016
SQ FT: 34,000
SALES (est): 4.6MM **Privately Held**
WEB: www.customfoldingwagons.com
SIC: 2531 Chairs, portable folding

(P-3621)
DANG THA
Also Called: Skyline Seating
13050 Hoover St, Westminster (92683-2388)
PHONE....................714 898-0989
Tha Dang, *Owner*
EMP: 13 **EST:** 1986
SQ FT: 3,000
SALES (est): 997.9K **Privately Held**
WEB: www.skylineseating.com
SIC: 2531 Seats, automobile

(P-3622)
DEFOE FURNITURE FOR KIDS INC
910 S Grove Ave, Ontario (91761-3435)
PHONE....................909 947-4459
John G Defoe, *President*
Narcisa Defoe, *Treasurer*
EMP: 16 **EST:** 1980
SQ FT: 17,000
SALES (est): 2.4MM **Privately Held**
WEB: www.defoefurniture4kids.com
SIC: 2531 School furniture

(P-3623)
ERA PRODUCTS INC
1130 Benedict Canyon Dr, Beverly Hills (90210-2726)
PHONE....................310 324-4908
Marlene Alter, *President*
Roy H Alter, *Vice Pres*
EMP: 16 **EST:** 1972
SQ FT: 56,792
SALES (est): 1.5MM **Privately Held**
WEB:
www.motorhomereplacementseats.com
SIC: 2531 Vehicle furniture

(P-3624)
FUTUREFLITE INC
806 Calle Plano, Camarillo (93012-8557)
PHONE....................818 653-2145
Andrew S Kanigowski, *CEO*
EMP: 20 **EST:** 1987
SALES (est): 3.6MM **Privately Held**
WEB: www.futureflite.com
SIC: 2531 Seats, aircraft

(P-3625)
LOUIS SARDO UPHOLSTERY INC (PA)
Also Called: Sardo Bus & Coach Upholstery
512 W Rosecrans Ave, Gardena
(90248-1515)
PHONE..................310 327-0532
Louis Sardo, *President*
Jeanie Sardo, *Vice Pres*
Betty Sahranavard, *Opers Staff*
Christine Steelman, *Assistant*
EMP: 55 **EST:** 1916
SQ FT: 10,000
SALES (est): 9.1MM **Privately Held**
WEB: www.sardobus.com
SIC: 2531 3713 7641 Seats, automobile; truck & bus bodies; reupholstery & furniture repair

(P-3626)
MORTECH MANUFACTURING
411 N Aerojet Dr, Azusa (91702-3253)
PHONE..................626 334-1471
Gino Joseph, *President*
Christy Haines, *CFO*
Paul Joseph, *Vice Pres*
Michael Kubacik, *Vice Pres*
Michael Hart, *Regl Sales Mgr*
◆ **EMP:** 82 **EST:** 1986
SQ FT: 43,000
SALES (est): 11.6MM **Privately Held**
WEB: www.mortechmfg.com
SIC: 2531 5087 Altars & pulpits; funeral directors' equipment & supplies

(P-3627)
NELSON ADAMS INC
160 N Cactus Ave, Rialto (92376-5725)
PHONE..................909 256-8938
Rafael Rangel, *President*
Eric Adler, *CEO*
◆ **EMP:** 15 **EST:** 2013
SQ FT: 40,000
SALES (est): 1.1MM **Privately Held**
WEB: www.nelsonadamsnaco.com
SIC: 2531 Chairs, table & arm

(P-3628)
NEWHOUSE UPHOLSTERY
Also Called: Newhouse Upholstery Mfg
2309 Edwards Ave, El Monte (91733-2041)
P.O. Box 3201 (91733-0201)
PHONE..................626 444-1370
Ed Stevenson, *President*
Maria Stevenson, *Corp Secy*
EMP: 22 **EST:** 1953
SQ FT: 18,000
SALES (est): 4.8MM **Privately Held**
WEB: www.newhouserv.com
SIC: 2531 Vehicle furniture

(P-3629)
ORBO CORPORATION
Also Called: Eurotec Seating
1000 S Euclid St, La Habra (90631-6806)
PHONE..................562 806-6171
Oscar Galvez, *President*
Ricardo Galvez, *Vice Pres*
Alex Osorio, *Accounts Exec*
EMP: 50 **EST:** 2001
SALES (est): 13.4MM **Privately Held**
SIC: 2531 Seats, automobile

(P-3630)
PACIFIC HOSPITALITY DESIGN INC
Also Called: PH Design
2620 S Malt Ave, Commerce (90040-3206)
PHONE..................323 278-7998
Gilberto Martinez, *CEO*
Ana Martinez, *Vice Pres*
EMP: 25 **EST:** 1979
SQ FT: 14,000
SALES (est): 1.7MM **Privately Held**
WEB: www.anamariadesigns.com
SIC: 2531 Public building & related furniture

(P-3631)
REDART CORPORATION
Also Called: Beard Seats
2549 Eastbluff Dr, Newport Beach
(92660-3500)
PHONE..................714 774-9444
Tim Sousamian, *President*

▲ **EMP:** 14 **EST:** 1961
SQ FT: 10,000
SALES (est): 261.3K **Privately Held**
SIC: 2531 2298 Seats, automobile; cargo nets

(P-3632)
STEARNS PARK
Also Called: Long Beach City of
4520 E 23rd St, Long Beach (90815-1806)
PHONE..................562 570-1685
Garcia Elyse, *Principal*
Elyse Garcia, *Supervisor*
EMP: 19 **EST:** 2001 **Privately Held**
WEB: www.longbeach.gov
SIC: 2531 Picnic tables or benches, park

(P-3633)
TALIMAR SYSTEMS INC
3105 W Alpine St, Santa Ana (92704-6911)
PHONE..................714 557-4884
David G Wesdell, *President*
Patty Boris, *Project Mgr*
Rosario Hernandez, *Purch Agent*
Mike Lee, *Marketing Staff*
▲ **EMP:** 37 **EST:** 1988
SQ FT: 11,000
SALES (est): 6MM **Privately Held**
WEB: www.talimarsystems.com
SIC: 2531 5712 7389 5932 Public building & related furniture; furniture stores; merchandise liquidators; office furniture, secondhand

(P-3634)
VILLA FURNITURE MFG CO
Also Called: Villa International
13760 Midway St, Cerritos (90703-2331)
PHONE..................714 535-7272
Andrew M Greenthal, *President*
Mike Ramirez, *Natl Sales Mgr*
Robert Long, *Sales Staff*
John Hermosillo, *Manager*
Luis Maldonado, *Manager*
▲ **EMP:** 125
SQ FT: 75,000
SALES (est): 21.8MM **Privately Held**
WEB: www.villainternational.com
SIC: 2531 2522 Vehicle furniture; office furniture, except wood

(P-3635)
VIRCO MFG CORPORATION (PA)
2027 Harpers Way, Torrance (90501-1524)
PHONE..................310 533-0474
Robert A Virtue, *Ch of Bd*
Douglas A Virtue, *President*
J Scott Bell, *COO*
Robert E Dose, *CFO*
Donald Rudkin, *Bd of Directors*
◆ **EMP:** 527 **EST:** 1950
SQ FT: 560,000
SALES (est): 152.8MM **Publicly Held**
WEB: www.virco.com
SIC: 2531 2522 2511 School furniture; chairs, portable folding; chairs, table & arm; office furniture, except wood; chairs, office: padded or plain, except wood; tables, office: except wood; wood household furniture

---

2541 Wood, Office & Store Fixtures

(P-3636)
ALL AMERICAN CABINETRY INC
Also Called: All American Sterile Coat
13901 Saticoy St, Van Nuys (91402-6521)
PHONE..................818 376-0500
Chris Zepatos, *President*
EMP: 22 **EST:** 1996
SALES (est): 2.3MM **Privately Held**
WEB: www.allamericancabinets.us
SIC: 2541 Cabinets, lockers & shelving

(P-3637)
AMTREND CORPORATION
1458 Manhattan Ave, Fullerton
(92831-5222)
PHONE..................714 630-2070
Hamid A Malik, *President*
Javeeda Malik, *CEO*
Rosa Rubio, *Human Res Mgr*

Luis Orozco, *Plant Mgr*
Robert Flores, *Manager*
EMP: 85
SQ FT: 45,000
SALES (est): 16.5MM **Privately Held**
WEB: www.amtrend.com
SIC: 2541 2521 7641 2512 Wood partitions & fixtures; wood office furniture; upholstery work; upholstered household furniture

(P-3638)
ARCHITECTURAL WOODWORKING CO
582 Monterey Pass Rd, Monterey Park
(91754-2417)
PHONE..................626 570-4125
John K Heydorff, *President*
John F Heydorff, *Shareholder*
Thomas C Heydorff, *CFO*
Richard A Schaub, *Admin Sec*
Edward Illig, *Director*
EMP: 100
SQ FT: 60,000
SALES (est): 13.6MM **Privately Held**
WEB: www.awcla.com
SIC: 2541 1751 Office fixtures, wood; carpentry work

(P-3639)
BLOCK TOPS INC (PA)
1321 S Sunkist St, Anaheim (92806-5614)
PHONE..................714 978-5080
Vanessa Bates, *CEO*
Nate Kolenski, *President*
Adrianne Mendoza, *COO*
Derrick Sellers, *Manager*
▲ **EMP:** 34
SQ FT: 10,000
SALES (est): 6.7MM **Privately Held**
WEB: www.blocktops.com
SIC: 2541 2519 3281 2821 Table or counter tops, plastic laminated; furniture, household: glass, fiberglass & plastic; cut stone & stone products; plastics materials & resins

(P-3640)
BRISTOL OMEGA INC
9441 Opal Ave Ste 2, Mentone
(92359-9900)
PHONE..................909 794-6862
Ralf G Zacky, *CEO*
EMP: 27 **EST:** 1993 **Privately Held**
WEB: www.bristolomega.com
SIC: 2541 1611 Wood partitions & fixtures; general contractor, highway & street construction

(P-3641)
CALIFORNIA MFG CABINETRY INC
Also Called: C M C
1474 E Francis St, Ontario (91761-5791)
PHONE..................909 930-3632
Miguel Jimenez, *President*
Mike Jimmez, *Vice Pres*
EMP: 15 **EST:** 1988
SALES (est): 2MM **Privately Held**
SIC: 2541 2434 2431 Cabinets, except refrigerated: show, display, etc.: wood; wood kitchen cabinets; millwork

(P-3642)
CLOSETS BY DESIGN INC
3860 Capitol Ave, City of Industry
(90601-1733)
PHONE..................562 699-9945
Frank Melkonian, *President*
Gerard Thompson, *CFO*
Nedda Viscovich, *Design Engr*
EMP: 30 **EST:** 1982
SALES (est): 3.9MM **Privately Held**
WEB: www.closetsbydesign.com
SIC: 2541 2521 Lockers, except refrigerated: wood; wood office filing cabinets & bookcases

(P-3643)
COLUMBIA SHOWCASE & CAB CO INC
11034 Sherman Way Ste A, Sun Valley
(91352-4915)
PHONE..................818 765-9710
Samuel M Patterson Jr, *CEO*

James E Barnett, *Co-COB*
Samuel M Patterson Sr, *Co-COB*
Joe Patterson, *Senior VP*
James Haley, *Project Mgr*
▲ **EMP:** 125 **EST:** 1950
SQ FT: 170,000
SALES (est): 14.5MM **Privately Held**
SIC: 2541 1542 Cabinets, except refrigerated: show, display, etc.: wood; commercial & office building contractors

(P-3644)
COMPATICO INC
1901 S Archibald Ave, Ontario
(91761-8548)
PHONE..................616 940-1772
John REA, *Shareholder*
Patrick Mullen, *Shareholder*
Richard Posthumus, *President*
William Boer, *Chairman*
Carrie Boer, *Corp Secy*
◆ **EMP:** 45 **EST:** 1989
SALES (est): 7.5MM **Privately Held**
WEB: www.compatico.com
SIC: 2541 Wood partitions & fixtures

(P-3645)
CUSTOM DISPLAYS INC
411 W 157th St, Gardena (90248-2118)
PHONE..................323 770-8074
Thomas Otani, *President*
Ben Hasuike, *Vice Pres*
EMP: 14 **EST:** 1970
SQ FT: 16,000
SALES (est): 2.5MM **Privately Held**
SIC: 2541 3827 3993 Display fixtures, wood; triplet magnifying instruments, optical; signs & advertising specialties

(P-3646)
F-J-E INC
Also Called: Jf Fixtures & Design
546 W Esther St, Long Beach
(90813-1529)
PHONE..................562 437-7466
Frank Ernandes, *President*
Barbara Ernandes, *Admin Sec*
Nancy Lombardo, *Purchasing*
Brian Summers, *Sales Staff*
EMP: 25
SQ FT: 26,000
SALES (est): 3.1MM **Privately Held**
WEB: www.jffixtures.com
SIC: 2541 2542 Store fixtures, wood; fixtures, store: except wood

(P-3647)
GREG IAN ISLANDS INC
Also Called: Igi
123b E Montecito Ave B, Sierra Madre
(91024-1923)
PHONE..................626 355-0019
EMP: 20
SALES (est): 1.8MM **Privately Held**
SIC: 2541 Mfg Outdoor Cabinets

(P-3648)
GRENEKER FURNITURE
3110 E 12th St, Los Angeles (90023-3616)
PHONE..................323 263-9000
Erik Johnson, *Owner*
Gerry Clark, *CTO*
Steve Beckman, *Human Res Mgr*
EMP: 13 **EST:** 1999
SQ FT: 100,000
SALES (est): 440.6K **Privately Held**
WEB: www.greneker.com
SIC: 2541 2542 Display fixtures, wood; fixtures: display, office or store: except wood

(P-3649)
HEMISPHERE DESIGN & MFG LLC
28895 Industry Dr, Valencia (91355-5419)
PHONE..................661 294-9500
Timothy Arnold, *Mng Member*
EMP: 15 **EST:** 2013
SALES (est): 3.9MM **Privately Held**
WEB: www.hemisphere-dm.com
SIC: 2541 7389 Store & office display cases & fixtures; design services

(P-3650)
HERITAGE CABINET CO INC
21740 Marilla St, Chatsworth (91311-4125)
PHONE..................818 786-4900

Robert Geyer, *Owner*
Kathy Geyer, *Corp Secy*
EMP: 18 **EST:** 1982
SQ FT: 12,000
SALES (est): 2.6MM **Privately Held**
WEB: www.heritagecabinet.com
SIC: 2541 5211 2521 2517 Cabinets, except refrigerated: show, display, etc.: wood; lumber & other building materials; wood office furniture; wood television & radio cabinets; wood kitchen cabinets; millwork

(P-3651)
IDEAL PRODUCTS INC
4501 Etiwanda Ave, Jurupa Valley (91752-1445)
P.O. Box 4090, Ontario (91761-1006)
PHONE.................................951 727-8600
Robert L Martin Jr, *CEO*
Virginia Martin, *Vice Pres*
EMP: 35 **EST:** 1976
SQ FT: 20,000
SALES (est): 7MM **Privately Held**
WEB: www.idealockers.com
SIC: 2541 Lockers, except refrigerated: wood

(P-3652)
IVARS DISPLAY (PA)
Also Called: Ivar's Displays
2314 E Locust Ct, Ontario (91761-7613)
PHONE.................................909 923-2761
Ivan Gundersen, *President*
Karl Gundersen, *CEO*
Jason Gundersen, *CFO*
Linda Pulice, *Vice Pres*
Rose Marie Aunario, *Accounts Mgr*
▲ **EMP:** 106 **EST:** 1966
SQ FT: 95,000
SALES (est): 16.3MM **Privately Held**
WEB: www.ivarsdisplay.com
SIC: 2541 2542 Store fixtures, wood; shelving, office & store: except wood

(P-3653)
J P B JEWELRY BOX CO (PA)
2428 Dallas St, Los Angeles (90031-1013)
PHONE.................................323 225-0500
Jerry Borodian, *Partner*
Josephine Borodian, *Partner*
▲ **EMP:** 15 **EST:** 1978
SQ FT: 14,000
SALES (est): 1MM **Privately Held**
WEB: www.jpbbox.com
SIC: 2541 2441 3172 Wood partitions & fixtures; nailed wood boxes & shook; cases, jewelry

(P-3654)
JUDITH VON HOPF INC
1525 W 13th St Ste H, Upland (91786-7528)
PHONE.................................909 481-1884
Judith P Hopf, *CEO*
Shana Wardle, *Sales Staff*
▲ **EMP:** 25 **EST:** 1976
SALES (est): 4MM **Privately Held**
WEB: www.judithvonhopf.com
SIC: 2541 Display fixtures, wood

(P-3655)
L & N FIXTURES INC
2214 Tyler Ave, El Monte (91733-2710)
PHONE.................................626 442-4778
Louis Pierotti, *President*
EMP: 20 **EST:** 1970
SQ FT: 16,000
SALES (est): 2MM **Privately Held**
WEB: www.lnfixtures.com
SIC: 2541 1799 2521 2434 Store fixtures, wood; office furniture installation; wood office furniture; wood kitchen cabinets

(P-3656)
LA CABINET & MILLWORK INC
Also Called: Bromack
3005 Humboldt St, Los Angeles (90031-1830)
PHONE.................................323 227-5000
Leonard Lumpkin, *President*
Kurt Webster, *Treasurer*
Oscar Gonzalez, *Vice Pres*
Brown S McPherson III, *Vice Pres*
Robert Rieger, *Vice Pres*

EMP: 25 **EST:** 2005
SQ FT: 17,000
SALES (est): 3.7MM **Privately Held**
SIC: 2541 1799 2434 1751 Counters or counter display cases, wood; counter top installation; wood kitchen cabinets; carpentry work

(P-3657)
LEGGETT & PLATT INCORPORATED
Also Called: Leggett & Platt 0302
29120 Commerce Center Dr # 1, Valencia (91355-5404)
PHONE.................................661 775-8500
EMP: 30
SALES (corp-wide): 3.7B **Publicly Held**
SIC: 2541 Mfg Wood Partitions/Fixtures
PA: Leggett & Platt, Incorporated
1 Leggett Rd
Carthage MO 64836
417 358-8131

(P-3658)
LEONARDS CARPET SERVICE INC (PA)
Also Called: Xgrass Turf Direct
1121 N Red Gum St, Anaheim (92806-2582)
PHONE.................................714 630-1930
Leonard Nagel, *President*
Joel Nagel, *CEO*
▲ **EMP:** 75 **EST:** 1970
SQ FT: 52,000
SALES (est): 27.4MM **Privately Held**
WEB: www.leonardscarpetservice.com
SIC: 2541 1771 1799 Table or counter tops, plastic laminated; flooring contractor; artificial turf installation

(P-3659)
NICO NAT MFG CORP
Also Called: Niconat Manufacturing
2624 Yates Ave, Commerce (90040-2622)
PHONE.................................323 721-1900
Jose Valdez, *CEO*
Francisco Valdez, *Shareholder*
Valerie Castillo, *Assistant*
EMP: 45 **EST:** 2008
SALES (est): 8.6MM **Privately Held**
WEB: www.niconat.co
SIC: 2541 Store & office display cases & fixtures

(P-3660)
OAK-IT INC
845 Sandhill Ave, Carson (90746-1210)
P.O. Box 4733, Downey (90241-1733)
PHONE.................................310 719-3999
Lori Barrett, *President*
Sean Kittiko, *Treasurer*
◆ **EMP:** 53 **EST:** 1983
SQ FT: 8,000
SALES (est): 1.2MM **Privately Held**
WEB: www.oakitinc.com
SIC: 2541 2431 5046 Store fixtures, wood; cabinets, except refrigerated: show, display, etc.: wood; millwork; store fixtures

(P-3661)
PACIFIC WESTLINE INC
1536 W Embassy St, Anaheim (92802-1016)
PHONE.................................714 956-2442
Daniel G McLeith, *CEO*
EMP: 90 **EST:** 1975
SQ FT: 62,000
SALES (est): 7.8MM **Privately Held**
WEB: www.pacificwestline.com
SIC: 2541 2431 Cabinets, except refrigerated: show, display, etc.: wood; millwork

(P-3662)
PYRAMID SYSTEMS INC
10105 8 3/4 Ave, Hanford (93230-4769)
PHONE.................................559 582-9345
David Gunter, *President*
Lori Pollard, *Exec VP*
Amber Ratt, *Admin Sec*
EMP: 24 **EST:** 1995
SQ FT: 12,000
SALES (est): 1.1MM **Privately Held**
WEB: www.pyrmfg.com
SIC: 2541 Wood partitions & fixtures

(P-3663)
SCIENTIFIC SURFACE INDS INC
Also Called: Ssi Surfaces
855 Rancho Conejo Blvd, Newbury Park (91320-1714)
PHONE.................................805 499-5100
David Marquez, *COO*
Lori Lynch, *Department Mgr*
EMP: 16 **EST:** 2009
SQ FT: 10,000
SALES (est): 1.1MM **Privately Held**
WEB: www.ssisurfaces.com
SIC: 2541 Counter & sink tops

(P-3664)
SHOW OFFS
1696 W Mill St Unit 10, Colton (92324-1074)
PHONE.................................909 885-5223
Dave Snavely, *Owner*
EMP: 14 **EST:** 1989
SQ FT: 18,000
SALES (est): 3.2MM **Privately Held**
WEB: www.showoffsdisplay.com
SIC: 2541 2542 5046 Display fixtures, wood; racks, merchandise display or storage: except wood; store fixtures

(P-3665)
SISTONE INC
15530 Lanark St, Van Nuys (91406-1411)
PHONE.................................818 988-9918
Yair Sisso, *President*
EMP: 15 **EST:** 1999
SALES (est): 1.4MM **Privately Held**
WEB: www.sistoneinc.com
SIC: 2541 Counter & sink tops

(P-3666)
SPALINGER ENTERPRISES INC
Also Called: Skyline Cabinet & Millworks
800 S Mount Vernon Ave, Bakersfield (93307-2889)
PHONE.................................661 834-4550
David Spalinger, *President*
Melody Spalinger, *Treasurer*
J W Spalinger, *Vice Pres*
▲ **EMP:** 35 **EST:** 1948
SQ FT: 8,500
SALES (est): 5.3MM **Privately Held**
WEB: www.skylinecabinets.com
SIC: 2541 Cabinets, except refrigerated: show, display, etc.: wood

(P-3667)
SW FIXTURES INC
3940 Valley Blvd Ste C, Walnut (91789-1541)
PHONE.................................909 595-2506
Daniel Zachary, *President*
Brian Welsh, *Opers Mgr*
Daniel Farinella, *Sr Project Mgr*
EMP: 18
SQ FT: 22,500
SALES (est): 3.4MM **Privately Held**
WEB: www.swfixtures.com
SIC: 2541 2431 Display fixtures, wood; planing mill, millwork

(P-3668)
TECHNIQUE DESIGNS INC
63665 19th Ave, North Palm Springs (92258-0541)
P.O. Box 550, Morongo Valley (92256-0550)
PHONE.................................760 904-6223
Bruce Watts, *President*
Danelle Watts, *Admin Sec*
EMP: 14 **EST:** 1986
SQ FT: 6,000
SALES (est): 2.9MM **Privately Held**
WEB: www.techniquedesignsinc.com
SIC: 2541 Wood partitions & fixtures

(P-3669)
TEMEKA ADVERTISING INC
Also Called: Temeka Group
9073 Pulsar Ct, Corona (92883-7357)
PHONE.................................951 277-2525
Michael D Wilson, *CEO*
Paul Mieboer, *Shareholder*
Marlene Kelly, *CFO*
Tommy Bradfield, *Marketing Staff*
Chris Isley, *Marketing Staff*
▲ **EMP:** 55
SQ FT: 24,000

SALES (est): 10MM **Privately Held**
WEB: www.temekagroup.com
SIC: 2541 Store & office display cases & fixtures

(P-3670)
V TWEST INC
16222 Phoebe Ave, La Mirada (90638-5610)
PHONE.................................714 521-2167
Douglas Edward Clausen, *Branch Mgr*
EMP: 13
SALES (corp-wide): 434.9MM **Privately Held**
WEB: www.vtindustries.com
SIC: 2541 Counter & sink tops
HQ: V T.West Inc.
1000 Industrial Park
Holstein IA 51025

(P-3671)
WALLACE WOOD PRODUCTS
Also Called: Corte Custom Case
1247 S Buena Vista St C, San Jacinto (92583-4664)
PHONE.................................951 654-9311
Roy Wallace, *Owner*
EMP: 16 **Privately Held**
WEB: www.spinolution.com
SIC: 2541 Wood partitions & fixtures
PA: Wallace Wood Products
1247 S Buena Vista St C
San Jacinto CA 92583

(P-3672)
YOSHIMASA DISPLAY CASE INC
108 Pico St, Pomona (91766-2137)
PHONE.................................213 637-9999
Toro Hayashi, *President*
Michael Y Yoo, *Principal*
Alma Kim, *Manager*
Tesia Yi, *Manager*
▲ **EMP:** 35 **EST:** 2011
SQ FT: 15,000
SALES (est): 2.5MM **Privately Held**
WEB: www.yoshimasausa.com
SIC: 2541 3564 Store & office display cases & fixtures; aircurtains (blower)

2542 Partitions & Fixtures, Except Wood

(P-3673)
ABTECH INCORPORATED
3420 W Fordham Ave, Santa Ana (92704-4422)
PHONE.................................714 550-9961
James Herr, *CEO*
Cheryl Herr, *Treasurer*
▲ **EMP:** 56 **EST:** 1992
SQ FT: 11,000
SALES (est): 6.7MM **Privately Held**
WEB: www.abtech.net
SIC: 2542 3448 Partitions & fixtures, except wood; prefabricated metal buildings; buildings, portable: prefabricated metal; panels for prefabricated metal buildings

(P-3674)
ACCURATE LAMINATED PDTS INC
1826 Dawns Way, Fullerton (92831-5323)
PHONE.................................714 632-2773
Daniel Dunn, *President*
Patricia Dunn, *Vice Pres*
Aaron Grim, *Project Mgr*
Carlos Muro, *Project Mgr*
Brian Vigneault, *Project Mgr*
EMP: 30 **EST:** 1989
SQ FT: 5,000
SALES (est): 6MM **Privately Held**
WEB: www.accuratelaminated.com
SIC: 2542 Bar fixtures, except wood; cabinets: show, display or storage: except wood

PRODUCTS & SVCS

(P-3675)
ADVANCED EQUIPMENT CORPORATION (PA)
2401 W Commonwealth Ave, Fullerton
(92833-2999)
PHONE..................................714 635-5350
Wesley B Dickson, *Owner*
W Dickson, *President*
W Scott Dickson, *CEO*
Lynn Stanco, *Corp Secy*
Frank Manning, *Senior VP*
◆ EMP: 50 EST: 1957
SQ FT: 51,000
SALES (est): 10.1MM **Privately Held**
WEB: www.advancedequipment.com
SIC: 2542 2541 Partitions for floor attachment, prefabricated: except wood; wood partitions & fixtures

(P-3676)
AVCA FIXTURE SYSTEM INC
Also Called: Whittier Millwork Co
6203 Southwind Dr, Whittier (90601-3841)
PHONE..................................562 693-3214
EMP: 15 EST: 1950
SQ FT: 11,800
SALES (est): 2.4MM **Privately Held**
SIC: 5712 2542 Ret Furniture Mfg Partitions/Fixtures-Nonwood

(P-3677)
BURKE DISPLAY SYSTEMS INC
55 S Peak, Laguna Niguel (92677-2903)
PHONE..................................949 248-0091
Robert Burke, *President*
EMP: 13 EST: 1991
SQ FT: 1,000
SALES (est): 537.8K **Privately Held**
WEB: www.burkedisplays.com
SIC: 2542 Fixtures, store: except wood

(P-3678)
CAL PARTITIONS INC
23814 President Ave, Harbor City
(90710-1390)
PHONE..................................310 539-1911
Alan Anderson, *President*
Sarah Anderson, *Treasurer*
Sami Anderson, *Sales Staff*
EMP: 30 EST: 1959
SQ FT: 13,000
SALES (est): 1.4MM **Privately Held**
WEB: www.calpartitionsinc.com
SIC: 2542 5046 3231 2631 Partitions for floor attachment, prefabricated: except wood; partitions; products of purchased glass; paperboard mills; wood partitions & fixtures; office furniture, except wood

(P-3679)
CARDENAS ENTERPRISES INC
Also Called: J C Rack Systems
339 W Norman Ave, Arcadia (91007-8042)
PHONE..................................323 588-0137
EMP: 17
SALES (est): 1MM **Privately Held**
WEB: www.jcrack.com
SIC: 2542 Mfg Partitions/Fixtures-Nonwood

(P-3680)
CTA FIXTURES INC
5721 Santa Ana St Ste B, Ontario
(91761-8617)
PHONE..................................909 390-6744
Carlos Gutierrez, *CEO*
▲ EMP: 62 EST: 1994
SQ FT: 90,000
SALES (est): 8.7MM **Privately Held**
WEB: www.ctafixtures.com
SIC: 2542 Partitions & fixtures, except wood

(P-3681)
CUTTING EDGE CREATIVE LLC
9944 Flower St, Bellflower (90706-5411)
PHONE..................................562 907-7007
Jennifer Franklin, *Mng Member*
Daniel Esquer, *Prdtn Mgr*
Ward Lookabaugh,
Andres Tamayo, *Manager*
▲ EMP: 75 EST: 1996

SALES (est): 8.9MM **Privately Held**
WEB: www.edgecreativeco.com
SIC: 2542 3496 7319 Racks, merchandise display or storage: except wood; miscellaneous fabricated wire products; display advertising service

(P-3682)
FELBRO INC
3666 E Olympic Blvd, Los Angeles
(90023-3147)
PHONE..................................323 263-8686
Howard Feldner, *Ch of Bd*
Norman Feldner, *CEO*
Jeff Feldner, *Vice Pres*
Conrad Natac, *Controller*
Jeffrey Feldner, *VP Mfg*
▲ EMP: 180 EST: 1945
SQ FT: 75,000
SALES (est): 25.1MM **Privately Held**
WEB: www.felbrodisplays.com
SIC: 2542 Racks, merchandise display or storage: except wood

(P-3683)
FIELD MANUFACTURING CORP (PA)
1751 Torrance Blvd Ste H, Torrance
(90501-1726)
PHONE..................................310 781-9292
Patrick Field, *President*
▲ EMP: 36 EST: 1955
SQ FT: 20,000
SALES (est): 8.2MM **Privately Held**
WEB: www.field-manufacturing.com
SIC: 2542 3089 Partitions & fixtures, except wood; injection molding of plastics

(P-3684)
HANNIBAL MATERIAL HANDLING INC
2230 E 38th St, Vernon (90058-1629)
PHONE..................................323 587-4060
Blanton Bartlett, *President*
Heidy Moon, *Vice Pres*
Steve Roger, *Vice Pres*
▼ EMP: 214 EST: 1980
SQ FT: 163,000
SALES (est): 53.7MM
SALES (corp-wide): 20.1B **Publicly Held**
WEB: www.hannibalindustries.com
SIC: 2542 Partitions & fixtures, except wood
HQ: Hannibal Industries, Inc.
3851 S Santa Fe Ave
Vernon CA 90058
323 513-1200

(P-3685)
HUFCOR CALIFORNIA INC (HQ)
Also Called: Hufcor Airwall Since 1900
2380 E Artesia Blvd, Long Beach
(90805-1708)
P.O. Box 1149, Bellflower (90707-1149)
PHONE..................................562 634-3116
Andy Espineira, *President*
J Michael Borden, *CEO*
Mike Borden, *Chairman*
Frank Scott, *Treasurer*
Sally Mann, *Sales Staff*
EMP: 56 EST: 1987
SQ FT: 87,000
SALES (est): 57.1MM
SALES (corp-wide): 233.7MM **Privately Held**
WEB: www.hufcorworldwide.com
SIC: 2542 5046 Partitions & fixtures, except wood; partitions
PA: Hufcor, Inc.
2101 Kennedy Rd
Janesville WI 53545
608 756-1241

(P-3686)
IDX LOS ANGELES LLC
Also Called: West Coast Mfg & Whsng
5005 E Philadelphia St, Ontario
(91761-2816)
PHONE..................................909 212-8333
Graham Fownes, *General Mgr*
◆ EMP: 109 EST: 2012
SALES (est): 36.5MM
SALES (corp-wide): 5.1B **Publicly Held**
WEB: www.idxcorporation.com
SIC: 2542 Partitions & fixtures, except wood

PA: Ufp Industries, Inc.
2801 E Beltline Ave Ne
Grand Rapids MI 49525
616 364-6161

(P-3687)
JCM INDUSTRIES INC (PA)
Also Called: Advance Storage Products
15302 Pipeline Ln, Huntington Beach
(92649-1138)
PHONE..................................714 902-9000
John Vr Krummell, *President*
Ken Blankenhorn, *President*
John Warren, *CFO*
Jeff Howard, *Vice Pres*
Logan Kebeli, *Vice Pres*
▼ EMP: 21 EST: 1970
SQ FT: 10,000
SALES (est): 44.7MM **Privately Held**
SIC: 2542 Racks, merchandise display or storage: except wood

(P-3688)
MAGNA-POLE PRODUCTS INC (PA)
Also Called: Hang-UPS Unlimited
1904 14th St Ste 107, Santa Monica
(90404-4600)
PHONE..................................310 453-3806
Scott Freeman, *President*
◆ EMP: 15 EST: 1962
SQ FT: 15,000 **Privately Held**
SIC: 2542 Partitions & fixtures, except wood

(P-3689)
NEW GREENSCREEN INCORPORATED
Also Called: Impac International
5500 Jurupa St, Ontario (91761-3668)
PHONE..................................800 767-9378
Kory Levoy, *Branch Mgr*
EMP: 42 **Privately Held**
WEB: www.premierenclosuresystems.com
SIC: 2542 3444 Cabinets: show, display or storage: except wood; sheet metalwork
PA: New Greenscreen, Incorporated
5500 Jurupa St
Ontario CA 91761

(P-3690)
PACIFIC MANUFACTURING MGT INC
Also Called: Greneker Solutions
3110 E 12th St, Los Angeles (90023-3616)
PHONE..................................323 263-9000
Erik Johnson, *President*
Steven Beckman, *COO*
David Naranjo, *Vice Pres*
Robert Ruckdeschel, *Sales Staff*
▲ EMP: 60 EST: 2003
SQ FT: 60,000
SALES (est): 11.2MM **Privately Held**
WEB: www.greneker.com
SIC: 2542 2541 Fixtures: display, office or store: except wood; display fixtures, wood

(P-3691)
PLASTIC TOPS INC
521 E Jamie Ave, La Habra (90631-6842)
PHONE..................................714 738-8128
Paul Ackerman, *President*
Gene Versluys, *Vice Pres*
EMP: 14 EST: 1972
SQ FT: 9,500
SALES (est): 3.1MM **Privately Held**
WEB: www.plastictops.com
SIC: 2542 8011 Counters or counter display cases: except wood; offices & clinics of medical doctors

(P-3692)
RACK INSTALLATIONS SVCS INC
1256 Brooks St Ste E, Ontario
(91762-3663)
PHONE..................................909 261-2243
Gabriel Caliana, *CEO*
EMP: 20 EST: 2018

SALES (est): 1MM **Privately Held**
SIC: 2542 1796 Partitions & fixtures, except wood; mail racks & lock boxes, postal service: except wood; garment racks: except wood; installing building equipment

(P-3693)
RAP SECURITY INC
4630 Cecilia St, Cudahy (90201-5814)
PHONE..................................323 560-3493
Angelo Palmer, *President*
Marki Leonard, *COO*
Bob Palmer, *Vice Pres*
◆ EMP: 55
SQ FT: 40,000
SALES (est): 7.6MM **Privately Held**
SIC: 2542 Fixtures, store: except wood

(P-3694)
REEVE STORE EQUIPMENT COMPANY (PA)
9131 Bermudez St, Pico Rivera
(90660-4507)
PHONE..................................562 949-2535
John Frackelton, *President*
Mary Ann Crysler, *CFO*
Mary Crysler, *CFO*
Robert Frackelton, *Vice Pres*
Jose Joya, *Human Resources*
▲ EMP: 100
SQ FT: 170,000
SALES (est): 16.2MM **Privately Held**
WEB: www.reeveco.com
SIC: 2542 3471 Counters or counter display cases: except wood; electroplating of metals or formed products

(P-3695)
SALSBURY INDUSTRIES INC (PA)
18300 Central Ave, Carson (90746-4008)
PHONE..................................323 846-6700
Dennis Fraher, *President*
Michael N Lobasso, *CFO*
John Fraher, *Chairman*
Eva Torres, *Treasurer*
Brian Fraher, *Vice Pres*
◆ EMP: 349 EST: 1936
SQ FT: 600,000
SALES (est): 94.7MM **Privately Held**
WEB: www.mailboxes.com
SIC: 2542 Locker boxes, postal service: except wood; postal lock boxes, mail racks & related products

(P-3696)
SAMSON PRODUCTS INC
Also Called: J L Industries
6285 Randolph St, Commerce
(90040-3514)
PHONE..................................323 726-9070
John Reissner, *President*
Robert Dunn, *President*
EMP: 43 EST: 1955
SQ FT: 20,000
SALES (est): 8.8MM
SALES (corp-wide): 142.6MM **Privately Held**
WEB: www.activarcpg.com
SIC: 2542 Cabinets: show, display or storage: except wood
PA: Activar, Inc.
9700 Newton Ave S
Bloomington MN 55431
952 392-8445

(P-3697)
STEVES PLATING CORPORATION
3111 N San Fernando Blvd, Burbank
(91504-2527)
PHONE..................................818 842-2184
Terry Knezevich, *CEO*
Roger C Knezevich, *Corp Secy*
EMP: 140 EST: 1956
SQ FT: 80,000
SALES (est): 15.1MM **Privately Held**
WEB: www.stevesplating.com
SIC: 2542 3446 3471 7692 Fixtures, store: except wood; ladders, for permanent installation: metal; railings, prefabricated metal; plating of metals or formed products; welding repair; fabricated pipe & fittings

(P-3698)
TEICHMAN ENTERPRISES INC
Also Called: T & H Store Fixtures
6100 Bandini Blvd, Commerce
(90040-3112)
PHONE...................323 278-9000
Ruth Teichman, *President*
Alan Teichman, *Treasurer*
Sol Teichman, *Treasurer*
Bernard Teichman, *Vice Pres*
Sidney Teichman, *Vice Pres*
▲ EMP: 50 EST: 1956
SALES (est): 9.5MM Privately Held
WEB: www.teichman.net
SIC: 2542 Fixtures: display, office or store:
except wood

(P-3699)
TURTLE STORAGE LTD
Also Called: American Bicycle Security Co
401 S Beckwith Rd, Santa Paula
(93060-3047)
P.O. Box 7359, Ventura (93006-7359)
PHONE...................805 933-3688
Thomas Volk, *President*
Thomas M Volk, *CEO*
Ron Reynolds, *Opers Mgr*
EMP: 20 EST: 1986
SQ FT: 16,000
SALES (est): 2.7MM Privately Held
WEB: www.ameribike.com
SIC: 2542 1799 Lockers (not refrigerated):
except wood; fiberglass work

(P-3700)
UNIWEB INC (PA)
222 S Promenade Ave, Corona
(92879-1743)
PHONE...................951 279-7999
Karl F Weber, *CEO*
Delia Guerrero, *Human Res Dir*
Brent Abbott, *Purch Agent*
Ernesto Lopez, *Prdtn Mgr*
Kathi Locy, *Sales Executive*
▲ EMP: 90
SQ FT: 170,000
SALES (est): 14.2MM Privately Held
WEB: www.uniwebinc.com
SIC: 2542 Fixtures: display, office or store:
except wood

(P-3701)
VERLO INDUSTRIES INC
5032 Apollo Cir, Los Alamitos
(90720-5102)
PHONE...................714 236-2191
Kreig Lopour, *President*
EMP: 16 EST: 1977
SALES (est): 1.6MM Privately Held
WEB: www.verloii.com
SIC: 2542 Racks, merchandise dis-
play or storage: except wood; office furni-
ture, except wood

(P-3702)
WBP ASSOCIATES INC
2017 Seaman Ave, South El Monte
(91733-2626)
PHONE...................626 575-0747
William Pope, *President*
Robert Pope, *Vice Pres*
EMP: 13 EST: 1982
SQ FT: 6,500
SALES (est): 1MM Privately Held
WEB: www.wbpassociates.com
SIC: 2542 1799 Counters or counter dis-
play cases: except wood; counter top in-
stallation

(P-3703)
**WESTERN PCF STOR
SOLUTIONS INC (PA)**
300 E Arrow Hwy, San Dimas
(91773-3339)
PHONE...................909 451-0303
Tom Rogers, *President*
Peter G Dunn, *Ch of Bd*
Angie Bosley, *COO*
Soheir Hakim, *CFO*
Mike Guerrero, *Vice Pres*
EMP: 100 EST: 1985
SQ FT: 165,000
SALES (est): 56MM Privately Held
WEB: www.wpss.com
SIC: 2542 Shelving, office & store: except
wood

2591 Drapery Hardware,
Window Blinds & Shades

(P-3704)
AERO SHADE CO INC (PA)
Also Called: A-Z Industries Div
8404 W 3rd St, Los Angeles (90048-4112)
PHONE...................323 938-2314
Jack Pitson, *President*
Shelly Soulema, *Treasurer*
Mario Soulema, *Vice Pres*
Ashleigh Boutelle, *Admin Asst*
EMP: 25 EST: 1942
SQ FT: 2,400
SALES (est): 3.4MM Privately Held
WEB: www.aeroshadeco.com
SIC: 5719 2591 5023 Window furnish-
ings; window shades; window shades

(P-3705)
**ALL STRONG INDUSTRY (USA)
INC (PA)**
326 Paseo Tesoro, Walnut (91789-2725)
PHONE...................909 598-6494
Pei-Hsiang Hsu, *Ch of Bd*
Frank Hsu, *Vice Pres*
◆ EMP: 30 EST: 1992
SQ FT: 52,000
SALES (est): 4.7MM Privately Held
SIC: 2591 Mini blinds; window shades

(P-3706)
ALUMINUM TECHNOLOGY INC
1455 Columbia Ave, Riverside
(92507-2013)
PHONE...................909 946-3697
Daniel Schwartz, *CEO*
EMP: 14 EST: 2016
SALES (est): 1.3MM Privately Held
SIC: 2591 Window blinds

(P-3707)
C & M WOOD INDUSTRIES
17229 Lemon St Ste D, Hesperia
(92345-5125)
PHONE...................760 949-3292
Calvin Lam, *President*
Roger McCarvel, *Vice Pres*
▲ EMP: 24 EST: 1987
SQ FT: 55,000
SALES (est): 1.1MM Privately Held
WEB: www.cmwood.com
SIC: 2591 Venetian blinds

(P-3708)
CENTURY BLINDS INC
300 S Promenade Ave, Corona
(92879-1754)
P.O. Box 77940 (92877-0131)
PHONE...................951 734-3762
Mitch Shapiro, *CEO*
Gene Sierra, *CIO*
Tracy Roy, *Info Tech Mgr*
Richard Cervantes, *Purch Mgr*
Alan Kramer, *Sales Mgr*
▲ EMP: 100 EST: 1992
SALES (est): 15MM Privately Held
WEB: www.hunterdouglas.se
SIC: 2591 3429 5719 5023 Blinds verti-
cal; manufactured hardware (general);
vertical blinds; vertical blinds
HQ: Hunter Douglas Scandinavia Ab
Kristineholmsvagen 14a
Alingsas 441 3
322 775-00

(P-3709)
ELWIN INC
6910 8th St, Buena Park (90620-1036)
PHONE...................714 752-6962
Josh W Kim, *CEO*
EMP: 20 EST: 2015
SALES (est): 1.7MM Privately Held
SIC: 2591 5719 Window blinds; window
shades

(P-3710)
**HD WINDOW FASHIONS INC
(DH)**
Also Called: M & B Window Fashions
1818 Oak St, Los Angeles (90015-3302)
PHONE...................213 749-6333

Wayne Gourlay, *President*
Dominique Au Yeung, *General Mgr*
Isha Garcia, *Human Res Mgr*
Tim Turner, *Supervisor*
▲ EMP: 500 EST: 1975
SQ FT: 200,000
SALES (est): 71.9MM Privately Held
WEB: www.hunterdouglas.com
SIC: 2591 Mini blinds; venetian blinds; win-
dow shades; blinds vertical
HQ: Hunter Douglas Inc.
1 Blue Hill Plz Ste 1569
Pearl River NY 10965
845 664-7000

(P-3711)
JC WINDOW FASHIONS INC
2438 Peck Rd, Whittier (90601-1604)
PHONE...................909 364-8888
Jennifer Chiao, *CEO*
▲ EMP: 28 EST: 2011
SALES (est): 4.7MM Privately Held
WEB: www.jcwindowfashions.com
SIC: 2591 Drapery hardware & blinds &
shades

(P-3712)
KITTRICH CORPORATION (PA)
1585 W Mission Blvd, Pomona
(91766-1233)
PHONE...................714 736-1000
Robert Friedland, *CEO*
Sloane Friedman, *Regional Mgr*
Marc Scouten, *Technology*
Anh Truong, *CPA*
Mary Kathryn, *Senior Buyer*
◆ EMP: 130 EST: 1978
SQ FT: 237,000
SALES (est): 114.9MM Privately Held
WEB: www.kittrich.com
SIC: 2591 2392 2381 Blinds vertical;
household furnishings; fabric dress &
work gloves

(P-3713)
L C PRINGLE SALES INC (PA)
Also Called: Pringle's Draperies
12020 Western Ave, Garden Grove
(92841-2913)
PHONE...................714 892-1524
Larry C Pringle, *President*
Pamela Pringle Skinner, *Corp Secy*
Susan Pringle Kusinsky, *Vice Pres*
Carolyn Pringle, *Vice Pres*
Curtis L Pringle, *Vice Pres*
EMP: 30 EST: 1968
SQ FT: 11,000
SALES (est): 2.8MM Privately Held
WEB: www.pringlesdraperies.com
SIC: 2591 7216 2391 7211 Blinds verti-
cal; mini blinds; curtain cleaning & repair;
draperies, plastic & textile: from pur-
chased materials; power laundries, family
& commercial

(P-3714)
ROLL-A-SHADE INC (PA)
12101 Madera Way, Riverside
(92503-4849)
PHONE...................951 245-5077
Tyrone Pereira, *President*
Ric Berg, *Vice Pres*
Harsh Wanigaratne, *CTO*
Yvette Flores, *Project Mgr*
Jay Gonzalez, *Project Mgr*
◆ EMP: 22 EST: 1996
SQ FT: 10,000
SALES (est): 10.4MM Privately Held
WEB: www.rollashade.com
SIC: 2591 1799 Window shades; window
treatment installation

(P-3715)
SOLEFFECT
13009 Los Nietos Rd, Santa Fe Springs
(90670-3013)
PHONE...................323 275-9945
Ron Divas, *Co-Owner*
Lynette Wilson, *Co-Owner*
EMP: 15 EST: 2019
SALES (est): 1.9MM Privately Held
WEB: www.soleffectshades.com
SIC: 2591 Drapery hardware & blinds &
shades

(P-3716)
SPEED-O-PIN INTERNATIONAL
1401 Freeman Ave, Long Beach
(90804-2518)
PHONE...................562 433-4911
Jeffrey Jacobson, *President*
EMP: 16 EST: 1952
SQ FT: 20,000
SALES (est): 354.1K Privately Held
SIC: 2591 2672 Drapery hardware &
blinds & shades; coated & laminated
paper

(P-3717)
VERTICAL DOORS INC
Also Called: Vdi Motor Sports
542 3rd St, Lake Elsinore (92530-2729)
PHONE...................951 273-1069
Rob Baum, *President*
Ginarose Chalico, *Sales Staff*
EMP: 24 EST: 2003
SALES (est): 2MM Privately Held
WEB: www.verticaldoors.com
SIC: 2591 Blinds vertical

(P-3718)
VERTICAL TANK INC
4807 Matterhorn Way, Bakersfield
(93312-5449)
P.O. Box 5190 (93388-5190)
PHONE...................415 686-8796
Travis Ellis, *Principal*
EMP: 14 EST: 2014
SALES (est): 1.4MM Privately Held
WEB: www.vertical-tanks.com
SIC: 2591 Blinds vertical

2599 Furniture & Fixtures,
NEC

(P-3719)
1PERFECTCHOICE
21908 Valley Blvd, Walnut (91789-0938)
PHONE...................909 594-8855
CHI Ching Lin, *CEO*
Brian Lin, *CFO*
EMP: 18 EST: 2014
SQ FT: 5,000
SALES (est): 14.3MM Privately Held
WEB: www.oneperfectchoice.com
SIC: 2599 5021 5712 Hospital furniture,
except beds; furniture; furniture stores

(P-3720)
6TH STREET PARTNERS LLC
3950 W 6th St Apt 201, Los Angeles
(90020-4251)
PHONE...................213 377-5277
Robert Kim,
EMP: 17 EST: 2015
SALES (est): 580K Privately Held
SIC: 2599 Bar, restaurant & cafeteria furni-
ture

(P-3721)
**ALEGACY FDSRVICE PDTS
GROUP IN**
12683 Corral Pl, Santa Fe Springs
(90670-4748)
PHONE...................562 320-3100
Jesse Gross, *Principal*
Brett Gross, *President*
Eric Gross, *Vice Pres*
Mark Gross, *Business Dir*
Kevin Pauls, *Regional Mgr*
◆ EMP: 60 EST: 2000
SQ FT: 130,000
SALES (est): 9.5MM Privately Held
WEB: www.alegacy.com
SIC: 2599 3263 Carts, restaurant equip-
ment; cookware, fine earthenware

(P-3722)
ARISTON HOSPITALITY INC
1124 Westminster Ave, Alhambra
(91803-1233)
PHONE...................626 458-8668
Tony Tsai, *CEO*
▲ EMP: 20 EST: 2006
SALES (est): 2.4MM Privately Held
WEB: www.aristonhospitality.com
SIC: 2599 2426 Furniture & fixtures; furni-
ture stock & parts, hardwood

(P-3723)
COMMERCIAL CSTM STING UPHL INC
12601 Western Ave, Garden Grove (92841-4014)
PHONE..................714 850-0520
Robert Francis, *CEO*
Kinga Ludwinek, *Project Mgr*
▲ EMP: 90 EST: 1988
SQ FT: 50,000
SALES (est): 21MM **Privately Held**
WEB: www.ccs-ind.com
SIC: 2599 Restaurant furniture, wood or metal

(P-3724)
DAVID HAID
8619 Crocker St, Los Angeles (90003-3516)
PHONE..................323 752-8096
EMP: 20 **Privately Held**
SIC: 2599 5199 Factory furniture & fixtures; advertising specialties
PA: David Haid
　3931 Topanga Canyon Blvd
　Malibu CA 90265

(P-3725)
ELEGANCE UPHOLSTERY INC
11803 Slauson Ave Unit A, Ontario (91762)
PHONE..................562 698-2584
Ricardo Vargas, *CEO*
Bob Christoff, *Project Mgr*
EMP: 16 EST: 2010
SALES (est): 2.2MM **Privately Held**
WEB: www.eleganceupholsteryinc.com
SIC: 2599 7641 Bar, restaurant & cafeteria furniture; restaurant furniture, wood or metal; bowling establishment furniture; re-upholstery & furniture repair; reupholstery

(P-3726)
ELITE CABINETRY INC
25755 Jefferson Ave, Murrieta (92562-6903)
PHONE..................951 698-5050
Paul Silva, *President*
EMP: 17 EST: 1995
SQ FT: 8,200
SALES (est): 781.3K **Privately Held**
WEB: www.elitecabinetryinc.com
SIC: 2599 Cabinets, factory

(P-3727)
ERGONOM CORPORATION (PA)
Also Called: E R G International
361 Bernoulli Cir, Oxnard (93030-5164)
PHONE..................805 981-9978
George Zaki, *CEO*
Roy Zaki, *President*
Alyssa Lugo, *Administration*
Sherry Beverly, *Accountant*
▲ EMP: 90 EST: 1981
SALES (est): 25.4MM **Privately Held**
SIC: 2599 2531 Hospital furniture, except beds; school furniture

(P-3728)
ERGONOM CORPORATION
Also Called: Erg International
390 Lombard St, Oxnard (93030-7209)
PHONE..................805 981-9978
Roy Zaki, *President*
EMP: 70
SALES (corp-wide): 25.4MM **Privately Held**
SIC: 2599 2531 Hospital furniture, except beds; school furniture
PA: Ergonom Corporation
　361 Bernoulli Cir
　Oxnard CA 93030
　805 981-9978

(P-3729)
FORBES INDUSTRIES DIV
1933 E Locust St, Ontario (91761-7608)
PHONE..................909 923-4559
Tim Sweetland, *President*
Peter Sweetland, *Vice Pres*
▼ EMP: 210 EST: 1919
SQ FT: 110,000

SALES (est): 31.3MM
SALES (corp-wide): 49.8MM **Privately Held**
WEB: www.forbesindustries.com
SIC: 2599 Carts, restaurant equipment
PA: The Winsford Corporation
　1933 E Locust St
　Ontario CA 91761
　909 923-4559

(P-3730)
GLP DESIGNS INC
Also Called: Antique Designs
916 W Hyde Park Blvd, Inglewood (90302-3308)
PHONE..................310 652-6800
Keith G Hudson, *Vice Pres*
Keith Hudson, *Vice Pres*
EMP: 13 EST: 2006
SALES (est): 383.7K **Privately Held**
WEB: www.hydeparkcustom.com
SIC: 2599 Furniture & fixtures

(P-3731)
IAC INDUSTRIES
8175 E Brookdale Ln, Anaheim (92807-2526)
PHONE..................714 990-8997
John Notti, *Opers Staff*
Navor Martin, *Production*
Jessica Urioste, *Marketing Staff*
Rosa Gomez, *Sales Staff*
Jessica Haderer, *Sales Staff*
EMP: 40
SALES (corp-wide): 17.9MM **Privately Held**
WEB: www.iacindustries.com
SIC: 2599 Bar furniture
PA: Iac Industries
　3831 S Bullard Ave
　Goodyear AZ 85338
　714 990-8997

(P-3732)
IMPORTLA LLC
1300 John Reed Ct Ste D, City of Industry (91745-2422)
PHONE..................626 336-8118
Billy Chen, *Manager*
Wen WEI, *CFO*
Michael Chen,
EMP: 15 EST: 2015
SALES (est): 3MM **Privately Held**
WEB: www.importla.com
SIC: 2599 Cabinets, factory

(P-3733)
JBI LLC (PA)
Also Called: Jbi Interiors
2650 E El Presidio St, Long Beach (90810-1142)
PHONE..................310 886-8034
Pete Jensen, *Manager*
Jean Reeves, *CFO*
Andy Braddy, *Exec VP*
Joseph Parisi, *Senior VP*
Shea Brownlow, *Vice Pres*
◆ EMP: 200 EST: 1968
SQ FT: 270,000
SALES (est): 63.1MM **Privately Held**
WEB: www.jbi-interiors.com
SIC: 2599 5046 Restaurant furniture, wood or metal; restaurant equipment & supplies

(P-3734)
KCI NEWPORT INC
15763 Ornelas St, Baldwin Park (91706-6610)
PHONE..................877 302-5302
Ziad Kassir, *Principal*
EMP: 15 EST: 2013
SALES (est): 1.1MM **Privately Held**
WEB: www.kcinewport.com
SIC: 2599 Hospital beds

(P-3735)
MASHINDUSTRIES INC
7150 Village Dr, Buena Park (90621-2261)
PHONE..................714 736-9600
Bernard Brucha, *CEO*
Robert Rivas, *Business Dir*
Michelle Blemel, *Admin Sec*
Isamar Munguia, *Engineer*
Diane Roberts, *Controller*
EMP: 47 EST: 2013 **Privately Held**

WEB: www.mashindustries.com
SIC: 2599 Factory furniture & fixtures

(P-3736)
PRODUCTION SYSTEMS GROUP INC
Also Called: Production Industries
895 Beacon St, Brea (92821-2905)
PHONE..................714 990-8997
EMP: 40
SQ FT: 50,000
SALES: 5MM
SALES (corp-wide): 12.6MM **Privately Held**
SIC: 2599 Mfg Furniture Specializing In Work Stations & Work Benches
PA: Iac Industries
　895 Beacon St
　Brea CA 85338
　714 990-8997

(P-3737)
PTM IMAGES LLC
10990 Wilshire Blvd # 140, Los Angeles (90024-3962)
PHONE..................310 881-8053
Jonathan Bass, *Manager*
EMP: 15 EST: 1995
SALES (est): 1.7MM **Privately Held**
WEB: www.ptmimages.com
SIC: 2599 Factory furniture & fixtures

(P-3738)
R & J FABRICATORS INC
1121 Railroad St Ste 102, Corona (92882-8219)
PHONE..................951 817-0300
James Ciarletta, *CEO*
Jay Warren Ciarletta, *Vice Pres*
EMP: 20 EST: 1982
SQ FT: 20,000
SALES (est): 3.6MM **Privately Held**
SIC: 2599 Restaurant furniture, wood or metal

(P-3739)
STAINLESS FIXTURES INC
3323 Russell St, Riverside (92501-2217)
PHONE..................909 622-1615
EMP: 18 EST: 1989
SALES (est): 1MM **Privately Held**
WEB: www.sfi-online.com
SIC: 2599 Restaurant furniture, wood or metal

(P-3740)
STAINLESS FIXTURES INC
1250 E Franklin Ave, Pomona (91766-5449)
PHONE..................909 622-1615
Randy Rodriguez, *President*
Lana Hammerton, *Controller*
Usama Cost, *Manager*
Steven Vasquez, *Manager*
EMP: 35 EST: 1989
SQ FT: 36,000
SALES (est): 12.5MM **Privately Held**
WEB: www.sfi-online.com
SIC: 2599 Restaurant furniture, wood or metal; hotel furniture

(P-3741)
SYC INTERNATIONAL INC
16027 Brookhurst St I305, Fountain Valley (92708-1551)
PHONE..................888 300-9168
Wai Sze Lau, *CEO*
EMP: 50 EST: 2019
SALES (est): 1.4MM **Privately Held**
SIC: 2599 Furniture & fixtures

(P-3742)
TAHITI CABINETS INC
5419 E La Palma Ave, Anaheim (92807-2022)
PHONE..................714 693-0618
Mark Ramsey, *President*
Lori Gudinas, *Planning Mgr*
Doreen Ramsey, *Admin Sec*
Steve Lichtenwalter, *Project Mgr*
Carrie Olson, *Project Mgr*
EMP: 58 EST: 1975
SQ FT: 32,000

SALES (est): 11.4MM **Privately Held**
WEB: www.tahiticabinets.com
SIC: 2599 2431 2434 Cabinets, factory; millwork; wood kitchen cabinets

2611 Pulp Mills

(P-3743)
GO2ZERO STRATEGIES LLC
6625 N Calle Eva Miranda, Irwindale (91702-2870)
PHONE..................626 840-1850
Judi Gregory, *Branch Mgr*
Jonathan Levy, *Project Mgr*
EMP: 18
SALES (corp-wide): 1.1MM **Privately Held**
WEB: www.go2zero.net
SIC: 2611 Pulp mills, mechanical & recycling processing
PA: Go2zero Strategies, Llc
　6625 N Calle Eva Miranda
　Irwindale CA 91702
　877 462-9376

(P-3744)
NEW GREEN DAY LLC
1710 E 111th St, Los Angeles (90059-1910)
P.O. Box 72147 (90002-0147)
PHONE..................323 566-7603
Brian Kelly, *CEO*
Virgialeo San Victors, *Accountant*
Randi Yamamoto, *Accountant*
David Holt,
Kirk Sanford, *Mng Member*
EMP: 25 EST: 2004
SQ FT: 25,000
SALES (est): 5.4MM **Privately Held**
WEB: www.ngdla.com
SIC: 2611 Pulp manufactured from waste or recycled paper

(P-3745)
WESTERN PACIFIC PULP AND PAPER (HQ)
9400 Hall Rd, Downey (90241-5365)
PHONE..................562 803-4401
Ralph Ho, *Ch of Bd*
Kevin Duncombe, *CEO*
Jim Forkey, *Vice Pres*
Karen Murray, *Vice Pres*
Phil Wijmer, *Vice Pres*
▼ EMP: 51 EST: 1983
SALES (est): 15.9MM
SALES (corp-wide): 22.5MM **Privately Held**
WEB: www.wppp.com
SIC: 2611 5093 Pulp manufactured from waste or recycled paper; waste paper
PA: Y. F. International
　180 Park Rd
　Burlingame CA 94010
　650 342-6560

2621 Paper Mills

(P-3746)
ACME UNITED CORPORATION
630 Young St, Santa Ana (92705-5633)
PHONE..................714 557-2001
EMP: 22
SALES (corp-wide): 164MM **Publicly Held**
WEB: www.acmeunited.com
SIC: 2621 Absorbent paper
PA: Acme United Corporation
　1 Waterview Dr Ste 200
　Shelton CT 06484
　800 835-2263

(P-3747)
ALLIED WEST PAPER CORP
11101 Etiwanda Ave # 100, Fontana (92337-6984)
PHONE..................909 349-0710
Ray Ovanessian, *CEO*
Eric Ovanessian, *Vice Pres*
Mike Ovanessian, *Vice Pres*
Greg Castillo, *Administration*
Tony Pyne, *Info Tech Mgr*
◆ EMP: 95 EST: 1989
SQ FT: 300,000

SALES (est): 48.3MM **Privately Held**
WEB: www.alliedwestpaper.com
SIC: 2621 Paper mills; pattern tissue; creping tissue; napkin stock, paper

(P-3748)
AMERICAN GRAPHIC BOARD INC
5880 E Slauson Ave, Commerce (90040-3018)
PHONE..................323 721-0585
Don Zeccola, *President*
Michael Carmody, *CFO*
Peter Kang, *Admin Sec*
▲ **EMP:** 48 **EST:** 2003
SQ FT: 135,000
SALES (est): 1.6MM **Privately Held**
SIC: 2621 Paper mills

(P-3749)
CROWN PAPER CONVERTING INC
1380 S Bon View Ave, Ontario (91761-4403)
P.O. Box 3277 (91761-0928)
PHONE..................909 923-5226
Bruce Hale, *Principal*
Lisa Hale, *Vice Pres*
EMP: 40 **EST:** 1983
SQ FT: 34,000
SALES (est): 9.7MM **Privately Held**
WEB: www.crownpaperconverting.com
SIC: 2621 Paper mills

(P-3750)
D D OFFICE PRODUCTS INC
Also Called: Liberty Paper
5025 Hampton St, Vernon (90058-2133)
P.O. Box 58026 (90058-0026)
PHONE..................323 582-3400
Alex Ismail, *CEO*
Anwar Lalani, *President*
Benazir Ismael, *CFO*
Cindy Flores, *Vice Pres*
Stephanie Scherping, *Admin Sec*
▲ **EMP:** 15 **EST:** 1986
SQ FT: 22,000
SALES (est): 63.8MM **Privately Held**
WEB: www.libertypp.com
SIC: 2621 5112 5044 5045 Printing paper; stationery & office supplies; office equipment; computers & accessories, personal & home entertainment; hardware; furniture

(P-3751)
EAGLE RIDGE PAPER LTD (HQ)
Also Called: Eagleridge Paper CA
100 S Anaheim Blvd # 250, Anaheim (92805-3848)
PHONE..................714 780-1799
Yeoh Khai Sun, *President*
▲ **EMP:** 178 **EST:** 2012
SALES (est): 6.8MM
SALES (corp-wide): 22.6MM **Privately Held**
WEB: www.eagleridgepaper.com
SIC: 2621 Printing paper
PA: Eagle Ridge Paper Ltd
20 Hereford St Unit 15
Brampton ON L6Y 0
888 324-5399

(P-3752)
ENVELOPMENTS INC
13091 Sandhurst Pl, Santa Ana (92705-2135)
PHONE..................714 569-3300
Mark A Smith, *CEO*
Holly Jakobs, *CFO*
Deborah Hefter, *Vice Pres*
Ramon Gomez, *Creative Dir*
Karen Huerta, *Supervisor*
▲ **EMP:** 39 **EST:** 1993
SALES (est): 5.4MM **Privately Held**
WEB: www.envelopments.com
SIC: 2621 5112 Stationery, envelope & tablet papers; stationery

(P-3753)
GLOBAL PAPER SOLUTIONS INC
100 S Anaheim Blvd # 250, Anaheim (92805-3848)
PHONE..................714 687-6102

CHI MI Chung, *President*
▲ **EMP:** 42 **EST:** 2004
SALES (est): 2.8MM **Privately Held**
WEB: www.globalpapersolutions.com
SIC: 2621 Paper mills

(P-3754)
GOODMAN NORTH AMERICA LLC
2001 E Orangethorpe Ave, Fullerton (92831-5326)
PHONE..................714 680-7460
Rick Tucker, *Branch Mgr*
Gary Hardesty, *Safety Mgr*
Lana Lint, *QC Mgr*
EMP: 100
SQ FT: 3,000 **Privately Held**
SIC: 2621 2676 Sanitary tissue paper; sanitary paper products
PA: Goodman North America Llc
18201 Von Karman Ave # 1
Irvine CA 92612

(P-3755)
HARVARD LABEL LLC
Also Called: Harvard Card Systems
111 Baldwin Park Blvd, City of Industry (91746-1402)
PHONE..................626 333-8881
Michael Tang, *CEO*
David Banducci, *President*
▲ **EMP:** 115 **EST:** 1996
SQ FT: 125,000
SALES (est): 38.1MM **Privately Held**
WEB: www.plicards.com
SIC: 2621 2675 2752 Greeting card paper; stencil cards, die-cut; made from purchased materials; cards, lithographed
PA: Plasticard - Locktech International, Llc
1220 Trade Dr
North Las Vegas NV 89030

(P-3756)
INNOVENT INC (PA)
4667 Macarthur Blvd # 220, Newport Beach (92660-1817)
PHONE..................949 387-7725
Yogesh Parmar, *CEO*
Daryl Asato, *Director*
EMP: 14 **EST:** 2013
SQ FT: 100
SALES (est): 1.6MM **Privately Held**
WEB: www.innoventinc.com
SIC: 2621 Sanitary tissue paper

(P-3757)
J R C INDUSTRIES INC
11804 Wakeman St, Santa Fe Springs (90670-2129)
PHONE..................562 698-0171
Leonard Fishelberg, *CEO*
EMP: 24 **EST:** 1976
SQ FT: 32,000
SALES (est): 1.1MM **Privately Held**
WEB: www.jrcindustries.com
SIC: 2621 Paper mills

(P-3758)
KEVIDKO INC
9903 Santa Monica Blvd # 982, Beverly Hills (90212-1671)
PHONE..................310 601-0060
Mehrdad Soleimani, *CEO*
EMP: 13 **EST:** 2012
SALES (est): 1.5MM **Privately Held**
WEB: www.kevidko.com
SIC: 2621 Packaging paper

(P-3759)
KUI CO INC
266 Calle Pintoresco, San Clemente (92672-7504)
PHONE..................949 369-7949
Terry Daum, *President*
Sandy Daum, *CFO*
Matthew McLaughlin, *Engineer*
Art Escalona, *Supervisor*
EMP: 40
SQ FT: 14,800
SALES (est): 3.5MM **Privately Held**
WEB: www.kuicoinc.com
SIC: 2621 3089 Molded pulp products; plastic processing

(P-3760)
LD PRODUCTS INC
Also Called: 4inkjets
3700 Cover St, Long Beach (90808-1782)
PHONE..................888 321-2552
Aaron Leon, *CEO*
Patrick Devane, *Senior VP*
Gary Conrado, *Business Mgr*
Matt Geisel, *VP Sales*
Frank Farina, *Marketing Staff*
◆ **EMP:** 193 **EST:** 1999
SQ FT: 25,000
SALES (est): 46.1MM **Privately Held**
WEB: www.ldproducts.com
SIC: 2621 5045 Stationery, envelope & tablet papers; printers, computer

(P-3761)
MAILING PROS INC
5261 Business Dr, Huntington Beach (92649-1221)
PHONE..................714 892-7251
Pedro Flores, *CEO*
Christopher West, *President*
EMP: 13 **EST:** 2000
SQ FT: 8,000
SALES (est): 2.6MM **Privately Held**
WEB: www.mailingprosinc.com
SIC: 2621 7331 3579 Printing paper; addressing service; mailing service; envelope stuffing, sealing & addressing machines; letter folding, stuffing & sealing machines

(P-3762)
NASHUA CORPORATION
Rittenhouse
13341 Cambridge St, Santa Fe Springs (90670-4903)
PHONE..................323 583-8828
EMP: 80
SQ FT: 57,600
SALES (corp-wide): 1.9B **Publicly Held**
SIC: 2621 Paper Mill
HQ: Nashua Corporation
59 Daniel Webster Hwy A
Merrimack NH 03054
603 880-1100

(P-3763)
NEW-INDY CONTAINERBOARD LLC (DH)
Also Called: International Paper
3500 Porsche Way Ste 150, Ontario (91764-4969)
P.O. Box 519, Port Hueneme (93044-0519)
PHONE..................909 296-3400
Richard Hartman, *CEO*
Mike Conkey, *Vice Pres*
Frederick Donatucci, *Vice Pres*
Patricia Hansen, *Asst Controller*
Todd Malaki, *Manager*
▲ **EMP:** 95 **EST:** 2012
SALES (est): 332.3K
SALES (corp-wide): 679.2MM **Privately Held**
WEB: www.newindycontainerboard.com
SIC: 2621 Paper mills

(P-3764)
NEW-INDY ONTARIO LLC
Also Called: New-Indy Containerboard
5100 Jurupa St, Ontario (91761-3618)
PHONE..................909 390-1055
Richard Hartman, *CEO*
Mike Conkey, *Vice Pres*
Tobias Pina, *Info Tech Dir*
Victor Kumpera, *Technical Mgr*
Beth Hindman, *Safety Mgr*
EMP: 110 **EST:** 2012
SALES (est): 114.5K
SALES (corp-wide): 679.2MM **Privately Held**
WEB: www.newindycontainerboard.com
SIC: 2621 Paper mills
HQ: New-Indy Containerboard Llc
3500 Porsche Way Ste 150
Ontario CA 91764
909 296-3400

(P-3765)
NEW-INDY OXNARD LLC
Also Called: New-Indy Containerboard
5936 Perkins Rd, Oxnard (93033-9044)
P.O. Box 519, Port Hueneme (93044-0519)
PHONE..................805 986-3881

Richard Hartman, *CEO*
Mike Conkey, *Vice Pres*
▲ **EMP:** 224 **EST:** 2012
SALES (est): 233.3K
SALES (corp-wide): 679.2MM **Privately Held**
WEB: www.newindycontainerboard.com
SIC: 2621 Paper mills
HQ: New-Indy Containerboard Llc
3500 Porsche Way Ste 150
Ontario CA 91764
909 296-3400

(P-3766)
OEM MATERIALS & SUPPLIES INC
1500 Ritchey St, Santa Ana (92705-4731)
PHONE..................714 564-9600
Randall K Johnson, *CEO*
Wendy R King, *President*
Ana Hernandez, *Purch Agent*
Brandy Murad, *Sales Staff*
Santiago Arciniega, *Manager*
EMP: 20 **EST:** 2008
SALES (est): 4.1MM **Privately Held**
WEB: www.oemmaterials.com
SIC: 2621 2631 5084 2671 Wrapping & packaging papers; container, packaging & boxboard; processing & packaging equipment; packaging paper & plastics film, coated & laminated

(P-3767)
PACON INC
4249 Puente Ave, Baldwin Park (91706-3420)
PHONE..................626 814-4654
Robert M Austin, *CEO*
Michael Austin, *Vice Pres*
Donald Arrowood, *General Mgr*
Ryan Dressler, *General Mgr*
Veronica Padilla, *Office Mgr*
◆ **EMP:** 103 **EST:** 1977
SQ FT: 44,000
SALES (est): 20.6MM **Privately Held**
WEB: www.paconinc.com
SIC: 2621 Paper mills

(P-3768)
PAPER SURCE CONVERTING MFG INC
Also Called: Soft-Touch Tissue
2015 E 48th St, Vernon (90058-2021)
PHONE..................323 583-3800
Jacob Khobian, *CEO*
▲ **EMP:** 50 **EST:** 1996
SQ FT: 55,000
SALES (est): 21.4MM **Privately Held**
WEB: www.papersourcemfg.com
SIC: 2621 Tissue paper; napkin stock, paper; facial tissue stock; toilet tissue stock

(P-3769)
SAN DIEGO DAILY TRANSCRIPT
34 Emerald Gln, Laguna Niguel (92677-9379)
P.O. Box 85469, San Diego (92186-5469)
PHONE..................619 232-4381
Ed Frederickson, *President*
EMP: 63 **EST:** 1886
SQ FT: 30,000
SALES (est): 10MM
SALES (corp-wide): 12.8MM **Privately Held**
WEB: www.sddt.com
SIC: 2621 4813 Printing paper;
PA: Calcomco, Inc.
5544 S Red Pine Cir
Kalamazoo MI 49009
313 885-9228

(P-3770)
SPECIALTY PAPER MILLS INC
8844 Millergrove Dr, Santa Fe Springs (90670-2004)
P.O. Box 3188 (90670-0188)
PHONE..................562 692-8737
Ronald Gabriel, *President*
Aldo De Soto, *Vice Pres*
Agnes Gabriel, *Admin Sec*
EMP: 200 **EST:** 1959
SQ FT: 45,000

PRODUCTS & SVCS

SALES (est): 32.1MM **Privately Held**
WEB: www.gabrielcontainer.com
SIC: 2621 2631 Paper mills; paperboard mills
PA: Gabriel Container
8844 Millergrove Dr
Santa Fe Springs CA 90670
562 699-1051

(P-3771)
SPILL MAGIC INC
630 Young St, Santa Ana (92705-5633)
PHONE..........................714 557-2001
Susan Wampler, *President*
David Wampler, *Vice Pres*
▲ **EMP:** 22 **EST:** 1995
SQ FT: 30,000
SALES (est): 5.2MM
SALES (corp-wide): 164MM **Publicly Held**
WEB: www.firstaidonly.com
SIC: 2621 Absorbent paper
PA: Acme United Corporation
1 Waterview Dr Ste 200
Shelton CT 06484
800 835-2263

2631 Paperboard Mills

(P-3772)
CALIFRNIA TRADE CONVERTERS INC
9816 Variel Ave, Chatsworth (91311-4316)
PHONE..........................818 899-1455
Carlos Martinez, *President*
EMP: 25 **EST:** 1997
SALES (est): 3.9MM **Privately Held**
SIC: 2631 2675 Paperboard mills; paper die-cutting

(P-3773)
LOS ANGELES BOARD MILLS INC
Also Called: Los Angeles Ppr Box & Bd Mills
1600 Barranca Pkwy, Irvine (92606-4823)
PHONE..........................323 685-8900
William H Kewell III, *President*
Carol A Kewell, *Corp Secy*
EMP: 53 **EST:** 1901
SALES (est): 2.1MM **Privately Held**
SIC: 2631 2652 2653 5113 Folding boxboard; packaging board; setup boxboard; setup paperboard boxes; boxes, corrugated: made from purchased materials; industrial & personal service paper; folding paperboard boxes

(P-3774)
MAXON AUTO CORPORATION
8599 Enterprise Way, Chino (91710-9306)
PHONE..........................626 400-6464
Xinxiang Wang, *CEO*
▲ **EMP:** 15 **EST:** 2014
SALES (est): 1.2MM **Privately Held**
SIC: 2631 Automobile board

(P-3775)
ONE UP MANUFACTURING LLC
550 E Airline Way, Gardena (90248-2502)
PHONE..........................310 749-8347
Nielson Ballon, *Mng Member*
Kavish Mehta,
Nathan Miller,
EMP: 25 **EST:** 2017
SALES (est): 500K **Privately Held**
SIC: 2631 Container, packaging & boxboard

(P-3776)
PACKAGING DIST ASSEMBLY GROUP
Also Called: Pda Group
24730 Avenue Rockefeller, Valencia (91355-3465)
PHONE..........................661 607-0600
▲ **EMP:** 14 **EST:** 2011
SALES (est): 4.4MM **Privately Held**
WEB: www.pda-valencia.com
SIC: 2631 Container, packaging & boxboard

(P-3777)
UP PACKAGING ENTERPRISE
3228 Gabriella St, West Covina (91792-2101)
PHONE..........................626 715-2838
Yumei LI, *Principal*
EMP: 16 **EST:** 2012
SALES (est): 75.9K **Privately Held**
WEB: www.enterprise.com
SIC: 2631 Container, packaging & boxboard

(P-3778)
ZAPP PACKAGING INC
1921 S Business Pkwy, Ontario (91761-8539)
PHONE..........................909 930-1500
Vincent Randazzo, *CEO*
William L Finn, *CEO*
Bruce Altshuler, *Corp Secy*
▲ **EMP:** 60 **EST:** 1931
SQ FT: 80,000
SALES (est): 12.7MM **Privately Held**
SIC: 2631 Folding boxboard; setup boxboard

2652 Set-Up Paperboard Boxes

(P-3779)
PACIFIC PAPER BOX COMPANY (PA)
3928 Encino Hills Pl, Encino (91436-3804)
PHONE..........................323 771-7733
Craig T Harrison, *CEO*
Bud Erhardt, *President*
EMP: 37 **EST:** 1939
SQ FT: 70,000
SALES (est): 5.1MM **Privately Held**
SIC: 2652 Boxes, newsboard, metal edged: made from purchased materials

(P-3780)
YEBO GROUP INC
Also Called: Yebo Printing
2652 Dow Ave, Tustin (92780-7208)
PHONE..........................949 502-3317
Andrew Tosh, *Principal*
Leah Covey, *Opers Staff*
Miguel Sampablo, *Opers Staff*
Marquez Michael, *Sales Mgr*
Martinez Anthony, *Sales Staff*
▲ **EMP:** 25 **EST:** 2008
SALES (est): 8.7MM **Privately Held**
WEB: www.customboxesandpackaging.com
SIC: 5943 2652 Stationery stores; boxes, newsboard, metal edged: made from purchased materials

2653 Corrugated & Solid Fiber Boxes

(P-3781)
ABEX DISPLAY SYSTEMS INC (PA)
Also Called: Abex Exhibit Systems
355 Parkside Dr, San Fernando (91340-3036)
PHONE..........................800 537-0231
Robbie Blumenfeld, *President*
Peter Blumenfeld, *Vice Pres*
Max Candiotty, *Vice Pres*
George Contorinis, *Executive*
Alan Go, *Information Mgr*
◆ **EMP:** 105 **EST:** 1982
SQ FT: 85,000
SALES (est): 9MM **Privately Held**
WEB: www.abex.com
SIC: 2653 2541 Display items, solid fiber: made from purchased materials; store & office display cases & fixtures

(P-3782)
ADVANCE PAPER BOX COMPANY
Also Called: Packaging Spectrum
6100 S Gramercy Pl, Los Angeles (90047-1397)
PHONE..........................323 750-2550
Martin Gardner, *CEO*

Carlo Mendoza, *CFO*
Nick Silk, *Treasurer*
Devan Gardner, *Vice Pres*
Poren Hsiao, *Engineer*
▲ **EMP:** 250 **EST:** 1924
SQ FT: 500,000
SALES (est): 52.9MM **Privately Held**
WEB: www.advancepaperbox.com
SIC: 2653 3082 2657 Boxes, corrugated: made from purchased materials; boxes, solid fiber: made from purchased materials; unsupported plastics profile shapes; folding paperboard boxes

(P-3783)
ANDROP PACKAGING INC
Also Called: Ontario Foam Products
4400 E Francis St, Ontario (91761-2327)
PHONE..........................909 605-8842
Cesar Flores, *President*
Larry Lippert, *Director*
▲ **EMP:** 23 **EST:** 1974
SQ FT: 52,000
SALES (est): 4.6MM **Privately Held**
WEB: www.androppkg.com
SIC: 2653 3086 Boxes, corrugated: made from purchased materials; plastics foam products

(P-3784)
AWARD PACKAGING SPC CORP
12855 Midway Pl, Cerritos (90703-2141)
PHONE..........................323 727-1200
Alfred Espinoza, *CEO*
Virginia S Espinoza, *Treasurer*
EMP: 28 **EST:** 1978
SQ FT: 800
SALES (est): 3MM **Privately Held**
SIC: 2653 Boxes, corrugated: made from purchased materials

(P-3785)
BAY CITIES CONTAINER CORP (PA)
5138 Industry Ave, Pico Rivera (90660-2550)
PHONE..........................562 948-3751
Greg A Tucker, *CEO*
Michael Musgrave, *COO*
Patrick Donohoe, *CFO*
Nanneke Dinklo, *Surgery Dir*
Johnathan Barragan, *IT/INT Sup*
▲ **EMP:** 152 **EST:** 1956
SALES (est): 111.9MM **Privately Held**
WEB: www.bay-cities.com
SIC: 2653 3993 5113 Boxes, corrugated: made from purchased materials; display items, corrugated: made from purchased materials; signs & advertising specialties; corrugated & solid fiber boxes; folding paperboard boxes

(P-3786)
BEST BOX COMPANY INC
Also Called: A1 Carton Co
8011 Beach St, Los Angeles (90001-3424)
PHONE..........................323 589-6088
Jay Kim, *President*
EMP: 22 **EST:** 1963
SQ FT: 38,000
SALES (est): 1.1MM **Privately Held**
WEB: www.best-box.com
SIC: 2653 Boxes, corrugated: made from purchased materials

(P-3787)
BLOWER-DEMPSAY CORPORATION
Also Called: Pacific Western Container
4044 W Garry Ave, Santa Ana (92704-6300)
PHONE..........................714 547-9266
Ken Ito, *Opers Mgr*
Tim Bynon, *General Mgr*
Dale Haskins, *Prdtn Mgr*
Manuel Pantoja, *Manager*
Mike Webb, *Manager*
EMP: 20
SQ FT: 30,000
SALES (corp-wide): 83.3MM **Privately Held**
WEB: www.pakwest.com
SIC: 2653 5199 5113 Boxes, corrugated: made from purchased materials; packaging materials; corrugated & solid fiber boxes

PA: Blower-Dempsay Corporation
4042 W Garry Ave
Santa Ana CA 92704
714 481-3800

(P-3788)
BLUE RIBBON CONT & DISPLAY INC
11106 Shoemaker Ave, Santa Fe Springs (90670-4647)
PHONE..........................562 944-1217
Kenneth G Overfield, *President*
EMP: 15 **EST:** 1991
SQ FT: 32,000
SALES (est): 2.3MM **Privately Held**
WEB: www.brcbox.com
SIC: 2653 5199 5113 Boxes, corrugated: made from purchased materials; packaging materials; boxes & containers

(P-3789)
BOXES R US INC
Also Called: Ultimate Paper Box Company
15051 Don Julian Rd, City o' Industry (91746-3302)
PHONE..........................626 820-5410
Janak P Patel, *President*
Dipak Patel, *Vice Pres*
Eric Haikara, *Sales Mgr*
Juan Montanez, *Manager*
Mark Perez, *Manager*
▲ **EMP:** 70 **EST:** 1996
SQ FT: 38,000
SALES (est): 18.7MM **Privately Held**
SIC: 2653 Boxes, corrugated: made from purchased materials

(P-3790)
C B SHEETS INC
13901 Carmenita Rd, Santa Fe Springs (90670-4916)
PHONE..........................562 921-1223
John Widera, *CEO*
Mackey Davis, *President*
EMP: 21 **EST:** 2001
SALES (est): 7.9MM
SALES (corp-wide): 22.9MM **Privately Held**
WEB: www.calbox.com
SIC: 2653 Boxes, corrugated: made from purchased materials
PA: California Box Company
13901 Carmenita Rd
Santa Fe Springs CA 90670
562 921-1223

(P-3791)
CALIFORNIA BOX II
8949 Toronto Ave, Rancho Cucamonga (91730-5412)
PHONE..........................909 944-9202
John Widera, *CEO*
Mackey Davis, *Vice Pres*
Joe Yocam, *Sales Staff*
Reed Gibbons, *Maintence Staff*
EMP: 45 **EST:** 1990
SQ FT: 100,000
SALES (est): 7.8MM **Privately Held**
WEB: www.calbox.com
SIC: 2653 5113 Boxes, corrugated: made from purchased materials; corrugated & solid fiber boxes

(P-3792)
CD CONTAINER INC
Also Called: Carton Design
7343 Paramount Blvd, Pico Rivera (90660-3713)
PHONE..........................562 948-1910
Juan De La Cruz, *President*
Jose De La Cruz, *CFO*
▲ **EMP:** 70 **EST:** 1987
SQ FT: 46,000
SALES (est): 9.7MM **Privately Held**
WEB: www.cdcontainerinc.com
SIC: 2653 Boxes, corrugated: made from purchased materials

(P-3793)
CITY PAPER BOX CO
652 E 61st St, Los Angeles (90001-1021)
PHONE..........................323 231-5990
Stanley Goodrich, *President*
Maurey Friedman, *Vice Pres*
Frieda Goodrich, *Vice Pres*
Michael Goodrich, *Vice Pres*

Abe Friedman, *Executive*
EMP: 16 **EST:** 1962
SQ FT: 9,000
SALES (est): 2.9MM **Privately Held**
WEB: www.citypaperbox.com
SIC: 2653 Boxes, corrugated: made from purchased materials

(P-3794)
COASTAL CONTAINER INC
8455 Loch Lomond Dr, Pico Rivera (90660-2508)
PHONE.................562 801-4595
Richard Rudell, *President*
Roberta Noble, *Treasurer*
EMP: 23 **EST:** 1993
SQ FT: 3,000
SALES (est): 6.2MM **Privately Held**
SIC: 2653 5113 Boxes, corrugated: made from purchased materials; corrugated & solid fiber boxes

(P-3795)
COMMANDER PACKAGING WEST INC
602 S Rockefeller Ave D, Ontario (91761-8191)
PHONE.................714 921-9350
Joseph F Kindlon, *Ch of Bd*
Brian R Webber, *President*
EMP: 37 **EST:** 1987
SQ FT: 48,000
SALES (est): 3.7MM **Privately Held**
WEB: www.commanderpackagingwest.com
SIC: 2653 7389 5113 Boxes, corrugated: made from purchased materials; packaging & labeling services; corrugated & solid fiber boxes
PA: Cano Container Corporation
3920 Enterprise Ct Ste A
Aurora IL 60504

(P-3796)
CORRU-KRAFT IV
1911 E Rosslynn Ave, Fullerton (92831-5141)
PHONE.................714 773-0124
Bob Dunford, *Principal*
Ron Vivian, *Sales Mgr*
George Zaldivar, *Supervisor*
EMP: 18 **EST:** 2008
SALES (est): 4.8MM **Privately Held**
WEB: www.bluestream.net
SIC: 2653 Boxes, corrugated: made from purchased materials

(P-3797)
CROCKETT GRAPHICS INC (PA)
Also Called: Folding Cartons
980 Avenida Acaso, Camarillo (93012-8759)
PHONE.................805 987-8577
Edward Randall Crockett, *President*
Rod K Rieth, *Treasurer*
Mike Mullens, *Vice Pres*
Dave Eisenberg, *Pub Rel Mgr*
Glen Brown, *Sales Staff*
▲ **EMP:** 60 **EST:** 1994
SALES (est): 17.1MM **Privately Held**
WEB: www.garedgraphics.com
SIC: 2653 Corrugated boxes, partitions, display items, sheets & pad

(P-3798)
CROWN CARTON COMPANY INC
1820 E 48th Pl, Vernon (90058-1946)
PHONE.................323 582-3053
Jeffrey P Marks, *President*
Kyle Johnson, *Vice Pres*
EMP: 20 **EST:** 1953
SQ FT: 28,000
SALES (est): 4.1MM **Privately Held**
WEB: www.crowncarton.com
SIC: 2653 Boxes, corrugated: made from purchased materials

(P-3799)
ECKO PRODUCTS GROUP LLC
Also Called: Ecko Print & Packaging
740 S Milliken Ave Ste C, Ontario (91761-7842)
PHONE.................909 628-5678
Eric Rogers, *CFO*
Christopher Hively, *President*

Eric Martinez, *Vice Pres*
Jennifer Pearce, *Accountant*
Glen Billups, *Sales Staff*
◆ **EMP:** 23 **EST:** 2002
SQ FT: 17,000
SALES (est): 7.4MM **Privately Held**
WEB: www.eckopg.com
SIC: 2653 5085 2759 Boxes, corrugated: made from purchased materials; abrasives & adhesives; commercial printing

(P-3800)
EMPIRE CONTAINER CORPORATION
1161 E Walnut St, Carson (90746-1382)
PHONE.................310 537-8190
Donald Simmons, *President*
Patrick Fox, *Shareholder*
Gregory V Hall, *Principal*
▲ **EMP:** 66 **EST:** 1970
SQ FT: 61,000
SALES (est): 7.4MM **Privately Held**
WEB: www.empirecontainercorp.com
SIC: 2653 3578 Boxes, corrugated: made from purchased materials; point-of-sale devices

(P-3801)
EXPRESS CONTAINER INC
560 Iowa St, Redlands (92373-8060)
P.O. Box 230 (92373-0064)
PHONE.................909 798-3857
Gilles Roy, *President*
EMP: 22 **EST:** 1984
SQ FT: 25,000
SALES (est): 4.8MM **Privately Held**
WEB: www.boxanything.com
SIC: 2653 Boxes, corrugated: made from purchased materials

(P-3802)
FRUIT GROWERS SUPPLY COMPANY (PA)
27770 N Entrmt Dr Fl 3 Flr 3, Valencia (91355)
PHONE.................888 997-4855
Jim Phillips, *CEO*
Charles Boyce, *CFO*
William O Knox, *Vice Pres*
Mark Lindgren, *Executive*
John W Eacker, *Regional Mgr*
◆ **EMP:** 50 **EST:** 1907
SQ FT: 10,000
SALES (est): 222.6MM **Privately Held**
WEB: www.fruitgrowerssupply.com
SIC: 2653 0811 5191 2448 Boxes, corrugated: made from purchased materials; timber tracts; farm supplies; fertilizer & fertilizer materials; pallets, wood; cardboard & products

(P-3803)
FRUIT GROWERS SUPPLY COMPANY
934 W Scranton Ave, Porterville (93257-8968)
PHONE.................559 783-6383
EMP: 26
SALES (corp-wide): 222.6MM **Privately Held**
WEB: www.fruitgrowerssupply.com
SIC: 2653 Boxes, corrugated: made from purchased materials
PA: Fruit Growers Supply Company Inc
27770 N Entrmt Dr Fl 3 Flr 3
Valencia CA 91355
888 997-4855

(P-3804)
FRUIT GROWERS SUPPLY COMPANY
Also Called: F G S Packing Services
674 E Myer Ave, Exeter (93221-9644)
PHONE.................559 592-6550
Bruce Adams, *Manager*
Michael Fontes, *Officer*
Dave Sorenson, *Technical Staff*
EMP: 26
SQ FT: 5,240
SALES (corp-wide): 222.6MM **Privately Held**
WEB: www.fruitgrowerssupply.com
SIC: 2653 Boxes, corrugated: made from purchased materials

PA: Fruit Growers Supply Company Inc
27770 N Entrmt Dr Fl 3 Flr 3
Valencia CA 91355
888 997-4855

(P-3805)
GABRIEL CONTAINER (PA)
Also Called: Recycled Paper Products
8844 Millergrove Dr, Santa Fe Springs (90670-2013)
P.O. Box 3188 (90670-0188)
PHONE.................562 699-1051
Ronald H Gabriel, *President*
Agnes Gabriel, *Admin Sec*
Felipe Avila, *Maint Spvr*
Anush Gabriel,
▲ **EMP:** 199 **EST:** 1935
SQ FT: 72,000
SALES (est): 32.1MM **Privately Held**
WEB: www.gabrielcontainer.com
SIC: 2653 2621 Boxes, corrugated: made from purchased materials; paper mills

(P-3806)
GEM BOX OF WEST
2430 S Hill St, Los Angeles (90007-2720)
PHONE.................213 748-4875
▲ **EMP:** 26
SQ FT: 135,000
SALES (est): 3.8MM **Privately Held**
SIC: 2653 5094 Mfg Corrugated/Solid Fiber Boxes Whol Jewelry/Precious Stones

(P-3807)
GENERAL CONTAINER
235 Radio Rd, Corona (92879-1725)
PHONE.................714 562-8700
Tim G Black, *CEO*
Scott Black, *CFO*
Patty Black, *Admin Sec*
Kimberly Howorth, *Admin Sec*
Debbie McMillen, *Accounting Mgr*
EMP: 72 **EST:** 1976
SALES (est): 19.6MM
SALES (corp-wide): 50.5MM **Privately Held**
WEB: www.usdisplaygroup.com
SIC: 2653 Boxes, corrugated: made from purchased materials
PA: U.S. Display Group, Inc.
810 S Washington St
Tullahoma TN 37388
931 455-9585

(P-3808)
GOLDEN WEST PACKG GROUP LLC (PA)
15400 Don Julian Rd, City of Industry (91745-1004)
PHONE.................888 501-5893
Brad Jordan, *President*
Ron Frederick, *VP Finance*
EMP: 381 **EST:** 2017
SALES (est): 317.1MM **Privately Held**
SIC: 2653 Boxes, corrugated: made from purchased materials

(P-3809)
GOLDENCORR SHEETS LLC
13890 Nelson Ave, City of Industry (91746-2050)
P.O. Box 90968 (91715-0968)
PHONE.................626 369-6446
Tom Anderson, *Mng Member*
John Perullo, *President*
Esau Ramirez, *Human Resources*
Katrina Boss, *Mfg Staff*
Curtis Warren, *Maintence Staff*
▲ **EMP:** 150
SALES (est): 49.1MM **Privately Held**
WEB: www.goldencorr.net
SIC: 2653 Corrugated boxes, partitions, display items, sheets & pad

(P-3810)
HARVEST CONTAINER COMPANY
24476 Road 216, Lindsay (93247-8222)
P.O. Box 697 (93247-0697)
PHONE.................559 562-1394
Dennis A Del Rio, *Principal*
Fred Lo Bue, *President*
Robert Reniers, *Corp Secy*
Phil Enghusen, *Executive*
Dennis Del Rio, *General Mgr*

▲ **EMP:** 45 **EST:** 1983
SQ FT: 104,000
SALES (est): 8.3MM **Privately Held**
WEB: www.harvestcontainer.com
SIC: 2653 Boxes, corrugated: made from purchased materials

(P-3811)
HERITAGE CONTAINER INC
4777 Felspar St, Riverside (92509-3040)
P.O. Box 605, Mira Loma (91752-0605)
PHONE.................951 360-1900
Richard Gabriel, *CEO*
Thomas Gabriel, *President*
Nancy Zuniga, *CFO*
Nancy Swanson, *Vice Pres*
Tom Gabriel, *Executive*
EMP: 100 **EST:** 1988
SQ FT: 95,000
SALES (est): 16.5MM **Privately Held**
WEB: www.heritagecontainer.com
SIC: 2653 5199 Boxes, corrugated: made from purchased materials; boxes, solid fiber: made from purchased materials; packaging materials

(P-3812)
HERITAGE PAPER CO (HQ)
2400 S Grand Ave, Santa Ana (92705-5211)
PHONE.................714 540-9737
Ron Scagliotti, *CEO*
Lenet Derksen, *CFO*
Diane Schmitz, *Admin Mgr*
Terri Sloane, *Department Mgr*
Hugh Lovelace, *Sales Mgr*
▲ **EMP:** 75 **EST:** 1976
SQ FT: 150,000
SALES (est): 40.1MM
SALES (corp-wide): 94.6MM **Privately Held**
WEB: www.heritagepaper.net
SIC: 2653 5199 Boxes, corrugated: made from purchased materials; packaging materials
PA: Pioneer Packing, Inc.
2430 S Grand Ave
Santa Ana CA 92705
714 540-9751

(P-3813)
JELLCO CONTAINER INC
1151 N Tustin Ave, Anaheim (92807-1736)
PHONE.................714 666-2728
Jeff Erselius, *President*
Rick Leininger, *CFO*
Jason Wilkerson, *Opers Mgr*
Ron Wassenaar, *Sales Staff*
Clara Rodriguez, *Clerk*
EMP: 72
SQ FT: 42,000
SALES (est): 24.6MM **Privately Held**
WEB: www.jellco.com
SIC: 2653 Boxes, corrugated: made from purchased materials

(P-3814)
JKV INC
Also Called: Atlantic Box & Carton Company
8343 Loch Lomond Dr, Pico Rivera (90660-2507)
PHONE.................562 948-3000
Michael Valov, *President*
Elena Valov, *Treasurer*
Jack Valov, *Admin Sec*
EMP: 40 **EST:** 1971
SQ FT: 30,000
SALES (est): 5.6MM **Privately Held**
WEB: www.atlanticboxncarton.com
SIC: 2653 Boxes, corrugated: made from purchased materials

(P-3815)
KAPSTONE ONTARIO
1790 Champagne Ave, Ontario (91761-3614)
PHONE.................909 390-0619
EMP: 13 **EST:** 2016
SALES (est): 2.2MM **Privately Held**
SIC: 2653 Corrugated & solid fiber boxes

(P-3816)
KAWEAH CONTAINER INC (HQ)
7101 Avenue 304, Visalia (93291-9479)
P.O. Box 6940 (93290-6940)
PHONE.................559 651-7846

Robert J Reeves, *CEO*
▲ **EMP:** 67 **EST:** 1988
SQ FT: 30,000
SALES (est): 22.1MM
SALES (corp-wide): 37.4MM **Privately Held**
WEB: www.kcboxes.com
SIC: 2653 Boxes, corrugated: made from purchased materials
PA: Wileman Bros. & Elliott, Inc.
40232 Road 128
Cutler CA 93615
559 651-8378

(P-3817)
LIBERTY CONTAINER COMPANY
Also Called: Key Container
4224 Santa Ana St, South Gate (90280-2557)
PHONE..........................323 564-4211
Robert J Watts, *President*
William J Watts, *Vice Pres*
Vanessa McLellan, *Admin Sec*
Milli Simmonds, *CIO*
Amanda De La Torre, *Sales Staff*
▲ **EMP:** 110 **EST:** 1956
SQ FT: 300,000
SALES (est): 20.4MM **Privately Held**
WEB: www.keycontainer.com
SIC: 2653 Boxes, corrugated: made from purchased materials

(P-3818)
LIFOAM INDUSTRIES LLC
15671 Industry Ln, Huntington Beach (92649-1536)
PHONE.........................714 891-5035
EMP: 60
SALES (corp-wide): 1.8B **Privately Held**
WEB: www.lifoam.com
SIC: 2653 Corrugated & solid fiber boxes
HQ: Lifoam Industries, Llc
1303 S Batesville Rd
Greer SC 29650
866 770-3626

(P-3819)
MENASHA PACKAGING COMPANY LLC
8110 Sorensen Ave, Santa Fe Springs (90670-2122)
PHONE.........................562 698-3705
EMP: 84
SALES (corp-wide): 1.6B **Privately Held**
WEB: www.menasha.com
SIC: 2653 Mfg Corrugated/Solid Fiber Boxes
HQ: Menasha Packaging Company, Llc
1645 Bergstrom Rd
Neenah WI 54956
920 751-1000

(P-3820)
MENASHA PACKAGING COMPANY LLC
1686 W Base Line Rd # 200, Rialto (92376-8604)
PHONE.........................909 442-0668
Erik Sgro, *Branch Mgr*
EMP: 14
SALES (corp-wide): 1.9B **Privately Held**
WEB: www.menasha.com
SIC: 2653 Boxes, corrugated: made from purchased materials
HQ: Menasha Packaging Company, Llc
1645 Bergstrom Rd
Neenah WI 54956
920 751-1000

(P-3821)
MONTEBELLO CONTAINER CO LLC (HQ)
16069 Shoemaker Ave, Cerritos (90703-2234)
PHONE.........................562 404-6221
Lawrence Vas,
Joseph Salcido, *Prdtn Mgr*
▲ **EMP:** 100 **EST:** 2015
SALES (est): 4.1MM **Privately Held**
WEB: www.montcc.com
SIC: 2653 Sheets, corrugated: made from purchased materials; corrugated boxes, partitions, display items, sheets & pad

(P-3822)
NUMATECH WEST (KMP) LLC
Also Called: Kmp Numatech Pacific
1201 E Lexington Ave, Pomona (91766-5520)
P.O. Box 357, Placentia (92871-0357)
PHONE.........................909 706-3627
John Neate, *Mng Member*
Robert Sliter, *General Mgr*
Rodelieta Clavin, *Controller*
▲ **EMP:** 100 **EST:** 1986
SQ FT: 65,000
SALES (est): 3.1MM
SALES (corp-wide): 19.3MM **Privately Held**
WEB: www.nwpackingonline.com
SIC: 2653 Boxes, corrugated: made from purchased materials
PA: Nw Packaging Llc
1201 E Lexington Ave
Pomona CA 91766
909 706-3627

(P-3823)
PACIFIC QUALITY PACKAGING CORP
660 Neptune Ave, Brea (92821-2909)
PHONE.........................714 257-1234
Frederick H Chau, *President*
Chris Chau, *Project Mgr*
▲ **EMP:** 65 **EST:** 1984
SQ FT: 44,000
SALES (est): 8MM **Privately Held**
WEB: www.pacificqp.com
SIC: 2653 3993 Boxes, corrugated: made from purchased materials; signs & advertising specialties

(P-3824)
PACIFIC SOUTHWEST CONT LLC
Also Called: PSC
9525 W Nicholas Ct, Visalia (93291-9468)
PHONE.........................559 651-5500
Don Mayol,
Bryan Smith, *Chief Mktg Ofcr*
Jeremy Reed, *Office Admin*
Nicolle Bermejo, *Project Mgr*
Jess Fauria, *Project Mgr*
EMP: 44
SALES (corp-wide): 143.5MM **Privately Held**
WEB: www.teampsc.com
SIC: 2653 Boxes, corrugated: made from purchased materials
PA: Pacific Southwest Container, Llc
4530 Leckron Rd
Modesto CA 95357
209 526-0444

(P-3825)
PNC PROACTIVE NTHRN CONT LLC
602 S Rockefeller Ave A, Ontario (91761-8190)
PHONE.........................909 390-5624
Gary Hartog, *Mng Member*
▲ **EMP:** 49 **EST:** 2005
SQ FT: 362,000
SALES (est): 3.6MM **Privately Held**
SIC: 2653 Boxes, corrugated: made from purchased materials
PA: Fourth Third Llc
375 Park Ave Ste 3304
New York NY

(P-3826)
SCOPE PACKAGING INC
Also Called: Sp
13400 Nelson Ave, City of Industry (91746-2331)
PHONE.........................714 998-4411
Mike E Flinn, *CEO*
Cindy Baker, *Vice Pres*
▲ **EMP:** 51 **EST:** 1966
SQ FT: 70,000
SALES (est): 3.8MM **Privately Held**
SIC: 2653 7389 Boxes, corrugated: made from purchased materials; packaging & labeling services

(P-3827)
SMURFIT KAPPA NORTH AMER LLC
440 Baldwin Park Blvd, City of Industry (91746-1407)
PHONE.........................626 322-2123
EMP: 413 **Privately Held**
SIC: 2653 2671 2657 Mfg Corrugated/Solid Fiber Boxes Mfg Packaging Paper/Film Mfg Folding Paperboard Boxes
HQ: Smurfit Kappa North America Llc
13400 Nelson Ave
City Of Industry CA 75062
626 333-6363

(P-3828)
SOUTHLAND CONTAINER CORP
Also Called: Concept Packaging Group
1600 Champagne Ave, Ontario (91761-3612)
PHONE.........................909 937-9781
Tom Heinz, *Branch Mgr*
EMP: 279
SALES (corp-wide): 371.1MM **Privately Held**
WEB: www.southlandcontainer.com
SIC: 2653 Boxes, corrugated: made from purchased materials
PA: Southland Container Corporation
493 Livingston Vernon Rd
Flora MS 39071
864 578-0085

(P-3829)
TEX RHINO INC
15080 Hilton Dr, Fontana (92336-4020)
PHONE.........................909 548-3910
Russell M Coleman, *President*
EMP: 15 **EST:** 2018
SALES (est): 2.8MM **Privately Held**
WEB: www.rhinotex.com
SIC: 2653 Sheets, corrugated: made from purchased materials

(P-3830)
US DISPLAY GROUP INC
235 Radio Rd, Corona (92879-1725)
PHONE.........................951 444-4567
Gabriel Perez, *Director*
EMP: 50
SALES (corp-wide): 50.5MM **Privately Held**
WEB: www.usdisplaygroup.com
SIC: 2653 Boxes, corrugated: made from purchased materials
PA: U.S. Display Group, Inc.
810 S Washington St
Tullahoma TN 37388
931 455-9585

(P-3831)
WESTERN CORRUGATED DESIGN INC
8741 Pioneer Blvd, Santa Fe Springs (90670-2021)
PHONE.........................562 695-9295
John Brendlinger, *CEO*
▲ **EMP:** 50 **EST:** 2004
SALES (est): 10.7MM **Privately Held**
SIC: 2653 Boxes, corrugated: made from purchased materials

(P-3832)
WESTROCK RKT COMPANY
536 S 2nd Ave, Covina (91723-3043)
PHONE.........................626 859-7633
EMP: 161
SALES (corp-wide): 16B **Publicly Held**
SIC: 2653 2679 Mfg Corrugated/Solid Fiber Boxes Mfg Converted Paper Products
HQ: Westrock Rkt Company
504 Thrasher St
Norcross GA 30328
770 448-2193

2655 Fiber Cans, Tubes & Drums

(P-3833)
CALIFORNIA COMPOSITE CONT CORP
22770 Perry St, Perris (92570-9725)
PHONE.........................951 940-9343
Jerry Martin, *President*
Richard Hull, *Vice Pres*
▲ **EMP:** 18 **EST:** 1983
SQ FT: 18,000
SALES (est): 4MM **Privately Held**
WEB: www.californiacomposite.com
SIC: 2655 Cans, fiber: made from purchased material

(P-3834)
CARAUSTAR CSTM PACKG GROUP INC
Also Called: Caraustar Custom Packg Group
6001 S Eastern Ave, Commerce (90040-3413)
PHONE.........................323 724-5989
EMP: 87
SALES (corp-wide): 4.5B **Publicly Held**
SIC: 2655 Fiber cans, drums & similar products
HQ: Caraustar Custom Packaging Group, Inc.
5000 Austell Powder Sprin
Austell GA 30106

(P-3835)
DORCO ELECTRONICS INC
Also Called: Dorco Fiberglass Products
13540 Larwin Cir, Santa Fe Springs (90670-5031)
PHONE.........................562 623-1133
Ted Casmer, *President*
Gary Dexter, *Vice Pres*
EMP: 16 **EST:** 1958
SQ FT: 7,000
SALES (est): 2.1MM **Privately Held**
WEB: www.dorco.com
SIC: 2655 Bobbins, fiber: made from purchased material

(P-3836)
GREEN PRODUCTS PACKAGING CORP
Also Called: California Composite Container
22770 Perry St, Perris (92570-9725)
PHONE.........................951 940-9343
Paul Z Rachina, *CEO*
Corina Rachina, *Corp Secy*
EMP: 14 **EST:** 2017
SQ FT: 28,000
SALES (est): 2.6MM **Privately Held**
WEB: www.californiacomposite.com
SIC: 2655 Ammunition cars or tubes, board laminated with metal foil

(P-3837)
GREIF BROS CORP
3042 Inland Empire Blvd, Ontario (91764-6549)
PHONE.........................909 941-4570
▼ **EMP:** 30 **EST:** 2009
SALES (est): 9.7MM
SALES (corp-wide): 4.5B **Publicly Held**
WEB: www.greif.com
SIC: 2655 Fiber cans, drums & similar products
PA: Greif, Inc.
425 Winter Rd
Delaware OH 43015
740 549-6000

(P-3838)
PLASTOPAN INDUSTRIES INC (PA)
812 E 59th St, Los Angeles (90001-1006)
PHONE.........................323 231-2225
Ronald D Miller, *President*
Martin L Miller, *Vice Pres*
Sofia G Miller, *Vice Pres*
Catherine M Bump, *Admin Sec*
Eric J Scala, *Accountant*
EMP: 30 **EST:** 1992
SQ FT: 48,000 **Privately Held**

SIC: 2655 Fiber cans, drums & similar products

(P-3839)
SGL COMPOSITES INC (DH)
1551 W 139th St, Gardena (90249-2603)
PHONE..............................424 329-5250
David Otterson, *CEO*
Jeff Schade, *Vice Pres*
Dominic Calamito, *Program Mgr*
Joe Greco, *Prdtn Mgr*
Brian Smith, *Supervisor*
▼ EMP: 20 EST: 1995
SALES (est): 30.5MM
SALES (corp-wide): 1B **Privately Held**
WEB: www.sglcarbon.com
SIC: 2655 Fiber cans, drums & similar products
HQ: Sgl Carbon, Llc
10715 David Taylor Dr # 460
Charlotte NC 28262
704 593-5100

(P-3840)
SPIRAL PPR TUBE & CORE CO INC
5200 Industry Ave, Pico Rivera (90660-2506)
PHONE..............................562 801-9705
George Hibard, *CEO*
Summer Hibard, *Vice Pres*
▲ EMP: 45
SQ FT: 40,000
SALES (est): 9.2MM **Privately Held**
WEB: www.spiralpaper.com
SIC: 2655 Fiber cans, drums & similar products

(P-3841)
TUBE-TAINER INC
8174 Byron Rd, Whittier (90606-2616)
PHONE..............................562 945-3711
Mike Mundia, *President*
▲ EMP: 45 EST: 1967
SQ FT: 44,000
SALES (est): 7.4MM **Privately Held**
WEB: www.tubetainer.com
SIC: 2655 Tubes, fiber or paper: made from purchased material

2656 Sanitary Food Containers

(P-3842)
LOLLICUP USA INC (HQ)
Also Called: Lollicup Tea Zone
6185 Kimball Ave, Chino (91708-9126)
PHONE..............................626 965-8882
Alan Yu, *President*
Ann Sabahat, *CFO*
Luis Amezcua, *Vice Pres*
Marvin Cheng, *Vice Pres*
Amy Tsen, *Vice Pres*
◆ EMP: 402 EST: 2000
SQ FT: 9,800
SALES (est): 156.2MM
SALES (corp-wide): 295.5MM **Publicly Held**
WEB: www.karatpackaging.com
SIC: 2656 Paper cups, plates, dishes & utensils
PA: Karat Packaging Inc.
6185 Kimball Ave
Chino CA 91708
626 965-8882

(P-3843)
SWC GROUP INC
Also Called: Carryoutsupplies.com
20529 E Walnut Dr N, Walnut (91789-2945)
PHONE..............................888 982-1628
Jimmy Chan, *CEO*
◆ EMP: 15 EST: 2004
SQ FT: 18,000
SALES (est): 2.4MM **Publicly Held**
WEB: www.carryoutsupplies.com
SIC: 2656 Sanitary food containers
PA: Sugarmade, Inc.
750 Royal Oaks Dr Ste 106
Monrovia CA

(P-3844)
YOCUP COMPANY
13711 S Main St, Los Angeles (90061-2165)
PHONE..............................310 884-9888
Jian Yin Liang, *President*
▲ EMP: 14 EST: 2009
SALES (est): 1.5MM **Privately Held**
WEB: www.shop.yocupco.com
SIC: 2656 Cups, paper: made from purchased material

2657 Folding Paperboard Boxes

(P-3845)
ABSOLUTE PACKAGING INC
1201 N Miller St, Anaheim (92806-1933)
PHONE..............................714 630-3020
Ramin Kohan, *President*
Sandy Kohan, *Controller*
EMP: 35 EST: 2020
SALES (est): 2.6MM **Privately Held**
SIC: 2657 5199 Folding paperboard boxes; packaging materials

(P-3846)
T & T BOX COMPANY INC
Also Called: Thomas Container & Packaging
1353 Philadelphia St, Pomona (91766-5554)
PHONE..............................909 465-0848
Thomas Murphy, *CEO*
Andy Murphy, *Vice Pres*
EMP: 22 EST: 1972
SQ FT: 60,000
SALES (est): 2MM **Privately Held**
WEB: www.thomascontainer.com
SIC: 2657 2653 Folding paperboard boxes; corrugated & solid fiber boxes

(P-3847)
YAVAR MANUFACTURING CO INC
Also Called: National Packaging Products
1900 S Tubeway Ave, Commerce (90040-1612)
PHONE..............................323 722-2040
Massoud Afari, *CEO*
Ben Afari, *Vice Pres*
Brandon Afari, *Vice Pres*
▲ EMP: 48 EST: 1998
SQ FT: 50,000
SALES (est): 14.4MM **Privately Held**
WEB: www.nationalpkg.com
SIC: 2657 2631 Folding paperboard boxes; folding boxboard

2671 Paper Coating & Laminating for Packaging

(P-3848)
AMCOR FLEXIBLES LLC
5416 Union Pacific Ave, Commerce (90022-5117)
PHONE..............................323 721-6777
Graeme Liebelt, *Branch Mgr*
EMP: 718
SALES (corp-wide): 12.4B **Privately Held**
SIC: 2671 2621 2821 3081 Plastic film, coated or laminated for packaging; packaging paper; plastics materials & resins; packing materials, plastic sheet; closures, stamped metal
HQ: Amcor Flexibles Llc
2150 E Lake Cook Rd
Buffalo Grove IL 60089
224 313-7000

(P-3849)
ATRA INTERNATIONAL TRADERS INC
3301 Leonis Blvd, Vernon (90058-3013)
PHONE..............................562 864-3885
Alex Patel, *President*
◆ EMP: 14 EST: 1988
SALES (est): 555.8K **Privately Held**
SIC: 2671 Packaging paper & plastics film, coated & laminated

(P-3850)
AUDIO VIDEO COLOR CORPORATION (PA)
17707 S Santa Fe Ave, E Rncho Dmngz (90221-5419)
PHONE..............................424 213-7500
Kali J Limath, *CEO*
Jim Hardiman, *President*
Guy Marrom, *Exec VP*
Griselda Rosales, *Accounting Mgr*
Jorge Anaya, *Warehouse Mgr*
▲ EMP: 281 EST: 1990
SQ FT: 78,000
SALES (est): 52.6MM **Privately Held**
SIC: 2671 Packaging paper & plastics film, coated & laminated

(P-3851)
BEU INDUSTRIES INC
2937 E Maria St, E Rncho Dmngz (90221-5801)
PHONE..............................310 885-9626
Jeffrey Beu, *President*
Ken Beu Jr, *Vice Pres*
EMP: 14 EST: 2004
SALES (est): 1.7MM **Privately Held**
SIC: 2671 Packaging paper & plastics film, coated & laminated

(P-3852)
CARRYOUT BAGS LLC (PA)
550 S 7th Ave, City of Industry (91746-3120)
PHONE..............................626 279-7000
Paul Cervino, *Mng Member*
Daniel Emrani,
EMP: 52 EST: 2006
SALES (est): 259.7K **Privately Held**
SIC: 2671 Plastic film, coated or laminated for packaging

(P-3853)
FEDERATED DIVERSIFIED SLS INC
Also Called: FDS Manufacturing Company Svcs
2200 S Reservoir St, Pomona (91766-6408)
PHONE..............................909 591-1733
Robert B Stevenson, *CEO*
EMP: 89 EST: 1957
SALES (est): 8.7MM **Privately Held**
SIC: 2671 2631 2653 3086 Packaging paper & plastics film, coated & laminated; paper coated or laminated for packaging; container, packaging & boxboard; packaging board; corrugated & solid fiber boxes; corrugated boxes, partitions, display items, sheets & pad; cups & plates, foamed plastic

(P-3854)
GLOBAL LINK SOURCING INC
41690 Corporate Center Ct, Murrieta (92562-7084)
PHONE..............................951 698-1977
Jullie Annet, *President*
Mike Deigan, *VP Bus Dvlpt*
Lanette Johnson, *Office Mgr*
Tony Montalbano, *Graphic Designe*
Miller Jeremy, *Sales Associate*
▲ EMP: 70 EST: 2006
SQ FT: 80,000
SALES (est): 15MM **Privately Held**
WEB: www.globallinksourcing.com
SIC: 2671 Packaging paper & plastics film, coated & laminated

(P-3855)
GREAT NORTHERN CORPORATION
Laminations West
12075 Cabernet Dr, Fontana (92337-7703)
PHONE..............................951 361-4770
EMP: 35
SALES (corp-wide): 294.9MM **Privately Held**
WEB: www.greatnortherncorp.com
SIC: 2671 Mfg Packaging Paper/Film
PA: Great Northern Corporation
395 Stroebe Rd
Appleton WI 54914
920 739-3671

(P-3856)
PAPERCUTTERS INC
6023 Bandini Blvd, Los Angeles (90040-2904)
PHONE..............................323 888-1330
Susan Feinstein, *President*
Joyce Feinstein, *Corp Secy*
Beth Feinstein, *Vice Pres*
▲ EMP: 21 EST: 1983
SQ FT: 20,000
SALES (est): 4.9MM **Privately Held**
WEB: www.papercutters.net
SIC: 2671 5113 Packaging paper & plastics film, coated & laminated; paper & products, wrapping or coarse

(P-3857)
QUALITY CONTAINER CORP
866 Towne Center Dr, Pomona (91767-5902)
P.O. Box 1297, Claremont (91711-1297)
PHONE..............................909 482-1850
Edward J Kaleff, *CEO*
EMP: 18 EST: 2004
SALES (est): 2.9MM **Privately Held**
SIC: 2671 Packaging paper & plastics film, coated & laminated

(P-3858)
THERMECH CORPORATION
Also Called: Thermech Engineering
1773 W Lincoln Ave Ste I, Anaheim (92801-6713)
PHONE..............................714 533-3183
Jim Shah, *CEO*
Richard Gorman, *President*
Shanu Doshi, *General Mgr*
Sonia Bounds, *Purchasing*
EMP: 23 EST: 1949
SQ FT: 24,000
SALES (est): 4.7MM **Privately Held**
WEB: www.thermech.com
SIC: 2671 3083 Packaging paper & plastics film, coated & laminated; plastic finished products, laminated

(P-3859)
TNT PACKAGING CORPORATION
300 Thor Pl, Brea (92821-4132)
PHONE..............................714 671-9012
EMP: 16 EST: 2017
SALES (est): 1.8MM **Privately Held**
WEB: www.4tntpack.com
SIC: 2671 Packaging paper & plastics film, coated & laminated

(P-3860)
TRANSCONTINENTAL ONTARIO INC
5601 Santa Ana St, Ontario (91761-8622)
PHONE..............................909 390-8866
Brian Reid, *CEO*
EMP: 46 EST: 2003
SALES (est): 27.5MM
SALES (corp-wide): 1.9B **Privately Held**
WEB: www.tctranscontinental.com
SIC: 2671 Paper coated or laminated for packaging
HQ: Transcontinental Us Llc
8600 W Bryn Mawr Ave
Chicago IL 60631
773 877-3300

(P-3861)
TRIUNE ENTERPRISES INC
Also Called: Triune Enterprises Mfg
13711 S Normandie Ave, Gardena (90249-2609)
PHONE..............................310 719-1600
John Christman, *CEO*
Sidney Arouh, *Vice Pres*
Donald Alhanati, *Admin Sec*
◆ EMP: 23 EST: 1996
SQ FT: 29,000
SALES (est): 4.4MM **Privately Held**
WEB: www.triuneent.com
SIC: 2671 5162 Plastic film, coated or laminated for packaging; resinous impregnated paper for packaging; plastics materials & basic shapes

(P-3862)
VINYL TECHNOLOGY INC
200 Railroad Ave, Monrovia (91016-4643)
PHONE..................................626 443-5257
Carlos A Mollura, *Ch of Bd*
Daniel Mullora, *CEO*
Haydee Mollura, *Corp Secy*
Rodney Mollura, *Exec VP*
Carlos Mollura Jr, *Vice Pres*
◆ **EMP: 200 EST:** 1981
SQ FT: 68,000
SALES (est): 51.8MM **Privately Held**
WEB: www.vinyltechnology.com
SIC: 2671 7389 Plastic film, coated or
laminated for packaging; sewing contrac-
tor

2672 Paper Coating & Laminating, Exc for Packaging

(P-3863)
AVERY DENNISON CORPORATION (PA)
207 N Goode Ave, Glendale (91203-1301)
PHONE..................................626 304-2000
Mitchell R Butier, *Ch of Bd*
Gregory S Lovins, *CFO*
Bradley A Alford, *Bd of Directors*
David Pyott, *Bd of Directors*
Patrick T Siewert, *Bd of Directors*
EMP: 8780 **EST:** 1946
SALES: 6.9B **Publicly Held**
WEB: www.averydennison.com
SIC: 2672 3081 3497 2678 Adhesive pa-
pers, labels or tapes: from purchased
material; gummed paper: made from
purchased materials; coated paper, ex-
cept photographic, carbon or abrasive;
unsupported plastics film & sheet; metal
foil & leaf; notebooks: made from pur-
chased paper

(P-3864)
AVERY DENNISON CORPORATION
50 Pointe Dr, Brea (92821-3648)
PHONE..................................714 674-8500
Rick Alonzo, *Manager*
Coleen Alberico, *Human Res Mgr*
Denisse Rodriguez, *Marketing Staff*
Colwin Chan, *Senior Mgr*
Steve Abernathy, *Manager*
EMP: 400
SALES (corp-wide): 6.9B **Publicly Held**
WEB: www.averydennison.com
SIC: 2672 3081 3497 2678 Adhesive pa-
pers, labels or tapes: from purchased
material; unsupported plastics film & sheet;
metal foil & leaf; stationery products; pens
& mechanical pencils; adhesives &
sealants
PA: Avery Dennison Corporation
207 N Goode Ave
Glendale CA 91203
626 304-2000

(P-3865)
AVERY DENNISON CORPORATION
2900 Bradley St, Pasadena (91107-1560)
PHONE..................................626 304-2000
Dave Edwards, *Vice Pres*
Elaine Sulzbach, *Applctn Conslt*
Michael Hiller, *Technician*
Cindelle Mills, *Technician*
Joseph Meckler, *Research*
EMP: 120
SQ FT: 67,580
SALES (corp-wide): 6.9B **Publicly Held**
WEB: www.averydennison.com
SIC: 2672 2679 Adhesive papers, labels
or tapes: from purchased material; coated
paper, except photographic, carbon or
abrasive; labels; paper: made from pur-
chased material
PA: Avery Dennison Corporation
207 N Goode Ave
Glendale CA 91203
626 304-2000

(P-3866)
AVERY DENNISON FOUNDATION
207 N Goode Ave Ste 500, Glendale
(91203-1301)
PHONE..................................626 304-2000
Alicia Maddox, *President*
EMP: 21 **EST:** 1978
SALES: 3.1MM **Privately Held**
SIC: 2672 Coated & laminated paper

(P-3867)
BECKERS FABRICATION INC
Also Called: B F I Labels
22465 La Palma Ave, Yorba Linda
(92887-3803)
PHONE..................................714 692-1600
Mark Becker, *CEO*
Dan Becker, *President*
David Beilfuss, *General Mgr*
James Monteverde, *Sales Staff*
James Steven, *Sales Staff*
EMP: 24 **EST:** 1981
SQ FT: 6,500
SALES (est): 6.3MM **Privately Held**
WEB: www.beckersfab.com
SIC: 2672 2759 Coated & laminated
paper; screen printing

(P-3868)
CINTON INC
Also Called: West Coast Labels
620 Richfield Rd, Placentia (92870-6727)
PHONE..................................714 961-8808
Salvatore Scaffide, *President*
Mike Taylor, *Officer*
Romona Scaffide, *Vice Pres*
Cindi Montgomery, *Admin Sec*
Mark Trahanovski, *Mktg Dir*
EMP: 46 **EST:** 1972
SQ FT: 23,000
SALES (est): 9MM **Privately Held**
SIC: 2672 2679 Coated & laminated
paper; labels, paper: made from pur-
chased material

(P-3869)
CLARIANT CORPORATION
926 S 8th St, Colton (92324-3500)
P.O. Box 610 (92324-0610)
PHONE..................................909 825-1793
Kenneth Golder, *President*
EMP: 32
SALES (corp-wide): 4.2B **Privately Held**
WEB: www.clariant.com
SIC: 2672 7389 5199 Coated & laminated
paper; packaging & labeling services;
packaging materials
HQ: Clariant Corporation
500 E Morehead St Ste 400
Charlotte NC 28202
704 331-7000

(P-3870)
EDWARDS ASSOC CMMNICATIONS INC (PA)
Also Called: Edwards Label
2277 Knoll Dr Ste A, Ventura (93003-5878)
PHONE..................................805 658-2626
Joel Horacio Gomez-Avila, *President*
John Edwards, *President*
Lisa Hernandez, *Engineer*
Daniel Martinez, *Senior Engr*
Garrett Boys, *Human Resources*
EMP: 150 **EST:** 1984
SQ FT: 44,000
SALES (est): 52.9MM **Privately Held**
WEB: www.edwardslabel.com
SIC: 2672 Labels (unprinted), gummed:
made from purchased materials; adhesive
papers, labels or tapes: from purchased
material

(P-3871)
GARY SIPOSS INC
633 Young St, Santa Ana (92705-5633)
PHONE..................................714 557-3830
Gary J Siposs, *President*
EMP: 13 **EST:** 2001
SALES (est): 389.3K **Privately Held**
SIC: 2672 Adhesive papers, labels or
tapes: from purchased material

(P-3872)
HARRIS INDUSTRIES INC (PA)
5181 Argosy Ave, Huntington Beach
(92649-1058)
P.O. Box 3269 (92605-3269)
PHONE..................................714 898-8048
William Helzer, *President*
Gail Helzer, *Corp Secy*
Toni Cameron, *Manager*
◆ **EMP:** 50 **EST:** 1987
SQ FT: 25,000
SALES (est): 13.3MM **Privately Held**
WEB: www.harrisind.com
SIC: 2672 Tape, pressure sensitive: made
from purchased materials

(P-3873)
PRECISION DYNAMICS CORPORATION (HQ)
Also Called: Pdc-Identicard
25124 Sprngfld Ct Ste 20, Valencia
(91355)
PHONE..................................818 897-1111
J Michael Nauman, *CEO*
Robin Barber, *Vice Pres*
Robert Case, *Vice Pres*
John Park, *Vice Pres*
Sean Souffie, *Vice Pres*
◆ **EMP:** 165 **EST:** 1956
SQ FT: 75,000
SALES (est): 53.7MM
SALES (corp-wide): 1.1B **Publicly Held**
WEB: www.pdcorp.com
SIC: 2672 2754 5047 3069 Adhesive pa-
pers, labels or tapes: from purchased ma-
terial; labels (unprinted), gummed: made
from purchased materials; labels: gravure
printing; instruments, surgical & medical;
tape, pressure sensitive: rubber
PA: Brady Corporation
6555 W Good Hope Rd
Milwaukee WI 53223
414 358-6600

(P-3874)
SEAL METHODS INC (PA)
11915 Shoemaker Ave, Santa Fe Springs
(90670-4717)
P.O. Box 2604 (90670-0604)
PHONE..................................562 944-0291
Eugene Welter, *Principal*
Ron McGuire, *COO*
Joseph Evans, *General Mgr*
Evelyn Joloya, *Office Mgr*
Geri Welter, *Admin Sec*
◆ **EMP:** 90 **EST:** 1974
SQ FT: 75,000
SALES (est): 42.9MM **Privately Held**
WEB: www.sealmethodsinc.com
SIC: 2672 3053 5085 Masking tape:
made from purchased materials; tape,
pressure sensitive: made from purchased
materials; gaskets, all materials; packing,
rubber; gaskets; seals, industrial

(P-3875)
SPINNAKER COATING LLC
566 Vanguard Way, Brea (92821-3928)
PHONE..................................714 482-1006
EMP: 103
SALES (corp-wide): 62.8MM **Privately Held**
WEB: www.spinnakercoating.com
SIC: 2672 Labels (unprinted), gummed:
made from purchased materials
PA: Spinnaker Coating, Llc
518 E Water St
Troy OH 45373
937 332-6500

(P-3876)
TAPE AND LABEL CONVERTERS INC
8231 Allport Ave, Santa Fe Springs
(90670-2105)
P.O. Box 398, Pico Rivera (90660-0398)
PHONE..................................562 945-3486
Toll Free:..................................888
Robert Varela Sr, *President*
Jeanette Verela, *Admin Sec*
Roger Varela, *Sales Staff*
EMP: 20 **EST:** 1996
SQ FT: 3,625

SALES (est): 3.6MM **Privately Held**
WEB: www.stickybiz.com
SIC: 2672 2782 2752 2671 Labels (unprinted), gummed: made from purchased
materials; blankbooks & looseleaf
binders; commercial printing, lithographic;
packaging paper & plastics film, coated &
laminated

(P-3877)
UPM RAFLATAC INC
1105 Auto Center Dr, Ontario (91761-2213)
PHONE..................................909 390-4657
Alan Punch, *Manager*
Eric Fiessinger, *General Mgr*
Krzysztof Minta, *General Mgr*
Toney Nabors, *Technician*
Guy Jones, *Technology*
EMP: 20 **Privately Held**
WEB: www.upmraflatac.com
SIC: 2672 2679 Coated & laminated
paper; labels, paper: made from pur-
chased material
HQ: Upm Raflatac, Inc.
400 Broadpointe Dr
Mills River NC 28759
828 651-4800

2673 Bags: Plastics, Laminated & Coated

(P-3878)
ASIA PLASTICS INC
9347 Rush St, South El Monte
(91733-2544)
PHONE..................................626 448-8100
Kent Ung, *CEO*
Hung Tran, *CFO*
Tracy Ung, *Corp Secy*
▲ **EMP:** 20 **EST:** 1982
SQ FT: 11,000
SALES (est): 2.1MM **Privately Held**
SIC: 2673 Plastic bags: made from pur-
chased materials

(P-3879)
CALIFORNIA PLASTX INC
1319 E 3rd St, Pomona (91766-2212)
PHONE..................................909 629-8288
Danny Farshadfar, *President*
Touraj Tour, *Vice Pres*
▼ **EMP:** 25 **EST:** 1994
SQ FT: 44,000
SALES (est): 4MM **Privately Held**
WEB: www.californiaplastix.com
SIC: 2673 3089 Garment & wardrobe
bags, (plastic film); extruded finished
plastic products

(P-3880)
CF&B MANUFACTURING INC
Also Called: Cleanroom Film & Bags
1405 N Manzanita St, Orange
(92867-3603)
P.O. Box 807, Atwood (92811-0807)
PHONE..................................714 744-8361
Michael Hoffman, *CEO*
Kyle Purcell, *CFO*
Brad Mello, *General Mgr*
Peggy Dichard, *Sales Staff*
EMP: 20 **EST:** 2004
SQ FT: 10,000
SALES (est): 8.7MM **Privately Held**
WEB: www.cleanroomfilm.com
SIC: 2673 Plastic bags: made from pur-
chased materials
HQ: C. P. Converters, Inc.
15 Grumbacher Rd
York PA 17406
717 764-1193

(P-3881)
CROWN POLY INC
5701 S Boyle Ave, Vernon (90058-3928)
PHONE..................................323 583-4570
Ebrahim Simhaee, *CEO*
Steve Williams, *CIO*
Jim Wells, *Technician*
Shivkumar Nistala, *Electrical Engi*
Steven Weinhandl, *Sales Mgr*
EMP: 14 **EST:** 1991

▲ = Import ▼=Export
◆ =Import/Export

SALES (est): 1MM Privately Held
WEB: www.crownpoly.com
SIC: 2673 Plastic bags: made from purchased materials

(P-3882)
CROWN POLY INC
Also Called: Pull-N-Pac
5700 Bickett St, Huntington Park (90255-2625)
PHONE...................323 268-1298
Ebrahim Simhaee, *CEO*
Galia Goldberg, *General Mgr*
Jim Wells, *Technician*
Greg Walker, *Sales Mgr*
Michael Nahin, *Sales Staff*
◆ **EMP:** 150 **EST:** 1991
SQ FT: 40,000
SALES (est): 84.2MM Privately Held
WEB: www.crownpoly.com
SIC: 2673 Plastic bags: made from purchased materials

(P-3883)
DURABAG COMPANY INC
1432 Santa Fe Dr, Tustin (92780-6417)
PHONE...................714 259-9811
Frank C S Huang, *Vice Pres*
Wendy SOO, *CFO*
Daniel Huang, *Vice Pres*
Richard Barnes, *CIO*
Loi Jenny, *Controller*
▲ **EMP:** 70
SQ FT: 150,000
SALES (est): 25.7MM Privately Held
WEB: www.durabag.net
SIC: 2673 Food storage & frozen food bags, plastic; trash bags (plastic film): made from purchased materials; plastic bags: made from purchased materials

(P-3884)
GREAT AMERICAN PACKAGING
4361 S Soto St, Vernon (90058-2311)
PHONE...................323 582-2247
Greg Gurewitz, *President*
Bruce Carter, *President*
Marlene Gurewitz, *CFO*
David Vogel, *Finance*
Cheryl Gartin, *Purch Agent*
EMP: 50 **EST:** 1966
SQ FT: 40,000
SALES (est): 13MM Privately Held
WEB: www.greatampack.com
SIC: 2673 3081 3082 Plastic bags: made from purchased materials; plastic film & sheet; unsupported plastics profile shapes

(P-3885)
LIBERTY PACKG & EXTRUDING INC
3015 Supply Ave, Commerce (90040-2709)
PHONE...................323 722-5124
Derek De Heras, *CEO*
Bonnie Hudson, *CEO*
Mary Anne Bove, *Treasurer*
Mary Hudson, *Vice Pres*
Lola Jones, *Principal*
EMP: 40 **EST:** 1986
SQ FT: 25,000
SALES (est): 6MM Privately Held
WEB: www.libertypkg.com
SIC: 2673 7389 Plastic & pliofilm bags; packaging & labeling services

(P-3886)
MERCURY PLASTICS INC (HQ)
14825 Salt Lake Ave, City of Industry (91746-3131)
PHONE...................626 961-0165
Benjamin Deutsch, *CEO*
Stanley Tzenkov, *Exec VP*
Kamyar Mirdamadi, *Vice Pres*
Rupesh Raman, *Technician*
Gabriella Gomez, *Human Resources*
▲ **EMP:** 415 **EST:** 1987
SQ FT: 140,000
SALES (est): 102.4MM Privately Held
WEB: www.mercplastics.com
SIC: 2673 2759 3089 Plastic bags: made from purchased materials; bags, plastic: printing; plastic containers, except foam

(P-3887)
MOHAWK WESTERN PLASTICS INC
1496 Arrow Hwy, La Verne (91750-5219)
P.O. Box 463 (91750-0463)
PHONE...................909 593-7547
John R Mordoff, *CEO*
J Christopher Mordoff, *President*
Dale Long, *Representative*
EMP: 40
SQ FT: 28,000
SALES (est): 10.1MM Privately Held
WEB: www.mohawkwestern.com
SIC: 2673 3081 Plastic bags: made from purchased materials; unsupported plastics film & sheet

(P-3888)
NORMAN PAPER AND FOAM CO INC
Also Called: Norman International
4501 S Santa Fe Ave, Vernon (90058-2129)
PHONE...................323 582-7132
Norman Levine, *President*
Christopher Werner, *CFO*
Ellen Levine, *Corp Secy*
Chris Werner, *Vice Pres*
Dawnn Winter, *Vice Pres*
▲ **EMP:** 23 **EST:** 1980
SQ FT: 40,000
SALES (est): 4.9MM Privately Held
WEB: www.normaninternational.com
SIC: 2673 2671 3086 Bags: plastic, laminated & coated; packaging paper & plastics film, coated & laminated; packaging & shipping materials, foamed plastic

(P-3889)
REPUBLIC BAG INC (PA)
580 E Harrison St, Corona (92879-1344)
PHONE...................951 734-9740
Richard Schroeder, *CEO*
Frecia Castro, *Officer*
Steven Fritz, *Vice Pres*
Mark Teo, *Principal*
▲ **EMP:** 80 **EST:** 1976
SQ FT: 59,000
SALES (est): 18.9MM Privately Held
WEB: www.republicbag.com
SIC: 2673 Plastic bags: made from purchased materials

(P-3890)
SORMA USA LLC
9810 W Ferguson Ave, Visalia (93291-2450)
PHONE...................559 651-1269
Rick Goddard, *Vice Pres*
Tracy Hart, *General Mgr*
Donna D Weems, *Controller*
Steve McCartha, *Plant Mgr*
Laura Pena, *Production*
▲ **EMP:** 350 **EST:** 1993
SALES (est): 41.3MM
SALES (corp-wide): 1.1MM Privately Held
WEB: www.sormausa.com
SIC: 2673 3565 Bags: plastic, laminated & coated; packaging machinery
HQ: Sorma Spa
Via Delle Mele 65
Cesena FC 47522
054 741-8611

(P-3891)
SUN PLASTICS INC
7140 E Slauson Ave, Commerce (90040-3663)
PHONE...................323 888-6999
Vahan Bagamian, *President*
Movses Shrikian, *Admin Sec*
EMP: 50 **EST:** 1979
SQ FT: 60,000
SALES (est): 14.3MM Privately Held
WEB: www.sunplastics.com
SIC: 2673 Plastic bags: made from purchased materials

(P-3892)
TDI2 CUSTOM PACKAGING INC
17391 Mount Cliffwood Cir, Fountain Valley (92708-4102)
PHONE...................714 751-6782
Stephen Deniger, *CEO*

Catharina Deniger, *Admin Sec*
Catrina Deniger, *Marketing Staff*
EMP: 17 **EST:** 1975
SQ FT: 19,000
SALES (est): 3.7MM Privately Held
WEB: www.tdicustompackaging.com
SIC: 2673 Plastic bags: made from purchased materials

(P-3893)
WESTERN STATES PACKAGING INC
13276 Paxton St, Pacoima (91331-2356)
PHONE...................818 686-6045
Richard Joyce, *President*
Mark Pickrell, *Vice Pres*
Carroll Pickrell, *Accountant*
Dinh Nguyen, *QC Mgr*
Lee Joice, *Sales Staff*
▲ **EMP:** 50 **EST:** 1995
SQ FT: 35,000
SALES (est): 10.7MM Privately Held
WEB: www.wspusa.com
SIC: 2673 5113 5162 Plastic bags: made from purchased materials; bags, paper & disposable plastic; plastics materials

---

2674 Bags: Uncoated Paper & Multiwall

(P-3894)
BAGCRAFTPAPERCON I LLC
Also Called: Papercon Packaging Division
515 Turnbull Canyon Rd, City of Industry (91745-1118)
PHONE...................626 961-6766
Hector Lourido, *Manager*
EMP: 100
SALES (corp-wide): 2.9B Publicly Held
WEB: www.bagcraft.com
SIC: 2674 2671 Bags: uncoated paper & multiwall; packaging paper & plastics film, coated & laminated
HQ: Bagcraftpapercon I, Llc
3900 W 43rd St
Chicago IL 60632
620 856-2800

(P-3895)
E-Z MIX INC (PA)
11450 Tuxford St, Sun Valley (91352-2638)
PHONE...................818 768-0568
William Frenzel, *CEO*
Sunjiv Parekh, *CEO*
Joel Castellanos, *Sales Staff*
EMP: 33 **EST:** 1992
SQ FT: 50,000
SALES (est): 14.2MM Privately Held
WEB: www.ezmixinc.com
SIC: 2674 Cement bags: made from purchased materials

(P-3896)
ENDPAK PACKAGING INC
9101 Perkins St, Pico Rivera (90660-4512)
PHONE...................562 801-0281
Edgar A Garcia, *CEO*
Carlos Garcia, *President*
EMP: 90 **EST:** 1992
SQ FT: 45,600
SALES (est): 16.7MM Privately Held
WEB: www.endpak.com
SIC: 2674 5199 Paper bags: made from purchased materials; packaging materials

(P-3897)
PACOBOND INC
9344 Glenoaks Blvd, Sun Valley (91352-1533)
PHONE...................818 768-5002
Arsine Seraydarian, *CEO*
Gerard Seradarian, *President*
▲ **EMP:** 50 **EST:** 1985
SALES (est): 9.6MM Privately Held
WEB: www.pacobond.com
SIC: 2674 5162 Shopping bags: made from purchased materials; plastics materials

---

2675 Die-Cut Paper & Board

(P-3898)
J J FOIL COMPANY INC
650 W Freedom Ave, Orange (92865-2537)
PHONE...................714 998-9920
Tiffany Dang, *President*
EMP: 32 **EST:** 1991
SQ FT: 18,000
SALES (est): 7.5MM Privately Held
WEB: www.jjfoil.com
SIC: 2675 2759 Paper die-cutting; embossing on paper

(P-3899)
K & D GRAPHICS
Also Called: K & D Graphics Prtg & Packg
1432 N Main St Ste C, Orange (92867-3450)
PHONE...................714 639-8900
Don Chew, *CEO*
Montri Chew, *CFO*
Bebe Chew, *Vice Pres*
Gus Chew, *Vice Pres*
Kim Chew, *Admin Sec*
▲ **EMP:** 48
SQ FT: 75,500
SALES (est): 7.9MM Privately Held
WEB: www.kdgpp.com
SIC: 2675 2752 Die-cut paper & board; commercial printing, offset

(P-3900)
PRESENTATION FOLDER INC
1130 N Main St, Orange (92867-3421)
PHONE...................714 289-7000
Joseph Tardie Jr, *President*
Joseph Tardie Sr, *Vice Pres*
◆ **EMP:** 45 **EST:** 1988
SQ FT: 70,000
SALES (est): 15.4MM Privately Held
WEB: www.presentationfolder.com
SIC: 2675 2759 2672 Folders, filing, die-cut: made from purchased materials; paper die-cutting; embossing on paper; coated & laminated paper

(P-3901)
TOPS SLT INC
8550 Chetle Ave Ste B, Whittier (90606-2662)
PHONE...................562 968-2000
EMP: 148
SALES (corp-wide): 10.4B Publicly Held
SIC: 2675 Mfg Die-Cut Paper/Paperboard
HQ: Tops Slt, Inc.
225 Broadhollow Rd 184w
Melville NY 11747
631 675-5700

2676 Sanitary Paper Prdts

(P-3902)
AXENT CORPORATION LIMITED
Also Called: Axent USA
3 Musick, Irvine (92618-1638)
PHONE...................949 900-4349
LI Feiyu, *Principal*
Keith Dagarin, *Vice Pres*
▲ **EMP:** 15 **EST:** 2008
SALES (est): 4.5MM Privately Held
WEB: www.wdiecoflush.com
SIC: 2676 2499 Sanitary paper products; seats, toilet

(P-3903)
DEPENDBLE INCONTINENCE SUP INC
Also Called: Dis
590 S Vincent Ave, Azusa (91702-5130)
PHONE...................626 812-0044
Mike Cholakian, *CEO*
Harry Kemangian, *CFO*
▲ **EMP:** 22 **EST:** 2003
SQ FT: 25,000
SALES (est): 831.9K Privately Held
SIC: 2676 Diapers, paper (disposable): made from purchased paper

(P-3904)
GEORGIA PACIFIC HOLDINGS INC
13208 Hadley St Apt 1, Whittier (90601-4531)
PHONE..................626 926-1474
Jorge Arroyo, *CEO*
EMP: 860 **EST:** 2008
SQ FT: 1,000
SALES (est): 155MM
SALES (corp-wide): 36.9B **Privately Held**
WEB: www.kochind.com
SIC: 2676 2656 2435 2821 Sanitary paper products; sanitary food containers; hardwood veneer & plywood; plastics materials & resins
PA: Koch Industries, Inc.
4111 E 37th St N
Wichita KS 67220
316 828-5500

(P-3905)
LIL O BLOSSOM INC
2025 W Balboa Blvd Ste A, Newport Beach (92663-4342)
PHONE..................949 675-3885
Lorie Collins, *CEO*
EMP: 15 **EST:** 2008
SALES (est): 937.7K **Privately Held**
WEB: www.liloblossom.com
SIC: 2676 Infant & baby paper products

(P-3906)
PRINCESS PAPER INC
4455 Fruitland Ave, Vernon (90058-3222)
PHONE..................323 588-4777
Abraham Hakimi, *President*
▲ **EMP:** 45 **EST:** 1989
SQ FT: 150,000
SALES (est): 12MM **Privately Held**
WEB: www.princesspaper.com
SIC: 2676 Towels, napkins & tissue paper products

(P-3907)
PROCTER & GAMBLE PAPER PDTS CO
800 N Rice Ave, Oxnard (93030-8910)
PHONE..................805 485-8871
Shirley Boone, *Manager*
Martin Boyd, *Technology*
Sokny Ea, *Human Res Mgr*
Mike Doyle, *Prdtn Mgr*
EMP: 1898
SALES (corp-wide): 76.1B **Publicly Held**
WEB: www.pg.com
SIC: 2676 Towels, paper: made from purchased paper
HQ: The Procter & Gamble Paper Products Company
1 Procter And Gamble Plz
Cincinnati OH 45202
513 983-1100

(P-3908)
RAEL INC
6940 Beach Blvd Unit D301, Buena Park (90621-6827)
PHONE..................800 573-1516
Aness Han, *CEO*
Yanghee Park, *President*
EMP: 20 **EST:** 2017
SALES (est): 4.8MM **Privately Held**
WEB: www.getrael.com
SIC: 2676 Feminine hygiene paper products

2677 Envelopes

(P-3909)
INLAND ENVELOPE COMPANY
150 N Park Ave, Pomona (91768-3835)
PHONE..................909 622-2016
Bernard Kloenne, *CEO*
Otilia Kloenne, *Admin Sec*
EMP: 55 **EST:** 1966
SQ FT: 45,000
SALES (est): 10MM **Privately Held**
WEB: www.inlandenvelope.com
SIC: 2677 Envelopes

(P-3910)
LA ENVELOPE INCORPORATED
1053 S Vail Ave, Montebello (90640-6019)
PHONE..................323 838-9300
Gary T Earls, *President*
Louise Earls, *Admin Sec*
John Mekosh, *Accounts Exec*
EMP: 35
SQ FT: 25,000
SALES (est): 7.5MM **Privately Held**
WEB: www.laenvelope.com
SIC: 2677 2752 Envelopes; commercial printing, offset

(P-3911)
SEABOARD ENVELOPE CO INC
15601 Cypress Ave, Irwindale (91706-2020)
P.O. Box 721, Corona Del Mar (92625-0721)
PHONE..................626 960-4559
Ronald Neidringhaus, *President*
Richard Riggle, *Vice Pres*
Valerie Niedringhaus, *Admin Sec*
EMP: 25 **EST:** 1939
SQ FT: 72,000
SALES (est): 4.3MM **Privately Held**
WEB: www.seaboardenvelope.com
SIC: 2677 Envelopes

(P-3912)
VISION ENVELOPE & PRTG CO INC (PA)
13707 S Figueroa St, Los Angeles (90061-1045)
PHONE..................310 324-7062
Mark Fisher, *Principal*
Michael J Leeny, *Vice Pres*
EMP: 50 **EST:** 1993
SQ FT: 45,000
SALES (est): 12MM **Privately Held**
WEB: www.vision-envelope.com
SIC: 2677 2752 Envelopes; commercial printing, offset

2678 Stationery Prdts

(P-3913)
AVERY PRODUCTS CORPORATION (DH)
50 Pointe Dr, Brea (92821-3648)
PHONE..................714 675-8500
Geoff Martin, *President*
Mark Cooper, *Vice Pres*
Jeff Lattanzio, *Vice Pres*
Allison Phillips, *Vice Pres*
Bohdan Sirota, *Admin Sec*
◆ **EMP:** 596 **EST:** 2012
SALES: 325.8MM
SALES (corp-wide): 4B **Privately Held**
WEB: www.avery.com
SIC: 2678 3951 2672 2891 Notebooks: made from purchased paper; markers, soft tip (felt, fabric, plastic, etc.); labels (unprinted), gummed: made from purchased materials; adhesives

(P-3914)
ETERNAL STAR CORPORATION
17813 S Main St Ste 101, Gardena (90248-3542)
PHONE..................310 768-1945
▲ **EMP:** 30
SQ FT: 250,000
SALES (est): 4.1MM **Privately Held**
SIC: 2678 2782 Mfg Stationery Products Mfg Blankbooks/Binders

(P-3915)
MILLS ASAP REPROGRAPHICS (PA)
495 Morro Bay Blvd, Morro Bay (93442-2143)
P.O. Box 1678 (93443-1678)
PHONE..................805 772-2019
Roger R Marlin, *Owner*
Vicki Marlin, *Manager*
Victoria Marlin, *Manager*
EMP: 13 **EST:** 1960
SQ FT: 4,000

SALES (est): 2MM **Privately Held**
WEB: www.asapreprographics.com
SIC: 2678 5943 5999 Memorandum books, notebooks & looseleaf filler paper; office forms & supplies; writing supplies; artists' supplies & materials

(P-3916)
PENCIL GRIP INC (PA)
21200 Superior St Ste A, Chatsworth (91311-4324)
P.O. Box 3787 (91313-3787)
PHONE..................310 315-3545
Alexander Provda, *President*
Asher Provda, *CEO*
Julia Boyle, *Vice Pres*
Theresa Baker, *Finance*
Steve George, *Director*
◆ **EMP:** 17 **EST:** 1991
SQ FT: 12,000
SALES (est): 5.6MM **Privately Held**
WEB: www.thepencilgrip.com
SIC: 2678 Stationery products

(P-3917)
PIPSTICKS INC
1304 Garden St Ste 1, San Luis Obispo (93401-3984)
PHONE..................805 439-1692
Nathan Vazquez, *CEO*
Maureen D Vazquez, *Principal*
EMP: 22 **EST:** 2016
SALES (est): 3MM **Privately Held**
WEB: www.pipsticks.com
SIC: 2678 Stationery products

(P-3918)
TREE HOUSE PAD & PAPER INC
2341 Pomona Rd Ste 108, Corona (92878-4373)
PHONE..................800 213-4184
David Moncrief, *President*
Darrin Monroe, *Vice Pres*
Daniel Anguiano, *Production*
EMP: 55 **EST:** 1998
SQ FT: 50,000
SALES (est): 10.8MM **Privately Held**
WEB: www.treehousepaper.com
SIC: 2678 Stationery products

(P-3919)
VIVA HOLDINGS LLC (PA)
Also Called: Viva Concepts
4210 Charter St, Vernon (90058-2520)
PHONE..................818 243-1363
Farid Tabibzadeh,
Melissa Jacobs, *COO*
Majid Tabibzadeh, *Principal*
Kashif Shaheed, *Purchasing*
Eiman Rahnama, *Director*
EMP: 18 **EST:** 2011
SALES (est): 14.7MM **Privately Held**
SIC: 2678 Memorandum books, except printed: purchased materials

(P-3920)
VIVA PRINT LLC (HQ)
1025 N Brand Blvd Ste 300, Glendale (91202-3633)
PHONE..................818 243-1363
Greg Hughes Sr, *CEO*
Greg Hughes Jr, *COO*
EMP: 17 **EST:** 2013
SQ FT: 28,000
SALES (est): 4.7MM
SALES (corp-wide): 14.7MM **Privately Held**
SIC: 2678 Memorandum books, except printed: purchased materials
PA: Viva Holdings, Llc
4210 Charter St
Vernon CA 90058
818 243-1363

2679 Converted Paper Prdts, NEC

(P-3921)
A PLUS LABEL INC
3215 W Warner Ave, Santa Ana (92704-5314)
PHONE..................714 229-9811
Nick Phan, *President*
Adrianna Cornejo, *Graphic Designe*

Christophe Nguyen, *Sales Staff*
Bushra Alwakza, *Manager*
EMP: 50 **EST:** 1995
SQ FT: 6,400
SALES (est): 9.2MM **Privately Held**
WEB: www.apluslabel.com
SIC: 2679 Tags & labels, paper

(P-3922)
APPLE PAPER CONVERTING INC
3800 E Miraloma Ave, Anaheim (92806-2108)
P.O. Box 768, Atwood (92811-0768)
PHONE..................714 632-3195
Jorge Daniel Podboj, *President*
Louis Salavar, *President*
George Podboj, *Vice Pres*
EMP: 20 **EST:** 2001
SALES (est): 2.1MM **Privately Held**
WEB: www.applepaperconverting.com
SIC: 2679 Paper products, converted

(P-3923)
ARTISTRY IN MOTION INC
19411 Londelius St, Northridge (91324-3512)
PHONE..................818 994-7388
Roger Wachtell, *CEO*
Richard Graves, *President*
▼ **EMP:** 22 **EST:** 1995
SALES (est): 2.9MM **Privately Held**
WEB: www.artistryinmotion.com
SIC: 2679 5947 Confetti: made from purchased material; gifts & novelties

(P-3924)
CALPACO PAPERS INC (PA)
3155 Universe Dr, Jurupa Valley (91752-3252)
PHONE..................323 767-2800
Paul Maier, *President*
Francis A Maier, *Chairman*
▲ **EMP:** 136 **EST:** 1968
SQ FT: 606,000
SALES (est): 13.7MM **Privately Held**
WEB: www.calpaco.com
SIC: 2679 5111 Paper products, converted; printing & writing paper

(P-3925)
CONTINENTAL DATALABEL INC
Also Called: American Single Sheets
211 Business Center Ct, Redlands (92373-4404)
PHONE..................909 307-3600
Patrick Flynn, *Branch Mgr*
Jackie Flynn, *Executive*
Anthony Acosta, *Branch Mgr*
McKenna Williams, *Admin Asst*
Ron Kruger, *CTO*
EMP: 15
SALES (corp-wide): 28.3MM **Privately Held**
WEB: www.datalabel.com
SIC: 2679 2672 Labels, paper: made from purchased material; coated & laminated paper
PA: Continental Datalabel, Inc.
1855 Fox Ln
Elgin IL 60123
847 742-1600

(P-3926)
DIETZGEN CORPORATION
1522 E Bentley Dr, Corona (92879-1741)
PHONE..................951 278-3259
Darren A Letang, *President*
EMP: 24 **Privately Held**
WEB: www.dietzgen.com
SIC: 2679 Paper products, converted
PA: Dietzgen Corporation
121 Kelsey Ln Ste G
Tampa FL 33619

(P-3927)
DIGITAL LABEL SOLUTIONS LLC
22745 Old Canal Rd, Yorba Linda (92887-4603)
PHONE..................714 982-5000
Joel H Mark, *CEO*
Sandy Petersen, *Vice Pres*
Suzie Dobyns, *Admin Sec*
EMP: 29 **EST:** 2006

SQ FT: 14,000
SALES (est): 6.3MM **Privately Held**
WEB: www.digitallabelsolutions.com
SIC: 2679 Tags & labels, paper
PA: Brook & Whittle Limited
20 Carter Dr
Guilford CT 06437

(P-3928)
ENCORR SHEETS LLC
5171 E Francis St, Ontario (91761-3661)
PHONE....................626 523-4661
Tim Benecke, *COO*
Kevin Miller, *Vice Pres*
Michael Soule, *Vice Pres*
Adam Shafer, *Business Dir*
EMP: 53 **EST:** 2016
SALES (est): 16.4MM **Privately Held**
SIC: 2679 Corrugated paper: made from
purchased material

(P-3929)
**FDS MANUFACTURING
COMPANY (PA)**
2200 S Reservoir St, Pomona
(91766-6408)
P.O. Box 3120 (91769-3120)
PHONE....................909 591-1733
Robert B Stevenson, *CEO*
Samuel B Stevenson, *Chairman*
Chuck O'Connor, *Vice Pres*
Kevin Stevenson, *Vice Pres*
Todd Lawrence, *Controller*
▲ **EMP:** 100 **EST:** 1950
SQ FT: 240,000
SALES (est): 19.1MM **Privately Held**
WEB: www.fdsmfg.com
SIC: 2679 3089 Corrugated paper: made
from purchased material; plastic contain-
ers, except foam

(P-3930)
GOLDEN KRAFT INC
15500 Valley View Ave, La Mirada
(90638-5230)
PHONE....................562 926-8888
Dan August, *General Mgr*
▲ **EMP:** 281 **EST:** 1982
SQ FT: 63,200
SALES (est): 9.1MM
SALES (corp-wide): 36.9B **Privately Held**
SIC: 2679 2631 Corrugated paper: made
from purchased material; paperboard
mills
HQ: Georgia-Pacific Corrugated Iii Llc
5645 W 82nd St
Indianapolis IN 46278

(P-3931)
NCLA INC
1388 W Foothill Blvd, Azusa (91702-2846)
PHONE....................562 926-6252
John McGee, *President*
EMP: 19 **EST:** 1997
SALES (est): 2MM **Privately Held**
WEB: www.nclainc.com
SIC: 2679 3083 Paper products, con-
verted; plastic finished products, lami-
nated

(P-3932)
**PACIFIC PPRBD CONVERTING
LLC (PA)**
8865 Utica Ave Ste A, Rancho Cucamonga
(91730-5144)
PHONE....................909 476-6466
Bill Donahue, *CEO*
Terry Esquivias, *Sales Executive*
EMP: 24 **EST:** 2016
SALES (est): 5.1MM **Privately Held**
WEB: www.pacificpaper.com
SIC: 2679 Paper products, converted

(P-3933)
POSITIVE CONCEPTS INC (PA)
Also Called: Ameri-Fax
2021 N Glassell St, Orange (92865-3305)
PHONE....................714 685-5800
Lambert C Thom, *CEO*
George Manzur, *President*
Ken Mount, *Exec VP*
Susan Lindsey, *Train & Dev Mgr*
Delanee Barajas, *Accounts Exec*
▼ **EMP:** 22 **EST:** 1989

SQ FT: 20,000
SALES (est): 9.5MM **Privately Held**
WEB: www.posconcepts.com
SIC: 2679 5084 Paper products, con-
verted; machine tools & accessories

(P-3934)
**PRIME CONVERTING
CORPORATION**
9121 Pttsbrgh Ave Ste 100, Rancho Cuca-
monga (91730)
P.O. Box 3207 (91729-3207)
PHONE....................909 476-9500
Robert J Nielsen, *President*
Jillian Smith, *Controller*
Joe Silva, *Accounts Mgr*
▲ **EMP:** 24 **EST:** 2003
SALES (est): 13.9MM **Privately Held**
WEB: www.primecc.com
SIC: 2679 Paper products, converted

(P-3935)
**PROGRESSIVE CONVERTING
INC**
280 W Bonita Ave, Pomona (91767-1850)
PHONE....................909 392-2201
Eric Briones, *Manager*
EMP: 18 **Privately Held**
WEB: www.pro-con.net
SIC: 2679 Paper products, converted
PA: Progressive Converting, Inc.
2430 E Glendale Ave
Appleton WI 54911

(P-3936)
PROGRESSIVE LABEL INC
2545 Yates Ave, Commerce (90040-2619)
P.O. Box 911430, Los Angeles (90091-
1238)
PHONE....................323 415-9770
Gus Garcia, *President*
David Lawrence, *Shareholder*
Adam Flores, *Vice Pres*
Julie Lawrence, *Admin Sec*
Leonel Salazar, *IT/INT Sup*
▲ **EMP:** 39 **EST:** 1988
SQ FT: 18,000
SALES (est): 7.2MM **Privately Held**
WEB: www.progressivelabel.com
SIC: 2679 2672 2671 2241 Tags & la-
bels, paper; coated & laminated paper;
packaging paper & plastics film, coated &
laminated; narrow fabric mills

(P-3937)
**QUADRIGA USA ENTERPRISES
INC**
Also Called: Commercial and Security Labels
28410 Witherspoon Pkwy, Valencia
(91355-4167)
PHONE....................888 669-9994
Aram Mehrabyan, *CEO*
Ashot Mehrabyan, *CFO*
Vahan Arakelyan, *General Mgr*
Mher Mehrabyan, *Admin Sec*
EMP: 14 **EST:** 2015
SQ FT: 18,200
SALES (est): 2.5MM **Privately Held**
WEB: www.usa.quadrigausa.com
SIC: 2679 5131 7389 2672 Tags & la-
bels, paper; labels; packaging & labeling
services; adhesive papers, labels or
tapes: from purchased material; labels &
seals: printing

(P-3938)
TAGTIME USA INC
4601 District Blvd, Vernon (90058-2731)
PHONE....................323 587-1555
Cort Johnson, *President*
Mindy Flynn, *COO*
Mindy Knox, *Vice Pres*
Mark Lonneker, *Vice Pres*
Jim Maier, *Vice Pres*
▲ **EMP:** 480 **EST:** 2001
SQ FT: 23,000
SALES (est): 28.5MM **Privately Held**
WEB: www.tagtimeusa.com
SIC: 2679 Labels, paper: made from pur-
chased material

(P-3939)
THOMPSON PIPE GROUP INC
3011 N Laurel Ave, Rialto (92377-3725)
PHONE....................909 822-0200
Kenneth D Thompson, *CEO*
Branimir Kovac, *Vice Pres*
Detlev Schlorke, *Vice Pres*
Colin Brown, *Business Mgr*
Kenneth Davis, *Business Mgr*
EMP: 29 **EST:** 2018
SALES (est): 5.3MM **Privately Held**
WEB: www.thompsonpipegroup.com
SIC: 2679 Pipes & fittings, fiber: made
from purchased material

(P-3940)
Z B P INC
Also Called: Z-Barten Productions
2871 E Pico Blvd, Los Angeles
(90023-3609)
PHONE....................323 266-3363
Dale Zabel, *President*
Nancy Andersen, *Principal*
Jane Berse, *Principal*
Paula Greenberg, *Principal*
Howard Kuykendall, *Principal*
▲ **EMP:** 16 **EST:** 1984
SQ FT: 20,000
SALES (est): 1.3MM **Privately Held**
WEB: www.confetti.com
SIC: 2679 2678 Novelties, paper: made
from purchased material; stationery prod-
ucts

2711 Newspapers: Publishing & Printing

(P-3941)
2100 FREEDOM INC (HQ)
625 N Grand Ave, Santa Ana (92701-4347)
PHONE....................714 796-7000
Richard E Mirman, *CEO*
Aaron Kushner, *CEO*
EMP: 100 **EST:** 2012
SALES (est): 371.7MM **Privately Held**
WEB: www.socalnewsgroup.com
SIC: 2711 2721 7313 2741 Newspapers,
publishing & printing; periodicals; news-
paper advertising representative; miscel-
laneous publishing; newspapers, home
delivery, not by printers or publishers;
PA: 2100 Trust, Llc
625 N Grand Ave
Santa Ana CA 92701
877 469-7344

(P-3942)
**5800 SUNSET PRODUCTIONS
INC**
Also Called: Tribune Studios
5800 W Sunset Blvd, Los Angeles
(90028-6607)
PHONE....................323 460-3987
EMP: 13
SALES (est): 3.4MM
SALES (corp-wide): 2B **Publicly Held**
SIC: 2711 Newspaper Publication
PA: Tribune Media Company
435 N Michigan Ave Fl 2
Chicago IL 60654
212 210-2786

(P-3943)
ACORN NEWSPAPER INC
30423 Canwood St Ste 108, Agoura Hills
(91301-4313)
PHONE....................818 706-0266
Jim Rule, *President*
Allison Montroy, *Adv Dir*
EMP: 35 **EST:** 1974
SQ FT: 3,000
SALES (est): 3MM **Privately Held**
SIC: 2711 Newspapers: publishing only,
not printed on site

(P-3944)
**AMPERSAND PUBLISHING LLC
(PA)**
Also Called: Santa Barbara News-Press Info
715 Anacapa St, Santa Barbara
(93101-2203)
P.O. Box 1359 (93102-1359)
PHONE....................805 564-5200

Wendy McCaw,
John A Royston, *Info Tech Dir*
Yoland Apodaca, *Human Res Dir*
Yolanda Apodaca, *Opers Staff*
Gabriele Huth, *Advt Staff*
EMP: 30 **EST:** 1856
SQ FT: 65,000
SALES (est): 20MM **Privately Held**
WEB: www.newspress.com
SIC: 2711 Newspapers: publishing only,
not printed on site

(P-3945)
**ANTELOPE VALLEY
NEWSPAPERS INC**
Also Called: Antelope Valley Press
44939 10th St W, Lancaster (93534-2313)
PHONE....................661 940-1000
Tammy Valdes, *Manager*
EMP: 29
SALES (corp-wide): 13.6MM **Privately
Held**
WEB: www.avpress.com
SIC: 2711 7313 2741 Newspapers: pub-
lishing only, not printed on site; newspa-
per advertising representative;
miscellaneous publishing
PA: Antelope Valley Newspapers Inc.
37404 Sierra Hwy
Palmdale CA
661 273-2700

(P-3946)
ARGONAUT
5355 Mcconnell Ave, Los Angeles
(90066-7025)
PHONE....................310 822-1629
David Asper Johnson, *President*
George Drury Smith, *CFO*
Rocki Davidson, *Sales Staff*
EMP: 26 **EST:** 1971
SQ FT: 10,000
SALES (est): 2MM **Privately Held**
WEB: www.argonautnews.com
SIC: 2711 Newspapers: publishing only,
not printed on site

(P-3947)
**ASIA-PACIFIC CALIFORNIA INC
(PA)**
Also Called: China Press, The
2121 W Mission Rd Ste 207, Alhambra
(91803-1431)
PHONE....................323 318-2254
Yining Xie, *President*
▲ **EMP:** 43 **EST:** 1991
SQ FT: 13,000
SALES (est): 5.9MM **Privately Held**
SIC: 2711 Newspapers, publishing & print-
ing

(P-3948)
ASIA-PACIFIC CALIFORNIA INC
Also Called: The China Press
923 E Valley Blvd Ste 203, San Gabriel
(91776-3684)
PHONE....................626 281-8500
Non Hiand, *General Mgr*
EMP: 35 **Privately Held**
SIC: 2711 Newspapers, publishing & print-
ing
PA: Asia-Pacific California, Inc.
2121 W Mission Rd Ste 207
Alhambra CA 91803

(P-3949)
**ASSOCIATED DESERT
NEWSPAPER (DH)**
Also Called: Imperial Valley Press
205 N 8th St, El Centro (92243-2301)
P.O. Box 2641 (92244-2641)
PHONE....................760 337-3400
Mayer Malone, *President*
David Leone, *President*
Teresa Zimmer, *CFO*
John Yanni, *Treasurer*
Clifford James, *Admin Sec*
EMP: 40 **EST:** 1950
SQ FT: 30,000
SALES (est): 22.4MM
SALES (corp-wide): 2.3B **Publicly Held**
WEB: www.ivpressonline.com
SIC: 2711 Newspapers, publishing & print-
ing; commercial printing & newspaper
publishing combined

**P
R
O
D
U
C
T
S
&
S
V
C
S**

HQ: Schurz Communications, Inc.
1301 E Douglas Rd Ste 200
Mishawaka IN 46545
574 247-7237

(P-3950)
ASSOCIATED STUDENTS UCLA
Also Called: Asucla Publications
308 Westwood Plz Ste 118, Los Angeles
(90095-8355)
PHONE..................310 825-2787
Arvli Ward, *Director*
Remington Lee, *Director*
EMP: 151
SALES (corp-wide): 54.7MM **Privately Held**
WEB: www.asucla.ucla.edu
SIC: 2711 2741 2721 Newspapers: publishing only, not printed on site; miscellaneous publishing; periodicals
PA: Associated Students U.C.L.A.
308 Westwood Plz
Los Angeles CA 90095
310 794-8836

(P-3951)
AUT INC
3925 Schaefer Ave, Chino (91710-5445)
PHONE..................909 393-9961
EMP: 13 EST: 2019
SALES (est): 679.9K **Privately Held**
SIC: 2711 Newspapers

(P-3952)
BALITA MEDIA INC
Also Called: Weekend Balita
2629 Foothill Blvd, La Crescenta
(91214-3511)
PHONE..................818 552-4503
Luchie Allen, *CEO*
Ruby Allen, *Principal*
Ramonsito Mendoza, *Admin Sec*
EMP: 18 EST: 1993
SALES (est): 3.9MM **Privately Held**
WEB: www.balita.com
SIC: 2711 Newspapers, publishing & printing

(P-3953)
BEVERLY HILLS COURIER INC
499 N Canon Dr Ste 100, Beverly Hills
(90210-6192)
PHONE..................310 278-1322
Clifton Smith, *President*
March Schwartz, *President*
Pat Wilkins, *Advt Staff*
Carole Dixon, *Editor*
EMP: 27 EST: 1965
SQ FT: 10,000
SALES (est): 1.4MM **Privately Held**
WEB: www.beverlyhillscourier.com
SIC: 2711 Newspapers, publishing & printing

(P-3954)
CALIFORNIA COMMUNITY NEWS LLC
Also Called: Burbank Leader
221 N Brand Blvd Fl 2, Glendale
(91203-2609)
PHONE..................818 843-8700
Danette Goulet, *Manager*
Will Fleet, *Publisher*
EMP: 56
SALES (corp-wide): 746.2MM **Privately Held**
SIC: 2711 Newspapers: publishing only, not printed on site
HQ: California Community News, Llc
2000 E 8th St
Los Angeles CA 90021

(P-3955)
CALIFORNIA COMMUNITY NEWS LLC (HQ)
2000 E 8th St, Los Angeles (90021-2474)
PHONE..................626 388-1017
Eddy Hartenstein, *President*
Judy Kendall, *Vice Pres*
Julie Xanders, *Admin Sec*
EMP: 349 EST: 1993

SALES (est): 63.4MM
SALES (corp-wide): 746.2MM **Privately Held**
WEB: www.tribpub.com
SIC: 2711 Newspapers, publishing & printing; commercial printing & newspaper publishing combined
PA: Tribune Publishing Company
560 W Grand Ave
Chicago IL 60654
312 222-9100

(P-3956)
CALIFRNIA NWSPAPERS LTD PARTNR (DH)
Also Called: Inland Valley Daily Bulletin
605 E Huntington Dr # 100, Monrovia
(91016-6352)
P.O. Box 1259, Covina (91722-0259)
PHONE..................626 962-8811
Ron Hasse, *President*
Jeanne White, *CFO*
Fran Conte, *Exec VP*
Jim Maurer, *Vice Pres*
Mark Welches, *Vice Pres*
EMP: 450 EST: 1997
SALES (est): 199.5MM
SALES (corp-wide): 1.8B **Privately Held**
WEB: www.medianewsgroup.com
SIC: 2711 Newspapers, publishing & printing

(P-3957)
CALIFRNIA NWSPAPERS LTD PARTNR
Also Called: Inland Valley Daily Bulletin
3200 E Guasti Rd Ste 100, Ontario
(91761-8661)
PHONE..................909 987-6397
Bob Balzer, *Manager*
Jim Maurer, *Vice Pres*
Christine Burt, *Executive Asst*
Veronica Nair, *Marketing Staff*
Don Sproul, *Manager*
EMP: 106
SALES (corp-wide): 1.8B **Privately Held**
SIC: 2711 Newspapers, publishing & printing
HQ: California Newspapers Limited Partnership
605 E Huntington Dr # 100
Monrovia CA 91016
626 962-8811

(P-3958)
CALIFRNIA NWSPAPERS LTD PARTNR
Also Called: Redlands Daily Facts
19 E Citrus Ave Ste 102, Redlands
(92373-4763)
PHONE..................909 793-3221
Peggy Del Torro, *Manager*
EMP: 106
SQ FT: 8,301
SALES (corp-wide): 1.8B **Privately Held**
SIC: 2711 7313 Newspapers, publishing & printing; newspaper advertising representative
HQ: California Newspapers Limited Partnership
605 E Huntington Dr # 100
Monrovia CA 91016
626 962-8811

(P-3959)
CAPISTRANO DISPATCH
34932 Calle Del Sol Ste B, Capistrano
Beach (92624-1664)
PHONE..................949 388-7700
Norb Garrett, *Executive Asst*
EMP: 19 EST: 1998
SALES (est): 260.6K **Privately Held**
WEB: www.thecapistranodispatch.com
SIC: 2711 Commercial printing & newspaper publishing combined; newspapers, publishing & printing

(P-3960)
CHAMPION PBLICATIONS CHINO INC
Also Called: Champion Newspapers
13179 9th St, Chino (91710-4216)
P.O. Box 607 (91708-0607)
PHONE..................909 628-5501
Allen P McCombs, *President*

Bill McCombs, *Treasurer*
Gretchen McCombs, *Vice Pres*
Linda Fenner, *Sales Staff*
Tom Hebert, *Senior Mgr*
EMP: 17 EST: 1887
SQ FT: 6,500
SALES (est): 5.1MM **Privately Held**
WEB: www.championnewspapers.com
SIC: 2711 Newspapers, publishing & printing
PA: Golden State Newspapers Llc
95 W 11th St Ste 101
Tracy CA 95376
209 835-3030

(P-3961)
CHURM PUBLISHING INC (PA)
Also Called: O.C. Metro Magazine
1451 Quail St Ste 201, Newport Beach
(92660-2741)
PHONE..................714 796-7000
Steve Churm, *President*
Chris Dahl, *CFO*
Brian O'Neill, *CFO*
Peter Churm, *Vice Pres*
Sherry Guyer, *Executive Asst*
EMP: 47 EST: 1982
SQ FT: 7,000
SALES (est): 8.5MM **Privately Held**
WEB: www.ocregister.com
SIC: 2711 Newspapers, publishing & printing

(P-3962)
CITY NEWS GROUP INC
22797 Barton Rd, Grand Terrace
(92313-5207)
PHONE..................909 370-1200
Margie Miller, *CEO*
EMP: 13 EST: 2006
SALES (est): 485.5K **Privately Held**
WEB: www.citynewsgroup.com
SIC: 2711 2621 7311 Newspapers: publishing only, not printed on site; catalog, magazine & newsprint papers; advertising agencies

(P-3963)
CIVIC CENTER NEWS INC
Also Called: Los Angeles Downtown News
1264 W 1st St, Los Angeles (90026-5831)
PHONE..................213 481-1448
Susan R Laris, *President*
Claudia Hernandez, *Production*
Michael Lamb, *Accounts Exec*
EMP: 19 EST: 1972
SQ FT: 2,366
SALES (est): 1.2MM **Privately Held**
WEB: www.ladowntownnews.com
SIC: 2711 Newspapers, publishing & printing

(P-3964)
CLAREMONT COURIER INC
114 Olive St, Claremont (91711-4924)
PHONE..................909 621-4761
Peter Weinberger, *President*
D Proffitt, *Accountant*
Mick Rhodes, *Editor*
EMP: 17 EST: 1955
SQ FT: 4,000
SALES (est): 3.1MM **Privately Held**
WEB: www.claremont-courier.com
SIC: 2711 Newspapers, publishing & printing

(P-3965)
COMMUNITY CLOSE-UP WESTMINSTER
1771 S Lewis St, Anaheim (92805-6439)
PHONE..................714 704-5811
EMP: 61
SALES (est): 6.6MM
SALES (corp-wide): 2.3B **Privately Held**
SIC: 2711 Newspapers-Publishing/Printing
HQ: Freedom Communications, Inc.
625 N Grand Ave
Santa Ana CA 92701
714 796-7000

(P-3966)
COMMUNITY MEDIA CORPORATION (PA)
Also Called: San Dego Nghborhood Newspapers
5119 Ball Rd, Cypress (90630-3645)
PHONE..................714 220-0292
Kathy Verdugo, *President*
Daniel Verdugo, *COO*
Linda Townson, *Vice Pres*
Franco Te, *Director*
EMP: 67 EST: 1993
SQ FT: 4,000
SALES (est): 1.6MM **Privately Held**
WEB: www.communitymediaus.com
SIC: 2711 Newspapers, publishing & printing

(P-3967)
CYCLE NEWS INC (PA)
Also Called: CN Publishing Group
17771 Mitchell N, Irvine (92614-6028)
PHONE..................949 863-7082
Sharon Clayton, *President*
Michelle Baird, *Editor*
EMP: 32 EST: 1965
SQ FT: 10,000
SALES (est): 5MM **Privately Held**
WEB: www.cyclenews.com
SIC: 2711 Newspapers, publishing & printing

(P-3968)
DAILY DOSES LLC (FA)
1130 S Shenandoah St, Los Angeles
(90035-2208)
PHONE..................858 220-0076
Daniel Andrade, *Principal*
EMP: 24 EST: 2012
SALES (est): 187.4K **Privately Held**
WEB: www.daily-doses.com
SIC: 2711 Newspapers, publishing & printing

(P-3969)
DAILY JOURNAL CORPORATION (PA)
915 E 1st St, Los Angeles (90012-4042)
PHONE..................213 229-5300
Gerald L Salzman, *President*
Charles T Munger, *Ch of Bd*
Veronica Espinoza, *Info Tech Dir*
Hoa To, *Controller*
Emma Sanchez, *Purchasing*
EMP: 209 EST: 1888
SQ FT: 34,000
SALES: 49.9MM **Publicly Held**
WEB: www.dailyjournal.com
SIC: 2711 2721 3713 73"2 Newspapers, publishing & printing; magazines: publishing & printing; newspaper advertising representative; prepackaged software

(P-3970)
DAILY SPORTS SEOUL USA INC
3550 Wilshire Blvd # 1912 Los Angeles
(90010-2403)
PHONE..................213 487-9331
Jang Hee Lee, *President*
Austin Park, *Marketing Mgr*
EMP: 18 EST: 1999
SALES (est): 2.2MM **Privately Held**
WEB: www.koreatowndaily.com
SIC: 2711 Commercial printing & newspaper publishing combined; newspapers, publishing & printing

(P-3971)
DAILYMEDIA INC (PA)
8 E Figueroa St Ste 220, Santa Barbara
(93101-2716)
PHONE..................541 821-5207
Scott Blum, *President*
Jessica Roady, *Bookkeeper*
EMP: 19 EST: 2005
SQ FT: 5,000
SALES (est): 1.1MM **Privately Held**
SIC: 2711 Newspapers, publishing & printing

(P-3972)
DESERT SUN PUBLISHING CO (DH)
Also Called: Desert Sun The
750 N Gene Autry Trl, Palm Springs (92262-5463)
P.O. Box 2734 (92263-2734)
PHONE..................................760 322-8889
Joe Myers, *Credit Mgr*
Joe Hong, *Education*
EMP: 200 **EST:** 1974
SQ FT: 30,621
SALES (est): 63.8MM
SALES (corp-wide): 3.4B **Publicly Held**
WEB: www.desertsun.com
SIC: 2711 Newspapers, publishing & printing
HQ: Gannett Media Corp.
7950 Jones Branch Dr
Mc Lean VA 22102
703 854-6000

(P-3973)
E Z BUY E Z SELL RECYCLER CORP (DH)
Also Called: Recycler Classified
4954 Van Nuys Blvd Ste 20, Sherman Oaks (91403-1719)
PHONE..................................310 886-7808
Niki Ruokosuo, *President*
Jim Fullmer, *VP Finance*
EMP: 200 **EST:** 1973
SQ FT: 13,000
SALES (est): 33.7MM
SALES (corp-wide): 4.5B **Publicly Held**
WEB:
www.recyclerclassifieds.blogspot.com
SIC: 2711 2741 Newspapers: publishing only, not printed on site; miscellaneous publishing
HQ: Tribune Media Company
515 N State St Ste 2400
Chicago IL 60654
312 222-3394

(P-3974)
EASY READER INC
832 Hermosa Ave, Hermosa Beach (90254-4116)
P.O. Box 427 (90254-0427)
PHONE..................................310 372-4611
Kevin Cody, *President*
Richard Barnes, *CIO*
Bondo Wyszpolski, *Editor*
EMP: 35 **EST:** 1970
SQ FT: 3,400
SALES (est): 3.2MM **Privately Held**
WEB: www.easyreadernews.com
SIC: 2711 Newspapers: publishing only, not printed on site

(P-3975)
EL CLASIFICADO (PA)
11205 Imperial Hwy, Norwalk (90650-2229)
PHONE..................................323 837-4095
Martha C Dela Torre, *President*
Joseph Badame, *President*
Gil Garcia, *CFO*
Robert Feugate, *IT/INT Sup*
Trevor Romero, *Production*
EMP: 61 **EST:** 1988
SALES (est): 31.3MM **Privately Held**
WEB: www.elclasificado.com
SIC: 2711 Newspapers, publishing & printing

(P-3976)
FOOTHILLS SUN-GAZETTE
Also Called: Foothills Advertiser
120 N E St, Exeter (93221-1729)
P.O. Box 7 (93221-0007)
PHONE..................................559 592-3171
Katie Byrne, *President*
Wsley Byrne, *Treasurer*
Reggie Ellis, *Vice Pres*
William Brown, *Principal*
EMP: 19 **EST:** 1984
SQ FT: 5,000
SALES (est): 2.3MM **Privately Held**
WEB: www.thesungazette.com
SIC: 2711 Newspapers, publishing & printing

(P-3977)
FREEDOM COMMUNICATIONS INC
Also Called: Orange County Register
22481 Aspan St, El Toro (92630-1630)
PHONE..................................949 454-7300
EMP: 50
SALES (corp-wide): 2.5B **Privately Held**
SIC: 2711 Newspapers-Publishing/Printing
HQ: Freedom Communications Inc
625 N Grand Ave
Santa Ana CA 92701
714 796-7000

(P-3978)
FREEDOM NEWSPAPERS INC
729 N Grand Ave, Santa Ana (92701-4350)
PHONE..................................714 796-7000
Richard E Mirman, *CEO*
EMP: 18 **EST:** 2009 **Privately Held**
WEB: www.yumasun.com
SIC: 2711 Newspapers, publishing & printing

(P-3979)
GANNETT STLLITE INFO NTWRK LLC
6060 Center Dr, Los Angeles (90045-1587)
PHONE..................................310 846-5870
EMP: 27
SALES (corp-wide): 3.4B **Publicly Held**
WEB: www.gannett.com
SIC: 2711 Newspapers, publishing & printing
HQ: Gannett Satellite Information Network, Llc
7950 Jones Branch Dr
Mc Lean VA 22102
703 854-6000

(P-3980)
GARDENA VALLEY NEWS INC
Also Called: Valley News Gardens
15005 S Vermont Ave, Gardena (90247-3004)
P.O. Box 219 (90248-0219)
PHONE..................................310 329-6351
George D Algie, *President*
Ruriko Yatabe, *Corp Secy*
Carlos Bueno, *Plant Mgr*
Robert Von Gorres, *Sales Mgr*
EMP: 40 **EST:** 1904
SQ FT: 8,200
SALES (est): 2.3MM **Privately Held**
WEB: www.gardenavalleynews.org
SIC: 2711 Commercial printing & newspaper publishing combined

(P-3981)
GATEHOUSE MEDIA LLC
Also Called: Victorville Daily Press
13891 Park Ave, Victorville (92392-2435)
PHONE..................................760 241-7744
Michael E Reed, *Branch Mgr*
EMP: 25
SALES (corp-wide): 3.4B **Publicly Held**
WEB: www.gannett.com
SIC: 2711 Commercial printing & newspaper publishing combined
HQ: Gatehouse Media, Llc
175 Sullys Trl Fl 3
Pittsford NY 14534
585 598-0030

(P-3982)
GAZETTE NEWSPAPERS INC
Also Called: Grunion Gazette
5225 E 2nd St, Long Beach (90803-5326)
PHONE..................................562 433-2000
Simmon Grief, *Principal*
Simon Grieve, *Editor*
Julie McKibbin, *Publisher*
EMP: 22 **EST:** 1977
SQ FT: 2,600
SALES (est): 1.1MM **Privately Held**
WEB: www.presstelegram.com
SIC: 2711 Newspapers, publishing & printing

(P-3983)
GRACE COMMUNICATIONS INC (PA)
Also Called: Metropolitan News Company
210 S Spring St, Los Angeles (90012-3710)
P.O. Box 86308 (90086-0308)
PHONE..................................213 628-4384
Joann W Grace, *President*
Roger M Grace, *Vice Pres*
EMP: 43 **EST:** 1901
SQ FT: 21,000
SALES (est): 8.8MM **Privately Held**
WEB: www.mnc.net
SIC: 2711 Newspapers, publishing & printing; newspapers: publishing only, not printed on site

(P-3984)
HANFORD SENTINEL INC
Also Called: Pulitzer Community Newspapers
300 W 6th St, Hanford (93230-4518)
P.O. Box 9 (93232-0009)
PHONE..................................559 582-0471
Randy Rickman, *President*
Mark Daniel, *Vice Pres*
Jennifer Vikjord, *Advt Staff*
Joyce Chambers, *Manager*
Jenny McGill, *Manager*
EMP: 321 **EST:** 1900
SQ FT: 16,000
SALES (est): 5.1MM
SALES (corp-wide): 618MM **Publicly Held**
WEB: www.hanfordsentinel.com
SIC: 2711 Commercial printing & newspaper publishing combined; newspapers, publishing & printing
HQ: Pulitzer Inc
900 N Tucker Blvd
Saint Louis MO 63101
314 340-8000

(P-3985)
HARRELL HOLDINGS (PA)
1707 Eye St Ste 102, Bakersfield (93301-5208)
P.O. Box 440 (93302-0440)
PHONE..................................661 322-5627
Richard Beene, *President*
Logan Molen, *COO*
Michelle Hirst, *CFO*
Virginia Fritts Moorhouse, *Chairman*
John Arthur, *Vice Pres*
EMP: 188
SALES (est): 29.7MM **Privately Held**
WEB: www.bakersfield.com
SIC: 2711 Commercial printing & newspaper publishing combined; newspapers, publishing & printing

(P-3986)
HI-DESERT PUBLISHING COMPANY
Also Called: Yuciapa & Calimesa News Mirror
35154 Yucaipa Blvd, Yucaipa (92399-4339)
P.O. Box 760 (92399-0760)
PHONE..................................909 795-8145
Jerry Bean, *Manager*
Garry Moore, *Executive*
Toebe Bush, *Publisher*
EMP: 34
SALES (corp-wide): 228.3MM **Privately Held**
WEB: www.hidesertstar.com
SIC: 2711 Newspapers, publishing & printing
HQ: Hi-Desert Publishing Company
56445 29 Palms Hwy
Yucca Valley CA 92284

(P-3987)
HI-DESERT PUBLISHING COMPANY
Also Called: Mountain News & Shopper
28200 Highway 189 O-1, Lake Arrowhead (92352-9700)
P.O. Box 2410 (92352-2410)
PHONE..................................909 336-3555
Harry Bradley, *Sales/Mktg Mgr*
EMP: 34

SALES (corp-wide): 228.3MM **Privately Held**
SIC: 2711 Commercial printing & newspaper publishing combined
HQ: Hi-Desert Publishing Company
56445 29 Palms Hwy
Yucca Valley CA 92284

(P-3988)
HI-DESERT PUBLISHING COMPANY (HQ)
56445 29 Palms Hwy, Yucca Valley (92284-2861)
PHONE..................................760 365-3315
Cindy Melland, *Publisher*
Stacy Moore, *Editor*
EMP: 70 **EST:** 1990
SALES (est): 10.3MM
SALES (corp-wide): 228.3MM **Privately Held**
WEB: www.hidesertstar.com
SIC: 2711 Newspapers, publishing & printing
PA: Brehm Communications, Inc.
16644 W Bernardo Dr # 300
San Diego CA 92127
858 451-6200

(P-3989)
HI-DESERT PUBLISHING COMPANY
Also Called: Big Bear Grizzly & Big Bear Lf
42007 Fox Farm Rd Ste 3b, Big Bear Lake (92315-2192)
PHONE..................................909 866-3456
Gerald Wright, *Manager*
EMP: 40
SALES (corp-wide): 228.3MM **Privately Held**
WEB: www.hidesertstar.com
SIC: 5994 2711 News dealers & newsstands; newspapers
HQ: Hi-Desert Publishing Company
56445 29 Palms Hwy
Yucca Valley CA 92284

(P-3990)
HOLLYWOOD REPORTER
6715 W Sunset Blvd, Los Angeles (90028-7107)
PHONE..................................323 525-2000
Janice Min, *Principal*
Carolyn Bernste n, *Exec Dir*
Kirsten Chuba, *Assistant*
EMP: 27 **EST:** 2010
SALES (est): 1.3MM **Privately Held**
WEB: www.hollywoodreporter.com
SIC: 2711 Newspapers, publishing & printing

(P-3991)
HOLLYWOOD REPORTER
100 N Crescent Dr Gl-1, Beverly Hills (90210-5408)
PHONE..................................323 525-2150
Janice Min, *President*
Ashley Lyle, *Executive Asst*
Steven Huizar, *Marketing Staff*
Chelsea Sageer, *Sales Staff*
Scott Roxborough, *Chief*
EMP: 22 **EST:** 2015
SALES (est): 1.1MM **Privately Held**
WEB: www.hollywoodreporter.com
SIC: 2711 Newspapers, publishing & printing

(P-3992)
HOLLYWOOD REPORTER LLC
100 N Crescent Dr Gl-1, Beverly Hills (90210-5408)
PHONE..................................323 525-2000
EMP: 33 **EST:** 2010
SALES (est): 323.6K **Privately Held**
SIC: 2711 Newspapers, publishing & printing

(P-3993)
HUGHES PRICE & SHARP INC
Also Called: Bargain Mart Classifieds
5200 Lankershim Blvd # 85, North Hollywood (91601-3155)
PHONE..................................865 675-6278
Jose Ortiz, *President*

A Eugene Hughes, *Treasurer*
EMP: 14 **EST:** 1973
SALES (est): 195.6K **Privately Held**
SIC: 2711 Newspapers: publishing only, not printed on site

(P-3994)
INLAND EMPIRE CMNTY NEWSPAPERS
Also Called: Rialto Record
1809 Commercenter W, San Bernardino (92408-3303)
P.O. Box 110, Colton (92324-0110)
PHONE..........................909 381-9898
William B Harrison, *President*
EMP: 19 **EST:** 1948
SQ FT: 4,000
SALES (est): 421.1K **Privately Held**
WEB: www.iecn.com
SIC: 2711 Newspapers: publishing only, not printed on site

(P-3995)
INLAND VALLEY NEWS INC
2009 Porter Field Way C, Upland (91786-2196)
PHONE..........................909 949-3099
Ta Lese Morrow, *CEO*
Ta Mia Morrow, *CFO*
Tommy Morrow, *Admin Sec*
▲ **EMP:** 17 **EST:** 1992
SALES (est): 1.7MM **Privately Held**
WEB: www.inlandvalleynews.com
SIC: 2711 Newspapers: publishing only, not printed on site

(P-3996)
INTERNATIONAL DAILY NEWS INC (PA)
870 Monterey Pass Rd, Monterey Park (91754-3688)
PHONE..........................323 265-1317
Jessica G Elnitiarta, *President*
Yopie Sioeng, *Manager*
▲ **EMP:** 20 **EST:** 1981
SQ FT: 10,000
SALES (est): 4.3MM **Privately Held**
WEB: www.chinesetoday.com
SIC: 2711 Newspapers, publishing & printing

(P-3997)
INVESTORS BUSINESS DAILY INC (HQ)
12655 Beatrice St, Los Angeles (90066-7303)
PHONE..........................310 448-6000
William O'Neil, *President*
Kathy Sherman, *Vice Pres*
Bree Miller, *Production*
Jonathan Regan, *Production*
Josh Kossack, *Producer*
▲ **EMP:** 200 **EST:** 1984
SQ FT: 180,000
SALES (est): 70.7MM
SALES (corp-wide): 335.6MM **Privately Held**
WEB: www.investors.com
SIC: 2711 Newspapers, publishing & printing
PA: Data Analysis Inc.
12655 Beatrice St
Los Angeles CA 90066
310 448-6800

(P-3998)
JOONG-ANG DAILY NEWS CAL INC (DH)
Also Called: Korea Daily
690 Wilshire Pl, Los Angeles (90005-3930)
PHONE..........................213 368-2500
Kae Hong Ko, *CEO*
In Taek Park, *President*
Don Lee, *COO*
Min Pak, *Vice Pres*
Joseph Kim, *Executive*
▲ **EMP:** 200 **EST:** 1974
SQ FT: 70,000
SALES (est): 92.1MM **Privately Held**
WEB: www.joongang.joins.com
SIC: 2711 Commercial printing & newspaper publishing combined

(P-3999)
KEVIN WHITE
Also Called: Habit Homes
9918 Ramona St Apt 1, Bellflower (90706-6947)
PHONE..........................562 231-6642
Kevin White, *Principal*
EMP: 15 **EST:** 2017
SALES (est): 310K **Privately Held**
WEB: www.bhpioneer.com
SIC: 2711 Newspapers, publishing & printing

(P-4000)
LA OPINION LP (HQ)
Also Called: Lozano Enterprises
915 Wilshire Blvd Ste 915 # 915, Los Angeles (90017-3474)
P.O. Box 71847 (90071-0847)
PHONE..........................213 891-9191
Monica C Lozano, *CEO*
Lozano Communications, *General Ptnr*
La Opini N, *Vice Pres*
Maria Amezcua, *Executive*
Laura Plascencia, *Executive*
EMP: 54 **EST:** 1926
SALES (est): 94.2MM **Privately Held**
WEB: www.laopinion.com
SIC: 2711 Newspapers, publishing & printing
PA: Impremedia, Llc
1 Metrotech Ctr Fl 18
Brooklyn NY 11201
212 807-4600

(P-4001)
LA OPINION LP
210 E Washington Blvd, Los Angeles (90015-3603)
PHONE..........................213 896-2222
Carlos Marina, *Manager*
EMP: 359
SALES (corp-wide): 94.2MM **Privately Held**
WEB: www.laopinion.com
SIC: 2711 Newspapers, publishing & printing
HQ: La Opinion, L.P.
915 Wilshire Blvd Ste 915 # 915
Los Angeles CA 90017
213 891-9191

(P-4002)
LA TIMES
202 W 1st St Ste 500, Los Angeles (90012-4401)
PHONE..........................213 237-2279
Raymond Jansen, *CEO*
Joyce Cruz, *Manager*
EMP: 28 **EST:** 2008
SALES (est): 1.5MM **Privately Held**
WEB: www.onnitimessquare.com
SIC: 2711 Newspapers, publishing & printing

(P-4003)
LOS ANGELES DAILY NEWS PUBG CO
21860 Burbank Blvd # 200, Woodland Hills (91367-6477)
PHONE..........................818 713-3883
EMP: 28 **EST:** 1999
SALES (est): 2.8MM
SALES (corp-wide): 1.8B **Privately Held**
WEB: www.dailynews.com
SIC: 2711 Newspapers, publishing & printing
HQ: Medianews Group, Inc.
101 W Colfax Ave Ste 1100
Denver CO 80202

(P-4004)
LOS ANGELES SENTINEL INC
Also Called: La Sentinel Newspaper
3800 Crenshaw Blvd, Los Angeles (90008-1813)
PHONE..........................323 299-3800
Jennifer Thomas, *President*
Brik Booker, *CEO*
Robert M Holds, *Counsel*
Bernard Lloyd, *Manager*
Cora Jackson, *Editor*
EMP: 51 **EST:** 1933

SALES (est): 6.8MM **Privately Held**
WEB: www.lasentinel.net
SIC: 2711 Newspapers, publishing & printing

(P-4005)
LOS ANGLES TMES CMMNCTIONS LLC (PA)
2300 E Imperial Hwy, El Segundo (90245-2813)
PHONE..........................213 237-5000
Ross Levinsohn, *CEO*
Don Reis, *Officer*
Jeff Balbien, *Vice Pres*
Crane Kenney, *Vice Pres*
Hillary Manning, *Vice Pres*
▲ **EMP:** 2302 **EST:** 1884
SQ FT: 162,000
SALES (est): 930.8MM **Privately Held**
WEB: www.latimes.com
SIC: 2711 Newspapers, publishing & printing

(P-4006)
LOS ANGLES TMES CMMNCTIONS LLC
Also Called: Lats International
145 S Spring St, Los Angeles (90012-4053)
PHONE..........................213 237-7987
EMP: 30
SALES (corp-wide): 769.2MM **Privately Held**
SIC: 2711 2741 Newspapers-Publishing/Printing Misc Publishing
PA: Los Angeles Times Communications, Llc
2300 E Imperial Hwy
El Segundo CA 90245
213 237-5000

(P-4007)
MALIBU TIMES INC
3864 Las Flores Canyon Rd, Malibu (90265-5295)
P.O. Box 1127 (90265-1127)
PHONE..........................310 456-5507
Arnold York, *President*
Karen York, *Vice Pres*
Emily Sawicki, *Manager*
EMP: 28 **EST:** 1946
SQ FT: 2,000
SALES (est): 3MM **Privately Held**
WEB: www.malibutimes.com
SIC: 2711 Newspapers: publishing only, not printed on site

(P-4008)
MAMMOTH MEDIA INC
1447 2nd St, Santa Monica (90401-3404)
PHONE..........................832 315-0833
Benoit Vatere, *CEO*
Mike Jones, *Chairman*
EMP: 64 **EST:** 2016
SALES (est): 7.5MM **Privately Held**
WEB: www.mammoth.la
SIC: 2711 Newspapers

(P-4009)
MEDIANEWS GROUP INC
Also Called: Daily News
24800 Ave Rockefeller, Valencia (91355-3467)
P.O. Box 4200, Woodland Hills (91365-4200)
PHONE..........................661 257-5200
EMP: 200
SALES (corp-wide): 4.3B **Privately Held**
SIC: 2711 2752 Newspapers-Publishing/Printing Lithographic Commercial Printing
HQ: Medianews Group, Inc.
101 W Colfax Ave Ste 1100
Denver CO 80202

(P-4010)
METROPOLITAN NEWS COMPANY
Also Called: Riverside Blltin Jrupa This We
3540 12th St, Riverside (92501-3802)
P.O. Box 60859, Los Angeles (90060-0859)
PHONE..........................951 369-5890
Roger Gray, *President*
EMP: 29 **EST:** 1998

SALES (est): 1.3MM **Privately Held**
WEB: www.mnc.net
SIC: 2711 Newspapers, publishing & printing

(P-4011)
NATIONAL MEDIA INC (HQ)
Also Called: Beach Reporter
609 Deep Valley Dr # 200, Rllng HLS Est (90274-3629)
P.O. Box 2609, Pls Vrds Pnsl (90274-8609)
PHONE..........................310 377-6877
Stephen C Laxineta, *President*
Simon M Tam, *President*
William Dean Singleton, *CEO*
EMP: 30 **EST:** 1983
SQ FT: 12,000
SALES (est): 16.1MM
SALES (corp-wide): 1.8B **Privately Held**
WEB: www.dailybreeze.com
SIC: 2711 Newspapers: publishing only, not printed on site
PA: Digital First Media, Llc
101 W Colfax Ave Fl 11
Denver CO 80202
303 954-6360

(P-4012)
NATIONAL MEDIA INC
Also Called: Beach Reporter, The
2615 Pcf Cast Hwy Ste 329 Hermosa Beach (90254)
PHONE..........................310 372-0388
Richard Frank, *Publisher*
Lisa Jacobs, *General Mgr*
Alejandro Gonzalez, *Graphic Designe*
Karina P Rodriguez, *Graphic Designe*
Robin Pittman, *Assistant*
EMP: 16
SALES (corp-wide): 1.8B **Privately Held**
WEB: www.dailybreeze.com
SIC: 2711 Newspapers: publishing only, not printed on site
HQ: National Media, Inc.
609 Deep Valley Dr # 200
Rllng Hls Est CA 90274
310 377-6877

(P-4013)
NEWLON ROUGE LLC
Also Called: Santa Monica Daily Press
1640 5th St Ste 218, Santa Monica (90401-3325)
P.O. Box 1380 (90406-1380)
PHONE..........................310 458-7737
Ross Furukawa, *President*
Rose Mann, *Executive*
Cindy Moreno, *Opers Staff*
David Ganforth,
Carolyn Sackariason,
EMP: 14 **EST:** 2001
SALES (est): 2.3MM **Privately Held**
WEB: www.smdp.com
SIC: 2711 Commercial printing & newspaper publishing combined newspapers, publishing & printing

(P-4014)
NEWS MEDIA INC
Also Called: Paso Robles Press
502 First St, Paso Robles (93446-3763)
P.O. Box 427 (93447-0427)
PHONE..........................805 237-6060
Richard D Reddick, *President*
Lana Loguidice, *Marketing Staff*
Sheri Potruch, *Marketing Staff*
EMP: 18 **EST:** 2000
SALES (est): 515.4K **Privately Held**
WEB: www.pasoroblespress.com
SIC: 2711 Newspapers, publishing & printing

(P-4015)
NGUOI VIET VTNAMESE PEOPLE INC (PA)
Also Called: Nguoi Viet Newspaper
14771 Moran St, Westminster (92683-5553)
PHONE..........................714 892-9414
Dat Pham, *Chairman*
Hoang Tong, *CEO*
Dieu Le, *Vice Pres*
▲ **EMP:** 30 **EST:** 1978
SQ FT: 10,000

SALES (est): 5.3MM **Privately Held**
WEB: www.nguoi-viet.com
SIC: 2711 5994 2741 Newspapers: publishing only, not printed on site; news dealers & newsstands; miscellaneous publishing

(P-4016)
NORTH COUNTY TIMES
28441 Rancho California R, Temecula (92590-3618)
PHONE.................................951 676-4315
Claude Reinke, *Manager*
EMP: 45
SALES (corp-wide): 618MM **Publicly Held**
SIC: 2711 Newspapers, publishing & printing
HQ: North County Times
350 Camino De La Reina
San Diego CA 92108
800 533-8830

(P-4017)
NORTHEAST NEWSPAPERS INC
621 W Beverly Blvd, Montebello (90640-3623)
PHONE.................................213 727-1117
Art Aguilar, *President*
Eastern Community Newspapers, *Shareholder*
Tom Morrison, *Vice Pres*
EMP: 32 **EST:** 1905
SALES (est): 2.5MM **Privately Held**
SIC: 2711 Newspapers, publishing & printing

(P-4018)
NOTICIERO SEMANAL ADVERTISING
Also Called: Porterville Recorder
115 E Oak Ave, Porterville (93257-3807)
P.O. Box 151 (93258-0151)
PHONE.................................559 784-5000
Paul Mauney, *Principal*
Joshua Resurreccion, *District Mgr*
Christina K Hansen, *Graphic Designe*
Terry Feagin, *Business Mgr*
Rick Elkins, *Publisher*
EMP: 18 **EST:** 2005
SALES (est): 2.3MM **Privately Held**
WEB: www.recorderonline.com
SIC: 2711 7313 Newspapers, publishing & printing; newspaper advertising representative

(P-4019)
OBSERVER GROUP NEWSPAPER
Also Called: Bakersfield News Observer
1219 20th St, Bakersfield (93301-4611)
PHONE.................................661 324-9466
Ellen Coley, *President*
James Luckey, *Editor*
EMP: 22 **EST:** 1977
SQ FT: 3,000 **Privately Held**
SIC: 2711 Commercial printing & newspaper publishing combined; newspapers, publishing & printing

(P-4020)
P E N INC
Also Called: News Publishers' Press
215 Allen Ave, Glendale (91201-2803)
PHONE.................................818 954-0775
Richard E Jutras, *CEO*
Jeffrey Jutras, *President*
Joven Calingo, *Info Tech Dir*
Robert Garcia, *Plant Mgr*
EMP: 18 **EST:** 1978
SQ FT: 11,000
SALES (est): 541.2K **Privately Held**
WEB: www.newspublisherspress.com
SIC: 2711 Newspapers: publishing only, not printed on site

(P-4021)
PACIFIC COAST BUS TIMES INC
14 E Carrillo St Ste A, Santa Barbara (93101-2769)
PHONE.................................805 560-6950
Henry Dubroff, *President*
Linda Brock, *Executive*
Sean McCullough, *Executive*
Debra Giles, *Office Mgr*
Jennifer Carusa, *Marketing Staff*

EMP: 19 **EST:** 1999
SQ FT: 2,200
SALES (est): 2.5MM **Privately Held**
WEB: www.pacbiztimes.com
SIC: 2711 Newspapers, publishing & printing

(P-4022)
PASADENA NEWSPAPERS INC (PA)
Also Called: Pasadena Star-News
2 N Lake Ave Ste 150, Pasadena (91101-1896)
PHONE.................................626 578-6300
Dean Singleton, *President*
Melene Alfonso, *Vice Pres*
▲ **EMP:** 190 **EST:** 1884
SQ FT: 80,000
SALES (est): 17.1MM **Privately Held**
WEB: www.pasadenastarnews.com
SIC: 2711 7313 Commercial printing & newspaper publishing combined; newspaper advertising representative

(P-4023)
PEOPLE MEDIA INC
8800 W Sunset Blvd 3, West Hollywood (90069-2105)
P.O. Box 25458, Dallas TX (75225-1458)
PHONE.................................800 600-7111
Josh Meyers, *CEO*
Mathew Domanski, *Director*
EMP: 13 **EST:** 2008
SALES (est): 108.2K **Privately Held**
WEB: www.peoplemedia.la
SIC: 2711 Commercial printing & newspaper publishing combined

(P-4024)
PRESS-ENTERPRISE COMPANY (PA)
3450 14th St, Riverside (92501-3862)
P.O. Box 792 (92502-0792)
PHONE.................................951 684-1200
Ronald Redfern, *President*
Ed Lasak, *CFO*
Sue Barry, *Vice Pres*
Kathy Weiermiller, *Vice Pres*
Erik Pedersen, *Editor*
▲ **EMP:** 700 **EST:** 2011
SQ FT: 190,000
SALES (est): 66.3MM **Privately Held**
WEB: www.discountednewspapers.com
SIC: 2711 Commercial printing & newspaper publishing combined; newspapers, publishing & printing

(P-4025)
RAFU SHIMPO
Also Called: L A Japanese Daily News
701 E 3rd St Ste 130, Los Angeles (90013-1789)
PHONE.................................213 629-2231
Michael M Komai, *President*
Gail Miyasaki, *Office Mgr*
Bryce Umemoto, *Admin Asst*
Gwen Muranaka, *Editor*
Mario Reyes, *Editor*
EMP: 31 **EST:** 1903
SQ FT: 20,000
SALES (est): 2.6MM **Privately Held**
WEB: www.rafunews.com
SIC: 2711 Newspapers, publishing & printing

(P-4026)
SANTA BARBARA INDEPENDENT INC
12 E Figueroa St, Santa Barbara (93101-2709)
PHONE.................................805 965-5205
M Partridge Poette, *President*
Marianne Partridge Poette, *President*
Tanya S Guiliacci, *Office Mgr*
Robert Leblanc, *Manager*
Brandi Rivera, *Publisher*
EMP: 40 **EST:** 1984
SQ FT: 5,000
SALES (est): 7.7MM **Privately Held**
WEB: www.independent.com
SIC: 2711 Newspapers, publishing & printing

(P-4027)
SIERRA VIEW INC
Also Called: News Review, The
109 N Sanders St, Ridgecrest (93555-3848)
PHONE.................................760 371-4301
Patricia Farris, *President*
Pat Farris, *Publisher*
EMP: 21 **EST:** 1976
SQ FT: 2,800
SALES (est): 450K **Privately Held**
SIC: 2711 Newspapers: publishing only, not printed on site

(P-4028)
SIGNAL
Also Called: Newhall Signal
26330 Diamond Pl Ste 100, Santa Clarita (91350-5819)
P.O. Box 801870 (91380-1870)
PHONE.................................661 259-1234
Charles Morris, *President*
Chris Budman, *Vice Pres*
Dawn Begley, *Executive*
Karen Bennett, *Graphic Designe*
Abner Gutierrez, *Graphic Designe*
EMP: 85 **EST:** 1919
SQ FT: 32,000
SALES (est): 6.3MM
SALES (corp-wide): 285.7MM **Privately Held**
WEB: www.signalscv.com
SIC: 2711 Newspapers, publishing & printing
PA: Morris Multimedia, Inc.
27 Abercorn St
Savannah GA 31401
912 233-1281

(P-4029)
SING TAO NEWSPAPERS LTD
Also Called: Sing Tao Nwspapers Los Angeles
17059 Green Dr, City of Industry (91745-1812)
PHONE.................................626 839-8200
EMP: 52 **Privately Held**
WEB: www.singtaonewscorp.com
SIC: 2711 Newspaper Publishers
PA: Sing Tao Limited
Sing Tao News Corporation Bldg
Tseung Kwan O NT

(P-4030)
SLO NEW TIMES INC
Also Called: New Times Media Group
1010 Marsh St, San Luis Obispo (93401-3630)
PHONE.................................805 546-8208
Bob Rucker, *CEO*
Jason Gann, *Adv Dir*
Georgia Shore, *Adv Dir*
Ikey Ipekjian, *Marketing Staff*
Jim Parsons, *Manager*
EMP: 28 **EST:** 1987
SALES (est): 4.3MM **Privately Held**
WEB: www.newtimesslo.com
SIC: 2711 Newspapers, publishing & printing

(P-4031)
SOUTHLAND PUBLISHING INC (PA)
Also Called: Ventura County Reporter
50 S Delacey Ave Ste 200, Pasadena (91105)
PHONE.................................626 584-1500
Michael Flannery, *President*
David Comden, *Vice Pres*
Chris Jay, *Author*
EMP: 13 **EST:** 1980
SALES (est): 1.4MM **Privately Held**
WEB: www.southlandpublishing.com
SIC: 2711 Newspapers, publishing & printing

(P-4032)
SUN COMPANY SAN BERNARDINO CAL (PA)
Also Called: San Bernardino County Sun, The
4030 Georgia Blvd, San Bernardino (92407-1847)
PHONE.................................909 889-9666
Bob Balzer, *President*

Rosemaria Altieri, *Vice Pres*
Jon Merendino, *Vice Pres*
Douglass H McCorkindale, *Principal*
Gustavo Ortiz, *MIS Dir*
EMP: 400 **EST:** 1964
SQ FT: 110,000
SALES (est): 42MM **Privately Held**
WEB: www.sbsun.com
SIC: 2711 Newspapers, publishing & printing

(P-4033)
TAKE A BREAK PAPER
263 W Olive Ave 307, Burbank (91502-1825)
PHONE.................................323 333-7773
Albert Moran, *Partner*
EMP: 30 **EST:** 2013
SALES (est): 961.7K **Privately Held**
WEB: www.takeabreakpaper.com
SIC: 2711 Newspapers, publishing & printing

(P-4034)
TAKUYO CORPORATION
Also Called: Light House
2958 Columbia St, Torrance (90503-3806)
PHONE.................................310 782-6927
Yoichi Komiyama, *President*
Yuzo Komiyama, *Vice Pres*
Takeshi Ueno, *Vice Pres*
Mayumi Ito, *Graphic Designe*
Satoko Yoshida, *Chief*
EMP: 15 **EST:** 1989
SQ FT: 6,647
SALES (est): 1.4MM **Privately Held**
WEB: www.us-utopia.com
SIC: 2711 Newspapers, publishing & printing

(P-4035)
TARGET MEDIA PARTNERS OPER LLC
5900 Wilshire Blvd # 550, Los Angeles (90036-5013)
PHONE.................................323 930-3123
Mark Schiffmacher, *CEO*
EMP: 13 **EST:** 2010
SALES (est): 310.7K **Privately Held**
WEB: www.targetmediapartners.com
SIC: 2711 Newspapers

(P-4036)
TEHACHAPI NEWS INC (PA)
Also Called: Southeast Kern Weekender
411 N Mill St, Tehachapi (93561-1351)
P.O. Box 1840 (93581-1840)
PHONE.................................661 822-6828
Al Criseli, *President*
William J Mead, *President*
Elizabeth S Mead, *Corp Secy*
Stephanie Garcia, *Business Mgr*
Betty J Autery, *Advt Staff*
EMP: 13 **EST:** 1943
SQ FT: 2,400
SALES (est): 1.1MM **Privately Held**
WEB: www.tehachapinews.com
SIC: 2711 Newspapers, publishing & printing

(P-4037)
THEWRAP
2260 S Centinela Ave # 150, Los Angeles (90064-1007)
PHONE.................................424 273-4787
Emily Vogel, *Manager*
EMP: 15 **EST:** 2016
SALES (est): 445.4K **Privately Held**
WEB: www.thewrap.com
SIC: 2711 Newspapers

(P-4038)
TIDINGS
Also Called: VIDA NUEVA
3424 Wilshire Blvd, Los Angeles (90010-2263)
PHONE.................................213 637-7360
Roger Mahoney, *President*
EMP: 34 **EST:** 1895
SALES (est): 2MM **Privately Held**
WEB: www.angelusnews.com
SIC: 2711 Newspapers: publishing only, not printed on site

(P-4039)
TRIBE MEDIA CORP
Also Called: Jewish Journal, The
3250 Wilshire Blvd, Los Angeles
(90010-1577)
PHONE..................213 368-1661
Rob Eshman, *Publisher*
Amanda Epstein, *Admin Asst*
Ginger Vick, *Admin Asst*
Lynn Pelkey, *Art Dir*
Tom Fields-Meyer, *Editor*
EMP: 27 **EST:** 1985
SQ FT: 4,500
SALES (est): 4.4MM **Privately Held**
WEB: www.jewishjournal.com
SIC: 2711 Newspapers, publishing & print-ing

(P-4040)
TXD INTERNATIONAL USA INC
2336 S Vineyard Ave A, Ontario
(91761-7767)
PHONE..................909 947-6568
Rodolfo J Galvez Cordova, *CEO*
Francisco Galvez Vernis, *Vice Pres*
Armando Herrera, *Admin Sec*
Jose Buitron, *Director*
Manny Carlo, *Accounts Mgr*
▲ **EMP:** 15 **EST:** 2003
SQ FT: 8,500
SALES (est): 1.5MM **Privately Held**
WEB: www.txdinternational.com
SIC: 2711 2752 2211 2262 Commercial printing & newspaper publishing com-bined; promotional printing, lithographic; print cloths, cotton; printing: manmade fiber & silk broadwoven fabrics; printing of narrow fabrics

(P-4041)
VENTURA COUNTY STAR
771 E Daily Dr Ste 300, Camarillo
(93010-0781)
PHONE..................805 437-0138
George H Cogswell III, *President*
EMP: 22 **EST:** 2005
SALES (est): 537.3K **Privately Held**
SIC: 2711 Newspapers: publishing only, not printed on site

(P-4042)
VILLLAGE NEWS INC
Also Called: Fallbrook Bonsall Village News
41740 Enterprise Cir S, Temecula
(92590-4881)
PHONE..................760 451-3488
Julie Reeder, *President*
Michelle Howard, *Advt Staff*
EMP: 32 **EST:** 1997
SQ FT: 1,500
SALES (est): 4.8MM **Privately Held**
WEB: www.villagenews.com
SIC: 2711 Newspapers, publishing & print-ing

(P-4043)
WAVE COMMUNITY NEWSPAPERS INC (PA)
Also Called: The Wave
3731 Wilshire Blvd # 840, Los Angeles
(90010-2830)
PHONE..................323 290-3000
Pluria Marshall, *President*
Andy Wiedlin, *Officer*
▲ **EMP:** 30 **EST:** 1970
SQ FT: 15,000
SALES (est): 4.9MM **Privately Held**
SIC: 2711 Commercial printing & newspa-per publishing combined; newspapers, publishing & printing

(P-4044)
WESTERN OUTDOORS PUBLICATIONS (PA)
Also Called: Western Outdoor News
1211 Puerta Del Sol # 270, San Clemente
(92673-6342)
P.O. Box 73370 (92673-0113)
PHONE..................949 366-0030
Robert Twilegar, *President*
Lori Twilegar, *Admin Sec*
Gloria Sievers, *Graphic Designe*
Chuck Buhagiar, *Sls & Mktg Exec*
Bill Egan, *Director*
EMP: 28 **EST:** 1953

SALES (est): 4.7MM **Privately Held**
WEB: www.wonews.com
SIC: 2711 2721 Newspapers: publishing only, not printed on site; periodicals

(P-4045)
WICK COMMUNICATIONS CO
Also Called: Kern Valley Sun
6404 Lake Isabella Blvd, Lake Isabella
(93240-9475)
P.O. Box 3074 (93240-3074)
PHONE..................760 379-3667
Cliff Urfeth, *Manager*
Mike Rand, *CFO*
Jillaine Eastridge, *Executive Asst*
Cindy Hefley, *Director*
EMP: 24
SALES (corp-wide): 87.6MM **Privately Held**
WEB: www.wickcommunications.com
SIC: 2711 Newspapers, publishing & print-ing
HQ: Wick Communications Co.
333 W Wilcox Dr Ste 302
Sierra Vista AZ 85635
520 458-0200

(P-4046)
WORLD JOURNAL LA LLC (HQ)
1588 Corporate Center Dr, Monterey Park
(91754-7624)
PHONE..................323 268-4982
James Guon, *CEO*
▲ **EMP:** 170 **EST:** 1981
SQ FT: 45,000
SALES (est): 36.6MM **Privately Held**
WEB: www.udngroup.com
SIC: 2711 Newspapers, publishing & print-ing

2721 Periodicals: Publishing & Printing

(P-4047)
18 MEDIA INC (PA)
Also Called: Gentry Magazine
200 N Pcf Cast Hwy Ste 11, El Segundo
(90245)
PHONE..................650 324-1818
Elsie Sloriani, *Ch of Bd*
Sloan Citron, *President*
Marilyn Kallins, *Executive*
Norene Sheehan, *Executive*
Elsie Floriani, *Exec Dir*
EMP: 13 **EST:** 1993
SALES (est): 1.9MM **Privately Held**
WEB: www.gentry.goldenstate.is
SIC: 2721 Magazines: publishing only, not printed on site

(P-4048)
ADAMS TRADE PRESS LP (PA)
Also Called: Adams Business Media
420 S Palm Canyon Dr, Palm Springs
(92262-7304)
PHONE..................760 318-7000
Mark Adams, *Partner*
EMP: 30 **EST:** 1994
SQ FT: 2,000
SALES (est): 4.1MM **Privately Held**
SIC: 2721 Magazines: publishing only, not printed on site

(P-4049)
ADVANSTAR COMMUNICATIONS INC
6200 Canoga Ave Fl 3, Woodland Hills
(91367-2450)
PHONE..................818 593-5000
Nora Ellingwood, *Vice Pres*
Jim Kovach, *Manager*
EMP: 14
SALES (corp-wide): 1.3B **Privately Held**
WEB: www.epay.advanstar.com
SIC: 2721 Magazines: publishing only, not printed on site
HQ: Advanstar Communications Inc.
2501 Colorado Ave Ste 280
Santa Monica CA 90404
310 857-7500

(P-4050)
AEROTECH NEWS AND REVIEW INC (PA)
Also Called: Astro News
220 E Avenue K4 Ste 4, Lancaster
(93535-4687)
P.O. Box 1332 (93584-1332)
PHONE..................661 945-5634
Paul Kinison, *President*
EMP: 42 **EST:** 1986
SALES (est): 5.6MM **Privately Held**
WEB: www.aerotechnews.com
SIC: 2721 2741 2752 Trade journals: publishing only, not printed on site; mis-cellaneous publishing; commercial print-ing, lithographic

(P-4051)
AFFLUENT TARGET MARKETING INC
Also Called: Affluent Living Publication
3855 E La Palma Ave # 250, Anaheim
(92807-1765)
P.O. Box 18507 (92817-8507)
PHONE..................714 446-6280
Wally Hicks, *President*
Joseph M Kootsey, *Vice Pres*
Deborah Mesna, *Executive*
Debbie Tarnoff, *Clerk*
EMP: 17 **EST:** 1980
SQ FT: 3,500
SALES (est): 3.1MM **Privately Held**
WEB: www.orangecountylivingmagazine.com
SIC: 2721 Magazines: publishing only, not printed on site

(P-4052)
APPAREL NEWS GROUP
Also Called: California Apparel News
110 E 9th St Ste A777, Los Angeles
(90079-1777)
PHONE..................213 327-1002
EMP: 40
SALES (est): 3.7MM
SALES (corp-wide): 4.5MM **Privately Held**
WEB: www.apparelnews.net
SIC: 2721 Periodicals-Publishing/Printing
PA: Mnm Corporation
110 E 9th St Ste A777
Los Angeles CA 90079
213 627-3737

(P-4053)
AUTO CLUB ENTERPRISES
Also Called: Westway Magazine
3333 Fairview Rd, Costa Mesa
(92626-1610)
PHONE..................714 885-2376
Tamara Hill, *Principal*
EMP: 176
SALES (corp-wide): 1.3B **Privately Held**
WEB: www.aaa.com
SIC: 2721 Periodicals
PA: Auto Club Enterprises
3333 Fairview Rd Msa451
Costa Mesa CA 92626
714 850-5111

(P-4054)
CBJ LP
Also Called: San Fernando Valley Bus Jurnl
21550 Oxnard St, Woodland Hills
(91367-7100)
PHONE..................818 676-1750
Pegi Matsuda, *Manager*
Khaled Abdelwahed, *Advt Staff*
Marc Harris, *Advt Staff*
Ellen Mazen, *Sales Staff*
EMP: 35
SALES (corp-wide): 21.4MM **Privately Held**
WEB: www.sfvbj.com
SIC: 2721 Magazines: publishing only, not printed on site
PA: Cbj, L.P.
7101 College Blvd # 1100
Shawnee Mission KS
913 451-9000

(P-4055)
CBJ LP
Also Called: Los Angeles Business Journal
11150 Santa Monica Blvd, Los Angeles
(90025-3380)
PHONE..................323 549-5225
Matt Toledo, *Branch Mgr*
Alexandra Davila, *Exec Dir*
Joshua Niv, *Research*
Tammi Dutro, *Controller*
Nina Bays, *Prdtn Dir*
EMP: 40
SALES (corp-wide): 21.4MM **Privately Held**
SIC: 2721 2711 8742 Periodicals: publish-ing only; trade journals: publishing only, not printed on site; newspapers; general management consultant
PA: Cbj, L.P.
7101 College Blvd # 1100
Shawnee Mission KS
913 451-9000

(P-4056)
CBJ LP
Also Called: Orange County Business Journal
18500 Von Karman Ave # 150, Irvine
(92612-0504)
PHONE..................949 833-8373
Janet Cox, *Manager*
Diana Leonard, *Vice Pres*
Angela Phillips, *Executive Asst*
Martin Nilchian, *MIS Staff*
Emily Santiago-Molina, *Research*
EMP: 40
SALES (corp-wide): 21.4MM **Privately Held**
WEB: www.ocbj.com
SIC: 2721 2711 7313 Trade journals: pub-lishing only, not printed on site; newspa-pers; newspaper advertising representative
PA: Cbj, L.P.
7101 College Blvd # 100
Shawnee Mission KS
913 451-9000

(P-4057)
CHALLENGE PUBLICATIONS INC
21835 Nordhoff St, Chatsworth
(91311-5712)
P.O. Box 2474 (91313-2474)
PHONE..................818 700-6868
Edwin A Schnepf, *President*
EMP: 13 **EST:** 1963
SQ FT: 30,000
SALES (est): 1.3MM **Privately Held**
WEB: www.challengeweb.com
SIC: 2721 Magazines: publishing only, not printed on site

(P-4058)
CHET COOPER
Also Called: C2 Publishing
1001 W 17th St, Costa Mesa (92627-4512)
P.O. Box 10878 (92627-0271)
PHONE..................949 854-8700
Chet Cooper, *Owner*
EMP: 14 **EST:** 1992
SALES (est): 968.8K **Privately Held**
WEB: www.abilitymagazine.com
SIC: 2721 Magazines: publishing only, not printed on site

(P-4059)
CLIQUE BRANDS INC (PA)
Also Called: Who What Wear
750 N San Vicente Blvd, West Hollywood
(90069-5788)
PHONE..................310 623-6916
Katherine Power, *CEO*
Hilary Kerr, *President*
Mika Onishi, *COO*
Karen Klein, *Vice Pres*
David Thomas, *CTO*
EMP: 31 **EST:** 2007
SQ FT: 2,200
SALES (est): 8.1MM **Privately Held**
WEB: www.cliquebrands.com
SIC: 2721 5621 Magazines: publishing only, not printed on site; women's spe-cialty clothing stores

(P-4060)
CREATIVE AGE PUBLICATIONS INC
Also Called: Nailpro
15975 High Knoll Rd, Encino (91436-3426)
PHONE...................................818 782-7328
Deborah Carver, *President*
Mindy Rosiejka, *CFO*
Trevor Cameron, *CIO*
Susie Q Susieq-, *Personnel Assit*
Francisco Abrego, *Production*
EMP: 50 **EST:** 1972
SALES (est): 9.4MM **Privately Held**
WEB: www.creativeage.com
SIC: 2721 2731 Magazines: publishing only, not printed on site; book publishing

(P-4061)
CURTCO MEDIA GROUP
29160 Heathercliff Rd # 1, Malibu
(90265-6310)
P.O. Box 6934 (90264-6934)
PHONE...................................310 589-7700
Samantha Brooks, *Principal*
Christina Frio, *Production*
Maryelena Voorhis, *Marketing Staff*
Daniel Borchert, *Director*
Brian Cash, *Director*
EMP: 28 **EST:** 2010
SALES (est): 1.3MM **Privately Held**
WEB: www.curtco.com
SIC: 2721 Magazines: publishing & printing

(P-4062)
CURTCO ROBB MEDIA LLC (PA)
29160 Heathercliff Rd # 1, Malibu
(90265-6310)
PHONE...................................310 589-7700
Stephen Colvin, *CEO*
William J Curtis, *Vice Ch Bd*
David Arnold, *Senior VP*
Colette Alderson, *Vice Pres*
Christopher Fabian,
EMP: 30 **EST:** 2001
SALES (est): 17.6MM **Privately Held**
WEB: www.robbreport.com
SIC: 2721 Magazines: publishing & printing

(P-4063)
D & S MEDIA GROUP INC
Also Called: Home Mag, The
16808 Armstrong Ave Ste 2, Irvine
(92606-2415)
PHONE...................................714 881-4700
Shaun A Harris, *Principal*
Deborah K Harris, *Principal*
Ralph T Harris, *Principal*
EMP: 15 **EST:** 2009
SQ FT: 1,800
SALES (est): 1.4MM **Privately Held**
WEB: www.thmsocal.com
SIC: 2721 Magazines: publishing & printing

(P-4064)
DAISY PUBLISHING COMPANY INC
Also Called: Hi-Torque Publications
25233 Anza Dr, Santa Clarita (91355-1289)
P.O. Box 957 (91380-9057)
PHONE...................................661 295-1910
Roland Hinz, *President*
Lila Hinz, *Vice Pres*
Carl Husfeld, *Safety Mgr*
Jeff Shoop, *Opers Staff*
Robb Mesecher, *Adv Dir*
EMP: 55 **EST:** 1969
SQ FT: 16,000
SALES (est): 8.4MM **Privately Held**
WEB: www.hi-torque.com
SIC: 2721 Magazines: publishing & printing

(P-4065)
DESERT PUBLICATIONS INC (PA)
Also Called: Desert Grafics
303 N Indian Canyon Dr, Palm Springs
(92262-6015)
P.O. Box 2724 (92263-2724)
PHONE...................................760 325-2333
Franklin Jones, *Principal*
Stuart Funk, *Creative Dir*
Phillip Large, *Creative Dir*
Greg Loring, *CTO*
Todd May, *Info Tech Dir*
EMP: 47 **EST:** 1965

SQ FT: 25,000
SALES (est): 11.8MM **Privately Held**
WEB: www.palmspringslife.com
SIC: 2721 7311 Magazines: publishing only, not printed on site; advertising agencies

(P-4066)
DISNEY PUBLISHING WORLDWIDE (DH)
500 S Buena Vista St, Burbank
(91521-0001)
PHONE...................................212 633-4400
R Russell Hampton Jr, *Chairman*
Robert W Hernandez, *Senior VP*
Melissa Lasdon, *Senior Mgr*
Sean Corrigan, *Director*
Kathleen Drumm, *Director*
▲ **EMP:** 100 **EST:** 1992
SALES (est): 146.3MM
SALES (corp-wide): 65.3B **Publicly Held**
WEB: www.disney.com
SIC: 2721 Magazines: publishing only, not printed on site
HQ: Disney Enterprises, Inc.
500 S Buena Vista St
Burbank CA 91521
818 560-1000

(P-4067)
DUNCAN MCINTOSH COMPANY INC (PA)
Also Called: Sea Magazine
18475 Bandilier Cir, Fountain Valley
(92708-7012)
P.O. Box 1337, Newport Beach (92659-0337)
PHONE...................................949 660-6150
Duncan R McIntosh, *CEO*
Teresa McIntosh, *Corp Secy*
Dave Kelsen, *Info Tech Dir*
Martha McKintosh, *Adv Mgr*
Susanne Diaz, *Sales Staff*
EMP: 35 **EST:** 1967
SQ FT: 15,728
SALES (est): 7.7MM **Privately Held**
WEB: www.duncanmcintoshco.com
SIC: 2721 7389 Magazines: publishing & printing; trade show arrangement

(P-4068)
ELISID MAGAZINE
1450 University Ave F168, Riverside
(92507-4467)
PHONE...................................619 990-9999
EMP: 20
SALES (est): 1.2MM **Privately Held**
SIC: 2721 Periodicals-Publishing/Printing

(P-4069)
ENTREPRENEUR MEDIA INC (PA)
Also Called: Entrepeneur Magazine
18061 Fitch, Irvine (92614-6018)
P.O. Box 19787 (92623-9787)
PHONE...................................949 261-2325
Ryan Shea, *CEO*
Neil Perlman, *President*
Joe Goodman, *CFO*
Deepa Shah, *Vice Pres*
Ronald Young, *Admin Sec*
▲ **EMP:** 80 **EST:** 1986
SQ FT: 30,000
SALES (est): 37MM **Privately Held**
WEB: www.entrepreneur.com
SIC: 2721 Magazines: publishing only, not printed on site

(P-4070)
FLAUNT MAGAZINE
1418 N Highland Ave, Los Angeles
(90028-7611)
PHONE...................................323 836-1044
Luis A Barajas Jr, *President*
Liam Casey, *Assoc Editor*
Yraima Martinez, *Editor*
Rhiyen Sharp, *Editor*
Angus Donohoo, *Senior Editor*
▲ **EMP:** 18 **EST:** 1998
SALES (est): 3.1MM **Privately Held**
WEB: www.flaunt.com
SIC: 2721 Magazines: publishing & printing

(P-4071)
GRAPHIC FILM GROUP LLC (PA)
1901 Avenue Of The Stars, Los Angeles
(90067-6001)
PHONE...................................310 887-6330
Scott Walterschied, *Chairman*
Ranford Schlei, *Chairman*
Randy Mendhlsohn, *Principal*
EMP: 15
SALES (est): 1MM **Privately Held**
WEB: www.graphicfilmgroup.com
SIC: 2721 7812 Television schedules: publishing & printing; video production

(P-4072)
HAYMARKET WORLDWIDE INC
17030 Red Hill Ave, Irvine (92614-5626)
PHONE...................................949 417-6700
Peter Foubister, *CEO*
▲ **EMP:** 56 **EST:** 1992
SQ FT: 4,000
SALES (est): 2.4MM
SALES (corp-wide): 174.1MM **Privately Held**
WEB: www.haymarket.com
SIC: 2721 Magazines: publishing only, not printed on site
HQ: Haymarket Media, Inc.
275 7th Ave Fl 10
New York NY 10001
646 638-6000

(P-4073)
HIC CORPORATION (PA)
Also Called: Heavy Duty Trucking
38 Executive Park Ste 300, Irvine
(92614-6755)
PHONE...................................949 261-1636
Doug Condra, *President*
Sean Thornton, *Sales Staff*
Jack Roberts, *Senior Editor*
EMP: 15 **EST:** 1947
SALES (est): 2.5MM **Privately Held**
WEB: www.truckinginfo.com
SIC: 2721 Magazines: publishing only, not printed on site

(P-4074)
INFOKOREA INC
Also Called: Radio Korea USA
626 S Kingsley Dr, Los Angeles
(90005-2318)
PHONE...................................213 487-1580
Fax: 213 487-7744
▲ **EMP:** 30
SALES (est): 2.3MM **Privately Held**
SIC: 2721 4832 Directory Publishing & Radio Broadcasting

(P-4075)
INLAND EMPIRE MEDIA GROUP INC
Also Called: Inland Empire Magazine
36095 Monte De Oro Rd, Temecula
(92592-8123)
PHONE...................................951 682-3026
Don Lorenzi, *President*
Richard Lorenzi, *Admin Sec*
Sandy Cartwright, *Regl Sales Mgr*
Lesleyanne Daniels, *Regl Sales Mgr*
EMP: 33 **EST:** 1972
SALES (est): 4.3MM **Privately Held**
WEB: www.inlandempiremagazine.com
SIC: 2721 Magazines: publishing & printing; magazines: publishing only, not printed on site

(P-4076)
KELLEY BLUE BOOK CO INC (DH)
195 Technology Dr, Irvine (92618-2402)
P.O. Box 19691 (92623-9691)
PHONE...................................949 770-7704
Jared Rowe, *CEO*
John Morrison, *CFO*
Leo Drew, *Vice Pres*
Adrianna Dehnadi, *Executive*
Brett Nanigian, *Surgery Dir*
EMP: 92 **EST:** 1926
SALES (est): 113.9MM
SALES (corp-wide): 1.6MM **Privately Held**
WEB: www.b2b.autotrader.com
SIC: 2721 Trade journals: publishing only, not printed on site

HQ: Autotrader.Com, Inc.
3003 Summit Blvd Fl 200
Brookhaven GA 30319
404 568-8000

(P-4077)
L F P INC (PA)
Also Called: Flynt, Larry Publishing
8484 Wilshire Blvd # 900, Beverly Hills
(90211-3218)
PHONE...................................323 651-3525
Larry Flynt, *Ch of Bd*
Michael H Klein, *President*
Alexander Behrens, *Vice Pres*
Liz Flynt, *Vice Pres*
William Liu, *Vice Pres*
▲ **EMP:** 100 **EST:** 1976
SQ FT: 10,000
SALES (est): 33.1MM **Privately Held**
WEB: www.larryflynt.com
SIC: 2721 Magazines: publishing only, not printed on site

(P-4078)
LA PARENT MAGAZINE (PA)
5855 Topanga Canyon Blvd # 210, Woodland Hills (91367-4671)
P.O. Box 8275, Calabasas (91372-8275)
PHONE...................................818 264-2222
Madelyn Calabrese, *Manager*
Cindy Hadash, *Opers Mgr*
Sheri McCrone, *Sales Staff*
Elena Epstein, *Manager*
EMP: 15 **EST:** 1978
SQ FT: 2,500
SALES (est): 1.2MM **Privately Held**
WEB: www.laparent.com
SIC: 2721 Magazines: publishing only, not printed on site

(P-4079)
LANDSCAPE COMMUNICATIONS INC
Also Called: Landscape Contract National
14771 Plaza Dr Ste A, Tustin (92780-2779)
P.O. Box 1126 (92781-1126)
PHONE...................................714 979-5276
George Schmok, *President*
Cynthia McCarthy, *Administration*
Chase Reed, *Analyst*
Nathan Schmok, *Advt Staff*
Mike Dahl, *Manager*
EMP: 25 **EST:** 1991
SQ FT: 1,618
SALES (est): 3.1MM **Privately Held**
WEB: www.landscapearchitect.com
SIC: 2721 Trade journals: publishing only, not printed on site

(P-4080)
LIFE MEDIA INC
Also Called: Black Media News
7657 Winnetka Ave Ste 504, Winnetka
(91306-2677)
PHONE...................................800 201-9440
EMP: 50
SALES (est): 10MM **Privately Held**
WEB: www.blackmedianews.net
SIC: 2721 Periodicals-Publishing/Printing

(P-4081)
LINE PUBLICATIONS INC
Also Called: Movieline Magazine
9800 S La Cienega Blvd # 10, Inglewood
(90301-4440)
PHONE...................................310 234-9501
EMP: 15
SALES (est): 1.4MM **Privately Held**
WEB: www.movieline.com
SIC: 2721 Magazine Publishing

(P-4082)
LOCALE LIFESTYLE MAGAZINE LLC
Also Called: Locale Magazine
2755 Bristol St Ste 295, Costa Mesa
(92626-5968)
P.O. Box 2971, Newport Beach (92659-0459)
PHONE...................................949 436-8910
Erik Hale, *CEO*
Mike Smith, *Vice Pres*
Reilly Kavanaugh, *Graphic Designe*
Ashley Hickson, *Mktg Dir*
Jason Kosky, *Marketing Mgr*
EMP: 26 **EST:** 2010

PRODUCTS & SVCS

SQ FT: 2,000
SALES (est): 3.3MM **Privately Held**
WEB: www.localemagazine.com
SIC: 2721 Magazines: publishing only, not printed on site

(P-4083)
LOS ANGELES BUS JURNL ASSOC
11150 Santa Monica Blvd # 350, Los Angeles (90025-3385)
PHONE..................................323 549-5225
Matt Toledo, *President*
Fabian Avellaneda, *Executive Asst*
Joshua Niv, *Research*
Samson Amore, *Finance*
Grigor Aleksanian, *Advt Staff*
EMP: 30 **EST:** 1975
SALES (est): 570.2K **Privately Held**
WEB: www.labusinessjournal.com
SIC: 2721 Magazines: publishing only, not printed on site

(P-4084)
LUNDBERG SURVEY INC
911 Via Alondra, Camarillo (93012-8048)
PHONE..................................805 383-2400
Trilby Lundberg, *President*
Netta Shelton, *COO*
Paul Kendall, *Info Tech Mgr*
Alex Wolff, *Prgrmr*
Charles Lundberg, *Project Mgr*
EMP: 28 **EST:** 1949
SALES (est): 2.6MM **Privately Held**
WEB: www.lundbergsurvey.com
SIC: 2721 8748 2741 Statistical reports (periodicals): publishing only; business consulting; miscellaneous publishing

(P-4085)
MAXWELL PETERSEN ASSOCIATES
Also Called: Dynamic Chiropractic
412 Olive Ave Ste 208, Huntington Beach (92648-5142)
PHONE..................................714 230-3150
Donald M Petersen, *President*
Becky Richmond, *Executive*
Randy Matthews, *Prgrmr*
Paulo Lapuz, *Graphic Designe*
Weeks Andrea, *Accountant*
EMP: 36 **EST:** 1977
SQ FT: 2,000
SALES (est): 4.1MM **Privately Held**
SIC: 2721 Magazines: publishing only, not printed on site

(P-4086)
MNM CORPORATION (PA)
Also Called: Apparel Newsgroup, The
110 E 9th St Ste A777, Los Angeles (90079-1777)
PHONE..................................213 627-3737
Martin Wernicke, *CEO*
Howard Greller, *Officer*
Ellen Mackin, *Principal*
Andrew Asch, *General Mgr*
Molly Rhodes, *General Mgr*
▲ **EMP:** 25 **EST:** 1985
SQ FT: 11,000
SALES (est): 9.6MM **Privately Held**
WEB: www.apparelnews.net
SIC: 2721 8721 Magazines: publishing only, not printed on site; accounting, auditing & bookkeeping

(P-4087)
MODEL LYFE
Also Called: Model Lyfe Magazine
5405 Wilshire Blvd, Los Angeles (90036-4203)
PHONE..................................224 325-5933
EMP: 15
SALES: 950K **Privately Held**
SIC: 2721 Periodicals

(P-4088)
OLD PROSPECTORS ASSN AMER LLC
Also Called: Gold Prospectors Assn Amer
25810 Jefferson Ave # 110, Murrieta (92562-6964)
P.O. Box 891509, Temecula (92589-1509)
PHONE..................................951 699-4749
Thomas Massie, *Mng Member*

Michael Lukes, *Finance Mgr*
Paul Louly, *Marketing Staff*
Anne Tolleson, *Sales Staff*
Richard Dixon, *Mng Member*
EMP: 32 **EST:** 1966
SALES (est): 4.4MM **Privately Held**
WEB: www.goldprospectors.org
SIC: 2721 4833 Magazines: publishing only, not printed on site; television broadcasting stations

(P-4089)
OMICS GROUP INC
5716 Corsa Ave Ste 110, Westlake Village (91362-7354)
PHONE..................................650 268-9744
Srinu B Gedela, *Branch Mgr*
EMP: 460
SALES (corp-wide): 109.6MM **Privately Held**
WEB: www.omicsonline.org
SIC: 2721 Trade journals: publishing & printing
PA: Omics Group Inc
2360 Corp Cir Ste 400
Henderson NV 89074
888 843-8169

(P-4090)
ORANGE COAST KOMMUNICATIONS
Also Called: Orange Coast Magazine
5900 Wilshire Blvd # 1000, Los Angeles (90036-5013)
PHONE..................................949 862-1133
Gary Thoe, *President*
Kevin Montague, *VP Sales*
Traci Takeda, *Marketing Staff*
Brandi Yates, *Marketing Staff*
Linda McCall, *Sales Staff*
EMP: 291 **EST:** 1975
SALES (est): 14.9MM
SALES (corp-wide): 39.7MM **Privately Held**
WEB: www.orangecoast.com
SIC: 2721 5812 Magazines: publishing only, not printed on site; eating places
HQ: Emmis Publishing, L.P.
40 Monument Cir Ste 100
Indianapolis IN 46204

(P-4091)
PAISANO PUBLICATIONS LLC (PA)
Also Called: V Twin Magazine
28210 Dorothy Dr, Agoura Hills (91301-2693)
PHONE..................................818 889-8740
John Lagana, *CEO*
Joseph Teresi, *Chairman*
Tammy Porter, *Executive*
Karen Johnson, *Controller*
Robert Davis,
EMP: 60 **EST:** 1971
SQ FT: 40,000
SALES (est): 8.6MM **Privately Held**
WEB: www.tattoomag.com
SIC: 2721 Magazines: publishing only, not printed on site

(P-4092)
PAISANO PUBLICATIONS INC
Also Called: V/ Twins
28210 Dorothy Dr, Agoura Hills (91301-2693)
P.O. Box 3000 (91376-3000)
PHONE..................................818 889-8740
Bill Prather, *President*
Robert Davis, *Treasurer*
Allen Ribakoff, *Vice Pres*
Joseph Teresi, *Admin Sec*
Beverly Jermyn, *Human Res Dir*
EMP: 52 **EST:** 1993
SALES (est): 3MM
SALES (corp-wide): 8.6MM **Privately Held**
WEB: www.tattoomag.com
SIC: 2721 7812 Magazines: publishing & printing; commercials, television: tape or film
PA: Paisano Publications, Llc
28210 Dorothy Dr
Agoura Hills CA 91301
818 889-8740

(P-4093)
PALM SPRINGS LIFE
303 N Indian Canyon Dr, Palm Springs (92262-6015)
P.O. Box 2724 (92263-2724)
PHONE..................................760 325-2333
Joan Braunstein, *Manager*
Todd May, *CIO*
EMP: 13 **EST:** 2016
SALES (est): 3.3MM **Privately Held**
WEB: www.palmspringslife.com
SIC: 2721 Magazines: publishing only, not printed on site

(P-4094)
PARTNER CONCEPTS INC
811 Camino Viejo, Santa Barbara (93108-2313)
PHONE..................................805 745-7199
William J Kasch, *President*
William L Coulson, *CFO*
EMP: 75 **EST:** 1983
SALES (est): 18.5MM **Privately Held**
SIC: 2721 Magazines: publishing only, not printed on site

(P-4095)
PENINSULA PUBLISHING INC
1602 Monrovia Ave, Newport Beach (92663-2808)
PHONE..................................949 631-1307
Nick Slevin, *President*
Georgina Slim, *Controller*
Nick Kosan, *Natl Sales Mgr*
Nicole Feenstra, *Marketing Staff*
EMP: 26 **EST:** 1998
SALES (est): 2.4MM **Privately Held**
WEB: www.penpubinc.com
SIC: 2721 Magazines: publishing & printing

(P-4096)
PENSKE BUSINESS MEDIA LLC (HQ)
11175 Santa Monica Blvd # 9, Los Angeles (90025-3368)
PHONE..................................310 321-5000
David Arnold, *Exec VP*
Anne Doyle, *Vice Pres*
Gillian Garcia, *Sales Staff*
Dana Harris, *Chief*
EMP: 67 **EST:** 2016
SALES (est): 3.8MM
SALES (corp-wide): 46.3MM **Privately Held**
WEB: www.indiewire.com
SIC: 2721 Periodicals
PA: Penske Media Corporation
11175 Santa Monica Blvd # 9
Los Angeles CA 90025
310 321-5000

(P-4097)
PLAYBOY ENTERPRISES INC
10960 Wilshire Blvd Fl 22, Los Angeles (90024-3808)
PHONE..................................310 424-1800
John Luther, *Manager*
David Israel, *COO*
Jared Dougherty, *Chief Mktg Ofcr*
Jenny Sade, *Officer*
George Akopov, *Vice Pres*
EMP: 79 **Publicly Held**
WEB: www.playboy.tv
SIC: 2721 Magazines: publishing & printing
HQ: Playboy Enterprises, Inc.
10960 Wilshire Blvd Fl 22
Los Angeles CA 90024
310 424-1800

(P-4098)
PLAYBOY ENTERPRISES INC (HQ)
10960 Wilshire Blvd Fl 22, Los Angeles (90024-3808)
PHONE..................................310 424-1800
Ben Kohn, *President*
Suhail Rizvi, *Ch of Bd*
David Israel, *COO*
Chris Riley, *Admin Sec*
▲ **EMP:** 348 **EST:** 1953
SQ FT: 45,000
SALES: 147MM **Publicly Held**
WEB: www.playboy.tv
SIC: 2721 Periodicals; magazines: publishing & printing

PA: Plby Group, Inc.
10960 Wilshire Blvd Fl 22
Los Angeles CA 90024
310 424-1800

(P-4099)
POLLSTAR LLC
Also Called: Pollstar.com
1100 Glendon Ave Ste 2100 (90024-3592)
PHONE..................................559 271-7900
Gary Bongiovanni, *President*
Gary Smith, *CEO*
Connor Chase, *Software Der*
Dean Olmstead, *Marketing Staff*
Jodi Di Pasquale, *Sales Staff*
EMP: 58 **EST:** 1981
SALES (est): 10.6MM **Privately Held**
WEB: www.pollstar.com
SIC: 2721 Magazines: publishing only, not printed on site

(P-4100)
PROMEDIA COMPANIES
Also Called: National Mustang Racers Assn
3518 W Lake Center Dr D, Santa Ana (92704-6979)
PHONE..................................714 444-2426
Steve Wolcott, *Partner*
James Lawrence, *Partner*
Judy Keaton, *Executive*
Steve W Wolcott, *Office Mgr*
Chris Vopat, *Opers Staff*
EMP: 35 **EST:** 1998
SQ FT: 3,000
SALES (est): 16.9MM **Privately Held**
WEB: www.promediapub.com
SIC: 2721 Magazines: publishing only, not printed on site

(P-4101)
QG PRINTING CORP
6688 Box Springs Blvd, Riverside (92507-0726)
PHONE..................................951 571-2500
Ken Eazell, *Manager*
EMP: 14
SALES (corp-wide): 2.9B **Publicly Held**
SIC: 2721 2752 Periodicals; commercial printing, lithographic
HQ: Qg Printing Corp.
N61w23044 Harrys Way
Sussex WI 53089

(P-4102)
R T C GROUP
Also Called: Cots Journal Magazine
905 Calle Amanecer # 150, San Clemente (92673-6226)
PHONE..................................949 226-2000
John Reardon, *Owner*
EMP: 21 **EST:** 1985
SALES (est): 1.9MM **Privately Held**
WEB: www.web2.twindom.com
SIC: 2721 Magazines: publishing only, not printed on site

(P-4103)
RACER MEDIA & MARKETING INC
17030 Red Hill Ave, Irvine (92614-5626)
PHONE..................................949 417-6700
William Sparks, *COO*
Paul Pfanner, *President*
John Chambers, *Sales Staff*
EMP: 14 **EST:** 2012
SQ FT: 4,500
SALES (est): 2.5MM **Privately Held**
WEB: www.racer.com
SIC: 2721 Magazines: publishing only, not printed on site

(P-4104)
REAL ESTATE TRAINERS INC
212 Twne Cntre Pl Ste 100, Anaheim (92806)
PHONE..................................800 282-2352
Jerry McHarg, *President*
EMP: 35 **EST:** 1972
SQ FT: 17,000
SALES (est): 245.2K
SALES (corp-wide): 4MM **Privately Held**
WEB: www.retrainersca.com
SIC: 8249 2721 Real estate & insurance school; periodicals

PA: Universal Training Corporation
2121 S Twne Cntre Pl Ste
Anaheim CA 92806
714 972-2211

(P-4105)
ROBB CURTCO MEDIA LLC
22741 Pcf Cast Hwy Ste 40, Malibu
(90265)
PHONE..................310 589-7700
EMP: 33
SALES (corp-wide): 17.6MM **Privately
Held**
WEB: www.robbreport.com
SIC: 2721 Magazines: publishing & printing
PA: Curtco Robb Media Llc
29160 Heathercliff Rd # 1
Malibu CA 90265
310 589-7700

(P-4106)
ROBB REPORT COLLECTION
29160 Heathercliff Rd # 200, Malibu
(90265-6306)
PHONE..................310 589-7700
John S Geer, *Principal*
Jeff Litvack, *COO*
Robert Crozier, *Exec VP*
Elyse Heckman, *Vice Pres*
Livia Hooson, *Marketing Staff*
EMP: 22 **EST:** 2008
SALES (est): 643.1K **Privately Held**
WEB: www.robbreport.com
SIC: 2721 Magazines: publishing & printing

(P-4107)
ROMAN CTHLIC DIOCESE OF
ORANGE
Also Called: Santa Mrgrita Cthlic High Schl
22062 Antonio Pkwy, Rcho STA Marg
(92688-1993)
PHONE..................949 766-6000
Mary B Dougherty, *Principal*
Andrea Aldridge, *Admin Sec*
Carolyn Bien, *Admin Sec*
Patricia Canfield, *Admin Sec*
Catherine Hassen, *Admin Sec*
EMP: 200
SQ FT: 142,959
SALES (corp-wide): 100.3MM **Privately
Held**
WEB: www.rcbo.org
SIC: 8211 2721 Catholic senior high
school; periodicals
PA: The Roman Catholic Diocese Of Or-
ange
13280 Chapman Ave
Garden Grove CA 92840
714 282-3000

(P-4108)
TOTAL BEAUTY MEDIA INC (HQ)
1158 26th St Ste 535, Santa Monica
(90403-4621)
PHONE..................310 295-9593
Emrah Kovacoglu, *CEO*
Ivan Ivankovich, *CFO*
Ann Marie Macdougall, *Vice Pres*
Beth Mayall, *Vice Pres*
EMP: 14 **EST:** 2007
SALES (est): 36.5K
SALES (corp-wide): 10.6MM **Privately
Held**
WEB: www.evolvemediallc.com
SIC: 2721 7389 Magazines: publishing &
printing; beauty shops
PA: Evolve Media, Llc
5140 W Goldleaf Cir G100
Los Angeles CA 90056
310 449-1890

(P-4109)
TWELVE SIGNS INC
Also Called: Starscroll
3369 S Robertson Blvd, Los Angeles
(90034-3309)
PHONE..................310 553-8000
Richard W Housman, *President*
H Kim, *Vice Pres*
EMP: 16 **EST:** 1967
SQ FT: 25,000
SALES (est): 591.1K **Privately Held**
SIC: 2721 Magazines: publishing only, not
printed on site

(P-4110)
UBM CANON LLC (DH)
2901 28th St Ste 100, Santa Monica
(90405-2975)
PHONE..................310 445-4200
Sally Shankland, *CEO*
Scott Schulman, *CEO*
Brian Field, *COO*
Rudolf Hotter, *COO*
David Cox, *CFO*
EMP: 188 **EST:** 1996
SQ FT: 50,000
SALES (est): 25.8MM
SALES (corp-wide): 1.3B **Privately Held**
WEB: www.informamarkets.com
SIC: 2721 7389 Magazines: publishing
only, not printed on site; trade show
arrangement
HQ: Informa Tech Holdings Llc
1983 Marcus Ave Ste 250
New Hyde Park NY 11042
516 562-7800

(P-4111)
WEIDER LEASING INC
21100 Erwin St, Woodland Hills
(91367-3712)
PHONE..................818 884-6800
EMP: 100
SQ FT: 32,000
SALES (est): 4.7MM **Privately Held**
SIC: 2721 Periodicals-Publishing/Printing

(P-4112)
WEST WORLD PRODUCTIONS
INC
420 N Camden Dr, Beverly Hills
(90210-4507)
PHONE..................310 276-9500
Yuri Spiro, *President*
EMP: 28 **EST:** 1980
SQ FT: 9,000
SALES (est): 1MM **Privately Held**
SIC: 2721 Trade journals: publishing only,
not printed on site

(P-4113)
WSR PUBLISHING INC (PA)
Also Called: Widescreen Review
27645 Commerce Center Dr, Temecula
(92590-2521)
P.O. Box 2587 (92593-2587)
PHONE..................951 676-4914
Gary Reber, *President*
Mary M Reber, *Exec VP*
Tricia Spears, *Assoc Editor*
EMP: 14 **EST:** 1992
SQ FT: 7,000 **Privately Held**
WEB: www.widescreenreview.com
SIC: 2721 5731 Magazines: publishing
only, not printed on site; radio, television
& electronic stores

(P-4114)
XBIZ
Also Called: Adnet Media
4929 Wilshire Blvd # 960, Los Angeles
(90010-3808)
PHONE..................310 820-0228
Alec Helmy, *Principal*
Mike Able, *CFO*
Dave Schultz, *Info Tech Dir*
Nick Yu, *Software Dev*
Rick Brenes, *Graphic Designe*
EMP: 14 **EST:** 2013
SALES (est): 442.6K **Privately Held**
WEB: www.xbiz.com
SIC: 2721 Magazines: publishing only, not
printed on site

(P-4115)
XPLAIN CORPORATION
Also Called: Mactech Magazine
705 Lakefield Rd Ste I, Westlake Village
(91361-5903)
P.O. Box 5200 (91359-5200)
PHONE..................805 494-9797
Neil Ticktin, *President*
Andrea Sniderman, *Ch of Bd*
EMP: 27 **EST:** 1992
SALES (est): 2.5MM **Privately Held**
WEB: www.xplain.com
SIC: 2721 5994 Magazines: publishing
only, not printed on site; magazine stand

(P-4116)
ZOASIS CORPORATION
1960 E Grand Ave Ste 555, El Segundo
(90245-5099)
PHONE..................800 745-4725
Douglas Drew, *CEO*
David Aucoin, *President*
Lisa Moise, *Vice Pres*
EMP: 21 **EST:** 1999
SQ FT: 7,000
SALES (est): 423.1K **Privately Held**
SIC: 2721 8742 7375 Periodicals: pub-
lishing only; marketing consulting serv-
ices; information retrieval services

2731 Books: Publishing &
Printing

(P-4117)
2006 SAGE PUBLICATIONS
2455 Teller Rd, Thousand Oaks
(91320-2218)
PHONE..................805 499-0721
Stephen Barr, *Principal*
Zimmerman Diane, *Education*
Joe Brown, *Manager*
EMP: 19 **EST:** 2012
SALES (est): 323.6K **Privately Held**
SIC: 2731 Book publishing

(P-4118)
ABC - CLIO INC (PA)
Also Called: ABC-Clio
147 Castilian Dr, Goleta (93117-5505)
P.O. Box 1911, Santa Barbara (93116-
1911)
PHONE..................805 968-1911
Ronald Boehm, *CEO*
Rick Lumsden, *Vice Pres*
Marlys Boehm, *Admin Sec*
Chris Martinich, *Software Dev*
Elissa Keith, *Credit Staff*
EMP: 115 **EST:** 1955
SALES (est): 30.9MM **Privately Held**
WEB: www.abc-clio.com
SIC: 2731 Books: publishing only

(P-4119)
ALFRED MUSIC GROUP INC (PA)
16320 Roscoe Blvd Ste 100, Van Nuys
(91406-1216)
PHONE..................818 891-5999
Steven Manus, *CEO*
Ron Manus, *President*
Elise Keil, *General Mgr*
Kristi Jacobsen, *Administration*
Christine Jones, *Administration*
EMP: 127 **EST:** 2008
SALES (est): 12.2MM **Privately Held**
WEB: www.alfred.com
SIC: 2731 Book music: publishing & print-
ing

(P-4120)
AVN MEDIA NETWORK INC
Also Called: Adult Video News
9400 Penfield Ave, Chatsworth
(91311-6549)
PHONE..................818 718-5788
Tony Rios, *CEO*
Janet Gibson, *COO*
Roy Karch, *Bd of Directors*
Jesse Dena, *Creative Dir*
Gary Miller, *Producer*
EMP: 30 **EST:** 1982
SQ FT: 15,000
SALES (est): 4.4MM **Privately Held**
WEB: www.avnmedianetwork.com
SIC: 2731 2721 Book publishing; periodi-
cals

(P-4121)
BERTELSMANN INC
Also Called: Arvato Services
29011 Commerce Center Dr, Valencia
(91355-4195)
PHONE..................661 702-2700
Janet Adams, *Manager*
Mark Ricks, *Technician*
EMP: 5003
SALES (corp-wide): 147.7MM **Privately
Held**
WEB: www.bertelsmann.com
SIC: 2731 Books: publishing only

HQ: Bertelsmann, Inc.
1745 Broadway Fl 20
New York NY 10019
212 782-1000

(P-4122)
BRIDGE PUBLICATIONS INC (PA)
Also Called: Bpi Records
5600 E Olympic Blvd, Commerce
(90022-5128)
PHONE..................323 888-6200
Blake Silber, *CEO*
Lis Astrupgaard, *President*
Tom Golan, *President*
Helen Lumbroso, *Vice Pres*
Irma Macias, *Vice Pres*
▲ **EMP:** 40 **EST:** 1981
SQ FT: 15,000
SALES (est): 23.5MM **Privately Held**
WEB: www.bridgepub.com
SIC: 2731 3652 Books: publishing only;
pre-recorded records & tapes

(P-4123)
CHICK PUBLICATIONS INC
8780 Archibald Ave, Rancho Cucamonga
(91730-4697)
P.O. Box 3500, Ontario (91761-1019)
PHONE..................909 987-0771
Jack T Chick, *President*
Ronald Rockney, *Treasurer*
George A Collins, *Vice Pres*
David Daniels, *Author*
◆ **EMP:** 27 **EST:** 1961
SQ FT: 10,000
SALES (est): 4.2MM **Privately Held**
WEB: www.chick.com
SIC: 2731 5961 Books: publishing only;
mail order house

(P-4124)
CORWIN PRESS INC (HQ)
2455 Teller Rd, Newbury Park
(91320-2218)
PHONE..................805 499-9734
Douglas Rife, *President*
Johnnie A James, *Senior VP*
Leigh Peake, *Vice Pres*
Lisa Shaw, *Exec Dir*
Karl Wogksch, *Accountant*
EMP: 206 **EST:** 1990
SALES (est): 6.5MM
SALES (corp-wide): 65.3MM **Privately
Held**
WEB: www.us.corwin.com
SIC: 2731 Books: publishing only
PA: Sage Publications, Inc.
2455 Teller Rd
Thousand Oaks CA 91320
805 499-0721

(P-4125)
CREATIVE TEACHING PRESS
INC (PA)
6262 Katella Ave, Cypress (90630-5204)
PHONE..................714 799-2100
James M Connelly, *CEO*
Luella Connelly, *Chairman*
Patrick Connelly, *Treasurer*
Ann Marie Hofmann, *Vice Pres*
Susan Connelly, *Admin Sec*
◆ **EMP:** 93 **EST:** 1965
SQ FT: 85,000
SALES (est): 12.6MM **Privately Held**
WEB: www.creativeteaching.com
SIC: 2731 Books: publishing only

(P-4126)
DISNEY BOOK GROUP LLC (DH)
Also Called: Hyperion Books For Children
500 S Buena Vista St, Burbank
(91521-0001)
PHONE..................818 560-1000
Russell R Hampton Jr, *President*
Marsha L Reed, *Admin Sec*
Liz Mushill, *Manager*
EMP: 57 **EST:** 1999
SALES (est): 3.8MM
SALES (corp-wide): 65.3B **Publicly Held**
WEB: www.thewaltdisneycompany.com
SIC: 2731 Book publishing

(P-4127)
DMZ STUDIO INC (PA)
Also Called: Local Hero Bookstore and Cafe
1211 Maricopa Hwy Ste 250, Ojai
(93023-3160)
PHONE...................................805 640-9240
Elio Zarmati, *CEO*
EMP: 15 **EST:** 2000
SQ FT: 2,000
SALES (est): 1MM **Privately Held**
SIC: 5942 2731 Book stores; books: publishing & printing

(P-4128)
EDUCATIONAL IDEAS INCORPORATED
Also Called: Ballard & Tighe Publishers
471 Atlas St, Brea (92821-3118)
P.O. Box 219 (92822-0219)
PHONE...................................714 990-4332
Dorothy Roberts, *Ch of Bd*
Mark Espinola, *CEO*
Sari Luoma, *Vice Pres*
Kent Roberts, *Admin Sec*
Rebecca Ratnam, *Manager*
◆ **EMP:** 55 **EST:** 1976
SQ FT: 12,000
SALES (est): 8.5MM **Privately Held**
WEB: www.ballard-tighe.com
SIC: 2731 Textbooks: publishing only, not printed on site

(P-4129)
GANDER PUBLISHING INC
450 Front St, Avila Beach (93424-3551)
P.O. Box 780 (93424-0780)
PHONE...................................805 541-5523
Nanci L Bell, *CEO*
▲ **EMP:** 21 **EST:** 1995
SQ FT: 5,000
SALES (est): 1.1MM **Privately Held**
WEB: www.ganderpublishing.com
SIC: 2731 Books: publishing only

(P-4130)
GARDEN GROVE UNIFIED SCHL DST
Also Called: Alamitos Intermediate School
12381 Dale St, Garden Grove
(92841-3219)
PHONE...................................714 663-6101
Christina Pflughoft, *Principal*
Kent Baird, *Principal*
Randy Sheetes, *Info Tech Mgr*
Dinah Barling, *Teacher*
Angelica Cortez, *Teacher*
EMP: 62
SALES (corp-wide): 658.3MM **Privately Held**
WEB: www.ggusd.us
SIC: 8211 2731 Public junior high school; book publishing
PA: Garden Grove Unified School District
10331 Stanford Ave
Garden Grove CA 92840
714 663-6000

(P-4131)
INTERVISUAL BOOKS INC
Also Called: Piggy Toes Press
9800 S La Cienega Blvd, Inglewood
(90301-4440)
PHONE...................................302 636-5400
Louis Perlman, *Ch of Bd*
Michael Silber, *President*
Thomas Yamamoto, *CFO*
Dorothea Deprisco-Wang, *Vice Pres*
▲ **EMP:** 15 **EST:** 1975
SQ FT: 9,200
SALES (est): 354.8K **Privately Held**
SIC: 2731 Books: publishing only

(P-4132)
JUDY O PRODUCTIONS INC
4858 W Pico Blvd Ste 331, Los Angeles
(90019-4225)
PHONE...................................323 938-8513
Judy Ostarch, *President*
▲ **EMP:** 28 **EST:** 1999
SALES (est): 1.5MM **Privately Held**
SIC: 2731 Book publishing

(P-4133)
LITTLE EINSTEINS LLC
500 S Buena Vista St, Burbank
(91521-0001)
P.O. Box 25020, Glendale (91221-5020)
PHONE...................................818 560-1000
Julie Aigner-Clark,
Susan McLain, *Vice Pres*
EMP: 72 **EST:** 1997
SQ FT: 6,000
SALES (est): 4.6MM
SALES (corp-wide): 65.3B **Publicly Held**
WEB: www.thewaltdisneycompany.com
SIC: 2731 3695 Books: publishing & printing; video recording tape, blank
HQ: Twdc Enterprises 18 Corp.
500 S Buena Vista St
Burbank CA 91521

(P-4134)
NARCOTICS ANNYMOUS WRLD SVCS I
Also Called: WORLD SERVICE OFFICE
19737 Nordhoff Pl, Chatsworth
(91311-6606)
P.O. Box 9999, Van Nuys (91409-9099)
PHONE...................................818 773-9999
Anthony Edmondson, *CEO*
Uschi Mueller, *Manager*
▲ **EMP:** 45 **EST:** 1953
SQ FT: 35,000
SALES (est): 6.5MM **Privately Held**
WEB: www.na.org
SIC: 2731 Books: publishing only; pamphlets: publishing only, not printed on site

(P-4135)
PRACTICE MANAGEMENT INFO CORP (PA)
Also Called: Pmic
4727 Wilshire Blvd # 302, Los Angeles
(90010-3806)
PHONE...................................323 954-0224
James B Davis, *President*
Greg Trupiano, *Exec VP*
Michelle Cuevas, *Opers Mgr*
Peggy Paladin, *Sales Staff*
Richard Uyeno, *Manager*
◆ **EMP:** 15 **EST:** 1988
SQ FT: 6,000
SALES (est): 5.6MM **Privately Held**
WEB: www.pmiconline.com
SIC: 2731 7372 Book publishing; business oriented computer software

(P-4136)
SADDLEBACK EDUCATIONAL INC
151 Kalmus Dr Ste J1, Costa Mesa
(92626-5973)
PHONE...................................714 640-5200
Arianne M McHugh, *President*
Tim McHugh, *President*
▲ **EMP:** 19 **EST:** 1982
SQ FT: 5,000
SALES (est): 3.9MM **Privately Held**
WEB: www.sdlback.com
SIC: 2731 5192 Books: publishing only; books

(P-4137)
SEQUOIA PARKS CONSERVANCY
Also Called: Sequoia Natural History Assn
47050 Generals Hwy # 10, Three Rivers
(93271-9502)
P.O. Box 10 (93271-0010)
PHONE...................................559 565-3759
Savannah Boiano, *Exec Dir*
Steve Baltzell, *Ch of Bd*
Dayna Higgins, *Comms Dir*
Elizabeth Gonzalez, *Admin Dir*
Wendy McLaren, *Human Res Mgr*
EMP: 20 **EST:** 1940
SQ FT: 3,000
SALES (est): 4.3MM **Privately Held**
WEB: www.sequoiaparksconservancy.org
SIC: 5942 2731 Book stores; books: publishing & printing; pamphlets: publishing & printing

(P-4138)
TASCHEN AMERICA LLC (PA)
6121 W Sunset Blvd, Los Angeles
(90028-6442)
PHONE...................................323 463-4441
Elissa Gomez, *Director*
Chris Forbes, *Office Mgr*
Meghan Clarke, *Administration*
Chiara Donati, *Administration*
Creed Poulson, *Pub Rel Mgr*
◆ **EMP:** 13 **EST:** 1995
SQ FT: 5,000
SALES (est): 8.1MM **Privately Held**
WEB: www.taschen.com
SIC: 2731 Books: publishing only

(P-4139)
THE MICROFILM COMPANY OF CAL
Also Called: Library Reproduction Service
14214 S Figueroa St, Los Angeles
(90061-1034)
PHONE...................................310 354-2610
Joan Miller, *President*
Peter Jones, *Vice Pres*
EMP: 18 **EST:** 1946
SQ FT: 7,000
SALES (est): 1MM **Privately Held**
SIC: 2731 7389 Books: publishing & printing; microfilm recording & developing service

(P-4140)
TOKYOPOP INC
5200 W Century Blvd Fl 7, Los Angeles
(90045-5926)
PHONE...................................323 920-5967
Stuart J Levy, *President*
John Parker, *Vice Pres*
Victor Chin, *Admin Sec*
◆ **EMP:** 90 **EST:** 1997
SQ FT: 8,699
SALES (est): 7.6MM **Privately Held**
WEB: www.tokyopop.com
SIC: 2731 3652 7812 7371 Books: publishing only; compact laser discs, prerecorded; video tape production; custom computer programming services; periodicals; entertainment promotion

(P-4141)
TORAH-AURA PRODUCTIONS INC
2710 Supply Ave, Commerce (90040-2704)
PHONE...................................323 585-1847
▲ **EMP:** 13 **EST:** 1982
SQ FT: 15,000
SALES (est): 1.3MM **Privately Held**
WEB: www.torahaura.com
SIC: 2731 Books-Publishing/Printing

(P-4142)
TRUCK CLUB PUBLISHING INC
7807 Telegraph Rd Ste H, Montebello
(90640-6528)
PHONE...................................323 726-8620
Miguel A Machuca, *President*
EMP: 16 **EST:** 2002
SALES (est): 1.2MM **Privately Held**
WEB: www.truckclubmagazine.com
SIC: 2731 Book publishing

(P-4143)
WEST PUBLISHING CORPORATION
Also Called: The Rutter Group
800 Crprate Pinte Ste 150, Culver City
(90230)
PHONE...................................800 747-3161
William Rutter, *Branch Mgr*
Bruce E Cooperman, *Partner*
Robert H Fairbank, *Partner*
Dennis L Greenwald, *Partner*
Mark Hagarty, *Partner*
EMP: 134
SALES (corp-wide): 10.6B **Publicly Held**
WEB: www.thomsonreuters.com
SIC: 2731 8111 Book publishing; general practice attorney, lawyer
HQ: West Publishing Corporation
610 Opperman Dr
Eagan MN 55123
651 687-7000

(P-4144)
WIXEN MUSIC PUBLISHING INC
24025 Park Sorrento # 130, Calabasas
(91302-4018)
PHONE...................................818 591-7355
Randall Wixen, *President*
Jennifer Suomi, *Administration*
Kim Stockemer, *Director*
EMP: 15 **EST:** 1978
SALES (est): 2.1MM **Privately Held**
WEB: www.wixenmusic.com
SIC: 2731 8111 Book music publishing & printing; legal services

(P-4145)
WORD FOR TODAY
3232 W Macarthur Blvd A, Santa Ana
(92704-6802)
PHONE...................................714 825-9673
Charles W Smith, *President*
Jeff Smith, *Vice Pres*
EMP: 92 **EST:** 1978
SQ FT: 19,000
SALES (est): 784.1K
SALES (corp-wide): 31.1MM **Privately Held**
WEB: www.shop.twft.com
SIC: 5961 2731 3652 Record &/or tape (music or video) club, mail order; books: publishing only; pre-recorded records & tapes
PA: Calvary Chapel Of Costa Mesa
3800 S Fairview St
Santa Ana CA 92704
714 979-4422

(P-4146)
WORKBOOK INC
110 N Doheny Dr, Beverly Hills
(90211-1811)
PHONE...................................323 856-0008
Alexis Scott, *Principal*
Heidi Goverman, *Sales Staff*
Andy Carey, *Art Dir*
Marie Oley, *Director*
Zach Thomas, *Editor*
▲ **EMP:** 18 **EST:** 2008
SALES (est): 7.4MM **Privately Held**
WEB: www.workbook.com
SIC: 2731 Book publishing

2741 Misc Publishing

(P-4147)
ACCEPTED CO
2229 S Canfield Ave, Los Angeles
(90034-1114)
PHONE...................................310 815-9553
Linda Abraham, *President*
Mark Abraham, *CFO*
Jen Weld, *Regl Sales Mgr*
Sara Wolff, *Marketing Staff*
Esmeralda Cardenal, *Dean*
EMP: 19 **EST:** 2002
SALES (est): 3.6MM **Privately Held**
WEB: www.accepted.com
SIC: 2741 Miscellaneous publishing

(P-4148)
ADVANCED PUBLISHING TECH INC
1105 N Hollywood Way, Burbank
(91505-2528)
PHONE...................................818 557-3035
D Kraai, *Owner*
Heidi Stein, *Sr Project Mgr*
EMP: 18 **Privately Held**
WEB: www.advpubtech.com
SIC: 2741 Miscellaneous publishing
PA: Advanced Publishing Technology, Inc.
123 S Victory Blvd
Burbank CA 91502

(P-4149)
AMERICAN HISTORIC INNS INC
249 Forest Ave, Laguna Beach
(92651-2104)
PHONE...................................949 499-8070
Deborah Sakach, *CEO*
Jamee Danihels, *Office Mgr*
EMP: 14 **EST:** 1981
SQ FT: 1,800

SALES (est): 590K **Privately Held**
WEB: www.iloveinns.com
SIC: 2741 7011 Directories: publishing only, not printed on site; hotels & motels

(P-4150)
AMERICAN SOC CMPSERS ATHORS PB
Also Called: Ascap
7920 W Sunset Blvd # 300, Los Angeles (90046-3300)
PHONE.................................323 883-1000
Daniel Gonzales, *General Mgr*
Mir Harris, *Director*
Moya Ashman, *Manager*
Ontario Haynes, *Manager*
EMP: 24
SALES (corp-wide): 152.7MM **Privately Held**
WEB: www.ascap.com
SIC: 2741 Miscellaneous publishing
PA: American Society Of Composers, Authors And Publishers
250 W 57th St Ste 1300
New York NY 10107
212 621-6000

(P-4151)
AMERICAN SYSTEM PUBLICATIONS
3018 Carmel St, Los Angeles (90065-1401)
P.O. Box 476, Pasadena (91102-0476)
PHONE.................................323 259-1867
Maureen Calney, *President*
EMP: 25 **EST:** 1987
SALES (est): 599.6K **Privately Held**
SIC: 2741 Miscellaneous publishing

(P-4152)
ASSOCIATED DESERT SHOPPERS INC (DH)
Also Called: The White Sheet
73400 Highway 111, Palm Desert (92260-3908)
PHONE.................................760 346-1729
Harold Paradis, *President*
Esperanza Barrett, *Treasurer*
Rey Verdugo Sr, *Vice Pres*
EMP: 75 **EST:** 1987
SQ FT: 4,000
SALES (est): 11.4MM
SALES (corp-wide): 2.3B **Publicly Held**
WEB: www.schurz.com
SIC: 2741 7313 Shopping news: publishing & printing; newspaper advertising representative
HQ: Schurz Communications, Inc.
1301 E Douglas Rd Ste 200
Mishawaka IN 46545
574 247-7237

(P-4153)
AUDIENCE INC
5670 Wilshire Blvd # 100, Los Angeles (90036-5686)
PHONE.................................323 413-2370
Oliver Luckett, *CEO*
Kate McLean, *President*
Jeffery Pressman, *COO*
EMP: 19 **EST:** 2011
SALES (est): 1.5MM **Privately Held**
WEB: www.theaudience.com
SIC: 2741 Miscellaneous publishing
PA: Al Ahli Holding Group
Dubai Al-Ain Road Route 66 Blue Glasses Building, Dubai Outlet C
Dubai

(P-4154)
AUTOMOTIVE LEASE GUIDE ALG INC
120 Broadway Ste 200, Santa Monica (90401-2385)
P.O. Box 61207, Santa Barbara (93160-1207)
PHONE.................................424 258-8026
James Nguyen, *President*
Michael Guthrie, *CFO*
Valeri Tompkins, *Vice Pres*
Jeff Swart, *Admin Sec*
Scott Watkinson, *Admin Sec*
EMP: 278 **EST:** 1972

SALES (est): 5.7MM **Publicly Held**
WEB: www.jdpowervalues.com
SIC: 2741 Guides: publishing only, not printed on site
PA: Truecar, Inc.
120 Broadway Ste 200
Santa Monica CA 90401

(P-4155)
BINGO PUBLISHERS INCORPORATED
24881 Alicia Pkwy Ste E, Laguna Hills (92653-4617)
PHONE.................................949 581-5410
Charles Sloan, *President*
EMP: 19 **EST:** 1990
SQ FT: 3,000
SALES (est): 1.1MM **Privately Held**
WEB: www.localbingohalls.com
SIC: 2741 Miscellaneous publishing

(P-4156)
BLAVITY INC
600 Wilshire Blvd # 1650, Los Angeles (90017-3228)
PHONE.................................818 669-9162
Morgan Rose Debaun, *CEO*
Abhisek Tibrewal, *Finance*
EMP: 44 **EST:** 2018
SALES (est): 5.9MM **Privately Held**
WEB: www.blavityinc.com
SIC: 2741

(P-4157)
BREMIK INTERNATIONAL INC
Also Called: Bremik Press
14403 S Main St, Gardena (90248-1913)
PHONE.................................310 715-6622
Alan Saloner, *President*
Gary Hesp, *Controller*
EMP: 55 **EST:** 1992
SQ FT: 17,500
SALES (est): 4.3MM **Privately Held**
WEB: www.bremik.com
SIC: 2741 Posters: publishing & printing

(P-4158)
BROWNTROUT PUBLISHERS INC (PA)
201 Continental Blvd # 200, El Segundo (90245-4514)
PHONE.................................424 290-6122
William Michael Brown, *CEO*
Gray Peterson, *Vice Pres*
Andrew Andersen, *General Mgr*
Femie Mueller, *Planning*
Jenna Burrow, *Project Mgr*
▲ **EMP:** 40 **EST:** 1993
SQ FT: 11,000
SALES (est): 13.9MM **Privately Held**
WEB: www.browntrout.com
SIC: 2741 Miscellaneous publishing

(P-4159)
BRUD INC
837 N Spring St Ste 101, Los Angeles (90012-2594)
PHONE.................................310 806-2283
Trevor McFedries, *President*
EMP: 17 **EST:** 2017
SALES (est): 1.3MM **Privately Held**
WEB: www.brud.fyi
SIC: 2741

(P-4160)
C PUBLISHING LLC
Also Called: C Magazine
1543 7th St Fl 2, Santa Monica (90401-2645)
PHONE.................................310 393-3800
Jennifer Smith Hale, *Info Tech Dir*
Sandy Hubbard, *Info Tech Dir*
Cameron Bird, *Director*
Autumn Okeefe, *Director*
Avery Travis, *Director*
EMP: 25 **EST:** 2005
SALES (est): 5.7MM **Privately Held**
WEB: www.magazinec.com
SIC: 2741 Miscellaneous publishing

(P-4161)
CAVIAR EXPRESS INC
820 Thompson Ave, Glendale (91201-2046)
P.O. Box 9984 (91226-0984)
PHONE.................................818 956-1566
Alex Avakian, *CEO*
Don Michaelson, *Owner*
EMP: 13 **EST:** 2003
SALES (est): 586.8K **Privately Held**
WEB: www.caviarexpress.com
SIC: 2741 5146 7299 Miscellaneous publishing; seafoods; personal shopping service

(P-4162)
CHINESE OVERSEAS MKTG SVC CORP (PA)
Also Called: Chinese Consumer Yellow Pages
3940 Rosemead Blvd, Rosemead (91770-1952)
PHONE.................................626 280-8588
Alan KAO, *President*
Gorden KAO, *Director*
Gordon KAO, *Director*
Ruby Lei, *Manager*
▲ **EMP:** 60 **EST:** 1982
SQ FT: 9,298
SALES (est): 1.5MM **Privately Held**
WEB: www.ccyp.com
SIC: 2741 7389 8742 Directories, telephone: publishing only, not printed on site; trade show arrangement; marketing consulting services

(P-4163)
COLBI TECHNOLOGIES INC
12841 Newport Ave, Tustin (92780-2711)
PHONE.................................714 505-9544
Charles Olsen, *Principal*
Larry Goshorn, *President*
Lettie Cowie, *CEO*
Francisco Javier Oseguera, *Vice Pres*
Jon Patterson, *Business Dir*
EMP: 43 **EST:** 2008
SALES (est): 4.1MM **Privately Held**
WEB: www.colbitech.com
SIC: 2741 Miscellaneous publishing

(P-4164)
COYNE COMPANIES LLC
2351 S 4th St, El Centro (92243-6004)
PHONE.................................760 353-1016
EMP: 14 **EST:** 2012
SALES (est): 513.5K **Privately Held**
SIC: 2741 Miscellaneous publishing

(P-4165)
DAISY SCOUT PUBLISHING
1200 N Barsten Way, Anaheim (92806-1822)
PHONE.................................714 630-6611
Athena Cox, *Owner*
EMP: 13 **EST:** 2014
SALES (est): 286.9K **Privately Held**
SIC: 2741 Miscellaneous publishing

(P-4166)
DANIELS INC (PA)
Also Called: Big Nickel
74745 Leslie Ave, Palm Desert (92260-2030)
PHONE.................................801 621-3355
Daniel Murphy, *President*
Dennis Porter, *Corp Secy*
EMP: 23 **EST:** 1968
SQ FT: 10,000
SALES (est): 2.1MM **Privately Held**
SIC: 2741 Shopping news: publishing & printing

(P-4167)
DIVERSIFIED PRINTERS INC
12834 Maxwell Dr, Tustin (92782-0914)
PHONE.................................714 994-3400
Kenneth Bittner, *President*
Paul R Nassar, *CFO*
Jerry Tominaga, *Exec VP*
EMP: 51 **EST:** 1986
SQ FT: 105,000
SALES (est): 9.8MM **Privately Held**
SIC: 2741 2759 2789 Directories: publishing & printing; commercial printing; bookbinding & related work

(P-4168)
ECT NEWS NETWORK INC
16133 Ventura Blvd # 700, Encino (91436-2403)
P.O. Box 18500 (91416-8500)
PHONE.................................818 461-9700
Richard Kern, *Principal*
Barry Cohen, *Executive*
EMP: 19 **EST:** 2004
SALES (est): 942.7K **Privately Held**
WEB: www.ectnews.com
SIC: 2741

(P-4169)
EL CLASIFICADO
1125 Goodrich Blvd, Commerce (90022-5104)
P.O. Box 227310, Los Angeles (90022-0750)
PHONE.................................323 278-5310
EMP: 100
SALES (corp-wide): 11.2MM **Privately Held**
SIC: 2741 Misc Publishing
PA: El Clasificado
11205 Imperial Hwy
Norwalk CA 90650
323 837-4095

(P-4170)
ELECTRIC SOLIDUS LLC
26565 Agoura Rd Ste 200, Calabasas (91302-1990)
PHONE.................................917 692-7764
Cory Klippsten,
EMP: 25 **EST:** 2019
SALES (est): 1.1MM **Privately Held**
SIC: 2741

(P-4171)
EXPRESS CHIPPING
418 Goetz Ave, Santa Ana (92707-3710)
PHONE.................................562 789-8058
Mike Pla, *Owner*
John Pla, *President*
EMP: 15 **EST:** 2014
SALES (est): 1.1MM **Privately Held**
WEB: www.chippingconcrete.com
SIC: 2741 Miscellaneous publishing

(P-4172)
FOODBEAST INC
220 E 4th St Ste 202, Santa Ana (92701-4652)
PHONE.................................949 344-2634
Geoff Kutnick, *CEO*
Elie Ayrouth, *President*
Rudolph Chaney, *CTO*
Hunter Anderson, *Internal Med*
Evan Lancaster, *Internal Med*
EMP: 16 **EST:** 2014
SALES (est): 2MM **Privately Held**
WEB: www.foodbeast.com
SIC: 2741

(P-4173)
FRONTIERS MEDIA LLC
Also Called: Frontiers Magazine
5657 Wilshire Blvd # 470, Los Angeles (90036-3736)
PHONE.................................323 930-3220
EMP: 50
SALES (est): 3.7MM **Privately Held**
SIC: 2741 Misc Publishing

(P-4174)
GLOBAL COMPLIANCE INC
Also Called: Compliance Poster
438 W Chestnut Ave Ste A, Monrovia (91016-1129)
P.O. Box 607 (91017-0607)
PHONE.................................626 303-6855
Patricia A Blum, *President*
Michael Blum, *CFO*
John Nielsen, *Corp Comm Staff*
Rene Fager, *Sr Project Mgr*
EMP: 25 **EST:** 1990
SALES (est): 4MM **Privately Held**
WEB: www.accupostdocs.com
SIC: 2741 Posters: publishing & printing

(P-4175)
GMM INC
Also Called: Creative Industry Handbooks
10152 Riverside Dr, Toluca Lake
(91602-2532)
PHONE..................................818 752-3200
Carl Rovsek, *President*
Blythe Rovsek, *Vice Pres*
EMP: 18 **EST:** 1988
SALES (est): 3.5MM **Privately Held**
WEB: www.creativehandbook.com
SIC: 2741 Newsletter publishing

(P-4176)
GOOD WORLDWIDE LLC
6380 Wilshire Blvd # 1500, Los Angeles
(90048-5003)
PHONE..................................323 206-6495
Ben Goldhirsh,
Michelle Medlock, *Manager*
EMP: 44 **EST:** 2010 **Privately Held**
WEB: www.good.is
SIC: 2741 Miscellaneous publishing

(P-4177)
GRAPHIQ LLC
101a Innovation Pl, Santa Barbara
(93108-2268)
P.O. Box 1259, Summerland (93067-1259)
PHONE..................................805 335-2433
Kevin Oconnor, *President*
Ivan Bercovich, *President*
Victoria Roebuck, *Executive*
Scott Leonard, *CTO*
Ignacio Ampuero, *Software Engr*
EMP: 120 **EST:** 2009
SALES (est): 17.2MM **Publicly Held**
WEB: www.graphiq.com
SIC: 2741 4813
PA: Amazon.Com, Inc.
410 Terry Ave N
Seattle WA 98109

(P-4178)
**GREAT EASTERN
ENTERTAINMENT CO**
610 W Carob St, Compton (90220-5210)
PHONE..................................310 638-5058
Kent Hsu, *President*
Gennie Yang, *Accounting Mgr*
▲ **EMP:** 24 **EST:** 1995
SQ FT: 6,000
SALES (est): 3.2MM **Privately Held**
WEB: www.geanimation.com
SIC: 2741 Posters: publishing & printing

(P-4179)
HALLMARK LABS LLC
3130 Wilshire Blvd # 400, Santa Monica
(90403-2346)
PHONE..................................424 210-3600
Steven Hawn, *President*
Paul Wang, *CFO*
Jeff McMillen, *Treasurer*
Kevin M Hartley, *Officer*
Albert Lai, *Senior VP*
EMP: 117 **EST:** 2017
SQ FT: 22,831
SALES (est): 13.3MM
SALES (corp-wide): 2.7B **Privately Held**
WEB: www.hallmarklabs.com
SIC: 5947 2741 8999 Greeting cards; ;
personal services
PA: Hallmark Cards, Incorporated
2501 Mcgee St
Kansas City MO 64108
816 274-5111

(P-4180)
**HOMEFACTS MANAGEMENT
LLC**
Also Called: Homefacts.com
1 Venture Ste 300, Irvine (92618-7416)
PHONE..................................949 502-8300
Cabell Cobbs, *Principal*
EMP: 15 **EST:** 2014
SQ FT: 3,750
SALES (est): 165.7K **Privately Held**
WEB: www.attomdata.com
SIC: 2741

(P-4181)
IBISWORLD INC (DH)
Also Called: Procurementiq
11755 Wilshire Blvd # 1100, Los Angeles
(90025-1549)
PHONE..................................310 496-6871
Justin Ruthven, *President*
EMP: 158 **EST:** 2000
SALES (est): 48.5MM **Privately Held**
WEB: www.ibisworld.com
SIC: 2741 Miscellaneous publishing

(P-4182)
**INDEPENDANT BOOK PUBLS
ASSN**
1020 Manhattan Beach Blvd, Manhattan
Beach (90266-5129)
PHONE..................................310 546-1818
Angela Bole, *Director*
EMP: 13 **EST:** 2011
SALES (est): 1.8MM **Privately Held**
SIC: 2741 Miscellaneous publishing

(P-4183)
INFORMA BUSINESS MEDIA INC
Sourceesb
16815 Von Karman Ave # 150, Irvine
(92606-2406)
PHONE..................................949 252-1146
EMP: 30
SALES (corp-wide): 3.1B **Privately Held**
SIC: 2741 Publishes Industrial Directories
HQ: Informa Business Media, Inc.
605 3rd Ave
New York NY 10158
212 204-4200

(P-4184)
IRON PRESS INCORPORATED
20201 Sw Birch St Ste 275, Newport Beach
(92660-1529)
PHONE..................................714 426-8088
Leonard Chan, *Principal*
EMP: 13 **EST:** 2011
SALES (est): 306.2K **Privately Held**
WEB: www.theironpress.com
SIC: 2741 Miscellaneous publishing

(P-4185)
J BEE NP PUBLISHING LTD
30423 Canwood St Ste 108, Agoura Hills
(91301-4313)
PHONE..................................818 706-0266
Richard Singer, *Advt Staff*
EMP: 13 **EST:** 1996
SALES (est): 257K **Privately Held**
WEB: www.theacorn.com
SIC: 2741 Miscellaneous publishing

(P-4186)
KETAB CORPORATION
Also Called: Persian Bks Englsh-Prsian Bks
12701 Van Nuys Blvd Ste H, Pacoima
(91331-7289)
PHONE..................................310 477-7477
Bijan Khalili, *CEO*
Parvin Ketab, *Agent*
◆ **EMP:** 22 **EST:** 1981
SQ FT: 5,000
SALES (est): 2.7MM **Privately Held**
WEB: www.ketab.com
SIC: 5942 2741 Books, foreign; directo-
ries: publishing only, not printed on site

(P-4187)
**LA XPRESS AIR & HEATING
SVCS**
6400 E Wash Blvd Ste 121, Commerce
(90040-1820)
PHONE..................................310 856-9678
Jesus A Chavez, *CEO*
EMP: 67 **EST:** 2013
SALES (est): 1.9MM **Privately Held**
SIC: 2741 Miscellaneous publishing

(P-4188)
M G A INVESTMENT CO INC
Also Called: Easy Ad Magazine
3211 Broad St Ste 201, San Luis Obispo
(93401-6770)
PHONE..................................805 543-9050
Jackie Koda, *Administration*
EMP: 15 **EST:** 1975
SQ FT: 2,000

SALES (est): 979.8K **Privately Held**
SIC: 2741 2721 Shopping news: publishing only, not printed on site; magazines:
publishing only, not printed on site

(P-4189)
**NATIONAL APPRAISAL GUIDES
INC**
Also Called: Nada Appraisal Guide
3186 Airway Ave Ste K, Costa Mesa
(92626-4650)
PHONE..................................714 556-8511
Donald D Christy Jr, *President*
Jody Christy, *Corp Secy*
Robin Lewis, *Vice Pres*
EMP: 33 **EST:** 1968
SQ FT: 20,000
SALES (est): 4.4MM **Privately Held**
WEB: www.nadaguides.com
SIC: 2741 Guides: publishing & printing

(P-4190)
NETMARBLE US INC
600 Wilshire Blvd # 1100, Los Angeles
(90017-3249)
PHONE..................................213 222-7712
Chul Min Sim, *CEO*
Nicole Kim, *Marketing Staff*
EMP: 66 **EST:** 2012
SQ FT: 2,500
SALES (est): 10MM **Privately Held**
WEB: www.netmarble.com
SIC: 2741 5734 Miscellaneous publishing;
software, computer games
PA: Netmarble Corporation
B3-2,7-39/F G-Valley Biz Plaza
Seoul 08393

(P-4191)
**NETWORK TELEVISION TIME
INC (PA)**
3929 Clearford Ct, Westlake Village
(91361-4106)
PHONE..................................877 468-8899
Bruce Arditte, *President*
EMP: 25 **EST:** 1999
SQ FT: 200
SALES (est): 1.8MM **Privately Held**
SIC: 2741 7374 7371 ; data processing &
preparation; custom computer program-
ming services

(P-4192)
NEXTCLIENTCOM INC
25000 Avenue Stanford # 125, Valencia
(91355-4593)
PHONE..................................661 222-7755
Lawrence J Tjan, *CEO*
David Morelli, *CFO*
Javier Pliego, *Vice Pres*
Delyn Thornton, *Vice Pres*
Karen E Sugihara, *Admin Sec*
EMP: 14 **EST:** 2000
SALES (est): 1.3MM **Privately Held**
WEB: www.nextclient.com
SIC: 2741 8742 7336 Newsletter publish-
ing; marketing consulting services; com-
mercial art & graphic design

(P-4193)
**PARROT COMMUNICATIONS
INTL INC**
Also Called: Parrot Media Network
26321 Ferry Ct, Santa Clarita
(91350-2998)
PHONE..................................818 567-4700
Robert W Mertz, *CEO*
Evan Harris, *Accounts Mgr*
Gina Norton, *Representative*
▲ **EMP:** 50 **EST:** 1989
SQ FT: 60,000
SALES (est): 7.6MM **Privately Held**
WEB: www.parrotmedia.com
SIC: 2741 7331 4822 7375 Directories:
publishing only, not printed on site; direct
mail advertising services; facsimile trans-
mission services; information retrieval
services; prepackaged software

(P-4194)
PLANETIZEN INC
3530 Wilshire Blvd # 1285, Los Angeles
(90010-2328)
PHONE..................................877 260-7526

Chris Steins, *President*
Cate Miller, *Opers Mgr*
James Brasuell, *Manager*
EMP: 24 **EST:** 2011
SALES (est): 733.8K **Privately Held**
WEB: www.planetizen.com
SIC: 2741

(P-4195)
PLAYBOY ENTERPRISES INTL
Also Called: Peei
10960 Wilshire Blvd Fl 22, Los Angeles
(90024-3808)
PHONE..................................310 424-1800
Christopher Pachler, *Exec VP*
Hugh Heffner, *Officer*
EMP: 100 **EST:** 1964
SALES (est): 22.2MM **Publicly Held**
WEB: www.playboy.tv
SIC: 2741 Miscellaneous publishing
HQ: Playboy Enterprises, Inc.
10960 Wilshire Blvd Fl 22
Los Angeles CA 90024
310 424-1800

(P-4196)
POST PUBLISHING LLC
620 W Elk Ave, Glendale (91204-1404)
PHONE..................................818 291-1100
William R Rittwage, *Mng Member*
Linda Romanello, *Manager*
EMP: 17 **EST:** 1998
SALES (est): 1.2MM **Privately Held**
WEB: www.postmagazine.com
SIC: 2741 Posters: publishing only, not
printed on site

(P-4197)
**PRIORITY POSTING AND PUBG
INC**
17501 Irvine Blvd Ste 1, Tustin
(92780-3103)
PHONE..................................714 338-2568
Thomas Haacker, *President*
Maureen Haacker, *Vice Pres*
EMP: 16 **EST:** 1993
SQ FT: 3,000
SALES (est): 1.3MM **Privately Held**
WEB: www.priorityposting.com
SIC: 2741 Miscellaneous publishing

(P-4198)
PRISON RIDE SHARE NETWORK
Also Called: Prison Rideshare Network
1541 S California Ave, Compton
(90221-4924)
PHONE..................................314 703-5245
Keisha Joseph-Beard, *Owner*
EMP: 20 **EST:** 2016
SALES (est): 741.7K **Privately Held**
SIC: 2741 8742 4729 Telephone & other
directory publishing; transportation con-
sultant; carpool/vanpool arrangement

(P-4199)
**PROTOTYPE INDUSTRIES INC
(PA)**
26035 Acero Ste 100, Mission Viejo
(92691-7951)
PHONE..................................949 680-4890
Irene Grigoriadis, *President*
Jose Alcid, *Software Engr*
Donna Warner, *Manager*
EMP: 29 **EST:** 1991
SQ FT: 4,000
SALES (est): 3.4MM **Privately Held**
WEB: www.prototypeindustries.com
SIC: 2741 2752 Miscellaneous publishing;
commercial printing, offset

(P-4200)
PUBLISH BRAND INC
15731 Graham St, Huntington Beach
(92649-1612)
PHONE..................................714 890-1908
Chuong Huynh, *Principal*
Will Tran, *CFO*
Michael Huynh, *Creative Dir*
EMP: 15 **EST:** 2013
SALES (est): 3.5MM **Privately Held**
WEB: www.publishbrand.com
SIC: 2741 Miscellaneous publishing

(P-4201)
RASPADOXPRESS
8610 Van Nuys Blvd, Panorama City
(91402-7205)
PHONE..............................818 892-6969
Oscar Limon, *Branch Mgr*
EMP: 36
SALES (corp-wide): 1.5MM **Privately Held**
WEB: www.raspadoxpress.com
SIC: 2741 Miscellaneous publishing
PA: Raspadoxpress
9765 Laurel Canyon Blvd
Pacoima CA 91331
818 890-4111

(P-4202)
SCRIBBLE PRESS INC
1109 Montana Ave, Santa Monica
(90403-1609)
P.O. Box 20743, New York NY (10021-0075)
PHONE..............................212 288-2928
EMP: 30
SALES (est): 2.2MM
SALES (corp-wide): 5.2MM **Privately Held**
SIC: 2741 Miscellaneous Publishing
PA: Make Meaning, Inc.
1100 La Avenida St Ste A
Mountain View CA 94043
646 307-5906

(P-4203)
SELF-REALIZATION FELLOWSHIP CH (PA)
Also Called: Self Realization Fellowship
3880 San Rafael Ave, Los Angeles
(90065-3219)
PHONE..............................323 225-2471
Faye Wright, *President*
Mrinalini Mata, *CEO*
Augusto Mendez, *Administration*
Brian Schadel, *Project Mgr*
Juan Garcia, *Production*
▲ **EMP:** 35 **EST:** 1935
SALES (est): 10.8MM **Privately Held**
WEB: www.hollywoodtemple.org
SIC: 8661 2741 Miscellaneous denomination church; miscellaneous publishing

(P-4204)
SIEMENS ENERGY INC
6 Journey Ste 200, Aliso Viejo
(92656-5321)
PHONE..............................949 448-0600
Ralph Sonnseld, *Branch Mgr*
Brian Morris, *Vice Pres*
EMP: 57
SALES (corp-wide): 32.3B **Privately Held**
WEB: www.new.siemens.com
SIC: 2741 Miscellaneous publishing
HQ: Siemens Energy, Inc.
4400 N Alafaya Trl
Orlando FL 32826
407 736-2000

(P-4205)
SONGS MUSIC PUBLISHING LLC
7656 W Sunset Blvd, Los Angeles
(90046-2724)
PHONE..............................323 939-3511
Carianne Marshall, *Branch Mgr*
EMP: 15 **Privately Held**
WEB: www.songspub.com
SIC: 2741 Miscellaneous publishing
PA: Songs Music Publishing, Llc
307 7th Ave Rm 904
New York NY 10001

(P-4206)
SPIDELL PUBLISHING INC
1134 N Gilbert St, Anaheim (92801-1401)
P.O. Box 61044 (92803-6144)
PHONE..............................714 776-7850
Lynn Freer, *President*
Kariann Asmus, *COO*
Tim Hilger, *CPA*
Anthony Abeyta, *Production*
Jansen Cudal, *Marketing Mgr*
EMP: 32 **EST:** 1975
SQ FT: 2,500

SALES (est): 4.2MM **Privately Held**
WEB: www.caltax.com
SIC: 2741 Guides: publishing only, not printed on site

(P-4207)
STORIES INTERNATIONAL INC
400 Corporate Pointe, Culver City
(90230-7615)
PHONE..............................310 242-8409
Tomoya Suzuki, *CEO*
Evan Cholfin, *Production*
EMP: 14 **EST:** 2013
SALES (est): 216.2K **Privately Held**
WEB: www.stories-llc.com
SIC: 2741 Miscellaneous publishing

(P-4208)
STUDIO SYSTEMS INC (PA)
5700 Wilshire Blvd # 600, Los Angeles
(90036-3659)
PHONE..............................323 634-3400
Gary Hiller, *President*
Colleen Damico, *Sales Staff*
EMP: 20 **EST:** 1999
SQ FT: 13,000
SALES (est): 5.1MM **Privately Held**
SIC: 2741 Miscellaneous publishing

(P-4209)
SUPERMEDIA LLC
1270 E Garvey St, Covina (91724-3658)
PHONE..............................626 331-9440
EMP: 254
SALES (corp-wide): 1.8B **Privately Held**
SIC: 2741 Misc Publishing
HQ: Supermedia Llc
2200 W Airfield Dr
Dfw Airport TX 75261
972 453-7000

(P-4210)
SWVL LLC
2118 Wilshire Blvd # 400, Santa Monica
(90403-5704)
PHONE..............................424 248-3677
James W Dovine III, *CEO*
EMP: 15 **EST:** 2016
SALES (est): 513.9K **Privately Held**
SIC: 5961 2741 Catalog & mail-order houses;

(P-4211)
TANZ PUBLISHING INC (PA)
94 Seton Rd, Irvine (92612-2113)
PHONE..............................949 231-2290
Ali Reza Sepassi, *Principal*
EMP: 27 **EST:** 2018
SALES (est): 147.6K **Privately Held**
SIC: 2741 Miscellaneous publishing

(P-4212)
TEACHER CREATED MATERIALS INC
5301 Oceanus Dr, Huntington Beach
(92649-1030)
P.O. Box 1040 (92647-1040)
PHONE..............................714 891-2273
Rachelle Cracchiolo, *CEO*
Corinne Burton, *President*
Samantha Ozbat, *President*
Rich Levitt, *COO*
Kimberly Carlton, *Officer*
◆ **EMP:** 110 **EST:** 1979
SQ FT: 10,000
SALES (est): 40.4MM **Privately Held**
WEB: www.teachercreatedmaterials.com
SIC: 2741 Miscellaneous publishing

(P-4213)
TEACHER CREATED RESOURCES INC
12621 Western Ave, Garden Grove
(92841-4014)
PHONE..............................714 230-7060
Mary Diane Smith, *CEO*
Dan Bauer, *Graphic Designe*
Tal Frink, *Human Res Mgr*
Amy Lascola, *VP Mktg*
Neri Garcia, *Advt Staff*
◆ **EMP:** 100 **EST:** 2004
SALES (est): 28.8MM **Privately Held**
WEB: www.teachercreated.com
SIC: 2741 Miscellaneous publishing

(P-4214)
TECHTURE INC ✪
1010 Wilshire Blvd # 120, Los Angeles
(90017-5662)
PHONE..............................323 347-6209
Muhammad Zubair Khan, *President*
Chris M Joseph, *Vice Pres*
EMP: 35 **EST:** 2021
SALES (est): 1.4MM **Privately Held**
SIC: 2741

(P-4215)
UMG COMMERCIAL SERVICES INC (DH)
Also Called: Umgd
2220 Colorado Ave, Santa Monica
(90404-3506)
PHONE..............................310 235-4700
Jim Urie, *President*
Lj Gutierrez, *Partner*
Sara Connally, *President*
Ron Spaulding, *President*
Trina Campbell, *Treasurer*
EMP: 76 **EST:** 1996
SALES (est): 211.9MM
SALES (corp-wide): 108MM **Privately Held**
SIC: 2741 Miscellaneous publishing
HQ: Vivendi Holding I Llc
1755 Broadway Frnt 2
New York NY 10019
212 445-3800

(P-4216)
UNIVERSAL MUSIC PUBLISHING INC
2100 Colorado Ave, Santa Monica
(90404-3504)
PHONE..............................310 235-4700
Jody Gerson, *CEO*
Stephen Dallas, *Senior VP*
Joy Murphy, *Senior VP*
Rakesh Nigam, *Vice Pres*
Matthew Dunn, *Administration*
EMP: 84 **EST:** 1999
SALES (est): 5MM **Privately Held**
WEB: www.universalmusic.com
SIC: 2741 Miscellaneous publishing

(P-4217)
VOYAGER LEARNING COMPANY
2060 Lynx Pl Unit G, Ontario (91761)
PHONE..............................909 923-3120
EMP: 16 **Publicly Held**
SIC: 2741 Misc Publishing
HQ: Voyager Learning Company
17855 Dallas Pkwy Ste 400
Dallas TX 75287
214 932-9500

(P-4218)
WARNER/CHAPPELL MUSIC INC (DH)
777 S Santa Fe Ave, Los Angeles
(90021-1750)
PHONE..............................310 441-8600
Cameron Strang, *CEO*
Scott Francis, *President*
Ira Pianko, *COO*
Brian Roberts, *CFO*
Edgar Miles Bronfman, *Chairman*
EMP: 110 **EST:** 1984
SALES (est): 113.4MM **Publicly Held**
WEB: www.wmg.com
SIC: 2741 Music book & sheet music publishing

(P-4219)
WB MUSIC CORP (DH)
10585 Santa Monica Blvd # 200, Los Angeles (90025-4926)
PHONE..............................310 441-8600
Leslie Bider, *CEO*
EMP: 125 **EST:** 1994
SALES (est): 40.9MM **Publicly Held**
WEB: www.wmg.com
SIC: 2741 Music, sheet: publishing only, not printed on site

2752 Commercial Printing: Lithographic

(P-4220)
365 PRINTING INC
14747 Artesia Blvd Ste 3a, La Mirada
(90638-6003)
PHONE..............................714 752-6990
Chang Lee, *President*
EMP: 15 **EST:** 2014
SQ FT: 3,300
SALES (est): 1.9MM **Privately Held**
WEB: www.365inlove.com
SIC: 2752 Commercial printing, lithographic

(P-4221)
4 GEN DIGITAL
3540 Cadillac Ave, Costa Mesa
(92626-1415)
PHONE..............................714 486-1150
Craig Thomas, *Principal*
Blake Thomas, *Accounts Exec*
EMP: 14 **EST:** 2014
SALES (est): 3.1MM **Privately Held**
WEB: www.4gendigital.com
SIC: 2752 Commercial printing, offset

(P-4222)
ACE COMMERCIAL INC
Also Called: Press Colorcom
10310 Pioneer Blvd Ste 1, Santa Fe
Springs (90670-3737)
PHONE..............................562 946-6664
Andrew H Choi, *CEO*
Juan Garcia, *Prdtn Mgr*
Ozzie Villalobos, *Manager*
Jeff Morgan, *Accounts Mgr*
Eugene Yoo, *Accounts Mgr*
EMP: 40 **EST:** 1988
SQ FT: 22,000
SALES (est): 9.5MM **Privately Held**
WEB: www.acecommercial.com
SIC: 2752 7331 2791 2789 Commercial printing, offset; direct mail advertising services; typesetting; bookbinding & related work; die-cut paper & board

(P-4223)
ADVANCED COLOR GRAPHICS
Also Called: Acg Ecopack
1921 S Business Pkwy, Ontario
(91761-8539)
PHONE..............................909 930-1500
Steve Thompson, *President*
Mike Mullens, *Vice Pres*
EMP: 60 **EST:** 1992
SQ FT: 70,000
SALES (est): 8MM **Privately Held**
SIC: 2752 Commercial printing, offset

(P-4224)
ADVANCED VSUAL IMAGE DSIGN LLC
Also Called: Avid Ink
229 N Sherman Ave, Irvine (92614)
PHONE..............................951 279-2138
Robert D Davis, *CEO*
Jennie Enholm,
▲ **EMP:** 24 **EST:** 1997
SQ FT: 20,000
SALES (est): 1.3MM **Privately Held**
SIC: 2752 Commercial printing, offset

(P-4225)
ALPHA PRINTING & GRAPHICS INC
12758 Schabarum Ave, Irwindale
(91706-6801)
PHONE..............................626 851-9800
Stacey Chen, *President*
Kelly Ngo, *CEO*
▲ **EMP:** 20 **EST:** 1990
SQ FT: 5,000
SALES (est): 4.3MM **Privately Held**
WEB: www.alphaprinting.com
SIC: 2752 Commercial printing, offset

(P-4226)
AM-PM PRINTING INC
Also Called: Quality Instant Printing
163 W Bonita Ave, San Dimas
(91773-3007)
PHONE..............................909 599-0811

Dennis Ostler, *President*
Patrick Meyers, *Treasurer*
Kathy Meyers, *Admin Sec*
EMP: 13 **EST:** 1978
SQ FT: 2,500
SALES (est): 1.3MM **Privately Held**
WEB: www.am-pm-printing-inc.hub.biz
SIC: 2752 7334 Commercial printing, off-
set; photocopying & duplicating services

(P-4227)
**AMERICAN PCF PRTRS
COLLEGE INC**
Also Called: Kenny The Printer
675 N Main St, Orange (92868-1103)
PHONE....................949 250-3212
David Smith, *CEO*
Cal Laird, *CFO*
EMP: 36 **EST:** 1981
SALES (est): 4.9MM **Privately Held**
SIC: 2752 Commercial printing, offset

(P-4228)
**AMERICAN PRINTING & DESIGN
LTD**
14622 Ventura Blvd # 102, Sherman Oaks
(91403-3600)
PHONE....................310 287-0460
Michael Kenner, *President*
EMP: 14 **EST:** 1981
SQ FT: 40,000
SALES (est): 311K **Privately Held**
WEB: www.americanspeedy.com
SIC: 2752 Commercial printing, offset; cat-
alogs, lithographed

(P-4229)
AMERICHIP INC (PA)
19032 S Vermont Ave, Gardena
(90248-4412)
PHONE....................310 323-3697
Timothy Clegg, *CEO*
Keven Clegg, *President*
Primoz Samardzija, *CFO*
John Clegg, *Vice Pres*
Michael Ronk, *Vice Pres*
▲ **EMP:** 48 **EST:** 1995
SQ FT: 30,000
SALES (est): 18.5MM **Privately Held**
WEB: www.americhip.com
SIC: 2752 Promotional printing, litho-
graphic

(P-4230)
ANCHORED PRINTS INC
635 N Eckhoff St Ste Q, Orange
(92868-1048)
PHONE....................714 929-9317
Samuel Schinhofen, *CEO*
Jacob Austell, *Opers Staff*
EMP: 23 **EST:** 2018
SALES (est): 2.6MM **Privately Held**
WEB: www.anchoredprints.com
SIC: 2752 Commercial printing, litho-
graphic

(P-4231)
ARROWHEAD PRESS INC
220 W Maple Ave Ste B, Monrovia
(91016-3393)
PHONE....................626 358-1168
Diana Marie Sims, *CEO*
Ken Shannon, *Marketing Staff*
Charlie Hodge, *Sales Staff*
Frances Harsono, *Manager*
EMP: 28 **EST:** 1973
SQ FT: 9,000
SALES (est): 3.1MM **Privately Held**
SIC: 2752 2789 Commercial printing, off-
set; bookbinding & related work

(P-4232)
AVION GRAPHICS INC
27192 Burbank, Foothill Ranch
(92610-2503)
PHONE....................949 472-0438
Craig Greiner, *President*
Mary Kay Swanson, *Shareholder*
Jason Walden, *Division VP*
Michele Morris, *Vice Pres*
John Jones, *Purchasing*
EMP: 33 **EST:** 1984
SQ FT: 6,800

SALES (est): 6.1MM **Privately Held**
WEB: www.aviongraphics.com
SIC: 2752 7336 3993 5999 Decals, lithographed; commercial art & graphic design; signs & advertising specialties;
decals; aircraft & parts

(P-4233)
AXIOMPRINT INC
Also Called: Axiom Designs & Printing
513 State St, Glendale (91203-1523)
PHONE....................747 888-7777
Garnik Bayatyan, *CEO*
Lilit Avagyants, *Manager*
▼ **EMP:** 17 **EST:** 2009
SALES (est): 2MM **Privately Held**
WEB: www.axiomprint.com
SIC: 2752 5999 2741 7312 Commercial
printing, offset; banners, flags, decals &
posters; banners; posters: publishing &
printing; poster advertising, outdoor; peri-
odicals: publishing & printing

(P-4234)
B AND Z PRINTING INC
1300 E Wakeham Ave B, Santa Ana
(92705-4145)
PHONE....................714 892-2000
Frank Buono, *President*
James Zimmer, *Admin Sec*
Beau Johnson, *Agent*
EMP: 45 **EST:** 1984
SQ FT: 40,000
SALES (est): 4MM **Privately Held**
WEB: www.bandzprinting.com
SIC: 2752 2789 Commercial printing, off-
set; bookbinding & related work

(P-4235)
B&D LITHO CALIFORNIA INC
325 N Ponderosa Ave, Ontario
(91761-1530)
PHONE....................909 390-0903
Steven J Gaynor, *CEO*
EMP: 19 **EST:** 2000
SALES (est): 2.5MM **Privately Held**
WEB: www.bndlithoca.com
SIC: 2752 Commercial printing, offset

(P-4236)
BARRYS PRINTING INC
Also Called: All About Printing
9005 Eton Ave Ste D, Canoga Park
(91304-6534)
PHONE....................818 998-8600
Barry Shapiro, *CEO*
EMP: 30 **EST:** 1996
SALES (est): 2.2MM **Privately Held**
WEB: www.barrysprinting.mfgpages.com
SIC: 2752 7334 Commercial printing, off-
set; photocopying & duplicating services

(P-4237)
**BOONE PRINTING & GRAPHICS
INC**
70 S Kellogg Ave Ste 8, Goleta
(93117-6408)
PHONE....................805 683-2349
Andrew Ochsner, *President*
Rob Grayson, *Creative Dir*
Dave Tanner, *General Mgr*
Lindsey Fugitt, *Project Mgr*
Mike Meyer, *Sales Staff*
EMP: 52 **EST:** 1988
SQ FT: 15,000
SALES (est): 8.1MM **Privately Held**
WEB: www.boonegraphics.net
SIC: 2752 Commercial printing, offset

(P-4238)
BOP INC
Also Called: Best Office Products
23575 Underwood Cir, Murrieta
(92562-4828)
PHONE....................909 598-5776
Victor Gamboa, *President*
Michelle Gamboa, *CFO*
EMP: 18 **EST:** 1980
SALES (est): 2.1MM **Privately Held**
SIC: 5943 2752 Office forms & supplies;
commercial printing, lithographic

(P-4239)
BOSS LITHO INC
2380 Peck Rd, City of Industry
(90601-1601)
PHONE....................626 912-7088
Jean Pierre Nataf, *President*
Kathy Greil, *Project Dir*
Brenda Scroggins, *Bookkeeper*
Tim Chen, *Marketing Staff*
EMP: 48 **EST:** 2010
SALES (est): 8MM **Privately Held**
WEB: www.bosslitho.com
SIC: 2752 Commercial printing, offset

(P-4240)
BREAKAWAY PRESS INC
9620 Topanga Canyon Pl A, Chatsworth
(91311-0868)
PHONE....................818 727-7388
Cynthia Friedman, *President*
Marc Friedman, *Vice Pres*
Carole Kimmel, *Office Mgr*
Jeni Wood, *Business Mgr*
EMP: 25 **EST:** 1993
SQ FT: 3,000
SALES (est): 2.5MM **Privately Held**
WEB: www.breakawaypress.com
SIC: 2752 Commercial printing, offset

(P-4241)
BRYAN PRESS INC
1011 S Stimson Ave, City of Industry
(91745-1630)
P.O. Box 92222 (91715-2222)
PHONE....................626 961-9257
K Bryan, *President*
Brad Bryan, *Sales Mgr*
EMP: 15 **EST:** 1996
SALES (est): 631.4K **Privately Held**
WEB: www.b-2print.com
SIC: 2752 Commercial printing, offset

(P-4242)
C & H LETTERPRESS INC
3400 W Castor St, Santa Ana
(92704-3910)
PHONE....................714 438-1350
Hernan A Pineda, *President*
Suzanne Harrison, *Treasurer*
EMP: 14 **EST:** 1999
SQ FT: 8,600
SALES (est): 7.2MM **Privately Held**
SIC: 2752 Commercial printing, offset

(P-4243)
C & L GRAPHICS INC
6825 Valjean Ave, Van Nuys (91406-4713)
PHONE....................818 785-8310
Charles Ball, *President*
Laurie Ball, *Corp Secy*
Erin Williams, *Manager*
EMP: 18 **EST:** 1985
SQ FT: 10,500
SALES (est): 2.5MM **Privately Held**
WEB: www.clgraphicsinc.com
SIC: 2752 Commercial printing, offset

(P-4244)
C4 LITHO LLC
27020 Daisy Cir, Yorba Linda (92887-4233)
PHONE....................714 259-1073
Su T Dang,
Stacey Dang,
EMP: 14 **EST:** 2006
SALES (est): 1MM **Privately Held**
WEB: www.c4usa.com
SIC: 2752 Commercial printing, offset

(P-4245)
**CAL SOUTHERN GRAPHICS
CORP (PA)**
8432 Steller Dr, Culver City (90232-2425)
PHONE....................310 559-3600
Timothy Toomey, *CEO*
Amir Saeed, *Controller*
Donya Tummey, *Purchasing*
Mark Armstrong, *Sales Staff*
Jonas Hanelin, *Sales Staff*
▲ **EMP:** 81 **EST:** 1959
SQ FT: 32,000
SALES (est): 20MM **Privately Held**
WEB: www.socalgraph.com
SIC: 2752 2759 2754 Lithographing on
metal; commercial printing; commercial
printing, gravure

(P-4246)
**CALIFORNIA OFFSET PRINTERS
INC**
Also Called: Cop Communications
5075 Brooks St, Montclair (91763-4804)
PHONE....................818 291-1100
John Hedlund, *Ch of Bd*
William R Rittwage, *President*
Joe Watson, *Executive*
Marine Zograbyan, *Receptionist*
EMP: 100
SQ FT: 55,000
SALES (est): 40.7MM **Privately Held**
WEB: www.copprints.com
SIC: 2752 2741 2721 Commercial print-
ing, offset; miscellaneous publishing; peri-
odicals

(P-4247)
**CALIFORNIA PRTG SOLUTIONS
INC**
1950 W Park Ave, Redlands (92373-3133)
P.O. Box 11451, San Bernardino (92423-
1451)
PHONE....................909 307-2032
Mark Smith, *President*
▲ **EMP:** 26 **EST:** 1996
SQ FT: 20,000
SALES (est): 1.1MM **Privately Held**
WEB: www.printingsolutions.tv
SIC: 2752 Commercial printing, offset

(P-4248)
CDR GRAPHICS INC (PA)
1207 E Washington Blvd, Los Angeles
(90021-3035)
PHONE....................310 474-7600
Homan Hadawi, *President*
Ralph Connor, *Manager*
EMP: 23 **EST:** 2010
SALES (est): 2.6MM **Privately Held**
WEB: www.cdrgraphics.com
SIC: 2752 Commercial printing, offset

(P-4249)
CH IMAGE INC
Also Called: Cater Line , The
15350 Valley Blvd, City of Industry
(91746-3335)
PHONE....................626 336-6063
▲ **EMP:** 15 **EST:** 1999
SALES (est): 1.2MM **Privately Held**
SIC: 2752 Lithographic Commercial Print-
ing

(P-4250)
CHALLENGE GRAPHICS INC
7661 Densmore Ave Ste 3 Van Nuys
(91406-2016)
PHONE....................818 892-0123
Robert F Ritter, *President*
Kathy Burtoft, *Treasurer*
Sally A Ritter, *Vice Pres*
Tara Curtis, *Admin Sec*
EMP: 31 **EST:** 1975
SALES (est): 2.5MM **Privately Held**
WEB: www.challenge-graphics.com
SIC: 2752 Commercial printing, offset

(P-4251)
**CHROMATIC INC
LITHOGRAPHERS**
127 Concord St, Glendale (91203-2456)
PHONE....................818 242-5785
Keith Sevigny, *President*
Mary Gene Sevigny, *CEO*
Michael Sevigny, *Vice Pres*
Mike Sevigny, *Vice Pres*
Sandy Orozco, *Admin Asst*
▲ **EMP:** 32 **EST:** 1969
SQ FT: 30,000
SALES (est): 6.2MM **Privately Held**
WEB: www.chromaticinc.com
SIC: 2752 Commercial printing, offset

(P-4252)
CHUP CORPORATION
Also Called: Color Digit
2990 Airway Ave Ste A, Costa Mesa
(92626-6037)
PHONE....................949 455-0676
Mohsen Kaeni, *President*
Hadi Kaeni, *Vice Pres*
Hamid Kaeni, *Admin Sec*
EMP: 15 **EST:** 1990

SQ FT: 11,000
SALES (est): 4.4MM **Privately Held**
SIC: 2752 2796 Commercial printing, off-set; color separations for printing

(P-4253)
CLASSIC LITHO & DESIGN INC
340 Maple Ave, Torrance (90503-2600)
PHONE.............................310 224-5200
Masoud Nikravan, *CEO*
Firouzeh Nikravan, *President*
Darioush Nikravan, *Vice Pres*
Cristian Salgado, *Sr Project Mgr*
Craig Elferdink, *Manager*
EMP: 30 **EST:** 1976
SQ FT: 12,500
SALES (est): 6.5MM **Privately Held**
WEB: www.classiclitho.com
SIC: 2752 Commercial printing, offset

(P-4254)
CLEAR IMAGE PRINTING INC
12744 San Fernando Rd # 200, Sylmar
(91342-3853)
PHONE.............................818 547-4684
Anthony Toven, *President*
Jessica Slepicka, *Executive*
Dejirlene Concha, *Bookkeeper*
Frank Hang, *Sales Staff*
Steve Milne, *Sales Staff*
EMP: 28 **EST:** 2007
SQ FT: 18,000
SALES (est): 7.5MM **Privately Held**
WEB: www.clearimageprinting.com
SIC: 2752 Commercial printing, offset

(P-4255)
COLOR INC
1600 Flower St, Glendale (91201-2319)
PHONE.............................818 240-1350
Barry D Hamm, *President*
James E Hamm, *Vice Pres*
EMP: 35 **EST:** 1968
SQ FT: 16,000
SALES (est): 2.8MM **Privately Held**
WEB: www.colorincorporated.com
SIC: 2752 2796 Color lithography; publication printing, lithographic; platemaking services

(P-4256)
COLOR SERVICE INC
40 E Verdugo Ave, Burbank (91502-1931)
PHONE.............................323 283-4793
Patrick F Seeholzer, *President*
Michael Mahoney, *Vice Pres*
EMP: 17 **EST:** 1957
SQ FT: 30,000
SALES (est): 1.1MM **Privately Held**
SIC: 2752 Commercial printing, offset

(P-4257)
COLORCOM INC
2437 S Eastern Ave, Commerce
(90040-1414)
PHONE.............................323 246-4640
John Youn, *President*
Young Kim, *Shareholder*
Alex Kang, *Production*
EMP: 57 **EST:** 1992
SALES (est): 6.5MM **Privately Held**
WEB: www.colorcom.net
SIC: 2752 Commercial printing, offset

(P-4258)
COLORFAST DYE & PRINT HSE INC
5075 Pacific Blvd, Vernon (90058-2215)
PHONE.............................323 581-1656
Enrique Ruiz, *President*
Jose Ramos, *Vice Pres*
EMP: 15 **EST:** 1999
SQ FT: 30,000
SALES (est): 512K **Privately Held**
SIC: 2752 2396 2269 Commercial printing, lithographic; screen printing on fabric articles; dyeing: raw stock yarn & narrow fabrics

(P-4259)
COLORFX INC
11050 Randall St, Sun Valley (91352-2621)
P.O. Box 12357, La Crescenta (91224-5357)
PHONE.............................818 767-7671
Razmik Avedissian, *CEO*

Arby Avedissan, *Vice Pres*
Yolanda Avedissan, *Admin Sec*
EMP: 50 **EST:** 1996
SQ FT: 28,000
SALES (est): 11.1MM **Privately Held**
WEB: www.colorfxweb.com
SIC: 2752 Commercial printing, offset

(P-4260)
CONTINENTAL GRAPHICS CORP
Also Called: Continental Data Graphics
4060 N Lakewood Blvd 8015fl, Long Beach
(90808-1700)
PHONE.............................714 827-1752
Warren Smith, *Manager*
Valerie Gill, *Train & Dev Mgr*
EMP: 55
SALES (corp-wide): 58.1B **Publicly Held**
WEB: www.cdgnow.com
SIC: 2752 7336 Promotional printing, lithographic; graphic arts & related design
HQ: Continental Graphics Corporation
4060 N Lakewood Blvd
Long Beach CA 90808
714 503-4200

(P-4261)
CONTINENTAL GRAPHICS CORP
Also Called: Continental Data Graphics
9302 Pttsbrgh Ave Ste 100, Rancho Cucamonga (91730)
PHONE.............................909 758-9800
Steve Meade, *Branch Mgr*
Robert Pahia, *Technical Staff*
EMP: 55
SALES (corp-wide): 58.1B **Publicly Held**
WEB: www.cdgnow.com
SIC: 2752 7336 Promotional printing, lithographic; graphic arts & related design
HQ: Continental Graphics Corporation
4060 N Lakewood Blvd
Long Beach CA 90808
714 503-4200

(P-4262)
CONTINENTAL GRAPHICS CORP
Also Called: Continental Data Graphics
222 N Pacific Coast Hwy # 300, El Segundo (90245-5648)
PHONE.............................310 662-2307
Mike Parvin, *Manager*
David Malmo, *Director*
EMP: 55
SALES (corp-wide): 58.1B **Publicly Held**
WEB: www.cdgnow.com
SIC: 2752 7336 Promotional printing, lithographic; graphic arts & related design
HQ: Continental Graphics Corporation
4060 N Lakewood Blvd
Long Beach CA 90808
714 503-4200

(P-4263)
COPY SOLUTIONS INC
919 S Fremont Ave Ste 398, Alhambra
(91803-4701)
PHONE.............................323 307-0900
Roger Zhao, *President*
Jacqueline Saavedra, *Director*
EMP: 20 **EST:** 1995
SQ FT: 5,000
SALES (est): 2.7MM **Privately Held**
WEB: www.copysolution.com
SIC: 2752 Commercial printing, offset

(P-4264)
CORPORATE GRAPHICS & PRINTING
335 Science Dr, Moorpark (93021-2092)
PHONE.............................805 529-5333
Harry A Stidham, *President*
Harry Stidham, *President*
John Bird, *Vice Pres*
Warren Bachtel, *Accounts Exec*
EMP: 17 **EST:** 2002
SQ FT: 20,000
SALES (est): 3MM **Privately Held**
WEB: www.corgfx.com
SIC: 2752 Commercial printing, offset

(P-4265)
COYLE REPRODUCTIONS INC (PA)
2850 Orbiter St, Brea (92821-6224)
PHONE.............................866 269-5373
Frank T Cutrone, *Ch of Bd*

Jason De Soto, *Exec VP*
Kiri Chhoy, *Administration*
Rosa Hernandez, *Human Res Mgr*
Gene Cutrone, *Purch Mgr*
EMP: 112 **EST:** 1963
SQ FT: 85,000
SALES (est): 20.3MM **Privately Held**
WEB: www.coylerepro.com
SIC: 2752 2759 Commercial printing, offset; screen printing; posters, including billboards: printing

(P-4266)
CREAMER PRINTING CO
1413 N La Brea Ave, Inglewood
(90302-1218)
PHONE.............................310 671-9491
Fred John Creamer III, *President*
Lawrence Creamer, *CFO*
Edmund J Creamer, *Corp Secy*
EMP: 15 **EST:** 1924
SQ FT: 10,000
SALES (est): 534.4K **Privately Held**
WEB: www.creamerprinting.com
SIC: 2752 2759 Commercial printing, offset; flexographic printing

(P-4267)
CREATIVE PRESS LLC (PA)
1350 S Caldwell Cir, Anaheim
(92805-6408)
PHONE.............................714 774-5060
Michael L Patton, *President*
Greg Bosdet, *President*
Seybert Tina, *Technology*
Kevin McHugh, *Foreman/Supr*
Tom Spence, *Marketing Mgr*
EMP: 64 **EST:** 2007
SQ FT: 31,000
SALES (est): 9.8MM **Privately Held**
WEB: www.creativepressinc.net
SIC: 2752 2791 2789 Commercial printing, offset; typesetting; bookbinding & related work

(P-4268)
CRESCENT INC
Also Called: Print Printing
1196 N Osprey Cir, Anaheim (92807-1709)
PHONE.............................714 992-6030
Reza Mohkami, *President*
Tahereh Mohkami, *Treasurer*
Ira Heshmati, *Vice Pres*
EMP: 25 **EST:** 1980
SQ FT: 10,000
SALES (est): 3MM **Privately Held**
SIC: 2752 7549 Commercial printing, offset; do-it-yourself garages

(P-4269)
CRESTEC USA INC
Also Called: Crestec Los Angeles
2410 Mira Mar Ave, Long Beach
(90815-1756)
PHONE.............................310 327-9000
Takeomi Kurisawa, *CEO*
Mike Burk, *Vice Pres*
Michael Fleder, *Engineer*
Isip Rene, *Controller*
Kim Petersen, *Supervisor*
▲ **EMP:** 50 **EST:** 1967
SALES (est): 10.2MM **Privately Held**
WEB: www.crestecusa.com
SIC: 2752 Commercial printing, offset
PA: Crestec Inc.
676, Kasaishindencho, Higashi-Ku
Hamamatsu SZO 431-3

(P-4270)
CUSTOM LITHOGRAPH
7006 Stanford Ave, Los Angeles
(90001-1583)
PHONE.............................323 778-7751
Robert D Hanel, *President*
John Sebourn, *CFO*
Pamela Sebourn, *Admin Sec*
EMP: 13 **EST:** 1958
SQ FT: 92,000
SALES (est): 571.1K **Privately Held**
WEB: www.customlithograph.com
SIC: 2752 Commercial printing, offset

(P-4271)
CYU LITHOGRAPHICS INC
Also Called: Choice Lithographics
6951 Oran Cir, Buena Park (90621-3305)
PHONE.............................888 878-9898
Michael Wang, *President*
Claire Tang, *Director*
Dory Rivera, *Manager*
▲ **EMP:** 25 **EST:** 1983
SQ FT: 13,000
SALES (est): 3.3MM **Privately Held**
SIC: 2752 2721 Color lithography; magazines: publishing only, not printed on site

(P-4272)
DAVID B ANDERSON
Also Called: Central Coast Printing
174 Suburban Rd Ste 100, San Luis Obispo
(93401-7522)
PHONE.............................805 489-0661
David B Anderson, *Owner*
Gail Speer, *Admin Sec*
EMP: 26 **EST:** 1978
SALES (est): 3.1MM **Privately Held**
SIC: 2752 Commercial printing, offset

(P-4273)
DBC PRINTING INCORPORATED
Also Called: Vanguard Printing
220 Bernoulli Cir, Oxnard (93030-8012)
PHONE.............................805 988-8855
Jeff D Cox, *CEO*
Justin Cox, *Sales Executive*
Dina Masters, *Accounts Mgr*
EMP: 14 **EST:** 1990
SQ FT: 14,000
SALES (est): 2.5MM **Privately Held**
SIC: 2752 Commercial printing, offset

(P-4274)
DELTA PRINTING SOLUTIONS INC
28210 Avenue Stanford, Valencia
(91355-3983)
PHONE.............................661 257-0584
Tony Richardson, *President*
Vicki Gorman, *Vice Pres*
Gary Lee, *Administration*
Matt Walter, *Data Proc Staff*
John Fritzenkotter, *Accounting Dir*
EMP: 130 **EST:** 2003
SQ FT: 100,000
SALES (est): 13.6MM **Privately Held**
WEB: www.sheridan.com
SIC: 2752 Commercial printing, lithographic

(P-4275)
DENNIS BOLTON ENTERPRISES INC
7285 Coldwater Canyon Ave, North Hollywood (91605-4204)
PHONE.............................818 982-1800
Dennis Bolton, *President*
Osvaldo Acosta, *Treasurer*
Max Guerrero, *Vice Pres*
Carlo Bernal, *Admin Sec*
EMP: 35 **EST:** 1971
SQ FT: 14,780
SALES (est): 2MM **Privately Held**
WEB: www.printingbydbe.com
SIC: 2752 7334 7311 Commercial printing, offset; photocopying & duplicating services; advertising consultant

(P-4276)
DIGITAL PRINTING SYSTEMS INC (PA)
2350 Panorama Ter, Los Angeles
(90039-2536)
PHONE.............................626 815-1888
Donald J Nores, *CEO*
Peter Young, *CEO*
Doug Gabriel, *CFO*
Joyce Nores, *Treasurer*
Jim Nores, *Vice Pres*
◆ **EMP:** 64 **EST:** 1971
SALES (est): 8.3MM **Privately Held**
WEB: www.dpstickets.com
SIC: 2752 Commercial printing, offset

(P-4277)
DIRECT EDGE SCREENWORKS INC
1221 N Lakeview Ave, Anaheim (92807-1830)
PHONE..................714 579-3686
Jennifer Brueckner, *CEO*
Ryan Clark, *President*
Ryan Bruecknru, *Vice Pres*
Nicksharo Oshiro, *Vice Pres*
Tim Standon, *Vice Pres*
EMP: 27 EST: 2008
SQ FT: 20,000
SALES (est): 1.2MM Privately Held
WEB: www.directedgemedia.com
SIC: 2752 Commercial printing, offset

(P-4278)
DOCUMEDIA GROUP (PA)
2082 Bus Ctr Dr Ste 257, Irvine (92612)
PHONE..................949 567-9930
James S Nolin, *CEO*
Lewis Lebeque, *President*
Pam Bierly, *Officer*
Jim Nolin, *Comptroller*
Lori Shaw, *Opers Mgr*
▲ EMP: 13 EST: 1999
SQ FT: 900
SALES (est): 1.7MM Privately Held
WEB: www.documediagroup.com
SIC: 2752 Commercial printing, offset

(P-4279)
DOCUMOTION RESEARCH INC
2020 S Eastwood Ave, Santa Ana (92705-5208)
PHONE..................714 662-3800
Joel Van Boom, *President*
EMP: 17 EST: 2010
SQ FT: 10,000
SALES (est): 3.2MM Privately Held
WEB: www.documotion.com
SIC: 2752 Commercial printing, lithographic

(P-4280)
DOT COPY INC
Also Called: DOT Graphics
9655 De Soto Ave, Chatsworth (91311-5013)
PHONE..................818 341-6666
Brian Whiteman, *CEO*
EMP: 56 EST: 1998
SALES (est): 5.2MM Privately Held
SIC: 2752 Commercial printing, offset

(P-4281)
DOT CORP (PA)
Also Called: DOT Fulfillment The
2525 Pullman St, Santa Ana (92705-5511)
PHONE..................714 708-5800
Richard Alvarez, *CIO*
Emily Saenz, *Business Mgr*
Sherry Gardner, *Credit Mgr*
Lisa Holmes, *Human Resources*
Heather Lantow, *Production*
▼ EMP: 27 EST: 2010
SALES (est): 8.9MM Privately Held
WEB: www.thedotcorp.com
SIC: 2752 Commercial printing, offset

(P-4282)
DOT CORP
1801 S Standard Ave, Santa Ana (92707-2465)
PHONE..................714 708-5960
Diana Ortiz, *Executive Asst*
Sherry Gardner, *Credit Mgr*
Robin Clark, *Director*
Ruben Gonzalez, *Director*
Kevin Omahony, *Manager*
EMP: 46
SALES (corp-wide): 8.9MM Privately Held
WEB: www.thedotcorp.com
SIC: 2752 Commercial printing, offset
PA: The Dot Corp
2525 Pullman St
Santa Ana CA 92705
714 708-5800

(P-4283)
DOT PRINTER INC (PA)
2424 Mcgaw Ave, Irvine (92614-5834)
PHONE..................949 474-1100
Bruce M Carson, *President*

Gregory Peterson, *President*
Stan Lowe, *COO*
Jim Voss, *CFO*
Laura Parker, *Senior VP*
▲ EMP: 95 EST: 1980
SQ FT: 40,000
SALES (est): 53MM Privately Held
WEB: www.thedotcorp.com
SIC: 2752 2732 3555 Commercial printing, offset; book printing; printing trades machinery

(P-4284)
DSJ PRINTING INC
1703 Stewart St, Santa Monica (90404-4021)
PHONE..................310 828-8051
Jeffrey L Vaughan, *President*
Ed Molina, *Vice Pres*
Jeffrey Vaughan Jr, *Vice Pres*
Stacie Vaughan, *Graphic Designe*
Brandon Vaughan, *Prdtn Mgr*
EMP: 13 EST: 1953
SQ FT: 3,000
SALES (est): 2.8MM Privately Held
WEB: www.dsjprinting.com
SIC: 2752 2759 Commercial printing, offset; letterpress printing

(P-4285)
EAGLE GRAPHICS INC (PA)
Also Called: Eagle Print Dynamics
1430 W Katella Ave, Orange (92867-3409)
PHONE..................714 978-2200
Tim Smith, *President*
John Gordon, *CFO*
Jeff Carte, *Vice Pres*
Kevin Welch, *Vice Pres*
Mandi Trevena, *Office Mgr*
EMP: 15 EST: 1971
SALES (est): 5.7MM Privately Held
WEB: www.eagle411.com
SIC: 2752 Commercial printing, lithographic

(P-4286)
EARTH PRINT INC
Also Called: Cr Print
31115 Via Colinas Ste 301, Westlake Village (91362-4507)
PHONE..................818 879-6050
Jim Friedl, *President*
Edward Corridori, *Admin Sec*
Mike Corridori, *VP Sales*
Michael Keane, *Manager*
EMP: 19 EST: 1994
SQ FT: 7,500
SALES (est): 3.5MM Privately Held
WEB: www.crprint.com
SIC: 2752 7334 Commercial printing, offset; photocopying & duplicating services

(P-4287)
ECLIPSE PRTG & GRAPHICS LLC
Also Called: James Litho
4462 E Airport Dr, Ontario (91761-7804)
PHONE..................909 390-2452
Jeff James, *Mng Member*
Deborah Whisler, *General Mgr*
Sue James,
EMP: 20 EST: 1999
SQ FT: 25,000
SALES (est): 3.4MM Privately Held
WEB: www.jameslitho.com
SIC: 2752 Commercial printing, offset

(P-4288)
ECON-O-PLATE INC
Also Called: Pacific Rim Printers & Mailers
5731 W Slauson Ave # 175, Culver City (90230-6595)
PHONE..................310 342-5900
Robert Brothers, *President*
Richard Gonzales, *President*
Brad Carl, *Treasurer*
EMP: 15 EST: 1969
SALES (est): 4.1MM Privately Held
WEB: www.pacrim.la
SIC: 2752 7331 Commercial printing, offset; mailing service

(P-4289)
EDGEWOOD PRESS INC
1130 N Main St, Orange (92867-3421)
PHONE..................714 516-2455

Carol Altvater, *President*
Ernest Altvater Jr, *Corp Secy*
John M Atwell, *Vice Pres*
EMP: 13 EST: 1958
SQ FT: 12,000
SALES (est): 531.2K Privately Held
WEB: www.schoolfolderfactory.com
SIC: 2752 Commercial printing, offset

(P-4290)
ELITE 4 PRINT INC
851 E Walnut St, Carson (90746-1214)
PHONE..................310 366-1344
Keith Kyong, *Principal*
▲ EMP: 20 EST: 2008
SALES (est): 2.2MM Privately Held
WEB: www.elite4print.com
SIC: 2752 Commercial printing, offset

(P-4291)
FAUST PRINTING INC
8656 Utica Ave Ste 100, Rancho Cucamonga (91730-4860)
P.O. Box 721713, Pinon Hills (92372-1713)
PHONE..................909 980-1577
Donald F Faust Jr, *President*
Greg Faust, *Shareholder*
Tom Faust, *Shareholder*
Rosemary Faust, *Ch of Bd*
Jim Buccholz, *CFO*
EMP: 18 EST: 1963
SQ FT: 20,000
SALES (est): 563K Privately Held
WEB: www.faustprinting.com
SIC: 2752 2796 Commercial printing, offset; letterpress plates, preparation of; embossing plates for printing

(P-4292)
FBPRODUCTIONS INC
12722 Riverside Dr Ste 204, Valley Village (91607)
PHONE..................818 773-9337
Frank Barbarino, *President*
David Wohl, *CEO*
Jerry Cheney, *Vice Pres*
Lupe Montenegro, *Purchasing*
EMP: 18 EST: 1989
SQ FT: 60,000
SALES (est): 979.7K Privately Held
SIC: 2752 2675 Commercial printing, offset; die-cut paper & board

(P-4293)
FGS-WI LLC
5401 Jurupa St, Ontario (91761-3621)
PHONE..................909 467-8300
Ron Roger, *Manager*
EMP: 21
SALES (corp-wide): 103.2MM Privately Held
WEB: www.fgs.com
SIC: 2752 Commercial printing, offset
HQ: Fgs-Wi, Llc
1101 S Janesville St
Milton WI 53563
608 373-6500

(P-4294)
FIREBRAND MEDIA LLC
Also Called: Laguna Beach Magazine
580 Broadway St Ste 301, Laguna Beach (92651-4328)
PHONE..................949 715-4100
Vincent Zepezauer, *Mng Member*
Steve Zepezauer, *CEO*
Sonia Chung, *Creative Dir*
Cindy Mendaros, *Office Mgr*
Scott Sanchez, *CTO*
EMP: 23 EST: 2015
SQ FT: 5,000
SALES (est): 4.2MM Privately Held
WEB: www.firebrandmediainc.com
SIC: 2752 Commercial printing, lithographic

(P-4295)
FISHER PRINTING INC (PA)
2257 N Pacific St, Orange (92865-2615)
PHONE..................714 998-9200
Thomas Fischer, *Chairman*
Will Fischer, *CEO*
Tom Scarpati, *COO*
John Klabacha, *Sales Dir*
Dario Martinez, *Marketing Staff*
EMP: 150 EST: 1933

SQ FT: 60,000
SALES (est): 60.1MM Privately Held
WEB: www.gofisher.net
SIC: 2752 Commercial printing, offset

(P-4296)
FOSTER PRINTING COMPANY INC
700 E Alton Ave, Santa Ana 92705-5610)
PHONE..................714 731-2000
Dennis M Blackburn, *CEO*
Steve Gutmann, *Plant Mgr*
EMP: 53 EST: 1988
SQ FT: 35,000
SALES (est): 9.7MM Privately Held
WEB: www.fosterprint.com
SIC: 2752 Commercial printing, offset

(P-4297)
FOX PRINTING COMPANY INC (PA)
18017 Chatsworth St, Granada Hills (91344-5608)
PHONE..................818 768-6110
Gary J Fox, *President*
Kathryn Fox, *Treasurer*
Todd Fox, *Vice Pres*
EMP: 15 EST: 1936
SALES (est): 1.4MM Privately Held
SIC: 2752 2759 Commercial printing, offset; commercial printing

(P-4298)
FPC GRAPHICS INC
2682 Market St, Riverside (92501-2126)
P.O. Box 192 (92502-0192)
PHONE..................951 686-0232
Michael S Vaughan, *President*
EMP: 25 EST: 1955
SQ FT: 35,000
SALES (est): 1.2MM Privately Held
WEB: www.fpcgraphics.com
SIC: 2752 7336 7311 2791 Commercial printing, offset; commercial art & graphic design; advertising agencies; typesetting

(P-4299)
FRANCHISE SERVICES INC (PA)
26722 Plaza, Mission Viejo (92691-8051)
PHONE..................949 348-5400
Don F Lowe, *Ch of Bd*
Daniel J Conger, *CFO*
Dan Beck, *Exec VP*
John Clampitt, *Vice Pres*
Knowlton Gabriel, *Vice Pres*
EMP: 20 EST: 1968
SQ FT: 44,000
SALES: 19.9MM Privately Held
WEB: www.franserv.com
SIC: 2752 6159 Commercial printing, lithographic; machinery & equipment finance leasing

(P-4300)
FULLERTON PRINTING INC
Also Called: Bixby Knolls Prtg & Graphics
315 N Lemon St, Fullerton (92832-2030)
PHONE..................714 870-7500
Donald Moreland, *President*
Bryan D Moreland, *Officer*
Jay Scott, *Officer*
EMP: 18 EST: 1951
SQ FT: 3,737
SALES (est): 1MM Privately Held
WEB: www.fullcoll.edu
SIC: 2752 Commercial printing, offset

(P-4301)
GALA DELUXE CORPORATION (PA)
979 S Meridian Ave, Alhambra (91803-1250)
PHONE..................626 283-4804
Ralph Sham, *Sales Staff*
EMP: 34 EST: 2017
SALES (est): 699.3K Privately Held
WEB: www.galadeluxe.com
SIC: 2752 Commercial printing, offset

(P-4302)
GEORGE CORIATY
Also Called: Sir Speedy
7240 Greenleaf Ave, Whittier (90602-1312)
PHONE..................562 698-7513

George Coriaty, *Owner*
EMP: 32 **EST:** 1979
SQ FT: 12,000
SALES: 12.4MM **Privately Held**
WEB: www.sirspeedy.com
SIC: 2752 7334 Commercial printing, lithographic; photocopying & duplicating services

(P-4303)
GOLDEN COLOR PRINTING INC
9353 Rush St, South El Monte
(91733-2544)
PHONE.................................626 455-0850
Deng-Muh Yen, *President*
EMP: 21 **EST:** 1996
SQ FT: 11,000
SALES (est): 1.2MM **Privately Held**
WEB: www.goldencolorprinting.com
SIC: 2752 Color lithography

(P-4304)
GOTPRINT
7651 N San Fernando Rd, Burbank
(91505-1073)
PHONE.................................877 922-7374
Kevin Schrader, *General Mgr*
Paul Kempf, *Prdtn Mgr*
Henrik Yekikan, *Director*
Yousif Hazboun, *Manager*
EMP: 13 **EST:** 2020
SALES (est): 654.8K **Privately Held**
WEB: www.gotprint.com
SIC: 2752 Commercial printing, lithographic

(P-4305)
GPA PRINTING CA LLC
9655 De Soto Ave, Chatsworth
(91311-5013)
PHONE.................................818 618-1500
Richard T Dixon,
EMP: 15 **EST:** 2019
SALES (est): 4.4MM **Privately Held**
WEB: www.gpaglobal.net
SIC: 2752 Commercial printing, lithographic

(P-4306)
GRAPHIC COLOR SYSTEMS INC
Also Called: Continental Colorcraft
1166 W Garvey Ave, Monterey Park
(91754-2511)
PHONE.................................323 283-3000
Andy Scheidegger, *President*
Maria Donhauser, *Treasurer*
Linda Clarke, *Vice Pres*
Kathleen Ryan, *Executive*
Ellen Crabb, *Project Mgr*
EMP: 52 **EST:** 1968
SQ FT: 28,000
SALES (est): 7.9MM **Privately Held**
WEB: www.continentalcolorcraft.com
SIC: 2752 2796 2791 2759 Commercial printing, offset; color separations for printing; typesetting; commercial printing

(P-4307)
GRAPHIC VISIONS INC
7119 Fair Ave, North Hollywood
(91605-6304)
PHONE.................................818 845-8393
Randall Avazian, *CEO*
Kenneth Langer, *President*
Jodi Shapiro, *Bookkeeper*
Michael Beauregard, *VP Mfg*
Fred Buck, *Accounts Mgr*
▲ **EMP:** 23 **EST:** 1940
SALES (est): 6.9MM **Privately Held**
WEB: www.graphicvisionsla.com
SIC: 2752 Commercial printing, offset

(P-4308)
H J S GRAPHICS
Also Called: Printing Connection , The
3533 Old Conejo Rd # 104, Newbury Park
(91320-2156)
PHONE.................................818 782-5490
Henry Steenackers, *President*
Erik Steenackers, *IT/INT Sup*
EMP: 15 **EST:** 1983
SALES (est): 1.9MM **Privately Held**
SIC: 2752 Commercial printing, offset

(P-4309)
HALL LETTER SHOP INC
5200 Rosedale Hwy, Bakersfield
(93308-6000)
PHONE.................................661 327-3228
Catherine A Dounies, *President*
Greg Dounies, *General Mgr*
EMP: 16 **EST:** 1963
SALES (est): 2.9MM **Privately Held**
WEB: www.hallprintmail.com
SIC: 2752 7331 2791 2789 Commercial printing, offset; mailing service; typesetting, computer controlled; binding only: books, pamphlets, magazines, etc.

(P-4310)
HANDBILL PRINTERS LP
820 E Parkridge Ave, Corona (92879-6611)
PHONE.................................951 547-5910
Don J Messick, *President*
Dane Messick, *Partner*
Kenneth Messick, *Partner*
Mark Messick, *Partner*
Michael Messick, *Partner*
EMP: 45 **EST:** 1984
SQ FT: 62,500
SALES (est): 8.9MM **Privately Held**
WEB: www.handbillprinters.com
SIC: 2752 7336 Commercial printing, offset; graphic arts & related design

(P-4311)
HARMAN PRESS INC
Also Called: Harman Envelopes
6840 Vineland Ave, North Hollywood
(91605-6409)
PHONE.................................818 432-0570
Jay Goldner, *President*
Phillip Goldner, *Vice Pres*
Deborah Goldner-Watson, *Admin Sec*
Sundee Shehyn, *Analyst*
Pilar Banas, *Purchasing*
EMP: 38 **EST:** 1963
SQ FT: 10,000
SALES (est): 8.6MM **Privately Held**
WEB: www.harmanpress.com
SIC: 2752 Commercial printing, offset

(P-4312)
HARRIS CONSTRUCTION INC
174 N Wetherly Dr, Beverly Hills
(90211-1813)
P.O. Box 2, Corinne UT (84307-0002)
PHONE.................................310 246-0188
Jenny Harris, *Principal*
David Gonzales, *Project Engr*
Mike Marsh, *Sr Project Mgr*
Anthony Aguilar, *Director*
Samantha Austin, *Clerk*
EMP: 14 **EST:** 2008
SALES (est): 123.2K **Privately Held**
WEB: www.harrisconstruction.com
SIC: 2752 Commercial printing, lithographic

(P-4313)
HAVANA GRAPHIC CENTER INC
Also Called: Zada International Printing
9250 Independence Ave # 109, Chatsworth
(91311-5904)
PHONE.................................818 841-3774
George Zada, *CEO*
Kenarique Zada, *Treasurer*
EMP: 24 **EST:** 1967
SALES (est): 1MM **Privately Held**
SIC: 2752 2759 Lithographing on metal; flexographic printing

(P-4314)
HELENS PLACE INC
Also Called: Printing Rsources Southern Cal
893 W 9th St, Upland (91786-4541)
PHONE.................................909 981-5715
Nancy De Diemar Jones, *President*
Patrick C Jones, *Corp Secy*
Jeannette Jacobson,
EMP: 21 **EST:** 1970
SQ FT: 5,400
SALES (est): 2MM **Privately Held**
WEB: www.printingresources.com
SIC: 2752 7331 Commercial printing, offset; mailing service

(P-4315)
HG GRAPHIC & PRINTING
4217 Gage Ave, Bell (90201-1212)
PHONE.................................323 412-3866
Humberto Granda, *Principal*
EMP: 14 **EST:** 2014
SALES (est): 356K **Privately Held**
WEB: www.hggraphicprinting.com
SIC: 2752 Commercial printing, offset

(P-4316)
HIGH FIVE INC
Also Called: Printech
625 Fee Ana St, Placentia (92870-6704)
PHONE.................................714 847-2200
Steve Kramer, *President*
Katherine Kramer, *Corp Secy*
Tina Kramer, *Office Mgr*
▼ **EMP:** 18 **EST:** 1987
SALES (est): 2.8MM **Privately Held**
WEB: www.printechusa.com
SIC: 2752 Commercial printing, offset

(P-4317)
HOUSE OF PRINTING INC
3336 E Colorado Blvd, Pasadena
(91107-3885)
PHONE.................................626 793-7034
Eugene F Pittroff Sr, *President*
Marguerite Pittroff, *Treasurer*
Walter E Pittroff, *Vice Pres*
Edna Pittroff, *Admin Sec*
EMP: 22 **EST:** 1942
SQ FT: 6,500
SALES (est): 2.7MM **Privately Held**
WEB: www.thehouseofprinting.com
SIC: 2752 2791 2789 Commercial printing, offset; typesetting; bookbinding & related work

(P-4318)
IDEAL GRAPHICS INC
580 S State College Blvd, Fullerton
(92831-5114)
PHONE.................................714 632-3398
Patric Fung, *President*
Frank Liang, *Vice Pres*
EMP: 18 **EST:** 1998
SALES (est): 1MM **Privately Held**
SIC: 2752 Offset & photolithographic printing

(P-4319)
IDEAL PRINTING CO INC
17855 Maclaren St, City of Industry
(91744-5799)
PHONE.................................626 964-2019
Richard Mancino, *President*
Yolanda Mancino, *Vice Pres*
EMP: 20 **EST:** 1961
SQ FT: 30,000
SALES (est): 1.9MM **Privately Held**
WEB: www.idealprintingcompany.com
SIC: 2752 Commercial printing, offset

(P-4320)
IKONICK LLC
705 W 9th St Apt 1404, Los Angeles
(90015-1696)
PHONE.................................516 680-7765
Mark Mastrandrea, *President*
EMP: 35 **EST:** 2017
SALES (est): 2.3MM **Privately Held**
WEB: www.checkout.ikonick.com
SIC: 2752 7336 Commercial printing, lithographic; commercial art & graphic design; graphic arts & related design

(P-4321)
IMAGE DISTRIBUTION SERVICES
3191 W Temple Ave Ste 180, Pomona
(91768-3254)
PHONE.................................909 599-7680
EMP: 16
SALES (corp-wide): 7MM **Privately Held**
WEB: www.fontissolutions.com
SIC: 2752 Commercial printing, offset
PA: Image Distribution Services Inc
19781 Pauling
Foothill Ranch CA 92610
949 754-9000

(P-4322)
IMAGE DISTRIBUTION SERVICES (PA)
Also Called: Image Printing Solutions
19781 Pauling, Foothill Ranch
(92610-2606)
P.O. Box 60119, City of Industry (91716-0119)
PHONE.................................949 754-9000
Joe Fries, *CEO*
William Kaszton, *President*
Chris Paul, *CFO*
Jim Spellman, *Vice Pres*
Rob Gerstley, *CIO*
EMP: 48
SALES (est): 7MM **Privately Held**
WEB: www.fontissolutions.com
SIC: 2752 5943 Commercial printing, offset; office forms & supplies

(P-4323)
IMAGE SQUARE INC
Also Called: Image Square Copy & Print
1627 Stanford St, Santa Monica
(90404-4113)
PHONE.................................310 586-2333
Kavian Soudbakhsh, *President*
Ashkan Soudbakhsh, *President*
Sepideh Soudbakhsh, *Admin Sec*
Thomas Allison, *Mktg Dir*
EMP: 21 **EST:** 1997
SQ FT: 2,400
SALES (est): 2.3MM **Privately Held**
WEB: www.imagesquareprinting.com
SIC: 2752 Commercial printing, offset

(P-4324)
IMAGEMOVER INC
10051 Bradley Ave, Pacoima (91331-2202)
PHONE.................................818 485-8840
Ben Taylor, *President*
EMP: 17 **EST:** 2009
SALES (est): 3.2MM **Privately Held**
WEB: www.imagemoverinc.com
SIC: 2752 Commercial printing, lithographic

(P-4325)
IMPACT PRINTING & GRAPHICS
15150 Sierra Bonita Ln, Chino
(91710-8903)
PHONE.................................909 614-1678
Bill McGinley, *President*
Sarah Jensen, *Human Resources*
Jason Edwards, *Manager*
EMP: 25 **EST:** 1995
SQ FT: 14,000
SALES (est): 4.4MM **Privately Held**
WEB: www.impactpkgco.com
SIC: 2752 Commercial printing, offset

(P-4326)
IMPERIAL PRINTERS (PA)
Also Called: Imperial Printers Rocket Copy
430 W Main St, El Centro (92243-3019)
PHONE.................................760 352-4374
Rudy Rodgruegos, *President*
Rodolfo Rodriguez, *Vice Pres*
Marvin Wieben Jr, *Vice Pres*
Frank Printers, *Art Dir*
EMP: 18 **EST:** 1977
SQ FT: 8,725
SALES (est): 3.8MM **Privately Held**
WEB: www.imperialprinters.com
SIC: 2752 2796 Commercial printing, offset; letterpress plates, preparation of

(P-4327)
IMPRESS COMMUNICATIONS INC
9320 Lurline Ave, Chatsworth
(91311-6041)
PHONE.................................818 701-8800
Paul Marino, *President*
Jeff Park, *COO*
Jeff Kaye, *CFO*
Marty Cooperstone, *Vice Pres*
Cameron Bowers, *Creative Dir*
▲ **EMP:** 92 **EST:** 1974
SQ FT: 50,000
SALES (est): 16.5MM **Privately Held**
WEB: www.impress1.com
SIC: 2752 7336 7319 Commercial printing, offset; commercial art & graphic design; display advertising service

(P-4328)
INDUSTRY COLOR PRINTING INC
11642 Washington Blvd, Whittier (90606-2425)
P.O. Box 1903, Rancho Cucamonga (91729-1903)
PHONE..................................626 961-2403
Rafael Osorio, *President*
Miriam Osorio, *Treasurer*
EMP: 15 **EST:** 1976
SALES (est): 737.8K **Privately Held**
WEB: www.icpprint.com
SIC: 2752 Commercial printing, offset

(P-4329)
INK & COLOR INC
Also Called: Acuprint
5920 Bowcroft St, Los Angeles (90016-4302)
PHONE..................................310 280-6060
Saman Sowlaty, *CEO*
Jane Corish, *Vice Pres*
Mojgan Sowalty, *Vice Pres*
Dena Limpert, *Bookkeeper*
Cris Zabka, *Marketing Staff*
▲ **EMP:** 30 **EST:** 1985
SQ FT: 17,000
SALES (est): 4.6MM **Privately Held**
WEB: www.acuprint.net
SIC: 2752 Commercial printing, offset

(P-4330)
INK SPOT INC
9737 Bell Ranch Dr, Santa Fe Springs (90670-2951)
PHONE..................................626 338-4500
Somsak Reuanglith, *CEO*
Som Reuanglith, *Graphic Designe*
Betty Ching, *Sales Staff*
EMP: 26 **EST:** 2004
SALES (est): 4.5MM **Privately Held**
WEB: www.inkspotinc.com
SIC: 2752 Commercial printing, offset

(P-4331)
INK SPOT DIGITAL PRINTING LLC (PA)
9825 Bell Ranch Dr, Santa Fe Springs (90670-2953)
PHONE..................................562 777-1666
Eric CU, *Mng Member*
EMP: 24 **EST:** 2017
SALES (est): 640.4K **Privately Held**
WEB: www.inkspotsndots.com
SIC: 2752 Commercial printing, offset

(P-4332)
INKOVATION INC
13659 Excelsior Dr, Santa Fe Springs (90670-5103)
PHONE..................................800 465-4174
Janak Savaliya, *President*
Carl Friesen, *Manager*
EMP: 21 **EST:** 2010
SALES (est): 1.6MM **Privately Held**
WEB: www.inkovation.net
SIC: 2752 Commercial printing, offset

(P-4333)
INKWRIGHT LLC
5822 Research Dr, Huntington Beach (92649-1348)
PHONE..................................714 892-3300
Danny Nichols,
EMP: 30 **EST:** 2010
SALES (est): 3.5MM **Privately Held**
WEB: www.inkwright.com
SIC: 2752 Offset & photolithographic printing

(P-4334)
INLAND LITHO LLC
Also Called: Inland Group
4305 E La Palma Ave, Anaheim (92807-1843)
PHONE..................................714 993-6000
Steve Urbanovitch, *Marketing Mgr*
Kathy Urbanovitch,
EMP: 60 **EST:** 1984
SQ FT: 40,000
SALES (est): 10.1MM **Privately Held**
WEB: www.inlandgroupllc.com
SIC: 2752 Commercial printing, offset

(P-4335)
INLAND MAILING SERVICES INC
Also Called: Advanced Mktg Print & Mail
160 W Fthill Pkwy Ste 105, Corona (92882)
PHONE..................................951 371-6245
Phillip K Adishian, *President*
Michelle Adishian, *Vice Pres*
EMP: 14 **EST:** 1989
SQ FT: 38,500
SALES (est): 523.8K **Privately Held**
SIC: 2752 7331 Commercial printing, offset; direct mail advertising services

(P-4336)
INSTANT WEB LLC
Also Called: Iwco Direct - Downey
7300 Flores St, Downey (90242-4010)
PHONE..................................562 658-2020
Jake Hertel, *Branch Mgr*
Laura Seyler, *Buyer*
Patricia Marvin, *Accounts Mgr*
EMP: 30
SALES (corp-wide): 613.7MM **Publicly Held**
WEB: www.iwco.com
SIC: 2752 Commercial printing, lithographic
HQ: Instant Web, Llc
7951 Powers Blvd
Chanhassen MN 55317
952 474-0961

(P-4337)
INSUA GRAPHICS INCORPORATED
9121 Glenoaks Blvd, Sun Valley (91352-2612)
PHONE..................................818 767-7007
Jose Miguel Insua, *CEO*
Albert Insua, *Treasurer*
Eric Insua, *Vice Pres*
Ernesto Vera, *Manager*
Karina Mondello, *Accounts Mgr*
◆ **EMP:** 35 **EST:** 1996
SQ FT: 28,000
SALES (est): 4.9MM **Privately Held**
WEB: www.insua.com
SIC: 2752 Commercial printing, offset

(P-4338)
INTEGRATED COMMUNICATIONS INC
208 N Broadway, Santa Ana (92701-4863)
PHONE..................................310 851-8066
Peter Levshin, *CEO*
David Humphrey, *President*
Bruce Chambers, *Accounts Exec*
▲ **EMP:** 24 **EST:** 1986
SALES (est): 4.1MM **Privately Held**
WEB: www.icla.com
SIC: 2752 Commercial printing, lithographic

(P-4339)
INTERLINK INC
Also Called: Precision Plastics Packaging
3845 E Coronado St, Anaheim (92807-1649)
PHONE..................................714 905-7700
Bob Bhagat, *President*
Hathin Bhagat, *Principal*
▲ **EMP:** 85
SQ FT: 50,000
SALES (est): 18MM **Privately Held**
WEB: www.pppc.com
SIC: 2752 Commercial printing, lithographic

(P-4340)
INTERNATIONAL PRTG & TYPSG INC
14535 Hamlin St, Van Nuys (91411-1608)
PHONE..................................818 787-6804
Todd M Wallace, *President*
Joyce Wallace, *CFO*
Richard Barnes, *CIO*
EMP: 13 **EST:** 1981
SQ FT: 3,000
SALES (est): 186K **Privately Held**
SIC: 2752 2791 Commercial printing, offset; typesetting, computer controlled

(P-4341)
J&L PRESS INC (PA)
1218 W 163rd St, Gardena (90247-4432)
PHONE..................................818 549-8344
Mark Iwakiri, *CEO*
John Iwakiri, *Vice Pres*
EMP: 15 **EST:** 1958
SQ FT: 6,700
SALES (est): 2.4MM **Privately Held**
SIC: 2752 Commercial printing, offset

(P-4342)
JD BUSINESS SOLUTIONS INC
Also Called: Printing Impressions
1351 Holiday Hill Rd, Goleta (93117-1815)
P.O. Box 1729 (93116-1729)
PHONE..................................805 962-8193
James Denion, *President*
Michael Gregory, *Principal*
Jeannine Denion, *Admin Sec*
Lynda Handgis, *Representative*
EMP: 25 **EST:** 1982
SQ FT: 9,000
SALES (est): 3MM **Privately Held**
SIC: 2752 Commercial printing, offset

(P-4343)
JEB-PHI INC
Also Called: PIP Printing
10417 Lakewood Blvd, Downey (90241-2744)
PHONE..................................562 861-0863
Bruce Pansky, *President*
Belinda Pansky, *Corp Secy*
Phillip Pansky, *Vice Pres*
Landy Pansky, *Sales Mgr*
EMP: 25 **EST:** 1970
SQ FT: 2,900
SALES (est): 3.2MM **Privately Held**
WEB: www.pip.com
SIC: 2752 Commercial printing, offset

(P-4344)
JSM PRODUCTIONS INC
Also Called: PIP Printing
537 E Florida Ave, Hemet (92543-4333)
PHONE..................................951 929-5771
John E Mullany, *President*
EMP: 17 **EST:** 1983
SQ FT: 3,500
SALES (est): 1MM **Privately Held**
WEB: www.pip.com
SIC: 2752 Commercial printing, offset

(P-4345)
K S PRINTING INC
710 E Parkridge Ave # 105, Corona (92879-1097)
PHONE..................................951 268-5180
Ralph Azar, *President*
▲ **EMP:** 13 **EST:** 1986
SQ FT: 20,000
SALES (est): 390.3K **Privately Held**
SIC: 2752 Commercial printing, offset

(P-4346)
K-1 PACKAGING GROUP (PA)
17989 Arenth Ave, City of Industry (91748-1126)
PHONE..................................626 964-9384
Mike Tsai, *President*
Lynn An, *Asst Admin*
Richard Barnes, *CIO*
Linda Tsai, *Project Mgr*
Adam Aguirre, *Graphic Designe*
◆ **EMP:** 113 **EST:** 1992
SALES (est): 24MM **Privately Held**
WEB: www.k1packaging.com
SIC: 2752 Offset & photolithographic printing

(P-4347)
K2 LABEL & PRINTING INC
633 Great Bend Dr, Diamond Bar (91765-2034)
PHONE..................................626 922-8108
Jack Dam, *Branch Mgr*
EMP: 41
SALES (corp-wide): 526.3K **Privately Held**
SIC: 2752 Commercial printing, lithographic
PA: K2 Label & Printing, Inc.
23535 Palomino Dr
Diamond Bar CA

(P-4348)
KELMSCOTT COMMUNICATIONS LLC
Also Called: Orange County Printing
2485 Da Vinci, Irvine (92614 5844)
PHONE..................................949 475-1900
Paz Calaci, *Branch Mgr*
Luis Delgadillo, *Production*
Kevin Elder, *Manager*
EMP: 320
SALES (corp-wide): 4.7B **Publicly Held**
WEB: www.mittera.com
SIC: 2752 Commercial printing, offset
HQ: Kelmscott Communications Llc
5858 Westheimer Rd # 410
Houston TX 77057
713 787-0977

(P-4349)
KINDRED LITHO INCORPORATED
10833 Bell Ct, Rancho Cucamonga (91730-4835)
PHONE..................................909 944-4015
Kurt Kindred, *President*
Cherie Kindred, *Admin Sec*
EMP: 40 **EST:** 1971
SQ FT: 8,000
SALES (est): 2MM **Privately Held**
SIC: 2752 Commercial printing, offset

(P-4350)
KM PRINTING PRODUCTION INC
218 Longden Ave, Irwindale (91706-1328)
PHONE..................................626 821-0008
Chim Moon Ming, *President*
Kerwin Ngo, *Vice Pres*
Wendy Lui, *Accounting Mgr*
EMP: 18 **EST:** 1994
SQ FT: 600
SALES (est): 2.8MM **Privately Held**
WEB: www.kmppi.com
SIC: 2752 Commercial printing, offset

(P-4351)
L T LITHO & PRINTING CO
16811 Noyes Ave, Irvine (92606-5122)
PHONE..................................949 466-8584
Craig Thomas, *President*
Mark Thomas, *CEO*
EMP: 19 **EST:** 1970
SQ FT: 16,000
SALES (est): 731K **Privately Held**
WEB: www.ltlitho.net
SIC: 2752 2759 Commercial printing, offset; commercial printing

(P-4352)
LA PRINTING & GRAPHICS INC
Also Called: L A Press
13951 S Main St, Los Angeles (90061-2140)
PHONE..................................310 527-4526
Kevin Sheu Chhim Kaing, *CEO*
Sheu C Kevin Kaing, *President*
Lor Yik, *Admin Sec*
EMP: 26 **EST:** 1989
SQ FT: 32,000
SALES (est): 4.8MM **Privately Held**
SIC: 2752 Commercial printing, offset

(P-4353)
LAVA PRODUCTS INC
3168 Airway Ave, Costa Mesa (92626-4608)
PHONE..................................949 951-7191
Michael Freitas, *CEO*
Rhonda Stutz, *COO*
David Howard, *Vice Pres*
Chris Joyce, *Sales Staff*
Nathan Stutz, *Manager*
▲ **EMP:** 22 **EST:** 1997
SQ FT: 13,500
SALES (est): 4.7MM **Privately Held**
WEB: www.lavapartners.com
SIC: 2752 Commercial printing, offset

(P-4354)
LAYTON PRINTING & MAILING
1538 Arrow Hwy, La Verne (91750-5318)
PHONE..................................909 592-4419
Michael Layton, *President*
Mary Ellen Layton, *Admin Sec*
EMP: 18 **EST:** 1996

SQ FT: 20,000
SALES (est): 3.4MM **Privately Held**
WEB: www.laytonprinting.com
SIC: 2752 Commercial printing, offset

(P-4355)
LEE MAXTON INC
Also Called: Minuteman Press
10844 Edison Ct, Rancho Cucamonga
(91730-3868)
PHONE..................909 483-0688
Kevin Browm, *President*
Dave McPherson, *President*
Maribel Brown, *Administration*
EMP: 15 **EST:** 2011
SALES (est): 942.7K **Privately Held**
WEB: www.mmprancho.com
SIC: 2752 Commercial printing, lithographic

(P-4356)
LEGAL VISION GROUP LLC
2030 Paddock Ln, Norco (92860-2663)
PHONE..................310 945-5550
Michelle Cano,
EMP: 30 **EST:** 2018
SALES (est): 1.2MM **Privately Held**
WEB: www.legalvisiongroup.com
SIC: 2752 7389 7374 7335 Commercial printing, lithographic; mailing & messenger services; data processing & preparation; commercial photography; title abstract offices

(P-4357)
LESTER LITHOGRAPH INC
1128 N Gilbert St, Anaheim (92801-1412)
PHONE..................714 491-3981
Robert Miller, *CEO*
Larry Lester, *COO*
Larita Miller, *CFO*
Jim Witt, *Exec VP*
James Witt, *Vice Pres*
EMP: 50 **EST:** 1980
SQ FT: 25,000
SALES (est): 8.8MM **Privately Held**
WEB: www.lesterlitho.com
SIC: 2752 Commercial printing, offset

(P-4358)
LETTERHEAD FACTORY INC
1007 E Dominguez St Ste H, Carson
(90746-7252)
PHONE..................310 538-3321
Richard W Rice, *CEO*
Jerry Loukatos, *Manager*
EMP: 15 **EST:** 1986
SQ FT: 5,000
SALES (est): 2.1MM **Privately Held**
WEB: www.letterheadfactory.com
SIC: 2752 Commercial printing, offset

(P-4359)
LICHER DIRECT MAIL INC
980 Seco St, Pasadena (91103-2816)
PHONE..................626 795-3333
Wayne Licher Sr, *President*
Besse Licher, *Treasurer*
Wayne Licher Jr, *Vice Pres*
Tony Huynh, *Prdtn Mgr*
EMP: 36 **EST:** 1946
SQ FT: 17,000
SALES (est): 3.1MM **Privately Held**
WEB: www.licherdm.com
SIC: 2752 7331 Commercial printing, offset; direct mail advertising services

(P-4360)
LITHOGRAPHIX INC (PA)
12250 Crenshaw Blvd, Hawthorne
(90250-3332)
PHONE..................323 770-1000
Herbert Zebrack, *President*
Gary Bates, *President*
Linh Bober, *CFO*
Victor Wolfe, *CFO*
Jeffrey Zebrack, *Corp Secy*
▲ **EMP:** 305 **EST:** 1949
SQ FT: 250,000
SALES (est): 77.4MM **Privately Held**
WEB: www.lithographix.com
SIC: 2752 2759 Commercial printing, offset; commercial printing

(P-4361)
LIVING WAY INDUSTRIES INC
Also Called: Creative Graphic Services
20734 Centre Pointe Pkwy, Santa Clarita
(91350-2966)
PHONE..................661 298-3200
Ronald Niner, *President*
Charlene E Niner, *Corp Secy*
Matt Hare, *Prdtn Mgr*
Malerie Leach, *Marketing Staff*
Omar Mejias, *Sales Staff*
EMP: 18 **EST:** 1970
SQ FT: 22,500
SALES (est): 3MM **Privately Held**
SIC: 2752 Commercial printing, lithographic

(P-4362)
LOMBARD ENTERPRISES INC
Also Called: Lombard Graphics
3619 San Gbriel Rver Pkwy, Pico Rivera
(90660-1403)
PHONE..................562 692-7070
Stephen R Lombard, *President*
Ross Lombard, *Vice Pres*
EMP: 20 **EST:** 1993
SQ FT: 10,000
SALES (est): 2.2MM **Privately Held**
WEB: www.lombardgraphics.com
SIC: 2752 Commercial printing, offset

(P-4363)
MADISN/GRHAM CLOR GRAPHICS INC
Also Called: Colorgraphics
150 N Myers St, Los Angeles (90033-2109)
PHONE..................323 261-7171
Cappy Childs, *CEO*
Chris Madison, *President*
Arthur Bell, *Vice Pres*
Terry Bell, *Admin Sec*
Stephanie Kruse, *Purch Agent*
▲ **EMP:** 380 **EST:** 1953
SQ FT: 96,000
SALES (est): 27.8MM **Privately Held**
WEB: www.colorgraphics.com
SIC: 2752 7336 2796 Commercial printing, offset; graphic arts & related design; platemaking services

(P-4364)
MAIL HANDLING GROUP INC
Also Called: Mail Handling Services
2840 Madonna Dr, Fullerton (92835-1830)
PHONE..................952 975-5000
Brian Ostenso, *President*
Michael Murphy, *CEO*
Todd Tume, *Info Tech Dir*
Michael Price, *Prgrmr*
Brian Gliniany, *IT/INT Sup*
EMP: 120 **EST:** 1977
SALES (est): 17.8MM **Privately Held**
SIC: 2752 7331 7374 Commercial printing, offset; mailing service; data processing service

(P-4365)
MAJESTIC PRINT INC
Also Called: Majestic Printing Systems
4017 Trail Creek Rd, Riverside
(92505-5863)
PHONE..................951 509-2539
Isaiah Rudy, *President*
EMP: 15 **EST:** 1981
SQ FT: 6,500 **Privately Held**
WEB: www.majesticprintinc.com
SIC: 2752 2759 Commercial printing, offset; commercial printing

(P-4366)
MAJOR FULFILLMENT LLC
13707 S Figueroa St, Los Angeles
(90061-1024)
PHONE..................310 204-1874
Hayden Fisher, *Mng Member*
Mike Leeny,
EMP: 17 **EST:** 2014
SALES (est): 5.6MM **Privately Held**
WEB: www.majorfulfillment.com
SIC: 2752 Commercial printing, offset

(P-4367)
MARRS PRINTING INC
Also Called: Mars Printing and Packaging
860 Tucker Ln, City of Industry
(91789-2914)
PHONE..................909 594-9459
Walter H Marrs, *CEO*
Jackie Marrs, *Treasurer*
Teresa Grigsby, *Vice Pres*
Teresa Grisby, *Vice Pres*
Scott Marrs, *Vice Pres*
EMP: 82 **EST:** 1971
SQ FT: 27,000
SALES (est): 15.2MM **Privately Held**
WEB: www.marrs.com
SIC: 2752 Commercial printing, offset

(P-4368)
MATSUDA HOUSE PRINTING INC
Also Called: B & G House of Printing
1825 W 169th St Ste A, Gardena
(90247-5270)
PHONE..................310 532-1533
Benjamin Matsuda, *CEO*
Patsy Matsuda, *Treasurer*
Darren Matsuda, *Vice Pres*
Rick Morimura, *Sales Staff*
▲ **EMP:** 31 **EST:** 1975
SALES (est): 4.4MM **Privately Held**
WEB: www.bgprinting.com
SIC: 2752 Lithographing on metal; commercial printing, offset

(P-4369)
MCPRINT CORP
Also Called: McPrint Direct
327 E Commercial St, Pomona
(91767-5505)
PHONE..................714 632-9966
Yusheng Shew, *President*
EMP: 13 **EST:** 2017
SALES (est): 877.4K **Privately Held**
WEB: www.mcprintdirect.com
SIC: 2752 2759 Commercial printing, offset; post cards, picture: printing

(P-4370)
MEKONG PRINTING INC
Also Called: Mk Printing
2421 W 1st St, Santa Ana (92703-3509)
PHONE..................714 558-9595
Hoan Truong, *CEO*
Nancy Luu, *Vice Pres*
EMP: 22 **EST:** 1986
SQ FT: 20,000
SALES (est): 3.4MM **Privately Held**
SIC: 2752 Commercial printing, offset

(P-4371)
MERIDIAN GRAPHICS INC
2652 Dow Ave, Tustin (92780-7208)
PHONE..................949 833-3500
David R Melin, *President*
David Melin, *President*
Craig Miller, *Corp Secy*
Paul Valencia, *Senior VP*
David Jernigan, *Vice Pres*
▲ **EMP:** 65 **EST:** 2000
SQ FT: 40,000
SALES (est): 16.3MM **Privately Held**
WEB: www.mglitho.com
SIC: 2752 2759 Commercial printing, offset; letterpress printing

(P-4372)
METRO DIGITAL PRINTING INC
3311 W Macarthur Blvd, Santa Ana
(92704-6803)
PHONE..................714 545-8400
Mike Jafari, *President*
Sally Shulkin, *Partner*
Sherri Taheri, *Treasurer*
EMP: 25 **EST:** 1986
SQ FT: 15,000
SALES (est): 1.2MM **Privately Held**
WEB: www.store.metrodigitalinc.com
SIC: 2752 Commercial printing, offset

(P-4373)
MICROPRINT INC
133 Puente Ave, City of Industry
(91746-2302)
PHONE..................626 369-1950
Stone Liu, *President*
Chung Chien Peng, *Shareholder*

Teresa Peng, *Shareholder*
TSE Hung Liu, *CEO*
MEI Wong Chen, *Admin Sec*
▲ **EMP:** 20 **EST:** 1995
SQ FT: 10,000
SALES (est): 2.8MM **Privately Held**
WEB: www.microprintinc.com
SIC: 2752 Commercial printing, offset

(P-4374)
MICROSCALE INDUSTRIES INC
18435 Bandilier Cir, Fountain Valley
(92708-7012)
PHONE..................714 593-1422
David Williams, *President*
David Khai-Vu, *Info Tech Dir*
Jay Peterson, *Marketing Staff*
EMP: 28 **EST:** 1933
SQ FT: 10,626
SALES (est): 1.4MM **Privately Held**
WEB: www.microscale.com
SIC: 2752 5945 Decals, lithographed; hobby, toy & game shops

(P-4375)
MOJAVE COPY & PRINTING INC
12402 Industrial Blvd E10, Victorville
(92395-5875)
PHONE..................760 241-7898
Howard Kack, *President*
EMP: 14 **EST:** 1987
SQ FT: 5,500
SALES (est): 2.4MM **Privately Held**
WEB: www.mojavecopy.com
SIC: 2752 Commercial printing, offset

(P-4376)
MOLINO COMPANY
Also Called: Melcast
13712 Alondra Blvd, Cerritos (90703-2316)
PHONE..................323 726-1000
Melchor Castano, *President*
EMP: 85 **EST:** 1976
SQ FT: 200,000
SALES (est): 8.8MM **Privately Held**
SIC: 2752 Commercial printing, offset

(P-4377)
MONARCH LITHO INC (PA)
1501 Date St, Montebello (90640-6324)
PHONE..................323 727-0300
Robert Lopez, *President*
Victor Neri, *Corp Secy*
George Lopez, *Vice Pres*
Mariano Balbuena, *Info Tech Dir*
Eddie Audelo, *Controller*
EMP: 50 **EST:** 1974
SQ FT: 153,000
SALES (est): 46.7MM **Privately Held**
WEB: www.monarchlitho.com
SIC: 2752 Commercial printing, offset; advertising posters, lithographed

(P-4378)
NATIONAL GRAPHICS LLC
Also Called: Jano Graphics
200 N Elevar St, Oxnard (93030-7969)
PHONE..................805 644-9212
Mike Scher, *President*
Ginna Caskey, *Sales Staff*
Alan Walsh, *Sales Staff*
Walsh Alan, *Manager*
Junior Gaona, *Manager*
EMP: 40 **EST:** 1960
SALES (est): 10MM **Privately Held**
WEB: www.janoprint.com
SIC: 2752 Commercial printing, offset

(P-4379)
NEWPORT MESA USD CAMPUS C
2985 Bear St, Costa Mesa (92626-4300)
PHONE..................714 424-8939
Mellissia Christensen, *Principal*
EMP: 16 **EST:** 2013
SALES (est): 962.6K **Privately Held**
SIC: 2752 Commercial printing, lithographic

(P-4380)
NIKNEJAD INC
Also Called: Colornet Press
6855 Hayvenhurst Ave, Van Nuys
(91406-4718)
PHONE..................310 477-0407
Kamran Niknejad, *President*

(PA)=Parent Co (HQ)=Headquarters (DH)=Div Headquarters
✪ = New Business established in last 2 years

2022 Southern California Business
Directory and Buyers Guide

P R O D U C T S & S V C S

199

Sima Fouladi, *Vice Pres*
Rashid Yassamy, *Vice Pres*
Temo Moreno, *Project Mgr*
Lisa Roman, *Accountant*
EMP: 40 **EST:** 1981
SQ FT: 5,000
SALES (est): 8.8MM **Privately Held**
WEB: www.colornetpress.com
SIC: 2752 7336 2791 Commercial printing, offset; graphic arts & related design; typesetting

(P-4381)
OCPC INC
Also Called: The Orange County Printing Co
2485 Da Vinci, Irvine (92614-5844)
PHONE...............................949 475-1900
Miguel Jacobowitz, *COO*
Moises Ramirez, *Info Tech Mgr*
Matt Schwartz, *Technology*
Bessie Konrad, *Controller*
Lac Pham, *Production*
EMP: 60 **EST:** 1986
SQ FT: 18,000
SALES (est): 10.1MM **Privately Held**
WEB: www.rrd.com
SIC: 2752 Commercial printing, offset

(P-4382)
ODCOMBE PRESS (NASHVILLE)
Also Called: Haynes Publications
859 Lawrence Dr, Newbury Park
(91320-2232)
PHONE...............................615 793-5414
John H Haynes, *Ch of Bd*
▲ **EMP:** 45 **EST:** 1993
SALES (est): 3.2MM
SALES (corp-wide): 2.6MM **Privately Held**
WEB: www.haynes.com
SIC: 2752 Commercial printing, lithographic
HQ: Haynes Group Limited
Sparkford
Yeovil
196 344-0635

(P-4383)
ORANGE COAST REPROGRAPHICS INC
Also Called: Mouse Graphics
659 W 19th St, Costa Mesa (92627-2715)
PHONE...............................949 548-5571
Constance Mary Lane, *CEO*
Rachel Harvey, *Manager*
EMP: 22 **EST:** 1947
SQ FT: 9,000
SALES (est): 4.3MM **Privately Held**
WEB: www.sendmouse.com
SIC: 2752 7336 2789 2759 Commercial printing, lithographic; commercial art & graphic design; bookbinding & related work; commercial printing

(P-4384)
PACER PRINT
9655 De Soto Ave, Chatsworth
(91311-5013)
PHONE...............................888 305-3144
Peter Varady, *CEO*
EMP: 17 **EST:** 2016
SALES (est): 1MM **Privately Held**
WEB: www.pacerprint.com
SIC: 2752 Commercial printing, lithographic

(P-4385)
PACIFIC WEST LITHO INC
3291 E Miraloma Ave, Anaheim
(92806-1910)
PHONE...............................714 579-0868
Chang Che Chou, *CEO*
Raymond Lai, *Info Tech Mgr*
John Brucheri, *Sales Mgr*
Paul Good, *Sales Staff*
EMP: 70 **EST:** 1984
SQ FT: 24,000
SALES (est): 10.4MM **Privately Held**
WEB: www.pacificwestlitho.com
SIC: 2752 Lithographing on metal; commercial printing, offset

(P-4386)
PARADISE PRINTING INC
13474 Pumice St, Norwalk (90650-5247)
PHONE...............................714 228-9628

Paul B Pistone, *CEO*
EMP: 30 **EST:** 1980
SQ FT: 48,000
SALES (est): 2.5MM **Privately Held**
WEB: www.paradiseprintingca.com
SIC: 2752 Commercial printing, offset

(P-4387)
PARS PUBLISHING CORP
Also Called: Grapheex
4485 Runway St, Simi Valley (93063-3436)
PHONE...............................818 280-0540
Mehran Kiankarimi, *President*
Mike Kian, *President*
Allan Yegani, *Treasurer*
Mahnaz Shidfar, *Vice Pres*
Vincent Fisher, *Admin Sec*
EMP: 14 **EST:** 1996
SQ FT: 40,000
SALES (est): 1.6MM **Privately Held**
WEB: www.grapheex.com
SIC: 2752 Commercial printing, offset

(P-4388)
PDF PRINT COMMUNICATIONS INC (PA)
2630 E 28th St, Long Beach (90755-2202)
PHONE...............................562 426-6978
Robert Albert Mullaney, *CEO*
Shirley Mullaney, *Treasurer*
Kevin J Mullaney, *Vice Pres*
Jeff Keller, *Production*
Leann Beltran, *Sales Staff*
EMP: 52 **EST:** 1973
SQ FT: 23,000
SALES (est): 16.9MM **Privately Held**
WEB: www.pdfpc.com
SIC: 2752 2761 Commercial printing, offset; manifold business forms

(P-4389)
PGI PACIFIC GRAPHICS INTL
14938 Nelson Ave, City of Industry
(91744-4330)
PHONE...............................626 336-7707
Yvonne Castillo Wasson, *CEO*
Kim Sankovich, *Partner*
Ricardo Wasson, *Vice Pres*
John Namy, *Sales Engr*
Gabe Weathers, *Manager*
EMP: 25 **EST:** 1989
SQ FT: 17,000
SALES (est): 5.4MM **Privately Held**
WEB: www.pacgraphics.com
SIC: 2752 2759 8742 7331 Commercial printing, offset; commercial printing; marketing consulting services; mailing service

(P-4390)
PHOTONIC CORP
5800 Uplander Way Ste 100, Culver City
(90230-6608)
PHONE...............................310 642-7975
Birendra Dutt, *President*
Dennis Mattock, *Sales Dir*
EMP: 15 **EST:** 2007
SALES (est): 359.1K **Privately Held**
WEB: www.apichip.com
SIC: 2752 Commercial printing, lithographic

(P-4391)
PINEGROVE INDUSTRIES INC
Also Called: Custom Printing
2001 Cabot Pl, Oxnard (93030-2666)
PHONE...............................805 485-3700
Charles Utts, *President*
Becky Utts, *Vice Pres*
Kristen Utts, *Accounting Mgr*
Kevin Mehle, *Representative*
EMP: 26 **EST:** 1975
SQ FT: 10,000
SALES (est): 1.8MM **Privately Held**
SIC: 2752 Commercial printing, offset

(P-4392)
POSTAL INSTANT PRESS INC (HQ)
Also Called: PIP PRINTING
26722 Plaza, Mission Viejo (92691-8051)
P.O. Box 9077 (92690-9077)
PHONE...............................949 348-5000
Dan Lowe, *Ch of Bd*
Richard Low, *President*
Dan Conger, *CFO*
Jyndhia Echevarria, *Vice Pres*

David C Rice, *Vice Pres*
EMP: 40
SQ FT: 25,000
SALES (est): 2.6MM
SALES (corp-wide): 19.9MM **Privately Held**
WEB: www.pip.com
SIC: 2752 6159 Commercial printing, offset; machinery & equipment finance leasing
PA: Franchise Services, Inc.
26722 Plaza
Mission Viejo CA 92691
949 348-5400

(P-4393)
PRECISION OFFSET INC
Also Called: Precision Services Group
15201 Woodlawn Ave, Tustin (92780-6418)
PHONE...............................949 752-1714
Lawrence Smith, *CEO*
Lorie Kluth, *President*
Greg Cocroft, *Vice Pres*
Faith Pantel, *Manager*
Dina Traylor, *Accounts Mgr*
EMP: 75 **EST:** 1979
SQ FT: 15,000
SALES (est): 20.8MM **Privately Held**
SIC: 2752 Commercial printing, offset

(P-4394)
PRIMARY COLOR SYSTEMS CORP (PA)
11130 Holder St, Cypress (90630-5162)
PHONE...............................949 660-7080
Daniel Hirt, *President*
Ronald Hirt, *Shareholder*
Vince Foxx, *Vice Pres*
Michael Gonzalez, *Vice Pres*
Drew Haygeman, *Vice Pres*
▲ **EMP:** 292 **EST:** 1984
SQ FT: 40,000
SALES (est): 61MM **Privately Held**
WEB: www.primarycolor.com
SIC: 2752 2759 Commercial printing, offset; commercial printing

(P-4395)
PRINTCOM INC
Also Called: Minuteman Press
14675 Titus St, Van Nuys (91402-4922)
PHONE...............................818 891-8282
Pamela K Berg, *President*
Kevin Berg, *CFO*
EMP: 13 **EST:** 1990
SQ FT: 5,100
SALES (est): 1.8MM **Privately Held**
WEB: www.printwithmmp.com
SIC: 2752 Commercial printing, lithographic

(P-4396)
PRINTERY INC
1762 Kaiser Ave, Irvine (92614-5706)
PHONE...............................949 757-1930
Massis Chahbazian, *CEO*
Joe Creazzo, *Sales Staff*
Isabel Packwood,
Mike Wilson, *Manager*
▲ **EMP:** 15 **EST:** 1989
SQ FT: 10,000
SALES (est): 4MM **Privately Held**
WEB: www.theprintery.com
SIC: 2752 Commercial printing, offset

(P-4397)
PRINTFIRM INC
21352 Nordhoff St Ste 104, Chatsworth
(91311-6908)
PHONE...............................818 992-1005
Masis Artounian, *President*
Alex Vartanian, *Manager*
EMP: 17 **EST:** 2000
SALES (est): 1.9MM **Privately Held**
WEB: www.printfirm.com
SIC: 2752 Commercial printing, offset

(P-4398)
PRINTING DIVISION INC
1933 N Main St, Orange (92865-4101)
PHONE...............................714 685-0111
Richard Baca, *CEO*
Sam Nooriala, *CFO*
EMP: 13 **EST:** 1997
SQ FT: 6,800

SALES (est): 605.8K **Privately Held**
WEB: www.printdivinc.com
SIC: 2752 Commercial printing, offset

(P-4399)
PRINTING ISLAND CORPORATION
11535 Martens River Cir, Fountain Valley
(92708-4201)
PHONE...............................714 668-1000
Philip Wang, *President*
Denise Pham, *Admin Sec*
EMP: 14 **EST:** 1985
SALES (est): 294K **Privately Held**
SIC: 2752 Commercial printing, offset

(P-4400)
PRINTING MANAGEMENT ASSOCIATES
17128 Edwards Rd, Cerritos (90703-2424)
P.O. Box 5037 (90703-5037)
PHONE...............................562 407-9977
Jeffrey Brady, *CEO*
Michael Lane, *President*
Clif McDougall, *Exec VP*
Rich Russell, *Vice Pres*
Adele Masuda, *Sales Staff*
▲ **EMP:** 19 **EST:** 1991
SQ FT: 12,600
SALES (est): 7MM **Privately Held**
WEB: www.printmgt.com
SIC: 2752 5111 Commercial printing, offset; printing paper

(P-4401)
PRINTING PALACE INC (PA)
2300 Lincoln Blvd, Santa Monica
(90405-2530)
PHONE...............................310 451-5151
Eli Albek, *President*
EMP: 19 **EST:** 1982
SQ FT: 8,000
SALES (est): 2.3MM **Privately Held**
WEB: www.printingpalace.com
SIC: 2752 Commercial printing, offset

(P-4402)
PRINTOGRAPH INC
7625 N San Fernando Rd, Burbank
(91505-1073)
PHONE...............................818 252-3000
Kristina Keshishyan, *Principal*
Shodja Talaee, *CFO*
Martin Ojeda, *Production*
EMP: 13 **EST:** 2014
SALES (est): 704.4K **Privately Held**
WEB: www.gotprint.com
SIC: 2752 Commercial printing, offset

(P-4403)
PRINTRUNNER LLC
Also Called: U-Nited Printing and Copy Ctr
8000 Haskell Ave, Van Nuys (91406-1321)
PHONE...............................888 296-5760
Dean Rabbani, *Mng Member*
Mike Zaya, *President*
Adam Berger, *CEO*
Brandon Kurtz, *Graphic Designe*
Kamie Davison, *Controller*
EMP: 32 **EST:** 1999
SQ FT: 50,000
SALES (est): 1.2MM **Privately Held**
WEB: www.printrunner.com
SIC: 2752 Commercial printing, offset

(P-4404)
PRINTS 4 LIFE
43145 Business Ctr Pkwy, Lancaster
(93535-4564)
PHONE...............................661 942-2233
EMP: 29 **EST:** 2016
SALES (est): 29.3MM **Privately Held**
WEB: www.learn4life.org
SIC: 2752 Commercial printing, lithographic

(P-4405)
PRINTXCEL - VISALIA
1424 E Tulare Ave, Visalia (93292-3647)
PHONE...............................559 636-6290
Jeff Trump, *General Mgr*
Betty Klaseus, *Sales Staff*
Donna Marquette, *Manager*
EMP: 17 **EST:** 2014

SALES (est): 1.6MM **Privately Held**
WEB: www.printxcel.com
SIC: 2752 Commercial printing, lithographic

(P-4406)
PRO DOCUMENT SOLUTIONS INC (PA)
Also Called: Pro Vote Solutions
1760 Commerce Way, Paso Robles (93446-3620)
PHONE..................................805 238-6680
George Phillips, *CEO*
Brad Stier, *President*
Noal Phillips, *COO*
Molly Comin, *CFO*
Diana Phillips, *Corp Secy*
▲ **EMP:** 50 **EST:** 1979
SQ FT: 35,000
SALES (est): 9.9MM **Privately Held**
WEB: www.prodocumentsolutions.com
SIC: 2752 Business forms, lithographed

(P-4407)
PRO MEDIA MERCHANTS
Also Called: Double Inks
3746 Foothill Blvd, La Crescenta (91214-1740)
PHONE..................................818 957-7114
Armen Issagholuian, *President*
David Hitzhusen, *Consultant*
▲ **EMP:** 13 **EST:** 2011
SALES (est): 524K **Privately Held**
SIC: 2752 Commercial printing, lithographic

(P-4408)
PROCESSORS MAILING INC
Also Called: Processors The
761 N Dodsworth Ave, Covina (91724-2408)
PHONE..................................626 358-5600
Anthony N Perone, *President*
Greg Hansen, *Prdtn Mgr*
Mark Perone, *Sales Mgr*
EMP: 21 **EST:** 1974
SQ FT: 8,000
SALES (est): 1.4MM **Privately Held**
WEB: www.theprocessors.com
SIC: 2752 7331 2791 Commercial printing, offset; mailing service; typesetting

(P-4409)
PROGRAPHICS INC
9200 Lower Azusa Rd, Rosemead (91770-1593)
PHONE..................................626 287-0417
Christina Stevens, *CEO*
Timothy Stevens, *President*
Elizabeth Cawley, *Vice Pres*
Jaime Colacio, *Vice Pres*
EMP: 40 **EST:** 1967
SQ FT: 23,000
SALES (est): 4.8MM **Privately Held**
WEB: www.prographicsllc.com
SIC: 2752 Commercial printing, offset

(P-4410)
PRPCO
Also Called: Poor Richard's Press
2226 Beebee St, San Luis Obispo (93401-5505)
PHONE..................................805 543-6844
Todd P Ventura, *President*
Mary Monroe, *CFO*
Richard C Blake, *Vice Pres*
Karen Evans, *Project Mgr*
Brian Burgess, *Accountant*
EMP: 35 **EST:** 2000
SALES (est): 6MM **Privately Held**
WEB: www.prpco.com
SIC: 2752 Commercial printing, offset

(P-4411)
Q TEAM
Also Called: Ryan Press
6400 Dale St, Buena Park (90621-3115)
PHONE..................................714 228-4465
Donna Quibodeaux, *President*
James Quibodeaux, *Treasurer*
Mike Quibodeaux, *Vice Pres*
Kip Dabbs, *Analyst*
EMP: 16
SQ FT: 13,000

SALES (est): 3.5MM **Privately Held**
WEB: www.ryanpress.com
SIC: 2752 Commercial printing, offset

(P-4412)
QG PRINTING IL LLC
Also Called: Quad Graphics
6688 Box Springs Blvd, Riverside (92507-0726)
PHONE..................................951 571-2500
Georg Decker, *Branch Mgr*
Tony Moyer, *Technology*
EMP: 114
SALES (corp-wide): 2.9B **Publicly Held**
SIC: 2752 Commercial printing, offset
HQ: Qg Printing Il Llc
N61w23044 Harrys Way
Sussex WI 53089

(P-4413)
QUEEN BEACH PRINTERS INC
937 Pine Ave, Long Beach (90813-4375)
P.O. Box 540 (90801-0540)
PHONE..................................562 436-8201
Nicholas W Edwards, *CEO*
William L Edwards Sr, *President*
Bill Edwards Jr, *COO*
William L Edwards Jr, *COO*
Virginia Noyes, *Vice Pres*
EMP: 30 **EST:** 1944
SQ FT: 25,000
SALES (est): 5.1MM **Privately Held**
WEB: www.qbprinters.com
SIC: 2752 7336 Commercial printing, offset; commercial art & graphic design

(P-4414)
RAINBOW MAGNETICS INCORPORATED
1 Whatney, Irvine (92618-2806)
PHONE..................................714 540-4777
Robert Knapp, *President*
Jennifer Knapp, *CFO*
◆ **EMP:** 14 **EST:** 1974
SQ FT: 13,174
SALES (est): 598.3K **Privately Held**
WEB: www.magneticattractions.com
SIC: 2752 3993 Commercial printing, offset; advertising novelties

(P-4415)
RAINTREE BUSINESS PRODUCTS INC
Also Called: B C T
23101 Terra Dr, Laguna Hills (92653-1320)
PHONE..................................949 859-0801
Joseph H Rachal Jr, *President*
Donna C Rachal, *Vice Pres*
EMP: 26 **EST:** 1981
SQ FT: 7,000
SALES (est): 639.6K **Privately Held**
WEB: www.bctlagunahills.com
SIC: 2752 Commercial printing, lithographic

(P-4416)
READY INDUSTRIES INC
Also Called: Ready Reproductions
1520 E 15th St, Los Angeles (90021-2712)
PHONE..................................213 749-2041
E H Reitz, *CEO*
Chuck Nix, *Treasurer*
EMP: 16 **EST:** 1968
SQ FT: 15,000
SALES (est): 2.2MM **Privately Held**
WEB: www.readyrepro.com
SIC: 2752 Photolithographic printing

(P-4417)
RED BRICK CORPORATION
Also Called: Design Printing
5364 Venice Blvd, Los Angeles (90019-5240)
PHONE..................................323 549-9444
Parviz Bina, *CEO*
Bijan Bina, *Vice Pres*
Wendy Galope, *Accountant*
Cindy Lauren, *Marketing Staff*
EMP: 18 **EST:** 1984
SQ FT: 8,000
SALES (est): 5.7MM **Privately Held**
WEB: www.dprintla.com
SIC: 2752 Commercial printing, offset

(P-4418)
RNJ PRINTING CORPORATION
116 23rd Pl, Manhattan Beach (90266-4301)
PHONE..................................310 638-7768
John Samuel Osten, *President*
Rose Cecola Osten, *CFO*
Alfredo Jimenez, *Manager*
Yvette Barnett, *Accounts Mgr*
EMP: 16 **EST:** 1977
SALES (est): 1.6MM **Privately Held**
WEB: www.mjprinting.com
SIC: 2752 2796 Commercial printing, offset; letterpress plates, preparation of

(P-4419)
SCHACHTEL CORPORATION (PA)
Also Called: Ctp Solutions
5236 Colodny Dr Ste 200, Agoura Hills (91301-2692)
PHONE..................................818 597-1222
Jack Schachtel, *President*
Jim Romano, *Exec VP*
Teresa Quan, *Controller*
Marill Bartz-Samuel, *Manager*
Deepa Rajaram, *Manager*
▼ **EMP:** 13 **EST:** 1990
SQ FT: 13,000
SALES (est): 8.3MM **Privately Held**
WEB: www.ctpsolutions.com
SIC: 5943 2752 7336 8721 Office forms & supplies; commercial printing, lithographic; graphic arts & related design; billing & bookkeeping service; check writing, signing & endorsing machines; commercial printing

(P-4420)
SEDAS PRINTING INC
5335 Santa Monica Blvd, Los Angeles (90029-1105)
PHONE..................................323 469-1034
John Rashidi, *President*
Seda Rashidi, *Vice Pres*
Eder Infante, *Graphic Designe*
EMP: 15 **EST:** 1984
SQ FT: 8,000
SALES (est): 2.2MM **Privately Held**
WEB: www.sedasprinting.com
SIC: 2752 Commercial printing, offset

(P-4421)
SELECT GRAPHICS
11931 Euclid St, Garden Grove (92840-2200)
PHONE..................................714 537-5250
Yung Phan, *Principal*
Laura Reeves, *Graphic Designe*
Christina Pham, *Accountant*
EMP: 15 **EST:** 1988
SQ FT: 2,703
SALES (est): 1.3MM **Privately Held**
WEB: www.selectgp.com
SIC: 2752 2759 Commercial printing, offset; commercial printing

(P-4422)
SHIFT CALENDARS INC
Also Called: Graphics United
809 N Glendora Ave, Covina (91724-2529)
PHONE..................................626 967-5862
Robert Breaux Jr, *President*
Brenda Moreno, *Office Mgr*
EMP: 15 **EST:** 1975
SQ FT: 6,500
SALES (est): 2.2MM **Privately Held**
SIC: 2752 Commercial printing, offset

(P-4423)
SID-MAR INC
Also Called: Stationery Exchange
23303 La Palma Ave, Yorba Linda (92887-4773)
PHONE..................................213 626-8121
Brian Rosenblum, *CEO*
Craig Rosenblum, *Vice Pres*
Darren Rosenblum, *Admin Sec*
EMP: 21 **EST:** 1976
SQ FT: 14,000
SALES (est): 1.5MM **Privately Held**
WEB: www.bluespaceinteriors.com
SIC: 5943 2752 Office forms & supplies; commercial printing, offset

(P-4424)
SIR SPEEDY INC (HQ)
26722 Plaza, Mission Viejo (92691-8051)
P.O. Box 9077 (92690-9077)
PHONE..................................949 348-5000
Don Lowe, *CEO*
Alison Trovarelli, *Managing Prtnr*
Richard Lowe, *President*
Andrew Dworin, *COO*
Dan Conger, *CFO*
EMP: 43
SQ FT: 44,000
SALES: 7.9MM
SALES (corp-wide): 19.9MM **Privately Held**
WEB: www.sirspeedy.com
SIC: 2752 Commercial printing, lithographic
PA: Franchise Services, Inc.
26722 Plaza
Mission Viejo CA 92691
949 348-5400

(P-4425)
SOUTHWEST OFFSET PRTG CO INC (PA)
13650 Gramercy Pl, Gardena (90249-2453)
PHONE..................................310 965-9154
Greg McDonald, *CEO*
Mark Franco, *President*
Jose Martinez, *President*
Art Spear, *CFO*
Bill Elliott, *Vice Pres*
▲ **EMP:** 275 **EST:** 1986
SQ FT: 45,000
SALES (est): 42.5MM **Privately Held**
WEB: www.southwestoffset.com
SIC: 2752 Commercial printing, offset

(P-4426)
STOUGHTON PRINTING CO
130 N Sunset Ave, City of Industry (91744-3595)
PHONE..................................626 961-3678
Jack Stoughton Jr, *President*
Clay Stoughton, *Vice Pres*
Rob Maushund, *Production*
EMP: 35 **EST:** 1952
SQ FT: 21,000
SALES (est): 4.7MM **Privately Held**
WEB: www.stoughtonprinting.com
SIC: 2752 Commercial printing, offset

(P-4427)
SUMI PRINTING & BINDING INC
Also Called: Sumi Office Services
1139 E Janis St, Carson (90746-1306)
PHONE..................................310 769-1600
Roland Sumi, *President*
John Castillo, *Plant Mgr*
EMP: 14 **EST:** 1989
SALES (est): 2.8MM **Privately Held**
WEB: www.sumiprinting.com
SIC: 2752 Commercial printing, offset

(P-4428)
SUPERIOR LITHOGRAPHICS INC
3055 Bandini Blvd, Vernon (90058-4109)
PHONE..................................323 263-8400
Douglas Rawson, *CEO*
Carol Rawson, *President*
Megan Simmons, *Vice Pres*
Ricardo Villa, *Technician*
Hector Romo, *Plant Mgr*
▲ **EMP:** 90 **EST:** 1982
SQ FT: 60,000
SALES (est): 22MM **Privately Held**
WEB: www.superiorlithographics.com
SIC: 2752 Commercial printing, offset

(P-4429)
SUPERPRINT LITHOGRAPHICS INC
8332 Secura Way, Santa Fe Springs (90670-2204)
PHONE..................................562 698-8001
Chao-Tung Chen, *CEO*
Roy Chen, *President*
Michael Chen, *General Mgr*
Erika Delun, *Accountant*
Sal Dipasquale, *Sales Staff*
EMP: 15 **EST:** 1978
SQ FT: 30,000

SALES (est): 3.9MM **Privately Held**
WEB: www.superprintla.com
SIC: 2752 Commercial printing, offset

(P-4430)
SUPREME GRAPHICS INC
1201 N Miller St, Anaheim (92806-1933)
PHONE..........................310 531-8300
Ramin Kohanteb, *President*
Jesse Rodriguez, *Supervisor*
EMP: 18 EST: 2005
SALES (est): 2.6MM **Privately Held**
WEB: www.supremegraphicsinc.com
SIC: 2752 Commercial printing, offset

(P-4431)
TAILGATE PRINTING INC
2930 S Fairview St, Santa Ana
(92704-6503)
PHONE..........................714 966-3035
Maria C Vega, *President*
Colleen Madrid, *Executive*
Jennifer Garcia, *Sales Staff*
EMP: 90 EST: 2008
SQ FT: 80,000
SALES (est): 9.4MM **Privately Held**
WEB: www.tailgatela.com
SIC: 2752 Commercial printing, offset

(P-4432)
TAJEN GRAPHICS INC
Also Called: Apollo Printing & Graphics
2100 W Lincoln Ave Ste B, Anaheim
(92801-5642)
PHONE..........................714 527-3122
Dhansukhlal Ratanjee, *President*
Sam Gasper, *Officer*
Ken Ratanjee, *Vice Pres*
Mike Alurac, *Sales Executive*
EMP: 30 EST: 1977
SQ FT: 1,800
SALES (est): 6.2MM **Privately Held**
WEB: www.sirspeedy-anaheim.com
SIC: 2752 2791 Commercial printing, off-
set; typesetting, computer controlled

(P-4433)
TAM PRINTING INC
2961 E White Star Ave, Anaheim
(92806-2630)
PHONE..........................714 224-4488
Tam Bui, *President*
Debbie Trinh, *Director*
CHI Trinh, *Manager*
EMP: 19 EST: 1986
SQ FT: 10,000
SALES (est): 3MM **Privately Held**
WEB: www.tamprinting.com
SIC: 2752 Commercial printing, offset

(P-4434)
TEC COLOR CRAFT (PA)
Also Called: TEC Color Craft Products
1860 Wright Ave, La Verne (91750-5824)
PHONE..........................909 392-9000
Edgar A Frenkiel, *CEO*
Jim Evans, *VP Sales*
Blake Frenkiel, *Marketing Mgr*
Tracie Hodgson, *Sales Staff*
Brian Evans, *Representative*
▲ EMP: 40 EST: 1960
SQ FT: 8,000
SALES (est): 5.5MM **Privately Held**
WEB: www.teccolorcraft.com
SIC: 2752 Commercial printing, offset

(P-4435)
TECHNOLOGY TRAINING CORP
Also Called: Avalon Communications
3238 W 131st St, Hawthorne (90250-5517)
PHONE..........................310 644-7777
Richard D Lytle, *President*
EMP: 54
SALES (corp-wide): 9.7MM **Privately
Held**
WEB: www.ttcus.com
SIC: 2752 7331 3577 Commercial print-
ing, offset; direct mail advertising serv-
ices; computer peripheral equipment
PA: Technology Training Corp
369 Van Ness Way Ste 735
Torrance CA 90501
310 320-8110

(P-4436)
THAI PRINT USA LLC (PA)
8666 Garvey Ave Ste C, Rosemead
(91770-3269)
PHONE..........................626 872-6600
Tanya Brown,
EMP: 13 EST: 2011
SALES (est): 138.2K **Privately Held**
SIC: 2752 Commercial printing, offset

(P-4437)
THE LIGATURE INC (HQ)
Also Called: Echelon Fine Printing
4909 Alcoa Ave, Vernon (90058-3022)
PHONE..........................323 585-6000
Tom Clifford, *Vice Pres*
Dave Meyer, *Vice Pres*
Linda H Pennell, *Admin Sec*
Denyse Owens, *VP Finance*
Joseph Fontana, *Director*
EMP: 50 EST: 1920
SQ FT: 47,415
SALES (est): 12.4MM
SALES (corp-wide): 3.6B **Privately Held**
WEB: www.echelonprint.com
SIC: 2752 2759 Commercial printing, off-
set; invitation & stationery printing & en-
graving
PA: Taylor Corporation
1725 Roe Crest Dr
North Mankato MN 56003
507 625-2828

(P-4438)
THOMAS BURT
Also Called: Ink Spots
5095 Brooks St, Montclair (91763-4804)
P.O. Box 2086, Arcadia (91077-2086)
PHONE..........................626 301-9065
Thomas Burt, *Owner*
EMP: 15 EST: 1987
SQ FT: 15,000
SALES (est): 1.8MM **Privately Held**
SIC: 2752 Commercial printing, offset

(P-4439)
TOUCH LITHO COMPANY
7215 E Gage Ave, Commerce
(90040-3812)
PHONE..........................562 927-8899
Michael Wu, *President*
Alex Wu, *Manager*
▲ EMP: 15
SQ FT: 6,000
SALES (est): 3.2MM **Privately Held**
WEB: www.touchlitho.com
SIC: 2752 Commercial printing, offset

(P-4440)
TREND OFFSET PRINTING SVCS INC
Also Called: TREND OFFSET PRINTING
SERVICES INCORPORATED
3791 Catalina St, Los Alamitos
(90720-2402)
PHONE..........................562 598-2446
Paul Rhilindger, *Manager*
Randy Ginsberg, *Vice Pres*
EMP: 425
SALES (corp-wide): 742.8MM **Privately
Held**
WEB: www.mittera.com
SIC: 2752 2732 Commercial printing, off-
set; books: printing & binding
HQ: Trend Offset Printing Services, Inc.
3701 Catalina St
Los Alamitos CA 90720
562 598-2446

(P-4441)
TU VETS PRINTING
5635 E Beverly Blvd, Los Angeles
(90022-2803)
PHONE..........................323 723-4569
Herman Waer III, *President*
Henry Ayala Jr, *Corp Secy*
Henry J Ayala Jr, *Admin Sec*
EMP: 17 EST: 1948
SQ FT: 7,500
SALES (est): 554.4K **Privately Held**
SIC: 2752 Commercial printing, offset; let-
ters, circular or form: lithographed

(P-4442)
TYPECRAFT INC
Also Called: Typecraft Wood & Jones
2040 E Walnut St, Pasadena (91107-5804)
PHONE..........................626 795-8093
D Harry Montgomery, *President*
Jeffrey J Gish, *Vice Pres*
Jeffrey Gish, *Vice Pres*
Jj Gish, *Vice Pres*
Mark Burks, *Plant Mgr*
EMP: 38 EST: 1947
SQ FT: 19,000
SALES (est): 6MM **Privately Held**
WEB: www.typecraft.com
SIC: 2752 Commercial printing, offset; cir-
culars, lithographed; posters, lithographed

(P-4443)
ULTIMATE PRINT SOURCE INC
Also Called: Printing 4him
2070 S Hellman Ave, Ontario (91761-8018)
PHONE..........................909 947-5292
Jeffrey J Ferrazzano, *CEO*
Edith Le Leux, *Treasurer*
Desiree Ferrazzano, *Vice Pres*
Jon Le Leux, *Admin Sec*
Michelle Melendez,
EMP: 30 EST: 1987
SQ FT: 20,000
SALES (est): 5.5MM **Privately Held**
WEB: www.ultimateprintsource.com
SIC: 2752 Commercial printing, offset

(P-4444)
UNI-SPORT INC
16933 Gramercy Pl, Gardena
(90247-5207)
PHONE..........................310 217-4587
Thomas Hebert, *President*
Jorge Hernandez, *Vice Pres*
Kris Beasley, *General Mgr*
Adrien Dotson, *Sales Staff*
Geovani Guerra, *Sales Staff*
◆ EMP: 25 EST: 2006
SQ FT: 10,000
SALES (est): 3MM **Privately Held**
WEB: www.uni-sport.com
SIC: 2752 Commercial printing, litho-
graphic

(P-4445)
UNIQUE IMAGE INC
19365 Bus Center Dr Ste 4, Northridge
(91324-3581)
PHONE..........................818 727-7785
Wafa Kanan, *President*
EMP: 13 EST: 1993
SQ FT: 15,400
SALES (est): 2.6MM **Privately Held**
WEB: www.uniqueimageinc.com
SIC: 2752 2741 7311 7331 Commercial
printing, lithographic; miscellaneous pub-
lishing; advertising agencies; direct mail
advertising services; commercial art &
graphic design; public relations services

(P-4446)
UNIVERSAL PRINTING SVCS INC
Also Called: Color Tech Commercial Printing
26012 Atlantic Ocean Dr, Lake Forest
(92630-8843)
PHONE..........................951 788-1500
Gregg Baxter, *President*
Sharon Baxter, *Vice Pres*
EMP: 16 EST: 1985
SQ FT: 2,800
SALES (est): 919.9K **Privately Held**
SIC: 2752 Commercial printing, offset

(P-4447)
V3 PRINTING CORPORATION
Also Called: V 3
200 N Elevar St, Oxnard (93030-7969)
PHONE..........................805 981-2600
David Wilson, *President*
Michael Szanger, *Vice Pres*
Dean Venturaprint, *Opers Staff*
Dave Loeppke, *Representative*
EMP: 80 EST: 1959
SQ FT: 4,000
SALES (est): 18MM **Privately Held**
WEB: www.printv3.com
SIC: 2752 Lithographing on metal

(P-4448)
VALLEY BUSINESS PRINTERS INC
Also Called: Valley Printers
6355 Topanga Canyon Blvd # 225, Wood-
land Hills (91367-2118)
PHONE..........................818 362-7771
Michael Flannery, *CEO*
Bruce Bolkin, *President*
Karen S Flannery, *Corp Secy*
Russell Sacks, *Sales Mgr*
▲ EMP: 92 EST: 1965
SALES (est): 9.2MM **Privately Held**
WEB: www.valleyprinters.net
SIC: 2752 2759 Commercial printing, off-
set; commercial printing

(P-4449)
VARIABLE IMAGE PRINTING
16540 Aston Ste A, Irvine (92606-4805)
PHONE..........................949 296-1444
Paul O Brien, *President*
Bob Stewart, *Vice Pres*
Kevin Lite, *Prdtn Mgr*
EMP: 14 EST: 2000
SQ FT: 12,400
SALES (est): 812.2K **Privately Held**
WEB: www.variableimageprinting.com
SIC: 2752 Commercial printing, offset

(P-4450)
VOMELA SPECIALTY COMPANY
9810 Bell Ranch Dr, Santa Fe Springs
(90670-2952)
PHONE..........................562 944-3853
Loren Maxwell, *Branch Mgr*
EMP: 42
SALES (corp-wide): 258MM **Privately
Held**
WEB: www.vomela.com
SIC: 2752 7336 Poster & decal printing,
lithographic; commercial art & graphic de-
sign
PA: Vomela Specialty Company
845 Minnehaha Ave E
Saint Paul MN 55106
651 228-2200

(P-4451)
W B MASON CO INC
5911 E Washington Blvd, Commerce
(90040-2412)
PHONE..........................888 926-2766
EMP: 30
SALES (corp-wide): 1B **Privately Held**
WEB: www.wbmason.com
SIC: 5943 5712 2752 Office forms & sup-
plies; office furniture; commercial printing,
lithographic
PA: W. B. Mason Co., Inc.
59 Ctr St
Brockton MA 02301
508 586-3434

(P-4452)
WANDA MATRANGA
Also Called: Printing Place, The
41651 Corporate Way Ste 5, Palm Desert
(92260-1987)
P.O. Box 12827 (92255-2827)
PHONE..........................760 773-4701
Wanda Matranga, *Owner*
Larry Espinola, *Project Mgr*
EMP: 13 EST: 1977
SQ FT: 7,000
SALES (est): 1.2MM **Privately Held**
SIC: 2752 Commercial printing, offset

(P-4453)
WE DO GRAPHICS INC
1150 N Main St, Orange (92867-3421)
PHONE..........................714 997-7390
Douglas K Le Mieux, *President*
Heidi G Le Mieux, *CFO*
Steven I Lehrer, *Vice Pres*
Kevin Magula, *Manager*
▲ EMP: 38 EST: 1980
SQ FT: 23,000
SALES (est): 6.3MM **Privately Held**
WEB: www.wedographics.com
SIC: 2752 Commercial printing, offset

(P-4454)
WEBER PRINTING COMPANY INC
1124 E Del Amo Blvd, Carson (90746-3180)
PHONE.................................310 639-5064
Richard M Weber, *President*
Lynda Slack, *CFO*
Steven Weber, *Vice Pres*
Kathleen McGuire, *Sales Staff*
EMP: 35 EST: 1946
SQ FT: 30,000
SALES (est): 4.8MM **Privately Held**
WEB: www.weberprint.com
SIC: 2752 Commercial printing, offset

(P-4455)
WEST COAST BUSINESS PRTRS INC
Also Called: West Coast Digital
9822 Independence Ave, Chatsworth (91311-4319)
PHONE.................................818 709-4980
Arthur Worthington, *President*
Patricia Worthington, *Admin Sec*
EMP: 17 EST: 1987
SQ FT: 10,000
SALES (est): 934.3K **Privately Held**
SIC: 2752 5112 2759 Commercial printing, offset; envelopes; commercial printing

(P-4456)
WESTATES INC
Also Called: Westates Automotive Promotions
6800 Orangethorpe Ave H, Buena Park (90620-1366)
PHONE.................................714 523-7600
Dale W Becker, *President*
Natalie Pohl, *Corp Secy*
Doug Pohl, *Vice Pres*
Gerald Mateo, *Production*
Keith Ana, *Sales Staff*
EMP: 28 EST: 1978
SQ FT: 12,900
SALES (est): 7.8MM **Privately Held**
WEB: www.westates.net
SIC: 5961 2752 Mail order house; commercial printing, offset

(P-4457)
WESTERN PRTG & GRAPHICS LLC (PA)
Also Called: Western Printing and Label
675 N Main St, Orange (92868-1103)
PHONE.................................714 532-3946
Aaron David Smith,
Cynthia Joan Smith,
Marina Evanov, *Accounts Mgr*
EMP: 22 EST: 1981
SALES (est): 3.3MM **Privately Held**
WEB: www.westprint.com
SIC: 2752 2791 2759 2741 Commercial printing, offset; typesetting; commercial printing; miscellaneous publishing

(P-4458)
WESTMINSTER PRESS INC
4906 W 1st St, Santa Ana (92703-3110)
PHONE.................................714 210-2881
Gary Tang, *CEO*
Thoai Tang, *Vice Pres*
Tri Tang, *Vice Pres*
▲ **EMP: 50 EST:** 1986
SQ FT: 10,000
SALES (est): 7.6MM **Privately Held**
SIC: 2752 Color lithography

(P-4459)
WESTROCK CP LLC
MPS Corona
2577 Research Dr, Corona (92882-7607)
PHONE.................................951 273-7900
Steven Voorhees, *CEO*
EMP: 64
SALES (corp-wide): 17.5B **Publicly Held**
WEB: www.westrock.com
SIC: 2752 Commercial printing, offset
HQ: Westrock Cp, Llc
1000 Abernathy Rd Ste 125
Atlanta GA 30328

(P-4460)
WIRZ & CO
444 Colton Ave, Colton (92324-3019)
PHONE.................................909 825-6970
Charles Fred Wirz, *Owner*
Michael Miller, *Analyst*
Kelly Gettings, *Sales Staff*
EMP: 18 EST: 1985
SQ FT: 8,000
SALES (est): 1.8MM **Privately Held**
WEB: www.wirzco.com
SIC: 2752 Commercial printing, offset

(P-4461)
WS PACKAGING-BLAKE PRINTERY
Also Called: Poor Richards Press
2224 Beebee St, San Luis Obispo (93401-5505)
PHONE.................................805 543-6844
Bruce Dickinson, *Branch Mgr*
EMP: 34
SQ FT: 3,500 **Privately Held**
SIC: 2752 2621 2791 Commercial printing, offset; wrapping paper; typesetting, computer controlled
HQ: Ws Packaging-Blake Printery
2222 Beebee St
San Luis Obispo CA 93401
805 543-6843

(P-4462)
WTPC INC
Also Called: World Trade Printing Company
12082 Western Ave, Garden Grove (92841-2913)
PHONE.................................714 903-2500
Joe Ratanjee, *CEO*
John Gratian, *General Mgr*
Felipe Delgado, *Prdtn Mgr*
Joe Ratangee, *Sales Executive*
Teresa King, *Marketing Staff*
▲ **EMP: 30 EST:** 1991
SQ FT: 25,000
SALES (est): 7.7MM **Privately Held**
WEB: www.wtpcenter.com
SIC: 2752 Commercial printing, offset

(P-4463)
X-IGENT PRINTING INC
1001 Goodrich Blvd, Commerce (90022-5102)
PHONE.................................323 837-9779
Omar Rodriguez, *President*
Hugo Cervantes, *Admin Sec*
Isabel Serrano, *Technology*
EMP: 15 EST: 2001
SQ FT: 6,000
SALES (est): 4.4MM **Privately Held**
WEB: www.xigentprints.com
SIC: 2752 Commercial printing, offset

(P-4464)
ZOO PRINTING INC (PA)
Also Called: Zoo Printing Trade Printer
1225 Los Angeles St, Glendale (91204-2403)
PHONE.................................310 253-7751
Dan Doron, *President*
Maria Camins, *Vice Pres*
Mark Larson, *Software Engr*
Shawn Mahoney, *Prgrmr*
Jeff Bentz, *Plant Mgr*
▲ **EMP: 83 EST:** 2001
SALES (est): 18.9MM **Privately Held**
WEB: www.zooprinting.com
SIC: 2752 Commercial printing, offset

2754 Commercial Printing: Gravure

(P-4465)
ALNA ENVELOPE COMPANY INC
1567 E 25th St, Los Angeles (90011-1887)
PHONE.................................323 235-3161
Al Azus, *President*
Hedi Azus, *Treasurer*
Max Candiotty, *Vice Pres*
James Arnold, *Finance Mgr*
Jose Caldera, *Prdtn Mgr*
EMP: 14 EST: 1955
SQ FT: 14,000

SALES (est): 513.8K **Privately Held**
WEB: www.alnaenvelope.com
SIC: 2754 2759 Envelopes: gravure printing; commercial printing

(P-4466)
ONEIL CAPITAL MANAGEMENT INC
12655 Beatrice St, Los Angeles (90066-7300)
PHONE.................................310 448-6400
William O Neil, *CEO*
Laura Dahlkamp, *President*
Linda Clapper, *Vice Pres*
Donna Dailey, *Vice Pres*
Bill Hickey, *VP Bus Dvlpt*
▲ **EMP: 152 EST:** 1973
SQ FT: 70,000
SALES (est): 51MM
SALES (corp-wide): 335.6MM **Privately Held**
WEB: www.oneildigitalsolutions.com
SIC: 2754 2732 2741 2711 Catalogs: gravure printing, not published on site; book printing; miscellaneous publishing; newspapers
PA: Data Analysis Inc.
12655 Beatrice St
Los Angeles CA 90066
310 448-6800

(P-4467)
QPE INC
Also Called: Quality Packaging and Engrg
1372 Mcgaw Ave, Irvine (92614-5539)
PHONE.................................949 263-0381
Kirk WEI, *President*
Rachel Lee, *CFO*
Joseph S Chiang, *Corp Secy*
Joseph Chiang, *Admin Sec*
▲ **EMP: 18 EST:** 1986
SQ FT: 10,000
SALES (est): 2.2MM **Privately Held**
WEB: www.qpeinc.com
SIC: 2754 7389 Labels: gravure printing; packaging & labeling services

(P-4468)
RESOURCE LABEL GROUP LLC
Also Called: Axiom Label & Packaging
1360 W Walnut Pkwy, Compton (90220-5029)
PHONE.................................310 603-8910
Kieron Delahunt, *Branch Mgr*
EMP: 50 Privately Held
WEB: www.resourcelabel.com
SIC: 2754 2752 Labels: gravure printing; commercial printing, lithographic
PA: Resource Label Group, Llc
147 Seaboard Ln
Franklin TN 37067

(P-4469)
WESTERN SHELD ACQUISITIONS LLC (PA)
Also Called: Western Shield Label
2146 E Gladwick St, Rancho Dominguez (90220-6203)
PHONE.................................310 527-6212
Graham C Weaver, *Mng Member*
Thomas Moyer, *President*
Frank Connelly, *CEO*
Rod Couser, *Vice Pres*
Jessica Cervantes, *Receptionist*
EMP: 18 EST: 1970
SQ FT: 17,000
SALES (est): 9.9MM **Privately Held**
WEB: www.westernshield.com
SIC: 2754 3172 2752 Labels: gravure printing; tobacco pouches; coupons, lithographed

2759 Commercial Printing

(P-4470)
4 OVER LLC (HQ)
5900 San Fernando Rd D, Glendale (91202-2773)
PHONE.................................818 246-1170
Zarik Megerdichian, *CEO*
Tina Hartounian, *President*
Russell Chance, *CFO*
Lala Elyasi, *Officer*

Yiannis Lykogiannis, *Vice Pres*
▲ **EMP: 162 EST:** 2001
SALES (est): 172.3MM **Privately Held**
WEB: www.4over.com
SIC: 2759 7336 Commercial printing; commercial art & graphic design

(P-4471)
4 OVER LLC
1225 Los Angeles St, Glendale (91204-2403)
PHONE.................................818 246-1170
Erika Takenaka, *Principal*
Dean Rossi, *Exec VP*
Amber Solorzano, *Admin Asst*
Alexandra Minchaca, *CIO*
Vahe Safaian, *Research*
EMP: 15
SALES (corp-wide): 172.3MM **Privately Held**
WEB: www.4over.com
SIC: 2759 Screen printing
HQ: 4 Over, Llc
5900 San Fernando Rd D
Glendale CA 91202
818 246-1170

(P-4472)
6480 CORPORATION
Also Called: First Press
7230 Coldwater Canyon Ave, North Hollywood (91605-4203)
PHONE.................................818 765-9670
Daniel Mamane, *President*
Richard Eliazar, *General Mgr*
EMP: 13 EST: 1992
SQ FT: 25,000
SALES (est): 838K **Privately Held**
SIC: 2759 3695 Bag, wrapper & seal printing & engraving; magnetic & optical recording media

(P-4473)
A F E INDUSTRIES INC (PA)
13233 Barton Cir, Whittier (90605-3255)
P.O. Box 3303, Santa Fe Springs (90670-1303)
PHONE.................................562 944-6889
Fred Elhami, *President*
Ruth Elhami, *Treasurer*
Tiffany Elhami, *Chief Mktg Ofcr*
EMP: 15 EST: 1981
SQ FT: 27,000
SALES (est): 18.9MM **Privately Held**
WEB: www.afeindustries.com
SIC: 2759 Screen printing; imprinting; letterpress printing

(P-4474)
ABC IMAGING OF WASHINGTON
17240 Red Hill Ave, Irvine (92614-5628)
PHONE.................................949 419-3728
Matthew Marshall, *Executive*
EMP: 17
SALES (corp-wide): 124.9MM **Privately Held**
WEB: www.abcimaging.com
SIC: 2759 Commercial printing
PA: Abc Imaging Of Washington, Inc
5290 Shawnee Rd Ste 300
Alexandria VA 22312
202 429-8870

(P-4475)
ABC IMAGING OF WASHINGTON
13573 Larwin Cir, Santa Fe Springs (90670-5032)
PHONE.................................562 375-7280
EMP: 17
SALES (corp-wide): 124.9MM **Privately Held**
WEB: www.abcimaging.com
SIC: 2759 Advertising literature: printing
PA: Abc Imaging Of Washington, Inc
5290 Shawnee Rd Ste 300
Alexandria VA 22312
202 429-8870

(P-4476)
ABF PRINTS INC
102 N Riverside Ave, Rialto (92376-5922)
PHONE.................................909 875-7163
Kevin M Danko, *CEO*
Matthew Danko, *Prdtn Mgr*
Victor Maglio, *Sales Executive*
Keith Sabo, *Sales Staff*

PRODUCTS & SVCS

EMP: 25 EST: 2005
SQ FT: 10,000
SALES (est): 2.5MM Privately Held
WEB: www.abfprints.com
SIC: 2759 7323 Commercial printing;
   credit reporting services

(P-4477)
ADCRAFT PRODUCTS CO INC
1230 S Sherman St, Anaheim
(92805-6455)
PHONE................................714 776-1230
Randy C Mottram, *President*
Keith A Mottram, *Vice Pres*
Jose Lujan, *Graphic Designe*
Jocelyn Sicat, *Accounting Mgr*
Sal Reyna, *Plant Mgr*
EMP: 27 EST: 1977
SALES (est): 7.1MM Privately Held
WEB: www.adcraftlabels.com
SIC: 2759 Labels & seals: printing

(P-4478)
ALL-STAR LETTERING INC
9419 Ann St, Santa Fe Springs
(90670-2613)
PHONE................................562 404-5995
Paul Possemato, *President*
Palma Possemato, *Treasurer*
Arcadio Aguayo, *Vice Pres*
Susan Possemato, *Vice Pres*
Henry Ojeda, *General Mgr*
EMP: 21 EST: 1969
SALES (est): 4.7MM Privately Held
WEB: www.allstarlettering.com
SIC: 2759 3555 2396 Screen printing;
   printing trades machinery; automotive &
   apparel trimmings

(P-4479)
AMERICAN ZABIN INTL INC
3933 S Hill St, Los Angeles (90037-1313)
PHONE................................213 746-3770
Alan Faiola, *CEO*
Steven Garfinkle, *President*
Eric Sedso, *Vice Pres*
Lola Chernova, *Executive*
◆ EMP: 32 EST: 1993
SQ FT: 18,000
SALES (est): 10MM Privately Held
WEB: www.zabin.com
SIC: 2759 Tags: printing

(P-4480)
ARACA MERCHANDISE LP
Araca Ink
459 Park Ave, San Fernando (91340-2525)
PHONE................................818 743-5400
Judy Courney, *Manager*
EMP: 97 Privately Held
WEB: www.araca.com
SIC: 2759 Screen printing
HQ: Araca Merchandise L.P.
   545 W 45th St Fl 10
   New York NY 10036

(P-4481)
ARTISAN NAMEPLATE AWARDS
CORP
Also Called: Weber Precision Graphics
2730 S Shannon St, Santa Ana
(92704-5232)
PHONE................................714 556-6222
Henry G Weber, *President*
Manny Estrada, *COO*
Margaret Weber, *Corp Secy*
Jeff Johnson, *Exec VP*
Ricardo Martinez, *Planning Mgr*
EMP: 33 EST: 1972
SQ FT: 12,160
SALES (est): 6.3MM Privately Held
WEB: www.weberpg.com
SIC: 2759 3479 Labels & seals: printing;
   coating of metals with plastic or resins

(P-4482)
ARTISAN SCREEN PRINTING
INC
1055 W 5th St, Azusa (91702-3313)
PHONE................................626 815-2700
Vasant N Doabria, *President*
C P Kheni, *Corp Secy*
Praful Bajaria, *Vice Pres*
▲ EMP: 120
SQ FT: 90,000

SALES (est): 15.3MM Privately Held
WEB: www.artisanscreen.com
SIC: 2759 Screen printing

(P-4483)
ASPE INC
42295 Avnida Alvrado Unit, Temecula
(92590)
PHONE................................951 296-2595
Alexander Szyszko, *CEO*
Matt Yeazel, *Sales Staff*
▲ EMP: 15 EST: 2011
SALES (est): 2MM Privately Held
WEB: www.aspesite.com
SIC: 2759 Screen printing

(P-4484)
BASIC BUSINESS FORMS INC
561 Kinetic Dr Ste A, Oxnard (93030-7947)
PHONE................................805 278-4551
EMP: 30
SALES (est): 2.7MM Privately Held
SIC: 2759 2761 Commercial Printing Mfg
   Manifold Business Forms

(P-4485)
BEYONDGREEN BTECH INC
DBA BYND
1202 E Wakeham Ave, Santa Ana
(92705-4145)
PHONE................................800 983-7221
Veejay Patell, *CEO*
Achyut Patel, *Vice Pres*
EMP: 15 EST: 2018
SQ FT: 8,500
SALES (est): 125K
SALES (corp-wide): 150K Privately Held
SIC: 2759 2875 3089 2656 Bags, plastic:
   printing; compost; injection molded fin-
   ished plastic products; injection molding
   of plastics; straws, drinking: made from
   purchased material; eating utensils, dis-
   posable plastic
PA: Prosourcing, Inc.
   12 Santa Catalina
   Rcho Sta Marg CA 92688
   949 246-6868

(P-4486)
BLACKBURN ALTON
INVSTMENTS LLC
Also Called: Foster Print
700 E Alton Ave, Santa Ana (92705-5610)
PHONE................................714 731-2000
Dennis M Blackburn,
EMP: 34 EST: 2011
SALES (est): 1.6MM Privately Held
SIC: 2759 Commercial printing

(P-4487)
BLC WC INC (PA)
Also Called: Imperial Marking Systems
13260 Moore St, Cerritos (90703-2228)
PHONE................................562 926-1452
Ernest Wong, *President*
Timothy Koontz, *CFO*
Donald Ingle, *Admin Sec*
Pat Ortiz, *Persnl Dir*
EMP: 120 EST: 1989
SQ FT: 60,000
SALES (est): 21.2MM Privately Held
WEB: www.resourcelabel.com
SIC: 2759 Labels & seals: printing

(P-4488)
BRIXEN & SONS INC
2100 S Fairview St, Santa Ana
(92704-4516)
PHONE................................714 566-1444
Martin Corey Brixen, *President*
Son Nguyen, *Treasurer*
Elizabeth Northrop, *Purch Agent*
Pam Drzymkowski, *Sales Staff*
Gabriel Oseguera, *Manager*
▲ EMP: 27 EST: 1992
SQ FT: 32,000
SALES (est): 5.9MM Privately Held
WEB: www.brixen.com
SIC: 2759 3993 Screen printing; signs &
   advertising specialties

(P-4489)
BROOK & WHITTLE LIMITED
Also Called: Label Impressions
1177 N Grove St, Anaheim (92806-2110)
PHONE................................714 634-3466

Remy Zada, *Branch Mgr*
EMP: 42 Privately Held
WEB: www.brookandwhittle.com
SIC: 2759 Labels & seals: printing
PA: Brook & Whittle Limited
   20 Carter Dr
   Guilford CT 06437

(P-4490)
C T L PRINTING INDS INC
Also Called: Cal Tape & Label
1741 W Lincoln Ave Ste A, Anaheim
(92801-6716)
PHONE................................714 635-2980
James Edward Hudson, *CEO*
J J Hudson, *Ch of Bd*
Dave Adams, *Principal*
EMP: 25 EST: 1960
SQ FT: 8,950
SALES (est): 5MM Privately Held
WEB:
www.ctlprintingindustries.openfos.com
SIC: 2759 Labels & seals: printing; decals:
   printing

(P-4491)
CAL SPRINGS LLC
6250 N Irwindale Ave, Irwindale
(91702-3208)
PHONE................................562 943-5599
▲ EMP: 54
SALES (est): 4.6MM Privately Held
SIC: 2759 3069 3751 5149 Promotional
   Product Water Bottle And Bicycle Para-
   phernalia Wholesale And Manufacture

(P-4492)
CCL LABEL (DELAWARE) INC
576 College Commerce Way, Upland
(91786-4377)
PHONE................................909 608-2260
Kieron Delahunt, *Manager*
EMP: 183
SALES (corp-wide): 4B Privately Held
SIC: 2759 Labels & seals: printing
HQ: Ccl Label (Delaware), Inc.
   15 Controls Dr
   Shelton CT 06484
   203 926-1253

(P-4493)
CEE JAY RESEARCH & SALES
LLC
920 W 10th St, Azusa (91702-1936)
PHONE................................626 815-1530
Bert Banta, *Mng Member*
EMP: 17 EST: 1988
SALES (est): 1MM Privately Held
WEB: www.cee-jay.com
SIC: 2759 2679 3429 Tags: printing; tags,
   paper (unprinted): made from purchased
   paper; manufactured hardware (general)

(P-4494)
CENTURY PUBLISHING
Also Called: Community Adviser Newspaper
218 N Murray St, Banning (92220-5512)
P.O. Box 727 (92220-0018)
PHONE................................951 849-4586
Gerald Bean, *Owner*
Art Reyes, *General Mgr*
Virginia Bradford, *Office Mgr*
EMP: 18 EST: 1908
SALES (est): 1.1MM Privately Held
WEB: www.recordgazette.net
SIC: 2759 7313 2711 Commercial print-
   ing; newspaper advertising representa-
   tive; newspapers

(P-4495)
CLAREMONT INST FOR THE
STUDY O (PA)
Also Called: CLAREMONT INSTITUTE, THE
1317 W Fthill Blvd Ste 12, Upland
PHONE................................909 981-2200
Michael Pack, *President*
Ryan Williams, *COO*
John Marini, *Bd of Directors*
Daniel C Palm, *Admin Sec*
Amanda Callanan, *Corp Comm Staff*
EMP: 13 EST: 1979
SQ FT: 3,600

SALES: 6.2MM Privately Held
WEB: www.claremont.org
SIC: 2759 8733 Publication printing; re-
   search institute

(P-4496)
CNM MARKETING INC
Also Called: Blankstylcom Vision Sport Mtrs
2569 Mccabe Way Ste 210, Irvine
(92614-5220)
PHONE................................866 792-5265
Mark Azzarito, *Administration*
EMP: 15 EST: 2008
SQ FT: 1,000
SALES (est): 2.7MM Privately Held
WEB: www.blankstyle.com
SIC: 2759 Screen printing

(P-4497)
COASTAL TAG & LABEL INC
13233 Barton Cir, Whittier (90605-3255)
P.O. Box 3303, Santa Fe Springs (90670-
1303)
PHONE................................562 946-4318
Fred Elhami, *President*
Ruth Elhami, *Admin Sec*
EMP: 94 EST: 1982
SALES (est): 10.6MM Privately Held
WEB: www.afeindustries.com
SIC: 2759 2672 2671 Labels & seals:
   printing; tags: printing; coated & lami-
   nated paper; packaging paper & plastics
   film, coated & laminated
PA: A F E Industries, Inc.
   13233 Barton Cir
   Whittier CA 90605

(P-4498)
COASTWIDE TAG & LABEL CO
INC
7647 Industry Ave, Pico Rivera
(90660-4301)
PHONE................................323 721-1501
Jay Sullivan, *President*
Jerry Sullivan, *Vice Pres*
EMP: 35 EST: 1946
SQ FT: 6,000
SALES (est): 1.2MM Privately Held
WEB: www.coastwidetag.com
SIC: 2759 Labels & seals: printing; tags:
   printing

(P-4499)
COLOR DEPOT INC
512 State St, Glendale (91203-1524)
PHONE................................818 500-9033
Thomas Hovsepian, *President*
Anna Hovsepian, *CFO*
Lilit Shamiryan, *Graphic Designe*
Narek Hovsepian, *Marketing Staff*
Tom Hovsepian, *Art Dir*
EMP: 14 EST: 1997
SQ FT: 2,800 Privately Held
WEB: www.colordepot.net
SIC: 2759 7336 2732 2752 Commercial
   printing; commercial art & graphic design;
   book printing; commercial printing, litho-
   graphic

(P-4500)
COLOR FX INC
8000 Haskell Ave, Van Nuys (91406-1321)
PHONE................................877 763-7671
EMP: 14 EST: 1995
SALES (est): 517.6K Privately Held
WEB: www.colorfxweb.com
SIC: 2759 Commercial printing

(P-4501)
COLORTECH LABEL INC
1230 S Sherman St, Anaheim
(92805-6455)
PHONE................................714 999-5545
Randy Montram, *President*
EMP: 17 EST: 1996
SALES (est): 205.7K Privately Held
WEB: www.adcraftlabels.com
SIC: 2759 Labels & seals: printing

(P-4502)
CORPORATE IMPRESSIONS LA INC
Also Called: Dorado Pkg
10742 Burbank Blvd, North Hollywood
(91601-2516)
PHONE...................................818 761-9295
Jennifer L Freund, *President*
Gary Gonzales, *Project Mgr*
Sandy Benson, *Business Mgr*
EMP: 27 EST: 1982
SQ FT: 10,000
SALES (est): 4.8MM **Privately Held**
WEB: www.impressionsla.com
SIC: 2759 7389 Screen printing; packaging & labeling services

(P-4503)
CORPRINT INCORPORATED
Also Called: Total Brand Delivery
4235 Mission Oaks Blvd, Camarillo
(93010)
PHONE...................................818 839-5316
Marc Lewis, *President*
Roberta Wollerman, *Products*
EMP: 15 EST: 1996
SALES (est): 691.8K **Privately Held**
SIC: 2759 Business forms: printing

(P-4504)
COSMO FIBER CORPORATION (PA)
1802 Santo Domingo Ave, Duarte
(91010-2933)
PHONE...................................626 256-6098
Sidney Ru, *President*
Sissy Ru, *Admin Sec*
Iris Kwok, *Manager*
◆ EMP: 39 EST: 1990
SQ FT: 4,000
SALES (est): 6MM **Privately Held**
WEB: www.cosmopromos.com
SIC: 2759 7389 Promotional printing; advertising, promotional & trade show services

(P-4505)
COUNTY OF ORANGE
Also Called: Public Fclities Resources Dept
1300 S Grand Ave Ste B, Santa Ana
(92705-4434)
PHONE...................................714 567-7444
Manny Apodaca, *Branch Mgr*
EMP: 25
SALES (corp-wide): 4.3B **Privately Held**
WEB: www.ocgov.com
SIC: 9199 2759 General government administration; ; commercial printing
PA: County Of Orange
333 W Santa Ana Blvd
Santa Ana CA 92701
714 834-6200

(P-4506)
CR & A CUSTOM APPAREL INC
Also Called: Cr & A Custom
312 W Pico Blvd, Los Angeles
(90015-2437)
PHONE...................................213 749-4440
Masoud RAD, *COO*
Carmen RAD, *President*
Rocio Morales, *Office Mgr*
Dino Maquiddang, *Controller*
Dennis Bise, *VP Opers*
◆ EMP: 30 EST: 1993
SQ FT: 26,500
SALES (est): 6.5MM **Privately Held**
WEB: www.cracustom.com
SIC: 2759 Posters, including billboards: printing

(P-4507)
DIGITAL ROOM HOLDINGS INC (PA)
Also Called: New Printing
8000 Haskell Ave, Van Nuys (91406-1321)
PHONE...................................310 575-4440
Michael Turner, *Officer*
Anthony Scott, *President*
Brett Zane, *CFO*
Lilie Rahimzadeh, *Vice Pres*
Alex Miller, *Planning*
▲ EMP: 147 EST: 2016

SALES (est): 82.4MM **Privately Held**
WEB: www.digitalroominc.com
SIC: 2759 7336 Commercial printing; graphic arts & related design

(P-4508)
DIRECT EDGE MEDIA INC (PA)
2900 E White Star Ave, Anaheim
(92806-2627)
PHONE...................................714 221-8686
Ryan Brueckner, *President*
Jim Hudgens, *Officer*
Ryan Clark, *Vice Pres*
Thomas Hsiao, *Vice Pres*
Jackie Vo, *Controller*
▲ EMP: 13 EST: 2001
SQ FT: 22,000
SALES (est): 15.7MM **Privately Held**
WEB: www.directedgemedia.com
SIC: 2759 7312 7336 2752 Letterpress & screen printing; outdoor advertising services; graphic arts & related design; commercial printing, lithographic

(P-4509)
DOING GOOD WORKS
12 Mauchly Ste B, Irvine (92618-2395)
P.O. Box 6392, Laguna Niguel (92607-6392)
PHONE...................................949 354-0400
Scott Henderson, *CEO*
Lisa Ullmann, *Business Dir*
EMP: 14 EST: 2015
SALES (est): 1.3MM **Privately Held**
WEB: www.doinggoodworks.com
SIC: 2759 7336 8742 5199 Commercial printing; package design; management consulting services; advertising specialties

(P-4510)
EARL HAYS PRESS
10707 Sherman Way, Sun Valley
(91352-5155)
PHONE...................................818 765-0700
Rafael Hernandez Jr, *Partner*
Paul Crumrine, *Partner*
EMP: 17 EST: 1929
SQ FT: 8,000
SALES (est): 1.5MM **Privately Held**
WEB: www.theearlhayspress.com
SIC: 2759 7829 Card printing & engraving, except greeting; motion picture distribution services

(P-4511)
EAS SENSORSENSE INC (PA)
13351 Riverside Dr Ste D, Sherman Oaks
(91423-2542)
PHONE...................................818 763-9186
Arthur Fuss, *President*
EMP: 27 EST: 1995
SQ FT: 16,000
SALES (est): 2.4MM **Privately Held**
SIC: 2759 Tags: printing

(P-4512)
ECLECTIC PRINTING & DESIGN LLC
1030 Ortega Way Ste A, Placentia
(92870-7161)
P.O. Box 6667, Fullerton (92834-6667)
PHONE...................................714 528-8040
Jeffrey Abraham, *President*
Jeff Abraham, *Owner*
EMP: 18 EST: 2007
SALES (est): 2.2MM **Privately Held**
WEB: www.eclecticprinting.com
SIC: 2759 Screen printing

(P-4513)
ELITE COLOR TECHNOLOGIES INC
851 E Walnut St, Carson (90746-1214)
PHONE...................................310 324-3040
Ki Kyong, *President*
▲ EMP: 17 EST: 2004
SQ FT: 15,000
SALES (est): 515K **Privately Held**
SIC: 2759 Commercial printing

(P-4514)
FLANNIGANS MERCHANDISING INC
15803 Stagg St, Van Nuys (91406-1922)
PHONE...................................818 785-7428

Nathan Boles, *President*
Arturo Verdin, *Prdtn Mgr*
EMP: 14 EST: 2002
SQ FT: 10,000
SALES (est): 1.3MM **Privately Held**
WEB: www.flannigans.org
SIC: 2759 Screen printing

(P-4515)
FOILFLEX PRODUCTS INC
25636 Avenue Stanford, Valencia
(91355-1117)
PHONE...................................661 702-0775
Michael Dekel, *President*
Ned Washburn, *Vice Pres*
Bleys Lieuallen, *Prdtn Mgr*
▲ EMP: 14 EST: 2004
SALES (est): 2.9MM **Privately Held**
WEB: www.foilflex.com
SIC: 2759 Flexographic printing

(P-4516)
G PRINTING INC
1815 Ayers Way, Burbank (91501-1106)
PHONE...................................818 246-1156
George Ouzounian, *President*
John Melkonian, *Vice Pres*
Tom Nichols, *Info Tech Dir*
Jonathan Feldman, *Opers Staff*
Gary Worth, *Opers Staff*
EMP: 28 EST: 1974
SALES (est): 952.7K **Privately Held**
SIC: 2759 Catalogs: printing

(P-4517)
G-2 GRAPHIC SERVICE INC
5510 Cleon Ave, North Hollywood
(91601-2835)
PHONE...................................818 623-3100
John C Beard, *CEO*
Joe Cotrupe, *President*
Pamela Beard-Cotrupe, *CEO*
Rob Cashman, *Vice Pres*
Scott Dewinkeleer, *Vice Pres*
◆ EMP: 52 EST: 1969
SQ FT: 35,000
SALES (est): 9.5MM **Privately Held**
WEB: www.g2online.com
SIC: 2759 7331 Commercial printing; direct mail advertising services

(P-4518)
GACHUPIN ENTERPRISES LLC
Also Called: Speedwear.com
5671 Engineer Dr, Huntington Beach
(92649-1123)
PHONE...................................714 375-4111
Kai Gachupin, *Owner*
Tony Bustamante, *Graphic Designe*
Will Marquez, *Prdtn Mgr*
Robert Fowler, *Sales Staff*
Joe Giustra, *Art Dir*
▲ EMP: 16 EST: 2010
SQ FT: 11,000
SALES (est): 2.7MM **Privately Held**
SIC: 2759 7389 3949 Screen printing; embroidering of advertising on shirts, etc.; sporting & athletic goods

(P-4519)
GEO LABELS INC
1180 E Francis St Ste G, Ontario
(91761-4802)
P.O. Box 3009 (91761-0901)
PHONE...................................909 923-6832
George Contreras, *President*
Elena Conteras, *Admin Sec*
EMP: 15 EST: 2004
SQ FT: 16,000
SALES (est): 1.5MM **Privately Held**
WEB: www.geolabelsinc.com
SIC: 2759 Labels & seals: printing

(P-4520)
GOLDEN APPLEXX CO INC
19805 Harrison Ave, Walnut (91789-2849)
PHONE...................................909 594-9788
Peter Lee, *President*
Jeff Lee, *Vice Pres*
Shio R Lee, *Vice Pres*
Shio-Ru Lee, *Vice Pres*
◆ EMP: 24 EST: 1986
SALES (est): 2.2MM **Privately Held**
WEB: www.goldenapplexx.com
SIC: 2759 2396 Promotional printing; automotive & apparel trimmings

(P-4521)
GOLDEN GROVE TRADING INC
Also Called: Crystal Castle
468 S Humane Way, Pomona
(91766-1035)
PHONE...................................909 718-8000
Werner Schulz, *President*
Yung Schulz, *Vice Pres*
Patricia Widklund, *Office Mgr*
Thomas Tran, *Sales Staff*
▲ EMP: 15 EST: 1983
SQ FT: 20,000
SALES (est): 2MM **Privately Held**
WEB: www.ggtrading.com
SIC: 2759 2395 5699 Letterpress & screen printing; embroidery & art needlework; customized clothing & apparel

(P-4522)
GRAPHIC TRENDS INCORPORATED
7301 Adams St, Paramount (90723-4007)
PHONE...................................562 531-2339
Kieu V Tran, *Principal*
Chris Jackson, *Info Tech Dir*
Cesar Arambula, *Supervisor*
EMP: 40 EST: 1983
SQ FT: 20,984
SALES (est): 7.6MM **Privately Held**
WEB: www.graphictrends.net
SIC: 2759 7336 Screen printing; graphic arts & related design

(P-4523)
GREAT WESTERN PACKAGING LLC
8230-8240 Haskell Ave, Van Nuys (91406)
PHONE...................................818 464-3800
Michael C Warner, *Mng Member*
Denise Scanlon, *Executive*
Howard Metz, *MIS Mgr*
Jim Crowfoot, *Site Mgr*
Victoria Warner Kaplan,
EMP: 68 EST: 1970
SALES (est): 9.3MM **Privately Held**
WEB: www.greatwesternpackaging.com
SIC: 2759 Commercial printing

(P-4524)
HB PRODUCTS LLC
5671 Engineer Dr, Huntington Beach
(92649-1123)
PHONE...................................714 799-6967
Robert Mannarelli,
Rick Ball, *VP Sales*
EMP: 20 EST: 2000
SALES (est): 3.4MM **Privately Held**
WEB: www.hbapparel.com
SIC: 2759 Screen printing

(P-4525)
ICON SCREENING INC
Also Called: Icon Screen Printing
1108 W Grove Ave, Orange (92865-4131)
PHONE...................................714 630-4266
Bryan Huber, *CEO*
Karen Neilsen, *Production*
Mike Zaremba, *Director*
EMP: 13 EST: 2011
SALES (est): 1.6MM **Privately Held**
WEB: www.iconscreening.com
SIC: 2759 Screen printing

(P-4526)
ID SUPPLY
1970 Placentia Ave, Costa Mesa
(92627-3421)
PHONE...................................714 728-6478
Brandon Ruddach, *CEO*
Brandon Rudach, *President*
EMP: 34 EST: 2017
SALES (est): 2.5MM **Privately Held**
WEB: www.idsupplyco.com
SIC: 2759 Screen printing

(P-4527)
IN HOUSE CUSTOM DECALS
Also Called: In House Stickers
2300 S Reservoir St # 308, Pomona
(91766-6458)
PHONE...................................909 613-1403
Frank Caldron, *Owner*
▲ EMP: 13 EST: 1996
SALES (est): 650.5K **Privately Held**
SIC: 2759 Decals: printing

PRODUCTS & SVCS

(P-4528)
INK FX CORPORATION
2031 S Lynx Ave, Ontario (91761-8011)
PHONE..................................909 673-1950
Joe Metz, *President*
Mike Machrone, *CEO*
Lydia Matz, *Executive*
EMP: 25
SQ FT: 12,000
SALES (est): 3.5MM **Privately Held**
WEB: www.inkfxcorp.myshopify.com
SIC: 2759 Screen printing

(P-4529)
INTERNTIONAL COLOR POSTERS INC
Also Called: ICP West
8081 Orangethorpe Ave, Buena Park (90621-3801)
PHONE..................................949 768-1005
Eric Guerineau, *President*
▲ EMP: 37 EST: 1985
SQ FT: 26,000
SALES (est): 1.2MM **Privately Held**
SIC: 2759 Screen printing

(P-4530)
INVESTMENT ENTERPRISES INC (PA)
Also Called: Great Western Litho
8230 Haskell Ave Ste 8240, Van Nuys (91406-1322)
PHONE..................................818 464-3800
Michael Warner, *President*
Denise Scanlon, *Vice Pres*
Jack Wickson, *Vice Pres*
EMP: 43 EST: 1970
SALES (est): 3.8MM **Privately Held**
SIC: 2759 Magazines: printing

(P-4531)
LABEL SPECIALTIES INC
704 Dunn Way, Placentia (92870-6805)
PHONE..................................714 961-8074
Michael A Gyure, *President*
Tom Wetterhus, *Vice Pres*
Debra Gyure, *Manager*
EMP: 33 EST: 1981
SQ FT: 11,000
SALES (est): 1.4MM **Privately Held**
WEB: www.labelspec.com
SIC: 2759 Labels & seals: printing

(P-4532)
LABELING HURST SYSTEMS LLC
Also Called: Hurst International
20747 Dearborn St, Chatsworth (91311-5914)
P.O. Box 5169 (91313-5169)
PHONE..................................818 701-0710
Aron Lichtenberg, *President*
Cory Murdock, *Regl Sales Mgr*
Alex Lichtenberg, *Sales Staff*
▲ EMP: 18 EST: 1995
SQ FT: 12,875
SALES (est): 6MM **Privately Held**
WEB: www.hurst-international.com
SIC: 2759 Labels & seals: printing

(P-4533)
LABELS-R-US INC
Also Called: Label Shoppe, The
1121 Fullerton Rd, City of Industry (91748-1232)
PHONE..................................626 333-4001
Rudolph Gaytan, *CEO*
Pete Stoeffler, *Vice Pres*
Geralyn Lambou, *Sales Staff*
EMP: 25 EST: 1991
SQ FT: 65,000
SALES (est): 3.9MM **Privately Held**
WEB: www.labelsrus.com
SIC: 5932 2759 Used merchandise stores; commercial printing

(P-4534)
LABELTRONIX LLC
Also Called: Rethink Label Systems
2419 E Winston Rd, Anaheim (92806-5544)
PHONE..................................800 429-4321
Daniel Blair,
Louie Mendoza, *Engineer*
John Adams, *Credit Mgr*
Christina Castillo, *Purchasing*
Meghan Lievanos, *Opers Staff*
▲ EMP: 73 EST: 1993
SQ FT: 48,000 **Privately Held**
WEB: www.labeltronix.com
SIC: 2759 Labels & seals: printing

(P-4535)
LAWEB OFFSET PRINTING INC
Also Called: Chinese-La Daily News
9639 Telstar Ave, El Monte (91731-3003)
PHONE..................................626 454-2469
Walter Chang, *President*
Ya-Tang Fu, *Shareholder*
CHI-Kwang Chiang, *Treasurer*
▲ EMP: 34 EST: 1990
SQ FT: 29,730
SALES (est): 1MM **Privately Held**
WEB: www.lawebprint.com
SIC: 2759 2752 Newspapers: printing; commercial printing, offset

(P-4536)
LCA PROMOTIONS INC
3073 Cicero Ct, Simi Valley (93063-1606)
PHONE..................................818 773-9170
Terrence R Aleck, *President*
EMP: 20 EST: 1992
SALES (est): 2MM **Privately Held**
WEB: www.lcapromotions.com
SIC: 2759 Screen printing

(P-4537)
LEGION CREATIVE GROUP
500 N Brand Blvd Ste 1800, Glendale (91203-3305)
PHONE..................................323 498-1100
Kathleen Fliller, *Owner*
Ian Leaman, *Managing Dir*
Jeff Barnett, *Director*
Zack Du, *Director*
Madoka Kogi, *Director*
EMP: 25 EST: 2015
SALES (est): 2.8MM **Privately Held**
WEB: www.legioncreative.us
SIC: 2759 Advertising literature: printing

(P-4538)
LIMPUS PRINTS INC
Also Called: Insight System Exchange
1820 S Santa Fe St, Santa Ana (92705-4815)
PHONE..................................714 545-5078
Pat Pester, *President*
EMP: 14 EST: 1997
SALES (est): 1.9MM **Privately Held**
WEB: www.limpusprints.com
SIC: 2759 Screen printing

(P-4539)
LITHOTECH INTERNATIONAL LLC
9950 Baldwin Pl, El Monte (91731-2204)
PHONE..................................626 443-4210
Shen Yen,
Shih-Yi Yang,
▲ EMP: 14 EST: 1998
SALES (est): 606.1K **Privately Held**
SIC: 2759 Commercial printing

(P-4540)
LOGOMART CORPORATION
600 W 15th St, Long Beach (90813-1508)
PHONE..................................714 458-3181
Samuel Liskey, *President*
EMP: 13 EST: 2019
SALES (est): 1.1MM **Privately Held**
SIC: 2759 7213 5047 Promotional printing; uniform supply; industrial safety devices: first aid kits & masks

(P-4541)
MARCO FINE ARTS GALLERIES INC
4860 W 147th St, Hawthorne (90250-6706)
PHONE..................................310 615-1818
Al Marco, *President*
Kristoff Honeymany, *CEO*
Scott Cornelius, *VP Bus Dvlpt*
Sean Macdonald, *Sales Staff*
▲ EMP: 41 EST: 1986
SQ FT: 10,000
SALES (est): 9.2MM **Privately Held**
WEB: www.marcofinearts.com
SIC: 2759 5199 5023 Commercial printing; art goods; frames & framing, picture & mirror

(P-4542)
MARTIN E-Z STICK LABELS
12921 Sunnyside Pl, Santa Fe Springs (90670-4645)
PHONE..................................562 906-1577
Francisco Martinez, *President*
Sylvia Martinez, *Treasurer*
Moncia Martinez, *Admin Sec*
EMP: 18 EST: 1979
SQ FT: 14,800
SALES (est): 3MM **Privately Held**
WEB: www.martinezsticklabels.com
SIC: 2759 Labels & seals: printing

(P-4543)
MATRIX DOCUMENT IMAGING INC
527 E Rowland St Ste 214, Covina (91723-3267)
PHONE..................................626 966-9959
Thomas Smith, *President*
Mercedes Uribe, *Vice Pres*
EMP: 24 EST: 2006
SALES (est): 2.9MM **Privately Held**
WEB: www.legal-records.com
SIC: 2759 8111 Laser printing; legal services

(P-4544)
MERRILL CORPORATION INC
10635 Santa Monica Blvd # 350, Los Angeles (90025-8300)
PHONE..................................310 552-5288
Fax: 310 552-5299
EMP: 25
SALES (corp-wide): 691.4MM **Privately Held**
SIC: 2759 Commercial Printing
PA: Merrill Corporation
　　1 Merrill Cir
　　Saint Paul MN 55402
　　651 646-4501

(P-4545)
MILLION CORPORATION
Also Called: Able Card Corporation
1300 W Optical Dr Ste 600, Irwindale (91702-3285)
PHONE..................................626 969-1888
Herman Ho, *CEO*
Donny Yu, *CFO*
Hector Dominguez, *Vice Pres*
Scott Killen, *Sales Mgr*
Kelly Wiser, *Cust Mgr*
EMP: 70 EST: 1989
SQ FT: 45,000
SALES (est): 11.3MM **Privately Held**
WEB: www.ablecard.com
SIC: 2759 Commercial printing
PA: First Nations Capital Partners, Llc
　　7676 Hazard Center Dr # 5
　　San Diego CA 92108

(P-4546)
NATIONWIDE LITHO INC
11728 Goldring Rd, Arcadia (91006-6006)
PHONE..................................626 542-0371
Pedro D Tomaz, *CEO*
Pedro Tomaz, *Principal*
EMP: 16 EST: 2008
SALES (est): 865.6K **Privately Held**
WEB: www.nationwidelitho.com
SIC: 2759 Commercial printing

(P-4547)
ONE STOP LABEL CORPORATION
1641 S Baker Ave, Ontario (91761-8025)
PHONE..................................909 230-9380
Maria Navarro, *President*
Jorge Navarro, *Vice Pres*
EMP: 27 EST: 1996
SQ FT: 12,000
SALES (est): 1.8MM **Privately Held**
WEB: www.onestoplabel.com
SIC: 2759 Labels & seals: printing

(P-4548)
ORANGE CIRCLE STUDIO CORP
Also Called: Studio OH
8687 Research Dr Ste 150, Irvine (92618-4290)
PHONE..................................949 727-0800
Daniel Whang, *CEO*
Scott Whang, *Chairman*
◆ EMP: 56
SQ FT: 10,000
SALES (est): 26MM **Privately Held**
WEB: www.orangecirclestudio.com
SIC: 2759 Calendars: printing

(P-4549)
ORANGE COUNTY LABEL CO INC
301 W Dyer Rd Ste D, Santa Ana (92707-3450)
PHONE..................................714 437-1010
Jerome Mattert, *President*
Jef Mattert, *Opers Staff*
EMP: 13 EST: 1995
SQ FT: 3,500
SALES (est): 2.6MM **Privately Held**
WEB: www.oclabel.com
SIC: 2759 Labels & seals: printing

(P-4550)
ORORA VISUAL LLC
1600 E Valencia Dr, Fullerton (92831-4735)
PHONE..................................714 879-2400
James R Hamel, *President*
Richard Williams, *President*
Christopher Zagala, *President*
Luis Jara, *Regional Mgr*
Sandra Bergeaux, *Project Mgr*
▲ EMP: 100
SALES (est): 13.2MM **Privately Held**
WEB: www.ororavisual.com
SIC: 2759 Screen printing

(P-4551)
PACIFIC CONTAINERPRINT INC
5951 Riverside Dr Apt 4, Chino (91710-4477)
PHONE..................................909 465-0365
Michael E Wever, *President*
Debra Wever, *Treasurer*
Daniel P Wever, *Vice Pres*
EMP: 28 EST: 1981
SQ FT: 9,300
SALES (est): 700K **Privately Held**
SIC: 2759 3993 Screen printing; signs & advertising specialties

(P-4552)
PACIFIC LABEL INC
1511 E Edinger Ave, Santa Ana (92705-4907)
PHONE..................................714 237-1276
Nick Valestrino, *President*
EMP: 22 EST: 1998
SQ FT: 22,000
SALES (est): 406.1K **Privately Held**
SIC: 2759 Labels & seals: printing

(P-4553)
PADYWELL CORP
835 Meridian St, Duarte (91010-3587)
PHONE..................................626 359-9149
▲ EMP: 20
SQ FT: 7,825
SALES (est): 1.4MM **Privately Held**
SIC: 2759 Commercial Printing

(P-4554)
PARADIGM LABEL INC
10258 Birtcher Dr, Jurupa Valley (91752-1827)
PHONE..................................951 372-9212
Curtis Harton, *CEO*
EMP: 15 EST: 2006
SQ FT: 15,000
SALES (est): 2.3MM **Privately Held**
WEB: www.paradigmlabel.com
SIC: 2759 Labels & seals: printing

(P-4555)
PAX TAG & LABEL INC
9528 Rush St Ste C, El Monte (91733-1551)
PHONE..................................626 579-2000
Michael Brown, *President*
Myrna Gutierrez, *Sales Executive*

Mike Vasco, *Manager*
EMP: 20 **EST:** 1994
SQ FT: 10,000
SALES (est): 2.3MM **Privately Held**
WEB: www.paxtag.com
SIC: 2759 2679 Tags: printing; tags, paper (unprinted): made from purchased paper

(P-4556)
POLYCRAFT INC
42075 Avenida Alvarado, Temecula (92590-3486)
PHONE.....................951 296-0860
William D Verstegen, *President*
Bryan Nealy, *Principal*
Patricia Verstegen, *Principal*
EMP: 20 **EST:** 1974
SQ FT: 21,000
SALES (est): 1.6MM **Privately Held**
WEB: www.polycraftinc.com
SIC: 2759 2671 Screen printing; packaging paper & plastics film, coated & laminated

(P-4557)
POSTCARD PRESS INC (PA)
Also Called: Next Day Flyers
8000 Haskell Ave, Van Nuys (91406-1321)
PHONE.....................855 898-9870
David Handmaker, *President*
◆ **EMP:** 31 **EST:** 1996
SALES (est): 12.7MM **Privately Held**
WEB: www.nextdayflyers.com
SIC: 2759 Visiting cards (including business): printing

(P-4558)
PRESIDENT ENTERPRISE INC
Also Called: Lotus Labels
655 Tamarack Ave, Brea (92821-3213)
PHONE.....................714 671-9577
George Wu, *President*
Shu-Feng T Wu, *Vice Pres*
Lindsey Hand, *Sales Staff*
Veronica Munoz,
▲ **EMP:** 20 **EST:** 1992
SALES (est): 4.7MM **Privately Held**
WEB: www.lotuslabels.net
SIC: 2759 Labels & seals: printing

(P-4559)
PRIMARY COLOR SYSTEMS CORP
401 Coral Cir, El Segundo (90245-4622)
PHONE.....................310 841-0250
Ed Philipps, *Branch Mgr*
Doug Hand, *Executive*
Ed Phillips, *Division Mgr*
Andres Iniestra, *Purch Mgr*
Steve Rowe, *Opers Mgr*
EMP: 39
SALES (corp-wide): 61MM **Privately Held**
WEB: www.primarycolor.com
SIC: 2759 2752 Commercial printing; commercial printing, lithographic
PA: Primary Color Systems Corporation
11130 Holder St
Cypress CA 90630
949 660-7080

(P-4560)
PROFESSNAL RPRGRAPHIC SVCS INC
Also Called: Pro Group
17731 Cowan, Irvine (92614-6009)
PHONE.....................949 748-5400
Cindy Kennedy, *President*
Thomas Brian Kennedy, *CFO*
EMP: 25 **EST:** 2008
SALES (est): 4.7MM **Privately Held**
WEB: www.professionalreprographic.mfg-pages.com
SIC: 2759 Commercial printing

(P-4561)
PROGRSSIVE INTGRATED SOLUTIONS
Also Called: Progressive Manufacturing
377 S Acacia Ave, Fullerton (92831-4748)
PHONE.....................714 237-0980
Rodney Dean Boehme, *President*
Doug Woodward, *Vice Pres*
EMP: 76 **EST:** 1988

SALES (est): 7.9MM **Privately Held**
WEB: www.progressiveusa.com
SIC: 2759 2752 Envelopes: printing; commercial printing, offset

(P-4562)
QUIKTURN PROF SCRNPRINTING INC
567 S Melrose St, Placentia (92870-6305)
PHONE.....................800 784-5419
Bill Allen, *CEO*
Stephanie Scharf, *Controller*
Emily Williams, *Controller*
EMP: 17 **EST:** 2015
SALES (est): 3.2MM **Privately Held**
WEB: www.quikturnusa.com
SIC: 2759 Screen printing

(P-4563)
RAINBOW SUBLYMATION INC
2438 E 11th St, Los Angeles (90021-2938)
PHONE.....................213 489-5001
▲ **EMP:** 37
SALES (est): 2.7MM **Privately Held**
SIC: 2759 Commercial Printing

(P-4564)
RANAR MANUFACTURING CORP
149 Lomita St, El Segundo (90245-4114)
PHONE.....................310 414-4122
Peter Gilbert, *President*
EMP: 14 **EST:** 1972
SQ FT: 9,500
SALES (est): 2MM **Privately Held**
WEB: www.ranar.com
SIC: 2759 Screen printing

(P-4565)
RAOUL TEXTILES INC
Also Called: Raouls Hnd-Scrned Yrdage Prntw
110 Los Aguajes Ave, Santa Barbara (93101-3818)
PHONE.....................805 965-1694
Sally McQuillan, *Mng Member*
Salley McQuillan, *President*
EMP: 16 **EST:** 1991
SALES (est): 983.3K **Privately Held**
WEB: www.raoultextiles.com
SIC: 2759 Screen printing

(P-4566)
RESPONSE ENVELOPE INC (PA)
1340 S Baker Ave, Ontario (91761-7742)
PHONE.....................909 923-5855
Jonas Ulrich, *CEO*
Wendy Antrim, *Vice Pres*
Philip Ulrich, *Vice Pres*
Lee Larson, *Plant Mgr*
Gary Hybl, *VP Sales*
▲ **EMP:** 104 **EST:** 1986
SQ FT: 85,000
SALES (est): 16.5MM **Privately Held**
WEB: www.response-envelope.com
SIC: 2759 2677 Envelopes: printing; envelopes

(P-4567)
RETAIL PRINT MEDIA INC
2355 Crenshaw Blvd # 135, Torrance (90501-3329)
PHONE.....................424 488-6950
Raymond Young, *CEO*
Karli Sikich, *COO*
Amy Scheibel, *Media Spec*
Rose Balleras, *Manager*
Angelina Jungo, *Account Dir*
EMP: 35 **EST:** 2015
SALES (est): 3.9MM **Privately Held**
WEB: www.retailprintmedia.com
SIC: 2759 7371 Advertising literature: printing; computer software writing services

(P-4568)
RJ ACQUISITION CORP (PA)
Also Called: Ad Art Company
3260 E 26th St, Vernon (90058-8008)
PHONE.....................323 318-1107
Joe M Demarco, *President*
Roger Keech, *CEO*
Todd Conrad, *Vice Pres*
Joseph Demarco, *Executive*
David Cardena, *Info Tech Dir*
▲ **EMP:** 215 **EST:** 1944

SQ FT: 200,000
SALES (est): 39.3MM **Privately Held**
WEB: www.adartco.com
SIC: 2759 Screen printing

(P-4569)
ROBINSON PRINTING INC
42685 Rio Nedo, Temecula (92590-3711)
PHONE.....................951 296-0300
David Robinson, *CEO*
Jeff Blount, *President*
Dennis Dibiasi, *President*
Mike Robinson, *President*
▲ **EMP:** 37 **EST:** 1981
SQ FT: 24,000
SALES (est): 6.9MM **Privately Held**
WEB: www.robinsonprinting.com
SIC: 2759 2621 Screen printing; packaging paper

(P-4570)
SAN BRNRDINO CMNTY COLLEGE DST
Also Called: Print Shop
701 S Mount Vernon Ave, San Bernardino (92410-2705)
PHONE.....................909 888-6511
Louie Chavira, *Supervisor*
EMP: 48
SALES (corp-wide): 46.5MM **Privately Held**
WEB: www.sbccd.edu
SIC: 2759 Commercial printing
PA: San Bernardino Community College District
550 E Hospitality Ln # 200
San Bernardino CA 92408
909 382-4000

(P-4571)
SCREEN ART INC
15162 Triton Ln, Huntington Beach (92649-1041)
PHONE.....................714 891-4185
James K Proctor, *President*
Kathryn Proctor, *Vice Pres*
EMP: 13 **EST:** 1989
SQ FT: 8,400
SALES (est): 740.5K **Privately Held**
WEB: www.screenartllc.com
SIC: 2759 Screen printing

(P-4572)
SCREEN PRINTERS RESOURCE INC
1251 Burton St, Fullerton (92831-5211)
PHONE.....................714 441-1155
Frank Sator, *President*
Tina Laguerra, *Technical Staff*
▲ **EMP:** 16 **EST:** 2000
SQ FT: 20,000
SALES (est): 4.1MM **Privately Held**
WEB: www.silkscreen-supplies.com
SIC: 2759 Screen printing

(P-4573)
SHORETT PRINTING INC (PA)
Also Called: Crown Printers
250 W Rialto Ave, San Bernardino (92408-1017)
PHONE.....................714 545-4689
Charles D Shorett Jr, *CEO*
Ken Martin, *Vice Pres*
John Shorett, *Vice Pres*
Mike Brusig, *Executive*
Vance Carriere, *Creative Dir*
EMP: 39 **EST:** 1970
SALES (est): 6.4MM **Privately Held**
WEB: www.crownconnect.com
SIC: 2759 2752 Commercial printing; commercial printing, offset

(P-4574)
SIRENA INCORPORATED
Also Called: Los Angeles Wraps
22717 S Western Ave, Torrance (90501-4952)
PHONE.....................866 548-5353
Brandon Park, *CEO*
EMP: 16 **EST:** 2010
SQ FT: 10,000
SALES (est): 1.5MM **Privately Held**
WEB: www.lawraps.com
SIC: 2759 Commercial printing

(P-4575)
SPECIALIZED SCREEN PRTG INC
18435 Bandilier Cir, Fountain Valley (92708-7012)
PHONE.....................714 964-1230
David Williams, *CEO*
Jim Keisker, *President*
Mark Brown, *Info Tech Dir*
Danielle Butler, *Sales Staff*
Joe Bottum, *Representative*
EMP: 18 **EST:** 1998
SQ FT: 20,000
SALES (est): 2.3MM **Privately Held**
WEB: www.specializedscreenprinting.com
SIC: 2759 2752 2396 Screen printing; commercial printing, lithographic; automotive & apparel trimmings

(P-4576)
SPINELLI GRAPHIC INC
10621 Bloomfield St Ste 2, Los Alamitos (90720-6729)
PHONE.....................562 431-3232
Joseph Spinelli, *President*
Renee Spinelli, *Admin Sec*
EMP: 17 **EST:** 1976
SALES (est): 754.9K **Privately Held**
WEB: www.spinelligraphics.com
SIC: 2759 2752 Screen printing; commercial printing, lithographic

(P-4577)
SUPER COLOR DIGITAL LLC (PA)
16761 Hale Ave, Irvine (92606-5006)
PHONE.....................949 622-0010
Peyman Rashtchi, *Mng Member*
Shahin Falah, *CFO*
Carl Steindler, *Executive*
Kellie Alcala, *Project Mgr*
Rebecca Lloyd, *Project Mgr*
▲ **EMP:** 25 **EST:** 2006
SQ FT: 48,043
SALES (est): 53MM **Privately Held**
WEB: www.supercolor.com
SIC: 2759 Commercial printing

(P-4578)
SUPERIOR PRINTING INC
Also Called: Superior Press
9440 Norwalk Blvd, Santa Fe Springs (90670-2928)
PHONE.....................888 590-7998
Robert Traut, *President*
Jason Traut, *Treasurer*
Colin Holden, *Vice Pres*
Frank Marquez, *Vice Pres*
Kevin Traut, *Admin Sec*
EMP: 95 **EST:** 1953
SQ FT: 32,000
SALES (est): 14.4MM **Privately Held**
WEB: www.superiorpress.com
SIC: 2759 5112 Commercial printing; business forms

(P-4579)
TARGET MDIA PRTNERS INTRCTIVE (HQ)
Also Called: Target Mdia Prtners Intractive
5200 Lankershim Blvd # 35, North Hollywood (91601-3155)
PHONE.....................323 930-3123
Dave Duckwitz, *CEO*
Mark Salcido, *Senior VP*
Boris Bronshteyn, *Vice Pres*
Eve Minogue, *Vice Pres*
Tom Minogue, *Vice Pres*
EMP: 15 **EST:** 1998
SALES (est): 9.9MM
SALES (corp-wide): 27MM **Privately Held**
WEB: www.targetmediapartners.com
SIC: 2759 7331 Commercial printing; direct mail advertising services
PA: Responsologix, Inc.
6991 E Camelback Rd B30
Scottsdale AZ 85251
408 220-6545

(P-4580)
TAYLOR GRAPHICS INC
1582 Browning, Irvine (92606-4807)
PHONE.....................949 752-5200
Dean S Taylor, *CEO*

Carla Spicer, *Admin Sec*
Gary Schulthess, *Supervisor*
EMP: 23 **EST:** 1950
SQ FT: 7,500
SALES (est): 5.7MM **Privately Held**
SIC: 2759 Screen printing

(P-4581)
TAYLOR TECHNOLOGY SERVICES INC
Nowdocs
3230 E Imperial Hwy # 302, Brea
(92821-6721)
PHONE.................714 986-1559
EMP: 137
SALES (corp-wide): 3.6B **Privately Held**
WEB: www.taylor.com
SIC: 2759 Commercial printing
HQ: Taylor Technology Services, Inc.
1725 Roe Crest Dr
North Mankato MN 56003

(P-4582)
TECHNICAL SCREEN PRINTING INC
677 N Hariton St, Orange (92868-1311)
PHONE.................714 541-8590
Robert Golino, *President*
Barbara Golino, *Vice Pres*
EMP: 17 **EST:** 1981
SQ FT: 18,000
SALES (est): 1.3MM **Privately Held**
WEB: www.technicalscreenprinting.com
SIC: 2759 2752 2396 Screen printing; commercial printing, lithographic; automotive & apparel trimmings

(P-4583)
TEMECULA T-SHIRT PRINTERS INC
41607 Enterprise Cir N A, Temecula
(92590-5684)
PHONE.................951 296-0184
Kenneth Dawkins, *President*
EMP: 15 **EST:** 2015
SALES (est): 1MM **Privately Held**
WEB: www.temeculatshirtprinters.com
SIC: 2759 Screen printing

(P-4584)
TJ GIANT LLC
12623 Cisneros Ln, Santa Fe Springs
(90670-3373)
PHONE.................562 906-1060
Peter D Ahn,
EMP: 15 **EST:** 2008
SQ FT: 1,500
SALES: 5.1MM **Privately Held**
WEB: www.tjgiant.com
SIC: 2759 Screen printing

(P-4585)
TRISAR INC
2200 W Orangewood Ave # 235, Orange
(92868-1975)
PHONE.................714 972-2626
James Bell, *President*
▲ **EMP:** 19 **EST:** 1979
SALES (est): 769.7K
SALES (corp-wide): 1.8B **Publicly Held**
WEB: www.amscan.com
SIC: 2759 2261 Screen printing; screen printing of cotton broadwoven fabrics
HQ: Amscan Inc.
80 Grasslands Rd Ste 3
Elmsford NY 10523
914 345-2020

(P-4586)
UNITECH DECO INC
Also Called: Unitech Industries
19731 Bahama St, Northridge
(91324-3304)
PHONE.................818 700-1373
Merle Wurm, *President*
Tina Wurm-Donikian, *Treasurer*
EMP: 14 **EST:** 1979
SQ FT: 9,000
SALES (est): 855.6K **Privately Held**
SIC: 2759 2789 2396 Bag, wrapper & seal printing & engraving; bookbinding & related work; automotive & apparel trimmings

(P-4587)
UNIVERSAL LABEL PRINTERS
Also Called: Unilabel
13003 Los Nietos Rd, Santa Fe Springs
(90670-3348)
P.O. Box 3648 (90670-1648)
PHONE.................562 944-0234
John Walsh, *President*
Patricia Walsh, *Treasurer*
Jack Walsh, *Vice Pres*
Kathleen Mulcahey, *Admin Sec*
EMP: 20 **EST:** 1956
SQ FT: 30,000
SALES (est): 1.3MM **Privately Held**
WEB: www.universallabel.com
SIC: 2759 Labels & seals: printing; tags: printing

(P-4588)
VENTURA PRINTING INC (PA)
Also Called: V3
200 N Elevar St, Oxnard (93030-7969)
PHONE.................805 981-2600
David Wilson, *President*
▲ **EMP:** 99 **EST:** 1946
WEB: www.venturaprint.com
SIC: 2759 Commercial printing

(P-4589)
VITACHROME GRAPHICS GROUP INC
3710 Park Pl, Montrose (91020-1623)
P.O. Box 2924, Santa Fe Springs (90670-0924)
PHONE.................818 957-0900
Gary Durbin, *President*
Tony Won, *Vice Pres*
Jeanne De Guzman, *Opers Mgr*
EMP: 45 **EST:** 1971
SQ FT: 43,000
SALES (est): 3.7MM **Privately Held**
WEB: www.adahotelsigns.com
SIC: 2759 Decals: printing; screen printing; labels & seals: printing

(P-4590)
VOMAR PRODUCTS INC
7800 Deering Ave, Canoga Park
(91304-5005)
PHONE.................818 610-5115
Paul Van Ostrand, *CEO*
Herbert Paul Van Ostrand, *President*
Jason Van Ostrand, *Vice Pres*
John Barmaan, *General Mgr*
Anh Nguyen, *IT/INT Sup*
EMP: 38 **EST:** 1961
SQ FT: 29,000
SALES (est): 6.1MM **Privately Held**
WEB: www.vomarproducts.com
SIC: 2759 3993 Commercial printing; name plates: except engraved, etched, etc.: metal

(P-4591)
WAVELINE CREATIVE LLC
1299 S Wells Rd, Ventura (93004-1901)
PHONE.................805 469-1549
Mitch Burroughs,
Blake Burroughs,
Daniel Freismuth,
EMP: 30 **EST:** 2019
SALES (est): 4.9MM **Privately Held**
SIC: 2759 Screen printing
PA: Dbm Holdings, Llc
5807 W 20th St
Greeley CO 80634
970 484-4110

(P-4592)
WES GO INC
Also Called: GP Color Imaging Group
8211 Lankershim Blvd, North Hollywood
(91605-1614)
PHONE.................818 504-1200
Wesley Adams, *CEO*
Thomas Wilhelm, *President*
Bisher Ahdab, *COO*
Jeff Bowman, *Manager*
▲ **EMP:** 24 **EST:** 2001
SALES (est): 5.2MM **Privately Held**
WEB: www.gpcolor.com
SIC: 2759 Posters, including billboards: printing

(P-4593)
WESTERN CONVERTING SPC INC
Also Called: Consolidated Design West
2886 Metropolitan Pl, Pomona
(91767-1854)
PHONE.................909 392-4578
Chad Junkin, *President*
Yvonne Schnyder, *Office Mgr*
EMP: 20 **EST:** 1980
SQ FT: 8,000 **Privately Held**
WEB: www.westernconverting.com
SIC: 2759 Commercial printing

(P-4594)
WESTERN DIE & PRINTING CORP
3109 Casitas Ave, Los Angeles
(90039-2410)
PHONE.................323 665-0474
Saied Toobian, *President*
▲ **EMP:** 15 **EST:** 2008
SALES (est): 791K **Privately Held**
WEB: www.western-die-printing-corp.business.site
SIC: 2759 Commercial printing

(P-4595)
WESTERN STATES ENVELOPE CORP
2301 Raymer Ave, Fullerton (92833-2514)
P.O. Box 2607 (92837-0607)
PHONE.................714 449-0909
Lisa Hoehle, *President*
Giovanni Portanova, *Maintence Staff*
Jing Zaide, *Maintence Staff*
EMP: 60 **EST:** 1968
SQ FT: 24,000
SALES (est): 8.9MM **Privately Held**
WEB: www.wseca.com
SIC: 2759 Commercial printing

(P-4596)
WILSONS ART STUDIO INC
Also Called: Solutions Unlimited
501 S Acacia Ave, Fullerton (92831-5101)
PHONE.................714 870-7030
William L Goetsch, *President*
Roberta C Goetsch, *Corp Secy*
N Jim Goetsch, *Vice Pres*
EMP: 63
SQ FT: 50,000
SALES (est): 8.1MM **Privately Held**
WEB: www.solutions-unlimited.net
SIC: 2759 2396 Screen printing; automotive & apparel trimmings

---
2761 Manifold Business Forms

(P-4597)
APPERSON INC (PA)
17315 Studebaker Rd # 209, Cerritos
(90703-2508)
PHONE.................562 356-3333
Kelly Doherty, *CEO*
William Apperson, *Ch of Bd*
Elizabeth Tejada, *COO*
Brian Apperson, *Vice Pres*
Helen Calvillo, *Administration*
▲ **EMP:** 70 **EST:** 1955
SQ FT: 80,080
SALES (est): 24.9MM **Privately Held**
WEB: www.apperson.com
SIC: 2761 Continuous forms, office & business

(P-4598)
BESTFORMS INC
1135 Avenida Acaso, Camarillo
(93012-8740)
PHONE.................805 388-0503
Joe Valdez, *President*
Irv Michlin, *President*
Joy Macfarlane, *CFO*
Patrick Valdez, *Vice Pres*
Lili Montijo, *General Mgr*
EMP: 48 **EST:** 1985
SQ FT: 31,000
SALES (est): 8.3MM **Privately Held**
WEB: www.bestforms.com
SIC: 2761 Manifold business forms

(P-4599)
COMPLYRIGHT DIST SVCS INC
3451 Jupiter Ct, Oxnard (93030-8957)
PHONE.................805 981-0992
Richard Roddis, *CEO*
Oscar Camacho, *Plant Mgr*
Letty Vasquez, *Cust Mgr*
Yesenia Cervantes, *Supervisor*
EMP: 44 **EST:** 2006
SALES (est): 11MM
SALES (corp-wide): 3.6B **Privately Held**
WEB: www.complyright.com
SIC: 2761 Manifold business forms
PA: Taylor Corporation
1725 Roe Crest Dr
North Mankato MN 56003
507 625-2828

(P-4600)
TAYLOR COMMUNICATIONS INC
8972 Cuyamaca St, Corona (92883-2102)
PHONE.................951 203-9011
Edward Arminta, *Branch Mgr*
EMP: 17
SALES (corp-wide): 3.6B **Privately Held**
WEB: www.taylor.com
SIC: 2761 Manifold business forms
HQ: Taylor Communications Inc.
1725 Roe Crest Dr
North Mankato MN 56003
866 541-0937

(P-4601)
TAYLOR COMMUNICATIONS INC
535 Anton Blvd Ste 530, Costa Mesa
(92626-1947)
PHONE.................714 708-2005
EMP: 17
SALES (corp-wide): 3.6B **Privately Held**
WEB: www.taylor.com
SIC: 2761 Manifold business forms
HQ: Taylor Communications, Inc.
1725 Roe Crest Dr
North Mankato MN 56003
866 541-0937

(P-4602)
TAYLOR COMMUNICATIONS INC
400 N Tustin Ave Ste 275, Santa Ana
(92705-3885)
PHONE.................714 664-8865
Don Chelius, *Manager*
EMP: 17
SALES (corp-wide): 3.6B **Privately Held**
WEB: www.taylor.com
SIC: 2761 Manifold business forms
HQ: Taylor Communications, Inc.
1725 Roe Crest Dr
North Mankato MN 56003
866 541-0937

(P-4603)
TST/IMPRESO CALIFORNIA INC
10589 Business Dr, Fontana (92337-8223)
PHONE.................909 357-7190
Marshall Sorokwasz, *President*
▲ **EMP:** 45 **EST:** 1990
SQ FT: 30,000
SALES (est): 1.9MM
SALES (corp-wide): 115.2MM **Publicly Held**
WEB: www.tstimpreso.com
SIC: 2761 Continuous forms, office & business
HQ: Tst/Impreso, Inc.
652 Southwestern Blvd
Coppell TX 75019
972 462-0100

(P-4604)
WRIGHT BUSINESS GRAPHICS LLC
Also Called: Wright Business Graphics Calif
13602 12th St Ste A, Chino (91710-5200)
P.O. Box 20489, Portland OR (97294-0489)
PHONE.................909 614-6700
Gene Snitker, *Principal*
Steve Dupas, *Cust Mgr*
EMP: 30
SALES (corp-wide): 357.3MM **Publicly Held**
WEB: www.wrightbg.com
SIC: 2761 Manifold business forms

▲ = Import ▼=Export
◆ =Import/Export

HQ: Wright Business Graphics Llc
18440 Ne San Rafael St
Portland OR 97230
800 547-8397

2771 Greeting Card Publishing

(P-4605)
SCHURMAN FINE PAPERS
22500 Town Cir, Moreno Valley
(92553-7509)
PHONE....................................951 653-1934
EMP: 158
SALES (corp-wide): 265.8MM **Privately Held**
SIC: 2771 Mfg Greeting Cards
PA: Schurman Retail Group
500 Chadbourne Rd
Fairfield CA 37072
707 428-0200

2782 Blankbooks & Looseleaf Binders

(P-4606)
ABISCO PRODUCTS CO
5925 E Washington Blvd, Commerce
(90040-2412)
PHONE....................................562 906-9330
EMP: 25
SQ FT: 10,000
SALES (est): 2.7MM **Privately Held**
WEB: www.abiscoproducts.com
SIC: 2782 2675 Mfg Blankbooks/Binders
Mfg Die-Cut Paper/Paperboard

(P-4607)
CHECKWORKS INC
315 Cloverleaf Dr Ste J, Baldwin Park
(91706-6510)
P.O. Box 60065, City of Industry (91716-
0065)
PHONE....................................626 333-1444
Aloysious J Uniack, *President*
Aloysious J Uniack, *President*
Christen Mc Kiernan, *Admin Sec*
EMP: 55 **EST:** 1995
SQ FT: 15,000
SALES (est): 6.8MM **Privately Held**
WEB: www.checkworks.com
SIC: 2782 Checkbooks

(P-4608)
CONTINENTAL BDR SPECIALTY CORP (PA)
407 W Compton Blvd, Gardena
(90248-1703)
PHONE....................................310 324-8227
Andrew Lisardi, *CEO*
Jack Gray, *Vice Pres*
Nancy Torres, *Purch Mgr*
▼ **EMP:** 120 **EST:** 1978
SQ FT: 31,000
SALES (est): 11.1MM **Privately Held**
WEB: www.continentalbinder.com
SIC: 2782 2759 2675 2396 Looseleaf
binders & devices; commercial printing;
die-cut paper & board; automotive & ap-
parel trimmings

(P-4609)
DELUXE CORPORATION
Also Called: Deluxe Check Printers
42933 Business Ctr Pkwy, Lancaster
(93535-4515)
PHONE....................................661 942-1144
EMP: 460
SQ FT: 67,253
SALES (corp-wide): 1.7B **Publicly Held**
WEB: www.sitekreator.com
SIC: 2782 2761 2759 Blankbooks And
Looseleaf Binders, Nsk
PA: Deluxe Corporation
3680 Victoria St N
Shoreview MN 55126
651 483-7111

(P-4610)
DOCUPAK INC
17515 Valley View Ave, Cerritos
(90703-7002)
PHONE....................................714 670-7944
William Lyons, *President*
John Flores, *CFO*
Pat Lyons, *Vice Pres*
George Loveridge, *Project Mgr*
EMP: 36 **EST:** 1993
SQ FT: 27,000
SALES (est): 5.2MM **Privately Held**
WEB: www.docupakinc.com
SIC: 2782 Looseleaf binders & devices

(P-4611)
PIONEER PHOTO ALBUMS INC (PA)
9801 Deering Ave, Chatsworth
(91311-4398)
P.O. Box 2497 (91313-2497)
PHONE....................................818 882-2161
Shell Plutsky, *CEO*
Jason Reubens, *President*
Eric Bisquera, *COO*
Tiffany Boxer, *Vice Pres*
Rick Collies, *Vice Pres*
◆ **EMP:** 150
SQ FT: 100,000
SALES (est): 16.6MM **Privately Held**
WEB: www.pioneerphotoalbums.com
SIC: 2782 Albums

(P-4612)
SHARON HAVRILUK
Also Called: American Mailing & Prtg Svc
1164 N Kraemer Pl, Anaheim (92806-1922)
PHONE....................................714 630-1313
Sharon Havriluk, *Owner*
Jennifer Hill, *COO*
EMP: 20 **EST:** 1966
SQ FT: 10,000
SALES (est): 1.6MM **Privately Held**
SIC: 2782 7331 Account books; mailing
list compilers; mailing service

(P-4613)
ULTRA PRO ACQUISITION LLC
6049 E Slauson Ave, Commerce
(90040-3007)
PHONE....................................323 725-1975
▲ **EMP:** 46 **EST:** 2007
SALES (est): 5MM **Privately Held**
WEB: www.marlinequity.com
SIC: 2782 Library binders, looseleaf
PA: Marlin Equity Partners, Llc
338 Pier Ave
Hermosa Beach CA 90254

(P-4614)
ULTRA PRO INTERNATIONAL LLC (PA)
Also Called: Jolly Roger Games
6049 E Slauson Ave, Commerce
(90040-3007)
PHONE....................................323 890-2100
Sheldon Rosenberg, *Managing Prtnr*
Dan Rowen, *Surgery Dir*
Nathan Hamill, *Associate Dir*
Justin Cole, *Project Mgr*
Carlos Pineda, *Engineer*
▲ **EMP:** 87 **EST:** 2011
SALES (est): 17.2MM **Privately Held**
WEB: www.ultrapro.com
SIC: 2782 Scrapbooks, albums & diaries

(P-4615)
VAGRANT RECORDS INC
6351 Wilshire Blvd # 101, Los Angeles
(90048-5021)
PHONE....................................323 302-0100
Richard A Egan, *President*
Jon Cohen, *Vice Pres*
EMP: 15 **EST:** 1993
SALES (est): 1.6MM **Privately Held**
WEB: www.vagrant.com
SIC: 2782 5735 Record albums; records

(P-4616)
WEST CAST HNDCRFTED ALBUMS INC
Also Called: West Coast Albums
1717 S Hoover St Ste 101, Los Angeles
(90006-4958)
PHONE....................................626 253-0335
Mohsen Saeedy, *CEO*
EMP: 20 **EST:** 2010
SALES (est): 54K **Privately Held**
WEB: www.westcoastalbums.com
SIC: 2782 Albums

2789 Bookbinding

(P-4617)
B J BINDERY INC
833 S Grand Ave, Santa Ana (92705-4117)
PHONE....................................714 835-7342
Naresh Arya, *CEO*
Renu Arya, *Vice Pres*
Yessica Cervantes, *Accounts Exec*
▲ **EMP:** 80 **EST:** 1970
SQ FT: 29,000
SALES (est): 8.4MM **Privately Held**
WEB: www.bjbindery.com
SIC: 2789 Binding only: books, pamphlets,
magazines, etc.

(P-4618)
KATER-CRAFTS INCORPORATED
Also Called: Book Binders
4860 Gregg Rd, Pico Rivera (90660-2107)
PHONE....................................562 692-0665
Bruce Kavin, *President*
Richard Kavin, *Vice Pres*
EMP: 40 **EST:** 1948
SQ FT: 20,000
SALES (est): 6MM **Privately Held**
WEB: www.katercrafts.com
SIC: 2789 Binding only: books, pamphlets,
magazines, etc.

(P-4619)
PACIFICO BINDERY INC
544 W Angus Ave, Orange (92868-1302)
PHONE....................................714 744-1510
Richard G Zinke, *President*
EMP: 15 **EST:** 1989
SALES (est): 824K **Privately Held**
WEB: www.pacificobindery.com
SIC: 2789 Binding only: books, pamphlets,
magazines, etc.

(P-4620)
ROSS BINDERY INC
15310 Spring Ave, Santa Fe Springs
(90670-5644)
PHONE....................................562 623-4565
George Jackson, *CEO*
Desiree Reyna, *Accounting Dir*
Karl Doerzapf, *Opers Staff*
Alex Cantabella, *Manager*
John Gaynor, *Manager*
▲ **EMP:** 120
SQ FT: 65,000
SALES (est): 16.6MM **Privately Held**
WEB: www.rossbindery.com
SIC: 2789 Pamphlets, binding

(P-4621)
S & S BINDERY INC
2366 1st St, La Verne (91750-5545)
PHONE....................................909 596-2213
Steve Thompson, *President*
Scott Fehrensen, *Vice Pres*
▼ **EMP:** 20 **EST:** 1998
SQ FT: 13,750
SALES (est): 2.3MM **Privately Held**
SIC: 2789 Binding only: books, pamphlets,
magazines, etc.

(P-4622)
SOUTHERN CAL BNDERY MILING INC
10661 Business Dr, Fontana (92337-8212)
PHONE....................................909 829-1949
Rex Miller, *President*
EMP: 18 **EST:** 1988
SQ FT: 51,000

SALES (est): 578.1K **Privately Held**
WEB: www.scbminc.com
SIC: 2789 7331 Binding & repair of books,
magazines & pamphlets; mailing service

2791 Typesetting

(P-4623)
AUTOMATION PRINTING CO (PA)
1230 Long Beach Ave, Los Angeles
(90021-2320)
PHONE....................................213 488-1230
David Tobman, *President*
Ann Tobman, *Corp Secy*
Jesse Lobato, *Executive*
Art Tolentino, *Opers Mgr*
Terry Harrison, *Sales Mgr*
EMP: 37 **EST:** 1949
SQ FT: 30,000
SALES (est): 3.4MM **Privately Held**
WEB: www.automation-123.com
SIC: 2791 2796 2759 2732 Typesetting;
platemaking services; commercial print-
ing; book printing; commercial printing,
offset

(P-4624)
CASTLE PRESS
1128 N Gilbert St, Anaheim (92801-1401)
PHONE....................................800 794-0858
Jay Bautista, *Manager*
Martin Callan, *Prgrmr*
Janice Ho, *Controller*
Lee Wong, *Warehouse Mgr*
EMP: 13 **EST:** 2016
SALES (est): 3.1MM **Privately Held**
WEB: www.castlepress.com
SIC: 2791 Typesetting

(P-4625)
GOLDING PUBLICATIONS
Also Called: Friday Flier
31558 Railroad Canyon Rd, Canyon Lake
(92587-9427)
PHONE....................................951 244-1966
Charles G Golding, *Owner*
Dona Jessup, *Executive*
Marti Norris, *Executive*
Sharon Rice, *Editor*
EMP: 17 **EST:** 1990
SALES (est): 1.2MM **Privately Held**
WEB: www.goldingpublications.com
SIC: 2791 Typesetting

(P-4626)
SYSTEMS PRINTING INC
14311 Chambers Rd, Tustin (92780-6911)
PHONE....................................714 832-4677
Kevin Williams, *President*
EMP: 13 **EST:** 1988
SQ FT: 3,600
SALES (est): 598.7K **Privately Held**
WEB: www.systemsprint.com
SIC: 2791 7334 2752 Typesetting; photo-
copying & duplicating services; commer-
cial printing, lithographic

(P-4627)
TS ENTERPRISES INC
Also Called: La Quinta Cliff House
78250 Highway 111, La Quinta
(92253-2074)
PHONE....................................760 360-5991
David Potesta, *Branch Mgr*
EMP: 26
SALES (corp-wide): 25.4MM **Privately Held**
WEB: www.tsrestaurants.com
SIC: 5812 5699 5261 2791 American
restaurant; custom tailor; lawn & garden
supplies; typesetting; gourmet food
stores; video repair
PA: T.S. Enterprises, Inc
225 W Plaza St Ste 300
Solana Beach CA 92075
858 720-2380

2796 Platemaking & Related Svcs

(P-4628)
AFT CORPORATION
Also Called: Andresen Digital Pre-Press
1815 Centinela Ave Unit C, Santa Monica
(90404-4203)
PHONE..............................310 576-1007
Andrew Andresen, *President*
William Andresen, *President*
Ann Verkuilen, *CFO*
Chuck Henk, *Treasurer*
Glen Rosuck, *Vice Pres*
EMP: 18 **EST:** 1994
SQ FT: 4,200
SALES (est): 5.6MM **Privately Held**
WEB: www.andresendigital.com
SIC: 2796 2791 7336 Color separations for printing; photocomposition, for the printing trade; creative services to advertisers, except writers

(P-4629)
EFFECTIVE GRAPHICS NC INC
40 E Verdugo Ave, Burbank (91502-1931)
PHONE..............................310 323-2223
Roger Sanders, *CEO*
David Curtis, *President*
Michael Vascellaro, *CFO*
Frank Franco, *Sales Mgr*
EMP: 25 **EST:** 1977
SQ FT: 47,970
SALES (est): 1.2MM **Privately Held**
SIC: 2796 2752 Color separations for printing; commercial printing, lithographic

(P-4630)
FLEXLINE INC
15405 Cornet St, Santa Fe Springs
(90670-5533)
PHONE..............................562 921-4141
John Bateman, *President*
William Hall, *Vice Pres*
EMP: 28 **EST:** 1991
SALES (est): 2.6MM **Privately Held**
WEB: www.flexlineinc.com
SIC: 2796 2759 3555 Platemaking services; commercial printing; printing plates

(P-4631)
GEMINI GEL LLC
8365 Melrose Ave, Los Angeles
(90069-5419)
PHONE..............................323 651-0513
Sidney B Felsen, *President*
Stanley Grinstein, *Treasurer*
Xavier Fumat, *Graphic Designe*
Renee Coppola, *Sales Staff*
EMP: 29 **EST:** 1966
SQ FT: 6,000
SALES (est): 3.7MM **Privately Held**
WEB: www.geminigel.com
SIC: 2796 2752 Etching on copper, steel, wood or rubber: printing plates; commercial printing, lithographic

(P-4632)
INDUSTRIAL PRINTERS CALIFORNIA
Also Called: Industrial Printing Group
3012 S Croddy Way, Santa Ana
(92704-6305)
PHONE..............................714 545-8484
Darcy H Hall, *President*
Dale Hall, *Corp Secy*
Howard Rettberg, *Vice Pres*
EMP: 18 **EST:** 1969
SQ FT: 30,000
SALES (est): 364.3K **Privately Held**
SIC: 2796 2759 2752 Platemaking services; commercial printing; catalogs, lithographed

(P-4633)
MASTER ARTS INC
Also Called: Master Arts Engraving
3737 E Miraloma Ave, Anaheim
(92806-2100)
PHONE..............................714 240-4550
Elgin Chalayan, *President*
Rick Workman, *General Mgr*
Mike Liberto, *Sales Mgr*
EMP: 15 **EST:** 1962

SQ FT: 10,000
SALES (est): 2.3MM **Privately Held**
WEB: www.masterartsgraphicsinc.com
SIC: 2796 3555 Platemaking services; printing plates

2812 Alkalies & Chlorine

(P-4634)
ARKEMA INC
Also Called: Arkema Coating Resins
19206 Hawthorne Blvd, Torrance
(90503-1505)
PHONE..............................310 214-5327
EMP: 43
SALES (corp-wide): 117MM **Privately Held**
WEB: www.arkema.com
SIC: 2812 2819 2869 2899 Chlorine, compressed or liquefied; caustic soda, sodium hydroxide; industrial inorganic chemicals; sodium compounds or salts, inorg., ex. refined sod. chloride; sodium sulfate, glauber's salt, salt cake; peroxides, hydrogen peroxide; industrial organic chemicals; solvents, organic; formaldehyde (formalin); metal treating compounds; plastics pipe
HQ: Arkema Inc.
900 1st Ave
King Of Prussia PA 19406
610 205-7000

(P-4635)
HILL BROTHERS CHEMICAL COMPANY
Also Called: Desert Brand
15017 Clark Ave, City of Industry
(91745-1409)
PHONE..............................626 333-2251
Ron Hill, *President*
Toni Dakovich, *Purch Mgr*
EMP: 18
SQ FT: 17,203
SALES (corp-wide): 125.4MM **Privately Held**
WEB: www.hillbrothers.com
SIC: 2812 2851 2819 Chlorine, compressed or liquefied; paints & allied products; industrial inorganic chemicals
PA: Hill Brothers Chemical Company
3000 E Birch St Ste 108
Brea CA 92821
714 998-8800

(P-4636)
JCI JONES CHEMICALS INC
1401 Del Amo Blvd, Torrance (90501-1630)
PHONE..............................310 523-1629
Mike Reddinton, *Manager*
EMP: 18
SALES (corp-wide): 196.9MM **Privately Held**
WEB: www.jcichem.com
SIC: 2812 2899 Alkalies; chlorine, compressed or liquefied; chemical preparations
PA: Jci Jones Chemicals, Inc.
1765 Ringling Blvd # 200
Sarasota FL 34236
941 330-1537

2813 Industrial Gases

(P-4637)
AIR LIQUIDE ELECTRONICS US LP
1502 W Anaheim St, Wilmington
(90744-2303)
PHONE..............................310 549-7079
EMP: 5002
SALES (corp-wide): 102.6MM **Privately Held**
WEB: www.airliquide.com
SIC: 2813 3564 8631 2819 Industrial gases; blowers & fans; labor unions & similar labor organizations; industrial inorganic chemicals
HQ: Air Liquide Electronics U.S. Lp
9101 Lyndon B Johnson Fwy # 800
Dallas TX 75243
972 301-5200

(P-4638)
AIR SOURCE INDUSTRIES
3976 Cherry Ave, Long Beach
(90807-3727)
PHONE..............................562 426-4017
Robert L Bowers, *CEO*
Jackie Villa, *Officer*
Richard Smith, *Vice Pres*
Donna Slott, *General Mgr*
EMP: 28 **EST:** 1938
SALES (est): 5.6MM **Privately Held**
WEB: www.air-source.com
SIC: 2813 5999 Industrial gases; convalescent equipment & supplies

(P-4639)
FOLLMER DEVELOPMENT INC
Also Called: Fd
840 Tourmaline Dr, Newbury Park
(91320-1205)
PHONE..............................805 498-4531
Christopher H Follmer, *CEO*
Garrett Follmer, *President*
Helen Follmer, *Corp Secy*
David McKenzie, *Vice Pres*
Dan Follmer, *Principal*
▼ **EMP:** 41 **EST:** 1974
SQ FT: 35,000
SALES (est): 20.7MM **Privately Held**
WEB: www.follmerdevelopment.com
SIC: 2813 Aerosols

(P-4640)
LINDE GAS & EQUIPMENT INC
Praxair
2006 E 223rd St Bldg 1, Long Beach
(90810-1609)
PHONE..............................310 816-9397
EMP: 25 **Privately Held**
SIC: 2813 Dry ice, carbon dioxide (solid)
HQ: Linde Gas & Equipment Inc.
10 Riverview Dr
Danbury CT 06810
203 837-2000

(P-4641)
LINDE GAS NORTH AMERICA LLC
Also Called: Lifegas
614 S Glenwood Pl, Burbank (91506-2820)
PHONE..............................626 855-8344
EMP: 19
SALES (corp-wide): 20.1B **Privately Held**
SIC: 2813 Mfg Nitrogen/ Oxygen
HQ: Linde Gas North America Llc
200 Somerset Corp Blvd # 7000
Bridgewater NJ 06810

(P-4642)
MESSER LLC
Also Called: Cryostar USA
13117 Meyer Rd, Whittier (90605-3555)
PHONE..............................562 903-1290
Mark Sutton, *Branch Mgr*
EMP: 16
SALES (corp-wide): 1.3B **Privately Held**
WEB: www.messeramericas.com
SIC: 2813 3561 Oxygen, compressed or liquefied; pumps & pumping equipment
HQ: Messer Llc
200 Smrst Corp Blvd # 7000
Bridgewater NJ 08807
800 755-9277

(P-4643)
MESSER LLC
2535 Del Amo Blvd, Torrance (90503-1706)
PHONE..............................310 533-8394
Jason Lacasella, *Branch Mgr*
EMP: 16
SALES (corp-wide): 1.3B **Privately Held**
WEB: www.messeramericas.com
SIC: 2813 Carbon dioxide
HQ: Messer Llc
200 Smrst Corp Blvd # 7000
Bridgewater NJ 08807
800 755-9277

(P-4644)
MESSER LLC
660 Baldwin Park Blvd, City of Industry
(91746-1501)
PHONE..............................626 855-8366
Mike Colvin, *Branch Mgr*
Daniel Kahan, *Area Mgr*

Luke Sakievich, *Manager*
EMP: 16
SALES (corp-wide): 1.3B **Privately Held**
WEB: www.messeramericas.com
SIC: 2813 Nitrogen
HQ: Messer Llc
200 Smrst Corp Blvd # 7000
Bridgewater NJ 08807
800 755-9277

2816 Inorganic Pigments

(P-4645)
RYVEC INC
251 E Palais Rd, Anaheim (92805-6239)
PHONE..............................714 520-5592
Michael Ryan, *CEO*
Lucy Toledo, *Admin Asst*
Phil Ellis, *Maintence Staff*
Kim Ceja, *Manager*
Carlos Gomez, *Manager*
◆ **EMP:** 25 **EST:** 1982
SQ FT: 43,000
SALES (est): 10.4MM **Privately Held**
WEB: www.ryvec.com
SIC: 2816 2865 2821 Color pigments; dyes & pigments; polyurethane resins

(P-4646)
SPECTRA COLOR INC
9116 Stellar Ct, Corona (92883-4923)
PHONE..............................951 277-0200
Robert Shedd, *President*
John Shedd, *Admin Sec*
Maria Conner, *Accountant*
▲ **EMP:** 42 **EST:** 1976
SQ FT: 40,000
SALES (est): 13.9MM **Privately Held**
WEB: www.spectracolor.com
SIC: 2816 3089 2821 Color pigments; coloring & finishing of plastic products; plastics materials & resins

(P-4647)
STANFORD MATERIALS CORPORATION
23661 Birtcher Dr, Lake Forest
(92630-1770)
PHONE..............................949 380-7362
▲ **EMP:** 13
SALES (est): 2.1MM **Privately Held**
SIC: 2816 Mfg Inorganic Figments

(P-4648)
VENATOR AMERICAS LLC
Davis Colors
3700 E Olympic Blvd, Los Angeles
(90023-3123)
P.O. Box 23100 (90023-0100)
PHONE..............................323 269-7311
Nick Paris, *Vice Pres*
Joe Hernandez, *Buyer*
EMP: 70
SQ FT: 540,000
SALES (corp-wide): 669.4MM **Privately Held**
WEB: www.huntsman.com
SIC: 2816 2865 Inorganic pigments; cyclic crudes & intermediates
HQ: Venator Americas Llc
10001 Woodloch Forest Dr
The Woodlands TX 77380
281 465-6700

2819 Indl Inorganic Chemicals, NEC

(P-4649)
ADVANCED CHEMICAL TECHNOLOGY
3540 E 26th St, Vernon (90058-4103)
PHONE..............................800 527-9607
Daniel Anthony Earley, *CEO*
Candi Delgadillo, *Purchasing*
EMP: 40 **EST:** 1996
SALES (est): 9.9MM **Privately Held**
WEB: www.actglobal.net
SIC: 2819 2899 5169 Industrial inorganic chemicals; antiscaling compounds, boiler; water treating compounds; anti-corrosion products; industrial chemicals

▲ = Import ▼=Export
◆ =Import/Export

(P-4650)
BIOLARGO INC (PA)
Also Called: Bio2
14921 Chestnut St, Westminster
(92683-5215)
P.O. Box 3950, Laguna Hills (92654-3950)
PHONE........................949 643-9540
Dennis P Calvert, *President*
Charles K Dargan II, *CFO*
Charles Dargan, *CFO*
Kenneth R Code, *Officer*
Joseph L Provenzano, *Vice Pres*
EMP: 18 **EST:** 1989
SQ FT: 9,000
SALES (est): 2.4MM **Publicly Held**
WEB: www.biolargo.com
SIC: 2819 Iodine, elemental

(P-4651)
CAL-PAC CHEMICAL CO INC
6231 Maywood Ave, Huntington Park
(90255-4530)
PHONE........................323 585-2178
Charles F Duane, *President*
EMP: 17 **EST:** 1955
SQ FT: 37,000
SALES (est): 2.5MM **Privately Held**
WEB: www.calpacchem.com
SIC: 2819 Industrial inorganic chemicals

(P-4652)
CALIFORNIA CARBON COMPANY INC
2825 E Grant St, Wilmington (90744-4033)
PHONE........................562 436-1962
Franklin Liu, *President*
Rita L Wu, *Treasurer*
Richard Liu, *Vice Pres*
▲ **EMP:** 42 **EST:** 1962
SQ FT: 10,000
SALES (est): 11.6MM **Privately Held**
WEB: www.californiacarbon.com
SIC: 2819 Carbides

(P-4653)
CALIFORNIA SILICA PRODUCTS LLC (PA)
1420 S Bon View Ave, Ontario
(91761-4405)
P.O. Box 3340 (91761-0934)
PHONE........................760 885-5358
Randall Humphreys, *Principal*
EMP: 48 **EST:** 2002
SALES (est): 952.5K **Privately Held**
WEB: www.calsilica.net
SIC: 2819 Silica compounds

(P-4654)
CALIFORNIA SILICA PRODUCTS LLC
12808 Rancho Rd, Adelanto (92301-2719)
PHONE........................909 947-0028
Randall Humphreys, *Branch Mgr*
EMP: 27
SALES (corp-wide): 952.5K **Privately Held**
WEB: www.calsilica.net
SIC: 2819 Silica compounds
PA: California Silica Products, Llc
1420 S Bon View Ave
Ontario CA 91761
760 885-5358

(P-4655)
CALIFORNIA SULPHUR COMPANY
2250 E Pacific Coast Hwy, Wilmington
(90744-2917)
P.O. Box 176 (90748-0176)
PHONE........................562 437-0768
John Babbitt, *Principal*
Cheryl Rocha, *Manager*
▼ **EMP:** 28 **EST:** 1958
SQ FT: 900
SALES (est): 6.1MM **Privately Held**
WEB: www.california-sulphur-company.com
SIC: 2819 Industrial inorganic chemicals

(P-4656)
CDTI ADVANCED MATERIALS INC (PA)
1641 Fiske Pl, Oxnard (93033-1862)
PHONE........................805 639-9458
Matthew Beale, *President*

Lon E Bell, *Ch of Bd*
Peter J Chase, *COO*
Tracy A Kern, *CFO*
Tracy Kern, *CFO*
EMP: 47
SALES (est): 28.3MM **Privately Held**
WEB: www.cdti.com
SIC: 2819 3823 Catalysts, chemical; industrial instrmnts msrmnt display/control process variable

(P-4657)
ECO SERVICES OPERATIONS CORP
20720 S Wilmington Ave, Long Beach
(90810-1034)
PHONE........................310 885-6719
Stephen Caro, *Plant Mgr*
Kelly Bowen, *Office Spvr*
EMP: 51
SALES (corp-wide): 1.1B **Publicly Held**
SIC: 2819 Sulfuric acid, oleum
HQ: Eco Services Operations Corp.
300 Lindenwood Dr
Malvern PA 19355
610 251-9118

(P-4658)
FLORIDE PRODUCTS LLC (PA)
2867 Vail Ave, Commerce (90040-2613)
PHONE........................323 201-4363
EMP: 23
SALES (est): 19.1MM **Privately Held**
SIC: 2819 Mfg Industrial Inorganic Chemicals

(P-4659)
GENERAL CARBON COMPANY
7542 Maie Ave, Los Angeles (90001-2637)
PHONE........................323 588-9291
Renee Aukers, *President*
Julio Negrete, *Vice Pres*
Mark Attwater, *Business Mgr*
▲ **EMP:** 25 **EST:** 1931
SQ FT: 10,000
SALES (est): 3.7MM **Privately Held**
WEB: www.generalcarboncompany.com
SIC: 2819 Industrial inorganic chemicals

(P-4660)
JM HUBER MICROPOWDERS INC
Also Called: Nutri Granulations
16024 Phoebe Ave, La Mirada
(90638-5606)
PHONE........................714 994-7855
Mike Marberry, *President*
EMP: 35
SQ FT: 45,000
SALES (corp-wide): 1.1B **Privately Held**
WEB: www.huber.com
SIC: 2819 Industrial inorganic chemicals
HQ: J.M. Huber Micropowders Inc.
3100 Cumberland Blvd Se # 600
Atlanta GA 30339
732 549-8600

(P-4661)
MATERIA INC (PA)
60 N San Gabriel Blvd, Pasadena
(91107-3748)
PHONE........................626 584-8400
Cliff Post, *President*
Scott Krog, *CFO*
Christopher Cruce, *Vice Pres*
Christopher J Cruce, *Vice Pres*
Neal Gilmore, *Vice Pres*
◆ **EMP:** 120 **EST:** 1998
SQ FT: 30,000
SALES (est): 44.6MM **Privately Held**
WEB: www.materia-inc.com
SIC: 2819 Catalysts, chemical

(P-4662)
MERELEX CORPORATION
Also Called: American Elements
10884 Weyburn Ave, Los Angeles
(90024-2917)
PHONE........................310 208-0551
Michael Silver, *President*
Scott Michel, *COO*
Annie Simons, *Officer*
Janet Walker, *Comms Dir*
Preston McKnight, *Human Resources*
▲ **EMP:** 22 **EST:** 1996

SALES (est): 5MM **Privately Held**
WEB: www.americanelements.com
SIC: 2819 Chemicals, high purity: refined from technical grade

(P-4663)
MORAVEK BIOCHEMICALS INC (PA)
577 Mercury Ln, Brea (92821-4831)
PHONE........................714 990-2018
Paul Moravek, *President*
Joseph Moravek, *President*
Lia Barnes, *COO*
Helen Moravek, *Corp Secy*
Megan Schmitz, *Office Mgr*
▲ **EMP:** 25 **EST:** 1976
SQ FT: 6,000
SALES (est): 9.3MM **Privately Held**
WEB: www.moravek.com
SIC: 2819 Industrial inorganic chemicals

(P-4664)
OMYA INC
7299 Crystal Creek Rd, Lucerne Valley
(92356-8646)
PHONE........................760 248-5200
Rainer Seidler, *CEO*
EMP: 100
SALES (corp-wide): 1B **Privately Held**
WEB: www.omya.com
SIC: 2819 8741 3281 Calcium compounds & salts, inorganic; management services; cut stone & stone products
HQ: Omya Inc.
9987 Carver Rd Ste 300
Blue Ash OH 45242
513 387-4600

(P-4665)
PCT-GW CARBIDE TOOLS USA INC
13701 Excelsior Dr, Santa Fe Springs
(90670-5104)
PHONE........................562 921-7898
Shamir Seth, *President*
▲ **EMP:** 19 **EST:** 2005
SALES (est): 484.7K **Privately Held**
SIC: 2819 Carbides

(P-4666)
PERIMETER SOLUTIONS LP
Wildfire Control Division
10667 Jersey Blvd, Rancho Cucamonga
(91730-5110)
PHONE........................909 983-0772
Vinayak Sharma, *Manager*
Craig McDonnell, *Business Mgr*
Melissa Kim, *Director*
Cheryl Canada Airbase, *Manager*
EMP: 20 **Privately Held**
WEB: www.icl-phos-spec.com
SIC: 2819 Industrial inorganic chemicals
HQ: Perimeter Solutions Lp
120 S Central Ave
Saint Louis MO 63105
314 983-7500

(P-4667)
PHIBRO-TECH INC
8851 Dice Rd, Santa Fe Springs
(90670-2515)
PHONE........................562 698-8036
Mark Alling, *Manager*
Alonso Alatorre, *Lab Dir*
Jeff Dorfman, *MIS Dir*
Jim Ferguson, *Maintence Staff*
Jerry Mesinger, *Manager*
EMP: 50
SALES (corp-wide): 833.3MM **Publicly Held**
WEB: www.pahc.com
SIC: 2819 2899 Inorganic metal compounds or salts; chemical preparations
HQ: Phibro-Tech, Inc.
300 Frank W Burr Blvd
Teaneck NJ 07666

(P-4668)
QUALITY CAR CARE PRODUCTS INC
2734 Huntington Dr, Duarte (91010-2301)
PHONE........................626 359-9174
Edward R Justice Jr, *President*
EMP: 44 **EST:** 1947

SQ FT: 25,000
SALES (est): 14MM **Privately Held**
SIC: 2819 Industrial inorganic chemicals

(P-4669)
SINGOD INVESTORS VI LLC
Also Called: Element Anheim Rsort Cnvntion
1600 S Clementine St, Anaheim
(92802-2901)
PHONE........................714 326-7800
Padmesh Patel, *Principal*
EMP: 55 **EST:** 2016
SALES (est): 6.9MM **Privately Held**
SIC: 2819 Elements

(P-4670)
SOLVAY USA INC
Also Called: Marchem Solvay Group
20851 S Santa Fe Ave, Long Beach
(90810-1130)
PHONE........................310 669-5300
Maria Johnson, *Manager*
EMP: 17
SALES (corp-wide): 13MM **Privately Held**
WEB: www.solvay.com
SIC: 2819 Industrial inorganic chemicals
HQ: Solvay Usa Inc.
504 Carnegie Ctr
Princeton NJ 08540
609 860-4000

(P-4671)
SONGS DCMMSSNING SOLUTIONS LLC
5000 Pacific Coast Hwy, San Clemente
(92674)
PHONE........................801 649-2223
William F Acton, *Principal*
EMP: 13 **EST:** 2018
SALES (est): 2.6MM **Privately Held**
WEB: www.songscommunity.com
SIC: 2819 Nuclear fuel scrap, reprocessing

(P-4672)
SPECIALTY MINERALS INC
Minerals Technology
6565 Meridian Rd, Lucerne Valley
(92356-8602)
P.O. Box 558 (92356-0558)
PHONE........................760 248-5300
Doug Mayger, *Branch Mgr*
Luke Kurtz, *Manager*
EMP: 150 **Publicly Held**
WEB: www.mineralstech.com
SIC: 2819 Industrial inorganic chemicals
HQ: Specialty Minerals Inc.
622 3rd Ave Fl 38
New York NY 10017

(P-4673)
US BORAX INC
14486 Borax Rd, Boron (93516-2017)
PHONE........................760 762-7000
Joe A Carrabba, *Branch Mgr*
Doug Batchelor, *MIS Dir*
Sheila Richardson, *Manager*
EMP: 900
SALES (corp-wide): 44.6B **Privately Held**
WEB: www.borax.com
SIC: 2819 Industrial inorganic chemicals
HQ: U.S. Borax Inc.
200 E Randolph St # 7100
Chicago IL 60601
773 270-6500

(P-4674)
VENUS LABORATORIES INC
Earth Friendly Products
11150 Hope St, Cypress (90630-5236)
PHONE........................714 891-3100
Firas Jamal, *Manager*
Victoria Nuevo-Celeste, *Vice Pres*
Belinda Diaz, *Purch Agent*
Monika Hanks, *Marketing Staff*
Noel Ebrahim, *Sales Staff*
EMP: 70
SALES (corp-wide): 76.7MM **Privately Held**
WEB: www.ecos.com
SIC: 2819 2844 2842 2841 Industrial inorganic chemicals; toilet preparations; specialty cleaning, polishes & sanitation goods; soap & other detergents

PRODUCTS & SVCS

PA: Venus Laboratories, Inc.
111 S Rohlwing Rd
Addison IL 60101
630 595-1900

2821 Plastics, Mtrls & Nonvulcanizable Elastomers

(P-4675)
ACP NOXTAT INC
1112 E Washington Ave, Santa Ana
(92701-4221)
PHONE..................714 547-5477
Anthony Floyd Richard, *President*
Tracee Huwe, *COO*
Anthony Richard, *Info Tech Dir*
EMP: 22 **EST:** 2004
SALES (est): 6.1MM **Privately Held**
WEB: www.noxtat.com
SIC: 2821 Plastics materials & resins

(P-4676)
AFFORDABLE PLAS & PACKG INC
739 E Francis St, Ontario (91761-5514)
PHONE..................909 972-1944
Rene J Villalpando, *CEO*
EMP: 13 **EST:** 2012
SALES (est): 1.6MM **Privately Held**
WEB: www.affordableplastics.com
SIC: 2821 Plastics materials & resins

(P-4677)
ALPHA CORPORATION OF TENNESSEE
Also Called: Alpha-Owens Corning
19991 Seaton Ave, Perris (92570-8724)
PHONE..................951 657-5161
John Mulrine, *Enginr/R&D Mgr*
EMP: 128
SALES (corp-wide): 166.7K **Privately Held**
SIC: 2821 Polyethylene resins
HQ: The Alpha Corporation Of Tennessee
955 Highway 57
Piperton TN 38017
901 854-2800

(P-4678)
APTCO LLC (PA)
31381 Pond Rd Bldg 2, Mc Farland
(93250-9795)
PHONE..................661 792-2107
Jim Banuelos, *Mng Member*
Scott Hakl,
◆ **EMP:** 99 **EST:** 1996
SALES (est): 16MM **Privately Held**
WEB: www.aptcollc.com
SIC: 2821 Thermoplastic materials

(P-4679)
B & B PLASTICS INC
1892 W Casmalia St, Rialto (92377-4112)
PHONE..................909 829-3606
Baltazar Mejia, *CEO*
Christy Dawson, *Human Resources*
Bacilo Mejia, *Sales Mgr*
Phillip Booker, *Sales Staff*
Martha Martinez, *Sales Staff*
EMP: 20 **EST:** 2014
SALES (est): 3.8MM **Privately Held**
WEB: www.bbplasticsinc.com
SIC: 2821 Thermoplastic materials

(P-4680)
BDC EPOXY SYSTEMS INC
12903 Sunshine Ave, Santa Fe Springs
(90670-4732)
P.O. Box 2445 (90670-0445)
PHONE..................562 944-6177
Fred Benson, *CEO*
Laura Benson, *CFO*
Matt Benson, *Vice Pres*
Patricia Ashford, *General Mgr*
Gene Vega, *Sales Mgr*
▲ **EMP:** 27 **EST:** 1976
SQ FT: 15,000
SALES (est): 5.2MM **Privately Held**
SIC: 2821 Epoxy resins

(P-4681)
BJB ENTERPRISES INC
14791 Franklin Ave, Tustin (92780-7215)
PHONE..................714 734-8450
Brian Stransky, *President*
Troy Peterson, *Technical Staff*
Joseph Castillo, *Mfg Staff*
Haylee Detroit, *Marketing Staff*
Michael Richard, *Marketing Staff*
EMP: 27 **EST:** 1970
SQ FT: 38,000
SALES (est): 7.1MM **Privately Held**
WEB: www.bjbenterprises.com
SIC: 2821 3087 5162 Polyurethane
resins; custom compound purchased
resins; plastics materials & basic shapes

(P-4682)
CGPC AMERICA CORPORATION
Also Called: Enduratex
1181 California Ave # 235, Corona
(92881-3304)
PHONE..................951 332-4100
Quentin Wu, *Ch of Bd*
Amy Pan, *CFO*
Dr Dean Lee, *Vice Pres*
Sonia Acosta, *Executive Asst*
Linda Ortiz, *Sales Staff*
▲ **EMP:** 22 **EST:** 1985
SQ FT: 52,000
SALES (est): 15.8MM **Privately Held**
WEB: www.enduratex.com
SIC: 2821 Plastics materials & resins
PA: China General Plastics Corporation
12th Floor , No.37 , Ji-Hu Rd.
Taipei City TAP 11492

(P-4683)
COASTAL ENTERPRISES
1925 W Collins Ave, Orange (92867-5426)
P.O. Box 4875 (92863-4875)
PHONE..................714 771-4969
Chuck Miller, *Owner*
Sheila Miller, *General Mgr*
Candy Cerneka, *Sales Staff*
Danny Lotz, *Manager*
▲ **EMP:** 20 **EST:** 1970
SQ FT: 25,000
SALES (est): 3.5MM **Privately Held**
WEB: www.precisionboard.com
SIC: 2821 Plastics materials & resins

(P-4684)
COSMIC PLASTICS INC (PA)
28410 Industry Dr, Valencia (91355-4108)
PHONE..................661 257-3274
George Luh, *CEO*
Edwin Luh, *Vice Pres*
Eddie Cantrell, *Manager*
Steve Castro, *Manager*
◆ **EMP:** 30
SQ FT: 846,000
SALES (est): 5MM **Privately Held**
WEB: www.cosmicplastics.com
SIC: 2821 Plastics materials & resins

(P-4685)
CROSSFIELD PRODUCTS CORP (PA)
Also Called: Dex-O-Tex Division
3000 E Harcourt St, Compton
(90221-5589)
PHONE..................310 886-9100
Richard Watt, *Ch of Bd*
W Brad Watt, *President*
Ronald Borum, *Exec VP*
Steven Schroeder, *Vice Pres*
◆ **EMP:** 47 **EST:** 1938
SQ FT: 23,000
SALES (est): 24.5MM **Privately Held**
WEB: www.crossfieldproducts.com
SIC: 2821 Plastics materials & resins

(P-4686)
CYTEC ENGINEERED MATERIALS INC
1191 N Hawk Cir, Anaheim (92807-1723)
PHONE..................714 632-8444
George Slayton, *Branch Mgr*
Martin Melgoza, *Purchasing*
EMP: 20

SALES (corp-wide): 13MM **Privately Held**
SIC: 2821 2822 Plastics materials &
resins; synthetic rubber
HQ: Cytec Engineered Materials Inc.
2085 E Tech Cir Ste 102
Tempe AZ 85284

(P-4687)
DOW CHEMICAL CO FOUNDATION
11266 Jersey Blvd, Rancho Cucamonga
(91730-5114)
P.O. Box 748 (91729-0748)
PHONE..................909 476-4127
Steve Rynders, *Principal*
EMP: 173
SALES (corp-wide): 38.5B **Publicly Held**
SIC: 2821 Thermoplastic materials
HQ: The Dow Chemical Company Foundation
2030 Dow Ctr
Midland MI 48674
989 636-1000

(P-4688)
ECOWISE INC
13538 Excelsior Dr Unit B, Santa Fe
Springs (90670-5616)
PHONE..................626 759-3997
Sheng Xu, *President*
EMP: 30 **EST:** 2019
SALES (est): 2.6MM **Privately Held**
SIC: 2821 Polyethylene resins

(P-4689)
ELASCO INC
Also Called: E Sales
11377 Markon Dr, Garden Grove
(92841-1402)
PHONE..................714 373-4767
Henry Larrucea, *President*
David Schindler, *President*
Gary Stull, *CFO*
Janet Lurrucea, *Vice Pres*
▲ **EMP:** 100 **EST:** 1979
SQ FT: 28,000
SALES (est): 20.6MM **Privately Held**
WEB: www.elascourethane.com
SIC: 2821 2891 2822 Polyurethane
resins; adhesives & sealants; synthetic
rubber

(P-4690)
ELASCO URETHANE INC
11377 Markon Dr, Garden Grove
(92841-1402)
PHONE..................714 895-7031
John Frasco, *CEO*
EMP: 34 **EST:** 2014
SALES (est): 1.3MM **Privately Held**
SIC: 2821 2891 2822 Polyurethane
resins; adhesives & sealants; synthetic
rubber

(P-4691)
ELITE GLOBAL SOLUTIONS INC
19732 Descartes, Foothill Ranch
(92610-2621)
PHONE..................949 709-4872
Garry Mazzone, *President*
Christine Mazzone, *Treasurer*
Marc Mazzone, *Treasurer*
Joel Gonzales, *Vice Pres*
Alexis Morgan, *Creative Dir*
▲ **EMP:** 14 **EST:** 2005
SALES (est): 3.1MM **Privately Held**
WEB: www.egsfoodservice.com
SIC: 2821 5023 Melamine resins,
melamine-formaldehyde; kitchenware

(P-4692)
FERCO COLOR INC
Also Called: Ferco Plastic Products
5498 Vine St, Chino (91710-5247)
PHONE..................909 930-0773
Jennifer Thaw, *President*
David De La Torre, *General Mgr*
EMP: 48 **EST:** 1989
SQ FT: 20,000
SALES (est): 1.2MM **Privately Held**
WEB: www.fercocolor.com
SIC: 2821 2865 Polyethylene resins; color
pigments, organic

(P-4693)
HENNIS ENTERPRISES INC
2646 Palma Dr Ste 430, Ventura
(93003-7798)
PHONE..................805 477-0257
Rodney Hennis, *President*
Christopher Hennis, *Treasurer*
EMP: 24 **EST:** 1975
SQ FT: 10,000
SALES (est): 2.9MM **Privately Held**
WEB: www.hennisinc.com
SIC: 2821 Polyurethane resins

(P-4694)
HOFFMAN PLASTIC COMPOUNDS INC
16616 Garfield Ave, Paramount
(90723-5305)
PHONE..................323 636-3346
Ronald P Hoffman, *President*
Susan Hoffman, *Treasurer*
Maria Hilario, *Financial Exec*
Larry Czyz, *Plant Mgr*
▲ **EMP:** 66
SQ FT: 46,000
SALES (est): 18.9MM **Privately Held**
WEB: www.hoffmanplastic.com
SIC: 2821 3087 Polyvinyl chloride resins
(PVC); custom compound purchased
resins

(P-4695)
HUNTSMAN ADVANCED MATERIALS AM
5121 W San Fernando Rd, Los Angeles
(90039-1011)
PHONE..................818 265-7221
Glenn Bauernschmidt, *Manager*
Gary Chapman, *Vice Pres*
Alonso Medina, *Production*
Carol Ottaway, *Director*
Matthew Austin, *Manager*
EMP: 120
SALES (corp-wide): 6B **Publicly Held**
WEB: www.huntsman.com
SIC: 2821 Plastics materials & resins
HQ: Huntsman Advanced Materials Americas Llc
10003 Woodloch Forest Dr # 260
The Woodlands TX 77380
281 719-6000

(P-4696)
INDORAMA VNTRES SSTNBLE SLTION
11591 Etiwanda Ave, Fontana
(92337-6927)
PHONE..................951 727-8318
John Wang, *CEO*
EMP: 28 **EST:** 2018
SALES (est): 15.3MM **Privately Held**
WEB: www.indoramaventures.com
SIC: 2821 Plastics materials & resins
PA: Indorama Ventures Public Company
Limited
75/102 Soi Sukhumvit 19, Asok Road
Wattana 10110

(P-4697)
INDUSPAC CALIFORNIA INC
Also Called: Pacific Foam
1550 Champagne Ave, Ontario
(91761-3600)
PHONE..................909 390-4422
Keith Tatum, *General Mgr*
EMP: 13 **Privately Held**
SIC: 2821 Polyethylene resins
HQ: Induspac California, Inc.
6818 Patterson Pass Rd A
Livermore CA 94550

(P-4698)
IP CORPORATION
Also Called: Silmar Division
12335 S Van Ness Ave, Hawthorne
(90250-3320)
PHONE..................323 757-1801
Doug Johnson, *Branch Mgr*
Amber Hunt, *Transportation*
EMP: 31
SQ FT: 56,425

▲ = Import ▼=Export
◆ =Import/Export

SALES (corp-wide): 208.4MM **Privately Held**
WEB: www.interplastic.com
SIC: **2821** 5169 Plastics materials & resins; synthetic resins, rubber & plastic materials
PA: Ip Corporation
1225 Willow Lake Blvd
Saint Paul MN 55110
651 481-6860

(P-4699)
JOES PLASTICS INC
Also Called: Joes Plastics
5725 District Blvd, Vernon (90058-5590)
PHONE....................................323 771-8433
Joe La Fountain Jr, *CEO*
▼ EMP: 40 EST: 1974
SQ FT: 130,000
SALES (est): 2MM **Privately Held**
SIC: **2821** Plastics materials & resins

(P-4700)
LINCOLN COMPOSITE MTLS INC
15422 Electronic Ln, Huntington Beach (92649-1334)
PHONE....................................714 898-8350
Scott Lincoln, *President*
EMP: 17 EST: 2013
SALES (est): 2.6MM **Privately Held**
WEB: www.lcmaterials.com
SIC: **2821** Plastics materials & resins

(P-4701)
MSRS INC
Also Called: Vm International
945 E Church St, Riverside (92507-1103)
PHONE....................................310 952-9000
Roya Vazin, *CEO*
Moe Il Afsari, *Manager*
◆ EMP: 120 EST: 1996
SQ FT: 250,000
SALES (est): 22.9MM **Privately Held**
SIC: **2821** 5023 Plastics materials & resins; kitchenware

(P-4702)
NATURAL ENVMTL PROTECTION CO
Also Called: Nepco
750 S Reservoir St, Pomona (91766-3815)
PHONE....................................909 620-8028
Young Su Shin, *President*
▲ EMP: 31 EST: 2006
SQ FT: 3,600
SALES (est): 20.6MM **Privately Held**
SIC: **2821** Polystyrene resins
PA: Kumsung Industrial Co.Ltd
57-6 Gubong-Gil, Donghwa-Myeon
Jangseong 57242

(P-4703)
NEW TECHNOLOGY PLASTICS INC
7110 Fenwick Ln, Westminster (92683-5248)
PHONE....................................562 941-6034
Gregory A Nelson, *President*
Robert Radtke, *Vice Pres*
Sandra Barratt, *Office Mgr*
Carol Fitzpatrick, *Administration*
Robert Molina, *Opers Mgr*
EMP: 35 EST: 1996
SALES (est): 6.1MM **Privately Held**
WEB: www.newtechnologyplastics.com
SIC: **2821** 5162 Molding compounds, plastics; plastics materials & basic shapes

(P-4704)
NORTH AMERICAN COMPOSITES CO
Also Called: Interplastic
4990 Vanderbilt St, Ontario (91761-2202)
PHONE....................................909 605-8977
Mark Prost, *Vice Pres*
David Englesgard, *Vice Pres*
Rick Whitt, *Technical Staff*
▲ EMP: 20 EST: 2000
SALES (est): 5MM **Privately Held**
WEB: www.nacomposites.com
SIC: **2821** Plastics materials & resins

(P-4705)
ORION PLASTICS CORPORATION
700 W Carob St, Compton (90220-5225)
PHONE....................................310 223-0370
Patricia Conkling, *Principal*
Fred Conkling, *President*
Daniel Gitzke, *Marketing Staff*
Mike Felix, *Director*
Wayne Moore, *Director*
▲ EMP: 75
SQ FT: 60,000
SALES (est): 26MM **Privately Held**
WEB: www.orionplastics.net
SIC: **2821** Plastics materials & resins

(P-4706)
PERFORMANCE MATERIALS CORP (HQ)
Also Called: Tencate Performance Composite
1150 Calle Suerte, Camarillo (93012-8051)
PHONE....................................805 482-1722
Thomas W Smith, *President*
Michelle Larios, *Admin Asst*
Bob Reynolds, *Mktg Dir*
◆ EMP: 100 EST: 1986
SQ FT: 50,000
SALES (est): 36.2MM **Privately Held**
WEB: www.toraytac.com
SIC: **2821** Plastics materials & resins

(P-4707)
PEXCO AEROSPACE INC
5451 Argosy Ave, Huntington Beach (92649-1038)
PHONE....................................714 894-9922
Julio Cuevas, *Plant Mgr*
Toni Cunningham, *Sales Executive*
EMP: 40
SALES (corp-wide): 4.8B **Publicly Held**
WEB: www.pexcoaerospace.com
SIC: **2821** Plastics materials & resins
HQ: Pexco Aerospace, Inc.
2405 S 3rd Ave
Union Gap WA 98903

(P-4708)
PLASKOLITE WEST LLC
Also Called: Continental Acrylics
2225 E Del Amo Blvd, Compton (90220-6303)
PHONE....................................310 637-2103
Rick Larkin, *CFO*
▲ EMP: 30 EST: 2000
SALES (est): 9.6MM
SALES (corp-wide): 307.8MM **Privately Held**
WEB: www.plaskolite.com
SIC: **2821** Acrylic resins
PA: Plaskolite, Llc
400 W Nationwide Blvd # 400
Columbus OH 43215
614 294-3281

(P-4709)
PLASTIC MART INC
43535 Gadsden Ave Ste F, Lancaster (93534-6147)
PHONE....................................310 268-1404
James Nahigian, *President*
Ralph Kafesjian, *Vice Pres*
Gary Phillips, *Admin Sec*
EMP: 13 EST: 1961
SALES (est): 1.2MM **Privately Held**
WEB: www.dshsolutions.org
SIC: **2821** 5211 5162 Plastics materials & resins; lumber & other building materials; plastics materials & basic shapes

(P-4710)
POLYCARBIN INC (PA) ✪
2640 N San Fernando Rd, Los Angeles (90065-1317)
PHONE....................................203 615-3797
EMP: 52 EST: 2021
SALES (est): 280.5K **Privately Held**
SIC: **2821** Molding compounds, plastics

(P-4711)
R K FABRICATION INC
1283 N Grove St, Anaheim (92806-2114)
PHONE....................................714 630-9654
Roger King, *CEO*
Sarah King, *Treasurer*

EMP: 18 EST: 1989
SQ FT: 10,000
SALES (est): 5.5MM **Privately Held**
WEB: www.rkfabrication.com
SIC: **2821** 3714 1799 Plastics materials & resins; exhaust systems & parts, motor vehicle; fiberglass work

(P-4712)
REICHHOLD LLC 2
Also Called: Reichhold Chemicals
237 S Motor Ave, Azusa (91702-3228)
PHONE....................................626 334-4974
Steward Fletcher, *Branch Mgr*
Eden Salywoda, *Manager*
EMP: 14
SALES (corp-wide): 2B **Privately Held**
WEB: www.reichhold.com
SIC: **2821** 2851 Plastics materials & resins; paints & allied products
HQ: Reichhold Llc 2
99 E Cottage Ave
Carpentersville IL 60110
847 836-3178

(P-4713)
RONCELLI PLASTICS INC
330 W Duarte Rd, Monrovia (91016-4584)
PHONE....................................800 250-6516
Gino Roncelli, *CEO*
Riley Cole, *President*
Lisa Isaguirre, *CFO*
Bingo Roncelli, *Corp Secy*
Rich Davis, *Info Tech Dir*
EMP: 61
SQ FT: 11,000
SALES (est): 18.6MM **Privately Held**
WEB: www.roncelli.com
SIC: **2821** Plastics materials & resins

(P-4714)
SAINT-GOBAIN PRFMCE PLAS CORP
7301 Orangewood Ave, Garden Grove (92841-1411)
PHONE....................................714 893-0470
Greg Maki, *Branch Mgr*
John Leary, *Manager*
EMP: 190
SALES (corp-wide): 2.1B **Privately Held**
WEB: www.plastics.saint-gobain.com
SIC: **2821** Plastics materials & resins
HQ: Saint-Gobain Performance Plastics Corporation
31500 Solon Rd
Solon OH 44139
440 836-6900

(P-4715)
SANDERS INDS HOLDINGS INC (HQ)
Also Called: Integrated Polymer Solutions
3701 E Conant St, Long Beach (90808-1783)
PHONE....................................562 354-2920
Rajeev Amara, *CEO*
▲ EMP: 15 EST: 1985
SQ FT: 55,000
SALES (est): 128.8MM
SALES (corp-wide): 653.4MM **Privately Held**
WEB: www.arcline.com
SIC: **2821** Plastics materials & resins
PA: Arcline Investment Management Lp
4 Embarcadero Ctr # 3460
San Francisco CA 94111
415 801-4570

(P-4716)
SILPAK INC (PA)
470 E Bonita Ave, Pomona (91767-1928)
PHONE....................................909 625-0056
Philip Galarneau, *President*
Janice A Galarneau, *Vice Pres*
Janice Galarneau, *Vice Pres*
Don Galarneau, *Sales Staff*
EMP: 13 EST: 1983
SQ FT: 13,850
SALES (est): 2.6MM **Privately Held**
WEB: www.silpak.com
SIC: **2821** Plastics materials & resins

(P-4717)
SK CHEMICALS AMERICA INC
3 Park Plz Ste 430, Irvine (92614-2579)
PHONE....................................949 336-8088

Michael Tae, *President*
▲ EMP: 16 EST: 2002
SALES (est): 1MM **Privately Held**
WEB: www.skchemicals.com
SIC: **2821** Plastics materials & resins

(P-4718)
SOUTHERN CALIFORNIA PLAS INC
3122 Maple St, Santa Ana (92707-4408)
PHONE....................................714 751-7084
Anthony Codet, *President*
▲ EMP: 54 EST: 1995
SQ FT: 240,000
SALES (est): 7.9MM **Privately Held**
WEB: www.unitindustriesgroup.com
SIC: **2821** Plastics materials & resins

(P-4719)
SOUTHLAND POLYMERS INC
14030 Gannet St, Santa Fe Springs (90670-5314)
PHONE....................................562 921-0444
Henry Hsi, *President*
Pantoja Robert, *Export Mgr*
Bob Campbell, *Sales Staff*
Francisco D 'angelo, *Manager*
◆ EMP: 26 EST: 1979
SQ FT: 64,000
SALES (est): 7.1MM **Privately Held**
WEB: www.southlandpolymers.com
SIC: **2821** 5162 Plastics materials & resins; plastics resins

(P-4720)
SPHERE ALLIANCE INC
Also Called: Advanced Aircraft Seal
3087 12th St, Riverside (92507-4904)
PHONE....................................951 352-2400
Daryl Silva, *CEO*
EMP: 37 EST: 2011
SALES (est): 5.5MM **Privately Held**
SIC: **2821** Plastics materials & resins

(P-4721)
TA AEROSPACE CO
Also Called: Ta Division
28065 Franklin Pkwy, Valencia (91355-4117)
PHONE....................................661 702-0448
Jim Sweeney, *President*
Ali Sarhang, *Info Tech Dir*
Chris Bair, *Production*
Hemant Gupta, *Director*
EMP: 180
SQ FT: 78,124
SALES (corp-wide): 4.8B **Publicly Held**
WEB: www.esterline.com
SIC: **2821** 3429 Elastomers, nonvulcanizable (plastics); clamps, metal
HQ: Ta Aerospace Co.
28065 Franklin Pkwy
Valencia CA 91355
661 775-1100

(P-4722)
TAMMY TAYLOR NAILS INC
2001 E Deere Ave, Santa Ana (92705-5724)
PHONE....................................949 250-9287
Tammy Taylor, *President*
Yvette Cotton, *Vice Pres*
Michael Knutson, *Sales Staff*
▼ EMP: 45 EST: 1982
SQ FT: 11,500
SALES (est): 8.6MM **Privately Held**
WEB: www.tammytaylornails.com
SIC: **2821** 7231 5087 Acrylic resins; beauty shops; beauty parlor equipment & supplies

(P-4723)
TECHMER PM INC
18420 S Laurel Park Rd, Compton (90220-6015)
PHONE....................................310 632-9211
John R Manuck, *President*
Ebrahim Mor, *CTO*
Anthony Chang, *Engineer*
Craig Burnett, *VP Opers*
Moonpil Choi, *Manager*
◆ EMP: 500 EST: 1982
SQ FT: 40,000
SALES (est): 61.8MM **Privately Held**
WEB: www.techmerpm.com
SIC: **2821** Plastics materials & resins

(P-4724)
TEKNOR COLOR COMPANY
Also Called: Teknor Apex
420 S 6th Ave, City of Industry
(91746-3128)
P.O. Box 2307, La Puente (91746-0307)
PHONE..............................626 336-7709
Tony Patrizio, *General Mgr*
EMP: 19
SALES (corp-wide): 1B **Privately Held**
WEB: www.teknorapex.com
SIC: 2821 3089 Plastics materials &
resins; plastic processing
HQ: Teknor Color Company Llc
505 Central Ave
Pawtucket RI 02861

(P-4725)
TUFF STUFF PRODUCTS
9600 Road 256, Terra Bella (93270-9732)
PHONE..............................559 535-5778
Maximilian B Lee, *President*
Victoria Lee, *CFO*
Max Lee, *Manager*
▲ **EMP:** 500 **EST:** 1999
SALES (est): 29MM **Privately Held**
WEB: www.tufftubs.com
SIC: 2821 Plastics materials & resins

(P-4726)
UREMET CORPORATION
7012 Belgrave Ave, Garden Grove
(92841-2808)
PHONE..............................657 257-4027
Steve Zamollo, *CEO*
Mark Moore, *President*
John Cockriel, *Vice Pres*
Matt Berry, *Design Engr*
Barbara Griffin, *Purchasing*
▲ **EMP:** 26 **EST:** 1989
SQ FT: 9,500
SALES (est): 9.8MM **Privately Held**
WEB: www.uremet.com
SIC: 2821 Polyurethane resins

(P-4727)
US BLANKS LLC (PA)
14700 S San Pedro St, Gardena
(90248-2001)
P.O. Box 486 (90248-0486)
PHONE..............................310 225-6774
Jeff Holtby,
Kimberly Thress,
▲ **EMP:** 48 **EST:** 2006
SALES (est): 7.8MM **Privately Held**
WEB: www.usblanks.com
SIC: 2821 Plastics materials & resins

(P-4728)
WELLMAN & COMPANY
12931 Venice Blvd, Los Angeles
(90066-3509)
PHONE..............................310 980-4918
Colin Wellman, *Principal*
EMP: 14 **EST:** 2019
SALES (est): 2MM **Privately Held**
WEB: www.wellmanam.com
SIC: 2821 Plastics materials & resins

(P-4729)
XERXES CORPORATION
1210 N Tustin Ave, Anaheim (92807-1617)
PHONE..............................714 630-0012
Rudy Tapia, *Manager*
Kathy Demuth, *CFO*
Jan R Arciszewski, *Vice Pres*
Gerardo Zendejas, *Vice Pres*
Shawn Roach, *VP Mfg*
EMP: 35
SALES (corp-wide): 899.6MM **Privately
Held**
WEB: www.zcl.com
SIC: 2821 5999 3444 Polystyrene resins;
fiberglass materials, except insulation;
sheet metalwork
HQ: Xerxes Corporation
7901 Xerxes Ave S Ste 201
Minneapolis MN 55431
952 887-1890

2822 Synthetic Rubber (Vulcanizable Elastomers)

(P-4730)
COI RUBBER PRODUCTS INC
19255 San Jose Ave Unit D, City of Industry
(91748-1418)
PHONE..............................626 965-9966
David Chao, *CEO*
EMP: 450 **EST:** 2013
SQ FT: 2,500
SALES (est): 22.5MM **Privately Held**
WEB: www.coirubber.com
SIC: 2822 Butadiene-acrylonitrile, nitrile
rubbers, NBR

(P-4731)
CRITICALPOINT CAPITAL LLC
Arlon Materials For Elec Div
9433 Hyssop Dr, Rancho Cucamonga
(91730-6107)
PHONE..............................909 987-9533
Roy Baulmer, *Branch Mgr*
EMP: 100
SALES (corp-wide): 60.3MM **Privately
Held**
WEB: www.criticalpointpartners.com
SIC: 2822 3672 2821 Silicone rubbers;
printed circuit boards; plastics materials &
resins
PA: Criticalpoint Capital, Llc
1230 Rosecrans Ave # 170
Manhattan Beach CA 90266
310 321-4400

(P-4732)
PUROSIL LLC (HQ)
708 S Temescal St Ste 101, Corona
(92879-2096)
P.O. Box 2467 (92878-2467)
PHONE..............................951 271-3900
Thomas Garrett, *President*
Shari Allen,
▲ **EMP:** 133 **EST:** 2009
SQ FT: 5,000
SALES (est): 18MM
SALES (corp-wide): 91.1MM **Privately
Held**
WEB: www.purosil.com
SIC: 2822 Silicone rubbers
PA: Mcp Industries, Inc.
708 S Temescal St Ste 101
Corona CA 92879
951 736-1881

(P-4733)
QUALITY RUBBER SOURCING INC
3988 Short St Ste 110, San Luis Obispo
(93401-7574)
P.O. Box 796, Santa Margarita (93453-
0796)
PHONE..............................805 544-7770
Brian Hotovec, *Principal*
▲ **EMP:** 15 **EST:** 2008
SALES (est): 759.4K **Privately Held**
WEB: www.qualityrubbersourcing.com
SIC: 2822 Synthetic rubber

2824 Synthetic Organic Fibers, Exc Cellulosic

(P-4734)
MATCHES INC
1700 E Araby St Ste 64, Palm Springs
(92264)
PHONE..............................760 899-1919
Jinle Chen, *Ch of Bd*
Xiqing Zhang, *COO*
Zhimeng Zhao, *CFO*
EMP: 359 **EST:** 2009
SALES (est): 10.4MM **Privately Held**
SIC: 2824 Polyester fibers

(P-4735)
ST PAUL BRANDS INC
11555 Monarch St Ste B, Garden Grove
(92841-1814)
PHONE..............................714 903-1000
Jimmy Ngo, *President*
Hieu Huynh, *Vice Pres*
Henry Smith, *Vice Pres*

Tracy Nguyen, *Marketing Staff*
▲ **EMP:** 25 **EST:** 2004
SALES (est): 2.6MM **Privately Held**
WEB: www.probactive.en.ec21.com
SIC: 2824 Protein fibers

(P-4736)
TURNER FIBERFILL INC
1600 Date St, Montebello (90640-6371)
P.O. Box 460 (90640-0460)
PHONE..............................323 724-7957
Paul Turner, *President*
▲ **EMP:** 35 **EST:** 2003
SALES (est): 5.4MM **Privately Held**
SIC: 2824 Polyester fibers

2833 Medicinal Chemicals & Botanical Prdts

(P-4737)
AMASS BRANDS INC
927 S Santa Fe Ave, Los Angeles
(90021-1726)
PHONE..............................619 204-2560
Alejandro Wiley, *Principal*
EMP: 28 **EST:** 2019
SALES (est): 11.1MM **Privately Held**
WEB: www.amass.com
SIC: 2833 Alkaloids & other botanical
based products

(P-4738)
BEACON MANUFACTURING INC
Also Called: North West Pharmanaturals
1000 Beacon St, Brea (92821-2938)
PHONE..............................714 529-0980
Jack L Brown, *CEO*
Patrick D K Brown, *CFO*
Johanna Lee, *Manager*
EMP: 20 **EST:** 2015
SQ FT: 25,000
SALES (est): 3.1MM **Privately Held**
WEB: www.northwestpn.com
SIC: 2833 Vitamins, natural or synthetic:
bulk, uncompounded

(P-4739)
CHROMADEX CORPORATION (PA)
10005 Muirlands Blvd G, Irvine
(92618-2538)
PHONE..............................949 419-0288
Robert Fried, *CEO*
Frank Jaksch Jr, *Ch of Bd*
Kevin Farr, *CFO*
Fadi Karam, *Chief Mktg Ofcr*
Ben Shichman, *Officer*
EMP: 31 **EST:** 2000
SQ FT: 15,000
SALES (est): 59.2MM **Publicly Held**
WEB: www.chromadex.com
SIC: 2833 Botanical products, medicinal:
ground, graded or milled

(P-4740)
CHULADA INC
Also Called: Chulada Spices Herbs & Snacks
640 S Flower St, Burbank (91502-2011)
PHONE..............................818 841-6536
Hector D Alvarez, *President*
Rey Sanchez, *Director*
EMP: 17 **EST:** 1982
SQ FT: 12,000
SALES (est): 2.6MM **Privately Held**
WEB: www.chuladaspicesherbssnacks.com
SIC: 2833 2099 Drugs & herbs: grading,
grinding & milling; seasonings & spices

(P-4741)
COSMO - PHARM INC
Also Called: Nature's Glory
11751 Vose St Ste 53, North Hollywood
(91605-5736)
PHONE..............................818 764-0246
Ashwin Patel, *President*
Urmila Patel, *Corp Secy*
Rajen Patel, *Exec VP*
▼ **EMP:** 17 **EST:** 1975
SQ FT: 45,000
SALES (est): 4.9MM **Privately Held**
SIC: 2833 2048 Vitamins, natural or syn-
thetic: bulk, uncompounded; prepared
feeds

(P-4742)
CREATONS GRDN NTFAL FD MKTS IN
Also Called: Cgnfm
24849 Anza Dr, Valencia (91355-1259)
PHONE..............................661 877-4280
Dino Guglielmelli, *President*
EMP: 18 **EST:** 1999
SALES (est): 769.7K **Privately Held**
SIC: 2833 Medicinals & botanicals

(P-4743)
ERBAVIVA INC
Also Called: Erba Organics
19831 Nordhoff Pl Ste 116, Chatsworth
(91311-6614)
PHONE..............................818 998-7112
Robin Brown, *CEO*
Anna C Brown, *Vice Pres*
Jason Lee, *Opers Mgr*
Gena Carletta-Craig, *Sales Staff*
Hector Alaniz, *Warehouse Mgr*
▲ **EMP:** 20 **EST:** 2010
SQ FT: 10,000
SALES (est): 4.5MM **Privately Held**
WEB: www.erbaviva.com
SIC: 2833 Organic medicinal chemicals:
bulk, uncompounded

(P-4744)
EVERGREEN LICENSING LLC
5737 Kanan Rd Ste 344, Agoura Hills
(91301-1601)
PHONE..............................844 270-2700
Bruce Friedman, *CEO*
EMP: 15 **EST:** 2014
SALES (est): 666.2K **Privately Held**
WEB: www.evergreen-licensing.com
SIC: 2833 8742 Vitamins, natural or syn-
thetic: bulk, uncompounded; business
consultant

(P-4745)
EVOLIFE SCIENTIFIC LLC
1452 E 33rd St, Signal Hill (90755-5200)
PHONE..............................888 750-0310
Alan Castro,
EMP: 23 **EST:** 2019
SALES (est): 1.4MM **Privately Held**
SIC: 2833 Medicinals & botanicals

(P-4746)
EXCELSIOR NUTRITION INC
Also Called: 4excelsior
1206 N Miller St Unit D, Anaheim
(92806-1960)
PHONE..............................657 999-5188
Yisheng Lin, *President*
Jennifer Wu, *CFO*
Jian Wu, *CFO*
Andre Wirawan, *Purchasing*
EMP: 48 **EST:** 2014
SQ FT: 78,000
SALES (est): 6MM **Privately Held**
WEB: www.4excelsior.com
SIC: 2833 Medicinals & botanicals

(P-4747)
GRAPEFRUIT BLVD INVSTMENTS INC
10866 Wilshire Blvd # 225, Los Angeles
(90024-4359)
PHONE..............................310 575-1175
Bradley J Yourist, *CEO*
Daniel J Yourist, *COO*
EMP: 14 **EST:** 2017
SALES (est): 3.4MM **Publicly Held**
SIC: 2833 5122 Medicinals & botanicals;
drugs, proprietaries & sundries
PA: Grapefruit Usa, Inc.
1000 N West St # 12003094
Wilmington DE 19801

(P-4748)
HERBAL SCIENCE NTL INC
655 S 6th Ave 208, La Puente
(91746-3026)
PHONE..............................626 333-9998
William Chang, *President*
▲ **EMP:** 17 **EST:** 1991
SALES (est): 857.4K **Privately Held**
WEB: www.hsusa.net
SIC: 2833 5499 Medicinals & botanicals;
spices & herbs

(P-4749)
IMP INTERNATIONAL INC (PA)
Also Called: Unichem Enterprises
1905 S Lynx Ave, Ontario (91761-8055)
PHONE................................909 321-1000
Chentao Hang, *President*
Mark Grieco, *Sales Dir*
Riley Bendel, *Regl Sales Mgr*
▲ **EMP:** 44 **EST:** 2005
SQ FT: 40,000
SALES (est): 6.4MM **Privately Held**
SIC: 2833 2869 Vitamins, natural or synthetic: bulk, uncompounded; sweeteners, synthetic

(P-4750)
INTERNTNAL MDCTION SYSTEMS LTD
Also Called: IMS
10642 El Poche St, South El Monte
(91733-3408)
PHONE................................626 459-5586
EMP: 13
SALES (corp-wide): 210.4MM **Publicly Held**
SIC: 2833 Mfg Medicinal/Botanical Products
HQ: International Medication Systems, Ltd.
1886 Santa Anita Ave
South El Monte CA 91733
626 442-6757

(P-4751)
KADENWOOD LLC
450 Nwport Ctr Dr Ste 550, Newport Beach (92660)
PHONE................................949 287-6703
Erick Dickens, *CEO*
Doug Weekes, *COO*
Mike Deidrick, *CFO*
Garrett Bain, *Officer*
Brian Newberry, *Security Dir*
EMP: 90 **EST:** 2019
SALES (est): 11MM **Privately Held**
WEB: www.kadenwoodbrands.com
SIC: 2833 Medicinals & botanicals

(P-4752)
MERCI LIFE LLC
321 N Pass Ave Ste 144, Burbank (91505-3859)
PHONE................................317 341-4109
Samantha Ford, *Manager*
EMP: 15 **EST:** 2020
SALES (est): 1.4MM **Privately Held**
SIC: 2833 Medicinals & botanicals

(P-4753)
MIDNIGHT MANUFACTURING LLC
2535 Conejo Spectrum St, Thousand Oaks (91320-1453)
PHONE................................714 833-6130
Kevin A Shaw, *President*
EMP: 25 **EST:** 2019
SALES (est): 2.5MM **Privately Held**
SIC: 2833 Medicinals & botanicals

(P-4754)
NITRO 2 GO INC
1420 Richardson St, San Bernardino (92408-2962)
PHONE................................909 864-4886
Jeff Diehl, *President*
▲ **EMP:** 16 **EST:** 1995
SQ FT: 6,000
SALES (est): 4.7MM **Privately Held**
WEB: www.nitro2go.com
SIC: 2833 Drugs & herbs: grading, grinding & milling

(P-4755)
NU-HEALTH PRODUCTS CO
Also Called: Nu Health Products
20875 Currier Rd, Walnut (91789-3081)
PHONE................................909 869-0666
Lynn Leung, *President*
Amanda Fu, *Purch Mgr*
▲ **EMP:** 25 **EST:** 1991
SQ FT: 12,000

SALES (est): 3.8MM **Privately Held**
WEB: www.nu-health.com
SIC: 2833 2048 5149 Vitamins, natural or synthetic: bulk, uncompounded; drugs & herbs: grading, grinding & milling; prepared feeds; organic & diet foods

(P-4756)
NUTRIPHARM USA INC
15046 Nelson Ave Ste 1, City of Industry (91744-4304)
PHONE................................626 962-9871
Zhong Wang, *President*
▲ **EMP:** 14 **EST:** 2003
SALES (est): 3.1MM **Privately Held**
WEB: www.nutripharmusa.com
SIC: 2833 Medicinals & botanicals

(P-4757)
OPTIMUM BIOENERGY INTL CORP
2463 Pomona Rd, Corona (92878-4331)
PHONE................................714 903-8872
Louis LI, *President*
Judy LI, *Vice Pres*
▲ **EMP:** 19 **EST:** 1994
SQ FT: 5,000
SALES (est): 2.9MM **Privately Held**
SIC: 2833 Vitamins, natural or synthetic: bulk, uncompounded

(P-4758)
ORGANIC BY NATURE INC (PA)
2610 Homestead Pl, Compton (90220-5610)
PHONE................................562 901-0177
Amy L Venner Hamdi, *CEO*
David Sandoval, *Founder*
Amelia Kanan, *Chief Mktg Ofcr*
Brandon Riddle, *Info Tech Mgr*
Rob Sepulveda, *Web Dvlpr*
▲ **EMP:** 37 **EST:** 1993
SQ FT: 30,000
SALES (est): 10.4MM **Privately Held**
WEB: www.ishoppurium.com
SIC: 2833 Adrenal derivatives

(P-4759)
PALETTE LIFE SCIENCES INC
27 E Cota St Ste 401, Santa Barbara (93101-7632)
PHONE................................805 869-7020
Per Lango, *CEO*
Ole Mikkelsen, *COO*
Hank Courson, *CFO*
Mary McEwen, *Office Mgr*
Amy Oppenheim, *Marketing Mgr*
EMP: 23 **EST:** 2018
SALES (est): 4.5MM **Privately Held**
WEB: www.palettelifesciences.com
SIC: 2833 Medicinal chemicals

(P-4760)
PHARMAVITE LLC (DH)
8531 Fallbrook Ave, West Hills (91304-3232)
PHONE................................818 221-6200
Jeff Boutelle, *CEO*
Rhonda Hoffman, *Chief Mktg Ofcr*
Dave Larson, *Division VP*
Tobe Cohen, *Exec VP*
Christine Darragh, *Exec VP*
▲ **EMP:** 300 **EST:** 2002
SQ FT: 45,000
SALES (est): 548.6MM **Privately Held**
WEB: www.pharmavite.com
SIC: 2833 2834 Vitamins, natural or synthetic: bulk, uncompounded; pharmaceutical preparations

(P-4761)
PROMEGA BIOSCIENCES LLC
277 Granada Dr, San Luis Obispo (93401-7396)
PHONE................................805 544-8524
Kristen Yetter, *Finance*
Irin Nahar, *Assoc VP*
Ruslan Arbit, *Research*
Sergiy Levin, *Research*
Poncho Meisenheimer, *Research*
EMP: 55 **EST:** 1999
SQ FT: 40,000

SALES (est): 33.3MM
SALES (corp-wide): 487.9MM **Privately Held**
WEB: www.promega.com
SIC: 2833 2835 Medicinal chemicals; in vitro & in vivo diagnostic substances
PA: Promega Corporation
2800 Woods Hollow Rd
Fitchburg WI 53711
608 274-4330

(P-4762)
RON TEEGUARDEN ENTERPRISES INC (PA)
Also Called: Dragon Herbs
5670 Wilshire Blvd # 1500, Los Angeles (90036-5660)
PHONE................................323 556-8188
Ron Teagarden, *President*
Jimmy Telles, *VP Bus Dvlpt*
Yanlin Teeguarden, *Principal*
Ricah Rejano, *Executive Asst*
Roy Rocha, *Sales Executive*
◆ **EMP:** 31 **EST:** 1994
SQ FT: 13,000
SALES (est): 5.6MM **Privately Held**
WEB: www.dragonherbs.com
SIC: 2833 5122 Drugs & herbs: grading, grinding & milling; medicinals & botanicals

(P-4763)
S&B PHARMA INC
Also Called: Norac Pharma
405 S Motor Ave, Azusa (91702-3232)
PHONE................................626 334-2908
Dr Daniel Levin, *President*
Michael Roth, *Business Dir*
Emerich Eisenreich, *Research*
Les Ordway, *Finance*
Lee Miller, *Opers Mgr*
▲ **EMP:** 66 **EST:** 2012
SALES (est): 10.3MM **Privately Held**
WEB: www.noracpharma.com
SIC: 2833 8731 2834 Medicinals & botanicals; commercial physical research; pharmaceutical preparations

(P-4764)
SPECTRUM LIFESCIENCES LLC (HQ)
18617 S Broadwick St, Rancho Dominguez (90220-6435)
PHONE................................310 885-4600
Tony Hunt, *CEO*
Jon Snodgres, *CFO*
EMP: 14 **EST:** 2017
SALES (est): 12.4MM
SALES (corp-wide): 366.2MM **Publicly Held**
WEB: www.repligen.com
SIC: 2833 Antibiotics
PA: Repligen Corporation
41 Seyon St Ste 100
Waltham MA 02453
781 250-0111

(P-4765)
STAUBER PRFMCE INGREDIENTS INC (HQ)
4120 N Palm St, Fullerton (92835-1026)
PHONE................................714 441-3900
Patrick Hawkins, *President*
Dan Stauber, *Officer*
Monica Mitchell, *Vice Pres*
Daniel Stauber, *Vice Pres*
Sheri Esswein, *VP Bus Dvlpt*
EMP: 66 **EST:** 1969
SALES (est): 59.4MM
SALES (corp-wide): 596.8MM **Publicly Held**
WEB: www.stauberusa.com
SIC: 2833 Medicinals & botanicals
PA: Hawkins, Inc.
2381 Rosegate
Roseville MN 55113
612 331-6910

(P-4766)
TIKUN OLAM ADELANTO LLC
541 S Spring St Unit 213, Los Angeles (90013-1657)
PHONE................................833 468-4586
David Librush, *Branch Mgr*
EMP: 17

SALES (corp-wide): 3.6MM **Privately Held**
WEB: www.tikunolam.com
SIC: 2833 Medicinals & botanicals
PA: Tikun Olam Adelanto Llc
16605 Koala Rd
Adelanto CA 92301
833 468-4586

(P-4767)
TIKUN OLAM ADELANTO LLC (PA)
16605 Koala Rd, Adelanto (92301-3925)
PHONE................................833 468-4586
David Librush, *Principal*
EMP: 19 **EST:** 2018
SALES (est): 3.6MM **Privately Held**
SIC: 2833 Medicinals & botanicals

(P-4768)
UNI-CAPS LLC
540 Lambert Rd, Brea (92821)
PHONE................................714 529-8400
Sang H Kim, *Mng Member*
Robert Kugh, *Director*
▲ **EMP:** 27 **EST:** 2006
SALES (est): 13.1MM **Privately Held**
WEB: www.unicapsllc.com
SIC: 2833 Vitamins, natural or synthetic: bulk, uncompounded

(P-4769)
WESTAR NUTRITION CORP (PA)
350 Paularino Ave, Costa Mesa (92626-4616)
PHONE................................949 645-6100
David Fan, *President*
Lucy Fan, *Vice Pres*
Joe Ramos, *Production*
▼ **EMP:** 20 **EST:** 1973
SQ FT: 55,000
SALES (est): 29.1MM **Privately Held**
WEB: www.westarnutrition.com
SIC: 2833 2834 2844 7389 Vitamins, natural or synthetic: bulk, uncompounded; pharmaceutical preparations; cosmetic preparations; packaging & labeling services

(P-4770)
WINNING LABORATORIES INC
Also Called: Natutac
16218 Arthur St, Cerritos (90703-2131)
PHONE................................562 921-6880
James Hao, *President*
Lydia Hao, *Vice Pres*
▲ **EMP:** 16 **EST:** 1981
SQ FT: 90,000
SALES (est): 4.1MM
SALES (corp-wide): 870.7MM **Privately Held**
WEB: www.winninglabs.com
SIC: 2833 Medicinals & botanicals
HQ: Silver Spur Corporation
16010 Shoemaker Ave
Cerritos CA 90703
562 921-6880

2834 Pharmaceuticals

(P-4771)
A Q PHARMACEUTICALS INC
11555 Monarch St Ste C, Garden Grove (92841-1814)
PHONE................................714 903-1000
Tracy Nguyen, *President*
Henry Smith, *Vice Pres*
▲ **EMP:** 30 **EST:** 2001
SQ FT: 3,000
SALES (est): 3.9MM **Privately Held**
WEB: www.aqpharmaceuticals.com
SIC: 2834 Pharmaceutical preparations

(P-4772)
ABBOTT
2375 Morse Ave, Irvine (92614-6233)
PHONE................................949 769-5018
Jocelyn Osoy, *Principal*
EMP: 13 **EST:** 2017
SALES (est): 3.5MM **Privately Held**
WEB: www.abbott.com
SIC: 2834 Pharmaceutical preparations

(P-4773)
ABBOTT VASCULAR INC
26531 Ynez Rd, Temecula (92591-4630)
PHONE..................................951 941-2400
Ronald Dollens, *Branch Mgr*
Ken Carlisle, *Vice Pres*
Cornel Ciurea, *Administration*
Schmitz Brian, *Business Anlyst*
Steve Hazelwood, *Business Anlyst*
EMP: 500
SALES (corp-wide): 34.6B Publicly Held
WEB: www.cardiovascular.abbott
SIC: 2834 Pharmaceutical preparations
HQ: Abbott Vascular Inc.
　　3200 Lakeside Dr
　　Santa Clara CA 95054
　　408 845-3000

(P-4774)
ABRAXIS BIOSCIENCE LLC
(DH)
11755 Wilshire Blvd Fl 20, Los Angeles
(90025-1543)
PHONE..................................800 564-0216
Leon O Moulder Jr,
Rick Rodgers Sr,
Patrick Soon-Shiong MD,
EMP: 232 EST: 2007
SALES (est): 130.1MM
SALES (corp-wide): 42.5B Publicly Held
SIC: 2834 Pharmaceutical preparations

(P-4775)
ACCOLADE PHARMA USA
13260 Temple Ave, City of Industry
(91746-1511)
PHONE..................................626 279-9699
Spencer Liu, *CEO*
Amy Chou, *Project Mgr*
Chu MAI Tan, *Finance*
Giant Lee, *Sales Dir*
Trina Phan, *Manager*
EMP: 20 EST: 2018
SALES (est): 4.2MM Privately Held
SIC: 2834 Pharmaceutical preparations

(P-4776)
ACTAVIS LLC
311 Bonnie Cir, Corona (92878-5182)
P.O. Box 1149 (92878-1149)
PHONE..................................909 270-1400
Allen Chao, *Branch Mgr*
Abigail Jenkins, *President*
Michel Feldman, *Officer*
Charles Thompson, *Officer*
Patrick Brunner, *Senior VP*
EMP: 79 Privately Held
WEB: www.actavis.com
SIC: 2834 Pharmaceutical preparations
HQ: Actavis Llc
　　5 Giralda Farms
　　Madison NJ 07940
　　862 261-7000

(P-4777)
ALCON MANUFACTURING LTD
(PA)
15800 Alton Pkwy, Irvine (92618-3818)
PHONE..................................949 753-1393
Ken Lickel, *Principal*
Rajkumar Narayanan, *Senior VP*
Sue-Jean Lin, *CIO*
John Pulera, *Software Engr*
Joseph Dull, *Buyer*
▲ EMP: 196 EST: 1945
SALES (est): 32.1MM Privately Held
WEB: www.alcon.com
SIC: 2834 8011 Veterinary pharmaceutical
　preparations; eyes, ears, nose & throat
　specialist: physician/surgeon

(P-4778)
ALLERGAN SALES LLC (DH)
2525 Dupont Dr, Irvine (92612-1599)
P.O. Box 19534 (92623-9534)
PHONE..................................862 261-7000
Brenton L Saunders, *President*
Matthew M Walsh, *CFO*
Alex Kelly, *Ch Credit Ofcr*
William Meury, *Ch Credit Ofcr*
A Robert D Bailey,
▲ EMP: 600 EST: 1986
SQ FT: 10,000

SALES (est): 1.3B Privately Held
WEB: www.allergan.com
SIC: 2834 Pharmaceutical preparations
HQ: Allergan, Inc.
　　5 Giralda Farms
　　Madison NJ 07940
　　862 261-7000

(P-4779)
ALLERGAN SPCLTY
THRPEUTICS INC
2525 Dupont Dr, Irvine (92612-1599)
PHONE..................................714 246-4500
David Pyott, *President*
William Meury, *Officer*
David Nicholson, *Officer*
Donna Beal, *Assoc VP*
Matthew Brady, *Assoc VP*
EMP: 1500 EST: 1997
SALES (est): 560.7MM Privately Held
WEB: www.allergan.com
SIC: 2834 Pharmaceutical preparations
HQ: Allergan, Inc.
　　5 Giralda Farms
　　Madison NJ 07940
　　862 261-7000

(P-4780)
ALLERGAN USA INC
Also Called: Pacific Communications
18581 Teller Ave, Irvine (92612-1627)
P.O. Box 19534 (92623-9534)
PHONE..................................714 427-1900
David E I Pyott, *CEO*
Craig Sullivan, *President*
Jeffrey L Edwards, *CFO*
James M Hindman, *Treasurer*
Kun Kim, *Vice Pres*
EMP: 2000 EST: 2007
SALES (est): 228.8MM Privately Held
WEB: www.pacificcommunications.com
SIC: 2834 Druggists' preparations (phar-
　maceuticals)
HQ: Allergan, Inc.
　　5 Giralda Farms
　　Madison NJ 07940
　　862 261-7000

(P-4781)
AMF PHARMA LLC
1909 S Campus Ave, Ontario (91761-5410)
PHONE..................................909 930-9599
Zi Meng,
Trung Bui, *Vice Pres*
Jeanne Liu, *Research*
EMP: 13 EST: 2012
SALES (est): 2.9MM Privately Held
WEB: www.amfpharma.com
SIC: 2834 Pharmaceutical preparations

(P-4782)
AMGEN USA INC (HQ)
1 Amgen Center Dr, Thousand Oaks
(91320-1799)
PHONE..................................805 447-1000
Kevin W Sharer, *CEO*
EMP: 93 EST: 2010
SALES (est): 27.3MM
SALES (corp-wide): 25.4B Publicly Held
WEB: www.amgen.com
SIC: 2834 Pharmaceutical preparations
PA: Amgen Inc.
　　1 Amgen Center Dr
　　Thousand Oaks CA 91320
　　805 447-1000

(P-4783)
AMPHASTAR
PHARMACEUTICALS INC (PA)
11570 6th St, Rancho Cucamonga
(91730-6025)
PHONE..................................909 980-9484
Jack Yongfeng Zhang, *CEO*
Mary Ziping Luo, *Ch of Bd*
William J Peters, *CFO*
Rick Koo, *Bd of Directors*
Rong Zhou, *Exec VP*
▲ EMP: 140 EST: 1996
SQ FT: 267,674
SALES (est): 349.8MM Publicly Held
WEB: www.amphastar.com
SIC: 2834 Pharmaceutical preparations

(P-4784)
ANABOLIC INCORPORATED
Also Called: Vitamer Laboratories
17802 Gillette Ave, Irvine (92614-6502)
P.O. Box 19516 (92623-9516)
PHONE..................................949 863-0340
Steven R Brown, *President*
Jane Drinkwalter, *Vice Pres*
Kari Cooper, *Opers Mgr*
Justin Duez, *Supervisor*
▲ EMP: 28 EST: 1959
SALES (est): 5.4MM Privately Held
SIC: 2834 Vitamin preparations

(P-4785)
ANABOLIC LABORATORIES INC
26021 Commercentre Dr, Lake Forest
(92630-8853)
P.O. Box 19516, Irvine (92623-9516)
PHONE..................................949 863-0340
Steven Brown, *President*
EMP: 20 EST: 1935
SALES (est): 3.4MM Privately Held
SIC: 2834 Pharmaceutical preparations

(P-4786)
ARBONNE INTERNATIONAL
LLC (DH)
9400 Jeronimo Rd, Irvine (92618-1907)
PHONE..................................949 770-2610
Tyler Whitehead, *CEO*
Alison Allen, *President*
Melody Allred, *President*
Carla Alvarado, *President*
Rebecca Banks, *President*
▲ EMP: 25 EST: 1984
SQ FT: 37,000
SALES (est): 775.3MM
SALES (corp-wide): 2.9MM Privately
Held
WEB: www.arbonne.com
SIC: 5999 5961 5499 2834 Cosmetics;
　cosmetics & perfumes, mail order; vitamin
　food stores; vitamin preparations; cos-
　metic sales, house-to-house
HQ: Groupe Rocher Operations
　　Lecc Laboratoire Europeen De Cre-
　　ation
　　La Gacilly 56200
　　299 297-474

(P-4787)
ARCUTIS BIOTHERAPEUTICS
INC
3027 Townsgate Rd Ste 300, Westlake Vil-
lage (91361-5873)
PHONE..................................805 418-5006
Todd Franklin Watanabe, *CEO*
Patrick J Heron, *Ch of Bd*
John W Smither, *CFO*
Kenneth A Lock, *Ch Credit Ofcr*
Howard G Welgus, *Chief Mktg Ofcr*
EMP: 53 EST: 2016
SQ FT: 4,741
SALES (est): 0 Privately Held
WEB: www.arcutis.com
SIC: 2834 Pharmaceutical preparations

(P-4788)
ASKGENE PHARMA INC
5217 Verdugo Way Ste A, Camarillo
(93012-8642)
PHONE..................................805 807-9868
Jeff Lu, *CEO*
Robert Wynner, *Principal*
Ray Chuang, *Director*
Ming LI, *Director*
EMP: 26 EST: 2012
SALES (est): 4.7MM Privately Held
WEB: www.ask-gene.com
SIC: 2834 Pharmaceutical preparations

(P-4789)
AURITEC PHARMACEUTICALS
INC
2285 E Foothill Blvd, Pasadena
(91107-3658)
PHONE..................................424 272-9501
Thomas Smith, *President*
Frederic Ransom, *President*
Amanda Malone, *Vice Pres*
Meredith Blake, *General Mgr*
Gary Ransom,
EMP: 13 EST: 2002
SQ FT: 250

SALES (est): 2MM Privately Held
WEB: www.auritecpharma.com
SIC: 2834 Proprietary drug products

(P-4790)
AVANIR PHARMACEUTICALS
INC (DH)
30 Enterprise Ste 200, Aliso Viejo
(92656-7112)
PHONE..................................949 389-6700
Rohan Palekar, *President*
Gregory J Flesher, *Senior VP*
Joao Siffert, *Senior VP*
Christine G Ocampo, *Vice Pres*
Bhavana Desai, *Surgery Dir*
EMP: 477 EST: 1988
SALES (est): 120.3MM Privately Held
WEB: www.avanir.com
SIC: 2834 Pharmaceutical preparations

(P-4791)
AVID BIOSERVICES INC (PA)
2642 Michelle Dr Ste 200, Tustin
(92780-7019)
PHONE..................................714 508-6000
Richard B Hancock, *President*
Joseph Carleone, *Ch of Bd*
Richard Richieri, *COO*
Daniel Hart, *CFO*
Timothy Compton, *Officer*
EMP: 167 EST: 1981
SQ FT: 183,000
SALES: 95.8MM Publicly Held
WEB: www.avidbio.com
SIC: 2834 Pharmaceutical preparations

(P-4792)
BAUSCH & LOMB
INCORPORATED
50 Technology Dr, Irvine (92618-2301)
PHONE..................................949 788-6000
EMP: 75
SALES (corp-wide): 5.7B Privately Held
SIC: 2834 Mfg Pharmaceutical Prepara-
　tions
HQ: Bausch & Lomb Incorporated
　　1 Bausch And Lomb Fl
　　Rochester NY 08807
　　585 338-5442

(P-4793)
BAXALTA INCORPORATED
4501 Colorado Blvd, Los Angeles
(90039-1103)
PHONE..................................818 240-5600
Raul Navarro, *Branch Mgr*
Giuseppe Accogli, *President*
Edwin Betancourt, *Vice Pres*
Jay Ehrlich, *Vice Pres*
Art Gibson, *Vice Pres*
EMP: 431 Privately Held
WEB: www.takeda.com
SIC: 2834 Pharmaceutical preparations
HQ: Baxalta Incorporated
　　1200 Lakeside Dr
　　Bannockburn IL 60015
　　224 940-2000

(P-4794)
BAXCO PHARMACEUTICAL INC
2393 Bateman Ave, Duarte (91010-3313)
PHONE..................................626 610-7088
Dennis Wong, *President*
Jim Lanzillo, *Partner*
Joseph Meuse, *COO*
Koki Luu, *CFO*
James Wang, *CFO*
▲ EMP: 17 EST: 2000
SALES (est): 5.2MM Privately Held
WEB: www.baxcoinc.com
SIC: 2834 Pharmaceutical preparations

(P-4795)
BAXTER INTERNATIONAL INC
550 N Brand Blvd Fl 14, Glendale
(91203-1952)
PHONE..................................818 550-4500
Tracy Kish, *Portfolio Mgr*
Kelly Tremmel, *Business Mgr*
EMP: 13
SALES (corp-wide): 11.3B Publicly Held
WEB: www.baxter.com
SIC: 2834 Pharmaceutical preparations

▲ = Import ▼=Export
◆ =Import/Export

PA: Baxter International Inc.
1 Baxter Pkwy
Deerfield IL 60015
224 948-2000

(P-4796)
BEAUTY & HEALTH INTERNATIONAL
7541 Anthony Ave, Garden Grove (92841-4005)
P.O. Box 890, Westminster (92684-0890)
PHONE....................714 903-9730
Charles G Myung, *President*
John Myuong, *Manager*
▲ **EMP:** 50 **EST:** 1993
SQ FT: 12,000
SALES (est): 6.4MM **Privately Held**
SIC: 2834 2844 5122 5149 Vitamin preparations; cosmetic preparations; vitamins & minerals; cosmetics; health foods; health & dietetic food stores

(P-4797)
BF SUMA PHARMACEUTICALS INC
5077 Walnut Grove Ave, San Gabriel (91776-2023)
PHONE....................626 285-8366
Chak Yeung Chan, *President*
Wendy Cheung, *Office Mgr*
Annie Cheng, *Controller*
▲ **EMP:** 14 **EST:** 2006
SQ FT: 10,000
SALES (est): 2.8MM **Privately Held**
SIC: 2834 Pharmaceutical preparations

(P-4798)
BIMEDA INC
5539 Ayon Ave, Irwindale (91706-2057)
PHONE....................626 815-1680
Tim Tynan, *Branch Mgr*
Fred Hetzel, *Manager*
Dan Witherspoon, *Manager*
EMP: 31
SALES (corp-wide): 2.6B **Privately Held**
WEB: www.bimedaus.com
SIC: 2834 3841 Veterinary pharmaceutical preparations; surgical & medical instruments
HQ: Bimeda Inc.
1 Tower Ln Ste 2250
Oakbrook Terrace IL 60181
630 928-0361

(P-4799)
BIORX PHARMACEUTICALS INC
Also Called: Biorx Laboratories
6465 Corvette St, Commerce (90040-1702)
PHONE....................323 725-3100
Amin Jack, *President*
EMP: 32 **EST:** 2010
SALES (est): 2.6MM **Privately Held**
WEB: www.biorxlabs.com
SIC: 2834 2844 Pharmaceutical preparations; toilet preparations

(P-4800)
BIOVAIL TECHNOLOGIES LTD
1 Enterprise, Aliso Viejo (92656-2606)
PHONE....................703 995-2400
David Tierney, *President*
EMP: 70 **EST:** 1988
SQ FT: 55,000
SALES (est): 7MM
SALES (corp-wide): 8.6B **Privately Held**
WEB: www.bauschhealth.com
SIC: 2834 8731 3841 2087 Pharmaceutical preparations; commercial physical research; surgical & medical instruments; flavoring extracts & syrups
PA: Bausch Health Companies Inc
2150 Boul Saint-Elzear O
Sainte-Rose QC H7L 4
514 228-1752

(P-4801)
BMS INVESTMENTS LLC
Also Called: Jiffy Lube
12626 Hackberry Ln, Moreno Valley (92553-4796)
PHONE....................714 376-2535
Byron Marroquin, *President*
David Orlando Marroquin, *Mng Member*
EMP: 17 **EST:** 2015

SALES (est): 1.5MM **Privately Held**
WEB: www.bms.com
SIC: 2834 Pharmaceutical preparations

(P-4802)
CALIMMUNE INC
129 N Hill Ave Ste 105, Pasadena (91106-1961)
PHONE....................310 806-6240
Mary Santos, *Manager*
EMP: 14 **Privately Held**
SIC: 2834 Pharmaceutical preparations
HQ: Calimmune, Inc.
35 N Lake Ave Ste 600
Pasadena CA 91101

(P-4803)
CANNDESCENT
3905 State St, Santa Barbara (93105-3138)
PHONE....................877 778-9587
Adrian Sedlin, *CEO*
Tom Digiovanni, *CFO*
Sam Arellano, *Chief Mktg Ofcr*
EMP: 17 **EST:** 2016
SALES (est): 5.1MM **Privately Held**
WEB: www.canndescent.com
SIC: 2834 Pharmaceutical preparations

(P-4804)
CAPRICOR THERAPEUTICS INC (PA)
8840 Wilshire Blvd Fl 2, Beverly Hills (90211-2606)
PHONE....................310 358-3200
Linda Marban, *President*
Frank Litvack, *Ch of Bd*
Anthony Bergmann, *CFO*
Deborah Ascheim, *Chief Mktg Ofcr*
Karen G Krasney, *Exec VP*
EMP: 19 **EST:** 2005
SALES: 310.2K **Publicly Held**
WEB: www.capricor.com
SIC: 2834 Pharmaceutical preparations

(P-4805)
CAPTEK SOFTGEL INTL INC
Also Called: Captek Pharma
14535 Industry Cir, La Mirada (90638-5814)
PHONE....................657 325-0412
Paul Hwang, *General Mgr*
Miguel Intencion, *Production*
EMP: 130
SALES (corp-wide): 203.2MM **Privately Held**
WEB: www.capteksoftgel.com
SIC: 2834 Pharmaceutical preparations
HQ: Captek Softgel International, Inc.
16218 Arthur St
Cerritos CA 90703

(P-4806)
CAPTEK SOFTGEL INTL INC (DH)
16218 Arthur St, Cerritos (90703-2131)
PHONE....................562 921-9511
Carl Bridges, *CEO*
Fon Wong, *CFO*
Danielle Conner, *Officer*
Tim Chiprich, *Vice Pres*
Mark Roff, *Admin Sec*
▲ **EMP:** 300 **EST:** 1995
SQ FT: 90,000
SALES (est): 203.2MM **Privately Held**
WEB: www.capteksoftgel.com
SIC: 2834 Vitamin, nutrient & hematinic preparations for human use
HQ: Captek Midco, Inc.
16218 Arthur St
Cerritos CA 90703
562 921-9511

(P-4807)
CG ONCOLOGY INC
400 Spectrum Center Dr # 20, Irvine (92618-4934)
PHONE....................949 409-3700
Arthur Kuan, *CEO*
Paola Grandi, *Officer*
Amy Steele, *Vice Pres*
Bing Kung, *VP Bus Dvlpt*
Maolu LI, *Project Mgr*
EMP: 33 **EST:** 2010

SALES (est): 2.9MM **Privately Held**
WEB: www.cgoncology.com
SIC: 2834 8733 Pharmaceutical preparations; biotechnical research, noncommercial

(P-4808)
CH LABORATORIES INC (PA)
1243 W 130th St, Gardena (90247-1501)
PHONE....................310 516-8273
Brid Nolan, *President*
EMP: 24 **EST:** 2001
SQ FT: 30,000
SALES (est): 4.4MM **Privately Held**
WEB: www.chlabs.com
SIC: 2834 Vitamin preparations

(P-4809)
COMPRHNSIVE CRDVSCLAR SPCALIST (PA)
220 S 1st St Ste 101, Alhambra (91801-3705)
PHONE....................626 281-8663
Peter Fung MD, *President*
EMP: 17 **EST:** 2002
SALES (est): 4.9MM **Privately Held**
WEB: www.ccsheartcare.com
SIC: 2834 8111 Drugs acting on the cardiovascular system, except diagnostic; legal services

(P-4810)
CONTINENTAL VITAMIN CO INC
Also Called: Cvc Specialties
4510 S Boyle Ave, Vernon (90058-2418)
PHONE....................323 581-0176
Ron Beckenfeld, *President*
Lillian Beckenfeld, *Vice Pres*
Dee Dee Garcia, *Admin Sec*
Laura Hernandez, *Controller*
Ron Deckenfield, *Sales Executive*
EMP: 60 **EST:** 1969
SQ FT: 80,000
SALES (est): 11.4MM **Privately Held**
WEB: www.cvc4health.com
SIC: 2834 5122 Vitamin preparations; vitamins & minerals

(P-4811)
COUGAR BIOTECHNOLOGY INC
10990 Wilshire Blvd # 1200, Los Angeles (90024-3919)
PHONE....................310 943-8040
Alan H Auerbach, *President*
Arie S Belldegrun MD, *Ch of Bd*
Charles Eyler, *Treasurer*
Gloria Lee MD, *Vice Pres*
Cheryl Collett, *Controller*
EMP: 58 **EST:** 2003
SQ FT: 7,300
SALES (est): 16.2MM
SALES (corp-wide): 82.5B **Publicly Held**
WEB: www.pumabiotechnology.com
SIC: 2834 Drugs affecting neoplasms & endocrine systems
PA: Johnson & Johnson
1 Johnson And Johnson Plz
New Brunswick NJ 08933
732 524-0400

(P-4812)
DAVID S TSAI DDS INC (PA)
400 Hillcrest Blvd, Arcadia (91006-2402)
PHONE....................626 358-9136
David S Tsai, *Owner*
EMP: 17 **EST:** 2015
SALES (est): 465.1K **Privately Held**
SIC: 2834 Pharmaceutical preparations

(P-4813)
DBV INC (PA)
314 N Vista St, Los Angeles (90036-5739)
PHONE....................323 857-5577
Jeffrey Best, *Principal*
EMP: 184 **EST:** 2008
SALES (est): 826.3K **Privately Held**
SIC: 2834 Pharmaceutical preparations

(P-4814)
DENDREON PHARMACEUTICALS INC
1700 Saturn Way, Seal Beach (90740-5618)
PHONE....................562 253-3931
EMP: 13

SALES (corp-wide): 215.7MM **Privately Held**
SIC: 2834 Mfg Pharmaceutical Preparations
HQ: Dendreon Pharmaceuticals Llc
1700 Saturn Way
Seal Beach CA 90740
562 252-7500

(P-4815)
DENDREON PHARMACEUTICALS LLC (HQ)
1700 Saturn Way, Seal Beach (90740-5618)
PHONE....................562 252-7500
Jason Oneill, *CEO*
Chris Carr, *CFO*
Matthew Kemp, *Ch Credit Ofcr*
Christina Yi, *Officer*
Bruce A Brown, *Senior VP*
EMP: 50 **EST:** 2015
SALES (est): 100MM **Privately Held**
WEB: www.dendreon.com
SIC: 2834 Pharmaceutical preparations

(P-4816)
DLC LABORATORIES INC
Also Called: De La Cruz Products
7008 Marcelle St, Paramount (90723-4839)
PHONE....................562 602-2184
Spero Kessaris, *President*
Sonia Perez, *Admin Asst*
Judy De Rocha, *Purchasing*
▲ **EMP:** 14 **EST:** 1963
SQ FT: 16,000
SALES (est): 4.4MM **Privately Held**
WEB: www.dlclabs.com
SIC: 2834 2844 Vitamin preparations; shampoos, rinses, conditioners: hair

(P-4817)
ESSENTIAL PHARMACEUTICAL CORP
1906 W Holt Ave, Pomona (91768-3351)
PHONE....................909 623-4565
Bruce Lin, *CEO*
PO Chia Lin, *Treasurer*
▲ **EMP:** 20 **EST:** 1986
SQ FT: 7,642
SALES (est): 4.2MM **Privately Held**
WEB: www.essentialpharmaceutical.com
SIC: 2834 Vitamin preparations; vitamin, nutrient & hematinic preparations for human use

(P-4818)
EVOLUS INC (PA)
520 Nwport Ctr Dr Ste 120, Newport Beach (92660)
PHONE....................949 284-4555
David Moatazedi, *President*
Vikram Malik, *Ch of Bd*
Crystal Muilenburg, *Chief Mktg Ofcr*
Rui Avelar, *Officer*
Lauren Silvernail, *Exec VP*
EMP: 116 **EST:** 2012
SQ FT: 17,758
SALES (est): 56.5MM **Publicly Held**
WEB: www.evolus.com
SIC: 2834 Pharmaceutical preparations

(P-4819)
EXPERT PHARMACEUTICAL LLC
1136 Samuelson St, City of Industry (91748-1221)
PHONE....................626 581-4008
Jianghua Liu, *Mng Member*
EMP: 14 **EST:** 2016
SALES (est): 3.4MM **Privately Held**
WEB: www.expertpharm.com
SIC: 2834 Tablets, pharmaceutical

(P-4820)
FAIRVIEW MTM PHARMA INC
Also Called: Mtm Pharmacy Fairview
1002 N Fairview St, Santa Ana (92703-1811)
PHONE....................714 881-0012
Denise T Le, *CEO*
Tina Quach, *President*
EMP: 14 **EST:** 2016
SALES (est): 675.7K **Privately Held**
SIC: 2834 Pharmaceutical preparations

PRODUCTS & SVCS

(P-4821)
FORTE BIOSCIENCES INC (PA)
1124 W Crson St Mrl Bldg, Torrance (90502)
PHONE................................310 618-6994
Paul A Wagner, *Ch of Bd*
Antony A Riley, *CFO*
Mohamed Ladha, *Vice Pres*
EMP: 28 **EST:** 2017 **Publicly Held**
SIC: 2834 Pharmaceutical preparations

(P-4822)
GENSIA SICOR INC (HQ)
19 Hughes, Irvine (92618-1902)
PHONE................................949 455-4700
Carlo Salvi, *Vice Chairman*
▲ **EMP:** 800 **EST:** 1986
SQ FT: 170,000
SALES (est): 139.6MM **Privately Held**
WEB: www.tevapharm.com
SIC: 2834 8731 Drugs acting on the cardiovascular system, except diagnostic; medical research, commercial

(P-4823)
GILEAD PALO ALTO INC
Also Called: Gilead Scientist
550 Cliffside Dr, San Dimas (91773-2978)
PHONE................................909 394-4000
Chris Beley, *CEO*
EMP: 37
SALES (corp-wide): 24.6B **Publicly Held**
WEB: www.gilead.com
SIC: 2834 Drugs acting on the cardiovascular system, except diagnostic
HQ: Alto Gilead Palo Inc
333 Lakeside Dr
Foster City CA 94404

(P-4824)
GILEAD SCIENCES INC
1800 Wheeler St, La Verne (91750-5801)
PHONE................................650 522-2771
Michael Lee, *Principal*
Carisia Lloyd, *Counsel*
Jason Willems, *Manager*
EMP: 99 **EST:** 1987
SALES (est): 9.3MM **Privately Held**
WEB: www.gilead.com
SIC: 2834 Pharmaceutical preparations

(P-4825)
GMP LABORATORIES AMERICA INC
2931 E La Jolla St, Anaheim (92806-1306)
PHONE................................714 630-2467
Mohammad Ishaq, *CEO*
Suhail Ishaq, *President*
Yusuf Ishaq, *Officer*
Shakil Ahmad, *Vice Pres*
Pauline Lynn, *Executive*
▲ **EMP:** 92 **EST:** 1994
SQ FT: 90,000
SALES (est): 23MM **Privately Held**
WEB: www.gmplabs.com
SIC: 2834 Pharmaceutical preparations

(P-4826)
GMP NUTRITION ENTERPRISES INC
13653 Central Ave, Chino (91710-5108)
PHONE................................909 628-8889
Ka Hung Wong, *CEO*
EMP: 13 **EST:** 2015
SALES (est): 1.1MM **Privately Held**
WEB: www.gmpglobalnutrition.com
SIC: 2834 Pharmaceutical preparations

(P-4827)
GSMS INC (PA)
5187 Camino Ruiz, Camarillo (93012-8601)
PHONE................................805 477-9866
Michael Bornitz, *President*
Anita Wrublevski, *Vice Pres*
Sonia De La Rosa, *General Mgr*
Sonia Espinoza, *Business Mgr*
Regina Coronado, *Analyst*
EMP: 78 **EST:** 2012
SALES (est): 61MM **Privately Held**
WEB: www.gsms.us
SIC: 2834 Pharmaceutical preparations

(P-4828)
H J HARKINS COMPANY INC
Also Called: Pharma Pac
1400 W Grand Ave Ste F, Grover Beach (93433-4221)
PHONE................................805 929-1333
Norma Jean Erenius, *CEO*
Charles Smith, *President*
Norma Erenius, *Officer*
Mary Graham, *Administration*
Leonard Lutz, *Technology*
EMP: 50 **EST:** 1984
SQ FT: 10,000
SALES (est): 6MM **Privately Held**
WEB: www.hjharkinscompanyinc.com
SIC: 2834 Pharmaceutical preparations

(P-4829)
HARPERS PHARMACY INC
Also Called: Ameripharma
132 S Anita Dr Ste 210, Orange (92868-3317)
PHONE................................877 778-3773
Andrew A Harper, *CEO*
Hayk Mnatsakanyan, *CFO*
Gor Mnatsakanyan, *Principal*
Tamara Geronaga, *Admin Mgr*
William Kirk, *Sales Mgr*
EMP: 187 **EST:** 2016
SALES (est): 25.9MM **Privately Held**
WEB: www.ameripharmaltc.com
SIC: 2834 Pharmaceutical preparations

(P-4830)
INSTACURE HEALING PRODUCTS
235 N Moorpark Rd # 2022, Thousand Oaks (91358-7001)
PHONE................................818 222-9600
David Traub, *Owner*
EMP: 33 **EST:** 2015
SQ FT: 6,000
SALES (est): 3MM **Privately Held**
WEB: www.instacure.net
SIC: 2834 Lip balms

(P-4831)
INTERNATIONAL VITAMIN CORP
Also Called: Adam Nutrition, A Division Ivc
11010 Hopkins St Ste B, Jurupa Valley (91752-3279)
PHONE................................951 361-1120
Iliu Elisara, *Branch Mgr*
Alfredo Ferradas, *Safety Mgr*
EMP: 125 **Privately Held**
SIC: 2834 Vitamin, nutrient & hematinic preparations for human use
PA: International Vitamin Corp
1 Park Plz Ste 800
Irvine CA 92614

(P-4832)
INTERNATIONAL VITAMIN CORP (PA)
Also Called: I V C
1 Park Plz Ste 800, Irvine (92614-5998)
PHONE................................949 664-5500
Steven Dai, *President*
Anita Khamvongsa, *CEO*
Glenn Davis, *COO*
Eva Pinto, *Treasurer*
Mike Richtmyer, *Exec VP*
▲ **EMP:** 72 **EST:** 2009
SQ FT: 166,000
SALES (est): 619.4MM **Privately Held**
SIC: 2834 5149 8099 Vitamin preparations; organic & diet foods; nutrition services

(P-4833)
INTERNTNAL MDCTION SYSTEMS LTD
Also Called: IMS
1886 Santa Anita Ave, South El Monte (91733-3414)
PHONE................................626 442-6757
Jack Zhang, *President*
Mary Luo Zhang, *COO*
Paul Yu, *Vice Pres*
Mary Zuniga, *Executive*
MEI Ho, *CIO*
▲ **EMP:** 720 **EST:** 1963

SALES (est): 228.8MM
SALES (corp-wide): 349.8MM **Publicly Held**
WEB: www.amphastar.com
SIC: 2834 2833 3841 Drugs acting on the central nervous system & sense organs; anesthetics, in bulk form; surgical & medical instruments
PA: Amphastar Pharmaceuticals Inc
11570 6th St
Rancho Cucamonga CA 91730
909 980-9484

(P-4834)
JAMES STEWART
Also Called: Diagnostic Reagents
8931 S Vermont Ave, Los Angeles (90044-4833)
PHONE................................323 778-1687
EMP: 22
SQ FT: 4,200
SALES (est): 2.1MM **Privately Held**
SIC: 2834 Distributing Pharmaceutical Solutions

(P-4835)
JARROW INDUSTRIES INC
12246 Hawkins St, Santa Fe Springs (90670-3365)
PHONE................................562 906-1919
Jarrow Rogovin, *Ch of Bd*
Mohammed Khalid, *President*
David Chen, *CFO*
Ben Khowong, *Treasurer*
Terrence Terr Lamb, *Technical Staff*
▲ **EMP:** 140 **EST:** 2000
SQ FT: 125,000
SALES (est): 45.4MM **Privately Held**
WEB: www.jarrowindustries.com
SIC: 2834 Vitamin preparations

(P-4836)
K-MAX HEALTH PRODUCTS CORP
1468 E Mission Blvd, Pomona (91766-2229)
PHONE................................909 455-0158
Lei Ye, *CEO*
Frances Fan, *CFO*
EMP: 24 **EST:** 1999
SALES (est): 2.4MM **Privately Held**
SIC: 2834 Vitamin, nutrient & hematinic preparations for human use

(P-4837)
KALYPSYS INC
333 S Grand Ave Ste 4070, Los Angeles (90071-1544)
P.O. Box 1390, Solana Beach (92075-7390)
PHONE................................858 552-0674
August Watanabe, *Ch of Bd*
John McKearn, *CEO*
David C Tiemeier, *COO*
EMP: 30 **EST:** 2001
SQ FT: 42,000
SALES (est): 2.1MM **Privately Held**
SIC: 2834 Pharmaceutical preparations

(P-4838)
KATE SOMERVILLE SKINCARE LLC (PA)
Also Called: Kate Smrvlle Skin Hlth Experts
144 S Beverly Dr Ste 500, Beverly Hills (90212-3023)
PHONE................................323 655-7546
Kate Somerville, *Mng Member*
Josie Padilla, *CFO*
Anne Grana, *Research*
Audrey TSE, *Graphic Designe*
Brian Edwards, *Business Mgr*
▲ **EMP:** 51 **EST:** 2005
SALES (est): 26.6MM **Privately Held**
WEB: www.katesomerville.com
SIC: 2834 5122 Pharmaceutical preparations; toiletries; cosmetics; perfumes

(P-4839)
KC PHARMACEUTICALS INC (PA)
3201 Producer Way, Pomona (91768-3916)
PHONE................................909 598-9499
L T Khouw, *Ch of Bd*
Joseph Sutedjo, *President*

Dr Pramuditya Oen, *CEO*
Linda Dao, *Vice Pres*
Marcello Ganda, *Technology*
▲ **EMP:** 90 **EST:** 1987
SQ FT: 20,000
SALES (est): 32.6MM **Privately Held**
WEB: www.kc-ph.com
SIC: 2834 Solutions, pharmaceutical; cough medicines; cold remedies; antacids

(P-4840)
KINDEVA DRUG DELIVERY LP
19901 Nordhoff St, Northridge (91324-3213)
P.O. Box 1001 (91328-1001)
PHONE................................818 341-1300
Carol Beesley, *Branch Mgr*
Meg Arce, *Admin Asst*
Amy Kuniyoshi, *Engineer*
Sal Briones, *Mfg Staff*
Mark Syrstad, *Manager*
EMP: 400 **Privately Held**
SIC: 2834 Pharmaceutical preparations
PA: Kindeva Drug Delivery L.P.
42 Water St W Bldg 75
Saint Paul MN 55107

(P-4841)
KINGDOMWAY USA LLC
2802 Dow Ave, Tustin (92730-7212)
PHONE................................714 832-9700
Gale Bensussen, *President*
EMP: 19 **EST:** 2015
SALES (est): 3.8MM **Privately Held**
WEB: www.kingdomway.com
SIC: 2834 Pharmaceutical preparations
PA: Xiamen Kingdomway Group Company
Haicang Xinyang Industrial Zone
Xiamen 36102

(P-4842)
KYTHERA BIOPHARMACEUTICALS INC (HQ)
30930 Russell Ranch Rd # 3, Westlake Village (91362-7378)
PHONE................................818 587-4500
A R D Bailey, *President*
A Robert D Bailey, *President*
John W Smither, *CFO*
Elisabeth A Sandoval, *Ch Credit Ofcr*
Frederick Beddingfield III, *Chief Mktg Ofcr*
EMP: 105 **EST:** 2005
SQ FT: 33,198
SALES (est): 23.6MM **Privately Held**
WEB: www.mykybella.com
SIC: 2834 Dermatologicals

(P-4843)
LEINER HEALTH PRODUCTS INC (HQ)
901 E 233rd St, Carson 90745-6204)
PHONE................................631 200-2000
Jeffrey A Nagel, *CEO*
Robert J La Ferriere, *President*
Crystal Wright, *President*
Michael Collins, *CFO*
Harvey Kamil, *Vice Ch Bd*
◆ **EMP:** 693 **EST:** 1952
SQ FT: 488,000
SALES (est): 127.4MM
SALES (corp-wide): 2.2B **Privately Held**
WEB: www.leiner.com
SIC: 2834 5122 Vitamin, nutrient & hematinic preparations for human use; vitamins & minerals
PA: The Nature's Bounty Co
110 Orville Dr
Bohemia NY 11716
631 200-2000

(P-4844)
LEINER HEALTH PRODUCTS INC
7366 Orangewood Ave, Garden Grove (92841-1412)
PHONE................................714 898-9936
James Smith, *Manager*
EMP: 101

SALES (corp-wide): 2.2B **Privately Held**
WEB: www.leiner.com
SIC: **2834** 2844 2833 5122 Vitamin, nutrient & hematinic preparations for human use; toilet preparations; medicinals & botanicals; vitamins & minerals
HQ: Leiner Health Products, Inc.
901 E 233rd St
Carson CA 90745
631 200-2000

(P-4845)
LEINER HEALTH PRODUCTS INC
27655b Avenue Hopkins, Valencia (91355-3493)
PHONE..................661 775-1422
EMP: 100 **Publicly Held**
SIC: **2834** Mfg Vitamins & Nutritional Products
HQ: Leiner Health Products, Inc.
901 E 233rd St
Carson CA 90745
631 200-2000

(P-4846)
LIEF ORGANICS LLC (PA)
Also Called: Lief Labs
28903 Avenue Paine, Valencia (91355-4169)
PHONE..................661 775-2500
Adel Villalobos, *CEO*
Helder Guimaraes, *CFO*
Nathan Cox, *VP Bus Dvlpt*
Victor Leyson, *VP Finance*
Shar Zega, *Human Resources*
EMP: 25 EST: 2008
SALES (est): 23.8MM **Privately Held**
WEB: www.lieflabs.com
SIC: **2834** Adrenal pharmaceutical preparations

(P-4847)
LIFEBLOOM CORPORATION
Also Called: B&A Health Products Co
925 W Lambert Rd Ste B, Brea (92821-2943)
PHONE..................562 944-6800
Sam Ahn, *CEO*
Chong Ahn, *President*
David Kim, *Purch Mgr*
Cathy Ahn, *Opers Mgr*
Mia Jin, *Manager*
◆ EMP: 20 EST: 2002
SALES (est): 4.6MM **Privately Held**
WEB: www.lifebloomcorp.com
SIC: **2834** Vitamin preparations

(P-4848)
M & L PHARMACEUTICALS INC
629 S Allen St, San Bernardino (92408-2250)
PHONE..................909 890-0078
Jorge Molina Jr, *President*
Guadalupe Molina, *Corp Secy*
EMP: 25 EST: 1991
SQ FT: 6,000
SALES (est): 3.5MM **Privately Held**
WEB: www.mlpharmaceutical.com
SIC: **2834** Vitamin preparations

(P-4849)
MANNKIND CORPORATION (PA)
30930 Russell Ranch Rd, Westlake Village (91362-7378)
PHONE..................818 661-5000
Michael E Castagna, *CEO*
Christopher Klatka, *Partner*
James S Shannon, *Ch of Bd*
Steven B Binder, *CFO*
Alejandro Galindo, *Ch Credit Ofcr*
▲ EMP: 165 EST: 1991
SQ FT: 24,475
SALES (est): 65.1MM **Publicly Held**
WEB: www.mannkindcorp.com
SIC: **2834** Pharmaceutical preparations

(P-4850)
MCGUFF PHARMACEUTICALS INC
2921 W Macarthur Blvd # 1, Santa Ana (92704-6909)
PHONE..................714 918-7277
Ronald M McGuff, *President*
Damon Jones, *Vice Pres*
Nicholas Hoang, *Pharmacist*
▲ EMP: 24 EST: 2002

SQ FT: 12,000
SALES (est): 7.7MM
SALES (corp-wide): 36.4MM **Privately Held**
WEB: www.mcguffpharmaceuticals.com
SIC: **2834** Pharmaceutical preparations
PA: Mcguff Company, Inc.
3524 W Lake Center Dr
Santa Ana CA 92704
714 545-2491

(P-4851)
MCKENNA LABS INC (PA)
1601 E Orangethorpe Ave, Fullerton (92831-5230)
PHONE..................714 687-6888
Dennis Alexander Owen, *President*
Jose Ramirez, *Vice Pres*
Irina Samofalova, *Vice Pres*
Lana Tennant, *Vice Pres*
Raymond Gamboa, *Technician*
◆ EMP: 39 EST: 1998
SQ FT: 62,000
SALES (est): 11.6MM **Privately Held**
WEB: www.mckennalabs.com
SIC: **2834** 2844 Pharmaceutical preparations; toilet preparations

(P-4852)
MED-PHARMEX INC
2727 Thompson Creek Rd, Pomona (91767-1861)
PHONE..................909 593-7875
Gerald Macedo, *CEO*
Avinash Ghanekar, *President*
▲ EMP: 111 EST: 1982
SQ FT: 18,000
SALES (est): 37.6MM **Privately Held**
WEB: www.medpharmex.com
SIC: **2834** Pharmaceutical preparations

(P-4853)
MURAD LLC (HQ)
2121 Park Pl Fl 1, El Segundo (90245-4843)
PHONE..................310 726-0600
Howard Murad MD,
Tikia Dixon, *Executive*
Ashley McDermott, *Executive*
Felicia Paradeis, *Executive*
Leah McGibeny, *Executive Asst*
▲ EMP: 160 EST: 1990
SQ FT: 8,000
SALES (est): 88.6MM
SALES (corp-wide): 59.9B **Privately Held**
WEB: www.murad.com
SIC: **2834** 5122 Vitamin, nutrient & hematinic preparations for human use; vitamin preparations; pharmaceuticals; proprietary (patent) medicines
PA: Unilever Plc
Unilever House
London
207 822-5252

(P-4854)
MYOGENIX INCORPORATED
4725 Allene Way, San Luis Obispo (93401-8734)
PHONE..................800 950-0348
Adam G Nielson, *President*
▲ EMP: 21 EST: 2002
SALES (est): 6.8MM **Privately Held**
WEB: www.myogenix.com
SIC: **2834** Pharmaceutical preparations

(P-4855)
NADIN COMPANY
1815 Flower St, Glendale (91201-2024)
PHONE..................818 500-8908
EMP: 25
SQ FT: 35,000
SALES (est): 2.2MM **Privately Held**
SIC: **2834** Mfg Pharmeuticals

(P-4856)
NATALS INC
Also Called: Ritual
5681 W Jefferson Blvd, Los Angeles (90016-3130)
PHONE..................310 866-8145
Katerina Schneider, *CEO*
Kadie Bowen, *Vice Pres*
Elizabeth Reifsnyder, *Vice Pres*
Kathryn Rogers, *Executive Asst*
Jack Hair, *Engineer*

EMP: 24 EST: 2015
SALES (est): 8.3MM **Privately Held**
WEB: www.ritual.com
SIC: **2834** Vitamin preparations

(P-4857)
NATROL LLC (PA)
21411 Prairie St, Chatsworth (91311-5829)
PHONE..................818 739-6000
Andrew Houlberg, *President*
Edgar Rodriguez, *Comp Lab Dir*
Michael Berinde, *Info Tech Mgr*
Ronald Verga, *Prgrmr*
Edgar Garcia, *Graphic Designe*
◆ EMP: 202 EST: 2014
SALES (est): 85.1MM **Privately Held**
WEB: www.natrol.com
SIC: **2834** Pharmaceutical preparations

(P-4858)
NBTY MANUFACTURING LLC
Also Called: Nature's Bounty
5115 E La Palma Ave, Anaheim (92807-2018)
PHONE..................714 765-8323
Steve Cahillane, *CEO*
Lily Mu, *Training Dir*
Scott Ludwig, *Recruiter*
Hans Lindgren,
Scott Rudolph,
▼ EMP: 224 EST: 1978
SALES (est): 49.4MM
SALES (corp-wide): 2.2B **Privately Held**
WEB: www.bountifulcompany.com
SIC: **2834** Vitamin preparations
PA: The Nature's Bounty Co
110 Orville Dr
Bohemia NY 11716
631 200-2000

(P-4859)
NEW GENERATION WELLNESS INC (PA)
Also Called: Nexgen Pharma
46 Corporate Park Ste 200, Irvine (92606-3120)
P.O. Box 19516 (92623-9516)
PHONE..................949 863-0340
Kyle Brown, *President*
Chris Limer, *President*
Mark Nishi, *CFO*
Gene Nakagawa, *Exec VP*
Jane Drinkwalter, *Vice Pres*
EMP: 190 EST: 1935
SQ FT: 50,000
SALES (est): 51.5MM **Privately Held**
WEB: www.nexgenpharma.com
SIC: **2834** Pharmaceutical preparations

(P-4860)
NEWHERE INC (PA)
Also Called: Cbdfx
19851 Nordhoff Pl Ste 105, Chatsworth (91311-6616)
PHONE..................888 991-7471
Ali Esmaili, *CEO*
Sam Fathfard, *Vice Pres*
Jeremy West, *VP Bus Dvlpt*
Jeff Brunell, *Marketing Staff*
Jameson Rodgers,
EMP: 46 EST: 2012
SALES (est): 9.1MM **Privately Held**
WEB: www.cbdfx.com
SIC: **2834** 2023 3999 5961 Vitamin preparations; dietary supplements, dairy & non-dairy based; ; catalog & mail-order houses; vitamin food stores;

(P-4861)
NHK LABORATORIES INC (PA)
12230 Florence Ave, Santa Fe Springs (90670-3806)
PHONE..................562 903-5835
Karim Amirul, *CEO*
Shafiel Ahmed, *CFO*
Shabbir Akand, *Vice Pres*
Nasima A Karim, *Vice Pres*
Nasima Karim, *Vice Pres*
▲ EMP: 94 EST: 1987
SQ FT: 90,000
SALES (est): 21.2MM **Privately Held**
WEB: www.nhklabs.com
SIC: **2834** 5122 Vitamin preparations; vitamins & minerals

(P-4862)
NITTO AVECIA PHARMA SVCS INC (DH)
10 Vanderbilt, Irvine (92618-2010)
PHONE..................949 951-4425
Raymond Kaczmarek, *President*
William Stowell, *CFO*
Adam Fox, *Exec VP*
Deniz Ozler, *Associate Dir*
Amber Sanchez, *Manager*
EMP: 156 EST: 2016
SQ FT: 62,000
SALES (est): 23.9MM **Privately Held**
WEB: www.aveciapharma.com
SIC: **2834** Pharmaceutical preparations

(P-4863)
NUTRAWISE HEALTH & BEAUTY CORP (PA)
9600 Toledo Way, Irvine (92618-1808)
PHONE..................949 900-2400
Darren Rude, *CEO*
Patty Terzo-Rude, *President*
Theresa Rude, *Treasurer*
Jerry Seidl, *Vice Pres*
Heidi Kaufman, *Planning*
EMP: 94 EST: 2009
SQ FT: 130,000
SALES (est): 48MM **Privately Held**
WEB: www.youtheory.com
SIC: **2834** Vitamin, nutrient & hematinic preparations for human use

(P-4864)
OBAGI COSMECEUTICALS LLC (PA)
Also Called: Obagi Medical
3760 Kilroy Arprt Way, Long Beach (90806-2443)
PHONE..................800 636-7546
Jamie Castle, *President*
Mark T Taylor, *Senior VP*
Lisa Errecart, *Vice Pres*
Michael Goodman, *Associate Dir*
Shawn Moyle, *Technology*
EMP: 101 EST: 1997
SQ FT: 30,884
SALES (est): 34.7MM **Privately Held**
WEB: www.obagi.com
SIC: **2834** Pharmaceutical preparations

(P-4865)
ONYX PHARMACEUTICALS INC
1 Amgen Center Dr, Newbury Park (91320-1730)
PHONE..................650 266-0000
Pablo Cagnoni, *President*
Helen Torley, *COO*
Matthew K Fust, *CFO*
Juergen Lasowski PHD, *Exec VP*
Suzanne M Shema Jdl, *Exec VP*
EMP: 741 EST: 2013
SQ FT: 297,111
SALES (est): 106.3MM
SALES (corp-wide): 25.4B **Publicly Held**
WEB: www.amgen.com
SIC: **2834** 8049 Drugs affecting parasitic & infective diseases; occupational therapist
PA: Amgen Inc.
1 Amgen Center Dr
Thousand Oaks CA 91320
805 447-1000

(P-4866)
OPIANT PHARMACEUTICALS INC
233 Wilshire Blvd Ste 280, Santa Monica (90401-1240)
PHONE..................310 598-5410
Roger Crystal, *CEO*
David O'Toole, *CFO*
Aziz Mottiwala, *Ch Credit Ofcr*
Matthew Ruth, *Officer*
Ben Atkins, *Vice Pres*
EMP: 16 EST: 2005
SQ FT: 1,500
SALES (est): 29.6MM **Privately Held**
WEB: www.opiant.com
SIC: **2834** Pharmaceutical preparations

(P-4867)
P & L DEVELOPMENT LLC
Also Called: Pl Development
11865 Alameda St, Lynwood (90262-4022)
PHONE..................323 567-2482

Jim Smith, *General Mgr*
EMP: 34 **Privately Held**
WEB: www.pldevelopments.com
SIC: 2834 2841 2844 Pharmaceutical preparations; soap & other detergents; toilet preparations
PA: P & L Development, Llc
609 Cantiague Rock Rd 2a
Westbury NY 11590

(P-4868)
PACIFIC SHORE HOLDINGS INC
Also Called: Nature-Cide
8236 Remmet Ave, Canoga Park
(91304-4156)
PHONE..................818 998-0996
Matthew Mills, *President*
Ronald J Tchorzewski, *CFO*
David E Toomey, *Exec VP*
Jennifer Mills, *Admin Sec*
▲ **EMP:** 24 **EST:** 1981
SQ FT: 13,000
SALES (est): 4.7MM **Privately Held**
WEB: www.pac-sh.com
SIC: 2834 2879 Pharmaceutical preparations; pesticides, agricultural or household
PA: Med-X, Inc.
8236 Remmet Ave
Canoga Park CA 91304
818 349-2870

(P-4869)
PELICAN BIOPHARMA LLC
23215 Early Ave, Torrance (90505-4002)
PHONE..................310 326-4700
EMP: 28 **EST:** 2013
SALES (est): 590K **Privately Held**
WEB: www.pelican.com
SIC: 2834 Pharmaceutical preparations

(P-4870)
PENINSULA LABORATORIES LLC
3132 Kashiwa St, Torrance (90505-4011)
PHONE..................310 539-4171
Kuno Sommer, *Principal*
Patricia Myhre, *Admin Asst*
Guenther Loidl, *CTO*
Joshua Kramer, *Project Mgr*
Rachel Yang, *Project Mgr*
EMP: 15 **EST:** 2013
SALES (est): 261.3K **Privately Held**
WEB: www.bachem.com
SIC: 2834 Pharmaceutical preparations

(P-4871)
PHARMA ALLIANCE GROUP INC
Also Called: Lab Ecx.com
28452 Constellation Rd, Valencia
(91355-5081)
PHONE..................661 294-7955
Marvin Delgado, *President*
Amit Marfatia, *Vice Pres*
Bharat Zaveri, *Vice Pres*
Vilma Delgado, *Admin Sec*
◆ **EMP:** 13 **EST:** 2000
SALES (est): 1.5MM **Privately Held**
WEB: www.pharma-alliance-group.net
SIC: 2834 Pharmaceutical preparations

(P-4872)
PHARMACEUTIC LITHO LABEL INC
3990 Royal Ave, Simi Valley (93063-3380)
PHONE..................805 285-5162
Timothy Laurence, *President*
Tom Moore, *President*
Lyuba Ross, *CFO*
Rick Machale, *Vice Pres*
Evelyn Phillips, *Manager*
▲ **EMP:** 85
SQ FT: 32,000
SALES (est): 28.3MM **Privately Held**
WEB: www.pharmaceuticlitho.com
SIC: 2834 Pharmaceutical preparations

(P-4873)
PHIL INTER PHARMA USA INC (PA)
8767 Lanyard Ct, Rancho Cucamonga
(91730-0804)
PHONE..................909 982-3670
Joog Hong, *President*
Rachel Park, *CFO*

Ji Park, *Principal*
◆ **EMP:** 13 **EST:** 2012
SQ FT: 10,000
SALES (est): 6MM **Privately Held**
WEB: www.philinterpharmausa.com
SIC: 2834 Vitamin preparations

(P-4874)
PHYTO TECH CORP (PA)
Also Called: Blue California Company
30111 Tomas, Rcho STA Marg
(92688-2125)
PHONE..................949 635-1990
Minwang Chen, *CEO*
▲ **EMP:** 24 **EST:** 1995
SQ FT: 50,000
SALES (est): 7.2MM **Privately Held**
WEB: www.bluecal-ingredients.com
SIC: 2834 Vitamin, nutrient & hematinic preparations for human use

(P-4875)
PROTAB LABORATORIES
25902 Towne Centre Dr, Foothill Ranch
(92610-3436)
PHONE..................949 635-1930
Min W Chen, *CEO*
Xiao Zhou, *Co-Owner*
Shafiqul Islam, *Vice Pres*
Randy L Pollan, *Vice Pres*
Sarah Mendoza, *Purchasing*
▲ **EMP:** 150 **EST:** 2004
SQ FT: 100,000
SALES (est): 31.4MM **Privately Held**
WEB: www.protablabs.com
SIC: 2834 2023 Vitamin preparations; dietary supplements, dairy & non-dairy based

(P-4876)
PUMA BIOTECHNOLOGY INC (PA)
10880 Wilshire Blvd # 2150, Los Angeles
(90024-4106)
P.O. Box 64945, Saint Paul MN (55164-0945)
PHONE..................424 248-6500
Alan H Auerbach, *Ch of Bd*
Maximo F Nougues, *CFO*
Charles R Eyler, *Treasurer*
Steven Lo, *Ch Credit Ofcr*
Adrian Senderowicz, *Bd of Directors*
EMP: 316 **EST:** 2007
SQ FT: 25,700
SALES (est): 225.1MM **Publicly Held**
WEB: www.pumabiotechnology.com
SIC: 2834 Pharmaceutical preparations

(P-4877)
PURETEK CORPORATION
7900 Nelson Rd Unit A, Panorama City
(91402-6828)
PHONE..................818 361-3949
Jeff Pressman, *Exec VP*
Greg Verbeck, *Officer*
Jeremy Smith, *Sales Staff*
EMP: 130 **Privately Held**
WEB: www.puretekcorp.com
SIC: 2834 2844 Pharmaceutical preparations; cosmetic preparations
PA: Puretek Corporation
1145 Arroyo St Ste D
San Fernando CA 91340

(P-4878)
PURETEK CORPORATION (PA)
1145 Arroyo St Ste D, San Fernando
(91340-1839)
PHONE..................818 361-3316
Barry Pressman, *CEO*
Dick Alston, *CFO*
Jeff Pressman, *Exec VP*
Amy Velasquez, *Administration*
Nikki Chew, *Research*
◆ **EMP:** 50 **EST:** 1991
SQ FT: 114,000
SALES (est): 38MM **Privately Held**
WEB: www.puretekcorp.com
SIC: 2834 Pharmaceutical preparations

(P-4879)
QUANTUM FOUR LABS LLC
3310 Fruitland Ave, Vernon (90058-3714)
PHONE..................213 217-9777
David E French, *CEO*

EMP: 15
SALES (est): 500K **Privately Held**
SIC: 2834 Pharmaceutical preparations

(P-4880)
REDWOOD SCIENTIFIC TECH INC
11450 Sheldon St, Sun Valley
(91352-1121)
PHONE..................310 693-5401
Jason E Cardiff, *President*
Jacques Poujade, *Treasurer*
M Salah Zaki, *Chief Mktg Ofcr*
Eunjung Cardiff, *Admin Sec*
Rhonda Pearlman, *General Counsel*
EMP: 24 **EST:** 2014
SALES (est): 2.9MM **Privately Held**
WEB: www.redwoodscientific.co
SIC: 2834 Druggists' preparations (pharmaceuticals)

(P-4881)
RESEARCH WAY LL LLC
Also Called: Research Way Partners
1900 Main St Ste 375, Irvine (92614-7332)
PHONE..................608 830-6300
Justin Komppa, *Senior Partner*
EMP: 14 **EST:** 2017
SALES (est): 1.8MM **Privately Held**
SIC: 2834 Tablets, pharmaceutical

(P-4882)
ROBINSON PHARMA INC
3701 W Warner Ave, Santa Ana
(92704-5218)
PHONE..................714 241-0235
Tam H Nguyen, *CEO*
EMP: 45 **Privately Held**
WEB: www.robinsonpharma.com
SIC: 2834 7389 Pharmaceutical preparations; packaging & labeling services
PA: Robinson Pharma, Inc.
3330 S Harbor Blvd
Santa Ana CA 92704

(P-4883)
ROBINSON PHARMA INC
2811 S Harbor Blvd, Santa Ana
(92704-5805)
PHONE..................714 241-0235
Tuoi Nguyen, *Sales Staff*
EMP: 45 **Privately Held**
WEB: www.robinsonpharma.com
SIC: 2834 Vitamin preparations
PA: Robinson Pharma, Inc.
3330 S Harbor Blvd
Santa Ana CA 92704

(P-4884)
ROBINSON PHARMA INC
2811 S Harbor Blvd, Santa Ana
(92704-5805)
PHONE..................714 241-0235
EMP: 45 **Privately Held**
WEB: www.robinsonpharma.com
SIC: 2834 Vitamin preparations
PA: Robinson Pharma, Inc.
3330 S Harbor Blvd
Santa Ana CA 92704

(P-4885)
ROBINSON PHARMA INC (PA)
3330 S Harbor Blvd, Santa Ana
(92704-6831)
PHONE..................714 241-0235
Tam Nguyen, *President*
Suliman Jahangiri, *Senior VP*
Rebecca Castillo, *Vice Pres*
Zue Delaney, *Vice Pres*
Neil Shah, *Vice Pres*
◆ **EMP:** 310 **EST:** 1989
SQ FT: 124,000
SALES (est): 207.9MM **Privately Held**
WEB: www.robinsonpharma.com
SIC: 2834 Medicines, capsuled or ampuled

(P-4886)
ROBINSON PHARMA INC
2811 S Harbor Blvd, Santa Ana
(92704-5805)
PHONE..................714 241-0235
Tam Nguyen, *President*
Rebecca Montes, *Vice Pres*

Whitmore Sandra, *Research*
Brandon Le, *Business Mgr*
Jennifer Pham, *Purchasing*
EMP: 45 **Privately Held**
WEB: www.robinsonpharma.com
SIC: 2834 Pharmaceutical preparations
PA: Robinson Pharma, Inc.
3330 S Harbor Blvd
Santa Ana CA 92704

(P-4887)
ROSE CHEM INTL - USA CORP
25 Rainbow Fls, Irvine (92603-3439)
PHONE..................678 510-8864
Minh Nguyen Thi Thanh, *CEO*
Son Ngoc Ha, *CFO*
Lich Thi Thanh Nguyen, *Admin Sec*
EMP: 30
SALES (est): 1.3MM **Privately Held**
SIC: 2834 Pharmaceutical preparations

(P-4888)
S K LABORATORIES INC
Also Called: S K Labs
5420 E La Palma Ave, Anaheim
(92807-2023)
PHONE..................714 695-9800
Bansi Patel, *President*
Ramila B Patel, *Admin Sec*
Marko Vukelic, *Manager*
▲ **EMP:** 100 **EST:** 1992
SQ FT: 60,000
SALES (est): 25MM **Privately Held**
WEB: www.sklabs.com
SIC: 2834 Pharmaceutical preparations

(P-4889)
S K PHARMACEUTICALS INC
31473 Rancho Viejo Rd, San Juan Capistrano (92675-1861)
PHONE..................949 235-5265
Hampar Karageozian, *CEO*
EMP: 14 **EST:** 2000
SALES (est): 433.4K **Privately Held**
SIC: 2834 Pharmaceutical preparations

(P-4890)
SAMSON PHARMACEUTICALS INC
5635 Smithway St, Commerce
(90040-1545)
PHONE..................323 722-3066
Jay Kassir, *President*
Ziad Kassir, *CFO*
Jennifer Chan, *Marketing Staff*
Elsa Sanchez, *Sales Staff*
▲ **EMP:** 40 **EST:** 2001
SALES (est): 9.3MM **Privately Held**
WEB: www.samsonpharmaceutical.com
SIC: 2834 Pharmaceutical preparations

(P-4891)
SENJU USA INC
21700 Oxnard St Ste 1070, Woodland Hills
(91367-8103)
PHONE..................818 719-7190
AG Katayama, *President*
EMP: 15 **EST:** 2007
SALES (est): 3.2MM **Privately Held**
WEB: www.senju-usa.com
SIC: 2834 Druggists' preparations (pharmaceuticals)
PA: Senju Pharmaceutical Co.,Ltd.
3-1-9, Kawaramachi, Chuo-Ku
Osaka OSK 541-0

(P-4892)
SENSORY NEUROSTIMULATION INC
Also Called: Relaxis
1235 Puerta Del Sol # 600, San Clemente
(92673-6309)
PHONE..................949 492-0550
Fred Burbank, *CEO*
Michael Jones, *COO*
Tiffany Jones, *Consultant*
EMP: 13 **EST:** 2008
SQ FT: 4,000
SALES (est): 326.4K **Privately Held**
WEB: www.myrelaxis.com
SIC: 2834 5122 Druggists' preparations (pharmaceuticals); drugs & drug proprietaries

(P-4893)

SHIRE-NPS PHARMACEUTICALS INC
4501 Colorado Blvd, Los Angeles
(90039-1103)
PHONE..................................818 241-3700
Khoa Tran, *Research*
EMP: 3166
SALES (corp-wide): 187MM **Privately Held**
WEB: www.takeda.com
SIC: 2834 Pharmaceutical preparations
PA: Shire-Nps Pharmaceuticals, Inc.
300 Shire Way
Lexington MA 02421
617 349-0200

(P-4894)

SIMPSON INDUSTRIES INC
Also Called: Simpsonsimpson Industries
1093 E Bedmar St, Carson (90746-3601)
PHONE..................................310 605-1224
Rick Simpson, *CEO*
Robert Simpson, *COO*
Oz Martinez, *QA Dir*
Lovie Ebro-Cassiero, *Purchasing*
EMP: 50 EST: 2011
SALES (est): 8.3MM **Privately Held**
SIC: 2834 Proprietary drug products

(P-4895)

SOFT GEL TECHNOLOGIES INC (HQ)
6982 Bandini Blvd, Commerce
(90040-3326)
PHONE..................................323 726-0700
Steve Holtby, *CEO*
Ronald Udell, *President*
Hiroshi Kishimoto, *CFO*
Tomo Kirimoto, *General Mgr*
Debra Schultz, *Office Mgr*
▲ EMP: 91 EST: 1994
SQ FT: 21,000
SALES (est): 27.2MM **Privately Held**
WEB: www.soft-gel.com
SIC: 2834 Medicines, capsuled or ampuled

(P-4896)

STANDARD HOMEOPATHIC COMPANY (PA)
Also Called: Hyland's Homeopathic
13301 S Main St, Los Angeles
(90061-1611)
P.O. Box 61067 (90061-0067)
PHONE..................................310 768-0700
Daniel M Krombach, *President*
Will Righeimer, *CEO*
Dan Krombach, *CFO*
Jeannine Taillac, *Admin Asst*
Mark Phillips, *Pharmacist*
▲ EMP: 100 EST: 1903
SQ FT: 150
SALES (est): 29.9MM **Privately Held**
WEB: www.hylands.com
SIC: 2834 5912 Pharmaceutical preparations; drug stores

(P-4897)

STASON PHARMACEUTICALS INC (PA)
Also Called: IMT-Stason Laboratories
11 Morgan, Irvine (92618-2005)
PHONE..................................949 380-0752
Harry Fan, *CEO*
Karl Weinrich, *Officer*
Amy Cheng, *Executive Asst*
Sue Liu, *Manager*
▲ EMP: 38 EST: 1994
SQ FT: 37,149
SALES (est): 11.9MM **Privately Held**
WEB: www.stasonpharma.com
SIC: 2834 Pharmaceutical preparations

(P-4898)

STERISYN INC
11969 Challenger Ct, Moorpark
(93021-7119)
PHONE..................................805 991-9694
Julie Anne, *Administration*
Timothy Henry, *CEO*
EMP: 30 EST: 2015
SALES (est): 2.5MM **Privately Held**
WEB: www.sterisyn.com
SIC: 2834 Pharmaceutical preparations

(P-4899)

SUHEUNG-AMERICA CORPORATION (HQ)
428 Saturn St, Brea (92821-1710)
PHONE..................................714 854-9882
Joo Hwan Yang, *President*
Ki Hoon Kim, *Principal*
Kevin Lee, *Technical Staff*
Jeff Pague, *Regl Sales Mgr*
▲ EMP: 47 EST: 1998
SALES (est): 25.4MM **Privately Held**
WEB: www.embocaps.com
SIC: 2834 2899 3769 Medicines, capsuled or ampuled; gelatin capsules; space capsules

(P-4900)

SUN TEN LABORATORIES INC
9250 Jeronimo Rd, Irvine (92618-1905)
PHONE..................................949 587-1238
Hong-Yen Hsu, *Principal*
EMP: 20 EST: 2016
SALES (est): 4.9MM **Privately Held**
WEB: www.sunten.com
SIC: 2834 Medicines, capsuled or ampuled

(P-4901)

TAKEDA PHARMACEUTICALS
Also Called: Takeda Thousand Oaks
1700 Rancho Conejo Blvd, Thousand Oaks
(91320-1424)
PHONE..................................805 375-6700
Bobby Riahi, *Mfg Staff*
EMP: 17 EST: 2019
SALES (est): 1.1MM **Privately Held**
WEB: www.takeda.com
SIC: 2834 Pharmaceutical preparations

(P-4902)

TALON THERAPEUTICS INC
157 Technology Dr, Irvine (92618-2402)
PHONE..................................949 788-6700
Joseph W Turgeon, *CEO*
EMP: 75 EST: 2002
SQ FT: 50,000
SALES (est): 4.3MM **Publicly Held**
WEB: www.sppirx.com
SIC: 2834 8731 Pharmaceutical preparations; commercial physical research
PA: Spectrum Pharmaceuticals, Inc.
11500 S Estrn Ave Ste 240
Henderson NV 89052

(P-4903)

TARGETED MEDICAL PHARMA INC (PA)
Also Called: Tmp
2980 N Beverly Glen Cir # 301, Los Angeles (90077-1735)
PHONE..................................310 474-9809
Marcus Charuvastra, *CEO*
Kerry N Weems, *Ch of Bd*
William B Horne, *CFO*
William Horne, *CFO*
Douglas P Gintz, *CIO*
EMP: 22 EST: 1996
SQ FT: 3,200
SALES (est): 7MM **Privately Held**
WEB: www.tmedpharma.com
SIC: 2834 Pharmaceutical preparations

(P-4904)

TEVA PARENTERAL MEDICINES INC
19 Hughes, Irvine (92618-1902)
P.O. Box 57049 (92619-7049)
PHONE..................................949 455-4700
Phillip Frost, *Ch of Bd*
Karin Shanahan, *CEO*
Amir Elstein, *Vice Ch Bd*
Nir Baron, *Senior VP*
Iris Beck-Codner, *Vice Pres*
▲ EMP: 830 EST: 1990
SQ FT: 148,000
SALES (est): 110.3MM **Privately Held**
WEB: www.tevausa.com
SIC: 2834 Pills, pharmaceutical
HQ: Teva Pharmaceuticals Usa, Inc.
400 Interpace Pkwy Ste A1
Parsippany NJ 07054
215 591-3000

(P-4905)

TIANCHENG INTL INC USA
2851 E Philadelphia St, Ontario
(91761-8553)
PHONE..................................909 947-5577
Lizhe Zhang, *CEO*
Zhang Guoji, *Ch of Bd*
Lance Ding, *General Mgr*
Fang Tan, *Business Mgr*
Fong Chauvin, *Manager*
▲ EMP: 15 EST: 2000
SQ FT: 25,000
SALES (est): 3.5MM **Privately Held**
WEB: www.tianchengusa.com
SIC: 2834 Pharmaceutical preparations
PA: Tianjin Tiancheng Pharmaceutical Co.,Ltd.
No.9 Liuming Road, Yangliuqing Town, Xiqing District
Tianjin 30038

(P-4906)

TITAN MEDICAL ENTERPRISES INC
Also Called: US Apothecary Crown Labs
11100 Greenstone Ave, Santa Fe Springs
(90670-4640)
PHONE..................................562 903-7236
James L McDaniel, *President*
James McDaniel, *President*
EMP: 15 EST: 1990
SQ FT: 12,000
SALES (est): 2.3MM **Privately Held**
SIC: 2834 Vitamin preparations

(P-4907)

UROVANT SCIENCES INC (HQ)
5281 California Ave # 100, Irvine
(92617-3218)
PHONE..................................949 226-6029
James Robinson, *CEO*
Ajay Bansal, *CFO*
Walt Johnston, *Senior VP*
Ted Chan, *Vice Pres*
Anne Blanco, *Associate Dir*
EMP: 40 EST: 2016
SQ FT: 8,000
SALES (est): 24.6MM **Privately Held**
WEB: www.urovant.com
SIC: 2834 Pharmaceutical preparations
PA: Sumitovant Biopharma, Inc.
151 W 42nd St Fl 15
New York NY 10036
716 235-5983

(P-4908)

US PHARMATECH INC
2927 Lomita Blvd Ste A, Torrance
(90505-5117)
PHONE..................................310 219-6003
Dongjun Lee, *President*
EMP: 15 EST: 2017
SALES (est): 5.4MM **Privately Held**
WEB: www.uspharmatech.com
SIC: 2834 Druggists' preparations (pharmaceuticals)

(P-4909)

VITA-HERB NUTRICEUTICALS INC
172 E La Jolla St, Placentia (92870-7111)
PHONE..................................714 632-3726
M Bing Baksh, *CEO*
Karen Brewer, *Administration*
David Rough, *Maintnce Staff*
Amelia Carrasco, *Supervisor*
▲ EMP: 35 EST: 1999
SQ FT: 11,000
SALES (est): 6.8MM **Privately Held**
WEB: www.vhni.com
SIC: 5499 2834 Vitamin food stores; pharmaceutical preparations

(P-4910)

VITABEST NUTRITION INC
Also Called: Vit Best
2906 S Tech Center Dr, Santa Ana
(92705-5657)
PHONE..................................714 368-1181
Gale Bensussen, *President*
Toni Clubb, *CFO*
Bing Jiang, *Admin Sec*
Janessa Sanchez, *Admin Asst*
Scott Blaska, *CIO*

(P-4911)

WAKUNAGA OF AMERICA CO LTD (HQ)
EMP: 275 EST: 2015
SQ FT: 200,000
SALES (est): 77.4MM **Privately Held**
WEB: www.kingdomway.com
SIC: 2834 Vitamin preparations
PA: Xiamen Kingdomway Group Company
Haicang Xinyang Industrial Zone
Xiamen 36102

(P-4911)

WAKUNAGA OF AMERICA CO LTD (HQ)
Also Called: Kyolic
23501 Madero, Mission Viejo (92691-2744)
PHONE..................................949 855-2776
Kazuhiko Nomura, *President*
Albert Dahbour, *Vice Pres*
Hiyoshi Sakai, *Vice Pres*
Kathy Comstock, *Admin Asst*
Rene King, *Info Tech Mgr*
◆ EMP: 64
SQ FT: 36,000
SALES: 31MM **Privately Held**
WEB: www.kyolic.com
SIC: 2834 Pharmaceutical preparations

(P-4912)

WEST COAST LABORATORIES INC
156 E 162nd St, Gardena (90248-2802)
PHONE..................................310 527-6163
Maurice Ovadia, *Manager*
EMP: 35
SQ FT: 4,000
SALES (corp-wide): 10.8MM **Privately Held**
WEB: www.westcoastlabsinc.com
SIC: 2834 Vitamin preparations
PA: West Coast Laboratories, Inc.
116 E Alondra Blvd
Gardena CA 90248
323 321-4774

(P-4913)

WEST COAST LABORATORIES INC (PA)
116 E Alondra Blvd, Gardena (90248-2806)
PHONE..................................323 321-4774
Maurice Ovadia, *President*
Jamil Shad, *Treasurer*
Naim Abdullah, *Vice Pres*
Larry Bridwell, *Vice Pres*
Anwar Abdullah, *Admin Sec*
EMP: 15 EST: 1967
SQ FT: 4,000
SALES (est): 10.8MM **Privately Held**
WEB: www.westcoastlabsinc.com
SIC: 2834 Vitamin preparations

(P-4914)

XENCOR INC
111 W Lemon Ave, Monrovia (91016-2809)
PHONE..................................626 305-5900
Bassil I Dahiyat, *President*
Robert Baltera, *Bd of Directors*
Paul Foster, *Chief Mktg Ofcr*
Allen Yang, *Chief Mktg Ofcr*
John R Desjarlais, *Senior VP*
EMP: 114 EST: 1997
SQ FT: 48,000
SALES (est): 122.6MM **Privately Held**
WEB: www.xencor.com
SIC: 2834 Pharmaceutical preparations

(P-4915)

YOUCARE PHARMA (USA) INC
132 Business Center Dr, Corona
(92878-3224)
P.O. Box 668 (92878-0668)
PHONE..................................951 258-3114
Weishi Yu, *CEO*
EMP: 60 EST: 2015
SQ FT: 160,000
SALES (est): 20.9MM **Privately Held**
WEB: www.youcareyk.com
SIC: 2834 Pharmaceutical preparations
PA: Youcare Pharmaceutical Group Co., Ltd.
No.6, Hongda Middle Road, Economic And Technology Development Zo
Beijing 10000

(PA)=Parent Co (HQ)=Headquarters (DH)=Div Headquarters
✿ = New Business established in last 2 years

2022 Southern California Business
Directory and Buyers Guide

221

PRODUCTS & SVCS

(P-4916)
ZELZAH PHARMACY INC (PA)
Also Called: Good Neighbor Pharmacy
17911 Ventura Blvd, Encino (91316-3618)
PHONE........................818 609-0692
Pejman Javaheri, *Principal*
EMP: 29 **EST:** 2007
SALES (est): 3.9MM **Privately Held**
WEB: www.zelzahrx.com
SIC: 2834 5912 Druggists' preparations
(pharmaceuticals); drug stores

2835 Diagnostic Substances

(P-4917)
ALERE SAN DIEGO INC
Also Called: Immunalysis
829 Towne Center Dr, Pomona
(91767-5901)
PHONE........................909 482-0840
Bob Funck, *Branch Mgr*
EMP: 16
SALES (corp-wide): 34.6B **Publicly Held**
WEB: www.globalpointofcare.abbott
SIC: 2835 3841 In vitro & in vivo diagnos-
tic substances; diagnostic apparatus,
medical
HQ: Alere San Diego, Inc.
9975 Summers Ridge Rd
San Diego CA 92121
858 455-4808

(P-4918)
BIOMERICA INC (PA)
17571 Von Karman Ave, Irvine
(92614-6207)
PHONE........................949 645-2111
Zackary Irani, *Ch of Bd*
Steve Sloan, *CFO*
Allen Barbieri, *Admin Sec*
▲ **EMP:** 62 **EST:** 1971
SQ FT: 22,000
SALES: 7.2MM **Publicly Held**
WEB: www.biomerica.com
SIC: 2835 In vitro & in vivo diagnostic sub-
stances; in vitro diagnostics; microbiology
& virology diagnostic products

(P-4919)
DIASORIN MOLECULAR LLC
11331 Valley View St, Cypress
(90630-5300)
PHONE........................562 240-6500
Carlo Rosa, *CEO*
Mauro Priolo, *CFO*
Michelle Tabb, *Officer*
Lezlie Kelzenberg, *Research*
Huong MAI, *Research*
EMP: 200 **EST:** 2016
SALES (est): 90MM
SALES (corp-wide): 408.1K **Privately
Held**
WEB: www.molecular.diasorin.com
SIC: 2835 5047 In vitro diagnostics; diag-
nostic equipment, medical
HQ: Diasorin Inc.
1951 Northwestern Ave S
Stillwater MN 55082
651 439-9710

(P-4920)
EPICUREN DISCOVERY
31 Journey Ste 100, Aliso Viejo
(92656-3334)
PHONE........................949 588-5807
Colleen Lohrman, *President*
Chelsea Bartolotta, *Vice Pres*
Tamara Miyao, *Vice Pres*
Janae Muzzy, *Vice Pres*
Kendall Clark, *Executive*
▲ **EMP:** 65 **EST:** 1999
SALES (est): 8.7MM **Privately Held**
WEB: www.epicuren.com
SIC: 2835 Enzyme & isoenzyme diagnostic
agents

(P-4921)
HELICA BIOSYSTEMS INC
3310 W Macarthur Blvd, Santa Ana
(92704-6804)
PHONE........................714 578-7830
Wondu Wolde Mariam, *President*
Wondu Wolde-Mariam, *Executive*
Jess Hinton, *Technician*

Ely Zaidler, *Technician*
Thu Huynh, *Research*
EMP: 17 **EST:** 1999
SQ FT: 7,500
SALES (est): 1.9MM **Privately Held**
WEB: www.helica.com
SIC: 2835 2836 In vitro diagnostics; bio-
logical products, except diagnostic

(P-4922)
HYGIENA LLC (PA)
941 Avenida Acaso, Camarillo
(93012-8700)
PHONE........................805 388-2383
Steven Nason, *CEO*
Susan Nason, *COO*
Ed Luterbach, *Officer*
Janice Stack, *Vice Pres*
Hugo Gonzalez, *Regional Mgr*
EMP: 300 **EST:** 2001
SQ FT: 30,000
SALES (est): 114.1MM **Privately Held**
WEB: www.hygiena.com
SIC: 2835 3812 8731 Microbiology & vi-
rology diagnostic products; search & de-
tection systems & instruments; biological
research

(P-4923)
**INTERNATIONAL IMMUNOLOGY
CORP**
25549 Adams Ave, Murrieta (92562-9747)
P.O. Box 972 (92564-0972)
PHONE........................951 677-5629
Shunsaku Shibota, *President*
▲ **EMP:** 30 **EST:** 1982
SQ FT: 20,000
SALES (est): 4MM **Privately Held**
WEB: www.iicsera.com
SIC: 2835 2836 In vitro & in vivo diagnos-
tic substances; biological products, ex-
cept diagnostic

(P-4924)
MONOCENT INC
9237 Eton Ave, Chatsworth (91311-5808)
PHONE........................424 310-0777
Shervin Taheri, *CEO*
EMP: 18 **EST:** 2019
SALES (est): 3.3MM **Privately Held**
WEB: www.monocent.com
SIC: 2835 In vitro diagnostics

(P-4925)
ONCOCYTE CORPORATION (PA)
15 Cushing, Irvine (92618-4220)
PHONE........................949 409-7600
Ronald Andrews, *President*
Cavan Redmond, *Ch of Bd*
Gisela Paulsen, *COO*
Mitchell Levine, *CFO*
Padma Sundar, *Ch Credit Ofcr*
EMP: 30 **EST:** 2009
SALES (est): 1.2MM **Publicly Held**
WEB: www.oncocyte.com
SIC: 2835 In vitro & in vivo diagnostic sub-
stances

(P-4926)
QUANTIMETRIX CORPORATION
2005 Manhattan Beach Blvd, Redondo
Beach (90278-1205)
PHONE........................310 536-0006
Monty Ban, *President*
Edward Cleek, *CEO*
Abdee Akhavan, *CFO*
Karen Yee-Lee, *Human Resources*
Dennis Bly, *Opers Staff*
EMP: 70
SQ FT: 86,400
SALES (est): 17.5MM **Privately Held**
WEB: www.quantimetrix.com
SIC: 2835 In vitro & in vivo diagnostic sub-
stances

(P-4927)
TECO DIAGNOSTICS
1268 N Lakeview Ave, Anaheim
(92807-1831)
PHONE........................714 693-7788
K C Chen, *President*
Stephen Chen, *General Mgr*
Hui-Ling Koh, *Research*
Aquil Merchant, *Research*
Dhaval Waghela, *Research*
◆ **EMP:** 70 **EST:** 1985

SQ FT: 40,000
SALES (est): 17MM **Privately Held**
WEB: www.tecodiagnostics.com
SIC: 2835 5049 In vitro & in vivo diagnos-
tic substances; laboratory equipment, ex-
cept medical or dental

2836 Biological Prdts, Exc Diagnostic Substances

(P-4928)
**ALTA ADVANCED
TECHNOLOGIES INC**
760 E Sunkist St, Ontario (91761-1861)
PHONE........................909 983-2973
Steven G Boland Jr, *President*
▲ **EMP:** 21 **EST:** 1988
SQ FT: 12,723
SALES (est): 1.3MM **Privately Held**
WEB: www.bhkinc.com
SIC: 2836 2851 3827 Biological products,
except diagnostic; coating, air curing; lens
coating equipment

(P-4929)
AMGEN INC (PA)
1 Amgen Center Dr, Thousand Oaks
(91320-1799)
PHONE........................805 447-1000
Robert A Bradway, *Ch of Bd*
Dana Dumford, *COO*
Peter H Griffith, *CFO*
Nancy A Grygiel, *Ch Credit Ofcr*
Jonathan P Graham, *Exec VP*
◆ **EMP:** 2577 **EST:** 1980
SALES (est): 25.4B **Publicly Held**
WEB: www.amgen.com
SIC: 2836 Biological products, except diag-
nostic

(P-4930)
**ARMATA PHARMACEUTICALS
INC (PA)**
4503 Glencoe Ave, Marina Del Rey
(90292-6372)
PHONE........................310 665-2928
Todd R Patrick, *CEO*
Brian Varnum, *President*
Steve R Martin, *CFO*
Duane Morris, *Vice Pres*
EMP: 25 **EST:** 1989
SQ FT: 35,500
SALES (est): 823K **Publicly Held**
WEB: www.armatapharma.com
SIC: 2836 Biological products, except diag-
nostic

(P-4931)
BACHEM AMERICAS INC (DH)
Also Called: Bachem California
3132 Kashiwa St, Torrance (90505-4087)
PHONE........................310 784-4440
Brian Gregg, *CEO*
Monica Mendoza, *Partner*
Jessica Novak, *Partner*
Michael Brenk, *CFO*
Peter Hutchings, *Vice Pres*
▲ **EMP:** 163 **EST:** 1971
SQ FT: 70,000
SALES (est): 100.4MM
SALES (corp-wide): 115.6MM **Privately
Held**
WEB: www.bachem.com
SIC: 2836 2834 Biological products, ex-
cept diagnostic; pharmaceutical prepara-
tions
HQ: Bachem Holding Ag
Hauptstrasse 144
Bubendorf BL 4416
585 952-021

(P-4932)
BACHEM BIOSCIENCE INC
3132 Kashiwa St, Torrance (90505-4087)
PHONE........................310 784-7322
Peter Grogg, *Ch of Bd*
Michael Pennington, *President*
Rolf Nyfeler, *CEO*
Cara Zeno, *Admin Asst*
Yao Lin, *Research*
▲ **EMP:** 45 **EST:** 1987

SALES (est): 7.8MM
SALES (corp-wide): 115.6MM **Privately
Held**
WEB: www.bachem.com
SIC: 2836 2899 Biological products, ex-
cept diagnostic; chemical preparations
HQ: Bachem Holding Ag
Hauptstrasse 144
Bubendorf BL 4416
585 952-021

(P-4933)
CAMBRIDGE EQUITIES LP
9922 Jefferson Blvd, Culver City
(90232-3506)
PHONE........................858 350-2300
EMP: 46 **EST:** 2011
SALES (est): 4.9MM **Privately Held**
SIC: 2836 Biological products, except diag-
nostic

(P-4934)
**FUJIFILM IRVINE SCIENTIFIC
INC (DH)**
Also Called: Irvine Scientific
1830 E Warner Ave, Santa Ana
(92705-5505)
PHONE........................949 261-7800
Yutaka Yamaguchi, *CEO*
Ryo Iguchi, *CFO*
Akiko Ohno, *Vice Pres*
Holden Harris, *Associate Dr*
Judy Malillo, *Admin Sec*
▲ **EMP:** 44 **EST:** 1970
SQ FT: 20,000
SALES (est): 124.9MM **Privately Held**
WEB: www.irvinesci.com
SIC: 2836 5047 Blood derivatives; culture
media; medical laboratory equipment

(P-4935)
**GRIFOLS BIOLOGICALS LLC
(DH)**
5555 Valley Blvd, Los Angeles
(90032-3520)
PHONE........................323 225-2221
Greg Rich, *CEO*
Max Debrouwer, *CFO*
David Bell, *Vice Pres*
Willie Zuniga, *Principal*
Ken Whitlow, *CIO*
▲ **EMP:** 363 **EST:** 2003
SALES (est): 185.5MM
SALES (corp-wide): 657.5MM **Privately
Held**
WEB: www.grifols.jobs
SIC: 2836 2834 Plasmas; pharmaceutical
preparations
HQ: Grifols Shared Services North Amer-
ica, Inc.
2410 Lillyvale Ave
Los Angeles CA 90032
323 225-2221

(P-4936)
INFRATAB
4347 Raytheon Rd Unit E, Oxnard
(93033-8225)
PHONE........................805 986-8880
Therese E Myers, *Principal*
Stanton Kaye, *Principal*
Prashanth Vanchy, *Director*
EMP: 15 **EST:** 2004
SQ FT: 15,000
SALES (est): 1.4MM **Privately Held**
WEB: www.infratab.com
SIC: 2836 Biological products, except diag-
nostic

(P-4937)
NITTOBO AMERICA INC
25549 Adams Ave, Murrieta (92562-9747)
PHONE........................951 677-5629
Eva Rafalik, *President*
Tatsuo Sakae, *Presiden*
Samantha Gallego, *Purchasing*
Wilson Feng, *Accounts Mgr*
◆ **EMP:** 150 **EST:** 1986
SQ FT: 3,049,200
SALES: 29.1MM **Privately Held**
WEB: www.nittobous.com
SIC: 2836 Biological products, except diag-
nostic

PA: Nitto Boseki Co., Ltd.
2-4-1, Kojimachi
Chiyoda-Ku TKY 102-0

(P-4938)
PROLACTA BIOSCIENCE INC (PA)
757 Baldwin Park Blvd, City of Industry
(91746-1504)
PHONE.................................626 599-9260
Scott A Elster, *CEO*
Tami D Ciranna, *CFO*
Victoria Niklas, *Chief Mktg Ofcr*
John Nelson, *Officer*
Joseph Fournell, *Vice Pres*
▼ **EMP:** 132 **EST:** 1999
SQ FT: 65,000
SALES (est): 130.3MM **Privately Held**
WEB: www.prolacta.com
SIC: 2836 Biological products, except diagnostic

(P-4939)
SOCIAL JUNKY INC ✪
7874 Palmetto Ave, Fontana (92336-2744)
PHONE.................................323 347-9847
Shannon Bryant, *CEO*
EMP: 43 **EST:** 2021
SALES (est): 1.6MM **Privately Held**
SIC: 2836 7389 Culture media;

2841 Soap & Detergents

(P-4940)
BRADFORD SOAP MEXICO INC
1778 Zinetta Rd Ste G, Calexico
(92231-9510)
PHONE.................................760 768-4539
John Howland, *CEO*
George Laredo, *Manager*
EMP: 493 **Privately Held**
WEB: www.bradfordsoap.com
SIC: 2841 Soap: granulated, liquid, cake, flaked or chip
HQ: Bradford Soap Mexico, Inc.
200 Providence St
West Warwick RI 02893
401 821-2141

(P-4941)
GOODWIN AMMONIA COMPANY (PA)
12102 Industry St, Garden Grove
(92841-2814)
PHONE.................................714 894-0531
Tom Goodwin, *CEO*
Janice Fleet, *Corp Secy*
Gary Goodwin, *Vice Pres*
Katrina Harper, *Planning*
◆ **EMP:** 15 **EST:** 1922
SQ FT: 58,000
SALES (est): 35.2MM **Privately Held**
WEB: www.goodwininc.com
SIC: 2841 5169 Soap & other detergents; chemicals & allied products

(P-4942)
GOODWIN AMMONIA COMPANY
Also Called: The Goodwin Company
12361 Monarch St, Garden Grove
(92841-2908)
PHONE.................................714 894-0531
Tom Goodwin, *President*
Cheryl Ramsey, *Admin Asst*
EMP: 68
SALES (corp-wide): 35.2MM **Privately Held**
WEB: www.goodwininc.com
SIC: 2841 Soap & other detergents
PA: The Goodwin Ammonia Company
12102 Industry St
Garden Grove CA 92841
714 894-0531

(P-4943)
KINGMAN INDUSTRIES INC
26370 Beckman Ct Ste A, Murrieta
(92562-1005)
PHONE.................................951 698-1812
Barbara Mandel, *CEO*
Paul Mandel Jr, *President*
Mitch Mayer, *President*
▲ **EMP:** 20 **EST:** 1974

SQ FT: 23,000
SALES (est): 4MM **Privately Held**
WEB: www.kingmanmyjoy.com
SIC: 2841 2869 5169 5122 Soap & other detergents; industrial organic chemicals; detergents & soaps, except specialty cleaning; cosmetics

(P-4944)
MISSION KLEENSWEEP PROD INC
Also Called: Mission Laboratories
13644 Live Oak Ln, Baldwin Park
(91706-1317)
PHONE.................................323 223-1405
Toll Free:.................................888
Helen Rosenbaum, *President*
EMP: 53 **EST:** 1936
SQ FT: 75,000
SALES (est): 7.1MM **Privately Held**
SIC: 2841 2842 Soap & other detergents; specialty cleaning, polishes & sanitation goods

(P-4945)
PANROSA ENTERPRISES INC
550 Monica Cir, Corona (92878-5496)
PHONE.................................951 339-5888
Peter Chengjian Pan, *President*
Howard Chow, *COO*
Jingwen Zhao, *CFO*
Belle Vasquez, *Office Mgr*
Chenyang Sun, *Admin Sec*
▲ **EMP:** 60 **EST:** 2003
SALES (est): 9.9MM **Privately Held**
WEB: www.panrosa.com
SIC: 2841 Soap & other detergents

(P-4946)
PROCTER & GAMBLE MFG CO
18125 Rowland St, City of Industry
(91748-1235)
PHONE.................................513 627-4678
Ashley Tucker, *Branch Mgr*
EMP: 206
SALES (corp-wide): 76.1B **Publicly Held**
WEB: www.pg.com
SIC: 2841 2079 2099 2844 Detergents, synthetic organic or inorganic alkaline; shortening & other solid edible fats; peanut butter; toilet preparations; cake mixes, prepared: from purchased flour
HQ: The Procter & Gamble Manufacturing Company
1 Procter And Gamble Plz
Cincinnati OH 45202
513 983-1100

(P-4947)
SHIFT PACKAGING LLC
14261 Proctor Ave Ste A, La Puente
(91746-2936)
PHONE.................................206 412-4253
Jeffrey Welch, *President*
EMP: 15 **EST:** 2020
SALES (est): 666.2K **Privately Held**
SIC: 2841 Soap & other detergents

(P-4948)
UNIVERSAL SURFACE TECHLGY INC
Also Called: UST
13023 S Main St, Los Angeles
(90061-1605)
PHONE.................................310 352-6969
Fax: 310 352-6970
▲ **EMP:** 35
SQ FT: 30,000
SALES (est): 4.8MM **Privately Held**
SIC: 2841 Mfg Soap/Other Detergents

(P-4949)
VERMONT FUEL INC
2202 S Vermont Ave, Los Angeles
(90007-1655)
PHONE.................................818 339-6623
EMP: 15 **EST:** 2010
SALES (est): 983.4K **Privately Held**
SIC: 2841 5199 Soap & other detergents; general merchandise, non-durable

---
2842 Spec Cleaning, Polishing & Sanitation Preparations

(P-4950)
2ND GEN PRODUCTIONS INC
Also Called: Mark V Products
400 El Sobrante Rd, Corona (92879-5755)
PHONE.................................800 877-6282
Mark Marchese, *CEO*
Dora Marchese, *President*
Frank Marchese, *Vice Pres*
Robert Marchese, *Admin Sec*
Winnie Sanchez, *Accounting Mgr*
EMP: 40 **EST:** 1961
SALES (est): 5.9MM **Privately Held**
WEB: www.mark-v.com
SIC: 2842 5013 Waxes for wood, leather & other materials; polishing preparations & related products; automotive supplies

(P-4951)
3D/INTERNATIONAL INC
20724 Cntre Pnte Pkwy Uni, Santa Clarita
(91350)
PHONE.................................661 250-2020
Tony Goren, *Manager*
EMP: 118
SALES (corp-wide): 3.9B **Publicly Held**
SIC: 2842 Automobile polish
HQ: 3d/International, Inc.
2200 West Loop S Ste 200
Houston TX 77027
713 871-7000

(P-4952)
AMREP INC (DH)
1555 S Cucamonga Ave, Ontario
(91761-4512)
PHONE.................................909 923-0430
Lou Purvis, *CEO*
Kevin J Gallagher, *CEO*
Mark R Bachmann, *CFO*
Steve Ford, *VP Bus Dvlpt*
Eric Mattson, *Executive*
◆ **EMP:** 180 **EST:** 1969
SQ FT: 125,000
SALES (est): 100.6MM **Privately Held**
WEB: www.amrepproducts.com
SIC: 2842 2079 2911 2869 Specialty cleaning preparations; sanitation preparations, disinfectants & deodorants; edible oil products, except corn oil; greases, lubricating; industrial organic chemicals; soap & other detergents; industrial inorganic chemicals

(P-4953)
AQUA MIX INC
250 Benjamin Dr, Corona (92879-6508)
PHONE.................................951 256-3040
Rick Baldini, *President*
Manuel G Magallanes, *Ch of Bd*
Jill Magallanes, *Vice Pres*
William Tran, *Vice Pres*
▼ **EMP:** 42 **EST:** 1981
SQ FT: 74,000
SALES (est): 3.2MM **Privately Held**
WEB: www.aquamix.stonebtb.com
SIC: 2842 2891 Specialty cleaning preparations; sealants
HQ: Custom Building Products Llc
7711 Center Ave Ste 500
Huntington Beach CA 92647
800 272-8786

(P-4954)
AUTO-CHLOR SYSTEM WASH INC
16141 Hart St, Van Nuys (91406-3904)
PHONE.................................818 376-0940
Brian Gate, *Manager*
Eric Fuss, *Sales Staff*
Raul Ortega, *Manager*
EMP: 15
SALES (corp-wide): 285.7MM **Privately Held**
WEB: www.autochlor.com
SIC: 2842 Laundry cleaning preparations
PA: Auto-Chlor System Of Washington, Inc.
450 Ferguson Dr
Mountain View CA 94043
650 967-3085

(P-4955)
AWESOME PRODUCTS INC (PA)
Also Called: La's Totally Awesome
6370 Altura Blvd, Buena Park
(90620-1001)
PHONE.................................714 562-8873
Loksarang D Hardas, *CEO*
Norma Martinez, *VP Opers*
Sanjay Sata, *VP Opers*
Tejas Shah, *Opers Mgr*
Sanjay Daftary, *VP Sales*
◆ **EMP:** 125 **EST:** 1983
SQ FT: 250,000
SALES (est): 48.7MM **Privately Held**
WEB: www.lastotallyawesome.com
SIC: 2842 Cleaning or polishing preparations

(P-4956)
B&D INVESTMENT PARTNERS INC (PA)
20950 Centre Pointe Pkwy, Santa Clarita
(91350-2975)
PHONE.................................661 255-0955
Glenn Mahler, *Corp Secy*
George D Stroesenreuther, *CFO*
◆ **EMP:** 48 **EST:** 1960
SQ FT: 100,000
SALES (est): 18.1MM **Privately Held**
WEB: www.bc-labs.com
SIC: 2842 2844 Cleaning or polishing preparations; toilet preparations

(P-4957)
BAF INDUSTRIES (PA)
Also Called: Pro Wax
1451 Edinger Ave Ste F, Tustin
(92780-6250)
PHONE.................................714 258-8055
Michael P Bell, *CEO*
Otis F Bell, *President*
Michael Bell, *Director*
▲ **EMP:** 42 **EST:** 1935
SQ FT: 44,000
SALES (est): 9.5MM **Privately Held**
WEB: www.prowax.com
SIC: 2842 Cleaning or polishing preparations

(P-4958)
BURNS ENVIRONMENTAL SERVICES
19360 Rinaldi St Ste 381, Northridge
(91326-1607)
PHONE.................................818 446-9869
Kayla Lelea, *Office Admin*
Caleb Lagos, *Project Mgr*
Sean Miles, *Project Mgr*
Stuart Melendez, *Business Mgr*
Lynn Frasco, *Manager*
EMP: 20 **EST:** 2005
SALES (est): 1.9MM **Privately Held**
WEB: www.burns-enviro.com
SIC: 2842 Specialty cleaning, polishes & sanitation goods

(P-4959)
BUSHNELL INDUSTRIES INC
7449 Avenue 304, Visalia (93291-9466)
P.O. Box 429, Goshen (93227-0429)
PHONE.................................559 651-9039
Robert Bushnell, *President*
EMP: 27 **EST:** 1986
SQ FT: 11,000
SALES (est): 2.2MM **Privately Held**
WEB: www.bushnellindustries.com
SIC: 2842 7699 Specialty cleaning, polishes & sanitation goods; agricultural equipment repair services

(P-4960)
CILAJET LLC
16425 Ishida Ave, Gardena (90248-2924)
PHONE.................................310 320-8000
Jaci Warren, *President*
Richard Barnes, *CFO*
Steve Hansler, *Accounts Exec*
EMP: 25 **EST:** 2001
SALES (est): 4.5MM **Privately Held**
WEB: www.cilajet.com
SIC: 2842 7542 Automobile polish; washing & polishing, automotive

---

(P-4961)
CLOROX MANUFACTURING COMPANY
2300 W San Bernardino Ave, Redlands
(92374-5000)
PHONE..................909 307-2756
EMP: 73
SALES (corp-wide): 7.3B **Publicly Held**
WEB: www.thecloroxcompany.com
SIC: 2842 Specialty cleaning, polishes & sanitation goods
HQ: Clorox Manufacturing Company
1221 Broadway
Oakland CA 94612

(P-4962)
GPS ASSOCIATES INC
1803 Carnegie Ave, Santa Ana (92705-5502)
PHONE..................949 408-3162
Joe Parisi, CEO
Shelley Gaudreau, COO
Renee Gaudreau, Principal
EMP: 49 EST: 1993
SALES (est): 8.4MM **Publicly Held**
WEB: www.guardrxhandsanitizer.com
SIC: 2842 Sanitation preparations, disinfectants & deodorants
PA: Mountain High Acquisitions Corp.
6501 E Greenway Pkwy # 10
Scottsdale AZ 85254
303 358-3840

(P-4963)
GRANITIZE PRODUCTS INC
11022 Vulcan St, South Gate (90280-7621)
P.O. Box 2306 (90280-9306)
PHONE..................562 923-5438
Tony Raymondo, CEO
Betty Raymondo, Corp Secy
Randy Bair, General Mgr
Joyce Bannon, Administration
Palacios Mayra, Purch Mgr
◆ EMP: 75 EST: 1930
SQ FT: 30,000
SALES (est): 19.8MM **Privately Held**
WEB: www.granitize.com
SIC: 2842 Automobile polish; cleaning or polishing preparations

(P-4964)
HOME & BODY COMPANY (PA)
Also Called: Direct Chemicals
5800 Skylab Rd, Huntington Beach (92647-2054)
PHONE..................714 842-8000
Hazem H Haddad, President
Nadene Haddad, Admin Sec
▲ EMP: 32 EST: 1997
SALES (est): 9.1MM **Privately Held**
WEB: www.homeandbodyco.com
SIC: 2842 2841 2899 2844 Bleaches, household: dry or liquid; textile soap; essential oils; face creams or lotions

(P-4965)
JASON MARKK INC (PA)
329 E 2nd St, Los Angeles (90012-4202)
PHONE..................213 687-7060
Jason M Angsuvarn, CEO
Happiness Brown, Executive Asst
Jino Jinowat, Manager
Franda Lay, Manager
▲ EMP: 33 EST: 2007
SALES (est): 4MM **Privately Held**
WEB: www.jasonmarkk.com
SIC: 2842 Shoe polish or cleaner

(P-4966)
KIK-SOCAL INC
9028 Dice Rd, Santa Fe Springs (90670-2520)
PHONE..................562 946-6427
Jeffrey M Nodland, CEO
Stratis Katsiris, President
William Smith, President
Ben W Kaak, CFO
Xochitl Padilla, Manager
EMP: 3000 EST: 1995
SQ FT: 3,000,000
SALES (est): 259.9MM
SALES (corp-wide): 111.1MM **Privately Held**
WEB: www.kikcorp.com
SIC: 2842 Bleaches, household: dry or liquid; fabric softeners; ammonia, household; cleaning or polishing preparations
HQ: Kik International Llc
2921 Corder St
Houston TX
713 747-8710

(P-4967)
LAB CLEAN INC
3627 Briggeman Dr, Los Alamitos (90720-2475)
PHONE..................714 689-0063
Mark Cunningham, CEO
Cathy Poe, Administration
Matthew Bays,
EMP: 25 EST: 2005
SQ FT: 40,000
SALES (est): 2.4MM **Privately Held**
WEB: www.bayescleaners.com
SIC: 2842 Cleaning or polishing preparations

(P-4968)
LMC ENTERPRISES (PA)
Also Called: Chemco Products Company
6401 Alondra Blvd, Paramount (90723-3758)
PHONE..................562 602-2116
Elaine S Cooper, CEO
Janis Utz, President
John D Grimes, COO
Shawn Carroll, CFO
Julie Petritsch, CFO
EMP: 70 EST: 1962
SQ FT: 15,000
SALES (est): 52.3MM **Privately Held**
WEB: www.chemcoprod.com
SIC: 2842 Cleaning or polishing preparations

(P-4969)
LMC ENTERPRISES
Also Called: Flo-Kem
19402 S Susana Rd, Compton (90221-5712)
PHONE..................310 632-7124
Elaine Cooper, CEO
John Grimes, COO
Steven Hamstrom, Executive
June Massa, General Mgr
Justin Foster, IT/INT Sup
EMP: 50
SQ FT: 20,000
SALES (corp-wide): 52.3MM **Privately Held**
WEB: www.chemcoprod.com
SIC: 2842 Cleaning or polishing preparations; floor waxes
PA: Lmc Enterprises
6401 Alondra Blvd
Paramount CA 90723
562 602-2116

(P-4970)
M P M BUILDING SERVICES INC
Also Called: Mpm & Associates
7011 Hayvenhurst Ave F, Van Nuys (91406-3822)
PHONE..................818 708-9676
Paul Davis, President
Mike Danesh, Vice Pres
Valerie Quijano, Project Mgr
Pedro Lombera, Supervisor
EMP: 26 EST: 1975
SQ FT: 35,000
SALES (est): 1.4MM **Privately Held**
WEB: www.mpmco.com
SIC: 2842 Specialty cleaning, polishes & sanitation goods

(P-4971)
MEGUIARS INC (HQ)
Also Called: Brilliant Solutions
17991 Mitchell S, Irvine (92614-6015)
PHONE..................949 752-8000
Barry J Meguiar, President
Michael W Meguiar, Ch of Bd
Mary Swanson, Principal
Catherine E Bayless, Admin Sec
Krista Pennington, Director
◆ EMP: 50 EST: 1901

SALES (est): 72.2MM
SALES (corp-wide): 32.1B **Publicly Held**
WEB: www.3m.com
SIC: 2842 Cleaning or polishing preparations; automobile polish; furniture polish or wax
PA: 3m Company
3m Center
Saint Paul MN 55144
651 733-1110

(P-4972)
MORGAN GALLACHER INC
Also Called: Custom Chemical Formulators
8707 Millergrove Dr, Santa Fe Springs (90670-2001)
PHONE..................562 695-1232
Harriet Von Luft, Ch of Bd
David M Smith, President
Tam Sarmiento, Principal
Sufian Phoa, VP Finance
▼ EMP: 46 EST: 1964
SQ FT: 100,000
SALES (est): 9.9MM **Privately Held**
WEB: www.morgan-gallacher.com
SIC: 2842 5169 Cleaning or polishing preparations; industrial chemicals

(P-4973)
NO PRSSURE PRSSURE WSHG SVCS L
41880 Kalmia St Ste 165, Murrieta (92562-8838)
PHONE..................951 477-1988
Lennix Gibson, Mng Member
EMP: 20 EST: 2015
SALES (est): 2MM **Privately Held**
SIC: 2842 0782 8744 4971 Specialty cleaning, polishes & sanitation goods; lawn & garden services; facilities support services; irrigation systems

(P-4974)
PACE INTERNATIONAL LLC
1104 N Nevada St, Visalia (93291)
PHONE..................559 651-4877
Gorge Lobisser,
Maria Madrigal, Planning
Veronica Pitre, CIO
Nancy Curbow, Technical Staff
Eric Gordon, Engineer
EMP: 14 **Privately Held**
WEB: www.paceint.com
SIC: 2842 2879 2873 2899 Specialty cleaning preparations; agricultural chemicals; plant foods, mixed: from plants making nitrog. fertilizers; water treating compounds; emulsifiers, except food & pharmaceutical; cutting oils, blending: made from purchased materials
HQ: Pace International, Llc
5661 Branch Rd
Wapato WA 98951
800 936-6750

(P-4975)
PATRIOT POLISHING COMPANY
47260 Wrangler Rd, Aguanga (92536-9518)
PHONE..................310 903-7409
Raymond Esfandi, CFO
EMP: 15 EST: 2016
SALES (est): 458K **Privately Held**
SIC: 2842 Metal polish

(P-4976)
PEERLESS MATERIALS COMPANY
4442 E 26th St, Vernon (90058-4318)
P.O. Box 33228, Los Angeles (90033-0228)
PHONE..................323 266-0313
Louis J Buty, President
Peter H Pritchard, Vice Pres
Peter Pritchard, Vice Pres
Terry Scott, Business Dir
Hank Hahn, Sales Associate
▲ EMP: 40 EST: 1967
SQ FT: 35,000
SALES (est): 4.5MM **Privately Held**
WEB: www.americantex.com
SIC: 2842 Sweeping compounds, oil or water absorbent, clay or sawdust

(P-4977)
SANITEK PRODUCTS INC
3959 Goodwin Ave, Los Angeles (90039-1187)
PHONE..................323 245-6781
Robert L Moseley, President
David Moseley, Treasurer
▲ EMP: 13 EST: 1941
SQ FT: 25,000
SALES (est): 2.4MM **Privately Held**
WEB: www.sanitek.com
SIC: 2842 2899 2992 2891 Sanitation preparations, disinfectants & deodorants; fire retardant chemicals; lubricating oils & greases; adhesives & sealants; agricultural chemicals; soap & other detergents

(P-4978)
SOAPTRONIC LLC
20562 Crescent Bay Dr, Lake Forest (92630-8845)
PHONE..................949 465-8955
Horst Binderbauer, Mng Member
Deepshikha Solomon, Manager
◆ EMP: 25
SALES (est): 6.8MM **Privately Held**
WEB: www.germstar.com
SIC: 2842 2841 Sanitation preparations, disinfectants & deodorants; soap & other detergents

(P-4979)
SUNSHINE MAKERS INC (PA)
Also Called: Simple Green
15942 Pacific Coast Hwy, Huntington Beach (92649-1894)
PHONE..................562 795-6000
Bruce P Fabrizio, President
Rosemary Concilio, CFO
Rose Concilio, Officer
Carol Chapin, Vice Pres
Rose Concilia, Vice Pres
▼ EMP: 51 EST: 1981
SQ FT: 25,000
SALES (est): 24.6MM **Privately Held**
WEB: www.simplegreen.com
SIC: 2842 Cleaning or polishing preparations

(P-4980)
SURF CITY GARAGE
5872 Engineer Dr, Huntington Beach (92649-1166)
PHONE..................714 894-1707
Timothy D Miller, President
Matt Rigdon, VP Bus Dvlpt
Matthew Rigdon, VP Business
▲ EMP: 14 EST: 2006
SQ FT: 22,000
SALES (est): 3.1MM **Privately Held**
WEB: www.surfcitygarage.com
SIC: 2842 Cleaning or polishing preparations

(P-4981)
ULTRA CHEM LABS CORP
4581 Brickell Privado St, Ontario (91761-7828)
PHONE..................909 605-1640
Christopher Shieh, President
Cesar Castro, Admin Sec
John Shieh, Research
▲ EMP: 15 EST: 2014
SQ FT: 19,000
SALES (est): 2.8MM **Privately Held**
WEB: www.ultrachemlabs.com
SIC: 2842 Floor waxes

(P-4982)
US CONTINENTAL MARKETING INC (PA)
310 Reed Cir, Corona (92879-1349)
PHONE..................951 808-8888
David Lee Williams, President
Kenny Wang, Analyst
Ida Marquez, QC Mgr
Crystal Stansil, Marketing Mgr
Veronica Sandoval, Cust Mgr
◆ EMP: 83 EST: 1988
SQ FT: 40,000
SALES (est): 18.9MM **Privately Held**
WEB: www.uscontinental.com
SIC: 2842 Leather dressings & finishes; shoe polish or cleaner

2843 Surface Active & Finishing Agents, Sulfonated Oils

(P-4983)
CHEMEOR INC
727 Arrow Grand Cir, Covina (91722-2148)
PHONE...........................626 966-3808
Yongchun Tang, *Ch of Bd*
Pat Mills, *CEO*
Patrick Shuler, *CFO*
Carl Aften, *Vice Pres*
Herb Juppe, *Vice Pres*
▲ **EMP:** 40 **EST:** 2005
SQ FT: 16,000
SALES (est): 7.6MM **Privately Held**
WEB: www.chemeor.com
SIC: 2843 1389 2911 Surface active agents; chemically treating wells; aromatic chemical products

(P-4984)
HENKEL US OPERATIONS CORP
20021 S Susana Rd, Compton (90221-5721)
PHONE...........................310 764-4600
Janet Pan, *Regional Mgr*
Selene Hernandez, *Technician*
Rose Guino, *Engineer*
Khanh Trinh, *Maintence Staff*
Lorretta Atkinson, *Manager*
EMP: 175
SALES (corp-wide): 22.7B **Privately Held**
WEB: www.henkel.com
SIC: 2843 Surface active agents
HQ: Henkel Us Operations Corporation
1 Henkel Way
Rocky Hill CT 06067
860 571-5100

(P-4985)
JUSTICE BROS DIST CO INC
Also Called: Justice Bros-J B Car Care Pdts
2734 Huntington Dr, Duarte (91010-2301)
PHONE...........................626 359-9174
Edward R Justice Sr, *Ch of Bd*
Edward R Justice Jr, *President*
Courtney Justice, *VP Mktg*
Robert Ventura, *Manager*
▲ **EMP:** 25 **EST:** 1947
SQ FT: 33,000
SALES (est): 4.7MM **Privately Held**
WEB: www.justicebrothers.com
SIC: 2843 2899 Surface active agents; chemical preparations

2844 Perfumes, Cosmetics & Toilet Preparations

(P-4986)
220 LABORATORIES LLC (HQ)
2375 3rd St, Riverside (92507-3306)
PHONE...........................951 683-2912
Yoram Fishman, *CEO*
Ian Fishman, *President*
Mike Herzog, *Vice Pres*
George Allison, *Info Tech Mgr*
Tamara Rayter, *VP Engrg*
▲ **EMP:** 145 **EST:** 1991
SQ FT: 130,000
SALES (est): 97.9MM
SALES (corp-wide): 766.3MM **Privately Held**
WEB: www.220labs.com
SIC: 2844 Cosmetic preparations
PA: Plz Aeroscience Corporation
2651 Warrenville Rd
Downers Grove IL 60515
630 628-3000

(P-4987)
ADONIS INC
475 N Sheridan St, Corona (92878-4021)
PHONE...........................951 432-3960
Helga Arminak,
Kenneth Hewlett, *Vice Pres*
Daniel Ramirez, *Vice Pres*
Joey Bilotta, *Business Mgr*
Rami Lkhoury,
EMP: 50 **EST:** 2017

SALES (est): 8.3MM **Privately Held**
WEB: www.adonismfg.com
SIC: 2844 Toilet preparations; cosmetic preparations

(P-4988)
AMERICAN INTL INDS INC
Also Called: Aii Beauty
2220 Gaspar Ave, Commerce (90040-1516)
PHONE...........................323 728-2999
David Eisenstein, *CEO*
Pedro Curiel, *Branch Mgr*
Ralph Turner, *Technical Staff*
Theresa Cooper, *Manager*
◆ **EMP:** 1100 **EST:** 1998
SQ FT: 224,000
SALES (est): 39.4MM **Privately Held**
WEB: www.aiibeauty.com
SIC: 2844 Toilet preparations

(P-4989)
ARCHIPELAGO INC
Also Called: Archipelago Botanicals
1548 18th St, Santa Monica (90404-3404)
PHONE...........................213 743-9200
David Klass, *CEO*
Chad Corzine, *Exec Dir*
Gregory Corzine, *Admin Sec*
Alexi Mintz, *CTO*
Gloria Rivera, *Prdtn Mgr*
◆ **EMP:** 110 **EST:** 1994
SALES (est): 21.7MM **Privately Held**
WEB: www.shoparchipelago.com
SIC: 2844 3999 Toilet preparations; candles

(P-4990)
AWARE PRODUCTS INC
9250 Mason Ave, Chatsworth (91311-6005)
PHONE...........................818 206-6700
Joe Pender, *President*
Jeff Baum, *Info Tech Dir*
Fernando Velasco, *Director*
Mynor Perez, *Manager*
EMP: 35 **EST:** 1971
SALES (est): 5.4MM **Privately Held**
SIC: 2844 Toilet preparations

(P-4991)
AWARE PRODUCTS LLC
Also Called: Voyant Beauty
9250 Mason Ave, Chatsworth (91311-6005)
PHONE...........................818 206-6700
Richard McEvoy, *CEO*
Bill Saracco, *CFO*
Michelle Jimenez, *Vice Pres*
Arturo Bejarano, *Creative Dir*
Ivette Orantes, *Research*
▲ **EMP:** 150 **EST:** 1973
SQ FT: 60,000
SALES (est): 49.5MM
SALES (corp-wide): 2B **Privately Held**
WEB: www.voyantbeauty.com
SIC: 2844 Hair preparations, including shampoos
PA: Voyant Beauty Holdings, Inc.
6710 River Rd
Hodgkins IL 60525
708 482-8881

(P-4992)
BIO CREATIVE ENTERPRISES
Also Called: Bio Creative Labs
350 Kalmus Dr, Costa Mesa (92626-6013)
PHONE...........................714 352-3600
Jason Freeman, *CEO*
▲ **EMP:** 15 **EST:** 2003
SALES (est): 4MM **Privately Held**
WEB: www.bclspa.com
SIC: 2844 Toilet preparations

(P-4993)
BLUE CROSS BEAUTY PRODUCTS INC
557 Jessie St, San Fernando (91340-2542)
PHONE...........................818 896-8681
Ray J Friedman, *Ch of Bd*
Mark Friedman, *President*
Lorraine Friedman, *Corp Secy*
▲ **EMP:** 19 **EST:** 1942
SQ FT: 12,000
SALES (est): 1MM **Privately Held**
SIC: 2844 Manicure preparations

(P-4994)
BLUEFIELD ASSOCIATES INC
14900 Hilton Dr, Fontana (92336-4026)
PHONE...........................909 476-6027
Iheatu N Obioha, *CEO*
Chimere K Obioha, *Vice Pres*
Tembi Sukuta, *Vice Pres*
Sunil Ram, *QC Mgr*
Chimere Obioha, *Marketing Staff*
◆ **EMP:** 30 **EST:** 1986
SQ FT: 30,000
SALES (est): 3.4MM **Privately Held**
WEB: www.bluefieldinc.com
SIC: 2844 5122 Cosmetic preparations; cosmetics, perfumes & hair products

(P-4995)
BOTANX LLC
3357 E Miraloma Ave # 156, Anaheim (92806-1937)
PHONE...........................714 854-1601
James McGee, *Mng Member*
▲ **EMP:** 50 **EST:** 2005
SALES (est): 8.7MM **Privately Held**
WEB: www.botanx.com
SIC: 2844 Cosmetic preparations

(P-4996)
BUDS COTTON INC
1240 N Fee Ana St, Anaheim (92807-1817)
P.O. Box 18073 (92817-8073)
PHONE...........................714 223-7800
Dewitt Paul, *Ch of Bd*
Barry Williams, *President*
Carol Aarsleff, *Accountant*
Matt Paul, *VP Sales*
▲ **EMP:** 22 **EST:** 1991
SQ FT: 30,000
SALES (est): 1.1MM **Privately Held**
WEB: www.cottonbuds.com
SIC: 2844 Toilet preparations

(P-4997)
CALI CHEM INC
Also Called: Be Beauty
14271 Corporate Dr Ste B, Garden Grove (92843-5000)
PHONE...........................714 265-3740
Tung Doan, *CEO*
Duc Doan, *President*
Brian Doan, *General Mgr*
Amy Doan, *Admin Sec*
Alex Dodi, *Purchasing*
▲ **EMP:** 25 **EST:** 2005
SQ FT: 50,000
SALES (est): 4.4MM **Privately Held**
WEB: www.bebeautyproducts.com
SIC: 2844 Face creams or lotions

(P-4998)
CALIFORNIA INTERFILL INC
8178 Mar Vista Ct, Riverside (92504-4324)
PHONE...........................951 351-2619
Thomas E Boyes, *President*
▲ **EMP:** 15 **EST:** 2000
SQ FT: 20,000
SALES (est): 3.2MM **Privately Held**
SIC: 2844 Cosmetic preparations

(P-4999)
CDM CORP
Also Called: Rozge Cosmoceutical
7922 Haskell Ave, Van Nuys (91406-1923)
P.O. Box 572643, Tarzana (91357-2643)
PHONE...........................818 787-4002
Mary Arshadi, *President*
▲ **EMP:** 15 **EST:** 2009
SQ FT: 30,000
SALES (est): 1.7MM **Privately Held**
WEB: www.tradeshowplace.com
SIC: 5999 2844 Toiletries, cosmetics & perfumes; cosmetic preparations

(P-5000)
CLASSIC COSMETICS INC (PA)
9530 De Soto Ave, Chatsworth (91311-5010)
PHONE...........................818 773-9042
Ida Csiszar, *CEO*
Frank Csiszar, *Treasurer*
Steve Csiszar, *Vice Pres*
Larry Tapia, *Vice Pres*
Israel Galindo, *Info Tech Mgr*
▲ **EMP:** 125 **EST:** 1988
SQ FT: 70,000

SALES (est): 24.9MM **Privately Held**
WEB: www.classiccosmetics.com
SIC: 2844 Cosmetic preparations

(P-5001)
CLM GROUP INC
20730 Dearborn St, Chatsworth (91311-5912)
PHONE...........................818 349-2549
Joseph Caputo, *CEO*
EMP: 25 **EST:** 2018
SALES (est): 1MM **Privately Held**
WEB: www.clmgroupus.com
SIC: 2844 Cosmetic preparations

(P-5002)
CORETEX PRODUCTS INC (PA)
1850 Sunnyside Ct, Bakersfield (93308-6823)
PHONE...........................661 834-6805
James Boone, *Chairman*
Brad Bierman, *President*
Richard B Bierman, *CEO*
Barbara Norton, *Comptroller*
Matt Brummett, *Prdtn Mgr*
▲ **EMP:** 14 **EST:** 1999
SQ FT: 14,000
SALES (est): 2.6MM **Privately Held**
WEB: www.coretexproducts.com
SIC: 2844 Suntan lotions & oils

(P-5003)
COSMETIC ENTERPRISES LTD
12848 Pierce St, Pacoima (91331-2524)
PHONE...........................818 896-5355
Richard Saute, *President*
Jesse Woods, *CFO*
Arda Saute, *Treasurer*
Paul Hwang, *Info Tech Mgr*
Faviola Morelos, *Info Tech Mgr*
▲ **EMP:** 19 **EST:** 1980
SQ FT: 65,000
SALES (est): 5.6MM **Privately Held**
WEB: www.cosmeticent.com
SIC: 2844 Hair preparations, including shampoos; cosmetic preparations

(P-5004)
COSMETIC GROUP USA INC
8430 Tujunga Ave, Sun Valley (91352-3934)
PHONE...........................818 767-2889
Andrea Chuchvara, *CEO*
Giselle Poinier, *Project Mgr*
Jeff Engels, *Engineer*
Jacob Maxwell, *Analyst*
Jocelyn Martinez, *Personnel Assit*
▼ **EMP:** 180 **EST:** 1984
SQ FT: 80,000
SALES (est): 47.4MM **Privately Held**
WEB: www.cosmeticgroupusa.com
SIC: 2844 Cosmetic preparations

(P-5005)
COSMO INTERNATIONAL CORP
Also Called: Cosmo International Fragrances
9200 W Sunset Blvd # 401, West Hollywood (90069-3502)
PHONE...........................310 271-1100
Axel Van Liempt, *Branch Mgr*
EMP: 63
SALES (corp-wide): 32.3MM **Privately Held**
WEB: www.cosmo-fragrances.com
SIC: 2844 Perfumes, natural or synthetic
PA: Cosmo International Corp
1341 W Newport Center Dr
Deerfield Beach FL 33442
954 798-4500

(P-5006)
COSMOBEAUTI LABS & MFG INC
Also Called: Cosmo Beauty Lab & Mfg
480 E Arrow Hwy, San Dimas (91773-3340)
PHONE...........................909 971-9832
Barbara Choi, *President*
Raymond Chung, *Purchasing*
Kenneth Lim, *Sales Staff*
▲ **EMP:** 15 **EST:** 2000
SQ FT: 10,000
SALES (est): 2MM **Privately Held**
SIC: 2844 Face creams or lotions

(PA)=Parent Co (HQ)=Headquarters (DH)=Div Headquarters
✿ = New Business established in last 2 years

2022 Southern California Business
Directory and Buyers Guide

225

P R O D U C T S & S V C S

(P-5007)
COSRICH GROUP INC
12243 Branford St, Sun Valley
(91352-1010)
PHONE..................................818 686-2500
EMP: 24
SALES (corp-wide): 1.7B **Privately Held**
WEB: www.ouchiesonline.com
SIC: 2844 Toilet preparations
HQ: Cosrich Group, Inc.
　　51 La France Ave 55
　　Bloomfield NJ 07003
　　866 771-7473

(P-5008)
COSWAY COMPANY INC
14805 S Maple Ave, Gardena
(90248-1994)
PHONE..................................310 527-9135
Jose Lozano, *Manager*
EMP: 30
SALES (corp-wide): 67.3MM **Privately
Held**
WEB: www.coswayco.com
SIC: 2844 5699 Face creams or lotions;
　　bathing suits
PA: Cosway Company, Inc.
　　20633 S Fordyce Ave
　　Carson CA 90810
　　310 900-4100

(P-5009)
COSWAY COMPANY INC (PA)
20633 S Fordyce Ave, Carson
(90810-1019)
PHONE..................................310 900-4100
Richard L Hough, *CEO*
Maggie Martinez, *Planning*
Radesh Narine, *Engrg Dir*
Deanna Simon, *Research*
Alex Mora, *Technology*
▲ EMP: 20 EST: 1963
SALES (est): 67.3MM **Privately Held**
WEB: www.coswayco.com
SIC: 2844 Face creams or lotions; cos-
　　metic preparations; shampoos, rinses,
　　conditioners: hair

(P-5010)
DEN-MAT CORPORATION (DH)
236 S Broadway St, Orcutt (93455-4605)
PHONE..................................805 922-8491
Robert L Ibsen, *CEO*
Noreen Freitas, *Exec VP*
▲ EMP: 500 EST: 1972
SQ FT: 2,500
SALES (est): 77.3MM
SALES (corp-wide): 167.3MM **Privately
Held**
WEB: www.denmat.com
SIC: 2844 3843 Toothpastes or powders,
　　dentifrices; dental materials

(P-5011)
DEN-MAT CORPORATION
21515 Vanowen St Ste 200, Canoga Park
(91303-2715)
PHONE..................................800 445-0345
Robert Brennis, *Manager*
Sam Danak, *Area Mgr*
Jonas Tucker, *Technician*
Jessica Fish, *Sales Mgr*
Sophia Skafidas, *Sales Staff*
EMP: 179
SALES (corp-wide): 167.3MM **Privately
Held**
SIC: 2844 Toothpastes or powders, denti-
　　frices
HQ: Den-Mat Corporation
　　236 S Broadway St
　　Orcutt CA 93455
　　805 922-8491

(P-5012)
DERMALOGICA LLC (HQ)
Also Called: Dermal Group, The
1535 Beachey Pl, Carson (90746-4005)
PHONE..................................310 900-4000
Aurelian Lis, *President*
Karlee Vilsack, *Associate Dir*
Raymond Wurwand, *Branch Mgr*
David Goldstein, *General Mgr*
Cirsten Hannken, *General Mgr*
◆ EMP: 150 EST: 1983
SQ FT: 52,000

SALES (est): 125.3MM
SALES (corp-wide): 59.9B **Privately Held**
WEB: www.dermalogica.com
SIC: 2844 Cosmetic preparations
PA: Unilever Plc
　　Unilever House
　　London
　　207 822-5252

(P-5013)
DIAMOND WIPES INTL INC (PA)
Also Called: D W I
4651 Schaefer Ave, Chino (91710-5542)
PHONE..................................909 230-9888
Lance Leonard, *CEO*
Karina Ochoa, *Partner*
Jessica Lum, *President*
Angie Injian, *Senior VP*
Vivian Kul, *Vice Pres*
▲ EMP: 91 EST: 1994
SALES (est): 55MM **Privately Held**
WEB: www.diamondwipes.com
SIC: 2844 Towelettes, premoistened

(P-5014)
DR HAROLD KATZ LLC
Also Called: Therabreath
5802 Willoughby Ave, Los Angeles
(90038-3012)
PHONE..................................323 993-8320
Harold Katz, *Fmly & Gen Dent*
Aurora Sacarello, *Executive Asst*
▲ EMP: 16 EST: 2002
SQ FT: 1,800
SALES (est): 5.1MM **Privately Held**
WEB: www.therabreath.com
SIC: 5961 2844 Catalog & mail-order
　　houses; mouthwashes

(P-5015)
DR SQUATCH INC
4065 Glencoe Ave Apt 300b, Marina Del
Rey (90292-6079)
PHONE..................................704 989-9024
Matt Karp, *Office Mgr*
Dan Larson, *Finance*
Martin Forde, *Sales Staff*
Kendra Jackson, *Director*
EMP: 30 EST: 2019
SALES (est): 9.4MM **Privately Held**
WEB: www.drsquatch.com
SIC: 2844 Toilet preparations

(P-5016)
DYNAMIC DESIGNS INC
Also Called: Dynamic Collections
42259 Rio Nedo, Temecula (92590-3709)
PHONE..................................951 302-1344
Ennio V Racineli, *CEO*
Stephen Scheele, *President*
Darlene Racinelli, *Vice Pres*
▲ EMP: 13 EST: 2001
SALES (est): 336.6K **Privately Held**
WEB: www.dynamicdsgns.com
SIC: 2844 Concentrates, perfume

(P-5017)
ECOLY INTERNATIONAL INC
Also Called: Sea Critters
5800 Bristol Pkwy Ste 700, Culver City
(90230-6993)
PHONE..................................818 718-6982
Jim Morrison, *CEO*
EMP: 15 EST: 1995
SQ FT: 2,200
SALES (est): 402.8K **Privately Held**
WEB: www.ecoly.com
SIC: 2844 5122 Hair preparations, includ-
　　ing shampoos; drugs, proprietaries & sun-
　　dries

(P-5018)
**EDDIES PERFUME & COSMTC
CO INC**
19859 Nordhoff St, Northridge
(91324-3331)
PHONE..................................818 341-1717
Edmund Zafrani, *President*
Haim Zafrani, *Principal*
◆ EMP: 14 EST: 1987
SQ FT: 15,000
SALES (est): 1.2MM **Privately Held**
WEB: www.eddiesperfume.com
SIC: 2844 5122 Perfumes, natural or syn-
　　thetic; drugs, proprietaries & sundries

(P-5019)
EVERBRANDS INC
401 N Oak St, Inglewood (90302-3314)
PHONE..................................855 595-2999
Michael Florman, *CEO*
Joshua Wallace, *President*
Camilo Triana, *Officer*
Lana Gailani, *Project Mgr*
▲ EMP: 20 EST: 2013
SQ FT: 6,000
SALES (est): 1.8MM **Privately Held**
WEB: www.eversmilewhite.com
SIC: 2844 Oral preparations; cosmetic
　　preparations

(P-5020)
EXQUISITE CORPORATION
Also Called: Exquisite Mfg & Filling Serv
5000 Rivergrade Rd, Baldwin Park
(91706-1405)
PHONE..................................626 856-0200
Lily Gozaly, *President*
▲ EMP: 17 EST: 1988
SQ FT: 20,000
SALES (est): 1MM **Privately Held**
SIC: 2844 Cosmetic preparations

(P-5021)
FNC MEDICAL CORPORATION
Also Called: Show Off Time
6000 Leland St, Ventura (93003-7605)
PHONE..................................805 644-7576
Samuel S Pattillo, *President*
Samuel Pattillo, *President*
Synora Pattillo, *Vice Pres*
EMP: 20 EST: 1992
SQ FT: 36,000
SALES (est): 4.7MM **Privately Held**
WEB: www.fncmedical.com
SIC: 2844 Cosmetic preparations

(P-5022)
FORMOLOGY LAB INC
9174 Deering Ave, Chatsworth
(91311-5801)
PHONE..................................424 452-0377
Oren Ezra, *CEO*
Tonnie Ventura-Reyes, *Purchasing*
EMP: 15 EST: 2017
SALES (est): 997.6K **Privately Held**
WEB: www.formologylab.com
SIC: 2844 Toilet preparations

(P-5023)
GIOVANNI COSMETICS INC
Also Called: Giovanni Hair Care & Cosmetics
2064 E University Dr, Rancho Dominguez
(90220-6419)
P.O. Box 6990, Beverly Hills (90212-6990)
PHONE..................................310 952-9960
Giovanni J Guidotti, *CEO*
Arthur Guidotti, *Owner*
Peter Stathis, *President*
Phu Huynh, *Purch Mgr*
Jorge Perez, *Production*
◆ EMP: 56 EST: 1979
SALES (est): 12.1MM **Privately Held**
WEB: www.giovannicosmetics.com
SIC: 2844 5122 5999 Cosmetic prepara-
　　tions; cosmetics, perfumes & hair prod-
　　ucts; cosmetics

(P-5024)
**GLAM AND GLITS NAIL DESIGN
INC**
Also Called: Kiara Sky Professional Nails
8700 Swigert Ct Unit 209, Bakersfield
(93311-9696)
PHONE..................................661 393-4800
Khoa Duong, *CEO*
▲ EMP: 65 EST: 2013
SALES (est): 7.3MM **Privately Held**
WEB: www.glamandglits.com
SIC: 2844 Manicure preparations

(P-5025)
GLOBAL SALES INC
Also Called: Aniise Skin Care
1732 Westwood Blvd, Los Angeles
(90024-5608)
PHONE..................................310 474-7700
Sheida Kimiabakhsh, *CEO*
Sharareh Kimiabakhsh, *Vice Pres*
Melange Skincare, *Vice Pres*
Vafa Khoshbin, *Principal*
▲ EMP: 25 EST: 2011

SALES (est): 4.3MM **Privately Held**
WEB: www.aniise.com
SIC: 2844 5999 Hair preparations, includ-
　　ing shampoos; face creams or lotions; toi-
　　letries, cosmetics & perfumes

(P-5026)
GORDON LABORATORIES INC
751 E Artesia Blvd, Carson (90746-1202)
PHONE..................................310 327-5240
Julie Christiansen, *CEO*
Michael Pereira, *CEO*
Prashant Ingle, *Vice Pres*
Marco Pereira, *Vice Pres*
Laura Gutierrez, *Research*
▲ EMP: 120 EST: 1919
SQ FT: 100,000
SALES (est): 25.1MM **Privately Held**
WEB: www.gordonlabsinc.com
SIC: 2844 Cosmetic preparations

(P-5027)
**GRAHAM WEBB
INTERNATIONAL INC (DH)**
6109 De Soto Ave, Woodland Hills
(91367-3709)
PHONE..................................760 918-3600
Rick Kornbluth, *President*
Thomas P Baumann, *Vice Pres*
EMP: 70 EST: 1989
SQ FT: 30,000
SALES (est): 57MM **Publicly Held**
WEB: www.us.wella.professionalstore.com
SIC: 2844 Hair preparations, including
　　shampoos
HQ: Wella Corporation
　　4500 Park Granada Ste 100
　　Calabasas CA 91302
　　818 999-5112

(P-5028)
GSCM VENTURES INC
Also Called: Pacific Naturals
12924 Pierce St, Pacoima (91331-2526)
PHONE..................................818 303-2600
Gary McNelley, *President*
Gary Neeley, *President*
David Rivero, *Vice Pres*
▼ EMP: 32 EST: 2002
SQ FT: 5,000
SALES (est): 1.7MM **Privately Held**
SIC: 2844 Toilet preparations

(P-5029)
HAIN CELESTIAL GROUP INC
Also Called: Jason's Natural
5630 Rickenbacker Rd, Bell (90201-6412)
PHONE..................................323 859-0553
David Vazquez, *Branch Mgr*
EMP: 150 **Publicly Held**
WEB: www.hain.com
SIC: 2844 Toilet preparations
PA: The Hain Celestial Group Inc
　　1111 Marcus Ave Ste 100
　　New Hyde Park NY 11042

(P-5030)
HLB90067 INC (PA)
Also Called: Haus Laboratories
2008 Park Pl Ste E, El Segundo
(90245-6118)
PHONE..................................626 689-8614
EMP: 14
SALES (est): 2.5MM **Privately Held**
SIC: 2844 Mfg Toilet Preparations

(P-5031)
IBG HOLDINGS INC
24841 Avenue Tibbitts, Valencia
(91355-3405)
PHONE..................................661 702-8680
Richard Mayne, *President*
Marissa Pomerantz, *Vice Pres*
▲ EMP: 20 EST: 2002
SQ FT: 5,000
SALES (est): 1.7MM **Privately Held**
SIC: 2844 Cosmetic preparations

(P-5032)
**INNOVATIVE COSMETIC LABS
INC**
9740 Cozycroft Ave, Chatsworth
(91311-4401)
PHONE..................................818 349-1121
EMP: 15

SALES (est): 3.4MM **Privately Held**
WEB: www.iclpl.com
SIC: 2844 Mfg Toilet Preparations

(P-5033)
INSPARATION INC
11950 Hertz Ave, Moorpark (93021-7145)
PHONE.................................805 553-0820
Lori Guy, *CEO*
Joe Guy, *Officer*
EMP: 38 **EST:** 1987
SALES (est): 5.4MM **Privately Held**
WEB: www.insparation.com
SIC: 2844 Cosmetic preparations

(P-5034)
JAFRA COSMETICS INTL INC (HQ)
2451 Townsgate Rd, Westlake Village (91361-2506)
PHONE.................................805 449-3000
Mauro Schnaidman, *President*
Connie Tang, *President*
James Christl, *CFO*
Hans Ter Pelle, *CFO*
Stacy Wolf, *Treasurer*
◆ **EMP:** 130 **EST:** 1956
SQ FT: 123,500
SALES (est): 132.6MM
SALES (corp-wide): 3.2B **Privately Held**
WEB: www.jafra.com
SIC: 5999 2844 Cosmetics; toilet preparations
PA: Vorwerk Se & Co. Kg
Muhlenweg 17-37
Wuppertal NW 42275
202 564-0

(P-5035)
JOICO LABORATORIES INC
5800 Bristol Pkwy, Culver City (90230-6696)
PHONE.................................626 321-4100
Sara Jones, *President*
Akira Mochizuki, *Exec VP*
Michele Homer, *Production*
Christina Stein, *Marketing Mgr*
Annie Hu, *Marketing Staff*
▲ **EMP:** 72 **EST:** 1976
SALES (est): 1.4MM **Privately Held**
WEB: www.joico.com
SIC: 2844 Hair preparations, including shampoos; cosmetic preparations

(P-5036)
JON DAVLER INC
9440 Gidley St, Temple City (91780-4211)
PHONE.................................626 941-6558
David J Sheen, *President*
Christina Yang, *Vice Pres*
◆ **EMP:** 24
SQ FT: 12,000
SALES (est): 3MM **Privately Held**
WEB: www.jondavler.com
SIC: 5999 2844 Cosmetics; toilet preparations

(P-5037)
KAMSUT INCORPORATED
Also Called: Kama Sutra
2151 Anchor Ct, Thousand Oaks (91320-1604)
PHONE.................................805 495-7479
Joseph Bolstad, *President*
Jacqueline Kane, *Vice Pres*
Christine Lawrence, *Controller*
Christine Marsden, *Sales Staff*
Sarah Grant, *Accounts Mgr*
▲ **EMP:** 20 **EST:** 1968
SQ FT: 8,000
SALES (est): 4.2MM **Privately Held**
WEB: www.kamasutra.com
SIC: 2844 Cosmetic preparations

(P-5038)
KDC/ONE COSMETIC LABS AMER INC
20245 Sunburst St, Chatsworth (91311-6219)
PHONE.................................818 998-3511
Nicholas Whitley, *CEO*
EMP: 199 **EST:** 2020

SALES (est): 106MM
SALES (corp-wide): 1.7B **Privately Held**
WEB: www.kdc-one.com
SIC: 2844 Shampoos, rinses, conditioners: hair
HQ: Kdc Us Holdings Inc.
1000 Robins Rd
Lynchburg VA 24504

(P-5039)
KIM LAUBE & COMPANY INC
Also Called: Kelco
2221 Statham Blvd, Oxnard (93033-3913)
PHONE.................................805 240-1300
Kim E Laube, *President*
Daqvid Stillmunks, *Purch Agent*
David Stillmunks, *Purch Agent*
▲ **EMP:** 40 **EST:** 1982
SALES (est): 8.1MM **Privately Held**
WEB: www.kimlaubeco.com
SIC: 2844 3999 Hair preparations, including shampoos; shampoos, rinses, conditioners: hair; hair clippers for human use, hand & electric; pet supplies

(P-5040)
KUM KANG TRADING USAINC
Also Called: Black N Gold
6433 Alondra Blvd, Paramount (90723-3758)
PHONE.................................562 531-6111
Yoon OH, *President*
◆ **EMP:** 25 **EST:** 1987
SQ FT: 20,000
SALES (est): 2.4MM **Privately Held**
SIC: 2844 Hair preparations, including shampoos

(P-5041)
LANZA RESEARCH INTERNATIONAL
429 Santa Monica Blvd # 5, Santa Monica (90401-3401)
PHONE.................................310 393-5227
Robert De Lanza, *President*
Jo-Ann Stamp, *Corp Secy*
Dana Story, *Exec VP*
EMP: 17 **EST:** 1983
SQ FT: 40,000
SALES (est): 651.8K **Privately Held**
WEB: www.lanza.com
SIC: 2844 5122 Shampoos, rinses, conditioners: hair; cosmetics

(P-5042)
LEE PHARMACEUTICALS
1434 Santa Anita Ave, South El Monte (91733-3312)
PHONE.................................626 442-3141
Ronald G Lee, *CEO*
Mike Agresti, *CFO*
▲ **EMP:** 82 **EST:** 1971
SALES (est): 9.6MM **Privately Held**
WEB: www.leepharmaceuticals.com
SIC: 2844 2834 3843 Manicure preparations; pharmaceutical preparations; enamels, dentists'

(P-5043)
LEMYN LLC
Also Called: Lemyn Organics
511 S Harbor Blvd, La Habra (90631-9374)
PHONE.................................714 617-2410
Jochen Ittstein, *Mng Member*
Lupe Marquez, *Manager*
Margaret Tavares, *Manager*
EMP: 14 **EST:** 2016
SALES (est): 1.8MM **Privately Held**
WEB: www.lemyn.com
SIC: 2844 5122 Cosmetic preparations; cosmetics

(P-5044)
LIQUID TECHNOLOGIES INC
14425 Yorba Ave, Chino (91710-5733)
PHONE.................................909 393-9475
John Maruszewski, *CEO*
Marc Tomberlin, *CFO*
▲ **EMP:** 30 **EST:** 1998
SALES (est): 9.8MM
SALES (corp-wide): 766.3MM **Privately Held**
WEB: www.liquidtek.com
SIC: 2844 Cosmetic preparations

PA: Plz Aeroscience Corporation
2651 Warrenville Rd
Downers Grove IL 60515
630 628-3000

(P-5045)
MASTEY DE PARIS INC
25413 Rye Canyon Rd, Valencia (91355-1269)
PHONE.................................661 257-4814
Stephen Mastey, *President*
Lesley Mastey, *Admin Sec*
EMP: 50 **EST:** 1976
SQ FT: 63,000
SALES (est): 4.5MM **Privately Held**
WEB: www.mastey.com
SIC: 2844 Hair preparations, including shampoos

(P-5046)
MELISSA TRINIDAD ✪
Also Called: Paisleyriversoapco
3589 Vine St, Paso Robles (93446-1014)
PHONE.................................805 536-0954
Melissa Trinidad, *Owner*
EMP: 21 **EST:** 2021
SALES (est): 882K **Privately Held**
SIC: 2844 Bath salts

(P-5047)
MERLE NORMAN COSMETICS INC (PA)
9130 Bellanca Ave, Los Angeles (90045-4772)
PHONE.................................310 641-3000
Jack B Nethercutt, *Ch of Bd*
Amy Hackbart, *COO*
Michael Cassidy, *CFO*
Helen Nethercutt, *Vice Ch Bd*
Carol Porta, *Vice Pres*
▲ **EMP:** 345 **EST:** 1974
SQ FT: 354,000
SALES (est): 64MM **Privately Held**
WEB: www.merlenorman.com
SIC: 2844 5999 Cosmetic preparations; cosmetics

(P-5048)
MOEHAIR USA INC
1061 S Melrose St Ste A, Placentia (92870-7136)
PHONE.................................888 663-7032
Imtiaz Rangrez, *CEO*
Jarrah Hala Al, *CEO*
▲ **EMP:** 15 **EST:** 2013
SALES (est): 2MM **Privately Held**
WEB: www.moehair.com
SIC: 2844 Hair preparations, including shampoos

(P-5049)
NAKED PRINCESS WORLDWIDE LLC (PA)
11766 Wilshire Blvd Fl 9, Los Angeles (90025-6538)
PHONE.................................310 271-1199
Jordana Woodland, *CEO*
Cari Deutsch, *Production*
▲ **EMP:** 14 **EST:** 2008
SALES (est): 2.4MM **Privately Held**
WEB: www.lemarchebynp.com
SIC: 2844 Cosmetic preparations

(P-5050)
NEUTRADERM INC
20660 Nordhoff St, Chatsworth (91311-6114)
PHONE.................................818 534-3190
Samuel D Raoof, *CEO*
Toora J Raoof, *Principal*
Bernardo MA, *Accountant*
▲ **EMP:** 25 **EST:** 2003
SALES (est): 11.6MM **Privately Held**
WEB: www.neutraderm.com
SIC: 2844 Cosmetic preparations

(P-5051)
OLA805 LLC (PA)
1482 E Valley Rd Ste 701, Santa Barbara (93108-1200)
PHONE.................................805 258-7680
Dean Christal, *CEO*
Tyler Krebs, *Vice Pres*
Sarah Wonsowski, *Marketing Staff*
Darcy Christal,
EMP: 13 **EST:** 2014

SALES (est): 2.8MM **Privately Held**
WEB: www.olaplex.com
SIC: 2844 Hair preparations, including shampoos

(P-5052)
OLAPLEX HOLDINGS INC (PA) ✪
1187 Coast Village Rd 1-52, Santa Barbara (93108-2737)
PHONE.................................310 691-0776
Jue Wong, *President*
Christine Dagousset, *Ch of Bd*
Eric Tiziani, *CFO*
Tiffany Walden,
EMP: 15 **EST:** 2021
SALES (est): 22.4MM **Publicly Held**
SIC: 2844 Toilet preparations; hair preparations, including shampoos; rinses, conditioners: hair

(P-5053)
ORAL ESSENTIALS INC
436 N Roxbury Dr, Beverly Hills (90210-5026)
PHONE.................................888 773-5273
Kourosh Maddahi, *CEO*
Caroline Heerwagon, *COO*
Linda Kloeffer, *CFO*
Justin Maddahi, *Chief Mktg Ofcr*
Sean Duggan, *Officer*
EMP: 13 **EST:** 2014
SALES (est): 2.5MM **Privately Held**
WEB: www.oralessentials.com
SIC: 2844 Toothpastes or powders, dentifrices

(P-5054)
ORLY INTERNATIONAL INC (PA)
Also Called: Sparitual
7710 Haskell Ave, Van Nuys (91406-1905)
PHONE.................................818 994-1001
Jeff Pink, *President*
Paula Siegel, *Purch Mgr*
Elina Gitig, *Manager*
◆ **EMP:** 99 **EST:** 1977
SQ FT: 65,000
SALES (est): 33.7MM **Privately Held**
WEB: www.orlybeauty.com
SIC: 2844 Cosmetic preparations

(P-5055)
PACIFIC WORLD CORPORATION (PA)
100 Technology Dr Ste 200, Irvine (92618-2466)
PHONE.................................949 598-2400
Peter Baldino, *CEO*
Stuart Noyes, *President*
Joseph Jaeger, *COO*
Desiree Garcia, *Exec Officer*
Andy Stameson, *Officer*
◆ **EMP:** 99 **EST:** 1947
SQ FT: 30,000
SALES (est): 28MM **Privately Held**
WEB: www.pacificworldcorp.com
SIC: 2844 3421 3999 5199 Cosmetic preparations; clippers, fingernail & toenail; fingernails, artificial; general merchandise, non-durable

(P-5056)
PANCO MENS PRODUCTS INC
45605 Citrus Ave, Indio (92201-3451)
PHONE.................................760 342-4368
Gene Pantuso, *President*
EMP: 23 **EST:** 1964
SQ FT: 40,000
SALES (est): 1.4MM **Privately Held**
SIC: 2844 Cosmetic preparations; face creams or lotions; lotions, shaving; shampoos, rinses, conditioners: hair

(P-5057)
PERSON & COVEY INC
616 Allen Ave, Glendale (91201-2014)
P.O. Box 25018 (91221-5018)
PHONE.................................818 937-5000
Lorne Person Jr, *CEO*
Lorne Person Sr, *Ch of Bd*
Vaheh Martyr, *Officer*
Sue Person, *Vice Pres*
William Marquardt, *MIS Dir*
EMP: 45 **EST:** 1941
SQ FT: 36,000

P R O D U C T S

&

S V C S

SALES (est): 9.4MM **Privately Held**
WEB: www.personandcovey.com
SIC: 2844 2834 Cosmetic preparations;
dermatologicals

(P-5058)
PETRA-1 LP
12386 Osborne Pl, Pacoima (91331-2013)
PHONE..................................866 334-3702
Benjamin Witham, *Partner*
Shannel Brooks, *Sales Staff*
EMP: 15 EST: 2016
SALES (est): 1.5MM **Privately Held**
WEB: www.petra-1.com
SIC: 2844 Toilet preparations

(P-5059)
**PHYSICANS FORMULA
HOLDINGS INC (HQ)**
22067 Ferrero, Walnut (91789-5214)
PHONE..................................626 334-3395
Ingrid Jackel, *CEO*
Jeffrey P Rogers, *President*
Leslie H Keegan, *Senior VP*
Chad Boise, *Exec Sec*
▲ EMP: 100 EST: 2003
SQ FT: 82,000
SALES (est): 28.3MM
SALES (corp-wide): 283.8MM **Privately
Held**
WEB: www.physiciansformula.com
SIC: 2844 5122 Cosmetic preparations;
drugs, proprietaries & sundries
PA: Markwins Beauty Brands, Inc.
22067 Ferrero
Walnut CA 91789
909 595-8898

(P-5060)
**PHYSICIANS FORMULA INC
(DH)**
22067 Ferrero, City of Industry
(91789-5214)
PHONE..................................626 334-3395
Ingrid Jackel, *Ch of Bd*
Jeff Rogers, *President*
Joseph J Jaeger, *CFO*
Rick Kirchhoff, *Vice Pres*
Richard John Almeida, *Manager*
▲ EMP: 57 EST: 1980
SQ FT: 82,800
SALES (est): 28.3MM
SALES (corp-wide): 283.8MM **Privately
Held**
WEB: www.physiciansformula.com
SIC: 2844 Cosmetic preparations

(P-5061)
**PHYSICIANS FORMULA COSMT
INC**
22067 Ferrero, City of Industry
(91789-5214)
PHONE..................................626 334-3395
Jeffrey P Rogers, *President*
Joseph J Jaeger, *CFO*
EMP: 62 EST: 1937
SALES (est): 2.4MM
SALES (corp-wide): 283.8MM **Privately
Held**
WEB: www.physiciansformula.com
SIC: 2844 Cosmetic preparations
HQ: Physicians Formula, Inc.
22067 Ferrero
City Of Industry CA 91789
626 334-3395

(P-5062)
PRESTIGE COSMETICS INC
17780 Gothard St, Huntington Beach
(92647-6216)
PHONE..................................714 375-0395
Sarjula Sanghvi, *President*
EMP: 16 EST: 1986
SQ FT: 10,000
SALES (est): 1.9MM **Privately Held**
WEB: www.prestigecosmetics.com
SIC: 2844 5122 Cosmetic preparations;
cosmetics

(P-5063)
**PROFESSIONAL SKIN CARE
INC (PA)**
Also Called: Only You Rx Skin Care
25028 Avenue Kearny, Valencia
(91355-1253)
P.O. Box 753, Lafayette (94549-0753)
PHONE..................................661 257-7771
James Paige, *President*
▲ EMP: 30 EST: 1977
SQ FT: 25,000
SALES (est): 2.2MM **Privately Held**
WEB: www.onlyyourx.com
SIC: 2844 5122 5087 Cosmetic prepara-
tions; drugs, proprietaries & sundries;
cosmetics; beauty parlor equipment &
supplies

(P-5064)
PROLABS FACTORY INC
15001 Oxnard St, Van Nuys (91411-2613)
PHONE..................................818 646-3677
EMP: 26 EST: 2020
SALES (est): 1.1MM **Privately Held**
SIC: 2844 Cosmetic preparations

(P-5065)
PURA NATURALS INC (HQ)
Also Called: Advanced Innvtive Rcovery Tech
23615 El Toro Rd Ste X300, Lake Forest
(92630-4707)
PHONE..................................949 273-8100
Robert Doherty, *CEO*
Derek Duhame, *President*
Daniel Kryger, *Bd of Directors*
Robert Switzer, *Admin Sec*
Jim Breech, *VP Sales*
EMP: 15 EST: 2013
SQ FT: 4,000
SALES: 377K
SALES (corp-wide): 9MM **Publicly Held**
WEB: www.puranaturalsproducts.com
SIC: 2844 Cosmetic preparations
PA: Advanced Innovative Recovery Tech-
nologies, Inc.
23615 El Toro Rd Ste 207
Lake Forest CA 92630
949 273-8100

(P-5066)
SAYDEL INC (PA)
Also Called: Nina Religion
2475 E Slauson Ave, Huntington Park
(90255-2887)
PHONE..................................323 585-2800
Santo Gil Orta, *Owner*
Michael Orta, *Vice Pres*
Griffin Jaime, *Teacher*
Trina Falk, *Nurse*
EMP: 15 EST: 1968
SQ FT: 11,000
SALES (est): 1.8MM **Privately Held**
WEB: www.saydel.com
SIC: 2844 5049 5999 Perfumes, natural
or synthetic; religious supplies; religious
goods

(P-5067)
SEPHORA CO LLC (PA)
6103 Obispo Ave, Long Beach
(90805-3799)
PHONE..................................760 798-7654
Oscar Sadegi, *Mng Member*
Corey Yribarren, *Officer*
◆ EMP: 14 EST: 2003
SQ FT: 20,000
SALES (est): 3MM **Privately Held**
SIC: 2844 Cosmetic preparations

(P-5068)
SHADOW HOLDINGS LLC (HQ)
Also Called: Bocchi Laboratories
26455 Ruether Ave, Santa Clarita
(91350-2621)
PHONE..................................661 252-3807
Joe Pender, *CEO*
John Lutes, *Opers Spvr*
Ayde Merida, *Director*
Ignacio Simonette, *Director*
Ray Tyndall, *Director*
EMP: 460 EST: 2007
SQ FT: 88,500
SALES (est): 105.7MM **Privately Held**
WEB: www.anneliesespasalon.com
SIC: 2844 Toilet preparations

(P-5069)
SHANI DARDEN SKINCARE INC
1800 Century Park E # 400, Los Angeles
(90067-1507)
PHONE..................................310 745-3150
Jessica Goldin, *CEO*
EMP: 21 EST: 2016
SALES (est): 1.7MM **Privately Held**
WEB: www.shanidarden.com
SIC: 2844 5122 5961 Toilet preparations;
cosmetics, perfumes & hair products; cos-
metics & perfumes, mail order

(P-5070)
SHEER DESIGN INC (PA)
6309 Esplanade, Playa Del Rey
(90293-7581)
PHONE..................................310 306-2121
Mark Friedland, *President*
EMP: 29 EST: 2012
SALES (est): 377.6K **Privately Held**
WEB: www.sheerdesignbeauty.com
SIC: 2844 Cosmetic preparations

(P-5071)
SPATZ CORPORATION
Also Called: Spatz Laboratories
1600 Westar Dr, Oxnard (93033-2423)
PHONE..................................805 487-2122
Joel Lynn Nelson, *CEO*
John Nelson, *COO*
George Jefferson, *CFO*
Laura Nelson, *Vice Pres*
Maria Zendejas, *Executive*
▲ EMP: 145 EST: 1954
SQ FT: 62,000
SALES (est): 44.4MM **Privately Held**
WEB: www.spatzlabs.com
SIC: 2844 3089 Cosmetic preparations;
plastic containers, except foam

(P-5072)
STEARNS CORPORATION
Also Called: Derma E
2280 Ward Ave Ste 100, Simi Valley
(93065-2075)
PHONE..................................805 582-2710
Brenda Wu, *President*
Linda Miles, *President*
Barbara Roll, *Officer*
Nayantara Viswanath, *Graphic Designe*
Molly Blake, *Sales Staff*
▲ EMP: 25 EST: 1981
SALES (est): 3.9MM **Privately Held**
WEB: www.dermae.com
SIC: 2844 Face creams or lotions
PA: Topix Pharmaceuticals Inc.
174 Route 109 Ste 2
West Babylon NY 11704

(P-5073)
THIBIANT INTERNATIONAL INC
Also Called: Kdc-One
20320 Prairie St, Chatsworth (91311-6026)
PHONE..................................818 709-1345
Wayne Swanton, *CEO*
Jim Illson, *CFO*
Rick Delao, *Vice Pres*
Nicholas Beugnot, *Admin Sec*
Carolina Fox, *Planning*
◆ EMP: 390 EST: 1976
SQ FT: 350,000
SALES (est): 160.7MM
SALES (corp-wide): 1.7B **Privately Held**
WEB: www.kdc-one.com
SIC: 2844 Cosmetic preparations
HQ: Kdc Us Holdings Inc.
1000 Robins Rd
Lynchburg VA 24504

(P-5074)
TRADEMARK COSMETICS INC
545 Columbia Ave, Riverside (92507-2183)
PHONE..................................951 683-2631
David Ryngler, *CEO*
Joy Boiani, *CFO*
Eko Handoko, *Vice Pres*
Jessica Burrola, *Purch Mgr*
▲ EMP: 38 EST: 1994
SQ FT: 38,000

SALES (est): 8.1MM **Privately Held**
WEB: www.trademarkcosmetics.com
SIC: 2844 7231 5999 5122 Hair preparations, including shampoos; beauty shops;
cosmetics; cosmetics

(P-5075)
TU-K INDUSTRIES INC
5702 Firestone Pl, South Gate
(90280-3714)
PHONE..................................562 927-3365
Arman Cornell, *Executive*
Alpin K Kaler, *President*
Eleanor Kaler, *Treasurer*
Gerri Cornell, *Officer*
Rafael Esparza, *Prdtn Mgr*
▲ EMP: 50 EST: 1970
SQ FT: 40,000
SALES (est): 5.5MM **Privately Held**
WEB: www.tukindustries.com
SIC: 2844 Cosmetic preparations

(P-5076)
**TWILA TRUE COLLABORATIONS
LLC**
27156 Burbank, Foothill Ranch
(92610-2503)
PHONE..................................949 258-9720
Twila True,
Paula Mauricio, *Vice Pres*
Daniella McBride, *Director*
EMP: 20 EST: 2018
SALES (est): 1.5MM **Privately Held**
WEB: www.twilatruecollaborations.com
SIC: 2844 2389 Toilet preparations; men's
miscellaneous accessories

(P-5077)
**UNIVERSAL PACKG SYSTEMS
INC (PA)**
Also Called: Paklab
14570 Monte Vista Ave, Chino
(91710-5743)
PHONE..................................909 517-2442
Jeffery Morlando, *CEO*
Alan Kristel, *COO*
Justine Garate, *Executive Asst*
William Wachtel, *Admin Sec*
Andrew Cheung, *Engineer*
◆ EMP: 750
SALES (est): 379.3MM **Privately Held**
WEB: www.paklab.com
SIC: 2844 7389 3565 2671 Cosmetic
preparations; packaging & labeling serv-
ices; bottling machinery: filling, capping,
labeling; plastic film, coated or laminated
for packaging

(P-5078)
URBAN DECAL LLC (HQ)
Also Called: Urban Decay Cosmetics
833 W 16th St, Newport Beach
(92663-2801)
PHONE..................................949 574-9712
Adel Hamdan, *Mng Member*
Elaine Mac Neil, *Senior VP*
Paul Blank, *Vice Pres*
Kimberly Bowers, *Vice Pres*
Carolea Fields, *Vice Pres*
◆ EMP: 34 EST: 1995
SQ FT: 6,500
SALES (est): 13.2MM
SALES (corp-wide): 5.7B **Privately Held**
WEB: www.loreal.fr
SIC: 2844 5122 Cosmetic preparations;
cosmetics, perfumes & hair products
PA: L'oreal
Kerastase Mizani L Ora Al Profession
Paris 75008
140 206-000

(P-5079)
**V MANUFACTURING LOGISTICS
INC**
20501 Earlgate St, Walnut (91789-2909)
PHONE..................................909 869-6200
Florence Nacino, *President*
Beatriz Betancourt, *Executive Asst*
▲ EMP: 20 EST: 2007
SALES (est): 2MM **Privately Held**
WEB: www.vmlcosmetics.com
SIC: 2844 Cosmetic preparations

228   2022 Southern California Business
Directory and Buyers Guide   ▲ = Import ▼=Export
◆ =Import/Export

(P-5080)
VEGE - KURL INC
Also Called: Vege-Tech Company
412 W Cypress St, Glendale (91204-2402)
PHONE..................................818 956-5582
Eric W Huffman, *President*
Helen Huffman, *Corp Secy*
James Morse, *VP Bus Dvlpt*
EMP: 60 **EST:** 1959
SALES (est): 17.1MM **Privately Held**
WEB: www.vegelabs.com
SIC: 2844 2833 5122 Shampoos, rinses, conditioners; hair; medicinals & botanicals; cosmetics, perfumes & hair products

(P-5081)
VERDE COSMETIC LABS LLC
19845 Nordhokk St, Northridge (91324)
PHONE..................................818 284-4080
John Mizialko, *President*
Linda Mile,
David Stearn,
EMP: 14 **EST:** 2017
SQ FT: 13,000
SALES (est): 1.5MM **Privately Held**
WEB: www.vclpl.com
SIC: 2844 Cosmetic preparations

(P-5082)
WESTRIDGE LABORATORIES INC
1671 E Saint Andrew Pl, Santa Ana (92705-4932)
PHONE..................................714 259-9400
Gregg Richard Haskell, *CEO*
John Speelman, *Vice Pres*
John Spielman, *Vice Pres*
Nelly Cuadra, *Accountant*
▲ **EMP:** 28 **EST:** 1993
SALES (est): 5.1MM **Privately Held**
WEB: www.westridgelabs.com
SIC: 2844 Cosmetic preparations

(P-5083)
WESTWOOD LABORATORIES INC (PA)
710 S Ayon Ave, Azusa (91702-5123)
PHONE..................................626 969-3305
Tony De Vos, *CEO*
Paul Schirmer, *President*
Rick Verhines, *COO*
Cheryl Kohorst, *CFO*
Arnel Garcia, *Manager*
▲ **EMP:** 46 **EST:** 2004
SALES (est): 13.4MM **Privately Held**
WEB: www.westwoodlabs.com
SIC: 2844 Toilet preparations

(P-5084)
YES TO INC
Also Called: Yes To Carrots
177 E Colo Blvd Ste 110, Pasadena (91105)
PHONE..................................626 365-1976
Ingrid Jackel, *CEO*
Lance Kalish, *Shareholder*
Ido Leffler, *Shareholder*
Geri Lieberman, *Chief Mktg Ofcr*
Jenn Stryker, *Marketing Staff*
▲ **EMP:** 40 **EST:** 2009
SQ FT: 3,000
SALES (est): 10.3MM **Privately Held**
WEB: www.yesto.com
SIC: 2844 5122 Face creams or lotions; cosmetic preparations; hair preparations, including shampoos; cosmetics

(P-5085)
YOUTH TO PEOPLE INC
708 Traction Ave, Los Angeles (90013-1814)
PHONE..................................309 648-5500
Joe Cloyes, *CEO*
Greg Gonzalez, *President*
Ricky Phan, *Planning*
Lauren Cummings, *Sales Staff*
Laura Cline, *Education*
EMP: 27 **EST:** 2018
SALES (est): 7.2MM **Privately Held**
WEB: www.youthtothepeople.com
SIC: 2844 Lotions, shaving

(P-5086)
ZO SKIN HEALTH INC (DH)
9685 Research Dr, Irvine (92618-4657)
PHONE..................................949 988-7524
Mark Williams, *CEO*
Kevin Cornett, *CFO*
Noelle Denlinger, *Vice Pres*
Frank Fazio, *Vice Pres*
Chris Kraneiss, *Vice Pres*
▲ **EMP:** 80 **EST:** 2006
SQ FT: 12,000
SALES (est): 38.3MM
SALES (corp-wide): 6.1B **Publicly Held**
WEB: www.zoskinhealth.com
SIC: 2844 Face creams or lotions
HQ: Blackstone Tactical Opportunities Advisors L.L.C.
345 Park Ave
New York NY 10154
212 583-5000

2851 Paints, Varnishes, Lacquers, Enamels

(P-5087)
AMERICA WOOD FINISHES INC
728 E 59th St, Los Angeles (90001-1004)
PHONE..................................323 232-8256
Manuel Padilla, *President*
Elvira Padilla, *Admin Sec*
▲ **EMP:** 23 **EST:** 2002
SALES (est): 1.3MM **Privately Held**
SIC: 2851 Paints, waterproof

(P-5088)
BEHR HOLDINGS CORPORATION (HQ)
3400 W Segerstrom Ave, Santa Ana (92704-6405)
PHONE..................................714 545-7101
Jeff Filley, *President*
EMP: 100 **EST:** 1997
SALES (est): 1.5B
SALES (corp-wide): 7.1B **Publicly Held**
WEB: www.behr.com
SIC: 2851 Paints & paint additives; stains: varnish, oil or wax; varnishes
PA: Masco Corporation
17450 College Pkwy
Livonia MI 48152
313 274-7400

(P-5089)
BEHR PROCESS CORPORATION (DH)
Also Called: Behr Paint Company
1801 E Saint Andrew Pl, Santa Ana (92705-5044)
PHONE..................................714 545-7101
Jeffrey D Filley, *President*
Jodi Allen, *Chief Mktg Ofcr*
Jonathan Sullivan, *Senior VP*
Greg Brod, *Vice Pres*
Lawrence F Leaman, *Vice Pres*
▼ **EMP:** 700 **EST:** 1947
SQ FT: 220,000
SALES (est): 1.5B
SALES (corp-wide): 7.1B **Publicly Held**
WEB: www.behr.com
SIC: 2851 Paints & paint additives; stains: varnish, oil or wax; varnishes

(P-5090)
BEHR SALES INC (HQ)
Also Called: Behr Paint Corp.
3400 W Segerstrom Ave, Santa Ana (92704-6405)
PHONE..................................714 545-7101
Jeffrey D Filley, *CEO*
Jonathan M Sullivan, *CFO*
Anthony Demiro, *Senior VP*
Jessica Barr, *Training Spec*
Erik Neely, *Training Spec*
EMP: 433 **EST:** 1948
SQ FT: 54,000
SALES (est): 594MM
SALES (corp-wide): 7.1B **Publicly Held**
WEB: www.behr.com
SIC: 2851 Paints & paint additives; stains: varnish, oil or wax

PA: Masco Corporation
17450 College Pkwy
Livonia MI 48152
313 274-7400

(P-5091)
CARDINAL PAINT AND POWDER INC
15010 Don Julian Rd, City of Industry (91746-3301)
PHONE..................................626 937-6767
Stanley W Ekstrom, *Branch Mgr*
Grant Morris, *Administration*
Connie Robles, *Production*
Daniel Morales, *Associate*
EMP: 96
SALES (corp-wide): 70MM **Privately Held**
WEB: www.cardinalpaint.com
SIC: 2851 Paints & allied products
PA: Cardinal Paint and Powder, Inc.
1900 Aerojet Way
North Las Vegas NV 89030
702 852-2333

(P-5092)
CONSOLIDATED COLOR CORPORATION
12316 Carson St, Hawaiian Gardens (90716-1604)
PHONE..................................562 420-7714
Michael J Muldown, *President*
Deborah Muldown, *Vice Pres*
Blessy Conde, *Technical Staff*
Matthew Muldown, *Purchasing*
EMP: 25 **EST:** 1993
SQ FT: 30,000
SALES (est): 2.6MM **Privately Held**
WEB: www.consolidatedcolorcorp.com
SIC: 2851 2865 Paints & paint additives; cyclic crudes & intermediates

(P-5093)
CONTINENTAL COATINGS INC
10938 Beech Ave, Fontana (92337-7260)
PHONE..................................909 355-1200
Robert Wang, *President*
Jack Keenan, *Vice Pres*
Joe Seaton, *Vice Pres*
Stephanie Varela, *Mng Member*
Mathilde Mendez, *Director*
▲ **EMP:** 16 **EST:** 1976
SQ FT: 20,000
SALES (est): 3.6MM **Privately Held**
WEB: www.continentalyca.com
SIC: 2851 Paints & paint additives

(P-5094)
CONTRACT TRANSPORTATION SYS CO
Also Called: Certified Distribution Svcs
12500 Slauson Ave Ste B2, Santa Fe Springs (90670-8618)
PHONE..................................562 696-3262
Chuck Huff, *Branch Mgr*
EMP: 34
SALES (corp-wide): 18.3B **Publicly Held**
SIC: 2851 Paints & allied products
HQ: Contract Transportation System Co.
101 W Prospect Ave
Cleveland OH 44115
216 566-2000

(P-5095)
DUNN-EDWARDS CORPORATION (HQ)
Also Called: Dunn-Dwrds Pints Wallcoverings
4885 E 52nd Pl, Vernon (90058-5584)
P.O. Box 30389, Los Angeles (90030-0389)
PHONE..................................888 337-2468
Karl Altergott, *President*
Curt Sanker, *Treasurer*
Dominic Gonzalez, *Vice Pres*
Gary Hoxie, *Vice Pres*
Monte Lewis, *Vice Pres*
◆ **EMP:** 150 **EST:** 1925
SQ FT: 141,000
SALES (est): 325.9MM **Privately Held**
WEB: www.dunnedwards.com
SIC: 5231 Paint; lacquer: bases, dopes, thinner

(P-5096)
DURA TECHNOLOGIES INC
2720 S Willow Ave Ste A, Bloomington (92316-3259)
P.O. Box 333 (92316-0333)
PHONE..................................909 877-8477
Douglas L Dennis, *President*
Gina L Dennis, *Vice Pres*
▲ **EMP:** 150 **EST:** 1977
SQ FT: 14,000
SALES (est): 16.2MM **Privately Held**
SIC: 2851 Paints & allied products

(P-5097)
EPMAR CORPORATION
13210 Barton Cir, Whittier (90605-3254)
PHONE..................................562 946-8781
Peter Weissman, *President*
Joe Matrange, *President*
Christine Rivera, *Accountant*
Ward Thompson, *Accountant*
◆ **EMP:** 38 **EST:** 1980
SQ FT: 26,000
SALES (est): 13.6MM
SALES (corp-wide): 1.4B **Publicly Held**
WEB: www.epmar.com
SIC: 2851 2891 2821 3087 Epoxy coatings; polyurethane coatings; adhesives & sealants; plastics materials & resins; custom compound purchased resins
PA: Quaker Chemical Corporation
901 E Hector St
Conshohocken PA 19428
610 832-4000

(P-5098)
FSI COATING TECHNOLOGIES INC
45 Parker Ste 100, Irvine (92618-1658)
PHONE..................................949 540-1140
Antonios Grigoriou, *President*
Richard Chang, *COO*
Reid Beeman, *Sales Staff*
EMP: 37 **EST:** 1986
SALES (est): 2.6MM **Privately Held**
WEB: www.fsicti.com
SIC: 2851 Paints & allied products; paints & paint additives; plastics base paints & varnishes; lacquers, varnishes, enamels & other coatings
HQ: Sdc Technologies, Inc.
45 Parker Ste 100
Irvine CA 92618
714 939-8300

(P-5099)
KRETUS INC
1055 W Struck Ave, Orange (92867-3527)
PHONE..................................714 694-2061
Ronald Webber, *President*
EMP: 15 **EST:** 2019
SALES (est): 1.1MM **Privately Held**
SIC: 2851 Paints & paint additives

(P-5100)
LAIRD COATINGS CORPORATION
Also Called: Coatings Resource
15541 Commerce Ln, Huntington Beach (92649-1601)
PHONE..................................714 894-5252
Edwin Laird, *CEO*
Jeff Laird, *President*
▲ **EMP:** 51 **EST:** 1976
SQ FT: 17,500
SALES (est): 11.4MM **Privately Held**
WEB: www.coatingsresource.com
SIC: 2851 2865 Paints & paint additives; dyes, synthetic organic

(P-5101)
LIFE PAINT COMPANY (PA)
12927 Sunshine Ave, Santa Fe Springs (90670-4732)
P.O. Box 2488 (90670-0488)
PHONE..................................562 944-6391
Ronald Sibbrel, *President*
Fred Benson, *Corp Secy*
Mike De La Vega, *Vice Pres*
▲ **EMP:** 38 **EST:** 1963
SQ FT: 30,000

SALES (est): 6.5MM **Privately Held**
WEB: www.lifespecialtycoatings.com
SIC: 2851 2899 2821 Paints & allied products; waterproofing compounds; thermosetting materials

(P-5102)
MASTER POWDER COATING INC
13721 Bora Dr, Santa Fe Springs (90670-5007)
PHONE...................................562 863-4135
Judith Flores, *CEO*
Dalila Flores, *Vice Pres*
Juan Renteria, *Vice Pres*
EMP: 21 EST: 2006
SALES (est): 4.3MM **Privately Held**
WEB: www.masterpowdercoating.com
SIC: 2851 Paints & allied products

(P-5103)
MONOPOLE INC
4661 Alger St, Los Angeles (90039-1127)
P.O. Box 250534, Glendale (91225-0534)
PHONE...................................818 500-8585
Antoine Abikhalil, *President*
▲ EMP: 15 EST: 1976
SQ FT: 40,000
SALES (est): 2.3MM **Privately Held**
WEB: www.monopoleinc.com
SIC: 2851 Paints & allied products

(P-5104)
MOTORSHIELD LLC
Also Called: Motoshieldpro
3364 Garfield Ave, Commerce (90040-3102)
PHONE...................................323 396-9200
Rick Fung,
Maria Ortega, *General Mgr*
EMP: 15 EST: 2016
SALES (est): 2.2MM **Privately Held**
WEB: www.motoshieldpro.com
SIC: 2851 Undercoatings, paint

(P-5105)
MULTICOAT PRODUCTS INC
23331 Antonio Pkwy, Rcho STA Marg (92688-2664)
PHONE...................................949 888-7100
Dave Maietta, *President*
John Dill, *Vice Pres*
EMP: 15 EST: 1995
SALES (est): 2.5MM **Privately Held**
WEB: www.multicoat.com
SIC: 2851 2899 3299 3479 Paints & paint additives; waterproofing compounds; stucco; painting, coating & hot dipping

(P-5106)
PAINT-CHEM INC
Also Called: Transchem Coatings
1680 Miller Ave, Los Angeles (90063-1613)
P.O. Box 151014 (90015-8014)
PHONE...................................213 747-7725
Amir Afshar, *President*
Eugene Golling, *Vice Pres*
Eddie Andrews, *Admin Sec*
EMP: 15 EST: 1970
SQ FT: 8,000
SALES (est): 2.3MM **Privately Held**
WEB: www.paint-chem.com
SIC: 2851 5198 Coating, air curing; paints

(P-5107)
POLY-FIBER INC (PA)
Also Called: Consolidated Aircraft Coatings
4343 Fort Dr, Riverside (92509-6784)
P.O. Box 3129 (92519-3129)
PHONE...................................951 684-4280
Jon Goldenbaum, *President*
Greg Albarin, *General Mgr*
Long Cao, *Research*
Phyllis Goldenbaum, *Manager*
Rudy Medina, *Manager*
EMP: 19 EST: 1992
SQ FT: 75,000
SALES (est): 2.1MM **Privately Held**
WEB: www.conaircraft.com
SIC: 2851 Undercoatings, paint

(P-5108)
PPG INDUSTRIES INC
11601 United St, Mojave (93501-7048)
PHONE...................................661 824-4532

Michelle Brown, *Purchasing*
Andrew Soehnlen, *Opers Mgr*
EMP: 24
SALES (corp-wide): 15.1B **Publicly Held**
WEB: www.ppg.com
SIC: 2851 Paints & allied products
PA: Ppg Industries, Inc.
    1 Ppg Pl
    Pittsburgh PA 15272
    412 434-3131

(P-5109)
PRODUCTS/TECHNIQUES INC
Also Called: P T I
3271 S Riverside Ave, Bloomington (92316-3515)
PHONE...................................909 877-3951
Steven Andrews, *President*
Ryan Andrews, *Officer*
Barry Boden, *Vice Pres*
Marissa Phelps, *Purchasing*
Sean Andrews, *Director*
EMP: 16 EST: 1947
SQ FT: 12,000
SALES (est): 4.1MM **Privately Held**
WEB: www.ptipaint.com
SIC: 2851 Coating, air curing

(P-5110)
R & S MANUFACTURING & SUP INC
16616 Garfield Ave, Paramount (90723-5305)
PHONE...................................909 622-5881
Ronald Hoffman, *Principal*
Susan Hoffman, *Admin Sec*
Sheryl Hoffman-Knitz, *Sales Staff*
EMP: 18 EST: 1976
SQ FT: 20,000
SALES (est): 3.8MM **Privately Held**
WEB: www.rsmfgsupply.com
SIC: 2851 Colors in oil, except artists'

(P-5111)
SDC TECHNOLOGIES INC (HQ)
45 Parker Ste 100, Irvine (92618-1658)
PHONE...................................714 939-8300
Antonios Grigoriou, *President*
Andreas Schneider, *President*
Richard Chang, *COO*
Miho Takemoto, *Admin Asst*
Jeremy Marchant, *Technical Staff*
▲ EMP: 25 EST: 1986
SQ FT: 16,800
SALES (est): 49.4MM **Privately Held**
WEB: www.sdctech.com
SIC: 2851 Paints & allied products; paints & paint additives; plastics base paints & varnishes; lacquers, varnishes, enamels & other coatings

(P-5112)
SIERRACIN CORPORATION (HQ)
12780 San Fernando Rd, Sylmar (91342-3796)
PHONE...................................818 741-1656
Barry N Gillespie, *CEO*
Michael H McGarry, *Exec VP*
Viktoras R Sekmakas, *Exec VP*
Frank S Sklarsky, *Exec VP*
David B Navikas, *Senior VP*
▲ EMP: 550 EST: 1952
SQ FT: 287,000
SALES (est): 178.2MM
SALES (corp-wide): 15.1B **Publicly Held**
WEB: www.ppgaerospace.com
SIC: 2851 Paints & allied products
PA: Ppg Industries, Inc.
    1 Ppg Pl
    Pittsburgh PA 15272
    412 434-3131

(P-5113)
SPECIALIZED MILLING CORP
Also Called: Specialty Finishes
10330 Elm Ave, Fontana (92337-7319)
PHONE...................................909 357-7890
Jack Neems, *President*
Seymour S Neems, *Ch of Bd*
Adele Neems, *Treasurer*
EMP: 39 EST: 1968
SQ FT: 11,000
SALES (est): 7.6MM **Privately Held**
SIC: 2851 Paints & allied products

(P-5114)
SPECIALTY COATINGS & CHEM INC
Also Called: Special-T
7360 Varna Ave, North Hollywood (91605-4008)
P.O. Box 32459, Los Angeles (90032-0459)
PHONE...................................818 983-0055
Alaistair Macdonald, *President*
W Daniel Ernt, *Vice Pres*
Larry Wick, *Admin Sec*
Billy Hernandez, *Info Tech Mgr*
▲ EMP: 34 EST: 1964
SQ FT: 15,000
SALES (est): 1.1MM **Privately Held**
WEB: www.special-tcoatings.com
SIC: 2851 Plastics base paints & varnishes; enamels; lacquer: bases, dopes, thinner

(P-5115)
TALYARPS CORPORATION
3465 S La Cienega Blvd, Los Angeles (90016-4409)
PHONE...................................310 559-2335
Fax: 310 836-6094
EMP: 25
SQ FT: 25,000
SALES (corp-wide): 33.6MM **Privately Held**
SIC: 2851 Mfg Industrial Paints
PA: Talyarps Corporation
    143 Sparks Ave
    Pelham NY 10803
    914 699-3030

(P-5116)
TEX-COAT LLC
417 E Weber Ave, Compton (90222-1424)
P.O. Box 73109, Los Angeles (90003-0109)
PHONE...................................323 233-3111
Stuart M Haines, *Ch of Bd*
Simon Reynolds, *Vice Pres*
Christy Hart, *Admin Dir*
David Alvarado, *Supervisor*
EMP: 21
SALES (corp-wide): 129.5MM **Privately Held**
WEB: www.texcote.com
SIC: 2851 Paints & paint additives; lacquers, varnishes, enamels & other coatings
HQ: Tex-Coat Llc
    2422 E 15th St
    Panama City FL 32405
    800 454-0340

(P-5117)
TUFF KOTE SYSTEMS INC
7033 Orangethorpe Ave B, Buena Park (90621-3300)
PHONE...................................714 522-7341
William Ritt, *President*
EMP: 13 EST: 2002
SQ FT: 2,000
SALES (est): 532.7K **Privately Held**
WEB: www.tuffkote.com
SIC: 2851 Paints & allied products

(P-5118)
VINYLVISIONS COMPANY LLC
Also Called: Trim Quick
1233 Enterprise Ct, Corona (92882-7126)
PHONE...................................800 321-8746
John P Halle, *Mng Member*
Helen Halle, *CFO*
EMP: 20 EST: 2001
SQ FT: 40,000
SALES (est): 5.2MM
SALES (corp-wide): 17.8MM **Privately Held**
WEB: www.vinylvisions.com
SIC: 2851 Vinyl coatings, strippable
PA: Halle-Hopper, Llc
    5380 E Larry Caldwell Dr
    Prescott AZ 86301
    951 284-7373

(P-5119)
VISTA PAINT CORPORATION (PA)
2020 E Orangethorpe Ave, Fullerton (92831-5327)
PHONE...................................714 680-3800
Eddie R Fischer, *President*

Jerome Fischer, *Vice Pres*
Joe Wittenberg, *VP Sales*
Chris Brown, *Sales Staff*
Morgan Ramirez, *Manager*
▲ EMP: 150 EST: 1956
SQ FT: 140,000
SALES (est): 101.1MM **Privately Held**
WEB: www.vistapaint.com
SIC: 5231 2851 Paint; paints & paint additives

2865 Cyclic-Crudes, Intermediates, Dyes & Org Pigments

(P-5120)
CARETEX INC
4581 Firestone Blvd, South Gate (90280-3343)
PHONE...................................323 567-5074
Richard Kang, *President*
EMP: 17 EST: 1987
SQ FT: 30,000
SALES (est): 388.3K **Privately Held**
SIC: 2865 2269 Dyes, synthetic organic; finishing plants

(P-5121)
COLOR SCIENCE INC
Also Called: C S I
1230 E Glenwood Pl, Santa Ana (92707-3000)
PHONE...................................714 434-1033
Jocelyn Eubank, *CEO*
Mark Hoffenberg, *President*
EMP: 45 EST: 1989
SQ FT: 9,000
SALES (est): 26.2MM **Privately Held**
WEB: www.modifiedplastics.com
SIC: 2865 Color pigments organic
PA: Modified Plastics, Inc.
    1240 E Glenwood Pl
    Santa Ana CA 92707
    714 546-4667

(P-5122)
PERMALITE PLASTICS CORP
Also Called: Mks Color Composite
3121 E Ana St, Compton (90221-5606)
PHONE...................................310 669-9492
Frederic Van Bergh, *President*
Richard Van Bergh, *Vice Pres*
EMP: 20 EST: 1946
SQ FT: 16,000
SALES (est): 3.5MM **Privately Held**
WEB: www.permaliteplastics.com
SIC: 2865 2891 Color pigments, organic; adhesives

2869 Industrial Organic Chemicals, NEC

(P-5123)
AEROJET ROCKETDYNE DE INC (HQ)
8900 De Soto Ave, Canoga Park (91304-1967)
P.O. Box 7922 (91309-7922)
PHONE...................................818 586-1000
Eileen P Drake, *CEO*
Scott Correll, *Vice Pres*
Pete Gleszer, *Vice Pres*
Bruce McLain, *Principal*
Joseph Rivetti, *Principal*
▲ EMP: 1581 EST: 2005
SALES (est): 652MM
SALES (corp-wide): 2B **Publicly Held**
WEB: www.rocket.com
SIC: 2869 3724 Rocket engine fuel, organic; aircraft engines & engine parts
PA: Aerojet Rocketdyne Holdings, Inc.
    222 N Pcf Cast Hwy Ste 50
    El Segundo CA 90245
    310 252-8100

(P-5124)
AEROJET ROCKETDYNE DE INC
9001 Lurline Ave, Chatsworth (91311-6122)
P.O. Box 7922, Canoga Park (91309-7922)
PHONE..............................818 586-1000
Helen Lubin, *Branch Mgr*
Mike Kutin, *Principal*
Bruce Janeski, *Program Mgr*
Brian Lariviere, *Program Mgr*
Michelle Boyte, *Executive Asst*
EMP: 115
SALES (corp-wide): 2B **Publicly Held**
WEB: www.rocket.com
SIC: 2869 3724 Rocket engine fuel, organic; aircraft engines & engine parts
HQ: Inc Aerojet Rocketdyne Of De
8900 De Soto Ave
Canoga Park CA 91304
818 586-1000

(P-5125)
ALTRA INC (PA)
5757 W Century Blvd # 70, Los Angeles (90045-6401)
PHONE..............................310 348-7244
Lawrence S Gross, *President*
Stefan I Pollack, *CFO*
▼ **EMP:** 60 **EST:** 2005
SALES (est): 4.8MM **Privately Held**
WEB: www.altrabiofuels.com
SIC: 2869 Ethyl alcohol, ethanol

(P-5126)
APPLIED NATURAL GAS FUELS INC
31111 Agoura Rd Ste 208, Westlake Village (91361-4464)
PHONE..............................818 450-3659
Kevin Markey, *Vice Pres*
Matt Morrissette, *Finance*
Candelario Andalon, *Controller*
Julie Swift, *Manager*
EMP: 13 **EST:** 2016
SALES (est): 10.8MM **Privately Held**
WEB: www.appliedlng.com
SIC: 2869 Fuels

(P-5127)
AST ENZYMES
4880 Murrieta St, Chino (91710-5100)
PHONE..............................800 608-1688
Luis Girarldy, *Director*
EMP: 14 **EST:** 2011
SALES (est): 483.1K **Privately Held**
WEB: www.astenzymes.com
SIC: 2869 Enzymes

(P-5128)
AVIENT COLORANTS USA LLC
14355 Ramona Ave, Chino (91710-5740)
PHONE..............................909 606-1325
Mike Urbano, *Branch Mgr*
EMP: 229 **Publicly Held**
SIC: 2869 Industrial organic chemicals
HQ: Avient Colorants Usa Llc
85 Industrial Dr
Holden MA 01520
508 829-6321

(P-5129)
CAL-INDIA FOODS INTERNATIONAL
Also Called: Specilty Enzymes Btechnologies
13591 Yorba Ave, Chino (91710-5071)
PHONE..............................909 613-1660
Vic Rathi, *President*
Jim Titus, *Sales Staff*
▲ **EMP:** 20 **EST:** 1982
SQ FT: 12,000
SALES (est): 6.2MM **Privately Held**
WEB: www.specialtyenzymes.com
SIC: 2869 Enzymes

(P-5130)
CALIFORNIA BIO-PRODUCTEX INC
13220 Crown Ave, Hanford (93230-9413)
PHONE..............................559 582-5308
Leo Wirzbicki, *President*
Stasia Wierzbicki, *Vice Pres*
EMP: 23 **EST:** 1990
SQ FT: 2,500
SALES (est): 3.6MM **Privately Held**
WEB: www.californiabioproductexinc.com
SIC: 2869 2099 Industrial organic chemicals; yeast

(P-5131)
CIRCLE GREEN INC
Also Called: Beneficial AG Services
8271 Chino Ave, Ontario (91761-9412)
PHONE..............................909 930-0200
Kevin Sutton, *CEO*
EMP: 16 **EST:** 2009
SALES (est): 4MM **Privately Held**
WEB: www.compostmulchservices.com
SIC: 2869 Laboratory chemicals, organic

(P-5132)
DNA HEALTH INSTITUTE LLC
Also Called: Dna Health Inst Cyrogenic Div
4562 Westinghouse St B, Ventura (93003-5797)
PHONE..............................805 654-9363
Noel Aguilar,
EMP: 15 **EST:** 2001
SALES (est): 5.8MM **Privately Held**
WEB: www.dnaskin.com
SIC: 2869 Laboratory chemicals, organic

(P-5133)
EDENIQ INC (PA)
6910 W Pershing Ct, Visalia (93291-7942)
PHONE..............................559 302-1777
Brian Thome, *CEO*
Scott Janssen, *CFO*
CAM Cast, *Vice Pres*
Peter Kilner, *Vice Pres*
Dan Michalopoulos, *Vice Pres*
▲ **EMP:** 99 **EST:** 2007
SALES (est): 14.6MM **Privately Held**
WEB: www.edeniq.com
SIC: 2869 Fuels

(P-5134)
ELASTPRO SILICONE SHEETING LLC
13937 Rosecrans Ave, Santa Fe Springs (90670-5209)
PHONE..............................562 348-2348
EMP: 17 **EST:** 2019
SALES (est): 2.9MM **Privately Held**
WEB: www.elastapro.com
SIC: 2869 Silicones

(P-5135)
EVERGREEN CHEMICALS USA LLC
1700 Lee Ave, Arcadia (91006-4638)
PHONE..............................626 821-9236
Qin Zhang, *President*
▲ **EMP:** 15 **EST:** 2012
SALES (est): 198.6K **Privately Held**
WEB: www.evgreen.us
SIC: 2869 Laboratory chemicals, organic

(P-5136)
FIRMENICH
424 S Atchison St, Anaheim (92805-4045)
PHONE..............................714 535-2871
Brian Kirckof, *Engineer*
Jerry Mutka, *Senior Engr*
Susan Lauritsen, *Controller*
Dustin Duimstra, *Purch Agent*
Jennifer Johnson, *QC Mgr*
EMP: 55 **EST:** 2017
SALES (est): 19.7MM **Privately Held**
WEB: www.firmenich.com
SIC: 2869 Industrial organic chemicals

(P-5137)
GFP ETHANOL LLC
Also Called: Calgren Renewable Fuels
11704 Road 120, Pixley (93256-9727)
P.O. Box E (93256-1005)
PHONE..............................559 757-3850
Lyle Schlyer, *President*
Tim Morillo, *Plant Mgr*
Bob Coleman, *Manager*
EMP: 34 **EST:** 2011
SALES (est): 11.3MM **Privately Held**
WEB: www.calgren.com
SIC: 2869 2046 Ethyl alcohol, ethanol; corn oil, crude
PA: Sjv Biodiesel, Llc
11704 Road 120
Pixley CA 93256
559 757-3850

(P-5138)
INNOVATIVE ORGANICS INC
4905 E Hunter Ave, Anaheim (92807-2058)
PHONE..............................714 701-3900
Robert E Futrell Jr, *President*
Douglas E Ward, *Vice Pres*
EMP: 24 **EST:** 1990
SQ FT: 30,000
SALES (est): 3.8MM **Privately Held**
WEB: www.ceramicsrefractories.saint-gobain.com
SIC: 2869 2899 Industrial organic chemicals; chemical preparations

(P-5139)
INTERNATIONAL ACADEMY OF FIN (PA)
Also Called: Cordova Industries
13177 Foothill Blvd, Sylmar (91342-4830)
P.O. Box 922079 (91392-2079)
PHONE..............................818 361-7724
Sam Cordova, *President*
Steven M Cordova, *President*
Rodrick Cordova, *Exec VP*
Sam Scott Cordova, *Vice Pres*
Steven Schector, *Vice Pres*
EMP: 24 **EST:** 1963
SQ FT: 6,000
SALES (est): 59MM **Privately Held**
SIC: 2869 3944 2879 Alcohols, industrial: denatured (non-beverage); video game machines, except coin-operated; insecticides, agricultural or household

(P-5140)
INTERNATIONAL SILICON COMPANY
3972 Barranca Pkwy J210, Irvine (92606-1204)
PHONE..............................929 291-0056
Hyuk Heo, *CEO*
Daniel Lee, *Co-Founder*
EMP: 30
SALES (est): 11.9MM **Privately Held**
SIC: 2869 Silicones

(P-5141)
LA SUPPLY COMPANY LLC
13700 Rosecrans Ave, Santa Fe Springs (90670-5027)
PHONE..............................714 735-9053
Sung-Lip Chun, *Mng Member*
Song-Tak Chun, *Mng Member*
◆ **EMP:** 15 **EST:** 1989
SQ FT: 24,000
SALES (est): 3.6MM **Privately Held**
WEB: www.la-supply.com
SIC: 2869 2865 Industrial organic chemicals; dyes & pigments

(P-5142)
NORAC INC (PA)
405 S Motor Ave, Azusa (91702-3232)
PHONE..............................626 334-2907
Wallace McCloskey, *President*
Richard Carlson, *Vice Pres*
Olive J Mc Closkey, *Principal*
Lee Miller, *Principal*
Jim Scholler, *Principal*
▼ **EMP:** 56 **EST:** 1953
SQ FT: 10,000
SALES (est): 50MM **Privately Held**
WEB: www.noracdev.com
SIC: 2869 Industrial organic chemicals

(P-5143)
PREMIER FUEL DISTRIBUTORS INC
156 E La Cadena Dr, Riverside (92507-8699)
PHONE..............................760 423-3610
Hugo Rodriguez, *CEO*
EMP: 150 **EST:** 2013
SALES (est): 19MM **Privately Held**
SIC: 2869 Fuels

(P-5144)
PROVIVI INC (PA)
1701 Colorado Ave, Santa Monica (90404-3436)
PHONE..............................310 828-2307
Pedro S L Coelho, *CEO*
Paul Kuc, *President*
Teri Quinn Gray, *COO*
Eduardo Sein, *CFO*

Peter Meinhold, *Officer*
EMP: 23 **EST:** 2012
SALES (est): 19.8MM **Privately Held**
SIC: 2869 Laboratory chemicals, organic

(P-5145)
PUREFORM GLOBAL INC
5700 Melrose Ave Apt 208, Los Angeles (90038-5603)
PHONE..............................310 666-4869
Chanel Perez, *Manager*
EMP: 15 **EST:** 2018
SALES (est): 2.3MM **Privately Held**
WEB: www.pureformglobal.com
SIC: 2869 Laboratory chemicals, organic

(P-5146)
SAINT-GOBAIN CERAMICS PLAS INC
Innovative Organics Division
4905 E Hunter Ave, Anaheim (92807-2058)
PHONE..............................714 701-3900
Robert E Futrell Jr, *Branch Mgr*
EMP: 150
SALES (corp-wide): 2.1B **Privately Held**
SIC: 2869 2899 Industrial organic chemicals; chemical preparations
HQ: Saint-Gobain Ceramics & Plastics, Inc.
20 Moores Rd
Malvern PA 19355

(P-5147)
SPECIALIZED PDTS & DESIGN INC
1428 N Manzanita St, Orange (92867-3662)
PHONE..............................714 289-1428
Dennis Bergdorf, *CEO*
Deborah Bergdorf, *Corp Secy*
EMP: 18 **EST:** 1998
SQ FT: 6,000
SALES (est): 1.2MM **Privately Held**
SIC: 2869 3069 Silicones; tubing, rubber

(P-5148)
SPECILTY ENZYMES BTECHNOLOGIES
Also Called: Seb
13591 Yorba Ave, Chino (91710-5071)
PHONE..............................909 613-1660
Vasant Rathi, *Principal*
Rajendra Newase, *Prdtn Mgr*
EMP: 17 **EST:** 2011
SALES (est): 7.1MM **Privately Held**
WEB: www.specialtyenzymes.com
SIC: 2869 Enzymes

(P-5149)
STRATOS RENEWABLES CORPORATION
Also Called: A Development Stage Company
9440 Santa Monica Blvd, Beverly Hills (90210-4653)
PHONE..............................310 402-5901
Thomas Snyder, *President*
Jorge Eduardo Aza, *COO*
Jorge Aza, *COO*
Julio Cesar Alonso, *CFO*
Sanjay Pai, *Officer*
EMP: 28 **EST:** 2004
SALES (est): 4MM **Privately Held**
WEB: www.stratosrenewables.com
SIC: 2869 0133 Ethyl alcohol, ethanol; sugarcane & sugar beets

(P-5150)
SWEEGEN INC
30452 Esperanza, Rcho STA Marg (92688-2144)
PHONE..............................949 635-1984
Steven Chen, *President*
Lucas Wenthe, *Admin Sec*
EMP: 13 **EST:** 2018
SALES (est): 2.3MM **Privately Held**
WEB: www.sweegen.com
SIC: 2869 Sweeteners, synthetic

(P-5151)
USL PARALLEL PRODUCTS CAL
12281 Arrow Rte, Rancho Cucamonga (91739-9601)
PHONE..............................909 980-1200
Gene Kiesel, *CEO*
Ken Reese, *President*

PRODUCTS & SVCS

Tim Cusson, *Vice Pres*
Bob Pasma, *Vice Pres*
Jim Russell, *Vice Pres*
▲ EMP: 35
SQ FT: 6,000
SALES (est): 10.6MM
SALES (corp-wide): 89.8MM **Privately Held**
WEB: www.parallelproducts.com
SIC: 2869 Alcohols, industrial: denatured (non-beverage)
PA: Parallel Environmental Services Corporation
401 Industry Rd
Louisville KY 40208
502 471-2444

(P-5152)
UTAK LABORATORIES INC
25020 Avenue Tibbitts, Valencia (91355-3447)
PHONE..................661 294-3935
James D Plutchak, *CEO*
Christina Plutchak, *Ch Credit Ofcr*
Kalyani Naik, *Buyer*
Kevin Kopp, *Opers Spvr*
Nicole Miller, *Mfg Staff*
EMP: 26 EST: 1974
SQ FT: 12,000
SALES (est): 7.4MM **Privately Held**
WEB: www.utak.com
SIC: 2869 Industrial organic chemicals

2873 Nitrogenous Fertilizers

(P-5153)
BWF BANDUCCI INC
Also Called: B W F
321 Industrial St, Bakersfield (93307-2705)
P.O. Box 81506 (93380-1506)
PHONE..................661 302-6625
Brian Banducci, *President*
Jeff Wise, *Controller*
Tricia Brown, *Manager*
EMP: 18 EST: 2006
SALES (est): 1MM **Privately Held**
WEB: www.bwfbanducci.com
SIC: 2873 Fertilizers: natural (organic), except compost

(P-5154)
CVR NITROGEN LP (HQ)
10877 Wilshire Blvd Fl 10, Los Angeles (90024-4251)
PHONE..................310 571-9800
Keith B Forman, *CEO*
John H Diesch, *President*
Jeffrey R Spain, *CFO*
Wilfred Bahl Jr, *Senior VP*
Julie Dawoodjee Cafarella, *Vice Pres*
EMP: 100 EST: 2015
SALES (est): 16.2MM **Publicly Held**
WEB: www.cvrpartners.com
SIC: 2873 Ammonium nitrate, ammonium sulfate

(P-5155)
GRO-POWER INC
15065 Telephone Ave, Chino (91710-9614)
PHONE..................909 393-3744
Brent Holden, *President*
Jack Engberg, *Vice Pres*
Ana Gonzales, *Office Mgr*
▼ EMP: 25 EST: 1966
SALES (est): 4.1MM **Privately Held**
WEB: www.gropower.com
SIC: 2873 0782 0721 Fertilizers: natural (organic), except compost; lawn & garden services; crop planting & protection

(P-5156)
HYPONEX CORPORATION
Also Called: Scotts- Hyponex
12273 Brown Ave, Jurupa Valley (92509-1828)
PHONE..................909 597-2811
Roclund White, *Branch Mgr*
EMP: 235
SALES (corp-wide): 4.1B **Publicly Held**
WEB: www.scotts.com
SIC: 2873 Fertilizers: natural (organic), except compost

HQ: Hyponex Corporation
14111 Scottslawn Rd
Marysville OH 43040
937 644-0011

(P-5157)
MAR VISTA RESOURCES LLC
745 North Ave, Corcoran (93212-1906)
P.O. Box 218 (93212-0218)
PHONE..................559 992-4535
Jay Irvine, *President*
Travis Cardoza, *Info Tech Mgr*
Joceline Alfaro, *Technician*
Marrs Gist, *Plant Mgr*
Jeremy Glick, *Plant Mgr*
▲ EMP: 13 EST: 2010
SALES (est): 3.1MM **Privately Held**
WEB: www.marvistaresources.com
SIC: 2873 Plant foods, mixed: from plants making nitrog. fertilizers

(P-5158)
NAC MFG INC
601 Kettering Dr, Ontario (91761-8153)
PHONE..................909 472-3033
Stanley Hsiao, *CEO*
Jeff Zhang, *Manager*
EMP: 15 EST: 2014
SQ FT: 106,000
SALES (est): 443.8K **Privately Held**
SIC: 2873 Fertilizers: natural (organic), except compost

(P-5159)
RED STAR FERTILIZER CO
17132 Hellman Ave, Eastvale (92880-9724)
PHONE..................909 597-4801
Donald C Mc Millan, *Ch of Bd*
Paul E Bernhard Jr, *President*
Michael Hughes, *Corp Secy*
EMP: 15 EST: 1927
SQ FT: 52,100
SALES (est): 1.8MM **Privately Held**
SIC: 2873 2421 Fertilizers: natural (organic), except compost; sawmills & planing mills, general

(P-5160)
RENTECH NTRGN PASADENA SPA LLC
10877 Wilshire Blvd # 71, Los Angeles (90024-4341)
PHONE..................310 571-9805
EMP: 28 EST: 1987
SALES (est): 1.8MM **Publicly Held**
SIC: 2873 Nitrogenous fertilizers
HQ: Cvr Nitrogen, Lp
10877 Wilshire Blvd Fl 10
Los Angeles CA 90024
310 571-9800

(P-5161)
TI INC
13802 Avenue 352, Visalia (93292-9543)
PHONE..................559 972-1475
Bryce Iden, *Principal*
EMP: 15 EST: 1984
SALES (est): 2.6MM **Privately Held**
SIC: 2873 Plant foods, mixed: from plants making nitrog. fertilizers

(P-5162)
WHITTIER FERTILIZER COMPANY
9441 Kruse Rd, Pico Rivera (90660-1492)
PHONE..................562 699-3461
Robert Osborn, *CEO*
Janet Osborn, *Treasurer*
Osborn Jim, *Vice Pres*
Jim Osborn, *General Mgr*
▲ EMP: 51 EST: 1930
SQ FT: 20,000
SALES (est): 9.9MM **Privately Held**
WEB: www.whittierfertilizer.com
SIC: 2873 5261 2875 Fertilizers: natural (organic), except compost; garden supplies & tools; fertilizers, mixing only

(P-5163)
WTB TECHNOLOGY
245 Industrial St, Bakersfield (93307-2703)
PHONE..................661 327-9604
Craig Waterman, *President*
EMP: 13 EST: 1990

SALES (est): 353.3K **Privately Held**
WEB: www.wtb.com
SIC: 2873 Nitrogenous fertilizers

2875 Fertilizers, Mixing Only

(P-5164)
JH BIOTECH INC (PA)
4951 Olivas Park Dr, Ventura (93003-7667)
P.O. Box 3538 (93006-3538)
PHONE..................805 650-8933
Hsinhung John Hsu, *President*
Jonathan Coleman, *Sales Staff*
◆ EMP: 23 EST: 1986
SQ FT: 3,000
SALES (est): 15.4MM **Privately Held**
WEB: www.jhbiotech.com
SIC: 2875 Fertilizers, mixing only

2879 Pesticides & Agricultural Chemicals, NEC

(P-5165)
AMERICAN VANGUARD CORPORATION (PA)
Also Called: Avd
4695 Macarthur Ct, Newport Beach (92660-1882)
PHONE..................949 260-1200
Eric G Wintemute, *Ch of Bd*
Ulrich G Trogele, *COO*
Ulrich Trogele, *COO*
David T Johnson, *CFO*
Lawrence Clark, *Bd of Directors*
◆ EMP: 205 EST: 1969
SQ FT: 19,953
SALES (est): 458.7MM **Publicly Held**
WEB: www.american-vanguard.com
SIC: 2879 Pesticides, agricultural or household

(P-5166)
AMVAC CHEMICAL CORPORATION (HQ)
4695 Macarthur Ct # 1200, Newport Beach (92660-8859)
PHONE..................323 264-3910
Eric C Wintemute, *President*
Timothy Donnelly, *President*
Bob Trogele, *COO*
David T Johnson, *CFO*
MO Jaber, *Bd of Directors*
◆ EMP: 36 EST: 1945
SQ FT: 152,000
SALES (est): 212.1MM
SALES (corp-wide): 458.7MM **Publicly Held**
WEB: www.amvac.com
SIC: 2879 Pesticides, agricultural or household
PA: American Vanguard Corporation
4695 Macarthur Ct
Newport Beach CA 92660
949 260-1200

(P-5167)
CELLU-CON INC
19994 Meredith Dr, Strathmore (93267-9691)
P.O. Box 185 (93267-0185)
PHONE..................559 568-0190
Duane Hilty, *President*
Carol Hilty, *Vice Pres*
John Yale, *Vice Pres*
EMP: 25 EST: 1979
SQ FT: 15,000
SALES (est): 4.1MM **Privately Held**
WEB: www.americanextracts.com
SIC: 2879 Soil conditioners

(P-5168)
CERTIS USA LLC
Also Called: Thermo Trilogy
720 5th St, Wasco (93280-1420)
PHONE..................661 758-8471
Michael Hillberry, *Principal*
Mike Allan, *Vice Pres*
Anne Webster, *Regional Mgr*
Mary Anne Price, *Technical Staff*
Bob Wilson, *Engineer*
EMP: 40 **Privately Held**
WEB: www.certisbio.com

SIC: 2879 5191 Pesticides, agricultural or household; insecticides
HQ: Certis U.S.A. L.L.C.
9145 Guilford Rd Ste 175
Columbia MD 21046

(P-5169)
DECCO US POST-HARVEST INC (HQ)
1713 S California Ave, Monrovia (91016-4623)
P.O. Box 120 (91017-0120)
PHONE..................800 221-0925
Francois Girin, *President*
Bill Eakle, *Opers Mgr*
◆ EMP: 41 EST: 2009
SALES (est): 18.1MM **Privately Held**
WEB: www.deccous.com
SIC: 2879 Agricultural chemicals

(P-5170)
GROW MORE INC
15600 New Century Dr, Gardena (90248-2129)
PHONE..................310 515-1700
John Atwill, *CEO*
William Haller, *Vice Pres*
Debbie Gerber, *Controller*
Anthony Sotak, *Safety Mgr*
Phil Nash, *Sales Staff*
◆ EMP: 62 EST: 1918
SQ FT: 43,560
SALES (est): 18.3MM **Privately Held**
WEB: www.growmore.com
SIC: 2879 2899 2873 2869 Agricultural chemicals; chemical preparations; water treating compounds; nitrogenous fertilizers; industrial organic chemicals; cyclic crudes & intermediates

(P-5171)
IE HORTICULTURE & CULTIVATION
56524 Sunset Dr, Yucca Valley (92284-5030)
PHONE..................909 295-1446
Jason Scott,
EMP: 14
SALES (est): 629K **Privately Held**
SIC: 2879 Agricultural chemicals

(P-5172)
SOUTHERN VALLEY CHEMICAL CO
101 Sycamore Rd, Arvin (93203-2341)
P.O. Box 181 (93203-0181)
PHONE..................661 366-3308
Christopher Carlson, *CEO*
Christopher C Carlson, *CEO*
Russel Carlson, *Corp Secy*
EMP: 13 EST: 1963
SQ FT: 13,400
SALES (est): 3.3MM **Privately Held**
SIC: 2879 Insecticides & pesticides

(P-5173)
TRICAL INC
28679 Rd 68, Visalia (93277)
PHONE..................559 651-0736
Dean Storkan, *President*
EMP: 22
SALES (corp-wide): 39.5MM **Privately Held**
WEB: www.trical.com
SIC: 2879 Agricultural chemicals
PA: Trical, Inc.
8100 Arroyo Cir
Gilroy CA 95020
831 637-0195

(P-5174)
TRICAL INC
1029 Railroad St, Corona (92882-2416)
PHONE..................951 737-6960
Joanne Vargas, *Manager*
EMP: 22
SALES (corp-wide): 39.5MM **Privately Held**
WEB: www.trical.com
SIC: 2879 Agricultural chemicals
PA: Trical, Inc.
8100 Arroyo Cir
Gilroy CA 95020
831 637-0195

(P-5175)
TRICAL INC
1667 Purdy Rd, Mojave (93501-7403)
PHONE.............................661 824-2494
Neil Adkins, *Branch Mgr*
EMP: 22
SALES (corp-wide): 39.5MM **Privately Held**
WEB: www.trical.com
SIC: 2879 Agricultural chemicals
PA: Trical, Inc.
8100 Arroyo Cir
Gilroy CA 95020
831 637-0195

2891 Adhesives & Sealants

(P-5176)
AC PRODUCTS INC
Also Called: Quaker
9930 Painter Ave, Whittier (90605-2759)
PHONE.............................714 630-7311
Peter Weissman, *President*
Joseph Matrange, *President*
Hugh H Muller, *Exec VP*
Sheldon I Weinstein, *Vice Pres*
◆ EMP: 35 EST: 1972
SQ FT: 28,000
SALES (est): 15.5MM
SALES (corp-wide): 1.4B **Publicly Held**
WEB: www.acpmaskants.com
SIC: 2891 2952 8731 Adhesives & sealants; coating compounds, tar; chemical laboratory, except testing
PA: Quaker Chemical Corporation
901 E Hector St
Conshohocken PA 19428
610 832-4000

(P-5177)
ADVANTAGE ADHESIVES INC
8345 White Oak Ave, Rancho Cucamonga (91730-3896)
PHONE.............................909 204-4990
Greg Lane, *President*
Erika Machado, *Receptionist*
▲ EMP: 26 EST: 1998
SQ FT: 25,620
SALES (est): 5.3MM **Privately Held**
WEB: www.advantageadhesives.com
SIC: 2891 Adhesives

(P-5178)
AXIOM MATERIALS INC
2320 Pullman St, Santa Ana (92705-5507)
PHONE.............................949 623-4400
John D Lincoln, *CEO*
Tom Cain, *CFO*
James Samuel Miele, *CFO*
Raj Dhawan, *Vice Pres*
Legrand Lewis, *Admin Sec*
▲ EMP: 35 EST: 2009
SQ FT: 15,000
SALES (est): 18.5MM **Privately Held**
WEB: www.axiommaterials.com
SIC: 2891 2295 Epoxy adhesives; resin or plastic coated fabrics

(P-5179)
CTS CEMENT MANUFACTURING CORP (PA)
12442 Knott St, Garden Grove (92841-2832)
PHONE.............................714 379-8260
Walter J Hoyle, *CEO*
Louis Priego, *Regional Mgr*
Nolan Reiter, *Design Engr*
John Kim, *Engineer*
Keith Lamy, *Engineer*
▼ EMP: 45 EST: 1978
SQ FT: 14,000
SALES (est): 50.6MM **Privately Held**
WEB: www.ctscement.com
SIC: 2891 Cement, except linoleum & tile

(P-5180)
CTS CEMENT MANUFACTURING CORP
2077 Linda Flora Dr, Los Angeles (90077-1406)
PHONE.............................310 472-4004
Sean Casey, *Regional Mgr*
Tommy Fasano, *Regional Mgr*
Logan Denton, *Technical Staff*

Richard Mize, *Technical Staff*
Michael Baker, *Engineer*
EMP: 13
SALES (corp-wide): 50.6MM **Privately Held**
WEB: www.ctscement.com
SIC: 2891 Cement, except linoleum & tile
PA: Cts Cement Manufacturing Corporation
12442 Knott St
Garden Grove CA 92841
714 379-8260

(P-5181)
CUSTOM BUILDING PRODUCTS LLC (DH)
7711 Center Ave Ste 500, Huntington Beach (92647-3076)
PHONE.............................800 272-8786
Don Devine, *CEO*
Thomas Peck Jr, *President*
Chuck Bloome, *COO*
Scott Hanson, *Vice Pres*
Dean Leffler, *Vice Pres*
◆ EMP: 65 EST: 2005
SQ FT: 15,000
SALES (est): 435.3MM **Privately Held**
WEB: www.custombuildingproducts.com
SIC: 2891 Adhesives & sealants
HQ: The Quikrete Companies Llc
5 Concourse Pkwy Ste 1900
Atlanta GA 30328
404 634-9100

(P-5182)
DAVCO ENTERPRISES INC
Also Called: Design Polymerics
3301 W Segerstrom Ave, Santa Ana (92704-6402)
PHONE.............................714 432-0600
Lyle R Davis, *President*
Matt Marowitz, *CFO*
Lisa Tomic, *Office Mgr*
Carl Busse, *Regl Sales Mgr*
John Hutchinson, *Manager*
▲ EMP: 13
SQ FT: 15,000
SALES (est): 3.8MM **Privately Held**
WEB: www.designpoly.com
SIC: 2891 Adhesives & sealants

(P-5183)
GENERAL SEALANTS
300 Turnbull Canyon Rd, City of Industry (91745-1009)
P.O. Box 3855 (91744-0855)
PHONE.............................626 961-0211
Bradley Boyle, *President*
Patricia Boyle, *Owner*
Patrick Boyle, *CFO*
Greg Hanson, *Purchasing*
Matthew Smiley, *Plant Mgr*
◆ EMP: 120 EST: 1964
SQ FT: 96,000
SALES (est): 16.1MM **Privately Held**
WEB: www.generalsealants.com
SIC: 2891 Adhesives

(P-5184)
HENKEL CHEMICAL MANAGEMENT LLC
Also Called: Henkel Electronic Mtls LLC
14000 Jamboree Rd, Irvine (92606-1730)
PHONE.............................888 943-6535
Benoit Pouliquen, *Vice Pres*
Paul R Berry, *President*
Alan P Syzdek, *President*
Soon Kim, *Technician*
Ruairi Okane, *Manager*
EMP: 170 EST: 2010
SQ FT: 75,000
SALES (est): 77.5MM
SALES (corp-wide): 22.7B **Privately Held**
WEB: www.henkel.de
SIC: 2891 Adhesives
PA: Henkel Ag & Co. Kgaa
Henkelstr. 67
Dusseldorf NW 40589
211 797-0

(P-5185)
INTERNATIONAL COATINGS CO INC (PA)
13929 166th St, Cerritos (90703-2431)
PHONE.............................562 926-1010
Stephen W Kahane, *CEO*
Herbert A Wells, *Ch of Bd*

Janet Wells, *Corp Secy*
Sonja Pulliam, *Office Mgr*
Jesse Pittman, *Prdtn Mgr*
◆ EMP: 40 EST: 1957
SQ FT: 50,000
SALES (est): 13.2MM **Privately Held**
WEB: www.internationalcoatings.com
SIC: 2891 2899 3555 2893 Adhesives; ink or writing fluids; printing trades machinery; printing ink; paints & allied products; plastics materials & resins

(P-5186)
IPS CORPORATION (PA)
Also Called: Weld-On Adhesives
455 W Victoria St, Compton (90220-6064)
PHONE.............................310 898-3300
Tracy Bilbrough, *CEO*
Will Barton, *CFO*
Gary Rosenfield, *Chief Mktg Ofcr*
Denise Maidment, *Finance Mgr*
Albert Paguio, *Finance Mgr*
◆ EMP: 180 EST: 1953
SQ FT: 22,000
SALES (est): 161.8MM **Privately Held**
WEB: www.ipscorp.com
SIC: 2891 Adhesives, plastic; cement, except linoleum & tile

(P-5187)
MITSUBISHI CHEMICAL CRBN FBR
1822 Reynolds Ave, Irvine (92614-5714)
PHONE.............................800 929-5471
Takashi Sasaki, *Vice Pres*
Mike Pierce, *Sales Mgr*
EMP: 110 **Privately Held**
WEB: www.mccfc.com
SIC: 2891 5169 Adhesives; chemical additives
HQ: Mitsubishi Chemical Carbon Fiber And Composites, Inc
5900 88th St
Sacramento CA 95828

(P-5188)
PACER TECHNOLOGY (HQ)
Also Called: Super Glue
3281 E Guasti Rd Ste 260, Ontario (91761-7642)
PHONE.............................909 987-0550
Ronald T Gravette, *Vice Pres*
Ron Gravette, *President*
E T Gravette, *CEO*
Kristine Wright, *CFO*
James Gallagher, *Vice Pres*
◆ EMP: 107 EST: 1975
SQ FT: 47,700
SALES (est): 29.7MM **Privately Held**
WEB: www.pacerprivatelabel.com
SIC: 2891 3089 3085 Adhesives & sealants; plastic containers, except foam; plastics bottles
PA: Cyan Holding Corporation
9420 Santa Anita Ave
Rancho Cucamonga CA 91730
909 987-0550

(P-5189)
PACKAGING SYSTEMS INC
26435 Summit Cir, Santa Clarita (91350-2991)
PHONE.............................661 253-5700
Raymond J Gray, *CEO*
Steve Gray, *President*
Patricia Gray, *Exec VP*
Stephanie Broadway, *Project Mgr*
Marie Whitehead, *Accounting Mgr*
▼ EMP: 42 EST: 1976
SQ FT: 25,700
SALES (est): 17MM **Privately Held**
WEB: www.pkgsys.net
SIC: 2891 Adhesives & sealants

(P-5190)
PLAS-TECH SEALING TECH LLC
252 Mariah Cir Fl 2, Corona (92879-1751)
PHONE.............................951 737-2228
Chad Miller, *Manager*
Charlotte Miller,
Craig Miller Sr,
Eve Miller,
▲ EMP: 15 EST: 1997
SQ FT: 16,000

SALES (est): 1.1MM **Privately Held**
SIC: 2891 Sealants

(P-5191)
PRC - DESOTO INTERNATIONAL INC (HQ)
Also Called: PPG Aerospace
24811 Ave Rockefeller, Valencia (91355-3468)
PHONE.............................661 678-4209
Michael H McGarry, *President*
Barry Gillespie, *CEO*
Ralph Dyba, *CFO*
Viktoras R Sekmakas, *Exec VP*
Frank S Sklarsky, *Exec VP*
▲ EMP: 320 EST: 1945
SQ FT: 200,000
SALES (est): 138.5MM
SALES (corp-wide): 15.1B **Publicly Held**
WEB: www.ppgaerospace.com
SIC: 2891 3089 Sealing compounds, synthetic rubber or plastic; adhesives; plastic containers, except foam
PA: Ppg Industries, Inc.
1 Ppg Pl
Pittsburgh PA 15272
412 434-3131

(P-5192)
PRC - DESOTO INTERNATIONAL INC
Also Called: PPG Aerospace
11601 United St, Mojave (93501-7048)
PHONE.............................661 824-4532
Dave Richardson, *Branch Mgr*
EMP: 130
SALES (corp-wide): 15.1B **Publicly Held**
WEB: www.ppgaerospace.com
SIC: 2891 Sealing compounds, synthetic rubber or plastic; adhesives
HQ: Prc - Desoto International, Inc.
24811 Ave Rockefeller
Valencia CA 91355
661 678-4209

(P-5193)
QSPAC INDUSTRIES INC (PA)
Also Called: Quality Service Pac Industry
15020 Marquardt Ave, Santa Fe Springs (90670-5704)
PHONE.............................562 407-3868
Jow-Lin Tang, *President*
Wu-Hsiung Chung, *CFO*
Gloria Chang, *Accountant*
Lisa Wang, *Human Res Mgr*
Eugena Lee, *Purch Agent*
◆ EMP: 52 EST: 2009
SQ FT: 96,000
SALES (est): 16.9MM **Privately Held**
WEB: www.qspac.com
SIC: 2891 Adhesives

(P-5194)
RELIABLE PACKAGING SYSTEMS INC
Also Called: Astro Packaging
1300 N Jefferson St, Anaheim (92807-1614)
PHONE.............................714 572-1094
Debra Lynn Dillon, *President*
Debra Dillon, *President*
Ryan Dillon, *Info Tech Mgr*
Todd Dice, *Engineer*
Ryan Davis, *Mktg Dir*
EMP: 17 EST: 1994
SQ FT: 5,500
SALES (est): 4.5MM **Privately Held**
SIC: 2891 3565 5084 5169 Adhesives & sealants; packaging machinery; packaging machinery & equipment; adhesives & sealants; consulting engineer

(P-5195)
RIVERSIDE LAMINATION CORP
3016 Kansas Ave Bldg 6, Riverside (92507-3456)
PHONE.............................951 682-0100
Theresa Santoro, *CEO*
Steve Hobbs, *Sales Executive*
EMP: 14 EST: 2008
SALES (est): 4.6MM **Privately Held**
WEB: www.riversidelaminations.com
SIC: 2891 Laminating compounds

(P-5196)
SIGNATURE FLEXIBLE PACKG LLC
19310 San Jose Ave, City of Industry
(91748-1419)
PHONE...................323 887-1997
Adrian Backer, *President*
Jeff Sewel, *Vice Pres*
Kelly Redding, *Admin Sec*
Armando Lira, *Technical Mgr*
Dio Brenes, *Technology*
▲ **EMP:** 82 **EST:** 1954
SALES (est): 18MM **Privately Held**
WEB: www.signatureflexible.com
SIC: 2891 2673 Adhesives & sealants;
bags: plastic, laminated & coated

(P-5197)
STIC-ADHESIVE PRODUCTS CO INC
3950 Medford St, Los Angeles
(90063-1675)
PHONE...................323 268-2956
Junho Suh, *President*
John Roberts, *General Mgr*
Bong Suh, *Info Tech Mgr*
EMP: 150 **EST:** 1975
SQ FT: 75,000
SALES (est): 13.3MM **Privately Held**
WEB: www.sticadhesive.com
SIC: 2891 2851 Adhesives; paints & allied
products

(P-5198)
TCK USA CORPORATION
2580 Corp Pl Ste F101, Monterey Park
(91754)
P.O. Box 1190, Alhambra (91802-1190)
PHONE...................323 269-2969
Wendy Chen, *President*
Frank Chen, *Vice Pres*
◆ **EMP:** 16 **EST:** 2000
SQ FT: 5,000
SALES (est): 850.6K **Privately Held**
WEB: www.tckgroup.com
SIC: 2891 Sealing compounds, synthetic
rubber or plastic

(P-5199)
TECHNICOTE INC
1141 California Ave, Corona (92881-7233)
PHONE...................951 372-0627
George Parker, *Manager*
Ivan Jurado, *Production*
EMP: 29
SQ FT: 2,000
SALES (corp-wide): 69.4MM **Privately
Held**
WEB: www.technicote.com
SIC: 2891 2675 Adhesives; die-cut paper
& board
PA: Technicote, Inc.
222 Mound Ave
Miamisburg OH 45342
800 358-4448

2892 Explosives

(P-5200)
ALPHA DYNO NOBEL
Also Called: Alpha Explosives
1682 Sabovich St Bldg A, Mojave
(93501-1600)
P.O. Box 920 (93502-0920)
PHONE...................661 824-1356
Richard Cross, *Manager*
Gerald Hackler, *General Mgr*
Danniell Edwards, *Administration*
EMP: 17 **Privately Held**
WEB: www.alphaexplosives.com
SIC: 2892 5169 Explosives; explosives
PA: Alpha Dyno Nobel
3400 Nader Rd
Lincoln CA 95648

2893 Printing Ink

(P-5201)
BOMARK INC
601 S 6th Ave, La Puente (91746-3026)
PHONE...................626 968-1666

Herman R Schowe Jr, *Ch of Bd*
H Mark Schowe, *COO*
Kathie Virgil, *CFO*
EMP: 31 **EST:** 1961
SQ FT: 21,000
SALES (est): 1.1MM **Privately Held**
SIC: 2893 Printing ink

(P-5202)
FARBOTECH COLOR INC
Also Called: K & E Printing Ink
1630 Yeager Ave, La Verne (91750-5853)
PHONE...................909 596-9330
Edd Butch, *President*
Fiona Cummings, *Vice Pres*
▲ **EMP:** 19 **EST:** 1985
SQ FT: 15,000
SALES (est): 1.4MM **Privately Held**
WEB: www.gw-inks.com
SIC: 2893 Printing ink

(P-5203)
**GANS INK AND SUPPLY CO INC
(PA)**
1441 Boyd St, Los Angeles (90033-3790)
P.O. Box 33806 (90033-0806)
PHONE...................323 264-2200
Jeffrey Koppelman, *President*
Sarah Christman, *Branch Mgr*
Tom Debartolo, *Branch Mgr*
Mike Fanton, *Branch Mgr*
Thomas Debartolo, *Division Mgr*
◆ **EMP:** 50 **EST:** 1950
SQ FT: 28,000
SALES (est): 21.5MM **Privately Held**
WEB: www.gansink.com
SIC: 2893 Printing ink

(P-5204)
HADDADS FINE ARTS INC
3855 E Miraloma Ave, Anaheim
(92806-2124)
PHONE...................714 996-2100
Paula Haddad, *President*
Craig Skeen, *Vice Pres*
Silvina Bates, *Sales Staff*
EMP: 23 **EST:** 1958
SQ FT: 17,000
SALES (est): 2MM **Privately Held**
WEB: www.haddadsfinearts.com
SIC: 2893 Lithographic ink

(P-5205)
INK DIRECT
17572 Griffin Ln, Huntington Beach
(92647-6791)
PHONE...................714 418-1999
Voravit Chaicharn, *Principal*
EMP: 14 **EST:** 2006
SALES (est): 1.1MM **Privately Held**
WEB: www.onlineinkdirect.com
SIC: 2893 Lithographic ink; ink or
writing fluids

(P-5206)
INK MAKERS INC
2121 Yates Ave, Commerce (90040-1911)
PHONE...................323 728-7500
EMP: 15
SQ FT: 15,000
SALES: 1.7MM **Privately Held**
SIC: 2893 Mfg Printing Ink

(P-5207)
INK MILL LLC
Also Called: Ink Mill Corp.
207 N Goode Ave Fl 5, Glendale
(91203-1364)
PHONE...................626 304-2000
Vikas Arora, *Mng Member*
Kevin Dyer, *Vice Pres*
◆ **EMP:** 13 **EST:** 2008
SALES (est): 6.9MM
SALES (corp-wide): 6.9B **Publicly Held**
WEB: www.inkmillcorp.com
SIC: 2893 Printing ink
PA: Avery Dennison Corporation
207 N Goode Ave
Glendale CA 91203
626 304-2000

(P-5208)
INKJETMADNESSCOM INC
Also Called: Inkgrabber.com
882 Patriot Dr Ste G, Moorpark
(93021-3544)
PHONE...................805 583-7755
Keith Ramirez, *President*
▲ **EMP:** 15 **EST:** 2002
SALES (est): 1.5MM **Privately Held**
SIC: 2893 Printing ink

(P-5209)
SELECT OFFICE SYSTEMS INC
1811 W Magnolia Blvd, Burbank
(91506-1725)
P.O. Box 11777 (91510-1777)
PHONE...................818 861-8320
Andrew Hunter Rouse, *CEO*
EMP: 13 **EST:** 2015
SALES (est): 1.1MM **Privately Held**
WEB: www.selectofficesystemsinc.com
SIC: 2893 Printing ink

2899 Chemical Preparations, NEC

(P-5210)
AMERICAN CONSUMER PRODUCTS LLC
2833 Leonis Blvd Ste 102, Vernon
(90058-3029)
PHONE...................323 289-6610
David Molayem, *President*
David Molayen, *President*
Kam Jahanbigloo, *Vice Pres*
Daryoosh Molayem, *Managing Dir*
◆ **EMP:** 33 **EST:** 1999
SALES (est): 7.5MM
SALES (corp-wide): 32.5MM **Privately
Held**
WEB: www.american-consumer-
products.com
SIC: 2899 2844 2834 Chemical prepara-
tions; cosmetic preparations; pharmaceu-
tical preparations
PA: Tabletops Unlimited, Inc.
23000 Avalon Blvd
Carson CA 90745
310 549-6000

(P-5211)
APOLLO TECHNOLOGIES INC
31441 Snta Margarita Pkwy, Rcho STA
Marg (92688-1836)
PHONE...................949 888-0573
Robert W Ricks, *President*
EMP: 23 **EST:** 1980
SALES (est): 3.4MM **Privately Held**
WEB: www.apollotechnologiesinc.com
SIC: 2899 Water treating compounds

(P-5212)
APOLLOTEK INTERNATIONAL INC
1702 Mcgaw Ave, Irvine (92614-5732)
PHONE...................800 787-1244
Jeff Hatamkhani, *CEO*
Crystal Nova, *Marketing Staff*
EMP: 21 **EST:** 2011
SALES (est): 5MM **Privately Held**
WEB: www.lefay.com
SIC: 2899 Water treating compounds

(P-5213)
BEST FORMULATIONS
938 Radecki Ct, City of Industry
(91748-1132)
PHONE...................626 912-9998
Michael Bach, *Vice Pres*
Donald R Steele, *Vice Pres*
Jennifer Monroy, *Admin Asst*
Evelyn Jimenez, *Purch Agent*
Joshua McCann, *Purch Agent*
▲ **EMP:** 18 **EST:** 2015
SALES (est): 6.3MM **Privately Held**
WEB: www.bestformulations.com
SIC: 2899 7389 2023 Gelatin capsules;
packaging & labeling services; dietary
supplements, dairy & non-dairy based

(P-5214)
CALIFORNIA RESPIRATORY CARE
16055 Ventura Blvd # 715, Encino
(91436-2601)
PHONE...................818 379-9999
EMP: 55
SALES (est): 4.1MM **Privately Held**
SIC: 2899 5047 5169 Chemical Prepara-
tions, Nec, Nsk

(P-5215)
CONTRBAND CTRL SPECIALISTS INC
Also Called: Zee Consulting
26 H St, Bakersfield (93304-2908)
P.O. Box 2365 (93303-2365)
PHONE...................661 322-3363
Gary Zvirblis, *President*
Moriah Mendenhall, *Opers Staff*
EMP: 20 **EST:** 1996
SALES (est): 3.4MM **Privately Held**
WEB: www.contrabandcontrol.com
SIC: 2899

(P-5216)
CYTEC ENGINEERED MATERIALS INC
645 N Cypress St, Orange 92867-6603)
PHONE...................714 630-9400
Ron Martin, *Branch Mgr*
Manuel Duchement, *Technology*
EMP: 130
SQ FT: 300,000
SALES (corp-wide): 13MM **Privately
Held**
SIC: 2899 Chemical preparations
HQ: Cytec Engineered Materials Inc.
2085 E Tech Cir Ste 102
Tempe AZ 85284

(P-5217)
DIAMON FUSION INTL INC
9361 Irvine Blvd, Irvine (92618-1669)
PHONE...................949 388-8000
Adam Zax, *President*
Denise Robinson, *CFO*
Russell Slaybaugh, *Vice Pres*
Ana Zax, *Export Mgr*
S Aguilar, *Opers Staff*
EMP: 16 **EST:** 1997
SQ FT: 4,500
SALES (est): 4.9MM **Privately Held**
WEB: www.dfisolutions.com
SIC: 2899 6794 Chemical preparations;
patent owners & lessors

(P-5218)
ENOVA SOLUTIONS INC
3553 Landco Dr Ste B, Bakersfield
(93308-6169)
P.O. Box 21988 (93390-1988)
PHONE...................661 327-2405
Richard Dyer, *President*
Jesse Holman, *Treasurer*
Michael Ripley, *Admin Sec*
EMP: 17 **EST:** 2006
SALES (est): 2.8MM **Privately Held**
WEB: www.enovaes.com
SIC: 2899 Oil treating compounds

(P-5219)
EVERSPRING CHEMICAL INC
11577 W Olympic Blvd, Los Angeles
(90064-1522)
PHONE...................310 707-1600
Marvin Lai, *CEO*
▲ **EMP:** 17 **EST:** 2005
SQ FT: 2,000
SALES (est): 2.6MM **Privately Held**
WEB: www.everspringchem.com
SIC: 2899 Chemical preparations

(P-5220)
FIREQUICK PRODUCTS INC
1137 Red Rock Inyokern Rd, Inyokern
(93527)
P.O. Box 910 (93527-0910)
PHONE...................760 377-5766
EMP: 13 **EST:** 2005
SALES (est): 1.7MM **Privately Held**
WEB: www.firequick.com
SIC: 2899 Flares

(P-5221)
FLAMEMASTER CORPORATION
Also Called: Chemseal
13576 Desmond St, Pacoima
(91331-2315)
P.O. Box 4510 (91333-4500)
PHONE....................................818 890-1401
Joseph Mazin, *CEO*
Mary Eason, *Treasurer*
Mary Kay Eason, *Corp Secy*
Gary Sokol, *Prdtn Mgr*
Eugenia Alonso, *Sales Staff*
▲ EMP: 28 EST: 1942
SALES (est): 7.4MM Privately Held
WEB: www.flamemaster.com
SIC: 2899 2819 1799 2891 Fire retardant
chemicals; industrial inorganic chemicals;
coating of metal structures at construction
site; sealing compounds, synthetic rubber
or plastic

(P-5222)
HEMOSURE INC
5358 Irwindale Ave, Baldwin Park
(91706-2086)
PHONE....................................888 436-6787
Dr John Wan, *President*
Sherry Wang, *Human Res Mgr*
Jay Polley, *Sales Staff*
EMP: 40 EST: 2003
SALES (est): 10.4MM Privately Held
WEB: www.hemosure.com
SIC: 2899 3841 Chemical preparations;
surgical & medical instruments
PA: W.H.P.M. Inc.
5358 Irwindale Ave
Irwindale CA 91706

(P-5223)
INDIO PRODUCTS INC
Cultural Heritage Candle Co
5331 E Slauson Ave, Commerce
(90040-2916)
PHONE....................................323 720-9117
Marty Mayer, *Owner*
Anna Riva, *Products*
EMP: 33
SALES (corp-wide): 26.7MM Privately
Held
WEB: www.indioproducts.com
SIC: 2899 3999 5199 5049 Incense; can-
dles; candles; religious supplies
PA: Indio Products, Inc.
12910 Mulberry Dr Unit A
Whittier CA 90602
323 720-1188

(P-5224)
INSULTECH LLC (PA)
3530 W Garry Ave, Santa Ana
(92704-6423)
PHONE....................................714 384-0506
Lisa Romero, *Mng Member*
Cheryl Case, *Accountant*
Pedro Alonso, *Production*
Selvyn Furtado, *Mfg Spvr*
Glenn Anderson, *Sales Staff*
◆ EMP: 60 EST: 1994
SQ FT: 30,000
SALES (est): 15.6MM Privately Held
WEB: www.insultech.com
SIC: 2899 Insulating compounds

(P-5225)
KIK POOL ADDITIVES INC
5160 E Airport Dr, Ontario (91761-7824)
PHONE....................................909 390-9912
John A Christensen, *President*
Brian Patterson, *CFO*
Brian P Patterson, *CFO*
David M Christensen, *Vice Pres*
Debra Schonk, *Vice Pres*
▲ EMP: 140 EST: 1958
SALES (est): 16.8MM Privately Held
WEB: www.kem-tek.com
SIC: 2899 3089 7389 5169 Chemical
preparations; plastic hardware & building
products; packaging & labeling services;
swimming pool & spa chemicals

(P-5226)
L M SCOFIELD COMPANY (DH)
12767 Imperial Hwy, Santa Fe Springs
(90670-4711)
PHONE....................................323 720-3000

Phillip J Arnold, *President*
Janet Dickinson, *Info Tech Dir*
Mike Decandia, *Marketing Staff*
CAM Villar, *Marketing Staff*
Stan Stratton, *Director*
◆ EMP: 50 EST: 1915
SQ FT: 36,000
SALES (est): 22.5MM
SALES (corp-wide): 8.6B Privately Held
WEB: www.usa.sika.com
SIC: 2899 Concrete curing & hardening
compounds
HQ: Sika Corporation
201 Polito Ave
Lyndhurst NJ 07071
201 933-8800

(P-5227)
LG NANOH2O INC
21250 Hawthorne Blvd # 33, Torrance
(90503-5506)
PHONE....................................424 218-4000
Jeff Green, *CEO*
Doug Barnes, *COO*
John Markovich, *CFO*
Michael Demartino, *Vice Pres*
Nicholas Dyner, *Vice Pres*
▲ EMP: 35 EST: 2005
SQ FT: 2,000
SALES (est): 7.3MM Privately Held
WEB: www.nanoh2o.com
SIC: 2899 Distilled water
PA: Lg Chem, Ltd.
128 Yeoui-Daero, Yeongdeungpo-Gu
Seoul 07336

(P-5228)
LUBRIZOL CORPORATION
30211 Ave D Las Bandras, Rancho Santa
Margari (92688)
PHONE....................................949 212-1863
EMP: 19
SALES (corp-wide): 182.1B Publicly
Held
SIC: 2899 Mfg Chemical Preparations
HQ: The Lubrizol Corporation
29400 Lakeland Blvd
Wickliffe OH 44092
440 943-4200

(P-5229)
LUCE COMMUNICATIONS LLC
Also Called: ABG Communications
22895 Eastpark Dr, Yorba Linda
(92887-4653)
PHONE....................................657 600-6812
Joel Luce, *CEO*
Dan Ablett, *President*
Vicki Ruff, *Vice Pres*
Humberto Quintanar, *Principal*
Dave Warren, *Network Mgr*
EMP: 53 EST: 1955
SALES (est): 14.3MM Privately Held
WEB: www.bridgecomsolutions.com
SIC: 2899 4822 7331 ; electronic mail;
mailing service

(P-5230)
MASTER BUILDERS LLC
Degussa Construction
9060 Haven Ave, Rancho Cucamonga
(91730-5405)
PHONE....................................909 987-1758
Dave Lougheed, *Manager*
EMP: 799
SALES (corp-wide): 2.1MM Privately
Held
WEB: www.master-builders-solutions.com
SIC: 2899 Chemical preparations
HQ: Master Builders, Llc
23700 Chagrin Blvd
Beachwood OH 44122
800 228-3318

(P-5231)
**MATSUI INTERNATIONAL CO
INC (HQ)**
Also Called: Unimark
1501 W 178th St, Gardena (90248-3203)
PHONE....................................310 767-7812
Masa Matsui, *President*
Elizabeth Botello, *Technical Staff*
Cody Corsano, *Technical Staff*
Sayaka Taira, *Human Resources*
Yoshi Haga, *Opers Mgr*

◆ EMP: 179 EST: 1987
SQ FT: 30,000
SALES (est): 26.3MM Privately Held
WEB: www.matsui-color.com
SIC: 2899 Ink or writing fluids

(P-5232)
MC PRODUCTS INC
23331 Antonio Pkwy, Rcho STA Marg
(92688-2664)
PHONE....................................949 888-7100
Dave Maietta, *President*
EMP: 31 EST: 2003
SQ FT: 36,000
SALES (est): 2.4MM Privately Held
SIC: 2899 Waterproofing compounds

(P-5233)
**MEDICAL CHEMICAL
CORPORATION**
Also Called: M C C
19250 Van Ness Ave, Torrance
(90501-1102)
P.O. Box 6217 (90504-0217)
PHONE....................................310 787-6800
Emmanuel Didier, *President*
Patrick Braden, *Senior VP*
Kris Kontis, *Vice Pres*
Andy Rocha, *Vice Pres*
Elizabeth Escobedo, *Human Res Mgr*
◆ EMP: 45 EST: 1954
SALES (est): 12.1MM Privately Held
WEB: www.med-chem.com
SIC: 2899 2841 Chemical preparations;
soap & other detergents

(P-5234)
**MOC PRODUCTS COMPANY INC
(PA)**
Also Called: Auto Edge Solutions
12306 Montague St, Pacoima
(91331-2279)
PHONE....................................818 794-3500
Mark Waco, *CEO*
Dave Waco, *Vice Pres*
Vidyalakshmi Raman, *Office Mgr*
Alan Hope, *Info Tech Dir*
Dean Puett, *Design Engr*
◆ EMP: 75
SQ FT: 100,000
SALES (est): 73.9MM Privately Held
WEB: www.mocproducts.com
SIC: 2899 7549 5169 Corrosion preven-
tive lubricant; automotive maintenance
services; chemicals & allied products

(P-5235)
NALCO COMPANY LLC
2111 E Dominguez St, Long Beach
(90810-1087)
PHONE....................................310 900-5400
James Ford, *Principal*
Todd Haverlock, *Executive*
Jerry Means, *Admin Mgr*
Fred Casey, *Plant Mgr*
Mohammad Zaheer, *Plant Supt*
▲ EMP: 58 EST: 2000
SALES (est): 8.1MM
SALES (corp-wide): 11.7B Publicly Held
WEB: www.ecolab.com
SIC: 2899 Chemical preparations
HQ: Nalco Holding Company
1601 W Diehl Rd
Naperville IL 60563
630 305-1000

(P-5236)
OLDE THOMPSON LLC
3250 Camino Del Sol, Oxnard
(93030-8998)
PHONE....................................805 983-0388
David Sugarman, *CEO*
Jeffrey M Shumway, *Chairman*
Larry Valenzuela, *General Mgr*
Marcus Merchant, *Info Tech Dir*
Debbie Harrison, *Technical Mgr*
◆ EMP: 225 EST: 1917
SQ FT: 88,000
SALES (est): 75.4MM Privately Held
WEB: www.oldethompson.com
SIC: 2899 2099 5149 Salt; seasonings &
spices; spices & seasonings

(P-5237)
**PACIFIC WTRPRFING RSTRTION
INC**
2845 Pomona Blvd, Pomona (91768-3242)
PHONE....................................909 444-3052
Ronald Bithell, *CEO*
Tony Bithell, *Vice Pres*
Brian Rhode, *Manager*
EMP: 27 EST: 2005
SALES (est): 4MM Privately Held
WEB: www.pacificwaterproofing.com
SIC: 2899 7641 Waterproofing com-
pounds; antique furniture repair & restora-
tion

(P-5238)
**PRESTONE PRODUCTS
CORPORATION**
Also Called: Kik Custom Products
19500 Mariner Ave, Torrance (90503-1644)
PHONE....................................424 271-4836
Raymond Yu, *Plant Mgr*
EMP: 30
SALES (corp-wide): 2B Privately Held
WEB: www.prestone.com
SIC: 2899 5531 5169 Antifreeze com-
pounds; automotive parts; anti-freeze
compounds
HQ: Prestone Products Corporation
6250 N River Rd Ste 6000
Rosemont IL 60018

(P-5239)
**PURE-CHEM PRODUCTS
COMPANY INC**
8371 Monroe Ave, Stanton (90680-2613)
PHONE....................................714 995-4141
Bruce Bereiter, *General Mgr*
William J Roe, *Exec VP*
EMP: 35 EST: 1973
SQ FT: 2,400
SALES (est): 4.3MM Privately Held
SIC: 2899 Chemical preparations

(P-5240)
RELTON CORPORATION
317 Rolyn Pl, Arcadia (91007-2838)
P.O. Box 60019 (91066-6019)
PHONE....................................800 423-1505
William Kinard, *Chairman*
Craig Kinard, *President*
Wm Craig Kinard, *CEO*
Kevin Kinard, *Treasurer*
Darcey Arena, *Vice Pres*
◆ EMP: 65 EST: 1946
SQ FT: 20,000
SALES (est): 11.3MM Privately Held
WEB: www.relton.com
SIC: 2899 3423 3546 2992 Chemical
preparations; masons' hand tools; power-
driven handtools; lubricating oils &
greases

(P-5241)
**ROYAL ADHESIVES &
SEALANTS LLC**
800 E Anaheim St, Wilmington
(90744-3637)
PHONE....................................310 830-9904
Theodore M Clark, *Mng Member*
Suanne Stevens, *Vice Pres*
Jeff Swindells, *Branch Mgr*
Michael Leuschner, *General Mgr*
Mel Miller, *General Mgr*
▲ EMP: 20 EST: 2006
SALES (est): 5.5MM
SALES (corp-wide): 2.7B Publicly Held
WEB: www.hbfuller.com
SIC: 2899 3479 Waterproofing com-
pounds; painting, coating & hot dipping
PA: H.B. Fuller Company
1200 Willow Lake Blvd
Saint Paul MN 55110
651 236-5900

(P-5242)
SIKA CORPORATION
12767 Imperial Hwy, Santa Fe Springs
(90670-4711)
PHONE....................................562 941-0231
Jerry Monarch, *Branch Mgr*
Jon Watson, *QC Dir*
Michael Winge, *Marketing Staff*
Evert Wells, *Maintence Staff*

P R O D U C T S & S V C S

EMP: 17
SQ FT: 26,186
SALES (corp-wide): 8.6B **Privately Held**
WEB: www.usa.sika.com
SIC: 2899 Concrete curing & hardening compounds
HQ: Sika Corporation
201 Polito Ave
Lyndhurst NJ 07071
201 933-8800

(P-5243)
SOUTH ORANGE COUNTY WW AUTH
34156 Del Obispo St, Dana Point (92629-2916)
PHONE..................949 234-5400
Brian Peck, *Principal*
Bruno Santos, *Prgrmr*
David Lloyd, *IT/INT Sup*
Jim Burror, *Opers Staff*
Katie Greenwood, *Manager*
EMP: 17 **EST:** 2004
SALES (est): 4.1MM **Privately Held**
WEB: www.socwa.com
SIC: 2899 Water treating compounds

(P-5244)
TRI SERVICE CO INC
2465 Loma Ave, South El Monte (91733-1415)
P.O. Box 3513 (91733-0513)
PHONE..................626 442-3270
Jeff Rein, *CEO*
Elinore Rein, *Corp Secy*
EMP: 31 **EST:** 1963
SQ FT: 8,300
SALES (est): 2.3MM **Privately Held**
SIC: 2899 7699 5084 Water treating compounds; boiler repair shop; industrial machinery & equipment

(P-5245)
UNITED PHARMA LLC
2317 Moore Ave, Fullerton (92833-2510)
PHONE..................714 738-8999
Bill Wang, *President*
Cathy Maranan, *Purchasing*
George Koo, *Prdtn Mgr*
Thanh Huynh, *Production*
Kamal Kho, *Asst Mgr*
▲ **EMP:** 130 **EST:** 2006
SQ FT: 53,000
SALES (est): 29.1MM **Privately Held**
WEB: www.unitedpharmallc.com
SIC: 2899 Gelatin: edible, technical, photographic or pharmaceutical

(P-5246)
URETHANE POLYMER INTERNATIONAL
10880 Poplar Ave, Fontana (92337-7336)
PHONE..................909 357-7200
James Bolotin, *Vice Pres*
Phyllis Smith, *Office Mgr*
Phyllis Smithjames, *Office Admin*
EMP: 16
SALES (corp-wide): 11.1MM **Privately Held**
WEB: www.urethanepolymers.com
SIC: 2899 Waterproofing compounds
HQ: Urethane Polymer International
3800 E 91st St
Cleveland OH 44105
216 430-3655

2911 Petroleum Refining

(P-5247)
ACCU-BLEND CORPORATION
364 Malbert St, Perris (92570-8336)
PHONE..................626 334-7744
Xia Wang, *CEO*
Kenny Wang, *President*
▲ **EMP:** 17 **EST:** 2005
SALES (est): 3.5MM **Privately Held**
WEB: www.accu-blend.com
SIC: 2911 Paraffin wax

(P-5248)
AIR PRODUCTS AND CHEMICALS INC
3700 W 190th St, Torrance (90504-5733)
PHONE..................310 212-2800

Pete Trelenberg, *Manager*
Thomas L Connor, *Vice Pres*
Brad Nack, *Project Mgr*
EMP: 15
SALES (corp-wide): 8.8B **Publicly Held**
WEB: www.airproducts.com
SIC: 2911 5541 Petroleum refining; gasoline service stations
PA: Air Products And Chemicals, Inc.
7201 Hamilton Blvd
Allentown PA 18195
610 481-4911

(P-5249)
CASTAIC TRUCK STOP INC
31611 Castaic Rd, Castaic (91384-3939)
PHONE..................661 295-1374
Sarkis Khrimian, *President*
Refe Dimmuck, *Opers Mgr*
EMP: 26 **EST:** 1994
SQ FT: 2,000
SALES (est): 3.9MM **Privately Held**
WEB: www.castaictrucksupply.com
SIC: 2911 7389 5812 Diesel fuels; flea market; American restaurant

(P-5250)
D-1280-X INC
Also Called: Omstar Environmental Products
126 N Marine Ave, Wilmington (90744-5723)
P.O. Box 6293, San Pedro (90734-6293)
PHONE..................310 835-6909
Roberta L Skaggs, *CEO*
Richard J Skaggs, *President*
Howard Sargent, *Exec VP*
EMP: 18 **EST:** 1989
SQ FT: 7,500
SALES (est): 2.5MM **Privately Held**
WEB: www.d-1280x.com
SIC: 2911 5169 Fuel additives; chemical additives

(P-5251)
DE MENNO-KERDOON TRADING CO (HQ)
2000 N Alameda St, Compton (90222-2702)
PHONE..................310 537-7100
Jim Ennis, *COO*
Jay Demel, *Vice Pres*
Jim Tice, *Mktg Dir*
N Bonnie Booth, *Manager*
EMP: 149 **EST:** 1990
SQ FT: 60,000
SALES (est): 37.8MM
SALES (corp-wide): 128.1MM **Privately Held**
WEB: www.worldoilcorp.com
SIC: 2911 Oils, fuel
PA: World Oil Marketing Company
9302 Garfield Ave
South Gate CA 90280
562 928-0100

(P-5252)
LION TANK LINE INC
5801 Randolph St, Commerce (90040-3415)
PHONE..................323 726-1966
Levon Termandjyan, *President*
EMP: 20 **EST:** 1992
SQ FT: 6,000
SALES (est): 1.4MM **Privately Held**
SIC: 2911 4213 Diesel fuels; liquid petroleum transport, non-local

(P-5253)
LOS ANGELES REFINING CO
2101 E Pacific Coast Hwy, Wilmington (90744-2914)
PHONE..................310 522-6000
EMP: 14 **EST:** 2003
SALES (est): 422.9K **Privately Held**
SIC: 2911 Petroleum refining

(P-5254)
M ARGESO & CO INC
2628 River Ave, Rosemead (91770-3302)
PHONE..................626 573-3000
G Douglas Orr, *President*
Jim Mallory, *Manager*
EMP: 17 **EST:** 2001
SALES (est): 3.1MM **Privately Held**
WEB: www.paramelt.com
SIC: 2911 Paraffin wax

(P-5255)
MOLECULUM
3128 Red Hill Ave, Costa Mesa (92626-4525)
PHONE..................714 619-5139
Ivan Krylov, *Regional Mgr*
EMP: 18 **EST:** 2015
SALES (est): 1.3MM **Privately Held**
WEB: www.moleculum.com
SIC: 2911 Aromatic chemical products

(P-5256)
PARAMOUNT PETROLEUM CORP (DH)
Also Called: Paramount Asphalt
14700 Downey Ave, Paramount (90723-4526)
PHONE..................562 531-2060
W S Lovejoy, *CEO*
Steve S Farkas, *President*
Glenn Clausen, *Vice Pres*
Kathryn Gleeson, *Vice Pres*
Allan Moret, *Vice Pres*
◆ **EMP:** 155 **EST:** 1980
SQ FT: 6,000
SALES (est): 77.5MM
SALES (corp-wide): 7.3B **Publicly Held**
WEB: www.ppcla.com
SIC: 2911 Petroleum refining

(P-5257)
PBF ENERGY WESTERN REGION LLC (DH)
111 W Ocean Blvd Ste 1500, Long Beach (90802-7907)
PHONE..................973 455-7500
Thomas J Nimbley, *CEO*
EMP: 239 **EST:** 2015
SALES (est): 414.7MM
SALES (corp-wide): 15.1B **Publicly Held**
WEB: www.pbfenergy.com
SIC: 2911 2992 Petroleum refining; lubricating oils

(P-5258)
R GAS LLC
30045 Road 196, Exeter (93221-9772)
PHONE..................559 592-2456
Franklin D Ross, *Principal*
EMP: 17 **EST:** 2006
SALES (est): 1.2MM **Privately Held**
SIC: 2911 Gases & liquefied petroleum gases

(P-5259)
RESIDUAL INCOME OPPRTNTIES INC
4580 E Thsand Oaks Blvd S, Westlake Village (91362)
PHONE..................818 991-1999
Reuven Cypers, *CEO*
EMP: 13 **EST:** 2013
SALES (est): 2.3MM **Privately Held**
SIC: 2911 Residues

(P-5260)
SAN JOAQUIN REFINING CO INC
3500 Shell St, Bakersfield (93308-5215)
P.O. Box 5576 (93388-5576)
PHONE..................661 327-4257
Kenneth E Fait, *Ch of Bd*
Majid Mojibi, *President*
Dorothy A Gribben, *Admin Sec*
David Pinkston, *Info Tech Mgr*
Jerry McKnight, *Project Mgr*
EMP: 130 **EST:** 1979
SQ FT: 15,000
SALES (est): 34.1MM **Privately Held**
WEB: www.sjr.com
SIC: 2911 Oils, fuel

(P-5261)
TESORO REFINING & MKTG CO LLC
5905 N Paramount Blvd, Long Beach (90805-3709)
PHONE..................562 728-2215
EMP: 56 **Publicly Held**
SIC: 2911 5541 Petroleum refining; gasoline service stations

HQ: Tesoro Refining & Marketing Company Llc
19100 Ridgewood Pkwy
San Antonio TX 78259
210 828-8484

(P-5262)
TORRANCE REFINING COMPANY LLC
3700 W 190th St, Torrance (90504-5733)
PHONE..................310 212-2800
Thomas J Nimbley, *CEO*
EMP: 600 **EST:** 2015
SALES (est): 373.6MM
SALES (corp-wide): 15.1B **Publicly Held**
WEB: www.pbfenergy.com
SIC: 2911 2992 Petroleum refining; lubricating oils
HQ: Pbf Energy Western Region Llc
111 W Ocean Blvd Ste 1500
Long Beach CA 90802
973 455-7500

(P-5263)
TRICOR REFINING LLC
1134 Manor St, Bakersfield (93308-3553)
P.O. Box 5877 (93388-5877)
PHONE..................661 393-7110
Majid Mojibi, *Mng Member*
Merlin Minghini, *Finance Mgr*
Don Brookes, *Mng Member*
Kenneth E Fait, *Mng Member*
Marilyn Vallembois, *Manager*
EMP: 28 **EST:** 2001
SALES (est): 9.7MM **Privately Held**
WEB: www.tricorrefining.com
SIC: 2911 Oils, fuel

(P-5264)
UBI ENERGY CORPORATION
9465 Wilshire Blvd # 300, Beverly Hills (90212-2612)
PHONE..................310 283-6978
EMP: 200
SALES: 120MM **Privately Held**
SIC: 2911 Petroleum Refiner

(P-5265)
ULTRAMAR INC
Also Called: Village Center Ultramar
9508 E Palmdale Blvd, Palmdale (93591-2202)
PHONE..................661 944-2496
Ken Berglund, *Manager*
EMP: 27
SALES (corp-wide): 64.9B **Publicly Held**
SIC: 2911 Petroleum refining
HQ: Ultramar Inc.
1 Valero Way
San Antonio TX 78249
210 345-2000

(P-5266)
VALERO REF COMPANY-CALIFORNIA
2401 E Anaheim St, Wilmington (90744-4009)
PHONE..................562 491-6754
Mark Thair, *Manager*
EMP: 1194
SALES (corp-wide): 64.9B **Publicly Held**
SIC: 2911 Petroleum refining
HQ: Valero Refining Company-California
1 Valero Way
San Antonio TX 78249
210 345-2000

(P-5267)
VENOCO INC
7979 Hollister Ave, Goleta (93117-2421)
PHONE..................805 961-2305
EMP: 40
SALES (corp-wide): 224.2MM **Privately Held**
SIC: 2911 5172 Petroleum Refiner Whol Petroleum Products
HQ: Venoco, Inc.
370 17th St Ste 3900
Denver CO 80202
303 626-8300

2951 Paving Mixtures & Blocks

(P-5268)
ADVANCED EROSION SERVICES
175 N Cawston Ave Ste 170, Hemet
(92545-5254)
PHONE..................951 929-8780
EMP: 15 EST: 2015
SALES (est): 3.4MM Privately Held
WEB: www.aeserosion.com
SIC: 2951 Asphalt paving mixtures & blocks

(P-5269)
CALMAT CO (DH)
Also Called: Vulcan Materials
500 N Brand Blvd Ste 500 # 500, Glendale
(91203-3319)
PHONE..................818 553-8821
Tom Hill, CEO
James W Smack, President
Danny R Shepherd, COO
Daniel F Sansone, CFO
Cindy Vu, Vice Pres
EMP: 150 EST: 1891
SQ FT: 40,000
SALES (est): 976.9MM Publicly Held
WEB: www.vulcanmaterials.com
SIC: 2951 1442 1429 3273 Asphalt & asphaltic paving mixtures (not from refineries); construction sand & gravel; igneous rock, crushed & broken-quarrying; ready-mixed concrete; commercial & industrial building operation; land subdividers & developers, residential
HQ: Legacy Vulcan, Llc
1200 Urban Center Dr
Vestavia AL 35242
205 298-3000

(P-5270)
DELTA TRADING LP
Also Called: Crimson Resource Management
17731 Millux Rd, Bakersfield (93311-9714)
PHONE..................661 834-5560
Mike Purdy, Partner
Rob McElroy, General Mgr
Ernie Martinez, Manager
EMP: 20 EST: 2004
SALES (est): 4.9MM Privately Held
WEB: www.deltatradinglp.com
SIC: 2951 Asphalt paving mixtures & blocks

(P-5271)
DESERT BLOCK CO INC
11374 Tuxford St, Sun Valley (91352-2636)
PHONE..................661 824-2624
Bill Fenzel, President
William Gapastione, Vice Pres
EMP: 33 EST: 1991
SALES (est): 6MM Privately Held
WEB: www.angelusblock.com
SIC: 2951 3272 Concrete, asphaltic (not from refineries); concrete products, precast

(P-5272)
GOLDSTAR ASPHALT PRODUCTS INC
1354 Jet Way, Perris (92571-7466)
PHONE..................951 940-1610
Jeff S Nelson, President
EMP: 32 EST: 1997
SALES (est): 2.8MM Privately Held
WEB: www.goldstarasphalt.com
SIC: 2951 Asphalt paving mixtures & blocks

(P-5273)
HUNTMIX INC
Also Called: Calmut Industrial Asphalt
500 N Brand Blvd Ste 500, Glendale
(91203-3319)
PHONE..................818 548-5200
Fax: 323 254-1191
EMP: 165
SQ FT: 70,000
SALES (est): 12MM
SALES (corp-wide): 2.9B Publicly Held
SIC: 2951 Mfg Asphalt Paving Materials

HQ: Calmat Co.
500 N Brand Blvd Ste 500
Glendale CA 91203
818 553-8821

(P-5274)
LEWIS BARRICADE INC
4000 Westerly Pl Ste 100, Newport Beach
(92660-2347)
PHONE..................661 363-0912
John R Lewis, President
Teresa Lewis, Corp Secy
EMP: 54 EST: 1998
SQ FT: 20,000
SALES (est): 1.8MM Privately Held
SIC: 2951 7353 Concrete, asphaltic (not from refineries); heavy construction equipment rental

(P-5275)
NPG INC (PA)
Also Called: Goldstar Asphalt Products
1354 Jet Way, Perris (92571-7466)
P.O. Box 1515 (92572-1515)
PHONE..................951 940-0200
Jeff Nelson, President
Sharon Nelson, Officer
Vicki Pritchett,
EMP: 55 EST: 1962
SQ FT: 6,900
SALES (est): 15.6MM Privately Held
WEB: www.npgasphalt.com
SIC: 2951 1799 1771 Asphalt & asphaltic paving mixtures (not from refineries); parking lot maintenance; driveway, parking lot & blacktop contractors

(P-5276)
PAVEMENT RECYCLING SYSTEMS INC
Also Called: West Coast Milling
46205 Division St, Lancaster (93535-5908)
PHONE..................661 948-5599
Steve Ward, Manager
Jolena Jordan, Administration
EMP: 60
SQ FT: 1,000 Privately Held
WEB: www.pavementrecycling.com
SIC: 2951 1611 Asphalt paving mixtures & blocks; surfacing & paving
PA: Pavement Recycling Systems, Inc.
10240 San Sevaine Way
Jurupa Valley CA 91752

(P-5277)
RECYCLED AGGREGATE MTLS CO INC (PA)
Also Called: Ramco
2655 1st St Ste 210, Simi Valley
(93065-1578)
PHONE..................805 522-1646
Dennis L Newman, President
Mark Heinzman, General Mgr
EMP: 18 EST: 2006
SALES (est): 3.3MM Privately Held
WEB: www.ramco.us.com
SIC: 2951 Concrete, asphaltic (not from refineries)

(P-5278)
WORLD OIL MARKETING COMPANY (PA)
9302 Garfield Ave, South Gate
(90280-3805)
P.O. Box 1966 (90280-1966)
PHONE..................562 928-0100
Robert S Roth, President
Dave Palmer, Treasurer
Christopher Norton, Officer
Sue Gornick, Vice Pres
Florence Roth, Vice Pres
EMP: 20 EST: 1977
SQ FT: 60,000
SALES (est): 128.1MM Privately Held
WEB: www.worldoilcorp.com
SIC: 5411 2951 5541 4213 Convenience stores; paving mixtures; gasoline service stations; liquid petroleum transport, non-local; petroleum haulage, local; asphalt or asphaltic materials, made in refineries

2952 Asphalt Felts & Coatings

(P-5279)
FONTANA PAPER MILLS INC
13733 Valley Blvd, Fontana (92335-5268)
P.O. Box 339 (92334-0339)
PHONE..................909 823-4100
George Thagard III, President
Jeff Thagard, Executive
Casey Tzeng, Executive
Ray G Thagard Jr, Admin Sec
Miguel Trejo, Manager
EMP: 56 EST: 1967
SQ FT: 28,000
SALES (est): 11.6MM Privately Held
WEB: www.fontanaroof.com
SIC: 2952 2621 Roofing materials; felts, building

(P-5280)
HCO HOLDING II CORPORATION
999 N Pacific Coast Hwy, El Segundo
(90245-2714)
PHONE..................310 955-9200
Brian C Strauss, President
Jeff Wedge, Vice Pres
Todd Skopic, Manager
EMP: 560 EST: 2005
SALES (est): 249.7MM
SALES (corp-wide): 254.1MM Privately Held
SIC: 2952 2821 2891 Roof cement: asphalt, fibrous or plastic; polyurethane resins; sealants
HQ: Hco Holding I Corporation
999 N Pacific Coast Hwy # 80
El Segundo CA 90245
323 583-5000

(P-5281)
HENRY COMPANY LLC (HQ)
999 N Pcf Cast Hwy Ste 80, El Segundo
(90245)
PHONE..................310 955-9200
Frank Ready, President
Jason Peel, CFO
Jerry Burch, Officer
Chris Yount, Senior VP
John Dobson, Vice Pres
◆ EMP: 100 EST: 2010
SALES (est): 212.6MM
SALES (corp-wide): 4.2B Publicly Held
WEB: www.henry.com
SIC: 2952 2821 2891 Roof cement: asphalt, fibrous or plastic; polyurethane resins; sealants
PA: Carlisle Companies Incorporated
16430 N Scottsdale Rd
Scottsdale AZ 85254
480 781-5000

(P-5282)
HNC PARENT INC (PA)
999 N Pacific Coast Hwy # 80, El Segundo
(90245-2714)
PHONE..................310 955-9200
Rob Newbold, Principal
Michael Com, Human Res Mgr
EMP: 100
SALES (est): 254.1MM Privately Held
SIC: 2952 2821 2891 Roof cement: asphalt, fibrous or plastic; polyurethane resins; sealants

(P-5283)
JAMES HARDIE TRADING CO INC
26300 La Alameda Ste 400, Mission Viejo
(92691-8372)
PHONE..................949 582-2378
Bryon G Borgardt, President
EMP: 160 EST: 1995
SALES (est): 30MM Privately Held
WEB: www.jameshardie.com
SIC: 2952 Siding materials
HQ: James Hardie Transition Co., Inc.
26300 La Alameda Ste 400
Mission Viejo CA 92691
949 348-1800

(P-5284)
LUNDAY-THAGARD COMPANY
9301 Garfield Ave, South Gate
(90280-3804)
P.O. Box 1519 (90280-1519)
PHONE..................562 928-6990
John Todorovich, Vice Pres
EMP: 369
SALES (corp-wide): 128.1MM Privately Held
SIC: 2952 2951 Roofing materials; asphalt paving mixtures & blocks
HQ: Lunday-Thagard Company
9302 Garfield Ave
South Gate CA 90280
562 928-7000

(P-5285)
REP-KOTE PRODUCTS INC
10938 Beech Ave, Fontana (92337-7260)
PHONE..................909 355-1288
Robert Wang, President
EMP: 15 EST: 1981
SQ FT: 20,000
SALES (est): 358.4K Privately Held
SIC: 2952 5084 Asphalt felts & coatings; water pumps (industrial)

(P-5286)
TROPICAL ASPHALT LLC (PA)
Also Called: Tropical Roofing Products CA
14435 Macaw St, La Mirada (90638-5210)
PHONE..................714 739-1408
Richard Zegelbone,
Michael King, Vice Pres
Yolanda Green, Controller
Omar Rivero, Purchasing
Edward Leshansky, Marketing Staff
EMP: 15 EST: 1998
SQ FT: 27,000
SALES (est): 9.7MM Privately Held
WEB: www.tropicalroofingproducts.com
SIC: 2952 Asphalt felts & coatings

2992 Lubricating Oils & Greases

(P-5287)
AOCLSC INC
Also Called: Aocusa
8015 Paramount Blvd, Pico Rivera
(90660-4811)
PHONE..................813 248-1988
Harry Barkett, Branch Mgr
EMP: 150
SALES (corp-wide): 46.9MM Privately Held
SIC: 2992 Lubricating oils
PA: Aoclsc, Inc.
1601 Mcclosky Blvd
Tampa FL 33605
813 248-1988

(P-5288)
AOCLSC INC
Also Called: Aocusa
3365 E Slauson Ave, Vernon (90058-3914)
PHONE..................562 776-4000
Stephen Milam, CEO
Alex Ip, Admin Asst
Richard Scott, Business Mgr
Vartan Vartanov, Director
Sharon Alvarenga, Manager
EMP: 30
SALES (corp-wide): 46.9MM Privately Held
SIC: 2992 Lubricating oils & greases
PA: Aoclsc, Inc.
1601 Mcclosky Blvd
Tampa FL 33605
813 248-1988

(P-5289)
CHAMPIONS CHOICE INC
1910 E Via Burton, Anaheim (92806-1228)
PHONE..................714 635-4491
Adam W Huber, Ch of Bd
Al Baudoin, President
Melodie Reguero, Treasurer
Patrick Huber, Vice Pres
Candace Baudoin, Admin Sec
EMP: 14 EST: 1977
SQ FT: 20,000

PRODUCTS & SVCS

SALES (est): 603.5K **Privately Held**
SIC: 2992 Lubricating oils

(P-5290)
CHEM ARROW CORP
13643 Live Oak Ln, Irwindale
(91706-1317)
P.O. Box 2366, Baldwin Park (91706-1198)
PHONE..................................626 358-2255
Alphonse Spalding, *Ch of Bd*
Hemith Mitchello, *President*
Alex Klubnikin, *Plant Mgr*
▼ EMP: 25 EST: 1977
SQ FT: 36,000
SALES (est): 5.5MM **Privately Held**
WEB: www.chemarrow.com
SIC: 2992 2899 Lubricating oils; rust arresting compounds, animal or vegetable oil base; fuel tank or engine cleaning chemicals; metal treating compounds; rust resisting compounds

(P-5291)
CHEMTOOL INCORPORATED
1300 Goodrick Dr, Tehachapi (93561-1508)
PHONE..................................661 823-7190
Bill Hart, *Manager*
EMP: 115
SALES (corp-wide): 245.5B **Publicly Held**
WEB: www.chemtool.com
SIC: 2992 2899 5172 Oils & greases, blending & compounding; chemical preparations; lubricating oils & greases
HQ: Chemtool Incorporated
801 W Rockton Rd
Rockton IL 61072
815 957-4140

(P-5292)
DEMENNO/KERDOON HOLDINGS
Also Called: D K Environmental
3650 E 26th St, Vernon (90058-4104)
PHONE..................................323 268-3387
Rodney Ananda, *Manager*
Bhavesh Shah, *Technician*
EMP: 16
SALES (corp-wide): 128.1MM **Privately Held**
SIC: 2992 4953 Oils & greases, blending & compounding; re-refining lubricating oils & greases; transmission fluid: made from purchased materials; refuse systems
HQ: Demenno/Kerdoon Holdings
9302 Garfield Ave
South Gate CA 90280
562 231-1550

(P-5293)
DEMENNO/KERDOON HOLDINGS (DH)
Also Called: Demenno-Kerdoon
9302 Garfield Ave, South Gate (90280-3805)
PHONE..................................562 231-1550
Robert Roth, *Ch of Bd*
Bruce Demenno, *CEO*
Steve Kerdoon, *COO*
Mark Snell, *Principal*
Roger Graves, *Safety Dir*
EMP: 67 EST: 1971
SQ FT: 21,000
SALES (est): 37.1MM
SALES (corp-wide): 128.1MM **Privately Held**
SIC: 2992 2911 Oils & greases, blending & compounding; re-refining lubricating oils & greases; transmission fluid: made from purchased materials; petroleum refining

(P-5294)
EVERGREEN HOLDINGS INC (PA)
18952 Macarthur Blvd # 410, Irvine (92612-1402)
PHONE..................................949 757-7770
Jacob Voogd, *Ch of Bd*
Gary Colbert, *President*
Jesus Romero, *CFO*
Atam Gossain, *Admin Sec*
▲ EMP: 20 EST: 1981
SQ FT: 6,200

SALES (est): 20.6MM **Privately Held**
SIC: 2992 4953 Re-refining lubricating oils & greases; liquid waste, collection & disposal

(P-5295)
EVERGREEN OIL INC (HQ)
Also Called: Evergreen Environmental Svcs
18025 S Broadway, Gardena (90248-3539)
PHONE..................................949 757-7770
Jake Voogd, *CEO*
Jesus Romero, *CFO*
George Lamont, *Exec VP*
Obert Gwaltney, *VP Opers*
EMP: 203 EST: 1983
SALES (est): 45.8MM
SALES (corp-wide): 3.1B **Publicly Held**
WEB: www.cleanharbors.com
SIC: 2992 2911 4953 Lubricating oils & greases; petroleum refining; refuse systems
PA: Clean Harbors, Inc.
42 Longwater Dr
Norwell MA 02061
781 792-5000

(P-5296)
EZ LUBE LLC
532 W Florida Ave, Hemet (92543-4007)
PHONE..................................951 766-1996
Richie Berling, *Manager*
EMP: 67
SALES (corp-wide): 22.5MM **Privately Held**
WEB: www.vioc.com
SIC: 2992 Lubricating oils
PA: Ez Lube, Llc
3540 Howard Way Ste 200
Costa Mesa CA

(P-5297)
LUBECO INC
6859 Downey Ave, Long Beach (90805-1967)
PHONE..................................562 602-1791
Steven Rossi, *President*
EMP: 45 EST: 1958
SQ FT: 20,000
SALES (est): 6.4MM **Privately Held**
WEB: www.lubecoinc.com
SIC: 2992 2851 Lubricating oils & greases; paints & allied products

(P-5298)
SALCO DYNAMIC SOLUTIONS INC (PA)
Also Called: Salco Oil
6248 Surfpoint Cir, Huntington Beach (92648-5590)
PHONE..................................714 374-7500
Lucy George, *CEO*
Scott George, *CFO*
EMP: 23 EST: 2003 **Privately Held**
WEB: www.salcooils.com
SIC: 2992 5172 5085 5084 Oils & greases, blending & compounding; petroleum products; industrial supplies; industrial machinery & equipment; machine tools, metal cutting type; machine tool accessories

(P-5299)
VAST ENTERPRISES
Also Called: Liquid Packaging
7739 Monroe St, Paramount (90723-5020)
PHONE..................................562 633-3224
Joe Mouren-Laurens, *CEO*
Dean Mouren-Laurens, *Vice Pres*
EMP: 13 EST: 1977
SQ FT: 18,000
SALES (est): 3.1MM **Privately Held**
WEB: www.liquidpackagingcompany.com
SIC: 2992 Transmission fluid: made from purchased materials

2999 Products Of Petroleum & Coal, NEC

(P-5300)
LUNDAY-THAGARD COMPANY (HQ)
Also Called: Ltr
9302 Garfield Ave, South Gate (90280-3805)
P.O. Box 1519 (90280-1519)
PHONE..................................562 928-7000
Bernard B Roth, *Ch of Bd*
Robert Roth, *President*
Austin Miller, *COO*
Larry Mori, *Vice Pres*
Steve Roth, *Vice Pres*
EMP: 106 EST: 1937
SQ FT: 16,000
SALES (est): 52MM
SALES (corp-wide): 128.1MM **Privately Held**
WEB: www.worldoilcorp.com
SIC: 2999 2951 2911 Coke; paving blocks; gases & liquefied petroleum gases
PA: World Oil Marketing Company
9302 Garfield Ave
South Gate CA 90280
562 928-0100

(P-5301)
RENTECH INC (PA)
10880 Wilshire Blvd # 1101, Los Angeles (90024-4112)
PHONE..................................310 571-9800
Keith Forman, *President*
Halbert S Washburn, *Ch of Bd*
Keith B Forman, *President*
Paul M Summers, *CFO*
Joseph V Herold, *Senior VP*
EMP: 274 EST: 1981
SQ FT: 600
SALES (est): 150.7MM **Privately Held**
WEB: www.rentechinc.com
SIC: 2999 2873 6794 Waxes, petroleum: not produced in petroleum refineries; nitrogenous fertilizers; patent buying, licensing, leasing

3011 Tires & Inner Tubes

(P-5302)
HSB HOLDINGS INC
14050 Day St, Moreno Valley (92553-9106)
PHONE..................................951 214-6590
Ohannes Beudjekian, *Ch of Bd*
Sarkis Beudjeaian, *CEO*
▲ EMP: 40 EST: 1989
SQ FT: 80,000
SALES (est): 5.2MM **Privately Held**
WEB: www.basrecycling.com
SIC: 3011 Tires, cushion or solid rubber

(P-5303)
ITW GLOBAL TIRE REPAIR INC
Also Called: Access Marketing
125 Venture Dr Ste 210, San Luis Obispo (93401-9105)
PHONE..................................805 489-0490
E Scott Santi, *Ch of Bd*
Rodney Cegelski, *Exec VP*
Ken Manning, *Analyst*
◆ EMP: 71 EST: 1993
SQ FT: 20,000
SALES (est): 16.4MM
SALES (corp-wide): 12.5B **Publicly Held**
WEB: www.slime.com
SIC: 3011 Tire & inner tube materials & related products
PA: Illinois Tool Works Inc.
155 Harlem Ave
Glenview IL 60025
847 724-7500

(P-5304)
MCLAREN INDUSTRIES INC (PA)
1515 W 190th St Ste 528, Gardena (90248-4900)
PHONE..................................310 212-1333
Richardson Doyle, *CEO*
George Valev, *CFO*

◆ EMP: 17 EST: 1997
SALES (est): 4.7MM **Privately Held**
WEB: www.mclarenindustries.com
SIC: 3011 Automobile tires, pneumatic

(P-5305)
SKAT-TRAK
654 Avenue K, Calimesa (92320-1115)
P.O. Box 518 (92320-0518)
PHONE..................................909 795-2505
Ken Stuart, *President*
Diane Stuart, *Corp Secy*
EMP: 26 EST: 1952
SQ FT: 3,000
SALES (est): 3.5MM **Privately Held**
WEB: www.skat-trak.com
SIC: 3011 3599 3366 Tires & inner tubes; propellers, ship & boat: machined; copper foundries

(P-5306)
TOYO TIRE HLDINGS AMERICAS INC (HQ)
5665 Plaza Dr Ste 200, Cypress (90630-5066)
PHONE..................................562 431-6502
Tomoshige Mizutani, *CEO*
Jeffrey Bootz, *Sales Staff*
Angelo Naval, *Sales Staff*
▲ EMP: 20 EST: 1988
SALES (est): 616.1MM **Privately Held**
WEB: www.toyotires.com
SIC: 3011 Automobile inner tubes

(P-5307)
YOKOHAMA CORP NORTH AMERICA (HQ)
Also Called: Yokohama Tire
1 Macarthur Pl Ste 800, Santa Ana (92707-5948)
PHONE..................................540 389-5426
Yasuo Tominaga, *CEO*
Takaharu Fushimi, *CFO*
Jim Hobbs, *Officer*
Brian Ballard, *Planning*
Patrick Huang, *Design Engr*
◆ EMP: 250 EST: 1917
SQ FT: 450,000
SALES (est): 710.6MM **Privately Held**
WEB: www.yokohamatire.com
SIC: 3011 5014 Tires & inner tubes; tires & tubes

3021 Rubber & Plastic Footwear

(P-5308)
FOUR STAR DISTRIBUTION
206 Calle Conchita, San Clemente (92672-5404)
PHONE..................................949 369-4420
Markus Bohi, *CEO*
Raul Ries, *President*
▲ EMP: 53 EST: 1991
SALES (est): 3.4MM **Privately Held**
SIC: 3021 Shoes, plastic soles molded to fabric uppers

(P-5309)
K-SWISS INC (HQ)
523 W 6th St Ste 534, Los Angeles (90014-1225)
PHONE..................................323 675-2700
Philip Jeong, *Ch of Bd*
Mark Miller, *President*
Barney Waters, *Chief Mktg Ofcr*
Helen Hong, *Vice Pres*
Brian Keating, *Vice Pres*
◆ EMP: 408 EST: 1990
SALES (est): 488.5MM **Privately Held**
WEB: www.kswiss.com
SIC: 3021 Rubber & plastics footwear

(P-5310)
K-SWISS SALES CORP
31248 Oak Crest Dr # 200, Westlake Village (91361-4693)
PHONE..................................818 706-5100
Cheryl Kuchinka, *President*
EMP: 57 EST: 1999
SALES (est): 3.6MM **Privately Held**
WEB: www.kswiss.com
SIC: 3021 Rubber & plastics footwear

HQ: K-Swiss Inc.
523 W 6th St Ste 534
Los Angeles CA 90014
323 675-2700

(P-5311)
NXT FACTORY INC (PA)
1923 Eastman Ave Ste 200, Ventura (93003-8085)
PHONE.................805 340-2340
EMP: 14 EST: 2017
SALES (est): 401.5K Privately Held
WEB: www.nexa3d.com
SIC: 3021 3143 3144 Protective footwear, rubber or plastic; men's footwear, except athletic; women's footwear, except athletic

(P-5312)
PLS DIABETIC SHOE COMPANY INC
21500 Osborne St, Canoga Park (91304-1522)
PHONE.................818 734-7080
Ambartsum Kumuryan, President
Konstandin Kumuryan, COO
▲ EMP: 32 EST: 2004
SQ FT: 24,031
SALES (est): 4.5MM Privately Held
WEB: www.pedorthiclab.com
SIC: 3021 Shoes, rubber or plastic molded to fabric

(P-5313)
PRINCIPLE PLASTICS
1136 W 135th St, Gardena (90247-1919)
P.O. Box 2408 (90247-0408)
PHONE.................310 532-3411
David Hoyt, President
Robert Hoyt, CFO
Russell Hokama,
▲ EMP: 27 EST: 1948
SQ FT: 28,000
SALES (est): 7.5MM Privately Held
WEB: www.sloggers.com
SIC: 3021 3949 2519 Galoshes, plastic; golf equipment; lawn & garden furniture, except wood & metal

(P-5314)
SKECHERS COLLECTION LLC
Also Called: Sketchers
228 Manhattan Beach Blvd, Manhattan Beach (90266-5347)
PHONE.................310 318-3100
Robert Greenberg, Mng Member
Mandy Dimiero, Vice Pres
Michael Macchione, Executive
Joshua Olkes, Executive
Charles Owen, Executive
◆ EMP: 20 EST: 1999
SALES (est): 6.9MM Publicly Held
WEB: www.investors.skechers.com
SIC: 3021 5661 Shoes, rubber or plastic molded to fabric; shoe stores
PA: Skechers U.S.A., Inc.
228 Manhattan Beach Blvd # 200
Manhattan Beach CA 90266

(P-5315)
SKECHERS USA INC
330 S Sepulveda Blvd, Manhattan Beach (90266-6828)
PHONE.................310 318-3100
Jeffrey Greenberg, Vice Pres
Ryan Rossler, Vice Pres
James Beirne, Director
Ally Barron, Manager
Brian Sanchez, Manager
EMP: 25 Publicly Held
WEB: www.skechers.com
SIC: 3021 3149 5661 Shoes, rubber or plastic molded to fabric; athletic shoes, except rubber or plastic; shoe stores
PA: Skechers U.S.A., Inc.
228 Manhattan Beach Blvd # 200
Manhattan Beach CA 90266

(P-5316)
SKECHERS USA INC II (HQ)
228 Manhattan Beach Blvd # 200, Manhattan Beach (90266-5356)
PHONE.................800 746-3411
Robert Greenberg, CEO

Carolina Santiago, General Mgr
David Lamberti, Office Mgr
Ed Jones, Business Mgr
Maria Hernandez, Manager
◆ EMP: 65 EST: 1994
SALES (est): 163.5MM Publicly Held
WEB: www.skechers.com
SIC: 5661 3021 Shoe stores; shoes, rubber or plastic molded to fabric

(P-5317)
SONICSENSORY INC (PA)
1163 Logan St, Los Angeles (90026-3210)
P.O. Box 24, Lake Peekskill NY (10537-0024)
PHONE.................213 336-3747
Susan Paley, CEO
Christopher Long, CFO
Eddie Borjas, CTO
Coady Humphries, Manager
EMP: 17 EST: 2012
SQ FT: 2,000
SALES (est): 3MM Privately Held
WEB: www.droplabs.com
SIC: 3021 Shoes, rubber or rubber soled fabric uppers

(P-5318)
SUMMER RIO CORP (PA)
17501 Rowland St, City of Industry (91748-1115)
PHONE.................626 854-1498
Qing LI, President
Irene Lee, Office Mgr
Lauren Schneider, Accounts Mgr
◆ EMP: 15 EST: 2000
SALES (est): 3.1MM Privately Held
WEB: www.formystore.com
SIC: 3021 Canvas shoes, rubber soled; shoes, plastic soles molded to fabric uppers; shoes, rubber or plastic molded to fabric; shoes, rubber or rubber soled fabric uppers

(P-5319)
VANS INC (DH)
Also Called: Vans Shoes
1588 S Coast Dr, Costa Mesa (92626-1549)
PHONE.................714 755-4000
Arthur I Carver, Senior VP
Scott J Blechman, CFO
Robert L Nagel, Senior VP
Allen E Black, Vice Pres
Craig E Gosselin, Vice Pres
▲ EMP: 263 EST: 1987
SQ FT: 185,000
SALES (est): 511.5MM
SALES (corp-wide): 9.2B Publicly Held
WEB: www.vans.com
SIC: 3021 2321 2329 2325 Canvas shoes, rubber soled; protective footwear, rubber or plastic; boots, rubber or rubber soled fabric; men's & boys' sports & polo shirts; polo shirts, men's & boys': made from purchased materials; men's & boys' sportswear & athletic clothing; jackets (suede, leatherette, etc.), sport: men's & boys'; slacks, dress: men's, youths' & boys'; shorts (outerwear): men's, youths' & boys'; hats, caps & millinery; canvas bags
HQ: Vf Outdoor, Llc
2701 Harbor Bay Pkwy
Alameda CA 94502
855 500-8639

3052 Rubber & Plastic Hose & Belting

(P-5320)
HPS PERFORMANCE PRODUCTS
15332 Valley Blvd, City of Industry (91746-3324)
PHONE.................626 747-9200
Hung Huynh, Principal
EMP: 13 EST: 2018
SALES (est): 464.2K Privately Held
WEB: www.hpsperformanceproducts.com
SIC: 3052 Air line or air brake hose, rubber or rubberized fabric

(P-5321)
NORTH AMERICAN FIRE HOSE CORP
Also Called: Nafhc
910 Noble Way, Santa Maria (93454-1506)
P.O. Box 1968 (93456-1968)
PHONE.................805 922-7076
Michael S Aubuchon, CEO
Virginia Aubuchon, Admin Sec
▲ EMP: 55 EST: 1980
SQ FT: 43,000
SALES (est): 6.4MM Privately Held
WEB: www.nafhc.com
SIC: 3052 Fire hose, rubber

(P-5322)
SANI-TECH WEST INC (HQ)
1020 Flynn Rd, Camarillo (93012-8705)
PHONE.................805 389-0400
Richard J Shor, President
Sherry Maxson, Vice Pres
John Nitsch, Administration
Bob Maxson, Design Engr
Ariana Argend, Technical Staff
EMP: 61 EST: 1991
SQ FT: 27,000
SALES (est): 45MM
SALES (corp-wide): 2.7B Privately Held
WEB: www.sani-techwest.com
SIC: 3052 3053 Rubber hose; gasket materials
PA: 3i Group Plc
16 Palace Street
London SW1E
207 928-3131

(P-5323)
TECHNICAL HEATERS INC
Also Called: Thermolab
10959 Tuxford St, Sun Valley (91352-2626)
PHONE.................818 361-7185
Bruce W Jones, President
EMP: 18 EST: 1969
SQ FT: 35,000
SALES (est): 3MM Privately Held
WEB: www.techheat.com
SIC: 3052 Plastic hose

(P-5324)
TK PAX INC
Also Called: P A X Industries
1561 Macarthur Blvd, Costa Mesa (92626-1407)
PHONE.................714 850-1330
Tom Kawaguchi, President
Randy Tamura, Vice Pres
Armando Martinez, General Mgr
Ann Mundine, Opers Staff
▲ EMP: 30 EST: 1985
SQ FT: 30,000
SALES (est): 5.4MM Privately Held
WEB: www.paxindusties.com
SIC: 3052 3053 Rubber hose; plastic hose; gaskets, all materials

(P-5325)
TTI FLOOR CARE NORTH AMER INC
13055 Valley Blvd, Fontana (92335-2603)
PHONE.................440 996-2802
Ross Verrocchi, Manager
EMP: 83 Privately Held
WEB: www.ttifloorcare.com
SIC: 3052 5722 Vacuum cleaner hose, plastic; vacuum cleaners
HQ: Tti Floor Care North America, Inc.
8405 Ibm Dr
Charlotte NC 28262

3053 Gaskets, Packing & Sealing Devices

(P-5326)
ABLE INDUSTRIAL PRODUCTS INC (PA)
2006 S Baker Ave, Ontario (91761-7709)
PHONE.................909 930-1585
Gilbert J Martinez, CEO
Gloria Martinez, Treasurer
Debbie Viramontes, Admin Sec
Rick Viramontes, Sales Staff
Tyrone Dizon, Manager

▲ EMP: 30 EST: 1974
SQ FT: 21,120
SALES (est): 11MM Privately Held
WEB: www.able123.com
SIC: 3053 3069 5085 Gaskets, all materials; weather strip, sponge rubber; industrial supplies; hose, belting & packing; adhesives, tape & plasters; abrasives

(P-5327)
ADVANCED SEALING (DH)
15500 Blackburn Ave, Norwalk (90650-6845)
PHONE.................562 802-7782
▲ EMP: 64
SQ FT: 35,000
SALES (est): 19MM Privately Held
WEB: www.advseal.com
SIC: 3053 3965 3052 2992 Mfg Gasket/Packing/Seals Mfg Fastener/Button/Pins Mfg Rubr/Plstc Hose/Belt Mfg Lubrictng Oil/Grease
HQ: Eriks North America, Inc.
650 Washington Rd Ste 500
Pittsburgh PA 15228
800 937-9070

(P-5328)
BRYANT RUBBER CORP (PA)
1580 W Carson St, Long Beach (90810-1455)
PHONE.................310 530-2530
Steven Bryant, Principal
William J Bryant, Shareholder
Norman Alexander, CFO
Ash Augustus, CFO
Brogan Bryant, Officer
EMP: 37 EST: 1971
SALES (est): 33.5MM Privately Held
WEB: www.bryantrubber.com
SIC: 3053 Gaskets, packing & sealing devices

(P-5329)
BRYANT RUBBER CORP
Also Called: Ingla Rubber Products
1083 W 251st St, Bellflower (90706)
PHONE.................310 530-2530
Caroline Johns, General Mgr
Saul Arias, Finance Asst
Julie Valdez, Human Res Mgr
Matt Kaminski, VP Sales
Marian Barker, Director
EMP: 113
SALES (corp-wide): 33.5MM Privately Held
WEB: www.bryantrubber.com
SIC: 3053 3061 Gaskets, packing & sealing devices; mechanical rubber goods
PA: Bryant Rubber Corp.
1580 W Carson St
Long Beach CA 90810
310 530-2530

(P-5330)
CALIBER SEALING SOLUTIONS INC (PA)
2780 Palisades Dr, Corona (92882-0631)
PHONE.................949 461-0555
Chris Byers, Mng Member
Jesse Estrada, Manager
▲ EMP: 19 EST: 1983
SALES (est): 2.6MM Privately Held
WEB: www.calibersealingsolutions.com
SIC: 3053 Gaskets, packing & sealing devices

(P-5331)
CANNON GASKET INC
7784 Edison Ave, Fontana (92336-3635)
PHONE.................909 355-1547
Billy Cannon, President
Billy Jr P Cannon, President
Candy Houle, Admin Sec
Mark Muto, Sales Mgr
Travis Cannon, Manager
▲ EMP: 27 EST: 1971
SQ FT: 10,000
SALES (est): 5.4MM Privately Held
WEB: www.cannongasket.com
SIC: 3053 Gaskets, all materials

(P-5332)
CHAVERS GASKET CORPORATION
23325 Del Lago Dr, Laguna Hills (92653-1309)
PHONE..............................949 472-8118
Lloyd Chavers, *President*
Gino Roncelli, *Admin Sec*
EMP: 25 **EST:** 1986
SQ FT: 13,000
SALES (est): 5.2MM **Privately Held**
WEB: www.chaversgasket.com
SIC: 3053 Gaskets, all materials

(P-5333)
CIASONS INDUSTRIAL INC
1615 Boyd St, Santa Ana (92705-5103)
PHONE..............................714 259-0838
Paul Hsieh, *President*
Samuel Hsieh, *CFO*
Grace S P Hsieh, *Admin Sec*
▲ **EMP:** 30 **EST:** 1985
SQ FT: 25,000
SALES (est): 2.5MM **Privately Held**
WEB: www.ciasons.com
SIC: 3053 3563 Packing: steam engines, pipe joints, air compressors, etc.; air & gas compressors

(P-5334)
D W MACK CO INC
900 W 8th St, Azusa (91702-2216)
P.O. Box 1247, Monrovia (91017-1247)
PHONE..............................626 969-1817
Danny J Mack, *President*
Joseph Demarco, *Vice Pres*
Dennis S Mack, *Admin Sec*
▲ **EMP:** 40 **EST:** 1979
SALES (est): 5.4MM **Privately Held**
WEB: www.dwmack.com
SIC: 3053 Gaskets, all materials

(P-5335)
DAR-KEN INC
Also Called: K & S Enterprises
10515 Rancho Rd, Adelanto (92301-3414)
PHONE..............................760 246-4010
Ken Mc Gilp, *Partner*
Darla Mc Gilp, *Partner*
Renee Berry, *QC Mgr*
EMP: 32 **EST:** 1965
SQ FT: 10,000
SALES (est): 2.2MM **Privately Held**
WEB: www.ksentusa.com
SIC: 3053 3728 Gaskets, packing & sealing devices; aircraft parts & equipment

(P-5336)
ERIKS NORTH AMERICA INC
15500 Blackburn Ave, Norwalk (90650-6845)
PHONE..............................562 802-7782
EMP: 74 **Privately Held**
WEB: www.eriksna.com
SIC: 3053 3965 3052 2992 Gaskets, all materials; fasteners; heater hose, rubber; lubricating oils; sealing compounds for pipe threads or joints; industrial valves
HQ: Eriks North America, Inc.
650 Washington Rd Ste 500
Pittsburgh PA 15228
800 937-9070

(P-5337)
FREUDENBERG-NOK GENERAL PARTNR
Also Called: International Seal Company
2041 E Wilshire Ave, Santa Ana (92705-4726)
PHONE..............................714 834-0602
John Hudspeth, *Manager*
EMP: 150
SQ FT: 28,928
SALES (corp-wide): 10.4B **Privately Held**
WEB: www.fst.com
SIC: 3053 Gaskets & sealing devices
HQ: Freudenberg-Nok General Partnership
47774 W Anchor Ct
Plymouth MI 48170
734 451-0020

(P-5338)
G F COLE CORPORATION (PA)
21735 S Western Ave, Torrance (90501-3718)
PHONE..............................310 320-0601
Fritz Cole, *President*
Cathy Cole, *Vice Pres*
Michelle Hafer, *Manager*
▼ **EMP:** 27 **EST:** 1982
SQ FT: 26,000
SALES (est): 4.5MM **Privately Held**
WEB: www.gfcole.com
SIC: 3053 3069 Gaskets, all materials; hard rubber & molded rubber products

(P-5339)
GASKET MANUFACTURING CO
8427 Secura Way, Santa Fe Springs (90670-2215)
PHONE..............................310 217-5600
Maureen E Labor, *CEO*
Dewain R Butler, *Ch of Bd*
Vince Labor, *Vice Pres*
Gustavo Ocegueda, *VP Mfg*
Rory Clark, *Marketing Staff*
EMP: 33 **EST:** 1937
SALES (est): 5.6MM **Privately Held**
WEB: www.gasketmfg.com
SIC: 3053 Gaskets, all materials
PA: Gasket Associates Lp
10816 Kurt St
Sylmar CA 91342

(P-5340)
HARBOR SEAL INCORPORATED
909 S Myrtle Ave, Monrovia (91016-3426)
PHONE..............................626 305-5754
Kunibert Gerhardt, *President*
Karen Edmonds, *Corp Secy*
Marie Gerhardt, *Vice Pres*
EMP: 15 **EST:** 1979
SQ FT: 10,000
SALES (est): 2MM **Privately Held**
WEB: www.harborsealinc.com
SIC: 3053 Gaskets, packing & sealing devices

(P-5341)
HUTCHINSON SEAL CORPORATION (DH)
Also Called: National O Rings
11634 Patton Rd, Downey (90241-5212)
PHONE..............................248 375-4190
Christian Groche, *President*
Tim Morton, *Vice Pres*
Ron Bonner, *Info Tech Mgr*
Robert Hanson, *VP Engrg*
▲ **EMP:** 856 **EST:** 1996
SQ FT: 125,000
SALES (est): 64MM
SALES (corp-wide): 4.6B **Publicly Held**
WEB: www.hutchinson-seal.com
SIC: 3053 Gaskets & sealing devices
HQ: Hutchinson Corporation
460 Fuller Ave Ne
Grand Rapids MI 49503
616 459-4541

(P-5342)
INDUSTRIAL GASKET AND SUP CO
Also Called: Gasketfab Division
23018 Normandie Ave, Torrance (90502-2691)
P.O. Box 4138 (90510-4138)
PHONE..............................310 530-1771
William P Hynes, *President*
Theresa Holmes, *Corp Secy*
Kevin P Treacy, *Vice Pres*
EMP: 23 **EST:** 1970
SQ FT: 11,000
SALES (est): 3MM **Privately Held**
SIC: 3053 5085 Gaskets, all materials; gaskets; seals, industrial

(P-5343)
INERTECH SUPPLY INC
641 Monterey Pass Rd, Monterey Park (91754-2418)
PHONE..............................626 282-2000
James Huang, *President*
Charlie C Miskell, *Vice Pres*
Bruce Wang, *Vice Pres*
Walter Lee, *Admin Sec*
Jean Okita, *Human Res Mgr*
▲ **EMP:** 75 **EST:** 1991
SQ FT: 14,000
SALES (est): 8.8MM **Privately Held**
WEB: www.inertech.com
SIC: 3053 5085 2891 Gasket materials; gaskets; adhesives & sealants

(P-5344)
J MILLER CO INC
Also Called: Miller Gasket Co
11537 Bradley Ave, San Fernando (91340-2519)
PHONE..............................818 837-0181
Dennis D Miller, *President*
Elaine Miller, *Corp Secy*
▲ **EMP:** 35 **EST:** 1961
SQ FT: 20,000
SALES (est): 3.5MM **Privately Held**
WEB: www.millergasket.com
SIC: 3053 Gaskets, all materials

(P-5345)
KIRKHILL INC
300 E Cypress St, Brea (92821-4007)
PHONE..............................714 529-4901
Kevin McHenry, *Manager*
EMP: 700
SALES (corp-wide): 4.8B **Publicly Held**
WEB: www.kirkhill.com
SIC: 3053 3728 2822 Gaskets, packing & sealing devices; aircraft parts & equipment; synthetic rubber
HQ: Kirkhill Inc.
300 E Cypress St
Brea CA 92821
714 529-4901

(P-5346)
KIRKHILL INC
Also Called: Haskon, Div of
300 E Cypress St, Brea (92821-4007)
PHONE..............................714 529-4901
Michael Harden, *Branch Mgr*
EMP: 700
SALES (corp-wide): 4.8B **Publicly Held**
WEB: www.kirkhill.com
SIC: 3053 3728 2822 Gaskets, packing & sealing devices; aircraft parts & equipment; synthetic rubber
HQ: Kirkhill Inc.
300 E Cypress St
Brea CA 92821
714 529-4901

(P-5347)
PARCO LLC (HQ)
1801 S Archibald Ave, Ontario (91761-7677)
PHONE..............................909 947-2200
Adam Morrison Burgener, *President*
Louis W Burgener, *Ch of Bd*
Angela L Garcia, *Vice Pres*
Angie Garcia, *Vice Pres*
W Carl Horn, *Vice Pres*
▲ **EMP:** 223 **EST:** 1989
SQ FT: 154,000
SALES (est): 50.2MM
SALES (corp-wide): 1.2B **Privately Held**
WEB: www.parcoinc.com
SIC: 3053 Gaskets, all materials
PA: Datwyler Fuhrungs Ag
Gotthardstrasse 31
Altdorf UR 6460
418 751-100

(P-5348)
POLYMER CONCEPTS TECH INC
13522 Manhasset Rd, Apple Valley (92308-5790)
P.O. Box 2738 (92307-0052)
PHONE..............................760 240-4999
Rob Girman, *President*
Dean Anderson, *CEO*
Michael Boylan, *General Mgr*
Juli Hunzeker, *Info Tech Mgr*
Tuan La, *Regl Sales Mgr*
EMP: 15 **EST:** 1995
SQ FT: 3,000
SALES (est): 1.9MM **Privately Held**
WEB: www.polymerconcepts.com
SIC: 3053 Gaskets & sealing devices

(P-5349)
ROETTELE INDUSTRIES
15485 Dupont Ave, Chino (91710-7605)
PHONE..............................909 606-8252
Mark Roettele, *President*
Maurice Roettele, *Ch of Bd*
Randal Roettele, *Treasurer*
Lon Roettele, *Vice Pres*
Maria Landino, *Human Resources*
▲ **EMP:** 19 **EST:** 1979
SQ FT: 15,000
SALES (est): 3.7MM **Privately Held**
WEB: www.roetteleindustries.com
SIC: 3053 5085 Gaskets, all materials; industrial supplies

(P-5350)
RPM PRODUCTS INC (PA)
Also Called: Rubber Plastic & Metal Pdts
30065 Comercio, Rcho STA Marg (92688-2106)
PHONE..............................949 888-8543
Mark Paolella, *President*
Suzanne Paolella, *Corp Secy*
▲ **EMP:** 35 **EST:** 1994
SALES (est): 18.2MM **Privately Held**
WEB: www.rpmproducts.com
SIC: 3053 3089 5085 Gaskets & sealing devices; injection molding of plastics; molding primary plastic; gaskets & seals

(P-5351)
SEAL SCIENCE INC (DH)
Also Called: S S I
17131 Daimler St, Irvine (92614-5508)
PHONE..............................949 253-3130
Frederick E Tuliper, *CEO*
Patricia Tuliper, *CFO*
Charles Gilson, *Technical Staff*
Piyush Kakar, *Director*
▲ **EMP:** 68 **EST:** 1985
SQ FT: 25,000
SALES (est): 16.3MM
SALES (corp-wide): 653.4MM **Privately Held**
WEB: www.sealscience.com
SIC: 3053 3089 3061 Gaskets, all materials; injection molding of plastics; mechanical rubber goods
HQ: Sanders Industries Holdings, Inc.
3701 E Conant St
Long Beach CA 90808
562 354-2920

(P-5352)
SEALING CORPORATION
7353 Greenbush Ave B, North Hollywood (91605-4004)
PHONE..............................818 765-7327
John Patterson, *President*
Adrian Patterson, *Corp Secy*
▲ **EMP:** 17 **EST:** 1973
SQ FT: 2,600
SALES (est): 1MM **Privately Held**
WEB: www.selcoseal.com
SIC: 3053 Gaskets, all materials

(P-5353)
SEWING COLLECTION INC
3113 E 26th St, Vernon (90058-8006)
PHONE..............................323 264-2223
Touraj Tour, *President*
Houshang Tour, *Vice Pres*
◆ **EMP:** 100 **EST:** 1991
SQ FT: 135,000
SALES (est): 24.3MM **Privately Held**
WEB: www.sewingcollection.com
SIC: 3053 5199 4953 Packing materials; packaging materials; recycling, waste materials

(P-5354)
SPIRA MANUFACTURING CORP
650 Jessie St, San Fernando (91340-2233)
PHONE..............................818 764-8222
George M Kunkel, *President*
Michael Kunkel, *General Mgr*
Bonnie Paul, *Admin Sec*
Joseph Sanchez, *Technical Staff*
Ernesto Nunez, *Buyer*
EMP: 30 **EST:** 1972
SQ FT: 15,000
SALES (est): 4.3MM **Privately Held**
WEB: www.spira-emi.com
SIC: 3053 Gaskets, all materials

(P-5355)
WEST COAST GASKET CO
300 Ranger Ave, Brea (92821-6217)
PHONE....................714 869-0123
Louis Russell, *Principal*
Jean Grey, *CEO*
Larry Thompson, *General Mgr*
Mikie Reed, *IT/INT Sup*
Christine Geraghty, *Human Res Mgr*
EMP: 75 EST: 1979
SQ FT: 50,000
SALES (est): 16MM **Privately Held**
WEB: www.westcoastgasket.com
SIC: 3053 3061 3469 5085 Gaskets, all
materials; mechanical rubber goods;
metal stampings; industrial supplies

3061 Molded, Extruded & Lathe-Cut Rubber Mechanical Goods

(P-5356)
CRM CO LLC (PA)
Also Called: C R M
1301 Dove St Ste 940, Newport Beach
(92660-2483)
PHONE....................949 263-9100
H Barry Takallou, *CEO*
▲ EMP: 43 EST: 1998
SALES (est): 9.9MM **Privately Held**
WEB: www.crmrubber.com
SIC: 3061 Mechanical rubber goods

(P-5357)
CRYSTAL TIPS HOLDINGS
8850 Research Dr, Irvine (92618-4223)
PHONE....................800 944-3939
Dave Sproat, *CEO*
EMP: 46 EST: 2017
SALES (est): 2.6MM **Privately Held**
WEB: www.crystaltip.com
SIC: 3061 Medical & surgical rubber tubing
(extruded & lathe-cut)

(P-5358)
J FLYING MANUFACTURING
11000 Brimhall Rd Ste E, Bakersfield
(93312-3022)
PHONE....................805 839-9229
Dennis Walrath, *President*
Sindy Walrath, *Vice Pres*
EMP: 16 EST: 1989
SALES (est): 824.9K **Privately Held**
SIC: 3061 3599 Mechanical rubber goods;
amusement park equipment

(P-5359)
MIKRON PRODUCTS INC
3701 E Conant St, Long Beach
(90808-1783)
PHONE....................909 545-8600
Nicholas Carone, *President*
Palma Carone, *Corp Secy*
Ed Duran, *Principal*
EMP: 22 EST: 1974
SALES (est): 1.1MM **Privately Held**
WEB: www.mikronpmpaerospace.com
SIC: 3061 Mechanical rubber goods

(P-5360)
R D RUBBER TECHNOLOGY CORP
12870 Florence Ave, Santa Fe Springs
(90670-4540)
PHONE....................562 941-4800
Walter V Hopkins Jr, *President*
Rosanne Dukowitz, *Exec VP*
Waler Hopkins, *CTO*
EMP: 27 EST: 1986
SQ FT: 15,600
SALES (est): 3.7MM **Privately Held**
WEB: www.rdrubber.com
SIC: 3061 Mechanical rubber goods

(P-5361)
RUBBERCRAFT CORP CAL LTD (DH)
Also Called: Rubber Teck Division
3701 E Conant St, Long Beach
(90808-1783)
PHONE....................562 354-2800
Marc Sanders, *CEO*

Eric Sanders, *CEO*
Nicholas Borrelli, *Engineer*
Nimi Fafowora, *Engineer*
Naomi Pikofsky, *Human Res Mgr*
EMP: 238 EST: 1984
SQ FT: 40,000
SALES (est): 50.9MM
SALES (corp-wide): 653.4MM **Privately Held**
WEB: www.rubbercraft.com
SIC: 3061 Appliance rubber goods (mechanical)
HQ: Sanders Industries Holdings, Inc.
3701 E Conant St
Long Beach CA 90808
562 354-2920

3069 Fabricated Rubber Prdts, NEC

(P-5362)
3 - D POLYMERS
13026 S Normandie Ave, Gardena
(90249-2126)
PHONE....................310 324-7694
David Johnson, *President*
Kathleen Johnson, *Corp Secy*
EMP: 19 EST: 1938
SQ FT: 11,000
SALES (est): 1.6MM **Privately Held**
WEB: www.3-dpolymers.com
SIC: 3069 3089 3061 Hard rubber &
molded rubber products; plastic processing; mechanical rubber goods

(P-5363)
ABBA ROLLER LLC (DH)
1351 E Philadelphia St, Ontario
(91761-5719)
PHONE....................909 947-1244
Jeffrey Garvens,
▲ EMP: 19 EST: 2010
SQ FT: 4,000
SALES (est): 4.8MM **Privately Held**
WEB: www.abbaroller.com
SIC: 3069 Roll coverings, rubber
HQ: Electro-Coatings, Inc.
216 Baywood St
Houston TX 77011
713 923-5935

(P-5364)
ACE CALENDERING ENTPS INC (PA)
Also Called: Midwest Rubber
1311 S Wanamaker Ave, Ontario
(91761-2237)
PHONE....................909 937-1901
Gary Holcomb, *CEO*
Fred Rodriguez, *President*
Bob Rich, *Vice Pres*
Ivan Rodriguez, *Purchasing*
EMP: 15 EST: 2001
SALES (est): 2.6MM **Privately Held**
WEB: www.acecalender.com
SIC: 3069 Sheets, hard rubber

(P-5365)
AMES RUBBER MFG CO INC
Also Called: Ames Industrial
4516 Brazil St, Los Angeles (90039-1002)
PHONE....................818 240-9313
Timothy L Brown, *CEO*
Pat Brown, *Corp Secy*
Maria Lepe, *Finance Mgr*
Tim Brown, *Manager*
▲ EMP: 30 EST: 1954
SQ FT: 20,000
SALES (est): 5.3MM **Privately Held**
WEB: www.amesrubberonline.com
SIC: 3069 3061 Medical & laboratory rubber sundries & related products; mechanical rubber goods

(P-5366)
BANDAG LICENSING CORPORATION
2500 E Thompson St, Long Beach
(90805-1836)
P.O. Box 140990, Nashville TN (37214-0990)
PHONE....................562 531-3880
EMP: 57
SQ FT: 310,000

SALES (est): 5.8MM **Privately Held**
WEB: www.bandag.com
SIC: 3069 Fabricated Rubber Products,
Nec, Nsk
HQ: Bridgestone Bandag, Llc
2000 Bandag Dr
Muscatine IA 52761
563 262-2511

(P-5367)
BRADEN COURT LLC
1517 W Braden Ct, Orange (92868-1125)
PHONE....................714 288-3936
Dan Richardson, *Manager*
EMP: 17 EST: 2005
SALES (est): 510.6K **Privately Held**
WEB: www.warco.com
SIC: 3069 Fabricated rubber products

(P-5368)
CA-WA CORP
1360 W 1st St, Pomona (91766-1305)
PHONE....................909 868-0630
Jim Sicilia, *CEO*
▲ EMP: 14 EST: 2006
SQ FT: 10,000
SALES (est): 370.4K **Privately Held**
SIC: 3069 Medical & laboratory rubber
sundries & related products

(P-5369)
CALIFORNIA GASKET AND RBR CORP (PA)
533 W Collins Ave, Orange (92867-5509)
PHONE....................310 323-4250
Scott H Franklin, *Vice Pres*
Armando Rodriguez, *Admin Sec*
Amelia Castro, *Sales Staff*
EMP: 35 EST: 1942
SQ FT: 51,000
SALES (est): 7.7MM **Privately Held**
WEB: www.calgasket.com
SIC: 3069 3053 3469 3061 Molded rubber products; rubber automotive products; gaskets; packing & sealing devices; metal stampings; appliance rubber goods (mechanical)

(P-5370)
CENTURY RUBBER COMPANY INC
719 Rooster Dr, Bakersfield (93307-9807)
PHONE....................661 366-7009
Steve Cozzetto, *President*
EMP: 13 EST: 1973
SQ FT: 7,500
SALES (est): 2.3MM **Privately Held**
WEB: www.centuryrubber.com
SIC: 3069 Molded rubber products

(P-5371)
CUSTOM GLASS FABRICATORS INC
15521 Vermont Ave, Paramount
(90723-4226)
PHONE....................562 529-2300
Moize Kapsi, *Principal*
Robert Perry, *General Mgr*
Phillip Price, *Project Mgr*
▲ EMP: 13 EST: 2013
SALES (est): 3.5MM **Privately Held**
WEB: www.customglass.us
SIC: 3069 Fabricated rubber products

(P-5372)
DEVOLL RUBBER MFG GROUP INC
Also Called: Devoll Rubber Mfg Group
18626 Phantom St, Victorville
(92394-7929)
PHONE....................760 246-0142
John De Voll, *CEO*
Stacy Devoll, *General Mgr*
Amanda De Voll, *Office Mgr*
Richard Barnes, *CIO*
EMP: 14 EST: 1964
SQ FT: 8,000
SALES (est): 2.6MM **Privately Held**
WEB: www.devollrubber.com
SIC: 3069 Medical & laboratory rubber
sundries & related products

(P-5373)
DURO ROLLER COMPANY INC
Also Called: Cal State Rubber
13006 Park St, Santa Fe Springs
(90670-4098)
PHONE....................562 944-8856
Maureen Wayda, *President*
Julie Wayda, *Vice Pres*
▲ EMP: 16 EST: 1973
SQ FT: 8,100
SALES (est): 2.3MM **Privately Held**
WEB: www.duroroller.com
SIC: 3069 3599 Molded rubber products;
rubber rolls & roll coverings; machine &
other job shop work

(P-5374)
DURO-FLEX RUBBER PRODUCTS INC
13215 Lakeland Rd, Santa Fe Springs
(90670-4522)
PHONE....................562 946-5533
John A Lozano, *President*
James West, *Sales Executive*
EMP: 30 EST: 1967
SQ FT: 6,000
SALES (est): 2.5MM **Privately Held**
WEB: www.duroflexrubber.com
SIC: 3069 Molded rubber products

(P-5375)
ENVIRNMNTAL MLDING CNCEPTS LLC
Also Called: E M C
14050 Day St, Moreno Valley (92553-9106)
PHONE....................951 214-6596
Sarkis Beudjekian, *Mng Member*
Anne Beudjekian,
◆ EMP: 15 EST: 1997
SQ FT: 15,000
SALES (est): 2MM **Privately Held**
WEB: www.emcmolding.com
SIC: 3069 Reclaimed rubber & specialty
rubber compounds

(P-5376)
FALCON WATERFREE TECH LLC (HQ)
2255 Barry Ave, Los Angeles (90064-1401)
PHONE....................310 209-7250
James Krug,
Ned Goldsmith, *Vice Pres*
Michelle Khalatian, *Vice Pres*
Dimitre Krouchev, *Controller*
Jake Jaskolski, *Sales Mgr*
◆ EMP: 20 EST: 2000
SALES (est): 10.7MM
SALES (corp-wide): 37.8MM **Privately Held**
WEB: www.falconwatertech.com
SIC: 3069 Pump sleeves, rubber
PA: Management Kingsley Llc Mapleton
9952 Santa Monica Blvd
Beverly Hills CA 90212
310 282-0780

(P-5377)
FLEX COMPANY (PA)
318 Lincoln Blvd Ste 200, Venice
(90291-2827)
PHONE....................424 209-2711
Lauren Schulte, *CEO*
Brian Wang, *Admin Sec*
EMP: 44 EST: 2015
SQ FT: 4,500
SALES (est): 5.9MM **Privately Held**
WEB: www.flexfits.com
SIC: 5999 3069 Toiletries, cosmetics &
perfumes; birth control devices, rubber

(P-5378)
GOOD-WEST RUBBER CORP (PA)
Also Called: Goodyear Rbr Co Southern Cal
9615 Feron Blvd, Rancho Cucamonga
(91730-4503)
PHONE....................909 987-1774
Christian Groche, *President*
Fred Ledesma, *Vice Pres*
Harold W Sears, *Vice Pres*
Patrick Sears, *Vice Pres*
Flynn Sears, *Technology*
▲ EMP: 145 EST: 1961
SQ FT: 56,000

SALES (est): 19.6MM **Privately Held**
WEB: www.goodwestlining.com
SIC: **3069** 3061 5531 Molded rubber products; mechanical rubber goods; automotive tires

(P-5379)
GOODWEST RUBBER LININGS INC
Also Called: Goodwest Linings & Coatings
8814 Industrial Ln, Rancho Cucamonga (91730-4528)
PHONE..................................888 499-0085
Ryan Sears, *President*
Larry Sears, *Corp Secy*
Fred Ledesma, *Vice Pres*
Patrick Sears, *Vice Pres*
EMP: 20 EST: 1995
SQ FT: 300,000
SALES (est): 5.7MM **Privately Held**
WEB: www.goodwestlining.com
SIC: **3069** Linings, vulcanizable rubber

(P-5380)
HEXPOL COMPOUNDING CA INC
Also Called: Valley Processing
491 Wilson Way, City of Industry (91744-3935)
PHONE..................................626 961-0311
Tracy Garrison, *President*
Ernie Ulmer, *CFO*
David Schlothauer, *Managing Dir*
EMP: 97 EST: 2011
SALES (est): 16.8MM
SALES (corp-wide): 1.5B **Privately Held**
SIC: **3069** Custom compounding of rubber materials
HQ: Hexpol Holding Inc.
14330 Kinsman Rd
Burton OH 44021
440 834-4644

(P-5381)
HITT COMPANIES
Also Called: Hitt Marking Devices I D Tech
3231 W Macarthur Blvd, Santa Ana (92704-6801)
PHONE..................................714 979-1405
Harold G Hitt, *President*
Ken Hitt, *Vice Pres*
Carol Billen, *General Mgr*
Heidi Hitt, *Admin Sec*
Tue Truong, *Manager*
▲ EMP: 24 EST: 1987
SQ FT: 10,000
SALES (est): 4MM **Privately Held**
WEB: www.hittcompanies.com
SIC: **3069** 3993 5199 Stationers' rubber sundries; signs & advertising specialties; badges

(P-5382)
HUTCHINSON AROSPC & INDUST INC
Also Called: Barry Controls Aerospace
4510 W Vanowen St, Burbank (91505-1135)
P.O. Box 7710 (91510-7710)
PHONE..................................818 843-1000
Grant Hintze, *CEO*
Arnaud Vaz, *President*
Neil O'Hara, *Chief Mktg Ofcr*
Max Maggi, *Exec VP*
Andre Guellec, *Vice Pres*
EMP: 156
SALES (corp-wide): 4.6B **Publicly Held**
WEB: www.hutchinsonai.com
SIC: **3069** Molded rubber products
HQ: Hutchinson Aerospace & Industry, Inc.
82 South St
Hopkinton MA 01748
508 417-7000

(P-5383)
INNOCOR WEST LLC
300-310 S Tippecanoe Ave, San Bernardino (92408)
PHONE..................................909 307-3737
Carol S Eicher, *CEO*
Doug Vaughan, *CFO*
Catarino Murillo, *Supervisor*
▲ EMP: 366 EST: 2003
SQ FT: 150,000

SALES (est): 5.9MM **Privately Held**
WEB: www.fxi.com
SIC: **3069** 5021 Pillows, sponge rubber; mattresses
HQ: Innocor, Inc.
200 Schulz Dr Ste 2
Red Bank NJ 07701

(P-5384)
INTERNATIONAL RUBBER PDTS INC (DH)
Also Called: Irp
1035 Calle Amanecer, San Clemente (92673-6260)
PHONE..................................909 947-1244
Rich McManus, *CEO*
Armando Lopez, *Purchasing*
Milinda Baltazar,
▲ EMP: 61 EST: 2003
SQ FT: 45,000
SALES (est): 23.5MM
SALES (corp-wide): 653.4MM **Privately Held**
WEB: www.irpi.com
SIC: **3069** Medical & laboratory rubber sundries & related products
HQ: Sanders Industries Holdings, Inc.
3701 E Conant St
Long Beach CA 90808
562 354-2920

(P-5385)
JJ ACQUISITIONS LLC
8501 Fllbrook Ave Ste 370, West Hills (91304)
PHONE..................................818 772-0100
Matthew Matsudaira, *Mng Member*
EMP: 41 EST: 2014
SALES (est): 7MM **Privately Held**
SIC: **3069** Toys, rubber

(P-5386)
KIRKHILL INC
12023 Woodruff Ave, Downey (90241-5603)
P.O. Box 7012 (90242-7012)
PHONE..................................562 803-1117
Robert L Harold, *Chairman*
Bruce Mekjian, *President*
Mike Brickner, *Vice Pres*
Gary Riopelle, *Principal*
Arlene Hite, *Admin Sec*
EMP: 95 EST: 1941
SQ FT: 173,000
SALES (est): 15.1MM **Privately Held**
WEB: www.hexpol.com
SIC: **3069** Acid bottles, rubber

(P-5387)
KIRKHILL RUBBER COMPANY
2500 E Thompson St, Long Beach (90805-1836)
PHONE..................................562 803-1117
David Schlothauer, *President*
Edward Reker, *President*
EMP: 99 EST: 2018
SALES (est): 19.9MM
SALES (corp-wide): 1.5B **Privately Held**
WEB: www.hexpol.com
SIC: **3069** Medical & laboratory rubber sundries & related products
HQ: Hexpol Holding Inc.
14330 Kinsman Rd
Burton OH 44021
440 834-4644

(P-5388)
LEONARDS MOLDED PRODUCTS INC
25031 Anza Dr, Valencia (91355-3414)
PHONE..................................661 253-2227
Randy Smith, *President*
Frank Smith, *Vice Pres*
Marty Kudlac, *Manager*
Sherry Wampler, *Manager*
EMP: 25 EST: 1984
SQ FT: 5,000
SALES (est): 2.7MM **Privately Held**
SIC: **3069** Molded rubber products

(P-5389)
LINE ONE LABORATORIES INC USA (PA)
9600 Lurline Ave, Chatsworth (91311-5107)
PHONE..................................818 886-2288
Budiman Lee, *President*
Robert Gruber, *Vice Pres*
▲ EMP: 131 EST: 1990
SQ FT: 22,000
SALES (est): 2.2MM **Privately Held**
WEB: www.lineonelabsusa.com
SIC: **3069** 5122 Medical & laboratory rubber sundries & related products; medical rubber goods

(P-5390)
MATZ RUBBER CO INC
1209 Chestnut St, Burbank (91506-1626)
PHONE..................................323 849-5170
Phillip Jensen, *President*
Jan Jensen, *Treasurer*
EMP: 17 EST: 1954
SQ FT: 12,000
SALES (est): 3.7MM **Privately Held**
WEB: www.matzabrasive.com
SIC: **3069** 3541 3291 Rubber covered motor mounting rings (rubber bonded); machine tools, metal cutting type; abrasive products

(P-5391)
MCP INDUSTRIES INC (PA)
Also Called: Mission Rubber Co
708 S Temescal St Ste 101, Corona (92879-2096)
P.O. Box 1839 (92878-1839)
PHONE..................................951 736-1881
Walter N Garrett, *CEO*
Charlotte Garrett, *Corp Secy*
Owen Garrett, *Vice Pres*
▲ EMP: 15 EST: 1950
SQ FT: 100,000
SALES (est): 91.1MM **Privately Held**
WEB: www.mcpind.com
SIC: **3069** 3259 3089 Molded rubber products; sewer pipe or fittings, clay; injection molding of plastics

(P-5392)
MITCHELL PROCESSING LLC
2778 Pomona Blvd, Pomona (91768-3222)
PHONE..................................909 519-5759
Mark Mitchell,
EMP: 20 EST: 2012
SQ FT: 100,000
SALES (est): 1.6MM **Privately Held**
WEB: www.mitchellsafetysurface.com
SIC: **3069** Custom compounding of rubber materials

(P-5393)
MITCHELL RUBBER PRODUCTS LLC (PA)
1880 Iowa Ave Ste 400, Riverside (92507-7405)
PHONE..................................951 681-5655
Theodore Ballou, *CEO*
Mark Mitchell, *Admin Sec*
Daniel Reyes, *QC Mgr*
Jackie Soto,
Trevor Ballou, *Manager*
◆ EMP: 120 EST: 1967
SALES (est): 36.5MM **Privately Held**
WEB: www.mitchellrubber.com
SIC: **3069** 2891 2822 Mats or matting, rubber; floor coverings, rubber; rubber automotive products; custom compounding of rubber materials; adhesives & sealants; synthetic rubber

(P-5394)
MOMENTUM MANAGEMENT LLC
Also Called: Bushman Products
1206 W Jon St, Torrance (90502-1208)
PHONE..................................310 329-2599
Justin Ross,
Conde Aumann, *Executive*
Keith Caggiano, *Principal*
Aumann Conde, *Principal*
Angela Lahmann, *Accounts Mgr*
▲ EMP: 15 EST: 2003

SALES (est): 3.2MM **Privately Held**
WEB: www.screamingo.com
SIC: **3069** Toys, rubber

(P-5395)
MORTAN INDUSTRIES INC
880 Columbia Ave Ste 2, Riverside (92507-2159)
PHONE..................................951 682-2215
John A Mortan, *President*
Frieda Mortan, *Vice Pres*
EMP: 16 EST: 1981
SQ FT: 22,000
SALES (est): 1.2MM **Privately Held**
WEB: www.mortanindustries.com
SIC: **3069** Hard rubber & molded rubber products

(P-5396)
NEWBY RUBBER INC
320 Industrial St, Bakersfield (93307-2706)
PHONE..................................661 327-5137
Kelly Newby, *President*
Lori Newby, *Admin Sec*
▼ EMP: 25 EST: 1958
SQ FT: 80,000
SALES (est): 5.9MM **Privately Held**
WEB: www.newbyrubber.com
SIC: **3069** Molded rubber products

(P-5397)
PACIFICTECH MOLDED PDTS INC
22805 Savi Ranch Pkwy, Yorba Linda (92887-4634)
PHONE..................................714 279-9928
Jane Xu, *President*
Mike Lou, *Project Mgr*
Fred Valenzuela, *Sales Mgr*
▲ EMP: 20 EST: 2006
SALES (est): 1.7MM **Privately Held**
WEB: www.pacifictechmold.com
SIC: **3069** Rubber automotive products

(P-5398)
PLAYMAX SURFACING INC
Also Called: Califrnia Rcrtion Instllations
1950 Compton Ave Ste 11, Corona (92881-6471)
P.O. Box 77372 (92877-0112)
PHONE..................................951 250-6039
Chris Wolf, *President*
EMP: 19 EST: 2014
SQ FT: 3,500
SALES (est): 2.1MM **Privately Held**
WEB: www.playmaxsurfacing.com
SIC: **3069** 5091 1752 1771 Flooring, rubber: tile or sheet; sporting & recreation goods; floor laying & floor work; flooring contractor; playground equipment; playground construction & equipment installation

(P-5399)
PMR PRECISION MFG & RBR CO INC
1330 Etiwanda Ave, Ontario (91761-8605)
PHONE..................................909 605-7525
Samuel Surh, *President*
George Y Surh, *Executive*
George Surh, *Executive*
Richard Surh, *General Mgr*
EMP: 30 EST: 1996
SQ FT: 36,800
SALES (est): 4MM **Privately Held**
WEB: www.pmrubbertech.com
SIC: **3069** 2295 Rubberized fabrics; coated fabrics, not rubberized

(P-5400)
PRO-TECH MATS INDUSTRIES INC
72370 Quarry Trl Ste A, Thousand Palms (92276-6647)
PHONE..................................760 343-3667
Randy Ernst, *President*
EMP: 14 EST: 1994
SQ FT: 5,650
SALES (est): 2MM **Privately Held**
WEB: www.protechmats.com
SIC: **3069** Medical & laboratory rubber sundries & related products

(P-5401)
PROMOTONAL DESIGN CONCEPTS INC
Also Called: Creative Inflatables
9872 Rush St, South El Monte
(91733-2635)
PHONE....................................626 579-4454
Adam Melendez, *CEO*
Gabby Aguilar, *Sales Executive*
◆ **EMP:** 71 **EST:** 1984
SALES (est): 7.8MM **Privately Held**
WEB: www.promotionaldesigngroup.com
SIC: 3069 7389 5092 2394 Balloons, advertising & toy: rubber; balloons, novelty & toy; toy novelties & amusements; canvas & related products; canvas awnings & canopies; shades, canvas: made from purchased materials

(P-5402)
PURUS INTERNATIONAL INC
82860 Avenue 45, Indio (92201-2396)
PHONE....................................760 775-4500
Dennis Baldwin, *President*
Jessica Baldwin, *CFO*
Eric Bookland, *Vice Pres*
Pablo Castro, *Production*
David Martinez, *Production*
◆ **EMP:** 19 **EST:** 2002
SQ FT: 3,000
SALES (est): 3.4MM **Privately Held**
WEB: www.purusint.com
SIC: 3069 2381 Mats or matting, rubber; glove linings, except fur

(P-5403)
R & R RUBBER MOLDING INC
2444 Loma Ave, South El Monte
(91733-1416)
P.O. Box 3533 (91733-0533)
PHONE....................................626 575-8105
Richard P Norman, *President*
Sixto Castillo, *General Mgr*
Lupe Frausto-Perez, *Vice Pres*
Antonio Morales, *Manager*
EMP: 35 **EST:** 1977
SQ FT: 6,100
SALES (est): 3.2MM **Privately Held**
WEB: www.rrrubber.com
SIC: 3069 Molded rubber products

(P-5404)
R & R SERVICES CORPORATION
Also Called: Geolabs Westlake Village
31119 Via Colinas Ste 502, Westlake Village (91362-3941)
PHONE....................................818 889-2562
Ronald Z Shmerling, *President*
Tim Casey, *Vice Pres*
Timothy Casey, *Marketing Staff*
EMP: 33 **EST:** 1983
SALES (est): 5.9MM **Privately Held**
SIC: 3069 8999 8711 Laboratory sundries: cases, covers, funnels, cups, etc.; geological consultant; engineering services

(P-5405)
R & S PROCESSING CO INC
15712 Illinois Ave, Paramount
(90723-4113)
P.O. Box 2037 (90723-8037)
PHONE....................................562 531-0738
Karen A Kelly, *President*
Anthony J Inga, *Corp Secy*
Linda M Inga, *Vice Pres*
Linda Inga, *Vice Pres*
Karen Kelly, *Executive*
EMP: 73 **EST:** 1959
SQ FT: 53,000
SALES (est): 9.2MM **Privately Held**
WEB: www.rsprocessing.com
SIC: 3069 Reclaimed rubber (reworked by manufacturing processes)

(P-5406)
ROGERS CORPORATION
Also Called: Diversified Silicone
13937 Rosecrans Ave, Santa Fe Springs
(90670-5209)
PHONE....................................562 404-8942
Brian Lindey, *General Mgr*
Brian Lindley, *Sales Mgr*
Diana Mendoza, *Director*
EMP: 60

SALES (corp-wide): 802.5MM **Publicly Held**
WEB: www.rogerscorp.com
SIC: 3069 Bags, rubber or rubberized fabric
PA: Rogers Corporation
2225 W Chandler Blvd
Chandler AZ 85224
480 917-6000

(P-5407)
RUBBERITE CORP (PA)
Also Called: Rubberite Cypress Spnge Rbr Pd
301 Goetz Ave, Santa Ana (92707-3707)
PHONE....................................714 546-6464
Greg Brooks, *President*
Barbara Ballou, *Corp Secy*
Terry Brooks, *Vice Pres*
Russell Miller, *Plant Mgr*
◆ **EMP:** 13 **EST:** 1949
SQ FT: 52,000
SALES (est): 1.9MM **Privately Held**
WEB: www.cypresssponge.com
SIC: 3069 Molded rubber products

(P-5408)
S AND H RUBBER COMPANY INC
1141 E Elm Ave, Fullerton (92831-5023)
PHONE....................................714 525-0277
Mike Haney, *President*
Stephen Haney, *President*
EMP: 28 **EST:** 1967
SQ FT: 5,406
SALES (est): 3.7MM **Privately Held**
WEB: www.shrubber.com
SIC: 3069 3061 Washers, rubber; mechanical rubber goods

(P-5409)
SANTA FE RUBBER PRODUCTS INC
12306 Washington Blvd, Whittier
(90606-2597)
PHONE....................................562 693-2776
William Krames, *President*
Mike Peterman, *Vice Pres*
EMP: 50 **EST:** 1966
SQ FT: 30,000
SALES (est): 7.6MM **Privately Held**
WEB: www.santaferubber.com
SIC: 3069 Molded rubber products

(P-5410)
SGT BOARDRIDERS INC
Also Called: Aleeda Wetsuits
7403 Slater Ave, Huntington Beach
(92647-6228)
PHONE....................................714 274-8000
Steve Terry, *President*
EMP: 13 **EST:** 1981
SQ FT: 6,000
SALES (est): 1.4MM **Privately Held**
SIC: 3069 Wet suits, rubber

(P-5411)
SHERCON INC
18704 S Ferris Pl, Rancho Dominguez
(90220-6400)
PHONE....................................800 228-3218
Keith Ennis, *CEO*
EMP: 60 **EST:** 1966
SQ FT: 50,000
SALES (est): 12MM
SALES (corp-wide): 1.8B **Privately Held**
WEB: www.caplugs.com
SIC: 3069 3089 2672 Tape, pressure sensitive: rubber; injection molded finished plastic products; coated & laminated paper
HQ: Protective Industries, Inc.
2150 Elmwood Ave
Buffalo NY 14207
716 876-9951

(P-5412)
SOUTH BAY CORPORATION
Also Called: Windy Balloon Company
1335 W 134th St, Gardena (90247-1904)
PHONE....................................310 532-5353
Ashhad S Khan, *CEO*
Wendy L Khan, *Vice Pres*
Sharon Aeder, *Admin Asst*
▲ **EMP:** 14 **EST:** 1993
SQ FT: 12,000

SALES (est): 1.4MM **Privately Held**
WEB: www.fastballoons.com
SIC: 3069 Balloons, advertising & toy: rubber

(P-5413)
SPANGLER INDUSTRIES INC
Also Called: A S I American
1711 N Delilah St, Corona (92879-1865)
P.O. Box 1445 (92878-1445)
PHONE....................................951 735-5000
Bernard D Spangler, *President*
Greg Spangler, *Vice Pres*
EMP: 165 **EST:** 1970
SQ FT: 37,897
SALES (est): 8.5MM **Privately Held**
SIC: 3069 Rubber bands

(P-5414)
TA AEROSPACE CO (DH)
28065 Franklin Pkwy, Valencia
(91355-4117)
PHONE....................................661 775-1100
Carol Marinello, *President*
Clare Cole, *Administration*
Ali Sarhang, *Info Tech Mgr*
Lev Baycher, *Research*
Laura Silva, *Purchasing*
▲ **EMP:** 250 **EST:** 1919
SQ FT: 100,000
SALES (est): 193.2MM
SALES (corp-wide): 4.8B **Publicly Held**
WEB: www.esterline.com
SIC: 3069 Reclaimed rubber & specialty rubber compounds
HQ: Esterline Technologies Corp
1301 E 9th St Ste 3000
Cleveland OH 44114
216 706-2960

(P-5415)
TIMEMED LABELING SYSTEMS INC (DH)
27770 N Entrmt Dr Ste 200, Valencia
(91355)
PHONE....................................818 897-1111
Cecil Kost, *CEO*
Patrick Singer, *President*
Tracey Carpentier, *COO*
Mark Segal, *CFO*
EMP: 100 **EST:** 1953
SQ FT: 75,000
SALES (est): 41.6MM
SALES (corp-wide): 1.1B **Publicly Held**
WEB: www.pdchealthcare.com
SIC: 3069 Tape, pressure sensitive: rubber
HQ: Precision Dynamics Corporation
25124 Sprngfeld Ct Ste 20
Valencia CA 91355
818 897-1111

(P-5416)
TINYINKLINGCOM LLC
Also Called: Matsmatsmats.com
6303 Owensmouth Ave Fl 10, Woodland Hills (91367-2262)
PHONE....................................877 777-6287
Mark Carmer,
▼ **EMP:** 21 **EST:** 2000
SALES (est): 5.1MM **Privately Held**
WEB: www.matsmatsmats.com
SIC: 3069 5199 Rubber floor coverings, mats & wallcoverings; general merchandise, non-durable

(P-5417)
UROCARE PRODUCTS INC
2735 Melbourne Ave, Pomona
(91767-1931)
PHONE....................................909 621-6013
Friedhelm Franke, *CEO*
Raymond Halsey-Franke, *President*
Sylvia Bender, *CFO*
Glenn Franke, *Admin Sec*
▲ **EMP:** 18 **EST:** 1975
SQ FT: 30,000
SALES (est): 3.1MM **Privately Held**
WEB: www.urocare.com
SIC: 3069 3089 Medical & laboratory rubber sundries & related products; injection molded finished plastic products

(P-5418)
US RUBBER RECYCLING INC
1231 Lincoln St, Colton (92324-3533)
PHONE....................................909 825-1200

Rick Snyder, *President*
Jr R Snyder, *Technology*
Stephanie Slater, *Manager*
▲ **EMP:** 22 **EST:** 1996
SQ FT: 30,000
SALES (est): 7.4MM **Privately Held**
WEB: www.usrubber.com
SIC: 3069 Acid bottles, rubber

(P-5419)
US RUBBER ROLLER COMPANY INC
1516 7th St, Riverside (92507-4421)
PHONE....................................951 682-2221
Jose Uribe, *President*
Lebizia Uribe, *Vice Pres*
Ramie Uribe, *Admin Sec*
EMP: 18 **EST:** 1994
SQ FT: 10,000
SALES (est): 2.4MM **Privately Held**
WEB: www.usrubberroller.com
SIC: 3069 Medical & laboratory rubber sundries & related products

(P-5420)
VAL PAK PRODUCTS
20731 Centre Pointe Pkwy, Santa Clarita
(91350-2967)
PHONE....................................661 252-0115
Ben Solakian, *Owner*
Ed Navickas, *Sales Mgr*
EMP: 14 **EST:** 1956
SQ FT: 33,700
SALES (est): 2.6MM **Privately Held**
WEB: www.val-pakproducts.com
SIC: 3069 Chlorinated rubbers, natural

(P-5421)
VIKING RUBBER PRODUCTS INC
2600 Homestead Pl, Compton
(90220-5610)
PHONE....................................310 868-5200
Rod Trujillo, *CEO*
Leigh Munsell, *President*
Ricardo Ordonez, *CFO*
EMP: 15 **EST:** 1981
SALES (est): 7.9MM
SALES (corp-wide): 653.4MM **Privately Held**
WEB: www.irpi.com
SIC: 3069 3061 Custom compounding of rubber materials; mechanical rubber goods
HQ: International Rubber Products, Inc.
1035 Calle Amanecer
San Clemente CA 92673

(P-5422)
VIP RUBBER COMPANY INC (PA)
540 S Cypress St, La Habra (90631-6127)
PHONE....................................562 905-3456
Bernardyne Louise Campana, *President*
Howard Vipperman, *Ch of Bd*
Deena Campana, *President*
Kathy Leclair, *CFO*
Dean Gillespie, *Vice Pres*
▲ **EMP:** 116 **EST:** 1970
SQ FT: 58,000
SALES (est): 30.6MM **Privately Held**
WEB: www.viprubber.com
SIC: 3069 3089 3061 Rubber hardware; sponge rubber & sponge rubber products; plastic hardware & building products; mechanical rubber goods

(P-5423)
VORSTEINER INC
Also Called: Nero
11621 Markon Dr, Garden Grove
(92841-1810)
PHONE....................................714 379-4600
Seung Bum Nam, *CEO*
Nina Yoo, *Opers Staff*
Vorsteiner Nero, *Products*
▲ **EMP:** 14 **EST:** 2008
SALES (est): 2.8MM **Privately Held**
WEB: www.vorsteiner.com
SIC: 5531 3089 Automotive parts; rubber automotive products; automotive parts, plastic

---

(PA)=Parent Co (HQ)=Headquarters (DH)=Div Headquarters
✪ = New Business established in last 2 years

(P-5424)
WEST AMERICAN RUBBER CO LLC (PA)
Also Called: Warco
1337 W Braden Ct, Orange (92868-1123)
P.O. Box 6146 (92863-6146)
PHONE..................................714 532-3355
Tim Hemstreet, *Mng Member*
Kelvin Baker, *CFO*
Ben Martinez, *Vice Pres*
Laquita Wilkerson, *Vice Pres*
Michael Ziegwied, *Vice Pres*
▲ **EMP:** 239 **EST:** 1910
SQ FT: 12,500
SALES (est): 52.1MM **Privately Held**
WEB: www.warco.com
SIC: 3069 3061 3053 Sheets, hard rubber; mechanical rubber goods; gaskets, all materials

(P-5425)
WEST AMERICAN RUBBER CO LLC
Also Called: Warco
750 N Main St, Orange (92868-1106)
P.O. Box 6146 (92863-6146)
PHONE..................................714 532-3355
Renan Mendez, *Vice Pres*
Laquita Wilkerson, *Vice Pres*
Bob Rich, *Marketing Mgr*
Ruth Vance, *Marketing Staff*
Ken Hemstreet, *Director*
EMP: 165
SALES (corp-wide): 52.1MM **Privately Held**
WEB: www.warco.com
SIC: 3069 Sheets, hard rubber
PA: West American Rubber Company Llc
1337 W Braden Ct
Orange CA 92868
714 532-3355

3081 Plastic Unsupported Sheet & Film

(P-5426)
ARLON GRAPHICS LLC
200 Boysenberry Ln, Placentia (92870-6413)
PHONE..................................714 985-6300
Andrew McNeill, *President*
Andrew Huddlestone, *President*
Rich Trombino, *Vice Pres*
Christina Lopez, *Engineer*
Serena Shishani, *Engineer*
◆ **EMP:** 150 **EST:** 2011
SALES (est): 56.1MM
SALES (corp-wide): 314.3MM **Privately Held**
WEB: www.arlon.com
SIC: 3081 Vinyl film & sheet
PA: Flexcon Company, Inc.
1 Flexcon Industrial Park
Spencer MA 01562
508 885-8200

(P-5427)
ARVINYL LAMINATES LP
233 N Sherman Ave, Corona (92882-1844)
PHONE..................................951 371-7800
Andy Peters, *Partner*
Linda Foster, *Sales Mgr*
EMP: 41 **EST:** 2011
SALES (est): 24.8MM **Privately Held**
WEB: www.arvinyl.com
SIC: 3081 Vinyl film & sheet

(P-5428)
C & R EXTRUSIONS
2618 River Ave, Rosemead (91770-3302)
PHONE..................................626 642-0244
Luis Michel, *President*
EMP: 17 **EST:** 1976
SALES (est): 866.7K **Privately Held**
SIC: 3081 Plastic film & sheet

(P-5429)
CREATIVE IMPRESSIONS INC
7697 9th St, Buena Park (90621-2898)
PHONE..................................714 521-4441
Marc D Abbott, *President*
▲ **EMP:** 26 **EST:** 1991
SQ FT: 8,000

SALES (est): 3.7MM **Privately Held**
WEB: www.emenucovers.com
SIC: 3081 Plastic film & sheet

(P-5430)
DINSMORE & ASSOCIATES INC
1681 Kettering, Irvine (92614-5613)
PHONE..................................714 641-7111
Jason Dinsmore, *CEO*
Nick Dario, *Accounts Mgr*
Philippe Servando, *Accounts Mgr*
▲ **EMP:** 15 **EST:** 2001
SALES (est): 4.6MM **Privately Held**
WEB: www.dinsmoreinc.com
SIC: 3081 8711 Film base, cellulose acetate or nitrocellulose plastic; machine tool design

(P-5431)
GRAFFITI SHIELD INC
2940 E Le Palma Ave Ste D, Anaheim (92806)
PHONE..................................714 575-1100
Jeffrey Green, *CEO*
Katelynne Green, *Finance*
EMP: 16 **EST:** 2013
SALES (est): 6.1MM **Privately Held**
WEB: www.graffiti-shield.com
SIC: 3081 Floor or wall covering, unsupported plastic

(P-5432)
LIFOAM INDUSTRIES LLC
Also Called: Lifoam Mfg
2340 E 52nd St, Vernon (90058-3444)
PHONE..................................323 587-1934
Dennis Bevans, *Branch Mgr*
EMP: 60
SQ FT: 40,000
SALES (corp-wide): 1.8B **Privately Held**
WEB: www.lifoam.com
SIC: 3081 3086 Packing materials, plastic sheet; plastics foam products
HQ: Lifoam Industries, Llc
1303 S Batesville Rd
Greer SC 29650
866 770-3626

(P-5433)
MERCURY PLASTICS INC
Poly Pak Packaging Division
2939 E Washington Blvd, Los Angeles (90023-4218)
PHONE..................................323 264-2400
Mark Freedman, *VP Finance*
Elizabeth Diaz, *Production*
EMP: 95 **Privately Held**
WEB: www.mercplastics.com
SIC: 3081 2677 Polyethylene film; envelopes
HQ: Mercury Plastics, Inc.
14825 Salt Lake Ave
City Of Industry CA 91746
626 961-0165

(P-5434)
MONTEBELLO PLASTICS LLC
601 W Olympic Blvd, Montebello (90640-5229)
P.O. Box 789 (90640-0789)
PHONE..................................323 728-6814
Timothy F Guth, *President*
Efrain Marmolejo, *Warehouse Mgr*
Evelyn Garcia, *Manager*
EMP: 50 **EST:** 1982
SQ FT: 25,000
SALES (est): 8.7MM **Privately Held**
WEB: www.montebelloplastics.com
SIC: 3081 2673 3089 Packing materials, plastic sheet; trash bags (plastic film): made from purchased materials; extruded finished plastic products

(P-5435)
NATIONWIDE PLASTIC PRODUCTS
16809 Gramercy Pl, Gardena (90247-5205)
PHONE..................................310 366-7585
Daniel Tai, *President*
John McGee, *CEO*
EMP: 16 **EST:** 2000
SQ FT: 10,000
SALES (est): 773.7K **Privately Held**
SIC: 3081 5093 Plastic film & sheet; plastics scrap

(P-5436)
NEXUS CALIFORNIA INC
4551 Brickell Privado St, Ontario (91761-7828)
PHONE..................................909 937-1000
Kariman Sholakh, *President*
Tamer Sholakh, *Vice Pres*
Cathy Sutphin, *Sales Staff*
Bill Trotta, *Manager*
▲ **EMP:** 26 **EST:** 1998
SQ FT: 23,512
SALES (est): 3MM **Privately Held**
WEB: www.nexuscalifornia.com
SIC: 3081 2673 Plastic film & sheet; plastic bags: made from purchased materials

(P-5437)
OCEANIA INC
14209 Gannet St, La Mirada (90638-5220)
PHONE..................................562 926-8886
Tai Leong, *CEO*
Angela Leung, *Vice Pres*
▲ **EMP:** 30 **EST:** 2014
SALES (est): 4.8MM **Privately Held**
SIC: 3081 Plastic film & sheet

(P-5438)
SIMPLEX STRIP DOORS LLC (PA)
Also Called: Simplex Isolation Systems
14500 Miller Ave, Fontana (92336-1696)
PHONE..................................800 854-7951
Jim Forschler, *Vice Pres*
Chris Lindlar, *Sales Staff*
Ward Patton, *Sales Staff*
▲ **EMP:** 30 **EST:** 1979
SQ FT: 28,000
SALES (est): 8.2MM **Privately Held**
WEB: www.simplex.is
SIC: 3081 Vinyl film & sheet

(P-5439)
TRAFFIC WORKS INC
5720 Soto St, Huntington Park (90255-2631)
PHONE..................................323 582-0616
Steve Josephson, *Owner*
▲ **EMP:** 20 **EST:** 1983
SQ FT: 20,000
SALES (est): 4.9MM **Privately Held**
WEB: www.trafficworksinc.com
SIC: 3081 2678 Packing materials, plastic sheet; stationery: made from purchased materials

(P-5440)
TRM MANUFACTURING INC
375 Trm Cir, Corona (92879-1758)
P.O. Box 77520 (92877-0117)
PHONE..................................951 256-8550
Ted Moore, *President*
Anaisa Moore, *Vice Pres*
Essie McBride, *Controller*
Dennis Waggoner, *Purchasing*
Lew Elwood, *Sales Staff*
▲ **EMP:** 200 **EST:** 1978
SQ FT: 200,000
SALES (est): 2.2MM **Privately Held**
WEB: www.trmmfg.com
SIC: 3081 Polyethylene film

(P-5441)
W PLASTICS INC
Also Called: Western Plastics Temecula
41573 Dendy Pkwy Ste 2543, Temecula (92590-3757)
PHONE..................................800 442-9727
Michael T F Cunningham, *President*
Thomas C Cunningham, *Treasurer*
Patrick Cunningham, *Vice Pres*
John Rimel, *Comp Spec*
Darlene Carter, *Purchasing*
◆ **EMP:** 35 **EST:** 1991
SQ FT: 65,000
SALES (est): 4.8MM **Privately Held**
WEB: www.wplastics.com
SIC: 3081 1799 Plastic film & sheet; food service equipment installation

(P-5442)
WESTERN SUMMIT MFG CORP
Also Called: Southern International Packg
30200 Cartier Dr, Rancho Palos Verdes (90275-5722)
PHONE..................................626 333-3333
Donald K Clark, *President*

EMP: 21 **EST:** 1978
SQ FT: 55,000
SALES (est): 482.3K **Privately Held**
SIC: 3081 2759 2673 Unsupported plastics film & sheet; commercial printing; bags: plastic, laminated & coated

3082 Plastic Unsupported Profile Shapes

(P-5443)
ALL WEST PLASTICS INC
5451 Argosy Ave, Huntington Beach (92649-1038)
PHONE..................................714 894-9922
L Scott Leishman, *President*
EMP: 22 **EST:** 1978
SQ FT: 35,000
SALES (est): 852.3K **Privately Held**
SIC: 3082 Unsupported plastics profile shapes

(P-5444)
BIRD B GONE LLC (PA)
1921 E Edinger Ave, Santa Ana (92705-4720)
PHONE..................................949 472-3122
Bruce Alan Donoho, *CEO*
Julianne Donoho, *President*
Terri Anne Meyer, *Marketing Staff*
Edward Mackay, *Mktg Coord*
◆ **EMP:** 17 **EST:** 1992
SQ FT: 7,100
SALES (est): 5.1MM **Privately Held**
WEB: www.birdbgone.com
SIC: 3082 Unsupported plastics profile shapes

(P-5445)
JSN PACKAGING PRODUCTS INC
9700 Jeronimo Rd, Irvine (92618-2019)
PHONE..................................949 458-0050
Jim Nagel, *President*
James H Nagel Jr, *CEO*
Sandra Nagel, *Treasurer*
EMP: 65 **EST:** 1985
SALES (est): 9.5MM **Privately Held**
WEB: www.jsn.com
SIC: 3082 3089 Tubes, unsupported plastic; caps, plastic

3083 Plastic Laminated Plate & Sheet

(P-5446)
A B C PLASTICS INC
Also Called: A B C Plastic Fabrication,
9132 De Soto Ave, Chatsworth (91311-4907)
PHONE..................................818 775-0065
Mark Walters, *President*
Ivan Jackovich, *Vice Pres*
Antonio Guerrero, *Prdtn Mgr*
▲ **EMP:** 15 **EST:** 1981
SQ FT: 8,000
SALES (est): 8MM **Privately Held**
WEB: www.abcplasticfab.com
SIC: 3083 7319 5046 3089 Plastic finished products, laminated; display advertising service; store fixtures; plastic processing

(P-5447)
ACRYLICORE INC
15902 S Broadway, Gardena (90248-2406)
PHONE..................................310 515-4846
Shane Nia, *President*
EMP: 14 **EST:** 1992
SQ FT: 7,500
SALES (est): 2.4MM **Privately Held**
WEB: www.shahrooz-art.com
SIC: 3083 Plastic finished products, laminated

(P-5448)
CUSTOM LAMINATORS INC
1350 S Claudina St, Anaheim (92805-6234)
P.O. Box 2744, Orange (92859-0744)
PHONE..................................714 778-0895

Stephen C Navelski, *President*
David Greene, *Opers Mgr*
EMP: 19 **EST:** 1977
SQ FT: 12,000
SALES (est): 407.5K **Privately Held**
WEB: www.aglinc.com
SIC: 3083 Laminated plastic sheets

(P-5449)
HARTERS SURFACES
12612 Osborne St 14, Pacoima
(91331-2128)
PHONE.................................818 899-9917
Gary Harter, *Owner*
EMP: 14 **EST:** 2002
SALES (est): 1.2MM **Privately Held**
WEB: www.hartersurfaces.com
SIC: 3083 Laminated plastics plate & sheet

(P-5450)
INNOVATIVE PLASTICS INC
5502 Buckingham Dr, Huntington Beach
(92649-5701)
PHONE.................................714 891-8800
Gary Elmer, *President*
EMP: 33 **EST:** 1989
SQ FT: 10,500
SALES (est): 1.6MM **Privately Held**
WEB: www.plasticfab.com
SIC: 3083 5947 3089 Plastic finished
products, laminated; gift, novelty & souvenir shop; plastic processing

(P-5451)
JOHNSON LAMINATING
COATING INC
20631 Annalee Ave, Carson (90746-3502)
PHONE.................................310 635-4929
Scott Davidson, *President*
Cristina Kovar, *Technician*
Ray Cruz, *Graphic Designe*
Beverly Hadley, *Accountant*
Kathy Truver, *Controller*
▲ **EMP:** 75 **EST:** 1960
SQ FT: 50,000
SALES (est): 22.6MM **Privately Held**
WEB: www.johnsonlaminating.com
SIC: 3083 3081 2891 1541 Laminated
plastic sheets; window sheeting, plastic;
unsupported plastics film & sheet; adhesives & sealants; food products manufacturing or packing plant construction;
silicones

(P-5452)
LINDSEY DOORS INC
Also Called: Lindsey Mfg
81101 Indio Blvd Ste D16, Indio
(92201-1920)
PHONE.................................760 775-1959
Pierre Letellier, *President*
Jacqueline Andrade, *Office Mgr*
Katherine Letellier, *Admin Sec*
Lucy Ramirez, *Administration*
EMP: 22 **EST:** 1996
SALES (est): 4MM **Privately Held**
WEB: www.lindseydoors.com
SIC: 3083 1521 Thermoplastic laminates:
rods, tubes, plates & sheet; single-family
housing construction

(P-5453)
LITE EXTRUSIONS MFG INC
15025 S Main St, Gardena (90248-1922)
PHONE.................................323 770-4298
Paul Puga, *President*
William Puga, *Corp Secy*
Barbara Puga, *Vice Pres*
Willy Puga, *Sales Executive*
EMP: 30 **EST:** 1973
SQ FT: 23,500
SALES (est): 2.6MM **Privately Held**
WEB: www.liteextrusions.com
SIC: 3083 Thermoplastic laminates: rods,
tubes, plates & sheet

(P-5454)
PARAMOUNT LAMINATES INC
(PA)
Also Called: Paramount Laminates & Cabinets
15527 Vermont Ave, Paramount
(90723-4295)
PHONE.................................562 531-7580
Dan Neeley, *President*
Wayne De Puy, *President*

Brian Depuy, *CEO*
Sheila De Puy, *Corp Secy*
EMP: 73 **EST:** 1966
SQ FT: 5,000
SALES (est): 682.9K **Privately Held**
WEB: www.paramountlaminate.com
SIC: 3083 Laminated plastics plate & sheet

(P-5455)
PHILLIPS BROS PLASTICS INC
17831 S Western Ave, Gardena
(90248-3681)
PHONE.................................310 532-8020
James Phillips, *President*
David Phillips, *General Mgr*
Alan Phillips, *VP Prdtn*
EMP: 19 **EST:** 1956
SQ FT: 28,000
SALES (est): 1.3MM **Privately Held**
SIC: 3083 3089 Plastic finished products,
laminated; injection molding of plastics

(P-5456)
PLASTIC INNOVATIONS INC
10513 San Sevaine Way, Jurupa Valley
(91752-3286)
PHONE.................................951 361-0251
Chinpan Patel, *CEO*
EMP: 18 **EST:** 2011
SQ FT: 22,000
SALES (est): 3.4MM **Privately Held**
WEB: www.plasticinnovations.com
SIC: 3083 Plastic finished products, laminated

(P-5457)
PLASTICOLOR MOLDED PDTS
INC (PA)
801 S Acacia Ave, Fullerton (92831-5398)
P.O. Box 6985 (92834-6985)
PHONE.................................714 525-3880
Matt Bagne, *President*
▲ **EMP:** 250 **EST:** 1971
SALES (est): 52.4MM **Privately Held**
WEB: www.plasticolorinc.com
SIC: 5531 3083 Automotive accessories;
plastic finished products, laminated

(P-5458)
PLASTICS RESEARCH
CORPORATION
Also Called: PRC
1400 S Campus Ave, Ontario (91761-4330)
PHONE.................................909 391-9050
Gene Gregory, *CEO*
Robert Black, *President*
Michael Maedel, *Exec VP*
▲ **EMP:** 100
SQ FT: 105,000
SALES (est): 27.5MM **Privately Held**
WEB: www.prccal.com
SIC: 3083 Laminated plastics plate & sheet

(P-5459)
PLASTIFAB INC
Also Called: Plastifab/Leed Plastics
1425 Palomares St, La Verne
(91750-5294)
PHONE.................................909 596-1927
Rick Donnelly, *President*
Tim Donnelly, *Vice Pres*
Jerri Kelly, *Executive*
Christopher Vaughn, *General Mgr*
Karen Aguirre, *Buyer*
EMP: 30 **EST:** 1977
SQ FT: 15,000
SALES (est): 4.9MM **Privately Held**
WEB: www.plastifabonline.com
SIC: 3083 5162 3089 Laminated plastic
sheets; plastics sheets & rods; plastic
processing

(P-5460)
PTM & W INDUSTRIES INC
10640 Painter Ave, Santa Fe Springs
(90670-4092)
PHONE.................................562 946-4511
Charles E Owen, *CEO*
William Ryan, *Vice Pres*
Matt Brown, *District Mgr*
Doug Mayer, *District Mgr*
John Peralta, *District Mgr*
▲ **EMP:** 25 **EST:** 1959
SQ FT: 25,000

SALES (est): 5.6MM **Privately Held**
WEB: www.ptm-w.com
SIC: 3083 2992 2891 2851 Plastic finished products, laminated; lubricating oils
& greases; adhesives & sealants; paints
& allied products; plastics materials &
resins

(P-5461)
REPET INC
14207 Monte Vista Ave, Chino
(91710-5724)
PHONE.................................909 594-5333
Shubin Zhao, *President*
Jennifer Chang, *Chairman*
Francisco Hernandez, *Project Mgr*
Nan Zhao, *Engineer*
▲ **EMP:** 145 **EST:** 2009
SALES (est): 22.2MM **Privately Held**
WEB: www.repetinc.com
SIC: 3083 Plastic finished products, laminated

(P-5462)
SCHAFFER LABORATORIES INC
Also Called: Western Plastic Products
8441 Monroe Ave, Stanton (90680-2615)
PHONE.................................714 202-1594
▲ **EMP:** 13
SQ FT: 9,000
SALES: 750K **Privately Held**
SIC: 3083 Mfg Laminated Plastic
Plate/Sheet Mfg Plastic Products

(P-5463)
SWISS PRODUCTIONS INC
2801 Golf Course Dr, Ventura
(93003-7610)
PHONE.................................805 654-8525
Kenneth Ray Putman, *CEO*
Michelle Rogers, *CFO*
Richard G Petrash, *Senior VP*
Michael Rodriguez, *Manager*
Timo Lunceford, *Assistant VP*
▲ **EMP:** 39 **EST:** 1982
SQ FT: 25,000
SALES (est): 4.5MM **Privately Held**
WEB: www.swissproductions.com
SIC: 3083 3469 3451 Plastic finished
products, laminated; metal stampings;
screw machine products

(P-5464)
VCLAD LAMINATES INC
2103 Seaman Ave, South El Monte
(91733-2628)
PHONE.................................626 442-2100
David Thomson, *President*
Anthony Cruz, *Manager*
▲ **EMP:** 20 **EST:** 2002
SALES (est): 2.1MM **Privately Held**
WEB: www.vclad.com
SIC: 3083 2434 Laminated plastic sheets;
wood kitchen cabinets

3084 Plastic Pipe

(P-5465)
ASSISVIS INC
10780 Mulberry Ave, Fontana
(92337-7062)
PHONE.................................909 628-2031
Ken Lam, *President*
EMP: 16 **EST:** 2012
SALES (est): 5.4MM **Privately Held**
WEB: www.assisvis.com
SIC: 3084 3089 Plastics pipe; plastic processing

(P-5466)
GEORG FISCHER HARVEL LLC
7001 Schirra Ct, Bakersfield (93313-2165)
PHONE.................................661 396-0653
EMP: 30
SALES (corp-wide): 3.5B **Privately Held**
SIC: 3084 Plastics pipe
HQ: Georg Fischer Harvel Llc
300 Kuebler Rd
Easton PA 18040
610 252-7355

(P-5467)
HANCOR INC
140 Vineland Rd, Bakersfield (93307-9515)
PHONE.................................661 366-1520

James Tingle, *Manager*
EMP: 42
SALES (corp-wide): 1.9B **Publicly Held**
WEB: www.adspipe.com
SIC: 3084 5051 Plastics pipe; pipe & tubing, steel
HQ: Hancor, Inc.
4640 Trueman Blvd
Hilliard OH 43026
614 658-0050

(P-5468)
KAKUICHI AMERICA INC
23540 Telo Ave, Torrance (90505-4013)
PHONE.................................310 539-1590
Yasuo Ogami, *CEO*
Kenichi Tanaka, *Principal*
▲ **EMP:** 100
SQ FT: 110,000
SALES (est): 29.1MM **Privately Held**
WEB: www.pacificecho.com
SIC: 3084 Plastics pipe
HQ: Kakuichi Co., Ltd.
1415, Midoricho, Tsuruga
Nagano NAG 380-0

(P-5469)
PACIFIC PLASTICS INC
111 S Berry St, Brea (92821-4827)
PHONE.................................714 990-9050
Anayat Raminfar, *President*
Rahim Arian, *Treasurer*
Farhad Bahremand, *Vice Pres*
Rahim Kashanian, *Vice Pres*
Aman Ramin, *Vice Pres*
▲ **EMP:** 71 **EST:** 1980
SQ FT: 32,000
SALES (est): 23.3MM **Privately Held**
WEB: www.pacificplasticsinc.com
SIC: 3084 Plastics pipe

(P-5470)
PW EAGLE INC
Also Called: JM Eagle
5200 W Century Blvd Fl 10, Los Angeles
(90045-5971)
PHONE.................................800 621-4404
EMP: 267
SALES (corp-wide): 978.3MM **Privately
Held**
SIC: 3084 Mfg Plastic Pipe
HQ: Pw Eagle, Inc.
5200 W Century Blvd
Los Angeles CA 90045
800 621-4404

(P-5471)
PW EAGLE INC
Also Called: P W Eagle
23711 Rider St, Perris (92570-7114)
PHONE.................................951 657-7400
EMP: 267
SALES (corp-wide): 978.3MM **Privately
Held**
SIC: 3084 3644 Mfg Plastic Pipe Mfg Nonconductive Wiring Devices
HQ: Pw Eagle, Inc.
5200 W Century Blvd
Los Angeles CA 90045
800 621-4404

(P-5472)
VALENCIA PIPE COMPANY
Also Called: Home-Flex
28305 Livingston Ave, Valencia
(91355-4164)
PHONE.................................661 257-3923
Andrew Dervin, *CEO*
Curt Meyer, *CFO*
Peter Dervin, *Vice Pres*
Uriel Sandoval, *Vice Pres*
Ian Howard, *Executive*
▲ **EMP:** 100 **EST:** 2007
SALES: 47.7MM **Privately Held**
WEB: www.valenciapipe.com
SIC: 3084 5074 3479 3312 Plastics pipe;
pipes & fittings, plastic; coating or wrapping steel pipe; iron & steel: galvanized,
pipes, plates, sheets, etc.

P R O D U C T S & S V C S

3085 Plastic Bottles

(P-5473)
ALTIUM PACKAGING LLC
Mayfair Plastics
1500 E 223rd St, Carson (90745-4316)
PHONE................................310 952-8736
Larry Lindsey, *Manager*
EMP: 19
SALES (corp-wide): 12.5B **Publicly Held**
WEB: www.altiumpkg.com
SIC: 3085 2656 Plastics bottles; sanitary food containers
HQ: Altium Packaging Llc
2500 Windy Ridge Pkwy Se # 1400
Atlanta GA 30339
678 742-4600

(P-5474)
CLASSIC CONTAINERS INC
1700 S Hellman Ave, Ontario (91761-7638)
PHONE................................909 930-3610
Manny G Hernandez Sr, *CEO*
Manny Hernandez Jr, *Treasurer*
Roberto Lopez, *Officer*
Ernie Hernandez, *Vice Pres*
Maria Hernandez, *Admin Sec*
EMP: 280 **EST:** 1988
SQ FT: 60,000
SALES (est): 25.2MM **Privately Held**
WEB: www.classiccontainers.com
SIC: 3085 5085 3089 Plastics bottles; industrial supplies; plastic containers, except foam

(P-5475)
GRAHAM PACKAGING CO EUROPE LLC
11555 Arrow Rte, Rancho Cucamonga (91730-4944)
PHONE................................909 989-5367
EMP: 147 **Privately Held**
SIC: 3085 Mfg Plastic Bottles
HQ: Graham Packaging Company Europe Llc
2401 Pleasant Valley Rd # 2
York PA 17601
717 849-8500

(P-5476)
MUNCHKIN INC (PA)
7835 Gloria Ave, Van Nuys (91406-1822)
PHONE................................800 344-2229
Steven Dunn, *CEO*
Paul Kirch, *Ch of Bd*
Andrew Keimach, *President*
Jeff Hale, *COO*
Gary Rolfes, *CFO*
◆ **EMP:** 123 **EST:** 1991
SQ FT: 63,000
SALES (est): 62.7MM **Privately Held**
WEB: www.munchkin.com
SIC: 3085 3069 5999 Plastics bottles; teething rings, rubber; infant furnishings & equipment

(P-5477)
NARAYAN CORPORATION
Also Called: Plastic Processing Co
13432 Estrella Ave, Gardena (90248-1513)
PHONE................................310 719-7330
Harshad Desai, *President*
▲ **EMP:** 37 **EST:** 2002
SALES (est): 2.8MM **Privately Held**
WEB: www.plasticprocessing.net
SIC: 3085 3089 Plastics bottles; bottle caps, molded plastic

(P-5478)
PLASCOR INC
972 Columbia Ave, Riverside (92507-2140)
PHONE................................951 328-1010
David Harrigan, *President*
Marie Harrigan, *Vice Pres*
▼ **EMP:** 135
SQ FT: 50,000
SALES (est): 39.3MM **Privately Held**
SIC: 3085 Plastics bottles

(P-5479)
PLAXICON HOLDING CORPORATION
Also Called: Plaxicon Co
10660 Acacia St, Rancho Cucamonga (91730-5409)
PHONE................................909 944-6868
Bill Williams, *CEO*
EMP: 5204 **EST:** 1983
SQ FT: 150,000
SALES (est): 2.8MM **Privately Held**
WEB: www.grahampackaging.com
SIC: 3085 3089 Plastics bottles; plastic containers, except foam
PA: Graham Packaging Company Europe Llc
700 Indian Springs Dr # 100
Lancaster PA 17601

(P-5480)
POLY-TAINER INC (PA)
Also Called: Custom Molded Devices
450 W Los Angeles Ave, Simi Valley (93065-1646)
PHONE................................805 526-3424
Julie Williams, *CEO*
Paul Strong, *President*
Louise Lipsum, *COO*
Tim Williams, *CFO*
Frank Cowles, *Vice Pres*
▲ **EMP:** 120 **EST:** 1970
SQ FT: 95,000
SALES (est): 52.5MM **Privately Held**
WEB: www.polytainer.com
SIC: 3085 Plastics bottles

(P-5481)
TRIPLE DOT CORP
3302 S Susan St, Santa Ana (92704-6841)
PHONE................................714 241-0888
Tony T Tsai, *President*
Elaine Chang, *Corp Secy*
Jason Tsai, *Vice Pres*
◆ **EMP:** 36 **EST:** 1990
SQ FT: 35,000
SALES (est): 6.8MM **Privately Held**
WEB: www.triple-dot.com
SIC: 3085 5085 3089 Plastics bottles; glass bottles; plastic containers, except foam

3086 Plastic Foam Prdts

(P-5482)
ABAD FOAM INC
6560 Caballero Blvd, Buena Park (90620-1130)
PHONE................................714 994-2223
Abad Chavez, *President*
Cesar Chavez, *COO*
Claire Alvarado, *Human Res Mgr*
Chris Wertz, *Sales Staff*
Jean Parrell,
▲ **EMP:** 50 **EST:** 1974
SALES (est): 8.2MM **Privately Held**
WEB: www.abadfoam.com
SIC: 3086 Plastics foam products

(P-5483)
ADVANCED FOAM INC
1745 W 134th St, Gardena (90249-2015)
PHONE................................310 515-0728
James Conley, *President*
Bettye Valadez, *General Mgr*
Susan L Conley, *Admin Sec*
EMP: 20 **EST:** 1983
SQ FT: 17,500
SALES (est): 7.5MM **Privately Held**
WEB: www.advancedfoam.com
SIC: 3086 3299 Packaging & shipping materials, foamed plastic; ornamental & architectural plaster work

(P-5484)
ADVANCED MATERIALS INC (HQ)
20211 S Susana Rd, Compton (90221-5725)
PHONE................................310 537-5444
Fax: 310 763-6869
▲ **EMP:** 19
SQ FT: 56,000

SALES (est): 2.5MM
SALES (corp-wide): 138.8MM **Publicly Held**
WEB: www.ami4.com
SIC: 3086 Mfg Plastic Foam Products
PA: Ufp Technologies, Inc.
100 Hale St
Newburyport MA 01950
978 352-2200

(P-5485)
AGRI-CEL INC
401 Road 192, Delano (93215-9598)
P.O. Box 100 (93216-0100)
PHONE................................661 792-2107
Louis Pandol, *President*
Jack Pandol, *Vice Pres*
Steve Pandol, *Vice Pres*
▲ **EMP:** 26 **EST:** 1980
SQ FT: 30,000
SALES (est): 1MM **Privately Held**
WEB: www.agri-cel.com
SIC: 3086 Packaging & shipping materials, foamed plastic

(P-5486)
ALLMAN PRODUCTS INC
21251 Deering Ct, Canoga Park (91304-5016)
P.O. Box 10625 (91309-1625)
PHONE................................818 715-0093
Allan Allman, *President*
▲ **EMP:** 21 **EST:** 1979
SQ FT: 8,000
SALES (est): 2.3MM **Privately Held**
WEB: www.allmanproducts.com
SIC: 3086 Plastics foam products

(P-5487)
ALTIUM PACKAGING LP
Also Called: A Division Continental Can Co
1217 E Saint Gertrude Pl, Santa Ana (92707-3029)
PHONE................................714 241-6640
Cesare Calabrese, *Branch Mgr*
Veronica Banuelos, *Purch Mgr*
EMP: 117
SALES (corp-wide): 12.5B **Publicly Held**
WEB: www.altiumpkg.com
SIC: 3086 3085 Plastics foam products; plastics bottles
HQ: Altium Packaging Lp
2500 Windy Ridge Pkwy Se # 1400
Atlanta GA 30339
678 742-4600

(P-5488)
AMFOAM INC (PA)
Also Called: American Foam & Packaging
15110 S Broadway, Gardena (90248-1822)
PHONE................................310 327-4003
Brian Leecing, *President*
Alex Gelbard, *Vice Pres*
Walter Hernandez, *Info Tech Dir*
David Wooldridge, *Info Tech Mgr*
Art Marquez, *Business Mgr*
▲ **EMP:** 59 **EST:** 1993
SQ FT: 42,000
SALES (est): 15.5MM **Privately Held**
WEB: www.amfoaminc.com
SIC: 3086 5199 Packaging & shipping materials, foamed plastic; foam rubber

(P-5489)
ARTISTIC COVERINGS INC
14135 Artesia Blvd, Cerritos (90703-7025)
PHONE................................562 404-9343
Troy Robinson, *President*
Michelle Robinson, *Vice Pres*
▲ **EMP:** 30 **EST:** 2000
SQ FT: 24,000
SALES (est): 5.4MM **Privately Held**
WEB: www.sportsvenuepadding.com
SIC: 3086 3949 2759 Padding, foamed plastic; track & field athletic equipment; commercial printing

(P-5490)
ATLAS FOAM PRODUCTS
12836 Arroyo St, Sylmar (91342-5304)
PHONE................................818 837-3626
Jeff Naples, *President*
Sandra Naples, *Admin Sec*
Jerry Davies, *Director*
EMP: 18 **EST:** 1957
SQ FT: 28,000

SALES (est): 3.4MM **Privately Held**
WEB: www.atlasfoam.com
SIC: 3086 Packaging & shipping materials, foamed plastic

(P-5491)
AXXION USA INC
8323 Canford St, Pico Rivera (90660-3701)
PHONE................................213 622-3717
Rodolfo Leija, *President*
Monica Elkhoury, *Regional Mgr*
EMP: 14 **EST:** 2013
SALES (est): 3.2MM **Privately Held**
SIC: 3086 5999 5199 Plastics foam products; foam & foam products; plastics foam

(P-5492)
BACK SUPPORT SYSTEMS INC
67688 San Andreas St, Desert Hot Springs (92240-6804)
P.O. Box 961 (92240-0907)
PHONE................................760 329-1472
Jeffrey A Kalatsky, *Presiden*
Jeffrey Kalatsky, *Manager*
▲ **EMP:** 17 **EST:** 1989
SQ FT: 9,800
SALES (est): 1.6MM **Privately Held**
WEB: www.rowlandsandnaylor.co.uk
SIC: 3086 5047 Plastics foam products; therapy equipment

(P-5493)
BOWERS & KELLY PRODUCTS INC
4572 E Eisenhower Cir, Anaheim (92807-1823)
PHONE................................714 630-1285
EMP: 26
SALES (est): 3.3MM **Privately Held**
SIC: 3086 Mfg Plastic Foam Products

(P-5494)
BUD WIL INC
Also Called: B W I
3224 E Radcliffe Ave, Anaheim (92806-2539)
PHONE................................714 630-1242
M Charles Williams, *President*
EMP: 21 **EST:** 1952
SALES (est): 1.9MM **Privately Held**
SIC: 3086 Plastics foam products

(P-5495)
CPD INDUSTRIES
Also Called: Custom Packaging Design
4665 State St, Montclair (91763-6130)
PHONE................................909 465-5596
Carlos Hurtado, *President*
Sergio Briceno, *CFO*
EMP: 29 **EST:** 1985
SQ FT: 22,000
SALES (est): 4.4MM **Privately Held**
WEB: www.cpdindustries.com
SIC: 3086 Packaging & shipping materials, foamed plastic

(P-5496)
DART CONTAINER CORP CALIFORNIA (PA)
150 S Maple Ctr, Corona (92880)
PHONE................................951 735-8115
Robert C Dart, *CEO*
Kevin Fox, *Treasurer*
John Scramling, *Technology*
Kris Stegall, *Production*
▲ **EMP:** 300 **EST:** 1937
SQ FT: 50,000
SALES (est): 51.4MM **Privately Held**
WEB: www.dartcontainer.com
SIC: 3086 Cups & plates, foamed plastic

(P-5497)
DIVERSIFIED PACKAGING INC
2221 S Anne St, Santa Ana (92704-4410)
PHONE................................714 850-9316
David A Hoyt, *President*
Kathleen Hoyt, *Corp Secy*
Donald Hoyt, *Vice Pres*
EMP: 14 **EST:** 1984
SALES (est): 642.7K **Privately Held**
SIC: 3086 7389 Packaging & shipping materials, foamed plastic; packaging & labeling services

(P-5498)
EDM INTRNATIONAL LOGISTICS INC
7211 Haven Ave Ste E368, Alta Loma (91701-6064)
PHONE...............................626 588-2299
Qun Wan, *CEO*
◆ EMP: 18 EST: 2006
SALES (est): 2.5MM Privately Held
SIC: 3086 Packaging & shipping materials, foamed plastic

(P-5499)
EPE INDUSTRIES USA INC (HQ)
Also Called: Epe USA
17835 Newhope St Ste G, Fountain Valley (92708-5428)
PHONE...............................800 315-0336
Troy Merrell, *CEO*
Toshio Yanagi, *CFO*
Darryl Lambert, *General Mgr*
Melissa Patrick, *Office Admin*
Dejana Salaj, *Project Mgr*
EMP: 18 EST: 2010
SALES (est): 62.2MM Privately Held
WEB: www.epeusa.com
SIC: 3086 Ice chests or coolers (portable), foamed plastic; packaging & shipping materials, foamed plastic; padding, foamed plastic

(P-5500)
FIVE STAR FOOD CONTAINERS INC
250 Eastgate Rd, Barstow (92311-3224)
PHONE...............................626 437-6219
Larry Luc, *President*
▲ EMP: 60 EST: 2016
SALES (est): 30MM Privately Held
SIC: 3086 Plastics foam products

(P-5501)
FOAM CONCEPTS INC
4729 E Wesley Dr, Anaheim (92807-1941)
PHONE...............................714 693-1037
Stephen C Ross, *Owner*
▲ EMP: 20 EST: 1995
SQ FT: 9,000
SALES (est): 2.4MM Privately Held
WEB: www.foamconcepts.net
SIC: 3086 Packaging & shipping materials, foamed plastic

(P-5502)
FOAM FACTORY INC
17515 S Santa Fe Ave, Compton (90221-5400)
PHONE...............................310 603-9808
Felipe Alcazar, *President*
▼ EMP: 45 EST: 1989
SQ FT: 40,000
SALES (est): 5MM Privately Held
SIC: 3086 3069 5199 5087 Insulation or cushioning material, foamed plastic; foam rubber; foams & rubber; upholsterers' equipment & supplies

(P-5503)
FOAM MOLDERS AND SPECIALTIES (PA)
Also Called: Foam Specialties
11110 Business Cir, Cerritos (90703-5523)
PHONE...............................562 924-7757
Daniel M Doke, *President*
Dan Doke, *President*
Norman Himel, *CFO*
Roukoz Elkhouri, *Vice Pres*
Rory Strammer, *Vice Pres*
▲ EMP: 80 EST: 1973
SQ FT: 35,600
SALES (est): 15.3MM Privately Held
WEB: www.foammolders.com
SIC: 3086 3089 Plastics foam products; thermoformed finished plastic products

(P-5504)
FOAM MOLDERS AND SPECIALTIES
20004 State Rd, Cerritos (90703-6495)
PHONE...............................562 924-7757
EMP: 50

SALES (corp-wide): 15.3MM Privately Held
WEB: www.foammolders.com
SIC: 3086 Packaging & shipping materials, foamed plastic
PA: Foam Molders And Specialties
11110 Business Cir
Cerritos CA 90703
562 924-7757

(P-5505)
FOAM PLASTICS & RBR PDTS CORP
Also Called: Case Club
4765 E Bryson St, Anaheim (92807-1901)
PHONE...............................714 779-0990
Kirk Plehn, *President*
Brent Plehn, *General Mgr*
Kirk Plehm, *Finance*
EMP: 15 EST: 1990
SQ FT: 10,000
SALES (est): 2.5MM Privately Held
WEB: www.caseclub.com
SIC: 3086 5099 Plastics foam products; cases, carrying

(P-5506)
FOAM-CRAFT INC
2441 Cypress Way, Fullerton (92831-5103)
PHONE...............................714 459-9971
Bruce Schneider, *President*
Michael Blatt, *Admin Sec*
▲ EMP: 165 EST: 1965
SQ FT: 110,000
SALES (est): 22.3MM
SALES (corp-wide): 510.3MM Privately Held
WEB: www.futurefoam.com
SIC: 3086 Plastics foam products
PA: Future Foam, Inc.
1610 Avenue N
Council Bluffs IA 51501
712 323-9122

(P-5507)
FUTURE FOAM INC
2451 Cypress Way, Fullerton (92831-5103)
PHONE...............................714 871-2344
Randall Lake, *Manager*
Kalie Lowder, *Assistant*
EMP: 30
SALES (corp-wide): 510.3MM Privately Held
WEB: www.futurefoam.com
SIC: 3086 Insulation or cushioning material, foamed plastic
PA: Future Foam, Inc.
1610 Avenue N
Council Bluffs IA 51501
712 323-9122

(P-5508)
FUTURE FOAM INC
2441 Cypress Way, Fullerton (92831-5103)
PHONE...............................714 459-9971
EMP: 165
SALES (corp-wide): 510.3MM Privately Held
WEB: www.futurefoam.com
SIC: 3086 Plastics foam products
PA: Future Foam, Inc.
1610 Avenue N
Council Bluffs IA 51501
712 323-9122

(P-5509)
GOLD VENTURE INC
Also Called: North American Foam & Packg
1050 S State College Blvd, Fullerton (92831-5335)
PHONE...............................909 623-1810
Fax: 909 865-6880
▲ EMP: 150
SQ FT: 95,000
SALES (est): 19.6MM
SALES (corp-wide): 459.1MM Privately Held
WEB: www.goldventure.com
SIC: 3086 Mfg Plastic Foam Products
PA: Future Foam, Inc.
1610 Avenue N
Council Bluffs IA 51501
712 323-9122

(P-5510)
HAN RIGID PLASTICS CORP USA
Also Called: D & M Plastics
980 W Cienega Ave, San Dimas (91773-2454)
PHONE...............................909 394-5832
▲ EMP: 16 EST: 2001
SALES (est): 768.4K Privately Held
SIC: 3086 Packaging & shipping materials, foamed plastic

(P-5511)
HUHTAMAKI INC
4209 Noakes St, Commerce (90023-4024)
PHONE...............................323 269-0151
Mark Pettigrew, *Branch Mgr*
George Clovis, *Maintence Staff*
EMP: 97
SALES (corp-wide): 3.9B Privately Held
WEB: www.huhtamaki.com
SIC: 3086 3089 2657 2656 Cups & plates, foamed plastic; plastic containers, except foam; folding paperboard boxes; sanitary food containers; disposable plates, cups, napkins & eating utensils; paperboard mills
HQ: Huhtamaki, Inc.
9201 Packaging Dr
De Soto KS 66018
913 583-3025

(P-5512)
INTER-PACKING INC
Also Called: Flexy Foam
12315 Colony Ave, Chino (91710-2092)
PHONE...............................909 465-5555
Alfonso Cardenas, *President*
EMP: 17 EST: 1985
SQ FT: 10,000
SALES (est): 3.7MM Privately Held
SIC: 3086 2653 Padding, foamed plastic; corrugated boxes, partitions, display items, sheets & pad

(P-5513)
MARKO FOAM PRODUCTS INC (PA)
7441 Vincent Cir, Huntington Beach (92648-1246)
PHONE...............................949 417-3307
Donald J Peterson, *Ch of Bd*
Tyson Peterson, *President*
Stacey Moss, *Admin Asst*
Ilir Bordoniqi, *Engineer*
▲ EMP: 30
SQ FT: 114,000
SALES (est): 13.8MM Privately Held
WEB: www.markofoam.com
SIC: 3086 5999 Packaging & shipping materials, foamed plastic; packaging materials: boxes, padding, etc.

(P-5514)
MULTI-LINK INTERNATIONAL CORP
12235 Los Nietos Rd, Santa Fe Springs (90670-2909)
PHONE...............................562 941-5380
SAI Hung Chan, *President*
Maria Villagomez, *Purch Agent*
▼ EMP: 20 EST: 1993
SQ FT: 45,000
SALES (est): 3.5MM Privately Held
WEB: www.multilinkintl.com
SIC: 3086 Plastics foam products

(P-5515)
PMC GLOBAL INC (PA)
12243 Branford St, Sun Valley (91352-1010)
PHONE...............................818 896-1101
Philip Kamins, *CEO*
Gary Kamins, *President*
Thian Cheong, *CFO*
Janette Whitt, *CFO*
Steven Cohen, *Vice Pres*
◆ EMP: 471 EST: 1996
SALES (est): 1.7B Privately Held
WEB: www.pmcglobalinc.com
SIC: 3086 3674 2865 2816 Plastics foam products; semiconductors & related devices; food dyes or colors, synthetic; color pigments; fiberglass insulation; industrial inorganic chemicals

---

(P-5516)
PMC LEADERS IN CHEMICALS INC (HQ)
12243 Branford St, Sun Valley (91352-1010)
PHONE...............................818 896-1101
Gary Kamins, *President*
EMP: 200
SQ FT: 180,000
SALES (est): 300MM
SALES (corp-wide): 1.7B Privately Held
WEB: www.pmcglobalinc.com
SIC: 3086 5169 Plastics foam products; chemicals & allied products
PA: Pmc Global, Inc.
12243 Branford St
Sun Valley CA 91352
818 896-1101

(P-5517)
POMONA QUALITY FOAM LLC
1279 Philadelphia St, Pomona (91766-5536)
PHONE...............................909 628-7844
Michael Clark,
Theodore Clark,
EMP: 67 EST: 2015
SQ FT: 70,000
SALES (est): 7.4MM Privately Held
WEB: www.pomonaqualityfoam.com
SIC: 3086 Plastics foam products

(P-5518)
QUALITY FOAM PACKAGING INC
31855 Corydon St, Lake Elsinore (92530-8501)
PHONE...............................951 245-4429
Noel A Castellon, *President*
Ruth Castellon, *Corp Secy*
James Barrett, *Vice Pres*
Jose Granda, *General Mgr*
Noel Castellon Jr, *Plant Mgr*
▲ EMP: 25
SQ FT: 56,000
SALES: 16MM Privately Held
WEB: www.qualityfoam.com
SIC: 3086 Packaging & shipping materials, foamed plastic

(P-5519)
QYCELL CORPORATION
600 Etiwanda Ave, Ontario (91761-8635)
PHONE...............................909 390-6644
Grant Kesler, *CEO*
Diana Santillan, *Sales Staff*
▲ EMP: 25 EST: 1990
SQ FT: 45,000
SALES (est): 14MM Privately Held
WEB: www.qycellfoam.com
SIC: 3086 Plastics foam products

(P-5520)
SABRED INTERNATIONAL PACKG INC
3740 Prospect Ave, Yorba Linda (92886-1742)
P.O. Box 566 (92885-0566)
PHONE...............................714 996-2800
Sabrina Sierra, *President*
Edward A Sierra, *Vice Pres*
EMP: 25 EST: 1991
SQ FT: 15,000
SALES (est): 1MM Privately Held
SIC: 3086 5199 5113 5087 Packaging & shipping materials, foamed plastic; packaging materials; corrugated & solid fiber boxes; janitors' supplies

(P-5521)
SLEEPCOMP WEST LLC
Also Called: Latexco West
10006 Santa Fe Springs Rd, Santa Fe Springs (90670-2922)
PHONE...............................562 946-3222
Roger Coffey, *President*
▲ EMP: 40 EST: 2002
SQ FT: 53,000
SALES (est): 4.4MM Privately Held
SIC: 3086 Plastics foam products

(P-5522)
SPECIALTY ENTERPRISES CO
Also Called: Seco Industries
6858 E Acco St, Commerce (90040-1902)
PHONE.................................323 726-9721
Charles De Heras, *President*
Yin Cheng,
▲ EMP: 100 EST: 1983
SQ FT: 60,000
SALES (est): 12.5MM **Privately Held**
SIC: 3086 3565 Plastics foam products; packaging machinery

(P-5523)
STYROTEK INC
345 Road 176, Delano (93215-9471)
P.O. Box 1180 (93216-1180)
PHONE.................................661 725-4957
Martin Caratan, *President*
Dale Arthur, *Corp Secy*
Verna Ransford, *Production*
▲ EMP: 110 EST: 1973
SQ FT: 18,500
SALES (est): 16.3MM **Privately Held**
WEB: www.styrotek.com
SIC: 3086 Packaging & shipping materials, foamed plastic

(P-5524)
TEMPO PLASTIC CO
1227 N Miller Park Ct, Visalia (93291-9343)
P.O. Box 44, Morro Bay (93443-0044)
PHONE.................................559 651-7711
Douglas B Rogers, *President*
Doug Rogers, *Sales Staff*
▲ EMP: 15 EST: 1960
SQ FT: 26,000
SALES (est): 1.1MM **Privately Held**
WEB: www.tempogloss.com
SIC: 3086 Packaging & shipping materials, foamed plastic; cups & plates, foamed plastic; ice chests or coolers (portable), foamed plastic

(P-5525)
TOPPER PLASTICS INC
Also Called: Tpi
461 E Front St, Covina (91723-1299)
PHONE.................................626 331-0561
Patricia Beery, *CEO*
Lewis Beery, *CFO*
Susan Beery, *Admin Sec*
EMP: 19 EST: 1962
SQ FT: 20,000
SALES (est): 1.7MM **Privately Held**
WEB: www.topperplastics.com
SIC: 3086 Packaging & shipping materials, foamed plastic

(P-5526)
UFP TECHNOLOGIES INC
20211 S Susana Rd, Compton (90221-5725)
PHONE.................................714 662-0277
Richard Tunila, *Branch Mgr*
Laura Huhn, *Purch Mgr*
EMP: 50
SALES (corp-wide): 179.3MM **Publicly Held**
WEB: www.ufpmedtech.com
SIC: 3086 Packaging & shipping materials, foamed plastic
PA: Ufp Technologies, Inc.
100 Hale St
Newburyport MA 01950
978 352-2200

(P-5527)
VEFO INC
3202 Factory Dr, Pomona (91768-3903)
PHONE.................................909 598-3856
Roger Voss, *President*
Pat Voss, *Admin Sec*
Elizabeth Hernandez, *Products*
EMP: 20 EST: 1970
SQ FT: 11,000
SALES (est): 3.3MM **Privately Held**
WEB: www.vefofoamshapes.com
SIC: 3086 Plastics foam products

3088 Plastic Plumbing Fixtures

(P-5528)
AQUATIC CO
1700 N Delilah St, Corona (92879-1893)
PHONE.................................714 993-1220
Gary Anderson, *President*
EMP: 240
SALES (corp-wide): 640.9MM **Privately Held**
WEB: www.aquaticbath.com
SIC: 3088 Plastics plumbing fixtures
HQ: Aquatic Co.
665 Industrial Rd
Savannah TN 38372

(P-5529)
AQUATIC CO
Lasco Bathware
8101 E Kaiser Blvd # 200, Anaheim (92808-2287)
PHONE.................................714 993-1220
Scott Hartman, *Manager*
Mike Seymour, *President*
Paul Van Slyke, *Finance*
Nicole Rogers, *Purchasing*
Kim Houseal, *Plant Mgr*
EMP: 110
SQ FT: 5,000
SALES (corp-wide): 640.9MM **Privately Held**
WEB: www.aquaticbath.com
SIC: 3088 1711 5211 Shower stalls, fiberglass & plastic; plumbing, heating, air-conditioning contractors; bathroom fixtures, equipment & supplies
HQ: Aquatic Co.
665 Industrial Rd
Savannah TN 38372

(P-5530)
AQUATIC INDUSTRIES INC
8101 E Kaiser Blvd # 200, Anaheim (92808-2287)
PHONE.................................800 877-2005
Anthony Reading, *CEO*
Margaret Voskamp, *Vice Pres*
Tamara Powell, *Human Resources*
Shirley Harris, *Clerk*
EMP: 20 EST: 1999
SQ FT: 78,004
SALES (est): 2.2MM **Privately Held**
WEB: www.aquaticbath.com
SIC: 3088 5999 3949 Plastics plumbing fixtures; hot tub & spa chemicals, equipment & supplies; sporting & athletic goods

(P-5531)
FIBER CARE BATHS INC
9832 Yucca Rd Ste A, Adelanto (92301-2471)
PHONE.................................760 246-0019
Harry R Kilpatrick, *CEO*
Mary Fernandez, *Administration*
Kaye Allen, *Controller*
Ivon Gonzalez, *Human Resources*
Danny Torres, *Plant Mgr*
EMP: 275 EST: 1996
SQ FT: 6,000
SALES (est): 56.7MM **Privately Held**
WEB: www.fibercarebaths.com
SIC: 3088 Shower stalls, fiberglass & plastic; tubs (bath, shower & laundry), plastic

(P-5532)
JACUZZI PRODUCTS CO (DH)
13925 City Center Dr # 200, Chino Hills (91709-5438)
PHONE.................................909 606-1416
Thomas D Koos, *CEO*
Philip Weeks, *President*
Destini Protich, *Marketing Staff*
▲ EMP: 120 EST: 1959
SALES (est): 105.2MM
SALES (corp-wide): 467.1K **Privately Held**
WEB: www.jacuzzibrands.com
SIC: 3088 Tubs (bath, shower & laundry), plastic; hot tubs, plastic or fiberglass

HQ: Jacuzzi Inc.
14525 Monte Vista Ave
Chino CA 91710
909 606-7733

(P-5533)
JACUZZI PRODUCTS CO
14525 Monte Vista Ave, Chino (91710-5721)
PHONE.................................909 548-7732
Jim Barry, *Manager*
Paresh Joshi, *Vice Pres*
Brianna Gonzales, *IT/INT Sup*
Bernice Gardner, *Credit Staff*
Joshua Gist, *Finance*
EMP: 340
SALES (corp-wide): 467.1K **Privately Held**
WEB: www.jacuzzibrands.com
SIC: 3088 5091 Tubs (bath, shower & laundry), plastic; fitness equipment & supplies
HQ: Jacuzzi Products Co.
13925 City Center Dr # 200
Chino Hills CA 91709
909 606-1416

(P-5534)
LE ELEGANT BATH INC
Also Called: American Bath Factory
13405 Estelle St, Corona (92879-1877)
P.O. Box 127 (92878-0127)
PHONE.................................951 734-0238
Richard Wheeler, *President*
Debbie Wheeler, *Admin Sec*
Joy Liesenfelt, *Controller*
Kathy McCue,
◆ EMP: 120 EST: 1984
SQ FT: 18,000
SALES (est): 22MM **Privately Held**
WEB: www.americanbathfactory.com
SIC: 3088 Tubs (bath, shower & laundry), plastic

(P-5535)
PAINTED RHINO INC
14310 Veterans Way, Moreno Valley (92553-9058)
PHONE.................................951 656-5524
Ryan Franklin, *President*
▲ EMP: 35 EST: 2007
SQ FT: 25,000
SALES (est): 3.7MM **Privately Held**
WEB: www.paintedrhino.com
SIC: 3088 Shower stalls, fiberglass & plastic

(P-5536)
SMITHS ACTION PLASTIC INC (PA)
Also Called: Action Plastics
645 S Santa Fe St, Santa Ana (92705-4143)
PHONE.................................714 836-4141
James A Smith, *President*
EMP: 15 EST: 1975
SQ FT: 5,000
SALES (est): 8.4MM **Privately Held**
WEB: www.action-plastics.com
SIC: 3088 5063 3089 Plastics plumbing fixtures; electrical fittings & construction materials; plastic processing

(P-5537)
VANTAGE ASSOCIATES INC
Glassform
12333 Los Nietos Rd, Santa Fe Springs (90670-2911)
PHONE.................................800 995-8322
Paul Roy, *CEO*
EMP: 25
SALES (corp-wide): 30.5MM **Privately Held**
WEB: www.vantageassoc.com
SIC: 3088 2519 Plastics plumbing fixtures; fiberglass & plastic furniture
PA: Vantage Associates Inc.
12333 Los Nietos Rd
Santa Fe Springs CA 90670
619 477-6940

(P-5538)
VORTEX WHIRLPOOL SYSTEMS INC
Also Called: Catalina Spas
26035 Jefferson Ave, Murrieta (92562-6983)
PHONE.................................951 940-4556
Boyd Cargill, *President*
▲ EMP: 15 EST: 1990
SQ FT: 100,000
SALES (est): 1.7MM **Privately Held**
WEB: www.catalinaspas.com
SIC: 3088 Hot tubs, plastic or fiberglass

3089 Plastic Prdts

(P-5539)
10 DAY PARTS INC
Also Called: Westfall Technik
235 Citation Cir, Corona (92878-5023)
PHONE.................................951 279-4810
Brian Laibach, *Director*
EMP: 35 EST: 2018
SALES (est): 6.3MM
SALES (corp-wide): 170MM **Privately Held**
WEB: www.westfalltechnik.com
SIC: 3089 Injection molding of plastics
PA: Westfall Technik, Inc.
3883 Howard Hughes Pkwy # 590
Las Vegas NV 89169
702 829-8681

(P-5540)
A & S MOLD AND DIE CORP
9705 Eton Ave, Chatsworth (91311-4306)
PHONE.................................818 341-5393
Arno Adlhoch, *CEO*
Karen Adlhoch, *Corp Secy*
Rina Caoyonan, *Accountant*
▲ EMP: 90 EST: 1969
SQ FT: 35,000
SALES (est): 11MM **Privately Held**
WEB: www.aandsmold.com
SIC: 3089 3544 Injection molding of plastics; special dies, tools, jigs & fixtures

(P-5541)
A&A GLOBAL IMPORTS LLC
Also Called: A&A Fulfillment Center
3389 E 50th St, Vernon (90058-3003)
PHONE.................................888 315-2453
David Aryan, *President*
Brian Anowns, *COO*
James Bunting, *CFO*
Adam Wolf, *Vice Pres*
Raymond Mesa, *Purchasing*
▲ EMP: 26 EST: 2011
SALES (est): 27.1MM **Privately Held**
WEB: www.aaglobalimports.com
SIC: 3089 3999 Injection molded finished plastic products;

(P-5542)
ACCENT PLASTICS INC (HQ)
13948 Mountain Ave, Chino (91710-9018)
PHONE.................................951 273-7777
Thomas A Pridonoff, *CEC*
Bonnie Pridonoff, *Admin Sec*
Josue Cordon, *Administration*
Denise Parks, *Director*
Paul Stephens, *Manager*
◆ EMP: 97 EST: 1965
SALES (est): 16.7MM
SALES (corp-wide): 18.3MM **Privately Held**
WEB: www.accentplastics.com
SIC: 3089 Injection molding of plastics
PA: Syntech Development And Manufacturing, Inc.
13948 Mountain Ave
Chino CA 91710
909 465-5554

(P-5543)
ACORN-GENCON PLASTICS LLC
13818 Oaks Ave, Chino (91710-7008)
PHONE.................................909 591-8461
Donald E Morris, *Mng Member*
Jacqueline Morovati, *General Mgr*
Martin Aguirre, *Plant Mgr*
Raul Ochoa, *Production*
Pamela Carlton, *Sales Mgr*

▲ EMP: 68
SQ FT: 94,000
SALES (est): 12.2MM
SALES (corp-wide): 90MM **Privately Held**
WEB: www.acorn-gencon.com
SIC: **3089** 3088 3821 3082 Injection molded finished plastic products; plastics plumbing fixtures; laboratory apparatus & furniture; unsupported plastics profile shapes
HQ: Acorn Plastics, Inc.
   13818 Oaks Ave
   Chino CA 91710
   909 591-8461

(P-5544)
ACTION ENTERPRISES INC
Also Called: Actionmold
1911 S Westside Dr, Anaheim (92805-6703)
PHONE..................714 978-0333
Bill Hall, *CEO*
Steve Burd, *CFO*
EMP: 15 EST: 1993
SALES (est): 1.4MM **Privately Held**
WEB: www.actionmold.com
SIC: **3089** Injection molding of plastics

(P-5545)
ACTION INNOVATIONS INC
Also Called: Action Mold and Tool Co
1911 S Westside Dr, Anaheim (92805-6703)
PHONE..................714 978-0333
Bill Hall, *CEO*
Stephen Burd, *President*
EMP: 14 EST: 1993
SQ FT: 15,000
SALES (est): 2.5MM **Privately Held**
WEB: www.actnmold.com
SIC: **3089** Injection molding of plastics

(P-5546)
ADVANCED CMPSITE PDTS TECH INC
Also Called: Acpt
15602 Chemical Ln, Huntington Beach (92649-1507)
PHONE..................714 895-5544
James C Leslie II, *President*
Jeff Jean, *Vice Pres*
Edgar Rodriguez, *Engineer*
Theada Burgess, *Controller*
Gerald Zierold, *Purch Mgr*
EMP: 45 EST: 1984
SQ FT: 25,300
SALES (est): 10.7MM **Privately Held**
WEB: www.acpt.com
SIC: **3089** 8748 Hardware, plastic; business consulting

(P-5547)
ADVANCED ENGRG MLDING TECH INC
6510 Box Springs Blvd B, Riverside (92507-0740)
P.O. Box 5620 (92517-5620)
PHONE..................888 264-0392
Donald Furness, *President*
Helen Furness, *Vice Pres*
▲ EMP: 20 EST: 1968
SQ FT: 12,000
SALES (est): 3.4MM **Privately Held**
WEB: www.aemt.com
SIC: **3089** Molding primary plastic; injection molding of plastics

(P-5548)
ADVANCED PLASTICS CORPORATION
1855 Rose Ave, San Marino (91108-3018)
PHONE..................626 286-7163
Ronald Printz, *Principal*
EMP: 14 EST: 2008
SALES (est): 212.7K **Privately Held**
WEB: www.advanced-plastics.com
SIC: **3089** 3083 Plastic processing; laminated plastics plate & sheet

(P-5549)
AGRI-LINK PLASTICS INC
296 E Wutchumna Ave, Woodlake (93286-9692)
P.O. Box 395 (93286-0395)
PHONE..................559 564-2889
James Taylor, *President*
EMP: 27 EST: 2007
SALES (est): 965.1K **Privately Held**
SIC: **3089** Injection molding of plastics

(P-5550)
AGSTAR SERVICES INC (PA)
13947 Santa Fe Ct, Bakersfield (93314-8355)
PHONE..................661 303-5556
Phillip Hailey, *Principal*
EMP: 15 EST: 2012
SALES (est): 559.4K **Privately Held**
WEB: www.agstarservices.com
SIC: **3089** Injection molded finished plastic products

(P-5551)
AKRA PLASTIC PRODUCTS INC
1504 E Cedar St, Ontario (91761-5761)
PHONE..................909 930-1999
R Wayne Callaway, *President*
Bentley Callaway, *Vice Pres*
Alex Semeczko, *Vice Pres*
EMP: 37 EST: 1972
SQ FT: 36,000
SALES (est): 6.6MM **Privately Held**
WEB: www.akraplastics.com
SIC: **3089** Injection molding of plastics; plastic processing

(P-5552)
ALLEN MOLD INC
1100 W Katella Ave Ste N, Orange (92867-3515)
PHONE..................714 538-6517
Clayton Allen, *President*
Mike Sillett, *Engineer*
EMP: 18 EST: 1997
SQ FT: 5,800
SALES (est): 2.7MM **Privately Held**
WEB: www.allenmold.com
SIC: **3089** Injection molding of plastics

(P-5553)
ALLEN UNITED INC
12711 Imperial Hwy, Santa Fe Springs (90670-4711)
PHONE..................562 944-5650
Gerald A Sampson, *President*
EMP: 16 EST: 1973
SALES (est): 443K **Privately Held**
SIC: **3089** Plastic containers, except foam

(P-5554)
ALLTEC INTEGRATED MFG INC
Also Called: New Age Enclosures
2240 S Thornburg St, Santa Maria (93455-1248)
PHONE..................805 595-3500
Randall Dennis, *CEO*
Justin Tomlinson, *Program Mgr*
Matthew Boyer, *Prgrmr*
Don Circosta, *Opers Staff*
Stan Ryland, *Sales Mgr*
◆ EMP: 40
SQ FT: 13,500
SALES (est): 9.3MM **Privately Held**
WEB: www.alltecmfg.com
SIC: **3089** 2821 Injection molding of plastics; plastics materials & resins

(P-5555)
ALTIUM HOLDINGS LLC
Also Called: California Plastics
12165 Madera Way, Riverside (92503-4849)
PHONE..................951 340-9390
Steve Thompson, *Manager*
EMP: 280
SALES (corp-wide): 510.8MM **Privately Held**
WEB: www.altiumpkg.com
SIC: **3089** Plastic containers, except foam
PA: Altium Holdings Llc
   2500 Windy Ridge Pkwy Se # 1400
   Atlanta GA 30339
   678 742-4600

(P-5556)
ALTIUM PACKAGING
4516 Azusa Canyon Rd, Irwindale (91706-2742)
PHONE..................626 856-2100
EMP: 60
SALES (corp-wide): 12.5B **Publicly Held**
WEB: www.altiumpkg.com
SIC: **3089** Plastic containers, except foam
HQ: Altium Packaging Llc
   2500 Windy Ridge Pkwy Se # 1400
   Atlanta GA 30339
   678 742-4600

(P-5557)
ALTIUM PACKAGING LLC
Also Called: Reid Plastics Customer Svcs
1070 Samuelson St, City of Industry (91748-1219)
PHONE..................888 425-7343
Fred Braham, *Principal*
Lidia Raya, *Technician*
Celestino Ramos, *Supervisor*
EMP: 19
SALES (corp-wide): 12.5B **Publicly Held**
WEB: www.altiumpkg.com
SIC: **3089** 3085 Plastic containers, except foam; plastics bottles
HQ: Altium Packaging Llc
   2500 Windy Ridge Pkwy Se # 1400
   Atlanta GA 30339
   678 742-4600

(P-5558)
ALTIUM PACKAGING LLC
1217 E Saint Gertrude Pl, Santa Ana (92707-3029)
PHONE..................714 241-6640
EMP: 19
SALES (corp-wide): 12.5B **Publicly Held**
WEB: www.altiumpkg.com
SIC: **3089** Plastic containers, except foam
HQ: Altium Packaging Llc
   2500 Windy Ridge Pkwy Se # 1400
   Atlanta GA 30339
   678 742-4600

(P-5559)
ALTIUM PACKAGING LP
Envision Plastics
14312 Central Ave, Chino (91710-5752)
PHONE..................909 590-7334
Jean Bina, *Sales Staff*
Lorena Hine, *Manager*
Budi Hoen, *Manager*
EMP: 117
SALES (corp-wide): 12.5B **Publicly Held**
WEB: www.altiumpkg.com
SIC: **3089** Plastic containers, except foam
HQ: Altium Packaging Lp
   2500 Windy Ridge Pkwy Se # 1400
   Atlanta GA 30339
   678 742-4600

(P-5560)
AMA PLASTICS (PA)
1100 Citrus St, Riverside (92507-1731)
PHONE..................951 734-5600
Mark Atchinson, *CEO*
Leni Pabulos, *Admin Asst*
Winkler Guada Bastida, *Engineer*
Jeff Fontaine, *Engineer*
Adam Fort, *Engineer*
◆ EMP: 200 EST: 1971
SQ FT: 92,000
SALES (est): 60.7MM **Privately Held**
WEB: www.westfalltechnik.com
SIC: **3089** 3544 Molding primary plastic; forms (molds), for foundry & plastics working machinery

(P-5561)
AMERICAN APPAREL ACC INC (PA)
10160 Olney St, El Monte (91731-2312)
PHONE..................626 350-3828
Lily Chang, *President*
Steve Bernstein, *Vice Pres*
▲ EMP: 20 EST: 2005
SQ FT: 5,000 **Privately Held**
SIC: **3089** Injection molding of plastics

(P-5562)
AMERICAN PLASTIC CARD CO
21550 Oxnard St Ste 300, Woodland Hills (91367-7109)
PHONE..................818 784-4224
Jim Akbar, *President*
James Alexander, *Vice Pres*
Peggy Peterson, *Vice Pres*
EMP: 15 EST: 1987
SQ FT: 50,000
SALES (est): 2.8MM **Privately Held**
WEB: www.apcci.com
SIC: **3089** 2759 Identification cards, plastic; commercial printing

(P-5563)
ANAHEIM CUSTOM EXTRUDERS INC
Also Called: Ace
1360 N Mccan St, Anaheim (92806-1316)
PHONE..................714 693-8508
William A Czapar, *Ch of Bd*
Chrintina Smith, *Exec VP*
EMP: 48 EST: 1977
SALES (est): 7.4MM **Privately Held**
WEB: www.acextrusions.com
SIC: **3089** 3082 Extruded finished plastic products; unsupported plastics profile shapes

(P-5564)
ANURA PLASTIC ENGINEERIGN
5050 Rivergrade Rd, Baldwin Park (91706-1405)
PHONE..................626 814-9684
Wolfgang Buehler, *CEO*
Anura Welikala, *President*
EMP: 21 EST: 1997
SQ FT: 35,000
SALES (est): 2.3MM **Privately Held**
SIC: **3089** Injection molding of plastics

(P-5565)
ARC PLASTICS INC
14010 Shoemaker Ave, Norwalk (90650-4536)
PHONE..................562 802-3299
Richard Renaudo, *President*
Olga Peralta, *Vice Pres*
EMP: 20 EST: 2002
SQ FT: 1,600
SALES (est): 4.8MM **Privately Held**
WEB: www.arcplastics.tripod.com
SIC: **3089** Injection molded finished plastic products; injection molding of plastics

(P-5566)
ARLON LLC
Arlon Adhesives-Films Division
2811 S Harbor Blvd, Santa Ana (92704-5805)
P.O. Box 5260 (92704-0260)
PHONE..................714 540-2811
Elmer Pruim, *President*
Lynne Kemp, *Vice Pres*
Rich Trombino, *Vice Pres*
Nicole Devaud, *CIO*
Kelly Kwo, *Technical Mgr*
EMP: 150
SQ FT: 124,478
SALES (corp-wide): 802.5MM **Publicly Held**
WEB: www.rogerscorp.com
SIC: **3089** 3081 2672 Plastic hardware & building products; unsupported plastics film & sheet; coated & laminated paper
HQ: Arlon Llc
   1100 Governor Lea Rd
   Bear DE 19701

(P-5567)
ARMORCAST PRODUCTS COMPANY INC
500 S Dupont Ave, Ontario (91761-1508)
PHONE..................909 390-1365
Paul Boghossian, *Branch Mgr*
EMP: 40
SALES (corp-wide): 4.1B **Publicly Held**
WEB: www.armorcastprod.com
SIC: **3089** 5092 Plastic processing; toys
HQ: Armorcast Products Company, Inc.
   9140 Lurline Ave
   Chatsworth CA 91311
   818 982-3600

(P-5568)
ARTHURMADE PLASTICS INC
Also Called: Kirk Containers
2131 Garfield Ave, Commerce
(90040-1805)
PHONE..................................323 721-7325
Kirk Marounian, *President*
Arthur Marounian, *Vice Pres*
Silva Marounian, *Vice Pres*
EMP: 75 EST: 1984
SQ FT: 20,000
SALES (est): 11.9MM **Privately Held**
SIC: 3089 Injection molding of plastics

(P-5569)
ARTISTIC PLASTICS INC
725 E Harrison St, Corona (92879-1350)
PHONE..................................951 808-9700
Diane Mixson, *President*
EMP: 19 EST: 2011
SALES (est): 950.5K **Privately Held**
WEB: www.tntplasticmolding.com
SIC: 3089 Injection molding of plastics

(P-5570)
ARZ TECH INC
1411 N Batavia St Ste 110, Orange
(92867-3526)
PHONE..................................714 642-9954
Xiaoyuan Zhang, *Principal*
◆ EMP: 14 EST: 2011
SALES (est): 2.3MM **Privately Held**
WEB: www.arztech.com
SIC: 3089 Injection molding of plastics

(P-5571)
**ASTROFOAM MOLDING
COMPANY INC**
4117 Calle Tesoro, Camarillo (93012-8760)
PHONE..................................805 482-7276
Anthony Bevan, *Ch of Bd*
Steven Bevan, *President*
Pamela R Bevan, *Corp Secy*
Christopher Bevan, *Vice Pres*
▲ EMP: 15 EST: 1969
SQ FT: 21,000
SALES (est): 2.2MM **Privately Held**
WEB: www.astrofoam.com
SIC: 3089 Injection molding of plastics

(P-5572)
B & S PLASTICS INC
Also Called: Waterway Plastics
2200 Sturgis Rd, Oxnard (93030-8978)
PHONE..................................805 981-0262
Bill Spears, *CEO*
Paul Shapiro, *COO*
Sandy Spears, *Corp Secy*
Jessie Garcia, *Purchasing*
Beto Heredia, *Opers Staff*
▲ EMP: 700 EST: 1973
SQ FT: 240,000
SALES (est): 228.8MM **Privately Held**
WEB: www.waterwayplastics.com
SIC: 3089 Injection molding of plastics

(P-5573)
**BACE MANUFACTURING INC
(HQ)**
Also Called: Spm
3125 E Coronado St, Anaheim
(92806-1915)
PHONE..................................714 630-6002
Richard R Harris, *President*
Shannon White, *Vice Pres*
EMP: 700 EST: 1989
SQ FT: 200,000
SALES (est): 101.9MM
SALES (corp-wide): 332.5MM **Privately
Held**
WEB: www.viantmedical.com
SIC: 3089 Injection molding of plastics;
molding primary plastic
PA: Medplast Group, Inc.
7865 Northcourt Rd # 100
Houston TX 77040
480 553-6400

(P-5574)
BALDA C BREWER INC (DH)
Also Called: C Brewer Company
4501 E Wall St, Ontario (91761-8143)
PHONE..................................714 630-6810
Christoph Klaus, *CEO*
Steve Holland, *President*

Harold Hee, *Vice Pres*
Tom Arttus, *Purch Mgr*
Shelley Hanst, *Manager*
▲ EMP: 170 EST: 1968
SQ FT: 60,000
SALES (est): 53MM
SALES (corp-wide): 562.9K **Privately
Held**
WEB: www.clere.de
SIC: 3089 3544 Molding primary plastic;
special dies, tools, jigs & fixtures
HQ: Clere Ag
Schluterstr. 45
Berlin 10707
302 130-0430

(P-5575)
**BARBER-WEBB COMPANY INC
(PA)**
3833 Medford St, Los Angeles
(90063-1997)
PHONE..................................541 488-4821
Donald B Barber Jr, *President*
James Barber, *Exec VP*
Wr Greenbecker, *Senior VP*
Donald Barber, *Executive*
Brian Barber, *Admin Sec*
▼ EMP: 30 EST: 1945
SQ FT: 106,000
SALES (est): 10.5MM **Privately Held**
WEB: www.barber-webb.com
SIC: 3089 Plastic processing

(P-5576)
BARNES PLASTICS INC
18903 Anelo Ave, Gardena (90248-4598)
PHONE..................................310 329-6301
Charles Walker, *CEO*
Scott Piepmeyer, *Vice Pres*
Kathy Choi, *Accounting Mgr*
▲ EMP: 30 EST: 1930
SQ FT: 30,000
SALES (est): 4.6MM **Privately Held**
WEB: www.barnesplastics.com
SIC: 3089 Injection molding of plastics

(P-5577)
BEEMAK PLASTICS LLC
Also Called: Beemak-Idl Display Products
16711 Knott Ave, La Mirada (90638-6013)
PHONE..................................800 421-4393
John Davis, *Mng Member*
Adam Sands, *Planning*
Andrew Marosi, *Design Engr*
Cynthia Franco, *Project Mgr*
Robert Ward, *Controller*
▲ EMP: 100 EST: 1951
SQ FT: 110,000
SALES (est): 25MM
SALES (corp-wide): 575.3MM **Privately
Held**
WEB: www.beemak.com
SIC: 3089 Injection molding of plastics
HQ: Deflecto, Llc
7035 E 86th St
Indianapolis IN 46250
317 849-9555

(P-5578)
**BENT MANUFACTURING CO
BDAA INC**
15442 Chemical Ln, Huntington Beach
(92649-1220)
PHONE..................................714 842-0600
Bruce Christopher Bent, *CEO*
EMP: 15 EST: 2013
SALES (est): 1.4MM **Privately Held**
WEB: www.bentmfg.com
SIC: 3089 3499 5093 Blow molded fin-
ished plastic products; barricades, metal;
barrels & drums

(P-5579)
BERICAP LLC
1671 Champagne Ave Ste B, Ontario
(91761-3650)
PHONE..................................905 634-2248
Steve Buckley, *President*
David Andison, *President*
Tarek Sultan, *General Mgr*
Frank Altenhofen, *Administration*
Okan Unal, *Research*
▲ EMP: 67 EST: 2001

SALES (est): 25.9MM
SALES (corp-wide): 533.7K **Privately
Held**
WEB: www.bericap.com
SIC: 3089 Injection molding of plastics
HQ: Bericap Holding Gmbh
Kirchstr. 5
Budenheim 55257
613 929-020

(P-5580)
BERRY GLOBAL INC
14000 Monte Vista Ave, Chino
(91710-5537)
PHONE..................................909 465-9055
Salama Elsayed, *Branch Mgr*
EMP: 200 **Publicly Held**
WEB: www.berryplastics.com
SIC: 3089 3081 Bottle caps, molded plas-
tic; unsupported plastics film & sheet
HQ: Berry Global, Inc.
101 Oakley St
Evansville IN 47710

(P-5581)
BOLERO INDS INC A CAL CORP
Also Called: Bolero Plastics
11850 Burke St, Santa Fe Springs
(90670-2536)
PHONE..................................562 693-3000
Daniel Imasdounian, *CEO*
Vasken Imasdounian, *Vice Pres*
Annie Imasdounian, *Admin Sec*
EMP: 20 EST: 1975
SQ FT: 19,500
SALES (est): 2.2MM **Privately Held**
WEB: www.boleroplastics.com
SIC: 3089 Injection molding of plastics;
thermoformed finished plastic products

(P-5582)
BOMATIC INC (HQ)
Also Called: Bmi
43225 Business Park Dr, Temecula
(92590-3648)
PHONE..................................909 947-3900
Kjeld R Hestehave, *President*
Borge Hestehave, *Ch of Bd*
Mary Ann, *CEO*
Kirk Franks, *CFO*
Kresten Hestehave, *Vice Pres*
▲ EMP: 40 EST: 1969
SQ FT: 35,000
SALES (est): 21.7MM **Privately Held**
WEB: www.bomatic.com
SIC: 3089 Plastic containers, except foam;
injection molding of plastics
PA: Universal Packaging West, Inc.
43225 Business Park Dr
Temecula CA 92590
909 947-3900

(P-5583)
BOMATIC INC
2181 E Francis St, Ontario (91761-7723)
PHONE..................................909 947-3900
Back Melon, *Manager*
EMP: 60
SALES (corp-wide): 21.7MM **Privately
Held**
WEB: www.bomatic.com
SIC: 3089 Plastic containers, except foam
HQ: Bomatic, Inc.
43225 Business Park Dr
Temecula CA 92590
909 947-3900

(P-5584)
BOTTLEMATE INC (PA)
2095 Leo Ave, Commerce (90040-1626)
PHONE..................................323 887-9009
Kai-Win Chuang, *CEO*
Anderson Chuang, *Vice Pres*
MEI-LI Chang, *Admin Sec*
Chen Katherine, *Accounts Exec*
▲ EMP: 23 EST: 1982
SQ FT: 25,000
SALES (est): 4.5MM **Privately Held**
WEB: www.bottlemate.com
SIC: 3089 5162 Blow molded finished
plastic products; plastics products

(P-5585)
**BRADLEY MANUFACTURING CO
INC**
Also Called: Bradley's Plastic Bag Co
9130 Firestone Blvd, Downey
(90241-5319)
PHONE..................................562 923-5556
Keith Smith, *President*
Richard Lane, *Corp Secy*
Doris Samala, *Office Mgr*
Robert Schneider, *Plant Mgr*
EMP: 28 EST: 1933
SQ FT: 30,000
SALES (est): 4.9MM **Privately Held**
WEB: www.bradleybag.com
SIC: 3089 3069 3083 2673 Plastic pro-
cessing; tubing, rubber; sheets, hard rub-
ber; laminated plastics plate & sheet;
bags: plastic, laminated & coated

(P-5586)
BUMBLE BEE PLASTICS INC
10140 Shoemaker Ave, Santa Fe Springs
(90670-3404)
PHONE..................................562 903-0833
EMP: 15
SALES (corp-wide): 1.6MM **Privately
Held**
SIC: 3089 Injection molding of plastics
PA: Bee Bumble Plastics Inc
3553 Atlantic Ave 328
Long Beach CA 90807
310 749-1655

(P-5587)
C & G PLASTICS
Also Called: C & G Mercury Plastics
12729 Foothill Blvd, Sylmar (91342-5314)
PHONE..................................818 837-3773
Greg Leighton, *President*
▲ EMP: 25 EST: 1963
SQ FT: 6,000
SALES (est): 1.5MM **Privately Held**
WEB: www.cgplastics.net
SIC: 3089 Injection molding of plastics

(P-5588)
C & R MOLDS INC
2737 Palma Dr, Ventura (93003-7651)
P.O. Box 5644 (93005-0644)
PHONE..................................805 658-7098
Randall Ohnemus, *President*
Marla Ohnemus, *Treasurer*
Sue Ohnemus, *Officer*
Steve Ohnemus, *Director*
▲ EMP: 24 EST: 1984
SQ FT: 12,000
SALES (est): 6.4MM **Privately Held**
WEB: www.crmolds.com
SIC: 3089 3544 Injection molding of plas-
tics; plastic hardware & building products;
special dies, tools, jigs & fixtures

(P-5589)
C & S PLASTICS
12621 Foothill Blvd, Sylmar (91342-5312)
PHONE..................................818 896-2489
Charles E Spears, *President*
Karen Spears, *Admin Sec*
EMP: 15 EST: 1979
SQ FT: 6,000
SALES (est): 2.3MM **Privately Held**
WEB: www.cnsplastics.com
SIC: 3089 Injection molding of plastics

(P-5590)
C G MOTOR SPORTS INC
5150 Eucalyptus Ave Ste A, Chino
(91710-9218)
PHONE..................................909 628-1440
Debbie Law, *President*
▲ EMP: 13 EST: 2006
SALES (est): 2.2MM **Privately Held**
SIC: 3089 Automotive parts, plastic

(P-5591)
C-PAK INDUSTRIES INC
4925 Hallmark Pkwy, San Bernardino
(92407-1870)
PHONE..................................909 880-6017
Arch Young, *President*
EMP: 28 EST: 1999
SQ FT: 25,000
SALES (est): 2.5MM **Privately Held**
WEB: www.c-pak.net
SIC: 3089 Injection molding of plastics

(P-5592)
CAL-MOLD INCORPORATED
Also Called: Pierco
3900 Hamner Ave, Eastvale (91752-1017)
PHONE..................951 361-6400
Erik Fleming, *President*
Edward T Fleming, *Chairman*
EMP: 37 **EST:** 1966
SQ FT: 170,000
SALES (est): 1.1MM **Privately Held**
SIC: 3089 Injection molding of plastics

(P-5593)
CAL-TRON CORPORATION
2290 Dixon Ln, Bishop (93514-8094)
PHONE..................760 873-8491
Dan J Pool, *President*
Colleen Pool, *Corp Secy*
EMP: 22 **EST:** 1963
SQ FT: 24,000
SALES (est): 2.5MM **Privately Held**
WEB: www.caltroncorp.com
SIC: 3089 Injection molded finished plastic products; injection molding of plastics

(P-5594)
CALIFORNIA FLEX CORPORATION (PA)
Also Called: Cal Flex
1318 1st St, San Fernando (91340-2804)
PHONE..................818 361-1169
Clifford A Schroeder, *President*
Jani Schroeder, *Corp Secy*
Nancie Hughes, *Administration*
Linda Gwin, *Human Res Dir*
◆ **EMP:** 52 **EST:** 1984
SQ FT: 18,500
SALES (est): 4.4MM **Privately Held**
SIC: 3089 Ducting, plastic

(P-5595)
CALIFORNIA PLASTIC CNTRS INC
2210 E Artesia Blvd, Long Beach (90805-1739)
PHONE..................562 423-3900
Jeff Vice, *President*
Steve Rockenbach, *CFO*
Gottfried Schmidt, *Admin Sec*
EMP: 15 **EST:** 2003
SQ FT: 20,000
SALES (est): 4.6MM **Privately Held**
WEB: www.california-plastic-containers-inc.hub.biz
SIC: 3089 Injection molding of plastics

(P-5596)
CALIFORNIA QUALITY PLAS INC
Also Called: Bel-Air Cases
2104 S Cucamonga Ave, Ontario (91761-5609)
PHONE..................909 930-5667
Erik Calcott, *Branch Mgr*
EMP: 20
SALES (corp-wide): 12.6MM **Privately Held**
WEB: www.calplastics.com
SIC: 3089 Plastic containers, except foam; boxes, plastic; flat panels, plastic; thermoformed finished plastic products
PA: California Quality Plastics, Inc.
2226 S Castle Harbour Pl
Ontario CA 91761
909 930-5535

(P-5597)
CAMBRO MANUFACTURING COMPANY (PA)
5801 Skylab Rd, Huntington Beach (92647-2051)
P.O. Box 2000 (92647-2000)
PHONE..................714 848-1555
Argyle Campbell, *CEO*
Greg Fischer, *Exec VP*
Nick Ditrolio, *Vice Pres*
Chris Fairgrief, *Vice Pres*
Jim Skelly, *Vice Pres*
◆ **EMP:** 500 **EST:** 1951
SQ FT: 300,000
SALES (est): 307.8MM **Privately Held**
WEB: www.cambro.com
SIC: 3089 Trays, plastic

(P-5598)
CANYON PLASTICS INC
28455 Livingston Ave, Valencia (91355-4173)
PHONE..................800 350-6325
Karshan A Gajera, *CEO*
Steven Cruz, *Vice Pres*
Olga Sepulveda, *Vice Pres*
Gunther Shia, *Administration*
Allan Hansen, *Project Mgr*
▲ **EMP:** 78 **EST:** 1982
SQ FT: 110,950
SALES (est): 17.3MM **Privately Held**
WEB: www.canyonplastics.com
SIC: 3089 3544 Plastic containers, except foam; injection molding of plastics; forms (molds), for foundry & plastics working machinery

(P-5599)
CAPCO/PSA
Also Called: California Art Products Co
11125 Vanowen St, North Hollywood (91605-6316)
PHONE..................818 762-4276
Zaven P Berberian, *President*
Andre Adidge, *General Mgr*
EMP: 25 **EST:** 1967
SQ FT: 18,000
SALES (est): 1.2MM **Privately Held**
WEB: www.californiaartproducts.com
SIC: 3089 2821 Planters, plastic; plastic containers, except foam; plastics materials & resins

(P-5600)
CAPLUGS
18704 S Ferris Pl, Rancho Dominguez (90220-6400)
PHONE..................310 537-2300
Alan Dettorre, *Engineer*
Liyang Zhang, *Purch Mgr*
EMP: 13 **EST:** 2019
SALES (est): 4.6MM **Privately Held**
WEB: www.caplugs.com
SIC: 3089 Injection molding of plastics

(P-5601)
CARR MANAGEMENT INC
22324 Temescal Canyon Rd, Corona (92883-4622)
PHONE..................951 277-4800
Nick Rende, *Branch Mgr*
EMP: 70 **Privately Held**
WEB: www.plasticind.com
SIC: 3089 Stock shapes, plastic
PA: Carr Management, Inc.
1 Tara Blvd Ste 303
Nashua NH 03062

(P-5602)
CCI INDUSTRIES INC (PA)
Also Called: Cool Curtain CCI
350 Fischer Ave Ste A, Costa Mesa (92626-4508)
PHONE..................714 662-3879
Michael Robinson, *President*
▲ **EMP:** 27 **EST:** 1976
SQ FT: 15,000
SALES (est): 3.6MM **Privately Held**
WEB: www.coolcurtain.com
SIC: 3089 3564 3496 Doors, folding: plastic or plastic coated fabric; aircurtains (blower); grilles & grillework, woven wire

(P-5603)
CCL TUBE INC (HQ)
2250 E 220th St, Carson (90810-1638)
PHONE..................310 635-4444
Andreas Iseli, *CEO*
April Ambrose, *Credit Mgr*
Sandra Pacay, *Production*
Michael Greaves, *Supervisor*
Duane Sleichter, *Supervisor*
▲ **EMP:** 179 **EST:** 1984
SQ FT: 300,000
SALES (est): 102.7MM
SALES (corp-wide): 4B **Privately Held**
WEB: www.ccllabel.com
SIC: 3089 Injection molded finished plastic products
PA: Ccl Industries Inc
111 Gordon Baker Rd Suite 801
Toronto ON M2H 3
416 756-8500

(P-5604)
CERTAINTEED CORONA INC
235 Radio Rd, Corona (92879-1725)
PHONE..................951 272-1300
EMP: 200
SQ FT: 128,000
SALES (est): 20.9MM
SALES (corp-wide): 332.4MM **Privately Held**
SIC: 3089 3442 Plastics Products, Nec, Nsk
HQ: Certainteed Llc
20 Moores Rd
Malvern PA 19355
610 893-5000

(P-5605)
CERTIFIED THERMOPLASTICS INC
Also Called: Certified Thermoplastics LLC
26381 Ferry Ct, Santa Clarita (91350-2998)
PHONE..................661 222-3006
Robert Duncan, *President*
Gilberto Latin, *Opers Mgr*
▲ **EMP:** 35 **EST:** 1978
SQ FT: 30,000
SALES (est): 9.5MM
SALES (corp-wide): 628.9MM **Publicly Held**
WEB: www.ctplastics.com
SIC: 3089 Injection molding of plastics
HQ: Ducommun Labarge Technologies, Inc.
1601 E Broadway Rd
Phoenix AZ 85040
480 998-0733

(P-5606)
CHUBBY GORILLA INC (PA)
4320 N Harbor Blvd, Fullerton (92835-1091)
PHONE..................844 365-5218
Ibraheim Hamsa Aboabdo, *CEO*
Eyad Aboabdo, *Vice Pres*
Dwain Sparks, *Director*
EMP: 29 **EST:** 2015
SALES (est): 4.8MM **Privately Held**
WEB: www.chubbygorilla.com
SIC: 3089 Closures, plastic

(P-5607)
CLEAR-AD INC
Also Called: Brochure Holders 4u
2410 W 3rd St, Santa Ana (92703-3519)
PHONE..................877 899-1002
Juan Diaz, *CEO*
Bruce Kelly, *Vice Pres*
John Diaz, *Executive*
Lauren Schlieser, *Sales Staff*
EMP: 30 **EST:** 1972
SQ FT: 17,006
SALES (est): 7.6MM **Privately Held**
WEB: www.brochureholders4u.com
SIC: 3089 3544 3993 3061 Injection molded finished plastic products; forms (molds), for foundry & plastics working machinery; displays & cutouts, window & lobby; medical & surgical rubber tubing (extruded & lathe-cut); advertising specialties

(P-5608)
CMP DISPLAY SYSTEMS INC
23301 Wilmington Ave, Carson (90745-6209)
PHONE..................805 499-3642
William M Hooker, *CEO*
Ken Collin, *President*
Bruce Miller, *Vice Pres*
EMP: 75 **EST:** 1980
SALES (est): 12.2MM
SALES (corp-wide): 628.9MM **Publicly Held**
WEB: www.cmp-displays.com
SIC: 3089 3823 3812 Injection molding of plastics; industrial instrmnts msrmnt display/control process variable; search & navigation equipment
HQ: Ducommun Labarge Technologies, Inc.
23301 Wilmington Ave
Carson CA 90745
310 513-7200

(P-5609)
COAST TO COAST MFG LLC
Also Called: Fire Windows and Doors
430 Nevada St, Perris (92373-4244)
P.O. Box 1503, Perris (92572-1503)
PHONE..................909 798-5024
John Seymour, *Mng Member*
EMP: 13 **EST:** 1998
SALES (est): 2.1MM **Privately Held**
WEB: www.coasttocoastmfg.com
SIC: 3089 Windows, plastic

(P-5610)
CODAN US CORPORATION
3501 S Harbor Blvd # 100, Santa Ana (92704-6919)
PHONE..................714 430-1300
Peter Schwark, *Ch of Bd*
Jeff Nielsen, *President*
Bernd J Larsen, *CEO*
Deon Miller, *Vice Pres*
Ruth Robertson, *Controller*
▲ **EMP:** 145 **EST:** 1971
SALES (est): 28.9MM
SALES (corp-wide): 192.5K **Privately Held**
WEB: www.codanusa.com
SIC: 3089 Molding primary plastic
HQ: Codan Medizinische Gerate Gmbh & Co Kg
Stig Husted-Andersen Str. 11
Lensahn 23738
436 351-11

(P-5611)
CONROY & KNOWLTON INC
320 S Montebello Blvd, Montebello (90640-5112)
PHONE..................323 665-5288
William A Conroy, *President*
Michelle Conroy, *Manager*
EMP: 21 **EST:** 1946
SQ FT: 17,000
SALES (est): 3.3MM **Privately Held**
WEB: www.conroyknowlton.com
SIC: 3089 Injection molding of plastics

(P-5612)
CONTAINER OPTIONS
1493 E San Bernardino Ave, San Bernardino (92408-2927)
PHONE..................909 478-0045
Patricia Shockey, *CEO*
EMP: 18 **EST:** 1995
SQ FT: 43,000
SALES (est): 2.7MM **Privately Held**
SIC: 3089 Plastic containers, except foam

(P-5613)
COOL-PAK LLC
401 N Rice Ave, Oxnard (93030-7936)
PHONE..................805 981-2434
Niall Kelly,
Anthony Toohey, *Sales Staff*
Jim Borchard,
Derek Goodin,
Patrick Larmon,
▲ **EMP:** 85 **EST:** 2001
SQ FT: 124,000
SALES (est): 28.2MM
SALES (corp-wide): 13.4B **Privately Held**
WEB: www.cool-pak.com
SIC: 3089 Plastic containers, except foam
HQ: Bunzl Distribution Usa, Llc
1 Cityplace Dr Ste 200
Saint Louis MO 63141
314 997-5959

(P-5614)
CORNUCOPIA TOOL & PLASTICS INC
448 Sherwood Rd, Paso Robles (93446-3554)
P.O. Box 1915 (93447-1915)
PHONE..................805 238-7660
Larry Horn, *President*
Art Horn, *Vice Pres*
EMP: 47 **EST:** 1969
SQ FT: 20,000
SALES (est): 10.1MM **Privately Held**
WEB: www.cornucopiaplastics.com
SIC: 3089 3544 Injection molding of plastics; industrial molds

(P-5615)
COSMETIC SPECIALTIES INTL LLC
550 E 3rd St, Oxnard　(93030-6020)
PHONE..............................805 487-6698
Michael J Musso, *President*
Mark Hauptman, *President*
Bruce Bellerose, *COO*
David Paneiko, *CFO*
Lisa Naylor, *Vice Pres*
▲ EMP: 102 EST: 1978
SALES (est): 27.1MM
SALES (corp-wide): 31.1MM **Privately Held**
WEB: www.csillc.com
SIC: 3089 Injection molded finished plastic products; injection molding of plastics
PA: Asparron Capital, Llc
　1701 W Northwest Hwy # 100
　Grapevine TX 76051
　817 865-6573

(P-5616)
COUNTRY PLASTICS INC
32501 Road 228, Woodlake (93286-9705)
PHONE..............................559 597-2556
Jay D Ayres, *President*
Jenny Ayres, *Corp Secy*
Shawn Howell, *Production*
▲ EMP: 17 EST: 1975
SQ FT: 3,000
SALES (est): 4.2MM **Privately Held**
WEB: www.countryplastics.net
SIC: 3089 Injection molding of plastics

(P-5617)
CRAFTECH EDM CORPORATION
Also Called: Crafttech
2941 E La Jolla St, Anaheim (92806-1306)
PHONE..............................714 630-8117
John Butler, *President*
Peggy Thomas, *CFO*
Alfredo Bonetto, *Senior VP*
John Ayers, *Vice Pres*
Douglas Barker, *Vice Pres*
▲ EMP: 220 EST: 1983
SQ FT: 35,000
SALES (est): 51.2MM **Privately Held**
WEB: www.craftechcorp.com
SIC: 3089 3559 Injection molding of plastics; plastics working machinery

(P-5618)
CREU LLC
12750 Baltic Ct, Rancho Cucamonga (91730-8957)
PHONE..............................909 483-4888
Anthony Quezada, *CEO*
EMP: 25 EST: 2014
SALES (est): 1.3MM **Privately Held**
SIC: 3089 5063 Automotive parts, plastic; lighting fixtures

(P-5619)
CYPRESS MANUFACTURING LLC
Also Called: Hitech Plastics and Molds
25620 Rye Canyon Rd Ste B, Valencia (91355-1140)
PHONE..............................818 477-2777
Robert Loranger, *Mng Member*
Chris Loranger, *Admn Asst*
Christine Loranger, *Administration*
Tae Youn, *Design Engr*
Arian Dart,
◆ EMP: 15 EST: 1987
SQ FT: 20,000
SALES (est): 2MM **Privately Held**
WEB: www.hitech-plastics.com
SIC: 3089 Injection molding of plastics

(P-5620)
CYTYDEL PLASTICS INC
17813 S Main St Ste 117, Gardena (90248-3542)
PHONE..............................310 523-2884
Aeran Lee, *President*
Chang Lee, *Treasurer*
◆ EMP: 18 EST: 1993
SQ FT: 10,200
SALES (est): 1MM **Privately Held**
SIC: 3089 Plastic processing

(P-5621)
DELAMO MANUFACTURING INC
7171 Telegraph Rd, Montebello (90640-6511)
PHONE..............................323 936-3566
Fred Morad, *CEO*
Helana Morad, *Business Dir*
Lily Lianawati-Koshi, *Mfg Staff*
EMP: 80 EST: 2008
SQ FT: 120,000
SALES (est): 7.8MM **Privately Held**
WEB: www.delamo-mfg.com
SIC: 3089 Plastic kitchenware, tableware & houseware

(P-5622)
DELFIN DESIGN & MFG INC
15672 Producer Ln, Huntington Beach (92649-1310)
PHONE..............................949 888-4644
John M Rief, *President*
Rita Williams, *Corp Secy*
Paul Iverson, *Exec VP*
▲ EMP: 28 EST: 1991
SALES (est): 4.8MM **Privately Held**
WEB: www.delfinfs.com
SIC: 3089 3083 Thermoformed finished plastic products; plastic finished products, laminated

(P-5623)
DEMOLDCO PLASTICS INC
3931 E Miraloma Ave, Anaheim (92806-6201)
PHONE..............................714 577-9391
Nick Trees, *President*
EMP: 32 EST: 1994
SQ FT: 6,600
SALES (est): 3.7MM **Privately Held**
SIC: 3089 Injection molding of plastics

(P-5624)
DESIGN WEST TECHNOLOGIES INC
2701 Dow Ave, Tustin (92780-7209)
PHONE..............................714 731-0201
Ryan Hur, *President*
Bryan Nguyen, *Planning*
John Mace, *CIO*
Hope Arakaki, *Info Tech Mgr*
Tony Figurski, *Prgrmr*
▲ EMP: 65 EST: 1994
SQ FT: 60,000
SALES (est): 16.2MM **Privately Held**
WEB: www.dwtusa.com
SIC: 3089 8711 Injection molded finished plastic products; electrical or electronic engineering

(P-5625)
DESIGNER SASH AND DOOR SYS INC
Also Called: Designer Fashion Door
45899 Via Tornado, Temecula (92590-3359)
PHONE..............................951 657-4179
Ross Eberhart, *President*
Kenneth McBride, *Treasurer*
EMP: 26 EST: 1988
SQ FT: 20,000
SALES (est): 1MM **Privately Held**
SIC: 3089 2431 5211 Windows, plastic; doors, wood; door & window products

(P-5626)
DIAL INDUSTRIES INC
Also Called: All-Power Plastics Div Dial
3616 Noakes St, Los Angeles (90023-3200)
PHONE..............................323 263-6878
Richard Oxford, *President*
Diana Ghiotto, *Manager*
EMP: 100
SALES (corp-wide): 17.9MM **Privately Held**
WEB: www.dialind.com
SIC: 3089 3354 Plastic kitchenware, tableware & houseware; aluminum extruded products
PA: Dial Industries, Inc.
　3628 Noakes St
　Los Angeles CA 90023
　323 263-6878

(P-5627)
DIVERSE OPTICS INC
10339 Dorset St, Rancho Cucamonga (91730-3067)
PHONE..............................909 593-9330
Erik Fleming, *President*
Letty Dela Cruz, *Sales Engr*
Letty Trevino, *Sales Engr*
Deborah De Melo, *Director*
EMP: 20 EST: 1987
SALES (est): 2.7MM **Privately Held**
WEB: www.diverseoptics.com
SIC: 3089 3827 Injection molding of plastics; lenses, optical: all types except ophthalmic

(P-5628)
DOMINO PLASTICS MFG INC
601 Gateway Ct, Bakersfield (93307-6827)
PHONE..............................661 396-3744
W Thomas Bathe III, *CEO*
Neil Conway, *President*
Suzanne Lostaunau, *Office Mgr*
Fabiola Rodriguez, *Office Mgr*
Mike Zavala, *Representative*
EMP: 21 EST: 1971
SQ FT: 16,000
SALES (est): 3.1MM **Privately Held**
WEB: www.dominoplastics.com
SIC: 3089 Billfold inserts, plastic

(P-5629)
DOREL JUVENILE GROUP INC
9950 Calabash Ave, Fontana (92335-5210)
PHONE..............................909 428-0295
Carrisa John, *Principal*
EMP: 32
SALES (corp-wide): 2.7B **Privately Held**
WEB: www.na.doreljuvenile.com
SIC: 3089 Plastic kitchenware, tableware & houseware
HQ: Dorel Juvenile Group, Inc.
　2525 State St
　Columbus IN 47201
　800 457-5276

(P-5630)
DOREL JUVENILE GROUP INC
Also Called: Cosco Home & Office Products
5400 Shea Center Dr, Ontario (91761-7892)
PHONE..............................909 390-5705
Rick Mc Cook, *Manager*
Edward Morales, *Supervisor*
EMP: 32
SALES (corp-wide): 2.7B **Privately Held**
WEB: www.na.doreljuvenile.com
SIC: 3089 Plastic kitchenware, tableware & houseware
HQ: Dorel Juvenile Group, Inc.
　2525 State St
　Columbus IN 47201
　800 457-5276

(P-5631)
DURA PLASTIC PRODUCTS INC (HQ)
533 E Third St, Beaumont (92223-2715)
P.O. Box 2097 (92223-0997)
PHONE..............................951 845-3161
Kevin Rost, *CEO*
Monica Rost, *CFO*
John Akamine, *Executive*
Peter Doan, *Engineer*
Marianna Gomez, *Accounting Dir*
◆ EMP: 100 EST: 1974
SQ FT: 150,000
SALES (est): 33MM **Privately Held**
WEB: www.duraplastics.com
SIC: 3089 Fittings for pipe, plastic

(P-5632)
EAGLE PRODUCTS - PLAST INDUST
10811 Fremont Ave, Ontario (91762-3912)
PHONE..............................909 465-1548
Henry Ngo, *President*
Thu Nguyen, *Corp Secy*
EMP: 14 EST: 1994
SQ FT: 6,100
SALES (est): 346.7K **Privately Held**
SIC: 3089 Injection molding of plastics

(P-5633)
ECOPLAST CORPORATION INC
13414 Slover Ave, Fontana (92337-6977)
PHONE..............................909 346-0450
Jose Perez, *President*
Massoud Forouzan, *CFO*
EMP: 32 EST: 1963
SQ FT: 40,000
SALES (est): 3.1MM **Privately Held**
SIC: 3089 Plastic containers, except foam

(P-5634)
EDCO PLASTICS INC
2110 E Winston Rd, Anaheim (92806-5534)
PHONE..............................714 772-1986
Edward A Contreras, *President*
Maria Contreras, *Vice Pres*
▲ EMP: 49 EST: 1984
SQ FT: 25,000
SALES (est): 9.1MM **Privately Held**
WEB: www.edcoplastics.com
SIC: 3089 Molding primary plastic; injection molding of plastics

(P-5635)
EDGE PLASTICS INC (PA)
Also Called: O D I
3016 Kansas Ave Bldg 3, Riverside (92507-3442)
PHONE..............................951 786-4750
Earl David Grimes, *President*
Holly Grimes, *Admin Sec*
Ralph Vasquez, *Controller*
◆ EMP: 27 EST: 1990
SQ FT: 23,000
SALES (est): 5.9MM **Privately Held**
WEB: www.odigrips.com
SIC: 3089 5199 5091 Injection molding of plastics; advertising specialties; bicycle parts & accessories

(P-5636)
EDRIS PLASTICS MFG INC
4560 Pacific Blvd, Vernon (90058-2208)
PHONE..............................323 581-7000
Hovanes Hovik Issaghollan, *CEO*
▲ EMP: 26 EST: 1991
SQ FT: 27,000
SALES (est): 6.6MM **Privately Held**
WEB: www.edrisplastics.com
SIC: 3089 Injection molding of plastics

(P-5637)
EE PAULEY PLASTIC EXTRUSION
17177 Navajo Rd, Apple Valley (92307-1046)
PHONE..............................760 240-3737
Ben Oehme, *Controller*
EMP: 17 EST: 2010
SALES (est): 2.9MM **Privately Held**
WEB: www.pauleyplastic.com
SIC: 3089 Injection molding of plastics

(P-5638)
EEP HOLDINGS LLC (PA)
4626 Eucalyptus Ave, Chino (91710-9215)
PHONE..............................909 597-7861
Earl E Payton, *CEO*
EMP: 370 EST: 2002
SALES (est): 497.4MM **Privately Held**
SIC: 3089 3544 Molding primary plastic; special dies, tools, jigs & fixtures

(P-5639)
EMBER TECHNOLOGIES INC
880 Hampshire Rd, Westlake Village (91361-2811)
PHONE..............................520 400-9337
Clayton Alexander, *CEO*
Phil Poel, *COO*
Tom Johnstone, *Chief Mkg Ofcr*
John Stone, *Officer*
Jolene Abbott, *Vice Pres*
EMP: 50 EST: 2017
SALES (est): 7.4MM **Privately Held**
WEB: www.ember.com
SIC: 3089 5999 Cups, plastic, except foam; electronic parts & equipment

(P-5640)
ENDUREQUEST CORPORATION
1813 Thunderbolt Dr, Porterville
(93257-9300)
PHONE..................................559 783-9220
Kenneth Dewing, *President*
Russell Sarno, *Vice Pres*
▲ EMP: 25 EST: 1991
SQ FT: 10,000
SALES (est): 4.6MM Privately Held
WEB: www.endurequest.com
SIC: 3089 Plastic hardware & building
products; injection molding of plastics

(P-5641)
**ENGINEERING MODEL ASSOC
INC (PA)**
Also Called: Ema
1020 Wallace Way, City of Industry
(91748-1027)
PHONE..................................626 912-7011
John Jay Wanderman, *President*
Leon Katz, *Admin Sec*
EMP: 25 EST: 1955
SQ FT: 28,000
SALES (est): 9.4MM Privately Held
SIC: 3089 5162 Plastic processing; plas-
tics products

(P-5642)
**EXPRESS SYSTEMS & ENGRG
INC**
41357 Date St, Murrieta (92562-7030)
PHONE..................................951 461-1500
Mike Arndt, *President*
Bill Oppertshauser, *Opers Mgr*
▲ EMP: 18 EST: 1991
SQ FT: 14,000
SALES (est): 1.9MM Privately Held
SIC: 3089 Injection molding of plastics

(P-5643)
EXTRUMED INC (DH)
Also Called: Vesta
547 Trm Cir, Corona (92879-1768)
PHONE..................................951 547-7400
Phil Estes, *President*
Eric R Schnur, *CEO*
Chris Guglielmi, *CFO*
EMP: 99 EST: 1990
SQ FT: 53,000
SALES (est): 35.3MM
SALES (corp-wide): 245.5B Publicly
Held
WEB: www.lubrizol.com
SIC: 3089 Injection molding of plastics
HQ: Vesta Intermediate Funding, Inc.
9900 S 57th St
Franklin WI 53132
414 423-0550

(P-5644)
**FAIRWAY INJECTION MOLDS
INC**
20109 Paseo Del Prado, Walnut
(91789-2665)
PHONE..................................909 595-2201
Brian Jones, *Managing Dir*
Perry Morgan, *CEO*
Dave Cockrell, *General Mgr*
Antonio Barrera, *Prgrmr*
James Gabel, *Prgrmr*
▲ EMP: 54
SQ FT: 31,147
SALES (est): 16MM Privately Held
WEB: www.fairwaymolds.com
SIC: 3089 Industrial molds

(P-5645)
**FISCHER MOLD
INCORPORATED**
393 Meyer Cir, Corona (92879-1078)
PHONE..................................951 279-1140
Robert Fischer, *President*
Mary Peterson, *Office Mgr*
Katie Stephenson, *Office Mgr*
Eleanor Fischer, *Admin Sec*
Ruthann Harris, *Prdtn Mgr*
▲ EMP: 60 EST: 1969
SQ FT: 32,000
SALES (est): 8.9MM Privately Held
WEB: www.fischermoldinc.com
SIC: 3089 3544 Injection molding of plas-
tics; special dies, tools, jigs & fixtures

(P-5646)
FIT-LINE INC
Also Called: Fit-Line Global
2901 S Tech Center Dr, Santa Ana
(92705-5657)
PHONE..................................714 549-9091
Ronni Levinson, *CEO*
George Alvarado, *Vice Pres*
▼ EMP: 50 EST: 1993
SQ FT: 4,500
SALES (est): 5.5MM Privately Held
WEB: www.fit-lineglobal.com
SIC: 3089 Fittings for pipe, plastic

(P-5647)
FLUIDMASTER INC (PA)
30800 Rancho Viejo Rd, San Juan Capis-
trano (92675-1564)
PHONE..................................949 728-2000
Robert Andersonschoepe, *CEO*
Michael Draves, *President*
Terry Bland, *CFO*
Robert Connell, *Exec VP*
Tawnya Cummiskey, *Vice Pres*
◆ EMP: 127 EST: 1957
SALES (est): 317.3MM Privately Held
WEB: www.fluidmaster.com
SIC: 3089 3432 1711 Injection molding of
plastics; plumbing fixture fittings & trim;
plumbing contractors

(P-5648)
G B REMANUFACTURING INC
2040 E Cherry Indus Cir, Long Beach
(90805-4410)
PHONE..................................562 272-7333
Michael J Kitching, *President*
F William Kitching, *Chairman*
Patricia Kitching, *Treasurer*
Joe Evert, *Engineer*
Laura Bungert, *Purchasing*
▲ EMP: 70 EST: 1986
SQ FT: 26,400
SALES (est): 9.8MM Privately Held
WEB: www.gbreman.com
SIC: 3089 Injection molded finished plastic
products

(P-5649)
GEIGER PLASTICS INC
16150 S Maple Ave A, Gardena
(90248-2837)
PHONE..................................310 327-9926
Charlotte May, *President*
Vangie Ramirez, *Corp Secy*
Adriana Formica-Garcia, *Office Mgr*
Michael Kamau, *Prdtn Mgr*
EMP: 20 EST: 1964
SQ FT: 10,000
SALES (est): 3.3MM Privately Held
WEB: www.geigerplastics.com
SIC: 3089 3559 Injection molding of plas-
tics; plastics working machinery

(P-5650)
GEMINI FILM & BAG INC (PA)
Also Called: Gemini Plastics
3574 Fruitland Ave, Maywood
(90270-2008)
P.O. Box 806, Atwood (92811-0806)
PHONE..................................323 582-0901
James Fruth, *President*
Brian Kunisch, *CFO*
EMP: 25 EST: 1966
SQ FT: 12,000
SALES (est): 2.5MM Privately Held
SIC: 3089 8742 Extruded finished plastic
products; manufacturing management
consultant

(P-5651)
GEO PLASTICS
2200 E 52nd St, Vernon (90058-3446)
PHONE..................................323 277-8106
Michael Abraham Morris, *CEO*
Justin Hunt, *Vice Pres*
Robert Burch, *Sales Staff*
Rita Adams, *Manager*
▲ EMP: 27 EST: 1992
SALES (est): 6.4MM Privately Held
WEB: www.geoplastics.com
SIC: 3089 Extruded finished plastic prod-
ucts

(P-5652)
**GIBRALTAR PLASTIC PDTS
CORP**
12885 Foothill Blvd, Sylmar (91342-5317)
PHONE..................................818 365-9318
Harvey J Jacobs, *President*
Keith Jacobs, *Vice Pres*
Adam Libarkin, *General Mgr*
Tom Lee, *Site Mgr*
EMP: 25 EST: 1964
SQ FT: 30,000
SALES (est): 8.5MM Privately Held
WEB: www.gibraltarplastic.com
SIC: 3089 Injection molded finished plastic
products; cases, plastic

(P-5653)
GILL CORPORATION (PA)
4056 Easy St, El Monte (91731-1054)
PHONE..................................626 443-6094
Stephen E Gill, *President*
Dave Cross, *COO*
Janet Caldwell, *CFO*
William Heinze, *CFO*
Irv Freund, *Vice Pres*
◆ EMP: 236 EST: 1945
SQ FT: 390,000
SALES (est): 225.8MM Privately Held
WEB: www.thegillcorp.com
SIC: 3089 3469 3272 2448 Laminating of
plastic; panels, building: plastic; honey-
combed metal; panels & sections, prefab-
ricated concrete; cargo containers, wood
& metal combination; aircraft

(P-5654)
**GKN ARSPACE TRNSPRNCY
SYSTEMS (DH)**
12122 Western Ave, Garden Grove
(92841-2915)
PHONE..................................714 893-7531
John Danley, *CEO*
Joakim Anderson, *CEO*
Mike McCann, *CEO*
Will Hoy, *CFO*
David Nguyen, *CFO*
▲ EMP: 359 EST: 1946
SQ FT: 324,000
SALES (est): 116.6MM
SALES (corp-wide): 11.6B Privately Held
WEB: www.gkntransparencysystems.com
SIC: 3089 3231 3827 3728 Windows,
plastic; windshields, plastic; mirrors, truck
& automobile; made from purchased
glass; optical instruments & lenses; air-
craft parts & equipment; unsupported
plastics film & sheet; plastics materials &
resins
HQ: Gkn America Corp.
1180 Peachtree St Ne # 2450
Atlanta GA 30309
630 972-9300

(P-5655)
**GOLDMAN GLOBAL
GREENFIELD INC**
2025 E 48th St, Vernon (90058-2021)
PHONE..................................323 589-3444
Michelle Choi, *President*
▲ EMP: 16 EST: 1997
SQ FT: 17,000
SALES (est): 518K Privately Held
SIC: 3089 Plastic processing

(P-5656)
**GRAND FUSION HOUSEWARES
LLC (PA)**
12 Partridge, Irvine (92604-4519)
PHONE..................................888 614-7263
Brendan Bauer, *CEO*
EMP: 41 EST: 2016
SQ FT: 1,000
SALES (est): 4.3MM Privately Held
SIC: 3089 3083 2869 Kitchenware, plas-
tic; laminated plastic sheets; silicones

(P-5657)
GRIFF INDUSTRIES INC
4515 Runway Dr, Lancaster (93536-8530)
PHONE..................................661 728-0111
Michael Griffin, *President*
◆ EMP: 19
SQ FT: 8,400

SALES (est): 3.8MM Privately Held
WEB: www.griffindustries.com
SIC: 3089 Injection molding of plastics

(P-5658)
GT STYLING CORP
2830 E Via Martens, Anaheim
(92806-1751)
PHONE..................................714 644-9214
Gregory Allen Knox, *CEO*
Jodee Jensen Smith, *Exec VP*
EMP: 27 EST: 2001
SALES (est): 1.6MM Privately Held
SIC: 3089 Molding primary plastic

(P-5659)
**HAMMERHEAD INDUSTRIES
INC**
5720 Nicolle St, Ventura (93003-7612)
PHONE..................................805 658-9922
Kenneth S Collin Jr, *President*
John Salentine, *Vice Pres*
Mark Bursek, *Principal*
▲ EMP: 26 EST: 1995
SQ FT: 8,000
SALES (est): 5.3MM Privately Held
WEB: www.gearkeeper.com
SIC: 3089 Injection molding of plastics

(P-5660)
**HERMAN ENGINEERING & MFG
INC**
4501 E Airport Dr Ste B, Ontario
(91761-7877)
P.O. Box 418, Oak Harbor OH (43449-
0418)
PHONE..................................909 483-1631
Donald B Donisthorpe, *President*
Tiffany Herrmann, *Manager*
▲ EMP: 15 EST: 1979
SQ FT: 30,000
SALES (est): 2.5MM Privately Held
SIC: 3089 Plastic containers, except foam

(P-5661)
**HI-REL PLASTICS & MOLDING
CORP**
7575 Jurupa Ave, Riverside (92504-1012)
PHONE..................................951 354-0258
Rakesh Bajaria, *CEO*
Dennis Sovalia, *President*
Harry Thummer, *CFO*
Rick Bajria, *Vice Pres*
Oscar Contreras, *Sales Staff*
▲ EMP: 50 EST: 1984
SQ FT: 15,000
SALES (est): 8MM Privately Held
WEB: www.hirelplastics.com
SIC: 3089 3549 3599 Injection molded
finished plastic products; assembly ma-
chines, including robotic; machine shop,
jobbing & repair

(P-5662)
HIGH SIERRA PLASTICS
375 Joe Smith Rd, Bishop (93514-8800)
PHONE..................................760 873-5600
Robert W Wilson, *Partner*
EMP: 15 EST: 1988
SALES (est): 551.9K Privately Held
WEB: www.highsierraplastics.com
SIC: 3089 3544 Blow molded finished
plastic products; plastic processing; ther-
moformed finished plastic products; in-
dustrial molds

(P-5663)
HIGHLAND PLASTICS INC
Also Called: Hi-Plas
3650 Dulles Dr, Jurupa Valley
(91752-3260)
PHONE..................................951 360-9587
James L Nelson, *Principal*
William B Warren, *CFO*
William Warren, *CFO*
Miguel Viguerias, *Purch Mgr*
Mark Murphy, *Purchasing*
◆ EMP: 130
SQ FT: 150,000
SALES (est): 31.8MM Privately Held
WEB: www.hiplas.com
SIC: 3089 Injection molding of plastics

(P-5664)
HOOD MANUFACTURING INC
Also Called: Thermobile
2621 S Birch St, Santa Ana (92707-3410)
PHONE....................714 979-7681
Michael Hood, *President*
Patrica Hood, *Admin Sec*
Michele Rauschenbach, *CIO*
EMP: 60 EST: 1948
SQ FT: 24,000 **Privately Held**
WEB: www.hoodmfg.com
SIC: 3089 3585 Injection molded finished plastic products; refrigeration & heating equipment

(P-5665)
HOOSIER INC
1152 California Ave, Corona (92881-3324)
P.O. Box 78926 (92877-0164)
PHONE....................951 272-3070
Robert G Simms, *CEO*
Mitchell McCall, *Vice Pres*
Shannon Sims, *Executive*
Willie Abundez, *Info Tech Mgr*
Cesar Mier, *Project Mgr*
EMP: 80 EST: 1979
SQ FT: 45,000
SALES (est): 22MM **Privately Held**
WEB: www.hoosierinc.com
SIC: 3089 Injection molding of plastics

(P-5666)
HOPE PLASTIC CO INC
5353 Strohm Ave, North Hollywood (91601-3526)
PHONE....................818 769-5560
Steven Borden, *President*
Bill Borden, *Treasurer*
Hope Borden, *Admin Sec*
▲ EMP: 20 EST: 1964
SQ FT: 17,000
SALES (est): 2.7MM **Privately Held**
WEB: www.hopeplastics.com
SIC: 3089 Injection molding of plastics

(P-5667)
HOUSEWARES INTERNATIONAL INC
Also Called: American Household Company
1933 S Broadway Ste 867, Los Angeles (90007-4523)
PHONE....................323 581-3000
Kamyar Solouki, *CEO*
Sean Solouki, *Vice Pres*
Norick Parseh, *Office Mgr*
Glenda Seale, *Administration*
Paula Love, *Accounting Mgr*
◆ EMP: 35 EST: 1988
SALES (est): 8.2MM **Privately Held**
WEB: www.housewaresintl.com
SIC: 3089 5023 Kitchenware, plastic; kitchenware

(P-5668)
HUSKY INJCTION MLDING SYSTEMS
5245 Maureen Ln, Moorpark (93021-7125)
PHONE....................805 523-9593
EMP: 99 **Privately Held**
WEB: www.husky.co
SIC: 3089 Injection molding of plastics
HQ: Husky Injection Molding Systems, Inc.
288 North Rd
Milton VT 05468
802 859-8000

(P-5669)
HUSKY INJCTION MLDING SYSTEMS
3505 Cadillac Ave Ste N4, Costa Mesa (92626-1433)
PHONE....................714 545-8200
Michael Smith, *Manager*
EMP: 99
SQ FT: 6,501 **Privately Held**
WEB: www.husky.co
SIC: 3089 Injection molding of plastics
HQ: Husky Injection Molding Systems, Inc.
288 North Rd
Milton VT 05468
802 859-8000

(P-5670)
IDEMIA AMERICA CORP
3150 E Ana St, Compton (90221-5607)
PHONE....................310 884-7900
Eric Daniele, *Director*
Liz Palmer, *Senior VP*
Anne Dang, *Software Engr*
Boris Galchenko, *Technician*
Vronique De Moura, *Project Mgr*
EMP: 161
SALES (corp-wide): 1.3B **Privately Held**
WEB: www.idemia.com
SIC: 3089 3083 Identification cards, plastic; plastic finished products, laminated
HQ: Idemia America Corp.
11951 Freedom Dr Ste 1800
Reston VA 20190
703 775-7800

(P-5671)
IGS MOLDING LLC
5093 Walnut Grove Ave, San Gabriel (91776-2023)
PHONE....................562 801-3522
EMP: 13
SALES (corp-wide): 610.4K **Privately Held**
WEB: www.igsmolding.com
SIC: 3089 Injection molding of plastics
PA: I.G.S. Molding Llc
1518 Ricardo St
Los Angeles CA 90033
626 642-8745

(P-5672)
INCA PLASTICS MOLDING CO INC
948 E Belmont St, Ontario (91761-4549)
PHONE....................909 923-3235
Howard L Haigh, *President*
Bill Odell, *Sales Mgr*
▲ EMP: 27 EST: 1960
SQ FT: 33,000
SALES (est): 3.8MM **Privately Held**
WEB: www.incaplastics.com
SIC: 3089 3714 3544 3443 Injection molding of plastics; motor vehicle parts & accessories; special dies, tools, jigs & fixtures; fabricated plate work (boiler shop)

(P-5673)
INCA PLASTICS MOLDING CO INC
17129 Koala Rd, Adelanto (92301-2248)
PHONE....................760 246-8087
Howard Haigh, *CEO*
EMP: 19 EST: 2016
SALES (est): 1.5MM **Privately Held**
SIC: 3089 Injection molding of plastics

(P-5674)
INLINE PLASTICS INC
1950 S Baker Ave, Ontario (91761-7755)
PHONE....................909 923-1033
Kelly Orr, *CEO*
Alfredo Perez, *Vice Pres*
Charlene Woodard, *Office Mgr*
EMP: 25 EST: 1996
SQ FT: 21,000
SALES (est): 5.2MM **Privately Held**
WEB: www.inlineplasticsinc.com
SIC: 3089 Injection molding of plastics

(P-5675)
INNOVATIVE TECHNOLOGIES GROUP ✪
10155 Sharon Cir, Rancho Cucamonga (91730-5300)
PHONE....................909 476-2555
Robert Fortune, *CEO*
Steve Hoare, *CFO*
Rania Bishay, *Office Mgr*
Brendon Heyes, *Admin Sec*
EMP: 13 EST: 2021
SALES (est): 893.1K **Privately Held**
SIC: 3089 Injection molding of plastics

(P-5676)
IPS INDUSTRIES INC
Also Called: Spectrum Bags
12641 166th St, Cerritos (90703-2101)
PHONE....................562 623-2555
Frank Su, *CEO*
Peter Hii, *CFO*
David Silva, *Exec VP*

Ben Tran, *Exec VP*
Betty Green, *Vice Pres*
◆ EMP: 80 EST: 1990
SQ FT: 150,000
SALES (est): 21.4MM **Privately Held**
WEB: www.ipspi.com
SIC: 3089 3629 Battery cases, plastic or plastic combination; battery chargers, rectifying or nonrotating

(P-5677)
J & L CSTM PLSTIC EXTRSONS INC
1532 Santa Anita Ave, South El Monte (91733-3314)
PHONE....................626 442-0711
Louis Salmon, *President*
Jaime Lizarraga, *Vice Pres*
Joe Montez, *Manager*
EMP: 30 EST: 1974
SALES (est): 4.2MM **Privately Held**
WEB: www.jlplastic.com
SIC: 3089 Plastic hardware & building products; plastic processing

(P-5678)
JACOBSON PLASTICS INC
1401 Freeman Ave, Long Beach (90804-2518)
PHONE....................562 433-4911
Jeff Jacobson, *President*
Linda Asher, *Executive*
Karen Catania, *Purchasing*
Anthony Gates, *Director*
▲ EMP: 75 EST: 1962
SQ FT: 25,000
SALES (est): 8.5MM **Privately Held**
WEB: www.jacobsonplastics.com
SIC: 3089 3544 Injection molding of plastics; special dies, tools, jigs & fixtures

(P-5679)
JASON TOOL AND ENGINEERING INC
7101 Honold Cir, Garden Grove (92841-1424)
PHONE....................714 895-5067
Jack Winterswyk, *President*
Curtis H Thompson, *Corp Secy*
▲ EMP: 30 EST: 1979
SQ FT: 30,000
SALES (est): 5.2MM **Privately Held**
WEB: www.jasontool.com
SIC: 3089 3544 Injection molding of plastics; dies, plastics forming

(P-5680)
JB BRANANNE INC
6 Orchard, Lake Forest (92630-8335)
PHONE....................949 215-7704
Jay Kim, *CEO*
EMP: 20 EST: 1993
SALES (est): 50MM **Privately Held**
WEB: www.jbbrananne.com
SIC: 3089 Automotive parts, plastic

(P-5681)
JB PLASTICS INC
1921 E Edinger Ave, Santa Ana (92705-4720)
PHONE....................714 541-8500
Joseph N Chiodo, *President*
Bruce Donoho, *Vice Pres*
Andres Estrada, *Manager*
EMP: 45 EST: 2000
SQ FT: 30,000
SALES (est): 7.9MM **Privately Held**
WEB: www.jb-plastics.com
SIC: 3089 Injection molding of plastics

(P-5682)
JDR ENGINEERING CONS INC (PA)
3122 Maple St, Santa Ana (92707-4408)
PHONE....................714 751-7084
Dionisio Rodriguez, *President*
Janet Rodriguez, *Vice Pres*
Paul Roberts, *Office Mgr*
Wesley Cirves, *Electrical Engi*
Joe Mullvain, *Electrical Engi*
▲ EMP: 108 EST: 1969
SQ FT: 25,000
SALES (est): 10MM **Privately Held**
SIC: 3089 Injection molding of plastics

(P-5683)
JET PLASTICS (PA)
941 N Eastern Ave, Los Angeles (90063-1307)
PHONE....................323 268-6706
Lee R Johnson, *President*
Lee Johnson, *President*
Lon Johnson, *Vice Pres*
Lowell Johnson, *Vice Pres*
Linda Huerta, *Office Mgr*
◆ EMP: 50
SQ FT: 30,000
SALES (est): 14.6MM **Privately Held**
WEB: www.jetplastics.com
SIC: 3089 Injection molding of plastics

(P-5684)
JG PLASTICS GROUP LLC
335 Fischer Ave, Costa Mesa (92626-4522)
PHONE....................714 751-4266
Dale Balough,
◆ EMP: 50 EST: 1975
SQ FT: 32,000
SALES (est): 9.2MM **Privately Held**
WEB: www.jgplastics.com
SIC: 3089 3544 Injection molding of plastics; special dies, tools, jigs & fixtures

(P-5685)
JOHNSON DOC ENTERPRISES
11933 Vose St, North Hollywood (91605-5786)
PHONE....................818 764-1543
Ronald Braverman, *President*
Chad Braverman, *COO*
Scott Watkins, *Vice Pres*
Rolando Del Real, *Technician*
Rhoda Francia, *Purchasing*
◆ EMP: 33 EST: 1987
SALES (est): 5MM **Privately Held**
WEB: www.docjohnson.com
SIC: 3089 Novelties, plastic

(P-5686)
JSN INDUSTRIES INC
9700 Jeronimo Rd, Irvine (92618-2019)
PHONE....................949 458-0050
James H Nagel Jr, *CEO*
Sandra Nagel, *Vice Pres*
EMP: 70 EST: 1984
SQ FT: 65,000
SALES (est): 11.4MM **Privately Held**
WEB: www.jsn.com
SIC: 3089 Injection molding of plastics

(P-5687)
KARAT PACKAGING INC (PA)
6185 Kimball Ave, Chino (91708-9126)
PHONE....................626 965-8882
Alan Yu, *Ch of Bd*
Joanne Wang, *COO*
Ann T Sabahat, *CFO*
Marvin Cheng, *Admin Sec*
Ron Gonzales, *Supervisor*
EMP: 52 EST: 2001
SALES (est): 295.5MM **Publicly Held**
WEB: www.karatpackaging.com
SIC: 3089 5113 Plastic containers, except foam; disposable plates, cups, napkins & eating utensils; cups, disposable plastic & paper; dishes, disposable plastic & paper; eating utensils, disposable plastic

(P-5688)
KELCOURT PLASTICS INC (DH)
Also Called: Kelpac Medical
1000 Calle Recodo, San Clemente (92673-6225)
PHONE....................949 361-0774
Neil Shillingford, *CEO*
Bob Carter, *Controller*
Julio Cueva, *Plant Mgr*
▲ EMP: 80 EST: 1982
SQ FT: 20,000
SALES (est): 20MM
SALES (corp-wide): 1.3B **Privately Held**
WEB: www.spectrumplastics.com
SIC: 3089 Injection molding of plastics
HQ: Pexco Llc
6470 E Johns Xing Ste 430
Johns Creek GA 30097
770 777-8540

▲ = Import ▼=Export
◆ =Import/Export

(P-5689)
KEPNER PLAS FABRICATORS INC
3131 Lomita Blvd, Torrance (90505-5158)
PHONE..................................310 325-3162
Frank Meyers, *CEO*
Meryl Bayley, *Admin Sec*
Jeff Zelin, *Purch Mgr*
Ben Cowart, *Sales Associate*
▲ **EMP:** 26 **EST:** 1960
SQ FT: 50,000
SALES (est): 4.1MM **Privately Held**
WEB: www.kepnerplastics.com
SIC: 3089 Molding primary plastic; plastic processing

(P-5690)
KING PLASTICS INC
840 N Elm St, Orange (92867-7908)
P.O. Box 6229 (92863-6229)
PHONE..................................714 997-7540
Larry E Lathrum, *CEO*
David Marlow, *Maintence Staff*
◆ **EMP:** 96 **EST:** 1962
SQ FT: 100,000
SALES (est): 15MM **Privately Held**
WEB: www.kingplastics.com
SIC: 3089 Plastic kitchenware, tableware & houseware

(P-5691)
KINGSEAL CORPORATION
12681 Corral Pl, Santa Fe Springs (90670-4748)
PHONE..................................562 944-3100
John Song, *President*
▲ **EMP:** 16 **EST:** 1981
SQ FT: 21,000
SALES (est): 2MM **Privately Held**
WEB: www.kingseal.com
SIC: 3089 3842 2499 Work gloves, plastic; gloves, safety; skewers, wood; toothpicks, wood

(P-5692)
KIRK API CONTAINERS
2131 Garfield Ave, Commerce (90040-1805)
PHONE..................................323 278-5400
Arthur Marounian, *Vice Pres*
Jerair Hovsepyan, *Warehouse Mgr*
Sam Gunashyan, *Maintence Staff*
Michael Mercado, *Manager*
▼ **EMP:** 43 **EST:** 2005
SALES (est): 9.8MM **Privately Held**
WEB: www.apikirkcontainers.com
SIC: 3089 Plastic containers, except foam

(P-5693)
KUSHCO HOLDINGS INC (PA)
6261 Katella Ave Ste 250, Cypress (90630-5200)
PHONE..................................714 462-4603
Nicholas Kovacevich, *Ch of Bd*
Rodrigo De Oliveira, *COO*
Stephen Christoffersen, *CFO*
Ryan Selewicz, *Exec VP*
Calvin Coy, *Vice Pres*
EMP: 67 **EST:** 2010
SQ FT: 23,600
SALES (est): 113.8MM **Privately Held**
WEB: www.kushsupplyco.com
SIC: 3089 5085 Plastic containers, except foam; industrial supplies

(P-5694)
L & H MOLD & ENGINEERING INC (PA)
Also Called: L & H Molds
140 Atlantic St, Pomona (91768-3285)
PHONE..................................909 930-1547
Stan Hillary, *CEO*
Steve Hillary, *President*
Brenda Bishop, *Admin Sec*
EMP: 23 **EST:** 1974
SQ FT: 6,000
SALES (est): 3.4MM **Privately Held**
SIC: 3089 Injection molding of plastics

(P-5695)
LAMSCO WEST INC
Also Called: Shimtech US
29101 The Old Rd, Santa Clarita (91355-1014)
PHONE..................................661 295-8620

Steve Griffith, *President*
Rick Casillas, *COO*
Scott Wilkinson, *CFO*
Favian Arellano, *Administration*
Frank Cortez, *Planning*
EMP: 99 **EST:** 1993
SQ FT: 31,280
SALES (est): 25.7MM
SALES (corp-wide): 140.1MM **Privately Held**
WEB: www.avantusaerospace.com
SIC: 3089 Injection molding of plastics
HQ: Avantus Aerospace, Inc.
29101 The Old-Rd
Valencia CA 91355
661 295-8620

(P-5696)
LANTIC INC
Also Called: Molded Interconnect Industries
27081 Burbank, Foothill Ranch (92610-2505)
PHONE..................................949 830-9951
Hung Vinh, *President*
Lien Pham, *Shareholder*
Hoi Vinh, *Shareholder*
Huy Vinh, *Shareholder*
Xuan L Cong, *Admin Sec*
▲ **EMP:** 22 **EST:** 1994
SQ FT: 10,700
SALES (est): 3.5MM **Privately Held**
WEB: www.moldedinterconnect.com
SIC: 3089 Injection molding of plastics

(P-5697)
LEHRER BRLLNPRFKTION WERKS INC (PA)
Also Called: Lbi - USA
20801 Nordhoff St, Chatsworth (91311-5925)
P.O. Box 3519 (91313-3519)
PHONE..................................818 407-1890
Keith Lehrer, *President*
Chett Lehrer, *Corp Secy*
Leo Yang, *Info Tech Mgr*
▲ **EMP:** 64 **EST:** 1949
SQ FT: 38,000
SALES (est): 5.5MM **Privately Held**
SIC: 3089 Cases, plastic

(P-5698)
LINER TECHNOLOGIES INC
Also Called: Flexi-Liner
4821 Chino Ave, Chino (91710-5132)
PHONE..................................909 594-6610
Tait Eyre, *President*
Angela Eyre, *Admin Sec*
Saul Jauregui, *Mktg Dir*
Dustin Goff, *Supervisor*
▼ **EMP:** 20
SQ FT: 20,000
SALES (est): 4.1MM **Privately Held**
WEB: www.flexi-liner.com
SIC: 3089 Plastic containers, except foam

(P-5699)
LINPAC USA HOLDINGS INC
10540 Talbert Ave, Fountain Valley (92708-6027)
PHONE..................................714 845-2845
Greg Toft, *President*
EMP: 53 **EST:** 2004
SALES (est): 5.3MM
SALES (corp-wide): 1.1B **Privately Held**
SIC: 3089 Plastic containers, except foam
HQ: Ropak Corporation
10540 Talbert Ave 200w
Fountain Valley CA 92708
714 845-2845

(P-5700)
LORITZ & ASSOCIATES INC
Also Called: L & A Plastics
24895 La Palma Ave, Yorba Linda (92887-5531)
PHONE..................................714 694-0200
Edward F Loritz, *CEO*
Ken Loritz, *President*
Anita Court, *Vice Pres*
◆ **EMP:** 35 **EST:** 1982
SQ FT: 6,000
SALES (est): 7.2MM **Privately Held**
SIC: 3089 Plastic processing

(P-5701)
M & A PLASTICS INC
11735 Sheldon St, Sun Valley (91352-1580)
PHONE..................................818 768-0479
Guillermo S Morales, *President*
Nancy M Morales, *Treasurer*
EMP: 17 **EST:** 1979
SQ FT: 20,000
SALES (est): 1.2MM **Privately Held**
WEB: www.maplastics.com
SIC: 3089 Injection molding of plastics

(P-5702)
MAGIC PLASTICS INC (PA)
25215 Avenue Stanford, Santa Clarita (91355-3923)
PHONE..................................800 369-0303
John Sarno, *CEO*
Patrick Madormo, *CFO*
Tony Madormo, *Vice Pres*
Nan Sarno, *Admin Sec*
Christina Downs, *Technology*
▲ **EMP:** 54 **EST:** 1985
SQ FT: 75,000
SALES (est): 13.7MM **Privately Held**
WEB: www.magicplastics.com
SIC: 3089 Injection molding of plastics

(P-5703)
MAKABI 26 INC
Also Called: Best Buy Imports
2850 E 44th St, Vernon (90058-2402)
PHONE..................................323 588-7666
Benham Makabi, *CEO*
EMP: 15 **EST:** 1998
SQ FT: 12,000
SALES (est): 521.7K **Privately Held**
WEB: www.bestbuyimportsusa.com
SIC: 3089 Plastic kitchenware, tableware & houseware

(P-5704)
MDI EAST INC (HQ)
Also Called: Molded Devices
6918 Ed Perkic St, Riverside (92504-1001)
PHONE..................................951 509-6918
Brian P Anderson, *President*
Jason Fairfield, *CFO*
Tobe Allenbrand, *Vice Pres*
Chuck Brider, *Vice Pres*
Penny Traxler, *Office Mgr*
EMP: 52 **EST:** 2009
SALES (est): 12.5MM
SALES (corp-wide): 26.3MM **Privately Held**
WEB: www.moldeddevices.com
SIC: 3089 Injection molding of plastics
PA: Molded Devices, Inc.
740 W Knox Rd
Tempe AZ 85284
480 785-9100

(P-5705)
MEDEGEN LLC (DH)
4501 E Wall St, Ontario (91761-8143)
P.O. Box 515111, Los Angeles (90051-5111)
PHONE..................................909 390-9080
Charles Stroupe, *CEO*
W Mark Dorris,
Paul M Ellis,
Jeffrey S Goble,
Michael E Stanley,
▲ **EMP:** 50 **EST:** 2001
SQ FT: 3,000
SALES (est): 135.6MM
SALES (corp-wide): 17.1B **Publicly Held**
WEB: www.bd.com
SIC: 3089 Injection molded finished plastic products

(P-5706)
MEDICAL EXTRUSION TECH INC (PA)
Also Called: M E T
26608 Pierce Cir Ste A, Murrieta (92562-1008)
PHONE..................................951 698-4346
Tom E Bauer, *CEO*
I Rikki Bauer, *Vice Pres*
Todd Wellman, *Technician*
EMP: 20 **EST:** 1990
SQ FT: 16,645

SALES (est): 9.9MM **Privately Held**
WEB: www.medicalextrusion.com
SIC: 3089 Injection molding of plastics

(P-5707)
MEDWAY PLASTICS CORPORATION
2250 E Cherry Indus Cir, Long Beach (90805-4414)
PHONE..................................562 630-1175
Thomas Hutchinson Jr, *CEO*
Mary Hutchinson, *CFO*
Gerry Hutchinson, *Vice Pres*
Rick Hutchinson, *Vice Pres*
Sheryl McDaniel, *Vice Pres*
◆ **EMP:** 196
SALES (est): 54.9MM **Privately Held**
WEB: www.medwayplastics.com
SIC: 3089 Injection molding of plastics

(P-5708)
MERRICK ENGINEERING INC (PA)
1275 Quarry St, Corona (92879-1707)
PHONE..................................951 737-6040
Abraham M Abdi, *President*
Katina Brown, *CFO*
Martha Sanchez, *Officer*
Roy Jorgensen, *Vice Pres*
Shannon Daugherty, *Branch Mgr*
◆ **EMP:** 250 **EST:** 1971
SQ FT: 150,000
SALES (est): 108.1MM **Privately Held**
WEB: www.merrickengineering.com
SIC: 3089 Injection molding of plastics

(P-5709)
MICRODYNE PLASTICS INC
1901 E Cooley Dr, Colton (92324-6322)
PHONE..................................909 503-4010
Judy Lopez, *CEO*
Ed Housmann, *CFO*
Tracey Kimberlin, *Security Dir*
Rhonda Torres, *Office Mgr*
Sofia Carbajal, *Technician*
▲ **EMP:** 100 **EST:** 1977
SQ FT: 33,000
SALES (est): 23.3MM **Privately Held**
WEB: www.microdyneplastics.com
SIC: 3089 Blow molded finished plastic products; injection molding of plastics

(P-5710)
MICROMOLD INC
2100 Iowa Ave, Riverside (92507-2413)
P.O. Box 51118 (92517-2118)
PHONE..................................951 684-7130
Robert Aust, *President*
Bill Tischler, *COO*
Ron Peterson, *Vice Pres*
Dave Dunn, *Mktg Dir*
EMP: 15 **EST:** 1979
SQ FT: 11,000
SALES (est): 2.6MM **Privately Held**
WEB: www.micromoldinc.com
SIC: 3089 Molding primary plastic; injection molding of plastics

(P-5711)
MILGARD MANUFACTURING LLC
Also Called: Milgard Windows
26879 Diaz Rd, Temecula (92590-3470)
PHONE..................................480 763-6000
Cory Hall, *Branch Mgr*
Herbert Cofer, *Manager*
EMP: 128
SALES (corp-wide): 822.1MM **Privately Held**
WEB: www.milgard.com
SIC: 3089 3442 5211 3231 Windows, plastic; sash, door or window: metal; door & window products; products of purchased glass; glass & glazing work; carpentry work
HQ: Milgard Manufacturing Llc
1010 54th Ave E
Tacoma WA 98424
253 922-4343

P R O D U C T S & S V C S

(P-5712)
MISSION CUSTOM EXTRUSION INC
10904 Beech Ave, Fontana (92337-7260)
P.O. Box 310302 (92331-0302)
PHONE..............................909 822-1581
Moses Tersaud, *President*
EMP: 25 **EST:** 2005
SQ FT: 23,400
SALES (est): 2.6MM **Privately Held**
WEB: www.missioncustomextrusions.com
SIC: 3089 Awnings, fiberglass & plastic combination

(P-5713)
MISSION PLASTICS INC
1930 S Parco Ave, Ontario (91761-8312)
PHONE..............................909 947-7287
Patrick Dauphinee, *CEO*
Charles Montes, *Corp Secy*
Gabriel Angulo, *Engineer*
Marc Aspiras, *Engineer*
Matthew Dauphinee, *Engineer*
▲ **EMP:** 120 **EST:** 1982
SQ FT: 20,000
SALES: 1.4MM **Privately Held**
WEB: www.missionplastics.com
SIC: 3089 Injection molding of plastics

(P-5714)
MODERN CONCEPTS INC
3121 E Ana St, E Rncho Dmngz (90221-5606)
PHONE..............................310 637-0013
Richard J Warpack, *President*
◆ **EMP:** 60 **EST:** 1983
SQ FT: 42,000
SALES (est): 10MM **Privately Held**
SIC: 3089 3087 Coloring & finishing of plastic products; custom compound purchased resins

(P-5715)
MODIFIED PLASTICS INC (PA)
1240 E Glenwood Pl, Santa Ana (92707-3000)
PHONE..............................714 546-4667
Robert Estep, *CEO*
Jocelyn Eubank, *Corp Secy*
Hernan Soto, *Engineer*
▲ **EMP:** 27 **EST:** 1976
SQ FT: 18,000
SALES (est): 26.2MM **Privately Held**
WEB: www.modifiedplastics.com
SIC: 3089 Injection molding of plastics; plastic processing

(P-5716)
MOLDED FIBER GL COMPANIES - W
Also Called: M F G West
9400 Holly Rd, Adelanto (92301-3900)
P.O. Box 675, Ashtabula OH (44005-0675)
PHONE..............................760 246-4042
Richard Morrison, *CEO*
Dave Denny, *Exec VP*
Jim Sommer, *Vice Pres*
Jose Cisneros, *Executive*
Jackie Thomas, *Executive*
▲ **EMP:** 100 **EST:** 1958
SQ FT: 66,000
SALES (est): 24.4MM
SALES (corp-wide): 360.8MM **Privately Held**
WEB: www.moldedfiberglass.com
SIC: 3089 Air mattresses, plastic
PA: Molded Fiber Glass Companies
2925 Mfg Pl
Ashtabula OH 44004
440 997-5851

(P-5717)
MOLDING CORPORATION AMERICA
10349 Norris Ave, Pacoima (91331-2220)
PHONE..............................818 890-7877
Mark Hurley, *CEO*
Sandra Rinder, *Vice Pres*
Sandy Rinder, *Vice Pres*
▲ **EMP:** 50 **EST:** 1967
SQ FT: 59,000
SALES (est): 6.3MM **Privately Held**
WEB: www.moldingcorp.com
SIC: 3089 Injection molding of plastics

(P-5718)
MOLDING INTL & ENGRG INC
Also Called: M I E
42136 Avenida Alvarado, Temecula (92590-3400)
PHONE..............................951 296-5010
Bradway B Adams, *CEO*
Sean Russell, *Broker*
EMP: 21 **EST:** 1985
SQ FT: 27,000
SALES (est): 1.1MM **Privately Held**
SIC: 3089 3544 2821 Injection molded finished plastic products; industrial molds; plastics materials & resins

(P-5719)
MONCO PRODUCTS INC
7562 Acacia Ave, Garden Grove (92841-4057)
PHONE..............................714 891-2788
Tom Monson, *President*
Jerry Monson, *Vice Pres*
▲ **EMP:** 47 **EST:** 1979
SQ FT: 15,000
SALES (est): 6.2MM **Privately Held**
WEB: www.moncoproducts.com
SIC: 3089 Injection molding of plastics

(P-5720)
MONSTER VENDING
Also Called: New Horizon Vending
8545 Devon Ln, Garden Grove (92844-1236)
PHONE..............................909 223-5522
J Rick Denet, *Owner*
EMP: 14 **EST:** 1980
SALES (est): 1.6MM **Privately Held**
WEB: www.monstervending.com
SIC: 3089 2631 Kitchenware, plastic; cardboard

(P-5721)
MORRIS ENTERPRISES INC
16799 Schoenborn St, North Hills (91343-6107)
PHONE..............................818 894-9103
Morris Weinberg, *President*
Benjamin Weinberg, *Vice Pres*
Simon Morrison, *CTO*
EMP: 16 **EST:** 1959
SQ FT: 5,000
SALES (est): 184.1K **Privately Held**
SIC: 3089 3676 3674 3577 Blow molded finished plastic products; molding primary plastic; electronic resistors; semiconductors & related devices; computer peripheral equipment

(P-5722)
NATIONAL DIVERSIFIED SALES INC (HQ)
Also Called: Nds
21300 Victory Blvd # 215, Woodland Hills (91367-2525)
P.O. Box 339, Lindsay (93247-0339)
PHONE..............................559 562-9888
Michael Gummeson, *President*
Randall Stott, *CFO*
Cindy Castaneda, *Vice Pres*
John Koehler, *VP Bus Dvlpt*
Mercedes Jimenez, *Admin Asst*
◆ **EMP:** 200 **EST:** 1978
SQ FT: 5,000
SALES (est): 210.5MM
SALES (corp-wide): 1.1B **Privately Held**
WEB: www.normagroup.com
SIC: 3089 Plastic hardware & building products
PA: Norma Group Se
Edisonstr. 4
Maintal HE 63477
618 140-30

(P-5723)
NATIONAL MEDICAL PRODUCTS INC
57 Parker, Irvine (92618-1605)
PHONE..............................949 768-1147
Dahyabhai Patel, *President*
Kaushik Patel, *CFO*
Jack Kay, *Research*
Sana Patel, *Sales Mgr*
EMP: 19 **EST:** 1989
SQ FT: 28,630

(P-5724)
NEOPACIFIC HOLDINGS INC
Also Called: Pro-Action Products
14940 Calvert St, Van Nuys (91411-2603)
PHONE..............................818 786-2900
Steve Chan, *President*
▲ **EMP:** 48 **EST:** 1981
SQ FT: 24,000
SALES (est): 8MM **Privately Held**
WEB: www.proactionproducts.com
SIC: 3089 Injection molding of plastics

(P-5725)
NEWLIGHT TECHNOLOGIES INC
14382 Astronautics Ln, Huntington Beach (92647-2081)
PHONE..............................714 556-4500
Mark Herrema, *CEO*
Evan Creelman, *COO*
Scott Wollack, *Vice Pres*
Scott William Wollack, *Vice Pres*
Kenton Kimmel, *CTO*
EMP: 29 **EST:** 2007
SALES (est): 11.6MM **Privately Held**
WEB: www.newlight.com
SIC: 3089 Plastic processing

(P-5726)
NEWPORT LAMINATES INC
3121 W Central Ave, Santa Ana (92704-5302)
PHONE..............................714 545-8335
Brad A Bollman, *President*
Wendy Bollman, *Vice Pres*
EMP: 40 **EST:** 1974
SQ FT: 24,000
SALES (est): 4.2MM **Privately Held**
WEB: www.newportlaminates.com
SIC: 3089 Fiber, vulcanized

(P-5727)
NEWPORT PLASTIC INC
Also Called: Country Weave
1525 E Edinger Ave, Santa Ana (92705-4907)
PHONE..............................714 549-1955
Kay Hale, *President*
Mike Williams, *COO*
EMP: 45 **EST:** 1969
SALES (est): 2.8MM
SALES (corp-wide): 5.2MM **Privately Held**
WEB: www.newportplastics.com
SIC: 3089 Injection molding of plastics
PA: Newport Plastics, Llc
1525 E Edinger Ave
Santa Ana CA 92705
800 854-8402

(P-5728)
NEWPORT PLASTICS LLC (PA)
1525 E Edinger Ave, Santa Ana (92705-4907)
PHONE..............................800 854-8402
Shirley Carlisle, *Principal*
Peter Bonin,
Kathleen Steck,
EMP: 25 **EST:** 1965
SQ FT: 8,000
SALES (est): 5.2MM **Privately Held**
WEB: www.newportplastics.com
SIC: 3089 Injection molding of plastics

(P-5729)
NORCO INJECTION MOLDING INC
Also Called: Norco Plastics
14325 Monte Vista Ave, Chino (91710-5726)
P.O. Box 2528 (91708-2528)
PHONE..............................909 393-4000
Jack Williams, *President*
John Williams, *General Mgr*
Leticia Babcock, *QC Mgr*
▲ **EMP:** 100 **EST:** 1974
SQ FT: 45,000
SALES (est): 7.2MM **Privately Held**
WEB: www.norco.biz
SIC: 3089 3544 Injection molding of plastics; special dies, tools, jigs & fixtures

(P-5730)
NORCO PLASTICS INC
14325 Monte Vista Ave, Chino (91710-5726)
P.O. Box 2528 (91708-2528)
PHONE..............................909 393-4000
John Williams, *CEO*
Jose Sotelo, *Maintence Staff*
Letty Babcock, *Director*
▲ **EMP:** 90 **EST:** 2010
SALES (est): 18.8MM **Privately Held**
WEB: www.norcoplastics.com
SIC: 3089 Plastic containers except foam; injection molding of plastics

(P-5731)
NORTON PACKAGING INC
5800 S Boyle Ave, Vernon (90058-3927)
PHONE..............................323 588-6167
Joe Schrick, *Branch Mgr*
Ed Arzola, *Manager*
EMP: 26
SALES (corp-wide): 55.5MM **Privately Held**
WEB: www.nortonpackaging.com
SIC: 3089 5162 Plastic containers, except foam; resins
PA: Norton Packaging, Inc.
20670 Corsair Blvd
Hayward CA 94545
510 786-1922

(P-5732)
NSA HOLDINGS INC
Also Called: Amerex Company
888 Marlborough Ave, Riverside (92507-2117)
PHONE..............................951 686-1400
Donald H Circosta, *President*
EMP: 14 **EST:** 1972
SQ FT: 15,500
SALES (est): 455K **Privately Held**
SIC: 3089 Injection molding of plastics

(P-5733)
NUCONIC PACKAGING LLC
4889 Loma Vista Ave, Vernon (90058-3216)
PHONE..............................323 588-9033
Alan Franz, *CEO*
Jason Farber, *Principal*
Ally Jacoby, *Office Mgr*
Francisco Diaz, *Opers Staff*
Skip Farber,
▲ **EMP:** 31 **EST:** 2008
SQ FT: 30,000
SALES (est): 9.7MM **Privately Held**
WEB: www.easypak.com
SIC: 3089 4783 Plastic containers, except foam; packing & crating
PA: Carlin Capital Partners, Llc
15760 Ventura Blvd # 700
Encino CA 91436

(P-5734)
P M REHRIG INC (HQ)
4010 E 26th St, Vernon (90058-4401)
PHONE..............................323 262-5145
William J Rehrig, *President*
Michael J Doka, *Ch of Bd*
James L Drew, *CFO*
Rajesh Luhar, *CFO*
Peter Jackson, *Senior VP*
◆ **EMP:** 150 **EST:** 1997
SQ FT: 200,000
SALES (est): 712.6MM **Privately Held**
WEB: www.rehrigpacific.com
SIC: 3089 2821 Cases, plastic; plasticizer/additive based plastic materials

(P-5735)
PACKLINE USA LLC
9555 Hyssop Dr, Rancho Cucamonga (91730-6124)
PHONE..............................909 392-8000
Diron M Ohanian, *Principal*
Karina Barajas, *Project Mgr*
Thomas Stedman, *Controller*
EMP: 13 **EST:** 2018
SALES (est): 1.3MM **Privately Held**
WEB: www.packlineusa.com
SIC: 3089 3221 Plastic containers, except foam; bottles for packing, bottling & canning: glass

(P-5736)
PANOB CORP
1531 E Cedar St, Ontario (91761-5762)
PHONE..............................909 947-8008
Arthur Graner Thorne, *President*
John Graner Thorne, *Treasurer*
Barbara Thorne, *Admin Sec*
EMP: 20 **EST:** 1953
SQ FT: 12,000
SALES (est): 607.7K
SALES (corp-wide): 5.5MM **Privately Held**
WEB: www.paramountpanels.com
SIC: 3089 3728 3613 Plastic processing; aircraft parts & equipment; switchgear & switchboard apparatus
PA: Paramount Panels, Inc.
     1531 E Cedar St
     Ontario CA 91761
     909 947-8008

(P-5737)
PARADIGM PACKAGING EAST LLC
Also Called: Paradigm Packaging West
9177 Center Ave, Rancho Cucamonga (91730-5312)
P.O. Box 10, Upland (91785-0010)
PHONE..............................909 985-2750
Steve Costecki, *Manager*
Juan Luna, *Prdtn Mgr*
Christina Perkins, *Regional*
EMP: 27
SALES (corp-wide): 101MM **Privately Held**
SIC: 3089 Plastic containers, except foam; caps, plastic
HQ: Paradigm Packaging East Llc
     141 5th St
     Saddle Brook NJ 07663
     201 909-3400

(P-5738)
PARAMOUNT PANELS INC (PA)
Also Called: California Plasteck
1531 E Cedar St, Ontario (91761-5762)
PHONE..............................909 947-8008
Arthur G Thorne, *President*
John Thorne, *Treasurer*
John Thorn, *Vice Pres*
John G Thorne, *Vice Pres*
Jorge Ramirez, *Engineer*
EMP: 32 **EST:** 1962
SQ FT: 12,000
SALES (est): 5.5MM **Privately Held**
WEB: www.paramountpanels.com
SIC: 3089 3812 3728 Plastic processing; search & navigation equipment; aircraft parts & equipment

(P-5739)
PARAMUNT PLSTIC FBRICATORS INC
Also Called: Paramount Fabricators
11251 Jersey Blvd, Rancho Cucamonga (91730-5147)
PHONE..............................909 987-4757
Peter M Smits, *President*
Rose I Smits, *Vice Pres*
James Grace, *Manager*
EMP: 24 **EST:** 1958
SQ FT: 60,000
SALES (est): 4.9MM **Privately Held**
WEB: www.paramountfabricators.com
SIC: 3089 Plastic containers, except foam

(P-5740)
PAULEY PLASTIC LLC
17177 Navajo Rd, Apple Valley (92307-1046)
PHONE..............................760 240-3737
Craig Oehme, *Manager*
EMP: 15 **EST:** 2020
SALES (est): 1.4MM **Privately Held**
WEB: www.pauleyplastic.com
SIC: 3089 Injection molding of plastics

(P-5741)
PEERLESS INJECTION MOLDING LLC
Also Called: Proplas Technologies
14321 Corp Dr, Garden Grove (92843)
PHONE..............................714 689-1920
Scott Taylor, *President*
Scott Munch, *General Mgr*

▲ **EMP:** 50 **EST:** 1977
SQ FT: 51,112
SALES (est): 11.6MM
SALES (corp-wide): 74.4MM **Privately Held**
SIC: 3089 Injection molding of plastics
PA: Comar, Inc.
     201 Laurel Rd Fl 2
     Voorhees NJ 08043
     856 692-6100

(P-5742)
PERFORMANCE ENGINEERED PDTS
Also Called: Honor Plastics
3270 Pomona Blvd, Pomona (91768-3282)
PHONE..............................909 594-7487
Dinesh Savalia, *CEO*
Steve Goldstein, *Vice Pres*
Robert Gomez, *Vice Pres*
Nirav Velani, *Engineer*
EMP: 48 **EST:** 2016
SQ FT: 42,000
SALES (est): 9MM **Privately Held**
WEB: www.honorplastics.com
SIC: 3089 Injection molding of plastics

(P-5743)
PERFORMNCE ENGINEERED PDTS INC
Also Called: P.E.P.
3270 Pomona Blvd, Pomona (91768-3282)
PHONE..............................909 594-7487
Patricia Dispenziere, *CEO*
Carl Dispenziere, *President*
Ann Campbell, *CFO*
▲ **EMP:** 70 **EST:** 1979
SQ FT: 47,000
SALES (est): 14.6MM **Privately Held**
SIC: 3089 3544 3441 Injection molding of plastics; special dies, tools, jigs & fixtures; fabricated structural metal

(P-5744)
PINNPACK PACKAGING LLC (DH)
875 Michigan Ave, Riverside (92507-1843)
PHONE..............................805 385-4100
Brian Weiss,
Fidel Cardenas, *Executive*
Cyrus Maroofian, *Project Engr*
Maria Aguiniga, *Purchasing*
Josefina Maldonado, *Safety Mgr*
EMP: 100 **EST:** 2016
SQ FT: 200,000
SALES (est): 26.5MM
SALES (corp-wide): 61.9MM **Privately Held**
WEB: www.pinnpack.com
SIC: 3089 Plastic containers, except foam

(P-5745)
PITBULL GYM INCORPORATED
Also Called: Art Plates
10782 Edison Ct, Rancho Cucamonga (91730-4845)
PHONE..............................909 980-7960
Gary John Vandenlangenberg, *President*
◆ **EMP:** 17 **EST:** 1988
SQ FT: 10,120
SALES (est): 4.5MM **Privately Held**
SIC: 3089 5072 Bottle caps, molded plastic; hardware

(P-5746)
PITTMAN PRODUCTS INTL INC
Also Called: Pittman Outdoors
650 S Jefferson St Ste D, Placentia (92870-6640)
PHONE..............................562 926-6660
James Pittman, *CEO*
▲ **EMP:** 15 **EST:** 1999
SALES (est): 3.2MM **Privately Held**
WEB: www.truckairbedz.com
SIC: 3089 Air mattresses, plastic

(P-5747)
PLASIDYNE ENGINEERING & MFG
3230 E 59th St, Long Beach (90805-4502)
P.O. Box 5578 (90805-0578)
PHONE..............................562 531-0510
Dean C Sutherland, *President*
EMP: 22 **EST:** 1969
SQ FT: 15,000

SALES (est): 2.3MM **Privately Held**
WEB: www.plasidyne.com
SIC: 3089 Injection molding of plastics

(P-5748)
PLASTHEC MOLDING INC
1945 S Grove Ave, Ontario (91761-5616)
PHONE..............................909 947-4267
Hector Carrion, *President*
James Downey, *Vice Pres*
EMP: 31 **EST:** 1978
SQ FT: 34,000
SALES (est): 2.8MM **Privately Held**
SIC: 3089 Injection molding of plastics

(P-5749)
PLASTIC AND METAL CENTER INC
23162 La Cadena Dr, Laguna Hills (92653-1405)
PHONE..............................949 770-0610
Faramarz Khaladj, *President*
Fred Carr, *Vice Pres*
Denise Khaladj, *Admin Sec*
Jim Aschtiani, *Engineer*
EMP: 25 **EST:** 1993
SQ FT: 20,000
SALES (est): 4.4MM **Privately Held**
WEB: www.plastic-metal.com
SIC: 3089 Injection molding of plastics; thermoformed finished plastic products

(P-5750)
PLASTIC DRESS-UP COMPANY
11077 Rush St, South El Monte (91733-3546)
PHONE..............................626 442-7711
Myron H Funk, *President*
◆ **EMP:** 82 **EST:** 1952
SQ FT: 130,000
SALES (est): 919.4K **Privately Held**
SIC: 3089 Novelties, plastic

(P-5751)
PLASTIC ENGINEERING TECH LLC
4502 Brickell Privado St, Ontario (91761-7827)
PHONE..............................909 390-1323
David Lilico,
▲ **EMP:** 23 **EST:** 2005
SALES (est): 931.6K **Privately Held**
SIC: 3089 Plastic hardware & building products

(P-5752)
PLASTIC FABRICATION TECH LLC
2320 E Cherry Indus Cir, Long Beach (90805-4417)
PHONE..............................773 509-1700
Jay Magness Jr,
Mary Hutchinson, *CFO*
EMP: 14 **EST:** 1997
SQ FT: 20,000
SALES (est): 347.9K **Privately Held**
SIC: 3089 Injection molding of plastics

(P-5753)
PLASTIC PROCESSING CORP
13432 Estrella Ave, Gardena (90248-1513)
PHONE..............................310 719-7330
Dagmer Schulte-Derne, *Ch of Bd*
Steve Rockenbach, *CFO*
▲ **EMP:** 16 **EST:** 1988
SQ FT: 20,000
SALES (est): 351.9K **Privately Held**
WEB: www.plasticprocessing.net
SIC: 3089 Blow molded finished plastic products

(P-5754)
PLASTIC SPECIALTIES & TECH INC
Action Technology
19555 Arenth Ave, City of Industry (91748-1403)
PHONE..............................909 869-8069
Roy Anderson, *Branch Mgr*
EMP: 130
SALES (corp-wide): 996.3MM **Privately Held**
SIC: 3089 Plastic containers, except foam

HQ: Plastic Specialties And Technologies Inc.
     101 Railroad Ave
     Ridgefield NJ 07657
     201 941-2900

(P-5755)
PLASTIC TECHNOLOGIES INC
Also Called: Blow Molded Products
4720 Felspar St, Riverside (92509-3068)
PHONE..............................951 360-6055
Meir Ben-David, *President*
Diane Ben-David, *Vice Pres*
Alec Lujan, *Engineer*
EMP: 50 **EST:** 2018
SALES (est): 5MM **Privately Held**
WEB: www.blowmoldedproducts.com
SIC: 3089 Injection molding of plastics

(P-5756)
PLASTICS DEVELOPMENT CORP
960 Calle Negocio, San Clemente (92673-6201)
PHONE..............................949 492-0217
Inder Jain, *President*
Vijay Jain, *Corp Secy*
Sanie Jain, *Vice Pres*
▲ **EMP:** 23 **EST:** 1969
SQ FT: 7,000
SALES (est): 3.5MM **Privately Held**
WEB: www.plasticsdev.com
SIC: 3089 Injection molding of plastics

(P-5757)
PLASTICS PLUS TECHNOLOGY INC
1495 Research Dr, Redlands (92374-4584)
PHONE..............................909 747-0555
Kathy Bodor, *President*
Rob Pellandini, *Information Mgr*
Linda Jenkins, *QC Mgr*
Kim Victorine, *Opers Staff*
EMP: 33 **EST:** 1980
SQ FT: 35,000
SALES (est): 7.9MM **Privately Held**
WEB: www.plasticsplus.com
SIC: 3089 3544 Injection molding of plastics; forms (molds), for foundry & plastics working machinery

(P-5758)
PLASTIJECT LLC
14811 Spring Ave, Santa Fe Springs (90670-5109)
PHONE..............................562 926-6705
EMP: 13 **EST:** 1997
SALES (est): 1.5MM **Privately Held**
SIC: 3089 Mfg Plastic Products

(P-5759)
PLASTIQUE UNIQUE INC
3383 Livonia Ave, Los Angeles (90034-3127)
PHONE..............................310 839-3968
Christine Galonska, *President*
Lionel Funes, *Vice Pres*
Silvia Totado, *Director*
EMP: 25 **EST:** 1970
SQ FT: 5,000
SALES (est): 2.5MM **Privately Held**
WEB: www.plastiqueuniqueinc.com
SIC: 3089 Injection molding of plastics

(P-5760)
PLASTO TECH INTERNATIONAL INC
4 Autry, Irvine (92618-2708)
PHONE..............................949 458-1880
Ben Khalaj, *President*
Jacqueline Khalaj, *CEO*
▲ **EMP:** 24 **EST:** 1985
SQ FT: 16,530
SALES (est): 6.2MM **Privately Held**
WEB: www.plastotech.com
SIC: 3089 5084 8711 7389 Injection molding of plastics; industrial machinery & equipment; consulting engineer; design, commercial & industrial; plastics sheets & rods

P R O D U C T S

&

S V C S

(P-5761)
PLASTOKER INC
Also Called: Mj-Pak
1690 Scenic Ave, Costa Mesa
(92626-1410)
PHONE.................714 598-5920
Michael Boggs, *General Mgr*
David Greenberg, *General Mgr*
Jason Greenberg, *General Mgr*
EMP: 13 **EST:** 2018
SALES (est): 709.9K **Privately Held**
SIC: 3089 Tumblers, plastic

(P-5762)
PLASTPRO 2000 INC (PA)
Also Called: Plastpro Doors
5200 W Century Blvd Fl 9, Los Angeles
(90045-5900)
PHONE.................310 693-8600
Franco An, *CEO*
Shirley Wang, *President*
Johnny MAI, *CFO*
Walter Wang, *Chairman*
Calvin Yang, *Purchasing*
◆ **EMP:** 126 **EST:** 1994
SALES (est): 16.6MM **Privately Held**
WEB: www.plastproinc.com
SIC: 3089 Fiberglass doors

(P-5763)
PLEXI FAB INC
1142 E Elm Ave, Fullerton (92831-5024)
PHONE.................714 447-8494
Abol Fazli, *President*
Mike Hall, *President*
Venis Hall, *Vice Pres*
◆ **EMP:** 13 **EST:** 1991
SQ FT: 20,000
SALES (est): 1.6MM **Privately Held**
WEB: www.plexifab.com
SIC: 3089 Injection molding of plastics

(P-5764)
POLYMASTERS INDUSTRIES INC
2821 Century Blvd, South Gate
(90280-5503)
PHONE.................213 564-7824
Raffi A Aposhian, *President*
Karnig Oughourlian, *Treasurer*
▲ **EMP:** 17 **EST:** 1940
SQ FT: 14,000
SALES (est): 2.9MM **Privately Held**
WEB: www.polymasters.com
SIC: 3089 3144 3143 Molding primary
plastic; women's footwear, except
athletic; men's footwear, except athletic

(P-5765)
POLYMER LOGISTICS INC
1725 Sierra Ridge Dr, Riverside
(92507-7133)
PHONE.................951 567-2900
Albert Terrazas, *Branch Mgr*
Amit Keren, *Info Tech Mgr*
Beatriz Cosin, *Business Mgr*
Joe Bortz, *Maintence Staff*
Mullens James, *Maintence Staff*
EMP: 60
SALES (corp-wide): 217.9MM **Privately
Held**
WEB: www.toscaltd.com
SIC: 3089 5085 5162 Pallets, plastic;
boxes, crates, etc., other than paper;
plastics materials & basic shapes
HQ: Polymer Logistics, Inc.
1175 Peachtree St Ne # 1900
Atlanta GA 30361

(P-5766)
POLYMERPAK LLC
6941 W Goshen Ave, Visalia (93291-8612)
PHONE.................559 651-1965
Michael Leraris, *Mng Member*
Virginia Chiu, *Accounting Mgr*
Jon Charles Buff, *
EMP: 130 **EST:** 2015
SALES (est): 11.6MM **Privately Held**
WEB: www.replanetpackaging.com
SIC: 3089 Plastic containers, except foam

(P-5767)
POLYTECH COLOR & COMPOUNDING
847 S Wanamaker Ave, Ontario
(91761-8152)
PHONE.................909 923-7008
Brian Cockren, *President*
EMP: 13 **EST:** 2000
SALES (est): 180.8K **Privately Held**
SIC: 3089 5169 Coloring & finishing of
plastic products; synthetic resins, rubber
& plastic materials

(P-5768)
POP PLASTICS ACRYLIC DISP INC
8211 Orangethorpe Ave, Buena Park
(90621-3811)
PHONE.................714 523-8500
Jeff Dougherty, *President*
David A Lewis, *COO*
Steven K North, *CFO*
▲ **EMP:** 13 **EST:** 2008
SQ FT: 15,000
SALES (est): 402.2K **Privately Held**
WEB: www.pop82.com
SIC: 3089 Plates, plastic

(P-5769)
PPP LLC
601 W Olympic Blvd, Montebello
(90640-5229)
P.O. Box 789 (90640-0789)
PHONE.................323 832-9627
Evelyn Garcia, *Mng Member*
Jan Voelkers, *Administration*
Ute Carstens, *Opers Staff*
EMP: 15 **EST:** 2001
SALES (est): 4MM **Privately Held**
WEB: www.ppp.net
SIC: 3089 Injection molding of plastics

(P-5770)
PRC COMPOSITES LLC (PA)
1400 S Campus Ave, Ontario (91761-4330)
PHONE.................909 391-2006
John Upsher, *Mng Member*
Gene Gregory, *
EMP: 51 **EST:** 2014
SALES (est): 18.1MM **Privately Held**
WEB: www.prccal.com
SIC: 3089 Plastic containers, except foam

(P-5771)
PRC COMPOSITES LLC
Also Called: Globe Plastics
13477 12th St, Chino (91710-5206)
PHONE.................909 464-1520
John Upsher, *Branch Mgr*
EMP: 20
SALES (corp-wide): 18.1MM **Privately
Held**
WEB: www.prccal.com
SIC: 3089 3544 Injection molding of plas-
tics; special dies, tools, jigs & fixtures
PA: Prc Composites, Llc
1400 S Campus Ave
Ontario CA 91761
909 391-2006

(P-5772)
PRECISE AEROSPACE MFG INC
Also Called: Precise Plastic Products
224 Glider Cir, Corona (92878-5033)
PHONE.................951 898-0500
Ronnie E Harwood, *CEO*
Roxanne Abdi, *President*
Mike Valeriano, *General Mgr*
Jon Atchison, *Foreman/Supr*
Sandy Armas, *Manager*
▲ **EMP:** 42 **EST:** 1965
SQ FT: 39,000
SALES (est): 9.3MM **Privately Held**
WEB: www.precisemfg.com
SIC: 3089 3544 Molding primary plastic;
industrial molds

(P-5773)
PRECISION MOLDED PRODUCTS INC
12660 Magnolia Ave, Riverside
(92503-4636)
PHONE.................951 354-0779
Chris Kozloski, *President*
Sabrina Kozloski, *CFO*

▲ **EMP:** 28 **EST:** 1967
SQ FT: 15,000
SALES (est): 3.8MM **Privately Held**
WEB: www.precisionmoldpro.com
SIC: 3089 3083 Injection molded finished
plastic products; laminated plastics plate
& sheet

(P-5774)
PREMIUM PLASTICS MACHINE INC
15956 Downey Ave, Paramount
(90723-5190)
PHONE.................562 633-7723
David Pennington, *President*
Michael Robert Pennington, *Exec VP*
Suzanne Pennington, *Vice Pres*
▲ **EMP:** 23 **EST:** 1976
SQ FT: 6,241
SALES (est): 2.3MM **Privately Held**
WEB: www.premiumplasticsmachine.com
SIC: 3089 Injection molding of plastics

(P-5775)
PREPRODUCTION PLASTICS INC
Also Called: P P I
210 Teller St, Corona (92879-1886)
PHONE.................951 340-9680
Koby Loosen, *President*
Barbara Loosen, *Corp Secy*
Ron Loosen, *Principal*
Paul Rice, *Engineer*
Neal Singh, *Controller*
▲ **EMP:** 50 **EST:** 1978
SQ FT: 45,000
SALES (est): 8.4MM **Privately Held**
WEB: www.ppiplastics.com
SIC: 3089 3544 Molding primary plastic;
forms (molds), for foundry & plastics
working machinery

(P-5776)
PRES-TEK PLASTICS INC (PA)
10700 7th St, Rancho Cucamonga
(91730-5404)
PHONE.................909 360-1600
Donna C Pursell, *CEO*
Ron Noggle, *Vice Pres*
Shawn Pecore, *General Mgr*
Lyndsay Petersen, *Office Mgr*
Luis Cardenas, *CIO*
EMP: 67 **EST:** 2005
SALES (est): 33.5MM **Privately Held**
WEB: www.prestekplastics.com
SIC: 3089 Injection molding of plastics

(P-5777)
PRETIUM PACKAGING LLC
5235 E Hunter Ave, Anaheim (92807-2004)
PHONE.................714 777-9580
Lisa Engert, *Manager*
Cynthia Melendez, *Plant Mgr*
Don Strader, *Plant Mgr*
Cescar Hernandaz, *Manager*
Samantha Newman, *Manager*
EMP: 150
SALES (corp-wide): 868.8MM **Privately
Held**
WEB: www.pretiumpkg.com
SIC: 3089 3544 3085 5113 Blow molded
finished plastic products; injection molded
finished plastic products; bottle caps,
molded plastic; industrial molds; plastics
bottles; bags, paper & disposable plastic
PA: Pretium Packaging, L.L.C.
13515 Barrett Parkway Dr # 150
Ballwin MO 63021
314 727-8200

(P-5778)
PRINCE LIONHEART INC (PA)
2421 Westgate Rd, Santa Maria
(93455-1075)
PHONE.................805 922-2250
Kelly Griffiths, *CEO*
Debbie Di Nardi, *Vice Pres*
Debbie Dinardi, *Vice Pres*
Hyde Smith, *Executive*
Michael McConnell, *Creative Dir*
▲ **EMP:** 40 **EST:** 1973
SQ FT: 80,000
SALES (est): 12.6MM **Privately Held**
WEB: www.princelionheart.com
SIC: 3089 Injection molding of plastics

(P-5779)
PRINCETON CASE-WEST INC
1444 W Mccoy Ln, Santa Maria
(93455-1005)
PHONE.................805 928-8840
Douglas Laggrenm, *President*
Jim Laggren, *Vice Pres*
EMP: 20 **EST:** 1964
SQ FT: 22,000
SALES (est): 1.8MM **Privately Held**
WEB: www.princetoncasewest.com
SIC: 3089 3161 Cases, plastic; luggage

(P-5780)
PRO DESIGN GROUP INC
438 E Alondra Blvd, Gardena
(90248-2902)
PHONE.................310 767-1032
Chris Raab, *President*
Christopher Allen Raab, *President*
Maria Chandler, *Vice Pres*
▲ **EMP:** 35 **EST:** 1990
SQ FT: 50,000
SALES (est): 8.5MM **Privately Held**
WEB: www.theprodesigngroup.com
SIC: 3089 Plastic kitchenware, tableware &
houseware; plastic processing

(P-5781)
PRODUCT DSIGN DEVELOPMENTS INC
15611 Container Ln, Huntington Beach
(92649-1532)
PHONE.................714 898-6895
Steven F Doke, *President*
EMP: 15 **EST:** 1993
SQ FT: 25,000
SALES (est): 2.1MM **Privately Held**
WEB: www.pddplasticforming.com
SIC: 3089 4724 Plastic containers, except
foam; travel agencies

(P-5782)
PRODUCTIVITY CALIFORNIA INC
Also Called: Pro Cal
10533 Sessler St, South Gate
(90280-7251)
PHONE.................562 923-3100
Gary Vollers, *President*
Don Uchiyama, *Admin Sec*
EMP: 170 **EST:** 1983
SQ FT: 100,000
SALES (est): 10MM
SALES (corp-wide): 510.3MM **Publicly
Held**
WEB: www.myersindustries.com
SIC: 3089 Plastic containers, except foam
PA: Myers Industries, Inc.
1293 S Main St
Akron OH 44301
330 253-5592

(P-5783)
PROTECTIVE INDUSTRIES INC
Also Called: Caplugs
18704 S Ferris Pl, Rancho Dominguez
(90220-6400)
PHONE.................310 537-2300
Fred Karam, *Branch Mgr*
Christopher Malone, *Comp Spec*
Liyang Zhang, *Purch Mgr*
Tom Valentine, *VP Sales*
Melanie Casey, *Marketing Staff*
EMP: 60
SALES (corp-wide): 1.8B **Privately Held**
WEB: www.caplugs.com
SIC: 3089 Injection molding of plastics
HQ: Protective Industries, Inc.
2150 Elmwood Ave
Buffalo NY 14207
716 876-9951

(P-5784)
PROULX MANUFACTURING INC
Also Called: Universal Products
11433 6th St, Rancho Cucamonga
(91730-6024)
PHONE.................909 980-0662
Richard Proulx, *President*
Raymond E Proulx, *CFC*
Lorraine Proulx, *Admin Sec*
◆ **EMP:** 45 **EST:** 1970

SALES (est): 6.5MM **Privately Held**
WEB: www.proulxmfg.com
SIC: 3089 Plastic hardware & building
products

(P-5785)
R & B PLASTICS INC
227 E Meats Ave, Orange (92865-3311)
PHONE..............................714 229-8419
Richard T Young, *President*
Nancy Young, *Vice Pres*
EMP: 14 EST: 1980
SQ FT: 10,000
SALES (est): 1.8MM **Privately Held**
WEB: www.r-bplastics.com
SIC: 3089 Injection molding of plastics

(P-5786)
RAKAR INCORPORATED
1700 Emerson Ave, Oxnard (93033-1847)
PHONE..............................805 487-2721
Theresa Padilla, *CEO*
Sarah Vibbart, *CFO*
Diego Padilla, *Exec VP*
Daniel Pittman, *Vice Pres*
Jamie Baker, *Office Mgr*
EMP: 48
SQ FT: 28,000
SALES (est): 9MM **Privately Held**
WEB: www.rakarinc.com
SIC: 3089 3544 Injection molding of plas-
tics; forms (molds), for foundry & plastics
working machinery

(P-5787)
RAMKO INJECTION INC
3551 Tanya Ave, Hemet (92545-9447)
PHONE..............................951 929-0360
Robert G Andrei, *President*
John Rathbone, *Vice Pres*
Lena Sinclair, *Vice Pres*
EMP: 100 EST: 2007
SALES (est): 18.6MM **Privately Held**
WEB: www.ramko-inj.com
SIC: 3089 3364 Blow molded finished
plastic products; nonferrous die-castings
except aluminum

(P-5788)
RAMTEC ASSOCIATES INC
Also Called: Con-Tech Plastics
3200 E Birch St Ste B, Brea (92821-6287)
PHONE..............................714 996-7477
Ralph Riehl, *President*
Vernon Meurer, *Vice Pres*
▲ EMP: 28 EST: 1984
SQ FT: 35,000
SALES (est): 6.8MM **Privately Held**
SIC: 3089 Molding primary plastic; injec-
tion molding of plastics

(P-5789)
REEVES EXTRUDED PRODUCTS INC
1032 Stockton Ave, Arvin (93203-2330)
PHONE..............................661 854-5970
Matthew Cobbs, *CEO*
Sandy Shelton, *Treasurer*
Beverly Palmer, *Admin Sec*
Steve Reeves, *Admin Sec*
EMP: 75 EST: 1967
SQ FT: 45,000
SALES (est): 13.9MM **Privately Held**
WEB: www.reevesextruded.com
SIC: 3089 Injection molding of plastics

(P-5790)
REHRIG PACIFIC HOLDINGS INC (PA)
4010 E 26th St, Vernon (90058-4477)
PHONE..............................323 262-5145
William J Rehrig, *CEO*
Sayre Peralta, *Partner*
Michael J Doka, *President*
James L Drew, *CFO*
Jeff Hentges, *Vice Pres*
EMP: 387 EST: 1998
SALES (est): 712.6MM **Privately Held**
WEB: www.rehrigpacific.com
SIC: 3089 2821 Cases, plastic; garbage
containers, plastic; molding primary plas-
tic; plasticizer/additive based plastic ma-
terials

(P-5791)
REINHOLD INDUSTRIES INC (DH)
12827 Imperial Hwy, Santa Fe Springs
(90670-4761)
PHONE..............................562 944-3281
Clarence Hightower, *CEO*
Carl Walker, *CFO*
Scott Walker, *Administration*
Rachelle Manganti, *Info Tech Mgr*
Victor Rodriguez, *Project Engr*
▲ EMP: 145
SQ FT: 130,000
SALES (est): 31.7MM **Publicly Held**
WEB: www.reinhold-ind.com
SIC: 3089 3764 2531 Molding primary
plastic; guided missile & space vehicle
propulsion unit parts; seats, aircraft

(P-5792)
RENY & CO INC
Also Called: Renymed
4505 Littlejohn St, Baldwin Park
(91706-2239)
PHONE..............................626 962-3078
Steve Raiken, *CEO*
Deanna Survillas, *Controller*
Stephanie Clemente-Finley, *Human Res Mgr*
Mary Heninger, *Plant Mgr*
Paula Estrada, *Manager*
EMP: 18 EST: 1985
SQ FT: 7,000
SALES (est): 8.5MM **Privately Held**
WEB: www.renymed.com
SIC: 3089 Plastic hardware & building
products

(P-5793)
RESINART CORPORATION
Also Called: Resinart Plastics
1621 Placentia Ave, Costa Mesa
(92627-4311)
PHONE..............................949 642-3665
Gary Uecker, *President*
Frank Uecker, *Treasurer*
Gene Chandler, *Vice Pres*
EMP: 40 EST: 1969
SQ FT: 15,000
SALES (est): 3.4MM **Privately Held**
WEB: www.resinart.com
SIC: 3089 Molding primary plastic; panels,
building: plastic

(P-5794)
REYRICH PLASTICS INC
1704 S Vineyard Ave, Ontario
(91761-7746)
PHONE..............................909 484-8444
Tina Richter, *President*
Sandy Reyes, *President*
EMP: 21 EST: 2012
SALES (est): 2.7MM **Privately Held**
WEB: www.reyrichplastics.com
SIC: 3089 Injection molding of plastics

(P-5795)
ROCKWEST TECHNOLOGY GROUP INC
3370 N San Fernando Rd, Los Angeles
(90051-1440)
PHONE..............................323 256-8700
Matt McDaniel, *Principal*
EMP: 19 **Publicly Held**
WEB: www.multicard.com
SIC: 3089 7382 Identification cards, plas-
tic; security systems services
HQ: Rockwest Technology Group, Inc.
7100 Broadway Ste 3k
Denver CO 80221

(P-5796)
ROLENN MANUFACTURING INC (PA)
2065 Roberta St, Riverside (92507-2644)
PHONE..............................951 682-1185
Thomas J Accatino, *President*
Christie Accatino, *Corp Secy*
Linda Lubken, *Prgrmr*
Aastha Bhardwaj, *Analyst*
Steven Romanini, *Prdtn Mgr*
EMP: 20 EST: 1965
SQ FT: 9,000

SALES (est): 12.9MM **Privately Held**
WEB: www.rolenn.com
SIC: 3089 3599 Injection molding of plastics; molding primary plastic; machine &
other job shop work

(P-5797)
RONCO PLASTICS INC
15022 Parkway Loop Ste B, Tustin
(92780-6529)
PHONE..............................714 259-1385
Ronald L Pearson, *President*
Alondra Barajas, *Administration*
EMP: 24 EST: 1976
SQ FT: 28,000
SALES (est): 6.5MM **Privately Held**
WEB: www.ronco-plastics.com
SIC: 3089 Injection molding of plastics;
septic tanks, plastic

(P-5798)
RONFORD PRODUCTS INC
1116 E 2nd St, Pomona (91766-2114)
PHONE..............................909 622-7446
Carl Higgins, *Manager*
Corri Steimle, *Bookkeeper*
EMP: 28
SALES (corp-wide): 4MM **Privately Held**
SIC: 3089 5093 Injection molding of plas-
tics; plastics scrap
PA: Ronford Products, Inc.
16616 Garfield Ave
Paramount CA 90723
562 408-1081

(P-5799)
ROPAK CORPORATION (DH)
Also Called: Ropak Packaging
10540 Talbert Ave 200w, Fountain Valley
(92708-6027)
PHONE..............................714 845-2845
Greg A Toft, *CEO*
◆ EMP: 448 EST: 1986
SQ FT: 12,000
SALES (corp-wide): 277MM
SALES (est): 1.1B **Privately Held**
WEB: www.mauserpackaging.com
SIC: 3089 Plastic containers, except foam

(P-5800)
ROTATIONAL MOLDING INC
Also Called: R M I
17038 S Figueroa St, Gardena
(90248-3089)
PHONE..............................310 327-5401
Mario Poma, *CEO*
Douglas Russell, *CFO*
Sherri Poma, *Human Res Mgr*
Chris Lariviere, *Sales Associate*
Peter Ramos, *Sales Staff*
EMP: 80 EST: 2010
SALES (est): 13.1MM **Privately Held**
WEB: www.rotationalmoldinginc.com
SIC: 3089 Plastic containers, except foam;
garbage containers, plastic
PA: Tank Holding Corp.
6940 O St Ste 100
Lincoln NE 68510

(P-5801)
ROTO DYNAMICS INC
1925 N Lime St, Orange (92865-4123)
PHONE..............................714 685-0183
Yogindra Saran, *CEO*
Rishi Saran, *Vice Pres*
EMP: 24 EST: 2005
SALES (est): 1.7MM **Privately Held**
WEB: www.rotodynamics.com
SIC: 3089 Plastic containers, except foam;
battery cases, plastic or plastic combina-
tion; boxes, plastic; cases, plastic

(P-5802)
ROTO LITE INC
84701 Avenue 48, Coachella (92236-1201)
PHONE..............................909 923-4353
Sandy Canzone, *President*
Dan Hammond, *Vice Pres*
John Hammond, *Admin Sec*
Kacey Hammond, *Marketing Mgr*
EMP: 30 EST: 2003
SALES (est): 8.8MM **Privately Held**
WEB: www.rotoliteinc.com
SIC: 3089 0781 Plastic containers, except
foam; landscape services

(P-5803)
ROTO POWER INC
191 Granite St Ste A, Corona
(92879-1286)
PHONE..............................951 751-9850
David Howey, *Officer*
Mayra Cepero, *Sales Staff*
EMP: 16 EST: 2016
SALES (est): 2.4MM **Privately Held**
WEB: www.roto-power.com
SIC: 3089 Injection molding of plastics

(P-5804)
ROTO WEST ENTERPRISES INC
15651 Container Ln, Huntington Beach
(92649-1532)
PHONE..............................714 899-2030
EMP: 15
SALES (est): 1.1MM **Privately Held**
SIC: 3089 Mfg Plastic Products

(P-5805)
ROYAL INTERPACK NORTH AMER INC
475 Palmyrita Ave, Riverside (92507-1812)
PHONE..............................951 787-6925
Radhika Shah, *CEO*
Tee Komsan, *President*
Visnau Chawla, *Principal*
Visanu Chawla, *Managing Dir*
Abu Hossain, *Administration*
▲ EMP: 45 EST: 2011
SALES (est): 24.6MM **Privately Held**
WEB: www.royalinterpackmidwest.com
SIC: 3089 Thermoformed finished plastic
products

(P-5806)
RPLANET ERTH LOS ANGLES HLDNGS
5300 S Boyle Ave, Vernon (90058-3921)
PHONE..............................833 775-2638
Robert Daviduk,
Rishi Moorjani, *Controller*
Andrew J Lopez, *Maintence Staff*
Daniel Gomez, *Supervisor*
EMP: 51 EST: 2015
SALES (est): 10.4MM **Privately Held**
WEB: www.rplanetearth.com
SIC: 3089 Injection molding of plastics

(P-5807)
RPM PLASTIC MOLDING INC
2821 E Miraloma Ave, Anaheim
(92806-1804)
PHONE..............................714 630-9300
Michael Ferik, *CEO*
Phil Hothan, *Admin Sec*
▲ EMP: 25 EST: 1995
SALES (est): 4.6MM **Privately Held**
WEB: www.rpmselect.com
SIC: 3089 Injection molding of plastics

(P-5808)
RSK TOOL INCORPORATED
410 W Carob St, Compton (90220-5213)
PHONE..............................310 537-3302
Ronald Kohagura, *President*
Mark Kohagura, *President*
Virginia Kohagura, *Vice Pres*
EMP: 35 EST: 1974
SQ FT: 27,000
SALES (est): 4.7MM **Privately Held**
WEB: www.rsktool.com
SIC: 3089 Injection molding of plastics

(P-5809)
S&B INDUSTRY INC
Also Called: Fxp Technologies
105 S Puente St, Brea (92821-3844)
PHONE..............................909 569-4155
Paul H Shiung, *President*
EMP: 40 **Privately Held**
SIC: 3089 Injection molded finished plastic
products
HQ: S&B Industry, Inc.
13301 Park Vista Blvd # 100
Fort Worth TX 76177

(P-5810)
SANDEE PLASTIC EXTRUSIONS
14932 Gwenchris Ct, Paramount
(90723-3423)
PHONE..............................323 979-4020

PRODUCTS & SVCS

Thomas Kunkel, *President*
Matt Andereck,
EMP: 22 **EST:** 1982
SQ FT: 14,000
SALES (est): 5.2MM
SALES (corp-wide): 15.4MM **Privately Held**
WEB: www.sandeeplastics.com
SIC: 3089 Injection molding of plastics
PA: Sandee Manufacturing Co.
10520 Waveland Ave
Franklin Park IL 60131
847 671-1335

(P-5811)
SANDIA PLASTICS INC
Also Called: Ultimate Solutions
15571 Container Ln, Huntington Beach
(92649-1530)
PHONE....................714 901-8400
William Allan, *CEO*
Bisson Monty, *President*
▲ **EMP:** 31 **EST:** 1996
SQ FT: 2,500
SALES (est): 6.2MM **Privately Held**
WEB: www.sandiaplastics.com
SIC: 3089 Injection molded finished plastic
products

(P-5812)
**SANTA CLARITA PLASTIC
MOLDING**
24735 Avenue Rockefeller, Valencia
(91355-3466)
PHONE....................661 294-2257
Walter Schrey, *President*
Thomas Schrey, *Principal*
EMP: 21 **EST:** 1998
SALES (est): 430.1K **Privately Held**
WEB: www.valenciaplastics.com
SIC: 3089 Injection molding of plastics

(P-5813)
SANTA FE EXTRUDERS INC
15315 Marquardt Ave, Santa Fe Springs
(90670-5709)
P.O. Box 524, Olney IL (62450-0524)
PHONE....................562 921-8991
Brick Pinckney, *President*
Jeanne Pinckney, *Corp Secy*
EMP: 18 **EST:** 1981
SQ FT: 30,000
SALES (est): 2.5MM **Privately Held**
WEB: www.sfext.com
SIC: 3089 3083 3081 2673 Extruded finished plastic products; laminated plastics plate & sheet; unsupported plastics film & sheet; bags: plastic, laminated & coated

(P-5814)
SANTA MONICA PLASTICS LLC
1602 Stanford St, Santa Monica
(90404-4114)
PHONE....................310 403-2849
Eric Warren, *Mng Member*
EMP: 14 **EST:** 2011
SALES (est): 1.2MM **Privately Held**
WEB: www.santamonicaplastics.com
SIC: 3089 Injection molded finished plastic
products

(P-5815)
SCR MOLDING INC
2340 Pomona Rd, Corona (92878-4329)
PHONE....................951 736-5490
Carl E Thompson, *President*
Richard H McCray, *Vice Pres*
Karen Thompson, *Admin Sec*
EMP: 22 **EST:** 1984
SQ FT: 21,000
SALES (est): 2.6MM **Privately Held**
WEB: www.scrmolding.com
SIC: 3089 Injection molding of plastics

(P-5816)
**SCULPTOR BODY MOLDING
(PA)**
10817 W Stallion Ranch Rd, Sunland
(91040-3702)
PHONE....................818 761-3767
Monica Canon Ferguson, *Principal*
Steve Ferguson, *Vice Pres*
EMP: 20 **EST:** 2006
SALES (est): 3.2MM **Privately Held**
SIC: 3089 Molding primary plastic

(P-5817)
SERCO MOLD INC (PA)
Also Called: Serpac Electronic Enclosures
2009 Wright Ave, La Verne (91750-5812)
PHONE....................626 331-0517
Patricia Ann Serio, *CEO*
Don Serio Jr, *Vice Pres*
George Boutros, *Opers Staff*
Jennifer McConnell, *Sales Mgr*
▲ **EMP:** 38 **EST:** 1978
SQ FT: 85,000
SALES (est): 11.5MM **Privately Held**
SIC: 3089 3544 5999 Injection molding of
plastics; industrial molds; electronic parts
& equipment

(P-5818)
SETCO LLC
4875 E Hunter Ave, Anaheim (92807-2005)
PHONE....................812 424-2904
Patty Harper, *Branch Mgr*
Richard Hofmann,
EMP: 150 **Publicly Held**
SIC: 3089 Plastic containers, except foam
HQ: Setco, Llc
101 Oakley St
Evansville IN 47710
812 424-2904

(P-5819)
**SIERRACIN/SYLMAR
CORPORATION**
Also Called: PPG Aerospace
12780 San Fernando Rd, Sylmar
(91342-3728)
PHONE....................818 362-6711
Barry Gillespie, *CEO*
◆ **EMP:** 600 **EST:** 1952
SQ FT: 300,000
SALES (est): 161.4MM
SALES (corp-wide): 15.1B **Publicly Held**
WEB: www.ppgaerospace.com
SIC: 3089 3812 3621 3231 Windshields,
plastic; search & navigation equipment;
motors & generators; products of purchased glass
PA: Ppg Industries, Inc.
1 Ppg Pl
Pittsburgh PA 15272
412 434-3131

(P-5820)
SKB CORPORATION (PA)
434 W Levers Pl, Orange (92867-3605)
PHONE....................714 637-1252
Steven A Kottman, *CEO*
Steve Kerpan, *Vice Pres*
David Sanderson, *Vice Pres*
Celso Nascimento, *Web Proj Mgr*
Don Weber, *VP Mfg*
◆ **EMP:** 350 **EST:** 1975
SALES (est): 57.3MM **Privately Held**
WEB: www.skbcases.com
SIC: 3089 3161 Cases, plastic; luggage

(P-5821)
SMART LLC
Also Called: Smart Wax
14108 S Western Ave, Gardena
(90249-3010)
PHONE....................310 674-8135
David Knotek, *CEO*
Sergio Galindo, *Vice Pres*
John Mansfield, *Vice Pres*
Paul Schneider, *Vice Pres*
Ivan Cabrera, *Purchasing*
▼ **EMP:** 40 **EST:** 2003
SALES (est): 11.6MM **Privately Held**
WEB: www.chemicalguys.com
SIC: 3089 5013 Automotive parts, plastic;
automotive supplies & parts

(P-5822)
SMITHCO PLASTICS INC (PA)
3330 W Harvard St, Santa Ana
(92704-3920)
PHONE....................714 545-9107
Stanley L Smith, *President*
Nancy Smith, *Treasurer*
Dan Smith, *Vice Pres*
EMP: 14 **EST:** 1977
SQ FT: 8,500
SALES (est): 1.3MM **Privately Held**
SIC: 3089 Injection molding of plastics;
plastic processing

(P-5823)
SNAPWARE CORPORATION
Also Called: Corningware Corelle & More
2325 Cottonwood Ave, Riverside
(92508-2309)
PHONE....................951 361-3100
Kris Malkoski, *CEO*
Ken Tran, *COO*
Grant Hartman, *Vice Pres*
Alex Yuan, *Technology*
Susan R Mercado, *Controller*
◆ **EMP:** 180
SALES (est): 43.8MM **Privately Held**
WEB: www.snapware.com
SIC: 3089 Plastic kitchenware, tableware &
houseware
HQ: Corelle Brands Llc
9525 Bryn Mawr Ave
Rosemont IL 60018
847 233-8600

(P-5824)
SONFARREL
3000 E La Jolla St, Anaheim (92806-1310)
PHONE....................714 630-7280
EMP: 26 **EST:** 1955
SALES (est): 6MM **Privately Held**
WEB: www.son-aero.com
SIC: 3089 Injection molding of plastics

(P-5825)
SPIN PRODUCTS INC
13878 Yorba Ave, Chino (91710-5518)
PHONE....................909 590-7000
Paul Burlingham, *President*
William Burlingham, *Vice Pres*
Gonzalo Banuelos, *Production*
▲ **EMP:** 24 **EST:** 1996
SQ FT: 96,000
SALES (est): 4.2MM **Privately Held**
WEB: www.spinproducts.com
SIC: 3089 Plastic containers, except foam

(P-5826)
**SR PLASTICS COMPANY LLC
(PA)**
640 Parkridge Ave, Norco (92860-3124)
PHONE....................951 520-9486
Larry Kaford, *Principal*
Larry Novak,
EMP: 64 **EST:** 2012
SALES (est): 6.3MM **Privately Held**
WEB: www.srplasticsmolding.com
SIC: 3089 Injection molding of plastics

(P-5827)
STAR PLASTIC DESIGN
25914 President Ave, Harbor City
(90710-3333)
PHONE....................310 530-7119
Dana Maltun, *President*
Maria Martinez, *Office Mgr*
Brooke Maltun, *VP Sales*
▲ **EMP:** 60 **EST:** 1980
SQ FT: 25,000
SALES (est): 8.5MM **Privately Held**
WEB: www.starplastic.com
SIC: 3089 Injection molding of plastics

(P-5828)
STAR SHIELD SOLUTIONS LLC
4315 Santa Ana St, Ontario (91761-7872)
PHONE....................866 662-4477
Gil Stanfill, *Mng Member*
Jim Kwon, *Marketing Staff*
EMP: 60 **EST:** 2007
SALES (est): 9.2MM **Privately Held**
WEB: www.starshieldsolutions.com
SIC: 3089 7389 Automotive parts, plastic;
financial services

(P-5829)
**STEVE LESHNER CLEAR
SYSTEMS**
13438 Wyandotte St, North Hollywood
(91605-4012)
PHONE....................818 764-9223
Steve Leshner, *Owner*
EMP: 14 **EST:** 1995
SQ FT: 5,000
SALES (est): 1MM **Privately Held**
WEB: www.clearsystemsonline.com
SIC: 3089 5211 Injection molding of plastics; closets, interiors & accessories

(P-5830)
**STONE CANYON INDUSTRIES
LLC (PA)**
1875 Century Park E # 320, Los Angeles
(90067-2253)
PHONE....................310 570-4869
James H Fordyce, *CEO*
James Fordyce, *Managing Ptnr*
Michael Neumann, *President*
Adam Cohn, *CEO*
Michael Salvator, *COO*
EMP: 35 **EST:** 2014
SALES (est): 1.1B **Privately Held**
WEB: www.stonecanyonllc.com
SIC: 3089 3411 Plastic containers, except
foam; metal cans

(P-5831)
STRAND ART COMPANY INC
4700 E Hunter Ave, Anaheim (92807-1919)
PHONE....................714 777-0444
Kevin Strand, *President*
Vicky Strand, *Admin Sec*
▲ **EMP:** 50 **EST:** 1974
SQ FT: 10,480
SALES (est): 5.7MM **Privately Held**
WEB: www.strandart.com
SIC: 3089 Injection molded finished plastic
products

(P-5832)
STRATASYS DIRECT INC (DH)
Also Called: Stratasys Direct Manufacturing
28309 Avenue Crocker, Valencia
(91355-1251)
PHONE....................661 295-4400
Joseph Allison, *CEO*
Peter Keller, *CFO*
Tom Smolders, *CFO*
Tom Vorgitch, *Vice Pres*
Andrew Latta, *Administration*
▲ **EMP:** 190 **EST:** 1991
SQ FT: 24,000
SALES (est): 106.5MM
SALES (corp-wide): 1.6B **Publicly Held**
WEB: www.stratasysdirect.com
SIC: 3089 Plastic processing; casting of
plastic

(P-5833)
SUPERIOR MOLD CO
1927 E Francis St, Ontario (91761-7719)
PHONE....................909 947-7028
Anthony Codet, *CEO*
Eleanor Yates, *QC Mgr*
EMP: 21 **EST:** 1972
SALES (est): 2.4MM **Privately Held**
WEB: www.unitindustriesgroup.com
SIC: 3089 Injection molding of plastics

(P-5834)
TALCO PLASTICS INC
3270 E 70th St, Long Beach (90805-1821)
PHONE....................562 630-1224
Ajit Ferera, *Manager*
Ajit Perera, *Vice Pres*
EMP: 64
SALES (corp-wide): 36.8MM **Privately
Held**
WEB: www.talcoplastics.com
SIC: 3089 4953 Extruded finished plastic
products; recycling, waste materials
PA: Talco Plastics, Inc.
1000 W Rincon St
Corona CA 92878
951 531-2000

(P-5835)
TAMSHELL CORP
237 Glider Cir, Corona (92878-5034)
PHONE....................951 272-9395
John Hernandez, *President*
Art Pierce, *Vice Pres*
Adam Bolt, *General Mgr*
Maricela Giles, *Office Mgr*
Silvia Tonelli, *Info Tech Mgr*
EMP: 95 **EST:** 1979
SQ FT: 20,000
SALES (est): 20.2MM **Privately Held**
WEB: www.tamshell.com
SIC: 3089 Caps, plastic; plastic hardware
& building products; hardware, plastic;
bearings, plastic

(P-5836)
TEKSUN INC
1549 N Poinsettia Pl # 1, Los Angeles
(90046-3662)
PHONE.................310 479-0794
David Meyer, *President*
EMP: 19 EST: 1938
SQ FT: 6,800
SALES (est): 2MM **Privately Held**
WEB: www.teksuninc.com
SIC: 3089 Injection molding of plastics; injection molded finished plastic products

(P-5837)
THERMODYNE INTERNATIONAL LTD
1841 S Business Pkwy, Ontario
(91761-8537)
PHONE.................909 923-9945
Gary S Ackerman, *Ch of Bd*
Scott Ackerman, *CFO*
◆ EMP: 110 EST: 1967
SQ FT: 57,500
SALES (est): 18.1MM **Privately Held**
WEB: www.thermodyne.com
SIC: 3089 3694 Plastic containers, except foam; engine electrical equipment

(P-5838)
THREE-D PLASTICS INC (PA)
Also Called: Three-D Traffics Works
430 N Varney St, Burbank (91502-1732)
PHONE.................323 849-1316
Frank J Dvoracek, *CEO*
Tim Trumbo, *COO*
Kathy Trumbo, *CFO*
Kathleen D Trumbo, *Corp Secy*
Joseph Dvoracek, *Vice Pres*
EMP: 34 EST: 1968
SQ FT: 40,000
SALES (est): 5.9MM **Privately Held**
WEB: www.3dplastics.com
SIC: 3089 Injection molding of plastics

(P-5839)
TNT PLASTIC MOLDING INC (PA)
725 E Harrison St, Corona (92879-1350)
PHONE.................951 808-9700
Diane Mixson, *President*
John Chadwick, *CFO*
Doug Chadwick, *Vice Pres*
Lynn Chadwick, *Vice Pres*
R J Jamaica, *Human Res Dir*
▲ EMP: 176 EST: 1979
SQ FT: 30,000
SALES (est): 28.5MM **Privately Held**
WEB: www.tntplasticmolding.com
SIC: 3089 Injection molding of plastics

(P-5840)
TOM YORK ENTERPRISES INC
Also Called: Kal Plastics
2050 E 48th St, Vernon (90058-2022)
PHONE.................323 581-6194
Tom York, *CEO*
EMP: 54 EST: 1958
SQ FT: 45,000
SALES (est): 4.7MM **Privately Held**
SIC: 3089 3993 Boxes, plastic; signs & advertising specialties

(P-5841)
TOTEX MANUFACTURING INC
3050 Lomita Blvd, Torrance (90505-5103)
PHONE.................310 326-2028
Tommy Tong, *President*
Helena Hui, *Controller*
Wayne WEI, *Accounts Mgr*
▲ EMP: 70 EST: 1998
SALES (est): 11.1MM **Privately Held**
WEB: www.totexusa.com
SIC: 3089 5063 Battery cases, plastic or plastic combination; batteries, dry cell

(P-5842)
TRIM-LOK INC (PA)
6855 Hermosa Cir, Buena Park
(90620-1151)
P.O. Box 6180 (90622-6180)
PHONE.................714 562-0500
Gary Whitener, *President*
Jack Hetherington, *Officer*
Balan Sorin, *Info Tech Mgr*
Garrett Brabant, *Engineer*

Rana Kim, *Accountant*
◆ EMP: 179 EST: 1971
SQ FT: 57,000
SALES (est): 53.6MM **Privately Held**
WEB: www.trimlok.com
SIC: 3089 Molding primary plastic

(P-5843)
TRINITY INTERNATIONAL INDS LLC
930 E 233rd St, Carson (90745-6203)
PHONE.................800 985-5506
Cze-Chao Tam, *Mng Member*
David Meehan, *Executive Asst*
Miguel Garcia, *Marketing Staff*
▲ EMP: 33 EST: 2007
SQ FT: 35,000
SALES (est): 3MM **Privately Held**
WEB: www.trinityii.com
SIC: 3089 2511 2542 Organizers for closets, drawers, etc.: plastic; storage chests, household: wood; racks, merchandise display or storage: except wood

(P-5844)
TRU-FORM PLASTICS INC
14600 Hoover St, Westminster
(92683-5346)
PHONE.................310 327-9444
Douglas W Sahm Sr, *CEO*
John D Evans, *COO*
Clauve Hurwicz, *CFO*
Anita Lorber, *Vice Pres*
▲ EMP: 35 EST: 1956
SQ FT: 1,000
SALES (est): 7.2MM **Privately Held**
WEB: www.tru-formplastics.com
SIC: 3089 Pallets, plastic; plastic processing

(P-5845)
TST MOLDING LLC
Also Called: All Amrcan Injction Mlding Svc
42322 Avenida Alvarado, Temecula
(92590-3445)
PHONE.................951 296-6200
Terry Voss, *Mng Member*
Tammy Richer, *Accounting Mgr*
Matthew Richards, *Opers Mgr*
Dave Hawley,
EMP: 27 EST: 2009
SALES (est): 4.9MM **Privately Held**
WEB: www.tstmolding.com
SIC: 3089 Injection molding of plastics

(P-5846)
TTL HOLDINGS LLC (HQ)
4626 Eucalyptus Ave, Chino (91710-9215)
PHONE.................909 597-7861
Earl E Payton, *Mng Member*
Liz Smith,
EMP: 494 EST: 2002
SALES (est): 497.4MM **Privately Held**
SIC: 3089 3544 Molding primary plastic: special dies, tools, jigs & fixtures

(P-5847)
UFO DESIGNS (PA)
5812 Machine Dr, Huntington Beach
(92649-1101)
PHONE.................714 892-4420
Jitendra Patel, *President*
Alfie Patel, *Vice Pres*
Hemant Patel, *VP Sales*
EMP: 16 EST: 1976
SQ FT: 35,000
SALES (est): 3.8MM **Privately Held**
WEB: www.ufodesign.com
SIC: 3089 Injection molding of plastics

(P-5848)
UFO INC
2110 Belgrave Ave, Huntington Park
(90255-2713)
P.O. Box 58192, Los Angeles (90058-0192)
PHONE.................323 588-5450
Efi Youavian, *President*
Efraim Youavian, *CEO*
Umar Farooq, *Prdtn Mgr*
▲ EMP: 50 EST: 1982
SQ FT: 65,000
SALES (est): 9.6MM **Privately Held**
WEB: www.ufobrand.com
SIC: 3089 2842 5199 Sponges, plastic; specialty cleaning, polishes & sanitation goods; foams & rubber

(P-5849)
UNCKS UNIQUE PLASTICS INC
1215 Brooks St, Ontario (91762-3609)
PHONE.................909 983-5181
Fax: 909 984-6376
EMP: 16
SALES (est): 1MM **Privately Held**
SIC: 3089 3544 Mfg Plastic Products Mfg Dies/Tools/Jigs/Fixtures

(P-5850)
UPLAND FAB INC
1445 Brooks St Ste L, Ontario
(91762-3665)
PHONE.................909 933-9185
Patsy Sapra, *CEO*
Jackson Sapra, *Shareholder*
Paul Sapra, *CEO*
Steven Sapra, *CFO*
Dawn Lancaster, *Office Mgr*
EMP: 24 EST: 1970
SQ FT: 12,000
SALES (est): 8.6MM **Privately Held**
WEB: www.uplandfab.com
SIC: 3089 Plastic & fiberglass tanks; plastic processing

(P-5851)
URBAN ARMOR GEAR LLC (HQ)
28202 Cabot Rd Ste 300, Laguna Niguel
(92677-1249)
PHONE.................949 329-0500
Scott W Hardy, *CEO*
Samuel Siu, *Co-CEO*
Steven Thomas, *Graphic Designe*
Joaquin Ramos, *Analyst*
Steve Armstrong, *Sales Staff*
▲ EMP: 36 EST: 2013
SALES (est): 12.1MM
SALES (corp-wide): 14.9MM **Privately Held**
WEB: www.urbanarmorgear.com
SIC: 3089 Cases, plastic
PA: Urban Armor Gear Holdings, Inc.
28202 Cabot Rd Ste 300
Laguna Niguel CA 92677
949 329-0500

(P-5852)
US POLYMERS INC (PA)
Also Called: Duramax Building Products
1057 S Vail Ave, Montebello (90640-6019)
PHONE.................323 728-3023
Viken Ohanesian, *CEO*
Vram Ohanesian, *CFO*
Haigan Ohanesian, *Treasurer*
Jacques Ohanesian, *Vice Pres*
Doug Robinson, *Purchasing*
◆ EMP: 100 EST: 1983
SQ FT: 70,000
SALES (est): 36.2MM **Privately Held**
WEB: www.uspolymersinc.com
SIC: 3089 3084 Shutters, plastic; plastics pipe

(P-5853)
USA EXTRUDED PLASTICS INC
965 E Discovery Ln, Anaheim
(92801-1147)
PHONE.................714 991-6061
Joseph Florimonte, *President*
Vida Aiona, *Vice Pres*
Linda Florimonte, *Admin Sec*
EMP: 16 EST: 1993
SQ FT: 11,000
SALES (est): 2.4MM **Privately Held**
WEB: www.usaextrudedplastics.com
SIC: 3089 Extruded finished plastic products

(P-5854)
UVM INC
Also Called: Global Packaging
511 S Harbor Blvd Ste G, La Habra
(90631-9375)
PHONE.................714 482-2914
Vinayak Upasani, *President*
Suvama Upasani, *Corp Secy*
Maria Kwok, *General Mgr*
▲ EMP: 14 EST: 1992
SQ FT: 1,400
SALES (est): 17.9MM **Privately Held**
SIC: 3089 3082 3221 3085 Tubs, plastic (containers); unsupported plastics profile shapes; glass containers; plastics bottles

(P-5855)
VALENCIA PLASTICS INC
Also Called: Valencia Mold
25611 Hercules St, Valencia (91355-5051)
PHONE.................661 257-0066
Luis Ruiz, *President*
EMP: 16 EST: 2009
SQ FT: 11,000
SALES (est): 1.9MM **Privately Held**
WEB: www.valenciaplastics.com
SIC: 3089 Injection molding of plastics

(P-5856)
VAN GRACE QUALITY INJECTION
Also Called: Crystal Tex Shoehorn
9164 Appleby St, Downey (90240-2915)
PHONE.................323 931-5255
EMP: 15
SQ FT: 2,000
SALES (est): 2.2MM **Privately Held**
SIC: 3089 Mfg Plastic Products

(P-5857)
VANDERVEER INDUSTRIAL PLAS LLC
515 S Melrose St, Placentia (92870-6337)
PHONE.................714 579-7700
Greg Geiss, *President*
EMP: 35 EST: 1951
SQ FT: 29,000
SALES (est): 5.6MM **Privately Held**
WEB: www.vanderveerplastics.com
SIC: 3089 Injection molding of plastics

(P-5858)
VANTAGE ASSOCIATES INC
12333 Los Nietos Rd, Santa Fe Springs
(90670-2911)
PHONE.................562 968-1400
Paul Roy, *CEO*
Eric Clack, *President*
Andrea Alpinieri Glover, *CFO*
Jess Jimenez, *Human Res Dir*
Dale Logsdon, *Manager*
EMP: 65
SQ FT: 20,000
SALES (corp-wide): 30.5MM **Privately Held**
WEB: www.vantageassoc.com
SIC: 3089 2499 5085 3621 Plastic processing; spools, reels & pulleys: wood; industrial supplies; motors & generators; aircraft parts & equipment; search & navigation equipment
PA: Vantage Associates Inc.
12333 Los Nietos Rd
Santa Fe Springs CA 90670
619 477-6940

(P-5859)
VOLANT COOL AIR INTAKES INC
10285 Indiana Ct, Rancho Cucamonga
(91730-5332)
PHONE.................909 476-7225
Anthony Quezada, *President*
▲ EMP: 28 EST: 1998
SQ FT: 12,000
SALES (est): 796.1K **Privately Held**
SIC: 3089 Molding primary plastic

(P-5860)
WADDINGTON NORTH AMERICA INC
Also Called: Wna City of Industry
1135 Samuelson St, City of Industry
(91748-1222)
PHONE.................626 913-4022
Mike Evans, *President*
Rodney Harano, *Controller*
Angie Knight, *Cust Mgr*
EMP: 112
SALES (corp-wide): 2.9B **Publicly Held**
WEB: www.novolex.com
SIC: 3089 Plastic kitchenware, tableware & houseware
HQ: Waddington North America, Inc.
50 E Rver Ctr Blvd Ste 65
Covington KY 41011

PRODUCTS & SVCS

(P-5861)
WCP INC
Also Called: West Coast Vinyl Windows
17730 Crusader Ave, Cerritos
(90703-2629)
PHONE..................562 653-9797
Charles Neubauer, *President*
▲ EMP: 95
SQ FT: 50,000
SALES (est): 20.4MM **Privately Held**
WEB: www.westcoastglass.com
SIC: 3089 3211 Windows, plastic; insulat-
ing glass, sealed units

(P-5862)
WEST-BAG INC
1161 Monterey Pass Rd, Monterey Park
(91754-3614)
PHONE..................323 264-0750
Luis Michel, *President*
Sixto Michel, *Vice Pres*
EMP: 30 EST: 1977
SQ FT: 12,000
SALES (est): 3.2MM **Privately Held**
WEB: www.west-bag.com
SIC: 3089 5149 Food casings, plastic;
sausage casings

(P-5863)
**WESTERN CASE
INCORPORATED**
231 E Alessandro Blvd, Riverside
(92508-5084)
PHONE..................951 214-6380
Toll Free:..................877   -
Paul F Queyrel, *CEO*
Steven Santos, *General Mgr*
Tarek Badawi, *Business Mgr*
▲ EMP: 60 EST: 1981
SALES (est): 13.4MM **Privately Held**
WEB: www.westerncase.com
SIC: 3089 3544 3444 Cases, plastic; spe-
cial dies, tools, jigs & fixtures; sheet met-
alwork

(P-5864)
**WESTLAKE ENGRG ROTO
FORM**
Also Called: Jaz Products
1041 E Santa Barbara St, Santa Paula
(93060-2820)
P.O. Box 3504, Westlake Village (91359-
0504)
PHONE..................805 525-8800
Wade Zimmerman, *President*
Pat Zimmerman, *Corp Secy*
Kim Fullerton, *Accounts Exec*
▲ EMP: 31 EST: 1969
SQ FT: 75,000
SALES (est): 1.6MM **Privately Held**
WEB: www.jazproducts.com
SIC: 3089 Planters, plastic; cases, plastic;
buoys & floats, plastic

(P-5865)
WHITE BOTTLE INC
10579 Dale Ave, Stanton (90680-2641)
PHONE..................949 788-1998
Arash Anvaripour, *Principal*
Robert W Thompson, *Principal*
Dante Torres, *Sales Staff*
▲ EMP: 20 EST: 2009
SALES (est): 2.9MM **Privately Held**
WEB: www.whitebottle.com
SIC: 3089 Plastic containers, except foam

(P-5866)
WNA COMET WEST INC
Also Called: Wna City of Industry
927 S Azusa Ave, City of Industry
(91748-1015)
PHONE..................626 913-0724
Mike Evans, *President*
Gabriella Flores, *Principal*
Rodney Harano, *Principal*
Janet Parga, *Principal*
▲ EMP: 230 EST: 1982
SALES (est): 31.4MM **Privately Held**
SIC: 3089 Plastic kitchenware, tableware &
houseware

3111 Leather Tanning & Finishing

(P-5867)
ANDREW ALEXANDER INC
Also Called: Falltech
1306 S Alameda St, Compton
(90221-4803)
PHONE..................323 752-0066
Michael Dancyger, *President*
Jeff Crosson, *CFO*
Steve Budrow, *Vice Pres*
Rob Luckey, *Regional Mgr*
Zachary Winters, *Engineer*
◆ EMP: 100 EST: 1992
SQ FT: 100,000
SALES (est): 25.3MM **Privately Held**
WEB: www.falltech.com
SIC: 3111 Harness leather

(P-5868)
CUSTOMFAB INC
7345 Orangewood Ave, Garden Grove
(92841-1411)
PHONE..................714 891-9119
Donald Alhanati, *President*
Sharon Davis, *Human Res Mgr*
Don Alhanati, *Mktg Dir*
Rhonda Alhanati, *Cust Mgr*
Trina Lamyuen, *Manager*
▲ EMP: 250 EST: 1991
SQ FT: 47,000
SALES (est): 45.8MM **Privately Held**
WEB: www.customfabusa.com
SIC: 3111 3842 Accessory products,
leather; surgical appliances & supplies

(P-5869)
**HERITAGE LEATHER COMPANY
INC**
4011 E 52nd St, Maywood (90270-2205)
PHONE..................323 983-0420
Jose C Munoz, *CEO*
Gustavo Gonzalez, *President*
Jose Munoz, *Advisor*
▲ EMP: 30 EST: 2000
SQ FT: 5,000
SALES (est): 2.7MM **Privately Held**
WEB: www.heritageleather.com
SIC: 3111 Belting leather

(P-5870)
**LA LA LAND PRODUCTION &
DESIGN**
1701 S Santa Fe Ave, Los Angeles
(90021-2904)
PHONE..................323 406-9223
Alexander M Zar, *CEO*
EMP: 45 EST: 2006
SQ FT: 30,000
SALES (est): 5.2MM **Privately Held**
SIC: 3111 Accessory products, leather

(P-5871)
LINEA PELLE INC (PA)
7107 Valjean Ave, Van Nuys (91406-3917)
PHONE..................310 231-9950
Wynn Katz, *President*
Mira Katz, *Vice Pres*
Michael Stafford, *Vice Pres*
Donna Basso, *Creative Dir*
Maria Salcedo, *Finance*
▲ EMP: 17 EST: 1987
SQ FT: 5,000
SALES (est): 2.6MM **Privately Held**
WEB: www.lineapelle.com
SIC: 3111 5621 Accessory products,
leather; dress shops

(P-5872)
SU MANO INC
16394 Downey Ave, Paramount
(90723-5500)
PHONE..................562 529-8835
Jeffrey Scott Kenney, *CEO*
Virginia Kenney, *Principal*
EMP: 23 EST: 2008
SALES (est): 528K **Privately Held**
WEB: www.sumano.com
SIC: 3111 Bookbinders' leather

3131 Boot & Shoe Cut Stock & Findings

(P-5873)
CYDWOQ INC
2102 Kenmere Ave, Burbank (91504-3413)
PHONE..................818 848-8307
Rafi Balouzian, *President*
Richard Delamarter, *Shareholder*
◆ EMP: 28 EST: 1996
SQ FT: 15,000
SALES (est): 4.6MM **Privately Held**
WEB: www.cydwoq.com
SIC: 3131 3199 Laces, shoe & boot:
leather; leather belting & strapping

(P-5874)
SOLE SOCIETY GROUP INC
11248 Playa Ct B, Culver City
(90230-6127)
P.O. Box 5206 (90231-5206)
PHONE..................310 220-0808
Andy Solomon, *Mng Member*
Talitha Peters,
▲ EMP: 200 EST: 2011
SALES (est): 32.3MM
SALES (corp-wide): 2.2B **Publicly Held**
WEB: www.solesociety.com
SIC: 3131 5661 5621 Boot & shoe acces-
sories; men's boots; women's boots;
ready-to-wear apparel, women's
HQ: Vcs Group Llc
1407 Broadway Frnt 3
New York NY 10018
203 413-6500

(P-5875)
SUNSPORTS LP
7 Holland, Irvine (92618-2506)
PHONE..................949 273-6202
Jamey Draper, *Partner*
▲ EMP: 21 EST: 1991
SQ FT: 85,000
SALES (est): 487.3K **Privately Held**
WEB: www.sunsportsapparel.com
SIC: 3131 2395 Footwear cut stock; em-
broidery products, except schiffli machine

3143 Men's Footwear, Exc Athletic

(P-5876)
**CAREISMATIC BRANDS INC
(PA)**
Also Called: Cherokee Uniform
9800 De Soto Ave, Chatsworth
(91311-4411)
PHONE..................818 671-2100
Michael Singer, *CEO*
David Byrnes, *Managing Prtnr*
Robert Pierpoint, *CFO*
Vanessa Teo, *CFO*
Lisa Hatfield, *Executive Asst*
◆ EMP: 203 EST: 1995
SQ FT: 140,000
SALES (est): 189.3MM **Privately Held**
WEB: www.careismatic.com
SIC: 3143 3144 5139 2339 Men's
footwear, except athletic; women's
footwear, except athletic; shoes; women's
& misses' outerwear; uniforms & vest-
ments; sweaters & sweater jackets: men's
& boys'

(P-5877)
SHOES FOR CREWS INTL INC
760 Baldwin Park Blvd, City of Industry
(91746-1503)
PHONE..................561 683-5090
EMP: 25
SALES (corp-wide): 19.9MM **Privately
Held**
SIC: 3143 3144 Warehouse For Men's
And Women's Slip Resistant Work Shoes
PA: Shoes For Crews International, Inc.
250 S Australian Ave # 1700
West Palm Beach FL 33401
561 683-5090

3144 Women's Footwear, Exc Athletic

(P-5878)
ALPARGATAS USA INC
Also Called: Havaianas
513 Boccaccio Ave, Venice (90291-4806)
PHONE..................646 277-7171
Marcio Moura, *CEO*
Afonso Fugiyama, *President*
Michele Kearns, *Marketing Staff*
Marlene Galicia, *Manager*
◆ EMP: 30 EST: 2006
SALES (est): 13.8MM **Privately Held**
WEB: www.alpargatas.com.br
SIC: 3144 Women's footwear, except ath-
letic
HQ: Alpargatas S/A
Av. Das Nacoes Unidas 14.261
Sao Paulo SP 04794

(P-5879)
EVOLUTION DESIGN LAB INC
Also Called: Jellypop
150 S Los Robles Ave # 1, Pasadena
(91101-2441)
PHONE..................626 960-8388
Jennet Chow, *CEO*
▲ EMP: 25 EST: 2009
SALES (est): 2.1MM **Privately Held**
WEB: www.jellypop-shoes.com
SIC: 3144 5139 Women's footwear, ex-
cept athletic; shoes

(P-5880)
IMPO INTERNATIONAL LLC
Also Called: Chili's
3510 Black Rd, Santa Maria (93455-5927)
P.O. Box 639 (93456-0639)
PHONE..................805 922-7753
Laura Ann Hopkins, *Mng Member*
Isabel Ruiz, *Director*
Lori Thompson, *Supervisor*
◆ EMP: 24 EST: 1968
SQ FT: 30,000
SALES (est): 4.6MM **Privately Held**
WEB: www.impo.com
SIC: 3144 Boots, canvas or leather:
women's; dress shoes, women's; san-
dals, women's

(P-5881)
MECO-NAG CORPORATION
Also Called: Dezario Shoe Company
7306 Laurel Canyon Blvd, North Hollywood
(91605-3710)
P.O. Box 16565 (91615-6565)
PHONE..................818 764-2020
Krikor Astourian, *President*
Vicki Astourian, *Vice Pres*
Cruz Martinez, *Admin Sec*
◆ EMP: 15 EST: 1986
SQ FT: 10,000
SALES (est): 310.8K **Privately Held**
SIC: 3144 Women's footwear, except ath-
letic

(P-5882)
ONNIK SHOE COMPANY INC
Also Called: Sergio Shoes
11443 Chandler Blvd, North Hollywood
(91601-2617)
P.O. Box 17018 (91615 7018)
PHONE..................818 506-5353
Vartan Vartanian, *President*
▲ EMP: 17 EST: 1973
SQ FT: 20,000
SALES (est): 657.7K **Privately Held**
SIC: 3144 Women's footwear, except ath-
letic

(P-5883)
SURGEON WORLDWIDE INC
3855 S Hill St, Los Angeles (90037-1415)
PHONE..................707 501-7962
Mariko Chambrone, *Vice Pres*
EMP: 27 EST: 2018
SALES (est): 1.8MM **Privately Held**
SIC: 3144 3143 Women's footwear, ex-
cept athletic; men's footwear, except ath-
letic

3149 Footwear, NEC

(P-5884)
NELSON SPORTS INC
12810 Florence Ave, Santa Fe Springs
(90670-4540)
PHONE..................................562 944-8081
Young Chu, *President*
Sook Hee Chu, *Admin Sec*
▲ **EMP:** 45 **EST:** 1986
SALES (est): 4.9MM **Privately Held**
WEB: www.madrock.com
SIC: 3149 3021 Athletic shoes, except rubber or plastic; rubber & plastics footwear

(P-5885)
SANTA FE FOOTWEAR CORPORATION
9988 Santa Fe Springs Rd, Santa Fe Springs (90670-2946)
PHONE..................................562 941-9689
Joel Tan, *President*
Joel O Tan, *President*
Debby Tio, *CFO*
Micah Gardner, *Opers Mgr*
▲ **EMP:** 15 **EST:** 1985
SQ FT: 30,000
SALES (est): 2MM **Privately Held**
SIC: 3149 3144 5139 Children's footwear, except athletic; women's footwear, except athletic; footwear

(P-5886)
SKECHERS USA INC (PA)
228 Manhattan Beach Blvd # 200, Manhattan Beach (90266-5356)
PHONE..................................310 318-3100
Robert Greenberg, *Ch of Bd*
Yasin Kavsak, *Managing Prtnr*
Michael Greenberg, *President*
David Weinberg, *COO*
John Vandemore, *CFO*
▲ **EMP:** 80 **EST:** 1992
SQ FT: 204,000
SALES (est): 4.6B **Publicly Held**
WEB: www.skechers.com
SIC: 3149 3021 Athletic shoes, except rubber or plastic; shoes, rubber or plastic molded to fabric

(P-5887)
SOLE TECHNOLOGY INC (PA)
Also Called: Etnies
26921 Fuerte, Lake Forest (92630-8149)
PHONE..................................949 460-2020
Pierre Senizergues, *President*
Paul Migaki, *COO*
Jeremiah Badell, *District Mgr*
Chuck Rios, *District Mgr*
Courtney Clair, *Executive Asst*
◆ **EMP:** 133 **EST:** 1996
SALES (est): 49.9MM **Privately Held**
WEB: www.soletechnology.com
SIC: 3149 5139 Athletic shoes, except rubber or plastic; footwear

3161 Luggage

(P-5888)
ANVIL CASES INC
1242 E Edna Pl Unit B, Covina
(91724-2540)
PHONE..................................626 968-4100
Joseph Calzone, *President*
Vincent Calzone, *Vice Pres*
Larry Hicks, *Executive*
Vint Calone, *Network Mgr*
▲ **EMP:** 125 **EST:** 1952
SALES (est): 20.3MM **Privately Held**
SIC: 3161 Musical instrument cases; cases, carrying
PA: Calzone, Ltd.
225 Black Rock Ave
Bridgeport CT 06605
203 367-5766

(P-5889)
BRIDGEPORT PRODUCTS INC
26895 Aliso Creek Rd, Aliso Viejo
(92656-5301)
PHONE..................................949 348-8800
Brent Foster, *President*

Jeffery Hahn, *Treasurer*
Ueli Gallizzi, *Officer*
Timothy Byk, *Vice Pres*
David Scott, *Admin Sec*
◆ **EMP:** 30 **EST:** 1999
SQ FT: 10,000
SALES (est): 1.4MM **Privately Held**
WEB: www.bridgeport-products.com
SIC: 3161 Traveling bags; cases, carrying

(P-5890)
ENCORE CASES INC
5260 Vineland Ave, North Hollywood
(91601-3221)
PHONE..................................818 768-8803
Gary A Peterson, *President*
▲ **EMP:** 27 **EST:** 1988
SALES (est): 3.3MM **Privately Held**
WEB: www.encorecases.com
SIC: 3161 Cases, carrying

(P-5891)
G & G QUALITY CASE CO INC
2025 E 25th St, Vernon (90058-1127)
P.O. Box 58541, Los Angeles (90058-0541)
PHONE..................................323 233-2482
Efren Guzman, *President*
Ben Germain, *Treasurer*
▲ **EMP:** 25 **EST:** 1978
SQ FT: 13,500
SALES (est): 7.8MM **Privately Held**
WEB: www.ggqualitycase.com
SIC: 3161 Musical instrument cases

(P-5892)
HAMMITT INC
2101 Pacific Coast Hwy, Hermosa Beach
(90254-2796)
PHONE..................................310 292-5200
Anthony Drockton, *Chairman*
Andrew Forbes, *CEO*
Tracy Jankowski, *Vice Pres*
Russell Travis, *Creative Dir*
Dan Goldman, *CTO*
▲ **EMP:** 51 **EST:** 2008
SQ FT: 3,600
SALES (est): 26.5MM **Privately Held**
WEB: www.hammitt.com
SIC: 3161 3171 Traveling bags; women's handbags & purses

(P-5893)
HSIAO & MONTANO INC
Also Called: Odyssey Innovative Designs
809 W Santa Anita Ave, San Gabriel
(91776-1016)
PHONE..................................626 588-2528
Mario Montano, *CEO*
John Hsiao, *Vice Pres*
Alice Jen, *Controller*
Dave Lopez, *Sales Dir*
Robert Rivera, *Supervisor*
▲ **EMP:** 50 **EST:** 1995
SALES (est): 9.8MM **Privately Held**
SIC: 3161 3648 5084 1751 Musical instrument cases; lighting equipment; woodworking machinery; cabinet & finish carpentry

(P-5894)
JAN-AL INNERPRIZES INC
Also Called: Jan-Al Cases
3339 Union Pacific Ave, Los Angeles
(90023-3812)
P.O. Box 23337 (90023-0337)
PHONE..................................323 260-7212
Miriam Alejandro, *President*
Jan Michael Alejandro, *Vice Pres*
Dianne Parker, *Executive*
Sal Funes, *Purch Mgr*
Jan Alejandro, *Sales Executive*
EMP: 30 **EST:** 1983
SQ FT: 16,000
SALES (est): 4.4MM **Privately Held**
WEB: www.janalcase.com
SIC: 3161 Luggage

(P-5895)
PMP PRODUCTS INC
Also Called: American Casuals
19827 Hamilton Ave, Torrance
(90502-1341)
PHONE..................................310 549-5122
Mariah Qian, *President*
EMP: 14 **EST:** 2015

SALES (est): 480.9K **Privately Held**
SIC: 3161 2231 Clothing & apparel carrying cases; apparel & outerwear broadwoven fabrics

(P-5896)
RJ SINGER INTERNATIONAL INC
Also Called: Ruben and Sharam
3737 Ross St, Vernon (90058-1635)
PHONE..................................323 735-1717
Reouben Melamed, *President*
Farshad Melamed, *Vice Pres*
Sam Abassi, *Human Res Mgr*
▲ **EMP:** 29 **EST:** 1947
SALES (est): 1.7MM **Privately Held**
WEB: www.rjsinger.com
SIC: 3161 2393 2335 2331 Cases, carrying; textile bags; women's, juniors' & misses' dresses; T-shirts & tops, women's: made from purchased materials; hats & caps

(P-5897)
TARGUS US LLC
1211 N Miller St, Anaheim (92806-1933)
PHONE..................................714 765-5555
Mikel H Williams, *CEO*
Victor Streufert, *CFO*
Lea Baltzinger, *Vice Pres*
Andrew Corkill, *Vice Pres*
Stan Mortensen, *Admin Sec*
EMP: 50 **EST:** 2015
SQ FT: 200,656
SALES (est): 11.9MM
SALES (corp-wide): 125.5MM **Privately Held**
WEB: www.us.targus.com
SIC: 3161 Cases, carrying
PA: Targus International Llc
1211 N Miller St
Anaheim CA 92806
714 765-5555

(P-5898)
TRAVELERS CHOICE TRAVELWARE
Also Called: Golden Pacific
2805 S Reservoir St, Pomona
(91766-6526)
PHONE..................................909 529-7688
Roger Yang, *CEO*
▲ **EMP:** 72 **EST:** 1993
SQ FT: 12,000
SALES (est): 15.2MM **Privately Held**
WEB: www.travelerchoice.com
SIC: 3161 Luggage

3171 Handbags & Purses

(P-5899)
COACH INC
3333 Bristol St Ste 2883, Costa Mesa
(92626-1821)
PHONE..................................949 365-0771
EMP: 15
SALES (corp-wide): 4.1B **Publicly Held**
SIC: 3171 Mfg Women's Handbags/Purses
PA: Coach, Inc.
516 W 34th St Bsmt 5
New York NY 10001
212 594-1850

(P-5900)
COACH INC
434 W Hillcrest Dr, Thousand Oaks
(91360-4222)
PHONE..................................805 496-9933
EMP: 15
SALES (corp-wide): 4.1B **Publicly Held**
SIC: 3171 Mfg Women's Handbags/Purses
PA: Coach, Inc.
516 W 34th St Bsmt 5
New York NY 10001
212 594-1850

(P-5901)
ISABELLE HANDBAGS INC
3155 Bandini Blvd Unit A, Vernon
(90058-4134)
PHONE..................................323 277-9888
Roye Xu, *President*
James LI, *Vice Pres*
▲ **EMP:** 35 **EST:** 2011
SQ FT: 2,000

SALES (est): 2.9MM **Privately Held**
WEB: www.emperiahandbags.com
SIC: 3171 5632 Handbags, women's; handbags

(P-5902)
NORTH RANCH MANAGEMENT CORP
9754 Deering Ave, Chatsworth
(91311-4301)
PHONE..................................800 410-2153
Richard Goldman, *CEO*
Denninger Linda, *Vice Pres*
Rodney Sohngen, *Vice Pres*
Linda Remollino, *Accounting Mgr*
Laura Barragan, *Merchandising*
▲ **EMP:** 70 **EST:** 2000
SALES (est): 11.3MM **Privately Held**
WEB: www.dreamproducts.com
SIC: 5719 3171 3172 4813 Housewares; women's handbags & purses; wallets;

(P-5903)
SBNW LLC (PA)
320 W 31st St, Los Angeles (90007-3806)
PHONE..................................213 234-5122
Jill Ause,
Jason Rimokh,
EMP: 110 **EST:** 2018
SALES (est): 14.8MM **Privately Held**
SIC: 3171 Handbags, women's

(P-5904)
URBAN EXPRESSIONS INC
5500 Union Pacific Ave, Commerce
(90022-5139)
PHONE..................................310 593-4574
Arash Vojdani, *President*
Farbod Shakouri, *Vice Pres*
Scott Roth, *Director*
Brian Chen, *Manager*
▲ **EMP:** 20 **EST:** 2005
SALES (est): 3.9MM **Privately Held**
WEB: www.urbanexpressions.net
SIC: 3171 5137 Handbags, women's; handbags

3172 Personal Leather Goods

(P-5905)
ALLEGRO PACIFIC CORPORATION
7250 Oxford Way, Commerce
(90040-3643)
PHONE..................................323 724-0101
▲ **EMP:** 16
SALES (est): 2MM **Privately Held**
SIC: 3172 Mfg Personal Leather Goods

(P-5906)
CASE WORLD CO
301 S Doubleday Ave, Ontario
(91761-1514)
PHONE..................................626 330-1000
Fax: 909 390-5222
EMP: 17
SALES (est): 1.6MM **Privately Held**
WEB: www.caseworld.tv
SIC: 3172 Mfg Personal Leather Goods

(P-5907)
GARYS LEATHER INC
Also Called: Gary's of California
12644 Bradford Pl, Granada Hills
(91344-1510)
PHONE..................................818 831-9977
Steven Matzdorff, *President*
Jeff Matzdorff, *Admin Sec*
EMP: 13 **EST:** 1973
SQ FT: 45,000
SALES (est): 243.2K **Privately Held**
SIC: 3172 Wallets; coin purses; key cases; card cases

(P-5908)
KOLTOV INC (PA)
300 S Lewis Rd Ste A, Camarillo
(93012-6620)
P.O. Box 2922 (93011-2922)
PHONE..................................805 764-0280
Joe Covrigaru, *CEO*
Brett Stone, *President*
Phillip Shieh, *Principal*
▲ **EMP:** 20 **EST:** 1983

SALES (est): 1.5MM Privately Held
SIC: 3172 5199 Personal leather goods;
leather, leather goods & furs

(P-5909)
LEATHER PRO INC
Also Called: Turtleback Case
12900 Bradley Ave, Sylmar (91342-3829)
PHONE................................818 833-8822
Brian Eremita, President
Tom Sutter, Vice Pres
Al Eremita, Admin Sec
▲ EMP: 24 EST: 2001
SQ FT: 13,000
SALES (est): 4.5MM Privately Held
WEB: www.turtlebackcase.com
SIC: 3172 Personal leather goods

(P-5910)
MALIBU LEATHER INC
510 W 6th St Ste 1002, Los Angeles
(90014-1311)
PHONE................................310 985-0707
Allen Cinoglu, President
EMP: 125 EST: 2009
SQ FT: 12,000
SALES (est): 3.8MM Privately Held
SIC: 3172 5199 5948 Personal leather
goods; leather, leather goods & furs; lug-
gage & leather goods stores

(P-5911)
RIDGE WALLET LLC
2448 Main St, Santa Monica (90405-3516)
PHONE................................818 636-2832
Daniel Kane, Mng Member
EMP: 15 EST: 2016
SALES (est): 614K Privately Held
WEB: www.ridgewallet.com
SIC: 3172 Wallets

3199 Leather Goods, NEC

(P-5912)
**CUSTOM LEATHERCRAFT MFG
LLC (DH)**
Also Called: CLC Work Gear
10240 Alameda St, South Gate
(90280-5551)
PHONE................................323 752-2221
Ron Pickens, CEO
Craig Anderson, CFO
Harry Karapetian, Vice Pres
Frank Gutierrez, Project Mgr
Stefanie Leary, Accounting Mgr
◆ EMP: 50
SQ FT: 150,000
SALES (est): 39.3MM
SALES (corp-wide): 1.4B Privately Held
WEB: www.goclc.com
SIC: 3199 2394 3111 Leather belting &
strapping; aprons: welders', blacksmiths',
etc.: leather; novelties, leather; canvas &
related products; glove leather
HQ: Hultafors Group Ab
J A Wettergrens Gata 7
Vastra Frolunda 421 3
337 237-400

(P-5913)
MASCORRO LEATHER INC
1303 S Gerhart Ave, Commerce
(90022-4256)
PHONE................................323 724-6759
Yolanda Mascorro, President
Antonio Mascorro, President
▲ EMP: 21 EST: 1977
SQ FT: 20,000
SALES (est): 1.1MM Privately Held
WEB: www.mascorroleather.com
SIC: 3199 Equestrian related leather arti-
cles

(P-5914)
OMAR LEATHER CO
4557 Valley Blvd, Los Angeles
(90032-3754)
PHONE................................323 227-5220
Maria M Rojas, Owner
EMP: 16 EST: 1972
SQ FT: 5,000
SALES (est): 786.8K Privately Held
SIC: 3199 Leather belting & strapping

(P-5915)
US DUTY GEAR INC
1946 S Grove Ave, Ontario (91761-5615)
PHONE................................909 391-8800
Jose Flores, CEO
Estela Flores, Vice Pres
EMP: 17 EST: 2015
SALES (est): 1.2MM Privately Held
WEB: www.usdutygear.com
SIC: 3199 Aprons: welders', blacksmiths',
etc.: leather

3211 Flat Glass

(P-5916)
**CARDINAL GLASS INDUSTRIES
INC**
Also Called: Cardinal C G
24100 Cardinal Ave, Moreno Valley
(92551-9545)
PHONE................................951 485-9007
Scott Paisley, Branch Mgr
Irene Orona, COO
Jennifer Gregg, Purch Agent
EMP: 35
SALES (corp-wide): 1B Privately Held
WEB: www.cardinalcorp.com
SIC: 3211 5039 3229 Flat glass; glass
construction materials; pressed & blown
glass
PA: Cardinal Glass Industries Inc
775 Pririe Ctr Dr Ste 200
Eden Prairie MN 55344
952 229-2600

(P-5917)
CEVIANS LLC
3128 Red Hill Ave, Costa Mesa
(92626-4525)
PHONE................................714 619-5135
Eric Lemay, President
Ben Phipps, Vice Pres
MAI Khuu, Controller
EMP: 55 EST: 2014
SALES (est): 10.1MM Privately Held
WEB: www.cevians.com
SIC: 3211 Flat glass

(P-5918)
GWLA ACQUISITION CORP (PA)
8600 Rheem Ave, South Gate
(90280-3333)
PHONE................................323 789-7800
Randy Steinberg, President
▲ EMP: 144 EST: 2002
SALES (est): 87.7MM Privately Held
SIC: 3211 3231 6719 Tempered glass;
mirrored glass; investment holding com-
panies, except banks

(P-5919)
INTELIGLAS CORPORATION
685 E California Blvd, Pasadena
(91106-3847)
PHONE................................626 722-8881
Richard Scott Martin, CEO
Robert Granadino, COO
EMP: 20 EST: 2018
SALES (est): 1.1MM Privately Held
WEB: www.inteliglas.com
SIC: 3211 7372 8748 Building glass, flat;
business oriented computer software; en-
ergy conservation consultant

(P-5920)
MEDILAND CORPORATION
Also Called: Premium Windows
7027 Motz St, Paramount (90723-4842)
PHONE................................562 630-9696
Carlos Landazuri, CEO
Jose Medina, Admin Sec
Kevin Vargas, Info Tech Mgr
Rosa Carrillo, Production
Daniel Delarosa, Sales Staff
▲ EMP: 79 EST: 2005
SALES (est): 9.1MM Privately Held
WEB: www.premiumwindows.com
SIC: 3211 3645 Window glass, clear &
colored; garden, patio, walkway & yard
lighting fixtures: electric

(P-5921)
SGC INTERNATIONAL INC
6489 Corvette St, Commerce
(90040-1702)
PHONE................................323 318-2998
Xinbo Huang, President
James Huang, Principal
▲ EMP: 15 EST: 1998
SALES (est): 2.3MM Privately Held
WEB: www.sgc-usa.com
SIC: 3211 5023 5039 Flat glass; frames &
framing, picture & mirror; exterior flat
glass: plate or window; interior flat glass:
plate or window

(P-5922)
SKYCO SKYLIGHTS INC
401 Goetz Ave, Santa Ana (92707-3709)
PHONE................................949 629-4090
Ryan Marshall, CEO
Robert Marshall, President
Gary Ritchie, Vice Pres
Leila Hale, Controller
EMP: 35 EST: 2014
SALES (est): 4.8MM Privately Held
WEB: www.skycoskylights.com
SIC: 3211 Skylight glass

(P-5923)
**SUNDOWN LIQUIDATING CORP
(PA)**
Also Called: Bristolite
401 Goetz Ave, Santa Ana (92707-3709)
PHONE................................714 540-8950
Randolph Heartfield, CEO
Rick Beets, President
Darryl Liyama, Technology
Joshua Keith, Engineer
Anthony Rossi, Engineer
◆ EMP: 154 EST: 1970
SQ FT: 100,000
SALES (est): 29.1MM Privately Held
SIC: 3211 Skylight glass

(P-5924)
TRANSIT CARE INC
7900 Nelson Rd, Panorama City
(91402-6827)
PHONE................................818 267-3002
William Baldwin, President
David Chaimowitz, CFO
▲ EMP: 15 EST: 1991
SQ FT: 20,000
SALES (est): 1.2MM Privately Held
SIC: 3211 Strengthened or reinforced
glass

(P-5925)
**US HORIZON MANUFACTURING
INC**
Also Called: U.S. Horizon Mfg
28539 Industry Dr, Valencia (91355-5424)
PHONE................................661 775-1675
Donald E Friest, CEO
Garrett A Russell, President
▲ EMP: 39 EST: 1998
SQ FT: 44,000
SALES (est): 5.8MM
SALES (corp-wide): 27.5B Privately Held
WEB: www.crl-arch.com
SIC: 3211 3429 Plate & sheet glass; man-
ufactured hardware (general)
HQ: C. R. Laurence Co., Inc.
2503 E Vernon Ave
Vernon CA 90058
323 588-1281

3221 Glass Containers

(P-5926)
ACME VIAL & GLASS CO
1601 Commerce Way, Paso Robles
(93446-3626)
PHONE................................805 239-2666
Debra C Knowles, President
Kay Anderson, Vice Pres
Angel Chairez, Opers Mgr
▲ EMP: 25 EST: 1942
SALES (est): 3.4MM Privately Held
WEB: www.acmevialglassa.openfos.com
SIC: 3221 3231 5113 Vials, glass; prod-
ucts of purchased glass; industrial & per-
sonal service paper

(P-5927)
ASEPTIC INNOVATIONS INC
4940 E Landon Dr, Anaheim 92807-1971)
PHONE................................714 584-2110
Noel Calma, CFO
EMP: 20 EST: 2016
SQ FT: 37,771
SALES (est): 1.3MM Privately Held
SIC: 3221 Glass containers

(P-5928)
CUSTOM PACK INC
11621 Cardinal Cir, Garden Grove
(92843-3814)
PHONE................................714 534-2201
EMP: 16
SALES (est): 659.1K
SALES (corp-wide): 1MM Privately Held
SIC: 3221 7389 Mfg Glass Containers
Business Services
PA: Custom Pack, Inc.
11661 Cardinal Cir
Garden Grove CA 92843
714 534-5353

(P-5929)
PACIFIC VIAL MFG INC
2738 Supply Ave, Commerce (90040-2704)
PHONE................................323 721-7004
Steven OH, Principal
▲ EMP: 40 EST: 2001
SQ FT: 30,000
SALES (est): 6.5MM Privately Held
WEB: www.pacificvial.com
SIC: 3221 Vials, glass

3229 Pressed & Blown
Glassware, NEC

(P-5930)
APUTURE IMAGING INDUSTRIES
1715 N Gower St, Los Angeles
(90028-5405)
PHONE................................626 295-6133
Bob Meesterman, Sales Staff
Jacob Robertson, Assistan
EMP: 15 EST: 2015
SALES (est): 155.1K Privately Held
WEB: www.aputure.com
SIC: 3229 Glass lighting equipment parts

(P-5931)
AVENUE LIGHTING
9000 Fullbright Ave, Chatsworth
(91311-6125)
PHONE................................800 798-0409
EMP: 17 EST: 2015
SALES (est): 257.8K Privately Held
WEB: www.avenuelighting.com
SIC: 3229 3646 3648 Glass lighting
equipment parts; commercial indusl & in-
stitutional electric lighting fixtures; lighting
equipment

(P-5932)
CARLEY (PA)
1502 W 228th St, Torrance (90501-5105)
PHONE................................310 325-8474
James A Carley, President
Margaret Tsang, CFO
Suzy Bush, MIS Staff
▲ EMP: 299 EST: 1974
SQ FT: 14,000
SALES (est): 27.9MM Privately Held
WEB: www.carleylamps.com
SIC: 3229 3646 3641 Lamp parts &
shades, glass; commercial indusl & insti-
tutional electric lighting fixtures; electric
lamps

(P-5933)
CDEQ INC
9421 Telfair Ave, Sun Valley (91352-1332)
PHONE................................818 767-5143
Chaim Dekel, President
EMP: 18 EST: 1995
SQ FT: 10,000
SALES (est): 1.1MM Privately Held
WEB: www.cdeq.com
SIC: 3229 Glassware, art or decorative

(P-5934)
DONOCO INDUSTRIES INC
Also Called: Encore Plastics
5642 Research Dr Ste B, Huntington Beach
(92649-1634)
P.O. Box 3208 (92605-3208)
PHONE....................714 893-7889
Richard Harvey, *CEO*
Donald Okada, *CFO*
George West, *Treasurer*
EMP: 25 **EST:** 1993
SQ FT: 12,000
SALES (est): 1.9MM **Privately Held**
WEB: www.encoreplastics.com
SIC: 3229 Tableware, glass or glass ceramic

(P-5935)
GLAS WERK INC
29710 Avnida De Las Bnder, Rancho Santa
Margari (92688)
PHONE....................949 766-1296
Maik Bollhorn, *President*
▲ **EMP:** 26 **EST:** 1987
SQ FT: 6,000
SALES (est): 3.1MM **Privately Held**
WEB: www.glaswerk.com
SIC: 3229 Scientific glassware

(P-5936)
IFIBER OPTIX INC
14450 Chambers Rd, Tustin (92780-6914)
PHONE....................714 665-9796
Sanjeev Jaiswal, *President*
Christopher Scheper, *Engineer*
▲ **EMP:** 25 **EST:** 2000
SQ FT: 5,731
SALES (est): 4MM **Privately Held**
WEB: www.ifiberoptix.com
SIC: 3229 Fiber optics strands

(P-5937)
IMPERIAL ENTERPRISES INC
9666 Owensmouth Ave Ste A, Chatsworth
(91311-8044)
PHONE....................818 886-5028
Galina Zingerman, *CEO*
Boris Zingerman, *Vice Pres*
Steven Zingerman, *Exec Dir*
▲ **EMP:** 23 **EST:** 1998
SQ FT: 13,000
SALES (est): 420.6K **Privately Held**
SIC: 3229 5023 Glassware, art or decorative; home furnishings

(P-5938)
ORBITS LIGHTWAVE INC
41 S Chester Ave, Pasadena (91106-3104)
PHONE....................626 513-7400
Yaakov Shevy, *CEO*
Allen Au, *Technician*
Drew Byers, *Engineer*
Rick Conner, *Director*
EMP: 36 **EST:** 1999
SQ FT: 9,700
SALES (est): 3.8MM **Privately Held**
WEB: www.orbitslightwave.com
SIC: 3229 Fiber optics strands

(P-5939)
PERFORMANCE COMPOSITES INC
1418 S Alameda St, Compton
(90221-4802)
PHONE....................310 328-6661
Francis Hu, *CEO*
Peter McNicol, *General Mgr*
Richard Craig, *Opers Mgr*
EMP: 106 **EST:** 1994
SQ FT: 46,000
SALES (est): 22.3MM **Privately Held**
WEB: www.performancecomposites.com
SIC: 3229 3624 3544 Glass fiber products; carbon & graphite products; special dies, tools, jigs & fixtures

(P-5940)
PRECISION GLASS BEVELLING INC
Also Called: Rbs Glass Designs
15201 Keswick St Ste A, Van Nuys
(91405-1014)
PHONE....................818 989-2727
Richard Sloan, *President*
Mike Latzer, *Vice Pres*

Peter Dallow, *Managing Dir*
▲ **EMP:** 16 **EST:** 1972
SQ FT: 7,000
SALES (est): 1.2MM **Privately Held**
SIC: 3229 5231 Pressed & blown glass; glass, leaded or stained

(P-5941)
SCI-TECH GLASSBLOWING INC
5555 Tech Cir, Moorpark (93021-1795)
P.O. Box 207 (93020-0207)
PHONE....................805 523-9790
Glenn Gaydick, *Shareholder*
Craig Gaydick, *Shareholder*
EMP: 17 **EST:** 1971
SQ FT: 4,600
SALES (est): 985.2K **Privately Held**
SIC: 3229 Pressed & blown glass

(P-5942)
SIMPLY STRAWS LLC
1725 Monrovia Ave Ste C3, Costa Mesa
(92627-4423)
PHONE....................855 787-2974
Cyndi Sladics, *President*
Teri Leigh, *Controller*
Chanelle Sladics
▲ **EMP:** 14 **EST:** 2011
SALES (est): 2.3MM **Privately Held**
WEB: www.simplystraws.com
SIC: 3229 Straws, glass

(P-5943)
SPOTLITE AMERICA CORPORATION (PA)
9937 Jefferson Blvd # 110, Culver City
(90232-3528)
PHONE....................310 829-0200
Halston Mikail, *CEO*
▲ **EMP:** 47 **EST:** 2014
SQ FT: 17,000
SALES (est): 5.9MM **Privately Held**
WEB: www.spotlite-usa.com
SIC: 3229 3699 Bulbs for electric lights; electrical equipment & supplies

(P-5944)
ZEONS INC
291 S Cienega Blvd 102, Beverly Hills
(90211)
PHONE....................323 302-8299
Naved Jafry, *President*
EMP: 312
SQ FT: 3,500
SALES (est): 13MM **Privately Held**
SIC: 3229 1629 6211 Insulators, electrical; glass; power plant construction; investment certificate sales; oil & gas lease brokers

---

3231 Glass Prdts Made Of Purchased Glass

(P-5945)
ALAN LEM & CO INC
Also Called: Advance Aqua Tanks
515 W 130th St, Los Angeles (90061-1180)
PHONE....................310 538-4282
Alan Y Lem, *President*
Irma Alvarado, *CFO*
Yvonne Chua, *Purch Mgr*
EMP: 27 **EST:** 1986
SQ FT: 11,000
SALES (est): 2.5MM **Privately Held**
WEB: www.advanceaquatanks.com
SIC: 3231 Aquariums & reflectors, glass

(P-5946)
BANANAFISH PRODUCTIONS INC
1536 W Embassy St, Anaheim
(92802-1016)
PHONE....................714 956-2129
Dan Iman, *President*
Jerry Smith, *Principal*
EMP: 17 **EST:** 1981
SQ FT: 4,500
SALES (est): 300K **Privately Held**
SIC: 3231 Ornamental glass: cut, engraved or otherwise decorated

(P-5947)
CARDINAL GLASS INDUSTRIES INC
Also Called: Cardinal Cg Company
1125 E Lanzit Ave, Los Angeles
(90059-1559)
PHONE....................323 319-0070
EMP: 44
SALES (corp-wide): 1B **Privately Held**
WEB: www.cardinalcorp.com
SIC: 3231 Products of purchased glass
PA: Cardinal Glass Industries Inc
775 Pririe Ctr Dr Ste 200
Eden Prairie MN 55344
952 229-2600

(P-5948)
CARLOS SHOWER DOORS INC
300 Kentucky St, Bakersfield (93305-4230)
P.O. Box 6009 (93386-6009)
PHONE....................661 204-6689
Phillip Calvillo, *President*
Loni Amado, *President*
Edward Amado, *Vice Pres*
Steven Amado, *Vice Pres*
Phillip C Calvillo, *Admin Sec*
EMP: 28 **EST:** 1947
SQ FT: 10,000
SALES (est): 765.8K **Privately Held**
WEB: www.carlosshowerdoors.com
SIC: 3231 Doors, glass: made from purchased glass; insulating glass: made from purchased glass

(P-5949)
CUSTOM INDUSTRIES INC
1371 N Miller St, Anaheim (92806-1412)
PHONE....................714 779-9101
Thomas McAfee, *President*
▲ **EMP:** 21 **EST:** 1992
SALES (est): 4.5MM **Privately Held**
WEB: www.customglassindustries.com
SIC: 3231 Doors, glass: made from purchased glass

(P-5950)
CV WNDOWS DORS RIVERSIDE INC
Also Called: Cv of Riverside
6676 Lance Dr, Riverside (92507-0769)
P.O. Box 802813, Santa Clarita (91380-2813)
PHONE....................951 784-8766
Kevin Grossman, *CEO*
EMP: 15 **EST:** 2002
SALES (est): 720K **Privately Held**
SIC: 3231 3211 3442 2431 Doors, glass: made from purchased glass; window glass, clear & colored; window & door frames; windows & window parts & trim, wood

(P-5951)
DA-LY GLASS CORP
Also Called: Western Glass Co
1193 W 2nd St, Pomona (91766-1308)
PHONE....................323 589-5461
William J Dake, *President*
▲ **EMP:** 20 **EST:** 1950
SQ FT: 25,000
SALES (est): 673.1K **Privately Held**
SIC: 3231 3281 3211 1411 Laminated glass: made from purchased glass; decorated glassware: chipped, engraved, etched, etc.; cut stone & stone products; flat glass; dimension stone

(P-5952)
E & R GLASS CONTRACTORS INC
5369 Brooks St, Montclair (91763-4539)
PHONE....................909 624-1763
Eric Dryden, *President*
Russ Dryden, *Vice Pres*
EMP: 22 **EST:** 2003
SQ FT: 800
SALES (est): 2.6MM **Privately Held**
SIC: 3231 Products of purchased glass

(P-5953)
GAFFOGLIO FMLY MTLCRAFTERS INC (PA)
Also Called: Camera Ready Cars
11161 Slater Ave, Fountain Valley
(92708-4921)
PHONE....................714 444-2000
George Gaffoglio, *CEO*
Ruben Gaffoglio, *President*
Mike Alexander, *COO*
EMP: 108 **EST:** 1979
SQ FT: 94,000
SALES (est): 17.2MM **Privately Held**
WEB: www.metalcrafters.com
SIC: 3231 3711 3365 Mirrors, truck & automobile: made from purchased glass; automobile assembly, including specialty automobiles; aerospace castings, aluminum

(P-5954)
GLASSPLAX
26605 Madison Ave, Murrieta
(92562-8909)
PHONE....................951 677-4800
Steve Tortomasi, *President*
▲ **EMP:** 18 **EST:** 1984
SALES (est): 1.2MM **Privately Held**
WEB: www.glassplax.com
SIC: 3231 5094 Ornamental glass: cut, engraved or otherwise decorated; trophies

(P-5955)
GLASSWERKS LA INC (HQ)
Also Called: Glasswerks Group
8600 Rheem Ave, South Gate
(90280-3333)
PHONE....................888 789-7810
Randy Steinberg, *President*
Ruben Huerta, *Admin Sec*
Bryan Colliver, *IT/INT Sup*
Lucy Castillo, *Credit Staff*
Joshua Lopez, *Sales Executive*
▲ **EMP:** 280 **EST:** 1949
SQ FT: 100,000
SALES (est): 72.3MM **Privately Held**
WEB: www.glasswerks.com
SIC: 3231 3211 Mirrored glass; flat glass

(P-5956)
GP MERGER SUB INC
Also Called: Glaspro
9401 Ann St, Santa Fe Springs
(90670-2613)
PHONE....................562 946-7722
Joseph Green, *President*
Bishop McNeill, *Chief Mktg Ofcr*
Delia Torres, *Mfg Dir*
McNeill Bishop, *Mktg Dir*
Phil Gonzalez, *Sales Staff*
◆ **EMP:** 85 **EST:** 1986
SQ FT: 75,000
SALES (est): 16.8MM **Privately Held**
WEB: www.glas-pro.com
SIC: 3231 Laminated glass: made from purchased glass

(P-5957)
INDUSTRIAL GLASS PRODUCTS INC
4229 Union Pacific Ave, Los Angeles
(90023-4016)
PHONE....................323 526-7125
Esther Ramirez, *President*
▲ **EMP:** 15 **EST:** 1990
SQ FT: 10,000 **Privately Held**
WEB: www.iglassprod.com
SIC: 3231 5039 Products of purchased glass; glass construction materials

(P-5958)
INNOVATIVE STRUCTURAL GL INC
Also Called: I S G
40220 Pierce Dr, Three Rivers
(93271-9332)
P.O. Box 775 (93271-0775)
PHONE....................559 561-7000
Manuel Marinos, *CEO*
Cynthia Marinos, *CFO*
Julie Gray, *Controller*
Lisa Taviano, *Purchasing*
▲ **EMP:** 56 **EST:** 1998
SQ FT: 100,000

SALES (est): 4MM **Privately Held**
WEB: www.structuralglass.com
SIC: 3231 Products of purchased glass

(P-5959)
INVENIOS LLC
320 N Nopal St, Santa Barbara
(93103-3225)
PHONE.....................................805 962-3333
Paul Then, *President*
EMP: 83 EST: 2017
SALES (est): 5.4MM
SALES (corp): 11.3B **Publicly Held**
WEB: www.invenios.com
SIC: 3231 Products of purchased glass
PA: Corning Incorporated
1 Riverfront Plz
Corning NY 14831
607 974-9000

(P-5960)
JANEL GLASS COMPANY INC
2960 Marsh St, Los Angeles (90039-2911)
P.O. Box 39849 (90039-0849)
PHONE.....................................323 661-8621
Fax: 323 661-8738
EMP: 50
SQ FT: 27,000
SALES (est): 5.4MM **Privately Held**
SIC: 3231 Mfg Products-Purchased Glass

(P-5961)
LARRY MTHVIN INSTALLATIONS INC (HQ)
Also Called: L M I
501 Kettering Dr, Ontario (91761-8150)
PHONE.....................................909 563-1700
Larry Methvin, *CEO*
Tom Forsythe, *Executive*
Danielle Endsley, *Administration*
Mary Duran, *Human Resources*
Michele Dantuono, *Personnel Assit*
▲ EMP: 200 EST: 1975
SQ FT: 28,000
SALES (est): 51MM
SALES (corp-wide): 2.4B **Publicly Held**
WEB: www.larrymethvin.com
SIC: 3231 3431 1751 Doors, glass: made
from purchased glass; shower stalls,
metal; carpentry work
PA: Patrick Industries, Inc.
107 W Franklin St
Elkhart IN 46516
574 294-7511

(P-5962)
LIPPERT COMPONENTS MFG INC
Hehr Glass Co
1021 Walnut Ave, Pomona (91766-6528)
PHONE.....................................909 628-5557
Pete Adams, *Manager*
EMP: 50
SALES (corp-wide): 2.8B **Publicly Held**
WEB: www.lci1.com
SIC: 3231 5231 Doors, glass: made from
purchased glass; glass
HQ: Lippert Components Manufacturing,
Inc.
3501 County Road 6 E
Elkhart IN 46514
574 535-1125

(P-5963)
MILGARD MANUFACTURING LLC
Also Called: Milgard-Simi Valley
355 E Easy St, Simi Valley (93065-1801)
PHONE.....................................805 581-6325
Wayne Ramay, *Branch Mgr*
Christopher Davis, *Plant Mgr*
Kenny Lopez, *Production*
Cal Mc Clure, *Maintence Staff*
Calvin Mc Clure, *Maintence Staff*
EMP: 128
SALES (corp-wide): 822.1MM **Privately Held**
WEB: www.milgard.com
SIC: 3231 5031 3442 Products of pur-
chased glass; metal doors, sash & trim;
metal doors, sash & trim
HQ: Milgard Manufacturing Llc
1010 54th Ave E
Tacoma WA 98424
253 922-4343

(P-5964)
NEW GLASPRO INC
9401 Ann St, Santa Fe Springs
(90670-2613)
PHONE.....................................800 776-2368
Joseph Green, *President*
EMP: 23 EST: 2005
SALES (est): 1.1MM **Privately Held**
WEB: www.glas-pro.com
SIC: 3231 Products of purchased glass

(P-5965)
NEWPORT INDUSTRIAL GLASS INC
Also Called: Glass Fabrication and Dist
8610 Central Ave, Stanton (90680-2720)
P.O. Box 127 (90680-0127)
PHONE.....................................714 484-7500
Ray Larsen, *Director*
Pilin Chung, *Shareholder*
EMP: 22 EST: 1983
SALES (est): 1.1MM **Privately Held**
WEB: www.newportglass.com
SIC: 3231 3827 3851 5039 Products of
purchased glass; mirrors, optical; lens
grinding, except prescription: ophthalmic;
protective eyeware; exterior flat glass:
plate or window

(P-5966)
OLDCASTLE BUILDINGENVELOPE INC
5631 Ferguson Dr, Commerce
(90022-5132)
P.O. Box 22243, Los Angeles (90022-0243)
PHONE.....................................323 722-2007
Luis Soto, *Principal*
Kristin Tharp, *President*
Carol Ohmann, *Bd of Directors*
Lina M Ingalls, *Executive*
Steven Fields, *CTO*
EMP: 51
SQ FT: 200,000
SALES (corp-wide): 27.5B **Privately Held**
WEB: www.obe.com
SIC: 3231 5231 Tempered glass: made
from purchased glass; insulating glass:
made from purchased glass; glass
HQ: Oldcastle Buildingenvelope, Inc.
5005 Lyndon B Johnson Fwy # 1050
Dallas TX 75244
214 273-3400

(P-5967)
PAI GP INC
Also Called: Pai Enterprises
5914 Crenshaw Blvd, Los Angeles
(90043-3030)
PHONE.....................................323 549-5355
Robert Johnson, *President*
Michael Woodman, *CFO*
▲ EMP: 77 EST: 2000
SQ FT: 4,000
SALES (est): 4.7MM **Privately Held**
SIC: 3231 Products of purchased glass

(P-5968)
PRL GLASS SYSTEMS INC
14760 Don Julian Rd, City of Industry
(91746-3107)
PHONE.....................................877 775-2586
EMP: 74 **Privately Held**
WEB: www.prlglass.com
SIC: 3231 Products of purchased glass
PA: Prl Glass Systems, Inc.
13644 Nelson Ave
City Of Industry CA 91746

(P-5969)
SREAM INC
12869 Temescal Canyon Rd A, Corona
(92883-4021)
PHONE.....................................951 245-6999
Jarir Farraj, *CEO*
Steve Rodriguez, *COO*
EMP: 34 EST: 2013
SALES (est): 3MM **Privately Held**
WEB: www.liquidsciglass.com
SIC: 3231 5231 Products of purchased
glass; glass

(P-5970)
TRIVIEW GLASS INDUSTRIES LLC
279 Shawnan Ln, La Habra (90631-8087)
PHONE.....................................626 363-7980
Alexander A Kastaniuk, *CEO*
Jorge Galvan, *Maintence Staff*
▲ EMP: 99
SALES (est): 17.2MM **Privately Held**
WEB: www.triview-glass.squarespace.com
SIC: 3231 Products of purchased glass

(P-5971)
TWED-DELLS INC
Also Called: California Glass & Mirror Div
1900 S Susan St, Santa Ana (92704-3924)
PHONE.....................................714 754-6900
Corey M Myer Jr, *President*
Gayle Myer, *Admin Sec*
▲ EMP: 38 EST: 1980
SQ FT: 45,000
SALES (est): 5.3MM **Privately Held**
WEB: www.tbmglass.com
SIC: 3231 Mirrored glass

(P-5972)
ZADRO INC
14462 Astronautics Ln # 101, Huntington
Beach (92647-2077)
PHONE.....................................714 892-9200
Elizabeth Zadro, *President*
EMP: 20 EST: 2007
SALES (est): 576.5K **Privately Held**
SIC: 3231 Mirrored glass

(P-5973)
ZADRO PRODUCTS INC
14462 Astronautics Ln # 101, Huntington
Beach (92647-2077)
PHONE.....................................714 892-9200
Zlatko Zadro, *President*
Becky Zadro, *Vice Pres*
Charlotte Shmavonian, *Human Resources*
Alex Zadro, *Opers Mgr*
Brad Everett, *Opers Staff*
◆ EMP: 35 EST: 1986
SQ FT: 22,000
SALES (est): 6.2MM **Privately Held**
WEB: www.zadroinc.com
SIC: 3231 3641 Mirrored glass; electric
lamps

3241 Cement, Hydraulic

(P-5974)
CALPORTLAND COMPANY
Also Called: California Portland Cement
9350 Oak Creek Rd, Mojave (93501-7738)
PHONE.....................................661 824-2401
Bruce Shaffer, *Branch Mgr*
Steve Troy, *Engineer*
Luz Rocha, *Credit Staff*
Jessica Nunez, *Analyst*
Jake Nieman, *Plant Mgr*
EMP: 130 **Privately Held**
WEB: www.calportland.com
SIC: 3241 5032 5211 Masonry cement;
brick, stone & related material; cement
HQ: Calportland Company
2025 E Financial Way
Glendora CA 91741

(P-5975)
CALPORTLAND COMPANY (DH)
Also Called: Arizona Portland Cement
2025 E Financial Way, Glendora
(91741-4692)
P.O. Box 5025 (91740-0885)
PHONE.....................................626 852-6200
Michio Kimura, *Ch of Bd*
James A Repman, *President*
Allen Hamblen, *CEO*
James A Wendoll, *CFO*
Noboru Kasai, *Vice Ch Bd*
▲ EMP: 77 EST: 1891
SQ FT: 28,000
SALES (est): 864.1MM **Privately Held**
WEB: www.calportland.com
SIC: 3241 3273 5032 Portland cement;
ready-mixed concrete; brick, stone & re-
lated material

HQ: Taiheiyo Cement U.S.A., Inc.
2025 E Fincl Way Ste 200
Glendora CA 91741
626 852-6200

(P-5976)
HEADWATERS CONSTRUCTION INC
Also Called: Louis W Osborn Co.
16005 Phoebe Ave, La Mirada
(90638-5607)
PHONE.....................................714 523-1530
Rudy Valverde, *General Mgr*
EMP: 24 EST: 1962
SQ FT: 18,000
SALES (est): 618.6K **Privately Held**
SIC: 3241 Cement, hydraulic

(P-5977)
JAMES HARDIE BUILDING PDTS INC
26300 La Alameda Ste 400, Mission Viejo
(92691-8372)
PHONE.....................................949 348-1800
Louis Gries, *President*
Kirk Williams, *Officer*
Jill Rogers, *Vice Pres*
Bryan Cummings, *Administration*
Jason Fang, *Administration*
EMP: 86
SQ FT: 97,250 **Privately Held**
WEB: www.jameshardie.com
SIC: 3241 Natural cement
HQ: James Hardie Building Products Inc.
231 S La Salle St # 2000
Chicago IL 60604
312 291-5072

(P-5978)
LEHIGH CEMENT WEST INC
13573 E Tehachapi Blvd, Tehachapi
(93561-8155)
PHONE.....................................661 822-4445
Axel Conrads, *Manager*
Ron Hibdon, *President*
Jaromir Vojtech, *Engineer*
Troy Beavor, *Production*
Garrett Fong, *Production*
EMP: 130
SALES (corp-wide): 6MM **Privately Held**
WEB: www.lehighhanson.com
SIC: 3241 3273 2951 1442 Portland ce-
ment; ready-mixed concrete; asphalt
paving mixtures & blocks; construction
sand & gravel
PA: Lehigh Cement West Inc.
300 E John Carpenter Fwy
Irving TX

(P-5979)
MITSUBISHI CEMENT CORPORATION
5808 State Highway 18, Lucerne Valley
(92356-8179)
PHONE.....................................760 248-7373
Jim Russell, *Branch Mgr*
Irene Rudow, *Admin Asst*
Ryan Barnett, *Project Eng*
Leandro Galaz, *Human Res Mgr*
Tom Gepford, *QC Mgr*
EMP: 175 **Privately Held**
WEB: www.mitsubishicement.com
SIC: 3241 Portland cement
HQ: Mitsubishi Cement Corporation
151 Cassia Way
Henderson NV 89014
702 932-3900

(P-5980)
MITSUBISHI CEMENT CORPORATION
1150 Pier F Ave, Long Beach (90802-6252)
PHONE.....................................562 495-0600
Marty Marcum, *Manager*
EMP: 428 **Privately Held**
WEB: www.mitsubishicement.com
SIC: 3241 Cement, hydraulic
HQ: Mitsubishi Cement Corporation
151 Cassia Way
Henderson NV 89014
702 932-3900

(P-5981)
NATIONAL CEMENT COMPANY INC (HQ)
15821 Ventura Blvd # 475, Encino (91436-2935)
PHONE....................818 728-5200
James E Rotch, *Ch of Bd*
Rod Gonzales, *Credit Mgr*
Denise Taylor, *Finance*
Eddie Reaves, *Production*
▲ EMP: 38 EST: 1920
SQ FT: 11,446
SALES (est): 1.1B
SALES (corp-wide): 521.8MM **Privately Held**
WEB: www.nationalcement.com
SIC: 3241 3273 Portland cement; ready-mixed concrete
PA: Vicat
　　Les Trois Vallons
　　L Isle D Abeau 38080
　　474 275-900

3251 Brick & Structural Clay Tile

(P-5982)
ARTO BRICK / CALIFORNIA PAVERS
Also Called: Arto Brick and Cal Pavers
15209 S Broadway, Gardena (90248-1823)
PHONE....................310 768-8500
Arto Alajian, *CEO*
Patrick Blake, *Vice Pres*
Mike Oleson, *General Mgr*
Reza Tabarrok, *Opers Staff*
Stephanie Morgan, *Sales Mgr*
EMP: 40 EST: 1966
SQ FT: 18,000
SALES (est): 4.6MM **Privately Held**
WEB: www.arto.com
SIC: 3251 Brick & structural clay tile

(P-5983)
CLAY CASTAIC MANUFACTURING CO
Also Called: Castaic Brick
32201 Castaic Lake Dr, Castaic (91384-4134)
P.O. Box 8 (91310-0008)
PHONE....................661 259-3066
Mike Mallow, *CEO*
Annette Mallow, *Treasurer*
Nick Gupta, *Controller*
Dan Navarro, *Controller*
Al Pinto, *Sales Staff*
EMP: 13 EST: 1957
SQ FT: 10,000
SALES (est): 1.4MM **Privately Held**
WEB: www.granbrique.com
SIC: 3251 Brick clay: common face, glazed, vitrified or hollow

3253 Ceramic Tile

(P-5984)
B & W TILE CO INC (PA)
Also Called: B & W Tile Manufacturing
14600 S Western Ave, Gardena (90249-3399)
PHONE....................310 538-9579
Joe Logan, *Vice Pres*
Ralph Logan, *President*
Joseph Logan, *Vice Pres*
▲ EMP: 35 EST: 1948
SQ FT: 32,000
SALES (est): 3MM **Privately Held**
WEB: www.bwtile.com
SIC: 5713 3253 Floor tile; floor tile, ceramic; wall tile, ceramic

(P-5985)
CONCEPT STUDIO INC
3195 Red Hill Ave Ste G, Costa Mesa (92626-3430)
PHONE....................949 759-0606
Richard Goddard, *President*
Karen Bishop, *Vice Pres*
▲ EMP: 14 EST: 1988
SQ FT: 5,000

SALES (est): 1.7MM **Privately Held**
WEB: www.conceptstudioinc.com
SIC: 3253 Ceramic wall & floor tile

(P-5986)
ELYSIUM TILES INC
Also Called: Elysium Ceramics
1160 N Anaheim Blvd, Anaheim (92801-2502)
PHONE....................714 991-7885
Yue Zhou, *CEO*
▲ EMP: 17 EST: 2012
SALES (est): 4.3MM **Privately Held**
WEB: www.elysiumtiles.com
SIC: 3253 Mosaic tile, glazed & unglazed: ceramic

3255 Clay Refractories

(P-5987)
B & B REFRACTORIES INC
12121 Los Nietos Rd, Santa Fe Springs (90670-2907)
PHONE....................562 946-4535
John Svet, *President*
Jeanette Svet, *Vice Pres*
▲ EMP: 22 EST: 1965
SQ FT: 50,000
SALES (est): 1MM **Privately Held**
WEB: www.bbrefractories.com
SIC: 3255 Clay refractories

3259 Structural Clay Prdts, NEC

(P-5988)
EAGLE ROOFING PRODUCTS FLA LLC
3546 N Riverside Ave, Rialto (92377-3802)
PHONE....................909 822-6000
Robert C Burlingame, *Mng Member*
Travis Rozas, *Sales Staff*
Raquel Viquez, *Sales Staff*
Joe H Anderson Jr,
M D Anderson,
EMP: 53 EST: 2006
SALES (est): 9.6MM **Privately Held**
WEB: www.eagleroofing.com
SIC: 3259 Roofing tile, clay

(P-5989)
MALIBU CERAMIC WORKS
903 Fairbanks Ave, Long Beach (90813-2861)
P.O. Box 1406, Topanga (90290-1406)
PHONE....................310 455-2485
Robert Harris, *President*
EMP: 13 EST: 1989
SALES (est): 2MM **Privately Held**
WEB: www.malibuceramicworks.com
SIC: 3259 1743 Adobe brick; tile installation, ceramic

(P-5990)
MARUHACHI CERAMICS AMERICA INC
1985 Sampson Ave, Corona (92879-6006)
PHONE....................800 736-6221
Yoshihiro Suzuki, *President*
Linda Hanson, *CFO*
Sharon Suzuki, *Executive*
Ama Santana, *Accountant*
▲ EMP: 22 EST: 1983
SQ FT: 83,250
SALES (est): 5MM **Privately Held**
WEB: www.mca-tile.com
SIC: 3259 Roofing tile, clay

3261 China Plumbing Fixtures & Fittings

(P-5991)
BBK SPECIALTIES INC
24147 Del Monte Dr # 297, Valencia (91355-3855)
PHONE....................661 255-2857
EMP: 15
SALES (est): 1.6MM **Privately Held**
SIC: 3261 3431 Mfg Vitreous Plumbing Fixtures Mfg Metal Sanitary Ware

(P-5992)
LOTUS HYGIENE SYSTEMS INC
1621 E Saint Andrew Pl, Santa Ana (92705-4932)
PHONE....................714 259-8805
Xiang Liu, *President*
▲ EMP: 20 EST: 2005
SQ FT: 10,000
SALES (est): 2MM **Privately Held**
WEB: www.lotusseats.com
SIC: 3261 Vitreous plumbing fixtures

(P-5993)
TUBULAR SPECIALTIES MFG INC
Also Called: T S M
13011 S Spring St, Los Angeles (90061-1685)
PHONE....................310 515-4801
Marcia Lynn Hemphill, *CEO*
L C Huntley, *Ch of Bd*
Arif Mansuri, *Treasurer*
Debbie Mansuri, *Sales Mgr*
Allie Hahe, *Director*
▲ EMP: 62 EST: 1966
SQ FT: 38,000
SALES (est): 8.5MM **Privately Held**
WEB: www.calltsm.com
SIC: 3261 2656 3446 Bathroom accessories/fittings, vitreous china or earthenware; sanitary food containers; railings, prefabricated metal

3262 China, Table & Kitchen Articles

(P-5994)
SKY ONE INC
Also Called: Vertex China
1793 W 2nd St, Pomona (91766-1253)
PHONE....................909 622-3333
Hoi Shum, *President*
Gary Dallas, *Vice Pres*
Ken Joyce, *Vice Pres*
Whitney Ngok, *Credit Staff*
Rick LI, *Controller*
▲ EMP: 19 EST: 1976
SQ FT: 14,000
SALES (est): 3.8MM **Privately Held**
SIC: 3262 Dishes, commercial or household: vitreous china

3263 Earthenware, Whiteware, Table & Kitchen Articles

(P-5995)
BROMWELL COMPANY (PA)
8605 Santa Monica Blvd, Los Angeles (90069-4109)
PHONE....................800 683-2626
Sean Bandawat, *President*
EMP: 30 EST: 1819
SALES (est): 506.7K **Privately Held**
WEB: www.jacobbromwell.com
SIC: 3263 Semivitreous table & kitchenware

(P-5996)
MASTERS IN METAL INC
131 Lombard St, Oxnard (93030-5161)
PHONE....................805 988-1992
Wayne R Haddox, *President*
Dennis Haddox, *Vice Pres*
Jeannette Garcia, *Manager*
▲ EMP: 39 EST: 1996
SQ FT: 11,000
SALES (est): 4MM **Privately Held**
WEB: www.mastersinmetal.com
SIC: 3263 3952 Commercial tableware or kitchen articles, fine earthenware; sizes, gold & bronze: artists'

3264 Porcelain Electrical Splys

(P-5997)
ALTA PROPERTIES INC
Channel Industries
839 Ward Dr, Santa Barbara (93111-2920)
PHONE....................805 967-0171
Kathy Woodard, *Executive*
Danny Chan, *General Mgr*
Richard Barnes, *CIO*
Dan Szubra, *Electrical Engi*
Don Bossard, *Engineer*
EMP: 105
SALES (corp-wide): 71.9MM **Privately Held**
SIC: 3264 Porcelain electrical supplies
PA: Alta Properties, Inc.
　　879 Ward Dr
　　Santa Barbara CA 93111
　　805 967-0171

(P-5998)
ALTA PROPERTIES INC (PA)
Also Called: Ctg
879 Ward Dr, Santa Barbara (93111-2920)
P.O. Box 90326 (93190-0326)
PHONE....................805 967-0171
Robert F Carlson, *CEO*
Paul J Downey, *CFO*
Randy Copperman, *Vice Pres*
Gary Douville, *Vice Pres*
Mark Shaw, *Vice Pres*
▲ EMP: 167 EST: 1983
SQ FT: 21,000
SALES (est): 71.9MM **Privately Held**
SIC: 3264 3699 3823 3679 Porcelain electrical supplies; underwater sound equipment; infrared instruments, industrial process type; transducers, electrical

(P-5999)
MAGNET SALES & MFG CO INC (HQ)
Also Called: Integrated Magnetics
11250 Playa Ct, Culver City (90230-6127)
PHONE....................310 391-7213
Anil Nanji, *President*
Shankar RAO, *COO*
Rene Robles, *Planning Mgr*
Will Effertz, *Administration*
Ben Pendleton, *Info Tech Mgr*
▲ EMP: 75 EST: 1930
SQ FT: 45,000
SALES (est): 42MM
SALES (corp-wide): 49.8MM **Privately Held**
WEB: www.intemag.com
SIC: 3264 3621 Porcelain electrical supplies; servomotors, electric; coils, for electric motors or generators; torque motors, electric
PA: Integrated Technologies Group, Inc.
　　11250 Playa Ct
　　Culver City CA 90230
　　310 391-7213

3269 Pottery Prdts, NEC

(P-6000)
ASDAK INTERNATIONAL
Also Called: Oggi Corp
1809 1/2 N Orngethorpe Pa, Anaheim (92801-1141)
PHONE....................714 449-0733
Ajit Das, *President*
Barbara Das, *CFO*
Paul Williamson, *Vice Pres*
◆ EMP: 26 EST: 1992
SQ FT: 29,000
SALES (est): 1.7MM **Privately Held**
SIC: 3269 Pottery cooking & kitchen articles

(P-6001)
BERNEY-KARP INC
3350 E 26th St, Vernon (90058-4145)
PHONE....................323 260-7122
Morry Karp, *President*
Anna Ramos, *Vice Pres*
Vicky Salaises, *Sales Staff*
▲ EMP: 74 EST: 1970
SQ FT: 80,000

SALES (est): 7.4MM **Privately Held**
WEB: www.berneykarp.openfos.com
SIC: 3269 Pottery cooking & kitchen arti-
cles

(P-6002)
CLAY DESIGNS INC
6435 Green Valley Cir # 1, Culver City
(90230-7047)
PHONE..............................562 432-3991
James L Camm, *President*
▲ EMP: 19 EST: 1974
SALES (est): 824.7K **Privately Held**
SIC: 3269 Figures: pottery, china, earthen-
ware & stoneware; stoneware pottery
products

(P-6003)
GAINEY CERAMICS INC
1200 Arrow Hwy, La Verne (91750-5217)
P.O. Box 1513, Monrovia (91017-5513)
PHONE..............................909 596-4464
Steve Gainey, *CEO*
▲ EMP: 28 EST: 1952
SQ FT: 75,500
SALES (est): 669.6K **Privately Held**
SIC: 3269 Flower pots, red earthenware

(P-6004)
HAGEN-RENAKER INC (PA)
914 W Cienega Ave, San Dimas
(91773-2415)
P.O. Box 427 (91773-0427)
PHONE..............................909 599-2341
Susan Renaker Nikas, *President*
Mary Lou Salas, *Treasurer*
EMP: 80 EST: 1946
SQ FT: 88,964
SALES (est): 8.2MM **Privately Held**
WEB: www.hagenrenaker.com
SIC: 3269 0181 Figures: pottery, china,
earthenware & stoneware; nursery stock,
growing of

(P-6005)
PERIMETRICS LLC
11661 San Vicente Blvd # 800, Los Angeles
(90049-5116)
P.O. Box 907, Kirkland WA (98083-0907)
PHONE..............................310 826-4905
Robert Hayman, *Mng Member*
Nyla Sheikh, *Vice Pres*
EMP: 16 EST: 2003
SALES (est): 1.2MM **Privately Held**
WEB: www.haymanproperties.com
SIC: 3269 Cones, pyrometric: earthenware

(P-6006)
**SANTA BARBARA DESIGN
STUDIO (PA)**
1600 Pacific Ave, Oxnard (93033-2746)
P.O. Box 6087, Santa Barbara (93160-
6087)
PHONE..............................805 966-3883
Raymond Markow, *CEO*
Brenda Ross, *Planning*
◆ EMP: 53 EST: 1972
SQ FT: 2,400
SALES (est): 7MM **Privately Held**
WEB: www.sb-designstudio.com
SIC: 3269 5719 Art & ornamental ware,
pottery; pottery

(P-6007)
YF MANUFACTURE INC
2455 Maple Ave, Pomona (91767-2232)
PHONE..............................626 768-0029
Peihua Ninci, *President*
EMP: 15 EST: 2015
SALES (est): 493.3K **Privately Held**
SIC: 3269 Pottery products

3271 Concrete Block & Brick

(P-6008)
AIR-VOL BLOCK INC
1 Suburban Rd, San Luis Obispo
(93401-7523)
P.O. Box 931 (93406-0931)
PHONE..............................805 543-1314
Robert J Miller, *President*
Richard Ayres, *Vice Pres*
Steve Henderson, *Sales Staff*
Erik Geil,

Mike Lutzow, *Supervisor*
EMP: 40
SQ FT: 1,400
SALES (est): 7.8MM **Privately Held**
WEB: www.airvolblock.com
SIC: 3271 Blocks, concrete or cinder: stan-
dard

(P-6009)
ANGELUS BLOCK CO INC (PA)
11374 Tuxford St, Sun Valley (91352-2678)
PHONE..............................714 637-8594
Mario Antonini, *President*
Edward Antonini, *President*
Marla Richmond, *CFO*
Doug Gapastione, *Executive*
Lindsay Barto, *Associate Dir*
▲ EMP: 50 EST: 1946
SQ FT: 2,000
SALES (est): 39.9MM **Privately Held**
WEB: www.angelusblock.com
SIC: 5211 3271 Concrete & cinder block;
blocks, concrete or cinder: standard

(P-6010)
MUTH DEVELOPMENT CO INC
Also Called: Orco Block
11100 Beach Blvd, Stanton (90680-3219)
PHONE..............................714 527-2239
Richard Muth, *President*
Dwayne Gleason, *Vice Pres*
Lynn Muth, *Vice Pres*
Tom Ruggeri, *Controller*
Carla Hansen, *Sales Staff*
EMP: 14 EST: 1996
SALES (est): 273.5K **Privately Held**
WEB: www.orco.com
SIC: 3271 Concrete block & brick

(P-6011)
**ORCO BLOCK & HARDSCAPE
(PA)**
11100 Beach Blvd, Stanton (90680-3219)
PHONE..............................714 527-2239
Richard J Muth, *CEO*
Eldon La Bossiere, *Office Mgr*
Mary M Muth, *Admin Sec*
Tim O 'connor, *VP Human Res*
Robert Gleason, *Plant Mgr*
EMP: 60 EST: 1946
SQ FT: 5,000
SALES (est): 52.2MM **Privately Held**
WEB: www.orco.com
SIC: 3271 Architectural concrete: block,
split, fluted, screen, etc.; blocks, concrete
or cinder: standard

(P-6012)
ORCO BLOCK & HARDSCAPE
26380 Palomar Rd, Romoland
(92585-9811)
PHONE..............................951 928-3619
Fax: 951 928-3153
EMP: 28
SALES (corp-wide): 33.6MM **Privately
Held**
SIC: 3271 3272 Mfg Concrete Block/Brick
Mfg Concrete Products
PA: Orco Block & Hardscape
11100 Beach Blvd
Stanton CA 90680
714 527-2239

(P-6013)
**WESTERN STATES WHOLESALE
INC (PA)**
Also Called: C-Cure
1420 S Bon View Ave, Ontario
(91761-4405)
P.O. Box 3340 (91761-0934)
PHONE..............................909 947-0028
Randall Humphreys, *CEO*
Donna Humphreys, *Treasurer*
Robert Humphreys, *Vice Pres*
Lydi Godsey, *Sales Executive*
▲ EMP: 70 EST: 1995
SQ FT: 60,000
SALES (est): 26MM **Privately Held**
WEB: www.wswcorp.com
SIC: 3271 5072 5032 5211 Concrete
block & brick; bolts; nuts (hardware);
screws; drywall materials; lumber prod-
ucts

3272 Concrete Prdts

(P-6014)
**ACKER STONE INDUSTRIES
INC (DH)**
13296 Temescal Canyon Rd, Corona
(92883-5299)
PHONE..............................951 674-0047
Giora Ackerstein, *Ch of Bd*
Travis Caffarelli, *Site Mgr*
Marco Aparicio, *Opers Mgr*
Veronica Trinkle, *Production*
Ron Ehrler, *Sales Mgr*
▲ EMP: 50 EST: 1987
SQ FT: 14,000
SALES (est): 11MM **Privately Held**
WEB: www.ackerstein.co.il
SIC: 3272 3271 Concrete products, pre-
cast; paving blocks, concrete; blocks,
concrete: landscape or retaining wall

(P-6015)
AMERICAN DATA VAULT INC
21346 Road 140, Tulare (93274-9363)
PHONE..............................559 686-2838
Mark E Hoffman, *Principal*
EMP: 14 EST: 2010
SALES (est): 563.3K **Privately Held**
SIC: 3272 Burial vaults, concrete or pre-
cast terrazzo

(P-6016)
**AMERON INTERNATIONAL
CORP**
1020 B St, Fillmore (93015-1024)
PHONE..............................425 258-2616
William Miner, *Branch Mgr*
EMP: 115
SALES (corp-wide): 6B **Publicly Held**
SIC: 3272 Cylinder pipe, prestressed or
pretensioned concrete
HQ: Ameron International Corporation
7909 Parkwood Circle Dr
Houston TX 77036
713 375-3700

(P-6017)
**AMERON INTERNATIONAL
CORP**
Ameron Pole Products & Systems
1020 B St, Fillmore (93015-1024)
PHONE..............................805 524-0223
West Allison, *Manager*
EMP: 100
SALES (corp-wide): 6B **Publicly Held**
SIC: 3272 3648 3646 3441 Concrete
products, precast; lighting equipment;
commercial indusl & institutional electric
lighting fixtures; fabricated structural
metal; steel pipe & tubes
HQ: Ameron International Corporation
7909 Parkwood Circle Dr
Houston TX 77036
713 375-3700

(P-6018)
AUBURN TILE INC
545 W Main St, Ontario (91762-3718)
P.O. Box 10 (91762-8010)
PHONE..............................909 984-2841
Udo Helferich, *President*
Steve Helferich, *Vice Pres*
EMP: 20 EST: 1958
SQ FT: 6,000
SALES (est): 2.5MM **Privately Held**
WEB: www.auburntile.com
SIC: 3272 Roofing tile & slabs, concrete

(P-6019)
AVILAS GARDEN ART (PA)
14608 Merrill Ave, Fontana (92335-4219)
PHONE..............................909 350-4546
Ralph G Avila, *Owner*
EMP: 60 EST: 1981
SQ FT: 7,000
SALES (est): 8.8MM **Privately Held**
WEB: www.avilasgardenart.com
SIC: 3272 5261 5211 5199 Precast ter-
razo or concrete products; lawn orna-
ments; masonry materials & supplies;
statuary

(P-6020)
**CALIFRNIA PRCAST STONE
MFG INC**
1796 Karen Ct, Hemet (92545-1644)
P.O. Box 40 (92546-0040)
PHONE..............................951 657-7913
Quint Mumford, *President*
John Mumford, *Vice Pres*
EMP: 16 EST: 1998
SQ FT: 7,700
SALES (est): 2.4MM **Privately Held**
WEB: www.californiaprecast.com
SIC: 3272 Concrete products, precast

(P-6021)
**CENTINELA CONSULTING
GROUP INC**
Also Called: Enderle Vault Co
720 E Florence Ave, Inglewood
(90301-1406)
PHONE..............................310 674-2115
Walter Birch, *President*
EMP: 19 EST: 1963
SQ FT: 14,000
SALES (est): 604.9K **Privately Held**
SIC: 3272 Burial vaults, concrete or pre-
cast terrazzo

(P-6022)
**CLARK - PACIFIC
CORPORATION**
131 Los Angeles St, Irwindale (91706)
PHONE..............................626 962-8751
Ed Wopschall, *Branch Mgr*
Gilbert Torres, *Purch Mgr*
EMP: 28
SALES (corp-wide): 243.7MM **Privately
Held**
WEB: www.clarkpacific.com
SIC: 3272 Concrete products, precast
PA: Clark - Pacific Corporation
710 Riverpoint Ct Ste 100
West Sacramento CA 95605
916 371-0305

(P-6023)
**CLARK - PACIFIC
CORPORATION**
9367 Holly Rd, Adelanto (92301-3910)
PHONE..............................626 962-8755
EMP: 28
SALES (corp-wide): 243.7MM **Privately
Held**
WEB: www.clarkpacific.com
SIC: 3272 5032 Concrete products, pre-
cast; brick, stone & related material
PA: Clark - Pacific Corporation
710 Riverpoint Ct Ste 100
West Sacramento CA 95605
916 371-0305

(P-6024)
**CLARK - PACIFIC
CORPORATION**
Also Called: Tecon Pacific
13592 Slover Ave, Fontana (92337-6978)
PHONE..............................909 823-1433
Donald Clark, *Owner*
Simon Peters, *Executive*
Jim Lewis, *Business Dir*
Geene Alhady, *Exec Dir*
Nick Hamann, *Project Mgr*
EMP: 28
SALES (corp-wide): 243.7MM **Privately
Held**
WEB: www.clarkpacific.com
SIC: 3272 5211 Concrete products, pre-
cast; masonry materials & supplies
PA: Clark - Pacific Corporation
710 Riverpoint Ct Ste 100
West Sacramento CA 95605
916 371-0305

(P-6025)
**CORESLAB STRUCTURES LA
INC**
150 W Placentia Ave, Perris (92571-3200)
PHONE..............................951 943-9119
Mario Franciosa, *CEO*
Lou Franciosa, *President*
Richard Burke, *Vice Pres*
Jorgen Clausen, *Vice Pres*
Neil Drews, *Vice Pres*
EMP: 200 EST: 1955

SQ FT: 25,000
SALES (est): 46.1MM
SALES (corp-wide): 27.3MM **Privately Held**
WEB: www.coreslab.com
SIC: **3272** Concrete products, precast
HQ: Coreslab Holdings U S Inc
332 Jones Rd Suite 1
Stoney Creek ON
905 643-0220

(P-6026)
CREATIVE STONE MFG INC (PA)
Also Called: Coronado Stone Products
11191 Calabash Ave, Fontana
(92337-7018)
PHONE..................................909 357-8295
Melton Bacon, *President*
Scott Ebersole, *Vice Pres*
Amy Toledo, *Comptroller*
Bob Ratkovic, *Production*
▲ EMP: 180 EST: 1962
SQ FT: 10,000
SALES (est): 58.1MM **Privately Held**
WEB: www.coronado.com
SIC: **3272** Siding, precast stone

(P-6027)
DO IT RIGHT PRODUCTS LLC (PA)
44321 62nd St W, Lancaster (93536-7533)
PHONE..................................661 722-9664
Elana K Sherve, *Principal*
EMP: 30 EST: 2008
SALES (est): 2.2MM **Privately Held**
SIC: **3272** Concrete products

(P-6028)
EDESSA INC
Also Called: Thompson Building Materials
11027 Cherry Ave, Fontana (92337-7118)
PHONE..................................909 823-1377
Fax: 909 823-8409
▲ EMP: 23
SALES (est): 4.2MM **Privately Held**
SIC: **3272** 5032 Mfg Concrete Products
Whol Brick/Stone Material

(P-6029)
EISEL ENTERPRISES INC
714 Fee Ana St, Placentia (92870-6705)
PHONE..................................714 993-1706
Lyle Eisel, *President*
Janis Eisel, *Corp Secy*
April Davis, *Vice Pres*
Kim Webster, *Vice Pres*
EMP: 22 EST: 1970
SQ FT: 4,000
SALES (est): 3.3MM **Privately Held**
WEB: www.eiselenterprises.com
SIC: **3272** Meter boxes, concrete

(P-6030)
ELK CORPORATION OF TEXAS
6200 Zerker Rd, Shafter (93263-9612)
PHONE..................................661 391-3900
Gus Freshwater, *Vice Pres*
EMP: 163
SALES (corp-wide): 4.4B **Privately Held**
SIC: **3272** 2952 Precast terrazo or concrete products; asphalt felts & coatings
HQ: Elk Corporation Of Texas
14911 Quorum Dr Ste 600
Dallas TX 75254

(P-6031)
EMPIRE PRE-CAST INC
19473 Grand Ave, Lake Elsinore
(92530-6341)
PHONE..................................951 609-1590
Carol Stahl, *Owner*
EMP: 22 EST: 2000
SALES (est): 5.6MM **Privately Held**
WEB: www.empireprecast.net
SIC: **3272** Precast terrazo or concrete products

(P-6032)
FARLEY PAVING STONE CO INC
Also Called: Farley Interlocking Pav Stones
75135 Sheryl Ave Ste A, Palm Desert
(92211-5114)
P.O. Box 10946 (92255-0946)
PHONE..................................760 773-3960
Shon Farley, *Vice Pres*

Charissa Farley, *President*
Hector Gonzalez, *Vice Pres*
Kimberly Ellis, *Sales Mgr*
Farrah Rizzo, *Sales Mgr*
EMP: 70 EST: 1985
SQ FT: 900
SALES (est): 7.5MM **Privately Held**
WEB: www.farleypavers.com
SIC: **3272** 3531 3281 Paving materials, prefabricated concrete; pavers; curbing, paving & walkway stone; paving blocks, cut stone

(P-6033)
FIORE STONE INC
1814 Commercenter W Ste E, San
Bernardino (92408-3332)
PHONE..................................909 424-0221
Bruce Raabe, *President*
EMP: 45 EST: 2009
SALES (est): 5.7MM **Privately Held**
WEB: www.fiorestone.com
SIC: **3272** Concrete products, precast

(P-6034)
FORMS AND SURFACES COMPANY LLC
Also Called: Lightform
6395 Cindy Ln, Carpinteria (93013-2909)
PHONE..................................805 684-8626
J Roger Flannery,
George Hickmann, *CFO*
Matthew Vizzini, *Vice Pres*
Luke Dawson, *Administration*
Meredith Morin, *Design Engr*
EMP: 150 EST: 1975
SQ FT: 63,000
SALES (est): 17.7MM **Privately Held**
WEB: www.forms-surfaces.com
SIC: **3272** 3531 3446 3429 Building materials, except block or brick: concrete; construction machinery; architectural metalwork; manufactured hardware (general); prefabricated wood buildings

(P-6035)
GEORGE L THROOP CO
Also Called: Do It Best
444 N Fair Oaks Ave, Pasadena
(91103-3619)
P.O. Box 92405 (91109-2405)
PHONE..................................626 796-0285
Jeffrey Throop, *President*
Ann T Comey, *Corp Secy*
George L Throop III, *Vice Pres*
Rosalind Stratman, *Manager*
Maria Zepeda, *Manager*
▲ EMP: 32 EST: 1921
SQ FT: 10,500
SALES (est): 13.4MM **Privately Held**
WEB: www.throop.com
SIC: **3272** 5211 5251 Concrete products; millwork & lumber; cement; hardware

(P-6036)
J & R CONCRETE PRODUCTS INC
440 W Markham St, Perris (92571-8138)
PHONE..................................951 943-5855
Raul Ramirez, *President*
EMP: 42 EST: 1981
SQ FT: 40,000
SALES (est): 4.9MM **Privately Held**
WEB: www.jrconcreteproducts.com
SIC: **3272** Meter boxes, concrete

(P-6037)
JENSEN ENTERPRISES INC
Also Called: Jensen Precast
14221 San Bernardino Ave, Fontana
(92335-5232)
PHONE..................................909 357-7264
Carol Kohanle, *Manager*
Paul Olivas, *CFO*
Walter Hahne, *Vice Pres*
Josh Myers, *Vice Pres*
Mark Voiselle, *Regional Mgr*
EMP: 300
SALES (corp-wide): 237.2MM **Privately Held**
WEB: www.jensenprecast.com
SIC: **3272** 7699 5211 5039 Concrete products, precast; waste cleaning services; masonry materials & supplies; septic tanks; concrete forms, sheet metal

PA: Jensen Enterprises, Inc.
9895 Double R Blvd
Reno NV 89521
775 352-2700

(P-6038)
KTI INCORPORATED
Also Called: Rialto Concrete Products
3011 N Laurel Ave, Rialto (92377-3725)
PHONE..................................909 434-1888
Kenneth D Thompson, *CEO*
Daniel J Deming, *President*
Jerry Cowden, *Vice Pres*
EMP: 100 EST: 1987
SQ FT: 400
SALES (est): 21.4MM **Privately Held**
WEB: www.thompsonpipegroup.com
SIC: **3272** Concrete products, precast

(P-6039)
MID-STATE CONCRETE PDTS INC
1625 E Donovan Rd Ste C, Santa Maria
(93454-2519)
P.O. Box 219 (93456-0219)
PHONE..................................805 928-2855
Ralph Vander Veen, *President*
Pat Vander Veen, *Vice Pres*
Anneke Vander Veen, *General Mgr*
Carl Vanswearingen, *Engineer*
Anne Gagne, *Controller*
EMP: 23 EST: 1975
SQ FT: 2,000
SALES (est): 4.9MM **Privately Held**
WEB: www.midstateconcrete.com
SIC: **3272** Concrete products, precast; covers, catch basin: concrete; manhole covers or frames, concrete; septic tanks, concrete

(P-6040)
NEWBASIS LLC
2626 Kansas Ave, Riverside (92507-2600)
PHONE..................................951 787-0600
Karl Stockbridge,
EMP: 150 EST: 2020
SALES (est): 33.2MM **Privately Held**
SIC: **3272** Concrete products
PA: Capital Precast Holdings Llc
250 W Nottingham Dr # 120
San Antonio TX

(P-6041)
NEWBASIS WEST LLC
2626 Kansas Ave, Riverside (92507-2600)
PHONE..................................951 787-0600
Karl Stockbridge, *CEO*
Jennifer Ewing, *CFO*
Kim Ruiz, *Controller*
◆ EMP: 115 EST: 1989
SALES (est): 25.8MM **Privately Held**
WEB: www.newbasis.com
SIC: **3272** Manhole covers or frames, concrete; tanks, concrete; meter boxes, concrete; concrete products, precast
PA: Echo Rock Ventures, Inc.
370 Hammond Dr
Auburn CA 95603
530 823-9600

(P-6042)
NEWMAN AND SONS INC (PA)
2655 1st St Ste 210, Simi Valley
(93065-1578)
PHONE..................................805 522-1646
Dennis L Newman, *President*
EMP: 40 EST: 1938
SQ FT: 12,500
SALES (est): 2.5MM **Privately Held**
WEB: www.ramco.us
SIC: **3272** Paving materials, prefabricated concrete

(P-6043)
NUCAST INDUSTRIES INC
Also Called: Robbins Precast
23220 Park Canyon Dr, Corona
(92883-6006)
PHONE..................................951 277-8888
David Minasian, *Principal*
Anthony Minasian, *Principal*
EMP: 51 EST: 1974
SQ FT: 5,000

SALES (est): 2.6MM **Privately Held**
WEB: www.robbinsprecast.com
SIC: **3272** 5211 Concrete products, precast; masonry materials & supplies

(P-6044)
OLDCAST PRECAST (DH)
Also Called: Riverside Foundary
2434 Rubidoux Blvd, Riverside
(92509-2144)
PHONE..................................951 788-9720
Thomas D Lynch, *Ch of Bd*
John R Waren, *President*
EMP: 35 EST: 1966
SQ FT: 7,000
SALES (est): 19.3MM
SALES (corp-wide): 27.5B **Privately Held**
WEB: www.inland-concrete.com
SIC: **3272** 3271 Concrete products, precast; concrete block & brick
HQ: Oldcastle Infrastructure, Inc.
7000 Central Pkwy Ste 800
Atlanta GA 30328
770 270-5000

(P-6045)
OLDCASTLE INFRASTRUCTURE INC
Also Called: Carson Industries Division
2434 Rubidoux Blvd, Riverside
(92509-2144)
PHONE..................................951 788-9720
EMP: 35
SALES (corp-wide): 27.5B **Privately Held**
WEB: www.oldcastleinfrastructure.com
SIC: **3272** Mfg Concrete Products
HQ: Oldcastle Infrastructure, Inc.
7000 Central Pkwy Ste 800
Atlanta GA 30328
770 270-5000

(P-6046)
OVER & OVER READY MIX INC
Also Called: Borges Rock Product
8216 Tujunga Ave, Sun Valley
(91352-3932)
P.O. Box 309, Moorpark (93020-0309)
PHONE..................................818 983-1588
Ed Borges, *President*
EMP: 52 EST: 2001
SALES (est): 1.5MM **Privately Held**
WEB: www.ooreadymix.com
SIC: **3272** 3273 Concrete products; ready-mixed concrete

(P-6047)
PACIFIC STONE DESIGN INC
1201 E Wakeham Ave, Santa Ana
(92705-4145)
PHONE..................................714 836-5757
Scott Sterling, *President*
Kathy Sterling, *CFO*
Brad Sterling, *Sales Staff*
EMP: 45 EST: 1996
SQ FT: 40,000
SALES (est): 7MM **Privately Held**
WEB: www.pacificstone.net
SIC: **3272** Concrete products, precast

(P-6048)
PARAGON BUILDING PRODUCTS INC (PA)
2191 5th St Ste 111, Norco (92860-1966)
P.O. Box 99 (92860-0099)
PHONE..................................951 549-1155
Jeffrey M Goodman, *President*
Jack Goodman, *CEO*
Richard Goodman, *Corp Secy*
Ben Hazelton, *Manager*
▲ EMP: 25 EST: 1984
SQ FT: 16,500
SALES (est): 22.7MM **Privately Held**
WEB: www.paragonbp.us
SIC: **3272** 3271 5032 Dry mixture concrete; concrete block & brick; brick, concrete; paving blocks, concrete; brick, stone & related material

(P-6049)
PORTERVILLE CONCRETE PIPE INC
474 S Main St, Porterville (93257-5324)
P.O. Box 408 (93258-0408)
PHONE..................................559 784-6187
Vincent Jurkovich, *President*

Steve Jurkovich, *Corp Secy*
Nick Jurkovich, *Executive*
EMP: 21 **EST:** 1924
SQ FT: 1,500
SALES (est): 2MM **Privately Held**
WEB: www.porterville.
SIC: 3272 Pipe, concrete or lined with concrete

(P-6050)
PRECAST INNOVATIONS INC
1670 N Main St, Orange (92867-3405)
PHONE......................714 921-4060
Chester Valdovinos, *President*
EMP: 28 **EST:** 2011
SQ FT: 20,000
SALES (est): 4MM **Privately Held**
WEB: www.precastinnovations.com
SIC: 3272 1791 Concrete products, precast; precast concrete structural framing or panels, placing of

(P-6051)
PRECISION TILE CO
Also Called: Penrose Coping Company
11140 Penrose St, Sun Valley (91352-2724)
P.O. Box 1612, Canyon Country (91386-1612)
PHONE......................818 767-7673
Brad Rose, *President*
Patricia Rose, *Treasurer*
Wallace Rose, *Vice Pres*
EMP: 19 **EST:** 1958
SQ FT: 4,000
SALES (est): 903.6K **Privately Held**
SIC: 3272 1743 Copings, concrete; tile installation, ceramic

(P-6052)
PRIME FORMING & CNSTR SUPS INC
Also Called: Fitzgerald Formliners
1500a E Chestnut Ave, Santa Ana (92701-6321)
PHONE......................714 547-6710
Edward Fitzgerald, *President*
Brian Sheehan, *General Mgr*
Ton Khuat, *Prgrmr*
John Schmidt, *Project Mgr*
Eric Lundberg, *Sales Mgr*
EMP: 46 **EST:** 1988
SQ FT: 30,000
SALES (est): 8.7MM **Privately Held**
SIC: 3272 Concrete products

(P-6053)
QUIKRETE CALIFORNIA LLC
Also Called: Quickrete
3940 Temescal Canyon Rd, Corona (92883-5618)
PHONE......................951 277-3155
John O Winshester, *Mng Member*
Luis Morales, *Human Res Dir*
Paul Ferraguto, *Sales Staff*
Tom Taylor, *Maintence Staff*
EMP: 130 **EST:** 2004
SALES (est): 31.3MM **Privately Held**
WEB: www.quikrete.com
SIC: 3272 Concrete products
HQ: The Quikrete Companies Llc
5 Concourse Pkwy Ste 1900
Atlanta GA 30328
404 634-9100

(P-6054)
RIVER VALLEY PRECAST INC
14796 Washington Dr, Fontana (92335-6263)
PHONE......................928 764-3839
Darryl Kerr, *President*
EMP: 15 **EST:** 2003
SALES (est): 708.6K **Privately Held**
SIC: 3272 Precast terrazzo or concrete products

(P-6055)
RMR PRODUCTS INC (PA)
11011 Glenoaks Blvd Ste 1, Pacoima (91331-1634)
PHONE......................818 890-0896
David McKendrick, *CEO*
Jim McKendrick, *President*
EMP: 25 **EST:** 1984
SQ FT: 3,200

SALES (est): 1.9MM **Privately Held**
WEB: www.chimneyproductsinc.com
SIC: 3272 Chimney caps, concrete

(P-6056)
SISSELL BROS
4322 E 3rd St, Los Angeles (90022-1501)
PHONE......................323 261-0106
John F Foote, *President*
Joan M Foote, *Treasurer*
Dorothy Sissell, *Vice Pres*
EMP: 29 **EST:** 1930
SQ FT: 7,000
SALES (est): 4.1MM **Privately Held**
SIC: 3272 Burial vaults, concrete or precast terrazzo

(P-6057)
SOUTHWEST CONCRETE PRODUCTS
519 S Benson Ave, Ontario (91762-4002)
PHONE......................909 983-9789
Bob Dzajkich, *President*
Natalie Dzajkich, *Treasurer*
Eileen Dzajkich, *Admin Sec*
▲ **EMP:** 94 **EST:** 1966
SQ FT: 25,000
SALES (est): 12.3MM **Privately Held**
SIC: 3272 5032 Manhole covers or frames, concrete; brick, stone & related material
PA: Taiheyo Kenkou Center Co.,Ltd.
164-2, Rokuchome, Yotsukuramachi
Iwaki FSM 979-0

(P-6058)
SPEC FORMLINERS INC
1038 E 4th St, Santa Ana (92701-4751)
PHONE......................714 429-9500
Stephen A Deering, *CEO*
Anthony Zaha, *Vice Pres*
Mike Castillo, *Sales Staff*
Chris Duzich, *Sales Staff*
EMP: 26 **EST:** 1996
SQ FT: 23,000
SALES (est): 8.2MM **Privately Held**
WEB: www.specformliners.com
SIC: 3272 Concrete products

(P-6059)
STEPSTONE INC (PA)
17025 S Main St, Gardena (90248-3125)
PHONE......................310 327-7474
Gordon S McWilliams, *CEO*
Paul Mitchell, *President*
Fred Samaniego, *Prdtn Mgr*
Kelsy Carrington, *Production*
EMP: 50 **EST:** 1963
SQ FT: 15,000
SALES (est): 12.7MM **Privately Held**
WEB: www.stepstoneinc.com
SIC: 3272 Concrete products, precast; burial vaults, concrete or precast terrazzo

(P-6060)
STEPSTONE INC
13238 S Figueroa St, Los Angeles (90061-1140)
PHONE......................310 327-7474
Kelsy Carrington, *Branch Mgr*
Jason Rochester, *Engineer*
EMP: 25
SALES (corp-wide): 12.7MM **Privately Held**
WEB: www.stepstoneinc.com
SIC: 3272 Concrete products, precast
PA: Stepstone, Inc.
17025 S Main St
Gardena CA 90248
310 327-7474

(P-6061)
STRUCTURECAST
8261 Mccutchen Rd, Bakersfield (93311-9407)
PHONE......................661 833-4490
Brent Dezember, *President*
Rick Treatch, *CFO*
Ann Dzember, *Corp Secy*
Amy Nakanishi, *Administration*
Glenn McMillan, *Project Mgr*
EMP: 100 **EST:** 1997
SQ FT: 10,000

SALES (est): 9.5MM **Privately Held**
WEB: www.structurecast.com
SIC: 3272 1791 Precast terrazzo or concrete products; precast concrete structural framing or panels, placing of

(P-6062)
UNITED MEMORIAL PRODUCTS INC
Also Called: United Memorial/Matthews Intl
4845 Pioneer Blvd, Whittier (90601-1842)
P.O. Box 721 (90608-0721)
PHONE......................562 699-3578
Joseph Bartolacci, *Owner*
Mac Sharrock, *General Mgr*
▲ **EMP:** 39 **EST:** 1993
SALES (est): 12.3MM
SALES (corp-wide): 1.5B **Publicly Held**
WEB: www.matw.com
SIC: 3272 3281 Concrete stuctural support & building material; cut stone & stone products
PA: Matthews International Corporation
2 N Shore Ctr Ste 200
Pittsburgh PA 15212
412 442-8200

(P-6063)
UTILITY VAULT CO
4491 S K St, Tulare (93274-7160)
PHONE......................559 688-6686
Rosemary Bettencourt, *Manager*
EMP: 20 **EST:** 1974
SALES (est): 295.3K **Privately Held**
SIC: 3272 Burial vaults, concrete or precast terrazzo

(P-6064)
VAULT PREP INC
2500 Broadway Ste F125, Santa Monica (90404-3080)
PHONE......................310 971-9091
John Duda, *CEO*
Danielle Kirschbaum, *Partner*
EMP: 20 **EST:** 2012
SALES (est): 2.4MM **Privately Held**
WEB: www.vault-prep.com
SIC: 3272 8748 Burial vaults, concrete or precast terrazzo; testing service, educational or personnel

3273 Ready-Mixed Concrete

(P-6065)
A & A READY MIXED CONCRETE INC (PA)
4621 Teller Ave 130, Newport Beach (92660-2165)
PHONE......................949 253-2800
Kurt Caillier, *President*
Jaret Ramirez, *COO*
John Gaeta, *CFO*
Randy Caillier, *Corp Secy*
Michael Krussman, *Vice Pres*
▲ **EMP:** 45 **EST:** 1956
SQ FT: 8,000
SALES (est): 103.9MM **Privately Held**
WEB: www.aareadymix.com
SIC: 3273 Ready-mixed concrete

(P-6066)
ALLIANCE READY MIX INC (PA)
915 Sheridan Rd, Arroyo Grande (93420-5834)
P.O. Box 1163 (93421-1163)
PHONE......................805 343-0360
Brandt Robertson, *President*
EMP: 70 **EST:** 2006
SALES (est): 6MM **Privately Held**
SIC: 3273 Ready-mixed concrete

(P-6067)
ALPHA MATERIALS INC
6170 20th St, Riverside (92509-2031)
PHONE......................951 788-5150
Brian Oaks, *President*
EMP: 36 **EST:** 2002
SQ FT: 1,200
SALES (est): 8.6MM **Privately Held**
WEB: www.alpha-materials-inc.com
SIC: 3273 Ready-mixed concrete

(P-6068)
AMERICAN READY MIX INC
1141 W Graaf Ave, Ridgecrest (93555-2307)
P.O. Box 1138 (93556-1138)
PHONE......................760 446-4556
Leroy Ladd, *President*
Donna Ladd, *Vice Pres*
EMP: 15 **EST:** 1977
SQ FT: 500
SALES (est): 1.6MM **Privately Held**
WEB: www.americanreadymix.net
SIC: 3273 Ready-mixed concrete

(P-6069)
ARROW TRANSIT MIX
507 E Avenue L12, Lancaster (93535-5417)
PHONE......................661 945-7600
H D Follendore, *President*
Christine Follendore, *Admin Sec*
Charla Anderson, *Bookkeeper*
Donny Thompson, *Accounts Mgr*
EMP: 35 **EST:** 1998
SQ FT: 7,200
SALES (est): 4.5MM **Privately Held**
WEB: www.arrowtransitmix.com
SIC: 3273 Ready-mixed concrete

(P-6070)
ASSOCIATED READY MIX CON INC
8946 Bradley Ave, Sun Valley (91352-2601)
PHONE......................818 504-3100
Tim Sullivan, *Manager*
EMP: 24 **Privately Held**
WEB: www.aareadymix.com
SIC: 3273 Ready-mixed concrete
PA: Associated Ready Mix Concrete, Inc.
4621 Teller Ave Ste 130
Newport Beach CA 92660

(P-6071)
ASSOCIATED READY MIX CON INC (PA)
4621 Teller Ave Ste 130, Newport Beach (92660-2165)
PHONE......................949 253-2800
Kurt Caillier, *President*
Randy Caillier, *Corp Secy*
Chris Pizano, *Vice Pres*
Jaret Ramirez, *Info Tech Mgr*
Harvey Sanders, *Safety Mgr*
EMP: 40 **EST:** 1996
SALES (est): 17.8MM **Privately Held**
WEB: www.assocrmc.com
SIC: 3273 Ready-mixed concrete

(P-6072)
B & B RED-I-MIX CONCRETE INC
Also Called: B & B Services
590 Live Oak Ave, Baldwin Park (91706-1315)
PHONE......................626 359-8371
Mike Gatherer, *President*
EMP: 15 **EST:** 1961
SQ FT: 4,400
SALES (est): 230K **Privately Held**
SIC: 3273 Ready-mixed concrete

(P-6073)
BEACON CONCRETE INC
Also Called: Lighthouse Trucking
1597 S Bluff Rd, Montebello (90640-6601)
PHONE......................323 889-7775
Lou Earlabaugh, *President*
Suzanne Earlabaugh, *Vice Pres*
EMP: 20 **EST:** 1993
SALES (est): 1.2MM **Privately Held**
WEB: www.beaconconcrete.com
SIC: 3273 Ready-mixed concrete

(P-6074)
CAL PORTLAND CEMENT CO
Also Called: Calportland
695 S Rancho Ave, Colton (92324-3242)
PHONE......................909 423-0436
EMP: 23
SALES (est): 3.3MM **Privately Held**
WEB: www.calportland.com
SIC: 3273 Central-Mixed Concrete

(P-6075)
CALIFORNIA CONCRETE RDYMX INC (PA)
2715 E Mayfair Ave, Orange (92867-7244)
PHONE..........................714 401-4382
Robert Clouser, *President*
EMP: 46 EST: 2014
SALES (est): 1MM **Privately Held**
WEB: www.caconcrete.com
SIC: 3273 Ready-mixed concrete

(P-6076)
CAPITAL READY MIX INC
11311 Pendleton St, Sun Valley (91352-1530)
PHONE..........................818 771-1122
Tigran Aneian, *CEO*
EMP: 32 EST: 2014
SALES (est): 7.5MM **Privately Held**
SIC: 3273 Ready-mixed concrete

(P-6077)
CATALINA PACIFIC CONCRETE
19030 Normandie Ave, Torrance (90502-1009)
PHONE..........................310 532-4600
Patrick E Greene, *President*
EMP: 20 EST: 1969
SQ FT: 1,500
SALES (est): 287.7K **Privately Held**
SIC: 3273 Ready-mixed concrete

(P-6078)
CEMEX CEMENT INC
25220 Black Mtn Quar Rd, Apple Valley (92307-9341)
PHONE..........................760 381-7616
Luis Lopez, *Branch Mgr*
EMP: 200 **Privately Held**
WEB: www.cemexusa.com
SIC: 3273 Ready-mixed concrete
HQ: Cemex Cement, Inc.
10100 Katy Fwy Ste 300
Houston TX 77043
713 650-6200

(P-6079)
CEMEX CNSTR MTLS PCF LLC
Also Called: Readymix -Redlands Rm Dual
8203 Alabama Ave, Highland (92346-4255)
PHONE..........................909 335-3105
Erick Garcia, *Branch Mgr*
EMP: 17 **Privately Held**
SIC: 3273 Ready-mixed concrete
HQ: Cemex Construction Materials Pacific, Llc
1501 Belvedere Rd
West Palm Beach FL 33406
561 833-5555

(P-6080)
CEMEX CNSTR MTLS PCF LLC
Also Called: Readymix -Fontana Rm
13200 Santa Ana Ave, Fontana (92337-8215)
PHONE..........................909 355-8754
EMP: 15 **Privately Held**
SIC: 3273 Mfg Ready Mixed Concrete
HQ: Cemex Construction Materials Pacific, Llc
1501 Belvedere Rd
West Palm Beach FL 33406
561 833-5555

(P-6081)
CEMEX MATERIALS LLC
23200 Temescal Canyon Rd, Corona (92883-5041)
PHONE..........................951 277-2420
Jim Nanfeldt, *Manager*
EMP: 95 **Privately Held**
SIC: 3273 Ready-mixed concrete
HQ: Cemex Materials Llc
1501 Belvedere Rd
West Palm Beach FL 33406
561 833-5555

(P-6082)
CEMEX MATERIALS LLC
1201 S La Cadena Dr, Colton (92324-3343)
PHONE..........................909 825-1500
Lindsey Hank, *Manager*
EMP: 95 **Privately Held**
SIC: 3273 Ready-mixed concrete

HQ: Cemex Materials Llc
1501 Belvedere Rd
West Palm Beach FL 33406
561 833-5555

(P-6083)
CEMEX USA INC
8731 Orange St, Redlands (92374-1779)
PHONE..........................909 798-1144
EMP: 120
SALES (corp-wide): 15.4B **Privately Held**
SIC: 3273 Mfg Ready-Mixed Concrete
HQ: Cemex U.S.A., Inc.
929 Gessner Rd Ste 1900
Houston TX 77024
713 650-6200

(P-6084)
CEMEX USA INC
4120 Jurupa St Ste 202, Ontario (91761-1423)
PHONE..........................909 974-5500
Mike Bauder, *Principal*
EMP: 19 EST: 2010
SALES (est): 4.7MM **Privately Held**
WEB: www.cemexusa.com
SIC: 3273 Ready-mixed concrete

(P-6085)
CONCRETE HOLDING CO CAL INC
15821 Ventura Blvd # 475, Encino (91436-2915)
PHONE..........................818 788-4228
Don Unmacht, *President*
Dominique Bidet, *Vice Pres*
EMP: 737 EST: 1988
SQ FT: 4,000
SALES (est): 22.5MM
SALES (corp-wide): 521.8MM **Privately Held**
WEB: www.nationalcement.com
SIC: 3273 Ready-mixed concrete
HQ: National Cement Company, Inc.
15821 Ventura Blvd # 475
Encino CA 91436
818 728-5200

(P-6086)
CORONET CONCRETE PRODUCTS INC (PA)
Also Called: Desert Redi Mix
83801 Avenue 45, Indio (92201-3311)
PHONE..........................760 398-2441
James Richert, *CEO*
EMP: 22 EST: 1982
SQ FT: 2,000
SALES (est): 8.3MM **Privately Held**
SIC: 3273 3272 Ready-mixed concrete; concrete products; manhole covers or frames, concrete

(P-6087)
CPC SERVICES INC
2025 E Fincl Way Ste 200, Glendora (91741)
PHONE..........................626 852-6200
James Repman, *President*
Ron White, *Info Tech Mgr*
David Carichner, *Engineer*
Chris Stoltz, *Sales Dir*
Eric Decrescenzo, *Sales Staff*
EMP: 49 EST: 2002
SALES (est): 707.7K **Privately Held**
SIC: 3273 Ready-mixed concrete

(P-6088)
CROOKSHANKS SALES CO
Also Called: CSC Ranch
2375 Dairy Ave, Corcoran (93212-3503)
P.O. Box 338 (93212-0338)
PHONE..........................559 992-5077
Jason Proctor, *President*
Donna Proctor, *President*
Morris Proctor, *Treasurer*
Dorothy Crookshanks, *Vice Pres*
Laura Snodgrass, *Admin Sec*
EMP: 32 EST: 1952
SQ FT: 2,500
SALES (est): 3.3MM **Privately Held**
SIC: 3273 0191 3275 Ready-mixed concrete; general farms, primarily crop; agricultural gypsum

(P-6089)
DENNIE MANNING CONCRETE INC
Also Called: D & K Concrete Co
15815 Arrow Blvd, Fontana (92335-3245)
PHONE..........................909 823-7521
Steve Mogan, *President*
Denise Manning, *Corp Secy*
L G Manning, *Vice Pres*
EMP: 13 EST: 1923
SQ FT: 1,000
SALES (est): 1.9MM **Privately Held**
WEB: www.dkconcreteco.com
SIC: 3273 Ready-mixed concrete

(P-6090)
DIVERSIFIED MINERALS INC
Also Called: Dmi Ready Mix
1100 Mountain View Ave F, Oxnard (93030-7213)
PHONE..........................805 247-1069
James W Price, *President*
Sharron Price, *Corp Secy*
▲ EMP: 44 EST: 1990
SQ FT: 44,482
SALES (est): 8.7MM **Privately Held**
WEB: www.dmicement.com
SIC: 3273 4013 3531 3241 Ready-mixed concrete; railroad terminals; bituminous, cement & concrete related products & equipment; batching plants, for aggregate concrete & bulk cement; pozzolana cement

(P-6091)
GARY BALE REDI-MIX CON INC
16131 Construction Cir W, Irvine (92606-4410)
PHONE..........................949 786-9441
Kyle Goerlitz, *CEO*
Austin Eminhizer, *Opers Staff*
EMP: 80 EST: 1968
SALES (est): 10.8MM **Privately Held**
WEB: www.garybaleredimix.com
SIC: 3273 Ready-mixed concrete

(P-6092)
GIBBEL BROS INC
Also Called: True Cast Concrete Products
11145 Tuxford St, Sun Valley (91352-2632)
PHONE..........................323 875-1367
Gregory Gibbel, *President*
EMP: 20 EST: 1965
SQ FT: 1,500
SALES (est): 1.4MM **Privately Held**
SIC: 3273 3271 Ready-mixed concrete; blocks, concrete or cinder: standard

(P-6093)
GIBSON AND SCHAEFER INC (PA)
1126 Rock Wood Rd, Heber (92249)
P.O. Box 1539 (92249-1539)
PHONE..........................619 352-3535
Don Gibson, *President*
Maria Schaefer, *Treasurer*
P M Schaefer, *Vice Pres*
Rhoberta Gibson, *Admin Sec*
EMP: 50 EST: 1989
SQ FT: 1,440
SALES (est): 11.1MM **Privately Held**
WEB: www.gibsonandschaeferinc.com
SIC: 3273 5032 Ready-mixed concrete; gravel

(P-6094)
HI-GRADE MATERIALS CO
6500 E Avenue T, Littlerock (93543-1722)
P.O. Box 1050 (93543-1050)
PHONE..........................661 533-3100
Rod Elderton, *Manager*
Skye Ostoich, *Administration*
Gary Hulburt, *Sales Staff*
EMP: 88
SALES (corp-wide): 63.9MM **Privately Held**
WEB: www.robar.com
SIC: 3273 Ready-mixed concrete
HQ: Hi-Grade Materials Co.
17671 Bear Valley Rd
Hesperia CA
760 244-9325

(P-6095)
HOLLIDAY ROCK TRUCKING INC
2300 W Base Line St, San Bernardino (92410-1002)
PHONE..........................888 273-2200
Frederick N Holliday, *Branch Mgr*
EMP: 60
SALES (corp-wide): 7.2MM **Privately Held**
WEB: www.hollidayrock.com
SIC: 3273 Ready-mixed concrete
PA: Holliday Trucking Inc.
1401 N Benson Ave
Upland CA 91786
909 982-1553

(P-6096)
HOLLIDAY TRUCKING INC (PA)
1401 N Benson Ave, Upland (91786-2166)
PHONE..........................909 982-1553
Frederick N Holliday, *President*
Penny Holliday, *President*
Ronald Chambers, *Vice Pres*
John Holliday, *Vice Pres*
Eric Adams, *Technology*
EMP: 60 EST: 1964
SQ FT: 2,000
SALES (est): 7.2MM **Privately Held**
WEB: www.hollidayrock.com
SIC: 3273 4212 Ready-mixed concrete; local trucking, without storage

(P-6097)
JF READY MIX INC
4038 N Woodgrove Ave, Covina (91722-3932)
PHONE..........................626 818-1204
Jesus Flores, *Principal*
EMP: 18 EST: 2011
SALES (est): 1.2MM **Privately Held**
SIC: 3273 Ready-mixed concrete

(P-6098)
LEBATA INC
Also Called: A & A Ready Mix Concrete
4621 Teller Ave Ste 130, Newport Beach (92660-2165)
PHONE..........................949 253-2800
Kurt Caillier, *President*
Jaret Ramirez, *COO*
John Gaeta, *CFO*
Randy Caillier, *Vice Pres*
Don Baillie, *Plant Mgr*
EMP: 30 EST: 1987
SALES (est): 3.6MM **Privately Held**
SIC: 3273 Ready-mixed concrete

(P-6099)
LYNCH READY MIX CONCRETE CO
Also Called: Mission Ready Mix
11011 Azahar St Ste 4, Ventura (93004-1944)
PHONE..........................805 647-2817
Robert A Lynch, *President*
Laverne Lynch, *Vice Pres*
EMP: 19 EST: 1989
SQ FT: 500
SALES (est): 4.1MM **Privately Held**
WEB: www.statereadymix.com
SIC: 3273 Ready-mixed concrete

(P-6100)
NATIONAL CEMENT CO CAL INC (DH)
15821 Ventura Blvd # 475, Encino (91436-2935)
PHONE..........................818 728-5200
Steven Weiss, *President*
Pragati Kapoor, *CFO*
Dominique Bidet, *Treasurer*
▲ EMP: 100 EST: 1987
SQ FT: 12,000
SALES (est): 270.3MM
SALES (corp-wide): 521.8MM **Privately Held**
WEB: www.nationalcement.com
SIC: 3273 3241 Ready-mixed concrete; cement, hydraulic
HQ: National Cement Company, Inc.
15821 Ventura Blvd # 475
Encino CA 91436
818 728-5200

PRODUCTS & SVCS

(P-6101)
NATIONAL READY MIX
15821 Ventura Blvd # 475, Encino
(91436-4778)
PHONE.................818 728-5200
Edward I Doucette, *Principal*
EMP: 16 **EST:** 2011
SALES (est): 1.3MM **Privately Held**
WEB: www.nationalcement.com
SIC: 3273 Ready-mixed concrete

(P-6102)
NATIONAL READY MIXED CON CO (DH)
15821 Ventura Blvd # 475, Encino
(91436-4778)
PHONE.................818 728-5200
Tim Toland, *CEO*
Don Unmacht, *Vice Pres*
▲ **EMP:** 20 **EST:** 1946
SQ FT: 40,000
SALES (est): 45.3MM
SALES (corp-wide): 521.8MM **Privately Held**
WEB: www.nationalcement.com
SIC: 3273 Ready-mixed concrete
HQ: National Cement Company Of California, Inc.
15821 Ventura Blvd # 475
Encino CA 91436
818 728-5200

(P-6103)
NAVAJO CONCRETE INC
Also Called: Navajo Rock & Block
2484 Ramada Dr, Paso Robles
(93446-3949)
P.O. Box 117, Templeton (93465-0117)
PHONE.................805 238-0955
Fax: 805 238-0140
EMP: 15
SQ FT: 144
SALES (est): 1.8MM **Privately Held**
SIC: 3273 Ready Mix Concrete

(P-6104)
PACIFIC AGGREGATES INC
28251 Lake St, Lake Elsinore
(92530-1635)
PHONE.................951 245-2460
Kai Chin, *CEO*
Barry Coley, *Vice Pres*
Dale Kline, *Vice Pres*
Kim Chan, *Controller*
Jose Rodriguez, *Purchasing*
▲ **EMP:** 75 **EST:** 2002
SQ FT: 1,000
SALES (est): 12.6MM
SALES (corp-wide): 372.8MM **Privately Held**
WEB: www.pacificaggregates.com
SIC: 3273 Ready-mixed concrete
PA: Castle & Cooke, Inc.
10000 Stockdale Hwy # 300
Bakersfield CA 93311
818 879-6700

(P-6105)
PUENTE READY MIX SERVICES INC (PA)
209 N California Ave, City of Industry
(91744-4324)
P.O. Box 3345 (91744-0345)
PHONE.................626 968-0711
Mark Keuning, *Ch of Bd*
Ronald A Biang, *President*
Rick Dachman, *Vice Pres*
Kevin Keuning, *Vice Pres*
Marcia Biang, *Admin Sec*
EMP: 22 **EST:** 1949
SQ FT: 5,000
SALES (est): 6.3MM **Privately Held**
WEB: www.puentereadymix.com
SIC: 3273 Ready-mixed concrete

(P-6106)
RANCHO READY MIX
28251 Lake St, Lake Elsinore
(92530-1635)
PHONE.................951 674-0488
William Summers, *President*
Mal Gatherer, *Corp Secy*
Barry Coley, *Vice Pres*
Pat Dempsey, *General Mgr*
EMP: 52 **EST:** 1976

SQ FT: 1,000
SALES (est): 14.7MM **Privately Held**
WEB: www.ieranchoreadymix.com
SIC: 3273 Ready-mixed concrete

(P-6107)
ROBAR ENTERPRISES INC (PA)
17671 Bear Valley Rd, Hesperia
(92345-4902)
PHONE.................760 244-5456
Jonathan D Hove, *CEO*
Al Calvanico, *CFO*
Robert E Hove, *Chairman*
Lori Clifton, *Vice Pres*
Sean McGill, *Branch Mgr*
EMP: 150 **EST:** 1981
SQ FT: 26,000
SALES (est): 63.9MM **Privately Held**
WEB: www.robar.com
SIC: 3273 5051 3441 Ready-mixed concrete; steel; building components, structural steel

(P-6108)
ROBERTSONS RDYMX LTD A CAL LTD (HQ)
200 S Main St Ste 200 # 200, Corona
(92882-2212)
P.O. Box 3600 (92878-3600)
PHONE.................951 493-6500
Jon Troesh, *Partner*
Greg Edwards, *Partner*
Roger Hortick, *Officer*
Don Rubidoux, *General Mgr*
Curt Perales, *Info Tech Mgr*
▲ **EMP:** 85 **EST:** 1991
SQ FT: 22,008
SALES (est): 511.7MM **Privately Held**
WEB: www.rrmca.com
SIC: 3273 3531 5032 2951 Ready-mixed concrete; bituminous, cement & concrete related products & equipment; asphalt plant, including gravel-mix type; concrete plants; asphalt mixture; paving mixtures; concrete mixtures; asphalt paving mixtures & blocks; construction sand & gravel

(P-6109)
ROBERTSONS RDYMX LTD A CAL LTD
200 S Main St Ste 200 # 200, Corona
(92882-2212)
PHONE.................800 834-7557
Robert Burmeister, *President*
Darrin Dragna, *Sales Staff*
EMP: 73 **Privately Held**
WEB: www.rrmca.com
SIC: 3273 Ready-mixed concrete
HQ: Robertson's Ready Mix, Ltd., A California Limited Partnership
200 S Main St Ste 200 # 200
Corona CA 92882
951 493-6500

(P-6110)
ROBERTSONS RDYMX LTD A CAL LTD
27401 3rd St, Highland (92346-4242)
PHONE.................909 425-2930
Dennis Troesh, *President*
EMP: 73 **Privately Held**
WEB: www.rrmca.com
SIC: 3273 Ready-mixed concrete
HQ: Robertson's Ready Mix, Ltd., A California Limited Partnership
200 S Main St Ste 200 # 200
Corona CA 92882
951 493-6500

(P-6111)
ROBERTSONS READY MIX LTD
9635 C Ave, Hesperia (92345-6047)
PHONE.................760 244-7239
EMP: 73 **Privately Held**
WEB: www.rrmca.com
SIC: 3273 Ready-mixed concrete
HQ: Robertson's Ready Mix, Ltd., A California Limited Partnership
200 S Main St Ste 200 # 200
Corona CA 92882
951 493-6500

(P-6112)
ROBERTSONS READY MIX LTD
7900 Moss Ave, California City
(93505-4311)
PHONE.................760 373-4815
EMP: 73 **Privately Held**
WEB: www.rrmca.com
SIC: 3273 Ready-mixed concrete
HQ: Robertson's Ready Mix, Ltd., A California Limited Partnership
200 S Main St Ste 200 # 200
Corona CA 92882
951 493-6500

(P-6113)
SHORT LOAD CONCRETE INC
605 E Commercial St, Anaheim
(92801-2511)
PHONE.................714 524-7013
Ryan Van Derhook, *President*
Colby Zethraeus, *Foreman/Supr*
EMP: 20 **EST:** 1996
SALES (est): 3.8MM **Privately Held**
WEB: www.shortloadconcrete.com
SIC: 3273 Ready-mixed concrete

(P-6114)
SOUTH VALLEY MATERIALS INC
1132 N Belmont Rd, Exeter (93221-9669)
PHONE.................559 594-4142
EMP: 17
SALES (corp-wide): 20.8B **Privately Held**
WEB: www.lehighhanson.com
SIC: 3273 Ready-mixed concrete
HQ: South Valley Materials, Inc.
114 E Shaw Ave Ste 100
Fresno CA 93710
559 277-7060

(P-6115)
SOUTH VALLEY MATERIALS INC
7761 Hanford Armona Rd, Hanford
(93230-9343)
P.O. Box 26240, Fresno (93729-6240)
PHONE.................559 582-0532
David Vickers, *Branch Mgr*
EMP: 17
SALES (corp-wide): 20.8B **Privately Held**
WEB: www.lehighhanson.com
SIC: 3273 Ready-mixed concrete
HQ: South Valley Materials, Inc.
114 E Shaw Ave Ste 100
Fresno CA 93710
559 277-7060

(P-6116)
SPRAGUES ROCK AND SAND COMPANY (PA)
Also Called: Spragues Ready Mix
230 Longden Ave, Irwindale (91706-1328)
PHONE.................626 445-2125
Carole Cotter, *Ch of Bd*
Michael Toland, *President*
Jerry Anctil, *CFO*
Gerald Anctil, *Treasurer*
Juli Paez, *Corp Secy*
EMP: 22 **EST:** 1953
SQ FT: 2,100
SALES (est): 7.6MM **Privately Held**
WEB: www.srmconcrete.com
SIC: 3273 Ready-mixed concrete

(P-6117)
SPRAGUES ROCK AND SAND COMPANY
Also Called: Spragues Ready Mix Concrete
5400 Bennett Rd, Simi Valley (93063-5135)
PHONE.................805 522-7010
Michael Toland, *Manager*
EMP: 14
SALES (corp-wide): 7.6MM **Privately Held**
WEB: www.srmconcrete.com
SIC: 3273 Ready-mixed concrete
PA: Spragues' Rock And Sand Company
230 Longden Ave
Irwindale CA 91706
626 445-2125

(P-6118)
STANDARD CONCRETE PRODUCTS INC (HQ)
Also Called: Associated Ready Mix Concrete
13550 Live Oak Ln, Baldwin Park
(91706-1318)
P.O. Box 15326, Santa Ana (92735-0326)
PHONE.................310 829-4537
David Hummel, *President*
Brian Serra, *Vice Pres*
EMP: 20 **EST:** 1986
SQ FT: 2,400
SALES (est): 32.7MM
SALES (corp-wide): 103.9MM **Privately Held**
WEB: www.standard-concrete.com
SIC: 3273 Ready-mixed concrete
PA: A & A Ready Mixed Concrete, Inc.
4621 Teller Ave Ste 130
Newport Beach CA 92660
949 253-2800

(P-6119)
STATE READY MIX INC (PA)
1011 Azahar St Ste 1, Ventura (93004)
PHONE.................805 647-2817
Russell Cochran, *CEO*
Robert A Lynch, *President*
EMP: 30 **EST:** 1988
SALES (est): 5.8MM **Privately Held**
WEB: www.statereadymix.com
SIC: 3273 Ready-mixed concrete

(P-6120)
SUPERIOR READY MIX CONCRETE LP
802 E Main St, El Centro (92243-9474)
P.O. Box 400 (92244-0400)
PHONE.................760 352-4341
Donald Lee, *Branch Mgr*
EMP: 52
SALES (corp-wide): 205.2MM **Privately Held**
WEB: www.superiorrm.cloudflareaccess.com
SIC: 3273 Ready-mixed concrete
PA: Superior Ready Mix Concrete L.P.
1564 Mission Rd
Escondido CA 92029
760 745-0556

(P-6121)
SUPERIOR READY MIX CONCRETE LP
24635 Temescal Canyon Rd, Corona
(92883-5422)
PHONE.................951 277-3553
Justine Moss, *Branch Mgr*
EMP: 52
SALES (corp-wide): 205.2MM **Privately Held**
WEB: www.superiorrm.cloudflareaccess.com
SIC: 3273 Ready-mixed concrete
PA: Superior Ready Mix Concrete L.P.
1564 Mission Rd
Escondido CA 92029
760 745-0556

(P-6122)
SUPERIOR READY MIX CONCRETE LP
Also Called: Hemet Ready Mix
1130 N State St, Hemet (92543-1510)
PHONE.................951 658-9225
Wayne Heckerman, *Principal*
EMP: 52
SALES (corp-wide): 205.2MM **Privately Held**
WEB: www.superiorrm.cloudflareaccess.com
SIC: 3273 5211 Ready-mixed concrete; masonry materials & supplies
PA: Superior Ready Mix Concrete L.P.
1564 Mission Rd
Escondido CA 92029
760 745-0556

(P-6123)
SUPERIOR READY MIX CONCRETE LP
72270 Varner Rd, Thousand Palms
(92276-3341)
PHONE.................760 343-3418
Mark Higgins, *Manager*

Dennis McGovern, *Supervisor*
EMP: 52
SALES (corp-wide): 205.2MM **Privately Held**
WEB:
www.superiorrm.cloudflareaccess.com
SIC: 3273 Ready-mixed concrete
PA: Superior Ready Mix Concrete L.P.
1564 Mission Rd
Escondido CA 92029
760 745-0556

(P-6124)
TROESH READYMIX INC
2280 Hutton Rd, Nipomo (93444-9448)
PHONE..................805 928-3764
Steve Troesh, *President*
Renee Troesh, *Vice Pres*
EMP: 26 **EST:** 1984
SALES (est): 1.2MM **Privately Held**
WEB: www.troeshcoleman.com
SIC: 3273 Ready-mixed concrete

(P-6125)
VULCAN CONSTRUCTION MTLS LLC
35800 146th St E, Pearblossom (93553)
PHONE..................661 810-2285
James McConnell, *Branch Mgr*
EMP: 17 **Publicly Held**
WEB: www.vulcanmaterials.com
SIC: 3273 Ready-mixed concrete
HQ: Vulcan Construction Materials, Llc
1200 Urban Center Dr
Vestavia AL 35242
205 298-3000

(P-6126)
WATERCRAFT MIX INC
2018 N Bahama Ave, Los Angeles
(90059-3458)
PHONE..................310 884-9755
Karla Y Moran, *Branch Mgr*
EMP: 24
SALES (corp-wide): 187.7K **Privately Held**
SIC: 3273 Ready-mixed concrete
PA: Watercraft Mix , Inc
26 Diplomat Pkwy
Hallandale Beach FL 33009
562 547-9759

(P-6127)
WERNER CORPORATION
Also Called: Foster Sand & Gravel
25050 Maitri Rd, Corona (92883-5105)
P.O. Box 77850 (92877-0128)
PHONE..................951 277-4586
Mark Miller, *Manager*
EMP: 20
SALES (corp-wide): 16.3MM **Privately Held**
WEB: www.wernercorp.net
SIC: 3273 Ready-mixed concrete
PA: Werner Corporation
25555 Maitri Rd
Corona CA 92883
951 277-3900

(P-6128)
WESTWOOD BUILDING MATERIALS CO
15708 Inglewood Ave, Lawndale
(90260-2544)
PHONE..................310 643-9158
Craig St John, *President*
Jose Garcia, *Sales Associate*
David Hernandez, *Sales Associate*
Ron Johnson, *Sales Associate*
Liza Peitzmeier, *Manager*
EMP: 36
SQ FT: 23,500
SALES (est): 9.8MM **Privately Held**
WEB: www.westwoodbm.com
SIC: 3273 Ready-mixed concrete

3275 Gypsum Prdts

(P-6129)
NATIONAL GYPSUM MFG OFFICE
1850 Pier B St, Long Beach (90813-2604)
PHONE..................562 435-4465
EMP: 18 **EST:** 2019

SALES (est): 1.2MM **Privately Held**
WEB: www.nationalgypsum.com
SIC: 3275 Gypsum products

(P-6130)
PABCO BUILDING PRODUCTS LLC
Also Called: Pabco Paper
4460 Pacific Blvd, Vernon (90058-2206)
PHONE..................323 581-6113
Mike Willoughby, *Branch Mgr*
EMP: 53
SALES (corp-wide): 1.1B **Privately Held**
WEB: www.pabcogypsum.com
SIC: 3275 Gypsum products
HQ: Pabco Building Products, Llc
10600 White Rock Rd Ste 1
Rancho Cordova CA 95670
510 792-1577

(P-6131)
UNITED STATES GYPSUM COMPANY
401 Van Ness Ave, Torrance (90501-1422)
PHONE..................908 232-8900
Matt Craig, *Manager*
Ali Al-Saihati, *Department Mgr*
Kumar Natesaiyer, *General Mgr*
Roni Gleason, *Admin Asst*
Garrett Thorne, *Admin Asst*
EMP: 100
SQ FT: 71,800
SALES (corp-wide): 10.7B **Privately Held**
WEB: www.usg.com
SIC: 3275 Gypsum products
HQ: United States Gypsum Company
550 W Adams St Ste 1300
Chicago IL 60661
312 606-4000

(P-6132)
UNITED STATES GYPSUM COMPANY
3810 Evan Hewes Hwy, Imperial
(92251-9529)
P.O. Box 2450, El Centro (92244-2450)
PHONE..................760 358-3200
George Keelan, *Finance*
EMP: 70
SALES (corp-wide): 10.7B **Privately Held**
WEB: www.usg.com
SIC: 3275 Gypsum products
HQ: United States Gypsum Company
550 W Adams St Ste 1300
Chicago IL 60661
312 606-4000

3281 Cut Stone Prdts

(P-6133)
AMERICAN MARBLE & GRANITE CO (PA)
4084 Whittier Blvd, Los Angeles
(90023-2527)
P.O. Box 23156 (90023-0156)
PHONE..................323 268-7979
John Vega, *President*
EMP: 14 **EST:** 1894
SQ FT: 600
SALES (est): 2.5MM **Privately Held**
WEB: www.amgmemorials.com
SIC: 3281 5999 Tombstones, cut stone
(not finishing or lettering only); tomb-
stones

(P-6134)
AMERICAN MARBLE & ONYX CO INC
10321 S La Cienega Blvd, Los Angeles
(90045-6109)
PHONE..................323 776-0900
Frederick Gherardi, *President*
Susan Gibbs, *Treasurer*
Steve Gherardi, *Vice Pres*
▲ **EMP:** 26 **EST:** 1933
SQ FT: 30,000
SALES (est): 1.6MM **Privately Held**
WEB: www.amocmarble.com
SIC: 3281 1743 Marble, building: cut &
shaped; marble installation, interior

(P-6135)
BEST-WAY MARBLE & TILE CO INC
Also Called: Best Way Marble
5037 Telegraph Rd, Los Angeles
(90022-4922)
PHONE..................323 266-6794
Shelley Herrera, *President*
Carl Palma, *Assistant*
Carlos Vidaurri, *Supervisor*
◆ **EMP:** 28 **EST:** 1981
SQ FT: 16,000
SALES (est): 3.5MM **Privately Held**
WEB: www.bestwaymarble.com
SIC: 3281 1743 Table tops, marble; mar--
ble installation, interior

(P-6136)
CARNEVALE & LOHR INC
6521 Clara St, Bell Gardens (90201-5634)
PHONE..................562 927-8311
Louie Carnevale, *CEO*
Michael Carnevale, *CFO*
David Carnevale, *Principal*
Edmund B Lohr IV, *Principal*
▲ **EMP:** 25 **EST:** 1958
SALES (est): 3.7MM **Privately Held**
WEB: www.carnevaleandlohr.com
SIC: 3281 1741 Cut stone & stone prod-
ucts; marble masonry, exterior construc-
tion

(P-6137)
COAST FLAGSTONE CO
1810 Colorado Ave, Santa Monica
(90404-3412)
PHONE..................310 829-4010
Timothy Wang, *Owner*
EMP: 70 **EST:** 2010
SALES (est): 4MM **Privately Held**
WEB: www.bourgetbros.com
SIC: 3281 Flagstones

(P-6138)
FAIRPRICE ENTERPRISES INC
Also Called: Fair Price Carpets
1070 Center St, Riverside (92507-1016)
PHONE..................951 684-8578
Kurt Ritz, *CEO*
Donovan Ritz, *President*
Marlene Ritz, *Corp Secy*
Krystal Gonzales, *Human Resources*
Debbie Snyder, *Purchasing*
EMP: 60 **EST:** 1957
SQ FT: 28,000 **Privately Held**
WEB: www.fairpricecarpets.com
SIC: 5713 3281 2426 5032 Carpets;
granite, cut & shaped; flooring, hardwood;
ceramic wall & floor tile; wood kitchen
cabinets; flooring contractor

(P-6139)
GL VENTURA INC
12595 Foothill Blvd, Sylmar (91342-5310)
PHONE..................818 890-1886
John Ventura, *President*
EMP: 23 **EST:** 1996
SQ FT: 8,000
SALES (est): 2.1MM **Privately Held**
WEB: www.glventura.com
SIC: 3281 5032 Marble, building: cut &
shaped; marble building stone

(P-6140)
MANTELS & MORE CORP
2909 Tanager Ave, Commerce
(90040-2723)
PHONE..................323 869-9764
Gourdikian Raffi, *Principal*
EMP: 17 **EST:** 2010
SALES (est): 2.1MM **Privately Held**
SIC: 3281 Stone, quarrying & processing
of own stone products

(P-6141)
PRECISION GRANITE USA INC
Also Called: Precision Granite Company
174 N Aspan Ave, Azusa (91702-4224)
P.O. Box 427, Whittier (90608-0427)
PHONE..................562 696-8328
John De Leon, *President*
▲ **EMP:** 14 **EST:** 1984
SQ FT: 11,904
SALES (est): 400K **Privately Held**
WEB: www.precisiongraniteusa.com
SIC: 3281 Granite, cut & shaped

(P-6142)
REGAL CULTURED MARBLE INC
1239 E Franklin Ave, Pomona
(91766-5450)
P.O. Box 780534, Maspeth NY (11378-
0534)
PHONE..................909 802-2388
Phillip K Black, *President*
David Sklar, *Vice Pres*
EMP: 17 **EST:** 1968
SQ FT: 12,000
SALES (est): 586.3K **Privately Held**
SIC: 3281 2821 Bathroom fixtures, cut
stone; plastics materials & resins

(P-6143)
RUGGERI MARBLE AND GRANITE INC
16001 S San Pedro St C, Gardena
(90248-2543)
PHONE..................310 513-2155
Andre Ruggeri, *President*
Robert Ruggeri, *Treasurer*
Giovanna F MWC, *Office Mgr*
◆ **EMP:** 80 **EST:** 1991
SQ FT: 6,650
SALES (est): 8.1MM **Privately Held**
WEB: www.ruggeri-marble-granite-
inc.hub.biz
SIC: 3281 5032 Marble, building: cut &
shaped; granite, cut & shaped; ceramic
wall & floor tile

(P-6144)
SAMPLE TILE AND STONE INC
1410 Richardson St, San Bernardino
(92408-2962)
PHONE..................951 776-8562
Curtis Sample, *CEO*
Brian Lyman, *Sales Mgr*
Abby Johnson, *Accounts Mgr*
EMP: 45
SQ FT: 13,500
SALES: 6MM **Privately Held**
SIC: 3281 5032 1411 1743 Cut stone &
stone products; table tops, marble; lime-
stone; limestone & marble dimension
stone; terrazzo, tile, marble, mosaic work;
marble installation, interior; marble ma-
sonry, exterior construction; stone masonry

(P-6145)
SIX ELEVEN LIMITED INC
11921 Sherman Way, North Hollywood
(91605-3726)
PHONE..................818 764-5810
George Gruber, *President*
Mort Braustein, *Principal*
EMP: 19 **EST:** 1986
SALES (est): 245.5K **Privately Held**
SIC: 3281 Bathroom fixtures, cut stone

(P-6146)
STANDRIDGE GRANITE CORPORATION
9437 Santa Fe Springs Rd, Santa Fe
Springs (90670-2684)
PHONE..................562 946-6334
Deborah Deleon, *President*
Steven Piel, *Plant Mgr*
EMP: 30 **EST:** 1965
SQ FT: 24,000
SALES (est): 4.8MM **Privately Held**
WEB: www.standridgegranite.com
SIC: 3281 1411 Granite, cut & shaped; di-
mension stone

(P-6147)
STONE IMAGE INC
7311 Fulton Ave, North Hollywood
(91605-4114)
PHONE..................561 547-1177
Leo Exler, *President*
Stephanie Exler, *Treasurer*
▼ **EMP:** 16 **EST:** 1996
SQ FT: 1,200
SALES (est): 504K **Privately Held**
WEB: www.stoneimagedesign.com
SIC: 3281 5032 Cut stone & stone prod-
ucts; brick, stone & related material

PRODUCTS & SVCS

(P-6148)
SULLIVANS STONE FACTORY INC
83778 Avenue 45, Indio (92201-3310)
PHONE...................................760 347-5535
Robert J Sullivan, *President*
▲ EMP: 25 EST: 2004
SALES (est): 2.2MM **Privately Held**
WEB: www.sullivansstonefactory.com
SIC: 3281 Granite, cut & shaped

(P-6149)
SUPERIOR STONE PRODUCTS INC
923 E Arlee Pl, Anaheim (92805-5645)
PHONE...................................714 635-7775
Costandi Awadalla, *President*
EMP: 15 EST: 2014
SALES (est): 1MM **Privately Held**
WEB: www.superiorstoneproductsinc.com
SIC: 3281 Cut stone & stone products

3291 Abrasive Prdts

(P-6150)
ARROW ABRASIVE COMPANY INC
12033 1/2 Regentview Ave, Downey (90241-5517)
P.O. Box 118, Borrego Springs (92004-0118)
PHONE...................................562 869-2282
Alan Bates, *President*
Linda Bates, *Treasurer*
Michael Bates, *Vice Pres*
EMP: 26 EST: 1976
SQ FT: 5,000
SALES (est): 1.4MM **Privately Held**
WEB: www.arrowabrasive.com
SIC: 3291 Wheels, grinding: artificial

(P-6151)
BUFF AND SHINE MFG INC
2139 E Del Amo Blvd, Rancho Dominguez (90220-6301)
PHONE...................................310 886-5111
Richard Umbrell, *President*
Elizabeth Umbrell, *Vice Pres*
◆ EMP: 40 EST: 1987
SQ FT: 25,792
SALES (est): 8.7MM **Privately Held**
WEB: www.buffandshine.com
SIC: 3291 Buffing or polishing wheels, abrasive or nonabrasive

(P-6152)
FALCON ABRASIVE MFG INC
5490 Brooks St, Montclair (91763-4520)
P.O. Box 713, Walnut (91788-0713)
PHONE...................................909 598-3078
Steve De La Torre, *President*
Rosemarie De Latorre, *Corp Secy*
▼ EMP: 24 EST: 1986
SQ FT: 6,900
SALES (est): 2.1MM **Privately Held**
WEB: www.falconabrasive.com
SIC: 3291 5085 Wheels, abrasive; industrial supplies

(P-6153)
GRITON INDUSTRIES INC (PA)
10821 Capital Ave, Garden Grove (92843-4953)
PHONE...................................714 554-8875
Eric Cheng, *President*
◆ EMP: 17 EST: 1983
SQ FT: 10,000
SALES (est): 1.6MM **Privately Held**
WEB: www.griton.com
SIC: 3291 Abrasive products

(P-6154)
MAGNUM ABRASIVES INC
758 S Allen St, San Bernardino (92408-2210)
PHONE...................................909 890-1100
Manuel Acuna, *President*
Richard Frenkel, *Vice Pres*
▲ EMP: 20 EST: 1985
SQ FT: 13,400

SALES (est): 2.8MM **Privately Held**
WEB: www.magnumabrasives.com
SIC: 3291 5085 Abrasive products; abrasives

(P-6155)
MAVERICK ABRASIVES CORPORATION
4340 E Miraloma Ave, Anaheim (92807-1886)
PHONE...................................714 854-9531
Rami Aryan, *President*
Junior Lucatero, *General Mgr*
Gregory Becker, *Marketing Staff*
Jesse Rodriguez, *Sales Staff*
◆ EMP: 60 EST: 1997
SQ FT: 15,000
SALES (est): 10.1MM **Privately Held**
WEB: www.maverickabrasives.com
SIC: 3291 Abrasive products

(P-6156)
MK TOOL AND ABRASIVE INC
4710 S Eastern Ave, Los Angeles (90040-2913)
PHONE...................................562 776-8818
Olinda Kapila, *President*
Rajiv Kapila, *Vice Pres*
Pete Barton, *Sales Staff*
▲ EMP: 14 EST: 1988
SQ FT: 15,000
SALES (est): 1.8MM **Privately Held**
WEB: www.mktool.net
SIC: 3291 3541 5251 Synthetic abrasives; abrasive buffs, bricks, cloth, paper, stones, etc.; machine tools, metal cutting type; builders' hardware

(P-6157)
PEARLMAN ENTERPRISES INC (DH)
6210 Garfield Ave, Commerce (90040-3613)
PHONE...................................800 969-5561
Daniel Davidenko, *CEO*
Eric Aguirre, *CFO*
John Waterworth, *CFO*
EMP: 100 EST: 2006
SALES (est): 69.3MM **Privately Held**
WEB: www.pearlabrasive.com
SIC: 3291 3843 3991 3421 Wheels, abrasive; abrasive points, wheels & disks, dental; brushes, household or industrial; razor blades & razors; fabricated structural metal
HQ: Pearlman Holdings, Inc.
3950 Steve Reynolds Blvd
Norcross GA 30093
800 458-6222

(P-6158)
SUPREME ABRASIVES
Also Called: Continental Machine Tool Co
1021 Fuller St, Santa Ana (92701-4212)
PHONE...................................949 250-8644
William W Taylor, *CEO*
Robert Longman, *Vice Pres*
▲ EMP: 40 EST: 1958
SQ FT: 20,000
SALES (est): 4.5MM **Privately Held**
SIC: 3291 Wheels, abrasive

(P-6159)
TECHNIFEX PRODUCTS LLC
25261 Rye Canyon Rd, Valencia (91355-1203)
PHONE...................................661 294-3800
Montgomery C Lunde, *CEO*
Rockne J Hall, *Chairman*
Joe Ortiz, *Vice Pres*
John Polk, *Vice Pres*
Jim Sharits, *Vice Pres*
▲ EMP: 25 EST: 1999
SALES (est): 4.7MM **Privately Held**
WEB: www.technifex.com
SIC: 3291 Steel wool

(P-6160)
VIBRA FINISH CO (PA)
Also Called: Vibrahone
2220 Shasta Way, Simi Valley (93065-1831)
PHONE...................................805 578-0033
Haskel Hall, *President*
Jerry Rindal, *Vice Pres*
▲ EMP: 20 EST: 1924

SQ FT: 41,000
SALES (est): 4.8MM **Privately Held**
WEB: www.vibrafinish.com
SIC: 3291 Abrasive products

(P-6161)
WESTERN ABRASIVES INC
4383 Fruitland Ave, Vernon (90058-3119)
PHONE...................................323 588-1245
EMP: 16
SQ FT: 36,000
SALES (est): 2MM **Privately Held**
SIC: 3291 Abrasive Products, Nsk

(P-6162)
YEAGER ENTERPRISES CORP
Also Called: Pasco
7100 Village Dr, Buena Park (90621-2261)
PHONE...................................714 994-2040
Joseph O'Mera, *CEO*
David M Yeager, *President*
Joan F Yeager, *Vice Pres*
▲ EMP: 81 EST: 1920
SQ FT: 55,000
SALES (est): 9.1MM **Privately Held**
WEB: www.cgwabrasives.com
SIC: 3291 Abrasive products

3292 Asbestos products

(P-6163)
FRANCO AMERICAN CORPORATION
Also Called: Franco American Textile
1051 Monterey Pass Rd, Monterey Park (91754-3612)
PHONE...................................323 268-2345
Roland Jones, *President*
▲ EMP: 17 EST: 2007
SALES (est): 2.3MM **Privately Held**
WEB: www.franco-american.com
SIC: 3292 Asbestos textiles, except insulating material

(P-6164)
H2 ENVIRONMENTAL
13122 6th St, Chino (91710-4105)
PHONE...................................909 628-0369
Amy Disantiago, *Owner*
EMP: 18 EST: 1995
SALES (est): 6MM **Privately Held**
WEB: www.h2environmental.com
SIC: 3292 1799 Asbestos products; asbestos removal & encapsulation

3295 Minerals & Earths: Ground Or Treated

(P-6165)
CLAY LAGUNA CO (HQ)
14400 Lomitas Ave, City of Industry (91746-3018)
PHONE...................................626 330-0631
Jonathan W Brooks, *Principal*
Laurie Brooks, *Corp Secy*
Elizabeth Steinhoff, *Credit Staff*
Rosanne Sloane, *Sales Mgr*
Rosemarie Copado, *Marketing Staff*
◆ EMP: 100 EST: 1976
SQ FT: 110,000
SALES (est): 9.9MM
SALES (corp-wide): 20.9MM **Privately Held**
WEB: www.lagunaclay.com
SIC: 3295 5032 Clay, ground or otherwise treated; tile & clay products
PA: Jon Brooks, Inc.
14400 Lomitas Ave
City Of Industry CA 91746
626 330-0631

(P-6166)
DESICCARE INC
3400 Pomona Blvd, Pomona (91768-3236)
PHONE...................................909 444-8272
Shaneen Aros, *CFO*
Jack Schrader, *Vice Pres*
Marcus Dukes, *General Mgr*
Ted Intyre, *VP Engrg*
Ted McIntyre, *VP Engrg*
EMP: 28 **Privately Held**
WEB: www.desiccare.com

SIC: 3295 Desiccants, clay: activated
PA: Desiccare, Inc.
3930 W Windmill Ln # 100
Las Vegas NV 89139

(P-6167)
JON BROOKS INC (PA)
Also Called: Laguna Clay Company
14400 Lomitas Ave, City of Industry (91746-3018)
PHONE...................................626 330-0631
Jon Brooks, *President*
Laurie Brooks, *Corp Secy*
◆ EMP: 100 EST: 1981
SQ FT: 117,000
SALES (est): 20.9MM **Privately Held**
WEB: www.lagunaclay.com
SIC: 3295 5085 Clay, ground or otherwise treated; refractory material

(P-6168)
SGL TECHNIC LLC (DH)
Also Called: Inc Polycarbon
28176 Avenue Stanford, Valencia (91355-1119)
PHONE...................................661 257-0500
Ken Mamon, *President*
Brian Green, *Vice Pres*
Kathy Vanschoonhoven, *Vice Pres*
Hrair Torosian, *IT/INT Sup*
Jay Tumuluri, *Controller*
▲ EMP: 76 EST: 1967
SQ FT: 130,000
SALES (est): 13.7MM
SALES (corp-wide): 1B **Privately Held**
WEB: www.sglcarbon.com
SIC: 3295 3624 Graphite, natural: ground, pulverized, refined or blended; carbon & graphite products
HQ: Sgl Carbon, Llc
10715 David Taylor Dr # 460
Charlotte NC 28262
704 593-5100

3296 Mineral Wool

(P-6169)
C A SCHROEDER INC (PA)
Also Called: Casco Mfg
1318 1st St, San Fernando (91340-2804)
PHONE...................................818 365-9561
Susan A Knudsen, *CEO*
Clifford A Schroeder, *President*
Alf Knudsen, *Sales Mgr*
Robert Voorhees, *Sales Staff*
Keith Thomas, *Director*
EMP: 42 EST: 1969
SQ FT: 18,500
SALES (est): 7.1MM **Privately Held**
WEB: www.casco-flex.com
SIC: 3296 3585 3444 3433 Fiberglass insulation; refrigeration & heating equipment; sheet metalwork; heating equipment, except electric

(P-6170)
CONSOLIDATED FIERGLS PDTS CO
Also Called: Conglas
3801 Standard St, Bakersfield (93308-5230)
PHONE...................................661 323-6026
Daron J Thomas, *CEO*
Jack Pfeffer, *Vice Ch Bd*
EMP: 60 EST: 1972
SQ FT: 20,000
SALES (est): 10.2MM **Privately Held**
SIC: 3296 Fiberglass insulation

(P-6171)
INSULFAB INC
4725 Calle Alto, Camarillo (93012-8538)
PHONE...................................805 482-2751
Sieg Borck, *President*
William Brown, *Corp Secy*
Ernest Sieger, *Vice Pres*
Jason Cherry, *Maint Spv*
Rachael Greathouse, *Manager*
EMP: 21 EST: 1979
SQ FT: 23,000
SALES (est): 1.6MM **Privately Held**
SIC: 3296 Insulation: rock wool, slag & silica minerals

(P-6172)
ROCK STRUCTURES-RIP RAP
11126 Silverton Ct, Corona (92881-5626)
PHONE..................................951 371-1112
Antonio Paredes, *Owner*
EMP: 30 **EST:** 2003
SQ FT: 3,500 **Privately Held**
WEB: www.rock-structures.com
SIC: 3296 Insulation: rock wool, slag & silica minerals

(P-6173)
UPF CORPORATION
3747 Standard St, Bakersfield
(93308-5228)
PHONE..................................661 323-8227
Jack Pfeffer, *President*
Michael Pipkin, *Programmer Anys*
Sloane Thomas, *Opers Staff*
Mike Rushing, *Supervisor*
▼ **EMP:** 23 **EST:** 1988
SALES (est): 5.7MM **Privately Held**
WEB: www.upf-usa.com
SIC: 3296 Fiberglass insulation

3297 Nonclay Refractories

(P-6174)
SIMONS BRICK CORPORATION
4301 Firestone Blvd, South Gate
(90280-3318)
PHONE..................................951 279-1000
John Williams, *President*
EMP: 38 **EST:** 1989
SQ FT: 24,000
SALES (est): 2MM
SALES (corp-wide): 1.1B **Privately Held**
WEB: www.basalite.com
SIC: 3297 5211 Brick refractories; brick
HQ: Basalite Building Products, Llc
2150 Douglas Blvd Ste 260
Roseville CA 95661
707 678-1901

3299 Nonmetallic Mineral Prdts, NEC

(P-6175)
3M TECHNICAL CERAMICS INC (HQ)
1922 Barranca Pkwy, Irvine (92606-4826)
PHONE..................................949 862-9600
Joel P Moskowitz, *CEO*
Mike Lipscombe, *President*
Jerrold J Pellizzon, *CFO*
Thomas A Cole, *Vice Pres*
Peter Hartl, *Vice Pres*
◆ **EMP:** 824 **EST:** 1967
SQ FT: 99,000
SALES (est): 284MM
SALES (corp-wide): 32.1B **Publicly Held**
WEB: www.ceradyne.com
SIC: 3299 3671 Ceramic fiber; cathode ray tubes, including rebuilt
PA: 3m Company
3m Center
Saint Paul MN 55144
651 733-1110

(P-6176)
ALS GARDEN ART INC (PA)
311 W Citrus St, Colton (92324-1412)
PHONE..................................909 424-0221
Donald Bracci, *President*
EMP: 290 **EST:** 1949
SQ FT: 305,000
SALES (est): 17MM **Privately Held**
WEB: www.alsgardenart.com
SIC: 3299 3272 Statuary: gypsum, clay, papier mache, metal, etc.; concrete products

(P-6177)
APPROVED NETWORKS LLC (PA)
Also Called: Approved Optics
6 Orchard Ste 150, Lake Forest
(92630-8352)
PHONE..................................800 590-9535
Michael Rapp, *CEO*
Ron Beale, *CFO*
Kurt Dumteman, *Vice Pres*

Jeff Motts, *Executive*
Thomas Horton, *Managing Dir*
EMP: 59 **EST:** 2010
SQ FT: 9,500
SALES (est): 123MM **Privately Held**
WEB: www.approvednetworks.com
SIC: 3299 Art goods: plaster of paris, papier mache & scagliola

(P-6178)
BURLINGAME INDUSTRIES INC
Also Called: Eagle Roofing Products Co
2352 N Locust Ave, Rialto (92377-5000)
PHONE..................................909 355-7000
Robert Burlingame, *President*
Seamus Burlingame, *Exec VP*
Christopher Schott, *Project Mgr*
Estella Martinez, *Human Res Mgr*
Steve Saldate, *Production*
EMP: 64
SQ FT: 76,704
SALES (corp-wide): 120.4MM **Privately Held**
WEB: www.eagleroofing.com
SIC: 3299 3272 2952 Tile, sand lime; concrete products; asphalt felts & coatings
PA: Burlingame Industries, Incorporated
3546 N Riverside Ave
Rialto CA 92377
909 355-7000

(P-6179)
CHINA MASTER USA ENTRMT CO
17890 Castleton St # 230, City of Industry
(91748-1756)
PHONE..................................626 810-9372
Richard Wang, *Mng Member*
EMP: 20 **EST:** 1991
SALES (est): 222.7K **Privately Held**
WEB: www.chinamasterusa.com
SIC: 3299 Ceramic fiber

(P-6180)
FOUNDRY SERVICE & SUPPLIES INC
2029 S Parco Ave, Ontario (91761-5700)
PHONE..................................909 284-5000
Curt Parnell, *CEO*
Joel Leathers, *Vice Pres*
◆ **EMP:** 24 **EST:** 1962
SQ FT: 40,000
SALES (est): 4.5MM **Privately Held**
WEB: www.foundryservice.com
SIC: 3299 Art goods: plaster of paris, papier mache & scagliola

(P-6181)
JP WEAVER & COMPANY
941 Air Way, Glendale (91201-3001)
PHONE..................................818 500-1740
Lenna Tyler Kast, *President*
Adam Kast, *Director*
EMP: 31 **EST:** 1914
SQ FT: 10,000
SALES (est): 2MM **Privately Held**
WEB: www.jpweaver.com
SIC: 3299 2431 Moldings, architectural: plaster of paris; millwork

(P-6182)
MERLEX STUCCO INC
Also Called: Merlex Stucco Mfg
2911 N Orange Olive Rd, Orange
(92865-1699)
PHONE..................................877 547-8822
Steve Combs, *President*
◆ **EMP:** 17 **EST:** 1963
SQ FT: 30,000
SALES (est): 971.5K **Privately Held**
WEB: www.merlex.com
SIC: 3299 Stucco

(P-6183)
OMEGA PRODUCTS CORP
282 S Anita Dr Fl 3, Orange (92868-3308)
P.O. Box 1149 (92856-0149)
PHONE..................................714 935-0900
Todd Martin, *Manager*
EMP: 39
SALES (corp-wide): 90.1MM **Privately Held**
WEB: www.omega-products.com
SIC: 3299 Stucco

HQ: Omega Products Corp.
8111 Fruitridge Rd
Sacramento CA 95826
916 635-3335

(P-6184)
OPAL SERVICE INC (PA)
282 S Anita Dr, Orange (92868-3308)
P.O. Box 1149 (92856-0149)
PHONE..................................714 935-0900
Kenneth R Thompson, *CEO*
Dylan Budd, *Sales Staff*
▲ **EMP:** 30 **EST:** 1962
SQ FT: 1,200
SALES (est): 90.1MM **Privately Held**
SIC: 3299 5031 5211 Stucco; doors & windows; lumber & other building materials

(P-6185)
PAREX USA INC (DH)
2150 Eastridge Ave, Riverside
(92507-0720)
PHONE..................................714 778-2266
Rodrigo Lacerda, *President*
Nicolas Corcia, *CFO*
Gregory Wiedbusch, *Division VP*
Timothy McDonald, *Vice Pres*
Dannie Castro, *Info Tech Mgr*
◆ **EMP:** 30 **EST:** 1926
SALES (est): 118MM
SALES (corp-wide): 8.6B **Privately Held**
WEB: www.parexusa.com
SIC: 3299 5031 Stucco; building materials, interior

(P-6186)
PAREX USA INC
Also Called: La Habra Stucco
2150 Eastridge Ave, Riverside
(92507-0720)
PHONE..................................951 653-3549
Brian Carrier, *Manager*
Jenny Thai, *Accountant*
Jessica Kennedy, *Sales Staff*
EMP: 43
SALES (corp-wide): 8.6B **Privately Held**
WEB: www.parexusa.com
SIC: 5211 3299 Lumber & other building materials; stucco
HQ: Parex Usa, Inc.
2150 Eastridge Ave
Riverside CA 92507
714 778-2266

3312 Blast Furnaces, Coke Ovens, Steel & Rolling Mills

(P-6187)
AMERICAN PLANT SERVICES INC (PA)
6242 N Paramount Blvd, Long Beach
(90805-3714)
P.O. Box 727 (90801-0727)
PHONE..................................562 630-1773
George M Bragg, *President*
Mary-Ann Pool, *Treasurer*
Duane Evans, *CIO*
EMP: 34 **EST:** 1981
SALES (est): 5.2MM **Privately Held**
SIC: 3312 Blast furnaces & steel mills

(P-6188)
ARTSONS MANUFACTURING COMPANY
11121 Garfield Ave, South Gate
(90280-7505)
PHONE..................................323 773-3469
Jeffery A Winders, *CEO*
Jeffrey A Winders, *CEO*
Steve Winders, *CFO*
Art L Winders, *Vice Pres*
▲ **EMP:** 28 **EST:** 1958
SALES (est): 4.8MM **Privately Held**
WEB: www.artsonswire.com
SIC: 3312 Wire products, steel or iron

(P-6189)
BROWN-PACIFIC INC
Also Called: B P W
13639 Bora Dr, Santa Fe Springs
(90670-5010)
PHONE..................................562 921-3471

Ron R Nagele, *CEO*
Claudia Nagele, *Vice Pres*
Kenneth Brown, *Principal*
EMP: 32 **EST:** 1967
SQ FT: 35,000
SALES (est): 5.4MM **Privately Held**
WEB: www.brownpacific.com
SIC: 3312 3355 3357 3356 Bar, rod & wire products; wire; aluminum: made in rolling mills; bars, rolled, aluminum; nonferrous wiredrawing & insulating; nonferrous rolling & drawing; cold finishing of steel shapes; steel wire & related products

(P-6190)
CALABASAS TMS CENTER
2950 Sycamore Dr, Simi Valley
(93065-1232)
PHONE..................................805 261-0824
EMP: 35
SALES (corp-wide): 326.7K **Privately Held**
WEB: www.calabasasbehavioralhealth.com
SIC: 3312 Blast furnaces & steel mills
PA: Calabasas Tms Center Inc.
23622 Calabasas Rd # 301
Calabasas CA 91302
818 921-4300

(P-6191)
CALIFORNIA AMFORGE CORPORATION
750 N Vernon Ave, Azusa (91702-2231)
PHONE..................................626 334-4931
William Taylor, *Branch Mgr*
Lee Edwards, *General Mgr*
Roberto Facio, *Supervisor*
Stacey Salas, *Supervisor*
EMP: 102
SQ FT: 20,000
SALES (corp-wide): 29.8MM **Privately Held**
WEB: www.cal-amforge.com
SIC: 3312 3462 Forgings, iron & steel; iron & steel forgings
PA: California Amforge Corporation
750 N Vernon Ave
Azusa CA 91702
626 334-4931

(P-6192)
CALIFORNIA STEEL INDS INC (PA)
Also Called: Si
14000 San Bernardino Ave, Fontana
(92335-5259)
P.O. Box 5080 (92334-5080)
PHONE..................................909 350-6300
Marcelo Botelho, *President*
Hiroshi Adachi, *Ch of Bd*
Tadaaki Yamaguchi, *Ch of Bd*
Ricardo Bernardes, *Exec VP*
Brett Guge, *Exec VP*
▲ **EMP:** 1017 **EST:** 1983
SALES (est): 201.4MM **Privately Held**
WEB: www.californiasteel.com
SIC: 3312 3317 Slabs, steel; plate, sheet & strip, except coated products; pipes, wrought: welded, lock joint or heavy riveted

(P-6193)
CALIFORNIA STEEL INDS INC
1 California Steel Way, Fontana (92335)
PHONE..................................909 350-6300
Kyle Schulty, *Branch Mgr*
Rene Reed, *Administration*
Brian Mathers, *Technician*
Debbie Moore, *Regl Sales Mgr*
Mindy Harris, *Supervisor*
EMP: 48
SALES (corp-wide): 201.4MM **Privately Held**
WEB: www.californiasteel.com
SIC: 3312 3317 Slabs, steel; plate, sheet & strip, except coated products; pipes, wrought: welded, lock joint or heavy riveted
PA: California Steel Industries, Inc.
14000 San Bernardino Ave
Fontana CA 92335
909 350-6300

(P-6194)
CALPIPE INDUSTRIES LLC
923 Calpipe Rd, Santa Paula (93060-9155)
PHONE.....................................562 803-4388
Francisco Hernandez, *Principal*
EMP: 50 **Publicly Held**
WEB: www.calbond.com
SIC: 3312 Pipes & tubes
HQ: Calpipe Industries, Llc
    12160 Woodruff Ave
    Downey CA 90241
    -

(P-6195)
CARTER HOLT HARVEY INC HOLDINGS
1230 Railroad St, Corona (92882-1837)
PHONE.....................................951 272-8180
John Miller, *President*
EMP: 32 EST: 1994
SQ FT: 60,000
SALES (est): 4.3MM **Privately Held**
WEB: www.chhwood.com
SIC: 3312 Blast furnaces & steel mills
HQ: Qeynos New Zealand Limited
    173 Captain Springs Road
    Auckland 1061

(P-6196)
CHAPALA IRON & MANUFACTURING
1301 Callens Rd, Ventura (93003-5602)
PHONE.....................................805 654-9803
Patrick Davis, *Owner*
EMP: 21 EST: 1973
SQ FT: 3,600
SALES (est): 7.1MM **Privately Held**
WEB: www.chapalairon.com
SIC: 3312 3446 Blast furnaces & steel
mills; architectural metalwork

(P-6197)
COAST CUTTERS CO
105 N 9th Ave, Upland (91786-5412)
PHONE.....................................626 444-2965
EMP: 14 EST: 2015
SALES (est): 733.9K **Privately Held**
WEB: www.coastcutters.com
SIC: 3312 5072 Tool & die steel; power
tools & accessories

(P-6198)
DESIGN SHAPES IN STEEL INC
10315 Rush St, South El Monte
(91733-3341)
PHONE.....................................626 579-2032
Peter Costruba II, *President*
EMP: 35 EST: 1979
SQ FT: 10,000
SALES (est): 12.3MM **Privately Held**
WEB: www.design-shapes-in-steel.busi-
ness.site
SIC: 3312 3446 3444 Primary finished or
semifinished shapes; architectural metal-
work; sheet metalwork

(P-6199)
EASYFLEX INC
Also Called: Easy Flex
2700 N Main St Ste 800, Santa Ana
(92705-6672)
PHONE.....................................888 577-8999
Sunmin Kim OH, *President*
Hun Kim, *General Mgr*
Ryan Park, *Sales Mgr*
Daniel Kim, *Sales Associate*
Gl Lee, *Sales Associate*
◆ EMP: 25 EST: 2005
SALES (est): 6.5MM **Privately Held**
WEB: www.easyflexusa.com
SIC: 3312 Stainless steel

(P-6200)
ENGENSE INC
Also Called: Dfndr Armor
2255 Pleasant Valley Rd G, Camarillo
(93012-8569)
PHONE.....................................805 484-8317
David Fernandez, *President*
EMP: 17 EST: 2013
SALES (est): 2MM **Privately Held**
WEB: www.engense.com
SIC: 3312 Armor plate

(P-6201)
FLOW DYNAMICS INC
1215 E Acacia St Ste 104, Ontario
(91761-4003)
PHONE.....................................909 930-5522
John McCarthy, *President*
Philip Espinoza, *Vice Pres*
EMP: 16 EST: 2004
SQ FT: 2,222
SALES (est): 4.8MM **Privately Held**
WEB: www.flowdynamicsonline.com
SIC: 3312 Stainless steel

(P-6202)
GRAND PRIX ROAD TRENDS INC (PA)
Also Called: Grand Prix Performance
1718 Newport Blvd, Costa Mesa
(92627-3010)
PHONE.....................................949 645-7022
Jerry Palanjian, *President*
Denis Parent, *Technology*
EMP: 17 EST: 1972
SQ FT: 2,500
SALES (est): 3.3MM **Privately Held**
WEB: www.grandprixperformance.com
SIC: 5531 3312 Automotive tires; automo-
tive accessories; wheels

(P-6203)
HARDY FRAMES INC
Also Called: My Tech USA
250 Klug Cir, Corona (92878-5409)
PHONE.....................................951 245-9525
Clifford Grant, *Branch Mgr*
EMP: 100
SALES (corp-wide): 11.1MM **Privately
Held**
WEB: www.hardyframe.com
SIC: 3312 Stainless steel
PA: Hardy Frames, Inc.
    1732 Palma Dr Ste 200
    Ventura CA 93003
    805 477-0793

(P-6204)
LINCOLN IRON WORKS
507 7th St, Santa Monica (90402-2707)
PHONE.....................................310 684-2543
EMP: 22 EST: 2012
SALES (est): 2.1MM **Privately Held**
SIC: 3312 Blast Furnace-Steel Works

(P-6205)
MAC PRODUCTS INC
Also Called: Mac Performance Exhaust
43214 Black Deer Loop # 113, Temecula
(92590-3473)
PHONE.....................................951 296-3077
Mack Jones Sr, *President*
Mack Jones Jr, *Corp Secy*
▲ EMP: 24 EST: 1969
SQ FT: 56,000
SALES (est): 2.6MM **Privately Held**
SIC: 3312 3751 3714 Tubes, steel & iron;
motorcycles, bicycles & parts; motor vehi-
cle parts & accessories

(P-6206)
MANLEY LABORATORIES INC
Also Called: Manufacturing
13880 Magnolia Ave, Chino (91710-7027)
PHONE.....................................909 627-4256
Eveanna Manley, *President*
Eveanna Manley-Collins, *CEO*
Gamaliel Ibarra, *COO*
▲ EMP: 40 EST: 1993
SQ FT: 11,000
SALES (est): 6.5MM **Privately Held**
WEB: www.manley.com
SIC: 3312 3663 3651 Tool & die steel;
radio & TV communications equipment;
audio electronic systems

(P-6207)
PACIFIC TOLL PROCESSING INC
Also Called: P T P
24724 Wilmington Ave, Carson
(90745-6127)
PHONE.....................................310 952-4992
Anthony J Camasta, *CEO*
Mark Proner, *Exec VP*
EMP: 47 EST: 1999
SQ FT: 101,000
SALES (est): 11.8MM **Privately Held**
WEB: www.pacifictoll.com
SIC: 3312 4785 Structural & rail mill prod-
ucts; toll road operation

(P-6208)
PASO ROBLES TANK INC (HQ)
825 26th St, Paso Robles (93446-1242)
P.O. Box 3229 (93447-3229)
PHONE.....................................805 227-1641
Shawn P Owens, *CEO*
Janna M Cullis, *CFO*
Dawn M Roiz, *CFO*
Shane P Wombles, *Admin Sec*
Desiree Brumley, *Project Mgr*
▲ EMP: 63 EST: 2000
SALES (est): 39.1MM
SALES (corp-wide): 61MM **Privately
Held**
WEB: www.pasoroblestank.com
SIC: 3312 3443 Blast furnaces & steel
mills; tanks, standard or custom fabri-
cated: metal plate
PA: Associated Construction And Engineer-
ing, Inc.
    23222 Peralta Dr Ste 206
    Laguna Hills CA 92653
    949 455-2682

(P-6209)
R S R STEEL FABRICATION INC
11040 I Ave, Hesperia (92345-5214)
PHONE.....................................760 244-2210
Hector Grijalva, *President*
Ruth Grijalva, *Vice Pres*
EMP: 26 EST: 1993
SQ FT: 12,000
SALES (est): 6.1MM **Privately Held**
SIC: 3312 Structural shapes & pilings,
steel

(P-6210)
RTM PRODUCTS INC
13120 Arctic Cir, Santa Fe Springs
(90670-5508)
PHONE.....................................562 926-2400
Robert M Thierjung, *Principal*
EMP: 23 EST: 2007
SALES (est): 4.6MM **Privately Held**
WEB: www.rtmproducts.com
SIC: 3312 Tool & die steel & alloys; tool &
die steel

(P-6211)
SEARING INDUSTRIES INC
8901 Arrow Rte, Rancho Cucamonga
(91730-4410)
P.O. Box 3059 (91729-3059)
PHONE.....................................909 948-3030
Lee Searing, *President*
Margaret Cantu, *Exec VP*
Richard Searing, *Exec VP*
Mmargaret Cantu, *Vice Pres*
Annie Wood, *Office Mgr*
◆ EMP: 120 EST: 1985
SQ FT: 265,000
SALES (est): 30.9MM **Privately Held**
WEB: www.searingindustries.com
SIC: 3312 3317 Tubes, steel & iron; hot-
rolled iron & steel products; steel pipe &
tubes

(P-6212)
SMITH BROS STRL STL PDTS INC
Also Called: Smith Bros Cstm Met Fbrication
1535 Potrero Ave, South El Monte
(91733-3016)
PHONE.....................................626 350-1872
Christopher Smith, *President*
Chris Smith, *President*
Reginald Smith, *Vice Pres*
EMP: 18 EST: 1976
SQ FT: 30,000
SALES (est): 2.4MM **Privately Held**
SIC: 3312 Structural shapes & pilings,
steel

(P-6213)
STATE PIPE & SUPPLY INC
Westcoast Pipe Lining Division
2180 N Locust Ave, Rialto (92377-4166)
PHONE.....................................909 356-5670
Kenneth Walker, *Manager*
Ivan Vukosav, *Sales Staff*
EMP: 50 **Privately Held**
WEB: www.statepipe.com
SIC: 3312 Blast furnaces & steel mills;
coke produced in chemical recovery coke
ovens
HQ: State Pipe & Supply, Inc.
    183 S Cedar Ave
    Rialto CA 92376
    909 877-9999

(P-6214)
STRADA WHEELS INC
560 S Magnolia Ave, Ontario (91762-4011)
PHONE.....................................626 336-1634
Enrico Aiello, *President*
Joyce Aiello, *Vice Pres*
Maria Yneguez, *General Mgr*
▲ EMP: 14 EST: 2006
SALES (est): 2.6MM **Privately Held**
WEB: www.stradawheels.com
SIC: 3312 5014 Wheels; tires & tubes

(P-6215)
TAMCO (HQ)
Also Called: CMC Steel California
12459 Arrow Rte, Rancho Cucamonga
(91739-9807)
PHONE.....................................909 899-0660
Chia Yuan Wang, *CEO*
Vilmar Babot, *CFO*
Harley Scardoelli, *Admin Sec*
◆ EMP: 347 EST: 1974
SQ FT: 150,000
SALES (est): 96.6MM
SALES (corp-wide): 6.7B **Publicly Held**
WEB: www.tamcosteel.com
SIC: 3312 Blast furnaces & steel mills
PA: Commercial Metals Company
    6565 N Macarthur Blvd # 800
    Irving TX 75039
    214 689-4300

(P-6216)
TMS INTERNATIONAL
1521 Railroad St, Glendale (91204-2717)
PHONE.....................................818 894-1414
▲ EMP: 14 EST: 2010
SALES (est): 344.1K **Privately Held**
WEB: www.tmsinternational.com
SIC: 3312 Blast furnaces & steel mills

(P-6217)
WAYNE TOOL & DIE CO
15853 Olden St, Sylmar (91342-1249)
PHONE.....................................818 364-1611
Kenneth E Ruggles, *President*
EMP: 19 EST: 1978
SQ FT: 1,200
SALES (est): 275.5K **Privately Held**
SIC: 3312 Tool & die steel

(P-6218)
WHEEL AND TIRE CLUB INC
Also Called: Discounted Wheel Warehouse
1301 Burton St, Fullerton (92831-5212)
PHONE.....................................714 422-3505
Naeem Niamat, *President*
◆ EMP: 35 EST: 2013
SQ FT: 42,000
SALES (est): 5.4MM **Privately Held**
WEB:
www.discountedwheelwarehouse.com
SIC: 3312 Locomotive wheels, rolled

3313 Electrometallurgical Prdts

(P-6219)
R D MATHIS COMPANY
2840 Gundry Ave, Signal Hill (90755-1813)
P.O. Box 92916, Long Beach (90809-2916)
PHONE.....................................562 426-7049
Robert Lumley, *President*
Barbara Bennett, *Treasurer*
Kirk Bennett, *Vice Pres*
EMP: 25 EST: 1963
SQ FT: 10,000
SALES (est): 3.2MM **Privately Held**
WEB: www.rdmathis.com
SIC: 3313 8711 3567 3443 Molybdenum
silicon, not made in blast furnaces; engi-
neering services; industrial furnaces &
ovens; fabricated plate work (boiler shop);
fabricated structural metal

3315 Steel Wire Drawing & Nails & Spikes

(P-6220)
CAL STATE SITE SERVICES
4518 Industrial St, Simi Valley
(93063-3411)
PHONE.................................800 499-5757
Daniel Sanchez, *Opers Staff*
EMP: 20 EST: 2014
SALES (est): 1.9MM **Privately Held**
WEB: www.rentfenceandtoilets.com
SIC: 3315 5099 3431 Fencing made in
wiredrawing plants; toilets, portable; bath-
room fixtures, including sinks

(P-6221)
D & D TECHNOLOGIES USA INC
17531 Metzler Ln, Huntington Beach
(92647-6242)
PHONE.................................949 852-5140
▼ EMP: 29
SALES: 12MM **Privately Held**
SIC: 3315 Mfg Steel Wire/Related Prod-
ucts
HQ: D & D Technologies Pty. Limited
U6 4 Aquatic Dr
Frenchs Forest NSW 2086
-

(P-6222)
DAVIS WIRE CORPORATION (HQ)
5555 Irwindale Ave, Irwindale
(91706-2046)
PHONE.................................626 969-7651
Jim Baske, *President*
Emily Heisley, *Ch of Bd*
Hak Kim, *CFO*
Carolyn Webb, *Administration*
▲ EMP: 150 EST: 1927
SQ FT: 265,000
SALES (est): 101.2MM **Privately Held**
WEB: www.daviswire.com
SIC: 3315 Wire, ferrous/iron; wire prod-
ucts, ferrous/iron: made in wiredrawing
plants

(P-6223)
DOOR SERVICE COMPANY
Also Called: Patton Door and Gate
680 S Williams Rd, Palm Springs
(92264-1549)
PHONE.................................760 320-0788
Fax: 760 323-9553
EMP: 15 EST: 2007
SALES (est): 1.2MM **Privately Held**
SIC: 3315 1751 Mfg Steel Wire/Related
Products Carpentry Contractor

(P-6224)
EAST WEST ENTERPRISES
Also Called: Service Chemicals
20545 Belshaw Ave, Carson (90746-3505)
PHONE.................................310 632-9933
Eugene Livshin, *Partner*
Michael Goldenstein, *Principal*
EMP: 26 EST: 1990
SQ FT: 30,000
SALES (est): 619.2K **Privately Held**
SIC: 3315 Hangers (garment), wire

(P-6225)
HALSTEEL INC (DH)
4190 Santa Ana St Ste A, Ontario
(91761-1527)
P.O. Box 90100, San Bernardino (92427-
1100)
PHONE.................................909 937-1001
Rebecca Kalis, *President*
Donald Halstead, *Treasurer*
Ed Halstead, *Vice Pres*
EMP: 118 EST: 1996
SQ FT: 100,000
SALES (est): 4.1MM
SALES (corp-wide): 164.8MM **Privately Held**
WEB: www.treeisland.com
SIC: 3315 5051 Nails, steel: wire or cut;
staples, steel: wire or cut; nails
HQ: Tree Island Industries Ltd
3933 Boundary Rd
Richmond BC V6V 1
604 524-3744

(P-6226)
HAMROCK INC
12400 Wilshire Blvd # 1180, Los Angeles
(90025-1058)
PHONE.................................562 944-0255
Stephen R Hamrock, *Principal*
Jerry Hamrock, *Vice Pres*
Marty Hamrock, *Purchasing*
▲ EMP: 250 EST: 1976
SALES (est): 39.7MM **Privately Held**
WEB: www.hamrock.com
SIC: 3315 2542 3496 3317 Wire & fabri-
cated wire products; racks, merchandise
display or storage: except wood; miscella-
neous fabricated wire products; steel pipe
& tubes

(P-6227)
HOGAN CO INC
2741 S Lilac Ave, Bloomington
(92316-3213)
PHONE.................................909 421-0245
Kraig B Hogan, *President*
Deelinda Garcia, *Manager*
◆ EMP: 20 EST: 1939
SQ FT: 9,150
SALES (est): 4.1MM **Privately Held**
WEB: www.hoganco.com
SIC: 3315 3531 Spikes, steel: wire or cut;
bituminous, cement & concrete related
products & equipment

(P-6228)
INWESCO INCORPORATED (PA)
746 N Coney Ave, Azusa (91702-2239)
PHONE.................................626 334-7115
David L Morris, *CEO*
Jeremy Acheson, *Vice Pres*
EMP: 65 EST: 1967
SQ FT: 30,000
SALES (est): 25MM **Privately Held**
WEB: www.inwesco.com
SIC: 3315 Steel wire & related products

(P-6229)
MERCHANTS METALS LLC
6466 Mission Blvd, Riverside (92509-4128)
PHONE.................................951 686-1888
Rob Sisco, *Manager*
EMP: 27
SQ FT: 8,750 **Privately Held**
WEB: www.merchantsmetals.com
SIC: 3315 3496 Fence gates posts & fit-
tings: steel; miscellaneous fabricated wire
products
HQ: Merchants Metals Llc
211 Perimeter Center Pkwy
Atlanta GA 30346
770 741-0300

(P-6230)
MK MAGNETICS INC
17030 Muskrat Ave, Adelanto
(92301-2258)
PHONE.................................760 246-6373
Magne Stangenes, *President*
John Stangenes, *Vice Pres*
Jay Runge, *Admin Sec*
Bryce E Kelchner, *Info Tech Dir*
William Jahnke, *Technical Staff*
▲ EMP: 53 EST: 2003
SQ FT: 45,000
SALES (est): 11.1MM
SALES (corp-wide): 26.9MM **Privately Held**
WEB: www.mkmagnetics.com
SIC: 3315 Steel wire & related products
PA: Stangenes Industries, Inc.
1052 E Meadow Cir
Palo Alto CA 94303
650 855-9926

(P-6231)
PRO DETENTION INC
Also Called: Viking Products
2238 N Glassell St Ste E, Orange
(92865-2742)
PHONE.................................714 881-3680
Mike Peterson, *CEO*
Josh McRea, *Opers Staff*
David Peterson, *Sales Staff*
▲ EMP: 70 EST: 2012
SALES (est): 7.8MM **Privately Held**
WEB:
SIC: 3315 Wire & fabricated wire products

(P-6232)
ROBERT P MARTIN COMPANY
Also Called: Bob Martin Co
2209 Seaman Ave, South El Monte
(91733-2630)
PHONE.................................323 686-2220
Robert P Martin Jr, *CEO*
Naomi Martin, *President*
EMP: 14 EST: 1947
SQ FT: 14,000
SALES (est): 2MM **Privately Held**
WEB: www.bobmartinco.com
SIC: 3315 3357 Wire & fabricated wire
products; nonferrous wiredrawing & insu-
lating

(P-6233)
SAFELAND INDUSTRIAL SUPPLY INC (PA)
8949 9th St Ste 130, Rancho Cucamonga
(91730-4470)
PHONE.................................909 786-1967
Lijun Zhang, *President*
▲ EMP: 43 EST: 2006
SALES (est): 2.9MM **Privately Held**
WEB: www.safelandindustrial.com
SIC: 3315 3312 Steel wire & related prod-
ucts; stainless steel

(P-6234)
SOUTH BAY WIRE & CABLE CO LLC ✪
54125 Maranatha Dr, Idyllwild (92549)
PHONE.................................951 659-2183
Richard Martin Jr,
EMP: 78 EST: 2021
SALES (est): 2.2MM **Privately Held**
SIC: 3315 Wire & fabricated wire products

(P-6235)
SWAN FENCE INCORPORATED
600 W Manville St, Compton (90220-5508)
PHONE.................................310 669-8000
Shigehiro Hatake, *President*
Jun Ando, *Admin Sec*
EMP: 25 EST: 1988
SQ FT: 50,000
SALES (est): 7.8MM **Privately Held**
WEB: www.swanfence.com
SIC: 5211 3315 Fencing; fence gates
posts & fittings: steel
PA: Koiwa Kanaami Co., Ltd.
3-20-14, Nishiasakusa
Taito-Ku TKY 111-0

(P-6236)
TREE ISLAND WIRE (USA) INC (DH)
Also Called: TI Wire
3880 Valley Blvd, Walnut (91789-1515)
P.O. Box 90100, San Bernardino (92427-
1100)
PHONE.................................909 594-7511
Amar S Doman, *Ch of Bd*
Dale R Maclean, *CEO*
Nancy Davies, *CFO*
Stephen Ogden, *Vice Pres*
▲ EMP: 250 EST: 1980
SALES (est): 59.3MM
SALES (corp-wide): 164.8MM **Privately Held**
WEB: www.treeisland.com
SIC: 3315 Steel wire & related products
HQ: Tree Island Industries Ltd
3933 Boundary Rd
Richmond BC V6V 1
604 524-3744

(P-6237)
TREE ISLAND WIRE (USA) INC
Industrial Alloys
13470 Philadelphia Ave, Fontana
(92337-7700)
PHONE.................................909 594-7511
Rebecca Kalis, *Branch Mgr*
EMP: 146
SALES (corp-wide): 164.8MM **Privately Held**
WEB: www.treeisland.com
SIC: 3315 Wire, steel: insulated or ar-
mored

HQ: Tree Island Wire (Usa), Inc.
3880 Valley Blvd
Walnut CA 91789

(P-6238)
TREE ISLAND WIRE (USA) INC
K-Lath
3880 W Valley Blvd, Pomona (91769)
PHONE.................................909 595-6617
Ken Stufford, *Manager*
EMP: 146
SALES (corp-wide): 164.8MM **Privately Held**
WEB: www.treeisland.com
SIC: 3315 Wire, steel: insulated or ar-
mored
HQ: Tree Island Wire (Usa), Inc.
3880 Valley Blvd
Walnut CA 91789

(P-6239)
US HANGER COMPANY LLC
17501 S Denver Ave, Gardena
(90248-3410)
PHONE.................................310 323-8030
Gene Livshin, *Mng Member*
▲ EMP: 47 EST: 2008
SALES (est): 3.6MM **Privately Held**
SIC: 3315 5199 Hangers (garment), wire;
clothes hangers

(P-6240)
WAVENET INC (PA)
707 E Sepulveda Blvd, Carson
(90745-6032)
PHONE.................................310 885-4200
Ylhong Jang, *President*
Kevin Chang, *COO*
Young Moon, *Accounting Mgr*
Sam Hen, *Manager*
Andre Jones, *Accounts Mgr*
▲ EMP: 18 EST: 1990
SQ FT: 29,000
SALES (est): 3MM **Privately Held**
WEB: www.wavenetcable.com
SIC: 3315 Wire & fabricated wire products

(P-6241)
WIRETECH INC (PA)
6440 Canning St, Commerce (90040-3122)
PHONE.................................323 722-4933
William Hillpot, *President*
Garry Goodson, *Exec VP*
Irene I Sanchez, *Controller*
Jorge Balderas, *Sales Staff*
Elio Estrada, *Sales Staff*
▲ EMP: 87 EST: 2001
SALES (est): 22.2MM **Privately Held**
WEB: www.wiretechincorporated.word-
press.com
SIC: 3315 Steel wire & related products

3316 Cold Rolled Steel Sheet, Strip & Bars

(P-6242)
CALSTRIP INDUSTRIES INC (PA)
3030 Dulles Dr, Jurupa Valley
(91752-3240)
PHONE.................................323 726-1345
Thomas B Nelis, *Chairman*
Jon Nelis, *CEO*
Crystal Velasquez, *Admin Asst*
EMP: 40 EST: 1939
SQ FT: 135,000
SALES (est): 160MM **Privately Held**
WEB: www.calstripsteel.com
SIC: 3316 Strip steel, cold-rolled: from pur-
chased hot-rolled

(P-6243)
KIP STEEL INC
1650 Valley Ln, Fullerton (92833-1718)
PHONE.................................714 461-1051
EMP: 25
SALES (corp-wide): 635.8K **Privately Held**
WEB: www.kipsteel.com
SIC: 3316 Cold finishing of steel shapes

PRODUCTS & SVCS

PA: Kip Steel, Inc.
21314 Twisted Willow Ln
Katy TX 77450
714 461-1051

(P-6244)
REMINGTON ROLL FORMING INC
2445 Chico Ave, El Monte (91733-1612)
P.O. Box 9325 (91733-0979)
PHONE...................626 350-5196
Thomas Henry, *President*
EMP: 25 **EST:** 1987
SQ FT: 25,000
SALES (est): 2MM **Privately Held**
SIC: 3316 Cold finishing of steel shapes

3317 Steel Pipe & Tubes

(P-6245)
CHARMAN MANUFACTURING INC
5681 S Downey Rd, Vernon (90058-3719)
PHONE...................213 489-7000
Shahab Namvar, *President*
Shawn Namvar, *President*
Ezra Namvar, *Vice Pres*
David Namvar, *Purchasing*
▲ **EMP:** 16 **EST:** 2006
SALES (est): 6.9MM **Privately Held**
WEB: www.charmaninc.com
SIC: 3317 Steel pipe & tubes

(P-6246)
CONTECH ENGNERED SOLUTIONS INC
950 S Coast Dr Ste 145, Costa Mesa
(92626-7833)
PHONE...................714 281-7883
EMP: 89
SALES (corp-wide): 119.2MM **Privately Held**
WEB: www.conteches.com
SIC: 3317 Steel pipe & tubes
PA: Contech Engineered Solutions Inc.
9025 Ctr Pinte Dr Ste 400
West Chester OH 45069
513 645-7000

(P-6247)
CRITERION AUTOMATION INC
1722 Production Cir, Riverside
(92509-1717)
PHONE...................951 683-2400
Chris Carda, *President*
Brad Laeger, *Vice Pres*
EMP: 13 **EST:** 2006
SALES (est): 3.2MM **Privately Held**
WEB: www.criterionautomation.com
SIC: 3317 5719 Steel pipe & tubes; metalware

(P-6248)
HANNIBAL INDUSTRIES INC (HQ)
3851 S Santa Fe Ave, Vernon
(90058-1712)
PHONE...................323 513-1200
Blanton Bartlett, *President*
Eric Andres, *CFO*
Wai Joe, *CFO*
Heidy Moon, *CFO*
Reed Reynolds, *Officer*
◆ **EMP:** 180 **EST:** 1985
SQ FT: 285,000
SALES (est): 140.6MM
SALES (corp-wide): 20.1B **Publicly Held**
WEB: www.hannibalindustries.com
SIC: 3317 Tubes, seamless steel
PA: Nucor Corporation
1915 Rexford Rd Ste 400
Charlotte NC 28211
704 366-7000

(P-6249)
IMPERIAL PIPE SERVICES LLC
12375 Brown Ave, Riverside (92509-1868)
PHONE...................951 682-3307
Leonard Shapiro,
Bob Raber,
Steve Teller,
Albert Chico, *Manager*
Mike Mayes, *Manager*
EMP: 21 **EST:** 2002

SALES (est): 11.9MM
SALES (corp-wide): 98.4MM **Privately Held**
WEB: www.imperialpipe.com
SIC: 3317 Steel pipe & tubes
PA: Shapco Inc.
1666 20th St Ste 100
Santa Monica CA 90404
310 264-1666

(P-6250)
MARUICHI AMERICAN CORPORATION
11529 Greenstone Ave, Santa Fe Springs
(90670-4622)
PHONE...................562 903-8600
Wataru Morita, *President*
Teruo Horikawa, *Ch of Bd*
Takuhiro Ishihara, *CFO*
Tak Ishihara, *Exec VP*
Makoto Ishikawa, *Vice Pres*
▲ **EMP:** 96 **EST:** 1978
SQ FT: 240,000
SALES (est): 21.9MM **Privately Held**
WEB: www.macsfs.com
SIC: 3317 Pipes, seamless steel
PA: Maruichi Steel Tube Ltd.
5-1-60, Namba, Chuo-Ku
Osaka OSK 542-0

(P-6251)
PRIMUS PIPE AND TUBE INC (DH)
5855 Obispo Ave, Long Beach
(90805-3715)
PHONE...................562 808-8000
Tommy Grahn, *President*
Scott Templeton, *Exec VP*
Karl Almond, *Vice Pres*
Domenick Di Giallonardo, *Vice Pres*
Roy Harrison, *Vice Pres*
▲ **EMP:** 35 **EST:** 1967
SQ FT: 120,000
SALES (est): 50.4MM **Privately Held**
WEB: www.tachen.com
SIC: 3317 Steel pipe & tubes
HQ: Ta Chen International, Inc.
5855 Obispo Ave
Long Beach CA 90805
562 808-8000

(P-6252)
ROSCOE MOSS MANUFACTURING CO (PA)
Also Called: Roscoe Moss Company
4360 Worth St, Los Angeles (90063-2536)
P.O. Box 31064 (90031-0064)
PHONE...................323 261-4185
Roscoe Moss Jr, *Ch of Bd*
Robert A Vanvaler, *President*
Tony Creque, *CFO*
Luis Ramirez, *CFO*
George E Moss, *Vice Ch Bd*
◆ **EMP:** 90 **EST:** 1913
SQ FT: 20,000
SALES (est): 35.3MM **Privately Held**
WEB: www.roscoemoss.com
SIC: 3317 Well casing, wrought: welded,
lock joint or heavy riveted; tubes,
wrought: welded or lock joint

(P-6253)
SUPERIOR TECH INC
Also Called: Superior Technologies
13850 Benson Ave, Chino (91710-7005)
PHONE...................909 364-2300
Peter Chifo, *Principal*
Allen Roe, *Opers Staff*
EMP: 13 **EST:** 2007
SALES (est): 1.9MM **Privately Held**
WEB: www.superior-tech.net
SIC: 3317 Tubes, wrought: welded or lock joint

(P-6254)
TUBE ONE INDUSTRIES INC
4055 Garner Rd, Riverside (92501-1043)
PHONE...................951 300-2998
Kimber Liu, *CEO*
Susan Liu, *Vice Pres*
Richard Liu, *Regl Sales Mgr*
Patrick Liu, *Manager*
▲ **EMP:** 15 **EST:** 1991
SQ FT: 46,000

SALES (est): 3.4MM **Privately Held**
WEB: www.tubeone.us
SIC: 3317 Steel pipe & tubes

(P-6255)
VEST INC
6023 Alcoa Ave, Vernon (90058-3954)
P.O. Box 58827, Los Angeles (90058-0827)
PHONE...................800 421-6370
Yoshiki Murakami, *President*
Sean McCaughan, *President*
Iwaki Sugimoto, *President*
Hideki Matsumoto, *CFO*
Kaz Sawai, *General Mgr*
▲ **EMP:** 77 **EST:** 1970
SQ FT: 312,000
SALES (est): 23.1MM **Privately Held**
WEB: www.vestinc.com
SIC: 3317 3547 Tubes, wrought: welded
or lock joint; rolling mill machinery
HQ: Shoji Jfe America Holdings Inc
301 E Ocean Blvd Ste 1750
Long Beach CA 90802
562 637-3500

3321 Gray Iron Foundries

(P-6256)
ALHAMBRA FOUNDRY COMPANY LTD
Also Called: Afco
1147 S Meridian Ave, Alhambra
(91803-1218)
P.O. Box 469 (91802-0469)
PHONE...................626 289-4294
Arzhang Baghkhanian, *CEO*
James Wright, *Vice Pres*
Mike Smalski, *General Mgr*
Sam Wong, *Safety Mgr*
▲ **EMP:** 46 **EST:** 1984
SQ FT: 48,370
SALES (est): 10MM **Privately Held**
WEB: www.alhambrafoundry.com
SIC: 3321 3312 5051 Gray iron castings;
structural shapes & pilings, steel; iron &
steel (ferrous) products

(P-6257)
FOX HILLS INDUSTRIES
5831 Research Dr, Huntington Beach
(92649-1385)
PHONE...................714 893-1940
John Burk, *President*
Doug Reichard, *President*
Raj Mittal, *Vice Pres*
Frank Reilly, *Vice Pres*
▲ **EMP:** 42 **EST:** 1947
SQ FT: 20,000
SALES (est): 4MM **Privately Held**
WEB: www.onesourcecc.com
SIC: 3321 3366 3365 3322 Ductile iron
castings; castings (except die): brass; alu-
minum foundries; malleable iron foundries

(P-6258)
GLOBE IRON FOUNDRY INC
5649 Randolph St, Commerce
(90040-3489)
PHONE...................323 723-8983
John M Pratto, *President*
Othon Garcia, *Officer*
Jeff Pratto, *Vice Pres*
John Pratto Jr, *Vice Pres*
EMP: 70 **EST:** 1929
SQ FT: 58,000
SALES (est): 10.7MM **Privately Held**
WEB: www.globeiron.com
SIC: 3321 3543 3369 Gray iron castings;
ductile iron castings; industrial patterns;
nonferrous foundries

(P-6259)
JDH PACIFIC INC (PA)
14821 Artesia Blvd, La Mirada
(90638-6006)
PHONE...................562 926-8088
Donald Hu, *President*
Jon Elgas, *Opers Mgr*
Jerry Higgs, *Sr Project Mgr*
Daniel Evans, *Director*
Sophia Shen, *Supervisor*
▲ **EMP:** 30 **EST:** 1989
SQ FT: 103,000

SALES (est): 30.1MM **Privately Held**
WEB: www.jdhpacific.com
SIC: 3321 3324 3599 3462 Gray iron
castings; commercial investment castings, ferrous; crankshafts & camshafts,
machining; iron & steel forgings; machinery forgings, ferrous

(P-6260)
THOMPSON GUNDRILLING INC
13840 Saticoy St, Van Nuys (91402-6582)
PHONE...................323 873-4045
Michael Thompson, *President*
Virginia Ramsey, *CFO*
Robert Thompson, *Director*
EMP: 39 **EST:** 1973
SQ FT: 32,000
SALES (est): 5.3MM **Privately Held**
WEB: www.thompsongundrilling.com
SIC: 3321 Gray & ductile iron foundries

3322 Malleable Iron Foundries

(P-6261)
COVERT IRON WORKS
7821 Otis S Ave, Huntington Park (90255)
PHONE...................323 560-2792
Fax: 323 560-8351
EMP: 19 **EST:** 1923
SQ FT: 20,000
SALES (est): 2.2MM **Privately Held**
WEB: www.covertironworks.com
SIC: 3322 3321 Malleable iron Foundry
Gray/Ductile Iron Foundry

(P-6262)
STEVEN HANDELMAN STUDIOS (PA)
Also Called: Handelman, Steven Studios
716 N Milpas St, Santa Barbara
(93103-3029)
PHONE...................805 884-9070
Steven Handelman, *Owner*
EMP: 41 **EST:** 1973
SALES (est): 5.3MM **Privately Held**
WEB: www.stevenhandelmanstudios.com
SIC: 3322 Malleable iron foundries

3324 Steel Investment Foundries

(P-6263)
CAST PARTS INC (DH)
Also Called: Cpp-Pomona
4200 Valley Blvd, Walnut (91789-1408)
PHONE...................909 595-2252
Steve Clodfelter, *President*
Ali Ghavami, *COO*
EMP: 185 **EST:** 2000
SQ FT: 300,000
SALES (est): 53.5MM
SALES (corp-wide): 789.9MM **Privately Held**
WEB: www.cppcorp.com
SIC: 3324 3365 Steel investment
foundries; aluminum foundries
HQ: Consolidated Precision Products Corp.
1621 Euclid Ave Ste 1850
Cleveland OH 44115
216 453-4800

(P-6264)
CAST PARTS INC
Also Called: Cpp-City of Industry
16800 Chestnut St, City of Industry
(91748-1017)
PHONE...................626 937-3444
David Atwood, *Branch Mgr*
John Grace, *Engineer*
EMP: 160
SALES (corp-wide): 789.9MM **Privately Held**
WEB: www.cppcorp.com
SIC: 3324 Aerospace investment castings,
ferrous
HQ: Cast Parts, Inc.
4200 Valley Blvd
Walnut CA 91789
909 595-2252

(P-6265)
CFI HOLDINGS CORP
Also Called: Consolidated Foundries
4200 Valley Blvd, Pomona (91765)
PHONE..................................909 595-2252
Debbie Comstock, *Principal*
EMP: 63 EST: 1979
SALES (est): 240.1K **Privately Held**
WEB: www.cppcorp.com
SIC: 3324 3365 Steel investment
foundries; aluminum foundries

(P-6266)
HOWMET CORPORATION
900 E Watson Center Rd, Carson
(90745-4201)
PHONE..................................310 847-8152
EMP: 126
SALES (corp-wide): 5.2B **Publicly Held**
WEB: www.theplayhouseatwhitelake.org
SIC: 3324 Commercial investment cast-
ings, ferrous
HQ: Howmet Corporation
1 Misco Dr
Whitehall MI 49461
231 894-5686

(P-6267)
**HOWMET GLOBL FSTNING
SYSTEMS I**
Rosan / Eagle Products
800 S State College Blvd, Fullerton
(92831-5334)
PHONE..................................714 871-1550
Craig Brown, *Manager*
EMP: 100
SALES (corp-wide): 5.2B **Publicly Held**
SIC: 3324 3365 Aerospace investment
castings, ferrous; aerospace castings,
aluminum
HQ: Howmet Global Fastening Systems
Inc.
3990a Heritage Oak Ct
Simi Valley CA 93063
805 426-2270

(P-6268)
**LISI AEROSPACE NORTH AMER
INC**
2600 Skypark Dr, Torrance (90505-5314)
PHONE..................................310 326-8110
Christian Darville, *CEO*
Maria Cruz, *Technology*
◆ EMP: 900 EST: 2009
SALES (est): 90.4MM
SALES (corp-wide): 177.9K **Privately
Held**
WEB: www.lisi-aerospace.com
SIC: 3324 Aerospace investment castings,
ferrous
HQ: Hi-Shear Corporation
2600 Skypark Dr
Torrance CA 90505
310 784-4025

(P-6269)
MCDANIEL INC
10807 Monte Vista Ave, Montclair
(91763-6113)
PHONE..................................909 591-8353
Timothy McDaniel, *President*
Shelly McDaniel, *Vice Pres*
EMP: 16
SALES (est): 4.3MM **Privately Held**
WEB: www.mcdanielinc.net
SIC: 3324 Steel investment foundries

(P-6270)
MILLER CASTINGS INC (PA)
2503 Pacific Park Dr, Whittier
(90601-1680)
PHONE..................................562 695-0461
Ralph Miller, *President*
Hadi Khandehroo, *CEO*
Dwight Macbain, *Vice Pres*
Christina Pacheco, *Administration*
Adrian Zuniga, *Administration*
▲ EMP: 330 EST: 1973
SQ FT: 40,000
SALES (est): 39.4MM **Privately Held**
WEB: www.millercastings.com
SIC: 3324 Steel investment foundries

(P-6271)
NET SHAPES INC
1336 E Francis St Ste B, Ontario
(91761-5723)
PHONE..................................909 947-3231
Joseph S Cannone, *President*
Patty Holguin, *Production*
Sonja Norvaez, *Sales Executive*
Sonia Narvaez, *Sales Staff*
Cordy Champan, *Director*
EMP: 120 EST: 1986
SQ FT: 43,500
SALES (est): 24.2MM **Privately Held**
WEB: www.netshapes.com
SIC: 3324 Steel investment foundries

(P-6272)
PAC FOUNDRY INC
8333 Wilcox Ave, Cudahy (90201-5919)
PHONE..................................323 773-2363
Steve Gallardo, *Plant Mgr*
EMP: 14 EST: 2015
SALES (est): 2.3MM **Privately Held**
WEB: www.cppcorp.com
SIC: 3324 Steel investment foundries

(P-6273)
PAC-RANCHO INC (DH)
11000 Jersey Blvd, Rancho Cucamonga
(91730-5103)
PHONE..................................909 987-4721
Steve Clodfelter, *President*
Ali Ghavami, *Vice Pres*
EMP: 180 EST: 1984
SQ FT: 55,000
SALES (est): 44.3MM
SALES (corp-wide): 789.9MM **Privately
Held**
WEB: www.cppcorp.com
SIC: 3324 3354 3369 Commercial invest-
ment castings, ferrous; aluminum ex-
truded products; nonferrous foundries
HQ: Consolidated Precision Products Corp.
1621 Euclid Ave Ste 1850
Cleveland OH 44115
216 453-4800

(P-6274)
**SIERRA TECHNICAL SERVICES
INC**
Also Called: STS
101 Commercial Way Unit D, Tehachapi
(93561-1427)
PHONE..................................661 823-1092
Roger Hayes, *President*
Debra Hayes, *Vice Pres*
Barbara Davidson, *Planning*
Walter Byers, *Engineer*
Kevin O 'brien, *Business Mgr*
EMP: 15 EST: 2006
SQ FT: 7,000
SALES (est): 1.8MM **Privately Held**
WEB: www.sierratechnicalservices.com
SIC: 3324 8711 Aerospace investment
castings, ferrous; engineering services

3325 Steel Foundries, NEC

(P-6275)
**DAMERON ALLOY FOUNDRIES
(PA)**
6330 Gateway Dr Ste B, Cypress
(90630-4836)
PHONE..................................310 631-5165
John W Dameron, *President*
Augustin Huerta, *Exec VP*
Joseph De Julio, *Vice Pres*
Christina Dameron, *Admin Mgr*
Kevin Burkhart, *Senior Engr*
▲ EMP: 100 EST: 1946
SQ FT: 5,000
SALES (est): 20.5MM **Privately Held**
WEB: www.dameron.net
SIC: 3325 3324 Steel foundries; commer-
cial investment castings, ferrous

(P-6276)
ENER-TECH METALS INC
7815 Somerset Blvd, Paramount
(90723-4212)
P.O. Box 137 (90723-0137)
PHONE..................................562 529-5034
Franklin Dees, *CEO*
Larry Boren, *Principal*

Randall Dees, *Principal*
Paz Gualvez, *Principal*
David C Brayton, *General Mgr*
EMP: 67 EST: 1986
SQ FT: 120,000
SALES (est): 6.6MM **Privately Held**
SIC: 3325 Alloy steel castings, except in-
vestment

(P-6277)
METAL CAST INC
Also Called: Metalcast
2002 W Chestnut Ave, Santa Ana
(92703-4341)
P.O. Box 3099 (92703-0099)
PHONE..................................714 285-9792
Rigoberto Urquiza, *President*
EMP: 30 EST: 1999
SQ FT: 12,000
SALES (est): 2.6MM **Privately Held**
WEB: www.metalcast.com
SIC: 3325 Alloy steel castings, except in-
vestment

(P-6278)
**WEST COAST FOUNDRY LLC
(HQ)**
2450 E 53rd St, Huntington Park (90255)
PHONE..................................323 583-1421
Michael Bargani, *President*
John Heine, *CFO*
Toni Banuelos, *Manager*
▲ EMP: 20 EST: 1972
SQ FT: 18,000
SALES (est): 10.6MM
SALES (corp-wide): 179.2MM **Privately
Held**
WEB: www.westcoastfoundry.com
SIC: 3325 Alloy steel castings, except in-
vestment
PA: Speyside Equity Fund I Lp
430 E 86th St
New York NY 10028
212 994-0308

(P-6279)
**WEST COAST STEEL & PROC
LLC (PA)**
Also Called: Steelco USA
3534 Philadelphia St, Chino (91710-2088)
PHONE..................................909 393-8405
Erik Gamm,
Jim Patel, *Controller*
Farris Eramya, *Sales Mgr*
EMP: 193 EST: 2006
SALES (est): 40.3MM **Privately Held**
WEB: www.steelcousa.com
SIC: 3325 Steel foundries

3334 Primary Production Of
Aluminum

(P-6280)
**ADVANCED PATTERN & MOLD
INC**
1720 S Balboa Ave, Ontario (91761-7773)
PHONE..................................909 930-3444
Dan Hilger, *Partner*
Chris Vanderhagen, *Partner*
EMP: 15 EST: 1996
SQ FT: 10,400
SALES (est): 2.2MM **Privately Held**
SIC: 3334 Primary aluminum

(P-6281)
HOWMET AEROSPACE INC
3016 Lomita Blvd, Torrance (90505-5103)
PHONE..................................212 836-2674
Daniel Oawster, *Business Anlyst*
Michael Zion, *Controller*
Izzy Blanco, *Production*
Ramon Garcia, *Manager*
John Golonka, *Manager*
EMP: 356
SALES (corp-wide): 5.2B **Publicly Held**
WEB: www.howmet.com
SIC: 3334 Primary aluminum
PA: Howmet Aerospace Inc.
201 Isabella St Ste 200
Pittsburgh PA 15212
412 553-1950

(P-6282)
INOVATIV INC
1500 W Mckinley St, Azusa (91702-3218)
PHONE..................................626 969-5300
Patrick Blewett, *CEO*
Tracy Barbosa, *Office Mgr*
Darren Yokota, *Manager*
EMP: 40 EST: 2013
SALES (est): 6.2MM **Privately Held**
WEB: www.inovativ.com
SIC: 3334 Primary aluminum

(P-6283)
**KAISER ALUMINUM
CORPORATION (PA)**
27422 Portola Pkwy # 350, Foothill Ranch
(92610-2837)
PHONE..................................949 614-1740
Keith Harvey, *President*
Janice Coburn, *COO*
Lauralee Martin, *Bd of Directors*
Alfred Osborne, *Bd of Directors*
Neal West, *Officer*
▼ EMP: 60 EST: 1946
SQ FT: 36,000
SALES (est): 1.1B **Publicly Held**
WEB: www.kaseraluminum.com
SIC: 3334 3353 3354 3355 Primary alu-
minum; aluminum sheet, plate & foil; alu-
minum rod & bar; bars, extruded,
aluminum; rods, extruded, aluminum;
wire, aluminum: made in rolling mills;
cable, aluminum: made in rolling mills

(P-6284)
**MAURICE & MAURICE ENGRG
INC**
17579 Mesa St Ste B4, Hesperia
(92345-8308)
P.O. Box 403682 (92340-3682)
PHONE..................................760 949-5151
Jennifer Thomas, *CEO*
Aron Maurice, *Treasurer*
Jennifer Maurice, *Admin Sec*
EMP: 27 EST: 1973
SQ FT: 22,000
SALES (est): 2MM **Privately Held**
SIC: 3334 Primary aluminum

3339 Primary Nonferrous
Metals, NEC

(P-6285)
**COMMODITY RESOURCE
ENVMTL INC**
Also Called: Commodity Rsource Enviromen-
tal
11847 United St, Mojave (93501-7047)
PHONE..................................661 824-2416
Mike Kelsey, *General Mgr*
Don Buckles, *Vice Pres*
Amy Consul, *Manager*
Chuck Yohn, *Manager*
EMP: 40
SALES (corp-wide): 20MM **Privately
Held**
WEB: www.creweb.com
SIC: 3339 3341 Precious metals; second-
ary nonferrous metals
PA: Commodity Resource & Environmental,
Inc.
116 E Prospect Ave
Burbank CA 91502
818 843-2811

(P-6286)
PCC ROLLMET INC
1822 Deere Ave, Irvine (92606-4817)
PHONE..................................949 221-5333
Ken Buck, *President*
Mark Donegan, *Ch of Bd*
Shawn Hagel, *CFO*
EMI Donis, *Vice Pres*
EMP: 70 EST: 2011
SALES (est): 22.3MM
SALES (corp-wide): 245.5B **Publicly
Held**
WEB: www.rollmetusa.com
SIC: 3339 Nickel refining (primary)
HQ: Precision Castparts Corp.
4650 Sw Mcdam Ave Ste 300
Portland OR 97239
503 946-4800

(P-6287)
RBC LUBRON BEARING SYSTEMS INC (HQ)
13141 Molette St, Santa Fe Springs
(90670-5523)
PHONE.................714 841-3007
Robert James Jr, *Sales Staff*
Brenda Leonard, *Info Tech Mgr*
EMP: 18 **EST:** 2009
SALES (est): 2.9MM
SALES (corp-wide): 608.9MM **Publicly Held**
WEB: www.rbclubron.com
SIC: 3339 Antifriction bearing metals, lead-base
PA: Rbc Bearings Incorporated
102 Willenbrock Rd Bldg B
Oxford CT 06478
203 267-7001

(P-6288)
WESTERN MESQUITE MINES INC
6502 E Us Highway 78, Brawley
(92227-9306)
PHONE.................928 341-4653
Randall Oliphant, *Chairman*
Cory Atiyeh, *President*
Robert Gallagher, *CEO*
W Hanson P Geo, *Vice Pres*
Penny Brian, *Admin Sec*
EMP: 20 **EST:** 1985
SALES (est): 14MM
SALES (corp-wide): 842.5MM **Privately Held**
WEB: www.equinoxgold.com
SIC: 3339 Gold refining (primary)
PA: Equinox Gold Corp
700 West Pender St Suite 1501
Vancouver BC V6C 1
604 558-0560

3341 Secondary Smelting & Refining Of Nonferrous Metals

(P-6289)
A D S GOLD INC
3843 E Eagle Dr, Anaheim (92807-1705)
PHONE.................714 632-1888
Patrick Joe Lopez, *CEO*
EMP: 14 **EST:** 1983
SQ FT: 8,600
SALES (est): 3.9MM **Privately Held**
WEB: www.adsgold.com
SIC: 3341 Secondary nonferrous metals

(P-6290)
CUSTOM ALLOY SALES INC (PA)
Also Called: Custom Alloy Light Metals
13181 Crssrads Pkwy N Ste, City of Industry (91746)
PHONE.................626 369-3641
Brandon Cox, *CEO*
Tim Chisum, *CFO*
Kenneth J Cox, *Chairman*
Nicholas Drakos, *Vice Pres*
Brett Jordan, *Vice Pres*
◆ **EMP:** 15 **EST:** 1969
SALES (est): 30.1MM **Privately Held**
WEB: www.customalloysales.com
SIC: 3341 5051 Aluminum smelting & refining (secondary); zinc

(P-6291)
DAVID H FELL & CO INC (PA)
6009 Bandini Blvd, Los Angeles
(90040-2967)
PHONE.................323 722-9992
Larry Fell, *CEO*
Lawrence Fell, *President*
Sondra Fell, *Treasurer*
Amanda Rudman, *Executive Asst*
Janet Itterly, *Regl Sales Mgr*
▼ **EMP:** 24 **EST:** 1973
SQ FT: 18,000
SALES (est): 14.7MM **Privately Held**
WEB: www.dhfco.com
SIC: 3341 5094 Secondary precious metals; bullion, precious metals

(P-6292)
ESPERER HOLDINGS INC (PA)
3820 State St, Santa Barbara
(93105-3182)
PHONE.................805 880-4220
D Stephen Sorensen, *CEO*
RI Chung, *Executive Asst*
Ian Kindberg, *Controller*
EMP: 17 **EST:** 2011
SALES (est): 7.2MM **Privately Held**
WEB: www.espererholdings.com
SIC: 3341 3911 Secondary precious metals; jewelry, precious metal

(P-6293)
GEMINI INDUSTRIES INC
2311 Pullman St, Santa Ana (92705-5585)
PHONE.................949 250-4011
M Elguindy, *CEO*
Melinda Munoz, *CFO*
McGee Rick, *CFO*
Munib Razzaq, *Vice Pres*
Diana Keiffer, *Admin Sec*
▲ **EMP:** 75
SQ FT: 150,000
SALES (est): 16.4MM **Privately Held**
WEB: www.gemini-catalyst.com
SIC: 3341 Secondary precious metals; platinum group metals, smelting & refining (secondary)

(P-6294)
HERAEUS PRCOUS MTLS N AMER LLC (DH)
15524 Carmenita Rd, Santa Fe Springs
(90670-5610)
PHONE.................562 921-7464
Roland Gerner, *Mng Member*
Todd England, *Engineer*
Franklin Soto, *Opers Mgr*
Diniz Cordeiro, *Prdtn Mgr*
Denise Diaz, *Production*
▲ **EMP:** 200 **EST:** 1970
SQ FT: 71,000
SALES (est): 138.3MM
SALES (corp-wide): 355.8K **Privately Held**
WEB: www.heraeus.com
SIC: 3341 2899 Gold smelting & refining (secondary); silver smelting & refining (secondary); platinum group metals, smelting & refining (secondary); chemical preparations; salt
HQ: Heraeus Holding Gesellschaft Mit Beschrankter Haftung
Heraeusstr. 12-14
Hanau HE 63450
618 135-0

(P-6295)
ON-GARD METALS INC
8638 Cleta St, Downey (90241-5201)
PHONE.................562 622-9057
Dick Gard, *President*
EMP: 13 **EST:** 1989
SQ FT: 6,000
SALES (est): 716.4K **Privately Held**
SIC: 3341 Aluminum smelting & refining (secondary)

(P-6296)
THOROCK METALS INC
1213 S Pacific Coast Hwy, Redondo Beach
(90277-4905)
PHONE.................310 537-1597
Holly Kadota, *President*
Holly M Kadota, *President*
Craig Mock, *CFO*
Jeff Mock, *Exec VP*
EMP: 26 **EST:** 1968
SQ FT: 50,000
SALES (est): 1.2MM **Privately Held**
WEB: www.thorockmetals.com
SIC: 3341 Aluminum smelting & refining (secondary)

(P-6297)
TST INC (PA)
Also Called: Alpase
13428 Benson Ave, Chino (91710-5258)
PHONE.................951 685-2155
Andrew G Stein, *CEO*
Robert A Stein, *Ch of Bd*
James Davidson, *CFO*
Greg Levine, *Vice Pres*
Maria Vasquez, *Manager*
◆ **EMP:** 260 **EST:** 1961
SQ FT: 123,000
SALES (est): 58.1MM **Privately Held**
WEB: www.tst-inc.com
SIC: 3341 5093 Aluminum smelting & refining (secondary); metal scrap & waste materials

3351 Rolling, Drawing & Extruding Of Copper

(P-6298)
C F W RESEARCH & DEV CO
Also Called: Cfw Precision Metal Components
338 S 4th St, Grover Beach (93433-1999)
P.O. Box 446 (93483-0446)
PHONE.................805 489-8750
Michael A Greenelsh, *President*
Kathryn Greenelsh, *Corp Secy*
Harlan Silva, *Vice Pres*
EMP: 16 **EST:** 1976
SQ FT: 10,000
SALES (est): 5MM
SALES (corp-wide): 11MM **Privately Held**
WEB: www.cfwpmc.com
SIC: 3351 Wire, copper & copper alloy
PA: California Fine Wire Co.
338 S 4th St
Grover Beach CA 93433
805 489-5144

3353 Aluminum Sheet, Plate & Foil

(P-6299)
HOWMET AEROSPACE INC
1550 Gage Rd, Montebello (90640-6614)
PHONE.................323 728-3901
Greg Walker, *Manager*
EMP: 135
SALES (corp-wide): 5.2B **Publicly Held**
WEB: www.howmet.com
SIC: 3353 Aluminum sheet & strip
PA: Howmet Aerospace Inc.
201 Isabella St Ste 200
Pittsburgh PA 15212
412 553-1950

(P-6300)
KAISER ALUMINUM FAB PDTS LLC (HQ)
Also Called: Kafp
27422 Portola Pkwy # 200, Foothill Ranch
(92610-2831)
PHONE.................949 614-1740
Jack A Hockema, *President*
Joseph P Bellino, *CFO*
Emily Liggett, *Bd of Directors*
John M Donnan, *Vice Pres*
Dave Rickman, *Vice Pres*
◆ **EMP:** 2200 **EST:** 2006
SALES (est): 984MM
SALES (corp-wide): 1.1B **Publicly Held**
WEB: www.kaiseraluminum.com
SIC: 3353 3334 3354 3355 Aluminum sheet, plate & foil; primary aluminum; aluminum rod & bar; wire, aluminum: made in rolling mills
PA: Kaiser Aluminum Corporation
27422 Portola Pkwy # 350
Foothill Ranch CA 92610
949 614-1740

(P-6301)
MATERIAL SCIENCES CORPORATION
Also Called: MSC-La
3730 Capitol Ave, City of Industry
(90601-1731)
PHONE.................562 699-4550
Patrick Murley, *CEO*
EMP: 45
SALES (corp-wide): 120.8MM **Privately Held**
WEB: www.materialsciencescorp.com
SIC: 3353 Aluminum sheet, plate & foil
PA: Material Sciences Corporation
6855 Commerce Blvd
Canton MI 48187
734 207-4444

(P-6302)
SOUTHWIRE INC
Also Called: Alflex
20250 S Alameda St, Compton
(90221-6207)
PHONE.................310 886-8300
Jorge Eulloqui, *Manager*
EMP: 500
SALES (corp-wide): 1.7B **Privately Held**
SIC: 3353 3644 3315 Coils, sheet aluminum; electric conduits & fittings; cable, steel: insulated or armored
HQ: Southwire Inc
11695 Pacific Ave
Fontana CA 92337
310 884-8500

(P-6303)
SOUTHWIRE INC (HQ)
Also Called: Electrical Products Division
11695 Pacific Ave, Fontana (92337-8225)
PHONE.................310 884-8500
Mark Kaminski, *COO*
John Wasz, *President*
Ron Williams, *Vice Pres*
Monique Renna, *Production*
Dwayne Johnson, *Manager*
EMP: 15 **EST:** 1984
SQ FT: 210,000
SALES (est): 92.5MM
SALES (corp-wide): 1.7B **Privately Held**
WEB: www.southwire.com
SIC: 3353 3644 3315 Coils, sheet aluminum; electric conduits & fittings; cable, steel: insulated or armored
PA: Southwire Company, Llc
1 Southwire Dr
Carrollton GA 30119
770 832-4242

3354 Aluminum Extruded Prdts

(P-6304)
BUILDIT ENGINEERING CO INC
3074 N Lima St, Burbank (91504-2012)
PHONE.................818 244-6666
Barry Alberts, *President*
Pat Alberts, *Treasurer*
Scott Alberts, *Vice Pres*
▲ **EMP:** 15 **EST:** 1973
SQ FT: 8,000
SALES (est): 1.8MM **Privately Held**
WEB: www.builditengineering.com
SIC: 3354 3312 8711 Aluminum extruded products; stainless steel; engineering services

(P-6305)
CENTURY AMERICAN ALUMINUM INC
1001 S Doubleday Ave, Ontario
(91761-1564)
PHONE.................909 390-2384
Trang Trong, *Principal*
▲ **EMP:** 20 **EST:** 2009
SALES (est): 687.6K **Privately Held**
SIC: 3354 Aluminum extruded products

(P-6306)
DARFIELD INDUSTRIES INC (PA)
4626 Sperry St, Los Angeles (90039-1018)
PHONE.................818 247-8350
Rosanne M Kusar, *Ch of Bd*
Jennifer K Hillman, *President*
Angelica K Clark, *Treasurer*
EMP: 14 **EST:** 1957
SQ FT: 64,980
SALES (est): 5.1MM **Privately Held**
WEB: www.sunvalleyextrusion.com
SIC: 3354 Aluminum extruded products

(P-6307)
FRY REGLET CORPORATION (PA)
14013 Marquardt Ave, Santa Fe Springs
(90670-5018)
P.O. Box 665, La Mirada (90637-0665)
PHONE.................800 237-9773
Stephen Reed, *CEO*
Avon M Hall, *President*
James Tuttle, *CFO*

Martha Alvarez, *Administration*
Richard Barnes, *CIO*
EMP: 75 **EST:** 1945
SQ FT: 20,000
SALES (est) 54MM **Privately Held**
WEB: www.fryreglet.com
SIC: 3354 Aluminum extruded products

(P-6308)
GEMINI ALUMINUM CORPORATION
3255 Pomona Blvd, Pomona (91768-3291)
P.O. Box 1462, Sandpoint ID (83864-0866)
PHONE..................................909 595-7403
Alan J Hardy, *President*
Healani Hardy, *Admin Sec*
EMP: 27 **EST:** 1976
SQ FT: 10,000
SALES (est): 3.1MM **Privately Held**
WEB: www.gemini-aluminum-corp.hub.biz
SIC: 3354 Aluminum rod & bar

(P-6309)
GLOBAL TRUSS AMERICA LLC
4295 Charter St, Vernon (90058-2520)
PHONE..................................323 415-6225
Charles Davies, *Mng Member*
Kenneth Kahn, *General Mgr*
Tony Gomez, *Sales Staff*
◆ **EMP:** 55 **EST:** 2004
SQ FT: 60,000
SALES (est): 16MM **Privately Held**
WEB: www.globaltruss.com
SIC: 3354 Aluminum extruded products

(P-6310)
HYDRO EXTRUSION USA LLC
18111 Railroad St, City of Industry (91748-1216)
PHONE..................................626 964-3411
Matt Zundel, *Sales Dir*
Brian Echavarria, *Manager*
EMP: 300
SALES (corp-wide): 16.1B **Privately Held**
SIC: 3354 Aluminum extruded products
HQ: Hydro Extrusion Usa, Llc
    6250 N River Rd Ste 5000
    Rosemont IL 60018

(P-6311)
LUXFER INC
1995 3rd St, Riverside (92507-3483)
PHONE..................................951 684-5110
Brian McGuire, *Manager*
Mark Trudgeon, *Vice Pres*
Graham Wardlow, *Managing Dir*
Matt Shufran, *General Mgr*
Deborah Simsen, *General Mgr*
EMP: 31
SALES (corp-wide): 378MM **Privately Held**
WEB: www.luxfercylinders.com
SIC: 3354 3728 Aluminum extruded products; aircraft parts & equipment
HQ: Luxfer Inc.
    3016 Kansas Ave Bldg 1
    Riverside CA 92507
    951 684-5110

(P-6312)
MERIT ALUMINUM INC (PA)
2480 Railroad St, Corona (92878-5418)
PHONE..................................951 735-1770
Michael Rapport, *CEO*
Evan Rapport, *Vice Pres*
Vincent Lee, *Human Res Mgr*
Daniel Salguero, *Manager*
▲ **EMP:** 179 **EST:** 1990
SQ FT: 58,000
SALES (est): 39.3MM **Privately Held**
WEB: www.meritaluminum.com
SIC: 3354 Aluminum extruded products

(P-6313)
NEAL FEAY COMPANY
Also Called: Troy Metal Products
133 S La Patera Ln, Goleta (93117-3291)
PHONE..................................805 967-4521
Neal C Rasmussen, *CEO*
N J Rasmussen, *Corp Secy*
Alex Rasmussen, *Vice Pres*
Jose Mendoza, *Design Engr*
Brad Babineaux, *Engineer*
EMP: 60 **EST:** 1944
SQ FT: 50,000

SALES (est): 10.5MM **Privately Held**
WEB: www.nealfeay.com
SIC: 3354 3469 Tube, extruded or drawn, aluminum; electronic enclosures, stamped or pressed metal

(P-6314)
PARAMOUNT EXTRUSIONS COMPANY (PA)
6833 Rosecrans Ave, Paramount (90723-3152)
P.O. Box 847 (90723-0847)
PHONE..................................562 634-3291
Charles E Munson, *CEO*
Leslie C Munson, *President*
Frank Fry, *Vice Pres*
Gary Munson, *Admin Sec*
Mike Thrush, *Sales Mgr*
▲ **EMP:** 29 **EST:** 1963
SQ FT: 2,000
SALES (est): 8.5MM **Privately Held**
WEB: www.paramountextrusions.com
SIC: 3354 3312 Aluminum extruded products; blast furnaces & steel mills

(P-6315)
PRL ALUMINUM INC
14760 Don Julian Rd, City of Industry (91746-3107)
PHONE..................................626 968-7507
Roberto Landeros, *CEO*
Aamer Javaid, *Info Tech Dir*
John Triviso, *Sales Associate*
Eva Alcala, *Sales Staff*
David Olague, *Sales Staff*
EMP: 100 **EST:** 2004
SALES (est): 17.5MM **Privately Held**
WEB: www.prlglass.com
SIC: 3354 Aluminum extruded products
PA: Prl Glass Systems, Inc.
    13644 Nelson Ave
    City Of Industry CA 91746

(P-6316)
SAMUEL SON & CO (USA) INC
Also Called: Sierra Aluminum
2345 Fleetwood Dr, Riverside (92509-2410)
PHONE..................................951 781-7800
David Baresh, *Vice Pres*
Tim Lara, *Vice Pres*
Candy Burgess, *Executive Asst*
Richard Barnes, *CIO*
Lorena Picazo, *IT/INT Sup*
EMP: 24
SALES (corp-wide): 1.8B **Privately Held**
WEB: www.samuel.com
SIC: 3354 Aluminum extruded products
HQ: Samuel, Son & Co. (Usa) Inc.
    1401 Davey Rd Ste 300
    Woodridge IL 60517
    630 783-8900

(P-6317)
SAPA EXTRUSIONS INC
2821 E Philadelphia St A, Ontario (91761-8522)
PHONE..................................909 947-7682
EMP: 166
SALES (corp-wide): 80MM **Privately Held**
SIC: 3354 Mfg Aluminum Extruded Products
HQ: Sapa Extrusions, Inc.
    9600 Bryn Mawr Ave # 250
    Rosemont IL 60018
    412 299-2286

(P-6318)
SUN VALLEY PRODUCTS INC
Also Called: Sun Valley Extrusion
4640 Sperry St, Los Angeles (90039-1018)
PHONE..................................818 247-8350
Kerry Dodge, *Branch Mgr*
EMP: 20
SALES (corp-wide): 5.1MM **Privately Held**
WEB: www.sunvalleyextrusion.com
SIC: 3354 Aluminum extruded products
HQ: Sun Valley Products, Inc.
    4626 Sperry St
    Los Angeles CA 90039
    818 247-8350

(P-6319)
SUN VALLEY PRODUCTS INC (HQ)
4626 Sperry St, Los Angeles (90039-1018)
PHONE..................................818 247-8350
Jennifer K Hillman, *President*
Rosanne M Kusar, *Ch of Bd*
Angelica K Clark, *Treasurer*
EMP: 40 **EST:** 1960
SQ FT: 64,980
SALES (est): 5.1MM **Privately Held**
WEB: www.sunvalleyextrusion.com
SIC: 3354 Aluminum extruded products
PA: Darfield Industries, Inc.
    4626 Sperry St
    Los Angeles CA 90039
    818 247-8350

(P-6320)
SUPERIOR METAL SHAPES INC
4730 Eucalyptus Ave, Chino (91710-9255)
PHONE..................................909 947-3455
David A Stockton, *President*
Tom Gracia, *QC Mgr*
Yasushi Shimabukuro, *Consultant*
EMP: 40 **EST:** 1983
SQ FT: 64,000
SALES (est): 7MM **Privately Held**
WEB: www.superiormetalshapes.net
SIC: 3354 Shapes, extruded aluminum

(P-6321)
UNIVERSAL MLDING EXTRUSION INC (DH)
Also Called: Umex
9151 Imperial Hwy, Downey (90242-2808)
PHONE..................................562 401-1015
Dominick L Baione, *CEO*
Sonia Prines, *Sales Staff*
Sylvia Bramasco, *Receptionist*
◆ **EMP:** 197 **EST:** 1988
SALES (est): 73.8MM **Privately Held**
WEB: www.umextrude.com
SIC: 3354 Aluminum extruded products
HQ: Universal Molding Company
    9151 Imperial Hwy
    Downey CA 90242
    310 886-1750

(P-6322)
US POLYMERS INC
5910 Bandini Blvd, Commerce (90040-2963)
PHONE..................................323 727-6888
Vram Ohanesiam, *Manager*
Vic Yeager, *Sales Staff*
Elisa Klatch, *Consultant*
Katie Parker, *Supervisor*
EMP: 100
SALES (corp-wide): 36.2MM **Privately Held**
WEB: www.uspolymersinc.com
SIC: 3354 5719 Aluminum extruded products; window furnishings
PA: U.S. Polymers, Inc.
    1057 S Vail Ave
    Montebello CA 90640
    323 728-3023

(P-6323)
VISTA METALS CORP (PA)
13425 Whittram Ave, Fontana (92335-2999)
PHONE..................................909 823-4278
Andrew Primack, *CEO*
Raymond Alpert, *Corp Secy*
Steve Chevlin, *Exec VP*
Robert Praefke, *Exec VP*
Ket Tran, *Administration*
◆ **EMP:** 234 **EST:** 1968
SQ FT: 17,000
SALES (est): 60.7MM **Privately Held**
WEB: www.vistametals.com
SIC: 3354 3341 Aluminum extruded products; aluminum smelting & refining (secondary)

3355 Aluminum Rolling & Drawing, NEC

(P-6324)
ARCADIA INC (PA)
Also Called: Arcadia Norcal
2301 E Vernon Ave, Vernon (90058-8052)
PHONE..................................323 269-7300
James Schladen, *CEO*
Khan Chow, *CFO*
Dan Spielberger, *General Mgr*
James Allen, *Project Mgr*
Julian Basurto, *Project Mgr*
▲ **EMP:** 250
SQ FT: 50,000
SALES (est): 116.8MM **Privately Held**
WEB: www.arcadiainc.com
SIC: 3355 Extrusion ingot, aluminum: made in rolling mills

(P-6325)
DIACK 1 INC
19437 Windrose Dr, Rowland Heights (91748-3994)
PHONE..................................626 961-2491
Thomas Gonzalez, *President*
Russell Serrano, *CFO*
Consuelo Diack, *Vice Pres*
Russ Seranno, *Sales Mgr*
A Diack, *Sales Staff*
EMP: 34 **EST:** 1953
SALES (est): 3.4MM **Privately Held**
WEB: www.showcasesbydiack.com
SIC: 3355 Aluminum rolling & drawing

(P-6326)
DURALUM PRODUCTS INC
4001 Greystone Dr, Ontario (91761-3100)
PHONE..................................951 736-4500
Ron Cull, *Manager*
Cheryl Anson, *Manager*
Lisa Bays, *Sales Staff*
EMP: 15
SALES (corp-wide): 13.1MM **Privately Held**
WEB: www.duralum.com
SIC: 3355 Aluminum rolling & drawing
PA: Duralum Products, Inc.
    8269 Alpine Ave
    Sacramento CA 95826
    916 452-7021

(P-6327)
INTERSTATE STEEL CENTER CO
7001 S Alameda St, Los Angeles (90001-2204)
PHONE..................................323 583-0855
Leon Banks, *President*
William Korth, *Admin Sec*
EMP: 50 **EST:** 1972
SQ FT: 53,000
SALES (est): 6.4MM **Privately Held**
SIC: 3355 3312 Coils, wire aluminum: made in rolling mills; blast furnaces & steel mills

(P-6328)
METALS USA BUILDING PDTS LP (DH)
955 Columbia St, Brea (92821-2923)
PHONE..................................713 946-9000
Charles Canning, *Partner*
Robert McPherson, *Partner*
▲ **EMP:** 700 **EST:** 1960
SQ FT: 60,000
SALES (est): 270.4MM
SALES (corp-wide): 8.8B **Publicly Held**
WEB: www.metalsusa.com
SIC: 3355 5031 1542 Structural shapes, rolled, aluminum; building materials, exterior; commercial & office buildings, renovation & repair
HQ: Metals Usa, Inc.
    800 W Cypress Creed Rd St
    Fort Lauderdale FL 33309
    215 673-3595

(P-6329)
METALS USA BUILDING PDTS LP
1951 S Parco Ave Ste C, Ontario (91761-8315)
PHONE..................................800 325-1305
Steve Brang, *Manager*

P R O D U C T S & S V C S

EMP: 142
SALES (corp-wide): 8.8B **Publicly Held**
SIC: 3355 Structural shapes, rolled, aluminum
HQ: Metals Usa Building Products Lp
955 Columbia St
Brea CA 92821
713 946-9000

(P-6330)
WERNER SYSTEMS INC
Also Called: Woodbridge Glass
14321 Myford Rd, Tustin (92780-7022)
PHONE.....................714 838-4444
Virgina Siciliani, *CEO*
Vito Siciliani, *Director*
▲ EMP: 20 EST: 1984
SQ FT: 58,000
SALES (est): 4.6MM **Privately Held**
WEB: www.woodbridgeglass.com
SIC: 3355 Aluminum rolling & drawing

3356 Rolling, Drawing-Extruding Of Nonferrous Metals

(P-6331)
DYNAMET INCORPORATED
16052 Beach Blvd Ste 221, Huntington Beach (92647-3855)
PHONE.....................714 375-3150
Tom Proteau, *Manager*
EMP: 37
SALES (corp-wide): 1.4B **Publicly Held**
WEB: www.ir.carpentertechnology.com
SIC: 3356 Titanium & titanium alloy bars, sheets, strip, etc.
HQ: Dynamet Incorporated
195 Museum Rd
Washington PA 15301
724 228-1000

(P-6332)
GRANDIS METALS INTL CORP
Also Called: Grandis Titanium
29752 Ave De Las Bndra, Rcho STA Marg (92688-2615)
PHONE.....................949 459-2621
Vasily T Semeniuta, *President*
Igor Krjenitski, *Vice Pres*
Theodore Semeniuta, *Vice Pres*
Shawn Young, *Director*
◆ EMP: 15 EST: 1995
SALES (est): 885.7K **Privately Held**
SIC: 3356 Titanium

(P-6333)
INTERSPACE BATTERY INC (PA)
2009 W San Bernardino Rd, West Covina (91790-1006)
PHONE.....................626 813-1234
Paul Godber, *Ch of Bd*
Donald W Godber, *President*
Richard Murrietta, *Manager*
EMP: 22 EST: 1970
SQ FT: 36,000
SALES (est): 3.5MM **Privately Held**
WEB: www.concordebattery.com
SIC: 3356 3691 Battery metal; storage batteries

(P-6334)
MAGNESIUM INTERNATIONAL INC (PA)
2798 Redwing Cir, Costa Mesa (92626-4843)
PHONE.....................808 741-9712
EMP: 14 EST: 2015
SALES (est): 126.8K **Privately Held**
SIC: 3356 Magnesium

(P-6335)
NEW CNTURY MTALS SOUTHEAST INC
Also Called: Rti Los Angeles
15723 Shoemaker Ave, Norwalk (90650-6863)
PHONE.....................562 356-6804
Jeremy S Halford, *CEO*
Marie T Batz, *Admin Sec*
EMP: 543 EST: 1998

SALES (est): 3.5MM
SALES (corp-wide): 5.2B **Publicly Held**
SIC: 3356 Titanium; titanium & titanium alloy bars, sheets, strip, etc.; titanium & titanium alloy: rolling, drawing or extruding
HQ: Rmi Titanium Company, Llc
1000 Warren Ave
Niles OH 44446
330 652-9952

(P-6336)
OCEANIA INTERNATIONAL LLC
Also Called: Stanford Advanced Materials
23661 Birtcher Dr, Lake Forest (92630-1770)
PHONE.....................949 407-8904
Alexander Chen, *Mng Member*
Arnie Pell, *Vice Pres*
Maria Wang, *Mfg Staff*
Norman Zhang, *Sales Mgr*
Alex Zheng, *Manager*
▲ EMP: 40 EST: 2012
SALES (est): 3.6MM **Privately Held**
WEB: www.samaterials.com
SIC: 3356 3313 Titanium & titanium alloy bars, sheets, strip, etc.; zirconium & zirconium alloy bars, sheets, strip, etc.; ferromolybdenum; ferrosilicon, not made in blast furnaces; ferrotungsten

(P-6337)
P KAY METAL INC (PA)
Also Called: P K Metal
2448 E 25th St, Los Angeles (90058-1209)
PHONE.....................323 585-5058
Larry Kay, *President*
Sharon Kay, *Treasurer*
Cindy Flame, *Admin Sec*
▲ EMP: 44 EST: 1977
SALES (est): 10.5MM **Privately Held**
WEB: www.pkaymetal.com
SIC: 3356 Lead & lead alloy bars, pipe, plates, shapes, etc.

(P-6338)
UMC ACQUISITION CORP (PA)
Also Called: Universal Molding Company
9151 Imperial Hwy, Downey (90242-2808)
PHONE.....................562 940-0300
Dominick L Baione, *Ch of Bd*
Edward L Koch III, *President*
Neil Smith, *Vice Pres*
Kristin Salters, *Project Mgr*
Abbie Scheliga, *Project Mgr*
EMP: 50 EST: 1998
SQ FT: 62,000
SALES (est): 129.5MM **Privately Held**
SIC: 3356 3354 3471 3479 Nonferrous rolling & drawing; aluminum extruded products; anodizing (plating) of metals or formed products; aluminum coating of metal products

(P-6339)
UNIVERSAL MOLDING COMPANY (HQ)
9151 Imperial Hwy, Downey (90242-2808)
PHONE.....................310 886-1750
Dominick L Baione, *Ch of Bd*
Carol Hansen, *COO*
Tom Webster, *Executive*
Geno Ackerman, *General Mgr*
Gerald Moore, *General Mgr*
EMP: 160 EST: 1952
SQ FT: 62,000
SALES (est): 123MM **Privately Held**
WEB: www.universalmold.com
SIC: 3356 3354 3448 3471 Nonferrous rolling & drawing; aluminum extruded products; screen enclosures; anodizing (plating) of metals or formed products; aluminum coating of metal products; sheet metalwork

(P-6340)
VSMPO TIRUS US
2850 E Cedar St, Ontario (91761-8514)
PHONE.....................909 230-9020
Dave Richardson, *Owner*
David Richardson, *Vice Pres*
Bob Randolph, *Administration*
Sandra Tejas, *Administration*
Lauren Barker, *Sales Staff*
◆ EMP: 47 EST: 2012

SALES (est): 54.3MM **Privately Held**
WEB: www.vsmpo-tirus.com
SIC: 3356 Titanium
HQ: Vsmpo-Tirus, U.S., Inc.
1745 Shea Center Dr # 330
Highlands Ranch CO 80129
720 746-1023

(P-6341)
VSMPO-TIRUS US INC
Also Called: West Coast Service Center
2850 E Cedar St, Ontario (91761-8514)
PHONE.....................909 230-9020
Dave Richardson, *Manager*
EMP: 24 **Privately Held**
WEB: www.vsmpo-tirus.com
SIC: 3356 Titanium
HQ: Vsmpo-Tirus, U.S., Inc.
1745 Shea Center Dr # 330
Highlands Ranch CO 80129
720 746-1023

3357 Nonferrous Wire Drawing

(P-6342)
BEE WIRE & CABLE INC
2850 E Spruce St, Ontario (91761-8550)
PHONE.....................909 923-5800
Arjan Bera, *President*
Kiran Kaneria, *Treasurer*
Nalin Kaneria, *Admin Sec*
▲ EMP: 26 EST: 1979
SQ FT: 34,400
SALES (est): 2.7MM **Privately Held**
SIC: 3357 Building wire & cable, nonferrous

(P-6343)
BELDEN INC
Also Called: Coast Custom Cable
1048 E Burgrove St, Carson (90746-3514)
PHONE.....................310 639-9473
Michael Dugar, *Branch Mgr*
Gregg McAfee, *Manager*
Marc Tousignant, *Manager*
EMP: 750
SALES (corp-wide): 1.8B **Publicly Held**
WEB: www.belden.com
SIC: 3357 3699 Coaxial cable, nonferrous; electrical equipment & supplies
PA: Belden Inc.
1 N Brentwood Blvd Fl 15
Saint Louis MO 63105
314 854-8000

(P-6344)
BROADATA COMMUNICATIONS INC
2545 W 237th St Ste K, Torrance (90505-5229)
PHONE.....................310 530-1416
Freddie Lin, *President*
Patty Shaw, *CFO*
Gary Fong, *Design Engr*
Kevin Hsu, *Controller*
Daniel Laconsay, *Controller*
◆ EMP: 54 EST: 2000
SQ FT: 10,000
SALES: 13.2MM **Privately Held**
WEB: www.broadatacom.com
SIC: 3357 3663 Fiber optic cable (insulated); television broadcasting & communications equipment

(P-6345)
CALIFORNIA INSULATED WIRE &
3050 N California St, Burbank (91504-2004)
PHONE.....................818 569-4930
Bill Boyd, *President*
Lois Boyd, *Corp Secy*
Bruce Boyd, *Vice Pres*
Micheal Boyd, *Vice Pres*
Sergio Fajardo, *Plant Mgr*
EMP: 60 EST: 1978
SQ FT: 26,000
SALES (est): 16.2MM **Privately Held**
WEB: www.ciwinc.com
SIC: 3357 Communication wire; fiber optic cable (insulated)

(P-6346)
CALMONT ENGRG & ELEC CORP (PA)
Also Called: Calmont Wire & Cable
420 E Alton Ave, Santa Ana (92707-4278)
PHONE.....................714 549-0336
Barbara Monteleone, *President*
Blanche F Chilcote, *Corp Secy*
Clark Alano, *VP Engrg*
Hung Tran, *Engineer*
Heather Priest, *Controller*
EMP: 36 EST: 1970
SQ FT: 24,000
SALES (est): 5.4MM **Privately Held**
WEB: www.calmont.com
SIC: 3357 3061 Nonferrous wiredrawing & insulating; medical & surgical rubber tubing (extruded & lathe-cut)

(P-6347)
CENTURY WIRE & CABLE INC
7400 E Slauson Ave, Commerce (90040-3300)
PHONE.....................800 999-5566
David Lifschitz, *CEO*
Rowdy Oxford, *Principal*
William Suddarth, *Principal*
Bob Arthur, *Accountant*
Carl Tom, *VP Mktg*
EMP: 100 EST: 1982
SALES (est): 25.2MM
SALES (corp-wide): 166.1MM **Privately Held**
WEB: www.centurywire.com
SIC: 3357 5063 Nonferrous wiredrawing & insulating; electrical apparatus & equipment
HQ: Gehr Industries, Inc.
7400 E Slauson Ave
Commerce CA 90040
323 728-5558

(P-6348)
COAST 2 COAST CABLES LLC
3162 E La Palma Ave Ste D, Anaheim (92806-2810)
PHONE.....................714 666-1062
Lynn Swearingen, *Mng Member*
EMP: 45 EST: 2007
SQ FT: 14,040
SALES (est): 4MM
SALES (corp-wide): 20.9MM **Privately Held**
WEB: www.lynnelec.com
SIC: 3357 Aluminum wire & cable; fiber optic cable (insulated)
PA: Lynn Electronics, Llc
1390 Welsh Rd
North Wales PA 19454
215 355-8200

(P-6349)
FIBEROPTIC SYSTEMS INC
60 Moreland Rd Ste A, Simi Valley (93065-1643)
PHONE.....................805 579-6600
Sanford S Stark, *President*
Kathy Hanau, *CFO*
Mark Helmick, *Engineer*
Suzanne Burmester, *Controller*
Gloria Morales, *QC Mgr*
EMP: 29 EST: 1982
SQ FT: 14,000
SALES (est): 4.3MM **Privately Held**
WEB: www.fiberopticsystems.com
SIC: 3357 3229 Fiber optic cable (insulated); fiber optics strands

(P-6350)
GEHR INDUSTRIES INC (HQ)
Also Called: Gehr Group
7400 E Slauson Ave, Commerce (90040-3300)
PHONE.....................323 728-5558
David Lifschitz, *CEO*
Mark Goldman, *COO*
Joel Golbin, *Vice Pres*
William Suddarth, *Vice Pres*
Carlton Tom, *Vice Pres*
▲ EMP: 140 EST: 1966
SQ FT: 260,000

SALES (est): 66.9MM
SALES (corp-wide): 166.1MM **Privately Held**
WEB: www.gehrindustries.com
SIC: 3357 5063 5072 5085 Nonferrous wiredrawing & insulating; electrical apparatus & equipment; hardware; industrial supplies
PA: The Gehr Group Inc
7400 E Slauson Ave
Commerce CA 90040
323 728-5558

(P-6351)
GLOBAL MFG SOLUTIONS LLC
2100 E Valencia Dr Ste D, Fullerton (92831-4811)
PHONE..............................562 356-3222
Mike Lin, *Mng Member*
Tom Liu, *Vice Pres*
Eugene Tsai,
▲ **EMP:** 20 **EST:** 1997
SQ FT: 10,000
SALES (est): 1.9MM **Privately Held**
WEB: www.cablesys.com
SIC: 3357 Communication wire

(P-6352)
JEB HOLDINGS CORP
42033 Rio Nedo, Temecula (92590-3705)
P.O. Box 67, Idyllwild (92549-0067)
PHONE..............................951 296-9900
Gordon Brown, *President*
EMP: 23
SALES (corp-wide): 19.1MM **Privately Held**
WEB: www.southbaycable.com
SIC: 3357 Nonferrous wiredrawing & insulating
PA: Jeb Holdings Corp.
54125 Maranatha Dr
Idyllwild CA 92549
951 659-2183

(P-6353)
MX ELECTRONICS MFG INC (HQ)
Also Called: Interconnect Solutions
1651 E Saint Andrew Pl, Santa Ana (92705-4932)
PHONE..............................714 258-0200
Lawrence Reusing, *President*
Mike Anderson, *CFO*
◆ **EMP:** 56 **EST:** 2000
SQ FT: 40,000
SALES (est): 25.1MM
SALES (corp-wide): 49.5MM **Privately Held**
WEB: www.mx-emi.com
SIC: 3357 Aluminum wire & cable
PA: Memory Experts International Inc
2321 Rue Cohen
Saint-Laurent QC H4R 2
514 333-5010

(P-6354)
OKONITE COMPANY INC
2900 Skyway Dr, Santa Maria (93455-1897)
PHONE..............................805 922-6682
Rick Flory, *Branch Mgr*
Barbara Schuck, *District Mgr*
Elbert Bustle, *Plant Engr*
Mario Castellanos, *Manager*
Michael Rauscher, *Supervisor*
EMP: 100
SQ FT: 10,000
SALES (corp-wide): 531.2MM **Privately Held**
WEB: www.okonite.com
SIC: 3357 Nonferrous wiredrawing & insulating
PA: The Okonite Company Inc
102 Hilltop Rd
Ramsey NJ 07446
201 825-0300

(P-6355)
PRIME WIRE & CABLE INC (HQ)
1330 Valley Vista Dr, Diamond Bar (91765-3910)
PHONE..............................888 445-9955
Juhng-Shyu Shieh, *CEO*
Bob Fredette, *Vice Pres*
Jerzy Marcinkowsky, *Engineer*
Rosa Hu, *Purch Dir*

Shen-Fu Lin, *Director*
▲ **EMP:** 103 **EST:** 1981
SQ FT: 150,000
SALES: 74.9MM **Privately Held**
WEB: www.primewirecable.com
SIC: 3357 Building wire & cable, nonferrous

(P-6356)
QPC FIBER OPTIC LLC
27612 El Lazo, Laguna Niguel (92677-3913)
PHONE..............................949 361-8855
Steven J Wilkes, *President*
David Olsen, *CFO*
EMP: 30 **EST:** 1999
SQ FT: 1,400
SALES (est): 7.3MM **Privately Held**
WEB: www.qpcfiber.com
SIC: 3357 Fiber optic cable (insulated)

(P-6357)
STANDARD WIRE & CABLE CO (PA)
Also Called: American Wire Sales
2050 E Vista Bella Way, Rancho Dominguez (90220-6109)
PHONE..............................310 609-1811
Russell J Skrable, *President*
Dick Hampikian, *Ch of Bd*
Jerry Gaither, *Info Tech Mgr*
◆ **EMP:** 22 **EST:** 1947
SQ FT: 45,500
SALES: 10.8MM **Privately Held**
WEB: www.standard-wire.com
SIC: 3357 5063 Coaxial cable, nonferrous; wire & cable; electronic wire & cable; power wire & cable

(P-6358)
VICTOR WIRE & CABLE CORP
12915 S Spring St, Los Angeles (90061-1631)
PHONE..............................310 842-9933
Mimi Feldman, *President*
EMP: 13 **EST:** 2009
SALES (est): 282.1K **Privately Held**
WEB: www.victorwire.com
SIC: 3357 Nonferrous wiredrawing & insulating

(P-6359)
VICTOR WIRE AND CABLE LLC
12915 S Spring St, Los Angeles (90061-1631)
PHONE..............................310 842-9933
Robert Smith, *General Mgr*
EMP: 18 **EST:** 1954
SQ FT: 20,000
SALES (est): 2.8MM **Privately Held**
WEB: www.victorwire.com
SIC: 3357 Nonferrous wiredrawing & insulating

(P-6360)
WIRE TECHNOLOGY CORPORATION
9527 Laurel St, Los Angeles (90002-2653)
P.O. Box 1608, South Gate (90280-1608)
PHONE..............................310 635-6935
Rachel Mendoza, *President*
Darlene Delange, *Vice Pres*
Robert Mendoza, *Principal*
EMP: 25 **EST:** 1970
SQ FT: 4,000
SALES (est): 3MM **Privately Held**
WEB: www.wiretechnologycorp.com
SIC: 3357 Nonferrous wiredrawing & insulating

3363 Aluminum Die Castings

(P-6361)
AEROTEC ALLOYS INC
10632 Alondra Blvd, Norwalk (90650-5301)
PHONE..............................562 809-1378
Robert W Franklin, *CEO*
Mitchell Frahm, *Vice Pres*
Derek Franklin, *Vice Pres*
Shery Franklin, *Vice Pres*
Shelly Murphy, *Manager*
EMP: 50
SQ FT: 18,000

SALES (est): 14.3MM **Privately Held**
WEB: www.aerotecalloys.com
SIC: 3363 3312 3365 3325 Aluminum die-castings; blast furnaces & steel mills; aluminum foundries; steel foundries

(P-6362)
ALLOY DIE CASTING CO
Also Called: ADC Aerospace
6550 Caballero Blvd, Buena Park (90620-1130)
PHONE..............................714 521-9800
Rick Simpson, *CEO*
Eric Sanders, *President*
Mihai Tiplea, *CFO*
Wim Huijs, *Vice Pres*
Courtney Jacobian, *Engineer*
EMP: 135 **EST:** 1939
SQ FT: 55,000
SALES (est): 21.5MM **Privately Held**
WEB: www.adc-aerospace.com
SIC: 3363 Aluminum die-castings

(P-6363)
ALUMINUM DIE CASTING CO INC
10775 San Sevaine Way, Jurupa Valley (91752-1146)
PHONE..............................951 681-3900
Steve Bennett, *CEO*
James Bennett, *Shareholder*
Rudy Bennett, *Vice Pres*
Rob Gusman, *Vice Pres*
Carolyn Hibbs,
EMP: 65
SQ FT: 31,000
SALES (est): 14.9MM **Privately Held**
WEB: www.adc3900.com
SIC: 3363 3364 Aluminum die-castings; nonferrous die-castings except aluminum

(P-6364)
HYATT DIE CAST ENGRG CORP - S
12250 Industry St, Garden Grove (92841-2816)
PHONE..............................714 622-2131
Mike Senter, *Branch Mgr*
EMP: 39
SALES (corp-wide): 26.8MM **Privately Held**
WEB: www.hyattdiecast.com
SIC: 3363 Aluminum die-castings
PA: Hyatt Die Cast And Engineering Corporation - South
4656 Lincoln Ave
Cypress CA 90630
714 826-7550

(P-6365)
KENWALT DIE CASTING CORP
Also Called: Kenwait Die Casting Company
8719 Bradley Ave, Sun Valley (91352-2799)
PHONE..............................818 768-5800
Ken Zaucha Sr, *President*
Rose Zaucha, *Shareholder*
Gabby Cheherlian, *Admin Asst*
Justin Robertson, *Sales Associate*
▼ **EMP:** 25 **EST:** 1974
SQ FT: 20,000
SALES (est): 3.5MM **Privately Held**
WEB: www.kenwalt.com
SIC: 3363 Aluminum die-castings

(P-6366)
MAGNESIUM ALLOY PDTS CO INC
2420 N Alameda St, Compton (90222-2895)
P.O. Box 4668 (90224-4668)
PHONE..............................310 605-1440
J W Long, *President*
M B Long, *Admin Sec*
EMP: 46 **EST:** 1945
SQ FT: 90,000
SALES (est): 8.3MM **Privately Held**
WEB: www.magnesiumalloy.com
SIC: 3363 Aluminum die-castings

(P-6367)
MAGNESIUM ALLOY PRODUCTS CO LP
2420 N Alameda St, Compton (90222-2895)
PHONE..............................323 636-2276
Richard Killen, *Partner*
James Long, *Partner*
EMP: 50 **EST:** 1956
SALES (est): 4.5MM **Privately Held**
WEB: www.magnesiumalloy.com
SIC: 3363 Aluminum die-castings

(P-6368)
PACIFIC DIE CASTING CORP
6155 S Eastern Ave, Commerce (90040-3401)
PHONE..............................323 725-1308
Jeff Orlandini, *Vice Pres*
Sonny Yun, *Shareholder*
▲ **EMP:** 150 **EST:** 1954
SQ FT: 8,000
SALES (est): 23.1MM **Privately Held**
WEB: www.pacdiecast.com
SIC: 3363 Aluminum die-castings

(P-6369)
PERFORMANCE ALUMINUM PRODUCTS
520 S Palmetto Ave, Ontario (91762-4121)
PHONE..............................909 391-4131
John Reed, *President*
▲ **EMP:** 20 **EST:** 1985
SALES (est): 2.4MM **Privately Held**
WEB: www.perfalum.com
SIC: 3363 Aluminum die-castings

(P-6370)
PIONEER DIECASTERS INC
4209 Chevy Chase Dr, Los Angeles (90039-1294)
PHONE..............................323 245-6561
Carl H Spahr, *President*
Gretchen Perry, *Admin Sec*
EMP: 17 **EST:** 1949
SQ FT: 18,000 **Privately Held**
SIC: 3363 3364 5051 Aluminum die-castings; zinc & zinc-base alloy die-castings; aluminum bars, rods, ingots, sheets, pipes, plates, etc.

(P-6371)
SEA SHIELD MARINE PRODUCTS
Also Called: American Zinc Enterprises
20832 Currier Rd, Walnut (91789-3017)
PHONE..............................909 594-2507
Wendell Walter Godwin, *CEO*
Shelley Lopez, *CFO*
Alicia Vongoeben, *Administration*
▲ **EMP:** 45 **EST:** 1971
SQ FT: 25,000
SALES (est): 9.7MM **Privately Held**
WEB: www.seashieldmarine.com
SIC: 3363 3364 Aluminum die-castings; magnesium & magnesium-base alloy die-castings

(P-6372)
VENUS ALLOYS INC (PA)
1415 S Allec St, Anaheim (92805-6306)
PHONE..............................714 635-8800
E K Venugopal, *President*
Kousalya Venugopal, *Admin Sec*
EMP: 24 **EST:** 1989
SQ FT: 20,000
SALES (est): 6.3MM **Privately Held**
SIC: 3363 3364 Aluminum die-castings; brass & bronze die-castings

---

3364 Nonferrous Die Castings, Exc Aluminum

(P-6373)
ALCAST MFG INC
2910 Fisk Ln, Redondo Beach (90278-5437)
PHONE..............................310 542-3581
EMP: 30

PRODUCTS & SVCS

SALES (corp-wide): 4.9MM **Privately Held**
WEB: www.alcast-foundry.com
SIC: **3364** 3363 Brass & bronze die-castings; aluminum die-castings
PA: Alcast Mfg, Inc.
　　7355 E Slauson Ave
　　Commerce CA 90040
　　310 542-3581

(P-6374)
AMERICAN DIE CASTING INC
14576 Fontlee Ln, Fontana (92335-2599)
PHONE...................909 356-7768
Walter Mueller, *President*
Marjorie Mueller, *Treasurer*
Marjorie N Mueller, *Treasurer*
Jeffrey Mueller, *Vice Pres*
Bob Ray, *Sales Engr*
EMP: 50 EST: 1992
SQ FT: 20,000
SALES (est): 7MM **Privately Held**
WEB: www.americandiecasting.com
SIC: **3364** 3363 Zinc & zinc-base alloy die-castings; brass & bronze die-castings; lead & zinc die-castings; aluminum die-castings

(P-6375)
CALIFORNIA DIE CASTING INC
1820 S Grove Ave, Ontario (91761-5613)
PHONE...................909 947-9947
Dan C Lane, *President*
Roy Herring, *Corp Secy*
Jerry C Holland, *Vice Pres*
Cathy Delapena, *Administration*
Tom Thomas, *Info Tech Dir*
EMP: 49 EST: 1996
SQ FT: 3,000
SALES (est): 10.7MM **Privately Held**
WEB: www.caldiecast.com
SIC: **3364** 3363 Nonferrous die-castings except aluminum; aluminum die-castings

(P-6376)
CUSTOM DESIGN IRON WORKS INC
9182 Kelvin Ave, Chatsworth (91311-5901)
PHONE...................818 700-9182
Shaia Schuchmacher, *President*
Beverly Schuchmacher, *Vice Pres*
EMP: 13 EST: 1981
SQ FT: 4,980
SALES (est): 2.4MM **Privately Held**
WEB: www.cdiw.com
SIC: **3364** 1799 Nonferrous die-castings except aluminum; ornamental metal work

(P-6377)
DEL MAR INDUSTRIES (PA)
Also Called: Del Mar Die Casting Co
12901 S Western Ave, Gardena (90249-1917)
P.O. Box 881, Venice (90294-0881)
PHONE...................323 321-0600
D R Taylor, *CEO*
Susan Davis, *Shareholder*
Louis A Cuhrt, *CFO*
Judith Taylor, *Admin Sec*
EMP: 100 EST: 1968
SQ FT: 68,000
SALES (est): 13.4MM **Privately Held**
WEB: www.delmarindustries.com
SIC: **3364** Zinc & zinc-base alloy die-castings; magnesium & magnesium-base alloy die-castings

(P-6378)
DEL MAR INDUSTRIES
Gardena Plating Co
12901 S Western Ave, Gardena (90249-1917)
PHONE...................310 327-2634
Fax: 310 327-2904
EMP: 25 **Privately Held**
SIC: **3364** 3471 Mfg Nonferrous Die-Castings Plating/Polishing Service
PA: Del Mar Industries
　　12901 S Western Ave
　　Gardena CA 90249
　　323 321-0600

(P-6379)
DYNACAST LLC
25952 Commercentre Dr, Lake Forest (92630-8815)
PHONE...................949 707-1211
John Hess, *Branch Mgr*
Thinh Pho, *Exec VP*
Adam Scichitano, *Engineer*
Zachary Southworth, *Engineer*
Dawn Howard, *Human Res Mgr*
EMP: 140
SALES (corp-wide): 1.5B **Privately Held**
WEB: www.dynacast.com
SIC: **3364** Nonferrous die-castings except aluminum
HQ: Dynacast Us Holdings, Inc.
　　14045 Balntyn Corp Pl
　　Charlotte NC 28277
　　704 927-2790

(P-6380)
FTG AEROSPACE INC (DH)
20740 Marilla St, Chatsworth (91311-4407)
PHONE...................818 407-4024
Michael Labrador, *President*
▼ EMP: 42 EST: 2011
SQ FT: 13,000
SALES (est): 21MM
SALES (corp-wide): 77.4MM **Privately Held**
WEB: www.ftgcorp.com
SIC: **3364** Nonferrous die-castings except aluminum
HQ: Firan Technology Group (Usa) Corporation
　　20750 Marilla St
　　Chatsworth CA 91311
　　818 407-4024

(P-6381)
WHITEFOX DEFENSE TECH INC
833 Buckley Rd, San Luis Obispo (93401-8130)
PHONE...................805 225-4506
Mark Kulam, *President*
Walter Stockwell, *Vice Pres*
Andrew D 'ambrosio, *CIO*
Teyvon Brooks, *Engineer*
Nora Beaubien, *Human Resources*
EMP: 32 EST: 2016
SALES (est): 7.9MM **Privately Held**
WEB: www.whitefoxdefense.com
SIC: **3364** Nonferrous die-castings except aluminum

3365 Aluminum Foundries

(P-6382)
ADM WORKS LLC
1343 E Wilshire Ave, Santa Ana (92705-4420)
PHONE...................714 245-0536
Jimmy Garcia, *Office Admin*
Javier Valbibieso,
EMP: 23 EST: 2004
SALES (est): 3.1MM **Privately Held**
WEB: www.adm-works.com
SIC: **3365** 7389 8711 Aerospace castings, aluminum; design services; engineering services

(P-6383)
AIRCRAFT FOUNDRY CO INC
Also Called: Afco
5316 Pacific Blvd, Huntington Park (90255-2596)
PHONE...................323 587-3171
Ronald Caliva, *President*
Don Caliva, *Treasurer*
Ken Caliva, *Vice Pres*
Glenn Caliva, *Admin Sec*
EMP: 42 EST: 1942
SQ FT: 16,000
SALES (est): 1.6MM **Privately Held**
WEB: www.aircraftfoundry.com
SIC: **3365** Aluminum & aluminum-based alloy castings

(P-6384)
ALCAST MFG INC (PA)
7355 E Slauson Ave, Commerce (90040-3626)
PHONE...................310 542-3581
Kiwon Ban, *CEO*

SOO Ban, *Treasurer*
Lily Martinez, *Admin Sec*
Johnna Schulz, *Mfg Staff*
▲ EMP: 25 EST: 1986
SALES: 4.9MM **Privately Held**
WEB: www.alcast-foundry.com
SIC: **3365** 3366 3544 3369 Aluminum & aluminum-based alloy castings; brass foundry; special dies, tools, jigs & fixtures; nonferrous foundries; nonferrous die-castings except aluminum; fabricated structural metal

(P-6385)
ALUMISTAR INC
Also Called: Pacific Cast Products
520 S Palmetto Ave, Ontario (91762-4121)
PHONE...................562 633-6673
Peter Lake, *President*
Krista Lake, *Human Res Mgr*
▲ EMP: 26 EST: 1982
SALES (est): 4.8MM **Privately Held**
WEB: www.pacificcastproducts.com
SIC: **3365** Aluminum & aluminum-based alloy castings

(P-6386)
ANGELUS ALUMINUM FOUNDRY CO
3479 E Pico Blvd, Los Angeles (90023-3084)
PHONE...................323 268-0145
Edward E Vena, *President*
Henry L Vena, *Vice Pres*
Judy Vena, *Admin Sec*
EMP: 21 EST: 1953
SQ FT: 12,800
SALES (est): 5.4MM **Privately Held**
SIC: **3365** Aluminum & aluminum-based alloy castings

(P-6387)
BUDDY BAR CASTING LLC
10801 Sessler St, South Gate (90280-7222)
PHONE...................562 861-9664
Edward W Barksdale Sr,
Bill Fell, *President*
Ty Barksdale, *Corp Secy*
John Fell, *Vice Pres*
Mike McKeen, *Vice Pres*
▲ EMP: 130 EST: 1953
SQ FT: 25,000
SALES (est): 18.4MM **Privately Held**
WEB: www.buddybarcasting.com
SIC: **3365** Aluminum foundries

(P-6388)
CALIDAD INC
1730 S Balboa Ave, Ontario (91761-7773)
PHONE...................909 947-3937
Don Cornell, *President*
Daniel Garcia, *Vice Pres*
Rito Garcia, *Administration*
Danielle Antinora, *Bookkeeper*
EMP: 30 EST: 1986
SQ FT: 10,000
SALES (est): 4.1MM **Privately Held**
WEB: www.calidadinc.com
SIC: **3365** 3324 Aluminum foundries; steel investment foundries

(P-6389)
CONSOLIDATED FOUNDRIES INC
Also Called: Cpp Cudahy
8333 Wilcox Ave, Cudahy (90201-5919)
P.O. Box 1099 (90201-7099)
PHONE...................323 773-2363
Steve Gallardo, *Branch Mgr*
Colin Schmidt, *Engineer*
Natalia Figueroa MBA, *Human Res Mgr*
EMP: 130
SALES (corp-wide): 789.9MM **Privately Held**
WEB: www.cppcorp.com
SIC: **3365** 3324 Aluminum foundries; steel investment foundries
HQ: Consolidated Foundries, Inc.
　　1621 Euclid Ave Ste 1850
　　Cleveland OH 44115

(P-6390)
CYTEC ENGINEERED MATERIALS INC
Also Called: Solvay Composite Materials
1440 N Kraemer Blvd, Anaheim (92806-1404)
PHONE...................714 632-1174
Ron Martin, *Branch Mgr*
Austin Liu, *Technician*
Paul Clark, *Technology*
Keith Hwang, *Project Engr*
Scott Low, *Engineer*
EMP: 125
SQ FT: 135,055
SALES (corp-wide): 13MM **Privately Held**
SIC: **3365** 2891 2851 2823 Aerospace castings, aluminum; adhesives & sealants; paints & allied products; cellulosic manmade fibers
HQ: Cytec Engineered Materials Inc.
　　2085 E Tech Cir Ste 102
　　Tempe AZ 85284

(P-6391)
DC PARTNERS INC (PA)
Also Called: Soligen 2006
19329 Bryant St, Northridge (91324-4114)
PHONE...................714 558-9444
Yehoram Uziel, *President*
Alecia Wagner, *Principal*
EMP: 32 EST: 2005
SALES (est): 7.7MM **Privately Held**
WEB: www.soligen2006.com
SIC: **3365** 3599 Aluminum foundries; machine & other job shop work

(P-6392)
DOWELL ALUMINUM FOUNDRY INC
11342 Hartland St, North Hollywood (91605-6387)
PHONE...................323 877-9645
Lynn F Dompe, *President*
EMP: 29 EST: 1954
SQ FT: 17,000
SALES (est): 2.9MM **Privately Held**
SIC: **3365** 3369 Aluminum & aluminum-based alloy castings; nonferrous foundries

(P-6393)
DWA ALUMINUM COMPOSITES USA INC
21100 Superior St, Chatsworth (91311-4308)
PHONE...................818 998-1504
Mark R Van Den Bergh, *CEO*
Gary Wolfe, *COO*
J J Shah, *CFO*
Neel Shah, *Project Mgr*
Cory Smith, *QC Mgr*
EMP: 20 EST: 2013
SQ FT: 40,000
SALES (est): 4.5MM **Privately Held**
WEB: www.dwa-usa.com
SIC: **3365** Aluminum & aluminum-based alloy castings

(P-6394)
EMPLOYEE OWNED PCF CAST PDTS I
Also Called: Aluminum Casting Company
520 S Palmetto Ave, Ontario (91762-4121)
PHONE...................562 633-6673
Alex B Hall, *President*
EMP: 19 EST: 2000
SALES (est): 677.7K **Privately Held**
SIC: **3365** Aluminum & aluminum-based alloy castings

(P-6395)
FONTANA FOUNDRY CORPORATION
8306 Cherry Ave, Fontana (92335-3026)
PHONE...................909 822-6128
Jeffrey Ritz, *Chief Mktg Ofcr*
Susan Ritz, *CFO*
EMP: 35 EST: 1946
SQ FT: 11,500
SALES (est): 4.2MM **Privately Held**
WEB: www.fontanafoundry.com
SIC: **3365** Aluminum & aluminum-based alloy castings

(P-6396)
GC INTERNATIONAL INC (PA)
Also Called: Alj
4671 Calle Carga, Camarillo (93012-8560)
PHONE..................805 389-4631
Mark Griffith, *President*
Richard R Carlson, *President*
F Willard Griffith, *CEO*
Terry Carlson, *Vice Pres*
Mark R Griffith, *Vice Pres*
▼ **EMP:** 43
SQ FT: 45,000
SALES (est): 14.3MM **Publicly Held**
WEB: www.aljcast.com
SIC: 3365 3695 3369 3061 Aluminum &
aluminum-based alloy castings; magnetic
disks & drums; lead, zinc & white metal;
appliance rubber goods (mechanical);
amusement park equipment

(P-6397)
INTERORBITAL SYSTEMS
1394 Barnes St Bldg 7, Mojave
(93501-1673)
P.O. Box 662 (93502-0662)
PHONE..................661 965-0771
Randa Milliron, *CEO*
Roderick Milliron, *President*
EMP: 16 **EST:** 1996
SQ FT: 6,000
SALES (est): 1.5MM **Privately Held**
WEB: www.interorbital.com
SIC: 3365 3764 Aerospace castings, alu-
minum; guided missile & space vehicle
propulsion unit parts

(P-6398)
LYNWOOD PATTERN SERVICE
INC
603 S Hope Ave, Ontario (91761-1824)
P.O. Box 536, Lynwood (90262-0536)
PHONE..................310 631-2225
Jose Alvarez, *President*
Benjamen Alvarez, *Vice Pres*
Jason Alvarez, *CIO*
Carlos Alvarez, *Manager*
EMP: 34 **EST:** 1944
SQ FT: 4,000
SALES (est): 3.7MM **Privately Held**
WEB: www.lynwoodpattern.com
SIC: 3365 3543 Aluminum & aluminum-
based alloy castings; foundry patternmak-
ing

(P-6399)
MAGPARTS (DH)
Also Called: Cpp-Azusa
1545 W Roosevelt St, Azusa (91702-3281)
PHONE..................626 334-7897
Richard H Emerson, *President*
L Scott Mac Donald, *Vice Pres*
Ellen E Skatvold, *Admin Sec*
Ivan Gastelum, *Technician*
Stephen A Mac Donald, *Site Mgr*
EMP: 138 **EST:** 1958
SQ FT: 100,000
SALES (est): 25MM
SALES (corp-wide): 789.9MM **Privately
Held**
WEB: www.magparts.com
SIC: 3365 3369 Aluminum & aluminum-
based alloy castings; magnesium &
magnes.-base alloy castings, exc. die-
casting
HQ: Consolidated Precision Products Corp.
1621 Euclid Ave Ste 1850
Cleveland OH 44115
216 453-4800

(P-6400)
OASIS ALLOY WHEELS INC
Also Called: Oasis Metal Works
400 S Lemon St, Anaheim (92805-3816)
PHONE..................714 533-3286
EMP: 13
SQ FT: 10,000
SALES (est): 2MM **Privately Held**
WEB: www.oasiswheels.com
SIC: 3365 Aluminum Foundry

(P-6401)
SONFARREL AEROSPACE LLC
3010 E La Jolla St, Anaheim (92806-1310)
PHONE..................714 630-7280
Jeffrey Greer,
Bunmee Duong, *Purchasing*

Ken Anderson,
Michael Deitrick, *Director*
EMP: 96 **EST:** 2018
SALES (est): 12.6MM **Privately Held**
WEB: www.son-aero.com
SIC: 3365 Aerospace castings, aluminum

(P-6402)
VAN BRUNT FOUNDRY INC
5136 Chakemco St, South Gate
(90280-6443)
PHONE..................323 569-2832
Richard Ledesma, *President*
EMP: 17 **EST:** 1963
SQ FT: 10,000
SALES (est): 1.3MM **Privately Held**
SIC: 3365 Aluminum & aluminum-based
alloy castings

3366 Copper Foundries

(P-6403)
ACME CASTINGS INC
6009 Santa Fe Ave, Huntington Park
(90255-2723)
PHONE..................323 583-3129
Lee Lewis, *President*
Ruth Lewis, *Corp Secy*
EMP: 26 **EST:** 1963
SQ FT: 25,000
SALES (est): 1.1MM **Privately Held**
WEB: www.acme-castings.com
SIC: 3366 3325 3365 3322 Copper
foundries; alloy steel castings, except in-
vestment; aluminum foundries; malleable
iron foundries

(P-6404)
AMERICAN FINE ARTS
FOUNDRY LLC
2520 N Ontario St Ste A, Burbank
(91504-4708)
PHONE..................818 848-7593
Brett Barney,
Angel Meza, *Purchasing*
Chris Delling, *Mktg Dir*
EMP: 14 **EST:** 1981
SQ FT: 3,000
SALES (est): 4.7MM **Privately Held**
WEB: www.afafoundry.com
SIC: 3366 3544 Castings (except die):
bronze; forms (molds), for foundry & plas-
tics working machinery

(P-6405)
ART BRONZE INC
11275 San Fernando Rd, San Fernando
(91340-3422)
PHONE..................818 897-2222
Ian G Killips, *CEO*
EMP: 30 **EST:** 1971
SQ FT: 11,400
SALES (est): 4.8MM **Privately Held**
WEB: www.artbronze.com
SIC: 3366 3312 Bronze foundry; stainless
steel

(P-6406)
CSB INDUSTRIES CORP
268 Benton Ct, Walnut (91789-5212)
PHONE..................626 964-4058
Yining Sun, *President*
▲ **EMP:** 13 **EST:** 2009
SALES (est): 1.8MM **Privately Held**
SIC: 3366 Bushings & bearings

(P-6407)
FLEETWOOD CONTINENTAL
INC
19451 S Susana Rd, Compton
(90221-5713)
PHONE..................310 609-1477
David J Forster, *President*
Sheila Polendey, *Sales Staff*
▲ **EMP:** 75 **EST:** 1965
SQ FT: 5,000
SALES (est): 10.4MM **Privately Held**
WEB: www.fleetcon.com
SIC: 3366 3823 3561 3523 Castings (ex-
cept die): bronze; turbine flow meters, in-
dustrial process type; pumps & pumping
equipment; farm machinery & equipment

(P-6408)
GALAXY DIE AND ENGINEERING
INC
Also Called: Galaxy Bearing Company
24910 Avenue Tibbitts, Valencia
(91355-3426)
PHONE..................661 775-9301
Jawahar Saini, *President*
Hamid Baig, *Shareholder*
Sooltan Ali Bhoy, *Shareholder*
Malkiat Saini, *Shareholder*
Elizabeth Krueger, *General Mgr*
EMP: 40 **EST:** 1958
SQ FT: 30,000
SALES (est): 3.2MM **Privately Held**
WEB: www.galaxybearing.com
SIC: 3366 3575 Bushings & bearings;
computer terminals

(P-6409)
MONTCLAIR BRONZE INC (PA)
5621 State St, Montclair (91763-6241)
P.O. Box 2009 (91763-0509)
PHONE..................909 986-2664
Dan Griffiths, *CEO*
Wayne Freeberg, *President*
Dan Griffiths, *CEO*
Thomas Freeberg, *Admin Sec*
Tom Freeberg, *Opers Staff*
EMP: 28 **EST:** 1963
SQ FT: 8,000
SALES (est): 7.9MM **Privately Held**
WEB: www.montclairbronze.com
SIC: 3366 3599 Bronze foundry; machine
shop, jobbing & repair

(P-6410)
PAC FOUNDRIES INC
Also Called: Prime Alloy Steel Casting
705 Industrial Way, Port Hueneme
(93041-3505)
PHONE..................805 986-1308
Steve Clodfelter, *President*
EMP: 163 **EST:** 1978
SALES (est): 13.2MM
SALES (corp-wide): 789.9MM **Privately
Held**
WEB: www.cppcorp.com
SIC: 3366 Copper foundries
HQ: Consolidated Precision Products Corp.
1621 Euclid Ave Ste 1850
Cleveland OH 44115
216 453-4800

3369 Nonferrous Foundries:
Castings, NEC

(P-6411)
ALLIEDSIGNAL AROSPC SVC
CORP (HQ)
Also Called: Allied Signal Aerospace
2525 W 190th St, Torrance (90504-6002)
PHONE..................310 323-9500
Bernd F Kessler, *President*
James V Gelly, *Treasurer*
Mary Beth Orson, *Vice Pres*
Lois H Fuchs, *Asst Treas*
David A Cohen, *Asst Sec*
EMP: 100 **EST:** 2003
SALES (est): 209.7MM
SALES (corp-wide): 32.6B **Publicly Held**
WEB: www.honeywell.com
SIC: 3369 3822 3812 3769 Nonferrous
foundries; auto controls regulating residntl
& coml environmt & applncs; search &
navigation equipment; guided missile &
space vehicle parts & auxiliary equip-
ment; fabricated plate work (boiler shop)
PA: Honeywell International Inc.
855 S Mint St
Charlotte NC 28202
704 627-6200

(P-6412)
CAST PARTNER
4658 W Washington Blvd, Los Angeles
(90016-1743)
PHONE..................323 876-9000
Fridlizius Theo, *President*
Tabitha Lawrence, *Opers Mgr*
Olivia Crawford, *Agent*
EMP: 16 **EST:** 2013

SALES (est): 1.3MM **Privately Held**
WEB: www.castpartner.com
SIC: 3369 Nonferrous foundries

(P-6413)
CAST-RITE INTERNATIONAL
INC (PA)
515 E Airline Way, Gardena (90248-2501)
PHONE..................310 532-2080
Donald E Dehaan, *CEO*
Howard Watkins, *CFO*
Wynn Chapman, *Vice Pres*
◆ **EMP:** 90 **EST:** 1961
SQ FT: 59,330
SALES (est): 25.7MM **Privately Held**
WEB: www.cast-rite.com
SIC: 3369 Zinc & zinc-base alloy castings,
except die-castings

(P-6414)
DELT INDUSTRIES INC
90 W Easy St Ste 2, Simi Valley
(93065-6206)
P.O. Box 940067 (93094-0067)
PHONE..................805 579-0213
Estelle Lee, *President*
Jerry Martin, *Vice Pres*
Debra Schultz, *Admin Sec*
Michael Hixon, *Manager*
EMP: 18 **EST:** 1994
SQ FT: 10,000
SALES (est): 2.5MM **Privately Held**
WEB: www.deltindustries.com
SIC: 3369 5088 Nonferrous foundries;
transportation equipment & supplies

(P-6415)
EXCELITY
Also Called: Solara Engineering
11127 Dora St, Sun Valley (91352-3339)
PHONE..................818 767-1000
Shaun Tan, *President*
EMP: 37 **EST:** 2003
SALES (est): 1.5MM **Privately Held**
SIC: 3369 3812 Aerospace castings, non-
ferrous: except aluminum; acceleration in-
dicators & systems components,
aerospace

(P-6416)
FENICO PRECISION CASTINGS
INC
7805 Madison St, Paramount
(90723-4220)
PHONE..................562 634-5000
Don Tomeo, *President*
Sherry Tomeo, *CFO*
▲ **EMP:** 75 **EST:** 1987
SQ FT: 20,000
SALES (est): 8.6MM **Privately Held**
WEB: www.fenicocastings.com
SIC: 3369 3324 3322 Machinery
castings, nonferrous: ex. alum., copper,
die, etc.; copper foundries; steel invest-
ment foundries; malleable iron foundries

(P-6417)
FS - PRECISION TECH CO LLC
3025 E Victoria St, Compton (90221-5616)
PHONE..................310 638-0595
Juan Molina,
Betty Ruffalo, *Info Tech Mgr*
Issa Nassar, *Engineer*
Marina Ramirez, *Human Resources*
Israel M Sanchez,
▲ **EMP:** 100 **EST:** 2004
SALES (est): 23.7MM **Privately Held**
WEB: www.fs-precision.com
SIC: 3369 Titanium castings, except die-
casting
PA: Fs-Elliott Company, Inc.
5710 Mellon Rd
Export PA 15632

(P-6418)
ORLANDINI ENTPS PCF DIE
CAST
6155 S Eastern Ave, Commerce
(90040-3401)
PHONE..................323 725-1332
Jeff Orlandini, *President*
Vincent Orlandini, *Principal*
▲ **EMP:** 125 **EST:** 1955
SQ FT: 45,000

SALES (est): 11.6MM **Privately Held**
WEB: www.pacdiecast.com
SIC: 3369 3363 Machinery castings, nonferrous: ex. alum., copper, die, etc.; aluminum die-castings

(P-6419)
PAC FOUNDRIES INC
705 Industrial Way, Port Hueneme
(93041-3505)
PHONE..................805 488-6451
Steve Clodfelter, *Owner*
Kinjal Patel, *QC Mgr*
EMP: 230 EST: 1966
SQ FT: 12,770
SALES (est): 30.8MM
SALES (corp-wide): 789.9MM **Privately
Held**
SIC: 3369 Castings, except die-castings,
precision
HQ: Consolidated Foundries, Inc.
1621 Euclid Ave Ste 1850
Cleveland OH 44115

(P-6420)
PANKL AEROSPACE SYSTEMS
16615 Edwards Rd, Cerritos (90703-2437)
PHONE..................562 207-6300
Horst Rieger, *CEO*
Harry Glieder, *President*
Lynn Ngo, *Administration*
Stefan Seidel, *CTO*
Alexander Aigner, *Technical Staff*
EMP: 75 EST: 2000
SQ FT: 63,040
SALES (est): 19.2MM
SALES (corp-wide): 2.4B **Privately Held**
WEB: www.pankl.com
SIC: 3369 3724 Aerospace castings, non-
ferrous: except aluminum; aircraft engines
& engine parts
HQ: Pankl Holdings, Inc.
1902 Mcgaw Ave
Irvine CA 92614

(P-6421)
PASSWORD ENTERPRISE INC
3200 E 29th St, Long Beach (90806-2321)
P.O. Box 90729 (90809-0729)
PHONE..................562 988-8889
Sophead Naing, *CEO*
Adam Chu, *Director*
EMP: 25 EST: 2013
SQ FT: 32,000
SALES (est): 4.2MM **Privately Held**
WEB: www.passwordmm.com
SIC: 5961 3369 Automotive supplies &
equipment, mail order; aerospace cast-
ings, nonferrous: except aluminum

(P-6422)
SYNERTECH PM INC
11711 Monarch St, Garden Grove
(92841-1830)
PHONE..................714 898-9151
Charles Barre, *CEO*
Kristen Barre, *President*
Victor Samarov, *Vice Pres*
Catherine Crawford, *Admin Asst*
Kevin Barre, *QC Mgr*
◆ EMP: 17 EST: 2000
SQ FT: 20,000
SALES (est): 3.7MM **Privately Held**
WEB: www.synertechpm.com
SIC: 3369 Aerospace castings, nonferrous:
except aluminum

(P-6423)
TECHNI-CAST CORP
11220 Garfield Ave, South Gate
(90280-7586)
PHONE..................562 923-4585
Bryn Jhan Van Hiel II, *President*
Donald Van Hiel, *Vice Pres*
Lynne Van Hiel, *Vice Pres*
Elaine M Kay, *Admin Sec*
Roberta Kennedy, *Controller*
▲ EMP: 80 EST: 1954
SQ FT: 60,000

SALES (est): 19.3MM **Privately Held**
WEB: www.techni-cast.com
SIC: 3369 3599 3364 3325 Lead, zinc &
white metal; machinery castings, nonferrous: ex. alum., copper, die, etc.; machine
shop, jobbing & repair; nonferrous die-
castings except aluminum; steel foundries

3398 Metal Heat Treating

(P-6424)
ABRASIVE FINISHING CO
Also Called: Afco
14920 S Main St, Gardena (90248-1985)
P.O. Box 2292 (90247-0292)
PHONE..................310 323-7175
William Swanson, *President*
EMP: 18 EST: 1957
SQ FT: 2,600
SALES (est): 1.2MM **Privately Held**
WEB: www.afco.la
SIC: 3398 3471 Shot peening (treating
steel to reduce fatigue); plating & polish-

(P-6425)
ACCURATE STEEL TREATING
INC
10008 Miller Way, South Gate
(90280-5496)
PHONE..................562 927-6528
Ronald Loyns, *President*
Mike Bastin, *Vice Pres*
Geoff Monti, *Vice Pres*
Al Lozano, *Manager*
EMP: 38 EST: 1962
SQ FT: 10,000
SALES (est): 8.4MM **Privately Held**
WEB: www.accuratesteeltreating.com
SIC: 3398 Metal heat treating

(P-6426)
ADB INDUSTRIES
Also Called: Subsidy of Be Aerospace
1400 Manhattan Ave, Fullerton
(92831-5222)
PHONE..................310 679-9193
Brian Dietz, *President*
Brad Beckmann, *Sales Staff*
EMP: 255 EST: 1961
SQ FT: 50,000
SALES (est): 5.5MM
SALES (corp-wide): 56.5B **Publicly Held**
SIC: 3398 8711 7692 3444 Brazing
(hardening) of metal; engineering serv-
ices; welding repair; sheet metalwork
HQ: Tsi Group, Inc.
94 Tide Mill Rd
Hampton NH 03842

(P-6427)
AEROCRAFT HEAT TREATING
CO INC
15701 Minnesota Ave, Paramount
(90723-4120)
PHONE..................562 674-2400
David W Dickson, *CEO*
Robert Lyddon, *Vice Pres*
EMP: 57 EST: 1947
SQ FT: 18,000
SALES (est): 14.2MM
SALES (corp-wide): 245.5B **Publicly
Held**
WEB: www.aerocraft-ht.com
SIC: 3398 Metal heat treating
HQ: Precision Castparts Corp.
4650 Sw Mcdam Ave Ste 300
Portland OR 97239
503 946-4800

(P-6428)
AL-MAG HEAT TREAT
9735 Alpaca St, South El Monte
(91733-3028)
PHONE..................626 442-8570
Don Dees, *President*
EMP: 16 EST: 1961
SQ FT: 12,000
SALES (est): 1.6MM **Privately Held**
WEB: www.almagheattreat.com
SIC: 3398 Metal heat treating

(P-6429)
AREMAC HEAT TREATING INC
330 S 9th Ave, City of Industry
(91746-3311)
P.O. Box 90068 (91715-0068)
PHONE..................626 333-3898
B E Kopaskie, *President*
Bernard E Kopaskie, *President*
D R Butler, *Vice Pres*
Ed Grott, *General Mgr*
Jan Kopaskie, *Admin Sec*
EMP: 38 EST: 1967
SQ FT: 14,000
SALES (est): 8.8MM **Privately Held**
WEB: www.aremac.com
SIC: 3398 Metal heat treating

(P-6430)
ASTRO ALUMINUM TREATING
CO
11040 Palmer Ave, South Gate
(90280-7497)
PHONE..................562 923-4344
Mark R Dickson, *President*
Sabino Luevano, *Executive*
Mike Burns, *Controller*
Mark Streiff, *Controller*
Josh Hansen, *Opers Mgr*
EMP: 90 EST: 1977
SQ FT: 4,800
SALES (est): 19MM **Privately Held**
SIC: 3398 Metal heat treating

(P-6431)
BODYCOTE THERMAL PROC
INC
515 W Apra St Ste A, Rancho Dominguez
(90220-5523)
PHONE..................310 604-8000
Jose Catano, *Branch Mgr*
Tracy Glende, *President*
Seth Walradth, *Office Mgr*
Mike Naylor, *Analyst*
Sandra Furguson, *Recruiter*
EMP: 21
SALES (corp-wide): 795.2MM **Privately
Held**
WEB: www.bodycote.com
SIC: 3398 Metal heat treating
HQ: Bodycote Thermal Processing, Inc.
12750 Merit Dr Ste 1400
Dallas TX 75251
214 904-2420

(P-6432)
BODYCOTE USA INC
2900 S Sunol Dr, Vernon (90058-4315)
PHONE..................323 264-0111
Adam Hoeker, *Vice Pres*
John Peacock, *Engineer*
EMP: 2267
SQ FT: 31,717
SALES (corp-wide): 795.2MM **Privately
Held**
WEB: www.bodycote.com
SIC: 3398 Metal heat treating
HQ: Bodycote Usa, Inc.
12750 Merit Dr Ste 1400
Dallas TX 75251
214 904-2420

(P-6433)
BODYCOTE W CAST ANLYTCAL
SVC I
Also Called: Metal Analysis
9840 Alburtis Ave, Santa Fe Springs
(90670-3208)
PHONE..................562 948-2225
Ian Nichol, *President*
Mark Batgaz, *Vice Pres*
Dana Cornelius, *Sales Staff*
Shaylyn Herrera, *Assistant*
EMP: 39 EST: 1967
SQ FT: 13,500
SALES (est): 500.4K **Privately Held**
WEB: www.bodycote.com
SIC: 3398 Metal heat treating

(P-6434)
BURBANK STEEL TREATING
INC
415 S Varney St, Burbank (91502-2194)
PHONE..................818 842-0975
Mildred Bennett, *Ch of Bd*
Larry Bennett, *President*

Kenneth Bennett, *Vice Pres*
Oscar Osornio, *QC Mgr*
EMP: 45 EST: 1969
SQ FT: 16,000
SALES (est): 7.9MM **Privately Held**
WEB: www.burbanksteel.com
SIC: 3398 Metal heat treating

(P-6435)
CALSTRIP STEEL
CORPORATION (HQ)
3030 Dulles Dr, Jurupa Valley
(91752-3240)
PHONE..................323 838-2097
Thomas B Nelis, *President*
Douglas Clark, *Vice Pres*
Robert Grattan, *Sales Mgr*
Tommy Rodriguez, *Manager*
▲ EMP: 76 EST: 1930
SQ FT: 190,000
SALES (est): 18.4MM
SALES (corp-wide): 160MM **Privately
Held**
WEB: www.calstripsteel.com
SIC: 3398 3316 Metal heat treating; strip
steel, cold-rolled: from purchased hot-
rolled
PA: Calstrip Industries, Inc.
3030 Dulles Dr
Jurupa Valley CA 91752
323 726-1345

(P-6436)
COAST HEAT TREATING CO
1767 Industrial Way, Los Angeles
(90023-4394)
PHONE..................323 263-6944
Frank Garcia, *President*
EMP: 18 EST: 1953
SQ FT: 10,000
SALES (est): 1.5MM **Privately Held**
SIC: 3398 Metal heat treating

(P-6437)
CONTINENTAL HEAT TREATING
INC
10643 Norwalk Blvd, Santa Fe Springs
(90670-3821)
PHONE..................562 944-8808
James Stull, *President*
Dennis Hugie, *Principal*
Don Lowman, *Principal*
Ken Nelson, *Principal*
Shaun Radford, *General Mgr*
EMP: 62 EST: 1957
SQ FT: 20,000
SALES (est): 9.9MM **Privately Held**
WEB: www.continentalht.com
SIC: 3398 Metal heat treating

(P-6438)
COOK INDUCTION HEATING CO
INC
4925 Slauson Ave, Maywood (90270-3094)
P.O. Box 430 (90270-0430)
PHONE..................323 560-1327
Keith Doolittle, *CEO*
Richard Egkan, *Vice Pres*
EMP: 21 EST: 1945
SQ FT: 24,500
SALES (est): 2.5MM **Privately Held**
WEB: www.cookinduction.com
SIC: 3398 3728 Metal heat treating; air-
craft assemblies, subassemblies & parts

(P-6439)
DIVERSFIED MTLLRGICAL SVCS
INC
Also Called: Varco Heat Treating
12101 Industry St, Garden Grove
(92841-2813)
P.O. Box 5500 (92846-0500)
PHONE..................714 895-7777
Don A Gay, *President*
Winston E Mote, *Vice Pres*
EMP: 39 EST: 1908
SQ FT: 28,000
SALES (est): 2.8MM **Privately Held**
WEB: www.varcoheat.com
SIC: 3398 4924 3479 Metal heat treating;
natural gas distribution; coating of metals
& formed products

(P-6440)
HI TECH HEAT TREATING INC
331 W 168th St, Gardena (90248-2732)
PHONE..................................310 532-3705
Alastair Oldfield, *President*
EMP: 15 **EST:** 1998
SALES (est): 879.6K **Privately Held**
SIC: 3398 Metal heat treating

(P-6441)
INTERNTONAL METALLURGICAL SVCS
Also Called: Scarrott Metallurgical Co
6371 Arizona Cir, Los Angeles
(90045-1201)
PHONE..................................310 645-7300
Dave Scarrott, *President*
Ralph Jones, *Vice Pres*
Laura Farrell, *Accounting Mgr*
German Nunez, *QC Mgr*
EMP: 19 **EST:** 1977
SQ FT: 8,000
SALES (est): 4.7MM **Privately Held**
WEB: www.scarrott.com
SIC: 3398 Brazing (hardening) of metal

(P-6442)
KITTYHAWK INC
11651 Monarch St, Garden Grove
(92841-1816)
PHONE..................................714 895-5024
Dennis Poor, *President*
Brandon Creason, *Sales Mgr*
EMP: 29 **EST:** 1995
SALES (est): 1.2MM **Privately Held**
WEB: www.kittyhawkinc.com
SIC: 3398 Metal heat treating

(P-6443)
KITTYHAWK PRODUCTS CA LLC
11651 Monarch St, Garden Grove
(92841-1816)
PHONE..................................714 895-5024
Brandon Creason, *Principal*
Daniel Bednar, *Principal*
Kimberly Dickerson, *Principal*
EMP: 25 **EST:** 2019
SALES (est): 1MM **Privately Held**
WEB: www.kittyhawkinc.com
SIC: 3398 Metal heat treating

(P-6444)
KPI SERVICES INC
Also Called: Kittyhawk Products
11651 Monarch St, Garden Grove
(92841-1816)
PHONE..................................714 895-5024
Charles Barre, *CEO*
Dennis Poor, *President*
Lois Barre, *Corp Secy*
Steve Belloise, *Vice Pres*
Dee Dee Poor, *Vice Pres*
▲ **EMP:** 35 **EST:** 1995
SQ FT: 12,500
SALES (est): 4.7MM **Privately Held**
WEB: www.kittyhawkinc.com
SIC: 3398 Metal heat treating

(P-6445)
METAL IMPROVEMENT COMPANY LLC
E/M Coatings Solutions
6940 Farmdale Ave, North Hollywood
(91605-6210)
PHONE..................................818 983-1952
Brent Taylor, *Branch Mgr*
EMP: 85
SALES (corp-wide): 2.3B **Publicly Held**
WEB: www.cwst.com
SIC: 3398 Shot peening (treating steel to
reduce fatigue)
HQ: Metal Improvement Company, Llc
80 E Rte 4 Ste 310
Paramus NJ 07652
201 843-7800

(P-6446)
METAL IMPROVEMENT COMPANY LLC
Also Called: Para Tech Coating
35 Argonaut Ste A1, Laguna Hills
(92656-4151)
PHONE..................................949 855-8010
Bill Gleason, *Manager*
Patricia Langraphi, *QC Mgr*

EMP: 30
SALES (corp-wide): 2.3B **Publicly Held**
WEB: www.cwst.com
SIC: 3398 Shot peening (treating steel to
reduce fatigue)
HQ: Metal Improvement Company, Llc
80 E Rte 4 Ste 310
Paramus NJ 07652
201 843-7800

(P-6447)
METAL IMPROVEMENT COMPANY LLC
E/M Coatings Services
20751 Superior St, Chatsworth
(91311-4416)
PHONE..................................818 407-6280
Brent Taylor, *Branch Mgr*
David Garduno, *Finance Mgr*
EMP: 96
SALES (corp-wide): 2.3B **Publicly Held**
WEB: www.cwst.com
SIC: 3398 Shot peening (treating steel to
reduce fatigue)
HQ: Metal Improvement Company, Llc
80 E Rte 4 Ste 310
Paramus NJ 07652
201 843-7800

(P-6448)
NEWTON HEAT TREATING CO INC
19235 E Walnut Dr N, City of Industry
(91748-1494)
P.O. Box 8010, Rowland Heights (91748-
0010)
PHONE..................................626 964-6528
Greg Newton, *President*
Scott Sockwell, *Executive*
Joe Osequera, *General Mgr*
Linda Malcor, *Admin Sec*
Linda Medina, *Controller*
EMP: 71 **EST:** 1968
SQ FT: 1,900
SALES (est): 7.6MM **Privately Held**
WEB: www.newtonheattreating.com
SIC: 3398 8734 3444 Metal heat treating;
X-ray inspection service, industrial; sheet
metalwork

(P-6449)
PALMDALE HEAT TREATING INC
38834 17th St E, Palmdale (93550-3915)
P.O. Box 901237 (93590-1237)
PHONE..................................661 274-8604
Jon Fishel, *President*
Janette Gorman, *Treasurer*
Catherine Battaglia, *Corp Secy*
James Rodgers, *Vice Pres*
EMP: 13 **EST:** 1993
SQ FT: 5,000
SALES (est): 515K **Privately Held**
SIC: 3398 Metal heat treating

(P-6450)
PEEN-RITE INC
11662 Sheldon St, Sun Valley
(91352-1597)
PHONE..................................818 767-3676
Bill Swanson, *President*
Richard Bluth, *Vice Pres*
Tillie Bluth, *Admin Sec*
Tito Garcia, *Production*
EMP: 24 **EST:** 1965
SQ FT: 13,000
SALES (est): 3.1MM **Privately Held**
WEB: www.peenrite.com
SIC: 3398 Shot peening (treating steel to
reduce fatigue)

(P-6451)
PRO TECH THERMAL SERVICES
1954 Tandem, Norco (92860-3607)
PHONE..................................951 272-5808
Brian Grier, *President*
Nathan Smith, *Principal*
Carolyn Dearborn, *Accountant*
John Chorich, *Plant Supt*
Keith Grier, *Sales Staff*
EMP: 33 **EST:** 1997
SQ FT: 4,000
SALES (est): 6.9MM **Privately Held**
WEB: www.protechthermal.com
SIC: 3398 Metal heat treating

(P-6452)
QUALITY HEAT TREATING INC
3305 Burton Ave, Burbank (91504-3199)
PHONE..................................818 840-8212
James G Stull, *President*
Howard Galass, *Opers Mgr*
William Duarte, *QC Mgr*
EMP: 34 **EST:** 1945
SQ FT: 20,000
SALES (est): 3.6MM **Privately Held**
WEB: www.qualityht.com
SIC: 3398 3471 Metal heat treating; sand
blasting of metal parts

(P-6453)
SUPREME STEEL TREATING INC
2466 Seaman Ave, El Monte (91733-1926)
PHONE..................................626 350-5865
Neal Begerow, *President*
Irene Jimenez, *Executive*
EMP: 20 **EST:** 1982
SQ FT: 5,400
SALES (est): 3.8MM **Privately Held**
WEB: www.supremesteeltreating.com
SIC: 3398 Metal heat treating

(P-6454)
TEAM INC
Also Called: Team Industrial Services
1515 240th St, Harbor City (90710-1308)
PHONE..................................310 514-2312
Bill Pigeon, *Manager*
Lisa Grigsby, *Admin Asst*
Chuck Morissette, *Comp Spec*
Frede Maxwell, *Director*
Linda Duncan, *Assistant*
EMP: 21
SALES (corp-wide): 852.5MM **Publicly
Held**
WEB: www.teaminc.com
SIC: 3398 3567 Metal heat treating; heat-
ing units & devices, industrial: electric;
fuel-fired furnaces & ovens
HQ: Team, Inc.
5095 Paris St
Denver CO 80239

(P-6455)
THERMAL-VAC TECHNOLOGY INC
1221 W Struck Ave, Orange (92867-3531)
PHONE..................................714 997-2601
Steve Driscol, *CEO*
Aaron Anderson, *President*
Harry Rowe, *Exec Dir*
Eric Chen, *Engineer*
Shannon Driscol, *Opers Mgr*
EMP: 41 **EST:** 1985
SQ FT: 26,800
SALES (est): 8.7MM **Privately Held**
WEB: www.thermalvac.com
SIC: 3398 Brazing (hardening) of metal

(P-6456)
TRI-J METAL HEAT TREATING CO (PA)
327 E Commercial St, Pomona
(91767-5505)
PHONE..................................909 622-9999
Debra Cramer, *Admin Sec*
Albert W James Jr, *President*
Robert L James, *Vice Pres*
Lena James, *Admin Sec*
▲ **EMP:** 19 **EST:** 1976
SQ FT: 17,500
SALES (est): 2.9MM **Privately Held**
WEB: www.trijonline.com
SIC: 3398 Annealing of metal

(P-6457)
VALLEY METAL TREATING INC
355 S East End Ave, Pomona
(91766-2312)
PHONE..................................909 623-6316
James G Stull, *President*
Doug Kriezel, *QC Mgr*
EMP: 38 **EST:** 1986
SQ FT: 8,000
SALES (est): 4.1MM **Privately Held**
WEB: www.valleymt.net
SIC: 3398 Metal heat treating

3399 Primary Metal Prdts, NEC

(P-6458)
CAPCO UNLIMITED
591 Apollo St, Brea (92821-3127)
P.O. Box 434 (92822-0434)
PHONE..................................714 257-0154
Chuck Sprag, *Principal*
EMP: 13 **EST:** 1998
SALES (est): 213.1K **Privately Held**
SIC: 3399 Iron ore recovery from open
hearth slag

(P-6459)
MELLING TOOL RUSH METALS LLC
Also Called: Melling Sintered Metals
16100 S Figueroa St, Gardena
(90248-2617)
PHONE..................................580 725-3295
Mark Melling, *CEO*
▲ **EMP:** 32 **EST:** 2003
SQ FT: 48,000
SALES (est): 2.1MM
SALES (corp-wide): 206.3MM **Privately
Held**
WEB: www.melling.com
SIC: 3399 Powder, metal
PA: Melling Tool Co.
2620 Saradan Dr
Jackson MI 49202
517 787-8172

(P-6460)
MICRO SURFACE ENGR INC (PA)
Also Called: Ball TEC
1550 E Slauson Ave, Los Angeles
(90011-5099)
P.O. Box 58611 (90011)
PHONE..................................323 582-7348
Eugene A Gleason Jr, *President*
Eugene A Gleason III, *Corp Secy*
Helen Gleason, *Vice Pres*
Patricia Johnson, *Finance Dir*
Tony Velazquez, *Prdtn Mgr*
EMP: 35 **EST:** 1952
SQ FT: 46,000
SALES (est): 9.3MM **Privately Held**
WEB: www.precisionballs.com
SIC: 3399 Steel balls

(P-6461)
PRECISION PWDRED MET PARTS INC
145 Atlantic St, Pomona (91768-3286)
PHONE..................................909 595-5656
Maurice Bridgman, *President*
David Connelly, *Treasurer*
Quan Nguyen, *Chief Engr*
▲ **EMP:** 48 **EST:** 1978
SQ FT: 25,000
SALES (est): 8MM **Privately Held**
WEB: www.precisionpm.com
SIC: 3399 Powder, metal

(P-6462)
RONMAN PRODUCTS INC
8440 Kass Dr, Buena Park (90621-3822)
PHONE..................................714 735-3146
Robert J Wilkinson, *CEO*
Carmen Wilkinson, *President*
Olivia Gonsalves, *Credit Mgr*
Mark Strobel, *Purch Mgr*
Shane Lemmer, *Purchasing*
▲ **EMP:** 15 **EST:** 1962
SQ FT: 22,000
SALES (est): 4.4MM **Privately Held**
WEB: www.ronman.com
SIC: 3399 Metal fasteners

(P-6463)
UNITED METAL PRODUCTS INC
Also Called: Ump
234 N Sherman Ave, Corona (92882-1843)
PHONE..................................951 739-9535
Bernie Smokowski, *President*
Jacqueline Lowery, *Corp Secy*
Ryan Jones, *Vice Pres*
Patricia Smokowski, *Vice Pres*
Jim Murphy, *General Mgr*
EMP: 14

SALES (est): 2.7MM **Privately Held**
WEB: www.unitedmetalproducts.info
SIC: 3399 Metal fasteners

3411 Metal Cans

(P-6464)
JOSEPH COMPANY INTL INC
1711 Langley Ave, Irvine (92614-5679)
PHONE....................................949 474-2200
Mitchell J Joseph, *President*
Scott Berger, *Exec VP*
Matteo Joseph, *Technical Staff*
▲ **EMP:** 20 **EST:** 2010
SQ FT: 18,000
SALES (est): 3.9MM **Privately Held**
WEB: www.chillcan.com
SIC: 3411 Food & beverage containers

(P-6465)
METAL CONTAINER CORPORATION
7155 Central Ave, Riverside (92504-1400)
PHONE....................................951 354-0444
Bob Parker, *Branch Mgr*
EMP: 158
SALES (corp-wide): 1.2B **Privately Held**
WEB: www.metal-containers.com
SIC: 3411 Can lids & ends, metal
HQ: Metal Container Corporation
　　3636 S Geyer Rd Ste 100
　　Saint Louis MO 63127
　　314 577-2000

(P-6466)
METAL CONTAINER CORPORATION
10980 Inland Ave, Jurupa Valley (91752-1127)
PHONE....................................951 360-4500
Otto Sosapavon, *Principal*
EMP: 158
SALES (corp-wide): 1.2B **Privately Held**
WEB: www.metal-containers.com
SIC: 3411 Aluminum cans
HQ: Metal Container Corporation
　　3636 S Geyer Rd Ste 100
　　Saint Louis MO 63127
　　314 577-2000

(P-6467)
NOKA LLC
15332 Antioch St Ste 199, Pacific Palisades (90272-3603)
PHONE....................................214 455-3888
Ryan Werner, *Principal*
Adam Steiner, *Principal*
EMP: 13 **EST:** 2011
SALES (est): 6MM **Privately Held**
WEB: www.nokaorganics.com
SIC: 3411 Food & beverage containers

(P-6468)
SILGAN CONTAINERS CORPORATION (DH)
21600 Oxnard St Ste 1600, Woodland Hills (91367-3609)
PHONE....................................818 710-3700
Anthony J Allott, *CEO*
Thomas J Snyder, *Ch of Bd*
James D Beam, *President*
R Phillip Silver, *Vice Ch Bd*
Joseph Heaney, *Vice Pres*
◆ **EMP:** 100 **EST:** 1987
SALES (est): 577.8MM **Publicly Held**
WEB: www.silgancontainers.com
SIC: 3411 Food containers, metal
HQ: Silgan Containers Llc
　　21600 Oxnard St Ste 1600
　　Woodland Hills CA 91367
　　818 710-3700

(P-6469)
SILGAN CONTAINERS LLC (HQ)
21600 Oxnard St Ste 1600, Woodland Hills (91367-5082)
PHONE....................................818 710-3700
Thomas Snyder, *President*
Ron Ford, *CFO*
Richard Brewer, *Senior VP*
Daniel Carson, *Senior VP*
Michael Beninato, *Vice Pres*
◆ **EMP:** 100 **EST:** 1997

SALES (est): 1.7B **Publicly Held**
WEB: www.silgancontainers.com
SIC: 3411 Food containers, metal

(P-6470)
SILGAN CONTAINERS MFG CORP (DH)
21600 Oxnard St Ste 1600, Woodland Hills (91367-5082)
PHONE....................................818 710-3700
Thomas Snyder, *Principal*
Jason Tallinger, *Dept Chairman*
Paul Goldberger, *Director*
Carl Antone, *Manager*
Mike Dean, *Supervisor*
EMP: 263 **EST:** 1997
SALES (est): 494.6MM **Publicly Held**
WEB: www.silgancontainers.com
SIC: 3411 Metal cans
HQ: Silgan Containers Llc
　　21600 Oxnard St Ste 1600
　　Woodland Hills CA 91367
　　818 710-3700

3412 Metal Barrels, Drums, Kegs & Pails

(P-6471)
B STEPHEN COOPERAGE INC
10746 Vernon Ave, Ontario (91762-4039)
P.O. Box 9537 (91762-9537)
PHONE....................................909 591-2929
Toll Free:....................................877 -
Mike Stephen, *CEO*
Ben Stephen, *President*
EMP: 15 **EST:** 1952
SQ FT: 174,240
SALES (est): 1.5MM **Privately Held**
WEB: www.bstephencooperage.com
SIC: 3412 Metal barrels, drums & pails

3421 Cutlery

(P-6472)
COLD STEEL INC (PA)
6060 Nicolle St, Ventura (93003-7600)
P.O. Box 535189, Grand Prairie TX (75053-5189)
PHONE....................................805 650-8481
Lynn C Thompson, *President*
Evelyn Hernandez, *Executive Asst*
Tyler Bullis, *Marketing Mgr*
Tracy Miles,
Gene Ortega, *Director*
◆ **EMP:** 18 **EST:** 1980
SQ FT: 7,000
SALES (est): 6.6MM **Privately Held**
WEB: www.coldsteel.com
SIC: 5961 3421 Catalog sales; knives: butchers', hunting, pocket, etc.

3423 Hand & Edge Tools

(P-6473)
ADVANCED CUTTING TOOLS INC
17741 Metzler Ln, Huntington Beach (92647-6246)
PHONE....................................714 842-9376
Stjepan Herceg, *President*
EMP: 30 **EST:** 1987
SQ FT: 10,200
SALES (est): 2.5MM **Privately Held**
WEB: www.advancedcuttingtools.com
SIC: 3423 3545 5251 Hand & edge tools; machine tool accessories; tools

(P-6474)
CALIFORNIA FLEXRAKE CORP
9620 Gidley St, Temple City (91780-4215)
PHONE....................................626 443-4026
John P McGuire, *President*
▲ **EMP:** 25 **EST:** 1946
SALES (est): 3.7MM **Privately Held**
WEB: www.flexrake.com
SIC: 3423 Garden & farm tools, including shovels

(P-6475)
CRAFTSMAN CUTTING DIES INC (PA)
Also Called: Ccd
2273 E Via Burton, Anaheim (92806-1222)
PHONE....................................714 776-8995
Thomas Hughes, *President*
David Chidester, *CFO*
Cathy Ong-Chan, *Corp Secy*
Ronald Ong, *Vice Pres*
▲ **EMP:** 22 **EST:** 1986
SQ FT: 11,000
SALES (est): 2.8MM **Privately Held**
WEB: www.craftsmancuttingdies.com
SIC: 3423 3544 Cutting dies, except metal cutting; special dies, tools, jigs & fixtures

(P-6476)
CRAFTSMAN UNITY LLC
2273 E Via Burton, Anaheim (92806-1222)
PHONE....................................714 776-8995
Graham Butler, *Mng Member*
EMP: 175 **EST:** 1986
SALES (est): 9.4MM **Privately Held**
SIC: 3423 Cutting dies, except metal cutting

(P-6477)
DURSTON MANUFACTURING COMPANY
Also Called: Vim Tools
1395 Palomares St, La Verne (91750-5241)
P.O. Box 340 (91750-0340)
PHONE....................................909 593-1506
Donovan Norton, *CEO*
James Maloney, *President*
Mary Dills, *Accounting Mgr*
▲ **EMP:** 18 **EST:** 1946
SQ FT: 29,000
SALES (est): 2.2MM **Privately Held**
WEB: www.vimtools.com
SIC: 3423 Mechanics' hand tools

(P-6478)
EQH LIMITED INC
5440 Mcconnell Ave, Los Angeles (90066-7037)
PHONE....................................310 736-4130
Eric Golden, *President*
EMP: 14 **EST:** 2007
SALES (est): 467.3K **Privately Held**
SIC: 3423 3523 Tools or equipment for use with sporting arms; planting, haying, harvesting & processing machinery

(P-6479)
FLEX-MATE INC
Also Called: D & G Manufacturing
1855 E 29th St Ste E, Signal Hill (90755-1919)
PHONE....................................562 426-7169
Theresa Gleason, *President*
EMP: 14 **EST:** 1998
SQ FT: 6,000
SALES (est): 483K **Privately Held**
SIC: 3423 Hand & edge tools

(P-6480)
FUN PROPERTIES INC (PA)
Also Called: PEC Tool
2645 Maricopa St, Torrance (90503-5144)
PHONE....................................310 787-4500
Richard A Luboviski, *CEO*
Bernard Brooks, *Treasurer*
Julie Hood, *Vice Pres*
Sandy Luboviski, *Vice Pres*
Sandra Molioo, *Human Res Dir*
◆ **EMP:** 53 **EST:** 1960
SQ FT: 68,000
SALES (est): 4.5MM **Privately Held**
WEB: www.pec.tools
SIC: 3423 Hand & edge tools

(P-6481)
GARDEN PALS INC
21753 Birch Hill Dr, Diamond Bar (91765-3106)
PHONE....................................909 605-0200
WEI Chun Hsu, *CEO*
Robert Deal, *COO*
◆ **EMP:** 20 **EST:** 1990

SALES (est): 4.6MM **Privately Held**
WEB: www.formosatools.com
SIC: 3423 Garden & farm tools, including shovels
PA: Formosa Tools Co., Ltd.
　　No. 22, Yanhai Rd., Sec. 2
　　Fushing Hsiang CHA 50645

(P-6482)
HALEX CORPORATION (HQ)
4200 Santa Ana St Ste A, Ontario (91761-1539)
PHONE....................................909 629-6219
Mark Chichak, *President*
◆ **EMP:** 43 **EST:** 2002
SALES (est): 40.9MM
SALES (corp-wide): 903.2MM **Publicly Held**
WEB: www.gcpat.com
SIC: 3423 Carpet layers' hand tools
PA: Gcp Applied Technologies Inc.
　　62 Whittemore Ave
　　Cambridge MA 02140
　　617 876-1400

(P-6483)
KAL-CAMERON MANUFACTURING CORP (HQ)
Also Called: Pro American Premium Tools
4265 Puente Ave, Baldwin Park (91706-3420)
PHONE....................................626 338-7308
John Toshima, *Ch of Bd*
EMP: 100 **EST:** 1983
SQ FT: 32,000
SALES (est): 9.2MM
SALES (corp-wide): 24.3MM **Privately Held**
WEB: www.americankal.com
SIC: 3423 Mechanics' hand tools
PA: American Kal Enterprises, Inc.
　　4265 Puente Ave
　　Baldwin Park CA 91706
　　626 338-7308

(P-6484)
KEMPER ENTERPRISES INC
13595 12th St, Chino (91710-5208)
P.O. Box 696 (91708-0696)
PHONE....................................909 627-6191
Herbert H Stampfl, *President*
Herbert Stampfl, *Executive*
Librado Cortez, *Admin Sec*
Dolores Maufras, *Sales Mgr*
Debbie Biessener, *Director*
▲ **EMP:** 26 **EST:** 1947
SQ FT: 30,000
SALES (est): 1.4MM **Privately Held**
WEB: www.kempertools.com
SIC: 3423 Hand & edge tools

(P-6485)
LARIN CORP
5651 Schaefer Ave, Chino (91710-9048)
PHONE....................................909 464-0605
Shouyun Zhang, *President*
▲ **EMP:** 20 **EST:** 1989
SQ FT: 50,000
SALES (est): 2.1MM **Privately Held**
WEB: www.larincorp.com
SIC: 3423 Jacks: lifting, screw or ratchet (hand tools)

(P-6486)
MEISEI TOOLS LLC
948 Tourmaline Dr, Thousand Oaks (91320-1206)
PHONE....................................805 497-2626
John Lippert, *CFO*
J Spiegel, *Mng Member*
EMP: 14 **EST:** 2018
SALES (est): 2MM **Privately Held**
WEB: www.meiseitools.com
SIC: 3423 3541 Mechanics' hand tools; machine tool replacement & repair parts, metal cutting types

(P-6487)
NUPLA LLC
11912 Sheldon St, Sun Valley (91352-1509)
PHONE....................................818 768-6800
Ronald Ortiz,
▲ **EMP:** 120 **EST:** 2002
SQ FT: 160,000

SALES (est): 24MM
SALES (corp-wide): 26.6MM **Privately Held**
WEB: www.nuplatools.com
SIC: **3423** 3089 Hand & edge tools; handles, brush or tool: plastic
PA: Saunders Midwest Llc
29 E Madison St Ste 900
Chicago IL 60602
312 372-3690

(P-6488)
PACIFIC HANDY CUTTER INC (DH)
Also Called: PHC
17819 Gillette Ave, Irvine (92614-6501)
PHONE.................................714 662-1033
Mark Marinovich, *CEO*
▲ EMP: 34 EST: 1960
SQ FT: 16,000
SALES (est): 7.6MM
SALES (corp-wide): 148.4MM **Privately Held**
WEB: www.phcsafety.com
SIC: **3423** 3421 Hand & edge tools; cutlery
HQ: Phc Sharp Holdings, Inc.
17819 Gillette Ave
Irvine CA 92614
714 662-1033

(P-6489)
SHARP PROFILES LLC
828 W Cienega Ave, San Dimas (91773-2489)
PHONE.................................760 246-9446
EMP: 15
SALES (est): 3.8MM **Privately Held**
SIC: **3423** Mfg Hand/Edge Tools

(P-6490)
STANLEY ACCESS TECH LLC
15750 Jurupa Ave, Fontana (92337-7329)
PHONE.................................909 628-9272
John Rapisarda, *Manager*
EMP: 20
SALES (corp-wide): 14.5B **Publicly Held**
WEB: www.stanleyaccess.com
SIC: **3423** Hand & edge tools
HQ: Stanley Access Technologies Llc
65 Scott Swamp Rd
Farmington CT 06032

(P-6491)
TOUGHBUILT INDUSTRIES INC (PA)
25371 Cmmrcntre Dr Dte 20 20 Dte, Lake Forest (92630)
PHONE.................................949 528-3100
Michael Panosian, *Ch of Bd*
Zareh Khachatoorian, *COO*
Manu Ohri, *CFO*
Tod Egan, *Vice Pres*
Joshua Keeler, *Vice Pres*
EMP: 14 EST: 2012
SQ FT: 8,300
SALES (est): 39.4MM **Publicly Held**
WEB: www.toughbuilt.com
SIC: **3423** 3429 3069 Hand & edge tools; manufactured hardware (general); kneeling pads, rubber

---

3425 Hand Saws & Saw Blades

(P-6492)
DIAMOND K2
23911 Garnier St Ste C, Torrance (90505-7523)
P.O. Box 346 (90508-0346)
PHONE.................................310 539-6116
Les Kuzmick, *Ch of Bd*
Richard Kirby, *President*
Monty Baswell, *Sales Staff*
Gary Ferras, *Sales Staff*
EMP: 21 EST: 1993
SQ FT: 7,600
SALES (est): 2.8MM **Privately Held**
WEB: www.k2diamond.com
SIC: **3425** 3531 5082 Saw blades & handsaws; construction machinery; concrete processing equipment

(P-6493)
WESTERN SAW MANUFACTURERS INC
3200 Camino Del Sol, Oxnard (93030-8998)
PHONE.................................805 981-0999
Kevin Baron, *CEO*
Kraig Baron, *President*
Frank Baron, *CEO*
Nancy Pounds, *Corp Secy*
Steve Williams, *Info Tech Dir*
◆ EMP: 50 EST: 1930
SQ FT: 70,000
SALES (est): 10.8MM **Privately Held**
WEB: www.westernsaw.com
SIC: **3425** 3546 Saw blades & handsaws; power-driven handtools

---

3429 Hardware, NEC

(P-6494)
ACCURIDE INTERNATIONAL INC (PA)
12311 Shoemaker Ave, Santa Fe Springs (90670-4721)
PHONE.................................562 903-0200
Scott E Jordan, *CEO*
Sid Kalantar, *Vice Pres*
Karen Chown, *Administration*
Mario Rojas, *Info Tech Dir*
Todd Watanabe, *Electrical Engi*
▲ EMP: 47
SALES (est): 369.2MM **Privately Held**
WEB: www.accuride.com
SIC: **3429** Manufactured hardware (general)

(P-6495)
ACTRON MANUFACTURING INC
1841 Railroad St, Corona (92878-5012)
PHONE.................................951 371-0885
Frank Rechberg, *CEO*
Dow Rechberg, *Corp Secy*
EMP: 93
SQ FT: 30,000
SALES (est): 16.6MM **Privately Held**
WEB: www.actronmfginc.com
SIC: **3429** Aircraft hardware

(P-6496)
ADVANCED VEHICLE MFG INC (PA)
892 W 10th St, Azusa (91702-1935)
PHONE.................................866 622-8628
Lawrence Brennan, *CEO*
EMP: 17 EST: 2014
SALES (est): 101.2K **Privately Held**
WEB: www.avmfg.com
SIC: **3429** Motor vehicle hardware

(P-6497)
ALARIN AIRCRAFT HINGE INC
Also Called: Commerce
6231 Randolph St, Commerce (90040-3514)
PHONE.................................323 725-1666
Gregory A Sanders, *President*
Maria Dolores Castaneda, *Office Mgr*
Jaden Luu, *Prgrmr*
Lola Castaneda, *Human Res Mgr*
Joce Tonnu, *Director*
EMP: 25
SQ FT: 11,000
SALES (est): 4.7MM **Privately Held**
WEB: www.alarin.com
SIC: **3429** 3728 Aircraft hardware; aircraft parts & equipment

(P-6498)
ASCO SINTERING CO
2750 Garfield Ave, Commerce (90040-2610)
P.O. Box 911157 (90091-1157)
PHONE.................................323 725-3550
Neil Moore, *CEO*
Robert Lebrun, *CFO*
Danny Rosales, *Technician*
▲ EMP: 33 EST: 1971
SQ FT: 69,000
SALES (est): 6.7MM **Privately Held**
WEB: www.ascosintering.com
SIC: **3429** 3714 Manufactured hardware (general); motor vehicle parts & accessories

(P-6499)
ASSA ABLOY ACC DOOR CNTRLS GRO
4226 Transport St, Ventura (93003-5627)
PHONE.................................805 642-2600
EMP: 80
SALES (corp-wide): 10.1B **Privately Held**
WEB: www.assaabloydooraccessories.us
SIC: **3429** 3466 Locks or lock sets; door opening & closing devices, except electrical; crowns & closures
HQ: Assa Abloy Accessories And Door Controls Group, Inc.
1902 Airport Rd
Monroe NC 28110
877 974-2255

(P-6500)
AUTOMOTIVE RACING PRODUCTS INC (PA)
Also Called: A R P
1863 Eastman Ave, Ventura (93003-8084)
PHONE.................................805 339-2200
Gary Holzapfel, *CEO*
Mike Holzapfel, *President*
Kelly Schau, *CFO*
Robert Florine, *Exec VP*
Robert Flourin, *Vice Pres*
▲ EMP: 65 EST: 1975
SQ FT: 10,000
SALES: 59.5K **Privately Held**
WEB: www.arp-bolts.com
SIC: **3429** 3714 3452 Manufactured hardware (general); motor vehicle parts & accessories; bolts, nuts, rivets & washers

(P-6501)
AUTOMOTIVE RACING PRODUCTS INC
Also Called: A R P
1760 E Lemonwood Dr, Santa Paula (93060-9510)
PHONE.................................805 525-1497
Michael Holzapsel, *Branch Mgr*
Art Venegas, *Technology*
Michael Thorson, *Mfg Staff*
Chris Raschke, *Sales Dir*
Midstokke Lynette, *Representative*
EMP: 43
SALES (corp-wide): 59.5K **Privately Held**
WEB: www.arp-bolts.com
SIC: **3429** Manufactured hardware (general)
PA: Automotive Racing Products, Inc.
1863 Eastman Ave
Ventura CA 93003
805 339-2200

(P-6502)
AVANTUS AEROSPACE INC
14957 Gwenchris Ct, Paramount (90723-3423)
PHONE.................................562 633-6626
Brian Williams, *Branch Mgr*
EMP: 50
SALES (corp-wide): 140.1MM **Privately Held**
SIC: **3429** 3452 Metal fasteners; bolts, nuts, rivets & washers
HQ: Avantus Aerospace, Inc.
29101 The Old Rd
Valencia CA 91355
661 295-8620

(P-6503)
AVIBANK MFG INC
Avk Industrial Products
25323 Rye Canyon Rd, Valencia (91355-1205)
PHONE.................................661 257-2329
James M Wolpert, *General Mgr*
EMP: 85
SQ FT: 23,000
SALES (corp-wide): 245.5B **Publicly Held**
WEB: www.avibank.com
SIC: **3429** 3541 3452 Manufactured hardware (general); machine tools, metal cutting type; bolts, nuts, rivets & washers
HQ: Avibank Mfg., Inc.
11500 Sherman Way
North Hollywood CA 91605
818 392-2100

(P-6504)
B & B SPECIALTIES INC (PA)
4321 E La Palma Ave, Anaheim (92807-1887)
PHONE.................................714 985-3000
Bruce Borchardt, *President*
Thomas Rutan, *VP Bus Dvlpt*
John Curiel, *Prgrmr*
Max Mendia, *Mfg Mgr*
Cruz Diaz, *Sales Staff*
▲ EMP: 90 EST: 1971
SQ FT: 40,000
SALES (est): 22.6MM **Privately Held**
WEB: www.bbspecialties.com
SIC: **3429** 3452 Metal fasteners; bolts, nuts, rivets & washers

(P-6505)
BAIER MARINE COMPANY INC
2920 Airway Ave, Costa Mesa (92626-6008)
PHONE.................................800 455-3917
Mark Smith, *President*
Danielle Rockmaker, *Sales Mgr*
Felice Lineberry, *Manager*
◆ EMP: 20 EST: 2007 **Privately Held**
WEB: www.baiermarine.com
SIC: **3429** Manufactured hardware (general)

(P-6506)
BALDWIN HARDWARE CORPORATION (DH)
Also Called: Baldwin Brass
19701 Da Vinci, Foothill Ranch (92610-2622)
PHONE.................................949 672-4000
David R Lumley, *CEO*
▲ EMP: 816 EST: 1944
SQ FT: 300,000
SALES (est): 131.4MM
SALES (corp-wide): 3.9B **Publicly Held**
WEB: www.baldwinhardware.com
SIC: **3429** Builders' hardware
HQ: Spectrum Brands, Inc.
3001 Deming Way
Middleton WI 53562
608 275-3340

(P-6507)
BATON LOCK & HARDWARE CO INC
Also Called: Baton Security
14275 Commerce Dr, Garden Grove (92843-4944)
PHONE.................................714 265-3636
Hwei Ying Chen, *President*
Fong Shiang Hsu, *President*
Sharron Hsu, *Vice Pres*
WEI Hsu, *Vice Pres*
Meiling Hu, *Managing Dir*
◆ EMP: 22 EST: 1971
SQ FT: 15,025
SALES (est): 654.9K **Privately Held**
SIC: **3429** Keys, locks & related hardware; locks or lock sets

(P-6508)
CAESAR HARDWARE INTL LTD
4985 Hallmark Pkwy, San Bernardino (92407-1870)
PHONE.................................800 306-3829
Chao Xu, *CEO*
EMP: 20 EST: 2012
SALES (est): 7MM **Privately Held**
WEB: www.caesarhardware.com
SIC: **3429** 3999 5021 Fireplace equipment, hardware: andirons, grates, screens; atomizers, toiletry; outdoor & lawn furniture
PA: Yuyao Super Wing Foreign Trade Co., Ltd
Room 1401, Yangguang International Mansion, No.55, Yuli Road
Yuyao

(P-6509)
CAL-JUNE INC (PA)
Also Called: Jim-Buoy
5238 Vineland Ave, North Hollywood (91601-3221)
P.O. Box 9551 (91609-1551)
PHONE.................................323 877-4164
James H Robertson, *President*

Jennifer D Jacobson, *President*
Andrea Robertson, *Vice Pres*
Melini Stevens, *Vice Pres*
◆ **EMP:** 76 **EST:** 1966
SQ FT: 3,000
SALES (est): 9MM **Privately Held**
WEB: www.jimbuoy.com
SIC: 3429 Marine hardware

(P-6510)
CALIFORNIA SCREW PRODUCTS CORP
14957 Gwenchris Ct, Paramount
(90723-3423)
P.O. Box 228 (90723-0228)
PHONE..................562 633-6626
Eric Stoltz, *Exec Dir*
Dennis Suedkamp, *CEO*
Pio Granados, *Engineer*
Letitia Serrano, *Human Res Dir*
Vikki Errett, *Purchasing*
EMP: 75 **EST:** 1966
SQ FT: 20,000
SALES (est): 9.4MM **Privately Held**
WEB: www.calscrew.net
SIC: 3429 3452 Metal fasteners; bolts, nuts, rivets & washers

(P-6511)
CALMEX FIREPLACE EQP MFG INC
Also Called: Calmex Fireplace Equip Mfg
13629 Talc St, Santa Fe Springs
(90670-5113)
PHONE..................716 645-2901
Maria Hirshal, *President*
Rosa Franco, *Vice Pres*
EMP: 20 **EST:** 1964
SQ FT: 15,000
SALES (est): 507.3K **Privately Held**
SIC: 3429 Fireplace equipment, hardware: andirons, grates, screens

(P-6512)
CONSOLIDATED AEROSPACE MFG LLC
630 E Lambert Rd, Brea (92821-4119)
PHONE..................714 989-2802
Bill Herdrich, *Vice Pres*
Jennifer Bailey, *Manager*
EMP: 32 **EST:** 2014
SALES (est): 5.1MM **Privately Held**
WEB: www.camaerospace.com
SIC: 3429 Metal fasteners

(P-6513)
CRD MFG INC
615 Fee Ana St, Placentia (92870-6704)
PHONE..................714 871-3300
Timothy Carroll, *CEO*
Alex Horowitz, *Opers Mgr*
EMP: 49 **EST:** 2011
SALES (est): 3.1MM **Privately Held**
WEB: www.crdmfg.com
SIC: 3429 3699, Motor vehicle hardware; welding machines & equipment, ultrasonic

(P-6514)
CUSTOM HARDWARE MFG INC
2112 E 4th St Ste 228g, Santa Ana
(92705-3840)
PHONE..................714 547-7440
▲ **EMP:** 45
SQ FT: 4,500
SALES: 3.4MM **Privately Held**
WEB: www.chmi.com
SIC: 3429 Mfg Hardware

(P-6515)
DOVAL INDUSTRIES INC
Also Called: Doval Industries Co
3961 N Mission Rd, Los Angeles
(90031-2931)
PHONE..................323 226-0335
Cruz Sandoval, *CEO*
▲ **EMP:** 65 **EST:** 1985
SALES (est): 4.7MM **Privately Held**
WEB: www.marksandoval.com
SIC: 3429 5072 2759 Keys, locks & related hardware; hardware; screen printing

(P-6516)
EVOLECTRIC INCORPORATED
2330 E Artesia Blvd, Long Beach
(90805-1740)
PHONE..................714 260-7022
Jakson Alvarez, *Administration*
William Beverley, *Mng Member*
EMP: 14 **EST:** 2019
SALES (est): 1MM **Privately Held**
WEB: www.evolectricnow.com
SIC: 3429 Motor vehicle hardware

(P-6517)
FRAMELESS HARDWARE COMPANY LLC
4361 Firestone Blvd, South Gate
(90280-3340)
PHONE..................888 295-4531
Donald Friese Jr, *Mng Member*
EMP: 23 **EST:** 2020
SALES (est): 5.5MM **Privately Held**
WEB: www.ccbpwin.com
SIC: 3429 1793 2591 Builders' hardware; glass & glazing work; drapery hardware & blinds & shades

(P-6518)
FXC CORPORATION (PA)
3050 Red Hill Ave, Costa Mesa
(92626-4524)
PHONE..................714 556-7400
Irene Chevrier, *CEO*
William Hawkins, *CFO*
Michael Urban, *Materials Mgr*
EMP: 21
SQ FT: 26,000
SALES (est): 12.4MM **Privately Held**
WEB: www.fxcguardian.com
SIC: 3429 2399 Parachute hardware; parachutes

(P-6519)
GARHAUER MARINE CORPORATION
1062 W 9th St, Upland (91786-5726)
PHONE..................909 985-9993
William Felgenhauer, *President*
Mary Felgenhauer, *Admin Sec*
EMP: 20 **EST:** 1971
SQ FT: 10,000
SALES (est): 3.9MM **Privately Held**
WEB: www.garhauermarine.com
SIC: 3429 Marine hardware

(P-6520)
HARTWELL CORPORATION (DH)
Also Called: Hasco
900 Richfield Rd, Placentia (92870-6788)
PHONE..................714 993-4200
Dain Miller, *President*
Joseph Juby, *Vice Pres*
Susan Martian, *General Mgr*
Liz Rodriguez, *Executive Asst*
John Boyer, *Project Leader*
▲ **EMP:** 200 **EST:** 1939
SQ FT: 134,000
SALES (est): 173.5MM
SALES (corp-wide): 4.8B **Publicly Held**
WEB: www.hartwellcorp.com
SIC: 3429 Aircraft hardware

(P-6521)
HOLLYWOOD BED SPRING MFG INC (PA)
5959 Corvette St, Commerce
(90040-1601)
PHONE..................323 887-9500
Larry Harrow, *CEO*
Jason Harrow, *President*
Jon Mullinax, *Vice Pres*
Andrea Harrow, *Admin Sec*
Ruben Gomez, *Production*
◆ **EMP:** 89 **EST:** 1945
SQ FT: 55,000
SALES (est): 17.5MM **Privately Held**
WEB: www.hollywoodbed.com
SIC: 3429 2515 2511 2514 Manufactured hardware (general); mattresses & bedsprings; wood household furniture; frames for box springs or bedsprings: metal

(P-6522)
JONATHAN ENGNRED SLUTIONS CORP (HQ)
250 Commerce Ste 100, Irvine
(92602-1341)
PHONE..................714 665-4400
Jack Frickel, *President*
Eric Hersom, *CFO*
Jason Ciancarulo, *Vice Pres*
Barbara Boyko, *Program Mgr*
Joe Meitch, *Regional Mgr*
▲ **EMP:** 44 **EST:** 1954
SQ FT: 120,000
SALES (est): 60.7MM
SALES (corp-wide): 258.1MM **Privately Held**
WEB: www.jonathanengr.com
SIC: 3429 3562 Manufactured hardware (general); ball bearings & parts
PA: Jll Partners, Llc
245 Park Ave Rm 1601
New York NY 10167
212 286-8600

(P-6523)
K & W MANUFACTURING CO INC
23107 Temescal Canyon Rd, Corona
(92883-6001)
PHONE..................951 277-3300
Gerald W Keck, *President*
Denise Jure, *Vice Pres*
Carolyn Keck, *Admin Sec*
German Salomon, *Prdtn Mgr*
EMP: 20 **EST:** 1982
SQ FT: 15,000
SALES (est): 1.3MM **Privately Held**
WEB: www.k-and-w-mfg.com
SIC: 3429 3631 Fireplace equipment, hardware: andirons, grates, screens; barbecues, grills & braziers (outdoor cooking)

(P-6524)
LIGHT COMPOSITE CORPORATION
Also Called: Forespar
22322 Gilberto, Rcho STA Marg
(92688-2102)
PHONE..................949 858-8820
Robert R Foresman, *President*
Marilyn Holst, *Treasurer*
Bill Hana, *Vice Pres*
Juin Foresman, *Principal*
Alan Massey, *Sales Staff*
▼ **EMP:** 35 **EST:** 1991
SALES (est): 3.3MM **Privately Held**
WEB: www.forespar.com
SIC: 3429 Marine hardware

(P-6525)
LOCK AMERICA INC
Also Called: Mr Lock
9168 Stellar Ct, Corona (92883-4923)
PHONE..................951 277-5180
Ming Shiao, *President*
Frank Minnella, *CEO*
Watson Visuwan, *Vice Pres*
Candice Smith, *Technology*
Dan Walsh, *Manager*
◆ **EMP:** 19
SQ FT: 11,500
SALES (est): 3.3MM **Privately Held**
WEB: www.laigroup.com
SIC: 3429 5099 Keys, locks & related hardware; locks & lock sets

(P-6526)
MID-WEST WHOLESALE HARDWARE CO
Also Called: Banner Solutions
1641 S Sunkist St, Anaheim (92806-5813)
PHONE..................714 630-4751
Terry Olson, *Branch Mgr*
EMP: 22
SALES (corp-wide): 30.6MM **Privately Held**
WEB: www.bannersolutions.com
SIC: 3429 5072 Manufactured hardware (general); hardware
PA: Mid-West Wholesale Hardware Co Inc
1000 Century Dr
Kansas City MO 64120
816 245-1142

(P-6527)
MOELLER MFG & SUP LLC
630 E Lambert Rd, Brea (92821-4119)
PHONE..................714 999-5551
Stevens Chevillotte, *President*
Peter George, *CEO*
Debbie Comstock, *Director*
EMP: 45 **EST:** 1978
SALES (est): 14MM
SALES (corp-wide): 14.5B **Publicly Held**
WEB: www.camaerospace.com
SIC: 3429 3452 Aircraft hardware; washers, metal
HQ: Consolidated Aerospace Manufacturing, Llc
1425 S Acacia Ave
Fullerton CA 92831
714 989-2797

(P-6528)
MONADNOCK COMPANY
Also Called: Lisi Aerospace
16728 Gale Ave, City of Industry
(91745-1803)
PHONE..................626 964-6581
Christian Darville, *CEO*
Michael Reyes, *Vice Pres*
Sudhir Panchal, *Technician*
Hans Ecke, *Engineer*
Joseph Sockett, *Engineer*
▼ **EMP:** 190 **EST:** 1987
SQ FT: 90,000
SALES (est): 51MM
SALES (corp-wide): 177.9K **Privately Held**
WEB: www.hi-shear.com
SIC: 3429 Aircraft hardware; metal fasteners
HQ: Hi-Shear Corporation
2600 Skypark Dr
Torrance CA 90505
310 784-4025

(P-6529)
MONOGRAM AEROSPACE FAS INC
3423 Garfield Ave, Commerce
(90040-3103)
PHONE..................323 722-4760
David Adler, *President*
John P Schaefer, *CEO*
Sean Hoskins, *Vice Pres*
Jeniffer Avila, *Administration*
Michelle Mullin, *Sales Mgr*
▲ **EMP:** 250 **EST:** 1990
SQ FT: 97,500
SALES (est): 70.9MM
SALES (corp-wide): 769.9MM **Publicly Held**
WEB: www.trsaero.com
SIC: 3429 3452 Manufactured hardware (general); bolts, metal; rivets, metal; screws, metal
PA: Trimas Corporation
38505 Woodward Ave # 200
Bloomfield Hills MI 48304
248 631-5450

(P-6530)
NUSET INC
2432 Peck Rd, City of Industry
(90601-1604)
PHONE..................626 246-1668
Caron Ng, *CEO*
EMP: 20 **EST:** 2017
SALES (est): 1.3MM **Privately Held**
WEB: www.nusetlock.com
SIC: 3429 Keys, locks & related hardware

(P-6531)
ORION ORNAMENTAL IRON INC
6918 Tujunga Ave, North Hollywood
(91605-6212)
PHONE..................818 752-0688
Sunil Patel, *CEO*
Atul Patel, *President*
Elizabeth Andonegui, *Executive*
Ben Oru, *Technology*
▲ **EMP:** 40 **EST:** 1983
SQ FT: 30,000
SALES (est): 3.3MM **Privately Held**
WEB: www.ironartbyorion.com
SIC: 3429 Builders' hardware

(P-6532)
PACIFIC LOCK COMPANY (PA)
25605 Hercules St, Valencia (91355-5051)
PHONE..............................661 294-3707
Gregory B Waugh, *President*
Patty Yang, *CFO*
Joshua Fleagane, *Vice Pres*
John Van Duzee, *Manager*
▲ **EMP:** 29 **EST:** 1998
SQ FT: 18,000
SALES (est): 3.2MM **Privately Held**
WEB: www.paclock.com
SIC: 3429 3699 5099 Keys & key blanks;
security devices; locks & lock sets

(P-6533)
R C PRODUCTS CORP
22322 Gilberto, Rcho STA Marg
(92688-2102)
PHONE..............................949 858-8820
Robert R Foresman, *President*
Marilyn Holst, *Admin Sec*
EMP: 37 **EST:** 1991
SQ FT: 40,000
SALES (est): 1.3MM
SALES (corp-wide): 9.5MM **Privately
Held**
WEB: www.forespar.com
SIC: 3429 Marine hardware
PA: Forespar Products Corp.
22322 Gilberto
Rcho Sta Marg CA 92688
949 858-8820

(P-6534)
RPC LEGACY INC
Also Called: Terry Hinge & Hardware
14600 Arminta St, Van Nuys (91402-5902)
PHONE..............................818 787-9000
Authur William, *Branch Mgr*
EMP: 15
SALES (corp-wide): 16.1MM **Privately
Held**
WEB: www.rockfordprocess.com
SIC: 3429 Manufactured hardware (gen-
eral)
PA: Rpc Legacy, Inc.
2020 7th St
Rockford IL 61104
815 966-2000

(P-6535)
SATURN FASTENERS INC
425 S Varney St, Burbank (91502-2193)
PHONE..............................818 973-1807
Raymond D Barker Jr, *President*
Laura Elaine Barker, *Chairman*
Valentin Espinoza, *Planning*
Noora Youssif, *QC Mgr*
Debbie Jones, *Sales Staff*
▲ **EMP:** 112
SQ FT: 38,000
SALES (est): 16.8MM **Privately Held**
WEB: www.saturnfasteners.com
SIC: 3429 5085 5072 3452 Metal fasten-
ers; industrial supplies; bolts, nuts &
screws; bolts, nuts, rivets & washers
HQ: Acument Global Technologies, Inc.
6125 18 Mile Rd
Sterling Heights MI 48314
586 254-3900

(P-6536)
SNAPNRACK INC
775 Fiero Ln Ste 200, San Luis Obispo
(93401-7904)
PHONE..............................877 732-2860
Lyn Cowgill, *Opers Mgr*
Ryan Work, *General Mgr*
Kevin Hooper, *Engineer*
David McLaughlin, *Engineer*
Greg McPheeters, *Engineer*
EMP: 19 **EST:** 2014
SALES (est): 2MM **Privately Held**
WEB: www.snapnrack.com
SIC: 3429 Clamps, couplings, nozzles &
other metal hose fittings

(P-6537)
**SOLID-SCOPE MACHINING CO
INC**
17925 Adria Maru Ln, Carson
(90746-1401)
PHONE..............................310 523-2366
Patsy Rhinehart, *President*
Robert Rhinehart, *Vice Pres*

EMP: 16 **EST:** 1979
SQ FT: 6,000
SALES (est): 1.8MM **Privately Held**
WEB: www.solid-scope.com
SIC: 3429 3728 Aircraft hardware; aircraft
parts & equipment

(P-6538)
SPEP ACQUISITION CORP (PA)
Also Called: Sierra Pacific Engrg & Pdts
4041 Via Oro Ave, Long Beach
(90810-1458)
P.O. Box 5246, Carson (90749-5246)
PHONE..............................310 608-0693
David Mochalski, *CEO*
Shaffiq Rahim, *CFO*
Larry Mirick, *Chairman*
Ed Zarate, *Executive*
Jhonny Cuyuch, *Engineer*
◆ **EMP:** 70
SQ FT: 48,300
SALES (est): 20.6MM **Privately Held**
WEB: www.spep.com
SIC: 3429 8711 5072 Manufactured hard-
ware (general); engineering services;
hardware

(P-6539)
STAR DIE CASTING INC
12209 Slauson Ave, Santa Fe Springs
(90670-2605)
PHONE..............................562 698-0627
Jer Ming Yu, *President*
MEI H Yu, *Treasurer*
Mark Chen, *QC Mgr*
▲ **EMP:** 80 **EST:** 1980
SQ FT: 13,290
SALES (est): 5.4MM **Privately Held**
WEB: www.stargroupglobal.com
SIC: 3429 3364 3544 Builders' hardware;
nonferrous die-castings except aluminum;
special dies & tools

(P-6540)
TOMORROWS HEIRLOOMS INC
Also Called: Stone Manufacturing Company
1636 W 135th St, Gardena (90249-2506)
P.O. Box 1325 (90249-0325)
PHONE..............................310 323-6720
Amit V Patel, *President*
Sumi Patel, *Treasurer*
Kumar V Patel, *Vice Pres*
EMP: 21 **EST:** 1957
SQ FT: 22,000
SALES (est): 2.6MM **Privately Held**
WEB: www.stonemfg.com
SIC: 3429 Fireplace equipment, hardware:
andirons, grates, screens

(P-6541)
TOP LINE MFG INC
7032 Alondra Blvd, Paramount
(90723-3926)
P.O. Box 739 (90723-0739)
PHONE..............................562 633-0605
Anne Graffy, *CEO*
Bill Watermen, *Officer*
Salim Khan, *Bookkeeper*
▲ **EMP:** 29 **EST:** 1982
SQ FT: 20,000
SALES (est): 4.9MM **Privately Held**
WEB: www.toplinemfg.com
SIC: 3429 Motor vehicle hardware; bicycle
racks, automotive; luggage racks, car top

(P-6542)
TUL INC
663 Brea Canyon Rd Ste 6, Walnut
(91789-3045)
PHONE..............................909 444-0577
Ted Chen, *President*
▲ **EMP:** 14 **EST:** 2008
SALES (est): 1.1MM **Privately Held**
WEB: www.powercolor.com
SIC: 3429 Manufactured hardware (gen-
eral)

(P-6543)
UMPCO INC
7100 Lampson Ave, Garden Grove
(92841-3914)
P.O. Box 5158 (92846-0158)
PHONE..............................714 897-3531
Dan Miller, *CEO*
EMP: 75
SQ FT: 60,000

SALES (est): 20.6MM **Privately Held**
WEB: www.umpco.com
SIC: 3429 Clamps, metal

(P-6544)
**WESTERN HARDWARE
COMPANY**
161 Commerce Way, Walnut (91789-2719)
PHONE..............................909 595-6201
Gayle E Pacheco, *President*
Lucy Arechiga, *Manager*
▲ **EMP:** 25 **EST:** 1968
SALES (est): 2.8MM **Privately Held**
WEB: www.westernhardware.com
SIC: 3429 Manufactured hardware (gen-
eral)

(P-6545)
YOUNG ENGINEERS INC
25841 Commercentre Dr, Lake Forest
(92630-8812)
P.O. Box 278 (92609-0278)
PHONE..............................949 581-9411
Pat Wells, *President*
David Owen, *Vice Pres*
Sam Fries, *Data Proc Exec*
Richard Switzer, *Engineer*
John Pumphrey, *Natl Sales Mgr*
EMP: 64 **EST:** 1963
SQ FT: 26,000
SALES (est): 9.5MM
SALES (corp-wide): 218.1MM **Privately
Held**
WEB: www.youngengineers.com
SIC: 3429 Aircraft hardware
PA: Novaria Group, L.L.C.
6300 Ridglea Pl Ste 800
Fort Worth TX 76116
817 381-3810

3431 Enameled Iron & Metal
Sanitary Ware

(P-6546)
ALTMANS PRODUCTS LLC (HQ)
7136 Kittyhawk Ave Apt 4, Los Angeles
(90045-2137)
PHONE..............................310 559-4093
Edgardo Flores, *CEO*
▲ **EMP:** 31 **EST:** 1984
SQ FT: 1,300
SALES (est): 12.5MM **Privately Held**
WEB: www.altmansproducts.com
SIC: 3431 Sinks: enameled iron, cast iron
or pressed metal

(P-6547)
HYDRO SYSTEMS INC (PA)
29132 Avenue Paine, Valencia
(91355-5402)
PHONE..............................661 775-0686
Scott G Steinhardt, *President*
Larry Burroughs, *Vice Pres*
Dave Ortwein, *Vice Pres*
Debbie Steinhardt, *Vice Pres*
Kevin Steinhardt, *VP Opers*
EMP: 94 **EST:** 1979
SQ FT: 90,000
SALES (est): 18.9MM **Privately Held**
WEB: www.hydrosystem.com
SIC: 3431 3432 3088 Bathtubs: enam-
eled iron, cast iron or pressed metal;
plumbing fixture fittings & trim; plastics
plumbing fixtures

(P-6548)
**MAG AEROSPACE INDUSTRIES
LLC**
Also Called: Mag Aerospace Industries, Inc.
1500 Glenn Curtiss St, Carson
(90746-4012)
P.O. Box 11189 (90749-1189)
PHONE..............................801 400-7944
Sebastien Weber, *President*
Mark Scott, *CFO*
Tim Birbeck, *Vice Pres*
Mike Nieves, *Vice Pres*
James Durso, *Executive*
◆ **EMP:** 350 **EST:** 1989
SQ FT: 150,000

SALES (est): 103.3MM
SALES (corp-wide): 639.8MM **Privately
Held**
WEB: www.safran-group.com
SIC: 3431 3728 Plumbing fixtures: enam-
eled iron cast iron or pressed metal; air-
craft parts & equipment
PA: Safran
2 Bd Du General Martial Valin
Paris 75015
140 608-080

(P-6549)
SEACHROME CORPORATION
1906 E Dominguez St, Long Beach
(90810-1002)
PHONE..............................310 427-8010
Sam C Longo Jr, *CEO*
Sam C Longo Sr, *Corp Secy*
Jan Phan, *Human Res Mgr*
Daniel Sowinski, *Inv Control Mgr*
Doug Carmichael, *Natl Sales Mgr*
▲ **EMP:** 112 **EST:** 1983
SQ FT: 50,000
SALES (est): 22.1MM **Privately Held**
WEB: www.seachrome.com
SIC: 3431 5072 3842 3429 Bathroom fix-
tures, including sinks; builders' hardware;
surgical appliances & supplies; manufac-
tured hardware (general)

3432 Plumbing Fixture
Fittings & Trim, Brass

(P-6550)
ACORNVAC INC
Also Called: Acorn Vac
13818 Oaks Ave, Chino (91710-7008)
PHONE..............................909 902-1141
Donald E Morris, *CEO*
Tom Zinn, *Engrg Dir*
Gina Jones, *Technology*
Carlos Galeazzi, *Engineer*
Craig Johnson, *Natl Sales Mgr*
EMP: 20 **EST:** 2000
SALES: 11.2MM
SALES (corp-wide): 90MM **Privately
Held**
WEB: www.acornvac.com
SIC: 3432 Plastic plumbing fixture fittings,
assembly
PA: Acorn Engineering Company
15125 Proctor Ave
City Of Industry CA 91746
800 488-8999

(P-6551)
ALL-AMERICAN MFG CO
2201 E 51st St, Vernon (90058-2814)
PHONE..............................323 581-6293
John F Norton, *President*
▲ **EMP:** 16 **EST:** 1938
SQ FT: 20,000
SALES (est): 1MM **Privately Held**
SIC: 3432 3469 Plumbing fixture fittings &
trim; stamping metal for the trade

(P-6552)
**AMERICAN BRASS & ALUM
FNDRY CO**
2060 Garfield Ave, Commerce
(90040-1804)
P.O. Box 80304, Los Angeles (90040)
PHONE..............................800 545-9988
Tony Orapallo Jr, *President*
Robert A Orapallo, *Vice Pres*
◆ **EMP:** 20 **EST:** 1931
SQ FT: 15,000
SALES (est): 2.3MM **Privately Held**
WEB: www.abainc.net
SIC: 3432 Plumbers' brass goods: drain
cocks, faucets, spigots, etc.; plastic
plumbing fixture fittings, assembly

(P-6553)
BRASSTECH INC (HQ)
Also Called: Newport Brass
2001 Carnegie Ave, Santa Ana
(92705-5531)
PHONE..............................949 417-5207
John V Halso, *CEO*
Tim Carr, *Research*
John Crvarich, *VP Finance*
Rachel Kissinger, *Accountant*

Mike Garwood, *Buyer*
◆ **EMP:** 335 **EST:** 1987
SQ FT: 70,000
SALES (est): 100.6MM
SALES (corp-wide): 7.1B **Publicly Held**
WEB: www.brasstech.com
SIC: 3432 Plumbing fixture fittings & trim
PA: Masco Corporation
    17450 College Pkwy
    Livonia MI 48152
    313 274-7400

(P-6554)
CALIFORNIA FAUCETS INC
    5231 Argosy Ave, Huntington Beach
    (92649-1015)
    PHONE....................657 400-1639
Blas Ramierez, *Branch Mgr*
EMP: 39 **Privately Held**
WEB: www.calfaucets.com
SIC: 3432 Faucets & spigots, metal & plastic
PA: California Faucets, Inc.
    5271 Argosy Ave
    Huntington Beach CA 92649

(P-6555)
CALIFORNIA FAUCETS INC (PA)
    5271 Argosy Ave, Huntington Beach
    (92649-1015)
    PHONE....................714 890-0450
Jeff Silverstein, *CEO*
Sonia Silverstein, *Corp Secy*
Gabriele Head, *Executive*
Armando Cayeros, *Department Mgr*
Lindi Otte, *Executive Asst*
◆ **EMP:** 36 **EST:** 1988
SALES (est): 19.3MM **Privately Held**
WEB: www.calfaucets.com
SIC: 3432 Faucets & spigots, metal & plastic

(P-6556)
CHAMPION-ARROWHEAD LLC
    5147 Alhambra Ave, Los Angeles
    (90032-3413)
    PHONE....................323 221-9137
Jim Shearer, *Mng Member*
Pamela Braun, *Sales Staff*
▲ **EMP:** 22 **EST:** 1936
SQ FT: 4,000
SALES (est): 5.8MM **Privately Held**
WEB: www.arrowheadbrass.com
SIC: 3432 Plumbing fixture fittings & trim

(P-6557)
CISCOS SHOP INC
    2911 E Miraloma Ave # 17, Anaheim
    (92806-1838)
    PHONE....................657 230-9158
Francisco Chavez, *Partner*
EMP: 13 **EST:** 2015
SALES (est): 512.5K **Privately Held**
WEB: www.ciscosshop.com
SIC: 3432 Plumbing fixture fittings & trim

(P-6558)
COLLICUTT ENERGY SERVICES INC
    12349 Hawkins St, Santa Fe Springs
    (90670-3366)
    PHONE....................562 944-4413
    Toll Free:....................866 -
Tim Rahman, *Branch Mgr*
EMP: 21
SQ FT: 77,000
SALES (corp-wide): 33.5MM **Privately Held**
WEB: www.collicutt.com
SIC: 3432 Plumbing fixture fittings & trim
HQ: Collicutt Energy Services Inc.
    940 Riverside Pkwy Ste 80
    West Sacramento CA 95605

(P-6559)
COLUMBIA SANITARY PRODUCTS INC
Also Called: Columbia Products Co
    1622 Browning, Irvine (92606-4809)
    PHONE....................949 474-0777
Dorothy Lazier, *CEO*
Paul Escalera, *President*
▲ **EMP:** 20 **EST:** 1949
SQ FT: 20,000

SALES (est): 10MM **Privately Held**
WEB: www.columbiasinks.com
SIC: 3432 Plumbing fixture fittings & trim

(P-6560)
FISHER MANUFACTURING CO (PA)
    1900 S O St, Tulare (93274-6850)
    P.O. Box 60 (93275-0060)
    PHONE....................559 685-5200
Ray Fisher Jr, *President*
Kay Fisher, *Shareholder*
Karen Lauterbach, *Shareholder*
Kathleen Sebahar, *Shareholder*
Scott Ball, *Vice Pres*
◆ **EMP:** 37 **EST:** 1936
SQ FT: 50,000
SALES (est): 8.7MM **Privately Held**
WEB: www.fisher-mfg.com
SIC: 3432 Plumbers' brass goods: drain cocks, faucets, spigots, etc.

(P-6561)
G T WATER PRODUCTS INC
    5239 N Commerce Ave, Moorpark
    (93021-1763)
    PHONE....................805 529-2900
George Tash, *President*
Russell Reasner, *Vice Pres*
Steve Schmitt, *Vice Pres*
Julie Shipley, *Vice Pres*
Debra Tash, *Vice Pres*
▲ **EMP:** 17 **EST:** 1971
SQ FT: 20,000
SALES (est): 3.8MM **Privately Held**
WEB: www.gtwaterproducts.com
SIC: 3432 Plumbing fixture fittings & trim

(P-6562)
GMS LANDSCAPES INC
    207 Camino Leon, Camarillo (93012-8635)
    PHONE....................805 402-3925
Sarah Corbin, *President*
EMP: 85 **EST:** 2017
SALES (est): 2.9MM **Privately Held**
SIC: 3432 0781 Plumbing fixture fittings & trim; landscape services

(P-6563)
PLUMBING PRODUCTS COMPANY INC
Also Called: Trim To Trade
    77551 El Duna Ct Ste I, Palm Desert
    (92211-4147)
    PHONE....................760 343-3306
Gary Yavitz, *President*
Jessie Yavitz, *Corp Secy*
◆ **EMP:** 13 **EST:** 1947
SQ FT: 36,000
SALES (est): 2.7MM **Privately Held**
WEB: www.trimtothetrade.com
SIC: 3432 3431 Plumbers' brass goods: drain cocks, faucets, spigots, etc.; bathroom fixtures, including sinks

(P-6564)
PRICE PFISTER INC
Also Called: Pfister Faucets
    19701 Da Vinci, Foothill Ranch
    (92610-2622)
    PHONE....................949 672-4003
James M Loree, *President*
Craig A Douglas, *Treasurer*
Bruce Beatt, *Admin Sec*
EMP: 149 **EST:** 1983
SALES (est): 11.8MM
SALES (corp-wide): 3.9B **Publicly Held**
WEB: www.pfisterfaucets.com
SIC: 3432 Plumbing fixture fittings & trim
HQ: Spectrum Brands Legacy, Inc.
    3001 Deming Way
    Middleton WI 53562

(P-6565)
PRICE PFISTER INC (DH)
Also Called: Price Pfister Brass Mfg
    19701 Da Vinci, Lake Forest (92610-2622)
    PHONE....................949 672-4000
Gregory John Gluchowski, *CEO*
▲ **EMP:** 800 **EST:** 1910
SQ FT: 127,612

SALES (est): 128.8MM
SALES (corp-wide): 3.9B **Publicly Held**
WEB: www.pfisterfaucets.com
SIC: 3432 Faucets & spigots, metal & plastic; plumbers' brass goods: drain cocks, faucets, spigots, etc.
HQ: Spectrum Brands, Inc.
    3001 Deming Way
    Middleton WI 53562
    608 275-3340

(P-6566)
SANTEC INC
    3501 Challenger St Fl 2, Torrance
    (90503-1697)
    PHONE....................310 542-0063
Nicolas Chen, *CEO*
James S Chen, *Principal*
▲ **EMP:** 50 **EST:** 1981
SQ FT: 32,000
SALES (est): 8.2MM **Privately Held**
WEB: www.santecfaucet.com
SIC: 3432 Faucets & spigots, metal & plastic

3433 Heating Eqpt

(P-6567)
ADVANCED CONSERVATION TECHNOLO
Also Called: Act Inc Dmand Kontrols Systems
    3176 Pullman St Ste 119, Costa Mesa
    (92626-3317)
    PHONE....................714 668-1200
Larry Acker, *CEO*
Donna-Marie Acker, *President*
Kristine Parker, *Vice Pres*
Tina Cook, *Purch Mgr*
EMP: 16 **EST:** 1990
SQ FT: 7,000
SALES (est): 3MM **Privately Held**
WEB: www.gothotwater.com
SIC: 3433 Boilers, low-pressure heating: steam or hot water

(P-6568)
AMERICAN SOLAR LLC
    8484 Wilshire Blvd, Beverly Hills
    (90211-3227)
    PHONE....................323 250-1307
Meir Yaniv, *CEO*
EMP: 30
SALES (est): 1MM **Privately Held**
SIC: 3433 Solar heaters & collectors

(P-6569)
CAPITAL COOKING EQUIPMENT INC
    1025 E Bedmar St, Carson (90746-3601)
    PHONE....................562 903-1168
Surjit Kalsi, *Co-COB*
Surya Kalsi, *COO*
Roberto Bernal, *Co-COB*
Alejandro Bernal, *Exec VP*
Raul Chita, *Exec VP*
▲ **EMP:** 47 **EST:** 2001
SALES (est): 7.9MM **Privately Held**
WEB: www.capital-cooking.com
SIC: 3433 3631 Stoves, wood & coal burning; gas ranges, domestic

(P-6570)
GC AERO INC
    21143 Hawthorne Blvd # 13, Torrance
    (90503-4615)
    PHONE....................310 539-7600
Jim Cowherd, *President*
Michael Monteiro, *Sales Staff*
▲ **EMP:** 14 **EST:** 1968
SQ FT: 11,500
SALES (est): 412.2K **Privately Held**
WEB: www.gcaero.com
SIC: 3433 3674 3822 3672 Heating equipment, except electric; integrated circuits, semiconductor networks, etc.; temperature controls, automatic; printed circuit boards

(P-6571)
INDUSTRIAL MANUFACTURING INC
    10110 Norwalk Blvd, Santa Fe Springs
    (90670-3326)
    P.O. Box 3163 (90670-0163)
    PHONE....................562 941-5888
Eddie Cerda, *President*
EMP: 13 **EST:** 1996
SQ FT: 15,700
SALES (est): 225.1K **Privately Held**
SIC: 3433 Radiators, except electric

(P-6572)
INFRARED DYNAMICS INC
    3830 Prospect Ave, Yorba Linda
    (92886-1742)
    PHONE....................714 572-4050
Robert Cowan, *President*
▲ **EMP:** 27 **EST:** 1959
SQ FT: 23,500
SALES (est): 5.7MM **Privately Held**
WEB: www.infradyne.com
SIC: 3433 5075 Heating equipment, except electric; warm air heating equipment & supplies

(P-6573)
RASMUSSEN IRON WORKS INC
    12028 Philadelphia St, Whittier
    (90601-3925)
    PHONE....................562 696-8718
Theodore Rasmussen, *President*
Irene Rasmussen, *Vice Pres*
Rett Rasmussen, *Vice Pres*
T E Rasmussen, *Vice Pres*
Ray Vazla, *Vice Pres*
▲ **EMP:** 62 **EST:** 1907
SQ FT: 40,000
SALES (est): 7.8MM **Privately Held**
WEB: www.radiantpatioheater.com
SIC: 3433 Logs, gas fireplace

(P-6574)
RAYPAK INC (DH)
    2151 Eastman Ave, Oxnard (93030-5194)
    PHONE....................805 278-5300
Kevin McDonald, *Vice Pres*
Mike Inlow, *Acting CFO*
Tom Nickel, *Officer*
Rich Corcoran, *Vice Pres*
Kevin Ruppelt, *Vice Pres*
▲ **EMP:** 320 **EST:** 1949
SQ FT: 250,000
SALES (est): 85MM **Privately Held**
WEB: www.raypak.com
SIC: 3433 Heaters, swimming pool: oil or gas
HQ: Rheem Manufacturing Company Inc
    1100 Abernathy Rd Ste 17
    Atlanta GA 30328
    770 351-3000

(P-6575)
SCHEU MANUFACTURING CO (PA)
    297 Stowell St, Upland (91786-6624)
    P.O. Box 250 (91785-0250)
    PHONE....................909 982-8933
Leland C Scheu, *Ch of Bd*
Daniel N League Jr, *Shareholder*
Allyn Scheu, *President*
▲ **EMP:** 15 **EST:** 1930
SQ FT: 7,000
SALES (est): 7.1MM **Privately Held**
SIC: 3433 Space heaters except electric

(P-6576)
SOLARRESERVE LLC (PA)
    520 Broadway Fl 6, Santa Monica
    (90401-2420)
    PHONE....................310 315-2200
Tom Georgis, *CEO*
Kevin Smith, *CEO*
Tim Rosenzweig, *CFO*
Alistair Jessop, *Senior VF*
Stephen Mullennix, *Senior VP*
EMP: 19 **EST:** 2007
SALES (est): 6.8MM **Privately Held**
WEB: www.solarreserve.com
SIC: 3433 1711 4911 Solar heaters & collectors; solar energy contractor; electric services

3441 Fabricated Structural Steel

(P-6577)
A & A FABRICATION & POLSG CORP
12031 Philadelphia St, Whittier (90601-3926)
PHONE.................562 696-0441
Amanda Henderson, *President*
EMP: 16 EST: 1999
SQ FT: 14,000
SALES (est): 2.3MM **Privately Held**
WEB: www.aafabpolishing.com
SIC: 3441 Fabricated structural metal

(P-6578)
ABLE IRON WORKS
222 Hershey St, Pomona (91767-5810)
PHONE.................909 397-5300
Stephen Holmes, *CEO*
Darcy Schultz, *Office Mgr*
Oscar Tapia, *Director*
EMP: 20 EST: 1993
SQ FT: 12,000
SALES (est): 5MM **Privately Held**
WEB: www.ableironwork.com
SIC: 3441 Fabricated structural metal

(P-6579)
ABSOLUTE MACHINING INC
20622 Superior St Unit 4, Chatsworth (91311-4432)
PHONE.................818 709-7367
Tim Ohanlon, *Owner*
EMP: 15 EST: 1996
SALES (est): 4.2MM **Privately Held**
WEB: www.absolutemachininginc.com
SIC: 3441 Fabricated structural metal

(P-6580)
ACCURATE METAL PRODUCTS INC
4276 Campbell St, Riverside (92509-2617)
PHONE.................951 360-3594
Elanor Quintero, *President*
Tony Schmidt, *Admin Sec*
EMP: 15 EST: 1997
SALES (est): 1.4MM **Privately Held**
WEB: www.accuratemetalinc.com
SIC: 3441 Fabricated structural metal

(P-6581)
ADVANCED PRECISION INC
13445 Yorba Ave, Chino (91710-5055)
PHONE.................909 591-4244
Craig G Rohde, *CFO*
EMP: 17 EST: 2013
SALES (est): 2.6MM **Privately Held**
WEB: www.advanced-precision.com
SIC: 3441 Fabricated structural metal

(P-6582)
AEROFAB CORPORATION
4001 E Leaverton Ct, Anaheim (92807-1610)
PHONE.................714 635-0902
Matthew Owen, *President*
George Robinson, *Vice Pres*
EMP: 17 EST: 2007
SQ FT: 10,000
SALES (est): 3.5MM **Privately Held**
WEB: www.aerofab-corp.com
SIC: 3441 Fabricated structural metal

(P-6583)
AFAKORI INC
Also Called: AAF Steel Structural
29390 Hunco Way, Lake Elsinore (92530-2757)
PHONE.................949 859-4277
Amir A Fakori, *President*
Luz Marina Agreda, *Admin Sec*
▲ EMP: 20 EST: 2001
SQ FT: 15,000
SALES (est): 4.6MM **Privately Held**
WEB: www.afakori.com
SIC: 3441 Building components, structural steel

(P-6584)
AG MACHINING INC
609 Science Dr, Moorpark (93021-2005)
PHONE.................805 531-9555
Angel Garcia, *President*
Bryan Garcia, *Vice Pres*
Eddie Garcia, *Vice Pres*
Raul Mollapaza, *Design Engr*
▲ EMP: 85 EST: 1986
SQ FT: 117,000
SALES (est): 15.8MM **Privately Held**
WEB: www.agm.us.com
SIC: 3441 3444 Fabricated structural metal; sheet metalwork; metal housings, enclosures, casings & other containers; pipe, sheet metal; restaurant sheet metalwork

(P-6585)
AMAZING STEEL COMPANY
Also Called: Mitchellamazing
4564 Mission Blvd, Montclair (91763-6106)
PHONE.................909 590-0393
Jim Mitchell, *President*
EMP: 20 EST: 1985
SQ FT: 25,000
SALES (est): 1.8MM **Privately Held**
WEB: www.mitchellamazing.com
SIC: 3441 7692 7699 Fabricated structural metal; welding repair; hydraulic equipment repair

(P-6586)
AMERICAN METAL & PAINT INC
Also Called: Nappcote
9030 Owensmouth Ave, Canoga Park (91304-1416)
PHONE.................818 882-6333
Youssef J Mikhail, *President*
EMP: 15
SQ FT: 14,000
SALES (est): 3MM **Privately Held**
SIC: 3441 3479 Fabricated structural metal; coating of metals & formed products

(P-6587)
ANDERSON CHRNESKY STRL STL INC
Also Called: Acss
353 Risco Cir, Beaumont (92223-2676)
PHONE.................951 769-5700
Kevin Charneskey, *President*
Kevin Charnesky, *President*
EMP: 72 EST: 1984
SQ FT: 6,600
SALES (est): 14.7MM **Privately Held**
WEB: www.acssteelinc.com
SIC: 3441 Fabricated structural metal

(P-6588)
BELL BROS STEEL INC
1510 Palmyrita Ave, Riverside (92507-1629)
PHONE.................951 784-0903
James Bell, *President*
EMP: 45 EST: 2001
SQ FT: 1,400
SALES (est): 5.5MM **Privately Held**
WEB: www.bellbrossteel.com
SIC: 3441 Fabricated structural metal

(P-6589)
BELLOWS MFG & RES INC
864 Arroyo St, San Fernando (91340-1832)
PHONE.................818 838-1333
Arteom Art Bulgadarian, *CEO*
David Galloway, *Engineer*
EMP: 30 EST: 2005
SQ FT: 28,000
SALES (est): 4MM **Privately Held**
WEB: www.bellowsmfg.com
SIC: 3441 Fabricated structural metal

(P-6590)
BLAZING INDUSTRIAL STEEL INC
9040 Jurupa Rd, Riverside (92509-3106)
PHONE.................951 360-8340
Fernando Herrera, *President*
Roberta Calderon, *Treasurer*
Mike Calderon, *Vice Pres*
Brad McGlothlin, *General Mgr*
EMP: 42 EST: 1985

SQ FT: 100,000
SALES (est): 4MM **Privately Held**
WEB: www.blazingindustrial.com
SIC: 3441 Fabricated structural metal

(P-6591)
BOYD CORPORATION (PA)
Also Called: Boyd Construction
5832 Ohio St, Yorba Linda (92886-5323)
P.O. Box 6012, Anaheim (92816-0012)
PHONE.................714 533-2375
Mitch Aiello, *President*
EMP: 149 EST: 1980
SALES (est): 19.1MM **Privately Held**
WEB: www.boydcorp.com
SIC: 3441 2891 Fabricated structural metal; adhesives

(P-6592)
BRASS UNIQUE INC
9948 Hayward Way, South El Monte (91733-3193)
PHONE.................626 444-8977
Yi-Tai Soong, *President*
EMP: 24 EST: 1991
SQ FT: 15,000
SALES (est): 3.7MM **Privately Held**
WEB: www.brassunique.com
SIC: 3441 Fabricated structural metal for ships

(P-6593)
BRUNTON ENTERPRISES INC
Also Called: Plas-Tal Manufacturing Co
8815 Sorensen Ave, Santa Fe Springs (90670-2636)
PHONE.................562 945-0013
Sean P Brunton, *CEO*
John W Brunton Jr, *President*
Alan Baker, *Vice Pres*
Patrick Scott, *Network Mgr*
Douglas Ferguson, *Project Mgr*
EMP: 125 EST: 1947
SQ FT: 45,000
SALES (est): 27.5MM **Privately Held**
WEB: www.plas-tal.com
SIC: 3441 Fabricated structural metal

(P-6594)
C A BUCHEN CORP
9231 Glenoaks Blvd, Sun Valley (91352-2688)
PHONE.................818 767-5408
John Oster, *CEO*
Ryan Chapman, *Vice Pres*
EMP: 25 EST: 1962
SQ FT: 22,500
SALES (est): 6.6MM **Privately Held**
WEB: www.cabuchen.com
SIC: 3441 1791 3312 Fabricated structural metal; structural steel erection; iron & steel: galvanized, pipes, plates, sheets, etc.

(P-6595)
CAC FABRICATION INC
9710 Owensmouth Ave Ste C, Chatsworth (91311-8077)
PHONE.................818 882-2626
David Agins, *President*
EMP: 16 EST: 1999
SQ FT: 5,000
SALES (est): 637.5K **Privately Held**
SIC: 3441 Fabricated structural metal

(P-6596)
CALCON STEEL CONSTRUCTION INC
Also Called: Hamilton Iron Works
1226 W 196th St, Torrance (90502-1101)
PHONE.................310 768-8094
Sung Nam, *President*
Hannah Nam, *Admin Sec*
EMP: 19 EST: 1989
SQ FT: 50,000
SALES (est): 1.3MM **Privately Held**
WEB: www.hamiltoniw.com
SIC: 3441 Fabricated structural metal

(P-6597)
CALCRAFT CORPORATION
Also Called: Calcraft Company
1426 S Willow Ave, Rialto (92376-7720)
PHONE.................909 879-2900
Daniel Steven Ensman, *President*
Gloria Ensman, *Admin Sec*

Joe Ensman, *Human Resources*
Jeff Brown, *Sales Staff*
Brett Ensman, *Maintence Staff*
EMP: 15 EST: 2004
SQ FT: 30,000
SALES (est): 4.4MM **Privately Held**
WEB: www.calcraft.com
SIC: 3441 Fabricated structural metal

(P-6598)
CANYON STEEL FABRICATORS INC
8314 Sultana Ave, Fontana (92335-3265)
PHONE.................951 683-2352
Thomas J Baggett, *President*
Ray Magnon, *Vice Pres*
Doug Magnon, *Admin Sec*
Heather Johnston, *Manager*
EMP: 22 EST: 2007
SALES (est): 3.2MM **Privately Held**
WEB: www.canyonsteelfab.com
SIC: 3441 Fabricated structural metal

(P-6599)
CAPITOL STEEL FABRICATORS INC
3565 Greenwood Ave, Commerce (90040-3305)
PHONE.................323 721-5460
James Moreland, *President*
Eric Jonkey, *Shareholder*
Janice Moreland, *Vice Pres*
Trevor Smith, *Vice Pres*
Carol Chavez, *Office Mgr*
EMP: 25 EST: 1984
SQ FT: 10,000
SALES (est): 7.1MM **Privately Held**
WEB: www.capitolsteel.com
SIC: 3441 Fabricated structural metal

(P-6600)
CK STEEL INC
19826 S Alameda St, Compton (90221-6211)
PHONE.................310 638-0855
Chin Kim, *President*
EMP: 13 EST: 2015
SALES (est): 2.3MM **Privately Held**
WEB: www.cksteel.org
SIC: 3441 Fabricated structural metal

(P-6601)
COLUMBIA ALUMINUM PRODUCTS LLC
1150 W Rincon St, Corona (92878-9601)
PHONE.................323 728-7361
Drew D Mumford, *Owner*
Grant Palenske, *Vice Pres*
▲ EMP: 70 EST: 1989
SALES (est): 8.8MM **Privately Held**
WEB:
www.columbiaaluminumproductsllc.com
SIC: 3441 Fabricated structural metal

(P-6602)
COLUMBIA STEEL INC
2175 N Linden Ave, Rialto (92377-4445)
PHONE.................909 874-8840
Gustavo Waldemar Theisen, *CEO*
Charmaine Helenihi, *CFO*
William Young, *Chairman*
Luis Theisen, *Vice Pres*
Patrick Garrett, *Info Tech Mgr*
EMP: 75 EST: 1975
SQ FT: 63,384
SALES (est): 24.4MM **Privately Held**
WEB: www.csirialto.com
SIC: 3441 Building components, structural steel

(P-6603)
COMMERCIAL SHTMTL WORKS INC
Also Called: CSM Metal Fabricating & Engrg
1800 S San Pedro St, Los Angeles (90015-3711)
PHONE.................213 748-7321
Jack L Gardener, *President*
Wade Hilton, *Project Mgr*
Tommy Campos, *Sales Staff*
Tyler Brown, *Director*
▲ EMP: 27 EST: 1916
SQ FT: 22,000

SALES (est): 6MM **Privately Held**
WEB: www.csmworks.com
SIC: 3441 Fabricated structural metal

(P-6604)
COMPLETE METAL FABRICATION INC
596 E Main St, El Centro (92243-9471)
P.O. Box 1529 (92244-1529)
PHONE..................................760 353-0260
Jesse Ray Riddle, *CEO*
Arita Riddle, *Info Tech Mgr*
EMP: 19 **EST:** 2012
SALES (est): 1.2MM **Privately Held**
WEB: www.cmfab.biz
SIC: 3441 Fabricated structural metal

(P-6605)
CONSTEEL INDUSTRIAL INC
15435 Woodcrest Dr, Whittier
(90604-3236)
PHONE..................................562 806-4575
Luis Lagarica, *CEO*
Maria Torres, *CFO*
Russ Lambert, *Admin Sec*
Frankie Alamintos, *Director*
Robert Geronca, *Director*
EMP: 27 **EST:** 2012
SALES (est): 8.2MM **Privately Held**
SIC: 3441 Fabricated structural metal

(P-6606)
CORBELL PRODUCTS INC (PA)
14650 Hawthorne Ave, Fontana
(92335-2509)
PHONE..................................909 574-9139
Frank Stavinski, *President*
Elaine Lucero, *Treasurer*
EMP: 45 **EST:** 1997
SQ FT: 26,000
SALES (est): 2.8MM **Privately Held**
SIC: 3441 Fabricated structural metal

(P-6607)
CORCORAN SAWTELLE ROSPRIM INC
Also Called: Sawtelle & Rosprim Machine Sp
542 Otis Ave, Corcoran (93212-1823)
PHONE..................................559 992-2117
Terry Kwast, *President*
EMP: 29 **EST:** 1944
SQ FT: 35,000
SALES (est): 5.2MM **Privately Held**
WEB: www.sawtelleandrosprim.com
SIC: 3441 3599 Fabricated structural
metal; machine shop, jobbing & repair

(P-6608)
CRAFTECH METAL FORMING INC
24100 Water Ave Ste B, Perris
(92570-6738)
PHONE..................................951 940-6444
Richard L Shaw, *President*
Gerry Day, *Manager*
EMP: 40 **EST:** 1996
SQ FT: 26,000
SALES (est): 4.2MM **Privately Held**
WEB: www.craftechmetal.com
SIC: 3441 3499 3444 Fabricated struc-
tural metal; fire- or burglary-resistive prod-
ucts; sheet metalwork

(P-6609)
CROSNO CONSTRUCTION INC
819 Sheridan Rd, Arroyo Grande
(93420-5833)
PHONE..................................805 343-7437
Wade Crosno, *President*
Jaime Crosno, *CFO*
Mike Whitney, *Vice Pres*
EMP: 48 **EST:** 2004
SQ FT: 5,000
SALES (est): 11.7MM **Privately Held**
WEB: www.crosnoconstruction.com
SIC: 3441 Fabricated structural metal

(P-6610)
CUSTOM IRON CORPORATION
26895 Aliso Creek Rd, Aliso Viejo
(92656-5301)
PHONE..................................949 939-4379
Michael Knee, *President*
Susan Smock, *Project Engr*
Cathy Baglio, *Controller*

EMP: 23 **EST:** 2013
SALES (est): 7MM **Privately Held**
WEB: www.customironcorp.com
SIC: 3441 Fabricated structural metal

(P-6611)
CUSTOM STEEL FABRICATION INC
Also Called: C & J Industries
11966 Rivera Rd, Santa Fe Springs
(90670-2232)
PHONE..................................562 907-2777
John Toscano, *President*
Carole Toscano, *CEO*
Tracy Delong, *Sales Staff*
EMP: 17 **EST:** 2006
SQ FT: 3,400
SALES (est): 2.8MM **Privately Held**
WEB: www.cnjindustries.com
SIC: 3441 Fabricated structural metal

(P-6612)
CW INDUSTRIES
1735 Santa Fe Ave, Long Beach
(90813-1242)
PHONE..................................562 432-5421
Craig Wildvank, *Principal*
Branden Wildvank, *Project Mgr*
EMP: 37 **EST:** 2006
SALES (est): 4.2MM **Privately Held**
WEB: www.cwindustries.us
SIC: 3441 3548 5084 Building compo-
nents, structural steel; welding apparatus;
oil refining machinery, equipment & sup-
plies

(P-6613)
D & M STEEL INC
13020 Pierce St, Pacoima (91331-2528)
PHONE..................................818 896-2070
Michael Atia, *President*
David Dagni, *Vice Pres*
EMP: 37 **EST:** 1980
SQ FT: 16,500
SALES (est): 9.5MM **Privately Held**
WEB: www.d-msteel.com
SIC: 3441 Fabricated structural metal

(P-6614)
D D WIRE CO INC (PA)
4335 Temple City Blvd, Temple City
(91780-4229)
PHONE..................................626 442-0459
Wes Berry, *President*
James Howe, *COO*
David Berry, *CFO*
Dorsey Wire, *Principal*
Elizabeth D Berry, *Admin Sec*
EMP: 22
SQ FT: 24,000
SALES (est): 3.4MM **Privately Held**
WEB: www.ddwire.com
SIC: 3441 3469 Fabricated structural
metal; stamping metal for the trade

(P-6615)
D&A METAL FABRICATION INC
16129 Runnymede St, Van Nuys
(91406-2913)
PHONE..................................818 780-8231
Jenny Anastasiu, *Office Mgr*
Anca Morgan, *Vice Pres*
EMP: 16 **EST:** 2014
SALES (est): 1.3MM **Privately Held**
WEB: www.dametalfabrication.com
SIC: 3441 Fabricated structural metal

(P-6616)
EW CORPRTION INDUS FABRICATORS (PA)
1002 E Main St, El Centro (92243)
P.O. Box 2189 (92244-2189)
PHONE..................................760 337-0020
Tiberio R Esparza, *President*
◆ **EMP:** 69 **EST:** 1973
SQ FT: 100,000
SALES (est): 15MM **Privately Held**
WEB: www.ewcorporation.com
SIC: 3441 Fabricated structural metal

(P-6617)
FABCO STEEL FABRICATION INC
14688 San Bernardino Ave, Fontana
(92335-5319)
P.O. Box 8636, Alta Loma (91701-0636)
PHONE..................................909 350-1535
John E Schick, *President*
Rich Schick, *CFO*
Doug Schick, *Vice Pres*
Toni Lamb, *Manager*
EMP: 35 **EST:** 1979
SQ FT: 30,000
SALES (est): 5.9MM **Privately Held**
WEB: www.fabcosteel.com
SIC: 3441 Fabricated structural metal

(P-6618)
GENERAL STEEL FABRICATORS INC
12179 Branford St Ste B, Sun Valley
(91352-5733)
PHONE..................................818 897-1300
Mehrad Maleki, *President*
EMP: 25 **EST:** 2003
SALES (est): 2.6MM **Privately Held**
SIC: 3441 Fabricated structural metal

(P-6619)
GOLDEN GATE STEEL INC
19826 S Alameda St, Compton
(90221-6211)
PHONE..................................310 638-0855
Yohann Chang, *President*
Joenne Kim, *Office Mgr*
EMP: 15 **EST:** 1990
SALES (est): 1.4MM **Privately Held**
SIC: 3441 Building components, structural
steel

(P-6620)
GRATING PACIFIC INC (PA)
3651 Sausalito St, Los Alamitos
(90720-2436)
PHONE..................................562 598-4314
Ronald S Robertson, *President*
Jeffrey Robertson, *Vice Pres*
Bryan Miller, *Sales Engr*
Brett Robertson, *Sales Staff*
Charles Demeyer, *Associate*
▲ **EMP:** 20 **EST:** 1971
SQ FT: 40,000
SALES (est): 25.9MM **Privately Held**
WEB: www.gratingpacific.com
SIC: 3441 3446 Fabricated structural
metal; architectural metalwork

(P-6621)
HITECH METAL FABRICATION CORP
Also Called: H M F
1705 S Claudina Way, Anaheim
(92805-6544)
PHONE..................................714 635-3505
Ba V Nguyen, *President*
Matthew Vu, *Vice Pres*
Lucia Coronel, *Administration*
EMP: 60 **EST:** 1989
SQ FT: 42,850
SALES (est): 9.8MM **Privately Held**
SIC: 3441 Fabricated structural metal

(P-6622)
INDUSTRIAL MACHINE & MFG CO
Also Called: Immco
2626 Seaman Ave, El Monte (91733-1930)
PHONE..................................626 444-0181
Diane Teresa, *President*
Ron Teresa, *Corp Secy*
David Teresa, *Vice Pres*
Mark Teresa, *Vice Pres*
EMP: 41 **EST:** 1959
SQ FT: 5,500
SALES (est): 2.5MM **Privately Held**
WEB: www.immcohandtrucks.com
SIC: 3441 3569 3537 Fabricated struc-
tural metal; assembly machines, non-met-
alworking; industrial trucks & tractors

(P-6623)
INTEGRAL ENGRG FABRICATION INC
520 Hofgaarden St, City of Industry
(91744-5529)
PHONE..................................626 369-0958
John Zheng, *CEO*
Sonny Nguyen, *General Mgr*
Son T Nguyen, *Admin Sec*
EMP: 25 **EST:** 2003
SQ FT: 20,000
SALES (est): 4.3MM **Privately Held**
WEB: www.integralfab.com
SIC: 3441 Fabricated structural metal

(P-6624)
JAMAC STEEL INC
1037 S Sultana Ave, Ontario (91761-3338)
PHONE..................................909 983-7592
William J McKernan, *CEO*
Maggie Mc Kernan, *Vice Pres*
EMP: 20 **EST:** 1988
SALES (est): 6.5MM **Privately Held**
WEB: www.jamacsteel.com
SIC: 3441 Fabricated structural metal

(P-6625)
JOHASEE REBAR INC
26365 Earthmover Cir, Corona
(92883-5270)
PHONE..................................661 589-0972
Mike Hill Sr, *CEO*
Michael Hill Jr, *COO*
Tamara L Chapman, *CFO*
EMP: 47 **EST:** 1979
SALES (est): 13.2MM
SALES (corp-wide): 66.5MM **Privately
Held**
WEB: www.johaseerebar.com
SIC: 3441 1791 Fabricated structural
metal; concrete reinforcement, placing of
PA: Lms Holdings (Ab) Ltd
7452 132 St
Surrey BC V3W 4
604 598-9930

(P-6626)
KERN STEEL FABRICATION INC (PA)
627 Williams St, Bakersfield (93305-5445)
PHONE..................................661 327-9588
Tom Champness, *President*
Terri Benyon, *Vice Pres*
Larkin McKenzie, *Vice Pres*
Yolanda De Leon, *Office Mgr*
Richard Barnes, *CIO*
◆ **EMP:** 62 **EST:** 1959
SQ FT: 50,000
SALES (est): 22.6MM **Privately Held**
WEB: www.kernsteel.com
SIC: 3441 3728 4581 3412 Fabricated
structural metal; aircraft parts & equip-
ment; aircraft maintenance & repair serv-
ices; metal barrels, drums & pails

(P-6627)
KSU CORPORATION
3 Emmy Ln, Ladera Ranch (92694-1521)
PHONE..................................951 409-7055
Luz Marina Agreda, *CEO*
EMP: 15 **EST:** 2015
SALES (est): 1.1MM **Privately Held**
SIC: 3441 Building components, structural
steel

(P-6628)
LEVEL 23 FAB
2117 S Anne St, Santa Ana (92704-4408)
PHONE..................................714 979-2323
Monica Arias, *Office Mgr*
EMP: 20 **EST:** 2017
SALES (est): 3.3MM **Privately Held**
WEB: www.lvl23.com
SIC: 3441 Fabricated structural metal

(P-6629)
LINDBLADE METALWORKS INC
Also Called: Lindblade Metal Works
14355 Macaw St, La Mirada (90638-5208)
PHONE..................................714 670-7172
Vernon Lindblade, *CEO*
Marilyn Lindblade, *Vice Pres*
Tim Hostetler, *Sales Associate*
EMP: 20 **EST:** 1973
SQ FT: 16,250

SALES (est): 3.1MM **Privately Held**
WEB: www.lindblademetalworks.com
SIC: **3441** Fabricated structural metal

(P-6630)
M AND M STAMPING CORP
13821 Oaks Ave, Chino (91710-7009)
PHONE..................................909 590-2704
Juan Uribe Sr, *President*
Juan Uribe Jr, *Vice Pres*
EMP: 15 EST: 2015
SQ FT: 8,000
SALES (est): 2MM **Privately Held**
WEB: www.mandmstamping.com
SIC: **3441 3444** Fabricated structural
metal; sheet metalwork

(P-6631)
MADISON INC OF OKLAHOMA
18000 Studebaker Rd, Cerritos
(90703-2679)
PHONE..................................918 224-6990
John Samuel Frey, *President*
Barbara Cruncleton, *Corp Secy*
Robert E Hansen, *Vice Pres*
EMP: 67 EST: 1946
SALES (est): 22.7MM
SALES (corp-wide): 118.8MM **Privately Held**
WEB: www.madisonind.com
SIC: **3441 1541 3448 3444** Fabricated
structural metal; prefabricated building
erection, industrial; prefabricated metal
buildings; sheet metalwork
PA: John S. Frey Enterprises
1900 E 64th St
Los Angeles CA 90001
323 583-4061

(P-6632)
MAXIMUM QUALITY METAL PDTS INC
Also Called: Max Q
1017 E Acacia St, Ontario (91761-4554)
PHONE..................................909 902-5018
John Kim, *President*
Paul Kim, *Admin Sec*
EMP: 20 EST: 1998
SQ FT: 10,000
SALES (est): 4.9MM **Privately Held**
WEB: www.maxqmetalproducts.com
SIC: **3441** Fabricated structural metal

(P-6633)
MAYA STEELS FABRICATION INC
301 E Compton Blvd, Gardena
(90248-2015)
PHONE..................................310 532-8830
Meir Amsalam, *CEO*
Yechiel Yogev, *CEO*
Yogev Yechiel, *Treasurer*
Sara Haddad, *Vice Pres*
Jorge Santana, *Purch Agent*
EMP: 64 EST: 1982
SQ FT: 65,000
SALES (est): 11.1MM **Privately Held**
WEB: www.mayasteel.com
SIC: **3441** Building components, structural steel

(P-6634)
MCWHIRTER STEEL INC
42211 7th St E, Lancaster (93535-5400)
PHONE..................................661 951-8998
David McWhirter, *President*
Angela McWhirter, *CFO*
Christina Swan, *Admin Asst*
Greg Liske, *Sr Project Mgr*
Nathan McWhirter, *Director*
EMP: 95 EST: 1992
SQ FT: 21,000
SALES (est): 14.1MM **Privately Held**
WEB: www.mcwhirtersteel.com
SIC: **3441 1791** Fabricated structural
metal; structural steel erection; iron work, structural

(P-6635)
MEDSCO FABRICATION & DIST INC
958 N Eastern Ave, Los Angeles
(90063-1308)
PHONE..................................323 263-0511
Michael Nevarez, *Chairman*

John Millan, *COO*
Jim Stock, *CFO*
EMP: 56 EST: 2001
SALES (est): 8MM **Privately Held**
WEB:
www.medscosheetmetalfabrication.com
SIC: **3441 3446** Fabricated structural
metal; architectural metalwork

(P-6636)
MERRIMANS INCORPORATED
32195 Dunlap Blvd, Yucaipa (92399-1728)
P.O. Box 547, Calimesa (92320-0547)
PHONE..................................909 795-5301
Tod Merriman, *President*
Elaine Onken, *CFO*
Janice Merriman, *Vice Pres*
Lisa Merriman, *Vice Pres*
EMP: 30 EST: 1965
SQ FT: 5,000
SALES (est): 4.3MM **Privately Held**
WEB: www.merrimansinc.com
SIC: **3441 5271 1521** Building compo-
nents, structural steel; mobile home parts
& accessories; general remodeling, sin-
gle-family houses

(P-6637)
METAL SUPPLY LLC
11810 Center St, South Gate (90280-7832)
PHONE..................................562 634-9940
Dion Genchi, *President*
Bruce E Hubert, *Owner*
Deann Jenki, *General Mgr*
Barbara Hubert, *Admin Sec*
Julio Alfaro, *Engineer*
▼ EMP: 63 EST: 1961
SQ FT: 50,000
SALES (est): 19.1MM **Privately Held**
WEB: www.metalsupply.com
SIC: **3441 5051** Fabricated structural
metal; iron & steel (ferrous) products; alu-
minum bars, rods, ingots, sheets, pipes,
plates, etc.

(P-6638)
METALS USA BUILDING PDTS LP
6450 Caballero Blvd Ste A, Buena Park
(90620-1007)
PHONE..................................714 522-7852
Tom Bush, *Branch Mgr*
Bob Pechiney, *Sales Mgr*
EMP: 81
SALES (corp-wide): 8.8B **Publicly Held**
SIC: **3441 3444** Fabricated structural
metal; sheet metalwork
HQ: Metals Usa Building Products Lp
955 Columbia St
Brea CA 92821
713 946-9000

(P-6639)
MILLERS FAB & WELD CORP
6100 Industrial Ave, Riverside
(92504-1120)
PHONE..................................951 359-3100
James Miller, *President*
Marina Rodocker, *Manager*
EMP: 21 EST: 1964
SQ FT: 2,100
SALES (est): 2.5MM **Privately Held**
WEB: www.millersfab.net
SIC: **3441** Fabricated structural metal

(P-6640)
MITCHELL FABRICATION
Also Called: Amazing Steel
4564 Mission Blvd, Montclair (91763-6106)
PHONE..................................909 590-0393
Jim Mitchell, *President*
Steven Miks, *Mfg Staff*
▲ EMP: 30 EST: 1985
SQ FT: 35,000
SALES (est): 4MM **Privately Held**
WEB: www.mitchellamazing.com
SIC: **3441** Fabricated structural metal

(P-6641)
MJM EXPERT PIPE FBRCATION WLDG
3404 Wrenwood St, Bakersfield
(93309-9331)
PHONE..................................661 330-8698
Michael J Martin, *Owner*
EMP: 20

SALES (est): 500K **Privately Held**
SIC: **3441** Fabricated structural metal

(P-6642)
MSI STRUCTURAL STEEL LLC
11810 Center St, South Gate (90280-7832)
PHONE..................................562 473-0066
Dion Genchi, *Mng Member*
EMP: 38 EST: 2019
SALES (est): 6.3MM **Privately Held**
WEB: www.msistructuralsteel.com
SIC: **3441 1791 1541** Fabricated struc-
tural metal; structural steel erection; steel
building construction

(P-6643)
MUHLHAUSER ENTERPRISES INC (PA)
Also Called: Muhlhauser Steel
25825 Adams Ave, Murrieta (92562-0601)
P.O. Box 159, Bloomington (92316-0159)
PHONE..................................909 877-2792
William C Muhlhauser, *President*
Gisela Muhlhauser, *Corp Secy*
EMP: 29 EST: 1961
SALES (est): 14.9MM **Privately Held**
WEB: www.msisteel.com
SIC: **3441 1791** Building components,
structural steel; structural steel erection

(P-6644)
MUHLHAUSER STEEL INC
25825 Adams Ave, Murrieta (92562-0601)
P.O. Box 159, Bloomington (92316-0159)
PHONE..................................909 877-2792
William Muhlhauser, *President*
Zigfried Muhlhauser, *Senior VP*
EMP: 20 EST: 1988
SALES (est): 10.6MM
SALES (corp-wide): 14.9MM **Privately Held**
WEB: www.msisteel.com
SIC: **3441 1791** Building components,
structural steel; structural steel erection
PA: Muhlhauser Enterprises, Inc.
25825 Adams Ave
Murrieta CA 92562
909 877-2792

(P-6645)
MYWI FABRICATORS INC
2115-2119 Edwards Ave, South El Monte
(91733)
PHONE..................................626 279-6994
Henry Yue, *President*
Jeanne Yue, *Admin Sec*
Dan Sewell, *Project Mgr*
Keith Jourdian, *Project Engr*
EMP: 18 EST: 1993
SQ FT: 5,000
SALES (est): 4.1MM **Privately Held**
WEB: www.mywifabricators.com
SIC: **3441** Fabricated structural metal

(P-6646)
PACIFIC COAST IRONWORKS INC
8831 Miner St, Los Angeles (90002-1835)
PHONE..................................323 585-1320
Andrew Larkin Jr, *President*
Ron David, *Treasurer*
Max Gonzalez, *Vice Pres*
Mike Larkin, *Vice Pres*
EMP: 17 EST: 1991
SQ FT: 22,000
SALES (est): 2.8MM **Privately Held**
WEB: www.pacificcoastironworks.com
SIC: **3441** Fabricated structural metal

(P-6647)
PARK STEEL CO INC
515 E Pine St, Compton (90222-2817)
P.O. Box 4787 (90224-4787)
PHONE..................................310 638-6101
Gregory M Park, *President*
Sally O Park, *Treasurer*
Randy Park, *Admin Sec*
EMP: 18 EST: 1980
SQ FT: 70,000
SALES (est): 3MM **Privately Held**
WEB: www.parksteel.net
SIC: **3441 1791** Bridge sections, prefabri-
cated highway; concrete reinforcement,
placing of

(P-6648)
PERPETUAL MOTION GROUP INC
11939 Sherman Rd, North Hollywood
(91605-3717)
PHONE..................................818 982-4300
Joe Rando, *Principal*
EMP: 14 EST: 2010
SQ FT: 55,000
SALES (est): 620.3K **Privately Held**
SIC: **3441** Fabricated structural metal

(P-6649)
POLARIS SALES INC
Also Called: Pro Armor
12885 Wildflower Ln, Riverside
(92503-9772)
PHONE..................................951 343-9270
Scott W Wine, *CEO*
Jeremy Brown, *Purch Agent*
Elisha Raphael, *Production*
▲ EMP: 15 EST: 1998
SALES (est): 961.1K **Privately Held**
SIC: **3441** Fabricated structural metal

(P-6650)
PRECISION IRON WORKS
4815 Slauson Ave, Maywood (90270-3018)
PHONE..................................562 220-2303
Julie Ramos, *President*
EMP: 14 EST: 2016
SALES (est): 2.6MM **Privately Held**
WEB: www.precisionironworks.co
SIC: **3441** Fabricated structural metal

(P-6651)
PRECISION METAL CRAFTS
16920 Gridley Pl, Cerritos (90703-1740)
PHONE..................................562 468-7080
Coleman Conard III, *Owner*
EMP: 26 EST: 2006
SQ FT: 24,100
SALES (est): 2.3MM **Privately Held**
WEB: www.precisionmetalcrafts.com
SIC: **3441** Fabricated structural metal

(P-6652)
PRECISION WELDING INC
241 Enterprise Pkwy, Lancaster
(93534-7201)
PHONE..................................661 729-3436
David R Jones, *President*
David Jones, *President*
EMP: 23 EST: 1995
SQ FT: 10,000
SALES (est): 4.2MM **Privately Held**
WEB: www.precisionweldingla.com
SIC: **3441 1799** Fabricated structural
metal; welding on site

(P-6653)
PREMIER STEEL STRUCTURES INC
13345 Estelle St, Corona (92879-1881)
PHONE..................................951 356-6655
Armando Rodarte, *President*
EMP: 30 EST: 2016
SALES (est): 4.9MM **Privately Held**
SIC: **3441** Fabricated structural metal

(P-6654)
R & D STEEL INC
1136 S Santa Fe Ave, Compton
(90221-4337)
PHONE..................................310 631-6183
Joie A Dunyon, *President*
Jim Dunyon, *Corp Secy*
▲ EMP: 30 EST: 1979
SQ FT: 8,000
SALES (est): 4.1MM **Privately Held**
WEB: www.rdsteelinc.com
SIC: **3441** Fabricated structural metal

(P-6655)
R & I INDUSTRIES INC
2910 S Archibald Ave A, Ontario
(91761-7323)
PHONE..................................909 923-7747
William Franklin Rowan Sr, *CEO*
Ardith Rowan, *Treasurer*
William Franklin Rowan Jr, *Vice Pres*
Paula Rowan, *Sales Mgr*
EMP: 40 EST: 1978
SQ FT: 12,000

SALES (est): 6.7MM **Privately Held**
WEB: www.rimetal.com
SIC: **3441** Building components, structural steel

(P-6656)
R & R FABRICATIONS INC
13438 Lambert Rd, Whittier (90605-2454)
PHONE..........................562 693-0500
Rodney Galan, *President*
EMP: 20 EST: 2005
SALES (est): 3.6MM **Privately Held**
WEB: www.rrfabrications.com
SIC: **3441** Fabricated structural metal

(P-6657)
R & R METAL FABRICATORS
14846 Ramona Blvd, Baldwin Park (91706-3436)
PHONE..........................626 960-6400
Martha Rodriguez, *Manager*
EMP: 15 EST: 2009
SALES (est): 1.1MM **Privately Held**
SIC: **3441** Fabricated structural metal

(P-6658)
RAILMAKERS INC
864 W 18th St, Costa Mesa (92627-4411)
PHONE..........................949 642-6506
John Hawley, *President*
David C Hawley, *Treasurer*
EMP: 14 EST: 1969
SQ FT: 10,000
SALES (est): 1.9MM **Privately Held**
WEB: www.railmakers.com
SIC: **3441** Fabricated structural metal

(P-6659)
RELIABLE BUILDING PRODUCTS INC
9301 Rayo Ave, South Gate (90280-3612)
PHONE..........................323 566-5000
Jeff Palmer, *President*
Nikki Reagan, *Vice Pres*
EMP: 26 EST: 1989
SQ FT: 135,910
SALES (est): 7.5MM **Privately Held**
SIC: **3441** Fabricated structural metal

(P-6660)
RND CONTRACTORS INC
14796 Jurupa Ave Ste A, Fontana (92337-7232)
PHONE..........................909 429-8500
Nancy Sauter, *President*
Angel Vargas, *Plant Mgr*
Dylan Sauter, *Production*
Justin Dunn, *Manager*
EMP: 40 EST: 2007
SALES (est): 6.7MM **Privately Held**
WEB: www.rndcontractorsinc.com
SIC: **3441** Fabricated structural metal

(P-6661)
SCHROEDER IRON CORPORATION
8417 Beech Ave, Fontana (92335-1200)
PHONE..........................909 428-6471
Linda Schroeder, *President*
Jason Hampton, *Project Mgr*
Ezequiel Ruvalcaba, *Engineer*
EMP: 30 EST: 1993
SQ FT: 23,000
SALES (est): 16.4MM **Privately Held**
WEB: www.schroederiron.com
SIC: **3441** Building components, structural steel

(P-6662)
SIMPLEX SUPPLIES INC
Also Called: JC Supply & Manufacturing
1370 Valley Vista Dr # 200, Diamond Bar (91765-3911)
PHONE..........................618 594-6450
Neysa Schwend, *Manager*
Glenn Eder, *VP Bus Dvlpt*
Benita Blanchard, *Office Mgr*
Shakenna Morris, *Admin Asst*
Manuel Gonzalez, *VP Opers*
EMP: 38
SALES (corp-wide): 39.4MM **Privately Held**
WEB: www.tycosimplexgrinnell.com
SIC: **3441 3479** Building components, structural steel; painting, coating & hot dipping

PA: Simplex Supplies, Inc.
9020 W 35w Service Dr Ne
Minneapolis MN 55449
763 398-0040

(P-6663)
SPARTAN INC
3030 M St, Bakersfield (93301-2137)
PHONE..........................661 327-1205
John Wood, *President*
Louis Stern, *CEO*
Tami Black, *CFO*
Teresa Wood, *Treasurer*
John D Clemmey, *Vice Pres*
▼ EMP: 65 EST: 2002
SQ FT: 125,000
SALES (est): 10.2MM **Privately Held**
WEB: www.spartaninc.net
SIC: **3441 8711** Fabricated structural metal; engineering services

(P-6664)
SS METAL FABRICATORS
2501 S Birch St, Santa Ana (92707-3408)
PHONE..........................949 631-4272
Kim Harding, *Owner*
EMP: 17 EST: 1985
SALES (est): 3.5MM **Privately Held**
WEB: www.ssmetalfabricators.com
SIC: **3441** Fabricated structural metal

(P-6665)
STAINLESS PROCESS SYSTEMS INC
1650 Beacon Pl, Oxnard (93033-2433)
PHONE..........................805 483-7100
Mark Hayman, *President*
Dennis Ziegler, *Prdtn Mgr*
EMP: 14 EST: 2007
SQ FT: 27,126
SALES (est): 2.6MM **Privately Held**
WEB: www.stainlessprocesssystems.com
SIC: **3441** Fabricated structural metal

(P-6666)
STEEL-TECH INDUSTRIAL CORP
1268 Sherborn St, Corona (92879-2090)
PHONE..........................951 270-0144
Michael R Black, *President*
Braebon Black, *Vice Pres*
Elise Roberts, *Office Mgr*
Linda Black, *Admin Sec*
EMP: 47 EST: 1984
SQ FT: 15,000
SALES (est): 8MM **Privately Held**
WEB: www.steeltech.org
SIC: **3441** Fabricated structural metal

(P-6667)
TAN SET CORPORATION
Also Called: Specialty Metal Fabrication
1 S Fairview Ave, Goleta (93117-3364)
PHONE..........................805 967-4567
Tanis M Hammond, *President*
Seth Hammond, *Vice Pres*
EMP: 13 EST: 1973
SQ FT: 15,000
SALES (est): 256.7K **Privately Held**
SIC: **3441** Fabricated structural metal

(P-6668)
THIN METAL SALES INC
5721 Schaefer Ave, Chino (91710-7004)
PHONE..........................909 393-2273
EMP: 14 EST: 1979
SALES (est): 1MM **Privately Held**
WEB: www.thinmetalsales.com
SIC: **3441** Fabricated structural metal

(P-6669)
TITAN METAL FABRICATORS INC (PA)
352 Balboa Cir, Camarillo (93012-8644)
PHONE..........................805 487-5050
Steve Muscarella, *President*
Debi Otto, *CFO*
Tom Muscarella, *Vice Pres*
Jim Ramirez, *Vice Pres*
Dan Yingling, *Info Tech Mgr*
▲ EMP: 69 EST: 1998
SQ FT: 15,000
SALES (est): 33.8MM **Privately Held**
WEB: www.titanmf.com
SIC: **3441** Fabricated structural metal

(P-6670)
TL FAB LP
2921 E Coronado St, Anaheim (92806-2502)
PHONE..........................562 802-3980
Joseph Schmidt, *Principal*
Javier Hernandez, *Project Mgr*
Dean Rick, *Project Mgr*
Allyssa Rogers, *Sr Project Mgr*
▲ EMP: 117
SALES (est): 3.4MM **Privately Held**
WEB: www.tlfab.com
SIC: **3441** Building components, structural steel

(P-6671)
TOBIN STEEL COMPANY INC
817 E Santa Ana Blvd, Santa Ana (92701-3909)
P.O. Box 717 (92702-0717)
PHONE..........................714 541-2268
Linda A Robin, *CEO*
Carl Tobin, *President*
Jim Tobin, *Vice Pres*
Steve Tobin, *Vice Pres*
Linda Tobin, *Controller*
EMP: 65 EST: 1978
SQ FT: 20,000
SALES (est): 11.4MM **Privately Held**
WEB: www.tobinsteel.com
SIC: **3441** Building components, structural steel

(P-6672)
TOLAR MANUFACTURING CO INC
258 Mariah Cir, Corona (92879-1751)
PHONE..........................951 808-0081
Gary Tolar, *President*
Rhonda Tolar, *Vice Pres*
Carlos Garcia, *Engineer*
Eli Meza, *Engineer*
Chris Mendoza, *Accountant*
▲ EMP: 40 EST: 1991
SQ FT: 22,000
SALES (est): 8.5MM **Privately Held**
WEB: www.tolarmfg.com
SIC: **3441 3599 3448** Fabricated structural metal; machine shop, jobbing & repair; prefabricated metal buildings

(P-6673)
TRIAD BELLOWS DESIGN & MFG INC
2897 E La Cresta Ave, Anaheim (92806-1817)
PHONE..........................714 204-4444
Michael G Moore, *President*
Julianne Moore, *CFO*
Paul Kattenbach, *General Mgr*
David Rivera, *Sales Engr*
EMP: 26
SALES (est): 2.4MM **Privately Held**
WEB: www.triadbellows.com
SIC: **3441** Fabricated structural metal

(P-6674)
TRUSSWORKS INTERNATIONAL INC
1275 E Franklin Ave, Pomona (91766-5450)
PHONE..........................714 630-2772
Michael Farrell, *President*
Ali Shantyaei, *Vice Pres*
Pam Tudor, *Executive*
Anastasiya Heydari, *Finance Dir*
Behnam Firoozfard, *Purchasing*
EMP: 60 EST: 2007
SALES (est): 9.2MM **Privately Held**
WEB: www.twifab.com
SIC: **3441 3446 1791** Fabricated structural metal; architectural metalwork; stairs, fire escapes, balconies, railings & ladders; fences, gates, posts & flagpoles; stairs, staircases, stair treads; prefabricated metal; building front installation metal

(P-6675)
UNIVERSAL STEEL SERVICES INC
5034 Heintz St, Baldwin Park (91706-1816)
P.O. Box 2428, Irwindale (91706-1232)
PHONE..........................626 960-1455

Ramon T Lopez, *CEO*
Meira Carrasco, *Manager*
EMP: 54 EST: 2001
SALES (est): 5MM **Privately Held**
WEB: www.universalsteelservices.com
SIC: **3441** Building components, structural steel

(P-6676)
US TOWER CORP
1099 W Ropes Ave, Woodlake (93286-1806)
PHONE..........................559 564-6000
Everett Cook, *Manager*
Shana Sawyer, *General Mgr*
Jan Wilson, *Planning*
Devin Aldridge, *Engineer*
Remigio Fernandez, *Engineer*
EMP: 52
SALES (corp-wide): 13.6MM **Privately Held**
WEB: www.ustower.com
SIC: **3441** Tower sections, radio & television transmission
PA: Us Tower Corp.
1099 W Ropes Ave
Woodlake CA 93286
785 524-9966

(P-6677)
US TOWER CORP (PA)
1099 W Ropes Ave, Woodlake (93286-1806)
P.O. Box 285, Lincoln KS (67455-0285)
PHONE..........................785 524-9966
Bruce Kopitar, *President*
Chuck Diehl, *Vice Pres*
Dee Wenger, *Executive*
Heidi Mendez, *Executive Asst*
Josh Wollberg, *Safety Mgr*
▲ EMP: 30 EST: 1985
SALES (est): 13.6MM **Privately Held**
WEB: www.ustower.com
SIC: **3441** Tower sections, radio & television transmission

(P-6678)
V & F FABRICATION COMPANY INC
13902 Seaboard Cir, Garden Grove (92843-3910)
PHONE..........................714 265-0630
Vinh Nguyen, *President*
Vinh Van Nguyen, *CEO*
Bao Truong, *Managing Dir*
Sen Truong, *Admin Sec*
Yvonne Nguyen, *Buyer*
▲ EMP: 35 EST: 1989
SALES (est): 8.5MM **Privately Held**
SIC: **3441 3599 3769 3444** Fabricated structural metal; machine shop, jobbing & repair; guided missile & space vehicle parts & auxiliary equipment; sheet metalwork

(P-6679)
VALENCE SURFACE TECH LLC
7718 Adams St, Paramount (90723-4202)
PHONE..........................562 531-7666
Chris Celtruda, *Branch Mgr*
EMP: 18
SALES (corp-wide): 103MM **Privately Held**
WEB: www.valencesurfacetech.com
SIC: **3441** Fabricated structural metal
PA: Valence Surface Technologies Llc
1790 Hughes Landing Blvd
The Woodlands TX 77380
888 540-0878

(P-6680)
VIRGIL WALKER INC
Also Called: Auton Motorized Systems
24856 Avenue Rockefeller, Valencia (91355-3467)
P.O. Box 801960, Santa Clarita (91380-1960)
PHONE..........................661 797-4101
Arthur Walker, *CEO*
James Famiglietti, *Sales Staff*
EMP: 15 EST: 2010
SALES (est): 2.3MM **Privately Held**
WEB: www.auton.com
SIC: **3441** Fabricated structural metal

(P-6681)
WADCO INDUSTRIES INC
Also Called: Wadco Steel Sales
2625 S Willow Ave, Bloomington
(92316-3258)
PHONE...................................909 874-7800
David D Scheibel, *CEO*
Salvador Arratia, *President*
Scott Brown, *Treasurer*
Anthony Salazar, *Vice Pres*
EMP: 47 **EST:** 1979
SQ FT: 50,000
SALES (est): 9.5MM **Privately Held**
WEB: www.wadcoindustries.com
SIC: 3441 5051 Building components,
structural steel; steel

(P-6682)
WEISER IRON INC
64 Sundance Dr, Pomona (91766-4894)
PHONE...................................909 429-4600
David Metoyer, *President*
Carmela Metoyer, *Corp Secy*
EMP: 28 **EST:** 1985
SALES (est): 1.6MM **Privately Held**
WEB: www.weiseriron.com
SIC: 3441 Fabricated structural metal

(P-6683)
WESTCO INDUSTRIES INC
Also Called: Corbell Products
2625 S Willow Ave, Bloomington
(92316-3258)
PHONE...................................909 874-8700
David Schibel, *President*
Viva Dasilva, *Project Engr*
Erick Maravilla, *Representative*
▲ **EMP:** 25 **EST:** 2005
SQ FT: 25,000
SALES (est): 1.6MM **Privately Held**
WEB: www.westcoind.com
SIC: 3441 Fabricated structural metal

(P-6684)
WILKINS DESIGN AND MFG INC
Also Called: Wilschur Design and Mfg
2619 Oak St, Santa Ana (92707-3720)
PHONE...................................714 564-3351
Paul Wilkins, *President*
EMP: 30 **EST:** 2003
SQ FT: 11,000
SALES (est): 4.5MM **Privately Held**
WEB: www.wilschur.com
SIC: 3441 Fabricated structural metal

(P-6685)
ZIA AAMIR
Also Called: Bridge Metals
2043 Imperial St, Los Angeles
(90021-3203)
PHONE...................................714 337-7861
Aamir Zia, *Owner*
EMP: 25 **EST:** 2017
SALES (est): 1.5MM **Privately Held**
WEB: www.bridgemetals.com
SIC: 3441 Fabricated structural metal

3442 Metal Doors, Sash, Frames, Molding & Trim

(P-6686)
ACCENT INDUSTRIES INC (PA)
Also Called: Accent Awnings
1600 E Saint Gertrude Pl, Santa Ana
(92705-5312)
PHONE...................................714 708-1389
Karl Desmarais, *CEO*
Bonanken Alonzo, *Manager*
▲ **EMP:** 29 **EST:** 1993
SQ FT: 26,000
SALES (est): 3.1MM **Privately Held**
WEB: www.accentawnings.com
SIC: 3442 3444 2394 5999 Shutters,
door or window: metal; awnings &
canopies; canvas & related products;
awnings

(P-6687)
ACTIVE WINDOW PRODUCTS
Also Called: Z Industries
5431 W San Fernando Rd, Los Angeles
(90039-1088)
P.O. Box 39125 (90039-0125)
PHONE...................................323 245-5185

Michael Schoenfeld, *President*
Rosa Castro, *Treasurer*
▲ **EMP:** 53 **EST:** 1952
SQ FT: 96,000
SALES: 10.8MM **Privately Held**
WEB: www.activewindowproducts.com
SIC: 3442 Storm doors or windows, metal

(P-6688)
ADVANCE OVERHEAD DOOR INC
15829 Stagg St, Van Nuys (91406-1969)
PHONE...................................818 781-5590
Leland S Groshong, *President*
Don Henderson, *Treasurer*
Marguerite Groshong, *Admin Sec*
EMP: 26 **EST:** 1956
SQ FT: 25,000
SALES (est): 1.3MM **Privately Held**
SIC: 3442 2431 Garage doors, overhead:
metal; garage doors, overhead: wood

(P-6689)
ADVANCED ARCHITECTURAL FRAMES
Also Called: Advance Architectural
17102 Newhope St, Fountain Valley
(92708-8223)
PHONE...................................424 209-6018
EMP: 33
SQ FT: 4,000
SALES: 6.4MM **Privately Held**
SIC: 3442 5211 Mfg Metal
Doors/Sash/Trim Ret Lumber/Building
Materials

(P-6690)
ANEMOSTAT DOOR PRODUCTS INC
1220 E Watson Center Rd, Carson
(90745-4206)
PHONE...................................310 835-7500
EMP: 14 **EST:** 2015
SALES (est): 888.6K **Privately Held**
WEB: www.anemostat-hvac.com
SIC: 3442 Louver doors, metal

(P-6691)
ARCADIA INC
2323 Firestone Blvd, South Gate
(90280-2684)
PHONE...................................310 665-0490
EMP: 40
SALES (corp-wide): 116.8MM **Privately Held**
WEB: www.arcadiainc.com
SIC: 3442 Window & door frames
PA: Arcadia Inc.
2301 E Vernon Ave
Vernon CA 90058
323 269-7300

(P-6692)
B & B DOORS AND WINDOWS INC
11455 Ilex Ave, San Fernando
(91340-3430)
PHONE...................................818 837-8480
Jeffrey C Brothers, *CEO*
Lori Brothers, *Treasurer*
EMP: 16 **EST:** 1996
SQ FT: 7,200
SALES (est): 2.6MM **Privately Held**
WEB: www.bandbdoor.com
SIC: 3442 5031 Window & door frames;
doors & windows

(P-6693)
BEST ROLL-UP DOOR INC
13202 Arctic Cir, Santa Fe Springs
(90670-5510)
PHONE...................................562 802-2233
Edward Choi, *President*
▲ **EMP:** 20 **EST:** 1978
SQ FT: 15,000
SALES (est): 2.3MM **Privately Held**
WEB: www.bestrollup.com
SIC: 3442 Rolling doors for industrial build-
ings or warehouses, metal

(P-6694)
COASTAL DOORS
21818 S Wilmington Ave, Carson
(90810-1642)
PHONE...................................562 665-5585

Brock William Livesey, *CEO*
EMP: 19 **EST:** 2019
SQ FT: 2,200
SALES (est): 2.5MM **Privately Held**
WEB: www.coastal-corp.com
SIC: 5211 3442 Garage doors, sale & in-
stallation; garage doors, overhead: metal;
rolling doors for industrial buildings or
warehouses, metal

(P-6695)
DOOR COMPONENTS INC
Also Called: DCI Hollow Metal On Demand
7980 Redwood Ave, Fontana (92336-1638)
PHONE...................................909 770-5700
Robert Briggs, *President*
David Bowen, *COO*
Sheryl Briggs, *CFO*
Ronald Green, *Vice Pres*
Cindi Bowen, *Info Tech Mgr*
EMP: 200 **EST:** 1981
SQ FT: 45,000
SALES (est): 41.8MM **Privately Held**
WEB: www.dcihollowmetal.com
SIC: 3442 Metal doors

(P-6696)
EDEY MANUFACTURING CO INC
Also Called: Edey Door
2159 E 92nd St, Los Angeles (90002-2509)
PHONE...................................323 566-6151
Fax: 323 566-0262
EMP: 21
SQ FT: 54,000
SALES (est): 1.3MM **Privately Held**
WEB: www.edeydoors.com
SIC: 3442 Mfg Metal Doors/Sash/Trim

(P-6697)
ELIZABETH SHUTTERS INC
525 S Rancho Ave, Colton (92324-3240)
P.O. Box 1345 (92324-0827)
PHONE...................................909 825-1531
Dean Frost, *CEO*
Maren Frost, *CFO*
Maggie Castaneda, *Accountant*
EMP: 45
SQ FT: 51,000
SALES (est): 7.6MM **Privately Held**
WEB: www.elizabethshutters.com
SIC: 3442 5023 5211 2431 Shutters,
door or window: metal; window furnish-
ings; door & window products; millwork

(P-6698)
EUROLINE STEEL WINDOWS
Also Called: Euroline Steel Windows & Doors
22600 Savi Ranch Pkwy E, Yorba Linda
(92887-4606)
PHONE...................................877 590-2741
Elyas Balta, *CEO*
Cristian Contreras, *Accountant*
Melanie Caswell, *Senior Buyer*
Chris Rogers, *Opers Staff*
Brace Lake, *Sales Mgr*
▲ **EMP:** 27 **EST:** 2013
SALES (est): 10.8MM **Privately Held**
WEB: www.eurolinesteelwindows.com
SIC: 3442 Window & door frames

(P-6699)
FANBOYS WINDOW FACTORY INC (PA)
10750 Saint Louis Dr, El Monte
(91731-2028)
PHONE...................................626 280-8787
Lili Bell, *CEO*
Jeff Bell, *COO*
EMP: 21 **EST:** 2015
SQ FT: 10,000
SALES (est): 2MM **Privately Held**
SIC: 3442 Window & door frames

(P-6700)
FLEX TRIM INDUSTRIES INC (PA)
210 E Citrus Ave, Redlands (92373-5215)
P.O. Box 589, Troy AL (36081-0589)
PHONE...................................909 748-6578
Allen A Jones, *Ch of Bd*
Mary Kay Jones, *Corp Secy*
EMP: 66 **EST:** 1984
SQ FT: 25,000
SALES (est): 929.2K **Privately Held**
SIC: 3442 Moldings & trim, except automo-
bile: metal

(P-6701)
G & G DOOR PRODUCTS INC
7600 Stage Rd, Buena Park (90621-1226)
PHONE...................................714 228-2008
Bernie Gabel, *President*
Chad Gabel, *Vice Pres*
Kenda Gabel, *Vice Pres*
Lynette Bleeker, *Admin Sec*
Elizabeth Caputo, *Administration*
EMP: 35 **EST:** 1995
SQ FT: 13,500
SALES (est): 5.1MM **Privately Held**
WEB: www.ggdoor.net
SIC: 5211 3442 Doors, storm: wood or
metal; metal doors, sash & trim

(P-6702)
J T WALKER INDUSTRIES INC
Also Called: Rite Screen
9322 Hyssop Dr, Rancho Cucamonga
(91730-6103)
PHONE...................................909 481-1909
Dan Harvey, *President*
EMP: 24
SQ FT: 36,929
SALES (corp-wide): 250.9MM **Privately Held**
WEB: www.mihvac.com
SIC: 3442 Screen & storm doors & win-
dows
PA: J. T. Walker Industries, Inc.
1310 N Hercules Ave Ste A
Clearwater FL 33765
727 461-0501

(P-6703)
JOANKA INC
Also Called: M & A Custom Doors
25510 Frampton Ave, Harbor City
(90710-2907)
PHONE...................................310 326-8940
Manuel A Valenzuela, *President*
EMP: 16 **EST:** 1998
SQ FT: 4,640
SALES (est): 248.1K **Privately Held**
SIC: 3442 Window & door frames

(P-6704)
KAWNEER COMPANY INC
925 Marlborough Ave, Riverside
(92507-2138)
PHONE...................................951 410-4779
EMP: 77
SALES (corp-wide): 5.6B **Publicly Held**
WEB: www.kawneer.com
SIC: 3442 Metal doors, sash & trim
HQ: Kawneer Company, Inc.
555 Guthridge Ct
Norcross GA 30092
770 449-5555

(P-6705)
L & L LOUVERS INC
12355 Doherty St, Riverside (92503-4842)
PHONE...................................951 735-9300
Terry Green, *President*
Robert Hammond, *Vice Pres*
EMP: 21 **EST:** 1988
SQ FT: 11,000
SALES (est): 2.8MM **Privately Held**
WEB: www.louver1.com
SIC: 3442 Louvers, shutters, jalousies &
similar items

(P-6706)
LAWRENCE ROLL UP DOORS INC (PA)
4525 Littlejohn St, Baldwin Park
(91706-2239)
PHONE...................................626 962-4163
Paul Weston Freberg, *CEO*
Rachael Aguilar, *Human Res Mgr*
Roger Garcia, *Production*
◆ **EMP:** 35 **EST:** 1925
SQ FT: 35,000
SALES (est): 17.4MM **Privately Held**
WEB: www.lawrencedoors.com
SIC: 3442 3446 Rolling doors for industrial
buildings or warehouses, metal; architec-
tural metalwork

(P-6707)
LINDSAY WINDOWS
CALIFORNIA LLC
13510 Central Rd, Apple Valley
(92308-6561)
P.O. Box 999 (92307-0017)
PHONE..................................760 247-1082
Geoff Roise, *Managing Prtnr*
EMP: 15 **EST:** 2016
SALES (est): 5MM **Privately Held**
WEB: www.lindsaywindows.com
SIC: 3442 Metal doors, sash & trim; sash,
   door or window: metal

(P-6708)
M N M MANUFACTURING INC
3019 E Harcourt St, Compton
(90221-5503)
PHONE..................................310 898-1099
Matt Klein, *President*
Elizabeth Klein, *Vice Pres*
Suzanne Figueroa, *Executive*
Marlene Klein, *Admin Sec*
EMP: 60 **EST:** 1980
SQ FT: 24,000
SALES (est): 4.4MM **Privately Held**
WEB: www.mnmmfg.com
SIC: 3442 Sash, door or window: metal

(P-6709)
METAL TITE PRODUCTS (PA)
Also Called: Krieger Speciality Products
4880 Gregg Rd, Pico Rivera (90660-2107)
PHONE..................................562 695-0645
Robert J McCluney, *President*
Charles Mc Cluney, *Shareholder*
James Mc Cluney, *Shareholder*
A W Mc Cluney, *Ch of Bd*
William Mc Cluney, *Executive*
EMP: 58 **EST:** 1966
SQ FT: 39,000
SALES (est): 10MM **Privately Held**
WEB: www.kriegerproducts.com
SIC: 3442 1751 Metal doors; window &
   door frames; window & door (prefabri-
   cated) installation

(P-6710)
MILLWORKS ETC INC
Also Called: Steel Works Etc
1250 Commercial Ave, Oxnard
(93030-7457)
PHONE..................................805 499-3400
Robin W Shattuck, *CEO*
◆ **EMP:** 25 **EST:** 1985
SALES (est): 5.3MM **Privately Held**
WEB: www.millworksetc.com
SIC: 3442 Window & door frames

(P-6711)
MURRAYS HARDWARE
Also Called: Ace Hardware
210 S Main St, Santa Ana (92701-5708)
PHONE..................................714 543-4023
Bruce Alexander Hichman, *Owner*
Doug Payan, *General Mgr*
EMP: 17 **EST:** 1948
SQ FT: 6,800
SALES (est): 3.1MM **Privately Held**
WEB: www.acehardware.com
SIC: 5251 5211 3442 Hardware; win-
   dows, storm: wood or metal; screens,
   window, metal

(P-6712)
PRECISE IRON DOORS INC
12331 Foothill Blvd, Sylmar (91342-6003)
PHONE..................................818 338-6269
EMP: 20 **EST:** 2015
SALES (est): 2.1MM **Privately Held**
WEB: www.preciseirondoors.com
SIC: 3442 5031 5999 Metal doors; metal
   doors, sash & trim; miscellaneous retail
   stores

(P-6713)
QUANEX SCREENS LLC
13611 Santa Ana Ave, Fontana
(92337-8203)
PHONE..................................909 349-0600
Dewayne Williams, *Vice Pres*
Darrell Woodland, *Site Mgr*
EMP: 17 **Publicly Held**
WEB: www.quanex.com
SIC: 3442 Screen doors, metal

HQ: Quanex Screens Llc
   1800 West Loop S Ste 1500
   Houston TX 77027
   713 961-4600

(P-6714)
R & S AUTOMATION INC
283 W Bonita Ave, Pomona (91767-1848)
PHONE..................................800 962-3111
Jerry Bradfield, *Manager*
Brad Goepner, *Manager*
EMP: 27
SALES (corp-wide): 3MM **Privately Held**
WEB: www.rsoperators.com
SIC: 3442 3446 5031 5063 Metal doors;
   grillwork, ornamental metal; doors; door
   frames, all materials; motor controls,
   starters & relays: electric; door & window
   repair
PA: R & S Automation, Inc.
   2041 W Avenue 140th
   San Leandro CA 94577
   510 357-4110

(P-6715)
R & S MFG SOUTHERN CAL INC
Also Called: R & S Mfg
283 W Bonita Ave, Pomona (91767-1848)
PHONE..................................909 596-2090
Ray Rodney, *CEO*
EMP: 14 **EST:** 1986
SQ FT: 15,000
SALES (est): 3MM
SALES (corp-wide): 12.9MM **Privately
Held**
WEB: www.rsdoorproducts.com
SIC: 3442 5031 Rolling doors for industrial
   buildings or warehouses, metal; doors &
   windows
HQ: R & S Manufacturing, Inc.
   33955 7th St
   Union City CA 94587
   510 429-1788

(P-6716)
**R & S OVERHEAD DOOR OF SO
CAL**
Also Called: Door Doctor
1617 N Orangethorpe Way, Anaheim
(92801-1228)
PHONE..................................714 680-0600
David Fowler, *President*
Kellie Cruz, *General Mgr*
EMP: 25 **EST:** 1991
SALES (est): 3.2MM **Privately Held**
SIC: 3442 7699 1731 3446 Rolling doors
   for industrial buildings or warehouses,
   metal; door & window repair; access con-
   trol systems specialization; gates, orna-
   mental metal

(P-6717)
R LANG COMPANY
Also Called: Truframe
8240 W Doe Ave, Visalia (93291-9263)
P.O. Box 7960 (93290-7960)
PHONE..................................559 651-0701
Richard A Lang, *President*
Judith D Lang, *Corp Secy*
Heather Simon, *HR Admin*
Esmeralda Hernandez, *Purchasing*
◆ **EMP:** 75 **EST:** 1967
SALES (est): 12.8MM **Privately Held**
WEB: www.rollaway.com
SIC: 3442 3444 3211 5031 Screen
   doors, metal; skylights; sheet metal; flat
   glass; windows

(P-6718)
SAN JOAQUIN WINDOW INC
Also Called: ATI Windows
1455 Columbia Ave, Riverside
(92507-2013)
PHONE..................................909 946-3697
Stephen Schwartz, *CEO*
Daniel Schwartz, *President*
Debbie Schwartz, *Sales Staff*
EMP: 120 **EST:** 1992
SQ FT: 190,000
SALES (est): 14.2MM **Privately Held**
SIC: 3442 5211 Metal doors, sash & trim;
   door & window products

(P-6719)
**SECURITY METAL PRODUCTS
CORP (DH)**
5678 Concours, Ontario (91764-5394)
PHONE..................................310 641-6690
Chris Holloway, *CEO*
Ann Webster, *Administration*
EMP: 18 **EST:** 2010
SALES (est): 5.9MM
SALES (corp-wide): 10.1B **Privately Held**
WEB: www.secmet.com
SIC: 3442 Metal doors

(P-6720)
STEELWORKS ETC INC
1250 Commercial Ave, Oxnard
(93030-7457)
PHONE..................................805 487-3000
EMP: 13 **EST:** 2015
SALES (est): 1.7MM **Privately Held**
WEB: www.steelworksetc.com
SIC: 3442 Metal doors, sash & trim

(P-6721)
TJE COMPANY
Also Called: Onyx Shutters
18343 Gale Ave, City of Industry
(91748-1201)
PHONE..................................909 869-7777
Sylvia Lee, *CEO*
Philip Kim, *Vice Pres*
◆ **EMP:** 21 **EST:** 2007
SALES (est): 3.1MM **Privately Held**
WEB: www.onyxshutters.com
SIC: 3442 Shutters, door or window: metal

(P-6722)
**TORRANCE STEEL WINDOW CO
INC**
1819 Abalone Ave, Torrance (90501-3704)
PHONE..................................310 328-9181
Dong K Lim, *President*
Gabriel Mena, *CFO*
▲ **EMP:** 24 **EST:** 1964
SQ FT: 32,000
SALES (est): 5.5MM **Privately Held**
WEB: www.torrancesteelwindow.com
SIC: 3442 Window & door frames

3443 Fabricated Plate Work

(P-6723)
ACD LLC (DH)
Also Called: A C D
2321 Pullman St, Santa Ana (92705-5512)
PHONE..................................949 261-7533
James Estes, *Managing Dir*
Richard S Young, *Executive*
Joseph Gardner, *Administration*
Vanessa Murillo, *Administration*
Matt Rockwood, *Administration*
◆ **EMP:** 107 **EST:** 1978
SQ FT: 52,000
SALES (est): 50.4MM **Privately Held**
WEB: www.nikkisoceig.com
SIC: 3443 3559 Cryogenic tanks, for liq-
   uids & gases; cryogenic machinery, in-
   dustrial
HQ: Cryogenic Industries, Inc.
   27710 Jefferson Ave # 301
   Temecula CA 92590
   951 677-2081

(P-6724)
**AERO-CLSSICS HEAT TRNSF
PDTS I**
1677 Curtiss Ct, La Verne (91750-5848)
PHONE..................................909 596-1630
Paul Saurenman, *CEO*
Ernie Ruiz, *Prdtn Mgr*
EMP: 15 **EST:** 2007
SALES (est): 4.5MM **Privately Held**
WEB: www.aero-classics.com
SIC: 3443 Heat exchangers: coolers (after,
   inter), condensers, etc.

(P-6725)
**ASC PROCESS SYSTEMS
INTERNATI**
28402 Livingston Ave, Valencia
(91355-4172)
PHONE..................................818 833-0088
David C Mason, *CEO*

EMP: 14 **EST:** 2011
SALES (est): 188.2K **Privately Held**
WEB: www.aschome.com
SIC: 3443 3585 Autoclaves, industrial;
   heating & air conditioning combination
   units

(P-6726)
ASCO LP
1749 Stergios Rd, Calexico (92231-9657)
PHONE..................................877 208-4316
EMP: 107
SALES (corp-wide): 16.7B **Publicly Held**
SIC: 3443 3491 3492 3625 Fabricated
   plate work (boiler shop); solenoid valves;
   fluid power valves & hose fittings; control
   equipment, electric; switches, except
   electronic
HQ: Asco, L.P.
   160 Park Ave
   Florham Park NJ 07932
   800 972-2726

(P-6727)
ATCO RUBBER PRODUCTS INC
3080 12th St, Riverside (92507-4903)
PHONE..................................951 788-4345
Bertha Almanza, *Branch Mgr*
EMP: 44 **Publicly Held**
WEB: www.atcoflex.com
SIC: 3443 Fabricated plate work (boiler
   shop)
HQ: Atco Rubber Products, Inc.
   7101 Atco Dr
   Fort Worth TX 76118
   817 595-2894

(P-6728)
BA HOLDINGS INC (DH)
3016 Kansas Ave Bldg 1, Riverside
(92507-3445)
PHONE..................................951 684-5110
John S Rhodes, *CEO*
EMP: 30 **EST:** 1996
SALES (est): 110.2MM
SALES (corp-wide): 378MM **Privately
Held**
WEB: www.mediluxcylinders.com
SIC: 3443 3728 Cylinders, pressure: metal
   plate; aircraft parts & equipment

(P-6729)
BASIC INDUSTRIES INTL INC
Also Called: Pacific Metal Products
10850 Wilshire Blvd, Los Angeles
(90024-4305)
PHONE..................................951 226-1500
John Wallace, *President*
Steven W Burge, *Director*
EMP: 200 **EST:** 2000
SALES (est): 36.8MM **Privately Held**
WEB: www.biidemexico.com
SIC: 3443 3446 Fabricated plate work
   (boiler shop); architectural metalwork

(P-6730)
BORIN MANUFACTURING INC
5741 Buckingham Pkwy B, Culver City
(90230-6520)
PHONE..................................310 822-1000
Frank William Borin, *CEO*
Gregg Steele, *Vice Pres*
EMP: 40 **EST:** 1976
SALES (est): 9.9MM **Privately Held**
WEB: www.borin.com
SIC: 3443 3561 3494 3317 Fabricated
   plate work (boiler shop); pumps & pump-
   ing equipment; valves & pipe fittings; steel
   pipe & tubes; telephone & telegraph ap-
   paratus; oil & gas field machinery

(P-6731)
BRYANT FUEL SYSTEMS LLC
1300 32nd St, Bakersfield (93301-2144)
PHONE..................................661 334-5462
Donald David Wells,
Eric Deavers, *Vice Pres*
Jeff Peacon, *Vice Pres*
Michelle Miller, *Human Resources*
EMP: 29 **EST:** 2019
SALES (est): 5.2MM **Privately Held**
WEB: www.bryantfuelsystems.com
SIC: 3443 Air coolers, metal plate

(P-6732)
CALIFORNIA METAL & SUPPLY INC
10230 Freeman Ave, Santa Fe Springs (90670-3410)
PHONE..................................800 707-6061
Kenneth Lee, *CEO*
Kenneth M Lee, *CEO*
Loreley Beltran, *Executive*
Henry Pena, *General Mgr*
Will Beutjer, *Business Mgr*
◆ **EMP:** 16
SQ FT: 35,000
SALES (est): 11.7MM **Privately Held**
WEB: www.californiametal.com
SIC: 3443 3469 3599 5051 Metal parts; machine parts, stamped or pressed metal; machine shop, jobbing & repair; metals service centers & offices; ferrous metals; nonferrous metal sheets, bars, rods, etc.; aluminum bars, rods, ingots, sheets, pipes, plates, etc.

(P-6733)
CATALINA CYLINDERS INC (PA)
7300 Anaconda Ave, Garden Grove (92841-2930)
PHONE..................................714 890-0999
Gregory Keeler, *CEO*
Roark Keeler, *CFO*
Richard Hill, *Vice Pres*
Bob Lance, *Executive*
Rick Hill, *General Mgr*
EMP: 91 **EST:** 2014
SALES (est): 21.8MM **Privately Held**
WEB: www.catalinacylinders.com
SIC: 3443 3491 Fabricated plate work (boiler shop); compressed gas cylinder valves

(P-6734)
CJI PROCESS SYSTEMS INC
Also Called: Lee Ray Sandblasting
12000 Clark St, Santa Fe Springs (90670-3709)
PHONE..................................562 777-0614
Archie Cholakian, *President*
John Cholakian, *Vice Pres*
Paul Tombakian, *Chief Engr*
▼ **EMP:** 70 **EST:** 1982
SQ FT: 35,000
SALES (est): 22.9MM **Privately Held**
WEB: www.cjiprocesssystems.com
SIC: 3443 3441 3444 Tanks, lined: metal plate; fabricated structural metal; sheet metalwork

(P-6735)
CMT SHEET METAL
22732 Granite Way Ste C, Laguna Hills (92653-1263)
PHONE..................................949 679-9868
Wes Hinze, *CEO*
Wes Hinze Jr, *President*
Gayle Hinze, *Admin Sec*
EMP: 15 **EST:** 2000
SALES (est): 3MM **Privately Held**
SIC: 3443 Boiler & boiler shop work

(P-6736)
COMMERCIAL METAL FORMING INC
341 W Collins Ave, Orange (92867-5505)
PHONE..................................714 532-6321
William Kowal, *President*
Donald E Washdewicz, *Vice Pres*
Phil Smith, *Engineer*
Tamara Fiorenza, *Regl Sales Mgr*
Steve Zaborsky, *Sales Staff*
▲ **EMP:** 53 **EST:** 2003
SALES (est): 6.1MM **Privately Held**
WEB: www.cmforming.com
SIC: 3443 Fabricated plate work (boiler shop)

(P-6737)
COMPUTRUS INC
250 Klug Cir, Corona (92878-5409)
PHONE..................................951 245-9103
William Turnbull, *President*
Scott R Carroll, *Vice Pres*
EMP: 35 **EST:** 1984

SALES (est): 9.9MM
SALES (corp-wide): 245.5B **Publicly Held**
WEB: www.computrusinc.com
SIC: 3443 Truss plates, metal
HQ: Mitek Industries, Inc.
16023 Swinly Rdg
Chesterfield MO 63017
314 434-1200

(P-6738)
CONSOLIDATED FABRICATORS CORP (PA)
Also Called: CF
14620 Arminta St, Van Nuys (91402-5902)
PHONE..................................818 901-1005
Michael J Melideo, *CEO*
Jeff Lombardi, *President*
Brian A Atwater, *COO*
Robert Cardenas, *Engineer*
Renee Fernandez, *Sales Staff*
▲ **EMP:** 110
SQ FT: 150,000
SALES: 106.8MM **Privately Held**
WEB: www.con-fab.com
SIC: 3443 5051 3444 Dumpsters, garbage; steel; studs & joists, sheet metal

(P-6739)
COOK AND COOK INCORPORATED
Also Called: Royal Welding & Fabricating
1000 E Elm Ave, Fullerton (92831-5022)
PHONE..................................714 680-6669
Wallace F Cook, *President*
Patricia Cook, *Vice Pres*
Seyung Kim, *Executive*
Veronica Covarrubias, *Human Resources*
EMP: 30 **EST:** 1967
SQ FT: 30,000
SALES (est): 7.1MM **Privately Held**
WEB: www.royalwelding.com
SIC: 3443 3599 3444 Industrial vessels, tanks & containers; amusement park equipment; sheet metalwork

(P-6740)
DESIGN FORM INC
8250 Electric Ave, Stanton (90680-2640)
PHONE..................................714 952-3700
Glenn Baldwin, *CEO*
EMP: 39 **EST:** 1980
SQ FT: 7,000
SALES (est): 3.2MM **Privately Held**
SIC: 3443 Tanks, standard or custom fabricated: metal plate

(P-6741)
DUNWEIZER MACHINE INC
Also Called: Dunweizer Mch & Fabrication
8338 Allport Ave, Santa Fe Springs (90670-2108)
P.O. Box 3046 (90670-0046)
PHONE..................................562 698-7787
Dennis Schweizer, *President*
Jim Van Eperen, *Marketing Staff*
EMP: 19 **EST:** 1976
SQ FT: 20,000
SALES (est): 6.1MM **Privately Held**
WEB: www.dunweizer.com
SIC: 3443 3599 Fabricated plate work (boiler shop); machine shop, jobbing & repair

(P-6742)
HAYDEN PRODUCTS LLC
Also Called: Hayden Industrial Products
1393 E San Bernardino Ave, San Bernardino (92408-2964)
PHONE..................................951 736-2600
Harold Lehon, *Mng Member*
Peter Camenzind, *Co-Owner*
James Neitz, *President*
Sue Misenhelter, *Administration*
Greg Loper, *Info Tech Mgr*
▲ **EMP:** 80
SQ FT: 55,000
SALES (est): 29.4MM **Privately Held**
WEB: www.haydenindustrial.com
SIC: 3443 Heat exchangers, condensers & components

(P-6743)
MELCO STEEL INC
1100 W Foothill Blvd, Azusa (91702-2818)
PHONE..................................626 334-7875

Michel Kashou, *President*
Joann Reese, *Corp Secy*
Mazin Kashou, *Vice Pres*
Tom Rockecharlie, *Vice Pres*
EMP: 30 **EST:** 1971
SQ FT: 25,500
SALES (est): 6.8MM **Privately Held**
WEB: www.melcosteel.com
SIC: 3443 Vessels, process or storage (from boiler shops): metal plate; autoclaves, industrial

(P-6744)
P-W WESTERN INC
9415 Kruse Rd, Pico Rivera (90660-1430)
PHONE..................................562 463-9055
Timothy Place, *CEO*
Emilia Gonzales, *Finance*
EMP: 95 **EST:** 1963
SQ FT: 60,000
SALES (est): 11.5MM
SALES (corp-wide): 25.9MM **Privately Held**
SIC: 3443 Cable trays, metal plate
HQ: P-W Industries Inc
9415 Kruse Rd
Pico Rivera CA 90660
562 463-9055

(P-6745)
PACIFIC STEAM EQUIPMENT INC
Also Called: P S E Boilers
11748 Slauson Ave, Santa Fe Springs (90670-2227)
PHONE..................................562 906-9292
William S Shanahan MD, *President*
David Kang, *Vice Pres*
Shin Duk Kang, *Vice Pres*
Santiago A Kuan, *Sales Mgr*
▲ **EMP:** 25 **EST:** 1954
SQ FT: 22,500
SALES (est): 4.4MM **Privately Held**
WEB: www.pacificsteam.com
SIC: 3443 5074 3582 2841 Tanks, standard or custom fabricated: metal plate; boilers: industrial, power, or marine; plumbing & hydronic heating supplies; steam fittings; commercial laundry equipment; soap & other detergents

(P-6746)
PACIFIC TANK & CNSTR INC
17995 E Highway 46, Shandon (93461-9636)
PHONE..................................805 237-2929
Tom Yanaga, *Manager*
Dan Oliveira, *Manager*
EMP: 30 **Privately Held**
WEB: www.pacifictank.net
SIC: 3443 Fabricated plate work (boiler shop)
PA: Pacific Tank & Construction, Inc.
31551 Avnida Los Cerritos
San Juan Capistrano CA 92675

(P-6747)
PLUCKYS DUMP RENTAL LLC
10136 Bowman Ave, South Gate (90280-6131)
PHONE..................................323 540-3510
Jonathan Cortes,
EMP: 45
SALES (est): 1.5MM **Privately Held**
SIC: 3443 Dumpsters, garbage

(P-6748)
QUALITY VESSEL ENGINEERING INC
8515 Chetle Ave, Santa Fe Springs (90670-2205)
PHONE..................................562 696-2100
John Gill, *President*
EMP: 15 **EST:** 2006
SALES (est): 537K **Privately Held**
WEB: www.qvessel.com
SIC: 3443 Cylinders, pressure: metal plate

(P-6749)
RICHFIELD ENGINEERING INC
Also Called: L W Lefort
1135 Fee Ana St, Placentia (92870-6761)
PHONE..................................714 524-3741
Don Robinson, *President*
EMP: 40 **EST:** 1995

SQ FT: 40,000
SALES (est): 1.6MM
SALES (corp-wide): 6.5MM **Privately Held**
WEB: www.robinsonmfginc.com
SIC: 3443 Metal parts
PA: Robinson Manufacturing, Inc.
1136 Richfield Rd
Placentia CA 92870
714 524-7395

(P-6750)
ROY E HANSON JR MFG (PA)
Also Called: Hanson Tank
1600 W Washington Blvd, Los Angeles (90021-3123)
P.O. Box 30507 (90030-0507)
PHONE..................................213 747-7514
Jonathan Goss, *CEO*
Roy E Hanson Jr, *Shareholder*
Johnathan Goss, *CEO*
Thys Dorenbosch, *Treasurer*
Cliff Jones, *Vice Pres*
▼ **EMP:** 81 **EST:** 1932
SQ FT: 55,000
SALES (est): 11.7MM **Privately Held**
WEB: www.hansontank.com
SIC: 3443 Fuel tanks (oil, gas, etc.): metal plate

(P-6751)
S BRAVO SYSTEMS INC
Also Called: Bravo Support
2929 Vail Ave, Commerce (90040-2615)
PHONE..................................323 888-4133
Paola Bravo Recendez, *CEO*
Micah Nelson, *Vice Pres*
Paula Recendez, *Executive*
Max Cohen, *Design Engr*
Christy Linares, *Human Resources*
▲ **EMP:** 26 **EST:** 1986
SQ FT: 40,000
SALES (est): 13.6MM **Privately Held**
WEB: www.sbravo.com
SIC: 3443 Containers, shipping (bombs, etc.): metal plate

(P-6752)
SID E PARKER BOILER MFG CO INC
Also Called: Parker Boiler Co
5930 Bandini Blvd, Commerce (90040-2903)
PHONE..................................323 727-9800
Sid D Danenhauer, *Ch of Bd*
Ed Marchak, *CFO*
Greg G Danenhauer, *Vice Pres*
Bob Keith, *Technical Staff*
Mike McDonald, *Engineer*
◆ **EMP:** 66 **EST:** 1939
SQ FT: 80,000
SALES (est): 14.6MM **Privately Held**
WEB: www.parkerboiler.com
SIC: 3443 3433 Boilers: industrial, power, or marine; heating equipment, except electric

(P-6753)
SOLACE CST LLC (HQ)
11111 Santa Monica Blvd, Los Angeles (90025-3333)
PHONE..................................310 919-5401
Christopher S Brothers, *Mng Member*
EMP: 100 **EST:** 2017
SALES (est): 239.5MM **Privately Held**
WEB: www.solacecap.com
SIC: 3443 Tanks, lined: metal plate
PA: Solace Capital Partners, L.P.
11111 Santa Monica Blvd # 1275
Los Angeles CA 90025
310 919-5401

(P-6754)
SOUTH GATE ENGINEERING LLC
13477 Yorba Ave, Chino (91710-5055)
PHONE..................................909 628-2779
Peter Morin,
William Paolino, *Mng Member*
EMP: 115 **EST:** 1947
SALES (est): 24.8MM **Privately Held**
WEB: www.southgateengineering.com
SIC: 3443 Vessels, process or storage (from boiler shops): metal plate; heat exchangers: coolers (after, inter), condensers, etc.

PRODUCTS & SVCS

(P-6755)
SPX CORPORATION
17815 Newhope St Ste M, Fountain Valley
(92708-5426)
PHONE...................714 434-2576
EMP: 99
SALES (corp-wide): 1.4B **Publicly Held**
SIC: 3443 Mfg Fabricated Plate Work
PA: Spx Corporation
13320a Balntyn Corp Pl
Charlotte NC 28277
980 474-3700

(P-6756)
**STRUCTURAL COMPOSITES
INDS LLC (HQ)**
Also Called: SCI
336 Enterprise Pl, Pomona (91768-3244)
PHONE...................909 594-7777
Ken Miller, *Mng Member*
◆ EMP: 155 EST: 2007
SALES (est): 32MM
SALES (corp-wide): 378MM **Privately
Held**
WEB: www.luxfer.com
SIC: 3443 Tanks, lined: metal plate
PA: Luxfer Holdings Plc
Ancorage Gateway
Salford LANCS M50 3
161 300-0611

(P-6757)
SUPERIOR STORAGE TANK INC
14700 Industry Cir, La Mirada
(90638-5817)
PHONE...................714 226-1914
Griff Williams, *CEO*
Rob Henderson, *COO*
EMP: 15 EST: 2010
SALES (est): 2.2MM **Privately Held**
WEB: www.superior-tanks.com
SIC: 3443 7692 Fuel tanks (oil, gas, etc.):
metal plate; welding repair

(P-6758)
SUPERIOR TANK CO INC (PA)
Also Called: Stci
9500 Lucas Ranch Rd, Rancho Cuca-
monga (91730-5724)
PHONE...................909 912-0580
Jesus Eric Marquez, *President*
Lewis A Marquez, *Treasurer*
Huel L Loden, *Branch Mgr*
Amber Crespo, *Executive Asst*
George Marquez, *Admin Sec*
◆ EMP: 50 EST: 1984
SQ FT: 53,392
SALES (est): 30.4MM **Privately Held**
WEB: www.superiortank.com
SIC: 3443 3494 1791 1794 Fuel tanks
(oil, gas, etc.): metal plate; water tanks,
metal plate; valves & pipe fittings; struc-
tural steel erection; excavation work

(P-6759)
TAIT & ASSOCIATES INC
2131 S Dupont Dr, Anaheim (92806-6102)
PHONE...................714 560-8222
Jim Streipz, *Branch Mgr*
Trevor Tait, *Managing Dir*
Andy Tait, *Regional Mgr*
Pat Banbury, *Technician*
Guillermina Benavides, *Project Mgr*
EMP: 36
SALES (corp-wide): 30.1MM **Privately
Held**
WEB: www.tait.com
SIC: 3443 Fuel tanks (oil, gas, etc.): metal
plate
PA: Tait & Associates, Inc.
701 Parkcenter Dr
Santa Ana CA 92705
866 584-0283

(P-6760)
**THERMAL EQUIPMENT
CORPORATION**
Also Called: TEC
2030 E University Dr, Compton
(90220-6410)
PHONE...................310 328-6600
Nancy Huffman, *President*
Osvaldo Lopez, *Engineer*
Mike Courtney, *Director*
▼ EMP: 45 EST: 1969

SQ FT: 45,000
SALES (est): 12.7MM **Privately Held**
WEB: www.thermalequipment.com
SIC: 3443 3821 2842 Autoclaves, industrial; process vessels, industrial: metal
plate; vessels, process or storage (from
boiler shops): metal plate; laboratory apparatus & furniture; specialty cleaning,
polishes & sanitation goods
PA: Km3 Holdings, Inc.
2030 E University Dr
Rancho Dominguez CA 90220

(P-6761)
**THERMLLY ENGNRED
MNFCTRED PDTS**
Also Called: T E M P
543 W 135th St, Gardena (90248-1505)
PHONE...................310 523-9934
Robert Greenwood, *President*
Binh Vinh, *Vice Pres*
▲ EMP: 27 EST: 1994
SQ FT: 50,000
SALES (est): 7.4MM **Privately Held**
WEB: www.greenwoodcncfin.com
SIC: 3443 Heat exchangers, condensers &
components

(P-6762)
THOMPSON TANK INC
8029 Phlox St, Downey (90241-4816)
P.O. Box 790, Lakewood (90714-0790)
PHONE...................562 869-7711
David B Thompson, *President*
Robert I Grue, *Treasurer*
EMP: 19 EST: 1993
SQ FT: 225,000
SALES (est): 4.6MM **Privately Held**
WEB: www.thompsontank.com
SIC: 3443 7699 3715 3713 Tanks, stan-
dard or custom fabricated: metal plate;
tank repair & cleaning services; truck trail-
ers; truck & bus bodies

(P-6763)
UNIVERSAL DEFENSE
412 Cucamonga Ave, Claremont
(91711-5019)
P.O. Box 1372 (91711-1372)
PHONE...................909 626-4178
EMP: 20
SALES (est): 1.7MM **Privately Held**
SIC: 3443 Military Equipment

(P-6764)
UTTAM COMPOSITES LLC
11700 Monarch St, Garden Grove
(92841-1819)
PHONE...................714 894-5300
Mary Leonard, *Branch Mgr*
EMP: 16 **Privately Held**
SIC: 3443 Cylinders, pressure: metal plate
HQ: Uttam Composites, Llc
1409 Post Oak Blvd
Houston TX 77056
202 644-3222

(P-6765)
**WAGNER PLATE WORKS WEST
INC (PA)**
Also Called: P V T Supply
14015 Garfield Ave, Paramount
(90723-2137)
PHONE...................562 531-6050
Jack Brian Purtell, *President*
EMP: 22 EST: 1994
SQ FT: 60,000
SALES (est): 7.5MM **Privately Held**
SIC: 3443 5051 Tanks, lined: metal plate;
pipe & tubing, steel

(P-6766)
WATERCREST INC
4850 E Airport Dr, Ontario (91761-7818)
PHONE...................909 390-3944
Jeremiah B Robins, *CEO*
Gary F Johnson, *President*
▲ EMP: 39 EST: 1996
SQ FT: 29,000
SALES (est): 1.6MM **Privately Held**
SIC: 3443 Heat exchangers, condensers &
components

(P-6767)
**WELLS STRUTHERS
CORPORATION**
Also Called: Tei Struthers Wells
10375 Slusher Dr, Santa Fe Springs
(90670-3748)
PHONE...................814 726-1000
John C Wallace, *President*
John M Carey, *Vice Pres*
Burton M Abrams, *Admin Sec*
EMP: 30 EST: 1937
SQ FT: 30,000
SALES (est): 2.2MM **Privately Held**
SIC: 3443 Heat exchangers, plate type;
heat exchangers: coolers (after, inter),
condensers, etc.; pressurizers or auxiliary
equipment, nuclear: metal plate

3444 Sheet Metal Work

(P-6768)
10 GAUGE SHEET METAL INC
1101 Endeavor Dr, Upland (91786-1506)
PHONE...................909 208-4525
Collette Grafius, *Principal*
EMP: 15 EST: 2018
SALES (est): 4MM **Privately Held**
WEB: www.10gaugesheetmetal.com
SIC: 3444 Sheet metalwork

(P-6769)
**5H SHEET METAL FABRICATION
INC**
1826 W Business Center Dr, Orange
(92867-7904)
PHONE...................714 633-7544
Hoa Nguyen, *CEO*
Helena Nguyen, *CFO*
Hoa Thi Nguyen, *Admin Sec*
EMP: 15 EST: 1998
SQ FT: 10,000
SALES (est): 2.3MM **Privately Held**
WEB: www.5hfab.com
SIC: 3444 Sheet metalwork

(P-6770)
**A & M SCULPTURED METALS
LLC**
Also Called: A & M Sculpture Lighting
1781 N Indiana St, Los Angeles
(90063-2523)
PHONE...................323 263-2221
Jerry Orlandini,
EMP: 23 EST: 1986
SQ FT: 10,000
SALES (est): 3.1MM **Privately Held**
WEB: www.ryanwoodfellowship.org
SIC: 3444 Sheet metalwork

(P-6771)
A-1 METAL PRODUCTS INC
2707 Supply Ave, Commerce (90040-2703)
PHONE...................323 721-3334
Jerry Calsbeek, *President*
Patricia Calsbeek, *Corp Secy*
Cathy C Calsbeek, *Technical Staff*
EMP: 24 EST: 1952
SQ FT: 40,000
SALES (est): 2.6MM **Privately Held**
WEB: www.a1metalproducts.com
SIC: 3444 Sheet metal specialties, not
stamped

(P-6772)
**ABC PRECISION SHEET METAL
INC**
13378 Monte Vista Ave, Chino
(91710-5147)
PHONE...................951 741-6667
EMP: 13 EST: 2019
SALES (est): 1.6MM **Privately Held**
WEB: www.abcprecisionsheetmetal.com
SIC: 3444 Sheet metalwork

(P-6773)
ABLE SHEET METAL INC (PA)
614 N Ford Blvd, Los Angeles
(90022-1195)
PHONE...................323 269-2181
Dmitri Triphon, *CEO*
Gurgen Tovmasyan, *COO*
Ingrid Anderson, *Office Mgr*
Sharon Cohn, *Technology*

Greg Avalos, *Sales Staff*
◆ EMP: 40 EST: 2001
SQ FT: 25,000
SALES (est): 7.9MM **Private y Held**
WEB: www.ablemetal.com
SIC: 3444 Sheet metal specialties, not
stamped

(P-6774)
ADVANCED METAL MFG INC
49 Strathearn Pl, Simi Valley (93065-1653)
PHONE...................805 322-4161
Scott Stewart, *CEO*
Gina Stewart, *Controller*
▲ EMP: 34 EST: 2010
SALES (est): 10.6MM **Privately Held**
SIC: 3444 Sheet metalwork

(P-6775)
AERO BENDING COMPANY
560 Auto Center Dr Ste A, Palmdale
(93551-4485)
PHONE...................661 948-2363
Robert Burns, *President*
Cory Conner, *QC Mgr*
EMP: 80
SQ FT: 26,000
SALES (est): 10.8MM **Privately Held**
WEB: www.aerobendingco.com
SIC: 3444 5088 Sheet metalwork; aircraft
engines & engine parts

(P-6776)
**AERO PRECISION
ENGINEERING**
11300 Hindry Ave, Los Angeles
(90045-6228)
PHONE...................310 642-9747
Sherry L Martinez, *President*
John Segotta, *Prgrmr*
Tom Segotta, *Exec Sec*
EMP: 45
SQ FT: 55,000
SALES (est): 9.8MM **Privately Held**
WEB: www.aeroprecisioneng.com
SIC: 3444 3599 Sheet metal specialties,
not stamped; machine shop, jobbing & re-
pair

(P-6777)
**AIRCRAFT STAMPING
COMPANY INC**
1285 Paseo Alicia, San Dimas
(91773-4407)
PHONE...................323 283-1239
Michael Nolan, *President*
Linda Nolan, *Shareholder*
EMP: 19 EST: 1943
SQ FT: 17,900
SALES (est): 1.1MM **Privately Held**
WEB: www.aircraftstamping.com
SIC: 3444 3469 Sheet metal specialties,
not stamped; metal stampings

(P-6778)
ALL-WAYS METAL INC
401 E Alondra Blvd, Gardena
(90248-2901)
PHONE...................310 217-1177
Shirley Pickens, *President*
Scott Pickens, *Vice Pres*
EMP: 30
SQ FT: 29,000
SALES (est): 7.1MM **Privately Held**
WEB: www.allwaysmetal.com
SIC: 3444 Sheet metal specialties, not
stamped

(P-6779)
**ALLIANCE METAL PRODUCTS
INC**
20844 Plummer St, Chatsworth
(91311-5004)
PHONE...................818 709-1204
Dan L Rowlett Jr, *CEO*
EMP: 212 EST: 2002
SQ FT: 2,000
SALES (est): 14.7MM **Privately Held**
WEB: www.alliancemp.com
SIC: 3444 Sheet metal specialties, not
stamped

(P-6780)
ALPHA PRODUCTIONS INCORPORATED
5830 W Jefferson Blvd # 1, Los Angeles (90016-3109)
PHONE....................310 559-1364
Missak Azirian, *President*
John Forker, *Controller*
Cliff Gimbert, *Opers Staff*
▲ EMP: 15 EST: 1978
SQ FT: 25,000
SALES (est): 2.5MM **Privately Held**
WEB: www.alphaproductions.com
SIC: 3444 Awnings, sheet metal

(P-6781)
AMD INTERNATIONAL TECH LLC
Also Called: International Rite-Way Pdts
1725 S Campus Ave, Ontario (91761-4346)
PHONE....................909 985-8300
Ravinder Joshi,
George Ruben, *Program Mgr*
EMP: 25 EST: 1994
SQ FT: 17,000
SALES (est): 2.9MM **Privately Held**
WEB: www.360.3f2.myftpupload.com
SIC: 3444 1761 Sheet metal specialties, not stamped; sheet metalwork

(P-6782)
AMERICAN AIRCRAFT PRODUCTS INC
Also Called: A A P
15411 S Broadway, Gardena (90248-2207)
PHONE....................310 532-7434
Gerald R Tupper, *President*
Robert Lourenco, *Mfg Staff*
EMP: 67 EST: 1975
SQ FT: 54,000
SALES (est): 12.3MM **Privately Held**
WEB: www.americanaircraft.com
SIC: 3444 3599 Sheet metalwork; machine shop, jobbing & repair

(P-6783)
AMERICAN COFFEE URN MFG CO INC
Also Called: A C U Precision Sheet Metal
5178 Western Way, Perris (92571-7422)
PHONE....................951 943-1495
Jeff Johs, *President*
Andy Johs, *Vice Pres*
EMP: 13 EST: 1960
SQ FT: 9,280
SALES (est): 2MM **Privately Held**
WEB: www.acumetalfab.com
SIC: 3444 Sheet metalwork

(P-6784)
AMERICAN RANGE CORPORATION
13592 Desmond St, Pacoima (91331-2315)
PHONE....................818 897-0808
Shane Demirjian, *President*
Alexander Qi, *CFO*
Mourad Demirjian, *Vice Pres*
Richard Lenning, *Vice Pres*
Guillermo Melendrez, *Technical Staff*
▲ EMP: 120 EST: 1989
SQ FT: 125,000
SALES (est): 26.2MM **Privately Held**
WEB: www.americanrange.com
SIC: 3444 3631 Hoods, range: sheet metal; household cooking equipment

(P-6785)
ANGELUS SHEET METAL MFG INC
Also Called: Angelus Sheet Metal & Plbg Sup
1355 Carroll Ave, Los Angeles (90026-5109)
PHONE....................323 221-4191
Ronald S Coutin, *President*
Leonard Coutin, *Manager*
EMP: 14 EST: 1932
SALES (est): 471.4K **Privately Held**
SIC: 3444 Sheet metalwork

(P-6786)
ANOROC PRECISION SHTMTL INC
19122 S Santa Fe Ave, Compton (90221-5910)
PHONE....................310 515-6015
Roxanne Zavala, *CEO*
Pete Corona, *Vice Pres*
Pete J Corona, *VP Engrg*
EMP: 25 EST: 1978
SQ FT: 15,000
SALES (est): 4.1MM **Privately Held**
WEB: www.anoroc.com
SIC: 3444 Sheet metal specialties, not stamped

(P-6787)
ARROYO HOLDINGS INC (PA)
898 N Fair Oaks Ave, Pasadena (91103-3068)
PHONE....................626 765-9340
Michael C Doyle, *President*
EMP: 31 EST: 1985
SALES (est): 15.7MM **Privately Held**
SIC: 3444 3669 8111 Sheet metalwork; pedestrian traffic control equipment; will, estate & trust law

(P-6788)
ARTISTIC WELDING
Also Called: Precision Sheet Metal
505 E Gardena Blvd, Gardena (90248-2915)
PHONE....................310 515-4922
George R Sandoval, *President*
Mary Sandoval, *General Mgr*
Christine Segura, *Purch Agent*
EMP: 65 EST: 1974
SQ FT: 85,000
SALES (est): 8.6MM **Privately Held**
WEB: www.artistic-welding.com
SIC: 3444 Sheet metalwork

(P-6789)
ATLAS SHEET METAL INC
19 Musick, Irvine (92618-1638)
PHONE....................949 600-8787
James M Odlum, *President*
Wendy Carter, *Admin Asst*
EMP: 17 EST: 1998
SQ FT: 5,500
SALES (est): 4.3MM **Privately Held**
WEB: www.atlassheetmetal.com
SIC: 3444 Sheet metalwork

(P-6790)
AZACHOROK CONTRACT SVCS LLC
320 Grand Cypress Ave # 502, Palmdale (93551-3622)
PHONE....................661 951-6566
Loren Peterson,
EMP: 14 EST: 1996
SQ FT: 12,000
SALES (est): 2MM **Privately Held**
SIC: 3444 3663 Sheet metalwork; airborne radio communications equipment; carrier equipment, radio communications

(P-6791)
B & CAWNINGS INC
Also Called: B & C Industries
3082 E Miraloma Ave, Anaheim (92806-1810)
PHONE....................714 632-3303
CHI Le, *Chairman*
Buu Pham, *President*
Jeff Pham, *Vice Pres*
Chris Walker, *Vice Pres*
Christopher Walker, *Vice Pres*
▲ EMP: 26 EST: 1984
SQ FT: 7,000
SALES (est): 1.9MM **Privately Held**
WEB: www.bcawnings.com
SIC: 3444 Awnings, sheet metal

(P-6792)
BARZILLAI MANUFACTURING CO INC
1410 S Cucamonga Ave, Ontario (91761-4509)
PHONE....................909 947-4200
Ray Richmond, *President*
Garrett Zopf, *Treasurer*
EMP: 17 EST: 2003

SQ FT: 5,200
SALES (est): 2.2MM **Privately Held**
SIC: 3444 Sheet metalwork

(P-6793)
BASMAT INC (PA)
Also Called: McStarlite
1531 240th St, Harbor City (90710-1308)
PHONE....................310 325-2063
John W Basso, *CEO*
John Allen Basso, *President*
Henry Matadlu, *President*
Tim Benfer, *COO*
Sharon Stelter, *Officer*
▲ EMP: 100 EST: 1952
SQ FT: 42,000
SALES (est): 22.7MM **Privately Held**
WEB: www.mcstarlite.com
SIC: 3444 Sheet metalwork

(P-6794)
BAY CITIES TIN SHOP INC
Also Called: Bay Cities Metal Products
301 E Alondra Blvd, Gardena (90248-2809)
PHONE....................310 660-0351
Henry Kamberg, *CEO*
Gary Mugford, *President*
Debra Childress, *Vice Pres*
Ben Hanfling, *Vice Pres*
Guillermo Patino, *Vice Pres*
EMP: 43 EST: 1947
SALES (est): 5.9MM **Privately Held**
WEB: www.bcmet.com
SIC: 3444 Sheet metal specialties, not stamped

(P-6795)
BEND-TEK INC
2205 S Yale St, Santa Ana (92704-4426)
PHONE....................714 210-8966
Melinda Nguyen, *CEO*
Mac Le, *Officer*
Eric Tran, *Officer*
EMP: 100
SQ FT: 7,000
SALES (est): 11MM **Privately Held**
WEB: www.bendtekinc.com
SIC: 3444 Pipe, sheet metal

(P-6796)
BLEEKER BROTHERS INC1
10868 Drury Ln, Lynwood (90262-1834)
PHONE....................310 639-4367
Charles Bleeker, *President*
EMP: 16 EST: 1952
SQ FT: 30,000
SALES (est): 674.7K **Privately Held**
SIC: 3444 3567 3563 Booths, spray: prefabricated sheet metal; sheet metal specialties, not stamped; industrial furnaces & ovens; air & gas compressors

(P-6797)
BOOZAK INC
Also Called: K Squared Metals
508 Chaney St Ste A, Lake Elsinore (92530-2797)
PHONE....................951 245-6045
Kevin Kluzak, *President*
Kevin Booth, *Vice Pres*
Shanon Martinez, *Accounts Mgr*
EMP: 45 EST: 2004
SALES (est): 4.6MM **Privately Held**
SIC: 3444 Sheet metalwork

(P-6798)
BROADWAY AC HTG & SHTMTL
Also Called: Broadway Sheet Metal
7855 Burnet Ave, Van Nuys (91405-1010)
PHONE....................818 781-1477
Alexander Merzel, *President*
Anna Merzel, *CFO*
Vince Lombardo, *Admin Sec*
Shannon Maybin, *Sales Staff*
EMP: 35 EST: 1926
SQ FT: 7,000
SALES (est): 2.5MM **Privately Held**
WEB: www.broadwaysm.com
SIC: 3444 Sheet metalwork

(P-6799)
C & J METAL PRODUCTS INC
6323 Alondra Blvd, Paramount (90723-3750)
PHONE....................562 634-3101

Roy L Chapman, *President*
Isabelle Chapman, *Corp Secy*
▲ EMP: 27 EST: 1946
SQ FT: 37,000
SALES (est): 1MM **Privately Held**
WEB: www.cjmetals.com
SIC: 3444 Ventilators, sheet metal

(P-6800)
C&O MANUFACTURING COMPANY INC
9640 Beverly Rd, Pico Rivera (90660-2137)
PHONE....................562 692-7525
Cesar Gonzalez, *President*
Luz Rivera, *Officer*
Oscar Valdez, *Vice Pres*
EMP: 67 EST: 1995
SQ FT: 22,000
SALES (est): 9.6MM **Privately Held**
WEB: www.cnomfg.com
SIC: 3444 Sheet metal specialties, not stamped

(P-6801)
CAL PAC SHEET METAL INC
2720 S Main St Ste B, Santa Ana (92707-3404)
PHONE....................714 979-2733
Marushkah Kurtz, *CEO*
Bob Catalano, *Vice Pres*
Carolyn Miller, *Principal*
Art Soto, *Production*
Craig Faucher, *Manager*
EMP: 40
SQ FT: 5,000
SALES (est): 8.8MM **Privately Held**
WEB: www.calpacsheetmetal.com
SIC: 3444 Sheet metal specialties, not stamped

(P-6802)
CALIFORNIA EXPANDED MET PDTS (PA)
Also Called: Cemco
13191 Crssrads Pkwy N Ste, City of Industry (91746)
PHONE....................626 369-3564
Raymond E Poliquin, *CEO*
Richard Poliquin, *President*
Michael Wu, *CFO*
Tom Porter, *Exec VP*
Michael Herring, *Project Mgr*
◆ EMP: 68 EST: 1982
SQ FT: 40,000
SALES (est): 78.1MM **Privately Held**
WEB: www.cemcosteel.com
SIC: 3444 Sheet metalwork

(P-6803)
CALIFORNIA HYDROFORMING CO INC
850 Lawson St, City of Industry (91748-1103)
PHONE....................626 912-0036
David Bonafede, *President*
David Wickey, *Vice Pres*
Krisie Panagiotou, *Office Mgr*
EMP: 15
SQ FT: 17,500
SALES (est): 3.1MM **Privately Held**
WEB: www.californiahydroforming.com
SIC: 3444 3469 Sheet metalwork; stamping metal for the trade

(P-6804)
CAPTIVE-AIRE SYSTEMS INC
2915 Red Hill Ave C106, Costa Mesa (92626-5916)
PHONE....................714 957-1500
Robert L Luddy, *Branch Mgr*
EMP: 22
SALES (corp-wide): 401.1MM **Privately Held**
WEB: www.captiveaire.com
SIC: 3444 Sheet metalwork
PA: Captive-Aire Systems, Inc.
4641 Paragon Park Rd # 104
Raleigh NC 27616
919 882-2410

(P-6805)
CAPTIVE-AIRE SYSTEMS INC
1123 Washington Ave, Santa Monica
(90403-4159)
PHONE..................310 876-8505
Alex Barr, *Technical Staff*
EMP: 22
SALES (corp-wide): 401.1MM **Privately Held**
WEB: www.captiveaire.com
SIC: 3444 Sheet metalwork
PA: Captive-Aire Systems, Inc.
　4641 Paragon Park Rd # 104
　Raleigh NC 27616
　919 882-2410

(P-6806)
CAPTIVE-AIRE SYSTEMS INC
2510 Cloudcrest Way, Riverside
(92507-3027)
PHONE..................951 231-5102
EMP: 22
SALES (corp-wide): 401.1MM **Privately Held**
WEB: www.captiveaire.com
SIC: 3444 Restaurant sheet metalwork
PA: Captive-Aire Systems, Inc.
　4641 Paragon Park Rd # 104
　Raleigh NC 27616
　919 882-2410

(P-6807)
CARTEL INDUSTRIES LLC
17152 Armstrong Ave, Irvine (92614-5718)
PHONE..................949 474-3200
William Penick,
Vickie Chukiat, *Human Res Mgr*
Kirby Unfried, *QC Mgr*
Rich Collins, *Production*
Gant Penick,
▲ EMP: 49 EST: 1971
SQ FT: 30,000
SALES (est): 11MM **Privately Held**
WEB: www.cartelind.com
SIC: 3444 Sheet metal specialties, not
　stamped

(P-6808)
CLARKWESTERN DIETRICH BUILDING
Also Called: Clarkdietrich Building Systems
6510 General Rd, Riverside (92509-0103)
PHONE..................951 360-3500
Clark Dietrich, *Owner*
Reymundo Rangel, *Programmer Anys*
EMP: 17 **Privately Held**
WEB: www.clarkdietrich.com
SIC: 3444 8711 3081 Studs & joists,
　sheet metal; engineering services; vinyl
　film & sheet
HQ: Clarkwestern Dietrich Building Sys-
　tems Llc
　9050 Cntre Pnte Dr Ste 40
　West Chester OH 45069

(P-6809)
COAST SHEET METAL INC
990 W 17th St, Costa Mesa (92627-4403)
PHONE..................949 645-2224
Wayne Chambers, *President*
Marna Chambers, *Vice Pres*
EMP: 35 EST: 1960
SQ FT: 3,800
SALES (est): 2.6MM **Privately Held**
WEB: www.coastsheetmetal.com
SIC: 3444 Sheet metalwork

(P-6810)
COMPUMERIC ENGINEERING INC
Also Called: Bearsaver
1390 S Milliken Ave, Ontario (91761-1585)
PHONE..................909 605-7666
Jeannie Hankins, *CEO*
David Moore, *COO*
Brad Genco, *Info Tech Dir*
Cory Coulter, *Marketing Staff*
EMP: 45 EST: 1989
SQ FT: 30,000
SALES (est): 7.3MM **Privately Held**
WEB: www.compumeric.com
SIC: 3444 Sheet metalwork

(P-6811)
COMPUTER METAL PRODUCTS CORP
Also Called: Vline Industries
370 E Easy St, Simi Valley (93065-1802)
PHONE..................805 520-6966
Jim Visage, *President*
Angel Angeles, *COO*
Karen Bender, *CFO*
Dan Messervey, *Info Tech Dir*
Fran Dobrich, *Controller*
EMP: 90 EST: 1971
SQ FT: 25,000
SALES (est): 10.2MM **Privately Held**
WEB: www.computermetal.com
SIC: 3444 Sheet metalwork

(P-6812)
COPP INDUSTRIAL MFG INC
2837 Metropolitan Pl, Pomona
(91767-1897)
PHONE..................909 593-7448
Sanjaya Amarasinghe, *CEO*
Brian Hershman, *President*
Larry R Marvin, *CEO*
Rick Rose, *Prdtn Mgr*
EMP: 20 EST: 1964
SQ FT: 15,000
SALES (est): 5.4MM **Privately Held**
WEB: www.coppmfg.com
SIC: 3444 Sheet metalwork

(P-6813)
COY INDUSTRIES INC
Also Called: E R C Company
2970 E Maria St, E Rncho Dmngz
(90221-5802)
PHONE..................310 603-2970
Michael Coy, *President*
James Patrick Coy, *Corp Secy*
Mike Barton, *Info Tech Mgr*
Thomas Gazzillo, *QC Mgr*
EMP: 95 EST: 1972
SQ FT: 50,000
SALES (est): 11.9MM **Privately Held**
WEB: www.ercco.com
SIC: 3444 3469 Sheet metal specialties,
　not stamped; metal stampings

(P-6814)
CPC FABRICATION INC
2904 Oak St, Santa Ana (92707-3723)
PHONE..................714 549-2426
Thomas Baker, *CEO*
Stacey Sarver, *Office Mgr*
Lyn Baker, *Admin Sec*
Jonathan Edwards, *Opers Staff*
EMP: 37 EST: 1980
SQ FT: 15,000
SALES (est): 2.5MM **Privately Held**
WEB: www.cpcfab.com
SIC: 3444 Sheet metal specialties, not
　stamped

(P-6815)
DAAZE INC
Also Called: C&H Metal Products
1714 S Grove Ave Ste B, Ontario
(91761-4550)
PHONE..................626 442-4961
Jeanet Alvarez, *CFO*
Octavio Hurtado III, *Principal*
EMP: 13 EST: 1982
SQ FT: 28,000
SALES (est): 2.7MM **Privately Held**
SIC: 3444 Sheet metalwork

(P-6816)
DANRICH WELDING CO INC
7001 Jackson St, Paramount (90723-4834)
PHONE..................562 634-4811
Richard Schenk, *President*
EMP: 36 EST: 1970
SQ FT: 10,800
SALES (est): 2.6MM **Privately Held**
WEB: www.danrichwelding.com
SIC: 3444 7692 Sheet metalwork; welding
　repair

(P-6817)
DECRA ROOFING SYSTEMS INC (DH)
1230 Railroad St, Corona (92882-1837)
PHONE..................951 272-8180
Willard C Hudson Jr, *President*

Lance Buck, *COO*
Chad Colton, *Vice Pres*
Rion Hollingsworth, *Regional Mgr*
Mike Schaufler, *Regional Mgr*
◆ EMP: 70 EST: 1998
SQ FT: 60,000
SALES (est): 35.8MM **Privately Held**
WEB: www.decra.com
SIC: 3444 Metal roofing & roof drainage
　equipment
HQ: Fletcher Building Holdings Usa, Inc.
　1230 Railroad St
　Corona CA 92882
　951 272-8180

(P-6818)
DELAFOIL HOLDINGS INC (PA)
18500 Von Karman Ave # 450, Irvine
(92612-0504)
PHONE..................949 752-4580
Drew Adams, *Managing Dir*
EMP: 261 EST: 1999
SALES (est): 17.1MM **Privately Held**
SIC: 3444 Radiator shields or enclosures,
　sheet metal

(P-6819)
DELTA FABRICATION INC
9600 De Soto Ave, Chatsworth
(91311-5012)
PHONE..................818 407-4000
Chava Ostrowsky, *CEO*
Joe Ostrowsky, *President*
Chris Martin, *CTO*
Julie Cremeans, *Controller*
EMP: 90 EST: 1996
SQ FT: 20,000
SALES (est): 15MM **Privately Held**
WEB: www.deltahi-tech.com
SIC: 3444 Sheet metalwork

(P-6820)
DIMIC STEEL TECH INC
145 N 8th Ave, Upland (91786-5402)
PHONE..................909 946-6767
Miles Dimic, *President*
Anna Dimic, *CFO*
Marija Goodale, *Officer*
Ana Dimic, *Sales Mgr*
Ronald Rusk, *Manager*
▲ EMP: 24 EST: 1973
SQ FT: 45,000
SALES (est): 4.8MM **Privately Held**
WEB: www.dimicsteeltech.com
SIC: 3444 Sheet metal specialties, not
　stamped

(P-6821)
DOKA USA LTD
Also Called: Conesco Industries
6901 Central Ave, Riverside (92504-1407)
PHONE..................951 509-0023
Peter Franceschina, *Principal*
EMP: 13
SALES (corp-wide): 1.6B **Privately Held**
WEB: www.doka.com
SIC: 3444 Concrete forms, sheet metal
HQ: Doka Usa Ltd.
　214 Gates Rd
　Little Ferry NJ 07643
　201 641-6500

(P-6822)
DUR-RED PRODUCTS
4900 Cecilia St, Cudahy (90201-5993)
PHONE..................323 771-9000
Russell Smith, *President*
Linda Harrison, *Corp Secy*
EMP: 50 EST: 1961
SQ FT: 135,000
SALES (est): 5.7MM **Privately Held**
WEB: www.dur-red.com
SIC: 3444 3446 Sheet metalwork; archi-
　tectural metalwork

(P-6823)
E & S PRCSION SHTMETAL MFG INC
19298 Mclane St, North Palm Springs
(92258)
P.O. Box 581136 (92258-1136)
PHONE..................760 329-1607
Steve Egresits, *President*
Margit R Egresits, *Corp Secy*
Frank Egresits, *Vice Pres*
EMP: 24 EST: 1986

SQ FT: 10,000
SALES (est): 3.1MM **Privately Held**
WEB: www.esprecisionmfg.com
SIC: 3444 Sheet metal specialties, not
　stamped

(P-6824)
EDWARDS SHEET METAL SUPPLY INC
7810 Burnet Ave, Van Nuys (91405-1009)
PHONE..................818 785-8600
Edward Der-Mesropian, *President*
Jacqueline Der-Mesropian, *Corp Secy*
EMP: 25 EST: 1985
SQ FT: 20,000
SALES (est): 3.2MM **Privately Held**
WEB: www.edwardssheetmetalsupply.com
SIC: 3444 Booths, spray: prefabricated
　sheet metal

(P-6825)
EMPIRE SHEET METAL INC
1215 S Bon View Ave, Ontario
(91761-4402)
PHONE..................909 923-2927
Martin Layman, *President*
EMP: 32 EST: 1999
SALES (est): 3.7MM **Privately Held**
WEB: www.empiresheetmetal.com
SIC: 3444 Sheet metalwork

(P-6826)
EPIC SHEET METAL INC
1720 Industrial Ave, Norco (92860-2949)
PHONE..................714 679-5917
EMP: 13 EST: 2018
SALES (est): 2.6MM **Privately Held**
SIC: 3444 Sheet metalwork

(P-6827)
EQUIPMENT DESIGN & MFG INC
119 Explorer St, Pomona (91768-3278)
PHONE..................909 594-2229
Rick Clewett, *CEO*
Steve Clewett, *Vice Pres*
Ryan Clewett, *Admin Sec*
Jack Cave, *Engineer*
Pete Morin, *Engineer*
EMP: 55 EST: 1976
SQ FT: 27,400
SALES (est): 6.5MM **Privately Held**
WEB: www.equipmentdesign.net
SIC: 3444 Sheet metalwork

(P-6828)
ESM AEROSPACE INC
1203 W Isabel St, Burbank (91506-1407)
PHONE..................818 841-3653
Jerome Flament, *President*
Rina Flament, *Admin Sec*
Eric Isaacson, *QC Mgr*
EMP: 25
SQ FT: 8,900
SALES (est): 2.9MM **Privately Held**
WEB: www.esmaerospace.com
SIC: 3444 Casings, sheet metal

(P-6829)
ESPANA METAL CRAFT INC
7600 Ventura Canyon Ave, Van Nuys
(91402-6372)
PHONE..................818 988-4988
Salvador J Espana, *President*
Catalina Espana, *Owner*
EMP: 16 EST: 1990
SQ FT: 7,300
SALES (est): 3.5MM **Privately Held**
WEB: www.espanametal.com
SIC: 3444 Sheet metalwork

(P-6830)
EUGENIOS SHEET METAL INC
2151 Maple Privado, Ontario (91761-7603)
PHONE..................909 923-2002
Eugenio M Lozano, *President*
EMP: 35 EST: 1983
SQ FT: 10,000
SALES (est): 2.7MM **Privately Held**
WEB: www.eugeniossheetmetal.com
SIC: 3444 Sheet metalwork

(P-6831)
EURMAX CANOFY INC
9460 Telstar Ave Ste 2, El Monte
(91731-2904)
PHONE..................626 279-1622

Yan Shen, *CEO*
◆ **EMP:** 13 **EST:** 2015
SALES (est): 576.9K **Privately Held**
WEB: www.eurmax.com
SIC: 3444 Canopies, sheet metal

(P-6832)
EXCEL SHEET METAL INC (PA)
Also Called: Excel Bridge Manufacturing Co.
12001 Shoemaker Ave, Santa Fe Springs
(90670-4718)
PHONE..................................562 944-0701
Craig E Vasquez, *CEO*
Jeffrey Vasquez, *Vice Pres*
Matt Brooks, *QC Mgr*
▼ **EMP:** 57 **EST:** 1952
SQ FT: 16,000
SALES (est): 7.4MM **Privately Held**
WEB: www.excelsheetmetal.com
SIC: 3444 1622 Sheet metalwork; bridge
construction

(P-6833)
EXHAUST CENTER INC
Also Called: Eci Fuel Systems
1794 W 11th St, Upland (91786-3504)
PHONE..................................951 685-8602
Greg S Mitchell, *CEO*
Robert Mitchell, *CFO*
Cesar Martinez, *Supervisor*
EMP: 15 **EST:** 1977
SQ FT: 15,000
SALES (est): 5MM **Privately Held**
WEB: www.ecifuelsystems.com
SIC: 3444 Sheet metalwork

(P-6834)
EXPRESS SHEET METAL PRODUCT
10131 Flora Vista St, Bellflower
(90706-4804)
PHONE..................................562 925-9340
Ramon Castaneda, *President*
Emma Lara, *Office Mgr*
EMP: 21 **EST:** 2002
SQ FT: 6,000
SALES (est): 2.7MM **Privately Held**
SIC: 3444 Sheet metalwork

(P-6835)
F T B & SON INC
11551 Markon Dr, Garden Grove
(92841-1808)
PHONE..................................714 891-8003
Frank Taylor Brown, *CEO*
Kathy M Ayers, *CFO*
Ray Mena, *Prgrmr*
EMP: 42 **EST:** 1972
SQ FT: 37,000
SALES (est): 1.8MM **Privately Held**
WEB: www.ftbson.com
SIC: 3444 Ducts, sheet metal

(P-6836)
FABRICATION NETWORK INC
Also Called: Fabnet
5410 E La Palma Ave, Anaheim
(92807-2023)
PHONE..................................714 393-5282
Robert F Denham, *President*
Donald V Eide, *CFO*
EMP: 16 **EST:** 1990
SQ FT: 45,000
SALES (est): 532.6K **Privately Held**
WEB: www.thefabricatornetwork.com
SIC: 3444 3599 Metal housings, enclo-
sures, casings & other containers; form-
ing machine work, sheet metal; machine
shop, jobbing & repair

(P-6837)
FABTRONIC INC
5026 Calmview Ave, Baldwin Park
(91706-1899)
PHONE..................................626 962-3293
Carlos Duarte, *President*
David Thompson, *Vice Pres*
▼ **EMP:** 20 **EST:** 1976
SQ FT: 26,000
SALES (est): 2.8MM **Privately Held**
WEB: www.fabtronics.com
SIC: 3444 3829 Sheet metal specialties,
not stamped; fare registers for street cars,
buses, etc.

(P-6838)
FACILITY MAKERS INC
345 W Freedom Ave, Orange
(92865-2647)
P.O. Box 60066, Irvine (92602-6002)
PHONE..................................714 544-1702
Cameron Kazemi, *CEO*
EMP: 20 **EST:** 2009
SALES (est): 3.5MM **Privately Held**
SIC: 3444 1542 3446 Sheet metal spe-
cialties, not stamped; culverts, sheet
metal; commercial & office building, new
construction; architectural metalwork

(P-6839)
FLETCHER BLDG HOLDINGS USA INC (DH)
1230 Railroad St, Corona (92882-1837)
PHONE..................................951 272-8180
Willard Hudson, *President*
Steve Jones, *CFO*
John Miller, *Vice Pres*
Shanna Amsbry, *Administration*
◆ **EMP:** 70 **EST:** 1998
SQ FT: 60,000
SALES (est): 40.4MM **Privately Held**
WEB: www.decra.com
SIC: 3444 Metal roofing & roof drainage
equipment

(P-6840)
FORTERRA PIPE & PRECAST LLC
30781 San Diego St, Shafter (93263-9764)
PHONE..................................661 746-3527
Deloras Thornberg, *Principal*
EMP: 22
SALES (corp-wide): 1.5B **Publicly Held**
WEB: www.forterrabp.com
SIC: 3444 3531 Sheet metalwork; asphalt
plant, including gravel-mix type
HQ: Forterra Pipe & Precast, Llc
511 E John Carpenter Fwy
Irving TX 75062
469 458-7973

(P-6841)
FOUR SEASONS REST EQP INC
412 Jenks Cir, Corona (92878-5006)
PHONE..................................951 278-9100
Larry Kaye, *President*
EMP: 22 **EST:** 1975
SQ FT: 19,000
SALES (est): 5.2MM **Privately Held**
SIC: 3444 Restaurant sheet metalwork

(P-6842)
GARD INC
Also Called: Reliable Sheet Metal Works
524 E Walnut Ave, Fullerton (92832-2540)
PHONE..................................714 738-5891
Arthur Schade, *President*
Dan Schade, *Corp Secy*
Arthur Schade Jr, *Vice Pres*
EMP: 20 **EST:** 1956
SQ FT: 12,000
SALES (est): 2.3MM **Privately Held**
WEB: www.reliablesheetmetal.com
SIC: 3444 Sheet metal specialties, not
stamped

(P-6843)
GENERAL FORMING CORPORATION
640 Alaska Ave, Torrance (90503-5100)
PHONE..................................310 326-0624
Ward Olson, *CEO*
Charles E Vegher, *CEO*
Joanne Vegher, *Vice Pres*
Efrain Partida, *Prgrmr*
Matthew Rudshagen, *Prgrmr*
EMP: 43 **EST:** 1956
SALES (est): 9.3MM **Privately Held**
WEB: www.generalformingcorporation.com
SIC: 3444 3812 3769 Sheet metal spe-
cialties, not stamped; search & navigation
equipment; guided missile & space vehi-
cle parts & auxiliary equipment

(P-6844)
GERARD ROOF PRODUCTS LLC (DH)
Also Called: Gerard Roofing Technologies
721 Monroe Way, Placentia (92870-6309)
PHONE..................................714 529-0407

Donald P Newman, *Mng Member*
EMP: 71 **EST:** 2014
SALES (est): 26.3MM **Privately Held**
WEB: www.headwaters.com
SIC: 3444 Sheet metalwork

(P-6845)
GKN AEROSPACE CAMARILLO INC
3030 Redhll Ave, Santa Ana (92705-5823)
PHONE..................................805 383-6684
Richard Oldfield, *CEO*
David Lind, *President*
Bernd Hermann, *CFO*
▲ **EMP:** 19
SALES (est): 6.6MM
SALES (corp-wide): 14.1B **Privately Held**
WEB: www.gkn.com
SIC: 3444 Sheet metalwork
HQ: Gkn Limited
Po Box 4128
Redditch WORCS B90 8

(P-6846)
GRAYD-A PRCSION MET FBRICATORS
13233 Florence Ave, Santa Fe Springs
(90670-4509)
PHONE..................................562 944-8951
William Gray Jr, *President*
Jo Dell Gray, *Corp Secy*
William Gray III, *Vice Pres*
EMP: 20 **EST:** 1964
SQ FT: 17,500
SALES (est): 4.2MM **Privately Held**
WEB: www.grayd-a.com
SIC: 3444 Sheet metal specialties, not
stamped

(P-6847)
GREAT PACIFIC ELBOW COMPANY
13900 Sycamore Way, Chino (91710-7016)
PHONE..................................909 606-5551
EMP: 24 **EST:** 2018
SALES (est): 3MM **Privately Held**
WEB: www.greatpacificelbow.com
SIC: 3444 3827 Elbows, for air ducts,
stovepipes, etc.: sheet metal; telescopes:
elbow, panoramic, sighting, fire control,
etc.

(P-6848)
HAIMETAL DUCT INC
625 Arroyo St, San Fernando
(91340-2219)
PHONE..................................818 768-2315
Rouben Hovsepian, *President*
EMP: 42 **EST:** 1980
SQ FT: 10,000
SALES (est): 1.3MM **Privately Held**
SIC: 3444 Ducts, sheet metal; ventilators,
sheet metal

(P-6849)
HALLMARK METALS INC
600 W Foothill Blvd, Glendora
(91741-2403)
PHONE..................................626 335-1263
Joseph Allen Zerucha, *CEO*
Scott Schoenick, *President*
Marina Carmona, *Treasurer*
David Peifer, *Vice Pres*
Candice Schoenick, *Vice Pres*
EMP: 28 **EST:** 1959
SQ FT: 23,000
SALES (est): 4.8MM **Privately Held**
WEB: www.hallmarkmetals.com
SIC: 3444 3469 Sheet metalwork; ma-
chine parts, stamped or pressed metal

(P-6850)
HAMILTON METALCRAFT INC
848 N Fair Oaks Ave, Pasadena
(91103-3046)
PHONE..................................626 795-4811
Sandra Stahler, *President*
EMP: 25 **EST:** 1966
SQ FT: 10,000
SALES (est): 2.5MM **Privately Held**
WEB: www.hmetal.com
SIC: 3444 Casings, sheet metal

(P-6851)
HI-CRAFT METAL PRODUCTS
606 W 184th St, Gardena (90248-4282)
PHONE..................................310 323-6949
Bill Gerich, *CEO*
Jennifer Gerich, *Shareholder*
Ted Gerich, *Shareholder*
Liz Gallagher, *Corp Secy*
Edward P Gerich, *Vice Pres*
EMP: 20 **EST:** 1948
SQ FT: 11,000
SALES (est): 4.4MM **Privately Held**
WEB: www.hicraftmetal.com
SIC: 3444 3469 Sheet metal specialties,
not stamped; metal stampings

(P-6852)
INFINITY KITCHEN PRODUCTS INC
Also Called: Infinity Stainless Products
7750 Scout Ave, Bell Gardens
(90201-4942)
PHONE..................................562 806-5771
Serafin Valdez, *President*
Rachel Haasis, *Sales Staff*
▲ **EMP:** 15 **EST:** 1999
SQ FT: 25,000
SALES (est): 1.7MM **Privately Held**
WEB: www.infinitystainless.com
SIC: 3444 Restaurant sheet metalwork

(P-6853)
INLAND METAL TRADING INC
41187 Sandalwood Cir, Murrieta
(92562-7003)
PHONE..................................833 396-0740
Kristopher Lanham, *President*
EMP: 22 **EST:** 2018
SALES (est): 6.5MM **Privately Held**
WEB: www.inlandmetal.wpengine.com
SIC: 3444 5039 Ducts, sheet metal; metal
buildings

(P-6854)
INNOVTIVE DSIGN SHTMTL PDTS IN
Also Called: Innovative Emergency Equipment
616 Mrlbrugh Ave Unit S-1, Riverside
(92507)
PHONE..................................951 222-2270
EMP: 16 **EST:** 2015
SALES (est): 1.4MM **Privately Held**
WEB: www.idsmp.com
SIC: 3444 3699 3647 3641 Forming machine work, sheet metal; skylights, sheet
metal; trouble lights; dome lights, automotive; flasher lights, automotive; pilot lights,
radio

(P-6855)
INTERNATIONAL WEST INC
Also Called: Continental Industries
1025 N Armando St, Anaheim
(92806-2606)
PHONE..................................714 632-9190
Jeffery Aaron Hayden, *President*
Tami Hayden, *CFO*
Perez Ryan, *Prgrmr*
Ricardo Diaz, *Manager*
EMP: 64 **EST:** 1985
SQ FT: 8,500
SALES (est): 14.1MM **Privately Held**
WEB: www.continental-ind.com
SIC: 3444 Sheet metalwork

(P-6856)
JBW PRECISION INC
2650 Lavery Ct, Newbury Park
(91320-1581)
PHONE..................................805 499-1973
David Ogden, *President*
Dawn Spalding, *Corp Secy*
Jack Ogden, *Vice Pres*
Rhonda Ogden, *Marketing Mgr*
EMP: 23 **EST:** 1969
SQ FT: 2,500
SALES (est): 4.1MM **Privately Held**
WEB: www.jbwprecision.com
SIC: 3444 Sheet metal specialties, not
stamped

(P-6857)
JEFFREY FABRICATION LLC
Also Called: C & J Metal Prducts
6323 Alondra Blvd, Paramount
(90723-3750)
PHONE...................562 634-3101
Lilly Chang, *Mng Member*
EMP: 50 EST: 2011
SALES (est): 3.1MM Privately Held
WEB: www.cjmetals.com
SIC: 3444 Sheet metalwork

(P-6858)
JET MANUFACTURING INC
Also Called: PRISM AEROSPACE DBA JET
MANUFACTURING
13445 Estelle St, Corona (92879-1877)
PHONE...................951 736-9316
Eric S Cunningham, *CEO*
Blake Conlin, *Program Mgr*
Melissa Noyola, *Buyer*
▲ EMP: 55 EST: 1997
SQ FT: 45,000
SALES (est): 4MM Privately Held
WEB: www.jetmanufacturing.com
SIC: 3444 3724 Sheet metalwork; jet as-
sisted takeoff devices (JATO)

(P-6859)
KARL M SMITH INC
1204 Dairy Ave, Corcoran (93212-2500)
PHONE...................559 992-4109
Pauline Smith, *President*
Karl M Smith, *Vice Pres*
EMP: 15 EST: 1970
SQ FT: 11,000
SALES (est): 989.6K Privately Held
WEB: www.karlmsmithinc.com
SIC: 3444 Sheet metalwork

(P-6860)
**KB SHEETMETAL FABRICATION
INC**
17371 Mount Wynne Cir B, Fountain Valley
(92708-4107)
PHONE...................714 979-1780
Cong Nguyen, *President*
Thu Huynh, *General Mgr*
Dawne Connell, *QA Dir*
Joyce Lorenz, *Sales Staff*
EMP: 25 EST: 2001
SQ FT: 12,000
SALES (est): 4.8MM Privately Held
WEB: www.kb-sheetmetal.com
SIC: 3444 3441 Sheet metalwork; fabri-
cated structural metal

(P-6861)
KEITH E ARCHAMBEAU SR INC
Also Called: American Precision Sheet Metal
20615 Plummer St, Chatsworth
(91311-5112)
PHONE...................818 718-6110
Keith Archambeau Jr, *President*
Angie Pimentel, *Officer*
John Wetlsch, *Vice Pres*
Ludvin Solorzano, *Engineer*
Hector Jimenez, *Senior Buyer*
EMP: 20 EST: 1986
SQ FT: 10,000
SALES (est): 3.7MM Privately Held
WEB: www.americanprecision.net
SIC: 3444 Sheet metal specialties, not
stamped

(P-6862)
LANEAIRE
1121 California Ave, Corona (92881-7233)
PHONE...................951 808-3658
EMP: 14 EST: 2018
SALES (est): 780.9K Privately Held
WEB: www.lane-aire.com
SIC: 3444 Sheet metalwork

(P-6863)
LE PETIT SHEET METAL INC
720 N Georgia Ave, Azusa (91702-2206)
PHONE...................626 334-4415
Amidou Diakite, *CEO*
EMP: 19 EST: 2015
SALES (est): 950.1K Privately Held
SIC: 3444 Sheet metalwork

(P-6864)
LYNAM INDUSTRIES INC
13050 Santa Ana Ave, Fontana
(92337-6948)
PHONE...................951 360-1919
Troy Lindstrom, *President*
Frany Montalvo, *Technology*
Ezequiel Correa, *Engineer*
Jade Robbins, *Analyst*
Ito Dennis, *Opers Mgr*
▲ EMP: 85 EST: 1989
SQ FT: 39,000
SALES (est): 14.3MM Privately Held
WEB: www.lynaminc.com
SIC: 3444 Sheet metal specialties, not
stamped

(P-6865)
M & M SERVICE
972 E 1st St, Pomona (91766-2101)
PHONE...................909 802-2050
Miguel Martinez, *Principal*
EMP: 14 EST: 2003
SALES (est): 1.3MM Privately Held
SIC: 3444 Sheet metalwork

(P-6866)
M-5 STEEL MFG INC (PA)
11778 San Marino St Ste A, Rancho Cuca-
monga (91730-6016)
PHONE...................323 263-9383
Douglas Linkon, *CEO*
Henry Casas, *Info Tech Mgr*
John Lucero, *Director*
Quinn Phan, *Clerk*
▲ EMP: 46 EST: 1970
SALES (est): 5.4MM Privately Held
WEB: www.m5steel.com
SIC: 3444 3443 Gutters, sheet metal; fab-
ricated plate work (boiler shop)

(P-6867)
MARVIC INC
7945 Deering Ave, Canoga Park
(91304-5009)
PHONE...................818 992-0078
Victoria Santos, *President*
Frank J Ramirez, *Vice Pres*
Farid Kanji, *CPA*
EMP: 15 EST: 1984
SQ FT: 7,400
SALES (est): 1.4MM Privately Held
SIC: 3444 Sheet metalwork

(P-6868)
MASTER ENTERPRISES INC
Also Called: A B C Restaurant Equipment Co
2025 Lee Ave, South El Monte
(91733-2505)
PHONE...................626 442-1821
Brian Kim Lien, *CEO*
Wen Lin, *Treasurer*
Thanh Quach, *Admin Sec*
EMP: 20 EST: 1988
SQ FT: 20,000
SALES (est): 2.5MM Privately Held
WEB: www.chineserange.com
SIC: 3444 5087 Restaurant sheet metal-
work; restaurant supplies

(P-6869)
MASTER FAB INC
9210 Stellar Ct, Corona (92883-4906)
PHONE...................951 277-4772
Kenneth Scheel, *President*
Troy Jackson, *Admin Sec*
EMP: 16 EST: 1980
SQ FT: 11,000
SALES (est): 1.9MM Privately Held
WEB: www.masterfabca.com
SIC: 3444 Sheet metalwork

(P-6870)
MATERIAL SUPPLY INC (PA)
Also Called: MSI Hvac
11700 Industry Ave, Fontana (92337-6934)
PHONE...................951 801-5004
Dion Quinn, *CEO*
Bob Billiu, *Vice Pres*
Jon Dautrich, *Vice Pres*
Robert Hascall, *Vice Pres*
Linda Heyd, *Principal*
▲ EMP: 170 EST: 1986
SQ FT: 80,000

SALES (est): 107MM Privately Held
WEB: www.msihvac.com
SIC: 3444 5075 7623 1711 Metal ventilating equipment; warm air heating & air
conditioning; air filters; ventilating equipment & supplies; air conditioning repair;
heating & air conditioning contractors

(P-6871)
**MATTHEWS MANUFACTURING
INC**
3301 E 14th St, Los Angeles (90023-3801)
PHONE...................323 980-4373
Benyamin Mikhael-Ford, *President*
Fiyodor Mikhael-Ford, *Corp Secy*
Fred Mikhael-Ford, *Vice Pres*
EMP: 14 EST: 1996
SQ FT: 20,000
SALES (est): 830.8K Privately Held
SIC: 3444 3599 Sheet metalwork; ma-
chine shop, jobbing & repair

(P-6872)
MAYONI ENTERPRISES
10320 Glenoaks Blvd, Pacoima
(91331-1699)
PHONE...................818 896-0026
Isaac Benyehuda, *CEO*
Isaac Glazer, *Vice Pres*
EMP: 60 EST: 1984
SQ FT: 17,000
SALES (est): 7.3MM Privately Held
WEB: www.mayoni.com
SIC: 3444 3581 Sheet metal specialties,
not stamped; automatic vending ma-
chines

(P-6873)
MCMILLIN MFG CORP
Also Called: McMillin Wire Products
40 E Verdugo Ave, Burbank (91502-1931)
PHONE...................323 981-8585
Bruce Goodman, *President*
EMP: 37 EST: 1968
SQ FT: 42,000
SALES (est): 1.3MM Privately Held
SIC: 3444 3496 3441 3315 Sheet metal-
work; miscellaneous fabricated wire prod-
ucts; fabricated structural metal; steel
wire & related products

(P-6874)
**MEADOWS SHEET METAL AND
AC INC**
Also Called: Meadows Mechanical
333 Crown Vista Dr, Gardena
(90248-1705)
PHONE...................310 615-1125
Madonna Rose, *CEO*
Dennis Johnson, *CFO*
Thomas Nolan, *Exec VP*
Manny Garcia, *Project Mgr*
Kevin Leeker, *Project Mgr*
EMP: 50 EST: 1949
SQ FT: 5,000
SALES (est): 11.6MM Privately Held
SIC: 3444 1711 Sheet metalwork; heating
& air conditioning contractors

(P-6875)
METAL ENGINEERING INC
1642 S Sacramento Ave, Ontario
(91761-8052)
PHONE...................626 334-1819
Arthur A Valenzuela, *President*
Wendy Linares, *Admin Asst*
Petra Markoski, *Opers Staff*
EMP: 23 EST: 2002
SQ FT: 14,000
SALES (est): 2.8MM Privately Held
WEB: www.metaleng.com
SIC: 3444 1761 Awnings & canopies;
sheet metalwork

(P-6876)
**METAL-FAB SERVICES INDUST
INC**
2500 E Miraloma Way, Anaheim
(92806-1608)
PHONE...................714 630-7771
Carlos Mondragon, *President*
Sandy Mondragon, *Office Mgr*
▲ EMP: 34 EST: 2003
SQ FT: 28,000

SALES (est): 8.4MM Privately Held
WEB: www.metalfabsi.com
SIC: 3444 Sheet metal specialties, not
stamped

(P-6877)
METALPRO INDUSTRIES INC
28064 Avenue Stanford H, Santa Clarita
(91355-1158)
PHONE...................661 294-0764
Robert Theberge, *President*
Edmundo Gomez, *Treasurer*
Mark Theberge, *Vice Pres*
Arlan Sams, *Admin Sec*
Mark Kappes, *Administration*
EMP: 21 EST: 1994
SQ FT: 13,000
SALES (est): 3.7MM Privately Held
SIC: 3444 Sheet metal specialties, not
stamped

(P-6878)
MMP SHEET METAL INC
501 Commercial Way, La Habra
(90631-6170)
PHONE...................562 691-1055
Frank Varanelli, *President*
Csaba Fodor, *Manager*
EMP: 30 EST: 1977
SQ FT: 8,500
SALES (est): 2.9MM Privately Held
WEB: www.mmp-sheetmetal.com
SIC: 3444 Sheet metal specialties, not
stamped

(P-6879)
**MODERN-AIRE VENTILATING
INC**
Also Called: Modern Aire Ventilating
7319 Lankershim Blvd, North Hollywood
(91605-3895)
PHONE...................818 765-9870
Steven Herman, *President*
Robert Delmazo, *Vice Pres*
Jennifer Cifelli, *Office Mgr*
Bruce Milligan, *Plant Mgr*
EMP: 23 EST: 1956
SQ FT: 20,000
SALES (est): 3.7MM Privately Held
WEB: www.modernaire.com
SIC: 3444 3645 Hoods, range: sheet
metal; residential lighting fixtures

(P-6880)
**MODULAR METAL
FABRICATORS INC**
24600 Nandina Ave, Moreno Valley
(92551-9537)
PHONE...................951 242-3154
E E Gearing, *CEO*
Don Gearing, *President*
John Wingate, *Treasurer*
Mike Beam, *Exec VP*
Pat Geary, *Director*
▲ EMP: 130
SQ FT: 200,000
SALES (est): 25.2MM Privately Held
WEB: www.modularmetalfabricators.com
SIC: 3444 Pipe, sheet metal

(P-6881)
**NEW GREENSCREEN
INCORPORATED**
Impac International
11445 Pacific Ave, Fontana (92337-8227)
PHONE...................951 685-9660
Kory Lavoy, *Division Mgr*
EMP: 63 Privately Held
WEB: www.impac-international.com
SIC: 3444 3315 Housings for business
machines, sheet metal; steel wire & re-
lated products
PA: New Greenscreen, Incorporated
5500 Jurupa St
Ontario CA 91761

(P-6882)
OC METALS INC
2720 S Main St Ste B, Santa Ana
(92707-3404)
PHONE...................714 668-0783
Marushka Kurtz, *CEO*
Mari Kurtz, *President*
Oc Pio, *Sales Staff*

Brent Catalano, *Master*
EMP: 20
SQ FT: 23,000
SALES (est): 4.6MM **Privately Held**
WEB: www.ocmetals.com
SIC: 3444 Sheet metalwork

(P-6883)
OLDCASTLE INFRASTRUCTURE INC
19940 Hansen Ave, Nuevo (92567-9649)
PHONE..................................951 928-8713
EMP: 30
SALES (corp-wide): 27.5B **Privately Held**
WEB: www.oldcastleinfrastructure.com
SIC: 3444 Metal housings, enclosures, casings & other containers
HQ: Oldcastle Infrastructure, Inc.
7000 Central Pkwy Ste 800
Atlanta GA 30328
770 270-5000

(P-6884)
ORTRONICS INC
Also Called: Electrorack
1443 S Sunkist St, Anaheim (92806-5626)
PHONE..................................714 776-5420
Mark Panico, *President*
James Laperriere, *Treasurer*
Robert Julian, *Vice Pres*
Valerie Alsante, *Admin Sec*
Torres Julie, *Sales Mgr*
▲ **EMP:** 120 **EST:** 1955
SQ FT: 50,000
SALES (est): 24MM
SALES (corp-wide): 25.9MM **Privately Held**
WEB: www.electrorack.com
SIC: 3444 3679 Sheet metalwork; power supplies, all types: static
HQ: Legrand Holding, Inc.
60 Woodlawn St
West Hartford CT 06110
860 233-6251

(P-6885)
OXNARD PRCSION FABRICATION INC
Also Called: O P F
2200 Teal Club Rd, Oxnard (93030-8640)
PHONE..................................805 985-0447
David Garza, *President*
Robert Valles, *Vice Pres*
EMP: 30 **EST:** 1987
SQ FT: 107,000
SALES (est): 3.5MM **Privately Held**
WEB: www.opfinc.com
SIC: 3444 3469 3443 Sheet metal specialties, not stamped; metal stampings; fabricated plate work (boiler shop)

(P-6886)
P T INDUSTRIES INC
3220 Industry Dr, Signal Hill (90755-4014)
PHONE..................................562 961-3431
Kim Nguyen, *President*
Thuy Nguyen, *Admin Sec*
EMP: 19 **EST:** 1999
SQ FT: 19,000
SALES (est): 3MM **Privately Held**
WEB: www.ptindustriesinc.com
SIC: 3444 Sheet metal specialties, not stamped

(P-6887)
PACIFIC AWARD METALS INC (HQ)
1450 Virginia Ave, Baldwin Park (91706-5819)
PHONE..................................626 814-4410
Brian J Lipke, *CEO*
W Brent Taylor, *President*
Frank Fulford, *VP Sales*
EMP: 100 **EST:** 2001
SQ FT: 110,000
SALES (est): 132.7MM
SALES (corp-wide): 1B **Publicly Held**
WEB: www.gibraltar1.com
SIC: 3444 3312 Sheet metalwork; blast furnaces & steel mills
PA: Gibraltar Industries, Inc.
3556 Lake Shore Rd # 100
Buffalo NY 14219
716 826-6500

(P-6888)
PACIFIC AWARD METALS INC
10302 Birtcher Dr, Jurupa Valley (91752-1829)
PHONE..................................360 694-9530
Mark Shaff, *Systems Mgr*
Chuck Griffin, *Mktg Dir*
EMP: 40
SALES (corp-wide): 1B **Publicly Held**
SIC: 3444 3443 Concrete forms, sheet metal; fabricated plate work (boiler shop)
HQ: Pacific Award Metals, Inc.
1450 Virginia Ave
Baldwin Park CA 91706
626 814-4410

(P-6889)
PACIFIC DUCT INC
5499 Brooks St, Montclair (91763-4563)
PHONE..................................909 635-1335
Riad M Wahid, *President*
George Bobo, *Supervisor*
▲ **EMP:** 46 **EST:** 1996
SQ FT: 15,000
SALES (est): 6.6MM **Privately Held**
WEB: www.pacificduct.com
SIC: 3444 5075 5039 Metal ventilating equipment; warm air heating & air conditioning; air ducts, sheet metal

(P-6890)
PCI INDUSTRIES INC
6501 Potello St, Commerce (90040)
PHONE..................................323 728-0004
Greg Skilley, *Vice Pres*
EMP: 37
SALES (corp-wide): 51.2MM **Privately Held**
WEB: www.pottorffcorporate.com
SIC: 3444 3564 Metal ventilating equipment; filters, air: furnaces, air conditioning equipment, etc.
PA: Pci Industries, Inc.
5101 Blue Mound Rd
Fort Worth TX 76106
817 509-2300

(P-6891)
PINNACLE PRECISION SHTMTL CORP (PA)
5410 E La Palma Ave, Anaheim (92807-2023)
PHONE..................................714 777-3129
David Oddo, *President*
Paul Oddo, *Shareholder*
Brian McLaughlin, *Vice Pres*
Angela Carlson, *Human Res Mgr*
EMP: 183 **EST:** 1973
SALES (est): 25.4MM **Privately Held**
WEB:
www.pinnacleprecisionsheetmetal.com
SIC: 3444 Sheet metalwork

(P-6892)
PNA CONSTRUCTION TECH INC
301 Espee St Ste E, Bakersfield (93301-2659)
PHONE..................................661 326-1700
Matt Wilen, *Principal*
Frank Barron, *Plant Mgr*
Crystal Parmley, *Manager*
EMP: 33
SALES (corp-wide): 8.9MM **Privately Held**
WEB: www.pna-inc.com
SIC: 3444 Concrete forms, sheet metal
PA: P.N.A. Construction Technologies, Inc.
1349 W Bryn Mawr Ave
Itasca IL 60143
770 668-9500

(P-6893)
PRECISE INDUSTRIES INC
610 Neptune Ave, Brea (92821-2909)
PHONE..................................714 482-2333
Terry D Wells, *President*
Jose Quintana, *Program Mgr*
Robert L Wells, *Admin Sec*
Dave Trubey, *Info Tech Dir*
Jan Van Der Kolk, *Prgrmr*
▲ **EMP:** 120 **EST:** 2004
SQ FT: 78,000

SALES (est): 16.6MM **Privately Held**
WEB: www.preciseind.com
SIC: 3444 3679 3599 Sheet metalwork; electronic circuits; machine & other job shop work

(P-6894)
PRECISION STEEL PRODUCTS INC
Also Called: Steel Products International
13124 Avalon Blvd, Los Angeles (90061-2738)
PHONE..................................310 523-2002
Raul De Latorre, *President*
Deborah De Latorre, *Admin Sec*
EMP: 22 **EST:** 1994
SQ FT: 24,000
SALES (est): 3.7MM **Privately Held**
WEB: www.steelproducts.biz
SIC: 3444 3441 Sheet metalwork; fabricated structural metal

(P-6895)
PRISM AEROSPACE
3087 12th St, Riverside (92507-4904)
PHONE..................................951 582-2850
Eng Tan, *CEO*
Peng Tan, *President*
Umesh Lad, *General Mgr*
EMP: 50 **EST:** 2014
SQ FT: 100,000
SALES (est): 8.1MM **Privately Held**
WEB: www.prismaerospace.com
SIC: 3444 3812 Forming machine work, sheet metal; aircraft/aerospace flight instruments & guidance systems; acceleration indicators & systems components, aerospace

(P-6896)
QUALITY FABRICATION INC (PA)
9631 Irondale Ave, Chatsworth (91311-5009)
PHONE..................................818 407-5015
Pradeep Kumar, *CEO*
John Rajaranam, *Project Leader*
Akash Kadam, *Engineer*
▲ **EMP:** 98 **EST:** 1980
SALES (est): 12.3MM **Privately Held**
WEB: www.quality-fab.com
SIC: 3444 Sheet metal specialties, not stamped

(P-6897)
R & R DUCTWORK LLC
12820 Lakeland Rd, Santa Fe Springs (90670-4515)
PHONE..................................562 944-9660
Brian Klebowski, *Mng Member*
EMP: 18 **EST:** 1997
SQ FT: 14,000
SALES (est): 1.5MM **Privately Held**
WEB: www.rrductwork.com
SIC: 3444 Ducts, sheet metal

(P-6898)
RADIATION PROTECTION & SPC INC
Also Called: RPS
1531 W Orangewood Ave, Orange (92868-2006)
PHONE..................................714 771-7702
John Jory, *President*
EMP: 15 **EST:** 2008
SALES (est): 2.1MM **Privately Held**
SIC: 3444 Radiator shields or enclosures, sheet metal

(P-6899)
RAMDA METAL SPECIALTIES INC
13012 Crenshaw Blvd, Gardena (90249-1544)
PHONE..................................310 538-2136
Daniel Guevara, *CEO*
EMP: 25 **EST:** 1985
SQ FT: 25,000 **Privately Held**
WEB: www.ramdametal.com
SIC: 3444 Metal housings, enclosures, casings & other containers

(P-6900)
RAYCO BURIAL PRODUCTS INC
Also Called: Rayco B Products
1601 Raymond Ave, Monrovia (91016-4690)
PHONE..................................626 357-1996
Geza Dala, *President*
Valerie Dala, *Treasurer*
Ilene Sakamoto, *Vice Pres*
Martin Dala, *Admin Sec*
EMP: 20 **EST:** 1961
SQ FT: 20,000
SALES (est): 720.6K **Privately Held**
SIC: 3444 Sheet metal specialties, not stamped

(P-6901)
RDFABRICATORS INC
11880 Western Ave, Stanton (90680-3438)
PHONE..................................714 634-2078
Raymond D Foye, *President*
EMP: 18 **EST:** 1979
SQ FT: 12,000 **Privately Held**
SIC: 3444 Sheet metal specialties, not stamped

(P-6902)
RIGOS EQUIPMENT MFG LLC
Also Called: Rigos Sheet Metal
14501 Joanbridge St, Baldwin Park (91706-1749)
PHONE..................................626 813-6621
Yury Anguiano, *Executive*
Christian Zapata, *Engineer*
EMP: 23 **EST:** 1977
SQ FT: 3,600
SALES (est): 4.9MM **Privately Held**
WEB: www.rigosequipment.com
SIC: 3444 Sheet metalwork

(P-6903)
ROBERT F CHAPMAN INC
43100 Exchange Pl, Lancaster (93535-4524)
PHONE..................................661 940-9482
Tim Mitchell, *CEO*
John H Mitchell, *President*
Nelson Barrios, *Vice Pres*
Paulette Mitchell, *Admin Sec*
Mario Lua, *Business Mgr*
EMP: 53
SQ FT: 62,000
SALES (est): 10.5MM **Privately Held**
WEB: www.robertfchapman.com
SIC: 3444 3549 Sheet metalwork; metalworking machinery

(P-6904)
ROYAL MANUFACTURING INDS INC
600 W Warner Ave, Santa Ana (92707-3347)
PHONE..................................714 668-9199
Robert Rieck, *President*
EMP: 14 **EST:** 1989
SQ FT: 9,000
SALES (est): 3.7MM **Privately Held**
WEB: www.royalmfgind.com
SIC: 3444 Sheet metalwork

(P-6905)
RUSS INTERNATIONAL INC
1658 W 132nd St, Gardena (90249-2006)
PHONE..................................310 329-7121
Randy Carter, *CEO*
Edmond Russ, *Chairman*
Joshua Bettencourt, *Technology*
Louise Moore, *Manager*
▲ **EMP:** 22 **EST:** 1952
SQ FT: 20,000
SALES (est): 4.2MM **Privately Held**
WEB: www.russ-international.com
SIC: 3444 Sheet metal specialties, not stamped

(P-6906)
SA SERVING LINES INC
Also Called: G A Systems
226 W Carleton Ave, Orange (92867-3608)
PHONE..................................714 848-7529
Steve Aderson, *CEO*
Pat Devalle, *CFO*
Virginia Anderson, *Treasurer*
EMP: 22 **EST:** 2011

SALES (est): 9.2MM **Privately Held**
WEB: www.gasystemsmfg.com
SIC: 3444 Metal housings, enclosures, casings & other containers

(P-6907)
SE-GI PRODUCTS INC
20521 Teresita Way, Lake Forest (92630-8142)
PHONE....................951 737-8320
◆ **EMP:** 21
SALES (est): 4MM **Privately Held**
SIC: 3444 Mfg Sheet Metalwork

(P-6908)
SHEET METAL PROTOTYPE INC
19420 Londelius St, Northridge (91324-3511)
PHONE....................818 772-2715
Jane E Lamborn, *President*
EMP: 32 **EST:** 1983
SQ FT: 7,500
SALES (est): 2.3MM **Privately Held**
WEB: www.sheetmetalprototypeinc.com
SIC: 3444 Sheet metal specialties, not stamped

(P-6909)
SHEET METAL SERVICE
2310 E Orangethorpe Ave, Anaheim (92806-1231)
PHONE....................714 446-0196
Miguel Nunez, *President*
EMP: 18 **EST:** 1991
SQ FT: 10,000
SALES (est): 4.1MM **Privately Held**
WEB: www.smsfab.com
SIC: 3444 Sheet metalwork

(P-6910)
SHEET METAL SPECIALISTS LLC
11698 Warm Springs Rd, Riverside (92505-5862)
PHONE....................951 351-6828
Michael Uranga,
Sandy Sligar,
EMP: 34 **EST:** 2000
SQ FT: 18,000
SALES (est): 2.5MM **Privately Held**
WEB: www.sheetmetalspecialists.com
SIC: 3444 Sheet metal specialties, not stamped

(P-6911)
SHEETMETAL ENGINEERING
1780 Voyager Ave, Simi Valley (93063-3301)
PHONE....................805 306-0390
Kenneth Chamberlain, *President*
Kathy Chou, *CFO*
David Reed, *Vice Pres*
Dave L Reed, *Technology*
Tony Zapata, *Manager*
EMP: 25 **EST:** 1983
SQ FT: 21,000
SALES (est): 4.2MM **Privately Held**
WEB: www.sheetmetaleng.com
SIC: 3444 1799 Sheet metal specialties, not stamped; welding on site

(P-6912)
SHOWERDOORDIRECT LLC
20100 Normandie Ave, Torrance (90502-1211)
PHONE....................310 327-8060
Adam Slutske,
▲ **EMP:** 21 **EST:** 2010
SALES (est): 1.7MM
SALES (corp-wide): 14.2MM **Privately Held**
WEB: www.showerdoordirect.com
SIC: 3444 Bins, prefabricated sheet metal; radiator shields or enclosures, sheet metal
PA: Century Shower Door Co., Inc.
20100 Normandie Ave
Torrance CA 90502
310 327-8060

(P-6913)
SMS FABRICATIONS INC
11698 Warm Springs Rd, Riverside (92505-5862)
PHONE....................951 351-6828
Michael A Uranga, *CEO*

Sandy Sligar, *President*
Scott Sligar, *Vice Pres*
EMP: 36 **EST:** 2003
SALES (est): 7.2MM **Privately Held**
WEB: www.sheetmetalspecialists.com
SIC: 3444 Sheet metalwork

(P-6914)
SOMAR CORPORATION
13006 Halldale Ave, Gardena (90249-2118)
PHONE....................310 329-1446
Martin Torres, *President*
Ramona Torres, *Office Mgr*
EMP: 20 **EST:** 1980
SQ FT: 32,000
SALES (est): 1.2MM **Privately Held**
WEB: www.posseproduct.com
SIC: 3444 3353 Sheet metalwork; aluminum sheet, plate & foil

(P-6915)
SPAN-O-MATIC INC
825 Columbia St, Brea (92821-2917)
PHONE....................714 256-4700
Wolfgang Arnold, *President*
Erik A Arnold, *CEO*
Lynda Arnold, *CFO*
Carl Arnold, *Vice Pres*
Karl Arnold, *Vice Pres*
EMP: 40 **EST:** 1972
SQ FT: 50,000
SALES (est): 7.6MM **Privately Held**
WEB: www.spanomatic.com
SIC: 3444 Sheet metalwork

(P-6916)
SPECIALTY FABRICATIONS INC
2674 Westhills Ct, Simi Valley (93065-6234)
PHONE....................805 579-9730
Mark Zimmerman, *President*
Randy Zimmerman, *Corp Secy*
EMP: 49 **EST:** 1978
SQ FT: 80,000
SALES (est): 8.6MM **Privately Held**
WEB: www.specfabinc.com
SIC: 3444 3599 Sheet metalwork; machine & other job shop work

(P-6917)
SPRAY ENCLOSURE TECH INC
Also Called: Spray Tech
1427 N Linden Ave, Rialto (92376-8601)
PHONE....................909 419-7011
Tyler Rand, *President*
▲ **EMP:** 30 **EST:** 1994
SQ FT: 59,000
SALES (est): 7.3MM **Privately Held**
WEB: www.spraytech.com
SIC: 3444 Booths, spray: prefabricated sheet metal

(P-6918)
STEELDYNE INDUSTRIES
Also Called: ABC Sheet Metal
2871 E La Cresta Ave, Anaheim (92806-1817)
PHONE....................714 630-6200
Jeff Duveneck, *President*
Richard Duveneck, *Vice Pres*
Brad Gnegy, *General Mgr*
Brian Appel, *Engineer*
Adrian Duardo, *Sales Staff*
EMP: 40 **EST:** 1995
SQ FT: 20,000
SALES (est): 9.1MM **Privately Held**
WEB: www.abcsheetmetal.com
SIC: 3444 Sheet metal specialties, not stamped

(P-6919)
STEIN INDUSTRIES INC (PA)
4005 Artesia Ave, Fullerton (92833-2519)
PHONE....................714 522-4560
Rudi Steinhilber, *CEO*
Theodore Steinhilber, *President*
Dave Spivy, *CFO*
EMP: 27 **EST:** 1982
SQ FT: 30,800
SALES (est): 6MM **Privately Held**
SIC: 3444 2599 Sheet metalwork; work benches, factory

(P-6920)
STOLL METALCRAFT INC
24808 Anza Dr, Valencia (91355-1258)
PHONE....................661 295-0401
Gunter Stoll, *President*
Frank Meacham, *Program Mgr*
EMP: 105 **EST:** 1973
SQ FT: 45,000
SALES (est): 24.7MM **Privately Held**
WEB: www.stoll-metalcraft.com
SIC: 3444 Sheet metal specialties, not stamped

(P-6921)
STRETCH FORMING CORPORATION
Also Called: Sfc
804 S Redlands Ave, Perris (92570-2478)
PHONE....................951 443-0911
Brian D Geary, *CEO*
Rick Remias, *Program Mgr*
Jim Lowther, *General Mgr*
Shawn Johnston, *Engineer*
Steve Hoefler, *QC Mgr*
▲ **EMP:** 85 **EST:** 2009
SQ FT: 97,000
SALES (est): 14.2MM **Privately Held**
WEB: www.stretchformingcorp.com
SIC: 3444 Sheet metalwork

(P-6922)
SUPERIOR DUCT FABRICATION INC
1683 Mount Vernon Ave, Pomona (91768-3300)
PHONE....................909 620-8565
Mike Hilgert, *CEO*
Kerry Bootke, *Vice Pres*
Branden Avila, *Administration*
Karine Stepanian, *Credit Mgr*
Tiffany Martin, *Sales Mgr*
◆ **EMP:** 107 **EST:** 2002
SQ FT: 3,900
SALES (est): 25.6MM **Privately Held**
WEB: www.sdfab.com
SIC: 3444 Ducts, sheet metal

(P-6923)
SUPERIOR METAL FABRICATORS INC
4768 Felspar St, Riverside (92509-3038)
PHONE....................951 360-2474
Ron Didonanto, *President*
Dave Anderson, *Vice Pres*
EMP: 29 **EST:** 1977
SQ FT: 10,000
SALES (est): 2.7MM **Privately Held**
WEB: www.superiormetalfabricators.net
SIC: 3444 Sheet metalwork

(P-6924)
SWIFT FAB
515 E Alondra Blvd, Gardena (90248-2903)
PHONE....................310 366-7295
Robert Senter, *Owner*
Carla Senter, *General Mgr*
EMP: 18 **EST:** 1988
SQ FT: 6,000
SALES (est): 2.4MM **Privately Held**
WEB: www.swiftfab.com
SIC: 3444 Sheet metal specialties, not stamped

(P-6925)
SWIFT-COR PRECISION INC
344 W 157th St, Gardena (90248-2135)
PHONE....................310 354-1207
Sam Longo Jr, *President*
Tony Serge, *CFO*
EMP: 30 **EST:** 1981
SQ FT: 100,000
SALES (est): 892.4K **Privately Held**
WEB: www.impresaaerospace.com
SIC: 3444 Sheet metalwork

(P-6926)
T & F SHEET MTLS FAB MCHNING I
15607 New Century Dr, Gardena (90248-2128)
PHONE....................310 516-8548
Thomas Medina, *President*
Hector Medina, *Vice Pres*
EMP: 32 **EST:** 2005

SQ FT: 9,800
SALES (est): 3.5MM **Privately Held**
WEB: www.tnfsheetmetal.com
SIC: 3444 Sheet metalwork

(P-6927)
TALINS INC
17800 S Main St Ste 121, Gardena (90248-3511)
PHONE....................310 378-3715
George Talbott, *Owner*
EMP: 13 **EST:** 1977
SQ FT: 3,200
SALES (est): 918.7K **Privately Held**
SIC: 3444 Sheet metalwork

(P-6928)
TED RIECK ENTERPRISES INC
Also Called: Royal Metal
1228 S Wright St, Santa Ana (92705-4507)
PHONE....................714 542-4763
Ted Rieck, *President*
Penny Rieck, *Vice Pres*
EMP: 14 **EST:** 1981
SQ FT: 9,000
SALES (est): 2.5MM **Privately Held**
SIC: 3444 Sheet metalwork

(P-6929)
TEE -N -JAY MANUFACTURING INC
9145 Glenoaks Blvd, Sun Valley (91352-2612)
PHONE....................818 504-2961
Jeff Berns, *President*
Tamara Berns, *Corp Secy*
Sandi Hollingsworth, *Office Mgr*
Jessica Berns-Hall, *Purch Mgr*
Buyer Sandi, *Sales Staff*
EMP: 20 **EST:** 1973
SQ FT: 10,187
SALES (est): 2.4MM **Privately Held**
WEB: www.tee-n-jay.com
SIC: 3444 Sheet metalwork

(P-6930)
TFC MANUFACTURING INC
4001 Watson Plaza Dr, Lakewood (90712-4034)
PHONE....................562 426-9559
Majid Shahbazi, *President*
Hamid Sharifat, *Vice Pres*
Baldo Marquez, *Purchasing*
Jim Hagani, *Mktg Coord*
EMP: 81
SQ FT: 28,500
SALES (est): 22MM **Privately Held**
WEB: www.tfcmfg.com
SIC: 3444 Sheet metalwork

(P-6931)
TJ COMPOSITES INC
Also Called: Martin Enterprises
7231 Boulder Ave, Highland (92346-3313)
PHONE....................951 928-8713
EMP: 30
SQ FT: 2,000
SALES (est): 11.4MM **Privately Held**
WEB: www.martinfrp.com
SIC: 3444 Mfg Sheet Metalwork

(P-6932)
TN SHEET METAL INC
18385 Bandilier Cir, Fountain Valley (92708-7001)
PHONE....................714 593-0100
Thony Quang Nguyen, *CEO*
▲ **EMP:** 19 **EST:** 2001
SQ FT: 12,035
SALES (est): 3.7MM **Privately Held**
WEB: www.tnsheetmetal.com
SIC: 3444 Ducts, sheet metal

(P-6933)
TREND TECHNOLOGIES LLC (DH)
4626 Eucalyptus Ave, Chino (91710-9215)
P.O. Box 515001, Los Angeles (90051-5001)
PHONE....................909 597-7861
Earl Payton, *Mng Member*
Tai Chen, *CFO*
Jeffrey Stump, *Vice Pres*
Barb Raftree, *Admin Asst*
Liz Perez, *Administration*
▲ **EMP:** 220

SQ FT: 125,000
SALES (est): 145.2MM **Privately Held**
WEB: www.trendtechnologies.com
SIC: 3444 3469 3499 3089 Metal housings, enclosures, casings & other containers; electronic enclosures, stamped or pressed metal; aquarium accessories, metal; injection molding of plastics
HQ: Ttl Holdings, Llc
4626 Eucalyptus Ave
Chino CA 91710
909 597-7861

(P-6934)
TRI PRECISION SHEETMETAL INC
845 N Elm St, Orange (92867-7909)
PHONE...........................714 632-8838
Ross Morrow, *President*
Rob Morrow, *CFO*
EMP: 40 **EST:** 1988
SALES (est): 7.9MM **Privately Held**
WEB: www.triprecision.com
SIC: 3444 Housings for business machines, sheet metal; sheet metal specialties, not stamped

(P-6935)
TRIO METAL STAMPING INC
15318 Proctor Ave, City of Industry (91745-1023)
PHONE...........................626 336-1228
Damian Rickard, *CEO*
Rudy Hernandez, *COO*
Georgia Boris, *Corp Secy*
Cindy Hansen, *Purch Mgr*
EMP: 53 **EST:** 1947
SQ FT: 75,000
SALES (est): 5.9MM **Privately Held**
WEB: www.triometalstamping.com
SIC: 3444 3469 Sheet metalwork; stamping metal for the trade

(P-6936)
UNITED DURALUME PRODUCTS INC
350 S Raymond Ave, Fullerton (92831-4689)
PHONE...........................714 773-4011
Mike Winston Adams, *CEO*
EMP: 15 **EST:** 1970
SQ FT: 128,600
SALES (est): 3.2MM **Privately Held**
SIC: 3444 1521 Awnings & canopies; patio & deck construction & repair

(P-6937)
US PRECISION SHEET METAL INC
Also Called: U S Precision Manufacturing
4020 Garner Rd, Riverside (92501-1006)
PHONE...........................951 276-2611
Amanda Hawkins, *CEO*
Ray Mayo, *President*
Sal Giulano, *Vice Pres*
EMP: 68 **EST:** 1981
SQ FT: 25,000
SALES (est): 7.3MM **Privately Held**
WEB: www.usprecision.net
SIC: 3444 Sheet metal specialties, not stamped

(P-6938)
VALLEY PRECISION METAL PRODUCT
Also Called: Valley Engravers
27771 Avenue Hopkins, Santa Clarita (91355-1223)
PHONE...........................661 607-0100
Toll Free:...........................888 -
Howard R Vermillion Jr, *President*
EMP: 25 **EST:** 1999
SQ FT: 15,000
SALES (est): 8.2MM **Privately Held**
WEB: www.veiaerospace.com
SIC: 3444 3599 Sheet metalwork; machine shop, jobbing & repair
PA: Valley Precision Metal Products, Inc.
27771 Avenue Hopkins
Valencia CA 91355
661 607-0100

(P-6939)
VERSAFAB CORP (PA)
15919 S Broadway, Gardena (90248-2489)
PHONE...........................800 421-1822
Edward Penfold Jr, *Ch of Bd*
Joe Flynn, *President*
Jon Ross, *General Mgr*
Florentino Moreno, *Elder*
EMP: 40 **EST:** 1982
SQ FT: 35,000
SALES: 10.2MM **Privately Held**
WEB: www.versafabcorp.com
SIC: 3444 3465 3496 3469 Sheet metalwork; moldings or trim, automobile: stamped metal; miscellaneous fabricated wire products; metal stampings

(P-6940)
VTS SHEETMETAL SPECIALIST CO
1041 N Grove St, Anaheim (92806-2015)
PHONE...........................714 237-1420
Tom Bonnett, *President*
SA H Vo, *Admin Sec*
EMP: 31 **EST:** 1986
SQ FT: 21,300
SALES (est): 5.6MM **Privately Held**
WEB: www.vtsfab.com
SIC: 3444 Metal housings, enclosures, casings & other containers

(P-6941)
WEST COAST CUSTOM SHEET METAL
8125 Lankershim Blvd, North Hollywood (91605-1612)
PHONE...........................818 252-7500
George Vartan, *President*
EMP: 36 **EST:** 2001
SALES (est): 3MM **Privately Held**
WEB:
www.westcoastcustomsheetmetal.com
SIC: 3444 Sheet metalwork

(P-6942)
WESTERN SHEET METALS INC
280 E Harrison St, Corona (92879-1309)
PHONE...........................951 272-3600
Albert Rivera, *President*
Matt Rola, *General Mgr*
EMP: 27 **EST:** 1993
SALES (est): 5.2MM **Privately Held**
WEB: www.westernsheetmetals.com
SIC: 3444 Sheet metalwork

(P-6943)
WILL-MANN INC
225 E Santa Fe Ave, Fullerton (92832-1917)
P.O. Box 976 (92836-0976)
PHONE...........................714 870-0350
Manfred Frischmuth, *President*
Sabina Andrassy, *Treasurer*
Lore Frischmuth, *Vice Pres*
EMP: 40 **EST:** 1968
SQ FT: 30,000
SALES (est): 4.8MM **Privately Held**
WEB: www.will-mann.com
SIC: 3444 7692 3471 Sheet metal specialties, not stamped; welding repair; plating & polishing

(P-6944)
WINBO USA INC
2120 California Ave Ste 2, Corona (92881-3301)
PHONE...........................951 738-9978
Eddie Cheung, *President*
▲ **EMP:** 40 **EST:** 2004
SALES (est): 1.6MM **Privately Held**
SIC: 3444 Machine guards, sheet metal

3446 Architectural & Ornamental Metal Work

(P-6945)
A AND M ORNAMENTAL IRON & WLDG
1611 Railroad St, Corona (92878-5003)
PHONE...........................951 734-6730
Michael J Tallick, *Owner*
EMP: 14 **EST:** 1984
SQ FT: 4,000

SALES (est): 2MM **Privately Held**
WEB: www.anmironworks.com
SIC: 3446 Architectural metalwork

(P-6946)
A/C FOLDING GATES INC
1374 E 9th St, Pomona (91766-3831)
PHONE...........................909 629-3026
Clifton G Adams, *Owner*
Kristina Simmons, *General Mgr*
EMP: 13 **EST:** 1984
SQ FT: 16,000
SALES (est): 2.1MM **Privately Held**
WEB: www.acfoldinggates.com
SIC: 3446 1799 Gates, ornamental metal; fence construction

(P-6947)
ACE IRON INC
929 Howard St, Marina Del Rey (90292-5518)
PHONE...........................510 324-3300
Aejaz Sareshwala, *President*
EMP: 28 **EST:** 2000
SQ FT: 60,000
SALES (est): 1.5MM **Privately Held**
WEB: www.nycreditinc.com
SIC: 3446 3441 1791 Fences or posts, ornamental iron or steel; building components, structural steel; structural steel erection

(P-6948)
ADF INCORPORATED
Also Called: Able Design and Fabrication
1550 W Mahalo Pl, Rancho Dominguez (90220-5422)
PHONE...........................310 669-9700
Lou Mannick, *President*
Brian Webster, *Info Tech Dir*
Mercedes Chavez, *Human Res Mgr*
Mayra Herrera, *Purchasing*
EMP: 30 **EST:** 1993
SQ FT: 23,000
SALES (est): 7.5MM **Privately Held**
WEB: www.able-design.com
SIC: 3446 Partitions & supports/studs, including accoustical systems

(P-6949)
ALABAMA METAL INDUSTRIES CORP
Also Called: Amico Fontana
11093 Beech Ave, Fontana (92337-7268)
P.O. Box 310353 (92331-0353)
PHONE...........................909 350-9280
Lilly Mc Donalds, *Branch Mgr*
EMP: 70
SALES (corp-wide): 1B **Publicly Held**
WEB: www.amicoglobal.com
SIC: 3446 Open flooring & grating for construction
HQ: Alabama Metal Industries Corporation
3245 Fayette Ave
Birmingham AL 35208
205 787-2611

(P-6950)
ARCHITECTURAL ENTERPRISES INC
Also Called: Hi-Tech Iron Works
5821 Randolph St, Commerce (90040-3415)
PHONE...........................323 268-4000
Tom Lee, *President*
John S Lee, *Treasurer*
Alma Gutierrez, *Admin Sec*
EMP: 40 **EST:** 1984
SQ FT: 20,000
SALES (est): 6MM **Privately Held**
SIC: 3446 Fences or posts, ornamental iron or steel; gates, ornamental metal

(P-6951)
ATR TECHNOLOGIES INCORPORATED
Also Called: Aluminum Tube Railings
805 Towne Center Dr, Pomona (91767-5901)
PHONE...........................909 399-9724
Donald Terry, *President*
Debbie Terry, *Partner*
Dave C Terry, *Treasurer*
Debra L Terry, *Admin Sec*
Bert Roark, *Sales Mgr*

▼ **EMP:** 15 **EST:** 1963
SQ FT: 15,800
SALES (est): 2.2MM **Privately Held**
WEB: www.atr-technologies.com
SIC: 3446 Architectural metalwork

(P-6952)
BAY ORNAMENTAL IRON INC
757 Newton Way, Costa Mesa (92627-4277)
PHONE...........................949 548-1015
Fax: 949 423-0084
EMP: 24
SQ FT: 4,000
SALES (est): 3.5MM **Privately Held**
WEB: www.bayornamentaliron.com
SIC: 3446 Mfg Architectural Metalwork

(P-6953)
BRADFIELD MANUFACTURING INC
2633 E Mardi Gras Ave, Anaheim (92806-3243)
PHONE...........................714 543-8348
Gerry L Bradfield, *President*
Nola Read, *Treasurer*
Roderick S Bradfield, *Vice Pres*
EMP: 15 **EST:** 1952
SQ FT: 12,000
SALES (est): 871.7K **Privately Held**
SIC: 3446 Stairs, staircases, stair treads: prefabricated metal

(P-6954)
CANTERBURY DESIGNS INC
Also Called: Canterbury International
6195 Maywood Ave, Huntington Park (90255-3213)
PHONE...........................323 936-7111
Larry Snyder, *President*
Laura Snyder, *Treasurer*
Tom Price, *General Mgr*
John Flanton, *Mfg Staff*
▲ **EMP:** 20 **EST:** 1964
SALES (est): 2.2MM **Privately Held**
WEB: www.canterbury-designs.com
SIC: 3446 3873 Architectural metalwork; clocks, assembly of

(P-6955)
CHALLENGER ORNAMENTAL IR WORKS
437 W Palmer Ave, Glendale (91204-2407)
PHONE...........................818 507-7030
Nerses Espanosian, *President*
EMP: 18 **EST:** 1987
SQ FT: 6,500
SALES (est): 1MM **Privately Held**
SIC: 3446 Architectural metalwork; gates, ornamental metal; railings, prefabricated metal; grillwork, ornamental metal

(P-6956)
COLUMBIA FABRICATING CO INC
5079 Gloria Ave, Encino (91436-1553)
PHONE...........................818 247-4220
Joseph Goldberg, *CEO*
Dalia Goldberg, *CFO*
EMP: 50 **EST:** 1983
SQ FT: 19,000
SALES (est): 1.7MM **Privately Held**
SIC: 3446 Architectural metalwork

(P-6957)
CRANEVEYOR MIDWEST CORP
13730 Central Ave, Chino (91710-5503)
PHONE...........................909 627-6801
Mike Williams, *Branch Mgr*
Hector Valiente, *CFO*
Paola Alfaro, *General Mgr*
Daniel Farden, *Sales Staff*
Dan Kelley, *Sales Staff*
EMP: 30
SALES (corp-wide): 27MM **Privately Held**
WEB: www.craneveyor.com
SIC: 3446 3536 Railings, bannisters, guards, etc.: made from metal pipe; hoists, cranes & monorails
PA: Craneveyor Corp.
1524 Potrero Ave
El Monte CA 91733
626 442-1524

(P-6958)
CURRAN ENGINEERING COMPANY INC
28727 Industry Dr, Valencia (91355-5414)
P.O. Box 26, Castaic (91310-0026)
PHONE....................................800 643-6353
Douglas M Curran, *CEO*
Patrick Curran, *President*
EMP: 20
SQ FT: 20,000
SALES (est): 3.7MM **Privately Held**
WEB: www.curranengineering.com
SIC: 3446 5399 Architectural metalwork; Army-Navy goods

(P-6959)
CUSTOM IRON DESIGN (PA)
522 E Banning St, Compton (90222-1416)
PHONE....................................310 537-5936
Carlos M Lozano, *Owner*
EMP: 18 **EST:** 1996
SALES (est): 259.4K **Privately Held**
SIC: 3446 Architectural metalwork

(P-6960)
DENNISON INC
Also Called: Maxxon Company
17901 Railroad St, City of Industry (91748-1113)
PHONE....................................626 965-8917
Dennis MA, *President*
◆ **EMP:** 47 **EST:** 1990
SQ FT: 26,000 **Privately Held**
SIC: 3446 Architectural metalwork

(P-6961)
EUROCRAFT ARCHTECTURAL MET INC
5619 Watcher St, Bell Gardens (90201-1632)
PHONE....................................323 771-1323
John Fechter, *President*
David Sawez, *Vice Pres*
Kris Debruyne, *Prdtn Mgr*
EMP: 30 **EST:** 1976
SQ FT: 30,000
SALES (est): 4.3MM **Privately Held**
WEB: www.eurocraftmetal.com
SIC: 3446 Architectural metalwork

(P-6962)
FORMS AND SURFACES INC
6395 Cindy Ln, Carpinteria (93013-2909)
PHONE....................................805 684-8626
George Hickmann, *Branch Mgr*
S Updates, *Bd of Directors*
Lauren Flannery, *Vice Pres*
Karen Tullis, *Vice Pres*
Amanda Reynolds, *Purch Agent*
EMP: 80
SALES (corp-wide): 103.1MM **Privately Held**
WEB: www.forms-surfaces.com
SIC: 3446 Architectural metalwork
PA: Forms And Surfaces, Inc.
30 Pine St
Pittsburgh PA 15223
412 781-9003

(P-6963)
GOLDEN STATE GRATING INC
8224 Goldmine Ave, Fontana (92335-3258)
PHONE....................................909 854-2489
Juan Castro, *President*
German Garciaparra, *Vice Pres*
Lucy Castro, *Admin Sec*
Rocky Castro, *Sales Staff*
EMP: 15 **EST:** 1987
SQ FT: 8,000
SALES (est): 1.8MM **Privately Held**
WEB: www.goldenstategrating.com
SIC: 3446 Gratings, tread: fabricated metal

(P-6964)
J TALLEY CORPORATION (PA)
Also Called: Talley Metal Fabrication
989 W 7th St, San Jacinto (92582-3813)
P.O. Box 850 (92581-0850)
PHONE....................................951 654-2123
Joe Brown Talley, *CEO*
Eloy Ochoa, *CFO*
Michael Terry, *General Mgr*
Scott Kinney, *Project Mgr*
Mike McKinnis, *Project Mgr*
EMP: 86 **EST:** 1963

SQ FT: 13,400
SALES (est): 18.2MM **Privately Held**
WEB: www.talleymetalfabrication.com
SIC: 3446 3444 Railings, prefabricated metal; sheet metalwork

(P-6965)
JAGUARS WROGHT IRON
Also Called: Jaguar Mfg Cstm Wrought Ir
300 Union Ave, Bakersfield (93307-1555)
PHONE....................................661 323-5015
Josh Hubble, *Owner*
EMP: 13 **EST:** 1969
SQ FT: 5,000
SALES (est): 1.3MM **Privately Held**
WEB: www.jaguarwroughtiron.com
SIC: 3446 Architectural metalwork

(P-6966)
JANSEN ORNAMENTAL SUPPLY CO
10926 Schmidt Rd, El Monte (91733-2708)
PHONE....................................626 442-0271
Mike Jansen, *CEO*
Harry Jansen, *President*
John Jansen, *Admin Sec*
Alain Duhart, *Warehouse Mgr*
▲ **EMP:** 30
SQ FT: 22,000
SALES (est): 6.6MM **Privately Held**
WEB: www.jansensupply.com
SIC: 3446 Architectural metalwork

(P-6967)
JMI STEEL INC
8983 San Fernando Rd, Sun Valley (91352-1410)
PHONE....................................818 768-3955
Martin J Blaha, *President*
EMP: 28 **EST:** 1989
SQ FT: 11,000
SALES (est): 4.3MM **Privately Held**
SIC: 3446 Fences or posts, ornamental iron or steel

(P-6968)
JONES IRON WORKS
2658 Griffith Park Blvd, Los Angeles (90039-2520)
PHONE....................................323 386-2368
EMP: 15 **EST:** 2013
SQ FT: 5,000
SALES (est): 890K **Privately Held**
SIC: 3446 Mfg Architectural Metalwork

(P-6969)
K & J WIRE PRODUCTS CORP
1220 N Lance Ln, Anaheim (92806-1812)
PHONE....................................714 816-0360
Klaus Borutzki, *President*
Barbara Borutzki, *Corp Secy*
EMP: 30 **EST:** 1989
SQ FT: 21,000
SALES (est): 1.2MM **Privately Held**
WEB: www.kjwire.com
SIC: 3446 3496 5046 3315 Architectural metalwork; miscellaneous fabricated wire products; store fixtures & display equipment; wire & fabricated wire products

(P-6970)
KAWNEER COMPANY INC
Also Called: Brite Vue Div
7200 W Doe Ave, Visalia (93291-9296)
PHONE....................................559 651-4000
Norris McElroy, *Branch Mgr*
Lee Bawanan, *Manager*
EMP: 116
SQ FT: 200,000
SALES (corp-wide): 5.6B **Publicly Held**
WEB: www.kawneer.com
SIC: 3446 Architectural metalwork
HQ: Kawneer Company, Inc.
555 Guthridge Ct
Norcross GA 30092
770 449-5555

(P-6971)
LAVI INDUSTRIES (PA)
27810 Avenue Hopkins, Valencia (91355-3409)
PHONE....................................877 275-5284
Gavriel Lavi, *President*
Yariv Blumkine, *COO*
Susan Lavi, *Vice Pres*
Yoni Lavi, *Vice Pres*

Chuck Wurl, *Executive*
◆ **EMP:** 80 **EST:** 1979
SQ FT: 80,000
SALES (est): 29.1MM **Privately Held**
WEB: www.lavi.com
SIC: 3446 Railings, bannisters, guards, etc.: made from metal pipe

(P-6972)
LD STEEL INC
15517 Illinois Ave, Paramount (90723-4110)
PHONE....................................213 632-8073
Jose L Morales, *CEO*
EMP: 13 **EST:** 2013
SALES (est): 683.4K **Privately Held**
WEB: www.ldsteelinc.com
SIC: 3446 Fences or posts, ornamental iron or steel

(P-6973)
LNI CUSTOM MANUFACTURING INC
15542 Broadway Center St, Gardena (90248-2137)
PHONE....................................310 978-2000
Scott Blakely, *CEO*
William Chica, *Prdtn Mgr*
EMP: 50 **EST:** 1995
SALES (est): 8.5MM **Privately Held**
WEB: www.lnisigns.com
SIC: 3446 5046 Architectural metalwork; neon signs

(P-6974)
LUR INC
Also Called: Lumar Metals
9936 Albany Ave, Rancho Cucamonga (91701-5919)
PHONE....................................909 623-4999
Marlene Racca, *President*
Cindy Rowland, *Office Mgr*
EMP: 15 **EST:** 1986
SALES (est): 3.2MM **Privately Held**
SIC: 3446 Architectural metalwork

(P-6975)
METAL X DIRECT INC
1555 Mesa Verde Dr E 11g, Costa Mesa (92626-5112)
PHONE....................................949 336-0055
Sean Lancona, *President*
EMP: 14 **EST:** 2012
SALES (est): 1MM **Privately Held**
SIC: 3446 3441 Architectural metalwork; building components, structural steel

(P-6976)
RAMI DESIGNS INC
24 Hammond Ste E, Irvine (92618-1680)
PHONE....................................949 588-8288
Ron Taybi, *President*
John Rodriguez, *Sr Project Mgr*
EMP: 19 **EST:** 1982
SQ FT: 6,000
SALES (est): 6MM **Privately Held**
WEB: www.ramidesigns.com
SIC: 3446 3299 3229 Architectural metalwork; architectural sculptures: gypsum, clay, papier mache, etc.: glass furnishings & accessories

(P-6977)
RINCON IRON INC
Also Called: Rincon Ironworks
531 Montgomery Ave, Oxnard (93036-1066)
PHONE....................................805 455-2904
Rick Sanchez, *CEO*
▲ **EMP:** 15 **EST:** 2001
SQ FT: 5,000
SALES (est): 1.2MM **Privately Held**
WEB: www.rinconiron.com
SIC: 3446 Architectural metalwork

(P-6978)
SANIE MANUFACTURING COMPANY
2600 S Yale St, Santa Ana (92704-5228)
PHONE....................................714 751-7700
Mendi Haidarali, *President*
Mohammad Haidari, *Vice Pres*
Tony Azadi, *Manager*
Elia Briones, *Contractor*
EMP: 18 **EST:** 1981
SQ FT: 8,900

SALES (est): 6MM **Privately Held**
WEB: www.saniemfg.com
SIC: 3446 Fences or posts, ornamental iron or steel

(P-6979)
SAPPHIRE MANUFACTURING INC
505 Porter Way, Placentia (92870-6454)
PHONE....................................714 401-3117
Hector Garibay, *CEO*
Hayley Misetich, *General Mgr*
Andrea Dorelli, *VP Sales*
EMP: 20 **EST:** 2015
SQ FT: 25,000
SALES (est): 2.4MM **Privately Held**
WEB: www.sapphirecleanrooms.com
SIC: 3446 7371 Fences or posts, ornamental iron or steel; computer software development & applications

(P-6980)
SURCO PRODUCTS INC
14001 S Main St, Los Angeles (90061-2196)
PHONE....................................310 323-2520
Ludwig Surkin, *President*
Uri Surkin, *Vice Pres*
Amir Surkin, *Manager*
▲ **EMP:** 16 **EST:** 1971
SQ FT: 20,000
SALES (est): 3MM **Privately Held**
WEB: www.surcoinc.com
SIC: 3446 3429 Ladders, for permanent installation: metal; luggage racks, car top

(P-6981)
TAJIMA USA DISSOLVING CORP
Also Called: Tajima /Crl
2503 E Vernon Ave, Vernon (90058-1826)
PHONE....................................323 588-1281
Bernard P Harris, *Ch of Bd*
EMP: 79 **EST:** 1999
SALES (est): 10.7MM
SALES (corp-wide): 27.5B **Privately Held**
WEB: www.crl-arch.com
SIC: 3446 Architectural metalwork
HQ: C. R. Laurence Co., Inc.
2503 E Vernon Ave
Vernon CA 90058
323 588-1281

(P-6982)
THORNTON STEEL & IR WORKS INC
1323 S State College Pkwy, Anaheim (92806-5242)
PHONE....................................714 491-8800
Ken Thornton, *CEO*
Steven Braseny, *President*
Richard Salcedo, *Vice Pres*
EMP: 17 **EST:** 1997
SQ FT: 12,200
SALES (est): 4.6MM **Privately Held**
WEB: www.thorntonsteelironworks.com
SIC: 3446 Architectural metalwork

(P-6983)
TJS METAL MANUFACTURING INC
10847 Drury Ln, Lynwood (90262-1833)
PHONE....................................310 604-1545
Jose Antonio Gallegos, *CEO*
EMP: 26 **EST:** 1999
SQ FT: 30,000
SALES (est): 9.3MM **Privately Held**
WEB: www.tjsmetal.com
SIC: 3446 Architectural metalwork

(P-6984)
WEIS/ROBART PARTITIONS INC
Also Called: Michigan Metal Partitions
3501 E La Palma Ave, Anaheim (92806-2117)
PHONE....................................714 666-0822
John R Penner, *President*
Eleanor Penner, *Treasurer*
Beverly Booms, *Vice Pres*
Sarah Michener, *Vice Pres*
Donald Harms, *Admin Sec*
EMP: 15 **EST:** 1876
SQ FT: 8,000
SALES (est): 1.2MM **Privately Held**
WEB: www.weisrobart.com
SIC: 3446 Partitions, ornamental metal

3448 Prefabricated Metal Buildings & Cmpnts

(P-6985)
ACORN ENGINEERING COMPANY (PA)
Also Called: Morris Group International
15125 Proctor Ave, City of Industry (91746-3327)
P.O. Box 3527 (91744-0527)
PHONE..........................800 488-8999
Donald E Morris, *President*
Charles C Fredricks, *Treasurer*
Kathryn Morris, *Treasurer*
Keith Marshall, *Exec VP*
Vince Conti, *Vice Pres*
◆ **EMP:** 702 **EST:** 1955
SQ FT: 120,000
SALES: 90MM **Privately Held**
WEB: www.acorneng.com
SIC: 3448 3431 3442 Buildings, portable: prefabricated metal; plumbing fixtures: enameled iron cast iron or pressed metal; metal doors

(P-6986)
ALLIED MDULAR BLDG SYSTEMS INC (PA)
642 W Nicolas Ave, Orange (92868-1316)
PHONE..........................714 516-1188
Kevin Peithman, *CEO*
Raj Singh, *COO*
Richard Navarro, *Treasurer*
Cathy Peithman, *Admin Sec*
Shirley Espiritu, *Materials Dir*
EMP: 38 **EST:** 1996
SQ FT: 35,000
SALES (est): 14MM **Privately Held**
WEB: www.alliedmodular.com
SIC: 3448 Prefabricated metal buildings

(P-6987)
BARNS AND BUILDINGS INC
23100 Wildomar Trl, Wildomar (92595-9699)
P.O. Box 1555 (92595-1555)
PHONE..........................951 678-4571
Russell Greer, *CEO*
Barret Hilzer, *COO*
EMP: 18 **EST:** 1982
SQ FT: 40,000
SALES (est): 1MM **Privately Held**
WEB: www.fcpbuildings.com
SIC: 3448 1541 5083 Prefabricated metal components; steel building construction; livestock equipment

(P-6988)
BLUESCOPE BUILDINGS N AMER INC
Also Called: Butler Manufacturing
7440 W Doe Ave, Visalia (93291-9296)
P.O. Box 1590 (93279-1590)
PHONE..........................559 651-5300
Juan Carlos Garcia, *Branch Mgr*
EMP: 200 **Privately Held**
WEB: www.bluescopeconstruction.com
SIC: 3448 Prefabricated metal buildings
HQ: Bluescope Buildings North America, Inc.
1540 Genessee St
Kansas City MO 64102

(P-6989)
CALIFORNIA RAMP WORKS INC
273 N Benson Ave, Upland (91786-5614)
PHONE..........................909 949-1601
Brian Moore, *President*
Joseph M Ciaglia Jr, *Director*
EMP: 13 **EST:** 2008
SALES (est): 1MM **Privately Held**
SIC: 3448 Ramps: prefabricated metal

(P-6990)
CLAMSHELL STRUCTURES INC
Also Called: Clamshell Buildings
300 Graves Ave Ste B, Oxnard (93030-8938)
PHONE..........................805 988-1340
Gregory J Mangan, *CEO*
Michael R Kane, *Vice Pres*
Dean Daddario, *Analyst*

Jennie Westling, *Manager*
EMP: 15 **EST:** 1982
SQ FT: 46,000
SALES: 5.9MM
SALES (corp-wide): 1MM **Privately Held**
WEB: www.clamshell.com
SIC: 3448 Prefabricated metal buildings
PA: Clamshell Holdings, Inc.
300 Graves Ave Ste B
Oxnard CA 93030
805 988-1340

(P-6991)
CRATE MODULAR INC
3025 E Dominguez St, Carson (90810-1437)
PHONE..........................310 405-0829
Rich Rozycki, *CEO*
Moises Bada, *Treasurer*
Natasaha Deski, *Vice Pres*
Celina Valadez, *Purch Mgr*
EMP: 99 **EST:** 2018
SALES (est): 17.2MM **Privately Held**
WEB: www.cratemodular.com
SIC: 3448 Prefabricated metal buildings

(P-6992)
DURACOLD REFRIGERATION MFG LLC
1551 S Primrose Ave, Monrovia (91016-4542)
PHONE..........................626 358-1710
Harold Monsher, *General Ptnr*
Ben Monsher, *Partner*
Bruce Podgur, *Sales Staff*
EMP: 22 **EST:** 1996
SQ FT: 25,000
SALES (est): 2.1MM **Privately Held**
WEB: www.arcticwalkins.com
SIC: 3448 3585 Prefabricated metal components; refrigeration & heating equipment

(P-6993)
FCP INC (PA)
23100 Wildomar Trl, Wildomar (92595-9699)
P.O. Box 1555 (92595-1555)
PHONE..........................951 678-4571
Russell J Greer, *CEO*
Barret Hilzer, *COO*
Stephen Evans, *General Mgr*
Stuart Wilson, *Opers Mgr*
Kathy Cvelbar, *Consultant*
EMP: 84 **EST:** 1982
SQ FT: 200,000
SALES (est): 15MM **Privately Held**
WEB: www.fcpbuildings.com
SIC: 3448 1541 Prefabricated metal components; steel building construction

(P-6994)
FCP INC
4125 Market St Ste 14, Ventura (93003-5643)
P.O. Box 1217, Carpinteria (93014-1217)
PHONE..........................805 684-1117
Barryet Hilzer, *President*
Mike Regan, *Division Mgr*
Melanie Fennell, *Executive Asst*
Manuel Mejia, *Project Mgr*
EMP: 16
SALES (corp-wide): 15MM **Privately Held**
WEB: www.fcpbuildings.com
SIC: 3448 1541 Prefabricated metal components; steel building construction
PA: Fcp, Inc.
23100 Wildomar Trl
Wildomar CA 92595
951 678-4571

(P-6995)
FOUR SEASONS BUILDING PRODUCTS
6450 Caballero Blvd, Buena Park (90620-1007)
PHONE..........................714 522-7852
Dawn Cole, *Materials Mgr*
Ron Williams, *Sales Staff*
EMP: 16 **EST:** 2018
SALES (est): 3.8MM **Privately Held**
WEB: www.fourseasonsbp.com
SIC: 3448 Buildings, portable: prefabricated metal

(P-6996)
GCN SUPPLY LLC
9070 Bridgeport Pl, Rancho Cucamonga (91730-5530)
PHONE..........................909 643-4603
Gustavo Chona, *Mng Member*
Gus Chona, *Opers Staff*
EMP: 50 **EST:** 2015
SALES (est): 10MM **Privately Held**
WEB: www.gcnsupply.com
SIC: 3448 2671 Prefabricated metal buildings; plastic film, coated or laminated for packaging

(P-6997)
H ROBERTS CONSTRUCTION
2165 W Gaylord St, Long Beach (90813-1033)
PHONE..........................562 590-4825
Kathleen F Roberts, *President*
Ken Kenedy, *Opers Mgr*
EMP: 51
SQ FT: 1,100
SALES (est): 8.2MM **Privately Held**
WEB: www.robertsconstructionllc.net
SIC: 3448 Buildings, portable: prefabricated metal

(P-6998)
HAZMAT CHEMICAL STORAGE INC (PA)
13681 Newport Ave Ste 8, Tustin (92780-7815)
P.O. Box 15605, Santa Ana (92735-0605)
PHONE..........................714 480-1290
George Aumond, *President*
EMP: 13 **EST:** 2005
SALES (est): 1.2MM **Privately Held**
WEB: www.hazmatchemicalstorage.com
SIC: 3448 Prefabricated metal buildings

(P-6999)
JOHN L CONLEY INC
Also Called: Conley's Mfg & Sales
4344 Mission Blvd, Montclair (91763-6017)
PHONE..........................909 627-0981
John L Conley, *CEO*
Tom Conley, *President*
Dean Conley, *Vice Pres*
Howard Davis, *Vice Pres*
Armando Maciel, *Technical Staff*
◆ **EMP:** 75 **EST:** 1946
SALES (est): 20.6MM **Privately Held**
WEB: www.conleys.com
SIC: 3448 3441 Greenhouses: prefabricated metal; buildings, portable: prefabricated metal; fabricated structural metal

(P-7000)
JTS MODULAR INC
7001 Mcdivitt Dr Ste B, Bakersfield (93313-2030)
P.O. Box 41765 (93384-1765)
PHONE..........................661 835-9270
Dene Hurlbert, *President*
Phillip Engler, *Vice Pres*
Lee Hawkins, *Vice Pres*
John Hurlbert, *Vice Pres*
Lilibeth Lopez, *Admin Asst*
EMP: 50 **EST:** 2000
SQ FT: 4,000
SALES (est): 8.5MM **Privately Held**
WEB: www.jtsmodular.com
SIC: 3448 Prefabricated metal buildings

(P-7001)
MADISON INDUSTRIES (HQ)
18000 Studebaker Rd # 305, Cerritos (90703-2681)
PHONE..........................323 583-4061
John Frey Jr, *President*
John Samuel Frey, *President*
Barbara Cruncleton, *CFO*
Mike Eyestone, *General Mgr*
Ernesto Anaya, *Project Mgr*
EMP: 26 **EST:** 1974
SQ FT: 24,000
SALES (est): 13.7MM
SALES (corp-wide): 118.8MM **Privately Held**
WEB: www.madisonind.com
SIC: 3448 3441 1542 Prefabricated metal buildings; fabricated structural metal; non-residential construction

PA: John S. Frey Enterprises
1900 E 64th St
Los Angeles CA 90001
323 583-4061

(P-7002)
MCELROY METAL MILL INC
17031 Koala Rd, Adelanto (92301-2246)
PHONE..........................760 246-5545
Pete Nadler, *Manager*
Jose Orozco, *Supervisor*
EMP: 62
SQ FT: 37,700
SALES (corp-wide): 362MM **Privately Held**
WEB: www.mcelroymetal.com
SIC: 3448 Prefabricated metal components
PA: Mcelroy Metal Mill, Inc.
1500 Hamilton Rd
Bossier City LA 71111
318 747-8000

(P-7003)
MORIN CORPORATION
Also Called: Morin West
10707 Commerce Way, Fontana (92337-8216)
PHONE..........................909 428-3747
Ilhan Eser, *Vice Pres*
Katarina Cox, *Sales Staff*
Joe Tibbetts, *Manager*
Randy Badenhop, *Supervisor*
EMP: 40 **Privately Held**
WEB: www.kingspan.com
SIC: 3448 Prefabricated metal buildings
HQ: Morin Corporation
685 Middle St
Bristol CT 06010

(P-7004)
MORRIS GROUP INTERNATIONAL (PA)
15125 Proctor Ave, City of Industry (91746-3327)
P.O. Box 3527 (91744-0527)
PHONE..........................626 336-4561
Donald E Morris, *President*
Ann Luong, *Vice Pres*
Mike Polis, *Vice Pres*
Charles White, *Vice Pres*
Jim Widmer, *Vice Pres*
EMP: 152 **EST:** 2012
SALES (est): 6.5MM **Privately Held**
WEB: www.morrisgroup.co
SIC: 3448 3431 3842 3442 Buildings, portable: prefabricated metal; plumbing fixtures: enameled iron cast iron or pressed metal; grafts, artificial: for surgery; metal doors

(P-7005)
MTN GOVERNMENT SERVICES INC (DH)
1821 E Dyer Rd Ste 125, Santa Ana (92705-5894)
PHONE..........................954 538-4000
Peg Grayson, *President*
Christian M Mezger, *CFO*
Margaret Grayson, *Vice Pres*
Catherine Melquist, *Vice Pres*
Michael Shakarji, *Vice Pres*
EMP: 15 **EST:** 2009
SALES (est): 10MM **Privately Held**
WEB: www.emcconnected.com
SIC: 3448 Prefabricated metal buildings

(P-7006)
ORANGE COUNTY ERECTORS INC
517 E La Palma Ave, Anaheim (92801-2536)
PHONE..........................714 502-8455
Richard Lewis, *CEO*
Sandra Lewis, *Senior VP*
Andy Arango, *Prgrmr*
Bryan Jurgenson, *Human Res Mgr*
Keith Bell, *Director*
EMP: 50 **EST:** 1975
SQ FT: 80,000
SALES (est): 17.6MM **Privately Held**
WEB: www.ocerectors.com
SIC: 3448 3441 1791 Buildings, portable: prefabricated metal; fabricated structural metal; structural steel erection

PRODUCTS & SVCS

(P-7007)
PROGRESSIVE MARKETING PDTS INC
4571 Avenida Del Este, Yorba Linda (92886-3002)
PHONE..................714 888-1700
Leonard Dozier, *CEO*
Kathy Bent, *CFO*
Richard Pierro, *Co-CEO*
Tiffany Dozier, *Exec VP*
Sam Malik, *Exec VP*
◆ EMP: 80 EST: 1977
SALES (est): 19.9MM **Privately Held**
WEB: www.gamberjohnson.com
SIC: 3448 Prefabricated metal buildings

(P-7008)
STELL INDUSTRIES INC
Also Called: C-Thru Sunrooms
1951 S Parco Ave Ste B, Ontario (91761-8315)
PHONE..................951 369-8777
Gary P Stell Jr, *CEO*
Jason S Albany, *President*
Mike Leigh, *President*
EMP: 50 EST: 1947
SALES (est): 8.4MM **Privately Held**
SIC: 3448 Sunrooms, prefabricated metal

(P-7009)
T M P SERVICES INC (PA)
2929 Kansas Ave, Riverside (92507-2639)
PHONE..................951 213-3900
Prentiss Tarver Jr, *Shareholder*
Shari Taylor, *President*
Diana Quevedo, *Sales Staff*
EMP: 22 EST: 1993
SQ FT: 32,000
SALES (est): 5.9MM **Privately Held**
WEB: www.tmpservices.com
SIC: 3448 Ramps: prefabricated metal

(P-7010)
TOLCO INCORPORATED
Also Called: Viking Fabrication
6480 Box Springs Blvd, Riverside (92507-0744)
PHONE..................951 656-3111
Patrick Shaughnessy, *Principal*
Chris Sharp, *Opers Mgr*
EMP: 19 EST: 2003
SALES (est): 1.1MM **Privately Held**
WEB: www.vikinggroupinc.com
SIC: 3448 Prefabricated metal buildings

(P-7011)
UNITED CARPORTS LLC
7280 Sycamore Canyon Blvd # 1, Riverside (92508-2316)
PHONE..................800 757-6742
Ryan Spates, *Mng Member*
Garrett Spates, *Vice Pres*
EMP: 18 EST: 2011
SQ FT: 5,000
SALES (est): 2.4MM **Privately Held**
WEB: www.unitedcarports.com
SIC: 3448 Prefabricated metal buildings

3449 Misc Structural Metal Work

(P-7012)
3G REBAR INC
6400 Price Way, Bakersfield (93308-5119)
PHONE..................661 588-0294
John Michael Dean, *President*
EMP: 15 EST: 2011
SQ FT: 5,600
SALES (est): 3.5MM **Privately Held**
SIC: 3449 Bars, concrete reinforcing: fabricated steel

(P-7013)
ACME SCREW PRODUCTS
7950 S Alameda St, Huntington Park (90255-6697)
PHONE..................323 581-8611
EMP: 25
SQ FT: 13,500
SALES (est): 4.3MM **Privately Held**
WEB: www.acme-screw.com
SIC: 3449 Mfg Misc Structural Metalwork

(P-7014)
AMC MACHINING INC
1540 Commerce Way, Paso Robles (93446-3524)
P.O. Box 665 (93447-0665)
PHONE..................805 238-5452
Alex Camp, *President*
Nicole Prizmich, *Manager*
EMP: 21 EST: 2007
SQ FT: 10,000
SALES (est): 4MM **Privately Held**
WEB: www.amcmachining.com
SIC: 3449 Miscellaneous metalwork

(P-7015)
BACKSTAGE EQUIPMENT INC
Also Called: Backstage Studio Equip
8052 Lankershim Blvd, North Hollywood (91605-1609)
PHONE..................818 504-6026
Cary Griffith, *President*
EMP: 13 EST: 1979
SQ FT: 9,801
SALES (est): 2.2MM **Privately Held**
WEB: www.backstageweb.com
SIC: 3449 3646 Miscellaneous metalwork; commercial indusl & institutional electric lighting fixtures

(P-7016)
CALIFORNIA STEEL PRODUCTS INC
10851 Drury Ln, Lynwood (90262-1833)
PHONE..................310 603-5645
Enrique Garcia, *President*
Ricardo Moctezuma, *Vice Pres*
EMP: 17 EST: 1993
SALES (est): 2.2MM **Privately Held**
SIC: 3449 3452 3312 Miscellaneous metalwork; bolts, metal; rods, iron & steel: made in steel mills

(P-7017)
CARLSON ARTS LLC
11230 Peoria St, Sun Valley (91352-1632)
PHONE..................818 767-1500
Peter M Carlson, *Principal*
EMP: 13 EST: 2010
SALES (est): 1.6MM **Privately Held**
WEB: www.carlsonbakerarts.com
SIC: 3449 Miscellaneous metalwork

(P-7018)
CMC STEEL US LLC
Also Called: Gerdau Ameristeel
12459 Arrow Rte, Rancho Cucamonga (91739-9807)
PHONE..................909 646-7827
EMP: 13
SALES (corp-wide): 6.7B **Publicly Held**
WEB: www.cmc.com
SIC: 3449 Bars, concrete reinforcing: fabricated steel
HQ: Cmc Steel Us, Llc
    6565 N Macarthur Blvd # 8
    Irving TX 75039
    214 689-4300

(P-7019)
DB BUILDING FASTENERS INC (PA)
Also Called: Db Building Fasteners
5555 E Gibralter, Ontario (91764-5121)
P.O. Box 4407, Rancho Cucamonga (91729-4407)
PHONE..................909 581-6740
Brent Dooley, *President*
Andrew Cohn, *Corp Secy*
John Dooley III, *Vice Pres*
Marco Ramos, *Sales Staff*
Danny Cintron, *Warehouse Mgr*
▲ EMP: 18 EST: 1992
SALES (est): 4.1MM **Privately Held**
WEB: www.selfdrillers.com
SIC: 3449 Miscellaneous metalwork

(P-7020)
FAB SERVICES WEST INC
10007 Elm Ave, Fontana (92335-6318)
PHONE..................909 350-7500
EMP: 62 EST: 2011

SALES (est): 9.8MM
SALES (corp-wide): 339.9MM **Privately Held**
WEB: www.fabservices.net
SIC: 3449 Miscellaneous metalwork
HQ: Fab Holding Llc
    3335 Susan St
    Costa Mesa CA 92626
    949 236-5520

(P-7021)
H WAYNE LEWIS INC
Also Called: Amber Steel Co.
312 S Willow Ave, Rialto (92376-6313)
P.O. Box 900 (92377-0900)
PHONE..................909 874-2213
H Wayne Lewis, *CEO*
Kriss Lewis, *COO*
Janet Lewis, *Treasurer*
Dan Bergen, *Vice Pres*
Robin Sanders, *Admin Sec*
EMP: 40 EST: 1983
SQ FT: 8,100
SALES (est): 6.1MM **Privately Held**
WEB: www.ambersteelco.com
SIC: 3449 Bars, concrete reinforcing: fabricated steel

(P-7022)
ICSN INC (PA)
17565 Cedarwood Dr, Riverside (92503-7037)
PHONE..................951 687-2305
Joon Hee Lee, *President*
▲ EMP: 18 EST: 2000
SALES (est): 1.2MM **Privately Held**
WEB: www.icsngroup.com
SIC: 3449 Miscellaneous metalwork

(P-7023)
INNOVATIVE METAL INDS INC
Also Called: Southwest Data Products
1330 Riverview Dr, San Bernardino (92408-2944)
PHONE..................909 796-6200
Kelly Brodhagan, *Principal*
▲ EMP: 100 EST: 2006
SQ FT: 150,000
SALES (est): 23.6MM **Privately Held**
WEB: www.imiac.com
SIC: 3449 Curtain wall, metal

(P-7024)
LMS REINFORCING STEEL USA LP (PA)
Also Called: LMS Reinforcing Steel Group
26365 Earthmover Cir, Corona (92883-5270)
PHONE..................604 598-9930
Norm Streu, *President*
Janice Comeau, *CFO*
Mike Schutz, *Vice Pres*
EMP: 49 EST: 2016
SALES (est): 7.6MM **Privately Held**
SIC: 3449 Bars, concrete reinforcing: fabricated steel

(P-7025)
NI INDUSTRIES INC
7300 E Slauson Ave, Commerce (90040-3627)
PHONE..................309 283-3355
David Adler, *President*
Brian McGuire, *President*
Anil Shanehg, *Vice Pres*
▲ EMP: 90 EST: 1930
SQ FT: 30,000
SALES (est): 5.8MM
SALES (corp-wide): 769.9MM **Publicly Held**
WEB: www.trimascorp.com
SIC: 3449 Miscellaneous metalwork
PA: Trimas Corporation
    38505 Woodward Ave # 200
    Bloomfield Hills MI 48304
    248 631-5450

(P-7026)
VISTA STEEL CO INC (PA)
6100 Francis Botello Rd, Goleta (93117-3259)
PHONE..................805 964-4732
Maria Di Maggio, *President*
EMP: 50 EST: 1969
SQ FT: 600

SALES (est): 6.8MM **Privately Held**
WEB: www.vistasteelcompany.com
SIC: 3449 Bars, concrete reinforcing: fabricated steel

(P-7027)
VOLTEGE INC (PA)
11 Pastora, Foothill Ranch (92610-1730)
PHONE..................949 273-3822
Blake Hardin, *CEO*
EMP: 25 EST: 2016
SALES (est): 1.8MM **Privately Held**
SIC: 3449 Miscellaneous metalwork

3451 Screw Machine Prdts

(P-7028)
ABEL AUTOMATICS LLC
Also Called: Abel Reels
165 N Aviador St, Camarillo 93010-8484)
PHONE..................805 388-3721
David Dragoo, *Ch of Bd*
Margie Hanley, *Office Mgr*
◆ EMP: 30 EST: 1980
SQ FT: 16,000
SALES (est): 2.7MM **Privately Held**
WEB: www.abelreels.com
SIC: 3451 3949 Screw machine products; reels, fishing

(P-7029)
ALGER PRECISION MACHINING LLC
724 S Bon View Ave, Ontario (91761-1913)
PHONE..................909 986-4591
Duane Femrite, *Principal*
Jeffrey Rowlette, *CIO*
Jeff Rowlette, *Information Mgr*
Maria Aguirre, *Accounting Mgr*
Carl Boyd, *Director*
▲ EMP: 160 EST: 1986
SQ FT: 35,000
SALES (est): 33.5MM **Privately Held**
WEB: www.algerprecision.com
SIC: 3451 Screw machine products

(P-7030)
ALPHA OMEGA SWISS INC
23305 La Palma Ave, Yorba Linda (92887-4773)
PHONE..................714 692-8009
Dale La Rock, *President*
Randy L Jones, *Vice Pres*
Robert Palmer, *General Mgr*
EMP: 18 EST: 1980
SQ FT: 15,500
SALES (est): 1.4MM **Privately Held**
WEB: www.alphaomegaswiss.com
SIC: 3451 3599 Screw machine products; machine shop, jobbing & repair

(P-7031)
ANWRIGHT CORPORATION
10225 Glenoaks Blvd, Pacoima (91331-1605)
P.O. Box 330940 (91333-0940)
PHONE..................818 896-2465
Lloyd Anderson, *President*
David Richardson, *Vice Pres*
Elva Guadiana, *Bookkeeper*
Carol Lane, *Purch Mgr*
Roy Burnett, *QC Mgr*
EMP: 48 EST: 1968
SQ FT: 15,000
SALES (est): 3.9MM **Privately Held**
WEB: www.anwright.com
SIC: 3451 3599 Screw machine products; machine shop, jobbing & repair

(P-7032)
ATHANOR GROUP INC
921 E California St, Ontario (91761-1918)
PHONE..................909 467-1205
Duane L Femrite, *President*
Richard Krause, *Vice Pres*
EMP: 17 EST: 1958
SQ FT: 35,600
SALES (est): 180.2K **Privately Held**
SIC: 3451 Screw machine products

(P-7033)
COLUMBIA SCREW PRODUCTS INC
3403 S Main St Unit B, Santa Ana (92707-4325)
PHONE.................714 549-1171
William E Gorham, *President*
Dolores Gorham, *Treasurer*
Candy Gorham, *Manager*
EMP: 20 **EST:** 1954
SALES (est): 800K **Privately Held**
SIC: 3451 Screw machine products

(P-7034)
CRELLIN MACHINE COMPANY
Also Called: BT Screw Products
114 W Elmyra St, Los Angeles (90012-1819)
PHONE.................323 225-8101
Richard Kirkendall, *President*
EMP: 21 **EST:** 1900
SQ FT: 22,000
SALES (est): 404.3K **Privately Held**
SIC: 3451 3541 Screw machine products; machine tools, metal cutting type

(P-7035)
FASTENER INNOVATION TECH INC
Also Called: F I T
19300 S Susana Rd, Compton (90221-5711)
PHONE.................310 538-1111
Larry Valeriano, *President*
Irma Preston, *Purch Agent*
EMP: 99 **EST:** 1979
SQ FT: 65,000
SALES (est): 20.6MM
SALES (corp-wide): 140.1MM **Privately Held**
WEB: www.fitfastener.com
SIC: 3451 3728 3452 3429 Screw machine products; aircraft parts & equipment; bolts, nuts, rivets & washers; manufactured hardware (general)
HQ: Avantus Aerospace, Inc.
29101 The Old Rd
Valencia CA 91355
661 295-8620

(P-7036)
GLENCO MANUFACTURING COMPANY
707 S Hope Ave, Ontario (91761-1826)
PHONE.................909 984-3348
Fax: 909 988-5970
EMP: 50
SQ FT: 15,027
SALES (est): 8.8MM **Privately Held**
WEB: www.glencomfg.com
SIC: 3451 Mfg Screw Machine Products

(P-7037)
GT PRECISION INC
Also Called: Alard Machine Products
1629 W 132nd St, Gardena (90249-2005)
PHONE.................310 323-4374
Gregg Thompson, *CEO*
Andrew Lozano, *Planning*
Emiliano Barajas, *Supervisor*
Francisco Garcia, *Supervisor*
Mike Guizar, *Supervisor*
▲ **EMP:** 107
SQ FT: 11,700
SALES (est): 23MM **Privately Held**
WEB: www.alardmachine.com
SIC: 3451 Screw machine products

(P-7038)
M & R ENGINEERING CO
227 E Meats Ave, Orange (92865-3311)
PHONE.................714 991-8480
Natalia Sephton, *President*
Maureen Derseweh, *General Mgr*
EMP: 15 **EST:** 1973
SQ FT: 32,000
SALES (est): 4MM **Privately Held**
WEB: www.m-reng.com
SIC: 3451 3541 Screw machine products; lathes; lathes, metal cutting & polishing

(P-7039)
ONYX INDUSTRIES INC (PA)
Also Called: Quad R Tech
1227 254th St, Harbor City (90710-2912)
PHONE.................310 539-8830
Vladimir Reil, *CEO*
Ed Oberg, *Officer*
Babamet Sharma, *Technology*
Frank Kova, *Plant Mgr*
▲ **EMP:** 100
SQ FT: 30,000
SALES (est): 14.5MM **Privately Held**
WEB: www.studex.com
SIC: 3451 Screw machine products

(P-7040)
ONYX INDUSTRIES INC
521 W Rosecrans Ave, Gardena (90248-1514)
PHONE.................310 851-6161
Siamak Maghoul, *Branch Mgr*
Frank Kova, *Plant Mgr*
Qiana Phelps, *Manager*
EMP: 100
SALES (corp-wide): 14.5MM **Privately Held**
WEB: www.onyxindustries.com
SIC: 3451 Screw machine products
PA: Onyx Industries Inc.
1227 254th St
Harbor City CA 90710
310 539-8830

(P-7041)
PRECISION TECHNOLOGY AND MFG
3147 Durahart St, Riverside (92507-3463)
PHONE.................951 788-0252
Jose Pompa, *President*
Lorraine Pagones, *Corp Secy*
Juan Pompa, *Vice Pres*
EMP: 25 **EST:** 1987
SQ FT: 9,000
SALES (est): 645.5K **Privately Held**
WEB: www.p-t-c.com
SIC: 3451 3643 Screw machine products; contacts, electrical

(P-7042)
PRICE MANUFACTURING CO INC
372 N Smith Ave, Corona (92878-4371)
P.O. Box 1209 (92878-1209)
PHONE.................951 371-5660
Robert P Schiffmacher, *CEO*
Ively Schiffmacher, *Corp Secy*
EMP: 32 **EST:** 1979
SQ FT: 15,600
SALES (est): 4.2MM **Privately Held**
WEB: www.pricemfg.com
SIC: 3451 Screw machine products

(P-7043)
R&R MACHINE PRODUCTS INC
760 W Mill St, San Bernardino (92410-3348)
PHONE.................909 885-7500
Eric Reiser, *President*
Belinda Reiser, *Corp Secy*
Karl Reiser, *Vice Pres*
EMP: 18 **EST:** 1980
SQ FT: 5,000
SALES (est): 1MM **Privately Held**
SIC: 3451 3643 Screw machine products; electric connectors

(P-7044)
SORENSON ENGINEERING INC (PA)
32032 Dunlap Blvd, Yucaipa (92399-1767)
PHONE.................909 795-2434
David L Sorenson, *President*
Paul Sewell, *Principal*
Robert Lunderville, *Design Engr*
Grant Feenstra, *Engineer*
Christopher Richardson, *Engineer*
◆ **EMP:** 169 **EST:** 1956
SQ FT: 61,000
SALES (est): 45.3MM **Privately Held**
WEB: www.sorensoneng.com
SIC: 3451 Screw machine products

(P-7045)
SWISS-MICRON INC
22361 Gilberto Ste A, Rcho STA Marg (92688-2103)
PHONE.................949 589-0430
Kurt Sollberger, *CEO*
Beverley Sollberger, *Vice Pres*
Wayne Twigg, *Finance*
Casey Colliflower, *Purch Mgr*
Alan McManus, *Prdtn Mgr*
EMP: 53 **EST:** 1984
SQ FT: 16,000 **Privately Held**
WEB: www.swissmicron.com
SIC: 3451 Screw machine products

(P-7046)
TL MACHINE INC
14272 Commerce Dr, Garden Grove (92843-4942)
PHONE.................714 554-4154
Thanh X Ly, *President*
Thanh Ly, *President*
Quynh Nguyen, *Executive*
Tuyen Ly, *Admin Sec*
Kevin Nguyen, *Data Proc Exec*
▲ **EMP:** 90 **EST:** 2001
SQ FT: 39,126
SALES (est): 20.8MM **Privately Held**
WEB: www.tlmachine.com
SIC: 3451 3561 3593 3728 Screw machine products; pumps & pumping equipment; fluid power cylinders & actuators; aircraft parts & equipment; aircraft; guided missiles & space vehicles

(P-7047)
TRIUMPH PRECISION PRODUCTS
Also Called: TP Products
13636 Vaughn St Ste A, San Fernando (91340-3052)
PHONE.................818 897-4700
Victor Linares, *President*
Javier Cervantes, *Vice Pres*
Jesus Cervantes, *Admin Sec*
EMP: 20 **EST:** 1967
SQ FT: 19,500
SALES (est): 1MM **Privately Held**
SIC: 3451 Screw machine products

(P-7048)
UNIVERSAL SCREW PRODUCTS
20421 Earl St, Torrance (90503-2414)
P.O. Box 14241 (90503-8241)
PHONE.................310 371-1170
Ken Shank, *President*
Michael Flannigan, *Admin Sec*
EMP: 17 **EST:** 1970
SQ FT: 6,000
SALES (est): 330.8K **Privately Held**
SIC: 3451 Screw machine products

(P-7049)
V M P INC
24830 Avenue Tibbitts, Valencia (91355-3404)
PHONE.................661 294-9934
Betty Schreiner, *President*
Steve Schreiner, *Treasurer*
Robert Schreiner Jr, *Vice Pres*
Suzanne St George, *Admin Sec*
Lisa Romero, *Director*
▲ **EMP:** 16 **EST:** 1960
SQ FT: 25,000
SALES (est): 2.4MM **Privately Held**
WEB: www.vmpinc.com
SIC: 3451 Screw machine products

(P-7050)
WESTERN SCREW PRODUCTS INC
11770 Slauson Ave, Santa Fe Springs (90670-2269)
PHONE.................562 698-5793
Lester P Kovats, *President*
William Doolittle, *Corp Secy*
Margaret K Doolittle, *Vice Pres*
Lester Kovats, *Vice Pres*
Steve Kovats, *Vice Pres*
EMP: 50 **EST:** 1940
SQ FT: 30,000
SALES (est): 5.3MM **Privately Held**
WEB: www.westernscrew.com
SIC: 3451 Screw machine products

(P-7051)
WYATT PRECISION MACHINE INC
3301 E 59th St, Long Beach (90805-4503)
PHONE.................562 634-0524
Dennis Allison, *President*
Allen Harmon, *Vice Pres*
Paul Layton, *Vice Pres*
EMP: 47 **EST:** 1952
SQ FT: 14,000
SALES (est): 4.8MM **Privately Held**
WEB: www.wyattprecisionmachine.com
SIC: 3451 Screw machine products

(P-7052)
ZENITH SCREW PRODUCTS INC
10910 Painter Ave, Santa Fe Springs (90670-4552)
P.O. Box 2747 (90670-0747)
PHONE.................562 941-0281
Kenneth Miller, *President*
Donald S Miller, *Ch of Bd*
Connie Miller, *Treasurer*
Keith L Miller, *Vice Pres*
EMP: 20 **EST:** 1953
SQ FT: 7,000
SALES (est): 2.2MM **Privately Held**
WEB: www.zspinc.com
SIC: 3451 Screw machine products

3452 Bolts, Nuts, Screws, Rivets & Washers

(P-7053)
3-V FASTENER CO INC
630 E Lambert Rd, Brea (92821-4119)
PHONE.................949 888-7700
Peter George, *CEO*
Jacqueline Ramos, *Human Resources*
Wayne Ysol, *QC Dir*
Robert Cantillo, *Supervisor*
EMP: 56 **EST:** 1982
SQ FT: 18,500
SALES (est): 13.5MM
SALES (corp-wide): 14.5B **Publicly Held**
WEB: www.camaerospace.com
SIC: 3452 Bolts, metal; nuts, metal; screws, metal
HQ: Consolidated Aerospace Manufacturing, Llc
1425 S Acacia Ave
Fullerton CA 92831
714 989-2797

(P-7054)
A J FASTENERS INC
Also Called: Pacific Hardware Sales
2800 E Miraloma Ave, Anaheim (92806-1803)
PHONE.................714 630-1556
Lawrence Roa, *President*
▲ **EMP:** 20 **EST:** 1975
SQ FT: 15,000
SALES (est): 2.4MM **Privately Held**
WEB: www.ajfasteners.com
SIC: 3452 5072 3429 Screws, metal; screws; metal stampings

(P-7055)
ANILLO INDUSTRIES INC (PA)
2090 N Glassell St, Orange (92865-3306)
P.O. Box 5586 (92863-5586)
PHONE.................714 637-7000
Kurt Hilton Koch, *President*
Mark Koch, *Vice Pres*
David Hultquist, *Manager*
EMP: 27 **EST:** 1957
SQ FT: 80,000
SALES (est): 6.4MM **Privately Held**
WEB: www.anilloinc.com
SIC: 3452 3325 3499 3429 Washers; bushings, cast steel; except investment; shims, metal; manufactured hardware (general)

(P-7056)
B&B HARDWARE INC
Also Called: Sealtight Technology
5370 Hollister Ave Ste 2, Santa Barbara (93111-2399)
P.O. Box 60840 (93160-0840)
PHONE.................805 683-6700
Larry Bogatz, *President*

PRODUCTS & SVCS

Diana Bogatz, *Vice Pres*
▲ **EMP:** 15 **EST:** 1990
SQ FT: 4,000
SALES (est): 1.4MM **Privately Held**
WEB: www.sealtighttechnology.com
SIC: 3452 5085 Bolts, nuts, rivets & washers; industrial supplies

(P-7057)
BLUE CIRCLE CORP
7520 Monroe St, Paramount (90723-4922)
PHONE..................................562 531-2711
Ronald E Anderson, *President*
Chris Anderson, *Vice Pres*
Jeffrey Anderson, *Vice Pres*
Walda Anderson, *Admin Sec*
EMP: 15 **EST:** 1971
SQ FT: 13,000
SALES (est): 1.4MM **Privately Held**
SIC: 3452 3365 Bolts, metal; aluminum & aluminum-based alloy castings

(P-7058)
BRILES AEROSPACE INC
1559 W 135th St, Gardena (90249-2219)
PHONE..................................310 701-2087
Michael P Briles, *President*
EMP: 95 **EST:** 2012
SQ FT: 22,000
SALES (est): 900K **Privately Held**
WEB: www.brilesaerospace.com
SIC: 3452 Bolts, nuts, rivets & washers

(P-7059)
BUTLER INC
2140 S Dupont Dr, Anaheim (92806-6101)
PHONE..................................310 323-3114
John Hollern, *President*
Cynthia Hollern, *Vice Pres*
EMP: 16 **EST:** 1974
SALES (est): 505.5K **Privately Held**
WEB: www.butlerbolt.com
SIC: 3452 Bolts, metal

(P-7060)
CBS FASTENERS INC
1345 N Brasher St, Anaheim (92807-2046)
PHONE..................................714 779-6368
Vic Luna, *President*
Michael Seibert, *Partner*
Gerald Bozarth, *President*
Machado Rosa, *Info Tech Dir*
Nathanial Luna, *Director*
EMP: 49 **EST:** 1978
SQ FT: 10,400
SALES (est): 7.1MM **Privately Held**
WEB: www.cbsfasteners.com
SIC: 3452 Bolts, metal; screws, metal

(P-7061)
CYI PINS LTD
6211 Sierra Ave Ste 147, Fontana (92336-1216)
PHONE..................................626 600-9017
Leslie Chen, *Principal*
EMP: 15
SALES (est): 586.5K **Privately Held**
SIC: 3452 Pins

(P-7062)
DOUBLECO INCORPORATED
Also Called: R & D Fasteners
9444 9th St, Rancho Cucamonga (91730-4509)
P.O. Box 250, Upland (91785-0250)
PHONE..................................909 481-0799
Craig Scheu, *President*
Miguel Rojas, *Manager*
EMP: 100
SQ FT: 30,000
SALES (est): 25.6MM **Privately Held**
WEB: www.rdfast.com
SIC: 3452 5072 Bolts, metal; bolts

(P-7063)
DUNCAN BOLT CO
5555 E Gibralter, Ontario (91764-5121)
PHONE..................................909 581-6740
Brent Dooley, *Manager*
EMP: 13
SALES (corp-wide): 29.5MM **Privately Held**
WEB: www.duncanbolt.com
SIC: 3452 Bolts, nuts, rivets & washers

PA: Duncan Bolt Co.
8535 Dice Rd
Santa Fe Springs CA 90670
562 698-8800

(P-7064)
DUPREE INC
Also Called: Stake Fastener
14395 Ramona Ave, Chino (91710-5740)
P.O. Box 1797 (91708-1797)
PHONE..................................909 597-4889
Jim Pon, *President*
James D Dupree, *Vice Pres*
Deborah Stewart, *Sales Executive*
▲ **EMP:** 31 **EST:** 1958
SQ FT: 60,000
SALES (est): 5.4MM **Privately Held**
WEB: www.dupreeinc.com
SIC: 3452 6512 Bolts, metal; gate hooks; commercial & industrial building operation

(P-7065)
FEDERAL MANUFACTURING CORP
9825 De Soto Ave, Chatsworth (91311-4412)
PHONE..................................818 341-9825
Helen Rainey, *President*
Arthur Rainey, *President*
Paul Rainey, *Vice Pres*
Collyn Rankin, *Engineer*
Steve Rainey, *Sales Staff*
EMP: 42 **EST:** 1951
SQ FT: 36,000
SALES (est): 7.9MM **Privately Held**
WEB: www.federalmanufacturing.com
SIC: 3452 3812 3462 3429 Bolts, metal; search & navigation equipment; iron & steel forgings; manufactured hardware (general)

(P-7066)
HI-SHEAR CORPORATION (DH)
2600 Skypark Dr, Torrance (90505-5373)
PHONE..................................310 784-4025
Christian Darville, *CEO*
▲ **EMP:** 600 **EST:** 1943
SQ FT: 180,000
SALES (est): 224.1MM
SALES (corp-wide): 177.9K **Privately Held**
WEB: www.hi-shear.com
SIC: 3452 3429 Bolts, nuts, rivets & washers; aircraft hardware
HQ: Lisi Aerospace
42 A 52
Paris 75012
140 198-200

(P-7067)
HUCK INTERNATIONAL INC
Also Called: Arconic Fastening Systems
900 E Watson Center Rd, Carson (90745-4201)
PHONE..................................310 830-8200
Jim Dawn, *Manager*
Willie Charukul, *Engineer*
Sanja Stajic, *Senior Mgr*
Hai-Tao Wang, *Manager*
EMP: 203
SALES (corp-wide): 5.2B **Publicly Held**
SIC: 3452 Nuts, metal
HQ: Huck International, Inc.
3724 E Columbia St
Tucson AZ 85714
520 519-7400

(P-7068)
INSTRUMENT BEARING FACTORY USA
19360 Rinaldi St, Northridge (91326-1607)
PHONE..................................818 989-5052
EMP: 50
SQ FT: 30,000
SALES (est): 2.6MM **Privately Held**
SIC: 3452 5085 Bolts, Nuts, Rivets, And Washers

(P-7069)
JW MANUFACTURING INC
Also Called: Arconic Fstening Systems Rings
12989 Bradley Ave, Sylmar (91342-3830)
PHONE..................................805 498-4594
Jacob Wood, *President*
▲ **EMP:** 21 **EST:** 1943
SQ FT: 40,000

SALES (est): 525.3K **Privately Held**
SIC: 3452 5072 Nuts, metal; bolts, nuts & screws

(P-7070)
MS AEROSPACE INC
13928 Balboa Blvd, Sylmar (91342-1086)
PHONE..................................818 833-9095
Michel Szostak, *CEO*
Jerome Taieb, *CFO*
James Cole, *Vice Pres*
Jim Cole, *Vice Pres*
Michelle Szostak, *VP Bus Dvlpt*
EMP: 302 **EST:** 1992
SALES (est): 86.2MM **Privately Held**
WEB: www.msaerospace.com
SIC: 3452 3728 Bolts, nuts, rivets & washers; aircraft parts & equipment

(P-7071)
NYLOK LLC
Also Called: Nylok Western Fastener
313 N Euclid Way, Anaheim (92801-6738)
PHONE..................................714 635-3993
Scott Plantiga, *Manager*
Miguel Sanchez, *Business Dir*
Nick Moore, *CIO*
Lillian Perez, *QC Mgr*
David Deanda, *Mfg Staff*
EMP: 45
SALES (corp-wide): 32.2MM **Privately Held**
WEB: www.nylok.com
SIC: 3452 Bolts, nuts, rivets & washers
PA: Nylok, Llc
15260 Hallmark Ct
Macomb MI 48042
586 786-0100

(P-7072)
POWER FASTENERS INC
650 E 60th St, Los Angeles (90001-1012)
P.O. Box 512056 (90051-0056)
PHONE..................................323 232-4362
Patrick Harrington, *President*
▲ **EMP:** 30 **EST:** 1991
SQ FT: 35,000
SALES (est): 2.8MM **Privately Held**
WEB: www.041d6c8.netsolhost.com
SIC: 3452 3448 Bolts, nuts, rivets & washers; prefabricated metal components

(P-7073)
RISCO INC
390 Risco Cir, Beaumont (92223-2676)
PHONE..................................951 769-2899
Joseph A Frainee II, *CEO*
Cynthia R Frainee, *Vice Pres*
Lisa Frainee, *Vice Pres*
Michael Wilcox, *Opers Staff*
Claudette Sousa, *Assistant VP*
EMP: 30 **EST:** 1964
SQ FT: 30,000
SALES (est): 6.4MM **Privately Held**
WEB: www.risco-fasteners.com
SIC: 3452 Bolts, metal; rivets, metal

(P-7074)
SCHRILLO COMPANY LLC
16750 Schoenborn St, North Hills (91343-6192)
PHONE..................................818 894-8241
Edward Schrillo, *Mng Member*
Donna Talamantez, *Treasurer*
Anthony Schrillo, *Exec VP*
Jeri Nowlen, *Admin Sec*
Alex Harris, *Project Mgr*
▲ **EMP:** 40
SQ FT: 60,000
SALES (est): 8.8MM **Privately Held**
WEB: www.schrillo.com
SIC: 3452 Screws, metal

(P-7075)
SPS TECHNOLOGIES LLC
Air Industries
12570 Knott St, Garden Grove (92841-3932)
PHONE..................................714 892-5571
Michael Wu, *Controller*
Erik Harsch, *Purch Mgr*
EMP: 50
SALES (corp-wide): 245.5B **Publicly Held**
WEB: www.pccfasteners.com
SIC: 3452 Bolts, metal

HQ: Sps Technologies, Llc
301 Highland Ave
Jenkintown PA 19046
215 572-3000

(P-7076)
STUD WELDING SYSTEMS INC
15306 Proctor Ave, City of Industry (91745-1023)
PHONE..................................626 330-7434
Gary Edward, *CEO*
EMP: 18 **EST:** 1967
SALES (est): 759.7K **Privately Held**
SIC: 3452 3548 Rivets, metal; welding apparatus

(P-7077)
SUNLAND AEROSPACE FASTENERS
12920 Pierce St, Pacoima (91331-2526)
PHONE..................................818 485-8929
Jack Wilson, *CEO*
EMP: 45 **EST:** 2012
SQ FT: 11,000
SALES (est): 4.9MM **Privately Held**
WEB: www.sunlandaerospace.com
SIC: 3452 Bolts, nuts, rivets & washers

(P-7078)
TROJAN RIVET
1835 Dana St, Glendale (91201-2044)
PHONE..................................818 245-1065
Debbie Kukta, *President*
EMP: 14 **EST:** 2010
SALES (est): 402.5K **Privately Held**
WEB: www.nationalrivet.com
SIC: 3452 Bolts, nuts, rivets & washers

(P-7079)
TWIST TITE MFG INC
13344 Cambridge St, Santa Fe Springs (90670-4904)
PHONE..................................562 229-0990
Spiro Aykias, *CEO*
Martha Leonard, *Admin Mgr*
EMP: 32 **EST:** 1994
SQ FT: 18,200
SALES (est): 4.5MM **Privately Held**
WEB: www.twisttite.com
SIC: 3452 Bolts, nuts, rivets & washers

(P-7080)
VALLEY-TODECO INC (DH)
Also Called: Arconic Fastening Systems
12975 Bradley Ave, Sylmar (91342-3852)
PHONE..................................800 992-4444
Jim Cotello, *President*
▲ **EMP:** 120 **EST:** 1995
SQ FT: 105,000
SALES (est): 38.6MM
SALES (corp-wide): 5.2B **Publicly Held**
SIC: 3452 5085 Bolts, nuts, rivets & washers; fasteners, industria; nuts, bolts, screws, etc.
HQ: Howmet Global Fastening Systems Inc.
3990a Heritage Oak Ct
Simi Valley CA 93063
805 426-2270

3462 Iron & Steel Forgings

(P-7081)
ADVANCED STRUCTURAL TECH INC
Also Called: Asa
950 Richmond Ave, Oxnard (93030-7212)
PHONE..................................805 204-9133
Robert Melsness, *President*
Douglas Jones, *Treasurer*
Benjamin Konrad, *Vice Pres*
April Pence, *Engineer*
Dawn Fowler, *Human Res Mgr*
▼ **EMP:** 135 **EST:** 2009
SALES (est): 36.3MM **Privately Held**
WEB: www.astforgetech.com
SIC: 3462 Aircraft forgings, ferrous

(P-7082)
AJAX FORGE COMPANY (PA)
1956 E 48th St, Vernon (90058-2006)
PHONE..................................323 582-6307
Fred Goble, *President*
Steve Mc Elrath, *Shareholder*

Carol Mc Neal, *Controller*
EMP: 19 **EST:** 1939
SQ FT: 10,000
SALES (est): 2.6MM **Privately Held**
WEB: www.ajaxforge.com
SIC: 3462 Iron & steel forgings

(P-7083)
CONTINENTAL FORGE COMPANY (PA)
412 E El Segundo Blvd, Compton (90222-2317)
PHONE..........................310 603-1014
Margaret A Haueisen, *CEO*
Marilyn Larick, *Info Tech Mgr*
Ramon Sandoval, *Human Res Mgr*
Walter Viera, *Sales Mgr*
EMP: 100 **EST:** 1968
SQ FT: 27,000
SALES (est): 19.7MM **Privately Held**
WEB: www.cforge.com
SIC: 3462 Iron & steel forgings

(P-7084)
ESCO INDUSTRIES INC
1755 Iowa Ave Bldg A, Riverside (92507-0525)
P.O. Box 52568 (92517-3568)
PHONE..........................951 782-2130
Chung LI Lin, *President*
Mark McClendon, *Sales Mgr*
▲ **EMP:** 15 **EST:** 1990
SALES (est): 47.1MM **Privately Held**
WEB: www.escousa.com
SIC: 3462 Automotive & internal combustion engine forgings

(P-7085)
FIRTH RIXSON INC
11711 Arrow Rte, Rancho Cucamonga (91730-4902)
PHONE..........................909 483-2200
EMP: 21
SALES (corp-wide): 23.9B **Publicly Held**
SIC: 3462 Mfg Iron/Steel Forgings
HQ: Firth Rixson, Inc.
   1616 Harvard Ave 53
   Newburgh Heights OH 44105
   860 760-1040

(P-7086)
FORGED METALS INC
Also Called: Arconic Fstening Systems Rings
10685 Beech Ave, Fontana (92337-7212)
PHONE..........................909 350-9260
Torben Kaese, *CEO*
Scott Burdette, *Sales Mgr*
◆ **EMP:** 200 **EST:** 1982
SQ FT: 4,800
SALES (est): 55.8MM
SALES (corp-wide): 5.2B **Publicly Held**
WEB: www.arconic.com
SIC: 3462 Iron & steel forgings
PA: Howmet Aerospace Inc.
   201 Isabella St Ste 200
   Pittsburgh PA 15212
   412 553-1950

(P-7087)
INDEPENDENT FORGE COMPANY
692 N Batavia St, Orange (92868-1221)
PHONE..........................714 997-7337
Rosemary Ruiz, *President*
Joe Ramirez, *Vice Pres*
Gloria Lopez, *Admin Sec*
Patricia Taoipu, *Analyst*
Andrew Flores, *Sales Staff*
▲ **EMP:** 40 **EST:** 1975
SQ FT: 11,900
SALES (est): 4.9MM **Privately Held**
WEB: www.independentforge.com
SIC: 3462 Iron & steel forgings

(P-7088)
IRONWOOD FABRICATION INC
Also Called: SOUTH COAST IRON
215 Industry Ave, La Habra (90631-6817)
PHONE..........................714 576-7320
Sean Michael, *President*
Sean D Michael, *Principal*
EMP: 18 **EST:** 2018
SALES (est): 1.2MM **Privately Held**
WEB: www.ironwoodfabrication.com
SIC: 3462 1791 Iron & steel forgings; structural steel erection

(P-7089)
JAZ DISTRIBUTION INC
8485 Artesia Blvd Ste B, Buena Park (90621-4195)
PHONE..........................714 521-3888
Tavis Tan, *President*
Mark Uchinao, *Vice Pres*
▲ **EMP:** 15 **EST:** 1999
SALES (est): 915.3K **Privately Held**
SIC: 3462 5013 Railroad wheels, axles, frogs or other equipment: forged; automotive supplies & parts

(P-7090)
KIMS WELDING AND IRON WORKS
Also Called: Kim's Fence
2331 E Orangethorpe Ave, Fullerton (92831-5330)
PHONE..........................714 680-7700
David S Kim, *President*
EMP: 19 **EST:** 1982
SQ FT: 5,000
SALES (est): 714.4K **Privately Held**
WEB: www.kimironworks.com
SIC: 3462 1799 Ornamental metal forgings, ferrous; welding on site

(P-7091)
MATTCO FORGE INC (HQ)
16443 Minnesota Ave, Paramount (90723-4985)
PHONE..........................562 634-8635
Robert Lewis, *President*
Andrew Fite, *CFO*
David Garcia, *Engineer*
Steven Saari, *Engineer*
Diana Marin, *Analyst*
▲ **EMP:** 50 **EST:** 1998
SQ FT: 150,000
SALES (est): 11.1MM
SALES (corp-wide): 18.6MM **Privately Held**
WEB: www.mattcoforge.com
SIC: 3462 Iron & steel forgings
PA: Mattco Forge Holdings, Llc
   16443 Minnesota Ave
   Paramount CA 90723
   562 634-8635

(P-7092)
PACIFIC FORGE INC
10641 Etiwanda Ave, Fontana (92337-6991)
PHONE..........................909 390-0701
Ronald D Browne, *President*
Jacqueline Dyer, *Vice Pres*
Debby Croulet, *Controller*
Roger Griffin, *Sales Staff*
John P Silk, *Sales Staff*
EMP: 55 **EST:** 1955
SQ FT: 34,816
SALES (est): 11.4MM
SALES (corp-wide): 474.5MM **Privately Held**
WEB: www.pacificforge.com
SIC: 3462 3463 Iron & steel forgings; nonferrous forgings
PA: Avis Industrial Corporation
   1909 S Main St
   Upland IN 46989
   765 998-8100

(P-7093)
PARAMOUNT FORGE INC
1721 E Colon St, Wilmington (90744-2210)
P.O. Box 205 (90748-0205)
PHONE..........................323 775-6803
Donald Ferguson, *President*
EMP: 20 **EST:** 1962
SALES (est): 1.6MM **Privately Held**
SIC: 3462 Iron & steel forgings

(P-7094)
PERFORMANCE FORGE INC
7401 Telegraph Rd, Montebello (90640-6500)
PHONE..........................323 722-3460
Wayne Ramay, *President*
Kevin Ramay, *Business Mgr*
EMP: 30 **EST:** 2012
SALES (est): 4.6MM **Privately Held**
WEB: www.performance-forge.com
SIC: 3462 Iron & steel forgings

(P-7095)
PREMIER GEAR & MACHINING INC
2360 Pomona Rd, Corona (92878-4329)
P.O. Box 2799 (92878-2799)
PHONE..........................951 278-5505
Steve Golden, *President*
Huy Nguyen, *Treasurer*
Edward Florian, *Purchasing*
Marshall Jarnagan, *Purchasing*
David Diaz, *Clerk*
EMP: 25 **EST:** 1986
SQ FT: 21,000
SALES (est): 5.2MM **Privately Held**
WEB: www.premiergearinc.com
SIC: 3462 3599 Iron & steel forgings; machine shop, jobbing & repair

(P-7096)
PRESS FORGE COMPANY
7700 Jackson St, Paramount (90723-5073)
P.O. Box 1432 (90723-1432)
PHONE..........................562 531-4962
Jeffrey M Carlton, *CEO*
Michael Buxton, *President*
Mike Buxton, *President*
▲ **EMP:** 80 **EST:** 1978
SQ FT: 32,726
SALES (est): 21MM
SALES (corp-wide): 245.5B **Publicly Held**
WEB: www.pressforge.com
SIC: 3462 Iron & steel forgings
HQ: Precision Castparts Corp.
   4650 Sw Mcdam Ave Ste 300
   Portland OR 97239
   503 946-4800

(P-7097)
RUBICON GEAR INC
225 Citation Cir, Corona (92878-5023)
PHONE..........................951 356-3800
Cheryl A Edwards, *Ch of Bd*
Ryan B Edwards, *President*
Randy Palinski, *Vice Pres*
Frank Salazar, *Admin Sec*
Trevor Riordan, *Engineer*
EMP: 68 **EST:** 1970
SQ FT: 25,000
SALES (est): 10MM **Privately Held**
WEB: www.rubicon-gear.com
SIC: 3462 Gears, forged steel

(P-7098)
SCODAN SYSTEMS INC
12373 Barringer St, South El Monte (91733-4141)
PHONE..........................626 444-1020
Eric Yang, *President*
Hector Pinedo, *Vice Pres*
EMP: 17 **EST:** 2003
SQ FT: 10,000
SALES (est): 1.1MM **Privately Held**
SIC: 3462 Automotive & internal combustion engine forgings

(P-7099)
TIMKEN GEARS & SERVICES INC
Also Called: Philadelphia Gear
12935 Imperial Hwy, Santa Fe Springs (90670-4715)
PHONE..........................310 605-2600
Tony Tartaglio, *Branch Mgr*
EMP: 19
SALES (corp-wide): 3.5B **Publicly Held**
WEB: www.philagear.com
SIC: 3462 Gear & chain forgings; gears, forged steel; anchors, forged
HQ: Timken Gears & Services Inc.
   935 1st Ave Ste 200
   King Of Prussia PA 19406

(P-7100)
VALLEY FORGE ACQUISITION CORP
444 S Motor Ave, Azusa (91702-3231)
PHONE..........................626 969-8701
Michael K Holmes, *President*
Michael Holmes, *President*
EMP: 15
SQ FT: 37,000

SALES (est): 3.3MM
SALES (corp-wide): 50.8MM **Privately Held**
WEB: www.tuffli.com
SIC: 3462 Iron & steel forgings
PA: Tuffli Company Incorporated
   2245 W 190th St
   Torrance CA 90504
   310 326-4747

(P-7101)
VI-STAR GEAR CO INC
7312 Jefferson St, Paramount (90723-4094)
PHONE..........................323 774-3750
Thomas R Redfield, *President*
Chris Redfield, *Treasurer*
Pete Gutierrez, *General Mgr*
EMP: 30 **EST:** 1960
SQ FT: 12,000
SALES (est): 3.4MM **Privately Held**
WEB: www.vistargear.com
SIC: 3462 3728 Iron & steel forgings; gears, aircraft power transmission

3463 Nonferrous Forgings

(P-7102)
ALUM-ALLOY CO INC
603 S Hope Ave, Ontario (91761-1824)
PHONE..........................909 986-0410
David Howell, *CEO*
Clark Howell, *President*
Marilyn Howell, *Treasurer*
EMP: 40 **EST:** 1961
SQ FT: 20,000
SALES (est): 3MM **Privately Held**
WEB: www.alumalloy.com
SIC: 3463 3365 Aluminum forgings; aluminum foundries

(P-7103)
LINDSEY MANUFACTURING CO
Also Called: Lindsey Systems
760 N Georgia Ave, Azusa (91702-2249)
P.O. Box 877 (91702-0877)
PHONE..........................626 969-3471
Keith E Lindsey, *President*
Frederick Findley, *CFO*
Lela Lindsey, *Admin Sec*
Sergio Cortez, *Project Engr*
Marwa Elsahragty, *Project Engr*
▲ **EMP:** 110 **EST:** 1947
SQ FT: 60,000
SALES (est): 25.2MM **Privately Held**
WEB: www.lindsey-usa.com
SIC: 3463 3644 Pole line hardware forgings, nonferrous; noncurrent-carrying wiring services

(P-7104)
LUXFER INC
Superform USA
6825 Jurupa Ave, Riverside (92504-1039)
PHONE..........................951 351-4100
Michael Reynolds, *Vice Pres*
Greg Cope, *Finance*
EMP: 38
SALES (corp-wide): 378MM **Privately Held**
WEB: www.luxfercylinders.com
SIC: 3463 Aluminum forgings
HQ: Luxfer Inc.
   3016 Kansas Ave Bldg 1
   Riverside CA 92507
   951 684-5110

(P-7105)
QUALITY ALUMINUM FORGE LLC
793 N Cypress St, Orange (92867-6605)
PHONE..........................714 639-8191
Michael S Lipscomb,
Brian Valparaiso, *General Mgr*
Brian Pam, *Info Tech Dir*
Michelle Meyer, *Human Res Mgr*
Annette Stevens, *Buyer*
EMP: 230 **EST:** 2011
SALES (est): 55.3MM
SALES (corp-wide): 113.5MM **Publicly Held**
WEB: www.sifco.com
SIC: 3463 Aluminum forgings

PA: Sifco Industries, Inc.
970 E 64th St
Cleveland OH 44103
216 881-8600

(P-7106)
SIERRA ALLOYS COMPANY
Also Called: STS Metals
5467 Ayon Ave, Irwindale (91706-2044)
PHONE..........................626 969-6711
Craig Culaciati, *CEO*
Jeff Augustyn, *Exec VP*
Ed Brennan, *Vice Pres*
Scott Brennan, *Sales Staff*
Zach Suddarth, *Sales Staff*
▲ **EMP:** 52 **EST:** 1974
SQ FT: 75,000
SALES (est): 17.2MM **Privately Held**
SIC: 3463 3494 3312 Nonferrous forgings; valves & pipe fittings; blast furnaces & steel mills

(P-7107)
SUPERFORM USA INCORPORATED
6825 Jurupa Ave, Riverside (92504-1039)
P.O. Box 5375 (92517-5375)
PHONE..........................951 351-4100
Michael Reynolds, *Vice Pres*
▼ **EMP:** 29 **EST:** 1985
SQ FT: 25,000
SALES (est): 5.3MM
SALES (corp-wide): 378MM **Privately Held**
WEB: www.neosintl.com
SIC: 3463 Aluminum forgings
HQ: Luxfer Inc.
3016 Kansas Ave Bldg 1
Riverside CA 92507
951 684-5110

(P-7108)
TURBINE ENG CMPNENTS TECH CORP
Also Called: Tech Powers
8839 Pioneer Blvd, Santa Fe Springs (90670-2007)
P.O. Box 2966 (90670-0966)
PHONE..........................562 908-0200
Ronald L Patlian, *Branch Mgr*
William McCormick, *Vice Chairman*
Alexander Terenzi, *Program Mgr*
Sami Hermes, *General Mgr*
John Johnston, *General Mgr*
EMP: 105
SALES (corp-wide): 232.9MM **Privately Held**
SIC: 3463 3599 Engine or turbine forgings, nonferrous; machine shop, jobbing & repair
PA: Turbine Engine Components Technologies Corporation
1211 Old Albany Rd
Thomasville GA 31792
229 228-2600

(P-7109)
WEBER METALS INC
16706 Garfield Ave, Paramount (90723-5315)
PHONE..........................562 602-0260
John R Creed, *CEO*
Paul Dennis, *CFO*
Paul R Dennis, *CFO*
Dawn Kazoleas, *Vice Pres*
Ricardo Guzman, *Technician*
◆ **EMP:** 500 **EST:** 1962
SQ FT: 270,000
SALES (est): 112.8MM
SALES (corp-wide): 3B **Privately Held**
WEB: www.webermetals.com
SIC: 3463 Aluminum forgings
PA: Otto Fuchs Beteiligungen Kg
Derschlager Str. 26
Meinerzhagen NW 58540
235 473-0

(P-7110)
WJB BEARINGS INC
535 Brea Canyon Rd, City of Industry (91789-3001)
PHONE..........................909 598-6238
John Jun Jiang, *CEO*
Josephine Chien, *Officer*
▲ **EMP:** 25 **EST:** 1992
SQ FT: 30,000

SALES (est): 4.4MM **Privately Held**
WEB: www.wjbbearing.com
SIC: 3463 5085 Bearing & bearing race forgings, nonferrous; bearings

3465 Automotive Stampings

(P-7111)
APOLLO METAL SPINNING CO INC
15315 Illinois Ave, Paramount (90723-4108)
PHONE..........................562 634-5141
George Di Matteo, *President*
Josephine Di Matteo, *Corp Secy*
Laura Rodriguez, *Manager*
EMP: 15 **EST:** 1968
SQ FT: 4,650 **Privately Held**
WEB: www.apollometalspinning.com
SIC: 3465 3469 5015 Hub caps, automobile: stamped metal; spinning metal for the trade; automotive parts & supplies, used

(P-7112)
ORIGINAL PARTS GROUP INC (PA)
Also Called: Chevelle Classics Parts & ACC
1770 Saturn Way, Seal Beach (90740-5618)
PHONE..........................562 594-1000
David Harry Leonard, *President*
Joe Rittel, *CFO*
Anthony M Genty, *Vice Pres*
Gus Stewart, *Vice Pres*
Steve Lekutis, *General Mgr*
▲ **EMP:** 86 **EST:** 1984
SQ FT: 100,000
SALES (est): 33.8MM **Privately Held**
WEB: www.opgi.com
SIC: 5531 3465 Automotive parts; body parts, automobile: stamped metal

(P-7113)
SALEEN AUTOMOTIVE INC (PA)
2735 Wardlow Rd, Corona (92882-2869)
PHONE..........................800 888-8945
Steve Saleen, *Ch of Bd*
Amy Boylan, *President*
David Fiene, *CFO*
EMP: 21 **EST:** 2011
SALES (est): 13.7MM **Publicly Held**
WEB: www.saleen.com
SIC: 3465 3711 Body parts, automobile: stamped metal; automobile assembly, including specialty automobiles; automobile bodies, passenger car, not including engine, etc.

(P-7114)
T-REX TRUCK PRODUCTS INC
Also Called: T-Rex Grilles
2365 Railroad St, Corona (92878-5411)
PHONE..........................800 287-5900
Behrouz Mizban, *President*
Paco Gonzalez, *Director*
Juan Crespo, *Supervisor*
▼ **EMP:** 55 **EST:** 1995
SQ FT: 45,000
SALES (est): 10MM **Privately Held**
WEB: www.trexbillet.com
SIC: 3465 Automotive stampings

(P-7115)
TROY SHEET METAL WORKS INC (PA)
Also Called: Troy Products
1024 S Vail Ave, Montebello (90640-6020)
PHONE..........................323 720-4100
Carl Moses Kahalewai, *CEO*
Paul Alvarado, *Shareholder*
Marci Norkin, *Shareholder*
Carol Stewart, *Shareholder*
Rigo Guadiana, *CFO*
EMP: 80 **EST:** 1930
SQ FT: 16,000
SALES (est): 16.2MM **Privately Held**
WEB: www.troyproducts.com
SIC: 3465 3444 3714 3564 Automotive stampings; sheet metalwork; motor vehicle parts & accessories; blowers & fans

3469 Metal Stampings, NEC

(P-7116)
A & J MANUFACTURING COMPANY
70 Icon, Foothill Ranch (92610-3000)
PHONE..........................714 544-9570
Barry Lyerly, *CEO*
Janice Lyerly, *Vice Pres*
Ian Amstedter, *Info Tech Dir*
Mike Gates, *Engineer*
EMP: 32
SQ FT: 40,000
SALES (est): 7.8MM **Privately Held**
WEB: www.aj-racks.com
SIC: 3469 Electronic enclosures, stamped or pressed metal

(P-7117)
A-W ENGINEERING COMPANY INC
8528 Dice Rd, Santa Fe Springs (90670-2590)
PHONE..........................562 945-1041
Guy Hansen, *President*
Anthony Giangrande, *Treasurer*
EMP: 36
SQ FT: 38,000
SALES (est): 8.2MM **Privately Held**
WEB: www.aw-eng.com
SIC: 3469 3544 Stamping metal for the trade; special dies & tools

(P-7118)
AAA STAMPING INC
1630 Shearwater St, Ontario (91761-5710)
P.O. Box 4027 (91761-1001)
PHONE..........................909 947-4151
Tom Hendrickson, *President*
Sal Chico, *Vice Pres*
EMP: 19 **EST:** 1974
SQ FT: 15,100
SALES (est): 3.6MM **Privately Held**
SIC: 3469 Stamping metal for the trade

(P-7119)
ACRONTOS MANUFACTURING INC
Also Called: Al Industries
1641 E Saint Gertrude Pl, Santa Ana (92705-5311)
PHONE..........................714 850-9133
Ngoc V Hoang, *President*
Daisy L Pierce, *Engineer*
EMP: 30 **EST:** 1991
SQ FT: 22,000
SALES (est): 5.1MM **Privately Held**
SIC: 3469 3599 3441 Stamping metal for the trade; machine & other job shop work; fabricated structural metal

(P-7120)
ACTION STAMPING INC
517 S Glendora Ave, Glendora (91741-6212)
P.O. Box 778 (91740-0778)
PHONE..........................626 914-7466
Henry Reynolds, *CEO*
Terry Reynolds, *President*
▲ **EMP:** 42 **EST:** 1982
SQ FT: 55,000
SALES (est): 3.1MM **Privately Held**
WEB: www.actionstamping.com
SIC: 3469 Stamping metal for the trade

(P-7121)
ALCO TECH INC
Also Called: Crome Gallery
12750 Raymer St Unit 2, North Hollywood (91605-4227)
PHONE..........................818 503-9209
Ben Tavakkoli, *President*
EMP: 21 **EST:** 2000
SALES (est): 1MM **Privately Held**
WEB: www.alcoproduction.com
SIC: 3469 3479 7692 4581 Metal stampings; painting, coating & hot dipping; welding repair; aircraft maintenance & repair services

(P-7122)
ALL NEW STAMPING CO
10801 Lower Azusa Rd, El Monte (91731-1307)
P.O. Box 5948 (91734-1948)
PHONE..........................626 443-8813
Donald Schuil, *President*
Robert Larson, *Corp Secy*
EMP: 150
SQ FT: 40,000
SALES: 13MM **Privately Held**
WEB: www.allnewstamping.com
SIC: 3469 3441 3444 Stamping metal for the trade; fabricated structural metal; sheet metal specialties, not stamped

(P-7123)
AMITY WASHER & STAMPING CO
10926 Painter Ave, Santa Fe Springs (90670-4529)
PHONE..........................562 941-1259
James M Mc Ginley, *President*
Nancy Wilson, *Admin Sec*
EMP: 14 **EST:** 1958
SQ FT: 15,000
SALES (est): 244.7K **Privately Held**
SIC: 3469 3544 Stamping metal for the trade; special dies, tools, jigs & fixtures

(P-7124)
APT METAL FABRICATORS INC
11164 Bradley Ave, Pacoima (91331-2405)
PHONE..........................818 896-7478
Dennis M Vigo, *President*
Susan Vigo, *Corp Secy*
Monica Gutierrez, *Site Mgr*
Tom Chindlund, *Plant Mgr*
Dennis Vigo, *Manager*
▼ **EMP:** 26 **EST:** 1975
SQ FT: 18,000
SALES (est): 2.7MM **Privately Held**
WEB: www.aptmetal.com
SIC: 3469 Stamping metal for the trade

(P-7125)
ASCENT MANUFACTURING LLC
2545 W Via Palma, Anaheim (92801-2624)
PHONE..........................714 540-6414
Travis Mullen, *CEO*
David Kramer, *VP Sales*
EMP: 34 **EST:** 2001
SQ FT: 17,000
SALES (est): 6.3MM **Privately Held**
WEB: www.ascentmfg.com
SIC: 3469 1796 Machine parts, stamped or pressed metal; machinery installation

(P-7126)
BANDEL MFG INC
4459 Alger St, Los Angeles (90039-1292)
PHONE..........................818 246-7493
Ed Finley, *President*
Chester Carlson, *Exec VP*
EMP: 23 **EST:** 1947
SQ FT: 15,000
SALES (est): 5.1MM **Privately Held**
WEB: www.bandel.com
SIC: 3469 Stamping metal for the trade

(P-7127)
BERRY-PERUSSI INC
Also Called: Associated Engineering Company
25131 Arctic Ocean Dr, Lake Forest (92630-8852)
P.O. Box 7 (92609-0007)
PHONE..........................949 461-7000
Roberto Perussi, *President*
Jerry Berry, *Vice Pres*
Ruben Perussi, *Admin Sec*
EMP: 40 **EST:** 1972
SQ FT: 4,600
SALES (est): 3.5MM **Privately Held**
SIC: 3469 Machine parts, stamped or pressed metal

(P-7128)
BINDER METAL PRODUCTS INC
14909 S Broadway, Gardena (90248-1817)
P.O. Box 2306 (90247-0106)
PHONE..........................800 233-0896
Steve Binder, *President*
Eric Bono, *COO*
Adam Binder, *General Mgr*
Ana Weber, *Controller*

Anna Weber, *Controller*
▲ **EMP:** 75 **EST:** 1925
SQ FT: 35,000
SALES (est): 18.3MM **Privately Held**
WEB: www.bindermetal.com
SIC: 3469 Stamping metal for the trade

(P-7129)
BLOOMERS METAL STAMPINGS INC
28615 Braxton Ave, Valencia (91355-4112)
PHONE....................661 257-2955
Matt Holland, *CEO*
Perry Bloomer, *President*
Ella H Bloomer, *CFO*
EMP: 30 **EST:** 1976
SQ FT: 25,000
SALES (est): 3.9MM **Privately Held**
WEB: www.bloomersmetal.com
SIC: 3469 Stamping metal for the trade

(P-7130)
BRAXTON CARIBBEAN MFG CO INC
2641 Walnut Ave, Tustin (92780-7005)
P.O. Box 425 (92781-0425)
PHONE....................714 508-3570
Thomas Ordway, *President*
Robert Dionne, *Principal*
Joesph Triano, *Principal*
EMP: 62 **EST:** 1972
SALES (est): 8.7MM **Privately Held**
WEB: www.braxtonmfg.com
SIC: 3469 Stamping metal for the trade

(P-7131)
BRICE TOOL & STAMPING
1170 N Van Home Way, Anaheim (92806-2506)
PHONE....................714 630-6400
Russel Brice, *President*
EMP: 15 **EST:** 1956
SQ FT: 10,000
SALES (est): 1.6MM **Privately Held**
WEB: www.bricetool.com
SIC: 3469 3544 Stamping metal for the trade; dies, steel rule

(P-7132)
C&C METAL FORM & TOOLING INC
Also Called: Promag
10654 Garfield Ave, South Gate (90280-7334)
PHONE....................562 861-9554
Chris Chiang, *President*
Kristina Kessler, *Sales Executive*
Drew Kelley, *Marketing Staff*
EMP: 13 **EST:** 1954
SALES (est): 2.7MM **Privately Held**
WEB: www.promagindustries.com
SIC: 3469 5941 3482 7389 Stamping metal for the trade; sporting goods & bicycle shops; small arms ammunition; design services

(P-7133)
CABRAC INC
13250 Paxton St, Pacoima (91331-2356)
PHONE....................818 834-0177
Hans Kaufmann, *President*
Sue Kaufmann, *Executive*
EMP: 20 **EST:** 1973
SQ FT: 20,000
SALES (est): 2.4MM **Privately Held**
WEB: www.cabrac.com
SIC: 3469 Electronic enclosures, stamped or pressed metal

(P-7134)
CAMISASCA AUTOMOTIVE MFG INC
20341 Hermana Cir, Lake Forest (92630-8701)
PHONE....................949 452-0195
Henry Camisasca, *CEO*
EMP: 20
SALES (corp-wide): 7.4MM **Privately Held**
WEB: www.camincusa.com
SIC: 3469 Automobile license tags, stamped metal

PA: Camisasca Automotive Manufacturing, Inc.
20352 Hermana Cir
Lake Forest CA 92630
949 452-0195

(P-7135)
CAMISASCA AUTOMOTIVE MFG INC (PA)
20352 Hermana Cir, Lake Forest (92630-8701)
PHONE....................949 452-0195
Henry Camisasca, *CEO*
Georgann Camisasca, *CFO*
Virginia Close, *Office Mgr*
Kody Gergis, *Engineer*
John Nowland, *Prdtn Mgr*
▲ **EMP:** 20 **EST:** 1982
SQ FT: 16,000
SALES (est): 7.4MM **Privately Held**
WEB: www.camincusa.com
SIC: 3469 Automobile license tags, stamped metal

(P-7136)
CKD INDUSTRIES INC
501 E Jamie Ave, La Habra (90631-6842)
PHONE....................714 871-5600
Rolf Hess, *President*
Rose Hess, *Vice Pres*
EMP: 19 **EST:** 1986
SQ FT: 15,000
SALES (est): 1.9MM **Privately Held**
SIC: 3469 8711 3544 Metal stampings; designing: ship, boat, machine & product; special dies & tools

(P-7137)
CUDOFORM INC
802 Calle Plano, Camarillo (93012-8557)
PHONE....................805 617-0818
Ryan Vallance, *CEO*
Elizabeth Lee, *CFO*
Robbie Slemaker, *Human Res Mgr*
EMP: 15 **EST:** 2019
SALES (est): 1.2MM **Privately Held**
SIC: 3469 Machine parts, stamped or pressed metal

(P-7138)
CYGNET STAMPNG & FABRICTNG INC
916 Western Ave, Glendale (91201-2353)
PHONE....................818 240-7574
Ron Ernst, *Manager*
Sandy Irwin, *Purchasing*
Scott McGrath, *Manager*
EMP: 20
SALES (corp-wide): 5MM **Privately Held**
WEB: www.cygnetstamping.com
SIC: 3469 Stamping metal for the trade
PA: Cygnet Stamping And Fabricating, Inc., A Swan Technologies Corporation
613 Justin Ave
Glendale CA 91201
818 240-7574

(P-7139)
CYGNET STAMPNG & FABRICTNG INC (PA)
613 Justin Ave, Glendale (91201-2326)
PHONE....................818 240-7574
Marko Swan, *President*
E Michael Swan, *Vice Pres*
John Swan, *Vice Pres*
Christyne Cerrie, *Manager*
EMP: 20 **EST:** 1976
SQ FT: 28,000
SALES (est): 5MM **Privately Held**
WEB: www.cygnetstamping.com
SIC: 3469 Stamping metal for the trade

(P-7140)
DAVID ENGINEERING & MFG INC
Also Called: David Engineering & Mfg
1230 Quarry St, Corona (92879-1708)
P.O. Box 77035 (92877-0101)
PHONE....................951 735-5200
Mike David, *CEO*
Michael David, *President*
Sarah Caoile, *Technology*
Dene Winstead, *Sales Staff*
EMP: 30 **EST:** 2003

SALES (est): 5MM **Privately Held**
WEB: www.davidengineering.com
SIC: 3469 3544 Stamping metal for the trade; special dies & tools

(P-7141)
DECCO GRAPHICS INC
24411 Frampton Ave, Harbor City (90710-2107)
PHONE....................310 534-2861
Harry B Line, *President*
Phil Kielty, *Cust Mgr*
EMP: 30 **EST:** 1979
SQ FT: 5,000
SALES (est): 3.8MM **Privately Held**
WEB: www.deccographics.com
SIC: 3469 2759 Stamping metal for the trade; commercial printing

(P-7142)
DIAMOND PERFORATED METALS INC
Also Called: Amico - Diamond Perforated
7300 W Sunnyview Ave, Visalia (93291-9605)
PHONE....................559 651-1889
Brian Lipke, *CEO*
Guy Anderson, *Vice Pres*
Joe Smith, *Vice Pres*
Stephen Seitz, *Sales Staff*
EMP: 78 **EST:** 1956
SQ FT: 80,000
SALES (est): 39.8MM
SALES (corp-wide): 1B **Publicly Held**
WEB: www.diamondperf.com
SIC: 3469 Perforated metal, stamped
PA: Gibraltar Industries, Inc.
3556 Lake Shore Rd # 100
Buffalo NY 14219
716 826-6500

(P-7143)
EAGLEWARE MANUFACTURING CO INC
12683 Corral Pl, Santa Fe Springs (90670-4748)
PHONE....................562 320-3100
Brett L Gross, *President*
Eric Gross, *Vice Pres*
▲ **EMP:** 32 **EST:** 1963
SQ FT: 130,000
SALES (est): 4MM **Privately Held**
SIC: 3469 3421 Stamping metal for the trade; household cooking & kitchen utensils, metal; cooking ware, except porcelain enamelled; cutlery

(P-7144)
ENTERPRISES INDUSTRIES INC
7500 Tyrone Ave, Van Nuys (91405-1447)
PHONE....................818 989-6103
Tony Magnome, *President*
Rolando Loera, *Ch of Bd*
Frank Ramirez III, *Vice Pres*
Livino D Ribaya Jr, *Vice Pres*
Charles E Shaw, *Vice Pres*
EMP: 130 **EST:** 1971
SALES (est): 10.1MM **Privately Held**
SIC: 3469 Stamping metal for the trade

(P-7145)
EXCEL INDUSTRIES INC
Also Called: Accu-Tek
1601 Fremont Ct, Ontario (91761-8309)
PHONE....................909 947-4867
William Kohout, *President*
EMP: 22 **EST:** 1975
SALES (est): 2.4MM **Privately Held**
WEB: www.accu-tekfirearms.com
SIC: 3469 3484 3542 3496 Metal stampings; small arms; machine tools, metal forming type; miscellaneous fabricated wire products

(P-7146)
GASKET MANUFACTURING ENGRG INC
8427 Secura Way, Santa Fe Springs (90670-2215)
PHONE....................310 217-5060
Ramon Cardenas, *CEO*
Juan Ramirez, *Principal*
Maureen Labor, *Director*
EMP: 16 **EST:** 2020

SALES (est): 1.6MM **Privately Held**
WEB: www.gasketmanufacturers.org
SIC: 3469 Metal stampings

(P-7147)
GLOBAL PCCI (GPC) (PA)
2465 Campus Dr Ste 100, Irvine (92612-1502)
PHONE....................757 637-9000
Sherri Bovino, *Partner*
Robert W Urban,
EMP: 120 **EST:** 1989
SQ FT: 10,000
SALES (est): 41.7MM **Privately Held**
SIC: 3469 4499 Metal stampings; salvaging, distressed vessels & cargoes

(P-7148)
GONZALEZ KITCHEN SUPPLIES INC (PA)
959 W State St Ste F, Ontario (91762-4102)
PHONE....................909 460-0581
Alfredo Gonzalez, *CEO*
EMP: 19 **EST:** 2008
SALES (est): 105.8K **Privately Held**
SIC: 3469 Household cooking & kitchen utensils, metal

(P-7149)
HANMAR LLC (PA)
Also Called: Metalite Manufacturing
11441 Bradley Ave, Pacoima (91331-2304)
PHONE....................818 890-2802
John Schachtner, *CEO*
Hannes Michael Schachtner, *CEO*
Joe Sauceda, *Program Mgr*
Joey Sauceda, *QC Mgr*
EMP: 88 **EST:** 1969
SQ FT: 25,000
SALES (est): 17MM **Privately Held**
WEB: www.hanmarllc.com
SIC: 3469 Spinning metal for the trade; stamping metal for the trade

(P-7150)
HOME PARADISE LLC
Also Called: Cabinet Home
10932 Klingerman St Ste C, El Monte (91733-2711)
PHONE....................626 284-9999
Jian Q Chen, *President*
Patrice Wang, *Mktg Dir*
▲ **EMP:** 17 **EST:** 2005
SALES (est): 3.2MM **Privately Held**
WEB: www.homeparadiserg.com
SIC: 3469 1799 Kitchen fixtures & equipment, porcelain enameled; kitchen fixtures & equipment: metal, except cast aluminum; kitchen & bathroom remodeling

(P-7151)
HOUSTON BAZZ CO
Also Called: Bazz Houston Co
12700 Western Ave, Garden Grove (92841-4017)
PHONE....................714 898-2666
Javier Castro, *President*
Chester O Houston, *Corp Secy*
Ray Mena, *Prgrmr*
Eric Pham, *Engineer*
Maziar Salimi, *Engineer*
▲ **EMP:** 85 **EST:** 1957
SQ FT: 50,000
SALES (est): 19.2MM **Privately Held**
WEB: www.bhisolutions.com
SIC: 3469 3495 3493 Machine parts, stamped or pressed metal; mechanical springs, precision; steel springs, except wire

(P-7152)
IMPERIAL CAL PRODUCTS INC
425 Apollo St, Brea (92821-3110)
PHONE....................714 990-9100
Shari Bittel, *President*
Kathy Flentye, *Vice Pres*
Armando Garay, *Opers Mgr*
Janet Dirisio, *Marketing Staff*
▲ **EMP:** 35 **EST:** 1961
SQ FT: 35,000
SALES (est): 3.8MM **Privately Held**
WEB: www.imperialhoods.com
SIC: 3469 Kitchen fixtures & equipment: metal, except cast aluminum

PRODUCTS & SVCS

(P-7153)
INNOVATIVE STAMPING INC
Also Called: Innovative Systems
2068 E Gladwick St, Compton
(90220-6202)
P.O. Box 5327 (90224-5327)
PHONE..........................310 537-6996
Gerald L Czaban, *President*
Kim Stevenson, *Vice Pres*
▼ EMP: 32 EST: 1976
SQ FT: 128,000
SALES (est): 5MM **Privately Held**
WEB: www.innovative-sys.com
SIC: 3469 Stamping metal for the trade

(P-7154)
IPT HOLDING INC (PA)
751 S Kellogg Ave, Goleta (93117-3806)
PHONE..........................805 683-3414
Stephen Braunheim, *President*
Ron Williams, *CFO*
EMP: 64 EST: 2002
SALES (est): 21.6MM **Privately Held**
WEB: www.intriplex.com
SIC: 3469 Stamping metal for the trade

(P-7155)
KAGA (USA) INC
2620 S Susan St, Santa Ana (92704-5816)
PHONE..........................714 540-2697
Masaaki Nozaki, *President*
Fumio Shiina, *Treasurer*
Takashi Nozaki, *Vice Pres*
Nobuharu Nozaki, *Admin Sec*
Asami Fujioka, *Accountant*
▲ EMP: 30 EST: 1981
SQ FT: 38,400
SALES (est): 6.3MM **Privately Held**
WEB: www.kagainc.com
PA: Kaga,Inc.
140, Ni, Ota, Tsubatamachi
Kahoku-Gun ISH 929-0

(P-7156)
KB DELTA INC
Also Called: KB Delta Comprsr Valve Parts
3340 Fujita St, Torrance (90505-4017)
PHONE..........................310 530-1539
Boris Giourof, *CEO*
Katarina Giourof, *Vice Pres*
Victor Guerra, *Manager*
Mauricio Rodriguez, *Manager*
◆ EMP: 37 EST: 1982
SQ FT: 5,500
SALES (est): 6.4MM **Privately Held**
WEB: www.kbdelta.com
SIC: 3469 5085 7699 Machine parts,
stamped or pressed metal; industrial sup-
plies; compressor repair

(P-7157)
KITCHEN EQUIPMENT MFG CO INC
Also Called: Kemco
2102 Maple Privado, Ontario (91761-7602)
PHONE..........................909 923-3153
David Rodriguez, *President*
EMP: 43 EST: 1984
SQ FT: 15,000
SALES (est): 7MM **Privately Held**
SIC: 3469 3431 Kitchen fixtures & equip-
ment, porcelain enameled; metal sanitary
ware

(P-7158)
KITCOR CORPORATION
9959 Glenoaks Blvd, Sun Valley
(91352-1085)
PHONE..........................323 875-2820
Kent Kitchen, *Principal*
Alice Kitchen, *Treasurer*
Bob Kitchen, *Vice Pres*
Jim Kitchen, *Vice Pres*
Kimberly Schulman, *Office Mgr*
EMP: 35
SQ FT: 42,000
SALES (est): 9.1MM **Privately Held**
WEB: www.kitcor.com
SIC: 3469 Kitchen fixtures & equipment:
metal, except cast aluminum

(P-7159)
KOPYKAKE ENTERPRISES INC (PA)
Also Called: Mayer Baking Co
3699 W 240th St, Torrance (90505-6002)
PHONE..........................310 373-8906
Gerald G Mayer, *President*
Greg Mayer, *Vice Pres*
Rick Mayer, *Vice Pres*
Gary A Newland, *Plant Mgr*
Bill Connelly, *Manager*
▲ EMP: 19 EST: 1970
SQ FT: 22,000
SALES (est): 9.5MM **Privately Held**
WEB: www.kopykake.com
SIC: 3469 2051 Kitchen fixtures & equip-
ment: metal, except cast aluminum; bak-
ery: wholesale or wholesale/retail
combined

(P-7160)
LARRY SPUN PRODUCTS INC
1533 S Downey Rd, Los Angeles
(90023-4042)
PHONE..........................323 881-6300
Hilario F Hurtado, *CEO*
George Acevedo, *Sales Dir*
EMP: 49 EST: 1958
SQ FT: 6,000
SALES (est): 7.5MM **Privately Held**
WEB: www.larryspunproducts.com
SIC: 3469 Spinning metal for the trade

(P-7161)
LOCK-RIDGE TOOL COMPANY INC
2000 Pomona Blvd, Pomona (91768-3323)
PHONE..........................909 865-8309
Keith Clark, *President*
Penney Clark, *Corp Secy*
Ashford Clark, *Vice Pres*
▲ EMP: 52 EST: 1962
SQ FT: 21,000
SALES (est): 9.9MM **Privately Held**
WEB: www.lockridgetool.com
SIC: 3469 Stamping metal for the trade

(P-7162)
LUPPEN HOLDINGS INC (PA)
Also Called: METAL PRODUCTS ENGI-
NEERING
3050 Leonis Blvd, Vernon (90058-2914)
PHONE..........................323 581-8121
Luppe R Luppen, *Ch of Bd*
Paula Luppen, *Treasurer*
Ray Woodmansee, *Vice Pres*
Raymond Woodmansee, *VP Engrg*
▲ EMP: 23 EST: 1940
SQ FT: 40,000
SALES (est): 688.3K **Privately Held**
WEB: www.metalproductseng.com
SIC: 3469 3578 3596 Stamping metal for
the trade; change making machines;
scales & balances, except laboratory

(P-7163)
MC WILLIAM & SON INC
Also Called: California Tool & Die
421 S Irwindale Ave, Azusa (91702-3217)
PHONE..........................626 969-1821
Dan McWilliam, *President*
Dana Matejka, *Corp Secy*
EMP: 19 EST: 1967
SQ FT: 26,000
SALES (est): 4.2MM **Privately Held**
WEB: www.californiatool-die.com
SIC: 3469 3544 Stamping metal for the
trade; special dies, tools, jigs & fixtures

(P-7164)
MC-KINLEY WELDING CORP
Also Called: Mc Welco Products
6730 Santa Fe Ave E, Hesperia
(92345-5768)
PHONE..........................760 244-8876
Riley E Mc Kinley Jr, *President*
James Mc Kinley, *Vice Pres*
EMP: 22 EST: 1945
SQ FT: 22,000
SALES (est): 2.7MM **Privately Held**
WEB: www.mcwelco.com
SIC: 3469 3499 Boxes: tool, lunch, mail,
etc.: stamped metal; safes & vaults, metal

(P-7165)
METCO MANUFACTURING INC
Also Called: Metco Fourslide Manufacturing
17540 S Denver Ave, Gardena
(90248-3411)
PHONE..........................310 516-6547
Jack Bishop, *President*
Dana Beisel, *Vice Pres*
Darryl Scholl, *Vice Pres*
Kathy Phipps, *Executive*
Amanda Trinidad, *Executive Asst*
EMP: 29 EST: 1980
SQ FT: 11,200
SALES (est): 4.8MM **Privately Held**
WEB: www.metcofourslide.com
SIC: 3469 Stamping metal for the trade

(P-7166)
MICRO MATRIX SYSTEMS (PA)
Also Called: M M S
1899 Salem Ct, Claremont (91711-2638)
PHONE..........................909 626-8544
Grant P Zarbock, *CEO*
Kerry Zarbock, *Vice Pres*
Kimberly Henderson, *Human Res Mgr*
▲ EMP: 24 EST: 1968
SALES (est): 2.7MM **Privately Held**
WEB: www.mmsys.biz
SIC: 3469 Stamping metal for the trade

(P-7167)
NANOPRECISION PRODUCTS INC
802 Calle Plano, Camarillo (93012-8557)
PHONE..........................310 597-4991
Michael K Barnoski, *CEO*
Ian Brown, *Info Tech Mgr*
Shawn Matsuda, *Technical Staff*
Meirong Shi, *Technical Staff*
Ren Yang, *Engineer*
EMP: 25 EST: 2002
SALES (est): 8.8MM **Privately Held**
WEB: www.nanoprecision.com
SIC: 3469 3721 Stamping metal for the
trade; research & development on aircraft
by the manufacturer

(P-7168)
NATIONAL METAL STAMPINGS INC
42110 8th St E, Lancaster (93535-5444)
PHONE..........................661 945-1157
William T Bloomer, *President*
Madeleine J Bloomer, *Corp Secy*
Tiffany Drake, *Vice Pres*
John Doyle, *General Mgr*
Irving Hernandez, *General Mgr*
▲ EMP: 70 EST: 1979
SQ FT: 20,000
SALES (est): 8.2MM **Privately Held**
WEB: www.nationalmetal.com
SIC: 3469 Stamping metal for the trade

(P-7169)
NELLXO LLC ✪
5990 Bald Eagle Dr, Fontana (92336-4573)
PHONE..........................909 320-8501
Shanelle Downs, *Mng Member*
EMP: 37 EST: 2021
SALES (est): 881.7K **Privately Held**
SIC: 3469 7389 Household cooking &
kitchen utensils, metal;

(P-7170)
ORANGE MTAL SPNNING STMPING IN
2601 Orange Ave, Santa Ana (92707-3724)
P.O. Box 80070, Rcho STA Marg (92688-
0070)
PHONE..........................714 754-0770
Mario Haber, *President*
Enrique Haber, *Vice Pres*
Elsa Haber, *Admin Sec*
EMP: 30 EST: 1984
SQ FT: 10,000
SALES (est): 1.1MM **Privately Held**
WEB: www.orangemetal.com
SIC: 3469 Stamping metal for the trade

(P-7171)
P P MFG CO INC
13130 Arctic Cir, Santa Fe Springs
(90670-5508)
PHONE..........................562 921-3640
Ronald Burr, *President*
Glenn Burr, *Treasurer*
EMP: 26 EST: 1948
SQ FT: 10,000
SALES (est): 3.7MM **Privately Held**
SIC: 3469 3544 Stamping metal for the
trade; special dies & tools

(P-7172)
PACIFIC METAL STAMPINGS INC
28415 Witherspoon Pkwy, Valencia
(91355-4174)
PHONE..........................661 257-7656
Brian Schlotfelt, *CEO*
Scott Schlotfelt, *Vice Pres*
▲ EMP: 30 EST: 1954
SQ FT: 21,000
SALES (est): 4MM **Privately Held**
WEB: www.pacificmetalstampings.com
SIC: 3469 Stamping metal for the trade

(P-7173)
PACIFIC PRECISION METALS INC
Also Called: Tubing Seal Cap Co
1100 E Orangethorpe Ave # 253, Anaheim
(92801-1164)
P.O. Box 51481, Ontario (91761-0081)
PHONE..........................951 226-1500
Ajay N Thakkar, *President*
EMP: 130 EST: 1941
SQ FT: 2,063
SALES (est): 24.7MM **Privately Held**
WEB: www.triyar.com
SIC: 3469 3429 2599 871 Stamping
metal for the trade; door locks, bolts &
checks; cabinets, factory; machine tool
design; metal household furniture
PA: Triyar Sv, Llc
10850 Wilshire Blvd
Los Angeles CA 90024

(P-7174)
PLATESCAN INC
20101 Sw Birch St Ste 250, Newport Beach
(92660-1770)
PHONE..........................949 851-1600
Robert Pinzler, *Vice Pres*
EMP: 14 EST: 2009 **Privately Held**
SIC: 3469 Automobile license tags,
stamped metal

(P-7175)
PRECISION STAMPG SOLUTIONS INC
500 Egan Ave, Beaumont (92223-2191)
PHONE..........................951 845-1174
EMP: 50
SALES (est): 11MM **Privately Held**
WEB: www.precisionstampinginc.com
SIC: 3469 Metal Stampings, Nec, Nsk

(P-7176)
PROFESSIONAL FINISHING SYSTEMS
Also Called: Pfs
12341 Gladstone Ave, Sylmar
(91342-5319)
PHONE..........................818 365-8888
Vern Coley, *CEO*
Pat Ramnarine, *Vice Pres*
EMP: 17 EST: 1980
SQ FT: 14,000
SALES (est): 3.1MM **Privately Held**
WEB: www.profinishing.com
SIC: 3469 5084 3471 Machine parts,
stamped or pressed metal; machine tools
& metalworking machinery; plating & pol-
ishing

(P-7177)
PROFORMANCE MANUFACTURING INC
1922 Elise Cir, Corona (92879-1882)
PHONE..........................951 279-1230
Robert Morales, *President*
Debbie Fox, *Info Tech Mgr*
EMP: 20 EST: 1987
SQ FT: 21,000

SALES (est): 3.6MM Privately Held
WEB: www.proformancemfg.com
SIC: 3469 3599 3451 3312 Machine parts, stamped or pressed metal; machine & other job shop work; screw machine products; blast furnaces & steel mills; special dies, tools, jigs & fixtures

(P-7178)
PROTOTYPE & SHORT-RUN SVCS INC
Also Called: Pass
1310 W Collins Ave, Orange (92867-5415)
PHONE..................714 449-9661
Jack Mc Devitt, *President*
John McDevitt, *General Mgr*
Lorene Schmdt, *Office Mgr*
Doug Eschen, *Admin Asst*
Florence Lulu Montoya, *Manager*
EMP: 25 EST: 1989
SQ FT: 6,700
SALES (est): 6MM Privately Held
WEB: www.prototype-shortrun.com
SIC: 3469 Stamping metal for the trade

(P-7179)
RSR METAL SPINNING INC
850 E Edna Pl, Covina (91723-1410)
PHONE..................626 814-2339
Russell Spencer, *President*
Jenny Spencer, *Admin Sec*
EMP: 16 EST: 1979
SQ FT: 6,800
SALES (est): 4.4MM Privately Held
WEB: www.rsrmetalspinning.net
SIC: 3469 Stamping metal for the trade

(P-7180)
SERRA MANUFACTURING CORP (PA)
3039 E Las Hermanas St, Compton (90221-5575)
PHONE..................310 537-4560
Sylvia G Hernandez, *Ch of Bd*
John B Hernandez, *Ch of Bd*
Kris Hernandez, *President*
Dominick Pellegrino, *CFO*
Roy Cerda, *Vice Pres*
EMP: 56 EST: 1959
SQ FT: 23,916
SALES: 616.3K Privately Held
WEB: www.serramfg.com
SIC: 3469 Stamping metal for the trade

(P-7181)
SESSA MANUFACTURING & WELDING
2932 Golf Course Dr, Ventura (93003-7689)
PHONE..................805 644-2284
Michael J Sessa, *CEO*
Lea Sessa, *Shareholder*
EMP: 47 EST: 1980
SQ FT: 15,500
SALES (est): 4.1MM Privately Held
WEB: www.sessamfg.com
SIC: 3469 Stamping metal for the trade

(P-7182)
SKM INDUSTRIES INC
Also Called: Job Shop Managers
28966 Hancock Pkwy, Valencia (91355-1069)
PHONE..................661 294-8373
Sanjeev Kapoor, *President*
▲ EMP: 14 EST: 1992
SQ FT: 4,300
SALES (est): 3.3MM Privately Held
WEB: www.skmindustries.com
SIC: 3469 Machine parts, stamped or pressed metal

(P-7183)
SPECIALTY INTERNATIONAL INC
11144 Penrose St Ste 11, Sun Valley (91352-5601)
PHONE..................818 768-8810
Anthony J Magnone, *President*
Jack McConnell, *Vice Pres*
▲ EMP: 41 EST: 1978
SALES (est): 1.7MM Privately Held
WEB: www.specialtyinternational.com
SIC: 3469 Metal stampings

(P-7184)
SUNSTONE COMPONENTS GROUP INC (HQ)
Also Called: Sun Stone Sales
42136 Avenida Alvarado, Temecula (92590-3400)
PHONE..................951 296-5010
Bradway B Adams, *CEO*
David Bernard, *CFO*
EMP: 57 EST: 1990
SALES (est): 15.2MM
SALES (corp-wide): 46.1MM Privately Held
WEB: www.4scg.com
SIC: 3469 Metal stampings
PA: Pancon Corporation
350 Revolutionary Dr
East Taunton MA 02718
781 297-6000

(P-7185)
TEAM MANUFACTURING INC
2625 Homestead Pl, Rancho Dominguez (90220-5610)
PHONE..................310 639-0251
Ed Ellis, *CEO*
Nancy Craig, *CFO*
James Cheatham, *Vice Pres*
Luis Almanza, *Manager*
▲ EMP: 50 EST: 1975
SQ FT: 34,000
SALES (est): 7.9MM Privately Held
WEB: www.teammfg.com
SIC: 3469 3544 Stamping metal for the trade; die sets for metal stamping (presses)

(P-7186)
TRU-FORM INDUSTRIES INC (PA)
Also Called: Tru Form Industries
14511 Anson Ave, Santa Fe Springs (90670-5393)
PHONE..................562 802-2041
Vernon M Hildebrandt, *CEO*
Vern Hildebrandt, *Info Tech Mgr*
Cindy Suer, *Human Res Mgr*
Dave Meek, *QC Mgr*
Mark Tiedeman, *Sales Executive*
▲ EMP: 68 EST: 1974
SQ FT: 50,000
SALES (est): 9.5MM Privately Held
WEB: www.tru-form.com
SIC: 3469 3496 3429 Metal stampings; clips & fasteners, made from purchased wire; manufactured hardware (general)

(P-7187)
USG CEILINGS PLUS LLC
6711 E Washington Blvd, Commerce (90040-1801)
PHONE..................323 724-8166
Nancy Mercolino, *President*
EMP: 27 EST: 2017
SALES (est): 9.6MM
SALES (corp-wide): 10.7B Privately Held
WEB: www.usg.com
SIC: 3469 Architectural panels or parts, porcelain enameled
HQ: Usg Corporation
550 W Adams St
Chicago IL 60661
312 436-4000

(P-7188)
VANGUARD TOOL & MFG CO INC
Also Called: Vanguard Tool & Manufacturing
8388 Utica Ave, Rancho Cucamonga (91730-3849)
PHONE..................909 980-9392
Robert A Scudder, *President*
Connie Scudder, *Vice Pres*
EMP: 49 EST: 1970
SQ FT: 47,000
SALES (est): 8.8MM Privately Held
WEB: www.vanguardtoolmfg.net
SIC: 3469 Stamping metal for the trade

(P-7189)
VERDUGO TOOL & ENGRG CO INC
20600 Superior St, Chatsworth (91311-4414)
PHONE..................818 998-1101
Kevin Gresiak, *President*
Keith Gresiak, *Vice Pres*
Johny Abarca, *Manager*
EMP: 19 EST: 1957
SQ FT: 15,000
SALES (est): 3.3MM Privately Held
WEB: www.verdugotool.com
SIC: 3469 3544 Stamping metal for the trade; special dies & tools

(P-7190)
VORWERK LLC
Also Called: Thermomix
3255 E Thousand Oaks Blvd B, Thousand Oaks (91362-3452)
PHONE..................805 413-0800
Louis Ross, *President*
EMP: 52 EST: 2016
SALES (est): 5.1MM
SALES (corp-wide): 3.2B Privately Held
WEB: www.corporate.vorwerk.com
SIC: 3469 Kitchen fixtures & equipment: metal, except cast aluminum
PA: Vorwerk Se & Co. Kg
Muhlenweg 17-37
Wuppertal NW 42275
202 564-0

(P-7191)
WALKER CORPORATION
1555 S Vintage Ave, Ontario (91761-3655)
P.O. Box 2146, Bakersfield (93303-2146)
PHONE..................909 390-4300
Randall Walker, *Vice Pres*
EMP: 47 EST: 2015
SALES (est): 9.6MM Privately Held
WEB: www.walkercorp.com
SIC: 3469 Stamping metal for the trade

(P-7192)
WALKER SPRING & STAMPING CORP
1555 S Vintage Ave, Ontario (91761-3655)
PHONE..................909 390-4300
Lang Walker, *Ch of Bd*
Bruce Walker, *President*
Carmen Prieto, *CFO*
Randy Walker, *Vice Pres*
James D Walker Jr, *VP Mfg*
▲ EMP: 110 EST: 1954
SQ FT: 108,000
SALES (est): 19.8MM Privately Held
SIC: 3469 3495 Stamping metal for the trade; precision springs

(P-7193)
WEST COAST MANUFACTURING INC
1822 Western Ave, Stanton (90680)
PHONE..................714 897-4221
Patrick Hundley, *President*
Minerva Hundley, *Vice Pres*
Ann Marie Lind, *Manager*
▲ EMP: 26
SQ FT: 8,000
SALES (est): 5.9MM Privately Held
WEB: www.westcoastmfg.com
SIC: 3469 Machine parts, stamped or pressed metal

(P-7194)
WEST COAST METAL STAMPING INC
550 W Crowther Ave, Placentia (92870-6312)
PHONE..................714 792-0322
Jerome R Reinhart, *President*
Dan A Totoiu, *Vice Pres*
Crystal Johnson, *Office Mgr*
EMP: 32 EST: 1966
SQ FT: 58,000
SALES (est): 5MM Privately Held
WEB: www.wcmetalstamping.com
SIC: 3469 Stamping metal for the trade

3471 Electroplating, Plating, Polishing, Anodizing & Coloring

(P-7195)
AAA PLATING & INSPECTION INC
424 E Dixon St, Compton (90222-1420)
PHONE..................323 979-8930
Gerald Wahlin, *CEO*
Charles Schwan, *Corp Secy*
Gladys Diaz, *Engineer*
Marie Reed, *Human Res Mgr*
Brenda Carrillo, *Purch Agent*
EMP: 95 EST: 1958
SQ FT: 50,000
SALES (est): 9.9MM Privately Held
WEB: www.aaaplating.com
SIC: 3471 8734 Anodizing (plating) of metals or formed products; metallurgical testing laboratory

(P-7196)
ACCURATE PLATING COMPANY
2811 Alcazar St, Los Angeles (90033-1108)
P.O. Box 33348 (90033-0348)
PHONE..................323 268-8567
Dennis Orr, *President*
Rigo Rodriguez, *Vice Pres*
EMP: 30 EST: 1949
SQ FT: 18,000
SALES (est): 3.4MM Privately Held
WEB: www.accurateplatingco.com
SIC: 3471 Electroplating of metals or formed products

(P-7197)
ACTIVE PLATING INC
1411 E Pomona St, Santa Ana (92705-4802)
PHONE..................714 547-0356
Keith Korta, *President*
EMP: 20 EST: 1984
SQ FT: 6,000
SALES (est): 1.5MM Privately Held
WEB: www.activeplating.com
SIC: 3471 Electroplating of metals or formed products

(P-7198)
ADVANCED TECH PLATING
1061 N Grove St, Anaheim (92806-2015)
PHONE..................714 630-7093
Meliton Gomez, *President*
Danny Gomez, *Sales Associate*
EMP: 15 EST: 2001
SQ FT: 9,706
SALES (est): 1.3MM Privately Held
SIC: 3471 Electroplating of metals or formed products

(P-7199)
AERO MFG & PLTG CO LLC
Also Called: Automation Plating
927 Thompson Ave, Glendale (91201-2011)
PHONE..................818 241-2844
William Wiggins, *Chairman*
Peter Wiggins, *Chairman*
Kaera Milano, *Marketing Staff*
EMP: 20 EST: 1958
SQ FT: 65,000
SALES (est): 920K Privately Held
WEB: www.apczinc.com
SIC: 3471 Electroplating of metals or formed products

(P-7200)
AERODYNAMIC PLATING CO
13620 S Saint Andrews Pl, Gardena (90249-2480)
PHONE..................310 329-7959
Joe Reynoso Jr, *President*
Joe Reynoso Sr, *Treasurer*
EMP: 22 EST: 1967
SQ FT: 5,500
SALES (est): 2MM Privately Held
SIC: 3471 Electroplating of metals or formed products

PRODUCTS & SVCS

(P-7201)
AGUILAR WILLIAMS INC
Also Called: Tool & Jig Plating Co
7635 Baldwin Pl, Whittier (90602-1024)
PHONE....................................562 693-2736
Jesus Aguilar, *President*
Michael Williams, *Treasurer*
Leonor Oropeza, *Admin Sec*
EMP: 15 **EST:** 1993
SALES (est): 1.1MM **Privately Held**
SIC: 3471 Electroplating of metals or
  formed products

(P-7202)
ALCO PLATING CORP (PA)
Also Called: Modern Plating
1400 Long Beach Ave, Los Angeles
(90021-2794)
PHONE....................................213 749-7561
E Edward Manzetti, *President*
Emil Edward Manzetti, *President*
David Manzetti, *Vice Pres*
▲ **EMP:** 50 **EST:** 1929
SQ FT: 65,000
SALES (est): 6.1MM **Privately Held**
WEB: www.alconickelchrome.com
SIC: 3471 Electroplating of metals or
  formed products

(P-7203)
ALERT PLATING COMPANY
9939 Glenoaks Blvd, Sun Valley
(91352-1023)
PHONE....................................818 771-9304
David La Liberte, *President*
Maurice La Liberte, *Ch of Bd*
Ed Lee, *Treasurer*
Mussaddiq Hussain, *Vice Pres*
Shirley La Liberte, *Admin Sec*
EMP: 45 **EST:** 1968
SQ FT: 22,000
SALES (est): 8.4MM **Privately Held**
SIC: 3471 Finishing, metals or formed
  products

(P-7204)
**ALL METALS PROC SAN DIEGO
INC**
Also Called: AMC
8401 Standustrial St, Stanton
(90680-2688)
PHONE....................................714 828-8238
EMP: 120
SQ FT: 27,000
SALES (est): 16.2MM **Privately Held**
WEB: www.allmetalsprocessing.com
SIC: 3471 3479 8734 Plating And Polish-
  ing

(P-7205)
**ALL MTALS PROC ORANGE
CNTY LLC**
8401 Standustrial St, Stanton
(90680-2619)
PHONE....................................714 828-8238
Scott Christman, *CFO*
Derek Watson, *Managing Prtnr*
Michael Coburn, *CEO*
Bob Wolfsberger, *Vice Pres*
Rose Blikian,
EMP: 125 **EST:** 2015
SALES (est): 19.3MM **Privately Held**
WEB: www.allmetalsprocessing.com
SIC: 3471 3479 8734 Electroplating of
  metals or formed products; enameling, in-
  cluding porcelain, of metal products; X-
  ray inspection service, industrial

(P-7206)
ALLBLACK CO INC
13090 Park St, Santa Fe Springs
(90670-4032)
PHONE....................................562 946-2955
Juan F Guerrero, *President*
Lorena Guerrero, *Corp Secy*
Jose Hernandez, *Plant Mgr*
▲ **EMP:** 39 **EST:** 1992
SQ FT: 12,000
SALES (est): 5.1MM **Privately Held**
WEB: www.allblackco-inc.com
SIC: 3471 Electroplating of metals or
  formed products

(P-7207)
**ALLIANCE CHEMICAL &
ENVMTL**
Also Called: Alliance Finishing and Mfg
1721 Ives Ave, Oxnard (93033-1866)
PHONE....................................805 385-3330
Mark Hyman, *President*
Heather Hyman, *Vice Pres*
Bill Morgan, *QC Mgr*
EMP: 16 **EST:** 1991
SQ FT: 15,600
SALES (est): 2.7MM **Privately Held**
WEB: www.alliance-finishing.com
SIC: 3471 Electroplating of metals or
  formed products

(P-7208)
**ALPHA POLISHING
CORPORATION (PA)**
Also Called: General Plating
1313 Mirasol St, Los Angeles
(90023-3108)
PHONE....................................323 263-7593
Alan Olick, *President*
Trinidad Gonzales, *Vice Pres*
Dilip Patel, *Office Mgr*
Luis Casillas, *Manager*
EMP: 60 **EST:** 1940
SQ FT: 7,500
SALES (est): 8.5MM **Privately Held**
WEB: www.generalplatingco.net
SIC: 3471 3911 Plating of metals or
  formed products; polishing, metals or
  formed products; pins (jewelry), precious
  metal

(P-7209)
ALUMIN-ART PLATING CO INC
803 W State St, Ontario (91762-4130)
PHONE....................................909 983-1866
David Rudy, *President*
Barbara Newman, *Treasurer*
Joyce Clements, *Vice Pres*
Jerry Newman, *Engineer*
Isaac Rudy, *Safety Mgr*
EMP: 15 **EST:** 1961
SQ FT: 6,500
SALES (est): 1MM **Privately Held**
WEB: www.anopros.com
SIC: 3471 Electroplating of metals or
  formed products

(P-7210)
ANADITE CAL RESTORATION TR
Also Called: Metal Finishing Division
10647 Garfield Ave, South Gate
(90280-7391)
P.O. Box 1399 (90280-1399)
PHONE....................................562 861-2205
Margie Gutierrez, *Branch Mgr*
EMP: 111
SALES (corp-wide): 1.6MM **Privately
Held**
SIC: 3471 Finishing, metals or formed
  products
PA: Anadite California Restoration Trust
    711 W Hurst Blvd
    Hurst TX 76053
    817 282-9171

(P-7211)
ANAPLEX CORPORATION
15547 Garfield Ave, Paramount
(90723-4033)
PHONE....................................714 522-4481
Carmen Campbell, *CEO*
Bernie Kerper, *President*
Julio Valdivieso, *Bd of Directors*
EMP: 48 **EST:** 1962
SQ FT: 38,000
SALES (est): 6MM **Privately Held**
WEB: www.anaplexcorp.com
SIC: 3471 Plating of metals or formed
  products; finishing, metals or formed
  products

(P-7212)
ANODIZING INDUSTRIES INC
5222 Alhambra Ave, Los Angeles
(90032-3403)
P.O. Box 32459 (90032-0459)
PHONE....................................323 227-4916
Eugene J Golling, *President*
Amir Afshar, *Vice Pres*
▲ **EMP:** 30 **EST:** 1980

SQ FT: 8,000
SALES (est): 4.3MM **Privately Held**
WEB: www.anodizingindustries.com
SIC: 3471 3479 2396 Anodizing (plating)
  of metals or formed products; cleaning,
  polishing & finishing; painting of metal
  products; automotive & apparel trimmings

(P-7213)
ANODYNE INC
2230 S Susan St, Santa Ana (92704-4493)
PHONE....................................714 549-3321
Ralph Adams, *President*
Patti Kientz, *Vice Pres*
Odon Figueroa, *General Mgr*
Erika Cortez, *Planning*
Gary Fox, *Director*
EMP: 49 **EST:** 1960
SQ FT: 30,000
SALES (est): 5.6MM **Privately Held**
WEB: www.anodyne.aero
SIC: 3471 8734 Anodizing (plating) of met-
  als or formed products; testing laborato-
  ries

(P-7214)
AQUARIAN COATINGS CORP
2244 N Pacific St, Orange (92865-2616)
PHONE....................................714 632-0230
Ronald Marquez, *President*
Rose Marquez, *Vice Pres*
Chris Brady, *Manager*
EMP: 14 **EST:** 1974
SALES (est): 1.2MM **Privately Held**
WEB: www.aquariancoatings.openfos.com
SIC: 3471 Electroplating of metals or
  formed products

(P-7215)
**ARTISTIC PLTG & MET FINSHG
INC**
2801 E Miraloma Ave, Anaheim
(92806-1804)
PHONE....................................619 661-1691
Kipton Kahler, *President*
EMP: 43 **EST:** 1992
SQ FT: 44,573
SALES (est): 1MM **Privately Held**
SIC: 3471 Chromium plating of metals or
  formed products

(P-7216)
ARTURO CAMPOS
Also Called: A&A Plating
796 Palmyrita Ave Ste B, Riverside
(92507-1824)
PHONE....................................951 300-2111
Arturo Campos, *Owner*
▼ **EMP:** 14 **EST:** 2007
SQ FT: 3,680
SALES (est): 1MM **Privately Held**
SIC: 3471 Plating of metals or formed
  products

(P-7217)
**ASSOCIATED PLATING
COMPANY**
9636 Ann St, Santa Fe Springs
(90670-2902)
PHONE....................................562 946-5525
Michael Evans, *President*
Jon Shulkin, *Shareholder*
Diane Crane, *Vice Pres*
Randy Roth, *Plant Engr*
Theresa Flores,
▲ **EMP:** 49 **EST:** 1952
SQ FT: 18,000
SALES (est): 4.2MM **Privately Held**
WEB: www.associatedplating.com
SIC: 3471 Finishing, metals or formed
  products; electroplating of metals or
  formed products

(P-7218)
**ASTRO CHROME AND POLSG
CORP**
8136 Lankershim Blvd, North Hollywood
(91605-1611)
PHONE....................................818 781-1463
Jesse Gonzalez, *President*
Eazi Tamen, *General Mgr*
EMP: 23 **EST:** 1981
SQ FT: 3,000

SALES (est): 1.3MM **Privately Held**
WEB: www.astropowdercoating.com
SIC: 3471 Plating of metals or formed
  products

(P-7219)
**AUTOMATION PLATING
CORPORATION**
927 Thompson Ave, Glendale
(91201-2011)
PHONE....................................323 245-4951
William D Wiggins, *Co-COB*
Peter K Wiggins, *CEO*
Pat Kinzy, *COO*
Marcia Mitchell, *CFO*
Edward Lee, *Admin Sec*
EMP: 40 **EST:** 1941
SQ FT: 65,000
SALES (est): 5MM **Privately Held**
WEB: www.apczinc.com
SIC: 3471 Plating of metals or formed
  products

(P-7220)
B & C PLATING CO
1507 S Sunol Dr, Los Angeles
(90023-4031)
PHONE....................................323 263-6757
Dick Patel, *President*
Suresh Sheth, *Admin Sec*
EMP: 17 **EST:** 1985
SQ FT: 10,000
SALES (est): 971.5K **Privately Held**
WEB: www.bandcplating.com
SIC: 3471 2899 Plating of metals or
  formed products; chemical preparations

(P-7221)
**BARRY AVENUE PLATING CO
INC**
2210 Barry Ave, Los Angeles (90064-1488)
PHONE....................................310 478-0078
Chuck Kearsley, *President*
Charles B Kearsley IV, *President*
Charles Kearsley, *CFO*
Ken Kearsley, *Vice Pres*
Kenneth F Kearsley, *Vice Pres*
▼ **EMP:** 88 **EST:** 1951
SQ FT: 26,000
SALES: 16.7MM **Privately Held**
WEB: www.barryavenueplating.com
SIC: 3471 Electroplating of metals or
  formed products

(P-7222)
BHC INDUSTRIES INC
239 E Greenleaf Blvd, Compton
(90220-4913)
PHONE....................................310 632-2000
Gary Barken, *President*
EMP: 25 **EST:** 2000
SQ FT: 20,000
SALES (est): 2.7MM **Privately Held**
WEB: www.barkenshardchrome.com
SIC: 3471 Electroplating of metals or
  formed products

(P-7223)
BLACK OXIDE INDUSTRIES INC
1745 N Orangethorpe Park, Anaheim
(92801-1139)
PHONE....................................714 870-9610
Pete Mata, *President*
Evelyn Mata, *Corp Secy*
Edward Mata, *Vice Pres*
EMP: 35 **EST:** 1974
SALES (est): 3.7MM **Privately Held**
WEB: www.blackoxideindustries.com
SIC: 3471 3479 Electroplating of metals or
  formed products; coating of metals &
  formed products

(P-7224)
**BLAIRS METAL POLSG PLTG CO
INC**
17760 Crusader Ave, Cerritos
(90703-2629)
PHONE....................................562 860-7106
Keith W Blair, *CEO*
Keith Blair, *Vice Pres*
EMP: 27 **EST:** 1950
SQ FT: 10,000

SALES (est): 1.2MM **Privately Held**
WEB: www.blairsmetalpolishing.net
SIC: **3471** Electroplating of metals or formed products

(P-7225)
BODYCOTE THERMAL PROC INC
3370 Benedict Way, Huntington Park (90255-4517)
PHONE...................323 583-1231
Chris Hall, *Branch Mgr*
EMP: 87
SQ FT: 16,694
SALES (corp-wide): 795.2MM **Privately Held**
WEB: www.bodycote.com
SIC: **3471 3398** Plating & polishing; metal heat treating
HQ: Bodycote Thermal Processing, Inc.
12750 Merit Dr Ste 1400
Dallas TX 75251
214 904-2420

(P-7226)
BOWMAN PLATING CO INC
2631 E 126th St, Compton (90222-1599)
P.O. Box 5205 (90224-5205)
PHONE...................310 639-4343
Mac Esfandi, *President*
John Esfandi, *Shareholder*
Cyrus Gipoor, *Shareholder*
Dan Cunningham, *Exec VP*
Brad Simpson, *Vice Pres*
EMP: 150 EST: 1952
SALES (est): 18.5MM **Privately Held**
WEB: www.bowmanplating.com
SIC: **3471** Electroplating of metals or formed products

(P-7227)
BRITE PLATING CO INC
1313 Mirasol St, Los Angeles (90023-3108)
PHONE...................323 263-7593
Alan Olick, *CEO*
Kashiam Patel, *Vice Pres*
EMP: 18 EST: 1950
SQ FT: 60,000
SALES (est): 1.1MM **Privately Held**
WEB: www.generalplatingco.net
SIC: **3471** Plating of metals or formed products

(P-7228)
BRONZE-WAY PLATING CORPORATION (PA)
3301 E 14th St, Los Angeles (90023-3893)
PHONE...................323 266-6933
Sarkis Mikhael-Fard, *President*
Benjamin Mikhael-Fard, *Vice Pres*
Fiyodor Mikhael-Fard, *Vice Pres*
Fred Mikhael-Fard, *Vice Pres*
EMP: 44 EST: 1956
SQ FT: 27,000
SALES (est): 3.2MM **Privately Held**
WEB: www.generalplatingco.net
SIC: **3471** Electroplating of metals or formed products

(P-7229)
BURBANK PLATING SERVICE CORP
13561 Desmond St, Pacoima (91331-2394)
PHONE...................818 899-1157
Robert Scheer, *President*
Andy Scheer, *Vice Pres*
Midge Churchill, *Bookkeeper*
▲ EMP: 17 EST: 1965
SQ FT: 20,000
SALES (est): 1.6MM **Privately Held**
WEB: www.burbankplating.com
SIC: **3471** Electroplating of metals or formed products

(P-7230)
BURLINGTON ENGINEERING INC
220 W Grove Ave, Orange (92865-3204)
PHONE...................714 921-4045
Karen Corbell, *President*
David Corbell, *Vice Pres*
EMP: 19 EST: 1979
SQ FT: 18,000

SALES (est): 1.5MM **Privately Held**
WEB: www.burlingtoneng.com
SIC: **3471 3398** Plating & polishing; metal heat treating

(P-7231)
C C M D INC
Also Called: Hytech Processing
700 Centinela Ave, Inglewood (90302-2414)
PHONE...................310 673-5532
Michael S Graves, *President*
Odette Graves, *CFO*
EMP: 23 EST: 1983
SQ FT: 7,000
SALES (est): 3MM **Privately Held**
WEB: www.hytechprocessing.com
SIC: **3471** Finishing, metals or formed products

(P-7232)
CADILLAC PLATING INC
1147 W Struck Ave, Orange (92867-3529)
PHONE...................714 639-0342
Adan Ibarra, *President*
Lupe Ibarra, *Treasurer*
Alfred Ibarra, *Assistant VP*
EMP: 21 EST: 1972
SQ FT: 6,000
SALES (est): 1.6MM **Privately Held**
WEB: www.cadillacplating.com
SIC: **3471** Plating of metals or formed products; electroplating of metals or formed products

(P-7233)
CAL-AURUM INDUSTRIES
15632 Container Ln, Huntington Beach (92649-1533)
PHONE...................714 898-0996
Paul A Ginder, *President*
Chuck Tygard, *Vice Pres*
Vern Marken, *Executive*
Jason Nations, *Purch Mgr*
Allison Hinkley, *Materials Mgr*
EMP: 35
SQ FT: 25,000
SALES (est): 4.8MM **Privately Held**
WEB: www.cal-aurum.com
SIC: **3471** Electroplating of metals or formed products

(P-7234)
CAL-TRON PLATING INC
11919 Rivera Rd, Santa Fe Springs (90670-2209)
PHONE...................562 945-1181
Carl Troncale Jr, *CEO*
Carl Troncale Sr, *Ch of Bd*
EMP: 45 EST: 1961
SQ FT: 15,000 **Privately Held**
WEB: www.cal-tronplating.com
SIC: **3471** Electroplating of metals or formed products; polishing, metals or formed products

(P-7235)
CALIFORNIA METAL PROCESSING CO
1518 W Slauson Ave # 1530, Los Angeles (90047-1230)
PHONE...................323 753-2247
Terry Andersen, *Partner*
Merry Anderson, *Ltd Ptnr*
Robert Gates, *Ltd Ptnr*
Thelma Gates, *Ltd Ptnr*
EMP: 20 EST: 1952
SQ FT: 10,800
SALES (est): 2.9MM **Privately Held**
WEB: www.calmetal.com
SIC: **3471 8734** Plating of metals or formed products; testing laboratories

(P-7236)
CARTER PLATING INC
1842 N Keystone St, Burbank (91504-3417)
PHONE...................818 842-1325
Val T Romney Sr, *President*
Earlene Romney, *Vice Pres*
EMP: 24 EST: 1953
SQ FT: 2,400
SALES (est): 1.9MM **Privately Held**
WEB: www.carterplating.com
SIC: **3471** Plating of metals or formed products

(P-7237)
CEMCOAT INC
4928 W Jefferson Blvd, Los Angeles (90016-3923)
PHONE...................323 733-0125
Farzaneh Aalam, *President*
Mike Aalam, *Vice Pres*
EMP: 27 EST: 1966
SQ FT: 14,500
SALES (est): 1.5MM **Privately Held**
WEB: www.cemcoat.com
SIC: **3471** Plating of metals or formed products

(P-7238)
CERTIFIED STEEL TREATING CORP
2454 E 58th St, Vernon (90058-3592)
PHONE...................323 583-8711
Janice Davis, *President*
Pauline Nicolls, *Shareholder*
Dante Germano, *CFO*
Jeff Davis, *General Mgr*
Chuck Groves, *General Mgr*
EMP: 42 EST: 1947
SQ FT: 30,000
SALES (est): 7.5MM **Privately Held**
SIC: **3471 3398** Sand blasting of metal parts; annealing of metal

(P-7239)
CHROMAL PLATING COMPANY
Also Called: Chromal Plating & Grinding
1748 Workman St, Los Angeles (90031-3395)
PHONE...................323 222-0119
Ethel Bokelman, *President*
Robin Osborn, *CFO*
Robin Ospoin, *CFO*
Robin Bokelman, *Corp Secy*
Ray F Bokelman Jr, *Vice Pres*
EMP: 28 EST: 1946
SQ FT: 20,625
SALES (est): 4.1MM **Privately Held**
WEB: www.chromal.com
SIC: **3471 3999** Electroplating of metals or formed products; custom pulverizing & grinding of plastic materials

(P-7240)
COAST TO COAST MET FINSHG CORP
401 S Raymond Ave, Alhambra (91803-1532)
PHONE...................626 282-2122
Gildardo Bernal, *President*
David Bernal, *Vice Pres*
Maria Diaz, *Office Mgr*
EMP: 25 EST: 1978
SQ FT: 20,000
SALES (est): 3.4MM **Privately Held**
WEB: www.ctclightingmfg.com
SIC: **3471 3646 3645** Finishing, metals or formed products; commercial indusl & institutional electric lighting fixtures; residential lighting fixtures

(P-7241)
COASTLINE METAL FINISHING CORP
7061 Patterson Dr, Garden Grove (92841-1414)
PHONE...................714 895-9099
Tracy Glende, *CEO*
Jamie Mitchell, *CFO*
Matthew Alty, *Vice Pres*
Rosa Vazquez, *Supervisor*
EMP: 83 EST: 1987
SQ FT: 18,600
SALES (est): 9.3MM **Privately Held**
WEB: www.valencesurfacetech.com
SIC: **3471** Finishing, metals or formed products; electroplating & plating; anodizing (plating) of metals or formed products

(P-7242)
CONNELL PROCESSING INC
3094 N Avon St, Burbank (91504-2003)
PHONE...................818 845-7661
Stephen Lee, *President*
David Augustine, *Vice Pres*
EMP: 27 EST: 1946
SQ FT: 25,000 **Privately Held**
WEB: www.connellprocessing.com

SIC: **3471** Electroplating of metals or formed products

(P-7243)
CONTINUOUS COATING CORP (PA)
Also Called: Clinch-On Cornerbead Company
520 W Grove Ave, Orange (92865-3210)
PHONE...................714 637-4642
Ralph M Scott, *President*
Kenneth N Harel, *Corp Secy*
EMP: 72
SQ FT: 84,000
SALES (est): 14MM **Privately Held**
WEB: www.continuouscoating.com
SIC: **3471 3444 7389** Electroplating of metals or formed products; sheet metal specialties, not stamped; metal slitting & shearing

(P-7244)
CP AUTO PRODUCTS INC
3901 Medford St, Los Angeles (90063-1608)
P.O. Box 63915 (90063-0915)
PHONE...................323 266-3850
Tom Longo, *President*
▲ EMP: 32 EST: 1955
SQ FT: 100,000
SALES (est): 1.2MM **Privately Held**
WEB: www.derale.com
SIC: **3471 3714 3564** Plating of metals or formed products; motor vehicle parts & accessories; blowers & fans

(P-7245)
DANCO ANODIZING INC (PA)
Also Called: Danco Metal Surfacing
44 La Porte St, Arcadia (91006-2827)
P.O. Box 660727 (91066-0727)
PHONE...................626 445-3303
Sherri Vivian Scherer, *President*
David Tatge, *Treasurer*
Ross Tiamson, *General Mgr*
George Saunders, *QC Mgr*
Lavaughn Daniel, *Marketing Mgr*
EMP: 40 EST: 1971
SQ FT: 10,000
SALES (est): 15.6MM **Privately Held**
WEB: www.danco.net
SIC: **3471** Electroplating of metals or formed products

(P-7246)
DANCO ANODIZING INC
1750 E Monticello Ct, Ontario (91761-7740)
PHONE...................909 923-0562
Joe Galvan, *Manager*
EMP: 102
SALES (corp-wide): 15.6MM **Privately Held**
WEB: www.danco.net
SIC: **3471** Anodizing (plating) of metals or formed products
PA: Danco Anodizing, Inc.
44 La Porte St
Arcadia CA 91006
626 445-3303

(P-7247)
DILLON AIRCRAFT DEBURRING INC
11771 Sheldon St, Sun Valley (91352-1506)
PHONE...................818 768-0801
Pedro Dillon, *President*
Consuelo Dillon, *Treasurer*
Alejandra Dillon, *Vice Pres*
EMP: 14 EST: 1993
SQ FT: 4,000
SALES (est): 613.2K **Privately Held**
SIC: **3471** Cleaning, polishing & finishing

(P-7248)
DUNHAM METAL PROCESSING CO
936 N Parker St, Orange (92867-5580)
P.O. Box 3736 (92857-0736)
PHONE...................714 532-5551
Charles H Dunham, *Owner*
EMP: 46 EST: 1960

PRODUCTS & SVCS

SALES (est): 1.9MM **Privately Held**
WEB: www.dunhammetalprocessing.com
SIC: 3471 2396 3341 Anodizing (plating) of metals or formed products; plating of metals or formed products; automotive & apparel trimmings; secondary nonferrous metals

(P-7249)
E M E INC
Also Called: Electro Machine & Engrg Co
500 E Pine St, Compton (90222-2818)
P.O. Box 4998 (90224-4998)
PHONE.....................310 639-1621
Wesley Turnbow, *CEO*
Steven Turnbow, *President*
Randy Turnbow, *Chairman*
Jesus Alanis, *Engineer*
Ricardo Osorio, *Opers Mgr*
EMP: 125 EST: 1962
SQ FT: 65,000
SALES (est): 13.5MM **Privately Held**
WEB: www.emeplating.com
SIC: 3471 2899 Anodizing (plating) of metals or formed products; chemical preparations

(P-7250)
ELECTRODE TECHNOLOGIES INC
Also Called: Reid Metal Finishing
3110 W Harvard St Ste 14, Santa Ana (92704-3940)
PHONE.....................714 549-3771
Tim A Grandcolas, *President*
Jose Ramirez, *Officer*
Susie Underwood, *General Mgr*
Ivan Padron, *Admin Sec*
Tim Grandcolas,
▲ EMP: 40 EST: 1978
SQ FT: 10,000
SALES (est): 5.9MM **Privately Held**
SIC: 3471 Finishing, metals or formed products

(P-7251)
ELECTROLIZING INC
1947 Hooper Ave, Los Angeles (90011-1354)
P.O. Box 11900 (90011-0900)
PHONE.....................213 749-7876
Susan B Grant, *President*
Jack Morgan, *Vice Pres*
Janet James, *Sales Staff*
Gary Kennard, *Maintence Staff*
EMP: 26 EST: 1947
SQ FT: 10,000
SALES (est): 3.5MM **Privately Held**
WEB: www.electrolizingofla.com
SIC: 3471 Electroplating of metals or formed products

(P-7252)
ELECTROLURGY INC
1121 Duryea Ave, Irvine (92614-5519)
PHONE.....................949 250-4494
Eron G Eklund, *President*
June Eklund, *Ch of Bd*
Sean Eklund, *Vice Pres*
Stefni Gritten, *Controller*
Trina McClain, *Controller*
EMP: 68 EST: 1969
SQ FT: 25,000
SALES (est): 13.3MM **Privately Held**
WEB: www.electrolurgy.com
SIC: 3471 3429 Electroplating of metals or formed products; anodizing (plating) of metals or formed products; polishing, metals or formed products; marine hardware

(P-7253)
ELECTROMATIC
14025 Stage Rd, Santa Fe Springs (90670-5225)
PHONE.....................562 623-9993
Diego Alvizo, *Manager*
EMP: 15
SALES (corp-wide): 3.7MM **Privately Held**
WEB: www.electromatic.com
SIC: 3471 Electroplating of metals or formed products

PA: Electromatic
789 S Kellogg Ave
Goleta CA 93117
805 964-9880

(P-7254)
ELECTRON PLATING III INC
13932 Enterprise Dr, Garden Grove (92843-4021)
PHONE.....................714 554-2210
Jose Luis Padilla Sr, *President*
Luis Padilla Sr, *President*
EMP: 30 EST: 1988
SQ FT: 10,000
SALES (est): 1.5MM **Privately Held**
WEB: www.electronplating.com
SIC: 3471 Electroplating of metals or formed products; plating of metals or formed products

(P-7255)
ELECTRONIC CHROME GRINDING INC
9128 Dice Rd, Santa Fe Springs (90670-2545)
PHONE.....................562 946-6671
Philip Reed, *President*
Jeannette Goble, *Corp Secy*
Dale Reed, *Vice Pres*
Mike Reed, *Vice Pres*
Debbie Scheibel, *Controller*
EMP: 22 EST: 1956
SQ FT: 55,000
SALES (est): 2.2MM **Privately Held**
WEB: www.ecgrinding.com
SIC: 3471 3599 Electroplating of metals or formed products; machine shop, jobbing & repair

(P-7256)
ELECTRONIC PRECISION SPC INC
545 Mercury Ln, Brea (92821-4831)
PHONE.....................714 256-8950
Henry Brown, *President*
EMP: 34 EST: 1980
SQ FT: 4,000
SALES (est): 4.6MM **Privately Held**
WEB: www.elecprec.com
SIC: 3471 Electroplating of metals or formed products

(P-7257)
ELITE METAL FINISHING LLC (PA)
540 Spectrum Cir, Oxnard (93030-8988)
PHONE.....................805 983-4320
Joe Hansen, *President*
Joel Clemons, *QC Mgr*
Greg Hansen, *Production*
George Hansen,
Sergio Rodriguez, *Manager*
EMP: 96 EST: 2001
SQ FT: 55,000
SALES (est): 20.1MM **Privately Held**
WEB: www.elitemetalfinishing.com
SIC: 3471 8734 Plating of metals or formed products; testing laboratories; metallurgical testing laboratory

(P-7258)
ELITE METAL FINISHING LLC
3430 Galaxy Pl, Oxnard (93030-8984)
PHONE.....................805 983-4320
EMP: 23
SALES (corp-wide): 20.1MM **Privately Held**
WEB: www.elitemetalfinishing.com
SIC: 3471 Electroplating of metals or formed products
PA: Elite Metal Finishing, L.L.C.
540 Spectrum Cir
Oxnard CA 93030
805 983-4320

(P-7259)
FINE QUALITY METAL FINSHG INC
1640 Daisy Ave, Long Beach (90813-1525)
PHONE.....................562 983-7425
Edna Bolour, *President*
Cy Gipoor, *Shareholder*
Manoucher Esfandi, *Treasurer*
EMP: 15 EST: 1981
SQ FT: 6,000

SALES (est): 2.5MM **Privately Held**
WEB: www.finequalitymetalfinishing.com
SIC: 3471 Electroplating of metals or formed products

(P-7260)
FLORENCE INTERNATIONAL CO INC
Also Called: Dixon Hard Chrome
11645 Pendleton St, Sun Valley (91352-2502)
PHONE.....................818 767-9650
Ronald Dixon, *President*
Donald Dixon, *Vice Pres*
Lawrence Dixon, *Vice Pres*
EMP: 24 EST: 1955
SQ FT: 15,000
SALES (est): 343.9K **Privately Held**
WEB: www.dixonhardchrome.com
SIC: 3471 8734 Plating of metals or formed products; chromium plating of metals or formed products; testing laboratories

(P-7261)
GCG CORPORATION
Also Called: Gcg Precision Metal Finishing
608 Ruberta Ave, Glendale (91201-2335)
PHONE.....................818 247-8508
Eugene Cockran, *President*
Gene Cockran, *Vice Pres*
EMP: 30 EST: 1966
SQ FT: 13,000
SALES (est): 1MM **Privately Held**
SIC: 3471 Electroplating of metals or formed products

(P-7262)
GEORGE INDUSTRIES
4116 Whiteside St, Los Angeles (90063-1619)
PHONE.....................323 264-6660
Jeff Briggs, *President*
EMP: 380 EST: 1953
SQ FT: 38,200
SALES (est): 55.4MM
SALES (corp-wide): 2.9B **Publicly Held**
WEB: www.valmontcoatings.com
SIC: 3471 3479 Anodizing (plating) of metals or formed products; cleaning & descaling metal products; plating of metals or formed products; aluminum coating of metal products
PA: Valmont Industries, Inc.
1 Valmont Plz Ste 500
Omaha NE 68154
402 963-1000

(P-7263)
GLOBAL METAL SOLUTIONS INC
2150 Mcgaw Ave, Irvine (92614-0912)
PHONE.....................949 872-2995
Mario Robles, *President*
Thomas Linovitz, *CFO*
Pamela Bennett, *Office Mgr*
Edgar Vargas, *QC Mgr*
EMP: 35 EST: 2016
SALES (est): 2.8MM **Privately Held**
WEB: www.gms1.net
SIC: 3471 Polishing, metals or formed products

(P-7264)
GRANATH & GRANATH INC
Also Called: Sonic Plating Company
1930 W Rosecrans Ave, Gardena (90249-2930)
P.O. Box 5387 (90249-5387)
PHONE.....................310 327-5740
Richard E Granath Jr, *President*
Richard E Granath Sr, *Vice Pres*
Tina Mc Vey, *Admin Sec*
EMP: 24 EST: 1964
SQ FT: 40,000
SALES (est): 1.3MM **Privately Held**
WEB: www.sonicplatingco.com
SIC: 3471 Anodizing (plating) of metals or formed products; plating of metals or formed products

(P-7265)
GSP METAL FINISHING INC
16520 S Figueroa St, Gardena (90248-2625)
PHONE.....................818 744-1328

Mike Palatas, *Vice Pres*
EMP: 35 EST: 2019
SALES (est): 3MM **Privately Held**
WEB: www.gspmf.com
SIC: 3471 Plating & polishing

(P-7266)
HENRYS METAL POLISHING INC
9856 Rush St, South El Monte (91733-2635)
PHONE.....................323 263-9701
Danny Reese, *President*
EMP: 14 EST: 1952
SALES (est): 1.4MM **Privately Held**
WEB: www.henrysmetalpolishing.com
SIC: 3471 Electroplating of metals or formed products

(P-7267)
HIGHTOWER PLATING & MFG CO
Also Called: Hightower Metals
2090 N Glassell St, Orange (92865-3306)
P.O. Box 5586 (92863-5586)
PHONE.....................714 637-9110
Kurt Koch, *President*
Mark Koch, *Vice Pres*
EMP: 50 EST: 1957
SQ FT: 8,000
SALES (est): 4.4MM **Privately Held**
SIC: 3471 Plating of metals or formed products

(P-7268)
HIXSON METAL FINISHING
829 Production Pl, Newport Beach (92663-2809)
PHONE.....................800 900-9798
Carl Blazik, *Principal*
Douglas Greene, *President*
Al Gonyer, *Managing Dir*
Tina Matinpour, *Executive Asst*
Tanya Cameron, *Admin Asst*
EMP: 143 EST: 1960
SQ FT: 38,000
SALES (est): 14.1MM **Privately Held**
WEB: www.hmfgroup.com
SIC: 3471 Finishing, metals or formed products

(P-7269)
INDUSTRIAL METAL FINISHING INC
1941 Petra Ln, Placentia (92870-6749)
PHONE.....................714 628-8808
Robert E Hayden, *President*
EMP: 26 EST: 1991
SQ FT: 12,000
SALES (est): 2.7MM **Privately Held**
WEB: www.indmetfin.com
SIC: 3471 3398 Finishing, metals or formed products; shot peening (treating steel to reduce fatigue)

(P-7270)
INTERNTIONAL PHOTO PLATES CORP
Also Called: Nanofilm
2641 Townsgate Rd Ste 100, Westlake Village (91361-2724)
PHONE.....................805 496-5031
Valdis Sneberg, *President*
Dale Burow, *Vice Pres*
Maria Flores, *Executive*
Dorothy Cesari, *Admin Sec*
Luis Flores, *Analyst*
▲ EMP: 38 EST: 1989
SQ FT: 8,000
SALES (est): 4.2MM **Privately Held**
SIC: 3471 2796 Plating & polishing; platemaking services

(P-7271)
INVECO INC
Also Called: Mighty Green
440 Fair Dr Ste 200, Costa Mesa (92626-6222)
PHONE.....................949 378-3850
Dennis D'Alessio, *President*
EMP: 30 EST: 2013
SALES (est): 18MM **Privately Held**
SIC: 3471 Cleaning, polishing & finishing

(P-7272)
J P TURGEON & SONS INC
7758 Scout Ave, Bell (90201-4942)
PHONE....................323 773-3105
David E Turgeon, *President*
Robert L Turgeon, *Treasurer*
Joseph Phillip Turgeon Jr, *Vice Pres*
Charles D Turgeon, *Admin Sec*
▲ **EMP:** 13 **EST:** 1946
SQ FT: 9,200
SALES (est): 630.9K **Privately Held**
SIC: 3471 Polishing, metals or formed
products; buffing for the trade

(P-7273)
JCR AIRCRAFT DEBURRING LLC
Also Called: Jcr Deburring
221 Foundation Ave, La Habra
(90631-6812)
PHONE....................714 870-4427
Juan Carlos Ruiz, *CEO*
David Escoto, *General Mgr*
Paul Castellanos, *Maintence Staff*
Omar Ruiz, *Opers Staff*
EMP: 80
SALES (est): 10.8MM **Privately Held**
WEB: www.jcrindustries.com
SIC: 3471 3541 3444 3542 Electroplating
of metals or formed products; deburring
machines; forming machine work, sheet
metal; machine tools, metal forming type

(P-7274)
JD PROCESSING INC
2220 Cape Cod Way, Santa Ana
(92703-3563)
PHONE....................714 972-8161
Thomas Scimeca, *CEO*
Luis Magana, *Planning*
Gonzalo Magana, *Prdtn Mgr*
EMP: 50 **EST:** 2014
SALES (est): 5MM **Privately Held**
WEB: www.jdprocessinginc.com
SIC: 3471 3559 Anodizing (plating) of met-
als or formed products; anodizing equip-
ment

(P-7275)
KEN HOFFMANN INC
Also Called: Palm Springs Plating
345 Del Sol Rd, Palm Springs
(92262-1607)
P.O. Box 4488 (92263-4488)
PHONE....................760 325-6012
Ken Hoffmann, *President*
Lidia Castro, *Office Admin*
EMP: 26 **EST:** 1976
SQ FT: 4,200
SALES (est): 5.3MM **Privately Held**
WEB: www.psplating.com
SIC: 3471 Electroplating of metals or
formed products

(P-7276)
KRYLER CORP
Also Called: Pecific Grinding
1217 E Ash Ave, Fullerton (92831-5019)
PHONE....................714 871-9611
Chet Krygier Jr, *President*
Phyllis Krygier, *Admin Sec*
EMP: 30 **EST:** 1977
SQ FT: 900
SALES (est): 2.5MM **Privately Held**
WEB: www.krylercorporation.com
SIC: 3471 Chromium plating of metals or
formed products

(P-7277)
LORTZ & SON MFG CO
Also Called: Lortz Manufacturing
4042 Patton Way, Bakersfield
(93308-5030)
PHONE....................281 241-9418
Nathan C Lortz, *President*
Steven E Fisher, *Shareholder*
Nathan Lortz, *General Mgr*
Mike Miller, *General Mgr*
Karen Lortz, *Admin Sec*
EMP: 137 **EST:** 1939
SQ FT: 50,000
SALES (est): 6.7MM **Privately Held**
SIC: 3471 3443 7692 3441 Plating & pol-
ishing; fabricated plate work (boiler shop);
welding repair; fabricated structural metal

(P-7278)
M & R PLATING CORPORATION
12375 Montague St, Pacoima
(91331-2214)
PHONE....................818 896-2700
Andres Rauda, *CEO*
EMP: 17 **EST:** 1976
SQ FT: 11,000
SALES (est): 1.8MM **Privately Held**
WEB: www.m-rplatingcorp.com
SIC: 3471 Electroplating of metals or
formed products

(P-7279)
M P C INDUSTRIAL PRODUCTS INC
Also Called: M P C Industries
2150 Mcgaw Ave, Irvine (92614-0912)
PHONE....................949 863-0106
Paul F Queyrel, *Chairman*
John A Spencer, *CFO*
Edgar Vargas, *QC Mgr*
Ed Lara, *Opers Staff*
▲ **EMP:** 46 **EST:** 1952
SQ FT: 55,000
SALES (est): 5MM **Privately Held**
SIC: 3471 3541 Polishing, metals or
formed products; grinding, polishing, buff-
ing, lapping & honing machines

(P-7280)
METAL CHEM INC
21514 Nordhoff St, Chatsworth
(91311-5822)
PHONE....................818 727-9951
Carlos Pongo, *President*
Guillermo Aguilera, *Vice Pres*
Brenda Tapia, *General Mgr*
EMP: 30 **EST:** 1997
SALES (est): 2.8MM **Privately Held**
WEB: www.metalcheminc.com
SIC: 3471 3443 Plating of metals or
formed products; fabricated plate work
(boiler shop)

(P-7281)
METAL PREPARATIONS
1000 E Ocean Blvd Unit 41, Long Beach
(90802-8507)
PHONE....................213 628-5176
Jeff Savage, *President*
Jason Savage, *Vice Pres*
EMP: 30 **EST:** 1961
SQ FT: 32,000
SALES (est): 199.1K **Privately Held**
WEB: www.metalprepinc.com
SIC: 3471 Cleaning & descaling metal
products; polishing, metals or formed
products

(P-7282)
METAL SURFACES INTL LLC
6060 Shull St, Bell Gardens (90201-6297)
P.O. Box 5001 (90202-5001)
PHONE....................562 927-1331
Charles K Bell, *CEO*
Sam Bell, *COO*
Raul Trujillo, *MIS Mgr*
Lala Khachatrian, *Engineer*
Nel Wallace, *Human Res Mgr*
EMP: 150 **EST:** 1954
SQ FT: 85,000
SALES (est): 25.7MM **Privately Held**
WEB: www.metalsurfaces.com
SIC: 3471 Electroplating of metals or
formed products

(P-7283)
MORRELLS ELECTRO PLATING INC
Also Called: Morrell's Metal Finishing
432 E Euclid Ave, Compton (90222-2899)
P.O. Box 3085 (90223-3085)
PHONE....................310 639-1024
Cyrus Gipoor, *President*
EMP: 30 **EST:** 1948
SQ FT: 20,000
SALES (est): 7.2MM **Privately Held**
WEB: www.morrellsplating.com
SIC: 3471 Electroplating of metals or
formed products; chromium plating of
metals or formed products

(P-7284)
MULTICHROME COMPANY INC (PA)
Also Called: Microplate
1013 W Hillcrest Blvd, Inglewood
(90301-2019)
PHONE....................310 216-1086
Steven A Peterman, *President*
Tina Sangaspar, *Manager*
EMP: 31 **EST:** 1962
SQ FT: 5,000
SALES (est): 3MM **Privately Held**
WEB: www.multiplate.com
SIC: 3471 Electroplating of metals or
formed products

(P-7285)
NASMYTH TMF INC
29102 Hancock Pkwy, Valencia
(91355-1066)
PHONE....................818 954-9504
Peter Smith, *CEO*
Geoff Folkes, *Exec VP*
EMP: 54 **EST:** 2014
SQ FT: 10,000
SALES (est): 6.9MM **Privately Held**
WEB: www.technicalmetalfinishing.com
SIC: 3471 3479 Anodizing (plating) of met-
als or formed products; coating of metals
& formed products
PA: Nasmyth Group Limited
Nasmyth House
Coventry W MIDLANDS

(P-7286)
NDT METAL FINISHING INC
11370 Luddington St, Sun Valley
(91352-3106)
PHONE....................818 807-1381
David M Colin, *Principal*
Herman Guerra, *Vice Pres*
EMP: 13 **EST:** 2008
SALES (est): 1.1MM **Privately Held**
SIC: 3471 Finishing, metals or formed
products

(P-7287)
NEUTRON PLATING INC
2993 E Blue Star St, Anaheim
(92806-2511)
PHONE....................714 632-9241
Manuel Zavala, *President*
Glafira Zavala, *Treasurer*
Manuel Zavala Jr, *Vice Pres*
Sylvia Cassillas, *Admin Sec*
EMP: 16 **EST:** 1983
SQ FT: 16,000
SALES (est): 1.2MM **Privately Held**
SIC: 3471 Electroplating of metals or
formed products; anodizing (plating) of
metals or formed products

(P-7288)
NORMANDY REFINISHERS INC
355 S Rosemead Blvd, Pasadena
(91107-4955)
PHONE....................626 792-9202
Gregory Sarkisian, *President*
Doris Sarkisian, *Vice Pres*
EMP: 22 **EST:** 1948
SQ FT: 2,000
SALES (est): 356.7K **Privately Held**
SIC: 3471 3431 Decorative plating & fin-
ishing of formed products; bathroom fix-
tures, including sinks

(P-7289)
OLD SPC INC
202 W 140th St, Los Angeles (90061-1006)
PHONE....................310 533-0748
Mary McMeans, *CEO*
Jesus Diaz, *Corp Secy*
Donna Martinez, *Vice Pres*
John Behm, *QC Mgr*
Scott McLean, *Maintence Staff*
EMP: 25 **EST:** 1999
SQ FT: 60,000
SALES (est): 5.3MM **Privately Held**
WEB: www.spectrumplating.com
SIC: 3471 Electroplating of metals or
formed products

(P-7290)
OMNI METAL FINISHING INC (PA)
11665 Coley River Cir, Fountain Valley
(92708-4279)
PHONE....................714 979-9414
Victor M Salazar, *President*
Victor Loyola, *CFO*
Filiberto Hernandez, *Treasurer*
Mark Obrien, *General Mgr*
Ramiro Salazar, *Admin Sec*
EMP: 99 **EST:** 1980
SQ FT: 34,000
SALES (est): 15.7MM **Privately Held**
WEB: www.omnimetal.com
SIC: 3471 Electroplating of metals or
formed products

(P-7291)
OPTI-FORMS INC
42310 Winchester Rd, Temecula
(92590-4810)
PHONE....................951 296-1300
Ralph C Dawson, *CEO*
Clint Tinker, *Chairman*
Kevin Thompson, *Exec VP*
Robert Brunson, *Vice Pres*
Sean Ewing, *Supervisor*
EMP: 52 **EST:** 1984
SQ FT: 61,000
SALES (est): 11MM **Privately Held**
SIC: 3471 3827 Plating of metals or
formed products; optical instruments &
lenses

(P-7292)
ORANGE COUNTY PLATING CO INC
940 N Parker St 960, Orange
(92867-5581)
PHONE....................714 532-4610
Lawrence J Honikel, *President*
Jeanne T Honikel, *Corp Secy*
Daniel L Honikel, *Vice Pres*
EMP: 14 **EST:** 1959
SQ FT: 12,000
SALES (est): 1.2MM **Privately Held**
WEB: www.ocplating.com
SIC: 3471 Electroplating of metals or
formed products

(P-7293)
PENTRATE METAL PROCESSING
3517 E Olympic Blvd, Los Angeles
(90023-3976)
PHONE....................323 269-2121
John J.Grana, *President*
Nick Grana, *Corp Secy*
Vincent Grana, *Vice Pres*
Mary Grana, *Administration*
Frank Grana, *Purchasing*
EMP: 30 **EST:** 1945
SQ FT: 18,000
SALES (est): 3MM **Privately Held**
WEB: www.calelectro.com
SIC: 3471 Electroplating of metals or
formed products; plating of metals or
formed products

(P-7294)
PLASMA RGGEDIZED SOLUTIONS INC
5452 Business Dr, Huntington Beach
(92649-1226)
PHONE....................714 893-6063
Bob Marla, *Branch Mgr*
Migel Clemente, *Engineer*
EMP: 27 **Privately Held**
WEB: www.plasmarugged.com
SIC: 3471 3479 Electroplating & plating;
coating of metals & formed products
PA: Plasma Ruggedized Solutions, Inc.
2284 Ringwood Ave Ste A
San Jose CA 95131

(P-7295)
PLATERONICS PROCESSING INC
9164 Independence Ave, Chatsworth
(91311-5902)
PHONE....................818 341-2191
Joseph Roter, *President*
Lee F Roter, *Corp Secy*

P R O D U C T S & S V C S

Marvin Roter, *Vice Pres*
EMP: 35 **EST:** 1959
SQ FT: 6,500 **Privately Held**
WEB: www.plateronics.com
SIC: 3471 5051 Finishing, metals or formed products; metals service centers & offices

(P-7296)
PRECIOUS METALS PLATING CO INC
2635 Orange Ave, Santa Ana (92707-3738)
PHONE.................................714 546-6271
Chad Wayne Bird, *President*
Betty Bird, *Admin Sec*
Jeff Kennedy, *QC Mgr*
EMP: 15 **EST:** 1957
SQ FT: 6,500
SALES (est): 2.1MM **Privately Held**
WEB: www.pmplating.com
SIC: 3471 Electroplating of metals or formed products

(P-7297)
PRECISION ANODIZING & PLTG INC
Also Called: P A P
1601 N Miller St, Anaheim (92806-1469)
PHONE.................................714 996-1601
Jose A Salazar, *CEO*
Kimberly Hayner, *Principal*
Tracy Betow, *Human Res Dir*
Kim Hayner, *Human Res Mgr*
Jordan Salazar, *Purchasing*
EMP: 89 **EST:** 1971
SQ FT: 44,000
SALES (est): 8.7MM **Privately Held**
WEB:
www.precisionanodizingandplating.com
SIC: 3471 Electroplating of metals or formed products

(P-7298)
PRIDE METAL POLISHING INC
10822 Saint Louis Dr, El Monte (91731-2030)
PHONE.................................626 350-1326
Rod Lowell, *President*
EMP: 19 **EST:** 1977
SQ FT: 15,000
SALES (est): 1.5MM **Privately Held**
WEB: www.pridepolishing.com
SIC: 3471 Electroplating of metals or formed products

(P-7299)
PRIME PLATING AEROSPACE INC
11321 Goss St, Sun Valley (91352-3206)
P.O. Box 1843 (91353-1843)
PHONE.................................818 768-9100
Fred Schmidt, *President*
EMP: 24 **EST:** 2012
SALES (est): 668.7K **Privately Held**
WEB: www.prime-plating.com
SIC: 3471 Electroplating of metals or formed products; plating of metals or formed products

(P-7300)
QUAKER CITY PLATING
Also Called: Quaker City Plating & Silvrsm
11729 Washington Blvd, Whittier (90606-2498)
P.O. Box 2406 (90610-2406)
PHONE.................................562 945-3721
Michael Crain, *Managing Prtnr*
Angelo Dirado, *Managing Prtnr*
Fred Mose, *CFO*
Lourdes Ortiz, *CIO*
Ena Wiley, *Sales Staff*
▲ **EMP:** 220 **EST:** 1937
SQ FT: 48,000
SALES (est): 27.3MM **Privately Held**
WEB: www.qcpent.com
SIC: 3471 Plating of metals or formed products

(P-7301)
QUALITY CONTROL PLATING INC
4425 E Airport Dr Ste 113, Ontario (91761-7815)
PHONE.................................909 605-0206
Jay J Singh, *Vice Pres*

Mona Singh, *President*
EMP: 22 **EST:** 1991
SQ FT: 3,500
SALES (est): 1.5MM **Privately Held**
SIC: 3471 Plating of metals or formed products

(P-7302)
R L ANODIZING
Also Called: R L Anodizing & Plating
11331 Penrose St, Sun Valley (91352-3109)
PHONE.................................818 252-3804
Raymond Lane, *Owner*
EMP: 19 **EST:** 1997
SALES (est): 1.4MM **Privately Held**
SIC: 3471 Electroplating of metals or formed products

(P-7303)
RAVLICH ENTERPRISES LLC
Also Called: Spectrum Plating Company
202 W 140th St, Los Angeles (90061-1006)
PHONE.................................310 533-0748
Anthony Ravlich, *Branch Mgr*
EMP: 41
SALES (corp-wide): 15MM **Privately Held**
WEB: www.neutronicstamping.com
SIC: 3471 Plating & polishing
PA: Ravlich Enterprises, Llc
100 Business Center Dr
Corona CA 92878
714 964-8900

(P-7304)
RAVLICH ENTERPRISES LLC (PA)
Also Called: Neutronic Stamping & Plating
100 Business Center Dr, Corona (92878-3224)
PHONE.................................714 964-8900
Anthony Ravlich, *CEO*
Nicholas Ravlich, *CFO*
Carmen Pinedo, *Executive*
Silvia Saiz, *Admin Asst*
Robert Soltero, *Controller*
EMP: 27 **EST:** 2003
SQ FT: 27,000
SALES (est): 15MM **Privately Held**
WEB: www.neutronicstamping.com
SIC: 3471 3469 Electroplating of metals or formed products; metal stampings

(P-7305)
RD METAL POLISHING INC
244 Pioneer Pl, Pomona (91768-3275)
PHONE.................................909 594-8393
Ron Delgado Jr, *President*
Ranulfo M Delgado Sr, *Vice Pres*
EMP: 15 **EST:** 1981
SQ FT: 11,000
SALES (est): 1.2MM **Privately Held**
SIC: 3471 Polishing, metals or formed products

(P-7306)
REAL PLATING INC
1245 W 2nd St, Pomona (91766-1310)
PHONE.................................909 623-2304
Juan Real, *CEO*
EMP: 25 **EST:** 2007
SQ FT: 5,264
SALES (est): 3.2MM **Privately Held**
WEB: www.realplating.com
SIC: 3471 Electroplating of metals or formed products

(P-7307)
S & K PLATING INC
2727 N Compton Ave, Compton (90222-1097)
PHONE.................................310 632-7141
Mardig Tchakalian, *President*
Hagop Chakalian, *General Mgr*
EMP: 18 **EST:** 1957
SQ FT: 7,500
SALES (est): 1.1MM **Privately Held**
WEB: www.skplating.com
SIC: 3471 Electroplating of metals or formed products

(P-7308)
SAFE PLATING INC
18001 Railroad St, City of Industry (91748-1215)
PHONE.................................626 810-1872
Magdy Seif, *President*
Mario Gomez, *COO*
Victor Rodriguez, *Safety Mgr*
Kevin Folden, *Manager*
EMP: 58 **EST:** 1979
SQ FT: 35,000
SALES (est): 11.1MM **Privately Held**
WEB: www.safeplatinginc.com
SIC: 3471 Electroplating of metals or formed products

(P-7309)
SANTA ANA PLATING (PA)
1726 E Rosslynn Ave, Fullerton (92831-5111)
PHONE.................................310 923-8305
Tony Kakuk, *President*
Michael F Gustin, *Owner*
EMP: 55 **EST:** 1954
SQ FT: 17,100
SALES (est): 4.5MM **Privately Held**
SIC: 3471 Finishing, metals or formed products; plating of metals or formed products

(P-7310)
SANTOSHI CORPORATION
Also Called: Alum-A-Coat
2439 Seaman Ave, El Monte (91733-1936)
PHONE.................................626 444-7118
Hershad Shah, *President*
Raksha Shah, *Vice Pres*
Alicia Moreno, *Sales Staff*
EMP: 33 **EST:** 1971
SQ FT: 15,000
SALES (est): 6.3MM **Privately Held**
WEB: www.alumacoat.com
SIC: 3471 Coloring & finishing of aluminum or formed products

(P-7311)
SCHMIDT INDUSTRIES INC
Also Called: Prime Plating
11321 Goss St, Sun Valley (91352-3206)
P.O. Box 1843 (91353-1843)
PHONE.................................818 768-9100
Fred Schmidt, *President*
Jennifer Schmidt, *Admin Sec*
EMP: 90 **EST:** 1986
SQ FT: 30,000
SALES (est): 10.5MM **Privately Held**
WEB: www.prime-plating.com
SIC: 3471 Electroplating of metals or formed products

(P-7312)
SOUTHWEST PLATING CO INC
1344 W Slauson Ave, Los Angeles (90044-2897)
PHONE.................................323 753-3781
Gus Brigantino, *Owner*
EMP: 15 **EST:** 1945
SALES (est): 1MM **Privately Held**
SIC: 3471 Plating of metals or formed products

(P-7313)
SOVEREIGN ARTS MET FINSHG LLC
Also Called: Blooddiamond.gallery
1336 N Mccadden Pl, Los Angeles (90028-7710)
PHONE.................................714 742-9944
Michael B Johnson,
EMP: 17 **EST:** 2018
SALES (est): 2.9MM **Privately Held**
SIC: 3471 Finishing, metals or formed products

(P-7314)
STABILE PLATING COMPANY INC
1150 E Edna Pl, Covina (91724-2592)
PHONE.................................626 339-9091
David Crest, *President*
Eric Crest, *Vice Pres*
Steve Crest, *Vice Pres*
Steven Crest, *Vice Pres*
Stephanie Esqueda, *Office Mgr*
EMP: 22 **EST:** 1959

SQ FT: 6,000
SALES (est): 1.5MM **Privately Held**
WEB:
SIC: 3471 3444 3353 Plating of metals or formed products; sheet metalwork; aluminum sheet, plate & foil

(P-7315)
STAINLESS MICRO-POLISH INC
1286 N Grove St, Anaheim (92806-2113)
PHONE.................................714 632-8903
Robert Maculsay, *President*
Elizabeth Maculsay, *Treasurer*
EMP: 30 **EST:** 1979
SQ FT: 10,000
SALES (est): 2MM **Privately Held**
WEB: www.stainlessmicropolish.com
SIC: 3471 Polishing, metals or formed products

(P-7316)
STANDARD METAL PRODUCTS INC
1541 W 132nd St, Gardena (90249-2107)
P.O. Box 7636, Torrance (90504-9036)
PHONE.................................310 532-9861
Danny Corrales Jr, *CEO*
Dan Corrales Sr, *Corp Secy*
Jo Ann Stanley, *Bookkeeper*
EMP: 31 **EST:** 1972
SQ FT: 24,000
SALES (est): 1.2MM **Privately Held**
WEB: www.sheet-metal.com
SIC: 3471 3444 Cleaning, polishing & finishing; sheet metalwork

(P-7317)
STUART-DEAN CO INC
14731 Franklin Ave Ste L, Tustin (92780-7221)
PHONE.................................714 544-4460
Steven Materazzo, *Manager*
Irvin Villasenor, *Opers Mgr*
EMP: 13
SALES (corp-wide): 65.4MM **Privately Held**
WEB: www.stuartdean.com
SIC: 3471 Polishing, metals or formed products
PA: Stuart-Dean Co. Inc.
4350 10th St
Long Island City NY 11101
212 273-6900

(P-7318)
SUPERIOR CONNECTOR PLATING INC
Also Called: Superior Plating
1901 E Cerritos Ave, Anaheim (92805-6427)
PHONE.................................714 774-1174
Juan Martin, *President*
Rosa Martin, *Director*
EMP: 22 **EST:** 1994
SQ FT: 7,500
SALES (est): 3.1MM **Privately Held**
WEB: www.superiorplatingca.com
SIC: 3471 Electroplating of metals or formed products

(P-7319)
SUPERIOR METAL FINISHING INC
1733 W 134th St, Gardena (90249-2015)
PHONE.................................310 464-8010
William Leffingwell Sr, *President*
Duane O'Reilly, *Corp Secy*
EMP: 14 **EST:** 1973
SQ FT: 5,290
SALES (est): 1.6MM **Privately Held**
SIC: 3471 Finishing, metals or formed products

(P-7320)
SUPERIOR PLATING INC
9001 Glenoaks Blvd, Sun Valley (91352-2040)
PHONE.................................818 252-1088
EMP: 35
SALES (est): 2.7MM **Privately Held**
SIC: 3471 Metal Plating

(P-7321)
TECHNIC INC
1170 N Hawk Cir, Anaheim (92807-1789)
PHONE..................................714 632-0200
Mike Chicos, *Opers-Prdtn-Mfg*
Jeff Cannis, *Technical Mgr*
Maria Coe, *Human Res Mgr*
EMP: 30
SALES (corp-wide): 159.5MM **Privately Held**
WEB: www.technic.com
SIC: 3471 2899 3678 3672 Plating of metals or formed products; plating compounds; electronic connectors; printed circuit boards; precious metals; semiconductor devices
PA: Technic, Inc.
47 Molter St
Cranston RI 02910
401 781-6100

(P-7322)
TEMECULA QUALITY PLATING INC
42147 Roick Dr, Temecula (92590-3695)
PHONE..................................951 296-9875
Duc Vo, *President*
Dat Vo, *Vice Pres*
EMP: 32 EST: 2011
SALES (est): 2.7MM **Privately Held**
WEB: www.temeculaplating.com
SIC: 3471 Electroplating of metals or formed products; anodizing (plating) of metals or formed products

(P-7323)
TRIDENT PLATING INC
10046 Romandel Ave, Santa Fe Springs (90670-3424)
PHONE..................................562 906-2556
Maty Rodriguez, *President*
Ian Holmber, *Corp Secy*
Juan Carlos Rodriguez, *Vice Pres*
EMP: 28 EST: 1981
SQ FT: 18,197
SALES (est): 2MM **Privately Held**
WEB: www.tridentplating.com
SIC: 3471 Electroplating of metals or formed products

(P-7324)
TRIUMPH PROCESSING INC
Also Called: Valence Lynwood
2605 Industry Way, Lynwood (90262-4007)
PHONE..................................323 563-1338
Peter Labarbera, *CEO*
Richard C III, *CEO*
Jose De Santiago, *Manager*
Jess Lozano, *Manager*
Derek Ruhl, *Manager*
EMP: 103 EST: 1968
SQ FT: 140,000
SALES (est): 18.1MM
SALES (corp-wide): 103MM **Privately Held**
WEB: www.triumphgroup.com
SIC: 3471 3398 3356 Anodizing (plating) of metals or formed products; finishing, metals or formed products; polishing, metals or formed products; metal heat treating; nonferrous rolling & drawing
PA: Valence Surface Technologies Llc
1790 Hughes Landing Blvd
The Woodlands TX 77380
888 540-0878

(P-7325)
U M S INC
Also Called: A C Plating
317 Mount Vernon Ave, Bakersfield (93307-2743)
PHONE..................................661 324-5454
Robert D McBride, *President*
Tori McBride, *Manager*
EMP: 26 EST: 1968
SQ FT: 15,000
SALES (est): 1.2MM **Privately Held**
WEB: www.acplating.com
SIC: 3471 Plating of metals or formed products

(P-7326)
ULTRAMET
12173 Montague St, Pacoima (91331-2210)
PHONE..................................818 899-0236

Andrew Duffy, *CEO*
James Kaplan, *Shareholder*
Richard B Kaplan, *Shareholder*
Walter Abrams, *Admin Sec*
Celia Thorp, *Purch Mgr*
▲ EMP: 79 EST: 1970
SQ FT: 43,000
SALES (est): 16MM **Privately Held**
WEB: www.ultramet.com
SIC: 3471 8731 Electroplating & plating; commercial physical research

(P-7327)
UNIVERSAL METAL PLATING
704 S Taylor Ave, Montebello (90640-5562)
PHONE..................................626 969-7932
Guadalupe Martinez, *Partner*
EMP: 15
SALES (corp-wide): 1.8MM **Privately Held**
WEB: www.universalmetalplating.com
SIC: 3471 Chromium plating of metals or formed products
PA: Universal Metal Plating
1526 W 1st St
Irwindale CA 91702
626 969-7931

(P-7328)
V & M PLATING CO
14024 Avalon Blvd, Los Angeles (90061-2692)
PHONE..................................310 532-5633
Anthony Babiak, *President*
Timothy Babiak, *Vice Pres*
▲ EMP: 19 EST: 1948
SQ FT: 7,500
SALES (est): 1.2MM **Privately Held**
WEB: www.vmplating.com
SIC: 3471 Electroplating of metals or formed products

(P-7329)
VALLEY PLATING WORKS INC
5900 Sheila St, Commerce (90040-2403)
PHONE..................................323 838-9211
David Cullen, *Principal*
EMP: 14 EST: 2009
SALES (est): 78.3K **Privately Held**
WEB: www.valleyplating.com
SIC: 3471 Plating of metals or formed products

(P-7330)
VIRGIL M STUTZMAN INC
Also Called: Stutzman Plating
5045 Exposition Blvd, Los Angeles (90016-3913)
P.O. Box 78457 (90016-0457)
PHONE..................................323 732-9146
Virgil M Stutzman, *President*
Joseph C Stutzman, *Corp Secy*
James D Stutzman, *Vice Pres*
EMP: 19 EST: 1967
SQ FT: 4,000
SALES (est): 2.7MM **Privately Held**
WEB: www.stutzmanplating.com
SIC: 3471 5051 3369 3364 Electroplating of metals or formed products; metals service centers & offices; nonferrous foundries; nonferrous die-castings except aluminum

(P-7331)
WE FIVE-R CORPORATION
Also Called: Bank C Plating Co
1507 S Sunol Dr, Los Angeles (90023-4031)
PHONE..................................323 263-6757
Dick Patel, *President*
◆ EMP: 22 EST: 1950
SQ FT: 8,000
SALES (est): 483.5K **Privately Held**
SIC: 3471 Electroplating of metals or formed products

(P-7332)
WEST VALLEY PLATING INC
21061 Superior St Ste A, Chatsworth (91311-4330)
PHONE..................................818 709-1684
Josephina Campos, *President*
EMP: 15 EST: 2000

SALES (est): 2.1MM **Privately Held**
SIC: 3471 Plating of metals or formed products; electroplating of metals or formed products

---

3479 Coating & Engraving, NEC

(P-7333)
A & R POWDER COATING INC
1198 N Grove St Ste B, Anaheim (92806-2136)
PHONE..................................714 630-0709
Jack Rainwater, *President*
Everett Ryan, *President*
EMP: 17 EST: 1993
SQ FT: 5,500
SALES (est): 1.7MM **Privately Held**
SIC: 3479 Coating of metals & formed products

(P-7334)
A-1 ENGRAVING CO INC
8225 Phlox St, Downey (90241-4880)
PHONE..................................562 861-2216
Jack E Young, *President*
Grace Young, *Corp Secy*
Don Schram, *Vice Pres*
EMP: 21 EST: 1966
SQ FT: 22,900
SALES (est): 1.1MM **Privately Held**
WEB: www.a-1engraving.com
SIC: 3479 Engraving jewelry silverware, or metal; etching & engraving

(P-7335)
ABACUS POWDER COATING
1829 Tyler Ave, South El Monte (91733-3617)
PHONE..................................626 443-7556
Esther Davidoff, *President*
EMP: 25 EST: 2006
SALES (est): 2.2MM **Privately Held**
WEB: www.abacuspowder.com
SIC: 3479 Coating of metals & formed products

(P-7336)
ADFA INCORPORATED
Also Called: A&A Jewelry Supply
319 W 6th St, Los Angeles (90014-1703)
PHONE..................................213 627-8004
Robert Adem, *President*
Naim Farah, *Vice Pres*
▲ EMP: 45 EST: 1986
SALES (est): 5.5MM **Privately Held**
WEB: www.aajewelry.com
SIC: 3479 3548 3172 Engraving jewelry silverware, or metal; electric welding equipment; cases, jewelry

(P-7337)
ADVANCE POWDER COATINGS LLC
169 W Mindanao St, Bloomington (92316-2946)
PHONE..................................909 543-0014
Aaron Michael Ruiz, *Mng Member*
EMP: 15 EST: 2019
SALES (est): 2MM **Privately Held**
WEB: www.advancepowder.com
SIC: 3479 Coating of metals & formed products

(P-7338)
AERO POWDER COATING INC
710 Monterey Pass Rd, Monterey Park (91754-3607)
PHONE..................................323 264-6405
Phillip Kontos, *President*
EMP: 24 EST: 1977
SQ FT: 27,000
SALES (est): 2.8MM **Privately Held**
SIC: 3479 Coating of metals & formed products

(P-7339)
AIRCOAT INC
13405 S Broadway, Los Angeles (90061-1127)
PHONE..................................310 527-2258
Francisco Ramirez, *President*
EMP: 27 EST: 1995
SQ FT: 20,000

SALES (est): 1.3MM **Privately Held**
WEB: www.aircoat.com
SIC: 3479 Painting of metal products; painting, coating & hot dipping

(P-7340)
AJ SPECIAL COATINGS INC
17881 Bangor Ave, Hesperia (92345-6932)
PHONE..................................760 646-2813
Efrain Ortega, *Principal*
EMP: 13 EST: 2014
SALES (est): 869.3K **Privately Held**
SIC: 3479 Metal coating & allied service

(P-7341)
AMERICAN ETCHING & MFG
13730 Desmond St, Pacoima (91331-2706)
PHONE..................................323 875-3910
Gary Kipka, *President*
Frances D Torre, *Officer*
Frances Torre, *Officer*
Chris Kipka, *Opers Staff*
EMP: 45 EST: 1972
SQ FT: 20,000
SALES (est): 5.3MM **Privately Held**
WEB: www.aemetch.com
SIC: 3479 Etching on metals

(P-7342)
ANDREWS POWDER COATING INC
10138 Canoga Ave, Chatsworth (91311-3005)
PHONE..................................818 700-1030
Scott Andrews, *President*
Sandee Andrews, *CFO*
Tc Carter, *Sales Staff*
EMP: 20 EST: 1991
SALES (est): 2.6MM **Privately Held**
WEB: www.powdercoater.com
SIC: 3479 Coating of metals & formed products

(P-7343)
ANOCHEM COATINGS
4525 W 1st St Ste B, Santa Ana (92703-3170)
PHONE..................................949 322-3280
Toan Nguyen, *Principal*
EMP: 16 EST: 2016
SALES (est): 1.1MM **Privately Held**
SIC: 3479 Metal coating & allied service

(P-7344)
APPLIED COATINGS & LININGS
3224 Rosemead Blvd, El Monte (91731-2807)
PHONE..................................626 280-6354
EMP: 24
SQ FT: 150,000
SALES (est): 2.7MM **Privately Held**
WEB: www.appliedcoatings.com
SIC: 3479 3471 Coating/Engraving Service Plating/Polishing Service

(P-7345)
APPLIED POWDERCOAT INC
3101 Camino Del Sol, Oxnard (93030-8999)
PHONE..................................805 981-1991
Victor Anselmo, *President*
J Michael Hagan, *Ch of Bd*
Debbi Anselmo, *Controller*
George Grippo, *Plant Mgr*
Deborah Anselmo, *Manager*
EMP: 45 EST: 1989
SQ FT: 30,000
SALES (est): 5.7MM **Privately Held**
WEB: www.appliedpowder.com
SIC: 3479 Coating of metals & formed products

(P-7346)
ARNACO INDUSTRIAL COATINGS
8445 Warvale St, Pico Rivera (90660-4316)
PHONE..................................562 222-1022
Edawrd Gomez, *President*
Jose Vasquez, *Principal*
EMP: 20 EST: 2016
SALES (est): 2.8MM **Privately Held**
WEB: www.aicindustrialcoatings.com
SIC: 3479 Coating of metals & formed products

P
R
O
D
U
C
T
S
&
S
V
C
S

(P-7347)
ATLAS GALVANIZING LLC
2639 Leonis Blvd, Vernon (90058-2203)
PHONE................................323 587-6247
Victor Bruno Jr,
Patricia New,
EMP: 36 **EST:** 1936
SQ FT: 20,000
SALES (est): 3.7MM **Privately Held**
WEB: www.atlasgalv.com
SIC: 3479 Coating of metals & formed
products

(P-7348)
BELL POWDER COATING INC
4747 Mcgrath St, Ventura (93003-6495)
P.O. Box 7117 (93006-7117)
PHONE................................805 658-2233
Carl Bell, *President*
Judith Bell, *Vice Pres*
EMP: 15 **EST:** 1986
SQ FT: 16,500
SALES (est): 1.5MM **Privately Held**
SIC: 3479 Coating of metals & formed
products

(P-7349)
BESTWAY INTERNATIONAL GROUP
Also Called: Bestway Powder
14797 Carmenita Rd, Norwalk
(90650-5230)
PHONE................................562 921-7100
Henry Pak, *CEO*
Shao Jia Kong, *CFO*
Young Kwon, *Admin Sec*
▲ **EMP:** 15 **EST:** 2003
SALES (est): 312.5K **Privately Held**
SIC: 3479 Hot dip coating of metals or
formed metals

(P-7350)
BRIGHT SHARK POWDER COATING
4530 Schaefer Ave, Chino (91710-5539)
PHONE................................909 591-1385
Rosalva Garcia, *Partner*
EMP: 17 **EST:** 1989
SQ FT: 9,600
SALES (est): 6MM **Privately Held**
WEB: www.brightshark.net
SIC: 3479 Coating of metals & formed
products

(P-7351)
CALWEST GALVANIZING CORP
2226 E Dominguez St, Carson
(90810-1086)
PHONE................................310 549-2200
Toll Free:..............................888 -
Isaac Malbonado, *General Mgr*
Isaac Maldonado, *Manager*
▲ **EMP:** 40 **EST:** 1984
SQ FT: 20,000
SALES (est): 14.8MM
SALES (corp-wide): 2.9B **Publicly Held**
WEB: www.valmontcoatings.com
SIC: 3479 3317 Galvanizing of iron, steel
or end-formed products; steel pipe &
tubes
PA: Valmont Industries, Inc.
1 Valmont Plz Ste 500
Omaha NE 68154
402 963-1000

(P-7352)
CERTIFIED ENAMELING INC (PA)
3342 Emery St, Los Angeles (90023-3810)
PHONE................................323 264-4403
Vicki Ziegel, *CEO*
Glenn Ziegel, *CFO*
Adrian Quijano, *General Mgr*
Rocio Tinajero, *Prdtn Mgr*
EMP: 92 **EST:** 1953
SQ FT: 50,000
SALES (est): 11.8MM **Privately Held**
WEB: www.certifiedenameling.com
SIC: 3479 Coating of metals & formed
products

(P-7353)
COATINGS BY SANDBERG INC
856 N Commerce St, Orange
(92867-7900)
PHONE................................714 538-0888
Nona Sandberg, *President*
Gerald Sandberg, *Admin Sec*
Don McKinney, *Nurse*
EMP: 14 **EST:** 1997
SQ FT: 12,000
SALES (est): 2.6MM **Privately Held**
WEB: www.cbs-dichroic.com
SIC: 3479 Coating of metals & formed
products

(P-7354)
COLOR-TEC INDUS FINSHG INC
11231 Ilex Ave, Pacoima (91331-2725)
PHONE................................818 897-2669
Michael Cabral, *Owner*
EMP: 19 **EST:** 1979
SQ FT: 6,000
SALES (est): 1.9MM **Privately Held**
WEB: www.colortecinc.com
SIC: 3479 Coating of metals & formed
products

(P-7355)
CREST COATING INC
1361 S Allec St, Anaheim (92805-6304)
PHONE................................714 635-7090
Michael D Erickson, *CEO*
Bonnie George, *Vice Pres*
Louie Munet, *Buyer*
Andrew Starritt, *Opers Mgr*
Jeff Erickson, *Sales Mgr*
▲ **EMP:** 60 **EST:** 1968
SQ FT: 55,000
SALES (est): 13MM **Privately Held**
WEB: www.crestcoating.com
SIC: 3479 Coating of metals & formed
products

(P-7356)
CUSTOM ENAMELERS INC
18340 Mount Baldy Cir, Fountain Valley
(92708-6181)
PHONE................................714 540-7884
Ronald Folmer, *President*
Janet Folmer, *Treasurer*
Daryl Folmer, *Vice Pres*
EMP: 21 **EST:** 1957
SQ FT: 27,000
SALES (est): 1.1MM **Privately Held**
WEB: www.customenamelersinc.com
SIC: 3479 Coating of metals & formed
products

(P-7357)
DENMAC INDUSTRIES INC
7616 Rosecrans Ave, Paramount
(90723-2508)
P.O. Box 2144 (90723-8144)
PHONE................................562 634-2714
Mark Plechot, *President*
Maurice Plechot, *CFO*
James Campangna, *Vice Pres*
▲ **EMP:** 40
SQ FT: 20,000
SALES (est): 5.5MM **Privately Held**
WEB: www.denmac-ind.com
SIC: 3479 Coating of metals & formed
products

(P-7358)
DRYWIRED DEFENSE LLC
9606 Santa Monica Blvd # 4, Beverly Hills
(90210-4427)
PHONE................................310 684-3891
Alex Nesic, *Vice Pres*
Samantha Gonzalez, *Pub Rel Dir*
EMP: 15 **EST:** 2012
SQ FT: 4,000
SALES (est): 329.9K **Privately Held**
WEB: www.drywired.com
SIC: 3479 3672 Coating electrodes; coat-
ing, rust preventive; printed circuit boards

(P-7359)
DURA COAT PRODUCTS INC (PA)
5361 Via Ricardo, Riverside (92509-2414)
PHONE................................951 341-6500
Myung K Hong, *CEO*
Suzanne Faust, *COO*
Lorrie Y Hong, *Admin Sec*

Paul Daugherty, *Technical Staff*
Dexter Sunderman, *Technical Staff*
◆ **EMP:** 64 **EST:** 1986
SQ FT: 29,000
SALES (est): 43.1MM **Privately Held**
WEB: www.duracoatproducts.com
SIC: 3479 2851 Aluminum coating of
metal products; coating of metals &
formed products; paints & allied products

(P-7360)
DURABLE COATING INC
28716 Garnet Canyon Dr, Santa Clarita
(91390-4296)
PHONE................................805 299-8850
EMP: 13
SALES (corp-wide): 96.5K **Privately Held**
WEB: www.durablecoatinginc.com
SIC: 3479 Coating of metals & formed
products
PA: Durable Coating Inc.
21163 Centre Pointe Pkwy
Santa Clarita CA

(P-7361)
EEMUS MANUFACTURING CORP
16750 Pocono St, La Puente (91744-3335)
PHONE................................626 443-8841
Gitte Simionian, *President*
Richard Mitchell, *Vice Pres*
Art Arteaga, *Principal*
EMP: 14 **EST:** 1975
SALES (est): 1.5MM **Privately Held**
WEB: www.eemusmfg.com
SIC: 3479 Etching on metals

(P-7362)
ENGINEERED APPLICATION LLC
4727 E 49th St, Vernon (90058-2703)
PHONE................................323 585-2894
Gil Hestmark,
EMP: 15 **EST:** 1997
SALES (est): 2.2MM **Privately Held**
WEB: www.engineeredapps.com
SIC: 3479 Coating of metals & formed
products

(P-7363)
ETS EXPRESS LLC (DH)
420 Lombard St, Oxnard (93030-5100)
PHONE................................805 278-7771
Sharon Eyal, *President*
Gabriel Marcial, *CFO*
Derek Hansen, *Vice Pres*
Ely Eastman, *Engineer*
Jason Shepherd, *Controller*
▲ **EMP:** 28 **EST:** 1998
SQ FT: 40,000
SALES (est): 23.1MM
SALES (corp-wide): 23.1MM **Privately
Held**
WEB: www.etsexpress.com
SIC: 3479 3231 Etching & engraving; cut
& engraved glassware: made from pur-
chased glass
HQ: Leedsworld, Inc.
400 Hunt Valley Rd
New Kensington PA 15068
724 334-9000

(P-7364)
EXCLUSIVE POWDER COATINGS INC
24922 Anza Dr Ste C, Valencia
(91355-1230)
P.O. Box 803307, Santa Clarita (91380-
3307)
PHONE................................661 294-9812
Mark Kier, *CEO*
▲ **EMP:** 22 **EST:** 1999
SQ FT: 8,500
SALES (est): 1.7MM **Privately Held**
WEB: www.e-powdercoating.com
SIC: 3479 Coating of metals & formed
products

(P-7365)
FLETCHER COATING CO
426 W Fletcher Ave, Orange (92865-2612)
PHONE................................714 637-4763
Kurtis Breeding, *CEO*
Melinda Lujan, *Admin Dir*
Bernardo Gomez, *Maintence Staff*
John Bejarano, *Manager*
▲ **EMP:** 50 **EST:** 1971

SQ FT: 37,500
SALES (est): 5.5MM **Privately Held**
WEB: www.fletcherkote.com
SIC: 3479 Coating of metals & formed
products

(P-7366)
FUSION FINISH LLC (PA)
19200 S Reyes Ave, Compton
(90221-5812)
PHONE................................562 773-5303
EMP: 35 **EST:** 2018
SALES (est): 1.1MM **Privately Held**
WEB: www.fusionfinishwheels.com
SIC: 3479 Coating of metals & formed
products

(P-7367)
GEBE ELECTRONIC SERVICES INC
4112 W Jefferson Blvd, Los Angeles
(90016-4125)
PHONE................................323 731-2439
R O Fergus Sr, *President*
R O Fergus Jr, *Treasurer*
Gregory Fergus, *Vice Pres*
EMP: 16 **EST:** 1957
SQ FT: 10,500
SALES (est): 714.7K **Privately Held**
SIC: 3479 Bonderizing of metal or metal
products; coating of metals & formed
products

(P-7368)
GEMTECH INDS GOOD EARTH MFG
Also Called: Gemtech International
2737 S Garnsey St, Santa Ana
(92707-3340)
P.O. Box 15506 (92735-0506)
PHONE................................714 848-2517
Shig Shiwota, *President*
Maya Shiwota, *Vice Pres*
David Shiwota, *Managing Dir*
▲ **EMP:** 24 **EST:** 1971
SQ FT: 10,500
SALES (est): 3MM **Privately Held**
WEB: www.gemtechcoatings.com
SIC: 3479 Coating of metals & formed
products

(P-7369)
GRAND-WAY FABRI-GRAPHIC INC
22550 Lamplight Pl, Santa Clarita
(91350-5729)
PHONE................................818 206-8560
Marlene Kane, *President*
EMP: 18 **EST:** 1965
SQ FT: 10,500
SALES (est): 1.1MM **Privately Held**
SIC: 3479 Etching & engraving; painting of
metal products

(P-7370)
H-D SPECIALTY GROUPS INC
Also Called: Coatings Hub
5913 E Washington Blvd, Commerce
(90040-2412)
PHONE................................323 516-6186
EMP: 13 **EST:** 2015
SALES (est): 3.3MM **Privately Held**
WEB: www.coatingshub.com
SIC: 3479 Painting, coating & hot dipping

(P-7371)
HAI ADVNCED MTL SPCIALISTS INC
Also Called: H A I
1688 Sierra Madre Cir, Placentia
(92870-6628)
PHONE................................714 414-0575
Daren J Gansert, *President*
Debra Gansert, *Vice Pres*
Mark Enyeart, *Manager*
▲ **EMP:** 15 **EST:** 2003
SQ FT: 10,000
SALES (est): 4MM **Privately Held**
WEB: www.haiinc.com
SIC: 3479 Coating of metals & formed
products

(P-7372)
HALEY INDUS CTINGS LININGS INC
2919 Tanager Ave, Commerce (90040-2723)
PHONE..................................323 588-8086
Yvonne P Haley, *President*
EMP: 21 EST: 1993
SALES (est): 3.3MM **Privately Held**
WEB: www.haleyindustrial.com
SIC: 3479 1771 Coating of metals & formed products; flooring contractor

(P-7373)
HIGH TECH COATINGS INC
Also Called: High-Tech Coatings
1724 S Santa Fe St, Santa Ana (92705-4813)
PHONE..................................714 547-2122
Dan C Hilton, *Owner*
Sharon Hilton, *Human Res Mgr*
EMP: 13 EST: 1984
SQ FT: 8,500
SALES (est): 2.5MM **Privately Held**
WEB: www.hightechcoatingsinc.com
SIC: 3479 Coating of metals & formed products

(P-7374)
INLAND PACIFIC COATINGS INC
3556 Lytle Creek Rd, Lytle Creek (92358-9776)
PHONE..................................909 822-0594
Ciro Hernandez, *Principal*
EMP: 20 EST: 2012
SALES (est): 1.8MM **Privately Held**
SIC: 3479 1721 7389 Metal coating & allied service; painting & paper hanging;

(P-7375)
INLAND POWDER COATING CORP
Also Called: Prs Industries
1656 S Bon View Ave Ste F, Ontario (91761-4419)
P.O. Box 3427 (91761-0943)
PHONE..................................909 947-1122
David Paul Flatten, *President*
Debbie Flatten, *Corp Secy*
Jason Flatten, *Sales Staff*
EMP: 104
SQ FT: 83,000
SALES (est): 16.9MM **Privately Held**
WEB: www.inlandpowder.com
SIC: 3479 3471 Coating of metals & formed products; sand blasting of metal parts

(P-7376)
INTEGRATED POLYMER INDS INC
9741 Irvine Center Dr, Irvine (92618-4324)
PHONE..................................949 788-1050
Ergun Kirlikovali, *President*
Juliana Kirlikovali, *Vice Pres*
EMP: 23 EST: 1985
SALES (est): 1.1MM **Privately Held**
WEB: www.integratedpolymer.com
SIC: 3479 Coating of metals & formed products

(P-7377)
ISLAND POWDER COATING
1830 Tyler Ave, South El Monte (91733-3618)
PHONE..................................626 279-2460
Joe Graham, *Owner*
EMP: 30 EST: 1994
SALES (est): 4.2MM **Privately Held**
WEB: www.abacuspowder.com
SIC: 3479 Coating of metals & formed products

(P-7378)
JES DISC GRINDING INC
2824 Metropolitan Pl, Pomona (91767-1854)
PHONE..................................909 596-3823
John Schmidt, *President*
Ray Schmidt, *Vice Pres*
EMP: 16 EST: 1984
SQ FT: 12,000

SALES (est): 602.7K **Privately Held**
WEB: www.jesgrinding.com
SIC: 3479 Coating of metals & formed products

(P-7379)
KENNEDY NAME PLATE CO
4501 Pacific Blvd, Vernon (90058-2207)
PHONE..................................323 585-0121
William J Kennedy Jr, *President*
Mike Kennedy, *Vice Pres*
William Kennedy, *Manager*
EMP: 25 EST: 1921
SQ FT: 36,000
SALES (est): 2.6MM **Privately Held**
WEB: www.tpx.com
SIC: 3479 7336 3993 3444 Name plates: engraved, etched, etc.; silk screen design; signs & advertising specialties; sheet metalwork; coated & laminated paper; packaging paper & plastics film, coated & laminated

(P-7380)
KENS SPRAY EQUIPMENT INC (DH)
Also Called: Alloy Processing
1900 W Walnut St, Compton (90220-5019)
PHONE..................................310 635-9995
Joseph I Snowden, *Principal*
Brian Leibl, *President*
Sandra Jeglum, *Corp Secy*
EMP: 132 EST: 1979
SQ FT: 37,000
SALES (est): 33.9MM
SALES (corp-wide): 245.5B **Publicly Held**
WEB: www.precast.com
SIC: 3479 Painting of metal products
HQ: Precision Castparts Corp.
4650 Sw Mcdam Ave Ste 300
Portland OR 97239
503 946-4800

(P-7381)
LICENSE FRAME INC
Also Called: Baron & Baron
15462 Electronic Ln, Huntington Beach (92649-1334)
PHONE..................................714 903-7550
Catherine Baron, *President*
Peter Baron, *Vice Pres*
▲ EMP: 13 EST: 1997
SALES (est): 1.3MM **Privately Held**
WEB: www.licenseframe.com
SIC: 3479 Engraving jewelry silverware, or metal

(P-7382)
LINABOND INC
1161 Avenida Acaso, Camarillo (93012-8720)
PHONE..................................805 484-7373
Richard Bertram, *President*
German Gilli, *Vice Pres*
Georgia Dreifus, *Admin Sec*
▲ EMP: 23 EST: 1984
SQ FT: 23,000
SALES (est): 1.6MM **Privately Held**
WEB: www.linabond.com
SIC: 3479 Coating of metals with plastic or resins

(P-7383)
LOS ANGELES GALVANIZING CO
2518 E 53rd St, Huntington Park (90255-2505)
PHONE..................................323 583-2263
Lance Michael Rosenkranz, *CEO*
Jamie Rosenkranz, *Vice Pres*
Lance Rosenkranz, *Vice Pres*
Tim Rosenkranz, *Vice Pres*
EMP: 58 EST: 1932
SQ FT: 26,000
SALES (est): 9.7MM **Privately Held**
WEB: www.lagalvanizing.com
SIC: 3479 Coating of metals & formed products

(P-7384)
LUSTER COTE INC
10841 Business Dr, Fontana (92337-8235)
PHONE..................................909 355-9995
Jan Niblett, *President*
Robert Young, *Data Proc Staff*

EMP: 14 EST: 1984
SQ FT: 29,000
SALES (est): 1.1MM **Privately Held**
WEB: www.lustercote.com
SIC: 3479 3444 Coating of metals & formed products; awnings, sheet metal

(P-7385)
MABEL BAAS INC
Also Called: Royal Coatings
3960 Royal Ave, Simi Valley (93063-3380)
PHONE..................................805 520-8075
Marilyn Teperson, *President*
Rachel A Davis, *Credit Staff*
EMP: 50 EST: 1991
SALES (est): 5.7MM **Privately Held**
WEB: www.royalcoatings.com
SIC: 3479 Coating of metals & formed products; painting, coating & hot dipping

(P-7386)
MATSON COMPANY
213 N Olive St, Ventura (93001-2515)
PHONE..................................805 643-7166
William Matson, *Principal*
Ann Matson, *Admin Sec*
EMP: 13 EST: 2009
SALES (est): 1MM **Privately Held**
WEB: www.matsonindustrialfinishing.com
SIC: 3479 Hot dip coating of metals or formed products

(P-7387)
MERCURY METAL DIE & LTR CO INC (PA)
Also Called: Hts Division
600 3rd St Ste A, Lake Elsinore (92530-2748)
P.O. Box 86 (92531-0086)
PHONE..................................951 674-8717
Hugh Mosbacher, *President*
▲ EMP: 15 EST: 1946
SQ FT: 10,000
SALES (est): 2.4MM **Privately Held**
SIC: 3479 3953 3544 Engraving jewelry silverware, or metal; marking devices; diamond dies, metalworking

(P-7388)
METAL COATERS CALIFORNIA INC
Also Called: Metal Coaters System
9123 Center Ave, Rancho Cucamonga (91730-5312)
PHONE..................................909 987-4681
Norman C Chambers, *CEO*
Dick Klein, *President*
Joan Hoesl, *QC Mgr*
EMP: 75 EST: 1998
SALES (est): 21.5MM
SALES (corp-wide): 4.6B **Publicly Held**
WEB: www.metalcoaters.com
SIC: 3479 Painting of metal products
PA: Cornerstone Building Brands, Inc.
5020 Weston Pkwy
Cary NC 27513
281 897-7788

(P-7389)
NANOFLOWX LLC
3364 Garfield Ave, Commerce (90040-3102)
PHONE..................................323 396-9200
Yu Ting Huang, *Mng Member*
EMP: 25 EST: 2015
SALES (est): 4MM **Privately Held**
WEB: www.nanoflowx.com
SIC: 3479 Aluminum coating of metal products

(P-7390)
NELSON NAME PLATE COMPANY (DH)
Also Called: Nelson-Miller
2800 Casitas Ave, Los Angeles (90039-2942)
PHONE..................................323 663-3971
Hosmel Galan, *CEO*
Jim Kaldem, *President*
Mark Steffen, *CFO*
Shane Mast, *IT/INT Sup*
Mark Segal, *Credit Mgr*
▲ EMP: 182 EST: 1946
SQ FT: 52,000

SALES (est): 43.2MM **Privately Held**
WEB: www.nelson-miller.co
SIC: 3479 3993 Name plates: engraved, etched, etc.; signs & advertising specialties
HQ: Nm Holdco, Inc.
2800 Casitas Ave
Los Angeles CA 90039
323 663-3971

(P-7391)
NORM HARBOLDT
Also Called: Primo Sandblasting
17592 Gothard St, Huntington Beach (92647-6214)
PHONE..................................714 596-4242
Norm Harboldt, *President*
Brenda Curet-Chandler, *Marketing Staff*
EMP: 14 EST: 1999
SQ FT: 10,000
SALES (est): 2.3MM **Privately Held**
WEB: www.primo-powder.com
SIC: 3479 Coating of metals & formed products

(P-7392)
NYD LIVET TECHNOLOGIES INC
Also Called: Matson Industrial Finishing
213 N Olive St, Ventura (93001-2515)
PHONE..................................805 643-7166
Alan Anderson, *President*
EMP: 13 EST: 2020.
SALES (est): 2MM **Privately Held**
WEB: www.matsonindustrialfinishing.com
SIC: 3479 Painting of metal products

(P-7393)
PAINT SPECIALISTS INC
8629 Bradley Ave, Sun Valley (91352-3303)
P.O. Box 1124 (91353-1124)
PHONE..................................818 771-0552
Mike Kim, *President*
EMP: 13 EST: 1981
SQ FT: 15,000
SALES (est): 316.8K **Privately Held**
SIC: 3479 Coating of metals & formed products; painting of metal products

(P-7394)
PDU LAD CORPORATION (PA)
Also Called: Plastic Dress-Up
11165 Valley Spring Ln, North Hollywood (91602-2646)
P.O. Box 3897, South El Monte (91733-0897)
PHONE..................................626 442-7711
Loren Funk, *CEO*
Dennis Funk, *COO*
Allen Greenblat, *Treasurer*
Catherine M Garcia, *Vice Pres*
Darnise Smallwood, *Executive*
◆ EMP: 66 EST: 1990
SALES (est): 21.1MM **Privately Held**
WEB: www.pducat.com
SIC: 3479 Name plates: engraved, etched, etc.

(P-7395)
PEARSON ENGINEERING CORP
Also Called: Vaga Industries
2505 Loma Ave, South El Monte (91733-1417)
PHONE..................................626 442-7436
Jeff Trost, *President*
EMP: 15 EST: 1965
SQ FT: 10,000
SALES (est): 1.9MM **Privately Held**
WEB: www.vaga.com
SIC: 3479 Etching, photochemical

(P-7396)
PELTEK HOLDINGS INC
35 Argonaut Ste A1, Laguna Hills (92656-4151)
PHONE..................................949 855-8010
Jeffrey Stewart, *President*
Paul Stewart, *Vice Pres*
Joyce Stewart, *Admin Sec*
Patricia Langraphi, *QA Dir*
Bien Rabaya, *QA Dir*
▲ EMP: 30 EST: 1974
SQ FT: 10,560

PRODUCTS & SVCS

SALES (est): 2.9MM **Privately Held**
SIC: 3479 5169 Bonderizing of metal or metal products; chemicals & allied products

(P-7397)
PERFORMANCE POWDER INC
2940 E La Jolla St Ste A, Anaheim (92806-1349)
PHONE..................714 632-0600
Kevin Aaberg, *President*
Robert Goldberg, *Vice Pres*
Bob Goldberg, *General Mgr*
EMP: 29 EST: 1993
SALES (est): 5.5MM **Privately Held**
WEB: www.performancepowder.com
SIC: 3479 Coating of metals & formed products; painting of metal products

(P-7398)
PLASMA COATING CORPORATION
1900 W Walnut St, Compton (90220-5019)
PHONE..................310 532-1951
James M Emery, *President*
Willard A Emery, *Vice Pres*
EMP: 22 EST: 1972
SALES (est): 5.2MM
SALES (corp-wide): 245.5B **Publicly Held**
WEB: www.pccaero.com
SIC: 3479 Coating of metals & formed products
HQ: Southwest United Industries, Inc.
422 S Saint Louis Ave
Tulsa OK 74120
918 587-4161

(P-7399)
PLASMA COATING TECH INC
24971 Avenue Stanford, Valencia (91355-1278)
PHONE..................661 670-8810
Kamleswar Uphazya, *President*
EMP: 13 EST: 2017
SALES (est): 1.8MM **Privately Held**
WEB: www.plasmacoatingtech.com
SIC: 3479 Coating of metals & formed products

(P-7400)
PLASMA TECHNOLOGY INCORPORATED (PA)
Also Called: P T I
1754 Crenshaw Blvd, Torrance (90501-3384)
PHONE..................310 320-3373
Robert Donald Dowell, *CEO*
Andy D 'amato, *Vice Pres*
Satish Dixit, *Vice Pres*
Richard Petersen, *MIS Mgr*
Sterling McNulty, *Engineer*
▲ EMP: 73
SQ FT: 40,000
SALES (est): 12.3MM **Privately Held**
WEB: www.ptise.com
SIC: 3479 Coating of metals & formed products

(P-7401)
POWDERCOAT SERVICES LLC
1747 W Lincoln Ave Ste K, Anaheim (92801-6770)
PHONE..................714 533-2251
Ravi RAO, *President*
Annalee Binswanger, *Office Mgr*
Jesse Herrera, *Office Mgr*
Kay Monteleone, *Prdtn Mgr*
▲ EMP: 38 EST: 1981
SQ FT: 75,000
SALES (est): 7.1MM
SALES (corp-wide): 8.4MM **Privately Held**
WEB: www.powdercoatservices.com
SIC: 3479 7211 Coating of metals & formed products; power laundries, family & commercial
PA: Meridian General Capital Fund Ii, L.P.
46 Peninsula Ctr Ste 2
Rllng Hls Est CA 90274
310 818-4500

(P-7402)
PROCESSES BY MARTIN INC
12150 Alameda St, Lynwood (90262-4005)
PHONE..................310 637-1855
Irene Romero, *President*
Cathleen Fuentes, *Treasurer*
EMP: 45 EST: 1993
SQ FT: 200,000
SALES (est): 3.9MM **Privately Held**
WEB: www.processesbymartin.com
SIC: 3479 Coating of metals & formed products

(P-7403)
PVD COATINGS LLC
5271 Argosy Ave, Huntington Beach (92649-1015)
PHONE..................714 899-4892
Red Silversterstein, *Mng Member*
EMP: 18 EST: 2002
SALES (est): 1.7MM **Privately Held**
WEB: www.pvdcoatings.net
SIC: 3479 Coating of metals & formed products

(P-7404)
PYRAMID POWDER COATING INC
12251 Montague St, Pacoima (91331-2212)
PHONE..................818 768-5898
Quasim Riaz, *President*
EMP: 15 EST: 1991
SQ FT: 9,000
SALES (est): 1MM **Privately Held**
WEB: www.pyramidpowder.com
SIC: 3479 Coating of metals & formed products

(P-7405)
QUALITY PAINTING CO
19136 San Jose Ave, Rowland Heights (91748-1415)
PHONE..................626 964-2529
Louise J Merkel, *President*
Ronald Merkel, *Treasurer*
James H Merkel, *Vice Pres*
EMP: 17 EST: 1974
SQ FT: 15,000
SALES (est): 600K **Privately Held**
SIC: 3479 Coating of metals with plastic or resins; painting of metal products; varnishing of metal products

(P-7406)
RGF ENTERPRISES INC
220 Citation Cir, Corona (92878-5022)
PHONE..................951 734-6922
Rodney G Fisher, *President*
EMP: 26 EST: 1976
SQ FT: 15,000
SALES (est): 3.2MM **Privately Held**
WEB: www.rgfcoatings.com
SIC: 3479 Coating of metals & formed products

(P-7407)
RTS POWDER COATING INC (PA)
15121 Sierra Bonita Ln, Chino (91710-8904)
PHONE..................909 393-5404
Donald D Reed Sr, *President*
EMP: 20 EST: 1991
SQ FT: 8,100
SALES (est): 3.6MM **Privately Held**
SIC: 3479 Coating of metals & formed products

(P-7408)
SBIF INC
Also Called: Santa Barbara Indus Finshg
873 S Kellogg Ave, Goleta (93117-3805)
PHONE..................805 683-1711
Shelby See Jr, *President*
Rochelle See, *Corp Secy*
EMP: 24 EST: 1971
SQ FT: 6,750
SALES (est): 1.7MM **Privately Held**
WEB: www.sbifin.com
SIC: 3479 7336 Painting of metal products; silk screen design

(P-7409)
SCIENTIFIC SPRAY FINISHES INC
315 S Richman Ave, Fullerton (92832-2195)
PHONE..................714 871-5541

Carlos A Lopez, *President*
Sharon Lopez, *Corp Secy*
EMP: 23 EST: 1964
SQ FT: 15,000
SALES (est): 2.6MM **Privately Held**
WEB: www.scispray.com
SIC: 3479 3399 Coating of metals & formed products; powder, metal

(P-7410)
SHMAZE INDUSTRIES INC
Also Called: Shmaze Custom Coatings
20792 Canada Rd, Lake Forest (92630-6732)
PHONE..................949 583-1448
Michael Shamassian, *President*
Joanne Shamassian, *Treasurer*
Scott Howard, *Program Mgr*
James McPartland, *Technician*
EMP: 50 EST: 1987
SQ FT: 21,500
SALES (est): 6.9MM **Privately Held**
WEB: www.shmaze.com
SIC: 3479 Coating of metals with plastic or resins

(P-7411)
SOCCO PLASTIC COATING COMPANY
11251 Jersey Blvd, Rancho Cucamonga (91730-5147)
PHONE..................909 987-4753
Peter M Smits Jr, *President*
Rose Smits, *Vice Pres*
EMP: 25 EST: 1945
SQ FT: 60,000
SALES (est): 3.3MM **Privately Held**
WEB: www.soccoplastics.com
SIC: 3479 3444 3088 2851 Coating of metals with plastic or resins; sheet metalwork; plastics plumbing fixtures; paints & allied products

(P-7412)
SPECIALTY COATING SYSTEMS INC
4435 E Airport Dr Ste 100, Ontario (91761-7816)
PHONE..................909 390-8818
Steven Frease, *Branch Mgr*
EMP: 93 **Privately Held**
WEB: www.scscoatings.com
SIC: 3479 Coating of metals & formed products
HQ: Specialty Coating Systems, Inc.
7645 Woodland Dr
Indianapolis IN 46278

(P-7413)
SPECILZED CRMIC PWDR CTING INC
Also Called: Specialized Coating
5862 Research Dr, Huntington Beach (92649-1348)
PHONE..................714 901-2628
Lee Crecelius, *President*
EMP: 19 EST: 2004
SALES (est): 1.1MM **Privately Held**
WEB: www.specializedcoating.com
SIC: 3479 Coating of metals & formed products

(P-7414)
SPRAYLINE ENTERPRISES INC
10774 Grand Ave, Ontario (91762-4007)
PHONE..................909 627-8411
Phil Merenda, *President*
Russ Guthrie, *Treasurer*
Candy Merenda, *Vice Pres*
Darlene Guthrie, *Principal*
EMP: 14 EST: 1977
SQ FT: 9,000
SALES (est): 500K **Privately Held**
WEB: www.sprayline.com
SIC: 3479 Painting of metal products

(P-7415)
ST PIERRE GONZALEZ ENTERPRISES
419 E La Palma Ave, Anaheim (92801-2534)
PHONE..................714 491-2191
Jose Gonzalez, *President*
EMP: 17 EST: 2005

SALES (est): 781.8K **Privately Held**
SIC: 3479 Painting, coating & hot dipping

(P-7416)
STEELSCAPE LLC
11200 Arrow Rte, Rancho Cucamonga (91730-4805)
PHONE..................909 987-4711
Ron Hurst, *Branch Mgr*
Nouh Anies, *Engineer*
Belinda Glenz, *Accountant*
Brenda Eubanks, *HR Admin*
Shaun Page, *Marketing Staff*
EMP: 28
SALES (corp-wide): 99.7MM **Privately Held**
WEB: www.steelscape.com
SIC: 3479 Coating of metals & formed products
PA: Steelscape, Llc
222 W Kalama River Rd
Kalama WA 98625
360 673-8200

(P-7417)
SUNDIAL INDUSTRIES INC
Also Called: Powder Painting Ey Sundial
8421 Telfair Ave, Sun Valley (91352-3926)
PHONE..................818 767-4477
Toll Free:..................866
Hasu Bhakta, *President*
Naseen Khan, *Corp Secy*
Gurtreet Riaz, *Vice Pres*
▲ EMP: 30 EST: 1980
SQ FT: 13,000
SALES (est): 4.3MM **Privately Held**
WEB: www.powdercoatingca.com
SIC: 3479 Coating of metals & formed products

(P-7418)
SUNDIAL POWDER COATINGS INC
Also Called: Bottle Coatings
8421 Telfair Ave, Sun Valley (91352-3926)
PHONE..................818 767-4477
Hasu Bhakta, *CEO*
EMP: 25
SALES (est): 4.1MM **Privately Held**
WEB: www.sundialpowdercoating.com
SIC: 3479 Coating of metals & formed products

(P-7419)
THERM-O-NAMEL INC
2780 Mrtin Lther King Jr, Lynwood (90262-1857)
PHONE..................310 631-7866
Grant Kinsman, *President*
Colleen Kinsman, *Corp Secy*
Byron Kinsman, *Vice Pres*
Sylvia Kinsman, *Vice Pres*
EMP: 25 EST: 1950
SQ FT: 15,000
SALES (est): 1.8MM **Privately Held**
WEB: www.therm-o-namel.com
SIC: 3479 3555 2851 2759 Painting of metal products; coating of metals & formed products; printing trades machinery; paints & allied products; commercial printing; automotive & apparel trimmings

(P-7420)
TIODIZE CO INC (PA)
5858 Engineer Dr, Huntington Beach (92649-1166)
PHONE..................714 898-4377
Thomas R Adams, *CEO*
Lynnette Cubbin, *Purch Mgr*
Terry Parks, *Manager*
EMP: 17 EST: 1966
SQ FT: 26,000
SALES (est): 9.1MM **Privately Held**
WEB: www.tiodize.com
SIC: 3479 Coating of metals & formed products

(P-7421)
TITANIUM COATING SERVICES INC
720 N Valley St Ste G-H, Anaheim (92801-3830)
PHONE..................714 860-4229
Mahesh Sukumaran, *Principal*
EMP: 14 EST: 2017

SALES (est): 1.2MM **Privately Held**
WEB: www.pvdamerica.com
SIC: 3479 Coating of metals & formed products

(P-7422)
ULTIMATE METAL FINISHING CORP
6150 Sheila St, Commerce (90040-2407)
PHONE......................323 890-9100
John Ondrasik, *President*
James M Sales, *General Mgr*
EMP: 44 EST: 1983
SQ FT: 4,800
SALES (est): 943.4K
SALES (corp-wide): 20.2MM **Privately Held**
WEB: www.precisionwire products.com
SIC: 3479 Coating of metals & formed products
PA: Precision Wire Products, Inc.
6150 Sheila St
Commerce CA 90040
323 890-9100

(P-7423)
UNITED WESTERN ENTERPRISES INC
Also Called: Uwe
850 Flynn Rd Ste 200, Camarillo (93012-8783)
PHONE......................805 389-1077
Gerald Williams, *President*
Mike Lynch, *Vice Pres*
Charles Boone, *Opers Mgr*
EMP: 29 EST: 1969
SQ FT: 21,000
SALES (est): 4.1MM **Privately Held**
WEB: www.uweinc.com
SIC: 3479 Etching, photochemical

(P-7424)
VALMONT COATINGS INC
Also Called: Valmont Ctngs Clwest Glvnizing
2226 E Dominguez St, Long Beach (90810-1008)
PHONE......................310 549-2200
Corey Wraguen, *General Mgr*
EMP: 16 EST: 2016
SALES (est): 3.6MM **Privately Held**
WEB: www.valmontcoatings.com
SIC: 3479 Coating of metals & formed products

(P-7425)
WESTERN EDGE INC
37957 Sierra Hwy, Palmdale (93550-5375)
PHONE......................661 947-3900
Kris E Johnson, *Owner*
EMP: 15 EST: 2004
SALES (est): 1.2MM **Privately Held**
WEB: www.palmdaleautoshop.com
SIC: 3479 Painting of metal products

(P-7426)
WM J MATSON COMPANY
213 N Olive St, Ventura (93001-2515)
PHONE......................805 684-9410
William J Matson, *President*
Ann Matson, *Vice Pres*
EMP: 16 EST: 1983
SQ FT: 5,000
SALES (est): 1MM **Privately Held**
WEB: www.matsonindustrialfinishing.com
SIC: 3479 Coating of metals & formed products

3483 Ammunition, Large

(P-7427)
FIELD TIME TARGET TRAINING LLC
Also Called: Ft3 Tactical
8230 Electric Ave, Stanton (90680-2640)
P.O. Box 1219 (90680-1219)
PHONE......................714 677-2841
Michael R Kaplan, *Mng Member*
Forest Meadows, *General Mgr*
James Ward, *Mfg Mgr*
EMP: 24 EST: 2010
SALES (est): 3.5MM **Privately Held**
WEB: www.fieldtimetargetandtraining.com
SIC: 3483 7999 Ammunition, except for small arms; shooting range operation

---

3484 Small Arms

(P-7428)
KAK INDUSTRY LLC
2241 Celsius Ave, Oxnard (93030-5189)
PHONE......................805 981-4734
EMP: 21
SALES (corp-wide): 5.2MM **Privately Held**
WEB: www.kakindustry.com
SIC: 3484 3482 Machine guns & grenade launchers; cores, bullet: 30 mm. & below
PA: Kak Industry Llc
1709 Ne Misty Ln
Lees Summit MO 64086
816 524-8280

(P-7429)
PHOENIX ARMS
4231 E Brickell St, Ontario (91761-1512)
PHONE......................909 937-6900
Dave Brazeau, *Owner*
▲ **EMP: 21 EST:** 1992
SALES (est): 1.3MM **Privately Held**
WEB: www.phoenix-arms.com
SIC: 3484 Guns (firearms) or gun parts, 30 mm. & below

(P-7430)
SAI INDUSTRIES
Also Called: Standard Armament
631 Allen Ave, Glendale (91201-2013)
PHONE......................818 842-6144
Curtis Correll, *CEO*
Gary Correll, *President*
Kriti Ahuja, *Officer*
Marcene Correll, *Vice Pres*
Cathy Joens, *Admin Sec*
◆ **EMP:** 40
SQ FT: 24,000
SALES: 5MM **Privately Held**
WEB: www.standardarmament.com
SIC: 3484 Guns (firearms) or gun parts, 30 mm. & below

(P-7431)
TENCATE ADVANCED ARMOR USA INC (DH)
120 Cremona Dr Ste 130, Goleta (93117-3159)
PHONE......................805 845-4085
Joseph Dobriski, *President*
Matt Hisaka, *Technology*
Will Littlefield, *Plant Mgr*
Jean Auguste, *Director*
EMP: 86 EST: 2007
SALES (est): 17.9MM
SALES (corp-wide): 355.8K **Privately Held**
WEB: www.tencate.com
SIC: 3484 Small arms
HQ: Tencate Advanced Armour Holding B.V.
De Entree 143
Amsterdam
546 544-911

3489 Ordnance & Access, NEC

(P-7432)
ARMTEC DEFENSE PRODUCTS CO (DH)
85901 Avenue 53, Coachella (92236-2607)
PHONE......................760 398-0143
Robert W Cremin, *CEO*
Neal Brune, *Vice Pres*
Miguel Badena, *Admin Asst*
Kellie Young, *Administration*
Kent Rogers, *Info Tech Dir*
◆ **EMP: 330 EST:** 1968
SQ FT: 108,000
SALES (est): 110MM
SALES (corp-wide): 4.8B **Publicly Held**
WEB: www.armtecdefense.com
SIC: 3489 Artillery or artillery parts, over 30 mm.
HQ: Esterline Technologies Corp
1301 E 9th St Ste 3000
Cleveland OH 44114
216 706-2960

(P-7433)
NETWORKS ELECTRONIC CO LLC
9750 De Soto Ave, Chatsworth (91311-4409)
PHONE......................818 341-0440
Tamara Marie Christen,
Andrew Campany, *Officer*
Andrew D Campany, *Officer*
Syed Khadri, *Project Engr*
Lucy Lopez, *Manager*
▼ **EMP: 26 EST:** 2005
SQ FT: 25,000
SALES (est): 6.2MM **Privately Held**
WEB: www.networkselectronic.com
SIC: 3489 Ordnance & accessories

(P-7434)
ROBERTS RESEARCH LABORATORY
23150 Kashiwa Ct, Torrance (90505-4027)
PHONE......................310 320-7310
David Roberts, *President*
A L Roberts, *President*
Kathryn Roberts, *Corp Secy*
David E Roberts, *Vice Pres*
EMP: 15 EST: 1964
SQ FT: 10,000
SALES (est): 2MM **Privately Held**
SIC: 3489 8731 Ordnance & accessories; commercial research laboratory

(P-7435)
VECTOR LAUNCH LLC (PA)
15261 Connector Ln, Huntington Beach (92649-1117)
PHONE......................202 888-3063
Jim Penrose, *CEO*
Robert Spalding, *President*
Stephanie Koster, *CFO*
Eric Besnard, *Vice Pres*
Robert Cleave, *Risk Mgmt Dir*
EMP: 117 EST: 2016
SALES (est): 32.2MM **Privately Held**
WEB: www.vector-launch.com
SIC: 3489 Rocket launchers

3491 Industrial Valves

(P-7436)
A & G INSTR SVC CLIBRATION INC
1227 N Tustin Ave, Anaheim (92807-1616)
PHONE......................714 630-7400
Bill Arnould, *President*
Humberto Mexia, *Vice Pres*
EMP: 15 EST: 1987
SQ FT: 4,100
SALES (est): 1MM **Privately Held**
WEB: www.a-and-g.com
SIC: 3491 7699 Process control regulator valves; professional instrument repair services

(P-7437)
ADVANCED PROCESS SERVICES INC
4350 E Washington Blvd, Commerce (90023-4410)
PHONE......................323 278-6530
Somjit Burdi, *CEO*
Thomas Burdi, *Vice Pres*
Richard Smith, *Engineer*
EMP: 38 EST: 2001
SALES (est): 1.6MM **Privately Held**
WEB: www.advprocserv.com
SIC: 3491 Process control regulator valves

(P-7438)
BERMINGHAM CNTRLS INC A CAL CO (PA)
11144 Business Cir, Cerritos (90703-5523)
PHONE......................562 860-0463
Gregory Gass, *President*
Edwin Bonner, *CFO*
Kevin Mulholland, *Vice Pres*
Zabel James, *Sales Engr*
EMP: 37 EST: 1961
SQ FT: 20,000

SALES (est): 15MM **Privately Held**
WEB: www.bermingham.com
SIC: 3491 3823 5084 Industrial valves; industrial instrmnts msrmnt display/control process variable; industrial machinery & equipment

(P-7439)
C C I
22591 Avenida Empresa, Rcho STA Marg (92688-2003)
PHONE......................910 616-7426
Ed Villalva, *Manager*
EMP: 33 EST: 2017
SALES (est): 2.1MM **Privately Held**
SIC: 3491 Industrial valves

(P-7440)
CIRCOR AEROSPACE INC (HQ)
2301 Wardlow Cir, Corona (92878-5101)
P.O. Box 2824, Spartanburg SC (29304-2824)
PHONE......................951 270-6200
Scott Buckhout, *CEO*
Carl Nasca, *President*
Renuka Ayer, *Vice Pres*
Steve Cartolano, *Vice Pres*
Christopher Celtruda, *Vice Pres*
◆ **EMP: 245 EST:** 1947
SQ FT: 100,000
SALES (est): 68.6MM
SALES (corp-wide): 773.2MM **Publicly Held**
WEB: www.circoraerospace.com
SIC: 3491 3494 3769 5085 Pressure valves & regulators, industrial; plumbing & heating valves; guided missile & space vehicle parts & auxiliary equipment; seals, industrial
PA: Circor International, Inc.
30 Corporate Dr Ste 200
Burlington MA 01803
781 270-1200

(P-7441)
CONTROL COMPONENTS INC (DH)
Also Called: IMI CCI
22591 Avenida Empresa, Rcho STA Marg (92688-2012)
PHONE......................949 858-1877
Wayne Prokop, *CEO*
Abhijit RAO, *CFO*
Marla Lindly, *Admin Asst*
Monique Brotzman, *Administration*
David Fordyce, *Prgrmr*
◆ **EMP: 365 EST:** 1961
SQ FT: 75,000
SALES (est): 128.6MM
SALES (corp-wide): 2.4B **Privately Held**
WEB: www.controlcomponentsinc.com
SIC: 3491 Process control regulator valves
HQ: Imi Americas Inc.
5400 S Delaware St
Littleton CO 80120
763 488-5400

(P-7442)
CURTISS-WRIGHT FLOW CONTROL
Penny & Giles
28965 Avenue Penn, Valencia (91355-4185)
PHONE......................626 851-3100
EMP: 160
SALES (corp-wide): 2.4B **Publicly Held**
SIC: 3491 Mfg Industrial Valves
HQ: Curtiss-Wright Flow Control Corporation
1966 Broadhollow Rd Ste E
Farmingdale NY 11735
631 293-3800

(P-7443)
DANCO VALVE COMPANY
15230 Lakewood Blvd, Bellflower (90706-4240)
PHONE......................562 925-2588
Mike Dante, *President*
EMP: 30 EST: 1985
SQ FT: 27,000
SALES (est): 1.1MM **Privately Held**
WEB: www.dantevalve.com
SIC: 3491 5085 Industrial valves; industrial supplies

PRODUCTS & SVCS

(P-7444)
FCKINGSTON CO
Also Called: Storm Manufacturing
23201 Normandie Ave, Torrance
(90501-5050)
PHONE..................................310 326-8287
Joe Taormina, *President*
Rick Ward, *Information Mgr*
Mike Ray, *VP Sales*
▲ **EMP:** 23 **EST:** 1908
SQ FT: 32,500
SALES (est): 2MM **Privately Held**
WEB: www.kingstonvalves.com
SIC: 3491 3494 Industrial valves; plumb-
ing & heating valves

(P-7445)
HUDSON VALVE CO INC
5630 District Blvd # 108, Bakersfield
(93313-2109)
PHONE..................................661 831-6208
EMP: 20
SQ FT: 3,027
SALES (est): 1.9MM **Privately Held**
SIC: 3491 Mfg Industrial Valves

(P-7446)
**INTERNTNAL PLYMR
SOLUTIONS INC**
Also Called: Ipolymer
5 Studebaker, Irvine (92618-2013)
PHONE..................................949 458-3731
Michael Siino, *President*
Patrick P Lee, *CEO*
Richard Ryan, *CFO*
Mark O'Donnell, *Treasurer*
Dan Foulds, *Production*
EMP: 33
SQ FT: 18,000
SALES (est): 8MM **Privately Held**
WEB: www.ipolymer.com
SIC: 3491 3674 Industrial valves; semi-
conductors & related devices

(P-7447)
**J-M MANUFACTURING
COMPANY INC (PA)**
Also Called: JM Eagle
5200 W Century Blvd, Los Angeles
(90045-5928)
PHONE..................................800 621-4404
Walter Wang, *CEO*
Neal Gordon, *Vice Pres*
Ien CHI, *Creative Dir*
Shirley Wang, *Principal*
Taylor Matsunaga, *CIO*
◆ **EMP:** 150
SQ FT: 24,000
SALES (est): 998.2MM **Privately Held**
WEB: www.jmeagle.com
SIC: 3491 3084 2821 Water works
valves; plastics pipe; polyvinyl chloride
resins (PVC)

(P-7448)
JAMES JONES COMPANY
1470 S Vintage Ave, Ontario (91761-3646)
PHONE..................................909 418-2558
Jerry Schnelzer, *General Mgr*
Terry Martinez, *Office Mgr*
◆ **EMP:** 3988 **EST:** 1892
SQ FT: 68,000
SALES (est): 6.1MM
SALES (corp-wide): 964.1MM **Publicly
Held**
WEB: www.joneswaterproducts.com
SIC: 3491 3494 Fire hydrant valves; pipe
fittings
HQ: Mueller Group, Llc
1200 Abernathy Rd
Atlanta GA 30328
770 206-4200

(P-7449)
**LITTLE FIREFIGHTER
CORPORATION**
Also Called: Firefighter Gas Safety Pdts
204 S Center St, Santa Ana (92703-4302)
PHONE..................................714 834-0410
Tod Minato, *President*
EMP: 16 **EST:** 2000
SQ FT: 8,000
SALES (est): 3.5MM **Privately Held**
WEB: www.littlefirefighter.com
SIC: 3491 Gas valves & parts, industrial

(P-7450)
LUBRICATION SCIENTIFICS INC
Also Called: All Technology Machine
17651 Armstrong Ave, Irvine (92614-5727)
PHONE..................................714 557-0664
Richard T Hanley, *President*
Adam Rinderer, *Opers Staff*
EMP: 15 **EST:** 1993
SQ FT: 6,000
SALES (est): 3.9MM **Privately Held**
WEB: www.lubricationscientifics.com
SIC: 3491 Industrial valves

(P-7451)
**PACIFIC SEISMIC PRODUCTS
INC**
233 E Avenue H8, Lancaster (93535-1821)
PHONE..................................661 942-4499
Etsuko Ikegaya, *President*
Shigeko I Aramaki, *Corp Secy*
EMP: 24 **EST:** 1989
SQ FT: 10,000
SALES (est): 2.6MM **Privately Held**
WEB: www.pspvalves.com
SIC: 3491 Industrial valves

(P-7452)
**STORM MANUFACTURING
GROUP INC**
23201 Normandie Ave, Torrance
(90501-5050)
PHONE..................................310 326-8287
Dale Philippi, *CEO*
Russell Kneipp, *President*
Gary Wilfert, *CFO*
Richard G Ward, *Vice Pres*
Rick Ward, *Vice Pres*
▲ **EMP:** 74 **EST:** 1908
SQ FT: 41,936
SALES (est): 13.8MM
SALES (corp-wide): 77.2MM **Privately
Held**
WEB: www.bucknersuperior.com
SIC: 3491 3494 Industrial valves; sprinkler
systems, field
PA: Storm Industries, Inc.
23223 Normandie Ave
Torrance CA 90501
310 534-5232

3492 Fluid Power Valves &
Hose Fittings

(P-7453)
ACOUSTICFAB LLC (DH)
28150 Industry Dr, Valencia (91355-4100)
PHONE..................................661 257-2242
Joseph W Brown,
James Will Brown,
EMP: 100 **EST:** 2008
SQ FT: 12,000
SALES (est): 7.7MM
SALES (corp-wide): 2.4B **Publicly Held**
WEB: www.ittaerospace.com
SIC: 3492 3812 3728 Control valves, air-
craft: hydraulic & pneumatic; acceleration
indicators & systems components, aero-
space; aircraft body & wing assemblies &
parts
HQ: Itt Aerospace Controls Llc
28150 Industry Dr
Valencia CA 91355
315 568-7258

(P-7454)
**CIRCOR INSTRMENTATION
TECH INC**
2301 Wardlow Cir, Corona (92878-5101)
PHONE..................................951 270-6200
Andy Brandenburg, *General Mgr*
Robert Jones, *IT/INT Sup*
Mark Gaines, *Controller*
EMP: 18
SALES (corp-wide): 2.9B **Publicly Held**
WEB: www.circortechnologies.com
SIC: 3492 Control valves, fluid power: hy-
draulic & pneumatic; hose & tube fittings
& assemblies, hydraulic/pneumatic
HQ: Crane Instrumentation & Sampling,
Inc.
405 Centura Ct
Spartanburg SC 29303
864 574-7966

(P-7455)
CRANE CO
3201 Walnut Ave, Long Beach
(90755-5225)
PHONE..................................562 426-2531
Kevin McKown, *Manager*
Brenda Watters, *President*
Ej Jabbour, *Sales Staff*
Steve Booher, *Manager*
Carlos Davila, *Manager*
EMP: 110
SALES (corp-wide): 2.9B **Publicly Held**
WEB: www.craneco.com
SIC: 3492 Fluid power valves & hose fit-
tings
PA: Crane Co.
100 1st Stamford Pl # 300
Stamford CT 06902
203 363-7300

(P-7456)
ELECTROFILM MFG CO LLC
Also Called: Hartzell Aerospace
28150 Industry Dr, Valencia (91355-4100)
PHONE..................................661 257-2242
Daniel L Oconnell,
Julius Mekwinski, *Vice Pres*
James W Brown III,
Joseph W Brown,
Matthew Jesch,
EMP: 80 **EST:** 2008
SQ FT: 43,000
SALES (est): 20MM
SALES (corp-wide): 2.4B **Publicly Held**
WEB: www.ittaerospace.com
SIC: 3492 3728 3812 Control valves, air-
craft: hydraulic & pneumatic; aircraft body
& wing assemblies & parts; aircraft
assemblies, subassemblies & parts; aircraft
power transmission equipment; accel-
eration indicators & systems components,
aerospace
HQ: Itt Aerospace Controls Llc
28150 Industry Dr
Valencia CA 91355
315 568-7258

(P-7457)
FABER ENTERPRISES INC
14800 S Figueroa St, Gardena
(90248-1719)
PHONE..................................310 323-6200
Kevin M Stein, *CEO*
Esther Faber, *Ch of Bd*
Ronald E Spencer, *President*
Marilyn Spencer, *Corp Secy*
Loretta Appel, *Vice Pres*
EMP: 110 **EST:** 1947
SALES (est): 8MM **Privately Held**
WEB: www.pccfluidfittings.com
SIC: 3492 Control valves, aircraft: hy-
draulic & pneumatic

(P-7458)
**INDUSTRIAL TUBE COMPANY
LLC**
28150 Industry Dr, Valencia (91355-4100)
PHONE..................................661 295-4000
Farrokh Batliwala,
Bronwyn Wilber, *Sales Staff*
Daniel L Oconnell,
EMP: 99 **EST:** 2008
SQ FT: 28,000
SALES (est): 24.9MM
SALES (corp-wide): 2.4B **Publicly Held**
WEB: www.ittaerospace.com
SIC: 3492 3728 3812 Control valves, air-
craft: hydraulic & pneumatic; aircraft body
& wing assemblies & parts; aircraft as-
semblies, subassemblies & parts; aircraft
power transmission equipment; accel-
eration indicators & systems components,
aerospace
HQ: Itt Aerospace Controls Llc
28150 Industry Dr
Valencia CA 91355
315 568-7258

(P-7459)
S & H MACHINE INC
9928 Hayward Way, South El Monte
(91733-3114)
PHONE..................................626 448-5062
David Fisher, *President*

EMP: 23
SALES (corp-wide): 7.3MM **Privately
Held**
WEB: www.shmachine.com
SIC: 3492 3728 Fluid power valves &
hose fittings; aircraft parts & equipment
PA: S & H Machine, Inc.
900 N Lake St
Burbank CA 91502
818 846-9847

(P-7460)
**SPENCER AEROSPACE MFG
LLC**
28510 Industry Dr, Valencia (91355-5442)
PHONE..................................805 452-3536
Steven Spencer, *President*
Dale Metcalf, *Sales Staff*
Marco Ortega, *Manager*
EMP: 68 **EST:** 2013
SQ FT: 1,000
SALES (est): 5.2MM **Privately Held**
WEB: www.spenceraero.com
SIC: 3492 Hose & tube fittings & assem-
blies, hydraulic/pneumatic

3493 Steel Springs, Except
Wire

(P-7461)
AMERICAN SPRING INC
321 W 135th St, Los Angeles (90061-1001)
PHONE..................................310 324-2181
Ty Kehlenbec, *President*
▲ **EMP:** 16 **EST:** 2004
SQ FT: 25,000
SALES (est): 2.4MM **Privately Held**
WEB: www.americanspring.com
SIC: 3493 3446 Coiled flat springs;
acoustical suspension systems, metal

(P-7462)
ARGO SPRING MFG CO INC
13930 Shoemaker Ave, Norwalk
(90650-4597)
PHONE..................................800 252-2740
Gene Fox, *President*
Kay Greathouse, *Corp Secy*
Michael Fox, *Vice Pres*
▲ **EMP:** 55 **EST:** 1966
SQ FT: 20,000
SALES (est): 7.2MM **Privately Held**
WEB: www.argospringmfg.com
SIC: 3493 3495 3469 3599 Coiled flat
springs; wire springs; stamping metal for
the trade; custom machinery; springs;
miscellaneous fabricated wire products

(P-7463)
EIBACH INC
Also Called: Eibach Springs, Inc.
264 Mariah Cir, Corona (92879-1706)
PHONE..................................951 256-8300
Greg Cooley, *President*
Sieglinde Eibach, *Corp Secy*
Gary Peek, *Vice Pres*
Sonny Tran, *Info Tech Mgr*
Michael Coulombe, *Design Engr*
◆ **EMP:** 60 **EST:** 1987
SQ FT: 52,000
SALES (est): 15.4MM
SALES (corp-wide): 73MM **Privately
Held**
WEB: www.eibach.com
SIC: 3493 Steel springs, except wire
HQ: Heinrich Eibach Gmbh
Am Lennedamm 1
Finnentrop NW 57413
272 151-10

(P-7464)
JUENGERMANN INC
Also Called: Spring Industries
1899 Palma Dr Ste A, Ventura
(93003-5739)
PHONE..................................805 644-7165
Peter Juengermann, *President*
EMP: 40 **EST:** 1974
SQ FT: 21,600
SALES (est): 4.8MM **Privately Held**
WEB: www.springind.com
SIC: 3493 3495 Steel springs, except
wire; wire springs

(P-7465)
MATTHEW WARREN INC
Also Called: Helical Products
901 W Mccoy Ln, Santa Maria
(93455-1109)
P.O. Box 1069 (93456-1069)
PHONE...................................805 928-3851
Leroy McChesney, *Branch Mgr*
Josh Mendez, *Technician*
Kyle Sitton, *Design Engr*
EMP: 30
SALES (corp-wide): 1B **Privately Held**
WEB: www.mw-ind.com
SIC: 3493 Helical springs, hot wound: rail-
road equipment etc.; hot wound springs,
except wire; cold formed springs; coiled
flat springs
HQ: Matthew Warren, Inc.
3426 Toringdon Way # 100
Charlotte NC 28277
847 349-5760

(P-7466)
MATTHEW WARREN INC
Also Called: Century Spring
5959 Triumph St, Commerce (90040-1609)
PHONE...................................800 237-5225
Bill Cook, *Principal*
Crystal Wiemals, *Admin Asst*
Ayda Mashhadchi, *Engineer*
Gordon Braid, *QC Mgr*
George Contorinis, *Marketing Mgr*
EMP: 75
SALES (corp-wide): 1B **Privately Held**
WEB: www.mw-ind.com
SIC: 3493 Coiled flat springs; cold formed
springs; helical springs, hot wound: rail-
road equipment etc.; hot wound springs,
except wire
HQ: Matthew Warren, Inc.
3426 Toringdon Way # 100
Charlotte NC 28277
847 349-5760

(P-7467)
SCHELLINGER SPRING INC
8477 Utica Ave, Rancho Cucamonga
(91730-3809)
PHONE...................................909 373-0799
Dean Schellinger, *President*
EMP: 32 EST: 1954
SQ FT: 12,000
SALES (est): 2.9MM **Privately Held**
SIC: 3493 Steel springs, except wire

(P-7468)
SUPERSPRINGS
INTERNATIONAL INC
505 Maple St, Carpinteria (93013-2070)
PHONE...................................805 745-5553
Gerry Lamberti, *CEO*
Adam Weisner, *Chief Mktg Ofcr*
Denise Kono, *Admin Asst*
Ryan Dougan, *Controller*
Robbie Overby, *Bookkeeper*
EMP: 32 EST: 1998
SALES (est): 4.3MM **Privately Held**
WEB: www.superspringsinternational.com
SIC: 3493 Automobile springs

3494 Valves & Pipe Fittings, NEC

(P-7469)
ALLAN AIRCRAFT SUPPLY CO
LLC
11643 Vanowen St, North Hollywood
(91605-6128)
PHONE...................................818 765-4992
Robert Kahmann, *Mng Member*
Bob Kahmann, *General Mgr*
Michael Kahmann, *Info Tech Dir*
Mary Katz, *Controller*
Brian Heurkins, *Prdtn Mgr*
EMP: 45 EST: 1952
SQ FT: 30,000
SALES (est): 9MM **Privately Held**
WEB: www.allanaircraft.com
SIC: 3494 Pipe fittings

(P-7470)
ANCO INTERNATIONAL INC
19851 Cajon Blvd, San Bernardino
(92407-1828)
PHONE...................................909 887-2521
Marjorie A Nielsen, *President*
EMP: 36
SQ FT: 13,500
SALES (est): 8.2MM **Privately Held**
WEB: www.ancointernational.com
SIC: 3494 3599 3492 Valves & pipe fit-
tings; machine shop, jobbing & repair;
fluid power valves & hose fittings

(P-7471)
BRASSCRAFT
MANUFACTURING CO
Also Called: Brasscraft Corona
215 N Smith Ave, Corona (92878-3241)
PHONE...................................951 735-4375
Val Perillo, *Branch Mgr*
EMP: 23
SALES (corp-wide): 7.1B **Publicly Held**
WEB: www.brasscraft.com
SIC: 3494 3432 5074 Valves & pipe fit-
tings; plumbing fixture fittings & trim;
plumbing fittings & supplies
HQ: Brasscraft Manufacturing Company
39600 Orchard Hill Pl
Novi MI 48375
248 305-6000

(P-7472)
DIE CRAFT STAMPING INC
Also Called: Gorlitz Sewer and Drain
10132 Norwalk Blvd, Santa Fe Springs
(90670-3326)
PHONE...................................562 944-2395
Gerd Kruger, *President*
Edward A Dzwonkowski, *Agent*
▲ EMP: 14 EST: 1974
SQ FT: 20,000
SALES (est): 430.8K **Privately Held**
WEB: www.gorlitz.com
SIC: 3494 Couplings, except pressure &
soil pipe

(P-7473)
FEDERAL INDUSTRIES INC
Also Called: FI
645 Hawaii St, El Segundo (90245-4814)
PHONE...................................310 297-4040
AVI Wacht, *President*
Asher Bartov, *CEO*
Mark Overturf, *Engineer*
EMP: 15 EST: 1981
SALES (est): 3.3MM **Privately Held**
WEB: www.fedindustries.com
SIC: 3494 3728 Valves & pipe fittings; air-
craft parts & equipment

(P-7474)
GRISWOLD CONTROLS LLC
(PA)
1700 Barranca Pkwy, Irvine (92606-4824)
P.O. Box 19612 (92623-9612)
PHONE...................................949 559-6000
Brooks Sherman, *CEO*
Doris Meyers, *Admin Sec*
Jesse Teasley, *Info Tech Mgr*
Stefan Tuineag, *Engineer*
Larry Abts, *Finance*
◆ EMP: 100 EST: 1960
SALES (est): 22MM **Privately Held**
WEB: www.griswoldcontrols.com
SIC: 3494 3491 Valves & pipe fittings; in-
dustrial valves

(P-7475)
RAIN BIRD CORPORATION (PA)
970 W Sierra Madre Ave, Azusa
(91702-1873)
PHONE...................................626 812-3400
Anthony La Fetra, *President*
Bret Ramsey, *Regional Mgr*
Truong Richard Hai, *Software Engr*
Kenny Phong, *Project Engr*
Frank Atmoko, *Engineer*
◆ EMP: 125 EST: 1933
SALES (est): 445.6MM **Privately Held**
WEB: www.rainbird.com
SIC: 3494 3432 3523 Sprinkler systems,
field; lawn hose nozzles & sprinklers; farm
machinery & equipment

(P-7476)
RWS RESEARCH &
DEVELOPMENT INC
Also Called: Spears Manufacturing
15853 Olden St, Sylmar (91342-1249)
P.O. Box 9203 (91392-9203)
PHONE...................................818 364-6766
EMP: 13 EST: 2008
SALES (est): 403.4K **Privately Held**
SIC: 3494 Valves & pipe fittings

(P-7477)
VACCO INDUSTRIES (DH)
10350 Vacco St, South El Monte
(91733-3399)
PHONE...................................626 443-7121
Antonio E Gonzalez, *CEO*
Anthony Gonzelas, *Vice Pres*
Robert Mc Creadie, *Vice Pres*
Edgard Roa, *Program Mgr*
Carmen Wellever, *Program Mgr*
EMP: 248 EST: 1954
SALES (est): 91.6MM **Publicly Held**
WEB: www.vacco.com
SIC: 3494 3492 3728 Valves & pipe fit-
tings; fluid power valves & hose fittings;
aircraft parts & equipment
HQ: Esco Technologies Holding Llc
9900 Clayton Rd Ste A
Saint Louis MO 63124
314 213-7200

(P-7478)
VALTERRA PRODUCTS LLC
(PA)
15230 San Fernando Missio, Mission Hills
(91345-1121)
PHONE...................................818 898-1671
Dennis Lunder, *Principal*
Harvey Hal, *CFO*
George Grengs, *Principal*
Dan Otero, *Administration*
Debbie Krejci, *Sales Mgr*
▲ EMP: 20 EST: 1981
SQ FT: 50,000
SALES (est): 45MM **Privately Held**
WEB: www.valterra.com
SIC: 3494 3088 3949 3432 Valves & pipe
fittings; plastics plumbing fixtures; skate-
boards; plumbing fixture fittings & trim

(P-7479)
WILLIAMS MFG AERO
MACHINING
12727 Foothill Blvd, Sylmar (91342-5314)
PHONE...................................818 898-2272
Oscar Pineda, *President*
EMP: 13 EST: 1974
SQ FT: 7,400
SALES (est): 570.6K **Privately Held**
WEB: www.williamsmanufacturing.com
SIC: 3494 Pipe fittings

3495 Wire Springs

(P-7480)
AARD INDUSTRIES INC
Also Called: Aard Spring & Stamping
42075 Avenida Alvarado, Temecula
(92590-3486)
PHONE...................................951 296-0844
William Verstegen, *President*
EMP: 22 EST: 1970
SQ FT: 5,000
SALES (est): 1.6MM **Privately Held**
WEB: www.aard.com
SIC: 3495 3469 Wire springs; metal
stampings

(P-7481)
ADVANEX AMERICAS INC (HQ)
5780 Cerritos Ave, Cypress (90630-4741)
PHONE...................................714 995-4519
Kiyoshi Kato, *Ch of Bd*
Yuichi Kato, *President*
James F Grueser, *Exec VP*
Rhonda Brabbin, *IT/INT Sup*
Antonio Aguilar, *Project Engr*
▲ EMP: 211 EST: 1966
SQ FT: 52,000
SALES (est): 32.1MM **Privately Held**
WEB: www.advanexusa.com
SIC: 3495 Wire springs

(P-7482)
ATLAS SPRING MFGCORP
10635 Santa Monica Blvd, Los Angeles
(90025-8300)
PHONE...................................310 532-6200
Melvin Bayer, *President*
Stan Grietzer, *Corp Secy*
Jeff Miller, *Vice Pres*
Mary Ann Lamascus, *General Mgr*
EMP: 35 EST: 1932
SQ FT: 100,000
SALES (est): 1.7MM **Privately Held**
SIC: 3495 Upholstery springs, unassem-
bled

(P-7483)
BAL SEAL ENGINEERING LLC
(DH)
19650 Pauling, Foothill Ranch
(92610-2610)
PHONE...................................949 460-2100
Richard Dawson, *CEO*
Hugh Cook, *President*
Sean McCarthy, *CFO*
Peter J Balsells, *Chairman*
Jacques Naviaux, *Chairman*
▲ EMP: 441 EST: 1959
SQ FT: 325,000
SALES (est): 101.5MM
SALES (corp-wide): 784.4MM **Publicly Held**
WEB: www.balseal.com
SIC: 3495 3053 Wire springs; gaskets &
sealing devices
HQ: Kaman Acquisition Usa, Inc.
1332 Blue Hills Ave
Bloomfield CT 06002
860 243-7100

(P-7484)
C & M SPRING ENGRG CO INC
5244 Las Flores Dr, Chino (91710-9610)
P.O. Box 2559 (91708-2559)
PHONE...................................909 597-2030
Paul Lockhart, *President*
EMP: 31 EST: 1962
SQ FT: 15,000
SALES (est): 4.5MM **Privately Held**
WEB: www.cmspring.com
SIC: 3495 3496 Mechanical springs, preci-
sion; miscellaneous fabricated wire prod-
ucts

(P-7485)
CLIO INC
Also Called: B&B Spring Co
12981 166th St, Cerritos (90703-2104)
PHONE...................................562 926-3724
Jerome M Johnson, *President*
Reva J Johnson, *CEO*
EMP: 46 EST: 1954
SQ FT: 2,000
SALES (est): 4.1MM **Privately Held**
WEB: www.cliosprings.com
SIC: 3495 3679 Wire springs; transducers,
electrical

(P-7486)
FOREMOST SPRING COMPANY
INC
Also Called: Foremost Spring & Mfg
11876 Burke St, Santa Fe Springs
(90670-2536)
PHONE...................................562 923-0791
Forrest Gardner, *President*
Christine Brown, *Vice Pres*
Jesus Silva, *Admin Sec*
EMP: 15 EST: 1968
SQ FT: 20,000
SALES (est): 2.2MM **Privately Held**
WEB: www.foremostspring.com
SIC: 3495 3469 3493 Mechanical springs,
precision; stamping metal for the trade;
steel springs, except wire

(P-7487)
ICONN ENGINEERING LLC
6882 Preakness Dr, Huntington Beach
(92648-1567)
PHONE...................................714 696-8826
Elaine Wang,
Jay Huang, *President*
EMP: 25 EST: 2011

SALES (est): 1.6MM **Privately Held**
WEB: www.iconneng.com
SIC: 3495 Wire springs

(P-7488)
ORLANDO SPRING CORP
5341 Argosy Ave, Huntington Beach
(92649-1036)
PHONE................................562 594-8411
Frank Mauro, *President*
Zachary Fischer, *CEO*
Todd Crow, *CFO*
Jenna Gibson, *Sales Staff*
Victor Bautista, *Manager*
EMP: 40
SQ FT: 20,000
SALES (est): 8.4MM **Privately Held**
WEB: www.orlandospring.com
SIC: 3495 Wire springs

(P-7489)
PRAXIS MUSICAL INSTRUMENTS INC
19122 S Vermont Ave, Gardena
(90248-4413)
PHONE................................714 532-6655
Jong Ho Park, *President*
◆ **EMP:** 16 **EST:** 2005
SALES (est): 2.6MM **Privately Held**
WEB: www.sterlingbymusicman.com
SIC: 3495 Instrument springs, precision

(P-7490)
PRECISION COIL SPRING COMPANY
10107 Rose Ave, El Monte (91731-1898)
PHONE................................626 444-0561
Albert H Goering, *CEO*
Bert Goering, *President*
Gustavo Arenas, *Vice Pres*
William Turek, *Vice Pres*
Cheryl Hyland, *VP Accounting*
EMP: 100
SQ FT: 45,000
SALES (est): 26.1MM **Privately Held**
WEB: www.pcspring.com
SIC: 3495 Wire springs

(P-7491)
REV CO SPRING MFANUFACTURING
9915 Alburtis Ave, Santa Fe Springs
(90670-3209)
PHONE................................562 949-1958
Evelyn Valles, *President*
Vicky Garcia, *Corp Secy*
Rudy Valles, *Vice Pres*
EMP: 19 **EST:** 1973
SQ FT: 6,000
SALES (est): 4MM **Privately Held**
WEB: www.revcospring.com
SIC: 3495 Precision springs

(P-7492)
STECHER ENTERPRISES INC
Also Called: C&F Wire Products
8536 Central Ave, Stanton (90680-2718)
PHONE................................714 484-6900
Fred Stecher, *Director*
Tammy Stecher, *President*
Carol Stecher, *Vice Pres*
EMP: 15 **EST:** 1995
SQ FT: 10,000
SALES (est): 1.6MM **Privately Held**
WEB: www.stecher.openfos.com
SIC: 3495 Instrument springs, precision

(P-7493)
SUPERIOR SPRING COMPANY
1260 S Talt Ave, Anaheim (92806-5533)
PHONE................................714 490-0881
Robert De Long Jr, *President*
Robert Uphus, *COO*
Tom Pruett, *General Mgr*
Marilyn Spearman, *General Mgr*
John Wake, *Administration*
EMP: 25 **EST:** 1958
SQ FT: 17,000
SALES (est): 4.6MM **Privately Held**
WEB: www.superiorspring.com
SIC: 3495 Wire springs

3496 Misc Fabricated Wire Prdts

(P-7494)
AMERICAN WIRE INC
784 S Lugo Ave, San Bernardino
(92408-2236)
PHONE................................909 884-9990
Bambang Rahardjanoto, *CEO*
▲ **EMP:** 19 **EST:** 1991
SQ FT: 12,000
SALES (est): 3.7MM **Privately Held**
WEB: www.americanwirecorp.com
SIC: 3496 Mesh, made from purchased wire

(P-7495)
ANAHEIM WIRE PRODUCTS INC
1009 E Vermont Ave, Anaheim
(92805-5618)
PHONE................................714 563-8300
Michael Lewis, *President*
▲ **EMP:** 20 **EST:** 1985
SQ FT: 14,000
SALES (est): 4.3MM **Privately Held**
WEB: www.anaheimwire.online
SIC: 3496 Miscellaneous fabricated wire products

(P-7496)
CALIFORNIA WIRE PRODUCTS CORP
Also Called: Cal-Monarch
1316 Railroad St, Corona (92882-1840)
PHONE................................951 371-7730
John G Frei, *CEO*
Samuel A Agajanian, *President*
Francis Estaris, *CFO*
Sam Agajanian, *Principal*
Kenny Kuhns, *Prdtn Mgr*
▲ **EMP:** 30 **EST:** 1948
SQ FT: 34,000
SALES (est): 5.2MM **Privately Held**
WEB: www.cawire.com
SIC: 3496 2542 Screening, woven wire: made from purchased wire; partitions for floor attachment, prefabricated: except wood

(P-7497)
CIRCLE W ENTERPRISES INC
Also Called: Wirenetics Co
27737 Avenue Hopkins, Valencia
(91355-1223)
PHONE................................661 257-2400
Howard Weiss, *CEO*
Michael Weiss, *President*
Phyllis G Weiss, *CEO*
Mark Lee, *Vice Pres*
▲ **EMP:** 50 **EST:** 1969
SQ FT: 65,000
SALES (est): 13.9MM
SALES (corp-wide): 165.9MM **Privately Held**
WEB: www.bjgelectronics.com
SIC: 3496 Miscellaneous fabricated wire products
PA: B.J.G. Electronics, Inc.
141 Remington Blvd
Ronkonkoma NY 11779
631 737-1234

(P-7498)
CLOSETMAID LLC
5150 Edison Ave Ste C, Chino
(91710-5786)
PHONE................................909 590-4444
Ken Graper, *Branch Mgr*
EMP: 29
SALES (corp-wide): 2.2B **Publicly Held**
WEB: www.closetmaid.com
SIC: 3496 Miscellaneous fabricated wire products
HQ: Closetmaid Llc
13485 Veterans Way # 200
Orlando FL 32827
352 401-6000

(P-7499)
COVE FOUR-SLIDE STAMPING CORP (PA)
Also Called: Cove West Division
355 S Hale Ave, Fullerton (92831-4805)
PHONE................................516 379-4232
Barry Jaffe, *Principal*
Marjorie R Jaffee, *Admin Sec*
Lynne Maltz, *Controller*
◆ **EMP:** 75 **EST:** 1960
SQ FT: 50,000
SALES (est): 10.4MM **Privately Held**
WEB: www.covewestusa.com
SIC: 3496 3469 Miscellaneous fabricated wire products; metal stampings

(P-7500)
EJAY FILTRATION INC
3036 Durahart St, Riverside (92507-3446)
P.O. Box 5268 (92517-5268)
PHONE................................951 683-0805
Jerry Green, *CEO*
Cheryl Young, *President*
Jennifer Hall, *Vice Pres*
Bob Rostig, *Vice Pres*
Kavin McNabb, *QA Dir*
EMP: 33 **EST:** 1988
SQ FT: 14,000
SALES (est): 3.5MM **Privately Held**
WEB: www.ejayfiltration.com
SIC: 3496 Mesh, made from purchased wire

(P-7501)
FITTINGS THAT FIT INC
4628 Mission Blvd, Montclair (91763-6135)
PHONE................................909 248-2808
Eric C Wang, *President*
▲ **EMP:** 15 **EST:** 1947
SALES (est): 2.2MM **Privately Held**
WEB: www.ftf99.com
SIC: 3496 Fencing, made from purchased wire

(P-7502)
FRANKLIN RENFRO
525 Brooks St, Ontario (91762-3702)
PHONE................................909 984-5500
Franklin Renfro, *Principal*
EMP: 19 **EST:** 2018
SALES (est): 254.4K **Privately Held**
WEB: www.rfcwireforms.com
SIC: 3496 Miscellaneous fabricated wire products

(P-7503)
K METAL PRODUCTS INC
Also Called: Benchmark Engineering Div of
11935 Baker Pl, Santa Fe Springs
(90670-2551)
PHONE................................562 693-5425
EMP: 200
SQ FT: 54,000
SALES (est): 12.5MM **Privately Held**
SIC: 3496 3444 2542 3498 Mfg Misc Fab Wire Prdts Mfg Sheet Metalwork Mfg Nonwd Partition/Fixt

(P-7504)
NASHVILLE WIRE PDTS MFG CO LLC
10727 Commerce Way Ste C, Fontana
(92337-8246)
PHONE................................714 736-0081
George Alvarez, *Executive Asst*
▲ **EMP:** 22 **EST:** 2006
SALES (est): 347.5K **Privately Held**
WEB: www.nashvillewire.com
SIC: 3496 Miscellaneous fabricated wire products

(P-7505)
OUTDOOR GALORE INC (PA)
6801 White Ln Ste A1, Bakersfield
(93309-0301)
PHONE................................661 831-8662
Timothy S Clark, *CEO*
▲ **EMP:** 17 **EST:** 2011
SALES (est): 237K **Privately Held**
WEB: www.outdoor-galore.com
SIC: 3496 2421 3433 Grilles & grillework, woven wire; outdoor wood structural products; unit heaters, domestic

(P-7506)
PACIFIC WIRE PRODUCTS INC
10725 Vanowen St, North Hollywood
(91605-6402)
PHONE................................818 755-6400
Charles L Swick, *President*
EMP: 25 **EST:** 1984
SQ FT: 28,000 **Privately Held**

WEB: www.prontoproducts.com
SIC: 3496 Miscellaneous fabricated wire products

(P-7507)
PHIFER INCORPORATED
Also Called: Phifer Western
14408 Nelson Ave, City of Industry
(91744-3513)
PHONE................................626 968-0438
Joel Hartig, *Manager*
EMP: 119
SQ FT: 23,182
SALES (corp-wide): 555.9MM **Privately Held**
WEB: www.phifer.com
SIC: 3496 Miscellaneous fabricated wire products
PA: Phifer Incorporated
4400 Kauloosa Ave
Tuscaloosa AL 35401
205 345-2120

(P-7508)
PRECISION WIRE PRODUCTS INC (PA)
6150 Sheila St, Commerce (90040-2407)
PHONE................................323 890-9100
Vladimir John Ondrasik Jr, *Principal*
V John Ondrasik, *President*
Crystal McLaughlin, *Safety Dir*
◆ **EMP:** 200 **EST:** 1946
SQ FT: 200,000
SALES (est): 20.2MM **Privately Held**
WEB: www.precisionwireproducts.com
SIC: 3496 Grocery carts, made from purchased wire

(P-7509)
R & B WIRE PRODUCTS INC
2902 W Garry Ave, Santa Ana
(92704-6510)
PHONE................................714 549-3355
Richard G Rawlins, *President*
Keys Mike, *General Mgr*
Pedro Contreras, *Technology*
Steve Votaw, *Purch Mgr*
Frank Rowe, *VP Sls/Mktg*
◆ **EMP:** 35 **EST:** 1948
SQ FT: 20,000
SALES (est): 9.6MM **Privately Held**
WEB: www.rbwire.com
SIC: 3496 Miscellaneous fabricated wire products

(P-7510)
RAMPONE INDUSTRIES LLC
2761 Dow Ave, Tustin (92780-7209)
PHONE................................949 581-8701
Horacio Rampone,
Kirk Blackman, *Sales Staff*
▲ **EMP:** 30 **EST:** 2003
SALES (est): 4.3MM **Privately Held**
WEB: www.ramponeindustries.com
SIC: 3496 Miscellaneous fabricated wire products

(P-7511)
RAPID MANUFACTURING A (PA)
8080 E Crystal Dr, Anaheim (92807-2524)
PHONE................................714 974-2432
Joseph Lang, *Partner*
David L Lang, *Partner*
Adriana Dominguez, *Program Mgr*
Lucky Liu, *Program Mgr*
Julio Rubi, *Program Mgr*
EMP: 180 **EST:** 1979
SQ FT: 19,500
SALES (est): 89.9MM **Privately Held**
WEB: www.rapidmfg.com
SIC: 3496 Miscellaneous fabricated wire products

(P-7512)
RFC WIRE FORMS INC
525 Brooks St, Ontario (91762-3702)
PHONE................................909 467-0559
Donald C Kemby, *CEO*
Ryan Gonzales, *General Mgr*
Christine Kemby, *Admin Sec*
Amber Magana, *Admin Asst*
Jay Munoz, *Controller*
▲ **EMP:** 70 **EST:** 1946
SQ FT: 29,000

▲ = Import ▼=Export
◆ =Import/Export

SALES (est): 8.7MM **Privately Held**
WEB: www.rfcwireforms.com
SIC: 3496 Miscellaneous fabricated wire products

(P-7513)
RPS INC
20331 Corisco St, Chatsworth (91311-6120)
PHONE..................818 350-8088
Travis Miller, *President*
EMP: 25 EST: 2017
SQ FT: 1,000
SALES (est): 2MM **Privately Held**
WEB: www.radprosys.com
SIC: 3496 7389 Miscellaneous fabricated wire products; design services

(P-7514)
STANDARD CABLE USA INC
Also Called: Conductive
23126 Arroyo Vis, Rcho STA Marg (92688-2608)
PHONE..................949 888-0842
Selvin KAO, *Vice Pres*
Ann Tai, *Treasurer*
Salvin KAO, *Vice Pres*
Sarah Hought, *Technology*
Philip Deguzman, *Engineer*
▲ EMP: 15 EST: 1999
SQ FT: 10,000
SALES (est): 4.5MM **Privately Held**
WEB: www.standard-cable.com
SIC: 3496 Miscellaneous fabricated wire products

(P-7515)
SYNERGISTIC RESEARCH INC
11208 Young River Ave, Fountain Valley (92708-4109)
PHONE..................949 476-0000
Theodore Denney III, *President*
▲ EMP: 15 EST: 1999
SALES (est): 3MM **Privately Held**
WEB: www.synergisticresearch.com
SIC: 3496 Cable, uninsulated wire: made from purchased wire

(P-7516)
SYSTEMS WIRE & CABLE LIMITED
1165 N Stanford Ave, Los Angeles (90059-3516)
PHONE..................310 532-7870
Ueli Burkhardt, *CEO*
Robert Gaisford, *Vice Pres*
Jennifer Harman, *Office Mgr*
Pete Burkhardt, *Admin Sec*
EMP: 13 EST: 1985
SQ FT: 15,000
SALES (est): 3.3MM **Privately Held**
WEB: www.systemswire.com
SIC: 3496 Cable, uninsulated wire: made from purchased wire

(P-7517)
T AND T INDUSTRIES INC (PA)
1835 Dawns Way Ste A, Fullerton (92831-5301)
PHONE..................714 284-6555
John Vaughn, *President*
John Mayberry, *Officer*
Yannik Soll, *Vice Pres*
Claudio Gonzalez, *Sales Staff*
▲ EMP: 13 EST: 1943
SQ FT: 10,000
SALES (est): 11.8MM **Privately Held**
WEB: www.twistems.com
SIC: 3496 Clips & fasteners, made from purchased wire

(P-7518)
TOP-SHELF FIXTURES LLC
5263 Schaefer Ave, Chino (91710-5554)
P.O. Box 2470 (91708-2470)
PHONE..................909 627-7423
Alonso Munoz, *Mng Member*
Tony Russo, *Engineer*
Steve Prochnow, *Controller*
Barbara Bandini, *Human Resources*
Dennis Poudel, *Sales Staff*
EMP: 95 EST: 2002
SQ FT: 90,000

SALES (est): 20.9MM **Privately Held**
WEB: www.topshelffixtures.com
SIC: 3496 Miscellaneous fabricated wire products

(P-7519)
TREE ISLAND WIRE (USA) INC
Also Called: Tree Island Wire USA
5080 Hallmark Pkwy, San Bernardino (92407-1835)
P.O. Box 90100 (92427-1100)
PHONE..................909 899-1673
Daryl Young, *Manager*
EMP: 55
SALES (corp-wide): 164.8MM **Privately Held**
WEB: www.treeisland.com
SIC: 3496 Miscellaneous fabricated wire products
HQ: Tree Island Wire (Usa), Inc.
3880 Valley Blvd
Walnut CA 91789

(P-7520)
UNIVERSAL WIRE INC
1705 S Campus Ave, Ontario (91761-4346)
PHONE..................626 285-2288
Mahesh Vaghasia, *President*
Himat Desai, *CFO*
Rashmikant Vaghasia, *Vice Pres*
Parshottam Lakhani, *Admin Sec*
▲ EMP: 14 EST: 1958
SQ FT: 15,000
SALES (est): 2.5MM **Privately Held**
WEB: www.uwireinc.com
SIC: 3496 Miscellaneous fabricated wire products

(P-7521)
US RIGGING SUPPLY CORP
1600 E Mcfadden Ave, Santa Ana (92705-4310)
PHONE..................714 545-7444
Richard T Walker, *CEO*
Rick Nicholson, *Purch Mgr*
Paul Ottone, *Opers Staff*
Eddie Arias, *Sales Staff*
Roy Mader, *Sales Staff*
▲ EMP: 50 EST: 1974
SQ FT: 20,000
SALES (est): 8.9MM **Privately Held**
WEB: www.usrigging.com
SIC: 3496 5051 Miscellaneous fabricated wire products; rope, wire (not insulated)

(P-7522)
WHITMOR PLSTIC WIRE CABLE CORP (PA)
Also Called: Whitmor Wire and Cable
27737 Avenue Hopkins, Santa Clarita (91355-1223)
PHONE..................661 257-2400
Michael Weiss, *President*
Mark Lee, *Vice Pres*
Stella Reaza, *Principal*
Mike McGuire, *General Mgr*
Clark Alano, *Controller*
▼ EMP: 50
SQ FT: 50,000
SALES (est): 14.8MM **Privately Held**
WEB: www.wireandcable.com
SIC: 3496 5063 3357 Cable, uninsulated wire: made from purchased wire; electrical apparatus & equipment; nonferrous wiredrawing & insulating

(P-7523)
WHITMOR PLSTIC WIRE CABLE CORP
Also Called: Whitmor Wirenetics
28420 Stanford Ave, Valencia (91355)
PHONE..................661 257-2400
Jeff Siebert, *Vice Pres*
Tony Retamozo, *Sales Staff*
EMP: 42
SALES (corp-wide): 14.8MM **Privately Held**
WEB: www.wireandcable.com
SIC: 3496 5063 Cable, uninsulated wire: made from purchased wire; electrical apparatus & equipment
PA: Whitmor Plastic Wire And Cable Corp.
27737 Avenue Hopkins
Santa Clarita CA 91355
661 257-2400

(P-7524)
WYREFAB INC
15711 S Broadway, Gardena (90248-2401)
P.O. Box 3767 (90247-7467)
PHONE..................310 523-2147
Charles Nick, *President*
John P Massey, *Corp Secy*
EMP: 42 EST: 1948
SQ FT: 55,000
SALES (est): 5.5MM **Privately Held**
WEB: www.wyrefab.com
SIC: 3496 Miscellaneous fabricated wire products

3497 Metal Foil & Leaf

(P-7525)
FRM-USA LLC
Also Called: Framing Fabrics International
6001 Santa Monica Blvd, Los Angeles (90038-1807)
PHONE..................323 469-9006
Chaim Neuberg, *CEO*
Rommel Villa, *Vice Pres*
Larry Neuberg, *Principal*
EMP: 14 EST: 1999
SQ FT: 15,000
SALES (est): 406.2K **Privately Held**
WEB: www.nnigroup.com
SIC: 3497 Metal foil & leaf

3498 Fabricated Pipe & Pipe Fittings

(P-7526)
AEROFIT LLC
1425 S Acacia Ave, Fullerton (92831-5317)
PHONE..................714 521-5060
Jordan A Law, *Mng Member*
Devin Paglinawan, *Engineer*
Myrone Vasquez, *Business Mgr*
Paul Dallura, *Human Res Mgr*
Cecilia Donan, *Personnel Assit*
▲ EMP: 150 EST: 1968
SQ FT: 67,000
SALES (est): 46.8MM
SALES (corp-wide): 14.5B **Publicly Held**
WEB: www.camaerospace.com
SIC: 3498 Pipe fittings, fabricated from purchased pipe
HQ: Consolidated Aerospace Manufacturing, Llc
1425 S Acacia Ave
Fullerton CA 92831
714 989-2797

(P-7527)
AMERIFLEX INC
Also Called: Mw Components - Corona
2390 Railroad St, Corona (92878-5410)
PHONE..................951 737-5557
John Bagnuolo, *CEO*
Chester Kwasniak, *CFO*
▲ EMP: 76 EST: 1981
SQ FT: 32,000
SALES (est): 18.3MM
SALES (corp-wide): 1B **Privately Held**
WEB: www.mwcomponents.com
SIC: 3498 3494 3674 Fabricated pipe & fittings; valves & pipe fittings; semiconductors & related devices
HQ: Mw Industries, Inc.
9501 Tech Blvd Ste 401
Rosemont IL 60018
847 349-5760

(P-7528)
B F MCGILLA INC
Also Called: Advance Pipe Bending & Fabg Co
2020 E Slauson Ave, Huntington Park (90255-2726)
PHONE..................323 581-8288
Gary McCray, *President*
Peter Bowman, *Corp Secy*
Malcolm Field, *Vice Pres*
EMP: 20 EST: 1976
SQ FT: 4,100
SALES (est): 2.5MM **Privately Held**
WEB: www.advancepipebending.com
SIC: 3498 Tube fabricating (contract bending & shaping)

(P-7529)
BAKER COUPLING COMPANY INC
2929 S Santa Fe Ave, Vernon (90058-1425)
PHONE..................323 583-3444
Ramendra Satyarthi, *President*
▲ EMP: 35 EST: 1982
SQ FT: 65,000
SALES (est): 6.4MM **Privately Held**
WEB: www.bakercoupling.com
SIC: 3498 Couplings, pipe: fabricated from purchased pipe; pipe fittings, fabricated from purchased pipe

(P-7530)
BASSANI MANUFACTURING
Also Called: Bassani Exhaust
2900 E La Jolla St, Anaheim (92806-1305)
PHONE..................714 630-1821
Darryl Bassani, *President*
Becky Bassani, *Corp Secy*
Geoff Adams, *Research*
▲ EMP: 46 EST: 1969
SQ FT: 20,791
SALES (est): 9.4MM **Privately Held**
WEB: www.bassani.com
SIC: 3498 3599 Fabricated pipe & fittings; machine shop, jobbing & repair

(P-7531)
CAL PIPE MANUFACTURING INC (PA)
Also Called: Calpipe Security Bollards
12160 Woodruff Ave, Downey (90241-5606)
PHONE..................562 803-4388
Dan Markus, *President*
Sheri Caine-Markus, *Vice Pres*
Mike Lang, *Manager*
▲ EMP: 37 EST: 1986
SQ FT: 125,000
SALES (est): 5.5MM **Privately Held**
WEB: www.calpipebollards.com
SIC: 3498 Tube fabricating (contract bending & shaping)

(P-7532)
COTT TECHNOLOGIES INC
14923 Proctor Ave, La Puente (91746-3206)
PHONE..................626 961-3399
Gilbert L Decardenas, *President*
George C Salmas, *Vice Pres*
EMP: 16 EST: 1996
SALES (est): 631.5K **Privately Held**
SIC: 3498 Piping systems for pulp paper & chemical industries

(P-7533)
CRYOWORKS INC
3309 Grapevine St, Jurupa Valley (91752-3503)
PHONE..................951 360-0920
Timothy L Mast, *President*
Tamara Sipos, *CFO*
Donna J Mast, *Vice Pres*
David Dickens, *Manager*
EMP: 58 EST: 2009
SALES (est): 6.5MM **Privately Held**
WEB: www.cryoworks.net
SIC: 3498 1711 Fabricated pipe & fittings; plumbing contractors

(P-7534)
CUSTOM PIPE & FABRICATION INC (HQ)
10560 Fern Ave, Stanton (90680-2648)
P.O. Box 978 (90680-0978)
PHONE..................800 553-3058
Danny Daniel, *CEO*
Leonard Shapiro, *Treasurer*
David Pyle, *Branch Mgr*
Donna Vogt, *Accountant*
Danny Campos, *Sales Mgr*
▲ EMP: 60 EST: 1972
SQ FT: 8,000
SALES (est): 77.7MM
SALES (corp-wide): 98.4MM **Privately Held**
WEB: www.custompipe.com
SIC: 3498 Tube fabricating (contract bending & shaping)

PA: Shapco Inc.
1666 20th St Ste 100
Santa Monica CA 90404
310 264-1666

(P-7535)
EDMUND A GRAY CO (PA)
2277 E 15th St, Los Angeles (90021-2852)
PHONE....................213 625-0376
Lawrence Gray Jr, *CEO*
Patricia Gray, *Treasurer*
Lawrence Gray III, *Vice Pres*
Alma Corral, *Executive*
Tony Delgatto, *Sales Mgr*
▲ EMP: 108 EST: 1910
SQ FT: 50,000
SALES (est): 13.6MM **Privately Held**
WEB: www.eagray.com
SIC: 3498 Pipe fittings, fabricated from
purchased pipe

(P-7536)
**EPS CORPORATE HOLDINGS
INC (DH)**
3100 Dnald Dglas Loop Hng, Santa Monica
(90405)
PHONE....................310 204-7238
Greg Boiko, *President*
Alan Shapiro, *Principal*
Trish Dougherty, *Admin Sec*
EMP: 166 EST: 1993
SQ FT: 200,000
SALES (est): 49.6MM **Privately Held**
WEB: www.expresspipe.com
SIC: 3498 5074 Pipe fittings, fabricated
from purchased pipe; plumbing & hy-
dronic heating supplies
HQ: Express Pipe & Supply Co., Llc
1235 S Lewis St
Santa Monica CA 90404
310 204-7238

(P-7537)
**EXPRESS PIPE & SUPPLY CO
LLC (DH)**
Also Called: Expressions Home Gallery
1235 S Lewis St, Santa Monica (90404)
PHONE....................310 204-7238
Greg Boiko, *President*
EMP: 100 EST: 2012
SALES (est): 78.2MM **Privately Held**
WEB: www.expresspipe.com
SIC: 3498 5074 Pipe fittings, fabricated
from purchased pipe; plumbing & hy-
dronic heating supplies
HQ: Morsco Supply, Llc
15850 Dallas Pkwy Fl 2
Dallas TX 75248
877 709-2227

(P-7538)
FLO-MAC INC
1846 E 60th St, Los Angeles (90001-1420)
P.O. Box 1078, Huntington Park (90255-
1078)
PHONE....................323 583-8751
Larry Smith, *President*
Mark Smith, *Treasurer*
Scott Crane, *Vice Pres*
EMP: 24 EST: 1974
SQ FT: 14,000
SALES (est): 4.3MM **Privately Held**
WEB: www.flo-mac.net
SIC: 3498 Pipe fittings, fabricated from
purchased pipe

(P-7539)
ILCO INDUSTRIES INC
1308 W Mahalo Pl, Compton (90220-5418)
PHONE....................310 631-8655
Elias Awad, *President*
EMP: 35 EST: 1936
SQ FT: 23,000
SALES (est): 8.3MM **Privately Held**
WEB: www.ilcoind.com
SIC: 3498 3492 Manifolds, pipe: fabri-
cated from purchased pipe; pipe fittings,
fabricated from purchased pipe; pipe sec-
tions fabricated from purchased pipe;
tube fabricating (contract bending & shap-
ing); hose & tube fittings & assemblies,
hydraulic/pneumatic

(P-7540)
LEVCO FAB INC
10757 Fremont Ave, Ontario (91762-3910)
PHONE....................909 465-0840
Ben Levacy, *President*
Gail Levacy, *CFO*
EMP: 22 EST: 1995
SQ FT: 6,000
SALES (est): 3.3MM **Privately Held**
SIC: 3498 Tube fabricating (contract bend-
ing & shaping)

(P-7541)
MD STAINLESS SERVICES
8241 Phlox St, Downey (90241-4841)
PHONE....................562 904-7022
Marvin Davis, *President*
Sunshine Olsen, *Treasurer*
Mike Greene, *Project Mgr*
Clay Guinaldo, *Purch Mgr*
EMP: 20 EST: 1988
SQ FT: 15,000
SALES (est): 5.7MM **Privately Held**
WEB: www.mdstainless.com
SIC: 3498 1711 Fabricated pipe & fittings;
process piping contractor

(P-7542)
ONE-WAY MANUFACTURING INC
1195 N Osprey Cir, Anaheim (92807-1709)
PHONE....................714 630-8833
Sue Huang, *CEO*
Ike Huang, *COO*
EMP: 23 EST: 2005
SQ FT: 19,400
SALES (est): 3.9MM **Privately Held**
WEB: www.onewaymfg.com
SIC: 3498 3599 1541 7692 Tube fabri-
cating (contract bending & shaping); ma-
chine & other job shop work; truck &
automobile assembly plant construction;
welding repair; mechanical engineering;
fluxes: brazing, soldering, galvanizing &
welding

(P-7543)
RUSSELL FABRICATION CORP
Also Called: American Fabrication
4940 Gilmore Ave, Bakersfield
(93308-6150)
PHONE....................661 861-8495
Kevin Russell, *President*
EMP: 45 EST: 1985
SALES (est): 9.5MM **Privately Held**
WEB: www.americanfabandpowdercoat-
ing.com
SIC: 3498 3444 Fabricated pipe & fittings;
sheet metalwork

(P-7544)
**TRINITY PROCESS SOLUTIONS
INC**
4740 E Bryson St, Anaheim (92807-1901)
PHONE....................714 701-1112
Jack Brunner, *President*
Candace Brunner, *Vice Pres*
Richard Barnes, *CIO*
EMP: 20 EST: 2005
SQ FT: 13,000
SALES (est): 6.4MM **Privately Held**
WEB: www.trinityprocesssolutions.com
SIC: 3498 3317 8711 Fabricated pipe &
fittings; welded pipe & tubes; engineering
services

(P-7545)
TRYMAX
5900 E Lerdo Hwy, Shafter (93263-4023)
PHONE....................661 391-1572
Jim Garner, *Owner*
▲ EMP: 14 EST: 2010
SALES (est): 1.2MM **Privately Held**
WEB: www.jdrush.com
SIC: 3498 Fabricated pipe & fittings

(P-7546)
TUBE BENDING LLC
4747 Citrus Dr, Pico Rivera (90660-2034)
PHONE....................562 692-5829
Richard Alvarez,
Robyn Marquez, *Administration*
Beatrice Alvarez,
EMP: 15 EST: 2004
SQ FT: 6,460

SALES (est): 2.2MM **Privately Held**
SIC: 3498 Tube fabricating (contract bending & shaping)

(P-7547)
WESSEX INDUSTRIES INC
8619 Red Oak St, Rancho Cucamonga
(91730-4820)
PHONE....................562 944-5760
Archie Castillo, *President*
Linne A Castillo, *CFO*
Edward Mojica, *Vice Pres*
EMP: 25 EST: 1985
SQ FT: 30,000
SALES (est): 3.9MM **Privately Held**
SIC: 3498 8742 Pipe fittings, fabricated
from purchased pipe; pipe sections fabri-
cated from purchased pipe; management
consulting services

3499 Fabricated Metal Prdts, NEC

(P-7548)
**AMERICAN SECURITY
PRODUCTS CO**
Also Called: Amsec
11925 Pacific Ave, Fontana (92337-8231)
P.O. Box 317001 (92331-7001)
PHONE....................951 685-9680
Dave Lazier, *CEO*
Tom Cassutt, *CFO*
Thomas Cassutt, *Bd of Directors*
Tony Maniaci, *Vice Pres*
Robert Sallee, *Vice Pres*
◆ EMP: 220 EST: 1953
SQ FT: 150,000
SALES (est): 56.9MM **Privately Held**
WEB: www.americansecuritysafes.com
SIC: 3499 1731 Safes & vaults, metal;
safety & security specialization

(P-7549)
ARTISAN HOUSE INC
8238 Lankershim Blvd, North Hollywood
(91605-1613)
PHONE....................818 767-7476
Dennis Damore, *Branch Mgr*
EMP: 30
SALES (corp-wide): 2.7MM **Privately
Held**
WEB: www.artisanhouse.com
SIC: 3499 Novelties & specialties, metal
PA: Artisan House, Inc.
3750 Cohasset St
Burbank CA 91505
818 565-5030

(P-7550)
BEY-BERK INTERNATIONAL (PA)
9145 Deering Ave, Chatsworth
(91311-5802)
PHONE....................818 773-7534
Kurken Y Berksanlar, *President*
Serop Beylerian, *Vice Pres*
◆ EMP: 23 EST: 1980
SQ FT: 19,800
SALES (est): 2.8MM **Privately Held**
WEB: www.bey-berk.com
SIC: 3499 3873 Novelties & giftware, in-
cluding trophies; clocks, assembly of

(P-7551)
**CHATSWORTH PRODUCTS INC
(PA)**
Also Called: C P I
9353 Winnetka Ave, Chatsworth
(91311-6033)
PHONE....................818 735-6100
Michael Custer, *CEO*
Larry Renaud, *President*
Tom Jorgenson, *CFO*
Larry Varblow, *Corp Secy*
Ted Behrens, *Exec VP*
◆ EMP: 25 EST: 1990
SALES (est): 107.7MM **Privately Held**
WEB: www.chatsworth.com
SIC: 3499 2542 Machine bases, metal;
partitions & fixtures, except wood

(P-7552)
DEC FABRICATORS INC
16916 Gridley Pl, Cerritos (90703-1740)
PHONE....................562 403-3626
William Befort, *President*
EMP: 14 EST: 1992
SQ FT: 20,000
SALES (est): 1.2MM **Privately Held**
WEB: www.decfabricators.com
SIC: 3499 2434 Furniture parts, metal;
wood kitchen cabinets

(P-7553)
**DO IT AMERICAN MFG
COMPANY LLC**
137 Vander St, Corona (92878-3252)
PHONE....................951 254-9204
Moises Vasquez, *Mng Member*
Kathy Armstrong, *Marketing Staff*
John Armstrong,
Alicia Macias,
EMP: 16 EST: 2008
SQ FT: 20,000
SALES (est): 4.8MM **Privately Held**
WEB: www.doitamerican.net
SIC: 3499 3545 8711 Machine bases,
metal; machine tool accessories; engi-
neering services

(P-7554)
**DOT BLUE SAFES
CORPORATION**
2707 N Garey Ave, Pomona (91767-1809)
PHONE....................909 445-8888
Berge Jalakian, *CEO*
Melodye Joy Henderson, *Project Mgr*
Vickie Thomas, *Sales Staff*
Kevin Trimble, *Director*
◆ EMP: 42 EST: 2004
SQ FT: 90,000
SALES (est): 11.1MM **Privately Held**
WEB: www.bluedotsafes.com
SIC: 3499 8741 Safes & vaults, metal;
management services

(P-7555)
ECOOLTHING CORP
Also Called: Cool Things
1321 E Saint Gertrude Pl, Santa Ana
(92705-5241)
P.O. Box 6022, Irvine (926 6-6022)
PHONE....................714 368-4791
Connie Wang, *President*
Linda Wang, *Vice Pres*
▲ EMP: 50 EST: 2001
SQ FT: 10,000 **Privately Held**
SIC: 3499 5199 Novelties & giftware, in-
cluding trophies; gifts & novelties

(P-7556)
EVANS INDUSTRIES INC
Darnell-Rose Div
17915 Railroad St, City of Industry
(91748-1113)
PHONE....................626 912-1688
Bob Batistic, *Manager*
Rick Chichester, *Chief Mktg Ofcr*
Brent Bargar, *Vice Pres*
Greg Belanger, *Technical Staff*
Ryan Bargar, *Sales Staff*
EMP: 33
SALES (corp-wide): 39.4MM **Privately
Held**
SIC: 3499 5072 Wheels: wheelbarrow,
stroller, etc.: disc, stamped metal; casters
& glides
HQ: Evans Industries, Inc
3150 Livernois Rd Ste 170
Troy MI 48083
313 259-2266

(P-7557)
**EXECUTIVE SAFE AND SEC
CORP**
Also Called: Amphion
10722 Edison Ct, Rancho Cucamonga
(91730-4845)
PHONE....................909 947-7020
Scott C Denton, *President*
Robyn Denton, *COO*
George Chenarides, *Vice Pres*
◆ EMP: 30 EST: 1999
SQ FT: 11,000

SALES (est): 6.2MM **Privately Held**
WEB: www.amphion.biz
SIC: 3499 5072 7382 5099 Safes & vaults, metal; security devices, locks; confinement surveillance systems maintenance & monitoring; locks & lock sets

(P-7558)
GS PROMO INC (PA)
20829 Valley Blvd, Walnut (91789-2540)
PHONE..................................626 223-4755
Jingyi Guo, *CEO*
EMP: 43 **EST:** 2016
SALES (est): 386.4K **Privately Held**
WEB: www.gs-jj.com
SIC: 3499 Novelties & giftware, including trophies

(P-7559)
INTEGRATED TECH GROUP INC (PA)
11250 Playa Ct, Culver City (90230-6127)
PHONE..................................310 391-7213
Anil Anji, *CEO*
EMP: 168 **EST:** 2006
SQ FT: 50,000
SALES (est): 49.8MM **Privately Held**
WEB: www.intetechgroup.com
SIC: 3499 Magnetic shields, metal

(P-7560)
IPME
Also Called: International Port MGT Entp
19523 S Susana Rd, Compton (90221-5715)
PHONE..................................866 237-6302
◆ **EMP:** 50
SQ FT: 3,000
SALES (est): 7.2MM **Privately Held**
WEB: www.goipme.com
SIC: 3499 Fabricated Metal Products, Nec, Nsk

(P-7561)
J & J PRODUCTS INC
Also Called: J & J Co
9134 Independence Ave, Chatsworth (91311-5902)
PHONE..................................818 998-4250
Peter Hauber, *President*
David Kline, *Controller*
Connie Dickinson, *Manager*
Gabi Girard, *Manager*
EMP: 17 **EST:** 1994
SQ FT: 6,400
SALES (est): 1.3MM **Privately Held**
WEB: www.jandjproducts.com
SIC: 3499 5091 3089 Ammunition boxes, metal; hunting equipment & supplies; plastic processing

(P-7562)
L A PROPOINT INC
10870 La Tuna Canyon Rd, Sun Valley (91352-2009)
PHONE..................................818 767-6800
Mark Riddlesperger, *President*
James Hartman, *Vice Pres*
Brad Powers, *Technical Mgr*
John Williams, *Technical Staff*
Oscar Arevalo, *Prdtn Mgr*
▼ **EMP:** 30 **EST:** 2002
SQ FT: 28,000
SALES (est): 6.2MM **Privately Held**
WEB: www.lapropoint.com
SIC: 3499 3449 Metal household articles; miscellaneous metalwork

(P-7563)
MAGNETIC COMPONENT ENGRG INC (PA)
Also Called: M C E
2830 Lomita Blvd, Torrance (90505-5101)
PHONE..................................310 784-3100
Linda Montgomerie, *CEO*
Brian Beeler, *Executive*
Slava Trosman, *Prgrmr*
▲ **EMP:** 93 **EST:** 1973
SQ FT: 50,000
SALES (est): 13.3MM **Privately Held**
WEB: www.xyz.mceproducts.com
SIC: 3499 3677 Magnets, permanent: metallic; electronic coils, transformers & other inductors

(P-7564)
MATERIAL CONTROL INC
Also Called: Cotterman Company
6901 District Blvd Ste A, Bakersfield (93313-2071)
PHONE..................................661 617-6033
Tony Ortiz, *Branch Mgr*
EMP: 74
SALES (corp-wide): 48MM **Privately Held**
WEB: www.materialcontrolinc.com
SIC: 3499 Metal ladders
PA: Material Control, Inc.
   130 Seltzer Rd
   Croswell MI 48422
   630 892-4274

(P-7565)
MESA SAFE COMPANY INC
337 W Freedom Ave, Orange (92865-2647)
P.O. Box 52282, Irvine (92619-2282)
PHONE..................................714 202-8000
George L Vicente, *President*
Chris Nakao, *Vice Pres*
Mary Croinin, *Admin Sec*
Aguilera Erik, *Technician*
Jared Norton, *Technician*
◆ **EMP:** 40 **EST:** 2003
SQ FT: 75,000
SALES (est): 4.7MM **Privately Held**
WEB: www.mesasafe.com
SIC: 3499 5044 Safes & vaults, metal; vaults & safes

(P-7566)
MICHAEL D WILSON INC
Also Called: Strathmore Ladder
19774 Orange Belt Dr, Strathmore (93267-9798)
P.O. Box 307 (93267-0307)
PHONE..................................559 568-1115
Michael D Wilson, *President*
Gary Wilson, *Treasurer*
Jeanie Wilson, *Vice Pres*
Garry Wilson, *General Mgr*
EMP: 20 **EST:** 1936
SQ FT: 7,800
SALES (est): 2.1MM **Privately Held**
WEB: www.wilsonmichaeldc.openfos.com
SIC: 3499 Ladders, portable: metal

(P-7567)
PNK ENTERPRISES INC
Also Called: Anderson Trophy Company
12901 Saticoy St, North Hollywood (91605-3508)
PHONE..................................818 765-3770
Wesley Starnes, *President*
EMP: 21 **EST:** 1965
SALES (est): 1.1MM **Privately Held**
WEB: www.andersontrophy.com
SIC: 5999 3499 Trophies & plaques; trophies, metal, except silver

(P-7568)
PSM INDUSTRIES INC (PA)
14000 Avalon Blvd, Los Angeles (90061-2636)
PHONE..................................888 663-8256
Craig Paullin, *CEO*
Mary Sherrill, *Treasurer*
Susan Paullin, *Admin Sec*
Greg Jones, *Engineer*
Michael Daley, *QC Mgr*
▲ **EMP:** 60 **EST:** 1956
SALES (est): 64.8MM **Privately Held**
WEB: www.psmindustries.com
SIC: 3499 Friction material, made from powdered metal

(P-7569)
QUALITY MAGNETICS CORPORATION
18025 Adria Maru Ln, Carson (90746-1403)
P.O. Box 1238, Desert Hot Springs (92240-0947)
PHONE..................................310 632-1941
William K Buckley, *CEO*
Chante Buckley, *CFO*
Jimmie Miller, *Vice Pres*
▲ **EMP:** 23 **EST:** 1991
SQ FT: 27,000

SALES (est): 1.7MM **Privately Held**
SIC: 3499 3299 Magnets, permanent: metallic; ceramic fiber

(P-7570)
SKLAR BOV SOLUTIONS INC
3137 E 26th St, Vernon (90058-8006)
PHONE..................................323 266-7111
Darin Brown, *Exec VP*
EMP: 26
SALES (corp-wide): 12MM **Privately Held**
WEB: www.bovsolutions.com
SIC: 3499 Aerosol valves, metal
PA: Sklar Bov Solutions, Inc.
   1233 E Norvell Bryant Hwy
   Hernando FL 34442
   352 746-6731

(P-7571)
SPORTSMEN STEEL SAFE FABG CO (PA)
Also Called: Sportsman Steel Gun Safe
6311 N Paramount Blvd, Long Beach (90805-3301)
PHONE..................................562 984-0244
Kevin Hand, *CEO*
Chris Cude, *CFO*
Ernie Vonepp, *Representative*
Fernando Raphael, *Relations*
▲ **EMP:** 20 **EST:** 1988
SQ FT: 30,000
SALES (est): 4.5MM **Privately Held**
WEB: www.sportsmansteelsafes.com
SIC: 3499 5999 Safes & vaults, metal; safety supplies & equipment

(P-7572)
TDA MAGNETICS LLC
1175 W Victoria St, Rancho Dominguez (90220-5813)
PHONE..................................424 213-1585
Tracy Moon, *President*
Jeff Calvert, *Opers Staff*
EMP: 13 **EST:** 2015
SALES (est): 1.3MM **Privately Held**
WEB: www.tdamagnetics.com
SIC: 3499 Magnets, permanent: metallic

(P-7573)
TROPI-CON FOODS INC
3691 Noakes St, Los Angeles (90023-3244)
PHONE..................................949 472-2200
EMP: 18
SALES (corp-wide): 291.7K **Privately Held**
WEB: www.tropicon.com
SIC: 3499 Novelties & specialties, metal
PA: Tropi-Con Foods, Inc.
   17748 Sky Park Cir # 255
   Irvine CA 92614
   949 472-2200

(P-7574)
VAULT PRO
13607 Pumice St, Santa Fe Springs (90670-5105)
PHONE..................................800 299-6929
Tony Darling, *Principal*
Dick Slater, *CFO*
▲ **EMP:** 17 **EST:** 2013
SALES (est): 1.6MM **Privately Held**
WEB: www.vaultprousa.com
SIC: 3499 Fabricated metal products

(P-7575)
VESUKI INC
Also Called: V R Gifts
1350 W Lambert Rd Ste A, Brea (92821-2886)
PHONE..................................562 245-4000
Suru Manek, *President*
Kishorlal Manek, *Vice Pres*
▲ **EMP:** 18 **EST:** 1987
SALES (est): 3.5MM **Privately Held**
SIC: 5947 3499 5199 5088 Greeting cards; gift shop; magnets, permanent: metallic; gifts & novelties; aeronautical equipment & supplies; aircraft & heavy equipment repair services; aviation &/or aeronautical engineering

(P-7576)
VIGILANT DRONE DEFENSE INC
1055 W 7th St Fl 33, Los Angeles (90017-2577)
PHONE..................................424 275-8282
Paul Tremaine, *President*
Bob Kroutil, *COO*
EMP: 20 **EST:** 2017
SALES (est): 1.3MM **Privately Held**
WEB: www.vigilantdronedefense.com
SIC: 3499 3728 Target drones, for use by ships: metal; target drones

(P-7577)
WESTERN FAB INC
Also Called: Western Fabricators
9823 E Ave, Hesperia (92345-6280)
PHONE..................................760 949-1441
Bryon Porter, *President*
Mandi Porter, *Corp Secy*
Tina Thompson, *Office Mgr*
EMP: 15 **EST:** 1990
SQ FT: 4,800
SALES (est): 2MM **Privately Held**
WEB: www.westernfabricators.com
SIC: 3499 Welding tips, heat resistant: metal

(P-7578)
Z MANUFACTURING INC
2679 Sierra Way, La Verne (91750-5642)
PHONE..................................909 593-2191
Steve Ziolkowski, *President*
Jeanette Ziolkowski, *Admin Sec*
EMP: 20 **EST:** 1985
SQ FT: 30,000
SALES (est): 1.2MM **Privately Held**
WEB: www.zmanufacturinginc.com
SIC: 3499 8711 3751 Reels, cable: metal; engineering services; motorcycles, bicycles & parts

---

3511 Steam, Gas & Hydraulic Turbines & Engines

(P-7579)
BAE SYSTEMS CONTROLS INC
5140 W Goldleaf Cir G100, Los Angeles (90056-1666)
PHONE..................................323 642-5000
Karla Scherer, *CIO*
Gerardo Cornejo, *Technician*
Stephanie Carrera, *Accounting Dir*
EMP: 17
SALES (corp-wide): 25.6B **Privately Held**
SIC: 3511 3721 3812 3728 Turbines & turbine generator sets; aircraft; search & navigation equipment; aircraft parts & equipment
HQ: Bae Systems Controls Inc.
   1098 Clark St
   Endicott NY 13760
   607 770-2000

(P-7580)
CAPSTONE GREEN ENERGY CORP (PA)
16640 Stagg St, Van Nuys (91406-1630)
PHONE..................................818 734-5300
Darren R Jamison, *President*
Holly A Van Deursen, *Ch of Bd*
Frederick S Hencken III, *CFO*
Gary Mayo, *Bd of Directors*
James D Crouse, *Officer*
◆ **EMP:** 119 **EST:** 1988
SQ FT: 79,000
SALES: 67.6MM **Publicly Held**
WEB: www.capstonegreenenergy.com
SIC: 3511 Turbines & turbine generator sets

(P-7581)
CLIPPER WINDPOWER PLC
6305 Carpinteria Ave # 300, Carpinteria (93013-2968)
PHONE..................................805 690-3275
Mauricio Quintana, *President*
Josh Fox, *Admin Sec*
David Wheatley, *Engineer*
Matt Shaffer, *Controller*
Ken Klosterman, *Buyer*
EMP: 740 **EST:** 2005

P R O D U C T S & S V C S

SALES (est): 66.3MM **Privately Held**
WEB: www.clipperwind.com
SIC: 3511 Turbines & turbine generator sets

(P-7582)
ENER-CORE POWER INC (HQ)
30100 Town Center Dr O, Laguna Niguel (92677-2064)
PHONE................................949 428-3300
Alain Castro, *CEO*
Boris Maslov, *President*
Wes Kimmel, *CFO*
Charles Cherington, *Bd of Directors*
Patrick Connelly, *Bd of Directors*
EMP: 14 **EST:** 2012
SALES (est): 9.1MM **Publicly Held**
WEB: www.ener-core.com
SIC: 3511 Turbines & turbine generator sets
PA: Ener-Core, Inc.
30100 Town Center Dr
Laguna Niguel CA 92677
949 732-4400

(P-7583)
ENERGENT CORPORATION
1831 Carnegie Ave, Santa Ana (92705-5528)
PHONE................................949 885-0365
Lance G Hays, *President*
EMP: 13 **EST:** 2002
SALES (est): 1.7MM **Privately Held**
WEB: www.energent.net
SIC: 3511 Turbines & turbine generator sets

(P-7584)
ENERGENT CORPORATION
2321 Pullman St, Santa Ana (92705-5506)
PHONE................................949 885-0365
Dicran Sahabian, *Administration*
Patrick Boyle, *Engineer*
Phillip Welch, *Engineer*
Connie Tang, *Buyer*
EMP: 15 **EST:** 2015
SALES (est): 624.9K **Privately Held**
WEB: www.energent.net
SIC: 3511 Turbines & turbine generator sets

(P-7585)
GE WIND ENERGY LLC (HQ)
13000 Jameson Rd, Tehachapi (93561-8157)
PHONE................................661 822-6835
J R Spriggle,
◆ **EMP:** 400 **EST:** 2002
SALES (est): 549.3MM
SALES (corp-wide): 79.6B **Publicly Held**
WEB: www.ge.com
SIC: 3511 Turbines & turbine generator sets
PA: General Electric Company
5 Necco St
Boston MA 02210
617 443-3000

(P-7586)
GE WIND ENERGY LLC
13681 Chantico Rd, Tehachapi (93561-8188)
PHONE................................661 823-6423
Gerlad Turk, *Manager*
John Hornbeck, *Engineer*
Kelly Chambers, *Facilities Mgr*
EMP: 89
SALES (corp-wide): 79.6B **Publicly Held**
SIC: 3511 Turbines & turbine generator sets
HQ: Ge Wind Energy, Llc
13000 Jameson Rd
Tehachapi CA 93561
661 822-6835

(P-7587)
LA TURBINE (HQ)
28557 Industry Dr, Valencia (91355-5424)
PHONE................................661 294-8290
John Maskaluk, *CEO*
Danny Mascari, *President*
David Dorough, *CFO*
Dominique Maskaluk, *CFO*
Julie Stalmans, *Executive Asst*
▼ **EMP:** 69 **EST:** 2003
SQ FT: 90,000

SALES (est): 19.6MM **Publicly Held**
WEB: www.laturbine.com
SIC: 3511 Turbines & turbine generator sets & parts

(P-7588)
OEM PARTS NETWORK INC
10763 Bell Ct, Rancho Cucamonga (91730-4834)
PHONE................................909 944-8030
Todd Stutesman, *CEO*
EMP: 14 **EST:** 2009
SALES (est): 4.6MM **Privately Held**
WEB: www.oempartsnetwork.com
SIC: 3511 Turbines & turbine generator sets & parts

(P-7589)
TURBINE REPAIR SERVICES LLC (PA)
1838 E Cedar St, Ontario (91761-7763)
PHONE................................909 947-2256
Victor M Sanchez, *Mng Member*
Dave Meyer,
Danny Sanchez,
Cesar Siordia,
Michael Dorrel, *Mng Member*
EMP: 87 **EST:** 2000
SQ FT: 12,000
SALES (est): 16.3MM **Privately Held**
WEB: www.turbinerepairservices.com
SIC: 3511 Turbines & turbine generator sets

(P-7590)
WEPOWER LLC
32 Journey Ste 250, Aliso Viejo (92656-5329)
PHONE................................866 385-9463
Marvin Winkler, *Mng Member*
Howard Makler, *President*
Thomas Schiff,
Kevin B Donovan, *Director*
▲ **EMP:** 21 **EST:** 2008
SALES (est): 638K **Privately Held**
SIC: 3511 Turbines & turbine generator set units, complete

3519 Internal Combustion Engines, NEC

(P-7591)
CUMMINS PACIFIC LLC
9520 Stewart And Gray Rd, Downey (90241-5559)
PHONE................................866 934-4373
Susan Morales, *Principal*
Courtney Cheek, *Opers Staff*
EMP: 15
SALES (corp-wide): 19.8B **Publicly Held**
WEB: www.cummins.com
SIC: 3519 Internal combustion engines
HQ: Cummins Pacific, Llc
1939 Deere Ave
Irvine CA 92606

(P-7592)
CUMMINS PACIFIC LLC
3061 S Riverside Ave, Bloomington (92316-3527)
PHONE................................909 877-0433
Brandon Daste, *Principal*
EMP: 15
SALES (corp-wide): 19.8B **Publicly Held**
WEB: www.cummins.com
SIC: 3519 Internal combustion engines
HQ: Cummins Pacific, Llc
1939 Deere Ave
Irvine CA 92606

(P-7593)
CUMMINS PACIFIC LLC (HQ)
1939 Deere Ave, Irvine (92606-4818)
PHONE................................949 253-6000
Mark Yragui, *President*
Robert Bogen, *Engineer*
▲ **EMP:** 85 **EST:** 2002

SALES (est): 133.4MM
SALES (corp-wide): 19.8B **Publicly Held**
WEB: www.cummins.com
SIC: 3519 5063 7538 Internal combustion engines; generators; general automotive repair shops
PA: Cummins Inc.
500 Jackson St
Columbus IN 47201
812 377-5000

(P-7594)
CUMMINS PACIFIC LLC
3958 Transport St, Ventura (93003-5128)
PHONE................................805 644-7281
Dan Elliott, *Manager*
Tom Powers, *Sales Mgr*
EMP: 15
SALES (corp-wide): 19.8B **Publicly Held**
WEB: www.cummins.com
SIC: 3519 5063 Internal combustion engines; generators
HQ: Cummins Pacific, Llc
1939 Deere Ave
Irvine CA 92606

(P-7595)
GALE BANKS ENGINEERING
Also Called: Banks Power Products
546 S Duggan Ave, Azusa (91702-5136)
PHONE................................626 969-9600
Gale C Banks III, *President*
Vicki L Banks, *Vice Pres*
▲ **EMP:** 195 **EST:** 1970
SQ FT: 121,000
SALES (est): 53.3MM **Privately Held**
WEB: www.bankspower.com
SIC: 3519 3714 Parts & accessories, internal combustion engines; motor vehicle parts & accessories

(P-7596)
HIGH TECH MACHINE SHOP S-CORP
15149 Boyle Ave, Fontana (92337-7209)
PHONE................................909 356-5437
Susie Sanchez, *Owner*
Elias Sanchez, *Co-Owner*
EMP: 13 **EST:** 2015
SALES (est): 1.2MM **Privately Held**
SIC: 3519 Diesel engine rebuilding

(P-7597)
RACING BEAT INC
4789 E Wesley Dr, Anaheim (92807-1941)
PHONE................................714 779-8677
James Mederer, *President*
▲ **EMP:** 22 **EST:** 1971
SQ FT: 7,500
SALES (est): 3.5MM **Privately Held**
WEB: www.racingbeat.com
SIC: 3519 Parts & accessories, internal combustion engines

(P-7598)
SOUTHWEST PRODUCTS CORPORATION
2875 Cherry Ave, Signal Hill (90755-1908)
PHONE................................360 887-7400
Jason Hair, *Branch Mgr*
Holly Boranian, *Finance Mgr*
EMP: 15
SALES (corp-wide): 18.1MM **Privately Held**
WEB: www.southwestproducts.com
SIC: 3519 Diesel engine rebuilding
HQ: Southwest Products Corporation
11690 N 132nd Ave
Surprise AZ 85379
306 887-7400

(P-7599)
SUZUKI MOTOR OF AMERICA INC (HQ)
Also Called: Suzuki USA
3251 E Imperial Hwy, Brea (92821-6795)
P.O. Box 1100 (92822-1100)
PHONE................................714 996-7040
Takeshi Hayasaki, *President*
Suzanne Miller, *COO*
Robert Alsip, *Trustee*
Takuya Sato, *Exec VP*
Art Hashima, *Vice Pres*
◆ **EMP:** 250

SALES (est): 173MM **Privately Held**
WEB: www.suzuki.com
SIC: 5511 3519 3799 Automobiles, new & used; outboard motors; recreational vehicles

(P-7600)
TRACY INDUSTRIES INC
Also Called: Genuine Parts Distributors
3200 E Guasti Rd Ste 100, Ontario (91761-8661)
P.O. Box 1260 (91762-0260)
PHONE................................562 692-9034
Timothy Engvall, *CEO*
Rob McFarlane, *Partner*
Erma Jean Tracy, *Vice Pres*
David Rosenberger, *Admin Sec*
Steffani Bolhofner, *Marketing Staff*
▲ **EMP:** 216 **EST:** 1946
SALES (est): 142MM **Privately Held**
SIC: 3519 7538 Internal combustion engines; engine rebuilding: automotive

(P-7601)
TRANSONIC COMBUSTION INC
461 Calle San Pablo, Camarillo (93012-8506)
PHONE................................805 465-5145
Wolfgang Bullmer, *President*
Timothy Noonan, *CFO*
Mike Cheiky, *CTO*
EMP: 40 **EST:** 2006
SALES (est): 7.1MM **Privately Held**
WEB: www.tscombustion.com
SIC: 3519 Internal combustion engines

3523 Farm Machinery & Eqpt

(P-7602)
AG SPRAY EQUIPMENT INC
4618 Saco Rd, Bakersfield (93308-9626)
PHONE................................661 391-9081
Jared Schweitzer, *Asst Mgr*
Dennis Grumling, *Manager*
EMP: 17 **EST:** 2014
SALES (est): 1.1MM **Privately Held**
WEB: www.agspray.com
SIC: 3523 Farm machinery & equipment

(P-7603)
ALBERS MFG CO INC (PA)
Also Called: Albers Dairy Equipment. Inc
14323 Albers Way, Chino (91710-1134)
PHONE................................909 597-5537
Teo Albers Jr, *President*
◆ **EMP:** 21 **EST:** 1949
SQ FT: 10,000
SALES (est): 4.9MM **Privately Held**
SIC: 3523 Barn stanchions & standards

(P-7604)
AMARILLO WIND MACHINE LLC
20513 Avenue 256, Exeter (93221-9656)
P.O. Box 96809, Chicago IL (60693-6809)
PHONE................................559 592-4256
Steven Chaloupka, *President*
EMP: 18 **EST:** 1989
SQ FT: 12,000
SALES (est): 7.5MM
SALES (corp-wide): 245.3B **Publicly Held**
WEB: www.amarillowind.com
SIC: 3523 7699 Farm machinery & equipment; agricultural equipment repair services
HQ: Amarillo Gear Company Llc
2401 W Sundown Ln
Amarillo TX 79118
806 622-1273

(P-7605)
B W IMPLEMENT CO
288 W Front St, Buttonwillow (93206)
P.O. Box 758 (93206-0758)
PHONE................................661 764-5254
John C Blair, *President*
Julien Parsons, *Treasurer*
Alene Parsons, *Admin Sec*
EMP: 22 **EST:** 1948
SQ FT: 85,000
SALES (est): 4.4MM **Privately Held**
WEB: www.bwimp.com
SIC: 3523 5083 5999 Tractors, farm; farm implements; farm machinery

---

(P-7606)
BRAZEAU THOROUGHBRED FARMS LP
30500 State St, Hemet (92543-9258)
PHONE..................951 201-2278
Nadine Anderson, *Branch Mgr*
EMP: 28
SALES (corp-wide): 39.7K **Privately Held**
WEB:
www.brazeauthoroughbredfarms.com
SIC: 3523 0291 0752 Harvesters, fruit, vegetable, tobacco, etc.; animal specialty farm, general; boarding services, horses: racing & non-racing
PA: Brazeau Thoroughbred Farms, L.P.
660 Camino De Los Mares
San Clemente CA
-

(P-7607)
BRITZ FERTILIZERS INC
12498 11th Ave, Hanford (93230-9523)
PHONE..................559 582-0942
Keith Roberts, *Manager*
EMP: 63
SALES (corp-wide): 104.2MM **Privately Held**
SIC: 3523 2873 Spreaders, fertilizer; nitrogenous fertilizers
HQ: Britz Fertilizers Inc.
3265 W Figarden Dr
Fresno CA 93711
559 448-8000

(P-7608)
CAGECO INC
16225 Beaver Rd, Adelanto (92301-3908)
PHONE..................800 605-4859
Mike Alexander, *President*
EMP: 38 **EST:** 2012
SALES (est): 3.4MM **Privately Held**
WEB: www.cactushorsecorrals.com
SIC: 3523 Barn, silo, poultry, dairy & livestock machinery

(P-7609)
DOUBLE K INDUSTRIES INC
9711 Mason Ave, Chatsworth (91311-5208)
PHONE..................818 772-2887
Greg Crisp, *CEO*
Rich Warfield, *Purch Mgr*
Michael Beavers,
Danita Adkins, *Manager*
▲ **EMP:** 19 **EST:** 2008
SALES (est): 4.1MM **Privately Held**
WEB: www.doublekindustries.com
SIC: 3523 Farm machinery & equipment

(P-7610)
DOWDYS SALES AND SERVICES INC
15185 Avenue 224, Tulare (93274-9305)
PHONE..................559 688-6973
Brad Dowdy, *President*
Melinda Dowdy, *Corp Secy*
Chris Ince, *Parts Mgr*
EMP: 15 **EST:** 1987
SALES (est): 2.2MM **Privately Held**
WEB: www.dowdys.com
SIC: 3523 Farm machinery & equipment

(P-7611)
EXETER MERCANTILE COMPANY
Also Called: Ace Hardware
258 E Pine St, Exeter (93221-1750)
P.O. Box 67 (93221-0067)
PHONE..................559 592-2121
Robert G Schelling, *President*
Sidney Schelling Jr, *Corp Secy*
Brian Schelling, *Vice Pres*
Staci Smith, *Office Mgr*
Bryan Helin, *Materials Mgr*
▲ **EMP:** 19 **EST:** 1916
SQ FT: 22,000
SALES (est): 4.4MM **Privately Held**
WEB: www.exetermercantile.com
SIC: 3523 3537 5072 5251 Tractors, farm; industrial trucks & tractors; hardware; hardware

(P-7612)
INVELOP INC
Also Called: Double K Industries
9711 Mason Ave, Chatsworth (91311-5208)
PHONE..................818 772-2887
Gregory S Crisp, *President*
Grant Parrinello, *Engineer*
Valerie Crisp, *Marketing Staff*
◆ **EMP:** 28 **EST:** 1982
SQ FT: 20,700
SALES (est): 2.4MM **Privately Held**
SIC: 3523 Clippers, for animal use: hand or electric; pet supplies; veterinarians' instruments & apparatus

(P-7613)
MARIE EDWARD VINEYARDS INC
6901 E Brundage Ln, Bakersfield (93307-3057)
PHONE..................661 363-5038
Matthew E Brock, *President*
Amanda Shannon, *Marketing Staff*
EMP: 35 **EST:** 1988
SALES (est): 3.3MM **Privately Held**
WEB: www.wvv.brockstrailersinc.com
SIC: 3523 5013 7539 5511 Trailers & wagons, farm; trailer parts & accessories; trailer repair; trucks, tractors & trailers: new & used; utility trailers; welding on site

(P-7614)
NIKKEL IRON WORKS CORPORATION
17045 S Central Vly Hwy, Shafter (93263-2704)
P.O. Box 1597 (93263-1597)
PHONE..................661 746-4904
Andrew Cummings, *President*
Shirley Cummings, *Corp Secy*
EMP: 17 **EST:** 1924
SQ FT: 26,000
SALES (est): 3.5MM **Privately Held**
WEB: www.nikkelironworks.com
SIC: 3523 Farm machinery & equipment

(P-7615)
NYX INDUSTRIES INC
Also Called: Salco Products
9452 Resenda Ave, Fontana (92335-2541)
PHONE..................909 937-3923
Gabriel Hermida, *CEO*
Cindy Chavez, *President*
▲ **EMP:** 13 **EST:** 1967
SALES (est): 2.5MM **Privately Held**
WEB: www.salcodrip.com
SIC: 3523 Irrigation equipment, self-propelled

(P-7616)
QUINN COMPANY
Also Called: Caterpillar Authorized Dealer
3359 Pomona Blvd, Pomona (91768-3235)
PHONE..................888 987-8466
Blake Quinn, *CEO*
EMP: 15 **EST:** 2007
SALES (est): 1.1MM **Privately Held**
WEB: www.quinncompany.com
SIC: 3523 7353 5082 Tractors, farm; heavy construction equipment rental; construction & mining machinery

(P-7617)
RANDELL EQUIPTMENT & MFG
Also Called: Randell Equipment & Mfg
1408 S Lexington St, Delano (93215-9783)
PHONE..................661 725-6380
Lee Brown, *Vice Pres*
▼ **EMP:** 14 **EST:** 1980
SALES (est): 755.7K **Privately Held**
WEB: www.randellequipment.com
SIC: 3523 Sprayers & spraying machines, agricultural

(P-7618)
RUSSELL KC & SON
375 E Paige Ave, Tulare (93274-8902)
PHONE..................559 686-3236
EMP: 13 **EST:** 2006
SQ FT: 17,100
SALES (est): 512.8K **Privately Held**
SIC: 3523 Dairy equipment (farm)

(P-7619)
SIGNATURE CONTROL SYSTEMS
16485 Laguna Canyon Rd # 130, Irvine (92618-3848)
PHONE..................949 580-3640
Brian Smith, *President*
Jane Smith, *Vice Pres*
◆ **EMP:** 100 **EST:** 2000
SQ FT: 7,000
SALES (est): 9.2MM **Privately Held**
WEB: www.signaturecontrolsystems.com
SIC: 3523 Irrigation equipment, self-propelled

(P-7620)
SPECIALIZED DAIRY SERVICE INC
Also Called: S D S
1710 E Philadelphia St, Ontario (91761-7705)
PHONE..................909 923-3420
Joe T Trujillo, *CEO*
Joe Trujillo, *Vice Pres*
EMP: 22 **EST:** 2004
SQ FT: 25,000
SALES (est): 7.7MM **Privately Held**
WEB: www.sdsdairy.com
SIC: 3523 3556 5083 Dairy equipment (farm); dairy & milk machinery; dairy machinery & equipment

(P-7621)
SPRAYING DEVICES INC
Also Called: S D I
447 E Caldwell Ave, Visalia (93277-7609)
P.O. Box 3107 (93278-3107)
PHONE..................559 734-5555
William S Bennet II, *President*
Denise Bennett, *Vice Pres*
EMP: 17 **EST:** 1982
SQ FT: 16,000
SALES (est): 4.3MM **Privately Held**
WEB: www.sprayingdevices.com
SIC: 3523 Farm machinery & equipment

(P-7622)
STORM INDUSTRIES INC (PA)
23223 Normandie Ave, Torrance (90501-5050)
PHONE..................310 534-5232
Dale R Philippi, *CEO*
Kenneth J Harrisberger, *Ch of Bd*
Guy E Marge, *Ch of Bd*
Georgia Claessens, *Corp Secy*
Elizabeth McGovern, *Vice Pres*
▲ **EMP:** 100 **EST:** 1977
SALES (est): 77.2MM **Privately Held**
WEB: www.stormind.com
SIC: 3523 6552 Irrigation equipment, self-propelled; subdividers & developers

(P-7623)
UMBRLA INC
3242 Halladay St Ste 202, Santa Ana (92705-5648)
PHONE..................888 909-5564
Frank Knuettel II, *CEO*
EMP: 52 **EST:** 2019
SALES (est): 14.2MM **Publicly Held**
WEB: www.unrivaledbrands.com
SIC: 3523 Farm machinery & equipment
PA: Unrivaled Brands, Inc.
3242 Halladay St Ste 202
Santa Ana CA 92705
-

(P-7624)
UNRIVALED BRANDS INC (PA)
3242 Halladay St Ste 202, Santa Ana (92705-5648)
PHONE..................888 909-5564
Frank Knuettel II, *CEO*
Nicholas Kovacevich, *Ch of Bd*
Oren Schauble, *President*
Uri Kenig, *COO*
Jeffrey Batliner, *CFO*
EMP: 39 **EST:** 2008
SALES (est): 14.2MM **Publicly Held**
WEB: www.unrivaledbrands.com
SIC: 3523 Farm machinery & equipment

(P-7625)
VAL PLASTIC USA L L C
4570 Eucalyptus Ave Ste C, Chino (91710-9200)
PHONE..................909 390-9600
Dablu Kundu, *General Mgr*
▲ **EMP:** 15 **EST:** 1992
SQ FT: 11,000
SALES (est): 2.2MM **Privately Held**
WEB: www.valplasticusa.com
SIC: 3523 Fertilizing, spraying, dusting & irrigation machinery

(P-7626)
WARREN & BAERG MFG INC
39950 Road 108, Dinuba (93618-9518)
PHONE..................559 591-6790
Robert Baerg, *Chairman*
Randy R Baerg, *President*
Robert L Baerg, *Chairman*
Richard Barnes, *CIO*
Louis Garcia, *Engineer*
▲ **EMP:** 30 **EST:** 1968
SQ FT: 15,000
SALES (est): 5.8MM **Privately Held**
WEB: www.warrenbaerg.com
SIC: 3523 Planting, haying, harvesting & processing machinery

(P-7627)
WELDCRAFT INDUSTRIES INC
18794 Avenue 96, Terra Bella (93270-9630)
P.O. Box 11104 (93270-1104)
PHONE..................559 784-4322
Gerald R Micke, *President*
Dixie L Micke, *Vice Pres*
EMP: 17 **EST:** 1972
SALES (est): 4.5MM **Privately Held**
WEB: www.weldcraftindustries.com
SIC: 3523 5191 Harvesters, fruit, vegetable, tobacco, etc.; farm supplies

---

3524 Garden, Lawn Tractors & Eqpt

(P-7628)
MCLANE MANUFACTURING INC
6814 Foster Bridge Blvd, Bell Gardens (90201-2032)
PHONE..................562 633-8158
Elmer E Malchow, *Ch of Bd*
Olivia Osorio, *Treasurer*
Ronald Mc Lane, *Vice Pres*
Jorge Valdez, *Opers Staff*
▲ **EMP:** 65 **EST:** 1942
SALES (est): 10MM **Privately Held**
WEB: www.mclaneedgers.com
SIC: 3524 Lawnmowers, residential: hand or power

(P-7629)
POWER - TRIM CO
6060 Phyllis Dr, Cypress (90630-5243)
P.O. Box 18380, Irvine (92623-8380)
PHONE..................714 523-8560
James O Dykes, *CEO*
Philip Shearer, *Vice Pres*
Barbara Dykes, *Admin Sec*
▼ **EMP:** 15
SALES: 6.5MM **Privately Held**
WEB: www.powertrim.com
SIC: 3524 5083 Edgers, lawn; lawn & garden machinery & equipment

(P-7630)
SCOTTS TEMECULA OPERATIONS LLC (DH)
42375 Remington Ave, Temecula (92590-2512)
PHONE..................951 719-1700
Jim Hagedorn, *CEO*
Barry Sanders, *President*
Luis Talavera, *Engineer*
Bob Bawcombe, *Opers Staff*
Thomas Hart, *Sales Mgr*
▲ **EMP:** 249 **EST:** 1953
SQ FT: 400,000
SALES (est): 74.7MM
SALES (corp-wide): 4.1B **Publicly Held**
WEB: www.scotts.com
SIC: 3524 Lawn & garden equipment

PRODUCTS & SVCS

HQ: The Scotts Company Llc
14111 Scottslawn Rd
Marysville OH 43040
937 644-0011

(P-7631)
SPYDER MANUFACTURING INC
545 Porter Way, Placentia (92870-6454)
PHONE...............................714 528-8010
Gary J Monnig, *President*
Marc J Paquet, *Corp Secy*
Jules P Paquet, *Vice Pres*
Matthew Monnig, *Prdtn Mgr*
▲ EMP: 13
SQ FT: 11,000
SALES (est): 3.4MM **Privately Held**
WEB: www.spyderman.com
SIC: 3524 Lawn & garden equipment

(P-7632)
TRU-CUT INC
141 E 157th St, Gardena (90248-2508)
PHONE...............................310 630-0422
Nabi Merchant, *CEO*
▲ EMP: 35 EST: 1953
SQ FT: 28,620
SALES (est): 4.9MM **Privately Held**
WEB: www.trucutmower.com
SIC: 3524 5083 Lawn & garden mowers &
accessories; lawn & garden machinery &
equipment

3531 Construction Machinery & Eqpt

(P-7633)
ADEL PARK LLC
1432 Edinger Ave Ste 120, Tustin
(92780-6293)
PHONE...............................213 321-2030
Adel Park, *Mng Member*
EMP: 15 EST: 2016
SALES (est): 1MM **Privately Held**
SIC: 3531 Concrete plants

(P-7634)
AMERICAN COMPACTION EQP INC
Also Called: Compaction American
29380 Hunco Way, Lake Elsinore
(92530-2757)
PHONE...............................949 661-2921
Richard S Anderson, *CEO*
Monty Ihde, *President*
Kelly Ihde, *Corp Secy*
Darryl Kanell, *Vice Pres*
Mike Shoemaker, *Vice Pres*
▲ EMP: 24 EST: 1987
SQ FT: 8,500
SALES (est): 15.3MM **Privately Held**
WEB: www.acewheels.com
SIC: 3531 7353 Soil compactors: vibra-
tory; heavy construction equipment rental
HQ: Cascade Corporation
2201 Ne 201st Ave
Fairview OR 97024
503 669-6300

(P-7635)
AUTOBAHN CONSTRUCTION INC
933 N Batavia St Ste A, Orange
(92867-5501)
PHONE...............................714 769-7025
Ali Solehjou, *President*
EMP: 15 EST: 2006
SALES (est): 3.5MM **Privately Held**
WEB: www.autobahnconstruction.com
SIC: 3531 Road construction & mainte-
nance machinery

(P-7636)
BLACK DIAMOND BLADE COMPANY (PA)
Also Called: Cutting Edge Supply
234 E O St, Colton (92324-3466)
PHONE...............................800 949-9014
John Brenner, *CEO*
Franklin J Brenner Sr, *President*
Hoby Brenner, *Treasurer*
Franklin Brennerc, *Admin Sec*
◆ EMP: 35 EST: 1950
SQ FT: 16,000

SALES (est): 21.8MM **Privately Held**
WEB: www.cuttingedgesupply.com
SIC: 3531 Blades for graders, scrapers,
dozers & snow plows

(P-7637)
CAMLEVER INC
954 S East End Ave, Pomona
(91766-3837)
PHONE...............................909 629-9669
John Z Harris, *President*
Vanessa Rolden, *Admin Sec*
EMP: 22 EST: 1965
SQ FT: 2,500
SALES (est): 3.4MM **Privately Held**
WEB: www.camleverinc.com
SIC: 3531 3799 3312 Construction ma-
chinery; wheelbarrows; blast furnaces &
steel mills

(P-7638)
CAVOTEC INET US INC
5665 Corporate Ave, Cypress
(90630-4727)
PHONE...............................714 947-0005
Mike Larkin, *President*
Dorothy Chen, *CFO*
Sandra Torres, *Info Tech Mgr*
Mike Majewski, *VP Sales*
Johan Svensson, *Pub Rel Mgr*
▼ EMP: 70 EST: 2011
SALES (est): 24MM
SALES (corp-wide): 2.8MM **Privately
Held**
SIC: 3531 Airport construction machinery
HQ: Cavotec Us Holdings, Inc.
5665 Corporate Ave
Cypress CA 90630
714 545-7900

(P-7639)
COMMUNITY MANUFACTURING INC
5880 E Slauson Ave 2nd, Commerce
(90040-3018)
PHONE...............................323 720-8811
Jason Chauncey, *President*
EMP: 17 EST: 2016
SALES (est): 766.2K **Privately Held**
WEB: www.communitymfg.com
SIC: 3531 Asphalt plant, including gravel-
mix type

(P-7640)
COUNTY OF LOS ANGELES
Also Called: Public Works, Dept of
14959 Proctor Ave, La Puente
(91746-3206)
PHONE...............................626 968-3312
Mike Lee, *Manager*
EMP: 19
SALES (corp-wide): 25.2B **Privately Held**
WEB: www.lacounty.gov
SIC: 3531 9111 Road construction & main-
tenance machinery; bituminous batching
plants; executive offices
PA: County Of Los Angeles
500 W Temple St Ste 437
Los Angeles CA 90012
213 974-1101

(P-7641)
COUNTY OF LOS ANGELES
Also Called: Public Works, Dept of
3637 Winter Canyon Rd, Malibu
(90265-4834)
PHONE...............................310 456-8014
Mark Sanchez, *Manager*
Danny Knittle, *Administration*
EMP: 19
SALES (corp-wide): 25.2B **Privately Held**
WEB: www.lacounty.gov
SIC: 3531 9621 Graders, road (construc-
tion machinery); regulation, administration
of transportation
PA: County Of Los Angeles
500 W Temple St Ste 437
Los Angeles CA 90012
213 974-1101

(P-7642)
CROWN PAVERS INC
2434 W Valley Blvd Ste C, Alhambra
(91803)
PHONE...............................323 636-3365
Manuel Corona, *Branch Mgr*

EMP: 19
SALES (corp-wide): 242.8K **Privately
Held**
WEB: www.crownpavers.net
SIC: 3531 Pavers
PA: Crown Pavers, Inc.
429 S Hidalgo Ave
Alhambra CA

(P-7643)
GROUND HOG INC
1470 Victoria Ct, San Bernardino
(92408-2831)
P.O. Box 290 (92402-0290)
PHONE...............................909 478-5700
Edward Carlson, *President*
Jack Carlson, *Corp Secy*
Allen Carlson, *Natl Sales Mgr*
Lee Carlson, *Nurse*
▼ EMP: 25 EST: 1948
SQ FT: 52,000
SALES (est): 4.3MM **Privately Held**
WEB: www.groundhoginc.com
SIC: 3531 Posthole diggers, powered

(P-7644)
H & L TOOTH COMPANY (PA)
1540 S Greenwood Ave, Montebello
(90640-6536)
P.O. Box 48, Owasso OK (74055-0048)
PHONE...............................323 721-5146
Richard L Launder, *Ch of Bd*
Brian L Launder, *Vice Pres*
▲ EMP: 85 EST: 1931
SQ FT: 220,000
SALES (est): 13.2MM **Privately Held**
WEB: www.hltooth.com
SIC: 3531 Bucket or scarifier teeth; con-
struction machinery attachments

(P-7645)
JLG INDUSTRIES INC
Also Called: Jlg Serviceplus
7820 Lincoln Ave, Riverside (92504-4443)
PHONE...............................951 358-1915
Eric Golden, *Manager*
Howard Kaplan, *Vice Pres*
Neil Harris, *Project Engr*
EMP: 114
SALES (corp-wide): 7.7B **Publicly Held**
WEB: www.jlg.com
SIC: 3531 Cranes
HQ: Jlg Industries, Inc.
1 Jlg Dr
Mc Connellsburg PA 17233
717 485-5161

(P-7646)
MIXMOR INC
3131 Casitas Ave, Los Angeles
(90039-2499)
PHONE...............................323 664-1941
Michael K McNamara, *CEO*
Ann B Mc Namara, *Corp Secy*
Frank Tatreau, *Vice Pres*
Twila Bassett, *Administration*
David Ojeda, *Engineer*
EMP: 19 EST: 1935
SQ FT: 17,000
SALES (est): 3.5MM **Privately Held**
WEB: www.mixmor.com
SIC: 3531 Construction machinery

(P-7647)
MJ DIAZ BACKHOE SERVICE INC
968 White Ranch Cir, Corona
(92881-4742)
PHONE...............................951 496-4949
Manuel Jose Diaz, *Principal*
EMP: 13 EST: 2010
SALES (est): 2.3MM **Privately Held**
SIC: 3531 Backhoes

(P-7648)
OCEAN PAVERS INC
12 Endless Vis, Aliso Viejo (92656-8043)
PHONE...............................949 340-6363
Dieter Meltvedt, *Principal*
EMP: 14 EST: 2011
SALES (est): 1.8MM **Privately Held**
WEB: www.oceanpavers.com
SIC: 3531 Pavers

(P-7649)
SCHAMAS MFG COINC
6356 N Irwindale Ave, Irwindale
(91702-3210)
PHONE...............................626 334-6870
William Schaeffler, *President*
Ralph Mason, *Vice Pres*
EMP: 19 EST: 1987
SQ FT: 5,000
SALES (est): 1.7MM **Privately Held**
SIC: 3531 5084 Construction machinery;
materials handling machinery

(P-7650)
SILO CITY INC
1401 S Union Ave, Bakersfield
(93307-4141)
PHONE...............................661 387-0179
Michael Clift, *CEO*
Russell Cox, *Safety Mgr*
▲ EMP: 30 EST: 2001
SQ FT: 174,240
SALES (est): 1.9MM **Privately Held**
SIC: 3531 Bituminous, cement & concrete
related products & equipment

(P-7651)
STURGEON SERVICES INTL INC
Ssi
3511 Gilmore Ave, Bakersfield
(93308-6205)
P.O. Box 936 (93302-0936)
PHONE...............................661 322-4408
Ollie Sturgeon, *Branch Mgr*
EMP: 400 **Privately Held**
WEB: www.sturgeonservices.com
SIC: 3531 Construction machinery
PA: Sturgeon Services International, Inc.
3511 Gilmore Ave
Bakersfield CA 93308

(P-7652)
SUPERIOR INTERLOCKING PAVERS
27305 Live Oak Rd Ste A, Castaic
(91384-4520)
PHONE...............................818 838-0833
Albert Cedano, *President*
EMP: 13 EST: 2000
SALES (est): 1.7MM **Privately Held**
WEB: www.superiorpavers.com
SIC: 3531 Pavers

(P-7653)
TOMS BACKHOE SERVICES INC
2026 Roanoke St, San Jacinto
(92582-6919)
PHONE...............................951 634-4075
Thomas W Smith, *Administration*
EMP: 14 EST: 2015
SALES (est): 878.7K **Privately Held**
WEB: www.tomsbackhoe.net
SIC: 3531 Backhoes

(P-7654)
TRAVIS SNYDER
Also Called: Advantage Backhoes
27248 Hwy 189 Ste Ab-06, Blue Jay
(92317)
P.O. Box 647, Crestline (92325-0647)
PHONE...............................909 338-6302
Travis Snyder, *Principal*
EMP: 26 EST: 2006
SALES (est): 7.5MM **Privately Held**
SIC: 3531 Backhoes

(P-7655)
TRIO ENGINEERED PRODUCTS INC (HQ)
505 W Foothill Blvd, Azusa (91702-2345)
PHONE...............................626 851-3966
Michael Francis Burke, *CEO*
Eugene Xue, *Vice Pres*
◆ EMP: 25 EST: 2002
SALES (est): 10.2MM
SALES (corp-wide): 2.6B **Privately Held**
WEB: www.global.weir
SIC: 3531 Construction machinery attach-
ments; aggregate spreaders
PA: Weir Group Plc(The)
1 West Regent Street
Glasgow G2 1F
141 637-7111

(P-7656)
US SAWS INC (PA)
Also Called: U S Saw & Blades
3702 W Central Ave, Santa Ana
(92704-5832)
PHONE..................................860 668-2402
Bruce Root, *CEO*
C W Duncan, *President*
Bill Glynn, *Vice Pres*
Duncan C Warren, *CIO*
Stephanie Box, *Marketing Staff*
▲ **EMP:** 18 **EST:** 2004
SQ FT: 4,000
SALES (est): 7MM **Privately Held**
WEB: www.ussaws.com
SIC: 3531 5082 Blades for graders, scrapers, dozers & snow plows; road construction & maintenance machinery

(P-7657)
V AND L BACK HOE SERVICE INC
447 N Hagar St, San Fernando
(91340-2323)
PHONE..................................818 898-1997
Gerardo Gomez, *Principal*
EMP: 13 **EST:** 2007
SALES (est): 613.6K **Privately Held**
SIC: 3531 Backhoes

(P-7658)
VOLVO CONSTRUCTION EQP & SVCS
22099 Knabe Rd, Corona (92883-7111)
PHONE..................................951 277-7620
Mike Franks, *Owner*
EMP: 26 **EST:** 2007
SALES (est): 7.4MM
SALES (corp-wide): 39.1B **Privately Held**
WEB: www.volvocars.com
SIC: 3531 Construction machinery
HQ: Saba Holding Company, Llc
312 Volvo Way
Shippensburg PA 17257
717 532-9181

(P-7659)
WESTERN EQUIPMENT MFG INC
Also Called: Western Equipment Mfg
1160 Olympic Dr, Corona (92881-3390)
PHONE..................................951 284-2000
Kenneth R Thompson, *CEO*
William Weihl, *President*
▲ **EMP:** 29 **EST:** 2010
SALES (est): 5.1MM **Privately Held**
WEB: www.western-emi.com
SIC: 3531 Finishers & spreaders (construction equipment)

3532 Mining Machinery & Eqpt

(P-7660)
CAVOTEC US HOLDINGS INC (HQ)
Also Called: Cavotec Inet
5665 Corporate Ave, Cypress
(90630-4727)
PHONE..................................714 545-7900
Michael Larkin, *President*
Glenn Withers, *CFO*
Daniel Foster, *Treasurer*
Rene Meldem, *Officer*
Memed Uzel, *Vice Pres*
EMP: 37 **EST:** 2008
SALES (est): 28.5MM
SALES (corp-wide): 2.8MM **Privately Held**
WEB: www.cavotec.com
SIC: 3532 3569 Drills, bits & similar equipment; filters
PA: Cavotec Sa
Via Giovan Battista Pioda 14
Lugano TI 6900
919 114-010

(P-7661)
POLYALLOYS INJECTED METALS INC
14000 Avalon Blvd, Los Angeles
(90061-2636)
PHONE..................................310 715-9800
Craig Paulin, *CEO*

Angel Rosell, *Technician*
Eden Ines, *Controller*
Juan Camarillo, *Purch Mgr*
Quintin Castro, *Purchasing*
EMP: 75 **EST:** 2001
SALES (est): 11.6MM
SALES (corp-wide): 64.8MM **Privately Held**
WEB: www.psmindustries.com
SIC: 3532 Amalgamators (metallurgical or mining machinery)
PA: Psm Industries, Inc.
14000 Avalon Blvd
Los Angeles CA 90061
888 663-8256

(P-7662)
SOTEC USA LLC
3076 S Edenglen Ave, Ontario
(91761-2626)
PHONE..................................909 525-5861
Gang Ye, *Mng Member*
EMP: 24 **Privately Held**
WEB: www.sotecusa.com
SIC: 3532 Crushing, pulverizing & screening equipment
HQ: Sotec Usa Llc
17870 Castleton St # 338
City Of Industry CA 91748
909 930-2792

(P-7663)
SPAULDING EQUIPMENT COMPANY (PA)
Also Called: Spaulding Crusher Parts
75 Paseo Adelanto, Perris (92570-9343)
P.O. Box 1807 (92572-1807)
PHONE..................................951 943-4531
George E Spaulding, *Ch of Bd*
James Michael Spaulding, *President*
Fred Stemrich, *Corp Secy*
Norman Vetter, *Vice Pres*
◆ **EMP:** 47 **EST:** 1966
SALES (est): 9.2MM **Privately Held**
WEB: www.spauldingequipment.com
SIC: 3532 5082 7699 Mineral beneficiation equipment; mineral beneficiation machinery; industrial machinery & equipment repair

(P-7664)
WEBER DRILLING CO INC
401 Hindry Ave, Inglewood (90301-2015)
PHONE..................................310 670-7708
Marlene Wood, *President*
Ronald Wood, *Vice Pres*
EMP: 25 **EST:** 1947
SQ FT: 7,000
SALES (est): 2.2MM **Privately Held**
SIC: 3532 Drills & drilling equipment, mining (except oil & gas)

3533 Oil Field Machinery & Eqpt

(P-7665)
AQUEOS CORPORATION
2550 Eastman Ave, Ventura (93003-7714)
PHONE..................................805 676-4330
Theodore Roche, *Branch Mgr*
Sattech Aqueos, *Technician*
Jason Kleinschmidt, *Technician*
Erik Zawacki, *Project Mgr*
Ashley Touchet, *Accountant*
EMP: 95
SALES (corp-wide): 31.5MM **Privately Held**
WEB: www.aqueossubsea.com
SIC: 3533 Oil & gas field machinery
PA: Aqueos Corporation
418 Chapala St Ste E
Santa Barbara CA 93101
805 364-0570

(P-7666)
AQUEOS CORPORATION (PA)
418 Chapala St Ste E, Santa Barbara
(93101-8056)
PHONE..................................805 364-0570
Theodore Roche IV, *President*
Eric Legendre, *COO*
Bradley Parro, *CFO*
Michael Pfau, *Admin Sec*
Ryan Holm, *Technician*

EMP: 76 **EST:** 2000
SQ FT: 23,000
SALES (est): 31.5MM **Privately Held**
WEB: www.aqueossubsea.com
SIC: 3533 Oil & gas field machinery

(P-7667)
DAWSON ENTERPRISES (PA)
Also Called: Cavins Oil Well Tools
2853 Cherry Ave, Signal Hill (90755-1908)
P.O. Box 6039, Long Beach (90806-0039)
PHONE..................................562 424-8564
James M Dawson, *CEO*
Harry Dawson, *President*
Jim Dawson, *Executive*
Jim Moore, *Executive*
Robert Phillips, *Purch Mgr*
◆ **EMP:** 36 **EST:** 1928
SQ FT: 19,000
SALES (est): 9.6MM **Privately Held**
WEB: www.cavins.com
SIC: 3533 7359 Bits, oil & gas field tools: rock; garage facility & tool rental

(P-7668)
DOWNHOLE STABILIZATION INC
3515 Thomas Way, Bakersfield
(93308-6215)
P.O. Box 2467 (93303-2467)
PHONE..................................661 631-1044
Jim Calanchini, *President*
Diane Calanchini, *Corp Secy*
Jacob Banducci, *Vice Pres*
Ralph Bravo, *Vice Pres*
John Calanchini, *Vice Pres*
▲ **EMP:** 38 **EST:** 1989
SQ FT: 8,800
SALES (est): 9.9MM **Privately Held**
WEB: www.downholestabilization.com
SIC: 3533 5082 3599 1389 Drilling tools for gas, oil or water wells; construction & mining machinery; wellpoints (drilling equipment); amusement park equipment; machine shop, jobbing & repair; construction, repair & dismantling services; oil field services

(P-7669)
FARLEY MACHINE INC
7800 Davin Park Dr, Bakersfield
(93308-7230)
PHONE..................................661 397-4987
Paul J Farley, *President*
Winney Farley, *Corp Secy*
J B Rogers, *Vice Pres*
EMP: 25 **EST:** 1977
SALES (est): 1.1MM **Privately Held**
SIC: 3533 Oil field machinery & equipment; water well drilling equipment

(P-7670)
GLOBAL ELASTOMERIC PDTS INC
5551 District Blvd, Bakersfield
(93313-2126)
PHONE..................................661 831-5380
Phil W Embury, *President*
Sandy Embury, *Vice Pres*
Jim Pickering, *Safety Mgr*
Tom Pelle, *QC Mgr*
Zachary Ellis, *Sales Staff*
▲ **EMP:** 55 **EST:** 1963
SQ FT: 20,000
SALES (est): 8.3MM **Privately Held**
WEB: www.globaleee.com
SIC: 3533 5084 Oil & gas field machinery; oil refining machinery, equipment & supplies

(P-7671)
HYDRIL COMPANY
3237 Patton Way, Bakersfield
(93308-5717)
PHONE..................................661 588-9332
Ken Steinke, *Branch Mgr*
EMP: 62
SALES (corp-wide): 183.7K **Privately Held**
WEB: www.tenaris.com
SIC: 3533 Oil field machinery & equipment
HQ: Hydril Company
302 Mccarty St
Houston TX 77029

(P-7672)
KBA ENGINEERING LLC
2157 Mohawk St, Bakersfield
(93308-6020)
P.O. Box 1200 (93302-1200)
PHONE..................................661 323-0487
Richard C Jones, *Mng Member*
Sean McNally, *Vice Pres*
Kelly Stogden, *Vice Pres*
Rick Jones, *Executive*
Tina Fregeau, *Controller*
EMP: 95
SQ FT: 45,000
SALES (est): 19.6MM **Privately Held**
WEB: www.kbaeng.com
SIC: 3533 3462 Oil & gas field machinery; gear & chain forgings

(P-7673)
LASALLE INTL HLDINGS GROUP INC
9667 Owensmouth Ave, Chatsworth
(91311-4819)
P.O. Box 7396, Northridge (91327-7396)
PHONE..................................818 233-8000
Pierre Yenokian, *President*
Jan Papazian, *CFO*
◆ **EMP:** 14 **EST:** 2001
SQ FT: 70,000
SALES (est): 1MM **Privately Held**
WEB: www.lasalleint.com
SIC: 3533 5047 1382 Oil & gas field machinery; medical & hospital equipment; oil & gas exploration services; geological exploration, oil & gas field

(P-7674)
OIL COUNTRY MANUFACTURING INC
300 W Stanley Ave, Ventura (93001-1395)
PHONE..................................805 643-1200
Ed Patterson III, *General Mgr*
Robert M Nelson, *Vice Pres*
Michael Lettini, *Consultant*
◆ **EMP:** 119 **EST:** 1980
SQ FT: 100,000
SALES (est): 2.5MM **Privately Held**
SIC: 3533 5084 Oil field machinery & equipment; industrial machinery & equipment

(P-7675)
RDR PRECISION TECH INC
11000 Kern Canyon Rd A, Bakersfield
(93306-8324)
PHONE..................................661 322-8450
Richard Riggs, *President*
EMP: 13 **EST:** 2008
SQ FT: 3,000
SALES (est): 450K **Privately Held**
WEB: www.rdrprecision.com
SIC: 3533 Oil & gas drilling rigs & equipment

(P-7676)
SOUTH COAST SCREEN AND CASING
19112 S Santa Fe Ave, Compton
(90221-5910)
PHONE..................................310 632-3200
Tyson Scimo, *CEO*
EMP: 18 **EST:** 2011
SALES (est): 1.1MM **Privately Held**
WEB: www.southcoastsc.com
SIC: 3533 Oil & gas drilling rigs & equipment; drill rigs

3534 Elevators & Moving Stairways

(P-7677)
ELEVATOR RESEARCH & MFG CO
1417 Elwood St, Los Angeles
(90021-2812)
PHONE..................................213 746-1914
Frank Edward Park, *President*
Lynn Park, *Vice Pres*
David Alvarez, *General Mgr*
Rogers Barnet, *General Mgr*
Clive Mann, *General Mgr*
EMP: 49 **EST:** 1964
SQ FT: 5,000

P R O D U C T S & S V C S

SALES (est): 17.7MM
SALES (corp-wide): 72.6MM **Privately Held**
WEB: www.elevatorresearch.com
SIC: **3534** Elevators & equipment
PA: Dewhurst Plc
　　Unit 9
　　Feltham MIDDX
　　208 744-8200

(P-7678)
GAL MANUFACTURING CO LLC
Also Called: Bore-Max
3380 Gilman Rd, El Monte (91732-3201)
PHONE...................................626 443-8616
Bret Sturm, *Branch Mgr*
EMP: 14
SALES (corp-wide): 1.6B **Privately Held**
WEB: www.gal.com
SIC: **3534** Elevators & equipment
HQ: G.A.L. Manufacturing Company, Llc
　　50 E 153rd St
　　Bronx NY 10451
　　718 292-9000

(P-7679)
GMS ELEVATOR SERVICES INC
401 Borrego Ct, San Dimas (91773-2971)
PHONE...................................909 599-3904
G Matthew Simpkins, *President*
Nate Simpkins, *General Mgr*
Pamela Simpkins, *Admin Sec*
Shea Nolan, *Project Mgr*
Leo Martinez, *Sales Mgr*
EMP: 35 EST: 1987
SQ FT: 4,000
SALES (est): 7.9MM **Privately Held**
WEB: www.gmselevator.com
SIC: **3534** 1796 Elevators & equipment;
　　elevator installation & conversion

(P-7680)
OTIS ELEVATOR COMPANY
5733 Hollister Ave Ste B, Goleta
(93117-3470)
PHONE...................................805 683-3979
Lange Patty, *Branch Mgr*
EMP: 33
SALES (corp-wide): 12.7B **Publicly Held**
WEB: www.otis.com
SIC: **3534** Elevators & equipment
HQ: Otis Elevator Company
　　341 Southport Cir Ste B
　　Virginia Beach VA 23452
　　860 676-6000

(P-7681)
TL SHIELD & ASSOCIATES INC
Also Called: Inclinator of California
1030 Arroyo St, San Fernando
(91340-1822)
P.O. Box 6845, Thousand Oaks (91359-6845)
PHONE...................................818 509-8228
Thomas Louis Shield, *President*
Greg Sawyer, *Area Mgr*
Ron Woodward, *Administration*
EMP: 35 EST: 1982
SQ FT: 2,000
SALES (est): 9.8MM **Privately Held**
WEB: www.tlshield.com
SIC: **3534** 1796 Elevators & equipment;
　　elevator installation & conversion

(P-7682)
WINTER & BAIN MFG INC (PA)
1417 Elwood St, Los Angeles
(90021-2812)
PHONE...................................213 749-3568
Henry Spencer, *Owner*
Henry W Spencer, *President*
EMP: 16 EST: 1984
SQ FT: 8,000
SALES (est): 2.5MM **Privately Held**
SIC: **3534** Elevators & moving stairways

3535 Conveyors & Eqpt

(P-7683)
AIR TUBE TRANSFER SYSTEMS INC
Also Called: A T T
715 N Cypress St, Orange (92867-6605)
　PHONE...................................714 363-0700

Rick Blodgett, *President*
EMP: 48 EST: 1996
SQ FT: 10,000
SALES (est): 5.3MM **Privately Held**
SIC: **3535** 1796 7699 3494 Pneumatic
　　tube conveyor systems; machinery instal-
　　lation; industrial equipment services;
　　valves & pipe fittings

(P-7684)
AMERICAN ULTRAVIOLET WEST INC
Also Called: Lesco
23555 Telo Ave, Torrance (90505-4012)
PHONE...................................310 784-2930
Meredith C Stines, *President*
▲ EMP: 21 EST: 1978
SQ FT: 22,775
SALES (est): 4.7MM **Privately Held**
WEB: www.americanultraviolet.com
SIC: **3535** 5065 Conveyors & conveying
　　equipment; electronic parts

(P-7685)
APEX CONVEYOR CORP
27455 Bostik Ct, Temecula (92590-3698)
P.O. Box 812, Murrieta (92564-0812)
PHONE...................................951 304-7808
Dave Hill,
Barbara Hill,
EMP: 20 EST: 1995
SALES (est): 3.7MM **Privately Held**
WEB: www.apexconveyor.com
SIC: **3535** Conveyors & conveying equip-
　　ment

(P-7686)
APEX CONVEYOR SYSTEMS INC
27455 Bostik Ct, Temecula (92590-3698)
PHONE...................................951 304-7808
Greg King, *President*
Wenda King, *Admin Sec*
EMP: 14 EST: 2015
SALES (est): 1.3MM **Privately Held**
WEB: www.apexconveyor.com
SIC: **3535** Belt conveyor systems, general
　　industrial use

(P-7687)
CASE AUTOMATION CORPORATION
208 Jason Ct, Corona (92879-6101)
PHONE...................................951 493-6666
Don Nielsen, *President*
EMP: 16 EST: 1972
SQ FT: 15,000
SALES (est): 3.3MM **Privately Held**
WEB: www.caseautomation.com
SIC: **3535** 5084 Conveyors & conveying
　　equipment; industrial machinery & equip-
　　ment

(P-7688)
CONVEYOR MFG & SVC INC
771 Marylind Ave, Claremont (91711-3531)
PHONE...................................909 621-0406
Jesus Dehorta, *President*
Josefina Dehorta, *Corp Secy*
EMP: 15 EST: 1989
SQ FT: 30,000
SALES (est): 4.6MM **Privately Held**
WEB: www.conveyormfg.com
SIC: **3535** Conveyors & conveying equip-
　　ment

(P-7689)
CONVEYOR SERVICE & ELECTRIC
9550 Ann St, Santa Fe Springs
(90670-2616)
PHONE...................................562 777-1221
Patricia Moseley, *Partner*
Efren Alcantar, *Partner*
Richard Moseley, *Partner*
Vicky Voss, *Office Mgr*
Manuel Alcantar, *Engineer*
EMP: 23 EST: 1995
SQ FT: 13,000
SALES (est): 2.6MM **Privately Held**
WEB: www.conserel.com
SIC: **3535** 1796 Conveyors & conveying
　　equipment; machinery installation

(P-7690)
DEAMCO CORPORATION
6520 E Washington Blvd, Commerce
(90040-1822)
PHONE...................................323 890-1190
Armen Hovannesian, *President*
Nick Kanian, *Principal*
Armando Galan, *Sales Staff*
◆ EMP: 33 EST: 1977
SQ FT: 55,000
SALES (est): 5.8MM **Privately Held**
WEB: www.deamco.com
SIC: **3535** Conveyors & conveying equip-
　　ment

(P-7691)
INGALLS CONVEYORS INC
1005 W Olympic Blvd, Montebello
(90640-5121)
PHONE...................................323 837-9900
Toll Free:.................................888 -
Maged Labib Nakla, *CEO*
Steve Ingalls, *President*
Colleen Ingalls, *Admin Sec*
Mag Nakla, *Sales Engr*
EMP: 21 EST: 1976
SQ FT: 174,000
SALES (est): 5.3MM **Privately Held**
WEB: www.ingallsconveyors.com
SIC: **3535** 8711 Conveyors & conveying
　　equipment; consulting engineer

(P-7692)
RCI RACK CNVYOR INSTLLTION INC
39700 Grand Ave, Cherry Valley
(92223-4603)
PHONE...................................909 381-4818
Walt Thompson, *President*
Sheri Thompson, *CFO*
EMP: 23 EST: 2005
SALES (est): 4.4MM **Privately Held**
WEB: www.rackconveyorinc.com
SIC: **3535** 1796 Belt conveyor systems,
　　general industrial use; millwright

(P-7693)
SCREW CONVEYOR PACIFIC CORP
7807 W Doe Ave, Visalia (93291-9275)
PHONE...................................559 651-2131
Randy Smith, *Principal*
EMP: 112
SALES (corp-wide): 12.7MM **Privately Held**
WEB: www.screwconveyor.com
SIC: **3535** Conveyors & conveying equip-
　　ment
PA: Screw Conveyor Pacific Corp
　　700 Hoffman St
　　Hammond IN 46327
　　219 931-1450

(P-7694)
SDI INDUSTRIES INC (PA)
13000 Pierce St, Pacoima (91331-2528)
PHONE...................................818 890-6002
Krish Nathan, *CEO*
Mark Conrad, *CFO*
David Paneiko, *CFO*
Barron Desanctis, *Vice Pres*
Rick Dimaio, *Vice Pres*
▲ EMP: 150 EST: 1978
SQ FT: 80,000
SALES (est): 56.5MM **Privately Held**
WEB: www.sdi.systems
SIC: **3535** 3537 8748 8711 Conveyors &
　　conveying equipment; industrial trucks &
　　tractors; business consulting; engineering
　　services; machinery installation

(P-7695)
SHADECRAFT INC
116 W Del Mar Blvd, Pasadena
(91105-2508)
PHONE...................................818 502-0700
Armen Gharabegian, *CEO*
Kelly Sarahgrace, *COO*
Edgar Kirakosyan, *Manager*
EMP: 20 EST: 2013
SALES (est): 5.3MM **Privately Held**
WEB: www.shadecraft.com
SIC: **3535** Robotic conveyors

(P-7696)
TIG/M LLC
9160 Jordan Ave, Chatsworth
(91311-5707)
PHONE...................................818 709-8500
Alvaro Villa, *CEO*
Brad Read, *President*
David Hall, *CFO*
Bradley Read,
EMP: 30 EST: 2005
SQ FT: 2,000 **Privately Held**
WEB: www.tig-m.com
SIC: **3535** Trolley conveyors

3536 Hoists, Cranes & Monorails

(P-7697)
CRANEVEYOR CORP (PA)
1524 Potrero Ave, El Monte (91733-3017)
P.O. Box 3727 (91733-0727)
PHONE...................................626 442-1524
Frank Gaetano Trimboli, *CEO*
Greg Bischoff, *President*
Tim Chavez, *Vice Pres*
Lisa Swoboda, *Executive*
Amber Corona, *Project Mgr*
▲ EMP: 90 EST: 1946
SQ FT: 47,320
SALES (est): 27MM **Privately Held**
WEB: www.craneveyor.com
SIC: **3536** 3446 Cranes, overhead travel-
　　ing; monorail systems; railings, bannis-
　　ters, guards, etc.: made from metal pipe

(P-7698)
MOBILE EQUIPMENT COMPANY
Also Called: Mobile Equipment Appraisers
3610 Gilmore Ave, Bakersfield
(93308-6208)
PHONE...................................661 327-8476
Evelyn Stanfill, *President*
Felecia Stanfill, *Corp Secy*
Paul J Faulconer, *Vice Pres*
Gary Stanfill, *General Mgr*
EMP: 20 EST: 1960
SQ FT: 18,580
SALES (est): 4.6MM **Privately Held**
WEB: www.wwvv.mobile-equipment.com
SIC: **3536** 8748 3559 Cranes, overhead
　　traveling; safety training service; automo-
　　tive related machinery

(P-7699)
NATIONAL FUEL CELL RES CTR
1002 Health Sciences Rd, Irvine
(92617-3010)
PHONE...................................949 824-1509
Israel Christie, *Controller*
Nichole Berchtold, *Research*
Alice Szekunda, *Opers Staff*
Marissa Sapalala, *Pathologist*
EMP: 16 EST: 2017
SALES (est): 689.9K **Privately Held**
WEB: www.uci.edu
SIC: **3536** Hoists, cranes & monorails

(P-7700)
WESTMONT INDUSTRIES LLC (PA)
10805 Painter Ave Uppr, Santa Fe Springs
(90670-4526)
PHONE...................................562 944-6137
Diane Henderson, *President*
David Chetwood, *CFO*
Eric Henderson, *Vice Pres*
Lina Gomez, *Admin Asst*
Raymond Tan, *IT/INT Sup*
▼ EMP: 41 EST: 1951
SALES (est): 22.8MM **Privately Held**
WEB: www.westmont.com
SIC: **3536** 3533 Cranes, industrial plant;
　　oil & gas field machinery

3537 Indl Trucks, Tractors, Trailers & Stackers

(P-7701)
ACCLAIMED TRUCKING CORP (PA)
1106 El Monte Dr, Simi Valley (93065-4226)
PHONE..................................805 577-7611
Bruce Howard, *President*
EMP: 13 EST: 2018
SALES (est): 527K **Privately Held**
SIC: 3537 Trucks, tractors, loaders, carriers & similar equipment

(P-7702)
ANCRA INTERNATIONAL LLC
Aircraft Systems Division
601 S Vincent Ave, Azusa (91702-5102)
PHONE..................................626 765-4818
Ed Dugic, *Manager*
Tony Cardinale, *President*
Edward Moradians, *Engineer*
EMP: 24 **Privately Held**
WEB: www.ancra.com
SIC: 3537 2298 Industrial trucks & tractors; cargo nets
HQ: Ancra International Llc
601 S Vincent Ave
Azusa CA 91702

(P-7703)
ANCRA INTERNATIONAL LLC (HQ)
601 S Vincent Ave, Azusa (91702-5102)
PHONE..................................626 765-4800
Steve Frediani, *CEO*
Nelson Fong, *CFO*
Jim Calico, *VP Bus Dvlpt*
John Czarnecki, *Regional Mgr*
Victor Bassly, *QA Dir*
▲ EMP: 130 EST: 1996
SALES (est): 101MM **Privately Held**
WEB: www.ancra.com
SIC: 3537 Lift trucks, industrial: fork, platform, straddle, etc.; loading docks: portable, adjustable & hydraulic

(P-7704)
ANGEL LIFT INC
10662 Mina St, Whittier (90605-3433)
PHONE..................................310 871-6115
Angel Cabral Jr, *Principal*
EMP: 15 EST: 2004
SALES (est): 1.7MM **Privately Held**
SIC: 3537 Forklift trucks

(P-7705)
ANTHONY WELDED PRODUCTS INC (PA)
1447 S Lexington St, Delano (93215-9700)
P.O. Box 299, Simi Valley (93062-0299)
PHONE..................................661 721-7211
Frank S Salvucci Sr, *Chairman*
Elsie Salvucci, *President*
EMP: 20 EST: 1958
SQ FT: 25,000
SALES (est): 5.8MM **Privately Held**
WEB: www.anthonycarts.com
SIC: 3537 3444 3443 Dollies (hand or power trucks), industrial except mining; sheet metalwork; fabricated plate work (boiler shop)

(P-7706)
CIMC REEFER TRAILER INC (PA)
22101 Alessandro Blvd, Moreno Valley (92553-8215)
PHONE..................................951 218-1414
Xiaoyi Wang, *CEO*
▲ EMP: 169 EST: 2009
SALES (est): 8.3MM **Privately Held**
SIC: 3537 Truck trailers, used in plants, docks, terminals, etc.

(P-7707)
CROWN EQUIPMENT CORPORATION
Also Called: Crown Lift Trucks
4061 Via Oro Ave, Long Beach (90810-1458)
PHONE..................................310 952-6600
Tom Labrador, *Branch Mgr*
EMP: 64
SALES (corp-wide): 3.6B **Privately Held**
WEB: www.crown.com
SIC: 3537 Lift trucks, industrial: fork, platform, straddle, etc.
PA: Crown Equipment Corporation
44 S Washington St
New Bremen OH 45869
419 629-2311

(P-7708)
DYNAPRO
Also Called: Dynapro Logistics
255 E Santa Clara St # 2, Arcadia (91006-7226)
PHONE..................................626 898-4411
Manny Ochoa, *CFO*
EMP: 15 EST: 2015
SQ FT: 40,000
SALES (est): 1.8MM **Privately Held**
SIC: 3537 4214 4225 7549 Loading docks: portable, adjustable & hydraulic; local trucking with storage; general warehousing & storage; trailer maintenance

(P-7709)
HYDRAULIC SHOP INC
2753 S Vista Ave, Bloomington (92316-3269)
PHONE..................................909 875-9336
Christopher O Kirk, *President*
EMP: 20 EST: 2006
SQ FT: 4,500
SALES (est): 2.8MM **Privately Held**
WEB: www.hydraulicshopinc.com
SIC: 3537 Industrial trucks & tractors

(P-7710)
INDUSTRIAL DESIGN PRODUCTS INC
2700 Pomona Blvd, Pomona (91768-3222)
P.O. Box 7846, Norco (92860-8095)
PHONE..................................909 468-0693
Richard Fleischhacker Jr, *President*
Jose Pizarro, *Exec VP*
EMP: 31 EST: 1999
SQ FT: 14,000
SALES (est): 3.4MM **Privately Held**
WEB: www.idp-inc.com
SIC: 3537 5084 2542 Platforms, stands, tables, pallets & similar equipment; materials handling machinery; pallet racks: except wood

(P-7711)
J&S GOODWIN INC (HQ)
5753 E Sta Ana Cyn G355, Anaheim (92807-3230)
PHONE..................................714 956-4040
Arthur J Goodwin, *CEO*
Scott Currie, *COO*
Mark McGregor, *CFO*
Adam Navarro, *General Mgr*
Sharon Goodwin, *Admin Sec*
◆ EMP: 179 EST: 1989
SQ FT: 3,000
SALES (est): 40.6MM
SALES (corp-wide): 7B **Publicly Held**
WEB: www.polaris.com
SIC: 3537 5088 5084 Trucks, tractors, loaders, carriers & similar equipment; golf carts; materials handling machinery
PA: Polaris Inc.
2100 Highway 55
Medina MN 55340
763 542-0500

(P-7712)
JE THOMSON & COMPANY LLC
Also Called: Carousel USA
15206 Ceres Ave, Fontana (92335-4311)
PHONE..................................626 334-7190
John Thomson,
Richard Barnes, *CIO*
▲ EMP: 15 EST: 2004

SALES (est): 5.3MM **Privately Held**
WEB: www.carousel-usa.com
SIC: 3537 3535 Tables, lift: hydraulic; trolley conveyors; bulk handling conveyor systems; robotic conveyors

(P-7713)
KARRIOR ELECTRIC VEHICLES INC
Also Called: Karrior Indus Elc Vehicles
570 W 184th St, Gardena (90248-4202)
PHONE..................................310 515-7600
George Kettel, *President*
EMP: 16 EST: 1988
SQ FT: 12,000
SALES (est): 1.3MM **Privately Held**
WEB: www.karrior.com
SIC: 3537 7629 Industrial trucks & tractors; electrical equipment repair services

(P-7714)
KEY MATERIAL HANDLING INC
4790 Alamo St, Simi Valley (93063-1837)
PHONE..................................805 520-6007
Richard Galbraith, *President*
Kimberly Galbraith, *Treasurer*
John Galbraith, *Vice Pres*
▲ EMP: 18 EST: 1992
SQ FT: 2,000
SALES (est): 1.2MM **Privately Held**
WEB: www.keymaterial.com
SIC: 3537 4953 5084 5021 Platforms, stands, tables, pallets & similar equipment; trucks, tractors, loaders, carriers & similar equipment; hazardous waste collection & disposal; conveyor systems; shelving

(P-7715)
PAPE MATERIAL HANDLING INC
2600 Peck Rd, City of Industry (90601-1620)
P.O. Box 60007 (91716-0007)
PHONE..................................562 692-9311
Steve Smith, *Manager*
Jordan Pape, *President*
Chris Wetle, *President*
William Mc Kinley, *Div Sub Head*
Jim Mir, *General Mgr*
EMP: 100 **Privately Held**
WEB: www.papemh.com
SIC: 3537 5084 Forklift trucks; industrial machinery & equipment
HQ: Pape' Material Handling, Inc.
355 Goodpasture Island Rd
Eugene OR 97401

(P-7716)
POWER PT INC (PA)
Also Called: AAA Pallet
1500 Crafton Ave Bldg 100, Mentone (92359-1315)
PHONE..................................951 490-4149
Tyson Paulis, *CEO*
EMP: 19 EST: 2018
SALES (est): 2.9MM **Privately Held**
SIC: 3537 Platforms, stands, tables, pallets & similar equipment

(P-7717)
SHRED-TECH USA LLC
1100 S Grove Ave, Ontario (91761-4572)
PHONE..................................909 923-2783
Robert L Dibenedetto,
EMP: 14 EST: 2008
SQ FT: 64,000
SALES (est): 234.5K **Privately Held**
WEB: www.shred-tech.com
SIC: 3537 Industrial trucks & tractors

(P-7718)
SUPERIOR TRAILER WORKS
13700 Slover Ave, Fontana (92337-7067)
PHONE..................................909 350-0185
Jack N Pocock, *CEO*
Jay Pocock, *Treasurer*
Mike Espinosa, *Sales Staff*
▲ EMP: 50 EST: 1935
SQ FT: 4,000
SALES (est): 7.6MM **Privately Held**
WEB: www.superiortrailerworks.com
SIC: 3537 7539 Industrial trucks & tractors; trailer repair

(P-7719)
TAYLOR-DUNN MANUFACTURING CO (DH)
2114 W Ball Rd, Anaheim (92804-5498)
PHONE..................................714 956-4040
Keith Simon, *CEO*
Christopher Ferreira, *Engineer*
Bill Manning, *Sales Mgr*
Brian Maclean, *Sales Staff*
Adam Navarro, *Sales Staff*
◆ EMP: 100 EST: 1949
SQ FT: 145,000
SALES (est): 40.3MM
SALES (corp-wide): 7B **Publicly Held**
WEB: www.taylor-dunn.com
SIC: 3537 Trucks, tractors, loaders, carriers & similar equipment
HQ: Polaris Sales Inc.
2100 Highway 55
Hamel MN 55340
763 542-0500

3541 Machine Tools: Cutting

(P-7720)
AEROSPACE TOOL GRINDING
14020 Shoemaker Ave, Norwalk (90650-4536)
P.O. Box 1536 (90651-1536)
PHONE..................................562 802-3339
Alonzo Burgos, *President*
Azzie Burgos, *Vice Pres*
EMP: 21 EST: 1987
SALES (est): 1.2MM **Privately Held**
SIC: 3541 5251 Machine tools, metal cutting type; tools

(P-7721)
APT MANUFACTURING LLC
Also Called: Stellar Engineering
2899 E Coronado St Ste E, Anaheim (92806-2535)
PHONE..................................714 632-0040
James Mullion,
EMP: 16 EST: 2012
SALES (est): 2.4MM **Privately Held**
SIC: 3541 3451 Plasma process metal cutting machines; screw machine products

(P-7722)
BERNHARDT AND BERNHARDT INC
Also Called: Protool Co
14771 Myford Rd Ste D, Tustin (92780-7206)
PHONE..................................714 544-0708
Norbert Bernhardt, *President*
EMP: 21 EST: 1980
SQ FT: 4,600
SALES (est): 1MM **Privately Held**
WEB: www.protoolco.com
SIC: 3541 Numerically controlled metal cutting machine tools

(P-7723)
CERATIZIT LOS ANGELES LLC
1401 W Walnut St, Rancho Dominguez (90220-5012)
PHONE..................................310 464-8050
Mark Nunez, *President*
Salvador Nunez, *Vice Pres*
Carmen Nunez, *Admin Sec*
▲ EMP: 85 EST: 2016
SQ FT: 46,000
SALES (est): 18.9MM
SALES (corp-wide): 6.5MM **Privately Held**
WEB: www.bestcarbide.com
SIC: 3541 Machine tools, metal cutting type
PA: Ceratizit S.A.
Route De Holzem 101
Mamer 8232
312 085-1

(P-7724)
CREMACH TECH INC (PA)
Also Called: Creative Machine Technology
369 Meyer Cir, Corona (92879-1078)
PHONE..................................951 735-3194
Mike McNeeley, *CEO*
Jae Wan Choi, *Vice Pres*
Steve Lehman, *General Mgr*

Justin Choi, *Technology*
Jessica Doty, *Production*
EMP: 135 **EST:** 1994
SQ FT: 34,000
SALES (est): 19.3MM **Privately Held**
WEB: www.cmtus.com
SIC: 3541 8711 Machine tools, metal cutting type; designing: ship, boat, machine & product

(P-7725)
CTD MACHINES INC
7355 E Slauson Ave, Commerce (90040-3626)
PHONE....................213 689-4455
Kiwon Ban, *General Mgr*
Thomas Orlando, *President*
Ellen Orlando, *Corp Secy*
Seymour Lehrer, *Vice Pres*
Shirley Lehrer, *Vice Pres*
EMP: 18 **EST:** 1967
SALES (est): 4.7MM **Privately Held**
WEB: www.ctdsaw.com
SIC: 3541 Cutoff machines (metalworking machinery)

(P-7726)
D G INDUSTRIES
226 Viking Ave, Brea (92821-3818)
P.O. Box 696 (92822-0696)
PHONE....................714 990-3787
David Gillanders, *President*
▲ **EMP:** 13 **EST:** 1978
SQ FT: 5,500
SALES (est): 2.1MM **Privately Held**
WEB: www.dgindustries.com
SIC: 3541 Screw machines, automatic

(P-7727)
DAC INTERNATIONAL INC
Also Called: D A C
6390 Rose Ln, Carpinteria (93013-2998)
PHONE....................805 684-8307
Kenneth R Payne, *President*
Yuvi Murphy, *Purchasing*
Mike Marie, *Regl Sales Mgr*
Brad Sutphin, *Regl Sales Mgr*
David Golden, *Sales Staff*
▲ **EMP:** 34 **EST:** 1999
SQ FT: 17,500
SALES (est): 10MM **Privately Held**
WEB: www.dac-intl.com
SIC: 3541 Machine tools, metal cutting type

(P-7728)
DOLLAR SHAVE CLUB INC (HQ)
13335 Maxella Ave, Marina Del Rey (90292-5619)
PHONE....................310 975-8528
Jason Goldberger, *CEO*
Alec Brownstein, *Vice Pres*
Carly Jansen, *Vice Pres*
David Kujda, *Vice Pres*
John Milligan, *Vice Pres*
EMP: 386 **EST:** 2011
SALES (est): 104.7MM
SALES (corp-wide): 59.9B **Privately Held**
WEB: www.dollarshaveclub.com
SIC: 3541 3991 2844 Shaving machines (metalworking); shaving brushes; shaving preparations
PA: Unilever Plc
Unilever House
London
207 822-5252

(P-7729)
DORINGER MANUFACTURING CO INC
13400 Estrella Ave, Gardena (90248-1513)
PHONE....................310 366-7766
William Bailey, *President*
Lisa Pomeroy, *Treasurer*
EMP: 15 **EST:** 1982
SQ FT: 50,000
SALES (est): 3.6MM
SALES (corp-wide): 6MM **Privately Held**
WEB: www.doringer.com
SIC: 3541 Machine tools, metal cutting type
PA: Cold Saws Of America, Inc.
13400 Estrella Ave
Gardena CA
310 366-7766

(P-7730)
DOWNEY GRINDING CO
12323 Bellflower Blvd, Downey (90242-2829)
P.O. Box 583 (90241-0583)
PHONE....................562 803-5556
Larry Sequeira, *President*
Darla Sequeira, *Corp Secy*
Steve Schofield, *Vice Pres*
Steve Shailer, *Info Tech Mgr*
▲ **EMP:** 38 **EST:** 1960
SQ FT: 27,000
SALES (est): 2.9MM **Privately Held**
WEB: www.downeygrinding.com
SIC: 3541 3599 Machine tools, metal cutting type; machine shop, jobbing & repair

(P-7731)
ENSIGN US DRLG CAL INC (HQ)
7001 Charity Ave, Bakersfield (93308-5824)
PHONE....................661 589-0111
Selby Porter, *President*
Michael Nuss, *Exec VP*
EMP: 163 **EST:** 1962
SALES (est): 11.5MM
SALES (corp-wide): 1.2B **Privately Held**
WEB: www.ensignusd.com
SIC: 3541 Drilling & boring machines
PA: Ensign Energy Services Inc
400 5 Ave Sw Suite 1000
Calgary AB T2P 0
403 262-1361

(P-7732)
GERMAN KNIFE INC
4184 E Conant St, Long Beach (90808-1789)
PHONE....................310 900-1081
Brian Kim, *President*
Chuyan Ker, *Shareholder*
Frank Sun, *Shareholder*
▲ **EMP:** 13 **EST:** 1998
SALES (est): 345.1K **Privately Held**
SIC: 3541 Lathes, metal cutting & polishing

(P-7733)
I & I DEBURRING INC
14504 Carmenita Rd Ste A, Norwalk (90650-5290)
PHONE....................562 802-0058
Gary Wollum, *President*
Gary Klema, *Principal*
EMP: 15 **EST:** 1985
SQ FT: 4,300
SALES (est): 1MM **Privately Held**
WEB: www.i-i-deburring.com
SIC: 3541 Machine tools, metal cutting type

(P-7734)
JWC CARBIDE INC
33700 Calle Vis, Temecula (92592-9189)
PHONE....................714 540-8870
Fax: 714 668-8600
EMP: 14
SQ FT: 5,900
SALES (est): 2.2MM **Privately Held**
WEB: www.jwccarbide.com
SIC: 3541 Machine Shop

(P-7735)
K-V ENGINEERING INC
2411 W 1st St, Santa Ana (92703-3509)
PHONE....................714 229-9977
Duong Vu, *President*
Christie Vu, *CFO*
Hien Dao, *Program Mgr*
EMP: 60 **EST:** 1984
SQ FT: 22,000
SALES (est): 5.9MM **Privately Held**
WEB: www.kvengineering.com
SIC: 3541 3542 Milling machines; machine tools, metal forming type; punching & shearing machines; press brakes; riveting machines

(P-7736)
MELFRED BORZALL INC
2712 Airpark Dr, Santa Maria (93455-1418)
PHONE....................805 614-4344
Dick Melsheimer, *Principal*
Eric Melsheimer, *Executive*
Alan Bonn, *Export Mgr*
Roscoe Brister, *Sales Staff*
Michael Harmon, *Manager*

▲ **EMP:** 40
SQ FT: 30,000
SALES (est): 7.7MM **Privately Held**
WEB: www.melfredborzall.com
SIC: 3541 Machine tools, metal cutting type

(P-7737)
MONARCH PRCISION DEBURRING INC
1514 E Edinger Ave Ste C, Santa Ana (92705-4918)
PHONE....................714 258-0342
Russ Little, *President*
EMP: 15 **EST:** 1968
SQ FT: 6,100
SALES (est): 1.1MM **Privately Held**
WEB:
www.monarchprecisiondeburring.com
SIC: 3541 Machine tools, metal cutting type

(P-7738)
PAPCO SCREW PRODUCTS INC
Also Called: Papco Parts
9410 De Soto Ave Ste A, Chatsworth (91311-4993)
PHONE....................818 341-2266
Norman J Grencius, *President*
EMP: 13 **EST:** 1972
SQ FT: 6,000
SALES (est): 2.4MM **Privately Held**
WEB: www.papcoparts.com
SIC: 3541 3451 Screw machines, automatic; screw machine products

(P-7739)
PRECISION DEBURRING SERVICES
4440 Manning Rd, Pico Rivera (90660-2164)
PHONE....................562 944-4497
Darren Smith, *President*
▲ **EMP:** 20 **EST:** 1984
SALES (est): 1.1MM **Privately Held**
WEB: www.pdsdeburring.com
SIC: 3541 Machine tools, metal cutting type

(P-7740)
PRECON INC
Also Called: Precon Gage
3131 E La Palma Ave, Anaheim (92806-2895)
PHONE....................714 630-7632
James Von Zabern, *President*
Audrey Von Zabern, *Treasurer*
EMP: 27 **EST:** 1970
SQ FT: 10,500
SALES (est): 1.2MM **Privately Held**
WEB: www.precon-inc.com
SIC: 3541 3545 3823 3471 Deburring machines; saws & sawing machines; grinding machines, metalworking; gauges (machine tool accessories); industrial instrmnts msrmnt display/control process variable; plating & polishing

(P-7741)
R H STRASBAUGH (PA)
825 Buckley Rd, San Luis Obispo (93401-8192)
PHONE....................805 541-6424
Alan Strasbaugh, *President*
Allan Paterson, *President*
Eric Jacobson, *Vice Pres*
Bill Kalenian, *Vice Pres*
Brad Diaz, *VP Opers*
EMP: 77 **EST:** 1964
SQ FT: 135,000
SALES (est): 16.9MM **Publicly Held**
WEB: www.gainliftoff.com
SIC: 3541 3559 5065 Grinding, polishing, buffing, lapping & honing machines; grinding machines, metalworking; semiconductor manufacturing machinery; electronic parts & equipment

(P-7742)
REPUBLIC MACHINERY CO INC (PA)
Also Called: Lagun Engineering Solutions
800 Sprucelake Dr, Harbor City (90710-1607)
PHONE....................310 518-1100

Vivian Bezic, *CEO*
Joseph Bezic, *President*
Bryan Muhlenbruch, *Executive*
Gary Trapani, *Technical Staff*
Nicole Bezic, *Controller*
◆ **EMP:** 29 **EST:** 1969
SQ FT: 30,000
SALES (est): 6.2MM **Privately Held**
WEB: www.lagun.com
SIC: 3541 3542 3549 3545 Drilling & boring machines; arbor presses; extruding machines (machine tools); metal; metalworking machinery; machine knives, metalworking; drilling machine attachments & accessories

(P-7743)
ROTHENBERGER USA LLC
955 Monterey Pass Rd, Monterey Park (91754-3610)
PHONE....................323 268-1381
Glen Schlueter, *Manager*
EMP: 13 **EST:** 1955
SALES (est): 309.1K **Privately Held**
WEB: www.rothenberger.com
SIC: 3541 Machine tools, metal cutting type

(P-7744)
RYTAN INC
1648 W 134th St, Gardena (90249-2014)
PHONE....................310 328-6553
Carol J Silbaugh, *CEO*
Nicole Silbaugh, *Manager*
▲ **EMP:** 18 **EST:** 1983
SQ FT: 20,400
SALES (est): 2.7MM **Privately Held**
WEB: www.rytan.com
SIC: 3541 Keysetting machines

(P-7745)
S L FUSCO INC (PA)
1966 E Via Arado, Rancho Dominguez (90220-6100)
P.O. Box 5924, Compton (90224-5924)
PHONE....................310 868-1010
Jerald C Rosin, *CEO*
Eric Rosin, *President*
Arlene Rosin, *Vice Pres*
Arnaldo Rodriguez, *Info Tech Dir*
Omar Sanchez, *Purch Agent*
◆ **EMP:** 45 **EST:** 1941
SQ FT: 40,000
SALES (est): 24.6MM **Privately Held**
WEB: www.slfusco.com
SIC: 3541 Machine tools, metal cutting type

(P-7746)
S S SCHAFFER CO INC
Also Called: Steel Services Co
5637 District Blvd, Vernon (90058-5518)
PHONE....................323 560-1430
Steven Schaffer Jr, *President*
Marcia Schaffer, *Treasurer*
Caroline Sallenbach, *Vice Pres*
William Salenbach, *Admin Sec*
EMP: 15 **EST:** 1940
SQ FT: 30,000
SALES (est): 1.8MM **Privately Held**
SIC: 3541 Grinding machines, metalworking

(P-7747)
SOUTHWESTERN INDUSTRIES INC (PA)
Also Called: Trak Machine Tools
2615 Homestead Pl, Rancho Dominguez (90220-5610)
P.O. Box 9066, Compton (90224-9066)
PHONE....................310 608-4422
Richard Leonhard, *CEO*
Stephen Pinto, *President*
Tom Copeland, *Vice Pres*
Brian Napolitano, *Executive*
Charlie Cooper, *Regional Mgr*
▲ **EMP:** 70 **EST:** 1951
SALES (est): 47.6MM **Privately Held**
WEB: www.southwesternindustries.com
SIC: 3541 Machine tools, metal cutting type

(P-7748)
SUPERTEC MACHINERY INC
Also Called: St Supertec
6435 Alondra Blvd, Paramount
(90723-3758)
PHONE....................562 220-1675
Johnny KAO, *CEO*
Randy Chu, *President*
Rafael Vasquez, *Engineer*
Yanlin Qiao, *Accountant*
Edgar Bustos, *Regl Sales Mgr*
▲ **EMP:** 15 **EST:** 1994
SQ FT: 8,420
SALES (est): 2.9MM **Privately Held**
WEB: www.supertecusa.com
SIC: 3541 3542 7389 Grinding, polishing,
buffing, lapping & honing machines;
grinding machines, metalworking; ma-
chine tools, metal forming type; grinding,
precision: commercial or industrial

(P-7749)
TESCO PRODUCTS
25601 Avenue Stanford, Santa Clarita
(91355-1103)
PHONE....................661 257-0153
Mark Terry, *CEO*
EMP: 27 **EST:** 1946
SQ FT: 2,500
SALES (est): 785.7K **Privately Held**
WEB: www.tescoproductsinc.com
SIC: 3541 5032 Grinding, polishing, buff-
ing, lapping & honing machines; brick,
stone & related material

(P-7750)
US UNION TOOL INC (HQ)
1260 N Fee Ana St, Anaheim (92807-1817)
PHONE....................714 521-6242
Hideo Hirano, *President*
Robert Smallwood, *President*
Sherry Smith, *Database Admin*
John McCandlish, *Manager*
▲ **EMP:** 45 **EST:** 1981
SQ FT: 44,000
SALES (est): 10.9MM **Privately Held**
WEB: www.uniontool.co.jp
SIC: 3541 Machine tools, metal cutting
type

(P-7751)
VALLEY CUTTING SYSTEM INC
1455 N Belmont Rd, Exeter (93221-9669)
P.O. Box 607, Three Rivers (93271-0607)
PHONE....................559 684-1229
Ed Earnest, *Manager*
▲ **EMP:** 13 **EST:** 2010
SALES (est): 1.5MM **Privately Held**
WEB: www.valleycuttingsystems.com
SIC: 3541 Cutoff machines (metalworking
machinery)

(P-7752)
WESTERN FIBER CO INC
4234a Sandrini Rd, Arvin (93203-9200)
P.O. Box 22665, Bakersfield (93390-2665)
PHONE....................661 854-5556
John Scarrone, *President*
▲ **EMP:** 20 **EST:** 2002
SALES (est): 1.9MM **Privately Held**
WEB: www.westernfiber.com
SIC: 3541 Electrical discharge erosion ma-
chines

3542 Machine Tools: Forming

(P-7753)
AMBRIT INDUSTRIES INC
432 Magnolia Ave, Glendale (91204-2406)
PHONE....................818 243-1224
Paul Yaussi, *President*
Louis A Yaussi, *Corp Secy*
Michelle Taylor, *Manager*
EMP: 38 **EST:** 1946
SQ FT: 9,184
SALES (est): 3MM **Privately Held**
WEB: www.ambritindustries.com
SIC: 3542 3363 Die casting machines;
aluminum die-castings

(P-7754)
AMERICAN PNEUMATIC TOOLS INC
Also Called: APT
1000 S Grand Ave, Santa Ana
(92705-4122)
PHONE....................562 204-1555
Kim Eads, *President*
Dan O Brien, *CFO*
▲ **EMP:** 16 **EST:** 1938
SQ FT: 15,000
SALES (est): 1.8MM **Privately Held**
WEB: www.apt-tools.com
SIC: 3542 3541 3546 3532 Machine
tools, metal forming type; machine tools,
metal cutting type; power-driven hand-
tools; mining machinery; hand & edge
tools

(P-7755)
AMERICAN PRECISION HYDRAULICS
5601 Research Dr, Huntington Beach
(92649-1620)
PHONE....................714 903-8610
Susan Smith, *President*
Steve Smith, *Vice Pres*
Judith Spirtos, *QC Mgr*
EMP: 23 **EST:** 1996
SQ FT: 6,500
SALES (est): 2.6MM **Privately Held**
WEB:
www.americanprecisionassembly.com
SIC: 3542 Presses: hydraulic & pneumatic,
mechanical & manual

(P-7756)
BROTHERS MACHINE & TOOL INC
11095 Inland Ave, Jurupa Valley
(91752-1155)
PHONE....................951 361-9454
Jose E Razo, *President*
EMP: 20 **Privately Held**
SIC: 3542 Machine tools, metal forming
type
PA: Brothers Machine & Tool, Inc.
11098 Inland Ave
Jurupa Valley CA 91752

(P-7757)
BROTHERS MACHINE & TOOL INC (PA)
11098 Inland Ave, Jurupa Valley
(91752-1154)
PHONE....................951 361-2909
Jose E Razzo, *President*
Jose L Razzo, *Treasurer*
Jose F Razzo, *Vice Pres*
EMP: 15 **EST:** 1990
SALES (est): 2MM **Privately Held**
SIC: 3542 Machine tools, metal forming
type

(P-7758)
CIRCLE INDUSTRIAL MFG CORP
Also Called: Cim
2727 N Slater Ave, Compton (90222-1028)
PHONE....................310 638-5101
Debra Cosio, *Branch Mgr*
EMP: 14
SALES (corp-wide): 5.1MM **Privately
Held**
WEB: www.circleindustrial.com
SIC: 3542 Sheet metalworking machines
PA: Circle Industrial Mfg. Corporation
1613 W El Segundo Blvd
Compton CA 90222
310 638-5101

(P-7759)
MAGNETIC METALS CORPORATION
2475 W La Palma Ave, Anaheim
(92801-2610)
PHONE....................714 828-4625
Linda Cannon, *Branch Mgr*
EMP: 226
SQ FT: 50,400
SALES (corp-wide): 39.5MM **Privately
Held**
WEB: www.magneticmetals.com
SIC: 3542 Magnetic forming machines

PA: Magnetic Metals Corporation
1950 Marlton Pike E # 103
Cherry Hill NJ 08003
856 964-7842

(P-7760)
MEDLIN RAMPS
14903 Marquardt Ave, Santa Fe Springs
(90670-5128)
PHONE....................877 463-3546
Mark Medlin, *Principal*
▲ **EMP:** 42 **EST:** 1990
SQ FT: 10,000
SALES (est): 7MM **Privately Held**
WEB: www.medlinramps.com
SIC: 3542 5084 3441 Machine tools,
metal forming type; materials handling
machinery; fabricated structural metal

(P-7761)
MJC ENGINEERING AND TECH INC
15401 Assembly Ln, Huntington Beach
(92649-1329)
PHONE....................714 890-0618
Carl Lorentzen, *President*
Bernd Hermann, *CFO*
Gro Jensen, *CFO*
Per Carlson, *Vice Pres*
Percy Carlson, *Vice Pres*
◆ **EMP:** 18 **EST:** 1993
SQ FT: 10,000
SALES (est): 4.9MM **Privately Held**
WEB: www.mjcengineering.com
SIC: 3542 Spinning machines, metal

(P-7762)
NUGIER PRESS COMPANY INC
Also Called: Nugier Hydraulics
18031 La Salle Ave, Gardena
(90248-3606)
PHONE....................310 515-6025
Gary Livick, *President*
EMP: 29 **EST:** 1994
SALES (est): 1MM **Privately Held**
WEB: www.nugierfroom.com
SIC: 3542 5084 Presses: hydraulic &
pneumatic, mechanical & manual; indus-
trial machinery & equipment

(P-7763)
PHI (PA)
Also Called: PHI Hydraulics
14955 Salt Lake Ave, City of Industry
(91746-3133)
PHONE....................626 968-9680
Yuriy Rakhlin, *President*
Jim Voigt, *Engineer*
Tommy Duong, *Sales Mgr*
▼ **EMP:** 18 **EST:** 2010
SQ FT: 25,930
SALES (est): 3.8MM **Privately Held**
WEB: www.phihydraulics.com
SIC: 3542 3549 Presses: hydraulic &
pneumatic, mechanical & manual; metal-
working machinery

(P-7764)
PRECISION FASTENER TOOLING INC
11530 Western Ave, Stanton (90680-3490)
PHONE....................714 898-8558
Charles Boyles, *President*
James Azevedo, *Vice Pres*
EMP: 35 **EST:** 1981
SQ FT: 10,000
SALES (est): 2.6MM **Privately Held**
WEB: www.precisionfastenertooling.com
SIC: 3542 3544 Bulldozers (metalworking
machinery); special dies, tools, jigs & fix-
tures

(P-7765)
RAY CHINN CONSTRUCTION INC
424 24th St, Bakersfield (93301-4104)
PHONE....................661 327-2731
Raymond Dean Chinn, *President*
EMP: 23 **EST:** 2005
SALES (est): 2.4MM **Privately Held**
SIC: 3542 Mechanical (pneumatic or hy-
draulic) metal forming machines

(P-7766)
SAMTECH AUTOMOTIVE USA INC
Also Called: Samtech International
1130 E Dominguez St, Carson
(90746-3518)
PHONE....................310 638-9955
Yoshiki Sakaguchi, *President*
Don Zimmerman, *Vice Pres*
Harry Fujii, *General Mgr*
Hisashi Fujii, *General Mgr*
Huu Nguyen, *Engineer*
▲ **EMP:** 50 **EST:** 1996
SQ FT: 27,812
SALES (est): 11MM **Privately Held**
WEB: www.samtechintl.com
SIC: 3542 Machine tools, metal forming
type
PA: Samtech Corp.
1000-18, Emmyocho
Kashiwara OSK 582-0
-

(P-7767)
UNIVERSAL PUNCH CORP
4001 W Macarthur Blvd, Santa Ana
(92704-6307)
P.O. Box 26879 (92799-6879)
PHONE....................714 556-4488
Kenneth L Williams, *President*
Joan Williams, *CFO*
Kevin Williams, *Vice Pres*
Klint Williams, *Engineer*
▲ **EMP:** 55 **EST:** 1974
SQ FT: 52,000
SALES (est): 8.7MM **Privately Held**
WEB: www.concentricitygage.com
SIC: 3542 3545 3544 3452 Punching &
shearing machines; machine tool acces-
sories; special dies, tools, jigs & fixtures;
bolts, nuts, rivets & washers

(P-7768)
US INDUSTRIAL TOOL & SUP CO
Also Called: Usit Co
14083 S Normandie Ave, Gardena
(90249-2614)
PHONE....................310 464-8400
Keith Rowland, *CEO*
Sally Kovarik, *Vice Pres*
▲ **EMP:** 47 **EST:** 1955
SQ FT: 35,000
SALES (est): 8.8MM **Privately Held**
WEB: www.ustool.com
SIC: 3542 3546 Machine tools, metal
forming type; power-driven handtools

(P-7769)
WEST COAST-ACCUDYNE INC
Also Called: Accudyne Engineering & Eqp
7180 Scout Ave, Bell (90201-3202)
P.O. Box 2159 (90202-2159)
PHONE....................562 927-2546
George F Schofhauser, *President*
Jill Wigney, *Corp Secy*
Kurt Anderegg, *Vice Pres*
Luman Burton, *Chief Engr*
▲ **EMP:** 20 **EST:** 1954
SALES (est): 3.3MM **Privately Held**
WEB: www.accudyneeng.com
SIC: 3542 5084 Presses: forming, stamp-
ing, punching, sizing (machine tools); ma-
chine tools & accessories

(P-7770)
XY CORP INC
Also Called: E P S Products
1258 Montalvo Way Ste A, Palm Springs
(92262-5441)
PHONE....................760 323-0333
Jerry Good, *President*
Greg Good, *Vice Pres*
EMP: 15 **EST:** 1991
SQ FT: 14,000
SALES (est): 2.3MM **Privately Held**
SIC: 3542 3299 Presses: hydraulic &
pneumatic, mechanical & manual; orna-
mental & architectural plaster work

3543 Industrial Patterns

(P-7771)
HP CORE CO INC
1264 Indian Springs Dr, Glendora
(91741-2336)
PHONE.....................................323 582-1688
Ken Catalfo, *President*
Charles Catalfo, *Vice Pres*
Sunny Sohrabian, *Manager*
EMP: 26 EST: 1964
SALES (est): 1.6MM **Privately Held**
SIC: 3543 Foundry cores

3544 Dies, Tools, Jigs, Fixtures & Indl Molds

(P-7772)
A N TOOL & DIE
518 S Fair Oaks Ave, Pasadena
(91105-2690)
PHONE.....................................626 795-3238
Dorothy Nettleton, *President*
John Nettleton, *Vice Pres*
Leigha Nettleton, *Human Res Mgr*
EMP: 14 EST: 1948
SQ FT: 6,000
SALES (est): 1.9MM **Privately Held**
WEB: www.antoolindie.com
SIC: 3544 Special dies & tools

(P-7773)
ACE CLEARWATER ENTERPRISES INC
1614 Kona Dr, Compton (90220-5412)
PHONE.....................................310 538-5380
James D Dodson, *Branch Mgr*
EMP: 32
SALES (corp-wide): 32.6MM **Privately Held**
WEB: www.aceclearwater.com
SIC: 3544 3728 3769 Special dies, tools, jigs & fixtures; aircraft parts & auxiliary equipment
PA: Ace Clearwater Enterprises, Inc.
19815 Magellan Dr
Torrance CA 90502
310 323-2140

(P-7774)
ALCO MANUFACTURING INC
207 E Alton Ave, Santa Ana (92707-4416)
PHONE.....................................714 549-5007
Frank Reuland, *President*
Ingrid Reuland, *Corp Secy*
EMP: 15 EST: 1980
SQ FT: 11,000
SALES (est): 1.9MM **Privately Held**
WEB: www.alcomanufacturinginc.com
SIC: 3544 3469 3444 Special dies & tools; stamping metal for the trade; sheet metalwork

(P-7775)
AMBRIT ENGINEERING CORPORATION
2640 Halladay St, Santa Ana (92705-5649)
PHONE.....................................714 557-1074
Terrence Saul, *CEO*
John F Mattimoe, *President*
Thomas W Vickers, *Corp Secy*
Carl Suiter, *Program Mgr*
Lisa Jane, *Executive Asst*
▲ EMP: 65
SQ FT: 32,000
SALES (est): 17.9MM **Privately Held**
WEB: www.ambritengineering.com
SIC: 3544 Forms (molds), for foundry & plastics working machinery

(P-7776)
AMERICAN PLASTIC PRODUCTS INC
9243 Glenoaks Blvd, Sun Valley
(91352-2614)
PHONE.....................................818 504-1073
Roupen Yegavian, *President*
Varosh Petrosian, *Vice Pres*
▲ EMP: 75 EST: 1991
SQ FT: 35,000

SALES (est): 9MM **Privately Held**
SIC: 3544 Special dies & tools

(P-7777)
ART MOLD DIE CASTING INC
11872 Sheldon St, Sun Valley
(91352-1507)
PHONE.....................................818 767-6464
Leo Benavides, *President*
Arman Sarkissian, *Vice Pres*
EMP: 44 EST: 1965
SQ FT: 14,000
SALES (est): 1.4MM **Privately Held**
WEB: www.artmoldinc.com
SIC: 3544 3369 3363 Industrial molds; nonferrous foundries; aluminum die-castings

(P-7778)
ATS TOOL INC
Also Called: Ats Workholding
30222 Esperanza, Rcho STA Marg
(92688-2121)
PHONE.....................................949 888-1744
William Murphy, *President*
Sean Murphy, *Vice Pres*
Mike Harper, *Engineer*
▲ EMP: 59 EST: 1991
SALES (est): 3.3MM **Privately Held**
WEB: www.ats-s.com
SIC: 3544 Jigs & fixtures

(P-7779)
AVIS ROTO DIE CO
1560 N San Fernando Rd, Los Angeles
(90065-1225)
P.O. Box 65617 (90065-0617)
PHONE.....................................323 255-7070
Avetis Iskanian, *CEO*
Hasmik Iskanian, *Admin Sec*
Hasmik Iskanian, *Human Res Mgr*
Ron Lee, *Sales Staff*
Karine Atanesian, *Director*
EMP: 30 EST: 1982
SQ FT: 32,000
SALES (est): 4.6MM **Privately Held**
WEB: www.avisrd.com
SIC: 3544 Paper cutting dies

(P-7780)
AW DIE ENGRAVING INC
8550 Roland St, Buena Park (90621-3199)
PHONE.....................................714 521-7910
Arnold Werdin, *President*
Art Chavez, *Vice Pres*
EMP: 30 EST: 1972
SQ FT: 9,000
SALES (est): 2.9MM **Privately Held**
WEB: www.awdie.com
SIC: 3544 Dies & die holders for metal cutting, forming, die casting

(P-7781)
B & R MOLD INC
4564 E Los Angeles Ave C, Simi Valley
(93063-3428)
PHONE.....................................805 526-8665
Brent Robinson, *President*
Stephen Yamani, *Executive*
EMP: 20 EST: 1986
SALES (est): 4.9MM **Privately Held**
WEB: www.brmold.com
SIC: 3544 Industrial molds

(P-7782)
BARROT CORPORATION
1881 Kaiser Ave, Irvine (92614-5707)
PHONE.....................................949 852-1640
Jesus Barrot, *President*
Robert Barrot, *Treasurer*
Carlos Barrot, *Vice Pres*
James Barrot, *Admin Sec*
EMP: 22 EST: 1983
SQ FT: 15,000
SALES (est): 4.1MM **Privately Held**
WEB: www.barrotcorp.com
SIC: 3544 3769 Special dies & tools; guided missile & space vehicle parts & auxiliary equipment

(P-7783)
BUCY DIE CASTING
4122 W Burbank Blvd, Burbank
(91505-2121)
PHONE.....................................818 843-5044
EMP: 13

SALES (est): 1.9MM **Privately Held**
WEB: www.bucycast.com
SIC: 3544 Mfg Dies/Tools/Jigs/Fixtures

(P-7784)
CACO-PACIFIC CORPORATION (PA)
813 N Cummings Rd, Covina
(91724-2597)
PHONE.....................................626 331-3361
Robert G Hoffmann, *President*
Manfred Hoffman, *Ch of Bd*
Thom Williams, *Admin Sec*
◆ EMP: 142 EST: 1985
SQ FT: 45,000
SALES (est): 20.8MM **Privately Held**
WEB: www.cacopacific.com
SIC: 3544 Industrial molds

(P-7785)
CAST-RITE CORPORATION
515 E Airline Way, Gardena (90248-2593)
PHONE.....................................310 532-2080
Donald De Haan, *President*
Howard Watkins, *CFO*
Wynn Chapman, *Vice Pres*
Donald Dehaan, *General Mgr*
Marcela Toro, *Human Res Mgr*
▲ EMP: 98 EST: 1941
SQ FT: 74,712
SALES (est): 19.4MM
SALES (corp-wide): 25.7MM **Privately Held**
WEB: www.cast-rite.com
SIC: 3544 3471 3363 Special dies & tools; plating & polishing; aluminum die-castings
PA: Cast-Rite International, Inc.
515 E Airline Way
Gardena CA 90248
310 532-2080

(P-7786)
CHARLES MEISNER INC
201 Sierra Pl Ste A, Upland (91786-5668)
PHONE.....................................909 946-8216
Charles Meisner, *President*
Carol Meisner, *Corp Secy*
Tara Meisner, *Purchasing*
EMP: 25 EST: 1972
SQ FT: 19,000
SALES (est): 4MM **Privately Held**
WEB: www.charlesmeisnerinc.com
SIC: 3544 3599 Special dies & tools; machine shop, jobbing & repair

(P-7787)
CHIP-MAKERS TOOLING SUPPLY INC
7352 Whittier Ave, Whittier (90602-1131)
PHONE.....................................562 698-5840
Stephen Smith, *CEO*
Paul Hartman, *President*
Patty Rivera, *Treasurer*
EMP: 17 EST: 1990
SQ FT: 10,000
SALES (est): 2.2MM **Privately Held**
WEB: www.chip-makers.com
SIC: 3544 Special dies & tools

(P-7788)
CJ ENTERPRISES
Also Called: Precision Enterprises
11530 Western Ave, Stanton (90680-3435)
PHONE.....................................714 898-8558
Chuck Boyles, *Partner*
EMP: 17 EST: 1991
SALES (est): 788.5K **Privately Held**
SIC: 3544 Special dies, tools, jigs & fixtures

(P-7789)
COAST AEROSPACE MFG INC
950 Richfield Rd, Placentia (92870-6732)
PHONE.....................................714 893-8066
Louis Ponce, *President*
David Rodriguez, *President*
Steven Castillo, *Vice Pres*
Frank Fleck, *Vice Pres*
Richard Stiller, *Prgrmr*
EMP: 43 EST: 1999

SALES (est): 9.1MM **Privately Held**
WEB: www.coastaero.com
SIC: 3544 3441 3728 3291 Special dies & tools; fabricated structural metal; aircraft parts & equipment; abrasive products; screw machine products; computer peripheral equipment

(P-7790)
COLBRIT MANUFACTURING CO INC
9666 Owensmouth Ave Ste G Chatsworth
(91311-8050)
PHONE.....................................818 709-3608
Gerardo Cruz, *President*
Marina Cruz, *Vice Pres*
▲ EMP: 30 EST: 1979
SQ FT: 6,000
SALES (est): 4.5MM **Privately Held**
WEB: www.colbrit.com
SIC: 3544 Special dies & tools

(P-7791)
COMPUTED TOOL & ENGRG INC
2910 E Ricker Way, Anaheim (92806-2526)
PHONE.....................................714 630-3911
Oscar Torres, *President*
Isabel Torres, *Admin Sec*
EMP: 31 EST: 1983
SQ FT: 8,825
SALES (est): 752.5K **Privately Held**
WEB: www.computedtool.com
SIC: 3544 Special dies & tools

(P-7792)
CONCRETE MOLD CORPORATION
Also Called: Besser Company
2121 E Del Amo Blvd, Compton
(90220-6301)
PHONE.....................................310 537-5171
Bradley Gardner, *President*
EMP: 100 EST: 1960
SQ FT: 30,000
SALES (est): 2.7MM
SALES (corp-wide): 213.4MM **Privately Held**
WEB: www.besser.com
SIC: 3544 Industrial molds
PA: Besser Company
801 Johnson St
Alpena MI 49707
989 354-4111

(P-7793)
CRENSHAW DIE AND MFG CORP
7432 Prince Dr, Huntington Beach
(92647-4553)
PHONE.....................................949 475-5505
James V Ireland, *CEO*
Dale Congelliere, *President*
Sharon Piers, *CFO*
EMP: 55 EST: 1962
SQ FT: 38,000
SALES (est): 9.3MM **Privately Held**
WEB: www.crenshawdiemfg.com
SIC: 3544 Special dies & tools

(P-7794)
DAUNTLESS INDUSTRIES INC
Also Called: Dauntless Molds
806 N Grand Ave, Covina (91724-2418)
PHONE.....................................626 966-4494
George R Payton, *President*
Norm Holt, *General Mgr*
EMP: 25 EST: 1975
SQ FT: 15,000
SALES (est): 5MM **Privately Held**
WEB: www.dauntlessmolds.com
SIC: 3544 Special dies & tools

(P-7795)
DIE CAST MODEL MADNESS
743 N Mentor Ave, Pasadena
(91104-4624)
PHONE.....................................626 791-0364
Juan Hasbun, *Principal*
EMP: 13 EST: 2010
SALES (est): 201.9K **Privately Held**
SIC: 3544 Special dies & tools

(P-7796)
DIE SHOP
7302 Adams St, Paramount (90723-4008)
PHONE.....................................562 630-4400
Hector Ramirez, *Owner*

Hector J Ramirez, *Principal*
Veronica Raaff,
▲ **EMP:** 15 **EST:** 1997
SQ FT: 4,000
SALES (est): 2.1MM **Privately Held**
WEB: www.tdsfinishing.com
SIC: 3544 Special dies & tools

(P-7797)
DIVERSIFIED MFG TECH INC
Also Called: Dmt
149 Via Trevizio, Corona (92879-1773)
PHONE..................................714 577-7000
Michael McMillian, *President*
Tim Baber, *Vice Pres*
EMP: 14 **EST:** 2011
SALES (est): 2MM **Privately Held**
WEB: www.roembkedmt.com
SIC: 3544 3089 Industrial molds; injection
molding of plastics

(P-7798)
EDCO DIE INC
2199 W Arrow Rte, Upland (91786-7610)
PHONE..................................909 985-4417
Dennis Ortis, *President*
Joyce Ortis, *Corp Secy*
EMP: 32 **EST:** 1966
SQ FT: 23,000
SALES (est): 352K **Privately Held**
WEB: www.excoengusa.com
SIC: 3544 Special dies & tools

(P-7799)
EDRO ENGINEERING INC (DH)
Also Called: Voestalpine High Prfmce Mtls
20500 Carrey Rd, Walnut (91789-2417)
PHONE..................................909 594-5751
Eric Henn, *President*
Laurinda Diaz, *Shareholder*
Guy Recendez, *COO*
Mike Guscott, *Vice Pres*
Terry Henn, *Vice Pres*
◆ **EMP:** 80 **EST:** 1976
SQ FT: 60,000
SALES (est): 20MM
SALES (corp-wide): 13.6B **Privately Held**
WEB: www.edro.com
SIC: 3544 3599 Special dies & tools; ma-
chine shop, jobbing & repair
HQ: Voestalpine High Performance Metals
Corporation
2505 Millennium Dr
Elgin IL 60124
877 992-8764

(P-7800)
EDRO SPECIALTY STEELS INC
20500 Carrey Rd, Walnut (91789-2417)
PHONE..................................800 368-3376
Terry Henn, *President*
Kevin Ewing, *CFO*
Kristopher Welch, *Vice Pres*
Ivgen Simsek, *Sales Mgr*
▲ **EMP:** 15 **EST:** 2014
SALES (est): 2.3MM **Privately Held**
WEB: www.edro.com
SIC: 3544 Special dies & tools

(P-7801)
FELIX TOOL & ENGINEERING
14535 Bessemer St, Van Nuys
(91411-2804)
PHONE..................................830 947-4601
John Felix, *President*
EMP: 14 **EST:** 1962
SQ FT: 6,000
SALES (est): 278.4K **Privately Held**
WEB: www.felixtool.com
SIC: 3544 3469 Special dies, tools, jigs &
fixtures; metal stampings

(P-7802)
G E SHELL CORE CO
8346 Salt Lake Ave, Cudahy (90201-5817)
P.O. Box 1099, Bell Gardens (90201-7099)
PHONE..................................323 773-4242
Raul Rivera, *General Mgr*
EMP: 43 **EST:** 1967
SALES (est): 267.5K **Privately Held**
SIC: 3544 Industrial molds

(P-7803)
GEMINI MFG & ENGRG INC
1020 E Vermont Ave, Anaheim
(92805-5617)
PHONE..................................714 999-0010
Sandra Lowry, *President*
Sandy Lowry, *Officer*
David Lowry, *Vice Pres*
Mike Clavin, *Prdtn Mgr*
Veronica Buso, *Manager*
EMP: 20 **EST:** 1979
SQ FT: 40,000
SALES (est): 2.5MM **Privately Held**
WEB: www.geminimfg.com
SIC: 3544 3599 Subpresses, metalwork-
ing; machine shop, jobbing & repair

(P-7804)
GMS MOLDS (PA)
729 E 223rd St, Carson (90745-4111)
PHONE..................................310 684-1168
Bradley Gardner, *Owner*
Laurie Sharp, *Office Mgr*
Rafael Fernandez, *Engineer*
EMP: 23 **EST:** 2010
SALES (est): 2.4MM **Privately Held**
WEB: www.gmsmolds.com
SIC: 3544 Industrial molds

(P-7805)
GRUBER SYSTEMS INC
29071 The Old Rd, Valencia (91355-1083)
PHONE..................................661 257-0464
John Hoskinson, *Ch of Bd*
Katherine Pavard, *President*
Jim Thiessen, *President*
Diana Arima, *Treasurer*
Steve Miller, *Vice Pres*
◆ **EMP:** 45 **EST:** 1968
SALES (est): 10.4MM **Privately Held**
WEB: www.grubersystems.com
SIC: 3544 3842 3531 3537 Industrial
molds; whirlpool baths, hydrotherapy
equipment; construction machinery; in-
dustrial trucks & tractors

(P-7806)
HIGHTOWER METAL PRODUCTS
2090 N Glassell St, Orange (92865-3306)
P.O. Box 5586 (92863-5586)
PHONE..................................714 637-7000
Kurt Koch, *President*
Mark Koch, *Vice Pres*
EMP: 66 **EST:** 1945
SQ FT: 20,000
SALES (est): 6.4MM **Privately Held**
SIC: 3544 Special dies & tools

(P-7807)
HUGHES BROS AIRCRAFTERS INC
11010 Garfield Pl, South Gate
(90280-7512)
PHONE..................................323 773-4541
Susan Hughes, *President*
James P Hughes, *Vice Pres*
Michael Hall, *General Mgr*
Gerry Imes, *QC Mgr*
Tim Whitaker, *Manager*
EMP: 43
SQ FT: 15,000
SALES (est): 7.3MM **Privately Held**
WEB: www.hbai.com
SIC: 3544 3449 3444 Die sets for metal
stamping (presses); plastering acces-
sories, metal; sheet metalwork

(P-7808)
IDEA TOOLING AND ENGRG INC
13915 S Main St, Los Angeles
(90061-2151)
PHONE..................................310 608-7488
Peter Janner, *President*
Inga Janner, *Treasurer*
Monica Janner, *Vice Pres*
Moe Sumbulan, *Vice Pres*
▲ **EMP:** 56 **EST:** 1973
SALES (est): 6.9MM **Privately Held**
WEB: www.ideatooling.com
SIC: 3544 3061 Special dies & tools; me-
chanical rubber goods

(P-7809)
JW MOLDING INC
2523 Calcite Cir, Newbury Park
(91320-1204)
PHONE..................................805 499-2682
Ralf Wolters, *President*
Bridgette Wolters, *Admin Sec*
EMP: 15 **EST:** 1980
SQ FT: 16,000
SALES (est): 2.7MM **Privately Held**
WEB: www.jwmolding.com
SIC: 3544 3089 Forms (molds), for
foundry & plastics working machinery; in-
jection molding of plastics

(P-7810)
KINGSON MOLD & MACHINE INC
1350 Titan Way, Brea (92821-3707)
PHONE..................................714 871-0221
Gregory S Rex, *CEO*
Theresa Hitt, *Office Mgr*
EMP: 36 **EST:** 1977
SQ FT: 8,500
SALES (est): 6.1MM **Privately Held**
WEB: www.kingsonmold.com
SIC: 3544 5031 Industrial molds; molding,
all materials

(P-7811)
KIPE MOLDS INC
340 E Crowther Ave, Placentia
(92870-6419)
PHONE..................................714 572-9576
George B Kipe Jr, *President*
Rebbeca L Kipe, *Treasurer*
George B Kipe Sr, *Admin Sec*
Dana King, *Manager*
EMP: 15 **EST:** 1970
SQ FT: 15,000
SALES (est): 2.2MM **Privately Held**
WEB: www.kipemolds.com
SIC: 3544 Industrial molds

(P-7812)
LEE MACHINE PRODUCTS
Also Called: Pneumatic Tube Carrier
2030 Central Ave, Duarte (91010-2913)
PHONE..................................626 301-4105
Thomas Young, *President*
EMP: 15 **EST:** 1965
SQ FT: 7,100
SALES (est): 180.6K **Privately Held**
SIC: 3544 3535 3949 7699 Special dies,
tools, jigs & fixtures; pneumatic tube con-
veyor systems; tennis equipment & sup-
plies; industrial machinery & equipment
repair

(P-7813)
M I T INC
Also Called: Morin Industrial Technology
15202 Pipeline Ln, Huntington Beach
(92649-1136)
PHONE..................................714 899-6066
Rene Morin, *President*
EMP: 24 **EST:** 1974
SQ FT: 12,000
SALES (est): 2.4MM **Privately Held**
SIC: 3544 Forms (molds), for foundry &
plastics working machinery

(P-7814)
MACDONALD CARBIDE CO
525 S Prospero Dr, West Covina
(91791-2931)
PHONE..................................626 960-4034
Amy Mac Donald, *President*
◆ **EMP:** 20 **EST:** 1967
SALES (est): 2.5MM **Privately Held**
WEB: www.macdonaldcarbide.com
SIC: 3544 3545 Special dies & tools; ma-
chine tool accessories

(P-7815)
MAGOR MOLD LLC
420 S Lone Hill Ave, San Dimas
(91773-4600)
PHONE..................................909 592-3663
Wolfgang Buhler, *President*
Martin Schottli, *Vice Pres*
Pam Strobel, *Executive Asst*
Chris Twardowski, *Prgrmr*
Dan Agnew, *Manager*
▲ **EMP:** 68 **EST:** 1967
SQ FT: 15,000

SALES (est): 10.2MM **Privately Held**
WEB: www.schoettli.com
SIC: 3544 Industrial molds

(P-7816)
MOLD VISION INC
18351 Pasadena St, Lake Elsinore
(92530-2766)
PHONE..................................951 245-8020
Greg Yocum, *President*
Charles Premananthan, *Vice Pres*
EMP: 14 **EST:** 1998
SALES (est): 2.6MM **Privately Held**
WEB: www.moldvision.net
SIC: 3544 Special dies & tools

(P-7817)
MR MOLD & ENGINEERING CORP
1150 Beacon St, Brea (92821-2936)
PHONE..................................714 996-5511
Richard Finnie II, *President*
Marilyn Finnie, *Vice Pres*
Ashley Cupp, *Office Mgr*
Rick Finnie, *Engineer*
Ricardo Rodriguez, *Purchasing*
EMP: 31 **EST:** 1985 **Privately Held**
WEB: www.mrmold.com
SIC: 3544 Special dies & tools; jigs & fix-
tures

(P-7818)
NIRON INC
20541 Earlgate St, Walnut (91789-2909)
PHONE..................................909 598-1526
Glen Nieberle, *President*
Cheryl Nieberle, *Admin Sec*
EMP: 27 **EST:** 1974
SQ FT: 17,000
SALES (est): 2.6MM **Privately Held**
WEB: www.niron.com
SIC: 3544 3089 Industrial molds; injection
molding of plastics

(P-7819)
OLIPHANT TOOL COMPANY
15652 Chemical Ln, Huntington Beach
(92649-1507)
PHONE..................................714 903-6336
William Oliphant, *Owner*
EMP: 13 **EST:** 1983
SQ FT: 12,000
SALES (est): 808.9K **Privately Held**
WEB: www.oliphanttool.com
SIC: 3544 7699 Special dies & tools; in-
dustrial tool grinding

(P-7820)
PACE PUNCHES INC
297 Goddard, Irvine (92618-4604)
PHONE..................................949 428-2750
Edward W Pepper, *President*
▲ **EMP:** 55 **EST:** 1978
SQ FT: 30,000
SALES (est): 8.9MM **Privately Held**
WEB: www.pacepunches.com
SIC: 3544 Punches, forming & stamping

(P-7821)
PACIFIC DIE SERVICES INC
7626 Baldwin Pl, Whittier (90602-1001)
PHONE..................................562 907-4463
Eric Syndinos, *President*
EMP: 21 **EST:** 1992
SQ FT: 5,000
SALES (est): 1.3MM **Privately Held**
SIC: 3544 Dies, steel rule

(P-7822)
PDC LLC
Also Called: Precision Diecut
4675 Vinita Ct, Chino (91710-5731)
PHONE..................................626 334-5000
Steve Gasparelli, *Mng Member*
Renee Goetz, *VP Finance*
Patti L W McGlasson,
EMP: 20 **EST:** 2010
SQ FT: 11,000
SALES (est): 4.9MM **Privately Held**
WEB: www.pdcintl.com
SIC: 3544 Special dies & tools

P R O D U C T S & S V C S

(P-7823)
PHILIPS TOOL & DIE INC
Also Called: Busy Bee Tooling
1620 S Marigold Ave, Ontario
(91761-4551)
PHONE..................909 947-8712
Robert F Phillips, *Principal*
Linda Warsinski, *Office Mgr*
Keith Phillips, *Sales Mgr*
EMP: 29 **EST:** 1970
SALES (est): 1MM **Privately Held**
SIC: 3544 Special dies & tools

(P-7824)
POPE PLASTICS INC
9134 Independence Ave, Chatsworth
(91311-5902)
PHONE..................818 701-1850
EMP: 40
SQ FT: 30,000
SALES (est): 6.5MM **Privately Held**
SIC: 3544 Mfg Dies/Tools/Jigs/Fixtures

(P-7825)
PRECISE DIE AND FINISHING
9400 Oso Ave, Chatsworth (91311-6020)
PHONE..................818 773-9337
David Rewers, *CEO*
EMP: 27 **EST:** 2016
SQ FT: 15,000
SALES (est): 7.5MM **Privately Held**
WEB: www.precisedf.com
SIC: 3544 Special dies & tools

(P-7826)
PRECISION FORGING DIES INC
10710 Sessler St, South Gate
(90280-7221)
PHONE..................562 861-1878
Dan Kloss, *President*
Edmond Kloss, *General Mgr*
EMP: 30 **EST:** 2001
SALES (est): 4.5MM **Privately Held**
WEB: www.precisionforgingdies.com
SIC: 3544 Special dies & tools

(P-7827)
PRESTIGE MOLD INCORPORATED
11040 Tacoma Dr, Rancho Cucamonga
(91730-4857)
PHONE..................909 980-6600
Donna C Pursell, *CEO*
Donna Koebel, *CFO*
Lance Spangler, *Vice Pres*
Joanne Dickinson, *Administration*
David Mernin, *Info Tech Mgr*
▲ **EMP:** 98 **EST:** 1982
SQ FT: 28,500
SALES (est): 33.5MM **Privately Held**
WEB: www.prestigemold.com
SIC: 3544 Industrial molds
PA: Pres-Tek Plastics, Inc.
10700 7th St
Rancho Cucamonga CA 91730
909 360-1600

(P-7828)
PUNCH PRESS PRODUCTS INC
Also Called: Auto Trend Products
2035 E 51st St, Vernon (90058-2818)
PHONE..................323 581-7151
Delmo Molinari, *Chairman*
CJ Matiszik, *President*
Miguel Moncada, *Prdtn Mgr*
▲ **EMP:** 67
SQ FT: 150,000
SALES (est): 15.6MM **Privately Held**
WEB: www.punch-press.com
SIC: 3544 3469 3471 Special dies & tools; metal stampings; plating & polishing

(P-7829)
PYRAMID MOLD & TOOL
10155 Sharon Cir, Rancho Cucamonga
(91730-5300)
PHONE..................909 476-2555
Stephen M Hoare, *President*
Tony May, *Vice Pres*
Brandan Heyes, *Admin Sec*
Steve Helt, *Purchasing*
Brandon Heyes, *Foreman/Supr*
EMP: 42 **EST:** 1995
SQ FT: 30,300

SALES (est): 6MM **Privately Held**
WEB: www.pyramidmold.com
SIC: 3544 Industrial molds

(P-7830)
SANTA FE ENTERPRISES INC
Also Called: SFE
11654 Pike St, Santa Fe Springs
(90670-2938)
PHONE..................562 692-7596
David Warner, *President*
Bob Becker, *Vice Pres*
Jay Swartz, *QC Mgr*
Liz Warner, *Manager*
EMP: 27 **EST:** 1980
SQ FT: 20,000
SALES (est): 5MM **Privately Held**
WEB: www.santafeenterprises.com
SIC: 3544 Special dies & tools

(P-7831)
SCHREY & SONS MOLD CO INC
24735 Avenue Rockefeller, Valencia
(91355-3466)
PHONE..................661 294-2260
Walter Schrey, *President*
Gertrude Schrey, *Corp Secy*
Thomas Schrey, *Vice Pres*
William Schrey, *Vice Pres*
James Vincent, *IT/INT Sup*
EMP: 35 **EST:** 1969
SQ FT: 53,000
SALES (est): 6.3MM **Privately Held**
WEB: www.schrey.com
SIC: 3544 Industrial molds; special dies & tools

(P-7832)
STAINLESS INDUSTRIAL COMPANIES
11111 Santa Monica Blvd, Los Angeles
(90025-3333)
PHONE..................310 575-9400
Anthony Pritzker, *President*
▲ **EMP:** 97 **EST:** 1998
SALES (est): 8.8MM
SALES (corp-wide): 245.5B **Publicly Held**
WEB: www.unitedrentals.com
SIC: 3544 Special dies & tools
HQ: The Marmon Group Llc
181 W Madison St Ste 2600
Chicago IL 60602

(P-7833)
STAR DIE CASTING INC
19215 Woodlands Dr, Huntington Beach
(92648-5558)
PHONE..................714 536-2999
MEI Hwa Yu, *Principal*
EMP: 13 **EST:** 2010
SALES (est): 119.5K **Privately Held**
WEB: www.stargroupglobal.com
SIC: 3544 Special dies & tools

(P-7834)
SUPERIOR JIG INC
1540 N Orangethorpe Way, Anaheim
(92801-1289)
PHONE..................714 525-4777
John Morrissey, *President*
Tracy Reed, *Treasurer*
Reed Tracy, *Admin Sec*
Joshua Fitzgerald, *Prgrmr*
Jay SJI, *Project Mgr*
EMP: 22 **EST:** 1960
SQ FT: 14,000
SALES (est): 5MM **Privately Held**
WEB: www.rocketprecision.com
SIC: 3544 3599 Special dies & tools; machine shop, jobbing & repair

(P-7835)
T & S DIE CUTTING
13301 Alondra Blvd Ste A, Santa Fe
Springs (90670-5563)
PHONE..................562 802-1731
James Good, *Owner*
EMP: 15 **EST:** 1977
SQ FT: 16,000
SALES (est): 989K **Privately Held**
WEB: www.tandsdiecutting.com
SIC: 3544 Dies, steel rule

(P-7836)
TARPIN CORPORATION
Also Called: Western Forge Die
5361 Business Dr, Huntington Beach
(92649-1223)
PHONE..................714 891-6944
Harold Jermakian, *President*
EMP: 33 **EST:** 1981
SALES (est): 5MM **Privately Held**
WEB: www.westernforgedie.com
SIC: 3544 Dies, steel rule; special dies & tools

(P-7837)
THUNDERBIRD INDUSTRIES INC
695 W Terrace Dr, San Dimas
(91773-2917)
PHONE..................909 394-1633
Donald Serio, *President*
EMP: 18 **EST:** 1985
SQ FT: 20,000
SALES (est): 1.3MM **Privately Held**
SIC: 3544 3089 Industrial molds; injection molding of plastics

(P-7838)
TRIO TOOL & DIE CO (PA)
3340 W El Segundo Blvd, Hawthorne
(90250-4892)
PHONE..................310 644-4431
John Arroues, *President*
Dale Norton, *Office Mgr*
EMP: 16 **EST:** 1954
SQ FT: 9,200
SALES (est): 2.7MM **Privately Held**
WEB: www.triotoolanddie.com
SIC: 3544 Dies & die holders for metal cutting, forming, die casting; special dies & tools

(P-7839)
UNITED CALIFORNIA CORPORATION
12200 Woodruff Ave, Downey
(90241-5608)
P.O. Box 4250 (90241-1250)
PHONE..................562 803-1521
Dale L Bethke, *President*
Fred Clauson, *General Mgr*
Billie Huckins, *Admin Sec*
Lyle Mata, *Info Tech Mgr*
Mike Sohn, *Engineer*
EMP: 56 **EST:** 1974
SQ FT: 85,000
SALES (est): 1.5MM **Privately Held**
WEB: www.ucc-udb.com
SIC: 3544 Special dies & tools

(P-7840)
UPM INC
Also Called: Universal Plastic Mold
13245 Los Angeles St, Baldwin Park
(91706-2295)
PHONE..................626 962-4001
Jason Dowling, *CEO*
Steve Dowling, *President*
Don Ashleigh, *Vice Pres*
Cinthya Guevara, *Purch Mgr*
Jose Cortez, *QC Mgr*
◆ **EMP:** 290 **EST:** 1962
SQ FT: 100,000
SALES (est): 44.9MM **Privately Held**
WEB: www.upminc.com
SIC: 3544 3089 Forms (molds), for foundry & plastics working machinery; injection molding of plastics

(P-7841)
US STEEL RULE DIES INC
Also Called: M D D
40 E Verdugo Ave, Burbank (91502-1931)
PHONE..................562 921-0690
David Reynolds, *President*
EMP: 19 **EST:** 1978
SALES (est): 2.1MM **Privately Held**
WEB: www.ussrd.com
SIC: 3544 Special dies & tools

(P-7842)
VALCO PLANER WORKS INC
Also Called: Valco Precision Works
6131 Maywood Ave, Huntington Park
(90255-3213)
PHONE..................323 582-6355
Leonel F Valerio, *President*
Carlos Valerio, *Corp Secy*

Leonel G Valerio Jr, *Vice Pres*
Oscar Valerio, *General Mgr*
Leslie Valerio, *Purchasing*
▼ **EMP:** 25 **EST:** 1953
SQ FT: 10,000
SALES (est): 4.6MM **Privately Held**
SIC: 3544 3545 Special dies, tools, jigs & fixtures; machine tool accessories

(P-7843)
WAGNER DIE SUPPLY INC (PA)
2041 Elm Ct, Ontario (91761-7619)
PHONE..................909 947-3044
Ellsworth Knutson, *President*
John Knutson, *Treasurer*
Mike Knutson, *Vice Pres*
Tom Knutson, *Admin Sec*
▲ **EMP:** 36 **EST:** 1947
SALES (est): 9.8MM **Privately Held**
WEB: www.wagnerdiesupply.com
SIC: 3544 Dies, steel rule; special dies & tools

3545 Machine Tool Access

(P-7844)
ACCU-GRINDING INC
Also Called: Westcoast Tool Products
8518 Glencrest Dr, Sun Valley
(91352-3544)
PHONE..................818 768-4497
Ruben Cortez, *President*
Rubin Cortez, *President*
Antonette Cortez, *Manager*
EMP: 15 **EST:** 1980
SALES (est): 588.9K **Privately Held**
WEB: www.accugrinding.com
SIC: 3545 3599 Drill bushings (drilling jig); machine shop, jobbing & repair

(P-7845)
AMERICAN QUALITY TOOLS INC
12650 Magnolia Ave Ste E, Riverside
(92503-4690)
PHONE..................951 280-4700
Mukesh Aghi, *President*
Rakesh Aghi, *Vice Pres*
▲ **EMP:** 45 **EST:** 1989
SQ FT: 22,000
SALES (est): 6.9MM **Privately Held**
WEB: www.cobracarbide.com
SIC: 3545 Cutting tools for machine tools

(P-7846)
ATS WORKHOLDING LLC
Also Called: Ats Systems
30222 Esperanza, Rcho STA Marg
(92688-2121)
PHONE..................800 321-1833
Kenneth Erkenbrack, *President*
Charles A Goad, *CEO*
Wu Robert, *CFO*
Carlos Hernandez, *Principal*
Jeff Toegel, *Regional Mgr*
▲ **EMP:** 67 **EST:** 1981
SQ FT: 22,840
SALES (est): 10.3MM **Privately Held**
WEB: www.ats-s.com
SIC: 3545 Milling machine attachments (machine tool accessories)

(P-7847)
CALIFORNIA REAMER COMPANY INC
12747 Los Nietos Rd, Santa Fe Springs
(90670-3007)
P.O. Box 2427, Lake Arrowhead (92352-2427)
PHONE..................562 946-6377
David J Neptune, *President*
EMP: 13 **EST:** 1960
SQ FT: 5,500
SALES (est): 363.7K **Privately Held**
SIC: 3545 Reamers, machine tool

(P-7848)
CAMPBELL ENGINEERING INC
20412 Barents Sea Cir, Lake Forest
(92630-8807)
PHONE..................949 859-3306
James Campbell, *President*
Carolyn Campbell, *Principal*
Lisa Parsons, *Office Mgr*

Margo Montgomery, *Office Admin* .
Bob Lynch, *Purchasing*
EMP: 24 **EST:** 1994
SQ FT: 3,800
SALES (est): 2MM **Privately Held**
WEB: www.campbellcnc.com
SIC: 3545 3541 Precision measuring tools; lathes, metal cutting & polishing

(P-7849)
COASTAL CNTING INDUS SCALE INC
Also Called: Actionpac Scales & Automation
1621 Fiske Pl, Oxnard (93033-1862)
PHONE...................................805 487-0403
John W Dishion, *CEO*
Bryan Chandler, *Officer*
Daniel Barker, *Technician*
Jerry Dorhn, *Technician*
Chris Meza, *Technician*
▲ **EMP:** 22
SQ FT: 22,000
SALES (est): 5.2MM **Privately Held**
WEB: www.actionpacscales.com
SIC: 3545 3565 Machine tool accessories; packaging machinery

(P-7850)
COORSTEK INC
4544 Mcgrath St, Ventura (93003-6492)
PHONE...................................805 644-5583
EMP: 100
SALES (corp-wide): 829.3MM **Privately Held**
SIC: 3545 Mfg Machine Tool Accessories
HQ: Coorstek, Inc.
14143 Denver Ste 400
Golden CO 80401
303 271-7000

(P-7851)
CRAIG TOOLS INC
142 Lomita St, El Segundo (90245-4113)
PHONE...................................310 322-0614
William B Cleveland, *President*
Don Tripler, *Exec VP*
▼ **EMP:** 37 **EST:** 1958
SQ FT: 13,000
SALES (est): 5.6MM **Privately Held**
WEB: www.craigtools.com
SIC: 3545 Precision tools, machinists'

(P-7852)
CURRY COMPANY LLC
Also Called: Carbro Company
15724 Condon Ave, Lawndale (90260-2531)
P.O. Box 278 (90260-0278)
PHONE...................................310 643-8400
Patrick Curry, *Mng Member*
EMP: 40 **EST:** 2019
SALES (est): 8.4MM
SALES (corp-wide): 23.3MM **Privately Held**
WEB: www.carbrousa.com
SIC: 3545 End mills; files, machine tool; reamers, machine tool
PA: Fullerton Tool Company, Inc.
121 Perry St
Saginaw MI 48602
989 799-4550

(P-7853)
DIAMOTEC INC
22104 S Vt Ave Ste 104, Torrance (90502-2156)
PHONE...................................310 539-4994
Varoujan Kundakjian, *President*
Alex Kundakjian, *Vice Pres*
Rod Shahinian, *Vice Pres*
Houry Abacyan, *Admin Sec*
EMP: 13 **EST:** 1976
SALES (est): 1.2MM **Privately Held**
WEB: www.diamotec.com
SIC: 3545 Tools & accessories for machine tools

(P-7854)
GUHRING INC
15581 Computer Ln, Huntington Beach (92649-1605)
PHONE...................................714 841-3582
EMP: 47
SALES (corp-wide): 1.2B **Privately Held**
WEB: www.guhring.com
SIC: 3545 Cutting tools for machine tools

HQ: Guhring, Inc.
1445 Commerce Ave
Brookfield WI 53045
262 784-6730

(P-7855)
KEMPTON MACHINE WORKS INC
4070 E Leaverton Ct, Anaheim (92807-1610)
PHONE...................................714 990-0596
Greg Kempton, *President*
EMP: 26 **EST:** 1983
SQ FT: 14,000
SALES (est): 2.7MM **Privately Held**
SIC: 3545 3599 Tools & accessories for machine tools; machine shop, jobbing & repair

(P-7856)
MERCURY BROACH COMPANY INC
2546 Seaman Ave, El Monte (91733-1986)
PHONE...................................626 443-5904
Mark Eberlein, *President*
EMP: 19 **EST:** 1961
SQ FT: 7,000
SALES (est): 2.2MM **Privately Held**
WEB: www.mercurybroach.wordpress.com
SIC: 3545 Broaches (machine tool accessories)

(P-7857)
MEYCO MACHINE AND TOOL INC
11579 Martens River Cir, Fountain Valley (92708-4201)
P.O. Box 9659 (92728-9659)
PHONE...................................714 435-1546
Manuel Gomez, *CEO*
Victor Salazar, *Vice Pres*
Lorena Estrada, *Principal*
Max Gomez, *Principal*
Edith Martinez, *Principal*
EMP: 38 **EST:** 1996
SQ FT: 12,500 **Privately Held**
WEB: www.meycomachine.com
SIC: 3545 Tools & accessories for machine tools

(P-7858)
MKKR INC
Also Called: Matko
430 E Parkcenter Cir N, San Bernardino (92408-2869)
P.O. Box 8891, Redlands (92375-2091)
PHONE...................................909 890-5994
Matthew Curtis, *President*
Rowena Rivera-Curtis, *Vice Pres*
EMP: 20 **EST:** 1989
SQ FT: 23,500
SALES (est): 1.5MM **Privately Held**
WEB: www.matko.com
SIC: 3545 Scales, measuring (machinists' precision tools)

(P-7859)
MUELLER GAGES COMPANY
318 Agostino Rd, San Gabriel (91776-2505)
P.O. Box 310 (91778-0310)
PHONE...................................626 287-2911
Rhett Mueller, *President*
Sandra Mueller, *Admin Sec*
EMP: 23 **EST:** 1949
SQ FT: 10,500
SALES (est): 1.3MM **Privately Held**
WEB: www.muellergage.com
SIC: 3545 Precision tools, machinists'

(P-7860)
ORANGE VISE COMPANY LLC
940 S Via Rodeo, Placentia (92870-6775)
PHONE...................................714 482-3952
Eric Sun, *CEO*
EMP: 15 **EST:** 2012
SALES (est): 5.8MM **Privately Held**
WEB: www.orangevise.com
SIC: 3545 Vises, machine (machine tool accessories)

(P-7861)
PENNOYER-DODGE CO
6650 San Fernando Rd, Glendale (91201-1745)
P.O. Box 5105 (91221-1017)
PHONE...................................818 547-2100
Hazel Dodge, *President*
Karen Dodge, *Admin Sec*
EMP: 40 **EST:** 1946
SALES (est): 5.1MM **Privately Held**
WEB: www.pdgage.com
SIC: 3545 8734 5084 3643 Gauges (machine tool accessories); precision tools, machinists'; calibration & certification; instruments & control equipment; current-carrying wiring devices; special dies, tools, jigs & fixtures

(P-7862)
PIONEER BROACH COMPANY (PA)
6434 Telegraph Rd, Commerce (90040-2593)
PHONE...................................323 728-1263
Gary M Ezor, *CEO*
Robert Ezor, *Vice Pres*
Karin Ezor, *Admin Sec*
▲ **EMP:** 50 **EST:** 1939
SQ FT: 22,000
SALES (est): 7.8MM **Privately Held**
WEB: www.pioneerbroach.com
SIC: 3545 3599 3541 Broaches (machine tool accessories); machine shop, jobbing & repair; machine tools, metal cutting type

(P-7863)
PRECISION CUTTING TOOLS INC
5572 Fresca Dr, La Palma (90623-1007)
PHONE...................................562 921-7898
Audrey Sheth, *CEO*
Edward Cortez, *Prgrmr*
▲ **EMP:** 30 **EST:** 1979
SALES (est): 4.3MM **Privately Held**
WEB: www.pct-imc.com
SIC: 3545 3541 Cutting tools for machine tools; drilling machine tools (metal cutting)

(P-7864)
PRO TOOL SERVICES INC
1704 Sunnyside Ct, Bakersfield (93308-6859)
P.O. Box 80235 (93380-0235)
PHONE...................................661 393-9222
Ron Jacobs, *President*
Mark Gardner, *Treasurer*
Mark Gardener, *Corp Secy*
Jaime Pena, *Foreman/Supr*
EMP: 47 **EST:** 2000
SQ FT: 4,000
SALES (est): 4MM **Privately Held**
SIC: 3545 Tools & accessories for machine tools

(P-7865)
QUALITY GRINDING CO INC
6800 Caballero Blvd, Buena Park (90620-1136)
P.O. Box 5968 (90622-5968)
PHONE...................................714 228-2100
Cornel Feceu, *President*
Yvonne Ramirez, *Accounting Mgr*
EMP: 16 **EST:** 1946
SQ FT: 29,000
SALES (est): 1.6MM **Privately Held**
WEB: www.qualitygrinding.net
SIC: 3545 3599 Precision tools, machinists'; machine shop, jobbing & repair

(P-7866)
RAFCO-BRICKFORM LLC (PA)
Also Called: Rafco Products Brickform
11061 Jersey Blvd, Rancho Cucamonga (91730-5135)
PHONE...................................909 484-3399
Robert Freis, *Mng Member*
Bob Meador, *Sales Mgr*
Mark Harrington, *Sales Staff*
Matt Bissantti, *Mng Member*
Stanley Zawadzki, *Manager*
▲ **EMP:** 72 **EST:** 1973
SQ FT: 79,000
SALES (est): 17.7MM **Privately Held**
SIC: 3545 5169 Machine tool accessories; adhesives, chemical

(P-7867)
SCIENTIFIC CUTTING TOOLS INC
220 W Los Angeles Ave, Simi Valley (93065-1650)
PHONE...................................805 584-9495
Dale Christopher, *President*
Prudence Kenzie, *CFO*
Tom Keleman, *Officer*
Jan Kaye, *Vice Pres*
Jeff Kaye, *General Mgr*
EMP: 37 **EST:** 1963
SALES (est): 6MM **Privately Held**
WEB: www.sct-usa.com
SIC: 3545 Machine tool accessories

(P-7868)
SEV-CAL TOOL INC
3231 Halladay St, Santa Ana (92705-5628)
PHONE...................................714 549-3347
James F Severance, *President*
William E Severance, *Corp Secy*
Naomi Severance, *Vice Pres*
EMP: 15 **EST:** 1940
SQ FT: 8,000
SALES (est): 1.3MM **Privately Held**
WEB: www.sevcal.com
SIC: 3545 3541 3423 Cutting tools for machine tools; machine tools, metal cutting type; hand & edge tools

(P-7869)
SOUTHLAND TOOL MFG INC
1430 N Hundley St, Anaheim (92806-1322)
PHONE...................................714 632-8198
David Pryor, *President*
▲ **EMP:** 16 **EST:** 2010
SALES (est): 2.3MM **Privately Held**
WEB: www.southlandtool.com
SIC: 3545 Machine tool accessories

(P-7870)
STADCO (PA)
Also Called: Standard Tool & Die Co
107 S Avenue 20, Los Angeles (90031-1709)
PHONE...................................323 227-8888
Doug Paletz, *President*
Bob Parsi, *COO*
Bret Matta, *Vice Pres*
Christian Cazares, *Technician*
Craig Sliwa, *Engineer*
EMP: 149 **EST:** 1945
SQ FT: 15,000
SALES (est): 30MM **Privately Held**
WEB: www.stadco.com
SIC: 3545 3599 Precision tools, machinists'; machine shop, jobbing & repair

(P-7871)
STARRETT KINEMETRIC ENGRG INC
26052 Merit Cir Ste 103, Laguna Hills (92653-7004)
PHONE...................................949 348-1213
Douglas Starrett, *President*
Mark Arenal, *Managing Dir*
Ken Knicker, *IT/INT Sup*
EMP: 26 **EST:** 2007
SALES (est): 5MM
SALES (corp-wide): 219.6MM **Publicly Held**
WEB: www.starrett.com
SIC: 3545 Machine tool accessories
PA: The L S Starrett Company
121 Crescent St
Athol MA 01331
978 249-3551

(P-7872)
SWISSMANN ENGINEERING INC
14019 Park Palisades Dr, Bakersfield (93306-7684)
PHONE...................................760 223-0663
Thomas Brady, *President*
Linda Brady, *Corp Secy*
EMP: 13 **EST:** 1999
SALES (est): 319.7K **Privately Held**
WEB: www.swissmann.com
SIC: 3545 5084 Machine tool accessories; industrial machinery & equipment

PRODUCTS & SVCS

(P-7873)
SYGMA INC
13168 Flores St, Santa Fe Springs
(90670-4023)
PHONE...................562 906-8880
Jimmy Fung, *CEO*
◆ EMP: 28 EST: 1992
SQ FT: 10,000
SALES (est): 784.5K **Privately Held**
WEB: www.sygmatools.com
SIC: 3545 Machine tool accessories

(P-7874)
TOSCO - TOOL SPECIALTY COMPANY
1011 E Slauson Ave, Los Angeles
(90011-5296)
P.O. Box 512157 (90051-0157)
PHONE...................323 232-3561
Jerry Tetzlaff, *President*
Ted Tetzlaff, *Vice Pres*
▲ EMP: 25 EST: 1943
SQ FT: 19,500 **Privately Held**
WEB: www.toolspecialty.com
SIC: 3545 Machine tool accessories

(P-7875)
UNITED DRILL BUSHING CORP
Also Called: United California
12200 Woodruff Ave, Downey
(90241-5608)
P.O. Box 4250 (90241-1250)
PHONE...................562 803-1521
Dale L Bethke, *President*
Billie Huckins, *Admin Sec*
Lyle Mata, *Info Tech Dir*
Erma Parrish, *Controller*
Teresa Walsh, *Sales Mgr*
EMP: 150 EST: 1964
SQ FT: 80,000
SALES (est): 24.9MM **Privately Held**
WEB: www.ucc-udb.com
SIC: 3545 3544 Drill bushings (drilling jig);
drilling machine attachments & accessories; tools & accessories for machine tools; special dies, tools, jigs & fixtures

(P-7876)
VERTEX DIAMOND TOOL CO INC
940 W Cienega Ave, San Dimas
(91773-2454)
PHONE...................909 599-1129
Tony Pontone, *CEO*
Loretta Pontone Houchin, *President*
Kenneth Houchin, *Vice Pres*
EMP: 24 EST: 1977
SQ FT: 13,000
SALES (est): 3MM **Privately Held**
WEB: www.vertexdiamondtoom.mfg-pages.com
SIC: 3545 Diamond cutting tools for turning, boring, burnishing, etc.

(P-7877)
VIKING PRODUCTS INC
20 Doppler, Irvine (92618-4306)
PHONE...................949 379-5100
Marc Kaplan, *CEO*
EMP: 40 EST: 1981
SQ FT: 12,000
SALES (est): 4.8MM **Privately Held**
WEB: www.vikingproducts.com
SIC: 3545 Precision measuring tools

(P-7878)
WESTERN GAGE CORPORATION
3316 Maya Linda Ste A, Camarillo
(93012-8776)
PHONE...................805 445-1410
Donald E Moors, *President*
Nanette Moors, *Corp Secy*
Ann Christansen, *Executive*
Sharon Garcia, *Executive*
Suzette Pedler, *Admin Asst*
EMP: 24 EST: 1968
SQ FT: 22,000
SALES (est): 3.6MM **Privately Held**
WEB: www.westerngage.com
SIC: 3545 Gauges (machine tool accessories)

3546 Power Hand Tools

(P-7879)
BLACK & DECKER (US) INC
Also Called: Dewalt Service Center 148
9020 Alondra Blvd, Bellflower
(90706-4206)
PHONE...................562 925-7551
Fax: 562 925-2561
EMP: 14
SALES (corp-wide): 11.4B **Publicly Held**
SIC: 3546 Mfg Power-Driven Handtools
HQ: Black & Decker (U.S.) Inc.
1000 Stanley Dr
New Britain CT 06053
860 225-5111

(P-7880)
BLACK & DECKER CORPORATION
3949 E Guasti Rd Ste A, Ontario
(91761-1549)
PHONE...................909 390-5548
EMP: 15
SALES (corp-wide): 11B **Publicly Held**
SIC: 3546 Mfg Power-Driven Handtools
HQ: The Black & Decker Corporation
701 E Joppa Rd
Towson MD 21286
410 716-3900

(P-7881)
GEORGE JUE MFG CO INC
Also Called: Paramont Metal & Supply Co
8140 Rosecrans Ave, Paramount
(90723-2794)
PHONE...................562 634-8181
Vincent Jue, *CEO*
George Jue, *President*
Elenor Sylva, *Admin Sec*
Rocky Chernow, *Sales Mgr*
◆ EMP: 60 EST: 1946
SQ FT: 80,000
SALES (est): 12.8MM **Privately Held**
SIC: 3546 Drills & drilling tools

(P-7882)
MK DIAMOND PRODUCTS INC (PA)
1315 Storm Pkwy, Torrance (90501-5041)
PHONE...................310 539-5221
Robert J Delahaut, *President*
Richard Narehood, *COO*
Brian Delahaut, *Vice Pres*
John Yenny, *General Mgr*
Steve Nichols, *Sales Staff*
◆ EMP: 207
SQ FT: 35,000
SALES (est): 44.8MM **Privately Held**
WEB: www.mkdiamond.com
SIC: 3546 3425 Saws & sawing equipment; saw blades & handsaws

(P-7883)
SHG HOLDINGS CORP (PA)
Also Called: Zephyr Tool Group
201 Hindry Ave, Inglewood (90301-1519)
PHONE...................310 410-4907
Bernard J Kersulis, *President*
EMP: 29 EST: 1991
SQ FT: 53,000
SALES (est): 15.5MM **Privately Held**
WEB: www.zephyrmanufacturing.com
SIC: 3546 Power-driven handtools

(P-7884)
ZEPHYR MANUFACTURING CO INC
Also Called: Zephyr Tool Group
201 Hindry Ave, Inglewood (90301-1519)
PHONE...................310 410-4907
Ray Chin, *VP Finance*
Andy Fuller, *Engineer*
Robert Szanter, *Finance*
Jack McAfee, *Analyst*
Tom Houstan, *VP Mfg*
▲ EMP: 100 EST: 1939
SQ FT: 60,000
SALES (est): 15.5MM **Privately Held**
WEB: www.zephyrmanufacturing.com
SIC: 3546 3545 3423 Power-driven handtools; machine tool accessories; hand & edge tools

PA: Shg Holdings Corp
201 Hindry Ave
Inglewood CA 90301

3547 Rolling Mill Machinery & Eqpt

(P-7885)
JOHN LIST CORPORATION
Also Called: Protocast
9732 Cozycroft Ave, Chatsworth
(91311-4498)
PHONE...................818 882-7848
John List, *President*
Susan List, *Vice Pres*
Natalie Mandelbaumn, *General Mgr*
EMP: 47
SQ FT: 16,000
SALES (est): 8.3MM **Privately Held**
WEB: www.protocastjlc.com
SIC: 3547 3365 3369 3366 Ferrous & nonferrous mill equipment, auxiliary; aluminum & aluminum-based alloy castings; nonferrous foundries; copper foundries

(P-7886)
OLD COUNTRY MILLWORK INC
Also Called: O C M
5855 Hooper Ave, Los Angeles
(90001-1280)
PHONE...................323 234-2940
Gerard J Kilgallon, *CEO*
Patrick Macdougall, *CFO*
Tim Kilgallon, *Executive*
Cory Robinson, *Marketing Staff*
Robert Macropoulos, *Sales Staff*
▲ EMP: 38
SQ FT: 36,000
SALES (est): 9.3MM **Privately Held**
WEB: www.ocmcoil.com
SIC: 3547 3479 Rolling mill machinery; painting, coating & hot dipping

(P-7887)
ROBINSON ENGINEERING CORP
3575 Grapevine St, Jurupa Valley
(91752-3505)
PHONE...................951 361-8000
Peter Robinson, *President*
Zora Robinson, *Vice Pres*
EMP: 18 EST: 1968
SQ FT: 20,000
SALES (est): 375.9K **Privately Held**
SIC: 3547 Rolling mill machinery

3548 Welding Apparatus

(P-7888)
AMADA WELD TECH INC (DH)
1820 S Myrtle Ave, Monrovia (91016-4833)
PHONE...................626 303-5676
David Fawcett, *President*
Barbara Kuntz, *Chief Mktg Ofcr*
David Cielinski, *Vice Pres*
James Malloy, *Vice Pres*
Kunio Minejima, *Vice Pres*
◆ EMP: 159 EST: 1994
SQ FT: 70,000
SALES (est): 56.5MM **Privately Held**
WEB: www.amadaweldtech.com
SIC: 3548 3699 3829 Soldering equipment, except hand soldering irons; laser welding, drilling & cutting equipment; measuring & controlling devices

(P-7889)
CREATIVE PATHWAYS INC
20815 Higgins Ct, Torrance (90501-1830)
PHONE...................310 530-1965
Timothy Rohrberg, *President*
Patrica Rohrberg, *Admin Sec*
Patricia Rohrberg, *Opers Staff*
EMP: 35 EST: 1969
SQ FT: 29,000
SALES (est): 4MM **Privately Held**
WEB: www.creativepathways.com
SIC: 3548 Welding & cutting apparatus & accessories

(P-7890)
DIAMOND GROUND PRODUCTS INC
2651 Lavery Ct, Newbury Park
(91320-1502)
PHONE...................305 498-3837
James C Elizarraz, *President*
▲ EMP: 30 EST: 1992
SQ FT: 40,000
SALES (est): 5.9MM **Privately Held**
WEB: www.diamondground.com
SIC: 3548 Electrodes, electric welding; welding & cutting apparatus & accessories

(P-7891)
LODESTONE LLC
Also Called: Weldstone Portable Welders
4769 E Wesley Dr, Anaheim 92807-1941)
PHONE...................714 970-0900
Richard H Barden, *President*
Yip Ye, *Opers Mgr*
Susan Barden, *Mktg Coord*
Patricia Walck,
EMP: 15 EST: 2007
SALES (est): 950K **Privately Held**
WEB: www.lodestonepacific.com
SIC: 3548 8742 Welding apparatus; management consulting services

(P-7892)
M K PRODUCTS INC
Also Called: Mk Manufacturing
16882 Armstrong Ave, Irvine (92606-4975)
PHONE...................949 798-1425
Chris Westlake, *President*
Joseph J Lapaglia, *CFO*
Rick Dietz, *Vice Pres*
Leslie McCurdy, *Executive Asst*
Barbara Pierce, *Admin Sec*
▲ EMP: 81 EST: 1966
SQ FT: 80,000
SALES (est): 18.5MM **Privately Held**
WEB: www.mkproducts.com
SIC: 3548 Electric welding equipment

(P-7893)
ONEX RF INC
1824 Flower Ave, Duarte (91010-2931)
PHONE...................626 358-6639
Onik Bogosyan, *President*
EMP: 16 EST: 1991
SALES (est): 3.1MM **Privately Held**
WEB: www.onexrf.com
SIC: 3548 Welding apparatus

(P-7894)
PERKINS
Also Called: Perkins Family Restaurant
7312 Varna Ave Ste A, North Hollywood
(91605-4008)
PHONE...................818 764-9293
EMP: 21
SALES (est): 1.4MM **Privately Held**
SIC: 3548 Mfg Welding Apparatus

(P-7895)
SIKAMA INTERNATIONAL INC
118 E Gutierrez St, Santa Barbara
(93101-2314)
P.O. Box 40298 (93140-0298)
PHONE...................805 962-1000
Sigurd R Wathne, *President*
Mariellen Wathne, *Treasurer*
Kail S Wathne, *Vice Pres*
Kail Wathne, *Vice Pres*
EMP: 13 EST: 1982
SQ FT: 9,300
SALES (est): 2MM **Privately Held**
WEB: www.sikama.com
SIC: 3548 Soldering equipment, except hand soldering irons

(P-7896)
TECHNICAL DEVICES COMPANY
560 Alaska Ave, Torrance (90503-3904)
PHONE...................310 618-8437
Douglas N Winther, *CEO*
Rey Malazo, *CFO*
EMP: 48
SQ FT: 35,000

SALES (est): 5.6MM
SALES (corp-wide): 8.3MM **Privately Held**
WEB: www.technicaldev.com
SIC: 3548 3471 3544 3423 Soldering equipment, except hand soldering irons; cleaning, polishing & finishing; special dies & tools; hand & edge tools
PA: Winther Technologies, Inc.
560 Alaska Ave
Torrance CA 90503
310 618-8437

(P-7897)
WINTHER TECHNOLOGIES INC (PA)
Also Called: Technical Devices
560 Alaska Ave, Torrance (90503-3904)
PHONE......................310 618-8437
Douglas N Winther, *President*
Julie Fields, *Purch Mgr*
▲ **EMP:** 46 **EST:** 1986
SQ FT: 32,000
SALES (est): 8.3MM **Privately Held**
WEB: www.technicaldev.com
SIC: 3548 3544 3542 3471 Soldering equipment, except hand soldering irons; special dies & tools; machine tools, metal forming type; cleaning & descaling metal products

3549 Metalworking Machinery, NEC

(P-7898)
ADAPT AUTOMATION INC
1661 Palm St Ste A, Santa Ana (92701-5190)
PHONE......................714 662-4454
Case Van Mechelen, *Principal*
Case V Mechelen, *CEO*
Tia V Mechelen, *Corp Secy*
Peter Smit, *Vice Pres*
EMP: 34 **EST:** 1988
SQ FT: 50,000
SALES (est): 7.3MM **Privately Held**
WEB: www.adaptautomation.com
SIC: 3549 Assembly machines, including robotic

(P-7899)
ASSEMBLY AUTOMATION INDUSTRIES
1849 Business Center Dr, Duarte (91010-2902)
PHONE......................626 303-2777
Francis E Frost, *CEO*
Elizabeth Frost, *Treasurer*
Jill Chastain, *Manager*
EMP: 28 **EST:** 1978
SQ FT: 10,000
SALES (est): 5.2MM **Privately Held**
WEB: www.assemblyauto.com
SIC: 3549 Metalworking machinery

(P-7900)
BMCI INC
Also Called: Bergandi Machinery Company
1689 S Parco Ave, Ontario (91761-8308)
P.O. Box 3790 (91761-0977)
PHONE......................951 361-8000
Scott Barsotti, *President*
Gary Costanzo, *COO*
Jose Garcia, *Vice Pres*
▼ **EMP:** 45 **EST:** 1994
SQ FT: 45,000
SALES (est): 8.3MM **Privately Held**
WEB: www.bergandi.com
SIC: 3549 3548 Wiredrawing & fabricating machinery & equipment, ex. die; welding apparatus

(P-7901)
EUBANKS ENGINEERING CO (PA)
1921 S Quaker Ridge Pl, Ontario (91761-8041)
P.O. Box 8490, Rancho Cucamonga (91701-0490)
PHONE......................909 483-2456
David C Eubanks, *Principal*
Maria Sanders, *General Mgr*
EMP: 23 **EST:** 1951

SQ FT: 34,000
SALES (est): 6.6MM **Privately Held**
WEB: www.eubanks.com
SIC: 3549 3825 Wiredrawing & fabricating machinery & equipment, ex. die; test equipment for electronic & electrical circuits

(P-7902)
GOLDEN STATE ENGINEERING INC
15338 Garfield Ave, Paramount (90723-4092)
PHONE......................562 634-3125
Alexandra Rostovski, *CEO*
Eugenio Rostovski, *President*
Mary Saguini, *CEO*
Tom Scroggin, *Vice Pres*
Daniel Soto, *Engineer*
EMP: 120
SQ FT: 65,000
SALES (est): 28.2MM **Privately Held**
WEB: www.goldenstateeng.com
SIC: 3549 3541 3451 8711 Metalworking machinery; grinding, polishing, buffing, lapping & honing machines; screw machine products; engineering services; bolts, nuts, rivets & washers

(P-7903)
HART SALES LLC
Also Called: Pirtek Sfo
74959 Jasmine Way, Indian Wells (92210-7237)
PHONE......................650 532-9200
Ellen Patricia Hart, *Principal*
EMP: 13 **EST:** 2011
SALES (est): 3.3MM **Privately Held**
SIC: 3549 Wiredrawing & fabricating machinery & equipment, ex. die

(P-7904)
KME CNC INC
17200 Red Hill Ave, Irvine (92614-5628)
PHONE......................714 345-5816
Jerome Mezzasalma, *CEO*
Thomas Johansen, *Opers Staff*
EMP: 13 **EST:** 2015
SALES (est): 1.2MM **Privately Held**
WEB: www.kmecnc.com
SIC: 3549 Rotary slitters (metalworking machines)

(P-7905)
LTD TECH INC
2630 Lavery Ct Ste B, Newbury Park (91320-1534)
PHONE......................805 480-1886
Lonny Deboisblanc, *President*
Bonnie Deboisblanc, *CFO*
▲ **EMP:** 16 **EST:** 2002
SQ FT: 5,000
SALES (est): 1MM **Privately Held**
WEB: www.ltdtechnology.com
SIC: 3549 Assembly machines, including robotic

(P-7906)
UBTECH ROBOTICS CORP
767 S Alameda St Ste 330, Los Angeles (90021-1665)
PHONE......................213 261-7153
John Rhee, *CEO*
Ling LI, *Technical Staff*
Christina Truong, *Controller*
Max MAI, *Senior Mgr*
Michele McGriff, *Director*
EMP: 30 **EST:** 2015
SALES (est): 10MM **Privately Held**
WEB: www.ubtrobot.com
SIC: 3549 Assembly machines, including robotic
PA: Ubtech Robotics Corp Ltd.
Floor 16,22, Building C1, Nanshan Zhiyuan, No. 1001, Xueyuan Ave Shenzhen 51810

(P-7907)
WALLNER EXPAC INC (PA)
Also Called: W T E
1274 S Slater Cir, Ontario (91761-1522)
PHONE......................909 481-8800
Sophia Wallner, *Ch of Bd*
Michael Wallner, *CEO*
Paul Wallner, *Vice Pres*

Susie Harney, *Purch Mgr*
◆ **EMP:** 55 **EST:** 1959
SALES (est): 29.7MM **Privately Held**
WEB: www.expac.com
SIC: 3549 3542 Metalworking machinery; machine tools, metal forming type

3552 Textile Machinery

(P-7908)
DILCO INDUSTRIAL INC
205 E Bristol Ln, Orange (92865-2715)
PHONE......................714 998-5266
Jay R Dille Jr, *President*
Rene Dille, *General Mgr*
Brieana Phillips, *Office Mgr*
Tina Dille, *Admin Sec*
EMP: 15 **EST:** 1974
SQ FT: 6,000
SALES (est): 3.1MM **Privately Held**
WEB: www.dilco.com
SIC: 3552 3993 Silk screens for textile industry: signs & advertising specialties

(P-7909)
LYTLE SCREEN PRINTING INC
21572 Surveyor Cir, Huntington Beach (92646-7067)
PHONE......................714 969-2424
Tim McMillen, *President*
Mark Lytle, *President*
EMP: 18 **EST:** 1988
SQ FT: 6,000
SALES (est): 1.6MM **Privately Held**
WEB: www.lysphb.com
SIC: 3552 7336 2759 Silk screens for textile industry; silk screen design; screen printing

(P-7910)
P&Y T-SHRTS SILK SCREENING INC
Also Called: American Printworks
2126 E 52nd St, Vernon (90058-3448)
P.O. Box 58742, Los Angeles (90058-0742)
PHONE......................323 585-4604
Yossi Zaga, *President*
Lupe Avalos, *Office Mgr*
EMP: 38 **EST:** 1984
SQ FT: 35,000
SALES (est): 5.4MM **Privately Held**
SIC: 3552 5136 Silk screens for textile industry; shirts, men's & boys'

(P-7911)
PALACE TEXTILE INC
Also Called: Palace Textiles
8453 Terradell St, Pico Rivera (90660-5042)
PHONE......................323 587-7756
▲ **EMP:** 52
SQ FT: 26,000
SALES: 3.5MM **Privately Held**
SIC: 3552 2391 2211 Mfg Textile Machinery Mfg Curtains/Draperies Cotton Broadwoven Fabric Mill

(P-7912)
TAJIMA USA INC
19925 S Susana Rd, Compton (90221-5726)
PHONE......................310 604-8200
Ron Krasn tz, *President*
▲ **EMP:** 36 **EST:** 1996
SQ FT: 25,000
SALES (est): 1.6MM **Privately Held**
WEB: www.tajima.com
SIC: 3552 Embroidery machines
PA: Tajima Industries Ltd.
3-19-22, Shirakabe, Higashi-Ku Nagoya AIC 461-0

3553 Woodworking Machinery

(P-7913)
WESTERN MOTOR WORKS INC
8332 Osage Ave, Los Angeles (90045-4401)
PHONE......................310 382-6896
Hamid Baher, *President*

EMP: 16 **EST:** 2005
SALES (est): 1MM **Privately Held**
SIC: 3553 Woodworking machinery

3554 Paper Inds Machinery

(P-7914)
ELLISON EDUCATIONAL EQP INC (PA)
Also Called: Sizzix
25862 Commercentre Dr, Lake Forest (92630-8877)
PHONE......................949 598-8822
Richard Birse, *CEO*
Kristin Highberg, *CEO*
▲ **EMP:** 59 **EST:** 1995
SQ FT: 132,000
SALES (est): 17.7MM **Privately Held**
WEB: www.ellisoneducation.com
SIC: 3554 Cutting machines, paper

(P-7915)
MERQBIZ LLC
300 N Cntntl Blvd Ste 640, El Segundo (90245)
PHONE......................855 637-7249
Alex Viscosi,
John Fox,
Kelly Kessler, *Manager*
Todd Burnstein, *Accounts Mgr*
EMP: 35 **EST:** 2016
SALES (est): 4.3MM **Privately Held**
WEB: www.voith.com
SIC: 5961 3554 ; paper industries machinery

3555 Printing Trades Machinery & Eqpt

(P-7916)
ANAJET LLC
1100 Valencia Ave, Tustin (92780-6428)
PHONE......................714 662-3200
Chase Roh, *President*
John Ballard, *Regional Mgr*
Michael Johnstone, *Regional Mgr*
Haziel Mitchell, *Regional Mgr*
Adam Tipre, *Regional Mgr*
▲ **EMP:** 20 **EST:** 2005
SALES (est): 6.7MM **Privately Held**
WEB: www.ricohdtg.com
SIC: 3555 Printing trades machinery

(P-7917)
CAL PLATE (PA)
17110 Jersey Ave, Artesia (90701-2694)
PHONE......................562 403-3000
Richard Borelli, *President*
Carlos Ponce, *COO*
Rick Sharlow, *Business Mgr*
EMP: 67 **EST:** 1966
SQ FT: 33,000
SALES (est): 10.1MM **Privately Held**
WEB: www.calplate.com
SIC: 3555 3423 3544 Printing plates; cutting dies, except metal cutting; special dies, tools, jigs & fixtures

(P-7918)
IMPERIAL RUBBER PRODUCTS INC
5691 Gates St, Chino (91710-7603)
PHONE......................909 393-0528
Ronald Hill, *CEO*
Bob Schwartz, *President*
Steve Huff, *Vice Pres*
▲ **EMP:** 35 **EST:** 1989
SQ FT: 20,000
SALES (est): 5.8MM **Privately Held**
WEB: www.imperialrubber.com
SIC: 3555 Printing trades machinery

(P-7919)
KERNING DATA SYSTEMS INC
21628 Lassen St, Chatsworth (91311-4152)
PHONE......................818 882-8712
Quentin Leef, *President*
Rohn Schoss, *Materials Mgr*
EMP: 14 **EST:** 1986

PRODUCTS & SVCS

SALES (est): 3MM **Privately Held**
WEB: www.kerningdata.com
SIC: **3555** 1731 Printing trades machinery;
computer installation

(P-7920)
LITH-O-ROLL CORPORATION
9521 Telstar Ave, El Monte (91731-2994)
P.O. Box 5328 (91734-1328)
PHONE..............................626 579-0340
Rita Sepe, *President*
Jeff Espett, *Vice Pres*
Gilbert Cruz, *Technical Staff*
Chris Murray, *Engineer*
Edward Gump, *Manager*
EMP: 50 EST: 1957
SQ FT: 30,000
SALES (est): 9.4MM **Privately Held**
WEB: www.lithoroll.com
SIC: **3555** Printing trades machinery

(P-7921)
ONE TOUCH SOLUTIONS INC
Also Called: One Touch Office Technology
370 Amapola Ave Ste 106, Torrance
(90501-7241)
PHONE..............................310 320-6868
William Rees, *CEO*
Jayson Beasley, *COO*
Mark Stratton, *CFO*
Breanna Rees, *Sales Staff*
Ron Perez, *Director*
EMP: 15 EST: 2005
SQ FT: 5,182
SALES (est): 6.1MM **Privately Held**
WEB: www.1touchoffice.com
SIC: **3555** Printing trades machinery

(P-7922)
PACIFIC BARCODE INC
27531 Enterprise Cir W 201c, Temecula
(92590-4888)
PHONE..............................951 587-8717
Michael Meadors, *President*
Michelle Meadors, *Vice Pres*
Sandy Kucera, *Technology*
Buckley Ross, *Opers Mgr*
Phil Peretz, *Sales Mgr*
EMP: 28 EST: 1999
SQ FT: 8,600
SALES (est): 6.1MM **Privately Held**
WEB: www.pacificbarcode.com
SIC: **3555** 2759 3565 3577 Printing
trades machinery; commercial printing; la-
beling machines, industrial; bar code
(magnetic ink) printers

(P-7923)
PARA-PLATE & PLASTICS CO INC
Also Called: Para Plate
15910 Shoemaker Ave, Cerritos
(90703-2200)
PHONE..............................562 404-3434
Shane Pearson, *President*
Robert J Clapp, *President*
John Greenamyer, *Treasurer*
Steve Binnard, *Vice Pres*
Barbara Kishiyama, *Controller*
EMP: 27 EST: 1945
SQ FT: 17,000
SALES (est): 2.7MM **Privately Held**
WEB: www.paraplate.com
SIC: **3555** 7336 2796 Printing plates;
commercial art & graphic design;
platemaking services

(P-7924)
PIC MANUFACTURING INC
410 Sherwood Rd, Paso Robles
(93446-3554)
P.O. Box 665 (93447-0665)
PHONE..............................805 238-5451
Michael D Camp, *President*
EMP: 18 EST: 1962
SQ FT: 9,000
SALES (est): 689.7K **Privately Held**
WEB: www.picmanufacturing.com
SIC: **3555** Printing trade parts & attach-
ments

(P-7925)
RIMA ENTERPRISES INC
Also Called: Rima-System
16417 Ladona Cir, Huntington Beach
(92649-2133)
PHONE..............................714 893-4534
Horst K Steinhart, *CEO*
Venu Sunkara, *Executive*
John Kipp, *Technical Mgr*
Jeff Schwarz, *Engineer*
Jeffrey Schwarz, *Engineer*
▲ EMP: 62 EST: 1970
SALES (est): 7.4MM **Privately Held**
SIC: **3555** Bookbinding machinery

(P-7926)
THISTLE ROLLER CO INC
209 Van Norman Rd, Montebello
(90640-5393)
PHONE..............................323 685-5322
Lizbeth Karpynec, *CEO*
Eric Karpynetz, *Vice Pres*
Eric W Karpynetz, *Vice Pres*
▲ EMP: 35 EST: 1957
SQ FT: 45,000
SALES (est): 9.5MM **Privately Held**
WEB: www.thistleroller.com
SIC: **3555** 3312 2796 Printing trades ma-
chinery; blast furnaces & steel mills;
platemaking services

3556 Food Prdts Machinery

(P-7927)
AVALON MFG CO INCOIRPORATED
509 Bateman Cir, Corona (92878-4012)
PHONE..............................951 340-0280
Bill Enger, *President*
Troy Enger, *Vice Pres*
Kyle Enger, *Engineer*
EMP: 14 EST: 1976
SQ FT: 19,277
SALES (est): 4.2MM **Privately Held**
WEB: www.avalonmfg.com
SIC: **3556** Bakery machinery
PA: Enger, Inc.
509 Bateman Cir
Corona CA 92878

(P-7928)
BIOSYNTHETIC TECHNOLOGIES LLC (HQ)
Also Called: Lubrigreen
2 Park Plz Ste 200, Irvine (92614-8569)
P.O. Box 856, Malta MT (59538-0856)
PHONE..............................949 390-5910
Allen Barbieri,
Bruce Marley, *Vice Pres*
Travis Thompson, *Research*
John Hopkins, *Manager*
EMP: 13 EST: 2004
SQ FT: 4,800
SALES (est): 4.4MM **Publicly Held**
WEB: www.biosynthetic.com
SIC: **3556** Oilseed crushing & extracting
machinery

(P-7929)
CAPNA FABRICATION
Also Called: Capna Systems
16501 Ventura Blvd # 400, Encino
(91436-2007)
PHONE..............................888 416-6777
Vitaly Mekk, *CEO*
Gene Galyuk, *CTO*
Aj Smith, *Technical Staff*
EMP: 30 EST: 2017
SALES (est): 3.6MM **Privately Held**
WEB: www.capnasystems.com
SIC: **3556** Oilseed crushing & extracting
machinery

(P-7930)
CASA HERRERA INC (PA)
2655 Pine St, Pomona (91767-2115)
PHONE..............................909 392-3930
Michael L Herrera, *CEO*
Alfred J Herrera, *President*
Ronald L Meade, *President*
Susan A Herrera, *Treasurer*
Frank J Herrera, *Exec VP*
◆ EMP: 130 EST: 1970

SQ FT: 100,000
SALES (est): 26.2MM **Privately Held**
WEB: www.casaherrera.com
SIC: **3556** Food products machinery

(P-7931)
FOOD & BEV INNOVATIONS LLC
1801 Century Park E # 1420, Los Angeles
(90067-2316)
PHONE..............................888 491-3772
Jeffrey R Jetton, *President*
Andrew Craig, *Vice Pres*
Stan Levitsky, *Vice Pres*
Tyler Williams, *Vice Pres*
Aaron Boone, *Sales Staff*
EMP: 15 EST: 2012
SALES (est): 5MM **Privately Held**
SIC: **3556** Beverage machinery

(P-7932)
FOODTOOLS CONSOLIDATED INC (PA)
315 Laguna St, Santa Barbara
(93101-1716)
PHONE..............................805 962-8383
Martin Grano, *Ch of Bd*
Matt Browne, *Vice Pres*
Doug Petrovich, *Vice Pres*
Tashia Honcharenko, *Office Mgr*
Angel Huerta, *Engineer*
◆ EMP: 20 EST: 1983
SQ FT: 8,500
SALES (est): 11.2MM **Privately Held**
WEB: www.foodtools.com
SIC: **3556** 2679 Slicers, commercial, food;
paper products, converted

(P-7933)
FOTIS AND SON IMPORTS INC
15451 Electronic Ln, Huntington Beach
(92649-1333)
PHONE..............................714 894-9022
Peter Georgatsos, *President*
Laura Georgatsos, *Treasurer*
Russ Hillas, *Exec VP*
Eleni Hillas, *Principal*
Jose Agustin, *Manager*
▲ EMP: 50 EST: 1976
SQ FT: 34,000
SALES (est): 9.8MM **Privately Held**
WEB: www.fotisandsonimports.com
SIC: **3556** Food products machinery

(P-7934)
FPEC CORPORATION A CAL CORP (PA)
Also Called: Food Processing Equipment Co
13623 Pumice St, Santa Fe Springs
(90670-5105)
PHONE..............................562 802-3727
Alan Davison, *CEO*
Ethel Davison, *Corp Secy*
Terry Lovett, *Planning*
Tom Kearney, *Controller*
Margo Blunk, *Human Res Mgr*
EMP: 18 EST: 1969
SQ FT: 18,000
SALES (est): 8.1MM **Privately Held**
WEB: www.fpec.com
SIC: **3556** Food products machinery

(P-7935)
FRESH VENTURE FOODS LLC
1205 Craig Dr, Santa Maria (93458-4917)
P.O. Box 1023 (93456-1023)
PHONE..............................805 928-3374
John Schaefer, *Mng Member*
Veronica Dodd, *Human Res Dir*
Harold Reyes, *Opers Dir*
Jeff Lundberg,
Luis Martinez, *Manager*
EMP: 239 EST: 2012
SQ FT: 70
SALES (est): 28.8MM **Privately Held**
WEB: www.freshventurefoods.com
SIC: **3556** Dehydrating equipment, food
processing

(P-7936)
G & I ISLAS INDUSTRIES INC (PA)
Also Called: G & I Industries
12860 Schabarum Ave, Baldwin Park
(91706-6801)
P.O. Box 1262 (91706-7262)
PHONE..............................626 960-5020
Gonzalo R Islas, *CEO*
Sara Islas, *Vice Pres*
Gonzalo Islas, *Sales Staff*
Frankie Goeyvaerts, *Property Mgr*
▲ EMP: 23 EST: 1988
SQ FT: 12,500
SALES (est): 8.1MM **Privately Held**
WEB: www.giislasindustries.com
SIC: **3556** 5084 Bakery machinery; food
industry machinery

(P-7937)
GOLDEN PACIFIC SEAFOODS INC
700 S Raymond Ave, Fullerton
(92831-5233)
PHONE..............................714 589-8888
Tony Zavala, *President*
EMP: 45 EST: 2016
SALES (est): 10MM **Privately Held**
SIC: **3556** Meat, poultry & seafood pro-
cessing machinery

(P-7938)
HUD INDUSTRIES
2104 W Rosecrans Ave, Gardena
(90249-2990)
PHONE..............................310 327-7110
Pete Breum Jr, *President*
EMP: 13 EST: 1974
SQ FT: 20,000
SALES (est): 2.4MM **Privately Held**
WEB: www.hud.gov
SIC: **3556** Food products machinery

(P-7939)
INTERSTATE MEAT CO INC
Also Called: Sterling Pacific Meat Co.
6114 Scott Way, Commerce (90040-3518)
PHONE..............................323 838-9400
James T Asher, *President*
Ricky Willis, *Officer*
Luis Munoz, *Vice Pres*
Carmen Regalado, *Sales Staff*
Tony Cuevas, *Director*
EMP: 47 EST: 1996
SALES (est): 6MM **Privately Held**
WEB: www.sterlingpacificmeat.com
SIC: **3556** Meat processing machinery

(P-7940)
J C FORD COMPANY (HQ)
Also Called: JC Ford
901 S Leslie St, La Habra (90631-6841)
PHONE..............................714 871-7361
Scott D Ruhe, *CEO*
Connie Ruhe, *Treasurer*
Nicole Ruhe, *Vice Pres*
Nelson Grande, *Technician*
Orlando Hurtado, *Engineer*
◆ EMP: 94 EST: 1945
SQ FT: 80,000
SALES (est): 23.9MM **Privately Held**
WEB: www.jcford.com
SIC: **3556** Food products machinery

(P-7941)
JUICY WHIP INC
1668 Curtiss Ct, La Verne (91750-5848)
PHONE..............................909 392-7500
Gus Stratton, *President*
▲ EMP: 28 EST: 1981
SQ FT: 23,000
SALES (est): 8.1MM **Privately Held**
WEB: www.juicywhip.com
SIC: **3556** 2033 Beverage machinery; fruit
juices: fresh; fruit juices: concentrated,
hot pack

(P-7942)
LAWRENCE EQUIPMENT LEASING INC (PA)
2034 Peck Rd, El Monte (91733-3727)
PHONE..............................626 442-2894
John Lawrence, *CEO*
Jack Kirkpatrick, *Shareholder*
John Kirkpatrick, *Vice Pres*

Linda Lawrence, *Vice Pres*
Glenn Shelton, *Vice Pres*
▲ **EMP:** 190 **EST:** 1981
SQ FT: 50,000
SALES (est): 83.5MM **Privately Held**
WEB: www.lawrenceequipment.com
SIC: 3556 Flour mill machinery

(P-7943)
MACHINE BUILDING SPC INC
Also Called: Conveyor Concepts
1977 Blake Ave, Los Angeles (90039-3832)
PHONE.................................323 666-8289
Charles Conaway, *Ch of Bd*
Dennis James Conaway, *President*
Sharon Conaway, *Treasurer*
Frank Coryell, *Vice Pres*
Sandra Conaway, *Admin Sec*
EMP: 25 **EST:** 1960
SQ FT: 17,000
SALES (est): 3MM **Privately Held**
WEB: www.machinebuildingspecialties.com
SIC: 3556 3535 Bakery machinery; belt conveyor systems, general industrial use

(P-7944)
MEAT PACKERS BUTCHERS SUP INC
Also Called: Mpbs Industries
2820 E Washington Blvd, Los Angeles (90023-4274)
PHONE.................................323 268-8514
Jimmy Jin, *CEO*
Shaofa Jin, *Ch of Bd*
Bob Maxwell, *Vice Pres*
▲ **EMP:** 17 **EST:** 1939
SQ FT: 16,000
SALES (est): 4.1MM **Privately Held**
WEB: www.mpbs.com
SIC: 3556 Food products machinery

(P-7945)
MIGHTY SOY INC
1227 S Eastern Ave, Los Angeles (90022-4809)
PHONE.................................323 266-6969
Maung Myint, *President*
Gin Yee Lee, *Vice Pres*
EMP: 14 **EST:** 1980
SQ FT: 8,000
SALES (est): 2.6MM **Privately Held**
WEB: www.mightysoy.com
SIC: 3556 2099 2075 Smokers, food processing equipment; food preparations; soybean oil mills

(P-7946)
NATIONAL BAND SAW COMPANY
1055 W Avenue L12, Lancaster (93534-7045)
PHONE.................................661 294-9552
Harley Frank, *President*
Norman Frank, *Ch of Bd*
▲ **EMP:** 17 **EST:** 1953
SQ FT: 12,000
SALES (est): 3.4MM **Privately Held**
WEB: www.nbsparts.com
SIC: 3556 Meat processing machinery

(P-7947)
PACIFIC PACKAGING MCHY LLC
Also Called: Pack West Machinery
200 River Rd, Corona (92878-1435)
PHONE.................................951 393-2200
Gerald Carpino, *CEO*
Jerry Carpino, *President*
Charlie Booth, *Design Engr*
Angela Carpino, *Purch Mgr*
▲ **EMP:** 25 **EST:** 1962
SQ FT: 30,000
SALES (est): 5MM **Privately Held**
WEB: www.pacificpak.com
SIC: 3556 3565 Food products machinery; packaging machinery
HQ: Pro Mach, Inc.
50 E Rvrcnter Blvd Ste 18
Covington KY 41011
513 831-8778

(P-7948)
PACKERS MANUFACTURING INC
4212 W Hemlock Ave, Visalia (93277-6902)
PHONE.................................559 732-4886
Dwight Plumley, *President*
Teddy A Plumley, *Treasurer*
Doug Ohlemeier, *Editor*
EMP: 15 **EST:** 1958
SQ FT: 22,250
SALES (est): 577.2K **Privately Held**
WEB: www.thepacker.com
SIC: 3556 7699 Packing house machinery; industrial machinery & equipment repair

(P-7949)
R & A TECHNICAL INC
232 N Sherman Ave Ste D, Corona (92882-1877)
P.O. Box 399 (92878-0399)
PHONE.................................951 549-6945
Robert Louis Carlos Jr, *CEO*
EMP: 16 **EST:** 2010
SALES (est): 3.5MM **Privately Held**
WEB: www.ratech.info
SIC: 3556 Dehydrating equipment, food processing

(P-7950)
RBM CONVEYOR SYSTEMS INC
1432 Royal Blvd, Glendale (91207-1236)
PHONE.................................909 620-1333
Roobik Kureghian, *President*
Armine Kureghian, *Treasurer*
▲ **EMP:** 20 **EST:** 1980
SALES (est): 3MM **Privately Held**
SIC: 3556 8711 3537 3535 Food products machinery; engineering services; industrial trucks & tractors; conveyors & conveying equipment

(P-7951)
SC BEVERAGE INC
2300 Peck Rd, City of Industry (90601-1601)
PHONE.................................562 463-8918
Gilbert Ortega, *President*
Christopher Munguia, *Vice Pres*
Christina Mendoza, *Accounting Dir*
EMP: 14 **EST:** 1999
SALES (est): 2.2MM **Privately Held**
SIC: 3556 Brewers' & maltsters' machinery

(P-7952)
SHAVER SPECIALTY CO INC
20608 Earl St, Torrance (90503-3009)
PHONE.................................310 370-6941
George Shaver, *President*
Ronald Shaver, *Vice Pres*
▲ **EMP:** 22 **EST:** 1937
SQ FT: 20,000
SALES (est): 4MM **Privately Held**
WEB: www.shaverkeenkutter.com
SIC: 3556 3599 Choppers, commercial, food; machine shop, jobbing & repair

(P-7953)
SUPERIOR FOOD MACHINERY INC
8311 Sorensen Ave, Santa Fe Springs (90670-2125)
PHONE.................................562 949-0396
Danny Reyes, *President*
Polo Reyes, *President*
Marc Reyes, *Vice Pres*
Patricia Ruan, *Accountant*
EMP: 23 **EST:** 1975
SQ FT: 14,000
SALES (est): 4.9MM **Privately Held**
WEB: www.superiorinc.com
SIC: 3556 Food products machinery

(P-7954)
TRIPLE E MANUFACTURING
Also Called: Ernst Mfg
2121 S Union Ave, Bakersfield (93307-4155)
P.O. Box 70155 (93387-0155)
PHONE.................................661 831-7553
Martin W Etcheverry, *President*
Rick Etcheverry, *Treasurer*
EMP: 20 **EST:** 1938
SQ FT: 40,000

SALES (est): 1.1MM **Privately Held**
SIC: 3556 3565 Packing house machinery; packaging machinery

(P-7955)
VONS COMPANIES INC
Also Called: Vons 2560
1758 W Grand Ave, Grover Beach (93433-2293)
PHONE.................................805 481-2492
Jim Clark, *Manager*
EMP: 91
SALES (corp-wide): 69.6B **Publicly Held**
SIC: 5411 5912 3556 Supermarkets, chain; drug stores; food products machinery
HQ: The Vons Companies Inc
5918 Stoneridge Mall Rd
Pleasanton CA 94588
925 467-3000

(P-7956)
WILLIAM BOUNDS LTD
23625 Madison St, Torrance (90505-6004)
P.O. Box 1547 (90505-0547)
PHONE.................................310 375-0505
Helen Bounds, *President*
Sharon Bounds, *Vice Pres*
◆ **EMP:** 20 **EST:** 1963
SQ FT: 18,000
SALES (est): 1.7MM **Privately Held**
WEB: www.wmboundsltd.com
SIC: 3556 8733 Food products machinery; noncommercial research organizations

---

3559 Special Ind Machinery, NEC

(P-7957)
3650 INDUSTRY AVENUE LLC
100 Bayview Cir Ste 310, Newport Beach (92660-8910)
PHONE.................................949 509-5000
Daniel L Webb, *Administration*
EMP: 13 **EST:** 2013
SALES (est): 443.4K **Privately Held**
SIC: 3559 Special industry machinery

(P-7958)
ACME CRYOGENICS INC
Also Called: Cryogenic Experts
531 Sandy Cir, Oxnard (93036-0971)
PHONE.................................805 981-4500
Robert Worcester Jr, *Branch Mgr*
EMP: 30
SALES (corp-wide): 57.9MM **Privately Held**
WEB: www.acmecryo.com
SIC: 3559 Cryogenic machinery, industrial
PA: Acme Cryogenics, Inc.
2801 Mitchell Ave
Allentown PA 18103
610 966-4488

(P-7959)
AERO CLASSICS INC
1677 Curtiss Ct, La Verne (91750-5848)
PHONE.................................909 596-1630
James Potter, *President*
Skid Saurenman, *Accountant*
Ernie Ruiz, *Prdtn Mgr*
EMP: 20 **EST:** 1976
SALES (est): 2.5MM **Privately Held**
WEB: www.aero-classics.com
SIC: 3559 Sewing machines & hat & zipper making machinery

(P-7960)
AMERGENCE TECHNOLOGY INC
295 Brea Canyon Rd, Walnut (91789-3049)
PHONE.................................909 859-8400
Shavonne Tran, *President*
▲ **EMP:** 29 **EST:** 2006
SQ FT: 40,000
SALES (est): 2MM **Privately Held**
WEB: www.amergenceinc.com
SIC: 3559 Recycling machinery

(P-7961)
AMREP MANUFACTURING CO LLC
1555 S Cucamonga Ave, Ontario (91761-4512)
PHONE.................................877 468-9278
Martin Bryant, *CEO*
EMP: 500 **EST:** 2019
SALES (est): 37.3MM **Privately Held**
WEB: www.amrepproducts.com
SIC: 3559 Semiconductor manufacturing machinery

(P-7962)
AUTOTECHBIZCOM INC
23551 Commerce Center Dr I, Laguna Hills (92653-1513)
PHONE.................................949 245-7033
EMP: 13
SQ FT: 1,500
SALES (est): 2.2MM **Privately Held**
SIC: 3559 7359 Equipment Rental/Leasing

(P-7963)
AVANZATO TECHNOLOGY CORP
5335 Mcconnell Ave, Los Angeles (90066-7025)
PHONE.................................312 509-0506
Carissa Davino, *CEO*
Jeremy Green, *Director*
EMP: 20 **EST:** 2016
SALES (est): 1.4MM **Privately Held**
SIC: 3559 5065 Electronic component making machinery; electronic parts

(P-7964)
BARKENS HARDCHROME INC
239 E Greenleaf Blvd, Compton (90220-4913)
PHONE.................................310 632-2000
Gary Barken, *CEO*
Carol Barken, *Vice Pres*
Chanell Eteuati, *Office Mgr*
Ken Ames, *Manager*
EMP: 25 **EST:** 1942
SQ FT: 60,000
SALES (est): 5MM **Privately Held**
WEB: www.barkenshardchrome.com
SIC: 3559 5082 Metal finishing equipment for plating, etc.; oil field equipment

(P-7965)
BENDPAK INC (PA)
1645 E Lemonwood Dr, Santa Paula (93060-9651)
PHONE.................................805 933-9970
Donald Ray Henthorn, *President*
Jeffery Kritzer, *Senior VP*
Elizabeth Serrato, *Administration*
Abraham Viveros,
Lyle Simpson, *Director*
◆ **EMP:** 150 **EST:** 1979
SQ FT: 30,000
SALES: 69.8MM **Privately Held**
WEB: www.bendpak.com
SIC: 3559 3537 Automotive related machinery; automotive maintenance equipment; industrial trucks & tractors

(P-7966)
BIJAN RAD INC
Also Called: Sysparc
16125 Cantlay St, Van Nuys (91406-3416)
PHONE.................................818 902-1606
Bijan RAD, *CEO*
◆ **EMP:** 18 **EST:** 1986
SQ FT: 9,000
SALES (est): 2.7MM **Privately Held**
WEB: www.sysparc.com
SIC: 3559 1731 Parking facility equipment & supplies; access control systems specialization

(P-7967)
BOOM INDUSTRIAL INC
167 University Pkwy, Pomona (91768-4301)
PHONE.................................909 495-3555
Huiwen Chen, *CEO*
Robert Lane, *Engineer*
EMP: 60 **EST:** 2016

PRODUCTS & SVCS

SALES (est): 6.2MM **Privately Held**
WEB: www.boomindustrial.com
SIC: **3559** 3069 Rubber working machinery, including tires; rubber automotive products; castings, rubber

(P-7968)
COSMODYNE LLC
Also Called: Nikkiso Cosmodyne
3010 Old Ranch Pkwy # 300, Seal Beach (90740-2750)
PHONE...................................562 795-5990
Peter Wagner, *President*
George Win, *Project Mgr*
Dustin Semark, *Project Engr*
Eduardo Zapata, *Project Engr*
Thomas Gloss, *Engineer*
◆ **EMP: 35 EST:** 1997
SQ FT: 125,000
SALES (est): 15.2MM **Privately Held**
WEB: www.cosmodyne.com
SIC: **3559** 3443 Smelting & refining machinery & equipment; cryogenic machinery, industrial; cryogenic tanks, for liquids & gases
HQ: Cryogenic Industries, Inc.
27710 Jefferson Ave # 301
Temecula CA 92590
951 677-2081

(P-7969)
CRYOPORT SYSTEMS LLC (HQ)
Also Called: Cryoport Systems, Inc.
19000 Macarthur Blvd # 80, Irvine (92612-1438)
PHONE...................................949 540-7204
Jerrell W Shelton, *President*
Robert S Stefanovich, *CFO*
Bret Bollinger, *Officer*
Dee Kelly, *Vice Pres*
John Phillips, *Vice Pres*
EMP: 16 EST: 1999
SQ FT: 28,000
SALES (est): 16.3MM **Publicly Held**
WEB: www.cryoport.com
SIC: **3559** Cryogenic machinery, industrial

(P-7970)
CRYST MARK INC A SWAN TECHNO C
Also Called: Crystal Mark
613 Justin Ave, Glendale (91201-2326)
PHONE...................................818 240-7520
John Swan, *President*
E Michael Swan, *Vice Pres*
Marko S Swan, *Vice Pres*
Pauline Swan, *Asst Sec*
EMP: 40
SQ FT: 18,000
SALES (est): 9.6MM **Privately Held**
WEB: www.crystalmarkinc.com
SIC: **3559** 3471 Semiconductor manufacturing machinery; screening equipment, electric; sand blasting of metal parts

(P-7971)
CUSTOM METAL FINISHING CORP
17804 S Western Ave, Gardena (90248-3620)
P.O. Box 368 (90248-0368)
PHONE...................................310 532-5075
David Alverez, *President*
Larry Alvarez, *Shareholder*
Victor Alvarez, *Shareholder*
Kelly Alverez, *Treasurer*
Lilly Alvarez, *Vice Pres*
EMP: 23 EST: 1978
SQ FT: 7,500
SALES (est): 1.2MM **Privately Held**
WEB: www.1800deburring.com
SIC: **3559** 3471 Metal finishing equipment for plating, etc.; plating & polishing

(P-7972)
ENVIROKINETICS INC (PA)
101 S Milliken Ave, Ontario (91761-7836)
PHONE...................................909 621-7599
Henry Seal, *President*
Long Le, *Vice Pres*
Cheryl Fogarty, *Manager*
Tim Geyer, *Supervisor*
EMP: 15 EST: 2000
SQ FT: 6,000

SALES (est): 7.9MM **Privately Held**
WEB: www.envirokinetics.com
SIC: **3559** Petroleum refinery equipment

(P-7973)
EXCELLON ACQUISITION LLC (HQ)
Also Called: Excellon Automation Co
20001 S Rancho Way, Compton (90220-6318)
PHONE...................................310 668-7700
Bailey Su,
Tom Wilson, *Executive*
Barbara Tilk, *Buyer*
EMP: 38 EST: 1962
SQ FT: 35,000
SALES (est): 11.4MM **Privately Held**
WEB: www.excellon.com
SIC: **3559** Semiconductor manufacturing machinery

(P-7974)
FANUC AMERICA CORPORATION
Also Called: Fanuc Robotics West
25951 Commercentre Dr, Lake Forest (92630-8805)
PHONE...................................949 595-2700
Mike Hollingsworth, *Manager*
James Farmer, *District Mgr*
Josh Cantrell, *Engineer*
Don Trend, *Engineer*
Michael Rabina, *Opers Mgr*
EMP: 75 Privately Held
WEB: www.fanucamerica.com
SIC: **3559** 3548 3569 Metal finishing equipment for plating, etc.; electric welding equipment; robots, assembly line: industrial & commercial
HQ: Fanuc America Corporation
3900 W Hamlin Rd
Rochester Hills MI 48309
248 377-7000

(P-7975)
FC MANAGEMENT SERVICES
Also Called: PC Recycle
2001 Anchor Ct Ste B, Newbury Park (91320-1616)
PHONE...................................805 499-0050
Fulton Connor, *President*
Jill North, *Manager*
EMP: 21 EST: 2017
SALES (est): 2.5MM **Privately Held**
WEB: www.pcrecycle.us
SIC: **3559** Electronic component making machinery

(P-7976)
FLAT PLANET INC
618 Hampton Dr, Venice (90291-8625)
PHONE...................................310 392-0683
Michael Lee Simpson, *CEO*
EMP: 20 EST: 2006
SALES (est): 200K **Privately Held**
SIC: **3559** Tobacco products machinery

(P-7977)
FLIGHT MICROWAVE CORPORATION
410 S Douglas St, El Segundo (90245-4628)
PHONE...................................310 607-9819
Rolf Kich, *President*
Mike Callas, *CFO*
Mark Van Alstyne, *Vice Pres*
Amy Meyer, *Finance*
Richard Bennett, *Director*
EMP: 30 EST: 2004
SQ FT: 8,000
SALES (est): 2.9MM **Privately Held**
WEB: www.flightmicrowave.com
SIC: **3559** Electronic component making machinery

(P-7978)
FLIR MOTION CTRL SYSTEMS INC
6769 Hollister Ave, Goleta (93117-3001)
PHONE...................................650 692-3900
Philip Kahn, *President*
David Gaw, *Vice Pres*
Johnny Johnson, *Engineer*
▼ **EMP: 67 EST:** 1992
SQ FT: 6,000

SALES (est): 11.9MM
SALES (corp-wide): 3B **Publicly Held**
WEB: www.flir.com
SIC: **3559** 3541 Semiconductor manufacturing machinery; robots for drilling, cutting, grinding, polishing, etc.
HQ: Teledyne Flir, Llc
27700 Sw Parkway Ave
Wilsonville OR 97070
503 498-3547

(P-7979)
GARAGE EQUIPMENT SUPPLY INC
16000 Ventura Blvd # 1000, Encino (91436-2762)
PHONE...................................805 530-0027
Danette Henthorn, *CEO*
Gary Henthorn, *President*
Mike Oconnell, *Empl Benefits*
▲ **EMP: 15 EST:** 2003
SALES (est): 4.9MM **Privately Held**
SIC: **3559** Automotive maintenance equipment

(P-7980)
GLASTAR CORPORATION
8425 Canoga Ave, Canoga Park (91304-2607)
PHONE...................................818 341-0301
Lorie Mitchell, *President*
George Lopez, *Buyer*
EMP: 20 EST: 1978
SQ FT: 14,000
SALES (est): 2.5MM **Privately Held**
WEB: www.glastar.com
SIC: **3559** 3563 3231 Glass making machinery: blowing, molding, forming, etc.; spraying & dusting equipment; products of purchased glass

(P-7981)
INDIE RIDGE INC
4701 Arrow Hwy, Montclair (91763-1229)
PHONE...................................323 207-9181
Stephen Lauria, *CEO*
EMP: 14 EST: 2017
SALES (est): 732.5K **Privately Held**
SIC: **3559** Boots, shoes & leather working machinery

(P-7982)
INDUSTRIAL DYNAMICS CO LTD (PA)
Also Called: Filtec
3100 Fujita St, Torrance (90505-4007)
P.O. Box 2945 (90509-2945)
PHONE...................................310 325-5633
David Storey, *President*
Bob Catalanotti, *COO*
Dan Leo, *CFO*
Nick Newman, *Officer*
Denise Baker, *Vice Pres*
▲ **EMP: 214 EST:** 1960
SQ FT: 155,000
SALES (est): 56.4MM **Privately Held**
WEB: www.filtec.com
SIC: **3559** 3829 Screening equipment, electric; measuring & controlling devices

(P-7983)
INDUSTRIAL TOOLS INC
1111 S Rose Ave, Oxnard (93033-2499)
PHONE...................................805 483-1111
Donald O Murphy, *President*
John E Anderson, *Ch of Bd*
Lauren Bowen, *COO*
Kay Nolan, *CFO*
Adam Roof, *Info Tech Dir*
EMP: 50 EST: 1961
SQ FT: 65,000
SALES (est): 8.8MM **Privately Held**
WEB: www.iti-abrasives.com
SIC: **3559** 3545 3544 3541 Semiconductor manufacturing machinery; machine tool accessories; special dies, tools, jigs & fixtures; machine tools, metal cutting type

(P-7984)
INNOVATED SOLUTIONS INC
Also Called: Integrated Solutions
7201 Garden Grove Blvd C, Garden Grove (92841-4220)
PHONE...................................949 222-1088
Joe Whann, *President*
◆ **EMP: 15 EST:** 2002

SQ FT: 1,600
SALES (est): 1.3MM **Privately Held**
SIC: **3559** Ammunition & explosives, loading machinery

(P-7985)
JGM AUTOMOTIVE TOOLING INC
Also Called: Motec USA
5355 Industrial Dr, Huntington Beach (92649-1516)
PHONE...................................714 895-7001
James Munn, *CEO*
EMP: 23 EST: 1980
SQ FT: 8,000
SALES (est): 1.1MM **Privately Held**
WEB: www.jgm.com
SIC: **3559** 5531 Automotive maintenance equipment; automobile & truck equipment & parts

(P-7986)
JOHN CURRIE PERFORMANCE GROUP
Also Called: Rockjock
1592 Jenks Dr, Corona (92878-5008)
PHONE...................................714 367-1580
Stephen E Blaine, *Ch of Bd*
EMP: 22 EST: 2019
SALES (est): 2.5MM **Privately Held**
WEB: www.currieenterprises.com
SIC: **3559** Automotive maintenance equipment

(P-7987)
KVR INVESTMENT GROUP INC
Also Called: Pacific Plating
12113 Branford St, Sun Valley (91352-5710)
PHONE...................................818 896-1102
Rakesh Bajaria, *President*
Benny Kadhrota, *Treasurer*
Ken Pansuria, *Vice Pres*
Harry Thummar, *Vice Pres*
EMP: 60 EST: 1997
SALES (est): 8.1MM **Privately Held**
SIC: **3559** 3471 Metal finishing equipment for plating, etc.; plating & polishing

(P-7988)
MEGA MACHINERY INC
6688 Doolittle Ave, Riverside (92503-1432)
PHONE...................................951 300-9300
Richard Risch, *President*
Roger Blaney, *Vice Pres*
EMP: 30 EST: 1991
SQ FT: 20,000
SALES (est): 3.2MM **Privately Held**
WEB: www.mega.biz
SIC: **3559** Plastics working machinery

(P-7989)
MEI RIGGING & CRATING LLC
Also Called: Dunkel Bros. Machinery Moving
14555 Alondra Blvd, La Mirada (90638-5602)
PHONE...................................714 712-5888
Patrick Moore, *COO*
Seth Christensen, *CFO*
Terry Shain, *General Mgr*
Sondra Ludwick, *Human Resources*
EMP: 60
SALES (est): 5.4MM **Privately Held**
WEB: www.meirigimgcrating.com
SIC: **3559** Special industry machinery

(P-7990)
MERITEK ELECTRONICS CORP (PA)
5160 Rivergrade Rd, Baldwin Park (91706-1406)
PHONE...................................626 373-1728
Pa-Shih Oliver Su, *CEO*
Su Oliver, *Administration*
Brent Robinson, *Natl Sales Mgr*
Armando Mendez, *Sales Staff*
Sandy Mecusa, *Manager*
◆ **EMP: 74 EST:** 1993
SQ FT: 60,000
SALES (est): 26.1MM **Privately Held**
WEB: www.meritekusa.com
SIC: **3559** 5065 Electronic component making machinery; electronic parts

(P-7991)
MOREHOUSE-COWLES LLC
Also Called: Epworth Morehouse Cowles
13930 Magnolia Ave, Chino (91710-7029)
PHONE.................................909 627-7222
Michael E Pfau,
Khanh Nguyen, *Engineer*
EMP: 25 **EST:** 2004
SALES (est): 6.7MM
SALES (corp-wide): 6.3B **Publicly Held**
WEB: www.morehousecowles.com
SIC: 3559 Chemical machinery & equipment
HQ: Nusil Technology Llc
1050 Cindy Ln
Carpinteria CA 93013
805 684-8780

(P-7992)
NORCHEM CORPORATION (PA)
5649 Alhambra Ave, Los Angeles
(90032-3107)
PHONE.................................323 221-0221
Gevork Minissian, *CEO*
Kevin Minissian, *Vice Pres*
Chris Aguilar, *Project Mgr*
Martin Mora, *Project Mgr*
Vaughn Minissian, *Opers Staff*
▲ **EMP:** 53 **EST:** 1980
SQ FT: 50,000
SALES (est): 10.6MM **Privately Held**
WEB: www.norchemcorp.com
SIC: 3559 2842 2841 Chemical machinery & equipment; laundry cleaning preparations; soap & other detergents

(P-7993)
PEABODY ENGINEERING & SUP INC
13435 Estelle St, Corona (92879-1877)
PHONE.................................951 734-7711
Mark Peabody, *CEO*
Larry Peabody, *President*
Cheryl Peabody, *General Mgr*
Amber Trujillo, *CTO*
Maria Custodio, *Project Mgr*
◆ **EMP:** 25 **EST:** 1952
SQ FT: 32,400
SALES (est): 6.3MM **Privately Held**
WEB: www.4peabody.com
SIC: 3559 5084 Chemical machinery & equipment; industrial machinery & equipment

(P-7994)
PHILLIPS 66 CO CARBON GROUP
2555 Willow Rd, Arroyo Grande
(93420-5731)
PHONE.................................805 489-4050
Michael Eckert, *Purchasing*
Isaac Castillo, *Maintence Staff*
Robert Canton, *Supervisor*
EMP: 29 **EST:** 2004
SALES (est): 2.6MM **Privately Held**
SIC: 3559 Petroleum refinery equipment

(P-7995)
STARCO ENTERPRISES INC (PA)
Also Called: Four Star Chemical
3137 E 26th St, Vernon (90058-8006)
PHONE.................................323 266-7111
George D Stroesenreuther, *CEO*
Ross Sklar, *Co-CEO*
Mireya Flores, *Human Resources*
Kelli Read,
▲ **EMP:** 74 **EST:** 1973
SQ FT: 25,000
SALES (est): 16.3MM **Privately Held**
WEB: www.fourstarchemical.com
SIC: 3559 5169 5191 Degreasing machines, automotive & industrial; specialty cleaning & sanitation preparations; farm supplies

(P-7996)
SUSS MICROTEC INC (HQ)
2520 Palisades Dr, Corona (92882-0632)
PHONE.................................408 940-0300
Frank Averdung, *President*
Franz Richter, *Ch of Bd*
Stefan Schneidewind, *Ch of Bd*
Wilfried Bair, *President*
Peter Szafir, *President*
EMP: 130 **EST:** 1980
SALES (est): 40MM
SALES (corp-wide): 298.1MM **Privately Held**
WEB: www.suss.com
SIC: 3559 3825 3674 Semiconductor manufacturing machinery; instruments to measure electricity; semiconductors & related devices
PA: SUss Microtec Se
SchleiBheimer Str. 90
Garching B. Munchen BY 85748
893 200-70

(P-7997)
TRADEMARK PLASTICS INC
807 Palmyrita Ave, Riverside (92507-1805)
PHONE.................................909 941-8810
Erin Carty, *President*
Kay Walker, *Executive Asst*
Renato Valz-Brenta, *Project Mgr*
Sandra Hinojosa, *Human Res Mgr*
Robby Sinor, *Marketing Mgr*
◆ **EMP:** 150 **EST:** 1988
SQ FT: 100,000
SALES (est): 31.4MM **Privately Held**
WEB: www.trademarkplastics.com
SIC: 3559 3089 Plastics working machinery; injection molding of plastics

(P-7998)
ULTRA TEC MANUFACTURING INC
1025 E Chestnut Ave, Santa Ana
(92701-6425)
PHONE.................................714 542-0608
Joseph I Rubin, *President*
Maxine Rubin, *Corp Secy*
Robert Rubin, *Vice Pres*
Bobby Macneil, *CTO*
Heenal Patel, *Manager*
EMP: 15 **EST:** 1966
SQ FT: 7,000
SALES (est): 2.5MM **Privately Held**
WEB: www.ultratecusa.com
SIC: 3559 3541 Synthetic filament extruding machines; grinding, polishing, buffing, lapping & honing machines

(P-7999)
UNITED SURFACE SOLUTIONS LLC
11901 Burke St, Santa Fe Springs
(90670-2507)
PHONE.................................562 693-0202
Ken Bagdasarian, *CEO*
Lance Childers, *Plant Mgr*
EMP: 27 **EST:** 2010
SQ FT: 20,000
SALES (est): 4.7MM **Privately Held**
WEB: www.deburring.com
SIC: 3559 3541 Metal finishing equipment for plating, etc.; deburring machines

(P-8000)
VIZUALOGIC LLC
1493 E Bentley Dr Ste 102, Corona
(92879-5102)
PHONE.................................407 509-3421
Malek Tawil,
Kevin Velasquez, *Design Engr*
Robert Lorrey, *Opers Staff*
Janis Patterson,
Steven Cicilian, *Manager*
EMP: 200 **EST:** 2015
SQ FT: 3,000
SALES (est): 20MM **Privately Held**
WEB: www.vizualogicdirect.com
SIC: 3559 Automotive related machinery

(P-8001)
WALCO INC
9017 Arrow Rte, Rancho Cucamonga
(91730-4412)
PHONE.................................909 483-3333
James Wilkinson, *CEO*
Mary Martin, *Opers Mgr*
EMP: 18 **EST:** 2009
SALES (est): 3.1MM **Privately Held**
WEB: www.walcomachine.com
SIC: 3559 Ammunition & explosives, loading machinery

(P-8002)
ZEBRASCI INC (PA)
27973 Diaz Rd, Temecula (92590-3484)
PHONE.................................800 217-3032
Adam Kalbermatten, *CEO*
Robert Schultheis, *President*
Greg Wolfe, *CEO*
Brandon Chase, *Principal*
EMP: 17 **EST:** 2009
SALES (est): 5.5MM **Privately Held**
WEB: www.zebrasci.com
SIC: 3559 8071 8731 Pharmaceutical machinery; testing laboratories; biotechnical research, commercial

---

3561 Pumps & Pumping Eqpt

(P-8003)
AQUASTAR POOL PRODUCTS INC
Also Called: Aquastar Pool Productions
2340 Palma Dr Ste 104, Ventura
(93003-8091)
PHONE.................................877 768-2717
Olaf Mjelde, *CEO*
Sarah Reimer, *Admin Sec*
Edward Mjelde, *Marketing Staff*
Chris Freihaut, *Sales Staff*
▲ **EMP:** 31 **EST:** 2003
SALES (est): 4.4MM **Privately Held**
WEB: www.aquastarpoolproducts.com
SIC: 3561 Pumps, domestic: water or sump

(P-8004)
AQUATEC INTERNATIONAL INC
Also Called: Aquatec Water Systems
17422 Pullman St, Irvine (92614-5527)
PHONE.................................949 225-2200
Bryan Hausner, *CEO*
Sami Levi, *CFO*
Ivar Schoenmeyr, *Corp Secy*
Isak Levi, *Vice Pres*
Laura Alvarez, *Controller*
▲ **EMP:** 95 **EST:** 1986
SQ FT: 30,000
SALES (est): 20.5MM **Privately Held**
WEB: www.aquatec.com
SIC: 3561 Pumps & pumping equipment

(P-8005)
CASCADE PUMP COMPANY
10107 Norwalk Blvd, Santa Fe Springs
(90670-3354)
P.O. Box 2767 (90670-0767)
PHONE.................................562 946-1414
T W Summerfield, *CEO*
John Summerfield, *CFO*
Scott Summerfield, *Vice Pres*
Baltazar Hernandez, *Project Mgr*
Summerfield Brian, *Engineer*
EMP: 60 **EST:** 1948
SQ FT: 120,000
SALES (est): 13.6MM **Privately Held**
WEB: www.cascadepump.com
SIC: 3561 3594 Pumps, domestic: water or sump; fluid power pumps & motors

(P-8006)
COASTAL PRODUCTS COMPANY INC
2157 Mohawk St, Bakersfield
(93308-6020)
P.O. Box 1200 (93302-1200)
PHONE.................................661 323-0487
Dorothy Jones, *President*
Richard Jones, *General Mgr*
EMP: 29 **EST:** 1994
SQ FT: 2,500
SALES (est): 786.7K **Privately Held**
SIC: 3561 Pumps & pumping equipment

(P-8007)
CODYSALES INC
1393 Dodson Way Ste A, Riverside
(92507-2073)
P.O. Box 56099 (92517-0999)
PHONE.................................951 786-3650
Marius J A Pastoor, *President*
EMP: 18 **EST:** 2005
SALES (est): 2.7MM **Privately Held**
SIC: 3561 Cylinders, pump

(P-8008)
CRYOSTAR USA LLC
13117 Meyer Rd, Whittier (90605-3555)
PHONE.................................562 903-1290
Jose Moreno,
Kathleen Pogue, *Administration*
Loreen Smith, *Administration*
Bruno Brethes, *Technical Staff*
Edra Ivora, *CPA*
▲ **EMP:** 77 **EST:** 2013
SALES (est): 10MM **Privately Held**
WEB: www.cryostar.com
SIC: 3561 Pump jacks & other pumping equipment
HQ: Cryostar Sas
2 Rue De L Industrie
Hesingue 68220
389 702-727

(P-8009)
CURLIN MEDICAL INC (HQ)
15662 Commerce Ln, Huntington Beach
(92649-1604)
PHONE.................................714 897-9301
Martin Berarei, *President*
▲ **EMP:** 75 **EST:** 1998
SALES (est): 5.9MM
SALES (corp-wide): 2.8B **Publicly Held**
WEB: www.moog.com
SIC: 3561 Pumps & pumping equipment
PA: Moog Inc.
400 Jamison Rd
Elma NY 14059
716 652-2000

(P-8010)
FLOWSERVE CORPORATION
2300 E Vernon Ave Stop 76, Vernon
(90058-1609)
PHONE.................................323 584-1890
Rick Soldo, *Branch Mgr*
John Atten, *Vice Pres*
John Ondrejack, *Regional Mgr*
Woody Lawman, *General Mgr*
Rebecca Todd, *General Mgr*
EMP: 342
SALES (corp-wide): 3.7B **Publicly Held**
WEB: www.flowserve.com
SIC: 3561 Pumps & pumping equipment
PA: Flowserve Corporation
5215 N Ocnnor Blvd Ste 70 Connor
Irving TX 75039
972 443-6500

(P-8011)
GOULDS PUMPS
3951 Capitol Ave, City of Industry
(90601-1734)
PHONE.................................562 949-2113
Mike Suess, *Manager*
Michael Traber, *Buyer*
▲ **EMP:** 16 **EST:** 2010
SALES (est): 2.9MM **Privately Held**
SIC: 3561 Pumps & pumping equipment

(P-8012)
GRISWOLD PUMP COMPANY
22069 Van Buren St, Grand Terrace
(92313-5607)
PHONE.................................909 422-1700
Dale Pavlovich, *President*
Michael Boul, *Vice Pres*
Dave Spitzer, *Vice Pres*
Edward Vaughn, *Vice Pres*
◆ **EMP:** 25 **EST:** 1996
SQ FT: 25,000
SALES (est): 5.9MM
SALES (corp-wide): 100.8MM **Privately Held**
WEB: www.psgdover.com
SIC: 3561 5084 Industrial pumps & parts; industrial machinery & equipment
PA: Psg California Llc
22069 Van Buren St
Grand Terrace CA 92313
909 422-1700

(P-8013)
GROVER SMITH MFG CORP
Also Called: Grover Manufacturing
9717 Factorial Way, South El Monte
(91733-1724)
P.O. Box 986, Montebello (90640-0986)
PHONE.................................323 724-3444
Marilyn Schirmer, *President*
W Michael Meeker, *Ch of Bd*

Lino Paras, *Treasurer*
EMP: 30 **EST:** 1925
SALES (est): 3.2MM **Privately Held**
WEB: www.grovermfg.com
SIC: 3561 3569 Pumps & pumping equipment; lubrication equipment, industrial

(P-8014)
HASKEL INTERNATIONAL LLC (HQ)
100 E Graham Pl, Burbank (91502-2076)
PHONE..................818 843-4000
Chris Krieps, *CEO*
Steve Quigley, *Electrical Engi*
Veldma Crosby, *Accounting Mgr*
Alan Mann, *Senior Buyer*
Joseph Llamas, *Buyer*
▲ **EMP:** 125 **EST:** 1986
SQ FT: 78,000
SALES (est): 51MM
SALES (corp-wide): 4.9B **Publicly Held**
WEB: www.haskel.com
SIC: 3561 3594 5084 5085 Pumps & pumping equipment; fluid power pumps; hydraulic systems equipment & supplies; hose, belting & packing; valves, pistons & fittings; electrical equipment & supplies
PA: Ingersoll Rand Inc.
800 Beaty St Ste A
Davidson NC 28036
704 896-4000

(P-8015)
HYDRAFORCE INCORPORATED
7383 Orangewood Dr, Riverside (92504-1027)
PHONE..................951 689-3987
Javier Soto, *CEO*
Mark Decklar, *Engineer*
Ricardo Michel, *Manager*
EMP: 14 **EST:** 1990
SQ FT: 4,000
SALES (est): 1.6MM **Privately Held**
SIC: 3561 Cylinders, pump

(P-8016)
LOS ANGLES PUMP VALVE PDTS INC
Also Called: Los Angeles Brass Products
2528 E 57th St, Huntington Park (90255-2521)
P.O. Box 2007 (90255-1307)
PHONE..................323 277-7788
Santos J Pinto, *President*
Phil Pinto, *Vice Pres*
EMP: 20 **EST:** 1975
SQ FT: 11,000
SALES (est): 2.4MM **Privately Held**
WEB: www.la-pv.com
SIC: 3561 Pump jacks & other pumping equipment

(P-8017)
MJW INC
Also Called: American Lab and Systems
1328 W Slauson Ave, Los Angeles (90044-2824)
PHONE..................323 778-8900
Mike Curry, *President*
Linda Curry, *Vice Pres*
Shane Curry, *General Mgr*
Diana Isaac, *Office Mgr*
EMP: 65 **EST:** 1978
SQ FT: 30,000
SALES (est): 7.2MM **Privately Held**
WEB: www.americanlabs.com
SIC: 3561 Industrial pumps & parts

(P-8018)
PENGUIN PUMPS INCORPORATED
Also Called: Filter Pump Industries
7932 Ajay Dr, Sun Valley (91352-5315)
PHONE..................818 504-2391
Jerome S Hollander, *President*
Sonya E Hollander, *Corp Secy*
Mitchell A Hollander, *Vice Pres*
Mark Brien, *General Mgr*
▲ **EMP:** 50 **EST:** 1972
SQ FT: 20,000
SALES (est): 9.7MM **Privately Held**
WEB: www.filterpump.com
SIC: 3561 3569 Pumps & pumping equipment; filters, general line: industrial

(P-8019)
PHOENIX PUMPS CALIFORNIA INC
5143 Azusa Canyon Rd, Baldwin Park (91706-1833)
PHONE..................858 278-2223
Jeffrey Smith, *CEO*
EMP: 20 **EST:** 2009
SALES (est): 857.8K **Privately Held**
WEB: www.phoenixpumps.com
SIC: 3561 Pump jacks & other pumping equipment

(P-8020)
POLARIS E-COMMERCE INC
1941 E Occidental St, Santa Ana (92705-5115)
PHONE..................714 907-0582
Insoo Hwang, *CEO*
▲ **EMP:** 25 **EST:** 2010
SALES (est): 3.3MM **Privately Held**
WEB: www.officesmartlabels.com
SIC: 3561 Industrial pumps & parts

(P-8021)
PREFERRED PUMP INC
1740 Carlotti Dr, Santa Maria (93454-1505)
PHONE..................805 922-8510
Randy Lyne, *President*
EMP: 15 **EST:** 2001
SALES (est): 132.7K **Privately Held**
WEB: www.preferredpump.com
SIC: 3561 Pumps & pumping equipment

(P-8022)
PSG CALIFORNIA LLC (PA)
Also Called: Wilden Pump
22069 Van Buren St, Grand Terrace (92313-5607)
PHONE..................909 422-1700
Denny L Buskirk, *Mng Member*
Philip Behrman, *Technician*
Christa Toscano, *Human Res Dir*
Linda Anderson, *Purch Dir*
Anastasia Gozaly, *Export Mgr*
◆ **EMP:** 295 **EST:** 1998
SQ FT: 153,000
SALES (est): 100.8MM **Privately Held**
WEB: www.psgdover.com
SIC: 3561 Industrial pumps & parts

(P-8023)
REED LLC
Also Called: Reed Manufacturing
13822 Oaks Ave, Chino (91710-7008)
PHONE..................909 287-2100
James W Shea, *President*
Cliff KAO, *Vice Pres*
Shiletha Hancik, *Accountant*
Ivan Ward, *Materials Mgr*
Norma Payan, *Manager*
◆ **EMP:** 40 **EST:** 1957
SQ FT: 69,000
SALES (est): 10MM **Privately Held**
WEB: www.reedpumps.com
SIC: 3561 3531 Pumps & pumping equipment; bituminous, cement & concrete related products & equipment

(P-8024)
SULZER PUMP SERVICES (US) INC
Also Called: Sulzer Bingham Pumps
9856 Jordan Cir, Santa Fe Springs (90670-3303)
P.O. Box 3904 (90670-1904)
PHONE..................562 903-1000
Tim Voyles, *Manager*
Shea Wiley, *Project Mgr*
Jay McClain, *Manager*
EMP: 22
SQ FT: 18,968
SALES (corp-wide): 3.6B **Privately Held**
SIC: 3561 Pumps & pumping equipment
HQ: Sulzer Pump Services (Us) Inc.
101 Old Underwood Rd G
La Porte TX 77571
281 417-7110

(P-8025)
TOTAL PROCESS SOLUTIONS LLC
1400 Norris Rd, Bakersfield (93308-2232)
PHONE..................661 829-7910
Eddie L Rice, *Mng Member*

Stan Ellis, *Mng Member*
Travis Ellis, *Mng Member*
Joey L Taylor, *Mng Member*
EMP: 30 **EST:** 2012
SALES (est): 6.5MM **Privately Held**
SIC: 3563 Cylinders, pump; air & gas compressors including vacuum pumps

---

3562 Ball & Roller Bearings

(P-8026)
AMERICAN METAL BEARING COMPANY
7191 Acacia Ave, Garden Grove (92841-5297)
PHONE..................714 892-5527
Alfred A Anawati, *CEO*
Jim Demaio, *Corp Secy*
Michael Litton, *Vice Pres*
Tom Nguyen, *Design Engr*
Dave Aston, *Engineer*
▲ **EMP:** 21 **EST:** 1921
SQ FT: 40,000
SALES (est): 9.9MM
SALES (corp-wide): 24.2MM **Privately Held**
WEB: www.ambco.net
SIC: 3562 7699 3568 Ball bearings & parts; roller bearings & parts; rebabbitting; power transmission equipment
PA: Marisco, Ltd.
91-607 Malakole St
Kapolei HI 96707
808 682-1333

(P-8027)
CLEAN WAVE MANAGEMENT INC
Also Called: Impact Bearing
1291 Puerta Del Sol, San Clemente (92673-6310)
PHONE..................949 361-5356
Richard D Kay Jr, *CEO*
Stanley Truong, *QC Mgr*
Michael Bartlett, *Manager*
◆ **EMP:** 30 **EST:** 1995
SQ FT: 20,000
SALES (est): 4.8MM **Privately Held**
WEB: www.impactbearing.com
SIC: 3562 Ball bearings & parts

(P-8028)
INDUSTRIAL TCTNICS BRINGS CORP (DH)
18301 S Santa Fe Ave, E Rncho Dmngz (90221-5519)
PHONE..................310 537-3750
Michael J Hartnett, *CEO*
Daniel Molnar, *Counsel*
Ricardo Perez, *Manager*
EMP: 149 **EST:** 1990
SQ FT: 70,000
SALES (est): 57.8MM
SALES (corp-wide): 608.9MM **Publicly Held**
WEB: www.rbcbearings.com
SIC: 3562 5085 Roller bearings & parts; bearings
HQ: Roller Bearing Company Of America, Inc.
102 Willenbrock Rd
Oxford CT 06478
203 267-7001

(P-8029)
NEXT POINT BEARING GROUP LLC
28364 Avenue Crocker, Valencia (91355-1250)
PHONE..................818 988-1880
Mark Mickelson, *Mng Member*
James Leguizamon, *Engineer*
Ron Foster, *Opers Staff*
Javier Perez, *Sales Staff*
John Burroughs,
▲ **EMP:** 28 **EST:** 2012
SQ FT: 27,000
SALES (est): 8.2MM **Privately Held**
WEB: www.nextpointbearing.com
SIC: 3562 5085 Ball & roller bearings; bearings

(P-8030)
SCHAEFFLER GROUP USA INC
34700 Pcf Cast Hwy Ste 20, Capistrano Beach (92624)
PHONE..................949 234-9799
Rich Peterson, *Branch Mgr*
Kevin Marx, *Manager*
EMP: 237
SALES (corp-wide): 66.3B **Privately Held**
WEB: www.schaeffler.us
SIC: 3562 Ball & roller bearings
HQ: Schaeffler Group Usa Inc.
308 Springhill Farm Rd
Fort Mill SC 29715
803 548-8500

(P-8031)
SPECIALTY MOTIONS INC
5480 Smokey Mountain Way, Yorba Linda (92887-4247)
PHONE..................951 735-8722
Thomas Corey, *CEO*
Dorothy Corey, *CFO*
EMP: 20 **EST:** 1990
SQ FT: 13,000
SALES (est): 2.1MM **Privately Held**
SIC: 3562 5085 Ball & roller bearings; bearings

3563 Air & Gas Compressors

(P-8032)
C M AUTOMOTIVE SYSTEMS INC (PA)
120 Commerce Way, Walnut (91789-2714)
PHONE..................909 869-7912
Chander Mittal, *President*
Sameer Mittal, *CFO*
▲ **EMP:** 23 **EST:** 1986
SALES (est): 4.4MM **Privately Held**
WEB: www.cmautomotive.com
SIC: 3563 Air & gas compressors

(P-8033)
COMPUVAC INDUSTRIES INC
18381 Mount Langley St, Fountain Valley (92708-6904)
PHONE..................949 574-5085
David Donnelly, *President*
Jean Yoo, *Office Mgr*
▲ **EMP:** 16 **EST:** 2001
SQ FT: 13,000
SALES (est): 2.9MM **Privately Held**
WEB: www.compuvacind.com
SIC: 3563 Vacuum (air extraction) systems, industrial

(P-8034)
KOBELCO COMPRESSORS AMER INC
301 N Smith Ave, Corona (92878-3242)
PHONE..................951 739-3030
EMP: 75 **Privately Held**
WEB: www.kobelcocompressors.com
SIC: 3563 Air & gas compressors
HQ: Kobelco Compressors America, Inc.
1450 W Rincon St
Corona CA 92878

(P-8035)
KOBELCO COMPRESSORS AMER INC (DH)
1450 W Rincon St, Corona (92878-9205)
PHONE..................951 739-3030
Makoto Motoyoshi, *President*
Edelvais Di Rosa, *Admin Asst*
Baishali Chatterjee, *Electrical Engi*
Diego Ferreira, *Engineer*
Jon Golan, *Engineer*
◆ **EMP:** 260 **EST:** 1990
SALES (est): 83.3MM **Privately Held**
WEB: www.kobelcocompressors.com
SIC: 3563 Air & gas compressors including vacuum pumps

(P-8036)
NU VENTURE DIVING CO
Also Called: Nuvair
1600 Beacon Pl, Oxnard (93033-2433)
PHONE..................805 815-4044
Glenn Huebner, *CEO*
Glenn A Huebner, *CEO*

Janet Huebner, *CFO*
Craig Huebner, *Mktg Dir*
◆ **EMP:** 22 **EST:** 1988
SQ FT: 27,000
SALES (est): 5.5MM **Privately Held**
WEB: www.nuvair.com
SIC: 3563 Air & gas compressors

(P-8037)
PTB SALES INC (PA)
1361 Mountain View Cir, Azusa
(91702-1649)
PHONE....................626 334-0500
Patrick T Blackwell, *CEO*
Gavin Riley, *CFO*
Brendan Riley, *Vice Pres*
Dean Scarborough, *Admin Sec*
Carmen Williams, *Accountant*
▲ **EMP:** 32 **EST:** 1995
SQ FT: 16,000
SALES (est): 8.4MM **Privately Held**
WEB: www.ptbsales.com
SIC: 3563 3679 Vacuum (air extraction) systems, industrial; power supplies, all types: static

---

3564 Blowers & Fans

(P-8038)
ADWEST TECHNOLOGIES INC (HQ)
4222 E La Palma Ave, Anaheim
(92807-1816)
PHONE....................714 632-8595
Brian Cannon, *Vice Pres*
Craig Bayer, *President*
Maryann Erickson, *Vice Pres*
Richard Whitford, *Vice Pres*
EMP: 35 **EST:** 1988
SQ FT: 23,500
SALES (est): 7.4MM **Publicly Held**
WEB: www.cecoenviro.com
SIC: 3564 3585 3826 Air purification equipment; heating equipment, complete; thermal analysis instruments, laboratory type

(P-8039)
AIR BLAST INC
2050 Pepper St, Alhambra (91801-3162)
P.O. Box 367, San Gabriel (91778-0367)
PHONE....................626 576-0144
Carl Von Wolffradt, *President*
Patty Von Wolffradt, *Corp Secy*
Justine Von Wolffradt, *Administration*
Judy Doland, *Opers Staff*
EMP: 21 **EST:** 1976
SQ FT: 4,100
SALES (est): 1MM **Privately Held**
WEB: www.dipbraze.com
SIC: 3564 Turbo-blowers, industrial; blowing fans: industrial or commercial

(P-8040)
AIR CLEANING SYSTEMS INC
3633 Pomona Blvd, Pomona (91768-3277)
PHONE....................909 620-7114
George Bunting, *CEO*
James Bunting, *President*
EMP: 19 **EST:** 1972
SQ FT: 7,445
SALES (est): 1.6MM **Privately Held**
WEB: www.acs-cal.com
SIC: 3564 Blowing fans: industrial or commercial

(P-8041)
ATLAS COPCO MAFI-TRENCH CO LLC (DH)
3037 Industrial Pkwy, Santa Maria
(93455-1807)
PHONE....................805 352-0112
James T Reilly,
Abraham Garza, *Engineer*
William Hall, *Engineer*
John Oyen, *Buyer*
Rodney Little, *Natl Sales Mgr*
◆ **EMP:** 208 **EST:** 1975
SQ FT: 90,000

SALES (est): 110.4MM
SALES (corp-wide): 11.5B **Privately Held**
WEB: www.atlascopco.us
SIC: 3564 3533 8744 Turbo-blowers, industrial; oil & gas field machinery; facilities support services

(P-8042)
CAMFIL FARR INC
3625 Del Amo Blvd Ste 260, Torrance
(90503-1688)
PHONE....................973 616-7300
Frank Shahin, *Principal*
Geeta Taneja, *Sr Corp Ofcr*
John Vissers, *Vice Pres*
Leland Thierry, *Branch Mgr*
Mike Danford, *Info Tech Dir*
EMP: 18 **EST:** 2010
SALES (est): 789.5K **Privately Held**
SIC: 3564 Blowers & fans

(P-8043)
CENTRAL BLOWER CO
211 S 7th Ave, City of Industry
(91746-3288)
PHONE....................626 330-3182
David Roger Petersen, *President*
Mary Petersen, *Shareholder*
Eleanor Petersen, *Vice Pres*
EMP: 20 **EST:** 1979
SQ FT: 24,000
SALES (est): 3.6MM **Privately Held**
WEB: www.centralblower.com
SIC: 3564 Exhaust fans: industrial or commercial; blowing fans: industrial or commercial

(P-8044)
CLOUDBURST INC
707 E Hueneme Rd, Oxnard (93033-8654)
PHONE....................805 986-4125
Michael Davis, *CEO*
▲ **EMP:** 18 **EST:** 1992
SQ FT: 7,000
SALES (est): 1.5MM **Privately Held**
WEB: www.cloudburst.com
SIC: 3564 3585 Blowing fans: industrial or commercial; refrigeration & heating equipment

(P-8045)
COWAY USA INC
Also Called: Woongjin Coway USA Inc.
4221 Wilshire Blvd # 308, Los Angeles
(90010-3501)
PHONE....................213 486-1600
Hong Rae Gim, *President*
Hosuk Yoon, *CFO*
Jackie Choi, *Mktg Dir*
John Ko, *Sales Mgr*
Carolyn Lee, *Sales Mgr*
▲ **EMP:** 39
SQ FT: 4,200
SALES (est): 7.6MM **Privately Held**
WEB: www.coway-usa.com
SIC: 5999 3564 Water purification equipment; air purification equipment
PA: Coway Co., Ltd.
136-23 Yugumagoksa-Ro, Yugu-Eup
Gongju 32508

(P-8046)
ECW TECHNOLOGY INC
609 Deep Valley Dr, Rllng HLS Est
(90274-3629)
PHONE....................310 373-0082
REA-Tiing Liu, *President*
Wen Bow, *CFO*
EMP: 15 **EST:** 1995
SQ FT: 3,000
SALES (est): 373K **Privately Held**
SIC: 3564 5169 Air purification equipment; chemicals, industrial & heavy

(P-8047)
ENVION LLC
14724 Ventura Blvd Fl 200, Sherman Oaks
(91403-3514)
PHONE....................818 217-2500
Craig Shandler,
▲ **EMP:** 85 **EST:** 2003
SQ FT: 36,000

SALES (est): 7.3MM
SALES (corp-wide): 20.3MM **Privately Held**
WEB: www.envion.com
SIC: 3564 Air purification equipment
PA: Sylmark Inc.
7821 Orion Ave Ste 200
Van Nuys CA 91406
818 217-2000

(P-8048)
IQAIR NORTH AMERICA INC
14351 Firestone Blvd, La Mirada
(90638-5527)
PHONE....................877 715-4247
Glory Z Dolphin, *CEO*
Frank Hammes, *President*
Tiffany Allegretti, *Pub Rel Mgr*
▲ **EMP:** 48 **EST:** 1991
SQ FT: 40,000
SALES (esi): 24.1MM
SALES (corp-wide): 165.6K **Privately Held**
WEB: www.iqair.com
SIC: 3564 8742 5999 Air cleaning systems; air purification equipment; materials mgmt. (purchasing, handling, inventory) consultant; air purification equipment
PA: Icleen Entwicklungs- Und Vertriebsanstalt Fur Umweltprodukte C/O Jgt Treuunternehmen Reg. Vaduz

(P-8049)
M D H BURNER & BOILER CO INC
12106 Center St, South Gate (90280-8046)
PHONE....................562 630-2875
Mauro Donate, *CEO*
EMP: 18 **EST:** 1992
SQ FT: 5,000
SALES (est): 2.9MM **Privately Held**
SIC: 3564 7699 3443 Air purification equipment; boiler repair shop; fabricated plate work (boiler shop); heating equipment, except electric

(P-8050)
MACROAIR TECHNOLOGIES INC (PA)
Also Called: Macro Air Technologies
794 S Allen St, San Bernardino
(92408-2210)
PHONE....................909 890-2270
Edward Boyd, *CEO*
John Jamison, *Technology*
Brian Sirin, *Prdtn Mgr*
Marc Johnson, *Regl Sales Mgr*
Amber Jimenez, *Sales Staff*
◆ **EMP:** 45 **EST:** 1979
SQ FT: 15,000
SALES (est): 23.1MM **Privately Held**
WEB: www.macroairfans.com
SIC: 3564 Ventilating fans: industrial or commercial

(P-8051)
MARS AIR SYSTEMS LLC
14716 S Broadway, Gardena (90248-1814)
PHONE....................310 532-1555
EMP: 75 **EST:** 2009
SALES (est): 7.2MM **Privately Held**
SIC: 3564 Mfg Blowers/Fans

(P-8052)
POLLUTION CTRL SPECIALISTS INC
1354 Ritchey St, Santa Ana (92705-4727)
PHONE....................949 474-0137
Steve Fleischman, *President*
Andrea Stevens, *Office Mgr*
EMP: 14 **EST:** 2006
SALES (est): 3.1MM **Privately Held**
WEB: www.pollutioncontrolspecialists.com
SIC: 3564 Air cleaning systems

(P-8053)
QC MANUFACTURING INC
26040 Ynez Rd, Temecula (92591-6033)
PHONE....................951 325-6340
Dane Stevenson, *President*
Chris Bell, *IT/INT Sup*
Dave Heisel, *Engineer*
Laura Salvatore, *Finance*

▲ **EMP:** 65 **EST:** 2009
SALES (est): 20.1MM **Privately Held**
WEB: www.quietcoolsystems.com
SIC: 3564 Blowers & fans

(P-8054)
SUNON INC (PA)
Also Called: Eme Fan & Motor
1075 W Lambert Rd Ste A, Brea
(92821-2944)
PHONE....................714 255-0208
Yin Su Hong, *CEO*
Christie Chin, *Marketing Mgr*
Xotchil Castro, *Sales Staff*
Roxy Yang, *Sales Staff*
▲ **EMP:** 30 **EST:** 1998
SQ FT: 22,000
SALES (est): 3.3MM **Privately Held**
WEB: www.sunonusa.com
SIC: 3564 Blowers & fans

(P-8055)
SUPERIOR FILTRATION PDTS LLC
3401 Space Center Ct 811b, Jurupa Valley
(91752-1128)
PHONE....................951 681-1700
Julie Haight, *Manager*
EMP: 13
SALES (corp-wide): 19MM **Privately Held**
WEB: www.superiorfiltrationproducts.com
SIC: 3564 Blowers & fans
PA: Superior Filtration Products, Llc
160 N 400 W
North Salt Lake UT 84054
801 621-5200

(P-8056)
TERRA UNIVERSAL INC
800 S Raymond Ave, Fullerton
(92831-5234)
PHONE....................714 526-0100
G H Sadaghiani, *CEO*
Leo Nguyen, *Design Engr*
Khanh Tran, *Design Engr*
Vinh Luu, *Engineer*
Phillip Pavlovich, *Engineer*
▲ **EMP:** 195 **EST:** 1975
SQ FT: 88,000
SALES (est): 79.6MM **Privately Held**
WEB: www.terrauniversal.com
SIC: 3564 3567 3569 3572 Purification & dust collection equipment; air purification equipment; filters, air: furnaces, air conditioning equipment, etc.; ventilating fans: industrial or commercial; heating units & devices, industrial: electric; filters; computer storage devices; refrigeration equipment, complete; clean room supplies

(P-8057)
TMC FLUID SYSTEMS INC
Also Called: Socal Cleaning & Insulation
1228 Village Way Ste H, Santa Ana
(92705-4747)
PHONE....................714 553-0944
Dilva Mian, *President*
▲ **EMP:** 17 **EST:** 2011
SQ FT: 2,000
SALES (est): 1.6MM **Privately Held**
WEB: www.tmcfluidsystems.com
SIC: 3564 Blowers & fans

(P-8058)
TRI-DIM FILTER CORPORATION
15271 Fairfield Ranch Rd # 150, Chino Hills
(91709-8864)
PHONE....................626 826-5893
Scott Breckenridge, *Manager*
Rodney Payne, *Webmaster*
Karla Harrison, *Export Mgr*
Louis Flores, *Consultant*
EMP: 30
SALES (corp-wide): 4.6B **Privately Held**
WEB: www.tridim.com
SIC: 3564 Filters, air: furnaces, air conditioning equipment, etc.
HQ: Tri-Dim Filter Corporation
93 Industrial Dr
Louisa VA 23093
540 967-2600

(P-8059)
US TOYO FAN CORPORATION (HQ)
16025 Arrow Hwy Ste F, Irwindale (91706-2063)
P.O. Box 1941, Burbank (91507-1941)
PHONE..................................626 338-1111
William Jacobs, *President*
Arnold Weisman, *Corp Secy*
Robert Rosenthal, *Vice Pres*
▲ EMP: 76 EST: 1981
SQ FT: 10,000
SALES (est): 10.4MM
SALES (corp-wide): 66.3MM **Privately Held**
WEB: www.ustoyofan.descoindustries.com
SIC: 3564 Blowers & fans
PA: Desco Industries, Inc.
    3651 Walnut Ave
    Chino CA 91710
    909 627-8178

(P-8060)
VENTUREDYNE LTD
Climet Instruments Company
1320 W Colton Ave, Redlands (92374-2864)
P.O. Box 1760 (92373-0543)
PHONE..................................909 793-2788
Ray Felbinger, *Manager*
Rosalinda Saavedra, *Admin Asst*
John R Grater, *Data Proc Staff*
Manuel Patino, *Engineer*
Angel Adams, *Human Res Mgr*
EMP: 65
SALES (corp-wide): 0 **Privately Held**
WEB: www.venturedyne.com
SIC: 3564 3829 3825 3823 Blowing fans: industrial or commercial; measuring & controlling devices; instruments to measure electricity; industrial instrmnts msrmnt display/control process variable; relays & industrial controls
PA: Venturedyne, Ltd.
    600 College Ave
    Pewaukee WI 53072
    262 691-9900

(P-8061)
VORTECH ENGINEERING INC
1650 Pacific Ave, Oxnard (93033-2746)
PHONE..................................805 247-0226
Jim Middlebrook, *CEO*
Randolf Riley, *President*
Fermin Lopez, *Purchasing*
Chuck Richwine, *QC Mgr*
Brian Ellis, *Sales Staff*
▲ EMP: 42 EST: 2001
SALES (est): 11MM **Privately Held**
WEB: www.vortechsuperchargers.com
SIC: 3564 Blowing fans: industrial or commercial

(P-8062)
WEMS INC (PA)
Also Called: Wems Electronics
4650 W Rosecrans Ave, Hawthorne (90250-6898)
P.O. Box 528 (90251-0528)
PHONE..................................310 644-0251
Ronald Hood, *CEO*
Carroll Whitney, *President*
Mike Macbrair, *Vice Pres*
Gina Simons, *Executive Asst*
Charles Wilson, *Admin Sec*
EMP: 84 EST: 1960
SQ FT: 78,000
SALES (est): 20.4MM **Privately Held**
WEB: www.wems.com
SIC: 3564 3612 6513 Blowers & fans; transformers, except electric; apartment building operators

3565 Packaging Machinery

(P-8063)
BELCO PACKAGING SYSTEMS INC
910 S Mountain Ave, Monrovia (91016-3641)
PHONE..................................626 357-9566
Helen V Misik, *CEO*
A Michael Misik, *President*
Jan Hirsch, *Accountant*

Keira Ambles, *Controller*
Rob Powalski, *Opers Mgr*
▲ EMP: 25
SQ FT: 35,000
SALES (est): 8.4MM **Privately Held**
WEB: www.belcopackaging.com
SIC: 3565 Packing & wrapping machinery

(P-8064)
BOYD & BOYD INDUSTRIES (PA)
3500 Chester Ave, Bakersfield (93301-1630)
PHONE..................................661 631-8400
Jerry Boyd, *Owner*
◆ EMP: 14 EST: 1988
SQ FT: 30,000
SALES (est): 1MM **Privately Held**
WEB: www.boydandboyd.net
SIC: 3565 5084 3535 Packaging machinery; packaging machinery & equipment; unit handling conveying systems

(P-8065)
CAN LINES ENGINEERING INC (PA)
Also Called: C L E
9839 Downey Norwalk Rd, Downey (90241-5596)
PHONE..................................562 861-2996
Donald Koplien, *CEO*
Keenan Koplien, *President*
Erik Koplien, *Vice Pres*
Karla Ladera, *Admin Asst*
Mark Hodge, *Controller*
EMP: 91 EST: 1960
SQ FT: 40,000
SALES (est): 30.6MM **Privately Held**
WEB: www.canlines.com
SIC: 3565 3556 Canning machinery, food; bottling machinery: filling, capping, labeling; food products machinery

(P-8066)
COLIMATIC USA INC
1792 Kaiser Ave, Irvine (92614-5706)
PHONE..................................949 600-6440
Francesco Libretti, *President*
▲ EMP: 16 EST: 2005
SALES (est): 1.5MM **Privately Held**
WEB: www.colimaticusa.com
SIC: 3565 Packaging machinery

(P-8067)
CVC TECHNOLOGIES INC
10861 Business Dr, Fontana (92337-8235)
PHONE..................................909 355-0311
Sheng Hui Yang, *CEO*
K Joe Yang, *President*
Erick Collins, *Engineer*
▲ EMP: 21 EST: 1998
SQ FT: 29,000
SALES (est): 5.7MM **Privately Held**
WEB: www.cvcusa.com
SIC: 3565 Labeling machines, industrial
PA: Cvc Technologies Inc.
    No. 190, Gongye 9th Rd.
    Taichung City 41280

(P-8068)
FOOD MACHINERY SALES INC
Also Called: Serpa Packaging Solutions
7020 W Sunnyview Ave, Visalia (93291-9639)
PHONE..................................559 651-2339
Fernando M Serpa, *President*
Joseph Scalia, *CFO*
Manuela Parreira, *Admin Sec*
Juan Ramirez, *Project Mgr*
Allen O'Neal, *Electrical Engi*
◆ EMP: 100 EST: 1985
SQ FT: 62,000
SALES (est): 28.6MM **Privately Held**
WEB: www.serpapackaging.com
SIC: 3565 Carton packing machines
HQ: Pro Mach, Inc.
    50 E Rvrcnter Blvd Ste 18
    Covington KY 41011
    513 831-8778

(P-8069)
FUTURE COMMODITIES INTL INC
Also Called: Best Pack Packaging Systems
1425 S Campus Ave, Ontario (91761-4366)
PHONE..................................909 987-4258

David L Lim, *President*
Chery C Lim, *Exec VP*
Matthew Lim, *Vice Pres*
Edward Stevens, *Technician*
Vivien Dizon, *Accounting Mgr*
▲ EMP: 27 EST: 1984
SQ FT: 27,500
SALES (est): 6.8MM **Privately Held**
WEB: www.bestpack.com
SIC: 3565 Packaging machinery

(P-8070)
HANNAN PRODUCTS CORP (PA)
220 N Smith Ave, Corona (92878-3240)
PHONE..................................951 735-1587
Henry H Jenkins, *President*
Nancy P Jenkins, *Shareholder*
Alfred Ramos, *CFO*
Lawrence Jenkins, *Vice Pres*
Elena Nicklaus, *Manager*
EMP: 16 EST: 1966
SQ FT: 36,000
SALES (est): 5.1MM **Privately Held**
WEB: www.hannanpak.com
SIC: 3565 3053 3554 3549 Packaging machinery; packing materials; paper industries machinery; cutting & slitting machinery

(P-8071)
HIS INDUSTRIES INC
Also Called: Phoenix Engineering
1202 W Shelley Ct, Orange (92868-1239)
PHONE..................................949 383-4308
Lynn Worthington, *President*
▲ EMP: 20 EST: 1997
SQ FT: 6,000
SALES (est): 2.6MM **Privately Held**
WEB: www.pouchmachines.com
SIC: 3565 Packaging machinery

(P-8072)
JACKSAM CORPORATION
Also Called: JACKSAM CORP BLACKOUT
4440 Von Karman Ave # 220, Newport Beach (92660-2011)
PHONE..................................800 605-3580
Mark Adams, *President*
Michael Sakala, *CFO*
David Hall, *Exec VP*
Sebastian Alidad, *Software Dev*
Malachi Bodine, *Project Mgr*
EMP: 25 EST: 1989
SALES (est): 3.2MM **Privately Held**
WEB: www.convectium.com
SIC: 3565 Bottling machinery: filling, capping, labeling

(P-8073)
M & O PERRY INDUSTRIES INC
412 N Smith Ave, Corona (92878-4303)
PHONE..................................951 734-9838
Phillip Osterhaus, *CEO*
Robbin Driscoll, *Administration*
Cheng Lee, *Engineer*
Joy Tsai, *Analyst*
Detlef Teubert, *Marketing Staff*
▲ EMP: 40
SQ FT: 20,000
SALES (est): 10.2MM **Privately Held**
WEB: www.moperry.com
SIC: 3565 8711 7629 5084 Packaging machinery; engineering services; electrical repair shops; conveyor systems

(P-8074)
MAF INDUSTRIES INC (HQ)
36470 Highway 99, Traver (93673-7120)
P.O. Box 218 (93673-0218)
PHONE..................................559 897-2905
Thomas Blanc, *President*
Philippe Blanc, *Vice Pres*
Florian Best, *Department Mgr*
Raul Mejia, *Admin Sec*
Allen White, *Technical Staff*
▲ EMP: 80 EST: 1989
SQ FT: 30,000
SALES (est): 27.4MM **Privately Held**
WEB: www.mafindustries.com
SIC: 3565 5084 Packing & wrapping machinery; food industry machinery

(P-8075)
P R P MULTISOURCE INC
3836 Wacker Dr, Jurupa Valley (91752-1147)
PHONE..................................951 681-6100
Phil Woss, *President*
Kurt Fisch, *Treasurer*
Daniel Landeros, *Buyer*
▲ EMP: 20 EST: 1994
SQ FT: 25,000
SALES (est): 2.6MM **Privately Held**
WEB: www.multisource.us
SIC: 3565 5084 Vacuum packaging machinery; packaging machinery & equipment

(P-8076)
PACKAGING HOLDINGS INC
1030 N Anderson Rd, Exeter (93221-9341)
PHONE..................................831 634-0940
John McKernan, *CEO*
EMP: 24 EST: 2009
SALES (est): 4.3MM
SALES (corp-wide): 5.2B **Publicly Held**
WEB: www.sonoco.com
SIC: 3565 Packaging machinery
PA: Sonoco Products Company
    1 N 2nd St
    Hartsville SC 29550
    843 383-7000

(P-8077)
PACKLINE TECHNOLOGIES INC
5929 Avenue 408, Dinuba (93618-9791)
P.O. Box 636, Kingsburg (93631-0636)
PHONE..................................559 591-3150
Lorin R Reed, *President*
Jim Moshier, *General Mgr*
Brent Willems, *Sales Staff*
EMP: 30
SALES (est): 9.7MM **Privately Held**
WEB: www.packlinetech.com
SIC: 3565 5084 Packaging machinery; packaging machinery & equipment

(P-8078)
SYSTEMS TECHNOLOGY INC
Also Called: Delaware Systems Technology
1350 Riverview Dr, San Bernardino (92408-2944)
PHONE..................................909 799-9950
David R Landon, *CEO*
John G Stjohn, *CEO*
Allyn Peterson, *Engineer*
▲ EMP: 65 EST: 1998
SQ FT: 43,000
SALES (est): 9.4MM **Privately Held**
WEB: www.systems-technology-inc.com
SIC: 3565 Packing & wrapping machinery

(P-8079)
UNITED BAKERY EQUIPMENT CO INC (PA)
Also Called: Hartman Slice Div
19216 S Laurel Park Rd, Rancho Dominguez (90220-6008)
PHONE..................................310 635-8121
Dulce Sohm, *CFO*
Mike Bastasch, *Executive*
Todd Edmunds, *CTO*
Johny Tusi, *Engineer*
Jeff Samoff, *Human Res Mgr*
◆ EMP: 99 EST: 1966
SALES (est): 19.1MM **Privately Held**
WEB: www.ubeusa.com
SIC: 3565 3556 Packaging machinery; bakery machinery

(P-8080)
VANOMATION INC
9241 Research Dr, Irvine (92618-4286)
PHONE..................................877 228-2992
Van Le, *CEO*
EMP: 22 EST: 2012
SQ FT: 1,200
SALES (est): 3MM **Privately Held**
WEB: www.vanomation.com
SIC: 3565 Packaging machinery

(P-8081)
W J ELLISON CO INC
Also Called: Pack West Machinery Co
200 River Rd, Corona (92878-1435)
PHONE..................................626 814-4766
William J Ellison, *President*
Janice K Ellison, *Vice Pres*

EMP: 42 EST: 1971
SQ FT: 20,000
SALES (est): 3.4MM Privately Held
WEB: www.packwest.com
SIC: 3565 Packaging machinery

3566 Speed Changers, Drives & Gears

(P-8082)
MARPLES GEARS INC
808 W Santa Anita Ave, San Gabriel
(91776-1017)
PHONE..................626 570-1744
James A Phillips IV, CEO
Jeff Goff, General Mgr
EMP: 23 EST: 1937
SQ FT: 5,000
SALES (est): 3.9MM Privately Held
WEB: www.marplesgears.com
SIC: 3566 Speed changers, drives & gears

3567 Indl Process Furnaces & Ovens

(P-8083)
AMARK INDUSTRIES INC (PA)
600 W Esplanade Ave, San Jacinto
(92583-4903)
PHONE..................951 654-7351
Pepper Renshaw, President
Gordon Moss, CFO
EMP: 36 EST: 1961
SALES (est): 9.4MM Privately Held
WEB: www.ramacorporation.com
SIC: 3567 Heating units & devices, industrial: electric

(P-8084)
ASC PROCESS SYSTEMS INC
28402 Livingston Ave, Valencia
(91355-4172)
PHONE..................818 833-0088
David C Mason, President
Dave Mason, President
Gudrun Mason, CFO
Tony Page, Managing Dir
Ty Vorwaller, General Mgr
◆ EMP: 250 EST: 1988
SQ FT: 41,000
SALES (est): 46.6MM Privately Held
WEB: www.aschome.com
SIC: 3567 3585 3563 7378 Industrial furnaces & ovens; heating & air conditioning combination units; vacuum pumps, except laboratory; computer peripheral equipment repair & maintenance; fabricated plate work (boiler shop)

(P-8085)
CALDESSO LLC
Also Called: Therm Core Products
439 S Stoddard Ave, San Bernardino
(92401-2025)
PHONE..................909 888-2882
Andrew Cameron, CEO
P Anthony Panico, COO
▲ EMP: 65 EST: 2010
SQ FT: 23,500
SALES (est): 5.6MM Privately Held
SIC: 5999 3567 Hot tub & spa chemicals, equipment & supplies; heating units & devices, industrial: electric

(P-8086)
CIRCLE INDUSTRIAL MFG CORP (PA)
Also Called: Cim Services
1613 W El Segundo Blvd, Compton
(90222-1024)
PHONE..................310 638-5101
Ronald M La Forest, President
Karen Forest, Treasurer
Karen La Forest, Treasurer
John La Forest, Vice Pres
EMP: 23 EST: 1953
SQ FT: 3,500

SALES (est): 5.1MM Privately Held
WEB: www.circleindustrial.com
SIC: 3567 3542 3535 3444 Industrial furnaces & ovens; sheet metalworking machines; conveyors & conveying equipment; sheet metalwork

(P-8087)
DELTA T THERMAL SOLUTIONS
8323 Loch Lomond Dr, Pico Rivera
(90660-2507)
PHONE..................800 928-5828
Cameron Jolly, Principal
EMP: 13 EST: 2010
SALES (est): 445K Privately Held
WEB: www.deltat.com
SIC: 3567 Heating units & devices, industrial: electric

(P-8088)
DICK FARRELL INDUSTRIES INC
Also Called: D.F. Industries
5071 Lindsay Ct, Chino (91710-5757)
PHONE..................909 613-9424
Timothy Farrell, Principal
Richard Farrell, Vice Pres
Lisa Van Den Berg, Admin Sec
▲ EMP: 17
SQ FT: 25,000
SALES (est): 4.3MM Privately Held
WEB: www.dickf.openfos.com
SIC: 3567 3312 7699 Industrial furnaces & ovens; ferroalloys, produced in blast furnaces; industrial machinery & equipment repair

(P-8089)
HEATER DESIGNS INC
2211 S Vista Ave, Bloomington
(92316-2921)
PHONE..................909 421-0971
James Fan, Chairman
Tom Odendahl, President
EMP: 30 EST: 1986
SQ FT: 14,500
SALES (est): 2.2MM Privately Held
WEB: www.heaterdesigns.com
SIC: 3567 Heating units & devices, industrial: electric

(P-8090)
INDUCTION TECHNOLOGY CORP
22060 Bear Valley Rd, Apple Valley
(92308-7209)
PHONE..................760 246-7333
Micahei T Dicken, President
Michael T Dicken, President
Marilyn Dicken, Admin Sec
Adam Estrada, Engineer
Tom Van Norman, Controller
EMP: 21 EST: 1979
SQ FT: 25,000
SALES (est): 4.7MM Privately Held
WEB: www.inductiontech.com
SIC: 3567 7699 Induction heating equipment; industrial machinery & equipment repair

(P-8091)
INDUSTRIAL PROCESS EQP INC
Also Called: I P E
1700 Industrial Ave, Norco (92860-2949)
PHONE..................714 447-0171
Michael J Waggoner, CEO
James Waggoner, President
Amanda Weller, Manager
▼ EMP: 16 EST: 1984
SQ FT: 30,220
SALES (est): 4.9MM Privately Held
SIC: 3567 Industrial furnaces & ovens

(P-8092)
JHAWAR INDUSTRIES LLC
Also Called: G-M Enterprises
525 Klug Cir, Corona (92878-5452)
PHONE..................951 340-4646
Suresh Jhawar, CEO
Paul Warg, CFO
Veena Jhawar, Exec VP
John Kemper, Engineer
John Talone, Sales Staff
▼ EMP: 41 EST: 1975
SQ FT: 50,000

SALES (est): 20MM Privately Held
SIC: 3567 Vacuum furnaces & ovens

(P-8093)
L C MILLER COMPANY
717 Monterey Pass Rd, Monterey Park
(91754-3606)
PHONE..................323 268-3611
Dolores Naimy, President
Dave Vito, COO
Victor De Lucia, Vice Pres
EMP: 27 EST: 1956
SQ FT: 14,000
SALES (est): 2.6MM Privately Held
WEB: www.lcmiller.com
SIC: 3567 3546 3625 3398 Heating units & devices, industrial: electric; saws & sawing equipment; industrial electrical relays & switches; metal heat treating

(P-8094)
LAVA HEAT ITALIA
940 W Washington Blvd, Los Angeles
(90015-3312)
PHONE..................310 559-1700
Zioni George, Principal
▲ EMP: 13 EST: 2013
SALES (est): 3.2MM Privately Held
WEB: www.lavaheat.com
SIC: 3567 Heating units & devices, industrial: electric

(P-8095)
LOCHABER CORNWALL INC
Also Called: Furnace Pros
675 N Eckhoff St Ste D, Orange
(92868-1000)
PHONE..................714 935-0302
James Clark, President
Katherine Clark, Treasurer
EMP: 13 EST: 2007
SALES (est): 1MM Privately Held
WEB: www.furnacepros.com
SIC: 3567 Electrical furnaces, ovens & heating devices, exc. induction

(P-8096)
PACIFIC KILN INSULATIONS INC
14370 Veterans Way, Moreno Valley
(92553-9058)
PHONE..................951 697-4422
Joel Fritz, President
▲ EMP: 30 EST: 1978
SQ FT: 10,000
SALES (est): 4.2MM Privately Held
WEB: www.pacifickiln.com
SIC: 3567 Fuel-fired furnaces & ovens

(P-8097)
RAMA CORPORATION
600 W Esplanade Ave, San Jacinto
(92583-4999)
PHONE..................951 654-7351
Peggy Renshaw, President
Marilyn Renshaw, Vice Pres
Michael Dailey, Administration
EMP: 45 EST: 1947
SQ FT: 25,000
SALES (est): 8.3MM
SALES (corp-wide): 9.4MM Privately Held
WEB: www.ramacorporation.com
SIC: 3567 3634 Heating units & devices, industrial: electric; electric housewares & fans
PA: Amark Industries, Inc.
600 W Esplanade Ave
San Jacinto CA 92583
951 654-7351

(P-8098)
SILQ TECHNOLOGIES CORPORATION
607 Charles E Young Dr E, Los Angeles
(90095)
PHONE..................310 806-9202
Jack Kavanaugh, CEO
EMP: 15 EST: 2018
SALES (est): 1MM Privately Held
WEB: www.hydrophilix.com
SIC: 3567 Metal melting furnaces, industrial: electric

(P-8099)
THERMTRONIX CORPORATION (PA)
17129 Muskrat Ave, Adelanto
(92301-2260)
P.O. Box 100 (92301-0100)
PHONE..................760 246-4500
Robert Nealon, President
Deborah Nealon, Admin Sec
▲ EMP: 21 EST: 1984
SQ FT: 12,000
SALES (est): 2.7MM Privately Held
WEB: www.thermtronix.com
SIC: 3567 Metal melting furnaces, industrial: electric

(P-8100)
TP SOLAR INC
Also Called: Tpsi
16310 Downey Ave, Paramount
(90723-5500)
PHONE..................562 808-2171
Alex Rey, President
Peter Ragay, Vice Pres
▼ EMP: 16 EST: 2005
SQ FT: 4,000
SALES (est): 1.1MM Privately Held
WEB: www.tpsifurnaces.com
SIC: 3567 Industrial furnaces & ovens

(P-8101)
W P KEITH CO INC
8323 Loch Lomond Dr, Pico Rivera
(90660-2588)
PHONE..................562 948-3636
Carol N Keith, CEO
Wendell P Keith Jr, President
Bernd Matzer, Engineer
Charlie Birks, Sales Mgr
Debbie Ennis, Assistant
▲ EMP: 25 EST: 1954
SQ FT: 19,200
SALES (est): 7.3MM Privately Held
WEB: www.keithcompany.com
SIC: 3567 Kilns; metal melting furnaces, industrial: fuel-fired; metal melting furnaces, industrial: electric

---

3568 Mechanical Power Transmission Eqpt, NEC

(P-8102)
ANACO INC
1001 El Camino Ave, Corona (92879-1756)
PHONE..................951 372-2732
Leon Nolen III, President
Jack Dunaway, Technical Staff
Tina Velasquez, Human Res Mgr
Lupe Lopez, Purch Mgr
Angelina Halverson, Sales Staff
▲ EMP: 140 EST: 1986
SALES (est): 41.3MM
SALES (corp-wide): 970.3MM Privately Held
WEB: www.anaco-husky.com
SIC: 3568 Couplings, shaft: rigid, flexible, universal joint, etc.
PA: Mcwane, Inc.
2900 Highway 280 S # 300
Birmingham AL 35223
205 414-3100

(P-8103)
ATR SALES INC
Also Called: Atra-Flex
110 E Garry Ave, Santa Ana (92707-4201)
PHONE..................714 432-8411
Jerry Hauck, CEO
Tom Arutunian, Shareholder
Raymond Hoyt, Corp Secy
Tony Hauck, Opers Staff
EMP: 26 EST: 1980
SQ FT: 12,000 Privately Held
WEB: www.atra-flex.com
SIC: 3568 Couplings, shaft: rigid, flexible, universal joint, etc.

(P-8104)
INDU-ELECTRIC NORTH AMER INC (PA)
27756 Avenue Hopkins, Valencia
(91355-1222)
PHONE..................310 578-2144

Martin Gerber, *CEO*
Robert Franco, *Warehouse Mgr*
▲ **EMP:** 47 **EST:** 2002
SQ FT: 11,000
SALES (est): 8.9MM **Privately Held**
WEB: www.indu-electric.com
SIC: 3568 5063 Power transmission equipment; power transmission equipment, electric

(P-8105)
INDUSTRIAL SPROCKETS GEARS INC
13650 Rosecrans Ave, Santa Fe Springs (90670-5025)
PHONE..................................323 233-7221
Max R Patridge, *CEO*
Mark Partridge, *Treasurer*
Monty Patridge, *Vice Pres*
Connie Patridge-Eason, *Admin Sec*
EMP: 21 **EST:** 1971
SQ FT: 18,000
SALES (est): 4.6MM **Privately Held**
WEB:
www.industrialsprocketsandgears.com
SIC: 3568 3566 3462 Drives, chains & sprockets; sprockets (power transmission equipment); drives, high speed industrial, except hydrostatic; iron & steel forgings

(P-8106)
PRECISION BABBITT CO INC
1007 S Whitemarsh Ave, Compton (90220-4439)
PHONE..................................562 531-9173
Michael Machala, *President*
EMP: 15 **EST:** 1969
SQ FT: 3,200
SALES (est): 859.3K **Privately Held**
WEB: www.precisionbabbitt.com
SIC: 3568 7699 Bearings, plain; rebabbitting

(P-8107)
REMANFCTURED CONVERTER MBL LLC
Also Called: Remanufactured Converter MBL
582 N Batavia St, Orange (92868-1219)
PHONE..................................714 744-8988
Desmond Tan,
Jeronimo Bustillos,
Gustavo Magana,
EMP: 19 **EST:** 1998
SQ FT: 7,000
SALES (est): 1.2MM **Privately Held**
SIC: 3568 Chain, power transmission

(P-8108)
REXNORD INDUSTRIES LLC
14650 Miller Ave, Fontana (92336-1694)
PHONE..................................814 969-3665
EMP: 16 **EST:** 2006
SALES (est): 184.6K **Privately Held**
WEB: www.rexnord.com
SIC: 3568 Couplings, shaft: rigid, flexible, universal joint, etc.

(P-8109)
RNOVATE INC
Also Called: Rnc
834 S Broadway, Los Angeles (90014-3501)
PHONE..................................213 489-1617
John Parros, *CEO*
▲ **EMP:** 18 **EST:** 1990
SQ FT: 20,000
SALES (est): 573.6K **Privately Held**
WEB: www.rnovate.com
SIC: 3568 Belting, chain

(P-8110)
WEST COAST YAMAHA INC
Also Called: West Coast Motor Sports
1622 Illinois Ave, Perris (92571-9374)
PHONE..................................951 943-2061
Gerald Morris Langston, *CEO*
Margret McKinley, *Corp Secy*
EMP: 25 **EST:** 1998
SALES (est): 2.3MM **Privately Held**
WEB: www.yamaha.com
SIC: 3568 5571 5561 Power transmission equipment; motorcycle dealers; recreational vehicle dealers

3569 Indl Machinery & Eqpt, NEC

(P-8111)
AKM FIRE INC
18322 Oxnard St, Tarzana (91356-1502)
PHONE..................................818 343-8208
Yaakov Azran, *President*
Mary Azran, *Admin Sec*
EMP: 14 **EST:** 2004
SALES (est): 2.1MM **Privately Held**
SIC: 3569 1711 Sprinkler systems, fire: automatic; fire sprinkler system installation

(P-8112)
AVX FILTERS CORPORATION
11144 Penrose St Ste 7, Sun Valley (91352-2756)
PHONE..................................818 767-6770
John Gilbertson, *President*
Linda Shoemake, *Executive*
Jody Jeppson, *Cust Mgr*
▲ **EMP:** 90 **EST:** 1981
SQ FT: 25,000
SALES (est): 14.7MM **Privately Held**
WEB: www.avx.com
SIC: 3569 3675 Filters; electronic capacitors
HQ: Kyocera Avx Components Corporation
1 Avx Blvd
Fountain Inn SC 29644
864 967-2150

(P-8113)
CAPTIVE OCEAN REEF ENTPS INC (PA)
1011 S Linwood Ave, Santa Ana (92705-4323)
PHONE..................................714 543-4100
Leng Sy, *Principal*
EMP: 63 **EST:** 2015
SALES (est): 116.4K **Privately Held**
SIC: 3569 General industrial machinery

(P-8114)
CHAD INDUSTRIES INCORPORATED
1565 S Sinclair St, Anaheim (92806-5934)
PHONE..................................714 938-0080
Scott W Klimczak, *President*
Wayne Rapp, *Admin Sec*
▲ **EMP:** 40 **EST:** 1973
SQ FT: 31,000
SALES (est): 5.1MM **Privately Held**
WEB: www.jabil.com
SIC: 3569 Robots, assembly line: industrial & commercial

(P-8115)
CLAYTON MANUFACTURING COMPANY (PA)
Also Called: Clayton Industries
17477 Hurley St, City of Industry (91744-5106)
PHONE..................................626 443-9381
John Clayton, *President*
Alexander Smirnoff, *CFO*
Boyd A Calvin, *Senior VP*
Allen L Cluer, *Vice Pres*
Phyllis Nielson, *Vice Pres*
▲ **EMP:** 147 **EST:** 1930
SQ FT: 215,000
SALES (est): 88.1MM **Privately Held**
WEB: www.claytonindustries.com
SIC: 3569 3829 3511 Generators: steam, liquid oxygen or nitrogen; dynamometer instruments; turbines & turbine generator sets

(P-8116)
CLAYTON MANUFACTURING INC (HQ)
17477 Hurley St, City of Industry (91744-5106)
PHONE..................................626 443-9381
William Clayton Jr, *CEO*
John Clayton, *President*
Boyd A Calvin, *Treasurer*
Allen L Cluer, *Vice Pres*
Tim Pressley, *Manager*
▼ **EMP:** 80 **EST:** 1930
SQ FT: 215,000

SALES (est): 24MM
SALES (corp-wide): 88.1MM **Privately Held**
WEB: www.claytonindustries.com
SIC: 3569 3829 Generators: steam, liquid oxygen or nitrogen; dynamometer instruments
PA: Clayton Manufacturing Company
17477 Hurley St
City Of Industry CA 91744
626 443-9381

(P-8117)
CLOUD COMPANY (PA)
4855 Morabito Pl, San Luis Obispo (93401-8748)
PHONE..................................805 549-8093
James H Rucker, *Ch of Bd*
David L Rucker, *President*
Mike Kemp, *Executive*
Karen Rucker, *Admin Sec*
Seanah Muindi, *Data Proc Staff*
EMP: 24 **EST:** 1954
SQ FT: 7,000
SALES (est): 2.9MM **Privately Held**
WEB: www.tankcleaningmachines.com
SIC: 3569 Liquid automation machinery & equipment

(P-8118)
CODE-IN-MOTION LLC
1307 Calle Avanzado, San Clemente (92673-6351)
PHONE..................................949 361-2633
Jovan Zivkovic,
Mani Arbabi, *Administration*
Wally Popovich, *Purch Mgr*
Hubert Schroeder, *VP Sales*
Dan Popovich,
EMP: 15 **EST:** 2004
SALES (est): 4.1MM **Privately Held**
WEB: www.code-in-motion.com
SIC: 3569 3565 Robots, assembly line: industrial & commercial; labeling machines, industrial

(P-8119)
DELTA TAU DATA SYSTEMS INC CAL (HQ)
Also Called: Omron Delta Tau
9200 Oakdale Ave Fl 9, Chatsworth (91311-6506)
PHONE..................................818 998-2095
Yasuto Ikuta, *President*
Tamara Dimitri, *Treasurer*
Steve Fierro, *Engineer*
Akira Ohmori, *Engineer*
Sina Sattari, *Chief Engr*
EMP: 129 **EST:** 1976
SALES (est): 45MM **Privately Held**
WEB: www.automation.omron.com
SIC: 3569 7372 3625 3577 Robots, assembly line: industrial & commercial; prepackaged software; relays & industrial controls; computer peripheral equipment

(P-8120)
DESCHNER CORPORATION
3211 W Harvard St, Santa Ana (92704-3976)
PHONE..................................714 557-1261
Joe Alessi, *President*
Toby Ryan, *CEO*
Frank Solis, *CFO*
EMP: 26 **EST:** 1958
SQ FT: 21,600
SALES (est): 2MM **Privately Held**
WEB: www.deschner.com
SIC: 3569 3594 Liquid automation machinery & equipment; fluid power pumps & motors

(P-8121)
ENTEGRIS GP INC
4175 Santa Fe Rd, San Luis Obispo (93401-8159)
PHONE..................................805 541-9299
Bertrand Loy, *President*
◆ **EMP:** 130 **EST:** 1975
SQ FT: 50,000
SALES (est): 47.1MM
SALES (corp-wide): 1.8B **Publicly Held**
WEB: www.entegris.com
SIC: 3569 Gas producers, generators & other gas related equipment

PA: Entegris, Inc.
129 Concord Rd
Billerica MA 01821
978 436-6500

(P-8122)
FIREBLAST GLOBAL INC
545 Monica Cir, Corona (92878-5447)
PHONE..................................951 277-8319
Richard Egelin, *CEO*
Rick Egelin, *Director*
EMP: 25 **EST:** 2000
SALES (est): 6.3MM **Privately Held**
WEB: www.fireblast.com
SIC: 3569 8711 Firefighting apparatus; engineering services

(P-8123)
FIREQUICK PRODUCTS INC
1137 Red Rock Inyokern Rd, Inyokern (93527)
P.O. Box 910 (93527-0910)
PHONE..................................760 371-4279
Beth Sumners, *President*
Beth J Sumners, *President*
Bill Sumners, *Vice Pres*
EMP: 20 **EST:** 2004
SALES (est): 1.3MM **Privately Held**
WEB: www.firequick.com
SIC: 3569 Firefighting apparatus & related equipment

(P-8124)
HONEYBEE ROBOTICS LTD
2408 Lincoln Ave, Altadena (91001-5436)
PHONE..................................303 774-7613
EMP: 42
SALES (corp-wide): 696.3MM **Privately Held**
WEB: www.honeybeerobotics.com
SIC: 3569 Filters
HQ: Honeybee Robotics, Ltd.
Ste 121 63 F Bldg 128
Brooklyn NY 11205
212 966-0661

(P-8125)
HONEYBEE ROBOTICS LTD
398 W Washington Blvd, Pasadena (91103-2000)
PHONE..................................510 207-4555
Stephen Gorvan, *Branch Mgr*
William Cervantes, *Projec Engr*
Dean Bergman, *Director*
EMP: 42
SALES (corp-wide): 696.3MM **Privately Held**
WEB: www.honeybeerobotics.com
SIC: 3569 Filters
HQ: Honeybee Robotics, Ltd.
Ste 121 63 F Bldg 128
Brooklyn NY 11205
212 966-0661

(P-8126)
JEREMYWELL INTERNATIONAL INC
14 Vanderbilt, Irvine (92618-2010)
PHONE..................................949 588-6888
Stephanie Chang, *Principal*
▲ **EMP:** 17 **EST:** 2013
SALES (est): 4.6MM **Privately Held**
WEB: www.jeremywellindustry.com
SIC: 3569 General industrial machinery
PA: Hangzhou Fuhua Co., Ltd.
181, Fengqi Road
Hangzhou

(P-8127)
KNIGHT LLC (HQ)
15340 Barranca Pkwy, Irvine (92618-2215)
PHONE..................................949 595-4800
George Noa, *President*
Richard Yanez, *Vice Pres*
Rick Yanez, *Vice Pres*
Chris March, *Regl Sales Mgr*
Charles Sarno,
▲ **EMP:** 100 **EST:** 1972
SQ FT: 46,000

SALES (est): 28.8MM
SALES (corp-wide): 2.3B **Publicly Held**
WEB: www.knightequip.com
SIC: 3569 3582 3589 Liquid automation machinery & equipment; commercial laundry equipment; dishwashing machines, commercial
PA: Idex Corporation
3100 Sanders Rd Ste 301
Northbrook IL 60062
847 498-7070

(P-8128)
LUBRICATION SCIENTIFICS LLC
17651 Armstrong Ave, Irvine (92614-5727)
PHONE.................................714 557-0664
Richard Hanley, *Mng Member*
Christopher Longnecker, *Opers Staff*
James Schoen, *Marketing Mgr*
EMP: 48 **EST:** 2014
SALES (est): 7.1MM **Privately Held**
WEB: www.lubricationscientifics.com
SIC: 3569 Lubricating equipment

(P-8129)
MAHMOOD IZADI INC
Also Called: Solatron Enterprises
3115 Lomita Blvd, Torrance (90505-5108)
PHONE.................................310 325-0463
Mahmood Izadi, *President*
EMP: 15 **EST:** 1962
SQ FT: 9,500
SALES (est): 1.6MM **Privately Held**
WEB: www.solatron.com
SIC: 3569 Assembly machines, non-metalworking; testing chambers for altitude, temperature, ordnance, power

(P-8130)
MYERS MIXERS LLC
8376 Salt Lake Ave, Cudahy (90201-5817)
PHONE.................................323 560-4723
Gary Myers,
Cary Buller,
EMP: 41 **EST:** 2014
SALES (est): 4.3MM **Privately Held**
WEB: www.myersmixers.com
SIC: 3569 Centrifuges, industrial

(P-8131)
NATIONAL FILTER MEDIA CORP
17130 Muskrat Ave Ste B, Adelanto (92301-2473)
PHONE.................................760 246-4551
EMP: 52
SALES (corp-wide): 658.7MM **Privately Held**
SIC: 3569 Mfg General Industrial Machinery
HQ: The National Filter Media Corporation
691 N 400 W
Salt Lake City UT 84103
801 363-6736

(P-8132)
ONEX ENTERPRISES CORPORATION
Also Called: Onex Automation
1824 Flower Ave, Duarte (91010-2931)
PHONE.................................626 358-6639
Onik Bogosyan, *President*
Edwin Thomassien, *CFO*
▲ **EMP:** 16 **EST:** 1991
SALES (est): 2.7MM **Privately Held**
WEB: www.onexrf.com
SIC: 3569 5084 Robots, assembly line: industrial & commercial; robots, industrial

(P-8133)
PACIFIC CONSOLIDATED INDS LLC
Also Called: PCI
12201 Magnolia Ave, Riverside (92503-4820)
PHONE.................................951 479-0860
Bob Eng, *Mng Member*
Andy Barrs, *Managing Prtnr*
Paul Stevens, *CFO*
Tarik Naheiri, *Vice Pres*
Soeren Schmitz, *Vice Pres*
◆ **EMP:** 77 **EST:** 2003
SQ FT: 85,000
SALES (est): 29.1MM **Privately Held**
WEB: www.pcigases.com
SIC: 3569 1382 Gas separators (machinery); oil & gas exploration services

PA: Pci Holding Company, Inc.
12201 Magnolia Ave
Riverside CA 92503
951 479-0860

(P-8134)
PC VAUGHAN MFG CORP
Also Called: Rostar Filters
1278 Mercantile St, Oxnard (93030-7522)
PHONE.................................805 278-2555
Jeff Starin, *President*
Steve Day, *Opers Mgr*
EMP: 141 **EST:** 1979
SQ FT: 40,000
SALES (est): 13.2MM **Privately Held**
WEB: www.rostarfilters.com
SIC: 3569 Filters

(P-8135)
PCI HOLDING COMPANY INC (PA)
12201 Magnolia Ave, Riverside (92503-4820)
PHONE.................................951 479-0860
Bob Eng, *CEO*
Tarik Naheiri, *President*
EMP: 14 **EST:** 2012
SALES (est): 29.1MM **Privately Held**
WEB: www.pcigases.com
SIC: 3569 1382 Gas separators (machinery); oil & gas exploration services

(P-8136)
PHENIX TECHNOLOGY CORPORATION
3453 Durahart St, Riverside (92507-3452)
PHONE.................................951 272-4938
Raymond Russell, *President*
Nicole Clesceri, *CFO*
Shaun Russell, *Natl Sales Mgr*
Jessica Jimenez, *Sales Staff*
EMP: 24 **EST:** 1971
SALES (est): 4.2MM **Privately Held**
WEB: www.phenixfirehelmets.com
SIC: 3569 Firefighting apparatus & related equipment

(P-8137)
POLLEY INC (PA)
Also Called: Kelco Sales & Engineering
11936 Front St, Norwalk (90650-2911)
P.O. Box 305 (90651-0305)
PHONE.................................562 868-9861
Tracy Polley, *President*
Martin Blake, *Office Mgr*
Nyals Polley, *VP Prdtn*
Gay Blake, *Clerk*
▲ **EMP:** 19 **EST:** 1950
SQ FT: 24,000
SALES (est): 2.7MM **Privately Held**
WEB: www.wheelblast.com
SIC: 3569 5084 Assembly machines, non-metalworking; industrial machinery & equipment

(P-8138)
SENJU FIRE PROTECTION CORP
Also Called: Senju Sprinkler
30 Muller Ste 112, Irvine (92618-4679)
PHONE.................................949 333-1281
Mitsuhiro Uchimura, *President*
▲ **EMP:** 16 **EST:** 2015
SALES (est): 4.4MM **Privately Held**
SIC: 3569 Sprinkler systems, fire: automatic

(P-8139)
SPINTEK FILTRATION INC
10863 Portal Dr, Los Alamitos (90720-2508)
PHONE.................................714 236-9190
William A Greene, *CEO*
Patricia Kirk, *Vice Pres*
Jason D Gilmour, *Engineer*
Gigi Gonzalez, *Buyer*
Justin Rodriguez, *Marketing Staff*
◆ **EMP:** 15
SQ FT: 3,000
SALES (est): 3.7MM **Privately Held**
WEB: www.spintek.com
SIC: 3569 3069 8711 Filters & strainers, pipeline; roofing, membrane rubber; engineering services

(P-8140)
STEARNS PRODUCT DEV CORP (PA)
Also Called: Doughpro
20281 Harvill Ave, Perris (92570-7235)
PHONE.................................951 657-0379
Steven Raio, *President*
Caroline De Jong, *Admin Mgr*
Brian Raines, *Engineer*
Tommy Srioudom, *Engineer*
Debra Ludolph, *Controller*
▲ **EMP:** 91 **EST:** 1971
SQ FT: 50,000
SALES (est): 12MM **Privately Held**
WEB: www.proluxe.com
SIC: 3569 3444 Assembly machines, non-metalworking; sheet metalwork

(P-8141)
WALIN GROUP INC
Also Called: Brilliant AV
2950 Grace Ln Ste C, Costa Mesa (92626-4170)
P.O. Box 2074, Orange (92859-0074)
PHONE.................................714 444-5980
Matthew James Walin, *CEO*
Steve Stary, *Exec VP*
Brian Beach, *Project Mgr*
Siobahn Haut, *Human Res Dir*
EMP: 15 **EST:** 2011
SALES (est): 6MM **Privately Held**
WEB: www.brilliantav.com
SIC: 3569 3699 3645 3651 Liquid automation machinery & equipment; security devices; security control equipment & systems; residential lighting fixtures; home entertainment equipment, electronic

(P-8142)
WASSER FILTRATION INC (PA)
Also Called: Pacific Press
1215 N Fee Ana St, Anaheim (92807-1804)
PHONE.................................714 696-6450
Sean Duby, *President*
Daren Berk, *Project Mgr*
▲ **EMP:** 80
SQ FT: 20,000
SALES (est): 16.6MM **Privately Held**
WEB: www.pacpress.com
SIC: 3569 5084 Filters, general line: industrial; filters & strainers, pipeline; industrial machinery & equipment

(P-8143)
WATER FILTER EXCHANGE INC
Also Called: American Filter Company
875 N Todd Ave, Azusa (91702-2224)
PHONE.................................818 808-2541
Alex Chividian, *CEO*
Mireille Chividian, *CEO*
EMP: 16 **EST:** 2010
SQ FT: 5,000
SALES (est): 1.7MM **Privately Held**
SIC: 3569 5999 Filters; filters, general line: industrial; water purification equipment

---

3571 Electronic Computers

(P-8144)
A S A ENGINEERING INC
Also Called: Micro Express
8 Hammond Ste 105, Irvine (92618-1601)
PHONE.................................949 460-9911
Art Afshar, *President*
K C Shabak, *Vice Pres*
◆ **EMP:** 17 **EST:** 1986
SQ FT: 2,000
SALES (est): 1.1MM **Privately Held**
SIC: 3571 5963 Personal computers (microcomputers); direct selling establishments

(P-8145)
ACME PORTABLE MACHINES INC
1330 Mountain View Cir, Azusa (91702-1648)
PHONE.................................626 610-1888
James Cheng, *President*
Jay Hwang, *COO*
Myles Kelvin, *General Mgr*
Martin Yen, *General Mgr*

Chih Kuo, *Mktg Dir*
▲ **EMP:** 30 **EST:** 1994
SQ FT: 12,200
SALES (est): 7.2MM **Privately Held**
WEB: www.acmeportable.com
SIC: 3571 Electronic computers

(P-8146)
ADVANCED KEYBOARD TECH INC
Also Called: Akt
2501 Golden Hill Rd # 200, Paso Robles (93446-6391)
PHONE.................................805 237-2055
Joel Stark, *President*
Jeffrey C Stark, *Vice Pres*
EMP: 16 **EST:** 1998
SQ FT: 2,000
SALES (est): 514K **Privately Held**
SIC: 3571 Electronic computers

(P-8147)
ALLHEALTH
515 S Figueroa St # 1300, Los Angeles (90071-3301)
PHONE.................................213 538-0762
John R Cochran, *CEO*
EMP: 18 **EST:** 1998
SALES (est): 1.4MM **Privately Held**
WEB: www.allhealthinc.com
SIC: 3571 7381 Electronic computers; security guard service

(P-8148)
AMERICAN RELIANCE INC
Also Called: Amrel
789 N Fair Oaks Ave, Pasadena (91103-3045)
PHONE.................................626 443-6818
Edward Chen, *CEO*
Kalvin Chen, *Vice Pres*
Shelly Chen, *Admin Sec*
Ed Chen, *Personnel*
Michelle Chen, *Purch Mgr*
▲ **EMP:** 45 **EST:** 1985
SALES (est): 10.2MM **Privately Held**
WEB: www.amrel.com
SIC: 3571 Electronic computers

(P-8149)
APPLE TREE INTERNATIONAL CORP
10700 Business Dr, Fontana (92337-8201)
PHONE.................................626 679-7025
Min Xiao, *CEO*
EMP: 24 **EST:** 2014
SQ FT: 170,000
SALES (est): 5.5MM **Privately Held**
SIC: 3571 Electronic computers

(P-8150)
CEMTROL INC
3035 E La Jolla St, Anaheim (92806-1303)
PHONE.................................714 666-6606
Sharon Paz, *President*
Steve Smith, *Design Engr*
Stephen Cheng, *Engineer*
Samuel Paz, *Engineer*
Dimitri Droulias, *Prdtn Mgr*
EMP: 15 **EST:** 2010
SALES (est): 3.3MM **Privately Held**
WEB: www.cemtrol.com
SIC: 3571 Electronic computers

(P-8151)
CENTENT COMPANY
3879 S Main St, Santa Ana (92707-5787)
PHONE.................................714 979-6491
August Freimanis, *Partner*
Mariss Freimanis, *Partner*
Josh Dieterich, *Managing Dir*
Leonids Freimanis, *General Mgr*
Luke Freimanis, *General Mgr*
EMP: 15 **EST:** 1972
SQ FT: 2,500
SALES (est): 1.2MM **Privately Held**
WEB: www.centent.com
SIC: 3571 5063 Computers, digital, analog or hybrid; electrical apparatus & equipment

(P-8152)
CYBERNET MANUFACTURING INC
5 Holland Ste 201, Irvine (92618-2574)
PHONE...................................949 600-8000
Pouran Shoaee, *CEO*
Michael Scott, *Technical Staff*
Jeff Salem, *Purch Dir*
Joe Divino, *VP Mktg*
Tina Jo Wentz, *Marketing Staff*
◆ EMP: 720 EST: 1996
SALES (est): 70.6MM Privately Held
WEB: www.cybernetman.com
SIC: 3571 3577 Electronic computers;
computer peripheral equipment

(P-8153)
DYNABOOK AMERICAS INC (HQ)
5241 California Ave # 100, Irvine
(92617-3052)
PHONE...................................949 583-3000
Ikuaki Takayama, *President*
James Robbins, *President*
Lisa Allen, *Vice Pres*
Takayuki Tono, *Vice Pres*
Eric Paulsen, *Marketing Staff*
EMP: 298 EST: 2018
SALES (est): 51.4MM Privately Held
WEB: www.us.dynabook.com
SIC: 3571 Electronic computers

(P-8154)
EDGE SOLUTIONS CONSULTING INC (PA)
5126 Clareton Dr Ste 160, Agoura Hills
(91301-4529)
P.O. Box 661480, Arcadia (91066-1480)
PHONE...................................818 591-3500
Marti Reeder, *President*
Marti R Hedge, *President*
Jeremy Johnson, *VP Bus Dvlpt*
Kathy Valencia, *Principal*
Kailee Holt, *Business Anlyst*
EMP: 60 EST: 1999
SQ FT: 600
SALES (est): 17.6MM Privately Held
WEB:
www.edgesolutionsandconsulting.com
SIC: 3571 Mainframe computers

(P-8155)
GARNER HOLT PRODUCTIONS INC
1255 Research Dr, Redlands (92374-4541)
PHONE...................................909 799-3030
Garner L Holt, *President*
Andrew Garner, *Partner*
Michelle Berg, *Vice Pres*
Eduardo Medina, *Technician*
Victor Martin, *Project Mgr*
EMP: 50 EST: 1977
SQ FT: 50,000
SALES (est): 12.3MM Privately Held
WEB: www.garnerholt.com
SIC: 3571 Electronic computers

(P-8156)
GATEWAY INC (DH)
7565 Irvine Center Dr # 150, Irvine
(92618-4933)
PHONE...................................949 471-7000
Ed Coleman, *CEO*
Bradly Shaw, *President*
John Goldsberry, *CFO*
Craig Calle, *Treasurer*
Michael R Tyler, *Senior VP*
◆ EMP: 250 EST: 1985
SQ FT: 98,000
SALES (est): 495.5MM Privately Held
WEB: www.gway.org
SIC: 3571 3577 Personal computers (mi-
crocomputers); computer peripheral
equipment

(P-8157)
GATEWAY US RETAIL INC
7565 Irvine Center Dr, Irvine (92618-4918)
PHONE...................................949 471-7000
Wayne R Inouye, *President*
Brian Firestone, *Exec VP*
▲ EMP: 67 EST: 1998
SQ FT: 147,000

SALES (est): 9.9MM Privately Held
WEB: www.gway.org
SIC: 3571 3577 5045 Electronic computers; computer peripheral equipment; computers, peripherals & software
HQ: Gateway, Inc.
7565 Irvine Center Dr # 150
Irvine CA 92618
949 471-7000

(P-8158)
I/O MAGIC CORPORATION
4 Marconi, Irvine (92618-2525)
PHONE...................................949 707-4800
Tony Shahbaz, *CEO*
Steve Gillings, *CFO*
Hamie Harardi, *Purch Mgr*
EMP: 15 EST: 2000
SALES (est): 407.7K Privately Held
WEB: www.iomagic.com
SIC: 3571 3652 Computers, digital, analog
or hybrid; compact laser discs, prere-
corded

(P-8159)
INDUSTRIAL CPU SYSTE
111 W Dyer Rd Ste D, Santa Ana
(92707-3425)
P.O. Box 93445, Los Angeles (90093-0445)
PHONE...................................714 957-2815
Mehrdad Ayati, *Principal*
EMP: 14 EST: 2001
SALES (est): 655.6K Privately Held
WEB: www.icpu.com
SIC: 3571 Electronic computers

(P-8160)
INDUSTRIAL CPU SYSTEMS INTL
Also Called: Icpu
2225 S Grand Ave, Santa Ana
(92705-5235)
P.O. Box 93445, Los Angeles (90093-0445)
PHONE...................................714 957-2815
Mehrdad Ayati, *President*
EMP: 13 EST: 1990
SQ FT: 7,000
SALES (est): 471.8K Privately Held
SIC: 3571 7371 Electronic computers;
computer software systems analysis &
design, custom

(P-8161)
INNERS TASKS LLC
Also Called: Remstek Corp
27708 Jefferson Ave # 201, Temecula
(92590-2641)
PHONE...................................951 225-9696
Jason Patrick, *Mng Member*
James Stewart, *Mng Member*
Ryan Wetmore, *Mng Member*
EMP: 38 EST: 2015
SALES (est): 1.9MM Privately Held
SIC: 3571 Electronic computers

(P-8162)
INTERNATIONAL BUS MCHS CORP
Also Called: IBM
400 N Brand Blvd Fl 7, Glendale
(91203-2364)
PHONE...................................818 553-8100
Stephen Akuginow, *Technology*
Winnifer Jefferson, *Manager*
Pete Densmore, *Consultant*
EMP: 700
SALES (corp-wide): 73.6B Publicly Held
WEB: www.ibm.com
SIC: 3571 Minicomputers
PA: International Business Machines Cor-
poration
1 New Orchard Rd Ste 1 # 1
Armonk NY 10504
914 499-1900

(P-8163)
ISTARUSA GROUP
727 Phillips, Rowland Heights
(91748-1147)
PHONE...................................888 989-1189
Kuo An Wang, *CEO*
EMP: 23 EST: 2020
SALES (est): 2.4MM Privately Held
SIC: 3571 Electronic computers

(P-8164)
MAGNELL ASSOCIATE INC
Also Called: Newegg.com
17708 Rowland St, City of Industry
(91748-1119)
PHONE...................................626 271-1320
Fred Chang, *President*
EMP: 48
SALES (corp-wide): 2.2B Privately Held
WEB: www.abs.com
SIC: 3571 5961 5045 Personal comput-
ers (microcomputers); computers & pe-
ripheral equipment, mail order;
computers, peripherals & software
HQ: Magnell Associate, Inc.
17560 Rowland St
City Of Industry CA 91748

(P-8165)
MC2 SABTECH HOLDINGS INC
Also Called: Ixi Technology
22705 Savi Ranch Pkwy, Yorba Linda
(92887-4604)
PHONE...................................714 221-5000
Michael Carter, *CEO*
Thomas Bell, *CFO*
Carl Wallace, *Officer*
Jeff Norris, *Engineer*
Bryan Pippins, *Engineer*
EMP: 40 EST: 1984
SQ FT: 40,000
SALES (est): 15.3MM Privately Held
SIC: 3571 3672 Electronic computers;
printed circuit boards

(P-8166)
MEDIATEK USA INC
1 Ada Ste 200, Irvine (92618-5341)
PHONE...................................408 526-1899
EMP: 33
SALES (corp-wide): 13MM Privately
Held
WEB: www.mediatek.com
SIC: 3571 3674 Electronic computers;
semiconductors & related devices
PA: Mediatek Usa Inc.
2840 Junction Ave
San Jose CA 95134
408 526-1899

(P-8167)
MICRO/SYS INC
158 W Pomona Ave, Monrovia
(91016-4558)
PHONE...................................818 244-4600
Susan Wooley, *President*
James K Finster, *Vice Pres*
EMP: 30 EST: 1976
SALES (est): 3.5MM Privately Held
WEB: www.embeddedsys.com
SIC: 3571 3674 Electronic computers;
semiconductors & related devices

(P-8168)
MYRICOM INC
3871 E Colo Blvd Ste 101, Pasadena
(91107)
PHONE...................................626 821-5555
Nanette Boden, *President*
Robert Henigson, *Ch of Bd*
Rick Patton, *CFO*
Mike McPherson, *Vice Pres*
Dave Brandt, *Production*
◆ EMP: 23 EST: 1994
SQ FT: 17,000
SALES (est): 1.3MM Privately Held
WEB: www.cspi.com
SIC: 3571 Electronic computers

(P-8169)
ORANGE LOGIC LLC (PA)
19100 Von Karman Ave # 900, Irvine
(92612-6597)
PHONE...................................949 396-2233
Charles Facredyn,
Will Strain, *Project Mgr*
Bianca Ragsdale, *Technical Staff*
Barbara Frye, *Human Resources*
Eric Jochim, *Marketing Staff*
EMP: 63 EST: 2012
SALES (est): 8.2MM Privately Held
WEB: www.orangelogic.com
SIC: 3571 Electronic computers

(P-8170)
PREMIO INC (PA)
918 Radecki Ct, City of Industry
(91748-1132)
PHONE...................................626 839-3100
Crystal Tsao, *CEO*
Tom Tsao, *President*
John Lam, *Vice Pres*
Wai Lee, *Executive*
Ken Szeto, *General Mgr*
▲ EMP: 120 EST: 1989
SQ FT: 140,000
SALES: 41.5MM Privately Held
WEB: www.premioinc.com
SIC: 3571 7373 7378 Personal comput-
ers (microcomputers); computer inte-
grated systems design; computer
maintenance & repair

(P-8171)
PSITECH INC
18368 Bandilier Cir, Fountain Valley
(92708-7001)
PHONE...................................714 964-7818
John T Kerr, *Ch of Bd*
John S Kerr, *Shareholder*
EMP: 18 EST: 1980
SQ FT: 6,000
SALES (est): 1MM Privately Held
WEB: www.psitech.com
SIC: 3571 3577 Personal computers (mi-
crocomputers); computer peripheral
equipment

(P-8172)
RNBS CORPORATION
Also Called: Rugged Notebooks
725 S Paseo Prado, Anaheim
(92807-4949)
PHONE...................................714 998-1828
Alan Shad, *President*
Paul Valles, *Executive*
EMP: 20 EST: 2000
SALES (est): 4.4MM Privately Held
SIC: 5961 3571 Computers & peripheral
equipment, mail order; electronic comput-
ers; computers, digital, analog or hybrid

(P-8173)
ROSEWILL INC
17560 Rowland St, City of Industry
(91748-1114)
PHONE...................................800 575-9885
EMP: 643
SALES (corp-wide): 2.2B Privately Held
WEB: www.rosewill.com
SIC: 3571 5045 Electronic computers;
computers, peripherals & software
HQ: Rosewill, Inc.
17708 Rowland St
City Of Industry CA 91748

(P-8174)
S E P E INC
Also Called: Fax Star
245 Fischer Ave Ste C4, Costa Mesa
(92626-4538)
PHONE...................................714 241-7373
Michel J Remion, *President*
Patty King, *Admin Sec*
EMP: 32 EST: 1984
SQ FT: 5,000
SALES (est): 595.2K Privately Held
WEB: www.faxstar.com
SIC: 3571 7371 4822 Electronic comput-
ers; computer software development; fac-
simile transmission services

(P-8175)
SOLARFLARE COMMUNICATIONS INC (PA)
7505 Irvine Center Dr, Irvine (92618-2991)
PHONE...................................949 581-6830
Russell Stern, *President*
David Parry, *President*
Mary Jane Abalos, *CFO*
John Hamm, *Bd of Directors*
Andre Chartrand, *Vice Pres*
EMP: 97 EST: 2001
SQ FT: 22,097
SALES (est): 55.5MM Privately Held
WEB: www.xilinx.com
SIC: 3571 Electronic computers

(P-8176)
SOURCE CODE LLC
Also Called: Aberdeen
9808 Alburtis Ave, Santa Fe Springs
(90670-3208)
PHONE..................562 903-1500
EMP: 48 **Privately Held**
WEB: www.sourcecode.com
SIC: **3571 3572** Electronic computers;
computer storage devices
PA: Source Code, Llc
232 Vanderbilt Ave
Norwood MA 02062

(P-8177)
SYNERGY MICROSYSTEMS INC
(DH)
28965 Avenue Penn, Valencia
(91355-4185)
PHONE..................858 452-0020
Chris Wiltsey, *Director*
EMP: 70 EST: 1985
SALES (est): 22.4MM
SALES (corp-wide): 2.3B **Publicly Held**
WEB: www.curtisswright.com
SIC: **3571** Computers, digital, analog or
hybrid
HQ: Curtiss-Wright Controls, Inc.
15801 Brixham Hill Ave # 200
Charlotte NC 28277
704 869-4600

(P-8178)
TOSHIBA AMER INFO SYSTEMS
INC
225 Sonoma Aisle, Irvine (92618-3908)
PHONE..................949 300-9435
Akitsugu Nonaka, *President*
CHI Le, *IT/INT Sup*
Don Hanson, *Engineer*
Yasushi Kawakura, *Manager*
EMP: 67 **Privately Held**
WEB: www.toshibaproductregistration.com
SIC: **3571 3577 3861** Electronic comput-
ers; computer peripheral equipment; pho-
tocopy machines
HQ: Toshiba America Information Systems,
Inc.
1251 Ave Of The Amrcas St
New York NY 10020
949 583-3000

(P-8179)
TOSHIBA AMER INFO SYSTEMS
INC
9740 Irvine Blvd Fl 1, Irvine (92618-1651)
PHONE..................949 583-3000
Bill Goodwin, *Manager*
Kensuke Kani, *Vice Pres*
Lee Smith, *Planning*
George Dyer, *Project Mgr*
Maciek Brzeski, *VP Mktg*
EMP: 120 **Privately Held**
WEB: www.toshibaproductregistration.com
SIC: **3571** Electronic computers
HQ: Toshiba America Information Systems,
Inc.
1251 Ave Of The Amrcas St
New York NY 10020
949 583-3000

(P-8180)
UNITEK TECHNOLOGY INC
10211 Bellegrave Ave, Jurupa Valley
(91752-1919)
PHONE..................909 930-5700
Yubo Ho, *President*
EMP: 15 EST: 1990
SQ FT: 21,000
SALES (est): 2.6MM **Privately Held**
WEB: www.unitektechnologyinc.com
SIC: **3571 5734** Electronic computers;
computer & software stores

(P-8181)
VINCI BRANDS LLC ✪
1775 Flight Ste 300, Irvine (92606)
PHONE..................949 838-5111
Brian Stech, *CEO*
EMP: 169 EST: 2021
SALES (est): 11.8MM **Privately Held**
SIC: **3571 3676** Electronic computers;
electronic resistors

(P-8182)
VMC HOLDINGS GROUP CORP
9667 Owensmouth Ave # 202, Chatsworth
(91311-4819)
P.O. Box 7396, Northridge (91327-7396)
PHONE..................818 993-1466
Pierre Yenokian, *President*
Chris Geudo, *CFO*
Dorothy Yenokian, *Vice Pres*
EMP: 49 EST: 1980
SQ FT: 8,500
SALES (est): 1.3MM **Privately Held**
WEB: www.vmcholdings.com
SIC: **3571** Electronic computers

(P-8183)
VOICEBOARD CORPORATION
473 Post St, Camarillo (93010-8553)
PHONE..................805 389-3100
Greg Peacock, *President*
EMP: 28 EST: 1989
SQ FT: 10,000
SALES (est): 4MM **Privately Held**
WEB: www.tacticalcommunications.com
SIC: **3571** Electronic computers

(P-8184)
VOLTEDGE LLC
500 Nwport Ctr Dr Ste 910, Newport Beach
(92660)
PHONE..................949 877-8900
Chris Richards,
Steve Chon, *Vice Pres*
EMP: 15 EST: 2018
SALES (est): 2.7MM **Privately Held**
WEB: www.voltedge.mx
SIC: **3571 1531 5961** Electronic comput-
ers; ; computer equipment & electronics,
mail order

(P-8185)
XMULTIPLE TECHNOLOGIES
(PA)
Also Called: Xmultiple/Xrjax
543 Country Club Dr B-128, Simi Valley
(93065-0637)
PHONE..................805 579-1100
Alan Pocrass, *CEO*
Jeremy Chiu, *President*
Luke Flowers, *Vice Pres*
Emrich Kollar, *Vice Pres*
Drew Storberg, *Vice Pres*
▲ EMP: 49 EST: 1982
SALES (est): 4.1MM **Privately Held**
WEB: www.xmultiple.com
SIC: **3571 3663 3661 3577** Electronic
computers; multiplex equipment; tele-
phone & telegraph apparatus; computer
peripheral equipment

3572 Computer Storage Devices

(P-8186)
AKIWA TECHNOLOGY INC
13021 Arctic Cir, Santa Fe Springs
(90670-5505)
PHONE..................562 407-2782
Bill Lin, *President*
Jochen Becky Lai, *CFO*
Chungching Liang, *Vice Pres*
John Liang, *Engineer*
Cyndee Wang, *Accountant*
▲ EMP: 14 EST: 2002
SQ FT: 14,000
SALES (est): 4.1MM **Privately Held**
WEB: www.akiwa.com
SIC: **3572** Computer storage devices
PA: Guanghsing Industrial Co., Ltd.
No. 10-2, Lane 17, Nanshan Rd., Sec.
3
Taoyuan City TAY 33851

(P-8187)
ALLSTAR MICROELECTRONICS
INC
Also Called: Allstarshop.com
30191 Avendia De Las, Rancho Santa Mar-
gari (92688)
PHONE..................949 546-0888
Ming-Chyi Chiang, *President*
Wayne Liu, *Finance*

EMP: 18 EST: 1995
SQ FT: 12,843
SALES (est): 4.7MM **Privately Held**
WEB: www.allstarshop.com
SIC: **3572** Computer storage devices

(P-8188)
BNL TECHNOLOGIES INC
Also Called: Fantom Drives
20525 Manhattan Pl, Torrance
(90501-1825)
PHONE..................310 320-7272
Behzad Eshghieh, *CEO*
Hamid Khorsand, *Ch of Bd*
Nasser Ahdout, *CFO*
Atoosa Karimi-Bakabadi, *Sales Mgr*
Jennifer Ahdout, *Med Doctor*
▲ EMP: 26 EST: 1998
SALES (est): 9.4MM **Privately Held**
SIC: **3572** Computer storage devices

(P-8189)
CALDIGIT INC
1941 E Miraloma Ave Ste B, Placentia
(92870-6770)
PHONE..................714 572-6668
PO Hung Chen, *CEO*
▲ EMP: 15 EST: 2006
SALES (est): 2.2MM **Privately Held**
WEB: www.caldigit.com
SIC: **3572** Disk drives, computer; magnetic
storage devices, computer

(P-8190)
CAMEO TECHNOLOGIES INC
20511 Lake Forest Dr, Lake Forest
(92630-7741)
PHONE..................949 672-7000
Matthew Massingel, *CEO*
EMP: 25 EST: 2012
SALES (est): 5.2MM
SALES (corp-wide): 16.9B **Publicly Held**
WEB: www.westerndigital.com
SIC: **3572** Disk drives, computer
HQ: Western Digital Technologies, Inc.
5601 Great Oaks Pkwy
San Jose CA 95119

(P-8191)
CAPSA SOLUTIONS LLC
14000 S Broadway, Los Angeles
(90061-1018)
PHONE..................800 437-6633
Jeff Strickler, *CFO*
EMP: 38
SALES (corp-wide): 181.5MM **Privately
Held**
WEB: www.capsahealthcare.com
SIC: **3572** Computer storage devices
PA: Capsa Solutions Llc
4253 Ne 189th Ave
Portland OR 97230
503 766-2324

(P-8192)
CENTON ELECTRONICS INC
(PA)
27 Journey Ste 100, Aliso Viejo
(92656-3320)
PHONE..................949 855-9111
Jennifer Miscione, *CEO*
Gene Miscione, *President*
Janet Miscione, *Vice Pres*
Mark Miscione, *Purch Mgr*
Laura Miscione, *Sales Staff*
◆ EMP: 60 EST: 1978
SQ FT: 20,000
SALES (est): 15.1MM **Privately Held**
WEB: www.centon.com
SIC: **3572 5734 7379** Computer storage
devices; computer software & acces-
sories; computer related consulting serv-
ices

(P-8193)
CERTANCE LLC (HQ)
Also Called: Quantum Corporation
141 Innovation Dr, Irvine (92617-3211)
PHONE..................949 856-7800
Howard L Matthews, *President*
Donald L Waite, *Chairman*
Roy Owen, *Senior Engr*
Mary J Randles, *Marketing Staff*
New Suez Aquisition Corp,
EMP: 300 EST: 2000

SALES (est): 128.1MM
SALES (corp-wide): 402.9MM **Publicly
Held**
WEB: www.quantum.com
SIC: **3572** Computer tape drives & compo-
nents
PA: Quantum Corporation
224 Airport Pkwy Ste 550
San Jose CA 95110
408 944-4000

(P-8194)
CHENBRO MICOM (USA) INC
2800 Jurupa St, Ontario (91761-2903)
PHONE..................909 937-0100
MEI CHI Chen, *President*
▲ EMP: 20 EST: 1983
SALES (est): 5.8MM **Privately Held**
WEB: www.chenbro.com
SIC: **3572** Computer storage devices
PA: Chenbro Micom Co., Ltd.
15f, No. 150, Jian 1st Rd.
New Taipei City TAP 23511

(P-8195)
COMPUCASE CORPORATION
Also Called: Orion Tech
16720 Chestnut St Ste C, City of Industry
(91748-1038)
PHONE..................626 336-6588
Doung Fu Hsu, *President*
Aaron Tao, *COO*
Phillip Liu, *Manager*
▲ EMP: 1500 EST: 1995
SQ FT: 30,000
SALES (est): 113MM **Privately Held**
WEB: www.hecgroupusa.com
SIC: **3572** Computer storage devices
PA: Compucase Enterprise Co., Ltd.
No. 225, Lane 54, An Ho Rd., Sec. 2
Tainan City 70967

(P-8196)
DATADIRECT NETWORKS INC
(PA)
Also Called: D D N
9351 Deering Ave, Chatsworth
(91311-5858)
PHONE..................818 700-7600
Alex Bouzari, *CEO*
Yvonne Walker, *Partner*
Paul Bloch, *President*
Gordon Manning, *President*
Ian Angelo, *CFO*
▲ EMP: 120 EST: 1988
SQ FT: 50,000
SALES (est): 214.7MM **Privately Held**
WEB: www.ddn.com
SIC: **3572 7374** Computer auxiliary stor-
age units; data processing service

(P-8197)
DEALSADAY INC
1819 Floradale Ave, South El Monte
(91733-3605)
PHONE..................626 964-4266
or Chan, *CEO*
Gary Yeung, *General Mgr*
Kevin Nguyen, *Opers Mgr*
EMP: 15 EST: 2014
SALES (est): 3MM **Privately Held**
WEB: www.dealsaday.com
SIC: **3572 5045 5734** Computer storage
devices; printers, computer; computer pe-
ripheral equipment; computer software &
accessories

(P-8198)
EP HOLDINGS INC
Also Called: Ep Memory
30442 Esperanza, Rcho STA Marg
(92688-2144)
PHONE..................949 713-4600
Eric Krantz, *CEO*
EMP: 20 EST: 2005
SALES (est): 6.7MM **Privately Held**
SIC: **3572** Computer storage devices

(P-8199)
GIGAMEM LLC
9 Spectrum Pointe Dr, Lake Forest
(92630-2242)
PHONE..................949 461-9999
Keller J Lee, *Mng Member*

▲ **EMP:** 15 **EST:** 1996
SQ FT: 9,500
SALES (est): 5.2MM
SALES (corp-wide): 9.6MM **Privately Held**
WEB: www.membay.com
SIC: 3572 Computer storage devices
PA: Memoryten, Inc.
2995 Mead Ave
Santa Clara CA 95051
408 516-4141

(P-8200)
GLOBALVISION SYSTEMS INC
9401 Oakdale Ave Ste 100, Chatsworth
(91311-6512)
PHONE.........................888 227-7967
Oliver Song, *CEO*
Anthony Sager, *Engineer*
Scott Grant, *Manager*
James Vela, *Accounts Mgr*
EMP: 17 **EST:** 1996
SALES (est): 1.3MM **Privately Held**
WEB: www.gv-systems.com
SIC: 3572 Computer disk & drum drives &
components

(P-8201)
GST INC
3419 Via Lido Ste 164, Newport Beach
(92663-3908)
PHONE.........................949 510-1142
David Breisacher, *CEO*
▼ **EMP:** 56 **EST:** 2002
SQ FT: 10,000
SALES (est): 749.7K **Privately Held**
WEB: www.gstinc.com
SIC: 3572 Computer storage devices

(P-8202)
H CO COMPUTER PRODUCTS (PA)
Also Called: Thinkcp Technologies
16812 Hale Ave, Irvine (92606-5021)
PHONE.........................949 833-3222
Ali Hojreh, *CEO*
Mark Hojreh, *CFO*
Bryon Strachan, *Division Mgr*
Saed Hojreh, *Admin Sec*
Mohammad Hojreh, *Director*
◆ **EMP:** 25 **EST:** 1987
SQ FT: 15,600
SALES (est): 10.4MM **Privately Held**
WEB: www.thinkcp.com
SIC: 3572 3577 Computer storage de-
vices; computer peripheral equipment

(P-8203)
I/OMAGIC CORPORATION (PA)
20512 Crescent Bay Dr, Lake Forest
(92630-8847)
PHONE.........................949 707-4800
Tony Shahbaz, *Ch of Bd*
Mary St George, *Treasurer*
Paula Lecossois, *Marketing Staff*
▲ **EMP:** 30 **EST:** 1992
SQ FT: 52,000
SALES (est): 8.7MM **Privately Held**
WEB: www.iomagic.com
SIC: 3572 3651 Computer storage de-
vices; home entertainment equipment,
electronic

(P-8204)
IN WIN DEVELOPMENT USA INC
188 Brea Canyon Rd, Walnut
(91789-3086)
PHONE.........................909 348-0588
Wen Hsien Lai, *President*
Paul Hao, *Vice Pres*
Irene Huang, *Marketing Staff*
▲ **EMP:** 20 **EST:** 1989
SQ FT: 50,000
SALES (est): 4.9MM **Privately Held**
WEB: www.in-win.com
SIC: 3572 Computer tape drives & compo-
nents
PA: In Win Development Inc.
57, Lane 350, Nan Shang Rd.,
Taoyuan City TAY 33392

(P-8205)
INNOVATIVE DIVERSFD TECH INC
Also Called: Disk Faktory
18062 Irvine Blvd Ste 304, Tustin
(92780-3329)
PHONE.........................949 455-1701
EMP: 28
SQ FT: 7,800
SALES (est): 4.4MM **Privately Held**
WEB: www.burncd.com
SIC: 3572 7371 Mfg Computer Storage
Devices Custom Computer Programing

(P-8206)
LGARDE INC
15181 Woodlawn Ave, Tustin (92780-6487)
PHONE.........................714 259-0771
Gayle D Bilyeu, *Ch of Bd*
Constantine Cassapakis, *President*
Bill Davidson, *COO*
Alan R Hirasuna, *Treasurer*
Linden Bolisay, *Security Dir*
EMP: 24 **EST:** 1971
SQ FT: 19,000
SALES (est): 4.8MM **Privately Held**
WEB: www.lgarde.com
SIC: 3572 8731 2822 3769 Tape
recorders for computers; engineering lab-
oratory, except testing; acrylic rubbers,
polyacrylate; guided missile & space vehi-
cle parts & auxiliary equipment; radio &
TV communications equipment

(P-8207)
LUMAFORGE LLC AN OWC COMPANY ✪
1311 S Flower St, Burbank (91502-2026)
PHONE.........................818 741-2858
Josh Minney, *CEO*
Eric Altman, *CTO*
EMP: 14 **EST:** 2021
SALES (est): 3.6MM **Privately Held**
WEB: www.lumaforge.com
SIC: 3572 7819 Computer storage de-
vices; services allied to motion pictures
HQ: Other World Computing, Inc.
8 Galaxy Way
Woodstock IL 60098

(P-8208)
MEMORY EXPERTS INTL USA INC (HQ)
1651 E Saint Andrew Pl, Santa Ana
(92705-4932)
PHONE.........................714 258-3000
Guadulupe Reusing, *Ch of Bd*
Lawrence Reusing, *President*
Gerard Reusing, *CEO*
Rino Lampasona, *Vice Pres*
Julian Reusing, *Vice Pres*
▲ **EMP:** 27 **EST:** 1996
SQ FT: 40,000
SALES (est): 15MM
SALES (corp-wide): 49.5MM **Privately Held**
WEB: www.memoryexpertsinc.com
SIC: 3572 3577 Computer storage de-
vices; computer peripheral equipment
PA: Memory Experts International Inc
2321 Rue Cohen
Saint-Laurent QC H4R 2
514 333-5010

(P-8209)
MTI TECHNOLOGY CORPORATION (PA)
15461 Red Hill Ave # 200, Tustin
(92780-7314)
PHONE.........................949 251-1101
EMP: 200
SQ FT: 25,000
SALES (est): 54.8MM **Privately Held**
WEB: www.mti.com
SIC: 3572 3571 7372 3674 Mfg Com-
puter Storage Dvc Mfg Electronic Com-
puters

(P-8210)
NGD SYSTEMS INC
355 Goddard Ste 200, Irvine (92618-4642)
PHONE.........................949 870-9148
Mohammad Nader Salessi, *CEO*
Bill Haberlin, *Security Dir*

Hermes Costa, *Software Engr*
Siavash Rezaei, *Software Engr*
Michael Doostdar, *Engineer*
EMP: 30 **EST:** 2016
SALES (est): 3MM **Privately Held**
WEB: www.ngdsystems.com
SIC: 3572 Computer storage devices

(P-8211)
POSTVISION INC
Also Called: Archion
2605 E Fthill Blvd Ste 10, Glendora
(91740)
PHONE.........................818 840-0777
Reuben Lima, *CEO*
Mark Bianchi, *CEO*
Daniel Stern, *Exec VP*
James A Tucci, *CTO*
EMP: 17 **EST:** 1998
SQ FT: 6,000
SALES (est): 2.1MM **Privately Held**
SIC: 3572 Computer storage devices

(P-8212)
PSSC LABS
20432 N Sea Cir, Lake Forest
(92630-8806)
PHONE.........................949 380-7288
Janice Lesser, *President*
Larry Lesser, *Vice Pres*
Harrison Angus, *Executive*
Kurtis Henderson, *Comp Tech*
Sean Bradley, *Director*
▲ **EMP:** 15 **EST:** 1990
SQ FT: 2,500
SALES (est): 3.7MM **Privately Held**
WEB: www.pssclabs.com
SIC: 3572 5734 Computer storage de-
vices; computer & software stores

(P-8213)
QUALSTAR CORPORATION (PA)
1267 Flynn Rd, Camarillo (93012-8013)
PHONE.........................805 583-7744
David J Wolenski, *Ch of Bd*
Steven N Bronson, *President*
Louann L Negrete, *CFO*
Yvonne Ramos, *Admin Asst*
Kevin Yi, *Technical Staff*
EMP: 17 **EST:** 1984
SQ FT: 15,160
SALES (est): 13.4MM **Publicly Held**
WEB: www.qualstar.com
SIC: 3572 3695 Tape storage units, com-
puter; magnetic & optical recording media

(P-8214)
QUANTUM ALLIANCE INC
511 E Mountain St, Glendale (91207-1421)
PHONE.........................818 415-2085
Sabrina Tilimian, *Branch Mgr*
EMP: 16
SALES (corp-wide): 94.4K **Privately Held**
SIC: 3572 Computer storage devices
PA: Quantum Alliance Inc.
700 N Central Ave Ste 560
Glendale CA

(P-8215)
RADIAN MEMORY SYSTEMS INC
5010 N Pkwy Ste 205, Calabasas (91302)
PHONE.........................818 222-4080
Michael Jadon, *CEO*
Yossi Goldfill, *Software Engr*
Margaret Lachinian, *Senior Engr*
Brian Dexheimer, *Director*
Ted Samford, *Director*
EMP: 26 **EST:** 2011
SALES (est): 10MM **Privately Held**
WEB: www.radianmemory.com
SIC: 3572 Computer storage devices

(P-8216)
SHAXON INDUSTRIES INC
4852 E La Palma Ave, Anaheim
(92807-1911)
PHONE.........................714 779-1140
Bekir Aydinoglu, *CEO*
Christina Rodriguez, *Corp Secy*
Alex Medina, *Engineer*
Amy Prep, *Human Res Mgr*
Steven Frankenberg, *Purch Mgr*
▲ **EMP:** 85 **EST:** 1978
SQ FT: 30,000

SALES (est): 15.4MM **Privately Held**
WEB: www.shaxon.com
SIC: 3572 5045 3678 3661 Computer
storage devices; computers & accessories, personal & home entertainment;
electronic connectors; telephone & telegraph apparatus; pressed & blown glass

(P-8217)
SHOP4TECHCOM
Also Called: Leda Multimedia
13745 Seminole Dr, Chino (91710-5515)
PHONE.........................909 248-2725
Danny Wang, *President*
▲ **EMP:** 45 **EST:** 1999
SQ FT: 25,500
SALES (est): 5.3MM **Privately Held**
WEB: www.shop4tech.com
SIC: 3572 5731 Computer tape drives &
components; video recorders, players,
disc players & accessories
PA: Plc Multimedia, Inc.
398 Lemon Creek Dr Ste K
Walnut CA 91789
909 248-2680

(P-8218)
SILICON TECH INC
Also Called: Silicontech
3009 Daimler St, Santa Ana (92705-5812)
PHONE.........................949 476-1130
Manouch Moshayedi, *CEO*
Mark Moshayedi, *President*
Mike Moshayedi, *President*
EMP: 370 **EST:** 1998
SALES (est): 10.8MM
SALES (corp-wide): 16.9B **Publicly Held**
WEB: www.westerndigital.com
SIC: 3572 Computer storage devices
HQ: Stec, Inc.
3355 Michelson Dr Ste 100
Irvine CA 92612

(P-8219)
STEC INC (HQ)
3355 Michelson Dr Ste 100, Irvine
(92612-5694)
PHONE.........................415 222-9996
Stephen D Milligan, *President*
Faheem Hayat, *President*
▲ **EMP:** 340 **EST:** 1990
SQ FT: 73,100
SALES (est): 165.6MM
SALES (corp-wide): 16.9E **Publicly Held**
WEB: www.westerndigital.com
SIC: 3572 3674 3577 Computer storage
devices; semiconductors & related de-
vices; computer peripheral equipment
PA: Western Digital Corporation
5601 Great Oaks Pkwy
San Jose CA 95119
408 717-6000

(P-8220)
STEC INTERNATIONAL HOLDING INC
3001 Daimler St, Santa Ana (92705-5812)
PHONE.........................949 476-1180
Manouch Moshayedi, *Principal*
EMP: 161 **EST:** 2010
SALES (est): 6.7MM
SALES (corp-wide): 16.9B **Publicly Held**
SIC: 3572 Computer storage devices
HQ: Stec, Inc.
3355 Michelson Dr Ste 100
Irvine CA 92612

(P-8221)
SYPRIS DATA SYSTEMS INC (HQ)
160 Via Verde, San Dimas (91773-3901)
PHONE.........................909 962-9400
Darrell Robertson, *President*
▲ **EMP:** 50 **EST:** 1957
SQ FT: 30,000
SALES (est): 180.3MM
SALES (corp-wide): 82.3MM **Publicly Held**
WEB: www.sypris.com
SIC: 3572 3651 Computer tape drives &
components; tape recorders: cassette,
cartridge or reel: household use

PA: Sypris Solutions, Inc.
101 Bullitt Ln Ste 450
Louisville KY 40222
502 329-2000

(P-8222)
US CRITICAL LLC (PA)
6 Orchard Ste 150, Lake Forest
(92630-8352)
PHONE..................................949 916-9326
Thomas Horton, *Director*
John Lightman, *CEO*
Kurt Dunteman, *Vice Pres*
Angela Lunt, *Opers Mgr*
EMP: 64 **EST:** 2013
SQ FT: 12,000
SALES (est): 7.8MM **Privately Held**
WEB: www.uscritical.com
SIC: 3572 Computer disk & drum drives & components

(P-8223)
ZADARA STORAGE INC
9245 Research Drv Irvine, Irvine (92618)
PHONE..................................949 251-0360
Nelson Nahum, *CEO*
Nir Ben Zvi, *COO*
Scott Hebert, *Officer*
Yair Hershko, *Vice Pres*
Doug Jury, *Vice Pres*
▲ **EMP:** 59 **EST:** 2011
SQ FT: 11,000
SALES (est): 6.7MM **Privately Held**
WEB: www.zadara.com
SIC: 3572 Computer storage devices

3575 Computer Terminals

(P-8224)
GATEWAY MANUFACTURING LLC
7565 Irvine Center Dr, Irvine (92618-4918)
PHONE..................................949 471-7000
Gary Fan, *Principal*
EMP: 33 **EST:** 2002
SALES (est): 2.9MM **Privately Held**
WEB: www.gway.org
SIC: 3575 Computer terminals
HQ: Gateway, Inc.
7565 Irvine Center Dr # 150
Irvine CA 92618
949 471-7000

(P-8225)
IMC NETWORKS CORP (PA)
25531 Commercentre Dr, Lake Forest
(92630-8873)
PHONE..................................949 465-3000
Jerry Roby, *Ch of Bd*
Michael Dailey, *President*
Brad Worsham, *Administration*
▲ **EMP:** 68 **EST:** 1988
SQ FT: 35,000
SALES (est): 10.6MM **Privately Held**
WEB: www.imcnetworks.com
SIC: 3575 3577 Computer terminals, monitors & components; computer peripheral equipment

(P-8226)
LANSTREETCOM
Also Called: Tricir Technologies
1216 John Reed Ct, City of Industry
(91745-2404)
PHONE..................................626 964-2000
Michael Jen, *President*
EMP: 14 **EST:** 2000
SALES (est): 1.2MM **Privately Held**
WEB: www.lanstreet.com
SIC: 3575 Computer terminals, monitors & components

(P-8227)
LIKOM CASEWORKS USA INC (HQ)
17800 Castleton St # 220, City of Industry
(91748-1749)
P.O. Box 370070, El Paso TX (79937-0070)
PHONE..................................210 587-7824
Kim Ming Chow, *CEO*
◆ **EMP:** 49 **EST:** 1999

SALES (est): 14.1MM **Privately Held**
WEB: www.liongroup.com.my
SIC: 3575 3469 Computer terminals, monitors & components; metal stampings

(P-8228)
SGB ENTERPRISES INC
24844 Anza Dr Ste A, Valencia
(91355-1286)
PHONE..................................661 294-8306
Joseph Padula, *President*
Chuck Burkholder, *CFO*
Marvin Beiter, *Vice Pres*
Andrew Ormond, *Software Engr*
Ankit Prajapati, *Engineer*
EMP: 22 **EST:** 1991
SQ FT: 9,600
SALES (est): 6MM **Privately Held**
WEB: www.sgbent.com
SIC: 3575 5999 3728 3699 Cathode ray tube (CRT), computer terminal; training materials, electronic; aircraft training equipment; flight simulators (training aids), electronic

(P-8229)
TRANSPARENT PRODUCTS INC
28064 Avenue Stanford E, Valencia
(91355-1160)
PHONE..................................661 294-9787
Fred Bonyadian, *President*
John McVay, *President*
Brenda Captol, *Manager*
▲ **EMP:** 50 **EST:** 1992
SQ FT: 18,000
SALES (est): 7.3MM **Privately Held**
WEB: www.touchpage.com
SIC: 3575 7371 Computer terminals, monitors & components; computer software systems analysis & design, custom

(P-8230)
USEDMAC INC
665 E Los Angeles Ave, Simi Valley
(93065-1849)
PHONE..................................866 769-4777
Rozita Heidari, *President*
Reza Heidari, *Vice Pres*
EMP: 13 **EST:** 2009
SALES (est): 304.2K **Privately Held**
WEB: www.usedmac.com
SIC: 3575 Keyboards, computer, office machine

(P-8231)
WIDE USA CORPORATION
2210 E Winston Rd, Anaheim
(92806-5536)
PHONE..................................714 300-0540
Is Kang, *President*
Hyo Sung Lee, *Exec VP*
Mark Uchino, *Manager*
▲ **EMP:** 14 **EST:** 2007
SQ FT: 8,700
SALES (est): 615.6K **Privately Held**
WEB: www.wideusacorp.com
SIC: 3575 Computer terminals, monitors & components

3577 Computer Peripheral Eqpt, NEC

(P-8232)
ADD-ON COMPUTER PERIPHERAL INC
15775 Gateway Cir, Tustin (92780-6470)
PHONE..................................949 546-8200
James Patton, *CEO*
Matthew McCormick, *Vice Pres*
Denise Gonzalez, *Opers Staff*
Brent Loomis,
Thomas Virden, *Director*
▲ **EMP:** 130 **EST:** 2000
SQ FT: 11,000
SALES (est): 23.1MM **Privately Held**
WEB: www.addonnetworks.com
SIC: 3577 5045 Computer peripheral equipment; computers, peripherals & software

(P-8233)
ADDICE INC (PA)
19977 Harrison Ave, City of Industry
(91789-2848)
PHONE..................................626 617-7779
Hsing Yueh Chang, *CEO*
▲ **EMP:** 59 **EST:** 2012
SALES (est): 441.5K **Privately Held**
WEB: www.addiceinc.com
SIC: 3577 5734 Computer output to microfilm units; computer peripheral equipment

(P-8234)
AMAG TECHNOLOGY INC (DH)
2205 W 126th St Ste B, Hawthorne
(90250-3367)
PHONE..................................310 518-2380
Matt Barnette, *Ch of Bd*
N Keith Whitelock, *Ch of Bd*
Robert A Sawyer Jr, *President*
Robert Causee, *CFO*
Gary Thorington-Jones, *Treasurer*
▲ **EMP:** 49 **EST:** 1971
SALES (est): 20.4MM **Privately Held**
WEB: www.amag.com
SIC: 3577 Decoders, computer peripheral equipment
HQ: G4s Technology Limited
International Drive
Tewkesbury GLOS GL20
168 429-9400

(P-8235)
AOT ELECTRONICS INC
Also Called: Orbit Systems
2 Argos, Laguna Niguel (92677-9003)
PHONE..................................949 600-6335
Omar Turbi, *President*
Renee Laviolette, *CFO*
◆ **EMP:** 16 **EST:** 1987
SALES (est): 1MM **Privately Held**
WEB: www.aotelectronics.com
SIC: 3577 5065 Printers & plotters; communication equipment; electronic parts

(P-8236)
ATEN TECHNOLOGY INC
Also Called: Iogear
15365 Barranca Pkwy, Irvine (92618-2216)
PHONE..................................949 428-1111
Kevin Sun-Chung Chen, *President*
Holly Garcia, *Vice Pres*
Richard Cheng, *Info Tech Mgr*
Chris Wdowiak, *Info Tech Mgr*
Mishel Trujillo, *Accountant*
▲ **EMP:** 80 **EST:** 1996
SALES (est): 29.9MM **Privately Held**
WEB: www.iogear.com
SIC: 3577 Computer peripheral equipment
PA: Aten International Co., Ltd.
3f, No. 125, Sec. 2, Datong Rd.
New Taipei City TAP 22183

(P-8237)
BDR INDUSTRIES INC
Also Called: Rnd Enterprises
9700 Owensmouth Ave Lbby, Chatsworth
(91311-8073)
PHONE..................................818 341-2112
Scott Riddle, *Branch Mgr*
David Chittum, *Business Anlyst*
EMP: 20
SALES (corp-wide): 25.8MM **Privately Held**
SIC: 3577 Computer peripheral equipment
PA: B.D.R. Industries, Inc.
820 E Avenue L12
Lancaster CA 93535
661 940-8554

(P-8238)
BELKIN INTERNATIONAL INC (DH)
Also Called: Belkin Components
12045 Waterfront Dr, Playa Vista
(90094-2999)
PHONE..................................310 751-5100
Christopher Lu, *CEO*
Chester Pipkin, *Ch of Bd*
Jasjit Jay Singh, *CFO*
Stephen Lau, *Program Mgr*
David Nguyen, *Regional Mgr*
◆ **EMP:** 450 **EST:** 1983
SQ FT: 218,000

SALES (est): 580.9MM **Privately Held**
WEB: www.belkin.com
SIC: 3577 5045 5065 Computer peripheral equipment; computers & accessories, personal & home entertainment; intercommunication equipment, electronic; communication equipment

(P-8239)
BEST DATA PRODUCTS INC
Also Called: Diamond Multimedia
21541 Blythe St, Canoga Park
(91304-4910)
PHONE..................................818 534-1414
Bruce Zaman, *President*
Shirley Zaman, *CFO*
Jonh Macalino, *Controller*
▲ **EMP:** 85 **EST:** 1983
SALES (est): 16.9MM **Privately Held**
WEB: www.diamondmm.com
SIC: 3577 Computer peripheral equipment

(P-8240)
BIXOLON AMERICA INC
13705 Cimarron Ave, Gardena
(90249-2463)
PHONE..................................858 764-4580
Chan Young Hwang, *CEO*
Yon H Son, *President*
Chris Lee, *Network Tech*
Rosa Jeong, *Accounting Mgr*
David Roberts, *VP Sls/Mktg*
◆ **EMP:** 38 **EST:** 2005
SQ FT: 26,000
SALES (est): 10.5MM **Privately Held**
WEB: www.bixolonusa.com
SIC: 3577 Printers, computer
PA: Bixolon Co., Ltd
7,8/F
Seongnam 13494

(P-8241)
CABLE DEVICES INCORPORATED (HQ)
Also Called: Cable Exchange
3008 S Croddy Way, Santa Ana
(92704-6305)
PHONE..................................714 554-4370
Marvin S Edwards, *CEO*
Mark Olson, *CFO*
Maria Rangel, *Executive*
Dan Bowlin, *Admin Sec*
Frank B Wyatt, *Admin Sec*
▲ **EMP:** 150 **EST:** 1979
SQ FT: 24,516
SALES (est): 10.1MM **Publicly Held**
WEB: www.commscope.com
SIC: 3577 Computer peripheral equipment

(P-8242)
CALIFORNIA DIGITAL INC (PA)
6 Saddleback Rd, Rolling Hills
(90274-5141)
P.O. Box 3399, Torrance (90510-3399)
PHONE..................................310 217-0500
Terry Reiter, *President*
Floyd Pothoven, *Vice Pres*
Wade Wood, *Vice Pres*
EMP: 67 **EST:** 1973
SQ FT: 30,000
SALES (est): 4.2MM **Privately Held**
WEB: www.florod.com
SIC: 3577 3571 3699 Computer peripheral equipment; mainframe computers; electrical equipment & supplies

(P-8243)
CARDLOGIX
16 Hughes Ste 100, Irvine (92618-1948)
PHONE..................................949 380-1312
Walter Lim, *Ch of Bd*
Bruce Ross, *President*
Ken Indorf, *Vice Pres*
Arthur Krause, *Vice Pres*
Gary Colston, *Software Engr*
▲ **EMP:** 19 **EST:** 1994
SQ FT: 6,000
SALES (est): 2.8MM **Privately Held**
WEB: www.cardlogix.com
SIC: 3577 3089 Computer peripheral equipment; panels, building: plastic

(P-8244)
CD ALEXANDER LLC
2802 Willis St, Santa Ana (92705-5714)
P.O. Box 15101 (92735-0101)
PHONE..............................949 250-3306
Anthony Gonzalez, *Mng Member*
Agustin Hernandez,
EMP: 23 **EST:** 1982
SQ FT: 19,000
SALES (est): 4MM **Privately Held**
WEB: www.cdalexander.com
SIC: 3577 3444 Computer peripheral equipment; sheet metalwork

(P-8245)
CIPHERTEX LLC
Also Called: Ciphertex Data Security
9301 Jordan Ave Ste 105a, Chatsworth (91311-5863)
PHONE..............................818 773-8989
Jerry Kaner, *CEO*
Paul Espinosa, *Info Tech Dir*
Michael Rabinovici, *Sales Staff*
Brad Maryman,
Stan Stahl,
▲ **EMP:** 18 **EST:** 2009
SALES (est): 2MM **Privately Held**
WEB: www.ciphertex.com
SIC: 3577 3572 Computer peripheral equipment; computer storage devices

(P-8246)
CONVERGING SYSTEMS INC
32420 Nautilus Dr Ste 100, Pls Vrds Pnsl (90275-6002)
PHONE..............................310 544-2628
Craig Douglass, *President*
EMP: 15 **EST:** 1996
SALES (est): 2.6MM **Privately Held**
WEB: www.convergingsystems.com
SIC: 3577 3679 Computer peripheral equipment; video triggers, except remote control TV devices

(P-8247)
CRITICAL IO LLC
36 Executive Park Ste 150, Irvine (92614-4715)
PHONE..............................949 553-2200
John Staub, *Mng Member*
Erich Fischer, *Vice Pres*
Ron Godshalk, *Vice Pres*
Dustin Brazeau, *Sr Software Eng*
Ken Neeld,
EMP: 13 **EST:** 2002
SQ FT: 2,500
SALES (est): 2.8MM **Privately Held**
WEB: www.criticalio.com
SIC: 3577 5045 Computer peripheral equipment; computer software

(P-8248)
CS SYSTEMS INC
Also Called: Cs Electronics
16781 Noyes Ave, Irvine (92606-5123)
PHONE..............................949 475-9100
Christian Schwartz, *President*
Rebecca Martin, *CFO*
Gayle Schwartz, *CFO*
Ray Club, *Administration*
Eric Belson, *Accounts Mgr*
▲ **EMP:** 25 **EST:** 1982
SQ FT: 33,200
SALES (est): 3.6MM **Privately Held**
WEB: www.cs-electronics.com
SIC: 3577 3677 Computer peripheral equipment; coil windings, electronic

(P-8249)
DATAMETRICS CORPORATION
Also Called: DMC
25 E Easy St, Simi Valley (93065-7707)
PHONE..............................805 577-9710
Carl Stella, *President*
Harry Altery, *Vice Pres*
Roger Lazer, *Admin Sec*
EMP: 45 **EST:** 1980
SQ FT: 45,000
SALES (corp-wide): 12MM **Privately Held**
WEB: www.datametrics.com
SIC: 3577 7373 Printers, computer; value-added resellers, computer systems

PA: Rugged Information Technology Equipment Corporation
25 E Easy St
Simi Valley CA 93065
805 577-9710

(P-8250)
DELPHI DISPLAY SYSTEMS INC
3550 Hyland Ave, Costa Mesa (92626-1438)
PHONE..............................714 825-3400
Ken Neeld, *CEO*
Michael Deson, *CEO*
David Skinner, *Vice Pres*
Anita Maldonado, *Accountant*
Michael Pierce, *Sales Staff*
▲ **EMP:** 55 **EST:** 1997
SQ FT: 10,000
SALES (est): 10.7MM **Privately Held**
WEB: www.delphidisplay.com
SIC: 3577 Computer peripheral equipment

(P-8251)
DSS NETWORKS INC
24462 Redlen St, Lake Forest (92630-3848)
PHONE..............................949 981-3473
Anita Svay, *CEO*
Jerry Marcinko, *President*
Sam Svay, *Vice Pres*
EMP: 15 **EST:** 2000
SQ FT: 4,000
SALES (est): 574.8K **Privately Held**
WEB: www.dssnetworks.com
SIC: 3577 Computer peripheral equipment

(P-8252)
EFAXCOM (DH)
Also Called: Jetfax
6922 Hollywood Blvd Fl 5, Los Angeles (90028-6125)
PHONE..............................323 817-3207
Ronald Brown, *President*
John H Harris, *Vice Pres*
Gary P Kapner, *Vice Pres*
Dan Gallo, *Risk Mgmt Dir*
Rebecca Conley, *Sales Staff*
EMP: 80 **EST:** 1988
SALES (est): 24.5MM
SALES (corp-wide): 1.4B **Publicly Held**
WEB: www.ceoj2global.com
SIC: 3577 Computer peripheral equipment

(P-8253)
EFAXCOM
Also Called: J2 Global Communications
5385 Hollister Ave # 208, Santa Barbara (93111-2389)
PHONE..............................805 692-0064
Stephen Zendjahas, *Manager*
Alison Baxter, *Executive*
Vartan Mangasaryan, *Administration*
Christine Anderson, *Sales Staff*
Girlie Cabral, *Manager*
EMP: 41
SALES (corp-wide): 1.4B **Publicly Held**
WEB: www.ceoj2global.com
SIC: 3577 Computer peripheral equipment
HQ: Efax.Com
6922 Hollywood Blvd Fl 5
Los Angeles CA 90028
323 817-3207

(P-8254)
ENCRYPTED ACCESS CORPORATION
1730 Redhill Ave, Irvine (92697-0001)
PHONE..............................714 371-4125
Hirihisa Matsunaga, *Branch Mgr*
EMP: 20 **Privately Held**
SIC: 3577 Punch card equipment: readers, tabulators, sorters, etc.
PA: Encrypted Access Corporation
600 Anton Blvd Fl 11
Costa Mesa CA

(P-8255)
EPSON AMERICA INC (DH)
Also Called: Seiko Epson
3131 Katella Ave, Los Alamitos (90720-2335)
P.O. Box 93012, Long Beach (90809-3012)
PHONE..............................800 463-7766
John Lang, *President*
John D Lang, *President*

Mike Isrgig, *Vice Pres*
Genevieve Walker, *Vice Pres*
Sandra Tea, *Executive*
◆ **EMP:** 510 **EST:** 1975
SQ FT: 163,000
SALES (est): 359.4MM **Privately Held**
WEB: www.epson.com
SIC: 3577 Computer peripheral equipment

(P-8256)
FINIS LLC
Also Called: Incipio, LLC
3347 Michelson Dr Ste 100, Irvine (92612-0661)
P.O. Box 17192 (92623-7192)
PHONE..............................949 250-4929
Joseph Sklencar,
Alain Lo, *Senior Buyer*
Sean Tanaka, *Buyer*
Ching Phung, *Sales Dir*
Lance Garcia, *Sales Mgr*
EMP: 80 **EST:** 2015
SALES (est): 26.1MM
SALES (corp-wide): 55.4MM **Privately Held**
WEB: www.incipio.com
SIC: 3577 Computer peripheral equipment
PA: Incipio Technologies, Inc.
3347 Michelson Dr Ste 100
Irvine CA 92612
949 250-4929

(P-8257)
FORESEESON CUSTOM DISPLAYS INC (PA)
2210 E Winston Rd, Anaheim (92806-5536)
PHONE..............................714 300-0540
Insik Kang, *President*
Richard Barnes, *Admin Asst*
Robert Tran, *Technology*
Jin Han, *Engineer*
Isabell Park, *Opers Staff*
▲ **EMP:** 20 **EST:** 2000
SQ FT: 8,000
SALES (est): 3.8MM **Privately Held**
WEB: www.foreseesonusa.com
SIC: 3577 Computer peripheral equipment

(P-8258)
GIZMAC ACCESSORIES LLC
4025 Spencer St Ste 102, Torrance (90503-2499)
PHONE..............................310 320-5563
Timothy Cave,
▲ **EMP:** 14 **EST:** 2005
SALES (est): 2.3MM **Privately Held**
WEB: www.xrackpro2.com
SIC: 3577 Computer peripheral equipment

(P-8259)
GOODIX TECHNOLOGY INC
133 Technology Dr Ste 200, Irvine (92618-2465)
PHONE..............................858 554-0352
Fan Zhang, *CEO*
Bo Pi, *Admin Sec*
EMP: 15 **EST:** 2014
SALES (est): 2.7MM **Privately Held**
WEB: www.goodix.com
SIC: 3577 Computer peripheral equipment

(P-8260)
HALL RESEARCH TECHNOLOGIES LLC (PA)
1163 Warner Ave, Tustin (92780-6458)
PHONE..............................714 641-6607
Jason Schwartz, *CEO*
Gail Haghjoo, *CFO*
George Sarkissian, *CFO*
Robert Tarr, *Technical Staff*
Wayne Childs, *Business Mgr*
◆ **EMP:** 17 **EST:** 1984
SQ FT: 18,200
SALES (est): 12.2MM **Privately Held**
WEB: www.halltechav.com
SIC: 3577 Computer peripheral equipment

(P-8261)
HOLDEN INDUSTRIAL INC
280 S Lemon Ave Unit 1608, Walnut (91788-2657)
PHONE..............................909 919-5505
EMP: 20 **EST:** 2014

SALES (est): 85.8K **Privately Held**
WEB: www.holdenindustriesinc.com
SIC: 3577 Computer peripheral equipment

(P-8262)
HP IT SERVICES INCORPORATED
1506 W Flower Ave, Fullerton (92833-3952)
PHONE..............................714 844-7737
Brian White, *CEO*
EMP: 25 **EST:** 2019
SALES (est): 250K **Privately Held**
SIC: 3577 7372 7382 Computer peripheral equipment; operating systems computer software; confinement surveillance systems maintenance & monitoring

(P-8263)
INCIPIO TECHNOLOGIES INC (PA)
Also Called: Incipio Group
3347 Michelson Dr Ste 100, Irvine (92612-0661)
P.O. Box 17192 (92623-7192)
PHONE..............................949 250-4929
Brian Stech, *CEO*
Stephen Finney, *CFO*
Steve Finney, *CFO*
Joe Sklencar, *CFO*
Rusty Everett, *Exec VP*
◆ **EMP:** 45 **EST:** 2000
SALES (est): 55.4MM **Privately Held**
WEB: www.incipio.com
SIC: 3577 Computer peripheral equipment

(P-8264)
INDUSTRIAL ELCTRN C ENGNERS IN
Also Called: Iee
7723 Kester Ave, Van Nuys (91405-1105)
PHONE..............................818 787-0311
Thomas Whinfrey, *Presiden*
Elena Valderrama, *CFO*
Donald G Gumpertz, *Chairman*
Jim Foti, *Vice Pres*
Michael Tubbs, *Vice Pres*
▲ **EMP:** 100 **EST:** 1947
SQ FT: 131,000
SALES (est): 24.8MM **Privately Held**
WEB: www.ieeinc.com
SIC: 3577 3575 Graphic displays, except graphic terminals; keyboards, computer, office machine

(P-8265)
INFINEON TECH AMERICAS CORP
Interntnal Rctfier/Hexget Amer
41915 Business Park Dr, Temecula (92590-3637)
PHONE..............................951 375-6008
Marc Rougee, *Branch Mgr*
Dale Suddon, *Treasurer*
Chuck Hitchcock, *Business Dir*
Travis Miller, *Network Mgr*
Rajesh Kotian, *Software Engr*
EMP: 710
SALES (corp-wide): 10.1B **Privately Held**
WEB: www.infineon.com
SIC: 3577 3674 Computer peripheral equipment; semiconductor circuit networks
HQ: Infineon Technologies Americas Corp.
101 N Pacific Coast Hwy
El Segundo CA 90245
310 726-8200

(P-8266)
INNOVATIVE TECH & ENGRG INC
Also Called: Innov8v
2691 Richter Ave Ste 124, Irvine (92606-5124)
PHONE..............................949 955-2501
Hassan Siddiqi, *President*
EMP: 22 **EST:** 1997
SQ FT: 2,200
SALES (est): 917.1K **Privately Held**
WEB: www.innov8v.com
SIC: 3577 5961 1731 5999 Computer peripheral equipment; computers & peripheral equipment, mail order; safety & security specialization; audio-visual equipment & supplies

(P-8267)
INPUT/OUTPUT TECHNOLOGY INC
28415 Industry Dr Ste 520, Valencia (91355-4161)
PHONE..................................661 257-1000
Ted Drapala, *President*
EMP: 20 **EST:** 1977
SALES (est): 2.3MM **Privately Held**
WEB: www.iotechnology.com
SIC: 3577 3823 Input/output equipment, computer; industrial instrmnts msrmnt display/control process variable

(P-8268)
INSTRUMENTATION TECH SYSTEMS
Also Called: Its
19360 Business Center Dr, Northridge (91324-3547)
PHONE..................................818 886-2034
Paul Hightower, *CEO*
Don C Janess, *Vice Pres*
▼ **EMP:** 29 **EST:** 1978
SQ FT: 8,200
SALES (est): 2.7MM **Privately Held**
WEB: www.itsamerica.com
SIC: 3577 Encoders, computer peripheral equipment

(P-8269)
INTERNET MACHINES CORPORATION (PA)
30501 Agoura Rd Ste 203, Agoura Hills (91301-4389)
PHONE..................................818 575-2100
Christopher Hoogenboom, *CEO*
Frank Knuettel II, *CFO*
Chris Haywood, *Vice Pres*
Aloke Gupta, *VP Mktg*
Brian Fitzgerald, *VP Sales*
EMP: 70 **EST:** 1999
SQ FT: 18,500
SALES (est): 6.7MM **Privately Held**
WEB: www.internetmachines.com
SIC: 3577 Computer peripheral equipment

(P-8270)
KINGSTON DIGITAL INC (HQ)
17600 Newhope St, Fountain Valley (92708-4220)
PHONE..................................714 435-2600
John Tu, *President*
David Sun, *Principal*
▲ **EMP:** 232 **EST:** 2007
SALES (est): 29MM
SALES (corp-wide): 452.5MM **Privately Held**
WEB: www.kingston.com
SIC: 3577 Computer peripheral equipment
PA: Kingston Technology Company, Inc.
17600 Newhope St
Fountain Valley CA 92708
714 435-2600

(P-8271)
KINGSTON TECHNOLOGY CORP (PA)
17600 Newhope St, Fountain Valley (92708-4298)
PHONE..................................714 435-2600
John Tu, *CEO*
David Sun, *COO*
Joe Maloney, *Treasurer*
Mike Chen, *Vice Pres*
David Kuan, *Vice Pres*
▲ **EMP:** 500 **EST:** 1987
SALES (est): 651.4MM **Privately Held**
WEB: www.kingston.com
SIC: 3577 Computer peripheral equipment

(P-8272)
LANTRONIX INC (PA)
7535 Irvine Center Dr # 10, Irvine (92618-2962)
PHONE..................................949 453-3990
Paul H Pickle, *President*
Bernhard Bruscha, *Ch of Bd*
Jeremy R Whitaker, *CFO*
Roger Holliday, *Vice Pres*
Mohammed F Hakam, *VP Engrg*
▲ **EMP:** 251 **EST:** 1989
SQ FT: 27,000

SALES: 71.4MM **Publicly Held**
WEB: www.lantronix.com
SIC: 3577 Data conversion equipment, media-to-media: computer

(P-8273)
LASERGRAPHICS INC
Also Called: Lasergraphics General Business
20 Ada, Irvine (92618-2303)
PHONE..................................949 753-8282
Mihai Demetrescu PHD, *President*
David Boyd, *CFO*
Stefan Demetrescu, *Senior VP*
Stefan Demetrescu PHD, *Senior VP*
▲ **EMP:** 40 **EST:** 1981
SQ FT: 20,000
SALES (est): 6.9MM **Privately Held**
WEB: www.lasergraphics.com
SIC: 3577 7371 3823 Graphic displays, except graphic terminals; custom computer programming services; industrial instrmnts msrmnt display/control process variable

(P-8274)
LEXMARK INTERNATIONAL INC
575 Anton Blvd Fl 3, Costa Mesa (92626-7169)
PHONE..................................714 641-1007
EMP: 35
SALES (corp-wide): 2.5B **Privately Held**
SIC: 3577 Mfg Business Machines
PA: Lexmark International, Inc.
740 W New Circle Rd
Lexington KY 40511
859 232-2000

(P-8275)
LOGICUBE INC (PA)
19755 Nordhoff Pl, Chatsworth (91311-6606)
PHONE..................................888 494-8832
Farid Emrani, *President*
Jack M Schuster, *Ch of Bd*
Jeffrey Schuster, *CFO*
Chris Hernandez, *Opers Staff*
Chris M Hernandez, *Opers Staff*
▲ **EMP:** 20 **EST:** 1993
SALES (est): 5.4MM **Privately Held**
WEB: www.logicube.com
SIC: 3577 Computer peripheral equipment

(P-8276)
LOGITECH INC
3 Jenner Ste 180, Irvine (92618-3835)
PHONE..................................510 795-8500
Darrell Bracken, *Branch Mgr*
Navi Cohen, *Engineer*
Bruce Sanders, *Sales Staff*
Phoebe Ou, *Senior Mgr*
Jennifer Treopaldo, *Director*
EMP: 219
SALES (corp-wide): 2.9B **Privately Held**
WEB: www.logitech.com
SIC: 3577 Computer peripheral equipment
HQ: Logitech Inc.
7700 Gateway Blvd
Newark CA 94560
510 795-8500

(P-8277)
LYNN PRODUCTS INC
Also Called: Pureformance Cables
2645 W 237th St, Torrance (90505-5269)
PHONE..................................310 530-5966
Hsinyu Lin, *President*
Chun MEI Shei, *Treasurer*
Eric Tseng, *Vice Pres*
Chen Huei Tseng, *Admin Sec*
Estelle Chiang, *Purch Mgr*
▲ **EMP:** 1000 **EST:** 1982
SQ FT: 35,000
SALES (est): 50.5MM **Privately Held**
WEB: www.lynnprod.com
SIC: 3577 3357 Computer peripheral equipment; fiber optic cable (insulated)

(P-8278)
MAGIC RAM INC
3540 Wilshire Blvd # 716, Los Angeles (90010-3934)
PHONE..................................213 380-5555
Eddie Mirarooni, *Ch of Bd*
Meheran Navidbakhsh, *CFO*
Alan Nouray, *Vice Pres*
EMP: 16 **EST:** 1988

SQ FT: 65,000
SALES (est): 7MM **Privately Held**
WEB: www.magicram.com
SIC: 3577 Computer peripheral equipment

(P-8279)
MAGTEK INC (PA)
1710 Apollo Ct, Seal Beach (90740-5617)
PHONE..................................562 546-6400
Ann Marle Hart, *President*
Sam Kamel, *President*
Mike Brierley, *Vice Pres*
Lou Struett, *Exec VP*
Louis E Struett, *Exec VP*
▲ **EMP:** 200 **EST:** 1972
SQ FT: 48,000
SALES (est): 53.2MM **Privately Held**
WEB: www.magtek.com
SIC: 3577 3674 Readers, sorters or inscribers, magnetic ink; encoders, computer peripheral equipment; semiconductors & related devices

(P-8280)
MARWAY POWER SYSTEMS INC (PA)
Also Called: Marway Power Solutions
1721 S Grand Ave, Santa Ana (92705-4808)
P.O. Box 30118 (92735-8118)
PHONE..................................714 917-6200
Paul Patel, *President*
Kevin Jacobs, *CFO*
Tim Bishop, *Technical Staff*
Rudy Sanchez, *Project Engr*
Garen Manucharyan, *Electrical Engi*
◆ **EMP:** 39 **EST:** 1979
SQ FT: 33,400
SALES (est): 9.3MM **Privately Held**
WEB: www.marway.com
SIC: 3577 8711 Computer peripheral equipment; engineering services

(P-8281)
METROMEDIA TECHNOLOGIES INC
311 Parkside Dr, San Fernando (91340-3036)
PHONE..................................818 552-6500
Paul Havig, *Branch Mgr*
EMP: 20
SALES (corp-wide): 43.2MM **Privately Held**
WEB: www.circlegraphicsonline.com
SIC: 3577 Graphic displays, except graphic terminals
PA: Metromedia Technologies, Inc.
810 7th Ave Fl 29
New York NY 10019
212 273-2100

(P-8282)
MOTION ENGINEERING INC (HQ)
Also Called: M E I
33 S La Patera Ln, Santa Barbara (93117-3214)
PHONE..................................805 696-1200
Robert Steele, *CTO*
EMP: 60 **EST:** 1987
SQ FT: 21,000
SALES (est): 10.6MM
SALES (corp-wide): 22.2B **Publicly Held**
WEB: www.motioneng.com
SIC: 3577 8711 3823 Computer peripheral equipment; engineering services; industrial instrmnts msrmnt display/control process variable
PA: Danaher Corporation
2200 Penn Ave Nw Ste 800w
Washington DC 20037
202 828-0850

(P-8283)
MOXA AMERICAS INC
601 Valencia Ave Ste 100, Brea (92823-6357)
PHONE..................................714 528-6777
Tein Shun, *CEO*
Ben Chen, *President*
Steve Won, *Exec VP*
Clark Ko, *Vice Pres*
CC Peng, *Vice Pres*
▲ **EMP:** 50 **EST:** 2002
SQ FT: 8,000

SALES (est): 26.7MM **Privately Held**
WEB: www.moxa.com
SIC: 3577 Input/output equipment, computer
HQ: Moxa Inc.
13f, No. 3, Xinbei Blvd., Sec. 4,
New Taipei City TAP 24250

(P-8284)
MPD HOLDINGS INC
Also Called: Mousepad Designs
16200 Commerce Way, Cerritos (90703-2324)
PHONE..................................562 777-1051
Glenn M Boghosian, *President*
▲ **EMP:** 34 **EST:** 1993
SALES (est): 5MM **Privately Held**
SIC: 3577 Computer peripheral equipment

(P-8285)
MYGNAR INC (PA)
2525 Main St Ste 300, Santa Monica (90405-3687)
PHONE..................................626 676-5415
Tim Feess, *CEO*
William Africano, *Admin Sec*
EMP: 16 **EST:** 2014
SQ FT: 5,000
SALES (est): 3.5MM **Privately Held**
WEB: www.gnarbox.com
SIC: 3577 Printers & plotters

(P-8286)
NEXA3D INC
Also Called: Nexa 3d
1923 Eastman Ave Ste 200, Ventura (93003-8085)
PHONE..................................805 465-9001
AVI Reichental, *CEO*
Kenyon Whetsell, *Engineer*
Orhun Oskay, *Mng Member*
Robert Rhoades, *Manager*
EMP: 29 **EST:** 2014
SALES (est): 2.7MM **Privately Held**
WEB: www.nexa3d.com
SIC: 3577 Computer peripheral equipment

(P-8287)
OLEA KIOSKS INC
13845 Artesia Blvd, Cerritos (90703-9000)
PHONE..................................562 924-2644
Francisco Olea, *CEO*
Shauna Olea, *Administration*
Craig Bennett, *Engineer*
Craig Keefner, *Manager*
Tania Rollins, *Accounts Exec*
▲ **EMP:** 54 **EST:** 1977
SQ FT: 50,000
SALES (est): 13.9MM **Privately Held**
WEB: www.olea.com
SIC: 3577 Computer peripheral equipment

(P-8288)
OMNIPRINT INC
1923 E Deere Ave, Santa Ana (92705-5715)
PHONE..................................949 833-0080
Fardin Mostafavi, *President*
Kuma Lin, *Vice Pres*
James Yee, *Design Engr*
▲ **EMP:** 24 **EST:** 1984
SQ FT: 22,000
SALES (est): 2.6MM **Privately Held**
WEB: www.omniprintinc.com
SIC: 3577 5045 Printers & plotters; printers, computer

(P-8289)
OPTIMA TECHNOLOGY CORPORATION
17062 Murphy Ave, Irvine (92614-5914)
PHONE..................................949 253-5768
Barry Eisler, *Branch Mgr*
EMP: 343 **EST:** 2014
WEB: www.optimatech.com
SIC: 3577 Computer peripheral equipment
PA: Optima Technology Corporation
2222 Michelson Dr # 1830
Irvine CA

(P-8290)
PHOTO SCIENCES
INCORPORATED (PA)
2542 W 237th St, Torrance (90505-5217)
PHONE..............................310 634-1500
Kyle Stogsdill, *CEO*
L J Stogsdill, *Chairman*
Wade Walsh, *Treasurer*
Jeff Platts, *Vice Pres*
Maurice Muehle,
EMP: 33 EST: 1972
SQ FT: 35,000
SALES (est): 6MM **Privately Held**
WEB: www.photo-sciences.com
SIC: 3577 7335 Computer output to micro-
film units; still & slide file production

(P-8291)
PLUSTEK TECHNOLOGY INC
9830 Norwalk Blvd Ste 155, Santa Fe
Springs (90670-6107)
PHONE..............................714 670-7713
Karen Ku, *President*
Johnson Yang, *Vice Pres*
Maggie Su, *Director*
▲ EMP: 13 EST: 2005
SQ FT: 15,000
SALES (est): 2.3MM **Privately Held**
SIC: 3577 Optical scanning devices

(P-8292)
PRINCETON TECHNOLOGY INC
1691 Browning, Irvine (92606-4808)
PHONE..............................949 851-7776
Nasir Javed, *CEO*
▲ EMP: 30 EST: 1990
SQ FT: 14,000
SALES (est): 5.4MM **Privately Held**
WEB: www.princetonssd.com
SIC: 3577 5045 3674 Computer periph-
eral equipment; computers, peripherals &
software; semiconductors & related de-
vices

(P-8293)
PRINTRONIX LLC (PA)
7700 Irvine Center Dr # 700, Irvine
(92618-3042)
PHONE..............................714 368-2300
Werner Heid, *CEO*
Sean Irby, *Vice Pres*
Bill Matthewes, *Vice Pres*
Jenny Chua, *CIO*
Yali Fang, *Finance*
▲ EMP: 93 EST: 1974
SALES (est): 21MM **Privately Held**
WEB: www.printronix.com
SIC: 3577 Printers, computer

(P-8294)
PRINTRONIX HOLDING CORP
7700 Irvine Center Dr # 70, Irvine
(92618-2923)
PHONE..............................714 368-2300
Werner Heid, *CEO*
EMP: 20 EST: 2007
SALES (est): 2.8MM **Privately Held**
WEB: www.tallygenicom.com
SIC: 3577 6719 Printers, computer; in-
vestment holding companies, except
banks

(P-8295)
RAISE 3D TECHNOLOGIES INC
43 Tesla, Irvine (92618-4603)
PHONE..............................949 482-2040
Hua Feng, *CEO*
Marc Franz, *Vice Pres*
EMP: 23 EST: 2018
SALES (est): 3.5MM **Privately Held**
WEB: www.raise3d.com
SIC: 3577 7372 7336 Printers, computer;
prepackaged software; graphic arts & re-
lated design

(P-8296)
RANCHO TECHNOLOGY INC
10783 Bell Ct, Rancho Cucamonga
(91730-4834)
PHONE..............................909 987-3966
Hari Gupta, *President*
John Fobel Jr, *Vice Pres*
EMP: 13 EST: 1983

SALES (est): 1MM **Privately Held**
SIC: 3577 5045 Computer peripheral
equipment; computers, peripherals & software

(P-8297)
RGB SYSTEMS INC (PA)
Also Called: Extron Electronics
1025 E Ball Rd Ste 100, Anaheim
(92805-5957)
PHONE..............................714 491-1500
Andrew C Edwards, *President*
Ron Tucci, *President*
Ivan Perez, *Officer*
Mohit Shah, *Admin Sec*
Cindy Amesquita, *Web Dvlpr*
◆ EMP: 185 EST: 1983
SQ FT: 160,000
SALES (est): 174.4MM **Privately Held**
WEB: www.extron.com
SIC: 3577 Computer output to microfilm
units

(P-8298)
RICOH PRTG SYSTEMS AMER
INC (HQ)
2390 Ward Ave Ste A, Simi Valley
(93065-1897)
PHONE..............................805 578-4000
Osamu Namikawa, *President*
John Harman, *Partner*
Hiroyuki Kajiyama, *President*
Leonard Stone, *Vice Pres*
Jim Obrien, *Administration*
◆ EMP: 400 EST: 1962
SQ FT: 97,400
SALES (est): 120.2MM **Privately Held**
WEB: www.rpsa.ricoh.com
SIC: 3577 3861 3955 Printers, computer;
toners, prepared photographic (not made
in chemical plants); ribbons, inked: type-
writer, adding machine, register, etc.

(P-8299)
RUGGED INFO TECH EQP CORP
(PA)
Also Called: Ritec
25 E Easy St, Simi Valley (93065-7707)
PHONE..............................805 577-9710
Carl C Stella, *President*
Harry P Alteri, *Senior VP*
Roger Lazer, *Admin Sec*
Willie Roland, *Engineer*
Vincent Stella, *VP Finance*
◆ EMP: 41 EST: 1996
SQ FT: 25,000
SALES (est): 12MM **Privately Held**
WEB: www.ritecrugged.com
SIC: 3577 Computer peripheral equipment

(P-8300)
SEAGRA TECHNOLOGY INC (PA)
14252 Culver Dr, Irvine (92604-0317)
PHONE..............................949 419-6796
Atul Talati, *President*
Timothy Lipsky, *CEO*
Tim Lipsky, *CTO*
▲ EMP: 34 EST: 2007
SQ FT: 1,200
SALES (est): 500K **Privately Held**
WEB: www.seagra.com
SIC: 3577 Computer peripheral equipment

(P-8301)
SENSATA TECHNOLOGIES INC
Also Called: BEI Industrial Encoders
1461 Lawrence Dr, Thousand Oaks
(91320-1303)
PHONE..............................805 716-0322
Glenn Avolio, *Sales Mgr*
Mohana Sambasivam, *Administration*
Mat Bagneski, *Engineer*
Rene Garcia, *Engineer*
Eli Morales, *Engineer*
EMP: 70
SALES (corp-wide): 3B **Privately Held**
WEB: www.sensata.com
SIC: 3577 3827 3663 Optical scanning
devices; optical instruments & lenses;
radio & TV communications equipment
HQ: Sensata Technologies, Inc.
529 Pleasant St
Attleboro MA 02703

(P-8302)
SHARPDOTS LLC
Also Called: Sharp Dots.com
3733 San Gabriel River Pk, Pico Rivera
(90660-1458)
PHONE..............................626 599-9696
John Tan,
EMP: 16 EST: 2000
SALES (est): 2.7MM **Privately Held**
WEB: www.sharpdots.com
SIC: 3577 Printers, computer

(P-8303)
SOLE SOURCE TECHNOLOGY
LLC
1968 S Coast Hwy 680, Laguna Beach
(92651-3681)
PHONE..............................949 500-3371
Kelly Pieropan, *President*
John Harriman, *COO*
Steven Golan, *Executive*
Chris Keyes, *Executive*
Jody Shaffer, *Executive*
EMP: 13 EST: 2007
SALES (est): 3.5MM **Privately Held**
WEB: www.solesourcetech.us
SIC: 3577 5045 Computer peripheral
equipment; computer peripheral equip-
ment

(P-8304)
SYNCHRONIZED
TECHNOLOGIES INC
Also Called: Synchrotech
7536 Tyrone Ave, Van Nuys (91405-1447)
PHONE..............................213 368-3760
Eric Hartouni, *President*
John Melikian, *Treasurer*
▲ EMP: 15 EST: 1991
SALES (est): 1.9MM **Privately Held**
WEB: www.synchrotech.com
SIC: 3577 Computer peripheral equipment

(P-8305)
TOPAZ SYSTEMS INC (PA)
875 Patriot Dr Ste A, Moorpark
(93021-3351)
PHONE..............................805 520-8282
Anthony Zank, *President*
Mike Ambrose, *Vice Pres*
Tomlinson Rauscher, *Vice Pres*
Angelica Revolorio, *Admin Asst*
Oliver Lan, *Sr Software Eng*
▲ EMP: 31 EST: 1995
SQ FT: 16,000
SALES (est): 10.4MM **Privately Held**
WEB: www.topazsystems.com
SIC: 3577 7371 Graphic displays, except
graphic terminals; custom computer pro-
gramming services

(P-8306)
TOYE CORPORATION
9230 Deering Ave, Chatsworth
(91311-5803)
P.O. Box 3997 (91313-3997)
PHONE..............................818 882-4000
Gordon Morris, *President*
▲ EMP: 37 EST: 1941
SQ FT: 5,000
SALES (est): 1.3MM **Privately Held**
WEB: www.toyecorp.com
SIC: 3577 Computer peripheral equipment

(P-8307)
TRANSPARENT DEVICES INC
Also Called: Cybertouch
853 Lawrence Dr, Newbury Park
(91320-2232)
PHONE..............................805 499-5000
Abraham Gohari, *President*
Sergio Loera, *Production*
Dina De Falco, *Manager*
EMP: 32 EST: 1982
SQ FT: 25,000
SALES (est): 5.3MM **Privately Held**
WEB: www.cybertouch.com
SIC: 3577 Graphic displays, except
graphic terminals

(P-8308)
TRI-NET TECHNOLOGY INC
21709 Ferrero, Walnut (91789-5209)
PHONE..............................909 598-8818
Tom Chung, *President*

Lisa Chung, *CFO*
Akinori Ogawa, *Vice Pres*
Cynthia Hsu, *Vice Pres*
Sandra Niko, *Sales Staff*
▲ EMP: 100 EST: 1992
SQ FT: 35,000
SALES (est): 9.2MM **Privately Held**
WEB: www.tnthomevue.net
SIC: 3577 3571 Computer peripheral
equipment; electronic computers

(P-8309)
US COMPUTERS INC
Also Called: U S Technical Institute
181 W Orangethorpe Ave C, Placentia
(92870-6931)
PHONE..............................714 528-0514
Uzma Sheikh, *President*
Saleem Sheikh, *Vice Pres*
Amin Iftikhar, *Technical Staff*
Sonny Vo, *Technical Staff*
Nicholas Mirkovich, *Sales Staff*
EMP: 19 EST: 1997
SQ FT: 3,500
SALES (est): 3MM **Privately Held**
WEB: www.uscomputersinc.com
SIC: 3577 8249 Computer peripheral
equipment; vocational schools

(P-8310)
VIEWSONIC CORPORATION (PA)
10 Pointe Dr Ste 200, Brea (92821-7620)
PHONE..............................909 444-8888
James Chu, *Ch of Bd*
Jeff Volpe, *President*
Sung Yi, *CFO*
Brian Igoe, *Vice Pres*
Caroline Lin, *Vice Pres*
◆ EMP: 140 EST: 1987
SQ FT: 298,050
SALES (est): 541.8MM **Privately Held**
WEB: www.viewsonic.com
SIC: 3577 3575 5045 Computer periph-
eral equipment; computer terminals, mon-
itors & components; computer peripheral
equipment

(P-8311)
WESTERN TELEMATIC INC
5 Sterling, Irvine (92618-2517)
PHONE..............................949 586-9950
Daniel Morrison, *CEO*
Herbert Hoover III, *Ch of Bd*
Everett Sykes, *Vice Pres*
Matoula Senethavong, *IT/ NT Sup*
Brian Ross, *Opers Mgr*
▲ EMP: 50 EST: 1964
SQ FT: 24,000
SALES (est): 10.1MM **Privately Held**
WEB: www.wti.com
SIC: 3577 5065 Computer peripheral
equipment; electronic parts & equipment

(P-8312)
WINIT AMERICA INC
381 Brea Canyon Rd, Walnut
(91789-3060)
PHONE..............................626 606-0308
Sarah Kearns, *Marketing Mgr*
Erik Willey, *Sales Staff*
Bonny Cheng, *Director*
EMP: 13 EST: 2018
SALES (est): 3MM **Privately Held**
SIC: 3577 Computer peripheral equipment

3578 Calculating & Accounting Eqpt

(P-8313)
COMMUNITY MERCH
SOLUTIONS LLC
Also Called: CMS
27201 Puerta Real Ste 120, Mission Viejo
(92691-8555)
PHONE..............................877 956-9258
EMP: 35
SALES: 2.9MM **Privately Held**
SIC: 3578 Mfg Calculating Equipment

(P-8314)
FRONTECH N FUJITSU AMER INC (DH)
Also Called: Ffna
27121 Twne Cntre Dr Ste 1, Foothill Ranch (92610)
PHONE...................949 855-5500
Yoshihiko Masuda, *President*
Hiromi Ladino, *President*
Tatsuo Horibe, *CFO*
Pat Cathey, *Senior VP*
Larry Fandel, *Senior VP*
▲ **EMP:** 210 **EST:** 1990
SQ FT: 90,000
SALES (est): 225.2MM **Privately Held**
WEB: www.fujitsufrontechna.com
SIC: 3578 Calculating & accounting equipment

(P-8315)
MAGENSA LLC
1710 Apollo Ct, Seal Beach (90740-5617)
PHONE...................562 546-6689
EMP: 13 **EST:** 2009
SALES (est): 963.1K
SALES (corp-wide): 53.2MM **Privately Held**
WEB: www.magensa.net
SIC: 3578 Automatic teller machines (ATM)
PA: Magtek, Inc.
1710 Apollo Ct
Seal Beach CA 90740
562 546-6400

(P-8316)
PAYMENTMAX PROCESSING INC
600 Hampshire Rd Ste 120, Westlake Village (91361-2584)
P.O. Box 3847, Thousand Oaks (91359-0847)
PHONE...................805 557-1692
Tony Shap, *President*
EMP: 13 **EST:** 2004
SALES (est): 1MM **Privately Held**
WEB: www.paymentmax.com
SIC: 3578 Point-of-sale devices

(P-8317)
SUZHOU SOUTH
18351 Colima Rd Ste 82, Rowland Heights (91748-2791)
PHONE...................626 322-0101
Joel Wynne, *Director*
EMP: 300 **EST:** 2017
SALES (est): 16MM **Privately Held**
SIC: 3578 Banking machines

3579 Office Machines, NEC

(P-8318)
LYNDE-ORDWAY COMPANY INC
5402 Commercial Dr, Huntington Beach (92649-1232)
P.O. Box 8709, Fountain Valley (92728-8709)
PHONE...................714 957-1311
Thomas Ordway, *President*
Penny Ordway, *Admin Sec*
EMP: 18 **EST:** 1925
SALES (est): 3.4MM **Privately Held**
WEB: www.lynde-ordway.com
SIC: 3579 5999 5044 7359 Paper handling machines; coin wrapping machines; business machines & equipment; office equipment; equipment rental & leasing; industrial equipment services

(P-8319)
RICOH ELECTRONICS INC
17482 Pullman St, Irvine (92614-5527)
PHONE...................714 259-1220
Paul Bakonyi, *Manager*
EMP: 39
SQ FT: 49,359 **Privately Held**
WEB: www.rei.ricoh.com
SIC: 3579 3571 Mailing, letter handling & addressing machines; typing & word processing machines; paper handling machines; electronic computers
HQ: Ricoh Electronics, Inc.
1125 Hurricane Shoals Rd
Lawrenceville GA 30043
714 566-2500

(P-8320)
WHITTIER MAILING PRODUCTS INC (PA)
13019 Park St, Santa Fe Springs (90670-4005)
PHONE...................562 464-3000
Richard A Casford, *President*
Luis Contreras, *Vice Pres*
EMP: 31 **EST:** 1991
SQ FT: 5,000
SALES (est): 5.5MM **Privately Held**
WEB: www.wmpwebstore.com
SIC: 3579 Mailing, letter handling & addressing machines

3581 Automatic Vending Machines

(P-8321)
AQUA PRODUCTS INC
6351 Burnham Ave Ste B, Buena Park (90621-5204)
PHONE...................714 670-0691
Daniel Suh, *President*
Kathleen McClarnon, *CFO*
Miguel Bonaparte, *Executive*
◆ **EMP:** 13 **EST:** 1982
SALES (est): 1.1MM **Privately Held**
WEB: www.watervending.com
SIC: 3581 Automatic vending machines

(P-8322)
NUTRITION WITHOUT BORDERS LLC
Also Called: H.U.M.A.N. Healthy Vending
4641 Leahy St, Culver City (90232-3515)
PHONE...................310 845-7745
Sean Kelly,
Andrew Mackensen,
▼ **EMP:** 13 **EST:** 2008
SQ FT: 10,000
SALES (est): 871.3K **Privately Held**
SIC: 3581 5122 Automatic vending machines; vitamins & minerals

(P-8323)
OAK MANUFACTURING COMPANY INC
2850 E Vernon Ave, Vernon (90058-1804)
P.O. Box 58201, Los Angeles (90058-0201)
PHONE...................323 581-8087
James Hinton, *President*
EMP: 20 **EST:** 1948
SQ FT: 12,000
SALES (est): 2.7MM **Privately Held**
SIC: 3581 Automatic vending machines

3585 Air Conditioning & Heating Eqpt

(P-8324)
ACAPULCO RESTAURANTS INC
Also Called: Acapulco Mexican Restaurants
9405 Monte Vista Ave, Montclair (91763-1926)
PHONE...................909 621-3955
EMP: 75
SALES (corp-wide): 461MM **Privately Held**
SIC: 5812 3585 7299 Eating Place Mfg Refrigeration/Heating Equipment Misc Personal Services
HQ: Acapulco Restaurants, Inc.
4001 Via Oro Ave Ste 200
Long Beach CA 90810
310 513-7538

(P-8325)
ACCO ENGINEERED SYSTEMS INC
3121 N Sillect Ave # 104, Bakersfield (93308-6364)
PHONE...................661 631-1975
Sam Beasley, *Project Engr*
Noah Sadler, *Project Engr*
EMP: 17
SALES (corp-wide): 1.4B **Privately Held**
WEB: www.accoes.com
SIC: 3585 Air conditioning equipment, complete

PA: Acco Engineered Systems, Inc.
888 E Walnut St
Pasadena CA 91101
818 244-6571

(P-8326)
ACE HEATERS LLC
130 Klug Cir, Corona (92878-5424)
PHONE...................951 738-2230
Robin Cruse, *CEO*
William Newbauer III, *President*
EMP: 20 **EST:** 2016
SQ FT: 40,000
SALES (est): 3.4MM
SALES (corp-wide): 39.7MM **Privately Held**
WEB: www.aceheaters.com
SIC: 3585 3443 Heating equipment, complete; boiler & boiler shop work; boiler shop products: boilers, smokestacks, steel tanks; industrial vessels, tanks & containers
PA: Heh Holdings, Llc
45 Seymour St
Stratford CT

(P-8327)
ADVANCED AEROSPACE
10781 Forbes Ave, Garden Grove (92843-4977)
PHONE...................714 265-6200
Steve Flowers, *President*
Brad Pinson, *Engineer*
Joe St Amand, *Controller*
Gene Comfort, *Marketing Staff*
EMP: 17 **EST:** 1997
SALES (est): 459.2K **Privately Held**
SIC: 3585 Refrigeration equipment, complete

(P-8328)
ANTHONY INC (DH)
Also Called: Anthony International
12391 Montero Ave, Sylmar (91342-5370)
PHONE...................818 365-9451
Jeffrey Clark, *CEO*
David Lautenschaelger, *CFO*
Craig Little, *Senior VP*
Michael Murth, *Vice Pres*
John Patterson, *Vice Pres*
◆ **EMP:** 850 **EST:** 2012
SQ FT: 350,000
SALES (est): 510.7MM
SALES (corp-wide): 6.6B **Publicly Held**
WEB: www.anthonyintl.com
SIC: 3585 Refrigeration & heating equipment
HQ: Dover Refrigeration & Food Equipment, Inc.
3005 Highland Pkwy # 200
Downers Grove IL 60515
513 878-4400

(P-8329)
ARI INDUSTRIES INC
Also Called: Airdyne Refrigeration
17018 Edwards Rd, Cerritos (90703-2422)
PHONE...................714 993-3700
R Tony Bedi, *President*
Ruth Lee Bedi, *Vice Pres*
Ruth Bedi, *Vice Pres*
Ruth Lee, *Vice Pres*
Gary Altiero, *Manager*
EMP: 80
SQ FT: 20,000
SALES (est): 17.9MM **Privately Held**
WEB: www.airdyne.com
SIC: 3585 Refrigeration equipment, complete

(P-8330)
BIGFOGG INC (PA)
30818 Wealth St, Murrieta (92563-2534)
PHONE...................951 587-2460
Christopher Miehl, *President*
Chris Miehl, *President*
EMP: 17 **EST:** 2000
SALES (est): 1.5MM **Privately Held**
WEB: www.bigfogg.com
SIC: 3585 Air conditioning condensers & condensing units

(P-8331)
CALIFRNIA INDUS RFRGN MCHS INC
3197 Cornerstone Dr, Eastvale (91752-1028)
PHONE...................951 361-0040
Shahnaz Ghelani, *Corp Secy*
Rahim Ghelani, *President*
Mansoor Ghelani, *Vice Pres*
Mohamed Richi, *Technician*
EMP: 15 **EST:** 1984
SALES (est): 3MM **Privately Held**
WEB: www.caindustrial.com
SIC: 3585 5075 1711 1731 Air conditioning equipment, complete; compressors for refrigeration & air conditioning; compressors, air conditioning; heating & air conditioning contractors; general electrical contractor

(P-8332)
COMMERCIAL DISPLAY SYSTEMS LLC
Also Called: C D S
17341 Sierra Hwy, Canyon Country (91351-1625)
PHONE...................818 361-8160
Fernando Calderon, *Mng Member*
Nick Beswick, *Technology*
Robert Enriquez, *Technology*
Duane Beswick,
John T Karnes, *Mng Member*
EMP: 30 **EST:** 2002
SQ FT: 17,000
SALES (est): 5.7MM **Privately Held**
WEB: www.cdsdoors.net
SIC: 3585 Refrigeration & heating equipment

(P-8333)
COMPU AIRE INC
8167 Byron Rd, Whittier (90606-2615)
PHONE...................562 945-8971
Balbir Narang, *President*
Robert Narang, *Vice Pres*
Mahendra Ahir, *Engineer*
Jasmeen Narang, *Assistant*
▲ **EMP:** 150 **EST:** 1980
SQ FT: 75,000
SALES (est): 18MM **Privately Held**
WEB: www.compu-aire.com
SIC: 3585 Air conditioning units, complete: domestic or industrial

(P-8334)
COOLTEC REFRIGERATION CORP
1250 E Franklin Ave B, Pomona (91766-5449)
P.O. Box 1150 (91769-1150)
PHONE...................909 865-2229
Paul Bedi, *CEO*
George Share, *Corp Secy*
Katherine Sanchez, *Office Mgr*
EMP: 22 **EST:** 2005
SQ FT: 50,000
SALES (est): 5.6MM **Privately Held**
WEB: www.cooltecrefrigeration.com
SIC: 3585 Refrigeration equipment, complete

(P-8335)
CROWNTONKA CALIFORNIA INC
Also Called: Thermal Rite
6514 E 26th St, Commerce (90040-3240)
PHONE...................909 230-6720
Dave Jett, *General Mgr*
David Rodriguez, *Purch Mgr*
EMP: 46 **Privately Held**
WEB: www.everidge.com
SIC: 3585 Refrigeration & heating equipment
HQ: Crowntonka California, Inc.
15600 37th Ave N Ste 100
Minneapolis MN 55446
763 543-2386

(P-8336)
DATA AIRE INC (HQ)
230 W Blueridge Ave, Orange (92865-4225)
PHONE...................800 347-2473
Duncan Moffatt, *President*
Edward J Altieri, *Corp Secy*
▲ **EMP:** 164 **EST:** 1979

(PA)=Parent Co (HQ)=Headquarters (DH)=Div Headquarters
✪ = New Business established in last 2 years

2022 Southern California Business
Directory and Buyers Guide

365

PRODUCTS & SVCS

SALES (est): 51MM
SALES (corp-wide): 555.2MM **Privately Held**
WEB: www.dataaire.com
SIC: 3585 Air conditioning units, complete: domestic or industrial
PA: Construction Specialties Inc.
　3 Werner Way Ste 100
　Lebanon NJ 08833
　908 236-0100

(P-8337)
ENLINK GEOENERGY SERVICES INC
2630 Homestead Pl, Rancho Dominguez (90220-5610)
PHONE...........................424 242-1200
Mark Mizrahi, *President*
Howard Johnson, *CIO*
▲ EMP: 46 EST: 2004
SQ FT: 12,000
SALES (est): 1MM **Privately Held**
WEB: www.enlinkgeoenergy.com
SIC: 3585 Heat pumps, electric

(P-8338)
ENVIRO-INTERCEPT INC
7327 Varna Ave Unit 5, North Hollywood (91605-4183)
PHONE...........................818 982-6063
Fred Bonamici, *President*
Jim Watt, *Shareholder*
Carlos Alverado, *Vice Pres*
EMP: 19 EST: 1975
SQ FT: 11,500
SALES (est): 2.5MM **Privately Held**
SIC: 3585 Refrigeration & heating equipment

(P-8339)
EVERIDGE INC
Also Called: Thermalrite
8886 White Oak Ave, Rancho Cucamonga (91730-5106)
PHONE...........................909 605-6419
Chris Kahler, *Branch Mgr*
Steve Gills, *Vice Pres*
Mark Norvold, *Vice Pres*
Derek Johnson, *Cust Mgr*
Becky Murphy, *Accounts Mgr*
EMP: 75 **Privately Held**
WEB: www.everidge.com
SIC: 3585 Refrigeration & heating equipment
PA: Everidge, Inc.
　15600 37th Ave N Ste 100
　Plymouth MN 55446

(P-8340)
FERGUSON CO
6226 Cherry Ave, Long Beach (90805-3205)
P.O. Box 5849, Los Alamitos (90721-5849)
PHONE...........................562 428-3300
Rosa Bermeo, *Principal*
EMP: 15 EST: 2006
SALES (est): 4.1MM **Privately Held**
WEB: www.fpl-global.com
SIC: 3585 5078 Refrigeration equipment, complete; refrigeration equipment & supplies

(P-8341)
GOODMAN MANUFACTURING CO LP
15024 Anacapa Rd, Victorville (92392-2509)
PHONE...........................760 955-7770
Don Johnston, *Branch Mgr*
EMP: 292 **Privately Held**
WEB: www.goodmanmfg.com
SIC: 3585 Air conditioning equipment, complete
HQ: Goodman Manufacturing Company, Lp
　19001 Kermier Rd
　Waller TX 77484
　713 861-2500

(P-8342)
HUSSMANN CORPORATION
13770 Ramona Ave, Chino (91710-5423)
P.O. Box 5133 (91708-5133)
PHONE...........................909 590-4910
Mike Gleason, *General Mgr*
Lindsay Harrington, *Program Mgr*

Todd Blaufuss, *Area Mgr*
Richard Hill, *Area Mgr*
Roger Page, *Area Mgr*
EMP: 350 **Privately Held**
WEB: www.hussmann.com
SIC: 3585 7623 Refrigeration & heating equipment; refrigeration service & repair
HQ: Hussmann Corporation
　12999 St Charles Rock Rd
　Bridgeton MO 63044
　314 291-2000

(P-8343)
KOOLFOG INC (PA)
31290 Plantation Dr, Thousand Palms (92276-6604)
PHONE...........................760 321-9203
Bryan Roe, *President*
Mike Montez, *Project Mgr*
Robert Xanders, *Sales Mgr*
EMP: 17 EST: 1987
SQ FT: 4,000
SALES (est): 5.1MM **Privately Held**
WEB: www.koolfog.com
SIC: 3585 7819 Humidifiers & dehumidifiers; visual effects production

(P-8344)
LMW ENTERPRISES LLC
Also Called: Lrc Coil Company
10558 Norwalk Blvd, Santa Fe Springs (90670-3836)
PHONE...........................562 944-1969
EMP: 16
SALES (corp-wide): 3.6MM **Privately Held**
WEB: www.lrccoil.com
SIC: 3585 Refrigeration equipment, complete; condensers, refrigeration; evaporative condensers, heat transfer equipment
PA: Lmw Enterprises Llc
　3861 E 42nd Pl
　Yuma AZ 85365
　562 944-1969

(P-8345)
MESTEK INC
Also Called: Anemostat Products
1220 E Watson Center Rd, Carson (90745-4206)
PHONE...........................310 835-7500
Chang Hung, *Plant Mgr*
Blanca Olvera, *Executive*
Khalid Bu Khamsin, *Engineer*
Hari Thacker, *Controller*
Ben Cortez, *Mktg Dir*
EMP: 200
SALES (corp-wide): 689.9MM **Privately Held**
WEB: www.mestek.com
SIC: 3585 3549 3542 3354 Heating equipment, complete; metalworking machinery; punching, shearing & bending machines; shapes, extruded aluminum; mainframe computers; manufactured hardware (general)
PA: Mestek, Inc.
　260 N Elm St
　Westfield MA 01085
　470 898-4533

(P-8346)
R-COLD INC
1221 S G St, Perris (92570-2477)
PHONE...........................951 436-5476
Michael Mulcahy, *President*
Ernest Gaston, *CFO*
Joshua Elder, *Sales Staff*
EMP: 65 EST: 1982
SQ FT: 28,000
SALES (est): 10.8MM **Privately Held**
WEB: www.r-cold.com
SIC: 3585 1541 Refrigeration & heating equipment; industrial buildings & warehouses

(P-8347)
RAHN INDUSTRIES INCORPORATED (PA)
2630 Pacific Park Dr, Whittier (90601-1611)
PHONE...........................562 908-0680
John Hancock, *President*
Jeff Meier, *Vice Pres*
Claudia Maytum, *Admin Sec*
Ahmed Khalili, *Chief Engr*
Javier Sandoval, *QC Mgr*

▲ EMP: 58 EST: 1979
SQ FT: 25,000
SALES (est): 14.6MM **Privately Held**
WEB: www.rahnindustries.com
SIC: 3585 Refrigeration & heating equipment

(P-8348)
REFRIGERATOR MANUFACTURERS LLC
Also Called: Airdyne Refrigeration
17018 Edwards Rd, Cerritos (90703-2422)
PHONE...........................562 926-2006
Tony Bedi, *President*
Bill Hargraves, *Sales Mgr*
EMP: 47 EST: 2015
SALES (est): 5MM **Privately Held**
WEB: www.rmi-econocold.com
SIC: 3585 Condensers, refrigeration

(P-8349)
TEAM AIR INC (PA)
Also Called: Team Air Conditioning Eqp
12771 Brown Ave, Riverside (92509-1831)
PHONE...........................909 823-1957
Thirusenthil Nathan, *President*
Oliver Corbala, *Vice Pres*
EMP: 35 EST: 1999
SALES (est): 8.2MM **Privately Held**
WEB: www.teamairconditionequipment.com
SIC: 3585 Air conditioning equipment, complete

(P-8350)
THREE STAR RFRGN ENGRG INC
Also Called: Kool Star
21720 S Wilmington Ave, Long Beach (90810-1641)
PHONE...........................310 327-9090
James Pak, *President*
William So, *CFO*
Kyung Lee, *Admin Sec*
◆ EMP: 23 EST: 1989
SQ FT: 68,000
SALES (est): 1.3MM **Privately Held**
SIC: 3585 4222 Air conditioning condensers & condensing units; condensers, refrigeration; refrigerated warehousing & storage

(P-8351)
TRANE US INC
Also Called: Southern California Trane
3253 E Imperial Hwy, Brea (92821-6722)
PHONE...........................626 913-7123
John Clark, *Branch Mgr*
EMP: 100 **Privately Held**
WEB: www.trane.com
SIC: 3585 Heating & air conditioning combination units
HQ: Trane U.S. Inc.
　3600 Pammel Creek Rd
　La Crosse WI 54601
　608 787-2000

(P-8352)
TURBO COIL INC
1532 Sinaloa Ave, Pasadena (91104-2744)
PHONE...........................626 644-6254
Hector Delgadillo, *CEO*
EMP: 21 EST: 2013
SQ FT: 2,000
SALES (est): 696.6K **Privately Held**
SIC: 3585 Compressors for refrigeration & air conditioning equipment

(P-8353)
TURBO REFRIGERATION SYSTEMS
1740 Evergreen St, Duarte (91010-2845)
PHONE...........................626 599-9777
Hector Delgadillo, *CEO*
Jose Carbajal, *Principal*
Roberta Delgadillo, *Principal*
EMP: 13 EST: 2012
SQ FT: 4,000
SALES (est): 165.4K **Privately Held**
SIC: 3585 Condensers, refrigeration

(P-8354)
UTILITY REFRIGERATOR
12160 Sherman Way, North Hollywood (91605-5501)
P.O. Box 570782, Tarzana (91357-0782)
PHONE...........................818 764-6200
Michael Michrowski, *President*
Marshall Brown, *Officer*
Karl Bruno, *Sales Staff*
Geiger Russ, *Sales Staff*
Justin Smith, *Sales Staff*
▲ EMP: 22 EST: 2007
SALES (est): 2.5MM **Privately Held**
WEB: www.utilityrefrigerator.com
SIC: 3585 Parts for heating, cooling & refrigerating equipment

(P-8355)
VEGE-MIST INC
Also Called: Alco Designs
407 E Redondo Beach Blvd, Gardena (90248-2312)
PHONE...........................310 353-2300
Samuel Cohen, *CEO*
Liz Luna, *General Mgr*
Dick Warden, *Sales Staff*
▲ EMP: 61 EST: 1988
SQ FT: 8,000
SALES (est): 14.9MM **Privately Held**
SIC: 3585 2541 5074 2542 Humidifying equipment, except portable; store & office display cases & fixtures; water purification equipment; partitions & fixtures, except wood

(P-8356)
VENSTAR INC
9250 Owensmouth Ave, Chatsworth (91311-5853)
PHONE...........................818 341-8760
Steve Dushane, *President*
Scott Agnew, *Natl Sales Mgr*
▲ EMP: 15 EST: 1992
SALES (est): 3.5MM **Privately Held**
WEB: www.venstar.com
SIC: 3585 Refrigeration & heating equipment

(P-8357)
WESTAIRE ENGINEERING INC
5820 S Alameda St, Vernon (90058-3432)
PHONE...........................323 587-3347
Vazgen Galadjian, *President*
Shane Bekian, *Vice Pres*
Kevin Galadjian, *Vice Pres*
▲ EMP: 15 EST: 1993
SQ FT: 50,000
SALES (est): 2.5MM **Privately Held**
WEB: www.westaireengineering.com
SIC: 3585 5075 Air conditioning units, complete: domestic or industrial; ventilating equipment & supplies

(P-8358)
WHITES HVAC SERVICES INC
131 E Knotts St, Nipomo (93444-9423)
P.O. Box 365 (93444-0365)
PHONE...........................805 801-0167
Mike White, *President*
Georgia White, *CFO*
EMP: 15 EST: 1995
SALES (est): 1.2MM **Privately Held**
WEB: www.whiteshvacservicesinc.com
SIC: 3585 7389 Heating & air conditioning combination units;

(P-8359)
WILLIAMS FURNACE CO (DH)
Also Called: Williams Comfort Products
250 W Laurel St, Colton (92324-1435)
PHONE...........................562 450-3602
Michael Markowich, *President*
Joseph Sum, *Treasurer*
Ruth Ann Davis, *Vice Pres*
James Gidwitz, *Vice Pres*
Maribel Saffo, *Vice Pres*
▲ EMP: 173 EST: 1916
SQ FT: 400,000
SALES (est): 43.3MM
SALES (corp-wide): 113.2MM **Privately Held**
WEB: www.williamscomfortprod.com
SIC: 3585 3433 Refrigeration & heating equipment; heating equipment, except electric

HQ: Continental Materials Corporation
440 S La Salle St # 3100
Chicago IL 60605
312 541-7200

3589 Service Ind Machines, NEC

(P-8360)
AATECH
6666 Box Springs Blvd, Riverside
(92507-0726)
PHONE.....................................909 854-3200
Jerry McAuley, *President*
Darlene McAuley, *Vice Pres*
EMP: 13 **EST:** 1990
SALES (est): 1MM **Privately Held**
WEB: www.aatechwater.com
SIC: 3589 Water treatment equipment, industrial

(P-8361)
ADVANCED UV INC (PA)
16350 Manning Way, Cerritos
(90703-2224)
PHONE.....................................562 407-0299
Kiyomitsu Kevin Toma, *CEO*
▲ **EMP:** 38 **EST:** 1996
SQ FT: 30,000
SALES (est): 9.4MM **Privately Held**
WEB: www.advanceduv.com
SIC: 3589 Water purification equipment, household type; water treatment equipment, industrial

(P-8362)
AMIAD USA INC
Also Called: Amiad Filtration Systems
1251 Maulhardt Ave, Oxnard (93030-7990)
P.O. Box 5547 (93031-5547)
PHONE.....................................805 988-3323
Tom Akehurst, *President*
Issac Orlans, *Shareholder*
Yigal Schwartz, *Founder*
Lisa Charles, *Administration*
Wendy Paul, *Purchasing*
▲ **EMP:** 35 **EST:** 1981
SQ FT: 30,000
SALES (est): 7.6MM
SALES (corp-wide): 104.6MM **Privately Held**
WEB: www.amiad.com
SIC: 3589 Water treatment equipment, industrial
PA: Amiad Water Systems Ltd
Kibbutz
Amiad 12335
469 095-00

(P-8363)
AQUAFINE CORPORATION (HQ)
29010 Avenue Paine, Valencia
(91355-4198)
PHONE.....................................661 257-4770
Roberta Veloz, *Chairman*
Michael Murphy, *President*
Sarah Clarke, *Human Resources*
Darry McCloud, *Manager*
Jiawei Zhang, *Manager*
◆ **EMP:** 73 **EST:** 1949
SQ FT: 100,000
SALES (est): 23.8MM
SALES (corp-wide): 22.2B **Publicly Held**
WEB: www.danaher.com
SIC: 3589 Water treatment equipment, industrial
PA: Danaher Corporation
2200 Penn Ave Nw Ste 800w
Washington DC 20037
202 828-0850

(P-8364)
AQUAMOR LLC
Also Called: Watersentinel
42188 Rio Nedo, Temecula (92590-3717)
PHONE.....................................951 541-9517
Michael T Baird,
Mounir Ibrahim, *CFO*
Michael Pennington, *Vice Pres*
Cynthia Perez, *Admin Asst*
Will Mott, *Info Tech Mgr*
▲ **EMP:** 100 **EST:** 2004

SALES (est): 14.9MM **Privately Held**
WEB: www.aquamor.com
SIC: 3589 Water filters & softeners, household type

(P-8365)
AQUEOUS TECHNOLOGIES CORP
1678 N Maple St, Corona (92878-3206)
PHONE.....................................909 944-7771
Michael Konrad, *CEO*
Chad Cisneros, *Partner*
Cameron Heckman, *Accounting Mgr*
Rosendo Ramirez, *Manager*
▲ **EMP:** 23 **EST:** 1992
SQ FT: 15,000
SALES (est): 5.5MM **Privately Held**
WEB: www.aqueoustech.com
SIC: 3589 3829 5084 7699 High pressure cleaning equipment; water treatment equipment, industrial; physical property testing equipment; cleaning equipment, high pressure, sand or steam; industrial machinery & equipment repair

(P-8366)
AXEON WATER TECHNOLOGIES
40980 County Center Dr # 110, Temecula
(92591-6052)
PHONE.....................................760 723-5417
Augustin R Pavel, *President*
Patty Hinrichs, *CFO*
Jeanette Pavel, *Corp Secy*
Cristhian Paez, *Technician*
Taylor Ressel, *Design Engr*
◆ **EMP:** 85 **EST:** 1989
SQ FT: 47,000
SALES (est): 15.8MM **Privately Held**
WEB: www.axeonwater.com
SIC: 3589 5999 Water filters & softeners, household type; water purification equipment, household type; water purification equipment

(P-8367)
B&W CUSTOM RESTAURANT EQP INC
541 E Jamie Ave, La Habra (90631-6842)
PHONE.....................................714 578-0332
Nathan Bojorquez, *President*
EMP: 20 **EST:** 1990
SALES (est): 2.6MM **Privately Held**
WEB: www.bwcustom.com
SIC: 3589 8711 2599 Cooking equipment, commercial; industrial engineers; carts, restaurant equipment

(P-8368)
BARHENA INC
Also Called: Adamation
1085 Bixby Dr, Hacienda Heights
(91745-1704)
PHONE.....................................888 383-8800
EMP: 25 **EST:** 1957
SQ FT: 45,000
SALES (est): 2.7MM **Privately Held**
WEB: www.adamationinc.com
SIC: 3589 3952 Mfg Commercial Dish Washing Systems & Burnishing Machines
PA: Flow Grinding Corp.
70 Conn St
Woburn MA 01801

(P-8369)
BLUE DESERT INTERNATIONAL INC
Also Called: Hydro Quip
510 N Sheridan St Ste A, Corona
(92878-4024)
PHONE.....................................951 273-7575
Christopher W Kuttig, *President*
Jerri Freed, *Admin Sec*
Michael Staab, *Manager*
◆ **EMP:** 80 **EST:** 1994
SQ FT: 31,000
SALES (est): 16.4MM **Privately Held**
SIC: 3589 Swimming pool filter & water conditioning systems

(P-8370)
CHEMICAL METHODS ASSOC LLC (DH)
Also Called: CMA Dish Machines
12700 Knott St, Garden Grove
(92841-3938)
PHONE.....................................714 898-8781
Fred G Palmer, *President*
Fred Palmer, *Vice Pres*
Nancy Guzman, *General Mgr*
Steve Wingate, *General Mgr*
Joseph Nudel, *Design Engr*
▲ **EMP:** 30 **EST:** 1970
SQ FT: 50,000
SALES (est): 36.7MM
SALES (corp-wide): 2.6MM **Privately Held**
WEB: www.cmadishmachines.com
SIC: 3589 Dishwashing machines, commercial
HQ: Ali Group North America Corporation
101 Corporate Woods Pkwy
Vernon Hills IL 60061
847 215-6565

(P-8371)
CITY OF DELANO
Also Called: Delano Waste Water Treatment
1107 Lytle Ave, Delano (93215-9389)
PHONE.....................................661 721-3352
Bill Hylton, *Manager*
EMP: 30
SALES (corp-wide): 38.3MM **Privately Held**
WEB: www.cityofdelano.org
SIC: 3589 Water treatment equipment, industrial
PA: City Of Delano
1015 11th Ave
Delano CA 93215
661 721-3300

(P-8372)
CITY OF RIVERSIDE
Also Called: Water Treatment Plant
5950 Acorn St, Riverside (92504-1036)
PHONE.....................................951 351-6140
Richard Pallante, *General Mgr*
EMP: 39
SALES (corp-wide): 338.1MM **Privately Held**
WEB: www.riversideca.gov
SIC: 3589 9111 Water treatment equipment, industrial; mayors' offices
PA: City Of Riverside
3900 Main St Fl 7
Riverside CA 92522
951 826-5311

(P-8373)
CLEAN WATER TECHNOLOGY INC (HQ)
Also Called: CWT
13008 S Western Ave, Gardena
(90249-1920)
PHONE.....................................310 380-4648
Ariel Lechter, *CEO*
Gerald Friedman, *Admin Sec*
▲ **EMP:** 50 **EST:** 1996
SALES (est): 13.8MM
SALES (corp-wide): 149.5MM **Privately Held**
WEB: www.cwt-global.com
SIC: 3589 Water treatment equipment, industrial
PA: Marvin Engineering Co., Inc.
261 W Beach Ave
Inglewood CA 90302
310 674-5030

(P-8374)
CLEAR WATER CORPORATION INC
7848 San Fernando Rd B, Sun Valley
(91352-4367)
PHONE.....................................818 765-8293
Yarvin Gilboa, *President*
EMP: 14 **EST:** 1991
SALES (est): 1.8MM **Privately Held**
SIC: 3589 Water treatment equipment, industrial

(P-8375)
CM BREWING TECHNOLOGIES LLC
Also Called: Ss Brewtech
13681 Newport Ave Ste 8, Tustin
(92780-7815)
PHONE.....................................888 391-9990
Mitchell Thomson, *CEO*
Michael Fabian, *COO*
Jake Kucera, *Officer*
Curt Kucera, *CTO*
EMP: 15 **EST:** 2013
SALES (est): 3.9MM
SALES (corp-wide): 2.5B **Publicly Held**
WEB: www.middleby.com
SIC: 3589 5046 Coffee brewing equipment; coffee brewing equipment & supplies
PA: The Middleby Corporation
1400 Toastmaster Dr
Elgin IL 60120
847 741-3300

(P-8376)
COMCO INC
2151 N Lincoln St, Burbank (91504-3392)
PHONE.....................................818 333-8500
Colin Weightman, *President*
Anders Pineiro, *Info Tech Mgr*
Ozzy Cuellar, *Production*
EMP: 36
SQ FT: 12,500
SALES (est): 8MM **Privately Held**
WEB: www.comcoinc.com
SIC: 3589 3291 Sandblasting equipment; abrasive products

(P-8377)
COMPASS WATER SOLUTIONS INC (PA)
15542 Mosher Ave, Tustin (92780-6425)
PHONE.....................................949 222-5777
Thomas Farshler, *CEO*
Bill Tidmore, *CFO*
Collin Tovey, *Engineer*
Jade Trieu, *Accountant*
Trent Nieto, *Regl Sales Mgr*
▲ **EMP:** 50 **EST:** 1983
SQ FT: 3,000
SALES (est): 11MM **Privately Held**
WEB: www.compasswater.com
SIC: 3589 Water treatment equipment, industrial

(P-8378)
DE NORA WATER TECHNOLOGIES LLC
1230 Rosecrans Ave # 300, Manhattan
Beach (90266-2477)
PHONE.....................................310 618-9700
Marwan Nesicolaci, *Vice Pres*
Wayne De Freest, *Purch Agent*
EMP: 19 **Privately Held**
WEB: www.denora.com
SIC: 3589 Water treatment equipment, industrial
HQ: De Nora Water Technologies Llc
3000 Advance Ln
Colmar PA 18915
215 997-4000

(P-8379)
DYNAMIC COOKING SYSTEMS INC
Also Called: Fisher & Paykel
695 Town Center Dr # 180, Costa Mesa
(92626-1924)
PHONE.....................................714 372-7000
Laurence Mawhinney, *CEO*
Jeff Elder, *CFO*
Scott Davies, *Marketing Mgr*
Don Norton, *Regl Sales Mgr*
Sarah Howey, *Marketing Staff*
▲ **EMP:** 700 **EST:** 1987
SQ FT: 140,000
SALES (est): 113.7MM **Privately Held**
WEB: www.fisherpaykel.com
SIC: 3589 Cooking equipment, commercial
HQ: Fisher & Paykel Appliances Usa Holdings Inc.
695 Town Center Dr # 180
Costa Mesa CA 92626

(P-8380)
ENGINEERED FOOD SYSTEMS
2490 Anselmo Dr, Corona (92879-8089)
P.O. Box 28321, Anaheim (92809-0144)
PHONE....................................714 921-9913
Martin Olguin, *President*
Irma Olguin, *CFO*
▲ EMP: 25 EST: 2008
SQ FT: 18,000
SALES (est): 3.8MM **Privately Held**
WEB: www.efs-eng.com
SIC: 3589 5084 Food warming equipment,
commercial; food product manufacturing
machinery

(P-8381)
FILTRONICS INC
16872 Hale Ave Ste B, Irvine (92606-5064)
PHONE....................................714 630-5040
EMP: 19 EST: 1974
SALES (est): 1.2MM **Privately Held**
WEB: www.filtronics.com
SIC: 3589 Water treatment equipment, in-
dustrial

(P-8382)
G A SYSTEMS INC
226 W Carleton Ave, Orange (92867-3608)
PHONE....................................714 848-7529
Steven Anderson, *President*
Larry Wange, *Natl Sales Mgr*
EMP: 27 EST: 1968
SQ FT: 19,400
SALES (est): 2.3MM **Privately Held**
WEB: www.gasystemsmfg.com
SIC: 3589 Commercial cooking & food-
warming equipment

(P-8383)
GET
Also Called: Vita Science Health Products
2030 W 17th St, Long Beach (90813-1012)
PHONE....................................562 989-5400
Fax: 562 983-7717
EMP: 15
SQ FT: 28,000
SALES (est): 2.4MM **Privately Held**
WEB: www.get-inc.com
SIC: 3589 Mfg Service Industry Machinery

(P-8384)
GORLITZ SEWER & DRAIN INC
10132 Norwalk Blvd, Santa Fe Springs
(90670-3326)
PHONE....................................562 944-3060
James Kruger, *CEO*
Gerd Kruger, *President*
Elba Kruger, *Vice Pres*
▲ EMP: 30 EST: 1974
SQ FT: 33,300
SALES (est): 5.2MM **Privately Held**
WEB: www.gorlitz.com
SIC: 3589 Sewer cleaning equipment,
power

(P-8385)
HANNAH INDUSTRIES INC
Also Called: South Coast Water
401 S Santa Fe St, Santa Ana
(92705-4139)
P.O. Box 247, Orange (92856-6247)
PHONE....................................714 939-7873
Roy Hall, *President*
Hayley Jackson, *Office Mgr*
Hayley Castillo, *Manager*
Cristina Lomeli, *Manager*
EMP: 15
SQ FT: 15,000
SALES (est): 4.3MM **Privately Held**
WEB: www.sch2o.com
SIC: 3589 5074 Water treatment equip-
ment, industrial; water purification equip-
ment

(P-8386)
HYDRODEX LLC
31225 La Baya Dr, Westlake Village
(91362-4019)
PHONE....................................800 218-8813
Bassem Khoury,
EMP: 20 EST: 2019
SALES (est): 1.4MM **Privately Held**
WEB: www.hydrodex.com
SIC: 3589 Water treatment equipment, in-
dustrial

(P-8387)
**J F DUNCAN INDUSTRIES INC
(PA)**
Also Called: Duray
9301 Stewart And Gray Rd, Downey
(90241-5315)
PHONE....................................562 862-4269
Johnny F Wong, *CEO*
Don Durward, *Vice Pres*
Greg Rodriguez, *Project Mgr*
Jim Sharpe, *Project Mgr*
Dave Jensen, *Sr Project Mgr*
▲ EMP: 94 EST: 1988
SALES (est): 22MM **Privately Held**
WEB: www.durayduncan.com
SIC: 3589 Cooking equipment, commercial

(P-8388)
J L WINGERT COMPANY
11800 Monarch St, Garden Grove
(92841-2113)
P.O. Box 6207 (92846-6207)
PHONE....................................714 379-5519
Tommy Thomas, *CEO*
Reeve Thomas, *Principal*
Robert Anderson, *Sales Staff*
Itzel Luis,
EMP: 65 EST: 1965
SQ FT: 16,000
SALES (est): 9.4MM **Privately Held**
WEB: www.jlwingert.com
SIC: 3589 5084 Water treatment equip-
ment, industrial; industrial machinery &
equipment

(P-8389)
JACUZZI INC (DH)
Also Called: Jacuzzi Outdoor Products
14525 Monte Vista Ave, Chino
(91710-5721)
PHONE....................................909 606-7733
Roy A Jacuzzi, *Ch of Bd*
Donald C Devine, *President*
Thomas Koos, *CEO*
Ryan Sessler, *Vice Pres*
Ritchie Taylor, *Vice Pres*
◆ EMP: 110 EST: 1979
SALES (est): 808.2MM
SALES (corp-wide): 467.1K **Privately
Held**
WEB: www.jacuzzi.com
SIC: 3589 3088 Swimming pool filter &
water conditioning systems; hot tubs,
plastic or fiberglass
HQ: Jacuzzi Brands Llc
13925 City Center Dr # 200
Chino Hills CA 91709
909 606-1416

(P-8390)
JWC ENVIRONMENTAL INC
Also Called: Disposable Waste System
2600 S Garnsey St, Santa Ana
(92707-3339)
PHONE....................................714 662-5829
Steve Glomb, *CFO*
Robert Pepper, *Managing Dir*
Rob Sabol, *Research*
Jon Kimler, *Engineer*
Michael Wolf, *Sales Staff*
EMP: 100
SQ FT: 45,637
SALES (corp-wide): 3.6B **Privately Held**
WEB: www.jwce.com
SIC: 3589 Sewage treatment equipment
HQ: Jwc Environmental Inc.
2850 Redhill Ave Ste 125
Santa Ana CA 92705

(P-8391)
LAS COLINAS
600 S Jefferson St Ste M, Placentia
(92870-6634)
PHONE....................................714 528-8100
C Christine Licata, *President*
Catharine Christine Licata, *President*
Anthony Licata, *CFO*
David Everett, *Branch Mgr*
EMP: 15 EST: 2000
SALES (est): 2.1MM **Privately Held**
WEB: www.lascolinasco.com
SIC: 3589 1711 Asbestos removal equip-
ment; plumbing contractors

(P-8392)
**LIFESOURCE WATER SYSTEMS
INC (PA)**
523 S Fair Oaks Ave, Pasadena
(91105-2605)
PHONE....................................626 792-9996
B J Wright, *President*
Richard Boisclair, *Vice Pres*
Roger Crmc, *Vice Pres*
Tony Romaldo, *Vice Pres*
Nathan Anderson, *Regional Mgr*
EMP: 22
SQ FT: 10,000
SALES (est): 10.7MM **Privately Held**
WEB: www.lifesourcewater.com
SIC: 3589 5074 Water purification equip-
ment, household type; water filters & sof-
teners, household type; plumbing &
hydronic heating supplies

(P-8393)
M D MANUFACTURING INC
34970 Mcmurtrey Ave, Bakersfield
(93308-9578)
PHONE....................................661 283-7550
Raymond Stewart, *President*
◆ EMP: 19 EST: 1961
SQ FT: 34,000
SALES (est): 2.7MM **Privately Held**
WEB: www.builtinvacuum.com
SIC: 3589 Vacuum cleaners & sweepers,
electric; industrial

(P-8394)
**MANN+HMMEL WTR FLUID
SLTONS IN (DH)**
Also Called: Microdyn-Nadir Us, Inc.
93 S La Patera Ln, Goleta (93117-3246)
PHONE....................................805 964-8003
Peter Knappe, *President*
Kevin Edberg, *CFO*
Michael Kraus, *Info Tech Mgr*
Alfredo Rodriguez, *IT/INT Sup*
Nikhilesh Mehta, *Engineer*
◆ EMP: 90 EST: 1990
SQ FT: 40,000
SALES (est): 25.4MM
SALES (corp-wide): 4.6B **Privately Held**
WEB: www.microdyn-nadir.com
SIC: 3589 Water treatment equipment, in-
dustrial
HQ: Mann+Hummel Water & Fluid Solu-
tions Gmbh
Kasteler Str. 45
Wiesbaden HE 65203
611 962-6001

(P-8395)
MAR COR PURIFICATION INC
6351 Orangethorpe Ave, Buena Park
(90620-1340)
PHONE....................................800 633-3080
Sean West, *Branch Mgr*
Paul Felice, *Manager*
EMP: 29 **Privately Held**
WEB: www.mcpur.com
SIC: 3589 Water treatment equipment, in-
dustrial
HQ: Mar Cor Purification, Inc.
4450 Township Line Rd
Skippack PA 19474
800 633-3080

(P-8396)
**MAZZEI INJECTOR COMPANY
LLC**
500 Rooster Dr, Bakersfield (93307-9555)
PHONE....................................661 363-6500
Angelo Mazzei, *CEO*
Geoffrey Whynot, *President*
Mary Mazzei, *Bd of Directors*
Celia Cobar, *Vice Pres*
▲ EMP: 24 EST: 1978
SALES (est): 8MM
SALES (corp-wide): 8MM **Privately Held**
WEB: www.mazzei.net
SIC: 3589 Water treatment equipment, in-
dustrial
PA: Mazzei Injector Corporation
500 Rooster Dr
Bakersfield CA 93307
661 363-6500

(P-8397)
MEDIA BLAST & ABRASIVE INC
591 Apollo St, Brea (92821-3127)
PHONE....................................714 257-0484
Ronald Storer, *President*
EMP: 19 EST: 1997
SALES (est): 4.5MM **Privately Held**
WEB: www.mediablast.com
SIC: 3589 3822 Sandblasting equipment;
high pressure cleaning equipment; auto
controls regulating residntl & coml envi-
ronmt & applncs

(P-8398)
MEGUIARS INC
18001 Mitchell S, Irvine (92614-6007)
PHONE....................................651 733-1110
Mary Swanson, *President*
◆ EMP: 17 EST: 2014
SALES (est): 3.9MM
SALES (corp-wide): 32.1B **Publicly Held**
WEB: www.meguiarsonline.com
SIC: 3589 Car washing machinery
PA: 3m Company
3m Center
Saint Paul MN 55144
651 733-1110

(P-8399)
N/S CORPORATION (PA)
Also Called: NS Wash Systems
235 W Florence Ave, Inglewood
(90301-1293)
PHONE....................................310 412-7074
G Thomas Ennis Sr, *CEO*
Francis Penggardjaja, *Exec VP*
Regina Dominguez, *Project Engr*
Lumen Ong, *Controller*
Victor Sanchez, *Manager*
◆ EMP: 84 EST: 1967
SQ FT: 80,000
SALES (est): 26.3MM **Privately Held**
WEB: www.nswash.com
SIC: 3589 Car washing machinery

(P-8400)
**NALCO WTR PRTRTMENT
SLTONS LLC**
704 Richfield Rd, Placentia (92870-6760)
PHONE....................................714 792-0708
EMP: 28
SALES (corp-wide): 1.9B **Publicly Held**
SIC: 3589 Water treatment equipment, in-
dustrial
HQ: Nalco Water Pretreatment Solutions,
Llc
1601 W Diehl Rd
Naperville IL 60563
708 754-2550

(P-8401)
NIMBUS WATER SYSTEMS
42445 Avenida Alvarado, Temecula
(92590-3461)
P.O. Box 1478 (92593-1478)
PHONE....................................951 984-2800
Anthony Alexander Capone, *President*
Patricia Renee Capone, *CFO*
David See, *General Mgr*
EMP: 15 EST: 1968
SQ FT: 25,000
SALES (est): 4.8MM
SALES (corp-wide): 1B **Privately Held**
WEB: www.nimbuswater.com
SIC: 3589 Water purification equipment,
household type; water treatment equip-
ment, industrial
HQ: Kinetico Incorporated
10845 Kinsman Rd
Newbury OH 44065
440 564-9111

(P-8402)
OSMOSIS TECHNOLOGY INC
Also Called: Osmotik
6900 Hermosa Cir, Buena Park
(90620-1151)
PHONE....................................714 670-9303
Mike Joulakian, *President*
Sonia Joulakian, *Vice Pres*
Tina Hampe, *General Mgr*
EMP: 21 EST: 1984
SQ FT: 13,000

SALES (est): 2.9MM **Privately Held**
WEB: www.osmotik.com
SIC: **3589** Water filters & softeners, household type

(P-8403)
PENTAIR WATER POOL AND SPA INC
Also Called: Pentair Pool Products
10951 W Los Angeles Ave, Moorpark (93021-9744)
P.O. Box 8085 (93020-8085)
PHONE...................................805 553-5003
Diane Larkin, *Manager*
EMP: 48 **Privately Held**
WEB: www.pentair.com
SIC: **3589** 3561 3569 3648 Swimming pool filter & water conditioning systems; pumps, domestic: water or sump; heaters, swimming pool: electric; underwater lighting fixtures; sporting & athletic goods; swimming pool & hot tub service & maintenance
HQ: Pentair Water Pool And Spa, Inc.
1620 Hawkins Ave
Sanford NC 27330
919 566-8000

(P-8404)
PERFORMANCE WATER PRODUCTS INC
6902 Aragon Cir, Buena Park (90620-1118)
PHONE...................................714 736-0137
Kristopher Mecca, *President*
Kari Mecca, *Corp Secy*
John Mecca, *Vice Pres*
Mat Mecca, *Vice Pres*
Mike Mecca, *Director*
EMP: 17 EST: 1992
SQ FT: 51,000
SALES (est): 11.1MM **Privately Held**
WEB: www.performancewater.com
SIC: **5963** 3589 Bottled water delivery; water purification equipment, household type; water treatment equipment, industrial

(P-8405)
PRODUCT SOLUTIONS INC
1182 N Knollwood Cir, Anaheim (92801-1307)
PHONE...................................714 545-9757
Robert Kreaton, *CEO*
Judith Keaton, *Admin Sec*
▲ EMP: 50 EST: 1993
SQ FT: 25,000
SALES (est): 9.1MM **Privately Held**
WEB: www.fastproductsolutions.com
SIC: **3589** 3631 Commercial cooking & foodwarming equipment; household cooking equipment

(P-8406)
PURI TECH INC
Also Called: Everfilt
3167 Progress Cir, Jurupa Valley (91752-1112)
PHONE...................................951 360-8380
Barbara J Andrew, *President*
Amber Mills, *Administration*
Brian Tolson, *Senior Mgr*
EMP: 24 EST: 1979
SQ FT: 10,600
SALES (est): 1.4MM **Privately Held**
WEB: www.everfilt.com
SIC: **3589** 5074 Water treatment equipment, industrial; water purification equipment

(P-8407)
QMP INC
25070 Avenue Tibbitts, Valencia (91355-3447)
PHONE...................................661 294-6860
Freddy Vidal, *President*
Irma Vidal, *Vice Pres*
Tady Salaues, *VP Sales*
▲ EMP: 45 EST: 1994
SQ FT: 40,000
SALES (est): 10MM **Privately Held**
WEB: www.qmpusa.com
SIC: **3589** Sewage & water treatment equipment; water purification equipment, household type; water treatment equipment, industrial

(P-8408)
RANKIN-DELUX INC (PA)
3245 Corridor Dr, Eastvale (91752-1030)
PHONE...................................951 685-0081
L Vasan, *President*
William A Rankin, *Shareholder*
▲ EMP: 15 EST: 1965
SQ FT: 25,000
SALES (est): 2.4MM **Privately Held**
WEB: www.rankindelux.com
SIC: **3589** Cooking equipment, commercial

(P-8409)
S & S INSTALLATIONS INC
Also Called: Pacific Stainless
294 W Olive St, Colton (92324-1757)
PHONE...................................909 370-1730
Tom Skocilich, *President*
Ron Greg, *Vice Pres*
Robert Skocilich, *Vice Pres*
EMP: 22 EST: 1984
SQ FT: 12,000
SALES (est): 3.6MM **Privately Held**
SIC: **3589** 3556 3469 Food warming equipment, commercial; food products machinery; metal stampings

(P-8410)
SANSANI CLEANING SOLUTIONS LLC
551 E 64th St Apt 3, Long Beach (90805-2395)
PHONE...................................310 630-9033
Daven Trotter,
EMP: 15 EST: 2020
SALES (est): 615K **Privately Held**
SIC: **3589** Commercial cleaning equipment

(P-8411)
SANTA MONICA CITY OF
Also Called: City Snta Mnica Wtr Trtmnt Pla
1228 S Bundy Dr, Los Angeles (90025-1102)
PHONE...................................310 826-6712
Myriam Cardenas, *Branch Mgr*
Karen Evans, *Analyst*
Rathar Duong, *Associate*
EMP: 38
SQ FT: 2,500
SALES (corp-wide): 455.7MM **Privately Held**
WEB: www.santamonica.gov
SIC: **3589** Sewage & water treatment equipment
PA: City Of Santa Monica
1685 Main St
Santa Monica CA 90401
310 458-8411

(P-8412)
SEWER RODDING EQUIPMENT CO (PA)
Also Called: Flexible Video Systems
3217 Carter Ave, Marina Del Rey (90292-5554)
PHONE...................................310 301-9009
Patrick Crane, *CEO*
EMP: 25 EST: 1932
SQ FT: 24,000
SALES (est): 9.7MM **Privately Held**
SIC: **3589** Sewer cleaning equipment, power

(P-8413)
SEYCHELLE ENVMTL TECH INC
32963 Calle Perfecto, San Juan Capistrano (92675-4705)
PHONE...................................949 234-1999
Carl Palmer, *Branch Mgr*
Desiree Walton, *Sales Staff*
EMP: 13 **Publicly Held**
WEB: www.seychelle.com
SIC: **3589** Water treatment equipment, industrial
PA: Seychelle Environmental Technologies, Inc.
22 Journey
Aliso Viejo CA 92656

(P-8414)
SHEPARD BROS INC (PA)
503 S Cypress St, La Habra (90631-6126)
PHONE...................................562 697-1366
Ronald Shepard, *CEO*

Duane Shepard, *President*
Jon Wynkoop, *CFO*
Don Miller, *Vice Pres*
Manuel Solis, *Vice Pres*
▲ EMP: 119 EST: 1976
SQ FT: 57,830
SALES (est): 34.6MM **Privately Held**
WEB: www.shepardbros.com
SIC: **3589** 5169 Sewage & water treatment equipment; chemicals & allied products

(P-8415)
SNOWPURE LLC
Also Called: Snowpure Water Technologies
130 Calle Iglesia Ste A, San Clemente (92672-7535)
P.O. Box 73368 (92673-0113)
PHONE...................................949 240-2188
Michael Snow, *Mng Member*
Don Mettler, *Engineer*
Joe Ramirez, *Purchasing*
Janell Sanz, *Marketing Mgr*
Janell Cedarstrom, *Sales Mgr*
◆ EMP: 30 EST: 1979
SALES (est): 5MM **Privately Held**
WEB: www.snowpure.com
SIC: **3589** 5074 Water purification equipment, household type; water purification equipment

(P-8416)
SPECIALTY CAR WASH SYSTEM
146 Mercury Cir, Pomona (91768-3210)
PHONE...................................909 869-6300
Mike Martorano, *Owner*
EMP: 17 EST: 2007
SALES (est): 3.5MM **Privately Held**
WEB: www.scwsinc.com
SIC: **3589** Car washing machinery

(P-8417)
SPENUZZA INC (HQ)
Also Called: Imperial Mfg Co
1128 Sherborn St, Corona (92879-2089)
PHONE...................................951 281-1830
Peter Spenuzza, *CEO*
Jennifer Mullen, *Executive*
Linda Ramsey, *Human Res Dir*
Miguel Betancourt, *Plant Mgr*
Christina Barker, *Sales Staff*
◆ EMP: 117 EST: 1957
SQ FT: 100,000
SALES (est): 31.5MM
SALES (corp-wide): 2.5B **Publicly Held**
WEB: www.imperialrange.com
SIC: **3589** 3556 Cooking equipment, commercial; food products machinery
PA: The Middleby Corporation
1400 Toastmaster Dr
Elgin IL 60120
847 741-3300

(P-8418)
STERNO LLC (DH)
1880 Compton Ave Ste 101, Corona (92881-2780)
PHONE...................................800 669-6699
John Clark, *Mng Member*
David Amirault, *Vice Pres*
Scott Rylko, *Vice Pres*
Jacquelyn Kozar, *Human Resources*
Salvador Alvarado, *Purchasing*
▼ EMP: 32 EST: 2006
SALES (est): 55.4MM **Publicly Held**
WEB: www.sternopro.com
SIC: **3589** Commercial cooking & foodwarming equipment
HQ: The Sterno Group Companies Llc
1880 Compton Ave Ste 101
Corona CA 92881
951 682-9600

(P-8419)
STERNO GROUP COMPANIES LLC (HQ)
Also Called: Sterno Candle Lamp
1880 Compton Ave Ste 101, Corona (92881-2780)
PHONE...................................951 682-9600
Don Hinshaw, *CEO*
John Clark, *President*
Donna Moad, *President*
Craig Carnes, *Vice Pres*
Mike Pacharis, *Vice Pres*
◆ EMP: 50 EST: 2006

SQ FT: 110,000
SALES (est): 59.3MM **Publicly Held**
WEB: www.sternopro.com
SIC: **3589** 3634 2899 Food warming equipment, commercial; chafing dishes, electric; chemical preparations

(P-8420)
SUEZ WTS SERVICES USA INC
7777 Industry Ave, Pico Rivera (90660-4303)
PHONE...................................562 942-2200
Michael Dimick, *Branch Mgr*
Fred Valdes, *Sales Mgr*
Orlando Magana, *Supervisor*
EMP: 60
SQ FT: 32,091
SALES (corp-wide): 117.1MM **Privately Held**
WEB: www.suezwatertechnologies.com
SIC: **3589** Water treatment equipment, industrial
HQ: Suez Wts Services Usa, Inc.
4545 Patent Rd
Norfolk VA 23502
757 855-9000

(P-8421)
TIMBUCKTOO MANUFACTURING INC
Also Called: T M I
1633 W 134th St, Gardena (90249-2013)
PHONE...................................310 323-1134
Juen Lee, *CEO*
Kyu Lee, *President*
▲ EMP: 43 EST: 1974
SQ FT: 50,000
SALES (est): 4.5MM **Privately Held**
WEB: www.timbucktoomfg.com
SIC: **3589** Car washing machinery

(P-8422)
TOPPER MANUFACTURING CORP
23880 Madison St, Torrance (90505-6009)
PHONE...................................310 375-5000
Timothy A Beall, *CEO*
EMP: 15 EST: 2015
SQ FT: 11,000
SALES (est): 2.1MM **Privately Held**
SIC: **3589** Water filters & softeners, household type; water purification equipment, household type

(P-8423)
WATERHEALTH INTERNATIONAL INC
9601 Irvine Center Dr, Irvine (92618-4652)
PHONE...................................949 716-5790
Sanjay Bhatnagar, *CEO*
Mahendra Misra, *Research*
Raghavendra Alse, *Technology*
EMP: 66 EST: 1995
SQ FT: 2,000
SALES (est): 2.5MM **Privately Held**
WEB: www.waterhealth.com
SIC: **3589** Water treatment equipment, industrial

(P-8424)
WATERMAN VALVE LLC (HQ)
25500 Road 204, Exeter (93221-9655)
P.O. Box 458 (93221-0458)
PHONE...................................559 562-4000
Marcus Shiveley, *President*
Darryl Pauls, *Engineer*
Tyler Sestini, *Engineer*
Mike Yeckinevich, *Products*
Mike Duron, *Manager*
▲ EMP: 126
SQ FT: 175,000
SALES (est): 34.2MM
SALES (corp-wide): 970.3MM **Privately Held**
WEB: www.watermanusa.com
SIC: **3589** Water treatment equipment, industrial
PA: Mcwane, Inc.
2900 Highway 280 S # 300
Birmingham AL 35223
205 414-3100

(P-8425)
WESFAC INC (HQ)
Also Called: Wespac
9300 Hall Rd, Downey (90241-5309)
PHONE....................................562 861-2160
Don Hyatt, *President*
Julie Hyatt, *Corp Secy*
EMP: 100 EST: 1982
SQ FT: 55,000
SALES (est): 855.6K
SALES (corp-wide): 11.1MM **Privately Held**
WEB: www.omniteaminc.com
SIC: 3589 3431 Commercial cooking & foodwarming equipment; metal sanitary ware
PA: Omniment Industries, Inc
9300 Hall Rd
Downey CA 90241
562 923-9660

(P-8426)
WHITTIER FILTRATION INC (DH)
120 S State College Blvd, Brea (92821-5834)
PHONE....................................714 986-5300
Jim Brown, *President*
John M Santelli, *Corp Secy*
Sara Mendez, *Admin Asst*
◆ EMP: 21 EST: 1977
SQ FT: 80,000
SALES (est): 12.1MM
SALES (corp-wide): 622.8MM **Privately Held**
WEB: www.veoliawatertech.com
SIC: 3589 Water treatment equipment, industrial

(P-8427)
WILBUR CURTIS CO INC
6913 W Acco St, Montebello (90640-5403)
PHONE....................................323 837-2300
Bryan Morford, *CEO*
Kevin R Cutis, *President*
Norman Fujitaki, *CFO*
Steve Bradley, *Vice Pres*
Scott Grimes, *Vice Pres*
EMP: 189 EST: 2018
SALES (est): 14.8MM
SALES (corp-wide): 355.8K **Privately Held**
WEB: www.wilburcurtis.com
SIC: 3589 Coffee brewing equipment
HQ: Groupe Seb Retailing
112 Chemin Du Moulin Carron
Ecully 69130

(P-8428)
WILBUR CURTIS CO INC
6913 W Acco St, Montebello (90640-5403)
PHONE....................................323 837-2300
EMP: 275 EST: 1946
SQ FT: 170,000
SALES: 75MM **Privately Held**
SIC: 3589 Mfg Service Industry Machinery

(P-8429)
YARDNEY WATER MGT SYSTEMS INC (PA)
Also Called: Yardney Water MGT Systems
6666 Box Springs Blvd, Riverside (92507-0736)
PHONE....................................951 656-6716
Kenneth Phillips, *President*
Chris Phillips, *Vice Pres*
Tony Barrios, *Purchasing*
Jorge Gutierrez, *Indstl Engineer*
Jared Bramwell, *Natl Sales Mgr*
◆ EMP: 39 EST: 1948
SQ FT: 55,000
SALES (est): 7.1MM **Privately Held**
WEB: www.yardneyfilters.com
SIC: 3589 Water treatment equipment, industrial

(P-8430)
Z P M INC
5770 Thornwood Dr Ste C, Goleta (93117-3812)
PHONE....................................805 681-3511
Dwayne Morse, *President*
Marlow Baar, *Treasurer*
EMP: 22
SQ FT: 2,400

SALES (est): 1MM **Privately Held**
SIC: 3589 5999 Water treatment equipment, industrial; water purification equipment

3592 Carburetors, Pistons, Rings & Valves

(P-8431)
CP-CARRILLO INC
17401 Armstrong Ave, Irvine (92614-5723)
PHONE....................................949 567-9000
Barry Calvert, *Mng Member*
Ignacio Chavez, *Prgrmr*
EMP: 30
SALES (corp-wide): 2.4B **Privately Held**
WEB: www.cp-carrillo.com
SIC: 3592 3714 Pistons & piston rings; connecting rods, motor vehicle engine
HQ: Cp-Carrillo, Inc.
1902 Mcgaw Ave
Irvine CA 92614

(P-8432)
CP-CARRILLO INC (DH)
1902 Mcgaw Ave, Irvine (92614-0910)
PHONE....................................949 567-9000
Barry Calvert, *CEO*
Peter Calvert, *President*
Harry Glieder, *CFO*
Stefan Penz, *Program Mgr*
Ignacio Chavez, *Prgrmr*
▲ EMP: 160 EST: 2011
SQ FT: 31,840
SALES (est): 28.8MM
SALES (corp-wide): 2.4B **Privately Held**
WEB: www.cp-carrillo.com
SIC: 3592 3714 Pistons & piston rings; connecting rods, motor vehicle engine

(P-8433)
PACIFIC PISTON RING CO INC
3620 Eastham Dr, Culver City (90232-2411)
P.O. Box 927 (90232-0927)
PHONE....................................310 836-3322
Forest Shannon, *President*
Christina Davis, *Corp Secy*
Michael Shannon, *Vice Pres*
EMP: 58 EST: 1921
SQ FT: 35,000
SALES (est): 8MM **Privately Held**
WEB: www.pacificpistonring.com
SIC: 3592 Pistons & piston rings

(P-8434)
PROBE RACING COMPONENTS INC
Also Called: Kwikparts.com
5022 Onyx St, Torrance (90503-2742)
PHONE....................................310 784-2977
Larry M O'Neal, *CEO*
▲ EMP: 23 EST: 1987
SQ FT: 25,000
SALES (est): 1.3MM **Privately Held**
WEB: www.vigilanteparts.com
SIC: 3592 3463 Pistons & piston rings; engine or turbine forgings, nonferrous

(P-8435)
ROSS RACING PISTONS
625 S Douglas St, El Segundo (90245-4812)
PHONE....................................310 536-0100
Ken Roble, *President*
Joy Roble, *Treasurer*
J B Mills, *Vice Pres*
Chris Petrini, *Creative Dir*
Ivet Lopez, *Admin Asst*
EMP: 55 EST: 1979
SQ FT: 25,000
SALES (est): 5.1MM **Privately Held**
WEB: www.rosspistons.com
SIC: 3592 Pistons & piston rings

(P-8436)
RTR INDUSTRIES LLC
Also Called: Grant Piston Rings
3943 E La Palma Ave, Anaheim (92807-1714)
PHONE....................................714 996-0050
Romy Laxamana,
Sergio Esparza, *Marketing Mgr*

Ramon Diaz,
Thom Nguyen,
Craig Marder, *Manager*
▲ EMP: 45 EST: 2002
SALES (est): 6.8MM **Privately Held**
WEB: www.grantpistonrings.com
SIC: 3592 Pistons & piston rings

(P-8437)
SEABISCUIT MOTORSPORTS INC
10800 Valley View St, Cypress (90630-5016)
PHONE....................................714 898-9763
EMP: 30
SALES (corp-wide): 539.5MM **Privately Held**
WEB: www.wiseco.com
SIC: 3592 3714 Pistons & piston rings; motor vehicle parts & accessories
HQ: Seabiscuit Motorsports, Inc.
7201 Industrial Park Blvd
Mentor OH 44060
440 951-6600

3593 Fluid Power Cylinders & Actuators

(P-8438)
GENERAL GRINDING & MFG CO LLC
15100 Valley View Ave, La Mirada (90638-5226)
PHONE....................................562 921-7033
SE Heung Kim,
Rich Kim,
Silas Pak,
EMP: 30 EST: 1947
SQ FT: 25,000
SALES (est): 3MM **Privately Held**
WEB: www.generalgrinding.com
SIC: 3593 3599 3471 Fluid power cylinders, hydraulic or pneumatic; grinding castings for the trade; plating & polishing

(P-8439)
HYDRAULIC PNEUMATIC INC
Also Called: Hpi Cylinders
13766 Milroy Pl, Santa Fe Springs (90670-5131)
PHONE....................................562 926-1122
James Whitney, *President*
EMP: 13 EST: 1946
SQ FT: 18,000
SALES (est): 1.2MM **Privately Held**
SIC: 3593 3599 Fluid power cylinders, hydraulic or pneumatic; machine shop, jobbing & repair

(P-8440)
RTC ARSPACE - CHTSWRTH DIV INC (PA)
20409 Prairie St, Chatsworth (91311-6029)
PHONE....................................818 341-3344
James B Hart, *CEO*
BJ Schramm, *President*
Bill Hart, *Vice Pres*
Elizabeth Hart, *Vice Pres*
Robert McSweeney, *Engineer*
◆ EMP: 122 EST: 1958
SQ FT: 42,000
SALES (est): 25.3MM **Privately Held**
WEB: www.rtcaerospace.com
SIC: 3593 3594 3599 Fluid power cylinders & actuators; fluid power pumps & motors; machine shop, jobbing & repair

3594 Fluid Power Pumps & Motors

(P-8441)
ACURA SPA SYSTEMS INC
Also Called: Aquassage
2954 Rubidoux Blvd, Riverside (92509-2129)
PHONE....................................951 684-6667
Joseph G Elnar, *President*
Mirna Elnar, *Vice Pres*
▲ EMP: 15 EST: 1987

SALES (est): 1.6MM **Privately Held**
WEB: www.acuraspa.com
SIC: 5999 3594 Hot tub & spa chemicals, equipment & supplies; fluid power pumps & motors

(P-8442)
BERNELL HYDRAULICS INC (PA)
8810 Etiwanda Ave, Rancho Cucamonga (91739-9662)
P.O. Box 417 (91739-0417)
PHONE....................................909 899-1751
Terrance B Jones Sr, *Ch of Bc*
Rhonda A Garness, *President*
John S Clemons, *Vice Pres*
EMP: 28
SQ FT: 6,000
SALES (est): 9.4MM **Privately Held**
WEB: www.bernellhydraulics.com
SIC: 3594 5084 3621 3593 Pumps, hydraulic power transfer; hydraulic systems equipment & supplies; motors & generators; fluid power cylinders & actuators; pumps & pumping equipment; machine tools, metal forming type

(P-8443)
CRISSAIR INC
28909 Avenue Williams, Valencia (91355-4183)
PHONE....................................661 367-3300
Linda Bradley, *President*
Patrick Lacanfora, *Vice Pres*
Eric Grupp, *VP Bus Dvlpt*
Marc Diaz, *Executive*
Vivian Gonzales, *Administration*
EMP: 185 EST: 1954
SQ FT: 40,000
SALES (est): 47.6MM **Publicly Held**
WEB: www.crissair.com
SIC: 3594 3492 Motors, pneumatic; fluid power valves & hose fittings
PA: Esco Technologies Inc.
9900 Clayton Rd Ste A
Saint Louis MO 63124

(P-8444)
HYPERION MOTORS LLC
1032 W Taft Ave, Orange (92865-4119)
PHONE....................................714 363-5858
Angelo Kafantaris, *Principal*
EMP: 50 EST: 2011
SALES (est): 5.4MM **Privately Held**
SIC: 3594 Fluid power pumps & motors

(P-8445)
PARKER-HANNIFIN CORPORATION
16666 Von Karman Ave, Irvine (92606-4997)
PHONE....................................949 833-3000
Fax: 949 851-3341
EMP: 123
SALES (corp-wide): 13B **Publicly Held**
SIC: 3594 Mfg Full-Line Of Motion-Control Products Including Fluid Power Systems
PA: Parker-Hannifin Corporation
6035 Parkland Blvd
Cleveland OH 44124
216 896-3000

(P-8446)
WATERDANCE CORPORATION (PA)
Also Called: Waterdance West
7340 Melrose St, Buena Park (90621-3226)
PHONE....................................818 656-0005
Steve Greenthal, *President*
EMP: 27 EST: 2004
SALES (est): 1MM **Privately Held**
WEB: www.waterdancevalve.com
SIC: 3594 Fluid power pumps & motors

(P-8447)
WESTERN HYDROSTATICS INC (PA)
1956 Keats Dr, Riverside (92501-1747)
PHONE....................................951 784-2133
John Starke Scott, *President*
Barnett Totten, *Treasurer*
Tandy W Scott, *Vice Pres*
Robert June, *Sales Staff*
David Siegel, *Accounts Mgr*

▲ **EMP:** 29 **EST:** 1985
SALES (est): 5MM **Privately Held**
WEB: www.weshyd.com
SIC: 3594 7699 5084 Hydrostatic drives (transmissions); hydraulic equipment repair; hydraulic systems equipment & supplies

3596 Scales & Balances, Exc Laboratory

(P-8448)
JONEL ENGINEERING
500 E Walnut Ave, Fullerton (92832-2540)
P.O. Box 798 (92836-0798)
PHONE..................................714 879-2360
John Lawson, *CEO*
Mike Lawson, *President*
Frank Munoz, *IT/INT Sup*
Henry Brown, *Technician*
Ken Clay, *Technology*
▼ **EMP:** 20 **EST:** 1963
SQ FT: 8,000
SALES (est): 3.2MM **Privately Held**
WEB: www.jonel.com
SIC: 3596 5045 Weighing machines & apparatus; computers

3599 Machinery & Eqpt, Indl & Commercial, NEC

(P-8449)
3D MACHINE CO INC
4790 E Wesley Dr, Anaheim (92807-1941)
PHONE..................................714 777-8985
Maria Falcusan, *President*
Constantine Falcusan, *Vice Pres*
EMP: 30 **EST:** 1996
SQ FT: 3,300
SALES (est): 6.4MM **Privately Held**
WEB: www.3dmachineco.com
SIC: 3599 Machine shop, jobbing & repair

(P-8450)
A & A MACHINE & DEV CO INC
16625 Gramercy Pl, Gardena (90247-5201)
PHONE..................................310 532-7706
Arlene Hymovitz, *President*
Eric Hymovitz, *Vice Pres*
EMP: 18 **EST:** 1972
SQ FT: 12,000
SALES (est): 3.2MM **Privately Held**
WEB: www.aamach.com
SIC: 3599 Machine shop, jobbing & repair

(P-8451)
A & B AEROSPACE INC
612 S Ayon Ave, Azusa (91702-5122)
PHONE..................................626 334-2976
Kenneth Smith, *President*
Malcolm Smith, *Vice Pres*
Jack Badeau, *General Mgr*
Alton A Hebert, *Production*
EMP: 35 **EST:** 1950
SQ FT: 23,000
SALES (est): 5MM **Privately Held**
WEB: www.abaerospace.com
SIC: 3599 Machine shop, jobbing & repair

(P-8452)
A & D PRECISION MFG INC
4751 E Hunter Ave, Anaheim (92807-1940)
PHONE..................................714 779-2714
Dan Wiegel, *President*
Cheryl Frost, *Treasurer*
Anthony Brown, *Vice Pres*
Tony Brown, *Vice Pres*
EMP: 21 **EST:** 1988
SQ FT: 9,000
SALES (est): 2.1MM **Privately Held**
WEB: www.adprecisionmfg.com
SIC: 3599 3728 Machine shop, jobbing & repair; aircraft parts & equipment

(P-8453)
A & H ENGINEERING & MFG INC
Also Called: A & H Tool Engineering
17109 Edwards Rd, Cerritos (90703-2423)
PHONE..................................562 623-9717
Asher Sharoni, *President*
Tova Sharoni, *CFO*

EMP: 25 **EST:** 2005
SQ FT: 15,000
SALES (est): 1.3MM **Privately Held**
SIC: 3599 Grinding castings for the trade

(P-8454)
A & M ENGINEERING INC
15854 Salvatierra St, Irwindale (91706-6603)
PHONE..................................626 813-2020
Boris Beljak Sr, *President*
Anita Beljak, *Corp Secy*
Boris Beljak Jr, *Vice Pres*
Roy Beljak, *Vice Pres*
Mark Neiman, *General Mgr*
EMP: 80
SQ FT: 25,000
SALES (est): 15MM **Privately Held**
WEB: www.amengineeringinc.com
SIC: 3599 3812 3537 Machine shop, jobbing & repair; search & navigation equipment; industrial trucks & tractors

(P-8455)
A & R ENGINEERING CO INC
1053 E Bedmar St, Carson (90746-3601)
PHONE..................................310 603-9060
Murat Sehidoglu, *President*
Massimo Fuso, *Opers Mgr*
EMP: 72
SQ FT: 23,334
SALES (est): 11.5MM **Privately Held**
WEB: www.arengr.com
SIC: 3599 Machine shop, jobbing & repair

(P-8456)
A H MACHINE INC
214 N Cedar Ave, Inglewood (90301-1009)
PHONE..................................310 672-0016
M P Desai, *President*
Sam Patel, *Vice Pres*
EMP: 20 **EST:** 1973
SQ FT: 6,500
SALES (est): 693.5K **Privately Held**
SIC: 3599 Machine shop, jobbing & repair

(P-8457)
A&W PRECISION MACHINING INC
16320 S Main St, Gardena (90248-2822)
PHONE..................................310 527-7242
Walter Galich, *President*
Adelfo Varela, *Vice Pres*
EMP: 15 **EST:** 2006
SALES (est): 1.5MM **Privately Held**
SIC: 3599 Machine shop, jobbing & repair

(P-8458)
A-Z MFG INC
Also Called: AZ Manufacturing
3101 W Segerstrom Ave, Santa Ana (92704-5811)
PHONE..................................714 444-4446
Ann Lukas, *Principal*
Garry Lukas, *Vice Pres*
Gary Lukas, *Admin Sec*
EMP: 40 **EST:** 1993
SQ FT: 16,096 **Privately Held**
WEB: www.azmfginc.com
SIC: 3599 Machine shop, jobbing & repair

(P-8459)
ABEN MACHINE PRODUCTS INC
9550 Owensmouth Ave, Chatsworth (91311-4801)
PHONE..................................818 960-4502
Nabeel Saoud, *President*
Esdras Giron, *Vice Pres*
EMP: 17 **EST:** 1998
SALES (est): 2.5MM **Privately Held**
WEB: www.abenusa.com
SIC: 3599 Machine shop, jobbing & repair

(P-8460)
ABLE WIRE EDM INC
440 Atlas St Ste A, Brea (92821-3136)
PHONE..................................714 255-1967
John Marquardt, *President*
Brooke Snow, *Vice Pres*
Kenny Snow, *Vice Pres*
Barbara Marquardt, *Admin Sec*
Chris Marks, *Manager*
EMP: 15 **EST:** 1988
SQ FT: 5,500 **Privately Held**
WEB: www.ableedm.com

SIC: 3599 Machine shop, jobbing & repair; electrical discharge machining (EDM)

(P-8461)
ABSOLUTE EDM
43153 Business Park Dr, Temecula (92590-3628)
P.O. Box 985, Murrieta (92564-0985)
PHONE..................................951 694-5601
Stephen Bowles, *President*
EMP: 15 **EST:** 2007
SALES (est): 196.3K **Privately Held**
SIC: 3599 Machine shop, jobbing & repair

(P-8462)
ACC PRECISION INC
321 Hearst Dr, Oxnard (93030-5158)
PHONE..................................805 278-9801
Arturo Alfaro, *President*
Sandra Guida, *Sales Staff*
EMP: 15 **EST:** 2003
SQ FT: 6,000
SALES (est): 2MM **Privately Held**
WEB: www.accprecision.com
SIC: 3599 Machine shop, jobbing & repair

(P-8463)
ACCURATE PRFMCE MACHINING INC
2255 S Grand Ave, Santa Ana (92705-5206)
PHONE..................................714 434-7811
Robert Keith Fischer, *CEO*
Karen Fischer, *Treasurer*
Larry Taylor, *Vice Pres*
Chris Straub, *Office Mgr*
EMP: 21 **EST:** 1996
SQ FT: 3,200
SALES (est): 2.7MM **Privately Held**
WEB: www.cncapm.com
SIC: 3599 Machine shop, jobbing & repair

(P-8464)
ACE MACHINE SHOP INC
11200 Wright Rd, Lynwood (90262-3124)
PHONE..................................310 608-2277
Pedro Gallinucci, *President*
Lucia Gallinucci, *Vice Pres*
Silvia Durell, *Office Mgr*
Ricardo Gallinucci, *Project Engr*
Jeff Ducas, *Purchasing*
EMP: 70 **EST:** 1956
SQ FT: 35,000
SALES (est): 7MM **Privately Held**
WEB: www.aceconstructions.com
SIC: 3599 Machine shop, jobbing & repair

(P-8465)
ACKLEY METAL PRODUCTS INC
Also Called: Waco Products
1311 E Saint Gertrude Pl B, Santa Ana (92705-5216)
PHONE..................................714 979-7431
Paul Ackley, *President*
EMP: 20 **EST:** 1985
SQ FT: 3,200
SALES (est): 1.3MM **Privately Held**
WEB: www.ackleymetal.com
SIC: 3599 Machine shop, jobbing & repair

(P-8466)
ACRATECH INC
2502 Supply St, Pomona (91767-2113)
PHONE..................................909 392-7522
Scott Dordick, *President*
Patty Dordick, *Vice Pres*
EMP: 15 **EST:** 1991
SQ FT: 4,000
SALES (est): 1.3MM **Privately Held**
WEB: www.acratech.net
SIC: 3599 Machine & other job shop work

(P-8467)
ACRO-SPEC GRINDING CO INC
4134 Indus Way, Riverside (92503-4847)
PHONE..................................951 736-1199
Clifford Boss, *President*
Michelle Austin, *Vice Pres*
EMP: 14 **EST:** 1972
SQ FT: 7,000
SALES (est): 2.2MM **Privately Held**
WEB: www.acrospec.com
SIC: 3599 Machine shop, jobbing & repair

(P-8468)
ACUNA DIONISIO ABLE
Also Called: A & L Engineering
12629 Prairie Ave, Hawthorne (90250-4611)
PHONE..................................310 978-4741
Dionisio Abel Acuna, *Owner*
EMP: 15 **EST:** 1993
SQ FT: 3,700
SALES (est): 300K **Privately Held**
SIC: 3599 8711 5049 Machine shop, jobbing & repair; industrial engineers; engineers' equipment & supplies

(P-8469)
ADVANCED CERAMIC TECHNOLOGY
803 W Angus Ave, Orange (92868-1307)
PHONE..................................714 538-2524
Eric Roberts, *President*
Eric Andrew Roberts, *President*
Bill Roberts, *Vice Pres*
William Roberts, *Vice Pres*
Kelly Roberts, *Program Mgr*
EMP: 16
SQ FT: 9,900
SALES (est): 2.1MM **Privately Held**
WEB: www.advancedceramictech.com
SIC: 3599 Machine shop, jobbing & repair

(P-8470)
AERO CHIP INC
13563 Freeway Dr, Santa Fe Springs (90670-5633)
PHONE..................................562 404-6300
Solomon M Gavrila, *CEO*
Liviu Pribac, *Vice Pres*
Solomon Gavrila, *Info Tech Mgr*
Dinu Tiprigan, *Prgrmr*
George Stan, *QC Mgr*
EMP: 50 **EST:** 1988
SQ FT: 17,000
SALES (est): 9.9MM **Privately Held**
WEB: www.aerochip.com
SIC: 3599 Machine shop, jobbing & repair

(P-8471)
AERO DYNAMIC MACHINING INC
11841 Monarch St, Garden Grove (92841-2110)
PHONE..................................714 379-1073
David Nguyen, *President*
Wendy Nguyen, *CFO*
Kevin Tran, *Vice Pres*
John Fairris, *Technical Staff*
Rick Zulawski, *Export Mgr*
▲ **EMP:** 60 **EST:** 1998
SALES (est): 11MM **Privately Held**
WEB: www.aerodynamicinc.com
SIC: 3599 Machine shop, jobbing & repair

(P-8472)
AERO ENGINEERING INC
1020 E Elm Ave, Fullerton (92831-5022)
PHONE..................................714 879-6200
Brent Borden, *President*
EMP: 16 **EST:** 1978
SQ FT: 5,500
SALES (est): 2.5MM **Privately Held**
SIC: 3599 Machine shop, jobbing & repair

(P-8473)
AERO INDUSTRIES LLC
139 Industrial Way, Buellton (93427-9592)
P.O. Box 198 (93427-0198)
PHONE..................................805 688-6734
Dave Watkins, *Manager*
Francis Williams, *Site Mgr*
EMP: 340 **EST:** 2007
SALES (est): 3.2MM
SALES (corp-wide): 84.3MM **Privately Held**
WEB: www.aero-cnc.com
SIC: 3599 Machine shop, jobbing & repair
PA: Gavial Holdings, Inc.
     1435 W Mccoy Ln
     Santa Maria CA 93455
     805 614-0060

(P-8474)
AERO MECHANISM PRECISION INC
21700 Marilla St, Chatsworth (91311-4125)
PHONE..................................818 886-1855

Palminder Sehmbey, *President*
EMP: 34 **EST:** 1996
SQ FT: 8,000
SALES (est): 5.3MM **Privately Held**
WEB: www.aeromechanism.com
SIC: 3599 Machine shop, jobbing & repair

(P-8475)
AERO-K
10764 Lower Azusa Rd, El Monte
(91731-1306)
PHONE..................626 350-5125
Robert Krusic, *President*
Ryan Krusic, *Opers Staff*
EMP: 45 **EST:** 1983
SQ FT: 14,000
SALES (est): 6.2MM **Privately Held**
WEB: www.aero-k.com
SIC: 3599 Machine shop, jobbing & repair

(P-8476)
AERO-MECHANICAL ENGRG INC
6475 E Pcf Cast Hwy Ste 1, Long Beach
(90803)
PHONE..................323 682-0961
Anders Ahlstrom, *CEO*
John Ahlstrom, *President*
EMP: 16 **EST:** 1974
SQ FT: 4,150
SALES (est): 2.3MM **Privately Held**
WEB: www.redirect.name
SIC: 3599 Machine shop, jobbing & repair

(P-8477)
AERODYNAMIC ENGINEERING INC
15495 Graham St, Huntington Beach
(92649-1205)
PHONE..................714 891-2651
Bob Waddell, *CEO*
Alfred Mayer, *President*
Bob Waddell, *CEO*
Ewald Eisel, *Principal*
Gregory Somers, *Engineer*
▲ **EMP:** 40 **EST:** 1968
SQ FT: 12,000
SALES (est): 4.9MM **Privately Held**
WEB: www.aerodynamic.net
SIC: 3599 3769 Machine shop, jobbing & repair; guided missile & space vehicle parts & auxiliary equipment

(P-8478)
AERODYNE PRCSION MACHINING INC
5471 Argosy Ave, Huntington Beach
(92649-1038)
PHONE..................714 891-1311
Raymond Krispel, *President*
Veronica Schultz, *CFO*
Otto Schulz, *Vice Pres*
Jason Krispel, *General Mgr*
Mike Trollman, *Opers Mgr*
▲ **EMP:** 25 **EST:** 1986
SQ FT: 20,000
SALES (est): 2.9MM **Privately Held**
WEB: www.aerodyneprecision.com
SIC: 3599 Machine shop, jobbing & repair

(P-8479)
AEROLIANT MANUFACTURING INC
Also Called: Fordon Grind Industries
1613 Lockness Pl, Torrance (90501-5119)
PHONE..................310 257-1903
Patricia A Wiacek, *President*
Greg Wiacek, *Vice Pres*
EMP: 20
SQ FT: 7,200
SALES (est): 2.5MM **Privately Held**
WEB: www.amratec.com
SIC: 3599 Machine shop, jobbing & repair

(P-8480)
AEROSPACE AND COML TOOLING INC
Also Called: A C T
1866 S Lake Pl, Ontario (91761-5788)
PHONE..................909 930-5780
Oscar Borello, *President*
EMP: 16
SQ FT: 20,000

SALES (est): 3MM **Privately Held**
WEB: www.actooling.com
SIC: 3599 Machine shop, jobbing & repair

(P-8481)
AEROTECH PRECISION MACHINING
42541 6th St E Ste 17, Lancaster
(93535-5201)
PHONE..................661 802-7185
Jose Reyes, *CEO*
EMP: 15 **EST:** 2018
SALES (est): 1.4MM **Privately Held**
SIC: 3599 Machine shop, jobbing & repair

(P-8482)
AGA PRECISION SYSTEMS INC
122 E Dyer Rd, Santa Ana (92707-3732)
PHONE..................714 540-3163
Ralph E Wilson, *President*
Wesley Wilson, *CFO*
EMP: 33 **EST:** 1978
SQ FT: 14,100
SALES (est): 1MM **Privately Held**
WEB: www.agaprecisioninc.com
SIC: 3599 Machine shop, jobbing & repair

(P-8483)
AIR CRAFTORS ENGINEERING INC
4040 Cheyenne Ct, Chino (91710-5457)
PHONE..................909 900-0635
Tim Boucher, *President*
John Boucher, *Vice Pres*
EMP: 13 **EST:** 1976
SQ FT: 6,000
SALES (est): 310.3K **Privately Held**
SIC: 3599 Machine shop, jobbing & repair

(P-8484)
ALCO ENGRG & TOOLING CORP
Also Called: Alco Metal Fab
3001 Oak St, Santa Ana (92707-4235)
PHONE..................714 556-6060
Frank Vallefuoco, *President*
Angelo D'Eramo, *Corp Secy*
Tom Hare, *Vice Pres*
EMP: 40 **EST:** 1944
SQ FT: 32,000
SALES (est): 3.9MM **Privately Held**
SIC: 3599 Machine shop, jobbing & repair

(P-8485)
ALDO FRAGALE
Also Called: Turner Precision
17813 S Main St Ste 111, Gardena
(90248-3542)
PHONE..................310 324-0050
Aldo Fragale, *President*
EMP: 20 **EST:** 1984
SQ FT: 2,500
SALES (est): 1.5MM **Privately Held**
SIC: 3599 Machine shop, jobbing & repair

(P-8486)
ALL DIAMETER GRINDING INC
725 N Main St, Orange (92868-1105)
PHONE..................714 744-1200
Marvin W Goodwin, *President*
Barbara Goodwin, *Treasurer*
Jeff Goodwin, *Vice Pres*
EMP: 22 **EST:** 1960
SQ FT: 9,500
SALES (est): 11MM **Privately Held**
WEB: www.alldiametergrinding.com
SIC: 3599 Machine shop, jobbing & repair

(P-8487)
ALL STAR PRECISION
8739 Lion St, Rancho Cucamonga
(91730-4428)
PHONE..................909 944-8373
Scott Jackson, *Owner*
Ron Jackson, *Partner*
Beth Picciolo, *Office Mgr*
EMP: 23 **EST:** 2004
SALES (est): 2.5MM **Privately Held**
WEB: www.allstarprecision.com
SIC: 3599 Machine shop, jobbing & repair

(P-8488)
ALL4-PCB (NORTH AMERICA) INC
345 Mira Loma Ave, Glendale
(91204-2912)
PHONE..................866 734-9403
Torsten Reckert, *President*
Roland Lacap, *Vice Pres*
Linda Gonzalez, *Office Mgr*
Ralph Jacobo, *Technical Staff*
Conrad Micale, *Sales Staff*
▲ **EMP:** 17 **EST:** 2001
SQ FT: 4,000
SALES (est): 2.4MM **Privately Held**
WEB: www.all4-pcb.us
SIC: 3599 3545 3541 3672 Chemical milling job shop; milling machine attachments (machine tool accessories); chemical milling machines; printed circuit boards

(P-8489)
ALLESANDRO AUTOMATIC INC
1146 N Central Ave, Glendale
(91202-2506)
PHONE..................323 663-8253
Kenneth P Feria, *CEO*
Gordon Adams, *President*
EMP: 15 **EST:** 1946
SQ FT: 20,000
SALES (est): 673.1K **Privately Held**
SIC: 3599 3451 Machine shop, jobbing & repair; screw machine products

(P-8490)
ALLOY MACHINING AND HONING INC
2808 Supply Ave, Commerce (90040-2706)
PHONE..................323 726-8248
Paul Muscet, *President*
Nada Muscet, *Admin Sec*
EMP: 24 **EST:** 1991
SQ FT: 12,000
SALES (est): 1MM **Privately Held**
WEB: www.alloymachiningservices.com
SIC: 3599 Machine shop, jobbing & repair

(P-8491)
ALLOY MACHINING SERVICES INC
2808 Supply Ave, Commerce (90040-2706)
PHONE..................323 725-2545
Paul Muscet, *President*
Christina Constantino, *Vice Pres*
EMP: 16 **EST:** 2010
SALES (est): 1MM **Privately Held**
WEB: www.alloymachiningservices.com
SIC: 3599 Machine shop, jobbing & repair

(P-8492)
ALPHA AVIATION COMPONENTS INC (PA)
16772 Schoenborn St, North Hills
(91343-6108)
PHONE..................818 894-8801
Lidia Gorko, *President*
Jerry Gorko, *Vice Pres*
William Tudor, *Vice Pres*
Joanna Zapala, *Office Mgr*
Fred De La Fuente, *QC Mgr*
EMP: 34 **EST:** 1954
SQ FT: 18,000 **Privately Held**
WEB: www.alphaaci.com
SIC: 3599 3451 3728 Machine shop, jobbing & repair; screw machine products; aircraft parts & equipment

(P-8493)
ALPHA GRINDING INC
12402 Benedict Ave, Downey
(90242-3112)
PHONE..................562 803-1509
Yanick Herrouin, *President*
Kay Marcy, *Corp Secy*
Marc Herrouin, *Vice Pres*
Espie Cortes, *QC Mgr*
▲ **EMP:** 19 **EST:** 1964
SQ FT: 9,000
SALES (est): 522.6K **Privately Held**
WEB: www.amnginc.com
SIC: 3599 Machine shop, jobbing & repair

(P-8494)
AM-TEK ENGINEERING INC
1180 E Francis St Ste C, Ontario
(91761-4802)
PHONE..................909 673-1633
Boone Bounyaseng, *CEO*
Lauren Waters, *Opers Mgr*
EMP: 18 **EST:** 1998
SQ FT: 10,000
SALES (est): 2.8MM **Privately Held**
WEB: www.amtekeng.com
SIC: 3599 Machine shop, jobbing & repair

(P-8495)
AMERICAN DEBURRING INC
Also Called: A Fab
20742 Linear Ln, Lake Forest
(92630-7804)
PHONE..................949 457-9790
Robert L Campbell, *President*
Theresa Cook, *Admin Sec*
EMP: 25 **EST:** 1973
SQ FT: 11,000
SALES (est): 3MM **Privately Held**
WEB: www.afabcnc.com
SIC: 3599 Machine shop, jobbing & repair

(P-8496)
AMERICAN MFG NETWRK INC
Also Called: Amanet
7001 Eton Ave, Canoga Park (91303-2112)
PHONE..................818 786-1113
Robert Barbour, *Chairman*
Sandip Desai, *President*
Maria Garcia, *Purch Mgr*
Natalia Garzo, *Manager*
EMP: 14 **EST:** 1978
SQ FT: 4,000
SALES (est): 2.9MM **Privately Held**
WEB: www.amanet.com
SIC: 3599 3469 Machine shop, jobbing & repair; metal stampings

(P-8497)
AMERICAN PRCSION GRINDING MCH
456 Gerona Ave, San Gabriel
(91775-2938)
PHONE..................626 357-6610
Fax: 626 358-4365
EMP: 13
SQ FT: 3,500
SALES (est): 1.5MM **Privately Held**
SIC: 3599 Mfg Industrial Machinery

(P-8498)
APOGEE MANUFACTURING
28231 Avenue Crocker # 90, Valencia
(91355-1299)
PHONE..................661 467-0440
Chad Jensen, *President*
Glen Jelletich, *Vice Pres*
Heath Edie, *Sales Staff*
◆ **EMP:** 15 **EST:** 2003
SQ FT: 800
SALES (est): 2.3MM **Privately Held**
SIC: 3599 Machine shop, jobbing & repair

(P-8499)
ARAM PRECISION TOOL & DIE INC
9758 Cozycroft Ave, Chatsworth
(91311-4417)
P.O. Box 3696 (91313-3696)
PHONE..................818 998-1000
AVI Amichai, *President*
Rona Amichai, *Corp Secy*
EMP: 19 **EST:** 1979
SQ FT: 12,000
SALES (est): 2MM **Privately Held**
SIC: 3599 3451 Machine shop, jobbing & repair; screw machine products

(P-8500)
ARANDA TOOLING INC
13950 Yorba Ave, Chino (91710-5520)
PHONE..................714 379-6565
Pedro Aranda, *President*
Martha Aranda, *Corp Secy*
Micheal Dean, *Executive*
Carlos Aranda, *Technology*
Eric Nelson, *Engineer*
▲ **EMP:** 70 **EST:** 1976
SQ FT: 60,000

SALES (est): 23.8MM **Privately Held**
WEB: www.arandatooling.com
SIC: 3599 3469 3544 3465 Machine shop, jobbing & repair; metal stampings; special dies, tools, jigs & fixtures; automotive stampings

(P-8501)
AREMAC ASSOCIATES INC
2004 S Myrtle Ave, Monrovia (91016-4837)
PHONE....................626 303-8795
Scott Sher, *CEO*
Mariela Vinas, *Vice Pres*
EMP: 35 EST: 1963
SQ FT: 12,500
SALES (est): 3.3MM **Privately Held**
SIC: 3599 3444 Machine shop, jobbing & repair; sheet metalwork

(P-8502)
ARNOLD-GONSALVES ENGRG INC
5731 Chino Ave, Chino (91710-5226)
PHONE....................909 465-1579
Manuel Gonsalves, *President*
Mike Arnold, *Vice Pres*
EMP: 35 EST: 1969
SQ FT: 10,000
SALES (est): 2.5MM **Privately Held**
WEB: www.arnoldgonsalveseng.com
SIC: 3599 3444 Machine shop, jobbing & repair; sheet metal specialties, not stamped

(P-8503)
ARROW ENGINEERING
4946 Azusa Canyon Rd, Irwindale (91706-1940)
PHONE....................626 960-2806
John Beaman, *President*
Jim Ballantyne, *Vice Pres*
Julie Teeter, *Office Mgr*
Mark J Silk, *Agent*
EMP: 36 EST: 1974
SQ FT: 18,000
SALES (est): 3.7MM **Privately Held**
WEB: www.arrow-engineering.com
SIC: 3599 Machine shop, jobbing & repair

(P-8504)
ARROW SCREW PRODUCTS INC
941 W Mccoy Ln, Santa Maria (93455-1109)
PHONE....................805 928-2269
Robert Vine, *CEO*
Tim Vine, *Vice Pres*
Hoang Vine, *Admin Sec*
Ken Losee, *Manager*
EMP: 33 EST: 1956
SQ FT: 10,000
SALES (est): 4MM **Privately Held**
SIC: 3599 3541 Machine shop, jobbing & repair; machine tools, metal cutting type

(P-8505)
ASTRO MACHINE CO INC
3734 W 139th St, Hawthorne (90250-7597)
PHONE....................310 679-8291
William Skintauy, *President*
Ann Vellonakis, *Treasurer*
James Vellonakis, *Vice Pres*
Stasi Vellonakis, *Admin Sec*
Allen Boothe, *Mfg Mgr*
EMP: 14 EST: 1965
SQ FT: 5,000
SALES (est): 2.5MM **Privately Held**
WEB: www.astromachine.net
SIC: 3599 Machine shop, jobbing & repair

(P-8506)
AUGER INDUSTRIES INC
390 E Crowther Ave, Placentia (92870-6419)
PHONE....................714 577-9350
John Auger, *President*
Francoise Auger, *Shareholder*
EMP: 17 EST: 1969
SQ FT: 12,000
SALES (est): 2.4MM **Privately Held**
WEB: www.augerind.com
SIC: 3599 Machine shop, jobbing & repair

(P-8507)
AUTOMATION WEST INC
Also Called: Cameron Metal Cutting
1605 E Saint Gertrude Pl, Santa Ana (92705-5311)
PHONE....................714 556-7381
George Danenhauer, *President*
David Roberts, *Vice Pres*
Linda Bingham, *Admin Sec*
Dave Roberts, *Sales Staff*
▲ **EMP: 29 EST:** 1977
SQ FT: 7,200
SALES (est): 1.3MM **Privately Held**
SIC: 3599 7389 Machine shop, jobbing & repair; metal cutting services

(P-8508)
AVATAR MACHINE LLC
18100 Mount Washington St, Fountain Valley (92708-6121)
PHONE....................714 434-2737
Liem Do,
Frank Nguyen,
EMP: 23 EST: 2008
SALES (est): 2.5MM **Privately Held**
WEB: www.avatarmachine.com
SIC: 3599 5049 Machine shop, jobbing & repair; precision tools

(P-8509)
AVION TL MFG MACHINING CTR INC
29035 The Old Rd, Valencia (91355-1083)
PHONE....................661 257-2915
Patrick Beaudoin, *President*
Alison Horne, *General Mgr*
EMP: 16 EST: 1975
SQ FT: 6,000
SALES (est): 1.3MM **Privately Held**
WEB: www.aviontool.com
SIC: 3599 Machine shop, jobbing & repair

(P-8510)
AXXIS CORPORATION
1535 Nandina Ave, Perris (92571-7010)
PHONE....................951 436-9921
Brandy Tidball, *President*
Jo Olchawa, *Treasurer*
Susan Tidball, *Vice Pres*
Jonathan Fuerte, *Human Resources*
EMP: 35 EST: 2007
SALES (est): 4.6MM **Privately Held**
WEB: www.axxiscorp.us
SIC: 3599 Machine shop, jobbing & repair

(P-8511)
AZURE MICRODYNAMICS INC
19652 Descartes, Foothill Ranch (92610-2600)
PHONE....................949 699-3344
Stanislaw Sulek, *President*
Zyta Sulek, *Shareholder*
Christopher Hughes, *CFO*
Oliver Sulek, *Vice Pres*
EMP: 77 EST: 1997
SALES (est): 11.9MM **Privately Held**
WEB: www.azuremicrodynamics.com
SIC: 3599 3544 Machine shop, jobbing & repair; special dies, tools, jigs & fixtures

(P-8512)
B & B PIPE AND TOOL CO
2301 Parker Ln, Bakersfield (93308-6006)
PHONE....................661 323-8208
Joe Keller, *General Mgr*
EMP: 29
SALES (corp-wide): 11.4MM **Privately Held**
WEB: www.bbpipe.com
SIC: 3599 Machine shop, jobbing & repair
PA: B & B Pipe And Tool Co.
   3035 Walnut Ave
   Long Beach CA 90807
   562 424-0704

(P-8513)
B & W PRECISION INC
1260 Pioneer St Ste A, Brea (92821-3725)
P.O. Box 674, Yucca Valley (92286-0674)
PHONE....................714 447-0971
EMP: 19 EST: 1964
SQ FT: 25,000
SALES (est): 2.5MM **Privately Held**
WEB: www.bwprecision.com
SIC: 3599 Manufacturing Company

(P-8514)
B S K T INC
Also Called: S & S Precision Sheetmetal
8447 Canoga Ave, Canoga Park (91304-2607)
PHONE....................818 349-1566
Steve Kim, *President*
Suzanne Kim, *General Mgr*
EMP: 19 EST: 1997
SQ FT: 12,000
SALES (est): 316.3K **Privately Held**
SIC: 3599 Machine shop, jobbing & repair

(P-8515)
B&B MANUFACTURING CO (PA)
27940 Beale Ct, Santa Clarita (91355-1210)
PHONE....................661 257-2161
Kenneth Gentry, *CEO*
Fred Duncan, *President*
Jeff Lage, *Vice Pres*
Vanessa Shaffer, *Vice Pres*
Rick Talbert, *Vice Pres*
▲ **EMP: 199 EST:** 1961
SQ FT: 180,000
SALES (est): 55.7MM **Privately Held**
WEB: www.bbmfg.com
SIC: 3599 Machine shop, jobbing & repair

(P-8516)
BAKERSFIELD MACHINE CO INC
Also Called: BMC Industries
5605 N Chester Ave Ext, Bakersfield (93308)
P.O. Box 122 (93302-0122)
PHONE....................661 709-1992
John L Meyer, *President*
Alfred T Meyer Jr, *Vice Pres*
▲ **EMP: 55 EST:** 1924
SQ FT: 8,276
SALES (est): 9.6MM **Privately Held**
WEB: www.bmc-ind.com
SIC: 3599 Machine shop, jobbing & repair

(P-8517)
BAUMANN ENGINEERING
212 S Cambridge Ave, Claremont (91711-4843)
PHONE....................909 621-4181
Fred Baumann, *President*
Isolde Doll, *Admin Sec*
EMP: 85 EST: 1961
SQ FT: 18,057
SALES (est): 7.6MM **Privately Held**
WEB: www.becontrols.com
SIC: 3599 Machine shop, jobbing & repair

(P-8518)
BAYLESS ENGINEERING INC
Also Called: Bayless Engineering & Mfg
26140 Avenue Hall, Valencia (91355-4808)
PHONE....................661 257-3373
Earl Bayless, *President*
Rod Smith, *Vice Pres*
EMP: 235 EST: 1978
SALES (est): 32.2MM **Privately Held**
WEB: www.baylessmfg.com
SIC: 3599 3444 Machine shop, jobbing & repair; sheet metalwork

(P-8519)
BCI INC
Also Called: Upton Engineering & Mfg Co
1822 Belcroft Ave, South El Monte (91733-3703)
PHONE....................626 579-4234
Adam Bondra, *President*
June Bondra, *Vice Pres*
Edward Mantsch, *Senior Mgr*
EMP: 31 EST: 1976
SQ FT: 6,500
SALES (est): 3.5MM **Privately Held**
WEB: www.bostoncareer.org
SIC: 3599 5084 Machine shop, jobbing & repair; welding machinery & equipment

(P-8520)
BECHLER CAMS INC
1313 S State College Pkwy, Anaheim (92806-5298)
PHONE....................714 774-5150
Daniel Lennert, *President*
Laura Stearman, *Corp Secy*
Jim Humphrey, *Mfg Staff*
EMP: 16
SQ FT: 11,500

SALES: 2.8MM **Privately Held**
WEB: www.bechlercams.com
SIC: 3599 Machine shop, jobbing & repair

(P-8521)
BEDARD MACHINE INC
141 Viking Ave, Brea (92821-3817)
PHONE....................714 990-4846
Dennis Bedard, *President*
Sue Bedard, *CFO*
Jaymie Marklevits, *Mfg Staff*
EMP: 13 EST: 1979
SQ FT: 7,200
SALES (est): 2.1MM **Privately Held**
WEB: www.bedardmachineinc.com
SIC: 3599 Machine shop, jobbing & repair

(P-8522)
BEL-AIR MACHINING CO
151 E Columbine Ave, Santa Ana (92707-4401)
PHONE....................714 953-6616
Moon H Choi, *Owner*
EMP: 15 EST: 1984
SQ FT: 5,000
SALES (est): 1.9MM **Privately Held**
WEB: www.belairmachine.com
SIC: 3599 Machine shop, jobbing & repair

(P-8523)
BENDER CCP INC (PA)
Also Called: Bender US
2150 E 37th St Vernon, Vernon (90058)
P.O. Box 847, Benicia (94510-0847)
PHONE....................707 745-9970
Michael A Potter, *President*
Randall Potter, *Vice Pres*
WEI Wu, *Purchasing*
Michael Gonzales, *Opers Staff*
Ralph Duskin, *Manager*
▲ **EMP: 75 EST:** 2007
SALES (est): 14.6MM **Privately Held**
WEB: www.benderccp.com
SIC: 3599 Custom machinery

(P-8524)
BENDICK PRECISION INC
56 La Porte St, Arcadia (91006-2827)
PHONE....................626 445-0217
Christie Joseph, *President*
Benny Joseph, *Corp Secy*
David Quiring, *Purchasing*
EMP: 27 EST: 1975
SQ FT: 5,000
SALES (est): 1.9MM **Privately Held**
WEB: www.bendick.com
SIC: 3599 3061 Machine shop, jobbing & repair; medical & surgical rubber tubing (extruded & lathe-cut)

(P-8525)
BEONCA MACHINE INC
1680 Curtiss Ct, La Verne (91750-5848)
PHONE....................909 392-9991
Johann Bock, *President*
Danny Bock, *President*
Dennis Bock, *Vice Pres*
Picture L Bock, *Office Mgr*
Jame Bock, *Admin Sec*
EMP: 17 EST: 1973
SQ FT: 7,000
SALES (est): 2.6MM **Privately Held**
WEB: www.beoncamachine.com
SIC: 3599 Machine shop, jobbing & repair

(P-8526)
BERANEK LLC
2340 W 205th St, Torrance (90501-1436)
PHONE....................310 328-9094
Hector Beranek, *President*
Sean Holly, *CEO*
Vilma Beranek, *CFO*
Stephen Cook, *Vice Pres*
Tucker Cowden, *Vice Pres*
EMP: 36 EST: 1978
SQ FT: 20,000
SALES (est): 9.7MM
SALES (corp-wide): 33.7MM **Privately Held**
WEB: www.beranekinc.com
SIC: 3599 Machine shop, jobbing & repair
PA: J&E Precision Tool Holdings, Llc
   107 Valley Rd
   Southampton MA 01073
   413 527-8778

P
R
O
D
U
C
T
S
&
S
V
C
S

(P-8527)
BERNS BROS INC
Also Called: De Berns Company
1250 W 17th St, Long Beach (90813-1310)
PHONE..................................562 437-0471
Steven Berns, *President*
Steve Berns, *Vice Pres*
Sue Porter, *Vice Pres*
▲ EMP: 17 EST: 1957
SQ FT: 20,000 **Privately Held**
WEB: www.thebernscompany.com
SIC: 3599 Machine & other job shop work

(P-8528)
BISON ENGINEERING COMPANY INC
15535 Texaco Ave, Paramount
(90723-3921)
PHONE..................................562 408-1525
Lothar Maertens, *President*
Neil Thompson, *Vice Pres*
EMP: 13 EST: 1979
SQ FT: 40,000
SALES (est): 1.8MM **Privately Held**
WEB: www.bisonengineeringco.com
SIC: 3599 3728 Machine shop, jobbing & repair; aircraft parts & equipment

(P-8529)
BLAGA PRECISION INC
11650 Seaboard Cir, Stanton (90680-3426)
PHONE..................................714 891-9509
Gavril Blaga, *President*
▲ EMP: 37 EST: 1983
SQ FT: 3,600
SALES (est): 2.4MM **Privately Held**
WEB: www.blaga-precision-inc.hub.biz
SIC: 3599 Machine shop, jobbing & repair

(P-8530)
BOCK MACHINE COMPANY INC
2141 S Parco Ave, Ontario (91761-5769)
PHONE..................................909 947-7250
Jacob Bock, *President*
Jack Bock, *Vice Pres*
Roy Bock, *Vice Pres*
Wilma Bock, *Admin Sec*
EMP: 16 EST: 1973
SQ FT: 10,000
SALES (est): 329.9K **Privately Held**
SIC: 3599 Machine shop, jobbing & repair

(P-8531)
BOUDRAUX PRCSION MCHINING CORP
11762 Western Ave Ste G, Stanton
(90680-3481)
PHONE..................................714 894-4523
Mike Boudreaux, *President*
Steve Boudreaux, *Vice Pres*
EMP: 25 EST: 1990
SQ FT: 3,750
SALES (est): 1.7MM **Privately Held**
WEB: www.boudreaux-precision-machin-ing-ca.hub.biz
SIC: 3599 Machine shop, jobbing & repair

(P-8532)
BTI AEROSPACE & ELECTRONICS
Also Called: B T I Areospace & Electronics
13546 Vintage Pl, Chino (91710-5243)
PHONE..................................909 465-1569
Gary Rindfleisch, *President*
▲ EMP: 23 EST: 1997
SQ FT: 25,000
SALES (est): 525.2K **Privately Held**
SIC: 3599 3444 3769 Machine shop, jobbing & repair; sheet metalwork; guided missile & space vehicle parts & auxiliary equipment

(P-8533)
BUENA PARK TOOL & ENGRG INC
7661 Windfield Dr, Huntington Beach
(92647-7100)
PHONE..................................714 843-6215
Leo Gomez, *CEO*
Teresa Gomez, *President*
Leo Gomez Jr, *Vice Pres*
EMP: 15 EST: 1972
SQ FT: 11,000

SALES (est): 570.1K **Privately Held**
WEB: www.buenaparktool.com
SIC: 3599 7692 3544 Machine shop, jobbing & repair; welding repair; special dies, tools, jigs & fixtures

(P-8534)
BURTREE INC
13513 Sherman Way, Van Nuys
(91405-2899)
PHONE..................................818 786-4276
Cyrus Massoudi, *President*
Farah Massoudi, *Vice Pres*
Shawn Massoudi, *Mfg Staff*
EMP: 28 EST: 1955
SQ FT: 13,500
SALES (est): 2.4MM **Privately Held**
WEB: www.burtree.com
SIC: 3599 7699 Machine shop, jobbing & repair; professional instrument repair services

(P-8535)
C & C DIE ENGRAVING
12510 Mccann Dr, Santa Fe Springs
(90670-3337)
PHONE..................................562 944-3399
Salvador J Chavez, *Owner*
EMP: 26 EST: 1981
SQ FT: 10,000
SALES (est): 1.1MM **Privately Held**
WEB: www.cncdie.com
SIC: 3599 Machine shop, jobbing & repair

(P-8536)
C & D PRECISION COMPONENTS INC
Also Called: Trimatic
969 S Raymond Ave, Pasadena
(91105-3241)
PHONE..................................626 799-7109
Coleen Ganguin, *President*
Daniel A Ganguin, *Corp Secy*
EMP: 24 EST: 1964
SQ FT: 4,000
SALES (est): 1.2MM **Privately Held**
SIC: 3599 Machine shop, jobbing & repair

(P-8537)
C N C MACHINING INC
510 S Fairview Ave, Goleta (93117-3617)
PHONE..................................805 681-8855
Gary Brous, *President*
Greg Brous, *Vice Pres*
Shirley Brous, *Admin Sec*
EMP: 30 EST: 1985
SQ FT: 2,000
SALES (est): 2.3MM **Privately Held**
WEB: www.cncmachining.com
SIC: 3599 Machine shop, jobbing & repair

(P-8538)
CAD WORKS INC
16366 E Valley Blvd, La Puente
(91744-5546)
PHONE..................................626 336-5491
David Paquini, *President*
Cecilia Chavez, *CFO*
Avrahan Garcia, *Vice Pres*
Abraham Garcia, *Mktg Dir*
EMP: 20 EST: 2004
SQ FT: 10,000 **Privately Held**
WEB: www.cadworks.us
SIC: 3599 Machine shop, jobbing & repair

(P-8539)
CAL PRECISION INC
1720 S Bon View Ave, Ontario
(91761-4411)
PHONE..................................951 273-9901
Donna Loper, *President*
Andy Loper, *Vice Pres*
Charles Loper, *Vice Pres*
Bill Kearns, *Production*
EMP: 14 EST: 1998
SALES (est): 1.9MM **Privately Held**
WEB: www.calprecision.com
SIC: 3599 Machine shop, jobbing & repair

(P-8540)
CANADY MANUFACTURING CO INC
500 5th St, San Fernando (91340-2299)
PHONE..................................818 365-9181
Brian Koehn, *President*
Rodney Hull, *Owner*

Lyndi Munchhof, *Office Mgr*
Kimberlee Koehn, *Admin Asst*
Chris Munchhof, *Foreman/Supr*
EMP: 13 EST: 1943
SQ FT: 5,000
SALES (est): 2.2MM **Privately Held**
WEB: www.canadymfg.com
SIC: 3599 Machine shop, jobbing & repair

(P-8541)
CARDIC MACHINE PRODUCTS INC
17000 Keegan Ave, Carson (90746-1309)
PHONE..................................310 884-3400
Joseph Trumpio, *CEO*
Calvin Crockett, *Vice Pres*
EMP: 15 EST: 1951
SQ FT: 10,900
SALES (est): 3.6MM **Privately Held**
WEB: www.cardicmachine.com
SIC: 3599 Machine shop, jobbing & repair

(P-8542)
CARTER PUMP & MACHINE INC
635 G St, Wasco (93280-2023)
PHONE..................................661 393-8620
Chet Grooman, *President*
EMP: 31 EST: 1987
SQ FT: 6,000
SALES (est): 2.7MM **Privately Held**
SIC: 3599 7699 Machine shop, jobbing & repair; pumps & pumping equipment repair

(P-8543)
CAVALLO & CAVALLO INC
Also Called: Production Engineering & Mch
14955 Hilton Dr, Fontana (92336-2082)
PHONE..................................909 428-6994
Thomas H Kearns, *President*
EMP: 16 EST: 1967
SQ FT: 16,400
SALES (est): 2.4MM **Privately Held**
SIC: 3599 Machine shop, jobbing & repair

(P-8544)
CAVANAUGH MACHINE WORKS INC
1540 Santa Fe Ave, Long Beach
(90813-1239)
PHONE..................................562 437-1126
John Wells, *President*
Michael Wells, *Treasurer*
Mark Evans, *Controller*
EMP: 40 EST: 1946
SQ FT: 19,000
SALES (est): 4.3MM **Privately Held**
WEB: www.cavmachine.com
SIC: 3599 3731 3441 Machine shop, jobbing & repair; shipbuilding & repairing; fabricated structural metal

(P-8545)
CENCAL MACHINE COMPANY
19444 Colombo St, Bakersfield
(93308-9717)
PHONE..................................661 392-7831
EMP: 13 EST: 2019
SALES (est): 501.9K **Privately Held**
WEB: www.cencalmachine.com
SIC: 3599 Machine shop, jobbing & repair

(P-8546)
CENTERPOINT MFG CO INC
2625 N San Fernando Blvd, Burbank
(91504-3220)
PHONE..................................818 842-2147
John C Rotunno, *President*
Carmen Rotunno, *Vice Pres*
EMP: 40 EST: 1966
SQ FT: 12,000
SALES (est): 6.8MM **Privately Held**
WEB: www.centerpointmfgco.com
SIC: 3599 Machine shop, jobbing & repair

(P-8547)
CENTURY PARTS INC
913 W 223rd St, Torrance (90502-2246)
PHONE..................................310 328-0281
Lynn Hale, *CEO*
EMP: 18 EST: 1969
SQ FT: 12,500
SALES (est): 992.9K **Privately Held**
SIC: 3599 Machine shop, jobbing & repair

(P-8548)
CENTURY PRECISION ENGRG INC
2141 W 139th St, Gardena (90249-2451)
PHONE..................................310 538-0015
Myron Yoo, *President*
Salvador Jimenez, *Business Dir*
Bruce Lee, *Admin Sec*
Sonny Shin, *Engineer*
Jean Yoo, *Opers Mgr*
EMP: 25 EST: 1980
SQ FT: 20,000
SALES (est): 4.6MM **Privately Held**
WEB: www.centurype.com
SIC: 3599 Machine shop, jobbing & repair

(P-8549)
CHANNEL ISLNDS OPT-MCHNCAL ENG
1595 Walter St Ste 1, Ventura
(93003-5613)
PHONE..................................805 644-2153
Alan Cornelius, *President*
Roger Ransom, *Treasurer*
Mark Pennington, *Vice Pres*
EMP: 16 EST: 1982
SQ FT: 5,000
SALES (est): 1MM **Privately Held**
WEB: www.ciome.com
SIC: 3599 3827 Machine shop, jobbing & repair; optical elements & assemblies, except ophthalmic

(P-8550)
CHAPMAN ENGINEERING CORP
2321 Cape Cod Way, Santa Ana
(92703-3514)
PHONE..................................714 542-1942
Mary M Chapman, *CEO*
Ernest D Chapman, *Admin Sec*
EMP: 23 EST: 1978
SQ FT: 25,000
SALES (est): 1.4MM **Privately Held**
WEB: www.chapmanengineering.com
SIC: 3599 3469 Machine shop, jobbing & repair; metal stampings

(P-8551)
CHE PRECISION INC
2586 Calcite Cir, Newbury Park
(91320-1203)
PHONE..................................805 499-8885
Charles Holguin, *President*
Claude Holguin, *President*
Charlie Holguin, *Vice Pres*
▲ EMP: 20 EST: 1989
SALES (est): 2.5MM **Privately Held**
WEB: www.cheprecision.com
SIC: 3599 Machine shop, jobbing & repair

(P-8552)
CHEEK MACHINE CORP
1312 S Allec St, Anaheim (92805-6303)
PHONE..................................714 279-9486
Tatiana Cheek, *President*
Christopher Cheek, *Vice Pres*
Thuan Vu, *Prgrmr*
Van Vu, *Prgrmr*
Hilario Herrera, *Engineer*
EMP: 21 EST: 1994
SQ FT: 5,000
SALES (est): 3.3MM **Privately Held**
WEB: www.cheekmachine.com
SIC: 3599 Machine shop, jobbing & repair

(P-8553)
CHIPMASTERS MANUFACTURING INC (PA)
798 N Coney Ave, Azusa (91702-2239)
P.O. Box 697 (91702-0697)
PHONE..................................626 804-8178
Richard Jacobsen, *President*
Rick Standley, *Manager*
EMP: 16 EST: 1973
SQ FT: 15,400
SALES (est): 5MM **Privately Held**
WEB: www.chipmastersmfg.com
SIC: 3599 Machine shop, jobbing & repair

(P-8554)
CJ PRECISION INDUSTRIES INC
2817 Cherry Ave, Signal Hill (90755-1908)
PHONE..................................562 426-3708
Mike Vedder, *President*
Michael Vedder, *Vice Pres*

Thomas Vedder, *Vice Pres*
Cynthia Vedder, *Admin Sec*
EMP: 24 **EST:** 1980
SQ FT: 10,000
SALES (est): 1.3MM **Privately Held**
WEB: www.cjprecisionindustries.com
SIC: 3599 Machine shop, jobbing & repair

(P-8555)
CLASSIC WIRE CUT COMPANY INC
28210 Constellation Rd, Valencia
(91355-5000)
PHONE......................661 257-0558
Brett Bannerman, *Principal*
Marcy Martinez, *Executive Asst*
Rudy Tirado, *Prgrmr*
Craig Bannerman, *Engineer*
Wesley Horton, *Engineer*
▲ **EMP:** 150 **EST:** 1984
SQ FT: 80,000
SALES (est): 25.3MM **Privately Held**
WEB: www.classicwirecut.com
SIC: 3599 3841 Electrical discharge machining (EDM); surgical instruments & apparatus

(P-8556)
CM MACHINE INC
560 S Grand Ave, San Jacinto
(92582-3832)
PHONE......................951 654-6019
Carmel Tomoni, *President*
Michael Tomoni, *General Mgr*
EMP: 15 **EST:** 1993
SQ FT: 6,000
SALES (est): 910K **Privately Held**
WEB: www.cmmachineinc.com
SIC: 3599 Machine shop, jobbing & repair

(P-8557)
CNC INDUSTRIES INC
4965 Brooks St, Montclair (91763-4760)
PHONE......................909 445-0300
Bob Evans, *President*
Stephanie Evans, *Treasurer*
Danny Dodds, *Manager*
EMP: 14 **EST:** 1980
SQ FT: 33,000
SALES (est): 1MM **Privately Held**
WEB: www.cnc-ind.com
SIC: 3599 Machine shop, jobbing & repair

(P-8558)
CNI MFG INC
Also Called: Computer-Nozzles
15627 Arrow Hwy, Irwindale (91706-2004)
PHONE......................626 962-6646
Toby Argandona, *President*
David Argandona, *Vice Pres*
Yolanda Pullen, *Admin Sec*
Fred Key, *Engineer*
EMP: 24 **EST:** 1969
SQ FT: 32,200
SALES (est): 2.1MM **Privately Held**
WEB: www.cni-mfg.com
SIC: 3599 3443 Custom machinery; fabricated plate work (boiler shop)

(P-8559)
COAST COMPOSITES LLC (PA)
5 Burroughs, Irvine (92618-2804)
PHONE......................949 455-0665
Paul Walsh, *President*
Sharon Nelson, *Vice Pres*
Anthony Danna, *Program Mgr*
Christina Heins, *Program Mgr*
Jim Stanley, *Program Mgr*
◆ **EMP:** 298 **EST:** 1988
SQ FT: 60,000
SALES (est): 51.4MM **Privately Held**
WEB: www.ascentaerospace.com
SIC: 3599 Machine shop, jobbing & repair

(P-8560)
CODY CYLINDER SERVICE LLC
1393 Dodson Way Ste A, Riverside
(92507-2073)
P.O. Box 56099 (92517-0999)
PHONE......................951 786-3650
Art Pastour, *President*
Jolene Cody Patoor, *Vice Pres*
EMP: 21 **EST:** 2018

SALES (est): 3.5MM **Privately Held**
WEB: www.codycylinderservices.com
SIC: 3599 7379 Machine shop, jobbing & repair; tape recertification service

(P-8561)
COMPUTER ASSISTED MFG TECH LLC
Also Called: Camtech
8710-8750 Research Dr, Irvine (92618)
PHONE......................949 263-8911
Mike Dennis, *CEO*
EMP: 40 **EST:** 1982
SQ FT: 50,000
SALES (est): 9.2MM **Privately Held**
WEB: www.camtechcorp.com
SIC: 3599 Machine shop, jobbing & repair
HQ: Cam Holdco, Llc
  8710 Research Dr
  Irvine CA

(P-8562)
CONNELLY MACHINE WORKS
420 N Terminal St, Santa Ana
(92701-4999)
PHONE......................714 558-6855
Ray Connelly, *President*
Scott Connelly, *Vice Pres*
Aurora Contreras, *Manager*
EMP: 22
SQ FT: 17,000
SALES (est): 3.5MM **Privately Held**
WEB: www.connellymachine.com
SIC: 3599 3492 Machine shop, jobbing & repair; fluid power valves & hose fittings

(P-8563)
COOP ENGINEERING INC
Also Called: Ce Nut & Bolt
12930 Lakeland Rd, Santa Fe Springs
(90670-4517)
PHONE......................562 944-0171
Jeffrey Coop Jr, *President*
EMP: 22 **EST:** 1957
SQ FT: 900
SALES (est): 653.3K **Privately Held**
WEB: www.coopengineering.com
SIC: 3599 Machine shop, jobbing & repair

(P-8564)
CRESCO MANUFACTURING INC
Also Called: Crescomfg.com
1614 N Orangethorpe Way, Anaheim
(92801-1227)
PHONE......................714 525-2326
Jon Spielman, *President*
Alberta Spielman, *Vice Pres*
EMP: 40 **EST:** 1981
SQ FT: 14,000
SALES (est): 4.8MM **Privately Held**
WEB: www.petespielman.weebly.com
SIC: 3599 Machine shop, jobbing & repair

(P-8565)
CRUSH MASTER GRINDING CORP
755 Penarth Ave, Walnut (91789-3028)
PHONE......................909 595-2249
Sherman Durousseau, *President*
Jeanne Durousseau, *Admin Sec*
Donna Gilliam, *Mfg Staff*
EMP: 35 **EST:** 1976
SQ FT: 11,800
SALES (est): 2.9MM **Privately Held**
WEB: www.crushmastergrinding.com
SIC: 3599 Machine shop, jobbing & repair

(P-8566)
D G A MACHINE SHOP INC
Also Called: D G A Mch Sp Blnchard Grinding
5825 Ordway St, Riverside (92504-1132)
PHONE......................951 354-2113
Tony Diguglielmo, *President*
Angelo Diguglielmo, *CEO*
Angelo Diguglieilmo, *COO*
Angela Di Guglielmo, *Executive*
Barbara Goodell, *Admin Sec*
EMP: 15 **EST:** 1980
SALES (est): 2.3MM **Privately Held**
WEB: www.dgamachineshop.com
SIC: 3599 Machine shop, jobbing & repair

(P-8567)
D MILLS GRNDING MACHINING INC
6131 Quail Valley Ct, Riverside
(92507-0763)
PHONE......................951 697-6847
Anthony Puccio, *President*
Joe Puccio, *COO*
Gilles Madelmont, *CFO*
Jerry Long, *Mfg Mgr*
EMP: 150 **EST:** 1973
SQ FT: 14,000
SALES (est): 1.5MM
SALES (corp-wide): 43MM **Privately Held**
WEB: www.dmillsinc.com
SIC: 3599 Grinding castings for the trade; machine shop, jobbing & repair
PA: Manufacturing Solutions, Inc.
  1738 N Neville St
  Orange CA 92865
  714 453-0100

(P-8568)
DARCY AK CORPORATION
Also Called: AK Darcy
1760 Monrovia Ave Ste A22, Costa Mesa
(92627-4433)
PHONE......................949 650-5566
Darrell Gilbert, *CEO*
EMP: 15 **EST:** 1988
SQ FT: 9,000
SALES (est): 16MM **Privately Held**
SIC: 3599 5085 Machine shop, jobbing & repair; valves & fittings

(P-8569)
DELAFIELD CORPORATION (PA)
Also Called: Delafield Fluid Technology
1520 Flower Ave, Duarte (91010-2925)
PHONE......................626 303-0740
Nik Ray, *President*
Henry Custodia, *CFO*
Paul Burke, *Vice Pres*
Jim Martin, *Vice Pres*
Diana Martinez, *Branch Mgr*
◆ **EMP:** 120
SQ FT: 90,000
SALES (est): 40.4MM **Privately Held**
WEB: www.dftcorp.com
SIC: 3599 5085 3498 3492 Hose, flexible metallic; valves, pistons & fittings; tube fabricating (contract bending & shaping); fluid power valves & hose fittings; plumbing fixture fittings & trim; rubber & plastics hose & beltings

(P-8570)
DELTA HI-TECH
9600 De Soto Ave, Chatsworth
(91311-5012)
PHONE......................818 407-4000
Joe Ostrowsky, *CEO*
Chava Ostrowsky, *CFO*
Ilan Ostrowsky, *Exec VP*
Juan Casarrubias, *Vice Pres*
Gregory Elkhunovich, *Vice Pres*
▲ **EMP:** 130 **EST:** 1985
SQ FT: 40,000
SALES (est): 27.6MM **Privately Held**
WEB: www.deltahi-tech.com
SIC: 3599 Machine shop, jobbing & repair

(P-8571)
DESCO MANUFACTURING COMPANY (PA)
23031 Arroyo Vis Ste A, Rcho STA Marg
(92688-2618)
PHONE......................949 858-7400
Ralph L Fabian, *President*
William Cobble, *Vice Pres*
Jerry Woodbeck, *Area Mgr*
Ruth Sistrunk, *Office Mgr*
Tom Sistrunk, *Info Tech Mgr*
▲ **EMP:** 16 **EST:** 1962
SALES (est): 3.3MM **Privately Held**
WEB: www.descomfg.com
SIC: 3599 Custom machinery

(P-8572)
DIAL PRECISION INC
17235 Darwin Ave, Hesperia (92345-5178)
P.O. Box 402259 (92340-2259)
PHONE......................760 947-3557
Darryl L Tarullo, *Ch of Bd*

Steve Tarullo, *Engineer*
Tom Jordon, *Accounts Mgr*
EMP: 95 **EST:** 1958
SQ FT: 15,000
SALES (est): 5.9MM **Privately Held**
WEB: www.dialprecision.com
SIC: 3599 3545 Machine shop, jobbing & repair; machine tool accessories

(P-8573)
DOLSTRA AUTOMATIC PRODUCTS
14441 Edwards St, Westminster
(92683-3607)
PHONE......................714 894-2062
John Dolstra, *President*
Susan Dolstra, *Admin Sec*
EMP: 15 **EST:** 1973
SQ FT: 3,400
SALES (est): 505.7K **Privately Held**
SIC: 3599 Machine shop, jobbing & repair

(P-8574)
DOW HYDRAULIC SYSTEMS INC
2895 Metropolitan Pl, Pomona
(91767-1853)
PHONE......................909 596-6602
Richard P Dow, *President*
Bryan Dow, *Vice Pres*
Ryan K Dow, *Vice Pres*
Ryan Dow, *Vice Pres*
Keith Dow, *Principal*
EMP: 60 **EST:** 1968
SALES (est): 11.6MM **Privately Held**
WEB: www.dowhydraulics.com
SIC: 3599 3594 Machine shop, jobbing & repair; fluid power pumps & motors

(P-8575)
DUNSTAN ENTERPRISES INC
Also Called: Green's Metal Cutoff
11821 Slauson Ave, Santa Fe Springs
(90670-2219)
PHONE......................562 630-6292
Renee Dunstan, *President*
EMP: 16 **EST:** 2003
SALES (est): 1.8MM **Privately Held**
WEB: www.greensmetal.com
SIC: 3599 Machine shop, jobbing & repair

(P-8576)
DYNAMIC ENTERPRISES INC
Also Called: D E I
2081 Rancho Hills Dr, Chino Hills
(91709-4763)
PHONE......................562 944-0271
Mildred Sudduth, *President*
Deanna Mansfield, *Corp Secy*
Alan Sudduth, *Vice Pres*
◆ **EMP:** 21 **EST:** 1959
SALES (est): 4MM **Privately Held**
WEB: www.dynamic-ent.com
SIC: 3599 Machine shop, jobbing & repair

(P-8577)
DYNOMILL INC
2018 Edwards Ave, South El Monte
(91733-2036)
PHONE......................626 454-1805
Jonathan Nguyen, *President*
Steven Nguyen, *Vice Pres*
EMP: 16 **EST:** 2006
SALES (est): 1.3MM **Privately Held**
WEB: www.dynomill-us.com
SIC: 3599 Machine shop, jobbing & repair

(P-8578)
EJAYS MACHINE CO INC
1108 E Valencia Dr, Fullerton (92831-4627)
PHONE......................714 879-0558
Denise Eastin, *President*
Schuyler Eastin, *Treasurer*
Ramona Fodor, *Production*
EMP: 20 **EST:** 1965
SALES (est): 2.3MM **Privately Held**
WEB: www.ejaysmachine.com
SIC: 3599 Machine shop, jobbing & repair

(P-8579)
ELLINGSON INC
119 W Santa Fe Ave, Fullerton
(92832-1831)
PHONE......................714 773-1923
Thomas Ellingson, *President*
T C Ellingson, *CEO*

PRODUCTS & SVCS

Nancy Ellingson, *CFO*
Steve Ellingson, *Vice Pres*
Steven C Ellingson, *Admin Sec*
EMP: 49 **EST:** 1946
SQ FT: 7,500
SALES (est): 4.3MM Privately Held
WEB: www.ellingson-inc.com
SIC: 3599 Machine shop, jobbing & repair;
machine & other job shop work

(P-8580)
ELY CO INC
3046 Kashiwa St, Torrance (90505-4083)
PHONE..................310 539-5831
Walter Senff, *CEO*
Bill Senff, *Vice Pres*
Judith Senff, *Vice Pres*
Kurt Senff, *Admin Sec*
EMP: 36
SQ FT: 11,500
SALES (est): 6.8MM Privately Held
WEB: www.elyco.com
SIC: 3599 Machine shop, jobbing & repair

(P-8581)
ENERGY LINK INDUS SVCS INC
11439 S Enos Ln, Bakersfield
(93311-9452)
P.O. Box 10716 (93389-0716)
PHONE..................661 765-4444
James R Miller III, *CEO*
Matt Knight, *Shareholder*
West Moore, *Shareholder*
Ray Miller, *President*
David Sandoval, *Manager*
EMP: 34 **EST:** 2000
SALES (est): 8.2MM Privately Held
WEB: www.energylink1.com
SIC: 3599 7699 Bellows, industrial: metal;
compressor repair

(P-8582)
ENGINEERED PRODUCTS BY LEE LTD
Also Called: Precision Engineered Products
10444 Mcvine Ave, Sunland (91040-3102)
PHONE..................818 352-3322
Wallace K Lee, *President*
Christine Lee, *Office Mgr*
EMP: 13 **EST:** 1967
SQ FT: 7,000
SALES (est): 246K Privately Held
SIC: 3599 Machine shop, jobbing & repair

(P-8583)
ESM PLASTICS INC
13575 Yorba Ave, Chino (91710-5057)
P.O. Box 808 (91708-0808)
PHONE..................909 591-7658
Earl D Silva, *CEO*
Cheryl Silva, *Admin Sec*
EMP: 15 **EST:** 1983
SQ FT: 7,400
SALES (est): 2.3MM Privately Held
SIC: 3599 3089 Custom machinery; injection molding of plastics

(P-8584)
EXTRUDE HONE DEBURRING SVC INC
Also Called: Extrude Hone Abrsive Flow McHn
8800 Somerset Blvd, Paramount
(90723-4659)
PHONE..................562 531-2976
William Melendez, *President*
EMP: 20 **EST:** 1971
SQ FT: 11,000
SALES (est): 1MM Privately Held
WEB: www.extrudehoneafm.com
SIC: 3599 5084 Machine shop, jobbing & repair; machine tools & accessories; machinists' precision measuring tools

(P-8585)
F &L MACHINE INC
10490 Ilex Ave, Pacoima (91331-3137)
PHONE..................818 899-6738
Fabian Montes, *President*
George Montes, *Vice Pres*
EMP: 14 **EST:** 1986
SALES (est): 180K Privately Held
WEB: www.flmachineinc.com
SIC: 3599 Machine shop, jobbing & repair

(P-8586)
FARRELL BROTHERS HOLDING CORP
Also Called: Swiss Machine Products
1137 N Armando St, Anaheim
(92806-2609)
PHONE..................714 630-3417
Doug Farrell, *President*
Myra Farrell, *Treasurer*
Kevan Farrell, *Vice Pres*
Ruby Farrell, *Admin Sec*
EMP: 16 **EST:** 1966
SQ FT: 10,000
SALES (est): 1.7MM Privately Held
WEB: www.swissmachine.com
SIC: 3599 Machine shop, jobbing & repair

(P-8587)
FIBREFORM ELECTRONICS INC
Also Called: Fibreform Precision Machining
5341 Argosy Ave, Huntington Beach
(92649-1036)
PHONE..................714 898-9641
Zachary Fischer, *Ch of Bd*
Frank Mauro, *COO*
Todd Crow, *CFO*
Rovalier Thompson, *Vice Pres*
EMP: 30 **EST:** 1945
SQ FT: 30,000
SALES (est): 4.5MM Privately Held
WEB: www.fibreformprecision.com
SIC: 3599 Machine shop, jobbing & repair

(P-8588)
FIERRITO METAL STAMPING
12358 San Fernando Rd, Sylmar
(91342-5020)
PHONE..................818 362-6136
Henry Avila, *President*
Rosie Avila, *Manager*
EMP: 13 **EST:** 1974
SALES (est): 250K Privately Held
SIC: 3599 3469 Machine shop, jobbing & repair; metal stampings

(P-8589)
FINNTECH INC
1930 W 169th St, Gardena (90247-5254)
PHONE..................310 323-0790
Renny Laitio, *President*
Peter Laitio, *Chairman*
Leila Johnson, *Treasurer*
Kari Laitio, *Vice Pres*
EMP: 15 **EST:** 1978
SQ FT: 2,500
SALES (est): 572.3K Privately Held
SIC: 3599 Machine shop, jobbing & repair

(P-8590)
FONTAL CONTROLS INC
12725 Encinitas Ave, Sylmar (91342-3517)
PHONE..................818 833-1127
Oscar Fontal, *President*
Gladys Fontal, *Treasurer*
Fernando Fontal, *Vice Pres*
Cristian Fontal, *Admin Sec*
EMP: 24 **EST:** 1982
SQ FT: 14,200
SALES (est): 1.7MM Privately Held
WEB: www.fontalcontrols.com
SIC: 3599 Machine shop, jobbing & repair

(P-8591)
FORM GRIND CORPORATION
Also Called: Form Products
30062 Aventura, Rcho STA Marg
(92688-2010)
PHONE..................949 858-7000
Ernest Treichler, *CEO*
Gary Treichler, *Treasurer*
Joan Treichler, *Admin Sec*
Tammi Castro, *IT Executive*
Laurence Erickson, *Mfg Mgr*
EMP: 50 **EST:** 1963
SQ FT: 30,000
SALES (est): 2.7MM Privately Held
WEB: www.formgrind.com
SIC: 3599 5084 Machine shop, jobbing & repair; industrial machinery & equipment

(P-8592)
FORTNER ENG & MFG INC
918 Thompson Ave, Glendale
(91201-2079)
P.O. Box 30015, Salt Lake City UT (84130-0015)
PHONE..................818 240-7740
David W Fortner, *President*
Robert S Fortner, *General Mgr*
Jon Benoit, *Engineer*
Gary M Fortner, *Engineer*
Robert Fortner, *Human Res Mgr*
EMP: 30 **EST:** 1952
SQ FT: 24,000
SALES (est): 7.4MM
SALES (corp-wide): 363.7MM Privately Held
WEB: www.fortnereng.com
SIC: 3599 Machine shop, jobbing & repair
PA: Wencor Group, Llc
416 Dividend Dr
Peachtree City GA 30269
678 490-0140

(P-8593)
FRANK RUSSELL INC
341 Pacific Ave, Shafter (93263-2046)
PHONE..................661 324-5575
Andrew Russell, *President*
Cody Russell, *Parts Mgr*
EMP: 17 **EST:** 1939
SQ FT: 13,000
SALES (est): 2.5MM Privately Held
WEB: www.frankrussellinc.com
SIC: 3599 5251 Machine shop, jobbing & repair; hardware

(P-8594)
FRONTIER ENGRG & MFG TECH INC
Also Called: Frontier Technologies
800 W 16th St, Long Beach (90813-1413)
PHONE..................562 606-2655
John Tsai, *CEO*
Steve Hoekstra, *President*
▲ **EMP:** 46 **EST:** 1994
SQ FT: 30,000
SALES (est): 12.3MM Privately Held
WEB: www.ftmfg.com
SIC: 3599 8711 Machine shop, jobbing & repair; engineering services

(P-8595)
FUNTASTIC FACTORY INC
Also Called: Einflatables
19703 Meadows Cir, Cerritos (90703-7734)
PHONE..................562 777-1140
Ajay H Patel, *CEO*
Ross Andrizzi, *President*
EMP: 17 **EST:** 1994
SQ FT: 20,000
SALES (est): 720.3K Privately Held
SIC: 3599 Carnival machines & equipment, amusement park

(P-8596)
FUTURE TECH METALS INC
719 Palmyrita Ave, Riverside (92507-1811)
PHONE..................951 781-4801
Tim Gearhardt, *Owner*
Art Medina, *Co-Owner*
Fidel Felt, *Senior Engr*
EMP: 20
SALES (est): 4.7MM Privately Held
WEB: www.futuretechmetals.com
SIC: 3599 Machine shop, jobbing & repair

(P-8597)
G & H PRECISION INC
11950 Vose St, North Hollywood
(91605-5749)
P.O. Box 16123 (91615-6123)
PHONE..................818 982-3873
George Hallajian, *President*
Sevan Hallajian, *Vice Pres*
EMP: 14 **EST:** 1980
SQ FT: 12,000
SALES (est): 3MM Privately Held
WEB: www.ghprecision.com
SIC: 3599 Machine shop, jobbing & repair

(P-8598)
G P MANUFACTURING INC
Also Called: Protype
541 W Briardale Ave, Orange
(92865-4207)
PHONE..................714 974-0288
Greg Gilbert, *President*
Lewis Pearmain, *Vice Pres*
EMP: 16 **EST:** 1984
SQ FT: 13,500
SALES (est): 1.6MM Privately Held
SIC: 3599 3444 Machine shop, jobbing & repair; sheet metalwork

(P-8599)
GAMMA AEROSPACE LLC
1415 W 178th St, Gardena (90248-3201)
PHONE..................310 532-4480
EMP: 32
SALES (corp-wide): 25MM Privately Held
WEB: www.gammaaero.com
SIC: 3599 Machine shop, jobbing & repair
PA: Gamma Aerospace Llc
601 Airport Dr
Mansfield TX 76063
817 477-2193

(P-8600)
GARRETT PRECISION INC
25082 La Suen Rd, Laguna Hills
(92653-5102)
PHONE..................949 855-9710
Justin S Osborn, *CEO*
Dean Garrett, *President*
Lynn Garrett, *Vice Pres*
EMP: 19 **EST:** 1978
SQ FT: 6,500
SALES (est): 1.4MM Privately Held
SIC: 3599 Machine shop, jobbing & repair

(P-8601)
GBF ENTERPRISES INC
2709 Halladay St, Santa Ana (92705-5618)
PHONE..................714 979-7131
Cheryl Nowak, *President*
Mike Corbean, *QC Mgr*
Lisa Garrison, *Sales Staff*
Hart Candi, *Consultant*
EMP: 25 **EST:** 1976
SQ FT: 17,000
SALES (est): 4.3MM Privately Held
WEB: www.gbfenterprises.com
SIC: 3599 Machine shop, jobbing & repair

(P-8602)
GEARTECH SERVICES INC
1640 N Dillon St, Los Angeles
(90026-1204)
PHONE..................323 309-7861
Ross Breitenbach, *CEO*
EMP: 14 **EST:** 2013
SALES (est): 135.8K Privately Held
WEB: www.gear-tech.com
SIC: 3599 Machine shop, jobbing & repair

(P-8603)
GENERAL INDUSTRIAL REPAIR
7417 E Slauson Ave, Commerce
(90040-3307)
PHONE..................323 278-0873
Henry Biazus, *President*
Richard Biazus, *CEO*
Bob Arconado, *Sales Staff*
Robert Biazus, *Sales Staff*
Enrique Gaspar, *Manager*
EMP: 25 **EST:** 1995
SQ FT: 75,000
SALES (est): 5.3MM Privately Held
WEB: www.girepair.us
SIC: 3599 Machine shop, jobbing & repair

(P-8604)
GENERAL PRODUCTION SERVICES
670 Arroyo St, San Fernando
(91340-2220)
PHONE..................818 365-4211
Maria Hall, *President*
Loren S Hall, *Vice Pres*
EMP: 30 **EST:** 1975
SQ FT: 3,500
SALES (est): 1.5MM Privately Held
SIC: 3599 Machine shop, jobbing & repair

(P-8605)
GEORGE FISCHER INC (HQ)
5462 Irwindale Ave Ste A, Baldwin Park
(91706-2074)
PHONE..................................626 571-2770
Chris Blumer, *CEO*
Daniel Vaterlaus, *Vice Pres*
Georg Fischer, *Managing Dir*
Mark Gruber, *CIO*
Sander Luu, *Electrical Engi*
◆ EMP: 281 EST: 1954
SALES (est): 264.8MM
SALES (corp-wide): 3.5B **Privately Held**
WEB: www.signet-gf.com
SIC: 3599 5074 3829 3559 Electrical discharge machining (EDM); pipes & fittings, plastic; testing equipment: abrasion, shearing strength, etc.; foundry machinery & equipment
PA: Georg Fischer Ag
Amsler-Laffon-Strasse 9
Schaffhausen SH 8200
526 311-111

(P-8606)
GOEPPNER INDUSTRIES INC
22924 Lockness Ave, Torrance
(90501-5117)
PHONE..................................310 784-2800
Joanne Goeppner, *President*
EMP: 34 EST: 1972
SQ FT: 12,000
SALES (est): 1.3MM **Privately Held**
SIC: 3599 Machine shop, jobbing & repair

(P-8607)
GOLDEN WEST MACHINE INC
9930 Jordan Cir, Santa Fe Springs
(90670-3305)
PHONE..................................562 903-1111
Dan Goodman, *Principal*
Al Schlunegger, *Vice Pres*
Shane Downs, *General Mgr*
Sarah Goodman, *Finance Mgr*
EMP: 35 EST: 1982
SQ FT: 25,000
SALES (est): 5.4MM **Privately Held**
WEB: www.goldenwestmachine.com
SIC: 3599 7699 Machine shop, jobbing & repair; industrial machinery & equipment repair

(P-8608)
GP MACHINING INC
94 Commerce Dr, Buellton (93427-9500)
P.O. Box 2006 (93427-2006)
PHONE..................................805 686-0852
Julian Guerra, *President*
Robert Place, *Vice Pres*
EMP: 34 EST: 1995
SQ FT: 4,500
SALES (est): 3.8MM **Privately Held**
WEB: www.gpmachining.com
SIC: 3599 Machine shop, jobbing & repair

(P-8609)
GRACE MACHINE CO INC
4540 Cecilia St, Cudahy (90201-5812)
PHONE..................................323 771-6215
Guillermo Castellanos Sr, *President*
Ivon Rodriguez, *Treasurer*
Guillermo Castellanos Jr, *Vice Pres*
Grace Castellanos, *Admin Sec*
EMP: 19 EST: 1982
SALES (est): 707.7K **Privately Held**
SIC: 3599 Machine shop, jobbing & repair

(P-8610)
GRICO PRECISION INC
Also Called: Swiss House
128 S Valencia Ave Ste A, Glendora
(91741-3271)
PHONE..................................626 963-0368
Tom Grisham, *President*
Robert E Dill, *Vice Pres*
EMP: 16 EST: 1977
SALES (est): 445.5K **Privately Held**
SIC: 3599 Machine shop, jobbing & repair

(P-8611)
GSP PRECISION INC
650 Town Center Dr # 950, Costa Mesa
(92626-1989)
PHONE..................................818 845-2212
George Gottardi, *President*
Walter D Prezioso, *CEO*

Pablo Prezioso, *Admin Sec*
EMP: 37 EST: 1979
SQ FT: 6,000
SALES (est): 886.4K **Privately Held**
WEB: www.gsp-precision.com
SIC: 3599 Machine shop, jobbing & repair

(P-8612)
GUNDRILL TECH INC
10030 Greenleaf Ave, Santa Fe Springs
(90670-3414)
PHONE..................................562 946-9355
Joe Bati, *President*
Yolande Bati, *Vice Pres*
EMP: 15 EST: 1986
SALES (est): 537K **Privately Held**
WEB: www.gundrilltech.com
SIC: 3599 Machine shop, jobbing & repair

(P-8613)
H FAM ENGINEERING INC
2131 S Hellman Ave Ste F, Ontario
(91761-8004)
PHONE..................................909 930-5678
Joe Herrera, *President*
Raul Herrera, *Vice Pres*
EMP: 13 EST: 1986
SQ FT: 7,000
SALES (est): 730.4K **Privately Held**
SIC: 3599 Machine shop, jobbing & repair

(P-8614)
HELFER ENTERPRISES
Also Called: Helfer Tool Co
3030 Oak St, Santa Ana (92707-4236)
PHONE..................................714 557-2733
Bennie L Helfer, *President*
EMP: 47 EST: 1973
SQ FT: 12,000
SALES (est): 620.2K **Privately Held**
WEB: www.helfertool.com
SIC: 3599 5084 3545 3544 Machine shop, jobbing & repair; industrial machinery & equipment; machine tool accessories; special dies, tools, jigs & fixtures

(P-8615)
HERA TECHNOLOGIES LLC
1590 S Milliken Ave Ste D, Ontario
(91761-2326)
PHONE..................................951 751-6191
Didi Truong, *CEO*
Aaron Evans, *COO*
Eugene Chuck, *CFO*
EMP: 50 EST: 2015
SALES (est): 4.2MM **Privately Held**
WEB: www.heratechnologies.com
SIC: 3599 Machine shop, jobbing & repair

(P-8616)
HI TEMP FORMING CO
315 Arden Ave Ste 28, Glendale
(91203-1150)
PHONE..................................714 529-6556
Marvin Rosenberg, *President*
Jay Rosenberg, *Treasurer*
Doris Rosenberg, *Vice Pres*
EMP: 18 EST: 1959
SQ FT: 36,000
SALES (est): 711.7K **Privately Held**
SIC: 3599 3812 3769 Machine shop, jobbing & repair; search & navigation equipment; guided missile & space vehicle parts & auxiliary equipment

(P-8617)
HI-TECH LABELS INCORPORATED (PA)
Also Called: Hi-Tech Products
8530 Roland St, Buena Park (90621-3124)
PHONE..................................714 670-2150
Jeffrey T Ruch, *CEO*
Sandra Duckett, *CFO*
Alan Weissman, *General Mgr*
Jerry Oswald, *Engineer*
Jim Ruch, *Engineer*
▲ EMP: 33 EST: 1983
SQ FT: 24,000
SALES (est): 6.7MM **Privately Held**
WEB: www.hi-tech-medical-products.com
SIC: 3599 Machine shop, jobbing & repair

(P-8618)
HILL MARINE PRODUCTS LLC
Also Called: Signature Propellers
2683 Halladay St, Santa Ana (92705-5617)
PHONE..................................714 855-2986
Chad Hill, *Mng Member*
Ron Hill,
▲ EMP: 14 EST: 2011
SALES (est): 1.4MM **Privately Held**
WEB: www.hillmarine.com
SIC: 3599 7699 3732 Propellers, ship & boat: machined; marine propeller repair; boats, fiberglass: building & repairing

(P-8619)
HMCOMPANY
4464 Mcgrath St Ste 111, Ventura
(93003-7764)
PHONE..................................805 650-2651
Mark Woellert, *Owner*
EMP: 22 EST: 1977
SQ FT: 3,500
SALES (est): 766.9K **Privately Held**
WEB: www.hm-company.net
SIC: 3599 Machine shop, jobbing & repair

(P-8620)
HOEFNER CORPORATION
9722 Rush St, South El Monte
(91733-1777)
PHONE..................................626 443-3258
Gerald Hoefner, *President*
Karen Hoefner, *Admin Sec*
EMP: 20
SQ FT: 14,800
SALES (est): 3.7MM **Privately Held**
WEB: www.hoefnercorp.com
SIC: 3599 3429 Machine shop, jobbing & repair; manufactured hardware (general)

(P-8621)
HOLLAND & HERRING MFG INC
Also Called: H & H Manufacturing
661 E Monterey Ave, Pomona
(91767-5607)
PHONE..................................909 469-4700
Jerry C Holland, *President*
Anne M Herring, *Shareholder*
Bruce N Herring, *Shareholder*
Mark B Herring, *Shareholder*
Steven R Herring, *Shareholder*
EMP: 24 EST: 1991
SQ FT: 15,000
SALES (est): 2.7MM **Privately Held**
SIC: 3599 3471 Machine shop, jobbing & repair; cleaning, polishing & finishing

(P-8622)
HOUSTON ONTIC INC
20400 Plummer St, Chatsworth
(91311-5372)
PHONE..................................818 678-6555
Gareth Blackbird, *CFO*
Ewa Anson, *IT/INT Sup*
Ryan Klaseus, *Analyst*
Kathie Cerda, *Accountant*
John Yi, *Director*
EMP: 39 EST: 2016
SALES (est): 2.8MM **Privately Held**
WEB: www.ontic.com
SIC: 3599 Machine shop, jobbing & repair

(P-8623)
HTE ACQUISITION LLC
Also Called: Hi-Tech Engineering
4610 Calle Quetzal, Camarillo
(93012-8558)
PHONE..................................805 987-5449
Shaffiq Rahim, *President*
EMP: 20 EST: 2019
SQ FT: 15,000
SALES (est): 2.2MM **Privately Held**
WEB: www.htemfg.com
SIC: 3599 Machine shop, jobbing & repair

(P-8624)
HYTRON MFG CO INC
15582 Chemical Ln, Huntington Beach
(92649-1505)
PHONE..................................714 903-6701
James C Rehling, *President*
Cheryll Rehling, *Corp Secy*
Robert Rehling, *Vice Pres*
Deborah Strickland, *Vice Pres*
Ken Rehling, *Sales Executive*
EMP: 50 EST: 1963

SQ FT: 13,370
SALES (est): 7.9MM **Privately Held**
WEB: www.hytronmanufacturing.com
SIC: 3599 Machine shop, jobbing & repair

(P-8625)
I COPY INC
Also Called: Ibe Digital
11266 Monarch St Ste B, Garden Grove
(92841-1450)
PHONE..................................562 921-0202
Ronald Varing, *President*
EMP: 50 EST: 2001
SALES (est): 6.2MM **Privately Held**
SIC: 3599 5044 Amusement park equipment; duplicating machines; business machines & equipment

(P-8626)
INFINITE ENGINEERING INC
13682 Newhope St, Garden Grove
(92843-3712)
PHONE..................................714 534-4688
Simon Ho, *President*
Kelly Ho, *Vice Pres*
EMP: 15 EST: 2006
SALES (est): 477.8K **Privately Held**
WEB: www.infinitecncshop.com
SIC: 3599 Machine shop, jobbing & repair

(P-8627)
INTERNATIONAL PRECISION INC
Also Called: I P
9526 Vassar Ave, Chatsworth
(91311-4168)
P.O. Box 4839 (91313-4839)
PHONE..................................818 882-3933
Renee M Brendel-Konrad, *CEO*
Rene Velasquez, *Vice Pres*
Rene Konrad, *Purch Mgr*
Jean Chiredjian, *Sales Mgr*
Alan Beauregard, *Sales Staff*
◆ EMP: 22 EST: 1968
SQ FT: 12,000
SALES (est): 5.7MM **Privately Held**
WEB: www.intlprecision.com
SIC: 3599 3728 Machine shop, jobbing & repair; aircraft parts & equipment

(P-8628)
INTRA AEROSPACE LLC
10671 Civic Center Dr, Rancho Cucamonga
(91730-3804)
PHONE..................................909 476-0343
Robert Sayig, *Principal*
Sharon Nevius, *Office Mgr*
Amber Black, *Controller*
EMP: 35 EST: 2018
SALES (est): 3.6MM **Privately Held**
WEB: www.gear-tech.com
SIC: 3599 Machine shop, jobbing & repair

(P-8629)
INTRI-PLEX TECHNOLOGIES INC (HQ)
751 S Kellogg Ave, Goleta (93117-3806)
PHONE..................................805 683-3414
Lawney J Falloon, *CEO*
David Janes, *Ch of Bd*
Lawrence Ellis, *CFO*
Sal Penza, *CFO*
John Sullivan, *Vice Pres*
▲ EMP: 126 EST: 1987
SQ FT: 46,000
SALES (est): 20.9MM
SALES (corp-wide): 21.6MM **Privately Held**
WEB: www.intriplex.com
SIC: 3599 Machine shop, jobbing & repair
PA: Ipt Holding Inc
751 S Kellogg Ave
Goleta CA 93117
805 683-3414

(P-8630)
ISI DETENTION CONTG GROUP INC
Also Called: Argyle Precision
577 N Batavia St, Orange (92868-1218)
PHONE..................................714 288-1770
Zach Greene, *President*
Joe Chavez, *Vice Pres*
▲ EMP: 90 EST: 1993
SQ FT: 25,000

PRODUCTS & SVCS

SALES (est): 9.5MM **Privately Held**
SIC: **3599** 3444 Machine & other job shop work; sheet metal specialties, not stamped

(P-8631)
J & F MACHINE INC
6401 Global Dr, Cypress (90630-5227)
PHONE..............................714 527-3499
Micheline Varnum, *President*
Richard Varnum, *Vice Pres*
Oscar Ocampo, *Finance*
Bill Barcikowski, *Production*
EMP: 22 EST: 1977
SQ FT: 8,500
SALES (est): 3.2MM **Privately Held**
WEB: www.jandfmachine.com
SIC: **3599** Machine shop, jobbing & repair

(P-8632)
J & P PRECISION DEBURRING INC
9135 Alabama Ave Ste D, Chatsworth (91311-5882)
PHONE..............................818 998-6079
Steve Bastin, *President*
Judy Craig, *Vice Pres*
EMP: 13 EST: 1974
SQ FT: 3,860
SALES (est): 525.8K **Privately Held**
WEB: www.jandpdeburring.com
SIC: **3599** 3471 Machine shop, jobbing & repair; plating & polishing

(P-8633)
J & R MACHINE WORKS
45420 60th St W, Lancaster (93536-8322)
PHONE..............................661 945-8826
Jesse Alvarado, *Partner*
Rudy Alvarado, *Partner*
Jonathan Varela, *QC Mgr*
EMP: 22 EST: 1989
SQ FT: 3,500
SALES (est): 3.2MM **Privately Held**
WEB: www.jrmachineworks.com
SIC: **3599** Machine shop, jobbing & repair

(P-8634)
J & S INC
229 E Gardena Blvd, Gardena (90248-2800)
PHONE..............................310 719-7144
Joseph Brown, *President*
Sheryl Zamora, *CEO*
Margaret Brown, *Corp Secy*
EMP: 33 EST: 1981
SQ FT: 6,141
SALES (est): 2.6MM **Privately Held**
SIC: **3599** Machine shop, jobbing & repair

(P-8635)
J & S MACHINE
Also Called: J and S Machine
8112 Freestone Ave, Santa Fe Springs (90670-2114)
PHONE..............................562 945-6419
EMP: 30
SQ FT: 7,200
SALES: 1.5MM **Privately Held**
SIC: **3599** Mfg Industrial Machinery

(P-8636)
J B TOOL INC
350 E Orngthrp Ave Ste 6, Placentia (92870-6504)
PHONE..............................714 993-7173
Robert Barna, *President*
EMP: 13 EST: 1975
SQ FT: 12,000
SALES (est): 800K **Privately Held**
WEB: www.jbtoolinc.com
SIC: **3599** Machine shop, jobbing & repair

(P-8637)
JACK C DREES GRINDING CO INC
11815 Vose St B, North Hollywood (91605-5748)
PHONE..............................818 764-8301
Jack C Drees, *President*
Dann Drees, *Vice Pres*
EMP: 16 EST: 1957
SQ FT: 12,000

SALES (est): 2MM **Privately Held**
WEB: www.jackdreesgrinding.com
SIC: **3599** 7389 Grinding castings for the trade; grinding, precision: commercial or industrial

(P-8638)
JACO ENGINEERING
879 S East St, Anaheim (92805-5391)
PHONE..............................714 991-1680
H J Meagher, *President*
Barbara Meagher, *Vice Pres*
Kathy Gordon, *General Mgr*
Alejandra Reyes, *Administration*
David T Theobold, *Technical Staff*
EMP: 35
SQ FT: 10,000
SALES (est): 6.7MM **Privately Held**
WEB: www.jacoengineering.com
SIC: **3599** Machine shop, jobbing & repair

(P-8639)
JAFFA PRECISION ENGRG INC
12117 Madera Way, Riverside (92503-4849)
PHONE..............................951 278-8797
Raida Sayegh, *President*
Chris S Sayegh, *COO*
Mark Sayegh, *Manager*
EMP: 15 EST: 1986
SQ FT: 12,500 **Privately Held**
WEB: www.jaffaprecision.com
SIC: **3599** Machine shop, jobbing & repair

(P-8640)
JAR MACHINE FABRICATION INC
1031 W Kirkwall Rd, Azusa (91702-5127)
PHONE..............................626 939-1111
Tony Rubio, *President*
Jesus Rubio, *Manager*
EMP: 13 EST: 2012
SALES (est): 1.2MM **Privately Held**
WEB: www.jarmachine.com
SIC: **3599** Machine shop, jobbing & repair

(P-8641)
JCPM INC
Also Called: J C Precision
8576 Red Oak St, Rancho Cucamonga (91730-4822)
PHONE..............................909 484-9040
Carlos Cajas, *President*
Peter Cajas, *Treasurer*
EMP: 24 EST: 1995
SQ FT: 5,200
SALES (est): 2.9MM **Privately Held**
WEB: www.jcpm-inc.com
SIC: **3599** Machine shop, jobbing & repair

(P-8642)
JET CUTTING SOLUTIONS INC
10853 Bell Ct, Rancho Cucamonga (91730-4835)
PHONE..............................909 948-2424
Louis Mammolito, *President*
Thomas Ribas, *President*
Louis Mammooito, *CEO*
EMP: 45 EST: 2005
SALES (est): 5.3MM **Privately Held**
WEB: www.jetcuttingsolutions.com
SIC: **3599** Machine shop, jobbing & repair

(P-8643)
JMG MACHINE INC
17037 Industry Pl, La Mirada (90638-5819)
PHONE..............................714 522-6221
Juan Manuel Guillen, *CEO*
EMP: 20 EST: 1994
SQ FT: 10,000
SALES (est): 2.3MM **Privately Held**
WEB: www.jmgmachine.com
SIC: **3599** Machine shop, jobbing & repair

(P-8644)
JNS INDUSTRIES INC
2322 S Vineyard Ave Ste C, Ontario (91761-7775)
PHONE..............................909 923-8334
Janet Sheikh, *President*
Pamela Oates Sanders, *Manager*
EMP: 15 EST: 2000
SALES (est): 1.7MM **Privately Held**
WEB: www.jnsindustries.com
SIC: **3599** Machine shop, jobbing & repair

(P-8645)
JOHNSON MANUFACTURING INC
15201 Connector Ln, Huntington Beach (92649-1117)
PHONE..............................714 903-0393
Colleen Johnson, *CEO*
Allan Johnson, *Vice Pres*
Melody Johnson, *General Mgr*
Sylvia Culling, *Office Mgr*
EMP: 35 EST: 1981
SQ FT: 13,000
SALES (est): 5.6MM **Privately Held**
WEB: www.johnsonmfginc.com
SIC: **3599** Machine shop, jobbing & repair

(P-8646)
JOHNSON PRECISION PRODUCTS INC
1308 E Wakeham Ave, Santa Ana (92705-4145)
PHONE..............................714 824-6971
Paul Cronin, *President*
Rene Ramirez, *Manager*
EMP: 19 EST: 1961
SQ FT: 4,000
SALES (est): 4.9MM **Privately Held**
WEB:
www.johnsonprecisionmachining.com
SIC: **3599** Machine shop, jobbing & repair

(P-8647)
JR MACHINE COMPANY INC
13245 Florence Ave, Santa Fe Springs (90670-4509)
PHONE..............................562 903-9477
Gilbert Reyes, *President*
EMP: 29 EST: 1973
SQ FT: 12,000
SALES (est): 2.6MM **Privately Held**
SIC: **3599** Machine shop, jobbing & repair

(P-8648)
K-P ENGINEERING CORP
2126 S Lyon St Ste A, Santa Ana (92705-5328)
PHONE..............................714 545-7045
Kemal Pepic, *CEO*
EMP: 32 EST: 1980
SQ FT: 7,000
SALES (est): 1.8MM **Privately Held**
WEB: www.kpengineering.com
SIC: **3599** 8711 Machine shop, jobbing & repair; professional engineer

(P-8649)
KADAN CONSULTANTS INCORPORATED
5662 Research Dr, Huntington Beach (92649-1615)
PHONE..............................562 988-1165
Rhoda Sjoberg, *CEO*
Kody Sjoberg, *Consultant*
EMP: 15 EST: 2001
SQ FT: 17,000
SALES (est): 2.2MM **Privately Held**
WEB: www.kadaninc.net
SIC: **3599** 3728 3544 8711 Machine shop, jobbing & repair; aircraft parts & equipment; special dies, tools, jigs & fixtures; engineering services

(P-8650)
KAP MANUFACTURING INC
327 W Allen Ave, San Dimas (91773-1441)
PHONE..............................909 599-2525
Michael D' Amato, *CFO*
Kathleen D Amato, *President*
Michael D Amato, *CEO*
Bryan D'Amato, *Vice Pres*
Edgar Carranza, *Administration*
EMP: 27
SQ FT: 6,000
SALES (est): 5.3MM **Privately Held**
WEB: www.kapmfg.com
SIC: **3599** Machine shop, jobbing & repair

(P-8651)
KAY & JAMES INC
Also Called: J&S Machine Works
14062 Balboa Blvd, Sylmar (91342-1005)
PHONE..............................818 998-0357
Kye Sook So, *CEO*
Jung M So, *Vice Pres*
EMP: 75

SQ FT: 25,000
SALES (est): 14.3MM **Privately Held**
SIC: **3599** Machine shop, jobbing & repair

(P-8652)
KELLER ENGINEERING INC
3203 Kashiwa St, Torrance (90505-4020)
PHONE..............................310 326-6291
Kathy Keller, *President*
Claudia Keller Abate, *Treasurer*
Maya Keller Navarra, *Admin Sec*
EMP: 16 EST: 1972
SQ FT: 20,000
SALES (est): 602.9K **Privately Held**
SIC: **3599** Machine shop, jobbing & repair

(P-8653)
KELLY & THOME
228 San Lorenzo St, Pomona (91766-2336)
PHONE..............................909 623-2559
Warren C Kelly, *President*
Martha Lehr, *Office Mgr*
Sherry Caudill, *Admin Sec*
EMP: 17 EST: 1961
SQ FT: 6,000
SALES (est): 1.2MM **Privately Held**
WEB: www.kandt.com
SIC: **3599** Machine shop, jobbing & repair

(P-8654)
KILGORE MACHINE COMPANY INC
2312 S Susan St, Santa Ana (92704-4421)
PHONE..............................714 540-3659
Bryant Kilgore, *President*
Karen Galloway, *CFO*
Karen Sullivan, *CFO*
Doree Kilgore, *Vice Pres*
Lisa Damico, *Principal*
EMP: 22 EST: 1968
SQ FT: 8,000
SALES (est): 2.4MM **Privately Held**
WEB: www.kilgoremachinecompany.com
SIC: **3599** Machine shop, jobbing & repair

(P-8655)
KIMBERLY MACHINE INC
12822 Joy St, Garden Grove (92840-6350)
PHONE..............................714 539-0151
Tam Huynh, *CEO*
Matias Vergara, *Project Mgr*
Valencia Ngo, *Accountant*
EMP: 24 EST: 1974
SQ FT: 10,300
SALES: 4.6MM **Privately Held**
WEB: www.kimberlymachines.com
SIC: **3599** Machine shop, jobbing & repair

(P-8656)
KITCH ENGINEERING INC
12320 Montague St, Pacoima (91331-2213)
PHONE..............................818 897-7133
Steven Kitching, *President*
Kerri Kitching, *Vice Pres*
Terry Kitching, *Vice Pres*
Justin Kitching, *Production*
EMP: 30 EST: 1984
SQ FT: 6,000
SALES (est): 2.6MM **Privately Held**
WEB: www.kitchengineering.com
SIC: **3599** 3751 Machine shop, jobbing & repair; motorcycles, bicycles & parts

(P-8657)
KT ENGINEERING CORPORATION
2016 E Vista Bella Way, Rancho Dominguez (90220-6109)
PHONE..............................310 537-3818
John Tajirian, *CEO*
Joshua Chapman, *QC Mgr*
EMP: 16 EST: 1986
SQ FT: 3,500
SALES (est): 3.9MM **Privately Held**
WEB: www.ktengineering.com
SIC: **3599** 8711 Machine shop, jobbing & repair; aviation &/or aeronautical engineering

(P-8658)
L J R GRINDING CORP
Also Called: Ljr Blanchard Grinding
445 W 164th St, Gardena (90248-2726)
PHONE..............................310 532-7232

James Garon, *President*
Robert Margolis Jr, *Vice Pres*
EMP: 18 **EST:** 1968
SQ FT: 4,000
SALES (est): 1.2MM **Privately Held**
SIC: 3599 Machine shop, jobbing & repair

(P-8659)
LA GAUGE CO INC
7440 San Fernando Rd, Sun Valley
(91352-4398)
PHONE..................................818 767-7193
Harbans Bawa, *President*
Guillermo Olmedo, *Controller*
JD Caravantes, *Sales Associate*
EMP: 74 **EST:** 1954
SQ FT: 26,682
SALES (est): 16.8MM **Privately Held**
WEB: www.lagauge.com
SIC: 3599 Machine shop, jobbing & repair

(P-8660)
LANGE PRECISION INC
1106 E Elm Ave, Fullerton (92831-5024)
PHONE..................................714 870-5420
Gregory R Lange, *President*
Lisa Lange, *CFO*
EMP: 18
SQ FT: 35,000
SALES (est): 3.8MM **Privately Held**
WEB: www.langeprecision.com
SIC: 3599 Machine shop, jobbing & repair

(P-8661)
LANSAIR CORPORATION
25228 Anza Dr, Santa Clarita (91355-3496)
PHONE..................................661 294-9503
John Voshell, *President*
Eleanor Voshell, *Vice Pres*
EMP: 37 **EST:** 1966
SQ FT: 15,000
SALES (est): 2.2MM **Privately Held**
WEB: www.lansaircorp.com
SIC: 3599 Machine shop, jobbing & repair

(P-8662)
LASER INDUSTRIES INC
1351 Manhattan Ave, Fullerton
(92831-5216)
PHONE..................................714 532-3271
Robert Karim, *President*
Joseph Butterly, *Corp Secy*
John Krickl, *Vice Pres*
Gary Nadau, *Vice Pres*
Nancy Rodolf, *Project Mgr*
EMP: 65 **EST:** 1986
SQ FT: 17,500
SALES (est): 9MM **Privately Held**
WEB: www.laserindustries.com
SIC: 3599 Machine shop, jobbing & repair

(P-8663)
LIBERTY INDUSTRIES
10754 Lower Azusa Rd, El Monte
(91731-1391)
PHONE..................................626 575-3206
William Carter, *President*
EMP: 15 **EST:** 1966
SQ FT: 9,000 **Privately Held**
SIC: 3599 Machine shop, jobbing & repair;
machine & other job shop work

(P-8664)
LONG MACHINE INC
27450 Colt Ct, Temecula (92590-3673)
PHONE..................................951 296-0194
Larry Long, *President*
Vicki Long, *Vice Pres*
EMP: 21 **EST:** 1979
SQ FT: 15,000
SALES (est): 2.6MM **Privately Held**
WEB: www.longmachine.com
SIC: 3599 Machine shop, jobbing & repair

(P-8665)
LONGBAR GRINDING INC
13121 Arctic Cir, Santa Fe Springs
(90670-5571)
P.O. Box 3128 (90670-0128)
PHONE..................................562 921-1983
Joseph Kudron, *President*
Kade Kudron, *Finance Mgr*
EMP: 15 **EST:** 1967
SQ FT: 25,000

SALES (est): 2.2MM **Privately Held**
WEB: www.longbargrinding.com
SIC: 3599 Machine shop, jobbing & repair

(P-8666)
LOUIS LEVIN & SON INC
13550 Larwin Cir, Santa Fe Springs
(90670-5031)
PHONE..................................562 802-8066
Dale Waite, *President*
EMP: 21 **EST:** 1942
SQ FT: 6,500
SALES (est): 755.8K **Privately Held**
WEB: www.levinlathe.com
SIC: 3599 Machine shop, jobbing & repair

(P-8667)
LOWERS WLDG & FABRICATION INC
Also Called: Lowers Industrial Supply
10847 Painter Ave, Santa Fe Springs
(90670-4526)
P.O. Box 2985 (90670-0985)
PHONE..................................562 946-4521
Dawn Davis, *President*
Nora Lowers, *CFO*
Shawn Gunthner, *Project Mgr*
Sheri Lowers, *Purchasing*
EMP: 13 **EST:** 1975
SQ FT: 4,669
SALES (est): 5.1MM **Privately Held**
WEB: www.lowerswelding.com
SIC: 3599 7692 5085 5719 Machine
shop, jobbing & repair; welding repair; in-
dustrial supplies; metalware

(P-8668)
LURAN INC
24927 Avenue Tibbitts K, Valencia
(91355-1268)
PHONE..................................661 257-6303
Terry Decker, *President*
Leo Solano, *Foreman/Supr*
EMP: 25 **EST:** 1970
SQ FT: 20,000
SALES (est): 1MM **Privately Held**
WEB: www.luraninc.com
SIC: 3599 Machine shop, jobbing & repair

(P-8669)
LUSK QUALITY MACHINE PRODUCTS
39457 15th St E, Palmdale (93550-3445)
P.O. Box 901030 (93590-1030)
PHONE..................................661 272-0630
Randall J Lusk, *CEO*
Lloyd Lusk, *President*
EMP: 27 **EST:** 1971
SQ FT: 25,000
SALES (est): 5.1MM **Privately Held**
WEB: www.luskquality.com
SIC: 3599 3451 Machine shop, jobbing &
repair; screw machine products

(P-8670)
M & W MACHINE CORPORATION
Also Called: Capitol Machine Co
1642 E Edinger Ave Ste A, Santa Ana
(92705-5002)
PHONE..................................714 541-2652
George Nys, *President*
Sandra Nys, *Treasurer*
Mike Smith, *General Mgr*
Jason Nys, *Admin Sec*
EMP: 23 **EST:** 1965
SQ FT: 6,000
SALES (est): 1.1MM **Privately Held**
SIC: 3599 Machine shop, jobbing & repair

(P-8671)
M-INDUSTRIAL ENTERPRISES
Also Called: Project Management
11 Via Onagro, Rcho STA Marg
(92688-4126)
PHONE..................................949 413-7513
Zahid Nazarzai, *Owner*
EMP: 25 **EST:** 2001
SALES (est): 1.1MM **Privately Held**
SIC: 3599 Industrial machinery

(P-8672)
MACHINE PRECISION COMPONENTS
14014 Dinard Ave, Santa Fe Springs
(90670-4923)
PHONE..................................562 404-0500
Mauro Michel, *CEO*
EMP: 18 **EST:** 2004
SALES (est): 1.9MM **Privately Held**
WEB: www.mpcmachining.com
SIC: 3599 Machine shop, jobbing & repair

(P-8673)
MADSEN PRODUCTS INCORPORATED
Also Called: Huntington Beach Machining
15321 Connector Ln, Huntington Beach
(92649-1119)
PHONE..................................714 894-1816
Robert Madsen, *President*
Linda Adkison, *Vice Pres*
Erik Madsen, *Vice Pres*
Tiffany Ramirez, *Opers Mgr*
EMP: 16 **EST:** 1975
SQ FT: 11,345
SALES (est): 2.2MM **Privately Held**
WEB: www.madsenproductions.com
SIC: 3599 5961 Machine shop, jobbing &
repair; mail order house

(P-8674)
MAGNA TOOL INC
5594 Market Pl, Cypress (90630-4710)
PHONE..................................714 826-2500
Bob Melton, *President*
Cindy Melton, *CFO*
EMP: 20 **EST:** 1977
SQ FT: 8,500
SALES (est): 2.9MM **Privately Held**
WEB: www.magnatoolinc.com
SIC: 3599 Machine shop, jobbing & repair

(P-8675)
MANTI - MACHINE CO INC
11782 Western Ave Ste 15, Stanton
(90680-3466)
PHONE..................................714 902-1465
William G Vlieland, *President*
Dawn Harlow, *CFO*
BJ Vlieland, *Corp Secy*
EMP: 17 **EST:** 1966
SQ FT: 3,400
SALES (est): 396.4K **Privately Held**
SIC: 3599 Machine shop, jobbing & repair

(P-8676)
MAR ENGINEERING COMPANY
7350 Greenbush Ave, North Hollywood
(91605-4003)
PHONE..................................818 765-4805
Monte Markowitz, *CEO*
Samuel Markowitz, *President*
Barbara Markowitz, *Corp Secy*
Ian Goyanes, *Production*
Jeff Markowitz, *Director*
EMP: 26 **EST:** 1957
SQ FT: 12,000
SALES (est): 2.3MM **Privately Held**
WEB: www.marengineering.com
SIC: 3599 Machine shop, jobbing & repair

(P-8677)
MARONEY COMPANY
9016 Winnetka Ave, Northridge
(91324-3235)
PHONE..................................818 882-2722
John C Maroney Sr, *President*
Francine L Maroney, *Senior VP*
EMP: 17 **EST:** 1955
SQ FT: 12,500
SALES (est): 2.6MM **Privately Held**
WEB: www.maroneycompany.com
SIC: 3599 Machine shop, jobbing & repair

(P-8678)
MARTIN-CHANDLER INC
122 E Alondra Blvd, Gardena
(90248-2883)
PHONE..................................323 321-5119
Paul Fihn, *CEO*
Hans Haag, *Treasurer*
EMP: 18 **EST:** 1951
SQ FT: 5,000
SALES (est): 1.2MM **Privately Held**
SIC: 3599 Machine shop, jobbing & repair

(P-8679)
MARTINEZ AND TUREK INC
Also Called: Martinez & Turek
300 S Cedar Ave, Rialto (92376-9100)
PHONE..................................909 820-6800
Larry Tribe, *President*
Romeo Gabriel, *CFO*
Donald A Turek, *CFO*
Thomas J Martinez, *Vice Pres*
Thomas Martinez, *Vice Pres*
EMP: 120 **EST:** 1980
SQ FT: 139,000
SALES (est): 26.1MM **Privately Held**
WEB: www.martinezandturek.com
SIC: 3599 Machine shop, jobbing & repair

(P-8680)
MAUL MFG INC (PA)
3041 S Shannon St, Santa Ana
(92704-6320)
PHONE..................................714 641-0727
Tony Johnson, *President*
Lori Deorio, *Admin Sec*
EMP: 21 **EST:** 1975
SQ FT: 10,080
SALES (est): 5MM **Privately Held**
WEB: www.ysc-mmi.com
SIC: 3599 3491 3492 Machine shop, job-
bing & repair; solenoid valves; control
valves; aircraft: hydraulic & pneumatic

(P-8681)
MCCAIN & MCCAIN INC
Also Called: B&G Machine Shop
3801 Gilmore Ave, Bakersfield
(93308-6211)
PHONE..................................661 322-7764
Jim McCain, *President*
Gary McCain, *Vice Pres*
Steven Glover, *General Mgr*
EMP: 15 **EST:** 1951
SQ FT: 10,000
SALES (est): 1.9MM **Privately Held**
WEB: www.bgmach.com
SIC: 3599 Machine shop, jobbing & repair

(P-8682)
MCCOPPIN ENTERPRISES
Also Called: Accurate Manufacturing Com-
pany
6641 San Fernando Rd, Glendale
(91201-1702)
PHONE..................................818 240-4840
Richard J Mc Coppin, *President*
Carol Park, *Shareholder*
John Gagliardi, *Vice Pres*
Robert R Gagliardi, *Vice Pres*
EMP: 22 **EST:** 1945
SQ FT: 25,000
SALES (est): 3MM **Privately Held**
WEB: www.accuratemfgco.com
SIC: 3599 3544 3441 Machine shop, job-
bing & repair; dies & die holders for metal
cutting, forming, die casting; fabricated
structural metal

(P-8683)
MCGUIRE GRINDING INC
2754 Concrete Ct, Paso Robles
(93446-5936)
PHONE..................................805 238-9000
Scott McGuire, *CEO*
Rachel McGuire, *Principal*
EMP: 19 **EST:** 2006
SALES (est): 667.7K **Privately Held**
SIC: 3599 Machine shop, jobbing & repair

(P-8684)
MD ENGINEERING INC
1550 Consumer Cir, Corona (92878-3225)
PHONE..................................951 736-5390
Mike Morgan, *President*
Ryan Cortes, *Vice Pres*
Mario Bolanos, *QC Mgr*
Danny Vu, *QC Mgr*
EMP: 37 **EST:** 1999
SQ FT: 16,000
SALES (est): 7MM **Privately Held**
WEB: www.mde-us.com
SIC: 3599 Machine shop, jobbing & repair

(P-8685)
MECHANIZED ENTERPRISES INC
1140 N Kraemer Blvd Ste M, Anaheim (92806-1919)
PHONE..................714 630-5512
George Hansel, *President*
EMP: 17 EST: 1980
SQ FT: 12,000
SALES (est): 750.5K **Privately Held**
WEB: www.mechanizedenterprises.com
SIC: 3599 Machine shop, jobbing & repair

(P-8686)
MEDLIN AND SON ENGRG SVC INC
Also Called: Medlin & Sons
12484 Whittier Blvd, Whittier (90602-1017)
PHONE..................562 464-5889
George W Medlin II, *CEO*
Susan Medlin, *Admin Sec*
EMP: 45 EST: 1959
SQ FT: 26,000
SALES (est): 3MM **Privately Held**
WEB: www.medlinandson.com
SIC: 3599 Machine shop, jobbing & repair

(P-8687)
MEERKAT INC
434 S Yucca Ave, Rialto (92376-6300)
PHONE..................909 877-0093
Ronald J Vangrouw, *President*
Dave Vangrouw, *Treasurer*
Cindy Vangrouw, *Admin Sec*
EMP: 13 EST: 2001
SQ FT: 11,000
SALES (est): 2.1MM **Privately Held**
WEB: www.meerkatsalvagemachining.com
SIC: 3599 Machine shop, jobbing & repair

(P-8688)
MELKES MACHINE INC
9928 Hayward Way, South El Monte (91733-3114)
PHONE..................626 448-5062
Isabelle Melkesian, *President*
Brent Melkesian, *Vice Pres*
Paul Novacek, *Sales Staff*
EMP: 28 EST: 1960
SQ FT: 24,000
SALES (est): 676.9K **Privately Held**
WEB: www.melkes.com
SIC: 3599 Machine shop, jobbing & repair

(P-8689)
MERCURY ENGINEERING CORP
5630 Imperial Hwy, South Gate (90280-7420)
PHONE..................562 861-7816
David Barker, *President*
EMP: 24 EST: 1949
SQ FT: 10,000
SALES (est): 679.6K **Privately Held**
WEB: www.mercuryengineeringcorp.com
SIC: 3599 Machine shop, jobbing & repair

(P-8690)
MERRY AN CEJKA
Also Called: Scott Craft Co
4601 Cecilia St, Cudahy (90201-5813)
P.O. Box 430, Bell (90201-0430)
PHONE..................323 560-3949
Merry An Cejka, *Owner*
Robert Cejka, *Principal*
Amelia Leal-Lee, *Principal*
Veronica Zazueta, *Principal*
EMP: 25 EST: 1966
SQ FT: 12,000
SALES (est): 3MM **Privately Held**
WEB: www.scottcraftco.com
SIC: 3599 3544 Custom machinery; machine shop, jobbing & repair; special dies, tools, jigs & fixtures

(P-8691)
METAL CUTTING SERVICE INC
16233 Gale Ave, City of Industry (91745-1719)
PHONE..................626 968-4764
David Viel, *President*
Milon Viel, *CEO*
Earl Viel, *Corp Secy*
Curt Steen, *Plant Mgr*
Thomas Etchebarren, *Manager*
EMP: 18 EST: 1956

SQ FT: 32,000
SALES (est): 1.4MM **Privately Held**
WEB: www.metalcut.com
SIC: 3599 Machine shop, jobbing & repair

(P-8692)
METALORE INC
750 S Douglas St, El Segundo (90245-4901)
PHONE..................310 643-0360
Kenneth Hill, *President*
Phil Jones, *General Mgr*
Mandy Luiz, *Accountant*
Dennis Reed, *Mfg Mgr*
▲ EMP: 30 EST: 1961
SALES (est): 3.1MM **Privately Held**
WEB: www.metalore.com
SIC: 3599 Machine shop, jobbing & repair

(P-8693)
METRIC MACHINING (PA)
Also Called: Master Machine Products
3263 Trade Center Dr, Riverside (92507-3432)
PHONE..................909 947-9222
David Parker, *Principal*
Joan Parker, *Treasurer*
Tim Keleher, *CTO*
Steve Molenda, *Engineer*
Magdalena Lopez, *Controller*
▲ EMP: 50 EST: 1973
SQ FT: 45,000
SALES (est): 7MM **Privately Held**
WEB: www.metricorp.com
SIC: 3599 Machine shop, jobbing & repair

(P-8694)
MIKE DYELL MACHINE SHOP INC (PA)
160 S Linden Ave, Rialto (92376-6204)
P.O. Box 974 (92377-0974)
PHONE..................909 350-4101
Edith Dyell, *Partner*
Tom Bradley, *Partner*
Donna Larson, *Manager*
EMP: 17 EST: 1968
SQ FT: 20,000
SALES (est): 3.8MM **Privately Held**
WEB: www.dyellmachine.com
SIC: 3599 5084 7699 Machine shop, jobbing & repair; hydraulic systems equipment & supplies; hydraulic equipment repair

(P-8695)
MIKE KENNEY TOOL INC
Also Called: Mkt Innovations
2900 Saturn St Ste A, Brea (92821-1702)
PHONE..................714 577-9262
Mike Kenney, *President*
Ken Erkenbrack, *Vice Pres*
Tim Schneider, *Vice Pres*
Julie Kenney, *Admin Sec*
Nathaniel Wills, *Prgrmr*
▲ EMP: 37 EST: 1980
SALES (est): 3.6MM **Privately Held**
SIC: 3599 Machine shop, jobbing & repair

(P-8696)
MIKELSON MACHINE SHOP INC
2546 Merced Ave, South El Monte (91733-1924)
PHONE..................626 448-3920
James Michaelson, *President*
James M Mikelson, *President*
▼ EMP: 23 EST: 1967
SQ FT: 14,000
SALES (est): 4.3MM **Privately Held**
WEB: www.mikelson.net
SIC: 3599 Machine shop, jobbing & repair

(P-8697)
MILCO WIRE EDM INC
Also Called: Milco Waterjet
15221 Connector Ln, Huntington Beach (92649-1117)
PHONE..................714 373-0098
Steven R Miller, *President*
Julie Lindsey, *Office Mgr*
Chadd Miller, *Manager*
Katelyn Normand, *Assistant*
EMP: 17 EST: 1990
SQ FT: 14,000 **Privately Held**
WEB: www.milcowireedm.com

SIC: 3599 3541 Electrical discharge machining (EDM); machine tools, metal cutting type

(P-8698)
MILLIPART INC (PA)
412 W Carter Dr, Glendora (91740-5998)
PHONE..................626 963-4101
Scot Jamison, *President*
EMP: 18 EST: 1954
SQ FT: 4,000
SALES (est): 2.9MM **Privately Held**
WEB: www.millipart.com
SIC: 3599 Machine shop, jobbing & repair

(P-8699)
MILLWORX PRCSION MACHINING INC
506 Malloy Ct, Corona (92878-4045)
PHONE..................951 371-2683
Stacy Wilson, *President*
Terry Windust, *Vice Pres*
Carson Miller, *General Mgr*
Sharon M Daniel, *Administration*
Vincent Mitchell, *Opers Staff*
EMP: 22 EST: 2003
SQ FT: 3,500
SALES (est): 4.9MM **Privately Held**
WEB: www.millworxprecision.com
SIC: 3599 Machine shop, jobbing & repair

(P-8700)
MINI-FLEX CORPORATION
2472 Eastman Ave Ste 29, Ventura (93003-5774)
PHONE..................805 644-1474
Paul Jorgensen, *President*
◆ EMP: 13 EST: 1961
SQ FT: 8,500
SALES (est): 1.4MM **Privately Held**
WEB: www.mini-flex.com
SIC: 3599 Bellows, industrial: metal

(P-8701)
MITCO INDUSTRIES INC (PA)
2235 S Vista Ave, Bloomington (92316-2921)
PHONE..................909 877-0800
Larry Mitchell, *President*
Sammy Mitchell, *Corp Secy*
EMP: 26 EST: 1972
SQ FT: 11,000
SALES (est): 4.9MM **Privately Held**
WEB: www.mitcoind.com
SIC: 3599 3533 Machine shop, jobbing & repair; drilling tools for gas, oil or water wells

(P-8702)
MKT INNOVATIONS
Also Called: Cooljet Systems
2900 Saturn St Ste A, Brea (92821-1702)
PHONE..................714 524-7668
Mike Kenney, *CEO*
Kathy Jackson, *CFO*
John Kenney, *Vice Pres*
▲ EMP: 68 EST: 2002
SALES (est): 7.5MM **Privately Held**
WEB: www.mkti.com
SIC: 3599 3523 Machine shop, jobbing & repair; farm machinery & equipment

(P-8703)
MODERN ENGINE INC
701 Sonora Ave, Glendale (91201-2431)
PHONE..................818 409-9494
Vachagan Aslanian, *President*
Armond Aslanian, *Treasurer*
Razmik Aslanian, *Vice Pres*
Nora Aslanian, *Admin Sec*
Besi Estrada, *Manager*
▲ EMP: 43 EST: 1979
SQ FT: 26,000
SALES (est): 6.9MM **Privately Held**
WEB: www.meparts.com
SIC: 3599 7539 Machine shop, jobbing & repair; machine shop, automotive

(P-8704)
MODERN MANUFACTURING INC
4110 E La Palma Ave, Anaheim (92807-1814)
PHONE..................714 254-0156
▲ EMP: 26 EST: 2002
SQ FT: 20,000

SALES (est): 2.5MM **Privately Held**
WEB: www.modernmfginc.com
SIC: 3599 Mfg Industrial Machinery

(P-8705)
MOLNAR ENGINEERING INC
Also Called: Lee's Enterprise
20731 Marilla St, Chatsworth 91311-4408)
PHONE..................318 993-3495
Laszlo Molnar, *CEO*
Tom Molnar, *President*
Linda D Molnar, *Corp Secy*
Michael Molnar, *Manager*
▲ EMP: 37 EST: 1975
SQ FT: 12,000
SALES (est): 4.3MM **Privately Held**
WEB: www.leesenterprise.com
SIC: 3599 Machine shop, jobbing & repair

(P-8706)
MOMENI ENGINEERING LLC
15662 Commerce Ln, Huntington Beach (92649-1604)
PHONE..................714 897-9301
Ahmad Momeni, *Mng Member*
Joe Hobson, *Mfg Staff*
Sepehr Goudarzi, *Manager*
Yvonne Goodin, *Supervisor*
EMP: 28 EST: 1982
SQ FT: 14,000
SALES (est): 4.7MM **Privately Held**
WEB: www.momenieng.com
SIC: 3599 3841 Machine shop, jobbing & repair; surgical & medical instruments

(P-8707)
MONO ENGINEERING CORP
20977 Knapp St, Chatsworth (91311-5926)
PHONE..................818 772-4998
Siamak Morini, *CEO*
Roujebeh Azarahishin, *Controller*
Rouzbeh Azarakhshi, *Controller*
Siegfried Treichel, *Prdtn Mgr*
EMP: 50 EST: 1994
SQ FT: 40,000
SALES (est): 7.2MM **Privately Held**
WEB: www.monoengineering.com
SIC: 3599 3444 8711 Machine shop, jobbing & repair; sheet metalwork; industrial engineers

(P-8708)
MONTEREY MACHINE PRODUCTS
1504 W Industrial Park St, Covina (91722-3413)
PHONE..................626 967-2242
David Griffits, *Owner*
Dave Griffith, *Partner*
EMP: 14 EST: 1953
SQ FT: 2,400
SALES (est): 2.3MM **Privately Held**
WEB: www.montereymachine.net
SIC: 3599 Machine shop, jobbing & repair

(P-8709)
MOONEY INDS PRCSION MCHNING IN
8744 Remmet Ave, Canoga Park (91304-1588)
PHONE..................818 998-0199
Alan Mooney, *CFO*
Brian Mooney, *President*
Joyce Mooney, *Vice Pres*
Suzi McNutt, *Manager*
EMP: 15 EST: 1962
SQ FT: 9,000
SALES (est): 1.5MM **Privately Held**
SIC: 3599 Machine shop, jobbing & repair

(P-8710)
MORGAN PRODUCTS INC
28103 Avenue Stanford, Santa Clarita (91355-1106)
PHONE..................661 257-3022
Morris E Morgan, *President*
Mary O Morgan, *CFO*
William A Morgan, *Vice Pres*
▲ EMP: 21 EST: 1966
SQ FT: 3,250
SALES (est): 807.6K **Privately Held**
WEB: www.morganproducts.com
SIC: 3599 3561 Machine shop, jobbing & repair; pumps & pumping equipment

(P-8711)
MOTEK INDUSTRIES
14434 Joanbridge St, Baldwin Park
(91706-1746)
PHONE..............................626 960-6005
Julio Enriquez, *Owner*
EMP: 16 **EST:** 1958
SQ FT: 5,000
SALES (est): 518.3K **Privately Held**
WEB: www.motekprecision.com
SIC: 3599 Machine shop, jobbing & repair

(P-8712)
MUTH MACHINE WORKS (HQ)
8042 Katella Ave, Stanton (90680-3207)
PHONE..............................714 527-2239
Richard Muth, *President*
Peter G Muth, *Treasurer*
Lynn Muth, *Vice Pres*
Dwayne Gleason, *VP Opers*
▲ **EMP:** 20 **EST:** 1993
SQ FT: 2,000
SALES (est): 16.8MM
SALES (corp-wide): 52.2MM **Privately Held**
WEB: www.orco.com
SIC: 3599 Machine shop, jobbing & repair
PA: Orco Block & Hardscape
11100 Beach Blvd
Stanton CA 90680
714 527-2239

(P-8713)
MY MACHINE INC
5140 Commerce Dr, Baldwin Park
(91706-1450)
PHONE..............................626 214-9223
Jamie Scott Young, *CEO*
Pedro Ignico Martinez, *Vice Pres*
Bob Barker, *Sales Staff*
EMP: 15 **EST:** 2008
SALES (est): 1.9MM **Privately Held**
WEB: www.mymachineinc.com
SIC: 3599 Machine shop, jobbing & repair

(P-8714)
NC DYNAMICS INCORPORATED
Also Called: Ncdi
6925 Downey Ave, Long Beach
(90805-1823)
PHONE..............................562 634-7392
Kevin Minter, *CEO*
Randall L Bazz, *President*
Vince Braun, *President*
Chris Thompson, *Vice Pres*
Mike Perrin, *Program Mgr*
▲ **EMP:** 151 **EST:** 1979
SALES (est): 24.4MM
SALES (corp-wide): 110.7MM **Privately Held**
WEB: www.ncdynamics.com
SIC: 3599 Machine shop, jobbing & repair
PA: Harlow Aerostructures Llc
1501 S Mclean Blvd
Wichita KS 67213
316 265-5268

(P-8715)
NC DYNAMICS LLC
3401 E 69th St, Long Beach (90805-1872)
PHONE..............................562 634-7392
Phillip Friedman, *Principal*
EMP: 150 **EST:** 2017
SALES (est): 22.8MM
SALES (corp-wide): 110.7MM **Privately Held**
WEB: www.harlowair.com
SIC: 3599 Machine shop, jobbing & repair
PA: Harlow Aerostructures Llc
1501 S Mclean Blvd
Wichita KS 67213
316 265-5268

(P-8716)
NELSON ENGINEERING LLC
11600 Monarch St, Garden Grove
(92841-1817)
PHONE..............................714 893-7999
Ed McKenna,
▲ **EMP:** 20 **EST:** 1986
SQ FT: 17,600
SALES (est): 642K **Privately Held**
SIC: 3599 Machine shop, jobbing & repair

(P-8717)
NEXT INTENT INC
865 Via Esteban, San Luis Obispo
(93401-7178)
PHONE..............................805 781-6755
Rodney Babcock, *CEO*
Catherine B Babcock, *CFO*
Cayse Babcock, *CFO*
Jon-Erik Hylee, *Purchasing*
Ben Swan, *Purchasing*
EMP: 30 **EST:** 1996
SQ FT: 8,500
SALES (est): 4.9MM **Privately Held**
WEB: www.nextintent.com
SIC: 3599 Machine shop, jobbing & repair

(P-8718)
NICKSONS MACHINE SHOP INC
914 W Betteravia Rd, Santa Maria
(93455-1194)
P.O. Box 5200 (93456-5200)
PHONE..............................805 925-2525
EMP: 24
SQ FT: 23,800
SALES (est): 3.8MM **Privately Held**
WEB: www.nicksonsmachine.com
SIC: 3599 Industrial Machinery, Nec, Nsk

(P-8719)
NIEDWICK CORPORATION
Also Called: Niedwick Machine Co
967 N Eckhoff St, Orange (92867-5432)
P.O. Box 63851, Irvine (92602-6132)
PHONE..............................714 771-9999
Theodore R Niedwick, *President*
EMP: 45 **EST:** 1992
SQ FT: 8,200
SALES (est): 4.4MM **Privately Held**
WEB: www.niedwickmachine.com
SIC: 3599 Machine shop, jobbing & repair

(P-8720)
NOROTOS INC
201 E Alton Ave, Santa Ana (92707-4416)
PHONE..............................714 662-3113
Ronald Soto, *President*
John Soto, *Vice Pres*
Linda Soto, *Human Res Mgr*
▲ **EMP:** 116 **EST:** 1985
SQ FT: 12,000
SALES (est): 9MM **Privately Held**
WEB: www.norotos.com
SIC: 3599 3842 Machine shop, jobbing &
repair; surgical appliances & supplies

(P-8721)
NOTRON MANUFACTURING INC
801 Milford St, Glendale (91203-1520)
PHONE..............................818 247-7739
Theone Notron, *President*
James Notron, *Treasurer*
David Notron Jr, *Vice Pres*
▲ **EMP:** 19 **EST:** 1995
SQ FT: 13,000
SALES (est): 1.2MM **Privately Held**
WEB: www.notronmfg.com
SIC: 3599 5084 Machine & other job shop
work; pneumatic tools & equipment

(P-8722)
NUSPACE INC (HQ)
4401 E Donald Douglas Dr, Long Beach
(90808-1732)
PHONE..............................562 497-3200
Ian Ballinger, *CEO*
Lili Zhou, *CFO*
Larry Isom, *Vice Pres*
Manoj Bhatia, *VP Bus Dvlpt*
Ld Woodward, *Sales Staff*
◆ **EMP:** 35 **EST:** 1907
SQ FT: 60,000
SALES (est): 19.7MM **Privately Held**
SIC: 3599 Air intake filters, internal com-
bustion engine, except auto
PA: Ke Company Acquisition Corp.
4401 E Donald Douglas Dr
Long Beach CA 90808
562 497-3200

(P-8723)
O & S PRECISION INC
20630 Nordhoff St, Chatsworth
(91311-6114)
PHONE..............................818 718-8876
Scott Onasch, *CEO*
Gina Gomez, *Buyer*

EMP: 20 **EST:** 1996
SQ FT: 5,000
SALES (est): 8.3MM **Privately Held**
WEB: www.oands.com
SIC: 3599 Machine shop, jobbing & repair

(P-8724)
ODONNELL MANUFACTURING INC
14811 Via Defrancesco Ave, Riverside
(92508-9005)
P.O. Box 6245, Norco (92860-8041)
PHONE..............................562 944-9671
Steve O'Donnell, *President*
▲ **EMP:** 21 **EST:** 1985
SQ FT: 10,000
SALES (est): 639.4K **Privately Held**
SIC: 3599 Machine shop, jobbing & repair

(P-8725)
OEM LLC
311 S Highland Ave, Fullerton
(92832-2305)
PHONE..............................714 449-7500
John B Copp, *CEO*
Mary Quinlan, *Vice Pres*
John Woods, *Info Tech Dir*
Rogelio Sanchez, *Prdtn Mgr*
▲ **EMP:** 23 **EST:** 1985
SQ FT: 40,000
SALES (est): 4.4MM **Privately Held**
WEB: www.oempresssystems.com
SIC: 3599 Machine shop, jobbing & repair

(P-8726)
OMEGA PRECISION
13040 Telegraph Rd, Santa Fe Springs
(90670-4078)
PHONE..............................562 946-2491
Richard Venegas, *CEO*
Joseph M Venegas, *President*
Steve Venegas, *COO*
Richard M Venegas, *Corp Secy*
Chris Klosowski, *Human Resources*
EMP: 25 **EST:** 1965
SQ FT: 16,332
SALES (est): 4.9MM **Privately Held**
WEB: www.omegaprecision.us
SIC: 3599 Machine shop, jobbing & repair

(P-8727)
ORANGE COUNTY SCREW PDTS INC
2993 E La Palma Ave, Anaheim
(92806-2620)
PHONE..............................714 630-7433
Robert Andri, *President*
EMP: 20 **EST:** 1967
SQ FT: 8,000
SALES (est): 1.6MM **Privately Held**
SIC: 3599 3451 Machine shop, jobbing &
repair; screw machine products

(P-8728)
PACIFIC AEROSPACE MACHINE INC
3002 S Rosewood Ave, Santa Ana
(92703-3822)
PHONE..............................714 534-1444
Paul Nguyen, *CEO*
Kirk Nguyen, *Vice Pres*
EMP: 20 **EST:** 1997
SQ FT: 50,000
SALES (est): 1.2MM **Privately Held**
WEB: www.pacificmachine.net
SIC: 3599 Machine shop, jobbing & repair

(P-8729)
PACIFIC BROACH & ENGRG ASSOC
1513 N Kraemer Blvd, Anaheim
(92806-1407)
PHONE..............................714 632-5678
Steven R Yetzke, *President*
Michael Yetzke, *Vice Pres*
Elaine Montgomery, *Admin Sec*
▲ **EMP:** 19 **EST:** 1943
SQ FT: 18,000
SALES (est): 1.7MM **Privately Held**
WEB: www.bdlind.com
SIC: 3599 Machine shop, jobbing & repair

(P-8730)
PAMCO MACHINE WORKS INC
9359 Feron Blvd, Rancho Cucamonga
(91730-4516)
PHONE..............................909 941-7260
James Fredrick Wilkinson, *CEO*
Diane Wilkinson, *Admin Sec*
EMP: 20
SQ FT: 17,000
SALES (est): 5MM **Privately Held**
WEB: www.pamcomachine.com
SIC: 3599 3462 Machine shop, jobbing &
repair; iron & steel forgings

(P-8731)
PARAMOUNT GRINDING SERVICE
7311 Madison St Ste C, Paramount
(90723-4038)
P.O. Box 893 (90723-0893)
PHONE..............................562 630-6940
John F Jaramillo, *President*
Lisa Jaramillo, *Vice Pres*
EMP: 20 **EST:** 1981
SQ FT: 3,000
SALES (est): 1.1MM **Privately Held**
WEB: www.paramountgrind.com
SIC: 3599 Grinding castings for the trade

(P-8732)
PARAMOUNT MACHINE CO INC
10824 Edison Ct, Rancho Cucamonga
(91730-3868)
PHONE..............................909 484-3600
Gregory A Harsen, *President*
Gail Harsen, *Vice Pres*
Jessica Harsen, *Office Mgr*
Robert Llano, *Purchasing*
Jeff Musolino, *Manager*
EMP: 36 **EST:** 1964
SQ FT: 12,000
SALES (est): 5.7MM **Privately Held**
WEB: www.paramountmachine.com
SIC: 3599 Machine shop, jobbing & repair

(P-8733)
PARK ENGINEERING AND MFG CO
Also Called: Pem
6430 Roland St, Buena Park (90621-3122)
P.O. Box 2275 (90621-0775)
PHONE..............................714 521-4660
Joanna Tenney, *CEO*
Jeff Tenney, *President*
EMP: 30 **EST:** 1959
SQ FT: 6,000
SALES (est): 3.8MM **Privately Held**
WEB: www.park-engineering.com
SIC: 3599 Machine shop, jobbing & repair

(P-8734)
PAULCO PRECISION INC
Also Called: Precision Resources
13916 Cordary Ave, Hawthorne
(90250-7916)
PHONE..............................310 679-4900
Paul Ruby, *President*
Erika Mageo, *Office Mgr*
Bob Radecki, *Sales Mgr*
EMP: 16 **EST:** 1989
SQ FT: 15,000
SALES (est): 2.5MM **Privately Held**
WEB: www.precisionresources.com
SIC: 3599 Machine shop, jobbing & repair

(P-8735)
PDQ ENGINEERING INC
1199 Avenida Acaso Ste F, Camarillo
(93012-8739)
PHONE..............................805 482-1334
Shannon Clark, *President*
Elmer Clark, *Vice Pres*
Paul Jackson, *Executive*
Scott Jenkins, *Manager*
EMP: 26 **EST:** 1999
SQ FT: 10,000
SALES (est): 2.7MM **Privately Held**
SIC: 3599 Machine shop, jobbing & repair

(P-8736)
PEDAVENA MOULD AND DIE CO INC
12464 Mccann Dr, Santa Fe Springs
(90670-3335)
PHONE..............................310 327-2814

PRODUCTS & SVCS

Steve Scardenzan, *President*
Paul Weisbrich, *Admin Sec*
▲ **EMP:** 28 **EST:** 1964
SQ FT: 12,000
SALES (est): 5MM **Privately Held**
WEB: www.pmdprecision.com
SIC: 3599 Machine & other job shop work

(P-8737)
PENDARVIS MANUFACTURING INC
1808 N American St, Anaheim (92801-1001)
PHONE..................714 992-0950
Robert D Pendarvis, *CEO*
Brian Pendarvis, *General Mgr*
EMP: 25 **EST:** 1982
SQ FT: 8,000
SALES (est): 4.8MM **Privately Held**
WEB: www.pendarvismanufacturing.com
SIC: 3599 Machine shop, jobbing & repair

(P-8738)
PERFECTION MACHINE AND TL WORK
Also Called: Perfection Machine & Tl Works
1568 E 22nd St, Los Angeles (90011-1389)
PHONE..................213 749-5095
Steve Hix, *President*
Marlon Chavez, *Engineer*
Ronalyn Freitas, *Sales Staff*
Karen Hix, *Sales Staff*
▲ **EMP:** 22 **EST:** 1917
SQ FT: 93,000
SALES (est): 2.8MM **Privately Held**
WEB: www.pmtw.com
SIC: 3599 3469 3544 Machine shop, jobbing & repair; stamping metal for the trade; special dies, tools, jigs & fixtures

(P-8739)
PERFORMANCE MACHINE TECH INC
25141 Avenue Stanford, Valencia (91355-1227)
PHONE..................661 294-8617
Dennis Moran, *President*
Carolyn Moran, *Corp Secy*
EMP: 38 **EST:** 1995
SQ FT: 10,000
SALES (est): 6.4MM **Privately Held**
WEB: www.pmtinc.org
SIC: 3599 Machine shop, jobbing & repair

(P-8740)
PIEDRAS MACHINE CORPORATION
15154 Downey Ave Ste B, Paramount (90723-4595)
PHONE..................562 602-1500
Salvador Piedra, *President*
Ruben Piedra, *CFO*
Lucia Piedra, *Admin Sec*
EMP: 19 **EST:** 2006 **Privately Held**
WEB: www.piedrasmachine.business.site
SIC: 3599 Machine shop, jobbing & repair

(P-8741)
PRECISION ARCFT MACHINING INC
Also Called: Pamco
10640 Elkwood St, Sun Valley (91352-4631)
PHONE..................818 768-5900
Donald A Pisano, *President*
Kimberly Pisano, *CFO*
Joyce Pisano, *Treasurer*
Jim Asseltyne, *Sales Mgr*
▲ **EMP:** 50 **EST:** 1961
SQ FT: 6,500
SALES (est): 9.6MM **Privately Held**
WEB: www.pamco-usa.com
SIC: 3599 3678 Machine shop, jobbing & repair; electronic connectors

(P-8742)
PRECISION FRRITES CERAMICS INC
5432 Production Dr, Huntington Beach (92649-1525)
PHONE..................714 901-7622
Myung Sook Hong, *CEO*
Sung MO Hong, *President*
Frank Hong, *Vice Pres*
Ji SOO Lee, *Vice Pres*

Jennie Shiwota, *General Mgr*
EMP: 90 **EST:** 1975
SQ FT: 23,811
SALES (est): 9.6MM **Privately Held**
WEB: www.semiceramic.com
SIC: 3599 3264 3674 Machine shop, jobbing & repair; porcelain electrical supplies; semiconductors & related devices

(P-8743)
PRECISION WATERJET INC
4900 E Hunter Ave, Anaheim (92807-2057)
PHONE..................888 538-9287
Shane Strowski, *President*
Noemi Hernandez, *Sales Staff*
EMP: 39 **EST:** 2011
SALES (est): 7.8MM **Privately Held**
WEB: www.h2ojet.com
SIC: 3599 Machine shop, jobbing & repair

(P-8744)
PREMAC INC
Also Called: Precision Machining
625 Thompson Ave, Glendale (91201-2032)
PHONE..................818 241-8370
Michael Warme, *CEO*
Victoria Warme, *CFO*
Rainer H Warme, *Principal*
EMP: 14 **EST:** 1966
SQ FT: 6,000
SALES (est): 3MM **Privately Held**
SIC: 3599 Machine shop, jobbing & repair

(P-8745)
PRODUCTION LAPPING COMPANY
124 E Chestnut Ave, Monrovia (91016-3432)
PHONE..................626 359-0611
Hans Herzig, *President*
Steve Herzig, *President*
Trudy Herzig, *Admin Sec*
George Avelar, *Supervisor*
EMP: 21 **EST:** 1959
SQ FT: 4,500
SALES (est): 1.3MM **Privately Held**
WEB: www.productionlapping.com
SIC: 3599 Machine shop, jobbing & repair

(P-8746)
PRODUCTION LAPPING COMPANY
120 E Chestnut Ave, Monrovia (91016-3432)
PHONE..................626 359-0611
Stephan Herzig, *Vice Pres*
Hans J Herzig, *President*
Gertrude Herzig, *Corp Secy*
Seon Park, *General Mgr*
Melissa Lozada, *Manager*
EMP: 16 **EST:** 1968
SQ FT: 9,000
SALES (est): 1.5MM **Privately Held**
WEB: www.productionlapping.com
SIC: 3599 Machine shop, jobbing & repair

(P-8747)
PRONTO DRILLING INC (PA)
9501 Santa Fe Springs Rd, Santa Fe Springs (90670-2624)
PHONE..................562 777-0900
Miguel A Montanez, *President*
Elizabeth Patron,
EMP: 23 **EST:** 1976
SALES (est): 3.3MM **Privately Held**
WEB: www.prontodrilling.com
SIC: 3599 Machine shop, jobbing & repair

(P-8748)
PROTO SPACE ENGINEERING INC
2214 Loma Ave, South El Monte (91733-2518)
PHONE..................626 442-8273
Linda Dabbs, *CEO*
Michael Dabbs, *President*
Rosie Hernandez,
Rudy Sanchez, *Supervisor*
EMP: 37 **EST:** 1965
SQ FT: 24,000
SALES (est): 1.9MM **Privately Held**
WEB: www.psengr.com
SIC: 3599 Machine shop, jobbing & repair

(P-8749)
PSCMB REPAIRS INC
Also Called: Quality Industry Repair
12145 Slauson Ave, Santa Fe Springs (90670-2619)
PHONE..................626 448-7778
Stephany Castellanos, *CEO*
EMP: 40 **EST:** 2012
SALES (est): 4MM **Privately Held**
WEB: www.qir-usa.com
SIC: 3599 Machine shop, jobbing & repair

(P-8750)
PVA TEPLA AMERICA INC (HQ)
Also Called: Plasma Division
251 Corporate Terrace St, Corona (92879-6000)
PHONE..................951 371-2500
Bill Marsh, *President*
Anna Fuhrmann, *Executive Asst*
Kathryn Kingston, *Accounts Mgr*
EMP: 20 **EST:** 1971
SQ FT: 15,000
SALES (est): 9.8MM
SALES (corp-wide): 162MM **Privately Held**
WEB: www.pvateplaamerica.com
SIC: 3599 Custom machinery
PA: Pva Tepla Ag
　Im Westpark 10-12
　Wettenberg HE 35435
　641 686-900

(P-8751)
QMA INC
1645 E Lemonwood Dr, Santa Paula (93060-9651)
PHONE..................805 529-5395
Don Henghorne, *President*
Robert Roth, *CFO*
Roy Henriksson, *Ch Invest Ofcr*
Edward Campbell, *Managing Dir*
Emily Rudge, *Executive Asst*
EMP: 18 **EST:** 2001
SALES (est): 154.3K **Privately Held**
WEB: www.pgimquantitativesolutions.com
SIC: 3599 Machine shop, jobbing & repair

(P-8752)
QUALITASK INC
2840 E Gretta Ln, Anaheim (92806-2512)
PHONE..................714 237-0900
Som Suntharaphat, *President*
Eduvigis Suntharaphat, *Principal*
Deb Beds, *Admin Sec*
EMP: 26 **EST:** 1992
SQ FT: 13,100
SALES (est): 4.4MM **Privately Held**
WEB: www.qualitask.net
SIC: 3599 Machine shop, jobbing & repair

(P-8753)
QUALONTIME CORPORATION
19 Senisa, Irvine (92612-2112)
PHONE..................714 523-4751
Douglas J Siemer, *President*
EMP: 18 **EST:** 1968
SQ FT: 7,500
SALES (est): 487.8K **Privately Held**
SIC: 3599 Machine shop, jobbing & repair

(P-8754)
R C I P INC
Also Called: R C Industries
1476 N Hundley St, Anaheim (92806-1322)
PHONE..................714 630-1239
Robert Champlin, *CEO*
Leonel Huerta, *QC Mgr*
Daniel Ly, *Manager*
EMP: 16 **EST:** 1997
SQ FT: 4,400
SALES (est): 4.9MM **Privately Held**
WEB: www.rcind.net
SIC: 3599 Machine shop, jobbing & repair

(P-8755)
R M BAKER MACHINE AND TL INC
815 W Front St, Covina (91722-3613)
PHONE..................562 697-4007
Richard Baker, *President*
Faith Baker, *Admin Sec*
Candis Bright, *Accounting Mgr*
Kevin Huckins, *Opers Staff*
EMP: 16 **EST:** 1980
SQ FT: 6,700

SALES (est): 2.4MM **Privately Held**
WEB: www.rmbakermachine.com
SIC: 3599 Machine shop, jobbing & repair

(P-8756)
RA INDUSTRIES LLC
900 Glenneyre St, Laguna Beach (92651-2707)
PHONE..................714 557-2322
Robert J Follman,
Robin Follman, *Planning*
Almut Szamosi, *Purch Mgr*
Carole A Follman,
Robin Follman-Otta,
◆ **EMP:** 30 **EST:** 1969
SALES (est): 6.7MM **Privately Held**
WEB: www.ra-industries.com
SIC: 3599 3593 Machine shop, jobbing & repair; fluid power cylinders & actuators

(P-8757)
RALPH E AMES MACHINE WORKS
2301 Dominguez Way, Torrance (90501-6200)
PHONE..................310 328-8523
Mike Ames, *President*
Ron Ames, *Vice Pres*
Eric Anderson, *General Mgr*
Alfonso Olivar, *Planning Mgr*
Kevin Ames, *QC Mgr*
EMP: 45 **EST:** 1942
SQ FT: 11,000
SALES (est): 8.1MM **Privately Held**
WEB: www.amesmachine.com
SIC: 3599 Machine shop, jobbing & repair

(P-8758)
RAMP ENGINEERING INC
6850 Walthall Way, Paramount (90723-2028)
PHONE..................562 531-8030
Mark Scott, *CEO*
Robert C Scott, *Ch of Bd*
Lisa Scott, *CFO*
Nathan Scott, *Software Dev*
Raul Meza, *Buyer*
EMP: 24 **EST:** 1998
SQ FT: 12,000
SALES (est): 3.1MM **Privately Held**
WEB: www.rampengineering.com
SIC: 3599 Machine & other job shop work

(P-8759)
RAPID PRODUCT SOLUTIONS INC
2240 Celsius Ave Ste D, Oxnard (93030-8015)
PHONE..................805 485-7234
Max Gerdts, *President*
Richard Fitch, *President*
Douglas Wallis, *President*
Shawn Tester, *Sales Staff*
▲ **EMP:** 30 **EST:** 1998
SQ FT: 10,000
SALES (est): 4.1MM **Privately Held**
WEB: www.rapid-products.com
SIC: 3599 Machine shop, jobbing & repair

(P-8760)
RE BILT METALIZING CO
Also Called: Rebuilt Metalizing Chrome Pltg
2229 E 38th St, Vernon (90058-1628)
P.O. Box 58808, Los Angeles (90058-0808)
PHONE..................323 277-8200
Dave Dehota, *Owner*
EMP: 13 **EST:** 1965
SQ FT: 18,000
SALES (est): 606.7K **Privately Held**
SIC: 3599 Machine shop, jobbing & repair

(P-8761)
REDLINE PRCISION MACHINING INC
907 E Francis St, Ontario (91761-5631)
PHONE..................909 483-1273
Jon Bouch, *CEO*
Cheryl Bouch, *Admin Sec*
EMP: 15 **EST:** 1997
SQ FT: 10,000
SALES (est): 2MM **Privately Held**
WEB: www.redlineprecision.com
SIC: 3599 Machine shop, jobbing & repair

(P-8762)
REGAL MACHINE & ENGRG INC
5200 E 60th St, Maywood (90270-3557)
PHONE..................................323 773-7462
Val Darie, *President*
Donna Darie, *Persnl Dir*
EMP: 26 **EST:** 1985
SQ FT: 20,500
SALES (est): 736.2K **Privately Held**
WEB: www.regalmachine.com
SIC: 3599 3769 Machine shop, jobbing & repair; guided missile & space vehicle parts & auxiliary equipment

(P-8763)
REID PRODUCTS INC
21430 Waalew Rd, Apple Valley (92307-1026)
P.O. Box 1507 (92307-0028)
PHONE..................................760 240-1355
Kevin Reid, *President*
Cliff R Carter, *Treasurer*
Shelby Reid, *Vice Pres*
Steve Childs, *General Mgr*
Lisa Grinser, *Admin Sec*
EMP: 48 **EST:** 1980
SQ FT: 15,000
SALES (est): 10.4MM **Privately Held**
WEB: www.reidproducts.com
SIC: 3599 Machine shop, jobbing & repair

(P-8764)
REISNER ENTERPRISES INC
Also Called: Westcorp Engineering
1403 W Linden St, Riverside (92507-6804)
PHONE..................................951 786-9478
Tom Reisner, *President*
EMP: 19 **EST:** 1983
SQ FT: 9,000
SALES (est): 1.3MM **Privately Held**
SIC: 3599 Machine shop, jobbing & repair

(P-8765)
REMCO MCH & FABRICATION INC
1966 S Date Ave, Bloomington (92316-2442)
PHONE..................................909 877-3530
Jacque Lewis Russell, *CEO*
Jerry Gilson, *Vice Pres*
▲ **EMP:** 19 **EST:** 1979
SALES (est): 3.4MM **Privately Held**
WEB: www.remco-steel.com
SIC: 3599 3441 Machine shop, jobbing & repair; fabricated structural metal; building components, structural steel

(P-8766)
RESEARCH METAL INDUSTRIES INC
1970 W 139th St, Gardena (90249-2408)
PHONE..................................310 352-3200
Harish Brahmbhatt, *President*
Kamla Brahmbhatt, *Vice Pres*
Leigh Thompson, *General Mgr*
Elaine Thompson, *Executive Asst*
Steve Oldakowski, *Technology*
◆ **EMP:** 35 **EST:** 1964
SQ FT: 24,000
SALES (est): 8.5MM **Privately Held**
WEB: www.researchmetal.com
SIC: 3599 3469 Electrical discharge machining (EDM); spinning metal for the trade

(P-8767)
RICAURTE PRECISION INC
1550 E Mcfadden Ave, Santa Ana (92705-4308)
PHONE..................................714 667-0632
Luis Ricaurte, *CEO*
Marina Ricaurte, *President*
EMP: 22 **EST:** 1985
SQ FT: 72,000
SALES (est): 4.6MM **Privately Held**
WEB: www.ricaurteprecision.com
SIC: 3599 Machine shop, jobbing & repair

(P-8768)
RIGGINS ENGINEERING INC
13932 Saticoy St, Van Nuys (91402-6587)
PHONE..................................818 782-7010
Joe Grossnickle, *President*
Michael Riggins, *Vice Pres*
Nana Grossnickle, *Admin Sec*

Alex Alfaro Jr, *Manager*
John Grossnickle, *Manager*
EMP: 40 **EST:** 1967
SQ FT: 18,000
SALES (est): 6.1MM **Privately Held**
WEB: www.rigginseng.com
SIC: 3599 Machine shop, jobbing & repair

(P-8769)
RINCON ENGINEERING CORPORATION
6325 Carpinteria Ave, Carpinteria (93013-2901)
P.O. Box 87 (93014-0087)
PHONE..................................805 684-0935
Alberto Hugo, *CEO*
Roger Hugo, *President*
Richard Hugo, *Vice Pres*
Colleen Hugo CPA, *General Mgr*
Ed Preston, *Plant Mgr*
EMP: 43
SQ FT: 12,000
SALES (est): 8.1MM **Privately Held**
WEB: www.rinconengineering.com
SIC: 3599 3444 3441 Machine shop, jobbing & repair; sheet metalwork; fabricated structural metal

(P-8770)
RIVERSIDE MACHINE WORKS INC
6301 Baldwin Ave, Riverside (92509-6014)
PHONE..................................951 685-7416
Kerry Townsend, *President*
EMP: 14 **EST:** 1946
SQ FT: 7,500
SALES (est): 1.9MM **Privately Held**
WEB: www.riversidemachineworks.com
SIC: 3599 7692 3444 Machine shop, jobbing & repair; welding repair; sheet metalwork

(P-8771)
ROBERT H OLIVA INC
Also Called: Romakk Engineering
19863 Nordhoff St, Northridge (91324-3331)
PHONE..................................818 700-1035
Robert Oliva, *President*
Kim Oliva, *Vice Pres*
EMP: 25 **EST:** 1975
SQ FT: 4,000
SALES (est): 3.8MM **Privately Held**
SIC: 3599 Machine shop, jobbing & repair

(P-8772)
ROBERT W WIESMANTEL
Also Called: Cebe Co
15345 Allen St, Paramount (90723-4011)
P.O. Box 620 (90723-0620)
PHONE..................................562 634-0442
Robert W Wiesmantel, *Owner*
EMP: 16 **EST:** 1965
SQ FT: 24,000
SALES (est): 672.7K **Privately Held**
SIC: 3599 Machine shop, jobbing & repair

(P-8773)
ROBERTS PRECISION ENGRG INC
Also Called: Robert's Engineering
1345 S Allec St, Anaheim (92805-6304)
PHONE..................................714 635-4485
Robert Flores II, *President*
Rosalio Castellon, *Engineer*
EMP: 25 **EST:** 1979
SQ FT: 23,000
SALES (est): 4.2MM **Privately Held**
WEB: www.roberts-eng.com
SIC: 3599 Machine shop, jobbing & repair

(P-8774)
ROC-AIRE CORP
2198 Pomona Blvd, Pomona (91768-3332)
PHONE..................................909 784-3385
Thomas L Collins, *CEO*
Jason Collins, *Treasurer*
Jason L Collins, *Treasurer*
EMP: 22 **EST:** 1958
SQ FT: 52,000
SALES (est): 3.9MM **Privately Held**
WEB: www.rocaire.com
SIC: 3599 Machine shop, jobbing & repair

(P-8775)
RODRIGUEZ BROTHERS AUTO PARTS (PA)
812 N Anaheim Blvd, Anaheim (92805-1901)
PHONE..................................714 772-7278
Fermen Rodriguez, *Partner*
Ceasar Rodriguez, *Partner*
EMP: 15 **EST:** 1993
SALES (est): 1.6MM **Privately Held**
WEB: www.rodriguezbrosautoparts.com
SIC: 5531 3599 Automotive parts; machine shop, jobbing & repair

(P-8776)
RONLO ENGINEERING LTD
955 Flynn Rd, Camarillo (93012-8704)
PHONE..................................805 388-3227
Ronnie Lowe, *CEO*
Rick Slaney, *President*
Tracy Slaney, *Treasurer*
Karen Mc Master, *Vice Pres*
Jon Finn, *Mfg Staff*
EMP: 30
SQ FT: 23,650
SALES (est): 5.3MM **Privately Held**
WEB: www.ronlo.com
SIC: 3599 Machine shop, jobbing & repair

(P-8777)
ROTHLISBERGER MFG A CAL CORP
Also Called: R M I
14718 Arminta St, Van Nuys (91402-5904)
PHONE..................................818 786-9462
Jerry Rothlisberger, *President*
Korena Rothlisberger, *Admin Sec*
EMP: 16 **EST:** 1967
SQ FT: 8,000
SALES (est): 2.2MM **Privately Held**
WEB: www.rmi-mfg.com
SIC: 3599 Machine shop, jobbing & repair

(P-8778)
ROY & VAL TOOL GRINDING INC
10131 Canoga Ave, Chatsworth (91311-3006)
PHONE..................................818 341-2434
Val Goelz, *President*
Jim Tweety, *Vice Pres*
Mark Goelz, *Admin Sec*
EMP: 29 **EST:** 1966
SQ FT: 4,800
SALES (est): 1.1MM **Privately Held**
SIC: 3599 7389 Machine shop, jobbing & repair; grinding, precision: commercial or industrial

(P-8779)
ROZAK ENGINEERING INC
556 S State College Blvd, Fullerton (92831-5114)
PHONE..................................714 446-8855
Solomon Kilaghbian, *President*
EMP: 16 **EST:** 1981
SQ FT: 1,920
SALES (est): 551K **Privately Held**
WEB: www.rozak.com
SIC: 3599 Machine shop, jobbing & repair

(P-8780)
RPM GRINDING CO INC
Also Called: R P M Centerless Grinding
1755 Commerce St, Norco (92860-2934)
PHONE..................................951 273-0602
Rudy Miller, *CEO*
EMP: 19 **EST:** 1984
SQ FT: 10,500
SALES (est): 1.9MM **Privately Held**
WEB: www.rpmgrinding.com
SIC: 3599 Machine shop, jobbing & repair

(P-8781)
S & H MACHINE INC (PA)
900 N Lake St, Burbank (91502-1622)
PHONE..................................818 846-9847
Kenneth Fisher, *Vice Pres*
Pamela Fisher, *Vice Pres*
Daniel Wierman, *Executive Asst*
Yvonne Hernandez, *Human Res Mgr*
Arturo Martinez, *Mfg Mgr*
EMP: 13 **EST:** 1957
SQ FT: 17,107

SALES (est): 7.3MM **Privately Held**
WEB: www.shmachine.com
SIC: 3599 Machine shop, jobbing & repair

(P-8782)
S & S NUMERICAL CONTROL INC
Also Called: Satterfield Aerospace
19841 Nordhoff St, Northridge (91324-3331)
PHONE..................................818 341-4141
John Satterfield, *President*
Roberta J Satterfield, *Admin Sec*
Celeste Zabala, *Opers Mgr*
EMP: 20 **EST:** 1982
SQ FT: 9,000
SALES (est): 2.4MM **Privately Held**
WEB: www.ssnumerical.com
SIC: 3599 Machine shop, jobbing & repair

(P-8783)
S & S PRECISION MFG INC
2101 S Yale St, Santa Ana (92704-4424)
PHONE..................................714 754-6664
David Mosier, *President*
Andrew Cotrell, *Manager*
EMP: 45 **EST:** 1987
SQ FT: 10,000
SALES (est): 8.4MM **Privately Held**
WEB: www.ssprecisionmfg.com
SIC: 3599 Machine shop, jobbing & repair

(P-8784)
S R MACHINING INC
640 Parkridge Ave, Norco (92860-3124)
PHONE..................................951 520-9486
Lawrence T Kaford, *President*
EMP: 33 **EST:** 2003
SALES (est): 1.5MM **Privately Held**
WEB: www.srmachining.com
SIC: 3599 Machine shop, jobbing & repair

(P-8785)
S R MACHINING-PROPERTIES LLC
640 Parkridge Ave, Norco (92860-3124)
PHONE..................................951 520-9486
Lawrence Kaford, *President*
Larry Novak, *Vice Pres*
John Kneisly, *QC Mgr*
▲ **EMP:** 134 **EST:** 1998
SQ FT: 28,000
SALES (est): 10.4MM **Privately Held**
WEB: www.srmachining.com
SIC: 3599 3089 Machine shop, jobbing & repair; injection molding of plastics

(P-8786)
SANTA FE MACHINE WORKS INC
14578 Rancho Vista Dr, Fontana (92335-4277)
PHONE..................................909 350-6877
Todd Kelly, *President*
Dennis Kelly, *President*
Scott Kelly, *CFO*
Patricia Kelly, *Vice Pres*
Gilbert Robinson, *Vice Pres*
EMP: 29 **EST:** 1923
SQ FT: 30,000
SALES (est): 5.4MM **Privately Held**
WEB: www.santafemachine.com
SIC: 3599 Machine shop, jobbing & repair

(P-8787)
SANTOS PRECISION INC
2220 S Anne St, Santa Ana (92704-4411)
PHONE..................................714 957-0299
Francisco Santos, *President*
Evelyn Santos, *Corp Secy*
Richard Santos, *Vice Pres*
EMP: 41 **EST:** 1979
SQ FT: 14,800
SALES (est): 1.4MM **Privately Held**
WEB: www.santosprecision.com
SIC: 3599 Machine shop, jobbing & repair

(P-8788)
SARR INDUSTRIES INC
8975 Fullbright Ave, Chatsworth (91311-6124)
PHONE..................................818 998-7735
Richard L Joice Jr, *President*
Angela Suszka, *Corp Secy*
Sharon Mills-Roche, *Accountant*

EMP: 25 EST: 1984
SQ FT: 5,500
SALES (est): 1MM Privately Held
WEB: www.sarrindustries.com
SIC: 3599 Machine shop, jobbing & repair

(P-8789)
SCHNEIDERS MANUFACTURING INC
11122 Penrose St, Sun Valley
(91352-2724)
PHONE..................818 771-0082
Nick Schneider, *President*
Trudy Schneider, *Corp Secy*
Tom Schneider, *Vice Pres*
EMP: 30 EST: 1967
SQ FT: 18,000
SALES (est): 3.4MM Privately Held
WEB: www.schneidersmanufacturing.com
SIC: 3599 Machine shop, jobbing & repair

(P-8790)
SCREWMATIC INC
925 W 1st St, Azusa (91702-4222)
P.O. Box 518 (91702-0518)
PHONE..................626 334-7831
Louis E Zimmerli, *CEO*
Alice Zimmerli, *Vice Pres*
Jeff Clow, *Admin Sec*
Oscar Carpio, *Finance Mgr*
Jose Avalos, *Production*
EMP: 65 EST: 1953
SQ FT: 40,000
SALES (est): 8MM Privately Held
WEB: www.screwmaticinc.com
SIC: 3599 Machine shop, jobbing & repair

(P-8791)
SDI LLC
21 Morgan Ste 150, Irvine (92618-2086)
PHONE..................949 351-1866
Jon Korbonski, *President*
EMP: 20 EST: 2017
SALES (est): 1.6MM Privately Held
WEB: www.sdinetwork.com
SIC: 3599 Custom machinery

(P-8792)
SENGA ENGINEERING INC
1525 E Warner Ave, Santa Ana
(92705-5419)
PHONE..................714 549-8011
Roy Jones, *President*
Tyler Smyth, *Engineer*
Mike Irion, *Business Mgr*
Elvia Rodriguez, *Human Res Mgr*
EMP: 48 EST: 1976
SQ FT: 25,000
SALES (est): 9.6MM Privately Held
WEB: www.senga-eng.com
SIC: 3599 Machine shop, jobbing & repair

(P-8793)
SERRANO INDUSTRIES INC
9922 Tabor Pl, Santa Fe Springs
(90670-3300)
PHONE..................562 777-8180
Hoberto Serrano Jr, *President*
Bobby Serrano, *Vice Pres*
Maria Serrano, *Vice Pres*
Jorge Ballesteros, *Buyer*
EMP: 34 EST: 1990
SQ FT: 30,000
SALES (est): 7.7MM Privately Held
WEB: www.serrano-ind.com
SIC: 3599 Machine shop, jobbing & repair

(P-8794)
SHEFFIELD MANUFACTURING INC
13849 Magnolia Ave, Chino (91710-7028)
PHONE..................818 767-4948
Dave Hilton, *CEO*
EMP: 17 EST: 2013
SALES (est): 595.6K Privately Held
WEB: www.sheffield-mfg.com
SIC: 3599 3444 Machine shop, jobbing & repair; sheet metalwork

(P-8795)
SHERMAN CORPORATION
10803 Los Jardines E, Fountain Valley
(92708-3936)
PHONE..................310 671-2117
EMP: 27
SQ FT: 14,000

SALES (est): 3.8MM Privately Held
SIC: 3599 Machine Shop

(P-8796)
SMI CA INC
Also Called: Saeilo Manufacturing Inds
14340 Iseli Rd, Santa Fe Springs
(90670-5204)
PHONE..................562 926-9407
Katsuhiko Tsukamoto, *CEO*
David Tsukamoto, *President*
Erik Kawakami, *Corp Secy*
EMP: 26 EST: 1999
SQ FT: 10,000
SALES (est): 8.8MM
SALES (corp-wide): 34.6MM Privately Held
WEB: www.smi-ca.com
SIC: 3599 Machine shop, jobbing & repair
PA: Saeilo Enterprises Inc
   105 Kahr Ave
   Greeley PA 18425
   845 735-6500

(P-8797)
SOLO ENTERPRISE CORP
Also Called: Solo Golf
220 N California Ave, City of Industry
(91744-4323)
PHONE..................626 961-3591
Richard F Mugica, *CEO*
Edward Mugica, *Vice Pres*
Cheryl Haskett, *Accountant*
Edward A Mugica, *VP Mfg*
Frank Duardo, *Foreman/Supr*
EMP: 50 EST: 1966
SQ FT: 20,000
SALES (est): 5.7MM Privately Held
WEB: www.soloenterprisecorp.com
SIC: 3599 3812 Machine shop, jobbing & repair; search & navigation equipment

(P-8798)
SOUTHERN CAL TCHNICAL ARTS INC
370 E Crowther Ave, Placentia
(92870-6419)
PHONE..................714 524-2626
John H Robson IV, *President*
Matt Robson, *COO*
Kristi A Robson, *CFO*
Christine Robson, *Corp Secy*
Paul Kiralla, *Admin Asst*
EMP: 48 EST: 1970
SQ FT: 9,400
SALES (est): 5.1MM
SALES (corp-wide): 427.5MM Publicly Held
WEB: www.technicalarts.net
SIC: 3599 3827 Machine shop, jobbing & repair; optical instruments & lenses
PA: Nn, Inc.
   6210 Ardrey Kell Rd # 600
   Charlotte NC 28277
   980 264-4300

(P-8799)
SPARTAN MANUFACTURING CO
7081 Patterson Dr, Garden Grove
(92841-1435)
PHONE..................714 894-1955
R J Horton, *President*
Terry Danielson, *Vice Pres*
EMP: 26 EST: 1957
SQ FT: 16,000
SALES (est): 3.7MM Privately Held
WEB: www.spartanmfg.com
SIC: 3599 Machine shop, jobbing & repair

(P-8800)
SPEC ENGINEERING CO INC
13754 Saticoy St, Van Nuys (91402-6518)
PHONE..................818 780-3045
Gregory Viksman, *President*
Anna Viksman, *Vice Pres*
EMP: 25 EST: 1987
SQ FT: 5,200
SALES (est): 2.7MM Privately Held
WEB: www.specengco.com
SIC: 3599 3412 Machine shop, jobbing & repair; metal barrels, drums & pails

(P-8801)
SPECIALTY SURFACE GRINDING INC
345 W 131st St, Los Angeles (90061-1103)
PHONE..................310 538-4352
Piero Casadio, *President*
Jone Casadio, *Corp Secy*
EMP: 30 EST: 1967
SQ FT: 11,000
SALES (est): 877.6K Privately Held
WEB: www.specialtysurfacegrinding.com
SIC: 3599 Machine shop, jobbing & repair

(P-8802)
SPENCO MACHINE & MANUFACTURING
27556 Commerce Center Dr, Temecula
(92590-2518)
PHONE..................951 699-5566
Robert L Spencer, *Owner*
EMP: 14 EST: 1957
SQ FT: 11,000
SALES (est): 1.7MM Privately Held
WEB: www.spencomachine.com
SIC: 3599 Machine shop, jobbing & repair

(P-8803)
SUMMIT MACHINE LLC
2880 E Philadelphia St, Ontario
(91761-8523)
PHONE..................909 923-2744
▼ EMP: 120 EST: 2003
SQ FT: 103,000
SALES (est): 26.1MM
SALES (corp-wide): 245.5B Publicly Held
WEB: www.summitmachining.com
SIC: 3599 3728 Machine shop, jobbing & repair; aircraft parts & equipment
HQ: Precision Castparts Corp.
   4650 Sw Mcdam Ave Ste 300
   Portland OR 97239
   503 946-4800

(P-8804)
SUN PRECISION MACHINING INC
1651 Market St Ste A, Corona
(92880-1710)
PHONE..................951 817-0056
EMP: 17
SALES (est): 2.6MM Privately Held
SIC: 3599 Industrial Machinery, Nec, Nsk

(P-8805)
SUNVAIR INC (HQ)
29145 The Old Rd, Valencia (91355-1015)
PHONE..................661 294-3777
Robert Dann, *President*
Melba Waschak, *Corp Secy*
Edward Waschak, *Vice Pres*
Cindy Guzman, *Admin Asst*
April Harrison, *Financial Analy*
EMP: 54 EST: 1956
SQ FT: 26,000
SALES (est): 17.7MM
SALES (corp-wide): 30MM Privately Held
WEB: www.sunvair.com
SIC: 3599 7699 Machine shop, jobbing & repair; aircraft & heavy equipment repair services
PA: Sunvair Aerospace Group, Inc.
   29145 The Old Rd
   Valencia CA 91355
   661 294-3777

(P-8806)
SUPREME MACHINE PRODUCTS INC
302 Sequoia Ave, Ontario (91761-1543)
PHONE..................909 974-0349
Harold Hal Peterson, *President*
Isac Gomez, *Vice Pres*
Lyn Kaplan, *Manager*
EMP: 18
SQ FT: 7,800
SALES: 4.9MM Privately Held
WEB: www.suprememachineproducts.com
SIC: 3599 Machine shop, jobbing & repair

(P-8807)
SWISS WIRE EDM
3505 Cadillac Ave Ste J1, Costa Mesa
(92626-1432)
PHONE..................714 540-2903
Malcolm Schneer, *President*
Nola Schneer, *Vice Pres*
Richard Barnes, *CIO*
EMP: 15 EST: 1979
SQ FT: 10,000
SALES (est): 3.2MM Privately Held
WEB: www.swedm.com
SIC: 3599 Machine shop, jobbing & repair

(P-8808)
T & M MACHINING
331 Irving Dr, Oxnard (93030-5172)
PHONE..................805 983-6716
Mario Mangone, *President*
Kay Mangone, *Controller*
EMP: 20 EST: 1979
SALES (est): 2.4MM Privately Held
WEB: www.tmmachining.com
SIC: 3599 3544 Machine shop, jobbing & repair; special dies, tools, jigs & fixtures

(P-8809)
T E B INC
8754 Lion St, Rancho Cucamonga
(91730-4427)
PHONE..................909 941-8100
Michael Harding, *President*
EMP: 15 EST: 1961
SQ FT: 8,500
SALES (est): 1.7MM Privately Held
WEB: www.tebincca.com
SIC: 3599 Machine shop, jobbing & repair

(P-8810)
T/Q SYSTEMS INC
25131 Arctic Ocean Dr, Lake Forest
(92630-8852)
PHONE..................949 455-0478
Victor Buytkus, *President*
Scott Moebius, *Vice Pres*
Vic Buytkus, *Executive*
John Lopez, *Purch Mgr*
Shea Quinn, *QC Mgr*
EMP: 40 EST: 1988
SALES (est): 7.1MM Privately Held
WEB: www.tqsystems.net
SIC: 3599 Machine shop, jobbing & repair

(P-8811)
TCT ADVANCED MACHINING INC
2454 Fender Ave Ste C, Fullerton
(92831-4320)
PHONE..................714 871-9371
James Chang, *President*
EMP: 14 EST: 1999
SQ FT: 2,400
SALES (est): 1.8MM Privately Held
SIC: 3599 Machine shop, jobbing & repair

(P-8812)
TECFAR MANUFACTURING INC
8525 Telfair Ave, Sun Valley (91352-3928)
PHONE..................818 767-0677
Joe Simpson, *President*
Charles Ahn, *CEO*
Joe Richardson, *Prdtn Mgr*
EMP: 17 EST: 1976
SQ FT: 8,500
SALES (est): 900K Privately Held
WEB: www.tecfar.com
SIC: 3599 Machine shop, jobbing & repair

(P-8813)
TECHNICAL TROUBLE SHOOTING INC
27822 Fremont Ct B, Valencia
(91355-1130)
PHONE..................661 257-1202
Sergey Levkov, *President*
EMP: 15 EST: 1989
SQ FT: 15,000
SALES (est): 1.1MM Privately Held
SIC: 3599 Bellows, industrial: metal

(P-8814)
TECHNIFORM INTERNATIONAL CORP
375 S Cactus Ave, Rialto (92376-6320)
PHONE..................909 877-6886

Richard S Jones, *President*
EMP: 165 **EST:** 1989
SQ FT: 60,000
SALES (est): 3.4MM **Privately Held**
WEB: www.techniform.com
SIC: 3599 3469 3444 Machine shop, jobbing & repair; metal stampings; sheet metalwork

(P-8815)
TECNO INDUSTRIAL ENGRG INC
13528 Pumice St, Norwalk (90650-5249)
PHONE..................................562 623-4517
Juan Giner, *President*
Enrique Viano, *Vice Pres*
EMP: 27 **EST:** 1979
SQ FT: 17,000
SALES (est): 1.3MM **Privately Held**
SIC: 3599 3728 Machine shop, jobbing & repair; aircraft parts & equipment

(P-8816)
TEMECULA PRECISION FABRICATION
Also Called: Temecula Precision Mfg
42201 Sarah Way, Temecula (92590-3463)
PHONE..................................951 699-4066
Steve Leckband, *President*
Teri Leckband, *Vice Pres*
EMP: 13 **EST:** 2010
SALES (est): 1.6MM **Privately Held**
WEB: www.temeculaprecision.com
SIC: 3599 Machine shop, jobbing & repair

(P-8817)
THIESSEN PRODUCTS INC
Also Called: Jim's Machining
555 Dawson Dr Ste A, Camarillo (93012-5085)
PHONE..................................805 482-6913
Jim Thiessen, *President*
Jay R Thiessen, *Corp Secy*
Debra Thiessen, *Vice Pres*
Paul Platts, *Executive*
Mike Keelan, *Prdtn Mgr*
EMP: 130 **EST:** 1971
SQ FT: 44,000
SALES (est): 16MM **Privately Held**
WEB: www.jimsmachining.com
SIC: 3599 Machine shop, jobbing & repair

(P-8818)
THUNDERBOLT MANUFACTURING INC
641 S State College Blvd, Fullerton (92831-5115)
PHONE..................................714 632-0397
Minh Son To, *President*
Robin Tran, *Human Res Mgr*
EMP: 26 **EST:** 1990
SQ FT: 5,800
SALES (est): 2.9MM **Privately Held**
WEB: www.thunderboltmfg.com
SIC: 3599 Machine shop, jobbing & repair

(P-8819)
TIM GUZZY SERVICES INC
5136 Calmview Ave, Baldwin Park (91706-1803)
P.O. Box 1457 (91706-7457)
PHONE..................................626 813-0626
Tim Guzzy, *President*
Mariana Guzzy, *Vice Pres*
EMP: 22 **EST:** 1989
SQ FT: 5,500
SALES (est): 1.8MM **Privately Held**
WEB: www.guzzyrepair.com
SIC: 3599 Machine shop, jobbing & repair

(P-8820)
TMX ENGINEERING AND MFG CORP
2141 S Standard Ave, Santa Ana (92707-3034)
PHONE..................................714 641-5884
Souhil Toubia, *CEO*
Gus Toubia, *President*
Mauricio Escarcega, *Principal*
Steve Korn, *Principal*
Rae Devault, *General Mgr*
EMP: 75 **EST:** 1985
SQ FT: 23,000

SALES (est): 8.7MM **Privately Held**
WEB: www.tmxengineering.com
SIC: 3599 3728 3544 Machine shop, jobbing & repair; aircraft parts & equipment; special dies, tools, jigs & fixtures

(P-8821)
TOMI ENGINEERING INC
414 E Alton Ave, Santa Ana (92707-4242)
PHONE..................................714 556-1474
Michael F Falbo, *CEO*
Anthony Falbo, *President*
Andrea Seifert, *Purch Mgr*
Andrea Haller, *Purchasing*
EMP: 52 **EST:** 1975
SQ FT: 15,000
SALES (est): 8.4MM **Privately Held**
WEB: www.tomiengineering.com
SIC: 3599 Machine shop, jobbing & repair

(P-8822)
TORRANCE PRCSION MACHINING INC
Also Called: Torrance Manufacturing
9530 Owensmouth Ave Ste 8, Chatsworth (91311-8026)
PHONE..................................818 709-7838
Fred Torrance, *President*
Lajauna Torrance, *CFO*
EMP: 13 **EST:** 1975
SQ FT: 8,000
SALES (est): 2MM **Privately Held**
WEB: www.torranceprecision.com
SIC: 3599 Machine shop, jobbing & repair

(P-8823)
TOWER INDUSTRIES INC
Also Called: Allied Mechanical Products
1720 S Bon View Ave, Ontario (91761-4411)
PHONE..................................909 947-2723
Mark Slater, *Manager*
EMP: 110
SQ FT: 60,794
SALES (corp-wide): 35.5MM **Privately Held**
SIC: 3599 Machine shop, jobbing & repair
PA: Tower Industries, Inc.
1518 N Endeavor Ln Ste C
Anaheim CA 92801

(P-8824)
TREPANNING SPECIALITIES INC
Also Called: Trepanning Specialties
16201 Illinois Ave, Paramount (90723-4996)
PHONE..................................562 633-8110
Donald B Laughlin, *President*
Patricia Laughlin, *Vice Pres*
▲ **EMP:** 23 **EST:** 1973
SQ FT: 7,000
SALES (est): 2.1MM **Privately Held**
WEB: www.trepanningspec.com
SIC: 3599 Machine shop, jobbing & repair

(P-8825)
TRIANGLE TOOL & DIE CORP
13189 Flores St, Santa Fe Springs (90670-4041)
PHONE..................................562 944-2117
Michael J Beyer, *Principal*
Barbara Beyer, *Vice Pres*
EMP: 15 **EST:** 1968
SQ FT: 14,000
SALES (est): 3MM **Privately Held**
SIC: 3599 3542 Electrical discharge machining (EDM); die casting & extruding machines

(P-8826)
TRUE POSITION TECHNOLOGIES LLC
24900 Avenue Stanford, Valencia (91355-1272)
PHONE..................................661 294-0030
Allen Sumian, *President*
EMP: 82 **EST:** 1990
SQ FT: 25,000
SALES (est): 10.9MM
SALES (corp-wide): 204.2MM **Privately Held**
WEB: www.truepositiontech.com
SIC: 3599 Machine shop, jobbing & repair

PA: Hbd Industries, Inc.
5200 Upper Metro Pl # 110
Dublin OH 43017
614 526-7000

(P-8827)
TRUE PRECISION MACHINING INC
175 Indstrial Way Bellton Buellton, Buellton (93427)
PHONE..................................805 964-4545
Todd Ackert, *President*
Marvin Rodriguez, *General Mgr*
EMP: 22 **EST:** 1998
SQ FT: 17,000
SALES (est): 3MM **Privately Held**
WEB: www.trueprecisionmachining.com
SIC: 3599 Machine shop, jobbing & repair

(P-8828)
TSC PRECISION MACHINING INC
1311 E Saint Gertrude Pl A, Santa Ana (92705-5216)
PHONE..................................714 542-3182
Steve Salazar, *President*
EMP: 15 **EST:** 1994
SQ FT: 6,298
SALES (est): 2.3MM **Privately Held**
WEB: www.tscprecision.com
SIC: 3599 3452 8711 Machine shop, jobbing & repair; bolts, nuts, rivets & washers; screws, metal; mechanical engineering

(P-8829)
TT MACHINE CORP
11651 Anabel Ave, Garden Grove (92843-3708)
PHONE..................................714 534-5288
Al Tran, *Manager*
EMP: 19 **EST:** 2006
SALES (est): 1.2MM **Privately Held**
WEB: www.ttmachinecorp.com
SIC: 3599 Machine shop, jobbing & repair

(P-8830)
TURRET LATHE SPECIALISTS INC
875 S Rose Pl, Anaheim (92805-5337)
PHONE..................................714 520-0058
Robert McBride, *President*
EMP: 18 **EST:** 1973
SQ FT: 6,000
SALES (est): 2.3MM **Privately Held**
WEB: www.turretlathespecialists.com
SIC: 3599 Machine shop, jobbing & repair

(P-8831)
UNITED PRECISION CORP
20810 Plummer St, Chatsworth (91311-5004)
PHONE..................................818 576-9540
Robert Stanley Hawrylo, *CEO*
David Hawrylo, *Engineer*
Lidia Hawrylo, *Human Res Mgr*
EMP: 30 **EST:** 2014
SQ FT: 7,500
SALES (est): 4.2MM **Privately Held**
WEB: www.upc-usa.com
SIC: 3599 3812 Machine shop, jobbing & repair; defense systems & equipment

(P-8832)
UNIVERSAL PLANT SVCS CAL INC
20545 Belshaw Ave A, Carson (90746-3505)
PHONE..................................310 618-1600
Stewart Jones, *Brartch Mgr*
EMP: 58
SALES (corp-wide): 502.8MM **Privately Held**
WEB: www.universalplant.com
SIC: 3599 Custom machinery
HQ: Universal Plant Services Cal Inc
20545a Belshaw Ave
Carson CA 90746
310 618-1600

(P-8833)
US CORE PINS INC
2115 S Hathaway St, Santa Ana (92705-5238)
PHONE..................................714 540-2846
EMP: 18 **EST:** 2018

SALES (est): 569.7K **Privately Held**
WEB: www.uscorepins.com
SIC: 3599 Machine shop, jobbing & repair

(P-8834)
V & S ENGINEERING COMPANY LTD
5766 Research Dr, Huntington Beach (92649-1617)
PHONE..................................714 898-7869
Dino Dukovic, *President*
Dino Dokovic, *President*
EMP: 25 **EST:** 1979
SQ FT: 10,000
SALES (est): 1MM **Privately Held**
WEB: www.vseng.biz
SIC: 3599 Machine shop, jobbing & repair

(P-8835)
VALLEY PERFORATING LLC
3201 Gulf St, Bakersfield (93308-4905)
PHONE..................................661 324-4964
Mike Dover, *President*
Dorothy Reynolds, *Vice Pres*
Alice Lomas, *Admin Sec*
John Boyles, *Sales Staff*
EMP: 65 **EST:** 1970
SQ FT: 10,440
SALES (est): 9.6MM **Privately Held**
WEB: www.valleyperf.com
SIC: 3599 Machine shop, jobbing & repair

(P-8836)
VALLEY TOOL AND MACHINE CO INC
111 Explorer St, Pomona (91768-3278)
PHONE..................................909 595-2205
Chuck Rogers, *CEO*
Jim Rogers, *President*
Nancy Larson, *Corp Secy*
EMP: 38 **EST:** 1982
SQ FT: 34,000
SALES (est): 2.1MM **Privately Held**
WEB: www.valleytool-inc.com
SIC: 3599 7692 3544 Machine shop, jobbing & repair; welding repair; special dies, tools, jigs & fixtures

(P-8837)
VANS MANUFACTURING INC
330 E Easy St Ste C, Simi Valley (93065-7526)
PHONE..................................805 522-6267
Louis Tignac, *President*
EMP: 19 **EST:** 1976
SQ FT: 8,500
SALES (est): 2.3MM **Privately Held**
SIC: 3599 Machine shop, jobbing & repair

(P-8838)
VELLIOS MACHINE SHOP INC
Also Called: Vellios Automotive Machine Sp
4625 29th Mnhttan Bch Blv, Lawndale (90260)
PHONE..................................310 643-8540
Harry Vellios, *President*
Carolyn Vellios, *Corp Secy*
Mark Vellios, *Vice Pres*
EMP: 22 **EST:** 1975
SQ FT: 6,500
SALES (est): 1.7MM **Privately Held**
WEB: www.velliosmachineshop.com
SIC: 3599 3714 5013 Machine shop, jobbing & repair; rebuilding engines & transmissions, factory basis; automotive supplies & parts

(P-8839)
VENTURA HYDRULIC MCH WORKS INC
1555 Callens Rd, Ventura (93003-5606)
PHONE..................................805 656-1760
Fred H Malzacher, *President*
Ray Jenkins, *Vice Pres*
Elaine Z Malzacher, *Vice Pres*
EMP: 20 **EST:** 1965
SQ FT: 15,700
SALES (est): 4.5MM **Privately Held**
WEB: www.venturahydraulics.com
SIC: 3599 Machine shop, jobbing & repair

PRODUCTS & SVCS

(P-8840)
VESCIO THREADING CO
Also Called: Vescio Manufacturing Intl
14002 Anson Ave, Santa Fe Springs
(90670-5202)
PHONE...................562 802-1868
Gregory Vescio, *CEO*
Robert Vescio, *President*
Greg Vescio, *CEO*
Bob Vescio, *CFO*
Verna Vescio, *Corp Secy*
EMP: 73
SQ FT: 13,000
SALES (est): 16.3MM **Privately Held**
WEB: www.vesciothreading.com
SIC: 3599 Machine shop, jobbing & repair

(P-8841)
VIANH COMPANY INC
13841 A Better Way 10c, Garden Grove
(92843-3930)
PHONE...................714 590-9808
Tam Nguyen, *President*
Vianh Nguyen, *CFO*
Jimmy Nguyen, *Administration*
Ann P Parras, *Manager*
EMP: 26 **EST:** 1989
SQ FT: 8,000
SALES (est): 6.2MM **Privately Held**
WEB: www.vianhcompany.com
SIC: 3599 Machine shop, jobbing & repair

(P-8842)
W MACHINE WORKS INC
13814 Del Sur St, San Fernando
(91340-3440)
PHONE...................818 890-8049
Marzel Neckien, *President*
Randy Neckien, *Vice Pres*
Martha Clark, *Technology*
Randall Uyeno, *QC Mgr*
Michael Gonzaga, *Production*
EMP: 45 **EST:** 1977
SQ FT: 25,000
SALES (est): 9.1MM **Privately Held**
WEB: www.wmwcnc.com
SIC: 3599 Machine shop, jobbing & repair

(P-8843)
WAHLCO INC
15 Marconi Ste B, Irvine (92618-2779)
PHONE...................714 979-7300
Alonso Munoz, *CEO*
Robert R Wahler, *CEO*
Dennis Nickel, *CFO*
Delia Ross, *Officer*
Barry J Southam, *Exec VP*
◆ **EMP:** 106 **EST:** 1972
SQ FT: 54,000
SALES (est): 17.3MM **Privately Held**
WEB: www.wahlco.com
SIC: 3599 Custom machinery

(P-8844)
WALLACE E MILLER INC
Also Called: Micro-TEC
9155 Alabama Ave Ste B, Chatsworth
(91311-5867)
PHONE...................818 998-0444
Gary Case, *President*
Roxanne Case, *Vice Pres*
EMP: 34 **EST:** 1987
SQ FT: 8,000
SALES (est): 1.4MM **Privately Held**
WEB: www.wyndhamhotels.com
SIC: 3599 Machine shop, jobbing & repair

(P-8845)
WARD ENTERPRISES
10332 Trumbull St, California City
(93505-1550)
P.O. Box 803231, Santa Clarita (91380-3231)
PHONE...................661 251-4890
EMP: 15
SQ FT: 16,000
SALES (est): 1.1MM **Privately Held**
SIC: 3599 Machine Shop

(P-8846)
WATSONS PROFILING CORP
1460 S Balboa Ave, Ontario (91761-7609)
PHONE...................909 923-5500
James Watson, *President*
EMP: 13 **EST:** 1958

SALES (est): 2.2MM **Privately Held**
WEB: www.watsonsprofiling.com
SIC: 3599 Machine shop, jobbing & repair

(P-8847)
WEST BOND INC (PA)
1551 S Harris Ct, Anaheim (92806-5932)
PHONE...................714 978-1551
John C Price, *President*
Gary Phillips, *Vice Pres*
Phyllis Eppig, *Admin Sec*
Thanh Bui, *Electrical Engi*
Dave Mehrtens, *Prdtn Mgr*
▼ **EMP:** 47 **EST:** 1966
SQ FT: 38,000
SALES (est): 8.5MM **Privately Held**
WEB: www.westbond.com
SIC: 3599 Machine shop, jobbing & repair

(P-8848)
WEST COAST MACHINING INC
14560 Marquardt Ave, Santa Fe Springs
(90670-5121)
PHONE...................562 229-1087
Sonia Duran, *CEO*
Carolina Beas, *CFO*
Cheryl Buholzer, *Controller*
EMP: 15 **EST:** 1997
SQ FT: 18,000
SALES (est): 2.5MM **Privately Held**
WEB: www.westcoastmachining.com
SIC: 3599 Machine shop, jobbing & repair

(P-8849)
WESTCOAST GRINDING CORPORATION
Also Called: Accurate Double Disc Grinding
10517 San Fernando Rd, Pacoima
(91331-2624)
PHONE...................818 890-1841
William C Birch, *President*
EMP: 17 **EST:** 1974
SQ FT: 6,000
SALES (est): 982.3K **Privately Held**
WEB: www.accuratedoubledisc.com
SIC: 3599 Machine shop, jobbing & repair

(P-8850)
WESTERN PRECISION AERO LLC
11600 Monarch St, Garden Grove
(92841-1817)
PHONE...................714 893-7999
Ed McKenna, *Mng Member*
Norma Davis, *CFO*
EMP: 37 **EST:** 2009
SQ FT: 16,000
SALES (est): 5.4MM
SALES (corp-wide): 608.9MM **Publicly Held**
WEB: www.rbcbearings.com
SIC: 3599 Machine shop, jobbing & repair
PA: Rbc Bearings Incorporated
  102 Willenbrock Rd Bldg B
  Oxford CT 06478
  203 267-7001

(P-8851)
WHITTEN MACHINE
4770 S K St, Tulare (93274-7149)
PHONE...................559 686-3428
John Whitten, *President*
Larry Whitten, *Shareholder*
Steve Whitten, *Shareholder*
Geraldine Whitten, *Corp Secy*
Ron Whitten, *Vice Pres*
EMP: 13 **EST:** 1956
SALES (est): 1.5MM **Privately Held**
SIC: 3599 Machine shop, jobbing & repair

(P-8852)
WILCOX MACHINE CO
7180 Scout Ave, Bell Gardens
(90201-3202)
P.O. Box 2159, Bell (90202-2159)
PHONE...................562 927-5353
George Schofhauser, *President*
Jill Wigney, *Corp Secy*
Kurt Anderegg, *Vice Pres*
Tom Anderegg, *Vice Pres*
Karen Mathis, *Persnl Dir*
◆ **EMP:** 60 **EST:** 1955
SALES (est): 12.7MM **Privately Held**
WEB: www.wilcoxmachine.com
SIC: 3599 Machine shop, jobbing & repair; custom machinery

(P-8853)
WILLIS MACHINE INC
11000 Alto Dr, Oak View (93022-9569)
PHONE...................805 604-4500
Harlan Willis, *President*
EMP: 23 **EST:** 1977
SALES (est): 3.5MM **Privately Held**
WEB: www.willismachine.com
SIC: 3599 Machine shop, jobbing & repair

(P-8854)
WILMINGTON MACHINE INC
Also Called: Wilmington Ironworks
432 W C St, Wilmington (90744-5714)
PHONE...................310 518-3213
Walter C Richards III, *President*
Elva Richards, *Treasurer*
J W Richards, *Admin Sec*
EMP: 43 **EST:** 1920
SQ FT: 13,000
SALES (est): 2.4MM **Privately Held**
WEB: www.wilmingtonironworksinc.com
SIC: 3599 Machine shop, jobbing & repair

(P-8855)
WILSHIRE PRECISION PDTS INC
7353 Hinds Ave, North Hollywood
(91605-3704)
PHONE...................818 765-4571
Thomas G Lewis, *President*
Dana Lewis, *Corp Secy*
Shoshona Lewis, *Corp Secy*
Wendy Lewis, *Vice Pres*
John Seeley, *Managing Dir*
EMP: 31 **EST:** 1951
SQ FT: 10,000
SALES (est): 5.7MM **Privately Held**
WEB: www.wilshireprecision.com
SIC: 3599 3621 Machine shop, jobbing & repair; motors, electric; electric motor & generator auxillary parts

(P-8856)
WIRE CUT COMPANY INC
6750 Caballero Blvd, Buena Park
(90620-1134)
PHONE...................714 994-1170
Sydney Omar, *CEO*
Tina Thomas, *Corp Secy*
Milton M Thomas, *Principal*
EMP: 30 **EST:** 1978
SQ FT: 20,000
SALES (est): 4.4MM **Privately Held**
WEB: www.wirecutcompany.com
SIC: 3599 Machine shop, jobbing & repair

(P-8857)
WMC PRCSION MCHNING GRNDING
1234 E Ash Ave Ste A, Fullerton
(92831-5013)
PHONE...................714 773-0059
Richard Mourey, *President*
Leigh Thompson, *General Mgr*
EMP: 22 **EST:** 1951
SQ FT: 10,000
SALES (est): 791.5K **Privately Held**
SIC: 3599 Machine shop, jobbing & repair

(P-8858)
YOUNG MACHINE INC
Also Called: California Machine Specialties
12282 Colony Ave, Chino (91710-2095)
PHONE...................909 464-0405
Anand Jagani, *President*
Sophia Gomez, *Office Admin*
Gilbert Fresquez, *Consultant*
EMP: 19 **EST:** 1970
SQ FT: 11,000
SALES (est): 3.4MM **Privately Held**
WEB: www.calmachine.com
SIC: 3599 Machine shop, jobbing & repair

(P-8859)
ZET-TEK PRECISION MACHINING (PA)
Also Called: Zet-Tek Machining
22951 La Palma Ave, Yorba Linda
(92887-6701)
PHONE...................714 777-8770
Daniel Zettler, *CEO*
Mark Deischter, *CFO*
Sandra Rubino, *Vice Pres*
EMP: 15 **EST:** 1988
SQ FT: 25,000

SALES (est): 4.9MM **Privately Held**
SIC: 3599 3444 Machine shop, jobbing & repair; sheet metalwork

---

3612 Power, Distribution & Specialty Transformers

(P-8860)
ABB INC
Also Called: Automation Tech - Low Voltage
741 E Ball Rd, Anaheim (92805-5953)
PHONE...................714 630-4111
EMP: 63
SALES (corp-wide): 26.1B **Privately Held**
WEB: www.global.abb
SIC: 3612 Transformers, except electric
HQ: Abb Inc.
  305 Gregson Dr
  Cary NC 27511

(P-8861)
ABBOTT TECHNOLOGIES INC
8203 Vineland Ave, Sun Valley
(91352-3956)
PHONE...................818 504-0644
Kerima Marie Batte, *CEO*
Albert Rieker, *Opers Mgr*
John Batte, *Sales Associate*
Jackson Vick, *Sales Engr*
Mosrat Ahmed, *Manager*
EMP: 40 **EST:** 1961
SQ FT: 12,000
SALES (est): 9.6MM **Privately Held**
WEB: www.abbott-tech.com
SIC: 3612 3559 3677 Transformers, except electric; electronic component making machinery; transformers power supply, electronic type

(P-8862)
ALECTRO INC
Also Called: Protech Systems
6770 Central Ave Ste B, Riverside
(92504-1443)
PHONE...................909 590-9521
Jorge Rios, *CEO*
Gail A Stephens, *President*
Tim Stevens, *CEO*
Remy Hernandez, *Purch Dir*
EMP: 15 **EST:** 1978
SQ FT: 18,000
SALES (est): 2.3MM **Privately Held**
SIC: 3612 1731 Transformers, except electric; safety & security specialization

(P-8863)
CALIFORNIA PAK INTL INC
1700 S Wilmington Ave, Compton
(90220-5116)
PHONE...................310 223-2500
Edward Kwon, *President*
Byung Yull Kwon, *CEO*
Roy Kwon, *Business Dir*
Judy Kwon, *Finance Mgr*
Gary Hover, *Sales Executive*
▲ **EMP:** 20 **EST:** 1989
SQ FT: 15,000
SALES (est): 4MM **Privately Held**
WEB: www.calpaktravel.com
SIC: 3612 Distribution transformers, electric

(P-8864)
CALIFRNIA STATE UNIV CHNNEL IS
45 Rincon Dr Unit 104a, Camarillo
(93012-8423)
PHONE...................805 437-2670
Erik Blaine, *Exec Dir*
EMP: 93 **EST:** 1996
SQ FT: 5,000
SALES (est): 773.4K **Privately Held**
WEB: www.csuci.edu
SIC: 3612 Power & distribution transformers

(P-8865)
CGR/THOMPSON INDUSTRIES INC
7155 Fenwick Ln, Westminster
(92683-5218)
PHONE...................714 678-4200

Michael B Baughan, *CEO*
Vince Corti, *General Mgr*
Kevin Rowan, *Sales Staff*
EMP: 52 **EST:** 2001
SQ FT: 10,000
SALES (est): 14.2MM
SALES (corp-wide): 56.5B **Publicly Held**
WEB: www.beaerospace.com
SIC: 3612 Machine tool transformers
HQ: B/E Aerospace, Inc.
1400 Corporate Center Way
Wellington FL 33414
410 266-2048

(P-8866)
CPI ADVANCED INC
Also Called: Enaba-Kbw USA
14708 Central Ave, Chino (91710-9502)
PHONE...................909 597-5533
Charles Pyong Cha, *President*
Yarnee Arias, *Manager*
◆ **EMP:** 17 **EST:** 1991
SQ FT: 2,500
SALES (est): 1.6MM **Privately Held**
WEB: www.cpipower.com
SIC: 3612 Fluorescent lighting transformers

(P-8867)
DATATRONICS ROMOLAND INC
28151 Us Highway 74, Menifee
(92585-8916)
P.O. Box 1579 (92585-1579)
PHONE...................951 928-7700
Paul Y Siu, *CEO*
Bradley Turner, *Vice Pres*
Joyce Schlaman, *Executive*
Gisela Anderson, *Info Tech Mgr*
Chris Caroselli, *Senior Engr*
▲ **EMP:** 75 **EST:** 1971
SQ FT: 38,800
SALES (est): 16.3MM **Privately Held**
WEB: www.datatronics.com
SIC: 3612 3677 Transformers, except
electric; inductors, electronic

(P-8868)
DOW-ELCO INC
1313 W Olympic Blvd, Montebello
(90640-5010)
P.O. Box 669 (90640-0669)
PHONE...................323 723-1288
Linda Su, *President*
Cecile SE Kay, *Vice Pres*
Grace Park, *Admin Sec*
Ronald Cheung, *Director*
Annie Su, *Director*
EMP: 25 **EST:** 1946
SQ FT: 8,100
SALES (est): 2.4MM **Privately Held**
SIC: 3612 3829 3061 Vibrators, interrupter; measuring & controlling devices; mechanical rubber goods

(P-8869)
ENERGY CNVRSION APPLCTIONS INC
Also Called: Eca
582 Explorer St, Brea (92821-3108)
PHONE...................714 256-2166
Akbal Grewal, *CEO*
Zafar Arain, *Mktg Dir*
Robert De Luca, *Manager*
EMP: 17 **EST:** 1989
SQ FT: 10,000
SALES (est): 3.9MM **Privately Held**
WEB: www.eca-mfg.com
SIC: 3612 8748 Transformers, except
electric; telecommunications consultant

(P-8870)
FALCON ELECTRIC INC
5116 Azusa Canyon Rd, Baldwin Park
(91706-1846)
PHONE...................626 962-7770
Arthur Seredian, *CEO*
Ron Seredian, *Sales Staff*
▲ **EMP:** 13 **EST:** 1999
SALES (est): 3MM **Privately Held**
WEB: www.falconups.com
SIC: 3612 Transformers, except electric

(P-8871)
FORTRON/SOURCE CORPORATION (PA)
23181 Antonio Pkwy, Rcho STA Marg
(92688-2652)
PHONE...................949 766-9240
Jackson Wang, *President*
Tom Sullivan, *COO*
Charlie Shih, *Vice Pres*
Jeff Tseng, *Vice Pres*
Eunice Chen, *Buyer*
▲ **EMP:** 91 **EST:** 1983
SQ FT: 10,000
SALES (est): 5.7MM **Privately Held**
SIC: 3612 3679 3577 Transformers, except electric; power supplies, all types: static; computer peripheral equipment

(P-8872)
FULHAM CO INC
12705 S Van Ness Ave, Hawthorne
(90250-3322)
PHONE...................323 779-2980
Antony Corrie, *President*
James Cooke, *CFO*
Deborah Knuckles, *CFO*
Michael Bauer, *Vice Pres*
Mike Hu, *Vice Pres*
▲ **EMP:** 40 **EST:** 1994
SQ FT: 48,000
SALES (est): 11.4MM **Privately Held**
WEB: www.fulham.com
SIC: 3612 Ballasts for lighting fixtures
HQ: Fulham Company Gmbh
Torstr. 138
Berlin 10119

(P-8873)
GRAND GENERAL ACCESSORIES LLC
1965 E Vista Bella Way, Rancho
Dominguez (90220-6106)
PHONE...................310 631-2589
Shu-Hui Lin Huang, *CEO*
Sophia Huang, *Vice Pres*
Nan-Huang Huang, *Admin Sec*
Maggie Huang, *Project Mgr*
Pat Brewer, *Sales Mgr*
▲ **EMP:** 39 **EST:** 1984
SALES (est): 7.6MM **Privately Held**
WEB: www.grandgeneral.com
SIC: 3612 5531 3713 Transformers, except electric; truck equipment & parts; truck & bus bodies

(P-8874)
INNOVATIVE POWER INC
P.O. Box 1580 (92585-1580)
PHONE...................951 928-7700
EMP: 16 **EST:** 2012
SALES (est): 2.8MM **Privately Held**
WEB: www.datatronics.com
SIC: 3612 Transformers, except electric

(P-8875)
JACKSON ENGINEERING CO INC
9411 Winnetka Ave A, Chatsworth
(91311-6035)
PHONE...................818 886-9567
Ron Jackson, *President*
Dennis Elliott, *Vice Pres*
EMP: 40 **EST:** 1951
SQ FT: 10,000
SALES (est): 3MM **Privately Held**
WEB: www.custom-transformers.com
SIC: 3612 Electronic meter transformers

(P-8876)
JUSTIN INC
2663 Lee Ave, El Monte (91733-1411)
PHONE...................626 444-4516
Frank Justin Jr, *President*
Jeffrey Ross Justin, *CEO*
Jeff Justin, *Vice Pres*
Justin Drury, *Director*
EMP: 50 **EST:** 1956
SQ FT: 4,000
SALES (est): 9.1MM **Privately Held**
WEB: www.justininc.com
SIC: 3612 Specialty transformers

(P-8877)
LORAN INC
Also Called: Nightscaping Outdoor Lighting
1705 E Colton Ave, Redlands
(92374-4971)
PHONE...................405 340-0660
Lavesta Locklin, *President*
▲ **EMP:** 22 **EST:** 1959
SQ FT: 100,000
SALES (est): 1.1MM **Privately Held**
WEB: www.nightscaping.com
SIC: 3612 Transformers, except
electric; garden, patio, walkway & yard lighting fixtures: electric

(P-8878)
MGM TRANSFORMER CO
5701 Smithway St, Commerce
(90040-1583)
PHONE...................323 726-0888
Patrick Gogerchin, *President*
David Walker, *Officer*
Jim Gibson, *Vice Pres*
Luis Otero, *Vice Pres*
Jason Yan, *Info Tech Mgr*
◆ **EMP:** 70 **EST:** 1975
SQ FT: 40,000
SALES (est): 28.2MM **Privately Held**
WEB: www.mgmtransformer.com
SIC: 3612 Transformers, except electric

(P-8879)
MPS INDUSTRIES INCORPORATED (PA)
19210 S Vermont Ave # 405, Gardena
(90248-4431)
PHONE...................310 325-1043
Chiging Jean Wang, *President*
▲ **EMP:** 23 **EST:** 2004
SQ FT: 25,000
SALES (est): 3.9MM **Privately Held**
WEB: www.mpsind.com
SIC: 3612 3499 Power transformers, electric; magnets, permanent: metallic

(P-8880)
ON-LINE POWER INCORPORATED (PA)
Also Called: Power Services
14000 S Broadway, Los Angeles
(90061-1018)
PHONE...................323 721-5017
Abbie Gougerchian, *CEO*
Vivian Meza, *Administration*
▲ **EMP:** 46 **EST:** 1980
SQ FT: 36,000
SALES (est): 15MM **Privately Held**
WEB: www.onlinepower.com
SIC: 3612 3621 3613 3677 Transformers, except electric; motors & generators; regulators, power; electronic coils, transformers & other inductors

(P-8881)
PACIFIC TRANSFORMER CORP
5399 E Hunter Ave, Anaheim (92807-2054)
PHONE...................714 779-0450
Patrick A Thomas, *CEO*
Jim Richardson, *CFO*
Jackie Wood, *Executive*
Ray Artsdalen, *General Mgr*
Sean McDougall, *Electrical Engi*
▲ **EMP:** 205
SQ FT: 37,000
SALES (est): 16.9MM **Privately Held**
WEB: www.pactran.com
SIC: 3612 Power transformers, electric

(P-8882)
PIONEER CUSTOM ELEC PDTS CORP
10640 Springdale Ave, Santa Fe Springs
(90670-3843)
PHONE...................562 944-0626
Geo Murickan, *President*
Ian Ross, *Bd of Directors*
EMP: 68 **EST:** 2013
SALES (est): 14.1MM **Publicly Held**
WEB: www.pioneercep.com
SIC: 3612 Electronic meter transformers
PA: Pioneer Power Solutions, Inc.
400 Kelby St Ste 12
Fort Lee NJ 07024

(P-8883)
RING LLC (HQ)
1523 26th St, Santa Monica (90404-3507)
PHONE...................800 656-1918
Jamie Siminoff, *CEO*
Angela Kang, *Partner*
Matthew Lehman, *Vice Pres*
Ashar Khan, *Program Mgr*
Matthew Sauter, *Software Dev*
▲ **EMP:** 300 **EST:** 2013
SQ FT: 40,000
SALES (est): 181.5MM **Publicly Held**
WEB: www.ring.com
SIC: 3612 5065 Doorbell transformers, electric; security control equipment & systems

(P-8884)
SOMA MAGNETICS CORPORATION
585 S State College Blvd, Fullerton
(92831-5113)
PHONE...................714 447-0782
Harry Sidhu, *President*
Soma Sidhu, *Vice Pres*
EMP: 19 **EST:** 1990
SQ FT: 10,000
SALES (est): 3.7MM **Privately Held**
WEB: www.somamagnetics.com
SIC: 3612 3677 3496 5099 Transformers, except electric; inductors, electronic; cable, uninsulated wire: made from purchased wire; electronic parts & equipment; transformers, electric

(P-8885)
STREAMLINE AVIONICS INC
17672 Armstrong Ave, Irvine (92614-5728)
PHONE...................949 861-8151
Daniel Frahm, *President*
EMP: 22 **EST:** 2010
SALES (est): 3.2MM **Privately Held**
WEB: www.streamlineavionics.com
SIC: 3612 Transformers, except electric

(P-8886)
UTOPIA LIGHTING
2329 E Pacifica Pl, Compton (90220-6210)
PHONE...................310 327-7711
▲ **EMP:** 14
SALES (est): 2.4MM **Privately Held**
SIC: 3612 Mfg Transformers

(P-8887)
ZETTLER MAGNETICS INC
75 Columbia, Aliso Viejo (92656-5386)
PHONE...................949 831-5000
Gunther Rueb, *CEO*
▲ **EMP:** 190 **EST:** 1997
SQ FT: 80,000
SALES (est): 5.8MM **Privately Held**
WEB: www.zettler-group.com
SIC: 3612 Transformers, except electric
PA: Zettler Components, Inc.
75 Columbia
Orange CA 92868

3613 Switchgear & Switchboard Apparatus

(P-8888)
AGE INCORPORATED
14831 Spring Ave, Santa Fe Springs
(90670-5109)
PHONE...................562 483-7300
Vasken Imasdounian, *President*
Annie Imasdounian, *Corp Secy*
Daniel Imasdounian, *Vice Pres*
Jennifer Heinl, *Office Mgr*
Hannah Brown, *Admin Asst*
▲ **EMP:** 35 **EST:** 1975
SALES (est): 4.2MM **Privately Held**
WEB: www.agenameplate.com
SIC: 3613 3625 Control panels, electric; electric controls & control accessories, industrial

P R O D U C T S & S V C S

(P-8889)
CALHOUN & POXON COMPANY INC
5330 Alhambra Ave, Los Angeles (90032-3485)
P.O. Box 1481, South Pasadena (91031-1481)
PHONE................323 225-2328
Garrett Calhoun, *President*
Lois Calhoun, *Vice Pres*
EMP: 18 **EST:** 1958
SQ FT: 22,000
SALES (est): 1.1MM **Privately Held**
WEB: www.candpcontrols.com
SIC: 3613 Control panels, electric

(P-8890)
COBEL TECHNOLOGIES INC
822 N Grand Ave, Covina (91724-2418)
PHONE................626 332-2100
Mike Warner, *President*
EMP: 16 **EST:** 1985
SQ FT: 5,600
SALES (est): 3.7MM **Privately Held**
WEB: www.cobeltech.com
SIC: 3613 3625 Control panels, electric; relays & industrial controls

(P-8891)
CROWN TECHNICAL SYSTEMS (PA)
13470 Philadelphia Ave, Fontana (92337-7700)
PHONE................951 332-4170
Naim Siddiqui, *President*
Howard Siddiqui, *Vice Pres*
Scott Joines, *Department Mgr*
Nathan Aguilera, *Electrical Engi*
Richard Coronado, *Engineer*
▲ **EMP:** 200 **EST:** 1996
SQ FT: 92,000
SALES (est): 60.8MM **Privately Held**
WEB: www.crowntechnicalsystems.com
SIC: 3613 Control panels, electric

(P-8892)
CUSTOM CONTROL SENSORS LLC (PA)
Also Called: Custom Aviation Supply
21111 Plummer St, Chatsworth (91311-4905)
P.O. Box 2516 (91313-2516)
PHONE................818 341-4610
Henry P Acuff, *President*
Thomas Pilgrim, *CFO*
Joann D Acuff, *Corp Secy*
Paul Konrath, *Vice Pres*
Eric Calderon, *Admin Asst*
EMP: 269 **EST:** 1957
SALES (est): 53.5MM **Privately Held**
WEB: www.ccsdualsnap.com
SIC: 3613 3643 3625 Switches, electric power except snap, push button, etc.; current-carrying wiring devices; relays & industrial controls

(P-8893)
CUSTOM CONTROL SENSORS INTL
21111 Plummer St, Chatsworth (91311-4905)
PHONE................818 341-4610
Henry P Acuff, *Administration*
EMP: 23 **EST:** 2014
SALES (est): 332.1K **Privately Held**
WEB: www.ccsdualsnap.com
SIC: 3613 Switchgear & switchboard apparatus

(P-8894)
DATA LIGHTS RIGGING LLC
Also Called: Ratpac Dimmers
7508 Tyrone Ave, Van Nuys (91405-1447)
PHONE................818 786-0536
Craig Allen Brink,
Tom Sievers, *Exec VP*
Ruwan Dharmasiri, *Vice Pres*
Nick Stabile, *Vice Pres*
Zaira Castro, *Executive Asst*
EMP: 29 **EST:** 2014
SALES (est): 6.6MM **Privately Held**
WEB: www.ratpaccontrols.com
SIC: 3613 Switchgear & switchboard apparatus

(P-8895)
DAZ INC
Also Called: Duramar Interior Surfaces
2500 White Rd Ste B, Irvine (92614-6276)
PHONE................949 724-8800
Farhad Abdollahi, *President*
Tom Belcher, *Vice Pres*
Nikkisa Abdollahi, *Exec Dir*
▲ **EMP:** 15 **EST:** 2007
SQ FT: 60,000
SALES (est): 10MM **Privately Held**
SIC: 3613 Panelboards & distribution boards, electric

(P-8896)
ELECTRO SWITCH CORP
Also Called: Digitran
10410 Trademark St, Rancho Cucamonga (91730-5826)
PHONE................909 581-0855
Robert M Pineau, *President*
Daniel Walls, *Program Mgr*
George Nguyen, *Engineer*
Edgar Mancenido, *Purch Mgr*
Michael Koval, *Sales Mgr*
EMP: 34
SALES (corp-wide): 103.8MM **Privately Held**
SIC: 3613 3625 Switches, electric power except snap, push button, etc.; control panels, electric; industrial controls: push button, selector switches, pilot
HQ: Electro Switch Corp.
　　775 Pleasant St Ste 1
　　Weymouth MA 02189
　　781 335-1195

(P-8897)
ELECTRONIC STAMPING CORP
Also Called: Esc
19920 S Alameda St, Compton (90221-6210)
PHONE................310 639-2120
Hang Up Moon, *President*
Madhu RAO, *CEO*
▲ **EMP:** 18 **EST:** 1968
SQ FT: 42,000
SALES (est): 5.9MM **Privately Held**
WEB: www.electronic-stamping.com
SIC: 3613 3678 3469 Bus bar structures; electronic connectors; metal stampings

(P-8898)
HYDRA-ELECTRIC COMPANY (PA)
3151 N Kenwood St, Burbank (91505-1052)
PHONE................818 843-6211
David E Schmidt, *CEO*
Rene Acosta, *Project Engr*
Sara Esparza, *Project Engr*
Christopher Chavez, *Engineer*
Joanna Dizon, *Engineer*
EMP: 178 **EST:** 1950
SQ FT: 90,000
SALES (est): 18.5MM **Privately Held**
WEB: www.hydraelectric.com
SIC: 3613 Switches, electric power except snap, push button, etc.

(P-8899)
MARWELL CORPORATION
1094 Wabash Ave, Mentone (92359)
P.O. Box 139 (92359-0139)
PHONE................909 794-4192
Larry R Blackwell, *President*
Kelle A Blackwell, *Corp Secy*
Karrie Matcham, *Supervisor*
EMP: 18 **EST:** 1979
SQ FT: 3,500
SALES (est): 3.8MM **Privately Held**
WEB: www.marwellcorp.com
SIC: 3613 Panel & distribution boards & other related apparatus

(P-8900)
MITSUBISHI ELC PWR PDTS INC
1065 Bonita Ave, La Verne (91750-5109)
PHONE................909 447-8410
David Belding, *Regl Sales Mgr*
EMP: 45 **Privately Held**
WEB: www.meppi.com
SIC: 3613 Switchgear & switchboard apparatus

HQ: Mitsubishi Electric Power Products, Inc.
　　530 Keystone Dr
　　Warrendale PA 15086
　　724 772-2555

(P-8901)
MYERS POWER PRODUCTS INC (PA)
Also Called: Myers FSI
2950 E Philadelphia St, Ontario (91761-8545)
PHONE................909 923-1800
Diana Grootonk, *CEO*
Jose Cudal, *CFO*
Tom Donnelly, *CFO*
Tony Williams, *Vice Pres*
Conrad Pecile, *Executive*
◆ **EMP:** 130 **EST:** 2003
SQ FT: 40,000
SALES (est): 172MM **Privately Held**
WEB: www.myerspower.com
SIC: 3613 Switchgear & switchboard apparatus

(P-8902)
PANEL SHOP INC
Also Called: Electrical Systems
2800 Palisades Dr, Corona (92878-9427)
PHONE................951 739-7000
Michael Hellmers, *President*
Carol Crawford, *President*
David Hellmers, *President*
EMP: 38 **EST:** 1974
SQ FT: 36,000
SALES (est): 4.1MM **Privately Held**
WEB: www.eslsys.com
SIC: 3613 3625 Control panels, electric; relays & industrial controls

(P-8903)
PHAOSTRON INSTR ELECTRONIC CO
717 N Coney Ave, Azusa (91702-2205)
PHONE................626 969-6801
Paul R Mc Guirk, *President*
Jackie Cangialosi, *CFO*
Andrew McGuirk, *Vice Pres*
Jacqueline Cangialosi, *Admin Sec*
Rick White, *CTO*
EMP: 80 **EST:** 1937
SQ FT: 50,000
SALES (est): 12.1MM **Privately Held**
WEB: www.phaostron.com
SIC: 3613 Metering panels, electric; bus bar structures
PA: Westbase, Inc.
　　717 N Coney Ave
　　Azusa CA 91702

(P-8904)
POWER AIRE INC
8055 E Crystal Dr, Anaheim (92807-2523)
PHONE................800 526-7661
Harry Ellis Sr, *President*
Jean Blasko, *Treasurer*
Harry Ellis Jr, *Vice Pres*
Michael Ellis, *Vice Pres*
EMP: 13 **EST:** 1988
SQ FT: 3,800
SALES (est): 440.8K **Privately Held**
WEB: www.coastpneumatics.com
SIC: 3613 5084 Panel & distribution boards & other related apparatus; industrial machinery & equipment

(P-8905)
ROMAC SUPPLY CO INC
7400 Bandini Blvd, Commerce (90040-3339)
PHONE................323 721-5810
David B Rosenfield, *President*
Victoria Rosenfield, *Treasurer*
Lisa R Podolsky, *Vice Pres*
Phillip Rosenfield, *Vice Pres*
Pedro Estrada, *Executive*
EMP: 60 **EST:** 1955
SQ FT: 105,000
SALES (est): 20.8MM **Privately Held**
WEB: www.romacsupply.com
SIC: 3613 3621 3612 5063 Switchgear & switchgear accessories; motors & generators; transformers, except electric; motors, electric

(P-8906)
STACO SYSTEMS INC (HQ)
Also Called: Staco Switch
7 Morgan, Irvine (92618-2005)
PHONE................949 297-8700
Patrick Hutchins, *President*
Andy Bain, *Vice Pres*
Jeff Bowen, *Vice Pres*
Tom Lanni, *Vice Pres*
Brett Meinsen, *Vice Pres*
◆ **EMP:** 69 **EST:** 1957
SQ FT: 35,000
SALES (est): 17.2MM
SALES (corp-wide): 44.2MM **Privately Held**
WEB: www.stacosystems.com
SIC: 3613 Switches, electric power except snap, push button, etc.
PA: Components Corporation Of America
　　5950 Berkshire Ln # 1500
　　Dallas TX 75225
　　214 969-0166

(P-8907)
W A BENJAMIN ELECTRIC CO
1615 Staunton Ave, Los Angeles (90021-3118)
PHONE................213 749-7731
D E Benjamin, *President*
Mauricio Mena, *CIO*
Jack Clark, *Business Mgr*
EMP: 50 **EST:** 1911
SALES (est): 10.6MM **Privately Held**
WEB: www.benjaminelectric.com
SIC: 3613 Panelboards & distribution boards, electric; switchgear & switchgear accessories

(P-8908)
WEST COAST SWITCHGEAR (HQ)
13837 Bettencourt St, Cerritos (90703-1009)
PHONE................562 802-3441
Alfred P Cisternelli, *CEO*
▲ **EMP:** 93 **EST:** 2003
SQ FT: 20,000
SALES (est): 18.4MM
SALES (corp-wide): 134.5MM **Privately Held**
WEB: www.westcoastswitchgear.com
SIC: 3613 5063 Power circuit breakers; switchgear
PA: Resa Power, Llc
　　8300 Cypress Pkwy Ste 225
　　Houston TX 77070
　　832 900-8340

3621 Motors & Generators

(P-8909)
BARTA-SCHOENEWALD INC (PA)
Also Called: Advanced Motion Controls
3805 Calle Tecate, Camarillo (93012-5068)
PHONE................805 389-1935
Sandor Barta, *President*
Daniel Schoenewald, *Exec VP*
Danny Leclair, *Info Tech Mgr*
Bradley Radomski, *Network Enginr*
Chris Fournier, *Project Mgr*
▲ **EMP:** 119 **EST:** 1986
SQ FT: 86,000
SALES (est): 34.7MM **Privately Held**
WEB: www.a-m-c.com
SIC: 3621 3699 Servomotors, electric; electrical equipment & supplies

(P-8910)
CALNETIX TECHNOLOGIES LLC (HQ)
16323 Shoemaker Ave, Cerritos (90703-2244)
PHONE................562 293-1660
Vatche Artinian, *Chairman*
Herman Artinian, *CEO*
Ian Hart, *CFO*
Pana Shenoy, *Vice Pres*
Andrea Matiauda, *Admin Sec*
EMP: 29 **EST:** 2011

SALES (est): 22MM
SALES (corp-wide): 113.4MM Privately Held
WEB: www.calnetix.com
SIC: 3621 Motors & generators
PA: Calnetix, Inc.
16323 Shoemaker Ave
Cerritos CA 90703
562 293-1660

(P-8911)
COLE INSTRUMENT CORP
2650 S Croddy Way, Santa Ana
(92704-5238)
P.O. Box 25063 (92799-5063)
PHONE..................714 556-3100
Ric Garcia, *President*
Manuel Garcia, *Exec VP*
Carolyn Calles, *Vice Pres*
Roshan Sarode, *Design Engr*
Alan Hotchkiss, *Controller*
EMP: 70 EST: 1965
SQ FT: 16,000
SALES (est): 14.1MM Privately Held
WEB: www.cole-switches.com
SIC: 3621 3679 Motors & generators;
electronic switches

(P-8912)
DIRECT DRIVE SYSTEMS INC
621 Burning Tree Rd, Fullerton
(92833-1448)
PHONE..................714 872-5500
James Pribble, *CEO*
Michael Slater, *COO*
Robert Clark, *CFO*
Daryl Kobayashi, *Engineer*
EMP: 57 EST: 2005
SALES (est): 11.3MM
SALES (corp-wide): 489.9MM Privately
Held
WEB: www.technipfmc.com
SIC: 3621 Electric motor & generator parts
HQ: Fmc Technologies, Inc.
11740 Katy Fwy Enrgy Twr
Houston TX 77079
281 591-4000

(P-8913)
GLENTEK INC
208 Standard St, El Segundo
(90245-3818)
PHONE..................310 322-3026
Richard Vasak, *CEO*
Helen Sysel, *CFO*
Helen Vasak, *Corp Secy*
Melton Vasak, *Vice Pres*
Bill Vasak, *Information Mgr*
◆ EMP: 84 EST: 1964
SQ FT: 105,000
SALES (est): 12.5MM Privately Held
WEB: www.glentek.com
SIC: 3621 Motors & generators

(P-8914)
GOHZ INC
23555 Golden Springs Dr K1, Diamond Bar
(91765-2176)
PHONE..................800 603-1219
Zhuge Fusheng, *President*
Sameh Gouda, *Manager*
EMP: 30
SQ FT: 1,200
SALES (est): 5.1MM Privately Held
WEB: www.gohz.com
SIC: 3621 Frequency converters (electric
generators)

(P-8915)
HEEGER INC
Also Called: Lmb Heeger
2431 Strozier Ave, South El Monte
(91733-2017)
PHONE..................323 728-5108
Robert Heeger, *President*
EMP: 13 EST: 1946
SALES (est): 1.7MM Privately Held
WEB: www.lmbheeger.com
SIC: 3621 3469 3444 Motors & genera-
tors; metal stampings; sheet metalwork

(P-8916)
HI PERFRMNCE ELC VHCL SYSTEMS
620 S Magnolia Ave Ste B, Ontario
(91762-4030)
PHONE..................909 923-1973
Brian Guy Seymour, *CEO*
Toni Seymour, *Treasurer*
▲ EMP: 26 EST: 2002
SQ FT: 9,000
SALES (est): 5.4MM Privately Held
WEB: www.hpevs.com
SIC: 3621 Motors, electric

(P-8917)
HITACHI AUTOMOTIVE SYSTEMS
Also Called: Los Angeles Plant
6200 Gateway Dr, Cypress (90630-4842)
PHONE..................310 212-0200
EMP: 100 Privately Held
SIC: 3621 3714 Mfg Motors/Generators
Mfg Motor Vehicle Parts/Accessories
HQ: Hitachi Automotive Systems Americas,
Inc.
955 Warwick Rd
Harrodsburg KY 40330
859 734-9451

(P-8918)
IMAGE MICRO SPARE PARTS INC
6301 Chalet Dr, Commerce (90040-3705)
PHONE..................562 776-9808
Hassan Mohrekesh, *President*
Brian Buhro, *Vice Pres*
Levy Antal, *VP Bus Dvlpt*
EMP: 30 EST: 2015
SQ FT: 17,000
SALES (est): 4.3MM Privately Held
WEB: www.imagemicro.com
SIC: 3621 Generating apparatus & parts,
electrical

(P-8919)
INTEGRATED MAGNETICS INC
11250 Playa Ct, Culver City (90230-6127)
PHONE..................310 391-7213
Anil Nanji, *President*
EMP: 40 EST: 2012
SQ FT: 120,000
SALES (est): 7.7MM
SALES (corp-wide): 49.8MM Privately
Held
WEB: www.intemag.com
SIC: 3621 3679 3764 Rotors, for motors;
servomotors, electric; cores, magnetic;
rocket motors, guided missiles
PA: Integrated Technologies Group, Inc.
11250 Playa Ct
Culver City CA 90230
310 391-7213

(P-8920)
KOLLMORGEN CORPORATION
33 S La Patera Ln, Santa Barbara
(93117-3214)
PHONE..................805 696-1236
David Cline, *Engineer*
Jenne Liu, *Buyer*
Veronica Santangelo, *Manager*
EMP: 53
SALES (corp-wide): 1.7B Publicly Held
WEB: www.kollmorgen.com
SIC: 3621 Servomotors, electric
HQ: Kollmorgen Corporation
203a W Rock Rd
Radford VA 24141
540 639-9045

(P-8921)
LEOCH BATTERY CORPORATION (HQ)
19751 Descartes Unit A, Foothill Ranch
(92610-2620)
PHONE..................949 588-5853
Hui Peng, *President*
Dianne Dickey, *VP Bus Dvlpt*
Christine Johnson, *Sales Staff*
Daniel Martinez, *Sales Staff*
John McGovern, *Sales Staff*
◆ EMP: 100 EST: 2003

SALES (est): 194.4MM Privately Held
WEB: www.leoch.us
SIC: 3621 Storage battery chargers, motor
& engine generator type

(P-8922)
MAGICALL INC
4550 Calle Alto, Camarillo (93012-8509)
P.O. Box 3730 (93011-3730)
PHONE..................805 484-4300
Joel Wacknov, *CEO*
Justin Delarge, *Engineer*
Vicki Clifford, *Purch Mgr*
▲ EMP: 19 EST: 2004
SALES (est): 3.3MM Privately Held
WEB: www.magicall.biz
SIC: 3621 3612 3677 3679 Motors &
generators; power transformers, electric;
electronic coils, transformers & other in-
ductors; static power supply converters
for electronic applications

(P-8923)
MC CULLY MAC M CORPORATION
Also Called: Mac M McCully Co
12012 Hertz Ave, Moorpark (93021-7130)
PHONE..................805 529-0661
Guy Mc Cully, *President*
Martha L McCully, *Corp Secy*
Dan Snyder, *Vice Pres*
EMP: 35 EST: 1979
SQ FT: 8,000
SALES (est): 3.3MM Privately Held
WEB: www.mccullycorp.com
SIC: 3621 Motors, electric

(P-8924)
MOTOR TECHNOLOGY INC
2301 Wardlow Cir, Corona (92878-5101)
PHONE..................951 270-6200
Robert Buchwalder, *President*
Phyllis Buchwalder, *Corp Secy*
George Teets, *Manager*
EMP: 59 EST: 1977
SQ FT: 12,600
SALES (est): 14.7MM
SALES (corp-wide): 773.2MM Publicly
Held
WEB: www.circoraerospace.com
SIC: 3621 Motors, electric
PA: Circor International, Inc.
30 Corporate Dr Ste 200
Burlington MA 01803
781 270-1200

(P-8925)
NANTENERGY LLC
2040 E Mariposa Ave, El Segundo
(90245-5027)
PHONE..................310 905-4866
William Schmidt,
EMP: 75 EST: 2019
SALES (est): 1.8MM Privately Held
SIC: 3621 8731 Storage battery chargers,
motor & engine generator type; energy re-
search

(P-8926)
RENCO ENCODERS INC
26 Coromar Dr, Goleta (93117-3094)
PHONE..................805 968-1525
Robert Setbacken, *President*
EMP: 393 EST: 1991
SQ FT: 33,000
SALES (est): 17.2MM
SALES (corp-wide): 72K Privately Held
WEB: www.heidenhain.com
SIC: 3621 3827 Rotary converters (electri-
cal equipment); optical instruments &
lenses
HQ: Heidenhain Holding Inc
333 E State Pkwy
Schaumburg IL 60173

(P-8927)
RESMED MOTOR TECHNOLOGIES INC
9540 De Soto Ave, Chatsworth
(91311-5010)
PHONE..................818 428-6400
David B Sears, *CEO*
Michael Fliss, *President*
David Sears, *Vice Pres*
Ashwin Trivedi, *CIO*

Aleksandr Nagorny, *Engineer*
▲ EMP: 170 EST: 2002
SQ FT: 35,000
SALES (est): 52.3MM Publicly Held
WEB: www.resmed.com
SIC: 3621 3714 3841 Coils, for electric
motors or generators; collector rings, for
electric motors or generators; propane
conversion equipment, motor vehicle; sur-
gical & medical instruments
PA: Resmed Inc.
9001 Spectrum Center Blvd
San Diego CA 92123

(P-8928)
REULAND ELECTRIC CO (PA)
17969 Railroad St, City of Industry
(91748-1192)
P.O. Box 1464, La Puente (91749-1464)
PHONE..................626 964-6411
Noel C Reuland, *President*
William Kramer III, *CFO*
Howard Lees, *Vice Pres*
Dick Blumer, *Info Tech Dir*
Jaime Lopez, *Project Mgr*
▲ EMP: 130 EST: 1937
SQ FT: 100,000
SALES (est): 35.6MM Privately Held
WEB: www.reulandfoundry.com
SIC: 3621 3566 3363 3625 Motors, elec-
tric; drives, high speed industrial, except
hydrostatic; aluminum die-castings; elec-
tric controls & control accessories, indus-
trial; fluid power motors

(P-8929)
SEA ELECTRIC LLC
436 Alaska Ave, Torrance (90503-3902)
PHONE..................424 376-3660
Darin Damron, *Regl Sales Mgr*
EMP: 21 EST: 2020
SALES (est): 6.1MM Privately Held
WEB: www.sea-electric.com
SIC: 3621 Motors & generators

(P-8930)
SKURKA AEROSPACE INC (DH)
4600 Calle Bolero, Camarillo (93012-8575)
P.O. Box 2869 (93011-2869)
PHONE..................805 484-8884
Michael Lisman, *CEO*
Lisa Sabol, *CFO*
Halle Terrion, *Admin Sec*
Victoria Alonzo, *Administration*
Loren Hesz, *IT/INT Sup*
EMP: 139 EST: 1950
SQ FT: 70,000
SALES (est): 45.7MM
SALES (corp-wide): 4.8B Publicly Held
WEB: www.skurka-aero.com
SIC: 3621 3679 Motors, electric; transduc-
ers, electrical

(P-8931)
SOUTH AMERICAN IMAGING INC
2360 Eastman Ave Ste 110, Oxnard
(93030-7287)
PHONE..................805 824-4036
Rogelio Zavala, *CEO*
EMP: 14 EST: 2009
SALES (est): 700.5K Privately Held
SIC: 3621 Electric motor & generator parts

(P-8932)
SPECIALTY MOTORS INC
28420 Witherspoon Pkwy, Valencia
(91355-4167)
PHONE..................800 232-2612
EMP: 14 EST: 2008
SALES (est): 5MM Privately Held
WEB: www.specialtymotors.com
SIC: 3621 Motors & generators

(P-8933)
THINGAP INC
4035 Via Pescador, Camarillo
(93012-5050)
PHONE..................805 477-9741
John Baumann, *CEO*
Sarah Gallagher, *President*
Len Wedman, *President*
Donnie Harris, *Project Engr*
Travis Kenney, *Prdtn Mgr*
EMP: 30

SALES (est): 2.5MM **Privately Held**
WEB: www.thingap.com
SIC: 3621 Coils, for electric motors or generators

(P-8934)
VALLEY POWER SERVICES INC
425 S Hacienda Blvd, City of Industry (91745-1123)
PHONE.............................909 969-9345
Clark Lee, *President*
▲ EMP: 24 EST: 1999
SQ FT: 17,802
SALES (est): 3.1MM **Privately Held**
WEB: www.valleypowersystems.com
SIC: 3621 Motor housings

(P-8935)
VIENTO FUNDING II LLC
18101 Von Karman Ave 1700a, Irvine (92612-1012)
PHONE.............................609 524-4500
EMP: 13 EST: 2008
SALES (est): 28.8MM **Publicly Held**
WEB: www.nrg.com
SIC: 3621 Windmills, electric generating
PA: Nrg Energy, Inc.
　　910 Louisiana St
　　Houston TX 77002

3624 Carbon & Graphite Prdts

(P-8936)
ALLIANCE SPACESYSTEMS LLC
4398 Corporate Center Dr, Los Alamitos (90720-2537)
PHONE.............................714 226-1400
Rick Byrens, *President*
David Kang, *Vice Pres*
Gilbert Kwok, *Program Mgr*
Anthony Kenniston, *General Mgr*
Thalia Diaz, *Admin Asst*
EMP: 155 EST: 1997
SQ FT: 101,000
SALES (est): 25MM
SALES (corp-wide): 189.2MM **Privately Held**
WEB: www.alliancespacesystems.com
SIC: 3624 Carbon & graphite products
PA: Applied Composites Holdings, Llc
　　25692 Atlantic Ocean Dr
　　Lake Forest CA 92630
　　949 716-3511

(P-8937)
FRONTERA SOLUTIONS INC
1913 E 17th St Ste 210, Santa Ana (92705-8627)
PHONE.............................714 368-1631
Earl B Johnson, *President*
John Drake, *CFO*
Ben Rawski, *Vice Pres*
EMP: 14 EST: 2001
SALES (est): 530K **Privately Held**
SIC: 3624 3231 Fibers, carbon & graphite; insulating glass: made from purchased glass

(P-8938)
KBR INC
Also Called: Electro-Tech Machining Div
2000 W Gaylord St, Long Beach (90813-1032)
P.O. Box 92610, Rochester NY (14692-0610)
PHONE.............................562 436-9281
Ryan McMahon, *President*
▲ EMP: 32 EST: 1977
SQ FT: 39,000
SALES (est): 6.3MM **Privately Held**
WEB: www.etmgraphite.com
SIC: 3624 Carbon & graphite products

(P-8939)
SPACESYSTEMS HOLDINGS LLC
4398 Corporate Center Dr, Los Alamitos (90720-2537)
PHONE.............................714 226-1400
Terence Lyons, *CEO*
Rick Byrens, *President*
Jeffrey David Lassiter, *CFO*

EMP: 13 EST: 2012
SQ FT: 101,000
SALES (est): 303.9K **Privately Held**
SIC: 3624 Carbon & graphite products

3625 Relays & Indl Controls

(P-8940)
A P SEEDORFF & COMPANY INC
Also Called: Seedorff Acme
1338 N Knollwood Cir, Anaheim (92801-1311)
PHONE.............................714 252-5330
Kurt Simon, *President*
Helmut Simon, *Treasurer*
Ernie Gasteiger, *Prdtn Mgr*
EMP: 15
SQ FT: 10,000
SALES (est): 3.9MM **Privately Held**
WEB: www.seedorffacme.com
SIC: 3625 Resistance welder controls

(P-8941)
ABSOLUTE GRAPHIC TECH USA INC
Also Called: Agt
235 Jason Ct, Corona (92879-6199)
PHONE.............................909 597-1133
Steven J Barberi, *President*
Karina Stoltz, *CFO*
Lou Barberi, *Vice Pres*
Nick Cruz, *Tech Recruiter*
Joanne Teegarden, *Purchasing*
EMP: 49 EST: 2006
SQ FT: 25,800
SALES (est): 9MM **Privately Held**
WEB: www.agt-usa.com
SIC: 3625 3577 Industrial electrical relays & switches; printers & plotters

(P-8942)
AMERICAN RELAYS INC
43 Gingerwood, Irvine (92603-0102)
PHONE.............................562 926-2837
Hyo Lee, *President*
Richard Lenning, *Vice Pres*
Rick Lenning, *Vice Pres*
EMP: 21 EST: 1978
SALES (est): 2.8MM **Privately Held**
WEB: www.americanrelays.com
SIC: 3625 Relays, for electronic use

(P-8943)
ANAHEIM AUTOMATION INC
4985 E Landon Dr, Anaheim (92807-1972)
PHONE.............................714 992-6990
Faithe Reimbold, *Vice Pres*
Nannette Israel, *CFO*
Alan Harmon, *General Mgr*
Joann Witt, *Admin Sec*
Bill Jones, *Webmaster*
◆ EMP: 47 EST: 1966
SQ FT: 9,000
SALES (est): 11.4MM **Privately Held**
WEB: www.anaheimautomation.com
SIC: 3625 3545 3566 Control equipment, electric; machine tool accessories; speed changers, drives & gears

(P-8944)
BALBOA WATER GROUP LLC (HQ)
Also Called: Controlmyspa
3030 Airway Ave Ste B, Costa Mesa (92626-6036)
PHONE.............................714 384-0384
David J Cline, *President*
Jean-Pierr Parent, *Senior VP*
◆ EMP: 287 EST: 2007
SALES (est): 106.5MM
SALES (corp-wide): 523MM **Publicly Held**
WEB: www.balboawater.com
SIC: 3625 3599 Electric controls & control accessories, industrial; machine shop, jobbing & repair
PA: Helios Technologies, Inc.
　　1500 W University Pkwy
　　Sarasota FL 34243
　　941 362-1200

(P-8945)
CALIFORNIA ECONOMIZER
Also Called: Zonex Systems
5622 Engineer Dr, Huntington Beach (92649-1124)
PHONE.............................714 898-9963
Jeff Osheroff, *President*
Trey West, *Manager*
▲ EMP: 50 EST: 1988
SQ FT: 16,000
SALES (est): 6MM **Privately Held**
WEB: www.zonexproducts.com
SIC: 3625 3822 Control equipment, electric; auto controls regulating residntl & coml environmt & applncs

(P-8946)
CONTROL SWITCHES INTL INC
2425 Mira Mar Ave, Long Beach (90815-1757)
P.O. Box 92349 (90809-2349)
PHONE.............................562 498-7331
Margerate Turner, *Exec VP*
Susan Moore, *CFO*
Susie Moore, *CFO*
Judith Steward, *Vice Pres*
Peggy Turner, *Vice Pres*
EMP: 25 EST: 1977
SQ FT: 10,000
SALES (est): 3.4MM
SALES (corp-wide): 12.3MM **Privately Held**
WEB: www.controlswitches.com
SIC: 3625 Switches, electronic applications
PA: Control Switches, Inc.
　　2425 Mira Mar Ave
　　Long Beach CA 90815
　　562 498-7331

(P-8947)
CUSTOM CONTROL SENSORS INC
21111 Plummer St, Chatsworth (91311-4905)
PHONE.............................818 341-4610
EMP: 25 EST: 2015
SALES (est): 306.2K **Privately Held**
WEB: www.ccsdualsnap.com
SIC: 3625 Relays & industrial controls

(P-8948)
DOW-KEY MICROWAVE CORPORATION
4822 Mcgrath St, Ventura (93003-7718)
PHONE.............................805 650-0260
David Wightman, *President*
EMP: 150 EST: 1970
SQ FT: 26,000
SALES (est): 28.8MM
SALES (corp-wide): 6.6B **Publicly Held**
WEB: www.dowkey.com
SIC: 3625 3678 3643 3613 Switches, electronic applications; electronic connectors; current-carrying wiring devices; switchgear & switchboard apparatus
PA: Dover Corporation
　　3005 Highland Pkwy # 200
　　Downers Grove IL 60515
　　630 541-1540

(P-8949)
EAGLE ACCESS CTRL SYSTEMS INC
12953 Foothill Blvd, Sylmar (91342-4929)
PHONE.............................818 837-7900
Yossi Afriat, *CEO*
Oren Afriat, *CFO*
AVI Afriat, *Vice Pres*
◆ EMP: 22 EST: 1996
SQ FT: 13,000
SALES (est): 8.8MM **Privately Held**
WEB: www.eagleoperators.com
SIC: 3625 Control equipment, electric

(P-8950)
EATON ELECTRICAL INC
13201 Dahlia St, Fontana (92337-6971)
PHONE.............................951 685-5788
EMP: 22 **Privately Held**
SIC: 3625 Motor controls & accessories
HQ: Eaton Electrical Inc.
　　1000 Cherrington Pkwy
　　Moon Township PA 15108

(P-8951)
EMBEDDED SYSTEMS INC
Also Called: Esi Motion
2250a Union Pl, Simi Valley (93065-1660)
PHONE.............................805 624-6030
Earnie Beem, *President*
Sheila D'Angelo, *Vice Pres*
Sheila Dangelo, *General Mgr*
Matthew Strickler, *Electrical Engi*
Robert Gannon, *Engineer*
EMP: 40 EST: 2005
SALES (est): 9.7MM **Privately Held**
WEB: www.esimotion.com
SIC: 3625 Motor starters & controllers, electric

(P-8952)
FIRE AND SAFETY ELEC INC
Also Called: Phase Research
3160 Pullman St, Costa Mesa (92626-3315)
PHONE.............................714 850-1320
John M Ludutsky, *President*
Thomas M Mitchell, *Chairman*
▼ EMP: 16 EST: 1982
SQ FT: 5,400
SALES (est): 1MM **Privately Held**
WEB: www.phaseresearch.com
SIC: 3625 3873 Timing devices, electronic; watches, clocks, watchcases & parts

(P-8953)
GIGAVAC LLC (HQ)
6382 Rose Ln, Carpinteria (93013-2922)
PHONE.............................805 684-8401
Rick Danchuk, *President*
Scott Hickman, *Vice Pres*
Murray McTigue, *Engineer*
Monica Navarro, *Buyer*
Rick Vargeson, *Buyer*
▲ EMP: 14 EST: 2002
SALES (est): 10.1MM
SALES (corp-wide): 3B **Privately Held**
WEB: www.gigavac.com
SIC: 3625 Relays, electric power

(P-8954)
H2W TECHNOLOGIES INC
26380 Ferry Ct, Santa Clarita (91350-2998)
PHONE.............................661 291-1620
Fred Wilson, *CEO*
Mark Wilson, *President*
Alexander Hinds, *Exec VP*
EMP: 16
SQ FT: 12,000
SALES (est): 5.2MM **Privately Held**
WEB: www.h2wtech.com
SIC: 3625 Relays & industrial controls

(P-8955)
HONGFA AMERICA INC
20381 Hermana Cir, Lake Forest (92630-8701)
PHONE.............................714 669-2888
Guo Manjin, *CEO*
▲ EMP: 22 EST: 2015
SALES (est): 8.6MM **Privately Held**
WEB: www.hongfa.com
SIC: 3625 6719 Electric controls & control accessories, industrial; investment holding companies, except banks
PA: Xiamen Hongfa Electroacoustic Co., Ltd.
　　No.91-101, Sunban South Road, Beibu Industrial Zone, Jimei Xiamen 36100

(P-8956)
I/O CONTROLS CORPORATION (PA)
1357 W Foothill Blvd, Azusa (91702-2853)
PHONE.............................626 812-5353
Jeffrey Ying, *President*
Renee Chen, *Treasurer*
Renee Hsiaspin Ying, *Vice Pres*
Michael Kuang, *VP Engr*
Scott Shellman, *Technical Staff*
▲ EMP: 63 EST: 1982
SALES (est): 11.7MM **Privately Held**
WEB: www.cloud.iocontrols.com
SIC: 3625 3621 Control equipment, electric; control equipment for buses or trucks, electric

(P-8957)
ITT CANNON LLC
56 Technology Dr, Irvine (92618-2301)
PHONE..................714 557-4700
Doria London, *CFO*
Shawn Swenson, *Officer*
Mary Beth Gustafsson, *Senior VP*
Philip Bordages, *Vice Pres*
John Capela, *Vice Pres*
EMP: 132 **EST:** 2011
SALES (est): 35.1MM
SALES (corp-wide): 2.4B **Publicly Held**
WEB: www.ittcannon.com
SIC: 3625 Control equipment, electric
HQ: Itt Industries Holdings, Inc
1133 Westchester Ave N-100
White Plains NY 10604
914 641-2000

(P-8958)
ITT LLC
ITT Goulds Pumps
3951 Capitol Ave, City of Industry
(90601-1734)
P.O. Box 1254, La Puente (91749-1254)
PHONE..................562 908-4144
Shashank Patel, *General Mgr*
Tracey Featherly, *Project Mgr*
Todd Gerstenberger, *Facilities Mgr*
Karen Larue, *Director*
EMP: 75
SQ FT: 85,000
SALES (corp-wide): 2.4B **Publicly Held**
WEB: www.itt.com
SIC: 3625 Control equipment, electric
HQ: Itt Llc
1133 Westchester Ave N-100
White Plains NY 10604
914 641-2000

(P-8959)
M W SAUSSE & CO INC (PA)
Also Called: Vibrex
28744 Witherspoon Pkwy, Valencia
(91355-5425)
PHONE..................661 257-3311
Torbjorn Helland, *President*
Paul Azevedo, *Vice Pres*
Gregory Hall, *Vice Pres*
Dan Robinson, *Vice Pres*
▲ **EMP:** 59 **EST:** 1961
SQ FT: 12,000
SALES (est): 9.5MM **Privately Held**
WEB: www.vibrex.net
SIC: 3625 Control equipment, electric

(P-8960)
MICROSEMI CORP-POWER MGT GROUP
11861 Western Ave, Garden Grove
(92841-2119)
PHONE..................714 994-6500
James J Peterson, *President*
John W Hohener, *CFO*
Rob Warren, *Vice Pres*
David Goren, *Asst Sec*
EMP: 249 **EST:** 1977
SQ FT: 135,000
SALES (est): 27.3MM
SALES (corp-wide): 5.4B **Publicly Held**
WEB: www.microsemi.com
SIC: 3625 3677 3679 3613 Relays, for electronic use; electronic transformers; liquid crystal displays (LCD); switchgear & switchboard apparatus; transformers, except electric; computer peripheral equipment
HQ: Microsemi Corp.-Power Management Group Holding
11861 Western Ave
Garden Grove CA 92841
714 994-6500

(P-8961)
MOOG INC
Also Called: Moog Jon Street Warehouse
1218 W Jon St, Torrance (90502-1208)
PHONE..................310 533-1178
Alberto Bilalon, *Manager*
John P Yu, *Engineer*
Nick Ioppolo, *Manager*
EMP: 500

SALES (corp-wide): 2.8B **Publicly Held**
WEB: www.moog.com
SIC: 3625 8711 3812 Relays & industrial controls; aviation &/or aeronautical engineering; aircraft/aerospace flight instruments & guidance systems
PA: Moog Inc.
400 Jamison Rd
Elma NY 14059
716 652-2000

(P-8962)
SILVERON INDUSTRIES INC
182 S Brent Cir, City of Industry
(91789-3050)
PHONE..................909 598-4533
Steve Lee, *President*
Jae Lee, *Business Mgr*
Sam Kwon, *Purchasing*
Brad Yi, *Purchasing*
Eddy Kim, *Sales Staff*
▲ **EMP:** 16 **EST:** 1977
SQ FT: 24,000
SALES (est): 3MM **Privately Held**
SIC: 3625 5065 Industrial controls: push button, selector switches, pilot; electronic parts

(P-8963)
SPECIALTY CONCEPTS INC
2393 Teller Rd Ste 106, Newbury Park
(91320-6092)
PHONE..................818 998-5238
Terry Staler, *President*
EMP: 13 **EST:** 1981
SQ FT: 7,200
SALES (est): 2.8MM **Privately Held**
WEB: www.specialtyconcepts.com
SIC: 3625 Relays & industrial controls

(P-8964)
SYSTEM TECHNICAL SUPPORT CORP
960 Knox St Bldg B, Torrance
(90502-1086)
PHONE..................310 845-9400
Eric Leskly, *President*
▲ **EMP:** 20 **EST:** 1996
SQ FT: 10,000
SALES (est): 5.2MM **Privately Held**
WEB: www.systemtechnical.com
SIC: 3625 Relays & industrial controls

(P-8965)
UNIVERSAL CTRL SOLUTIONS CORP
Also Called: Dnf Controls
19770 Bahama St, Northridge
(91324-3303)
PHONE..................818 898-3380
Daniel Fogel, *CEO*
Rochelle Perito, *General Mgr*
Dan Fogel, *CTO*
Mark Kozlen, *Prgrmr*
Kent Stork, *Engineer*
▲ **EMP:** 15 **EST:** 1990
SALES (est): 4.5MM
SALES (corp-wide): 8.7MM **Privately Held**
WEB: www.dnfcontrols.com
SIC: 3625 Control equipment, electric
HQ: Tsl Professional Products Ltd.
Unit 1-2
Marlow BUCKS SL7 1
162 856-4610

(P-8966)
VISHAY TECHNO COMPONENTS LLC
Also Called: Vishay Spectro
4051 Greystone Dr, Ontario (91761-3100)
PHONE..................909 923-3313
Felix Zandman PHD, *President*
Robert A Freece, *Vice Pres*
William J Spiers, *Admin Sec*
▲ **EMP:** 134 **EST:** 1961
SQ FT: 30,000
SALES (est): 15.2MM
SALES (corp-wide): 2.5B **Publicly Held**
WEB: www.vishay.com
SIC: 3625 Resistors & resistor units
HQ: Vishay Dale Electronics, Llc
1122 23rd St
Columbus NE 68601
605 665-9301

(P-8967)
WOODWARD HRT INC (HQ)
25200 Rye Canyon Rd, Santa Clarita
(91355-1204)
PHONE..................661 294-6000
Thomas A Gendron, *CEO*
Martin V Glass, *President*
Lisa Tanner, *Vice Pres*
Shirl Pope, *Administration*
Louis Carrizales, *IT/INT Sup*
▲ **EMP:** 650 **EST:** 1954
SQ FT: 200,000
SALES (est): 224.8MM
SALES (corp-wide): 2.5B **Publicly Held**
WEB: www.woodward.com
SIC: 3625 3492 Actuators, industrial; electrohydraulic servo valves, metal
PA: Woodward, Inc.
1081 Woodward Way
Fort Collins CO 80524
970 482-5811

(P-8968)
ZBE INC
1035 Cindy Ln, Carpinteria (93013-2905)
PHONE..................805 576-1600
Zac Bogart, *President*
Rod Martinez, *Engineer*
Tim Sexton, *Sales Executive*
Tony Baker, *Marketing Staff*
Thomas Coniglio, *Manager*
▲ **EMP:** 45
SQ FT: 7,500
SALES (est): 7.5MM **Privately Held**
WEB: www.zbe.com
SIC: 3625 3861 3577 Electric controls & control accessories, industrial; photographic equipment & supplies; computer peripheral equipment

(P-8969)
ZMP AQUISITION CORPORATION
Also Called: Adams Rite Aerospace
4141 N Palm St, Fullerton (92835-1025)
PHONE..................714 278-6500
Charles Collins, *President*
EMP: 14 **EST:** 1986
SQ FT: 100,000
SALES (est): 308.7K **Privately Held**
WEB: www.adamsriteaerospace.org
SIC: 3625 3743 3728 3429 Electric controls & control accessories, industrial; railroad locomotives & parts, electric or nonelectric; aircraft parts & equipment; aircraft hardware

3629 Electrical Indl Apparatus, NEC

(P-8970)
ADVANCED CHARGING TECH INC
Also Called: A C T
17260 Newhope St, Fountain Valley
(92708-4210)
PHONE..................877 228-5922
Robert J Istwan, *President*
Tom Quinn, *Partner*
Anthony Capalino, *Admin Sec*
Nasser Kutkut, *CTO*
Gregg Heimendinger, *Sales Staff*
▲ **EMP:** 21 **EST:** 2008
SALES (est): 14MM **Privately Held**
WEB: www.act-chargers.com
SIC: 3629 3691 Battery chargers, rectifying or nonrotating; alkaline cell storage batteries

(P-8971)
AVEOX INC
2265 Ward Ave Ste A, Simi Valley
(93065-1864)
PHONE..................805 915-0200
David Palombo, *President*
Robin Loboda, *VP Human Res*
Krista Precourt, *Opers Staff*
Brian Dumlao, *Production*
Brian Davies, *Manager*
▲ **EMP:** 35 **EST:** 1992
SQ FT: 22,000

SALES (est): 21.4MM **Privately Held**
WEB: www.aveox.com
SIC: 3629 Electronic generation equipment

(P-8972)
CAPAX TECHNOLOGIES INC
24842 Avenue Tibbitts, Valencia
(91355-3404)
PHONE..................661 257-7666
Jagdish Patel, *President*
Nina Patel, *Corp Secy*
Hiran Patel, *Vice Pres*
Kira Patel, *VP Mktg*
EMP: 28 **EST:** 1988
SQ FT: 17,000
SALES (est): 2.6MM **Privately Held**
WEB: www.capaxtechnologies.com
SIC: 3629 3675 Capacitors, fixed or variable; electronic capacitors

(P-8973)
CHARGETEK INC
409 Calle San Pablo # 104, Camarillo
(93012-8565)
PHONE..................805 444-7792
Louis C Josephs, *President*
Terri Shackelford, *Sales Staff*
▲ **EMP:** 16 **EST:** 1996
SALES (est): 2.7MM **Privately Held**
WEB: www.chargetek.com
SIC: 3629 3679 3677 Battery chargers, rectifying or nonrotating; static power supply converters for electronic applications; transformers power supply, electronic type

(P-8974)
CONCURRENT HOLDINGS LLC
11150 Santa Monica Blvd # 8, Los Angeles
(90025-3380)
PHONE..................310 473-3065
Benjamin Teno, *Mng Member*
Edwin Negron-Carballo,
▲ **EMP:** 750 **EST:** 2012
SALES (est): 53.9MM
SALES (corp-wide): 96.2MM **Privately Held**
WEB: www.balmoralfunds.com
SIC: 3629 3679 Electronic generation equipment; harness assemblies for electronic use: wire or cable
PA: Balmoral Funds Llc
11150 Santa Monica Blvd
Los Angeles CA 90025
310 473-3065

(P-8975)
ENGINEERED MAGNETICS INC
Also Called: Aap Division
10524 S La Cienega Blvd, Inglewood
(90304-1116)
PHONE..................310 649-9000
Josh Shachar, *Ch of Bd*
Kathy Tran, *President*
Tony Truong, *Project Mgr*
Isabella Yi Sha LI, *Director*
Maya Vu, *Director*
EMP: 26 **EST:** 2000
SQ FT: 57,000
SALES (est): 6MM **Privately Held**
WEB: www.engineeredmagnetics.net
SIC: 3629 3812 3369 Power conversion units, a.c. to d.c.: static-electric; missile guidance systems & equipment; aerospace castings, nonferrous: except aluminum

(P-8976)
IAMPLUS LLC
809 N Cahuenga Blvd, Los Angeles
(90038-3703)
PHONE..................323 210-3852
Phil Molyneux, *President*
Rosemary Peschken, *CFO*
Will Adams, *Founder*
Chandrasekar Rathakrishnan, *Director*
EMP: 56 **EST:** 2012
SQ FT: 3,900
SALES (est): 4.8MM
SALES (corp-wide): 10.9MM **Privately Held**
WEB: www.iamplus.services
SIC: 3629 Electronic generation equipment

PA: I.Am.Plus Electronics, Inc.
809 N Cahuenga Blvd
Los Angeles CA 90038
323 210-3852

(P-8977)
INNOTEC GROUP INC
61 Moreland Rd, Simi Valley (93065-1662)
PHONE.................................616 772-5959
J Fredrick Cox, *President*
EMP: 14 EST: 1993
SALES (est): 374.7K **Privately Held**
WEB: www.innotecgroup.com
SIC: 5722 3629 Vacuum cleaners; power conversion units, a.c. to d.c.: static-electric

(P-8978)
INTERCONNECT SOLUTIONS CO LLC (PA)
17595 Mount Herrmann St, Fountain Valley (92708-4160)
PHONE.................................909 545-6140
Michael Engler, *CEO*
▲ EMP: 70 EST: 2018
SQ FT: 15,000
SALES (est): 24.3MM **Privately Held**
WEB: www.interconnectsolutions.com
SIC: 3629 Electronic generation equipment

(P-8979)
OHSUNG DISPLAY USA INC (HQ)
203 S Waterman Ave, El Centro (92243-2228)
PHONE.................................760 482-5788
Byunghee Jung, *CEO*
EMP: 30 EST: 2013
SALES: 13.7MM **Privately Held**
WEB: www.ohsungdp.com
SIC: 3629 Electronic generation equipment

(P-8980)
Q C M INC
Also Called: Veris Manufacturing
285 Gemini Ave, Brea (92821-3704)
PHONE.................................714 414-1173
Jay Cadler, *CEO*
Larry Ching, *Vice Pres*
Carlos Martinez, *Program Mgr*
Vicki Nguyen, *Program Mgr*
Bill McIlvene, *General Mgr*
▲ EMP: 45 EST: 2006
SALES (est): 20.6MM
SALES (corp-wide): 84.8MM **Privately Held**
WEB: www.verismfg.com
SIC: 3629 Electronic generation equipment
PA: Megatronics Us Ultimate Holdco Llc
32 Northwestern Dr
Salem NH 03079
603 499-4300

(P-8981)
ROI DEVELOPMENT CORP
Also Called: Newmar
15272 Newsboy Cir, Huntington Beach (92649-1202)
PHONE.................................714 751-0488
James Kaplan, *CTO*
EMP: 24
SALES (corp-wide): 10.8MM **Privately Held**
WEB: www.newmarpower.com
SIC: 3629 Battery chargers, rectifying or nonrotating
PA: Roi Development Corp.
2911 W Garry Ave
Santa Ana CA 92704
714 751-0488

(P-8982)
SCOTT ENGINEERING INC
5051 Edison Ave, Chino (91710-5716)
PHONE.................................909 594-9637
Luis Ernesto Lujan, *CEO*
Deborah N Davis, *CEO*
Jason J Huitrado, *CFO*
Mary Muro, *Accountant*
Paul Sapien, *Senior Buyer*
▲ EMP: 50 EST: 1967
SQ FT: 102,660

SALES (est): 16.3MM **Privately Held**
WEB: www.scott-eng.com
SIC: 3629 3613 Electronic generation equipment; switchgear & switchboard apparatus

(P-8983)
SKYWORKS SOLUTIONS INC
1767 Carr Rd Ste 105, Calexico (92231-9506)
PHONE.................................301 874-6408
David J Aldrich, *Branch Mgr*
Carlos Bori, *Vice Pres*
Ramon Cibrian, *Engineer*
Jesse Mercer, *Maintence Staff*
▲ EMP: 18
SALES (corp-wide): 3.3B **Publicly Held**
WEB: www.skyworksinc.com
SIC: 3629 Capacitors & condensers
PA: Skyworks Solutions, Inc.
5260 California Ave
Irvine CA 92617
949 231-3000

(P-8984)
XANTREX LLC (HQ)
15272 Newsboy Cir, Huntington Beach (92649-1202)
PHONE.................................800 241-3897
Bruce Maccallum, *Mng Member*
John Kalbfleisch, *Vice Pres*
EMP: 100 EST: 2018
SALES (est): 51.7MM
SALES (corp-wide): 90.2MM **Privately Held**
WEB: www.mission-critical-electronics.com
SIC: 3629 Inverters, nonrotating: electrical
PA: Mission Critical Electronics Llc
15272 Newsboy Cir
Huntington Beach CA 92649
714 751-0488

(P-8985)
YUTAKA ELECTRIC INTL INC
Also Called: Falcon Electric
5116 Azusa Canyon Rd, Baldwin Park (91706-1846)
PHONE.................................626 962-7770
Arthur Seredian, *President*
Jitsuo Mase, *Vice Pres*
▲ EMP: 17 EST: 1988
SQ FT: 10,000
SALES (est): 552.2K **Privately Held**
WEB: www.falconups.com
SIC: 3629 3612 Power conversion units, a.c. to d.c.: static-electric; power & distribution transformers

(P-8986)
ZPOWER LLC
4765 Calle Quetzal, Camarillo (93012-8546)
PHONE.................................805 445-7789
Ross E Dueber,
Herbert V Weigel II, *COO*
Dennis Dugan, *CFO*
Dennis J Dugan, *Vice Pres*
Barry A Freeman, *Vice Pres*
EMP: 210 EST: 1996
SALES (est): 56.9MM **Privately Held**
WEB: www.zpowerbattery.com
SIC: 3629 Battery chargers, rectifying or nonrotating

3631 Household Cooking Eqpt

(P-8987)
CAPTIVATE BRANDS USA INC
25541 Arctic Ocean Dr, Lake Forest (92630-8827)
PHONE.................................949 229-8927
Alan Taylor, *CEO*
EMP: 15 EST: 2018
SALES (est): 1MM **Privately Held**
SIC: 3631 Barbecues, grills & braziers (outdoor cooking)

(P-8988)
DACOR (DH)
14425 Clark Ave, City of Industry (91745-1235)
PHONE.................................626 799-1000
Stanley Michael Joseph, *Ch of Bd*

Steve Joseph, *President*
Charles J Huebner, *CEO*
Anthony B Joseph III, *Principal*
Peter Steuernagel, *Managing Dir*
◆ EMP: 100 EST: 1965
SQ FT: 40,000
SALES (est): 91.4MM **Privately Held**
WEB: www.dacor.com
SIC: 5719 3631 Kitchenware; convection ovens, including portable: household
HQ: Samsung Electronics America, Inc.
85 Challenger Rd
Ridgefield Park NJ 07660
201 229-4000

(P-8989)
DSP WINNER INC
1641 W Main St Ste 222, Alhambra (91801-1900)
PHONE.................................858 336-9471
Jinsong Zou, *President*
EMP: 15 EST: 2020
SALES (est): 587.6K **Privately Held**
SIC: 3631 Household cooking equipment

(P-8990)
DURO CORPORATION
Also Called: Nexrange Industries
17018 Evergreen Pl, City of Industry (91745-1819)
PHONE.................................626 839-6541
Saban Chang, *President*
Grace Cho,
▲ EMP: 15 EST: 2003
SQ FT: 10,000
SALES (est): 2.7MM **Privately Held**
WEB: www.nxrv1.azurewebsites.net
SIC: 3631 Gas ranges, domestic

(P-8991)
JADE RANGE LLC
Also Called: Jade Products
2650 Orbiter St, Brea (92821-6265)
PHONE.................................714 961-2400
Timothy J Fitzgerald, *CFO*
Rio Giardinieri, *President*
Martin M Lindsay, *Treasurer*
Deanna Cook, *Administration*
Armando Rodriguez, *Technical Staff*
▲ EMP: 120 EST: 1998
SALES (est): 31.5MM
SALES (corp-wide): 2.5B **Publicly Held**
WEB: www.jaderange.com
SIC: 3631 3589 Household cooking equipment; commercial cooking & foodwarming equipment
PA: The Middleby Corporation
1400 Toastmaster Dr
Elgin IL 60120
847 741-3300

(P-8992)
MAGMA PRODUCTS LLC
3940 Pixie Ave, Lakewood (90712-4136)
PHONE.................................562 627-0500
Jerry Mashburn, *COO*
Greg Schicora, *Vice Pres*
Gordon Andresen, *Info Tech Mgr*
Julio Ayala, *Purch Mgr*
James Mashburn, *Purchasing*
◆ EMP: 70 EST: 1976
SQ FT: 22,000
SALES (est): 9.7MM **Privately Held**
WEB: www.magmaproducts.com
SIC: 3631 3634 Barbecues, grills & braziers (outdoor cooking); griddles or grills, electric: household

(P-8993)
PACIFIC COAST MFG INC
5270 Edison Ave, Chino (91710-5719)
PHONE.................................909 627-7040
Bruce Doran, *President*
James Poremba, *Vice Pres*
▲ EMP: 72 EST: 2011
SQ FT: 40,000 **Privately Held**
WEB: www.pcmbbq.com
SIC: 3631 Barbecues, grills & braziers (outdoor cooking)

(P-8994)
ROYAL RANGE CALIFORNIA INC
Also Called: Royal Industries
3245 Corridor Dr, Eastvale (91752-1030)
PHONE.................................951 360-1600

L Vasan, *CEO*
Patricia Woods, *Vice Pres*
▼ EMP: 65 EST: 1995
SQ FT: 52,000
SALES (est): 9.4MM **Privately Held**
WEB: www.royalranges.com
SIC: 3631 Household cooking equipment

(P-8995)
SUPERIOR EQUIPMENT SOLUTIONS
1085 Bixby Dr, Hacienda Heights (91745-1704)
PHONE.................................323 722-7900
Jeffrey Bernstein, *CEO*
Edwin Hovsepian, *CFO*
Stephan Bernstein, *Principal*
Adrian Crisci, *Engineer*
Neil Silcock, *Engineer*
▲ EMP: 60 EST: 2001
SQ FT: 45,000
SALES (est): 750MM **Privately Held**
WEB: www.alfrescogrills.com
SIC: 3631 5046 Household cooking equipment; restaurant equipment & supplies

(P-8996)
TWIN EAGLES INC
13259 166th St, Cerritos (90703-2203)
PHONE.................................562 802-3488
Dante L Cantal, *President*
Epifania Cantal, *Vice Pres*
▲ EMP: 101 EST: 1999
SQ FT: 45,000
SALES (est): 26.9MM
SALES (corp-wide): 1.8B **Privately Held**
WEB: www.twineaglesgrills.com
SIC: 3631 Barbecues, grills & braziers (outdoor cooking)
HQ: Dometic Corporation
5600 N River Rd Ste 250
Rosemont IL 60018

3632 Household Refrigerators & Freezers

(P-8997)
CHINA MFG SOLUTIONS USA LLC (PA)
5199 E Pacific Coast Hwy, Long Beach (90804-3309)
PHONE.................................562 537-8788
Steve Farajian, *President*
EMP: 51 EST: 2009
SALES (est): 701.7K **Privately Held**
SIC: 3632 Household refrigerators & freezers

(P-8998)
REFRIDERATOR MANUFACTERS LLC
17018 Edwards Rd, Cerritos (90703-2422)
PHONE.................................562 229-0500
Tony Bedi,
EMP: 42 EST: 2014
SQ FT: 40,000
SALES (est): 10MM **Privately Held**
SIC: 3632 Freezers, home & farm

(P-8999)
REFRIGERATOR MANUFACTERS INC (PA)
Also Called: Econocold Refrigerators
17018 Edwards Rd, Cerritos (90703-2422)
PHONE.................................562 926-2006
Lawrence E Jaffe, *President*
Paula Donohoo, *President*
Russell E Anthony, *Exec VP*
Leo R Lewis, *Exec VP*
EMP: 20 EST: 1945
SQ FT: 40,000
SALES (est): 3.9MM **Privately Held**
WEB: www.rmi-econocold.com
SIC: 3632 3585 Household refrigerators & freezers; refrigeration & heating equipment

3634 Electric Household Appliances

(P-9000)
BRANDS REPUBLIC INC
10333 Rush St, South El Monte
(91733-3341)
PHONE..............................302 401-1195
EMP: 50
SALES (est): 1.6MM **Privately Held**
SIC: 3634 Electric housewares & fans

(P-9001)
CAPITAL BRANDS DIST LLC (PA)
11601 Wilshire Blvd # 360, Los Angeles
(90025-1700)
PHONE..............................310 996-7200
Richard Krause, *Mng Member*
Lenny Sands,
EMP: 62 EST: 2015
SALES (est): 65.1MM **Privately Held**
WEB: www.capitalbrands.com
SIC: 3634 Blenders, electric

(P-9002)
COSMO PRODUCTS LLC
5431 Brooks St, Montclair (91763-4563)
PHONE..............................888 784-3108
Steven Law, *Mng Member*
▲ EMP: 30 EST: 2014
SALES (est): 2.5MM **Privately Held**
WEB: www.cosmoappliances.com
SIC: 3634 Electric household cooking appliances

(P-9003)
CRYOGENIC INDUSTRIES INC
25720 Jefferson Ave, Murrieta
(92562-6929)
PHONE..............................951 677-2060
Peter Wagner, *CEO*
EMP: 200 EST: 2016
SALES (est): 16.6MM **Privately Held**
WEB: www.nikkisoceig.com
SIC: 3634 Vaporizers, electric: household

(P-9004)
ESMART MASSAGE INC
339 N Berry St, Brea (92821-3140)
PHONE..............................657 341-0360
Demitry Pevzner, *Vice Pres*
EMP: 15 EST: 2017
SALES (est): 1MM **Privately Held**
SIC: 3634 Massage machines, electric, except for beauty/barber shops

(P-9005)
FOLDIMATE INC
879 White Pine Ct, Oak Park (91377-4769)
PHONE..............................805 876-4418
Gal Rozov, *CEO*
Ori Kaplan, *COO*
EMP: 22 EST: 2012
SALES (est): 1.8MM **Privately Held**
WEB: www.foldimate.com
SIC: 3634 Personal electrical appliances

(P-9006)
INSEAT SOLUTIONS LLC
1871 Wright Ave, La Verne (91750-5817)
PHONE..............................562 447-1780
Arthur Liu,
Dickson Liu,
▲ EMP: 22 EST: 2000
SALES (est): 4.2MM **Privately Held**
WEB: www.relaxor.com
SIC: 3634 Massage machines, electric, except for beauty/barber shops

(P-9007)
KIZURE PRODUCT CO INC
Also Called: Kizure Hair Products & Irons
1950 N Central Ave, Compton
(90222-3102)
P.O. Box 2556, Gardena (90247-0120)
PHONE..............................310 604-0058
EMP: 33
SQ FT: 40,000
SALES (est): 2.3MM **Privately Held**
SIC: 3634 2844 Mfg Hair Products

(P-9008)
LUMA COMFORT LLC
6600 Katella Ave, Cypress (90630-5104)
PHONE..............................855 963-9247
Luke Peters, *President*
Mariella Peters, *Admin Sec*
Alwyn Liu, *Controller*
Adam Hart, *Marketing Staff*
▲ EMP: 50 EST: 2011
SQ FT: 30,000
SALES (est): 9.1MM **Privately Held**
SIC: 3634 Electric housewares & fans

(P-9009)
MJC AMERICA LTD (PA)
Also Called: Soleus International
20035 E Walnut Dr N, Walnut
(91789-2922)
P.O. Box 1507 (91788-1507)
PHONE..............................888 876-5387
Simon Chu, *CEO*
Teresa Kamiya, *Vice Pres*
◆ EMP: 35 EST: 1998
SQ FT: 100,000
SALES (est): 5.5MM **Privately Held**
WEB: www.soleusair.com
SIC: 3634 Electric housewares & fans

(P-9010)
PACIFIC ACCENT INCORPORATED
623 S Doubleday Ave, Ontario
(91761-1520)
PHONE..............................909 563-1600
Sophia Juang, *CEO*
▲ EMP: 14 EST: 2010
SQ FT: 600
SALES (est): 4MM **Privately Held**
SIC: 3634 Housewares, excluding cooking appliances & utensils

(P-9011)
SAMVCO
Also Called: Sam Israel Viner
14016 Bora Bora Way, Marina Del Rey
(90292-6889)
PHONE..............................310 980-5680
Sam Israel Viner, *Owner*
▲ EMP: 15 EST: 1982
SQ FT: 3,500
SALES (est): 1MM **Privately Held**
WEB: www.samvco.com
SIC: 3634 3714 Electric household cooking appliances; motor vehicle parts & accessories

(P-9012)
SWISS PARK BANQUET CENTER
Also Called: Disposable Chafing Equipment
1905 Workman Mill Rd, Whittier
(90601-1457)
PHONE..............................562 699-1525
Hugo Hunziker, *Owner*
EMP: 14 EST: 1978
SQ FT: 2,500
SALES (est): 1MM **Privately Held**
WEB: www.swisspark.com
SIC: 5812 3634 Caterers; chafing dishes, electric

3639 Household Appliances, NEC

(P-9013)
BRENTWOOD APPLIANCES INC
Also Called: Import
3088 E 46th St, Vernon (90058-2422)
PHONE..............................323 266-4600
Poorad B Panahi, *President*
Maurice Araghi, *Vice Pres*
John Yadgari, *Vice Pres*
◆ EMP: 36 EST: 2009
SQ FT: 65,000
SALES (est): 4.6MM **Privately Held**
WEB: www.brentwoodus.com
SIC: 3639 Major kitchen appliances, except refrigerators & stoves

(P-9014)
FISHER & PAYKEL APPLIANCES INC (DH)
695 Town Center Dr # 180, Costa Mesa
(92626-1902)
PHONE..............................949 790-8900
Peter Lockwell, *President*
Robert Hanna, *Principal*
Johnny Imperial, *Regional Mgr*
Kevin Wilson, *Opers Staff*
Dara Reiter, *Marketing Staff*
◆ EMP: 140 EST: 1996
SQ FT: 26,000
SALES (est): 52.1MM **Privately Held**
WEB: www.fisherpaykel.com
SIC: 3639 3631 5064 5078 Dishwashing machines, household; household cooking equipment; electric household appliances; refrigeration equipment & supplies

(P-9015)
HESTAN COMMERCIAL CORPORATION
3375 E La Palma Ave, Anaheim
(92806-2815)
PHONE..............................714 869-2380
Stanley Kin Sui Cheng, *CEO*
Eric Deng, *President*
Yvonne Juarez, *Vice Pres*
Richard Zirges, *Vice Pres*
John Van Den Nieuwen, *Managing Dir*
▲ EMP: 125 EST: 2013
SQ FT: 70,000
SALES (est): 22.4MM **Privately Held**
WEB: www.commercial.hestan.com
SIC: 3639 Major household appliances, except refrigerators & stoves
HQ: Meyer Corporation, U.S.
     1 Meyer Plz
     Vallejo CA 94590
     707 551-2800

(P-9016)
TAKAGI-AO SMITH T W H CO LLC
5 Whatney, Irvine (92618-2806)
PHONE..............................949 770-7171
Koji Matsumura, *Vice Pres*
EMP: 13 EST: 2010
SALES (est): 192.9K **Privately Held**
WEB: www.hotwater.com
SIC: 3639 Hot water heaters, household

(P-9017)
THERMA-TEK RANGE CORP
9121 Atlanta Ave Ste 331, Huntington
Beach (92646-6309)
PHONE..............................570 455-9491
EMP: 25
SQ FT: 30,000
SALES (est): 3.1MM **Privately Held**
SIC: 3639 Mfg Household Appliances

3641 Electric Lamps

(P-9018)
BHK INC
760 E Sunkist St, Ontario (91761-1861)
PHONE..............................909 983-2973
Steve Boland, *President*
Lyle Brady, *Engineer*
Walter Chapman, *Engineer*
Suzie Garcia, *Sales Staff*
▲ EMP: 14 EST: 2008
SALES (est): 1.3MM **Privately Held**
WEB: www.bhkinc.com
SIC: 3641 Health lamps, infrared or ultraviolet

(P-9019)
DASOL INC
Also Called: Coronet Lighting
16210 S Avalon Blvd, Gardena
(90248-2908)
P.O. Box 2065 (90247-0010)
PHONE..............................310 327-6700
Sol Smith, *Ch of Bd*
David Smith, *President*
Mark Smith, *Vice Pres*
Jim Bindman, *Executive*
Patt Peterson, *Executive*
◆ EMP: 225 EST: 1944
SQ FT: 120,000

SALES (est): 13.4MM **Privately Held**
SIC: 3641 Electric lamps & parts for generalized applications

(P-9020)
HOLLYWOOD LAMP & SHADE CO
Also Called: Kimberly Lighting
2928 Leonis Blvd, Vernon (90058-2916)
PHONE..............................323 585-3999
Fred Nadal, *President*
EMP: 23 EST: 1963
SALES (est): 2.1MM **Privately Held**
WEB: www.hollywoodlampandshade.com
SIC: 3641 3648 3645 Lamps, fluorescent, electric; lamps, incandescent filament, electric; lighting equipment; lamp shades, metal

(P-9021)
IWORKS US INC
2501 S Malt Ave, Commerce (90040-3203)
PHONE..............................323 278-8363
Eric Dortch, *CEO*
Karla Bretado, *Project Mgr*
Lisa Dortch, *Opers Staff*
◆ EMP: 53 EST: 1988
SQ FT: 35,000
SALES (est): 10.1MM **Privately Held**
WEB: www.iworksus.com
SIC: 3641 Electric lamps & parts for generalized applications

(P-9022)
LITEPANELS INC
20600 Plummer St, Chatsworth
(91311-5111)
PHONE..............................818 752-7009
Rudy Pohlert, *President*
Victor Chen, *Engineer*
Byron Brown, *Manager*
▲ EMP: 29 EST: 2008
SALES (est): 4.9MM
SALES (corp-wide): 386.3MM **Privately Held**
WEB: www.litepanels.com
SIC: 3641 Electric lamps
HQ: Vitec Group Holdings Limited
     Bridge House
     Richmond TW9 1
     208 332-4600

(P-9023)
RADIANCE LIGHTWORKS INC
4607 Lkview Cyn Rd Ste 50, Westlake Village (91361)
PHONE..............................818 879-1516
Clayton Alexander, *Administration*
EMP: 13 EST: 2016
SALES (est): 1.1MM **Privately Held**
WEB: www.radiancelightworks.com
SIC: 3641 Lamps, fluorescent, electric

(P-9024)
TIVOLI LLC
17110 Armstrong Ave, Irvine (92614-5718)
PHONE..............................714 957-6101
Marie Paris, *CEO*
Susan Larson, *CEO*
Nigel Coppins, *Financial Exec*
Rae Wang, *Controller*
Jim Hardaway, *Marketing Staff*
▲ EMP: 50 EST: 2003
SALES (est): 9.2MM **Privately Held**
WEB: www.tivolilighting.com
SIC: 3641 3646 Tubes, electric light; ceiling systems, luminous; fluorescent lighting fixtures, commercial; ornamental lighting fixtures, commercial

3643 Current-Carrying Wiring Devices

(P-9025)
AERO-ELECTRIC CONNECTOR INC (PA)
2280 W 208th St, Torrance (90501-1452)
PHONE..............................310 618-3737
Walter Neubauer, *Chairman*
Walter Neubauer Jr, *CEO*
Hasson Jamshidian, *Vice Pres*
EMP: 358 EST: 1982
SQ FT: 65,000

SALES (est): 35.6MM **Privately Held**
WEB: www.aero-electric.com
SIC: 3643 3678 Connectors & terminals for electrical devices; electronic connectors

(P-9026)
ALLAN KIDD
Also Called: AK Industries
3115 E Las Hermanas St, Compton (90221-5512)
PHONE..................................310 762-1600
Allan Kidd, *Owner*
Loni Miller, *Marketing Mgr*
EMP: 20 EST: 1995
SQ FT: 17,000
SALES (est): 2MM **Privately Held**
WEB: www.ak-ind.com
SIC: 3643 Electric connectors

(P-9027)
COAST AIR SUPPLY CO INC
26501 Summit Cir, Santa Clarita (91350-3049)
PHONE..................................310 472-5612
Fred W Sutherland, *CEO*
EMP: 17 EST: 1953
SQ FT: 15,000
SALES (est): 2.3MM **Privately Held**
WEB: www.coast-air-supply-co-inc.sbcontract.com
SIC: 3643 Current-carrying wiring devices

(P-9028)
CONNECTEC COMPANY INC (PA)
1701 Reynolds Ave, Irvine (92614-5711)
PHONE..................................949 252-1077
Rassool Kavezade, *CEO*
Lora Taleb, *CFO*
Mike Taleb, *Treasurer*
Francis Rios, *Admin Sec*
Laura Lopez, *Opers Mgr*
▲ EMP: 89 EST: 1988
SQ FT: 12,000
SALES (est): 21.2MM **Privately Held**
WEB: www.connectecco.com
SIC: 3643 3678 Electric connectors; electronic connectors

(P-9029)
COOPER INTERCONNECT INC (DH)
750 W Ventura Blvd, Camarillo (93010-8382)
PHONE..................................805 484-0543
Revathi Advaithi, *President*
David Atkinson, *General Mgr*
Tamra Kluczynski, *Info Tech Mgr*
John White, *Engineer*
EMP: 100 EST: 1945
SQ FT: 113,000
SALES (est): 1.3MM **Privately Held**
WEB: www.eatonelectrical.com
SIC: 3643 3678 Electric connectors; electronic connectors
HQ: Eaton Corporation
1000 Eaton Blvd
Cleveland OH 44122
440 523-5000

(P-9030)
CTC GLOBAL CORPORATION (PA)
2026 Mcgaw Ave, Irvine (92614-0911)
PHONE..................................949 428-8500
J D Sitton, *CEO*
John Mansfield, *President*
Anne McDowell, *President*
Gabriel Tashjian, *COO*
Matthew Natalizio, *Corp Secy*
▲ EMP: 248 EST: 2011
SALES (est): 100MM **Privately Held**
WEB: www.ctcglobal.com
SIC: 3643 Power line cable

(P-9031)
DATA SOLDER INC
2915 Kilson Dr, Santa Ana (92707-3716)
PHONE..................................714 429-9866
Irma Gomez, *President*
Guillermo Gomez, *Vice Pres*
EMP: 19 EST: 1997
SQ FT: 4,000

SALES (est): 1.1MM **Privately Held**
WEB: www.datasolder.com
SIC: 3643 Solderless connectors (electric wiring devices)

(P-9032)
DMC POWER INC (PA)
623 E Artesia Blvd, Carson (90746-1201)
PHONE..................................310 323-1616
Tony Ward, *CEO*
Eben Kane, *CFO*
Ed Cox, *Vice Pres*
Michael Yazdanpanah, *Vice Pres*
Lawrence Markey, *Regional Mgr*
▲ EMP: 93 EST: 2009
SQ FT: 40,000
SALES (est): 24.5MM **Privately Held**
WEB: www.dmcpower.com
SIC: 3643 Current-carrying wiring devices

(P-9033)
EARTHWISE PACKAGING INC
14281 Franklin Ave, Tustin (92780-7008)
PHONE..................................714 602-2169
Kenneth Loritz, *President*
Ken Loritz, *Project Mgr*
Kaori Van Oort, *Manager*
EMP: 13 EST: 2007
SALES (est): 1.6MM **Privately Held**
WEB: www.earthwisepackaging.com
SIC: 3643 Caps & plugs, electric: attachment

(P-9034)
ELECTRO ADAPTER INC
Also Called: Plating
20640 Nordhoff St, Chatsworth (91311-6189)
P.O. Box 2560 (91313-2560)
PHONE..................................818 998-1198
Ray Fish, *President*
Terrill Fish, *Admin Sec*
Ken Ivers, *Info Tech Mgr*
Gary Fish, *Technical Staff*
Ken Breach, *Opers Mgr*
EMP: 100 EST: 1969
SQ FT: 54,000
SALES (est): 12.1MM **Privately Held**
WEB: www.electro-adapter.com
SIC: 3643 Electric connectors
PA: Intritec
20640 Nordhoff St
Chatsworth CA 91311

(P-9035)
EMP CONNECTORS INC
2280 W 208th St, Torrance (90501-1452)
PHONE..................................310 533-6799
Walter Neubauer Jr, *President*
Erika Neubauer, *Principal*
EMP: 20 EST: 1987
SQ FT: 39,000
SALES (est): 1.7MM **Privately Held**
WEB: www.conesys.com
SIC: 3643 3678 3612 Electric connectors; electronic connectors; transformers, except electric

(P-9036)
ESL POWER SYSTEMS INC
2800 Palisades Dr, Corona (92878-9427)
PHONE..................................800 922-4188
Michael Hellmers, *President*
David Hellmers, *Vice Pres*
◆ EMP: 55
SQ FT: 36,000
SALES (est): 15.9MM **Privately Held**
WEB: www.eslpwr.com
SIC: 3643 Outlets, electric: convenience

(P-9037)
FOXLINK INTERNATIONAL INC (HQ)
3010 Saturn St Ste 200, Brea (92821-6220)
PHONE..................................714 256-1777
Ching Fan Pu, *CEO*
James Lee, *President*
▲ EMP: 44 EST: 1994

SALES (est): 12.8MM **Privately Held**
WEB: www.foxlink.com
SIC: 3643 3678 3679 3691 Current-carrying wiring devices; electronic connectors; electronic circuits; storage batteries; household audio & video equipment; computer peripheral equipment

(P-9038)
HI REL CONNECTORS INC
Also Called: Hirel Connectors
760 Wharton Dr, Claremont (91711-4800)
PHONE..................................909 626-1820
Fred Baumann, *CEO*
Frederick Bb Baumann, *CEO*
George Argiriadis, *Engineer*
David Neitzke, *Engineer*
Wes Beauvais, *Maintenance Staff*
EMP: 300 EST: 1967
SQ FT: 25,000
SALES (est): 58.1MM **Privately Held**
WEB: www.hirelco.net
SIC: 3643 3678 Connectors & terminals for electrical devices; electronic connectors

(P-9039)
J TECH INC
548 Amapola Ave, Torrance (90501-1472)
PHONE..................................310 533-6700
Jai IL Lee, *CEO*
John Vinke, *CFO*
Thinh Nguyen, *Engineer*
EMP: 15 EST: 2010
SALES (est): 611K **Privately Held**
WEB: www.j-tech.com
SIC: 3643 Electric connectors

(P-9040)
LIGHTNING DVERSION SYSTEMS LLC
16572 Burke Ln, Huntington Beach (92647-4538)
PHONE..................................714 841-1080
Dave Wilmot, *President*
EMP: 14 EST: 1982
SQ FT: 6,284
SALES (est): 3.5MM
SALES (corp-wide): 628.9MM **Publicly Held**
WEB: www.lightningdiversion.com
SIC: 3643 3812 Lightning protection equipment; antennas, radar or communications; radar systems & equipment
HQ: Ls Holdings Company, Llc
16572 Burke Ln
Huntington Beach CA 92647
714 841-1080

(P-9041)
LYNCOLE GRUNDING SOLUTIONS LLC
Also Called: Lyncole Xit Grounding
3547 Voyager St Ste 204, Torrance (90503-1673)
PHONE..................................310 214-4000
Elizabeth B Robertson,
Bronson Walker, *Info Tech Mgr*
Benjamin Du, *Engineer*
Larry Labayen, *Engineer*
Helen Knapp,
EMP: 25 EST: 1985
SQ FT: 10,000
SALES (est): 3.5MM **Privately Held**
WEB: www.vfclp.com
SIC: 3643 8711 Current-carrying wiring devices; consulting engineer

(P-9042)
MICRO PLASTICS INC
20821 Dearborn St, Chatsworth (91311-5916)
P.O. Box 189, San Marcos (92079-0189)
PHONE..................................818 882-0244
Lynda Eurton, *President*
Anacleto Gonzalez, *Vice Pres*
Agripina Eurton, *Admin Sec*
EMP: 20 EST: 1956
SQ FT: 11,000
SALES (est): 294.2K **Privately Held**
SIC: 3643 3089 Connectors & terminals for electrical devices; molding primary plastic

(P-9043)
NEWVAC LLC (HQ)
9330 De Soto Ave, Chatsworth (91311-4926)
PHONE..................................310 525-1205
Ted Anderson, *CEO*
Mike Davidson, *CFO*
Garrett Hoffman, *Vice Pres*
Heather Wynne, *Controller*
EMP: 100 EST: 2019
SQ FT: 44,000
SALES (est): 26.5MM
SALES (corp-wide): 130.9MM **Privately Held**
WEB: www.newvac-llc.com
SIC: 3643 Current-carrying wiring devices
PA: Adi American Distributors Llc
2 Emery Ave Ste 1
Randolph NJ 07869
973 328-1181

(P-9044)
PLT ENTERPRISES INC
Also Called: So-Cal Value Added
809 Calle Plano, Camarillo (93012-8516)
PHONE..................................805 389-5335
Pamela L Tunis, *President*
Marco Day, *Vice Pres*
Peter L Tunis, *Vice Pres*
Catherine Shanley, *Executive*
Peter Tunis Jr, *General Mgr*
EMP: 75 EST: 1996
SQ FT: 41,000
SALES (est): 10.1MM **Privately Held**
WEB: www.so-calvalueadded.com
SIC: 3643 3679 Current-carrying wiring devices; harness assemblies for electronic use: wire or cable

(P-9045)
PRECISION STAMPINGS INC (PA)
Also Called: P S I
500 Egan Ave, Beaumont (92223-2132)
PHONE..................................951 845-1174
Herman Viets, *Ch of Bd*
Peter Gailing, *Shareholder*
Frauke Roth, *Shareholder*
Keith Roth, *Shareholder*
Herta Viets, *Shareholder*
EMP: 32 EST: 1966
SQ FT: 25,000
SALES (est): 8.7MM **Privately Held**
WEB: www.precisionstampingsinc.com
SIC: 3643 5084 7539 Contacts, electrical; tool & die makers' equipment; machine shop, automotive

(P-9046)
SOURIAU USA INC (DH)
1750 Commerce Way, Paso Robles (93446-3620)
PHONE..................................805 238-2840
Rob Hanes, *President*
◆ EMP: 46 EST: 2003
SQ FT: 55,000
SALES (est): 35MM
SALES (corp-wide): 4.8E **Publicly Held**
WEB: www.souriau.com
SIC: 3643 Bus bars (electrical conductors)
HQ: Souriau
9 Rue De La Porte De Buc
Versailles 78000
130 847-799

(P-9047)
T MCGEE ELECTRIC INC
12375 Mills Ave Ste 2, Chino (91710-2082)
PHONE..................................909 591-6461
Trent McGee, *President*
EMP: 26 EST: 1950
SQ FT: 15,000
SALES (est): 4.1MM **Privately Held**
WEB: www.tmcgeeelectric.com
SIC: 3643 Solderless connectors (electric wiring devices); ground clamps (electric wiring devices)

(P-9048)
TECHNICAL RESOURCE INDUSTRIES (PA)
Also Called: T R I
12854 Daisy Ct, Yucaipa (92399-2026)
PHONE..................................909 446-1109
Reinhard Thalmayer, *President*

EMP: 25 **EST:** 1988
SQ FT: 5,000
SALES (est): 1.5MM **Privately Held**
SIC: 3643 Electric connectors

(P-9049)
WASCO SALES AND MARKETING INC
2245 A St, Santa Maria (93455-1008)
PHONE..........................805 739-2747
Ronald Way, *President*
Brenda Way, *Shareholder*
Dave Way, *Shareholder*
Dana Way, *Admin Sec*
Brian Wyss, *VP Sales*
◆ **EMP:** 20 **EST:** 1987
SQ FT: 9,000
SALES (est): 7.3MM **Privately Held**
WEB: www.wascoinc.com
SIC: 3643 Electric switches

3644 Noncurrent-Carrying Wiring Devices

(P-9050)
GUND COMPANY INC
4701 E Airport Dr, Ontario (91761-7817)
PHONE..........................909 890-9300
Ricardo Beinar, *Manager*
Victor Melendrez, *Prdtn Mgr*
Alan Delahoyde, *Regl Sales Mgr*
Lucero Betty, *Sales Staff*
EMP: 15
SALES (corp-wide): 100MM **Privately Held**
WEB: www.thegundcompany.com
SIC: 3644 Insulators & insulation materials, electrical
PA: The Gund Company Inc
   9333 Dielman Indus Dr
   Saint Louis MO 63132
   314 423-5200

(P-9051)
INDUSTRIAL INSULATIONS INC (PA)
10509 Business Dr Ste A, Fontana (92337-8249)
PHONE..........................909 574-7433
Barbara Malone, *CEO*
Terry M Grill, *President*
Eduardo Gomez, *CFO*
John Dodson, *Sales Executive*
▲ **EMP:** 14 **EST:** 1951
SQ FT: 53,000
SALES (est): 5.7MM **Privately Held**
WEB: www.industrialinsulations.com
SIC: 3644 Electric conduits & fittings

(P-9052)
PRECISION FIBERGLASS PRODUCTS
3105 Kashiwa St, Torrance (90505-4089)
PHONE..........................310 539-7470
Robby D Ross, *President*
Lucille Ross, *Vice Pres*
Randal A Ross, *Vice Pres*
EMP: 15 **EST:** 1968
SQ FT: 13,300
SALES (est): 2.4MM **Privately Held**
WEB: www.precisionfiberglassproducts.com
SIC: 3644 Insulators & insulation materials, electrical

(P-9053)
SAF-T-CO SUPPLY
Also Called: All American Pipe Bending
1300 E Normandy Pl, Santa Ana (92705-4138)
PHONE..........................714 547-9975
Patricia McDonald, *President*
Paul McDonald, *CFO*
Robyn Dague, *Vice Pres*
Patty McCabe, *Office Mgr*
Dallas Syfert, *Production*
EMP: 50 **EST:** 1987
SQ FT: 24,000

SALES (est): 14.1MM **Privately Held**
WEB: www.saftco.com
SIC: 3644 5063 5032 5074 Noncurrent-carrying wiring services; electrical apparatus & equipment; brick, stone & related material; pipes & fittings, plastic; hardware

(P-9054)
TODAY PVC BENDING INC
501 N Garfield St, Santa Ana (92701-4756)
PHONE..........................714 953-5707
Joe Castro, *President*
Juan Martinez, *Principal*
Marcellino Rios, *Principal*
EMP: 14 **EST:** 2011
SALES (est): 3.1MM **Privately Held**
WEB: www.todaypvcbending.com
SIC: 3644 Electric conduits & fittings

(P-9055)
WESTERN TUBE & CONDUIT CORP (HQ)
2001 E Dominguez St, Long Beach (90810-1088)
PHONE..........................310 537-6300
Barry Zekelman, *CEO*
Steve Gasparro, *Vice Pres*
Patrick Ongman, *General Mgr*
Kandice Wolenchuk, *CIO*
Kathy Bowden, *Prgrmr*
▲ **EMP:** 238 **EST:** 2004
SQ FT: 420,000
SALES (est): 57.4MM **Privately Held**
WEB: www.westerntube.com
SIC: 3644 3446 3317 Electric conduits & fittings; fences or posts, ornamental iron or steel; tubing, mechanical or hypodermic sizes: cold drawn stainless

---

3645 Residential Lighting Fixtures

(P-9056)
ALGER-TRITON INC
Also Called: Alger International
5600 W Jefferson Blvd, Los Angeles (90016-3131)
PHONE..........................310 229-9500
Mishel Michael, *Principal*
Tiffany Reiner, *Sales Staff*
◆ **EMP:** 28 **EST:** 1993
SALES (est): 5.5MM **Privately Held**
WEB: www.studio-at.com
SIC: 3645 Residential lighting fixtures

(P-9057)
AMERICAN NAIL PLATE LTG INC
Also Called: Anp Lighting
9044 Del Mar Ave, Montclair (91763-1627)
PHONE..........................909 982-1807
Harry Foster, *CEO*
Ron Foster, *Treasurer*
Joan Foster, *Vice Pres*
Bob Foster, *Admin Sec*
David Alvarado, *Sales Staff*
▲ **EMP:** 70 **EST:** 1976
SQ FT: 13,000
SALES (est): 10.7MM **Privately Held**
WEB: www.anplighting.com
SIC: 3645 3646 Residential lighting fixtures; commercial indusl & institutional electric lighting fixtures

(P-9058)
ANTHONY CALIFORNIA INC (PA)
14485 Monte Vista Ave, Chino (91710-5728)
PHONE..........................909 627-0351
Kuei-Lan Yeh, *CEO*
Cindy Chang, *Treasurer*
Darien Chung, *Sales Mgr*
◆ **EMP:** 28 **EST:** 1983
SALES (est): 5.5MM **Privately Held**
WEB: www.anthonyshowrooms.com
SIC: 3645 5063 5023 Residential lighting fixtures; lighting fixtures; lamps: floor, boudoir, desk

(P-9059)
ARTIVA USA INC
12866 Ann St Ste 1, Santa Fe Springs (90670-3064)
PHONE..........................562 298-8968
Jane Wang, *Manager*
EMP: 42 **Privately Held**
WEB: www.artivaus.com
SIC: 3645 5063 Residential lighting fixtures; lighting fixtures
PA: Artiva Usa Inc.
   13901 Magnolia Ave
   Chino CA 91710

(P-9060)
ARTIVA USA INC (PA)
13901 Magnolia Ave, Chino (91710-7030)
PHONE..........................909 628-1388
PO Y Webb, *President*
▲ **EMP:** 35 **EST:** 2008
SQ FT: 20,000 **Privately Held**
WEB: www.artivaus.com
SIC: 3645 5063 Residential lighting fixtures; lighting fixtures

(P-9061)
BASE LITE CORPORATION
Also Called: Baselite
12260 Eastend Ave, Chino (91710-2008)
PHONE..........................909 444-2776
Moaaa A Teixeira, *CEO*
Nick Jones, *Sales Executive*
EMP: 38
SQ FT: 10,000
SALES (est): 9.4MM **Privately Held**
WEB: www.baselite.com
SIC: 3645 3646 Residential lighting fixtures; commercial indusl & institutional electric lighting fixtures

(P-9062)
DMF INC
Also Called: Dmf Lighting
1118 E 223rd St, Carson (90745-4210)
PHONE..........................323 934-7779
Morteza Danesh, *CEO*
Ian Ibbitson, *COO*
Fariba Danesh, *Vice Pres*
Michael Danesh, *Vice Pres*
Andrew Wakefield, *Vice Pres*
▲ **EMP:** 51 **EST:** 1989
SQ FT: 8,000
SALES (est): 15MM **Privately Held**
WEB: www.dmflighting.com
SIC: 3645 5063 Residential lighting fixtures; lighting fixtures, commercial & industrial

(P-9063)
FEIT ELECTRIC COMPANY INC (PA)
4901 Gregg Rd, Pico Rivera (90660-2108)
PHONE..........................562 463-2852
Aaron Feit, *CEO*
Toby Feit, *CFO*
◆ **EMP:** 158 **EST:** 1978
SQ FT: 300,000
SALES (est): 65.6MM **Privately Held**
WEB: www.feit.com
SIC: 3645 3641 5023 3646 Residential lighting fixtures; electric light bulbs, complete; lamps, fluorescent, electric; home furnishings; commercial indusl & institutional electric lighting fixtures; pressed & blown glass

(P-9064)
GLOBALUX LIGHTING LLC
773 S Benson Ave, Ontario (91762-4750)
PHONE..........................909 591-7506
Esmail K Parekh, *Mng Member*
Gerardo Valdez, *Sales Staff*
Nausheen Tabani,
Esamail K Parekh, *Mng Member*
▲ **EMP:** 16 **EST:** 2011
SALES (est): 2.3MM **Privately Held**
WEB: www.globaluxlighting.com
SIC: 3645 3646 5063 Residential lighting fixtures; commercial indusl & institutional electric lighting fixtures; lighting fittings & accessories

(P-9065)
LIGHTCRAFT OTDOOR ENVIRONMENTS
Also Called: Lightclub USA
9811 Owensmouth Ave Ste 1, Chatsworth (91311-3800)
PHONE..........................818 349-2663
Bruce Dennis, *President*
Rachel Ciavarello, *Cust Svc Dir*
▲ **EMP:** 15 **EST:** 2004
SQ FT: 5,000
SALES (est): 1.3MM **Privately Held**
WEB: www.lightcraftoutdoor.com
SIC: 3645 5063 Garden, patio, walkway & yard lighting fixtures: electric; lighting fittings & accessories

(P-9066)
LIGHTS OF AMERICA INC
749 S Lemon Ave, Walnut (91789-2906)
PHONE..........................909 444-2000
Imran Vakil, *Manager*
EMP: 700
SALES (corp-wide): 84.6MM **Privately Held**
WEB: www.lightsofamerica.com
SIC: 3645 3646 Fluorescent lighting fixtures, residential; fluorescent lighting fixtures, commercial
PA: Lights Of America, Inc.
   13602 12th St Ste B
   Chino CA 91710
   909 594-7883

(P-9067)
LIGHTS OF AMERICA INC (PA)
13602 12th St Ste B, Chino (91710-5200)
PHONE..........................909 594-7883
Usman Vakil, *CEO*
Farooq Vakil, *Exec VP*
Elizabeth Gardner, *Managing Dir*
Kamran Mirza, *General Mgr*
Joan Munoz, *Human Res Dir*
◆ **EMP:** 500 **EST:** 1977
SQ FT: 210,000
SALES (est): 84.6MM **Privately Held**
WEB: www.lightsofamerica.com
SIC: 3645 3646 3641 Fluorescent lighting fixtures, residential; fluorescent lighting fixtures, commercial; electric lamps

(P-9068)
MAXIM LIGHTING INTL INC
247 Vineland Ave, City of Industry (91746-2319)
PHONE..........................626 956-4200
EMP: 20
SALES (corp-wide): 52.1MM **Privately Held**
WEB: www.maximlighting.com
SIC: 3645 Residential lighting fixtures
PA: Maxim Lighting International, Inc.
   253 Vineland Ave
   City Of Industry CA 91746
   626 956-4200

(P-9069)
NL&A COLLECTIONS INC
Also Called: Nova
6323 Maywood Ave, Huntington Park (90255-4531)
P.O. Box 661820, Los Angeles (90066-8820)
PHONE..........................323 277-6266
Daniel Edelist, *President*
Sabrina Westbrook, *Accounts Mgr*
◆ **EMP:** 40 **EST:** 1980
SQ FT: 48,675
SALES (est): 5MM **Privately Held**
WEB: www.novaofcalifornia.com
SIC: 3645 5023 Boudoir lamps; lamps: floor, boudoir, desk

(P-9070)
PHILIPS NORTH AMERICA LLC
11201 Iberia St Ste A, Jurupa Valley (91752-3280)
PHONE..........................909 574-1800
Kenneth Parivar, *Branch Mgr*
EMP: 101

SALES (corp-wide): 133.6MM **Privately Held**
WEB: www.usa.philips.com
SIC: **3645** 3648 3646 Residential lighting fixtures; garden, patio, walkway & yard lighting fixtures: electric; fluorescent lighting fixtures, residential; outdoor lighting equipment; decorative area lighting fixtures; underwater lighting fixtures; ceiling systems, luminous
HQ: Philips North America Llc
222 Jacobs St Fl 3
Cambridge MA 02141
978 659-3000

(P-9071)
TROY-CSL LIGHTING INC
14508 Nelson Ave, City of Industry (91744-3514)
P.O. Box 514310, Los Angeles (90051-4310)
PHONE...................................626 336-4511
David Littman, *CEO*
Steve Nadell, *President*
Anne Wilcox, *CFO*
Ian Wilcox, *Admin Sec*
◆ EMP: 80 EST: 1970
SALES (est): 21MM **Privately Held**
WEB: www.troylighting.hvlgroup.com
SIC: **3645** 3646 Wall lamps; ornamental lighting fixtures, commercial

(P-9072)
USPAR ENTERPRISES INC
2037 S Vineyard Ave, Ontario (91761-8066)
PHONE...................................909 591-7506
Khalid Parekh, *President*
Esmail K Parekh, *CEO*
Irfan Parekh, *Vice Pres*
▲ EMP: 19 EST: 1973
SQ FT: 50,000
SALES (est): 1.1MM **Privately Held**
WEB: www.uspar.com
SIC: **3645** 3646 3641 5063 Fluorescent lighting fixtures, residential; fluorescent lighting fixtures, commercial; electric lamps; lighting fixtures

(P-9073)
VIDESSENCE LLC (PA)
10768 Lower Azusa Rd, El Monte (91731-1306)
PHONE...................................626 579-0943
Toni Swarens, *President*
Gary Thomas, *Technical Staff*
Brian Fraser, *Sales Staff*
Lee Hedberg, *Manager*
▲ EMP: 25 EST: 1951
SQ FT: 35,000
SALES (est): 4.4MM **Privately Held**
WEB: www.videssence.com
SIC: **3645** 3648 Residential lighting fixtures; stage lighting equipment

(P-9074)
WANGS ALLIANCE CORPORATION
Also Called: Wac Lighting
1750 S Archibald Ave, Ontario (91761-1239)
PHONE...................................909 230-9401
Nina Chou, *Principal*
EMP: 20
SALES (corp-wide): 54.4MM **Privately Held**
WEB: www.waclighting.com
SIC: **3645** Residential lighting fixtures
PA: Wangs Alliance Corporation
44 Harbor Park Dr
Port Washington NY 11050
516 515-5000

(P-9075)
YAWITZ INC
Also Called: Evergreen Lighting
1379 Ridgeway St, Pomona (91768-2701)
PHONE...................................909 865-5599
John Klena, *CEO*
Victor Rosen, *Corp Secy*
George Cole III, *Vice Pres*
Mayte Arias, *Office Mgr*
Robert Allen, *Natl Sales Mgr*
▲ EMP: 42 EST: 1997
SQ FT: 23,000

SALES (est): 8.8MM **Privately Held**
WEB: www.evergreenlighting.com
SIC: **3645** 3646 Fluorescent lighting fixtures, residential; fluorescent lighting fixtures, commercial

3646 Commercial, Indl & Institutional Lighting Fixtures

(P-9076)
A V POLES AND LIGHTING INC
43827 Division St, Lancaster (93535-4061)
P.O. Box 9054 (93539-9054)
PHONE...................................661 945-2731
Luis Romero, *CEO*
Roberta Wood, *President*
▼ EMP: 20 EST: 2013
SQ FT: 12,000
SALES (est): 2.6MM **Privately Held**
WEB: www.avpolesandlighting.com
SIC: **3646** Commercial indusl & institutional electric lighting fixtures

(P-9077)
ACCLAIM LIGHTING LLC
6122 S Eastern Ave, Commerce (90040-3402)
PHONE...................................323 213-4626
Charles J Davies, *Principal*
Jennie Picard, *Administration*
Jodie Moore, *Project Mgr*
Alvaro Montiel, *Opers Mgr*
Blaine Engle, *Natl Sales Mgr*
▲ EMP: 18 EST: 2003
SALES (est): 4.9MM **Privately Held**
WEB: www.acclaimlighting.com
SIC: **3646** 3679 5063 Commercial indusl & institutional electric lighting fixtures; electronic loads & power supplies; wire & cable

(P-9078)
ARTE DE MEXICO INC
5506 Riverton Ave, North Hollywood (91601-2815)
PHONE...................................818 753-4510
David Staffers, *Manager*
EMP: 71
SALES (corp-wide): 22.5MM **Privately Held**
WEB: www.artedemexico.com
SIC: **3646** 3446 Commercial indusl & institutional electric lighting fixtures; architectural metalwork
PA: Arte De Mexico, Inc.
1000 Chestnut St
Burbank CA 91506
818 753-4559

(P-9079)
AUBREY INDUSTRIES
Also Called: Clarte Lighting
750 W Golden Grove Way, Covina (91722-3255)
PHONE...................................626 261-4242
Michael Brenton Aubrey, *CEO*
EMP: 13 EST: 2015
SALES (est): 2.5MM **Privately Held**
WEB: www.clartelighting.com
SIC: **3646** Ceiling systems, luminous

(P-9080)
C W COLE & COMPANY INC
Also Called: Cole Lighting
2560 Rosemead Blvd, South El Monte (91733-1593)
PHONE...................................626 443-2473
Russell W Cole, *Ch of Bd*
Stephen W Cole, *President*
Donald Cole, *Vice Pres*
Melissa Kelemen, *Administration*
Eric Vargas, *Design Engr*
EMP: 41 EST: 1911
SQ FT: 25,000
SALES (est): 9.5MM **Privately Held**
WEB: www.colelighting.com
SIC: **3646** Commercial indusl & institutional electric lighting fixtures

(P-9081)
CRYSTAL LIGHTING CORP
13182 Flores St, Santa Fe Springs (90670-4023)
PHONE...................................562 944-0223

Manolo Naranjo, *CEO*
Fabian Naranjo, *Treasurer*
Robert Naranjo, *Vice Pres*
◆ EMP: 14 EST: 1984
SQ FT: 10,000
SALES (est): 4MM **Privately Held**
WEB: www.crystallighting.us
SIC: **3646** 3645 Ornamental lighting fixtures, commercial; residential lighting fixtures

(P-9082)
DECO ENTERPRISES INC
Also Called: Deco Lighting
2917 Vail Ave, Commerce (90040-2615)
PHONE...................................323 726-2575
Saman Sinai, *Principal*
Benjamin Pouladian, *President*
Ben Peterson, *Vice Pres*
David Brown, *Planning*
Tyrone King, *Technician*
▲ EMP: 60 EST: 2005
SQ FT: 100,000
SALES (est): 19.8MM **Privately Held**
WEB: www.getdeco.com
SIC: **3646** Commercial indusl & institutional electric lighting fixtures

(P-9083)
EPTRONICS INC
19210 S Vermont Ave C, Gardena (90248-4426)
PHONE...................................310 536-0700
Chris Chen, *President*
Rudy Wiesinger, *Vice Pres*
Quincie Lane, *Office Admin*
James Blevons, *Manager*
Susan Gober, *Manager*
EMP: 13 EST: 2008
SALES (est): 1.1MM **Privately Held**
WEB: www.eptronics.com
SIC: **3646** Commercial indusl & institutional electric lighting fixtures

(P-9084)
FLUORESCENT SUPPLY CO INC
Also Called: Fsc
9120 Center Ave, Rancho Cucamonga (91730-5310)
PHONE...................................909 948-8878
Edward Yawitz, *CEO*
John Watkins, *President*
John Elwood, *CFO*
Chad Treadwell, *Senior VP*
Josh Bond, *Vice Pres*
▲ EMP: 41 EST: 1969
SQ FT: 80,000
SALES (est): 12.3MM **Privately Held**
WEB: www.fsclighting.com
SIC: **3646** 3645 Commercial indusl & institutional electric lighting fixtures; residential lighting fixtures

(P-9085)
FOCUS INDUSTRIES INC
Also Called: Focus Landscape
25301 Commercentre Dr, Lake Forest (92630-8808)
PHONE...................................949 830-1350
Stan Shibata, *President*
Luis Mejia, *CFO*
June Shibata, *Treasurer*
Linda Lindgren, *Human Res Mgr*
Yasmin Arroyo, *Marketing Staff*
▲ EMP: 100 EST: 1989
SQ FT: 40,000
SALES (est): 22.5MM **Privately Held**
WEB: www.focusindustries.com
SIC: **3646** 5063 Commercial indusl & institutional electric lighting fixtures; electrical apparatus & equipment

(P-9086)
GENERAL ELECTRIC COMPANY
11600 Philadelphia Ave, Mira Loma (91752-1135)
PHONE...................................951 360-2400
Fax: 951 360-3235
EMP: 50
SALES (corp-wide): 122B **Publicly Held**
SIC: **3646** Distribution Center
PA: General Electric Company
41 Farnsworth St
Boston MA 02210
617 443-3000

(P-9087)
HALLMARK LIGHTING LLC
1945 S Tubeway Ave, Commerce (90040-1611)
PHONE...................................818 885-5010
Christopher Larocca, *CEO*
Robert Godlewski, *President*
Julie Winfield, *Officer*
Leslie Livingston, *Vice Pres*
Dan Harrison, *Info Tech Dir*
◆ EMP: 80
SALES (est): 14MM **Privately Held**
WEB: www.hallmarklighting.com
SIC: **3646** 3645 3641 Commercial indusl & institutional electric lighting fixtures; wall lamps; electric lamps

(P-9088)
HAMILTON TECHNOLOGY CORP
14900 S Figueroa St, Gardena (90248-1715)
PHONE...................................310 217-1191
Mark Rambod, *President*
▲ EMP: 15 EST: 1983
SQ FT: 2,000
SALES (est): 2.8MM **Privately Held**
WEB: www.hamiltontechnology.com
SIC: **3646** Commercial indusl & institutional electric lighting fixtures

(P-9089)
HI-LITE MANUFACTURING CO INC
13450 Monte Vista Ave, Chino (91710-5149)
PHONE...................................909 465-1999
Dorothy A Ohai, *President*
Dorothy Ohai, *Vice Pres*
◆ EMP: 90
SQ FT: 157,000
SALES (est): 17.9MM **Privately Held**
WEB: www.hilitemfg.com
SIC: **3646** 3645 Commercial indusl & institutional electric lighting fixtures; residential lighting fixtures

(P-9090)
INTENSE LIGHTING LLC
3340 E La Palma Ave, Anaheim (92806-2814)
PHONE...................................714 630-9877
Kenny Eidsvold, *President*
Kenneth Eidsvold, *President*
Evelyn Gutierrez, *Project Mgr*
Aida Spremo, *Project Engr*
Jim Hicks, *Engineer*
◆ EMP: 80 EST: 2001
SQ FT: 153,000
SALES (est): 22.2MM
SALES (corp-wide): 1.4B **Privately Held**
WEB: www.intenselighting.com
SIC: **3646** 3645 Commercial indusl & institutional electric lighting fixtures; residential lighting fixtures
PA: Leviton Manufacturing Co., Inc.
201 N Service Rd
Melville NY 11747
631 812-6000

(P-9091)
LA SPEC INDUSTRIES INC
Also Called: Laspec Lighting
2315 E 52nd St, Vernon (90058-3499)
PHONE...................................323 588-8746
Jacob Melamed, *Principal*
J Melamed, *President*
Lacy Dorice, *Manager*
▲ EMP: 15 EST: 1984
SQ FT: 30,000
SALES (est): 3MM **Privately Held**
WEB: www.laspec.com
SIC: **3646** 3648 Commercial indusl & institutional electric lighting fixtures; decorative area lighting fixtures

(P-9092)
LAMPS PLUS INC
Also Called: Pacific Coast Lighting
4723 Telephone Rd, Ventura (93003-5242)
PHONE...................................805 642-9007
David Hillard, *Manager*
EMP: 16

SALES (corp-wide): 573.4MM Privately Held
WEB: www.lampsplus.com
SIC: 3646 5719 5064 Commercial indusl & institutional electric lighting fixtures; lamps & lamp shades; fans, household: electric
PA: Lamps Plus, Inc.
20250 Plummer St
Chatsworth CA 91311
818 886-5267

(P-9093)
LEDINGEDGE LIGHTING INC (PA)
4682 Calle Bolero Ste A, Camarillo (93012-8591)
P.O. Box 5669, Ventura (93005-0669)
PHONE..................................805 383-8493
William P Miller, CEO
Harold Moore, President
EMP: 14 EST: 2004
SALES (est): 1.5MM Privately Held
WEB: www.ledingedge.com
SIC: 3646 Commercial indusl & institutional electric lighting fixtures

(P-9094)
LF ILLUMINATION LLC
9200 Deering Ave, Chatsworth (91311-5803)
PHONE..................................818 885-1335
Jack Zukerman, CEO
Loren Kessel, President
Eileen S Cheng, CFO
Eileen Cheng, Exec VP
Terri Roberts, Vice Pres
▲ EMP: 51 EST: 2013
SALES (est): 9.7MM Privately Held
WEB: www.lfillumination.com
SIC: 3646 3645 5719 Commercial indusl & institutional electric lighting fixtures; residential lighting fixtures; lighting fixtures; lighting, lamps & accessories

(P-9095)
LIGHTWAY INDUSTRIES
28435 Industry Dr, Valencia (91355-4107)
PHONE..................................661 257-0286
Jeffrey Bargman, President
Gary N Patten, Vice Pres
Jared Duncan, CIO
Delia Cerpa, Purchasing
EMP: 38 EST: 1980
SQ FT: 22,300
SALES (est): 5.5MM Privately Held
WEB: www.lightwayind.com
SIC: 3646 3645 Commercial indusl & institutional electric lighting fixtures; residential lighting fixtures

(P-9096)
LUMINATION LIGHTING & TECH INC
1515 240th St, Harbor City (90710-1308)
PHONE..................................855 283-1100
EMP: 150
SALES (est): 4.9MM Privately Held
SIC: 3646 Commercial Lighting Fixtures, Nsk

(P-9097)
OPTIC ARTS HOLDINGS INC
716 Monterey Pass Rd, Monterey Park (91754-3607)
PHONE..................................213 250-6069
Jason Mullen, CEO
Mason Barker, COO
Jeffrey Shepherd, Regional Mgr
Christy Lee, General Mgr
Dorian L Hicklin, Admin Sec
EMP: 47 EST: 2011
SQ FT: 15,750
SALES (est): 10.4MM
SALES (corp-wide): 21.6MM Privately Held
WEB: www.luminii.com
SIC: 3646 3645 3648 Commercial indusl & institutional electric lighting fixtures; residential lighting fixtures; decorative area lighting fixtures
PA: Luminii Llc
7777 N Merrimac Ave
Niles IL 60714
224 333-6033

(P-9098)
PACIFIC LTG & STANDARDS CO
2815 Los Flores Blvd, Lynwood (90262-2416)
PHONE..................................310 603-9344
Frank Munoz, President
Enrique Garcia, Vice Pres
▲ EMP: 34 EST: 1982
SQ FT: 17,000
SALES (est): 5MM Privately Held
WEB: www.pacificlighting.com
SIC: 3646 Commercial indusl & institutional electric lighting fixtures

(P-9099)
PACLIGHTS LLC (PA)
15318 El Prado Rd, Chino (91710-7659)
P.O. Box 928, Chino Hills (91709-0031)
PHONE..................................800 980-6386
Tommy Zhen, CEO
Fiona Zhao, President
Janine Pothier, Accounts Mgr
▲ EMP: 19 EST: 2013
SQ FT: 20,000
SALES (est): 2.9MM Privately Held
WEB: www.paclights.com
SIC: 3646 Commercial indusl & institutional electric lighting fixtures

(P-9100)
PRUDENTIAL LIGHTING CORP (PA)
Also Called: P L M
1774 E 21st St, Los Angeles (90058-1082)
P.O. Box 58736 (90058-0736)
PHONE..................................213 477-1694
Stanely J Ellis, CEO
Jeffrey Ellis, President
Jolie Ellis, Corp Secy
Elliot Ellis, Vice Pres
David Haygood, Controller
▲ EMP: 120 EST: 1955
SQ FT: 112,000
SALES (est): 45.9MM Privately Held
WEB: www.prulite.com
SIC: 3646 Fluorescent lighting fixtures, commercial

(P-9101)
R W SWARENS ASSOCIATES INC
Also Called: Engineered Lighting Products
10768 Lower Azusa Rd, El Monte (91731-1306)
PHONE..................................626 579-0943
Toni Swarens, CEO
Lauri Maines, President
Jerry Caron, Purch Agent
Bruce Jahnig, Sales Staff
John Linell, Sales Staff
▲ EMP: 36 EST: 1984
SALES (est): 3MM Privately Held
WEB: www.elplighting.com
SIC: 3646 Commercial indusl & institutional electric lighting fixtures

(P-9102)
SAPPHIRE CHANDELIER LLC
505 Porter Way, Placentia (92870-6454)
PHONE..................................714 879-3660
Hector Garibay, Partner
Cheryl Kaye, Vice Pres
Hayley Hustedt,
▲ EMP: 61 EST: 2009
SQ FT: 10,000
SALES (est): 6.8MM Privately Held
WEB: www.sapphirechandelier.com
SIC: 3646 Commercial indusl & institutional electric lighting fixtures

(P-9103)
SUN & SUN INDUSTRIES INC
2101 S Yale St, Santa Ana (92704-4424)
PHONE..................................714 210-5141
Lynda Sun-Frederick, CEO
Duncan Frederick, President
Ken Flockblower, Vice Pres
EMP: 100 EST: 1995
SQ FT: 11,000
SALES (est): 24.7MM
SALES (corp-wide): 4.2MM Privately Held
WEB: www.sunindustries.com
SIC: 3646 Fluorescent lighting fixtures, commercial

(P-9104)
SUN VALLEY LTG STANDARDS INC
Also Called: US Architectural Lighting
660 W Avenue O, Palmdale (93551-3610)
PHONE..................................661 233-2000
Joseph Straus, President
Judith Straus, Vice Pres
EMP: 65 EST: 1984
SQ FT: 30,000
SALES (est): 2.7MM
SALES (corp-wide): 34.6MM Privately Held
WEB: www.usaltg.com
SIC: 3646 5063 3648 Ornamental lighting fixtures, commercial; electrical apparatus & equipment; lighting equipment
PA: U.S. Pole Company, Inc.
660 W Avenue O
Palmdale CA 93551
800 877-6537

(P-9105)
T-1 LIGHTING INC
9929 Pioneer Blvd, Santa Fe Springs (90670-3219)
PHONE..................................626 234-2328
Artur Saakyan, CEO
An Bao Vu, COO
Pang Chun Zhang, CFO
Selene Estrada, Manager
EMP: 16 EST: 2016
SQ FT: 19,660
SALES (est): 10MM Privately Held
WEB: www.t1-lighting.com
SIC: 3646 Commercial indusl & institutional electric lighting fixtures

(P-9106)
TEMPO LIGHTING INC
Also Called: Tempo Industries
1961 Mcgaw Ave, Irvine (92614-0909)
PHONE..................................949 442-1601
Dennis Pearson, CEO
Mike Bremser, Vice Pres
Ian Shaw, Vice Pres
Helen Bustamante, Admin Sec
Jignesh Bhagat, Engineer
▲ EMP: 31 EST: 1986
SQ FT: 27,000
SALES (est): 7.8MM Privately Held
WEB: www.tempollc.com
SIC: 3646 Commercial indusl & institutional electric lighting fixtures

(P-9107)
TRITON CHANDELIER INC
1301 Dove St Ste 900, Newport Beach (92660-2473)
PHONE..................................714 957-9600
Richard Cooley, President
▲ EMP: 13 EST: 1995
SQ FT: 10,000
SALES (est): 1.4MM Privately Held
SIC: 3646 Chandeliers, commercial

(P-9108)
US POLE COMPANY INC (PA)
Also Called: U S Architectural Lighting
660 W Avenue O, Palmdale (93551-3610)
PHONE..................................800 877-6537
Joseph Straus, President
Harvey Solis, Purch Mgr
Gabby Castro, Purch Agent
Daphne LI, Purch Agent
Ward Fulcher, Sales Staff
◆ EMP: 84 EST: 1984
SQ FT: 112,000
SALES (est): 34.6MM Privately Held
WEB: www.usaltg.com
SIC: 3646 Commercial indusl & institutional electric lighting fixtures

(P-9109)
VISION ENGRG MET STAMPING INC
114 Grand Cypress Ave, Palmdale (93551-3617)
PHONE..................................661 575-0933
Joseph Avila, CEO
EMP: 100

PA: Eco-Shift Power Corp
125 Mcgovern Dr Unit 10
Cambridge ON N3H 4
SQ FT: 72,000
SALES (est): 10.6MM Privately Held
WEB: www.visionengineering.com
SIC: 3646 Ceiling systems, luminous

(P-9110)
VISIONAIRE LIGHTING LLC
19645 S Rancho Way, Rancho Dominguez (90220-6028)
PHONE..................................310 512-6480
Bryan Fried, CEO
Cheryl Moorman, CFO
Darren Scharringhausen, Exec VP
Grover Salzer, Regional Mgr
Todd Alcock, Info Tech Mgr
◆ EMP: 95 EST: 2000
SQ FT: 36,000
SALES (est): 29.5MM Privately Held
WEB: www.visionairelighting.com
SIC: 3646 Commercial indusl & institutional electric lighting fixtures

(P-9111)
WESTERN ILLUMINATED PLAS INC
14451 Edwards St, Westminster (92683-3607)
PHONE..................................714 895-3067
Cornelius Crompvoets, President
Irene Crompvoets, Treasurer
Charles Crompvoets, Vice Pres
Sandra Crompvoets-Katanjian, Admin Sec
EMP: 20 EST: 1978
SQ FT: 8,800
SALES (est): 3.5MM Privately Held
WEB: www.westernplastics.com
SIC: 3646 1761 Ceiling systems, luminous; ceilings, metal: erection & repair

(P-9112)
YANKON INDUSTRIES INC (PA)
Also Called: Energetic Lighting
13445 12th St, Chino (91710-5206)
PHONE..................................909 591-2345
WEI Chen, CEO
David Liu, CEO
Kristen Tai, CFO
▲ EMP: 23 EST: 2009
SQ FT: 100,627
SALES (est): 4MM Privately Held
WEB: www.energeticlighting.com
SIC: 3646 Commercial indusl & institutional electric lighting fixtures

3647 Vehicular Lighting Eqpt

(P-9113)
AMP PLUS INC
Also Called: Elco Lighting
2042 E Vernon Ave, Vernon (90058-1613)
PHONE..................................323 231-2600
Steve Cohen, President
Brandon Cohen, Opers Staff
◆ EMP: 55 EST: 1991
SQ FT: 100,000
SALES (est): 9.5MM Privately Held
WEB: www.elcolighting.com
SIC: 3647 5063 3645 Vehicular lighting equipment; electrical apparatus & equipment; residential lighting fixtures

(P-9114)
DELTA TECH INDUSTRIES LLC
1901 S Vineyard Ave, Ontario (91761-7747)
PHONE..................................909 673-1900
Bogdan G Durian, Mng Member
Andrew Pierce, Opers Mgr
◆ EMP: 25 EST: 1978
SQ FT: 12,000
SALES (est): 6.7MM Privately Held
WEB: www.deltalights.com
SIC: 3647 Automotive lighting fixtures

(P-9115)
EXCELLENCE OPTO INC (PA)
Also Called: E O I
21858 Garcia Ln, Walnut (91789-0941)
PHONE..................................909 468-0550
Cheryl Huang, Ch of Bd
Fang-Yue Huang, President
Michael Hodgdon, Natl Sales Mgr
▲ EMP: 21 EST: 2001
SQ FT: 18,000

SALES (est): 7.3MM **Privately Held**
WEB: www.eoius.com
SIC: 3647　3669　3648　Automotive lighting fixtures; traffic signals, electric; street lighting fixtures

(P-9116)
JKL COMPONENTS CORPORATION
13343 Paxton St, Pacoima　(91331-2340)
PHONE..........................818 896-0019
Joseph Velas, *President*
Sara Velas, *Chief Mktg Ofcr*
Kent Koerting, *Principal*
Percy Andres, *Info Tech Mgr*
Larry Rushefsky, *Engineer*
EMP: 32 **EST:** 1974
SQ FT: 7,000
SALES (est): 4.4MM **Privately Held**
WEB: www.jkllamps.com
SIC: 3647　3827　3699　Automotive lighting fixtures; optical instruments & lenses; electrical equipment & supplies

(P-9117)
K C HILITES INC
13637 Cimarron Ave, Gardena
(90249-2461)
P.O. Box 155, Williams AZ　(86046-0155)
PHONE..........................928 635-2607
Michael Dehaas, *President*
Andy Wang, *Managing Prtnr*
Rosanna Marmolejo, *Graphic Designe*
Justin Padilla, *Cust Mgr*
◆ **EMP:** 36 **EST:** 1970
SQ FT: 25,000
SALES (est): 7.6MM **Privately Held**
WEB: www.kchilites.com
SIC: 3647　Vehicular lighting equipment

(P-9118)
SODERBERG MANUFACTURING CO INC
20821 Currier Rd, Walnut　(91789-3018)
PHONE..........................909 595-1291
B W Soderberg, *CEO*
Kathy Kirkeby, *Corp Secy*
Kari Levario, *Vice Pres*
Rick Soderberg, *Vice Pres*
Stephen Mandap, *Engrg Dir*
EMP: 85 **EST:** 1946
SALES (est): 9MM **Privately Held**
WEB: www.soderberg.aero
SIC: 3647　3812　Aircraft lighting fixtures; search & navigation equipment

(P-9119)
STREET GLOW INC
2710 E El Presidio St, Carson
(90810-1117)
PHONE..........................310 631-1881
EMP: 60　**Privately Held**
SIC: 3647　Mfg Vehicle Lighting Equipment
PA: Street Glow Inc
　　160 Gregg St Ste 7
　　Lodi NJ
　　973 709-9000

(P-9120)
SUNBEAM TRAILER PRODUCTS INC
5312 Production Dr, Huntington Beach
(92649-1523)
PHONE..........................714 373-5000
EMP: 20 **EST:** 1939
SQ FT: 11,000
SALES (est): 1.7MM **Privately Held**
SIC: 3647　Mfg Lighting Fixtures

3648 Lighting Eqpt, NEC

(P-9121)
ALL ACCESS STGING PRDCTONS INC (PA)
1320 Storm Pkwy, Torrance　(90501-5041)
PHONE..........................310 784-2464
Clive Forrester, *CEO*
Erik Eastland, *President*
Mishele Bay, *CFO*
Robert Achlimbari, *Vice Pres*
Ira Nguyen, *Executive*
▲ **EMP:** 64 **EST:** 1997
SQ FT: 42,000

SALES (est): 13.7MM **Privately Held**
WEB: www.allaccessinc.com
SIC: 3648　Stage lighting equipment

(P-9122)
AMERICAN GRIP INC
8468 Kewen Ave, Sun Valley　(91352-3118)
PHONE..........................818 768-8922
Lance Snoke, *President*
EMP: 25 **EST:** 1984
SQ FT: 15,000
SALES (est): 4.8MM **Privately Held**
WEB: www.americangrip.com
SIC: 3648　3861　Stage lighting equipment; stands, camera & projector

(P-9123)
AMERICAN POWER SOLUTIONS INC
14355 Industry Cir, La Mirada
(90638-5810)
PHONE..........................714 626-0300
Bansik Yoon, *CEO*
Ritchie Hwang, *Software Dev*
Wayne Kim, *Sales Staff*
Lawrence Noh, *Sales Staff*
Charleen White, *Sales Staff*
▲ **EMP:** 20 **EST:** 2001
SALES (est): 4.9MM **Privately Held**
WEB: www.americanpowersolutions.com
SIC: 3648　Lighting equipment

(P-9124)
BEGA NORTH AMERICA INC
1000 Bega Way, Carpinteria　(93013-2902)
PHONE..........................805 684-0533
Don Kinderdick, *CEO*
Mark Reed, *Vice Pres*
Scott Sorensen, *Vice Pres*
Phil Modglin, *CTO*
Scott Knouse, *Network Tech*
◆ **EMP:** 100 **EST:** 1985
SQ FT: 60,000
SALES (est): 28MM **Privately Held**
WEB: www.bega-us.com
SIC: 3648　3646　Outdoor lighting equipment; commercial indusl & institutional electric lighting fixtures

(P-9125)
BIRCHWOOD LIGHTING INC
3340 E La Palma Ave, Anaheim
(92806-2814)
PHONE..........................714 550-7118
Darrin Weedon, *President*
Linda Allen, *Admin Sec*
EMP: 25 **EST:** 1993
SQ FT: 1,900
SALES (est): 9.1MM
SALES (corp-wide): 1.4B **Privately Held**
WEB: www.birchwoodlighting.com
SIC: 3648　3646　3645　Decorative area lighting fixtures; commercial indusl & institutional electric lighting fixtures; residential lighting fixtures
PA: Leviton Manufacturing Co., Inc.
　　201 N Service Rd
　　Melville NY 11747
　　631 812-6000

(P-9126)
DANA CREATH DESIGNS LTD
3030 Kilson Dr, Santa Ana　(92707-4203)
PHONE..........................714 662-0111
Dana E Creath, *Partner*
James K Creath, *Partner*
Raylene R Creath, *Partner*
EMP: 30 **EST:** 1968
SALES (est): 4.2MM **Privately Held**
WEB: www.danacreathdesigns.com
SIC: 3648　3646　3645　Lighting equipment; commercial indusl & institutional electric lighting fixtures; residential lighting fixtures

(P-9127)
EEMA INDUSTRIES INC
Also Called: Liton Lighting
5461 W Jefferson Blvd, Los Angeles
(90016-3715)
PHONE..........................323 904-0200
Amir Esmail Zadeh, *President*
Steve Symonds, *Natl Sales Mgr*
Tony Phan, *Marketing Staff*
Noel Madrid, *Manager*
◆ **EMP:** 40 **EST:** 1998

SQ FT: 40,000
SALES (est): 7.3MM **Privately Held**
WEB: www.eemagroup.com
SIC: 3648　5063　Lighting equipment; electrical apparatus & equipment

(P-9128)
EIDIM GROUP INC
Also Called: EIDIM AV TECHNOLOGY
6905 Oslo Cir Ste J, Buena Park
(90621-4671)
PHONE..........................562 777-1009
Andrew W Bang, *CEO*
Tim Pak, *Director*
EMP: 14 **EST:** 1999
SQ FT: 6,000
SALES (est): 4MM **Privately Held**
WEB: www.eidim.com
SIC: 3648　3651　5064　5065　Stage lighting equipment; public address systems; video camera-audio recorders (camcorders); video equipment, electronic

(P-9129)
ELATION LIGHTING INC
Also Called: Elation Professional
6122 S Eastern Ave, Commerce
(90040-3402)
PHONE..........................323 582-3322
Toby Velazquez, *President*
James Keeley, *Technician*
Francisco Aguilera, *Technology*
Scott Kinnebrew, *Engineer*
Ireneusz Skoczowski, *Engineer*
▲ **EMP:** 60 **EST:** 1992
SQ FT: 50,000
SALES (est): 15MM **Privately Held**
WEB: www.elationlighting.com
SIC: 3648　Lighting equipment

(P-9130)
ELITE LIGHTING
5424 E Slauson Ave, Commerce
(90040-2919)
PHONE..........................323 888-1973
Babak Rashiddoust, *CEO*
Daniel Lubin, *Project Engr*
Oscar Ramirez, *Engineer*
Ben Jebraeili, *Purchasing*
Valeria Rodriguez, *Purchasing*
◆ **EMP:** 200 **EST:** 1998
SQ FT: 25,000
SALES (est): 53.4MM **Privately Held**
WEB: www.iuseelite.com
SIC: 3648　3646　3645　Lighting equipment; commercial indusl & institutional electric lighting fixtures; boudoir lamps

(P-9131)
EMAZING LIGHTS LLC
240 S Loara St, Anaheim　(92802-1020)
PHONE..........................626 628-6482
Brian Lim, *Principal*
Joel Ruiz, *Store Mgr*
Randolth Yuson, *Project Mgr*
Jose Mendez, *Graphic Designe*
Steven Polanco, *Graphic Designe*
▲ **EMP:** 23 **EST:** 2010
SALES (est): 5.7MM **Privately Held**
WEB: www.gloving.com
SIC: 3648　3229　Spotlights; bulbs for electric lights

(P-9132)
FNTECH
3000 W Segerstrom Ave, Santa Ana
(92704-6526)
PHONE..........................714 429-7833
Jeremy Muir, *CEO*
Richard Barnes, *CIO*
Steven Mortimer, *Technician*
Chris Scanlan, *Technician*
Adam Dohm, *Opers Staff*
EMP: 40 **EST:** 2010
SALES (est): 4.9MM **Privately Held**
WEB: www.fntech.com
SIC: 3648　Lighting equipment

(P-9133)
FOCUS LINE LLC
160 Delfern Dr, Los Angeles　(90077-3541)
PHONE..........................818 517-5171
Lisa Larian,
Farhad Larian,
EMP: 16 **EST:** 2013

SALES (est): 2.6MM **Privately Held**
SIC: 3648　Outdoor lighting equipment

(P-9134)
GALLAGHER RENTAL NC
15701 Heron Ave, La Mirada　(90638-5206)
PHONE..........................714 690-1559
Joseph Gallagher, *CEO*
Bobby Castro, *CIO*
Megan Gallagher, *Manager*
Christopher Soares, *Accounts Exec*
EMP: 30 **EST:** 2012
SALES (est): 3.8MM **Privately Held**
WEB: www.gallagherstaging.com
SIC: 3648　Stage lighting equipment

(P-9135)
GREENSHINE NEW ENERGY LLC
23661 Birtcher Dr, Lake Forest
(92630-1770)
PHONE..........................949 609-9636
Alex Chen, *Sales Mgr*
Scott Douglas, *General Mgr*
Kevin Laurent, *Project Mgr*
Heidi Emmert, *Sales Mgr*
◆ **EMP:** 100 **EST:** 2010
SQ FT: 200
SALES (est): 7.7MM **Privately Held**
WEB: www.streetlights-solar.com
SIC: 3648　Lighting equipment

(P-9136)
JIMWAY INC
Also Called: Altair Lighting
20101 S Santa Fe Ave, Compton
(90221-5917)
PHONE..........................310 886-3718
Hsing-Min Keng, *CEO*
Rocks Hao, *Executive*
Irene Wang, *Admin Sec*
Jennifer Williams, *Admin Asst*
Singh Chang, *Info Tech Mgr*
▲ **EMP:** 100 **EST:** 1982
SQ FT: 200,000
SALES (est): 19.8MM **Privately Held**
WEB: www.designsftn.com
SIC: 3648　3221　5063　Lighting equipment; glass containers; electrical apparatus & equipment

(P-9137)
LEDCONN CORP
301 Thor Pl, Brea　(92821-4133)
PHONE..........................714 256-2111
Tsanyu Wang, *President*
Wan Ting Huang, *CFO*
Denise Torres, *Office Admn*
Desiree Ortiz, *Project Mgr*
Stella Liao, *Accountant*
▲ **EMP:** 25 **EST:** 2008
SQ FT: 2,000
SALES (est): 5.5MM **Privately Held**
WEB: www.ledconn.com
SIC: 3648　3993　7389　Lighting equipment; signs & advertising specialties; interior decorating

(P-9138)
LG-LED SOLUTIONS LIMITED
15902 Halliburton Rd A, Hacienda Heights
(91745-3500)
PHONE..........................626 587-8506
Zegao Hu, *CEO*
EMP: 50 **EST:** 2015
SALES (est): 1.6MM **Privately Held**
SIC: 3648　Lighting equipment

(P-9139)
LUMENTON INC
Also Called: Lumenton Lighting
5461 W Jefferson Blvd, Los Angeles
(90016-3715)
PHONE..........................323 904-0202
A J Esmailzadeh, *President*
Sonny Guerrero, *Purchasing*
▲ **EMP:** 17 **EST:** 1997
SQ FT: 100,000
SALES (est): 1.5MM **Privately Held**
WEB: www.eemagroup.com
SIC: 3648　Outdoor lighting equipment

(P-9140)
MAG INSTRUMENT INC (PA)
2001 S Hellman Ave, Ontario (91761-8019)
P.O. Box 50600 (91761-1083)
PHONE..................................909 947-1006
Anthony Maglica, *CEO*
Brent Flaharty, *Officer*
Malissa Peace, *Officer*
John Maglica, *Vice Pres*
James Zecchini, *Vice Pres*
▲ EMP: 903 EST: 1955
SQ FT: 1,000,000
SALES (est): 99.2MM Privately Held
WEB: www.maglite.com
SIC: 3648 Flashlights

(P-9141)
NEW BEDFORD PANORAMEX CORP
Also Called: Nbp
1480 N Claremont Blvd, Claremont
(91711-3538)
PHONE..................................909 982-9806
Steven Robert Ozuna, *President*
Bryce Nielsen, *Admin Sec*
Victor Zamora, *Project Engr*
Fernando Ramirez, *Controller*
Ken Harter, *Mfg Mgr*
EMP: 35 EST: 1966
SQ FT: 65,000
SALES (est): 9.2MM Privately Held
WEB: www.nbpcorp.com
SIC: 3648 Airport lighting fixtures: runway approach, taxi or ramp

(P-9142)
PACIFIC COAST LIGHTING INC (HQ)
Also Called: Pacific Coast Lighting Group
20238 Plummer St, Chatsworth
(91311-5365)
PHONE..................................800 709-9004
Dennis K Swanson, *CEO*
Dick Idol, *Partner*
Adrienne Quarto, *President*
Clark Linstone, *CEO*
Manja Swanson, *Admin Sec*
◆ EMP: 240 EST: 1979
SQ FT: 100,000
SALES (est): 41.3MM
SALES (corp-wide): 573.4MM Privately Held
WEB: www.pacificcoastlighting.com
SIC: 3648 3641 5719 Lighting equipment; electric lamps; lighting fixtures
PA: Lamps Plus, Inc.
20250 Plummer St
Chatsworth CA 91311
818 886-5267

(P-9143)
PELICAN PRODUCTS INC (PA)
23215 Early Ave, Torrance (90505-4002)
PHONE..................................310 326-4700
Phil Gyori, *President*
Peter Pace, *Ch of Bd*
Dave Williams, *President*
John Padian, *COO*
Don Jordan, *CFO*
◆ EMP: 401 EST: 1976
SQ FT: 150,000
SALES (est): 180.8MM Privately Held
WEB: www.pelican.com
SIC: 3648 3161 3089 Flashlights; luggage; plastic containers, except foam

(P-9144)
PRIMUS LIGHTING INC
3570 Lexington Ave, El Monte
(91731-2608)
PHONE..................................626 442-4600
Jaime Calderon, *President*
EMP: 13 EST: 1999
SQ FT: 5,300
SALES (est): 2.3MM Privately Held
WEB: www.primuslighting.com
SIC: 3648 Outdoor lighting equipment

(P-9145)
PRIORITY LIGHTING INC
77551 El Duna Ct Ste H, Palm Desert
(92211-4147)
PHONE..................................800 709-1119
Daniel Hengstler, *Mng Member*
Cassandra Coll, *Natl Sales Mgr*

Daniel J Hengstler,
Chris Edwards, *Supervisor*
EMP: 18 EST: 2009
SALES (est): 2.6MM Privately Held
WEB: www.prioritylighting.com
SIC: 5719 3648 5063 Lighting fixtures; lighting equipment; lighting fittings & accessories

(P-9146)
SHIMADA ENTERPRISES INC
Also Called: Celestial Lighting
14009 Dinard Ave, Santa Fe Springs
(90670-4922)
PHONE..................................562 802-8811
Tak Shimada, *President*
Mick Shimada, *Vice Pres*
Louise Song, *Controller*
Miguel Martinez, *Purchasing*
▲ EMP: 30 EST: 1975
SQ FT: 11,000
SALES (est): 4.8MM Privately Held
SIC: 3648 Decorative area lighting fixtures

(P-9147)
STERIL-AIRE INC
2840 N Lima St, Burbank (91504-2506)
PHONE..................................818 565-1128
Robert Scheir, *President*
Maricela Jimenez Steri, *CIO*
Bob Culbert, *Engineer*
Jose Barba, *Purchasing*
Tim Jones, *Plant Mgr*
◆ EMP: 23 EST: 1995
SQ FT: 15,000
SALES (est): 4.9MM Privately Held
WEB: www.steril-aire.com
SIC: 3648 Ultraviolet lamp fixtures

(P-9148)
SUN POWER SOURCE (PA)
1650 Palma Dr, Ventura (93003-5749)
PHONE..................................805 644-2520
Sean Frye, *President*
Tammy Frye, *Vice Pres*
EMP: 15 EST: 1989
SQ FT: 1,850
SALES (est): 3.1MM Privately Held
SIC: 3648 7299 Sun tanning equipment, incl. tanning beds; tanning salon

(P-9149)
TEC LIGHTING INC
115 Arovista Cir, Brea (92821-3830)
PHONE..................................714 529-5068
Kamal S Hodhodc, *CEO*
David Hodhod, *President*
Paul Hebert, *COO*
Alex Platt, *Technician*
Moses Nuno, *Engineer*
▲ EMP: 15 EST: 2001
SALES (est): 7.5MM Privately Held
WEB: www.teclighting.com
SIC: 3648 Lighting equipment

(P-9150)
THIN-LITE CORPORATION
530 Constitution Ave, Camarillo
(93012-8595)
PHONE..................................805 987-5021
Alan Griffin, *President*
Lilian Cross Szymanek, *Co-President*
▲ EMP: 47 EST: 1970
SQ FT: 27,000
SALES (est): 7.7MM Privately Held
WEB: www.thinlite.com
SIC: 3648 3612 3646 Lighting equipment; transformers, except electric; fluorescent lighting fixtures, commercial

(P-9151)
TIVOLI INDUSTRIES INC
1550 E Saint Gertrude Pl, Santa Ana
(92705-5310)
PHONE..................................714 957-6101
Peter Jang, *CEO*
▲ EMP: 22 EST: 1991
SALES (est): 546K Privately Held
WEB: www.tivolilighting.com
SIC: 3648 Lighting equipment

(P-9152)
TOTAL STRUCTURES INC
1696 Walter St, Ventura (93003-5619)
PHONE..................................805 676-3322
Martijn Kuijper, *President*

Danielle Magdaleno, *Office Admin*
Theresa Kelley, *Admin Sec*
Ian Coles, *MIS Mgr*
Sarah Haden, *Controller*
◆ EMP: 32 EST: 1995
SQ FT: 24,000
SALES (est): 14.6MM Privately Held
WEB: www.totalstructures.com
SIC: 3648 3441 Lighting equipment; fabricated structural metal

(P-9153)
TRULY GREEN SOLUTIONS LLC
9601 Variel Ave, Chatsworth (91311-4914)
PHONE..................................818 206-4404
Rubina Jadwet, *CEO*
Jennifer Cataffo, *Admin Asst*
Johana Romero, *Cust Mgr*
▲ EMP: 25 EST: 2010
SALES (est): 4.5MM Privately Held
WEB: www.trulygreensolutions.com
SIC: 3648 Lighting equipment

3651 Household Audio & Video Eqpt

(P-9154)
ABSOLUTE USA INC
Also Called: Absolute Pro Music
1800 E Washington Blvd, Los Angeles
(90021-3127)
PHONE..................................213 744-0044
Mohammad K Razipour, *President*
Junior Perez, *Sales Executive*
Juan Barragan, *Sales Dir*
Jesse Rosales, *Sales Staff*
Sam Farzan, *Manager*
◆ EMP: 47 EST: 2002
SQ FT: 35,000
SALES (est): 9.6MM Privately Held
WEB: www.absolutepromusic.com
SIC: 3651 Audio electronic systems

(P-9155)
ACTI CORPORATION INC
Also Called: California Acti
3 Jenner Ste 160, Irvine (92618-3834)
PHONE..................................949 753-0352
Juber Chu, *President*
Kelvin Wong, *CFO*
Frank Fang, *Sales Staff*
Joe Hudak, *Sales Staff*
Christine Jan, *Sales Staff*
EMP: 20 EST: 2008
SALES (est): 4.9MM Privately Held
WEB: www.acti.com
SIC: 3651 3663 3699 Household audio & video equipment; cameras, television; security devices
PA: Acti Corporation
7f, No. 1, Alley 20, Lane 407, Tiding Blvd., Sec. 2
Taipei City TAP 11493

(P-9156)
ADAPTIVE TECH GROUP INC
Also Called: Atm Fly-Ware
1635 E Burnett St, Signal Hill (90755-3603)
PHONE..................................562 424-1100
Paul W Allen, *President*
Frans Olivier, *Sales Staff*
▲ EMP: 20
SALES (est): 4.3MM Privately Held
WEB: www.adaptivetechnologiesgroup.com
SIC: 5961 3651 Electronic kits & parts, mail order; household audio equipment

(P-9157)
ALURATEK INC
15241 Barranca Pkwy, Irvine (92618-2201)
PHONE..................................949 468-2046
John Wolikow, *CEO*
Akash Patel, *CFO*
Dave Song, *Vice Pres*
Andrew Wang, *Vice Pres*
Victor Wang, *Principal*
▲ EMP: 25 EST: 2006
SQ FT: 5,000

SALES (est): 3.5MM Privately Held
WEB: www.aluratek.com
SIC: 3651 5045 Home entertainment equipment, electronic; audio electronic systems; computers, peripherals & software

(P-9158)
ANACOM GENERAL CORPORATION
Also Called: Anacom Medtek
1240 S Claudina St, Anaheim
(92805-6232)
PHONE..................................714 774-8484
Daniel S Haines, *President*
William K Haines, *Chairman*
Dan Haines, *Executive*
Jennifer Smithson, *Human Res Mgr*
Shannon Williams, *Purch Agent*
▲ EMP: 48 EST: 1967
SQ FT: 20,000
SALES (est): 11.1MM Privately Held
WEB: www.anacom-medtek.com
SIC: 3651 3577 Speaker monitors; computer peripheral equipment

(P-9159)
APOGEE ELECTRONICS CORPORATION
1715 Berkeley St, Santa Monica
(90404-4104)
PHONE..................................310 584-9394
Betty A Bennett, *CEO*
Tina Franco, *Administration*
Pieter Kelchtermans, *Electrical Engi*
Joseph Nader, *Marketing Staff*
Chris Shapiro, *Sales Staff*
▲ EMP: 35 EST: 1985
SQ FT: 5,000
SALES (est): 8.2MM Privately Held
WEB: www.apogeedigital.com
SIC: 3651 3621 8748 Audio electronic systems; motors & generators; communications consulting

(P-9160)
AUDIONICS SYSTEM INC
21541 Nordhoff St Ste C, Chatsworth
(91311-6983)
PHONE..................................818 345-9599
Khalid Jaffer, *President*
Sameera Khalid, *Admin Sec*
Richard N Hofmann, *Manager*
▲ EMP: 14 EST: 1990
SQ FT: 6,000
SALES (est): 4.5MM Privately Held
WEB: www.audionicsystem.com
SIC: 3651 Household audio & video equipment

(P-9161)
BALTIC LTVIAN UNVRSAL ELEC LLC
Also Called: Blue Microphone
5706 Corsa Ave Ste 102, Westlake Village
(91362-4057)
PHONE..................................818 879-5200
John Maier, *CEO*
Bart E Thielen, *CFO*
Adam Bennett, *Engineer*
Mark Burleson, *Engineer*
Jonathan Vonrentzell, *Regl Sales Mgr*
▲ EMP: 35 EST: 1998
SQ FT: 6,300
SALES (est): 8.2MM
SALES (corp-wide): 2.9B Privately Held
WEB: www.bluedesigns.com
SIC: 3651 5731 Microphones; consumer electronic equipment
PA: Logitech International S.A.
Les Chatagnis
Apples VD
218 635-511

(P-9162)
BEATS ELECTRONICS LLC
Also Called: Beats By Dre
8600 Hayden Pl, Culver City (90232-2902)
PHONE..................................424 326-4679
Timothy Cook, *CEO*
Fabiola Torres, *Vice Pres*
Victoria Deldin, *Creative Dir*
Casey Ryder, *Creative Dir*
Curtis Wong, *Engineer*
▲ EMP: 500 EST: 2006

SALES (est): 136.9MM
SALES (corp-wide): 365.8B **Publicly Held**
WEB: www.beatsbydre.com
SIC: 3651 3679 Speaker systems; headphones, radio
PA: Apple Inc.
1 Apple Park Way
Cupertino CA 95014
408 996-1010

(P-9163)
BELKIN INC
12045 Waterfront Dr, Playa Vista (90094-2999)
PHONE.....................800 223-5546
Chester J Pipkin, *President*
George Platisa, *CFO*
Sunny Choi, *Vice Pres*
Vj Nalwad, *Vice Pres*
Chris Rising, *Vice Pres*
◆ **EMP:** 235 **EST:** 2003
SALES (est): 23.6MM **Privately Held**
WEB: www.belkin.com
SIC: 3651 Electronic kits for home assembly: radio, TV, phonograph
HQ: Belkin International, Inc.
12045 Waterfront Dr
Playa Vista CA 90094
310 751-5100

(P-9164)
BIG 5 ELECTRONICS INC
Also Called: Big Five Electronics
13452 Alondra Blvd, Cerritos (90703-2315)
PHONE.....................562 941-4669
Amina Bawaney, *CEO*
Latif Bawaney, *President*
Rizwan Bawaney, *CFO*
Cynthia Linares, *General Mgr*
Carlos Cortez, *VP Sls/Mktg*
▲ **EMP:** 22 **EST:** 2003
SQ FT: 4,500
SALES (est): 4.8MM **Privately Held**
WEB: www.big5electronics.com
SIC: 3651 5099 5065 Audio electronic systems; video & audio equipment; electronic parts & equipment

(P-9165)
BLUE MICROPHONES LLC
5706 Corsa Ave Ste 102, Westlake Village (91362-4057)
PHONE.....................818 879-5200
Fax: 818 879-7258
EMP: 17 **EST:** 2008
SALES (est): 2.4MM **Privately Held**
SIC: 3651 Mfg Home Audio/Video Equipment

(P-9166)
BOSS INTERNATIONAL LLC (PA)
Also Called: Boss Audio Systems
3451 Lunar Ct, Oxnard (93030-8976)
PHONE.....................805 988-0192
Soheil Rabbani, *Mng Member*
Steve Garcia, *CFO*
Sheila Rabbani, *Vice Pres*
Eva Loeffler, *Human Resources*
Juan Sequeira, *Opers Mgr*
▼ **EMP:** 79 **EST:** 2012
SALES (est): 27.9MM **Privately Held**
WEB: www.bossaudio.com
SIC: 3651 Audio electronic systems

(P-9167)
CONVOY TECHNOLOGIES LLC
3300 Irvine Ave Ste 300, Newport Beach (92660-3108)
PHONE.....................949 680-9400
Allan Hillyer, *Vice Pres*
Ron Harker, *Sales Staff*
EMP: 13 **EST:** 2019
SALES (est): 518.4K **Privately Held**
WEB: www.convoytechnologies.com
SIC: 3651 Household audio & video equipment

(P-9168)
CUSTOM AUTOSOUND MFG INC
1030 Williamson Ave, Fullerton (92833-2746)
PHONE.....................714 535-1091
Carlton Sprague, *President*
▲ **EMP:** 23 **EST:** 1976

SQ FT: 18,000
SALES (est): 1.4MM **Privately Held**
WEB: www.customautosoundmfg.com
SIC: 3651 Audio electronic systems

(P-9169)
DANA INNOVATIONS
Also Called: Sonance
991 Calle Amanecer, San Clemente (92673-6212)
PHONE.....................949 492-7777
ARI Supran, *CEO*
Scott Struthers, *President*
Mike Simmons, *CFO*
Geoffrey L Spencer, *Corp Secy*
Jason Sloan, *Officer*
◆ **EMP:** 59 **EST:** 1981
SQ FT: 42,320
SALES (est): 13.8MM **Privately Held**
WEB: www.sonance.com
SIC: 3651 5731 7629 Speaker systems; radio, television & electronic stores; electrical repair shops

(P-9170)
DAVENPORT INTERNATIONAL CORP
7230 Coldwater Canyon Ave, North Hollywood (91605-4203)
P.O. Box 16539 (91615-6539)
PHONE.....................818 765-6400
Daniel Mamane, *President*
▲ **EMP:** 13 **EST:** 1993
SQ FT: 50,000
SALES (est): 270.4K **Privately Held**
SIC: 3651 7819 7812 7334 Household audio & video equipment; reproduction services, motion picture production; motion picture & video production; photocopying & duplicating services

(P-9171)
DIGITAL PERIPH SOLUTIONS INC
Also Called: Q-See
160 S Old Springs Rd # 22, Anaheim (92808-1260)
PHONE.....................714 998-3440
Priti Sharma, *President*
Rajeev Sharma, *CFO*
Evelyn Stephens, *Human Res Mgr*
Bridget Melson, *Marketing Staff*
Wil Parker, *Marketing Staff*
▲ **EMP:** 40 **EST:** 2002
SQ FT: 30,000
SALES (est): 9MM **Privately Held**
SIC: 3651 7382 Video camera-audio recorders, household use; confinement surveillance systems maintenance & monitoring

(P-9172)
DTS LLC
5220 Las Virgenes Rd, Calabasas (91302-1064)
PHONE.....................818 436-1000
Jon Kirchner,
EMP: 26 **EST:** 2012
SALES (est): 4.6MM
SALES (corp-wide): 892MM **Publicly Held**
WEB: www.dts.com
SIC: 3651 3845 Audio electronic systems; audiological equipment, electromedical
HQ: Dts, Inc.
5220 Las Virgenes Rd
Calabasas CA 91302

(P-9173)
DWI ENTERPRISES
11081 Winners Cir Ste 100, Los Alamitos (90720-2894)
PHONE.....................714 842-2236
Fred Delgleize, *President*
Amanda Delgleize, *CFO*
Dave Dain, *Vice Pres*
Dan Delgleize, *Vice Pres*
Mike Delgleize, *Vice Pres*
◆ **EMP:** 25 **EST:** 1980
SQ FT: 9,500
SALES (est): 1.9MM **Privately Held**
WEB: www.dwienterprises.com
SIC: 3651 3669 Audio electronic systems; visual communication systems

(P-9174)
ELECTRONIC AUTO SYSTEMS INC
9855 Joe Vargas Way, South El Monte (91733-3107)
PHONE.....................626 280-3855
Chang Ye Tong, *President*
Virginia Young, *Treasurer*
Eduardo Lo, *Exec VP*
Julio Young, *Vice Pres*
◆ **EMP:** 13 **EST:** 1988
SQ FT: 9,000
SALES (est): 532.8K **Privately Held**
SIC: 3651 Speaker systems

(P-9175)
ETI SOUND SYSTEMS INC
Also Called: Eti B Si Professional
5300 Harbor St, Commerce (90040-3927)
PHONE.....................323 835-6660
Eli El-Kiss, *President*
AVI El-Kiss, *Vice Pres*
Todd Vucins, *Admin Sec*
Gustavo Afont, *Sales Staff*
◆ **EMP:** 45 **EST:** 1989
SALES (est): 7.8MM **Privately Held**
WEB: www.b-52pro.com
SIC: 3651 Speaker monitors

(P-9176)
FUNAI CORPORATION INC (HQ)
12489 Lakeland Rd, Santa Fe Springs (90670-3938)
PHONE.....................201 806-7635
Ryo Fukuda, *President*
George Kanazawa, *CFO*
Yoshi Kanazawa, *CFO*
Lori Vullo, *Financial Exec*
Lisa Green, *Manager*
▲ **EMP:** 25 **EST:** 2008
SALES (est): 12MM **Privately Held**
WEB: www.funai.us
SIC: 3651 Household audio & video equipment

(P-9177)
HARMAN PROFESSIONAL INC (DH)
8500 Balboa Blvd, Northridge (91329-0003)
P.O. Box 2200 (91328-2200)
PHONE.....................818 893-8411
Michelle Taigman, *CEO*
Buzz Goodwin, *Exec VP*
Diane Ettinger, *Vice Pres*
Mark Gander, *Executive*
Kevin Vass, *Controller*
◆ **EMP:** 300 **EST:** 2006
SALES (est): 132.6K **Privately Held**
WEB: www.harman.com
SIC: 3651 Audio electronic systems
HQ: Harman International Industries Incorporated
400 Atlantic St
Stamford CT 06901
203 328-3500

(P-9178)
HENRYS ADIO VSUAL SLUTIONS INC
Also Called: Audio Images
1582 Parkway Loop Ste F, Tustin (92780-6505)
PHONE.....................714 258-7238
Mark Ontiveros, *CEO*
Suzy Laros, *Controller*
Rick Gallagher, *Sr Project Mgr*
EMP: 30 **EST:** 1998
SQ FT: 5,400
SALES (est): 5.6MM **Privately Held**
WEB: www.audioimages.tv
SIC: 3651 Household audio & video equipment

(P-9179)
HONAV USA INC
3030 W Warner Ave, Santa Ana (92704-5311)
PHONE.....................858 634-0617
David Jacobs, *President*
▲ **EMP:** 15 **EST:** 2013
SALES (est): 2.8MM **Privately Held**
WEB: www.honavusa.com
SIC: 3651 Speaker systems

PA: Beijing Huajiang Culture Group Co., Ltd.
No.9, Chongwenmenwai Avenue,
Chongwen District
Beijing 10006

(P-9180)
HPV TECHNOLOGIES INC
3030 Orange Ave, Santa Ana 92707-4248)
PHONE.....................949 476-7000
Vahan Simidian, *President*
Phillip Hamilton, *Vice Pres*
▼ **EMP:** 13 **EST:** 1999
SALES (est): 944.2K **Privately Held**
WEB: www.getmad.com
SIC: 3651 Speaker systems

(P-9181)
INTERMED VIDEO TECH INC
38 Waterworks Way, Irvine (92618-3107)
PHONE.....................203 270-9100
Roland Soohoo, *President*
EMP: 21 **EST:** 1990
SQ FT: 10,000
SALES (est): 327.6K **Privately Held**
WEB: www.sekai-electronics.com
SIC: 3651 3844 Household audio & video equipment; X-ray apparatus & tubes

(P-9182)
MAGNASYNC/MOVIOLA CORPORATION
Also Called: Magnasync-Moviola
1400 W Burbank Blvd, Burbank (91506-1308)
PHONE.....................818 845-8066
EMP: 20
SALES (corp-wide): 41.2MM **Privately Held**
WEB: www.filmtools.com
SIC: 3651 Household audio & video equipment
PA: Magnasync/Moviola Corporation
1015 N Hollywood Way
Burbank CA
818 845-8066

(P-9183)
MEDIAPOINTE INC
3952 Camino Ranchero, Camarillo (93012-5066)
PHONE.....................805 480-3700
Stephen Villoria, *CEO*
Kevin Leehey, *Vice Pres*
Bobby Ross, *Mfg Dir*
Wesley Hair, *Director*
Kevin Bergner, *Manager*
EMP: 17 **EST:** 2011
SALES (est): 2.5MM **Privately Held**
WEB: www.mediapointe.com
SIC: 3651 Audio electronic systems

(P-9184)
MJ BEST VIDEOGRAPHER LLC
14005 S Berendo Ave Ap 3, Gardena (90247-2248)
PHONE.....................209 208-8432
John S Morris, *CEO*
EMP: 209 **EST:** 2020
SALES (est): 125K **Privately Held**
WEB: www.mjbestvideographer.com
SIC: 3651 Video camera-audio recorders, household use

(P-9185)
O W I INC
Also Called: Movits
17141 Kingsview Ave, Carson (90746-1207)
PHONE.....................310 515-1900
Ned Morioka, *CEO*
Craig Morioka, *President*
Kristin Martinez, *Treasurer*
Joseph Martinez, *Vice Pres*
June Morioka, *Admin Sec*
▲ **EMP:** 13 **EST:** 1979
SQ FT: 17,000
SALES (est): 2.5MM **Privately Held**
WEB: www.owi-inc.com
SIC: 3651 5064 3944 5099 Speaker systems; high fidelity equipment; electronic toys; robots, service or novelty

(P-9186)
QSC LLC (PA)
Also Called: Qsc Audio
1675 Macarthur Blvd, Costa Mesa
(92626-1468)
PHONE..................................800 854-4079
Joe Pham, *President*
Jatan Shah, *COO*
Aravind Yarlagadda, *Exec VP*
Barry Ferrell, *Senior VP*
Zora Boieux, *Vice Pres*
◆ EMP: 337 EST: 1979
SQ FT: 180,000
SALES (est): 116.1MM Privately Held
WEB: www.qsc.com
SIC: 3651 Household audio equipment

(P-9187)
RENKUS-HEINZ INC (PA)
19201 Cook St, Foothill Ranch
(92610-3501)
PHONE..................................949 588-9997
Harro Heinz, *President*
Roscoe L Anthony III, *CEO*
Monika Smetona, *CFO*
Karl Brunvoll, *Vice Pres*
Erika Heinz, *Admin Sec*
▲ EMP: 79 EST: 1979
SQ FT: 48,500
SALES (est): 14.5MM Privately Held
WEB: www.renkus-heinz.com
SIC: 3651 Audio electronic systems

(P-9188)
RIDER BEST INC (PA)
428 S 9th Ave, City of Industry
(91746-3313)
PHONE..................................626 336-8388
Xue Ying Zheng, *CEO*
▲ EMP: 22 EST: 2012
SALES (est): 604.9K Privately Held
SIC: 5734 3651 Computer software & accessories; speaker systems; microphones

(P-9189)
ROBOT-GXG INC
8960 Toronto Ave, Rancho Cucamonga
(91730-5411)
PHONE..................................660 324-0030
Xiwen Xu, *Principal*
EMP: 20 EST: 2019
SALES (est): 848.6K Privately Held
SIC: 3651 Home entertainment equipment, electronic

(P-9190)
ROCK-OLA MANUFACTURING CORP
Also Called: Antique Apparatus Company
1445 Sepulveda Blvd, Torrance
(90501-5004)
PHONE..................................310 328-1306
Glenn S Streeter, *President*
◆ EMP: 80 EST: 1994
SALES (est): 13.5MM Privately Held
WEB: www.rock-ola.com
SIC: 3651 Coin-operated phonographs, juke boxes; speaker systems

(P-9191)
RODE MICROPHONES LLC
2745 Raymond Ave, Signal Hill
(90755-2129)
P.O. Box 91028, Long Beach (90809-1028)
PHONE..................................310 328-7456
Mark Ludmer, *CEO*
Peter Freedmon, *President*
Brian Swbaringen, *District Mgr*
▲ EMP: 140 EST: 2001
SALES (est): 21.2MM Privately Held
WEB: www.rode.com
SIC: 3651 Microphones
HQ: Freedman Electronics Pty Ltd
107 Carnarvon St
Silverwater NSW 2128

(P-9192)
S2E INC
Also Called: Mee Audio
817 Lawson St, City of Industry
(91748-1104)
PHONE..................................626 965-1008
Martie Shieh, *President*
Jerry Hsieh, *Vice Pres*
Jerry Shieh, *Vice Pres*

Jones Mike, *Mktg Dir*
▲ EMP: 15 EST: 2005
SQ FT: 7,000
SALES (est): 2.3MM Privately Held
WEB: www.meeaudio.com
SIC: 3651 Household audio & video equipment

(P-9193)
SAILING INNOVATION (US) INC
17870 Castleton St # 220, City of Industry
(91748-1755)
PHONE..................................626 965-6665
Steven Goldsmith, *CEO*
Valen Tong, *CFO*
Kiran Smith, *Chief Mktg Ofcr*
Stephen A Gould, *Senior VP*
Lauren Van Heerden, *Vice Pres*
EMP: 3187 EST: 2014
SALES (est): 12.7MM Privately Held
SIC: 5945 3651 Toys & games; audio electronic systems

(P-9194)
SCOSCHE INDUSTRIES INC
1550 Pacific Ave, Oxnard (93033-2451)
P.O. Box 2901 (93034-2901)
PHONE..................................805 486-4450
Roger Alves, *CEO*
Steven R Klinger, *CFO*
Kasidy Alves, *Exec VP*
Vincent Alves, *Exec VP*
Scotia Alves, *Vice Pres*
◆ EMP: 150 EST: 1980
SQ FT: 83,000
SALES (est): 47.3MM Privately Held
WEB: www.scosche.com
SIC: 3651 Audio electronic systems

(P-9195)
SIGMATRONIX INC
2109 S Susan St, Santa Ana (92704-4416)
PHONE..................................714 436-1618
Michael Dang, *President*
EMP: 15 EST: 2005
SQ FT: 5,600
SALES (est): 1MM Privately Held
WEB: www.sigmatronix.com
SIC: 3651 Electronic kits for home assembly: radio, TV, phonograph

(P-9196)
SONOS INC (PA)
614 Chapala St, Santa Barbara
(93101-3312)
PHONE..................................805 965-3001
Patrick Spence, *CEO*
Michelangelo Volpi, *Ch of Bd*
David Perri, *COO*
Brittany Bagley, *CFO*
Edward Lazarus,
◆ EMP: 91 EST: 2002
SALES: 1.3B Publicly Held
WEB: www.sonos.com
SIC: 3651 Household audio & video equipment

(P-9197)
SOUND STORM LABORATORIES LLC
3451 Lunar Ct, Oxnard (93030-8976)
PHONE..................................805 983-8008
Nasrin Rouhani,
Cameron Arbani,
▲ EMP: 18 EST: 1998
SQ FT: 72,000
SALES (est): 528.6K Privately Held
WEB: www.soundstormlab.com
SIC: 3651 5731 Audio electronic systems; radio, television & electronic stores

(P-9198)
SYNG INC
120 Mildred Ave, Venice (90291-4227)
PHONE..................................770 354-0915
Christopher Stringer, *CEO*
Afrooz Family, *Principal*
Damon Way, *Principal*
EMP: 65 EST: 2018
SALES (est): 9.2MM Privately Held
WEB: www.syngspace.com
SIC: 3651 Loudspeakers, electrodynamic or magnetic

(P-9199)
TECHNICOLOR USA INC
Also Called: Technicolor Connected USA
4049 Industrial Pkwy Dr, Lebec
(93243-9719)
PHONE..................................661 496-1309
EMP: 523
SALES (corp-wide): 57.9MM Privately Held
SIC: 3651 Household audio & video equipment
HQ: Technicolor Usa, Inc.
6040 W Sunset Blvd
Hollywood CA 90028
317 587-4287

(P-9200)
TECHNICOLOR USA INC
1507 Railroad St, Glendale (91204-2774)
PHONE..................................818 500-9090
EMP: 143
SALES (corp-wide): 82MM Privately Held
SIC: 3651 Mfg Home Audio/Video Eqp
HQ: Technicolor Usa, Inc.
4 Research Way
Princeton NJ 90028
317 587-3000

(P-9201)
TECHNICOLOR USA INC
Also Called: Technicolor Content Services
440 W Los Feliz Rd, Glendale
(91204-2776)
PHONE..................................818 260-3651
EMP: 143
SALES (corp-wide): 115.5MM Privately Held
SIC: 3651 3861 3661 Mfg Home Audio/Video Eqp Mfg Photo Equip/Supplies
HQ: Technicolor Usa, Inc.
101 W 103rd St
Indianapolis IN 90028
317 587-3000

(P-9202)
THETA DIGITAL CORPORATION
1749 Chapin Rd, Montebello (90640-6609)
PHONE..................................818 572-4300
Neil Sinclair, *President*
▲ EMP: 28 EST: 1988
SQ FT: 12,000
SALES (est): 448.5K Privately Held
WEB: www.thetadigital.com
SIC: 3651 5731 Audio electronic systems; radio, television & electronic stores

(P-9203)
TOSHIBA AMER ELCTRNIC CMPNNTS (DH)
5231 California Ave, Irvine (92617-3073)
PHONE..................................949 462-7700
Hideya Yamaguchi, *CEO*
Hitoshi Otsuka, *President*
Satrajit Misra, *Officer*
Ichiro Hirata, *Exec VP*
Bill Bell, *Vice Pres*
◆ EMP: 300 EST: 1998
SQ FT: 100,000
SALES (est): 394.8MM Privately Held
WEB: www.toshiba.com
SIC: 3651 3631 3674 3679 Television receiving sets; video cassette recorders/players & accessories; microwave ovens, including portable: household; semiconductors & related devices; electronic circuits; electronic parts & equipment; video cassette recorders & accessories; high fidelity equipment
HQ: Toshiba America Inc
1251 Ave Of Amrcas Ste 41
New York NY 10020
212 596-0600

(P-9204)
ULTIMATE SOUND INC
1200 S Diamond Bar Blvd # 200, Diamond Bar (91765-2298)
PHONE..................................909 861-6200
Robert Chiu, *President*
Cindy Chiu, *Vice Pres*
Alex Chiu, *Bus Dvlpt Dir*
◆ EMP: 300 EST: 1978
SQ FT: 20,000

SALES (est): 15.8MM Privately Held
SIC: 3651 5731 Loudspeakers, electrodynamic or magnetic; amplifiers: radio, public address or musical instrument; radio, television & electronic stores

(P-9205)
VANDERSTEEN AUDIO
116 W 4th St, Hanford (93230-5021)
PHONE..................................559 582-0324
Richard J Vandersteen, *President*
Eneke Vandersteen, *Principal*
▲ EMP: 21 EST: 1977
SQ FT: 20,000
SALES (est): 2.1MM Privately Held
WEB: www.vandersteen.com
SIC: 3651 5731 Speaker systems; radio, television & electronic stores

(P-9206)
VANTAGE POINT PRODUCTS CORP (PA)
Also Called: Vpt Direct
9115 Dice Rd Ste 18, Santa Fe Springs
(90670-2538)
P.O. Box 2485 (90670-0485)
PHONE..................................562 946-1718
Donald R Burns, *CEO*
Mick Mulcahey, *President*
Mike Ackermann, *Sales Staff*
John Silva, *Manager*
▲ EMP: 59 EST: 1988
SQ FT: 62,000
SALES (est): 7.1MM Privately Held
WEB: www.thinkvp.com
SIC: 3651 Audio electronic systems

(P-9207)
VIZIO INC (PA)
39 Tesla, Irvine (92618-4603)
PHONE..................................855 833-3221
William Wang, *CEO*
Ken Lowe, *President*
Adam Townsend, *CFO*
Lisa Johnstone, *Chief Mktg Ofcr*
Derrick Beard, *Vice Pres*
◆ EMP: 154 EST: 2002
SQ FT: 27,300
SALES (est): 189.7MM Privately Held
WEB: www.vizio.com
SIC: 3651 Television receiving sets; compact disk players

(P-9208)
VIZIO HOLDING CORP
39 Tesla, Irvine (92618-4603)
PHONE..................................949 428-2525
William Wang, *Ch of Bd*
Ben Wong, *President*
Adam Townsend, *CFO*
Michael O'Donnell, *Risk Mgmt Dir*
Bill Baxter, *CTO*
EMP: 527 EST: 2003
SALES (est): 33.8MM Privately Held
WEB: www.vizio.com
SIC: 3651 Household audio & video equipment

(P-9209)
VTL AMPLIFIERS INC
4774 Murrieta St Ste 10, Chino
(91710-5155)
PHONE..................................909 627-5944
Luke Manley, *President*
▲ EMP: 24 EST: 2000
SQ FT: 6,000
SALES (est): 1.8MM Privately Held
WEB: www.vtl.com
SIC: 3651 Audio electronic systems

(P-9210)
WIRELESS TECHNOLOGY INC
Also Called: Wti
2064 Eastman Ave Ste 113, Ventura
(93003-7787)
PHONE..................................805 339-9696
Phil Fancher, *CEO*
Arlene Fancher, *CFO*
Len Harvey, *Executive*
David Malackowskit, *CIO*
David Scales, *CIO*
EMP: 30 EST: 1987
SQ FT: 7,000
SALES (est): 7,000 Privately Held
WEB: www.gotowti.com
SIC: 3651 Household audio & video equipment

3652 Phonograph Records & Magnetic Tape

(P-9211)
APPONBOARD
11620 Wilshire Blvd # 37, Los Angeles (90025-1706)
PHONE...................707 933-7729
Mike Seavers, *CEO*
Matt Chin, *Vice Pres*
Doug Manson, *Vice Pres*
Nathan Zhang, *Vice Pres*
Adam Piechowicz, *CTO*
EMP: 17 **EST:** 2019
SALES (est): 1.1MM **Privately Held**
WEB: www.apponboard.com
SIC: 3652 Pre-recorded records & tapes

(P-9212)
CMH RECORDS INC
Also Called: Vitamin Records
2898 Rowena Ave Ste 201, Los Angeles (90039-2096)
P.O. Box 39439 (90039-0439)
PHONE...................323 663-8098
David Haerle, *President*
EMP: 29 **EST:** 1975
SQ FT: 3,303
SALES (est): 2.6MM **Privately Held**
WEB: www.cmhrecords.com
SIC: 3652 7929 Phonograph records, pre-recorded; entertainers & entertainment groups

(P-9213)
DISC REPLICATOR INC
21137 Commerce Point Dr, Walnut (91789-3054)
PHONE...................909 385-0118
Jingtao Xie, *CEO*
Amelyn Binagy, *Manager*
EMP: 15 **EST:** 2014
SALES (est): 2MM **Privately Held**
WEB: www.discreplicator.com
SIC: 3652 Compact laser discs, pre-recorded

(P-9214)
DISCOPYLABS
Also Called: Dcl
4455 E Philadelphia St, Ontario (91761-2329)
PHONE...................909 390-3800
Larry Shaker, *Director*
Mike Schneider, *Vice Pres*
Shane Gauthier, *Design Engr*
Ricky Anaya, *Technology*
Michael Haas, *Inv Control Mgr*
EMP: 18
SALES (corp-wide): 75.4MM **Privately Held**
WEB: www.dclcorp.com
SIC: 3652 4225 7379 7389 Pre-recorded records & tapes; general warehousing & storage; ; ; materials mgmt. (purchasing, handling, inventory) consultant
PA: Discopylabs
48641 Milmont Dr
Fremont CA 94538
510 651-5100

(P-9215)
ENAS MEDIA INC
1316 Michillinda Ave, Arcadia (91006-1921)
PHONE...................626 962-1115
Nagapet Keshishian, *President*
Avetis Keshishian, *Vice Pres*
Serop Keshishian, *Vice Pres*
Nick Keshian, *Mfg Staff*
EMP: 22 **EST:** 1985
SALES (est): 1.5MM **Privately Held**
SIC: 3652 Phonograph records, pre-recorded

(P-9216)
ERIKA RECORDS INC
6300 Caballero Blvd, Buena Park (90620-1126)
PHONE...................714 228-5420
Liz Dunster, *President*
Erzsebet Dunster, *CEO*
Ashley Hernandez, *Receptionist*

▲ **EMP:** 20 **EST:** 1981
SALES (est): 4.9MM **Privately Held**
WEB: www.erikarecords.com
SIC: 3652 5735 Phonograph records, pre-recorded; compact laser discs, pre-recorded; records

(P-9217)
EXTREME GROUP HOLDINGS LLC
Also Called: Extreme Production Music
1531 14th St, Santa Monica (90404-3302)
PHONE...................310 899-3200
Emanuel Russell, *Branch Mgr*
EMP: 23 **Privately Held**
SIC: 3652 Pre-recorded records & tapes
HQ: Extreme Group Holdings Llc
25 Madison Ave
New York NY 10010

(P-9218)
GC INTERNATIONAL INC
Also Called: Al Johnson Company
4671 Calle Carga, Camarillo (93012-8560)
PHONE...................805 389-4631
Mark Griffith, *Principal*
Mark Giffith, *Vice Pres*
EMP: 15
SALES (corp-wide): 14.3MM **Publicly Held**
WEB: www.aljcast.com
SIC: 3652 3369 Phonograph record blanks; lead, zinc & white metal
PA: Gc International, Inc.
4671 Calle Carga
Camarillo CA 93012
805 389-4631

(P-9219)
GOSPEL RECORDINGS
41823 Enterprise Cir N # 200, Temecula (92590-5682)
PHONE...................951 719-1650
Colin Stott, *Exec Dir*
Mac Timm, *President*
Bill Cornthwaite, *Vice Pres*
Dale Rickards, *Exec Dir*
Doug Fletcher, *Technology*
EMP: 14 **EST:** 1943
SQ FT: 20,000
SALES (est): 1.5MM **Privately Held**
WEB: www.globalrecordings.net
SIC: 3652 Pre-recorded records & tapes

(P-9220)
HOLLYWOOD RECORDS INC
Also Called: Andanov Music
500 S Buena Vista St, Burbank (91521-0002)
PHONE...................818 560-5670
Abbey Konowitch, *General Mgr*
Lillian Matulic, *Vice Pres*
Michele Alexander, *Marketing Staff*
Tamala Hutcherson, *Manager*
EMP: 50 **EST:** 1990
SALES (est): 15.3MM
SALES (corp-wide): 65.3B **Publicly Held**
WEB: www.hollywoodrecords.com
SIC: 3652 Pre-recorded records & tapes
HQ: Walt Disney Music Company
500 S Buena Vista St
Burbank CA 91521
818 560-1000

(P-9221)
INSIGHT MANAGEMENT CORPORATION (PA)
1130 E Clark Ave, Santa Maria (93455-5178)
PHONE...................866 787-3588
Kevin Jasper, *CEO*
EMP: 31 **EST:** 2006
SALES (est): 3.9MM **Privately Held**
SIC: 3652 Pre-recorded records & tapes

(P-9222)
INTERNATIONAL DISC MFR INC
Also Called: IDM
4906 W 1st St, Santa Ana (92703-3110)
PHONE...................714 210-1780
Thoai Tang, *President*
Tri Tang, *Vice Pres*
Alvin Tang, *Maintence Staff*
EMP: 16 **EST:** 2000
SQ FT: 50,000

SALES (est): 316.2K **Privately Held**
SIC: 3652 Compact laser discs, pre-corded

(P-9223)
PRECISE MEDIA SERVICES INC
Also Called: Precise-Full Service Media
888 Vintage Ave, Ontario (91764-5392)
PHONE...................909 481-3305
Choy Tim Lee, *CEO*
Robert Miller, *President*
▲ **EMP:** 25 **EST:** 1991
SQ FT: 112,000
SALES (est): 5MM **Privately Held**
WEB: www.precisemedia.com
SIC: 3652 7819 Pre-recorded records & tapes; video tape or disk reproduction

(P-9224)
RAINBO RECORD MFG CORP (PA)
Also Called: Rainbo Records & Cassettes
8960 Eton Ave, Canoga Park (91304-1621)
P.O. Box 280700, Northridge (91328-0700)
PHONE...................818 280-1100
Jack Brown, *Principal*
Felipe Delgadillo, *Chief Engr*
Darren Norton, *Sales Executive*
Richard Flaherty, *Director*
▲ **EMP:** 50 **EST:** 1939
SQ FT: 50,000
SALES (est): 19.5MM **Privately Held**
WEB: www.rainborecords.com
SIC: 3652 5099 Compact laser discs, pre-recorded; compact discs

(P-9225)
RECORD TECHNOLOGY INC
486 Dawson Dr Ste 4s, Camarillo (93012-8049)
PHONE...................805 484-2747
Don Mac Innis, *President*
Melodie Mac Innis, *Vice Pres*
Sharon Waldron, *Admin Asst*
Rick Hoshamoto, *Plant Mgr*
Kathy Waldron,
▲ **EMP:** 28 **EST:** 1972
SQ FT: 30,000
SALES (est): 4.6MM **Privately Held**
WEB: www.recordtech.com
SIC: 3652 Master records or tapes, preparation of; phonograph record blanks; compact laser discs, prerecorded

3661 Telephone & Telegraph Apparatus

(P-9226)
ALSTON TASCOM INC
5171 Edison Ave Ste C, Chino (91710-5758)
PHONE...................909 517-3660
Wayne Scaggs, *President*
Richard Fung, *General Mgr*
Susan Reinhart, *Admin Asst*
Maxine Sage, *Accountant*
Joanne Scaggs, *Train & Dev Mgr*
EMP: 19 **EST:** 1962
SQ FT: 7,500
SALES (est): 2.5MM **Privately Held**
WEB: www.startel.com
SIC: 3661 Telephones & telephone apparatus

(P-9227)
BALAJI TRADING INC
Also Called: City of Industry
4850 Eucalyptus Ave, Chino (91710-9255)
PHONE...................909 444-7999
Mukesh Batta, *CEO*
Sandy Mawikere, *Manager*
▲ **EMP:** 91 **EST:** 2010
SALES (est): 9.9MM **Privately Held**
SIC: 3661 Headsets, telephone; telephone cords, jacks, adapters, etc.

(P-9228)
CALIENT TECHNOLOGIES INC (PA)
25 Castilian Dr, Goleta (93117-3026)
PHONE...................805 695-4800
Saiyed Atiq Raza, *CEO*
Jag Setlur, *COO*

Kevin Welsh, *Senior VP*
Erik Leonard, *Vice Pres*
Jitender Miglani, *Vice Pres*
▲ **EMP:** 30 **EST:** 1999
SQ FT: 150,000
SALES (est): 32MM **Privately Held**
WEB: www.calient.net
SIC: 3661 Fiber optics communications equipment

(P-9229)
CFBTEL
3151 Airway Ave Ste B2, Costa Mesa (92626-4622)
PHONE...................949 381-2525
Siamak Siyami, *Principal*
Mehrdad Sami, *Principal*
EMP: 13 **EST:** 2013
SALES (est): 1.4MM **Privately Held**
WEB: www.cfbtel.com
SIC: 3661 8748 1731 4813 Telephones & telephone apparatus; telecommunications consultant; voice, data & video wiring contractor; voice telephone communications

(P-9230)
CHANNELL COMMERCIAL CORP (PA)
33380 Zeiders Rd Ste 101, Menifee (92584-1406)
P.O. Box 9022, Temecula (92589-9022)
PHONE...................951 719-2600
William H Channell Jr, *CEO*
Jacqueline M Channell, *Ch of Bd*
Guy E Marge, *President*
Michael Perica, *Treasurer*
Wood Jack, *Vice Pres*
◆ **EMP:** 100 **EST:** 1996
SQ FT: 210,000
SALES (est): 174.8MM **Privately Held**
WEB: www.channell.com
SIC: 3661 3663 3088 3083 Telephone & telegraph apparatus; television broadcasting & communications equipment; plastics plumbing fixtures; laminated plastics plate & sheet

(P-9231)
COASTAL CONNECTIONS
2085 Sperry Ave Ste B, Ventura (93003-7452)
PHONE...................805 644-5051
Andy Devine, *President*
Nancy Devine, *Treasurer*
Toby Shepard, *Prgrmr*
Marisol Diaz, *Project Mgr*
◆ **EMP:** 37
SQ FT: 9,000
SALES: 3.9MM **Privately Held**
WEB: www.coastalcon.com
SIC: 3661 Fiber optics communications equipment

(P-9232)
EPIC TECHNOLOGIES LLC (HQ)
Also Called: Natel Engineering
9340 Owensmouth Ave, Chatsworth (91311-6915)
PHONE...................818 495-8617
Bhawnesh Mathur, *Mng Member*
James Angeloni, *Officer*
John Lowrey, *Officer*
James Howe, *Vice Pres*
Jay Klug, *Vice Pres*
▲ **EMP:** 200 **EST:** 2004
SQ FT: 52,000
SALES (est): 647.8MM
SALES (corp-wide): 1.1B **Privately Held**
WEB: www.neotech.com
SIC: 3661 3577 3679 Telephone & telegraph apparatus; computer peripheral equipment; electronic circuits
PA: Natel Engineering Company, Llc
9340 Owensmouth Ave
Chatsworth CA 91311
818 495-8617

(P-9233)
FONEGEAR LLC
13953 Ramona Ave, Chino (91710-5428)
P.O. Box 2606, Chino Hills (91709-0087)
PHONE...................909 627-7999
Hong Lip Yow,
Barb Zygolewski, *Controller*
Melissa Villa, *Manager*

▲ **EMP:** 15 **EST:** 2003
SALES (est): 2.3MM **Privately Held**
SIC: 3661 Carrier equipment, telephone or
telegraph

(P-9234)
GENERAL PHOTONICS CORP
14351 Pipeline Ave, Chino (91710-5642)
PHONE.................................909 590-5473
Steve Yao, *President*
James Shen, *President*
Bruce Pazouki, *Vice Pres*
Geoff Thompson, *General Mgr*
Ansel Belisle, *Engineer*
▲ **EMP:** 51 **EST:** 1995
SQ FT: 20,000
SALES (est): 3.1MM **Publicly Held**
WEB: www.lunainc.com
SIC: 3661 Fiber optics communications
equipment
HQ: Luna Technologies, Inc.
301 1st St Sw Ste 200
Roanoke VA 24011
540 769-8400

(P-9235)
INTERNTNAL CNNCTORS
CABLE CORP
Also Called: I C C
2100 E Valencia Dr Ste D, Fullerton
(92831-4811)
PHONE.................................888 275-4422
Mike Lin, *President*
Eugene Chyun Tsai, *Shareholder*
Chuck Dodson, *Opers Staff*
▲ **EMP:** 110 **EST:** 1984
SQ FT: 38,720
SALES (est): 12.7MM **Privately Held**
SIC: 3661 5065 Telephone & telegraph
apparatus; telephone & telegraphic equip-
ment; communication equipment

(P-9236)
LEADER ELECTRONICS (NA)
INC
2901 S Harbor Blvd, Santa Ana
(92704-6428)
PHONE.................................714 435-0505
Grace Vhiu, *President*
▲ **EMP:** 20 **EST:** 2004
SALES (est): 1MM **Privately Held**
WEB: www.lei.com.tw
SIC: 3661 Telephone cords, jacks,
adapters, etc.
PA: Leader Electronics Inc.
8f, No. 138, Lane 235, Baoqiao Rd.
New Taipei City TAP 23145

(P-9237)
LYNX PHTNIC NTWORKS A DEL
CORP
6303 Owensmouth Ave Fl 10, Woodland
Hills (91367-2262)
PHONE.................................818 802-0244
Daniel Tal, *CEO*
Michael Leigh, *President*
Beni Kopelovitz, *COO*
EMP: 22 **EST:** 1998
SQ FT: 30,000
SALES (est): 598.1K **Privately Held**
WEB: www.lynxpn.com
SIC: 3661 Fiber optics communications
equipment

(P-9238)
OCCAM NETWORKS INC (HQ)
6868 Cortona Dr, Santa Barbara
(93117-1360)
PHONE.................................805 692-2900
Carl Russo, *CEO*
Michael Ashby, *Exec VP*
EMP: 149 **EST:** 1996
SQ FT: 51,000
SALES (est): 25.1MM
SALES (corp-wide): 541.2MM **Publicly**
Held
WEB: www.calix.com
SIC: 3661 Carrier equipment, telephone or
telegraph
PA: Calix, Inc.
2777 Orchard Pkwy
San Jose CA 95134
408 514-3000

(P-9239)
OPTICAL ZONU CORPORATION
7510 Hazeltine Ave, Van Nuys
(91405-1419)
PHONE.................................818 780-9701
Meir Bartur, *President*
Frazad Ghadooshay, *Vice Pres*
Dillon Harr, *Engineer*
John Rice, *Engineer*
Hanoch Eldar, *VP Opers*
▲ **EMP:** 18 **EST:** 2003
SALES (est): 4.3MM **Privately Held**
WEB: www.opticalzonu.com
SIC: 3661 Fiber optics communications
equipment

(P-9240)
QUINTRON SYSTEMS INC (PA)
2105 S Blosser Rd, Santa Maria
(93458-7300)
PHONE.................................805 928-4343
Dominick Barry, *President*
David Wilhite, *President*
James E Mc Glothlin, *CEO*
Sharon Lewis, *CFO*
Elton L Hammers, *Treasurer*
EMP: 33 **EST:** 1970
SQ FT: 20,000
SALES (est): 16.8MM **Privately Held**
WEB: www.quintron.com
SIC: 3661 1731 Telephone & telegraph
apparatus; telephone & telephone equip-
ment installation

(P-9241)
RLH INDUSTRIES INC
936 N Main St, Orange (92867-5403)
PHONE.................................714 532-1672
James B Harris, *CEO*
Tristan A Harris, *Vice Pres*
Tim Harris, *General Mgr*
Carol E Harris, *Admin Sec*
Kele Williams, *Technician*
▲ **EMP:** 40 **EST:** 1988
SQ FT: 16,000
SALES (est): 8MM **Privately Held**
WEB: www.fiberopticlink.com
SIC: 3661 5065 5999 Telephone & tele-
graph apparatus; communication equip-
ment; telephone equipment & systems

(P-9242)
SIEMENS INDUSTRY INC
7485 Anaconda Ave, Garden Grove
(92841-2911)
PHONE.................................714 891-3964
EMP: 13
SALES (corp-wide): 67.4B **Privately Held**
WEB: www.siemens.com
SIC: 3661 Telephones & telephone appara-
tus
HQ: Siemens Industry, Inc.
1000 Deerfield Pkwy
Buffalo Grove IL 60089
847 215-1000

(P-9243)
SIEMENS MOBILITY INC
1026 E Lacy Ave, Anaheim (92805-5651)
PHONE.................................714 284-0206
David Hopping, *Branch Mgr*
EMP: 821
SALES (corp-wide): 67.4B **Privately Held**
SIC: 3661 Telephones & telephone appara-
tus
HQ: Siemens Mobility, Inc.
1 Penn Plz Ste 1100
New York NY 10119
212 672-4000

(P-9244)
VESTA SOLUTIONS INC (HQ)
42555 Rio Nedo, Temecula (92590-3726)
P.O. Box 9007 (92589-9007)
PHONE.................................951 719-2100
Gino Bonanotte, *CEO*
John Molloy, *President*
Uygar Gazioglu, *Treasurer*
Andrew Sinclair, *Senior VP*
Daniel Pekofske, *Vice Pres*
▲ **EMP:** 280 **EST:** 1967
SQ FT: 100,000

SALES (est): 96.4MM
SALES (corp-wide): 7.4B **Publicly Held**
WEB: www.vestapublicsafety.com
SIC: 3661 Telephone station equipment &
parts, wire
PA: Motorola Solutions, Inc.
500 W Monroe St Ste 4400
Chicago IL 60661
847 576-5000

(P-9245)
VIAVI SOLUTIONS INC
3601 Calle Tecate, Camarillo (93012-5056)
PHONE.................................805 465-1875
EMP: 75
SALES (corp-wide): 811.4MM **Publicly**
Held
SIC: 3661 Mfg Fiber Optic Tranceivers
PA: Viavi Solutions Inc.
6001 America Center Dr # 6
San Jose CA 85254
408 404-3600

(P-9246)
Y B S ENTERPRISES INC
Also Called: Electro-Comm
3116 W Vanowen St, Burbank
(91505-1237)
PHONE.................................818 848-7790
Y B Song, *President*
Grace Song, *Admin Sec*
Yung Kim, *VP Opers*
EMP: 13 **EST:** 1986
SQ FT: 30,000
SALES (est): 6.5MM **Privately Held**
SIC: 3661 Communication headgear, tele-
phone

3663 Radio & T V
Communications, Systs &
Eqpt, Broadcast/Studio

(P-9247)
24/7 STUDIO EQUIPMENT INC
Also Called: Hertz Entertainment Services
3111 N Kenwood St, Burbank
(91505-1041)
PHONE.................................818 840-8247
Lance Sorenson, *President*
Gary Mielke, *Vice Pres*
Floyd Griffin, *Cust Mgr*
EMP: 35 **EST:** 2006
SALES (est): 26.8MM
SALES (corp-wide): 5.2B **Privately Held**
WEB: www.hertz.com
SIC: 3663 Studio equipment, radio & tele-
vision broadcasting
PA: Hertz Global Holdings, Inc.
8501 Williams Rd Fl 3
Estero FL 33928
239 301-7000

(P-9248)
ACROAMATICS INC
Also Called: Telemetry Systems
125 Cremona Dr Ste 130, Goleta
(93117-5503)
PHONE.................................805 967-9909
Geoffrey Johnson, *President*
Patricia Johnson, *CFO*
Robert Danford, *Vice Pres*
John Foondle, *Vice Pres*
Mark Urish, *Chief Engr*
EMP: 15 **EST:** 1971
SALES (est): 2.6MM **Privately Held**
WEB: www.gdpspace.com
SIC: 3663 7373 Telemetering equipment,
electronic; computer integrated systems
design

(P-9249)
ADAPTIVE DIGITAL SYSTEMS
INC
20322 Sw Acacia St # 200, Newport Beach
(92660-1504)
PHONE.................................949 955-3116
Attila W Mathe, *President*
Ralph Boehringer, *Vice Pres*
Susan Cameron, *Admin Sec*
Anna Cameron, *Administration*
Christian Corb, *Engineer*
▲ **EMP:** 27
SQ FT: 6,500

SALES: 9.5MM **Privately Held**
WEB: www.adaptivedigitalsystems.com
SIC: 3663 Marine radio communications
equipment

(P-9250)
ALE USA INC
26801 Agoura Rd, Calabasas
(91301-5122)
PHONE.................................818 878-4816
Stanley Stopka, *Principal*
Michel Emelianoff, *CEO*
Stan Stopka, *Vice Pres*
Mounif Haffar, *CIO*
Alan Pullen, *Engineer*
EMP: 550 **EST:** 2014
SQ FT: 50,000
SALES (est): 166.8MM **Privately Held**
WEB: www.al-enterprise.com
SIC: 3663 3613 Mobile communication
equipment; switchgear & switchboard ap-
paratus
HQ: China Huaxin Post And Telecom Tech-
nologies Co., Ltd.
4g, Building 4, Changan Xingrong
Center, No.1 Courtyard, Naoshik
Beijing 10003
105 852-8866

(P-9251)
ALTINEX INC
500 S Jefferson St, Placentia (92870-6617)
PHONE.................................714 990-0877
Jack Gershfeld, *President*
Sergey Alayev, *Design Engr*
Ing Leu, *Accountant*
Jim Lewis, *Materials Mgr*
Tawn Chambers,
▲ **EMP:** 50 **EST:** 1993
SALES (est): 11.3MM **Privately Held**
WEB: www.altinex.com
SIC: 3663 3577 3651 5099 Radio & TV
communications equipment; computer pe-
ripheral equipment; household audio &
video equipment; video & audio equip-
ment

(P-9252)
AMPLIFIER TECHNOLOGIES
INC
1749 Chapin Rd, Montebello (90640-6609)
PHONE.................................323 278-0001
Morris Kessler, *President*
Robert McKinley, *Exec VP*
▲ **EMP:** 25 **EST:** 1981
SQ FT: 84,000
SALES (est): 6.1MM
SALES (corp-wide): 10.1MM **Privately**
Held
WEB: www.ati-amp.com
SIC: 3663 Television broadcasting & com-
munications equipment
PA: Macey Investment Corp.
1749 Chapin Rd
Montebello CA 90640
323 278-0001

(P-9253)
ANTCOM CORPORATION
367 Van Ness Way Ste 602, Torrance
(90501-6246)
PHONE.................................310 782-1076
Michael Ritter, *CEO*
Reid Doug, *Vice Pres*
Sean Huynh, *Vice Pres*
Doug Reid, *General Mgr*
Huynh Sean, *VP Engrg*
EMP: 45 **EST:** 1997
SQ FT: 15,000
SALES (est): 10.9MM
SALES (corp-wide): 4.5B **Privately Held**
WEB: www.antcom.com
SIC: 3663 Antennas, transmitting & com-
munications
HQ: Novatel Inc
10921 14 St Ne
Calgary AB T3K 2
403 295-4500

(P-9254)
APPLICA INC
11651 Vanowen St, North Hollywood
(91605-6128)
PHONE.................................818 565-0011
Albert Cohen, *President*
Shlomo Barash, *Treasurer*

James Viray, *General Mgr*
EMP: 19 **EST:** 2008
SALES (est): 1MM **Privately Held**
WEB: www.smartbalun.info
SIC: 3663 Radio & TV communications equipment

(P-9255)
ASTRA COMMUNICATIONS INC
1101 Chestnut St, Burbank (91506-1624)
P.O. Box 391 (91503-0391)
PHONE..............................818 859-7305
Scott Bassett, *President*
Craig Bassett, *Vice Pres*
Kim Walsh, *Admin Sec*
Jason Mullins, *Corp Comm Staff*
EMP: 25 **EST:** 1981
SQ FT: 11,000
SALES (est): 3.1MM **Privately Held**
WEB: www.astracomm.com
SIC: 3663 Mobile communication equipment

(P-9256)
BLITZZ TECHNOLOGY INC
53 Parker, Irvine (92618-1605)
PHONE..............................949 380-7709
▲ **EMP:** 25
SQ FT: 10,000
SALES: 4MM **Privately Held**
SIC: 3663 5065 Telecommunication Product Manufacturing & Whol

(P-9257)
BOEING COML SATELLITE SVCS INC (HQ)
900 N Pacific Coast Hwy, El Segundo (90245-2710)
PHONE..............................310 335-6682
Craig R Cooning, *CEO*
Eric Wendle, *Administration*
Dennis Truong, *Engineer*
EMP: 30 **EST:** 2014
SALES (est): 4.9MM
SALES (corp-wide): 58.1B **Publicly Held**
WEB: www.boeing.com
SIC: 3663 Airborne radio communications equipment
PA: The Boeing Company
100 N Riverside Plz
Chicago IL 60606
312 544-2000

(P-9258)
BOEING SATELLITE SYSTEMS INC (HQ)
900 N Pacific Coast Hwy, El Segundo (90245-2710)
P.O. Box 92919, Los Angeles (90009-2919)
PHONE..............................310 791-7450
Craig R Cooning, *President*
Dave Ryan, *Vice Pres*
Charles Toups, *Vice Pres*
Michael Cook, *Network Enginr*
John Ziavras, *Design Engr*
◆ **EMP:** 25 **EST:** 1995
SALES (est): 1.2B
SALES (corp-wide): 58.1B **Publicly Held**
WEB: www.boeing.com
SIC: 3663 Satellites, communications; space satellite communications equipment
PA: The Boeing Company
100 N Riverside Plz
Chicago IL 60606
312 544-2000

(P-9259)
CABLE AML INC (PA)
2271 W 205th St Ste 101, Torrance (90501-1449)
PHONE..............................310 222-5599
Francisco Bernues, *President*
Eddie Nakamura, *CFO*
Hyung Ahn, *Officer*
Norman Woods, *Admin Sec*
Sunil Naik, *Sales Staff*
▼ **EMP:** 13 **EST:** 1992
SQ FT: 15,000
SALES (est): 4.5MM **Privately Held**
WEB: www.cableaml.com
SIC: 3663 8711 Radio & TV communications equipment; consulting engineer

(P-9260)
CALAMP CORP (PA)
15635 Alton Pkwy Ste 250, Irvine (92618-7328)
PHONE..............................949 600-5600
Jeff Gardner, *President*
Amal M Johnson, *Ch of Bd*
Kurtis Binder, *CFO*
Nathan Lowstuter, *Senior VP*
Garo Sarkissian, *Senior VP*
◆ **EMP:** 262 **EST:** 1981
SQ FT: 16,000
SALES: 308.5MM **Publicly Held**
WEB: www.calamp.com
SIC: 3663 Microwave communication equipment

(P-9261)
CENTRON INDUSTRIES INC
441 W Victoria St, Gardena (90248-3528)
PHONE..............................310 324-6443
Yong W Kim, *CEO*
Hye S Kim, *Admin Sec*
Jae Han, *Purchasing*
◆ **EMP:** 37 **EST:** 1984
SQ FT: 10,000
SALES (est): 8.9MM **Privately Held**
WEB: www.centronind.com
SIC: 3663 Radio & TV communications equipment

(P-9262)
COASTLINE HIGH PRFMCE CTNGS LT
7181 Orangewood Ave, Garden Grove (92841-1409)
PHONE..............................714 372-3263
Phil Viljoen, *President*
EMP: 15 **EST:** 2003
SALES (est): 1.8MM **Privately Held**
WEB: www.coastlinehpc.com
SIC: 3663 Satellites, communications

(P-9263)
COBHAM EXETER INC
Also Called: Cobham Trivec-Avant Inc.
17831 Jamestown Ln, Huntington Beach (92647-7136)
PHONE..............................714 841-4976
Mike Kahn, *CEO*
Mike Berberet, *Vice Pres*
David Macy, *Vice Pres*
▲ **EMP:** 45 **EST:** 1981
SQ FT: 15,000
SALES (est): 9.9MM
SALES (corp-wide): 177.9K **Privately Held**
WEB: www.cobham.com
SIC: 3663 Antennas, transmitting & communications
HQ: Cobham Aes Holdings Inc.
2121 Crystal Dr 625
Arlington VA 22202

(P-9264)
CONNECT SYSTEMS INC
1802 Eastman Ave Ste 116, Ventura (93003-5759)
PHONE..............................805 642-7184
▲ **EMP:** 22
SQ FT: 10,000
SALES (est): 3.5MM **Privately Held**
WEB: www.connectsystems.com
SIC: 3663 Mfg Radio Communication Equipment

(P-9265)
CPI MALIBU DIVISION
3623 Old Conejo Rd # 205, Newbury Park (91320-2163)
PHONE..............................805 383-1829
Joel Littman, *CFO*
Elizabeth McKenzie, *QA Dir*
Eunice Szejn, *Info Tech Mgr*
Scott Hanchar, *Project Engr*
Marianne Davis, *Human Res Mgr*
EMP: 80 **EST:** 1975
SALES (est): 15.4MM **Privately Held**
WEB: www.cpii.com
SIC: 3663 Antennas, transmitting & communications

HQ: Communications & Power Industries Llc
811 Hansen Way
Palo Alto CA 94304

(P-9266)
D X COMMUNICATIONS INC
Also Called: Tpl Communications
8160 Van Nuys Blvd, Panorama City (91402-4806)
PHONE..............................323 256-3000
Richard H Myers, *CEO*
John Ehret, *President*
Richard Myers, *CEO*
Kathy Torres, *Sales Executive*
EMP: 28 **EST:** 1971
SALES (est): 3.3MM **Privately Held**
WEB: www.tplcom.com
SIC: 3663 Satellites, communications

(P-9267)
DJH ENTERPRISES
Also Called: Channel Vision Technology
23011 Moulton Pkwy Ste B6, Laguna Hills (92653-1222)
PHONE..............................714 424-6500
Darrel Eugene Hauk, *President*
◆ **EMP:** 35 **EST:** 1993
SALES (est): 6.4MM **Privately Held**
SIC: 3663 Radio & TV communications equipment

(P-9268)
DRACO BROADCAST INC
2000 N Lincoln St, Burbank (91504-3333)
PHONE..............................818 736-5788
Aaron Street, *General Mgr*
EMP: 21
SALES (corp-wide): 3.8MM **Privately Held**
WEB: www.dracobroadcast.com
SIC: 3663 Radio & TV communications equipment
PA: Draco Broadcast Inc
9265 Commerce Hwy
Pennsauken NJ 08110
856 324-2892

(P-9269)
DRANSE TECHNOLOGY INC
8605 Santa Monica Blvd # 795, West Hollywood (90069-4109)
PHONE..............................323 908-8554
Jian Bai, *Chairman*
EMP: 15
SALES (est): 50K **Privately Held**
SIC: 3663

(P-9270)
DYNAMIC SCIENCES INTL INC
9400 Lurline Ave Unit B, Chatsworth (91311-6022)
PHONE..............................818 226-6262
Eli Shiri, *President*
Robert Cook, *Vice Pres*
Oren Shiri, *VP Sales*
James Zheng, *Sales Mgr*
EMP: 35 **EST:** 1972
SQ FT: 20,000
SALES (est): 3.2MM **Privately Held**
SIC: 3663 Radio receiver networks

(P-9271)
EMPOWER RF SYSTEMS INC (PA)
316 W Florence Ave, Inglewood (90301-1104)
PHONE..............................310 412-8100
Barry Phelps, *Ch of Bd*
Jon Jacocks, *President*
Larisa Stanisic, *CFO*
Robert Lauria, *VP Bus Dvlpt*
Jan Deperry, *Office Mgr*
EMP: 76 **EST:** 1999
SQ FT: 30,000
SALES (est): 21MM **Privately Held**
WEB: www.empowerrf.com
SIC: 3663 Amplifiers, RF power & IF

(P-9272)
ESCAPE COMMUNICATIONS INC
2790 Skypark Dr Ste 203, Torrance (90505-5345)
PHONE..............................310 997-1300

Micheal Stewart, *President*
Gregory Caso PHD, *Exec VP*
James Nadeau, *Admin Sec*
Jim Nadeau, *Engineer*
EMP: 17 **EST:** 1998
SQ FT: 5,300
SALES (est): 3.8MM **Privately Held**
WEB: www.escapecom.com
SIC: 3663 8711 8731 Microwave communication equipment; engineering services; commercial physical research

(P-9273)
FEI-ZYFER INC (HQ)
7321 Lincoln Way, Garden Grove (92841-1428)
PHONE..............................714 933-4000
Steve Strang, *President*
Chris Staffery, *Vice Pres*
Joan Lauti, *Admin Asst*
Dydan Nguyen, *Administration*
Alexander Varkey, *Engineer*
EMP: 335 **EST:** 1997
SQ FT: 50,000
SALES (est): 61.4MM
SALES (corp-wide): 54.2MM **Publicly Held**
WEB: www.fei-zyfer.com
SIC: 3663 Television broadcasting & communications equipment; encryption devices
PA: Frequency Electronics, Inc.
55 Charles Lindbergh Blvd # 2
Uniondale NY 11553
516 794-4500

(P-9274)
FLEET MANAGEMENT SOLUTIONS INC
310 Commerce Ste 100, Irvine (92602-1360)
PHONE..............................800 500-6009
Tony Eales, *CEO*
Sheila Henley Roth, *CFO*
EMP: 26 **EST:** 2002
SALES (est): 16MM
SALES (corp-wide): 4.6B **Publicly Held**
WEB: www.fleetmanagementsolutions.com
SIC: 3663 4899 Radio & TV communications equipment; satellite earth stations
HQ: Teletrac Navman (Uk) Ltd
First Floor
Milton Keynes BUCKS MK7 6
123 475-9000

(P-9275)
GC TECHNOLOGY LLC (PA)
Also Called: Phonesuit
1223 Wilshire Blvd 425, Santa Monica (90403-5406)
PHONE..............................310 633-5095
Sumeet Gupta, *Mng Member*
Joe Carrillo, *VP Mktg*
Joseph Carillo,
▲ **EMP:** 14 **EST:** 2007
SALES (est): 1.1MM **Privately Held**
SIC: 3663 Mobile communication equipment

(P-9276)
HBC SOLUTIONS HOLDINGS LLC
10877 Wilshire Blvd Fl 18, Los Angeles (90024-4373)
PHONE..............................321 727-9100
Daniel Abrams, *Mng Member*
EMP: 49 **EST:** 2013
SALES (est): 492.8K **Privately Held**
SIC: 3663 Radio broadcasting & communications equipment; television broadcasting & communications equipment

(P-9277)
HILLSIDE CAPITAL INC
6222 Fallbrook Ave, Woodland Hills (91367-1601)
PHONE..............................650 367-2011
Becky Tran, *President*
EMP: 115 **EST:** 2008
SALES (est): 6.5MM **Privately Held**
SIC: 3663 Radio & TV communications equipment

(P-9278)
IMPAC TECHNOLOGIES INC
3050 Red Hill Ave, Costa Mesa
(92626-4524)
PHONE....................714 427-2000
Louis Parker, *President*
EMP: 31 EST: 1992
SQ FT: 24,000
SALES (est): 1.2MM **Privately Held**
WEB: www.ozgift.com
SIC: 3663 Radio & TV communications
equipment

(P-9279)
INTERSTATE ELECTRONICS CORP
604 E Vermont Ave, Anaheim
(92805-5607)
PHONE....................714 758-3395
Thomas Jackson, *Branch Mgr*
EMP: 85
SALES (corp-wide): 18.1B **Publicly Held**
SIC: 3663 3621 Telemetering equipment,
electronic; motors & generators
HQ: Interstate Electronics Corporation
602 E Vermont Ave
Anaheim CA 92805
714 758-0500

(P-9280)
JANTEQ CORP (PA)
9975 Toledo Way Ste 150, Irvine
(92618-1827)
PHONE....................949 215-2603
John A Porter, *President*
Mike Payne, *COO*
Alexey Romanov, *Engineer*
Christine Yang, *Controller*
Irene Guardado, *Purchasing*
EMP: 23 EST: 2005
SQ FT: 33,000
SALES: 29.3MM **Privately Held**
WEB: www.site.janteq.com
SIC: 3663 Radio & TV communications
equipment

(P-9281)
KATZ MILLENNIUM SLS & MKTG INC
Also Called: Clear Channel Radio Sales
5700 Wilshire Blvd # 100, Los Angeles
(90036-3659)
PHONE....................323 966-5066
Nathan Brown, *Manager*
EMP: 157 **Publicly Held**
WEB: www.raisingthevolume.com
SIC: 3663 Radio receiver networks
HQ: Katz Millennium Sales & Marketing Inc.
125 W 55th St Frnt 3
New York NY 10019

(P-9282)
KWORLD (USA) COMPUTER INC
499 Nibus Ste D, Brea (92821-3211)
PHONE....................626 581-0867
Chung-Chieh Wang, *President*
▲ EMP: 22 EST: 2002
SQ FT: 4,600
SALES (est): 2.5MM **Privately Held**
WEB: www.kworld-global.com
SIC: 3663 Cable television equipment
PA: Kworld Computer Co.,Ltd
6f, 113, Chien 2nd Rd.,
New Taipei City TAP 23585

(P-9283)
L3 TECHNOLOGIES INC
Electron Devices
3100 Lomita Blvd, Torrance (90505-5104)
PHONE....................650 591-8411
James D Benham, *President*
Carter Armstrong, *Vice Pres*
Mike Martin, *Engineer*
EMP: 398
SALES (corp-wide): 18.1B **Publicly Held**
WEB: www.l3harris.com
SIC: 3663 Telemetering equipment, elec-
tronic
HQ: L3 Technologies, Inc.
600 3rd Ave Fl 34
New York NY 10016
321 727-9100

(P-9284)
L3 TECHNOLOGIES INC
602 E Vermont Ave, Anaheim
(92805-5607)
PHONE....................714 758-4222
Robert Vanwechel, *Branch Mgr*
Henry Empeno, *Officer*
George Moore, *Administration*
Mike Sanders, *Software Engr*
Mark Bartholme, *Engineer*
EMP: 220
SALES (corp-wide): 18.1B **Publicly Held**
WEB: www.l3harris.com
SIC: 3663 Telemetering equipment, elec-
tronic
HQ: L3 Technologies, Inc.
600 3rd Ave Fl 34
New York NY 10016
321 727-9100

(P-9285)
L3 TECHNOLOGIES INC
Datron Advanced Tech Div
200 W Los Angeles Ave, Simi Valley
(93065-1650)
PHONE....................805 584-1717
John Digioia, *Branch Mgr*
Eli Kozikaro, *Software Engr*
Clarice Rivera, *Project Mgr*
Fernando Nocedal, *Engineer*
Virginia Goodrich, *Senior Mgr*
EMP: 100
SALES (corp-wide): 18.1B **Publicly Held**
WEB: www.l3harris.com
SIC: 3663 Satellites, communications
HQ: L3 Technologies, Inc.
600 3rd Ave Fl 34
New York NY 10016
321 727-9100

(P-9286)
LENNTEK CORPORATION
Also Called: Sonix
1610 Lockness Pl, Torrance (90501-5119)
PHONE....................310 534-2738
Danny Tsai, *Principal*
Arlene Sherren, *Marketing Staff*
Steven Reymond, *Sales Staff*
Karen Brown, *Accounts Mgr*
▲ EMP: 50 EST: 2007
SQ FT: 15,000 **Privately Held**
WEB: www.shopsonix.com
SIC: 3663 Mobile communication equip-
ment

(P-9287)
LOMA SCIENTIFIC INTERNATIONAL
3115 Kashiwa St, Torrance (90505-4010)
PHONE....................310 539-8655
J Patrick Loughboro, *President*
Jeff Loughboro, *Vice Pres*
Jeffrey Loughboro, *Vice Pres*
Jeff Lougheoro, *Manager*
EMP: 18 EST: 1957
SQ FT: 16,000
SALES (est): 1MM **Privately Held**
WEB: www.lomasci.com
SIC: 3663 Transmitting apparatus, radio or
television

(P-9288)
MACOM TECHNOLOGY SOLUTIONS INC
Also Called: Commercial Electronics Pho
4000 Macarthur Blvd # 101, Newport Beach
(92660-2546)
PHONE....................310 320-6160
EMP: 16 **Publicly Held**
WEB: www.macom.com
SIC: 3663 2752 3674 Mfg Radio/Tv Com-
munication Equipment Lithographic Com-
mercial Printing Mfg
Semiconductors/Related Devices
HQ: Macom Technology Solutions Inc.
100 Chelmsford St
Lowell MA 01851

(P-9289)
MARATHON PRODUCTIONS INC
2900 W Alameda Ave # 800, Burbank
(91505-4220)
PHONE....................818 748-1100
Kevin Woodward, *Manager*

EMP: 13 EST: 2014
SALES (est): 1.2MM **Privately Held**
SIC: 3663 Television broadcasting & com-
munications equipment

(P-9290)
MICROVOICE CORPORATION
Also Called: Microvoice Systems
345 Willis Ave, Camarillo (93010-8558)
PHONE....................805 389-2922
EMP: 50
SQ FT: 10,000
SALES (est): 4.1MM **Privately Held**
WEB: www.microvoice.com
SIC: 3663 Mfg Radio/Tv Communication
Equipment

(P-9291)
MICROWAVE DYNAMICS
16541 Scientific, Irvine (92618-4356)
PHONE....................949 679-7788
Shoja Peter Adel, *CEO*
Brian Adel, *Admin Sec*
EMP: 18 EST: 1992
SQ FT: 10,000
SALES (est): 2.5MM **Privately Held**
WEB: www.microwave-dynamics.com
SIC: 3663 5065 Microwave communica-
tion equipment; electronic parts & equip-
ment

(P-9292)
MISSION MICROWAVE TECH LLC
6060 Phyllis Dr, Cypress (90630-5243)
PHONE....................951 893-4925
Francis Auricchio, *CEO*
Michael Delisio, *CTO*
Chad Deckman, *Engineer*
Nate Schultz, *Engineer*
Joseph Nguyen, *Production*
EMP: 70 EST: 2014
SALES (est): 10.1MM **Privately Held**
WEB: www.missionmicrowave.com
SIC: 3663 Satellites, communications

(P-9293)
MOBILE VIDEO SYSTEMS INC (PA)
23905 Clinton Kth Rd, Wildomar
(92595-7897)
PHONE....................888 721-5777
Charles Merken, *CEO*
EMP: 13 EST: 2009
SALES (est): 1MM **Privately Held**
WEB: www.mobilevideosystems.net
SIC: 3663 Mobile communication equip-
ment

(P-9294)
MODULAR COMMUNICATIONS SYSTEMS
Also Called: Moducom
2629 Foothill Blvd, La Crescenta
(91214-3511)
PHONE....................818 764-1333
Robert A Moesch, *President*
Bernard Brandt, *Vice Pres*
Peter Hong, *Vice Pres*
Robert Moesch, *Principal*
Steve Simpkins, *Managing Dir*
EMP: 31 EST: 1978
SALES (est): 3.6MM **Privately Held**
WEB: www.moducom.com
SIC: 3663 Radio & TV communications
equipment

(P-9295)
MOPHIE INC (DH)
15495 Sand Canyon Ave # 400, Irvine
(92618-3153)
PHONE....................888 866-7443
Daniel Huang, *CEO*
▲ EMP: 180 EST: 2005
SALES (est): 37.3MM
SALES (corp-wide): 521.9MM **Privately Held**
WEB: www.zagg.com
SIC: 3663 Mobile communication equip-
ment

(P-9296)
MOSELEY ASSOCIATES INC (HQ)
82 Coromar Dr, Goleta (93117-3024)
PHONE....................805 968-9621
Jamal N Hamdani, *President*
Bruce Tarr, *CFO*
Rodney Bryant, *Director*
▲ EMP: 171 EST: 1961
SQ FT: 56,000
SALES (est): 21.8MM
SALES (corp-wide): 92.2MM **Privately
Held**
WEB: www.moseleysb.com
SIC: 3663 Radio & TV communications
equipment
PA: Axxcss Wireless Solutions Inc
82 Coromar Dr
Goleta CA 93117
805 968-9621

(P-9297)
MOTOBELL USA INC
260 Corporate Way, Upland (91786-4587)
PHONE....................909 608-2830
Ching Ting Lan, *President*
Julian Lin, *Accountant*
EMP: 15 EST: 1996
SALES (est): 1.2MM **Privately Held**
SIC: 3663 Pagers (one-way)

(P-9298)
MOTOROLA SOLUTIONS INC
6101 W Century Blvd, Los Angeles
(90045-5310)
PHONE....................954 723-4730
EMP: 142
SALES (corp-wide): 5.7B **Publicly Held**
SIC: 3663 Mfg Radio/Tv Communication
Equipment
PA: Motorola Solutions, Inc.
1303 E Algonquin Rd
Schaumburg IL 60661
847 576-5000

(P-9299)
MTI LABORATORY INC
Also Called: Mtil
201 Continental Blvd # 300, El Segundo
(90245-4500)
PHONE....................310 955-3700
Davis Kent, *President*
Alister Hsu, *CFO*
David Rutan, *Senior Engr*
Rose Perl, *Human Resources*
▼ EMP: 26 EST: 2006
SQ FT: 12,000
SALES (est): 6.7MM **Privately Held**
WEB: www.mtigroup.com
SIC: 3663 Microwave communication
equipment; mobile communication equip-
ment; radio broadcasting & communica-
tions equipment
PA: Microelectronics Technology, Inc.
No. 1, Chuangxin 2nd Rd., Science-
Based Industrial Park,
Hsinchu City 30076

(P-9300)
NAVCOM TECHNOLOGY INC (HQ)
20780 Madrona Ave, Torrance
(90503-3777)
PHONE....................310 381-2000
Tony Thelen, *CEO*
Craig Fawcept, *President*
Michael Linzy, *COO*
Alisobhani Jalal, *Principal*
Wolfgang Ritter, *Program Mgr*
EMP: 100 EST: 1997
SQ FT: 55,000
SALES (est): 20.3MM
SALES (corp-wide): 35.5B **Publicly Held**
WEB: www.navcomtech.com
SIC: 3663 8748 Satellites, communica-
tions; communications consulting
PA: Deere & Company
1 John Deere Pl
Moline IL 61265
309 765-8000

P R O D U C T S & S V C S

(P-9301)
NERDIST CHANNEL LLC
Also Called: Nerdist Industries
2900 W Alameda Ave # 15, Burbank
(91505-4220)
PHONE..................................818 333-2705
Peter Levin,
EMP: 30 **EST:** 2011
SALES (est): 2.6MM **Privately Held**
WEB: www.nerdist.com
SIC: 3663 Digital encoders

(P-9302)
NEVION USA INC
400 W Ventura Blvd # 155, Camarillo
(93010-9137)
PHONE..................................805 247-8575
Geir Bryn-Jensen, *CEO*
Eugene Keane, *President*
Petter Kvaal Djupvik, *COO*
Nils Fredriksen, *CFO*
Hans Hasselbach, *Officer*
EMP: 61 **EST:** 1996
SQ FT: 12,000
SALES (est): 12.7MM **Privately Held**
WEB: www.nevion.com
SIC: 3663 3669 3661 Radio & TV communications equipment; emergency alarms; telephones & telephone apparatus
HQ: Network Electronics Holdings, Inc.
     1600 Emerson Ave
     Oxnard CA 93033

(P-9303)
NORTHROP GRUMMAN SYSTEMS CORP
Space Systems Division
1 Space Park Blvd, Redondo Beach
(90278-1071)
PHONE..................................310 812-5149
Ronald Tom, *Branch Mgr*
Ellen Gerber, *Administration*
Dennis Long, *Info Tech Dir*
Scott Ninegar, *Info Tech Dir*
Steve Schwarzbek, *Info Tech Mgr*
EMP: 101 **Publicly Held**
WEB: www.northropgrumman.com
SIC: 3663 3674 3679 3761 Airborne radio communications equipment; satellites, communications; semiconductors & related devices; antennas, satellite; household use; guided missiles & space vehicles; guided missile & space vehicle propulsion unit parts; navigational systems & instruments
HQ: Northrop Grumman Systems Corporation
     2980 Fairview Park Dr
     Falls Church VA 22042
     703 280-2900

(P-9304)
OPHIR RF INC
5300 Beethoven St Fl 3, Los Angeles
(90066-7068)
PHONE..................................310 306-5556
Ilan Israely, *President*
Albert Barrios, *Vice Pres*
Jordan Ensminger, *Administration*
Mary Ellen Smith, *Materials Mgr*
EMP: 42 **EST:** 1992
SQ FT: 11,800
SALES (est): 10.8MM **Privately Held**
WEB: www.ophirrf.com
SIC: 3663 Amplifiers, RF power & IF

(P-9305)
OPTIM MICROWAVE INC
4020 Adolfo Rd, Camarillo (93012-6793)
PHONE..................................805 482-7093
Jack Peterson, *President*
Cynthia Espino, *Shareholder*
John Mahon, *Vice Pres*
Noah Chung, *General Mgr*
William Faust, *Admin Sec*
EMP: 18 **EST:** 1984
SQ FT: 15,000
SALES (est): 1.9MM **Privately Held**
WEB: www.optim-microwave.com
SIC: 3663 Antennas, transmitting & communications

(P-9306)
OPTODYNE INCORPORATION
21345 Hawthorne Blvd # 2, Torrance
(90503-5656)
PHONE..................................310 635-7481
Charles Wang, *CEO*
Lily Wang, *CFO*
Wang Lichen, *Vice Pres*
Lichen Wang, *Vice Pres*
▲ **EMP:** 25 **EST:** 1986
SALES (est): 3.6MM **Privately Held**
SIC: 3663 3829 3827 Light communications equipment; measuring & controlling devices; optical instruments & lenses

(P-9307)
OVATION R&G LLC (PA)
2850 Ocean Park Blvd # 225, Santa Monica
(90405-2955)
PHONE..................................310 430-7575
Charles D D Segars,
Ken Solomon, *Ch of Bd*
Phil Gilligan, *CFO*
Liz Janneman, *Exec VP*
John Malkin, *Exec VP*
EMP: 75 **EST:** 2009
SALES (est): 12.1MM **Privately Held**
WEB: www.ovationtv.com
SIC: 3663 Satellites, communications; television broadcasting & communications equipment

(P-9308)
PACIFIC WAVE SYSTEMS INC
2525 W 190th St, Torrance (90504-6002)
PHONE..................................714 893-0152
Carl Esposito, *CEO*
John J Tus, *CFO*
Victor Jay Miller, *Admin Sec*
Robert B Topolski, *Director*
EMP: 68 **EST:** 1992
SALES (est): 11.2MM **Privately Held**
WEB: www.pacificwavesystems.com
SIC: 3663 Satellites, communications

(P-9309)
PEARPOINT INC
39740 Garand Ln Ste B, Palm Desert
(92211-7176)
PHONE..................................760 343-7350
Paul Tistai, *CEO*
Vince Monteleone, *CFO*
EMP: 34 **EST:** 1987
SQ FT: 15,000
SALES (est): 4.4MM
SALES (corp-wide): 1.5B **Publicly Held**
WEB: www.pearpoint.com
SIC: 3663 3829 5065 Television closed circuit equipment; measuring & controlling devices; closed circuit television
HQ: Radiodetection Limited
     Western Drive
     Bristol BS14
     117 976-7776

(P-9310)
PHONESUIT INC
1431 7th St Ste 201, Santa Monica
(90401-2638)
PHONE..................................310 774-0282
Sumeet Gupta, *CEO*
Christopher Folk, *Vice Pres*
EMP: 25
SQ FT: 4,000
SALES (est): 10MM **Privately Held**
WEB: www.phonesuit.com
SIC: 3663 Mobile communication equipment

(P-9311)
RADIAN AUDIO ENGINEERING INC
2720 Kimball Ave, Pomona (91767-2200)
PHONE..................................714 288-8900
Richard Kontrimas, *CEO*
Raimonda Kontrimas, *Admin Sec*
Timothy Hanson, *Controller*
Dwight Tobiano, *Manager*
◆ **EMP:** 27 **EST:** 1988
SALES (est): 2.5MM **Privately Held**
WEB: www.radianaudio.com
SIC: 3663 5731 3651 Radio broadcasting & communications equipment; radio, television & electronic stores; household audio & video equipment

(P-9312)
ROSELM INDUSTRIES INC
2510 Seaman Ave, South El Monte
(91733-1928)
PHONE..................................626 442-6840
Conrad Arguijo, *President*
EMP: 20 **EST:** 1965
SQ FT: 13,000
SALES (est): 2.5MM **Privately Held**
SIC: 3663 Radio & TV communications equipment

(P-9313)
ROTATING PRCSION MCHANISMS INC
Also Called: RPM
8750 Shirley Ave, Northridge (91324-3409)
PHONE..................................818 349-9774
Kathy Flynn-Nikolai, *CEO*
Jerome Smith, *Shareholder*
Daniel P Flynn, *President*
Chris Shibel, *Officer*
Kathleen Nikolai, *Vice Pres*
EMP: 46 **EST:** 1986
SQ FT: 40,000
SALES (est): 11.3MM **Privately Held**
WEB: www.rpm-psi.com
SIC: 3663 Radio & TV communications equipment

(P-9314)
SALEM MUSIC NETWORK INC
4880 Santa Rosa Rd # 300, Camarillo
(93012-5190)
PHONE..................................805 987-0400
Stuart W Epperson, *Principal*
Lee Sandra, *Consultant*
EMP: 16 **EST:** 1992
SALES (est): 117.5K **Privately Held**
WEB: www.salemmedia.com
SIC: 3663 Radio broadcasting & communications equipment

(P-9315)
SECURE COMM SYSTEMS INC (HQ)
Also Called: Benchmark Secure Technology
1740 E Wilshire Ave, Santa Ana
(92705-4615)
PHONE..................................714 547-1174
Edward Hanrahan, *President*
Roop Lakkaraju, *CFO*
Kim Diulio, *Officer*
Michael Buseman, *Vice Pres*
Richard Crowell, *Principal*
▲ **EMP:** 148 **EST:** 2014
SQ FT: 38,000
SALES (est): 78.1MM
SALES (corp-wide): 2B **Publicly Held**
WEB: www.bench.com
SIC: 3663 3829 3577 3571 Encryption devices; vibration meters, analyzers & calibrators; computer peripheral equipment; electronic computers
PA: Benchmark Electronics, Inc.
     56 S Rockford Dr
     Tempe AZ 85281
     623 300-7000

(P-9316)
SEKAI ELECTRONICS INC (PA)
38 Waterworks Way, Irvine (92618-3107)
PHONE..................................949 783-5740
Roland Soohoo, *CEO*
Mattias Nilsson,
Douglas Cebik, *Director*
EMP: 28 **EST:** 1982
SQ FT: 7,000
SALES (est): 4.5MM **Privately Held**
WEB: www.sekai-electronics.com
SIC: 3663 5065 Radio & TV communications equipment; video equipment, electronic

(P-9317)
SIERRA AUTOMATED SYS/ENG CORP
2821 Burton Ave, Burbank (91504-3224)
PHONE..................................818 840-6749
Edward O Fritz, *President*
Ai Salci, *Vice Pres*
Al Salci, *Vice Pres*
Giovanni Morales, *General Mgr*
Dan Gaylord, *Software Engr*
EMP: 20 **EST:** 1987

SALES (est): 3.9MM **Privately Held**
WEB: www.sasaudio.com
SIC: 3663 Radio broadcasting & communications equipment

(P-9318)
SILVUS TECHNOLOGIES INC (PA)
10990 Wilshire Blvd # 1500, Los Angeles
(90024-3913)
PHONE..................................310 479-3333
Babak Daneshrad, *Chairman*
Phillip Duncan, *Officer*
Kathleen Cook, *Vice Pres*
Jimi Henderson, *Vice Pres*
Cyrus Naim, *Vice Pres*
EMP: 79 **EST:** 2004
SQ FT: 7,200
SALES (est): 30.9MM **Privately Held**
WEB: www.silvustechnologies.com
SIC: 3663 8731 Radio & TV communications equipment; commercial physical research

(P-9319)
STM NETWORKS INC
Also Called: Stm Wireless
2 Faraday, Irvine (92618-2737)
PHONE..................................949 273-6800
Emil Youssefzadeh, *CEO*
Faramarz Yousefzaheh, *Ch of Bd*
Albert Yousefzaheh, *Treasurer*
Umar Javed, *Senior VP*
Richard Forberg, *Vice Pres*
▲ **EMP:** 51 **EST:** 2001
SQ FT: 22,000
SALES (est): 2.9MM **Privately Held**
SIC: 3663 Satellites, communications

(P-9320)
SUNBRITETV LLC (DH)
2630 Townsgate Rd Ste F, Westlake Village
(91361-2780)
PHONE..................................805 214-7250
Cameron Hill, *Mng Member*
Jonathan Johnson, *Manager*
▲ **EMP:** 49 **EST:** 2010
SALES (est): 13.7MM
SALES (corp-wide): 855.6MM **Publicly Held**
WEB: www.sunbritetv.com
SIC: 3663 Transmitting apparatus, radio or television
HQ: Sunbrite Holding Corporation
     2001 Anchor Ct
     Thousand Oaks CA 91320
     805 214-7250

(P-9321)
TATUNG COMPANY AMERICA INC (HQ)
2850 E El Presidio St, Long Beach
(90810-1119)
PHONE..................................310 637-2105
Huei-Jihn Jih, *President*
Danny Huang, *CFO*
Mike Lee, *Vice Pres*
Alvin Ramali, *Info Tech Mgr*
Vivien Ho, *Project Mgr*
▲ **EMP:** 98 **EST:** 1972
SQ FT: 95,000
SALES (est): 27.8MM **Privately Held**
WEB: www.tatungusa.com
SIC: 3663 3575 3944 3651 Television closed circuit equipment; computer terminals, monitors & components; video game machines, except coin-operated; television receiving sets; video cassette recorders/players & accessories; refrigerators, mechanical & absorption: household; microwave ovens, cooking equipment), commercial

(P-9322)
TELEMTRY CMMNCTONS SYSTEMS INC
Also Called: TCS
10020 Remmet Ave, Chatsworth
(91311-3854)
PHONE..................................818 718-6248
Sarin Michel Roy, *President*
Mihail Mateescu, *Vice Pres*
EMP: 24 **EST:** 1999
SQ FT: 14,500

▲ = Import ▼=Export
◆ =Import/Export

SALES (est): 7MM **Privately Held**
WEB: www.tcs.la
SIC: **3663** Antennas, transmitting & communications

(P-9323)

TRICOM RESEARCH INC
17791 Sky Park Cir Ste J, Irvine
(92614-6150)
PHONE...............................949 250-6024
Paula Wright, *President*
John W Wright, *CFO*
Richard Taras, *Engineer*
EMP: 64 EST: 2012
SALES (est): 6.4MM **Privately Held**
WEB: www.tricomresearch.com
SIC: **3663** Radio & TV communications equipment

(P-9324)

ULTIMATTE CORPORATION
5828 Calvin Ave, Tarzana (91356-1111)
PHONE...............................818 993-8007
Lynne Sauve, *President*
Petro Vlahos, *Shareholder*
Paul Vlahos, *Treasurer*
Nina Michalko, *Admin Sec*
▲ EMP: 30 EST: 1976
SALES (est): 4.8MM **Privately Held**
WEB: www.blackmagicdesign.com
SIC: **3663 3651 7371** Television broadcasting & communications equipment; household audio & video equipment; computer software development & applications
PA: Blackmagic Design Pty Ltd
11 Gateway Ct
Port Melbourne VIC 3207

(P-9325)

VISLINK LLC
1158 N Gilbert St, Anaheim (92801-1401)
PHONE...............................714 998-2121
John Hawkins, *Manager*
Jen Poff, *Program Mgr*
Julie Winemiller, *Technical Staff*
George Latham, *Controller*
Belinda Marino, *Human Res Dir*
EMP: 40 **Publicly Held**
WEB: www.vislink.com
SIC: **3663** Microwave communication equipment
HQ: Vislink Llc
101 Bilby Rd Ste 15
Hackettstown NJ 07840
908 852-3700

(P-9326)

W B WALTON ENTERPRISES INC
4185 Hallmark Pkwy, San Bernardino
(92407-1832)
P.O. Box 9010 (92427-0010)
PHONE...............................951 683-0930
William B Walton Jr, *President*
Jane Walton, *Corp Secy*
Ray Powers, *Sales Staff*
EMP: 26 EST: 1979
SQ FT: 30,000
SALES (est): 6.3MM **Privately Held**
WEB: www.de-ice.com
SIC: **3663 1731** Satellites, communications; electrical work

(P-9327)

WATER ASSOCIATES LLC
Also Called: Redtrac
34929 Flyover Ct, Bakersfield
(93308-9725)
PHONE...............................661 281-6077
Jeff Young, *Mng Member*
Michael McAllister, *Business Mgr*
Bob Simonian, *Sales Mgr*
Michael Young,
EMP: 20 EST: 2002
SQ FT: 7,000
SALES (est): 4.1MM **Privately Held**
WEB: www.waterassociates.com
SIC: **3663 3523** Radio & TV communications equipment; irrigation equipment, self-propelled

(P-9328)

WV COMMUNICATIONS INC
1125 Bus Ctr Cir Ste A, Newbury Park
(91320)
PHONE...............................805 376-1820
Uri Yulzari, *President*
Jim Tranovich, *Vice Pres*
Ron Bosi, *Admin Sec*
Don Berryman, *Sales Staff*
▲ EMP: 40 EST: 1998
SQ FT: 18,000
SALES (est): 6.9MM **Privately Held**
WEB: www.wv-comm.com
SIC: **3663** Microwave communication equipment

(P-9329)

XCOM WIRELESS INC
2700 Rose Ave Ste E, Signal Hill
(90755-1929)
PHONE...............................562 981-0077
Dan Hyman, *President*
Peter Bogdanoff, *Shareholder*
Ardesta LLC, *Shareholder*
Mark Hyman, *Corp Secy*
Lance Harrison, *Technician*
EMP: 17 EST: 2000
SQ FT: 3,500
SALES (est): 1.2MM **Privately Held**
WEB: www.xcomwireless.com
SIC: **3663** Mobile communication equipment

(P-9330)

YAESU USA INC
6125 Phyllis Dr, Cypress (90630-5242)
PHONE...............................714 827-7600
Jun Hasegawa, *CEO*
Dennis Motschenbacher, *Exec VP*
Tim Factor, *Technical Staff*
Gary Doshay, *Credit Mgr*
Joann Ordonez, *Analyst*
▲ EMP: 40 EST: 2012
SALES (est): 4.5MM **Privately Held**
WEB: www.yaesu.com
SIC: **3663** Radio & TV communications equipment

3669 Communications Eqpt, NEC

(P-9331)

ANTAIRA TECHNOLOGIES LLC (PA)
780 Challenger St, Brea (92821-2924)
PHONE...............................714 386-7036
Frank Yang, *Finance Mgr*
Peter Szyszko, *Engineer*
Deena Patel, *Opers Mgr*
Andy Liao, *Opers Staff*
Chris Carson, *Sales Mgr*
▲ EMP: 26 EST: 2005
SQ FT: 10,000
SALES (est): 5.8MM **Privately Held**
WEB: www.antaira.com
SIC: **3669 5065** Intercommunication systems, electric; communication equipment

(P-9332)

ATI SOLUTIONS INC (PA)
Also Called: Ucview
18425 Napa St, Northridge (91325-3619)
PHONE...............................818 772-7900
Guy Avital, *CEO*
Leah Avital, *Vice Pres*
Deborah Camou, *General Mgr*
Ronny Contreras, *Engineer*
Eileen Dela Cruz, *Accountant*
EMP: 14 EST: 2002
SALES (est): 4.8MM **Privately Held**
WEB: www.uniguest.com
SIC: **3669** Visual communication systems

(P-9333)

BDFCO INC
Also Called: Damac
1926 Kauai Dr, Costa Mesa (92626-3542)
PHONE...............................714 228-2900
Frank J Kubat Jr, *CEO*
Robert Mc Clory, *Shareholder*
Damon Gejeian, *Vice Pres*
Daniel L Davis, *Admin Sec*
▲ EMP: 80 EST: 1984

SQ FT: 120,000
SALES (est): 12.2MM **Privately Held**
SIC: **3669** Intercommunication systems, electric

(P-9334)

BITMAX LLC (PA)
6255 W Sunset Blvd # 1515, Los Angeles
(90028-7416)
PHONE...............................323 978-7878
Nancy Bennett, *Mng Member*
Tony Rizkallah, *CTO*
Jeff Beaudoin, *Technician*
Andy Nguyen, *Technician*
David Baker, *Opers Mgr*
EMP: 21 EST: 1998
SQ FT: 7,500
SALES (est): 8MM **Privately Held**
WEB: www.bitmax.net
SIC: **3669 7929** Visual communication systems; entertainment service

(P-9335)

CANOGA PERKINS CORPORATION (HQ)
20600 Prairie St, Chatsworth (91311-6008)
PHONE...............................818 718-6300
Alfred Tim Champion, *President*
Gary Allport, *Vice Pres*
Vamsi M Rachapudi, *Software Engr*
Anhtuan Trinh, *IT/INT Sup*
Keith Wynn, *Technical Staff*
◆ EMP: 100 EST: 1965
SQ FT: 64,000
SALES (est): 29.2MM
SALES (corp-wide): 645.5MM **Privately Held**
WEB: www.canoga.com
SIC: **3669** Intercommunication systems, electric
PA: Rowan Technologies, Inc.
10 Indel Ave
Rancocas NJ 08073
609 267-9000

(P-9336)

COMPUTER SERVICE COMPANY
Also Called: Steiny & Company
210 N Delilah St, Corona (92879-1883)
PHONE...............................951 738-1444
Justin Cataldo, *Manager*
Gayle Kappelman, *Admin Sec*
EMP: 49
SALES (corp-wide): 7.1MM **Privately Held**
SIC: **3669 7629** Traffic signals, electric; electrical repair shops
PA: Computer Service Company
5463 Diaz St
Baldwin Park CA 91706
951 738-1444

(P-9337)

D-TECH OPTOELECTRONICS INC
18062 Rowland St, City of Industry
(91748-1205)
PHONE...............................626 956-1100
An Baoxin, *President*
EMP: 20 EST: 2007
SALES (est): 20MM **Privately Held**
WEB: www.dtechopto.com
SIC: **3669** Intercommunication systems, electric
HQ: Global Communication Semiconductors, Llc
23155 Kashiwa Ct
Torrance CA 90505
310 530-7274

(P-9338)

DETECTORS INCORPORATED
1800 E Miraloma Ave Ste A, Placentia
(92870-6743)
PHONE...............................714 982-5350
EMP: 16 EST: 2015
SALES (est): 1.1MM **Privately Held**
WEB: www.detectorsinc.com
SIC: **3669** Smoke detectors

(P-9339)

ECONOLITE CONTROL PRODUCTS INC (PA)
1250 N Tustin Ave, Anaheim (92807-1617)
P.O. Box 6150 (92816-0150)
PHONE...............................714 630-3700
Michael C Doyle, *CEO*
David St Amant, *President*
Snehasis Chakravarty, *Vice Pres*
Wayne Hagewood, *Vice Pres*
Douglas Wiersig, *Vice Pres*
▼ EMP: 160 EST: 1933
SQ FT: 95,000
SALES (est): 111.6MM **Privately Held**
WEB: www.econolite.com
SIC: **3669** Traffic signals, electric

(P-9340)

ESCO TECHNOLOGIES INC
501 Del Norte Blvd, Oxnard (93030-7983)
PHONE...............................805 604-3875
EMP: 32 **Publicly Held**
WEB: www.escotechnologies.com
SIC: **3669** Intercommunication systems, electric
PA: Esco Technologies Inc.
9900 Clayton Rd Ste A
Saint Louis MO 63124

(P-9341)

EXIGENT SENSORS LLC
11441 Markon Dr, Garden Grove
(92841-1404)
PHONE...............................949 439-1321
Jeff Buss, *Mng Member*
Brent Duchon
▲ EMP: 22 EST: 2007
SALES (est): 6.6MM **Privately Held**
SIC: **3669** Fire alarm apparatus, electric

(P-9342)

FIRE & GAS DETECTION TECH INC
4222 E La Palma Ave, Anaheim
(92807-1816)
PHONE...............................714 671-8500
Olden Carr, *President*
Michelle Cabbell, *Controller*
EMP: 15 EST: 2017
SALES (est): 2.1MM **Privately Held**
WEB: www.fg-detection.com
SIC: **3669** Fire detection systems, electric

(P-9343)

GENERAL MONITORS INC (DH)
26776 Simpatica Cir, Lake Forest
(92630-8128)
PHONE...............................949 581-4464
Nish Vartanian, *Vice Pres*
Richard Lamishaw, *CFO*
Karen Nguyen, *Prdtn Mgr*
Raymond Kolander, *Manager*
◆ EMP: 110 EST: 1961
SQ FT: 60,000
SALES (est): 63.1MM
SALES (corp-wide): 1.3B **Publicly Held**
WEB: www.us.msasafety.com
SIC: **3669 1799 3812** Fire detection systems, electric; gas leakage detection; infrared object detection equipment
HQ: Mine Safety Appliances Company, Llc
1000 Cranberry Woods Dr
Cranberry Township PA 16066
724 776-8600

(P-9344)

ITERIS INC (PA)
1700 Carnegie Ave Ste 100, Santa Ana
(92705-5551)
PHONE...............................949 270-9400
J Joseph Bergera, *President*
Douglas L Groves, *CFO*
Douglas Groves, *CFO*
Andy Schmidt, *CFO*
Pete Costello, *Assoc VP*
▲ EMP: 343 EST: 1969
SQ FT: 47,000
SALES: 117.1MM **Publicly Held**
WEB: www.iteris.com
SIC: **3669 7373 8711** Transportation signaling devices; systems software development services; engineering services; consulting engineer

P R O D U C T S   &   S V C S

(P-9345)
JTB SUPPLY COMPANY INC
1030 N Batavia St Ste A, Orange
(92867-5541)
PHONE.................714 639-9558
Jeff York, *President*
Tara Dunham, *Opers Mgr*
Mindy Myers, *Sales Staff*
EMP: 51 **EST:** 1998
SQ FT: 10,000
SALES (est): 5.2MM **Privately Held**
WEB: www.jtbsupplyco.com
SIC: 3669 Traffic signals, electric

(P-9346)
OPTEX INCORPORATED
18730 S Wilmington Ave # 100, Compton
(90220-5924)
PHONE.................800 966-7839
Makoto Kokobo, *CEO*
Tohru Kobayashi, *Ch of Bd*
James Quick, *President*
Michael La Chere, *CFO*
Hajime Yamasaki, *Vice Pres*
▲ **EMP:** 54 **EST:** 1992
SQ FT: 35,000
SALES (est): 12.3MM **Privately Held**
WEB: www.optexamerica.com
SIC: 3669 Emergency alarms
PA: Optex Group Company, Limited
4-7-5, Nionohama
Otsu SGA 520-0

(P-9347)
PALOMAR PRODUCTS INC
23042 Arroyo Vis, Rcho STA Marg
(92688-2617)
PHONE.................949 858-8836
Kevin Moschetti, *CEO*
Val Policky, *President*
Fred Ekstein, *Vice Pres*
Nick Moore, *Info Tech Mgr*
Rhonda Kiyomura, *Engineer*
EMP: 79 **EST:** 1997
SQ FT: 35,000
SALES (est): 23.2MM
SALES (corp-wide): 4.8B **Publicly Held**
WEB: www.transdigm.com
SIC: 3669 Intercommunication systems, electric
HQ: Esterline Technologies Corp
1301 E 9th St Ste 3000
Cleveland OH 44114
216 706-2960

(P-9348)
PI VARIABLES INC
3002 Dow Ave Ste 138, Tustin
(92780-7248)
PHONE.................949 415-9411
James Selevan, *CEO*
Kathleen Selevan, *President*
Daniel Selevan, *Prdtn Mgr*
EMP: 15
SALES (est): 3MM **Privately Held**
WEB: www.pi-lit.com
SIC: 3669 Traffic signals, electric

(P-9349)
Q4 SERVICES LLC
1108 W Barkley Ave, Orange (92868-1213)
PHONE.................949 421-7856
Mario Fernandez, *Principal*
EMP: 13 **EST:** 2018
SALES (est): 1.8MM **Privately Held**
WEB: www.q4services.com
SIC: 3669 Visual communication systems

(P-9350)
RAYTHEON APPLIED SIGNAL
160 N Rverview Dr Ste 300, Anaheim
(92808)
PHONE.................714 917-0255
John McGrory, *Branch Mgr*
Oliver Curtis, *Fellow*
Coronado Martha, *Fellow*
EMP: 57
SALES (corp-wide): 56.5B **Publicly Held**
WEB: www.raytheon.com
SIC: 3669 Signaling apparatus, electric
HQ: Raytheon Applied Signal Technology, Inc.
460 W California Ave
Sunnyvale CA 94086
408 749-1888

(P-9351)
RSG/AAMES SECURITY INC
3300 E 59th St, Long Beach (90805-4504)
PHONE.................562 529-5100
Louis J Finkle, *President*
Danielle Roberts, *Shareholder*
Michelle Reuven, *Office Mgr*
Susan Bulloch, *Manager*
▲ **EMP:** 44 **EST:** 1975
SQ FT: 17,000
SALES (est): 1.3MM **Privately Held**
WEB: www.rsgsecurity.com
SIC: 3669 Fire alarm apparatus, electric

(P-9352)
SIEMENS RAIL AUTOMATION CORP
9568 Archibald Ave, Rancho Cucamonga
(91730-5744)
PHONE.................909 532-5405
Jay Aslam, *Opers Mgr*
Michael Sayer, *Technical Staff*
Richard V Peel, *Mfg Staff*
EMP: 66
SALES (corp-wide): 67.4B **Privately Held**
WEB: www.siemens.com
SIC: 3669 Railroad signaling devices, electric
HQ: Siemens Rail Automation Corporation
2400 Nelson Miller Pkwy
Louisville KY 40223
800 626-2710

(P-9353)
SIERRA TRAFFIC SERVICE INC
225 W Loop Dr, Camarillo (93010-2038)
P.O. Box 222, Somis (93066-0222)
PHONE.................805 388-2474
Terry Quinones, *President*
EMP: 17 **EST:** 2003
SALES (est): 3.6MM **Privately Held**
SIC: 3669 Pedestrian traffic control equipment

(P-9354)
SIGTRONICS CORPORATION
178 E Arrow Hwy, San Dimas
(91773-3336)
PHONE.................909 305-9399
Mark Kelley, *President*
Tim Theis, *Vice Pres*
Frank M Sigona, *Principal*
Jane Sigona, *Principal*
Steve Daw, *Technology*
EMP: 20 **EST:** 1974
SQ FT: 12,000
SALES (est): 2.7MM **Privately Held**
WEB: www.sigtronics.com
SIC: 3669 Intercommunication systems, electric

(P-9355)
STATEWIDE SAFETY AND SIGNS I
522 Lindon Ln, Nipomo (93444-9222)
PHONE.................714 468-1919
Greg Grosch, *CEO*
Don Nicholas, *President*
Chris Burns, *CFO*
Mike Adams, *Branch Mgr*
Ronnie Rodriquez, *Branch Mgr*
EMP: 300 **EST:** 2012
SALES (est): 33MM **Privately Held**
WEB: www.statewidess.com
SIC: 3669 Pedestrian traffic control equipment

(P-9356)
TACTICAL COMMAND INDS INC (DH)
4700 E Airport Dr, Ontario (91761-7875)
PHONE.................925 219-1097
Scott O'Brien, *President*
Denise Hutchinson, *Vice Pres*
Aris Makris, *Vice Pres*
Leanne McKenzie, *Executive Asst*
Medine Lucy, *Administration*
EMP: 23 **EST:** 1996
SALES (est): 11.3MM
SALES (corp-wide): 404.6MM **Privately Held**
WEB: www.safariland.com
SIC: 3669 Intercommunication systems, electric

HQ: Safariland, Llc
13386 International Pkwy
Jacksonville FL 32218
904 741-5400

(P-9357)
TACTICAL COMMUNICATIONS CORP
473 Post St, Camarillo (93010-8553)
PHONE.................805 987-4100
Gregory Peacock, *CEO*
E Carey Walter, *CEO*
Greg Peacock, *CTO*
EMP: 25 **EST:** 2009
SQ FT: 11,000
SALES (est): 4MM **Privately Held**
WEB: www.tacticalcommunications.com
SIC: 3669 Intercommunication systems, electric

(P-9358)
UNICOM ELECTRIC INC
565 Brea Canyon Rd Ste A, Walnut
(91789-3004)
PHONE.................626 964-7873
Jeffrey Lo, *President*
Christopher Lin, *Engineer*
▲ **EMP:** 15 **EST:** 1986
SQ FT: 25,000
SALES (est): 1.2MM **Privately Held**
WEB: www.unicomlink.com
SIC: 3669 3678 3577 Intercommunication systems, electric; electronic connectors; computer peripheral equipment

(P-9359)
WALTON ELECTRIC CORPORATION
755 N Central Ave Ste A, Upland
(91786-9475)
P.O. Box 1599, Claremont (91711-8599)
PHONE.................909 981-5051
Tanyon D Dunkley, *CEO*
Don R Davis, *Exec VP*
Ron C Stickel, *Vice Pres*
Parker Dunkley, *Project Mgr*
EMP: 150 **EST:** 1985
SQ FT: 10,150
SALES (est): 35.1MM **Privately Held**
WEB: www.waltonelectriccorp.com
SIC: 3669 1731 Fire alarm apparatus, electric; electrical work; general electrical contractor

3671 Radio & T V Receiving Electron Tubes

(P-9360)
DCX-CHOL ENTERPRISES INC (PA)
Also Called: Smi, Scb
12831 S Figueroa St, Los Angeles
(90061-1157)
PHONE.................310 516-1692
Neal Castleman, *President*
Brian Gamberg, *Vice Pres*
Garret Hoffman, *Vice Pres*
Robin Serrano, *Program Mgr*
Pam Paonessa, *Administration*
▲ **EMP:** 80 **EST:** 1997
SQ FT: 50,000
SALES (est): 109.1MM **Privately Held**
WEB: www.dcxchol.com
SIC: 3671 Electron tubes

(P-9361)
DCX-CHOL ENTERPRISES INC
Teletronic Div Dcx-Chol Entp
12831 S Figueroa St, Los Angeles
(90061-1157)
PHONE.................310 516-1692
Neil Levy, *Director*
Zeev Goland, *Engineer*
EMP: 44
SALES (corp-wide): 109.1MM **Privately Held**
WEB: www.dcxchol.com
SIC: 3671 3679 Electron tubes; harness assemblies for electronic use: wire or cable

PA: Dcx-Chol Enterprises, Inc.
12831 S Figueroa St
Los Angeles CA 90061
310 516-1692

(P-9362)
DCX-CHOL ENTERPRISES INC
Also Called: Masterite Division
12831 S Figueroa St, Los Angeles
(90061-1157)
PHONE.................310 516-1692
Brian Gamberg, *Branch Mgr*
EMP: 16
SALES (corp-wide): 109.1MM **Privately Held**
WEB: www.dcxchol.com
SIC: 3671 3365 Electron tubes; aerospace castings, aluminum
PA: Dcx-Chol Enterprises, Inc.
12831 S Figueroa St
Los Angeles CA 90061
310 516-1692

(P-9363)
DCX-CHOL ENTERPRISES INC
12831 S Figueroa St, Los Angeles
(90061-1157)
PHONE.................310 525-1205
EMP: 46
SALES (corp-wide): 110.2MM **Privately Held**
WEB: www.dcxchol.com
SIC: 3671 3365 Electron Tubes, Nsk
PA: Dcx-Chol Enterprises, Inc.
12831 S Figueroa St
Los Angeles CA 90061
310 516-1692

(P-9364)
NEWVAC LLC
Also Called: Newvac Division
9330 Desoto Ave, Chatsworth (91311)
PHONE.................310 990-0401
Garrett Hoffman, *Branch Mgr*
EMP: 114
SALES (corp-wide): 130.9MM **Privately Held**
WEB: www.newvac-llc.com
SIC: 3671 3678 3679 Electron tubes; electronic connectors; harness assemblies for electronic use: wire or cable
HQ: Newvac, Llc
9330 De Soto Ave
Chatsworth CA 91311
310 525-1205

(P-9365)
NEWVAC LLC
Newvac Division
9330 De Soto Ave, Chatsworth
(91311-4926)
PHONE.................747 202-7333
Garrett Hoffman, *Branch Mgr*
Erik Laroe, *Vice Pres*
Jon Strafuss, *Vice Pres*
Ana Chavoya, *Administration*
Rupert Flecter, *Engineer*
EMP: 80
SALES (corp-wide): 130.9MM **Privately Held**
WEB: www.newvac-llc.com
SIC: 3671 3678 3679 3643 Electron tubes; electronic connectors; harness assemblies for electronic use: wire or cable; current-carrying wiring devices; noncurrent-carrying wiring services
HQ: Newvac, Llc
9330 De Soto Ave
Chatsworth CA 91311
310 525-1205

(P-9366)
PENTA FINANCIAL INC
Also Called: Penta Laboratories
14399 Princeton Ave, Moorpark
(93021-1481)
PHONE.................818 882-3872
Steve Sanett, *CEO*
▲ **EMP:** 33 **EST:** 1993
SQ FT: 28,000
SALES (est): 4.9MM **Privately Held**
WEB: www.pentalabs.com
SIC: 3671 3589 Electron tubes; microwave ovens (cooking equipment), commercial

(P-9367)
PENTA LABORATORIES LLC
2359 Knoll Dr Ste A, Ventura (93003-5876)
PHONE..................................818 882-3872
Susan E Sanett,
Wayne Coturri, *President*
Neil Towey, *Vice Pres*
John Grandinetti, *Sales Staff*
▲ **EMP:** 15 **EST:** 1951
SALES (est): 3.6MM **Privately Held**
SIC: 3671 5065 Electron tubes; electronic
tubes: receiving & transmitting or indus-
trial

(P-9368)
STELLANT SYSTEMS INC (HQ)
Also Called: Electron Devices
3100 Lomita Blvd, Torrance (90505-5104)
P.O. Box 2999 (90509-2999)
PHONE..................................310 517-6000
Michael Strianese, *CEO*
Mark Hyun Choi, *Vice Pres*
Roger Williams, *Executive*
▲ **EMP:** 100 **EST:** 2000
SALES (est): 115.7MM **Privately Held**
SIC: 3671 3764 Traveling wave tubes;
guided missile & space vehicle propulsion
unit parts

3672 Printed Circuit Boards

(P-9369)
A & M ELECTRONICS INC
25018 Avenue Kearny, Valencia
(91355-1253)
PHONE..................................661 257-3680
Ron Simpson, *President*
Tiffiny Simpson, *Vice Pres*
Dan Simpson, *Manager*
EMP: 30 **EST:** 1977
SQ FT: 12,000
SALES (est): 6.1MM **Privately Held**
WEB: www.aandmelectronics.com
SIC: 3672 Circuit boards, television & radio
printed

(P-9370)
ACCU-SEMBLY INC
1835 Huntington Dr, Duarte (91010-2635)
PHONE..................................626 357-3447
John Hykes, *CEO*
Jan Shimmin, *Shareholder*
John Shimmin, *Shareholder*
Marilyn Hykes, *Admin Dir*
Carlos Martinez, *Program Mgr*
▲ **EMP:** 95 **EST:** 1983
SQ FT: 15,000
SALES (est): 19.8MM **Privately Held**
WEB: www.accu-sembly.com
SIC: 3672 Printed circuit boards

(P-9371)
ACCURATE CIRCUIT ENGRG INC
Also Called: Ace
3019 Kilson Dr, Santa Ana (92707-4202)
PHONE..................................714 546-2162
Charles Lowe, *CEO*
James Hofer, *General Mgr*
Charels Lowe, *Info Tech Mgr*
Tim Waddell, *Engineer*
Michael Ciccoianni, *Controller*
▲ **EMP:** 70
SQ FT: 15,000
SALES (est): 7.2MM **Privately Held**
WEB: www.ace-pcb.com
SIC: 3672 Printed circuit boards

(P-9372)
ACCURATE ENGINEERING INC
8710 Telfair Ave, Sun Valley (91352-2530)
PHONE..................................818 768-3919
Shitalkumar Desai, *President*
Ramesh Jasani, *Shareholder*
Rush Patel, *President*
Gautam Jasani, *CFO*
Suresh Jasani, *Treasurer*
EMP: 25 **EST:** 1996
SQ FT: 15,000
SALES (est): 3MM **Privately Held**
WEB: www.accueng.com
SIC: 3672 Printed circuit boards

(P-9373)
ADVANCED CIRCUITS INC
17067 Cantara St, Van Nuys (91406-1112)
PHONE..................................818 345-1993
Ralph Richart, *Branch Mgr*
EMP: 16 **Publicly Held**
WEB: www.4pcb.com
SIC: 3672 Printed circuit boards
HQ: Advanced Circuits, Inc.
21101 E 32nd Pkwy
Aurora CO 80011
-

(P-9374)
ALLIED ELECTRONIC SERVICES
INC
1342 E Borchard Ave, Santa Ana
(92705-4413)
PHONE..................................714 245-2500
Dave Vadodaria, *President*
Bharati Vadodaria, *CFO*
EMP: 33 **EST:** 1988
SQ FT: 6,000
SALES (est): 2.3MM **Privately Held**
WEB: www.alliedelectronicsservices.com
SIC: 3672 Printed circuit boards

(P-9375)
ALMATRON ELECTRONICS INC
644 Young St, Santa Ana (92705-5633)
PHONE..................................714 557-6000
Margarito Alvarez, *President*
Margarita Alvarez, *Owner*
Daniel Mingolla, *Engineer*
Sergio Rivera, *Purch Agent*
EMP: 20 **EST:** 1984
SQ FT: 11,500
SALES (est): 5.7MM **Privately Held**
WEB: www.almatron.com
SIC: 3672 Circuit boards, television & radio
printed

(P-9376)
AMBAY CIRCUITS INC
Also Called: Delta Dvh Circuits
16117 Leadwell St, Van Nuys
(91406-3417)
PHONE..................................818 786-8241
Kana Khunti, *President*
EMP: 20 **EST:** 1973
SQ FT: 5,500
SALES (est): 2.9MM **Privately Held**
SIC: 3672 Circuit boards, television & radio
printed

(P-9377)
AMERICAN BOARD ASSEMBLY
INC
5456 Endeavour Ct, Moorpark
(93021-1705)
PHONE..................................805 523-0274
Cindy Murray, *CEO*
Gene Difabritis, *President*
▲ **EMP:** 140 **EST:** 1994
SQ FT: 11,000
SALES (est): 19.7MM **Privately Held**
WEB: www.americanboard.com
SIC: 3672 Printed circuit boards

(P-9378)
AMERICAN CIRCUIT TECH INC
(PA)
5330 E Hunter Ave, Anaheim (92807-2053)
PHONE..................................714 777-2480
Ravi Kheni, *President*
Labheu Zalavadia, *Vice Pres*
Ankur Kheni, *General Mgr*
Giradhar Butani, *Admin Sec*
Labhu Zalavadia, *Mfg Staff*
EMP: 39 **EST:** 1975
SQ FT: 22,000
SALES (est): 6.1MM **Privately Held**
WEB: www.excello.com
SIC: 3672 Circuit boards, television & radio
printed

(P-9379)
APPLIED CIRCUIT SOLUTIONS
INC
3232 S Fairview St, Santa Ana
(92704-6509)
PHONE..................................949 754-1545
Jim Kerchner, *President*
Steven Root, *Treasurer*
Kay Stone, *Office Mgr*

EMP: 15 **EST:** 1989
SQ FT: 20,000
SALES (est): 1.4MM **Privately Held**
SIC: 3672 Printed circuit boards

(P-9380)
APT ELECTRONICS INC
241 N Crescent Way, Anaheim
(92801-6704)
PHONE..................................714 687-6760
Tae Myoung Kim, *CEO*
Kelly Bui, *Sales Staff*
Jacques Bojoh, *Manager*
EMP: 112 **EST:** 1999
SQ FT: 20,000
SALES (est): 21.3MM **Privately Held**
WEB: www.aptelectronics.com
SIC: 3672 Printed circuit boards

(P-9381)
ARTURO GONZALEZ
Also Called: Vortex Electronics
13409 Harding St, San Fernando
(91340-1219)
PHONE..................................818 837-7221
Arturo Gonzalez, *Principal*
EMP: 18 **EST:** 2008
SALES (est): 97.5K **Privately Held**
SIC: 5999 3672 3679 8711 Electronic
parts & equipment; printed circuit boards;
electronic circuits; electrical or electronic
engineering

(P-9382)
ASROCK AMERICA INC
13848 Magnolia Ave, Chino (91710-7027)
PHONE..................................909 590-8308
James Teng, *President*
Eric Lin, *Technology*
JC Chung, *Sales Dir*
Sergio Sanchez, *Sales Staff*
Clarinda Huang, *Manager*
▲ **EMP:** 37 **EST:** 2003
SALES (est): 13.3MM **Privately Held**
WEB: www.asrock.com
SIC: 3672 Printed circuit boards
HQ: Firstplace International Limited
C/O: Offshore Incorporations Limited
Road Town

(P-9383)
ASTRONIC
2 Orion, Aliso Viejo (92656-4200)
PHONE..................................949 454-1180
Sang H Choi, *CEO*
Kristine Cynn, *COO*
OK Kay Choi, *Corp Secy*
Dolores Carreon, *Controller*
▲ **EMP:** 143 **EST:** 1976
SQ FT: 41,000
SALES (est): 27.9MM **Privately Held**
WEB: www.astronic-ems.com
SIC: 3672 1742 Printed circuit boards;
acoustical & insulation work

(P-9384)
AVANTEC MANUFACTURING
INC
1811 N Case St, Orange (92865-4234)
PHONE..................................714 532-6197
Alan E McNeeney, *CEO*
▲ **EMP:** 20 **EST:** 2003
SALES (est): 5.2MM **Privately Held**
WEB: www.avantecusa.com
SIC: 3672 Printed circuit boards

(P-9385)
BENCHMARK ELEC MFG
SLTONS MRPA
200 Science Dr, Moorpark (93021-2003)
PHONE..................................805 532-2800
EMP: 523 **EST:** 1986
SALES (est): 116.7MM
SALES (corp-wide): 2B **Publicly Held**
WEB: www.bench.com
SIC: 3672 Printed circuit boards
HQ: Benchmark Electronics Manufacturing
Solutions Inc.
5550 Hellyer Ave
San Jose CA 95138
805 222-1303

(P-9386)
CALPAK USA INC
13748 Prairie Ave, Hawthorne
(90250-7359)
PHONE..................................310 937-7335
Danish Qureshi, *President*
▲ **EMP:** 20 **EST:** 1978 **Privately Held**
WEB: www.calpak-usa.com
SIC: 3672 3679 8742 4813 Printed circuit
boards; commutators, electronic; man-
agement consulting services; telephone
communication, except radio

(P-9387)
CELESTICA AEROSPACE TECH
CORP
Also Called: Celestica-Aerospace
895 S Rockefeller Ave, Ontario
(91761-8145)
PHONE..................................512 310-7540
Jeffrey Bain, *President*
Thomas Lovelock, *President*
Leslie K Sladek, *Admin Sec*
Enrique Saenz, *Manager*
Andres Sosa, *Manager*
▲ **EMP:** 200 **EST:** 2002
SQ FT: 55,000
SALES (est): 50.9MM
SALES (corp-wide): 1.1B **Privately Held**
WEB: www.celestica.com
SIC: 3672 Printed circuit boards
HQ: Celestica Inc
1900-5140 Yonge St
North York ON M2N 6
416 448-5800

(P-9388)
CHOOSE MANUFACTURING CO
LLC
24 Passion Flower, Irvine (92618-2252)
PHONE..................................714 327-1698
Herbert Chiu, *Mng Member*
Anthony Chiu, *Manager*
▲ **EMP:** 20 **EST:** 2000
SALES (est): 3MM **Privately Held**
WEB: www.choosemfg.com
SIC: 3672 Printed circuit boards

(P-9389)
CIRCUIT AUTOMATION INC
32052 Sea Island Dr, Dana Point
(92629-3629)
PHONE..................................714 763-4180
Thomas Meeker, *President*
Sherlene Meeker, *CFO*
Masayuki Kojima, *Vice Pres*
Larry Lindland, *Sales Staff*
◆ **EMP:** 18 **EST:** 1980 **Privately Held**
WEB: www.s585017606.onlinehome.us
SIC: 3672 Printed circuit boards

(P-9390)
CIRCUIT EXPRESS INC
67 W Easy St Ste 129, Simi Valley
(93065-6204)
PHONE..................................805 581-2172
Himmat Desai, *CEO*
Vinny Kathrota, *Admin Sec*
Rash Vaghasia, *Engineer*
EMP: 26 **EST:** 1979
SQ FT: 5,000
SALES (est): 1.2MM **Privately Held**
WEB: www.circuitexpressinc.com
SIC: 3672 Circuit boards, television & radio
printed

(P-9391)
CIRCUIT SERVICES LLC
Also Called: Career Tech Circuit Services
9134 Independence Ave, Chatsworth
(91311-5902)
PHONE..................................818 701-5391
Marc Haugen, *CEO*
Vicky Penate, *Admin Asst*
Elcid Aranas, *Engineer*
Garo Dardarian, *Engineer*
Artin Minas, *Marketing Mgr*
EMP: 43 **EST:** 1998
SALES (est): 10.7MM
SALES (corp-wide): 60.6MM **Privately**
Held
WEB: www.careertech-usa.com
SIC: 3672 Printed circuit boards

PA: Lockwood Industries, Llc
28525 Industry Dr
Valencia CA 91355
661 702-6999

(P-9392)
CMS CIRCUIT SOLUTIONS INC
41549 Cherry St, Murrieta (92562-9193)
P.O. Box 1031 (92564-1031)
PHONE..................................951 698-4452
Clark M Steddom, *President*
Nelson Pisciotti, *Technical Staff*
EMP: 20 EST: 2005
SALES (est): 2.6MM **Privately Held**
WEB: www.cmscircuitsolutions.com
SIC: 3672 Circuit boards, television & radio
printed

(P-9393)
**COAST TO COAST CIRCUITS
INC (PA)**
Also Called: Speedy Circuits
5331 Mcfadden Ave, Huntington Beach
(92649-1204)
PHONE..................................714 891-9441
Edward Porter, *CEO*
Ronald Scott Lawhead, *CFO*
Michael Schlehr, *CFO*
Mike Schlehr, *CFO*
Albert Martinez, *Vice Pres*
◆ EMP: 41 EST: 1985
SQ FT: 40,000
SALES (est): 13.5MM **Privately Held**
WEB: www.coast2coastcircuits.com
SIC: 3672 Circuit boards, television & radio
printed

(P-9394)
CONCEPT DEVELOPMENT LLC
Also Called: CDI
1881 Langley Ave, Irvine (92614-5623)
PHONE..................................949 623-8000
James M Reardon, *President*
Young Ha, *Engineer*
EMP: 20 EST: 1972
SQ FT: 12,880
SALES (est): 5.1MM
SALES (corp-wide): 51.9MM **Publicly
Held**
WEB: www.cdvinc.com
SIC: 3672 Printed circuit boards
PA: One Stop Systems, Inc.
2235 Entp St Ste 110
Escondido CA 92029
760 745-9883

(P-9395)
**CORNELL PTRSON AROSPC
TECH LLC**
167 Del Mar Ave, Costa Mesa
(92627-1352)
PHONE..................................714 656-5376
Reginald Little, *Branch Mgr*
EMP: 16
SALES (corp-wide): 153.9K **Privately
Held**
SIC: 3672 7389 Printed circuit boards;
PA: Cornell Peterson Aerospace & Technol-
ogy, Llc
9114 Adams Ave
Huntington Beach CA

(P-9396)
**CREATION TECH CALEXICO INC
(HQ)**
Also Called: Aisling Industries
1778 Zinetta Rd Ste A, Calexico
(92231-9511)
P.O. Box 1833, El Centro (92244-1833)
PHONE..................................760 336-8543
Bhawnesh Mathur, *CEO*
Michael J Logue, *President*
Sergio Quiroz, *Vice Pres*
▲ EMP: 25 EST: 1985
SQ FT: 10,000
SALES (est): 108.9MM
SALES (corp-wide): 212.6MM **Privately
Held**
WEB: www.creationtech.com
SIC: 3672 3679 Printed circuit boards;
electronic circuits

(P-9397)
**DE LEON ENTPS ELEC SPCLIST
INC**
11934 Allegheny St, Sun Valley
(91352-1833)
PHONE..................................818 252-6690
Miguel De Leon, *President*
Ray Payne, *Manager*
▲ EMP: 24 EST: 1994
SQ FT: 11,000
SALES (est): 4.5MM **Privately Held**
WEB: www.deleonenterprises.com
SIC: 3672 Printed circuit boards

(P-9398)
DELTA D V H CIRCUITS INC
16117 Leadwell St, Van Nuys
(91406-3417)
PHONE..................................818 786-8241
Kana Khunai, *Owner*
EMP: 15 EST: 1994
SQ FT: 10,000
SALES (est): 1.2MM **Privately Held**
SIC: 3672 Printed circuit boards

(P-9399)
**DYNASTY ELECTRONIC
COMPANY LLC**
Also Called: Dec
1790 E Mcfadden Ave # 10, Santa Ana
(92705-4638)
PHONE..................................714 550-1197
Fredrick Rodenhuis, *Mng Member*
Frederik Rodenhuis, *Legal Staff*
Mark Clark,
Jason Schmidlkofer, *Consultant*
EMP: 65 EST: 2008
SQ FT: 10,000
SALES (est): 8.5MM **Privately Held**
WEB: www.dec-assembly.com
SIC: 3672 Printed circuit boards

(P-9400)
EMLINQ LLC
Also Called: Electronic Mfg Leaders & Qulty
2125 N Madera Rd Ste C, Simi Valley
(93065-7711)
PHONE..................................805 409-4807
Tamara Bitticks, *Mng Member*
Linda Hana, *Program Mgr*
Henok Tadesse, *Engineer*
Arun Pabby, *Purch Mgr*
Sandro Aquilina,
▲ EMP: 106 EST: 2007
SALES (est): 26.3MM **Privately Held**
WEB: www.emlinq.com
SIC: 3672 Printed circuit boards

(P-9401)
ETI PARTNERS IV LLC
901 Wshngton Blvd Ste 208, Marina Del
Rey (90292)
PHONE..................................949 273-4990
EMP: 20 EST: 2015
SALES (est): 1MM **Privately Held**
SIC: 3672 Printed circuit boards

(P-9402)
EXCELLO CIRCUITS INC
1924 Nancita Cir, Placentia (92870-6737)
PHONE..................................714 993-0560
Rax Ribadia, *President*
Sam Bhayani, *President*
Tushar Patel, *Vice Pres*
EMP: 47
SQ FT: 11,000
SALES (est): 5.1MM **Privately Held**
WEB: www.excello.com
SIC: 3672 Printed circuit boards

(P-9403)
**EXPERT ASSEMBLY SERVICES
INC**
Also Called: Expert Ems
14312 Chambers Rd Ste B, Tustin
(92780-6912)
PHONE..................................714 258-8880
Jack Quinn, *CEO*
Shelly Martin, *Manager*
EMP: 50 EST: 1997
SALES (est): 11.4MM **Privately Held**
WEB: www.expertassembly.com
SIC: 3672 Printed circuit boards

(P-9404)
**FABRICATED COMPONENTS
CORP**
Also Called: Summit Interconnect Orange
130 W Bristol Ln, Orange (92865-2640)
PHONE..................................714 974-8590
Shane Whiteside, *President*
▼ EMP: 140
SQ FT: 40,000
SALES (est): 24MM **Privately Held**
WEB: www.fabricatedcomponents.com
SIC: 3672 Printed circuit boards

(P-9405)
**FINE PTCH ELCTRNIC ASSMBLY
LLC**
5106 Azusa Canyon Rd, Irwindale
(91706-1846)
PHONE..................................626 337-2800
Ashish Sheladiya, *General Mgr*
Mayur Savalia,
EMP: 20 EST: 2004
SQ FT: 15,000 **Privately Held**
WEB: www.finepitchassembly.com
SIC: 3672 Printed circuit boards

(P-9406)
**FINELINE CIRCUITS &
TECHNOLOGY**
594 Apollo St Ste A, Brea (92821-3134)
PHONE..................................714 529-2942
Rick Bajaria, *President*
Ken Pansuria, *Vice Pres*
Vinny Kathrotia, *Admin Sec*
Sharon Long, *Accounting Mgr*
Blanca Martinez, *Sales Staff*
EMP: 30 EST: 1995
SQ FT: 20,000
SALES (est): 5.5MM **Privately Held**
WEB: www.finelinecircuits.com
SIC: 3672 Circuit boards, television & radio
printed

(P-9407)
FOXLINK WORLD CIRCUIT TECH
925 W Lambert Rd Ste C, Brea
(92821-2943)
PHONE..................................714 256-0877
EMP: 20
SQ FT: 6,000
SALES (est): 1.6MM **Privately Held**
SIC: 3672 Mfg Flex Circuits

(P-9408)
FTG CIRCUITS INC (DH)
20750 Marilla St, Chatsworth (91311-4407)
PHONE..................................818 407-4024
Brad Bourne, *CEO*
Michael Labrador, *President*
Joe Ricci, *CFO*
Ed Hanna, *Director*
▼ EMP: 88 EST: 1956
SQ FT: 38,000
SALES (est): 25.7MM
SALES (corp-wide): 77.4MM **Privately
Held**
WEB: www.ftgcorp.com
SIC: 3672 3644 Printed circuit boards; ter-
minal boards
HQ: Firan Technology Group (Usa) Corpo-
ration
20750 Marilla St
Chatsworth CA 91311
818 407-4024

(P-9409)
**GAVIAL ENGINEERING & MFG
INC**
1435 W Mccoy Ln, Santa Maria
(93455-1002)
PHONE..................................805 614-0060
Don Connors, *President*
Stanley D Connors, *CEO*
Ken Hicks, *General Mgr*
Ginny Pokotylo, *Human Res Mgr*
David Mullins, *Mfg Staff*
EMP: 50 EST: 2012
SQ FT: 25,000
SALES (est): 10.5MM
SALES (corp-wide): 84.3MM **Privately
Held**
WEB: www.gavial.com
SIC: 3672 3679 Printed circuit boards;
electronic circuits

PA: Gavial Holdings, Inc.
1435 W Mccoy Ln
Santa Maria CA 93455
805 614-0060

(P-9410)
GEERIRAJ INC
Also Called: Mer-Mar Electronics
7042 Santa Fe Ave E A1, Hesperia
(92345-5711)
PHONE..................................760 244-6149
Kanjibhai Ghadia, *President*
Suresh Patel, *Vice Pres*
Elmo Pinard, *Purch Mgr*
EMP: 28 EST: 1974
SQ FT: 22,000
SALES (est): 450K **Privately Held**
SIC: 3672 Printed circuit boards

(P-9411)
GOLDEN WEST TECHNOLOGY
1180 E Valencia Dr, Fullerton (92831-4627)
PHONE..................................714 738-3775
Dan P Rieth, *President*
Bill Frye, *Executive*
Jim Young, *Senior Buyer*
EMP: 60 EST: 1974
SQ FT: 30,000
SALES (est): 11.9MM **Privately Held**
WEB: www.goldenwesttech.com
SIC: 3672 Printed circuit boards

(P-9412)
GRAPHIC RESEARCH INC
9334 Mason Ave, Chatsworth
(91311-5295)
PHONE..................................818 886-7340
Govind R Vaghashia, *President*
Pete Vaghashia, *Vice Pres*
Fred Greear, *Manager*
▲ EMP: 50 EST: 1966
SQ FT: 42,000
SALES (est): 6.7MM **Privately Held**
WEB: www.graphicresearch.com
SIC: 3672 Printed circuit boards

(P-9413)
HUA XING PCBA LIMITED
Carlow Rd, Torrance (90505)
PHONE..................................310 626-7575
Penny Yu, *Accounts Mgr*
EMP: 30
SALES (est): 2MM **Privately Held**
WEB: www.pcba-pcb.com
SIC: 3672 Printed circuit boards

(P-9414)
IPC CAL FLEX INC
13337 South St 307, Cerritos (90703-7308)
PHONE..................................714 952-0373
Scott Kohno, *President*
EMP: 21 EST: 1980
SQ FT: 25,000
SALES (est): 1.6MM **Privately Held**
SIC: 3672 Printed circuit boards

(P-9415)
IRVINE ELECTRONICS INC
1601 Alton Pkwy Ste A, Irvine
(92606-4843)
PHONE..................................949 250-0315
Jane Zerounian, *President*
Vahan Zerounian, *CFO*
Onnig Zerounian, *Vice Pres*
David Bossley, *Engineer*
Toni Wilkerson, *QC Mgr*
EMP: 100 EST: 1969
SQ FT: 48,000 **Privately Held**
WEB: www.irvine-electronics.com
SIC: 3672 Circuit boards, television & radio
printed

(P-9416)
ISU PETASYS CORP
12930 Bradley Ave, Sylmar (91342-3829)
PHONE..................................818 833-5800
Yong Kyoun Kim, *President*
Arleen Masangkay, *CFO*
John Stephens, *VP Bus Dvlpt*
Dave Hwang, *CIO*
Ryan Ji, *Human Resources*
▲ EMP: 95 EST: 1997
SQ FT: 50,000
SALES (est): 21.1MM **Privately Held**
WEB: www.isupetasys.com
SIC: 3672 Printed circuit boards

PA: Isu Chemical Co., Ltd.
84 Sapyeong-Daero, Seocho-Gu
Seoul 06575

(P-9417)
JABIL INC
Also Called: Jabil Chad Automation
1565 S Sinclair St, Anaheim (92806-5934)
PHONE.....................714 938-0080
Babak Naderi, *Director*
Brandon Kim, *Sales Staff*
David Soden, *Sr Project Mgr*
Jose Luna, *Manager*
EMP: 50
SALES (corp-wide): 29.2B **Publicly Held**
WEB: www.jabil.com
SIC: 3672 Printed circuit boards
PA: Jabil Inc.
10560 Dr Mrtn Lther King
Saint Petersburg FL 33716
727 577-9749

(P-9418)
JMP ELECTRONICS INC
2685 Dow Ave Ste A1, Tustin (92780-7241)
PHONE.....................714 730-2086
Joseph Manea, *President*
Martha Manea, *Senior VP*
Petru Pantis, *Vice Pres*
▲ EMP: 34 EST: 1992
SQ FT: 12,500
SALES (est): 3.7MM **Privately Held**
WEB: www.jmpelectronics.com
SIC: 3672 Printed circuit boards

(P-9419)
KCA ELECTRONICS INC
Also Called: Summit Interconnect - Anaheim
223 N Crescent Way, Anaheim
(92801-6704)
PHONE.....................714 239-2433
Shane Whiteside, *President*
▲ EMP: 180 EST: 1992
SQ FT: 60,000
SALES (est): 34.6MM
SALES (corp-wide): 1.7B **Privately Held**
WEB: www.kcamerica.com
SIC: 3672 Circuit boards, television & radio
printed
HQ: Equity Hci Management L P
1730 Pennsylvania Ave Nw # 525
Washington DC

(P-9420)
KL ELECTRONICS INC
3083 S Harbor Blvd, Santa Ana
(92704-6448)
PHONE.....................714 751-5611
Khanh Ton, *President*
Michael Ton, *CEO*
Luon Ton, *Corp Secy*
EMP: 24 EST: 1981
SQ FT: 4,000
SALES (est): 1.7MM **Privately Held**
WEB: www.klelectronics.com
SIC: 3672 Printed circuit boards

(P-9421)
**LAMINATING COMPANY OF
AMERICA**
Also Called: Lcoa
20322 Windrow Dr Ste 100, Lake Forest
(92630-8150)
PHONE.....................949 587-3300
Tim Redfern, *President*
Brad Biddol, *CFO*
▲ EMP: 30 EST: 1971
SALES (est): 5.4MM **Privately Held**
WEB: www.lcoa.com
SIC: 3672 Printed circuit boards

(P-9422)
LARITECH INC
5898 Condor Dr, Moorpark (93021-2603)
PHONE.....................805 529-5000
William Larrick, *CEO*
Joel Butler, *COO*
Scott Ishii, *CFO*
Terry Gonzales, *Treasurer*
Carson Derry, *Program Mgr*
EMP: 111 EST: 2001
SQ FT: 13,000

SALES (est): 10MM **Privately Held**
WEB: www.laritech.com
SIC: 3672 Printed circuit boards

(P-9423)
**LOGI GRAPHICS
INCORPORATED**
17592 Metzler Ln, Huntington Beach
(92647-6241)
PHONE.....................714 841-3686
Greg Otterbach, *President*
Terri Otterbach, *Admin Sec*
EMP: 16 EST: 1994
SQ FT: 12,000
SALES (est): 1.4MM **Privately Held**
WEB: www.logipcbs.com
SIC: 3672 Printed circuit boards

(P-9424)
LORSER INDUSTRIES INC
9636 Arby Dr, Beverly Hills (90210-1202)
PHONE.....................619 917-4298
EMP: 44
SALES (corp-wide): 1MM **Privately Held**
WEB: www.lorserindustries.com
SIC: 3672 Circuit boards, television & radio
printed
PA: Lorser Industries Inc
1959 Kellogg Ave
Carlsbad CA 92008
760 438-6625

(P-9425)
MATRIX USA INC
2730 S Main St, Santa Ana (92707-3435)
PHONE.....................714 825-0404
Kieran Healy, *President*
George Potocska, *Controller*
Sunil Shah, *Manager*
▲ EMP: 25 EST: 2005
SALES (est): 5.1MM
SALES (corp-wide): 9.1MM **Privately
Held**
WEB: www.matrixelectronics.com
SIC: 3672 Printed circuit boards
HQ: Matrix Electronics Limited
1124 Mid-Way Blvd
Mississauga ON L5T 2
905 670-8400

(P-9426)
MAXTROL CORPORATION
1701 E Edinger Ave Ste B6, Santa Ana
(92705-5010)
PHONE.....................714 245-0506
Uri Ranon, *President*
Leo Pardo, *Vice Pres*
EMP: 40 EST: 1990
SQ FT: 5,000
SALES (est): 5MM **Privately Held**
WEB: www.maxtrol.com
SIC: 3672 Printed circuit boards

(P-9427)
**MEGA PLUS PCB
INCORPORATED**
1479 E Warner Ave, Santa Ana
(92705-5434)
PHONE.....................714 550-0265
Nadim S Kazempoor, *CEO*
Noorya Kazempoor, *Vice Pres*
EMP: 15 EST: 2002
SALES (est): 1.1MM **Privately Held**
WEB: www.megapluspcb.com
SIC: 3672 Printed circuit boards

(P-9428)
MERCURY SYSTEMS INC
400 Del Norte Blvd, Oxnard (93030-7997)
PHONE.....................805 388-1345
Stephen Bouchard, *CEO*
EMP: 110
SALES (corp-wide): 924MM **Publicly
Held**
WEB: www.mrcy.com
SIC: 3672 Printed circuit boards
PA: Mercury Systems, Inc.
50 Minuteman Rd
Andover MA 01810
978 256-1300

(P-9429)
MFLEX DELAWARE INC
101 Academy Ste 250, Irvine (92617-3035)
PHONE.....................949 453-6800
Reza A Meshgin, *CEO*

EMP: 1128 EST: 2019
SALES (est): 1.1MM **Privately Held**
WEB: www.mflex.com
SIC: 3672 Printed circuit boards
HQ: Multi-Fineline Electronix, Inc.
101 Academy Ste 250
Irvine CA 92617
949 453-6800

(P-9430)
**MULTI-FINELINE ELECTRONIX
INC (HQ)**
Also Called: Mflex
101 Academy Ste 250, Irvine (92617-3035)
PHONE.....................949 453-6800
Reza Meshgin, *President*
Tom Kampfer, *CFO*
Christine Besnard, *Exec VP*
Thomas Lee, *Exec VP*
Jay Desai, *Vice Pres*
EMP: 583
SQ FT: 20,171
SALES (est): 520.3MM **Privately Held**
WEB: www.mflex.com
SIC: 3672 Printed circuit boards

(P-9431)
MULTILAYER PROTOTYPES INC
Also Called: Mpi
2513 Teller Rd, Newbury Park
(91320-2220)
PHONE.....................805 498-9390
Steve Ferris, *President*
Dara Garza, *Corp Secy*
EMP: 19 EST: 1981
SQ FT: 11,000
SALES (est): 2.7MM **Privately Held**
WEB: www.mpi-pcb.com
SIC: 3672 Circuit boards, television & radio
printed

(P-9432)
MURRIETTA CIRCUITS
5000 E Landon Dr, Anaheim (92807-1978)
PHONE.....................714 970-2430
Andrew Murrietta, *CEO*
Albert G Murrietta, *President*
Albert A Murrieta, *COO*
Albert Murrietta, *COO*
Helen Murrietta, *Treasurer*
EMP: 101 EST: 1992
SQ FT: 48,500
SALES (est): 29.7MM **Privately Held**
WEB: www.murrietta.com
SIC: 3672 8711 Printed circuit boards; en-
gineering services

(P-9433)
**NASO INDUSTRIES
CORPORATION**
Also Called: Naso Technologies
3007 Bunsen Ave Ste Q, Ventura
(93003-7634)
PHONE.....................805 650-1231
Jahansooz Saleh, *CEO*
Soraya Saleh, *CEO*
Bryan Howe, *Vice Pres*
Namdar Saleh, *Vice Pres*
Mike White, *Vice Pres*
EMP: 40 EST: 1990
SQ FT: 20,000
SALES (est): 8.6MM **Privately Held**
WEB: www.naso.com
SIC: 3672 3599 Printed circuit boards;
machine shop, jobbing & repair

(P-9434)
**NATEL ENGINEERING
HOLDINGS INC**
9340 Owensmouth Ave, Chatsworth
(91311-6915)
PHONE.....................818 734-6500
EMP: 20 EST: 2015
SALES (est): 652.5K **Privately Held**
WEB: www.neotech.com
SIC: 3672 Printed circuit boards

(P-9435)
**ONCORE MANUFACTURING
SVCS INC**
Also Called: Neo Tech Natel Epic Oncore
9340 Owensmouth Ave, Chatsworth
(91311-6915)
PHONE.....................510 360-2222
Sudesh Arora, *CEO*

Walt Hussey, *COO*
Sajjad Malik, *Exec VP*
David Brakenwagen, *Senior VP*
Magdy Henry, *Vice Pres*
▲ EMP: 230 EST: 2007
SALES (est): 1.1MM
SALES (corp-wide): 1.1B **Privately Held**
WEB: www.neotech.com
SIC: 3672 Printed circuit boards
PA: Natel Engineering Company, Llc
9340 Owensmouth Ave
Chatsworth CA 91311
818 495-8617

(P-9436)
OSI ELECTRONICS INC (HQ)
12533 Chadron Ave, Hawthorne
(90250-4807)
PHONE.....................310 978-0516
Paul Morben, *President*
Bruce Macdonald, *President*
Alex Colquhoun, *COO*
Lou Campana, *Vice Pres*
Joe Beck, *Project Mgr*
▲ EMP: 146 EST: 1995
SQ FT: 60,000
SALES (est): 139.2MM
SALES (corp-wide): 1.1B **Publicly Held**
WEB: www.osielectronics.com
SIC: 3672 Printed circuit boards
PA: Osi Systems, Inc.
12525 Chadron Ave
Hawthorne CA 90250
310 978-0516

(P-9437)
PARPRO TECHNOLOGIES INC
Also Called: P T I
2700 S Fairview St, Santa Ana
(92704-5947)
PHONE.....................714 545-8886
Thomas Sparrvik, *CEO*
Keith Knight, *President*
Ngathuong Le, *COO*
Eduardo Serrano, *CFO*
Ken Haney, *Exec VP*
EMP: 190
SALES: 48.8MM **Privately Held**
WEB: www.parpro.com
SIC: 3672 Printed circuit boards
PA: Parpro Corporation
No. 67-1, Dongyuan Rd., Zhongli In-
dustrial Park
Taoyuan City TAY

(P-9438)
PHOTO FABRICATORS INC
7648 Burnet Ave, Van Nuys (91405-1043)
PHONE.....................818 781-1010
Steve L Brooks, *President*
John R Brooks, *Chairman*
Susan Brooks, *Corp Secy*
▲ EMP: 75 EST: 1973
SQ FT: 14,000
SALES (est): 7.8MM **Privately Held**
WEB: www.photofabricators.com
SIC: 3672 Circuit boards, television & radio
printed

(P-9439)
PIONEER CIRCUITS INC
3000 S Shannon St, Santa Ana
(92704-6387)
PHONE.....................714 641-3132
Robert Lee, *CEO*
James Y Lee, *President*
Ben Koo, *Vice Pres*
Enrique Hernandez, *Software Dev*
Byung Park, *Technology*
EMP: 290 EST: 1981
SQ FT: 50,000
SALES (est): 85.9MM **Privately Held**
WEB: www.pioneercircuits.com
SIC: 3672 3812 Printed circuit boards; de-
fense systems & equipment

(P-9440)
POWER CIRCUITS INC
2630 S Harbor Blvd, Santa Ana
(92704-5829)
PHONE.....................714 327-3000
Kenton K Alder, *President*
EMP: 179 EST: 1985

SALES (est): 11.9MM
SALES (corp-wide): 2.1B **Publicly Held**
WEB: www.ttm.com
SIC: 3672 Printed circuit boards
PA: Ttm Technologies, Inc.
　　200 Sandpointe Ave # 400
　　Santa Ana CA 92707
　　714 327-3000

(P-9441)
PRECISION CIRCUITS WEST INC
3310 W Harvard St, Santa Ana
(92704-3920)
PHONE...........................714 435-9670
Chatur Patel, *President*
Sam Akbari, *President*
Prabhudas Patel, *Admin Sec*
Ashwin Patel, *Director*
EMP: 13 **EST:** 1985
SQ FT: 12,000
SALES (est): 1.7MM **Privately Held**
WEB: www.pcwesti.com
SIC: 3672 Circuit boards, television & radio
　　printed

(P-9442)
PSC CIRCUITS INC
5160 Rivergrade Rd, Baldwin Park
(91706-1406)
PHONE...........................626 373-1728
Pashih Oliver Su, *President*
▲ **EMP:** 18 **EST:** 2000
SALES (est): 278.9K **Privately Held**
WEB: www.psccircuits.com
SIC: 3672 Printed circuit boards

(P-9443)
Q-FLEX INC
1301 E Hunter Ave, Santa Ana
(92705-4133)
PHONE...........................714 664-0101
Nayna Uka, *President*
Nalini Celio, *Corp Secy*
Pete Uka, *Vice Pres*
▲ **EMP:** 32 **EST:** 1988
SQ FT: 7,200
SALES (est): 3.5MM **Privately Held**
WEB: www.qflexinc.com
SIC: 3672 Printed circuit boards

(P-9444)
QUAL-PRO CORPORATION (HQ)
18510 S Figueroa St, Gardena
(90248-4519)
PHONE...........................310 329-7535
Brian Jeffrey Shane, *CEO*
Richard Fitzgerald, *COO*
Kirk Waldron, *CFO*
Monica Quijas, *Program Mgr*
Monica Sierra, *Program Mgr*
EMP: 199 **EST:** 1971
SQ FT: 55,000
SALES (est): 61.6MM **Privately Held**
WEB: www.qual-pro.com
SIC: 3672 Circuit boards, television & radio
　　printed

(P-9445)
R-F CIRCUITS AND ASSEMBLY INC
3533 Old Conejo Rd # 107, Newbury Park
(91320-6163)
PHONE...........................805 499-7788
Pankaj Patell, *President*
EMP: 13 **EST:** 2003
SALES (est): 1MM **Privately Held**
WEB: www.rfassembly.com
SIC: 3672 Printed circuit boards

(P-9446)
RACAAR CIRCUIT INDUSTRIES INC
9225 Alabama Ave Ste F, Chatsworth
(91311-5843)
PHONE...........................818 998-7566
Stephen Serup, *President*
Julie Serup, *Corp Secy*
EMP: 17 **EST:** 1979
SQ FT: 4,000
SALES (est): 1.3MM **Privately Held**
SIC: 3672 3433 Printed circuit boards;
　　heating equipment, except electric

(P-9447)
RELIABLE CIRCUITS MFG INC
Also Called: Electronic Mfg
3080 Lomita Blvd, Torrance (90505-5103)
PHONE...........................310 373-2174
Craig Carlson, *CEO*
EMP: 17 **EST:** 2017
SALES (est): 1.5MM **Privately Held**
WEB: www.rcmfginc.com
SIC: 3672 Printed circuit boards

(P-9448)
RIGIFLEX TECHNOLOGY INC
1166 N Grove St, Anaheim (92806-2109)
PHONE...........................714 688-1500
Dhiru Sorathia, *President*
Albert Hanson, *Associate*
EMP: 14 **EST:** 1992
SQ FT: 15,000
SALES (est): 3.6MM **Privately Held**
WEB: www.rigiflex.com
SIC: 3672 Printed circuit boards

(P-9449)
ROGER INDUSTRY
11552 Knott St Ste 5, Garden Grove
(92841-1833)
PHONE...........................714 896-0765
Shann-Mou Lee, *President*
Jiin-Sheue Lee, *Vice Pres*
▲ **EMP:** 16 **EST:** 1985
SQ FT: 10,000
SALES (est): 1.3MM **Privately Held**
SIC: 3672 3479 Printed circuit boards;
　　coating of metals with plastic or resins

(P-9450)
ROYAL FLEX CIRCUITS INC
15505 Cornet St, Santa Fe Springs
(90670-5511)
PHONE...........................562 404-0626
Milan Shah, *CEO*
EMP: 27 **EST:** 2013
SALES (est): 10.2MM
SALES (corp-wide): 11.4MM **Privately Held**
WEB: www.royalflexcircuits.com
SIC: 3672 Wiring boards
PA: Royal Circuit Solutions, Inc.
　　21 Hamilton Ct
　　Hollister CA 95023
　　831 636-7789

(P-9451)
SANMINA CORPORATION
Viking Modular Solutions
2950 Red Hill Ave, Costa Mesa
(92626-5935)
PHONE...........................714 913-2200
Hamid Shokrgovar, *President*
Nahum Gat, *Officer*
Rick Hazell, *Vice Pres*
Chip Bellisime, *Business Dir*
Tony Geria, *Business Dir*
EMP: 110 **Publicly Held**
WEB: www.sanmina.com
SIC: 3672 Printed circuit boards
PA: Sanmina Corporation
　　2700 N 1st St
　　San Jose CA 95134

(P-9452)
SECURE TECHNOLOGY COMPANY
Also Called: Lark Engineering
2000 W Corporate Way, Anaheim
(92801-5373)
PHONE...........................714 991-6500
Patrick Huang, *President*
EMP: 58 **EST:** 2016
SALES (est): 3.1MM
SALES (corp-wide): 2B **Publicly Held**
WEB: www.bench.com
SIC: 3672 Printed circuit boards
PA: Benchmark Electronics, Inc.
　　56 S Rockford Dr
　　Tempe AZ 85281
　　623 300-7000

(P-9453)
SEMI-KINETICS INC
20191 Windrow Dr Ste A, Lake Forest
(92630-8161)
PHONE...........................949 830-7364
Gary H Gonzalez, *CEO*

Justine Leedom, *Admin Asst*
Brandie Diaz, *Project Mgr*
▲ **EMP:** 95 **EST:** 1981
SALES (est): 18.3MM
SALES (corp-wide): 75MM **Privately Held**
WEB: www.semi-kinetics.com
SIC: 3672 Circuit boards, television & radio
　　printed
PA: Gonzalez Production Systems, Inc.
　　1670 Highwood E
　　Pontiac MI 48340
　　248 745-1200

(P-9454)
SMART ELEC & ASSEMBLY INC
2000 W Corporate Way, Anaheim
(92801-5373)
PHONE...........................714 772-2651
Robert Swelgin, *President*
Shou-Lee Wang, *CEO*
Dave Wopschall, *CFO*
Getaneh Bekele, *Vice Pres*
James Wang, *Admin Sec*
▲ **EMP:** 120 **EST:** 1994
SQ FT: 34,500
SALES (est): 22.6MM
SALES (corp-wide): 2B **Publicly Held**
WEB: www.bench.com
SIC: 3672 Printed circuit boards
HQ: Secure Communication Systems, Inc.
　　1740 E Wilshire Ave
　　Santa Ana CA 92705
　　714 547-1174

(P-9455)
SOLDERMASK INC
17905 Metzler Ln, Huntington Beach
(92647-6258)
PHONE...........................714 842-1987
Frank S Kurisu, *President*
Son Pham, *General Mgr*
Debbie Ashby, *Technology*
▲ **EMP:** 15 **EST:** 1985
SQ FT: 10,000
SALES (est): 2.6MM **Privately Held**
WEB: www.soldermask.com
SIC: 3672 3577 Printed circuit boards;
　　printers & plotters

(P-9456)
SOUTH COAST CIRCUITS INC
3506 W Lake Center Dr A, Santa Ana
(92704-6985)
PHONE...........................714 966-2108
Charles R Benson, *CEO*
Daniel Alderete, *Purch Agent*
Patrick Bacon, *Mfg Staff*
Jeff Rice, *Mfg Staff*
Brad Harline, *Director*
▲ **EMP:** 68 **EST:** 1982
SQ FT: 30,000
SALES (est): 9MM **Privately Held**
WEB: www.sccircuits.com
SIC: 3672 Circuit boards, television & radio
　　printed

(P-9457)
SUMMIT INTERCONNECT INC (HQ)
223 N Crescent Way, Anaheim
(92801-6704)
PHONE...........................714 239-2433
Shane Whiteside, *President*
EMP: 150 **EST:** 2016
SALES (est): 113.6MM
SALES (corp-wide): 1.7B **Privately Held**
WEB: www.summit-pcb.com
SIC: 3672 Printed circuit boards
PA: Goldberg Lindsay & Co. Llc
　　630 5th Ave Fl 30
　　New York NY 10111
　　212 651-1100

(P-9458)
TC COSMOTRONIC INC
4663 E Guasti Rd Ste A, Ontario
(91761-8196)
PHONE...........................949 660-0740
James R Savage, *CEO*
Tracyconrad Enriquez, *CFO*
EMP: 62 **EST:** 1969
SALES (est): 1.8MM **Privately Held**
SIC: 3672 Printed circuit boards

(P-9459)
TECHNOTRONIX INC
1381 N Hundley St, Anaheim (92806-1301)
PHONE...........................714 630-9200
Jayshree Kapuria, *CEO*
Chris Paris, *Sales Engr*
Ken Ghadia, *Manager*
EMP: 20 **EST:** 2012
SALES (est): 4.1MM **Privately Held**
WEB: www.technotronix.us
SIC: 3672 Printed circuit boards

(P-9460)
TRANSLINE TECHNOLOGY INC
1106 S Technology Cir, Anaheim
(92805-6329)
PHONE...........................714 533-8300
Kishor Patel, *President*
Larry Padmani, *Vice Pres*
John Tussant, *Technical Staff*
▲ **EMP:** 33 **EST:** 1996
SQ FT: 20,000
SALES (est): 4.8MM **Privately Held**
WEB: www.translinetech.com
SIC: 3672 Printed circuit boards

(P-9461)
TRANTRONICS INC
1822 Langley Ave, Irvine (92614-5624)
PHONE...........................949 553-1234
Tom Tran, *President*
John Pham, *Vice Pres*
Thien Luc, *Prgrmr*
EMP: 32
SALES (est): 6.8MM **Privately Held**
WEB: www.trantronics.com
SIC: 3672 3599 Printed circuit boards;
　　machine & other job shop work

(P-9462)
TRI-STAR LAMINATES INC
Also Called: Laminating Company of America
20322 Windrow Dr Ste 100, Lake Forest
(92630-8150)
PHONE...........................949 587-3200
Patrick Redfern, *President*
Rob Wassem, *President*
Ethan Morgan, *Technology*
EMP: 33 **EST:** 2000
SQ FT: 50,000
SALES (est): 5.2MM **Privately Held**
SIC: 3672 Printed circuit boards

(P-9463)
TTM PRINTED CIRCUIT GROUP INC (HQ)
2630 S Harbor Blvd, Santa Ana
(92704-5829)
PHONE...........................714 327-3000
Thomas T Edman, *President*
Steve Richards, *CFO*
▲ **EMP:** 1126 **EST:** 2006
SALES (est): 122.8MM
SALES (corp-wide): 2.1B **Publicly Held**
WEB: www.ttm.com
SIC: 3672 Printed circuit boards
PA: Ttm Technologies, Inc.
　　200 Sandpointe Ave # 400
　　Santa Ana CA 92707
　　714 327-3000

(P-9464)
TTM TECHNOLOGIES INC (PA)
200 Sandpointe Ave # 400, Santa Ana
(92707-5747)
PHONE...........................714 327-3000
Thomas T Edman, *President*
Robert E Klatell, *Ch of Bd*
Douglas L Soder, *President*
Brian W Barber, *COO*
Todd B Schull, *CFO*
EMP: 500 **EST:** 1978
SQ FT: 11,775
SALES (est): 2.1B **Publicly Held**
WEB: www.ttm.com
SIC: 3672 Printed circuit boards

(P-9465)
TTM TECHNOLOGIES INC
3140 E Coronado St, Anaheim
(92806-1914)
PHONE...........................714 688-7200
Sameer Desai, *Director*
Khris Bonilla, *Manager*
EMP: 290

SALES (corp-wide): 2.1B **Publicly Held**
WEB: www.ttm.com
SIC: 3672 Printed circuit boards
PA: Ttm Technologies, Inc.
200 Sandpointe Ave # 400
Santa Ana CA 92707
714 327-3000

(P-9466)
VECTOR ELECTRONICS & TECH INC
11115 Vanowen St, North Hollywood (91605-6371)
PHONE..................................818 985-8208
Rakesh Bajaria, *CEO*
Ken Pansuriah, *Vice Pres*
Jerry Rodriguez, *Vice Pres*
Viny Kathrotia, *Admin Sec*
▲ **EMP:** 25 **EST:** 2001
SALES (est): 4MM **Privately Held**
WEB: www.vectorelect.com
SIC: 3672 Printed circuit boards

(P-9467)
VEECO ELECTRO FAB INC
1176 N Osprey Cir, Anaheim (92807-1709)
PHONE..................................714 630-8020
EMP: 21
SQ FT: 10,000
SALES (est): 2.5MM **Privately Held**
SIC: 3672 7629 Printed Circuit Boards

(P-9468)
VINATRONIC INC
15571 Industry Ln, Huntington Beach (92649-1534)
PHONE..................................714 845-3480
Lan Nguyen, *CEO*
Kem Strano, *President*
Minhdy Le, *Office Mgr*
EMP: 18 **EST:** 1988
SQ FT: 13,000
SALES (est): 7.1MM **Privately Held**
WEB: www.vinatronic.com
SIC: 3672 Printed circuit boards

(P-9469)
WINONICS INC
Also Called: Bench 2 Bench Technologies
1257 S State College Blvd, Fullerton (92831-5336)
PHONE..................................714 626-3755
Tom Sciulli, *General Mgr*
Ira Rosenberg, *Admin Mgr*
Octavio Ruelas, *Prdtn Mgr*
Richard Encinas, *Sales Engr*
Xavier Pacheco, *Manager*
EMP: 120
SALES (corp-wide): 37.9MM **Privately Held**
WEB: www.winonics.com
SIC: 3672 Printed circuit boards
HQ: Winonics Inc.
660 N Puente St
Brea CA
714 256-8700

(P-9470)
YUN INDUSTRIAL CO LTD
Also Called: Y I C
161 Selandia Ln, Carson (90746-1412)
PHONE..................................310 715-1898
Ilun Yun, *President*
Stephen Yun, *Vice Pres*
William Yun, *Admin Sec*
Anthony Yun, *Engineer*
Alice Yu, *Sales Staff*
◆ **EMP:** 40 **EST:** 1990
SQ FT: 16,000
SALES (est): 5.8MM **Privately Held**
WEB: www.yic-assm.com
SIC: 3672 Printed circuit boards

3674 Semiconductors

(P-9471)
ABB ENTERPRISE SOFTWARE INC
4600 Colorado Blvd, Los Angeles (90039-1106)
PHONE..................................213 743-4819
Carol Clemons, *Branch Mgr*
Francesco Renelli, *Manager*
▲ **EMP:** 47

SALES (corp-wide): 26.1B **Privately Held**
WEB: www.global.abb
SIC: 3674 Microcircuits, integrated (semi-conductor)
HQ: Abb Inc.
305 Gregson Dr
Cary NC 27511

(P-9472)
ACCELERATED MEMORY PROD INC
Also Called: AMP
1317 E Edinger Ave, Santa Ana (92705-4416)
PHONE..................................714 460-9800
Richard McCauley, *President*
Cathleen McCauley, *Vice Pres*
Stephanie Rafferty, *Info Tech Mgr*
◆ **EMP:** 49 **EST:** 2007
SQ FT: 10,000
SALES (est): 5.6MM **Privately Held**
WEB: www.ampinc.com
SIC: 3674 Semiconductors & related devices

(P-9473)
ADEX ELECTRONICS INC
3 Watson, Irvine (92618-2716)
PHONE..................................949 597-1772
Casey Huang, *President*
Cheryl Roberts, *Treasurer*
▲ **EMP:** 15 **EST:** 1985
SQ FT: 10,330
SALES (est): 2.1MM **Privately Held**
WEB: www.adexelec.com
SIC: 3674 8711 Semiconductors & related devices; engineering services

(P-9474)
ADTECH PHOTONICS INC
Also Called: Adtech Optics
18007 Cortney Ct, City of Industry (91748-1203)
PHONE..................................626 956-1000
Mary Fong, *CEO*
Marvin Lee, *Administration*
Charles Luu, *Electrical Engi*
Jenyu Fan, *Director*
Mariano Troccoli, *Director*
EMP: 25 **EST:** 2012
SALES (est): 4MM **Privately Held**
WEB: www.atoptics.com
SIC: 3674 Semiconductors & related devices

(P-9475)
ADVANCED SEMICONDUCTOR INC
Also Called: A S I
7525 Ethel Ave Ste I, North Hollywood (91605-1912)
PHONE..................................818 982-1200
Fred Golob, *CEO*
Eloisa Betancourt, *Plant Mgr*
▲ **EMP:** 58
SQ FT: 9,000
SALES (est): 8.7MM **Privately Held**
WEB: www.advancedsemiconductor.com
SIC: 3674 Integrated circuits, semiconductor networks, etc.

(P-9476)
ADVANCED THERMAL SCIENCES CORP
3355 E La Palma Ave, Anaheim (92806-2815)
PHONE..................................714 688-4200
Bruce Thayer, *President*
Masashi Iwao, *Vice Pres*
Erin Carey, *Administration*
James Yoo, *Electrical Engi*
▲ **EMP:** 43 **EST:** 1997
SALES (est): 11.7MM
SALES (corp-wide): 56.5B **Publicly Held**
WEB: www.atschiller.com
SIC: 3674 Semiconductors & related devices
HQ: B/E Aerospace, Inc.
1400 Corporate Center Way
Wellington FL 33414
410 266-2048

(P-9477)
ADVANTEST TEST SOLUTIONS INC (DH)
4 Goodyear, Irvine (92618-2002)
PHONE..................................949 523-6900
Debbora Ahlgren, *Principal*
Jess Gillespie, *Sr Software Eng*
Jon Koopman, *Engineer*
Kevin Trapp, *Engineer*
EMP: 100 **EST:** 2018
SALES (est): 153.9MM **Privately Held**
WEB: www.advantest.com
SIC: 3674 Semiconductors & related devices

(P-9478)
AEROFLEX INCORPORATED
15375 Barranca Pkwy F10, Irvine (92618-2217)
PHONE..................................800 843-1553
Len Burrows, *Branch Mgr*
EMP: 78
SALES (corp-wide): 177.9K **Privately Held**
WEB: www.caes.com
SIC: 3674 Semiconductors & related devices
HQ: Aeroflex Incorporated
2121 Crystal Dr Ste 800
Arlington VA 22202
516 694-6700

(P-9479)
AGILE TECHNOLOGIES INC
2 Orion, Aliso Viejo (92656-4200)
PHONE..................................949 454-8030
Martin Munzer, *CEO*
David A Krohn, *President*
Rick Brooks, *Vice Pres*
Toni Sweeney, *Buyer*
EMP: 34 **EST:** 2002
SQ FT: 40,000
SALES (est): 3.4MM **Privately Held**
WEB: www.agiletech.org
SIC: 3674 Photoelectric magnetic devices

(P-9480)
AMERICAN ARIUM
17791 Fitch, Irvine (92614-6019)
PHONE..................................949 623-7090
Larry Traylor, *President*
Diane George, *CFO*
Diane Dirks, *Corp Secy*
Jassy Mukherjee, *Finance*
EMP: 40 **EST:** 1977
SQ FT: 32,330
SALES (est): 6MM **Privately Held**
WEB: www.asset-intertech.com
SIC: 3577 Microprocessors; computer logic modules; computer peripheral equipment

(P-9481)
AMERICAN SOLAR ADVANTAGE INC
Also Called: Asa Power BDH Engrg & Cnstr
13348 Monte Vista Ave, Chino (91710-5147)
PHONE..................................877 765-2388
Bobby D Harris, *President*
EMP: 20 **EST:** 2016
SALES (est): 3.5MM **Privately Held**
WEB: www.asa.solar
SIC: 3674 1731 Solar cells; electrical work

(P-9482)
APIC CORPORATION
5800 Uplander Way, Culver City (90230-6608)
PHONE..................................310 642-7975
James Chan, *Officer*
Birendra Dutt, *President*
Todd Shays, *COO*
William Hoker, *Vice Pres*
Denise Lortie, *Vice Pres*
EMP: 58 **EST:** 2001
SQ FT: 14,416
SALES (est): 17.7MM **Privately Held**
WEB: www.apichip.com
SIC: 3674 Semiconductors & related devices

(P-9483)
ASC GROUP INC
12243 Branford St, Sun Valley (91352-1010)
PHONE..................................818 896-1101
Chuck Rogers, *President*
Greg Cluse, *Director*
EMP: 727 **EST:** 1988
SQ FT: 80,000
SALES (est): 7.7MM
SALES (corp-wide): 1.7B **Privately Held**
WEB: www.pmcglobalinc.com
SIC: 3674 Semiconductors & related devices
HQ: Pmc, Inc.
12243 Branford St
Sun Valley CA 91352
818 896-1101

(P-9484)
ASI SEMICONDUCTOR INC
Also Called: A S I
7525 Ethel Ave, North Hollywood (91605-1912)
PHONE..................................818 982-1200
Steve Golob, *Principal*
Mike Lincoln, *COO*
Fred Golob, *Principal*
EMP: 25 **EST:** 2011
SQ FT: 15,000
SALES (est): 4.1MM **Privately Held**
WEB: www.advancedsemiconductor.com
SIC: 3674 Semiconductors & related devices

(P-9485)
ATOMICA CORP
Also Called: IMT Analytical
75 Robin Hill Rd, Goleta (93117-3108)
PHONE..................................805 681-2807
Eric Sigler, *CEO*
Mike Shillinger, *COO*
Peter Altavilla, *CFO*
Jim McGibbon, *CFO*
Richard Brossart, *Vice Pres*
EMP: 115 **EST:** 1987
SQ FT: 130,000
SALES (est): 42.8MM **Privately Held**
WEB: www.atomica.com
SIC: 3674 Semiconductors & related devices

(P-9486)
AVID IDNTIFICATION SYSTEMS INC (PA)
3185 Hamner Ave, Norco (92860-1937)
PHONE..................................951 371-7505
Hannis L Stoddard, *CEO*
Trade Show, *Vice Pres*
Peter Troesch, *Vice Pres*
Alejandro Herrera, *Program Mgr*
Mary Metzner, *Administration*
▲ **EMP:** 100 **EST:** 1986
SQ FT: 30,000
SALES (est): 12.9MM **Privately Held**
WEB: www.avidid.com
SIC: 3674 5999 Semiconductors & related devices; pets & pet supplies

(P-9487)
BAYWA RE SOLAR PROJECTS LLC (DH)
Also Called: Baywa R.E.renewable Energy
18575 Jamboree Rd Ste 850, Irvine (92612-2558)
PHONE..................................949 398-3915
Jam Attari,
Roberta Connors, *Vice Pres*
David Dunlap, *Vice Pres*
Vitaly Lee, *Vice Pres*
Jared Quient, *Vice Pres*
▲ **EMP:** 16 **EST:** 2014
SALES (est): 28.9MM
SALES (corp-wide): 20.2B **Privately Held**
WEB: www.baywa-re.com
SIC: 3674 Solar cells

(P-9488)
CAMDEN SOLAR LLC ✪
18575 Jamboree Rd Ste 850, Irvine (92612-2558)
PHONE..................................940 398-3915
Jamaal Knight,
EMP: 42 **EST:** 2021

PRODUCTS & SVCS

(PA)=Parent Co (HQ)=Headquarters (DH)=Div Headquarters
✪ = New Business established in last 2 years

SALES (est): 1.3MM Privately Held
SIC: 3674 Solar cells

(P-9489)
CHRONICLE TECHNOLOGY INC
3972 Barranca Pkwy, Irvine (92606-1204)
PHONE....................949 651-8968
John Cheng, *President*
Chuck Martin, *VP Bus Dvlpt*
EMP: 15 EST: 1996
SALES (est): 807.5K Privately Held
WEB: www.chronicle-tech.com
SIC: 3674 Semiconductors & related devices

(P-9490)
CLARIPHY COMMUNICATIONS INC (DH)
7585 Irvine Center Dr # 100, Irvine (92618-2985)
PHONE....................949 861-3074
Nariman Yousefi, *President*
William J Ruehle, *CFO*
Norman L Swenson, *CTO*
Linda Leeman, *Cust Mgr*
EMP: 119 EST: 2004
SALES (est): 23.5MM
SALES (corp-wide): 682.9MM Privately Held
WEB: www.marvell.com
SIC: 3674 Integrated circuits, semiconductor networks, etc.
HQ: Inphi Corporation
110 Rio Robles
San Jose CA 95134
408 217-7300

(P-9491)
CNT ACQUISITION CORP (DH)
1 Enterprise, Aliso Viejo (92656-2606)
PHONE....................949 380-6100
James J Peterson, *CEO*
EMP: 288 EST: 2014
SALES (est): 10.5MM
SALES (corp-wide): 5.4B Publicly Held
WEB: www.microsemi.com
SIC: 3674 Rectifiers, solid state
HQ: Microsemi Corporation
11861 Western Ave
Garden Grove CA 92841
949 380-6100

(P-9492)
CONEXANT SYSTEMS INC
1901 Main St Ste 300, Irvine (92614-0512)
PHONE....................949 483-5714
Jan Johannessen, *CEO*
Leonard Ching, *Engineer*
Ruben Espitia, *Engineer*
Norbert Schade, *Engineer*
LI Yu, *Asst Controller*
EMP: 15 EST: 2016
SALES (est): 604.1K Privately Held
WEB: www.conexantsystems.com
SIC: 3674 Semiconductors & related devices

(P-9493)
CONEXANT SYSTEMS LLC (HQ)
1901 Main St Ste 300, Irvine (92614-0512)
PHONE....................949 483-4600
Jan Johannessen, *CEO*
EMP: 307 EST: 2013
SQ FT: 140,000
SALES (est): 57.6MM
SALES (corp-wide): 1.3B Publicly Held
WEB: www.synaptics.com
SIC: 3674 5065 Semiconductors & related devices; semiconductor devices
PA: Synaptics Incorporated
1251 Mckay Dr
San Jose CA 95131
408 904-1100

(P-9494)
CONEXANT SYSTEMS WORLDWIDE INC
4000 Macarthur Blvd, Newport Beach (92660-2558)
PHONE....................949 483-4600
Sailesh Chittipeddi, *President*
Gerard Carrillo, *Controller*
EMP: 36 EST: 1997
SALES (est): 1.5MM Privately Held
SIC: 3674 Semiconductors & related devices

(P-9495)
COOPER MICROELECTRONICS INC
Also Called: CMI
1671 Reynolds Ave, Irvine (92614-5709)
PHONE....................949 553-8352
Kenneth B Cooper III, *President*
Lily Cooper, *Vice Pres*
Tim Delpadre, *Prdtn Mgr*
▲ EMP: 37 EST: 1985
SQ FT: 10,000
SALES (est): 5.1MM Privately Held
WEB: www.coopermicro.com
SIC: 3674 7371 Semiconductors & related devices; custom computer programming services

(P-9496)
COSEMI TECHNOLOGIES INC (HQ)
1370 Reynolds Ave Ste 100, Irvine (92614-5504)
PHONE....................949 623-9816
Samir Desai, *President*
Rob Smith, *Engineer*
Devang Parekh, *Senior Engr*
Nanette Young, *Controller*
Adrian Collins, *Marketing Staff*
EMP: 14 EST: 2006
SQ FT: 3,000
SALES (est): 4.9MM Privately Held
WEB: www.cosemi.com
SIC: 3674 Light sensitive devices
PA: Mobix Labs, Inc.
15420 Laguna Canyon Rd # 100
Irvine CA 92618
949 808-8888

(P-9497)
DATA CIRCLE INC
3333 Michelson Dr Ste 735, Irvine (92612-7679)
PHONE....................949 260-6569
Steve Oren, *CEO*
EMP: 18 EST: 1991
SQ FT: 12,000
SALES (est): 242.3K Privately Held
SIC: 3674 Integrated circuits, semiconductor networks, etc.

(P-9498)
DPA LABS INC
Also Called: Dpa Components International
2251 Ward Ave, Simi Valley (93065-7556)
PHONE....................805 581-9200
Douglas Young, *President*
Phil Young, *Vice Pres*
Philip Young, *Vice Pres*
Steve Green, *Executive*
Erika Young, *Administration*
EMP: 50 EST: 1979
SQ FT: 38,000
SALES (est): 8.6MM Privately Held
WEB: www.dpaci.com
SIC: 3674 8734 Semiconductors & related devices; testing laboratories

(P-9499)
DRS NTWORK IMAGING SYSTEMS LLC
10600 Valley View St, Cypress (90630-4833)
PHONE....................714 220-3800
Shawn Black,
Timothy Harrison, *President*
Kevin Balsley, *Webmaster*
EMP: 100 EST: 2009
SALES (est): 20.5MM
SALES (corp-wide): 10.2B Privately Held
WEB: www.leonardodrs.com
SIC: 3674 8731 Infrared sensors, solid state; commercial physical research
HQ: Leonardo Drs, Inc.
2345 Crystal Dr Ste 1000
Arlington VA 22202
703 416-8000

(P-9500)
EDISON OPTO USA CORPORATION
1809 Excise Ave Ste 201, Ontario (91761-8558)
PHONE....................909 284-9710
Wen-Jui Cheng, *CEO*
Adrian Cheng, *Principal*

Anny Chen, *Manager*
▲ EMP: 13 EST: 2010
SALES (est): 3MM Privately Held
WEB: www.edison-opto.com.tw
SIC: 3674 Light emitting diodes

(P-9501)
EFFICIENT PWR CONVERSION CORP (PA)
909 N Pacific Coast Hwy, El Segundo (90245-2724)
PHONE....................310 615-0279
Alexander Lidow, *CEO*
Massimo Marabotti, *CFO*
Robert Beach, *Vice Pres*
Jianjun Cao, *Vice Pres*
Steve Colino, *Vice Pres*
EMP: 60 EST: 2007
SQ FT: 2,700
SALES (est): 10.2MM Privately Held
SIC: 3674 Integrated circuits, semiconductor networks, etc.

(P-9502)
EMCORE CORPORATION (PA)
2015 Chestnut St, Alhambra (91803-1542)
PHONE....................626 293-3400
Jeffrey Rittichier, *CEO*
Stephen L Domenik, *Ch of Bd*
Thomas Minichiello, *CFO*
Tom Minichiello, *CFO*
Iain Black, *Senior VP*
▲ EMP: 230 EST: 1984
SQ FT: 75,000
SALES (est): 110.1MM Publicly Held
WEB: www.emcore.com
SIC: 3674 3559 Integrated circuits, semiconductor networks, etc.; metal oxide silicon (MOS) devices; wafers (semiconductor devices); semiconductor manufacturing machinery

(P-9503)
EMCORE CORPORATION
Emcore-Ortel Division
2015 Chestnut St, Alhambra (91803-1542)
PHONE....................626 293-3400
Hone Hu, *Vice Pres*
EMP: 175
SALES (corp-wide): 110.1MM Publicly Held
WEB: www.emcore.com
SIC: 3674 Semiconductors & related devices
PA: Emcore Corporation
2015 Chestnut St
Alhambra CA 91803
626 293-3400

(P-9504)
EPSON ELECTRONICS AMERICA INC (DH)
3131 Katella Ave, Los Alamitos (90720-2335)
PHONE....................408 922-0200
Koji Abe, *President*
Craig Hodowski, *Admin Sec*
▲ EMP: 32 EST: 1997
SALES (est): 11.2MM Privately Held
WEB: www.epson.com
SIC: 3674 5065 8731 Semiconductors & related devices; electronic parts & equipment; commercial physical research

(P-9505)
ESI INC
Also Called: Electronic Services
5710 W Manchester Ave, Los Angeles (90045-4423)
P.O. Box 90772 (90009-0772)
PHONE....................310 670-4974
Abraham Shiepe, *President*
L Dodzinksi, *CEO*
B Colwell, *Admin Sec*
EMP: 46 EST: 1954
SQ FT: 5,000
SALES (est): 2.3MM Privately Held
SIC: 3674 Integrated circuits, semiconductor networks, etc.

(P-9506)
ESSEX ELECTRONICS INC
1130 Mark Ave, Carpinteria (93013-2918)
PHONE....................805 684-7601
Stewart Frisch, *Ch of Bd*
Garrett Kaufman, *President*

Fred Zimmermann, *President*
Jesse Moore, *CEO*
Dean Benjamin, *Vice Pres*
▲ EMP: 23 EST: 1991
SQ FT: 7,000
SALES (est): 4.8MM Privately Held
WEB: www.keyless.com
SIC: 3674 Semiconductors & related devices

(P-9507)
FAIRCOM INC
Also Called: United Technology
951 Lawson St, City of Industry (91748-1121)
P.O. Box 8638, Rowland Heights (91748-0638)
PHONE....................626 820-9900
James Yuan, *President*
Sam Wood, *CFO*
Fanny Yuan, *Admin Sec*
Richard Curreri, *Engineer*
Hubert Cheng, *Manager*
EMP: 53 EST: 1980
SQ FT: 16,000
SALES (est): 2.5MM Privately Held
WEB: www.faircom.com
SIC: 3674 Modules, solid state

(P-9508)
FALKOR PARTNERS LLC
Also Called: Semicoa
333 Mccormick Ave, Costa Mesa (92626-3422)
PHONE....................714 721-8772
Allen Ronk, *CEO*
John Park, *Principal*
EMP: 28 EST: 2014
SQ FT: 24,000
SALES (est): 2.9MM Privately Held
WEB: www.semicoa.com
SIC: 3674 Semiconductors & related devices

(P-9509)
FULCRUM MICROSYSTEMS INC
26630 Agoura Rd, Calabasas (91302-1954)
PHONE....................818 871-8100
Robert R Nunn, *CEO*
Mike Zeile, *President*
Dale Bartos, *CFO*
Harry Liu, *Sr Software Eng*
Uri Cummings, *CTO*
EMP: 58 EST: 1999
SQ FT: 17,077
SALES (est): 13.1MM
SALES (corp-wide): 77.8B Publicly Held
WEB: www.fulcrummicro.com
SIC: 3674 Semiconductors & related devices
PA: Intel Corporation
2200 Mission College Blvd
Santa Clara CA 95054
408 765-8080

(P-9510)
GLOBAL COMM SEMICONDUCTORS LLC (HQ)
Also Called: G C S
23155 Kashiwa Ct, Torrance (90505-4026)
PHONE....................310 530-7274
Bau-Hsing Ann, *President*
Ta-Lun Huang, *Chairman*
Sam Wang, *Senior VP*
Tseng-Yang Hsu, *Surgery Dir*
Mark L Raggio, *Admin Sec*
EMP: 18 EST: 1997
SQ FT: 38,000
SALES (est): 20MM Privately Held
WEB: www.gcsincorp.com
SIC: 3674 Semiconductors & related devices

(P-9511)
GLOBAL LOCATE INC
5300 California Ave, Irvine (92617-3038)
PHONE....................949 926-5000
Anthony Maslowski, *President*
Tom Souvignier, *Engrg Dir*
Rajsekhar Chundru, *Manager*
EMP: 51 EST: 2008

SALES (est): 17MM
SALES (corp-wide): 23.8B **Publicly Held**
WEB: www.broadcom.com
SIC: **3674** Semiconductor diodes & rectifiers
HQ: Broadcom Corporation
1320 Ridder Park Dr
San Jose CA 95131

(P-9512)
HALCYON MICROELECTRONICS INC
5467 2nd St, Irwindale (91706-2072)
PHONE..................................626 814-4688
Patricia Martin, *CEO*
Dennis Martin, *President*
EMP: 31 EST: 1981
SQ FT: 9,100
SALES (est): 4.9MM **Privately Held**
WEB: www.halcyonmicro.com
SIC: **3674** Microcircuits, integrated (semiconductor)

(P-9513)
HANWHA Q CELLS AMERICA INC
400 Spectrum Center Dr # 14, Irvine (92618-4934)
PHONE..................................949 748-5996
Goo Min, *CEO*
Hwal Noh, *CFO*
Sunghoon Kim, *Admin Sec*
Gilson Cortes, *Engineer*
Kim-Ngan Tran, *Finance Asst*
EMP: 109 EST: 2009
SALES (est): 6.6MM
SALES (corp-wide): 69.4MM **Privately Held**
WEB: www.q-cells.us
SIC: **3674** Solar cells
PA: Hanwha Q Cells Americas Holdings Corp.
300 Spectrum Center Dr # 1250
Irvine CA 92618
949 748-5996

(P-9514)
HELIX SEMICONDUCTORS (PA)
9980 Irvine Center Dr, Irvine (92618-4364)
PHONE..................................949 748-6057
Harold A Blomquist, *President*
Randy Sandusky, *Senior VP*
Bud Courville, *Vice Pres*
Ken Harada, *Vice Pres*
Kevin Townsend, *Design Engr*
EMP: 52 EST: 2017
SALES (est): 5.7MM **Privately Held**
WEB: www.helixsemiconductors.com
SIC: **3674** Semiconductors & related devices

(P-9515)
INDIE SEMICONDUCTOR INC
32 Journey, Aliso Viejo (92656-5329)
PHONE..................................949 608-0854
Donald McClymont, *CEO*
Ichiro Aoki, *President*
Steven Machuga, *COO*
Thomas Schiller, *CFO*
Ellen Bancroft, *Admin Sec*
EMP: 199 EST: 2019
SQ FT: 14,881 **Privately Held**
SIC: **3674** Semiconductors & related devices

(P-9516)
INFINEON TECH AMERICAS CORP (HQ)
101 N Pacific Coast Hwy, El Segundo (90245-4318)
PHONE..................................310 726-8200
Oleg Khaykin, *CEO*
Ilan Daskal, *CFO*
Bernd Hops, *Officer*
Gary Tanner, *Officer*
Paul Johnson, *Exec Dir*
▲ EMP: 900 EST: 1979
SALES (est): 1B
SALES (corp-wide): 10.1B **Privately Held**
WEB: www.infineon.com
SIC: **3674** Integrated circuits, semiconductor networks, etc.

PA: Infineon Technologies Ag
Am Campeon 1-15
Neubiberg BY 85579
892 340-

(P-9517)
INFRAREDVISION TECHNOLOGY CORP
Also Called: I T C
140 Industrial Way, Buellton (93427-9507)
PHONE..................................805 686-8848
James Giacobazzi, *President*
Kenneth Hay, *Vice Pres*
EMP: 130 EST: 2000
SALES (est): 48.1MM
SALES (corp-wide): 1.4B **Publicly Held**
WEB: www.advancedenergy.com
SIC: **3674** Semiconductors & related devices
HQ: Lumasense Technologies, Inc.
888 Tasman Dr 100
Milpitas CA 95035
408 727-1600

(P-9518)
INPHI INTERNATIONAL PTE LTD
112 S Lakeview Canyon Rd, Westlake Village (91362-3925)
PHONE..................................805 719-2300
Ford Tamer, *President*
John Edmunds, *CFO*
EMP: 21 EST: 2017
SALES (est): 1.2MM **Privately Held**
WEB: www.marvell.com
SIC: **3674** Semiconductors & related devices

(P-9519)
INTEGRA TECHNOLOGIES INC
321 Coral Cir, El Segundo (90245-4620)
PHONE..................................310 606-0855
Paul Aken, *President*
Jeff Burger, *Vice Pres*
Jonathan Corrao, *General Mgr*
Nikita Patel, *Software Dev*
Apet Barsegyan, *Engineer*
EMP: 50 EST: 1997
SQ FT: 15,000
SALES (est): 16.5MM **Privately Held**
WEB: www.integratech.com
SIC: **3674** Modules, solid state

(P-9520)
INTERCONNECT SYSTEMS INTL LLC (DH)
Also Called: Interconnect Systems, Inc.
741 Flynn Rd, Camarillo (93012-8056)
PHONE..................................805 482-2870
Mark Gilliam, *President*
William P Miller, *President*
Louis Buldain, *Vice Pres*
Glen Griswold, *Vice Pres*
Thomas Casey, *Principal*
▲ EMP: 90 EST: 1987
SQ FT: 48,000
SALES (est): 43.6MM
SALES (corp-wide): 36.9B **Privately Held**
WEB: www.isipkg.com
SIC: **3674** Computer logic modules
HQ: Molex, Llc
2222 Wellington Ct
Lisle IL 60532
630 969-4550

(P-9521)
INTERNATIONAL RECTIFIER CORP (PA)
17885 Von Karman Ave # 100, Irvine (92614-5256)
PHONE..................................949 453-1008
Fax: 949 453-8748
EMP: 23
SQ FT: 6,000
SALES (est): 3.9MM **Privately Held**
SIC: **3674** 3672 Mfg Semiconductors/Related Devices Mfg Printed Circuit Boards

(P-9522)
INVENLUX CORPORATION
168 Mason Way Ste B5, City of Industry (91746-2339)
PHONE..................................626 277-4163
Chunhui Yan, *President*
EMP: 16 EST: 2008
SQ FT: 18,000

SALES (est): 1.1MM **Privately Held**
SIC: **3674** Light emitting diodes

(P-9523)
IOG PRODUCTS LLC
Also Called: Impact-O-Graph Devices
9737 Lurline Ave, Chatsworth (91311-4404)
PHONE..................................818 350-5070
Mark Newgreen,
Darryl Termine, *Vice Pres*
Ron Ginther, *Executive*
Brandon Collier, *Sales Staff*
Kristen Payton, *Cust Mgr*
EMP: 15 EST: 2010
SALES (est): 2.1MM **Privately Held**
WEB: www.impactograph.com
SIC: **3674** 3669 Radiation sensors; visual communication systems

(P-9524)
IRVINE SENSORS CORPORATION
3000 Airway Ave Ste A1, Costa Mesa (92626-6033)
PHONE..................................714 444-8700
John C Carson, *President*
Lisa Negele, *CFO*
Anthony Mastrangelo, *Vice Pres*
Jule Hughes, *Executive Asst*
James Justice, *Admin Sec*
EMP: 43 EST: 2013
SALES (est): 5.3MM **Privately Held**
WEB: www.irvine-sensors.com
SIC: **3674** 8731 Semiconductors & related devices; electronic research

(P-9525)
IXYS INTGRTED CRCITS DIV AV IN
145 Columbia, Aliso Viejo (92656-1413)
PHONE..................................949 831-4622
Nathan Zommer, *Ch of Bd*
Uzi Sasson, *CFO*
EMP: 132 EST: 1983
SQ FT: 28,000
SALES (est): 21.9MM
SALES (corp-wide): 1.4B **Publicly Held**
WEB: www.ixys.com
SIC: **3674** 7389 Microcircuits, integrated (semiconductor); design services
HQ: Ixys, Llc
1590 Buckeye Dr
Milpitas CA 95035
408 457-9000

(P-9526)
IXYS LONG BEACH INC (DH)
2500 Mira Mar Ave, Long Beach (90815-1758)
PHONE..................................562 296-6584
Nathan Zommer, *CEO*
Arnold Agbayani, *CFO*
Ray Segall, *General Mgr*
▲ EMP: 25 EST: 1980
SQ FT: 20,000
SALES (est): 11.2MM
SALES (corp-wide): 1.4B **Publicly Held**
WEB: www.littelfuse.com
SIC: **3674** 5065 Semiconductors & related devices; electronic parts & equipment
HQ: Ixys, Llc
1590 Buckeye Dr
Milpitas CA 95035
408 457-9000

(P-9527)
KS ELECTRONICS INC
Also Called: Ram Technologies
322 Paseo Sonrisa, Walnut (91789-2720)
PHONE..................................909 869-8826
David Cheng, *CEO*
EMP: 35 EST: 2004
SALES (est): 1.3MM **Privately Held**
WEB: www.ramtech2000.com
SIC: **3674** Magnetic bubble memory device; random access memory (RAM)

(P-9528)
KTC-TU CORPORATION
17600 Newhope St, Fountain Valley (92708-4220)
PHONE..................................714 435-2600
John Tu, *President*
EMP: 14 EST: 2001

SALES (est): 458.6K **Privately Held**
SIC: **3674** Magnetic bubble memory device

(P-9529)
LABARGE/STC INC
200 Sandpointe Ave # 700, Santa Ana (92707-5751)
PHONE..................................281 207-1400
Anthony J Reardon, *President*
Weems Turner, *Principal*
Bill Nolan, *Purch Agent*
EMP: 563 EST: 1985
SALES (est): 5.8MM
SALES (corp-wide): 628.9MM **Publicly Held**
SIC: **3674** Hybrid integrated circuits
HQ: Ducommun Labarge Technologies, Inc.
689 Craig Rd 200
Saint Louis MO 63141
314 997-0800

(P-9530)
LASER OPERATIONS LLC
Also Called: Qpc Laser
15632 Roxford St, Sylmar (91342-1265)
PHONE..................................818 986-0000
Morris Lichtenstein, *CEO*
Mikhail Leibov, *President*
Robert Lammert, *Vice Pres*
Kulya Ponek, *General Mgr*
Jeffrey Ungar, *CTO*
EMP: 27 EST: 2009
SQ FT: 40,320
SALES (est): 5MM **Privately Held**
WEB: www.qpclasers.com
SIC: **3674** Semiconductors & related devices

(P-9531)
LEDTRONICS INC
23105 Kashiwa Ct, Torrance (90505-4026)
PHONE..................................310 534-1505
Pervaiz Lodhie, *President*
Almas Lodhie, *Vice Pres*
Lei Vinoya, *Research*
Meena Zehra, *Purchasing*
Stanley Bouchereau, *Materials Mgr*
▲ EMP: 130 EST: 1983
SQ FT: 60,000
SALES (est): 22.6MM **Privately Held**
WEB: www.ledtronics.com
SIC: **3674** 3825 3641 Light emitting diodes; instruments to measure electricity; electric lamps

(P-9532)
LOCKWOOD INDUSTRIES LLC (PA)
Also Called: Fralock
28525 Industry Dr, Valencia (91355-5424)
PHONE..................................661 702-6999
Marc Haugen, *CEO*
Bobbi Booher, *CFO*
Scott Broderick, *Vice Pres*
Dinesh Kanawade, *Vice Pres*
David Leon, *Executive*
EMP: 198 EST: 1966
SQ FT: 62,500
SALES (est): 60.6MM **Privately Held**
WEB: www.fralock.com
SIC: **3674** 3842 3089 2891 Semiconductors & related devices; prosthetic appliances; plastic containers, except foam; sealants; laminated plastics plate & sheet

(P-9533)
LUMIO INC
6355 Topanga Canyon Blvd # 335, Woodland Hills (91367-2102)
PHONE..................................586 861-2408
Freddy Raitan, *CEO*
Mario Neves, *Senior VP*
Dan Gunders, *Vice Pres*
EMP: 19 EST: 2000
SALES (est): 768.6K **Privately Held**
WEB: www.lumio.com
SIC: **3674** Radiation sensors

(P-9534)
MACKENZIE LABORATORIES INC
1163 Nicole Ct, Glendora (91740-5387)
P.O. Box 1416 (91740-1416)
PHONE..................................909 394-9007
Nagy Khattar, *President*
Robert Satchell, *COO*

Nagy J Khattar, *Info Tech Dir*
Bob Satchell, *Research*
Eric Grayson, *Accountant*
▲ **EMP:** 31 **EST:** 1952
SQ FT: 20,000
SALES (est): 7.7MM **Privately Held**
WEB: www.macklabs.com
SIC: 3674 3663 Semiconductors & related devices; radio & TV communications equipment

(P-9535)
MARVELL SEMICONDUCTOR INC
15485 Sand Canyon Ave, Irvine (92618-3154)
PHONE..................949 614-7700
Robert E Romney, *Principal*
Susan Benington, *Office Mgr*
Stanley Cheong, *Engineer*
Joe Kriscunas, *Engineer*
EMP: 217
SALES (corp-wide): 682.9MM **Privately Held**
WEB: www.marvell.com
SIC: 3674 Semiconductors & related devices
HQ: Marvell Semiconductor, Inc.
5488 Marvell Ln
Santa Clara CA 95054

(P-9536)
MASIMO SEMICONDUCTOR INC
52 Discovery, Irvine (92618-3105)
PHONE..................603 595-8900
Mark P De Raad, *President*
Gerry Hammarth, *Treasurer*
Hugh Ferguson, *Accounts Mgr*
EMP: 13 **EST:** 2012
SALES (est): 8.7MM **Publicly Held**
WEB: www.masimosemiconductor.com
SIC: 3674 Light emitting diodes
PA: Masimo Corporation
52 Discovery
Irvine CA 92618

(P-9537)
MENLO MICROSYSTEMS INC
49 Discovery Ste 150, Irvine (92618-6710)
PHONE..................949 771-0277
Russ Garcia, *CEO*
Mark Czepiel, *CFO*
Jeff Baloun, *Vice Pres*
Don Peterson, *Senior Mgr*
EMP: 23 **EST:** 2015
SALES (est): 3.6MM **Privately Held**
WEB: www.menlomicro.com
SIC: 3674 Semiconductors & related devices

(P-9538)
MICRO ANALOG INC
1861 Puddingstone Dr, La Verne (91750-5825)
PHONE..................909 392-8277
Hung T Nguyen, *CEO*
Khanh Van Nguyen, *CFO*
KV Nguyen, *Vice Pres*
Tuan Nguyen, *Executive*
Connie Nguyen, *Office Mgr*
▲ **EMP:** 160
SQ FT: 27,000
SALES (est): 43.6MM **Privately Held**
WEB: www.micro-analog.com
SIC: 3674 Semiconductors & related devices

(P-9539)
MICRO GAGE
9537 Telstar Ave Ste 131, El Monte (91731-2912)
PHONE..................626 443-1741
Bruce Talmo, *President*
Martin Chinn, *Vice Pres*
Vicky Wu, *Exec Dir*
David Doong, *Pastor*
EMP: 35 **EST:** 1972
SQ FT: 9,000
SALES (est): 3MM **Privately Held**
SIC: 3674 Semiconductors & related devices

(P-9540)
MICROPLEX INC
1070 Ortega Way, Placentia (92870-7124)
PHONE..................714 630-8220
Clay Kucenas, *President*
Catherine A Kucenas, *Executive*
EMP: 18 **EST:** 1986
SQ FT: 10,500
SALES (est): 1.8MM **Privately Held**
WEB: www.microplexinc.com
SIC: 3674 Semiconductors & related devices

(P-9541)
MICROSEMI COMMUNICATIONS INC (DH)
Also Called: Catawba County Schools
4721 Calle Carga, Camarillo (93012-8560)
PHONE..................805 388-3700
Christopher R Gardner, *President*
Martin S McDermut, *CFO*
Brenda McHale, *Administration*
Jacob Nielsen, *CIO*
Tracy Kern, *Controller*
EMP: 139 **EST:** 1987
SQ FT: 111,000
SALES (est): 58.4MM
SALES (corp-wide): 5.4B **Publicly Held**
WEB: www.microsemi.com
SIC: 3674 Semiconductors & related devices
HQ: Microsemi Corporation
11861 Western Ave
Garden Grove CA 92841
949 380-6100

(P-9542)
MICROSEMI CORP - ANLOG MXED SG (DH)
Also Called: Linfinity Microelectronics
11861 Western Ave, Garden Grove (92841-2119)
PHONE..................714 898-8121
James Peterson, *CEO*
Paul Pickle, *COO*
John Hohener, *CFO*
Russ Garcia, *Exec VP*
Steve Litchfield, *Security Dir*
EMP: 1250 **EST:** 1968
SALES (est): 141.9MM
SALES (corp-wide): 5.4B **Publicly Held**
WEB: www.microsemi.com
SIC: 3674 Semiconductor circuit networks
HQ: Microsemi Corporation
11861 Western Ave
Garden Grove CA 92841
949 380-6100

(P-9543)
MICROSEMI CORP - HIGH PRFMCE T (DH)
11861 Western Ave, Garden Grove (92841-2119)
PHONE..................949 380-6100
James J Peterson, *CEO*
EMP: 100 **EST:** 2017
SALES (est): 109.9MM
SALES (corp-wide): 5.4B **Publicly Held**
WEB: www.microsemi.com
SIC: 3674 Rectifiers, solid state
HQ: Microsemi Corporation
11861 Western Ave
Garden Grove CA 92841
949 380-6100

(P-9544)
MICROSEMI CORPORATION (HQ)
11861 Western Ave, Garden Grove (92841-2119)
PHONE..................949 380-6100
James J Peterson, *CEO*
Paul H Pickle, *President*
John W Hohener, *CFO*
Frederick G Goerner, *Exec VP*
Steven G Litchfield, *Exec VP*
EMP: 50 **EST:** 1960
SALES: 1.8B
SALES (corp-wide): 5.4B **Publicly Held**
WEB: www.microsemi.com
SIC: 3674 Integrated circuits, semiconductor networks, etc.

PA: Microchip Technology Inc
2355 W Chandler Blvd
Chandler AZ 85224
480 792-7200

(P-9545)
MICROSS HOLDINGS INC
11150 Santa Monica Blvd, Los Angeles (90025-3380)
PHONE..................215 997-3200
F Michael Pisch, *CFO*
EMP: 99 **EST:** 2010
SALES (est): 4.9MM **Privately Held**
SIC: 3674 Semiconductors & related devices

(P-9546)
MINDSPEED TECHNOLOGIES LLC (HQ)
Also Called: Mindspeed Technologies, Inc.
4000 Macarthur Blvd, Newport Beach (92660-2558)
PHONE..................949 579-3000
Raouf Y Halim, *CEO*
Stephen N Ananias, *CFO*
Abdelnaser M Adas, *Senior VP*
Najabat H Bajwa, *Senior VP*
Gerald J Hamilton, *Senior VP*
EMP: 548 **EST:** 2002
SQ FT: 97,000
SALES (est): 70.3MM **Publicly Held**
WEB: www.macom.com
SIC: 3674 Semiconductors & related devices

(P-9547)
MORSE MICRO INC
40 Waterworks Way, Irvine (92618-3107)
PHONE..................949 501-7080
Michael De Nil, *CEO*
EMP: 85 **EST:** 2019
SALES (est): 5.2MM **Privately Held**
WEB: www.morsemicro.com
SIC: 3674 Integrated circuits, semiconductor networks, etc.

(P-9548)
NETLIST INC (PA)
175 Technology Dr Ste 150, Irvine (92618-2479)
PHONE..................949 435-0025
Chun K Hong, *Ch of Bd*
Gail Sasaki, *CFO*
Jun Cho, *Bd of Directors*
Soon Choi, *Bd of Directors*
Erin Hong, *Vice Pres*
EMP: 81 **EST:** 2000
SQ FT: 8,200
SALES: 47.2MM **Publicly Held**
WEB: www.netlist.com
SIC: 3674 Random access memory (RAM)

(P-9549)
NEWPORT FAB LLC
Also Called: Jazz Semiconductor
4321 Jamboree Rd, Newport Beach (92660-3007)
PHONE..................949 435-8000
Susanna Bennette,
Ori Galzur, *Vice Pres*
Noit Levy-Karoubi, *Vice Pres*
Hung Trinh, *Admin Sec*
Pohchee Hurwitz, *Prgrmr*
EMP: 99 **EST:** 2002
SALES (est): 33.2MM **Privately Held**
WEB: www.towersemi.com
SIC: 3674 Wafers (semiconductor devices)
HQ: Tower Semiconductor Newport Beach, Inc.
4321 Jamboree Rd
Newport Beach CA 92660
949 435-8000

(P-9550)
OMNISIL
5401 Everglades St, Ventura (93003-6523)
PHONE..................805 644-2514
David Clark, *President*
Karin Clark, *Corp Secy*
Dennis Strang, *Vice Pres*
▲ **EMP:** 21 **EST:** 1986
SQ FT: 9,800
SALES (est): 1.9MM **Privately Held**
WEB: www.omnisil.com
SIC: 3674 Silicon wafers, chemically doped

(P-9551)
OMTEK INC
3722 Calle Cita, Santa Barbara (93105-2411)
PHONE..................805 687-9629
EMP: 23
SQ FT: 15,000
SALES (est): 1.3MM **Privately Held**
SIC: 3674 Product Research/Development

(P-9552)
OPTO DIODE CORPORATION
1260 Calle Suerte, Camarillo 93012-8053)
PHONE..................305 465-8700
Mary Hagerty-Goldberg, *Principal*
Mike Silverstein, *Engineer*
Roger Forrest, *Education*
EMP: 24 **EST:** 1982
SALES (est): 7.4MM **Privately Held**
WEB: www.optodiode.com
SIC: 3674 Semiconductors & related devices

(P-9553)
ORTEL A DIVISION EMCORE CO (HQ)
2015 Chestnut St, Alhambra (91803-1542)
PHONE..................626 293-3400
Mary E Ortel, *President*
EMP: 126 **EST:** 2005
SALES (est): 4.6MM
SALES (corp-wide): 110.1MM **Publicly Held**
WEB: www.emcore.com
SIC: 3674 3559 Integrated circuits, semiconductor networks, etc.; semiconductor manufacturing machinery
PA: Emcore Corporation
2015 Chestnut St
Alhambra CA 91803
626 293-3400

(P-9554)
OSI OPTOELECTRONICS INC
Also Called: Advanced Photonix
1240 Avenida Acaso, Camarillo (93012-8727)
PHONE..................805 987-0146
Jean-Pierre Maufras, *General Mgr*
EMP: 50
SALES (corp-wide): 1.1B **Publicly Held**
WEB: www.osioptoelectronics.com
SIC: 3674 Semiconductors & related devices
HQ: Osi Optoelectronics, Inc.
12525 Chadron Ave
Hawthorne CA 90250

(P-9555)
OSI SYSTEMS INC (PA)
12525 Chadron Ave, Hawthorne (90250-4807)
PHONE..................310 978-0516
Deepak Chopra, *Ch of Bd*
Tina Cooley, *Partner*
Alan Edrick, *CFO*
Rick Merritt, *Officer*
Ajay Mehra, *Exec VP*
EMP: 325 **EST:** 1987
SQ FT: 88,000
SALES: 1.1B **Publicly Held**
WEB: www.osi-systems.com
SIC: 3674 3845 Integrated circuits, semiconductor networks, etc.; photoconductive cells; photoelectric cells, solid state (electronic eye); electromedical equipment; ultrasonic scanning devices, medical

(P-9556)
PAYTON TECHNOLOGY CORPORATION
17665 Newhope St Ste B, Fountain Valley (92708-8209)
PHONE..................714 885-8000
John Tu, *President*
David Sun, *COO*
John Leitgeb, *CIO*
Tim Westland, *Marketing Mgr*
Annette Chong, *Marketing Staff*
▲ **EMP:** 58 **EST:** 1999

SALES (est): 1.7MM **Privately Held**
WEB: www.kingston.com
SIC: 3674 Semiconductors & related devices

(P-9557)
PHYSPEED CORPORATION
4055 Mission Oaks Blvd, Camarillo (93012-5156)
PHONE.................805 259-3101
Yu Ruai, *Principal*
EMP: 14 EST: 2012
SALES (est): 374.7K
SALES (corp-wide): 478.6MM **Publicly Held**
WEB: www.physpeed.com
SIC: 3674 Semiconductors & related devices
PA: Maxlinear, Inc.
5966 La Place Ct Ste 100
Carlsbad CA 92008
760 692-0711

(P-9558)
PICO INSTRUMENTS LLC
23232 Peralta Dr Ste 121, Laguna Hills (92653-1437)
PHONE.................949 910-6448
Ruihong Han, *Principal*
EMP: 13 EST: 2005
SALES (est): 402.8K **Privately Held**
WEB: www.picoinstruments.com
SIC: 3674 Semiconductors & related devices

(P-9559)
PIEZO-METRICS INC (PA)
Also Called: Micron Instruments
4584 Runway St, Simi Valley (93063-3449)
PHONE.................805 522-4676
Herbert Chelner, *President*
Sharon Chelner, *Vice Pres*
Geoff Dunsterville, *General Mgr*
EMP: 25 EST: 1967
SQ FT: 9,000
SALES (est): 4.9MM **Privately Held**
WEB: www.microninstruments.com
SIC: 3674 3829 Strain gages, solid state; pressure transducers

(P-9560)
POLYFET RF DEVICES INC
1110 Avenida Acaso, Camarillo (93012-8725)
PHONE.................805 484-9582
S K Leong, *President*
EMP: 25 EST: 1984
SQ FT: 7,500
SALES (est): 3.9MM **Privately Held**
WEB: www.polyfet.com
SIC: 3674 Transistors

(P-9561)
PRINTEC HT ELECTRONICS LLC
501 Sally Pl, Fullerton (92831-5014)
PHONE.................714 484-7597
Nancy Cheng, *General Mgr*
Greg Morton, *Regional Mgr*
▲ EMP: 50 EST: 2011
SQ FT: 12,000
SALES (est): 10.5MM **Privately Held**
WEB: www.printec-ht.com
SIC: 3674 3629 Modules, solid state; electronic generation equipment
PA: Printec H. T. Electronics Corp.
No. 38, Liyan St.
New Taipei City TAP 23557

(P-9562)
QLOGIC LLC (DH)
15485 Sand Canyon Ave, Irvine (92618-3154)
PHONE.................949 389-6000
Syed Ali,
Raghib Hussain, *Exec VP*
Sanjaya Anand, *Vice Pres*
Stacey Helmick, *Program Mgr*
Connie Williams, *IT Executive*
▲ EMP: 138 EST: 1992
SQ FT: 161,000

SALES (est): 79.9MM
SALES (corp-wide): 682.9MM **Privately Held**
WEB: www.marvell.com
SIC: 3674 Integrated circuits, semiconductor networks, etc.

(P-9563)
QPC LASERS INC
15632 Roxford St, Sylmar (91342-1265)
PHONE.................818 986-0000
Hao Zhao, *CEO*
Grace Caminade-Lopez, *Marketing Staff*
EMP: 13 EST: 2013
SALES (est): 1.5MM **Privately Held**
WEB: www.qpclasers.com
SIC: 3674 Semiconductors & related devices

(P-9564)
REVASUM INC
825 Buckley Rd Ste 200, San Luis Obispo (93401-8193)
PHONE.................805 541-6424
Rebecca Shooter-Dodd, *President*
Pat Oconnor, *CFO*
Eric Jacobson, *Vice Pres*
Bill Kalenian, *Vice Pres*
Sarah Okada, *Vice Pres*
EMP: 106 EST: 2016
SALES (est): 18.1MM **Privately Held**
WEB: www.revasum.com
SIC: 3674 Semiconductors & related devices

(P-9565)
RF DIGITAL CORPORATION
1601 Pcf Cast Hwy Ste 290, Hermosa Beach (90254)
PHONE.................949 610-0008
Armen Kazanchian, *President*
Rod Landers, *COO*
EMP: 110 EST: 1999
SQ FT: 5,000
SALES (est): 14.7MM
SALES (corp-wide): 4.1B **Privately Held**
SIC: 3674 Modules, solid state
HQ: Heptagon Usa, Inc.
465 N Whisman Rd Ste 200
Mountain View CA 94043
650 336-7990

(P-9566)
ROCKLEY PHOTONICS INC (HQ)
234 E Colo Blvd Ste 600, Pasadena (91101)
PHONE.................626 304-9960
Andrew George Rickman, *CEO*
Al Benzoni, *Vice Pres*
David Nelson, *Vice Pres*
Aaron Zilkie, *Vice Pres*
Michael Greaves, *Administration*
EMP: 192 EST: 2013
SALES (est): 76.9MM
SALES (corp-wide): 20.1MM **Privately Held**
WEB: www.rockleyphotonics.com
SIC: 3674 Semiconductors & related devices
PA: Rockley Photonics Limited
Clarendon Business Centre
Oxford OXON OX2 6
186 529-2017

(P-9567)
S-ENERGY AMERICA INC (HQ)
1170 N Gilbert St, Anaheim (92801-1401)
PHONE.................949 281-7897
David Kim, *President*
EMP: 14 EST: 2011
SALES (est): 5.4MM **Privately Held**
WEB: www.s-energy.com
SIC: 3674 Solar cells

(P-9568)
SAC-TEC LABS INC (PA)
24301 Wilmington Ave, Carson (90745-6139)
PHONE.................310 375-5295
Robert Kunesh, *President*
Marylin Hafermalz, *Shareholder*
Manouk Ohanesyan, *Executive*
Charles Spencer, *Engineer*
James Ledger, *Controller*
EMP: 25 EST: 1991
SQ FT: 10,000

SALES (est): 2.4MM **Privately Held**
WEB: www.sactec.com
SIC: 3674 Semiconductors & related devices

(P-9569)
SEMICOA CORPORATION
333 Mccormick Ave, Costa Mesa (92626-3479)
PHONE.................714 979-1900
Thomas E Epley, *CEO*
Ramesh Ramchandani, *President*
Perry Denning, *COO*
Gary B Joyce, *CFO*
Chris Nixon, *Opers Staff*
▲ EMP: 60 EST: 2009
SALES (est): 9.2MM **Privately Held**
WEB: www.semicoa.com
SIC: 3674 Semiconductors & related devices

(P-9570)
SEMICONDUCTOR COMPONENTS INC
Also Called: SCI
1353 E Edinger Ave, Santa Ana (92705-4430)
PHONE.................714 547-6059
Archie L Brainard, *President*
EMP: 15 EST: 1959
SQ FT: 2,500
SALES (est): 386.5K **Privately Held**
SIC: 3674 Semiconductor circuit networks

(P-9571)
SEMICONDUCTOR EQUIPMENT CORP
Also Called: SEC
5154 Goldman Ave, Moorpark (93021-1760)
PHONE.................805 529-2293
Donald I Moore, *CEO*
Richard Folsom, *CFO*
Chris Ryding, *Sr Software Eng*
Teresa Scruggs, *Info Tech Mgr*
Teresa Musard, *Technology*
▲ EMP: 16 EST: 1974
SQ FT: 12,500
SALES (est): 3MM **Privately Held**
WEB: www.semicorp.com
SIC: 3674 Semiconductors & related devices

(P-9572)
SEMICONDUCTOR PROCESS EQP CORP
Also Called: Spec
27963 Franklin Pkwy, Valencia (91355-4110)
PHONE.................661 257-0934
Arnold J Gustin, *CEO*
Robin Douglas, *President*
Kevin McGillivray, *Vice Pres*
◆ EMP: 35 EST: 1986
SQ FT: 139,000
SALES (est): 7.2MM **Privately Held**
WEB: www.team-spec.com
SIC: 3674 Semiconductors & related devices

(P-9573)
SEMIQ INCORPORATED
20692 Prism Pl, Lake Forest (92630-7803)
PHONE.................949 273-4373
Sung Joon Kim, *President*
Josta Hogervorst, *Office Mgr*
EMP: 16 EST: 2010
SALES (est): 2.2MM **Privately Held**
SIC: 3674 Semiconductors & related devices

(P-9574)
SEMTECH CORPORATION (PA)
200 Flynn Rd, Camarillo (93012-8790)
PHONE.................805 498-2111
Mohan R Maheswaran, *President*
Rockell N Hankin, *Ch of Bd*
Emeka N Chukwu, *CFO*
James P Burra, *Vice Ch Bd*
Charles B Ammann, *Exec VP*
▲ EMP: 180 EST: 1960
SQ FT: 88,000

SALES (est): 595.1MM **Publicly Held**
WEB: www.semtech.com
SIC: 3674 Semiconductors & related devices

(P-9575)
SENSONETICS INC
11164 Young River Ave, Fountain Valley (92708-4109)
PHONE.................714 799-1616
Gary Sahagen, *CEO*
Laurie Childress, *Office Mgr*
◆ EMP: 17 EST: 1998
SQ FT: 8,000
SALES (est): 1.9MM **Privately Held**
WEB: www.sensonetics.com
SIC: 3674 Semiconductors & related devices

(P-9576)
SKYWORKS SOLUTIONS INC (PA)
5260 California Ave, Irvine (92617-3228)
PHONE.................949 231-3000
Liam K Griffin, *Ch of Bd*
Kris Sennesael, *CFO*
Bruce J Freyman, *Exec VP*
Carlos S Bori, *Senior VP*
Kari A Durham, *Senior VP*
▲ EMP: 750 EST: 1962
SQ FT: 218,500
SALES (est): 3.3B **Publicly Held**
WEB: www.skyworksinc.com
SIC: 3674 Integrated circuits, semiconductor networks, etc.

(P-9577)
SMT ELECTRONICS MFG INC
2630 S Shannon St, Santa Ana (92704-5230)
PHONE.................714 751-8894
Henry T Tran, *CEO*
EMP: 30 EST: 1995
SQ FT: 12,104
SALES (est): 1.4MM **Privately Held**
WEB: www.smtelectronics.com
SIC: 3674 3672 Integrated circuits, semiconductor networks, etc.; printed circuit boards

(P-9578)
SOLID STATE DEVICES INC
Also Called: Ssdi
14701 Firestone Blvd, La Mirada (90638-5918)
PHONE.................562 404-4474
Arnold N Applebaum, *President*
David Franz, *CFO*
Mike Faucher, *Officer*
Nita Soma, *Executive*
Eli Dexter, *Engineer*
▲ EMP: 110
SQ FT: 32,000
SALES (est): 22.9MM **Privately Held**
WEB: www.ssdi-power.com
SIC: 3674 Diodes, solid state (germanium, silicon, etc.)

(P-9579)
SOURCE PHOTONICS USA INC (PA)
8521 Fllbrook Ave Ste 200, West Hills (91304)
PHONE.................818 773-9044
Doug Wright, *CEO*
EMP: 249 EST: 1999
SALES (est): 14.7MM **Privately Held**
WEB: www.sourcephotonics.com
SIC: 3674 Semiconductors & related devices

(P-9580)
SOURCE PHOTONICS USA INC
8917 Fullbright Ave, Chatsworth (91311-6124)
PHONE.................818 407-5007
EMP: 19 **Privately Held**
WEB: www.sourcephotonics.com
SIC: 3674 Semiconductors & related devices
PA: Source Photonics Usa, Inc.
8521 Fllbrook Ave Ste 200
West Hills CA 91304

PRODUCTS & SVCS

(P-9581)
SPECTROLAB INC
12500 Gladstone Ave, Sylmar
(91342-5373)
P.O. Box 9209 (91392-9209)
PHONE......................818 365-4611
David Lillington, *President*
Paul Ballew, *CFO*
Nasser Karam, *Vice Pres*
Jeff Peacock, *Vice Pres*
Edward Ringo, *Vice Pres*
EMP: 400 **EST:** 1956
SQ FT: 50,000
SALES (est): 89.8MM
SALES (corp-wide): 58.1B **Publicly Held**
WEB: www.spectrolab.com
SIC: 3674 3679 Solar cells; power supplies, all types: static
HQ: Boeing Satellite Systems, Inc.
900 N Pacific Coast Hwy
El Segundo CA 90245

(P-9582)
SST TECHNOLOGIES
Also Called: Sst Vacuum Reflow Systems
9801 Everest St, Downey (90242-3113)
PHONE......................562 803-3361
Anthony Wilson, *President*
Ralph Burroughs, *CFO*
Jorge Garcia, *Purch Mgr*
Matt Vorona, *Regl Sales Mgr*
Alexander Voronel, *Sales Staff*
◆ **EMP:** 30 **EST:** 1969
SQ FT: 20,000
SALES (est): 7.4MM **Privately Held**
WEB: www.palomartechnologies.com
SIC: 3674 Semiconductors & related devices
PA: Palomar Technologies, Inc.
6305 El Camino Real
Carlsbad CA 92009

(P-9583)
STELLAR MICROELECTRONICS INC
9340 Owensmouth Ave, Chatsworth
(91311-6915)
PHONE......................661 775-3500
Sudesh Arora, *President*
V U Ngyen, *Engineer*
EMP: 239 **EST:** 1974
SQ FT: 140,000
SALES (est): 77.6MM
SALES (corp-wide): 1.1B **Privately Held**
WEB: www.neotech.com
SIC: 3674 Semiconductors & related devices
PA: Natel Engineering Company, Llc
9340 Owensmouth Ave
Chatsworth CA 91311
818 495-8617

(P-9584)
STMICROELECTRONICS INC
85 Enterprise Ste 300, Aliso Viejo
(92656-2614)
PHONE......................949 347-0717
EMP: 34
SALES (corp-wide): 7.4B **Privately Held**
SIC: 3674 Mfg Semiconducteres
HQ: Stmicroelectronics, Inc
750 Canyon Dr Ste 300
Coppell TX 75019
972 466-6000

(P-9585)
SUBSTANCE ABUSE PROGRAM
1370 S State St Ste A, Hemet (92543)
PHONE......................951 791-3350
Mark Thuve, *Business Mgr*
EMP: 30 **EST:** 2010
SALES (est): 1.3MM **Privately Held**
SIC: 3674 Semiconductors & related devices

(P-9586)
SUNCORE INC
15 Hubble Ste 200, Irvine (92618-4268)
PHONE......................949 450-0054
Steven Brimmer, *President*
Donald A Nevins, *Treasurer*
Michael Swan, *Vice Pres*
Arthur Kozak, *Principal*
Jennifer Mansoor, *Executive Asst*

▲ **EMP:** 31 **EST:** 2004
SQ FT: 5,000
SALES (est): 2.9MM **Privately Held**
WEB: www.suncoresolar.com
SIC: 3674 5063 5065 Solar cells; batteries; electronic parts & equipment

(P-9587)
SYMMETRY ELECTRONICS LLC (DH)
Also Called: Semiconductorstore.com
222 N Pacific Coast Hwy # 10, El Segundo
(90245-5615)
PHONE......................310 536-6190
Joe Caravana, *Co-Founder*
Scott Wing, *President*
Gil Zaharoni, *Co-Founder*
▲ **EMP:** 35 **EST:** 1997
SQ FT: 15,000
SALES (est): 19.3MM
SALES (corp-wide): 245.5B **Publicly Held**
WEB: www.semiconductorstore.com
SIC: 3674 Semiconductors & related devices
HQ: Tti, Inc.
2441 Northeast Pkwy
Fort Worth TX 76106
817 740-9000

(P-9588)
SYNTIANT CORP
7555 Irvine Center Dr # 200, Irvine
(92618-2912)
PHONE......................949 774-4887
Kurt Busch, *CEO*
Paul Henderson, *CFO*
Dave Garrett, *Vice Pres*
Stephen Bailey, *CTO*
Chris Stevens, *VP Sales*
EMP: 75 **EST:** 2017
SALES (est): 8MM **Privately Held**
WEB: www.syntiant.com
SIC: 3674 Semiconductors & related devices

(P-9589)
TERIDIAN SEMICONDUCTOR CORP (DH)
6440 Oak Cyn Ste 100, Irvine
(92618-5208)
PHONE......................714 508-8800
Mark Casper, *CEO*
John Silk, *Vice Pres*
Pete Todd, *Vice Pres*
David Gruetter, *CTO*
EMP: 90 **EST:** 1996
SALES (est): 27.8MM
SALES (corp-wide): 5.6B **Publicly Held**
WEB: www.maximintegrated.com
SIC: 3674 Semiconductors & related devices

(P-9590)
TERIDIAN SMICDTR HOLDINGS CORP (DH)
6440 Oak Cyn Ste 100, Irvine
(92618-5208)
PHONE......................714 508-8800
Gerald Fitch, *President*
John Silk, *Vice Pres*
David Gruetter, *CTO*
EMP: 100 **EST:** 2005
SALES (est): 27.8MM
SALES (corp-wide): 5.6B **Publicly Held**
WEB: www.maximintegrated.com
SIC: 3674 Semiconductors & related devices
HQ: Maxim Integrated Products, Inc.
160 Rio Robles
San Jose CA 95134
408 601-1000

(P-9591)
TEXAS INSTRUMENTS INCORPORATED
14351 Myford Rd, Tustin (92780-7074)
PHONE......................714 731-7110
EMP: 190
SALES (corp-wide): 12.2B **Publicly Held**
SIC: 3674 Mfg Semiconductors/Related Devices

PA: Texas Instruments Incorporated
12500 Ti Blvd
Dallas TX 75243
214 479-3773

(P-9592)
TOUCHDOWN TECHNOLOGIES INC
5188 Commerce Dr, Baldwin Park
(91706-1450)
PHONE......................626 472-6732
Haruo Matsuno, *President*
Patrick Flynn, *President*
Raffi Garabedian, *Vice Pres*
Brian Flowers, *Admin Sec*
▼ **EMP:** 50 **EST:** 1996
SQ FT: 30,000
SALES (est): 3.8MM **Privately Held**
SIC: 3674 Semiconductor diodes & rectifiers

(P-9593)
TOWER SEMICDTR NEWPORT BCH INC (DH)
Also Called: Towerjazz
4321 Jamboree Rd, Newport Beach
(92660-3007)
PHONE......................949 435-8000
Russell Ellwanger, *CEO*
Tom Foerster, *Partner*
Itzhak Edrei, *President*
Rafi Mor, *COO*
Oren Shirazi, *CFO*
▲ **EMP:** 700 **EST:** 2002
SQ FT: 300,000
SALES (est): 221.4MM **Privately Held**
WEB: www.towersemi.com
SIC: 3674 Wafers (semiconductor devices)

(P-9594)
TRANSPHORM INC (PA)
75 Castilian Dr Ste 200, Goleta
(93117-5580)
PHONE......................805 456-1300
Mario Riva, *CEO*
Primit Parikh, *COO*
Cameron McAulay, *CFO*
Umesh Mishra, *CTO*
EMP: 71 **EST:** 2017
SALES (est): 11.3MM **Privately Held**
WEB: www.transphormusa.com
SIC: 3674 Microcircuits, integrated (semiconductor)

(P-9595)
TWILIGHT TECHNOLOGY INC (PA)
325 N Shepard St, Anaheim (92806-2832)
P.O. Box 1149, Placentia (92871-1149)
PHONE......................714 257-2257
Randy Greene, *President*
James Donaghy, *Vice Pres*
Gale Greene, *Admin Sec*
Shannon Neeper, *Bookkeeper*
EMP: 19 **EST:** 1997
SQ FT: 12,000
SALES (est): 3.7MM **Privately Held**
WEB: www.twilighttechnology.com
SIC: 3674 Integrated circuits, semiconductor networks, etc.

(P-9596)
ULTRON SYSTEMS INC
5105 Maureen Ln, Moorpark (93021-1783)
PHONE......................805 529-1485
Aki Egerer, *President*
Aaron Chan, *Vice Pres*
▲ **EMP:** 17 **EST:** 1982
SQ FT: 8,000
SALES (est): 2.8MM **Privately Held**
WEB: www.ultronsystems.com
SIC: 3674 Semiconductors & related devices

(P-9597)
UNIREX CORP
Also Called: Unirex Technologies
2288 E 27th St, Vernon (90058-1131)
PHONE......................323 589-4000
Bijan Neman, *President*
Richard Engler, *Vice Pres*
Behzad Neman, *Vice Pres*
Vener Venerc, *Bookkeeper*
Herlinda F Garcia, *Sales Staff*
▲ **EMP:** 50 **EST:** 1985

SQ FT: 33,000
SALES (est): 6.6MM **Privately Held**
WEB: www.unirex.com
SIC: 3674 3572 Magnetic bubble memory device; computer storage devices

(P-9598)
US SENSOR CORP
1832 W Collins Ave, Orange (92867-5425)
PHONE......................714 639-1000
Roger W Dankert, *CEO*
Dan Dankert, *President*
Robert Ruppert, *Opers Staff*
EMP: 100 **EST:** 1989
SQ FT: 30,000
SALES (est): 20.9MM
SALES (corp-wide): 1.4B **Publicly Held**
WEB: www.littelfuse.com
SIC: 3674 3676 Semiconductors & related devices; thermistors, except temperature sensors
PA: Littelfuse, Inc.
8755 W Higgins Rd Ste 500
Chicago IL 60631
773 628-1000

(P-9599)
VENTURA TECHNOLOGY GROUP
855 E Easy St Ste 104, Simi Valley
(93065-1825)
PHONE......................805 581-0800
Douglas E Lafountaine, *President*
EMP: 33 **EST:** 1994
SQ FT: 7,400
SALES (est): 2.6MM **Privately Held**
WEB: www.venturatech.com
SIC: 3674 Random access memory (RAM); read-only memory (ROM)

(P-9600)
VISHAY THIN FILM LLC
Also Called: Vishay Spectoral Electronics
4051 Greystone Dr, Ontario (91761-3100)
PHONE......................909 923-3313
Robert Leon, *Mng Member*
Sheila Rigg, *Principal*
EMP: 18 **EST:** 2006
SALES (est): 461.2K **Privately Held**
SIC: 3674 Thin film circuits

(P-9601)
VISHAY TRANSDUCERS LTD
2930 Inland Empire Blvd # 100, Ontario
(91764-4802)
PHONE......................626 363-7500
Dubi Zandman, *CEO*
Philx Zanman, *General Ptr*
▲ **EMP:** 50 **EST:** 2002
SALES (est): 6MM
SALES (corp-wide): 269.3MM **Publicly Held**
WEB: www.vishaypg.com
SIC: 3674 Semiconductors & related devices
PA: Vishay Precision Group, Inc.
3 Great Valley Pkwy # 150
Malvern PA 19355
484 321-5300

(P-9602)
VITESSE MANUFACTURING & DEV
Also Called: Vitesse Semiconductor
11861 Western Ave, Garden Grove
(92841-2119)
PHONE......................805 388-3700
Chris Gardner, *Officer*
Jim Sullivan, *Treasurer*
Barbara Blick, *Engineer*
Nitish Jain, *Engineer*
Jun Suwandy, *Engineer*
EMP: 200 **EST:** 1984
SALES (est): 52.1MM
SALES (corp-wide): 5.4B **Publicly Held**
WEB: www.microsemi.com
SIC: 3674 Microcircuits, integrated (semiconductor)
HQ: Microsemi Communications, Inc.
4721 Calle Carga
Camarillo CA 93012
805 388-3700

(P-9603)
VOLTAGE MULTIPLIERS INC (PA)
Also Called: V M I
8711 W Roosevelt Ave, Visalia
(93291-9458)
PHONE....................559 651-1402
Dennis J Kemp, *President*
John Yakura, *Corp Secy*
Kenneth Hage, *Vice Pres*
Randy Bethel, *Electrical Engi*
Rodney Davenport, *Engineer*
EMP: 176 **EST:** 1980
SQ FT: 24,000
SALES (est): 29.7MM **Privately Held**
WEB: www.voltagemultipliers.com
SIC: 3674 Diodes, solid state (germanium,
silicon, etc.)

(P-9604)
W G HOLT INC
Also Called: Holt Integrated Circuits
23351 Madero, Mission Viejo (92691-2730)
PHONE....................949 859-8800
David Mead, *CEO*
Sandy Edberg, *CTO*
Chris Zenter, *Info Tech Dir*
James Yu, *Info Tech Mgr*
Chris Zentner, *Info Tech Mgr*
EMP: 65
SQ FT: 17,000
SALES (est): 12.7MM **Privately Held**
WEB: www.holtic.com
SIC: 3674 Integrated circuits, semiconduc-
tor networks, etc.

(P-9605)
WELDEX CORPORATION (PA)
6751 Katella Ave, Cypress (90630-5105)
PHONE....................714 761-2100
G W Goddard, *CEO*
William Jung, *President*
Nina Liddi, *Clerk*
▲ **EMP:** 299 **EST:** 1992
SQ FT: 15,000
SALES (est): 21.1MM **Privately Held**
WEB: www.cms.weldex.com
SIC: 3674 3663 Light emitting diodes; tel-
evision closed circuit equipment

(P-9606)
XCELERIUM INC
530 Technology Dr Ste 100, Irvine
(92618-1350)
PHONE....................949 244-3668
Raheel Khan, *Principal*
Abdelnaser Adas, *Principal*
EMP: 14 **EST:** 2020
SALES (est): 527.2K **Privately Held**
SIC: 3674 Semiconductors & related de-
vices

(P-9607)
XEL USA INC
Also Called: XEL Group
21 Argonaut Ste B, Aliso Viejo
(92656-4150)
PHONE....................949 425-8686
Paul Kuszka, *CEO*
EMP: 25 **EST:** 2008
SALES (est): 2.1MM **Privately Held**
WEB: www.xelgroup.com
SIC: 3674 Magnetic bubble memory device

(P-9608)
ZT PLUS
1321 Mountain View Cir, Azusa
(91702-1649)
PHONE....................626 208-3440
Sandy Grouf, *Principal*
▲ **EMP:** 14 **EST:** 2009
SALES (est): 514.9K **Privately Held**
SIC: 3674 Thermoelectric devices, solid
state

3675 Electronic Capacitors

(P-9609)
AMERICAN CAPACITOR
CORPORATION
5367 3rd St, Irwindale (91706-2085)
PHONE....................626 814-4444
Joseph Latourelle, *President*
EMP: 30 **EST:** 1979
SQ FT: 14,200

SALES (est): 1.7MM **Privately Held**
WEB: www.americancapacitor.com
SIC: 3675 5065 Electronic capacitors;
electronic parts & equipment

(P-9610)
INCA ONE CORPORATION
1632 1/2 W 134th St, Gardena
(90249-2014)
PHONE....................310 808-0001
Adriana Roberts, *President*
Tupac Roberts, *Vice Pres*
Elmer Toribio, *Purch Mgr*
Roger Fortier,
▲ **EMP:** 35 **EST:** 1971
SALES (est): 7.8MM **Privately Held**
WEB: www.inca-tvlifts.com
SIC: 3675 Electronic capacitors

(P-9611)
JOHANSON DIELECTRICS INC
(HQ)
4001 Calle Tecate, Camarillo (93012-5087)
PHONE....................805 389-1166
N Eric Johanson, *CEO*
Justin Greene, *CFO*
Tian Tan, *Engineer*
John Mayhew, *Analyst*
Aurelio Garcia, *Accounts Mgr*
▲ **EMP:** 193 **EST:** 1965
SALES (est): 26.4MM **Privately Held**
WEB: www.johansondielectrics.com
SIC: 3675 Electronic capacitors

(P-9612)
JOHANSON TECHNOLOGY INC
4001 Calle Tecate, Camarillo (93012-5087)
PHONE....................805 389-1166
John Petrinec, *CEO*
Jay Gerber, *Info Tech Mgr*
Rosalie Valerio, *Engineer*
Dave Pomerantz, *Accounting Mgr*
D Ick Crawford, *Plant Mgr*
▲ **EMP:** 159
SQ FT: 30,000
SALES (est): 21MM **Privately Held**
WEB: www.johansontechnology.com
SIC: 3675 5065 3674 Electronic capaci-
tors; electronic parts & equipment; semi-
conductors & related devices
PA: Johanson Ventures, Inc.
4001 Calle Tecate
Camarillo CA 93012

(P-9613)
NEWMAR POWER LLC
15272 Newsboy Cir, Huntington Beach
(92649-1202)
PHONE....................800 854-3906
Kevin Moschetti, *Mng Member*
EMP: 250 **EST:** 1979
SALES (est): 23.3MM
SALES (corp-wide): 90.2MM **Privately
Held**
WEB: www.poweringthenetwork.com
SIC: 3675 3678 3679 Electronic capaci-
tors; electronic connectors; electronic
switches
PA: Mission Critical Electronics Llc
15272 Newsboy Cir
Huntington Beach CA 92649
714 751-0488

(P-9614)
TRIGON COMPONENTS INC (PA)
935 Mariner St, Brea (92821-3827)
PHONE....................714 990-1367
Yeankai Chorng, *CEO*
Maria Chorng, *Office Mgr*
▲ **EMP:** 76 **EST:** 1998
SALES (est): 5MM **Privately Held**
WEB: www.trigoncomponents.com
SIC: 3675 5065 Condensers, electronic;
electronic parts & equipment

(P-9615)
VIRGIL WALKER INC
Also Called: Auton Motorized Systems
29102 Hancock Pkwy, Valencia
(91355-1066)
PHONE....................661 294-9142
Fax: 310 295-5639
◆ **EMP:** 32
SQ FT: 15,000

SALES (est): 4.6MM **Privately Held**
WEB: www.auton.com
SIC: 3675 Mfg Electronic Capacitors

3676 Electronic Resistors

(P-9616)
MICRO-OHM CORPORATION
1075 Hamilton Rd, Duarte (91010-2743)
PHONE....................626 357-5377
Byron Ritchey, *CEO*
Charles Schwab, *President*
Barbette Bowers, *Corp Secy*
Mark Craven, *Vice Pres*
▲ **EMP:** 18 **EST:** 1961
SALES (est): 1MM **Privately Held**
WEB: www.microohm.com
SIC: 3676 Electronic resistors

(P-9617)
RIEDON INC (PA)
300 Cypress Ave, Alhambra (91801-3001)
PHONE....................626 284-9901
Michael A Zoeller, *President*
Clay Callander, *CFO*
Duane Ebbert, *Vice Pres*
Greg Wood, *Vice Pres*
Phil Ebbert, *CIO*
▲ **EMP:** 150 **EST:** 1960
SQ FT: 12,000
SALES (est): 18.6MM **Privately Held**
WEB: www.riedon.com
SIC: 3676 Electronic resistors

3677 Electronic Coils & Transformers

(P-9618)
A M I/COAST MAGNETICS INC
5333 W Washington Blvd, Los Angeles
(90016-1191)
PHONE....................323 936-6188
Satya Dosaj, *CEO*
Phillis Dosaj, *Shareholder*
Dev Dosaj, *President*
Austin Dosaj, *Administration*
EMP: 49 **EST:** 1965
SQ FT: 25,000
SALES (est): 6.3MM **Privately Held**
SIC: 3677 3549 Electronic transformers;
coil winding machines for springs

(P-9619)
ALLIED COMPONENTS INTL
19671 Descartes, Foothill Ranch
(92610-2609)
PHONE....................949 356-1780
Neal McDonald, *President*
Ruben Ramirez, *CFO*
▲ **EMP:** 25 **EST:** 1992
SQ FT: 9,000
SALES (est): 3.8MM **Privately Held**
WEB: www.alliedcomponents.com
SIC: 3677 Electronic coils, transformers &
other inductors

(P-9620)
ASTRON CORPORATION
9 Autry, Irvine (92618-2768)
PHONE....................949 458-7277
Loren Pochirowski, *President*
William Pochirowski, *Officer*
▲ **EMP:** 40 **EST:** 1976
SQ FT: 18,000
SALES (est): 4.8MM **Privately Held**
WEB: www.astroncorp.com
SIC: 3677 3679 Transformers power sup-
ply, electronic type; electronic circuits

(P-9621)
BECKER SPECIALTY
CORPORATION
15310 Arrow Blvd, Fontana (92335-3249)
PHONE....................909 356-1095
Jack McGrew, *Branch Mgr*
Elisama Lara, *Engineer*
EMP: 20
SALES (corp-wide): 877.7MM **Privately
Held**
SIC: 3677 Electronic coils, transformers &
other inductors

HQ: Becker Specialty Corporation
2526 Delta Ln
Elk Grove Village IL 60007

(P-9622)
BOURNS INC (PA)
1200 Columbia Ave, Riverside
(92507-2129)
PHONE....................951 781-5500
Gordon L Bourns, *CEO*
Erik Meijer, *President*
Renee Byrom, *CFO*
James Heiken, *CFO*
Gregg Gibbons, *Exec VP*
◆ **EMP:** 171 **EST:** 1952
SQ FT: 205,000
SALES (est): 642.7MM **Privately Held**
WEB: www.bourns.com
SIC: 3677 3676 3661 3639 Electronic
transformers; electronic resistors; tele-
phone & telegraph apparatus; major
kitchen appliances, except refrigerators &
stoves; electronic circuits; connectors &
terminals for electrical devices

(P-9623)
BOURNS APL CORP (HQ)
1200 Columbia Ave, Riverside
(92507-2129)
PHONE....................951 781-5500
EMP: 62
SALES (est): 200.9K
SALES (corp-wide): 642.7MM **Privately
Held**
WEB: www.bourns.com
SIC: 3677 Electronic coils, transformers &
other inductors
PA: Bourns, Inc.
1200 Columbia Ave
Riverside CA 92507
951 781-5500

(P-9624)
COAST/DVNCED CHIP
MGNETICS INC
Also Called: Coast/A C M
4225 Spencer St, Torrance (90503-2421)
PHONE....................310 370-8188
Benjamin Nguyen, *CEO*
Allen Adams, *President*
Ben Nguyen, *CEO*
Lorenzo Acosta, *Prdtn Mgr*
Jessica Ortiz, *Agent*
EMP: 19 **EST:** 1952
SQ FT: 3,000 **Privately Held**
WEB: www.coastacm.com
SIC: 3677 Electronic coils, transformers &
other inductors

(P-9625)
COIL WINDING SPECIALIST INC
Also Called: Cws
353 W Grove Ave, Orange (92865-3205)
PHONE....................714 279-9010
James Lau, *President*
Kian Chow, *Vice Pres*
Benny Ortiz, *Opers Mgr*
◆ **EMP:** 15 **EST:** 2006
SQ FT: 1,000
SALES (est): 4.9MM **Privately Held**
WEB: www.coilws.com
SIC: 3677 Inductors, electronic

(P-9626)
CORONA MAGNETICS INC
Also Called: C M I
201 Corporate Terrace St, Corona
(92879-6000)
P.O. Box 1355 (92878-1355)
PHONE....................951 735-7558
Jay Paasch, *CEO*
Heike Paasch, *COO*
Susan Paasch, *Executive*
Ubaldo Jimenez, *Engineer*
Jane King, *Human Resources*
EMP: 120 **EST:** 1968
SQ FT: 17,000
SALES (est): 12.8MM **Privately Held**
WEB: www.corona-magnetics.com
SIC: 3677 3679 Transformers power sup-
ply, electronic type; electronic circuits

(P-9627)
CUSTOM SUPPRESSION INC
Also Called: Csi
26470 Ruether Ave Ste 106, Santa Clarita
(91350-2972)
PHONE..................................818 718-1040
Edward C McSweeney Jr, *President*
Genevieve Mc Sweeney, *Admin Sec*
Phil Haber, *Controller*
Dee Noxon, *Sales Staff*
EMP: 17 **EST:** 1986
SQ FT: 7,000
SALES (est): 1.1MM **Privately Held**
SIC: 3677 3678 Filtration devices, electronic; electronic connectors

(P-9628)
DSPM INC
Also Called: Digital Signal Power Mfg
1921 S Quaker Ridge Pl, Ontario
(91761-8041)
PHONE..................................714 970-2304
Milton Hanson, *President*
Carey Neill, *Controller*
Pedro Esparza, *Sales Staff*
▲ **EMP:** 20 **EST:** 2003
SQ FT: 30,000
SALES (est): 5MM **Privately Held**
WEB: www.dspmanufacturing.com
SIC: 3677 Transformers power supply, electronic type

(P-9629)
DUCOMMUN INCORPORATED
Dbp Microwave Div
1321 Mountain View Cir, Azusa
(91702-1649)
P.O. Box 1062, Rancho Santa Fe (92067-1062)
PHONE..................................626 812-9666
EMP: 35
SALES (corp-wide): 550.6MM **Publicly Held**
SIC: 3677 3674 3625 3613 Mfg Electromechanical Switch
PA: Ducommun Incorporated
200 Sandpointe Ave # 700
Santa Ana CA 92707
657 335-3665

(P-9630)
FRONTIER ELECTRONICS CORP
667 Cochran St, Simi Valley (93065-1939)
PHONE..................................805 522-9998
Jeannie Gu, *President*
Winston Gu, *Vice Pres*
Jean Pope, *Controller*
Roy Talley, *Sales Mgr*
Sara Shinall, *Director*
▲ **EMP:** 18 **EST:** 1985
SQ FT: 15,246
SALES (est): 3.3MM **Privately Held**
WEB: www.frontierusa.com
SIC: 3677 3674 Inductors, electronic; transformers power supply, electronic type; semiconductors & related devices

(P-9631)
GENERAL LINEAR SYSTEMS INC
4332 Artesia Ave, Fullerton (92833-2523)
PHONE..................................714 994-4822
Garrett Hartney, *President*
Annette Hartney, *Treasurer*
James Mynatt, *Vice Pres*
Bill Hartnet, *Sales Staff*
Maria Ortega, *Manager*
EMP: 18 **EST:** 1972
SQ FT: 4,000
SALES (est): 2.5MM **Privately Held**
WEB: www.coilwinder.com
SIC: 3677 Electronic coils, transformers & other inductors

(P-9632)
MAGNOTEK MANUFACTURING INC
6510 Box Springs Blvd, Riverside
(92507-0740)
PHONE..................................951 653-8461
Donald K Furness, *CEO*
▲ **EMP:** 30 **EST:** 1989
SQ FT: 500

SALES (est): 1MM **Privately Held**
WEB: www.magnotek.com
SIC: 3677 Electronic transformers

(P-9633)
MAGTECH & POWER CONVERSION INC
Also Called: Speciality Labs
1146 E Ash Ave, Fullerton (92831-5018)
PHONE..................................714 451-0106
Viet Pho, *President*
Linh Pho, *Vice Pres*
Hien Pham, *Manager*
EMP: 40 **EST:** 1981
SQ FT: 9,000
SALES (est): 1MM **Privately Held**
WEB: www.magtechpower.com
SIC: 3677 Electronic transformers

(P-9634)
MERCURY MAGNETICS INC
Also Called: Gulf Enterprises
10050 Remmet Ave, Chatsworth
(91311-3854)
PHONE..................................818 998-7791
Sergio Hamernik, *President*
Susan Hamernik, *Vice Pres*
Carlen Walth, *Prdtn Mgr*
▲ **EMP:** 20 **EST:** 1968
SQ FT: 21,000
SALES (est): 2.5MM **Privately Held**
WEB: www.mercurymagnetics.com
SIC: 3677 Electronic transformers

(P-9635)
MIL-SPEC MAGNETICS INC
169 Pacific St, Pomona (91768-3215)
PHONE..................................909 598-8116
Shelton Gunewardena, *CEO*
Tony Gunewardena, *President*
Kris Gunewardena, *Vice Pres*
Andrew Gunewardena, *Principal*
Chrishani Anderson, *QC Mgr*
EMP: 30 **EST:** 1990
SQ FT: 6,000
SALES (est): 1MM **Privately Held**
WEB: www.milspecmag.com
SIC: 3677 3675 Electronic transformers; inductors, electronic; electronic capacitors

(P-9636)
PARKER-HANNIFIN CORPORATION
Also Called: Water Purification
19610 S Rancho Way, Rancho Dominguez
(90220-6039)
PHONE..................................310 608-5600
Jaime Garcia, *Principal*
Austin Finnegan, *Project Engr*
EMP: 150
SALES (corp-wide): 13.7B **Publicly Held**
WEB: www.parker.com
SIC: 3677 Filtration devices, electronic
PA: Parker-Hannifin Corporation
6035 Parkland Blvd
Cleveland OH 44124
216 896-3000

(P-9637)
PAYNE MAGNETICS INC
854 W Front St, Covina (91722-3614)
PHONE..................................626 332-6207
George Payne, *Chairman*
Jon S Payne, *President*
▲ **EMP:** 100 **EST:** 1982
SQ FT: 6,600
SALES (est): 9.7MM **Privately Held**
WEB: www.payne-magnetics.com
SIC: 3677 3699 Electronic transformers; inductors, electronic; electrical equipment & supplies

(P-9638)
PREMIER MAGNETICS INC
20381 Barents Sea Cir, Lake Forest
(92630-8807)
PHONE..................................949 452-0511
James Earley, *President*
Leslie Earley, *Broker*
▲ **EMP:** 30 **EST:** 1991
SALES (est): 5.7MM **Privately Held**
WEB: www.premiermag.com
SIC: 3677 3612 Electronic coils, transformers & other inductors; specialty transformers

(P-9639)
PUROFLUX CORPORATION
2121 Union Pl, Simi Valley (93065-1661)
PHONE..................................805 579-0216
Henry Nmi Greenberg, *President*
Kevin Carter, *Engineer*
Juan Lopez, *Purchasing*
Santos Lopez, *Purchasing*
▼ **EMP:** 17 **EST:** 1994
SQ FT: 25,000
SALES (est): 3.3MM **Privately Held**
WEB: www.puroflux.com
SIC: 3677 3613 Filtration devices, electronic; control panels, electric

(P-9640)
R H BARDEN INC
Also Called: Lodestone Pacific
4769 E Wesley Dr, Anaheim (92807-1941)
PHONE..................................714 970-0900
Richard H Barden III, *President*
Maurice Holmes, *Manager*
◆ **EMP:** 15 **EST:** 1988
SQ FT: 12,000
SALES (est): 2.3MM **Privately Held**
WEB: www.lodestonepacific.com
SIC: 3677 Electronic coils, transformers & other inductors

(P-9641)
RAYCO ELECTRONIC MFG INC
1220 W 130th St, Gardena (90247-1502)
PHONE..................................310 329-2660
Mahendra P Patel, *CEO*
Steve Mardani, *Vice Pres*
Mayan Patel, *Vice Pres*
EMP: 50 **EST:** 1941
SQ FT: 20,000
SALES (est): 9.8MM **Privately Held**
WEB: www.raycoelectronics.com
SIC: 3677 3612 3621 Electronic transformers; filtration devices, electronic; transformers, except electric; motors & generators

(P-9642)
ROBERT M HADLEY COMPANY INC
4054 Transport St, Ventura (93003-8323)
PHONE..................................805 658-7286
E Christopher Waian, *CEO*
Jim Hadley, *President*
Mary Hadley Waian, *Admin Sec*
Huly Ibarra, *Admin Asst*
Steve Krause, *Engineer*
EMP: 80 **EST:** 1929
SQ FT: 28,000
SALES (est): 8MM **Privately Held**
WEB: www.rmhco.com
SIC: 3677 Transformers power supply, electronic type

(P-9643)
RODON PRODUCTS INC
15481 Electronic Ln Ste A, Huntington
Beach (92649-1355)
PHONE..................................714 898-3528
Robert W Bertels Jr, *President*
Sandra Bertels, *Vice Pres*
Steve Freeman, *Vice Pres*
EMP: 13 **EST:** 1969
SALES (est): 1MM **Privately Held**
WEB: www.rodonproducts.com
SIC: 3677 3679 Electronic coils, transformers & other inductors; electronic circuits

(P-9644)
SI MANUFACTURING INC
1440 S Allec St, Anaheim (92805-6305)
PHONE..................................714 956-7110
James R Reed, *President*
Ata Shafizadeh, *Vice Pres*
Sandra Oropeza, *Controller*
▲ **EMP:** 50 **EST:** 2000
SALES (est): 11.7MM **Privately Held**
WEB: www.simfg.com
SIC: 3677 8711 3612 3613 Electronic coils, transformers & other inductors; engineering services; transformers, except electric; switchgear & switchboard apparatus; electronic loads & power supplies

(P-9645)
TUR-BO JET PRODUCTS CO INC
5025 Earle Ave, Rosemead (91770-1197)
PHONE..................................626 285-1294
Richard Bloom, *President*
Richard L Bloom, *Vice Pres*
Viviana Gomez, *Project Mgr*
Meisha Chavez, *Engineer*
Negwa Brownfield, *Accounting Mgr*
▲ **EMP:** 95 **EST:** 1945
SQ FT: 27,000
SALES (est): 12.9MM **Privately Held**
WEB: www.tbj.aero
SIC: 3677 Coil windings, electronic

3678 Electronic Connectors

(P-9646)
ADVANCED GLOBAL TECH GROUP
8015 E Treeview Ct, Anaheim
(92808-1553)
PHONE..................................714 281-8020
▲ **EMP:** 21
SALES: 2.5MM **Privately Held**
SIC: 3678 3652 4813 0191 Mfg & Product Sourcing

(P-9647)
ALPHA PRODUCTS INC
351 Irving Dr, Oxnard (93030-5173)
PHONE..................................805 981-8666
Tony Gulrajani, *President*
Lilian Compandium, *Purch Agent*
◆ **EMP:** 34 **EST:** 1978
SQ FT: 12,000
SALES (est): 2.1MM **Privately Held**
WEB: www.alpha-products.com
SIC: 3678 5065 Electronic connectors; electronic parts & equipment

(P-9648)
CLEARPATHGPS LLC
3463 State St 494, Santa Barbara
(93105-2662)
PHONE..................................805 979-3442
Christopher Fowler,
Steve Wells, *Managing Prtn*
EMP: 20 **EST:** 2013
SALES (est): 400K **Privately Held**
WEB: www.clearpathgps.com
SIC: 3678 Electronic connectors

(P-9649)
COMPONENT EQUIPMENT CO INC
Also Called: Ceco
3050 Camino Del Sol, Oxnard
(93030-7275)
PHONE..................................805 988-8004
Bill Rigby, *President*
Thomas Conway, *Vice Pres*
EMP: 26 **EST:** 1979
SQ FT: 32,000
SALES (est): 2.9MM **Privately Held**
WEB: www.ceco-inc.com
SIC: 3678 Electronic connectors

(P-9650)
CORSAIR ELEC CONNECTORS INC
17100 Murphy Ave, Irvine (92614-5916)
PHONE..................................949 833-0273
Amir Saket, *President*
Brian Pace, *Engrg Dir*
Steve Simmons, *Controller*
Margot Rodelli, *Human Res Dir*
Francisco Mendez, *Director*
EMP: 140 **EST:** 2009
SQ FT: 34,554
SALES (est): 20.4MM **Privately Held**
WEB: www.corsairelectricalconnectors.com
SIC: 3678 Electronic connectors

(P-9651)
CRISTEK INTERCONNECTS INC (HQ)
5395 E Hunter Ave, Anaheim (92807-2054)
PHONE..................................714 696-5200
Keith Barclay, *President*
Julie Barker, *COO*
John Pollock, *Vice Pres*
Chris Frueh, *General Mgr*

Corey Krueger, *Administration*
EMP: 135 **EST:** 1985
SALES (est): 55.2MM
SALES (corp-wide): 152.9MM **Privately Held**
WEB: www.cristek.com
SIC: 3678 Electronic connectors
PA: Hermetic Solutions Group Inc.
8 Neshaminy Interplex Dr # 221
Feasterville Trevose PA 19053
215 645-9420

(P-9652)
CS MANFACTURING INDUS SVCS INC (PA)
619 Paulin Ave Ste 105, Calexico
(92231-2671)
P.O. Box 2914 (92232-2914)
PHONE 760 890-7746
Cesar Samaniego Silva, *President*
EMP: 13 **EST:** 2008
SQ FT: 1,000
SALES (est): 3.4MM **Privately Held**
WEB: www.csmanufacture.com
SIC: 3678 Electronic connectors

(P-9653)
DETORONICS CORP
13071 Rosecrans Ave, Santa Fe Springs
(90670-4930)
PHONE 626 579-7130
Kenneth S Clark, *CEO*
Marcia Baroda, *CFO*
Louie Salas, *QC Mgr*
Jamie Saltos, *Marketing Staff*
Jerry Flores, *Manager*
EMP: 37 **EST:** 1959
SQ FT: 20,000
SALES (est): 4.9MM **Privately Held**
WEB: www.detoronics.com
SIC: 3678 Electronic connectors

(P-9654)
FLEXIBLE MANUFACTURING LLC
Also Called: F M I
1719 S Grand Ave, Santa Ana
(92705-4808)
PHONE 714 259-7996
Frank Meza,
Tom Rendina, *CFO*
Ross Silberfarb, *Vice Pres*
Bart Pacetti, *Program Mgr*
Dave Silberfarb, *Opers Mgr*
▲ **EMP:** 100 **EST:** 2001
SQ FT: 15,000
SALES (est): 10.3MM **Privately Held**
WEB: www.4fmi.com
SIC: 3678 Electronic connectors

(P-9655)
GLEN-MAC SWISS CO
12848 Weber Way, Hawthorne
(90250-5537)
PHONE 310 978-4555
Torkom Postajian, *President*
Armen Postajian, *Corp Secy*
▲ **EMP:** 42 **EST:** 1963
SQ FT: 12,676
SALES (est): 1MM **Privately Held**
WEB: www.screwmachineshop.net
SIC: 3678 3429 3451 3599 Electronic connectors; manufactured hardware (general); screw machine products; machine shop, jobbing & repair

(P-9656)
I O INTERCONNECT LTD (PA)
Also Called: I/O Interconnect
1041 W 18th St Ste A101, Costa Mesa
(92627-4583)
PHONE 714 564-1111
Gary Kung, *CEO*
Roland Balusek, *Vice Pres*
▲ **EMP:** 50 **EST:** 1985
SALES (est): 80.3MM **Privately Held**
WEB: www.ioint.com
SIC: 3678 3679 Electronic connectors; harness assemblies for electronic use: wire or cable

(P-9657)
INFINITE ELECTRONICS INTL INC (DH)
17792 Fitch, Irvine (92614-6020)
PHONE 949 261-1920
Penny Cotner, *CEO*
Jim Dauw, *COO*
Scott Rosner, *CFO*
Terry G Jarniga, *Chairman*
David Quinn, *Officer*
▲ **EMP:** 420 **EST:** 1972
SQ FT: 40,000
SALES (est): 231.4MM
SALES (corp-wide): 1.8B **Privately Held**
WEB: www.infiniteelectronics.com
SIC: 3678 3357 3651 3643 Electronic connectors; coaxial cable, nonferrous; household audio & video equipment; current-carrying wiring devices
HQ: Infinite Electronics, Inc.
17792 Fitch
Irvine CA 92614
949 261-1920

(P-9658)
J-T E C H
548 Amapola Ave, Torrance (90501-1472)
PHONE 310 533-6700
Walter Naubauer Jr, *Principal*
EMP: 136 **EST:** 1987
SALES (est): 14.1MM **Privately Held**
SIC: 3678 Electronic connectors

(P-9659)
JOSLYN SUNBANK COMPANY LLC
1740 Commerce Way, Paso Robles
(93446-3620)
PHONE 805 238-2840
Angel Cruz, *Principal*
Eric Lardiere,
Marlo Oliver,
EMP: 500 **EST:** 1997
SQ FT: 80,000
SALES (est): 4.8MM **Privately Held**
WEB: www.joslyn-sunbank-company-llc-in-paso-robles-ca.cityfos.com
SIC: 3678 3643 5065 Electronic connectors; connectors & terminals for electrical devices; connectors, electronic
HQ: Eaton Corporation
1000 Eaton Blvd
Cleveland OH 44122
440 523-5000

(P-9660)
L & M MACHINING CORPORATION
550 S Melrose St, Placentia (92870-6327)
PHONE 714 414-0923
Mike MAI, *President*
Troy Ferreira, *Opers Mgr*
EMP: 70 **EST:** 1985
SQ FT: 31,000
SALES (est): 14.4MM **Privately Held**
WEB: www.lmcnc.com
SIC: 3678 Electronic connectors

(P-9661)
MIN-E-CON LLC
17312 Eastman, Irvine (92614-5522)
PHONE 949 250-0087
Wendell Jacob, *Mng Member*
Charles Rosell, *Engineer*
Jack N Mica, *Mfg Dir*
Karyn Finch, *Marketing Mgr*
John M Brown,
▼ **EMP:** 60 **EST:** 1974
SALES (est): 9.9MM **Privately Held**
WEB: www.min-e-con.com
SIC: 3678 Electronic connectors

(P-9662)
NEA ELECTRONICS INC
14370 White Sage Rd, Moorpark
(93021-8720)
PHONE 805 292-4010
Steven Perkins, *President*
EMP: 24 **EST:** 1995
SQ FT: 20,000

SALES (est): 5.7MM
SALES (corp-wide): 696.3MM **Privately Held**
WEB: www.ebad.com
SIC: 3678 3629 3592 Electronic connectors; battery chargers, rectifying or nonrotating; valves
HQ: Ensign-Bickford Aerospace & Defense Co
640 Hopmeadow St
Simsbury CT 06070
860 843-2289

(P-9663)
P-W WIRING SYSTEMS LLC
Also Called: Pw Wiring Systems
9415 Kruse Rd, Pico Rivera (90660-1430)
PHONE 562 463-9055
Steven Koundouriotis,
EMP: 18 **EST:** 1996
SALES (est): 429.4K **Privately Held**
SIC: 3678 Electronic connectors

(P-9664)
R KERN ENGINEERING & MFG CORP
13912 Mountain Ave, Chino (91710-9018)
PHONE 909 664-2440
Richard Kern, *CEO*
Roland A Kern, *Ch of Bd*
Helga Kern, *Treasurer*
Jose Nunez, *Vice Pres*
Kevin Nunez, *Info Tech Dir*
▲ **EMP:** 54 **EST:** 1966
SQ FT: 34,000
SALES (est): 12.7MM **Privately Held**
WEB: www.kerneng.com
SIC: 3678 3599 Electronic connectors; machine shop, jobbing & repair

(P-9665)
TEKTEST INC
Also Called: E-Z-Hook Test Products Div
225 N 2nd Ave, Arcadia (91006-3286)
P.O. Box 660729 (91066-0729)
PHONE 626 446-6175
Phelps M Wood, *President*
Beverly Wood, *Vice Pres*
EMP: 20 **EST:** 1970
SQ FT: 24,000
SALES (est): 2.5MM **Privately Held**
WEB: www.e-z-hook.com
SIC: 3678 Electronic connectors

(P-9666)
ULTI-MATE CONNECTOR INC
1872 N Case St, Orange (92865-4233)
PHONE 714 637-7099
Ross Sealfon, *President*
Bruce I Billington, *CEO*
Thierry Pombart, *Vice Pres*
Isabel Mendoza, *Purchasing*
Luke Brockman, *Sales Staff*
▲ **EMP:** 113
SQ FT: 11,000
SALES (est): 8MM **Privately Held**
WEB: www.ultimateconnector.com
SIC: 3678 Electronic connectors

(P-9667)
UNIT INDUSTRIES INC (PA)
3122 Maple St, Santa Ana (92707-4408)
PHONE 714 871-4161
Anthony Codet, *President*
J W Abouchar, *CEO*
Lizabeth Mulligan Codet, *Admin Sec*
EMP: 19 **EST:** 1963
SQ FT: 16,000
SALES (est): 8.9MM **Privately Held**
WEB: www.unitindustriesgroup.com
SIC: 3678 Electronic connectors

3679 Electronic Components, NEC

(P-9668)
3Y POWER TECHNOLOGY INC
80 Bunsen, Irvine (92618-4210)
PHONE 949 450-0152
Yuan Yu, *President*
▲ **EMP:** 17 **EST:** 1985
SQ FT: 13,800

SALES (est): 2.8MM **Privately Held**
WEB: www.3ypower.com
SIC: 3679 Power supplies, all types: static; electronic circuits

(P-9669)
A R ELECTRONICS INC
Also Called: Audiolink
31290 Plantation Dr, Thousand Palms
(92276-6604)
PHONE 760 343-1200
Larry N Rich, *President*
Larry Rich, *President*
Cheryl Rich, *Admin Sec*
EMP: 27 **EST:** 1985
SQ FT: 10,000
SALES (est): 998.9K **Privately Held**
SIC: 3679 5065 Electronic circuits; electronic parts & equipment

(P-9670)
ACCRATRONICS SEALS CORPORATION
Also Called: A T S
2211 Kenmere Ave, Burbank (91504-3493)
PHONE 818 843-1500
William Fisch, *CEO*
Corby Jones, *President*
Delbert Jones, *Vice Pres*
Deken Jones, *Admin Sec*
EMP: 72 **EST:** 1960
SQ FT: 10,000
SALES (est): 8.3MM **Privately Held**
WEB: www.accratronics.com
SIC: 3679 Hermetic seals for electronic equipment

(P-9671)
ADCO PRODUCTS INC
23091 Mill Creek Dr, Laguna Hills
(92653-1258)
PHONE 937 339-6267
George Adkins, *President*
Randy Adkins, *Vice Pres*
EMP: 41 **EST:** 1980
SQ FT: 12,500
SALES (est): 963.5K **Privately Held**
SIC: 3679 2499 Electronic circuits; harness assemblies for electronic use: wire or cable; surveyors' stakes, wood

(P-9672)
ALYN INDUSTRIES INC
Also Called: Electronic Source Company
16028 Arminta St, Van Nuys (91406-1808)
PHONE 818 988-7696
Scott J Alyn, *CEO*
Nina Ning, *Program Dir*
Bobby Ferdosi, *Director*
Paul Friedenreich, *Director*
Maria De Jesus, *Manager*
▼ **EMP:** 100 **EST:** 1994
SALES (est): 19.4MM **Privately Held**
WEB: www.electronic-source.com
SIC: 3679 Electronic circuits

(P-9673)
AMERICAN AUDIO COMPONENT INC
Also Called: AAC
20 Fairbanks Ste 198, Irvine (92618-1673)
PHONE 909 596-3788
David Plekenpol, *CEO*
Richard Monk, *CFO*
Mark Cooper, *Vice Pres*
Willie Maglonso, *Manager*
▲ **EMP:** 26 **EST:** 1996
SALES (est): 9.9MM **Privately Held**
WEB: www.aactechnologies.com
SIC: 3679 Transducers, electrical
HQ: Aac Acoustic Technologies (Shenzhen) Co., Ltd.
(Office), 6/F, Block A, Nanjing University Technology Research B
Shenzhen 51805

(P-9674)
AMSCO US INC
15341 Texaco Ave, Paramount
(90723-3946)
PHONE 562 630-0333
Mike Yazdi, *President*
Victor Yazdi, *Vice Pres*
Karina Vega, *Purch Dir*
Tarane Yazdi, *VP Opers*

EMP: 110 EST: 1998
SALES (est): 11.4MM Privately Held
WEB: www.amscous.com
SIC: 3679 Harness assemblies for electronic use: wire or cable

(P-9675)
ARTECH INDUSTRIES INC
1966 Keats Dr, Riverside (92501-1747)
PHONE..............................951 276-3331
Mansukh R Bera, *President*
Girish Bera, *CFO*
Madan Bera, *Vice Pres*
▲ EMP: 23 EST: 1985
SQ FT: 24,500
SALES (est): 6.2MM Privately Held
WEB: www.artechloadcell.com
SIC: 3679 Loads, electronic

(P-9676)
ASTRO SEAL INC
827 Palmyrita Ave Ste B, Riverside
(92507-1820)
PHONE..............................951 787-6670
Michael Hammer, *President*
Karen Upfold, *Opers Staff*
Roger Hammer, *Director*
▲ EMP: 34 EST: 1964
SQ FT: 42,000
SALES (est): 4.7MM Privately Held
WEB: www.astroseal.com
SIC: 3679 3678 Hermetic seals for electronic equipment; electronic connectors

(P-9677)
ATLAS MAGNETICS INC
1121 N Kraemer Pl, Anaheim (92806-1923)
PHONE..............................714 632-9718
Maurice Brear, *CEO*
Shanon Togneri, *Controller*
Perry Preece, *VP Opers*
Jennifer Timbers, *Production*
EMP: 21 EST: 2008
SALES (est): 2.2MM Privately Held
WEB: www.atlasmagnetic.net
SIC: 3679 3592 Solenoids for electronic applications; valves, aircraft

(P-9678)
AULT GLOBAL HOLDINGS INC (PA)
201 Shipyard Way Ste E, Newport Beach
(92663-4452)
PHONE..............................949 444-5464
Milton C Ault III, *Ch of Bd*
William B Horne, *President*
Kenneth S Cragun, *CFO*
Henry Nisser, *Exec VP*
EMP: 23 EST: 1969
SQ FT: 2,983
SALES (est): 23.8MM Publicly Held
WEB: www.aultglobal.com
SIC: 3679 Electronic switches

(P-9679)
AZ DISPLAYS INC
75 Columbia, Aliso Viejo (92656-5386)
PHONE..............................949 831-5000
Reiner Moegling, *President*
▲ EMP: 50 EST: 1996
SALES (est): 10.1MM Privately Held
WEB: www.azdisplays.com
SIC: 3679 Liquid crystal displays (LCD)
HQ: American Zettler Inc.
75 Columbia
Aliso Viejo CA 92656
949 831-5000

(P-9680)
BASIC ELECTRONICS INC
11371 Monarch St, Garden Grove
(92841-1406)
PHONE..............................714 530-2400
Nancy Balzano, *President*
Al Balzano, *Vice Pres*
Aurora Medina, *Info Tech Dir*
EMP: 48 EST: 1967
SQ FT: 20,000
SALES (est): 3.4MM Privately Held
WEB: www.basicelectronicsinc.com
SIC: 3679 3672 3613 Electronic circuits; power supplies, all types: static; printed circuit boards; switchgear & switchboard apparatus

(P-9681)
BEATS ELECTRONICS LLC (PA)
Also Called: Beats By Dr. Dre
8600 Hayden Pl, Culver City (90232-2902)
PHONE..............................424 268-3055
EMP: 13 EST: 2010
SALES (est): 6.1MM Privately Held
SIC: 3679 3651 Mfg Electronic Components Mfg Home Audio/Video Equipment

(P-9682)
BI-SEARCH INTERNATIONAL INC
17550 Gillette Ave, Irvine (92614-5610)
PHONE..............................714 258-4500
Kevin Kim, *President*
Yong Su Kim, *CFO*
Channie Suh, *General Mgr*
Freddy Aceves, *Engineer*
Ken Cho, *Purchasing*
◆ EMP: 60 EST: 1996
SQ FT: 45,000
SALES (est): 25.1MM Privately Held
WEB: www.bisearch.com
SIC: 3679 Liquid crystal displays (LCD)

(P-9683)
BIVAR INC
4 Thomas, Irvine (92618-2593)
PHONE..............................949 951-8808
Thomas Silber, *CEO*
Ricardo Pereyra, *Engineer*
Lito Salvacion, *Engineer*
Reid Rice, *VP Finance*
Judy Moussette, *Human Res Mgr*
▲ EMP: 40 EST: 1965
SQ FT: 26,040
SALES (est): 7MM Privately Held
WEB: www.bivar.com
SIC: 3679 Electronic circuits

(P-9684)
C & A TRANSDUCERS INC
14329 Commerce Dr, Garden Grove
(92843-4949)
PHONE..............................714 554-9188
Daniel Toledo, *President*
EMP: 14 EST: 1976
SQ FT: 6,000
SALES (est): 1.1MM Privately Held
WEB: www.ca-transducers.com
SIC: 3679 3677 3674 Transducers, electrical; electronic coils, transformers & other inductors; semiconductors & related devices

(P-9685)
C & S ASSEMBLY INC
1150 N Armando St, Anaheim
(92806-2609)
PHONE..............................866 779-8939
Sandra A Foley, *President*
Christopher Foley, *Vice Pres*
EMP: 55 EST: 1997
SQ FT: 12,000
SALES (est): 11.1MM Privately Held
WEB: www.cnsassembly.com
SIC: 3679 5063 Harness assemblies for electronic use: wire or cable; electronic wire & cable

(P-9686)
CAC INC
20322 Windrow Dr Ste 100, Lake Forest
(92630-8150)
PHONE..............................949 587-3328
Patrick Redfern, *President*
▲ EMP: 30 EST: 1994
SALES (est): 2.8MM Privately Held
SIC: 3679 Electronic circuits

(P-9687)
CAL SOUTHERN BRAIDING INC
Also Called: Scb Division
7450 Scout Ave, Bell Gardens
(90201-4932)
PHONE..............................562 927-5531
Neal Castleman, *President*
EMP: 60 EST: 1976
SQ FT: 38,000
SALES (est): 14MM
SALES (corp-wide): 109.1MM Privately Held
WEB: www.dcxchol.com
SIC: 3679 Harness assemblies for electronic use: wire or cable

PA: Dcx-Chol Enterprises, Inc.
12831 S Figueroa St
Los Angeles CA 90061
310 516-1692

(P-9688)
CARDIGAN ROAD PRODUCTIONS
1999 Ave Of The Sts 110, Los Angeles
(90067)
PHONE..............................310 289-1442
Marc Friedland, *President*
EMP: 14 EST: 2001
SALES (est): 170.9K Privately Held
SIC: 3679 Electronic circuits

(P-9689)
CARROS AMERICAS INC
Also Called: Innovista Sensors
2945 Townsgate Rd Ste 200, Westlake Village (91361-5866)
PHONE..............................805 267-7176
Eric Pilaud, *President*
Ben Watt, *CFO*
Tae Rhee, *Vice Pres*
Olivier Clozeau, *Research*
Duncan Hynd, *Sales Staff*
EMP: 150 EST: 2015
SALES (est): 65.7MM
SALES (corp-wide): 675.4K Privately Held
WEB: www.crouzet.com
SIC: 3679 3577 Electronic circuits; encoders, computer peripheral equipment
HQ: Lbo France Gestion
148 Rue De L Universite
Paris 75007
140 627-767

(P-9690)
CELESCO TRANSDUCER PRODUCTS
20630 Plummer St, Chatsworth
(91311-5111)
PHONE..............................818 701-2701
Hernan Cortez, *Principal*
▲ EMP: 15 EST: 2013
SALES (est): 321.8K Privately Held
SIC: 3679 1541 Transducers, electrical; industrial buildings & warehouses

(P-9691)
CIAO WIRELESS INC
4000 Via Pescador, Camarillo
(93012-5044)
PHONE..............................805 389-3224
Glen Wasylewski, *President*
Etzon Garcia, *Marketing Staff*
▼ EMP: 70
SQ FT: 42,000
SALES (est): 15.6MM Privately Held
WEB: www.ciaowireless.com
SIC: 3679 3699 Microwave components; pulse amplifiers

(P-9692)
CICON ENGINEERING INC (PA)
6633 Odessa Ave, Van Nuys (91406-5746)
PHONE..............................818 909-6060
Ali Kolahi, *President*
Farah Kolahi, *Shareholder*
Peter Boskovich, *COO*
Abdi Kolahi, *Vice Pres*
Neenev Amirkhas, *Program Mgr*
EMP: 178 EST: 1990
SQ FT: 50,000
SALES (est): 51.3MM Privately Held
WEB: www.cicon.com
SIC: 3679 Harness assemblies for electronic use: wire or cable

(P-9693)
CLARY CORPORATION
150 E Huntington Dr, Monrovia
(91016-3415)
PHONE..............................626 359-4486
John G Clary, *Ch of Bd*
Donald G Ash, *Treasurer*
Craig Bolden, *Engineer*
Steven Espiritu, *Engineer*
Leo Tran, *Finance Dir*
EMP: 40 EST: 1939
SQ FT: 26,000

SALES (est): 9.8MM Privately Held
WEB: www.clary.com
SIC: 3679 3612 Electronic loads & power supplies; power supplies, all types: static; transformers, except electric

(P-9694)
COASTAL COMPONENT INDS INC
Also Called: C C I
133 E Bristol Ln, Orange (92865-2749)
PHONE..............................714 685-6677
Ronna Coe, *Chairman*
Mark Coe, *President*
Donald B Coe, *CFO*
Donald Coe, *CEO*
Diana Romero, *Vice Pres*
EMP: 20 EST: 1990
SQ FT: 6,027
SALES (est): 5.5MM Privately Held
WEB: www.ccicoastal.com
SIC: 3679 5065 3643 3678 Electronic circuits; electronic parts & equipment; electric connectors; electronic connectors; relays & industrial controls; manufactured hardware (general)

(P-9695)
CONSOLIDATED DEVICES INC (HQ)
Also Called: CDI Torque Products
19220 San Jose Ave, City of Industry
(91748-1417)
PHONE..............................626 965-0668
Michael King, *President*
Gary Keefe, *CEO*
▲ EMP: 25 EST: 1968
SQ FT: 90,000
SALES (est): 21.5MM
SALES (corp-wide): 3.5B Publicly Held
WEB: www.cditorque.com
SIC: 5251 3679 3625 5072 Tools; transducers, electrical; control equipment, electric; hardware
PA: Snap-On Incorporated
2801 80th St
Kenosha WI 53143
262 656-5200

(P-9696)
CORELIS INC
13100 Alondra Blvd # 102, Cerritos
(90703-2262)
PHONE..............................562 926-6727
George Lafever, *CEO*
George La Fever, *Vice Pres*
Terri Martinez, *Administration*
Doug Brandon, *Sr Software Eng*
Brian Park, *Sr Software Eng*
EMP: 25 EST: 1991
SQ FT: 15,000
SALES (est): 6.7MM
SALES (corp-wide): 128.5MM Privately Held
WEB: www.corelis.com
SIC: 3679 Electronic circuits
PA: Electronic Warfare Associates, Inc.
13873 Park Center Rd 500s
Herndon VA 20171
703 904-5700

(P-9697)
CRUCIAL POWER PRODUCTS
14000 S Broadway, Los Angeles
(90061-1018)
PHONE..............................323 721-5017
Abbie Gougerchian, *Principal*
Alan Stone, *Vice Pres*
Martin Corral, *Manager*
EMP: 24 EST: 1992
SALES (est): 717.7K Privately Held
WEB: www.crucialpower.com
SIC: 3679 Electronic circuits

(P-9698)
CRYSTAL CAL LAB INC
3981 E Miraloma Ave, Anaheim
(92806-6201)
PHONE..............................714 991-1580
EMP: 26
SQ FT: 7,600
SALES (est): 3MM Privately Held
SIC: 3679 3825 Mfg Electronic Components Mfg Electrical Measuring Instruments

(P-9699)
CUSTOM SENSORS & TECH INC (HQ)
Also Called: C S T
1461 Lawrence Dr, Thousand Oaks (91320-1303)
PHONE..................805 716-0322
Martha Sullivan, *CEO*
Dawn Batey, *Vice Pres*
Remi Chazalmartin, *General Mgr*
Diane Amodia, *IT/INT Sup*
Jeffrey Cote, *Director*
▲ EMP: 2161 EST: 1997
SALES (est): 597.9MM
SALES (corp-wide): 3B **Privately Held**
WEB: www.sensata.com
SIC: 3679 Electronic circuits

(P-9700)
DCX-CHOL ENTERPRISES INC
Also Called: Scb Division of Dcx-Chol
7450 Scout Ave, Bell (90201-4932)
PHONE..................562 927-5531
Ben Dose, *Branch Mgr*
EMP: 44
SALES (corp-wide): 109.1MM **Privately Held**
WEB: www.dcxchol.com
SIC: 3679 Harness assemblies for electronic use: wire or cable
PA: Dcx-Chol Enterprises, Inc.
　12831 S Figueroa St
　Los Angeles CA 90061
　310 516-1692

(P-9701)
DYNALLOY INC
1562 Reynolds Ave, Irvine (92614-5612)
PHONE..................714 436-1206
Wayne Brown, *CEO*
Jess Brown, *Vice Pres*
EMP: 20 EST: 1989
SQ FT: 8,000
SALES (est): 4.3MM **Privately Held**
WEB: www.dynalloy.com
SIC: 3679 3357 5065 Electronic circuits; nonferrous wiredrawing & insulating; electronic parts

(P-9702)
DYTRAN INSTRUMENTS INC
21592 Marilla St, Chatsworth (91311-4137)
PHONE..................818 700-7818
Michael Change, *President*
Nicholas D Change II, *President*
Dave Change, *Vice Pres*
Anne Hackney, *Vice Pres*
Stacey Westfall, *Vice Pres*
EMP: 160
SQ FT: 8,000
SALES (est): 29.9MM **Privately Held**
WEB: www.dytran.com
SIC: 3679 3829 Transducers, electrical; measuring & controlling devices

(P-9703)
ECLIPTEK INC
24422 Avnida De La Crlota Carlota, Laguna Hills (92653)
PHONE..................714 433-1200
Cary Rosen, *CEO*
EMP: 15 EST: 1987
SALES (est): 3.8MM **Privately Held**
WEB: www.abracon.com
SIC: 3679 5065 3825 3677 Electronic crystals; electronic parts & equipment; instruments to measure electricity; electronic coils, transformers & other inductors

(P-9704)
ELECTRO SWITCH CORP
Also Called: Arga Cntrls A Unit Elctro Swtc
10410 Trademark St, Rancho Cucamonga (91730-5826)
PHONE..................909 581-0855
Kathy Brown, *Branch Mgr*
Aneta Montgomery, *Engineer*
Ray Feigenbaum, *Manager*
George Tango, *Manager*
EMP: 26
SALES (corp-wide): 103.8MM **Privately Held**
WEB: www.electroswitch.com
SIC: 3679 Transducers, electrical

HQ: Electro Switch Corp.
　775 Pleasant St Ste 1
　Weymouth MA 02189
　781 335-1195

(P-9705)
ELECTRO-SUPPORT SYSTEMS CORP
Also Called: IMS-Ess
27449 Colt Ct, Temecula (92590-3674)
P.O. Box 50067, Irvine (92619-0067)
PHONE..................951 676-2751
Richard Olson, *President*
Mark Bridgeford, *Admin Sec*
EMP: 51 EST: 1977
SQ FT: 12,500
SALES (est): 1MM **Privately Held**
WEB: www.esupportsys.com
SIC: 3679 3845 3728 Mfg Electronic Components Mfg Electromedical Equipment Mfg Aircraft Parts/Equipment

(P-9706)
ELECTRO-TECH PRODUCTS INC
2001 E Gladstone St Ste A, Glendora (91740-5381)
PHONE..................909 592-1434
Ramzi Bader, *President*
Suzane Bader, *CFO*
Christopher Bader, *Opers Staff*
▲ EMP: 30 EST: 1984
SQ FT: 11,000
SALES (est): 4.8MM **Privately Held**
WEB: www.etp-inc.com
SIC: 3679 Electronic circuits; power supplies, all types: static

(P-9707)
ELECTROCUBE INC (PA)
Also Called: Southern Electronics
3366 Pomona Blvd, Pomona (91768-3234)
PHONE..................909 595-1821
Langdon Clay Parrill, *President*
Don Duquette, *Vice Pres*
Donald Duquette, *Vice Pres*
Scott Wieland, *Principal*
William Jaacks, *Senior Engr*
◆ EMP: 61 EST: 1961
SQ FT: 27,000
SALES (est): 10MM **Privately Held**
WEB: www.electrocube.com
SIC: 3679 3675 Electronic circuits; electronic capacitors

(P-9708)
EMAC ASSEMBLY CORP
21615 Parthenia St, Canoga Park (91304-1517)
PHONE..................818 882-2999
Lupe Garcia, *President*
EMP: 13 EST: 2005
SALES (est): 917.6K **Privately Held**
WEB: www.emacassembly.com
SIC: 3679 3469 Electronic circuits; stamping metal for the trade

(P-9709)
EMI SOLUTIONS INC
13805 Alton Pkwy Ste B, Irvine (92618-1690)
PHONE..................949 206-9960
Julie Ydens, *Ch of Bd*
Bob Ydens, *President*
Robert Zarrow, *Business Dir*
Sue Lester, *Office Mgr*
Justin Von, *QC Mgr*
▼ EMP: 18 EST: 1997
SQ FT: 6,500
SALES (est): 3.7MM **Privately Held**
WEB: www.4emi.com
SIC: 3679 Electronic circuits

(P-9710)
EXPRESS MANUFACTURING INC (PA)
3519 W Warner Ave, Santa Ana (92704-5214)
PHONE..................714 979-2228
Chauk Pan Chin, *President*
Catherine Lee Chin, *Treasurer*
C M Chin, *Vice Pres*
CP Chin, *Vice Pres*
Stana Marko, *Vice Pres*
▲ EMP: 497 EST: 1982

SQ FT: 96,000
SALES (est): 126.4MM **Privately Held**
WEB: www.eminc.com
SIC: 3679 3672 Electronic circuits; printed circuit boards

(P-9711)
FABRICAST INC (PA)
2517 Seaman Ave, South El Monte (91733-1927)
P.O. Box 3176 (91733-0176)
PHONE..................626 443-3247
H Phelps Wood III, *President*
Phelps Wood, *CIO*
EMP: 21 EST: 1960
SQ FT: 6,250
SALES (est): 3.4MM **Privately Held**
WEB: www.fabricast.com
SIC: 3679 3621 Electronic circuits; motors & generators

(P-9712)
FEMA ELECTRONICS CORPORATION
22 Corporate Park, Irvine (92606-3112)
PHONE..................714 825-0140
Bob Cheng, *CEO*
Chinyun Cheng, *Treasurer*
Cliff Cheng, *Vice Pres*
George Cheng, *Vice Pres*
Michael Decrescio, *Chief*
▲ EMP: 30 EST: 2010
SQ FT: 3,000
SALES (est): 4MM **Privately Held**
WEB: www.femacorp.com
SIC: 3679 Electronic crystals

(P-9713)
FOX ENTERPRISES LLC (HQ)
Also Called: Fox Electronics
24422 Avnida De La Crlota Carlota, Laguna Hills (92653)
PHONE..................239 693-0099
Eugene Trefethen, *President*
John Fallisgaard, *Treasurer*
Eleanor J Fox, *Vice Pres*
Ross O Weiss, *Vice Pres*
Kathy Richie, *Opers Mgr*
EMP: 41 EST: 1979
SALES (est): 24.1MM **Privately Held**
WEB: www.abracon.com
SIC: 3679 5065 Quartz crystals, for electronic application; electronic parts

(P-9714)
GAR ENTERPRISES
Also Called: K.G.S.electronics
1396 W 9th St, Upland (91786-5724)
PHONE..................909 985-4575
Alex Morales, *Manager*
EMP: 28
SALES (corp-wide): 23MM **Privately Held**
WEB: www.kgselectronics.com
SIC: 3679 3621 3577 Electronic loads & power supplies; motors & generators; computer peripheral equipment
PA: Gar Enterprises
　418 E Live Oak Ave
　Arcadia CA 91006
　626 574-1175

(P-9715)
GAVIAL HOLDINGS INC (PA)
Also Called: Gavial Engineering & Mfg
1435 W Mccoy Ln, Santa Maria (93455-1002)
PHONE..................805 614-0060
Morgan Maxwell Connor, *CEO*
Cathy Castor, *Office Mgr*
George Ayala, *Project Engr*
Ramona Castano, *Opers Mgr*
Lloyd Todd, *QC Mgr*
EMP: 15 EST: 1981
SQ FT: 24,500
SALES (est): 84.3MM **Privately Held**
WEB: www.gavial.com
SIC: 3679 4911 6799 Electronic circuits; electric services; investors

(P-9716)
GENERAL POWER SYSTEMS INC
955 E Ball Rd, Anaheim (92805-5916)
PHONE..................714 956-9321
David Noyes, *President*

Frank Castle, *President*
Jim Edman, *Vice Pres*
William Powell, *Controller*
EMP: 30
SQ FT: 30,000
SALES (est): 7.3MM
SALES (corp-wide): 44.2MM **Privately Held**
WEB: www.ccoadallas.com
SIC: 3679 Power supplies, all types: static
PA: Components Corporation Of America
　5950 Berkshire Ln # 1500
　Dallas TX 75225
　214 969-0166

(P-9717)
GES US (NEW ENGLAND) INC
1051 S East St, Anaheim (92805-5749)
PHONE..................978 459-4434
Riachard Pelletier, *General Mgr*
EMP: 114 EST: 1986
SQ FT: 70,000
SALES (est): 8.1MM **Privately Held**
WEB: www.41ststreetdelifl.com
SIC: 3679 3672 Electronic circuits; printed circuit boards
HQ: Ges Investment Pte. Ltd.
　28 Marsiling Lane
　Singapore 73915

(P-9718)
GIGATERA COMMUNICATIONS
Also Called: KMW Communications
1818 E Orangethorpe Ave, Fullerton (92831-5324)
PHONE..................714 515-1100
Duk Y Kim, *Ch of Bd*
Burton Calloway, *Vice Pres*
Yeong Kim, *Vice Pres*
Sunghwan Lim, *Software Engr*
James Chang, *Engineer*
▲ EMP: 65 EST: 1995
SQ FT: 4,500
SALES (est): 10.7MM **Privately Held**
WEB: www.kmw.co.kr
SIC: 3679 5063 Electronic circuits; electrical apparatus & equipment
PA: Kmw Inc.
　21 Dongtan-Daero 25-Gil
　Hwaseong 18462

(P-9719)
GTRAN INC (PA)
829 Flynn Rd, Camarillo (93012-8702)
PHONE..................805 445-4500
Ray Yu, *President*
Deepak Mehrotra, *CEO*
Douglas Holmes, *Vice Pres*
▲ EMP: 46 EST: 1999
SQ FT: 226,000
SALES (est): 7.1MM **Privately Held**
WEB: www.gtran.com
SIC: 3679 Electronic circuits

(P-9720)
HARPER & TWO INC (PA)
2937 Cherry Ave, Signal Hill (90755-1910)
PHONE..................562 424-3030
Dan Kilstofte, *President*
Jim Quilty, *Admin Sec*
EMP: 18 EST: 1987
SALES (est): 2.7MM **Privately Held**
WEB: www.harperandtwo.com
SIC: 3679 Electronic circuits

(P-9721)
HARWIL PRECISION PRODUCTS
541 Kinetic Dr, Oxnard (93030-7923)
PHONE..................805 988-6800
Geoffrey Strand, *President*
Teresa Bowmar, *Treasurer*
Cynthia Strand, *Admin Sec*
Ellis Anderson, *Sales Executive*
EMP: 35 EST: 1957
SQ FT: 33,000
SALES (est): 5.5MM **Privately Held**
SIC: 3679 3625 3823 Electronic circuits; flow actuated electrical switches; industrial instrmnts msrmnt display/control process variable

(P-9722)
HERMETIC SEAL CORPORATION (DH)
Also Called: Ametek HCC
4232 Temple City Blvd, Rosemead
(91770-1592)
PHONE.................626 443-8931
Andrew Goldfarb, *President*
Ronda Ross, *Vice Pres*
Alfred Enu-Kwesi, *Technician*
EMP: 200 EST: 1945
SQ FT: 36,000
SALES (est): 69MM
SALES (corp-wide): 4.5B **Publicly Held**
WEB: www.ametek-ecp.com
SIC: 3679 3469 Hermetic seals for electronic equipment; metal stampings
HQ: Hcc Industries Leasing, Inc.
4232 Temple City Blvd
Rosemead CA 91770
626 443-8933

(P-9723)
I SOURCE TECHNICAL SVCS INC (PA)
5 Rancho Cir, Lake Forest (92630-8324)
PHONE.................949 453-1500
Irene Horvath, *President*
David Tuza, *General Mgr*
Dora Tuza, *Marketing Staff*
EMP: 14 EST: 1990
SALES (est): 2.5MM **Privately Held**
WEB: www.i-source.com
SIC: 3679 Electronic circuits

(P-9724)
IJ RESEARCH INC
2919 S Tech Center Dr, Santa Ana
(92705-5657)
PHONE.................714 546-8522
Rick Yoon, *President*
Robert Perez, *Production*
Carla Guzman, *Manager*
◆ EMP: 35 EST: 1988
SQ FT: 12,500
SALES (est): 5.4MM
SALES (corp-wide): 97.7MM **Privately Held**
WEB: www.ijresearch.com
SIC: 3679 Hermetic seals for electronic equipment
HQ: Superior Technical Ceramics Corporation
600 Industrial Park Rd
Saint Albans VT 05478
802 527-7726

(P-9725)
IMPACT LLC
22521 Avenida Empresa # 107, Rcho STA Marg (92688-2041)
PHONE.................714 546-6000
Phil Laney,
Tim Scanlon, *Vice Pres*
Irina Williams, *General Mgr*
EMP: 28 EST: 1998
SALES (est): 2.8MM **Privately Held**
WEB: www.digitalmarketing-online.com
SIC: 3679 3829 Electronic circuits; measuring & controlling devices

(P-9726)
INFINITE ELECTRONICS INC (HQ)
17792 Fitch, Irvine (92614-6020)
PHONE.................949 261-1920
Penny Cotner, *President*
Jim Dauw, *COO*
Emily Campbell, *Chief Mktg Ofcr*
Mike Braun, *Vice Pres*
Jeff Bsee, *Vice Pres*
EMP: 100 EST: 2007
SQ FT: 40,000
SALES (est): 369.3MM
SALES (corp-wide): 1.8B **Privately Held**
WEB: www.infiniteelectronics.com
SIC: 3679 Electronic circuits
PA: Warburg Pincus Llc
450 Lexington Ave Fl 32
New York NY 10017
212 878-0600

(P-9727)
INTERCONNECT SOLUTIONS CO LLC
17595 Mount Herrmann St, Fountain Valley
(92708-4160)
PHONE.................714 556-7007
Michael Engler, *Branch Mgr*
EMP: 119
SALES (corp-wide): 24.3MM **Privately Held**
WEB: www.interconnectsolutions.com
SIC: 3679 5065 Harness assemblies for electronic use: wire or cable; electronic parts & equipment
PA: Interconnect Solutions Company, Llc
17595 Mount Herrmann St
Fountain Valley CA 92708
909 545-6140

(P-9728)
INTERCTIVE DSPLAY SLUTIONS INC
490 Wald, Irvine (92618-4638)
PHONE.................949 727-1959
Brian Chung, *President*
Paul Kitzerow, *Senior VP*
Son Park, *Vice Pres*
Danny Lee, *Director*
Dione Randell-Page, *Manager*
▲ EMP: 26 EST: 2004
SALES (est): 15MM **Privately Held**
WEB: www.idsdisplay.com
SIC: 3679 Liquid crystal displays (LCD)

(P-9729)
INTERLINK ELECTRONICS INC (PA)
1 Jenner Ste 200, Irvine (92618-3844)
PHONE.................805 484-8855
Steven N Bronson, *Ch of Bd*
Ryan J Hoffman, *CFO*
Albert Lu, *Vice Pres*
Luis Garcia, *Engineer*
Garrett Hess, *Marketing Staff*
▲ EMP: 82 EST: 1985
SQ FT: 4,351
SALES (est): 6.8MM **Publicly Held**
WEB: www.interlinkelectronics.com
SIC: 3679 Electronic circuits

(P-9730)
INTERLOG CORPORATION
Also Called: Interlog Construction
1295 N Knollwood Cir, Anaheim
(92801-1310)
PHONE.................714 529-7808
Justin H Kwon, *CEO*
Paul Kim, *Executive*
Nathanael Kim, *Info Tech Mgr*
Andy Peng, *Engineer*
▲ EMP: 20 EST: 1989
SALES (est): 5.8MM **Privately Held**
WEB: www.interlogcorp.com
SIC: 3679 Electronic circuits

(P-9731)
IQD FREQUENCY PRODUCTS INC
592 N Tercero Cir, Palm Springs
(92262-6243)
PHONE.................408 250-1435
Neil Floodgate, *President*
EMP: 43 EST: 2010
SALES (est): 10.8MM
SALES (corp-wide): 17B **Privately Held**
WEB: www.iqdfrequencyproducts.com
SIC: 3679 Microwave components
HQ: Iqd Frequency Products Limited
Station Road
Crewkerne
146 027-0200

(P-9732)
J L COOPER ELECTRONICS INC
Also Called: Jlcooper
142 Arena St, El Segundo (90245-3901)
PHONE.................310 322-9990
James Loren Cooper, *President*
Mark Van Kirk, *Director*
▲ EMP: 48 EST: 1981
SALES (est): 9.7MM **Privately Held**
WEB: www.jlcooper.com
SIC: 3679 Recording & playback apparatus, including phonograph

(P-9733)
J R V PRODUCTS INC
1314 N Harbor Blvd # 302, Santa Ana
(92703-1300)
P.O. Box 5645, Orange (92863-5645)
PHONE.................714 259-9772
Curt Shoup, *President*
John Beckingham, *President*
▲ EMP: 20 EST: 1989
SQ FT: 6,000
SALES (est): 990K **Privately Held**
WEB: www.jrvproductsinc.com
SIC: 3679 Electronic switches; electronic circuits; electronic loads & power supplies

(P-9734)
JASPER ELECTRONICS
1580 N Kellogg Dr, Anaheim (92807-1902)
PHONE.................714 917-0749
Robert Nishimoto, *CEO*
Hiroshi Tango, *Chairman*
Jeanine Urban, *Purch Agent*
Rob Nishimoto, *Manager*
◆ EMP: 30 EST: 1995
SQ FT: 17,000
SALES (est): 5.5MM **Privately Held**
WEB: www.jasperelectronics.com
SIC: 3679 Electronic loads & power supplies; power supplies, all types: static

(P-9735)
JAXX MANUFACTURING INC
Also Called: Craig Kackert Design Tech
1912 Angus Ave, Simi Valley (93063-3494)
PHONE.................805 526-4979
Greg Liu, *President*
Veronica Liu, *Office Mgr*
Dan Smith, *Info Tech Mgr*
EMP: 45 EST: 2001
SALES (est): 7.9MM **Privately Held**
WEB: www.jaxxmfg.com
SIC: 3679 Electronic circuits

(P-9736)
JAYCO INTERFACE TECHNOLOGY INC
1351 Pico St, Corona (92881-3373)
PHONE.................951 738-2000
Hemant Mistry, *President*
Shaila RAO, *Treasurer*
EMP: 33 EST: 1980
SQ FT: 23,000
SALES (est): 4.6MM **Privately Held**
SIC: 3679 5065 Electronic circuits; electronic parts & equipment

(P-9737)
JAYCO/MMI INC
1351 Pico St, Corona (92881-3373)
PHONE.................951 738-2000
Shaila Mistry, *President*
Hemant Mistry, *Vice Pres*
EMP: 42 EST: 1992
SQ FT: 24,000
SALES (est): 3MM **Privately Held**
WEB: www.jaycopanels.com
SIC: 3679 5065 3577 2759 Electronic circuits; electronic parts & equipment; computer peripheral equipment; commercial printing; engineering services

(P-9738)
KAVLICO CORPORATION (DH)
1461 Lawrence Dr, Thousand Oaks
(91320-1303)
PHONE.................805 523-2000
Martha Sullivan, *President*
Eric Prisk, *Prgrmr*
Lisa Chung, *Technician*
Nicolas Cortes, *Engineer*
Magdalena Manlulu, *Production*
▼ EMP: 1390 EST: 1958
SQ FT: 284,000
SALES (est): 236.8MM
SALES (corp-wide): 3B **Privately Held**
WEB: www.sensata.com
SIC: 3679 3829 3823 Transducers, electrical; measuring & controlling devices; industrial instrmnts msrmnt display/control process variable
HQ: Custom Sensors & Technologies, Inc.
1461 Lawrence Dr
Thousand Oaks CA 91320
805 716-0322

(P-9739)
KRITECH CORPORATION (PA)
333 W 131st St, Los Angeles (90061-1103)
P.O. Box 88637 (90009-8637)
PHONE.................310 538-9940
EMP: 15
SQ FT: 6,000
SALES (est): 1.3MM **Privately Held**
SIC: 3679 3053 Electronic Components, Nec, Nsk

(P-9740)
LIBRA CABLE TECHNOLOGIES INC
Monterey Business Park 27, Torrance
(90503)
PHONE.................310 618-8182
Palle Gravesen Jensen, *CEO*
Anne Sletto, *Sales Staff*
EMP: 14 EST: 2013
SALES (est): 5.1MM **Privately Held**
WEB: www.libracabletechnologies.com
SIC: 3679 Harness assemblies for electronic use: wire or cable
PA: Electronic House Uab
Dariaus Ir Gireno G. 149
Vilnius LT-02

(P-9741)
LIGHTCROSS INC
2630 Corporate Pl, Monterey Park
(91754-7645)
PHONE.................626 236-4500
Robert Barron, *President*
Daniel Kim, *Corp Secy*
Tom Smith, *Vice Pres*
EMP: 13 EST: 2000
SQ FT: 23,000
SALES (est): 196.1K **Privately Held**
WEB: www.lightcross.com
SIC: 3679 Electronic circuits

(P-9742)
LUCIX CORPORATION (HQ)
800 Avenida Acaso Ste E, Camarillo
(93012-8758)
PHONE.................805 987-6645
Mark Shahriary, *President*
Cheryl Johnson, *CFO*
D Ick Fanucchi, *Vice Pres*
▲ EMP: 83 EST: 1999
SQ FT: 48,000
SALES (est): 46.5MM **Publicly Held**
WEB: www.lucix.com
SIC: 3679 8731 Microwave components; commercial physical research

(P-9743)
LUCIX CORPORATION
3883 Via Pescador, Camarillo
(93012-5053)
PHONE.................805 987-3677
Matthew Rose, *Manager*
EMP: 57 **Publicly Held**
WEB: www.lucix.com
SIC: 3679 8731 Microwave components; commercial physical research
HQ: Lucix Corporation
800 Avenida Acaso Ste E
Camarillo CA 93012
805 987-6645

(P-9744)
MAGNETIC DESIGN LABS INC
1636 E Edinger Ave Ste H, Santa Ana
(92705-5020)
PHONE.................714 558-3355
ABI Kazem, *Principal*
Judith Kazem, *President*
Judith A Kazem, *CEO*
Kamran Kazem, *Vice Pres*
Virginia Montoya, *Purch Mgr*
EMP: 15 EST: 1985
SQ FT: 6,000
SALES (est): 2.8MM **Privately Held**
WEB: www.magneticdesign.com
SIC: 3679 5065 Power supplies, all types: static; electronic parts & equipment

(P-9745)
MAGNETIC SENSORS CORPORATION
1365 N Mccan St, Anaheim (92806-1316)
PHONE.................714 630-8380

Charles Boudakian, *President*
M Amirkhizi, *COO*
Don Payne, *Vice Pres*
Brenda Crain, *Office Mgr*
Njteh Bourjlian, *CIO*
EMP: 43 **EST:** 1983
SQ FT: 15,000
SALES (est): 8.2MM **Privately Held**
WEB: www.magsensors.com
SIC: 3679 3677 Transducers, electrical; coil windings, electronic

(P-9746)
MASK TECHNOLOGY INC
2601 Oak St, Santa Ana (92707-3720)
PHONE....................714 557-3383
Andrew Holzmann, *President*
Joanne Deblis, *Director*
EMP: 22 **EST:** 1983
SQ FT: 9,800
SALES (est): 1.1MM **Privately Held**
WEB: www.masktek.com
SIC: 3679 Electronic circuits

(P-9747)
MEMBRANE SWITCH AND PANEL INC
3198 Arprt Loop Dr Ste K, Costa Mesa (92626)
PHONE....................714 957-6905
John B Corzine, *President*
EMP: 29 **EST:** 2007
SQ FT: 5,000
SALES (est): 2.1MM **Privately Held**
WEB: www.membraneusa.com
SIC: 3679 Antennas, receiving

(P-9748)
MERCURY UNITED ELECTRONICS INC
Also Called: Global Electronics Intl
9804 Cres Ctr Dr Ste 603, Rancho Cucamonga (91730-5782)
PHONE....................909 466-0427
Chih-Hsun Yen, *CEO*
Jason Yen, *President*
Jean Hsi, *Corp Secy*
Jyh Yaw Yen, *Vice Pres*
Marty Yen, *Sales Staff*
EMP: 17 **EST:** 1990
SQ FT: 8,460
SALES (est): 1.8MM **Privately Held**
WEB: www.mercuryunited.com
SIC: 3679 5065 Quartz crystals, for electronic application; paging & signaling equipment

(P-9749)
MICROFABRICA INC
7911 Haskell Ave, Van Nuys (91406-1909)
PHONE....................888 964-2763
Eric Miller, *Principal*
Uri Frodis, *Senior VP*
Richard Chen, *Vice Pres*
Paolo Cocchiglia, *Vice Pres*
Greg Schmitz, *Vice Pres*
EMP: 50 **EST:** 1999
SQ FT: 39,000
SALES (est): 12.4MM **Privately Held**
WEB: www.microfabrica.com
SIC: 3679 Electronic circuits

(P-9750)
MICROMETALS INC (PA)
5615 E La Palma Ave, Anaheim (92807-2109)
PHONE....................714 970-9400
Richard H Barden, *CEO*
Teresa Longridge, *Purch Agent*
George Bradley, *Safety Mgr*
Bill Kemper, *Mfg Mgr*
James Fisher, *VP Sales*
◆ **EMP:** 146 **EST:** 1951
SQ FT: 50,000
SALES (est): 37.3MM **Privately Held**
WEB: www.micrometals.com
SIC: 3679 Cores, magnetic

(P-9751)
MINATRONIC INC
1139 13th St, Paso Robles (93446-2644)
PHONE....................805 239-8864
Max Clinger, *President*
David Kudija, *Executive*
EMP: 18 **EST:** 1962

SALES (est): 508.9K **Privately Held**
SIC: 3679 5065 Electronic circuits; electronic parts & equipment

(P-9752)
MITSUBSHI ELC VSUAL SLTONS AME
Also Called: Mevsa
10833 Valley View St # 300, Cypress (90630-5046)
PHONE....................800 553-7278
Kenichiro Yamanishi, *Chairman*
Tadashi Hiraoka, *CEO*
Perry Pappous, *Admin Sec*
◆ **EMP:** 150 **EST:** 2011
SALES (est): 29.9MM **Privately Held**
WEB: www.me-vis.com
SIC: 3679 Liquid crystal displays (LCD)
PA: Mitsubishi Electric Corporation
2-7-3, Marunouchi
Chiyoda-Ku TKY 100-0

(P-9753)
MULTIMEDIA LED INC (PA)
4225 Prado Rd Ste 108, Corona (92878-7443)
PHONE....................951 280-7500
Steven Craig, *CEO*
Alex Birner, *President*
Rick Vanrensselaer, *Engineer*
Ernest Lai, *Controller*
▲ **EMP:** 14 **EST:** 2000
SALES (est): 1.6MM **Privately Held**
WEB: www.multimedialed.com
SIC: 3679 Electronic circuits

(P-9754)
MUZIK INC (PA)
9220 W Sunset Blvd # 112, West Hollywood (90069-3500)
PHONE....................646 345-6500
Jason Hardi, *CEO*
Joakim Ostarson, *COO*
Marc Greenspoon, *Officer*
EMP: 34 **EST:** 2013
SQ FT: 4,140
SALES (est): 3.8MM **Privately Held**
WEB: www.muzikconnect.com
SIC: 3679 Headphones, radio

(P-9755)
NATEL ENGINEERING COMPANY LLC (PA)
Also Called: Neo Tech
9340 Owensmouth Ave, Chatsworth (91311-6915)
PHONE....................818 495-8617
Sudesh K Arora, *President*
James Howe, *Vice Pres*
Mark Darrow, *Business Dir*
Anthony Lautieri, *Business Dir*
Rene Paredes, *General Mgr*
▲ **EMP:** 210
SQ FT: 200,000
SALES (est): 1.1B **Privately Held**
WEB: www.neotech.com
SIC: 3679 3674 Antennas, receiving; semiconductors & related devices

(P-9756)
NEWAYS INC
28202 Cabot Rd Ste 100, Laguna Niguel (92677-1247)
PHONE....................949 264-1542
EMP: 38
SALES (est): 1.9MM **Privately Held**
SIC: 3679 Mfg Electronic Components

(P-9757)
NEWVAC LLC
American Def Interconnect Div
9330 De Soto Ave, Chatsworth (91311-4926)
PHONE....................747 202-7333
Garrett Hoffman, *Vice Pres*
George Fry, *Manager*
EMP: 26
SALES (corp-wide): 130.9MM **Privately Held**
WEB: www.newvac-llc.com
SIC: 3679 Harness assemblies for electronic use: wire or cable

HQ: Newvac, Llc
9330 De Soto Ave
Chatsworth CA 91311
310 525-1205

(P-9758)
OCM PE HOLDINGS LP
333 S Grand Ave Fl 28, Los Angeles (90071-1530)
PHONE....................213 830-6213
Mark C J Twaalfhoven, *CEO*
John Frank, *Vice Chairman*
Antoine Autain, *Vice Pres*
Randi Becker, *Vice Pres*
Priya Bowe, *Vice Pres*
EMP: 10000 **EST:** 2012
SALES (est): 172.4MM **Privately Held**
SIC: 3679 3612 3663 Electronic circuits; transformers, except electric; antennas, transmitting & communications

(P-9759)
OMEGA LEADS INC
Also Called: Wire Harness & Cable Assembly
1509 Colorado Ave, Santa Monica (90404-3316)
PHONE....................310 394-6786
Jeff Sweet Sr, *President*
Carole Faxon, *Controller*
EMP: 20 **EST:** 1960
SQ FT: 7,200
SALES (est): 4MM **Privately Held**
WEB: www.omegaleads.com
SIC: 3679 Harness assemblies for electronic use: wire or cable

(P-9760)
OMNI CONNECTION INTL INC
126 Via Trevizio, Corona (92879-1772)
PHONE....................951 898-6232
Henry Cheng, *President*
Phyllis Ting, *Vice Pres*
Robert Liu, *Info Tech Dir*
▲ **EMP:** 410 **EST:** 1992
SQ FT: 65,000
SALES (est): 68.3MM
SALES (corp-wide): 5.7B **Privately Held**
WEB: www.omni-conn.com
SIC: 3679 Harness assemblies for electronic use: wire or cable
HQ: Electrical Components International, Inc.
1 Cityplace Dr Ste 450
Saint Louis MO 63141

(P-9761)
ONSHORE TECHNOLOGIES INC
2771 Plaza Del Amo # 802, Torrance (90503-9308)
PHONE....................310 533-4888
Max Van Orden, *President*
EMP: 25 **EST:** 1992
SALES (est): 5.3MM **Privately Held**
WEB: www.onshoretechnologies.com
SIC: 3679 Harness assemblies for electronic use: wire or cable

(P-9762)
OPTO 22
43044 Business Park Dr, Temecula (92590-3614)
PHONE....................951 695-3000
Mark Engman, *President*
Kathleen Roe, *Treasurer*
Benson Hougland, *Vice Pres*
Bob Sheffres, *Vice Pres*
Jonathan Fischer, *Software Dev*
◆ **EMP:** 200
SQ FT: 135,000
SALES (est): 49.7MM **Privately Held**
WEB: www.opto22.com
SIC: 3679 3823 3625 Electronic switches; industrial instrmnts msrmnt display/control process variable; relays & industrial controls

(P-9763)
ORBIT INTL INC
4965 Firenza Dr, Cypress (90630-3569)
PHONE....................909 468-5160
Teresa Chen, *Principal*
EMP: 26 **EST:** 2011
SALES (est): 6.4MM **Privately Held**
SIC: 3679 Electronic circuits

(P-9764)
POWERS HOLDINGS INC
Also Called: Curtis Industries
1601 Clancy Ct, Visalia (93291-9253)
PHONE....................559 651-2222
Edward Powers, *CEO*
EMP: 14
SALES (corp-wide): 35.1MM **Privately Held**
WEB: www.curtisind.com
SIC: 3679 3677 Electronic switches; filtration devices, electronic
PA: Powers Holdings, Inc.
2400 S 43rd St
Milwaukee WI 53219
414 649-4200

(P-9765)
PPST INC (PA)
17692 Fitch, Irvine (92614-6022)
PHONE....................800 421-1921
Kevin J Voelcker, *President*
John Trinh, *IT/INT Sup*
Huy Hoang, *Engineer*
Ana Rosete, *Purch Agent*
Eladio Ruiz, *Opers Spvr*
▲ **EMP:** 35 **EST:** 2003
SALES (est): 15.9MM **Privately Held**
WEB: www.ppst.com
SIC: 3679 Power supplies, all types: static

(P-9766)
PRECISION ENGINEERING INDS INC
Also Called: Precision Engineering Industry
11627 Cantara St, North Hollywood (91605-1604)
PHONE....................818 767-8590
Greg Kellzi, *President*
▲ **EMP:** 16 **EST:** 1986
SQ FT: 23,975
SALES (est): 389.8K **Privately Held**
WEB: www.ceopei.edu
SIC: 3679 5063 Electronic circuits; burglar alarm systems

(P-9767)
PRECISION HERMETIC TECH INC
1940 W Park Ave, Redlands (92373-8042)
PHONE....................909 381-6011
Daniel B Schachtel, *President*
Randy Hagen, *Design Engr*
Jimmy Padilla, *Engineer*
Sari Schachtel, *Finance*
Daniel Vassallo, *Marketing Staff*
EMP: 77 **EST:** 1989
SQ FT: 25,000
SALES (est): 15.5MM **Privately Held**
WEB: www.precisionhermetic.com
SIC: 3679 Hermetic seals for electronic equipment

(P-9768)
PRX INTERNATIONAL CORP (PA)
23332 Madero Ste H, Mission Viejo (92691-2733)
PHONE....................714 624-0789
Joanne N Kawata, *Principal*
EMP: 68 **EST:** 2002
SALES (est): 2MM **Privately Held**
WEB: www.prxint.com
SIC: 3679 Piezoelectric crystals

(P-9769)
QORVO CALIFORNIA INC
Also Called: Qorvo US
950 Lawrence Dr, Newbury Park (91320-1522)
PHONE....................805 480-5050
Charles J Abronson, *Ch of Bd*
Mark Lampenfeld, *President*
Paul O Daughenbaugh, *CEO*
Ralph G Quinsey, *Chairman*
Susan Liles, *Treasurer*
EMP: 49 **EST:** 1996
SQ FT: 11,000
SALES (est): 13.2MM
SALES (corp-wide): 4B **Publicly Held**
WEB: www.qorvo.com
SIC: 3679 Electronic circuits
HQ: Qorvo Us, Inc.
2300 Ne Brookwood Pkwy
Hillsboro OR 97124
336 664-1233

(P-9770)
RADARSONICS INC
1190 N Grove St, Anaheim (92806-2109)
PHONE....................................714 630-7288
Deborah Rhea, *President*
▲ **EMP:** 14 **EST:** 1967
SQ FT: 12,000
SALES (est): 1.8MM **Privately Held**
WEB: www.radarsonics.com
SIC: 3679 5099 Transducers, electrical; firearms & ammunition, except sporting

(P-9771)
REEDEX INC
15526 Commerce Ln, Huntington Beach (92649-1602)
PHONE....................................714 894-0311
Dan Reed, *President*
Ted Reed, *Vice Pres*
Stephanie Reed, *Office Mgr*
▲ **EMP:** 49 **EST:** 1972
SALES (est): 8.5MM **Privately Held**
WEB: www.reedex.com
SIC: 3679 Harness assemblies for electronic use: wire or cable

(P-9772)
RJA INDUSTRIES INC
Also Called: Automation Electronics
9640 Topanga Canyon Pl J, Chatsworth (91311-0880)
PHONE....................................818 998-5124
Robert Aiani, *President*
Lynn Aiani, *Corp Secy*
Chris Aiani, *Vice Pres*
Sandra Acnason, *Controller*
EMP: 28 **EST:** 1974
SQ FT: 10,000
SALES (est): 2.1MM **Privately Held**
WEB: www.automationelectronics.com
SIC: 3679 Harness assemblies for electronic use: wire or cable; electronic circuits

(P-9773)
ROCKER SOLENOID COMPANY
Also Called: Rocker Industries
5492 Bolsa Ave, Huntington Beach (92649-1021)
PHONE....................................310 534-5660
John W Perry, *President*
Francis E Goodyear, *CEO*
Raymond Hatashita, *Chairman*
Milton A Mather, *Vice Pres*
Alexia Perry, *Info Tech Mgr*
▼ **EMP:** 88 **EST:** 1954
SQ FT: 23,000
SALES (est): 18MM **Privately Held**
WEB: www.rockerindustries.com
SIC: 3679 3672 Solenoids for electronic applications; printed circuit boards

(P-9774)
ROGAR MANUFACTURING INC
Also Called: Ro Gar Mfg
866 E Ross Ave, El Centro (92243-9652)
PHONE....................................760 335-3700
Pat Lewis, *Principal*
Manuel Alvarez, *Manager*
EMP: 126
SALES (corp-wide): 17.6MM **Privately Held**
WEB: www.rogarmfg.com
SIC: 3679 Electronic circuits
PA: Rogar Manufacturing Incorporated
1520 Montague Expy
San Jose CA 95131
408 894-9800

(P-9775)
ROTECH ENGINEERING INC
1020 S Melrose St Ste A, Placentia (92870-7169)
PHONE....................................714 632-0532
Ralph Ono, *President*
EMP: 20 **EST:** 1994
SQ FT: 10,000
SALES (est): 2.4MM **Privately Held**
WEB: www.rotech-busbar.com
SIC: 3679 Electronic circuits

(P-9776)
RTIE HOLDINGS LLC
1800 E Via Burton, Anaheim (92806-1213)
PHONE....................................714 765-8200
Mark Schelbert,

Jonathan Smith,
EMP: 15 **EST:** 2010
SALES (est): 472.9K **Privately Held**
SIC: 3679 Electronic circuits

(P-9777)
S AND C PRECISION INC
5045 Calmview Ave, Baldwin Park (91706-1802)
PHONE....................................626 338-7149
Jose Sanchez, *President*
EMP: 25 **EST:** 1987
SQ FT: 3,000
SALES (est): 2.6MM **Privately Held**
SIC: 3679 3721 3599 Microwave components; aircraft; machine shop, jobbing & repair

(P-9778)
SAS MANUFACTURING INC
405 N Smith Ave, Corona (92878-4305)
PHONE....................................951 734-1808
Theo F Smit Jr, *CEO*
Sharon Smit, *Vice Pres*
Kristeen Painter, *Engineer*
Judy James, *Purchasing*
Harold E Welsh, *Purchasing*
EMP: 45 **EST:** 1990
SQ FT: 24,000
SALES (est): 8.1MM **Privately Held**
WEB: www.sasmanufacturing.com
SIC: 3679 Harness assemblies for electronic use: wire or cable

(P-9779)
SCEPTRE INC
Also Called: E-Scepter
16800 Gale Ave, City of Industry (91745-1804)
PHONE....................................626 369-3698
Stephen Liu, *CEO*
Kieu Dao, *Marketing Mgr*
▲ **EMP:** 50 **EST:** 1984
SALES (est): 9MM **Privately Held**
WEB: www.sceptre.com
SIC: 3679 Liquid crystal displays (LCD)

(P-9780)
SEASONIC ELECTRONICS INC
301 Aerojet Ave, Azusa (91702)
PHONE....................................626 969-9966
Hsiu-Cheng Chang, *CEO*
Vincent Chang, *Principal*
Simon Wu, *Sales Mgr*
Stella Lo, *Sales Staff*
▲ **EMP:** 14 **EST:** 2005
SALES (est): 2.1MM **Privately Held**
SIC: 3679 Electronic loads & power supplies

(P-9781)
SIGNATURE TECH GROUP INC
Also Called: A & A Electronic Assembly
11960 Borden Ave, San Fernando (91340-1808)
PHONE....................................818 890-7611
Victor Castro, *Owner*
EMP: 19 **EST:** 1984
SQ FT: 10,000
SALES (est): 3.6MM **Privately Held**
WEB: www.aapcbassembly.com
SIC: 3679 3672 Electronic circuits; printed circuit boards

(P-9782)
SKYLINE INTERNATIONAL INC
6663 Leanne St, Eastvale (91752-3479)
PHONE....................................714 290-8866
Rajinder Shoor, *CEO*
EMP: 15 **EST:** 2010
SALES (est): 1.3MM **Privately Held**
SIC: 3679 Electronic circuits

(P-9783)
SMITHS INTERCONNECT INC
375 Conejo Ridge Ave, Thousand Oaks (91361-4928)
PHONE....................................805 267-0100
Dave Moorehouse, *President*
Randy Klebe, *Finance*
Paul Harris, *VP Sls/Mktg*
Harold Aikins, *Manager*
EMP: 68
SALES (corp-wide): 3.3B **Privately Held**
WEB: www.smithsinterconnect.com
SIC: 3679 Microwave components

HQ: Smiths Interconnect, Inc.
4726 Eisenhower Blvd
Tampa FL 33634
813 901-7200

(P-9784)
SMITHS INTRCNNECT AMERICAS INC
1231 E Dyer Rd Ste 235, Santa Ana (92705-5665)
PHONE....................................714 371-1100
Dom Matos, *President*
Rick Marshall, *Vice Pres*
David Sanders, *IT/INT Sup*
Richard Johannes, *Engrg Dir*
Ian Dower, *Engineer*
EMP: 300
SALES (corp-wide): 3.3B **Privately Held**
WEB: www.smithsinterconnect.com
SIC: 3679 Microwave components
HQ: Smiths Interconnect Americas, Inc.
5101 Richland Ave
Kansas City KS 66106
913 342-5544

(P-9785)
SO-CAL VALUE ADDED LLC
809 Calle Plano, Camarillo (93012-8516)
PHONE....................................805 389-5335
Marco M Day, *Vice Pres*
Maribel Alejandre, *Purchasing*
EMP: 35 **EST:** 2018
SQ FT: 40,000
SALES (est): 4MM **Privately Held**
WEB: www.so-calvalueadded.com
SIC: 3679 3643 Harness assemblies for electronic use: wire or cable; current-carrying wiring devices

(P-9786)
STATEK CORPORATION (HQ)
512 N Main St, Orange (92868-1182)
PHONE....................................714 639-7810
Brian McCarthy, *President*
Shih Chuang, *COO*
Michae Dastmalchian, *COO*
Michael Dastmalchian, *Co-President*
Conrad Chapa, *Officer*
▲ **EMP:** 249 **EST:** 1970
SQ FT: 71,000
SALES (est): 52.9MM
SALES (corp-wide): 82.9MM **Privately Held**
WEB: www.statek.com
SIC: 3679 Electronic circuits; quartz crystals, for electronic application; oscillators
PA: Technicorp International Ii, Inc.
512 N Main St
Orange CA 92868
714 639-7810

(P-9787)
STRIKE TECHNOLOGY INC
Also Called: Wilorco
24311 Wilmington Ave, Carson (90745-6139)
PHONE....................................562 437-3428
Robert Kunesh, *Ch of Bd*
Cheryl Lefebvre, *Executive*
Cameron Stewart, *CTO*
John Hofland, *Info Tech Mgr*
Raul Deanda, *QC Mgr*
EMP: 25 **EST:** 2001
SQ FT: 9,800
SALES (est): 6MM **Privately Held**
WEB: www.wilorco.com
SIC: 3679 Static power supply converters for electronic applications

(P-9788)
SUNTSU ELECTRONICS INC
142 Technology Dr Ste 150, Irvine (92618-2429)
PHONE....................................949 783-7300
Casey Conlan, *President*
Jason Gann, *Admin Sec*
Shireen Balou, *Administration*
James Braithwaite, *Technical Staff*
Kh Mun, *Engineer*
▲ **EMP:** 38 **EST:** 2002
SQ FT: 14,000
SALES (est): 8MM **Privately Held**
WEB: www.suntsu.com
SIC: 3679 5065 Electronic circuits; recording & playback apparatus, including phonograph; electronic parts & equipment

(P-9789)
SURE POWER INC
Also Called: Martek Power
1111 Knox St, Torrance (90502-1034)
PHONE....................................310 542-8561
Maricela Sanchez, *Branch Mgr*
EMP: 18 **Privately Held**
SIC: 3679 Power supplies, all types: static
HQ: Sure Power, Inc.
10955 Sw Avery St
Tualatin OR 97062
503 692-5360

(P-9790)
TECH ELECTRONIC SYSTEMS INC
404 S Euclid Ave, Ontario (91762-4309)
PHONE....................................909 986-4395
Robert B Contreras, *CEO*
Jack Merrick, *COO*
Contreras Randy, *CIO*
Rick Ellington, *Prdtn Mgr*
Saul Burgos, *Manager*
EMP: 40 **EST:** 1991
SQ FT: 14,000
SALES (est): 6.5MM **Privately Held**
WEB: www.techelectronicsyst-ems.com
SIC: 3679 3499 Liquid crystal displays (LCD); locks, safe & vault: metal

(P-9791)
TEK ENTERPRISES INC
7730 Airport Bus Pkwy, Van Nuys (91406)
PHONE....................................818 785-5971
Tek T Tjia, *President*
Amy Tjia, *COO*
Anthony Fredrick, *Vice Pres*
EMP: 15 **EST:** 2002
SALES (est): 4.2MM **Privately Held**
WEB: www.tekenterprisesinc.com
SIC: 3679 3621 Harness assemblies for electronic use: wire or cable; coils, for electric motors or generators

(P-9792)
TELEDYNE DEFENSE ELEC LLC
Also Called: Teledyne Reynolds
1001 Knox St, Torrance (90502-1030)
PHONE....................................310 823-5491
Mark Kotilinek, *Branch Mgr*
James E Bailey, *Surgery Dir*
EMP: 160
SALES (corp-wide): 3B **Publicly Held**
WEB:
www.teledynedefenseelectronics.com
SIC: 3679 Microwave components
HQ: Teledyne Defense Electronics, Llc
1274 Terra Bella Ave
Mountain View CA 94043
650 691-9800

(P-9793)
TELEDYNE TECHNOLOGIES INC
Also Called: Teledyne Controls
501 Continental Blvd, El Segundo (90245-5036)
P.O. Box 1026 (90245-1026)
PHONE....................................310 765-3600
Masood Hassan, *Vice Pres*
Joe Allen, *President*
Shervin Malmir, *Program Mgr*
Mercedes Duhaylonsod, *Administration*
Cindy Madden, *Administration*
EMP: 300
SALES (corp-wide): 3B **Publicly Held**
WEB: www.teledyne.com
SIC: 3679 8731 3812 3519 Electronic circuits; commercial physical research; search & navigation equipment; internal combustion engines
PA: Teledyne Technologies Inc
1049 Camino Dos Rios
Thousand Oaks CA 91360
805 373-4545

(P-9794)
TELEDYNE TECHNOLOGIES INC (PA)
1049 Camino Dos Rios, Thousand Oaks (91360-2362)
PHONE....................................805 373-4545
Aldo Pichelli, *President*
Robert Mehrabian, *Ch of Bd*
Susan L Main, *CFO*
Stephen F Blackwood, *Treasurer*

Melanie S Cibik, *Ch Credit Ofcr*
EMP: 250 **EST:** 1960
SALES: 3B **Publicly Held**
WEB: www.teledyne.com
SIC: 3679 3761 3519 3724 Electronic circuits; guided missiles & space vehicles; internal combustion engines; gasoline engines; engines, diesel & semi-diesel or dual-fuel; aircraft engines & engine parts; research & development on aircraft engines & parts; aircraft control systems, electronic; navigational systems & instruments; semiconductors & related devices

(P-9795)
TELEDYNE TECHNOLOGIES INC
12964 Panama St, Los Angeles (90066-6534)
PHONE.....................310 822-8229
Bruce Gecks, *Manager*
Matthew Bakker, *President*
Jody Glasser, *President*
Patricia Zamora, *Officer*
Chris Webster, *Senior VP*
EMP: 360
SALES (corp-wide): 3B **Publicly Held**
WEB: www.teledyne.com
SIC: 3679 Electronic circuits
PA: Teledyne Technologies Inc
1049 Camino Dos Rios
Thousand Oaks CA 91360
805 373-4545

(P-9796)
THOMPSON MAGNETICS INC
Also Called: Auto Doctor
42255 Baldaray Cir Ste C, Temecula (92590-3632)
P.O. Box 2019 (92593-2019)
PHONE.....................951 676-0243
Howard M Thompson Sr, *Ch of Bd*
Betty J Thompson, *Corp Secy*
David Thompson, *Vice Pres*
Howard M Thompson Jr, *Vice Pres*
EMP: 22 **EST:** 1969
SQ FT: 16,000
SALES (est): 1.7MM **Privately Held**
SIC: 3679 7538 Cores, magnetic; general automotive repair shops

(P-9797)
TNP INSTRUMENTS INC
119 Star Of India Ln, Carson (90746-1415)
PHONE.....................310 532-2222
Vu Tran, *President*
EMP: 17 **EST:** 1990
SQ FT: 5,000
SALES (est): 845.1K **Privately Held**
SIC: 3679 5065 Liquid crystal displays (LCD); electronic parts & equipment

(P-9798)
TRI TEK ELECTRONICS INC
25358 Avenue Stanford, Valencia (91355-1214)
PHONE.....................661 295-0020
James Gillson, *President*
Josie Gillson, *CFO*
Anthony Lopez, *Principal*
Joe Fattrusso, *Purch Mgr*
Carl Rensner, *Purch Mgr*
EMP: 40 **EST:** 1987
SQ FT: 22,000
SALES (est): 12.2MM **Privately Held**
WEB: www.tritekusa.com
SIC: 3679 Harness assemblies for electronic use: wire or cable; electronic circuits

(P-9799)
TRUE VISION DISPLAYS INC
16402 Berwyn Rd, Cerritos (90703-2440)
PHONE.....................562 407-0630
Steven H Yu, *CEO*
Dj Shin, *Engineer*
▲ **EMP:** 14 **EST:** 2005
SQ FT: 30,460
SALES (est): 1.3MM **Privately Held**
WEB: www.tvdlcd.com
SIC: 3679 Liquid crystal displays (LCD)

(P-9800)
TT ELCTRNICS PWR SLTONS US INC
1330 E Cypress St, Covina (91724-2103)
PHONE.....................626 967-6021

Michael Joseph Leahan, *CEO*
Kumen Rey Call, *CFO*
Matthew Alexander Sweaney, *Admin Sec*
EMP: 120 **EST:** 2019
SALES (est): 24.2MM
SALES (corp-wide): 574.1MM **Publicly Held**
WEB: www.ttelectronics.com
SIC: 3679 Electronic circuits
PA: Tt Electronics Plc
Fourth Floor
Woking
193 282-5300

(P-9801)
VOICE ASSIST INC
Also Called: (A DEVELOPMENT STAGE COMPANY)
100 Spectrum Center Dr # 90, Irvine (92618-4962)
PHONE.....................949 655-6400
Michael Metcalf, *Ch of Bd*
EMP: 16 **EST:** 2008
SALES (est): 2.2MM **Privately Held**
WEB: www.voiceassist.com
SIC: 3679 Voice controls

(P-9802)
WAVESTREAM CORPORATION (HQ)
545 W Terrace Dr, San Dimas (91773-2915)
PHONE.....................909 599-9080
Robert Huffman, *CEO*
Nimrod Itach, *CFO*
James Rosenberg, *Officer*
Francis Auricchio, *Exec VP*
Kirk Green, *Vice Pres*
EMP: 103 **EST:** 2006
SQ FT: 33,000
SALES (est): 27.5MM **Privately Held**
WEB: www.wavestream.com
SIC: 3679 8731 Microwave components; commercial physical research

(P-9803)
WYVERN TECHNOLOGIES
1205 E Warner Ave, Santa Ana (92705-5431)
PHONE.....................714 966-0710
James J Weber, *President*
Jim Hunt, *Program Mgr*
EMP: 30 **EST:** 1984
SQ FT: 10,000 **Privately Held**
WEB: www.wyverncorp.com
SIC: 3679 Microwave components

(P-9804)
XIDAS INC
Also Called: Integra Devices
46 Waterworks Way, Irvine (92618-3107)
PHONE.....................949 930-0147
Paul Dhillon, *CEO*
James Spoto, *COO*
Mark Bachman, *CTO*
EMP: 19 **EST:** 2015
SALES (est): 5.5MM **Privately Held**
WEB: www.xidas.com
SIC: 3679 Microwave components; electronic switches

(P-9805)
XP POWER INC
Also Called: Switching Systems
1590 S Sinclair St, Anaheim (92806-5933)
PHONE.....................714 712-2642
Fred McKirigan, *Vice Pres*
Nannette Ruiz, *Purch Agent*
Calvin Sutherland, *Sales Staff*
Keith Wotton, *Manager*
EMP: 64 **Privately Held**
WEB: www.xppower.com
SIC: 3679 Power supplies, all types: static
HQ: Xp Power Inc.
305 Foster St Ste 4
Littleton MA 01460
800 253-0490

(P-9806)
Z-TRONIX INC
Also Called: Manufacturer
6327 Alondra Blvd, Paramount (90723-3750)
PHONE.....................562 808-0800
Kamran Jahangard-Mahboob, *CEO*
Roy R Jahangard, *President*

Harry Woldt, *Opers Staff*
Esperanza Camacho, *Manager*
◆ **EMP:** 20 **EST:** 1997
SQ FT: 18,000
SALES (est): 6.1MM **Privately Held**
WEB: www.z-tronix.com
SIC: 3679 5063 5065 Harness assemblies for electronic use: wire or cable; wire & cable; connectors, electronic

---

3691 Storage Batteries

(P-9807)
BATTERY TECHNOLOGY INC (PA)
Also Called: B T I
16651 E Johnson Dr, City of Industry (91745-2413)
PHONE.....................626 336-6878
Christopher Chu, *President*
Andy Tong, *Vice Pres*
Mike Tobin, *Sales Mgr*
Scott Carlson, *Sales Staff*
Kristen McKenrick, *Sales Staff*
▲ **EMP:** 83 **EST:** 1992
SQ FT: 20,000
SALES (est): 11.7MM **Privately Held**
WEB: www.batterytech.com
SIC: 3691 Storage batteries

(P-9808)
CALEB TECHNOLOGY CORPORATION
2905 Lomita Blvd, Torrance (90505-5106)
PHONE.....................310 257-4780
Thomas S Lin, *President*
Lily W Lin, *Treasurer*
Lily Lin, *Treasurer*
John Jiang, *Engineer*
EMP: 19 **EST:** 1998
SQ FT: 14,000
SALES (est): 1.2MM **Privately Held**
WEB: www.caleb-corp.com
SIC: 3691 Batteries, rechargeable

(P-9809)
ENEVATE CORPORATION
101 Theory Ste 200, Irvine (92617-3089)
PHONE.....................949 243-0399
Robert A Rango, *CEO*
John B Kennedy, *CFO*
Sameer V RAO, *CFO*
Heidi Anderson, *Officer*
Oscar Diaz, *Officer*
▲ **EMP:** 62 **EST:** 2005
SQ FT: 17,000
SALES (est): 29.1MM **Privately Held**
WEB: www.enevate.com
SIC: 3691 Storage batteries

(P-9810)
FRONT EDGE TECHNOLOGY INC
13455 Brooks Dr Ste A, Baldwin Park (91706-2254)
PHONE.....................626 856-8979
Simon Nieh, *President*
Roger Lin, *CFO*
Andy Shih, *Manager*
EMP: 26 **EST:** 1994
SQ FT: 18,000
SALES (est): 3.4MM **Privately Held**
WEB: www.frontedgetechnology.com
SIC: 3691 Batteries, rechargeable

(P-9811)
INDUSTRIAL BATTERY ENGRG INC
Also Called: I B E
9121 De Garmo Ave, Sun Valley (91352-2697)
PHONE.....................818 767-7067
Birger Holmquist, *CEO*
Michael Sloan, *President*
Javier Sanchez, *Corp Secy*
Ralph Holanov, *Vice Pres*
Derek Sloan, *Vice Pres*
EMP: 29 **EST:** 1951
SQ FT: 20,000
SALES (est): 4.3MM **Privately Held**
WEB: www.ibe-inc.com
SIC: 3691 3629 Storage batteries; electronic generation equipment

(P-9812)
ONECHARGE INC
Also Called: Onecharge Biz
12472 Industry St, Garden Grove (92841-2819)
PHONE.....................833 895-8624
Alexander Pisarev, *CEO*
Vladimir Karimov, *Officer*
Pat Bayers, *Regional Mgr*
Jerry Mastroianni, *CIO*
Mark D´amato, *Sales Mgr*
EMP: 50 **EST:** 2016
SQ FT: 8,500
SALES (est): 6.1MM **Privately Held**
WEB: www.onecharge.biz
SIC: 3691 Storage batteries

(P-9813)
POWERSTORM HOLDINGS INC
Also Called: Powerstorm Ess
31244 Palos Verdes Dr W # 245, Rancho Palos Verdes (90275-5370)
PHONE.....................424 327-2991
Michel J Freni, *Ch of Bd*
Shailesh Upreti, *Vice Pres*
EMP: 18 **EST:** 2011
SQ FT: 2,000
SALES (est): 722.7K **Privately Held**
WEB: www.powerstormcapital.com
SIC: 3691 4911 5063 Storage batteries; ; storage batteries, industrial

(P-9814)
TELEDYNE TECHNOLOGIES INC
Also Called: Teledyne Battery Products
840 W Brockton Ave, Redlands (92374-2902)
P.O. Box 7950 (92375-1150)
PHONE.....................909 793-3131
Greg Donahey, *Branch Mgr*
Christine Delmar, *Vice Pres*
Janak Rajpara, *Engineer*
Joe Barnhill, *Business Mgr*
Rob Dunn, *Analyst*
EMP: 58
SALES (corp-wide): 3B **Publicly Held**
WEB: www.teledyne.com
SIC: 3691 3692 Storage batteries; primary batteries, dry & wet
PA: Teledyne Technologies Inc
1049 Camino Dos Rios
Thousand Oaks CA 91360
805 373-4545

(P-9815)
TROJAN BATTERY HOLDINGS LLC (DH)
12380 Clark St, Santa Fe Springs (90670-3804)
PHONE.....................800 423-6569
Jeffrey Elder,
Chris Litras, *Vice Pres*
Dawnmarie Martin, *Senior Mgr*
EMP: 100 **EST:** 2013
SALES (est): 22.3MM
SALES (corp-wide): 427MM **Privately Held**
WEB: www.trojanbattery.com
SIC: 3691 3692 Lead acid batteries (storage batteries); primary batteries, dry & wet
HQ: Trojan Battery Company
12380 Clark St
Santa Fe Springs CA 90670
562 236-3000

3692 Primary Batteries: Dry & Wet

(P-9816)
B & B BATTERY (USA) INC (PA)
6415 Randolph St, Commerce (90040-3511)
PHONE.....................323 278-1900
Jack Liu, *President*
George Liu, *Vice Pres*
▲ **EMP:** 19 **EST:** 1995
SQ FT: 20,000
SALES (est): 2.8MM **Privately Held**
SIC: 3692 Primary batteries, dry & wet

(P-9817)
QUALLION LLC
12744 San Fernando Rd # 100, Sylmar (91342-3854)
PHONE...................818 833-2000
Alfred E Mann,
Jackie York, *CFO*
▲ EMP: 155 EST: 1998
SALES (est): 42.9MM
SALES (corp-wide): 2.9B **Publicly Held**
WEB: www.enersys.com
SIC: 3692 Primary batteries, dry & wet
PA: Enersys
2366 Bernville Rd
Reading PA 19605
610 208-1991

(P-9818)
SPECTRUM BRANDS INC
Also Called: Spectrum Brands Hhi
19701 Da Vinci, Lake Forest (92610-2622)
PHONE...................949 672-4003
Phil Szuba, *President*
Shawn Simmons, *Vice Pres*
Alston Williams, *Vice Pres*
Marie Miller, *Planning*
Amy Sun, *Info Tech Mgr*
EMP: 700
SQ FT: 150,000
SALES (corp-wide): 3.9B **Publicly Held**
SIC: 3692 Primary batteries, dry & wet
HQ: Spectrum Brands, Inc.
3001 Deming Way
Middleton WI 53562
608 275-3340

(P-9819)
TROJAN BATTERY COMPANY (HQ)
12380 Clark St, Santa Fe Springs (90670-3804)
PHONE...................562 236-3000
Armand Lauzon, *President*
Edward Dunlap, *CFO*
Phil Taylor, *Senior VP*
Yvonne Schroeder, *Vice Pres*
Gabriel Merlano, *Business Anlyst*
◆ EMP: 365 EST: 1925
SALES (est): 204.9MM
SALES (corp-wide): 427MM **Privately Held**
WEB: www.trojanbattery.com
SIC: 3692 3691 Primary batteries, dry & wet; lead acid batteries (storage batteries)
PA: C&D Technologies, Inc.
200 Precision Rd
Horsham PA 19044
215 619-2700

3694 Electrical Eqpt For Internal Combustion Engines

(P-9820)
BATTERY-BIZ INC
Also Called: Ebatts.com
1380 Flynn Rd, Camarillo (93012-8016)
PHONE...................800 848-6782
Ophir Marish, *CEO*
Yossi Jakubovits, *Admin Sec*
▲ EMP: 63 EST: 1988
SQ FT: 60,000
SALES (est): 12.4MM **Privately Held**
WEB: www.battery-biz.com
SIC: 3694 Battery charging generators, automobile & aircraft

(P-9821)
BYD ENERGY LLC
1800 S Figueroa St, Los Angeles (90015-3422)
PHONE...................661 949-2918
EMP: 30 EST: 2013
SALES (est): 5.8MM
SALES (corp-wide): 2.4MM **Privately Held**
WEB: www.byd.com
SIC: 3694 Engine electrical equipment
HQ: Byd Motors Llc
1800 S Figueroa St
Los Angeles CA 90015

(P-9822)
DSM&T CO INC
10609 Business Dr, Fontana (92337-8212)
PHONE...................909 357-7960
Sergio Corona, *CEO*
Shirley Shi, *Purchasing*
Alicia Rebolledo, *VP Opers*
Ezekiel Adeleke, *Manager*
Norma Raygoza, *Accounts Mgr*
▲ EMP: 170
SQ FT: 41,000
SALES (est): 49.5MM **Privately Held**
WEB: www.dsmt.com
SIC: 3694 3357 3634 3643 Harness wiring sets, internal combustion engines; nonferrous wiredrawing & insulating; heating pads, electric; connectors, electric cord

(P-9823)
ELECTRICAL REBUILDERS SLS INC (PA)
Also Called: Vapex-Genex-Precision
7603 Willow Glen Rd, Los Angeles (90046-1608)
PHONE...................323 249-7545
Mike Klapper, *President*
Mary Ann Klapper, *Corp Secy*
David Klapper, *Vice Pres*
▲ EMP: 75 EST: 1966
SALES (est): 6.5MM **Privately Held**
SIC: 3694 3592 3714 Distributors, motor vehicle engine; carburetors; motor vehicle brake systems & parts

(P-9824)
JET PERFORMANCE PRODUCTS INC
Also Called: Jet Transmission
17491 Apex Cir, Huntington Beach (92647-5728)
PHONE...................714 848-5500
Bryant Seller, *President*
Dan Nicholas, *Sales Executive*
EMP: 21 EST: 1968
SQ FT: 8,500
SALES (est): 4.3MM **Privately Held**
WEB: www.jetchip.com
SIC: 3694 3714 Automotive electrical equipment; motor vehicle parts & accessories

(P-9825)
LG BATTERY
8973 Lotta Ave, South Gate (90280-3516)
PHONE...................323 569-3116
Luis Gonzalez, *Principal*
EMP: 15 EST: 2007
SALES (est): 1.5MM **Privately Held**
SIC: 3694 Automotive electrical equipment

(P-9826)
MYOTEK INDUSTRIES INCORPORATED (PA)
1278 Glenneyre St Ste 431, Laguna Beach (92651-3103)
PHONE...................949 502-3776
Robert Harrington, *President*
▲ EMP: 90 EST: 1998
SQ FT: 1,800
SALES (est): 14.3MM **Privately Held**
WEB: www.myotek.com
SIC: 3694 5013 Automotive electrical equipment; automotive servicing equipment

(P-9827)
PARTS OUT INC (PA)
Also Called: Ats International
1875 Century Park E # 2200, Los Angeles (90067-2337)
PHONE...................626 560-1540
Siong Tan, *President*
▲ EMP: 13 EST: 2001
SQ FT: 100,000
SALES (est): 6MM **Privately Held**
SIC: 3694 Distributors, motor vehicle engine

(P-9828)
PERTRONIX INC
Also Called: Patriot Products
15601 Cypress Ave Unit B, Irwindale (91706-2120)
PHONE...................909 599-5955
Jack Porter, *Manager*
Paul Rogers, *Technical Staff*
Jesse Burgos, *Prdtn Mgr*
Linda Ratzloff, *Production*
Frank Van Es, *Manager*
EMP: 50
SALES (corp-wide): 13.8MM **Privately Held**
WEB: www.pertronixbrands.com
SIC: 3694 5013 Ignition apparatus, internal combustion engines; automotive supplies & parts
PA: Pertronix, Inc.
440 E Arrow Hwy
San Dimas CA 91773
909 599-5955

(P-9829)
PRECO AIRCRAFT MOTORS INC
1133 Mission St, South Pasadena (91030-3211)
P.O. Box 189 (91031-0189)
PHONE...................626 799-3549
Peter Kingston Jr, *President*
Peter Kingston Sr, *Chairman*
Linda D Kingston, *Vice Pres*
EMP: 18 EST: 1945
SQ FT: 10,000
SALES (est): 479.8K **Privately Held**
SIC: 3694 Motors, starting: automotive & aircraft

(P-9830)
URIMAN INC (HQ)
650 N Puente St, Brea (92821-2880)
PHONE...................714 257-2080
Jinho Choi, *CEO*
Kyung Hoon Park, *COO*
Young Hak Yun, *CFO*
Kyeong Ho Lee, *Principal*
Susie Chiang, *Accountant*
◆ EMP: 27 EST: 1983
SQ FT: 42,144
SALES (est): 46.8MM **Privately Held**
WEB: www.halla.co.kr
SIC: 3694 3625 3714 Alternators, automotive; starter, electric motor; power steering equipment, motor vehicle

(P-9831)
VANTAGE VEHICLE INTL INC
Also Called: Vantage Vehicle Group
1740 N Delilah St, Corona (92879-1893)
PHONE...................951 735-1200
Michael Pak, *President*
Brian Swan, *Technical Staff*
◆ EMP: 30 EST: 2002
SQ FT: 50,000
SALES (est): 7.5MM **Privately Held**
WEB: www.vantagevehicle.com
SIC: 3694 Distributors, motor vehicle engine

(P-9832)
XOS INC
3550 Tyburn St Unit 100, Los Angeles (90065-1427)
PHONE...................818 316-1890
Dakota Semler, *Ch of Bd*
Giordano Sordoni, *COO*
Kingsley Afemikhe, *CFO*
Robert Ferber, *CTO*
EMP: 188 EST: 2020
SALES (est): 2.6MM **Privately Held**
SIC: 3694 Automotive electrical equipment

3695 Recording Media

(P-9833)
ALPHALOGIX INC
5811 Mcfadden Ave, Huntington Beach (92649-1323)
PHONE...................714 901-1456
Robert D McCandless, *CEO*
EMP: 13 EST: 2005
SALES (est): 209.6K **Privately Held**
WEB: www.alphalogix.com
SIC: 3695 Computer software tape & disks: blank, rigid & floppy

(P-9834)
CD VIDEO MANUFACTURING INC
Also Called: C D Video
12650 Westminster Ave, Santa Ana (92706-2139)
PHONE...................714 265-0770
Minh T Nguyen, *President*
John Nguyen, *Marketing Staff*
Teresa Falkenstein, *Sales Staff*
Chris Newton, *Manager*
Dave Nickelson, *Manager*
▲ EMP: 60 EST: 1995
SQ FT: 11,000
SALES (est): 13.5MM **Privately Held**
WEB: www.cdvideomfg.com
SIC: 3695 3652 7819 Video recording tape, blank; compact laser discs, prerecorded; services allied to motion pictures

(P-9835)
FARSTONE TECHNOLOGY INC
184 Technology Dr Ste 205, Irvine (92618-2435)
PHONE...................949 336-4321
EMP: 110
SALES (est): 3.1MM **Privately Held**
WEB: www.farstone.com
SIC: 3695 Magnetic And Optical Recording Media

(P-9836)
HOFFMAN MAGNETICS INC
19528 Ventura Blvd, Tarzana (91356-2917)
PHONE...................818 717-5095
EMP: 20
SALES (est): 1.7MM **Privately Held**
SIC: 3695 Mfg Magnetic/Optical Recording Media

(P-9837)
MSE MEDIA SOLUTIONS INC
Also Called: M S E Media Solutions
5711 Sheila St, Commerce (90040-2211)
PHONE...................323 721-1656
Fernando Antonio Ruballos, *CEO*
▲ EMP: 14 EST: 1985
SALES (est): 856K **Privately Held**
WEB: www.msemedia.com
SIC: 3695 Video recording tape, blank

(P-9838)
SCENEWISE INC
Also Called: Comchoice
2201 Park Pl Ste 100, El Segundo (90245-5167)
PHONE...................310 466-7692
Bob D Hively, *Ch of Bd*
Duncan Wain, *President*
Leslie Hively, *Corp Secy*
EMP: 18 EST: 1977
SQ FT: 19,000
SALES (est): 813.3K **Privately Held**
WEB: www.scenewise.com
SIC: 3695 0971 Magnetic tape; game services

(P-9839)
SONY DADC US INC
4499 Glencoe Ave, Marina Del Rey (90292-6357)
PHONE...................310 760-8500
Geoff Cambel, *Branch Mgr*
EMP: 14 **Privately Held**
WEB: www.sonydadc.com
SIC: 3695 Audio range tape, blank
HQ: Sony Dadc Us Inc
1800 N Fruitridge Ave
Terre Haute IN 47804
812 462-8100

(P-9840)
TARGET TECHNOLOGY COMPANY LLC
564 Wald, Irvine (92618-4637)
PHONE...................949 788-0909
Han H Nee,
Valerie Genrelly, *Asst Controller*
Stephene Nguyen, *Accountant*
Paul Maye, *Sales Staff*
EMP: 50 EST: 1998
SALES (est): 8.6MM **Privately Held**
WEB: www.targettechnology.com
SIC: 3695 Magnetic & optical recording media

(P-9841)
TECHNICOLOR DISC SERVICES CORP (HQ)
3233 Mission Oaks Blvd, Camarillo (93012-5097)
PHONE..............................805 445-1122
Mary Fialkowski, *President*
O F Raimondo, *Executive*
▲ EMP: 200 EST: 1996
SQ FT: 62,000
SALES (est): 43MM
SALES (corp-wide): 57.9MM **Privately Held**
WEB: www.technicolor.com
SIC: 3695 7361 Computer software tape & disks: blank, rigid & floppy; employment agencies

(P-9842)
UNITED AUDIO VIDEO GROUP INC
7651 Densmore Ave, Van Nuys (91406-2043)
PHONE..............................818 980-6700
Miriam Newman, *President*
Lauri Newman, *Corp Secy*
Steven Newman, *Vice Pres*
Larry Schwartz, *General Mgr*
Karol Wagner-Loy, *Accounts Mgr*
▲ EMP: 29 EST: 1972
SALES (est): 1.3MM **Privately Held**
WEB: www.unitedavg.com
SIC: 3695 5065 Audio range tape, blank; tapes, audio & video recording

(P-9843)
UNITED MEDIA SERVICES INC
4955 E Hunter Ave, Anaheim (92807-2058)
PHONE..............................714 693-8168
David Lin, *President*
Louis Chase, *Shareholder*
Tomas Sung, *Controller*
Girija S Mohanty, *Assistant*
EMP: 120 EST: 1992
SQ FT: 41,000
SALES (est): 6.9MM **Privately Held**
SIC: 3695 Video recording tape, blank

(P-9844)
VIDA CORPORATION
17807 Maclaren St Ste A, City of Industry (91744-5700)
PHONE..............................626 839-4912
Eva Chang Hsu, *President*
Tony Hsu, *Vice Pres*
EMP: 13 EST: 1993
SQ FT: 40,000
SALES (est): 388.5K **Privately Held**
SIC: 3695 5099 Magnetic tape; video recording tape, blank; video cassettes, accessories & supplies

---

3699 Electrical Machinery, Eqpt & Splys, NEC

(P-9845)
A T PARKER INC (PA)
Also Called: Solar Electronics Company
10866 Chandler Blvd, North Hollywood (91601-2945)
PHONE..............................818 755-1700
Tom A Parker, *President*
Jo Ann Dennis, *Vice Pres*
Sue Parker, *Asst Sec*
▼ EMP: 22
SQ FT: 7,500
SALES (est): 3.1MM **Privately Held**
WEB: www.solar-emc.com
SIC: 3699 Electrical equipment & supplies

(P-9846)
A-Z EMISSIONS SOLUTIONS INC
Also Called: A-Z Bussales
1900 S Riverside Ave, Colton (92324-3344)
PHONE..............................951 781-1856
John Landherr, *President*
David Goudeau, *Principal*
Jeff Laliberte, *Principal*
Joshua Pearson, *Principal*
April Rosenquist, *Principal*
EMP: 28 EST: 1984

SALES (est): 334.4K **Privately Held**
WEB: www.a-zbus.com
SIC: 3699 Heat emission operating apparatus

(P-9847)
AAMP OF AMERICA
2500 E Francis St, Ontario (91761-7730)
PHONE..............................805 338-6800
Dennis Hill, *Owner*
Brad Chapple, *Exec VP*
Julie Julian, *Purchasing*
Don Tolson, *Director*
▲ EMP: 20 EST: 2009
SALES (est): 2.1MM **Privately Held**
WEB: www.aampglobal.com
SIC: 3699 Electrical equipment & supplies

(P-9848)
ADVANCED MANUFACTURING TECH
3140a E Coronado St, Anaheim (92806-1914)
PHONE..............................714 238-1488
Tom Lee, *Director*
Craig M Riedel, *CFO*
Wayne Wilson, *General Mgr*
EMP: 3805 EST: 1992
SQ FT: 54,000
SALES (est): 3.6MM **Privately Held**
WEB: www.mflex.com
SIC: 3699 Electrical equipment & supplies
HQ: Multi-Fineline Electronix, Inc.
    101 Academy Ste 250
    Irvine CA 92617
    949 453-6800

(P-9849)
AGENTS WEST INC
Also Called: Electrical Products Rep
6 Hughes Ste 210, Irvine (92618-2063)
PHONE..............................949 614-0293
Aldo Pellicciotti, *President*
Clyde Collins, *Treasurer*
Stephen Benshoof, *Vice Pres*
Robert Rathburn, *Admin Sec*
Christy Foster, *Controller*
EMP: 36 EST: 1978
SQ FT: 30,000
SALES (est): 4.9MM **Privately Held**
WEB: www.agentswest.com
SIC: 3699 5063 Electrical equipment & supplies; electrical apparatus & equipment; electrical supplies

(P-9850)
AITECH DEFENSE SYSTEMS INC
19756 Prairie St, Chatsworth (91311-6531)
PHONE..............................818 700-2000
Moshe Tal, *CEO*
Erez Konfino, *CFO*
Douglas Patterson, *Vice Pres*
Richard Layne, *Technology*
Vardan Antonyan, *Electrical Engi*
◆ EMP: 48
SQ FT: 22,000
SALES (est): 15.7MM **Privately Held**
WEB: www.aitechsystems.com
SIC: 3699 Electrical equipment & supplies
PA: Aitech Rugged Group, Inc.
    19756 Prairie St
    Chatsworth CA 91311

(P-9851)
AITECH RUGGED GROUP INC (PA)
19756 Prairie St, Chatsworth (91311-6531)
PHONE..............................818 700-2000
Moshe Tal, *CEO*
Erez Konfino, *CFO*
Joshua Baer, *Program Mgr*
Faris Alsaad, *Electrical Engi*
Rusty Deshazo, *Business Mgr*
EMP: 50
SALES (est): 29.9MM **Privately Held**
WEB: www.aitechsystems.com
SIC: 3699 Electrical equipment & supplies

(P-9852)
ALPHA LASER
1801 Railroad St, Corona (92878-5012)
PHONE..............................951 582-0285
Kaan Cakmak, *President*
Sule Cakmak, *Office Mgr*
EMP: 13 EST: 2014

SALES (est): 1.5MM **Privately Held**
WEB: www.alphalasercutting.com
SIC: 3699 Laser welding, drilling & cutting equipment

(P-9853)
ALTA PROPERTIES INC
Also Called: Sonatech Division
879 Ward Dr, Santa Barbara (93111-2920)
PHONE..............................805 683-1431
Karen Vaughn, *Administration*
John Mather, *Engineer*
Curt Garcia, *Manager*
Tom Ochi, *Manager*
EMP: 280
SALES (corp-wide): 71.9MM **Privately Held**
SIC: 3699 Electrical equipment & supplies
PA: Alta Properties, Inc.
    879 Ward Dr
    Santa Barbara CA 93111
    805 967-0171

(P-9854)
ALTA PROPERTIES INC
Sonatech
879 Ward Dr, Santa Barbara (93111-2920)
PHONE..............................805 690-5382
David Cooper, *Design Engr*
James Bartek, *Engineer*
Chuck Randall, *Engineer*
Peter Bonsignori, *QC Mgr*
EMP: 280
SALES (corp-wide): 71.9MM **Privately Held**
SIC: 3699 Underwater sound equipment
PA: Alta Properties, Inc.
    879 Ward Dr
    Santa Barbara CA 93111
    805 967-0171

(P-9855)
AMREX-ZETRON INC
Also Called: Amrex Electrotherapy Equipment
7034 Jackson St, Paramount (90723-4835)
PHONE..............................310 527-6868
George Bell, *President*
Jennifer Steffler, *Web Dvlpr*
▲ EMP: 23 EST: 1935
SQ FT: 20,000
SALES (est): 2MM **Privately Held**
WEB: www.amrexusa.com
SIC: 3699 3845 High-energy particle physics equipment; electromedical equipment

(P-9856)
ASCO POWER SERVICES INC
120 S Chaparral Ct # 200, Anaheim (92808-2237)
PHONE..............................714 283-4000
Les Baird, *Manager*
EMP: 19
SALES (corp-wide): 177.9K **Privately Held**
WEB: www.ascopower.com
SIC: 3699 Electrical equipment & supplies
HQ: Asco Power Services, Inc.
    160 Park Ave
    Florham Park NJ 07932

(P-9857)
CALSTAR SYSTEMS GROUP INC
Also Called: Quikstor
6345 Balboa Blvd Ste 105, Encino (91316-1517)
PHONE..............................818 922-2000
Dennis Levitt, *President*
Tony Gardner, *Vice Pres*
Oleg Shaidurov, *Software Dev*
April Lee, *Technical Staff*
Selena Canlas, *Accounting Mgr*
▲ EMP: 22 EST: 1982
SALES (est): 3.5MM **Privately Held**
SIC: 3699 7371 Security devices; computer software development

(P-9858)
CARTTRONICS LLC (HQ)
90 Icon, Foothill Ranch (92610-3000)
PHONE..............................888 696-2278
John R French, *President*
Rebecca Lawton, *Controller*
◆ EMP: 27 EST: 1997

SALES (est): 11.2MM
SALES (corp-wide): 29.9MM **Privately Held**
WEB: www.gatekeepersystems.com
SIC: 3699 7382 5065 Security devices; security systems services; security control equipment & systems
PA: Gatekeeper Systems, Inc.
    90 Icon
    Foothill Ranch CA 92610
    949 268-1414

(P-9859)
CED ANAHEIM 018
Also Called: California Electric Supply
1304 S Allec St, Anaheim (92805-6303)
PHONE..............................714 956-5156
Steve Richardson, *Manager*
Tom A Catullo, *Manager*
EMP: 19 EST: 2005
SALES (est): 3.4MM **Privately Held**
SIC: 3699 5063 Electrical equipment & supplies; electrical apparatus & equipment

(P-9860)
CLEAN AMERICA INC
Also Called: EDM Performance Accessories
1400 Pioneer St, Brea (92821-3720)
PHONE..............................562 694-5990
Jim E Swartzbaugh, *President*
Tom Adams, *Vice Pres*
Anthony Gonzalez, *Vice Pres*
Dan Dejohn, *Regl Sales Mgr*
Jesse Rodriguez, *Sales Staff*
▲ EMP: 15 EST: 1989
SQ FT: 14,000
SALES (est): 3.5MM **Privately Held**
WEB: www.edmperformance.com
SIC: 3699 Electrical equipment & supplies

(P-9861)
CODA ENERGY HOLDINGS LLC
111 N Artsakh Ave Ste 300, Glendale (91206-4097)
PHONE..............................626 775-3900
Paul Detering, *CEO*
Peter Nortman, *COO*
John Bryan, *Vice Pres*
Davnette Librando,
Edward Solar,
▲ EMP: 25 EST: 2013
SALES (est): 3.1MM **Privately Held**
WEB: www.codaenergy.com
SIC: 3699 Household electrical equipment

(P-9862)
COMPULOCKS BRANDS INC
9115 Dice Rd Ste 18, Santa Fe Springs (90670-2538)
PHONE..............................562 201-2913
Martin Noble, *President*
Noam Aviv, *VP Business*
Miriam Silver, *General Mgr*
Shahar Agassi, *Accounts Mgr*
EMP: 13 EST: 2013
SALES (est): 3.3MM **Privately Held**
WEB: www.compulocks.com
SIC: 3699 5065 7382 Security devices; security control equipment & systems; security systems services

(P-9863)
COZZIA USA LLC (HQ)
861 S Oak Park Rd, Covina (91724-3624)
PHONE..............................626 667-2272
Mark Holmes, *COO*
Jimmy Lo, *CFO*
▲ EMP: 19 EST: 2009
SQ FT: 5,500
SALES (est): 21MM **Privately Held**
WEB: www.cozziausa.com
SIC: 3699 Electrical equipment & supplies

(P-9864)
DISTRIBUTION ELECTRNICS VLUED
Also Called: Deva
2651 Dow Ave, Tustin (92780-7207)
PHONE..............................714 368-1717
Rodger Dale Baker, *CEO*
Ken Plock, *COO*
Maureen Supple, *Sales Staff*
Ivan Morales, *Manager*
◆ EMP: 23 EST: 1974
SQ FT: 13,800

PRODUCTS & SVCS

SALES (est): 15MM **Privately Held**
WEB: www.devainc.com
SIC: 3699 5065 Electrical equipment &
supplies; electronic parts & equipment
HQ: Deva, Inc.
555 Madison Ave Ste 1100
New York NY 10022
212 223-2466

(P-9865)
DOORKING INC (PA)
120 S Glasgow Ave, Inglewood
(90301-1502)
PHONE.......................310 645-0023
Thomas Richmond, *President*
Pat Kochie, *Vice Pres*
Susan Richmond, *Admin Sec*
Hilda Gonzalez, *Administration*
Mario Sanchez, *Info Tech Mgr*
◆ **EMP:** 185
SQ FT: 16,000
SALES (est): 55MM **Privately Held**
WEB: www.doorking.com
SIC: 3699 5065 3829 Security control
equipment & systems; security control
equipment & systems; measuring & con-
trolling devices

(P-9866)
EASTERNCCTV (USA) LLC
Also Called: Ens Security
525 Parriott Pl W, Hacienda Heights
(91745-1033)
PHONE.......................626 961-8810
Xianjie Xiong, *Mng Member*
EMP: 171
SALES (corp-wide): 15.6MM **Privately
Held**
WEB: www.easterncctv.com
SIC: 3699 Security devices
PA: Easterncctv (Usa), Llc
50 Commercial St
Plainview NY 11803
516 870-3779

(P-9867)
ELECTRIC GATE STORE INC
15342 Chatsworth St, Mission Hills
(91345-2041)
PHONE.......................818 361-6872
Sophia Franco, *Accounting Mgr*
EMP: 142
SALES (corp-wide): 9MM **Privately Held**
WEB: www.gatestore.com
SIC: 3699 Security devices
PA: Electric Gate Store, Inc.
421 Park Ave
San Fernando CA 91340
818 504-2300

(P-9868)
FAAC
357 S Acacia Ave Unit 357 # 357, Fullerton
(92831-4748)
PHONE.......................800 221-8278
Andrea Marcellan, *Branch Mgr*
EMP: 47
SALES (corp-wide): 2.9MM **Privately
Held**
SIC: 3699 Door opening & closing devices,
electrical
PA: Faac International, Inc.
3160 Murrell Rd
Rockledge FL 32955
904 448-8952

(P-9869)
FREEDOM PHOTONICS LLC
41 Aero Camino, Santa Barbara
(93117-3104)
PHONE.......................805 967-4900
Milan Mashanovitch,
Leif Johansson, *Officer*
Henry Garrett, *Senior Engr*
Miranda Tang, *Finance*
Leif Johansson,
EMP: 50 **EST:** 2005
SQ FT: 14,500
SALES (est): 7.7MM **Privately Held**
WEB: www.freedomphotonics.com
SIC: 3699 3827 3674 Laser systems &
equipment; optical test & inspection
equipment; light sensitive devices

(P-9870)
GATEKEEPER SYSTEMS INC (PA)
90 Icon, Foothill Ranch (92610-3000)
PHONE.......................949 268-1414
Robert Harling, *CEO*
Keith Kato, *CFO*
R J Brandes, *Vice Pres*
Steve Hannah, *Vice Pres*
James Auyang, *General Mgr*
▲ **EMP:** 35 **EST:** 1998
SQ FT: 15,000
SALES (est): 29.9MM **Privately Held**
WEB: www.gatekeepersystems.com
SIC: 3699 Security devices

(P-9871)
GORES RADIO HOLDINGS LLC
10877 Wilshire Blvd Fl 18, Los Angeles
(90024-4373)
PHONE.......................310 209-3010
Alex Gores, *President*
EMP: 68 **EST:** 2007
SALES (est): 6.2MM
SALES (corp-wide): 1.8B **Privately Held**
WEB: www.gores.com
SIC: 3699 7382 Security devices; security
systems services
PA: The Gores Group Llc
9800 Wilshire Blvd
Beverly Hills CA 90212
310 209-3010

(P-9872)
INNOVATIVETEK INC
1271 W 9th St, Upland (91786-5706)
PHONE.......................909 981-3401
Sandy Samudrala, *President*
Paul Trinh, *Vice Pres*
EMP: 16 **EST:** 2004
SALES (est): 3.1MM **Privately Held**
WEB: www.innovativetek.com
SIC: 3699 Electronic training devices

(P-9873)
INTEGRITY SECURITY SVCS LLC (DH)
30 W Sola St, Santa Barbara (93101-2508)
PHONE.......................805 965-6044
Jeffrey R Hazarian, *President*
Alan Meyer, *Vice Pres*
Greg Powell, *CTO*
Jason Isaacs, *General Counsel*
EMP: 13 **EST:** 2001
SALES (est): 4.5MM
SALES (corp-wide): 128.9MM **Privately
Held**
WEB: www.ghsiss.com
SIC: 3699 7371 Security control equip-
ment & systems; custom computer pro-
gramming services; computer software
systems analysis & design, custom; com-
puter software development
HQ: Green Hills Software Llc
30 W Sola St
Santa Barbara CA 93101
805 965-6044

(P-9874)
IRONWOOD ELECTRIC INC
1239 N Tustin Ave, Anaheim (92807-1603)
PHONE.......................714 630-2350
Raymond Chafe, *Principal*
Adam Daugherty, *Technician*
Luis Villalobos, *Project Mgr*
Ray Chafe, *Sales Staff*
Joey Hanson, *Superintendent*
EMP: 21 **EST:** 2011
SALES (est): 8.6MM **Privately Held**
WEB: www.ironwoodelectric.com
SIC: 3699 1731 Electrical equipment &
supplies; electrical work

(P-9875)
ITECH SMART HOME INC
1015 Concord Ave, Ventura (93004-2343)
PHONE.......................805 673-8414
Thomas Robinson, *President*
EMP: 13 **EST:** 2018

SALES (est): 2.4MM **Privately Held**
WEB: www.itechsmarthome.com
SIC: 3699 1731 5065 8611 Security control equipment & systems; voice, data &
video wiring contractor; security control
equipment & systems; contractors' association

(P-9876)
IWERKS ENTERTAINMENT INC
Also Called: Simex-Iwerks
27509 Avenue Hopkins, Santa Clarita
(91355-3910)
PHONE.......................661 678-1800
Gary Matus, *CEO*
Donald Stults, *COO*
Jeff Dahl, *CFO*
Mark Cornell, *Senior VP*
Daniela Aviles, *Purchasing*
EMP: 75 **EST:** 1986
SQ FT: 23,000
SALES (est): 9MM
SALES (corp-wide): 20.3MM **Privately
Held**
WEB: www.simex-iwerks.com
SIC: 3699 7819 Electrical equipment &
supplies; developing & printing of com-
mercial motion picture film
PA: Simex Inc
600-210 King St E
Toronto ON M5A 1
416 597-1585

(P-9877)
JACK J ENGEL MANUFACTURING INC
Also Called: Creative Automation
11641 Pendleton St, Sun Valley
(91352-2502)
PHONE.......................818 767-6220
Jack Engel, *President*
Jack J Engel, *President*
Ilene Rosen, *CFO*
Ilene Engel, *Treasurer*
Gary Helmers, *Vice Pres*
EMP: 27 **EST:** 1968
SQ FT: 15,000
SALES (est): 4.1MM **Privately Held**
WEB: www.creativedispensing.com
SIC: 3699 5063 Electrical equipment &
supplies; electrical supplies

(P-9878)
JANTEK ELECTRONICS INC
4820 Arden Dr, Temple City (91780-4001)
PHONE.......................626 350-4198
Danny Jan, *Vice Pres*
Joe Jan, *Exec VP*
Shirley Jan, *Controller*
◆ **EMP:** 18 **EST:** 1985
SQ FT: 5,700
SALES (est): 2.6MM **Privately Held**
WEB: www.jantek.com
SIC: 3699 8748 5063 Security control
equipment & systems; communications
consulting; electric alarms & signaling
equipment

(P-9879)
JBB INC
Also Called: Precision Waterjet
4900 E Hunter Ave, Anaheim (92807-2057)
PHONE.......................888 538-9287
Jack Budd, *President*
EMP: 24 **EST:** 1995
SALES (est): 2.5MM **Privately Held**
SIC: 3699 Laser welding, drilling & cutting
equipment

(P-9880)
KANEX
500 S Brea Blvd Unit B, Brea (92821-5383)
PHONE.......................714 332-1681
Kelvin Yan, *CEO*
Wendee Cadacio, *Accounting Mgr*
Tracy Thomas, *Marketing Staff*
▲ **EMP:** 25 **EST:** 1987
SALES (est): 4.3MM **Privately Held**
WEB: www.kanex.com
SIC: 3699 5065 Electrical equipment &
supplies; electronic parts & equipment

(P-9881)
KELLY PNEUMATICS INC
1611 Babcock St, Newport Beach
(92663-2805)
PHONE.......................800 704-7552
Ed Kelly, *President*
John McDaniel, *Mfg Staff*
Nick Dancz, *Sales Staff*
Phil Troilo,
▲ **EMP:** 20 **EST:** 2003
SALES (est): 5.1MM **Privately Held**
SIC: 3699 Electrical equipment & supplies

(P-9882)
KULICKE SFFA WEDGE BONDING INC
Also Called: Kulicke & Soffa Industries
1821 E Dyer Rd Ste 200, Santa Ana
(92705-5700)
PHONE.......................949 660-0440
Scott Kulicke, *President*
Pamela Riggs, *Executive Asst*
Chong Chen, *Engineer*
Ricky Ferrer, *Engineer*
Jay McCandless, *Engineer*
▲ **EMP:** 200 **EST:** 2008
SALES (est): 36.6MM
SALES (corp-wide): 623.1MM **Publicly
Held**
WEB: www.kns.com
SIC: 3699 Electrical equipment & supplies
PA: Kulicke And Soffa Industries, Inc.
1005 Virginia Dr
Fort Washington PA 19034
215 784-6000

(P-9883)
KYOCERA SLD LASER INC (HQ)
485 Pine Ave, Goleta (93117-3709)
PHONE.......................805 696-6999
Steven Denbaars, *CEO*
James Raring, *President*
Eric B Kim, *CEO*
Thomas Caulfield, *COO*
George Stringer, *Senior VP*
EMP: 57 **EST:** 2013
SQ FT: 3,000
SALES (est): 17.5MM **Privately Held**
WEB: www.kyocera-sldlaser.com
SIC: 3699 Laser systems & equipment

(P-9884)
L T SEROGE INC
Also Called: Laser Tech
7400 Jurupa Ave, Riverside (92504-1030)
PHONE.......................951 354-7141
Anthony Di Guglielmo, *CEO*
John Burd, *Human Res Dir*
Chuck Markley, *Manager*
EMP: 15 **EST:** 1989
SQ FT: 50,000
SALES (est): 3.6MM **Privately Held**
SIC: 3699 Laser welding, drilling & cutting
equipment

(P-9885)
LASER SPECTRUM INC
15 Mira Mesa, Rcho STA Marg
(92688-3418)
PHONE.......................949 726-2978
EMP: 40
SALES (corp-wide): 123.2K **Privately
Held**
WEB: www.laser-spectrum.com
SIC: 3699 Laser systems & equipment
PA: Laser Spectrum, Inc.
4605 Barranca Pkwy 101g
Irvine CA 92604
949 551-8225

(P-9886)
LASER SPECTRUM INC (PA)
4605 Barranca Pkwy 101g, Irvine
(92604-4767)
PHONE.......................949 551-8225
Dick S Lin, *Administration*
EMP: 17 **EST:** 2010
SALES (est): 123.2K **Privately Held**
SIC: 3699 Laser systems & equipment

(P-9887)
LASEROD TECHNOLOGIES LLC
20312 Gramercy Pl, Torrance
(90501-1511)
PHONE.......................310 328-5869
Charles T Moffitt, *Mng Member*

David V Adams Jr, *Mng Member*
▼ **EMP:** 20 **EST:** 2011
SQ FT: 8,000
SALES (est): 1.9MM **Privately Held**
WEB: www.laserod.com
SIC: 3699 Laser systems & equipment;
laser welding, drilling & cutting equipment

(P-9888)
LAX IN-FLITE SERVICES LLC
125 N Ash Ave, Inglewood (90301-1648)
PHONE.................................310 677-9885
Jonathan Glabman, *Mng Member*
EMP: 13 **EST:** 2015
SALES (est): 863.6K **Privately Held**
SIC: 3699 Flight simulators (training aids),
electronic

(P-9889)
LORENZ INC
Also Called: Karel Manufacturing
1749 Stergios Rd, Calexico (92231-9657)
PHONE.................................760 427-1815
Zaven Arakelian, *President*
Valorie Lorenz, *Office Mgr*
Isabel Garcia, *Info Tech Mgr*
▲ **EMP:** 45 **EST:** 1993
SQ FT: 73,000
SALES (est): 3.5MM **Privately Held**
SIC: 3699 Electrical equipment & supplies

(P-9890)
LOW VOLTAGE ARCHITECTURE INC
11715 San Vicente Blvd, Los Angeles
(90049-6628)
P.O. Box 1182, Malibu (90265-1182)
PHONE.................................310 573-7588
Matthew Denos, *President*
EMP: 13 **EST:** 2003
SALES (est): 923.3K **Privately Held**
WEB: www.lvainc.com
SIC: 3699 8712 Security control equip-
ment & systems; architectural services

(P-9891)
MEDIA KING INC
140 W Valley Blvd 201a, San Gabriel
(91776-3760)
PHONE.................................626 288-4558
▲ **EMP:** 22
SALES (est): 2.5MM **Privately Held**
SIC: 3699 Mfg Electrical Equipment/Sup-
plies

(P-9892)
MEGGITT SAFETY SYSTEMS INC (HQ)
Also Called: Meggitt Ctrl Systms-Vntura Cnt
1785 Voyager Ave, Simi Valley
(93063-3363)
PHONE.................................805 584-4100
Dennis Hutton, *President*
David Rivard, *Vice Pres*
Dolores Watai, *Vice Pres*
Kevin Wright, *Vice Pres*
Aimee Birkner, *General Mgr*
▲ **EMP:** 210 **EST:** 1999
SQ FT: 180,000
SALES (est): 118.2MM
SALES (corp-wide): 2.2B **Privately Held**
WEB: www.meggitt.com
SIC: 3699 3724 3728 Betatrons; exhaust
systems, aircraft; engine heaters, aircraft;
aircraft parts & equipment
PA: Meggitt Plc
Unit 2
Coventry W MIDLANDS CV7 9
120 259-7597

(P-9893)
MERCURY SECURITY PRODUCTS LLC
4811 Arprt Plz Dr Ste 300, Long Beach
(90815)
PHONE.................................562 986-9105
Joseph Grillo, *CEO*
Michael Serafin, *President*
Hing Hung, *Exec VP*
▲ **EMP:** 19 **EST:** 2012

SALES (est): 4.7MM
SALES (corp-wide): 10.1B **Privately Held**
WEB: www.mercury-security.com
SIC: 3699 8742 Security control equip-
ment & systems; industry specialist con-
sultants
HQ: Hid Global Corporation
611 Center Ridge Dr
Austin TX 78753

(P-9894)
MYE TECHNOLOGIES INC
28460 Westinghouse Pl, Valencia
(91355-0929)
PHONE.................................661 964-0217
Anthony Garcia, *President*
John Curtin, *CFO*
Ron Pace, *Vice Pres*
Virg Kasputis, *General Mgr*
Chris Hern, *Engineer*
▲ **EMP:** 45 **EST:** 2006
SQ FT: 5,000
SALES (est): 5.8MM **Privately Held**
WEB: www.myeinc.com
SIC: 3699 Electric sound equipment

(P-9895)
NUPHOTON TECHNOLOGIES INC
41610 Corning Pl, Murrieta (92562-7023)
PHONE.................................951 696-8366
Ramadas Pillai, *CEO*
Dan Vera, *COO*
Vish Govindan, *CFO*
Norm Nelson, *Vice Pres*
Sindu Pillai, *Vice Pres*
EMP: 16 **EST:** 1996
SQ FT: 12,000
SALES (est): 2.7MM **Privately Held**
WEB: www.nuphoton.com
SIC: 3699 Laser systems & equipment

(P-9896)
OSI LASERSCAN INC
12525 Chadron Ave, Hawthorne
(90250-4807)
PHONE.................................310 978-0516
Douglas Dillman, *Controller*
EMP: 34 **EST:** 2003
SALES (est): 6MM
SALES (corp-wide): 1.1B **Publicly Held**
WEB: www.osilaserscan.com
SIC: 3699 3674 Laser systems & equip-
ment; photoconductive cells
HQ: Osi Optoelectronics, Inc.
12525 Chadron Ave
Hawthorne CA 90250

(P-9897)
OSI SUBSIDIARY INC
12525 Chadron Ave, Hawthorne
(90250-4807)
PHONE.................................310 978-0516
Deepak Chopra, *CEO*
Ajay Mehra, *President*
Alan Edrick, *CFO*
Daniel Sexton, *Info Tech Mgr*
EMP: 152 **EST:** 1995
SALES (est): 19.3MM
SALES (corp-wide): 1.1B **Publicly Held**
WEB: www.osi-systems.com
SIC: 3699 Laser systems & equipment
PA: Osi Systems, Inc.
12525 Chadron Ave
Hawthorne CA 90250
310 978-0516

(P-9898)
PHANTOM ACCESS SYSTEMS LLC
631 Wald, Irvine (92618-4628)
PHONE.................................949 753-1280
Ali Tehranchi, *Mng Member*
Heidi Ropac, *Purchasing*
Chris Mazzuckis, *Natl Sales Mgr*
Bahar Tehranchi,
▲ **EMP:** 15 **EST:** 2003
SALES (est): 5.5MM
SALES (corp-wide): 7.3MM **Privately
Held**
WEB: www.vikingaccess.com
SIC: 3699 3625 Security control equip-
ment & systems; relays & industrial con-
trols; control equipment, electric

HQ: Faac International, Inc.
3160 Murrell Rd
Rockledge FL 32955
904 448-8952

(P-9899)
PHILATRON INTERNATIONAL (PA)
Also Called: Santa Fe Supply Company
15315 Cornet St, Santa Fe Springs
(90670-5531)
PHONE.................................562 802-0452
Phillip M Ramos Jr, *CEO*
Phillip M Ramos Sr, *Exec VP*
Phillip Ramos, *Exec VP*
Eloy Gallegos, *Executive*
Olga Basurto, *Office Mgr*
EMP: 137 **EST:** 1978
SQ FT: 100,000
SALES (est): 25.3MM **Privately Held**
WEB: www.philatron.com
SIC: 3699 3694 3357 Electrical equip-
ment & supplies; engine electrical equip-
ment; communication wire

(P-9900)
PRO-SYSTEMS FABRICATORS INC (PA)
Also Called: Pro Systems
14643 Hawthorne Ave, Fontana
(92335-2544)
PHONE.................................909 350-9147
Edith Sugarman, *President*
Lynn Sugarman, *Treasurer*
Trina Jackson, *Admin Sec*
▲ **EMP:** 15 **EST:** 1981
SQ FT: 11,000
SALES (est): 1.3MM **Privately Held**
WEB: www.prosystemsinc.org
SIC: 3699 3677 3564 Electrical equip-
ment & supplies; filtration devices, elec-
tronic; blowers & fans

(P-9901)
PRONTO LASER CUTTING INC
13323 S Normandie Ave, Gardena
(90249-2209)
PHONE.................................310 327-7820
Jorge Luis Flores, *CEO*
EMP: 13 **EST:** 2012
SALES (est): 1.5MM **Privately Held**
SIC: 3699 Laser welding, drilling & cutting
equipment

(P-9902)
PROTOTYPE EXPRESS LLC
3506 W Lake Center Dr D, Santa Ana
(92704-6985)
PHONE.................................714 751-3533
Bob Tavi, *Mng Member*
EMP: 18 **EST:** 1995
SQ FT: 7,000
SALES (est): 4.1MM **Privately Held**
WEB: www.prototypexpress.com
SIC: 3699 Electrical equipment & supplies

(P-9903)
QUARTON USA INC
Also Called: Infiniter
3230 Fallow Field Dr, Diamond Bar
(91765-3479)
PHONE.................................888 532-2221
Chao-CHI Huang, *President*
Cindy Lin, *Controller*
Mike Murphy, *Sales Mgr*
▲ **EMP:** 13 **EST:** 1998
SALES (est): 1.2MM **Privately Held**
WEB: www.quarton.com
SIC: 3699 Laser systems & equipment

(P-9904)
RAPISCAN SYSTEMS INC
3232 W El Segundo Blvd, Hawthorne
(90250-4823)
PHONE.................................310 978-1457
A Mehra, *Principal*
Peter Williamson, *Exec VP*
Robert Goodhouse, *Vice Pres*
Andreas Kotowski, *CTO*
Tejas Mehta, *Technology*
EMP: 23
SALES (corp-wide): 1.1B **Publicly Held**
WEB: www.rapiscansystems.com
SIC: 3699 Security control equipment &
systems

HQ: Rapiscan Systems, Inc.
2805 Columbia St
Torrance CA 90503

(P-9905)
RAYTHEON COMPANY
6380 Hollister Ave, Goleta (93117-3114)
PHONE.................................805 967-5511
Jack Gressingh, *General Mgr*
Randy Brown, *President*
Brian Hatt, *President*
Carl Jelinex, *Principal*
Adolph Schulbach, *Principal*
EMP: 200
SQ FT: 102,570
SALES (corp-wide): 56.5B **Publicly Held**
WEB: www.rtx.com
SIC: 3699 3812 Countermeasure simula-
tors, electric; search & navigation equip-
ment
HQ: Raytheon Company
870 Winter St
Waltham MA 02451
781 522-3000

(P-9906)
RELDOM CORPORATION
3241 Industry Dr, Signal Hill (90755-4013)
PHONE.................................562 498-3346
Peter Modler, *CEO*
EMP: 20 **EST:** 1979
SALES (est): 4.9MM **Privately Held**
WEB: www.reldom.com
SIC: 3699 Security devices

(P-9907)
RIGOLI ENTERPRISES INC
Also Called: Rignoli Pacific
1983 Potrero Grande Dr, Monterey Park
(91755-7420)
PHONE.................................626 573-0242
EMP: 14
SALES (est): 1.3MM **Privately Held**
WEB: www.mindpik.com
SIC: 3699 Mfg Electrical Equipment/Sup-
plies

(P-9908)
RIOT GLASS INC
17941 Brookshire Ln, Huntington Beach
(92647-7132)
PHONE.................................800 580-2303
Brad Campbell, *CEO*
Pat Glass, *Controller*
Andrew Gale, *Manager*
EMP: 30 **EST:** 2017
SALES (est): 3.9MM **Privately Held**
WEB: www.campbellwindowfilm.com
SIC: 3699 Security devices

(P-9909)
ROMEO SYSTEMS INC
Also Called: Romeo Power Technology
4380 Ayers Ave, Vernon (90058-4306)
PHONE.................................323 675-2180
Michael Patterson, *Chairman*
Lionel Selwood Jr, *CEO*
Criswell Choi, *COO*
Lauren Webb, *CFO*
Cody Boggs, *Vice Pres*
◆ **EMP:** 133 **EST:** 2014
SQ FT: 114,000
SALES (est): 7.2MM
SALES (corp-wide): 8.9MM **Publicly Held**
WEB: www.romeopower.com
SIC: 3699 8731 High-energy particle
physics equipment; energy research
PA: Romeo Power, Inc.
4380 Ayers Ave
Vernon CA 90058
833 467-2237

(P-9910)
SCHNEIDER ELC BUILDINGS LLC
Also Called: Invensys Climate Controls
100 W Victoria St, Long Beach
(90805-2147)
PHONE.................................310 900-2385
Michael Utzman, *Principal*
EMP: 124
SALES (corp-wide): 177.9K **Privately
Held**
SIC: 3699 Electrical equipment & supplies

PRODUCTS & SVCS

HQ: Schneider Electric Buildings, Llc
839 N Perryville Rd
Rockford IL 61107
815 381-5000

(P-9911)
SCHNEIDER ELECTRIC
1660 Scenic Ave, Costa Mesa
(92626-1410)
PHONE.....................949 713-9200
Tiffany Nicosia, *Principal*
Ema Soc, *Manager*
EMP: 17 **EST:** 2017
SALES (est): 5MM **Privately Held**
WEB: www.se.com
SIC: 3699 Electrical equipment & supplies

(P-9912)
SENFENG LASER USA INC ✪
5989 Rickenbacker Rd, Commerce
(90040-3029)
PHONE.....................562 319-8053
Bin Han, *CEO*
EMP: 15 **EST:** 2021
SALES (est): 958K **Privately Held**
SIC: 3699 Laser systems & equipment

(P-9913)
SERRA LASER AND WATERJET INC
1740 N Orangethorpe Park, Anaheim
(92801-1138)
PHONE.....................714 680-6211
Glenn Kline, *CEO*
EMP: 30 **EST:** 2012
SALES (est): 3.3MM **Privately Held**
WEB: www.serralaser.com
SIC: 3699 Laser welding, drilling & cutting equipment

(P-9914)
SKYGUARD LLC
2945 Townsgate Rd Ste 200, Westlake Village (91361-5866)
PHONE.....................703 262-0500
EMP: 25
SALES (est): 2.5MM **Privately Held**
SIC: 3699 Mfg Electrical Equipment/Supplies

(P-9915)
SONNET TECHNOLOGIES INC
8 Autry, Irvine (92618-2708)
PHONE.....................949 587-3500
Robert Farnsworth, *President*
Robert Rich, *Admin Sec*
Jason Konarzewski, *Engineer*
Martin Wagner, *Engineer*
Clara Valencia, *Sales Associate*
▲ **EMP:** 27
SQ FT: 17,000
SALES (est): 2.4MM **Privately Held**
WEB: www.sonnettech.com
SIC: 3699 Electrical equipment & supplies

(P-9916)
SOUNDCRAFT INC
Also Called: Secura Key
20301 Nordhoff St, Chatsworth
(91311-6128)
PHONE.....................818 882-0020
Joel Smulson, *President*
Martin Casden, *Vice Pres*
Joel B Smulson, *MIS Mgr*
Randy Watkins, *VP Rsch/Dvlpt*
Wayne Dow, *Technology*
▲ **EMP:** 35 **EST:** 1971
SQ FT: 12,000
SALES (est): 7.9MM **Privately Held**
WEB: www.securakey.com
SIC: 3699 1731 3829 Security control equipment & systems; safety & security specialization; measuring & controlling devices

(P-9917)
STRACON INC
1672 Kaiser Ave Ste 1, Irvine (92614-5700)
PHONE.....................949 851-2288
Son Pham, *President*
Liz Yeung, *Purch Mgr*
EMP: 17 **EST:** 1986
SQ FT: 10,000
SALES (est): 4.3MM **Privately Held**
WEB: www.straconinc.com
SIC: 3699 Electrical equipment & supplies

(P-9918)
SUMMIT ELECTRIC & DATA INC
27913 Smyth Dr, Valencia (91355-4034)
PHONE.....................661 775-9901
Ray Vasquez, *President*
EMP: 18 **EST:** 2010
SALES (est): 4.7MM **Privately Held**
WEB: www.summitelectservices.com
SIC: 3699 1731 Electrical equipment & supplies; electrical work

(P-9919)
SUSS MCRTEC PHTNIC SYSTEMS INC
2520 Palisades Dr, Corona (92882-0632)
PHONE.....................951 817-3700
Courtney T Sheets, *CEO*
Debbie Brown, *CFO*
Courtney Sheets, *Bd of Directors*
Debora Blanchard, *Admin Sec*
Steve Crawford, *Marketing Staff*
EMP: 90 **EST:** 1966
SALES (est): 18MM
SALES (corp-wide): 298.1MM **Privately Held**
WEB: www.suss.com
SIC: 3699 7389 Electrical equipment & supplies; business services
PA: SUss Microtec Se
SchleiBheimer Str. 90
Garching B. Munchen BY 85748
893 200-70

(P-9920)
SYSTON CABLE TECHNOLOGY CORP
15278 El Prado Rd, Chino (91710-7623)
PHONE.....................888 679-7866
Daniel Wong, *General Mgr*
Yulin Wang, *Principal*
Sam Liang, *Marketing Staff*
▲ **EMP:** 20 **EST:** 2014
SALES (est): 2MM **Privately Held**
WEB: www.systoncable.com
SIC: 3699 4841 3351 3651 Electrical equipment & supplies; cable television services; wire, copper & copper alloy; household audio & video equipment; audio electronic systems; video & audio equipment

(P-9921)
TACTICAL MICRO INC (DH)
1740 E Wilshire Ave, Santa Ana
(92705-4615)
PHONE.....................714 547-1174
Ed Hanrahan, *President*
John Moulton, *President*
Allen Romk, *CEO*
Michael Hayden, *CFO*
Tammy Jacobs, *Purch Agent*
▲ **EMP:** 44 **EST:** 2005
SQ FT: 14,000
SALES (est): 11.2MM
SALES (corp-wide): 2B **Publicly Held**
WEB: www.bench.com
SIC: 3699 Electrical equipment & supplies
HQ: Secure Communication Systems, Inc.
1740 E Wilshire Ave
Santa Ana CA 92705
714 547-1174

(P-9922)
TEKLINK SECURITY INC
Also Called: Securityman
4601 E Airport Dr, Ontario (91761-7869)
PHONE.....................909 230-6668
Sam Hsien Jung Yu, *President*
Mike Chen, *Vice Pres*
▲ **EMP:** 14 **EST:** 1999
SALES (est): 1.2MM **Privately Held**
WEB: www.securitymaninc.com
SIC: 3699 Security control equipment & systems

(P-9923)
TRIGON ELECTRONICS INC
22865 Savi Ranch Pkwy A, Yorba Linda
(92887-4626)
PHONE.....................714 633-7442
Milton L Sneller, *CEO*
Lorna R Sneller, *President*
EMP: 22 **EST:** 1979

SALES (est): 4MM **Privately Held**
WEB: www.trigonelectronics.com
SIC: 3699 Security control equipment & systems

(P-9924)
ULTRA-STEREO LABS INC
Also Called: U S L
181 Bonetti Dr, San Luis Obispo
(93401-7310)
PHONE.....................805 549-0161
James A Cashin, *President*
Jack Cashin, *President*
Alice Williams, *Vice Pres*
Dj Layland, *Info Tech Mgr*
Michael Aarons, *Engineer*
▲ **EMP:** 28 **EST:** 2016
SQ FT: 15,000
SALES (est): 4.8MM
SALES (corp-wide): 116.1MM **Privately Held**
WEB: www.qsc.com
SIC: 3699 Electric sound equipment
PA: Qsc, Llc
1675 Macarthur Blvd
Costa Mesa CA 92626
800 854-4079

(P-9925)
UNDERSEA SYSTEMS INTL INC
Also Called: Ocean Technology Systems
3133 W Harvard St, Santa Ana
(92704-3912)
PHONE.....................714 754-7848
Michael R Pelissier, *President*
Joe Kelly, *COO*
Jerry Peck, *Chairman*
Dennis Martinez, *Vice Pres*
Tiffany Heredia, *Office Mgr*
▲ **EMP:** 62
SQ FT: 18,000
SALES (est): 12.9MM **Privately Held**
WEB: www.oceantechnologysystems.com
SIC: 3699 8711 Underwater sound equipment; acoustical engineering; electrical or electronic engineering

(P-9926)
USA VISION SYSTEMS INC (HQ)
9301 Irvine Blvd, Irvine (92618-1669)
PHONE.....................949 583-1519
Kuang Cheng Tai, *President*
Mike Liu, *General Mgr*
Ray Lee, *Business Mgr*
Ryan Clark, *Accounts Mgr*
▲ **EMP:** 40 **EST:** 2003
SALES (est): 17.3MM **Privately Held**
WEB: www.geovision.com.tw
SIC: 3699 Security control equipment & systems

(P-9927)
VTI INSTRUMENTS CORPORATION (HQ)
2031 Main St, Irvine (92614-6509)
PHONE.....................949 955-1894
Paul Dhillon, *CEO*
Jasdeep Dhillon, *President*
Nelson Vogt, *Engineer*
Albert Rodriguez, *Opers Staff*
Lee Labo, *Mktg Dir*
▲ **EMP:** 44 **EST:** 1990
SQ FT: 11,500
SALES (est): 10.4MM
SALES (corp-wide): 4.5B **Publicly Held**
WEB: www.powerandtest.com
SIC: 3699 Electrical equipment & supplies
PA: Ametek, Inc.
1100 Cassatt Rd
Berwyn PA 19312
610 647-2121

(P-9928)
WEST COAST CHAIN MFG CO
Also Called: Key-Bak
4245 Pacific Privado, Ontario
(91761-1588)
P.O. Box 9088 (91762-9088)
PHONE.....................909 923-7800
Boake Paugh, *President*
Mike Winegar, *Vice Pres*
Nicholas Voss, *Marketing Staff*
▲ **EMP:** 50 **EST:** 1948
SQ FT: 31,000

SALES (est): 9.7MM **Privately Held**
WEB: www.keybak.com
SIC: 3699 Security devices

(P-9929)
WEST COAST CORPORATION
4245 Pacific Privado, Ontario
(91761-1588)
PHONE.....................909 923-7800
Boake Paugh, *President*
Marco Hernandez, *Opers Mgr*
▲ **EMP:** 21 **EST:** 1986
SALES (est): 7.2MM **Privately Held**
SIC: 3699 Security devices

(P-9930)
WESTGATE MFG INC
Also Called: Westgate Manufacturing
2462 E 28th St, Vernon (90058-1402)
PHONE.....................877 805-2252
Isaac Hadjyan, *CEO*
Eryeh Hadjian, *President*
Andrew Gonzales, *Officer*
Richard Siegel, *Vice Pres*
Mark Sakaue, *Administration*
▲ **EMP:** 75 **EST:** 2008
SALES (est): 2.5MM **Privately Held**
WEB: www.westgatemfg.com
SIC: 3699 5063 Electrical equipment & supplies; lighting fixtures

(P-9931)
XIRGO TECHNOLOGIES LLC
188 Camino Ruiz Fl 2, Camarillo
(93012-6700)
PHONE.....................805 319-4079
Roberto Piolanti, *CEO*
Mark Grout, *CFO*
Shawn Aleman, *Chief Mktg Ofcr*
Ken Boschwitz, *Vice Pres*
Michael Lavery, *VP Bus Dvlpt*
EMP: 62 **EST:** 2006
SALES (est): 14.9MM
SALES (corp-wide): 3B **Privately Held**
WEB: www.xirgo.com
SIC: 3699 Electronic training devices
HQ: Sensata Technologies Limited
2 Columbus Drive
Farnborough HANTS GU14

3711 Motor Vehicles & Car Bodies

(P-9932)
ALAN JOHNSON PRFMCE ENGRG INC
Also Called: Johnson Racing
1097 Foxen Canyon Rd, Santa Maria
(93454-9146)
PHONE.....................805 922-1202
Alan P Johnson, *President*
Allen Johnson, *Administration*
Todd Bastian, *Prdtn Mgr*
Mark Meza, *Sales Staff*
Terry Morrow, *Sales Staff*
▲ **EMP:** 24 **EST:** 1985
SQ FT: 25,000
SALES (est): 4.1MM **Privately Held**
WEB: www.alanjohnsonperformance.com
SIC: 3711 Motor vehicles & car bodies

(P-9933)
ALEPH GROUP INC
1900 E Alessndro Blvd # 105, Riverside
(92508-2311)
PHONE.....................951 213-4815
Jales Mello, *CEO*
Karina Resendiz, *Controller*
▼ **EMP:** 20 **EST:** 2012
SALES (est): 3.6MM **Privately Held**
WEB: www.alephgroupinc.com
SIC: 3711 Motor vehicles & car bodies

(P-9934)
AMERICAN HX AUTO TRADE INC
Also Called: U.S. Specialty Vehicles
4845 Via Del Cerro, Yorba Linda
(92887-2641)
PHONE.....................909 484-1010
Amy Lin, *Mng Member*
▲ **EMP:** 72 **EST:** 2010

▲ = Import ▼=Export
◆ =Import/Export

SALES (est): 5.6MM **Privately Held**
SIC: 3711 Automobile bodies, passenger car, not including engine, etc.

(P-9935)
ARTISAN VEHICLE SYSTEMS INC
742 Pancho Rd, Camarillo (93012-8576)
PHONE..................................805 402-6856
Michael Kasaba, *President*
Mike Mayhew, *Executive*
Nadine Erdmann, *General Mgr*
Joe Beck, *Project Mgr*
Kyle Hickey, *Research*
EMP: 60 EST: 2010
SALES (est): 18.9MM
SALES (corp-wide): 9.9B **Privately Held**
WEB: www.artisanvehicles.com
SIC: 3711 Personnel carriers (motor vehicles), assembly of
PA: Sandvik Ab
Hogbovagen 45
Sandviken 811 3
262 600-00

(P-9936)
BAATZ ENTERPRISES INC
Also Called: Tow Industries
2223 W San Bernardino Rd, West Covina (91790-1008)
PHONE..................................323 660-4866
Mark Ormonde Baatz, *CEO*
John O Baatz, *President*
Helen Baatz, *Corp Secy*
Juan Calvillo, *General Mgr*
Jessica Tow, *Admin Asst*
▼ EMP: 17 EST: 1988
SALES (est): 4.2MM **Privately Held**
WEB: www.towindustries.com
SIC: 3711 5013 7538 Motor vehicles & car bodies; truck parts & accessories; truck engine repair, except industrial

(P-9937)
BECKER AUTOMOTIVE DESIGNS INC
Also Called: Becker Automotive Design USA
1711 Ives Ave, Oxnard (93033-1866)
PHONE..................................805 487-5227
Howard Bernard Becker, *CEO*
Debra Becker, *Corp Secy*
Troy Becker, *Vice Pres*
Don Helm, *Technician*
Doug Cannon, *Engineer*
▲ EMP: 50 EST: 1996
SQ FT: 35,000
SALES (est): 9.1MM **Privately Held**
WEB: www.beckerautodesign.com
SIC: 3711 Cars, armored, assembly of

(P-9938)
BEN CLYMERS BODY SP PERRIS INC
12203 Magnolia Ave, Riverside (92503-4889)
PHONE..................................800 338-5872
Ben Clymer, *Principal*
EMP: 14 EST: 2013
SALES (est): 6.4MM **Privately Held**
WEB: www.benclymers.com
SIC: 3711 4119 Motor vehicles & car bodies; limousine rental, with driver

(P-9939)
CADILLAC MOTOR DIV AREA
30930 Russell Ranch Rd, Westlake Village (91362-7378)
PHONE..................................805 373-9575
Mike Jackson, *Manager*
EMP: 175 EST: 1955
SALES (est): 61.1MM **Publicly Held**
WEB: www.cadillac.com
SIC: 5511 3711 Automobiles, new & used; motor vehicles & car bodies
HQ: General Motors Llc
300 Renaissance Ctr L1
Detroit MI 48243

(P-9940)
COACHWORKS HOLDINGS INC
1863 Service Ct, Riverside (92507-2341)
PHONE..................................951 684-9585
Dale Carson, *President*
Terri L Carson, *Admin Sec*

EMP: 18 EST: 2007
SALES (est): 5.3MM
SALES (corp-wide): 105.7MM **Privately Held**
WEB: www.deere.com
SIC: 3711 Motor buses, except trackless trollies, assembly of
PA: D/T Carson Enterprises, Inc.
42882 Ivy St
Murrieta CA 92562
951 684-9585

(P-9941)
CWD LLC
Also Called: Centric Parts
14528 Bonelli St, City of Industry (91746-3022)
PHONE..................................626 961-5775
◆ EMP: 63
SALES (est): 29.1MM **Privately Held**
WEB: www.apcautotech.com
SIC: 3711 Mfg Motor Vehicle/Car Bodies

(P-9942)
CZV INC
Also Called: Czinger Vehicles
2395 Silver Lake Blvd # 8, Los Angeles (90039-3293)
PHONE..................................424 603-1450
Kevin Czinger, *CEO*
Jens Sverdrup, *COO*
EMP: 50 EST: 2010
SALES (est): 1MM **Privately Held**
WEB: www.czvinc.com
SIC: 3711 Automobile assembly, including specialty automobiles

(P-9943)
DEINY AUTOMOTIVE INC
13040 Bradley Ave, Sylmar (91342-3831)
PHONE..................................818 362-5865
Ken Sapper, *President*
Diana Deiny, *Vice Pres*
Frank Deiny Jr, *Vice Pres*
Joan Sapper, *Admin Sec*
▼ EMP: 16 EST: 1964
SQ FT: 14,000
SALES (est): 2.4MM **Privately Held**
WEB: www.1speedway.com
SIC: 3711 Chassis, motor vehicle

(P-9944)
ELDORADO NATIONAL CAL INC (HQ)
9670 Galena St, Riverside (92509-3089)
PHONE..................................951 727-9300
Peter Orthwein, *CEO*
◆ EMP: 350 EST: 1991
SQ FT: 62,000
SALES (est): 52.8MM **Publicly Held**
WEB: www.eldorado-ca.com
SIC: 3711 Buses, all types, assembly of

(P-9945)
FARADAY FTURE INTLLGENT ELC IN (PA)
18455 S Figueroa St, Gardena (90248-4503)
PHONE..................................424 276-7616
Carsten Breitfeld, *CEO*
Walter J McBride, *CFO*
Chui Tin Mok, *Exec VP*
Matthias Aydt, *Senior VP*
Benedikt Hartmann, *Senior VP*
EMP: 52 EST: 2014
SQ FT: 146,765
SALES (est): 248.1MM **Publicly Held**
SIC: 3711 Motor vehicles & car bodies

(P-9946)
FISKER AUTO & TECH GROUP LLC
3080 Airway Ave, Costa Mesa (92626-6034)
PHONE..................................714 723-3247
EMP: 233
SALES: 300K **Privately Held**
SIC: 3711 Mfg Motor Vehicle/Car Bodies

(P-9947)
FISKER GROUP INC (HQ)
1888 Rosecrans Ave # 1000, Manhattan Beach (90266-3795)
PHONE..................................833 434-7537
Henrik Fisker, *CEO*

John Finnucan, *Officer*
Dan Galves, *Vice Pres*
Martin Welch, *Vice Pres*
Natasha Fisker, *Marketing Staff*
EMP: 80 EST: 2016 **Publicly Held**
WEB: www.fiskerinc.com
SIC: 3711 Cars, electric, assembly of
PA: Fisker Inc.
1888 Rosecrans Ave # 1000
Manhattan Beach CA 90266
833 434-7537

(P-9948)
FISKER INC (PA)
1888 Rosecrans Ave # 1000, Manhattan Beach (90266-3795)
PHONE..................................833 434-7537
Henrik Fisker, *Ch of Bd* .
Geeta Gupta, *CFO*
Burkhard J Huhnke, *CTO*
EMP: 32 EST: 2016
SQ FT: 72,649 **Publicly Held**
SIC: 3711 Motor vehicles & car bodies

(P-9949)
GENERAL MOTORS LLC
3050 Lomita Blvd Bldg Ste, Torrance (90505-5103)
PHONE..................................313 556-5000
Nicholas Herron, *Branch Mgr*
Wayne WEI, *Accounts Mgr*
EMP: 14 **Publicly Held**
WEB: www.gm.com
SIC: 5511 3711 Automobiles, new & used; automobile assembly, including specialty automobiles; truck & tractor truck assembly; military motor vehicle assembly
HQ: General Motors Llc
300 Renaissance Ctr L1
Detroit MI 48243

(P-9950)
GLOBAL ENVIRONMENTAL PDTS INC
Also Called: Global Sweeping Solutions
5405 Industrial Pkwy, San Bernardino (92407-1803)
PHONE..................................909 713-1600
Walter Pusic, *Principal*
Sebastian Mentelski, *President*
Kevin Cruz, *Engineer*
Geoffrey Odfers, *Engineer*
James Labonte, *Buyer*
▲ EMP: 67 EST: 2011
SQ FT: 104,000
SALES (est): 10.9MM **Privately Held**
WEB: www.globalsweeper.com
SIC: 3711 Street sprinklers & sweepers (motor vehicles), assembly of

(P-9951)
GREENKRAFT INC
2530 S Birch St, Santa Ana (92707-3444)
PHONE..................................714 545-7777
George Gemayel, *Ch of Bd*
George Patrick, *COO*
Sosi Bardakjian, *CFO*
EMP: 18 EST: 2008
SQ FT: 51,942
SALES: 434.1K **Privately Held**
WEB: www.greenkraftinc.com
SIC: 3711 3519 Motor vehicles & car bodies; internal combustion engines

(P-9952)
GREENPOWER MOTOR COMPANY INC
8885 Haven Ave Ste 150, Rancho Cucamonga (91730-5199)
PHONE..................................909 308-0960
Fraser Atkinson, *CEO*
Henry Caouette, *Director*
Adrian Benavides, *Manager*
EMP: 33 EST: 2013
SALES (est): 9.7MM
SALES (corp-wide): 10.1MM **Privately Held**
WEB: www.greenpowermotor.com
SIC: 3711 Bus & other large specialty vehicle assembly
PA: Greenpower Motor Company Inc
209 Carrall St Suite 240
Vancouver BC V6B 2
604 563-4144

(P-9953)
HCHD
1175 S Grove Ave Ste 104, Ontario (91761-3470)
PHONE..................................909 923-8889
Hui Luo, *President*
EMP: 14 EST: 2014
SALES (est): 359.2K **Privately Held**
WEB: www.hcdcn.com
SIC: 3711 Automobile assembly, including specialty automobiles
PA: Huachangda Intelligent Equipment Group Co.,Ltd.
No.9, Dongyi Boulevard, Maojian District
Shiyan 44201

(P-9954)
ICC COLLISION CENTERS 6 INC
3131 S Standard Ave, Santa Ana (92705-5642)
PHONE..................................888 894-4079
EMP: 18 EST: 2017
SALES (est): 511.5K **Privately Held**
WEB: www.icccollision.com
SIC: 3711 Automobile bodies, passenger car, not including engine, etc.

(P-9955)
KARMA AUTOMOTIVE LLC
9950 Jeronimo Rd, Irvine (92618-2014)
PHONE..................................714 723-3247
Liang Zhou, *CEO*
Deborah Spirito, *President*
Ashoka Achuthan, *CFO*
Ronald Ashpes, *Vice Pres*
Rod Hanks, *Vice Pres*
EMP: 896 EST: 2014
SQ FT: 262,463
SALES (est): 243.1MM **Privately Held**
WEB: www.karmaautomotive.com
SIC: 3711 Motor vehicles & car bodies
HQ: Wanxiang America Corporation
88 Airport Rd
Elgin IL 60123

(P-9956)
KOVATCH MOBILE EQUIPMENT CORP
Also Called: Kme Fire
4725 Troy Ct, Jurupa Valley (92509-2019)
PHONE..................................951 685-1224
Ken Creese, *Branch Mgr*
John Whitney, *Manager*
EMP: 33 **Publicly Held**
SIC: 3711 Motor vehicles & car bodies
HQ: Kovatch Mobile Equipment Corp.
1 Industrial Complex
Nesquehoning PA 18240
570 669-9461

(P-9957)
MARTINS QUALITY TRUCK BODY INC
1831 W El Segundo Blvd, Compton (90222-1026)
PHONE..................................310 632-5978
Oscar Parra, *Principal*
Edith A Torres, *Principal*
EMP: 17 EST: 2012
SALES (est): 1.3MM **Privately Held**
SIC: 3711 Motor vehicles & car bodies

(P-9958)
MARVIN LAND SYSTEMS INC
Also Called: Marvin Group The
261 W Beach Ave, Inglewood (90302-2904)
PHONE..................................310 674-5030
Gerald M Friedman, *President*
Leon Tsimmerman, *CFO*
Bea English, *Executive Asst*
Mike Hershewe, *Info Tech Mgr*
Greg Golamirians, *Opers Staff*
▲ EMP: 44 EST: 1995
SQ FT: 200,000
SALES (est): 12.4MM
SALES (corp-wide): 149.5MM **Privately Held**
WEB: www.marvinland.com
SIC: 3711 Military motor vehicle assembly

PA: Marvin Engineering Co., Inc.
261 W Beach Ave
Inglewood CA 90302
310 674-5030

(P-9959)
MULLEN TECHNOLOGIES INC (PA)
1405 Pioneer St, Brea (92821-3721)
PHONE..................714 613-1900
David Michery, *CEO*
Mary Winter, *COO*
Jerry Alban, *CFO*
William Johnston, *Exec VP*
Eric Graciano, *Vice Pres*
EMP: 40 EST: 2014
SQ FT: 24,730
SALES (est): 10.3MM **Privately Held**
WEB: www.mullenusa.com
SIC: 3711 5013 Motor vehicles & car bodies; motor vehicle supplies & new parts

(P-9960)
NEW FLYER OF AMERICA INC
2880 Jurupa St, Ontario (91761-2903)
PHONE..................909 456-3566
Danny Hetzler, *General Mgr*
EMP: 44
SALES (corp-wide): 2.8B **Privately Held**
WEB: www.newflyer.com
SIC: 3711 Motor vehicles & car bodies
HQ: New Flyer Of America Inc.
6200 Glenn Carlson Dr
Saint Cloud MN 56301

(P-9961)
PHOENIX CARS LLC
Also Called: Phoenix Motorcars
1500 Lakeview Loop, Anaheim (92807-1819)
PHONE..................909 987-0815
Joseph Mitchell, *CEO*
Ira Feintuch, *Senior VP*
JP Aguirre, *Vice Pres*
Jose Paul, *VP Bus Dvlpt*
Yasmin Fallah, *Principal*
▲ EMP: 39 EST: 2009
SQ FT: 40,000
SALES (est): 10.5MM **Privately Held**
WEB: www.phoenixmotorcars.com
SIC: 3711 Cars, electric, assembly of
PA: Edisonfuture Inc.
4677 Old Ironsides Dr # 1
Santa Clara CA

(P-9962)
PROTERRA INC
393 Cheryl Ln, City of Industry (91789-3003)
PHONE..................864 438-0000
Rohit Seetharam, *Manager*
EMP: 402
SALES (corp-wide): 181.2MM **Publicly Held**
WEB: www.proterra.com
SIC: 3711 Automobile assembly, including specialty automobiles
HQ: Proterra Operating Company, Inc.
1815 Rollins Rd
Burlingame CA 94010
864 438-0000

(P-9963)
RACEPAK LLC
Also Called: Race Pak
30402 Esperanza, Rcho STA Marg (92688-2144)
PHONE..................888 429-4709
Fax: 949 709-5556
▲ EMP: 29
SQ FT: 6,000
SALES (est): 5.5MM **Privately Held**
WEB: www.csisensors.com
SIC: 3711 Mfg Motor Vehicle/Car Bodies

(P-9964)
SALEEN INCORPORATED (PA)
2735 Wardlow Rd, Corona (92882-2869)
PHONE..................714 400-2121
Paul Wilbur, *President*
Stephen Saleen, *CEO*
Brian Walsh, *Senior VP*
Michael Simmons, *Sales Staff*
EMP: 200 EST: 1984

SALES (est): 24.5MM **Privately Held**
WEB: www.saleen.com
SIC: 3711 Automobile assembly, including specialty automobiles; motor trucks, except off-highway, assembly of

(P-9965)
SHELBY CARROLL INTL INC (PA)
19021 S Figueroa St, Gardena (90248-4510)
PHONE..................310 538-2914
Carroll Shelby, *Principal*
ARI Kopmar, *Exec VP*
Schechner Gary, *VP Mktg*
Mike Lambert, *Relations*
EMP: 73 EST: 2009
SALES (est): 8.4MM **Privately Held**
WEB: www.carrollshelby.com
SIC: 3711 Motor vehicles & car bodies

(P-9966)
SHYFT GROUP INC
1130 S Vail Ave, Montebello (90640-6021)
PHONE..................323 276-1933
EMP: 26
SALES (corp-wide): 146.2MM **Publicly Held**
WEB: www.spartanmotors.com
SIC: 3711 Motor vehicles & car bodies
PA: The Shyft Group Inc
41280 Bridge St
Novi MI 48375
517 543-6400

(P-9967)
TCI ENGINEERING INC
Also Called: Total Cost Involved
1416 Brooks St, Ontario (91762-3613)
PHONE..................909 984-1773
Edward Moss, *President*
Sherlly Prakarsa, *CFO*
Ruben Perez, *Purchasing*
EMP: 54 EST: 1974
SQ FT: 25,000
SALES (est): 8.8MM **Privately Held**
WEB: www.totalcostinvolved.com
SIC: 3711 5531 3714 Chassis, motor vehicle; automotive & home supply stores; motor vehicle parts & accessories

(P-9968)
TEAM USA (PA)
2154 E 51st St, Vernon (90058-2817)
PHONE..................323 826-9888
Tony Hur, *President*
Andre Achay, *Manager*
◆ EMP: 19 EST: 1999
SQ FT: 9,000
SALES (est): 1.2MM **Privately Held**
SIC: 3711 5511 Automobile assembly, including specialty automobiles; new & used car dealers

(P-9969)
TIFFANY COACHWORKS INC
420 N Mckinley St 111-465, Corona (92879-8099)
PHONE..................951 657-2680
William Auden, *CEO*
James Powel, *CEO*
◆ EMP: 19 EST: 1992
SQ FT: 57,000
SALES (est): 251.6K **Privately Held**
WEB: www.tiffanylimo.com
SIC: 3711 Motor vehicles & car bodies

(P-9970)
TOYOTA LOGISTICS SERVICES INC (DH)
19001 S Western Ave, Torrance (90501-1106)
PHONE..................310 468-4000
Randy Pflughaupt, *CEO*
Allen Decarr, *President*
Robert Young, *Vice Pres*
Donald Esmond, *Principal*
Shawn Soper, *Executive Asst*
◆ EMP: 176 EST: 1981
SQ FT: 600
SALES (est): 201.8MM **Privately Held**
WEB: www.toyota.com
SIC: 5511 3711 Automobiles, new & used; motor vehicles & car bodies

HQ: Toyota Motor Sales Usa Inc
6565 Hdqtr Dr Apt W1 3c
Plano TX 75024
310 468-4000

(P-9971)
WARNER CHEMICAL MFG
14803 S Spring St, Gardena (90248-1943)
PHONE..................310 715-3000
David Velasco, *Ch of Bd*
EMP: 23 EST: 1999
SALES (est): 4.1MM **Privately Held**
WEB: www.warnerchemical.com
SIC: 3711 Automobile bodies, passenger car, not including engine, etc.

(P-9972)
WEST COAST UNLIMITED
Also Called: West Coast Airlines
11161 Pierce St, Riverside (92505-2713)
PHONE..................951 352-1234
H J Manning, *Manager*
L K Manning, *President*
EMP: 22 EST: 1953
SQ FT: 6,000
SALES (est): 604.9K **Privately Held**
SIC: 3711 7699 Fire department vehicles (motor vehicles), assembly of; fire control (military) equipment repair

(P-9973)
WIDE OPEN INDUSTRIES LLC
21088 Bake Pkwy Ste 100, Lake Forest (92630-2165)
PHONE..................949 635-2292
Christian Hammarskjold, *Mng Member*
EMP: 23 EST: 2009 **Privately Held**
WEB: www.wideopenbaja.com
SIC: 3711 3714 5012 Motor vehicles & car bodies; motor vehicle parts & accessories; automobiles & other motor vehicles

(P-9974)
XOS FLEET INC
Also Called: Xos Trucks
3550 Tyburn St, Los Angeles (90065-1427)
PHONE..................818 316-1890
Dakota Semler, *CEO*
Giordano Sordoni, *COO*
Kingsley Afemikhe, *CFO*
Kevin Damoa, *Vice Pres*
Saleh Mirheidari, *Vice Pres*
EMP: 50 EST: 2020
SALES (est): 2.6MM **Privately Held**
WEB: www.xostrucks.com
SIC: 3711 3713 Truck & tractor truck assembly; truck tractors for highway use, assembly of; truck bodies & parts

(P-9975)
ZEROTRUCK
3687 W Mcfadden Ave, Santa Ana (92704-1329)
PHONE..................714 675-7117
Tedd Abramson, *CEO*
EMP: 15 EST: 2011
SQ FT: 5,000
SALES (est): 190K **Privately Held**
SIC: 5531 3711 Batteries, automotive & truck; trucks, pickup, assembly of

3713 Truck & Bus Bodies

(P-9976)
ARMENCO CATRG TRCK MFG CO INC
11819 Vose St, North Hollywood (91605-5748)
PHONE..................818 768-0400
Gerhayr Djahani, *President*
Yres Mardros, *Vice Pres*
EMP: 25 EST: 1977
SQ FT: 6,000
SALES (est): 2.8MM **Privately Held**
WEB: www.cateringtruck.com
SIC: 3713 Truck bodies (motor vehicles)

(P-9977)
ARROW TRUCK BODIES & EQP INC
1639 S Campus Ave, Ontario (91761-4364)
PHONE..................909 947-3991
Raymond A Glaze, *President*

Keith Wysocki, *President*
Richard Rubio, *Corp Secy*
EMP: 18 EST: 1963
SQ FT: 33,980
SALES (est): 2.5MM **Privately Held**
SIC: 3713 Truck bodies (motor vehicles)

(P-9978)
CALIFORNIA SUPERTRUCKS INC
14385 Veterans Way, Moreno Valley (92553-9059)
PHONE..................951 656-2903
Chris Robinson, *President*
Tim Clark, *Vice Pres*
Bradley Myers, *Vice Pres*
EMP: 22 EST: 1996
SQ FT: 20,000
SALES (est): 4.8MM **Privately Held**
WEB: www.californiasupertrucks.com
SIC: 3713 3011 5014 5013 Truck bodies & parts; inner tubes, all types; pneumatic tires, all types; truck tires & tubes; truck parts & accessories

(P-9979)
COMMERCIAL TRUCK EQP CO LLC
12351 Bellflower Blvd, Downey (90242-2829)
PHONE..................562 803-4466
James E Anderson, *President*
Lorena Anderson, *COO*
Jose Franco, *Engineer*
Dan Hartman, *Sales Staff*
EMP: 56 EST: 2008
SALES (est): 3.9MM **Privately Held**
SIC: 3713 Truck bodies (motor vehicles)

(P-9980)
CTBLA INC
1740 Albion St, Los Angeles (90031-2520)
PHONE..................323 276-1933
Kam C Law, *President*
Peter Lee, *Treasurer*
Dana Pearce, *General Mgr*
Roland Tercero, *Sales Executive*
Miles Olsen, *Manager*
◆ EMP: 99 EST: 1995
SALES (est): 7.1MM **Privately Held**
SIC: 3713 Truck bodies (motor vehicles)

(P-9981)
DADEE MANUFACTURING LLC
911 N Poinsettia St, Santa Ana (92701-3827)
PHONE..................602 276-4390
Paul Campbell,
EMP: 22 EST: 2007
SALES (est): 3.8MM **Privately Held**
SIC: 3713 Garbage, refuse truck bodies

(P-9982)
DELTA STAG MANUFACTURING
Also Called: Delta-Stag Truck Body
1818 E Rosslynn Ave, Fullerton (92831-5140)
PHONE..................562 904-6444
George Cashman Sr, *President*
David Odell, *General Mgr*
EMP: 20 EST: 1997
SQ FT: 100,000
SALES (est): 1.4MM **Privately Held**
WEB: www.deltastag.com
SIC: 3713 7549 Truck bodies (motor vehicles); specialty motor vehicle bodies; automotive maintenance services

(P-9983)
DOUGLASS TRUCK BODIES INC
231 21st St, Bakersfield (33301-4138)
PHONE..................661 327-0258
Rick Douglass, *President*
Jean Raley, *Corp Secy*
Deborah Douglass, *Vice Pres*
Jennifer Rutledge, *Office Mgr*
Danny Owens, *Sales Mgr*
EMP: 24 EST: 1959
SQ FT: 5,000
SALES (est): 6.5MM **Privately Held**
WEB: www.douglasstruckbodies.com
SIC: 3713 Truck bodies (motor vehicles)

(P-9984)
DYNAFLEX PRODUCTS (PA)
Also Called: Exhaust Tech
6466 Gayhart St, Commerce (90040-2506)
PHONE..............................323 724-1555
Robert L McGovern, *President*
Gil Contreras, *Vice Pres*
Kynon Johnson, *Engineer*
Rich Schevis, *Engineer*
EMP: 75 **EST:** 1971
SQ FT: 64,000
SALES: 16.7MM **Privately Held**
WEB: www.dynaflexproducts.com
SIC: 3713 3498 3714 Truck & bus bodies; fabricated pipe & fittings; exhaust systems & parts, motor vehicle

(P-9985)
EBUS INC
9250 Washburn Rd, Downey (90242-2909)
PHONE..............................562 904-3474
Anders B Eklov, *Ch of Bd*
Chris Mejia, *Engineer*
Lou Ellen Pruden, *Controller*
EMP: 29 **EST:** 1983
SALES (est): 4.4MM **Privately Held**
WEB: www.ebus.com
SIC: 3713 Bus bodies (motor vehicles)

(P-9986)
ERF ENTERPRISES INC
Also Called: Colton Truck Terminal Garage
863 E Valley Blvd, Colton (92324-3125)
PHONE..............................909 825-4080
Ed Doltar, *President*
Rich Doltar, *Principal*
Fran Fields, *Principal*
EMP: 18 **EST:** 2019
SALES (est): 1.2MM **Privately Held**
SIC: 3713 Truck bodies (motor vehicles)

(P-9987)
FLEMING METAL FABRICATORS
2810 Tanager Ave, Commerce (90040-2716)
PHONE..............................323 723-8203
Wade M Fleming, *President*
Marc Fleming, *Vice Pres*
EMP: 30 **EST:** 1918
SQ FT: 36,000
SALES (est): 5.5MM **Privately Held**
WEB: www.flemingmetal.com
SIC: 3713 3441 3714 3577 Truck bodies & parts; fabricated structural metal; motor vehicle parts & accessories; computer peripheral equipment; electronic computers

(P-9988)
HARBOR TRUCK BODIES INC
Also Called: Harbor Truck Body
255 Voyager Ave, Brea (92821-6223)
PHONE..............................714 996-0411
Ken Lindt, *President*
John Houng, *Engineer*
Alex Ledezma, *Purchasing*
Alan Perkins, *Purchasing*
Kimberly Bellamy, *Sales Staff*
EMP: 79 **EST:** 1973
SQ FT: 50,000
SALES (est): 22.1MM **Privately Held**
WEB: www.harbortruck.com
SIC: 3713 7532 Truck bodies (motor vehicles); body shop, automotive

(P-9989)
HARDWARE IMPORTS INC
Also Called: Western Hardware Company
161 Commerce Way, Walnut (91789-2719)
P.O. Box 4177, Covina (91723-0017)
PHONE..............................909 595-6201
Gayle Pacheco, *President*
Robert Pacheco, *CFO*
◆ **EMP:** 19 **EST:** 1970
SQ FT: 6,000
SALES (est): 1.3MM **Privately Held**
WEB: www.westernhardware.com
SIC: 3713 3429 Truck & bus bodies; furniture hardware

(P-9990)
MCLELLAN EQUIPMENT INC
13221 Crown Ave, Hanford (93230-9508)
PHONE..............................559 582-8100
Scott McLellan, *Vice Pres*
Russ Huffman, *Prdtn Mgr*
Adrian Gonzalez, *Sales Staff*

EMP: 45
SALES (corp-wide): 11.5MM **Privately Held**
WEB: www.mclellanindustries.com
SIC: 3713 3532 7532 3312 Truck bodies (motor vehicles); truck beds; mining machinery; tops (canvas or plastic); installation or repair: automotive; blast furnaces & steel mills
PA: Mclellan Equipment, Inc.
   251 Shaw Rd
   South San Francisco CA 94080
   650 873-8100

(P-9991)
MCLELLAN INDUSTRIES INC
13221 Crown Ave, Hanford (93230-9508)
PHONE..............................650 873-8100
Victor Resendez, *Manager*
Shawn Quinn, *General Mgr*
Ranae Agurrie, *Sales Mgr*
Megan Ogle, *Sales Staff*
EMP: 80
SALES (corp-wide): 23.2MM **Privately Held**
WEB: www.mclellanindustries.com
SIC: 3713 Truck bodies (motor vehicles)
PA: Mclellan Industries, Inc.
   251 Shaw Rd
   South San Francisco CA 94080
   650 873-8100

(P-9992)
MCNEILUS TRUCK AND MFG INC
401 N Pepper Ave, Colton (92324-1817)
P.O. Box 1588 (92324-0849)
PHONE..............................909 370-2100
Liza Langley, *Branch Mgr*
EMP: 33
SALES (corp-wide): 7.7B **Publicly Held**
WEB: www.mcneilus.com
SIC: 3713 5511 3711 3531 Cement mixer bodies; pickups, new & used; truck & tractor truck assembly; construction machinery
HQ: Mcneilus Truck And Manufacturing, Inc.
   524 E Highway St
   Dodge Center MN 55927
   507 374-6321

(P-9993)
METRO TRUCK BODY INCORPORATED
1201 W Jon St, Torrance (90502-1288)
PHONE..............................310 532-5570
Vincent Rigali, *CEO*
Vincint X Rigali, *President*
Philip W Rigali, *CEO*
Sid Halushka, *Corp Secy*
Virginia Rigali, *Vice Pres*
▲ **EMP:** 47 **EST:** 1968
SQ FT: 20,000
SALES (est): 8MM **Privately Held**
WEB: www.metrotruckbody.com
SIC: 3713 7532 5012 5531 Truck bodies (motor vehicles); body shop, automotive; truck bodies; truck equipment & parts

(P-9994)
PHENIX ENTERPRISES INC (PA)
Also Called: Phenix Truck Bodies and Eqp
1785 Mount Vernon Ave, Pomona (91768-3330)
PHONE..............................909 469-0411
Rick Albertini, *CEO*
Norma E Albertini, *President*
Benjamin Albertini, *Chairman*
Paul Albertini, *Corp Secy*
Maria Anderson, *Sales Staff*
EMP: 39 **EST:** 1978
SQ FT: 100,000
SALES (est): 11.5MM **Privately Held**
WEB: www.phenixent.com
SIC: 3713 3711 Truck bodies (motor vehicles); motor vehicles & car bodies

(P-9995)
SKAUG TRUCK BODY WORKS
1404 1st St, San Fernando (91340-2795)
PHONE..............................818 365-9123
George L Skaug, *President*
William Reeves, *Vice Pres*
EMP: 18 **EST:** 1946
SQ FT: 3,200

SALES (est): 2.1MM **Privately Held**
SIC: 3713 Truck bodies (motor vehicles)

(P-9996)
SOUTHERN CAL TRCK BDIES SLS IN
1131 E 2nd St, Pomona (91766-2115)
PHONE..............................909 469-1132
Miguel Sanchez, *President*
Silvia Sanchez, *Admin Sec*
EMP: 15 **EST:** 2000
SQ FT: 6,035
SALES (est): 3.3MM **Privately Held**
WEB: www.socaltrkbodies.com
SIC: 3713 5531 Truck bodies (motor vehicles); automotive parts

(P-9997)
SPARTAN MOTORS GTB LLC
Also Called: Ultimaster
1130 S Vail Ave, Montebello (90640-6021)
PHONE..............................323 276-1933
Daryl Adams, *CEO*
EMP: 15 **EST:** 2019
SALES (est): 3.5MM **Privately Held**
SIC: 3713 Truck beds

(P-9998)
SPARTAN TRUCK COMPANY INC
12266 Branford St, Sun Valley (91352-1009)
PHONE..............................818 899-1111
Myan Spaccarelli, *President*
Ana Alfaro, *Office Mgr*
Joe Capistran, *Opers Spvr*
Dan Spaccarelli, *Sales Mgr*
EMP: 35 **EST:** 1972
SQ FT: 25,000
SALES (est): 3.7MM **Privately Held**
WEB: www.spartantruck.com
SIC: 3713 7532 3537 Garbage, refuse truck bodies; top & body repair & paint shops; industrial trucks & tractors

(P-9999)
SPECIALTY EQUIPMENT CO
1921 E Pomona St, Santa Ana (92705-5119)
PHONE..............................714 258-1622
Richard Page, *President*
EMP: 16 **EST:** 1978
SALES (est): 1.5MM **Privately Held**
WEB: www.specialtytruckequipment.com
SIC: 3713 3711 Truck bodies & parts; motor vehicles & car bodies

(P-10000)
VAHE ENTERPRISES INC
Also Called: Aa Leasing
750 E Slauson Ave, Los Angeles (90011-5236)
PHONE..............................323 235-6657
Vahe Karapetian, *CEO*
Clarence Stokes, *Asst Controller*
▲ **EMP:** 90 **EST:** 1976
SQ FT: 60,000
SALES (est): 11.4MM **Privately Held**
WEB: www.aacatertruck.com
SIC: 3713 7513 Truck bodies (motor vehicles); truck leasing, without drivers

(P-10001)
VAN MART INC (PA)
Also Called: Van Mart, The
15192 Goldenwest Cir, Westminster (92683-5222)
PHONE..............................949 698-2447
Duran Morley, *CEO*
EMP: 18 **EST:** 2020
SALES (est): 2.5MM **Privately Held**
WEB: www.thevanmart.com
SIC: 3713 5571 7532 Van bodies; motorcycle parts & accessories; van conversion

3714 Motor Vehicle Parts & Access

(P-10002)
A TERRYCABLE CALIFORNIA CORP
17376 Eucalyptus St, Hesperia (92345-5118)
PHONE..............................760 244-9351
Terry P Davis, *President*
Danielle Medley, *General Mgr*
EMP: 20 **EST:** 1971
SQ FT: 10,000
SALES (est): 1.6MM **Privately Held**
WEB: www.terrycable.com
SIC: 3714 Motor vehicle parts & accessories

(P-10003)
ACME HEADLINING CO
Also Called: Acme Auto Headlining
550 W 16th St, Long Beach (90813-1510)
P.O. Box 847 (90801-0847)
PHONE..............................562 432-0281
Bob Westmoreland, *Vice Pres*
Steve Acme, *General Mgr*
Don Young, *Director*
▲ **EMP:** 75 **EST:** 1948
SQ FT: 18,000
SALES: 7.2MM **Privately Held**
SIC: 3714 Tops, motor vehicle

(P-10004)
ACSCO PRODUCTS INC
313 N Lake St, Burbank (91502-1816)
PHONE..............................818 953-2240
Thomas W Mc Intyre, *President*
Yolanda Piroli, *Info Tech Mgr*
Luigi Cervantes, *Engineer*
EMP: 20 **EST:** 1963
SQ FT: 4,000
SALES (est): 3.9MM **Privately Held**
WEB: www.acsco.net
SIC: 3714 Motor vehicle parts & accessories

(P-10005)
ADVANCE ADAPTERS INC
4320 Aerotech Center Way, Paso Robles (93446-8529)
P.O. Box 247 (93447-0247)
PHONE..............................805 238-7000
Mike Partridge, *President*
John Partridge, *Vice Pres*
Scott Corgiat, *Executive*
Jeff Walston, *Design Engr*
Charles Althausen, *Engineer*
▲ **EMP:** 44 **EST:** 1971
SQ FT: 44,000
SALES (est): 6.1MM **Privately Held**
WEB: www.advanceadapters.com
SIC: 3714 Transmission housings or parts, motor vehicle

(P-10006)
ADVANCE ADAPTERS LLC
4320 Aerotech Center Way, Paso Robles (93446-8529)
PHONE..............................805 238-7000
Scott Corgiat, *Vice Pres*
Geno Burrell, *Technical Staff*
Kevin Dill, *Engineer*
Justin Alvarez, *Sales Staff*
EMP: 45 **EST:** 2017
SALES (est): 3.8MM **Privately Held**
WEB: www.advanceadapters.com
SIC: 3714 Motor vehicle parts & accessories; motor vehicle transmissions, drive assemblies & parts

(P-10007)
ADVANCED CLUTCH TECHNOLOGY INC
206 E Avenue K4, Lancaster (93535-4685)
PHONE..............................661 940-7555
Tracy Nunez, *CEO*
Dirk Starksen, *President*
Rich Barsamian, *Vice Pres*
Danette Starksen, *Admin Sec*
Dean Williams, *Supervisor*
▲ **EMP:** 30 **EST:** 1994
SQ FT: 18,000

SALES (est): 6.9MM **Privately Held**
WEB: www.advancedclutch.com
SIC: 3714 Clutches, motor vehicle

(P-10008)
ADVANCED FLOW ENGINEERING INC (PA)
Also Called: Afe Power
252 Granite St, Corona (92879-1283)
PHONE..........................951 493-7155
Shahriar Nick Niakan, *President*
David Howey, *CFO*
Chris Barron, *Vice Pres*
Eric Griffith, *Vice Pres*
Stuart Miyagishima, *Vice Pres*
▲ EMP: 85 EST: 1999
SQ FT: 60,000
SALES (est): 20.5MM **Privately Held**
WEB: www.afepower.com
SIC: 3714 Motor vehicle engines & parts

(P-10009)
ADVANTI RACING USA LLC (DH)
10721 Business Dr Ste 1, Fontana (92337-8252)
PHONE..........................951 272-5930
Raymond Chan, *Principal*
EMP: 15 EST: 2008
SALES (est): 6.6MM **Privately Held**
WEB: www.advantiwheel.com
SIC: 3714 Wheel rims, motor vehicle

(P-10010)
AEC GROUP INC
Also Called: Advantage Engrg & Chemistry
3600 W Carriage Dr, Santa Ana (92704-6416)
PHONE..........................714 444-1395
Mike Lau, *President*
Erik Waelput, *Vice Pres*
Scott Lau, *Marketing Mgr*
EMP: 15 EST: 2000
SQ FT: 12,000
SALES (est): 3.2MM **Privately Held**
WEB: www.aecgroup.net
SIC: 3714 Lubrication systems & parts, motor vehicle

(P-10011)
AGILITY FUEL SYSTEMS LLC (DH)
1815 Carnegie Ave, Santa Ana (92705-5527)
PHONE..........................949 236-5520
Kathleen Ligocki, *CEO*
Ron Eickeleman, *President*
William Nowicke, *COO*
Tom Russell, *CFO*
Scott Lucero, *Vice Pres*
▲ EMP: 213 EST: 2010
SALES (est): 109.7MM
SALES (corp-wide): 339.9MM **Privately Held**
WEB: www.hexagonagility.com
SIC: 3714 Fuel systems & parts, motor vehicle
HQ: Agility Fuel Solutions Llc
3335 Susan St Ste 100
Costa Mesa CA 92626
949 236-5520

(P-10012)
AIR FLOW RESEARCH HEADS INC
28611 Industry Dr, Valencia (91355-5413)
PHONE..........................661 257-8124
Rick Sperling, *President*
Chris Paul, *Plant Mgr*
Jess Ulloa, *Prdtn Mgr*
Jerami Patrick, *Sales Staff*
▲ EMP: 40 EST: 1970
SQ FT: 14,000
SALES (est): 6.2MM **Privately Held**
WEB: www.airflowresearch.com
SIC: 3714 Cylinder heads, motor vehicle

(P-10013)
AISIN WORLD CORP OF AMERICA
19801 S Vermont Ave, Torrance (90502-1127)
PHONE..........................310 326-8681
EMP: 297 **Privately Held**
WEB: www.aisinworld.com

SIC: 3714 Motor vehicle parts & accessories
HQ: Aisin World Corp. Of America
15300 Centennial Dr
Northville MI 48168

(P-10014)
AITA CLUTCH INC
960 S Santa Fe Ave, Compton (90221-4333)
PHONE..........................323 585-4140
Guillermo Rios, *President*
Albert Rios, *Treasurer*
Fred Rios, *Vice Pres*
EMP: 23 EST: 1982
SALES (est): 2MM **Privately Held**
SIC: 3714 5013 Clutches, motor vehicle; automotive supplies & parts

(P-10015)
ALLIED WHEEL COMPONENTS INC
Also Called: Raceline Wheels
12300 Edison Way, Garden Grove (92841-2810)
P.O. Box 5667 (92846-0667)
PHONE..........................714 893-4160
Bruce Higginson, *CEO*
Val Peura, *Office Mgr*
Maggie Aragon, *Human Res Dir*
Gina Alcala, *Sales Staff*
Priscilla Brewer, *Sales Staff*
◆ EMP: 38 EST: 1996
SQ FT: 91,000
SALES (est): 15.4MM **Privately Held**
WEB: www.alliedwheel.com
SIC: 5531 3714 Automotive tires; wheels, motor vehicle

(P-10016)
AMCOR INDUSTRIES INC
Also Called: Gorilla Automotive Products
2011 E 49th St, Vernon (90058-2801)
PHONE..........................323 585-2852
Peter J Schermer, *President*
▲ EMP: 25 EST: 1983
SQ FT: 30,000
SALES (est): 4MM **Privately Held**
WEB: www.gorilla-auto.com
SIC: 3714 3429 Motor vehicle wheels & parts; manufactured hardware (general)
PA: Wheel Pros, Llc
5347 S Valentia Way # 200
Greenwood Village CO 80111

(P-10017)
AMERICAN FABRICATION CORP (PA)
Also Called: American Best Car Parts
2891 E Via Martens, Anaheim (92806-1751)
PHONE..........................714 632-1709
Greg Knox, *President*
Jodee Jensen Smith, *Vice Pres*
Grant Hurner, *Consultant*
▲ EMP: 70 EST: 1974
SALES (est): 9.2MM **Privately Held**
WEB: www.teamxenon.com
SIC: 3714 Motor vehicle parts & accessories

(P-10018)
ARIAS INDUSTRIES INC
Also Called: Arias Pistons
275 Roswell Ave, Long Beach (90803-1538)
PHONE..........................310 532-9737
Nicholas Arias Jr, *President*
Carmen Arias, *Vice Pres*
EMP: 20 EST: 1969
SQ FT: 20,000
SALES (est): 1.7MM **Privately Held**
WEB: www.ariaspistons.com
SIC: 3714 Motor vehicle engines & parts

(P-10019)
AUTOMAX STYLING INC
16833 Krameria Ave, Riverside (92504-6118)
PHONE..........................951 530-1876
Guoxiang Zhou, *CEO*
William Cheng, *Buyer*
EMP: 40 EST: 2005
SQ FT: 100,000

SALES (est): 3.2MM **Privately Held**
WEB: www.blog.automaxstyling.com
SIC: 3714 Motor vehicle parts & accessories

(P-10020)
AUTOMOCO LLC
Also Called: B & M Racing & Prfmce Pdts
9142 Independence Ave, Chatsworth (91311-5902)
PHONE..........................707 544-4761
Brian Applegate, *President*
EMP: 26 EST: 1953
SALES (est): 1.6MM **Privately Held**
SIC: 3714 Transmission housings or parts, motor vehicle

(P-10021)
AZUSA ENGINEERING INC
1542 W Industrial Park St, Covina (91722-3487)
P.O. Box 2909 (91722-8909)
PHONE..........................626 966-4071
James M Patronite, *CEO*
Tom Patronite, *President*
Janice M Patronite, *Admin Sec*
David Stillwell, *Supervisor*
▲ EMP: 17 EST: 1960
SQ FT: 17,000
SALES (est): 2.3MM **Privately Held**
WEB: www.azusaeng.com
SIC: 3714 Transmission housings or parts, motor vehicle

(P-10022)
BAB STEERING HYDRAULICS (PA)
Also Called: Bab Hydraulics
14554 Whittram Ave, Fontana (92335-3108)
PHONE..........................208 573-4502
William Carlson, *President*
▲ EMP: 20 EST: 1989
SQ FT: 15,000
SALES (est): 4.3MM **Privately Held**
WEB: www.babsteering.com
SIC: 3714 3713 5084 Hydraulic fluid power pumps for auto steering mechanism; truck & bus bodies; hydraulic systems equipment & supplies

(P-10023)
BSST LLC
5462 Irwindale Ave Ste A, Irwindale (91706-2074)
PHONE..........................626 593-4500
Lon Bell,
Sandy Grouf, *CFO*
▲ EMP: 111 EST: 2000
SQ FT: 12,000
SALES (est): 1.7MM **Publicly Held**
WEB: www.gentherm.com
SIC: 3714 Heaters, motor vehicle
PA: Gentherm Incorporated
21680 Haggerty Rd Ste 101
Northville MI 48167

(P-10024)
BUNKER CORP (PA)
Also Called: Energy Suspension
1131 Via Callejon, San Clemente (92673-6230)
PHONE..........................949 361-3935
Donald Bunker, *CEO*
Boni Cambel, *Manager*
▼ EMP: 100 EST: 1985
SQ FT: 78,000
SALES (est): 22.1MM **Privately Held**
SIC: 3714 Motor vehicle body components & frame

(P-10025)
BUS SERVICES CORPORATION
Also Called: Trams International
6801 Suva St, Bell Gardens (90201-1937)
P.O. Box 788, Seal Beach (90740-0788)
PHONE..........................562 231-1770
Don Duffy, *President*
Linda Duffy, *Corp Secy*
Newton Montano, *Vice Pres*
Fabricio Alas, *Purch Mgr*
▼ EMP: 35 EST: 1989
SQ FT: 70,000

SALES (est): 6.7MM **Privately Held**
WEB: www.tramsinternational.com
SIC: 3714 Motor vehicle body components & frame

(P-10026)
BYD MOTORS LLC (HQ)
1800 S Figueroa St, Los Angeles (90015-3422)
PHONE..........................213 748-3980
Stella Li, *CEO*
Ke Li, *President*
Michael Auftin, *Vice Pres*
Sandra Itkoff, *Vice Pres*
Fred Ni, *Vice Pres*
▲ EMP: 39 EST: 2010
SALES (est): 5.8MM
SALES (corp-wide): 2.4MM **Privately Held**
WEB: www.en.byd.com
SIC: 3714 Motor vehicle electrical equipment
PA: Byd Us Holding Inc.
1800 S Figueroa St
Los Angeles CA 90015
213 748-3980

(P-10027)
C R LAURENCE CO INC (HQ)
Also Called: Crl
2503 E Vernon Ave, Vernon (90058-1826)
PHONE..........................323 588-1281
Arty Feles, *President*
Barbara Haaksma, *Senior VP*
Shirin Khosravi, *Senior VP*
Jacque Maples, *Senior VP*
Steve Whitcomb, *Senior VP*
◆ EMP: 380 EST: 1963
SQ FT: 170,000
SALES (est): 423.4MM
SALES (corp-wide): 27.5B **Privately Held**
WEB: www.crl-arch.com
SIC: 3714 5072 5039 Sun roofs, motor vehicle; hand tools; glass construction materials
PA: Crh Public Limited Company
Stonemasons Way
Dublin D16 K
140 410-00

(P-10028)
CANOO INC (PA)
19951 Mariner Ave, Torrance (90503-1672)
PHONE..........................424 271-2144
Ulrich Kranz, *CEO*
Tony Aquila, *Ch of Bd*
Paul Balciunas, *CFO*
Christian Treiber, *Senior VP*
Andrew Wolstan, *Admin Sec*
EMP: 211 EST: 2020
SALES (est): 2.5MM **Publicly Held**
WEB: www.hennessycapllc.com
SIC: 3714 Motor vehicle parts & accessories

(P-10029)
CENTER LINE WHEEL CORPORATION
Also Called: Center Line Performance Wheels
23 Corporate Plaza Dr # 150, Newport Beach (92660-7908)
PHONE..........................562 921-9637
Ray Lipper, *President*
▲ EMP: 47 EST: 1963
SALES (est): 2.9MM **Privately Held**
SIC: 3714 Wheels, motor vehicle

(P-10030)
CIRCLE RACING WHEELS INC (PA)
14955 Don Julian Rd, City of Industry (91746-3112)
PHONE..........................800 959-2100
Michael Stallings, *President*
Bob Strickland, *CFO*
Sherrie Stallings, *Corp Secy*
Paul Beterbide, *Supervisor*
EMP: 13 EST: 1989
SQ FT: 45,000
SALES (est): 2.8MM **Privately Held**
WEB: www.wheelvintiques.com
SIC: 3714 5013 Wheel rims, motor vehicle; wheels, motor vehicle

(P-10031)
CITYFREIGHTER INC (PA)
414 Olive St, Santa Barbara (93101-1720)
PHONE....................................805 455-1440
Michael Schoening, *President*
EMP: 28 **EST:** 2018
SALES (est): 62.3K **Privately Held**
SIC: 3714 Motor vehicle electrical equipment

(P-10032)
CODA AUTOMOTIVE INC
12101 W Olympic Blvd, Los Angeles (90064-1017)
PHONE....................................310 820-3611
Phil Murtaugh, *CEO*
EMP: 23 **Privately Held**
WEB: www.codaautomotive.com
SIC: 3714 Motor vehicle parts & accessories
PA: Coda Automotive, Inc.
2340 S Fairfax Ave
Los Angeles CA 90016

(P-10033)
CODA AUTOMOTIVE INC
14 Auto Center Dr, Irvine (92618-2802)
PHONE....................................949 830-7000
EMP: 23 **Privately Held**
WEB: www.codaautomotive.com
SIC: 3714 Motor vehicle parts & accessories
PA: Coda Automotive, Inc.
2340 S Fairfax Ave
Los Angeles CA 90016

(P-10034)
COGNITO COMPANY INC
34935 Flyover Ct, Bakersfield (93308-9725)
PHONE....................................661 588-8085
Justin W Lambert, *CEO*
EMP: 21 **EST:** 2006
SALES (est): 981.2K **Privately Held**
WEB: www.cognitomotorsports.com
SIC: 3714 Motor vehicle parts & accessories

(P-10035)
CONTINNTAL ADVNCED LDAR SLTONS
6307 Crpinteria Ave Ste A, Santa Barbara (93103)
PHONE....................................805 318-2072
Arnaud Lagandre, *Mng Member*
Kevin P Collins,
Bert Franks,
George R Jurch,
Rick Ledsinger,
EMP: 60 **EST:** 2017
SALES (est): 12.2MM
SALES (corp-wide): 44.6B **Privately Held**
WEB: www.asc3d.com
SIC: 3714 Motor vehicle brake systems & parts
HQ: Continental Automotive Systems, Inc.
1 Continental Dr
Auburn Hills MI 48326

(P-10036)
CRAIG MANUFACTURING COMPANY (PA)
8129 Slauson Ave, Montebello (90640-6621)
PHONE....................................323 726-7355
Craig Taslitt, *President*
Julie Taslitt Gross, *Vice Pres*
Caleib Lynch, *Sales Staff*
EMP: 60 **EST:** 1976
SQ FT: 16,000
SALES (est): 4.1MM **Privately Held**
SIC: 3714 Radiators & radiator shells & cores, motor vehicle

(P-10037)
CUMMINS PACIFIC LLC
4601 E Brundage Ln, Bakersfield (93307-2311)
PHONE....................................661 325-9404
Robert Bickie, *Branch Mgr*
Tim Schmidt, *Parts Mgr*
EMP: 26

SALES (corp-wide): 19.8B **Publicly Held**
WEB: www.cummins.com
SIC: 3714 Motor vehicle parts & accessories
HQ: Cummins Pacific, Llc
1939 Deere Ave
Irvine CA 92606

(P-10038)
CURRIE ENTERPRISES
382 N Smith Ave, Corona (92878-4371)
PHONE....................................714 528-6957
Raymond Currie, *President*
Charles Currie, *Vice Pres*
Charlie Currie, *Vice Pres*
John Currie, *Admin Sec*
Cody Peterman, *Representative*
◆ **EMP:** 50 **EST:** 1960
SQ FT: 13,000
SALES (est): 17.6MM **Privately Held**
WEB: www.currieenterprises.com
SIC: 3714 3599 Differentials & parts, motor vehicle; gears, motor vehicle; machine shop, jobbing & repair

(P-10039)
CWD LLC (DH)
Also Called: Centric Parts
21046 Figueroa St Ste B, Carson (90745-1906)
PHONE....................................310 218-1082
Marc Weinsweig, *Mng Member*
Dave Vallette, *Partner*
Brian Griffin, *Vice Pres*
James Tucci, *Vice Pres*
Frank Filipponio, *Comms Dir*
◆ **EMP:** 37 **EST:** 2000
SQ FT: 80,000
SALES (est): 121.8MM
SALES (corp-wide): 3.3B **Privately Held**
WEB: www.apcautotech.com
SIC: 3714 Motor vehicle parts & accessories

(P-10040)
D & S CUSTOM PLATING INC
11552 Anabel Ave, Garden Grove (92843-3707)
PHONE....................................714 537-5411
Fax: 714 537-5413
EMP: 13
SQ FT: 1,500
SALES (est): 1.3MM **Privately Held**
SIC: 3714 Manufactures Chrome Plating For Rims

(P-10041)
DANCHUK MANUFACTURING INC
3201 S Standard Ave, Santa Ana (92705-5640)
PHONE....................................714 540-4363
Arthur Danchuk, *President*
Daniel Danchuk, *CEO*
Tricia Sousa, *Marketing Staff*
Bobbie Black, *Sales Staff*
Mike Martin, *Director*
▲ **EMP:** 71
SQ FT: 33,000
SALES (est): 13.8MM **Privately Held**
WEB: www.danchuk.com
SIC: 3714 3465 Motor vehicle parts & accessories; automotive stampings

(P-10042)
DEE ENGINEERING INC
1893 S Lake Pl, Ontario (91761-8331)
PHONE....................................909 947-5616
Gary Fulton, *Vice Pres*
Daniel Dee, *Admin Sec*
Bob Harris, *Purchasing*
EMP: 25
SQ FT: 25,000
SALES (corp-wide): 7.5MM **Privately Held**
WEB: www.deeeng.com
SIC: 3714 Mufflers (exhaust), motor vehicle
PA: Dee Engineering, Inc.
1284 E 10 S
Lindon UT 84042
714 979-4990

(P-10043)
DEL WEST ENGINEERING INC (PA)
Also Called: Del West USA
28128 Livingston Ave, Valencia (91355-4115)
PHONE....................................661 295-5700
Al Sommer, *Chairman*
Mark Sommer, *President*
Rosemarie Chegwin, *Vice Pres*
Guido Keijzers, *Vice Pres*
Justin Borreta, *Engineer*
EMP: 120 **EST:** 1973
SQ FT: 50,000
SALES (est): 20.9MM **Privately Held**
WEB: www.delwestengineering.com
SIC: 3714 Motor vehicle parts & accessories

(P-10044)
DENSO PDTS & SVCS AMERICAS INC
41673 Corning Pl, Murrieta (92562-7023)
PHONE....................................951 698-3379
Yoshihiko Yamada, *President*
Kazu San, *Vice Pres*
Larry Huddleston, *Regional Mgr*
Nelson Parise, *Regional Mgr*
Sara Slovak, *Admin Sec*
EMP: 150 **Privately Held**
SIC: 3714 Motor vehicle parts & accessories
HQ: Denso Products And Services Americas, Inc.
3900 Via Oro Ave
Long Beach CA 90810
310 834-6352

(P-10045)
DG HOLDINGS INC
Also Called: Hewitt Industries
2367 W La Palma Ave, Anaheim (92801-3356)
PHONE....................................714 891-9300
David S Gathright, *CEO*
EMP: 14 **EST:** 2018
SALES (est): 1.1MM **Privately Held**
SIC: 3714 Motor vehicle engines & parts

(P-10046)
DIRECT WHEEL INC
Also Called: Versante
1000 E Garvey Ave, Monterey Park (91755-3031)
PHONE....................................909 390-2824
Ernie Alfonso, *CEO*
EMP: 15 **EST:** 2010
SALES (est): 2.1MM **Privately Held**
WEB: www.directwheel.net
SIC: 3714 Wheels, motor vehicle

(P-10047)
DONOVAN ENGINEERING CORP
Also Called: Donovan Aluminum Racing Engine
2305 Border Ave, Torrance (90501-3614)
PHONE....................................310 320-3772
Kathleen Donovan, *President*
Norman Woodruff, *Vice Pres*
EMP: 17 **EST:** 1959
SQ FT: 15,000
SALES (est): 1.7MM **Privately Held**
WEB: www.donovanengines.com
SIC: 3714 Motor vehicle engines & parts

(P-10048)
DOUGLAS TECHNOLOGIES GROUP INC (PA)
Also Called: Douglas Wheel
42092 Winchester Rd Ste B, Temecula (92590-4805)
PHONE....................................760 758-5560
Johnny Leach, *President*
◆ **EMP:** 38 **EST:** 1982
SQ FT: 60,000
SALES (est): 7.7MM **Privately Held**
WEB: www.dwtracing.com
SIC: 3714 Wheel rims, motor vehicle

(P-10049)
DYNATRAC PRODUCTS CO INC
7392 Count Cir, Huntington Beach (92647-4551)
PHONE....................................714 596-4461
Jim McGean, *President*

Dan Seldon, *Products*
Peter Le, *Manager*
EMP: 15 **EST:** 1988
SQ FT: 1,600
SALES (est): 3.8MM **Privately Held**
WEB: www.dynatrac.com
SIC: 3714 5013 5531 Motor vehicle transmissions, drive assemblies & parts; motor vehicle supplies & new parts; truck equipment & parts

(P-10050)
EDELBROCK HOLDINGS INC
2301 Dominguez Way, Torrance (90501-6200)
PHONE....................................310 781-2290
Dave Stinson, *Department Mgr*
Marcelo Yelin, *Human Res Mgr*
EMP: 161 **Privately Held**
WEB: www.edelbrock.com
SIC: 3714 Motor vehicle parts & accessories
HQ: Edelbrock Holdings, Inc.
8649 Hacks Cross Rd
Olive Branch MS 38654

(P-10051)
EDELBROCK HOLDINGS INC
1380 S Buena Vista St, San Jacinto (92583-4665)
PHONE....................................951 654-6677
EMP: 161 **Privately Held**
WEB: www.edelbrock.com
SIC: 3714 Motor vehicle parts & accessories
HQ: Edelbrock Holdings, Inc.
8649 Hacks Cross Rd
Olive Branch MS 38654

(P-10052)
EGR INCORPORATED (DH)
4000 Greystone Dr, Ontario (91761-3101)
PHONE....................................909 923-7075
John Whitten, *President*
Bryan Speer, *Vice Pres*
Juan Rubio, *Regl Sales Mgr*
▲ **EMP:** 104 **EST:** 1993
SQ FT: 70,000
SALES (est): 17.8MM **Privately Held**
WEB: www.egrusa.com
SIC: 3714 Motor vehicle parts & accessories

(P-10053)
ENDERLE FUEL INJECTION
1830 Voyager Ave, Simi Valley (93063-3348)
PHONE....................................805 526-3838
Kent H Enderle, *President*
Joan C Enderle, *Corp Secy*
Jim Rehfeld, *Vice Pres*
EMP: 20 **EST:** 1966
SQ FT: 18,000
SALES (est): 2.5MM **Privately Held**
WEB: www.enderlefuelsystems.com
SIC: 3714 Fuel systems & parts, motor vehicle

(P-10054)
ESSLINGER ENGINEERING INC
5946 Freedom Dr, Chino (91710-7014)
PHONE....................................909 539-0544
Dwaine E Esslinger, *President*
Dan Esslinger, *Vice Pres*
Elizabeth Esslinger, *Admin Sec*
Brian Axup, *Manager*
▲ **EMP:** 20 **EST:** 1969
SQ FT: 4,000
SALES (est): 4.3MM **Privately Held**
WEB: www.esslingerracing.com
SIC: 3714 Motor vehicle engines & parts

(P-10055)
EVANS WALKER ENTERPRISES
Also Called: Evans, Walker Racing
2304 Fleetwood Dr, Riverside (92509-2409)
P.O. Box 2469 (92516-2469)
PHONE....................................951 784-7223
Walker Evans, *President*
Phyllis Evans, *Corp Secy*
Randall Anderson, *Vice Pres*
Phillis Evans, *Executive*
John Searle, *Prdtn Mgr*

▲ EMP: 20 EST: 1978
SQ FT: 20,000
SALES (est): 13.2MM **Privately Held**
WEB: www.walkerevansracing.com
SIC: 3714 Motor vehicle parts & accessories

(P-10056)
EXHAUST GAS TECHNOLOGIES INC
15642 Dupont Ave Ste B, Chino (91710-7615)
PHONE.....................909 548-8100
Dennis Lawler, *President*
Maria Lawler, *Vice Pres*
EMP: 13 EST: 1993
SQ FT: 5,000
SALES (est): 1.9MM **Privately Held**
WEB: www.exhaustgas.com
SIC: 3714 3829 Exhaust systems & parts, motor vehicle; thermocouples

(P-10057)
FAB FOUR CORP
15392 Vermont St, Westminster (92683-6153)
PHONE.....................714 901-5300
Ronald Mendonca, *Principal*
EMP: 13 EST: 2010
SALES (est): 472.6K **Privately Held**
WEB: www.fabfours.com
SIC: 3714 Motor vehicle parts & accessories

(P-10058)
FCA US LLC
Also Called: Chrysler West Coast Bus Ctr
7700 Irvine Center Dr # 40, Irvine (92618-2923)
PHONE.....................949 450-5111
Chris Chandler, *Manager*
EMP: 14
SALES (corp-wide): 102.5B **Privately Held**
WEB: www.chrysler.com
SIC: 5511 3714 Automobiles, new & used; motor vehicle engines & parts
HQ: Fca Us Llc
1000 Chrysler Dr
Auburn Hills MI 48326

(P-10059)
FOOTE AXLE & FORGE LLC
250 W Duarte Rd Ste A, Monrovia (91016-7460)
PHONE.....................323 268-4151
Michael F Denton Sr, *Mng Member*
Michael Denton, *Vice Pres*
Sergio Rebollo, *Technical Staff*
Merrie N Denton,
▲ EMP: 32 EST: 1937
SALES (est): 3MM **Privately Held**
WEB: www.footeaxle.com
SIC: 3714 Differentials & parts, motor vehicle

(P-10060)
FORGIATO INC
11915 Wicks St, Sun Valley (91352-1908)
PHONE.....................747 271-7151
Nisan G Celik, *CEO*
Michel Grigory, *Software Dev*
Hemi Bandari, *Sales Staff*
John Bektas, *Sales Staff*
▲ EMP: 62 EST: 2006
SQ FT: 60,000
SALES (est): 15.8MM **Privately Held**
WEB: www.forgiato.com
SIC: 3714 Motor vehicle wheels & parts

(P-10061)
FRIEDL AXLE CORPORATION
2430 N Glassell St Ste Q, Orange (92865-2755)
PHONE.....................714 944-5749
EMP: 21 EST: 2016
SALES (est): 517.4K **Privately Held**
WEB: www.friedlaxle.com
SIC: 3714 Motor vehicle parts & accessories

(P-10062)
FRIEDL CORPORATION
Also Called: Axles Now
1291 N Patt St, Anaheim (92801-2550)
P.O. Box 3233, Orange (92857-0233)
PHONE.....................714 443-0122
Daniel Friedl, *CEO*
EMP: 22 EST: 2014
SQ FT: 5,000
SALES (est): 1.2MM **Privately Held**
WEB: www.instantaxles.com
SIC: 3714 Axles, motor vehicle

(P-10063)
FTG INC (PA)
Also Called: Filtration Technology Group
12750 Center Court Dr S # 280, Cerritos (90703-8593)
PHONE.....................562 865-9200
Pino Pathak, *President*
▲ EMP: 16 EST: 1992
SQ FT: 1,500
SALES (est): 4MM **Privately Held**
WEB: www.ftginc.com
SIC: 3714 5085 3069 3053 Filters: oil, fuel & air, motor vehicle; industrial supplies; bushings, rubber; castings, rubber; grommets, rubber; packing, rubber

(P-10064)
FUEL INJECTION ENGINEERING CO
Also Called: Hilborn Fuel Injection Company
22892 Glenwood Dr, Aliso Viejo (92656-1520)
P.O. Box 786, Dana Point (92629-0786)
PHONE.....................949 360-0909
Duane Hilborn, *President*
Edrias Snipes, *Vice Pres*
EMP: 13 EST: 1948
SALES (est): 353.6K **Privately Held**
WEB: www.holley.com
SIC: 3714 Motor vehicle parts & accessories

(P-10065)
GARRISON MANUFACTURING INC
3320 S Yale St, Santa Ana (92704-6447)
PHONE.....................714 549-4880
Venu Shan, *President*
Jake Ralli, *President*
Todd Ayala, *Sales Mgr*
EMP: 24 EST: 1974
SQ FT: 26,000
SALES (est): 3.7MM **Privately Held**
WEB: www.garrisonmfg.com
SIC: 3714 7699 5084 3593 Steering mechanisms, motor vehicle; motor vehicle steering systems & parts; industrial machinery & equipment repair; hydraulic systems equipment & supplies; fluid power cylinders & actuators

(P-10066)
GERHARDT GEAR CO INC
133 E Santa Anita Ave, Burbank (91502-1926)
PHONE.....................818 842-6700
Ronald J Gerhardt, *CEO*
Mitch Gerhardt, *President*
Kurht Gerhardt, *Vice Pres*
John Kim, *General Mgr*
EMP: 46 EST: 1937
SQ FT: 30,000
SALES (est): 9.5MM **Privately Held**
WEB: www.gerhardtgear.com
SIC: 3714 3728 3769 3462 Gears, motor vehicle; gears, aircraft power transmission; guided missile & space vehicle parts & auxiliary equipment; iron & steel forgings

(P-10067)
GIBSON PERFORMANCE CORPORATION
Also Called: Gibson Exhaust Systems
1270 Webb Cir, Corona (92879-5760)
PHONE.....................951 372-1220
Ronald Gibson, *President*
Victor Lopez, *Owner*
Julie Gibson, *CFO*
▲ EMP: 75 EST: 1990
SQ FT: 50,000

SALES (est): 10.5MM **Privately Held**
WEB: www.gibsonperformance.com
SIC: 3714 5013 Exhaust systems & parts, motor vehicle; motor vehicle supplies & new parts

(P-10068)
GRANATELLI MOTOR SPORTS INC
1000 Yarnell Pl, Oxnard (93033-2454)
PHONE.....................805 486-6644
Joseph R Granatelli, *CEO*
Joseph Granatelli, *General Mgr*
Jack Salgado, *Opers Mgr*
▲ EMP: 31 EST: 1998
SQ FT: 49,000
SALES (est): 2.8MM **Privately Held**
WEB: www.granatellimotorsports.com
SIC: 3714 Fuel systems & parts, motor vehicle

(P-10069)
GROVER PRODUCTS CO
3424 E Olympic Blvd, Los Angeles (90023-3000)
P.O. Box 23966 (90023-0966)
PHONE.....................323 263-9981
John Adam Roesch Jr, *CEO*
Shawn Chatman, *Engineer*
William Marting, *VP Sales*
▲ EMP: 100 EST: 1932
SQ FT: 60,000
SALES (est): 9.9MM **Privately Held**
WEB: www.airhorns.com
SIC: 3714 3494 5999 Motor vehicle brake systems & parts; valves & pipe fittings; plumbing & heating supplies

(P-10070)
HALDEX BRAKE PRODUCTS CORP
291 Kettering Dr, Ontario (91761-8132)
PHONE.....................909 974-1200
EMP: 14
SALES (corp-wide): 528.7MM **Privately Held**
SIC: 3714 Motor Vehicle Parts And Accessories
HQ: Haldex Brake Products Corporation
10930 N Pomona Ave
Kansas City MO 64153
816 891-2470

(P-10071)
HANNEMANN FIBERGLASS INC
1132 W Kirkwall Rd, Azusa (91702-5128)
PHONE.....................626 969-7317
Harold H Hannemann, *President*
EMP: 17 EST: 1967
SQ FT: 9,000
SALES (est): 3MM **Privately Held**
WEB: www.hannemannfiberglass.com
SIC: 3714 Motor vehicle parts & accessories

(P-10072)
HEDMAN MANUFACTURING (PA)
Also Called: Hedman Hedders
12438 Putnam St, Whittier (90602-1002)
PHONE.....................562 204-1031
Robert Bandergriff, *President*
Ron Funfar, *Vice Pres*
Phillip Wigginton, *Technical Staff*
David Barlow, *Sales Staff*
David Czaplicki, *Sales Staff*
▲ EMP: 45 EST: 1978
SALES (est): 20.4MM **Privately Held**
WEB: www.hedman.com
SIC: 3714 Exhaust systems & parts, motor vehicle

(P-10073)
HELLWIG PRODUCTS COMPANY INC
16237 Avenue 296, Visalia (93292-9675)
PHONE.....................559 734-7451
Donald Hellwig, *Ch of Bd*
Mark Hellwig, *President*
▲ EMP: 30 EST: 1946
SQ FT: 37,000
SALES (est): 10MM **Privately Held**
WEB: www.hellwigproducts.com
SIC: 3714 3493 3499 Motor vehicle parts & accessories; automobile springs; stabilizing bars (cargo), metal

(P-10074)
HITACHI ASTEMO OHIO MFG INC
1235 Graphite Dr, Corona (92881-7252)
PHONE.....................951 340-0702
Satoru Panno, *Branch Mgr*
EMP: 83 **Privately Held**
WEB: www.amshowa.com
SIC: 3714 Motor vehicle parts & accessories
HQ: Hitachi Astemo Ohio Manufacturing, Inc.
707 W Cherry St
Sunbury OH 43074
740 965-1133

(P-10075)
HNH MOTORSPORTS
350 S C St, Oxnard (93030-5809)
PHONE.....................305 487-0505
Hipolito Herrera, *Principal*
EMP: 14 EST: 2006
SALES (est): 934.5K **Privately Held**
WEB: www.hnhautosales.com
SIC: 3714 Propane conversion equipment, motor vehicle

(P-10076)
HT MULTINATIONAL INC
Also Called: Unisun Multinational
12851 Reservoir St Apt A, Chino (91710-2908)
PHONE.....................626 964-2686
Chunli Zhao, *CEO*
▲ EMP: 21 EST: 2011
SALES (est): 8.7MM **Privately Held**
WEB: www.chtcusa.com
SIC: 3714 3429 5072 Motor vehicle brake systems & parts; manufactured hardware (general); hardware
HQ: Sinatex, S.A. De C.V.
Industriales No. 1188 Pte.
Cajeme SON. 85210

(P-10077)
I3 ENTERPRISE INC
21912 Garcia Ln, Walnut (91789-0942)
PHONE.....................626 272-9538
Michael H Lee, *Administration*
EMP: 14 EST: 2015
SALES (est): 704.7K **Privately Held**
WEB: www.i3enterpriseinc.com
SIC: 3714 Motor vehicle parts & accessories

(P-10078)
IDDEA CALIFORNIA LLC
Also Called: Go Rhino
589 Apollo St, Brea (92821-3127)
PHONE.....................714 257-7389
Manuel Alvarez, *Mng Member*
Peter Taylor, *General Mgr*
Raul Penunuri, *Cust Svc Dir*
Benjamin Ramirez,
Ron Storer,
▲ EMP: 14 EST: 2003
SQ FT: 50,000
SALES (est): 5MM **Privately Held**
SIC: 3714 Motor vehicle parts & accessories

(P-10079)
IMPCO TECHNOLOGIES INC (HQ)
3030 S Susan St, Santa Ana (92704-6435)
PHONE.....................714 656-1200
Massimo Fracchia, *General Mgr*
Peter Chase, *COO*
Colleen Woo, *Vice Pres*
Luis Fournier, *Software Dev*
Marco Galvagno, *Engineer*
◆ EMP: 160 EST: 1958
SQ FT: 108,000
SALES (est): 52MM
SALES (corp-wide): 305.3MM **Privately Held**
WEB: www.impcotechnologies.com
SIC: 3714 3592 7363 Fuel systems & parts, motor vehicle; carburetors; engineering help service
PA: Westport Fuel Systems Inc
1750 75th Ave W Suite 101
Vancouver BC
604 718-2000

(P-10080)
INLAND EMPIRE DRV LINE SVC INC (PA)
4035 E Guasti Rd Ste 301, Ontario
(91761-1532)
PHONE..................................909 390-3030
Gregory Frick, *President*
Carolyn Frick, *Corp Secy*
Jeff Gilroy, *Vice Pres*
EMP: 16 **EST:** 1981
SQ FT: 7,500
SALES (est): 2.3MM **Privately Held**
WEB: www.iedls.com
SIC: 3714 7539 Drive shafts, motor vehicle; automotive repair shops; powertrain components repair services

(P-10081)
INNOVA ELECTRONICS CORPORATION
Also Called: Equipment & Tool Institute
17352 Von Karman Ave, Irvine
(92614-6204)
PHONE..................................714 241-6800
Ieon C Chenn, *President*
Kim Nguyen, *Admin Sec*
Luis Velazquez, *Technician*
Jane Skidmore, *Controller*
Beth Swiderski, *Marketing Staff*
EMP: 29 **EST:** 1990
SQ FT: 12,000
SALES (est): 9.1MM **Privately Held**
WEB: www.innova.com
SIC: 3714 Motor vehicle electrical equipment

(P-10082)
INOVIT INC
3630 Cypress Ave, El Monte (91731-2723)
PHONE..................................626 444-4775
Lauren Bronson, *CEO*
Yingshen Mao, *CEO*
▲ **EMP:** 16 **EST:** 2008
SQ FT: 20,000
SALES (est): 2.2MM **Privately Held**
WEB: www.inovit.com
SIC: 3714 Wheels, motor vehicle

(P-10083)
K & G LATIROVIAN INC (PA)
Also Called: Kahgo Truck Parts
8277 Lankershim Blvd, North Hollywood
(91605-1614)
PHONE..................................818 319-2862
Kabrail Latirovian, *CEO*
EMP: 25 **EST:** 2014
SALES (est): 554.2K **Privately Held**
WEB: www.kahgotruckparts.com
SIC: 3714 Motor vehicle parts & accessories

(P-10084)
KARBZ INC
Also Called: SSC Racing
77806 Flora Rd Ste E, Palm Desert
(92211-4108)
PHONE..................................760 567-9953
Joe Ramos, *President*
Jim Boltz, *Vice Pres*
▲ **EMP:** 25 **EST:** 1994
SQ FT: 40,000
SALES (est): 712.2K **Privately Held**
WEB: www.sscracing.com
SIC: 3714 Motor vehicle parts & accessories

(P-10085)
KENNEDY ENGINEERED PDTS INC
38830 17th St E, Palmdale (93550-3915)
PHONE..................................661 272-1147
Hobert Kennedy, *Owner*
▲ **EMP:** 20 **EST:** 1968
SQ FT: 5,900
SALES (est): 2.8MM **Privately Held**
WEB: www.kennedyeng.com
SIC: 3714 Motor vehicle parts & accessories

(P-10086)
KF FIBERGLASS INC (PA)
8247 Phlox St, Downey (90241-4841)
PHONE..................................562 869-1536
Ron Belk, *President*
David Ruiz, *Vice Pres*
EMP: 16 **EST:** 1965
SQ FT: 35,000
SALES (est): 1.4MM **Privately Held**
WEB: www.kffiberglass.com
SIC: 3714 Motor vehicle parts & accessories

(P-10087)
KING SHOCK TECHNOLOGY INC
12472 Edison Way, Garden Grove
(92841-2821)
PHONE..................................719 394-3754
Brett King, *CEO*
Lance King, *President*
Ross King, *CFO*
Sharon King, *Vice Pres*
Mike Eads, *General Mgr*
◆ **EMP:** 99 **EST:** 2001
SQ FT: 18,000
SALES (est): 17.8MM **Privately Held**
WEB: www.kingshocks.com
SIC: 3714 Motor vehicle body components & frame

(P-10088)
KRAFTWERKS PRFMCE GROUP LLC
2050 5th St, Norco (92860-1912)
PHONE..................................951 808-9888
David Hsu, *Principal*
EMP: 13 **EST:** 2007
SALES (est): 656.1K **Privately Held**
WEB: www.kraftwerksusa.com
SIC: 3714 Motor vehicle parts & accessories

(P-10089)
LAPCO WEST LLC
6901 Marlin Cir, La Palma (90623-1018)
PHONE..................................562 348-4850
Graem Elliot, *CEO*
EMP: 20 **EST:** 2004
SALES (est): 2.7MM **Privately Held**
WEB: www.lapcowest.com
SIC: 3714 Motor vehicle brake systems & parts

(P-10090)
LEET TECHNOLOGY INC
1427 S Robertson Blvd, Los Angeles
(90035-3401)
PHONE..................................877 238-4492
Ding Jung Long, *CEO*
Kamal Hamidon, *Officer*
Dai Song, *Co-Founder*
Ganesha Karuppiaya, *CTO*
EMP: 17 **EST:** 2013
SALES (est): 73.4K **Privately Held**
SIC: 3714 Motor vehicle parts & accessories

(P-10091)
LEXANI WHEEL CORPORATION
34420 Gateway Dr, Palm Desert
(92211-0843)
PHONE..................................951 368-7526
Frank J Hodges, *CEO*
Brian Pecen, *Sales Mgr*
Aaron Dewitt, *Marketing Staff*
Wallace Johnnie, *Sales Staff*
Sergio Suarez, *Sales Staff*
◆ **EMP:** 60 **EST:** 1996
SQ FT: 35,000
SALES (est): 10.8MM **Privately Held**
WEB: www.lexani.com
SIC: 3714 Motor vehicle parts & accessories

(P-10092)
LLOYD DESIGN CORPORATION
Also Called: Lloyd Mats
19731 Nordhoff St, Northridge
(91324-3330)
PHONE..................................818 768-6001
Lloyd S Levine, *CEO*
Brendan Dooley, *President*
Mary Freeman, *Research*
▲ **EMP:** 55 **EST:** 1974
SALES (est): 8.4MM **Privately Held**
WEB: www.lloydmats.com
SIC: 3714 Motor vehicle parts & accessories

(P-10093)
LOS ANGELES SLEEVE CO INC
Also Called: L.A. Sleeve
12051 Rivera Rd, Santa Fe Springs
(90670-2211)
PHONE..................................562 945-7578
Nick G Metchkoff, *President*
Sarah Metchkoff, *Shareholder*
James G Metchkoff, *Corp Secy*
David Metchkoff, *Vice Pres*
Dave Lasco, *Managing Dir*
▲ **EMP:** 29 **EST:** 1975
SQ FT: 33,000
SALES (est): 4.9MM **Privately Held**
WEB: www.lasleeve.com
SIC: 3714 Exhaust systems & parts, motor vehicle

(P-10094)
LSI PRODUCTS INC
12885 Wildflower Ln, Riverside
(92503-9772)
PHONE..................................951 343-9270
Alex Danze, *CEO*
▲ **EMP:** 16 **EST:** 1998
SALES (est): 1MM **Privately Held**
WEB: www.proarmor.com
SIC: 3714 Motor vehicle parts & accessories

(P-10095)
LUND MOTION PRODUCTS INC
Also Called: AMP Research
15651 Mosher Ave, Tustin (92780-6426)
PHONE..................................949 221-0023
Mitch Fogle, *President*
Eric Bajza, *Engineer*
Stephen Dougherty, *Controller*
Carolina Busciglio, *Cust Mgr*
Chris Peterson, *Agent*
EMP: 35 **Privately Held**
WEB: www.lundtruck.com
SIC: 3714 Motor vehicle parts & accessories
HQ: Lund Motion Products, Inc.
4325 Hamilton Mill Rd
Buford GA 30518
678 804-3767

(P-10096)
M E D INC
14001 Marquardt Ave, Santa Fe Springs
(90670-5088)
PHONE..................................562 921-0464
Steven Moore, *CEO*
Susan Lowe, *CFO*
Susan M Rattay, *Software Dev*
Jessica Moore, *Purch Mgr*
EMP: 70
SQ FT: 40,000
SALES (est): 16MM **Privately Held**
WEB: www.dme-mfg.com
SIC: 3714 3429 Exhaust systems & parts, motor vehicle; clamps, couplings, nozzles & other metal hose fittings

(P-10097)
MAGNUSON PRODUCTS LLC
Also Called: Magnuson Superchargers
1990 Knoll Dr Ste A, Ventura (93003-7309)
PHONE..................................805 642-8833
Kim Pendergast, *CEO*
Tim Krauskopf, *Exec VP*
Jeff Wright, *Executive*
Owen Peterson, *Project Mgr*
Tom Amick, *Engineer*
EMP: 49 **EST:** 1970
SQ FT: 45,600
SALES (est): 10.5MM **Privately Held**
WEB: www.magnusonsuperchargers.com
SIC: 3714 Motor vehicle parts & accessories

(P-10098)
MARGUS AUTOMOTIVE ELC EXCH
165 E Jefferson Blvd, Los Angeles
(90011-2330)
PHONE..................................323 232-5281
Donald Lopez, *President*
Carolyn Lopez, *CFO*
EMP: 14 **EST:** 1956
SQ FT: 28,570

(P-10099)
MARK CHRISTOPHER CHEVROLET INC (PA)
Also Called: Mark Christopher Hummer
2131 E Convention Ctr Way, Ontario
(91764-4495)
PHONE..................................909 321-5860
Chris Leggio, *CEO*
Loretta Holtz, *Corp Secy*
Shirley Leggid, *Vice Pres*
Matt Torrez, *Marketing Staff*
Joseph Gomez, *Sales Staff*
EMP: 149 **EST:** 1986
SQ FT: 15,000
SALES (est): 76.5MM **Privately Held**
WEB: www.markchristopher.com
SIC: 5511 5521 3714 Automobiles, new & used; used car dealers; motor vehicle parts & accessories

(P-10100)
MAXON INDUSTRIES INC
11921 Slauson Ave, Santa Fe Springs
(90670-2221)
P.O. Box 3434, Los Angeles (90078-3434)
PHONE..................................562 464-0099
Murray Lugash, *President*
Larry Lugash, *Exec VP*
Brenda Leung, *Vice Pres*
Tuck Maxon, *Vice Pres*
Casey Lugash, *Info Tech Dir*
EMP: 75 **EST:** 1957
SQ FT: 250,000
SALES (est): 9MM **Privately Held**
WEB: www.maxonlift.com
SIC: 3714 Motor vehicle parts & accessories

(P-10101)
MCO INC
13925 Benson Ave, Chino (91710-7024)
PHONE..................................909 627-3574
Leon O Martin, *President*
Vicki Martin, *Corp Secy*
EMP: 25 **EST:** 1972
SQ FT: 10,000
SALES (est): 1.8MM **Privately Held**
SIC: 3714 Frames, motor vehicle

(P-10102)
METRA ELECTRONICS CORPORATION
Also Called: Antenna Works
3201 E 59th St, Long Beach (90805-4501)
PHONE..................................562 470-6601
Steve Hertel, *Manager*
Richard Barnes, *Credit Staff*
Teri Lelasher, *Controller*
Andy Adkins, *Regl Sales Mgr*
Abe Agront, *Director*
EMP: 25
SALES (corp-wide): 114.3MM **Privately Held**
WEB: www.metraonline.com
SIC: 3714 Motor vehicle body components & frame
PA: Metra Electronics Corporation
460 Walker St
Holly Hill FL 32117
386 257-1186

(P-10103)
MID-WEST FABRICATING CO
Also Called: West Bent Bolt Division
8623 Dice Rd, Santa Fe Springs
(90670-2511)
PHONE..................................562 698-9615
Steve Petersen, *Manager*
EMP: 46
SQ FT: 40,000
SALES (corp-wide): 28MM **Privately Held**
WEB: www.midwestfab.com
SIC: 3714 3452 3316 3312 Tie rods, motor vehicle; bolts, nuts, rivets & washers; cold finishing of steel shapes; wire products, steel or iron

PA: Mid-West Fabricating Co.
313 N Johns St
Amanda OH 43102
740 969-4411

(P-10104)
MILODON INCORPORATED
2250 Agate Ct, Simi Valley (93065-1842)
PHONE..................805 577-5950
Steve Morrison, *President*
Tom Wilson, *Purchasing*
Barbara Dunkleberger, *Director*
▲ **EMP:** 40 **EST:** 1957
SQ FT: 32,000
SALES (est): 4.3MM **Privately Held**
WEB: www.milodon.com
SIC: 3714 Motor vehicle engines & parts

(P-10105)
MOBIS PARTS AMERICA LLC
10550 Talbert Ave 4, Fountain Valley
(92708-6031)
PHONE..................949 450-0014
H S Lee
Iris Dorris, *Engineer*
David Gault, *Marketing Staff*
Agustin Nunez, *Manager*
EMP: 28 **Privately Held**
WEB: www.mobisusa.com
SIC: 3714 Motor vehicle body components
& frame
HQ: Mobis Parts America, Llc
10550 Talbert Ave Fl 4
Fountain Valley CA 92708
786 515-1101

(P-10106)
**MOTORCAR PARTS OF
AMERICA INC (PA)**
Also Called: MPA
2929 California St, Torrance (90503-3914)
PHONE..................310 212-7910
Selwyn Joffe, *Ch of Bd*
David Lee, *CFO*
Rudolph Rudy, *Bd of Directors*
Doug Schooner, *Chief Mktg Ofcr*
Douglas Schooner, *Officer*
◆ **EMP:** 5353 **EST:** 1968
SQ FT: 231,000
SALES (est): 540.7MM **Publicly Held**
WEB: www.motorcarparts.com
SIC: 3714 3694 3625 Motor vehicle parts
& accessories; alternators, automotive;
starter, electric motor

(P-10107)
**MOTORSPORT AFTRMRKET
GROUP INC (PA)**
13861 Rosecrans Ave, Santa Fe Springs
(90670-5207)
PHONE..................917 838-4002
J A Lacy, *CEO*
Brian Etter, *President*
Scott Christman, *Admin Sec*
Michael Moore, *Admin Sec*
Janet Ryan Sexton, *Controller*
EMP: 13 **EST:** 2000
SALES (est): 251.1MM **Privately Held**
WEB: www.tucker.com
SIC: 3714 Motor vehicle parts & acces-
sories

(P-10108)
**NEW CENTURY INDUSTRIES
INC**
7231 Rosecrans Ave, Paramount
(90723-2501)
P.O. Box 1845 (90723-1845)
PHONE..................562 634-9551
Michael Mason, *CEO*
EMP: 50 **EST:** 1991
SQ FT: 32,000
SALES (est): 9.1MM **Privately Held**
SIC: 3714 3465 3469 Wheels, motor ve-
hicle; automotive stampings; stamping
metal for the trade

(P-10109)
NMSP INC (HQ)
Also Called: Advanced Engine Management
Inc
2205 W 126th St Ste A, Hawthorne
(90250-3367)
PHONE..................310 484-2322
Gregory Neuwirth, *President*

Peter Neuwirth, *Chairman*
Steve Santiago, *Executive*
Cynthia Isom, *General Mgr*
Joe Ippolito, *Technology*
◆ **EMP:** 83 **EST:** 1997
SQ FT: 78,000
SALES (est): 27.3MM
SALES (corp-wide): 174.3MM **Privately
Held**
WEB: www.holley.com
SIC: 3714 Motor vehicle engines & parts
PA: Holley Performance Products Inc.
1801 Russellville Rd
Bowling Green KY 42101
270 782-2900

(P-10110)
NMSP INC
1451 E 6th St, Corona (92879-1715)
PHONE..................951 734-2453
Darrell Contreras, *Manager*
EMP: 46
SALES (corp-wide): 174.3MM **Privately
Held**
SIC: 3714 Motor vehicle engines & parts
HQ: Nmsp, Inc.
2205 W 126th St Ste A
Hawthorne CA 90250
310 484-2322

(P-10111)
OFFENHAUSER SALES CORP
5300 Alhambra Ave, Los Angeles
(90032-3405)
P.O. Box 32219 (90032-0219)
PHONE..................323 225-1307
Fred C Offenhauser Jr, *President*
EMP: 13 **EST:** 1956
SQ FT: 15,000
SALES (est): 2.3MM **Privately Held**
WEB: www.offenhauser.co
SIC: 3714 Motor vehicle parts & acces-
sories

(P-10112)
PANKL HOLDINGS INC (DH)
1902 Mcgaw Ave, Irvine (92614-0910)
PHONE..................949 567-9000
Wolfgang Plasser, *President*
Harry Glieder, *CFO*
Thomas Karazmann, *CFO*
EMP: 100 **EST:** 1998
SQ FT: 31,840
SALES (est): 48MM
SALES (corp-wide): 2.4B **Privately Held**
WEB: www.pankl.com
SIC: 3714 3592 Connecting rods, motor
vehicle engine; pistons & piston rings
HQ: Pankl Racing Systems Ag
IndustriestraBe West 4
Kapfenberg 8605
386 233-9990

(P-10113)
**PARTS EXPEDITING AND DIST
CO**
Also Called: Pedco
10805 Artesia Blvd # 112, Cerritos
(90703-2678)
P.O. Box 59068, Norwalk (90652-0068)
PHONE..................562 944-3199
Virgil Cooley, *President*
Rachel Cooley, *Vice Pres*
EMP: 28 **EST:** 1975
SQ FT: 32,000
SALES (est): 1.1MM **Privately Held**
SIC: 3714 3519 Rebuilding engines &
transmissions, factory basis; internal com-
bustion engines

(P-10114)
**POWER PROS RACG EXHUST
SYSTEMS**
Also Called: Power Pros Exhaust Systems
817 S Lakeview Ave Ste J, Placentia
(92870-6718)
PHONE..................714 777-3278
Don Kistler, *President*
Thomas Kistler, *CEO*
EMP: 13 **EST:** 1984
SQ FT: 7,000
SALES (est): 373.6K **Privately Held**
SIC: 3714 5013 Exhaust systems & parts,
motor vehicle; motorcycle parts

(P-10115)
PRIME WHEEL CORPORATION
23920 Vermont Ave, Harbor City
(90710-1602)
PHONE..................310 326-5080
Eddie Chen, *Manager*
Philip Chen, *Vice Pres*
Elmer Lopez, *Engineer*
Daniel Arroyo, *Purchasing*
Berenice Sanchez, *Purchasing*
EMP: 453
SQ FT: 200,000
SALES (corp-wide): 315.6MM **Privately
Held**
WEB: www.primewheel.com
SIC: 3714 3471 5013 Motor vehicle
wheels & parts; plating & polishing; auto-
motive supplies & parts
PA: Prime Wheel Corporation
17705 S Main St
Gardena CA 90248
310 516-9126

(P-10116)
PRIME WHEEL CORPORATION
Also Called: Prime Wheel of Figueroa
17680 S Figueroa St, Gardena
(90248-3419)
PHONE..................310 819-4123
Peter Liang, *Branch Mgr*
EMP: 25
SALES (corp-wide): 315.6MM **Privately
Held**
WEB: www.primewheel.com
SIC: 3714 Wheels, motor vehicle
PA: Prime Wheel Corporation
17705 S Main St
Gardena CA 90248
310 516-9126

(P-10117)
**PRIME WHEEL CORPORATION
(PA)**
17705 S Main St, Gardena (90248-3516)
PHONE..................310 516-9126
Henry Chen, *CEO*
Tony Fan, *Shareholder*
Webb Carter, *Vice Chairman*
Mitchell M Tung, *President*
Phillip Chen, *Vice Pres*
◆ **EMP:** 600
SQ FT: 320,000
SALES (est): 315.6MM **Privately Held**
WEB: www.primewheel.com
SIC: 3714 Wheels, motor vehicle

(P-10118)
QF LIQUIDATION INC (PA)
Also Called: Quantum Technologies
25242 Arctic Ocean Dr, Lake Forest
(92630-8821)
PHONE..................949 930-3400
W Brian Olson, *President*
Bradley J Timon, *CFO*
Mark Arold, *Vice Pres*
Kenneth R Lombardo, *Vice Pres*
David M Mazaika, *Exec Dir*
◆ **EMP:** 128 **EST:** 2000
SQ FT: 156,000
SALES (est): 26.3MM **Privately Held**
WEB: www.qtww.com
SIC: 3714 3764 8711 Motor vehicle parts
& accessories; guided missile & space
vehicle propulsion unit parts; engineering
services

(P-10119)
**R3 PERFORMANCE PRODUCTS
INC**
531 Old Woman Springs Rd, Yucca Valley
(92284-1613)
PHONE..................760 909-0846
Roger Ketelslger, *CEO*
Robert Istwan, *CFO*
Nelson Kaitlyn, *Office Mgr*
EMP: 15 **EST:** 2017
SALES (est): 2.3MM **Privately Held**
WEB: www.r3pp.com
SIC: 3714 Shock absorbers, motor vehicle

(P-10120)
RACE TECHNOLOGIES LLC
17422 Murphy Ave, Irvine (92614-5922)
PHONE..................714 438-1118
Jaime Trimble,

▲ **EMP:** 14 **EST:** 1998
SALES (est): 2.3MM **Privately Held**
WEB: www.racetechnologies.com
SIC: 3714 5013 Motor vehicle brake sys-
tems & parts; automotive brakes

(P-10121)
RACEPAK LLC
30402 Esperanza, Rcho STA Marg
(92688-2144)
PHONE..................949 709-5555
Tom Tomlinson, *President*
Jeff Greene, *Vice Pres*
Brian Woodard, *Creative Dir*
Cameron Ferre, *Marketing Staff*
Tim McCullough, *Supervisor*
EMP: 28 **EST:** 2014
SALES (est): 8.9MM
SALES (corp-wide): 174.3MM **Privately
Held**
WEB: www.holley.com
SIC: 3714 Motor vehicle parts & acces-
sories
PA: Holley Performance Products Inc.
1801 Russellville Rd
Bowling Green KY 42101
270 782-2900

(P-10122)
RACING POWER COMPANY
815 Tucker Ln, Walnut (91789-2914)
PHONE..................909 468-3690
Te Ming Chung, *CEO*
Isaiah Roman, *Opers Staff*
Gil Burris, *Sales Staff*
Kimberly Tsui, *Manager*
▲ **EMP:** 20
SQ FT: 2,000
SALES (est): 3.9MM **Privately Held**
WEB: www.usrpc.com
SIC: 3714 Motor vehicle parts & acces-
sories

(P-10123)
**RAM OFF ROAD ACCESSORIES
INC**
3901 Medford St, Los Angeles
(90063-1608)
PHONE..................323 266-3850
Chris Foterek, *President*
William Longo, *Vice Pres*
EMP: 31 **EST:** 1989
SQ FT: 103,000
SALES (est): 1.2MM **Privately Held**
SIC: 3714 Motor vehicle body components
& frame

(P-10124)
RBW INDUSTRIES INC
5788 Schaefer Ave, Chino (91710-7003)
PHONE..................909 591-5359
Larry Relevino, *President*
Marilyn Blodgett, *Treasure*
Bob Arnett, *Vice Pres*
▲ **EMP:** 65 **EST:** 1970
SQ FT: 72,000
SALES (est): 5.6MM **Privately Held**
WEB: www.rbwindustries.com
SIC: 3714 3792 Fifth wheel, motor vehicle;
travel trailers & campers

(P-10125)
RICARDO DEFENSE INC (DH)
175 Cremona Dr Ste 140, Goleta
(93117-3197)
PHONE..................805 882-1884
Chester Gryzcan, *President*
Jonathan Dorny, *Vice Pres*
Brian Smith, *Vice Pres*
Linda Chalmers, *Executive Asst*
Harvey Lin, *Software Engr*
EMP: 100 **EST:** 1995
SALES (est): 17.5MM
SALES (corp-wide): 498MM **Privately
Held**
WEB: www.control-pt.com
SIC: 3714 8711 Motor vehicle brake sys-
tems & parts; consulting engineer

(P-10126)
RK SPORTS LLC (PA)
16761 Viewpoint Ln # 268, Huntington
Beach (92647-4781)
PHONE..................714 794-4400
EMP: 15 **EST:** 2018

SALES (est): 453K **Privately Held**
WEB: www.rksport.com
SIC: **3714** Motor vehicle parts & accessories

(P-10127)
RLV TUNED EXHAUST PRODUCTS INC
2351 Thompson Way Bldg A, Santa Maria (93455-1041)
PHONE..............................805 925-5461
Rodney L Verlengiere, *President*
Arthur R Verlengiere, *Corp Secy*
Art Verlengiere, *Vice Pres*
▲ EMP: 24 EST: 1978
SQ FT: 5,000
SALES (est): 6.4MM **Privately Held**
WEB: www.rlv.com
SIC: **3714** Exhaust systems & parts, motor vehicle

(P-10128)
ROLL ALONG VANS INC
1350 E Yorba Linda Blvd, Placentia (92870-3833)
PHONE..............................714 528-9600
Dan Williams, *Manager*
EMP: 34 EST: 1976
SQ FT: 40,400
SALES (est): 7MM **Privately Held**
WEB: www.rollalongvans.com
SIC: **3714** Motor vehicle parts & accessories

(P-10129)
ROMEO POWER INC (PA)
4380 Ayers Ave, Vernon (90058-4306)
PHONE..............................833 467-2237
Susan S Brennan, *President*
Robert S Mancini, *Ch of Bd*
Criswell Choi, *COO*
Lauren Webb, *CFO*
Hang Shi, *Vice Pres*
EMP: 48 EST: 2018
SQ FT: 113,000
SALES (est): 8.9MM **Publicly Held**
WEB: www.romeopower.com
SIC: **3714** Motor vehicle parts & accessories

(P-10130)
S&B FILTERS INC
15461 Slover Ave Ste A, Fontana (92337-1306)
PHONE..............................909 947-0015
Berry Carter, *President*
Steven Du, *Research*
Hugo Rivera, *Engineer*
Gompel Craig VA, *Engineer*
Gabriel Lopez, *Prdtn Mgr*
▲ EMP: 58 EST: 1981
SALES (est): 17.2MM **Privately Held**
WEB: www.sbfilters.com
SIC: **3714 3564** Filters: oil, fuel & air, motor vehicle; filters, air: furnaces, air conditioning equipment, etc.

(P-10131)
SANKO ELECTRONICS AMERICA INC (HQ)
20700 Denker Ave Ste A, Torrance (90501-6415)
PHONE..............................310 618-1677
Hironori Saigusa, *CEO*
Akio Saigusa, *President*
Toshiaki Yamashita, *President*
▲ EMP: 19 EST: 1988
SQ FT: 35,000
SALES (est): 8.4MM **Privately Held**
WEB: www.sankoelec.com
SIC: **3714** Motor vehicle parts & accessories

(P-10132)
SEDENQUIST-FRASER ENTPS INC
Also Called: Leisure Components
16730 Gridley Rd, Cerritos (90703-1730)
PHONE..............................562 924-5763
Jitu Patel, *President*
Veary Im, *Manager*
EMP: 49 EST: 1974
SQ FT: 22,000

SALES (est): 574K **Privately Held**
WEB: www.sftech.com
SIC: **3714 3089 3544** Motor vehicle parts & accessories; plastic processing; special dies, tools, jigs & fixtures

(P-10133)
SHEPARD-THOMASON COMPANY
901 S Leslie St, La Habra (90631-6841)
PHONE..............................714 773-5539
Thomas A Ruhe, *President*
Connie Ruhe, *Corp Secy*
EMP: 73 EST: 1913
SQ FT: 25,000
SALES (est): 1.3MM **Privately Held**
SIC: **3714** Clutches, motor vehicle
PA: Ruhe Corporation
901 S Leslie St
La Habra CA 90631

(P-10134)
SONUS GROUP LLC
43537 Ridge Park Dr # 100, Temecula (92590-3615)
PHONE..............................888 316-5351
Jon Cenoz, *Principal*
EMP: 14 EST: 2015
SALES (est): 1.3MM **Privately Held**
WEB: www.sonus-es.com
SIC: **3714** Motor vehicle parts & accessories

(P-10135)
SPECIAL DEVICES INCORPORATED
Also Called: Sdi
2655 1st St Ste 300, Simi Valley (93065-1580)
PHONE..............................805 387-1000
Yasuhiro Sakaki, *CEO*
Mike Mendonca, *COO*
Harry Rector, *CFO*
Nicholas J Bruge, *Ch Credit Ofcr*
Richard Richins, *Planning*
▲ EMP: 600 EST: 1959
SQ FT: 170,000
SALES (est): 77.7MM **Privately Held**
WEB: www.specialdevices.com
SIC: **3714** Motor vehicle parts & accessories
PA: Daicel Corporation
3-1, Ofukacho, Kita-Ku
Osaka OSK 530-0

(P-10136)
STULL INDUSTRIES INC
1315 W Flint St, Lake Elsinore (92530-3248)
PHONE..............................951 248-9789
William Stull, *President*
▲ EMP: 21 EST: 1974
SQ FT: 50,000
SALES (est): 1.3MM **Privately Held**
WEB: www.stullindustries.com
SIC: **3714** Motor vehicle body components & frame

(P-10137)
SUNNY AMERICA & GLOBAL AUTOTEC
2681 Dow Ave Ste A, Tustin (92780-7244)
PHONE..............................714 544-0400
Alex Han, *Owner*
▲ EMP: 20 EST: 2006
SALES (est): 857K **Privately Held**
WEB: www.xlautocorp.com
SIC: **3714** Motor vehicle engines & parts

(P-10138)
SUPERIOR INDS INTL HLDINGS LLC (HQ)
7800 Woodley Ave, Van Nuys (91406-1722)
PHONE..............................818 781-4973
Steven J Borick, *Ch of Bd*
Francisco S Uranga, *Bd of Directors*
Emory Brown, *Vice Pres*
Shawn Fergus, *Vice Pres*
Anita Belanger, *Executive*
▲ EMP: 139 EST: 2008

SALES (est): 24.2MM
SALES (corp-wide): 1.1B **Publicly Held**
WEB: www.supind.com
SIC: **3714** Motor vehicle wheels & parts
PA: Superior Industries International, Inc.
26600 Telg Rd Ste 400
Southfield MI 48033
248 352-7300

(P-10139)
TABC INC (DH)
6375 N Paramount Blvd, Long Beach (90805-3301)
PHONE..............................562 984-3305
Michael Bafan, *CEO*
Yoshiaki Nishino, *Treasurer*
Mike Bafan, *Mfg Staff*
◆ EMP: 798 EST: 1974
SQ FT: 8,820
SALES (est): 113.1MM **Privately Held**
WEB: www.toyota.com
SIC: **3714 3713 3469** Motor vehicle parts & accessories; truck beds; metal stampings

(P-10140)
TASKER METAL PRODUCTS
1823 S Hope St, Los Angeles (90015-4197)
P.O. Box 15368 (90015-0368)
PHONE..............................213 765-5400
Eugene L Golling, *President*
Rudi Verstegen, *Vice Pres*
Rudy Verstegen, *Vice Pres*
▲ EMP: 15 EST: 1941
SQ FT: 12,000
SALES (est): 1.9MM **Privately Held**
WEB: www.taskermetalproducts.com
SIC: **3714** Motor vehicle body components & frame; hoods, motor vehicle

(P-10141)
TILTON ENGINEERING INC
25 Easy St, Buellton (93427-9566)
P.O. Box 1787 (93427-1787)
PHONE..............................805 688-2353
Jason Wahl, *President*
Todd Cooper, *Vice Pres*
Madden Patty, *Office Admin*
Jon Conway, *Purch Agent*
▲ EMP: 50 EST: 1972
SQ FT: 15,000
SALES (est): 6.3MM **Privately Held**
WEB: www.tiltonracing.com
SIC: **3714** Motor vehicle parts & accessories

(P-10142)
TRANS-DAPT CALIFORNIA INC
12438 Putnam St, Whittier (90602-1002)
PHONE..............................562 921-0404
Robert Vandergriff, *President*
Ron Funfar, *Vice Pres*
Laura Funfar, *Office Mgr*
Jan Garner, *Admin Sec*
EMP: 40 EST: 1959
SQ FT: 37,000
SALES (est): 2.7MM **Privately Held**
WEB: www.hedman.com
SIC: **3714** Motor vehicle parts & accessories

(P-10143)
TRANSGO
Also Called: Transco
2621 Merced Ave, El Monte (91733-1905)
PHONE..............................626 443-7456
Gilbert W Younger, *Principal*
David Hardin, *General Mgr*
Darlene Hardin, *Admin Sec*
Sema Reyes, *Admin Sec*
Jim Mobley, *Technician*
EMP: 33 EST: 1976
SQ FT: 4,560
SALES (est): 6.9MM **Privately Held**
WEB: www.transgo.com
SIC: **3714** Motor vehicle parts & accessories

(P-10144)
TUBE TECHNOLOGIES INC
Also Called: TTI Performance Exhaust
1555 Consumer Cir, Corona (92878-3226)
PHONE..............................951 371-4878
Sam Davis, *President*
Trini Respico, *Corp Secy*

Tom Nakawatase, *Vice Pres*
Raul Rodriguez, *Vice Pres*
Elias Anthony, *Technology*
▲ EMP: 30 EST: 1988
SQ FT: 18,400
SALES (est): 2.6MM **Privately Held**
WEB: www.ttiexhaust.com
SIC: **3714 3498** Exhaust systems & parts, motor vehicle; tube fabricating (contract bending & shaping)

(P-10145)
TURBONETICS HOLDINGS INC
651 Via Alondra Ste 715, Camarillo (93012-8077)
PHONE..............................805 581-0333
Brad Lewis, *Vice Pres*
Greg Papp, *Finance Dir*
▲ EMP: 49 EST: 2006
SALES (est): 18.6MM **Publicly Held**
WEB: www.turboneticsinc.com
SIC: **3714** Motor vehicle parts & accessories
PA: Westinghouse Air Brake Technologies Corporation
30 Isabella St
Pittsburgh PA 15212

(P-10146)
U S WHEEL CORPORATION
Also Called: US Wheel
15702 Producer Ln, Huntington Beach (92649-1303)
PHONE..............................714 892-0021
Eliot Mason, *President*
Robert Williams, *Vice Pres*
Kristie Boerum, *Executive*
Virgil Ugale, *Sales Staff*
Larry Van Es, *Manager*
◆ EMP: 20 EST: 1986
SQ FT: 135,000
SALES (est): 8.1MM **Privately Held**
WEB: www.uswheel.com
SIC: **3714 5013** Wheels, motor vehicle; wheels, motor vehicle

(P-10147)
UFO DESIGNS
Also Called: S F Technology
16730 Gridley Rd, Cerritos (90703-1730)
PHONE..............................562 924-5763
Jitu Patel, *President*
EMP: 22
SALES (corp-wide): 3.8MM **Privately Held**
WEB: www.ufodesign.com
SIC: **3714 3089** Motor vehicle parts & accessories; plastic processing
PA: U.F.O. Designs
5812 Machine Dr
Huntington Beach CA 92649
714 892-4420

(P-10148)
ULTRA WHEEL COMPANY
Also Called: Platinum
586 N Gilbert St, Fullerton (92833-2549)
PHONE..............................714 449-7100
Sharon A Wood, *President*
Jim Smith, *Owner*
James Smith, *Shareholder*
Sharon Wood, *CFO*
Fred Dobler, *Vice Pres*
▼ EMP: 25 EST: 1984
SQ FT: 65,000
SALES (est): 5.2MM **Privately Held**
WEB: www.ultrawheel.com
SIC: **3714** Motor vehicle parts & accessories

(P-10149)
UNI FILTER INC
1468 Manhattan Ave, Fullerton (92831-5222)
PHONE..............................714 535-6933
Lanny R Mitchell, *President*
Kenneth E Mitchell, *Shareholder*
Robert A Nichols, *Shareholder*
Kathi Perry, *Treasurer*
Tom Gross, *Vice Pres*
EMP: 26 EST: 1971
SQ FT: 26,000

SALES (est): 5.5MM **Privately Held**
WEB: www.unifilter.com
SIC: **3714** Filters: oil, fuel & air, motor vehicle

(P-10150)
US HYBRID CORPORATION (HQ)
2660 Columbia St, Torrance (90503-3802)
PHONE..................310 212-1200
Gordon Abas Goodarzi, *CEO*
Don C Kang, *President*
Don Kang, *Vice Pres*
Kellyanne Leblanc, *Program Mgr*
Daniel Orlowski, *Program Mgr*
▲ EMP: 49 EST: 1999
SALES (est): 15.2MM **Publicly Held**
WEB: www.ushybrid.com
SIC: **3714** Motor vehicle engines & parts

(P-10151)
US MOTOR WORKS LLC (PA)
14722 Anson Ave, Santa Fe Springs
(90670-5306)
PHONE..................562 404-0488
Gil Benjaman,
Doron Goren, *COO*
Danny Chavez, *Executive*
Roger Sijder, *Engineer*
Ariel Loza, *Business Mgr*
◆ EMP: 131 EST: 1995
SQ FT: 37,000
SALES (est): 33.8MM **Privately Held**
WEB: www.usmotorworks.com
SIC: **3714** Water pump, motor vehicle

(P-10152)
US RADIATOR CORPORATION (PA)
4423 District Blvd, Vernon (90058-3111)
P.O. Box 5486, Huntington Park (90255-9486)
PHONE..................323 826-0965
Donald Armstrong, *President*
William Zimmerman, *Treasurer*
Tim Armstrong, *Vice Pres*
▲ EMP: 29 EST: 1956
SQ FT: 35,000
SALES (est): 2.5MM **Privately Held**
WEB: www.usradiator.com
SIC: **3714** Radiators & radiator shells & cores, motor vehicle

(P-10153)
VINTIQUE INC
1828 W Sequoia Ave, Orange
(92868-1018)
PHONE..................714 634-1932
Chad Looney, *President*
Judy Looney, *Treasurer*
Denise Looney, *Vice Pres*
▲ EMP: 27 EST: 1973
SQ FT: 17,000
SALES (est): 2.4MM **Privately Held**
WEB: www.vintiqueinc.com
SIC: **3714** Motor vehicle parts & accessories

(P-10154)
WAH HUNG GROUP INC (PA)
1000 E Garvey Ave, Monterey Park
(91755-3031)
PHONE..................626 571-8700
Man Kwong Ng, *CEO*
EMP: 29 EST: 2009
SALES (est): 8.4MM **Privately Held**
WEB: www.wahhunggroup.com
SIC: **3714** Wheel rims, motor vehicle

(P-10155)
WAH HUNG GROUP INC
283 E Garvey Ave, Monterey Park
(91755-1811)
PHONE..................626 571-8700
EMP: 22
SALES (corp-wide): 8.4MM **Privately Held**
WEB: www.wahhunggroup.com
SIC: **3714** Wheel rims, motor vehicle
PA: Wah Hung Group, Inc.
    1000 E Garvey Ave
    Monterey Park CA 91755
    626 571-8700

(P-10156)
WALKER PRODUCTS
14291 Commerce Dr, Garden Grove
(92843-4944)
PHONE..................714 554-5151
Chris Weaver, *General Mgr*
Alejandro Marquez, *Export Mgr*
Tresa Kaufman, *Production*
Adam Fell, *Marketing Staff*
Brad Kindness, *Sales Staff*
EMP: 50
SALES (corp-wide): 49.1MM **Privately Held**
WEB: www.walkerproducts.com
SIC: **3714** Motor vehicle parts & accessories
PA: Walker Products
    525 W Congress St
    Pacific MO 63069
    636 257-2400

(P-10157)
WEBCAM INC
Also Called: Web CAM
1815 Massachusetts Ave, Riverside
(92507-2616)
PHONE..................951 369-5144
Laurie Dunlap, *Vice Pres*
EMP: 13 EST: 1945
SQ FT: 6,000
SALES (est): 2.2MM **Privately Held**
WEB: www.webcamshafts.com
SIC: **3714** Camshafts, motor vehicle

(P-10158)
WILWOOD ENGINEERING
4700 Calle Bolero, Camarillo (93012-8561)
PHONE..................805 388-1188
William H Wood, *President*
Larry Wolff, *General Mgr*
Dave Brzozowski, *Software Dev*
Jill Domke, *IT/INT Sup*
Derek Zoetewey, *Technical Staff*
▲ EMP: 120 EST: 1977
SALES (est): 24.2MM **Privately Held**
WEB: www.wilwood.com
SIC: **3714** Motor vehicle parts & accessories

(P-10159)
WIPEX CORP (PA)
10808 Foothill Blvd, Rancho Cucamonga
(91730-3889)
PHONE..................909 714-4623
EMP: 97 EST: 2011
SALES (est): 236.2K **Privately Held**
SIC: **3714** Motor vehicle parts & accessories

(P-10160)
WSW CORP (PA)
Also Called: Waag
16000 Strathern St, Van Nuys
(91406-1316)
PHONE..................818 989-5008
Gary Waagenaar, *CEO*
Mike Calka, *President*
Jennifer Waagenaar, *Vice Pres*
▲ EMP: 45 EST: 1978
SQ FT: 55,000
SALES (est): 6.6MM **Privately Held**
WEB: www.waag.com
SIC: **3714** **5712** Motor vehicle parts & accessories; beds & accessories

(P-10161)
XRP INC (PA)
5630 Imperial Hwy, South Gate
(90280-7420)
PHONE..................562 861-4765
David Barker, *CEO*
Debbie Singer, *President*
EMP: 19 EST: 1989
SQ FT: 25,000
SALES (est): 3.6MM **Privately Held**
WEB: www.xrp.com
SIC: **5531** **3714** Automotive parts; fuel systems & parts, motor vehicle

(P-10162)
YINLUN TDI LLC (HQ)
4850 E Airport Dr, Ontario (91761-7818)
PHONE..................909 390-3944
Zack Yang, *President*
Joe Ding, *Vice Pres*
Jonathan Moyer, *Vice Pres*

Eric Williams, *Program Mgr*
Michael Bellemore, *General Mgr*
EMP: 234 EST: 2012
SQ FT: 85,000
SALES (est): 29.5MM
SALES (corp-wide): 960.8MM **Privately Held**
WEB: www.yinluntdi.com
SIC: **3714** Motor vehicle engines & parts
PA: Zhejiang Yinlun Machinery Co., Ltd.
    No.8, Shifeng East Rd., Fuxi Street,
    Tiantai County
    Taizhou 31720
    576 839-3833

3715 Truck Trailers

(P-10163)
ANDERSEN INDUSTRIES INC
17079 Muskrat Ave, Adelanto
(92301-2259)
PHONE..................760 246-8766
Steven Andersen, *CEO*
Neil Andersen, *Vice Pres*
Wayne Andersen, *Vice Pres*
Judy Moreno, *Office Mgr*
Judy McCalmon, *Admin Asst*
EMP: 25 EST: 1980
SQ FT: 110,000
SALES (est): 4.8MM **Privately Held**
WEB: www.andersenmp.com
SIC: **3715** **3441** **3444** Truck trailers; fabricated structural metal; hoppers, sheet metal

(P-10164)
BLACKSERIES CAMPERS INC
Also Called: Black Series Campers
19501 E Walnut Dr S, City of Industry
(91748-2318)
PHONE..................833 822-6737
Hongwei Qiu, *CEO*
Yichun Chen, *Admin Sec*
EMP: 20 EST: 2017
SALES (est): 1.1MM **Privately Held**
SIC: **3715** Truck trailers

(P-10165)
CIMC INTERMODAL EQUIPMENT LLC (DH)
10530 Sessler St, South Gate
(90280-7252)
PHONE..................562 904-8600
Frank Sonzela, *CEO*
Trevor Ash, *Vice Pres*
Jeff Shutts, *Info Tech Mgr*
Robert Horton, *Chief Engr*
Silvia Arellano, *Accounting Mgr*
▲ EMP: 70 EST: 2007
SALES (est): 33MM **Privately Held**
WEB: www.ciemanufacturing.com
SIC: **3715** **7539** Truck trailer chassis; trailer repair

(P-10166)
ERMM CORPORATION
Also Called: J & L Tank Co
5415 Mrtin Lther King Jr, Lynwood
(90262-3961)
PHONE..................310 635-0524
Norma Ritterbush, *President*
Michael Ritterbush, *Vice Pres*
EMP: 17 EST: 1968
SQ FT: 450,000
SALES (est): 2.1MM **Privately Held**
SIC: **3715** **3795** **5561** **7538** Truck trailers; tanks & tank components; recreational vehicle dealers; general automotive repair shops; motor vehicle parts & accessories

(P-10167)
OWEN TRAILERS INC
9020 Jurupa Rd, Riverside (92509-3106)
P.O. Box 36, La Habra (90633-0036)
PHONE..................951 361-4557
Loren Owen Jr, *President*
Angela P Owen, *Corp Secy*
EMP: 25 EST: 1946
SQ FT: 34,000 **Privately Held**
WEB: www.owentrailers.com
SIC: **3715** Truck trailers

(P-10168)
REFRIGERATED TRCK SOLUTIONS LLC
1115 E Dominguez St, Carson
(90746-3517)
PHONE..................323 594-4500
Frederick Lukken, *President*
EMP: 26 EST: 2015
SALES (est): 3.5MM **Privately Held**
SIC: **3715** Truck trailers

(P-10169)
UNITED STATES LOGISTICS GROUP
Also Called: US Logistics
2700 Rose Ave Ste A, Signal Hill
(90755-1929)
P.O. Box 10129, Glendale (91209-3129)
PHONE..................562 989-9555
Khachatur Khudikyan, *CEO*
EMP: 32 EST: 2009
SALES (est): 3.4MM **Privately Held**
WEB: www.uslginc.com
SIC: **3715** Truck trailers

(P-10170)
UTILITY TRAILER MFG CO (PA)
17295 Railroad St Ste A, City of Industry
(91748-1043)
PHONE..................626 964-7319
Paul F Bennett, *Ch of Bd*
Harold C Bennett, *President*
Craig M Bennett, *Senior VP*
Craig Bennett, *Vice Pres*
Jeffrey J Bennett, *Vice Pres*
◆ EMP: 300 EST: 1914
SQ FT: 50,000
SALES (est): 897.7MM **Privately Held**
WEB: www.utilitytrailer.com
SIC: **3715** Truck trailers

(P-10171)
UTILITY TRAILER MFG CO
Tautliner Division
17295 Railroad St Ste A, City of Industry
(91748-1043)
PHONE..................909 594-6026
Linda Baker, *Manager*
Clod Santiago, *Web Dvlpr*
Tom Cherian, *IT/INT Sup*
George Flynn, *Accountant*
Azim Khan, *Accountant*
EMP: 245
SALES (corp-wide): 897.7MM **Privately Held**
WEB: www.utilitytrailer.com
SIC: **3715** **5199** Truck trailers; tarpaulins
PA: Utility Trailer Manufacturing Company
    17295 Railroad St Ste A
    City Of Industry CA 91748
    626 964-7319

(P-10172)
UTILITY TRAILER MFG CO
Also Called: Utility Trlr Sls Southern Cal
15567 Valley Blvd, Fontana (92335-6351)
PHONE..................909 428-8300
Thayne Stanger, *Branch Mgr*
EMP: 245
SALES (corp-wide): 897.7MM **Privately Held**
WEB: www.utilitytrailer.com
SIC: **3715** Semitrailers for truck tractors
PA: Utility Trailer Manufacturing Company
    17295 Railroad St Ste A
    City Of Industry CA 91748
    626 964-7319

3716 Motor Homes

(P-10173)
FLEETWOOD MOTOR HOMES-CALIF INC (DH)
Also Called: Fleetwood Homes
3125 Myers St, Riverside (92503-5527)
P.O. Box 7638 (92513-7638)
PHONE..................951 354-3000
Edward B Caudill, *CEO*
Elden L Smith, *President*
Boyd R Plowman, *CFO*
Lyle N Larkin, *Treasurer*
Christopher J Braun, *Senior VP*
▲ EMP: 274 EST: 1976
SQ FT: 262,900

SALES (est): 47.3MM **Privately Held**
WEB: www.fleetwoodhomes.com
SIC: 3716 Motor homes
HQ: Fleetwood Enterprises, Inc.
1351 Pomona Rd Ste 230
Corona CA 92882
951 354-3000

(P-10174)
REXHALL INDUSTRIES INC
26857 Tannahill Ave, Canyon Country
(91387-3969)
PHONE.....................661 726-5470
William Jonathan Rex, *Ch of Bd*
James C Rex, *Vice Pres*
Cheryl Rex, *Admin Sec*
▲ **EMP:** 46
SQ FT: 120,000
SALES (est): 7.5MM **Privately Held**
WEB: www.rexhall.com
SIC: 3716 Motor homes

3721 Aircraft

(P-10175)
AERCAP US GLOBAL AVIATION LLC (HQ)
Also Called: Aercap Los Angeles
10250 Constellation Blvd, Los Angeles
(90067-6200)
PHONE.....................310 788-1999
Sean Sullivan,
Keith Helming, *CFO*
Dan Donahue, *Vice Pres*
Pamela Hendry, *Vice Pres*
Feifei Hong, *Vice Pres*
EMP: 100 **EST:** 2014
SALES (est): 244.5MM
SALES (corp-wide): 1B **Privately Held**
WEB: www.aercap.com
SIC: 3721 4581 6159 Aircraft; airport
leasing, if operating airport; equipment &
vehicle finance leasing companies
PA: Aercap Holdings N.V.
Onbekend Nederlands Adres
Onbekend
353 163-6065

(P-10176)
AMERICAN SCENCE TECH AS T CORP
2372 Morse Ave Ste 571, Irvine
(92614-6234)
PHONE.....................310 773-1978
Kinda Assouad, *Branch Mgr*
EMP: 85
SALES (corp-wide): 348MM **Privately Held**
SIC: 3721 3724 3761 3764 Aircraft; aircraft engines & engine parts; guided missiles & space vehicles; guided missile &
space vehicle propulsion unit parts;
guided missile & space vehicle parts &
auxiliary equipment
PA: American Science & Technology
(As&T) Corporation
50 California St Fl 21
San Francisco CA 94111
415 251-2800

(P-10177)
BOEING COMPANY
4000 N Lakewood Blvd, Long Beach
(90808-1700)
PHONE.....................562 496-1000
Nan Bouchard, *Vice Pres*
Troy Ball, *Partner*
Charles Chen, *Administration*
Joseph Bruschi, *Info Tech Mgr*
Christine Onan, *Info Tech Mgr*
EMP: 2000
SALES (corp-wide): 58.1B **Publicly Held**
WEB: www.boeing.com
SIC: 3721 Airplanes, fixed or rotary wing
PA: The Boeing Company
100 N Riverside Plz
Chicago IL 60606
312 544-2000

(P-10178)
BOEING COMPANY
4060 N Lakewood Blvd, Long Beach
(90808-1700)
P.O. Box 200 (90801-0200)
PHONE.....................562 593-5511
Linda Van Reeden, *Manager*
Troy Ball, *Partner*
Andrew Masson, *Managing Dir*
Carola Najera, *Office Admin*
Wael Elaref, *Project Mgr*
EMP: 1400
SALES (corp-wide): 58.1B **Publicly Held**
WEB: www.boeing.com
SIC: 3721 Airplanes, fixed or rotary wing
PA: The Boeing Company
100 N Riverside Plz
Chicago IL 60606
312 544-2000

(P-10179)
BOEING COMSATCOM SERVICES INC (HQ)
900 N Pacific Coast Hwy, El Segundo
(90245-2710)
PHONE.....................310 335-6682
Craig R Cooning, *CEO*
EMP: 83 **EST:** 2014
SALES (est): 2.2MM
SALES (corp-wide): 58.1B **Publicly Held**
WEB: www.boeing.com
SIC: 3721 Aircraft
PA: The Boeing Company
100 N Riverside Plz
Chicago IL 60606
312 544-2000

(P-10180)
BOEING INTLLCTUAL PRPRTY LCNSI
14441 Astronautics Ln, Huntington Beach
(92647-2080)
PHONE.....................562 797-2020
Chia-WEI Chow, *Vice Pres*
Lacey Jones, *Vice Pres*
Todd Mather, *Program Mgr*
Eric Muehle, *General Mgr*
Martin Parsons, *Administration*
EMP: 335 **EST:** 2011
SALES (est): 83.5MM
SALES (corp-wide): 58.1B **Publicly Held**
WEB: www.boeing.com
SIC: 3721 Airplanes, fixed or rotary wing;
helicopters; research & development on
aircraft by the manufacturer
PA: The Boeing Company
100 N Riverside Plz
Chicago IL 60606
312 544-2000

(P-10181)
BOEING SATELLITE SYSTEMS INC
2300 E Imperial Hwy, El Segundo
(90245-2813)
P.O. Box 92919, Los Angeles (90009-2919)
PHONE.....................310 568-2735
Steve Tsukamoto, *Manager*
Jesse Arroyo, *Manager*
EMP: 3487
SALES (corp-wide): 58.1B **Publicly Held**
WEB: www.boeing.com
SIC: 3721 Aircraft
HQ: Boeing Satellite Systems, Inc.
900 N Pacific Coast Hwy
El Segundo CA 90245

(P-10182)
CHIPTON-ROSS INC
420 Culver Blvd, Playa Del Rey
(90293-7706)
PHONE.....................310 414-7800
Judith Hinkley, *President*
Michelle Reposa, *Exec Dir*
Carla Bernal, *Administration*
Chris Guldimann, *CIO*
Mike Clinton, *Software Dev*
EMP: 100
SQ FT: 6,000

SALES: 9MM **Privately Held**
WEB: www.chiptonross.com
SIC: 3721 3731 8731 7363 Motorized
aircraft; military ships, building & repairing; commercial physical research; temporary help service; engineering services

(P-10183)
CLEAN WAVE MANAGEMENT INC
Also Called: Impact Bearing
1291 Puerta Del Sol, San Clemente
(92673-6310)
PHONE.....................949 488-2922
Fax: 949 488-2923
▲ **EMP:** 15
SALES (est): 2.1MM **Privately Held**
WEB: www.aircraftbearing.com
SIC: 3721 Mfg Aircraft

(P-10184)
COMAC AMERICA CORPORATION
4350 Von Karman Ave # 400, Newport
Beach (92660-2007)
PHONE.....................760 616-9614
WEI Ye, *CEO*
EMP: 15 **EST:** 2013
SALES (est): 8.2MM **Privately Held**
WEB: www.comacamerica.com
SIC: 3721 Aircraft
PA: Commercial Aircraft Corporation Of
China,Ltd.
No.25, Zhangyang Road, China Pilot
Free Trade Zone
Shanghai

(P-10185)
GENERAL ATOMIC AERON
73 El Mirage Airport Rd B, Adelanto
(92301-9540)
PHONE.....................760 388-8208
Gary Bener, *Branch Mgr*
Joseph Martin, *Technician*
Vincent Phong, *Senior Engr*
Daniel Woods, *Manager*
Dominic Grossman, *Supervisor*
EMP: 200
SQ FT: 34,425
WEB: www.ga-asi.com
SIC: 3721 Aircraft
HQ: General Atomics Aeronautical Sys-
tems, Inc.
14200 Kirkham Way
Poway CA 92064

(P-10186)
GENERAL ELECTRIC COMPANY
18000 Phantom St, Victorville
(92394-7913)
PHONE.....................760 530-5200
John Hardell, *Principal*
Tim Ashley, *Technician*
Noah Demerly, *Maintence Staff*
EMP: 50
SALES (corp-wide): 79.6B **Publicly Held**
WEB: www.ge.com
SIC: 3721 Aircraft
PA: General Electric Company
5 Necco St
Boston MA 02210
617 443-3000

(P-10187)
GKN AEROSPACE
12242 Western Ave, Garden Grove
(92841-2916)
PHONE.....................714 653-7531
Cedo Nedic, *Engineer*
Rhonda Stevenson, *Human Res Dir*
Lilian Wilkirson, *Human Res Dir*
Joanne Brabon, *Opers Staff*
Mike Wehmeyer, *Opers Staff*
EMP: 22 **EST:** 2016
SALES (est): 12.1MM **Privately Held**
WEB: www.gknaerospace.com
SIC: 3721 Aircraft

(P-10188)
GULF STREAMS
4150 E Donald Douglas Dr, Long Beach
(90808-1725)
PHONE.....................562 420-1818
Mike Kambourian, *Owner*

Jim Bunke, *Vice Pres*
Andrew Miller, *Network Analyst*
Daniel Neher, *Analyst*
Wayne Burk, *Senior Mgr*
▲ **EMP:** 26 **EST:** 1960
SALES (est): 6.8MM **Privately Held**
SIC: 3721 Aircraft

(P-10189)
GULFSTREAM AEROSPACE CORP GA
9818 Mina Ave, Whittier (90605-3035)
PHONE.....................562 907-9300
EMP: 930
SALES (corp-wide): 37.9B **Publicly Held**
SIC: 3721 Airplanes, fixed or rotary wing
HQ: Gulfstream Aerospace Corporation
(Georgia)
500 Gulfstream Rd
Savannah GA 31408
912 965-3000

(P-10190)
GULFSTREAM AEROSPACE CORP GA
16644 Roscoe Blvd, Van Nuys
(91406-1103)
PHONE.....................805 236-5755
EMP: 36
SALES (corp-wide): 37.9B **Publicly Held**
WEB: www.gulfstream.com
SIC: 3721 Aircraft
HQ: Gulfstream Aerospace Corporation
(Georgia)
500 Gulfstream Rd
Savannah GA 31408
912 965-3000

(P-10191)
GULFSTREAM AEROSPACE CORP GA
4150 E Donald Douglas Dr, Long Beach
(90808-1725)
PHONE.....................562 420-1818
Barry Russell, *Vice Pres*
Patrick Franssen, *Vice Pres*
Robby Odell, *Program Mgr*
Frank Defelice, *General Mgr*
Georgia Taylor, *Office Mgr*
EMP: 930
SALES (corp-wide): 37.9B **Publicly Held**
SIC: 3721 Aircraft
HQ: Gulfstream Aerospace Corporation
(Georgia)
500 Gulfstream Rd
Savannah GA 31408
912 965-3000

(P-10192)
JVR SHEETMETAL FABRICATION INC
Also Called: Talsco
7101 Patterson Dr, Garden Grove
(92841-1415)
PHONE.....................714 841-2464
Jose Castaneda, *CEO*
Jeff Piaskowski, *Production*
EMP: 33 **EST:** 2003
SQ FT: 1,000
SALES (est): 3.8MM **Privately Held**
WEB: www.talsco.com
SIC: 3721 Aircraft

(P-10193)
KAY AND ASSOCIATES INC
300 Reeves Blvd, Lemoore (93246-7400)
PHONE.....................559 410-0917
Gregory Kay, *President*
Dianna Chinn Heinz, *CFO*
EMP: 23 **EST:** 1960
SALES (est): 134.8K **Privately Held**
WEB: www.kayinc.com
SIC: 3721 Aircraft

(P-10194)
M & T AEROSPACE INC
10492 Trask Ave, Garden Grove
(92843-3234)
PHONE.....................714 591-5154
Minh Danh, *Administration*
EMP: 13 **EST:** 2014
SALES (est): 300.9K **Privately Held**
WEB: www.tjaerospace.com
SIC: 3721 Aircraft

(P-10195)
MADN AIRCRAFT HINGE
26911 Ruether Ave Ste Q, Santa Clarita
(91351-6513)
PHONE................................661 257-3430
Aroosh Shahbazian, *CEO*
EMP: 45 **EST:** 2020
SALES (est): 1.1MM **Privately Held**
WEB: www.madnaircrafthinge.com
SIC: 3721 3728 Aircraft; aircraft parts &
equipment

(P-10196)
NEXJET CORPORATION
180 E Ocean Blvd Ste 1010, Long Beach
(90802-4711)
PHONE................................562 395-3030
John D Macmillan, *CEO*
Thomas Reed, *Director*
EMP: 15 **EST:** 2004
SALES (est): 469.3K **Privately Held**
WEB: www.nexjet.com
SIC: 3721 Aircraft

(P-10197)
NORTHROP GRUMMAN SYSTEMS CORP
Also Called: Air Combat Systems
3520 E Avenue M, Palmdale (93550-7401)
PHONE................................661 272-7000
David G Hogarth, *Manager*
Shaun Donnelly, *Info Tech Mgr*
Philip Kitchin, *Engineer*
EMP: 300 **Publicly Held**
WEB: www.northropgrumman.com
SIC: 3721 3812 3761 Aircraft; search &
navigation equipment; guided missiles &
space vehicles
HQ: Northrop Grumman Systems Corporation
2980 Fairview Park Dr
Falls Church VA 22042
703 280-2900

(P-10198)
NORTHROP GRUMMAN SYSTEMS CORP
Also Called: Aerospace Systems
1 Space Park Blvd, Redondo Beach
(90278-1071)
PHONE................................310 812-1089
Gary Ervin, *Branch Mgr*
Theodore Lau, *Planning*
Philip Hutson, *Software Engr*
Thomas Le, *Software Engr*
Victor Pham, *Design Engr*
EMP: 305 **Publicly Held**
WEB: www.northropgrumman.com
SIC: 3721 3761 3728 3812 Airplanes,
fixed or rotary wing; research & development on aircraft by the manufacturer;
guided missiles, complete; guided missiles & space vehicles, research & development; fuselage assembly, aircraft; wing
assemblies & parts, aircraft; research &
dev by manuf., aircraft parts & auxiliary
equip; inertial guidance systems; gyroscopes; warfare counter-measure equipment; search & detection systems &
instruments; test equipment for electronic
& electrical circuits; aircraft servicing & repairing
HQ: Northrop Grumman Systems Corporation
2980 Fairview Park Dr
Falls Church VA 22042
703 280-2900

(P-10199)
NORTHROP GRUMMAN SYSTEMS CORP
1 Space Park Blvd D, Redondo Beach
(90278-1071)
PHONE................................310 812-4321
Bruce Gaines, *Principal*
Shawn Purvis, *President*
Lisa Kicklighter, *Vice Pres*
Steven Briese, *Program Mgr*
Thomas Parry, *Program Mgr*
EMP: 305 **Publicly Held**
WEB: www.northropgrumman.com

SIC: 3721 3761 3728 Airplanes, fixed or
rotary wing; research & development on
aircraft by the manufacturer; guided missiles, complete; guided missiles & space
vehicles, research & development; fuselage assembly, aircraft; wing assemblies
& parts, aircraft; research & dev by
manuf., aircraft parts & auxiliary equip
HQ: Northrop Grumman Systems Corporation
2980 Fairview Park Dr
Falls Church VA 22042
703 280-2900

(P-10200)
OVERAIR INC
3001 S Susan St, Santa Ana (92704-6434)
PHONE................................949 503-7503
Benjamin Tigner, *CEO*
EMP: 30 **EST:** 2019
SALES (est): 2.7MM **Privately Held**
WEB: www.overair.com
SIC: 3721 Research & development on air-
craft by the manufacturer

(P-10201)
QUALITY TECH MFG INC
170 W Mindanao St, Bloomington
(92316-2946)
PHONE................................909 465-9565
Rudolph A Gutierrez, *President*
Camilio Gutierrez, *Vice Pres*
Danielle Alacron, *Administration*
Chris Gutierrez, *Engineer*
Hernan Delgado, *Purchasing*
EMP: 37
SQ FT: 18,000
SALES (est): 6.5MM **Privately Held**
WEB: www.qualitytechmfg.com
SIC: 3721 Aircraft

(P-10202)
SCALED COMPOSITES LLC
1624 Flight Line, Mojave (93501-1663)
PHONE................................661 824-4541
Kevin Mickey, *President*
Mark Taylor, *CFO*
Cory Bird, *Vice Pres*
Ben Diachun, *Vice Pres*
Jason Kelley, *Vice Pres*
EMP: 500 **EST:** 1982
SQ FT: 160,000
SALES (est): 98.5MM **Publicly Held**
WEB: www.scaled.com
SIC: 3721 3999 8711 Aircraft; models, ex-
cept toy; aviation &/or aeronautical engi-
neering
HQ: Northrop Grumman Systems Corpora-
tion
2980 Fairview Park Dr
Falls Church VA 22042
703 280-2900

(P-10203)
SOARING AMERICA CORPORATION
Also Called: Mooney International
8354 Kimball Ave F360, Chino
(91708-9267)
PHONE................................909 270-2628
Cheng-Yuan Jerry Chen, *CEO*
Albert LI, *CFO*
EMP: 45 **EST:** 2012
SALES (est): 3.7MM **Privately Held**
SIC: 3721 3728 Research & development
on aircraft by the manufacturer; motorized
aircraft; research & dev by manuf., aircraft
parts & auxiliary equip

(P-10204)
SPORT KITES INC
Also Called: Wills Wing
500 W Blueridge Ave, Orange
(92865-4206)
PHONE................................714 998-6359
Steven Pearson, *President*
Michael Meier, *Vice Pres*
Linda Meier, *Admin Sec*
Rick Zimbelman, *Purch Mgr*
▲ **EMP:** 18 **EST:** 1973
SQ FT: 16,000
SALES (est): 3.5MM **Privately Held**
SIC: 3721 Hang gliders

(P-10205)
TALENTSCALE INC
28693 Old Town Front St, Temecula
(92590-2786)
PHONE................................760 458-7633
Douglas Poldrugo, *President*
Steve Santich, *President*
Richard Nester, *Vice Pres*
Kristin Wolfram, *Administration*
Amy Corothers, *Tech Recruiter*
EMP: 100 **EST:** 2008
SALES (est): 20MM
SALES (corp-wide): 533.8MM **Privately
Held**
WEB: www.talentscale.com
SIC: 3721 Motorized aircraft
HQ: Atlas Engineering West, Inc.
6280 Riverdale St
San Diego CA 92120
619 280-4321

(P-10206)
TRI MODELS INC
5191 Oceanus Dr, Huntington Beach
(92649-1026)
PHONE................................714 896-0823
Prince A Herzog Sr, *CEO*
Jeff Herzog, *President*
Douglas Carr, *General Mgr*
Sharmon Herzog, *Administration*
Michael Gideon, *Engineer*
▲ **EMP:** 58
SALES (est): 17.4MM **Privately Held**
WEB: www.trimodels.com
SIC: 3721 Airplanes, fixed or rotary wing

(P-10207)
WORLDWIDE AEROS CORP
1734 Aeros Way, Montebello (90640-6504)
PHONE................................818 344-3999
Igor Pasternak, *President*
Carrie Cass, *CFO*
Anatoliy Pasternak, *Vice Pres*
Aric Hirami, *Info Tech Mgr*
Ryohei Yamamoto, *Purch Mgr*
▲ **EMP:** 82 **EST:** 1987
SALES (est): 13.7MM **Privately Held**
WEB: www.aeroscraft.com
SIC: 3721 8711 Airships; aviation &/or
aeronautical engineering

3724 Aircraft Engines & Engine Parts

(P-10208)
3-D PRECISION MACHINE INC
42132 Remington Ave, Temecula
(92590-2547)
PHONE................................951 296-5449
Linda Luoma, *President*
Roy Luoma, *Founder*
EMP: 31 **EST:** 2006
SQ FT: 14,000
SALES (est): 2.7MM **Privately Held**
WEB: www.3dprecisionmachine.com
SIC: 3724 Research & development on air-
craft engines & parts

(P-10209)
AC&A ENTERPRISES LLC (HQ)
25671 Commercentre Dr, Lake Forest
(92630-8801)
PHONE................................949 716-3511
Justin Uchida, *CEO*
Alejandro Sorrentino, *CIO*
Justin Schultz,
Steve Smith, *Director*
▲ **EMP:** 121 **EST:** 2004
SALES (est): 33MM
SALES (corp-wide): 189.2MM **Privately
Held**
WEB: www.appliedcomposites.com
SIC: 3724 3511 Aircraft engines & engine
parts; turbines & turbine generator sets
PA: Applied Composites Holdings, Llc
25692 Atlantic Ocean Dr
Lake Forest CA 92630
949 716-3511

(P-10210)
ACCURATE GRINDING AND MFG CORP
807 E Parkridge Ave, Corona (92879-6609)
PHONE................................951 479-0909
Douglas Nilsen, *CEO*
Hans J Nilsen, *President*
David Nilsen, *Admin Sec*
Kristin Hicks, *Admin Asst*
▲ **EMP:** 35 **EST:** 1950
SQ FT: 15,000
SALES (est): 8.5MM **Privately Held**
WEB: www.accuratemanufacturing.net
SIC: 3724 3812 Aircraft engines & engine
parts; search & navigation equipment

(P-10211)
ADVANCED GRUND SYSTEMS ENGRG L (HQ)
Also Called: Agse
10805 Painter Ave, Santa Fe Springs
(90670-4526)
PHONE................................562 906-9300
Diane Henderson, *CEO*
Frank Judge, *COO*
David Chetwood, *CFO*
Nicholas Demonte, *CFO*
Ray Meier, *Vice Pres*
▲ **EMP:** 40 **EST:** 1973
SALES (est): 12.8MM
SALES (corp-wide): 22.8MM **Privately
Held**
WEB: www.agsecorp.com
SIC: 3724 Aircraft engines & engine parts
PA: Westmont Industries Llc
10805 Painter Ave Uppr
Santa Fe Springs CA 90670
562 944-6137

(P-10212)
AMERICA METAL MFG RESOURCES
Also Called: American Metal
1989 W Holt Ave, Pomona (91768-3352)
PHONE................................909 620-4500
Vikas Sharma, *President*
EMP: 25 **EST:** 2007
SQ FT: 6,000
SALES (est): 2.1MM **Privately Held**
SIC: 3724 3999 Aircraft engines & engine
parts; barber & beauty shop equipment

(P-10213)
DUCOMMUN AEROSTRUCTURES INC (HQ)
268 E Gardena Blvd, Gardena
(90248-2814)
PHONE................................310 380-5390
Anthony Reardon, *CEO*
◆ **EMP:** 450 **EST:** 1949
SQ FT: 300,000
SALES (est): 333.7MM
SALES (corp-wide): 628.9MM **Publicly
Held**
WEB: www.ducommun.com
SIC: 3724 3812 3728 Aircraft engines &
engine parts; search & navigation equip-
ment; aircraft parts & equipment
PA: Ducommun Incorporated
200 Sandpointe Ave # 700
Santa Ana CA 92707
657 335-3665

(P-10214)
DUCOMMUN AEROSTRUCTURES INC
1885 N Batavia St, Orange (92865-4105)
PHONE................................714 637-4401
Kent T Christensen, *Branch Mgr*
EMP: 114
SALES (corp-wide): 628.9MM **Publicly
Held**
WEB: www.ducommun.com
SIC: 3724 3812 3728 Aircraft engines &
engine parts; search & navigation equip-
ment; aircraft parts & equipment
HQ: Ducommun Aerostructures, Inc.
268 E Gardena Blvd
Gardena CA 90248
310 380-5390

▲ = Import ▼=Export
◆ =Import/Export

(P-10215)
GARRETT TRANSPORTATION I INC (HQ)
2525 W 190th St, Torrance (90504-6002)
PHONE...................................973 455-2000
Darius Adamczyk, *CEO*
EMP: 127 EST: 2018
SALES (est): 27.3MM
SALES (corp-wide): 3B **Privately Held**
SIC: 3724 Aircraft engines & engine parts
PA: Garrett Motion Inc.
47548 Halyard Dr
Plymouth MI 48170
734 359-5901

(P-10216)
HONEYWELL INTERNATIONAL INC
2525 W 190th St, Torrance (90504-6002)
PHONE...................................310 323-9500
Ken Defusco, *Branch Mgr*
Adam Elliott, *Administration*
EMP: 1000
SALES (corp-wide): 32.6B **Publicly Held**
WEB: www.honeywell.com
SIC: 3724 Aircraft engines & engine parts
PA: Honeywell International Inc.
855 S Mint St
Charlotte NC 28202
704 627-6200

(P-10217)
INTERNATIONAL WIND INC (PA)
137 N Joy St, Corona (92879-1321)
PHONE...................................562 240-3963
Cory Arendt, *President*
EMP: 49 EST: 2013
SALES (est): 7MM **Privately Held**
WEB: www.international-wind.com
SIC: 3724 8711 8742 Turbines, aircraft type; engineering services; aviation &/or aeronautical engineering; consulting engineer; management consulting services; maintenance management consultant

(P-10218)
IRISH INTERNATIONAL
5511 Skylab Rd, Huntington Beach (92647-2068)
PHONE...................................949 559-0930
Tom McFarland, *CEO*
Jude Dozor, *COO*
Mike Melancon, *CFO*
Mike McCarthy, *Officer*
Antonio Perez, *Admin Sec*
▲ EMP: 250 EST: 2015
SQ FT: 80,000
SALES (est): 9.3MM **Privately Held**
WEB: www.encoregroup.aero
SIC: 3724 Aircraft engines & engine parts

(P-10219)
JET/BRELLA INC
6849 Hayvenhurst Ave, Van Nuys (91406-4718)
PHONE...................................818 786-5480
William Onasch, *President*
EMP: 20 EST: 1992
SQ FT: 18,000
SALES (est): 2.9MM **Privately Held**
WEB: www.jetbrella.com
SIC: 3724 3728 5088 Aircraft engines & engine parts; aircraft parts & equipment; aircraft & parts

(P-10220)
LOGISTICAL SUPPORT LLC
Also Called: RTC Aerospace
20409 Prairie St, Chatsworth (91311-6029)
PHONE...................................818 341-3344
Jerry Hill,
Cinthia Hernandez, *Program Mgr*
EMP: 125 EST: 1997
SQ FT: 14,600
SALES (est): 12.7MM **Privately Held**
SIC: 3724 Aircraft engines & engine parts

(P-10221)
MARTON PRECISION MFG LLC
1365 S Acacia Ave, Fullerton (92831-5315)
PHONE...................................714 808-6523
Daniel J Marton, *President*
Mary Marton, *CFO*
Greg Carroll, *General Mgr*
Crystal Torres, *Purch Mgr*

Nandor Weisz, *Manager*
EMP: 47
SQ FT: 20,000
SALES (est): 7.5MM **Privately Held**
WEB: www.martoninc.com
SIC: 3724 3599 3827 Aircraft engines & engine parts; machine & other job shop work; optical instruments & apparatus

(P-10222)
PARKER-HANNIFIN CORPORATION
Fluid Systems Division
16666 Von Karman Ave, Irvine (92606-4997)
PHONE...................................949 833-3000
Matthew Stafford, *Manager*
Jesse Anaya, *Administration*
Alex Cruz, *CIO*
WEI Chiu, *Software Engr*
Dennis Dinh, *Technician*
EMP: 246
SALES (corp-wide): 13.7B **Publicly Held**
WEB: www.parker.com
SIC: 3724 3728 Aircraft engines & engine parts; aircraft parts & equipment
PA: Parker-Hannifin Corporation
6035 Parkland Blvd
Cleveland OH 44124
216 896-3000

(P-10223)
PRINCETON TOOL INC
Also Called: Paragon Precision
25620 Rye Canyon Rd Ste A, Valencia (91355-1139)
PHONE...................................661 257-1380
Kenneth Bevington III, *CEO*
EMP: 18
SALES (corp-wide): 20.3MM **Privately Held**
WEB: www.princetontool.com
SIC: 3724 Aircraft engines & engine parts
PA: Princeton Tool, Inc.
7830 Division Dr
Mentor OH 44060
440 290-8666

(P-10224)
SALVADOR RAMIREZ
Also Called: S & R Cnc Machining
25334 Avenue Stanford B, Valencia (91355-1214)
PHONE...................................661 702-1813
Salvador Ramirez, *Owner*
EMP: 14 EST: 1995
SQ FT: 2,700
SALES (est): 2.8MM **Privately Held**
WEB: www.srcncmachining.com
SIC: 3724 3714 3599 Aircraft engines & engine parts; motor vehicle parts & accessories; machine & other job shop work

(P-10225)
SIERRA AEROSPACE LLC
2263 Ward Ave, Simi Valley (93065-1863)
PHONE...................................805 526-8669
EMP: 16
SQ FT: 7,500
SALES (est): 2.6MM **Privately Held**
SIC: 3724 Mfg Military Aircraft Parts

(P-10226)
THERMAL STRUCTURES INC (DH)
2362 Railroad St, Corona (92878-5421)
PHONE...................................951 736-9911
Vaughn Barnes, *President*
Javier Garcia, *Engineer*
Bryan Krot, *Engineer*
Harold Hernandez, *Asst Controller*
Ron Daviau, *Buyer*
▲ EMP: 270 EST: 1952
SQ FT: 175,000
SALES (est): 84.7MM **Publicly Held**
WEB: www.thermalstructures.com
SIC: 3724 Aircraft engines & engine parts
HQ: Heico Aerospace Holdings Corp.
3000 Taft St
Hollywood FL 33021
954 987-4000

(P-10227)
THERMAL STRUCTURES INC
2380 Railroad St, Corona (92878-5471)
PHONE...................................951 256-8051

EMP: 20 **Publicly Held**
WEB: www.thermalstructures.com
SIC: 3724 Aircraft engines & engine parts
HQ: Thermal Structures, Inc.
2362 Railroad St
Corona CA 92878
951 736-9911

(P-10228)
TMJ PRODUCTS INC
515 S Palm Ave Ste 6, Alhambra (91803-1430)
PHONE...................................626 576-4063
Jones Tsui, *President*
S L Tsui, *Vice Pres*
▲ EMP: 14 EST: 1994
SQ FT: 1,600
SALES (est): 2.2MM **Privately Held**
SIC: 3724 Aircraft engines & engine parts

3728 Aircraft Parts & Eqpt, NEC

(P-10229)
A & A AEROSPACE INC
1442 Hayes Ave, Long Beach (90813-1124)
PHONE...................................562 901-6803
Arnie Puentes, *President*
Tom Osuna, *Purchasing*
EMP: 15 **Privately Held**
WEB: www.aaaerospace.net
SIC: 3728 Aircraft parts & equipment
PA: A & A Aerospace, Inc.
13649 Pumice St
Santa Fe Springs CA 90670

(P-10230)
A & A AEROSPACE INC
1987 W 16th St, Long Beach (90813-1136)
PHONE...................................562 901-6803
Arnie Puentes, *President*
EMP: 15 **Privately Held**
WEB: www.aaaerospace.net
SIC: 3728 Aircraft parts & equipment
PA: A & A Aerospace, Inc.
13649 Pumice St
Santa Fe Springs CA 90670

(P-10231)
A CDG BOEING COMPANY
4060 N Lakewood Blvd, Long Beach (90808-1700)
PHONE...................................562 608-2000
Bonnia Malone, *Executive Asst*
Dick Michael, *Administration*
Bruce Robinson, *Administration*
Daniel Edwards, *Info Tech Dir*
Robert Faicol, *Technical Staff*
EMP: 20 EST: 2019
SALES (est): 665.5K **Privately Held**
WEB: www.boeingservices.com
SIC: 3728 Aircraft parts & equipment

(P-10232)
A-INFO INC
60 Tesla, Irvine (92618-4603)
PHONE...................................949 346-7326
Linda Williams, *Asst Mgr*
Cissy Suh, *Sales Mgr*
EMP: 35 EST: 2017
SALES (est): 2.6MM **Privately Held**
SIC: 3728 3812 5049 Aircraft parts & equipment; antennas, radar or communications; analytical instruments; scientific instruments; scientific recording equipment

(P-10233)
ACE AIR MANUFACTURING
1430 W 135th St, Gardena (90249-2218)
PHONE...................................310 323-7246
Roger Brandt, *President*
Sheryl Cattaneo, *Office Mgr*
EMP: 17 EST: 1957
SQ FT: 12,000
SALES (est): 2.4MM **Privately Held**
WEB: www.aceairmfg.com
SIC: 3728 Aircraft parts & equipment

(P-10234)
ACE CLEARWATER ENTERPRISES INC (PA)
19815 Magellan Dr, Torrance (90502-1107)
PHONE...................................310 323-2140
James D Dodson, *President*
Kellie Johnson, *CEO*
Brad Haan, *Comms Dir*
Cesar Tello, *Administration*
George Saunders, *Engineer*
EMP: 100 EST: 1961
SALES (est): 32.6MM **Privately Held**
WEB: www.aceclearwater.com
SIC: 3728 3544 7692 3812 Aircraft parts & equipment; special dies, tools, jigs & fixtures; welding repair; search & navigation equipment; sheet metalwork

(P-10235)
ACROMIL LLC (HQ)
18421 Railroad St, City of Industry (91748-1233)
PHONE...................................626 964-2522
John T Cave II,
David Patterson, *Vice Pres*
Jon Konheim,
Gerald A Niznick,
EMP: 144 EST: 2015
SQ FT: 96,000
SALES (est): 28.9MM
SALES (corp-wide): 55.2MM **Privately Held**
WEB: www.acromil.com
SIC: 3728 Aircraft body & wing assemblies & parts
PA: Acromil Corporation
18421 Railroad St
City Of Industry CA 91748
626 964-2522

(P-10236)
ACROMIL LLC
1168 Sherborn St, Corona (92879-2089)
PHONE...................................951 808-9929
David Nguyen, *President*
EMP: 60
SALES (corp-wide): 55.2MM **Privately Held**
WEB: www.acromil.com
SIC: 3728 Aircraft body & wing assemblies & parts
HQ: Acromil, Llc
18421 Railroad St
City Of Industry CA 91748
626 964-2522

(P-10237)
ACROMIL CORPORATION (PA)
18421 Railroad St, City of Industry (91748-1281)
PHONE...................................626 964-2522
Gerald A Niznick, *President*
John Stock, *President*
Jon Konheim, *COO*
Jeanne Aguilera, *CFO*
Ed Hatcher, *Exec VP*
◆ EMP: 187 EST: 1961
SQ FT: 100,000
SALES (est): 55.2MM **Privately Held**
WEB: www.acromil.com
SIC: 3728 Aircraft body & wing assemblies & parts

(P-10238)
ACUFAST AIRCRAFT PRODUCTS INC
12445 Gladstone Ave, Sylmar (91342-5321)
PHONE...................................818 365-7077
Art Dovlatian, *President*
Victor Bme, *Vice Pres*
Jaime Salazar, *Vice Pres*
Davit Dovlatian, *Opers Staff*
EMP: 40 EST: 2006 **Privately Held**
WEB: www.acufastap.com
SIC: 3728 Aircraft parts & equipment

(P-10239)
ADAMS RITE AEROSPACE INC (DH)
4141 N Palm St, Fullerton (92835-1025)
PHONE...................................714 278-6500
John Schaefer, *President*
Jennifer Aniag, *Administration*
Faustino Gutierrez, *Administration*

PRODUCTS & SVCS

Kevin Tang, *Design Engr*
Rhoneil Ramos, *Technical Staff*
EMP: 198 **EST:** 1973
SQ FT: 100,000
SALES (est): 65.3MM
SALES (corp-wide): 4.8B **Publicly Held**
WEB: www.araero.com
SIC: 3728 Aircraft parts & equipment

(P-10240)
ADAPTIVE AEROSPACE CORPORATION
501 Bailey Ave, Tehachapi (93561-9012)
PHONE................................661 300-0616
Bill McCune, *CEO*
Sergio Arellano, *Engineer*
Duana M Pera, *Accountant*
Duana Pera, *Controller*
EMP: 25 **EST:** 2001 **Privately Held**
WEB: www.adapt.aero
SIC: 3728 Aircraft parts & equipment

(P-10241)
ADVANCED MTLS JOINING CORP (PA)
Also Called: Advanced Technology Co
2858 E Walnut St, Pasadena (91107-3755)
PHONE................................626 449-2696
Jean L De Silvestri, *President*
Mohammed Islam, *President*
Jeffrey Lesovsky, *Vice Pres*
Gilbert Figueroa, *Facilities Mgr*
EMP: 41 **EST:** 1971
SQ FT: 23,000
SALES (est): 10.2MM **Privately Held**
WEB: www.at-co.com
SIC: 3728 3724 Aircraft parts & equipment; aircraft engines & engine parts

(P-10242)
ADVEXURE LLC
2288 Westwood Blvd # 100, Los Angeles (90064-2000)
PHONE................................920 917-9566
EMP: 17 **EST:** 2017
SALES (est): 2.3MM **Privately Held**
WEB: www.advexure.com
SIC: 3728 Target drones

(P-10243)
AERO ENGRG & MFG CO CAL LLC
28217 Avenue Crocker, Valencia (91355-1249)
PHONE................................661 295-0875
Dennis L Junker, *CEO*
Lance R Junker, *President*
Richard Jucksch, *Vice Pres*
Bob Singley, *Info Tech Mgr*
Scott Morgan, *Engineer*
▼ **EMP:** 49 **EST:** 1948
SQ FT: 21,000
SALES (est): 11.7MM **Privately Held**
WEB: www.aeroeng.com
SIC: 3728 5088 Aircraft assemblies, sub-assemblies & parts; aircraft & parts

(P-10244)
AERO PACIFIC CORPORATION
Also Called: Merco Manufacturing Co
20445 E Walnut Dr N, Walnut (91789-2918)
PHONE................................714 961-9200
Mark Heasley, *President*
Angelica Sosa, *Vice Pres*
Matt Heasley, *Business Mgr*
Laura Cardenas, *Director*
EMP: 80
SALES (est): 15MM **Privately Held**
WEB: www.aeropacificcorp.com
SIC: 3728 Aircraft parts & equipment

(P-10245)
AERO SENSE INC
26074 Avenue Hall Ste 18, Valencia (91355-3445)
PHONE................................661 257-1608
Sohail Tabrizi, *President*
Ro Missaghian, *CFO*
Amin Mozaffarian, *Program Mgr*
▲ **EMP:** 15 **EST:** 2007
SALES (est): 3.2MM **Privately Held**
WEB: www.ascacorp.com
SIC: 3728 Aircraft parts & equipment

(P-10246)
AERO-CRAFT HYDRAULICS INC
392 N Smith Ave, Corona (92878-4371)
PHONE................................951 736-4690
Rod Guzman Sr, *President*
Suzane Treneer, *Ch of Bd*
Brad Davidson, *CFO*
Gabriel Rudd, *VP Business*
Carol Thoe, *Engineer*
EMP: 43
SQ FT: 16,500
SALES (est): 8.8MM **Privately Held**
WEB: www.aero-craft.com
SIC: 3728 5084 7699 Aircraft body & wing assemblies & parts; hydraulic systems equipment & supplies; aircraft & heavy equipment repair services

(P-10247)
AERO-NASCH AVIATION INC
6849 Hayvenhurst Ave, Van Nuys (91406-4718)
PHONE................................818 786-5480
William Onasch, *CEO*
Julian Gutierrez, *Prdtn Mgr*
Eddie Ester, *Manager*
EMP: 19 **EST:** 2000
SALES (est): 3.1MM **Privately Held**
WEB: www.aeronasch.com
SIC: 3728 Aircraft parts & equipment

(P-10248)
AEROSHEAR AVIATION SVCS INC (PA)
7701 Woodley Ave 200, Van Nuys (91406-1732)
PHONE................................818 779-1650
Lonnie Paschal, *CEO*
Christine Paschal, *CFO*
Ryan Hogan, *Manager*
EMP: 32 **EST:** 1996
SQ FT: 42,000
SALES (est): 5MM **Privately Held**
WEB: www.aeroshearaviation.com
SIC: 3728 3599 1799 Aircraft parts & equipment; machine shop, jobbing & repair; welding on site

(P-10249)
AEROSPACE DRIVEN TECH INC
2807 Catherine Way, Santa Ana (92705-5708)
PHONE................................949 553-1606
Kathleen F Freeman, *CEO*
Roger H Gottfried, *President*
Lauro Estudillo, *Vice Pres*
Rudy Caracoza, *Engineer*
Steven Lovelady, *QC Mgr*
EMP: 18 **EST:** 2002
SQ FT: 10,000
SALES (est): 3.1MM **Privately Held**
WEB: www.driven-technologies.com
SIC: 3728 Aircraft parts & equipment

(P-10250)
AEROSPACE DYNAMICS INTL INC (DH)
Also Called: ADI
25540 Rye Canyon Rd, Valencia (91355-1169)
PHONE................................661 257-3535
Joseph I Snowden, *CEO*
◆ **EMP:** 447 **EST:** 1989
SQ FT: 250,000
SALES (est): 87.9MM
SALES (corp-wide): 245.5B **Publicly Held**
WEB: www.precast.com
SIC: 3728 Aircraft parts & equipment
HQ: Precision Castparts Corp.
4650 Sw Mcdam Ave Ste 300
Portland OR 97239
503 946-4800

(P-10251)
AEROSPACE ENGINEERING LLC
2632 Saturn St, Brea (92821-6701)
PHONE................................714 996-8178
Mark Mahboubi,
EMP: 120 **EST:** 2008

SALES (est): 9.1MM **Privately Held**
WEB: www.aerospaceengineeringcorp.com
SIC: 3728 3541 3599 Aircraft parts & equipment; numerically controlled metal cutting machine tools; machine & other job shop work

(P-10252)
AEROSPACE ENGRG SUPPORT CORP
Also Called: J and L Industries
645 Hawaii St, El Segundo (90245-4814)
P.O. Box 999 (90245-0999)
PHONE................................310 297-4050
Asher Bartov, *CEO*
Abraham Wacht, *President*
EMP: 27 **EST:** 1987
SQ FT: 30,000
SALES (est): 4MM
SALES (corp-wide): 916.6MM **Privately Held**
WEB: www.aerospace.org
SIC: 3728 Aircraft parts & equipment
PA: The Aerospace Corporation
2310 E El Segundo Blvd
El Segundo CA 90245
310 336-5000

(P-10253)
AEROSPACE PARTS HOLDINGS INC
Also Called: Cadence Aerospace
3150 E Miraloma Ave, Anaheim (92806-1906)
PHONE................................949 877-3630
Ron Case, *CEO*
Mike Coburn, *COO*
Don Devore, *CFO*
EMP: 1175
SALES (est): 301MM **Privately Held**
WEB: www.cadenceaerospace.com
SIC: 3728 Aircraft parts & equipment

(P-10254)
AEROSPACE SERVICE & CONTROLS
28402 Livingston Ave, Valencia (91355-4172)
PHONE................................818 833-0088
Dave Mason, *President*
Andre Villa, *Admin Sec*
Nick Mason, *Project Mgr*
Carlos Plascencia, *Technology*
Jose Lopez, *Electrical Engi*
EMP: 17 **EST:** 2010
SALES (est): 4.8MM **Privately Held**
WEB: www.aschome.com
SIC: 3728 Aircraft parts & equipment

(P-10255)
AEROSPACE SYSTEMS STRCTRES LLC
Also Called: Alatus Aerosystems
423 Berry Way, Brea (92821-3115)
PHONE................................626 965-1630
EMP: 19 **EST:** 2018
SALES (est): 3MM **Privately Held**
WEB: www.triumphgroup.com
SIC: 3728 Aircraft parts & equipment

(P-10256)
AFTERMARKET SERVICES
28150 Industry Dr, Valencia (91355-4100)
PHONE................................610 251-1000
Jeffry D Frisby, *President*
Dave Coil, *Purch Agent*
Jaime Oca, *Supervisor*
EMP: 16 **EST:** 2011
SALES (est): 562.5K **Privately Held**
WEB: www.triumphgroup.com
SIC: 3728 Aircraft parts & equipment

(P-10257)
AHF-DUCOMMUN INCORPORATED (HQ)
Also Called: Ducommun Arostructures-Gardena
268 E Gardena Blvd, Gardena (90248-2814)
PHONE................................310 380-5390
Joseph C Berenato, *Principal*
◆ **EMP:** 250 **EST:** 1950
SQ FT: 105,000

SALES (est): 333.7MM
SALES (corp-wide): 628.9MM **Publicly Held**
WEB: www.ducommun.com
SIC: 3728 3812 3769 3469 Aircraft body & wing assemblies & parts; search & navigation equipment; guided missile & space vehicle parts & auxiliary equipment; metal stampings
PA: Ducommun Incorporated
200 Sandpointe Ave # 700
Santa Ana CA 92707
657 335-3665

(P-10258)
AIR COMPONENTS INC
10235 Indiana Ct, Rancho Cucamonga (91730-5332)
PHONE................................909 980-8224
David Blocker, *President*
Harlen Weener, *Treasurer*
Robert Ames, *Vice Pres*
Kim Smith, *Vice Pres*
Alton Herrera, *Sales Staff*
EMP: 20 **EST:** 1987
SQ FT: 7,800
SALES (est): 6.6MM **Privately Held**
WEB: www.aircomponentsinc.com
SIC: 3728 Aircraft parts & equipment

(P-10259)
AIRBORNE TECHNOLOGIES INC
999 Avenida Acaso, Camarillo (93012-8700)
P.O. Box 2210 (93011-2210)
PHONE................................805 389-3700
Christopher Celtruda, *CEO*
Richard Drinkward, *CFO*
EMP: 67 **EST:** 1980
SQ FT: 40,000
SALES: 15.1MM
SALES (corp-wide): 178.4MM **Privately Held**
WEB: www.goallclear.com
SIC: 3728 5088 7699 3812 Aircraft parts & equipment; aircraft equipment & supplies; aircraft & heavy equipment repair services; search & navigation equipment
PA: Kellstrom Holding Corporation
100 N Pcf Cast Hwy Ste 19
El Segundo CA 90245
561 722-7455

(P-10260)
AIRCRAFT HINGE INC
28338 Constellation Rd # 970, Santa Clarita (91355-5801)
PHONE................................661 257-3434
Doug Silva, *President*
Robbie Johnson, *President*
Brianne Dautel, *Office Mgr*
Terrina Arroyo, *Administration*
Brian Silva, *Production*
▲ **EMP:** 20 **EST:** 1986
SQ FT: 11,000
SALES (est): 4.1MM **Privately Held**
WEB: www.aircrafthinge.com
SIC: 3728 Aircraft parts & equipment

(P-10261)
AIRTECH INTERNATIONAL INC (PA)
Also Called: Airtech Advanced Mtls Group
5700 Skylab Rd, Huntington Beach (92647-2055)
PHONE................................714 899-8100
Jeff Dahlgren, *President*
Lynn Quach, *Vice Pres*
Audrey Dahlgren, *Admin Sec*
Mandy Elliott, *Administration*
Leo Beyers, *Info Tech Mgr*
◆ **EMP:** 130 **EST:** 1973
SQ FT: 150,000
SALES (est): 110.4MM **Privately Held**
WEB: www.airtechintl.com
SIC: 3728 3081 5083 2673 Aircraft parts & equipment; unsupported plastics film & sheet; aeronautical equipment & supplies; bags: plastic, laminated & coated; coated & laminated paper; packaging paper & plastics film, coated & laminated

▲ = Import ▼=Export
◆ =Import/Export

(P-10262)
ALATUS AEROSYSTEMS (PA)
423 Berry Way, Brea (92821-3115)
PHONE..................................610 965-1630
Scott Holland, *CEO*
Joe Zarrilli, *Treasurer*
Mike Hebermehl, *Exec VP*
Scott Scruggs, *Exec VP*
Bernhard Bertrams, *Managing Dir*
◆ **EMP:** 661 **EST:** 1953
SALES (est): 26.3MM **Privately Held**
WEB: www.alatusaero.com
SIC: 3728 3489 Aircraft parts & equipment; wing assemblies & parts, aircraft; alighting (landing gear) assemblies, aircraft; artillery or artillery parts, over 30 mm.

(P-10263)
ALATUS AEROSYSTEMS
Also Called: Triumph Structures - Brea
423 Berry Way, Brea (92821-3115)
PHONE..................................714 732-0559
Manny Chacon, *Manager*
David Meers, *COO*
Brittany Slater, *CFO*
Jack B Albanese, *Exec VP*
Mike Hebermehl, *Exec VP*
EMP: 87
SALES (corp-wide): 26.3MM **Privately Held**
WEB: www.alatusaero.com
SIC: 3728 3489 Aircraft parts & equipment; wing assemblies & parts, aircraft; alighting (landing gear) assemblies, aircraft; artillery or artillery parts, over 30 mm.
PA: Alatus Aerosystems
423 Berry Way
Brea CA 92821
610 965-1630

(P-10264)
ALATUS AEROSYSTEMS
423 Berry Way, Brea (92821-3115)
PHONE..................................626 498-7376
Richard Oak, *Manager*
James Wolters, *Vice Pres*
Hector Zaldivar, *Maint Spvr*
Alice Calzada, *Director*
Greg Rogozinski, *Manager*
EMP: 80
SALES (corp-wide): 26.3MM **Privately Held**
WEB: www.alatusaero.com
SIC: 3728 3489 Aircraft parts & equipment; wing assemblies & parts, aircraft; alighting (landing gear) assemblies, aircraft; artillery or artillery parts, over 30 mm.
PA: Alatus Aerosystems
423 Berry Way
Brea CA 92821
610 965-1630

(P-10265)
ALIGN AEROSPACE LLC (PA)
9401 De Soto Ave, Chatsworth (91311-4920)
PHONE..................................818 727-7800
Ian Cohen,
Matt Connor, *Vice Pres*
Ingrid Felix, *Executive Asst*
Pascale Rohde, *Administration*
Michelle Saint-Amand, *Business Anlyst*
EMP: 290 **EST:** 2011
SQ FT: 73,000
SALES (est): 148MM **Privately Held**
WEB: www.alignaero.com
SIC: 3728 Aircraft parts & equipment

(P-10266)
ALL POWER MANUFACTURING CO
13141 Molette St, Santa Fe Springs (90670-5500)
PHONE..................................562 802-2640
Michael J Hartnett, *Principal*
Karen Ford, *Controller*
EMP: 30
SALES (corp-wide): 608.9MM **Publicly Held**
WEB: www.rbcbearings.com
SIC: 3728 Aircraft parts & equipment

HQ: All Power Manufacturing Co
1 Tribiology Ctr
Oxford CT 06478
562 802-2640

(P-10267)
ALVA MANUFACTURING INC
236 E Orangethorpe Ave, Placentia (92870-6442)
PHONE..................................714 237-0925
Tam V Nguyen, *President*
Sarah Naguib, *Admin Asst*
Aryan Ghomi, *Project Engr*
Bill Davila, *Engineer*
MAI Truong, *Engineer*
EMP: 44 **EST:** 2011
SQ FT: 15,000
SALES (est): 5.1MM **Privately Held**
WEB: www.alvamanufacturing.com
SIC: 3728 3599 Aircraft parts & equipment; machine & other job shop work; machine shop, jobbing & repair

(P-10268)
AMG TORRANCE LLC (DH)
Also Called: Metric Precision
5401 Business Dr, Huntington Beach (92649-1225)
PHONE..................................310 515-2584
Omar Khan, *CEO*
Oliver Que, *Engineer*
Angelique Flores, *Controller*
EMP: 68 **EST:** 2009
SQ FT: 37,800
SALES (est): 22.4MM **Privately Held**
WEB: www.amg-mfg.com
SIC: 3728 Ailerons, aircraft
HQ: Aerospace Manufacturing Group Inc
5401 Business Dr
Huntington Beach CA 92649
714 894-9802

(P-10269)
AMRO FABRICATING CORPORATION
17101 Heacock St, Moreno Valley (92551-9560)
PHONE..................................951 842-6140
EMP: 49
SALES (corp-wide): 53.6MM **Privately Held**
SIC: 3728 Mfg Aircraft Parts Or Equipments
PA: Amro Fabricating Corporation
1430 Adelia Ave
South El Monte CA 91733
626 579-2200

(P-10270)
AMRO FABRICATING CORPORATION (PA)
1430 Amro Way, South El Monte (91733-3046)
PHONE..................................626 579-2200
John Hammond, *President*
Michael Riley, *CEO*
Steve M Riley, *Vice Pres*
Mike Riley, *Program Mgr*
Maria Robles, *Admin Asst*
EMP: 239 **EST:** 1977
SQ FT: 150,000
SALES (est): 29.7MM **Privately Held**
WEB: www.amrofab.com
SIC: 3728 3769 3544 5088 Aircraft parts & equipment; guided missile & space vehicle parts & auxiliary equipment; special dies, tools, jigs & fixtures; aircraft & space vehicle supplies & parts; guided missiles & space vehicles

(P-10271)
ANMAR PRECISION COMPONENTS INC
7424 Greenbush Ave, North Hollywood (91605-4005)
PHONE..................................818 764-0901
Bruno Mudy, *President*
Teresa Mudy, *Corp Secy*
Anthony Mudy, *Vice Pres*
EMP: 23 **EST:** 1983
SQ FT: 10,000
SALES (est): 2.5MM **Privately Held**
SIC: 3728 Aircraft parts & equipment

(P-10272)
APM MANUFACTURING (HQ)
Also Called: Anaheim Precision Mfg
1738 N Neville St, Orange (92865-4214)
PHONE..................................714 453-0100
Anthony Puccio, *CEO*
Joe Puccio, *COO*
Gilles Madelmont, *CFO*
Anthony Cortez, *Purch Mgr*
Cynthia Carrillo, *Sales Staff*
EMP: 146 **EST:** 1986
SQ FT: 57,000
SALES (est): 36.1MM
SALES (corp-wide): 43MM **Privately Held**
WEB: www.anaheimprecision.com
SIC: 3728 3429 3599 3444 Aircraft parts & equipment; aircraft body & wing assemblies & parts; aircraft landing assemblies & brakes; aircraft hardware; machine shop, jobbing & repair; sheet metalwork
PA: Manufacturing Solutions, Inc.
1738 N Neville St
Orange CA 92865
714 453-0100

(P-10273)
APPLIED CMPSITE STRUCTURES INC (HQ)
1195 Columbia St, Brea (92821-2922)
PHONE..................................714 990-6300
David Horner, *CEO*
Jorge Garcia, *CFO*
Bobby Breaux, *Vice Pres*
Teri Morales, *Executive*
Justin Uchida, *Principal*
EMP: 249 **EST:** 1975
SQ FT: 100,000
SALES (est): 44.5MM
SALES (corp-wide): 189.2MM **Privately Held**
WEB: www.appliedcomposites.com
SIC: 3728 Aircraft parts & equipment
PA: Applied Composites Holdings, Llc
25692 Atlantic Ocean Dr
Lake Forest CA 92630
949 716-3511

(P-10274)
APPROVED AERONAUTICS LLC
Also Called: Manufacturer and Distributor
9130 Pulsar Ct, Corona (92883-4630)
PHONE..................................951 200-3730
Anthony Janes, *CEO*
David A Janes Jr,
EMP: 27 **EST:** 1999
SALES (est): 6MM **Privately Held**
WEB: www.approvedaeronautics.com
SIC: 3728 Aircraft parts & equipment

(P-10275)
ARCH PRECISION COMPONENTS
Also Called: Aero Pacific Mfg
7100 Belgrave Ave, Garden Grove (92841-2809)
PHONE..................................714 961-9200
Mike McDonnell, *Production*
EMP: 50
SALES (corp-wide): 1.5B **Privately Held**
WEB: www.aeropacificcorp.com
SIC: 3728 Aircraft parts & equipment
HQ: Arch Precision Components Corp
2600 S Telg Rd Ste 180
Bloomfield Hills MI 48302
866 935-5771

(P-10276)
ARDEN ENGINEERING INC (DH)
3130 E Miraloma Ave, Anaheim (92806-1906)
PHONE..................................949 877-3642
Thomas Hutton, *CEO*
Michael J Stow, *President*
John R Meisenbach Sr, *CEO*
Michael Stow, *Vice Pres*
Mark Metsker, *Manager*
▲ **EMP:** 21 **EST:** 1971
SQ FT: 25,000
SALES (est): 33MM
SALES (corp-wide): 250.8MM **Privately Held**
WEB: www.cadenceaerospace.com
SIC: 3728 Aircraft body assemblies & parts

HQ: Arden Engineering Holdings, Inc.
1878 N Main St
Orange CA 92865
714 998-6410

(P-10277)
ARDEN ENGINEERING INC
1878 N Main St, Orange (92865-4117)
Rural Route 3130, Anaheim (92806)
PHONE..................................714 998-6410
Thorin Southworth, *Director*
Jim Edwards, *Controller*
EMP: 197
SALES (corp-wide): 250.8MM **Privately Held**
WEB: www.cadenceaerospace.com
SIC: 3728 Aircraft body assemblies & parts
HQ: Arden Engineering, Inc.
3130 E Miraloma Ave
Anaheim CA 92806
949 877-3642

(P-10278)
ARDEN ENGINEERING HOLDINGS INC (HQ)
1878 N Main St, Orange (92865-4117)
PHONE..................................714 998-6410
EMP: 100 **EST:** 2010
SALES (est): 33MM
SALES (corp-wide): 250.8MM **Privately Held**
WEB: www.cadenceaerospace.com
SIC: 3728 Aircraft body assemblies & parts
PA: Cadence Aerospace, Llc
3150 E Miraloma Ave
Anaheim CA 92806
949 877-3630

(P-10279)
ARROWHEAD PRODUCTS CORPORATION
4411 Katella Ave, Los Alamitos (90720-3599)
PHONE..................................714 828-7770
Andrew Whelan, *President*
Rich Weatherford, *COO*
Bill Gardner, *Vice Pres*
Dominic Ruiz, *Vice Pres*
Karen Saidiner, *Vice Pres*
▲ **EMP:** 640 **EST:** 1968
SQ FT: 250,000
SALES (est): 166.3MM
SALES (corp-wide): 590.4MM **Privately Held**
WEB: www.arrowheadproducts.net
SIC: 3728 Aircraft parts & equipment
HQ: Industrial Manufacturing Company Llc
8223 Brecksville Rd # 100
Brecksville OH 44141
440 838-4700

(P-10280)
ASTRO-TEK INDUSTRIES LLC
1198 N Kraemer Blvd, Anaheim (92806-1916)
PHONE..................................714 238-0022
Terry Smith, *President*
Timothy Smith, *Vice Pres*
Tim Smith, *General Mgr*
Erik Kaiser, *Purch Mgr*
Johanna Miller, *Production*
EMP: 80 **EST:** 2005
SQ FT: 50,000
SALES (est): 22.8MM **Privately Held**
WEB: www.astro-tek.com
SIC: 3728 3599 3548 3449 Aircraft parts & equipment; electrical discharge machining (EDM); welding apparatus; miscellaneous metalwork

(P-10281)
ASTURIES MANUFACTURING CO INC
310 Cessna Cir, Corona (92878-5009)
PHONE..................................951 270-1766
Manuel Perez, *President*
Luis Perez, *Vice Pres*
Carlos Gonzalez, *Maint Spvr*
Leah Perez, *Manager*
EMP: 25 **EST:** 1979
SQ FT: 50,850
SALES (est): 4.8MM **Privately Held**
SIC: 3728 3559 Aircraft parts & equipment; semiconductor manufacturing machinery

(P-10282)
AVANTUS AEROSPACE INC (DH)
29101 The Old Rd, Valencia (91355-1014)
PHONE..................................661 295-8620
Brian Williams, *CEO*
Dennis Suedkamp, *President*
Scott Wilkinson, *CFO*
EMP: 125 **EST:** 2015
SQ FT: 75,000
SALES (est): 111.7MM
SALES (corp-wide): 140.1MM **Privately Held**
WEB: www.avantusaerospace.com
SIC: 3728 Aircraft parts & equipment
HQ: Avantus Aerospace Limited
Unit 7 Millington Road
Hayes MIDDX UB3 4
208 571-0055

(P-10283)
AVCORP CMPSITE FABRICATION INC
1600 W 135th St, Gardena (90249-2506)
P.O. Box 1007 (90249-0007)
PHONE..................................310 970-5658
Marcus Maria Van Rooij, *President*
Hardeep Sidhu, *Info Tech Mgr*
Brendan Connelly, *Engineer*
Lito Martin, *Senior Engr*
Neil Kumar, *Controller*
EMP: 400 **EST:** 2015
SQ FT: 350,000
SALES (est): 100.2MM
SALES (corp-wide): 123.7MM **Privately Held**
WEB: www.avcorp.com
SIC: 3728 Aircraft parts & equipment
PA: Avcorp Industries Inc
10025 River Way
Delta BC V4G 1
604 582-1137

(P-10284)
AVIBANK MFG INC (DH)
11500 Sherman Way, North Hollywood (91605-5827)
P.O. Box 9909 (91609-1909)
PHONE..................................818 392-2100
Dan Welter, *President*
John Duran, *Vice Pres*
▲ **EMP:** 115 **EST:** 1945
SALES (est): 107.8MM
SALES (corp-wide): 245.5B **Publicly Held**
WEB: www.avibank.com
SIC: 3728 Aircraft parts & equipment
HQ: Sps Technologies, Llc
301 Highland Ave
Jenkintown PA 19046
215 572-3000

(P-10285)
B & E MANUFACTURING CO INC
12151 Monarch St, Garden Grove (92841-2927)
PHONE..................................714 898-2269
Emmanuel Neildez, *President*
Jerome Guilloteau, *Admin Sec*
EMP: 45 **EST:** 1981
SQ FT: 26,000
SALES (est): 14.2MM
SALES (corp-wide): 177.9K **Privately Held**
WEB: www.bandemfg.com
SIC: 3728 Aircraft parts & equipment
HQ: Lisi
6 Rue Juvenal Viellard
Grandvillars 90600

(P-10286)
B/E AEROSPACE INC
Also Called: Teklam Corporation
350 W Rincon St, Corona (92878-4004)
PHONE..................................951 278-4563
Gordon McKauley, *Branch Mgr*
EMP: 100
SALES (corp-wide): 56.5B **Publicly Held**
WEB: www.beaerospace.com
SIC: 3728 Aircraft parts & equipment
HQ: B/E Aerospace, Inc.
1400 Corporate Center Way
Wellington FL 33414
410 266-2048

(P-10287)
BAILEY INDUSTRIES INC
25256 Terreno Dr, Mission Viejo (92691-5528)
PHONE..................................949 461-0807
Nonny Bailey, *President*
EMP: 13 **EST:** 1982
SALES (est): 263.7K **Privately Held**
SIC: 3728 4783 2679 5088 Aircraft parts & equipment; packing & crating; labels, paper: made from purchased material; aircraft equipment & supplies

(P-10288)
BANDY MANUFACTURING LLC
3420 N San Fernando Blvd, Burbank (91504-2532)
P.O. Box 7716 (91510-7716)
PHONE..................................818 846-9020
Tom Fulton, *President*
Kevin L Cummings, *CEO*
Tom Hoffa, *Design Engr*
Tim Pugh, *Engineer*
Darren Stacy, *Engineer*
EMP: 93 **EST:** 1952
SQ FT: 60,000
SALES (est): 12.2MM **Privately Held**
WEB: www.bandymanufacturing.com
SIC: 3728 Aircraft parts & equipment

(P-10289)
BOEING ENCORE INTERIORS LLC
5511 Skylab Rd, Huntington Beach (92647-2068)
PHONE..................................949 559-0930
EMP: 29 **EST:** 2019
SALES (est): 27.4MM
SALES (corp-wide): 58.1B **Publicly Held**
WEB: www.encoregroup.aero
SIC: 3728 1799 Aircraft parts & equipment; renovation of aircraft interiors
PA: The Boeing Company
100 N Riverside Plz
Chicago IL 60606
312 544-2000

(P-10290)
C&H HYDRAULICS INC
Also Called: Acme Divac Industries
1585 Monrovia Ave, Newport Beach (92663-2806)
PHONE..................................949 646-6230
James F Andreae Jr, *CEO*
EMP: 28 **EST:** 1976
SQ FT: 8,000
SALES (est): 2.7MM **Privately Held**
WEB: www.chhyd.com
SIC: 3728 8734 3769 3812 Aircraft parts & equipment; testing laboratories; guided missile & space vehicle parts & auxiliary equipment; search & navigation equipment; current-carrying wiring devices; hydraulic equipment repair

(P-10291)
CADENCE AEROSPACE LLC (PA)
3150 E Miraloma Ave, Anaheim (92806-1906)
PHONE..................................949 877-3630
Olivier Jarrault, *CEO*
Brian Bentley, *CEO*
Kevin W Martin, *CEO*
Jeff M Capponi, *Senior VP*
Robert J Saia, *Senior VP*
EMP: 43 **EST:** 2010
SQ FT: 5,000
SALES (est): 250.8MM **Privately Held**
WEB: www.cadenceaerospace.com
SIC: 3728 Aircraft body assemblies & parts

(P-10292)
CADENCE AEROSPACE LLC
3130 E Miraloma Ave, Anaheim (92806-1906)
PHONE..................................425 353-0405
Larry Resnick, *CEO*
Mike Coburn, *COO*
Don Devore, *CFO*
John Seguin, *Vice Pres*
Eddie Torres, *Vice Pres*
EMP: 40 **EST:** 2013

(P-10293)
CAL TECH PRECISION INC
1830 N Lemon St, Anaheim (92801-1000)
PHONE..................................714 992-4130
Guy Haarlammert, *President*
Jay Simms, *Engineer*
Rey Martinez, *Materials Mgr*
Arsenio Uy, *Director*
▲ **EMP:** 99
SALES (est): 10.9MM **Privately Held**
WEB: www.caltechprecision.com
SIC: 3728 Aircraft parts & equipment

(P-10294)
CALIFORNIA COMPOSITES MGT INC
1935 E Occidental St, Santa Ana (92705-5115)
PHONE..................................714 258-0405
Fred Good, *Ch of Bd*
Steven Sim, *Engineer*
EMP: 30 **EST:** 1986
SQ FT: 30,000
SALES (est): 1.3MM **Privately Held**
WEB: www.ccdicomposites.com
SIC: 3728 3812 3624 Aircraft parts & equipment; search & navigation equipment; carbon & graphite products

(P-10295)
CANYON COMPOSITES INCORPORATED
1548 N Gemini Pl, Anaheim (92801-1152)
PHONE..................................714 991-8181
BJ Rutkoski, *President*
Eric Collins, *CFO*
Robert Gray, *Vice Pres*
Christy Crizer, *Executive*
Richard Barnes, *CIO*
EMP: 40
SQ FT: 31,500
SALES (est): 11.3MM **Privately Held**
WEB: www.canyoncomposites.com
SIC: 3728 8711 Aircraft parts & equipment; engineering services

(P-10296)
CANYON ENGINEERING PDTS INC
28909 Avenue Williams, Valencia (91355-4183)
PHONE..................................661 294-0084
Todd Strickland, *President*
Paul Knerr, *Vice Pres*
EMP: 88 **EST:** 1979
SQ FT: 70,000
SALES (est): 22MM **Publicly Held**
WEB: www.canyonengineering.com
SIC: 3728 Aircraft assemblies, subassemblies & parts
PA: Esco Technologies Inc.
9900 Clayton Rd Ste A
Saint Louis MO 63124

(P-10297)
CARDONA MANUFACTURING CORP
1869 N Victory Pl, Burbank (91504-3476)
PHONE..................................818 841-8358
Louis Cardona, *President*
Jo Ann Cardona, *Corp Secy*
Jo Cardona, *Office Mgr*
Joe Martinez, *Info Tech Mgr*
Mike Cardona, *Production*
EMP: 26 **EST:** 1971
SQ FT: 10,000
SALES (est): 3.6MM **Privately Held**
WEB: www.cardonamfg.com
SIC: 3728 3812 Aircraft parts & equipment; search & navigation equipment

(P-10298)
CAVOTEC DABICO US INC
5665 Corporate Ave, Cypress (90630-4727)
PHONE..................................714 947-0005
Gary Matthews, *President*
Christian Bernadotte, *Admin Sec*
Chris Clayton, *Accountant*
Dorothy Chen, *Controller*

Ernesto Acevedo, *Purch Mgr*
▲ **EMP:** 36 **EST:** 2008
SALES (est): 9.4MM **Privately Held**
WEB: www.dabico.com
SIC: 3728 Aircraft parts & equipment

(P-10299)
CHAUHAN INDUSTRIES INC
32 Wood Rd Ste A, Camarillo (93010-8399)
PHONE..................................805 484-1616
Raj Chauhan, *President*
EMP: 15 **EST:** 1993
SQ FT: 6,000
SALES (est): 1.8MM **Privately Held**
WEB: www.miamicraftspirits.com
SIC: 3728 Aircraft parts & equipment

(P-10300)
CHOL ENTERPRISES INC
12831 S Figueroa St, Los Angeles (90061-1157)
PHONE..................................310 516-1328
Neal Castleman, *President*
Brian Gamberg, *Vice Pres*
EMP: 21 **EST:** 1991
SQ FT: 25,000
SALES (est): 1MM **Privately Held**
WEB: www.dcxchol.com
SIC: 3728 3769 3678 3357 Aircraft assemblies, subassemblies & parts; guided missile & space vehicle parts & auxiliary equipment; electronic connectors; nonferrous wiredrawing & insulating

(P-10301)
COATING SPECIALTIES INC
Also Called: Aero Products Co.
815 E Rosecrans Ave, Los Angeles (90059-3510)
PHONE..................................310 639-6900
Mitchell Grant, *President*
William Johnson, *CEO*
EMP: 18 **EST:** 1973
SQ FT: 31,000
SALES (est): 6.6MM **Privately Held**
WEB: www.coatingspecialties.com
SIC: 3728 3812 Aircraft assemblies, subassemblies & parts; search & navigation equipment

(P-10302)
COMPOSITES HORIZONS LLC (DH)
1629 W Industrial Park St, Covina (91722-3418)
PHONE..................................626 331-0861
Jeff Hynes, *President*
Renee Fahmy, *Vice Pres*
Rod Wolfe, *Facilities Mgr*
▲ **EMP:** 140 **EST:** 1974
SQ FT: 25,000
SALES (est): 26.4MM
SALES (corp-wide): 245.5B **Publicly Held**
WEB: www.chi-covina.com
SIC: 3728 3844 2821 Aircraft parts & equipment; X-ray apparatus & tubes; plastics materials & resins
HQ: Precision Castparts Corp.
4650 Sw Mcdam Ave Ste 300
Portland OR 97239
503 946-4800

(P-10303)
CONTOUR ENGINEERING INC
2344 Pullman St, Santa Ana (92705-5507)
PHONE..................................562 630-0250
Michael Sherwood, *CEO*
EMP: 14 **EST:** 2006
SALES (est): 2.6MM **Privately Held**
SIC: 3728 Aircraft parts & equipment

(P-10304)
CORONADO MANUFACTURING INC
8991 Glenoaks Blvd, Sun Valley (91352-2038)
PHONE..................................818 768-5010
Allen F Gowing, *President*
Phillip Belmonte, *Vice Pres*
Eric Rathjen, *Production*
▼ **EMP:** 50 **EST:** 1959
SQ FT: 19,000

SALES (est): 13.3MM **Privately Held**
WEB: www.coronadomfg.com
SIC: 3728 5084 Military aircraft equipment & armament; aircraft assemblies, sub-assemblies & parts; industrial machine parts

(P-10305)
CTCOA LLC
Also Called: Consolidated Trading Co Amer
16818 Marquardt Ave, Cerritos
(90703-1045)
PHONE.....................562 407-5375
Mark Robinson, *CEO*
Matthew Kuhnau, *Principal*
Amaris Pham, *Sales Staff*
Elizabeth Espanta, *Accounts Mgr*
EMP: 36 **EST:** 2018
SALES (est): 7.3MM **Privately Held**
WEB: www.ctcoa.com
SIC: 3728 Aircraft parts & equipment

(P-10306)
D & D GEAR INCORPORATED
Also Called: Absolute Technologies
4890 E La Palma Ave, Anaheim
(92807-1911)
PHONE.....................714 692-6570
Bill Beverage, *President*
Don Beverage, *Vice Pres*
James Chavez, *Engineer*
Leonard Dye, *Engineer*
Scott Reid, *Engineer*
▲ **EMP:** 210 **EST:** 1969
SQ FT: 82,500
SALES (est): 40.4MM **Privately Held**
SIC: 3728 Aircraft parts & equipment

(P-10307)
D & S INDUSTRIES INC
4515 E Eisenhower Cir, Anaheim
(92807-1852)
PHONE.....................714 779-8074
David Pierce Jr, *President*
Lisa Wilson, *Manager*
EMP: 13 **EST:** 1980
SQ FT: 8,000
SALES (est): 2.8MM **Privately Held**
WEB: www.dsindustries.com
SIC: 3728 Aircraft parts & equipment

(P-10308)
DASCO ENGINEERING CORP
24747 Crenshaw Blvd, Torrance
(90505-5308)
PHONE.....................310 326-2277
Ward Olson, *President*
John Karle, *Vice Pres*
Glen Olson, *Vice Pres*
◆ **EMP:** 110 **EST:** 1964
SQ FT: 50,000
SALES (est): 19.5MM **Privately Held**
WEB: www.dascoeng.com
SIC: 3728 Aircraft body & wing assemblies & parts

(P-10309)
DESIGNED METAL CONNECTIONS INC (DH)
Also Called: Permaswage USA
14800 S Figueroa St, Gardena
(90248-1719)
PHONE.....................310 323-6200
Thomas McDonnell, *Vice Pres*
▲ **EMP:** 500 **EST:** 2004
SQ FT: 175,000
SALES (est): 78.5MM
SALES (corp-wide): 245.5B **Publicly Held**
WEB: www.pccfluidfittings.com
SIC: 3728 Aircraft parts & equipment
HQ: Precision Castparts Corp.
4650 Sw Mcdam Ave Ste 300
Portland OR 97239
503 946-4800

(P-10310)
DIAGNOSTIC SOLUTIONS INTL LLC
2580 E Philadelphia St C, Ontario
(91761-8093)
PHONE.....................909 930-3600
Brian Hatcher, *Mng Member*
Elena Buckley,
Gino Ela, *Manager*
EMP: 16 **EST:** 2007

SQ FT: 5,000
SALES (est): 4.7MM **Privately Held**
WEB: www.dsi-hums.com
SIC: 3728 Aircraft parts & equipment

(P-10311)
DJI SERVICE LLC
17301 Edwards Rd, Cerritos (90703-2427)
PHONE.....................818 235-0788
Hao Shen,
Brendan Schulman, *Vice Pres*
Mingyu Wang, *Vice Pres*
Samuel Robertson, *Technician*
Chris Gould, *Opers Mgr*
EMP: 15 **EST:** 2016
SALES (est): 4.9MM **Privately Held**
WEB: www.dji.com
SIC: 3728 Aircraft parts & equipment

(P-10312)
DPI LABS INC
1350 Arrow Hwy, La Verne (91750-5218)
PHONE.....................909 392-5777
Vicki Brown, *CEO*
Al Snow, *CFO*
Pam Archibald, *Vice Pres*
Greg Desmet, *Vice Pres*
Alfonso Loera. *Technician*
EMP: 35 **EST:** 1984
SALES (est): 5MM **Privately Held**
WEB: www.dpilabs.com
SIC: 3728 Aircraft parts & equipment

(P-10313)
DRETLOH AIRCRAFT SUPPLY INC (PA)
2830 E La Cresta Ave, Anaheim
(92806-1816)
PHONE.....................714 632-6982
Eugene Holte, *President*
Freda Holte, *Treasurer*
Randy Holte, *Vice Pres*
Mark Holte, *General Mgr*
Steve Fanelli, *Manager*
▲ **EMP:** 14 **EST:** 1975
SQ FT: 10,000
SALES (est): 3.2MM **Privately Held**
WEB: www.dretloh.com
SIC: 3728 5199 Aircraft parts & equipment; foam rubber

(P-10314)
DUCOMMUN AEROSTRUCTURES INC
801 Royal Oaks Dr, Monrovia
(91016-3630)
PHONE.....................626 358-3211
Maurice Harris, *General Mgr*
EMP: 30
SALES (corp-wide): 628.9MM **Publicly Held**
WEB: www.ducommun.com
SIC: 3728 Aircraft parts & equipment
HQ: Ducommun Aerostructures, Inc.
268 E Gardena Blvd
Gardena CA 90248
310 380-5390

(P-10315)
DUCOMMUN AEROSTRUCTURES INC
4001 El Mirage Rd, Adelanto (92301-9489)
PHONE.....................760 246-4191
Art McFarlan, *Manager*
EMP: 114
SQ FT: 1,152
SALES (corp-wide): 628.9MM **Publicly Held**
WEB: www.ducommun.com
SIC: 3728 Aircraft parts & equipment
HQ: Ducommun Aerostructures, Inc.
268 E Gardena Blvd
Gardena CA 90248
310 380-5390

(P-10316)
DUCOMMUN AEROSTRUCTURES INC
23301 Wilmington Ave, Carson
(90745-6209)
PHONE.....................310 513-7200
Eugene Conese Jr, *Director*
EMP: 114

SALES (corp-wide): 628.9MM **Publicly Held**
WEB: www.ducommun.com
SIC: 3728 Aircraft parts & equipment
HQ: Ducommun Aerostructures, Inc.
268 E Gardena Blvd
Gardena CA 90248
310 380-5390

(P-10317)
DUCOMMUN INCORPORATED (PA)
200 Sandpointe Ave # 700, Santa Ana
(92707-5759)
PHONE.....................657 335-3665
Stephen G Oswald, *President*
Christopher D Wampler, *CFO*
Rosalie F Rogers, *Officer*
Jerry L Redondo, *Senior VP*
Rajiv A Tata, *Vice Pres*
▲ **EMP:** 255 **EST:** 1849
SALES (est): 628.9MM **Publicly Held**
WEB: www.ducommun.com
SIC: 3728 3679 Aircraft body & wing assemblies & parts; microwave components

(P-10318)
DUCOMMUN LABARGE TECH INC (HQ)
Also Called: American Electronics
23301 Wilmington Ave, Carson
(90745-6209)
PHONE.....................310 513-7200
Stephen G Oswald, *CEO*
Douglas L Groves, *CFO*
Rose Rogers, *Officer*
Rose F Rogers, *Vice Pres*
Andy Wu, *General Mgr*
▲ **EMP:** 180 **EST:** 1958
SQ FT: 117,000
SALES (est): 65.4MM
SALES (corp-wide): 628.9MM **Publicly Held**
WEB: www.ducommun.com
SIC: 3728 3769 5065 3812 Aircraft parts & equipment; guided missile & space vehicle parts & auxiliary equipment; electronic parts & equipment; search & navigation equipment; current-carrying wiring devices; relays & industrial controls
PA: Ducommun Incorporated
200 Sandpointe Ave # 700
Santa Ana CA 92707
657 335-3665

(P-10319)
DUKES RESEARCH AND MFG INC
9060 Winnetka Ave, Northridge
(91324-3293)
PHONE.....................818 998-9811
Patricia Huffman, *President*
EMP: 35 **EST:** 1983
SALES (est): 326.9K **Privately Held**
SIC: 3728 Aircraft parts & equipment

(P-10320)
DYNAMATION RESEARCH INC
2301 Pontius Ave, Los Angeles
(90064-1809)
PHONE.....................909 864-2310
Gal Lipkin, *President*
EMP: 15 **EST:** 2006
SQ FT: 5,500
SALES (est): 3MM **Privately Held**
WEB: www.dynamationresearch.com
SIC: 3728 3812 Aircraft parts & equipment; search & navigation equipment

(P-10321)
DYNAMIC FABRICATION INC
2615 S Hickory St, Santa Ana
(92707-3713)
PHONE.....................714 662-2440
Andrew Crook, *President*
Olga Crook, *Treasurer*
Olga Garcia Crook, *Corp Secy*
Olga Garcia, *Controller*
EMP: 25 **EST:** 1991
SQ FT: 22,000
SALES (est): 5.1MM **Privately Held**
WEB: www.dynamicfab.com
SIC: 3728 3764 3761 3812 Aircraft parts & equipment; engines & engine parts, guided missile; guided missiles & space vehicles; defense systems & equipment

(P-10322)
ENCORE SEATS INC
Also Called: Lift By Encore
5511 Skylab Rd, Huntington Beach
(92647-2068)
PHONE.....................949 559-0930
Thomas McFarland, *CEO*
Mike Melancon, *CFO*
Aram Krikorian, *Vice Pres*
Crystal Kimberlin, *Technical Mgr*
Wade Delaney, *Project Engr*
EMP: 46 **EST:** 2015
SQ FT: 80,000
SALES (est): 5.5MM **Privately Held**
WEB: www.encoregroup.aero
SIC: 3728 Aircraft assemblies, subassemblies & parts; seat ejector devices, aircraft

(P-10323)
ENGINEERING JK AEROSPACE & DEF
23231 La Palma Ave, Yorba Linda
(92887-4768)
PHONE.....................714 499-9092
Jonathan Crisan, *President*
EMP: 25 **EST:** 2012
SALES (est): 3.2MM **Privately Held**
WEB: www.jke.aero
SIC: 3728 3724 Aircraft parts & equipment; aircraft engines & engine parts

(P-10324)
F & L TOOLS CORPORATION
Also Called: F & L Tls Precision Machining
245 Jason Ct, Corona (92879-6199)
PHONE.....................951 279-1555
Tracey Pratt, *President*
Larry Pratt, *President*
Daryl Pratt, *General Mgr*
Albert Cruz, *Prdtn Mgr*
Shawn Wolfe, *Sales Staff*
EMP: 18 **EST:** 1972
SQ FT: 8,100
SALES (est): 4.7MM **Privately Held**
SIC: 3728 Aircraft parts & equipment

(P-10325)
FARRAR GRINDING COMPANY
347 E Beach Ave, Inglewood (90302-3191)
PHONE.....................323 678-4879
Clarke Farrar, *President*
EMP: 35 **EST:** 1957
SQ FT: 6,000
SALES (est): 3.8MM **Privately Held**
WEB: www.farrar-grinding.com
SIC: 3728 3599 Aircraft parts & equipment; machine shop, jobbing & repair

(P-10326)
FERRA AEROSPACE INC
940 E Orngthrp Ave Ste A, Anaheim
(92801-1129)
PHONE.....................918 787-2220
Kim Oneal, *Purch Mgr*
Justin Jones, *Sales Mgr*
EMP: 33
SALES (corp-wide): 52MM **Privately Held**
WEB: www.ferra-group.com
SIC: 3728 Aircraft parts & equipment
HQ: Ferra Aerospace, Inc.
64353 E 290 Rd
Grove OK 74344
918 787-2220

(P-10327)
FLARE GROUP
Also Called: Aviation Equipment Processing
1571 Macarthur Blvd, Costa Mesa
(92626-1407)
PHONE.....................714 850-2080
Dennis Heider, *President*
Steve Osorio, *Vice Pres*
Daryl Silva, *Principal*
Eric Trainor, *Principal*
Jim Vinyard, *Principal*
EMP: 25 **EST:** 2010
SALES (est): 4MM **Privately Held**
WEB: www.aveprocessing.com
SIC: 3728 Aircraft parts & equipment; aircraft body assemblies & parts

(P-10328)
FLEXCO INC
6855 Suva St, Bell Gardens (90201-1999)
PHONE.....................562 927-2525

Erik Moller, *President*
Luke Coleman, *Manager*
EMP: 36 **EST:** 1966
SQ FT: 14,000
SALES (est): 5.5MM **Privately Held**
WEB: www.flexcoinc.com
SIC: 3728 3496 Aircraft parts & equipment; miscellaneous fabricated wire products

(P-10329)
FMH AEROSPACE CORP
Also Called: F M H
17072 Daimler St, Irvine (92614-5548)
PHONE..................714 751-1000
Rick Busch, *CEO*
Valerie Gorman, *CFO*
David Difranco, *Admin Sec*
▲ **EMP:** 100 **EST:** 1991
SQ FT: 15,000
SALES (est): 23.3MM
SALES (corp-wide): 4.5B **Publicly Held**
WEB: www.fmhaerospace.com
SIC: 3728 Aircraft parts & equipment
PA: Ametek, Inc.
1100 Cassatt Rd
Berwyn PA 19312
610 647-2121

(P-10330)
FORMING SPECIALTIES INC
1309 W Walnut Pkwy, Compton (90220-5030)
PHONE..................310 639-1122
Darrell E Madole, *President*
Kevin Herbert, *Vice Pres*
Louise Gillenwater, *Office Mgr*
Shannon Madole, *QC Mgr*
Dean Parlato, *QC Mgr*
EMP: 33 **EST:** 1976
SQ FT: 40,000
SALES (est): 3.4MM **Privately Held**
WEB: www.formingspecialties.com
SIC: 3728 3444 Aircraft parts & equipment; sheet metalwork

(P-10331)
FORREST MACHINING LLC
Also Called: Forrest Machining Inc.
27756 Avenue Mentry, Valencia (91355-3453)
PHONE..................661 257-0231
Tim Mickael, *CEO*
Joe Velazques, *Chief Mktg Ofcr*
Joe Velazquez, *Executive*
Andrew Kim, *Program Mgr*
Tony Montoya, *Program Mgr*
▲ **EMP:** 240 **EST:** 1979
SALES: 47.9MM
SALES (corp-wide): 70.8MM **Privately Held**
WEB: www.forrestmachining.com
SIC: 3728 Aircraft parts & equipment
PA: Dvsm, L.L.C.
760 Sw 9th Ave Ste 2300
Portland OR 97205
503 223-2721

(P-10332)
FRAZIER AVIATION INC
445 N Fox St, San Fernando (91340-2501)
PHONE..................818 898-1998
Robert L Frazier, *CEO*
Robert Frazier III, *President*
Charles E Ricard, *Vice Pres*
Tamara Druschen, *Administration*
Charles Ricard, *Administration*
EMP: 42 **EST:** 1956
SQ FT: 44,000
SALES (est): 10MM **Privately Held**
WEB: www.frazieraviation.com
SIC: 3728 5088 Aircraft body assemblies & parts; transportation equipment & supplies

(P-10333)
GALI CORPORATION
Also Called: Dynamation Research
2301 Pontius Ave, Los Angeles (90064-1809)
PHONE..................310 477-1224
Gal Lipkin, *CEO*
EMP: 26 **EST:** 1983

SALES (est): 1.4MM **Privately Held**
WEB: www.ntgalij.mfgpages.com
SIC: 3728 Aircraft parts & equipment; aircraft control instruments

(P-10334)
GEAR MANUFACTURING INC
Also Called: G M I
3701 E Miraloma Ave, Anaheim (92806-2123)
PHONE..................714 792-2895
Gary M Smith, *CEO*
Dave Mackley, *QC Mgr*
Juan Gomez, *Mfg Staff*
George Abbascia, *Sales Staff*
Brandon M Smith, *Sales Staff*
EMP: 50 **EST:** 1989
SQ FT: 26,500
SALES (est): 10.9MM **Privately Held**
WEB: www.gearmfg.com
SIC: 3728 3714 3566 3568 Gears, aircraft power transmission; bearings, motor vehicle; speed changers, drives & gears; power transmission equipment; motorcycles, bicycles & parts

(P-10335)
GFMI AEROSPACE & DEFENSE INC
17375 Mount Herrmann St, Fountain Valley (92708-4103)
PHONE..................714 361-4444
EMP: 30 **EST:** 2011
SALES (est): 2.6MM **Privately Held**
WEB: www.gfmiaero.com
SIC: 3728 8711 Mfg Aircraft Parts/Equipment Engineering Services

(P-10336)
GIDDENS INDUSTRIES INC (DH)
3130 E Miraloma Ave, Anaheim (92806-1906)
PHONE..................425 353-0405
Curt Schroeder, *President*
Kevin D Brown, *Principal*
Ron Case, *Principal*
Donald Devore, *Principal*
Michael F Finley, *Principal*
EMP: 150 **EST:** 1974
SALES (est): 68.5MM
SALES (corp-wide): 250.8MM **Privately Held**
WEB: www.cadenceaerospace.com
SIC: 3728 Aircraft parts & equipment
HQ: Giddens Holdings, Inc.
2600 94th St Sw Ste 150
Everett WA 98204
425 353-0405

(P-10337)
GLEDHILL/LYONS INC
Also Called: Accurate Technology
1521 N Placentia Ave, Anaheim (92806-1236)
PHONE..................714 502-0274
David M Lyons, *President*
Johnny Ledesma, *Purch Mgr*
EMP: 43 **EST:** 2000
SQ FT: 31,200
SALES (est): 8.7MM **Privately Held**
WEB: www.accuratetechnology.net
SIC: 3728 Aircraft parts & equipment

(P-10338)
GLOBAL AEROSPACE TECH CORP
25109 Rye Canyon Loop, Valencia (91355-5004)
PHONE..................818 407-5600
Steve Cormier, *CEO*
Don Spengler, *CFO*
EMP: 22 **EST:** 2006
SQ FT: 40,000
SALES (est): 3.6MM **Privately Held**
WEB: www.globalatcorp.com
SIC: 3728 Aircraft parts & equipment

(P-10339)
GLOBAL AEROSTRUCTURES
10291 Trademark St Ste C, Rancho Cucamonga (91730-5847)
PHONE..................909 987-4888
Becky Landa, *CEO*
Ernesto Guerra, *COO*
Michael Cabral, *General Mgr*
Mike Cabral, *Manager*

EMP: 15 **EST:** 2011
SQ FT: 10,000
SALES (est): 2MM **Privately Held**
WEB: www.gacone.com
SIC: 3728 Aircraft assemblies, subassemblies & parts

(P-10340)
GOODRICH CORPORATION
2727 E Imperial Hwy, Brea (92821-6713)
PHONE..................714 984-1461
Rob Gibbs, *General Mgr*
Lydia Kirk, *General Mgr*
Tedd Wong, *Engineer*
Reza Ghavam, *Manager*
EMP: 140
SALES (corp-wide): 56.5B **Publicly Held**
WEB: www.collinsaerospace.com
SIC: 3728 Aircraft parts & equipment
HQ: Goodrich Corporation
2730 W Tyvola Rd
Charlotte NC 28217
704 423-7000

(P-10341)
GST INDUSTRIES INC
9060 Winnetka Ave, Northridge (91324-3235)
PHONE..................818 350-1900
EMP: 24
SQ FT: 9,700
SALES (est): 2.3MM
SALES (corp-wide): 8.4MM **Privately Held**
WEB: www.gstindustries.net
SIC: 3728 Mfg Aircraft Parts/Equipment
PA: Infinity Aerospace, Inc.
9060 Winnetka Ave
Northridge CA 91324
818 998-9811

(P-10342)
HAGER MFG INC
14610 Industry Cir, La Mirada (90638-5815)
PHONE..................714 522-8870
Donald L Bowley, *President*
Patricia Bowley, *CFO*
EMP: 21 **EST:** 1969
SQ FT: 10,800
SALES (est): 1MM **Privately Held**
SIC: 3728 3599 Aircraft assemblies, subassemblies & parts; machine shop, jobbing & repair

(P-10343)
HANSEN ENGINEERING CO
Also Called: Plant 2
24050 Frampton Ave, Harbor City (90710-2197)
PHONE..................310 534-3870
EMP: 18 **EST:** 2019
SALES (est): 836.6K **Privately Held**
WEB: www.hansenengineering.com
SIC: 3728 Aircraft parts & equipment

(P-10344)
HELICOPTER TECH CO LTD PARTNR
12902 S Broadway, Los Angeles (90061-1118)
PHONE..................310 523-2750
Frank Palminteri, *President*
Gary Burdorf, *Vice Pres*
Robert Bouchard, *General Mgr*
James Fackler, *VP Opers*
◆ **EMP:** 24 **EST:** 1995
SQ FT: 197,000
SALES (est): 5.2MM **Privately Held**
WEB: www.helicoptertech.com
SIC: 3728 3721 Aircraft parts & equipment; helicopters

(P-10345)
HUTCHINSON AROSPC & INDUST INC
Also Called: ARS
4510 W Vanowen St, Burbank (91505-1135)
PHONE..................818 843-1000
Shano Cristilli, *Branch Mgr*
Armando Perez, *Design Engr*
Velimir Randic, *Engineer*
Roberto Sarjeant, *Engineer*
Ron Yeager, *Human Res Mgr*
EMP: 165

SALES (corp-wide): 4.6B **Publicly Held**
WEB: www.hutchinsonai.com
SIC: 3728 Aircraft parts & equipment
HQ: Hutchinson Aerospace & Industry, Inc.
82 South St
Hopkinton MA 01748
508 417-7000

(P-10346)
HYDRAULICS INTERNATIONAL INC (PA)
9201 Independence Ave, Chatsworth (91311-5905)
PHONE..................818 998-1231
Nicky Ghaemmaghami, *Ch of Bd*
Shah Banifazl, *CFO*
Jeffrey Riley, *Vice Pres*
Beth Wynn, *General Mgr*
Steve Petach, *Technician*
◆ **EMP:** 332 **EST:** 1976
SQ FT: 78,000
SALES (est): 107.6MM **Privately Held**
WEB: www.hiinet.com
SIC: 3728 Aircraft parts & equipment

(P-10347)
HYDRAULICS INTERNATIONAL INC
20961 Knapp St, Chatsworth (91311-5926)
PHONE..................818 998-1231
EMP: 21
SALES (corp-wide): 107.6MM **Privately Held**
WEB: www.hiinet.com
SIC: 3728 Mfg Aircraft Parts/Equipment
PA: Hydraulics International, Inc.
9201 Independence Ave
Chatsworth CA 91311
818 998-1231

(P-10348)
HYDRO-AIRE INC (DH)
3000 Winona Ave, Burbank (91504-2540)
PHONE..................818 526-2600
Brendan J Curran, *CEO*
Tazewell Rowe, *Treasurer*
Travis Bevelaqua, *IT/INT Sup*
Sean Santos, *Engineer*
Rigo Garcia Garcia, *Buyer*
▲ **EMP:** 432 **EST:** 1947
SQ FT: 173,000
SALES (est): 127.9MM
SALES (corp-wide): 2.9B **Publicly Held**
WEB: www.craneae.com
SIC: 3728 Aircraft parts & equipment

(P-10349)
HYDROFORM USA INCORPORATED
2848 E 208th St, Carson (90810-1101)
PHONE..................310 632-6353
Chester K Jablonski, *CEO*
George Curiel, *COO*
Ulrich Gottschling, *CFO*
Mauricio Salazar, *CFO*
Dcreativesouv Emmgutzrocha, *Administration*
▼ **EMP:** 154 **EST:** 1982
SQ FT: 95,000
SALES (est): 45.4MM **Privately Held**
WEB: www.hydroformusa.com
SIC: 3728 Aircraft parts & equipment

(P-10350)
IKHANA GROUP LLC
Also Called: Ikhana Aircraft Services
37260 Sky Canyon Dr # 20, Murrieta (92563-2680)
PHONE..................951 600-0009
Brian Raduenz, *CEO*
Scott Starkey, *Engineer*
▲ **EMP:** 120 **EST:** 2007
SALES (est): 24.9MM **Privately Held**
WEB: www.ikhanagroup.com
SIC: 3728 Flaps, aircraft wing
PA: Merlin Global Services, Llc
440 Stevens Ave Ste 150
Solana Beach CA 92075

(P-10351)
IMPRESA AEROSPACE LLC
344 W 157th St, Gardena (90248-2135)
PHONE..................310 354-1200
Steven F Loye,

Steve Loye, *CEO*
Marco Barrantes, *CFO*
Dennis Fitzgerald, *Vice Pres*
Jose Banuelos, *General Mgr*
EMP: 169 **EST:** 1987
SQ FT: 26,000
SALES (est): 42MM
SALES (corp-wide): 42.2MM **Privately Held**
WEB: www.impresaaerospace.com
SIC: 3728 3444 Aircraft parts & equipment; sheet metalwork
HQ: Impresa Acquisition Corporation
344 W 157th St
Gardena CA

(P-10352)
INFINITY AEROSPACE INC (PA)
9060 Winnetka Ave, Northridge
(91324-3235)
PHONE 818 998-9811
Chet Huffman, *CEO*
R Lloyd Huffman, *Ch of Bd*
Steve Lonngren, *President*
Oscar Gonzales, *Info Tech Mgr*
William Gavidia, *Sales Associate*
EMP: 50 **EST:** 1958
SQ FT: 30,000
SALES (est): 10.8MM **Privately Held**
SIC: 3728 Aircraft parts & equipment

(P-10353)
INFLIGHT WARNING SYSTEMS INC
Also Called: Iws Predictive Technologies
3940 Prospect Ave Ste P, Yorba Linda
(92886-1752)
PHONE 714 993-9394
EMP: 19
SQ FT: 6,000
SALES (est): 2.1MM **Privately Held**
WEB: www.astronics.com
SIC: 3728 Mfg Aircraft Parts/Equipment

(P-10354)
INTEGRAL AEROSPACE LLC
Also Called: Pcx Aerosystems - Santa Ana
2040 E Dyer Rd, Santa Ana (92705-5710)
PHONE 949 250-3123
Jeff Frisby, *President*
John Kutler, *Ch of Bd*
John Alves, *President*
Terence Lyons, *CEO*
Jeffrey Lassiter, *CFO*
EMP: 155 **EST:** 2016
SQ FT: 270,000
SALES (est): 50MM
SALES (corp-wide): 97.1MM **Privately Held**
WEB: www.integralaerospace.com
SIC: 3728 Aircraft parts & equipment
PA: Pcx Aerostructures, Llc
300 Fenn Rd
Newington CT 06111
860 666-2471

(P-10355)
INTERTRADE AVIATION CORP
5722 Buckingham Dr, Huntington Beach
(92649-1130)
PHONE 714 895-3335
Ted Newfield, *President*
Bill Stuckert, *QC Mgr*
▲ **EMP:** 19 **EST:** 1980
SQ FT: 65,000
SALES (est): 1.5MM **Privately Held**
WEB: www.interavco.com
SIC: 3728 5088 Aircraft assemblies, subassemblies & parts; transportation equipment & supplies

(P-10356)
IRISH INTERIORS INC (HQ)
Also Called: Lift By Encore
5511 Skylab Rd Ste 101, Huntington Beach
(92647-2071)
PHONE 949 559-0930
Thomas McFarland, *President*
▲ **EMP:** 130 **EST:** 1972
SQ FT: 42,000
SALES (est): 81.2MM
SALES (corp-wide): 58.1B **Publicly Held**
WEB: www.encoregroup.aero
SIC: 3728 1799 Aircraft parts & equipment; renovation of aircraft interiors

PA: The Boeing Company
100 N Riverside Plz
Chicago IL 60606
312 544-2000

(P-10357)
IRISH INTERIORS HOLDINGS INC
5511 Skylab Rd Ste 101, Huntington Beach
(92647-2071)
PHONE 562 344-1700
Karl Jonson, *Vice Pres*
EMP: 200
SALES (corp-wide): 58.1B **Publicly Held**
WEB: www.encoregroup.aero
SIC: 3728 Aircraft parts & equipment
HQ: Irish Interiors, Inc.
5511 Skylab Rd Ste 101
Huntington Beach CA 92647
949 559-0930

(P-10358)
IRISH INTERIORS HOLDINGS INC
1729 Apollo Ct, Seal Beach (90740-5617)
PHONE 949 559-0930
EMP: 20
SALES (corp-wide): 58.1B **Publicly Held**
WEB: www.encoregroup.aero
SIC: 3728 Aircraft parts & equipment
HQ: Irish Interiors, Inc.
5511 Skylab Rd Ste 101
Huntington Beach CA 92647
949 559-0930

(P-10359)
IRWIN AVIATION INC
Also Called: Aero Performance
225 Airport Cir, Corona (92878-5027)
PHONE 951 372-9555
James Irwin, *CEO*
Nanci Irwin, *Vice Pres*
EMP: 30 **EST:** 2014
SALES (est): 4.3MM **Privately Held**
WEB: www.aeroperformance.com
SIC: 3728 Aircraft parts & equipment

(P-10360)
ITT AEROSPACE CONTROLS LLC
ITT Aerospace Controls Unit S
28150 Industry Dr, Valencia (91355-4101)
PHONE 661 295-4000
Robert Briggs, *Manager*
Farrokh Batliwala, *President*
EMP: 300
SALES (corp-wide): 2.4B **Publicly Held**
WEB: www.ittaerospace.com
SIC: 3728 Aircraft parts & equipment
HQ: Itt Aerospace Controls Llc
28150 Industry Dr
Valencia CA 91355
315 568-7258

(P-10361)
JOHNSON CALDRAUL INC
Also Called: Cal-Draulics
220 N Delilah St Ste 101, Corona
(92879-1883)
PHONE 951 340-1067
Douglas Johnson, *President*
Kenneth W Johnson, *Vice Pres*
EMP: 30 **EST:** 1992
SQ FT: 12,000
SALES (est): 2.9MM **Privately Held**
SIC: 3728 3593 Aircraft parts & equipment; fluid power cylinders & actuators

(P-10362)
KIRKHILL INC (HQ)
Also Called: Sfs
300 E Cypress St, Brea (92821-4007)
PHONE 714 529-4901
Kevin Stein, *President*
EMP: 742 **EST:** 2018
SALES (est): 94MM
SALES (corp-wide): 4.8B **Publicly Held**
WEB: www.kirkhill.com
SIC: 3728 Aircraft parts & equipment
PA: Transdigm Group Incorporated
1301 E 9th St Ste 3000
Cleveland OH 44114
216 706-2960

(P-10363)
KLUNE INDUSTRIES INC (DH)
Also Called: PCC Aerostructures
7323 Coldwater Canyon Ave, North Hollywood (91605-4206)
PHONE 818 503-8100
Joseph I Snowden, *CEO*
Kenneth Ward, *CFO*
Pamela Mayes, *Purch Agent*
Lesley Del Rosario, *Accounts Exec*
▲ **EMP:** 358 **EST:** 1972
SQ FT: 125,000
SALES (est): 131.1MM
SALES (corp-wide): 245.5B **Publicly Held**
WEB: www.pccaero.com
SIC: 3728 Aircraft parts & equipment

(P-10364)
KS ENGINEERING INC
14948 Shoemaker Ave, Santa Fe Springs
(90670-5552)
PHONE 562 483-7788
Clifford Yu, *President*
Kap Yu, *Manager*
EMP: 15 **EST:** 1984
SQ FT: 14,000
SALES (est): 1.7MM **Privately Held**
WEB: www.walthers.com
SIC: 3728 Aircraft body & wing assemblies & parts

(P-10365)
LANIC ENGINEERING INC (PA)
Also Called: Lanic Aerospace
12144 6th St, Rancho Cucamonga
(91730-6111)
PHONE 877 763-0411
S Robert Leaming, *CEO*
Shaun Arnold, *President*
Tory Delgadillo, *Executive*
Lizbeth Vargas, *Program Mgr*
Rick Villanueva, *Buyer*
EMP: 23 **EST:** 1984
SQ FT: 30,000
SALES (est): 2.5MM **Privately Held**
WEB: www.lanicaerospace.com
SIC: 3728 3721 Aircraft parts & equipment; aircraft

(P-10366)
LAUNCHPINT ELC PRPLSION SLTONS
Also Called: Launchpoint Eps
5735 Hollister Ave Ste B, Goleta
(93117-6410)
PHONE 805 683-9659
Robert Reali, *Principal*
Dave Paden, *Vice Pres*
Brian Clark, *Principal*
Christopher Grieco, *Principal*
Vicki Young, *Principal*
EMP: 20 **EST:** 2018
SALES (est): 1.3MM **Privately Held**
WEB: www.launchpnt.com
SIC: 3728 Aircraft parts & equipment

(P-10367)
LEACH INTERNATIONAL CORP (DH)
6900 Orangethorpe Ave A, Buena Park
(90620-1390)
P.O. Box 5032 (90622-5032)
PHONE 714 736-7537
Richard Brad Lawrence, *CEO*
Mark Thek, *President*
Alain Durand, *Vice Pres*
Imtiaz Khan, *Project Engr*
Malcolm Critchley, *Engineer*
EMP: 500 **EST:** 1919
SALES (est): 175.5MM
SALES (corp-wide): 4.8B **Publicly Held**
WEB: www.transdigm.com
SIC: 3728 Aircraft parts & equipment
HQ: Esterline Technologies Corp
1301 E 9th St Ste 3000
Cleveland OH 44114
216 706-2960

(P-10368)
LLAMAS PLASTICS INC
12970 Bradley Ave, Sylmar (91342-3851)
PHONE 818 362-0371
Ricardo M Llamas, *CEO*
Oswald Llamas, *President*

Jeff Mabry, *Corp Secy*
Peter Delgado, *Program Mgr*
Sandy Johnson, *Data Proc Staff*
EMP: 105 **EST:** 1977
SQ FT: 37,000
SALES (est): 19.4MM **Privately Held**
WEB: www.llamas-plastics.com
SIC: 3728 3089 3083 Aircraft parts & equipment; plastic containers, except foam; laminated plastics plate & sheet

(P-10369)
LONG-LOK LLC
20531 Belshaw Ave, Carson (90746-3505)
PHONE 424 209-8726
EMP: 21
SALES (corp-wide): 9.6MM **Privately Held**
SIC: 3728 Research & dev by manuf., aircraft parts & auxiliary equip
PA: Long-Lok, Llc
10630 Chester Rd
Cincinnati OH 45215
336 343-7319

(P-10370)
LUXFER INC (DH)
Also Called: Luxfer Gas Cylinder
3016 Kansas Ave Bldg 1, Riverside
(92507-3445)
PHONE 951 684-5110
John Rhodes, *President*
Anthony Barnes, *President*
Micheal Edwards, *Vice Pres*
Adrian De La Barcena, *IT/INT Sup*
Bryan Nuesse, *Engineer*
◆ **EMP:** 70 **EST:** 1973
SQ FT: 120,000
SALES (est): 110.2MM
SALES (corp-wide): 378MM **Privately Held**
WEB: www.luxfercylinders.com
SIC: 3728 3354 Aircraft parts & equipment; shapes, extruded aluminum

(P-10371)
MANEY AIRCRAFT INC
1305 S Wanamaker Ave, Ontario
(91761-2237)
PHONE 909 390-2500
Martin T Bright, *CEO*
David A Ederer, *Shareholder*
Michael Neely, *Shareholder*
Julie Nethington-Walt, *Administration*
EMP: 30 **EST:** 1955
SQ FT: 14,700
SALES (est): 6.7MM **Privately Held**
WEB: www.maneyaircraft.com
SIC: 3728 5088 3829 3812 Aircraft assemblies, subassemblies & parts; aircraft & parts; aircraft & motor vehicle measurement equipment; search & navigation equipment; guided missile & space vehicle parts & auxiliary equipment; aircraft, self-propelled

(P-10372)
MARINO ENTERPRISES INC
Also Called: Gear Technology
10671 Civic Center Dr, Rancho Cucamonga
(91730-3804)
PHONE 909 476-0343
Thomas Marino, *President*
Sharon Nevius, *Office Mgr*
EMP: 35 **EST:** 1986
SQ FT: 16,320
SALES (est): 7.2MM **Privately Held**
WEB: www.gear-tech.com
SIC: 3728 3769 Gears, aircraft power transmission; guided missile & space vehicle parts & auxiliary equipment

(P-10373)
MASON ELECTRIC CO
13955 Balboa Blvd, Sylmar (91342-1084)
PHONE 818 361-3366
Steven Brune, *Vice Pres*
Leticia Moore, *Executive*
Veronica Diaz, *Admin Asst*
Andrew Steier, *IT/INT Sup*
Arturo Goche, *Project Engr*
EMP: 350 **EST:** 1968
SQ FT: 105,000

SALES (est): 66.7MM
SALES (corp-wide): 4.8B **Publicly Held**
WEB: www.masoncontrols.com
SIC: 3728 Aircraft parts & equipment
HQ: Esterline Technologies Corp
1301 E 9th St Ste 3000
Cleveland OH 44114
216 706-2960

(P-10374)
MASTER RESEARCH & MFG INC
13528 Pumice St, Norwalk (90650-5249)
PHONE..........................562 483-8789
Enrique Viano, *Vice Pres*
Ron Chaplin, *Manager*
EMP: 52 **EST:** 1977
SQ FT: 31,200
SALES (est): 5.4MM **Privately Held**
WEB: www.master-research.com
SIC: 3728 Aircraft body assemblies & parts

(P-10375)
MAVERICK AEROSPACE INC
3718 Capitol Ave, City of Industry
(90601-1731)
PHONE..........................714 578-1700
David Feltch, *CEO*
George Ono, *President*
Shane Davis, *Vice Pres*
Nigel Young, *Vice Pres*
EMP: 16 **EST:** 2002
SQ FT: 12,000
SALES (est): 2.3MM **Privately Held**
WEB: www.mavaero.com
SIC: 3728 Aircraft assemblies, subassemblies & parts

(P-10376)
MAVERICK AEROSPACE LLC
3718 Capitol Ave, City of Industry
(90601-1731)
PHONE..........................714 578-1700
Steve Crisanti, *CEO*
Val Darie, *Exec VP*
George Ono, *Vice Pres*
Mark Riker, *Business Dir*
Jennie Michel, *Executive Asst*
EMP: 85 **EST:** 2017
SQ FT: 40,000
SALES (est): 22.6MM **Privately Held**
WEB: www.maverickaerospace.net
SIC: 3728 3544 3761 3441 Aircraft parts
& equipment; special dies, tools, jigs &
fixtures; guided missiles & space vehi-
cles; fabricated structural metal; guided
missile & space vehicle parts & auxiliary
equipment; machine shop, jobbing & re-
pair

(P-10377)
MEGGITT DEFENSE SYSTEMS INC
9801 Muirlands Blvd, Irvine (92618-2521)
PHONE..........................949 465-7700
Roger Brum, *President*
Greg Brostek, *CFO*
John Braley, *Vice Pres*
Bob Bettwy, *VP Finance*
Denice Brown, *Human Res Mgr*
EMP: 353 **EST:** 1998
SQ FT: 153,000
SALES (est): 92.9MM
SALES (corp-wide): 2.2B **Privately Held**
WEB: www.meggittdefense.com
SIC: 3728 Military aircraft equipment & ar-
mament
PA: Meggitt Plc
Unit 2
Coventry W MIDLANDS CV7 9
120 259-7597

(P-10378)
MEGGITT NORTH HOLLYWOOD INC
10092 Foxrun Rd, Santa Ana (92705-1407)
PHONE..........................818 691-6258
Jen Larsen, *Branch Mgr*
Larry Purvis, *Engineer*
Michael Williams, *Engineer*
Curtis Johnson, *Manager*
EMP: 30
SALES (corp-wide): 2.2B **Privately Held**
WEB: www.meggittfuelling.com
SIC: 3728 Aircraft parts & equipment

HQ: Meggitt (North Hollywood), Inc.
12838 Saticoy St
North Hollywood CA 91605

(P-10379)
MEGGITT NORTH HOLLYWOOD INC (HQ)
Also Called: Meggitt Control Systems
12838 Saticoy St, North Hollywood
(91605-3505)
PHONE..........................818 765-8160
Dennis Hutton, *CEO*
Barney Rosenberg, *Vice Pres*
Jon Bonar, *General Mgr*
Eric G Lardiere, *Admin Sec*
Scott Kirkwood, *Administration*
▲ **EMP:** 230 **EST:** 1969
SQ FT: 10,000
SALES (est): 61.3MM
SALES (corp-wide): 2.2B **Privately Held**
WEB: www.meggittfuelling.com
SIC: 3728 Aircraft parts & equipment
PA: Meggitt Plc
Unit 2
Coventry W MIDLANDS CV7 9
120 259-7597

(P-10380)
MEGGITT SAFETY SYSTEMS INC
Also Called: Htl Manufacturing Div
1785 Voyager Ave, Simi Valley
(93063-3363)
PHONE..........................805 584-4100
Dennis Hutton, *President*
Karlisa Callwood, *Vice Pres*
Mark Davidson, *Vice Pres*
Regina Ford, *Vice Pres*
Alison G Obe, *Exec Dir*
EMP: 90
SALES (corp-wide): 2.2B **Privately Held**
WEB: www.meggitt.com
SIC: 3728 Aircraft parts & equipment
HQ: Meggitt Safety Systems, Inc.
1785 Voyager Ave
Simi Valley CA 93063
805 584-4100

(P-10381)
MEGGITT SAFETY SYSTEMS INC
Meggitt Ctrl Systms-Vntura Cnt
1785 Voyager Ave, Simi Valley
(93063-3363)
PHONE..........................805 584-4100
Jim Healy, *Director*
EMP: 200
SALES (corp-wide): 2.2B **Privately Held**
WEB: www.meggitt.com
SIC: 3728 Aircraft parts & equipment
HQ: Meggitt Safety Systems, Inc.
1785 Voyager Ave
Simi Valley CA 93063
805 584-4100

(P-10382)
MEGGITT-USA INC (HQ)
Also Called: Meggitt Polymers & Composites
1955 Surveyor Ave, Simi Valley
(93063-3369)
PHONE..........................805 526-5700
Eric Lardiere, *President*
Peter Stammers, *President*
Robert W Soukup, *Treasurer*
Barney Rosenberg, *Vice Pres*
Mathew Wootton, *Vice Pres*
▲ **EMP:** 288 **EST:** 1980
SQ FT: 3,000
SALES (est): 663.2MM
SALES (corp-wide): 2.2B **Privately Held**
WEB: www.meggitt.com
SIC: 3728 3829 3679 Aircraft parts &
equipment; vibration meters, analyzers &
calibrators; electronic switches
PA: Meggitt Plc
Unit 2
Coventry W MIDLANDS CV7 9
120 259-7597

(P-10383)
MEGGITT-USA SERVICES INC
1955 Surveyor Ave, Simi Valley
(93063-3369)
PHONE..........................805 526-5700
EMP: 19 **EST:** 2018

SALES (est): 5.1MM
SALES (corp-wide): 2.2B **Privately Held**
WEB: www.meggitt.com
SIC: 3728 Aircraft parts & equipment
PA: Meggitt Plc
Unit 2
Coventry W MIDLANDS CV7 9
120 259-7597

(P-10384)
MISSION CRTICAL COMPOSITES LLC
15400 Graham St Ste 102, Huntington
Beach (92649-1257)
PHONE..........................714 831-2100
Robert Hartman, *Mng Member*
Hartman Robert, *Managing Dir*
Jaime Rodriguez, *Technician*
Alex Cooper, *Engineer*
Julie Hagen, *Controller*
EMP: 22 **EST:** 2012
SALES (est): 2.2B **Privately Held**
WEB: www.missioncriticalcomposites.com
SIC: 3728 3721 3724 3761 Aircraft as-
semblies, subassemblies & parts; aircraft;
aircraft engines & engine parts; guided
missiles & space vehicles; guided missile
& space vehicle propulsion unit parts; air-
frame assemblies, guided missiles

(P-10385)
MULGREW ARCFT COMPONENTS INC
1810 S Shamrock Ave, Monrovia
(91016-4251)
PHONE..........................626 256-1375
Mike Houshiar, *CEO*
Adrian Velasquez, *Engineer*
EMP: 58
SQ FT: 45,000
SALES (est): 8.2MM **Privately Held**
WEB: www.mulgrewaircraft.com
SIC: 3728 Aircraft assemblies, subassem-
blies & parts

(P-10386)
NASCO AIRCRAFT BRAKE INC
Also Called: Meggitt Arcft Braking Systems
13300 Estrella Ave, Gardena (90248-1519)
PHONE..........................310 532-4430
Daniel Aron, *CEO*
Phil Friedman, *Corp Secy*
Sara Kruse, *Vice Pres*
Terry Jones, *Business Dir*
Darren Lovato, *Engrg Dir*
EMP: 100 **EST:** 1981
SQ FT: 25,000
SALES (est): 20.8MM
SALES (corp-wide): 2.2B **Privately Held**
WEB: www.nascoaircraft.com
SIC: 3728 Brakes, aircraft
HQ: Meggitt Aircraft Braking Systems Cor-
poration
1204 Massillon Rd
Akron OH 44306
330 796-4400

(P-10387)
NEILL AIRCRAFT CO
1260 W 15th St, Long Beach (90813-1390)
PHONE..........................562 432-7981
Judith L Carpenter, *President*
Brad Barnette, *Business Dir*
Brad Barnett, *General Mgr*
Gonzalo Rivas, *General Mgr*
Tom Hitchcock, *Engineer*
EMP: 275 **EST:** 1956
SQ FT: 150,000
SALES (est): 58.7MM **Privately Held**
WEB: www.neillaircraft.com
SIC: 3728 Aircraft body & wing assemblies
& parts

(P-10388)
NOTTHOFF ENGINEERING LA INC
5416 Argosy Ave, Huntington Beach
(92649-1039)
PHONE..........................714 894-9802
Kelly Kaller, *CEO*
Karen Ewing, *Admin Sec*
▲ **EMP:** 54 **EST:** 1941
SALES (est): 9.2MM **Privately Held**
WEB: www.notthoff.com
SIC: 3728 3599 Aircraft parts & equip-
ment; machine shop, jobbing & repair

(P-10389)
OTTO INSTRUMENT SERVICE INC (PA)
1441 Valencia Pl, Ontario (91761-7639)
PHONE..........................909 930-5800
William R Otto Jr, *President*
Lynne Amber Otto-Miller, *Treasurer*
Ben Rosenthal, *Exec VP*
Juergen Buettgenbach, *Vice Pres*
Lynnae Otto, *Vice Pres*
EMP: 45 **EST:** 1946
SQ FT: 36,800
SALES: 29.5MM **Privately Held**
WEB: www.ottoinstrument.com
SIC: 3728 5088 7699 Aircraft parts &
equipment; aircraft equipment & supplies;
aircraft flight instrument repair

(P-10390)
PACIFIC CONTOURS CORPORATION
5340 E Hunter Ave, Anaheim (92807-2053)
PHONE..........................714 693-1260
Tom Rapacz, *President*
Jon Stannard, *COO*
Tim Anderson, *CFO*
Ray Santillan, *Administration*
Charles Regan, *QC Mgr*
EMP: 60 **EST:** 1997
SQ FT: 36,000
SALES (est): 13MM **Privately Held**
WEB: www.pacificcontours.com
SIC: 3728 5088 Aircraft assemblies, sub-
assemblies & parts; aircraft & parts

(P-10391)
PACIFIC SKY SUPPLY INC
8230 San Fernando Rd, Sun Valley
(91352-3218)
PHONE..........................818 768-3700
Emilio B Perez, *CEO*
Emilio Perez, *President*
Denise Zelaya, *Officer*
Keith Aeschlimann, *Vice Pres*
Tannis Smith, *Vice Pres*
EMP: 59 **EST:** 1954
SQ FT: 27,000
SALES (est): 10.3MM **Privately Held**
WEB: www.pacsky.com
SIC: 3728 3724 5088 Aircraft parts &
equipment; aircraft engines & engine
parts; transportation equipment & sup-
plies

(P-10392)
PCA AEROSPACE INC (PA)
17800 Gothard St, Huntington Beach
(92647-6217)
PHONE..........................714 841-1750
Brian Murray, *CEO*
Gregory Ruffalo, *COO*
▲ **EMP:** 71
SQ FT: 58,000
SALES (est): 19MM **Privately Held**
SIC: 3728 3599 Aircraft parts & equip-
ment; machine shop, jobbing & repair

(P-10393)
PMC INC (HQ)
12243 Branford St, Sun Valley
(91352-1010)
PHONE..........................818 896-1101
Christopher Lette, *President*
EMP: 859 **EST:** 1962
SALES (est): 541.3MM
SALES (corp-wide): 1.7B **Privately Held**
WEB: www.pmcglobalinc.com
SIC: 3728 3724 Bodies, aircraft; engine
mount parts, aircraft
PA: Pmc Global, Inc.
12243 Branford St
Sun Valley CA 91352
818 896-1101

(P-10394)
PRECISION AEROSPACE CORP
11155 Jersey Blvd Ste A, Rancho Cuca-
monga (91730-5148)
PHONE..........................909 945-9604
Jim Hudson, *President*
Sandra Ryan, *Vice Pres*
EMP: 70
SQ FT: 50,000

SALES (est): 15.1MM **Privately Held**
WEB: www.pac.cc
SIC: **3728** Aircraft assemblies, subassemblies & parts

(P-10395)
PRECISION TUBE BENDING
13626 Talc St, Santa Fe Springs
(90670-5173)
PHONE.....................562 921-6723
Diane M Williams, *CEO*
Harry Rowe, *General Mgr*
Fred Mason, *CIO*
Byron Washington, *Buyer*
Ralph Inzuna, *Plant Mgr*
EMP: 98 EST: 1957
SQ FT: 60,000
SALES (est): 18.8MM **Privately Held**
WEB: www.precision-tube-bending.com
SIC: **3728** 3498 Aircraft parts & equipment; tube fabricating (contract bending & shaping)

(P-10396)
PROGRAMMED COMPOSITES INC
250 Klug Cir, Corona (92880-5409)
PHONE.....................951 520-7300
Fax: 951 520-7300
EMP: 250
SALES: 20MM
SALES (corp-wide): 3.1B **Publicly Held**
SIC: **3728** 3769 Mfg Aircraft Parts/Equipment Mfg Space Vehicle Equipment
PA: Orbital Atk, Inc.
45101 Warp Dr
Dulles VA 20166
703 406-5000

(P-10397)
PTI TECHNOLOGIES INC (DH)
501 Del Norte Blvd, Oxnard (93030-7983)
PHONE.....................805 604-3700
Rowland Ellis, *President*
Beth Kozlowski, *Vice Pres*
Jim Martin, *Vice Pres*
Joan Peters, *Admin Asst*
Josh Shea, *Administration*
▲ EMP: 212 EST: 1979
SQ FT: 225,000
SALES (est): 57.5MM **Publicly Held**
WEB: www.ptitechnologies.com
SIC: **3728** Aircraft parts & equipment
HQ: Esco Technologies Holding Llc
9900 Clayton Rd Ste A
Saint Louis MO 63124
314 213-7200

(P-10398)
Q1 TEST INC
1100 S Grove Ave Ste B2, Ontario
(91761-4574)
PHONE.....................909 390-9718
Allen Riley, *CEO*
Jason Riley, *President*
Candy Lopez, *Manager*
EMP: 21 EST: 2005
SQ FT: 10,500
SALES (est): 4.1MM **Privately Held**
WEB: www.q1testinc.com
SIC: **3728** Turret test fixtures, aircraft

(P-10399)
QPI HOLDINGS INC (HQ)
22906 Frampton Ave, Torrance
(90501-5035)
PHONE.....................310 539-2855
David J Hammond, *Principal*
EMP: 100 EST: 2014
SALES (est): 21.3MM
SALES (corp-wide): 250.8MM **Privately Held**
WEB: www.cadenceaerospace.com
SIC: **3728** Aircraft assemblies, subassemblies & parts
PA: Cadence Aerospace, Llc
3150 E Miraloma Ave
Anaheim CA 92806
949 877-3630

(P-10400)
QUALITY FORMING LLC
Also Called: Qfi Prv Aerospace
22906 Frampton Ave, Torrance
(90501-5035)
PHONE.....................310 539-2855

Mark Severns, *President*
Ray Ruiz, *Program Mgr*
Corby Carrera, *Administration*
Richard Barnes, *CIO*
Benjamin Rockwell, *Info Tech Mgr*
▲ EMP: 100 EST: 1972
SALES (est): 21.3MM
SALES (corp-wide): 250.8MM **Privately Held**
WEB: www.cadenceaerospace.com
SIC: **3728** Aircraft assemblies, subassemblies & parts
HQ: Qpi Holdings, Inc.
22906 Frampton Ave
Torrance CA 90501
310 539-2855

(P-10401)
RAYTHEON TECHNOLOGIES CORP
Also Called: Sensors and Integrated Systems
2727 E Imperial Hwy, Brea (92821-6713)
PHONE.....................714 984-1467
David Gitlin, *Branch Mgr*
Thomas Schinke, *Project Mgr*
Angela Pereda, *Engineer*
EMP: 14
SALES (corp-wide): 56.5B **Publicly Held**
WEB: www.utcaerospacesystems.com
SIC: **3728** Aircraft parts & equipment
PA: Raytheon Technologies Corporation
870 Winter St
Waltham MA 02451
781 522-3000

(P-10402)
ROBINSON HELICOPTER CO INC
2901 Airport Dr, Torrance (90505-6115)
PHONE.....................310 539-0508
Kurt L Robinson, *CEO*
Frank Robinson, *President*
Tim Goetz, *CFO*
Daniel Huesca, *Technical Staff*
Ken Martin, *Engineer*
◆ EMP: 970 EST: 1973
SQ FT: 260,000
SALES (est): 171.8MM **Privately Held**
WEB: www.robinsonheli.com
SIC: **3728** Aircraft parts & equipment

(P-10403)
ROCKWELL COLLINS INC
1757 Carr Rd Ste 100e, Calexico
(92231-9781)
PHONE.....................760 768-4732
Nicolas Pineda, *Manager*
Kim Powers, *Sr Software Eng*
Matthew Putman, *Design Engr*
Karla Meza, *Engineer*
Heriberto Montoya, *Engineer*
EMP: 25
SALES (corp-wide): 56.5B **Publicly Held**
WEB: www.rockwellcollins.com
SIC: **3728** Aircraft parts & equipment
HQ: Rockwell Collins, Inc.
400 Collins Rd Ne
Cedar Rapids IA 52498

(P-10404)
ROGERS HOLDING COMPANY INC
Also Called: V & M Precision Grinding Co.
1130 Columbia St, Brea (92821-2921)
PHONE.....................714 257-4850
Aldo Devile, *Principal*
Maynard Hallman, *Partner*
Tom Rogers, *Vice Pres*
William Fickling 1111, *Program Mgr*
EMP: 67 EST: 1946
SQ FT: 65,000
SALES (est): 9.1MM **Privately Held**
WEB: www.vmprecision.com
SIC: **3728** Alighting (landing gear) assemblies, aircraft

(P-10405)
RSA ENGINEERED PRODUCTS LLC
Also Called: Trimas Aerospace
110 W Cochran St Ste A, Simi Valley
(93065-6228)
PHONE.....................805 584-4150
Ray Scarcello, *CEO*

Scott Leeds, *CFO*
Leslie Fernandes, *Vice Pres*
Karen Linscott, *Administration*
Yvonne Schott, *Administration*
◆ EMP: 90 EST: 2012
SQ FT: 43,000
SALES (est): 27.8MM
SALES (corp-wide): 769.9MM **Publicly Held**
WEB: www.rsaeng.com
SIC: **3728** Aircraft parts & equipment
PA: Trimas Corporation
38505 Woodward Ave # 200
Bloomfield Hills MI 48304
248 631-5450

(P-10406)
SABRIN CORPORATION
Also Called: Astronics Company
2836 E Walnut St, Pasadena (91107-3755)
PHONE.....................626 792-3813
Julian Doherty, *CEO*
▲ EMP: 19 EST: 1961
SQ FT: 8,000
SALES (est): 3MM **Privately Held**
WEB: www.sabrin.com
SIC: **3728** 3444 3544 3499 Aircraft parts & equipment; sheet metalwork; special dies, tools, jigs & fixtures; punches, forming & stamping; shims, metal

(P-10407)
SAFRAN CABIN GALLEYS US INC (HQ)
17311 Nichols Ln, Huntington Beach
(92647-5721)
PHONE.....................714 861-7300
Matthew Stafford, *CEO*
Vincent Kozar, *CFO*
Frank Delos Santos, *Controller*
◆ EMP: 717 EST: 1986
SQ FT: 90,000
SALES (est): 289.6MM
SALES (corp-wide): 639.8MM **Privately Held**
WEB: www.safran-group.com
SIC: **3728** Aircraft parts & equipment
PA: Safran
2 Bd General Martial Valin
Paris 75015
140 608-080

(P-10408)
SAFRAN CABIN INC (HQ)
5701 Bolsa Ave, Huntington Beach
(92647-2063)
PHONE.....................714 934-0000
Christophe Bernardini, *CEO*
Norman Jordan, *CEO*
Jeff Henry, *CFO*
Scott Savian, *Exec VP*
Danny Martin, *Vice Pres*
▲ EMP: 500 EST: 1972
SQ FT: 150,000
SALES (est): 442.3MM
SALES (corp-wide): 639.8MM **Privately Held**
WEB: www.zodiacaerospace.com
SIC: **3728** Aircraft assemblies, subassemblies & parts
PA: Safran
2 Bd Du General Martial Valin
Paris 75015
140 608-080

(P-10409)
SAFRAN CABIN INC
11040 Warland Dr, Cypress (90630-5035)
PHONE.....................562 344-4780
Gary Reese, *Branch Mgr*
Chris Keating, *Principal*
Cynthia Pham, *Electrical Engi*
Ferdinand Lansangan, *Engineer*
Tim Morse, *Chief Engr*
EMP: 248
SALES (corp-wide): 639.8MM **Privately Held**
WEB: www.zodiacaerospace.com
SIC: **3728** Aircraft assemblies, subassemblies & parts
HQ: Safran Cabin Inc.
5701 Bolsa Ave
Huntington Beach CA 92647
714 934-0000

(P-10410)
SAFRAN CABIN MATERIALS LLC
1945 S Grove Ave, Ontario (91761-5616)
PHONE.....................909 947-4115
Lek Makpaiboon, *President*
EMP: 42 EST: 2013
SALES (est): 4.8MM
SALES (corp-wide): 639.8MM **Privately Held**
WEB: www.safran-group.com
SIC: **3728** Aircraft parts & equipment
PA: Safran
2 Bd Du General Martial Valin
Paris 75015
140 608-080

(P-10411)
SAFRAN SEATS SANTA MARIA LLC
2641 Airpark Dr, Santa Maria (93455-1415)
PHONE.....................805 922-5995
Klaus Koester, *Principal*
Sarah Nakhla, *Buyer*
▲ EMP: 650 EST: 2012
SALES (est): 132MM
SALES (corp-wide): 639.8MM **Privately Held**
WEB: www.weber.zodiac.com
SIC: **3728** Aircraft parts & equipment
HQ: Safran Seats Usa Llc
2000 Weber Dr
Gainesville TX 76240
940 668-4825

(P-10412)
SANDERS COMPOSITES INC (DH)
Also Called: Sanders Composites Industries
3701 E Conant St, Long Beach
(90808-1783)
PHONE.....................562 354-2800
Larry O'Toole, *CEO*
Larry O Toole, *CEO*
EMP: 49 EST: 1988
SQ FT: 44,400
SALES (est): 12.3MM
SALES (corp-wide): 653.4MM **Privately Held**
WEB: www.sanderscomposites.com
SIC: **3728** Aircraft assemblies, subassemblies & parts
HQ: Sanders Industries Holdings, Inc.
3701 E Conant St
Long Beach CA 90808
562 354-2920

(P-10413)
SANTA MONICA PROPELLER SVC INC
3135 Dnald Douglas Loop S, Santa Monica
(90405-3210)
PHONE.....................310 390-6233
Leonid Polyakov, *CEO*
▲ EMP: 15 EST: 1963
SQ FT: 11,000
SALES (est): 1.8MM **Privately Held**
WEB: www.santamonicapropeller.com
SIC: **3728** 5088 Aircraft propellers & associated equipment; aircraft assemblies, subassemblies & parts; aircraft & parts

(P-10414)
SEAMAN PRODUCTS OF CALIFORNIA
12329 Gladstone Ave, Sylmar
(91342-5319)
PHONE.....................818 768-4881
Carol Haisten, *President*
EMP: 14 EST: 1951
SQ FT: 13,000
SALES (est): 1.2MM **Privately Held**
WEB: www.seamanproducts.com
SIC: **3728** Aircraft assemblies, subassemblies & parts

(P-10415)
SEHANSON INC
2121 E Via Burton, Anaheim (92806-1220)
PHONE.....................714 778-1900
Stanley E Hanson, *President*
Chris Jones, *CFO*
Christopher J Jones, *CFO*
Judy Trumbull, *Executive*
Carla Reynolds,

EMP: 57 **EST:** 2000
SQ FT: 18,000
SALES (est): 13.3MM **Privately Held**
WEB: www.acraaerospace.com
SIC: 3728 3429 Aircraft parts & equipment; manufactured hardware (general)

(P-10416)
SENIOR OPERATIONS LLC
Senior Aerospace SSP
2980 N San Fernando Blvd, Burbank
(91504-2522)
PHONE..................818 260-2900
Launie Flemning, *Manager*
Sherille Varela, *President*
Venugopal Sunkara, *Officer*
Cedric Bray, *Vice Pres*
Vijay Rajaram, *Vice Pres*
EMP: 380
SALES (corp-wide): 975.5MM **Privately Held**
WEB: www.seniorflexonics.com
SIC: 3728 3599 Aircraft parts & equipment; bellows, industrial: metal
HQ: Senior Operations Llc
300 E Devon Ave
Bartlett IL 60103
630 372-3500

(P-10417)
SHIM-IT CORPORATION
1691 California Ave, Corona (92881-3375)
PHONE..................951 734-8300
Jennifer Steigner, *CEO*
Jeff Johnson, *President*
Diane Hesson, *Vice Pres*
Rosa Aleman, *General Mgr*
Edgar Tapia, *General Mgr*
EMP: 15 **EST:** 1961
SQ FT: 8,500
SALES (est): 1.5MM **Privately Held**
WEB: www.shim-it.com
SIC: 3728 3542 Aircraft parts & equipment; machine tools, metal forming type

(P-10418)
SKYLOCK INDUSTRIES
1290 W Optical Dr, Azusa (91702-3249)
PHONE..................201 637-9505
Jim Pease, *Principal*
Jeff Crevoiserat, *Principal*
EMP: 50 **EST:** 1973
SALES (est): 3.2MM **Privately Held**
SIC: 3728 Aircraft parts & equipment

(P-10419)
SKYLOCK INDUSTRIES LLC
1290 W Optical Dr, Azusa (91702-3249)
PHONE..................626 334-2391
Jeff Creoiserat, *Ch of Bd*
Jim Pease, *President*
Candy Perez, *Office Mgr*
Bill Phillips, *Project Engr*
Maria Ledesma, *Buyer*
EMP: 70
SQ FT: 14,000
SALES (est): 19.6MM **Privately Held**
WEB: www.skylock.com
SIC: 3728 Aircraft parts & equipment

(P-10420)
SOUTHWEST MACHINE & PLASTIC CO
Also Called: Southwest Plastics Co
620 W Foothill Blvd, Glendora
(91741-2403)
PHONE..................626 963-6919
W Thomas Jorgensen, *President*
Alfred D Jorgensen, *Vice Pres*
▲ **EMP:** 30 **EST:** 1937
SALES (est): 5MM **Privately Held**
WEB: www.southwestplastics.com
SIC: 3728 3089 3544 Aircraft parts & equipment; injection molding of plastics; special dies, tools, jigs & fixtures

(P-10421)
SPACE-LOK INC
13306 Halldale Ave, Gardena
(90249-2204)
P.O. Box 2919 (90247-1119)
PHONE..................310 527-6150
Scott F Wade, *President*
Jeffrey Wade, *CFO*
Kurt Thompson, *Engineer*
EMP: 138 **EST:** 1962

SALES (est): 31.8MM
SALES (corp-wide): 218.1MM **Privately Held**
WEB: www.space-lok.herokuapp.com
SIC: 3728 3542 3812 3452 Aircraft assemblies, subassemblies & parts; machine tools, metal forming type; search & navigation equipment; bolts, nuts, rivets & washers
HQ: Novaria Fastening Systems, Llc
6300 Ridglea Pl Ste 800
Fort Worth TX 76116
817 381-3810

(P-10422)
SPEC TOOL COMPANY
Also Called: Alice G Fink-Painter
11805 Wakeman St, Santa Fe Springs
(90670-2130)
P.O. Box 1056, Pico Rivera (90660-1056)
PHONE..................323 723-9533
Alice G Fink-Painter, *President*
D B Fink, *CEO*
Albert G Fink Jr, *Vice Pres*
EMP: 50 **EST:** 1954
SALES (est): 8.8MM **Privately Held**
WEB: www.spectoolgse.com
SIC: 3728 Aircraft parts & equipment

(P-10423)
STRATOFLIGHT (DH)
Also Called: Western Methods
25540 Rye Canyon Rd, Valencia
(91355-1109)
PHONE..................949 622-0700
Joseph I Snowden, *CEO*
▲ **EMP:** 76 **EST:** 2003
SALES (est): 28.2MM
SALES (corp-wide): 245.5B **Publicly Held**
WEB: www.pccaero.com
SIC: 3728 Aircraft parts & equipment
HQ: Precision Castparts Corp.
4650 Sw Mcdam Ave Ste 300
Portland OR 97239
503 946-4800

(P-10424)
SUNVAIR OVERHAUL INC
Also Called: A H Plating
29145 The Old Rd, Valencia (91355-1015)
PHONE..................661 257-6123
John Waschak, *CEO*
Robert Waschak, *Officer*
Timothy Waschak, *Officer*
EMP: 37 **EST:** 1978
SQ FT: 35,000
SALES (est): 1.3MM **Privately Held**
WEB: www.sunvair.com
SIC: 3728 5088 Alighting (landing gear) assemblies, aircraft; aircraft & parts

(P-10425)
SYMBOLIC DISPLAYS INC
1917 E Saint Andrew Pl, Santa Ana
(92705-5143)
PHONE..................714 258-2811
Candy Suits, *CEO*
Javier Gil, *Engineer*
Bill Ostashay, *Engineer*
▼ **EMP:** 76 **EST:** 1964
SQ FT: 15,860
SALES (est): 14MM **Privately Held**
WEB: www.symbolicdisplays.com
SIC: 3728 3812 3577 Aircraft parts & equipment; search & navigation equipment; computer peripheral equipment

(P-10426)
SYNERGETIC TECH GROUP INC
1712 Earhart, La Verne (91750-5826)
PHONE..................909 305-4711
Tony Espinoza, *CEO*
Kevin Jones, *Director*
Mary Jones, *Director*
Michelle Valdez, *Director*
Jeff Scofield, *Manager*
EMP: 27 **EST:** 1997
SQ FT: 2,400
SALES (est): 4.9MM **Privately Held**
WEB: www.synergetic-us.com
SIC: 3728 Aircraft parts & equipment

(P-10427)
TCA PRECISION PRODUCTS LLC
Also Called: V&M Prcsion Machining Grinding
1130 Columbia St, Brea (92821-2921)
PHONE..................714 257-4850
Gregory Felix,
Alyce Schreiber,
Joe Madrid, *Manager*
EMP: 14 **EST:** 2017
SALES (est): 3.1MM **Privately Held**
WEB: www.vmprecision.com
SIC: 3728 Aircraft parts & equipment

(P-10428)
THALES AVIONICS INC
48 Discovery, Irvine (92618-3151)
PHONE..................949 381-3033
Dominique Giannoni, *Owner*
Man Ng, *Program Mgr*
EMP: 21
SALES (corp-wide): 279.3MM **Privately Held**
SIC: 3728 Aircraft parts & equipment
HQ: Thales Avionics, Inc.
140 Centennial Ave
Piscataway NJ 08854
732 242-6300

(P-10429)
THALES AVIONICS INC
Also Called: Inflight Entrtmt & Connectivity
58 Discovery, Irvine (92618-3105)
PHONE..................949 790-2500
Brad Foreman, *Manager*
Ashvin Kamaraju, *Vice Pres*
Sonia Gupta, *Sr Software Eng*
Michael Miles, *Senior Engr*
Priti Arora, *Director*
EMP: 21
SALES (corp-wide): 279.3MM **Privately Held**
SIC: 3728 3663 Aircraft parts & equipment; radio & TV communications equipment
HQ: Thales Avionics, Inc.
140 Centennial Ave
Piscataway NJ 08854
732 242-6300

(P-10430)
THOMPSON INDUSTRIES LTD
Also Called: Thompson ADB Industries
7155 Fenwick Ln, Westminster
(92683-5218)
PHONE..................310 679-9193
Werner Lieberherr, *CEO*
EMP: 79 **EST:** 1965
SQ FT: 52,000
SALES (est): 11.6MM
SALES (corp-wide): 56.5B **Publicly Held**
WEB: www.beaerospace.com
SIC: 3728 Aircraft parts & equipment
HQ: B/E Aerospace, Inc.
1400 Corporate Center Way
Wellington FL 33414
410 266-2048

(P-10431)
TJ AEROSPACE INC
12601 Monarch St, Garden Grove
(92841-3918)
PHONE..................714 891-3564
Tien Dang, *CEO*
Tien N Dang, *CEO*
EMP: 23 **EST:** 2007
SQ FT: 6,000
SALES (est): 9MM **Privately Held**
WEB: www.tjaerospace.com
SIC: 3728 3541 Aircraft parts & equipment; machine tools, metal cutting type

(P-10432)
TMW CORPORATION (PA)
Also Called: Crown Discount Tools
15148 Bledsoe St, Sylmar (91342-3807)
PHONE..................818 362-5665
William Windette, *President*
Gary Berger, *Vice Pres*
EMP: 110 **EST:** 1973
SQ FT: 115,000
SALES (est): 10MM **Privately Held**
SIC: 3728 Aircraft landing assemblies & brakes

(P-10433)
TRI-FITTING MFG COMPANY
10414 Rush St, South El Monte
(91733-3344)
PHONE..................626 442-2000
Ralph Bernal, *President*
EMP: 15 **EST:** 1977
SQ FT: 13,000
SALES (est): 2.3MM **Privately Held**
WEB: www.trifittingmfg.com
SIC: 3728 3494 3492 Aircraft assemblies, subassemblies & parts; valves & pipe fittings; fluid power valves & hose fittings

(P-10434)
TRI-TECH PRECISION INC
1863 N Case St, Orange (92865-4234)
PHONE..................714 970-1363
Ernie Husted, *President*
EMP: 17 **EST:** 1989
SALES (est): 2MM **Privately Held**
WEB: www.tri-techprecision.com
SIC: 3728 3544 Aircraft parts & equipment; special dies, tools, jigs & fixtures

(P-10435)
TRIO MANUFACTURING INC
601 Lairport St, El Segundo (90245-5005)
PHONE..................310 640-6123
Michael Hunkins, *President*
Brian Hunkins, *Vice Pres*
Laura Matthews, *Office Mgr*
Alexis Lands, *Administration*
Miguel Rouillon, *Manager*
▲ **EMP:** 125
SALES (est): 27.3MM **Privately Held**
WEB: www.triomfg.com
SIC: 3728 3829 3812 3663 Aircraft parts & equipment; measuring & controlling devices; search & navigation equipment; radio & TV communications equipment

(P-10436)
TRIUMPH ACTTION SYSTEMS - VLNC
Also Called: Triumph Group
28150 Harrison Pkwy, Valencia
(91355-4109)
PHONE..................661 702-7537
Daniel J Crowley, *President*
Jim McCabe, *CFO*
Lance Turner, *Senior VP*
John B Wright II, *Senior VP*
Gary Tenison, *Vice Pres*
EMP: 250 **EST:** 2001
SALES (est): 49.2MM **Publicly Held**
WEB: www.triumphgroup.com
SIC: 3728 Aircraft parts & equipment
PA: Triumph Group, Inc.
899 Cassatt Rd Ste 210
Berwyn PA 19312

(P-10437)
TRIUMPH EQUIPMENT INC
13434 S Ontario Ave, Ontario
(91761-7956)
PHONE..................909 947-5983
Brigitte A De Laura, *President*
EMP: 16 **EST:** 2000
SQ FT: 2,700
SALES (est): 256.2K **Privately Held**
SIC: 3728 Aircraft parts & equipment

(P-10438)
TRIUMPH GROUP INC
2401 Portico Blvd, Calexico (92231-9547)
PHONE..................760 768-1700
Manuel Estrada, *Branch Mgr*
▲ **EMP:** 13 **Publicly Held**
WEB: www.triumphgroup.com
SIC: 3728 Aircraft parts & equipment
PA: Triumph Group, Inc.
899 Cassatt Rd Ste 210
Berwyn PA 19312

(P-10439)
TRIUMPH INSULATION SYSTEMS LLC
Also Called: Triumph Group
1754 Carr Rd Ste 103, Calexico
(92231-9509)
PHONE..................760 618-7543
Scott Holland,

Aaron Smith, *Mfg Staff*
William R Gresher,
Alan Haase,
Steven Yari,
▲ **EMP:** 900 **EST:** 1976
SALES (est): 206.8MM **Publicly Held**
WEB: www.triumphgroup.com
SIC: 3728 Aircraft parts & equipment
HQ: Triumph Aerospace Systems Group,
Inc.
899 Cassatt Rd Ste 210
Berwyn PA 19312

(P-10440)
UNITED TECHNOLOGIES CORP
Also Called: UTC Aerospace Systems
11120 Norwalk Blvd, Santa Fe Springs
(90670-3830)
PHONE..................562 944-6244
Louis R Chenevert, *CEO*
Dary Zeigler, *Technician*
EMP: 60 **EST:** 1934
SALES (est): 2.5MM **Privately Held**
SIC: 3728 3312 Brakes, aircraft; wheels

(P-10441)
VANTAGE ASSOCIATES INC
Also Called: Vantage Master Machine Company
12333 Los Nietos Rd, Santa Fe Springs
(90670-2911)
PHONE..................562 968-1400
Paul Roy, *Branch Mgr*
EMP: 40
SALES (corp-wide): 30.5MM **Privately Held**
WEB: www.vantageassoc.com
SIC: 3728 Aircraft assemblies, subassemblies & parts
PA: Vantage Associates Inc.
12333 Los Nietos Rd
Santa Fe Springs CA 90670
619 477-6940

(P-10442)
VENTURA AEROSPACE INC
31355 Agoura Rd, Westlake Village
(91361-4610)
PHONE..................818 540-3130
Mark L Snow, *CEO*
Michael Snow, *Admin Sec*
Troy Ingram, *Design Engr*
EMP: 16 **EST:** 1996
SQ FT: 2,000
SALES (est): 3.7MM **Privately Held**
WEB: www.venturaaerospace.com
SIC: 3728 Aircraft parts & equipment

(P-10443)
WESANCO INC
14870 Desman Rd, La Mirada
(90638-5746)
PHONE..................714 739-4989
Brain Szymanski, *CFO*
Sandra Alford, *Executive*
Tony Scialla, *Purchasing*
Tatiana Matsuhiro, *Sales Staff*
Alex Tinoco, *Sales Staff*
▲ **EMP:** 30 **EST:** 1973
SQ FT: 30,000
SALES (est): 12MM
SALES (corp-wide): 224.6MM **Privately Held**
WEB: www.zsi-foster.com
SIC: 3728 Oleo struts, aircraft
HQ: Zsi-Foster, Inc.
45065 Michigan Ave
Canton MI 48188

(P-10444)
WHITTAKER CORPORATION
1955 Surveyor Ave Fl 2, Simi Valley
(93063-3369)
PHONE..................805 526-5700
Erick Lardiere, *President*
▲ **EMP:** 40 **EST:** 1942
SQ FT: 276,000
SALES (est): 8MM
SALES (corp-wide): 2.2B **Privately Held**
WEB: www.whittakercorp.com
SIC: 3728 3669 7373 Aircraft parts & equipment; fire detection systems, electric; smoke detectors; systems integration services

PA: Meggitt Plc
Unit 2
Coventry W MIDLANDS CV7 9
120 259-7597

(P-10445)
WOODWARD HRT INC
Also Called: Woodward Duarte
1700 Business Center Dr, Duarte
(91010-2863)
PHONE..................626 359-9211
Don Grimes, *Manager*
Oshin Eskandarian, *Technology*
Kevin Sun, *Engineer*
Mark Williams, *Engineer*
Kristin M Williams, *Human Res Mgr*
EMP: 250
SALES (corp-wide): 2.5B **Publicly Held**
SIC: 3728 5084 Aircraft parts & equipment; hydraulic systems equipment & supplies
HQ: Woodward Hrt, Inc.
25200 Rye Canyon Rd
Santa Clarita CA 91355
661 294-6000

(P-10446)
YEAGER MANUFACTURING CORP (PA)
Also Called: Cummins Aerospace
2320 E Orangethorpe Ave, Anaheim
(92806-1223)
PHONE..................714 879-2800
William B Cummins, *CEO*
Sean Cummins, *President*
Dean Cummins, *Engineer*
Nieves Medina, *Train & Dev Mgr*
EMP: 30 **EST:** 1978
SQ FT: 35,000
SALES (est): 15.2MM **Privately Held**
WEB: www.yeager-manufacturing-corp.sb-contract.com
SIC: 3728 3812 3519 Aircraft parts & equipment; search & navigation equipment; internal combustion engines

(P-10447)
ZENITH MANUFACTURING INC
Also Called: Zipco
3087 12th St, Riverside (92507-4904)
PHONE..................818 767-2106
James Phoung, *President*
EMP: 25 **EST:** 2006
SQ FT: 47,000
SALES (est): 3MM **Privately Held**
WEB: www.zenithmfg.com
SIC: 3728 Aircraft parts & equipment

(P-10448)
ZODIAC AEROSPACE
11340 Jersey Blvd, Rancho Cucamonga
(91730-4919)
PHONE..................909 652-9700
Frederic Duval, *COO*
Arnaud Dermange, *CFO*
Fabrice De Winter, *Vice Pres*
Karen Dorado, *Administration*
John Kimberlin, *Engineer*
EMP: 17 **EST:** 2018
SALES (est): 711.5K **Privately Held**
WEB: www.zodiacaerospace.com
SIC: 3728 Aircraft parts & equipment

(P-10449)
ZODIAC WTR WASTE AERO SYSTEMS
Also Called: Monogram Systems
1500 Glenn Curtiss St, Carson
(90746-4012)
PHONE..................310 884-7000
David Conrad, *Vice Pres*
David Beach, *Design Engr*
Robert Wood, *VP Opers*
EMP: 129 **EST:** 1958
SALES (est): 15.3MM
SALES (corp-wide): 639.8MM **Privately Held**
WEB: www.safran-group.com
SIC: 3728 Aircraft parts & equipment
PA: Safran
2 Bd Du General Martial Valin
Paris 75015
140 608-080

(P-10450)
ZODIAK SERVICES AMERICA
6734 Valjean Ave, Van Nuys (91406-5818)
PHONE..................310 884-7200
Lou Pedonne, *President*
EMP: 42 **EST:** 2000
SQ FT: 10,000
SALES (est): 4.8MM
SALES (corp-wide): 639.8MM **Privately Held**
WEB: www.aircruisers.com
SIC: 3728 5088 Oxygen systems, aircraft; transportation equipment & supplies
HQ: Air Cruisers Company, Llc
1747 State Route 34
Wall Township NJ 07727
732 681-3527

3731 Shipbuilding & Repairing

(P-10451)
APR ENGINEERING INC
Also Called: Oceanwide Repairs
1812 W 9th St, Long Beach (90813-2614)
P.O. Box 9100 (90810-0100)
PHONE..................562 983-3800
Roy Herington, *President*
Trina Young, *Treasurer*
Nicholas Berry, *Purchasing*
Richard Lewis, *Superintendent*
Steve Parsons, *Superintendent*
▲ **EMP:** 33 **EST:** 1997
SALES (est): 5.6MM **Privately Held**
SIC: 3731 Shipbuilding & repairing

(P-10452)
LARSON AL BOAT SHOP
1046 S Seaside Ave, San Pedro
(90731-7334)
PHONE..................310 514-4100
Jack Wall, *CEO*
Larry Castenola, *CFO*
George Wall, *Vice Pres*
Gloria Wall, *Vice Pres*
Kelly Wall, *Asst Controller*
▲ **EMP:** 70 **EST:** 1903
SQ FT: 65,000
SALES (est): 24.5MM **Privately Held**
WEB: www.larsonboat.com
SIC: 3731 4493 Military ships, building & repairing; marinas

(P-10453)
MAXON CRS LLC
5400 W Rosecrans Ave # 105, Hawthorne
(90250-6682)
PHONE..................424 236-4660
Isaac Zaharoni, *President*
Tom Carmody,
Letty Mercado,
EMP: 21
SQ FT: 9,411
SALES (est): 855.5K **Privately Held**
WEB: www.maxontechnologies.com
SIC: 3731 Shipbuilding & repairing

(P-10454)
OC FLEET SERVICE INC
8270 Monroe Ave, Stanton (90680-2612)
PHONE..................714 460-8069
Russell Loud, *President*
Evell Stanley, *Vice Pres*
EMP: 14 **EST:** 2007
SQ FT: 150,000
SALES (est): 684.2K **Privately Held**
SIC: 3731 Shipbuilding & repairing

(P-10455)
VALIANT TECHNICAL SERVICES INC
1785 Utah Ave, Lompoc (93437-6020)
PHONE..................757 628-9500
Danny Schanick, *Manager*
EMP: 57
SQ FT: 5,734
SALES (corp-wide): 845.8MM **Privately Held**
SIC: 3731 Shipbuilding & repairing
HQ: Valiant Technical Services Inc.
4465 Guthrie Hwy
Clarksville TN 37040

(P-10456)
WALKER DESIGN INC
Also Called: Walker Engineering Enterprises
9255 San Fernando Rd, Sun Valley
(91352-1416)
PHONE..................818 252-7788
Robert A Walker Jr, *CEO*
Shari Goodgame, *CFO*
Michael Delillo, *Vice Pres*
Blaine Tornow, *Consultant*
▲ **EMP:** 33 **EST:** 1976
SQ FT: 29,800
SALES (est): 7.1MM **Privately Held**
WEB: www.walkerairsep.com
SIC: 3731 Lighters, marine: building & repairing

3732 Boat Building & Repairing

(P-10457)
AMERICAN HONDA MOTOR CO INC
Also Called: Acura Client Services
1919 Torrance Blvd, Torrance
(90501-2722)
PHONE..................800 382-2238
Grace Jean, *Marketing Staff*
Darin Chamberlain, *Sales Staff*
Brian Freeland, *Sales Staff*
Lindsey Willis, *Manager*
EMP: 14 **Privately Held**
WEB: www.honda.com
SIC: 5511 3732 Automobiles, new & used; jet skis
HQ: American Honda Motor Co., Inc.
1919 Torrance Blvd
Torrance CA 90501
310 783-2000

(P-10458)
ANACAPA MARINE SERVICES (PA)
Also Called: Anacapa Boatyard
151 Shipyard Way Ste 5, Newport Beach
(92663-4460)
PHONE..................805 985-1818
Richard Fairchild, *President*
Jj Marine Acquisition, *Principal*
EMP: 17 **EST:** 1973
SQ FT: 8,000
SALES (est): 2.2MM **Privately Held**
SIC: 3732 5088 Boat building & repairing; marine supplies

(P-10459)
BASIN MARINE INC
Also Called: Basin Marine Shipyard
829 Harbor Island Dr A, Newport Beach
(92660-7235)
PHONE..................949 673-0360
Paul Smith, *President*
Augie Gonzaleez, *Clerk*
▲ **EMP:** 24 **EST:** 1956
SQ FT: 44,000
SALES (est): 2.4MM **Privately Held**
WEB: www.basinmarine.com
SIC: 3732 5551 Boat building & repairing; marine supplies

(P-10460)
CATALINA YACHTS INC (PA)
Also Called: Morgan Marine
2259 Ward Ave, Simi Valley (93065-1880)
PHONE..................818 884-7700
Frank W Butler, *President*
Sharon Day, *Chief Mktg Ofcr*
Bob Defilippo, *Purch Agent*
◆ **EMP:** 50 **EST:** 1968
SALES (est): 29.4MM **Privately Held**
WEB: www.catalinayachts.com
SIC: 3732 5551 Sailboats, building & repairing; boat dealers

(P-10461)
COMMANDER BOATS
Also Called: Commander Boats-Mira Loma Mar
4020 Tyler St, Riverside (92503-3402)
PHONE..................951 273-0100
Shailendra H Singhal, *Owner*
EMP: 15 **EST:** 1984
SQ FT: 16,000

SALES (est): 1MM **Privately Held**
WEB: www.commanderboats.com
SIC: 5551 3732 Boat dealers; boats, fiberglass: building & repairing

(P-10462)
CRYSTALINER CORP
1626 Placentia Ave, Costa Mesa
(92627-4385)
PHONE.............................949 548-0292
Jerry Norek, *President*
Jack L Norek Jr, *Treasurer*
Dorothy La Rose, *Admin Sec*
EMP: 16 EST: 1956
SQ FT: 9,000
SALES (est): 267.9K **Privately Held**
SIC: 3732 5551 5088 Boat building & repairing; marine supplies; marine supplies

(P-10463)
DR RADON BOATBUILDING INC
Also Called: Radon Boats
67 Depot Rd, Goleta (93117-3430)
PHONE.............................805 692-2170
Donald Rae Radon, *CEO*
Linda Radon, *Corp Secy*
EMP: 14 EST: 1980
SQ FT: 20,000
SALES (est): 1.7MM **Privately Held**
WEB: www.radonboats.com
SIC: 3732 Fishing boats: lobster, crab, oyster, etc.: small

(P-10464)
GAMBOL INDUSTRIES INC
1825 W Pier D St, Long Beach
(90802-1033)
PHONE.............................562 901-2470
Robert A Stein, *President*
Nels Nelsen, *COO*
John Bridwell, *Vice Pres*
▲ EMP: 45 EST: 1992
SALES (est): 8.3MM **Privately Held**
WEB: www.gambolindustries.com
SIC: 3732 7699 4493 Yachts, building & repairing; boat repair; boat yards, storage & incidental repair

(P-10465)
HALLETT BOATS LLC
180 S Irwindale Ave, Azusa (91702-3211)
PHONE.............................626 969-8844
Nick Barron, *President*
Shirley Barron, *Corp Secy*
Gerald Barron, *Sales Mgr*
EMP: 17 EST: 1963
SQ FT: 21,000
SALES (est): 727.5K **Privately Held**
WEB: www.hallettboats.com
SIC: 3732 5091 Motorboats, inboard or outboard: building & repairing; boats, canoes, watercrafts & equipment

(P-10466)
INDEL ENGINEERING INC
Also Called: Marina Shipyard
6400 E Marina Dr, Long Beach
(90803-4618)
PHONE.............................562 594-0995
D E Bud Tretter, *President*
D E Tretter, *President*
Kurt Tretter, *Corp Secy*
Jerry Tretter, *Vice Pres*
Cyndee Allen, *General Mgr*
EMP: 35 EST: 1964
SQ FT: 3,000
SALES (est): 2.6MM **Privately Held**
SIC: 3732 Houseboats, building & repairing; motorboats, inboard or outboard: building & repairing

(P-10467)
MACGREGOR YACHT CORPORATION
1631 Placentia Ave, Costa Mesa
(92627-4355)
PHONE.............................310 621-2206
Roger Mac Gregor, *President*
Mary Lou Mac Gregor, *Corp Secy*
EMP: 31 EST: 1963
SQ FT: 10,000
SALES (est): 662.8K **Privately Held**
SIC: 3732 5551 Sailboats, building & repairing; boat dealers

(P-10468)
MAURER MARINE INC
873 W 17th St, Costa Mesa (92627-4308)
PHONE.............................949 645-7673
Craig Maurer, *President*
Jay S Maurer, *Vice Pres*
Garrett Maurer, *Parts Mgr*
EMP: 18
SALES (est): 4MM **Privately Held**
WEB: www.maurermarine.com
SIC: 3732 7389 Yachts, building & repairing; yacht brokers

(P-10469)
NAVIGATOR YACHTS AND PDTS INC
364 Malbert St, Perris (92570-8336)
PHONE.............................951 657-2117
Xia Wang, *CEO*
Jule Marshall, *Principal*
Cheryl Bond, *Director*
EMP: 22 EST: 1988
SQ FT: 30,000
SALES (est): 665.1K **Privately Held**
WEB: www.navigatoryachts.com
SIC: 3732 Yachts, building & repairing

(P-10470)
OCEAN PROTECTA INCORPORATED
1240 Pioneer St Ste B, Brea (92821-3714)
PHONE.............................714 891-2628
Edgar Chong Tan, *CEO*
Myron Reyes, *President*
Loretta Erickson, *Manager*
EMP: 50 EST: 2014
SALES (est): 4MM **Privately Held**
WEB: www.oceanprotecta.com
SIC: 3732 Boat building & repairing

(P-10471)
RJ AIRWASH LLC (PA)
6860 Canby Ave Ste 109, Reseda
(91335-8720)
PHONE.............................818 342-8800
Regina Bondoc,
EMP: 21 EST: 2012
SALES (est): 202.6K **Privately Held**
SIC: 3732 Boat building & repairing

(P-10472)
TBYCI LLC
Also Called: Boatyard-Channel Islands, The
3615 Victoria Ave, Oxnard (93035-4360)
PHONE.............................805 985-6800
Gregory Schem,
Craig Campbell, *General Mgr*
EMP: 16 EST: 2013
SQ FT: 7,500
SALES (est): 1.6MM **Privately Held**
WEB: www.tbyci.com
SIC: 3732 3731 Motorized boat, building & repairing; motorboats, inboard or outboard: building & repairing; sailboats, building & repairing; patrol boats, building & repairing; crew boats, building & repairing

(P-10473)
TOLLER ENTERPRISES INC (PA)
Also Called: Electra Craft
2251 Townsgate Rd, Westlake Village
(91361-2404)
PHONE.............................805 374-9455
Alex Toller, *President*
Cheryl Toller, *Admin Sec*
EMP: 39 EST: 1979
SALES (est): 7MM **Privately Held**
SIC: 5551 3732 Motor boat dealers; marine supplies; boat building & repairing

(P-10474)
VENTURA HARBOR BOATYARD INC
1415 Spinnaker Dr, Ventura (93001-4339)
PHONE.............................805 654-1433
Robert Bartosh, *President*
Dale Morris, *CFO*
Kim Morris, *Vice Pres*
Stephen James, *Admin Sec*
Joe Gonzalez, *Facilities Mgr*
EMP: 35 EST: 1986
SQ FT: 2,000

SALES (est): 4.8MM **Privately Held**
WEB: www.vhby.com
SIC: 3732 4493 Boat building & repairing; boat yards, storage & incidental repair

(P-10475)
WILLARD MARINE INC
1250 N Grove St, Anaheim (92806-2130)
PHONE.............................714 666-2150
Jordan Angle, *CEO*
Joseph Nangle, *Mfg Staff*
Cole Christensen, *Sales Associate*
Karen Jacquelin, *Director*
Annie Summers, *Director*
▲ EMP: 55 EST: 1957
SQ FT: 45,000
SALES (est): 18MM **Privately Held**
WEB: www.willardmarine.com
SIC: 3732 Boats, fiberglass: building & repairing

(P-10476)
WINDWARD YACHT & REPAIR INC
Also Called: Windward Yacht Center
13645 Fiji Way, Venice (90292-6986)
PHONE.............................310 823-4581
Jacob Wood, *President*
Arlen Wood, *Vice Pres*
▲ EMP: 14 EST: 1976
SQ FT: 5,000
SALES (est): 1.9MM **Privately Held**
WEB: www.windwardyachtcenter.com
SIC: 3732 Boat building & repairing

3743 Railroad Eqpt

(P-10477)
KINKISHARYO INTERNATIONAL LLC (HQ)
1960 E Grand Ave Ste 1210, El Segundo
(90245-5061)
PHONE.............................424 276-1803
Hideki Hatai, *President*
Akiyoshi Oba, *President*
Hiroshi Okamoto, *CFO*
Masaya Wakuda, *Vice Pres*
William Covino, *Principal*
▲ EMP: 19 EST: 1999
SQ FT: 6,000
SALES (est): 86.2MM **Privately Held**
WEB: www.kinkisharyo.com
SIC: 3743 3321 Train cars & equipment, freight or passenger; railroad car wheels & brake shoes, cast iron

(P-10478)
PACIFIC GREEN TRUCKING INC
512 E C St, Wilmington (90744-6618)
PHONE.............................310 830-4528
Adrian Zarate, *CEO*
EMP: 13 EST: 2009
SALES (est): 2.6MM **Privately Held**
WEB: www.pacificgreentruckinginc.com
SIC: 3743 Freight cars & equipment

(P-10479)
WOOJIN IS AMERICA INC
12521 Mccann Dr, Santa Fe Springs
(90670-3338)
PHONE.............................626 386-0101
Sharon Peck, *President*
Rich Lee, *Administration*
▲ EMP: 13 EST: 2011
SALES (est): 7.3MM **Privately Held**
WEB: www.wjis.co.kr
SIC: 3743 4789 Railroad equipment; railroad maintenance & repair services
HQ: Woojin Industrial Systems Co., Ltd.
95 Sari-Ro, Sari-Myeon
Goesan 28046

3751 Motorcycles, Bicycles & Parts

(P-10480)
ALL AMERICAN RACERS INC
Also Called: Dan Gurneys All Amercn Racers
2334 S Broadway, Santa Ana
(92707-3250)
P.O. Box 2186 (92707-0186)
PHONE.............................714 557-2116
Daniel S Gurney, *CEO*
Justin B Gurney, *CEO*
Kathleen A Weida, *Vice Pres*
Kathy Weida, *Vice Pres*
Ellen La Bond, *Accountant*
EMP: 162 EST: 1962
SQ FT: 25,000
SALES (est): 36.2MM **Privately Held**
WEB: www.allamericanracers.com
SIC: 3751 Motorcycles & related parts

(P-10481)
B & E ENTERPRISES
1380 N Mccan St, Anaheim (92806-1316)
PHONE.............................714 630-3731
Michael Banister, *President*
Edward Miller, *Vice Pres*
EMP: 13 EST: 1982
SQ FT: 9,100
SALES (est): 2MM **Privately Held**
WEB: www.tubebender.com
SIC: 3751 3714 3599 Frames, motorcycle & bicycle; motor vehicle parts & accessories; machine shop, jobbing & repair

(P-10482)
BARNETT TOOL & ENGINEERING
Also Called: Barnett Performance Products
2238 Palma Dr, Ventura (93003-8068)
PHONE.............................805 642-9435
Michael Taylor, *President*
Colleen Taylor, *CFO*
Victor Ibarra, *Design Engr*
EMP: 60 EST: 1948
SQ FT: 43,000
SALES (est): 11.5MM **Privately Held**
WEB: www.barnettclutches.com
SIC: 3751 Motorcycle accessories; motorcycles & related parts

(P-10483)
BELT DRIVES LTD
Also Called: B D L
505 W Lambert Rd, Brea (92821-3909)
PHONE.............................714 693-1313
Steve R Yetzke, *CEO*
Kathy Yetzke, *Shareholder*
EMP: 21 EST: 1990
SQ FT: 30,000
SALES (est): 5.3MM **Privately Held**
WEB: www.beltdrives.com
SIC: 3751 Motorcycles & related parts

(P-10484)
BILLS PIPES INC
226 N Maple St, Corona (92878-4313)
PHONE.............................951 371-1329
EMP: 15
SQ FT: 4,500
SALES (est): 2.1MM **Privately Held**
WEB: www.billspipes.com
SIC: 3751 Motorcycles, Bicycles, And Parts, Nsk

(P-10485)
C C I REDLANDS INC
Also Called: CCI
721 Nevada St Ste 308, Redlands
(92373-8053)
P.O. Box 365 (92373-0121)
PHONE.............................909 307-6500
Michael E Lyon, *President*
Michael Lyon, *President*
Robert Lyon, *Vice Pres*
EMP: 20 EST: 1988
SALES (est): 1MM **Privately Held**
WEB: www.redlands.edu
SIC: 3751 5091 Bicycles & related parts; bicycle equipment & supplies

(P-10486)
CEE BAILEYS AIRCRAFT PLASTICS
6900 W Acco St, Montebello (90640-5435)
P.O. Box 1028 (90640-1028)
PHONE.................................323 721-4900
Jeff Johnston, *CEO*
Ken Faire, *Vice Pres*
Bryan Elliot, *Controller*
EMP: 14 **EST:** 1997
SQ FT: 5,000
SALES (est): 874.5K **Privately Held**
WEB: www.ceebaileys.com
SIC: 3751 3728 3089 Motorcycle accessories; aircraft parts & equipment; windows, plastic

(P-10487)
CULT/CVLT LLC
1555 E Saint Gertrude Pl, Santa Ana (92705-5309)
PHONE.................................714 435-2858
Robert Morales, *Principal*
▲ **EMP:** 16 **EST:** 2009
SALES (est): 1.1MM **Privately Held**
SIC: 3751 Motorcycles, bicycles & parts

(P-10488)
CURRIE ACQUISITIONS LLC
Also Called: Currie Technologies
3850 Royal Ave Ste A, Simi Valley (93063-3267)
PHONE.................................805 915-4900
Larry Pizzi, *Mng Member*
Bob Davis,
Sam Khoury,
EMP: 14 **EST:** 2008
SALES (est): 2.6MM
SALES (corp-wide): 606.6MM **Privately Held**
WEB: www.accelgroup.com
SIC: 3751 5012 8742 Motor scooters & parts; motor scooters; marketing consulting services
PA: Accell Group N.V.
Industrieweg 4
Heerenveen 8444
513 638-703

(P-10489)
DAYTEC CENTER LLC
Also Called: Jpm Finishing Company
17469 Lemon St, Hesperia (92345-5151)
P.O. Box 401328 (92340-1328)
PHONE.................................760 995-3515
Phil Day,
▲ **EMP:** 15 **EST:** 1991
SQ FT: 40,000
SALES (est): 788.7K **Privately Held**
WEB: www.daytec.com
SIC: 3751 3479 Frames, motorcycle & bicycle; coating of metals with plastic or resins

(P-10490)
FMF RACING
Also Called: Flying Machine Factory
18033 S Santa Fe Ave, Compton (90221-5514)
PHONE.................................310 631-4363
Don Emler, *CEO*
Brian McHale, *COO*
Richard King, *CTO*
Gerald Castillo, *Controller*
Daniel Beck, *Human Res Mgr*
▲ **EMP:** 150 **EST:** 1985
SALES (est): 32.2MM **Privately Held**
WEB: www.fmfracing.com
SIC: 3751 5571 Motorcycle accessories; motorcycle parts & accessories

(P-10491)
HEADWINDS
Also Called: Tradewinds
805 W Hillcrest Blvd, Monrovia (91016-1530)
PHONE.................................626 359-8044
Joel Felty, *Owner*
Julie Felty, *Co-Owner*
EMP: 13 **EST:** 1991
SALES (est): 1.6MM **Privately Held**
WEB: www.headwinds.com
SIC: 3751 3599 Motorcycle accessories; machine shop, jobbing & repair

(P-10492)
HIGH END SEATING SOLUTIONS LLC
1919 E Occidental St, Santa Ana (92705-5115)
PHONE.................................714 259-0177
Lars Roulund, *CEO*
Bob Doyle, *Vice Pres*
Brian Smith, *CIO*
Sharon Wells, *Purch Mgr*
EMP: 25 **EST:** 1998
SQ FT: 23,000
SALES (est): 1.6MM **Privately Held**
WEB: www.dannygray.com
SIC: 3751 Saddles & seat posts, motorcycle & bicycle

(P-10493)
IMS PRODUCTS INC
6240 Box Springs Blvd E, Riverside (92507-0748)
P.O. Box 1088, Banning (92220-0008)
PHONE.................................951 653-7720
C H Wheat, *President*
Chris Hardin, *General Mgr*
EMP: 16 **EST:** 1976
SQ FT: 10,000
SALES (est): 2.6MM **Privately Held**
WEB: www.imsproducts.com
SIC: 3751 5571 Motorcycles & related parts; motorcycle accessories; motorcycle dealers

(P-10494)
JIM ONEAL DISTRIBUTING INC
Also Called: O'Neal U S A
799 Camarillo Springs Rd, Camarillo (93012-9468)
PHONE.................................805 426-3300
Frank Kashare, *President*
Samantha Honnold, *Manager*
▲ **EMP:** 40 **EST:** 1970
SALES (est): 38MM **Privately Held**
WEB: www.oneal.com
SIC: 5571 3751 Motorcycle dealers; motorcycles, bicycles & parts

(P-10495)
K & N ENGINEERING INC (PA)
Also Called: K&N
1455 Citrus St, Riverside (92507-1603)
P.O. Box 1329 (92502-1329)
PHONE.................................951 826-4000
Richard Bisson, *CEO*
MO Ayad, *Vice Pres*
Russ Rowan, *Vice Pres*
Mary Brennan, *Executive Asst*
Cesar Torres, *Administration*
◆ **EMP:** 565 **EST:** 1964
SQ FT: 270,000
SALES (est): 140.5MM **Privately Held**
WEB: www.knfilters.com
SIC: 3751 3599 3714 Handle bars, motorcycle & bicycle; air intake filters, internal combustion engine, except auto; filters: oil, fuel & air, motor vehicle

(P-10496)
KRAFT/TECH INC
661 Arroyo St, San Fernando (91340-2219)
PHONE.................................818 837-3520
Javier Mendoza, *President*
Christian Ascencio, *Sales Executive*
▲ **EMP:** 16 **EST:** 1990
SQ FT: 40,000
SALES (est): 1.8MM **Privately Held**
WEB: www.krafttechinc.com
SIC: 3751 Motorcycle accessories

(P-10497)
LOADED BOARDS INC
10575 Virginia Ave, Culver City (90232-3520)
PHONE.................................310 839-1800
Don Tashman, *CEO*
Maria Alarcon, *Accounting Mgr*
Brian Dolen, *Mktg Dir*
Dan Briggs, *Sales Mgr*
Kyle Chin, *Marketing Staff*
◆ **EMP:** 17 **EST:** 2002
SQ FT: 5,500
SALES (est): 1.8MM **Privately Held**
WEB: www.loadedboards.com
SIC: 3751 Bicycles & related parts; frames, motorcycle & bicycle

(P-10498)
MARKLAND INDUSTRIES INC (PA)
1111 E Mcfadden Ave, Santa Ana (92705-4103)
PHONE.................................714 245-2850
Donald R Markland, *President*
▲ **EMP:** 223 **EST:** 1978
SQ FT: 100,000
SALES (est): 28.1MM **Privately Held**
WEB: www.marklandindustries.com
SIC: 3751 Motorcycle accessories

(P-10499)
PRO CIRCUIT PRODUCTS INC (PA)
Also Called: Pro Circuit Products & Racing
2771 Wardlow Rd, Corona (92882-2869)
PHONE.................................951 738-8050
Mitchell C Payton, *Principal*
◆ **EMP:** 20 **EST:** 1978
SALES (est): 7.6MM **Privately Held**
WEB: www.procircuit.com
SIC: 5571 3751 Motorcycle parts & accessories; motorcycles & related parts

(P-10500)
SEGWAY INC
2350 W Valley Blvd, Alhambra (91803-1930)
PHONE.................................603 222-6000
Luke Gao, *CEO*
Ye Wang, *President*
Jason Barton, *Officer*
Francis Bridges, *Vice Pres*
Chen Huang, *Vice Pres*
◆ **EMP:** 120 **EST:** 2000
SQ FT: 200,000
SALES (est): 16.5MM
SALES (corp-wide): 5MM **Privately Held**
WEB: www.segway.com
SIC: 3751 Motor scooters & parts
HQ: Nunn Bo (Tianjin) Technology Co., Ltd.
No.3, Tianrui Road, Qiche Industries Park, Wu Qing District
Tianjin 30170

(P-10501)
SPYKE INC
12155 Pangborn Ave, Downey (90241-5624)
PHONE.................................562 803-1700
Steve Campbell, *President*
◆ **EMP:** 20 **EST:** 1996
SQ FT: 15,000
SALES (est): 1MM **Privately Held**
WEB: www.pertronixbrands.com
SIC: 3751 Motorcycles, bicycles & parts

(P-10502)
SUPER73 INC (PA)
16591 Noyes Ave, Irvine (92606-5102)
PHONE.................................949 313-6340
Legrand Crewse, *CEO*
Lee Lucian, *Production*
Ashley Garin, *Sr Project Mgr*
Taylor Fiore, *Manager*
▼ **EMP:** 28 **EST:** 2016
SALES (est): 2.8MM **Privately Held**
WEB: www.super73.com
SIC: 3751 5012 Motorcycles, bicycles & parts; motorcycles

(P-10503)
T3 MOTION INC
425 Klug Cir, Corona (92878-5406)
PHONE.................................951 737-7300
Lucy LI, *CEO*
William Tsumpes, *COO*
EMP: 25 **EST:** 2016
SALES (est): 1.2MM **Privately Held**
WEB: www.t3motion.com
SIC: 3751 Motorcycles, bicycles & parts

(P-10504)
T3 MOTION INC
425 Klug Cir, Corona (92878-5406)
PHONE.................................909 737-7300
▲ **EMP:** 37
SALES (est): 5.4MM **Privately Held**
WEB: www.t3motion.com
SIC: 3751 Motorcycles, Bicycles, And Parts, Nsk

(P-10505)
TOLEMAR INC
Also Called: Tolemar Manufacturing
5221 Oceanus Dr, Huntington Beach (92649-1028)
PHONE.................................714 362-8166
Steve Ramelot, *CEO*
Joe Adkins, *Controller*
▲ **EMP:** 18 **EST:** 1994
SQ FT: 25,000
SALES (est): 3.2MM **Privately Held**
WEB: www.tolemar.com
SIC: 3751 Motorcycles & related parts; motorcycle accessories

(P-10506)
TRICO SPORTS INC
13541 Desmond St, Pacoima (91331-2301)
PHONE.................................818 899-7705
Paul Yates, *President*
George R Yates, *Vice Pres*
▲ **EMP:** 33 **EST:** 1988
SQ FT: 60,000
SALES (est): 574.8K **Privately Held**
WEB: www.tricosports.com
SIC: 3751 Bicycles & related parts; saddles & seat posts, motorcycle & bicycle

(P-10507)
TWO BROTHERS RACING INC
167 Via Trevizio, Corona (92879-1773)
PHONE.................................714 550-6070
Craig A Erion, *President*
James Saechao, *Sales Staff*
Robert Salazar, *Manager*
◆ **EMP:** 18 **EST:** 1985
SALES (est): 4.9MM **Privately Held**
WEB: www.twobros.com
SIC: 3751 5013 Motorcycles & related parts; motorcycle parts

(P-10508)
V&H PERFORMANCE LLC
Also Called: Vance & Hines
13861 Rosecrans Ave, Santa Fe Springs (90670-5207)
PHONE.................................562 921-7461
Andrew Graves, *CEO*
Byron Hines, *Shareholder*
Mike Kennedy, *President*
Ken Draper, *Vice Pres*
Terry Vance, *Vice Pres*
▼ **EMP:** 65 **EST:** 1980
SQ FT: 12,000
SALES (est): 31.3MM
SALES (corp-wide): 251.1MM **Privately Held**
WEB: www.vanceandhines.com
SIC: 3751 5013 Motorcycles, bicycles & parts; motorcycle parts
PA: Motorsport Aftermarket Group, Inc.
13861 Rosecrans Ave
Santa Fe Springs CA 90670
917 838-4002

(P-10509)
WESTERN MFG & DISTRG LLC
Also Called: I.V. League Medical
835 Flynn Rd, Camarillo (93012-8702)
P.O. Box 7192, Rancho Santa Fe (92067-7192)
PHONE.................................805 988-1010
Bill Nichols,
Ryan Nichols, *Safety Mgr*
Donnell Nichols,
Zenaida Monima, *Manager*
EMP: 40 **EST:** 1970
SQ FT: 25,000
SALES (est): 4.8MM **Privately Held**
WEB: www.westernmanufacturinganddistributing.com
SIC: 3751 3841 3599 Motorcycles & related parts; motorcycle accessories; surgical & medical instruments; machine shop, jobbing & repair

(P-10510)
WILSON CYCLES SPORTS CORP
Also Called: CJ Wilson BMW Mtcyc Murrieta
26145 Jefferson Ave # 205, Murrieta (92562-9500)
PHONE.................................951 894-5545
George Berta, *General Mgr*
Sarah Galin, *Principal*

EMP: 21 EST: 2015
SALES (est): 2.1MM **Privately Held**
WEB: www.bmwgroup.com
SIC: 5511 3751 7699 Automobiles, new &
used; motorcycle accessories; motorcycle
repair service

(P-10511)
ZERO GRAVITY CORPORATION
Also Called: Zero Gravity Group
912 Pancho Rd Ste A, Camarillo
(93012-8597)
PHONE..............................805 388-8803
Glenn Cook, *President*
Langness Garrett, *Sales Dir*
◆ EMP: 35 EST: 1986
SQ FT: 2,800
SALES (est): 4.8MM **Privately Held**
WEB: www.zerogravity-racing.com
SIC: 3751 Motorcycle accessories

3761 Guided Missiles & Space Vehicles

(P-10512)
ABL SPACE SYSTEMS COMPANY
224 Oregon St, El Segundo (90245-4214)
P.O. Box 1608 (90245-6608)
PHONE..............................424 321-5049
Harrison O'Hanley, *CEO*
Dan Piemont, *CFO*
Daniel Piemont, *CFO*
Jacob Trudell-Lozano, *Technician*
Patrick Wilczynski, *Engineer*
EMP: 60 EST: 2017
SALES (est): 27.5MM **Privately Held**
WEB: www.ablspacesystems.com
SIC: 3761 Guided missiles & space vehi-
cles; space vehicles, complete

(P-10513)
BOEING COMPANY
14441 Astronautics Ln, Huntington Beach
(92647-2080)
PHONE..............................714 896-3311
James McNerney, *Branch Mgr*
R Gale Schluter, *Vice Pres*
Will Trafton, *Vice Pres*
Mike McAninch, *Engineer*
EMP: 368
SQ FT: 2,200,000
SALES (corp-wide): 58.1B **Publicly Held**
WEB: www.boeing.com
SIC: 3761 3769 Guided missiles & space
vehicles; guided missile & space vehicle
parts & auxiliary equipment
PA: The Boeing Company
100 N Riverside Plz
Chicago IL 60606
312 544-2000

(P-10514)
GALACTIC CO LLC (DH)
Also Called: Spaceship Company, The
16555 Spceship Landing Wa, Mojave
(93501-1534)
PHONE..............................661 824-6600
Michael Colglazier, *CEO*
Jon Campagna, *CFO*
Stephanie Ruiz, *Officer*
Enrico Palermo, *Vice Pres*
Tom Pugh, *Vice Pres*
EMP: 356 EST: 2006
SQ FT: 200,000
SALES (est): 94.4MM **Publicly Held**
SIC: 3761 Rockets, space & military, com-
plete

(P-10515)
MASTEN SPACE SYSTEMS INC
1570 Sabovich St 25, Mojave
(93501-1681)
PHONE..............................661 824-3423
Joel Scotkin, *CEO*
Shawn Mahoney, *COO*
David Masten, *CTO*
EMP: 25 EST: 2004
SQ FT: 6,000
SALES (est): 5.1MM **Privately Held**
WEB: www.masten-space.com
SIC: 3761 Guided missiles & space vehi-
cles

(P-10516)
ROCKET LAB USA INC
3881 Mcgowen St, Long Beach
(90808-1702)
PHONE..............................714 465-5737
Peter Beck, *Ch of Bd*
Adam Spice, *CFO*
Shaun O'Donnell, *Exec VP*
Andrew Bunker, *Vice Pres*
EMP: 592 EST: 2006
SALES (est): 35.1MM **Privately Held**
SIC: 3761 Guided missiles & space vehi-
cles; guided missiles & space vehicles,
research & development; rockets, space
& military, complete; space vehicles, com-
plete

(P-10517)
SPACE EXPLORATION TECH CORP
Also Called: Spacex
2700 Miner St, San Pedro (90731)
PHONE..............................714 330-8668
EMP: 48
SALES (corp-wide): 2B **Privately Held**
WEB: www.spacex.com
SIC: 3761 Rockets, space & military, com-
plete
PA: Space Exploration Technologies Corp.
1 Rocket Rd
Hawthorne CA 90250
310 363-6000

(P-10518)
SPACE EXPLORATION TECH CORP (PA)
Also Called: Spacex
1 Rocket Rd, Hawthorne (90250-6844)
PHONE..............................310 363-6000
Elon Musk, *CEO*
Gwynne Shotwell, *President*
Bret Johnsen, *CFO*
Richard Barnes, *Vice Pres*
Bob Reagan, *Vice Pres*
◆ EMP: 6389 EST: 2002
SQ FT: 964,000
SALES (est): 2B **Privately Held**
WEB: www.spacex.com
SIC: 3761 Rockets, space & military, com-
plete

(P-10519)
SPACEX LLC
12533 Crenshaw Blvd, Hawthorne
(90250-3302)
PHONE..............................310 970-5845
Brandon Rocco, *Partner*
Efrain Murillo, *Comp Tech*
Richard Perez, *Comp Tech*
Bruno Battolla, *Technician*
Nadia Castellanos, *Technician*
EMP: 302 EST: 2004
SALES (est): 8.4MM
SALES (corp-wide): 2B **Privately Held**
WEB: www.spacex.com
SIC: 3761 Guided missiles & space vehi-
cles
PA: Space Exploration Technologies Corp.
1 Rocket Rd
Hawthorne CA 90250
310 363-6000

(P-10520)
STELLAR EXPLORATION INC
835 Airport Dr, San Luis Obispo
(93401-8370)
PHONE..............................805 459-1425
Tomas Svitek, *President*
Iva Svitek, *Admin Sec*
Richard Barnes, *CIO*
Benjamin Scheinberg, *Design Engr*
Michael Erberich, *Engineer*
EMP: 21 EST: 2001
SQ FT: 3,000
SALES (est): 4.3MM **Privately Held**
WEB: www.stellar-exploration.com
SIC: 3761 Space vehicles, complete

(P-10521)
TAYCO ENGINEERING INC
10874 Hope St, Cypress (90630-5214)
P.O. Box 6034 (90630-0034)
PHONE..............................714 952-2240
Jay Chung, *President*
Ann Taylor, *COO*

Sheri T Nikolakopulos, *CFO*
Brent Taylor, *Vice Pres*
Lisa Taylor, *VP Bus Dvlpt*
EMP: 130 EST: 1971
SQ FT: 55,600
SALES (est): 15.8MM **Privately Held**
WEB: www.taycoeng.com
SIC: 3761 Guided missiles & space vehi-
cles

(P-10522)
TERRAN ORBITAL CORPORATION (PA)
15330 Barranca Pkwy, Irvine (92618-2215)
PHONE..............................212 496-2300
Anthony Previte, *CEO*
Jordi Puig-Suari, *Admin Sec*
EMP: 30 EST: 2014
SALES (est): 25.1MM **Privately Held**
WEB: www.terranorbital.com
SIC: 3761 3764 Space vehicles, complete;
guided missiles & space vehicles, re-
search & development; guided missile &
space vehicle engines, research & devel.

(P-10523)
TYVAK NN-SATELLITE SYSTEMS INC
15330 Barranca Pkwy, Irvine (92618-2215)
PHONE..............................949 753-1020
Christian Becker, *CEO*
Marco Villa, *COO*
Tiffany Atkins, *Officer*
Todd Mosher, *Vice Pres*
Matthew Gann, *Program Mgr*
EMP: 75 EST: 2011
SALES (est): 25.1MM **Privately Held**
WEB: www.tyvak.com
SIC: 3761 3764 Space vehicles, complete;
guided missiles & space vehicles, re-
search & development; guided missile &
space vehicle propulsion unit parts;
guided missile & space vehicle engines,
research & devel.
PA: Terran Orbital Corporation
15330 Barranca Pkwy
Irvine CA 92618
212 496-2300

(P-10524)
UNITED LAUNCH ALLIANCE LLC
1579 Utah Ave Bldg 7525, Vandenberg Afb
(93437)
PHONE..............................303 269-5876
Deborah Settit, *Principal*
Bill Sobczak, *Engineer*
Marshall Robbins, *Agent*
EMP: 215 **Privately Held**
WEB: www.ulalaunch.com
SIC: 3761 Guided missiles & space vehi-
cles
PA: United Launch Alliance, L.L.C.
9501 E Panorama Cir
Centennial CO 80112

(P-10525)
VENTURI ASTROLAB INC
12536 Chadron Ave, Hawthorne
(90250-4808)
PHONE..............................310 989-1264
Jaret Matthews, *CEO*
Tobias Ziegler, *Principal*
EMP: 13 EST: 2019
SALES (est): 2MM **Privately Held**
WEB: www.venturiastrolab.com
SIC: 3761 Guided missiles & space vehi-
cles

(P-10526)
VIRGIN ORBIT LLC (PA)
4022 E Conant St, Long Beach
(90808-1777)
PHONE..............................562 384-4400
Dan Hart Became, *CEO*
Dan Hart, *President*
Derrick Boston, *Officer*
Jon Campagna, *Vice Pres*
Mauricio Pena, *Vice Pres*
EMP: 583 EST: 2016
SQ FT: 150,000

SALES (est): 112.1MM **Privately Held**
WEB: www.virginorbit.com
SIC: 3761 3764 Guided missiles & space
vehicles; guided missile & space vehicle
propulsion unit parts

3764 Guided Missile/Space Vehicle Propulsion Units & parts

(P-10527)
MICROCOSM INC
3111 Lomita Blvd, Torrance (90505-5108)
PHONE..............................310 219-2700
James Wertz, *President*
Alice Wertz, *Corp Secy*
Dr Robert E Conger, *Vice Pres*
EMP: 40 EST: 1984
SQ FT: 50,000
SALES (est): 6MM **Privately Held**
WEB: www.smad.com
SIC: 3764 2731 3769 Guided missile &
space vehicle propulsion unit parts; book
publishing; guided missile & space vehi-
cle parts & auxiliary equipment

(P-10528)
PHASE FOUR INC
129 Sierra St, El Segundo (90245-4118)
PHONE..............................310 648-8454
Jonathan Jarvis, *CEO*
Jason Wallace, *Vice Pres*
Mazzin Ajamia, *Electrical Engi*
Austin Prater, *Engineer*
Robert Yegiazaryan, *Engineer*
EMP: 17 EST: 2015
SALES (est): 2.6MM **Privately Held**
WEB: www.phasefour.io
SIC: 3764 Guided missile & space vehicle
propulsion unit parts

(P-10529)
RELATIVITY SPACE INC
3500 E Burnett St, Long Beach
(90815-1730)
PHONE..............................424 393-4309
Timothy Ellis, *CEO*
Muhammad Shahzad, *CFO*
Alexander Kwan, *Vice Pres*
Caryn Schenewerk, *Vice Pres*
Jordan Noone, *CTO*
EMP: 376 EST: 2015
SQ FT: 10,000
SALES (est): 47.7MM **Privately Held**
WEB: www.relativityspace.com
SIC: 3764 7389 Guided missile & space
vehicle propulsion unit parts;

3769 Guided Missile/Space Vehicle Parts & Eqpt, NEC

(P-10530)
AMERICAN AUTOMATED ENGRG INC
Also Called: A A E Aerospace & Coml Tech
5382 Argosy Ave, Huntington Beach
(92649-1037)
PHONE..............................714 898-9951
Kenneth Christensen, *President*
Paihan Lee, *General Mgr*
EMP: 85 EST: 1967
SQ FT: 48,000
SALES (est): 26MM **Privately Held**
SIC: 3769 Guided missile & space vehicle
parts & auxiliary equipment

(P-10531)
CLIFFDALE MANUFACTURING LLC
Also Called: RTC Aerospace
20409 Prairie St, Chatsworth (91311-6029)
PHONE..............................818 341-3344
Brad Hart, *CEO*
Jerry Koger, *President*
Jerry Hill, *Vice Pres*
Tj Marshall, *Vice Pres*
Kelly Meier, *Manager*
EMP: 200 EST: 1943
SQ FT: 42,000

SALES (est): 16.8MM Privately Held
WEB: www.rtcaerospace.com
SIC: 3769 3599 Guided missile & space vehicle parts & auxiliary equipment; machine shop, jobbing & repair

(P-10532)
DW AND BB CONSULTING INC
11381 Bradley Ave, Pacoima (91331-2358)
PHONE...................................818 896-9899
David Wyckoff, President
Lee Brown, CFO
Ben Bensal, Vice Pres
Cynthia Ramirez, Human Res Mgr
Brandon Bell, Opers Staff
EMP: 70 EST: 1989
SQ FT: 10,000
SALES (est): 8.8MM Privately Held
WEB: www.kdlprecision.com
SIC: 3769 2822 3061 Guided missile & space vehicle parts & auxiliary equipment; silicone rubbers; oil & gas field machinery rubber goods (mechanical)

(P-10533)
HYDROMACH INC
20400 Prairie St, Chatsworth (91311-8129)
PHONE...................................818 341-0915
Norberto A Cusinato, CEO
Jos A Nicosia, Vice Pres
Jos Nicosia, Vice Pres
Jose Nicosia, Vice Pres
Anna M Cusinato, Admin Sec
EMP: 64 EST: 1976
SQ FT: 23,000
SALES (est): 5.6MM Privately Held
WEB: www.hydromach.com
SIC: 3769 3599 Guided missile & space vehicle parts & auxiliary equipment; machine shop, jobbing & repair

(P-10534)
LEDA CORPORATION
7080 Kearny Dr, Huntington Beach (92648-6254)
PHONE...................................714 841-7821
Joseph K Tung, President
David Tung, Vice Pres
David C Tung, Vice Pres
Dorothy Tung, Vice Pres
EMP: 30 EST: 1985
SQ FT: 15,000
SALES (est): 6.3MM Privately Held
WEB: www.ledacorp.net
SIC: 3769 Guided missile & space vehicle parts & aux eqpt, rsch & dev

(P-10535)
MICRO STEEL INC
7850 Alabama Ave, Canoga Park (91304-4905)
PHONE...................................818 348-8701
Lazar Hersko, President
Claudia Sceelo, Vice Pres
Tova Hersko, Admin Sec
EMP: 25 EST: 1986
SQ FT: 14,500 Privately Held
WEB: www.microsteel.net
SIC: 3769 Guided missile & space vehicle parts & auxiliary equipment

(P-10536)
STANFORD MU CORPORATION
Also Called: Airborne Components
20725 Annalee Ave, Carson (90746-3503)
PHONE...................................310 605-2888
Stanford Mu, President
Robert Friend, Exec VP
Lynn Price, Vice Pres
Edgar Maldonado, Project Engr
Anders Nilarp, Buyer
EMP: 40 EST: 1992
SALES (est): 7.5MM Privately Held
WEB: www.stanfordmu.com
SIC: 3769 3764 7699 Guided missile & space vehicle parts & auxiliary equipment; guided missile & space vehicle propulsion unit parts; propulsion units for guided missiles & space vehicles; aircraft & heavy equipment repair services

(P-10537)
VANTAGE ASSOCIATES INC (PA)
12333 Los Nietos Rd, Santa Fe Springs (90670-2911)
PHONE...................................619 477-6940

Mary Normand, CEO
Eric Clack, President
Andrea Alpinieri Glover, CFO
Mark Seaver, General Mgr
Jess Jimenez, Human Res Dir
EMP: 35 EST: 1980
SQ FT: 15,000
SALES (est): 30.5MM Privately Held
WEB: www.vantageassoc.com
SIC: 3769 2821 3728 3083 Guided missile & space vehicle parts & auxiliary equipment; plastics materials & resins; aircraft parts & equipment; laminated plastics plate & sheet

---

3792 Travel Trailers & Campers

(P-10538)
CARSON TRAILER INC (PA)
Also Called: Carson Trailer Sales
14831 S Maple Ave, Gardena (90248-1935)
PHONE...................................310 835-0876
William Modisette, President
Kevin Felber, Manager
Derik Sicard, Manager
EMP: 100 EST: 1991
SALES (est): 33MM Privately Held
WEB: www.carsontrailer.com
SIC: 5599 3792 Utility trailers; travel trailers & campers

(P-10539)
CUSTOM FIBREGLASS MFG CO
Also Called: Custom Hardtops
1711 Harbor Ave, Long Beach (90813-1300)
PHONE...................................562 432-5454
Hartmut W Schroeder, President
Joel Thiefburg, CFO
Robert L Edwards, Senior VP
Pete Lopa, Production
◆ EMP: 165 EST: 1966
SQ FT: 135,000
SALES (est): 32MM
SALES (corp-wide): 1.3B Privately Held
WEB: www.snugtop.com
SIC: 3792 Pickup covers, canopies or caps
HQ: Truck Accessories Group, Llc
28858 Ventura Dr
Elkhart IN 46517
574 522-5337

(P-10540)
FLEETWOOD TRAVEL TRLRS IND INC (DH)
3125 Myers St, Riverside (92503-5527)
P.O. Box 7638 (92513-7638)
PHONE...................................951 354-3000
Edward B Caudill, President
Boyd R Plowman, CFO
Lyle N Larkin, Treasurer
Christopher J Braun, Senior VP
Forrest D Theobald, Senior VP
EMP: 100 EST: 1971
SQ FT: 262,900
SALES (est): 10.2MM Privately Held
WEB: www.daytonatraveltrailers.com
SIC: 3792 Travel trailers & campers
HQ: Fleetwood Enterprises, Inc.
1351 Pomona Rd Ste 230
Corona CA 92882
951 354-3000

(P-10541)
FLEETWOOD TRAVEL TRLRS OF MD (DH)
3125 Myers St, Riverside (92503-5527)
P.O. Box 7638 (92513-7638)
PHONE...................................951 351-3500
Elden L Smith, President
Lyle N Larkin, Treasurer
Christopher J Braun, Senior VP
Forrest D Theobald, Senior VP
▲ EMP: 100 EST: 1969
SQ FT: 262,900
SALES (est): 5MM Privately Held
SIC: 3792 Travel trailers & campers
HQ: Fleetwood Enterprises, Inc.
1351 Pomona Rd Ste 230
Corona CA 92882
951 354-3000

(P-10542)
KENDON INDUSTRIES LLC
2990 E Miraloma Ave, Anaheim (92806-1807)
PHONE...................................714 630-7144
Frank Esposito, Mng Member
EMP: 20 EST: 2014
SALES (est): 10.1MM Privately Held
WEB: www.kendonusa.com
SIC: 5561 3792 Travel trailers: automobile, new & used; travel trailers & campers

(P-10543)
LIN CONSULTING LLC
Also Called: Airstream of Orange County
15086 Beach Blvd, Midway City (92655-1414)
PHONE...................................714 650-8595
Margaret Bayston, CEO
Ira Cohen, Principal
Ken Kaiden, Principal
Kent Caden, Manager
Dale Johnson, Manager
EMP: 20 EST: 2000
SALES (est): 5.3MM Privately Held
SIC: 3792 4725 Travel trailers & campers; tour operators

(P-10544)
MVP RV INC
40 E Verdugo Ave, Burbank (91502-1931)
PHONE...................................951 848-4288
Brad Williams, President
Pablo Carmona, COO
Roger Humeston, CFO
▲ EMP: 20 EST: 1996
SALES (est): 1.6MM Privately Held
SIC: 3792 Travel trailer chassis

(P-10545)
PACIFIC COACHWORKS INC
3411 N Perris Blvd Bldg 1, Perris (92571-3100)
PHONE...................................951 686-7294
Brett Bashaw, CEO
Michael Rhodes, Admin Sec
EMP: 155 EST: 2006
SALES (est): 27.6MM Privately Held
WEB: www.pacificcoachworks.com
SIC: 3792 Travel trailers & campers

(P-10546)
PROTO HOMES LLC
917 W 17th St, Los Angeles (90015-3317)
PHONE...................................310 271-7544
Frank Vafaee,
Garden Carpio, Office Mgr
Annaliza Larosa, Comptroller
Zachary Toering, Sales Staff
EMP: 40 EST: 2009
SQ FT: 8,000
SALES (est): 9MM Privately Held
WEB: www.protohomes.com
SIC: 3792 House trailers, except as permanent dwellings

(P-10547)
SHADOW INDUSTRIES INC
Also Called: Shadow Trailers
8941 Electric St, Cypress (90630-2240)
PHONE...................................714 995-4353
Fritz Stanley Owner, President
Petra Stanley, Director
EMP: 14 EST: 1990
SQ FT: 2,804 Privately Held
WEB: www.shadowtrailers.com
SIC: 3792 5599 Travel trailers & campers; utility trailers

3795 Tanks & Tank Components

(P-10548)
TIGER TANKS INC
3397 Edison Hwy, Bakersfield (93307-2234)
P.O. Box 21041 (93390-1041)
PHONE...................................661 363-8335
Toll Free:.............................888 -
Robert E Bimat, Ch of Bd
Darryck Selk, President
Bryan Lewis, CFO
Roger Burns, Vice Pres

Carol Bimat, Admin Sec
EMP: 30
SQ FT: 55,000
SALES (est): 5.9MM Privately Held
WEB: www.tigertanksinc.com
SIC: 3795 3443 Tanks & tank components; fabricated plate work (boiler shop)

3799 Transportation Eqpt, NEC

(P-10549)
DG PERFORMANCE SPC INC
4100 E La Palma Ave, Anaheim (92807-1814)
PHONE...................................714 961-8850
Mark W Dooley, President
William J Dooley, Ch of Bd
Joan K Dooley, Corp Secy
EMP: 100 EST: 1972
SQ FT: 25,000
SALES (est): 15.8MM Privately Held
WEB: www.dgperformance.com
SIC: 3799 3751 5012 5961 Recreational vehicles; motorcycles & related parts; recreation vehicles, all-terrain; fitness & sporting goods, mail order; motor vehicle parts & accessories; carburetors, pistons, rings, valves

(P-10550)
FLEETWOOD ENTERPRISES INC (DH)
1351 Pomona Rd Ste 230, Corona (92882-7165)
PHONE...................................951 354-3000
Nelson Potter, President
Christopher J Braun, Exec VP
Paul C Eskritt, Exec VP
Charley Lott, Exec VP
Todd L Inlander, Senior VP
EMP: 866 EST: 1950
SALES (est): 1.9B Privately Held
WEB: www.americanindustrial.com
SIC: 3799 2451 5561 Recreational vehicles; mobile homes; recreational vehicle parts & accessories

(P-10551)
GENESIS SUPREME RV INC (PA)
23129 Cajalco Rd, Perris (92570-7298)
PHONE...................................951 337-0254
Pablo Carmona, CEO
Sarah Johnson, Purchasing
EMP: 43 EST: 2012
SALES (est): 3MM Privately Held
WEB: www.genesissupremerv.com
SIC: 3799 Recreational vehicles

(P-10552)
HALL ASSOCIATES RACG PDTS INC
23104 Normandie Ave, Torrance (90502-2619)
PHONE...................................310 326-4111
Ammie Armstrong, CEO
Kennith C Hall, President
Amy Armstrong, COO
EMP: 17 EST: 1995
SQ FT: 7,000
SALES (est): 2.4MM Privately Held
WEB: www.hallassociatesmachine.com
SIC: 3799 8733 3699 Recreational vehicles; research institute; security devices

(P-10553)
NATIONAL SIGNAL INC
2440 Artesia Ave, Fullerton (92833-2543)
PHONE...................................714 441-7707
Marcos Fernandez, President
Lupe Mertinez, Vice Pres
Luis Jonas, Purch Mgr
Daniel Beurrier, Prdtn Mgr
Peggy Lominac, Cust Mgr
◆ EMP: 50 EST: 1971
SQ FT: 55,000
SALES (est): 12.8MM Privately Held
WEB: www.nationalsignalinc.net
SIC: 3799 Trailers & trailer equipment

(P-10554)
PREMIER TRAILER MFG INC
30517 Ivy Rd, Visalia (93291-9553)
P.O. Box 191 (93279-0191)
PHONE....................................559 651-2212
Gene A Cuelho Jr, *President*
Sally Cuelho, *Admin Sec*
EMP: 39 **EST:** 1996
SALES (est): 8.7MM **Privately Held**
SIC: 3799 Trailers & trailer equipment

(P-10555)
RAUDMANS CRAIG VICTORY CIRCLE
Also Called: Victory Circle Chassis & Parts
700 S Mount Vernon Ave # 10, Bakersfield
(93307-2893)
PHONE....................................661 833-4600
Les Denherder, *President*
Susan Denherder, *Vice Pres*
Marc Lundgren, *General Mgr*
Craig Raudman, *Assistant VP*
EMP: 21 **EST:** 1995
SQ FT: 47,000
SALES (est): 544.9K **Privately Held**
WEB: www.victorycircle.com
SIC: 5531 3799 Automotive parts; recreational vehicles

(P-10556)
UNIVERSAL TRAILERS INC
2750 Mulberry St, Riverside (92501-2531)
PHONE....................................951 784-0543
Nghiem Nguyen, *Principal*
Thuan Nguyen, *Principal*
EMP: 21 **EST:** 1999
SQ FT: 22,000
SALES (est): 1.9MM **Privately Held**
WEB: www.universaltrailers.com
SIC: 3799 5599 Trailers & trailer equipment; utility trailers

(P-10557)
WEBTEZ INC
Also Called: Modvans
1679 Donlon St Ste 202, Ventura
(93003-8302)
PHONE....................................805 856-6585
Pj Tezza, *President*
EMP: 16 **EST:** 2012
SALES (est): 2.2MM **Privately Held**
WEB: www.modvans.com
SIC: 3799 Recreational vehicles

3812 Search, Detection, Navigation & Guidance Systs & Instrs

(P-10558)
ACCUTURN CORPORATION
7189 Old 215 Frontage Rd, Moreno Valley
(92553-7903)
PHONE....................................951 656-6621
Ignatius C Araujo, *CEO*
Henri Rahmon, *Shareholder*
Mark Sayegh, *Shareholder*
Iggy Araujo, *President*
Connie Spencer, *Manager*
EMP: 26 **EST:** 1974
SQ FT: 15,000
SALES (est): 6.3MM **Privately Held**
WEB: www.accuturninc.com
SIC: 3812 3089 3599 Acceleration indicators & systems components, aerospace; automotive parts, plastic; machine shop, jobbing & repair

(P-10559)
AERO CHIP INTGRTED SYSTEMS INC
13565 Freeway Dr, Santa Fe Springs
(90670-5633)
PHONE....................................310 329-8600
Solomon M Gavrila, *President*
Solomon Gavrila, *Vice Pres*
Liviu Pribac, *Vice Pres*
George Varghese, *QC Mgr*
EMP: 13 **EST:** 2011
SQ FT: 50,000
SALES (est): 3MM **Privately Held**
WEB: www.aerochip.com
SIC: 3812 Acceleration indicators & systems components, aerospace

(P-10560)
AEROANTENNA TECHNOLOGY INC
20732 Lassen St, Chatsworth
(91311-4507)
PHONE....................................818 993-3842
Yosef Klein, *President*
Joe Klein, *President*
Carmela Klein, *Admin Sec*
▲ **EMP:** 140
SALES (est): 35.6MM **Publicly Held**
WEB: www.aeroantenna.com
SIC: 3663 Antennas, radar or communications; antennas, transmitting & communications
HQ: Heico Electronic Technologies Corp.
3000 Taft St
Hollywood FL 33021
954 987-6101

(P-10561)
AEROJET RCKETDYNE HOLDINGS INC (PA)
222 N Pcf Cast Hwy Ste 50, El Segundo
(90245)
P.O. Box 537012, Sacramento (95853-7012)
PHONE....................................310 252-8100
Eileen P Drake, *President*
Warren G Lichtenstein, *Ch of Bd*
Amy Gowder, *COO*
Daniel L Boehle, *CFO*
Huseyin Gulcu, *Treasurer*
EMP: 75 **EST:** 1915
SALES (est): 2B **Publicly Held**
WEB: www.aerojetrocketdyne.com
SIC: 3812 3764 3769 6552 Defense systems & equipment; propulsion units for guided missiles & space vehicles; guided missile & space vehicle parts & auxiliary equipment; subdividers & developers; real property lessors

(P-10562)
ALLIANT TCHSYSTEMS OPRTONS LLC
21250 Califa St, Woodland Hills
(91367-5001)
PHONE....................................818 887-8185
EMP: 33 **Publicly Held**
WEB: www.northropgrumman.com
SIC: 3812 Search & navigation equipment
HQ: Alliant Techsystems Operations Llc
2980 Fairview Park Dr
Falls Church VA 22042

(P-10563)
ALLIANT TCHSYSTEMS OPRTONS LLC
9401 Corbin Ave, Northridge (91324-2400)
PHONE....................................818 887-8195
Ronald Hill, *Principal*
Humberto De La Cruz, *Engineer*
EMP: 400 **EST:** 2002
SALES (est): 214.1MM **Publicly Held**
WEB: www.northropgrumman.com
SIC: 3812 Search & navigation equipment
HQ: Northrop Grumman Innovation Systems, Inc.
45101 Warp Dr
Dulles VA 20166

(P-10564)
ALLIANT TCHSYSTEMS OPRTONS LLC
9401 Corbin Ave, Northridge (91324-2400)
PHONE....................................818 887-8195
Albert Calabrese, *President*
EMP: 33 **Publicly Held**
WEB: www.northropgrumman.com
SIC: 3812 Search & navigation equipment
HQ: Alliant Techsystems Operations Llc
2980 Fairview Park Dr
Falls Church VA 22042

(P-10565)
AMETEK AMERON LLC
4750 Littlejohn St, Baldwin Park
(91706-2274)
PHONE....................................626 337-4640
EMP: 35
SALES (corp-wide): 3.5B **Publicly Held**
SIC: 3812 Mfg& Dist Aviation Products
HQ: Ametek Ameron, Llc
4750 Littlejohn St
Baldwin Park CA 91706
626 337-4640

(P-10566)
ANDURIL INDUSTRIES INC (PA)
2722 Michelson Dr Ste 150, Irvine
(92612-8904)
PHONE....................................949 891-1607
Brian Schimpf, *CEO*
Matthew Grimm, *COO*
Jadon Smith, *Engineer*
Phil Hall, *VP Finance*
Babak Siavoshy, *General Counsel*
EMP: 128 **EST:** 2017
SQ FT: 155,000
SALES (est): 25.2MM **Privately Held**
WEB: www.anduril.com
SIC: 3812 Search & navigation equipment

(P-10567)
APEX TECHNOLOGY HOLDINGS INC
Also Called: Apex Design Technology
2850 E Coronado St, Anaheim
(92806-2503)
PHONE....................................321 270-3630
Lance Schroeder, *President*
EMP: 513 **EST:** 2005
SQ FT: 80,000
SALES (est): 52.3MM **Privately Held**
WEB: www.apexholdings.tech
SIC: 3812 Acceleration indicators & systems components, aerospace

(P-10568)
ARETE ASSOCIATES (PA)
9301 Corbin Ave Ste 2000, Northridge
(91324-2508)
PHONE....................................818 885-2200
David Campion, *President*
Christopher Choi, *CFO*
Sallie Di Vincenzo,
Doug Deprospo, *Security Dir*
Mariana Genzman, *Admin Asst*
EMP: 125 **EST:** 1975
SQ FT: 170,000
SALES (est): 100MM **Privately Held**
WEB: www.arete.com
SIC: 3812 3827 Aircraft/aerospace flight instruments & guidance systems; sighting & fire control equipment, optical

(P-10569)
ARMTEC COUNTERMEASURES CO (DH)
85901 Avenue 53, Coachella (92236-2607)
PHONE....................................760 398-0143
Paul Heidenreich, *Vice Pres*
Freeman Swank, *Vice Pres*
Blanca Villagomez, *Admin Asst*
Mayela Daza, *Database Admin*
Miguel Ortega, *Design Engr*
◆ **EMP:** 227 **EST:** 2002
SQ FT: 100,000
SALES (est): 79.6MM
SALES (corp-wide): 4.8B **Publicly Held**
WEB: www.armtecdefense.com
SIC: 3812 Defense systems & equipment

(P-10570)
ASCENT AEROSPACE
1395 S Lyon St, Santa Ana (92705-4608)
PHONE....................................586 726-0500
Tanner Hansler, *Program Mgr*
Graham Mitchell, *Program Mgr*
Jim Sewell, *Program Mgr*
Jim Stanley, *Program Mgr*
Mario Castro, *Prgrmr*
EMP: 30 **EST:** 2020
SALES (est): 6.2MM **Privately Held**
WEB: www.ascentaerospace.com
SIC: 3812 Search & navigation equipment

(P-10571)
ATK SPACE SYSTEMS LLC (DH)
Also Called: Space Components
6033 Bandini Blvd, Commerce
(90040-2968)
PHONE....................................323 722-0222
Blake Larson, *President*
Daniel J Murphy, *CEO*
Ronald D Dittemore, *Senior VF*
James Armor, *Vice Pres*
Thomas R Wilson, *Vice Pres*
◆ **EMP:** 50 **EST:** 1963
SQ FT: 104,000
SALES (est): 722.6MM **Publicly Held**
WEB: www.northropgrumman.com
SIC: 3812 Search & navigation equipment

(P-10572)
ATK SPACE SYSTEMS LLC
600 Pine Ave, Goleta (93117-3803)
PHONE....................................805 685-2262
Blake Larson, *CEO*
Mark Marley, *Senior Buyer*
EMP: 100 **Publicly Held**
WEB: www.northropgrumman.com
SIC: 3812 Search & navigation equipment
HQ: Atk Space Systems Llc
6033 Bandini Blvd
Commerce CA 90040
323 722-0222

(P-10573)
ATK SPACE SYSTEMS LLC
1960 E Grand Ave Ste 1150, El Segundo
(90245-5166)
PHONE....................................310 343-3799
Dale Woolheater, *Branch Mgr*
Lee Cardenas, *Manager*
EMP: 100 **Publicly Held**
WEB: www.northropgrumman.com
SIC: 3812 Search & navigation equipment
HQ: Atk Space Systems Llc
6033 Bandini Blvd
Commerce CA 90040
323 722-0222

(P-10574)
BOEING SATELLITE SYSTEMS
2060 E Imperial Hwy Fl 1, E Segundo
(90245-3507)
PHONE....................................310 364-5088
EMP: 54
SALES (corp-wide): 96.1B **Publicly Held**
SIC: 3812 Mfg Search/Navigation Equipment
HQ: Boeing Satellite Systems International, Inc.
2260 E Imperial Hwy
El Segundo CA 90245
310 364-4000

(P-10575)
CAL-SENSORS INC (PA)
1260 Calle Suerte, Camarillo (93012-8053)
PHONE....................................707 303-3837
Craig A Hindman, *CEO*
Jane Howard, *General Mgr*
Uksun Hong, *Engineer*
Stewart Miller, *Engineer*
Karen Nissim, *Controller*
EMP: 38 **EST:** 1986
SQ FT: 14,800
SALES (est): 2.7MM **Privately Held**
WEB: www.optodiode.com
SIC: 3812 3674 Infrared object detection equipment; semiconductors & related devices

(P-10576)
COMPUTATIONAL SENSORS CORP
1042 Via Los Padres, Santa Barbara
(93111-1345)
PHONE....................................805 962-1175
EMP: 22 **EST:** 1999
SQ FT: 5,500
SALES: 3MM **Privately Held**
SIC: 3812 Mfg Search/Navigation Equipment

(P-10577)
CONDOR PACIFIC INDUSTRIES INC (PA)
905 Rancho Conejo Blvd, Newbury Park (91320-1716)
PHONE..................818 889-2150
Sidney Meltzner, *President*
David Axelrad, *General Mgr*
Chris Persico, *Chief Engr*
Cher Gibson, *Program Dir*
EMP: 34 **EST:** 2006
SALES (est): 5.6MM **Privately Held**
WEB: www.condorpacific.com
SIC: 3812 3728 Gyroscopes; aircraft parts & equipment

(P-10578)
CONSOLIDATED AEROSPACE MFG LLC (HQ)
Also Called: CAM
1425 S Acacia Ave, Fullerton (92831-5317)
PHONE..................714 989-2797
Dave Werner, *Mng Member*
Jordan Law,
EMP: 114 **EST:** 2012
SALES (est): 312.2MM
SALES (corp-wide): 14.5B **Publicly Held**
WEB: www.camaerospace.com
SIC: 3812 Search & navigation equipment
PA: Stanley Black & Decker, Inc.
1000 Stanley Dr
New Britain CT 06053
860 225-5111

(P-10579)
CPP IND
16800 Chestnut St, City of Industry (91748-1017)
PHONE..................909 595-2252
Alan Hill, *President*
EMP: 45 **EST:** 2010
SALES (est): 729.2K **Privately Held**
WEB: www.cppcorp.com
SIC: 3812 Acceleration indicators & systems components, aerospace

(P-10580)
CRANE AEROSPACE INC
Crane Aerospace & Electronics
3000 Winona Ave, Burbank (91504-2540)
PHONE..................818 526-2600
Brendan Curran, *President*
Bob Tavares, *President*
Gregg Robison, *Vice Pres*
Ben Hager, *Business Dir*
Douglas Hilderbrand, *Administration*
EMP: 21
SALES (corp-wide): 2.9B **Publicly Held**
WEB: www.craneco.com
SIC: 3812 Defense systems & equipment
HQ: Crane Aerospace, Inc.
100 Stamford Pl
Stamford CT 06902

(P-10581)
DC-001 INC
Also Called: Spartan
10541 Calle Lee Ste 125, Los Alamitos (90720-6784)
PHONE..................833 526-5332
Nathan Mintz, *Principal*
EMP: 14 **EST:** 2020
SALES (est): 465.5K **Privately Held**
SIC: 3812 Radar systems & equipment

(P-10582)
DECA INTERNATIONAL CORP
Also Called: Golf Buddy
10700 Norwalk Blvd, Santa Fe Springs (90670-3824)
PHONE..................714 367-5900
Seung Wook Jung, *CEO*
Chris Bartlow, *Sales Staff*
▲ **EMP:** 28 **EST:** 2005
SQ FT: 3,000
SALES (est): 4.9MM **Privately Held**
SIC: 3812 Navigational systems & instruments

(P-10583)
DG ENGINEERING CORP (PA)
Also Called: Schulz Engineering
13326 Ralston Ave, Sylmar (91342-7608)
PHONE..................818 364-9024
Gary Gilmore, *Ch of Bd*
Aret Demiral, *President*
▲ **EMP:** 29 **EST:** 1973
SQ FT: 7,000
SALES (est): 5.5MM **Privately Held**
WEB: www.dge-corp.com
SIC: 3812 3845 Aircraft control systems, electronic; electromedical equipment

(P-10584)
EARTHWISE BAG COMPANY INC
2819 Burton Ave, Burbank (91504-3224)
PHONE..................818 847-2174
Stanley Ekstrom, *President*
Lisa Garcia, *Executive Asst*
Ana Sintop, *Bookkeeper*
Don Borders, *Marketing Staff*
Kris Gates, *Manager*
EMP: 16 **EST:** 2006
SALES (est): 3.1MM **Privately Held**
WEB: www.earthwisebags.com
SIC: 3812 Cabin environment indicators

(P-10585)
EATON AEROSPACE LLC
E E M C O Div
2905 Winona Ave, Burbank (91504-2539)
PHONE..................818 550-4200
John H Morris, *Branch Mgr*
EMP: 111
SALES (corp-wide): 385.8MM **Privately Held**
WEB: www.eaton.com
SIC: 3812 3621 Acceleration indicators & systems components, aerospace; motors, electric
PA: Eaton Aerospace Llc
1000 Eaton Blvd
Cleveland OH 44122
216 523-5000

(P-10586)
EATON AEROSPACE LLC
9650 Jeronimo Rd, Irvine (92618-2024)
PHONE..................949 452-9500
Lily Bridenbaker, *Manager*
EMP: 25
SALES (corp-wide): 385.8MM **Privately Held**
WEB: www.eaton.com
SIC: 3812 3365 Acceleration indicators & systems components, aerospace; aerospace castings, aluminum
PA: Eaton Aerospace Llc
1000 Eaton Blvd
Cleveland OH 44122
216 523-5000

(P-10587)
ENSIGN-BICKFORD AROSPC DEF CO
14370 White Sage Rd, Moorpark (93021-8720)
P.O. Box 429 (93020-0429)
PHONE..................805 292-4000
Brendan Walsh, *Vice Pres*
Allison Loudon, *Program Mgr*
Robin Neeley, *Purch Mgr*
Cindy O 'connell, *Buyer*
EMP: 26
SALES (corp-wide): 696.3MM **Privately Held**
WEB: www.ebad.com
SIC: 3812 Search & navigation equipment
HQ: Ensign-Bickford Aerospace & Defense Co
640 Hopmeadow St
Simsbury CT 06070
860 843-2289

(P-10588)
FIRAN TECH GROUP USA CORP (HQ)
20750 Marilla St, Chatsworth (91311-4407)
PHONE..................818 407-4024
Brad Bourne, *President*
David Nelson, *Engineer*
Heather Levesque,
Jon Johnson, *Director*
William Porter, *Manager*
EMP: 106 **EST:** 2004
SALES (est): 46.7MM
SALES (corp-wide): 77.4MM **Privately Held**
WEB: www.ftgcorp.com
SIC: 3812 Aircraft control systems, electronic
PA: Firan Technology Group Corporation
250 Finchdene Sq
Toronto ON M1X 1
416 299-4000

(P-10589)
GARMIN INTERNATIONAL INC
135 S State College Blvd # 110, Brea (92821-5819)
PHONE..................909 444-5000
Bertrand Tignon, *Engineer*
Tyler Conrad, *Manager*
EMP: 89
SALES (corp-wide): 3.7B **Privately Held**
WEB: www.garmin.com
SIC: 3812 Navigational systems & instruments
HQ: Garmin International, Inc.
1200 E 151st St
Olathe KS 66062

(P-10590)
GOLDAK INC
15835 Monte St Ste 104, Sylmar (91342-7674)
P.O. Box 1988, Glendale (91209-1988)
PHONE..................818 240-2666
Dan Mulcahey, *President*
Jeanie Mulcahey, *CFO*
Thomas Mulcahey, *CFO*
Butch Mulcahey, *Vice Pres*
Chris Sanford, *General Mgr*
EMP: 25 **EST:** 1970
SQ FT: 3,000
SALES (est): 2.5MM **Privately Held**
WEB: www.goldak.com
SIC: 3812 Detection apparatus: electronic/magnetic field, light/heat

(P-10591)
INTELLISENSE SYSTEMS INC
21041 S Western Ave, Torrance (90501-1727)
PHONE..................310 320-1827
Frank Willis, *President*
Juan F Hodelin, *Vice Pres*
Chris Ulmer, *Vice Pres*
Jack McParlane, *Business Dir*
Jimmy Almodovar, *IT/INT Sup*
EMP: 146 **EST:** 2017
SQ FT: 43,000
SALES: 38.7MM **Privately Held**
WEB: www.intellisenseinc.com
SIC: 3812 Search & navigation equipment

(P-10592)
JARIET TECHNOLOGIES INC
103 W Torrance Blvd, Redondo Beach (90277-3633)
PHONE..................310 698-1001
Charles Harper, *CEO*
Trevor Roots, *CFO*
David Clark, *Vice Pres*
Monica Gilbert, *Vice Pres*
Matthew Hoppe, *Vice Pres*
EMP: 35 **EST:** 2015
SQ FT: 20,000
SALES (est): 5MM **Privately Held**
WEB: www.jariettech.com
SIC: 3812 Search & navigation equipment

(P-10593)
JEDCO INC
23529 Castle Rock, Mission Viejo (92692-1894)
PHONE..................949 699-2974
Marcel Cordi, *Principal*
David Gross, *Design Engr*
Jake Ernst, *Project Engr*
Eric Koster, *Engineer*
Larry Sharp, *Engineer*
EMP: 29 **EST:** 2010
SALES (est): 376.7K **Privately Held**
WEB: www.jedinc.com
SIC: 3812 Aircraft/aerospace flight instruments & guidance systems

(P-10594)
JENNINGS AERONAUTICS LLC
831 Buckley Rd, San Luis Obispo (93401-8130)
PHONE..................805 544-0932
John Purvis, *CEO*
Gordon Jennings, *President*
Samual Miller, *General Mgr*
Cameron Chapman, *Electrical Engi*
Elias Sullwold, *Engineer*
EMP: 41 **EST:** 1989
SQ FT: 19,000
SALES (est): 7.7MM
SALES (corp-wide): 1B **Privately Held**
WEB: www.jenaero.com
SIC: 3812 7371 3721 Electronic detection systems (aeronautical); aircraft control systems, electronic; defense systems & equipment; computer software development & applications; computer software development; aircraft
HQ: Uav Factory Usa, Llc
2777 Nw Lolo Dr Ste 130
Bend OR 97703
541 678-0515

(P-10595)
KRATOS INSTRUMENTS LLC
Also Called: Kratos Pressure Products
2201 Alton Pkwy, Irvine (92606-5033)
PHONE..................949 660-0666
Lewis Wise, *Principal*
Michael J Rogerson, *Plant Mgr*
EMP: 14 **EST:** 2014
SALES (est): 3.2MM **Privately Held**
SIC: 3812 Search & navigation equipment

(P-10596)
L3 TECHNOLOGIES INC
Ocean Systems Division
28022 Industry Dr, Valencia (91355-4191)
PHONE..................818 833-2500
Alex Miseirvitch, *Vice Pres*
Don Davis, *Vice Pres*
Jon Piatt, *Vice Pres*
John Tierney, *Vice Pres*
Robert Coates, *VP Bus Dvlpt*
EMP: 200
SALES (corp-wide): 18.1B **Publicly Held**
WEB: www.l3harris.com
SIC: 3812 Search & navigation equipment
HQ: L3 Technologies, Inc.
600 3rd Ave Fl 34
New York NY 10016
321 727-9100

(P-10597)
L3HARRIS TECHNOLOGIES INC
7821 Orion Ave, Van Nuys (91406-2029)
P.O. Box 7713 (91409-7713)
PHONE..................818 901-2523
J Malloy, *Vice Pres*
EMP: 350
SALES (corp-wide): 18.1B **Publicly Held**
WEB: www.l3harris.com
SIC: 3812 Search & navigation equipment
PA: L3harris Technologies, Inc.
1025 W Nasa Blvd
Melbourne FL 32919
321 727-9100

(P-10598)
LOCKHEED MARTIN CORPORATION
Also Called: Lockheed Martin Aeronautics Co
1011 Lockheed Way, Palmdale (93599-0001)
PHONE..................661 572-7428
Rick Baker, *Vice Pres*
John Petersen, *Project Mgr*
Jeffrey Doran, *Engineer*
Jermaine Mazant, *Engineer*
Jim Nicolas, *Engineer*
EMP: 4000 **Publicly Held**
WEB: www.lockheedmartin.com
SIC: 3812 Search & navigation equipment
PA: Lockheed Martin Corporation
6801 Rockledge Dr
Bethesda MD 20817

P
R
O
D
U
C
T
S

&

S
V
C
S

(P-10599)
MILLENNIUM SPACE SYSTEMS
INC (HQ)
2265 E El Segundo Blvd, El Segundo
(90245-4608)
PHONE......................................310 683-5840
Stan Dubyn, *CEO*
Tiffany Guthrie, *COO*
Laura White, *CFO*
EMP: 32 **EST:** 2001
SQ FT: 10,000
SALES (est): 67MM
SALES (corp-wide): 58.1B **Publicly Held**
WEB: www.millennium-space.com
SIC: 3812 Search & navigation equipment
PA: The Boeing Company
100 N Riverside Plz
Chicago IL 60606
312 544-2000

(P-10600)
MOOG INC
21339 Nordhoff St, Chatsworth
(91311-5819)
PHONE......................................818 341-5156
Ruben Nalbandian, *Engineer*
John Hoop, *Technician*
Phil Scott, *Technology*
Carmen Aguilar, *Engineer*
Robert Berning, *Engineer*
EMP: 150
SALES (corp-wide): 2.8B **Publicly Held**
WEB: www.moog.com
SIC: 3812 Aircraft control systems, electronic
PA: Moog Inc.
400 Jamison Rd
Elma NY 14059
716 652-2000

(P-10601)
MOOG INC
7406 Hollister Ave, Goleta (93117-2583)
PHONE......................................805 618-3900
Robert W Urban, *General Mgr*
Chris Leslie, *Program Mgr*
EMP: 300
SALES (corp-wide): 2.8B **Publicly Held**
WEB: www.moog.com
SIC: 3812 3492 3625 3769 Aircraft control systems, electronic; electrohydraulic servo valves, metal; relays & industrial controls; guided missile & space vehicle parts & auxiliary equipment; aircraft parts & equipment; motors & generators
PA: Moog Inc.
400 Jamison Rd
Elma NY 14059
716 652-2000

(P-10602)
MOOG INC
Also Called: Moog Aircraft Group
20263 S Western Ave, Torrance
(90501-1310)
PHONE......................................310 533-1178
Alberto Bilalon, *Manager*
Kraig Kayser, *COO*
Tim Baptist, *Administration*
Wilma Whitley, *Info Tech Mgr*
Tom Elwell, *Technology*
EMP: 450
SALES (corp-wide): 2.8B **Publicly Held**
WEB: www.moog.com
SIC: 3812 Search & navigation equipment
PA: Moog Inc.
400 Jamison Rd
Elma NY 14059
716 652-2000

(P-10603)
MTI DE BAJA INC
915 Industrial Way, San Jacinto
(92582-3890)
PHONE......................................951 654-2333
Monty Merkin, *CEO*
Mike Merkin, *Vice Pres*
EMP: 22 **EST:** 2009
SALES (est): 2.9MM **Privately Held**
WEB: www.mtibaja.com
SIC: 3812 Acceleration indicators & systems components, aerospace

(P-10604)
NAVCOM DEFENSE
ELECTRONICS INC (PA)
9129 Stellar Ct, Corona (92883-4924)
PHONE......................................951 268-9205
Clifford C Christ, *President*
David Eliasson, *CFO*
EMP: 45 **EST:** 1932
SQ FT: 61,000
SALES (est): 7MM **Privately Held**
WEB: www.navcom.com
SIC: 3812 Navigational systems & instruments

(P-10605)
NORTHROP GRMMAN INNVTION
SYSTE
9401 Corbin Ave, Northridge (91324-2400)
PHONE......................................818 887-8100
Bill J Zimmer, *Principal*
Brian Simon, *Chief Engr*
Judy Cho, *Analyst*
Steve Connell, *Manager*
Ed Dantes, *Manager*
EMP: 100 **Publicly Held**
WEB: www.northropgrumman.com
SIC: 3812 Search & navigation equipment
HQ: Northrop Grumman Innovation Systems, Inc.
45101 Warp Dr
Dulles VA 20166

(P-10606)
NORTHROP GRUMMAN
CORPORATION
Northrop Grumman Aviation
1 Hornet Way, El Segundo (90245-2804)
PHONE......................................310 332-1000
Ray Pollok, *Manager*
Badar Farooquee, *Officer*
Tim Frei, *Vice Pres*
Richard G Matthews, *Vice Pres*
Sam Badwan, *Executive*
EMP: 200 **Publicly Held**
WEB: www.northropgrumman.com
SIC: 3812 Search & navigation equipment
PA: Northrop Grumman Corporation
2980 Fairview Park Dr
Falls Church VA 22042

(P-10607)
NORTHROP GRUMMAN INTL INC
Also Called: Northrop Grumman Aerospace
2420 Santa Fe Ave, Redondo Beach
(90278-1115)
PHONE......................................310 812-4321
Txomin Presilla, *Project Engr*
EMP: 21 **Publicly Held**
WEB: www.northropgrumman.com
SIC: 3812 Radar systems & equipment
HQ: Northrop Grumman International, Inc.
2980 Fairview Park Dr
Falls Church VA 22042

(P-10608)
NORTHROP GRUMMAN INTL
TRDG INC
21240 Burbank Blvd, Woodland Hills
(91367-6680)
PHONE......................................818 715-3607
Tina Davis, *Administration*
EMP: 455 **EST:** 2014
SALES (est): 16.4MM **Publicly Held**
WEB: www.northropgrumman.com
SIC: 3812 Search & navigation equipment
HQ: Northrop Grumman International, Inc.
2980 Fairview Park Dr
Falls Church VA 22042

(P-10609)
NORTHROP GRUMMAN
SYSTEMS CORP
6411 W Imperial Hwy, Los Angeles
(90045-6307)
PHONE......................................310 556-4911
Mark Shea, *Principal*
EMP: 303 **Publicly Held**
WEB: www.northropgrumman.com
SIC: 3812 Search & navigation equipment

HQ: Northrop Grumman Systems Corporation
2980 Fairview Park Dr
Falls Church VA 22042
703 280-2900

(P-10610)
NORTHROP GRUMMAN
SYSTEMS CORP
Litton Navigation Systems Div
21240 Burbank Blvd Ms29, Woodland Hills
(91367-6680)
PHONE......................................818 715-4040
Bill Allison, *Division Pres*
Patricia Slater, *Program Mgr*
Cammy Reynoso, *Executive Asst*
Jim Kemp, *Admin Asst*
David Kesachekian, *Technology*
EMP: 1000 **Publicly Held**
WEB: www.northropgrumman.com
SIC: 3812 Search & navigation equipment
HQ: Northrop Grumman Systems Corporation
2980 Fairview Park Dr
Falls Church VA 22042
703 280-2900

(P-10611)
NORTHROP GRUMMAN
SYSTEMS CORP
1 Hornet Way Dept Mt00w5, El Segundo
(90245-2804)
PHONE......................................310 632-1846
Richard A Lautzenheiser, *Manager*
Kenneth L Bedingfield, *Vice Pres*
Randy Agura, *General Mgr*
Agura Randy, *General Mgr*
Leticia Razo, *General Mgr*
EMP: 200 **Publicly Held**
WEB: www.northropgrumman.com
SIC: 3812 Search & navigation equipment
HQ: Northrop Grumman Systems Corporation
2980 Fairview Park Dr
Falls Church VA 22042
703 280-2900

(P-10612)
NORTHROP GRUMMAN
SYSTEMS CORP
2601 Camino Del Sol, Oxnard
(93030-7996)
PHONE......................................805 684-6641
Kathy Warden, *CEO*
Richard Nelson, *President*
Alice Reed, *President*
Michael Chow, *Engineer*
Miller Kristen, *Recruiter*
EMP: 110 **EST:** 1999
SQ FT: 70,000
SALES (est): 35.8MM **Publicly Held**
WEB: www.northropgrumman.com
SIC: 3812 Search & navigation equipment
HQ: Northrop Grumman Systems Corporation
2980 Fairview Park Dr
Falls Church VA 22042
703 280-2900

(P-10613)
NORTHROP GRUMMAN
SYSTEMS CORP
2700 Camino Del Sol, Oxnard
(93030-7967)
PHONE......................................805 278-2074
Pierre Courduroux, *Branch Mgr*
Roman Reyes, *Analyst*
EMP: 200 **Publicly Held**
WEB: www.northropgrumman.com
SIC: 3812 Aircraft/aerospace flight instruments & guidance systems
HQ: Northrop Grumman Systems Corporation
2980 Fairview Park Dr
Falls Church VA 22042
703 280-2900

(P-10614)
NORTHROP GRUMMAN
SYSTEMS CORP
California Microwave Systems
21200 Burbank Blvd, Woodland Hills
(91367-6675)
PHONE......................................818 715-2597
Roy Medlin, *Opers Mgr*

Lisle Sherwin, *Engineer*
EMP: 200 **Publicly Held**
WEB: www.northropgrumman.com
SIC: 3812 Search & navigation equipment
HQ: Northrop Grumman Systems Corporation
2980 Fairview Park Dr
Falls Church VA 22042
703 280-2900

(P-10615)
NORTHROP GRUMMAN
SYSTEMS CORP
Bldg 806, Fort Irwin (92310)
PHONE......................................760 380-4268
EMP: 200 **Publicly Held**
WEB: www.northropgrumman.com
SIC: 3812 Search & navigation equipment
HQ: Northrop Grumman Systems Corporation
2980 Fairview Park Dr
Falls Church VA 22042
703 280-2900

(P-10616)
NORTHROP GRUMMAN
SYSTEMS CORP
Also Called: Weapons System Division
9401 Corbin Ave, Northridge (91324-2400)
PHONE......................................818 887-8110
Richard Nolan, *Branch Mgr*
Alice Reed, *Principal*
Cesar Dominguez, *Design Engr*
Daniel Ray, *Engineer*
Brian Simon, *Chief Engr*
EMP: 200 **Publicly Held**
WEB: www.northropgrumman.com
SIC: 3812 Search & navigation equipment
HQ: Northrop Grumman Systems Corporation
2980 Fairview Park Dr
Falls Church VA 22042
703 280-2900

(P-10617)
NORTHROP GRUMMAN
SYSTEMS CORP
6033 Bandini Blvd, Commerce
(90040-2968)
PHONE......................................714 240-6521
Alice Reed, *Principal*
Jocelyn Mendoza, *Engineer*
EMP: 200 **Publicly Held**
WEB: www.northropgrumman.com
SIC: 3812 Aircraft/aerospace flight instruments & guidance systems
HQ: Northrop Grumman Systems Corporation
2980 Fairview Park Dr
Falls Church VA 22042
703 280-2900

(P-10618)
NORTHROP GRUMMAN
SYSTEMS CORP
600 Pine Ave, Goleta (931 7-3803)
PHONE......................................714 240-6521
Alice Reed, *Principal*
EMP: 200 **Publicly Held**
WEB: www.northropgrumman.com
SIC: 3812 Aircraft/aerospace flight instruments & guidance systems
HQ: Northrop Grumman Systems Corporation
2980 Fairview Park Dr
Falls Church VA 22042
703 280-2900

(P-10619)
NORTHROP GRUMMAN
SYSTEMS CORP
2401 E El Segundo Blvd, El Segundo
(90245-4631)
PHONE......................................480 355-7716
Alice Reed, *Principal*
EMP: 200 **Publicly Held**
WEB: www.northropgrumman.com
SIC: 3812 Aircraft/aerospace flight instruments & guidance systems
HQ: Northrop Grumman Systems Corporation
2980 Fairview Park Dr
Falls Church VA 22042
703 280-2900

(P-10620)
NORTHROP GRUMMAN SYSTEMS CORP
Strategic Deterrent Systems
1467 Fairway Dr, Santa Maria
(93455-1404)
PHONE...................805 315-5728
EMP: 200 Publicly Held
WEB: www.northropgrumman.com
SIC: **3812** Inertial guidance systems
HQ: Northrop Grumman Systems Corporation
2980 Fairview Park Dr
Falls Church VA 22042
703 280-2900

(P-10621)
NORTHROP GRUMMAN SYSTEMS CORP
2550 Honolulu Ave, Montrose
(91020-1858)
PHONE...................818 249-5252
Arthur F Brown, *Enginr/R&D Mgr*
EMP: 200 Publicly Held
WEB: www.northropgrumman.com
SIC: **3812** Search & navigation equipment
HQ: Northrop Grumman Systems Corporation
2980 Fairview Park Dr
Falls Church VA 22042
703 280-2900

(P-10622)
NORTHROP GRUMMAN SYSTEMS CORP
Also Called: Northrop Grmman Elctrnic Syste
1100 W Hollyvale St, Azusa (91702-3305)
P.O. Box 296 (91702-0296)
PHONE...................626 812-1000
Carl Fischer, *Manager*
Benson Wu, *Administration*
James Lott, *Sr Ntwrk Engine*
Tatiana Armal, *Software Engr*
William Salinas, *Software Engr*
EMP: 200 Publicly Held
WEB: www.northropgrumman.com
SIC: **3812** Search & navigation equipment
HQ: Northrop Grumman Systems Corporation
2980 Fairview Park Dr
Falls Church VA 22042
703 280-2900

(P-10623)
NORTHROP GRUMMAN SYSTEMS CORP
Western Region
3520 E Avenue M, Palmdale (93550-7401)
PHONE...................661 540-0446
Jim Pace, *Branch Mgr*
EMP: 200 Publicly Held
WEB: www.northropgrumman.com
SIC: **3812** Search & navigation equipment
HQ: Northrop Grumman Systems Corporation
2980 Fairview Park Dr
Falls Church VA 22042
703 280-2900

(P-10624)
NORTHROP GRUMMAN SYSTEMS CORP
2477 Manhattan Beach Blvd, Redondo
Beach (90278-1544)
PHONE...................310 812-4321
Bruce R Gerding, *Vice Pres*
Herbert Sims, *Director*
EMP: 200 Publicly Held
WEB: www.northropgrumman.com
SIC: **3812** Search & navigation equipment
HQ: Northrop Grumman Systems Corporation
2980 Fairview Park Dr
Falls Church VA 22042
703 280-2900

(P-10625)
NORTHROP GRUMMAN SYSTEMS CORP
1111 W 3rd St, Azusa (91702-3328)
PHONE...................626 812-1464
Michael Clayton, *Manager*
EMP: 200 Publicly Held
WEB: www.northropgrumman.com

SIC: **3812** Search & navigation equipment
HQ: Northrop Grumman Systems Corporation
2980 Fairview Park Dr
Falls Church VA 22042
703 280-2900

(P-10626)
NORTHROP GRUMMAN SYSTEMS CORP
1 Hornet Way, El Segundo (90245-2804)
PHONE...................310 332-1000
Kevin Witherell, *Principal*
Jerry Edwards, *Manager*
EMP: 200 Publicly Held
WEB: www.northropgrumman.com
SIC: **3812** Search & navigation equipment
HQ: Northrop Grumman Systems Corporation
2980 Fairview Park Dr
Falls Church VA 22042
703 280-2900

(P-10627)
NORTHROP GRUMMAN SYSTEMS CORP
Also Called: Technical Services
862 E Hospitality Ln, San Bernardino
(92408-3530)
PHONE...................703 713-4096
Ben Overall, *Manager*
EMP: 200 Publicly Held
WEB: www.northropgrumman.com
SIC: **3812** Search & navigation equipment
HQ: Northrop Grumman Systems Corporation
2980 Fairview Park Dr
Falls Church VA 22042
703 280-2900

(P-10628)
NORWICH AERO PRODUCTS INC (DH)
6900 Orangethorpe Ave B, Buena Park
(90620-1390)
P.O. Box 109, Norwich NY (13815-0109)
PHONE...................607 336-7636
Curtis Reusser, *CEO*
Roger Alan Ross, *President*
Robert D George, *CFO*
Christoper Ainsworth, *VP Opers*
EMP: 24 EST: 1983
SQ FT: 56,000
SALES (est): 10.2MM
SALES (corp-wide): 4.8B Publicly Held
WEB: www.transdigm.com
SIC: **3812 3829 3823** Search & navigation equipment; measuring & controlling devices; temperature instruments: industrial process type
HQ: Esterline Technologies Corp
1301 E 9th St Ste 3000
Cleveland OH 44114
216 706-2960

(P-10629)
ONE STEP GPS LLC
675 Glenoaks Blvd Unit C, San Fernando
(91340-4803)
PHONE...................818 659-2031
Ryan Dale,
Kevin Kenneth Dale,
EMP: 28 EST: 2017
SALES (est): 3.2MM Privately Held
WEB: www.onestepgps.com
SIC: **3812** Search & navigation equipment

(P-10630)
ORBITAL SCIENCES LLC
Also Called: Space Systems Division
2401 E El Segundo Blvd, El Segundo
(90245-4631)
PHONE...................703 406-5000
Antonio Elias, *Exec VP*
Antonio L Elias, *Exec VP*
EMP: 343 Publicly Held
WEB: www.northropgrumman.com
SIC: **3812** Search & navigation equipment
HQ: Orbital Sciences Llc
2980 Fairview Park Dr
Falls Church VA 22042

(P-10631)
ORBITAL SCIENCES LLC
1151 W Reeves Ave, Ridgecrest
(93555-2313)
PHONE...................818 887-8345
David Rocca, *Branch Mgr*
EMP: 343 Publicly Held
WEB: www.northropgrumman.com
SIC: **3812** Search & navigation equipment
HQ: Orbital Sciences Llc
2980 Fairview Park Dr
Falls Church VA 22042

(P-10632)
ORBITAL SCIENCES LLC
Talo Rd Bldg 1555, Lompoc (93437)
P.O. Box 5159, Vandenberg Afb (93437-0159)
PHONE...................805 734-5400
Eric Denbrook, *Manager*
EMP: 343 Publicly Held
WEB: www.northropgrumman.com
SIC: **3812** Search & navigation equipment
HQ: Orbital Sciences Llc
2980 Fairview Park Dr
Falls Church VA 22042

(P-10633)
PACIFIC SCIENTIFIC COMPANY (DH)
Also Called: Electro Kinetics Division
1785 Voyager Ave, Simi Valley
(93063-3363)
PHONE...................805 526-5700
James Simpkins, *Principal*
James Healey, *General Mgr*
David Penner, *Finance Dir*
◆ **EMP: 23 EST: 1998**
SALES (est): 200.4MM
SALES (corp-wide): 2.2B Privately Held
WEB: www.hachultra.com
SIC: **3812 3669 3621 3694** Aircraft control systems, electronic; fire detection systems, electric; generators & sets, electric; motors, electric; servomotors, electric; alternators, automotive; water quality monitoring & control systems; control equipment, electric
HQ: Meggitt-Usa, Inc.
1955 Surveyor Ave
Simi Valley CA 93063
805 526-5700

(P-10634)
PANEL PRODUCTS INC
21818 S Wilmington Ave # 411, Long Beach
(90810-1642)
PHONE...................310 830-3331
Nabil Abdou, *CEO*
Sherine Attia, *Vice Pres*
Gerges Khalil, *Engineer*
Ken Patton, *Engineer*
Sherry Sidarous,
EMP: 20 EST: 1999
SALES (est): 4.7MM Privately Held
WEB: www.panelproductsinc.com
SIC: **3812** Aircraft control instruments

(P-10635)
PNEUDRAULICS INC
8575 Helms Ave, Rancho Cucamonga
(91730-4591)
PHONE...................909 980-5366
Michael Saville, *CEO*
Dain Miller, *President*
Antonio Gamez, *Technician*
Craig Aunchman, *Design Engr*
Ralph Palomino, *Design Engr*
▼ **EMP: 275 EST: 1956**
SQ FT: 48,000
SALES (est): 52.1MM
SALES (corp-wide): 4.8B Publicly Held
WEB: www.pneudraulics.com
SIC: **3812** Acceleration indicators & systems components, aerospace
PA: Transdigm Group Incorporated
1301 E 9th St Ste 3000
Cleveland OH 44114
216 706-2960

(P-10636)
RANTEC MICROWAVE SYSTEMS INC (PA)
31186 La Baya Dr, Westlake Village
(91362-4003)
PHONE...................818 223-5000
Carl Grindle, *CEO*
Carl E Grindle, *CEO*
Steven Chegwin, *CFO*
Steven B Chegwin, *Treasurer*
Graham R Wilson, *Admin Sec*
EMP: 55
SQ FT: 35,000
SALES (est): 12.5MM Privately Held
WEB: www.rantecantennas.com
SIC: **3812** Antennas, radar or communications

(P-10637)
RAYTHEON COMPANY
1921 Mariposa St, El Segundo (90245)
PHONE...................310 647-1000
David Wajsgras, *Branch Mgr*
Kenny Loo, *Engineer*
BAC Tran, *Engineer*
EMP: 100
SALES (corp-wide): 56.5B Publicly Held
WEB: www.rtx.com
SIC: **3812 4899** Sonar systems & equipment; satellite earth stations
HQ: Raytheon Company
870 Winter St
Waltham MA 02451
781 522-3000

(P-10638)
RAYTHEON COMPANY
1801 Hughes Dr, Fullerton (92833-2200)
P.O. Box 902, El Segundo (90245-0902)
PHONE...................714 446-2584
John Coarse, *Branch Mgr*
John Panetta, *Executive*
Moses Sun, *Program Mgr*
Tiep Tran, *Sr Software Eng*
David Heine, *Info Tech Mgr*
EMP: 15
SALES (corp-wide): 56.5B Publicly Held
WEB: www.rtx.com
SIC: **3812** Sonar systems & equipment
HQ: Raytheon Company
870 Winter St
Waltham MA 02451
781 522-3000

(P-10639)
RAYTHEON COMPANY
2000 E El Segundo Blvd, El Segundo
(90245-4501)
PHONE...................310 647-1000
John Jones, *Manager*
Crystal Daley, *Officer*
Joan Procopio, *Officer*
Jeff Wolske, *Vice Pres*
Bill Balcer, *Program Mgr*
EMP: 500
SALES (corp-wide): 56.5B Publicly Held
WEB: www.rtx.com
SIC: **3812** Defense systems & equipment
HQ: Raytheon Company
870 Winter St
Waltham MA 02451
781 522-3000

(P-10640)
RAYTHEON COMPANY
2000 E El Segundo Blvd, El Segundo
(90245-4501)
P.O. Box 902 (90245-0902)
PHONE...................310 647-9438
Rick Yuse, *Branch Mgr*
EMP: 10000
SALES (corp-wide): 56.5B Publicly Held
WEB: www.rtx.com
SIC: **3812** Defense systems & equipment
HQ: Raytheon Company
870 Winter St
Waltham MA 02451
781 522-3000

(P-10641)
ROGERSON AIRCRAFT CORPORATION (PA)
16940 Von Karman Ave, Irvine
(92606-4923)
PHONE...................949 660-0666

P
R
O
D
U
C
T
S

&

S
V
C
S

Michael J Rogerson, *President*
Gordon Neil, *President*
Jonathan C Smith, *CFO*
Milton R Pizinger, *Vice Pres*
EMP: 80 **EST:** 1975
SALES (est): 44.6MM **Privately Held**
WEB: www.rogerson.com
SIC: 3812 3545 3492 3728 Aircraft flight instruments; machine tool accessories; fluid power valves & hose fittings; fuel tanks, aircraft

(P-10642)
ROGERSON KRATOS
403 S Raymond Ave, Pasadena (91105-2609)
PHONE....................626 449-3090
Lawrence Smith, *CEO*
Cannon Mathews, *CFO*
Michael Rogerson, *Chairman*
Milton R Pizinger, *Vice Pres*
EMP: 160 **EST:** 1981
SQ FT: 28,000
SALES (est): 25.6MM
SALES (corp-wide): 44.6MM **Privately Held**
WEB: www.rogersonkratos.com
SIC: 3812 3825 3699 Aircraft flight instruments; instruments to measure electricity; electrical equipment & supplies
PA: Rogerson Aircraft Corporation
16940 Von Karman Ave
Irvine CA 92606
949 660-0666

(P-10643)
SENSOR SYSTEMS INC
8929 Fullbright Ave, Chatsworth (91311-6179)
PHONE....................818 341-5366
Mary E Bazar, *CEO*
Rafael Melero, *Vice Pres*
Si Robin, *Vice Pres*
Dennis E Bazar, *Admin Sec*
Alejandra Rosales, *Admin Asst*
EMP: 258 **EST:** 1961
SQ FT: 60,000
SALES (est): 51.6MM **Privately Held**
WEB: www.sensorantennas.com
SIC: 3812 Aircraft flight instruments

(P-10644)
TELEDYNE CONTROLS LLC
501 Continental Blvd, El Segundo (90245-5036)
P.O. Box 1026 (90245-1026)
PHONE....................310 765-3600
Aldo Pichelli, *CEO*
Robert Mehrabian, *Ch of Bd*
Masood Hassan, *President*
Susan L Main, *CFO*
George C Bobb III, *Ch Credit Ofcr*
EMP: 616 **EST:** 2015
SALES (est): 54MM
SALES (corp-wide): 3B **Publicly Held**
WEB: www.teledynecontrols.com
SIC: 3812 Search & navigation equipment
PA: Teledyne Technologies Inc
1049 Camino Dos Rios
Thousand Oaks CA 91360
805 373-4545

(P-10645)
TELETRAC NAVMAN US LTD (HQ)
310 Commerce Ste 100, Irvine (92602-1360)
PHONE....................866 527-9896
Tj Chung, *President*
Mike Henn, *CFO*
Richard Lilwall, *Vice Pres*
Bill Conroy, *Executive*
Bernard Davis, *Executive*
▲ **EMP:** 37 **EST:** 2007
SALES (est): 18.5MM
SALES (corp-wide): 2.7B **Publicly Held**
WEB: www.teletracnavman.com
SIC: 3812 Navigational systems & instruments
PA: Vontier Corporation
5438 Wade Park Blvd # 601
Raleigh NC 27607
984 275-6000

(P-10646)
TELETRONICS TECHNOLOGY CORP
Also Called: I A D S
190 Sierra Ct Ste A3, Palmdale (93550-7608)
PHONE....................661 273-7033
EMP: 22
SALES (corp-wide): 2.3B **Publicly Held**
WEB: www.curtisswrightds.com
SIC: 3812 Aircraft/aerospace flight instruments & guidance systems; electronic detection systems (aeronautical)
HQ: Teletronics Technology Corp
15 Terry Dr
Newtown PA 18940

(P-10647)
TMC ICE PROTECTION SYSTEMS LLC (PA)
Also Called: TMC Aero
10850 Wilshire Blvd # 12, Los Angeles (90024-4305)
PHONE....................951 677-6934
Bob Yari, *CEO*
Edward Rigney, *COO*
Michael Heaton, *Officer*
EMP: 20 **EST:** 2014
SQ FT: 10,000
SALES (est): 5.6MM **Privately Held**
SIC: 3812 8711 Acceleration indicators & systems components, aerospace; aviation &/or aeronautical engineering

(P-10648)
TMC ICE PROTECTION SYSTEMS LLC
Also Called: TMC Aero
25775 Jefferson Ave, Murrieta (92562-6903)
PHONE....................951 677-6934
Edward Rigney, *COO*
EMP: 20
SALES (corp-wide): 5.6MM **Privately Held**
SIC: 3812 8711 Aircraft/aerospace flight instruments & guidance systems; aviation &/or aeronautical engineering
PA: Tmc Ice Protection Systems Llc
10850 Wilshire Blvd # 12
Los Angeles CA 90024
951 677-6934

(P-10649)
TOWER MECHANICAL PRODUCTS INC
Also Called: Allied Mechanical Products
1720 S Bon View Ave, Ontario (91761-4411)
PHONE....................714 947-2723
Richard B Slater, *President*
Susan J Hardy, *Corp Secy*
James W Longcrier, *Vice Pres*
Chris Schley, *Program Mgr*
Robert Garcia, *Prgrmr*
EMP: 126 **EST:** 1953
SQ FT: 148,000
SALES (est): 24.2MM
SALES (corp-wide): 35.5MM **Privately Held**
WEB: www.alliedmech.com
SIC: 3812 Acceleration indicators & systems components, aerospace
PA: Tower Industries, Inc.
1518 N Endeavor Ln Ste C
Anaheim CA 92801

(P-10650)
TUFFER MANUFACTURING CO INC
163 E Liberty Ave, Anaheim (92801-1012)
PHONE....................714 526-3077
Cathy Kim, *President*
Ken Kim, *Vice Pres*
EMP: 39 **EST:** 1977
SQ FT: 12,000
SALES (est): 6.4MM **Privately Held**
WEB: www.tuffermfg.com
SIC: 3812 3599 Search & navigation equipment; machine shop, jobbing & repair

(P-10651)
UDASH CORPORATION (PA)
4511 Ish Dr, Simi Valley (93063-7667)
PHONE....................805 526-5222
George Melamed, *CEO*
Roset Melamed, *President*
Karmel Melamed, *Admin Sec*
EMP: 14 **EST:** 1981
SALES (est): 5.4MM **Privately Held**
WEB: www.udash.com
SIC: 5599 3812 Aircraft instruments, equipment or parts; defense systems & equipment

(P-10652)
VOTAW PRECISION TECHNOLOGIES
13153 Lakeland Rd, Santa Fe Springs (90670-4542)
P.O. Box 314, Seal Beach (90740-0314)
PHONE....................562 944-0661
Steve Lamb, *CEO*
David Takes, *President*
Jonathan Miller, *CFO*
Steve Crisanti, *Exec VP*
Ken Clack, *Vice Pres*
▲ **EMP:** 140 **EST:** 1964
SQ FT: 240,000
SALES (est): 40MM **Privately Held**
WEB: www.votaw.com
SIC: 3812 Acceleration indicators & systems components, aerospace; aircraft/aerospace flight instruments & guidance systems; navigational systems & instruments

3821 Laboratory Apparatus & Furniture

(P-10653)
BRIGHTSIDE SCIENTIFIC INC
3029 E South St Ste A, Long Beach (90805-3776)
PHONE....................626 453-6436
Moe Tamary, *Principal*
EMP: 15 **EST:** 2017
SALES (est): 570.6K **Privately Held**
WEB: www.brightsidesci.com
SIC: 3821 Laboratory apparatus, except heating & measuring

(P-10654)
CERA INC
14180 Live Oak Ave Ste I, Baldwin Park (91706-1350)
P.O. Box 1608 (91706-7608)
PHONE....................626 814-2688
Philip Dimson, *Owner*
◆ **EMP:** 21 **EST:** 1987
SQ FT: 2,000
SALES (est): 2.4MM **Privately Held**
SIC: 3821 Chemical laboratory apparatus

(P-10655)
CHEMAT TECHNOLOGY INC
Also Called: Chemat Vision
9036 Winnetka Ave, Northridge (91324-3235)
PHONE....................818 727-9786
Haixing Zheng, *CEO*
Yuhong Huang, *Administration*
Thomas Zhang, *Technical Staff*
Syed Haider, *Engineer*
CHI Zhang, *Engineer*
▲ **EMP:** 32 **EST:** 1990
SQ FT: 30,000
SALES (est): 5.6MM **Privately Held**
WEB: www.chemat.com
SIC: 3821 3827 Chemical laboratory apparatus; optical test & inspection equipment

(P-10656)
CLEATECH LLC
2106 N Glassell St, Orange (92865-3308)
PHONE....................714 754-6668
Sam Kashanchi,
Angelica Rosales, *Sales Staff*
EMP: 27 **EST:** 2010
SALES: 3.9MM **Privately Held**
WEB: www.cleatech.com
SIC: 3821 Laboratory apparatus & furniture

(P-10657)
EVERGREEN INDUSTRIES INC
Also Called: Evergreen Scientific
2300 E 49th St, Vernon (90058-2879)
P.O. Box 58248, Los Angeles (30058-0248)
PHONE....................323 583-1331
N Johnson, *Branch Mgr*
EMP: 60
SALES (corp-wide): 1.8B **Privately Held**
WEB: www.evergreensci.com
SIC: 3821 Laboratory apparatus & furniture
HQ: Evergreen Industries, Inc.
2254 E 49th St
Vernon CA 90058
323 583-1331

(P-10658)
GARDNER SYSTEMS INC
3321 S Yale St, Santa Ana (92704-6446)
PHONE....................714 668-9018
Joe Gardner, *President*
Claudia Gardner, *Treasurer*
▲ **EMP:** 15 **EST:** 1983
SQ FT: 8,000
SALES (est): 2MM **Privately Held**
WEB: www.gardner-systems.com
SIC: 3821 Laboratory apparatus & furniture

(P-10659)
HANSON LAB SOLUTIONS INC
747 Calle Plano, Camarillo (93012-8556)
PHONE....................805 498-3121
Mike Hanson, *Chief Mktg Ofc*
Joe Matta, *CEO*
Joseph F Matta, *COO*
Jon Ramirez, *Planning*
Jose Vazquez, *Project Mgr*
▲ **EMP:** 30 **EST:** 1971
SQ FT: 40,000
SALES (est): 7MM **Privately Held**
WEB: www.hansonlab.com
SIC: 3821 Laboratory furniture

(P-10660)
NEWPORT CORPORATION (HQ)
1791 Deere Ave, Irvine (92606-4814)
P.O. Box 19607 (92623-9607)
PHONE....................949 863-3144
Seth Bagshaw, *President*
Derek D'Antilio, *Treasurer*
Greg Reischlein, *Vice Pres*
Pete Williams, *Vice Pres*
Palmer Bryan, *Admin Sec*
◆ **EMP:** 1225 **EST:** 1938
SALES (est): 518.5MM
SALES (corp-wide): 2.3B **Publicly Held**
WEB: www.newport.com
SIC: 3821 3699 3827 3825 Worktables, laboratory; laser systems & equipment; optical instruments & lenses; mirrors, optical; prisms, optical; analytical optical instruments; laser scientific & engineering instruments
PA: Mks Instruments, Inc.
2 Tech Dr Ste 201
Andover MA 01810
978 645-5500

(P-10661)
NORTHRDGE TR-MD_ITY IMGING INC
Also Called: Trifoil Imaging
9449 De Soto Ave, Chatsworth (91311-4920)
PHONE....................818 709-2468
Kevin Parnham, *President*
Ryan Weirich, *CFO*
Wesley Moy, *General Mgr*
EMP: 15 **EST:** 2013
SALES (est): 4.3MM **Privately Held**
WEB: www.trifoilimaging.com
SIC: 3821 7699 Clinical laboratory instruments, except medical & dental; medical equipment repair, non-electric

3822 Automatic Temperature Controls

(P-10662)
BEAR STATE WATER HEATING LLC
43234 Bus Pk Dr Ste 105, Temecula
(92590-3604)
PHONE..................951 269-3753
Jose Luis Sevilla,
EMP: 15 **EST:** 2020
SALES (est): 1.3MM **Privately Held**
WEB: www.bearstatewaterheating.com
SIC: 3822 Water heater controls

(P-10663)
CATALYTIC SOLUTIONS INC (HQ)
1700 Fiske Pl, Oxnard (93033-1863)
PHONE..................805 486-4649
David Gann, *CEO*
Charlie Karl, *CEO*
Kevin McDonnell, *CFO*
Dan McGuire, *Vice Pres*
Steven Golden, *CTO*
▲ **EMP:** 96 **EST:** 1996
SQ FT: 75,000
SALES (est): 22.4MM **Privately Held**
WEB: www.catalyticsolutions.com
SIC: 3822 Auto controls regulating residntl
& coml environmt & applncs

(P-10664)
CHRONOMITE LABORATORIES INC
17451 Hurley St, City of Industry
(91744-5106)
P.O. Box 3527 (91744-0527)
PHONE..................310 534-2300
Donald E Morris, *CEO*
Edward Fabrizio, *Vice Pres*
Cesar Cordero, *Opers Staff*
Forrest Maynard, *Natl Sales Mgr*
Cathy Milostan, *Sales Staff*
▲ **EMP:** 34 **EST:** 1967
SALES: 7MM
SALES (corp-wide): 90MM **Privately Held**
WEB: www.chronomite.com
SIC: 3822 8731 3432 Water heater controls; commercial physical research; plumbing fixture fittings & trim
PA: Acorn Engineering Company
15125 Proctor Ave
City Of Industry CA 91746
800 488-8999

(P-10665)
ELECTRASEM CORP
372 Elizabeth Ln, Corona (92878-5028)
PHONE..................951 371-6140
Don S Edwards, *President*
▲ **EMP:** 89 **EST:** 1980
SALES (est): 5MM
SALES (corp-wide): 1.3B **Publicly Held**
WEB: www.us.msasafety.com
SIC: 3822 Electric heat proportioning controls, modulating controls
HQ: General Monitors, Inc.
26776 Simpatica Cir
Lake Forest CA 92630
949 581-4464

(P-10666)
GEM MOBILE TREATMENT SVCS INC (HQ)
2525 Cherry Ave Ste 105, Signal Hill
(90755-2054)
PHONE..................562 595-7075
Paul Anderson, *COO*
Shane Whittington, *CFO*
Pam Patterson, *Manager*
EMP: 123 **EST:** 1994
SALES (est): 29.6MM **Privately Held**
WEB: www.enais.com
SIC: 3822 1629 Vapor heating controls; waste water & sewage treatment plant construction

(P-10667)
PERTRONIX INC (PA)
440 E Arrow Hwy, San Dimas
(91773-3340)
PHONE..................909 599-5955
Thomas A Reh, *CEO*
Joh R Sherer, *Vice Pres*
Marvin Grebow, *CIO*
Bryan Porter, *Purch Agent*
▲ **EMP:** 40 **EST:** 1962
SQ FT: 22,000
SALES (est): 13.8MM **Privately Held**
WEB: www.pertronixbrands.com
SIC: 3822 3694 Auto controls regulating residntl & coml environmt & applncs; ignition apparatus, internal combustion engines

(P-10668)
SMARTLABS INC
Also Called: Smarthomepro
1621 Alton Pkwy Ste 100, Irvine
(92606-4846)
PHONE..................800 762-7846
Rob Lilleness, *CEO*
Mike Nunes, *CIO*
Chasen Beck, *Engineer*
Christopher Perez, *Engineer*
Isaac Sanz, *Marketing Staff*
◆ **EMP:** 85 **EST:** 1993
SQ FT: 59,230
SALES (est): 17.3MM **Privately Held**
WEB: www.smartlabsinc.com
SIC: 5999 3822 Electronic parts & equipment; auto controls regulating residntl & coml environmt & applncs

(P-10669)
T & L AIR CONDITIONING INC
164 W Live Oak Ave, Arcadia (91007-8562)
PHONE..................626 294-9888
Shinn Liu, *President*
EMP: 20 **EST:** 1996
SQ FT: 2,928
SALES (est): 2.9MM **Privately Held**
SIC: 3822 Air flow controllers, air conditioning & refrigeration

(P-10670)
TRUE FRESH HPP LLC
6535 Caballero Blvd B, Buena Park
(90620-8106)
PHONE..................949 922-8801
Nora Jones, *Accountant*
EMP: 18 **EST:** 2015
SALES (est): 8.9MM **Privately Held**
WEB: www.hppfs.com
SIC: 3822 Refrigeration controls (pressure)

(P-10671)
WESTERN ENVIRONMENTAL INC
62150 Gene Welmas Way, Mecca
(92254-6550)
PHONE..................760 396-0222
William Carr,
Ed Kennon, *Partner*
Tina Pudiaooa, *Office Mgr*
EMP: 30 **EST:** 2002
SALES (est): 3.6MM **Privately Held**
WEB: www.wei-mecca.com
SIC: 3822 Auto controls regulating residntl & coml environmt & applncs

(P-10672)
XPOWER MANUFACTURE INC
668 S 6th Ave, City of Industry
(91746-3025)
PHONE..................626 285-3301
Keidy Gu, *CEO*
Guogen Cui, *President*
Leslie Chen, *Info Tech Mgr*
▲ **EMP:** 40 **EST:** 2011
SALES (est): 6.3MM **Privately Held**
WEB: www.xpower.com
SIC: 3822 3999 3564 Air flow controllers, air conditioning & refrigeration; pet supplies; blowing fans: industrial or commercial
PA: Xinshengyuan Electrical Appliances Co., Ltd.
No.3, East Area No.3 Road, Xiantang Industrial Zone, Longjiang T
Foshan 52831

3823 Indl Instruments For Meas, Display & Control

(P-10673)
ADS LLC
Also Called: A D S Environmental Srvs
15205 Springdale St, Huntington Beach
(92649-1156)
PHONE..................714 379-9778
Paul Mitchell, *Manager*
EMP: 19
SALES (est): 2.3B **Publicly Held**
WEB: www.adsenv.com
SIC: 3823 8748 Flow instruments, industrial process type; environmental consultant
HQ: Ads Llc
340 The Bridge St Ste 204
Huntsville AL 35806
256 430-3366

(P-10674)
AMETEK AEROSPACE
17072 Daimler St, Irvine (92614-5548)
PHONE..................949 473-6754
EMP: 16 **EST:** 2019
SALES (est): 2.7MM **Privately Held**
WEB: www.ametek.com
SIC: 3823 Industrial instrmnts msrmnt display/control process variable

(P-10675)
AMETEK AMERON LLC (HQ)
Also Called: Mass Systems
4750 Littlejohn St, Baldwin Park
(91706-2274)
PHONE..................626 856-0101
Keith Marsicola, *Mng Member*
Michael Mallari, *Engineer*
Steve Tanner, *Mng Member*
Brenda Sperber, *Manager*
Susan Meller-Rojas, *Supervisor*
EMP: 55 **EST:** 1988
SQ FT: 2,600
SALES (est): 23MM
SALES (corp-wide): 4.5B **Publicly Held**
WEB: www.ametekmro.com
SIC: 3823 3999 3728 8711 Pressure gauges, dial & digital; fire extinguishers, portable; aircraft parts & equipment; industrial engineers; clothing, fire resistant & protective
PA: Ametek, Inc.
1100 Cassatt Rd
Berwyn PA 19312
610 647-2121

(P-10676)
ANALYTICAL INDUSTRIES INC
Also Called: Advanced Instruments
2855 Metropolitan Pl, Pomona
(91767-1853)
PHONE..................909 392-6900
Frank S Gregus, *President*
Patrick J Prindible, *Vice Pres*
Mohammad Razaq, *Vice Pres*
Francisco Millan, *Sales Mgr*
David Zendejas, *Sales Engr*
EMP: 45 **EST:** 1994
SQ FT: 15,000
SALES (est): 8.8MM **Privately Held**
WEB: www.aii1.com
SIC: 3823 Industrial instrmnts msrmnt display/control process variable

(P-10677)
ARGA CONTROLS INC
10410 Trademark St, Rancho Cucamonga
(91730-5826)
PHONE..................626 799-3314
Bob Pineau, *President*
Linda Halsey, *President*
EMP: 17 **EST:** 1970
SALES (est): 955.8K **Privately Held**
WEB: www.electroswitch.com
SIC: 3823 3829 3625 3613 Industrial instrmnts msrmnt display/control process variable; measuring & controlling devices; relays & industrial controls; switchgear & switchboard apparatus

(P-10678)
AUTOFLOW PRODUCTS CO
15915 S San Pedro St, Gardena
(90248-2555)
PHONE..................310 515-2866
EMP: 15
SQ FT: 6,500
SALES (est): 1.5MM **Privately Held**
WEB: www.autoflowproducts.com
SIC: 3823 3491 Mfg Process Control Instruments Mfg Industrial Valves

(P-10679)
BAMBECK SYSTEMS INC (PA)
1921 Carnegie Ave Ste 3a, Santa Ana
(92705-5510)
PHONE..................949 250-3100
Robert J Bambeck, *President*
Robert Deweerd, *Vice Pres*
Melinda Yoshida, *Finance*
EMP: 19 **EST:** 1980
SQ FT: 6,100
SALES (est): 3.2MM **Privately Held**
WEB: www.bambecksystems.com
SIC: 3823 Boiler controls: industrial, power & marine type

(P-10680)
BESTEST INTERNATIONAL
Also Called: Bestest Medical
181 W Orangethorpe Ave C, Placentia
(92870-6931)
PHONE..................714 974-8837
Pamela Bogart, *President*
John Bogart, *CFO*
Jim Roberts, *Manager*
EMP: 32 **EST:** 1988
SQ FT: 9,200
SALES (est): 2.8MM **Privately Held**
SIC: 3823 3841 Industrial instrmnts msrmnt display/control process variable; surgical & medical instruments

(P-10681)
BIODOT INC (HQ)
2852 Alton Pkwy, Irvine (92606-5104)
PHONE..................949 440-3685
Anthony Lemmo, *CEO*
David Gracie, *CFO*
Brian Kirk, *VP Bus Dvlpt*
Young Chen, *Info Tech Mgr*
Caroline Holohan, *Technical Staff*
EMP: 93 **EST:** 1994
SQ FT: 24,000
SALES (est): 19.4MM
SALES (corp-wide): 1B **Privately Held**
WEB: www.biodot.com
SIC: 3823 3826 Industrial instrmnts msrmnt display/control process variable; analytical instruments
PA: Ats Automation Tooling Systems Inc
730 Fountain St N Suite 2b
Cambridge ON N3H 4
519 653-6500

(P-10682)
CALIFRNIA ANLYTICAL INSTRS INC
Also Called: Cai
1312 W Grove Ave, Orange (92865-4136)
PHONE..................714 974-5560
R Pete Furton, *President*
Loren T Mathews, *Corp Secy*
Harold J Peper, *Exec VP*
Tim Sharp, *Technician*
Jim Mabe, *Design Engr*
EMP: 55
SQ FT: 26,400
SALES (est): 11.3MM **Privately Held**
WEB: www.gasanalyzers.com
SIC: 3823 Industrial instrmnts msrmnt display/control process variable

(P-10683)
CAMERON TECHNOLOGIES US LLC
Also Called: Cameron's Measurement Systems
4040 Capitol Ave, Whittier (90601-1735)
PHONE..................562 222-8440
Victor Hart, *Plant Mgr*
EMP: 27 **Publicly Held**
SIC: 3823 Industrial flow & liquid measuring instruments

PRODUCTS & SVCS

HQ: Cameron Technologies Us, Llc
1000 Mcclaren Woods Dr
Coraopolis PA 15108

(P-10684)
CBRITE INC
421 Pine Ave, Goleta (93117-3709)
PHONE..................................805 722-1121
Boo Nilsson, *President*
EMP: 23 EST: 2002
SALES (est): 777.1K **Privately Held**
SIC: 3823 8731 Industrial instrmnts
msrmnt display/control process variable;
electronic research

(P-10685)
CK TECHNOLOGIES INC (PA)
Also Called: Ckt
3629 Vista Mercado, Camarillo
(93012-8055)
PHONE..................................805 987-4801
Karl F Zimmerman, *President*
Heidi Zimmerman, *Vice Pres*
Heidi Zimmermann, *Info Tech Mgr*
EMP: 32 EST: 1987
SQ FT: 34,000
SALES (est): 9.6MM **Privately Held**
WEB: www.ckt.com
SIC: 3823 3825 5065 Water quality moni-
toring & control systems; instruments to
measure electricity; electronic parts &
equipment

(P-10686)
COMPUTATIONAL SYSTEMS INC
4301 Resnik Ct, Bakersfield (93313-4852)
PHONE..................................661 832-5306
Shannon Romine, *Branch Mgr*
EMP: 123
SALES (corp-wide): 16.7B **Publicly Held**
SIC: 3823 Industrial instrmnts msrmnt dis-
play/control process variable
HQ: Computational Systems, Incorporated
8000 West Florissant Ave
Saint Louis MO 63136
314 553-2000

(P-10687)
COSASCO INC
11841 Smith Ave, Santa Fe Springs
(90670-3226)
PHONE..................................562 949-0123
Aaron Heilbrun, *Vice Pres*
Dave Bowen, *VP Engrg*
Jeannine Hurlic, *QC Mgr*
Jim Robinson, *Mfg Staff*
Kathleen Rosario, *Marketing Mgr*
EMP: 97 EST: 2015
SALES (est): 6.7MM **Privately Held**
WEB: www.cosasco.com
SIC: 3823 Industrial instrmnts msrmnt dis-
play/control process variable

(P-10688)
CRYSTAL ENGINEERING CORP
708 Fiero Ln Ste 9, San Luis Obispo
(93401-7945)
P.O. Box 3033 (93403-3033)
PHONE..................................805 595-5477
David Porter, *President*
Matthew Haas, *Vice Pres*
Rose Dechant, *Buyer*
Nielson Sean, *Marketing Mgr*
Jeff Gartner, *Sales Staff*
▲ EMP: 38 EST: 1981
SALES (est): 11.9MM
SALES (corp-wide): 4.5B **Publicly Held**
WEB: www.ametekcalibration.com
SIC: 3823 Pressure gauges, dial & digital;
industrial process measurement equip-
ment
PA: Ametek, Inc.
1100 Cassatt Rd
Berwyn PA 19312
610 647-2121

(P-10689)
DELPHI CONTROL SYSTEMS INC
2806 Metropolitan Pl, Pomona
(91767-1854)
PHONE..................................909 593-8099
Beth A Barbonc, *President*
Scott Crail, *Vice Pres*
EMP: 15 EST: 1976

SQ FT: 11,000 **Privately Held**
WEB: www.delphicontrolsystems.com
SIC: 3823 3613 Industrial process control
instruments; control panels, electric

(P-10690)
DURO-SENSE CORP
869 Sandhill Ave, Carson (90746-1210)
PHONE..................................310 533-6877
Jay Waterman, *President*
Roger S Waterman, *Ch of Bd*
Steve Rossi, *Purchasing*
EMP: 15 EST: 1979
SQ FT: 8,000
SALES (est): 2MM **Privately Held**
WEB: www.duro-sense.com
SIC: 3823 Temperature instruments: indus-
trial process type

(P-10691)
ENDRESS + HAUSER INC
Also Called: Endresshouser Conducta
4123 E La Palma Ave # 20, Anaheim
(92807-1867)
PHONE..................................714 577-5600
Wolfgang Bable, *Branch Mgr*
Jackie Vice, *Vice Pres*
EMP: 14
SALES (corp-wide): 371.8MM **Privately
Held**
WEB: www.us.endress.com
SIC: 3823 Industrial instrmnts msrmnt dis-
play/control process variable
HQ: Endress + Hauser Inc
2350 Endress Pl
Greenwood IN 46143
317 535-7138

(P-10692)
ETI SYSTEMS
Also Called: Polaris Music
1800 Century Park E # 600, Los Angeles
(90067-1501)
PHONE..................................310 684-3664
Bill Tice, *President*
Gayle Tice, *Corp Secy*
Debbie Marshall, *Vice Pres*
Mike Wilkes, *Vice Pres*
David Thompson, *Manager*
EMP: 60 EST: 1962
SQ FT: 8,200
SALES (est): 5.4MM **Privately Held**
SIC: 3823 Potentiometric self-balancing
inst., except X-Y plotters; industrial
process control instruments

(P-10693)
FLOWMETRICS INC
9201 Independence Ave, Chatsworth
(91311-5905)
PHONE..................................818 407-3420
Hormoz Ghaemmaghami, *President*
Irfan Ahmed, *Sales Staff*
EMP: 18 EST: 1989
SQ FT: 4,000
SALES (est): 1MM **Privately Held**
WEB: www.flowmetrics.com
SIC: 3823 Industrial flow & liquid measur-
ing instruments

(P-10694)
FLUID POWER CTRL SYSTEMS INC
1400 E Valencia Dr, Fullerton (92831-4733)
PHONE..................................714 525-3727
Harsoyo Lukito, *President*
EMP: 16 EST: 2008
SALES (est): 557.4K **Privately Held**
SIC: 3823 Fluidic devices, circuits & sys-
tems for process control

(P-10695)
FUNDAMENTAL TECH INTL INC
Also Called: F T I
2900 E 29th St, Long Beach (90806-2315)
PHONE..................................562 595-0661
Maarten Propper, *CEO*
John Jacobson, *President*
▼ EMP: 21 EST: 1996
SQ FT: 20,000
SALES (est): 3.1MM **Privately Held**
SIC: 3823 Liquid analysis instruments, in-
dustrial process type

(P-10696)
FUTEK ADVANCED SENSOR TECH INC
10 Thomas, Irvine (92618-2702)
PHONE..................................949 465-0900
Javad Mokhberi, *CEO*
Javad Mokhbery, *CEO*
Niket Tyagi, *Vice Pres*
Diane Burgess, *Executive*
Pratik Thakur, *Executive*
▼ EMP: 140 EST: 1988
SQ FT: 23,000
SALES (est): 30MM **Privately Held**
WEB: www.futek.com
SIC: 3823 8711 Industrial instrmnts
msrmnt display/control process variable;
engineering services

(P-10697)
GEORG FISCHER SIGNET LLC
5462 Irwindale Ave Ste A, Baldwin Park
(91706-2074)
PHONE..................................626 571-2770
Charlotte Hill, *Mng Member*
Karen Brown, *Sales Staff*
Stephanie Camacho, *Sales Staff*
Veronica Duran, *Sales Staff*
Laura Esquivel, *Sales Staff*
▲ EMP: 90 EST: 1953
SALES (est): 20.6MM
SALES (corp-wide): 3.5B **Privately Held**
WEB: www.gfps.eu
SIC: 3823 Industrial instrmnts msrmnt dis-
play/control process variable
HQ: Georg Fischer Spa
Via Eugenio Villoresi 2/4
Agrate Brianza MB 20041

(P-10698)
GRAPHTEC AMERICA INC (DH)
17462 Armstrong Ave, Irvine (92614-5724)
PHONE..................................949 770-6010
Yasutaka Arakawa, *CEO*
Kenichi Sahara, *CFO*
Gary Polsinelli, *Technical Staff*
James Belcher, *Sales Staff*
Dominick Bizzari, *Sales Staff*
◆ EMP: 49 EST: 1949
SQ FT: 35,000
SALES (est): 16.5MM **Privately Held**
WEB: www.graphtecamerica.com
SIC: 3823 5064 Industrial instrmnts
msrmnt display/control process variable;
video cassette recorders & accessories

(P-10699)
HCC INDUSTRIES LEASING INC (HQ)
4232 Temple City Blvd, Rosemead
(91770-1552)
PHONE..................................626 443-8933
Richard Ferraid, *President*
EMP: 15 EST: 1945
SQ FT: 36,000
SALES (est): 218.7MM
SALES (corp-wide): 4.5B **Publicly Held**
WEB: www.ametek.com
SIC: 3823 Industrial instrmnts msrmnt dis-
play/control process variable
PA: Ametek, Inc.
1100 Cassatt Rd
Berwyn PA 19312
610 647-2121

(P-10700)
HEWITT INDUSTRIES LOS ANGELES
1455 Crenshaw Blvd # 290, Torrance
(90501-2438)
PHONE..................................714 891-9300
John T Hewitt, *President*
David Wishart, *Purch Mgr*
▲ EMP: 27 EST: 1955
SALES (est): 671.1K **Privately Held**
WEB: www.hewittindustries.com
SIC: 3823 3714 3625 Pyrometers, indus-
trial process type; temperature instru-
ments: industrial process type; motor
vehicle parts & accessories; relays & in-
dustrial controls

(P-10701)
I T I ELECTRO-OPTIC CORP (PA)
Also Called: Ccd
11500 W Olympic Blvd, Los Angeles
(90064-1524)
PHONE..................................310 445-8900
MEI Shi, *Ch of Bd*
Robert Nevins, *President*
Henry Hong, *Executive*
James Wang, *VP Finance*
John Sun, *Analyst*
▲ EMP: 20 EST: 1985
SQ FT: 5,000
SALES (est): 5.3MM **Privately Held**
WEB: www.itieo.com
SIC: 3823 Infrared instruments, industrial
process type

(P-10702)
I T I ELECTRO-OPTIC CORP
1500 E Olympic Blvd # 400, Los Angeles
(90021-1900)
PHONE..................................310 312-4526
John Sun, *Manager*
EMP: 20
SALES (corp-wide): 5.3MM **Privately
Held**
WEB: www.itieo.com
SIC: 3823 Infrared instruments, industrial
process type
PA: I T I Electro-Optic Corporation
11500 W Olympic Blvd
Los Angeles CA 90064
310 445-8900

(P-10703)
INNOVATIVE INTEGRATION INC
741 Flynn Rd, Camarillo (93012-8056)
PHONE..................................805 520-3300
Jim Henderson, *President*
Dan McLane, *Vice Pres*
Nora Henderson, *Marketing Staff*
Shant Moses, *Manager*
▲ EMP: 30 EST: 1988
SQ FT: 11,000
SALES (est): 4.9MM **Privately Held**
WEB: www.isipkg.com
SIC: 3823 3571 Industrial instrmnts
msrmnt display/control process variable;
electronic computers

(P-10704)
KING INSTRUMENT COMPANY INC
12700 Pala Dr, Garden Grove
(92841-3924)
PHONE..................................714 891-0008
Clyde F King, *President*
EMP: 50 EST: 1983
SQ FT: 46,000
SALES (est): 9.9MM **Privately Held**
WEB: www.kinginstrumentco.com
SIC: 3823 Flow instruments, industrial
process type

(P-10705)
KING NUTRONICS CORPORATION
6421 Independence Ave, Woodland Hills
(91367-2608)
PHONE..................................818 887-5460
J Robert King, *President*
Leslie King, *Admin Sec*
Dan Fredrickson, *Electrical Engi*
Amir Gnessin, *Engineer*
Chris Crocker, *Purch Mgr*
EMP: 20 EST: 1960
SQ FT: 21,000
SALES (est): 5.4MM **Privately Held**
WEB: www.kingnutronics.com
SIC: 3823 3825 Pressure measurement
instruments, industrial instruments to
measure electricity

(P-10706)
MCCROMETER INC (HQ)
3255 W Stetson Ave, Hemet (92545-7763)
PHONE..................................951 652-6811
Stephen Bell, *President*
Ian Rule, *Vice Pres*
Laura Cruc, *Buyer*
Ray Loo, *Regl Sales Mgr*
Betty Richter, *Cnty Cmsnr*
◆ EMP: 214 EST: 1996
SQ FT: 9,090

SALES (est): 65MM
SALES (corp-wide): 22.2B Publicly Held
WEB: www.mccrometer.com
SIC: 3823 Industrial instrmnts msrmnt display/control process variable
PA: Danaher Corporation
2200 Penn Ave Nw Ste 800w
Washington DC 20037
202 828-0850

(P-10707)
MICROCOOL
72216 Northshore St # 103, Thousand Palms (92276-2325)
PHONE..................................760 322-1111
Mike Lemche, *President*
Christopher Stanley, *Vice Pres*
James Murphy, *Admin Sec*
Melanie Ruiz, *Marketing Staff*
▲ EMP: 15 EST: 2007
SQ FT: 5,800
SALES (est): 3.1MM Privately Held
WEB: www.microcool.com
SIC: 3823 Humidity instruments, industrial process type

(P-10708)
MOORE INDUSTRIES - EUROPE INC (HQ)
16650 Schoenborn St, Sepulveda (91343-6196)
PHONE..................................818 894-7111
Leonard W Moore, *President*
Dermot Nolan, *CFO*
Nancy Nahamo, *Buyer*
Gonzalo Caldera, *Supervisor*
EMP: 13 EST: 1977
SQ FT: 40,000
SALES (est): 9.8MM
SALES (corp-wide): 39.3MM Privately Held
WEB: www.miinet.com
SIC: 3823 Industrial instrmnts msrmnt display/control process variable
PA: Moore Industries - International Inc.
16650 Schoenborn St
North Hills CA 91343
818 830-5518

(P-10709)
OLEUMTECH CORPORATION
19762 Pauling, Foothill Ranch (92610-2611)
PHONE..................................949 305-9009
Paul Gregory, *CEO*
Vrej ISA, *COO*
Brent McAdams, *Vice Pres*
Colin Miller, *Software Engr*
Jacky Leong, *Engineer*
EMP: 43
SQ FT: 55,000
SALES (est): 15MM Privately Held
WEB: www.oleumtech.com
SIC: 3823 Industrial instrmnts msrmnt display/control process variable

(P-10710)
PRESSURE PROFILE SYSTEMS INC
5757 W Century Blvd # 600, Los Angeles (90045-6429)
PHONE..................................310 641-8100
Denis A O'Connor, *CEO*
Jae S Son, *CEO*
Huan Tran, *COO*
Eli Yered, *CFO*
Steven Sanchez, *Treasurer*
EMP: 17 EST: 1996
SALES (est): 2.4MM Privately Held
WEB: www.pressureprofile.com
SIC: 3823 Industrial instrmnts msrmnt display/control process variable

(P-10711)
PRIMORDIAL DIAGNOSTICS INC
Also Called: Pulse Instruments
3233 Mission Oaks Blvd P, Camarillo (93012-5134)
PHONE..................................800 462-1926
Karan Khurana, *President*
Mridula Khurana, *CFO*
Michael Porath, *Vice Pres*
Jill Hartman, *Sales Staff*
John Snyder, *Manager*
EMP: 25 EST: 1985

SALES (est): 3.4MM Privately Held
SIC: 3823 5063 5074 Water quality monitoring & control systems; electrical apparatus & equipment; water purification equipment

(P-10712)
PROMACH FILLING SYSTEMS LLC
200 River Rd, Corona (92878-1435)
PHONE..................................951 393-2200
Luis Michel, *Project Mgr*
Teddy Pardo, *Project Mgr*
Mario Bele, *Engineer*
Ryan Grable, *Engineer*
Deven Weston, *Manager*
EMP: 25 EST: 2018
SALES (est): 3.9MM Privately Held
WEB: www.pacificpak.com
SIC: 3823 Industrial instrmnts msrmnt display/control process variable

(P-10713)
Q-MARK MANUFACTURING INC
Also Called: Quality Components Co
30051 Comercio, Rcho STA Marg (92688-2106)
PHONE..................................949 457-1913
Mark Osterstock, *President*
Sharon Starr, *Treasurer*
EMP: 14 EST: 1992
SQ FT: 5,120
SALES (est): 3MM Privately Held
WEB: www.cmms.com
SIC: 3823 3599 Industrial instrmnts msrmnt display/control process variable; machine shop, jobbing & repair

(P-10714)
QED INC
2920 Halladay St, Santa Ana (92705-5623)
PHONE..................................714 546-6010
Erik K Moller, *CEO*
Randy Heartfield, *President*
Mary C Heartfield, *Admin Sec*
Edward Dubois, *Prgrmr*
Chris Barr, *Engineer*
▲ EMP: 39 EST: 1960
SQ FT: 14,000
SALES (est): 5.6MM Privately Held
WEB: www.qedaero.com
SIC: 3823 3829 3812 Pressure gauges, dial & digital; accelerometers; pressure & vacuum indicators, aircraft engine; aircraft/aerospace flight instruments & guidance systems; aircraft flight instruments; aircraft control systems, electronic

(P-10715)
QUANTUM-DYNAMICS CO
6414 Independence Ave, Woodland Hills (91367-2607)
PHONE..................................818 719-0142
Arnold F Liu, *President*
Frederick F Liu, *President*
Lily Liu, *Corp Secy*
Arnold Liu, *Vice Pres*
EMP: 19 EST: 1960
SQ FT: 25,000
SALES (est): 1.7MM Privately Held
WEB: www.qdflow.com
SIC: 3823 8731 Flow instruments, industrial process type; engineering laboratory, except testing

(P-10716)
R G HANSEN & ASSOCIATES (PA)
5951 Encina Rd Ste 106, Goleta (93117-6251)
P.O. Box 160 (93116-0160)
PHONE..................................805 564-3388
Ian Wood, *President*
Lisa Drynan, *General Mgr*
Dan Swets, *Mfg Spvr*
EMP: 13 EST: 1972
SQ FT: 10,000
SALES (est): 1.1MM Privately Held
WEB: www.cryostat.com
SIC: 3823 Industrial instrmnts msrmnt display/control process variable

(P-10717)
RAIN MSTR IRRGTION SYSTEMS INC
5825 Jasmine St, Riverside (92504-1144)
P.O. Box 489 (92502-0489)
PHONE..................................805 527-4498
Jim Sieminski, *President*
John Torosiani, *Admin Sec*
EMP: 44 EST: 1982
SQ FT: 13,000
SALES (est): 5.3MM
SALES (corp-wide): 3.3B Publicly Held
WEB: www.rainmaster.com
SIC: 3823 Industrial instrmnts msrmnt display/control process variable
PA: The Toro Company
8111 Lyndale Ave S
Bloomington MN 55420
952 888-8801

(P-10718)
RENAU CORPORATION
Also Called: Renau Electronic Laboratories
9309 Deering Ave, Chatsworth (91311-5858)
PHONE..................................818 341-1994
Karol Renau, *CEO*
Christine Renau, *Admin Sec*
Christopher Domanski, *Project Mgr*
Paul Simmonds, *Business Mgr*
Marissa Garcia, *Purchasing*
▲ EMP: 20 EST: 1981
SQ FT: 10,000
SALES (est): 6MM Privately Held
WEB: www.renau.com
SIC: 3823 Controllers for process variables, all types; time cycle & program controllers, industrial process type

(P-10719)
ROHRBACK COSASCO SYSTEMS INC (DH)
11841 Smith Ave, Santa Fe Springs (90670-3226)
PHONE..................................562 949-0123
Bryan Sanderlin, *CEO*
David Price, *IT/INT Sup*
Long Sung, *Technology*
Tony Anderson, *Technical Staff*
Kevin Minegar, *Engineer*
▼ EMP: 71 EST: 1977
SQ FT: 37,000
SALES (est): 17.4MM
SALES (corp-wide): 1.8B Privately Held
WEB: www.cosasco.com
SIC: 3823 8742 Industrial instrmnts msrmnt display/control process variable; industry specialist consultants

(P-10720)
RONAN ENGINEERING COMPANY (PA)
Also Called: Ronan Engnrng/Rnan Msrment Div
28290 Avenue Stanford, Valencia (91355-3984)
P.O. Box 129, Castaic (91310-0129)
PHONE..................................661 702-1344
John A Hewitson, *CEO*
▼ EMP: 56
SQ FT: 50,000
SALES (est): 12.7MM Privately Held
WEB: www.ronan.com
SIC: 3823 3825 Industrial instrmnts msrmnt display/control process variable; measuring instruments & meters, electric

(P-10721)
SANTA BARBARA CONTROL SYSTEMS
Also Called: Chemtrol
5375 Overpass Rd, Santa Barbara (93111-3015)
PHONE..................................805 683-8833
Pablo Navarro, *President*
Jacques Steininger, *CEO*
Ron Akin, *Vice Pres*
Karen Blomsprand, *Office Mgr*
Karen Grigsby, *Office Mgr*
EMP: 19
SQ FT: 8,000

SALES: 5.6MM Privately Held
WEB: www.sbcontrol.com
SIC: 3823 3589 7699 Water quality monitoring & control systems; swimming pool filter & water conditioning systems; cash register repair

(P-10722)
SENSOSCIENTIFIC INC
685 Cochran St Ste 200, Simi Valley (93065-1921)
PHONE..................................800 279-3101
Ramin Rostami, *CEO*
Mike Zarei, *Vice Pres*
Vahid Zarie, *CTO*
Dan Skelly, *Technician*
Summer Hodge, *Accountant*
▲ EMP: 15 EST: 2005
SQ FT: 4,000
SALES (est): 5MM Privately Held
WEB: www.sensoscientific.com
SIC: 3823 Industrial instrmnts msrmnt display/control process variable

(P-10723)
SILENX CORPORATION
10606 Shoemaker Ave Ste A, Santa Fe Springs (90670-4071)
PHONE..................................562 941-4200
Peter Kim, *President*
Chris Kim, *Treasurer*
Annie Kim, *Accounts Mgr*
◆ EMP: 16 EST: 2003
SQ FT: 10,000
SALES (est): 1.5MM Privately Held
WEB: www.silenx.com
SIC: 3823 5063 Computer interface equipment for industrial process control; lighting fixtures, commercial & industrial

(P-10724)
SJ CONTROLS INC
2248 Obispo Ave Ste 203, Long Beach (90755-4026)
P.O. Box 91059 (90809-1059)
PHONE..................................562 494-1400
David J Olszewski, *President*
Frederick D Hesley Jr, *Chairman*
Stephen Czaus, *Vice Pres*
Jazmin Jones, *Office Mgr*
Raul Valles, *Prdtn Mgr*
EMP: 25 EST: 1974
SQ FT: 8,000
SALES (est): 2.5MM Privately Held
WEB: www.sjcontrols.com
SIC: 3823 5084 3824 Industrial instrmnts msrmnt display/control process variable; controlling instruments & accessories; fluid meters & counting devices

(P-10725)
SOFFA ELECTRIC INC
5901 Corvette St, Commerce (90040-1690)
PHONE..................................323 728-0230
Maryam Shams, *Exec Dir*
Adele N Soffa, *President*
Marlene Avila, *Office Mgr*
EMP: 48 EST: 1971
SQ FT: 36,000
SALES (est): 14.1MM Privately Held
WEB: www.soffaelectric.com
SIC: 3823 1731 8711 8742 Industrial instrmnts msrmnt display/control process variable; computer interface equipment for industrial process control; general electrical contractor; engineering services; automation & robotics consultant

(P-10726)
STAR-LUCK ENTERPRISE INC
11807 Harrington St, Bakersfield (93311-9278)
PHONE..................................661 665-9999
Xiaodong Zhou, *President*
Stephen Thompson, *Senior VP*
David Johnson, *Vice Pres*
Jing Guo, *Admin Sec*
◆ EMP: 14 EST: 2000
SQ FT: 11,800
SALES (est): 3.4MM Privately Held
SIC: 3823 Pressure measurement instruments, industrial

(P-10727)
SUEZ WATER INDIANA LLC
Also Called: West Bsin Wtr Rclamation Plant
1935 S Hughes Way, El Segundo
(90245-4729)
PHONE..................310 414-0183
Reza Nabegh, *Finance*
Henry Phan, *Buyer*
EMP: 35
SALES (corp-wide): 117.1MM **Privately Held**
SIC: 3823 Water quality monitoring & control systems
HQ: Suez Water Indiana Llc
461 From Rd Ste F
Paramus NJ 07652
201 767-9300

(P-10728)
TELEDYNE INSTRUMENTS INC
Also Called: Teledyne Analytical Instrs
16830 Chestnut St, City of Industry
(91748-1017)
PHONE..................626 934-1500
Tom Compas, *Branch Mgr*
Thomas Compas, *General Mgr*
Tony Ho, *Administration*
Robin Fong, *Technician*
John Reyes, *Design Engr*
EMP: 170
SQ FT: 70,000
SALES (corp-wide): 3B **Publicly Held**
WEB: www.teledyne.com
SIC: 3823 Industrial instrmnts msrmnt display/control process variable
HQ: Teledyne Instruments, Inc.
16830 Chestnut St
City Of Industry CA 91748
626 934-1500

(P-10729)
THERMOMETRICS CORPORATION (PA)
18714 Parthenia St, Northridge
(91324-3813)
PHONE..................818 886-3755
Jorge Hernandez, *President*
Victoria Dukes, *CFO*
Robert Hernandez, *Vice Pres*
Dan Dobbs, *Technician*
Tom Fishwick, *Engineer*
EMP: 28 EST: 1965
SQ FT: 16,897
SALES (est): 7.3MM **Privately Held**
WEB: www.thermometricscorp.com
SIC: 3823 Industrial instrmnts msrmnt display/control process variable

(P-10730)
TRANSLOGIC INCORPORATED
5641 Engineer Dr, Huntington Beach
(92649-1123)
PHONE..................714 890-0058
Donald Ross, *CEO*
Gregory Ross, *Admin Sec*
EMP: 41 EST: 1979
SALES (est): 4.5MM **Privately Held**
WEB: www.translogicinc.com
SIC: 3823 3829 Temperature instruments: industrial process type; thermocouples, industrial process type; measuring & controlling devices

(P-10731)
WORLD WATER INC
9848 Everest St, Downey (90242-3114)
P.O. Box 2331, Pico Rivera (90662-2331)
PHONE..................562 940-1964
Fernando Guerrero, *CEO*
Nadia Macedo, *Office Mgr*
EMP: 40 EST: 2006
SQ FT: 1,000
SALES (est): 4MM **Privately Held**
WEB: www.worldwaterinc.com
SIC: 3823 Water quality monitoring & control systems

(P-10732)
WORLDWIDE ENVMTL PDTS INC (PA)
Also Called: Imperials Sand Dunes
1100 Beacon St, Brea (92821-2936)
PHONE..................714 990-2700
William Oscar Delaney, *CEO*
James Delaney, *CFO*

Art Vasquez, *Vice Pres*
Raquel Alvarez, *Office Mgr*
Stephen Alford, *CIO*
EMP: 90 EST: 1991
SQ FT: 23,000
SALES (est): 20.1MM **Privately Held**
WEB: www.wep-inc.com
SIC: 3823 3694 Industrial instrmnts msrmnt display/control process variable; automotive electrical equipment

(P-10733)
XIRRUS INC
2545 W Hillcrest Dr # 220, Newbury Park
(91320-2217)
PHONE..................805 262-1600
Shane Buckley, *CEO*
Steve Degennaro, *CFO*
Jillian Mansolf, *Chief Mktg Ofcr*
Sam Bass, *Vice Pres*
John Hudson, *Vice Pres*
◆ EMP: 54 EST: 2004
SALES (est): 3.3MM **Privately Held**
WEB: www.cambiumnetworks.com
SIC: 3823 Computer interface equipment for industrial process control

(P-10734)
YOUNG ENGINEERING & MFG INC (PA)
560 W Terrace Dr, San Dimas
(91773-2914)
P.O. Box 3984 (91773-7984)
PHONE..................909 394-3225
Winston Young, *President*
Joanne Young, *Vice Pres*
Ken Krogen, *CTO*
Cheri Witherell, *Persnl Mgr*
Heidi Berger, *Marketing Staff*
◆ EMP: 21 EST: 1980
SQ FT: 55,000
SALES (est): 9.2MM **Privately Held**
WEB: www.youngeng.com
SIC: 3823 5084 8711 5074 Industrial instrmnts msrmnt display/control process variable; industrial machinery & equipment; consulting engineer; water purification equipment

3824 Fluid Meters & Counters

(P-10735)
BLUE-WHITE INDUSTRIES LTD (PA)
5300 Business Dr, Huntington Beach
(92649-1224)
PHONE..................714 893-8529
Robert E Gledhill, *President*
Cindy Henderson, *Corp Secy*
Rob Gledhill, *Vice Pres*
Robert E Gledhill III, *Vice Pres*
Jeanne Hendrickson, *Vice Pres*
▲ EMP: 70 EST: 1957
SQ FT: 48,000
SALES (est): 19.7MM **Privately Held**
WEB: www.blue-white.com
SIC: 3824 3561 3589 Water meters; industrial pumps & parts; sewage & water treatment equipment

(P-10736)
EMCOR GROUP INC
2 Cromwell, Irvine (92618-1816)
PHONE..................949 475-6020
Henry Magdaleno, *Principal*
Frank Ledda, *President*
Joe Ramos, *Credit Mgr*
EMP: 37 EST: 2011
SALES (est): 8MM **Privately Held**
WEB: www.emcorfacilities.com
SIC: 3824 Fluid meters & counting devices

(P-10737)
EMITCON INC
Also Called: Airex
1175 N Van Horne Way, Anaheim
(92806-2506)
PHONE..................714 632-8595
Jack M Preston, *President*
EMP: 15 EST: 1989
SQ FT: 45,000
SALES (est): 537.1K **Privately Held**
SIC: 3824 Integrating & totalizing meters for gas & liquids

(P-10738)
INTERSCAN CORPORATION
4590 Ish Dr Ste 110, Simi Valley
(93063-7682)
PHONE..................805 823-8301
Richard Shaw, *President*
Lorienne Shaw, *Treasurer*
Michael Shaw, *Vice Pres*
Gitty Gilani, *Manager*
Scott Richards, *Manager*
EMP: 23
SQ FT: 10,000
SALES (est): 5.2MM **Privately Held**
WEB: www.gasdetection.com
SIC: 3824 3829 Gas meters, domestic & large capacity: industrial; measuring & controlling devices

(P-10739)
MINDRUM PRECISION INC
Also Called: Mindrum Precision Products
10000 4th St, Rancho Cucamonga
(91730-5793)
PHONE..................909 989-1728
Diane Mindrum, *CEO*
Kurt Ponsor, *President*
Daniel Mindrum, *Treasurer*
Daphne Fulayter, *Admin Asst*
Matt Wade, *Project Mgr*
EMP: 49 EST: 1956
SQ FT: 30,000
SALES (est): 7.9MM **Privately Held**
WEB: www.mindrum.com
SIC: 3824 3827 3823 3264 Fluid meters & counting devices; optical instruments & lenses; industrial instrmnts msrmnt display/control process variable; porcelain electrical supplies; products of purchased glass

(P-10740)
ZENNER PERFORMANCE METERS INC
1910 E Westward Ave, Banning
(92220-6366)
P.O. Box 895 (92220-0019)
PHONE..................951 849-8822
Ron Gallon, *CEO*
▲ EMP: 22 EST: 2012
SALES (est): 6.8MM **Privately Held**
SIC: 3824 Water meters

3825 Instrs For Measuring & Testing Electricity

(P-10741)
ALTA PROPERTIES INC
International Transducer
869 Ward Dr, Santa Barbara (93111-2920)
PHONE..................805 683-2575
Brian Dolan, *Director*
EMP: 175
SALES (corp-wide): 71.9MM **Privately Held**
SIC: 3825 3812 Transducers for volts, amperes, watts, vars, frequency, etc.; search & navigation equipment
PA: Alta Properties, Inc.
879 Ward Dr
Santa Barbara CA 93111
805 967-0171

(P-10742)
ARBITER SYSTEMS INCORPORATED (PA)
1324 Vendels Cir Ste 121, Paso Robles
(93446-3806)
PHONE..................805 237-3831
Craig Armstrong, *President*
Bruce Roeder, *CFO*
Craig E Armstrong, *Technical Staff*
EMP: 30 EST: 1973
SQ FT: 15,000
SALES (est): 5.5MM **Privately Held**
WEB: www.arbiter.com
SIC: 3825 3829 3663 Test equipment for electronic & electric measurement; measuring & controlling devices; radio & TV communications equipment

(P-10743)
ASTRONICS TEST SYSTEMS INC (DH)
4 Goodyear, Irvine (92618-2002)
PHONE..................800 722-2528
James Mulato, *President*
David Burney, *Treasurer*
Ted Baker, *Vice Pres*
Jonathan Sinskie, *Vice Pres*
Jaime Moreno, *Engineer*
◆ EMP: 130 EST: 2014
SQ FT: 98,600
SALES (est): 110.5MM **Privately Held**
WEB: www.astronics.com
SIC: 3825 Test equipment for electronic & electric measurement
HQ: Advantest Test Solutions, Inc.
4 Goodyear
Irvine CA 92618
949 523-6900

(P-10744)
AZIMUTH ELECTRONICS INC
2605 S El Camino Real, San Clemente
(92672-3353)
PHONE..................949 492-6481
Kenneth C Johnson, *President*
Kenneth C Johnsen, *President*
John Cangiano, *Technician*
Melissa Johnsen, *Technical Staff*
Michael Anello, *Sales Staff*
EMP: 13 EST: 1964
SQ FT: 3,600
SALES (est): 1.6MM **Privately Held**
WEB: www.azimuth-electronics.com
SIC: 3825 7389 Test equipment for electronic & electrical circuits; design, commercial & industrial

(P-10745)
B&K PRECISION CORPORATION (PA)
22820 Savi Ranch Pkwy, Yorba Linda
(92887-4610)
PHONE..................714 921-9095
Victor Tolan, *CEO*
Linda Morton, *CFO*
Michelle Yeh, *Opers Staff*
Ayumu Tokiwa, *Marketing Staff*
▲ EMP: 21 EST: 1951
SQ FT: 17,000
SALES (est): 7.6MM **Privately Held**
WEB: www.bkprecision.com
SIC: 3825 5063 Instruments to measure electricity; electrical apparatus & equipment

(P-10746)
CHILICON POWER LLC (PA)
15415 W Sunset Blvd # 102, Pacific Palisades (90272-3546)
PHONE..................310 800-1396
Christopher R Jones,
Thomas Nelson, *VP Business*
Alexandre Kral,
David Sywensky, *Director*
▲ EMP: 24 EST: 2011
SALES (est): 1MM **Privately Held**
WEB: www.chiliconpower.com
SIC: 3825 Power measuring equipment, electrical

(P-10747)
CHROMA SYSTEMS SOLUTIONS INC (HQ)
19772 Pauling, Foothill Ranch
(92610-2611)
PHONE..................949 297-4848
Fred Sabatine, *President*
Jim Payne, *Vice Pres*
Abbas Ford, *Executive*
Philip Ngo, *Program Mgr*
Brittany Reis, *Administration*
▲ EMP: 85 EST: 2001
SQ FT: 25,000
SALES (est): 28.7MM **Privately Held**
WEB: www.chromausa.com
SIC: 3825 Measuring instruments & meters, electric

(P-10748)
DIVERSFIED TCHNCAL SYSTEMS INC (HQ)
1720 Apollo Ct, Seal Beach (90740-5617)
PHONE..................562 493-0158

Stephen D Pruitt, *CEO*
Steve Pruitt, *President*
Rollin White, *COO*
Kirsten Larsen, *CFO*
George M Beckage, *Vice Pres*
▲ **EMP:** 29 **EST:** 1990
SQ FT: 55,000
SALES (est): 8.9MM
SALES (corp-wide): 269.8MM **Publicly Held**
WEB: www.dtsweb.com
SIC: 3825 3679 3495 8731 Instruments to measure electricity; analog-digital converters, electronic instrumentation type; electronic circuits; clock springs, precision; commercial physical research
PA: Vishay Precision Group, Inc.
    3 Great Valley Pkwy # 150
    Malvern PA 19355
    484 321-5300

(P-10749)
ECLYPSE INTERNATIONAL CORP (PA)
341 S Maple St, Corona (92878-4307)
PHONE................................951 371-8008
Tom Day, *Ch of Bd*
Glen Coulter, *Shareholder*
C Alan Ferguson, *CEO*
David Hieger, *Program Mgr*
Dave Lamper, *General Mgr*
EMP: 15 **EST:** 1988
SQ FT: 2,000
SALES (est): 7.1MM **Privately Held**
WEB: www.eclypse.org
SIC: 3825 8711 Test equipment for electronic & electrical circuits; consulting engineer

(P-10750)
EQUUS PRODUCTS INC
17352 Von Karman Ave, Irvine (92614-6204)
PHONE................................714 424-6779
Ieon C Chen, *CEO*
Cynthia H Tsai, *CFO*
◆ **EMP:** 31 **EST:** 1982
SQ FT: 36,000
SALES (est): 4.7MM **Privately Held**
WEB: www.equus.com
SIC: 3825 3545 3714 Electrical power measuring equipment; machine tool accessories; motor vehicle parts & accessories

(P-10751)
ERP POWER LLC (PA)
893 Patriot Dr Ste E, Moorpark (93021-3357)
PHONE................................805 517-1300
Jeffrey Frank, *CEO*
Abdul Sher-Jan, *COO*
James Kingman, *Exec VP*
Andy Williams, *Exec VP*
Vachik Javadian, *Vice Pres*
EMP: 17 **EST:** 2005
SALES (est): 12.8MM **Privately Held**
WEB: www.erp-power.com
SIC: 3825 Energy measuring equipment, electrical

(P-10752)
ETA COMPUTE INC
340 N Westlake Blvd # 115, Westlake Village (91362-7027)
PHONE................................805 379-5121
Leon Bezdikian, *Vice Pres*
EMP: 32 **EST:** 2015
SALES (est): 5.4MM **Privately Held**
WEB: www.etacompute.com
SIC: 3825 3559 Semiconductor test equipment; semiconductor manufacturing machinery

(P-10753)
FIRST LEGAL NETWORK
1517 Beverly Blvd, Los Angeles (90026-5704)
PHONE 213 250-1111
Alex Martinez, *CEO*
Don Hoefnagel, *Exec VP*
Patty Holland, *Vice Pres*
Gina Tsai, *Vice Pres*
Jayson Giannone, *Regional Mgr*
EMP: 47 **EST:** 2015

SALES (est): 4.7MM **Privately Held**
WEB: www.firstlegal.com
SIC: 3825 4899 Network analyzers; communication signal enhancement network system

(P-10754)
FISCHER CSTM CMMUNICATIONS INC (PA)
19220 Normandie Ave B, Torrance (90502-1011)
PHONE................................310 303-3300
David Fischer, *President*
Allen Fischer, *Vice Pres*
EMP: 22 **EST:** 1971
SALES (est): 9MM **Privately Held**
WEB: www.fischercc.com
SIC: 3825 Digital test equipment, electronic & electrical circuits

(P-10755)
GOULD & BASS COMPANY INC
1431 W 2nd St, Pomona (91766-1299)
PHONE................................909 623-6793
John S Bass, *CEO*
Jeremy Basse, *Purchasing*
Lura Jackson, *Senior Buyer*
Jackson Lura, *Senior Buyer*
Ed Plachy, *QC Mgr*
EMP: 32 **EST:** 1971
SQ FT: 66,000
SALES (est): 4.9MM **Privately Held**
WEB: www.gould-bass.net
SIC: 3825 3535 3556 Test equipment for electronic & electric measurement; belt conveyor systems, general industrial use; packing house machinery

(P-10756)
I C I
Also Called: Intercom
11693 San Vicente Blvd, Los Angeles (90049-5105)
PHONE................................213 749-3709
Behzad Soroudi, *President*
Victoria Goosey, *Corp Secy*
Perry Bakhtiari, *Vice Pres*
EMP: 15 **EST:** 1983
SQ FT: 6,000
SALES (est): 1.3MM **Privately Held**
SIC: 3825 5063 Test equipment for electronic & electrical circuits; electrical supplies

(P-10757)
INTELLIGENT CMPT SOLUTIONS INC (PA)
8968 Fullbright Ave, Chatsworth (91311-6123)
PHONE................................818 998-5805
Uzi Kohavi, *President*
Gonen Ravid, *CEO*
▲ **EMP:** 25 **EST:** 1989
SQ FT: 21,000
SALES (est): 6.1MM **Privately Held**
WEB: www.ics-iq.com
SIC: 3825 3577 3572 Test equipment for electronic & electrical circuits; computer peripheral equipment; computer storage devices

(P-10758)
INTEPRO AMERICA LP (PA)
14662 Franklin Ave Ste E, Tustin (92780-7224)
PHONE................................714 953-2686
Gary Halmbacher,
Jennifer Hoare, *Office Mgr*
Armando Prado, *Regl Sales Mgr*
Eric Turner, *Sales Staff*
Andrew Engler, *Mktg Coord*
▲ **EMP:** 23 **EST:** 2006
SALES (est): 4.6MM **Privately Held**
WEB: www.inteproate.com
SIC: 3825 Frequency meters: electrical, mechanical & electronic

(P-10759)
INTERNATIONAL TRANDUCER CORP
Also Called: Channel Technologies Group
869 Ward Dr, Santa Barbara (93111-2920)
PHONE................................805 683-2575
R M Callahan, *Co-COB*
Kevin Ruelas, *President*

Robert F Carlson, *Co-COB*
Brian Dolan, *Director*
EMP: 160 **EST:** 1966
SALES (est): 25MM
SALES (corp-wide): 84.3MM **Privately Held**
WEB: www.gavial.com
SIC: 3825 3812 Transducers for volts, amperes, watts, vars, frequency, etc.; search & navigation equipment
PA: Gavial Holdings, Inc.
    1435 W Mccoy Ln
    Santa Maria CA 93455
    805 614-0060

(P-10760)
INTERSTATE ELECTRONICS CORP (DH)
Also Called: L-3 Interstate Electronics
602 E Vermont Ave, Anaheim (92805-5607)
P.O. Box 3117 (92803-3117)
PHONE................................714 758-0500
Thomas L Walsh, *President*
Carol Grogg, *Vice Pres*
Candace Lee, *Admin Sec*
David Boss, *Network Mgr*
Mario Razo, *Software Engr*
EMP: 275 **EST:** 1955
SQ FT: 235,700
SALES (est): 185.6MM
SALES (corp-wide): 18.1B **Publicly Held**
WEB: www.l3harris.com
SIC: 3825 3812 3679 Test equipment for electronic & electric measurement; navigational systems & instruments; liquid crystal displays (LCD)
HQ: L3 Technologies, Inc.
    600 3rd Ave Fl 34
    New York NY 10016
    321 727-9100

(P-10761)
INTERSTATE ELECTRONICS CORP
Also Called: Integrated Technical Services
600 E Vermont Ave, Anaheim (92805-5607)
PHONE................................714 758-0500
Robert Schembre, *Branch Mgr*
EMP: 71
SALES (corp-wide): 18.1B **Publicly Held**
SIC: 3825 Instruments to measure electricity
HQ: Interstate Electronics Corporation
    602 E Vermont Ave
    Anaheim CA 92805
    714 758-0500

(P-10762)
IXIA (HQ)
26601 Agoura Rd, Calabasas (91302-1959)
PHONE................................818 871-1800
Neil Dougherty, *President*
Jason Kary, *CFO*
Jeffrey LI, *Treasurer*
Matthew S Alexander, *Senior VP*
Andy Moorwood, *Vice Pres*
EMP: 1179 **EST:** 1997
SQ FT: 116,000
SALES: 484.8MM
SALES (corp-wide): 4.2B **Publicly Held**
WEB: www.support.ixiacom.com
SIC: 3825 7371 Network analyzers; custom computer programming services; software programming applications
PA: Keysight Technologies, Inc.
    1400 Fountaingrove Pkwy
    Santa Rosa CA 95403
    800 829-4444

(P-10763)
KLA CORPORATION
15061 Beach Blvd, Westminster (92683-6201)
PHONE................................714 893-2474
Anand K Patel, *President*
Saleem Ahmed, *Engineer*
Timothy Wong, *Engineer*
Frank Lopez, *Mfg Staff*
Kambia Torres, *Dean*
EMP: 17 **EST:** 2006

SALES (est): 183.8K **Privately Held**
WEB: www.kla-tencor.com
SIC: 3825 Instruments to measure electricity

(P-10764)
MARVIN TEST SOLUTIONS INC
1770 Kettering, Irvine (92614-5616)
PHONE................................949 263-2222
Loofie Gutterman, *President*
Leon Tsimmerman, *CFO*
Gerald Friedman, *Treasurer*
Jacob Newberry, *IT/INT Sup*
Nicolas Bricteux, *Engineer*
EMP: 96 **EST:** 1987
SQ FT: 31,000
SALES (est): 17.5MM
SALES (corp-wide): 149.5MM **Privately Held**
WEB: www.marvintest.com
SIC: 3825 Instruments to measure electricity
PA: Marvin Engineering Co., Inc.
    261 W Beach Ave
    Inglewood CA 90302
    310 674-5030

(P-10765)
MEREX INC
1283 Flynn Rd, Camarillo (93012-8013)
P.O. Box 3474, Chatsworth (91313-3474)
PHONE................................805 446-2700
Chester J Dopler, *CEO*
Ahmad Shams, *President*
Nathan Skop, *Exec VP*
EMP: 25 **EST:** 1984
SALES (est): 874K **Privately Held**
WEB: www.goallclear.com
SIC: 3825 Instruments to measure electricity

(P-10766)
N H RESEARCH INCORPORATED
16601 Hale Ave, Irvine (92606-5049)
PHONE................................949 474-3900
Peter Swartz, *President*
Shawn Brown, *Buyer*
Joan Johnston, *Buyer*
Mike Nolan, *Natl Sales Mgr*
▲ **EMP:** 75 **EST:** 1965
SQ FT: 29,000
SALES (est): 18.5MM **Privately Held**
WEB: www.nhresearch.com
SIC: 3825 3829 Test equipment for electronic & electrical circuits; measuring & controlling devices

(P-10767)
NEARFIELD SYSTEMS INC
19730 Magellan Dr, Torrance (90502-1104)
PHONE................................310 525-7000
Greg Hindman, *President*
Dan Slater, *Vice Pres*
Joy Lebbin, *Administration*
Kenneth Rivers, *Technology*
Dan Swan, *Engineer*
▼ **EMP:** 62 **EST:** 1988
SALES (est): 16.9MM
SALES (corp-wide): 4.5B **Publicly Held**
WEB: www.nsi-mi.com
SIC: 3825 3829 Test equipment for electronic & electric measurement; measuring & controlling devices
HQ: Nsi-Mi Technologies, Llc
    1125 Satellit Blvd Nw # 100
    Suwanee GA 30024
    678 475-8300

(P-10768)
PULSE INSTRUMENTS
1234 Francisco St, Torrance (90502-1200)
PHONE................................310 515-5330
Sylvia Kan, *President*
David Kan, *Vice Pres*
David T Kan, *Vice Pres*
Michael Woi, *Info Tech Dir*
Victor Nguyen, *Technology*
EMP: 23 **EST:** 1975
SQ FT: 15,000
SALES (est): 4.8MM **Privately Held**
WEB: www.pulseinstruments.com
SIC: 3825 3823 Pulse (signal) generators; industrial instrmnts msrmnt display/control process variable

(P-10769)
ROHDE & SCHWARZ USA INC
2255 N Ontario St Ste 150, Burbank
(91504-3186)
PHONE................................818 846-3600
Chris Dennison, *Comp Spec*
Amit Khanna, *Engineer*
Matt Hammond, *Business Mgr*
Erik Balladares, *Director*
EMP: 17
SALES (corp-wide): 2.8B **Privately Held**
WEB: www.rohde-schwarz.com
SIC: 3825 Instruments to measure electricity
HQ: Rohde & Schwarz Usa, Inc.
6821 Benjamin Franklin Dr
Columbia MD 21046
410 910-7800

(P-10770)
SIGNUM SYSTEMS CORPORATION
1211 Flynn Rd Unit 104, Camarillo
(93012-6208)
PHONE................................805 383-3682
Jerry Lewandowski, *President*
Robert Chyla, *Vice Pres*
◆ EMP: 17 EST: 1979
SQ FT: 6,000
SALES (est): 2.8MM
SALES (corp-wide): 43MM **Privately Held**
WEB: www.iar.com
SIC: 3825 3577 Test equipment for electronic & electrical circuits; computer peripheral equipment
PA: I.A.R. Systems Group Ab

Uppsala 750 2
841 092-000

(P-10771)
SPECTRUM INSTRUMENTS INC
570 E Arrow Hwy Ste D, San Dimas
(91773-3347)
PHONE................................909 971-9710
Thomas Verseput, *President*
Jeffrey Grous, *Director*
Donald REA, *Director*
EMP: 14 EST: 1993
SALES (est): 749.5K **Privately Held**
WEB: www.spectruminstruments.net
SIC: 3825 Frequency synthesizers

(P-10772)
STS INSTRUMENTS INC
17711 Mitchell N, Irvine (92614-6028)
P.O. Box 1805, Ardmore OK (73402-1805)
PHONE................................580 223-4773
Kevin Voelcker, *President*
William D Long, *Treasurer*
Barbara J Stinnett, *Admin Sec*
▲ EMP: 47 EST: 1954
SQ FT: 20,000
SALES (est): 1.6MM
SALES (corp-wide): 15.9MM **Privately Held**
WEB: www.stsinstruments.com
SIC: 3825 Test equipment for electronic & electrical circuits
PA: Ppst, Inc.
17692 Fitch
Irvine CA 92614
800 421-1921

(P-10773)
TASEON INC
515 S Flower St Fl 25, Los Angeles
(90071-2228)
PHONE................................408 240-7800
Albert Wong, *CEO*
Celeste Rogers, *VP Finance*
Sue Whitsett, *Finance*
▲ EMP: 17 EST: 2007
SQ FT: 21,000
SALES (est): 1.1MM **Privately Held**
SIC: 3825 Network analyzers

(P-10774)
TRI-NET INC
14721 Hilton Dr, Fontana (92336-4013)
PHONE................................909 483-3555
Rosemarie V Hall, *President*
James Franzone, *Senior VP*
James Hall, *Technology*
Rex Arnold, *Engineer*

EMP: 19 EST: 1991
SQ FT: 7,500
SALES (est): 1.6MM **Privately Held**
SIC: 3825 Test equipment for electronic & electric measurement

(P-10775)
WILCOMPUTE
38713 Tierra Subida Ave, Palmdale
(93551-4562)
PHONE................................818 674-0506
Paul Wilson, *CEO*
EMP: 14 EST: 2001
SALES (est): 1.6MM **Privately Held**
SIC: 3825 7389 Network analyzers;

3826 Analytical Instruments

(P-10776)
ACTION RESPONSE TEAM INC
114 Stony Creek Rd, Big Bear Lake
(92315-2486)
P.O. Box 1412 (92315-1412)
PHONE................................909 585-9019
Donald Bowman, *Principal*
EMP: 15 EST: 2009
SALES (est): 3.2MM **Privately Held**
WEB: www.actionresponse.com
SIC: 3826 Moisture analyzers

(P-10777)
ADVANCED MICRO INSTRUMENTS INC
Also Called: AMI
225 Paularino Ave, Costa Mesa
(92626-3313)
PHONE................................714 848-5533
Kenneth Biele, *CEO*
W William Layton, *Controller*
EMP: 23 EST: 1999
SQ FT: 2,500
SALES (est): 5.3MM **Privately Held**
WEB: www.amio2.com
SIC: 3826 Analytical instruments

(P-10778)
AG LABORATORY CONSULTING
2255 S Brdwy Ste 12, Santa Maria (93454)
PHONE................................805 739-5333
Eryn K Gray, *Managing Prtnr*
Aaron Evans, *Division Mgr*
EMP: 16 EST: 2014
SALES (est): 2.1MM **Privately Held**
WEB: www.aglaboratory.com
SIC: 3826 3821 Surface area analyzers; physics laboratory apparatus

(P-10779)
ANALYTIK JENA US LLC (DH)
2066 W 11th St, Upland (91786-3509)
P.O. Box 5015 (91785-5015)
PHONE................................909 946-3197
Monde Qhobosheane, *CEO*
Chris Griffith, *CFO*
Deeanne Gunnemann, *Vice Pres*
Alex Waluszko, *Business Dir*
Sean Gallagher, *Research*
◆ EMP: 100 EST: 2006
SQ FT: 42,000
SALES (est): 32.5MM
SALES (corp-wide): 371.8MM **Privately Held**
WEB: www.analytik-jena.us
SIC: 3826 3641 Analytical instruments; ultraviolet lamps
HQ: Analytik Jena Gmbh
Konrad-Zuse-Str. 1
Jena TH 07745
364 177-70

(P-10780)
ANASYS INSTRUMENTS CORP (PA)
325 Chapala St, Santa Barbara
(93101-3407)
PHONE................................805 730-3310
Roshan Shetty, *President*
Kevin Kjloer, *Exec VP*
Doug Gotthard, *Engineer*
Michael Sbaraglia, *Buyer*
Dean Dawson, *VP Mktg*
EMP: 14 EST: 2005
SQ FT: 3,000

SALES (est): 3.3MM **Privately Held**
WEB: www.anasysinstruments.com
SIC: 3826 Thermal analysis instruments, laboratory type

(P-10781)
APPLIED INSTRUMENT TECH INC
2121 Aviation Dr, Upland (91786-2195)
PHONE................................909 204-3700
Joseph Laconte, *President*
EMP: 40 EST: 2010
SALES (est): 8.7MM
SALES (corp-wide): 177.9K **Privately Held**
WEB: www.aitanalyzers.com
SIC: 3826 Analytical instruments
HQ: Schneider Electric Usa, Inc.
201 Wshngton St Ext Ste 2
Boston MA 02108
978 975-9600

(P-10782)
AUTONOMOUS MEDICAL DEVICES INC (PA)
10604 S La Cienega Blvd, Inglewood
(90304-1115)
PHONE................................424 331-0900
Frank Adell, *CEO*
Christopher Bissell, *CFO*
EMP: 23 EST: 2013
SQ FT: 3,750
SALES (est): 3.4MM **Privately Held**
SIC: 3826 Analytical instruments

(P-10783)
BECKMAN COULTER INC
15989 Cypress Ave, Chino (91708-9100)
PHONE................................909 597-3967
EMP: 82
SALES (corp-wide): 18.3B **Publicly Held**
SIC: 3826 3821 3841 Mfg Analytical Instr Mfg Lab Apparatus/Furn Mfg Surgical/Med Instr
HQ: Beckman Coulter, Inc.
250 S Kraemer Blvd
Brea CA 92821
714 993-5321

(P-10784)
BECKMAN INSTRUMENTS INC
2500 N Harbor Blvd, Fullerton
(92835-2600)
PHONE................................714 871-4848
John Collette, *President*
Steve Blanc, *District Mgr*
EMP: 52 EST: 1934
SALES (est): 1.8MM **Privately Held**
SIC: 3826 Analytical instruments

(P-10785)
BEMCO INC (PA)
2255 Union Pl, Simi Valley (93065-1661)
PHONE................................805 583-4970
Randy Jean Bruskrud, *President*
Brian Bruskrud, *Admin Sec*
Adam Christiansen, *Project Engr*
Matthew Lazarony, *Engineer*
Richard Behrendt, *Sales Engr*
EMP: 24 EST: 1951
SQ FT: 50,000
SALES (est): 6.7MM **Privately Held**
WEB: www.bemcoinc.com
SIC: 3826 Environmental testing equipment

(P-10786)
BIOPAC SYSTEMS INC
42 Aero Camino, Goleta (93117-3105)
PHONE................................805 685-0066
Alan Macy, *CEO*
Marc Wester, *CFO*
William McMullen, *Vice Pres*
Rodney Wagoner, *Sales Dir*
Brenda Dentinger, *Marketing Staff*
EMP: 40 EST: 1986
SQ FT: 16,000
SALES (est): 9.1MM **Privately Held**
WEB: www.biopac.com
SIC: 3826 Analytical instruments

(P-10787)
BIORAD INC
9500 Jeronimo Rd, Irvine (92618-2017)
PHONE................................949 598-1200
Alfredo Ornelas, *Program Mgr*

Alex Alzona, *General Mgr*
Kristin Lucero, *Software Engr*
Jia Tan, *Software Engr*
Zdravko Bradic, *Research*
EMP: 21 EST: 2011
SALES (est): 5MM **Privately Held**
WEB: www.bio-rad.com
SIC: 3826 Analytical instruments

(P-10788)
BROADLEY-JAMES CORPORATION
19 Thomas, Irvine (92618-2704)
PHONE................................949 829-5555
Scott Broadley, *President*
Leighton S Broadley, *CFO*
Robert Garrahy, *Vice Pres*
Dan Folwell, *General Mgr*
Catherine A Broadley, *Admin Sec*
EMP: 79 EST: 1967
SQ FT: 24,000
SALES (est): 16.1MM **Privately Held**
WEB: www.broadleyjames.com
SIC: 3826 3823 Analytical instruments; industrial process measurement equipment

(P-10789)
COMBIMATRIX CORPORATION (HQ)
310 Goddard Ste 150, Irvine (92618-4617)
PHONE................................949 753-0624
Mark McDonough, *Officer*
R Judd Jessup, *Ch of Bd*
Scott R Burell, *CFO*
Evan Cleaver, *Executive*
Natasa Dzidic, *Research*
EMP: 51 EST: 1995
SQ FT: 12,200
SALES: 12.8MM **Publicly Held**
WEB: www.combimatrix.com
SIC: 3826 8731 8071 Analytical instruments; biotechnical research, commercial; medical laboratories

(P-10790)
CONDITION MONITORING SVCS INC
855 San Ysidro Ln, Nipomo (93444-8500)
P.O. Box 278 (93444-0278)
PHONE................................888 359-3277
Kirk F Cormany, *President*
Fred Hull, *Analyst*
Lindsey Pillow, *Manager*
EMP: 21 EST: 2006
SALES (est): 2.5MM **Privately Held**
WEB: www.conditionmonitoringservices.com
SIC: 3826 Infrared analytical instruments

(P-10791)
DOE & INGALLS CAL OPER LLC
1060 Citrus St, Riverside (92507-1730)
PHONE................................951 801-7175
John Hollenbach, *Mng Member*
EMP: 36 EST: 2008
SQ FT: 43,000
SALES (est): 9.9MM
SALES (corp-wide): 32.2E **Publicly Held**
WEB: www.thermofisher.com
SIC: 3826 Analytical instruments
HQ: Doe & Ingalls Management, Llc
4813 Emperor Blvd Ste 300
Durham NC 27703

(P-10792)
ENDRESS & HAUSER CONDUCTA INC
Also Called: Endresshauser Conducta
4123 E La Palma Ave, Anaheim
(92807-1867)
PHONE................................800 835-5474
Manfred A Jagiella, *CEO*
Claude Genswein, *CFO*
Steve Anderson, *Vice Pres*
Joachim Hartmeyer, *Vice Pres*
Jason Huo, *Engineer*
EMP: 50 EST: 1976
SQ FT: 31,000

SALES (est): 12.5MM
SALES (corp-wide): 371.8MM **Privately Held**
WEB: www.analysis-oem.com
SIC: **3826** 3823 Water testing apparatus; industrial instrmnts msrmnt display/control process variable
HQ: Endress+Hauser Conducta Gmbh+Co. Kg
Dieselstr. 24
Gerlingen BW 70839
715 620-90

(P-10793)
ENTECH INSTRUMENTS INC
2207 Agate Ct, Simi Valley (93065-1839)
PHONE..............................805 527-5939
Daniel B Cardin, *CEO*
Jared Bossart, *Admin Sec*
Brian Vogel, *Design Engr*
Ziggy Cunanan, *Graphic Designe*
Jeff Schroeder, *Engineer*
▲ EMP: 55 EST: 1989
SQ FT: 25,000
SALES (est): 12.8MM **Privately Held**
WEB: www.entechinst.com
SIC: **3826** Environmental testing equipment

(P-10794)
FLIR COMMERCIAL SYSTEMS INC (DH)
6769 Hollister Ave, Goleta (93117-3001)
PHONE..............................805 964-9797
James J Cannon, *President*
Carol P Lowe, *CFO*
Jeffrey Frank, *Vice Pres*
Tim Fitzgibbons, *General Mgr*
Eric Ford, *Software Engr*
▲ EMP: 350 EST: 1996
SALES (est): 253.9MM
SALES (corp-wide): 3B **Publicly Held**
WEB: www.flir.com
SIC: **3826** Analytical instruments
HQ: Teledyne Flir, Llc
27700 Sw Parkway Ave
Wilsonville OR 97070
503 498-3547

(P-10795)
FLIR EOC LLC
Also Called: Flir Elctr-Ptcal Comp Bus Unit
2223 Eastman Ave Ste B, Ventura (93003-8050)
P.O. Box 6217 (93006-6217)
PHONE..............................805 642-4645
John Baumann, *General Mgr*
Sergio Stebeikin, *Planning*
Mabel Mora, *Production*
EMP: 30 EST: 2004
SQ FT: 7,264
SALES (est): 9.9MM
SALES (corp-wide): 3B **Publicly Held**
WEB: www.flir.com
SIC: **3826** Laser scientific & engineering instruments
HQ: Teledyne Flir, Llc
27700 Sw Parkway Ave
Wilsonville OR 97070
503 498-3547

(P-10796)
HAMILTON SUNDSTRAND CORP
Collins Aerospace
960 Overland Ct, San Dimas (91773-1742)
P.O. Box 2801, Pomona (91769-2801)
PHONE..............................909 593-5300
Bob Hertel, *Branch Mgr*
Thomas Nemec, *Vice Pres*
Jeffrey Ludwig, *Associate Dir*
Araceli Cortez, *Program Mgr*
Bryan Hunt, *Program Mgr*
EMP: 240
SALES (corp-wide): 56.5B **Publicly Held**
WEB: www.utcaerospacesystems.com
SIC: **3826** 3861 3812 Spectrometers; cameras, still & motion picture (all types); search & navigation equipment
HQ: Hamilton Sundstrand Corporation
1 Hamilton Rd
Windsor Locks CT 06096
860 654-6000

(P-10797)
HORIBA AMERICAS HOLDING INC (HQ)
9755 Research Dr, Irvine (92618-4626)
PHONE..............................949 250-4811
Juichi Saito, *CEO*
Pattie Jones, *Controller*
EMP: 1055 EST: 2017
SALES (est): 194.1MM **Privately Held**
WEB: www.horiba.com
SIC: **3826** Analytical instruments

(P-10798)
HORIBA INSTRUMENTS INC (DH)
Also Called: Horiba Automotive Test Systems
9755 Research Dr, Irvine (92618-4626)
PHONE..............................949 250-4811
Jai Hakhu, *Ch of Bd*
Pattie Jones, *Credit Staff*
▲ EMP: 195 EST: 1998
SQ FT: 80,000
SALES (est): 194.1MM **Privately Held**
WEB: www.horiba.com
SIC: **3826** 3829 3511 3825 Analytical instruments; measuring & controlling devices; turbines & turbine generator sets; instruments to measure electricity; diagnostic equipment, medical; medical laboratory equipment; hospital equipment & supplies; physician equipment & supplies; industrial process measurement equipment
HQ: Horiba Americas Holding Incorporated
9755 Research Dr
Irvine CA 92618
949 250-4811

(P-10799)
LAMBDA RESEARCH OPTICS INC
1695 Macarthur Blvd, Costa Mesa (92626-1440)
PHONE..............................714 327-0600
Mark Youn, *President*
James Choi, *Managing Dir*
▲ EMP: 65 EST: 1991
SQ FT: 3,500
SALES (est): 8.7MM **Privately Held**
WEB: www.lambda.cc
SIC: **3826** 3827 3229 Laser scientific & engineering instruments; optical instruments & lenses; pressed & blown glass

(P-10800)
MAKO INDUSTRIES SC INC
1280 N Red Gum St, Anaheim (92806-1820)
PHONE..............................714 632-1400
John Tittelfitz, *CEO*
Gunnar Bredek, *Vice Pres*
Gia Moy, *Office Mgr*
Tony Watterson, *Prdtn Mgr*
Rob Larsen, *Sales Staff*
▲ EMP: 41 EST: 2007
SALES (est): 4.4MM **Privately Held**
WEB: www.makoindustries.com
SIC: **3826** Environmental testing equipment

(P-10801)
MARBIL INDUSTRIES INC
2201 N Glassell St, Orange (92865-2701)
PHONE..............................714 974-4032
Allan V Thompson, *President*
William B Thomson Jr, *Shareholder*
EMP: 32 EST: 1972
SQ FT: 10,000
SALES (est): 1.7MM **Privately Held**
WEB: www.marbilindustries.com
SIC: **3826** Mass spectrometers

(P-10802)
MOTIONLOFT INC
13681 Newport Ave Ste 8, Tustin (92780-7815)
PHONE..............................415 580-7671
Joyce Reitman, *CEO*
Dan Daogaru, *President*
Alex Hill, *Software Engr*
Peter Kim, *Opers Staff*
Chris Garrison, *VP Sales*
EMP: 39 EST: 2010

SALES (est): 6MM **Privately Held**
WEB: www.motionloft.com
SIC: **3826** 7372 Analytical instruments; application computer software; business oriented computer software

(P-10803)
MP BIOMEDICALS LLC (HQ)
9 Goddard, Irvine (92618-4600)
PHONE..............................949 833-2500
Huanjie Wang, *CEO*
Tom Stankovich, *CFO*
Earl Simpson, *Officer*
Samson Chen, *Vice Pres*
Paul Tan, *Vice Pres*
▲ EMP: 20 EST: 2014
SALES (est): 105.5MM
SALES (corp-wide): 443.3MM **Privately Held**
WEB: www.mpbio.com
SIC: **3826** Analytical instruments
PA: Valiant Co.,Ltd
No.11, Wuzhishan Road, Economic Technology Development Zone
Yantai 26400
535 637-8873

(P-10804)
OSPREYDATA INC
32242 Paseo Adelanto C, San Juan Capistrano (92675-3610)
PHONE..............................619 971-4662
Tim Burke, *Vice Pres*
Scott Brown, *VP Bus Dvlpt*
Ron Frohock, *CTO*
Jingwen Zhang, *Software Dev*
Richard Wuest, *VP Sales*
EMP: 16 EST: 2018
SALES (est): 1.3MM **Privately Held**
WEB: www.ospreydata.com
SIC: **3826** Petroleum product analyzing apparatus

(P-10805)
OXFORD INSTRS ASYLUM RES INC (HQ)
7416 Hollister Ave, Santa Barbara (93117-2583)
PHONE..............................805 696-6466
Jason Cleveland, *CEO*
John Green, *President*
Roger Proksch, *President*
Richard Clark, *CFO*
Dick Clark, *Exec VP*
EMP: 55 EST: 2012
SALES (est): 11.7MM
SALES (corp-wide): 448.8MM **Privately Held**
WEB: www.afm.oxinst.com
SIC: **3826** Analytical instruments
PA: Oxford Instruments Plc
Tubney Woods
Abingdon OXON OX13
186 539-3200

(P-10806)
PHENOMENEX INC (HQ)
411 Madrid Ave, Torrance (90501-1430)
PHONE..............................310 212-0555
Farshad Mahjoor, *President*
Frank T McFaden, *CFO*
Kati Farkas, *Vice Pres*
Kevin Hughes, *Creative Dir*
Bert Rietveld, *Business Dir*
▲ EMP: 250 EST: 1982
SQ FT: 100,000
SALES (est): 132.1MM
SALES (corp-wide): 22.2B **Publicly Held**
WEB: www.phenomenex.com
SIC: **3826** Analytical instruments
PA: Danaher Corporation
2200 Penn Ave Nw Ste 800w
Washington DC 20037
202 828-0850

(P-10807)
PHOTOTHERMAL SPECTROSCOPY CORP
325 Chapala St, Santa Barbara (93101-3407)
PHONE..............................805 730-3310
Roshan Shetty, *President*
David Grigg, *Director*
Mustafa Kansiz, *Director*
Sergey Zayats, *Manager*
EMP: 15 EST: 2018

SALES (est): 1.5MM **Privately Held**
WEB: www.photothermal.com
SIC: **3826** Analytical instruments

(P-10808)
QUEST DIAGNOSTICS NICHOLS INST (HQ)
33608 Ortega Hwy, San Juan Capistrano (92675-2042)
PHONE..............................949 728-4000
Catherine T Doherty, *CEO*
Nicholas Conti, *Vice Pres*
Timothy Sharpe, *Vice Pres*
Dan Haemmerle, *Exec Dir*
Olga Shevchenko, *Prgrmr*
EMP: 1000 EST: 1971
SQ FT: 240,000
SALES (est): 240.8MM
SALES (corp-wide): 9.4B **Publicly Held**
WEB: www.questdiagnostics.com
SIC: **3826** 8071 Analytical instruments; testing laboratories
PA: Quest Diagnostics Incorporated
500 Plaza Dr Ste G
Secaucus NJ 07094
973 520-2700

(P-10809)
SAFEGUARD ENVIROGROUP INC
153 Lowell Ave, Glendora (91741-2449)
PHONE..............................626 512-7585
Brad Kovar, *Principal*
Bryan Covar, *COO*
Bryan Kovar, *COO*
EMP: 24 EST: 2005
SALES (est): 1.5MM **Privately Held**
WEB: www.safeguardenviro.com
SIC: **3826** Moisture analyzers

(P-10810)
SCREENING SYSTEMS INC (PA)
36 Blackbird Ln, Aliso Viejo (92656-1765)
P.O. Box 3931, Laguna Hills (92654-3931)
PHONE..............................949 855-1751
Susan L Baker, *President*
Susan Baker, *CFO*
Peter Baker, *Consultant*
EMP: 25 EST: 1979
SQ FT: 34,000
SALES (est): 2.5MM **Privately Held**
WEB: www.scrsys.com
SIC: **3826** 3829 Environmental testing equipment; measuring & controlling devices

(P-10811)
SHORE WESTERN MANUFACTURING
225 W Duarte Rd, Monrovia (91016-4545)
PHONE..............................626 357-3251
Donald Schroeder, *President*
Alice Schroeder, *Corp Secy*
D Schroeder, *Vice Pres*
Joe Schroeder, *Vice Pres*
Alec Schroeder, *Project Mgr*
▲ EMP: 34 EST: 1967
SQ FT: 16,000
SALES (est): 5.1MM **Privately Held**
WEB: www.shorewestern.com
SIC: **3826** Environmental testing equipment

(P-10812)
SPECTRASENSORS INC
11027 Arrow Rte, Rancho Cucamonga (91730-4866)
PHONE..............................909 980-4238
EMP: 24
SALES (corp-wide): 371.8MM **Privately Held**
WEB: www.spectrasensors.com
SIC: **3826** Analytical Instruments, Nsk
HQ: Spectrasensors, Inc.
4333 W Sam Houston Pkwy N
Houston TX 91730
713 466-3172

(P-10813)
SPECTRASENSORS INC (HQ)
11027 Arrow Rte, Rancho Cucamonga (91730-4866)
PHONE..............................909 948-4102
George Balogh, *CEO*
Jon McCullum, *CFO*

Alfred Feitisch, *Vice Pres*
Bryce Ford, *Vice Pres*
Jorge Jones, *Vice Pres*
EMP: 25 **EST:** 2001
SALES (est): 14.6MM
SALES (corp-wide): 371.8MM **Privately Held**
WEB: www.spectrasensors.com
SIC: 3826 Analytical instruments
PA: Endress+Hauser Ag
Kagenstrasse 2
Reinach BL 4153
617 157-700

(P-10814)
SPRITE INDUSTRIES INCORPORATED
Also Called: Sprite Showers
1791 Railroad St, Corona (92878-5011)
PHONE..............................951 735-1015
David K Farley, *President*
Kathleen Farley, *Vice Pres*
Doris Farley, *Admin Sec*
Bruni Grimaldi, *Auditor*
Sherry Farley, *VP Sales*
▲ **EMP:** 20 **EST:** 1974
SQ FT: 25,000
SALES (est): 3.9MM **Privately Held**
WEB: www.spritewater.com
SIC: 3826 3589 Water testing apparatus; water filters & softeners, household type

(P-10815)
SYAGEN TECHNOLOGY LLC
1251 E Dyer Rd Ste 140, Santa Ana (92705-5677)
PHONE..............................714 258-4400
Karen Bomba,
EMP: 52 **EST:** 1995
SQ FT: 5,000
SALES (est): 2.9MM
SALES (corp-wide): 3.3B **Privately Held**
WEB: www.smithsdetection.com
SIC: 3826 Analytical instruments
HQ: Smiths Detection Inc.
2202 Lakeside Blvd
Edgewood MD 21040
410 612-2625

(P-10816)
TELEDYNE INSTRUMENTS INC
Teledyne Hanson Research
9810 Variel Ave, Chatsworth (91311-4316)
PHONE..............................818 882-7266
Thomas Reslewic, *Branch Mgr*
Jason Stuckey, *Controller*
EMP: 31
SALES (corp-wide): 3B **Publicly Held**
WEB: www.teledyne.com
SIC: 3826 Analytical instruments
HQ: Teledyne Instruments, Inc.
16830 Chestnut St
City Of Industry CA 91748
626 934-1500

(P-10817)
TELEDYNE REDLAKE MASD LLC (DH)
1049 Camino Dos Rios, Thousand Oaks (91360-2362)
PHONE..............................805 373-4545
Edwin Roks, *President*
Daryl Goodwin, *Technician*
Gabor Nagy, *Engineer*
Emily Tsang, *Production*
Darryl Symonds, *Director*
EMP: 21 **EST:** 1999
SQ FT: 50,000
SALES (est): 13.1MM
SALES (corp-wide): 3B **Publicly Held**
WEB: www.photometrics.com
SIC: 3826 3861 3822 3812 Analytical instruments; photographic equipment & supplies; auto controls regulating residntl & coml environmt & applncs; search & navigation equipment
HQ: Teledyne Digital Imaging Us, Inc.
700 Technology Park Dr # 2
Billerica MA 01821
978 670-2000

(P-10818)
TETRA TECH EC INC
17885 Von Karman Ave # 500, Irvine (92614-5227)
PHONE..............................949 809-5000

Andrew Brack, *Branch Mgr*
EMP: 61
SALES (corp-wide): 2.9B **Publicly Held**
SIC: 3826 Environmental testing equipment
HQ: Tetra Tech Ec, Inc.
6 Century Dr Ste 3
Parsippany NJ 07054
973 630-8000

(P-10819)
THERMAL ID TECHNOLOGIES INC
2707 Saturn St, Brea (92821-6705)
PHONE..............................408 656-6809
Phuong V Pham, *CEO*
EMP: 17 **EST:** 2018
SALES (est): 2.8MM **Privately Held**
WEB: www.thermalidtech.com
SIC: 3826 Thermal analysis instruments, laboratory type

(P-10820)
WYATT TECHNOLOGY CORPORATION (PA)
6330 Hollister Ave, Goleta (93117-3115)
PHONE..............................805 681-9009
Philip J Wyatt, *CEO*
Clifford D Wyatt, *President*
Geofrey K Wyatt, *President*
Carolyn Walton, *President*
Dwight Kahng, *Vice Pres*
EMP: 118 **EST:** 1982
SQ FT: 30,000
SALES (est): 37.9MM **Privately Held**
WEB: www.wyatt.com
SIC: 3826 Laser scientific & engineering instruments

3827 Optical Instruments

(P-10821)
AAREN LABORATORIES LLC
1040 S Vintage Ave Ste A, Ontario (91761-3631)
PHONE..............................909 906-5400
Richard Aguilera, *Mng Member*
Malik Smith, *Opers Staff*
EMP: 16 **EST:** 2016
SALES (est): 2.1MM **Privately Held**
WEB: www.aarenlabs.com
SIC: 3827 Optical instruments & apparatus

(P-10822)
AAREN SCIENTIFIC INC (DH)
Also Called: Carl Zeiss Meditec,
1040 S Vintage Ave Ste A, Ontario (91761-3631)
PHONE..............................909 937-1033
Hans-Joachim Miesner, *President*
Stevens Chevillotte, *Treasurer*
Eric Desjardins, *Vice Pres*
Victor Garcia, *Vice Pres*
James Thornton, *Admin Sec*
▲ **EMP:** 104 **EST:** 2008
SQ FT: 15,000
SALES (est): 21.9MM **Privately Held**
WEB: www.aareninc.com
SIC: 3827 3851 Optical instruments & lenses; ophthalmic goods
HQ: Carl Zeiss Meditec, Inc.
5300 Central Pkwy
Dublin CA 94568
925 557-4100

(P-10823)
ABRISA INDUSTRIAL GLASS INC (HQ)
Also Called: Abrisa Glass & Coating
200 Hallock Dr, Santa Paula (93060-9646)
P.O. Box 85055, Chicago IL (60680-0851)
PHONE..............................805 525-4902
Rajiv Ahuja, *CEO*
Nilda Rohrbach, *Administration*
David Kwan, *Info Tech Dir*
Heather Swartz, *Credit Mgr*
Kiva Catalina, *Purch Agent*
▲ **EMP:** 90 **EST:** 1980
SQ FT: 93,000
SALES (est): 31.3MM **Privately Held**
WEB: www.abrisatechnologies.com
SIC: 3827 Optical instruments & lenses

(P-10824)
ABRISA TECHNOLOGIES
200 Hallock Dr, Santa Paula (93060-9646)
P.O. Box 489 (93061-0489)
PHONE..............................805 525-4902
Blake Fennell, *CEO*
Maarten Oostendorp, *CFO*
Maartin Ostendorp, *CFO*
Bob Miller, *Vice Pres*
Vincent Gutierrez, *Technology*
EMP: 38 **EST:** 2013
SALES (est): 7.8MM **Privately Held**
WEB: www.abrisatechnologies.com
SIC: 3827 Optical instruments & lenses

(P-10825)
ADVANCED SPECTRAL TECH INC
74 W Cochran St Ste A, Simi Valley (93065-6268)
PHONE..............................805 527-7657
Thomas Persico, *President*
Roy Brochtrup, *CEO*
Pedro Arteaga, *Electrical Engi*
Greg Kuric, *Opers Mgr*
EMP: 16 **EST:** 2013
SALES (est): 3.3MM **Privately Held**
WEB: www.advancedspectral.com
SIC: 3827 Optical test & inspection equipment

(P-10826)
APOLLO INSTRUMENTS INC
55 Peters Canyon Rd, Irvine (92606-1402)
P.O. Box 53636 (92619-3636)
PHONE..............................949 756-3111
Alice Z Gheen, *President*
Peter Wang, *Vice Pres*
Lydia Kim, *IT Specialist*
▲ **EMP:** 15 **EST:** 1992
SALES (est): 352.8K **Privately Held**
WEB: www.apolloinstruments.com
SIC: 3827 3822 Optical instruments & lenses; auto controls regulating residntl & coml environmt & applncs

(P-10827)
BUK OPTICS INC
Also Called: Precision Glass & Optics
3600 W Moore Ave, Santa Ana (92704-6835)
PHONE..............................714 384-9620
Daniel S Bukaty, *CEO*
Daniel Bukaty Jr, *President*
Dan Bukaty, *Vice Pres*
Michelle Callahan, *Purchasing*
▲ **EMP:** 42 **EST:** 1985
SQ FT: 25,000
SALES (est): 6.1MM **Privately Held**
WEB: www.pgo.com
SIC: 3827 Optical instruments & apparatus

(P-10828)
CARL ZEISS MEDITEC PROD LLC
1040 S Vintage Ave Ste A, Ontario (91761-3631)
PHONE..............................877 644-4657
Hans-Joachim Miesner, *President*
Paul Yun, *Treasurer*
James Thornton, *Admin Sec*
Min Qu, *Asst Treas*
EMP: 99 **EST:** 2017
SQ FT: 67,000
SALES (est): 12.5MM **Privately Held**
WEB: www.zeiss.com
SIC: 3827 Optical instruments & lenses
HQ: Carl Zeiss Meditec, Inc.
5300 Central Pkwy
Dublin CA 94568
925 557-4100

(P-10829)
CASCADE OPTICAL COATING INC
1225 E Hunter Ave, Santa Ana (92705-4131)
PHONE..............................714 543-9777
Ken Romo, *Vice Pres*
Lawrence D Hundsdoerfer, *President*
Claudia J Hundsdoerfer, *Corp Secy*
EMP: 13 **EST:** 1975
SQ FT: 8,500

SALES (est): 3.1MM **Privately Held**
WEB: www.c-optical.com
SIC: 3827 Lens coating equipment

(P-10830)
CELESTRON ACQUISITION LLC
2835 Columbia St, Torrance (90503-3877)
PHONE..............................310 328-9560
Dave Anderson, *CEO*
Paul Roth, *CFO*
Amir Cannon, *Vice Pres*
Ben Hauck, *Vice Pres*
Nic Kranke, *Administration*
◆ **EMP:** 77 **EST:** 2002
SALES (est): 31.7MM **Privately Held**
WEB: www.celestron.com
SIC: 3827 Telescopes: elbow, panoramic, sighting, fire control, etc.; lenses, optical: all types except ophthalmic
HQ: Sw Technology Corporation
2835 Columbia St
Torrance CA 90503
310 328-9560

(P-10831)
CELESTRON INTERNATIONAL
2835 Columbia St, Torrance (90503-3877)
PHONE..............................310 328-9560
Dave Anderson, *CEO*
▲ **EMP:** 28 **EST:** 1957
SALES (est): 4.2MM **Privately Held**
WEB: www.celestron.com
SIC: 3827 Optical instruments & lenses

(P-10832)
DELTRONIC CORPORATION
Also Called: Hi-Precision Grinding
3900 W Segerstrom Ave, Santa Ana (92704-6312)
PHONE..............................714 545-5800
Robert C Larzelere, *President*
Sterling Sander, *CFO*
Diane Larzelere, *Admin Sec*
Gilbert Leos, *Opers Mgr*
▼ **EMP:** 73 **EST:** 1955
SQ FT: 40,000
SALES (est): 15.2MM **Privately Held**
WEB: www.deltronic.com
SIC: 3827 3545 Optical comparators; gauges (machine tool accessories)

(P-10833)
ELECTRO OPTICAL INDUSTRIES
320 Storke Rd Ste 100, Goleta (93117-2992)
PHONE..............................805 964-6701
Stephen Scopatz, *General Mgr*
Thierry Campos, *President*
Maegan Piccolo, *Admin Asst*
Mike Moschitto, *Opers Mgr*
Brent Lindstrom, *Sales Dir*
EMP: 21
SALES (corp-wide): 1MM **Privately Held**
WEB: www.hgh-infrared-usa.com
SIC: 3827 Optical instruments & apparatus
PA: Electro Optical Industries, Inc.
320 Storke Rd Ste 100
Goleta CA 93117
805 964-6701

(P-10834)
ENHANCED VISION SYSTEMS INC (HQ)
15301 Springdale St, Huntington Beach (92649-1140)
PHONE..............................800 440-9476
Tom Tiernan, *CEO*
Scott Drake, *Vice Pres*
Michael Harbolt, *Technical Staff*
Bobbie Viszolay, *Graphic Designe*
Zinaida Sellona, *Controller*
◆ **EMP:** 77 **EST:** 1996
SALES (est): 21.7MM
SALES (corp-wide): 42.6MM **Privately Held**
WEB: www.enhancedvision.com
SIC: 3827 Optical instruments & lenses
PA: Freedom Scientific Blv Group, Llc
17757 Us Highway 19 N # 560
Clearwater FL 33764
727 803-8000

(P-10835)
GENERAL FIRE CONTROL
828 S Alma Ave, Los Angeles
(90023-1830)
P.O. Box 86454 (90086-0454)
PHONE.................................323 260-7015
Eddie Lucatero, *Principal*
EMP: 13 **EST:** 1999
SALES (est): 1MM **Privately Held**
WEB: www.generalfirecontrol.com
SIC: 3827 Aiming circles (fire control
equipment)

(P-10836)
GMTO CORPORATION
465 N Halstead St Ste 250, Pasadena
(91107-3226)
PHONE.................................626 204-0500
Robert Shelton, *President*
Dr Robert N Shelton, *President*
Alan Gordon, *CFO*
Javier Luna, *Officer*
Savannah Winans, *Executive Asst*
▲ **EMP:** 70
SQ FT: 40,000
SALES: 5.4MM **Privately Held**
WEB: www.gmto.org
SIC: 3827 8733 Telescopes: elbow,
panoramic, sighting, fire control, etc.; non-
commercial research organizations

(P-10837)
GOOCH AND HOUSEGO CAL
LLC
5390 Kazuko Ct, Moorpark (93021-1790)
PHONE.................................805 529-3324
Kenneth Neczypor, *Mng Member*
Mark Batzdorf, *Vice Pres*
Jon Fowler, *Vice Pres*
Janet Jones, *Executive*
Bill Dickey, *General Mgr*
EMP: 80 **EST:** 2008
SALES (est): 9.5MM
SALES (corp-wide): 159.5MM **Privately
Held**
WEB: www.gandh.com
SIC: 3827 3823 Optical instruments &
lenses; industrial instrmnts msrmnt dis-
play/control process variable
PA: Gooch & Housego Plc
Dowlish Ford
Ilminster TA19
146 025-6440

(P-10838)
HOYA HOLDINGS INC
Hoya Corporation USA
425 E Huntington Dr, Monrovia
(91016-3632)
PHONE.................................626 739-5200
Al Benzoni, *Vice Pres*
EMP: 94 **Privately Held**
WEB: www.hoyaoptics.com
SIC: 3827 Optical instruments & lenses
HQ: Hoya Holdings, Inc.
680 N Mccarthy Blvd # 120
Milpitas CA 95035

(P-10839)
I-COAT COMPANY LLC
12020 Mora Dr Ste 2, Santa Fe Springs
(90670-6082)
PHONE.................................562 941-9989
Arman Bernardi, *CEO*
Frances Peck, *Controller*
Janice Fields, *Marketing Staff*
▲ **EMP:** 50 **EST:** 2003
SQ FT: 6,000
SALES (est): 10MM
SALES (corp-wide): 1.7MM **Privately
Held**
WEB: www.icoatcompany.com
SIC: 3827 Optical instruments & lenses
HQ: Essilor Of America, Inc.
13555 N Stemmons Fwy
Dallas TX 75234

(P-10840)
II-VI AEROSPACE & DEFENSE
INC
14192 Chambers Rd, Tustin (92780-6908)
PHONE.................................714 247-7100
Mark Maiberger, *General Mgr*

Andrew Bryson, *Project Engr*
Bill Chadwick, *Engineer*
Mike Davis, *Engineer*
Binh Vu, *Engineer*
EMP: 60
SALES (corp-wide): 3.1B **Publicly Held**
WEB: www.iiviad.com
SIC: 3827 7389 8748 Optical instruments
& apparatus; design services; business
consulting
HQ: Ii-Vi Aerospace & Defense Inc
36570 Briggs Rd
Murrieta CA 92563
951 926-2994

(P-10841)
INFINITE OPTICS INC
1712 Newport Cir Ste F, Santa Ana
(92705-5118)
PHONE.................................714 557-2299
Geza Keller, *President*
Daniel Houston, *Vice Pres*
Denise Banionis, *Principal*
Steven Crawford, *Principal*
Joseph Goodhand, *Principal*
EMP: 24 **EST:** 2003
SQ FT: 12,860
SALES (est): 4.2MM **Privately Held**
WEB: www.infiniteoptics.com
SIC: 3827 Lens coating & grinding equip-
ment

(P-10842)
IRCAMERA LLC
30 S Calle Cesar Chavez, Santa Barbara
(93103-5652)
PHONE.................................805 965-9650
Steve McHugh, *Mng Member*
Matthew Kimak, *Director*
EMP: 20 **EST:** 2011
SALES (est): 5MM **Publicly Held**
WEB: www.sbir.com
SIC: 3827 3812 Optical test & inspection
equipment; infrared object detection
equipment
HQ: Santa Barbara Infrared, Inc.
30 S Calle Cesar Chavez D
Santa Barbara CA 93103
805 965-3669

(P-10843)
ISCOPE CORP
Also Called: American Scopes
14370 Myford Rd Ste 150, Irvine
(92606-1016)
PHONE.................................949 333-0001
Frank Dai, *President*
Fuling Dai, *Vice Pres*
▲ **EMP:** 18 **EST:** 2009
SQ FT: 500
SALES (est): 1.9MM
SALES (corp-wide): 258.7MM **Privately
Held**
WEB: www.amscope.com
SIC: 3827 Optical instruments & lenses;
cinetheodolites
HQ: United Scope Llc
14370 Myford Rd Ste 150
Irvine CA 92606
949 333-0001

(P-10844)
LENS TECHNOLOGY I LLC
Also Called: LTI
45 Parker Ste 100, Irvine (92618-1658)
PHONE.................................714 940-6602
John Quinn, *President*
Sung Tark, *Vice Pres*
John W Quinn III, *General Mgr*
James J Ryan,
EMP: 18 **EST:** 1989
SQ FT: 11,500
SALES (est): 698K **Privately Held**
WEB: www.sdctech.com
SIC: 3827 5049 Lens coating equipment;
optical goods

(P-10845)
LUMINIT LLC
1850 W 205th St, Torrance (90501-1526)
PHONE.................................310 320-1066
Engin Arik,
Seth Coe-Sullivan, *Vice Pres*
Ed Kaiser, *Vice Pres*
Stanley KAO, *VP Bus Dvlpt*
Karma Burns, *Executive Asst*

▲ **EMP:** 42 **EST:** 2001
SALES (est): 9.2MM **Privately Held**
WEB: www.luminitco.com
SIC: 3827 Optical instruments & lenses

(P-10846)
MARK OPTICS INC
1424 E Saint Gertrude Pl, Santa Ana
(92705-5271)
PHONE.................................714 545-6684
Julie A Houser, *President*
Judy A Chapman, *CFO*
Lily Sandoval, *Production*
▲ **EMP:** 20 **EST:** 1994
SALES (est): 4.1MM **Privately Held**
WEB: www.markoptics.com
SIC: 3827 Optical elements & assemblies,
except ophthalmic

(P-10847)
MEADE INSTRUMENTS CORP
27 Hubble, Irvine (92618-4209)
PHONE.................................949 451-1450
Wenjun Ni, *CEO*
Victor Aniceto, *President*
Sara Roe, *Administration*
Hector Martinez, *Controller*
Jimmy Nguyen, *Sales Staff*
▲ **EMP:** 92
SQ FT: 25,000
SALES (est): 21MM **Privately Held**
WEB: www.meade.com
SIC: 3827 Telescopes: elbow, panoramic,
sighting, fire control, etc.

(P-10848)
NCSTAR INC
18031 Cortney Ct, City of Industry
(91748-1203)
PHONE.................................866 627-8278
Miguel Escobar, *Graphic Designe*
Graham Piscopo, *Sales Staff*
Danny Samaniego, *Director*
EMP: 18 **EST:** 2014
SALES (est): 5.1MM **Privately Held**
WEB: www.ncstar.com
SIC: 3827 Optical instruments & lenses

(P-10849)
NEWPORT OPTICAL
INDUSTRIES (PA)
Also Called: Newport Glassworks
10564 Fern Ave, Stanton (90680-2648)
P.O. Box 127 (90680-0127)
PHONE.................................714 484-8100
Ray Larsen, *President*
▲ **EMP:** 20 **EST:** 1979
SQ FT: 12,000
SALES (est): 2.7MM **Privately Held**
SIC: 3827 5049 Lenses, optical: all types
except ophthalmic; optical goods

(P-10850)
ONDAX INC
850 E Duarte Rd, Monrovia (91016-4275)
PHONE.................................626 357-9600
Randy Heyler, *CEO*
Christophe Moser, *President*
James Carriere, *Business Dir*
Ryan Park, *Sales Staff*
Lawrence Ho, *Director*
EMP: 15 **EST:** 2000
SQ FT: 60,000
SALES (est): 3MM
SALES (corp-wide): 1.2B **Publicly Held**
WEB: www.coherent.com
SIC: 3827 Optical instruments & apparatus
PA: Coherent, Inc.
5100 Patrick Henry Dr
Santa Clara CA 95054
408 764-4000

(P-10851)
OPTICAL CORPORATION (DH)
9731 Topanga Canyon Pl, Chatsworth
(91311-4135)
PHONE.................................818 725-9750
Francis Dominic, *President*
EMP: 23 **EST:** 1932
SQ FT: 14,000
SALES (est): 11.3MM **Publicly Held**
SIC: 3827 Optical instruments & lenses
HQ: Excel Technology, Inc.
125 Middlesex Tpke
Bedford MA 01730
781 266-5700

(P-10852)
OPTOSIGMA CORPORATION
3210 S Croddy Way, Santa Ana
(92704-6348)
PHONE.................................949 851-5881
Scott Rudder, *President*
Guy Ear, *Ch of Bd*
Roger Matsunaga, *Senior VP*
Steve McNamee, *Vice Pres*
Hoganson Laury, *Admin Asst*
EMP: 25 **EST:** 1995
SQ FT: 13,000
SALES (est): 5MM **Privately Held**
WEB: www.optosigma.com
SIC: 3827 Optical instruments & lenses
PA: Sigma Koki Co., Ltd.
1-19-9, Midori
Sumida-Ku TKY 130-0

(P-10853)
PACIFIC QUARTZ INC
900 Glenneyre St, Laguna Beach
(92651-2707)
PHONE.................................714 546-8133
Greg Dickson, *CEO*
E Roy Dickson, *President*
Andy Tran, *Cust Svc Dir*
EMP: 30 **EST:** 1965
SALES (est): 5.7MM **Privately Held**
WEB: www.pacificquartz.com
SIC: 3827 Optical elements & assemblies,
except ophthalmic

(P-10854)
PARKS OPTICAL
80 W Easy St Ste 3, Simi Valley
(93065-1665)
P.O. Box 1859 (93062-1859)
PHONE.................................805 522-6722
Maurice Sweiss, *President*
Martin Jun, *CIO*
▲ **EMP:** 15 **EST:** 1954
SQ FT: 25,000
SALES (est): 353.7K **Privately Held**
WEB: www.parksoptical.com
SIC: 3827 5999 Binoculars; telescopes:
elbow, panoramic, sighting, fire control,
etc.; telescopes

(P-10855)
PHILIPS ELEC N AMER CORP
13700 Live Oak Ave, Baldwin Park
(91706-1319)
PHONE.................................626 480-0755
EMP: 150
SALES (corp-wide): 26B **Privately Held**
SIC: 3827 3641 Mfg Optical
Instruments/Lenses Mfg Electric Lamps
HQ: Philips Electronics North America Cor-
poration
3000 Minuteman Rd Ms1203
Andover MA 02141
978 687-1501

(P-10856)
PVP ADVANCED EO SYSTEMS
INC
14312 Franklin Ave # 100, Tustin
(92780-7011)
PHONE.................................714 508-2740
Bruce E Ferguson, *CEO*
John Le Blanc, *CFO*
Dave Brandt, *Engineer*
Geoff Miller, *Engineer*
Carole Leblanc, *Purchasing*
▲ **EMP:** 50
SQ FT: 21,000
SALES (est): 14.7MM **Privately Held**
WEB: www.advancedeo.systems
SIC: 3827 Optical instruments & apparatus

(P-10857)
REYNARD CORPORATION
1020 Calle Sombra, San Clemente
(92673-6227)
PHONE.................................949 366-8866
Forrest Reynard, *President*
Jean Reynard, *Vice Pres*
Randy Reynard, *Vice Pres*
Beth Kinchyk, *Executive*
Stephanie Easton, *Admin Asst*
EMP: 32 **EST:** 1984
SQ FT: 28,000

PRODUCTS & SVCS

SALES (est): 7.9MM **Privately Held**
WEB: www.reynardcorp.com
SIC: 3827 Mirrors, optical

(P-10858)
RRDS INC (PA)
12 Goodyear Ste 100, Irvine (92618-3764)
PHONE...................................949 482-6200
Troy Barnes, CEO
Maxwell Sun, President
Fred Bouman, Program Mgr
Charles Hallums, Manager
▲ EMP: 15 EST: 2014
SALES (est): 3.5MM **Privately Held**
WEB: www.rrds.com
SIC: 3827 5012 3949 5045 Optical instruments & lenses; automobiles & other motor vehicles; sporting & athletic goods; computers, peripherals & software; tanks & tank components; motor vehicle parts & accessories

(P-10859)
SCOPE CITY (PA)
2978 Topaz Ave, Simi Valley (93063-2168)
P.O. Box 1630 (93062-1630)
PHONE...................................805 522-6646
Maurice Sweiss, CEO
▲ EMP: 35 EST: 1980
SQ FT: 35,000
SALES (est): 5.3MM **Privately Held**
WEB: www.scopecity.com
SIC: 3827 Optical instruments & lenses

(P-10860)
SELLERS OPTICAL INC
Also Called: Precision Optical
320 Kalmus Dr, Costa Mesa (92626-6013)
PHONE...................................949 631-6800
Alan Mixon Lambert, Ch of Bd
Rod Randolph, President
Donny Miller, CFO
Paul Dimeck, Vice Pres
Alan Lambert Jr, Vice Pres
EMP: 57 EST: 1981
SQ FT: 17,000
SALES (est): 11.5MM **Privately Held**
WEB: www.precisionoptical.com
SIC: 3827 Optical instruments & apparatus

(P-10861)
SPECTRUM SCIENTIFIC INC
16692 Hale Ave Ste A, Irvine (92606-5052)
PHONE...................................949 260-9900
Daphnie Chakran, President
Stacey Truong, Office Mgr
Grant Decastro, Engineer
Steve Dandrea, Accounts Mgr
EMP: 27 EST: 2004
SALES (est): 6MM **Privately Held**
WEB: www.ssioptics.com
SIC: 3827 Optical instruments & lenses

(P-10862)
TFD INCORPORATED
Also Called: Thin Film Devices
1180 N Tustin Ave, Anaheim (92807-1732)
PHONE...................................714 630-7127
Saleem Shaikh, CEO
Joy Shaikh, CFO
Marge Lewis, Purchasing
Margie Lewis, Purchasing
Torin Shaikh, Prdtn Mgr
▲ EMP: 25 EST: 1984
SQ FT: 20,000
SALES (est): 5.7MM **Privately Held**
WEB: www.tfdinc.com
SIC: 3827 Optical instruments & lenses

(P-10863)
TWIN COAST METROLOGY INC (PA)
333 Wshngton Blvd Ste 362, Marina Del Rey (90292)
PHONE...................................310 709-2308
Eric Stone, President
Jason Remillard, Treasurer
Amy Remillard, Admin Sec
EMP: 15
SQ FT: 1,200
SALES (est): 1.6MM **Privately Held**
WEB: www.twincoastmetrology.com
SIC: 3827 Optical instruments & lenses

(P-10864)
UNITED SCOPE LLC (HQ)
Also Called: Amscope
14370 Myford Rd Ste 150, Irvine (92606-1016)
PHONE...................................949 333-0001
Larry Marmon, CEO
Frank Dai, CEO
Nathaniel Fasnacht, CFO
Mandy J Liu, CFO
Andrew Wu, Vice Pres
▲ EMP: 50 EST: 2013
SQ FT: 58,000
SALES (est): 11.5MM
SALES (corp-wide): 258.7MM **Privately Held**
WEB: www.unitedscope.com
SIC: 3827 Optical instruments & lenses; optical goods
PA: L Squared Capital Partners Llc
   3434 Via Lido Ste 300
   Newport Beach CA 92663
   949 398-0168

(P-10865)
WAVE PRECISION INC
5390 Kazuko Ct, Moorpark (93021-1790)
PHONE...................................805 529-3324
Kenneth L Scribner, President
Dennis B Hotchkiss, Vice Pres
EMP: 15 EST: 1974
SQ FT: 16,000
SALES (est): 773.8K **Privately Held**
WEB: www.waveprecision.com
SIC: 3827 Optical instruments & apparatus

(P-10866)
Z C & R COATING FOR OPTICS INC
1401 Abalone Ave, Torrance (90501-2889)
PHONE...................................310 381-3060
Rajiv Ahuja, CEO
Robert Cabrera, Vice Pres
James Barba, Technician
Jim Walker, Engineer
Fred Praudisch, VP Opers
EMP: 43 EST: 1979
SQ FT: 21,781
SALES (est): 8.6MM **Privately Held**
WEB: www.abrisatechnologies.com
SIC: 3827 Lens coating equipment
HQ: Abrisa Industrial Glass, Inc.
   200 Hallock Dr
   Santa Paula CA 93060
   805 525-4902

3829 Measuring & Controlling Devices, NEC

(P-10867)
AES NDT
1821 W 213th St Ste L, Torrance (90501-2847)
PHONE...................................310 947-6755
Adolfo Velasco, Branch Mgr
Adam Shideler, Vice Pres
EMP: 20
SALES (corp-wide): 2.1MM **Privately Held**
WEB: www.aesndt.com
SIC: 3829 Measuring & controlling devices
PA: Aes Ndt
   1821 W 213th St Ste L
   Torrance CA 90501
   310 953-9822

(P-10868)
ALVARADO MANUFACTURING CO INC
12660 Colony Ct, Chino (91710-2975)
PHONE...................................909 591-8431
Bret Armatas, CEO
Bill Voss, Executive
Ryan Lemen, Engineer
Adam McGuern, Marketing Mgr
Steve Shelton, Sales Staff
◆ EMP: 71 EST: 1955
SQ FT: 69,000
SALES (est): 24.7MM **Privately Held**
WEB: www.alvaradomfg.com
SIC: 3829 Turnstiles, equipped with counting mechanisms

(P-10869)
APPLIED TECHNOLOGIES ASSOC INC (HQ)
Also Called: A T A
3025 Buena Vista Dr, Paso Robles (93446-8555)
PHONE...................................805 239-9100
William B Wade, President
Chris Barker, Owner
George Walker, Vice Pres
Steve Hirst, Software Engr
Jason Andrus, Technician
▲ EMP: 127 EST: 1981
SALES (est): 32.2MM
SALES (corp-wide): 535.6MM **Privately Held**
WEB: www.secure.scientificdrilling.com
SIC: 3829 1381 Surveying instruments & accessories; drilling oil & gas wells
PA: Scientific Drilling International, Inc.
   16071 Grnspint Pk Dr Ste
   Houston TX 77060
   281 443-3300

(P-10870)
ASTRO HAVEN ENTERPRISES INC
555 Anton Blvd Ste 150, Costa Mesa (92626-7036)
P.O. Box 3637, San Clemente (92674-3637)
PHONE...................................949 215-3777
Priscilla Brotherson, President
David Brotherston, Chief
▼ EMP: 14 EST: 2007
SALES (est): 763.3K **Privately Held**
WEB: www.astrohaven.com
SIC: 3829 Measuring & controlling devices

(P-10871)
BARKSDALE INC (DH)
3211 Fruitland Ave, Vernon (90058-3717)
P.O. Box 58843, Los Angeles (90058-0843)
PHONE...................................323 583-6243
C Ian Dodd, President
Vivian Fahy, Vice Pres
Mary Barksdale, Principal
Jim Rogriguez, Engng Exec
Angel Ching, Engineer
▲ EMP: 148 EST: 1946
SQ FT: 115,000
SALES (est): 25.8MM
SALES (corp-wide): 2.9B **Publicly Held**
WEB: www.barksdale.com
SIC: 3829 3491 3823 3643 Measuring & controlling devices; industrial valves; industrial instrmnts msrmnt display/control process variable; current-carrying wiring devices

(P-10872)
BEI NORTH AMERICA LLC (DH)
1461 Lawrence Dr, Thousand Oaks (91320-1303)
PHONE...................................805 716-0642
Martha Sullivan, President
Jeffrey Cote, Vice Pres
Alison Roelke, Vice Pres
EMP: 103 EST: 2015
SALES (est): 54MM
SALES (corp-wide): 3B **Privately Held**
WEB: www.sensata.com
SIC: 3829 Measuring & controlling devices
HQ: Custom Sensors & Technologies, Inc.
   1461 Lawrence Dr
   Thousand Oaks CA 91320
   805 716-0322

(P-10873)
BRENNER-FIEDLER & ASSOC INC (PA)
Also Called: B F
4059 Flat Rock Dr, Riverside (92505-5859)
PHONE...................................562 404-2721
James Kloman, CEO
Frank Raya, Officer
Candace Bathurst, Executive
Aj Moreno, Executive
Luis Perez, Technician
EMP: 39 EST: 1957
SQ FT: 28,669
SALES (est): 12.7MM **Privately Held**
WEB: www.brenner-fiedler.com
SIC: 3829 5085 Accelerometers; pistons & valves; valves & fittings

(P-10874)
C J INSTRUMENTS INC
Also Called: Pace Transducer Co
P.O. Box 570430, Tarzana (91357-0430)
PHONE...................................818 996-4131
Charles Tucker, President
Joe Bisera, Principal
Marshal Canter, General Mgr
J Bisera, Research
B Barber, Purchasing
EMP: 20 EST: 1968
SQ FT: 1,500
SALES (est): 2MM **Privately Held**
SIC: 3829 3641 3679 2819 Pressure transducers; lead-in wires, electric lamp made from purchased wire; transducers, electrical; aluminum oxide

(P-10875)
CALIFORNIA DYNAMICS CORP (PA)
Also Called: Caldyn
5572 Alhambra Ave, Los Angeles (90032-3195)
PHONE...................................323 223-3882
Donald Benkert, President
Adell Benkert, President
▲ EMP: 24 EST: 1966
SQ FT: 30,000
SALES (est): 4.9MM **Privately Held**
WEB: www.caldyn.com
SIC: 3829 Vibration meters, analyzers & calibrators

(P-10876)
CARROS SENSORS SYSTEMS CO LLC (DH)
Also Called: BEI Industrial Encoders
1461 Lawrence Dr, Thousand Oaks (91320-1303)
PHONE...................................805 968-0782
Eric Pilaud, CEO
Jean-Yves Mouttet, Treasurer
Victor Copeland, Admin Sec
Jean-Yves Vo, CTO
Rene Garcia, Engineer
▲ EMP: 125 EST: 1990
SALES (est): 62.9MM
SALES (corp-wide): 3B **Privately Held**
WEB: www.sensata.com
SIC: 3829 Measuring & controlling devices

(P-10877)
DAVIDSON OPTRONICS INC
Also Called: Doi Venture
9087 Arrow Rte Ste 180, Rancho Cucamonga (91730-4451)
PHONE...................................626 962-5181
Eugene Dumitrascu, Ch of Bd
Dan State, President
Debra Richards, Admin Sec
Byron Seabolt, Sales Staff
EMP: 22 EST: 1932
SQ FT: 40,000
SALES (est): 11.9MM
SALES (corp-wide): 907.3MM **Privately Held**
WEB: www.davidsonoptronics.com
SIC: 3829 3827 Measuring & controlling devices; optical instruments & apparatus
HQ: Trioptics, Inc.
   9087 Arrow Rte Ste 180
   Rancho Cucamonga CA 91730
   626 962-5181

(P-10878)
ECKERT ZEGLER ISOTOPE PDTS INC
1800 N Keystone St, Burbank (91504-3417)
PHONE...................................661 309-1010
Karl Amlauer, Branch Mgr
Gurpreet Hayhre, Officer
Martin Hughes, Business Dir
Hugh Evans, Admin Sec
Eric Holmes, Technician
EMP: 27
SALES (corp-wide): 208.3MM **Privately Held**
SIC: 3829 Nuclear radiation & testing apparatus
HQ: Eckert & Ziegler Isotope Products, Inc.
   24937 Avenue Tibbits
   Valencia CA 91355
   661 309-1010

(P-10879)
ECKERT ZEGLER ISOTOPE PDTS INC (HQ)
Also Called: Isotope Products Lab
24937 Avenue Tibbitts, Valencia
(91355-3427)
PHONE..............................661 309-1010
Frank Yeager, *CEO*
Joe Hathcock, *President*
Karen Haskins, *Treasurer*
Cary Renquist, *Officer*
Audrey Townsend, *Human Res Mgr*
EMP: 45 **EST:** 1967
SQ FT: 40,000
SALES (est): 44.6MM
SALES (corp-wide): 208.3MM **Privately Held**
WEB: www.ezag.com
SIC: 3829 Nuclear radiation & testing apparatus
PA: Eckert & Ziegler Strahlen- Und Medizintechnik Ag
Robert-Rossle-Str. 10
Berlin BE 13125
309 410-840

(P-10880)
ECKERT ZEGLER ISOTOPE PDTS INC
1800 N Keystone St, Burbank
(91504-3417)
PHONE..............................661 309-1010
EMP: 30
SALES (corp-wide): 158.2MM **Privately Held**
SIC: 3829 Mfg Measuring/Controlling Devices
HQ: Eckert & Ziegler Isotope Products, Inc.
24937 Avenue Tibbitts
Valencia CA 91355
661 309-1010

(P-10881)
EMISSION METHODS INC
Also Called: Webber EMI
1307 S Wanamaker Ave, Ontario
(91761-2237)
PHONE..............................909 605-6800
Kenneth Parker, *President*
Andrew Jakubec, *Engineer*
EMP: 20 **EST:** 1975
SQ FT: 14,100
SALES (est): 4.2MM **Privately Held**
WEB: www.emissionmethods.openfos.com
SIC: 3829 3499 3599 Dynamometer instruments; aircraft & motor vehicle measurement equipment; novelties & specialties, metal; carnival machines & equipment, amusement park

(P-10882)
F & D FLORES ENTERPRISES INC
Also Called: Hardware Specialties
761 E Francis St, Ontario (91761-5514)
PHONE..............................909 975-4853
Frank Flores, *President*
Steve Saldana,
▲ **EMP:** 27 **EST:** 1921
SQ FT: 20,000
SALES (est): 2.8MM **Privately Held**
SIC: 3829 5031 3446 Automatic turnstiles & related apparatus; lumber, plywood & millwork; architectural metalwork

(P-10883)
FAR WEST TECHNOLOGY INC
330 S Kellogg Ave, Goleta (93117-3814)
PHONE..............................805 964-3615
John D Rickey, *CEO*
John Handloser Jr, *Exec VP*
Scot Larson, *Products*
▼ **EMP:** 17 **EST:** 1971
SQ FT: 6,100
SALES (est): 2.5MM **Privately Held**
WEB: www.fwt.com
SIC: 3829 Nuclear radiation & testing apparatus

(P-10884)
FLOWLINE INC
Also Called: Flowline Liquid Intelligence
10500 Humbolt St, Los Alamitos
(90720-2439)
PHONE..............................562 598-3015

Stephen E Olson, *Ch of Bd*
Scott Olson, *President*
Gary Niebish, *Executive*
Iris Chen, *Accounting Mgr*
Al Motevalli, *Sales Staff*
EMP: 25 **EST:** 1990
SQ FT: 8,000
SALES (est): 3.2MM **Privately Held**
WEB: www.flowline.com
SIC: 3829 5084 Measuring & controlling devices; industrial machinery & equipment

(P-10885)
GLA AGRICULTURAL ELEC INC
3563 Sueldo St Ste D, San Luis Obispo
(93401-7331)
PHONE..............................805 541-3758
Cynthia Green, *Owner*
Kelly McDonough, *Director*
EMP: 27 **EST:** 1967
SQ FT: 2,350
SALES (est): 1MM **Privately Held**
WEB: www.gla-ag.com
SIC: 3829 8748 Thermometers, including digital: clinical; salinity indicators, except industrial process type; business consulting

(P-10886)
H2SCAN CORPORATION
27215 Turnberry Ln Unit A, Valencia
(91355-1068)
PHONE..............................661 775-9575
Michael Allman, *CEO*
Dennis W Reid, *President*
Michael Nofal, *Vice Pres*
Shannon Cosman, *General Mgr*
Evelyn Howard, *Sr Software Eng*
EMP: 25
SQ FT: 10,000
SALES (est): 8.7MM **Privately Held**
WEB: www.h2scan.com
SIC: 3829 Hydrometers, except industrial process type

(P-10887)
HAMILTON SUNDSTRAND SPC SYSTMS
Also Called: Hsssi
960 Overland Ct, San Dimas (91773-1742)
PHONE..............................909 288-5300
Edward Francis, *Exec Dir*
Lawrence R McNamara, *President*
Gregory J Hayes, *CEO*
Eugene Dougherty, *Treasurer*
Clinton Gardiner, *Vice Pres*
EMP: 76 **EST:** 2002
SQ FT: 134,000
SALES (est): 20.2MM
SALES (corp-wide): 56.5B **Publicly Held**
WEB: www.collinsaerospace.com
SIC: 3829 Measuring & controlling devices
HQ: Goodrich Corporation
2730 W Tyvola Rd
Charlotte NC 28217
704 423-7000

(P-10888)
HILZ CABLE ASSEMBLIES INC
31889 Corydon St Ste 110, Lake Elsinore
(92530-8509)
PHONE..............................951 245-0499
Darlene Hilz, *President*
▲ **EMP:** 15 **EST:** 1997
SALES (est): 1.6MM **Privately Held**
SIC: 3829 Cable testing machines

(P-10889)
IMDEX TECHNOLOGY USA LLC
3474 Empresa Dr Ste 150, San Luis Obispo
(93401-7391)
PHONE..............................805 540-2017
George Vu,
Tim Price,
EMP: 20 **EST:** 2011
SQ FT: 3,500
SALES (est): 9.3MM **Privately Held**
WEB: www.imdexlimited.com
SIC: 3829 8711 Surveying instruments & accessories; engineering services
PA: Imdex Ltd
216 Balcatta Rd
Balcatta WA 6021

(P-10890)
INTERNATIONAL SENSOR TECH
3 Whatney Ste 100, Irvine (92618-2836)
PHONE..............................949 452-9000
Thomas Jack Chou, *President*
Daniel R Chuo, *CFO*
Doris Chou, *Corp Secy*
Tai CAM Luu, *Admin Sec*
▲ **EMP:** 33 **EST:** 1972
SQ FT: 20,000
SALES (est): 6.8MM **Privately Held**
WEB: www.intlsensor.com
SIC: 3829 Gas detectors

(P-10891)
INTERNTONAL SUPER SENSORS CORP
2300 S Reservoir St # 306, Pomona
(91766-6458)
PHONE..............................909 590-5054
Luis Eduardo Gallardo, *CEO*
EMP: 19 **EST:** 2008
SALES (est): 560.1K **Privately Held**
WEB: www.internationalsupersensors.com
SIC: 3829 Measuring & controlling devices

(P-10892)
IRROMETER COMPANY INC
Also Called: Watermark
1425 Palmyrita Ave, Riverside
(92507-1600)
PHONE..............................951 682-9505
Thomas C Penning, *President*
Samuel Legget, *Treasurer*
Alfred J Hawkins, *Vice Pres*
Jeremy Sullivan, *Vice Pres*
Diganta Adhikari, *Engineer*
EMP: 18
SQ FT: 9,000
SALES (est): 3.6MM **Privately Held**
WEB: www.irrometer.com
SIC: 3829 Measuring & controlling devices

(P-10893)
J L SHEPHERD AND ASSOC INC
1010 Arroyo St, San Fernando
(91340-1822)
PHONE..............................818 898-2361
Dorothy Shepherd, *President*
Joseph L Shepherd, *President*
Diana Shepherd, *Vice Pres*
Mary Shepherd, *Vice Pres*
▲ **EMP:** 27 **EST:** 1967
SQ FT: 15,000
SALES (est): 4.5MM **Privately Held**
WEB: www.jlshepherd.com
SIC: 3829 3844 Nuclear radiation & testing apparatus; irradiation equipment

(P-10894)
KAP MEDICAL
1395 Pico St, Corona (92881-3373)
PHONE..............................951 340-4360
Raj K Gowda, *President*
Enrik Tobon, *CFO*
Dave Lewis, *Vice Pres*
Dan Rosenmayer, *Vice Pres*
Jen Alberton, *Executive*
◆ **EMP:** 35 **EST:** 1999
SQ FT: 20,000
SALES (est): 7.4MM **Privately Held**
WEB: www.kapmedical.com
SIC: 3829 8711 Medical diagnostic systems, nuclear; consulting engineer

(P-10895)
KARL STORZ IMAGING INC (HQ)
Also Called: Optronics
1 S Los Carneros Rd, Goleta (93117-5506)
PHONE..............................805 968-5563
Miles Hartfield, *General Mgr*
Anthony Catalano, *Executive*
Ted Kapsalis, *Executive*
Aaron Taylor, *Executive*
Hosam Afifi, *Exec Dir*
EMP: 344 **EST:** 1984
SQ FT: 105,000
SALES (est): 136.5MM
SALES (corp-wide): 2.1B **Privately Held**
WEB: www.karlstorz.com
SIC: 3829 3841 Measuring & controlling devices; surgical & medical instruments
PA: Karl Storz Se & Co. Kg
Dr.-Karl-Storz-Str. 34
Tuttlingen BW 78532
746 170-80

(P-10896)
LOBBY TRAFFIC SYSTEMS INC
8583 Irvine Center Dr # 10, Irvine
(92618-4298)
PHONE..............................800 486-8606
EMP: 16 **EST:** 1982
SQ FT: 1,500
SALES (est): 1.5MM **Privately Held**
WEB: www.crowdcontrol.net
SIC: 3829 1731 Turnstiles, equipped with counting mechanisms; safety & security specialization

(P-10897)
MECHANIZED SCIENCE SEALS INC
Also Called: Ms Bellows
5322 Mcfadden Ave, Huntington Beach
(92649-1239)
PHONE..............................714 898-5602
Jon Hamren, *President*
Victoria Hamren, *Treasurer*
Chris Hamren, *Vice Pres*
Linda Welsh, *Office Mgr*
Robin Hamren, *Admin Sec*
EMP: 39 **EST:** 1964
SQ FT: 10,000
SALES (est): 2.9MM **Privately Held**
SIC: 3829 Measuring & controlling devices

(P-10898)
MINUS K TECHNOLOGY INC
460 Hindry Ave Ste C, Inglewood
(90301-2044)
PHONE..............................310 348-9656
David L Platus, *President*
Nancee Schwartz, *Admin Sec*
EMP: 110 **EST:** 1991
SQ FT: 2,500
SALES (est): 5.2MM **Privately Held**
WEB: www.minusk.com
SIC: 3829 Measuring & controlling devices

(P-10899)
NDT SYSTEMS INC
5542 Buckingham Dr Ste A, Huntington
Beach (92649-1158)
PHONE..............................714 893-2438
Grant Johnston, *CEO*
Gregory Smith, *President*
Greg Smith, *Executive*
Drew Courtright, *General Mgr*
Martin Leyba, *General Mgr*
EMP: 22 **EST:** 1974
SALES (est): 6.9MM
SALES (corp-wide): 7.5B **Privately Held**
WEB: www.ndtsystems.com
SIC: 3829 Ultrasonic testing equipment
HQ: Amec Foster Wheeler Limited
23rd Floor
London E14 5
203 215-1700

(P-10900)
OMNI OPTICAL PRODUCTS INC (PA)
17282 Eastman, Irvine (92614)
PHONE..............................714 634-5700
Ken Panique, *President*
Cindy Von Hershman, *Manager*
▲ **EMP:** 25 **EST:** 1986
SALES (est): 5.9MM **Privately Held**
SIC: 3829 Surveying instruments & accessories

(P-10901)
OPTIVUS PROTON THERAPY INC
1475 Victoria Ct, San Bernardino
(92408-2831)
P.O. Box 608, Loma Linda (92354-0608)
PHONE..............................909 799-8300
Jon W Slater, *CEO*
Daryl L Anderson, *CFO*
Patrick Dias, *Administration*
Dan Lafuze, *Sr Software Eng*
Michael Baumann, *Software Engr*
EMP: 75 **EST:** 1992
SQ FT: 35,000

P R O D U C T S & S V C S

SALES (est): 15.8MM **Privately Held**
WEB: www.optivus.com
SIC: **3829** 7371 8742 3699 Nuclear radiation & testing apparatus; custom computer programming services; maintenance management consultant; electrical equipment & supplies

(P-10902)
PACIFIC PRECISION LABS INC
Also Called: J M A R Precision Systems
9430 Lurline Ave, Chatsworth
(91311-6003)
PHONE..................818 700-8977
Chandu Vanjani, *President*
▲ EMP: 17 EST: 1985
SQ FT: 10,000
SALES (est): 6.6MM **Privately Held**
WEB: www.ppli.com
SIC: **3829** Measuring & controlling devices

(P-10903)
PHOENIX AERIAL SYSTEMS INC
10131 National Blvd, Los Angeles
(90034-3804)
PHONE..................323 577-3366
Grayson Omans, *President*
Ben Adler, *CTO*
Juan Rimola, *Prdtn Mgr*
EMP: 15 EST: 2013
SQ FT: 1,500
SALES (est): 500K **Privately Held**
WEB: www.phoenixlidar.com
SIC: **3829** Surveying instruments & accessories

(P-10904)
PROPRIETARY CONTROLS SYSTEMS
Also Called: P C S C
3830 Del Amo Blvd 102, Torrance
(90503-2119)
PHONE..................310 303-3600
Masami Kosaka, *President*
Robert K Takahashi, *Vice Pres*
▲ EMP: 45 EST: 1983
SALES (est): 7.9MM
SALES (corp-wide): 12.1MM **Privately Held**
SIC: **3829** 3669 Measuring & controlling devices; burglar alarm apparatus, electric
PA: Ttik, Inc.
　3541 Challenger St
　Torrance CA 90503
　310 303-3600

(P-10905)
QUALITY CONTROL SOLUTIONS INC
43339 Bus Pk Dr Ste 101, Temecula
(92590-3636)
PHONE..................951 676-1616
Louis Todd, *President*
Denise Todd, *Admin Sec*
EMP: 21 EST: 1979
SQ FT: 7,500
SALES (est): 2MM **Privately Held**
WEB: www.qc-solutions.com
SIC: **3829** 5084 Measuring & controlling devices; instruments & control equipment

(P-10906)
RADCAL CORPORATION
Also Called: M D H
426 W Duarte Rd, Monrovia (91016-4591)
PHONE..................626 357-7921
Curt Harkless, *CEO*
J Howard Marshall III, *Ch of Bd*
Kenneth Mettler, *CEO*
John Crawford, *CFO*
Bill Roche, *CFO*
▲ EMP: 35 EST: 1973
SQ FT: 10,000
SALES (est): 8.1MM **Privately Held**
WEB: www.radcal.com
SIC: **3829** Nuclear radiation & testing apparatus

(P-10907)
REDLINE DETECTION LLC (PA)
828 W Taft Ave, Orange (92865-4232)
PHONE..................714 579-6961
Zachary Parker, *CEO*
Gene Stauffer, *General Mgr*
Mark Hawkins, *Technical Staff*
Jason Ouimette, *Purchasing*

Steve Marek, *Manager*
▲ EMP: 33 EST: 2004
SQ FT: 21,000
SALES (est): 14.6MM **Privately Held**
WEB: www.redlinedetection.com
SIC: **3829** Liquid leak detection equipment

(P-10908)
SEMCO
1495 S Gage St, San Bernardino
(92408-2835)
PHONE..................909 799-9666
Shawn Martin, *Owner*
▲ EMP: 25 EST: 1994
SQ FT: 5,400 **Privately Held**
WEB: www.semcousa.com
SIC: **3829** 3599 Physical property testing equipment; machine shop, jobbing & repair

(P-10909)
SENSO-METRICS INC
4584 Runway St, Simi Valley (93063-3449)
PHONE..................805 527-3640
Gary Johnson, *President*
Joan P Evans, *Corp Secy*
John Smith, *Exec VP*
EMP: 14 EST: 1972
SQ FT: 16,288
SALES (est): 1.1MM **Privately Held**
WEB: www.senso-metrics.com
SIC: **3829** 5084 Measuring & controlling devices; industrial machinery & equipment

(P-10910)
SENTRAN L L C (PA)
4355 E Lowell St Ste F, Ontario
(91761-2225)
PHONE..................888 545-8988
Ken Kramer, *CEO*
Carlos Valdes, *COO*
Jorge Valdes, *Personnel*
Manuel Haro, *Buyer*
▲ EMP: 15 EST: 1998
SQ FT: 5,000
SALES (est): 3.2MM **Privately Held**
WEB: www.sentranllc.com
SIC: **3829** Measuring & controlling devices

(P-10911)
SOBERLINK HEALTHCARE LLC
16787 Beach Blvd 211, Huntington Beach
(92647-4848)
PHONE..................714 975-7200
Brad Keays, *CEO*
Casey Hanrahan, *Vice Pres*
Cooper Penney, *Business Mgr*
Jared Fenlason, *Manager*
EMP: 13 EST: 2015
SALES (est): 3.2MM **Privately Held**
WEB: www.soberlink.com
SIC: **3829** Breathalyzers

(P-10912)
SOILMOISTURE EQUIPMENT CORP
801 S Kellogg Ave, Goleta (93117-3886)
P.O. Box 30025, Santa Barbara (93130-0025)
PHONE..................805 964-3525
Whitney Skaling, *CEO*
Kenneth Macaulay, *CFO*
Percy E Skaling, *Principal*
Jan Skaling, *Admin Sec*
Richard Barnes, *CIO*
▲ EMP: 23 EST: 1950
SQ FT: 14,000
SALES (est): 4.8MM **Privately Held**
WEB: www.soilmoisture.com
SIC: **3829** Measuring & controlling devices

(P-10913)
STRUCTURAL DIAGNOSTICS INC
Also Called: S D I
650 Via Alondra, Camarillo (93012-8733)
PHONE..................805 987-7755
Paul R Teagle, *President*
Greg Patterson, *COO*
EMP: 33
SQ FT: 30,000
SALES (est): 4MM **Privately Held**
WEB: www.sdindt.com
SIC: **3829** Measuring & controlling devices

(P-10914)
SYSTEMS INTEGRATED LLC
2200 N Glassell St, Orange (92865-2702)
PHONE..................714 998-0900
Susan Corrales-Diaz,
John Holbrook, *Director*
EMP: 26 EST: 1999
SQ FT: 7,000
SALES (est): 1MM **Privately Held**
WEB: www.systemsintegrated.com
SIC: **3829** Measuring & controlling devices

(P-10915)
TELATEMP CORPORATION
2910 E La Palma Ave Ste C, Anaheim
(92806-2618)
PHONE..................714 414-0343
Daniel Stack, *President*
Evelyn Darringer, *Vice Pres*
Dan Stack, *Manager*
EMP: 22 EST: 1972
SQ FT: 3,200
SALES (est): 3MM **Privately Held**
WEB: www.telatemp.com
SIC: **3829** Thermometers & temperature sensors

(P-10916)
TEMPTRON ENGINEERING INC
7823 Deering Ave, Canoga Park
(91304-5006)
PHONE..................818 346-4900
Edward Skei, *President*
Beverly Skei, *Treasurer*
Tim Thierry, *General Mgr*
Nick Briach, *Engineer*
Pablo Cruz, *Prdtn Mgr*
EMP: 35 EST: 1971
SQ FT: 13,000
SALES (est): 2.9MM **Privately Held**
WEB: www.temptronengineeringinc.com
SIC: **3829** 3769 3823 Measuring & controlling devices; guided missile & space vehicle parts & auxiliary equipment; temperature instruments: industrial process type

(P-10917)
TRANSDUCER TECHNIQUES LLC
42480 Rio Nedo, Temecula (92590-3734)
PHONE..................951 719-3965
Randy A Baker, *Mng Member*
Leoncio Flores, *Technician*
Gary Mann, *Director*
EMP: 37 EST: 1978
SQ FT: 27,000
SALES (est): 8.4MM **Privately Held**
WEB: www.transducertechniques.com
SIC: **3829** Measuring & controlling devices; synchronizers, aircraft engine; alidades, surveying

(P-10918)
TRUTOUCH TECHNOLOGIES INC
2020 Iowa Ave Ste 102, Riverside
(92507-2417)
PHONE..................909 703-5963
Benjamin Ver Steeg, *CEO*
Oscar Lazaro, *Partner*
David Desrochers, *CFO*
Gerald Grafe, *Admin Sec*
Ries Robinson, *Director*
EMP: 17 EST: 2005
SQ FT: 5,000
SALES (est): 2.3MM **Privately Held**
SIC: **3829** Measuring & controlling devices

(P-10919)
UNITED TESTING SYSTEMS INC
1375 S Acacia Ave, Fullerton (92831-5315)
PHONE..................714 638-2322
Jim Neville, *CEO*
Paul Mumford, *Vice Pres*
Cliff Schaffer, *Vice Pres*
Syed Ahmed, *Managing Dir*
Andrew Nguyen, *Engineer*
▲ EMP: 31 EST: 1964
SALES: 7.9MM **Privately Held**
WEB: www.industrialphysics.com
SIC: **3829** 8734 5084 Hardness testing equipment; tensile strength testing equipment; calibration & certification; industrial machinery & equipment

(P-10920)
VANTARI MEDICAL LLC
15440 Laguna Canyon Rd # 26, Irvine
(92618-2138)
PHONE..................949 783-5300
Nick Arroyo, *CEO*
Phil Lamb, *CFO*
EMP: 18 EST: 2015
SALES (est): 621.7K **Privately Held**
SIC: **3829** Medical diagnostic systems, nuclear

(P-10921)
WELLBORE NAVIGATION INC (PA)
Also Called: Welnav
1240 N Jefferson St Ste M, Anaheim
(92807-1632)
PHONE..................714 259-7760
Charles Ron Adams, *President*
Sandy Adams, *Admin Sec*
EMP: 18 EST: 1981
SQ FT: 7,000
SALES (est): 2.4MM **Privately Held**
WEB: www.welnavinc.com
SIC: **3829** 1381 7371 Surveying instruments & accessories; directional drilling oil & gas wells; computer software development

---

3841 Surgical & Medical Instrs & Apparatus

(P-10922)
3GEN INC
31521 Rncho Vejo Rd Ste 1, San Juan
Capistrano (92675)
PHONE..................949 481-6384
John Bottjer, *President*
Nizar Mullani,
Thorsten Trotzenberg,
EMP: 13 EST: 2002
SQ FT: 3,000
SALES (est): 3.6MM **Privately Held**
WEB: www.dermlite.com
SIC: **3841** Surgical & medical instruments

(P-10923)
ACCLARENT INC
31 Technology Dr Ste 200, Irvine
(92618-2302)
PHONE..................650 687-5888
David Shepherd, *President*
Heather Wozniak, *Regional Mgr*
Andrew Drake, *Research*
Emily Maginnis, *Engineer*
George Matlock, *Engineer*
EMP: 400 EST: 2004
SALES (est): 97.4MM
SALES (corp-wide): 82.5B **Publicly Held**
SIC: **3841** Surgical & medical instruments
HQ: Ethicon Inc.
　1000 Route 202
　Raritan NJ 08869
　732 524-0400

(P-10924)
ACCUMEDICAL USA INC
3545 Harbor Gtwy S # 103, Costa Mesa
(92626-1457)
PHONE..................714 929-1020
Tai Tieu, *President*
EMP: 13 EST: 2019
SALES (est): 500K **Privately Held**
SIC: **3841** Medical instruments & equipment; blood & bone work

(P-10925)
ADVANCED STERLIZATION (HQ)
Also Called: A S P
33 Technology Dr, Irvine (92618-2346)
PHONE..................800 595-0200
Bernard Zovighian, *CEO*
EMP: 218 EST: 1991
SALES (est): 16MM
SALES (corp-wide): 4.6B **Publicly Held**
WEB: www.fortive.com
SIC: **3841** Surgical & medical instruments
PA: Fortive Corporation
　6920 Seaway Blvd
　Everett WA 98203
　425 446-5000

▲ = Import ▼=Export
◆ =Import/Export

(P-10926)
ALCON LENSX INC (DH)
15800 Alton Pkwy, Irvine (92618-3818)
PHONE..................................949 753-1393
Kevin J Buehler, *CEO*
Elaine Whitbeck,
Bob Lundberg, *Vice Pres*
Guy Holland, *Associate Dir*
Sean Niizuma, *Software Engr*
EMP: 134 **EST:** 2006
SQ FT: 20,000
SALES (est): 34.4MM
SALES (corp-wide): 6.8B **Privately Held**
WEB: www.alcon-inc.net
SIC: 3841 Surgical lasers
HQ: Alcon, Inc.
    1132 Ferris Rd
    Amelia OH 45102
    513 722-1037

(P-10927)
ALCON VISION LLC
24514 Sunshine Dr, Laguna Niguel
(92677-7826)
PHONE..................................949 753-6218
Simon Han, *Software Dev*
EMP: 194
SALES (corp-wide): 6.8B **Privately Held**
WEB: www.alcon.com
SIC: 3841 Surgical & medical instruments
HQ: Alcon Vision, Llc
    6201 South Fwy
    Fort Worth TX 76134
    817 293-0450

(P-10928)
ALCON VISION LLC
Also Called: Alcon Surgical
15800 Alton Pkwy, Irvine (92618-3818)
P.O. Box 19587 (92623-9587)
PHONE..................................949 753-6488
Kenneth Lickel, *Manager*
Steve Ambrose, *Associate Dir*
Sanjay Datta, *Associate Dir*
Adrian Castro, *Technician*
Fred Reed, *Project Mgr*
EMP: 600
SQ FT: 32,000
SALES (corp-wide): 6.8B **Privately Held**
WEB: www.alcon.com
SIC: 3841 3851 5049 Surgical & medical
instruments; ophthalmic goods; optical
goods
HQ: Alcon Vision, Llc
    6201 South Fwy
    Fort Worth TX 76134
    817 293-0450

(P-10929)
ALEPH GROUP INC
Also Called: A G I
6920 Sycamore Canyon Blvd, Riverside
(92507-0781)
PHONE..................................951 213-4815
EMP: 14
SALES: 3MM **Privately Held**
SIC: 3841 3843 8099 Mfg Surgical/Medical Instruments Mfg Dental
Equipment/Supplies Health/Allied Services

(P-10930)
ALL MANUFACTURERS INC
Also Called: Allied Harbor Aerospace Fas
1831 Commerce St Ste 101, Corona
(92878-5026)
PHONE..................................951 280-4200
Jon R Gerwin, *CEO*
Ron Gerwin, *President*
Diana Watson, *Bookkeeper*
Michael Rhodes, *Manager*
Ron Tucker, *Manager*
EMP: 197 **EST:** 1993 **Privately Held**
WEB: www.allied1.com
SIC: 3841 3694 Surgical & medical instruments; motors, starting: automotive & aircraft

(P-10931)
ALLIANCE MEDICAL PRODUCTS INC (DH)
Also Called: Siegfried Irvine
9342 Jeronimo Rd, Irvine (92618-1903)
PHONE..................................949 768-4690
Robert Hughes, *CEO*
Brian Jones, *COO*

Tom Lucas, *Vice Pres*
Calvin Witcher, *Info Tech Mgr*
Sara Hardy-Baloun, *Project Mgr*
▲ **EMP:** 117 **EST:** 2001
SQ FT: 55,000
SALES (est): 40.7MM
SALES (corp-wide): 49.3MM **Privately Held**
WEB: www.amp-us.com
SIC: 3841 7819 Medical instruments & equipment, blood & bone work; laboratory service, motion picture
HQ: Siegfried Usa Holding , Inc.
    33 Industrial Park Rd
    Pennsville NJ 08070
    856 678-3601

(P-10932)
AMO USA INC
1700 E Saint Andrew Pl, Santa Ana
(92705-4933)
PHONE..................................714 247-8200
Tom Frinzi, *President*
Kristen Featherstone, *Research*
Holly Clark, *Marketing Staff*
Kathryn Lockwood, *Senior Mgr*
Jing Jiang Hughes, *Manager*
EMP: 200 **EST:** 2002
SQ FT: 100,000
SALES (est): 1.1B
SALES (corp-wide): 82.5B **Publicly Held**
WEB: www.jnjvisionpro.com
SIC: 3841 3845 Surgical & medical instruments; laser systems & equipment, medical
HQ: Johnson & Johnson Surgical Vision, Inc.
    1700 E Saint Andrew Pl
    Santa Ana CA 92705
    714 247-8200

(P-10933)
ANELLO CORPORATION
Also Called: Transit Control Systems
111 E Garry Ave, Santa Ana (92707-4201)
PHONE..................................714 546-0561
Peter J Anello, *President*
P J Anello Jr, *Vice Pres*
Patricia J Anello, *Admin Sec*
Kay Higgins Riley, *Controller*
EMP: 21 **EST:** 1977
SQ FT: 19,000
SALES (est): 375.5K **Privately Held**
WEB: www.anellocorp.com
SIC: 3841 3663 3569 Surgical & medical instruments; radio & TV communications equipment; assembly machines, non-metalworking

(P-10934)
APPLIED CARDIAC SYSTEMS INC
1 Hughes Ste A, Irvine (92618-2021)
PHONE..................................949 855-9366
Loren A Manera, *CEO*
Tricia Meads, *CFO*
Susan Marcus, *Vice Pres*
Robert Wilks, *Admin Sec*
Mark Wright, *Engineer*
▲ **EMP:** 64 **EST:** 1981
SQ FT: 18,000
SALES (est): 10.7MM **Privately Held**
WEB: www.acsd4u.com
SIC: 3841 Diagnostic apparatus, medical

(P-10935)
APPLIED MANUFACTURING LLC
22872 Avenida Empresa, Rcho STA Marg
(92688-2650)
PHONE..................................949 713-8000
Tom Wachli, *President*
EMP: 1200 **EST:** 2017
SALES (est): 193.7MM
SALES (corp-wide): 699.8MM **Privately Held**
WEB: www.appliedmed.com
SIC: 3841 Surgical & medical instruments
HQ: Applied Medical Resources Corporation
    22872 Avenida Empresa
    Rcho Sta Marg CA 92688
    949 713-8000

(P-10936)
APPLIED MEDICAL CORPORATION (PA)
Also Called: Applied Medical Resources
22872 Avenida Empresa, Rcho STA Marg
(92688-2650)
PHONE..................................949 713-8000
Said Hilal, *CEO*
Tom Demarchi, *COO*
Hany Louis, *Officer*
Mary Stegwell, *Vice Pres*
Alison Frisella, *District Mgr*
EMP: 2282 **EST:** 1987
SALES (est): 699.8MM **Privately Held**
WEB: www.appliedmedical.com
SIC: 3841 Surgical & medical instruments

(P-10937)
APPLIED MEDICAL DIST CORP
22872 Avenida Empresa, Rcho STA Marg
(92688-2650)
PHONE..................................949 713-8000
Said Hilal, *CEO*
Stephen Stanley, *President*
EMP: 700 **EST:** 1998
SALES (est): 179.5MM
SALES (corp-wide): 699.8MM **Privately Held**
WEB: www.appliedmedical.com
SIC: 3841 Surgical & medical instruments
HQ: Applied Medical Resources Corporation
    22872 Avenida Empresa
    Rcho Sta Marg CA 92688
    949 713-8000

(P-10938)
APPLIED MEDICAL RESOURCES
30152 Esperanza, Rcho STA Marg
(92688-2120)
PHONE..................................949 459-1042
Stephanie Handra, *Engineer*
Maria Rivera, *Director*
Case Cassedy, *Manager*
Jim Champion, *Manager*
Rick Curtis, *Manager*
EMP: 21 **EST:** 2013
SALES (est): 2.1MM **Privately Held**
WEB: www.appliedmedical.com
SIC: 3841 Surgical & medical instruments

(P-10939)
APPLIED MEDICAL RESOURCES CORP (HQ)
Also Called: Applied Medical Distribution
22872 Avenida Empresa, Rcho STA Marg
(92688-2650)
PHONE..................................949 713-8000
Said S Hilal, *President*
Nabil Hilal, *President*
Gary Johnson, *President*
Stephen E Stanley, *President*
Michael Vaughn, *President*
▲ **EMP:** 3408 **EST:** 1987
SQ FT: 800,000
SALES (est): 544.1MM
SALES (corp-wide): 699.8MM **Privately Held**
WEB: www.appliedmedical.com
SIC: 3841 Surgical & medical instruments
PA: Applied Medical Corporation
    22872 Avenida Empresa
    Rcho Sta Marg CA 92688
    949 713-8000

(P-10940)
APRICOT DESIGNS INC
677 Arrow Grand Cir, Covina (91722-2146)
PHONE..................................626 966-3299
Felix Yiu, *CEO*
Tedd Wong, *CFO*
William Otsen, *Technology*
Steffen Dubois, *Engineer*
William Lein, *Engineer*
▲ **EMP:** 66 **EST:** 1989
SQ FT: 6,200
SALES (est): 10.7MM
SALES (corp-wide): 50.2MM **Privately Held**
WEB: www.sptlabtech.com
SIC: 3841 Surgical & medical instruments
HQ: Spt Labtech Limited
    Melbourn Science Park
    Royston HERTS SG8 6
    122 362-7555

(P-10941)
ASPEN MEDICAL PRODUCTS LLC
6481 Oak Cyn, Irvine (92618-5202)
P.O. Box 22116, Pasadena (91185-0001)
PHONE..................................949 681-0200
Jim Cloar, *President*
Kathryn Gray, *Officer*
Geof Garth, *Vice Pres*
Scott Hampson, *Vice Pres*
John Williamson, *Vice Pres*
▲ **EMP:** 70 **EST:** 1993
SQ FT: 52,000
SALES (est): 28.1MM
SALES (corp-wide): 221.2MM **Privately Held**
WEB: www.aspenmp.com
SIC: 3841 Surgical & medical instruments
PA: Cogr, Inc.
    140 E 45th St Fl 43
    New York NY 10017
    212 370-5600

(P-10942)
B BRAUN MEDICAL INC
2525 Mcgaw Ave, Irvine (92614-5841)
P.O. Box 19791 (92623-9791)
PHONE..................................610 691-5400
Keith Klaes, *Manager*
Joe Garcia, *Officer*
Lars Hahn, *Vice Pres*
Bruce Heugel, *Vice Pres*
Thomas McWhinney, *Vice Pres*
EMP: 1300
SALES (corp-wide): 2.6MM **Privately Held**
WEB: www.bbraunusa.com
SIC: 3841 Catheters
HQ: B. Braun Medical Inc.
    824 12th Ave
    Bethlehem PA 18018
    610 691-5400

(P-10943)
BAXALTA US INC
1700 Rancho Conejo Blvd, Thousand Oaks
(91320-1424)
PHONE..................................805 498-8664
Paul Marshall, *Manager*
Reyes Miguel, *Officer*
Shawn Galastian, *Project Engr*
Steven Badawi, *Engineer*
Daniel Kim, *Engineer*
EMP: 216 **Privately Held**
SIC: 3841 2835 2389 3842 Surgical & medical instruments; catheters; medical instruments & equipment, blood & bone work; surgical instruments & apparatus; blood derivative diagnostic agents; hospital gowns; surgical appliances & supplies; medical laboratory equipment; intravenous solutions
HQ: Baxalta Us Inc.
    1200 Lakeside Dr
    Bannockburn IL 60015
    224 948-2000

(P-10944)
BAXTER HEALTHCARE CORPORATION
Also Called: Baxter Medication Delivery
17511 Armstrong Ave, Irvine (92614-5725)
PHONE..................................949 474-6301
Michael Mussallem, *Manager*
Charles Mooney, *Research*
Patti Bosalet, *Human Res Dir*
Jairo Martinez, *Supervisor*
EMP: 250
SALES (corp-wide): 11.6B **Publicly Held**
WEB: www.baxter.com
SIC: 3841 Surgical & medical instruments
HQ: Baxter Healthcare Corporation
    1 Baxter Pkwy
    Deerfield IL 60015
    224 948-2000

(P-10945)
BECKMAN COULTER INC
Beckman Coulter Diagnostics
250 S Kraemer Blvd, Brea (92821-6232)
P.O. Box 8000 (92822-8000)
PHONE..................................818 970-2161
Albert Ziegler, *Manager*
Helen Lee, *Marketing Mgr*
EMP: 200

SALES (corp-wide): 22.2B **Publicly Held**
WEB: www.beckmancoulter.com
SIC: 3841 3821 Surgical & medical instruments; clinical laboratory instruments, except medical & dental
HQ: Beckman Coulter, Inc.
250 S Kraemer Blvd
Brea CA 92821
714 993-5321

(P-10946)
BIO-MEDICAL DEVICES INC
Also Called: Maxair Systems
17171 Daimler St, Irvine (92614-5508)
PHONE....................949 752-9642
Nick Herbert, *President*
Alan Davidner, *Shareholder*
Harry N Herbert, *CEO*
Ray Sadeghi, *General Mgr*
Tim Klink, *Engineer*
▲ **EMP:** 37 **EST:** 1988
SQ FT: 40,000
SALES (est): 9.5MM **Privately Held**
WEB: www.maxair-systems.com
SIC: 3841 2353 Surgical & medical instruments; hats, caps & millinery

(P-10947)
BIO-MEDICAL DEVICES INTL INC
17171 Daimler St, Irvine (92614-5508)
PHONE....................800 443-3842
Nicholas Herbert, *President*
Larry Green, *Engineer*
Allan Schultz, *Director*
EMP: 31 **EST:** 1998
SALES (est): 5.7MM **Privately Held**
WEB: www.maxair-systems.com
SIC: 3841 2353 Surgical & medical instruments; hats, caps & millinery

(P-10948)
BIOPLATE INC
570 S Melrose St, Placentia (92870-6327)
PHONE....................310 815-2100
Thomas Hopson, *President*
Tadeusz Wellisz, *Ch of Bd*
Lester Mazariegos, *Production*
Anthony Ruggiero, *Sales Executive*
Erin Hickey, *Marketing Mgr*
EMP: 21 **EST:** 1994
SALES (est): 2.8MM **Privately Held**
WEB: www.bioplate.com
SIC: 3841 Surgical & medical instruments

(P-10949)
BIOSEAL
167 W Orangethorpe Ave, Placentia (92870-6922)
PHONE....................714 528-4695
Bill Runion, *President*
Robert C Kopple, *Corp Secy*
Lauren Martin, *Human Resources*
Hailey Golden, *Sales Staff*
Blake Wood, *Sales Staff*
▲ **EMP:** 40 **EST:** 1988
SQ FT: 8,500
SALES (est): 9.4MM **Privately Held**
WEB: www.biosealnet.com
SIC: 3841 5047 Surgical & medical instruments; hospital equipment & furniture

(P-10950)
BIT GROUP USA INC (PA)
Also Called: Bit Medtech
6 Thomas Ste 100, Irvine (92618-2505)
PHONE....................949 238-1200
Marius Balger, *CEO*
Susanne Gottschalk, *CFO*
John Frazier, *Mfg Mgr*
▲ **EMP:** 69 **EST:** 1998
SALES (est): 14.8MM **Privately Held**
WEB: www.bit-group.com
SIC: 3841 8711 Surgical & medical instruments; engineering services

(P-10951)
BLUESTONE MEDICAL INC
Also Called: Onsight Ways Technology
2807 Villa Way, Newport Beach (92663-3728)
PHONE....................949 338-3723
Brad Barnes, *CEO*
EMP: 15
SALES: 691.8K **Privately Held**
SIC: 3841 Surgical & medical instruments

(P-10952)
BOSTON SCIENTIFIC CORPORATION
Also Called: Boston Scientific - Valencia
25155 Rye Canyon Loop, Valencia (91355-5004)
PHONE....................800 678-2575
Phill Tarves, *Manager*
Laura Lewis, *Vice Pres*
Lisa Welker-Finney, *Vice Pres*
Jennifer Rowland, *Admin Asst*
Suzanne Jamal, *Technician*
EMP: 45
SALES (corp-wide): 9.9B **Publicly Held**
WEB: www.bostonscientific.com
SIC: 3841 Surgical & medical instruments
PA: Boston Scientific Corporation
300 Boston Scientific Way
Marlborough MA 01752
508 683-4000

(P-10953)
BRIGHTWATER MEDICAL INC
42580 Rio Nedo, Temecula (92590-3727)
P.O. Box 1286, Murrieta (92564-1286)
PHONE....................951 290-3410
Harry Robert Smouse, *CEO*
Scott Shaw, *Finance*
EMP: 15 **EST:** 2014
SQ FT: 5,000
SALES (est): 3.6MM
SALES (corp-wide): 963.8MM **Publicly Held**
WEB: www.merit.com
SIC: 3841 Surgical & medical instruments
PA: Merit Medical Systems, Inc.
1600 W Merit Pkwy
South Jordan UT 84095
801 253-1600

(P-10954)
BRUIN BIOMETRICS LLC
10877 Wilshire Blvd # 1600, Los Angeles (90024-4371)
PHONE....................310 268-9494
Martin Burns,
Colin Priestly, *COO*
Scott Hayashi, *CFO*
Ryan Stearns, *Officer*
Aryeh Goldberg, *Exec VP*
EMP: 17 **EST:** 2009
SQ FT: 3,000
SALES (est): 4MM
SALES (corp-wide): 7.3B **Privately Held**
WEB: www.bruinbiometrics.com
SIC: 3841 Diagnostic apparatus, medical
HQ: Arjo Ab (Publ)

Malmo 201 2
103 354-500

(P-10955)
CALDERA MEDICAL INC
4360 Park Terrace Dr # 140, Westlake Village (91361-4634)
PHONE....................818 879-6555
Bryon L Merade, *Ch of Bd*
Jeff Hubauer, *COO*
David Hochman, *CFO*
Dan Keeffe, *Vice Pres*
Bahar Sutorius, *Vice Pres*
EMP: 70 **EST:** 2002
SQ FT: 25,000
SALES (est): 20.4MM **Privately Held**
WEB: www.calderamedical.com
SIC: 3841 Surgical & medical instruments

(P-10956)
CAPISTRANO LABS INC
150 Calle Iglesia Ste B, San Clemente (92672-7550)
PHONE....................949 492-0390
Paul Meyers, *President*
Matt Stabley, *Treasurer*
Mike Martnick, *Senior Buyer*
EMP: 24 **EST:** 1986
SQ FT: 8,000
SALES (est): 2.1MM **Privately Held**
WEB: www.capolabs.com
SIC: 3841 Diagnostic apparatus, medical

(P-10957)
CAREFUSION 202 INC (DH)
22745 Savi Ranch Pkwy, Yorba Linda (92887-4668)
PHONE....................800 231-2466

Dave Mowry, *CEO*
Michael A Lynch, *President*
EMP: 221 **EST:** 2001
SALES (est): 46.5MM
SALES (corp-wide): 1.8B **Privately Held**
WEB: www.vyaire.com
SIC: 3841 Surgical & medical instruments
HQ: Vyaire Medical Llc
26125 N Riverwoods Blvd # 1
Mettawa IL 60045
833 327-3284

(P-10958)
CAREFUSION 207 INC
1100 Bird Center Dr, Palm Springs (92262-8000)
PHONE....................760 778-7200
Edward Borkowski, *CFO*
Carol Zilm, *President*
Amarendra Duvvur, *Treasurer*
Mark Stauffer, *Officer*
Cathy Cooney, *Exec VP*
▲ **EMP:** 327 **EST:** 2005
SALES (est): 50.2MM
SALES (corp-wide): 1.8B **Privately Held**
WEB: www.vyaire.com
SIC: 3841 8741 Surgical & medical instruments; nursing & personal care facility management
PA: Vyaire Holding Company
26125 N Riverwoods Blvd
Mettawa IL 60045
872 757-0114

(P-10959)
CAROLINA LQUID CHMISTRIES CORP
510 W Central Ave Ste C, Brea (92821-3032)
P.O. Box 92249 (92822)
PHONE....................336 722-8910
Phil Shugart, *Branch Mgr*
Patricia Shugart, *Vice Pres*
Renalto Pena, *General Mgr*
Dan Browning, *Technical Staff*
Lori Nicholson, *Technical Staff*
EMP: 17 **Privately Held**
WEB: www.carolinachemistries.com
SIC: 3841 Surgical & medical instruments
PA: Carolina Liquid Chemistries Corporation
313 Gallimore Dairy Rd
Greensboro NC 27409

(P-10960)
CAS MEDICAL SYSTEMS INC (HQ)
1 Edwards Way, Irvine (92614-5688)
PHONE....................203 488-6056
Thomas Patton, *President*
Jeffery Baird, *CFO*
Karen Harris-Coleman, *Exec VP*
Paul Benni, *Security Dir*
Yuliya Eisenmann, *Graphic Designe*
EMP: 15 **EST:** 2018
SALES: 18.7MM
SALES (corp-wide): 4.3B **Publicly Held**
WEB: www.edwards.com
SIC: 3841 Diagnostic apparatus, medical
PA: Edwards Lifesciences Corp
1 Edwards Way
Irvine CA 92614
949 250-2500

(P-10961)
CHEN-TECH INDUSTRIES INC (DH)
Also Called: ATI Forged Products
9 Wrigley, Irvine (92618-2711)
PHONE....................949 855-6716
Richard Harshman, *CEO*
Shannon Ko, *President*
Alston Chung, *Engineer*
Jennifer Lindmeyer, *Sales Staff*
Eric Massey, *Senior Mgr*
EMP: 38
SQ FT: 18,000
SALES (est): 12.3MM **Publicly Held**
WEB: www.chen-tech.com
SIC: 3841 3769 3724 3463 Surgical & medical instruments; guided missile & space vehicle parts & auxiliary equipment; aircraft engines & engine parts; aluminum forgings

HQ: Ati Ladish Llc
5481 S Packard Ave
Cudahy WI 53110
414 747-2611

(P-10962)
CHROMOLOGIC LLC
1225 S Shamrock Ave, Monrovia (91016-4244)
PHONE....................626 381-9974
Naresh Menon, *Mng Member*
Richard Barnes, *CIO*
Edward Burns, *Engineer*
Justine Durano, *Engineer*
Robert Cartland, *Manager*
EMP: 28 **EST:** 2008
SALES (est): 3.2MM **Privately Held**
WEB: www.chromologic.com
SIC: 3841 Diagnostic apparatus, medical

(P-10963)
CLARIENT INC (DH)
Also Called: Clarient Diagnostic Services
31 Columbia, Aliso Viejo (92656-1460)
PHONE....................949 445-7300
Douglas M Vanoort, *Ch of Bd*
Christian Placinta, *Partner*
Steven C Jones, *President*
Michael J Pellini MD, *President*
Cynthia Collins, *CEO*
EMP: 365 **EST:** 1996
SQ FT: 78,000
SALES (est): 71.4MM
SALES (corp-wide): 444.4MM **Publicly Held**
WEB: www.neogenomics.com
SIC: 3841 3826 8071 Diagnostic apparatus, medical; magnetic resonance imaging apparatus; medical laboratories
HQ: Neogenomics Laboratories, Inc.
12701 Commwl Dr Ste 9
Fort Myers FL 33913
239 768-0600

(P-10964)
CLEARFLOW INC (PA)
16 Technology Dr Ste 150, Irvine (92618-2327)
PHONE....................714 916-5010
Paul Molloy, *President*
Al Diaz, *Exec VP*
Michael Elniski, *Vice Pres*
Edward Boyle Jr, *Principal*
Patty Miller, *Office Mgr*
EMP: 20 **EST:** 2008
SALES (est): 244K **Privately Held**
WEB: www.clearflow.com
SIC: 3841 3829 Surgical & medical instruments; thermometers, including digital: clinical

(P-10965)
CLEARVIEW ORTHOPEDIC DEV LLC
15550 Rockfield Blvd D, Irvine (92618-2720)
PHONE....................949 752-7885
Tom Gardner,
Chad Neault, *Ch Invest Ofcr*
Hartmut Loch, *Vice Pres*
Kim Lindsay-Stern, *Executive Asst*
Cheryl Klukas, *Legal Staff*
EMP: 19 **EST:** 2009
SALES (est): 4MM **Privately Held**
SIC: 3841 Surgical & medical instruments

(P-10966)
COMPOSITE MANUFACTURING INC
Also Called: CMI
970 Calle Amanecer Ste D, San Clemente (92673-6250)
PHONE....................949 361-7580
Roger Malcolm, *President*
Tim Salter, *CEO*
Louis Mahony, *CFO*
Kim Bobb, *Admin Asst*
Tawney Tucker, *Administration*
EMP: 36 **EST:** 1995
SQ FT: 16,000
SALES (est): 6.5MM **Privately Held**
WEB: www.carbonfiber.com
SIC: 3841 3624 Operating tables; carbon & graphite products

(P-10967)
DAVID KOPF INSTRUMENTS
7324 Elmo St, Tujunga (91042-2205)
P.O. Box 636 (91043-0636)
PHONE..................818 352-3274
Carl Koph, *CEO*
J David Kopf, *President*
Carol Kopf, *Treasurer*
Joanne Simmons, *Financial Exec*
Mark Neumann, *Purch Agent*
EMP: 28 **EST:** 1959
SQ FT: 13,836
SALES (est): 3.5MM **Privately Held**
WEB: www.kopfinstruments.com
SIC: 3841 Veterinarians' instruments & apparatus

(P-10968)
DESIGN CATAPULT
MANUFACTURING
17331 Newhope St, Fountain Valley
(92708-4343)
PHONE..................949 522-6789
Sam Iravantchi, *President*
William Wooten, *Principal*
EMP: 14 **EST:** 2018
SALES (est): 1.6MM **Privately Held**
WEB: www.dcmedmfg.com
SIC: 3841 Surgical & medical instruments

(P-10969)
DIALITY INC
181 Technology Dr Ste 150, Irvine
(92618-2484)
PHONE..................949 916-5851
Osman Khawar, *CEO*
Jahnavi Lokre, *COO*
Ather Khan, *CFO*
Aaron Mishkin, *Admin Sec*
Clayton Poppe, *CTO*
EMP: 18 **EST:** 2015
SALES (est): 3.4MM **Privately Held**
WEB: www.diality.com
SIC: 3841 Hemodialysis apparatus

(P-10970)
DIGITAL SURGERY SYSTEMS
INC
Also Called: True Digital Surgery
125 Cremona Dr 110, Goleta (93117-5503)
PHONE..................805 978-5400
Aidan Foley, *President*
Arthur Rice, *Chairman*
September Riharb, *Vice Pres*
J Flagg Flanagan,
Kevin Foley,
EMP: 34 **EST:** 2018
SALES (est): 5MM **Privately Held**
SIC: 3841 Surgical & medical instruments

(P-10971)
DITEC CO
Also Called: Ditec Mfg.
1019 Mark Ave, Carpinteria (93013-2912)
PHONE..................805 566-7800
Don L Cooper, *President*
Scott Cooper, *Vice Pres*
Deeanna Moore, *Human Res Mgr*
EMP: 19 **EST:** 1985
SQ FT: 10,000
SALES (est): 615.3K **Privately Held**
WEB: www.ditecmfg.com
SIC: 3841 3843 3545 Surgical instruments & apparatus; burs, dental; diamond cutting tools for turning, boring, burnishing, etc.

(P-10972)
DOSE MEDICAL CORPORATION
229 Avenida Fabricante, San Clemente
(92672-7531)
PHONE..................949 367-9600
Thomas W Burns, *CEO*
EMP: 15 **EST:** 2009
SALES (est): 1.3MM
SALES (corp-wide): 224.9MM **Publicly Held**
WEB: www.glaukos.com
SIC: 3841 Eye examining instruments & apparatus
PA: Glaukos Corporation
229 Avenida Fabricante
San Clemente CA 92672
949 367-9600

(P-10973)
EAGLE LABS LLC
10201a Trademark St Ste A, Rancho Cucamonga (91730-5849)
PHONE..................909 481-0011
Richard J De Camp, *President*
Rich De Camp, *Vice Pres*
Michael Decamp, *Vice Pres*
Richard Decamp, *Vice Pres*
Jenny Villa, *Vice Pres*
EMP: 65 **EST:** 1988
SQ FT: 30,000
SALES (est): 16.5MM
SALES (corp-wide): 18.2MM **Privately Held**
WEB: www.eaglelabs.com
SIC: 3841 Surgical & medical instruments
PA: Innovia Medical
815 Northwest Pkwy # 100
Saint Paul MN 55121
651 789-3939

(P-10974)
ECA MEDICAL INSTRUMENTS
(DH)
1107 Tourmaline Dr, Newbury Park
(91320-1208)
PHONE..................805 376-2509
John J Nino, *President*
Clint Elsemore, *VP Finance*
Joe Brendle, *Director*
Joe Nagle, *Director*
EMP: 21 **EST:** 1979
SQ FT: 14,982
SALES (est): 9.7MM **Publicly Held**
WEB: www.ecamedical.com
SIC: 3841 Surgical & medical instruments
HQ: Acas, Llc
2 Bethesda Metro Ctr # 1200
Bethesda MD 20814
301 951-6122

(P-10975)
EDGE SYSTEMS LLC (PA)
Also Called: Hydrafacial Company, The
2165 E Spring St, Long Beach
(90806-2114)
PHONE..................800 603-4996
Clint Carnell, *CEO*
Erin Morisey, *Partner*
Jeff Nardoci, *COO*
Joel Freedman, *CFO*
Randy Sieve, *CFO*
▲ **EMP:** 170 **EST:** 2012
SQ FT: 22,515
SALES (est): 74.1MM **Privately Held**
WEB: www.hydrafacial.com
SIC: 3841 Surgical & medical instruments

(P-10976)
EDWARDS LFSCIENCES
CARDIAQ LLC
1 Edwards Way, Irvine (92614-5688)
PHONE..................949 387-2615
Robrecht Michiels, *CEO*
J Brent Ratz, *President*
Jan Felberg, *Vice Pres*
Danny Baldo, *Engineer*
Julie Fan, *Analyst*
EMP: 56 **EST:** 2007
SALES (est): 6MM
SALES (corp-wide): 4.3B **Publicly Held**
WEB: www.edwards.com
SIC: 3841 Surgical & medical instruments
PA: Edwards Lifesciences Corp
1 Edwards Way
Irvine CA 92614
949 250-2500

(P-10977)
ELECTRONIC WAVEFORM LAB
INC
5702 Bolsa Ave, Huntington Beach
(92649-1128)
PHONE..................714 843-0463
Ryan Haney, *President*
William Heaney, *President*
Kim Zink, *CFO*
Patricia Heaney, *Treasurer*
Robert Heaney, *Vice Pres*
EMP: 25 **EST:** 1981
SALES (est): 5.1MM **Privately Held**
WEB: www.h-wave.com
SIC: 3841 Anesthesia apparatus

(P-10978)
ENDOLOGIX INC (PA)
2 Musick, Irvine (92618-1631)
PHONE..................949 595-7200
John Onopchenko, *CEO*
Daniel Lemaitre, *Ch of Bd*
Cindy Pinto, *CFO*
Matthew Thompson, *Chief Mktg Ofcr*
Tim Benner, *Officer*
▲ **EMP:** 291 **EST:** 1992
SQ FT: 129,000
SALES (est): 143.3MM **Privately Held**
WEB: www.endologix.com
SIC: 3841 Surgical & medical instruments; catheters

(P-10979)
ENDOLOGIX CANADA LLC
2 Musick, Irvine (92618-1631)
PHONE..................949 595-7200
John Onopchenko,
EMP: 79 **EST:** 2014
SALES (est): 13.2MM **Privately Held**
WEB: www.trivascular.com
SIC: 3841 Catheters
HQ: Trivascular, Inc.
2 Musick
Irvine CA 92618

(P-10980)
ENVVENO MEDICAL
CORPORATION
70 Doppler, Irvine (92618-4306)
PHONE..................949 261-2900
Robert A Berman, *CEO*
Craig Glynn, *CFO*
Marc H Glickman, *Chief Mktg Ofcr*
EMP: 19 **EST:** 1987
SQ FT: 14,507 **Privately Held**
WEB: www.envveno.com
SIC: 3841 Surgical & medical instruments

(P-10981)
EPICA MEDICAL INNOVATIONS
LLC
901 Calle Amanecer # 150, San Clemente
(92673-4219)
PHONE..................949 238-6323
Frank D'Amelio,
Jason Grace, *Project Mgr*
▲ **EMP:** 24
SQ FT: 4,441
SALES (est): 4.5MM
SALES (corp-wide): 20MM **Privately Held**
WEB: www.epicaanimalhealth.com
SIC: 3841 5047 Surgical & medical instruments; medical equipment & supplies
PA: Epica International, Inc.
901 Calle Amanecer # 150
San Clemente CA 92673
949 238-6323

(P-10982)
FLUID LINE TECHNOLOGY
CORP
9362 Eton Ave Ste A, Chatsworth
(91311-5888)
P.O. Box 3116 (91313-3116)
PHONE..................818 998-8848
Joseph Marcilese, *President*
Phillip Jaramilla, *Vice Pres*
▼ **EMP:** 25 **EST:** 1989
SQ FT: 17,000
SALES (est): 4.1MM **Privately Held**
WEB: www.fluidlinetech.com
SIC: 3841 2833 Surgical & medical instruments; medicinals & botanicals

(P-10983)
FREUDENBERG MEDICAL LLC
5050 Rivergrade Rd, Baldwin Park
(91706-1405)
PHONE..................626 814-9684
Coburn Pharr, *Manager*
Sven Rosenbeiger, *Vice Pres*
Susan Ward, *Vice Pres*
Hamlet Haroutonian, *Project Mgr*
Rajan Panneer, *Project Mgr*
EMP: 149
SALES (corp-wide): 10.4B **Privately Held**
WEB: www.inhealth.com
SIC: 3841 Surgical & medical instruments

HQ: Freudenberg Medical, Llc
1110 Mark Ave
Carpinteria CA 93013
805 684-3304

(P-10984)
FZIOMED INC (PA)
231 Bonetti Dr, San Luis Obispo
(93401-7376)
PHONE..................805 546-0610
John S Krelle, *President*
Ronald F Haynes, *Ch of Bd*
Collette Canning, *Executive*
Mark Miller, *Senior Engr*
Lucy Lopez, *Mfg Staff*
EMP: 39 **EST:** 1996
SQ FT: 36,000
SALES (est): 6.3MM **Privately Held**
WEB: www.fziomed.com
SIC: 3841 Surgical & medical instruments

(P-10985)
GLAUKOS CORPORATION (PA)
229 Avenida Fabricante, San Clemente
(92672-7531)
PHONE..................949 367-9600
Thomas W Burns, *President*
William J Link, *Ch of Bd*
Chris M Calcaterra, *COO*
Joseph E Gilliam, *CFO*
Michele M Allegretto, *Vice Pres*
EMP: 205 **EST:** 1998
SALES (est): 224.9MM **Publicly Held**
WEB: www.glaukos.com
SIC: 3841 Eye examining instruments & apparatus

(P-10986)
HAEMONETICS
MANUFACTURING INC (HQ)
1630 W Industrial Park St, Covina
(91722-3419)
PHONE..................626 339-7388
Neil Ryding, *CEO*
Katherine Angeles, *Manager*
◆ **EMP:** 195 **EST:** 2012
SQ FT: 61,313
SALES (est): 57.6MM
SALES (corp-wide): 988.4MM **Publicly Held**
WEB: www.haemonetics.com
SIC: 3841 Surgical & medical instruments
PA: Haemonetics Corporation
125 Summer St
Boston MA 02110
781 848-7100

(P-10987)
HEMODIALYSIS INC
Also Called: Hunnington Dialysis Center
806 S Fair Oaks Ave, Pasadena
(91105-2601)
PHONE..................626 792-0548
Susan Burkhart, *Manager*
EMP: 41
SALES (corp-wide): 11.9MM **Privately Held**
WEB: www.hemodialysis-inc.com
SIC: 3841 8011 Hemodialysis apparatus; hematologist
PA: Hemodialysis, Inc.
710 W Wilson Ave
Glendale CA 91203
818 500-8736

(P-10988)
HOYA SURGICAL OPTICS INC
15335 Frfeld Rnch Rd Ste, Chino Hills
(91709)
PHONE..................909 680-3900
Yasuro Mori, *CFO*
Bruno Chermette, *President*
Sandra Gulbicki, *Corp Comm Staff*
EMP: 20 **EST:** 2007
SALES (est): 2.3MM **Privately Held**
WEB: www.hoyasurgicaloptics.com
SIC: 3841 Surgical & medical instruments

(P-10989)
HYCOR BIOMEDICAL LLC
7272 Chapman Ave Ste A, Garden Grove
(92841-2103)
PHONE..................714 933-3000
Dick Aderman, *President*
Eric Whitters, *COO*
Phil Crusco, *Vice Pres*

Richard Hockins, *Vice Pres*
Monse Gallegos, *Marketing Staff*
▲ **EMP:** 120 **EST:** 1985
SQ FT: 76,000
SALES (est): 34.8MM
SALES (corp-wide): 188.1MM **Privately Held**
WEB: www.hycorbiomedical.com
SIC: 3841 2835 Surgical & medical instruments; in vitro & in vivo diagnostic substances
PA: Linden, Llc
111 S Wacker Dr Ste 3350
Chicago IL 60606
312 506-5657

(P-10990)
I-FLOW LLC
43 Discovery Ste 100, Irvine (92618-3773)
PHONE..........................800 448-3569
Donald Earhart, *President*
James J Dal Porto, *COO*
James R Talevich, *CFO*
EMP: 1100 **EST:** 1985
SQ FT: 66,675
SALES (est): 118.3MM
SALES (corp-wide): 19.1B **Publicly Held**
WEB: www.avanospainmanagement.com
SIC: 3841 Surgical instruments & apparatus
PA: Kimberly-Clark Corporation
351 Phelps Dr
Irving TX 75038
972 281-1200

(P-10991)
ICU MEDICAL INC (PA)
951 Calle Amanecer, San Clemente (92673-6212)
PHONE..........................949 366-2183
Vivek Jain, *Ch of Bd*
Dan Lee, *Partner*
Christian B Voigtlander, *COO*
Christian Voigtlander, *COO*
Brian Bonnell, *CFO*
▲ **EMP:** 3683 **EST:** 1984
SQ FT: 39,000
SALES (est): 1.2B **Publicly Held**
WEB: www.icumed.com
SIC: 3841 3845 IV transfusion apparatus; catheters; pacemaker, cardiac

(P-10992)
ICU MEDICAL SALES INC (HQ)
951 Calle Amanecer, San Clemente (92673-6212)
PHONE..........................949 366-2183
Vivek Jain, *CEO*
EMP: 100 **EST:** 2001
SQ FT: 39,000
SALES (est): 15.2MM
SALES (corp-wide): 1.2B **Publicly Held**
WEB: www.event-medical.com
SIC: 3841 IV transfusion apparatus
PA: Icu Medical, Inc.
951 Calle Amanecer
San Clemente CA 92673
949 366-2183

(P-10993)
INARI MEDICAL INC
9 Parker Ste 100, Irvine (92618-1666)
PHONE..........................877 927-4747
William Hoffman, *CEO*
Drew Hykes, *COO*
Mitchell Hill, *CFO*
Thomas Tu, *Chief Mktg Ofcr*
Eben Gordon, *Vice Pres*
EMP: 244 **EST:** 2011
SQ FT: 38,200
SALES (est): 139.6MM **Privately Held**
WEB: www.inarimedical.com
SIC: 3841 Surgical & medical instruments; catheters

(P-10994)
INNOVATIVE PRODUCT BRANDS INC
Also Called: Ipb
7045 Palm Ave, Highland (92346-3291)
PHONE..........................909 864-7477
Bryan Joe Tapocik, *CEO*
Stacy Kristine Tapocik, *Admin Sec*
▲ **EMP:** 20 **EST:** 2001

SALES (est): 3.7MM **Privately Held**
WEB: www.innovativeproductbrands.com
SIC: 3841 Surgical & medical instruments

(P-10995)
INOGEN INC (PA)
301 Coromar Dr, Goleta (93117-3286)
PHONE..........................805 562-0500
Nabil Shabshab, *President*
Heath Lukatch, *Ch of Bd*
Alison Bauerlein, *CFO*
George Parr, *Ch Credit Ofcr*
Stanislav Glezer, *Chief Mktg Ofcr*
◆ **EMP:** 208 **EST:** 2001
SQ FT: 46,000
SALES (est): 308.4MM **Publicly Held**
WEB: www.inogen.com
SIC: 3841 3842 7352 Surgical & medical instruments; surgical appliances & supplies; medical equipment rental

(P-10996)
IVANTIS INC (PA)
201 Technology Dr, Irvine (92618-2400)
PHONE..........................949 600-9650
David Van Meter, *President*
Todd Abraham, *Vice Pres*
Mike Chodzko, *Vice Pres*
Ken Galt, *Vice Pres*
Richard Hope, *Vice Pres*
EMP: 152 **EST:** 2008
SALES (est): 14.2MM **Privately Held**
WEB: www.ivantisinc.com
SIC: 3841 Ophthalmic instruments & apparatus

(P-10997)
J F FONG INC
Also Called: American Imex
16520 Aston, Irvine (92606-4805)
PHONE..........................949 553-8885
Joan F Fong, *President*
Joseph Fong, *Executive*
Ulrick Fong, *Controller*
▲ **EMP:** 13 **EST:** 1984
SQ FT: 8,000
SALES (est): 440.1K **Privately Held**
SIC: 3841 5047 Surgical & medical instruments; medical equipment & supplies

(P-10998)
JIT MANUFACTURING INC
1610 Commerce Way, Paso Robles (93446-3699)
PHONE..........................805 238-5000
Sharon Smith, *CEO*
EMP: 50
SALES (est): 1.4MM **Privately Held**
SIC: 3841 Medical instruments & equipment, blood & bone work

(P-10999)
KARL STORZ ENDSCPY-AMERICA INC
2151 E Grand Ave Ste 100, El Segundo (90245-2838)
PHONE..........................508 248-9011
Marsha Hunter, *Branch Mgr*
David Chatenever, *Vice Pres*
Patrick Furtaw, *Vice Pres*
Jeffrey Lersch, *Vice Pres*
Bill Wise, *Vice Pres*
EMP: 83
SALES (corp-wide): 2.1B **Privately Held**
WEB: www.karlstorz.com
SIC: 3841 Surgical & medical instruments
HQ: Karl Storz Endoscopy-America, Inc.
2151 E Grand Ave
El Segundo CA 90245
424 218-8100

(P-11000)
KARL STORZ ENDSCPY-AMERICA INC (HQ)
2151 E Grand Ave, El Segundo (90245-5017)
PHONE..........................424 218-8100
Charles Wilhelm, *CEO*
Sken Huang, *CFO*
John Okeefe, *Chairman*
Mark Green, *Vice Pres*
Scott Andrew, *Executive*
▲ **EMP:** 464 **EST:** 1971
SQ FT: 90,000

SALES (est): 280.8MM
SALES (corp-wide): 2.1B **Privately Held**
WEB: www.karlstorz.com
SIC: 3841 5047 Surgical & medical instruments; medical equipment & supplies
PA: Karl Storz Se & Co. Kg
Dr.-Karl-Storz-Str. 34
Tuttlingen BW 78532
746 170-80

(P-11001)
KARL STORZ ENDSCPY-AMERICA INC
1 N Los Carneros Rd, Goleta (93117)
PHONE..........................800 964-5563
Tony Chobot, *Manager*
EMP: 83
SALES (corp-wide): 2.1B **Privately Held**
WEB: www.karlstorz.com
SIC: 3841 3845 Suction therapy apparatus; endoscopic equipment, electromedical
HQ: Karl Storz Endoscopy-America, Inc.
2151 E Grand Ave
El Segundo CA 90245
424 218-8100

(P-11002)
KARL STORZ IMAGING INC
32 Aero Camino, Goleta (93117-3105)
PHONE..........................805 968-5563
EMP: 24
SALES (corp-wide): 2.1B **Privately Held**
WEB: www.karlstorz.com
SIC: 3841 Surgical & medical instruments
HQ: Karl Storz Imaging, Inc.
1 S Los Carneros Rd
Goleta CA 93117

(P-11003)
KENLOR INDUSTRIES INC
1560 E Edinger Ave Ste A1, Santa Ana (92705-4913)
PHONE..........................714 647-0770
Kamales Som PHD, *President*
Sudeep Banerjee, *Vice Pres*
EMP: 14 **EST:** 1989
SQ FT: 5,000
SALES (est): 1.2MM **Privately Held**
WEB: www.kenlor.com
SIC: 3841 2834 Surgical & medical instruments; pharmaceutical preparations

(P-11004)
KONG VETERINARY PRODUCTS
Also Called: KVP
16018 Adelante St Ste C, Irwindale (91702-3236)
PHONE..........................626 633-0077
Nancy Klinkhart, *President*
Herman Klinkhart, *Vice Pres*
Roger Klinkhart, *Vice Pres*
Alan McCool, *Purch Mgr*
Kristi Pray, *Buyer*
▲ **EMP:** 18 **EST:** 1960
SQ FT: 8,000
SALES (est): 550.2K **Privately Held**
SIC: 3841 3842 Surgical & medical instruments; surgical appliances & supplies

(P-11005)
KOOL BLAST GAS
3059 Scholarship, Irvine (92612-4420)
PHONE..........................949 420-9675
EMP: 13 **EST:** 2018
SALES (est): 604.2K **Privately Held**
WEB: www.koolblastgas.com
SIC: 3841 Surgical & medical instruments

(P-11006)
KOROS USA INC
610 Flinn Ave, Moorpark (93021-2008)
PHONE..........................805 529-0825
Tibor Koros, *President*
▲ **EMP:** 25 **EST:** 1974
SQ FT: 12,000
SALES (est): 4.9MM **Privately Held**
WEB: www.korosusa.com
SIC: 3841 Diagnostic apparatus, medical

(P-11007)
LIFE SCIENCE OUTSOURCING INC
Also Called: Medical Device Manufacturing
830 Challenger St, Brea (92821-2946)
PHONE..........................714 672-1090
Barry Kazemi, *President*
Charlie Ricci, *Vice Pres*
Andrew Gladd, *Program Mgr*
Darcy Adams, *Planning Mgr*
Ryan Kazemi, *Project Mgr*
◆ **EMP:** 80
SQ FT: 56,000
SALES (est): 20.1MM **Privately Held**
WEB: www.lso-inc.com
SIC: 3841 Surgical instruments & apparatus

(P-11008)
LIFEMED OF CALIFORNIA
13948 Mountain Ave, Chino (91710-9018)
P.O. Box 787 (91708-0787)
PHONE..........................300 543-3633
Thomas Hamon, *President*
Pat Brinker, *Vice Pres*
EMP: 24 **EST:** 1985
SQ FT: 10,000
SALES (est): 2.4MM **Privately Held**
WEB: www.lifemedofcalifornia.com
SIC: 3841 Hemodialysis apparatus

(P-11009)
LINKS MEDICAL PRODUCTS INC (PA)
9249 Research Dr, Irvine (92618-4286)
PHONE..........................949 753-0001
Thomas L Buckley, *CEO*
Patrick Buckley, *President*
Chad Muhr, *Marketing Staff*
Bob Milton, *Sales Staff*
Albert Nardozi, *Sales Staff*
▲ **EMP:** 26 **EST:** 1996
SALES (est): 3.6MM **Privately Held**
WEB: www.linksmed.com
SIC: 3841 Medical instruments & equipment, blood & bone work

(P-11010)
LISI AEROSPACE
2600 Skypark Dr, Torrance (90505-5314)
PHONE..........................310 326-8110
Jared Young, *Vice Pres*
Charles Carrara, *Technical Staff*
John Bullard, *Accountant*
Marissa Jara, *Hum Res Coord*
Lashanda Rollins, *Buyer*
EMP: 37 **EST:** 2019
SALES (est): 11.1MM **Privately Held**
WEB: www.lisi-aerospace.com
SIC: 3841 Surgical & medical instruments

(P-11011)
LOVEIS CORP
Also Called: Ladybug Medical Supply
9588 Topanga Canyon Blvd, Chatsworth (91311-4011)
PHONE..........................818 408-9504
Barry Wright Jr, *CEO*
EMP: 15
SALES (est): 42MM **Privately Held**
SIC: 3841 5047 Surgical & medical instruments; medical equipment & supplies

(P-11012)
MARLEE MANUFACTURING INC
4711 E Guasti Rd, Ontario (91761-8106)
PHONE..........................909 390-3222
Russell Wells, *President*
Shawn Cory, *President*
Larry Pettit, *Vice Pres*
Patricia Wells, *Vice Pres*
EMP: 39 **EST:** 1984
SQ FT: 41,000
SALES (est): 6.7MM **Privately Held**
WEB: www.marleemanufacturing.com
SIC: 3841 3599 Surgical & medical instruments; machine shop, jobbing & repair

(P-11013)
MASIMO AMERICAS INC
52 Discovery, Irvine (92618-3105)
PHONE..........................949 297-7000
Rick Fishel, *CEO*
Ron Coverston, *Vice Pres*
Stephen Cartwright, *Accounts Mgr*

EMP: 72 **EST:** 2004
SALES (est): 8.2MM **Publicly Held**
WEB: www.masimo.com
SIC: 3841 Surgical & medical instruments
PA: Masimo Corporation
52 Discovery
Irvine CA 92618

(P-11014)
MEDEDGE INC
11965 Venice Blvd Ste 407, Los Angeles (90066-3982)
P.O. Box 3028, Venice (90294-3028)
PHONE..................................310 745-2290
EMP: 16
SQ FT: 2,000
SALES (est): 1.2MM **Privately Held**
WEB: www.mededge-inc.com
SIC: 3841 Mfg Surgical/Medical Instruments

(P-11015)
MEDEIA INC
7 W Figueroa St Ste 215, Santa Barbara (93101-3189)
PHONE..................................800 433-4609
Slav Danev, *President*
EMP: 13 **EST:** 2010
SQ FT: 1,500
SALES: 2MM **Privately Held**
WEB: www.vitalscan.com
SIC: 3841 Surgical instruments & apparatus

(P-11016)
MEDICAL TACTILE INC
5500 W Rosecrans Ave A, Hawthorne (90250-6643)
PHONE..................................310 641-8228
Jae Son, *Chairman*
Denis O'Connor, *CEO*
Steven Sanchez, *Admin Sec*
David Ables, *CTO*
▼ **EMP:** 18 **EST:** 2004
SALES (est): 1MM **Privately Held**
WEB: www.mybexa.com
SIC: 3841 Diagnostic apparatus, medical

(P-11017)
MEDICOOL INC
20460 Gramercy Pl, Torrance (90501-1513)
PHONE..................................310 782-2200
Steve Yeager, *Principal*
Jay Lee, *COO*
Teresa Robba, *Manager*
▲ **EMP:** 17 **EST:** 1986
SQ FT: 15,000
SALES (est): 1.7MM **Privately Held**
WEB: www.medicool.com
SIC: 3841 Inhalators, surgical & medical

(P-11018)
MEDTRONIC ATS MEDICAL INC
1851 E Deere Ave, Santa Ana (92705-5720)
PHONE..................................949 380-9333
Walter Cuevas, *Branch Mgr*
EMP: 63 **Privately Held**
SIC: 3841 Surgical instruments & apparatus
HQ: Medtronic Ats Medical, Inc.
710 Medtronic Pkwy
Minneapolis MN 55432
763 553-7736

(P-11019)
MEDTRONIC MINIMED INC (DH)
18000 Devonshire St, Northridge (91325-1219)
PHONE..................................800 646-4633
Hooman Hakami, *CEO*
Mark Christensen, *CFO*
Nathan Chan, *Vice Pres*
Austin Domenici, *Vice Pres*
Eric P Geismar, *Vice Pres*
▲ **EMP:** 1200 **EST:** 1993
SQ FT: 250,000
SALES (est): 648.3MM **Privately Held**
WEB: www.medtronicdiabetes.com
SIC: 3841 Surgical & medical instruments
HQ: Medtronic, Inc.
710 Medtronic Pkwy
Minneapolis MN 55432
763 514-4000

(P-11020)
MEDTRONIC PS MEDICAL INC (DH)
5290 California Ave # 100, Irvine (92617-3229)
PHONE..................................805 571-3769
Austin Noll, *General Mgr*
Chris Eso, *Vice Pres*
Ashish Srivastava, *Info Tech Dir*
Megan Trobridge, *Project Mgr*
George Hallak, *Engineer*
◆ **EMP:** 200 **EST:** 1978
SALES (est): 66.7MM **Privately Held**
WEB: www.medtronic.com
SIC: 3841 Surgical & medical instruments
HQ: Medtronic, Inc.
710 Medtronic Pkwy
Minneapolis MN 55432
763 514-4000

(P-11021)
MERIT MEDICAL SYSTEMS INC
6 Journey Ste 125, Aliso Viejo (92656-5319)
PHONE..................................801 208-4793
Judy Wagner, *Branch Mgr*
EMP: 20
SALES (corp-wide): 963.8MM **Publicly Held**
WEB: www.merit.com
SIC: 3841 Surgical & medical instruments
PA: Merit Medical Systems, Inc.
1600 W Merit Pkwy
South Jordan UT 84095
801 253-1600

(P-11022)
METTLER ELECTRONICS CORP
1333 S Claudina St, Anaheim (92805-6266)
PHONE..................................714 533-2221
Stephen C Mettler, *CEO*
Mark Mettler, *President*
Danielle Barrante, *CFO*
Matthew Ferrari, *CFO*
Donna Mettler, *Admin Sec*
▲ **EMP:** 42 **EST:** 1957
SQ FT: 22,500
SALES (est): 6.3MM **Privately Held**
WEB: www.mettlerelectronics.com
SIC: 3841 Surgical & medical instruments

(P-11023)
MICRO THERAPEUTICS INC (HQ)
Also Called: Ev3 Neurovascular
9775 Toledo Way, Irvine (92618-1811)
PHONE..................................949 837-3700
Thomas C Wilder III, *President*
Thomas Berryman, *CFO*
EMP: 100 **EST:** 1993
SQ FT: 43,000
SALES (est): 78.4MM **Privately Held**
WEB: www.medtronic.com
SIC: 3841 Surgical & medical instruments

(P-11024)
MICROVENTION INC (DH)
Also Called: Microvention Terumo
35 Enterprise, Aliso Viejo (92656-2601)
PHONE..................................714 258-8000
Carsten Schroeder, *President*
Kazuaki Kitabatake, *Ch of Bd*
Sandra Show, *CEO*
Bill Hughes, *COO*
Matt Fitz, *Senior VP*
▲ **EMP:** 594 **EST:** 1997
SQ FT: 35,000
SALES (est): 222.4MM **Privately Held**
WEB: www.microvention.com
SIC: 3841 Surgical & medical instruments
HQ: Terumo Americas Holding, Inc.
265 Davidson Ave Ste 320
Somerset NJ 08873
732 302-4900

(P-11025)
MIERON INC
9160 Rose St, Bellflower (90706-6420)
PHONE..................................626 466-9040
Jessica Maslin, *CEO*
EMP: 14 **EST:** 2017
SALES (est): 758K **Privately Held**
WEB: www.mieronvr.com
SIC: 3841 Holders, surgical needle

(P-11026)
MONOBIND SALES INC (PA)
100 N Pointe Dr, Lake Forest (92630-2270)
PHONE..................................949 951-2665
Frederick Jerome, *President*
Dr Jay Singh, *Vice Pres*
Veronica Landa, *Admin Asst*
Susan Jerome, *Human Res Dir*
Joshua Buckingham, *Production*
▲ **EMP:** 36 **EST:** 1977
SQ FT: 18,000
SALES (est): 6.7MM **Privately Held**
WEB: www.monobind.com
SIC: 3841 Diagnostic apparatus, medical

(P-11027)
MPS MEDICAL INC
830 Challenger St Ste 200, Brea (92821-2946)
PHONE..................................714 672-1090
Barry A Kazemi, *CEO*
Ryan B Kazemi, *Opers Mgr*
Ryan Kazemi, *Opers Mgr*
EMP: 37 **EST:** 2014
SALES (est): 5.6MM
SALES (corp-wide): 12.4MM **Privately Held**
WEB: www.innovamedgroup.com
SIC: 3841 Surgical & medical instruments
PA: Innova Medical Group, Inc.
800 E Colo Blvd Ste 288
Pasadena CA 91101
760 330-6123

(P-11028)
NATIONAL ADVANCED ENDOSCOPY DE
22134 Sherman Way, Canoga Park (91303-1136)
PHONE..................................818 227-2720
Fawzia Dabiri, *CEO*
John Dawoodjee, *President*
Gayle Butler, *CFO*
EMP: 25 **EST:** 1994
SQ FT: 16,000 **Privately Held**
WEB: www.aed.md
SIC: 5999 3841 5047 7629 Medical apparatus & supplies; surgical & medical instruments; medical & hospital equipment; electrical repair shops

(P-11029)
NELLIX INC
2 Musick, Irvine (92618-1631)
PHONE..................................650 213-8700
Robert D Mitchell, *President*
Doug Hughes, *COO*
K T RAO, *Vice Pres*
Soyoung Park, *Accountant*
Kim Smith, *Manager*
EMP: 29 **EST:** 2001
SQ FT: 7,500
SALES (est): 10.2MM **Privately Held**
WEB: www.endologix.com
SIC: 3841 Surgical & medical instruments
PA: Endologix, Inc.
2 Musick
Irvine CA 92618

(P-11030)
NEOMEND INC
60 Technology Dr, Irvine (92618-2301)
PHONE..................................949 783-3300
David Renzi, *President*
Erik Reese, *President*
Ken Watson, *President*
Kevin Cousins, *CFO*
Pete Davis, *Vice Pres*
▼ **EMP:** 90 **EST:** 1999
SQ FT: 21,000
SALES (est): 17.4MM
SALES (corp-wide): 17.1B **Publicly Held**
WEB: www.bd.com
SIC: 3841 Surgical & medical instruments
HQ: C. R. Bard, Inc.
1 Becton Dr
Franklin Lakes NJ 07417
201 847-6800

(P-11031)
NEUROPTICS INC
9223 Research Dr, Irvine (92618-4286)
PHONE..................................949 250-9792
Kamran Siminou, *CEO*
William Worthen, *President*
Kathleen Pierson, *Vice Pres*
Jessica Fernandez, *Administration*
Duane Thexton, *Project Mgr*
▲ **EMP:** 45 **EST:** 1995
SALES (est): 8.2MM **Privately Held**
WEB: www.neuroptics.com
SIC: 3841 Surgical & medical instruments

(P-11032)
NEUROVASC TECHNOLOGIES INC
3 Jenner Ste 100, Irvine (92618-3827)
PHONE..................................949 258-9946
EMP: 19 **EST:** 2016
SALES (est): 1.5MM **Privately Held**
WEB: www.neurovasctechnologies.com
SIC: 3841 Surgical & medical instruments

(P-11033)
NEW WORLD MEDICAL INCORPORATED
10763 Edison Ct, Rancho Cucamonga (91730-4844)
PHONE..................................909 466-4304
A Mateen Ahmed, *President*
Omar Ahmed, *Vice Pres*
Joshua Betancur, *Administration*
Patrick Chen, *Research*
Nathan Collins, *Research*
EMP: 17 **EST:** 1990
SQ FT: 10,000
SALES (est): 5MM **Privately Held**
WEB: www.newworldmedical.com
SIC: 3841 Ophthalmic instruments & apparatus

(P-11034)
NEWPORT MEDICAL INSTRS INC
Also Called: Covidien
1620 Sunflower Ave, Costa Mesa (92626-1513)
PHONE..................................949 642-3910
Philippe Negre, *President*
Mike Weinstein, *Senior VP*
David Anderson, *Engineer*
Truc Le, *Engineer*
Debbie Sakell, *Regl Sales Mgr*
◆ **EMP:** 281 **EST:** 1981
SQ FT: 33,328
SALES (est): 18MM **Privately Held**
WEB: www.allenstethoscopes.com
SIC: 3841 3842 3845 Surgical & medical instruments; respirators; electromedical equipment
HQ: Covidien Limited
1st Floor
Dublin

(P-11035)
NOBLES MEDICAL TECH INC
17080 Newhope St, Fountain Valley (92708-4206)
PHONE..................................714 427-0398
Anthony A Nobles, *Principal*
Anthony Nobles, *Principal*
EMP: 42 **EST:** 2009
SALES (est): 6MM **Privately Held**
SIC: 3841 Medical instruments & equipment, blood & bone work

(P-11036)
NORDSON MEDICAL (CA) LLC
7612 Woodwind Dr, Huntington Beach (92647-7164)
PHONE..................................657 215-4200
David Zgonc, *Mng Member*
Donald Adams, *Business Anlyst*
Sherry Liu, *Engineer*
Carlos Moreno, *Engineer*
Monica Lopez, *Purchasing*
EMP: 51 **EST:** 1991
SQ FT: 40,000
SALES (est): 21.8MM
SALES (corp-wide): 2.1B **Publicly Held**
WEB: www.nordson.com
SIC: 3841 Surgical & medical instruments
PA: Nordson Corporation
28601 Clemens Rd
Westlake OH 44145
440 892-1580

(P-11037)
NOVASIGNAL CORP
2440 S Sepulveda Blvd # 1, Los Angeles
(90064-1784)
PHONE................................818 317-4999
Diane M Bryant, *CEO*
Henry Hewes, *COO*
Mark Hattendorf, *CFO*
Neil A Martin, *Chief Mktg Ofcr*
John Arant, *Vice Pres*
EMP: 14 **EST:** 2013
SQ FT: 3,000
SALES (est): 2.6MM **Privately Held**
WEB: www.novasignal.com
SIC: 3841 3845 Diagnostic apparatus,
medical; ultrasonic scanning devices,
medical

(P-11038)
NU-HOPE LABORATORIES INC
12640 Branford St, Pacoima (91331-3451)
P.O. Box 331150 (91333-1150)
PHONE................................818 899-7711
Bradley Johnson Galindo, *CEO*
Linda Bolden, *COO*
Estelle Galindo, *CFO*
Ronald Bolden, *Marketing Mgr*
Tonya Bray, *Sales Staff*
▲ **EMP:** 38 **EST:** 1959
SQ FT: 25,000
SALES (est): 5MM **Privately Held**
WEB: www.nu-hope.com
SIC: 3841 Surgical & medical instruments

(P-11039)
**NUVASIVE SPCLZED
ORTHPDICS INC**
101 Enterprise Ste 100, Aliso Viejo
(92656-2604)
PHONE................................949 837-3600
Edmund Roschak, *CEO*
Robert Krist, *CFO*
Blair Walker, *Vice Pres*
Jeff Rydin, *Security Dir*
EMP: 100 **EST:** 2007
SQ FT: 52,741
SALES (est): 21.3MM
SALES (corp-wide): 1.1B **Publicly Held**
WEB: www.nuvasive.com
SIC: 3841 Inhalation therapy equipment
PA: Nuvasive, Inc.
7475 Lusk Blvd
San Diego CA 92121
858 909-1800

(P-11040)
ORCHID MPS
3233 W Harvard St, Santa Ana
(92704-3917)
PHONE................................714 549-9203
Mark Deischter, *Vice Pres*
EMP: 100 **EST:** 2005
SALES (est): 5.5MM **Privately Held**
WEB: www.orchid-ortho.com
SIC: 3841 Surgical & medical instruments

(P-11041)
**P K ENGINEERING & MFG CO
INC**
200 E Shell Rd 2b, Ventura (93001-1261)
PHONE................................805 628-9556
William Kilbury, *President*
Robert Kilbury, *Vice Pres*
EMP: 16 **EST:** 1964
SQ FT: 8,700
SALES (est): 943.6K **Privately Held**
SIC: 3841 Surgical instruments & appara-
tus; saws, surgical

(P-11042)
**PETER BRASSELER HOLDINGS
LLC**
4837 Mcgrath St, Ventura (93003-6442)
PHONE................................805 658-2643
Laura Kriese, *Branch Mgr*
Fatima Lopez, *District Mgr*
Matt Maleski, *Manager*
Tyler Thorson, *Manager*
EMP: 66
SALES (corp-wide): 50.2MM **Privately
Held**
WEB: www.brasselerusa.com
SIC: 3841 Surgical & medical instruments

PA: Peter Brasseler Holdings, Llc
1 Brasseler Blvd
Savannah GA 31419
912 925-8525

(P-11043)
**PHARMACO-KINESIS
CORPORATION**
10604 S La Cienega Blvd, Inglewood
(90304-1115)
PHONE................................310 641-2700
Frank Adell, *Principal*
Thomas Chen, *Principal*
Peter Hirshfield, *Principal*
John Muthew, *Principal*
EMP: 26 **EST:** 2006
SALES (est): 4.9MM **Privately Held**
WEB: www.pharmaco-kinesis.com
SIC: 3841 Surgical & medical instruments

(P-11044)
**PHILLPS-MDISIZE COSTA MESA
LLC**
3545 Harbor Blvd, Costa Mesa
(92626-1406)
PHONE................................949 477-9495
Bob Frank, *General Mgr*
Hank Mancini, *Business Mgr*
EMP: 240 **EST:** 1997
SQ FT: 45,000
SALES (est): 57.2MM
SALES (corp-wide): 36.9B **Privately Held**
WEB: www.phillipsmedisize.com
SIC: 3841 Surgical & medical instruments
HQ: Molex, Llc
2222 Wellington Ct
Lisle IL 60532
630 969-4550

(P-11045)
PLASVACC USA INC
1535 Templeton Rd, Templeton
(93465-9694)
PHONE................................805 434-0321
Andrew McArthur, *President*
Heather Alspach, *Vice Pres*
McKinley Swan, *Technician*
Andrew Macarthur, *Sales Mgr*
Judy Sonne, *Manager*
EMP: 15 **EST:** 2005
SALES (est): 2.5MM **Privately Held**
WEB: www.plasvaccusa.com
SIC: 3841 Surgical & medical instruments

(P-11046)
PRANALYTICA INC
1101 Colorado Ave, Santa Monica
(90401-3009)
PHONE................................310 458-3345
C Kumar N Patel, *President*
Bonnie Pauly, *Technician*
Francis McGuire, *VP Finance*
Raj Parekh, *Director*
EMP: 15 **EST:** 1999
SQ FT: 7,350
SALES (est): 2.2MM **Privately Held**
WEB: www.pranalytica.com
SIC: 3841 3826 Surgical & medical instru-
ments; laser scientific & engineering in-
struments

(P-11047)
PRO-DEX INC (PA)
2361 Mcgaw Ave, Irvine (92614-5831)
PHONE................................949 769-3200
Richard L Van Kirk, *President*
Nicholas J Swenson, *Ch of Bd*
Alisha K Charlton, *CFO*
Salvador Sigman, *Engineer*
Jamie Wahl, *Engineer*
EMP: 120 **EST:** 1978
SQ FT: 28,000
SALES: 38MM **Publicly Held**
WEB: www.pro-dex.com
SIC: 3841 3843 7372 3594 Surgical &
medical instruments; dental equipment;
business oriented computer software; mo-
tors, pneumatic; business consulting

(P-11048)
**RADIOLOGY SUPPORT DEVICES
INC**
1904 E Dominguez St, Long Beach
(90810-1002)
PHONE................................310 518-0527

Matthew Alderson, *CEO*
EMP: 29 **EST:** 1989
SQ FT: 16,000
SALES (est): 4.2MM **Privately Held**
WEB: www.rsdphantoms.com
SIC: 3841 3844 Diagnostic apparatus,
medical; X-ray apparatus & tubes

(P-11049)
**REBOUND THERAPEUTICS
CORP**
13900 Alton Pkwy Ste 120, Irvine
(92618-1621)
PHONE................................949 305-8111
Jeffrey Valko, *CEO*
EMP: 26 **EST:** 2015
SALES (est): 5.6MM **Publicly Held**
WEB: www.integralife.com
SIC: 3841 Surgical & medical instruments
PA: Integra Lifesciences Holdings Corpora-
tion
1100 Campus Rd
Princeton NJ 08540

(P-11050)
**REVERSE MEDICAL
CORPORATION**
13700 Alton Pkwy Ste 167, Irvine
(92618-1618)
PHONE................................949 215-0660
Jeffrey Valko, *President*
Brian Strauss, *CTO*
EMP: 59 **EST:** 2007
SALES (est): 9.3MM **Privately Held**
WEB: www.reversemed.com
SIC: 3841 Surgical & medical instruments
HQ: Covidien Limited
1st Floor
Dublin

(P-11051)
**RMS/ENDLGIX SDWAYS
MERGER CORP**
2 Musick, Irvine (92618-1631)
PHONE................................949 595-7200
John Onopchenko, *CEO*
EMP: 23 **EST:** 2002
SALES (est): 979.1K **Privately Held**
WEB: www.endologix.com
SIC: 3841 Catheters
PA: Endologix, Inc.
2 Musick
Irvine CA 92618

(P-11052)
ROBERT P VON ZABERN
4121 Tigris Way, Riverside (92503-4844)
PHONE................................951 734-7215
Robert P Von Zabern, *Owner*
Christine Bedard Rimmer, *Office Mgr*
EMP: 13 **EST:** 1986
SQ FT: 1,500
SALES (est): 1MM **Privately Held**
WEB: www.vzs.net
SIC: 3841 Surgical instruments & appara-
tus

(P-11053)
ROX MEDICAL INC (PA)
150 Calle Iglesia Ste A, San Clemente
(92672-7550)
P.O. Box 4078, Dana Point (92629-9078)
PHONE................................949 276-8968
Mike Mackinnon, *CEO*
Keegan Harper, *Ch of Bd*
Jonathan Sackner-Bernstein, *Chief Mktg
Ofcr*
Paul A Sobotka, *Officer*
Peter Balmforth, *Sales Staff*
EMP: 19 **EST:** 2003
SQ FT: 3,500
SALES (est): 2.6MM **Privately Held**
WEB: www.roxmedical.com
SIC: 3841 Surgical & medical instruments

(P-11054)
SECHRIST INDUSTRIES INC
4225 E La Palma Ave, Anaheim
(92807-1844)
PHONE................................714 579-8400
Edward Pulwer, *CEO*
John Razzano, *CFO*

Monica Gutierrez, *Vice Pres*
Majid Mashayekh, *Vice Pres*
Chris Patrick, *Vice Pres*
◆ **EMP:** 79 **EST:** 1973
SQ FT: 74,000
SALES (est): 23MM
SALES (corp-wide): 240.9MM **Privately
Held**
WEB: www.sechristusa.com
SIC: 3841 Surgical & medical instruments
HQ: Wound Care Holdings, Llc
5220 Belfort Rd Ste 130
Jacksonville FL 32256
800 379-9774

(P-11055)
**SECOND SIGHT MEDICAL PDTS
INC**
13170 Telfair Ave, Sylmar (91342-3573)
PHONE................................318 833-5000
Scott Dunbar, *Acting CEO*
Gregg Williams, *Ch of Bd*
Jonathan Will McGuire, *President*
Patrick Ryan, *COO*
Stephen Okland, *Officer*
EMP: 108 **EST:** 1998
SQ FT: 17,290 **Privately Held**
WEB: www.secondsight.com
SIC: 3841 Ophthalmic instruments & appa-
ratus

(P-11056)
SEQUENT MEDICAL INC
35 Enterprise, Aliso Viejo (92656-2601)
PHONE................................949 830-9600
Thomas C Wilder, *President*
Kevin J Cousins, *CFO*
Andrew J Hykes, *Vice Pres*
Paul G Krell, *Vice Pres*
William R Patterson, *Vice Pres*
EMP: 65 **EST:** 2006
SALES (est): 10.9MM **Privately Held**
WEB: www.microvention.com
SIC: 3841 Surgical & medical instruments
HQ: Microvention, Inc.
35 Enterprise
Aliso Viejo CA 92656
714 258-8000

(P-11057)
SHEERVISION INC (PA)
4030 Palos Verdes Dr N # 04, Rllng HLS
Est (90274-2559)
PHONE................................310 265-8918
Suzanne Lewsadder, *CEO*
Martin Chaput, *COO*
Patrick Adams, *CFO*
Brandon Pope, *Opers Staf*
John F Guhl, *Regl Sales Mgr*
EMP: 13 **EST:** 1986
SQ FT: 3,090
SALES (est): 2.5MM **Privately Held**
WEB: www.sheervision.com
SIC: 3841 Surgical & medical instruments

(P-11058)
**SIEMENS HLTHCARE
DGNOSTICS INC**
Also Called: Siemens Medical Solutions
5210 Pacific Concourse Dr, Los Angeles
(90045-6900)
PHONE................................310 645-8200
Anthony Bihl, *Branch Mgr*
Ayesha Rasheed, *Research*
Christopher Goss, *Director*
Vickie Hedgpeth, *Manager*
Dion Wylie, *Manager*
EMP: 55
SALES (corp-wide): 67.4B **Privately Held**
WEB: www.siemens.com
SIC: 3841 5047 8011 8734 Diagnostic
apparatus, medical; diagnostic equip-
ment, medical; hematologist; X-ray in-
spection service, industrial
HQ: Siemens Healthcare Diagnostics Inc.
511 Benedict Ave
Tarrytown NY 10591
914 631-8000

(P-11059)
**SPECIALTEAM MEDICAL SVC
INC**
22445 La Palma Ave Ste F, Yorba Linda
(92887-3811)
PHONE................................714 694-0348
Terry Bagwell, *President*

Erick Bickett, *CFO*
Billy Teeple, *Vice Pres*
EMP: 17 **EST:** 1996
SQ FT: 7,000
SALES (est): 681.9K **Privately Held**
WEB: www.specialteam.com
SIC: 3841 Surgical & medical instruments

(P-11060)
SSCOR INC
11064 Randall St, Sun Valley (91352-2621)
PHONE....................818 504-4054
Samuel Say, *CEO*
Samuel D Say, *President*
Jonathan Kim, *Vice Pres*
Suzette George, *Office Mgr*
Betty Say, *Admin Sec*
▲ **EMP:** 16
SQ FT: 12,000
SALES (est): 3.3MM **Privately Held**
WEB: www.sscor.com
SIC: 3841 Suction therapy apparatus

(P-11061)
SWEDEN & MARTINA INC
600 Anton Blvd Ste 1134, Costa Mesa
(92626-7221)
PHONE....................844 862-7846
Elisabetta Martina, *President*
Lisa Loban, *Office Mgr*
EMP: 33 **EST:** 2014
SALES (est): 1.5MM **Privately Held**
SIC: 3841 Medical instruments & equip-
   ment, blood & bone work

(P-11062)
TECOMET INC
503 S Vincent Ave, Azusa (91702-5131)
PHONE....................626 334-1519
Wendy Clark, *Office Mgr*
Ava Tenorio, *QC Mgr*
EMP: 477
SALES (corp-wide): 832.8MM **Privately
Held**
WEB: www.tecomet.com
SIC: 3841 3444 Diagnostic apparatus,
   medical; surgical instruments & appara-
   tus; medical instruments & equipment,
   blood & bone work; sheet metalwork
HQ: Tecomet Inc.
   115 Eames St
   Wilmington MA 01887
   978 642-2400

(P-11063)
TENEX HEALTH INC
26902 Vista Ter, Lake Forest (92630-8123)
PHONE....................949 454-7500
William Maya`, *President*
Ivan Mijatovic, *CFO*
Jagi Gill, *Officer*
Bernard Morrey, *Officer*
▲ **EMP:** 70 **EST:** 2011
SQ FT: 15,000
SALES (est): 8MM **Privately Held**
WEB: www.tenexhealth.com
SIC: 3841 Surgical & medical instruments

(P-11064)
THERAPEUTIC INDUSTRIES INC
72096 Dunham Way Ste E, Thousand
Palms (92276-3320)
P.O. Box 92 (92276-0092)
PHONE....................760 343-2502
Chris Lehude, *President*
Merideth Laureno, *Bd of Directors*
Tammy Digrande, *Admin Asst*
Kurt Jara, *Foreman/Supr*
EMP: 15 **EST:** 2014
SALES (est): 1.8MM **Privately Held**
WEB: www.barihab.com
SIC: 3841 Surgical & medical instruments

(P-11065)
THI INC
1525 E Edinger Ave, Santa Ana
(92705-4907)
PHONE....................714 444-4643
Jim Willett, *CEO*
Barb Bitzer, *CFO*
Brandon Anaya, *Vice Pres*
Bob Banks, *General Mgr*
David Pak, *Info Tech Dir*
▲ **EMP:** 100 **EST:** 2000
SQ FT: 35,000

SALES (est): 21.7MM **Privately Held**
WEB: www.tenacore.com
SIC: 3841 7699 Surgical instruments &
   apparatus; surgical instrument repair

(P-11066)
TMJ SOLUTIONS INC
Also Called: TMJ Concepts
6059 King Dr, Ventura (93003-7607)
PHONE....................805 650-3391
Heather Wise, *President*
William Anspach, *Shareholder*
David Samson, *President*
Erik Rinde, *Engineer*
Grant Samson, *Marketing Staff*
EMP: 54 **EST:** 1996
SQ FT: 7,280
SALES (est): 5MM **Privately Held**
WEB: www.tmjconcepts.com
SIC: 3841 Surgical & medical instruments

(P-11067)
TRELLBORG SLING SLTIONS US INC (DH)
Also Called: Issac
2761 Walnut Ave, Tustin (92780-7051)
PHONE....................714 415-0280
William Reising, *CEO*
Ron Fraleigh, *President*
Tom Mazelin, *Vice Pres*
Kevin Beatty, *General Mgr*
Carli Wendland, *Engineer*
EMP: 150 **EST:** 1993
SQ FT: 1,600
SALES (est): 95.3MM
SALES (corp-wide): 3.8B **Privately Held**
WEB: www.trelleborg.com
SIC: 3841 Surgical & medical instruments
HQ: Trelleborg Corporation
   200 Veterans Blvd Ste 3
   South Haven MI 49090
   269 639-9891

(P-11068)
TRELLEBORG SEALING SOLUTIONS
3034 Propeller Dr, Paso Robles
(93446-9519)
PHONE....................805 239-4284
William E Reising, *Branch Mgr*
EMP: 85
SALES (corp-wide): 3.8B **Privately Held**
WEB: www.trelleborg.com
SIC: 3841 Surgical & medical instruments
HQ: Trelleborg Sealing Solutions Us, Inc.
   2761 Walnut Ave
   Tustin CA 92780

(P-11069)
TRIVASCULAR INC (DH)
2 Musick, Irvine (92618-1631)
PHONE....................707 543-8800
John Onopchenko, *CEO*
Joseph Humphrey, *VP Mfg*
EMP: 106 **EST:** 1998
SALES (est): 38.1MM **Privately Held**
WEB: www.trivascular.com
SIC: 3841 Surgical & medical instruments
HQ: Trivascular Technologies, Inc.
   2 Musick
   Irvine CA 92618
   707 543-8800

(P-11070)
TRIVASCULAR TECHNOLOGIES INC (HQ)
2 Musick, Irvine (92618-1631)
PHONE....................707 543-8800
John Onopchenko, *CEO*
Christopher G Chavez, *President*
Michael R Kramer, *CFO*
Michael V Chobotov, *CTO*
Robert G Whirley, *Development*
EMP: 100 **EST:** 2008
SQ FT: 110,000
SALES (est): 82.2MM **Privately Held**
WEB: www.trivascular.com
SIC: 3841 Surgical & medical instruments

(P-11071)
TRUEVISION SYSTEMS INC
Also Called: Truevision 3d Surgical
315 Bollay Dr Ste 101, Goleta
(93117-2948)
PHONE....................805 963-9700
A Burton Tripathi, *CEO*
Burton Tripathi, *Officer*
Robert Reali, *Vice Pres*
David Chu, *CIO*
Charles Morison, *Software Dev*
▲ **EMP:** 43 **EST:** 2003
SQ FT: 10,549
SALES (est): 13.6MM
SALES (corp-wide): 6.8B **Privately Held**
WEB: www.professional.myalcon.com
SIC: 3841 Surgical & medical instruments
HQ: Alcon, Inc.
   1132 Ferris Rd
   Amelia OH 45102
   513 722-1037

(P-11072)
UOC USA INC
15251 Alton Pkwy Ste 100, Irvine
(92618-2307)
PHONE....................949 328-3366
Calvin Lin, *President*
▲ **EMP:** 17 **EST:** 2012
SALES (est): 600K **Privately Held**
WEB: www.us.unitedorthopedic.com
SIC: 3841 Surgical & medical instruments
PA: United Orthopedic Corporation
   No. 57, Park Ave. 2 Science Park
   Hsinchu City

(P-11073)
VERRIX LLC
1330 Calle Avanzado # 200, San Clemente
(92673-6351)
P.O. Box 14795, Scottsdale AZ (85267-
4795)
PHONE....................949 668-1234
Cameron Rouns, *CEO*
Kok-Hwee Ng, *Vice Pres*
Tim Way, *Vice Pres*
Amy Brandmeyer, *Human Resources*
EMP: 15 **EST:** 2013
SQ FT: 10,000
SALES (est): 1.4MM **Privately Held**
WEB: www.verrix.com
SIC: 3841 Biopsy instruments & equipment

(P-11074)
VERTIFLEX INC
25155 Rye Canyon Loop, Valencia
(91355-5004)
PHONE....................442 325-5900
Earl Fender, *CEO*
EMP: 40 **EST:** 2004
SALES (est): 14.8MM
SALES (corp-wide): 9.9B **Publicly Held**
WEB: www.bostonscientific.com
SIC: 3841 Surgical & medical instruments
PA: Boston Scientific Corporation
   300 Boston Scientific Way
   Marlborough MA 01752
   508 683-4000

(P-11075)
VERTOS MEDICAL INC
95 Enterprise Ste 325, Aliso Viejo
(92656-2612)
PHONE....................949 349-0008
James M Corbett, *CEO*
Rebecca Colbert, *CFO*
Amy Scott, *Vice Pres*
Stephen E Paul, *VP Sales*
Bryan Taueg, *Sales Dir*
EMP: 62 **EST:** 2005
SQ FT: 25,000
SALES (est): 10.2MM **Privately Held**
WEB: www.vertosmed.com
SIC: 3841 3842 Medical instruments &
   equipment, blood & bone work; surgical
   appliances & supplies

(P-11076)
VIASYS RESPIRATORY CARE INC
1100 Bird Center Dr, Palm Springs
(92262-8099)
PHONE....................714 283-2228
Jamal Abdul-Hafiz, *Engineer*
Michael Hiller, *Purch Agent*

Mark Berryhill, *Director*
EMP: 13
SALES (est): 1.5MM **Privately Held**
SIC: 3841 Surgical & medical instruments

(P-11077)
VIASYS RESPIRATORY CARE INC
Also Called: Biosys Healthcare
22745 Savi Ranch Pkwy, Yorba Linda
(92887-4668)
PHONE....................714 283-2228
William B Ross, *President*
EMP: 82 **EST:** 1961
SQ FT: 120,000
SALES (est): 2.5MM
SALES (corp-wide): 17.1B **Publicly Held**
WEB: www.viasyshealthcare.com
SIC: 3841 Diagnostic apparatus, medical
HQ: Carefusion Corporation
   3750 Torrey View Ct
   San Diego CA 92130

3842 Orthopedic, Prosthetic & Surgical Appliances/Splys

(P-11078)
ADENNA LLC
2151 Michelson Dr Ste 260, Irvine
(92612-1369)
PHONE....................909 510-6999
Thomas Friedl, *CEO*
Patrick Fitzmaurice, *CFO*
Jesilyn Duke, *Vice Pres*
Janice Adkins, *Credit Mgr*
◆ **EMP:** 13 **EST:** 1997
SQ FT: 13,000
SALES (est): 6.8MM
SALES (corp-wide): 358.6MM **Privately
Held**
WEB: www.adenna.com
SIC: 3842 Surgical appliances & supplies
PA: The Tranzonic Companies
   26301 Curtiss Wright Pkwy # 200
   Richmond Heights OH 44143
   216 535-4300

(P-11079)
ADEX MEDICAL INC
6101 Quail Valley Ct D, Riverside
(92507-0764)
P.O. Box 97, Temecula (92593-0097)
PHONE....................951 653-9122
Michael M Ghafouri, *President*
EMP: 14 **EST:** 1996
SQ FT: 15,000
SALES (est): 533.7K **Privately Held**
WEB: www.adexmed.com
SIC: 3842 3843 5999 5047 Surgical ap-
   pliances & supplies; dental equipment &
   supplies; medical apparatus & supplies;
   medical & hospital equipment; industrial
   supplies

(P-11080)
ADVANCED ARM DYNAMICS (PA)
123 W Torrance Blvd # 203, Redondo
Beach (90277-3614)
PHONE....................310 372-3050
John Miguelez, *President*
Michelle Intintoli,
Misty Carver, *Principal*
Dan Conyers, *Principal*
Carol Sorrels, *Principal*
EMP: 40 **EST:** 1998
SALES (est): 12.6MM **Privately Held**
WEB: www.armdynamics.com
SIC: 3842 Prosthetic appliances

(P-11081)
ADVANCED BIONICS LLC (HQ)
Also Called: A B
12740 San Fernando Rd, Sylmar
(91342-3700)
PHONE....................661 362-1400
Rainer Platz, *CEO*
Paolo Gregorini, *Vice Pres*
Scott Hebl, *Vice Pres*
Tom Santogrossi, *Vice Pres*
Lisa Guzman, *Admin Sec*
EMP: 450 **EST:** 1997

SALES (est): 91.6MM
SALES (corp-wide): 2.9B **Privately Held**
WEB: www.advancedbionics.com
SIC: 3842 Hearing aids
PA: Sonova Holding Ag
    Laubisrutistrasse 28
    StAfa ZH 8712
    589 280-101

(P-11082)
ADVANCED BIONICS
CORPORATION (HQ)
28515 Westinghouse Pl, Valencia
(91355-4833)
PHONE....................661 362-1400
Rainer Platz, *CEO*
Jeffrey Goldberg, *Senior VP*
Christopher Bingham, *Vice Pres*
Brian Faldetta, *Vice Pres*
Paolo Gregorini, *Vice Pres*
▲ EMP: 595 EST: 2007
SALES (est): 130MM
SALES (corp-wide): 2.9B **Privately Held**
WEB: www.advancedbionics.com
SIC: 3842 Hearing aids
PA: Sonova Holding Ag
    Laubisrutistrasse 28
    StAfa ZH 8712
    589 280-101

(P-11083)
ADVANCED ORTHPDIC
SLUTIONS INC
Also Called: Aos
3203 Kashiwa St, Torrance (90505-4020)
PHONE....................310 533-9966
Gary Sohngen, *CEO*
Barry Hubbard, *Vice Pres*
Scott Epperly, *Design Engr*
Kazunori Miyahara, *Engineer*
Mark Steinhauer, *Engineer*
EMP: 34 EST: 2001
SALES (est): 5.5MM **Privately Held**
WEB: www.aosortho.com
SIC: 3842 Implants, surgical

(P-11084)
ALIGNMED INC
1936 E Deere Ave Ste 115, Santa Ana
(92705-5733)
PHONE....................866 987-5433
William Schultz, *President*
Eliana Schultz, *CFO*
Steven Whisler, *Sales Associate*
Vanessa Pimentel,
Bob Schultz, *Director*
▲ EMP: 18 EST: 2001
SALES (est): 2.9MM **Privately Held**
WEB: www.alignmed.com
SIC: 5999 3842 Orthopedic & prosthesis
    applications; braces, orthopedic

(P-11085)
AMERICAN MED O & P CLINIC
INC
4955 Van Nuys Blvd, Sherman Oaks
(91403-1801)
PHONE....................818 281-5747
Konstandin Kumuryan, *CEO*
EMP: 20 EST: 2020
SALES (est): 1.3MM **Privately Held**
WEB: www.americanop.com
SIC: 3842 Prosthetic appliances

(P-11086)
AMERICH CORPORATION (PA)
13222 Saticoy St, North Hollywood
(91605-3404)
PHONE....................818 982-1711
Edward Richmond, *President*
Dino Pacifici, *Vice Pres*
Greg Richmond, *Vice Pres*
Agustin Paz, *Technical Staff*
Lynn Hardy, *Opers Mgr*
▲ EMP: 120 EST: 1982
SALES (est): 26MM **Privately Held**
WEB: www.americh.com
SIC: 3842 3432 3431 3261 Whirlpool
    baths, hydrotherapy equipment; plumbing
    fixture fittings & trim; metal sanitary ware;
    vitreous plumbing fixtures

(P-11087)
ANSELL SNDEL MED
SOLUTIONS LLC
9301 Oakdale Ave Ste 300, Chatsworth
(91311-6539)
PHONE....................818 534-2500
Anthony B Lopez, *President*
Wendell Franke, *Associate Dir*
Stephanie Barth, *Principal*
Marilyn Norrie, *Marketing Staff*
◆ EMP: 32 EST: 2002
SQ FT: 14,600
SALES (est): 6.9MM **Privately Held**
WEB: www.ansell.com
SIC: 3842 Surgical appliances & supplies
PA: Ansell Limited
    678 Victoria St
    Richmond VIC 3121

(P-11088)
APPLIED ORTHOPEDIC DESIGN
Also Called: Nanoknee
860 Oak Park Blvd Ste 101, Arroyo Grande
(93420-1800)
PHONE....................805 481-3685
Thomas D Ferro, *President*
Christiana Ferro, *Project Mgr*
EMP: 19 EST: 2009
SALES (est): 1.6MM **Privately Held**
WEB: www.aodesign.net
SIC: 3842 Orthopedic appliances; braces,
    orthopedic

(P-11089)
ARS ENTERPRISES (PA)
15554 Minnesota Ave, Paramount
(90723-4119)
PHONE....................562 946-3505
Ben Hom, *Mng Member*
Michael D Dunn, *Ch of Bd*
Glenn Caster, *President*
Joe Morrissey, *Mfg Staff*
Marshall Geller, *Mng Member*
EMP: 14 EST: 1971
SQ FT: 11,000
SALES (est): 1.8MM **Privately Held**
WEB: www.ars-sterilizers.com
SIC: 3842 5074 Autoclaves, hospital &
    surgical; boilers, steam

(P-11090)
BIO CYBERNETICS
INTERNATIONAL
Also Called: Cybertech
2701 Kimball Ave, Pomona (91767-2268)
PHONE....................909 447-7050
▲ EMP: 15
SQ FT: 10,000
SALES (est): 2MM **Privately Held**
WEB: www.cybertechmedical.com
SIC: 3842 Mfg Surgical Appliances/Sup-
    plies

(P-11091)
BIOMECHANICAL SERVICES INC
20509 Earlgate St, Walnut (91789-2909)
PHONE....................714 990-5932
Greg Wolfe, *President*
Kevin Hasegawa, *Shareholder*
Brian Killeen, *Shareholder*
Dr William Sniechowski, *Shareholder*
Scott De Francisco, *Vice Pres*
EMP: 24 EST: 1987
SQ FT: 13,000
SALES (est): 4.3MM **Privately Held**
WEB: www.biomechanical.com
SIC: 3842 5999 Orthopedic appliances;
    orthopedic & prosthesis applications

(P-11092)
BOSTON SCNTFIC NRMDLATION
CORP (HQ)
25155 Rye Canyon Loop, Valencia
(91355-5004)
PHONE....................661 949-4310
Michael F Mahoney, *CEO*
Supratim Bose, *Exec VP*
Jeffrey D Capello, *Exec VP*
Kevin Ballinger, *Senior VP*
Wendy Carruthers, *Senior VP*
▲ EMP: 450 EST: 1993
SQ FT: 26,000

SALES (est): 92.7MM
SALES (corp-wide): 9.9B **Publicly Held**
WEB: www.bostonscientific.com
SIC: 3842 3841 5047 Hearing aids; surgi-
    cal & medical instruments; metabolism
    apparatus; surgical instruments & appara-
    tus; medical & hospital equipment; hear-
    ing aids
PA: Boston Scientific Corporation
    300 Boston Scientific Way
    Marlborough MA 01752
    508 683-4000

(P-11093)
BREATHE TECHNOLOGIES INC
15091 Bake Pkwy, Irvine (92618-2501)
PHONE....................949 988-7700
Lawrence A Mastrovich, *President*
John L Miclot, *Ch of Bd*
Paul J Lytle, *CFO*
Gary Berman, *Officer*
Rebecca Mabry, *Senior VP*
EMP: 39 EST: 2005
SALES (est): 24.4MM
SALES (corp-wide): 3B **Publicly Held**
WEB: www.breathetechnologies.com
SIC: 3842 Respirators; respiratory protec-
    tion equipment, personal
HQ: Hill-Rom, Inc.
    1069 State Route 46 E
    Batesville IN 47006
    812 934-7777

(P-11094)
DIAMOND GLOVES
1100 S Linwood Ave Ste A, Santa Ana
(92705-4345)
PHONE....................714 667-0506
John Te, *CEO*
Zion Ong, *Warehouse Mgr*
Rachel Lai,
Ken Te, *Director*
▲ EMP: 22 EST: 2009
SALES (est): 2.9MM **Privately Held**
WEB: www.diamondglove.com
SIC: 3842 Gloves, safety

(P-11095)
DYNAMICS ORTHTICS
PRSTHTICS IN
Also Called: Dynamics O&P
1830 W Olympic Blvd Ste 1, Los Angeles
(90006-3734)
PHONE....................213 383-9212
Peter J Sean, *CEO*
Sophia Sean, *Info Tech Mgr*
Sharon Sean, *Mktg Dir*
Sarah Morris, *Director*
EMP: 50 EST: 1988
SQ FT: 20,662
SALES (est): 6.5MM **Privately Held**
WEB: www.walkagain.com
SIC: 3842 Orthopedic appliances; limbs,
    artificial

(P-11096)
EDWARDS LFESCIENCES
FOUNDATION
1 Edwards Way, Irvine (92614-5688)
PHONE....................949 250-2806
EMP: 14 EST: 2018
SALES (est): 256.5K **Privately Held**
WEB: www.edwards.com
SIC: 3842 Surgical appliances & supplies

(P-11097)
EDWARDS LFSCNCES WRLD
TRADE CO (HQ)
1 Edwards Way, Irvine (92614-5688)
PHONE....................949 250-2500
Michael A Mussallem, *CEO*
EMP: 100 EST: 1999
SALES (est): 3.5MM
SALES (corp-wide): 4.3B **Publicly Held**
WEB: www.edwards.com
SIC: 3842 Surgical appliances & supplies
PA: Edwards Lifesciences Corp
    1 Edwards Way
    Irvine CA 92614
    949 250-2500

(P-11098)
EDWARDS LIFESCIENCES CORP
(PA)
1 Edwards Way, Irvine (92614-5688)
PHONE....................949 250-2500
Michael A Mussallem, *Ch of Bd*
Neal Chambers, *Managing Prtnr*
Scott B Ullem, *CFO*
Jean-Francois Beyrath, *Vice Pres*
Donald E Bobo Jr, *Vice Pres*
EMP: 1600 EST: 1958
SALES (est): 4.3B **Publicly Held**
WEB: www.edwards.com
SIC: 3842 Surgical appliances & supplies

(P-11099)
EDWARDS LIFESCIENCES CORP
PR
1 Edwards Way, Irvine (92614-5688)
PHONE....................949 250-2500
Michael A Mussallem, *CEO*
Dirksen J Lehman, *Vice Pres*
Christine Z McCauley, *Vice Pres*
Stanton J Rowe, *Vice Pres*
Scott B Ullem, *Vice Pres*
EMP: 56 EST: 1999
SALES (est): 3.9MM
SALES (corp-wide): 4.3B **Publicly Held**
WEB: www.edwards.com
SIC: 3842 Orthopedic appliances
PA: Edwards Lifesciences Corp
    1 Edwards Way
    Irvine CA 92614
    949 250-2500

(P-11100)
EMERGENT GROUP INC (DH)
10939 Pendleton St, Sun Valley
(91352-1522)
PHONE....................818 394-2800
Bruce J Haber, *CEO*
Louis Buther, *President*
William M McKay, *CFO*
EMP: 55 EST: 1996
SQ FT: 13,000
SALES (est): 23.7MM
SALES (corp-wide): 773.3MM **Publicly**
Held
WEB: www.uhs.com
SIC: 3842 7352 Surgical appliances &
    supplies; medical equipment rental
HQ: Agiliti Health, Inc.
    6625 W 78th St Ste 300
    Minneapolis MN 55439
    952 893-3200

(P-11101)
ENDOTEC INC
14525 Valley View Ave H, Santa Fe Springs
(90670-5237)
PHONE....................714 681-6306
Young B Shim, *CEO*
EMP: 35 EST: 1999
SQ FT: 5,900
SALES (est): 9.3MM **Privately Held**
WEB: www.cellumed.co.kr
SIC: 3842 Orthopedic appliances
PA: Cellumed Co., Ltd.
    Rm 402
    Seoul 08589

(P-11102)
ENTERPRISE PORTABLE
WELDING
68548 Iroquois St, Cathedral City
(92234-2026)
PHONE....................760 328-6316
Lauren Williams, *Owner*
EMP: 15 EST: 1994
SALES (est): 202.1K **Privately Held**
WEB: www.enterprise.com
SIC: 3842 Welders' hoods

(P-11103)
ETHICON INC
Advanced Sterilization Pdts
33 Technology Dr, Irvine (92618-2346)
PHONE....................949 581-5799
Charles Austin, *Branch Mgr*
Saheed Alam, *Engineer*
Betsy Decker, *Manager*
EMP: 300

SALES (corp-wide): 82.5B **Publicly Held**
SIC: 3842 Sutures, absorbable & non-absorbable
HQ: Ethicon Inc.
    1000 Route 202
    Raritan NJ 08869
    732 524-0400

(P-11104)
FERRACO INC (HQ)
Also Called: Human Dsgns Prsthtic Orthtic L
2933 Long Beach Blvd, Long Beach
(90806-1517)
PHONE..............................562 988-2414
Natalie Rose Cronin, *CEO*
Eric Ferraco, *President*
Brian Cronin, *CFO*
EMP: 24 EST: 1991
SALES (est): 8MM
SALES (corp-wide): 16MM **Privately Held**
WEB: www.humandesigns.com
SIC: 3842 Surgical appliances & supplies
PA: Arc-V, Inc.
    1639 N Hollywood Way
    Burbank CA 91505
    626 445-7797

(P-11105)
FOOT IN MOTION INC
Also Called: Kevin Orthopedic
2239 Business Way, Riverside
(92501-2231)
PHONE..............................312 752-0990
Kevin Rosenbloom, *President*
◆ EMP: 15 EST: 2008
SALES (est): 1.8MM **Privately Held**
WEB: www.footinmotion.com
SIC: 3842 Foot appliances, orthopedic

(P-11106)
FRANK STUBBS CO INC
1830 Eastman Ave, Oxnard (93030-8935)
PHONE..............................805 278-4300
Glenn Soensker, *CFO*
David Paul Pearson, *President*
Glenn Alan Slensker, *CFO*
Iliana Chan, *Credit Mgr*
EMP: 47 EST: 1966
SQ FT: 50,100
SALES (est): 2.6MM **Privately Held**
WEB: www.fstubbs.com
SIC: 3842 Supports: abdominal, ankle, arch, kneecap, etc.; personal safety equipment

(P-11107)
FREEDOM DESIGNS INC
2241 N Madera Rd, Simi Valley
(93065-1762)
PHONE..............................805 582-0077
Matthew E Monaghan, *Ch of Bd*
Kathleen P Leneghan, *CFO*
Rick Aimone, *Sales Staff*
Anna Gonzalez, *Sales Staff*
◆ EMP: 120 EST: 1981
SQ FT: 40,000
SALES (est): 20.9MM
SALES (corp-wide): 850.6MM **Publicly Held**
WEB: www.freedomdesigns.com
SIC: 3842 Wheelchairs
PA: Invacare Corporation
    1 Invacare Way
    Elyria OH 44035
    440 329-6000

(P-11108)
FREUDENBERG MEDICAL LLC (DH)
Also Called: Helix Medical
1110 Mark Ave, Carpinteria (93013-2918)
PHONE..............................805 684-3304
Jorg Schneewind, *CEO*
Thomas Vassalo, *President*
Steve Lents, *Vice Pres*
Melissa Tucker, *Vice Pres*
Susan Ward, *Vice Pres*
▲ EMP: 171 EST: 1984
SQ FT: 66,000
SALES (est): 130.5MM
SALES (corp-wide): 10.4B **Privately Held**
WEB: www.inhealth.com
SIC: 3842 Prosthetic appliances

(P-11109)
HANGER INC
Also Called: Hanger Clinic
201 S Buena Vista St, Burbank
(91505-4569)
PHONE..............................818 563-9590
EMP: 30
SALES (corp-wide): 1B **Publicly Held**
WEB: www.hangerclinic.com
SIC: 5999 3842 Ret Misc Merchandise Mfg Surgical Appliances/Supplies
PA: Hanger, Inc.
    10910 Domain Dr Ste 300
    Austin TX 78758
    512 777-3800

(P-11110)
HAWTHORNE DISTRIBUTION INC
Also Called: Hanger, The
6099 Malburg Way, Vernon (90058-3947)
PHONE..............................323 238-7738
Scott Palmer, *CEO*
EMP: 15 EST: 2014
SALES (est): 739.5K **Privately Held**
SIC: 3842 Surgical appliances & supplies

(P-11111)
HELIX MEDICAL
Also Called: Inhealth Technology
1009 Cindy Ln, Carpinteria (93013-2905)
PHONE..............................805 576-5458
Jorg Schneewind, *CEO*
Kevin Madden, *Info Tech Mgr*
Steven Yun, *Engineer*
◆ EMP: 14 EST: 2010
SALES (est): 607.3K **Privately Held**
SIC: 3842 Prosthetic appliances

(P-11112)
HONGRAY USA MEDICAL PDTS INC
2235 E Francis St, Ontario (91761-8083)
PHONE..............................909 590-1611
Kevin Kai Liu, *President*
Hao Gang, *Administration*
▲ EMP: 20 EST: 2008
SALES (est): 652.4K **Privately Held**
WEB: www.hongrayusa.com
SIC: 3842 Gloves, safety

(P-11113)
HUMAN DESIGNS PROSTHETIC (HQ)
49 E Foothill Blvd, Arcadia (91006-2307)
PHONE..............................562 988-2414
Natalie Rose Cronin, *CEO*
Eric Ferraco, *President*
Brian Cronin, *CFO*
EMP: 18 EST: 1995
SALES (est): 8MM
SALES (corp-wide): 16MM **Privately Held**
SIC: 3842 Surgical appliances & supplies
PA: Arc-V, Inc.
    1639 N Hollywood Way
    Burbank CA 91505
    626 445-7797

(P-11114)
IMPLANTECH ASSOCIATES INC
Also Called: Allied Bio Medical
6025 Nicolle St Ste B, Ventura
(93003-7602)
P.O. Box 392 (93002-0392)
PHONE..............................805 289-1665
William Binder, *President*
Robert Ramirez, *Graphic Designe*
Andrew Leicht, *Engineer*
Tina Post, *Engineer*
Karen Hawkins, *Marketing Staff*
EMP: 30 EST: 1989
SQ FT: 11,000
SALES (est): 4.4MM **Privately Held**
WEB: www.implantech.com
SIC: 3842 Implants, surgical

(P-11115)
INFAB LLC
1040 Avenida Acaso, Camarillo
(93012-8712)
PHONE..............................805 987-5255
Brittany Lepley, *CEO*
Justine Peterson, *President*
Daren Dickerson, *CFO*

Donald J Cusick, *Chairman*
Billy Morgan, *Vice Pres*
◆ EMP: 57 EST: 1980
SQ FT: 40,000
SALES: 12.3MM **Privately Held**
WEB: www.infabcorp.com
SIC: 3842 Radiation shielding aprons, gloves, sheeting, etc.

(P-11116)
INHEALTH TECHNOLOGIES
1110 Mark Ave, Carpinteria (93013-2918)
PHONE..............................800 477-5969
Ed Munoz, *Principal*
Bethany Anke, *Vice Pres*
Constantine Davlantes, *Vice Pres*
Melissa Tucker, *Vice Pres*
Ed Jesle, *Executive*
EMP: 20 EST: 2005
SALES (est): 2.2MM **Privately Held**
WEB: www.inhealth.com
SIC: 3842 Surgical appliances & supplies

(P-11117)
INTERPORE CROSS INTL INC (DH)
181 Technology Dr, Irvine (92618-2484)
PHONE..............................949 453-3200
Dan Hann, *President*
Greg Hartman, *CFO*
▲ EMP: 58 EST: 1975
SALES (est): 26.9MM
SALES (corp-wide): 7B **Publicly Held**
WEB: www.interpore.org
SIC: 3842 3843 Orthopedic appliances; surgical appliances & supplies; dental equipment & supplies
HQ: Biomet, Inc.
    345 E Main St
    Warsaw IN 46580
    574 267-6639

(P-11118)
JOA CORPORATION (PA)
Also Called: Johnsons Orthopedic
7254 Magnolia Ave, Riverside
(92504-3829)
PHONE..............................951 785-4411
William Kearney, *President*
Lesli Kearney, *CFO*
Joe Kearney, *Manager*
EMP: 15 EST: 1983
SQ FT: 6,000
SALES (est): 4.2MM **Privately Held**
WEB: www.johnsonsorthopedic.com
SIC: 3842 5999 8011 Braces, orthopedic; limbs, artificial; orthopedic & prosthesis applications; orthopedic physician

(P-11119)
JOHNSON & JOHNSON
15715 Arrow Hwy, Irwindale (91706-2006)
PHONE..............................909 839-8650
Cathy Somalis, *Manager*
Tzachi Levy, *Program Dir*
Paulette Malacara, *Manager*
EMP: 300
SALES (corp-wide): 82.5B **Publicly Held**
WEB: www.jnj.com
SIC: 3842 Dressings, surgical
PA: Johnson & Johnson
    1 Johnson And Johnson Plz
    New Brunswick NJ 08933
    732 524-0400

(P-11120)
KINAMED INC
820 Flynn Rd, Camarillo (93012-8701)
PHONE..............................805 384-2748
Clyde R Pratt, *President*
Vineet Sarin, *President*
Bob Bruce, *Vice Pres*
Roy Fiebiger, *Vice Pres*
Patrick Munz, *Executive*
EMP: 26 EST: 1987
SQ FT: 28,828
SALES (est): 8.4MM **Privately Held**
WEB: www.kinamed.com
SIC: 3842 Implants, surgical
PA: Vme Acquisition Corp.
    820 Flynn Rd
    Camarillo CA 93012

(P-11121)
KYOCERA MEDICAL TECH INC
1200 California St # 210, Redlands
(92374-2945)
PHONE..............................909 557-2360
Takahiro Kobayashi, *CEO*
EMP: 48 EST: 2019
SALES (est): 4.9MM **Privately Held**
WEB: www.kyocera-medical.com
SIC: 3842 Prosthetic appliances

(P-11122)
MBK ENTERPRISES INC
Also Called: MBK Tape Solutions
9959 Canoga Ave, Chatsworth
(91311-3002)
PHONE..............................818 998-1477
Jeffrey Kaminski, *President*
Marcella B Kaminski, *Corp Secy*
Rosma Dewi, *Executive*
Patti Kaminski, *Executive*
Kelly Weber-Williams, *Controller*
▲ EMP: 40 EST: 1972
SQ FT: 14,000
SALES (est): 12.2MM **Privately Held**
WEB: www.mbktape.com
SIC: 3842 Adhesive tape & plasters, medicated or non-medicated

(P-11123)
MEDICAL PACKAGING CORPORATION
Also Called: Hygenia
941 Avenida Acaso, Camarillo
(93012-8700)
PHONE..............................805 388-2383
Frederic L Nason, *President*
Susan Nason, *COO*
Susan J Nason, *Corp Secy*
Chris Feitel, *QC Mgr*
EMP: 100
SQ FT: 45,000
SALES (est): 19.4MM **Privately Held**
WEB: www.medicalpackaging.com
SIC: 3842 2835 Surgical appliances & supplies; in vitro & in vivo diagnostic substances

(P-11124)
MEGIDDO GLOBAL LLC
17101 Central Ave Ste 1c, Carson
(90746-1360)
PHONE..............................844 477-7007
Omer Nissani, *CEO*
EMP: 25 EST: 2017
SALES (est): 1.2MM **Privately Held**
WEB: www.megiddo-global.com
SIC: 3842 2393 2329 3728 Bulletproof vests; textile bags; field jackets, military; military aircraft equipment & armament; medical equipment & supplies

(P-11125)
MENTOR WORLDWIDE LLC (DH)
31 Technology Dr Ste 200, Irvine
(92618-2302)
PHONE..............................800 636-8678
David Shepherd, *President*
Dean Freed, *President*
Robert Hum, *President*
Flavia Pease,
Joshua H Levine, *Mng Member*
▲ EMP: 250 EST: 1969
SALES (est): 455.6MM
SALES (corp-wide): 82.5B **Publicly Held**
WEB: www.mentordirect.com
SIC: 3842 3845 3841 Surgical appliances & supplies; prosthetic appliances; implants, surgical; cosmetic restorations; ultrasonic medical equipment, except cleaning; medical instruments & equipment, blood & bone work
HQ: Ethicon Inc.
    1000 Route 202
    Raritan NJ 08869
    732 524-0400

(P-11126)
MOLDEX-METRIC INC
10111 Jefferson Blvd, Culver City
(90232-3509)
PHONE..............................310 837-6500
Mark Magidson, *CEO*
Debra Magidson, *Admin Sec*
Steve Wooley, *Info Tech Dir*
Jose Trujillo, *Info Tech Mgr*

(PA)=Parent Co (HQ)=Headquarters (DH)=Div Headquarters
✪ = New Business established in last 2 years

Larry Tutor, *IT/INT Sup*
◆ **EMP:** 500 **EST:** 1960
SQ FT: 80,000
SALES (est): 106.5MM **Privately Held**
WEB: www.moldex.com
SIC: 3842 Personal safety equipment; ear plugs

(P-11127)
MPS ANZON LLC
Also Called: Orchid Orthopedis
11911 Clark St, Arcadia (91006-6026)
PHONE............................626 471-3553
EMP: 237
SALES (est): 2.7MM
SALES (corp-wide): 496.9MM **Privately Held**
WEB: www.orchid-ortho.com
PA: Tulip Us Holdings, Inc.
    1489 Cedar St
    Holt MI 48842
    517 694-2300

(P-11128)
NEUROSTRUCTURES INC
199 Technology Dr Ste 110, Irvine (92618-2447)
PHONE............................800 352-6103
John Stephani, *CEO*
Moti Altarc, *Principal*
Tasha Hurd, *Opers Staff*
EMP: 13 **EST:** 2014
SALES (est): 1.6MM **Privately Held**
WEB: www.neurostructures.com
SIC: 3842 Braces, orthopedic

(P-11129)
NOBBE ORTHOPEDICS INC
3010 State St, Santa Barbara (93105-3304)
PHONE............................805 687-7508
Ralph W Nobbe, *President*
Bret Laurent, *President*
Erwin Nobbe, *Vice Pres*
Rolf Schiefel, *Vice Pres*
EMP: 213 **EST:** 1964
SQ FT: 2,850
SALES (est): 3.2MM
SALES (corp-wide): 1B **Publicly Held**
WEB: www.hangerclinic.com
SIC: 3842 2342 Cosmetic restorations; braces, orthopedic; trusses, orthopedic & surgical; supports: abdominal, ankle, arch, kneecap, etc.; corsets & allied garments
PA: Hanger, Inc.
    10910 Domain Dr Ste 300
    Austin TX 78758
    512 777-3800

(P-11130)
OMNICAL INC
557 Jessie St, San Fernando (91340-2542)
PHONE............................818 837-7531
Ron Tinero, *President*
Ellen Tinero, *Admin Sec*
EMP: 14 **EST:** 1975
SQ FT: 9,100
SALES (est): 1MM **Privately Held**
WEB: www.omnical.co
SIC: 3842 5047 Surgical appliances & supplies; medical & hospital equipment

(P-11131)
ORTHO ENGINEERING INC (PA)
17402 Chtswrth St Ste 200, Granada Hills (91344-7620)
PHONE............................310 559-5996
Avo Ashkharikian, *President*
EMP: 22 **EST:** 1991
SQ FT: 4,000 **Privately Held**
WEB: www.orthoengineering.com
SIC: 3842 Braces, orthopedic; prosthetic appliances

(P-11132)
OSSUR AMERICAS INC (HQ)
27051 Towne Centre Dr # 100, Foothill Ranch (92610-2819)
PHONE............................800 233-6263
Mahesh Mansukhani, *CEO*
Avanindra Chaturvedi, *CFO*
Christian Robinson, *Vice Pres*
Max Hansen, *Area Mgr*
Jeannine Neuman, *Area Mgr*

◆ **EMP:** 264 **EST:** 1984
SQ FT: 12,000
SALES (est): 101.6MM
SALES (corp-wide): 612.8MM **Privately Held**
WEB: www.ossur.com
SIC: 3842 Braces, orthopedic
PA: Ossur Hf.
    Grjothalsi 5
    Reykjavik
    425 340-0

(P-11133)
PASSY-MUIR INC (PA)
17992 Mitchell S Ste 200, Irvine (92614-6813)
PHONE............................949 833-8255
Cameron Jolly, *President*
Julie Kobak, *Vice Pres*
Stewart Goetz, *Marketing Staff*
Mike Harrell, *Director*
Allie Atkinson, *Consultant*
EMP: 30 **EST:** 1985
SQ FT: 1,200
SALES (est): 6.6MM **Privately Held**
WEB: www.passy-muir.com
SIC: 3842 Orthopedic appliances

(P-11134)
PAULSON MANUFACTURING CORP
46752 Rainbow Canyon Rd, Temecula (92592-5984)
PHONE............................951 676-2451
Roy Paulson, *President*
Joyce Paulson, *Corp Secy*
Thomas V Paulson, *Vice Pres*
Jason D 'amore, *Engineer*
Jason Damore, *Engineer*
▲ **EMP:** 100 **EST:** 1947
SQ FT: 42,000
SALES (est): 29.2MM **Privately Held**
WEB: www.paulsonmfg.com
SIC: 3842 Personal safety equipment

(P-11135)
PHILIPS RS NORTH AMERICA LLC
14101 Rosecrans Ave Ste F, La Mirada (90638-3551)
PHONE............................562 483-6805
Jimmy Gibbs, *Manager*
EMP: 13
SALES (corp-wide): 133.6MM **Privately Held**
WEB: www.usa.philips.com
SIC: 3842 7699 Surgical appliances & supplies; medical equipment repair, non-electric
HQ: Philips Rs North America Llc
    6501 Living Pl
    Pittsburgh PA 15206
    541 598-3832

(P-11136)
PROSTHTIC ORTHTIC GROUP ORNGE
26300 La Alameda Ste 120, Mission Viejo (92691-6380)
PHONE............................949 242-2237
Chad Marquis, *Principal*
EMP: 13 **EST:** 2017
SALES (est): 272.9K **Privately Held**
WEB: www.p-o-group.com
SIC: 3842 Prosthetic appliances

(P-11137)
RACING PLUS INC
Also Called: Parker Pumper Helmet Co
3834 Wacker Dr, Jurupa Valley (91752-1147)
PHONE............................951 360-5906
Harold Nicks, *President*
EMP: 21 **EST:** 1969
SQ FT: 9,200
SALES (est): 1MM **Privately Held**
WEB: www.racingplus.com
SIC: 3842 Helmets, space

(P-11138)
SAFARILAND LLC
4700 E Airport Dr, Ontario (91761-7875)
PHONE............................909 923-7300
Warren B Kanders, *Branch Mgr*
Patricia Coppedge, *Sales Staff*

Nick Gorsky, *Sales Staff*
Jorge Ponce, *Maintence Staff*
Robert Lukshis, *Sr Project Mgr*
EMP: 354
SALES (corp-wide): 404.6MM **Privately Held**
WEB: www.safariland.com
SIC: 3842 Bulletproof vests
HQ: Safariland, Llc
    13386 International Pkwy
    Jacksonville FL 32218
    904 741-5400

(P-11139)
SAS SAFETY CORPORATION
3031 Gardenia Ave, Long Beach (90807-5215)
PHONE............................562 427-2775
Patrick Larmon, *CEO*
James McCool, *Treasurer*
Julie Calvo, *Executive Asst*
Daniel Lett, *Admin Sec*
Nick Mlouk, *Info Tech Mgr*
◆ **EMP:** 60 **EST:** 1983
SQ FT: 90,000
SALES (est): 14.7MM **Privately Held**
WEB: www.sassafety.com
SIC: 3842 Personal safety equipment

(P-11140)
SHAMROCK MARKETING CO INC (HQ)
Also Called: Shamrock Manufacturing
5445 Daniels St, Chino (91710-9009)
PHONE............................909 591-8855
Emmy Tjoeng, *President*
Jeremy Sligh, *Technology*
Julia Ku, *Natl Sales Mgr*
Angela Yiu, *Sales Mgr*
Jeni Tjoeng, *Manager*
◆ **EMP:** 14 **EST:** 1997
SQ FT: 28,000
SALES (est): 8.6MM **Privately Held**
WEB: www.smcgloves.com
SIC: 3842 Gloves, safety

(P-11141)
SIENTRA INC (PA)
420 S Fairview Ave # 200, Santa Barbara (93117-3654)
PHONE............................805 562-3500
Ron Menezes, *President*
Andy Schmidt, *CFO*
Denise Dajles, *Vice Pres*
Jeffrey Jones, *Vice Pres*
Joann Kuhne, *Vice Pres*
EMP: 245 **EST:** 2003
SQ FT: 20,000
SALES (est): 71.2MM **Publicly Held**
WEB: www.sientra.com
SIC: 3842 Surgical appliances & supplies

(P-11142)
SUBCHONDRAL SOLUTIONS INC
1127 Wilshire Blvd, Los Angeles (90017-3901)
PHONE............................888 410-5622
Sheryl McCoy, *CFO*
EMP: 13 **EST:** 2013
SALES (est): 202.7K **Privately Held**
WEB: www.subchondralsolutions.com
SIC: 3842 Implants, surgical

(P-11143)
SUREFIRE LLC (PA)
18300 Mount Baldy Cir, Fountain Valley (92708-6122)
PHONE............................714 545-9444
John W Matthews, *President*
Sean Vo, *CFO*
Willie Hunt, *Vice Pres*
Alex SOO, *Vice Pres*
Joel Smith,
◆ **EMP:** 455 **EST:** 2000
SQ FT: 45,000
SALES (est): 158.9MM **Privately Held**
WEB: www.surefire.com
SIC: 3842 3484 3648 Ear plugs; guns (firearms) or gun parts, 30 mm. & below; flashlights

(P-11144)
SUTURA INC
17080 Newhope St, Fountain Valley (92708-4206)
PHONE............................714 427-0398
Anthony Nobles, *CEO*
David Kernan, *COO*
EMP: 28 **EST:** 1985
SQ FT: 20,000
SALES (est): 5.2MM
SALES (corp-wide): 28.7MM **Privately Held**
WEB: www.suturaus.com
SIC: 3842 Surgical appliances & supplies
PA: Whitebox Advisors Llc
    3033 Excelsior Blvd # 50
    Minneapolis MN 55416
    612 253-6001

(P-11145)
TOTAL RESOURCES INTL INC (PA)
420 S Lemon Ave, Walnut (91789-2956)
PHONE............................909 594-1220
George Rivera, *CEO*
Gregg Rivera, *President*
Merlyn Rivera, *Vice Pres*
Cecilia Nicdao, *Admin Asst*
Antoinette Hernandez, *Manager*
▲ **EMP:** 79 **EST:** 1993
SQ FT: 115,000
SALES (est): 21.1MM **Privately Held**
WEB: www.trikits.com
SIC: 3842 First aid, snake bite & burn kits

(P-11146)
TOWNSEND INDUSTRIES INC
4401 Stine Rd, Bakersfield (93313-2306)
PHONE............................661 837-1795
EMP: 65
SALES (corp-wide): 1.2MM **Privately Held**
SIC: 3842 Braces, orthopedic
HQ: Townsend Industries, Inc.
    4615 Shepard St
    Bakersfield CA 93313
    661 837-1795

(P-11147)
TOWNSEND INDUSTRIES INC
4833 N Hills Dr, Bakersfield (93308-1186)
PHONE............................661 837-1795
Rick Riley, *Branch Mgr*
EMP: 65
SALES (corp-wide): 1.2MM **Privately Held**
WEB: www.thuasneusa.com
SIC: 3842 Braces, orthopedic
HQ: Townsend Industries, Inc.
    4615 Shepard St
    Bakersfield CA 93313
    661 837-1795

(P-11148)
ULTIMATE EARS CONSUMER LLC
3 Jenner Ste 180, Irvine (92618-3835)
PHONE............................949 502-8340
Mindy Harvey, *Owner*
Damyanti Patel, *Production*
Melinda Harvey,
Daphne X LI, *Senior Mgr*
Aaron Berg, *Manager*
▲ **EMP:** 3235 **EST:** 2004
SALES (est): 12MM
SALES (corp-wide): 2.9B **Privately Held**
WEB: www.logitech.com
SIC: 3842 Hearing aids
HQ: Logitech, Inc.
    7700 Gateway Blvd
    Newark CA 94560
    510 795-8500

(P-11149)
US ARMOR CORPORATION
10715 Bloomfield Ave, Santa Fe Springs (90670-3913)
PHONE............................562 207-4240
Stephen Armellino, *President*
Susan L Armellino, *Corp Secy*
Ashley Cortez, *Admin Asst*
David Miller, *Engineer*
Ruth Castillo, *Controller*
▲ **EMP:** 45 **EST:** 1986
SQ FT: 14,000

SALES (est): 9.8MM **Privately Held**
WEB: www.usarmor.com
SIC: 3842 2326 5999 Bulletproof vests;
men's & boys' work clothing; safety supplies & equipment

(P-11150)
VISALIA CTR 4 AMBLTRY MED SRGR
Also Called: Visalia Cams
842 S Akers St, Visalia (93277-8309)
PHONE..................................559 740-4094
Burton Redd, *Partner*
EMP: 13 **EST:** 1983
SQ FT: 5,000
SALES (est): 231.9K **Privately Held**
SIC: 3842 Trusses, orthopedic & surgical

(P-11151)
VISION QUEST INDUSTRIES INC (PA)
Also Called: V Q Orthocare
18011 Mitchell S Ste A, Irvine
(92614-6863)
PHONE..................................949 261-6382
James W Knape, *CEO*
Kevin Lunau, *COO*
Bob Blachford, *CFO*
Joe Farrell, *Engineer*
▲ **EMP:** 100 **EST:** 1989
SQ FT: 35,500
SALES (est): 34.3MM **Privately Held**
SIC: 3842 5999 Braces, orthopedic; med-
ical apparatus & supplies

(P-11152)
VME ACQUISITION CORP (PA)
Also Called: Kinamad
820 Flynn Rd, Camarillo (93012-8701)
PHONE..................................805 384-2748
Clyde R Pratt, *President*
Lorraine Willis, *CFO*
Kimberly Deshong, *Accountant*
EMP: 15 **EST:** 1993
SQ FT: 14,000
SALES (est): 8.4MM **Privately Held**
SIC: 3842 7342 Surgical appliances &
supplies; disinfecting & pest control serv-
ices

(P-11153)
WEBER ORTHOPEDIC LP (PA)
Also Called: Hely & Weber Orthopedic
1185 E Main St, Santa Paula (93060-2954)
P.O. Box 832 (93061-0832)
PHONE..................................800 221-5465
Jim Weber, *Partner*
John P Hely, *Vice Pres*
Fred Mady, *Vice Pres*
Jim Buckhout, *General Mgr*
Greg Gumser, *Controller*
▲ **EMP:** 62 **EST:** 1982
SQ FT: 28,000
SALES (est): 10.8MM **Privately Held**
WEB: www.hely-weber.com
SIC: 3842 5047 Braces, orthopedic; ortho-
pedic equipment & supplies

(P-11154)
WHITEHALL MANUFACTURING INC
Also Called: A Division Acorn Engrg Co
15125 Proctor Ave, City of Industry
(91746-3327)
P.O. Box 3527 (91744-0527)
PHONE..................................626 336-4561
Donald E Morris, *President*
Kathryn L Morris, *Corp Secy*
William D Morris, *Vice Pres*
Steve Stormes, *Vice Pres*
EMP: 76 **EST:** 1946
SQ FT: 2,000
SALES (est): 812.8K
SALES (corp-wide): 90MM **Privately Held**
WEB: www.acorneng.com
SIC: 3842 Whirlpool baths, hydrotherapy
equipment
PA: Acorn Engineering Company
15125 Proctor Ave
City Of Industry CA 91746
800 488-8999

(P-11155)
XR LLC
15251 Pipeline Ln, Huntington Beach
(92649-1135)
PHONE..................................714 847-9292
ARI Suss,
Paul Suss, *CFO*
Lonnie Parker, *Marketing Mgr*
Rebecca Weinberg, *Marketing Staff*
Kelly Eberhard Allen,
▲ **EMP:** 27 **EST:** 2002
SQ FT: 68,000
SALES (est): 5MM **Privately Held**
WEB: www.xrllc.com
SIC: 3842 Personal safety equipment

(P-11156)
ZIMMER INTERMED INC
1647 Yeager Ave, La Verne (91750-5854)
PHONE..................................909 392-0882
Kelly Liebhart, *President*
EMP: 14 **EST:** 2008
SALES (est): 2.2MM **Privately Held**
SIC: 3842 Orthopedic appliances

(P-11157)
ZIMMER MELIA & ASSOCIATES INC (PA)
6832 Presidio Dr, Huntington Beach
(92648-3025)
PHONE..................................615 377-0118
K Michael Melia, *President*
Donna Talbot, *Business Mgr*
EMP: 58 **EST:** 2005
SALES (est): 6.8MM **Privately Held**
WEB: www.zimmerbiomet.com
SIC: 3842 Orthopedic appliances

3843 Dental Eqpt & Splys

(P-11158)
3M UNITEK CORPORATION
2724 Peck Rd, Monrovia (91016-5097)
PHONE..................................626 445-7960
Mary Jo Abler, *CEO*
Fred Palensky, *Vice Pres*
Erasmo Robles, *Engineer*
Joan Harp, *Train & Dev Mgr*
▲ **EMP:** 480 **EST:** 1948
SQ FT: 249,000
SALES (est): 83MM
SALES (corp-wide): 32.1B **Publicly Held**
WEB: www.3m.com
SIC: 3843 Orthodontic appliances; dental
hand instruments; dental laboratory
equipment
PA: 3m Company
3m Center
Saint Paul MN 55144
651 733-1110

(P-11159)
ALPHA DENTAL OF UTAH INC
12898 Towne Center Dr, Cerritos
(90703-8546)
PHONE..................................562 467-7759
Anthony S Barth, *Principal*
Angela Whitfield, *Exec Dir*
Shahab Haghnazari, *Systs Prg Mgr*
Susan Hammer, *Business Anlyst*
Shannon Contreras, *Project Mgr*
EMP: 24 **EST:** 2010
SALES (est): 421.8K **Privately Held**
WEB: www.delta.org
SIC: 3843 Dental equipment & supplies

(P-11160)
AURIDENT INC
610 S State College Blvd, Fullerton
(92831-5138)
P.O. Box 7200 (92834-7200)
PHONE..................................714 870-1851
Howard M Hoffman, *President*
Fredelle G Hoffman, *Corp Secy*
David H Fell, *Vice Pres*
Bruce Spivack, *Vice Pres*
Sangdon Choi, *Technician*
EMP: 30 **EST:** 1974
SQ FT: 2,700
SALES (est): 3.1MM **Privately Held**
WEB: www.aurident.com
SIC: 3843 Dental alloys for amalgams

(P-11161)
BELPORT COMPANY INC (PA)
Also Called: Gingi Pak
4825 Calle Alto, Camarillo (93012-8530)
P.O. Box 240 (93011-0240)
PHONE..................................805 484-1051
Jo Pennington, *President*
Lupe Becerra, *Cust Mgr*
EMP: 19 **EST:** 1954
SQ FT: 22,000
SALES (est): 5MM **Privately Held**
WEB: www.gingi-pak.com
SIC: 3843 Dental hand instruments; com-
pounds, dental; impression material, den-
tal

(P-11162)
BIOLASE INC
4225 Prado Rd Ste 102, Corona
(92878-7443)
PHONE..................................949 361-1200
Richard Whitt, *Manager*
EMP: 75
SALES (corp-wide): 22.7MM **Publicly Held**
WEB: www.biolase.com
SIC: 3843 Dental equipment & supplies
PA: Biolase, Inc.
27042 Twne Cntre Dr Ste 2
Lake Forest CA 92610
949 361-1200

(P-11163)
BIOLASE INC (PA)
27042 Twne Cntre Dr Ste 2, Lake Forest
(92610)
PHONE..................................949 361-1200
John R Beaver, *President*
Jonathan T Lord, *Ch of Bd*
EMP: 127 **EST:** 1984
SQ FT: 11,000
SALES (est): 22.7MM **Publicly Held**
WEB: www.biolase.com
SIC: 3843 3841 Dental equipment & sup-
plies; dental equipment; dental hand in-
struments; dental laboratory equipment;
surgical lasers

(P-11164)
CMP INDUSTRIES LLC (PA)
Also Called: Ticonium Division
18150 Rowland St, City of Industry
(91748-1224)
PHONE..................................518 434-3147
Devon Howe, *Mng Member*
Walter Pietro, *Mfg Dir*
Lenny Ricci, *Director*
◆ **EMP:** 40 **EST:** 1889
SALES (est): 13MM **Privately Held**
WEB: www.nobilium.com
SIC: 3843 Dental equipment & supplies

(P-11165)
CYBER MEDICAL IMAGING INC
Also Called: Xdr Radiology
11300 W Olympic Blvd, Los Angeles
(90064-1637)
PHONE..................................888 937-9729
Douglas Yoon, *CEO*
Joel Karafin, *Officer*
Adam Chen, *Senior VP*
Adam Duffy, *Sales Engr*
Matt Glass, *Cust Mgr*
EMP: 25 **EST:** 2003
SQ FT: 2,800
SALES (est): 6.1MM **Privately Held**
WEB: www.xdrradiology.com
SIC: 3843 Dental equipment & supplies

(P-11166)
DANVILLE MATERIALS LLC
4020 E Leaverton Ct, Anaheim
(92807-1610)
PHONE..................................714 399-0334
Greg Dorsman, *Manager*
Caroline Franklin, *Admin Asst*
EMP: 20
SALES (corp-wide): 23MM **Privately Held**
WEB: www.zestdent.com
SIC: 3843 Dental materials
HQ: Danville Materials, Llc
2875 Loker Ave E
Carlsbad CA 92010

(P-11167)
DENOVO DENTAL INC
5130 Commerce Dr, Baldwin Park
(91706-1450)
P.O. Box 548 (91706-0548)
PHONE..................................626 480-0182
Richard R Parker, *President*
Joseph Parker, *Vice Pres*
Jeanette Parker, *Admin Sec*
Rose Garcia, *Manager*
▼ **EMP:** 20 **EST:** 1981
SQ FT: 10,000
SALES (est): 4.8MM **Privately Held**
WEB: www.denovodental.com
SIC: 3843 5047 Dental equipment & sup-
plies; dental equipment & supplies

(P-11168)
DENTTIO INC
116 N Maryland Ave # 125, Glendale
(91206-4235)
PHONE..................................323 254-1000
Young Han, *CEO*
EMP: 16 **EST:** 2011
SALES (est): 2.2MM **Privately Held**
WEB: www.denttio.com
SIC: 3843 Dental equipment & supplies

(P-11169)
DIAMODENT INC
1580 N Harmony Cir, Anaheim
(92807-2092)
PHONE..................................888 281-8850
Kazem Jeff Rassoli, *President*
EMP: 21 **EST:** 2000
SALES (est): 2.4MM **Privately Held**
WEB: www.diamodent.com
SIC: 3843 Dental equipment & supplies

(P-11170)
DOCKUM RESEARCH LABORATORY INC
844 E Mariposa St, Altadena (91001-2421)
PHONE..................................626 794-1821
Greta Dockum, *President*
EMP: 13 **EST:** 1956
SQ FT: 5,000
SALES (est): 424.4K **Privately Held**
SIC: 3843 Dental equipment & supplies

(P-11171)
DRCOLLINS INC
26229 Enterprise Ct, Lake Forest
(92630-8412)
PHONE..................................888 583-6048
Colin Suzman, *CEO*
EMP: 50 **EST:** 2008
SALES (est): 1.4MM **Privately Held**
SIC: 3843 Dental equipment & supplies

(P-11172)
ENDODENT INC
851 Meridian St, Duarte (91010-3588)
PHONE..................................626 359-5715
EMP: 34
SQ FT: 10,000
SALES (est): 3MM **Privately Held**
WEB: www.endodent.com
SIC: 3843 Mfg Dental Supplies

(P-11173)
ENVISTA HOLDINGS CORPORATION (PA)
200 S Kraemer Blvd Bldg E, Brea
(92821-6208)
PHONE..................................714 817-7000
Amir Aghdaei, *President*
Scott Huennekens, *Ch of Bd*
Howard H Yu, *CFO*
Curt W Bludworth, *Senior VP*
Mark E Nance, *Senior VP*
EMP: 10305 **EST:** 2018
SALES (est): 2.2B **Publicly Held**
WEB: www.envistaco.com
SIC: 3843 Dental equipment & supplies

(P-11174)
EVOLVE DENTAL TECHNOLOGIES INC
5 Vanderbilt, Irvine (92618-2011)
PHONE..................................949 713-0909
Rodger Kurthy, *CEO*
Sharon Kurthy, *President*
EMP: 37 **EST:** 2007

SALES (est): 9.1MM **Privately Held**
WEB: www.korwhitening.com
SIC: 3843 Dental equipment & supplies

(P-11175)
HAND PIECE PARTS AND PRODUCTS
707 W Angus Ave, Orange (92868-1305)
PHONE..........................714 997-4331
Steve Bowen, *President*
Lyla Bowen, *Vice Pres*
Eric Shanebeck, *Engineer*
EMP: 30 EST: 1992
SQ FT: 18,000
SALES (est): 3MM **Privately Held**
WEB: www.handpieceparts.com
SIC: 3843 Dental materials

(P-11176)
IMPLANT DIRECT SYBRON INTL LLC (HQ)
22715 Savi Ranch Pkwy, Yorba Linda (92887-4609)
PHONE..........................818 444-3000
Roy Chang,
Ed Buthusiem,
Henrik J Roos,
Tom Stratton,
EMP: 15 EST: 2010
SALES (est): 15.2MM
SALES (corp-wide): 22.2B **Publicly Held**
WEB: www.danaher.com
SIC: 3843 Dental equipment & supplies
PA: Danaher Corporation
2200 Penn Ave Nw Ste 800w
Washington DC 20037
202 828-0850

(P-11177)
IMPLANT DIRECT SYBRON MFG LLC
3050 E Hillcrest Dr # 100, Westlake Village (91362-3195)
PHONE..........................818 444-3300
Gerald A Niznick,
Tom Stratton, *Executive*
Michael Claravino, *Principal*
David McKinney, *Info Tech Dir*
Patrick Abbott, *Design Engr*
EMP: 200 EST: 2010
SQ FT: 45,622
SALES (est): 62.9MM
SALES (corp-wide): 22.2B **Publicly Held**
WEB: www.implantdirect.com
SIC: 3843 Dental equipment & supplies
PA: Danaher Corporation
2200 Penn Ave Nw Ste 800w
Washington DC 20037
202 828-0850

(P-11178)
JENERIC/PENTRON INCORPORATED (HQ)
1717 W Collins Ave, Orange (92867-5422)
PHONE..........................203 265-7397
Gordon Cohen, *President*
Martin Schulman, *Exec VP*
EMP: 200 EST: 1977
SQ FT: 46,000
SALES (est): 57.4MM
SALES (corp-wide): 62.3MM **Privately Held**
WEB: www.pentron.com
SIC: 3843 Dental equipment
PA: Pentron Corporation
53 N Plains Industrial Rd
Wallingford CT 06492
203 265-7397

(P-11179)
KERR CORPORATION (DH)
1717 W Collins Ave, Orange (92867-5422)
P.O. Box 14247 (92863-1447)
PHONE..........................714 516-7400
Damien McDonald, *CEO*
Philip Read, *President*
Steve Semmelmayer, *President*
Alexander Wallstein, *President*
Steve Dunkerken, *Treasurer*
◆ EMP: 218 EST: 1891
SQ FT: 105,000

SALES (est): 314.5MM
SALES (corp-wide): 22.2B **Publicly Held**
WEB: www.kerrdental.com
SIC: 3843 Dental materials; dental laboratory equipment; impression material, dental; dental hand instruments

(P-11180)
KETTENBACH LP
16052 Beach Blvd Ste 221, Huntington Beach (92647-3855)
PHONE..........................877 532-2123
Daniel Parrilli, *Director*
John Pargee, *Sales Mgr*
Heather Resney, *Sales Staff*
Steve Scalbom, *Sales Staff*
Keith Ternora, *Sales Staff*
EMP: 26 EST: 1994
SALES (est): 4.5MM **Privately Held**
WEB: www.kettenbach-dental.us
SIC: 3843 5047 Dental equipment & supplies; dental equipment & supplies

(P-11181)
LACLEDE INC
Also Called: Laclede Research Center
2103 E University Dr, Rancho Dominguez (90220-6413)
PHONE..........................310 605-4280
Michael Pellico, *President*
Stephen Pellico, *Vice Pres*
Margie Lee, *Controller*
Harjinder Kang, *Prdtn Mgr*
Janis Usui, *Opers Staff*
◆ EMP: 35 EST: 1978
SQ FT: 25,000
SALES (est): 8.8MM **Privately Held**
WEB: www.laclede.com
SIC: 3843 Dental equipment

(P-11182)
NOBEL BIOCARE USA LLC
22715 Savi Ranch Pkwy, Yorba Linda (92887-4609)
PHONE..........................714 282-4800
EMP: 19 EST: 2017
SALES (est): 3.1MM
SALES (corp-wide): 22.2B **Publicly Held**
WEB: www.nobelbiocare.com
SIC: 3843 Dental equipment
PA: Danaher Corporation
2200 Penn Ave Nw Ste 800w
Washington DC 20037
202 828-0850

(P-11183)
ORMCO CORPORATION
1889 W Mission Blvd, Pomona (91766-1022)
PHONE..........................714 516-7400
Demetrio Ambriz, *Research*
Eugene Sirovskiy, *Technical Staff*
Jessica Guzman, *Engineer*
Chris Terdenge, *Manager*
Kees Wind, *Manager*
EMP: 277
SALES (corp-wide): 22.2B **Publicly Held**
WEB: www.ormco.com
SIC: 3843 Orthodontic appliances
HQ: Ormco Corporation
1717 W Collins Ave
Orange CA 92867
714 516-7400

(P-11184)
ORMCO CORPORATION
200 S Kraemer Blvd, Brea (92821-6208)
PHONE..........................909 962-5705
Nicholas Dasilva, *Marketing Staff*
EMP: 21
SALES (corp-wide): 22.2B **Publicly Held**
WEB: www.ormco.com
SIC: 3843 Orthodontic appliances
HQ: Ormco Corporation
1717 W Collins Ave
Orange CA 92867
714 516-7400

(P-11185)
ORMCO CORPORATION (HQ)
Also Called: Sybron Endo
1717 W Collins Ave, Orange (92867-5422)
PHONE..........................714 516-7400
Patrik Eriksson, *CEO*
Vicente Reynal, *President*
Jason R Davis, *Vice Pres*

Jessica Guzman, *Vice Pres*
Ryan Alexander, *District Mgr*
◆ EMP: 100 EST: 1975
SQ FT: 104,000
SALES (est): 126MM
SALES (corp-wide): 22.2B **Publicly Held**
WEB: www.ormco.com
SIC: 3843 Orthodontic appliances
PA: Danaher Corporation
2200 Penn Ave Nw Ste 800w
Washington DC 20037
202 828-0850

(P-11186)
ORTHODENTAL INTERNATIONAL INC
280 Campillo St Ste J, Calexico (92231-3200)
PHONE..........................760 357-8070
Armando Lozano, *President*
▲ EMP: 57 EST: 1994
SALES (est): 10.4MM
SALES (corp-wide): 3.3B **Publicly Held**
WEB: www.sirona.com
SIC: 3843 Orthodontic appliances
PA: Dentsply Sirona Inc.
13320b Balntyn Corp Pl
Charlotte NC 28277
844 848-0137

(P-11187)
PAC-DENT INC
670 Endeavor Cir, Brea (92821-2949)
PHONE..........................909 839-0888
Daniel Wang, *President*
EMP: 49 EST: 2003
SALES (est): 5.1MM **Privately Held**
SIC: 3843 Dental equipment & supplies

(P-11188)
PANADENT CORPORATION
580 S Rancho Ave, Colton (92324-3252)
PHONE..........................909 783-1841
Arlene Lee, *Ch of Bd*
Thomas E Lee, *President*
Robert Sarabia, *Sales Staff*
EMP: 20 EST: 1966
SQ FT: 1,200
SALES (est): 3.5MM **Privately Held**
WEB: www.panadent.com
SIC: 3843 Dental hand instruments

(P-11189)
PDMA VENTURES INC
Also Called: Zet-Tek Precision Machining
22951 La Palma Ave, Yorba Linda (92887-6701)
PHONE..........................714 777-8770
Charles Platt, *President*
Mark Deischter, *Vice Pres*
EMP: 35 EST: 2016
SALES (est): 5MM **Privately Held**
SIC: 3843 3842 3841 Dental equipment & supplies; surgical appliances & supplies; surgical & medical instruments

(P-11190)
PRIMOR HUNTINGTON PARK INC
6334 Pacific Blvd, Huntington Park (90255-4102)
PHONE..........................323 365-3200
Dianela Rosario, *Principal*
EMP: 14 EST: 2009
SALES (est): 311.5K **Privately Held**
SIC: 3843 Enamels, dentists'

(P-11191)
PROMA INC
730 Kingshill Pl, Carson (90746-1219)
PHONE..........................310 327-0035
Raymond Tai, *CEO*
Harold Tai, *Ch of Bd*
▲ EMP: 40 EST: 1967
SQ FT: 37,000
SALES (est): 3MM **Privately Held**
WEB: www.proma.us
SIC: 3843 Dental equipment & supplies

(P-11192)
RANIR LLC
Also Called: Dr. Fresh
6 Centerpointe Dr Ste 640, La Palma (90623-2587)
PHONE..........................866 373-7374
Kevin Parekh, *Branch Mgr*

EMP: 34 **Privately Held**
WEB: www.ranir.com
SIC: 3843 Dental equipment & supplies
HQ: Ranir, Llc
4701 East Paris Ave Se
Grand Rapids MI 49512
616 698-8880

(P-11193)
RAY FOSTER DENTAL EQUIPMENT
5421 Commercial Dr, Huntington Beach (92649-1231)
PHONE..........................714 897-7795
John Foster, *President*
Muriel Foster, *Corp Secy*
Mark Foster, *Vice Pres*
▲ EMP: 25 EST: 1938
SQ FT: 12,000
SALES (est): 2.2MM **Privately Held**
WEB: www.fosterdental.com
SIC: 3843 Dental equipment

(P-11194)
REPLACEMENT PARTS INDS INC
Also Called: RPI
625 Cochran St, Simi Valley 93065-1939)
P.O. Box 940250 (93094-0250)
PHONE..........................818 882-8611
Ira Lapides, *President*
Albert M Lapides, *Chairman*
Sherry Lapides, *Corp Secy*
Joan Woodlock, *Vice Pres*
Joan Woolock, *Executive*
◆ EMP: 25 EST: 1972
SQ FT: 15,000
SALES (est): 6.3MM **Privately Held**
WEB: www.rpiparts.com
SIC: 3843 3841 3821 Dental equipment; surgical & medical instruments; laboratory apparatus, except heating & measuring

(P-11195)
SELANE PRODUCTS INC (PA)
Also Called: Sml Space Maintainers Labs
9129 Lurline Ave, Chatsworth (91311-5922)
P.O. Box 2101 (91313-2101)
PHONE..........................818 998-7460
Rob Veis, *CEO*
Wendy Kayne, *Vice Pres*
Victor Peraza, *Info Tech Mgr*
Anna McNaught, *Graphic Designe*
Laura Urbanski, *Human Res Mgr*
▲ EMP: 60 EST: 1957
SQ FT: 12,000
SALES (est): 18.8MM **Privately Held**
WEB: www.smlglobal.com
SIC: 3843 8072 Orthodontic appliances; dental laboratories

(P-11196)
SONENDO INC (PA)
26061 Merit Cir Ste 102, Laguna Hills (92653-7010)
PHONE..........................949 766-3636
Bjarne Bergheim, *President*
Andrew Kirkpatrick, *COO*
Michael P Watts, *CFO*
Michael J Smith, *Ch Credit Ofcr*
Roy T Chen, *Officer*
EMP: 163 EST: 2006
SQ FT: 55,000
SALES: 15.4MM **Publicly Held**
WEB: www.sonendo.com
SIC: 3843 Dental equipment & supplies

(P-11197)
SYBRON DENTAL SPECIALTIES INC (HQ)
Also Called: Analytic Endodontics
1717 W Collins Ave, Orange (92867-5422)
PHONE..........................714 516-7400
Dan Even, *CEO*
Steven Semmelmayer, *President*
Henricus A M Van Duijnnoven, *CEO*
Leeann Jones, *Exec VP*
Mike Beaudoin, *Vice Pres*
◆ EMP: 250 EST: 1993
SQ FT: 16,000
SALES (est): 915.7MM
SALES (corp-wide): 22.2B **Publicly Held**
WEB: www.kerrdental.com
SIC: 3843 2834 Dental laboratory equipment; pharmaceutical preparations

PA: Danaher Corporation
2200 Penn Ave Nw Ste 800w
Washington DC 20037
202 828-0850

(P-11198)
TALLADIUM INC (PA)
27360 Muirfield Ln, Valencia (91355-1010)
PHONE..................................661 295-0900
Eddie Harms-, *CEO*
Geoff Harms, *CFO*
Amy Shaw, *Purchasing*
Steve Brennan, *Sales Mgr*
Jazz Cantu, *Sales Mgr*
◆ **EMP:** 26 **EST:** 1980
SQ FT: 9,000
SALES (est): 12MM **Privately Held**
WEB: www.talladium.com
SIC: 3843 3541 5047 Investment material, dental; milling machines; dental equipment & supplies

(P-11199)
TRUABUTMENT INC
17742 Cowan, Irvine (92614-6012)
PHONE..................................714 956-1488
Hyungick Kim, *CEO*
Sangho Yoo, *CFO*
Katie Lee, *Sales Associate*
Jay Kim, *Sales Staff*
Scott Ro, *Manager*
EMP: 59 **EST:** 2013
SQ FT: 1,800
SALES (est): 12MM **Privately Held**
WEB: www.truabutment.com
SIC: 3843 Dental equipment & supplies

(P-11200)
US DENTAL INC
Also Called: Young Dental
13043 166th St, Cerritos (90703-2201)
PHONE..................................562 404-3500
Young Hoon Park, *CEO*
EMP: 20 **EST:** 2015
SALES (est): 1.2MM **Privately Held**
WEB: www.usdentalinc.com
SIC: 3843 Dental equipment & supplies

(P-11201)
VIADE PRODUCTS INC
354 Dawson Dr, Camarillo (93012-8008)
PHONE..................................805 484-2114
Keith Zinser, *President*
Sandra Zinser, *Corp Secy*
John Menzie, *Vice Pres*
EMP: 28 **EST:** 1968
SQ FT: 8,000
SALES (est): 934.6K **Privately Held**
WEB: www.viade.com
SIC: 3843 5047 5999 Dental laboratory equipment; dental materials; dental laboratory equipment; medical apparatus & supplies

(P-11202)
VMC INTERNATIONAL LLC
Also Called: Vaniman Manufacturing
25799 Jefferson Ave, Murrieta (92562-6903)
P.O. Box 74, Fallbrook (92088-0074)
PHONE..................................760 723-1498
Don Vaniman, *Manager*
Kyle Galenza, *Vice Pres*
Nathan Frey, *Marketing Mgr*
EMP: 16
SQ FT: 7,000
SALES (est): 1.6MM **Privately Held**
WEB: www.vaniman.com
SIC: 3843 Dental equipment

(P-11203)
WESTSIDE RESOURCES INC
Also Called: Crystal Tip
8850 Research Dr, Irvine (92618-4223)
PHONE..................................800 944-3939
Donovan Berkely, *CEO*
Derek Jenkins, *Vice-Pres*
▲ **EMP:** 40 **EST:** 2000
SQ FT: 18,000
SALES (est): 4.8MM **Privately Held**
WEB: www.crystaltip.com
SIC: 3843 5047 Dental equipment & supplies; medical & hospital equipment

(P-11204)
ZYRIS INC
6868 Cortona Dr Ste A, Santa Barbara (93117-1362)
PHONE..................................805 560-9888
Sandra Hirsch, *CEO*
Catherine Gloster, *President*
James Hirsch, *President*
Sandra Y Hirsch, *CEO*
Rolando Mia, *Vice Pres*
▲ **EMP:** 50 **EST:** 2001
SQ FT: 10,200
SALES (est): 11.8MM **Privately Held**
WEB: www.zyris.com
SIC: 3843 5047 Dental equipment; dental equipment & supplies

3844 X-ray Apparatus & Tubes

(P-11205)
ASHTEL STUDIOS INC
Also Called: Ashtel Dental
1610 E Philadelphia St, Ontario (91761-5759)
PHONE..................................909 434-0911
Anish Patel, *President*
Jessica Reza, *Products*
Ruby Contreras, *Manager*
◆ **EMP:** 25 **EST:** 2002
SQ FT: 40,000
SALES: 132.2MM **Privately Held**
WEB: www.ashtelstudios.com
SIC: 3844 3991 5122 X-ray apparatus & tubes; toothbrushes, except electric; toothbrushes, except electric

(P-11206)
ASTROPHYSICS INC (PA)
21481 Ferrero, City of Industry (91789-5233)
PHONE..................................909 598-5488
Francois Zayek, *CEO*
John Pan, *CFO*
Tom Schorling, *Vice Pres*
John Whelan, *Vice Pres*
Elias Abdo, *Administration*
▼ **EMP:** 129 **EST:** 2002
SQ FT: 65,376
SALES (est): 59.6MM **Privately Held**
WEB: www.astrophysicsinc.com
SIC: 3844 X-ray apparatus & tubes

(P-11207)
CARR CORPORATION (PA)
1547 11th St, Santa Monica (90401-2999)
PHONE..................................310 587-1113
John Carr, *President*
Paul Carr, *Exec VP*
Reese Carr, *Vice Pres*
EMP: 25 **EST:** 1946
SQ FT: 25,000
SALES (est): 4.3MM **Privately Held**
WEB: www.carrcorporation.com
SIC: 3844 3861 3842 X-ray apparatus & tubes; processing equipment, photographic; surgical appliances & supplies

(P-11208)
IMMPORT THERAPEUTICS INC
Also Called: Antigen Discovery
1 Technology Dr Ste E309, Irvine (92618-2343)
PHONE..................................949 679-4068
Philip Felgner, *President*
Joseph Campo, *Project Mgr*
Angela Yee, *Controller*
David Camerini, *Director*
Douglas Molina, *Director*
EMP: 29 **EST:** 2002
SALES (est): 5.4MM **Privately Held**
WEB: www.antigendiscovery.com
SIC: 3844 Therapeutic X-ray apparatus & tubes

(P-11209)
RAPISCAN SYSTEMS INC (HQ)
2805 Columbia St, Torrance (90503-3804)
PHONE..................................310 978-1457
Deepak Chopra, *CEO*
Ajay Mehra, *President*
Eric Luiz, *CFO*
Ted Alston, *Vice Pres*
J Bare, *Vice Pres*

◆ **EMP:** 790 **EST:** 1993
SQ FT: 93,000
SALES (est): 150.6MM
SALES (corp-wide): 1.1B **Publicly Held**
WEB: www.rapiscansystems.com
SIC: 3844 X-ray apparatus & tubes
PA: Osi Systems, Inc.
12525 Chadron Ave
Hawthorne CA 90250
310 978-0516

(P-11210)
STRATEGIC MEDICAL VENTURES LLC (PA)
280 Newport Center Dr, Newport Beach (92660-7526)
PHONE..................................949 355-5212
Antony Clarke, *Mng Member*
Michael McKinnon
EMP: 19 **EST:** 2010
SALES (est): 2.1MM **Privately Held**
SIC: 3844 X-ray apparatus & tubes

(P-11211)
WILLICK ENGINEERING CO INC
12516 Lakeland Rd, Santa Fe Springs (90670-3940)
PHONE..................................562 946-4242
Dan Guerrero, *President*
Jose Ramirez, *Engineer*
Gus Guerrero, *Manager*
Lori Guerrero, *Manager*
◆ **EMP:** 16
SQ FT: 10,673
SALES (est): 3.4MM **Privately Held**
WEB: www.willick.com
SIC: 3844 3612 7629 X-ray apparatus & tubes; specialty transformers; electrical equipment repair, high voltage

(P-11212)
ZIEHM INSTRUMENTARIUM
4181 Latham St, Riverside (92501-1729)
PHONE..................................407 615-8560
Wolfram Klawitter, *President*
Richard Westrick, *Treasurer*
Lars Nillson, *Vice Pres*
Stan Talaba, *Vice Pres*
EMP: 33 **EST:** 1980
SQ FT: 11,000
SALES (est): 823.2K **Privately Held**
SIC: 3844 X-ray apparatus & tubes

3845 Electromedical & Electrotherapeutic Apparatus

(P-11213)
ADVANCED BIONICS LLC
26081 Avenue Hall, Valencia (91355-1241)
PHONE..................................310 819-4004
EMP: 48
SALES (corp-wide): 2.9B **Privately Held**
WEB: www.advancedbionics.com
SIC: 3845 Electromedical equipment
HQ: Advanced Bionics, Llc
12740 San Fernando Rd
Sylmar CA 91342

(P-11214)
BETA BIONICS INC
11 Hughes, Irvine (92618-1902)
PHONE..................................949 297-6635
Edward Damiano, *CEO*
Gibb Clarke, *CFO*
Serafina Raskin, *Vice Pres*
Michael Rosinko, *CTO*
David Lim, *Business Mgr*
EMP: 22 **EST:** 2016
SALES (est): 7.3MM **Privately Held**
WEB: www.betabionics.com
SIC: 3845 Patient monitoring apparatus

(P-11215)
BIOMED INSTRUMENTS INC
1511 Alto Ln, Fullerton (92831-2007)
PHONE..................................714 459-5716
EMP: 18
SQ FT: 3,000
SALES (est): 987.4K **Privately Held**
WEB: www.biomedinstruments.com
SIC: 3845 Mfg Electromedical Equipment

(P-11216)
BIONESS INC
25103 Rye Canyon Loop, Valencia (91355-5004)
PHONE..................................661 362-4850
Todd Cushman, *President*
Jim McHargue, *COO*
Dan Lutz, *CFO*
Alfred E Mann, *Chairman*
Eric Grigsby, *Chief Mktg Ofcr*
▲ **EMP:** 190 **EST:** 2004
SQ FT: 29,000
SALES (est): 33.5MM
SALES (corp-wide): 33.7MM **Publicly Held**
WEB: www.bioventus.com
SIC: 3845 5047 Transcutaneous electrical nerve stimulators (TENS); medical & hospital equipment; medical equipment & supplies
PA: Bioventus Inc.
4721 Emperor Blvd Ste 100
Durham NC 27703
919 474-6700

(P-11217)
BIOSENSE WEBSTER INC (HQ)
31 Technology Dr Ste 200, Irvine (92618-2302)
PHONE..................................909 839-8500
Uri Yaron, *CEO*
Gerianne T Sarte, *CFO*
Lynn Ho, *Executive*
Stephenie Orsini, *Business Dir*
Sharad Rathod, *Business Dir*
▲ **EMP:** 150 **EST:** 1980
SALES (est): 146MM
SALES (corp-wide): 82.5B **Publicly Held**
WEB: www.jnj.com
SIC: 3845 3841 Electromedical apparatus; surgical & medical instruments
PA: Johnson & Johnson
1 Johnson And Johnson Plz
New Brunswick NJ 08933
732 524-0400

(P-11218)
CHRISTIE MEDICAL HOLDINGS INC
Also Called: Veinviewer
10550 Camden Dr, Cypress (90630-4600)
PHONE..................................714 236-8610
George Pinho, *President*
Chris Schnee, *General Mgr*
Chris Marsh, *Administration*
Maz Zaeefjou, *Sales Staff*
Warren Vandrine, *Manager*
EMP: 27 **EST:** 2009
SALES (est): 9.3MM **Privately Held**
WEB: www.christiedigital.com
SIC: 3845 Electromedical equipment
HQ: Christie Digital Systems Usa, Inc.
10550 Camden Dr
Cypress CA 90630
714 236-8610

(P-11219)
CONVERSION DEVICES INC
15481 Electronic Ln Ste D, Huntington Beach (92649-1355)
PHONE..................................714 898-6551
Roland Roth, *President*
Alan Augusta, *VP Mktg*
EMP: 16 **EST:** 1981
SQ FT: 11,000
SALES (est): 3.1MM **Privately Held**
WEB: www.cdipower.com
SIC: 3845 3577 Electromedical apparatus; computer peripheral equipment

(P-11220)
DOLPHIN MEDICAL INC (HQ)
12525 Chadron Ave, Hawthorne (90250-4807)
PHONE..................................800 448-6506
Deepak Chopra, *President*
Thomas Scharf, *Vice Pres*
▲ **EMP:** 100 **EST:** 2001
SALES (est): 64.1MM
SALES (corp-wide): 1.1B **Publicly Held**
WEB: www.osi-systems.com
SIC: 3845 Ultrasonic medical equipment, except cleaning

P R O D U C T S & S V C S

PA: Osi Systems, Inc.
12525 Chadron Ave
Hawthorne CA 90250
310 978-0516

(P-11221)
EDWARDS LIFESCIENCES US INC
1 Edwards Way, Irvine (92614-5688)
PHONE..................949 250-2500
Michael A Mussallem, *CEO*
Dirksen J Lehman, *Vice Pres*
Christine Z McCauley, *Vice Pres*
Stanton J Rowe, *Vice Pres*
Scott B Ullem, *Vice Pres*
EMP: 154 EST: 2011
SALES (est): 33MM
SALES (corp-wide): 4.3B **Publicly Held**
WEB: www.edwards.com
SIC: 3845 Patient monitoring apparatus; pacemaker, cardiac
PA: Edwards Lifesciences Corp
1 Edwards Way
Irvine CA 92614
949 250-2500

(P-11222)
EXAM ROOM SUPPLY LLC
2419 Hrbour Blvd Unit 126, Ventura (93001)
PHONE..................805 298-3631
Charles Solomon, *Mng Member*
M Wash, *Mng Member*
EMP: 15 EST: 2016
SALES (est): 877.6K **Privately Held**
SIC: 3845 3841 5047 5999 Electromedical apparatus; diagnostic apparatus, medical; medical & hospital equipment; medical apparatus & supplies

(P-11223)
GIVEN IMAGING LOS ANGELES LLC
5860 Uplander Way, Culver City (90230-6608)
PHONE..................310 641-8492
Tom Parks PHD, *President*
Ron McIntyre, *CFO*
Eric Finkelman, *Vice Pres*
Truc Le, *Engineer*
Jeffrey Sawyer, *Marketing Staff*
◆ EMP: 175 EST: 2003
SALES (est): 31.1MM **Privately Held**
WEB: www.givenimaging.com
SIC: 3845 Electromedical equipment
PA: Given Imaging Ltd.
2 Hacarmel
Yokneam Illit

(P-11224)
INBODY CO LTD
13850 Cerritos Corprt Dr, Cerritos (90703-2467)
PHONE..................323 932-6503
Mary Nakamura, *District Mgr*
Alec Waheed, *District Mgr*
Dan Park, *Natl Sales Mgr*
Jeff Kim, *Marketing Staff*
Alexander Golubiewski, *Legal Staff*
EMP: 26
SALES (est): 5.3MM **Privately Held**
WEB: www.inbodyusa.com
SIC: 3845 Electromedical equipment

(P-11225)
JOHNSON JHNSON SRGCAL VSION IN (HQ)
Also Called: Johnson & Johnson Vision
1700 E Saint Andrew Pl, Santa Ana (92705-4933)
P.O. Box 25929 (92799-5929)
PHONE..................714 247-8200
Thomas Frinzi, *President*
Victor Chang, *President*
Wayne Markowitz, *Vice Pres*
Catherine Mazzacco, *Vice Pres*
Vince Scullin, *Vice Pres*
▲ EMP: 300 EST: 2001
SALES (est): 1.2B
SALES (corp-wide): 82.5B **Publicly Held**
WEB: www.jnjvisionpro.com
SIC: 3845 3841 Laser systems & equipment, medical; ophthalmic instruments & apparatus

PA: Johnson & Johnson
1 Johnson And Johnson Plz
New Brunswick NJ 08933
732 524-0400

(P-11226)
MASIMO CORPORATION
9600 Jeronimo Rd, Irvine (92618-2024)
PHONE..................949 297-7000
Joe Kiani, *Branch Mgr*
EMP: 50 **Publicly Held**
WEB: www.masimo.com
SIC: 3845 Electromedical equipment
PA: Masimo Corporation
52 Discovery
Irvine CA 92618

(P-11227)
MASIMO CORPORATION
40 Parker, Irvine (92618-1604)
PHONE..................949 297-7000
Joe Kiani, *Branch Mgr*
Bilal Muhsin, *Exec VP*
Vaughn Eldstrom, *Vice Pres*
Abelson Matthew, *Vice Pres*
Gordon Richman, *Vice Pres*
EMP: 50 **Publicly Held**
WEB: www.masimo.com
SIC: 3845 Electromedical equipment
PA: Masimo Corporation
52 Discovery
Irvine CA 92618

(P-11228)
MASIMO CORPORATION (PA)
52 Discovery, Irvine (92618-3105)
PHONE..................949 297-7000
Joe Kiani, *Ch of Bd*
Bilal Muhsin, *COO*
Micah Young, *CFO*
Tao Levy, *Exec VP*
Tom McClenahan, *Exec VP*
▲ EMP: 350 EST: 1989
SQ FT: 314,400
SALES (est): 1.1B **Publicly Held**
WEB: www.masimo.com
SIC: 3845 Patient monitoring apparatus; phonocardiographs

(P-11229)
MEDIVISION INC
Also Called: Medivision Optics
4883 E La Palma Ave # 503, Anaheim (92807-1957)
PHONE..................714 563-2772
Kevin May, *President*
EMP: 15 EST: 1994
SQ FT: 6,000
SALES (est): 2.7MM **Publicly Held**
WEB: www.medivisionusa.com
SIC: 3845 7699 5047 Endoscopic equipment, electromedical; scientific equipment repair service; physician equipment & supplies
PA: Hca Healthcare, Inc.
1 Park Plz
Nashville TN 37203

(P-11230)
MEDTRONIC 3F THERAPEUTICS INC
1851 E Deere Ave, Santa Ana (92705-5720)
PHONE..................949 399-1675
Donna Saito, *Branch Mgr*
EMP: 216 **Privately Held**
WEB: www.medtronic.com
SIC: 3845 3842 3841 Electromedical equipment; surgical appliances & supplies; surgical & medical instruments
HQ: Medtronic 3f Therapeutics, Inc.
710 Medtronic Pkwy
Minneapolis MN 55432
763 514-4000

(P-11231)
NXT BIOMEDICAL LLC
5270 California Ave # 300, Irvine (92617-3231)
PHONE..................201 658-6455
Stanton Rowe, *CEO*
Dr Robert Schwartz, *Principal*
Steven Hochberg, *Mng Member*

EMP: 17 EST: 2019
SALES (est): 2.8MM **Privately Held**
WEB: www.nxtbiomedical.com
SIC: 3845 Electromedical apparatus

(P-11232)
OPTEK GROUP INC
23 Corporate Plaza Dr # 150, Newport Beach (92660-7911)
PHONE..................949 629-2558
Allan Hsieh, *President*
Perry Hsieh, *Admin Sec*
EMP: 15 EST: 2006
SQ FT: 3,000
SALES (est): 1.4MM **Privately Held**
SIC: 3845 5084 Electromedical equipment; chemical process equipment

(P-11233)
PACESETTER INC
13150 Telfair Ave, Sylmar (91342-3573)
PHONE..................818 493-2715
Ignacio Machuca, *Branch Mgr*
Robb Gosling, *Vice Pres*
Lisa Servin, *Training Spec*
Evelyn Villalpando, *Clerk*
▲ EMP: 212
SALES (corp-wide): 34.6B **Publicly Held**
SIC: 3845 Defibrillator
HQ: Pacesetter, Inc.
15900 Valley View Ct
Sylmar CA 91342

(P-11234)
PACESETTER INC (DH)
Also Called: Ventritex
15900 Valley View Ct, Sylmar (91342-3585)
P.O. Box 9221 (91392-9221)
PHONE..................818 362-6822
Eric S Fain, *CEO*
Ronald A Matricaria, *President*
Dan Starks, *Bd of Directors*
Jorge Amely-Velez, *Senior Engr*
Bryan Brust, *Sales Staff*
▲ EMP: 725 EST: 1994
SALES (est): 398MM
SALES (corp-wide): 34.6B **Publicly Held**
WEB: www.cardiovascular.abbott
SIC: 3845 Defibrillator
HQ: St. Jude Medical, Inc.
1 Saint Jude Medical Dr
Saint Paul MN 55117
651 756-2000

(P-11235)
PACESETTER INC
4946 Florence Ave, Bell (90201-4319)
PHONE..................323 773-0591
Rosa Martinez, *Branch Mgr*
Suresh Pichumani, *Administration*
Khulood Cotta, *Gnrl Med Prac*
EMP: 212
SALES (corp-wide): 34.6B **Publicly Held**
SIC: 3845 Electromedical equipment
HQ: Pacesetter, Inc.
15900 Valley View Ct
Sylmar CA 91342

(P-11236)
R & D NOVA INC
833 Marlborough Ave 200, Riverside (92507-2133)
PHONE..................951 781-7332
Scott Snyder, *President*
Martin Clajus, *General Mgr*
Kevin Pham, *Engineer*
Elizabeth Meyer, *Accounting Mgr*
EMP: 15 EST: 1984
SQ FT: 4,000
SALES (est): 2.9MM
SALES (corp-wide): 14.2MM **Privately Held**
WEB: www.kromek.com
SIC: 3845 3812 Magnetic resonance imaging device, nuclear; search & detection systems & instruments
PA: Kromek Group Plc
Thomas Wright Way
Stockton-On-Tees
174 062-6050

(P-11237)
RESHAPE WEIGHTLOSS INC (HQ)
1001 Calle Amanecer, San Clemente (92673-6260)
PHONE..................949 429-6680
Barton P Bandy, *President*
Thomas Stankovich, *CFO*
Brendan O 'connell, *Vice Pres*
EMP: 30 EST: 2002
SQ FT: 14,479
SALES (est): 11.3MM
SALES (corp-wide): 1.5MM **Publicly Held**
WEB: www.reshapelifesciences.com
SIC: 3845 Electromedical equipment
PA: Reshape Lifesciences Inc.
5421 Avd Encinas Ste F
Carlsbad CA 92008
760 795-6558

(P-11238)
STRAND PRODUCTS INC (PA)
2233 Knoll Dr, Ventura (93003-7398)
P.O. Box 4610, Santa Barbara (93140-4610)
PHONE..................300 343-7985
Wesley Prunckle, *CEO*
James Wilson, *President*
John Hottinger, *Vice Pres*
Susana Loewe, *Vice Pres*
Hamahito Hokyo, *Engineer*
▲ EMP: 39 EST: 1972
SQ FT: 6,000
SALES (est): 5MM **Privately Held**
WEB: www.strandproducts.com
SIC: 3845 5063 Ultrasonic scanning devices, medical; wire & cable

(P-11239)
SYNERON INC (DH)
Also Called: Syneron Candela
3 Goodyear Ste A, Irvine (92618-2050)
PHONE..................866 259-6661
Shimon Eckhouse, *Ch of Bd*
Doron Gerstel, *President*
Shimon Eckhouse, *CEO*
Asaf Alperovitz, *CFO*
Fabian Tenenbaum, *CFO*
EMP: 138 EST: 2000
SALES (est): 102.5MM **Privately Held**
WEB: www.candelamedical.com
SIC: 3845 Laser systems & equipment, medical

(P-11240)
TAE LIFE SCIENCES US LLC (HQ)
19641 Da Vinci, Foothill Ranch (92610-2603)
PHONE..................949 830-2117
Bruce Bauer, *Mng Member*
Rob Hill,
Kendall Morrison,
Anna Theriault,
Sheri Langerman, *Director*
◆ EMP: 24 EST: 2017
SALES (est): 5.2MM
SALES (corp-wide): 54MM **Privately Held**
WEB: www.taelifesciences.com
SIC: 3845 2834 Laser systems & equipment, medical; pharmaceutical preparations
PA: Tae Technologies, Inc.
19631 Pauling
Foothill Ranch CA 92610
949 830-2117

(P-11241)
TRI-STAR TECHNOLOGIES INC
1111 E El Segundo Blvd, E. Segundo (90245-4202)
PHONE..................310 567-9243
Alex Kerner, *President*
EMP: 13 EST: 1985
SQ FT: 80,000
SALES (est): 4.4MM
SALES (corp-wide): 4.2B **Publicly Held**
WEB: www.tri-star-technologies.com
SIC: 3845 2836 3542 Laser systems & equipment, medical; plasmas; crimping machinery, metal
PA: Carlisle Companies Incorporated
16430 N Scottsdale Rd
Scottsdale AZ 85254
480 781-5000

▲ = Import ▼=Export
◆ =Import/Export

(P-11242)
TRIMEDYNE INC (PA)
519 N Smith Ave Ste 105, Corona
(92878-4315)
PHONE.................................949 951-3800
Glenn D Yeik, *President*
Jeffrey S Radner, *Corp Secy*
L Dean Crawford, *Vice Pres*
Glenn Yeik, *Branch Mgr*
Mary Isun, *Human Res Mgr*
EMP: 17 **EST:** 1980
SQ FT: 9,215
SALES (est): 5.3MM **Publicly Held**
WEB: www.trimedyne.com
SIC: 3845 7352 Laser systems & equipment, medical; medical equipment rental

(P-11243)
VIVOMETRICS INC
16030 Ventura Blvd # 470, Encino
(91436-2731)
PHONE.................................805 667-2225
Howard R Baker, *President*
EMP: 17 **EST:** 1999
SQ FT: 8,220
SALES (est): 563K **Privately Held**
SIC: 3845 3842 Patient monitoring apparatus; surgical appliances & supplies

---

3851 Ophthalmic Goods

(P-11244)
ADVANCED VISION SCIENCE INC
5743 Thornwood Dr, Goleta (93117-3801)
PHONE.................................805 683-3851
Khalid Mentak, *Ch of Bd*
Mike Lee, *IT/INT Sup*
Karen Krebaum, *Marketing Staff*
Alan Matthews, *Research Analys*
Gail Lorencz, *Manager*
EMP: 40 **EST:** 1976
SQ FT: 30,000
SALES (est): 9.2MM **Privately Held**
WEB: www.advancedvisionscience.com
SIC: 3851 3841 8011 Intraocular lenses; surgical & medical instruments; offices & clinics of medical doctors
PA: Santen Pharmaceutical Co., Ltd.
4-20, Ofukacho, Kita-Ku
Osaka OSK 530-0

(P-11245)
BARTON PERREIRA LLC
459 Wald, Irvine (92618-4639)
PHONE.................................949 305-5360
William G Barton,
Robert Fiddler, *CIO*
Patty Jo L Perreira,
Patty L Perreira,
▲ **EMP:** 25 **EST:** 2006
SALES (est): 4.2MM **Privately Held**
WEB: www.bartonperreira.com
SIC: 3851 Protective eyeware

(P-11246)
BAUSCH & LOMB INCORPORATED
15273 Alton Pkwy Ste 100, Irvine
(92618-2609)
PHONE.................................949 788-6000
Ron Zarella, *Branch Mgr*
Joe Distefano, *Exec Dir*
Michele Dougherty, *Admin Asst*
Nancy Fehrman, *CIO*
Debbie Kremer, *Info Tech Mgr*
EMP: 200
SALES (corp-wide): 8.6B **Privately Held**
WEB: www.bausch.com
SIC: 3851 Ophthalmic goods
HQ: Bausch & Lomb Incorporated
400 Somerset Corp Blvd
Bridgewater NJ 08807
585 338-6000

(P-11247)
CONTEX INC
Also Called: Contex Inc Contact Lenses
4505 Van Nuys Blvd, Van Nuys
(91403-2914)
PHONE.................................818 788-5836
Nick Stoyan, *President*
Ann Stoyan, *Vice Pres*

Gary Stoyan, *Vice Pres*
Glenn Stoyan, *Comp Tech*
Don Cando, *Consultant*
EMP: 16 **EST:** 1963
SQ FT: 5,000
SALES (est): 1.2MM **Privately Held**
WEB: www.oklens.com
SIC: 3851 8011 Contact lenses; offices & clinics of medical doctors

(P-11248)
DITA INC (PA)
Also Called: Dita Eyewear
1787 Pomona Rd, Corona (92878-4395)
PHONE.................................949 599-2700
Sukhmeet Dhillon, *President*
Shahid Ghani, *CFO*
Jennifer Bradley, *Vice Pres*
Ken Lockwood, *General Mgr*
Ovid Rijfkogel, *Professor*
▲ **EMP:** 21 **EST:** 1995
SQ FT: 3,000
SALES (est): 8.6MM **Privately Held**
WEB: www.dita.com
SIC: 3851 5995 Ophthalmic goods; optical goods stores

(P-11249)
DRAGON ALLIANCE INC
971 Calle Amanecer, San Clemente
(92673-4228)
PHONE.................................760 931-4900
William H Howard, *President*
Ryan Howard, *Admin Sec*
Westley Grant, *Sales Staff*
▲ **EMP:** 76 **EST:** 1993
SQ FT: 3,500
SALES (est): 21.5MM
SALES (corp-wide): 1.8B **Privately Held**
WEB: www.dragonalliance.com
SIC: 3851 Glasses, sun or glare
HQ: Marchon Eyewear, Inc.
201 Old Country Rd
Melville NY 11747
631 755-2020

(P-11250)
ELECTRIC VISUAL EVOLUTION LLC (PA)
950 Calle Amanecer # 101, San Clemente
(92673-4203)
PHONE.................................949 940-9125
Eric Crane, *CEO*
Steve Hurst, *VP Opers*
Derek Bradley, *Opers Staff*
Zachary Rierson, *Manager*
◆ **EMP:** 28 **EST:** 1999
SQ FT: 2,000
SALES (est): 5.3MM **Privately Held**
WEB: www.electriccalifornia.com
SIC: 3851 5094 5136 Glasses, sun or glare; watchcases; apparel belts; men's & boys'

(P-11251)
EXPRESS LENS LAB INC
17150 Newhope St Ste 305, Fountain Valley (92708-4251)
PHONE.................................714 545-1024
Brian Goldstone, *President*
EMP: 16 **EST:** 1993
SQ FT: 5,000
SALES (est): 1.2MM **Privately Held**
WEB: www.expresslenslab.com
SIC: 3851 8011 5049 Ophthalmic goods; offices & clinics of medical doctors; optical goods

(P-11252)
EYEBRAIN MEDICAL INC (PA)
Also Called: Neurolenses
3188 Airway Ave Ste F, Costa Mesa
(92626-4652)
PHONE.................................949 339-5157
Corley Davis, *President*
Danny Perales, *COO*
Thomas J Chirillo, *Ch Credit Ofcr*
Matt Swartz, *Vice Pres*
Ron Balance, *Sales Staff*
▲ **EMP:** 13 **EST:** 2012
SALES (est): 2.6MM **Privately Held**
WEB: www.neurolenses.com
SIC: 3851 Eyeglasses, lenses & frames

(P-11253)
EYEONICS INC
Also Called: Bausch & Lomb Surgical Div
15273 Alton Pkwy Ste 100, Irvine
(92618-2609)
PHONE.................................949 788-6000
Joseph F Gordon, *CEO*
Daniel Stein, *COO*
Julie Cronin, *Admin Asst*
David Buchanan, *Manager*
Mark Gregory, *Manager*
EMP: 50 **EST:** 1998
SALES (est): 18MM
SALES (corp-wide): 8.6B **Privately Held**
WEB: www.bausch.com
SIC: 3851 Ophthalmic goods
HQ: Bausch & Lomb Incorporated
400 Somerset Corp Blvd
Bridgewater NJ 08807
585 338-6000

(P-11254)
KH9100 LLC
Also Called: Lab, The
3073 N California St, Burbank
(91504-2005)
PHONE.................................818 972-2580
Hye Won Kim,
Peter Wang, *Accountant*
EMP: 14 **EST:** 2016
SALES (est): 2MM **Privately Held**
SIC: 3851 Ophthalmic goods

(P-11255)
MEDENNIUM INC (PA)
9 Parker Ste 150, Irvine (92618-1691)
PHONE.................................949 789-9000
Jacob Feldman, *President*
James R Zullo, *CFO*
Loi Diep, *Manager*
EMP: 39 **EST:** 1998
SQ FT: 20,000
SALES (est): 5.5MM **Privately Held**
WEB: www.medennium.com
SIC: 3851 Intraocular lenses

(P-11256)
OAKLEY INC (DH)
1 Icon, Foothill Ranch (92610-3000)
PHONE.................................949 951-0991
Colin Baden, *President*
Jim Jannard, *Ch of Bd*
D Scott Olivet, *Ch of Bd*
Don Krause, *President*
Gianluca Tagliabue, *CFO*
◆ **EMP:** 900 **EST:** 1994
SQ FT: 550,000
SALES (est): 984MM
SALES (corp-wide): 1.7MM **Privately Held**
WEB: www.oakley.com
SIC: 3851 2339 3873 3143 Ophthalmic goods; women's & misses' outerwear; watches, clocks, watchcases & parts; men's footwear, except athletic; rubber & plastics footwear; women's & misses' blouses & shirts

(P-11257)
OAKLEY SALES CORP
1 Icon, Foothill Ranch (92610-3000)
PHONE.................................949 672-6925
Link Newcomb, *President*
Dane Howell, *Sales Mgr*
◆ **EMP:** 108 **EST:** 2001
SQ FT: 400,000
SALES (est): 9.5MM
SALES (corp-wide): 1.7MM **Privately Held**
WEB: www.oakley.com
SIC: 3851 Glasses, sun or glare
HQ: Oakley, Inc.
1 Icon
Foothill Ranch CA 92610
949 951-0991

(P-11258)
OASIS MEDICAL INC (PA)
510-528 S Vermont Ave, Glendora (91741)
P.O. Box 1137 (91740-1137)
PHONE.................................909 305-5400
Norman Delgado, *Ch of Bd*
Craig Delgado, *President*
Arlene Delgado, *Treasurer*
James Boore, *Regional Mgr*
Kevin Shamolian, *Engineer*

◆ **EMP:** 55 **EST:** 1987
SQ FT: 14,000
SALES (est): 14.7MM **Privately Held**
WEB: www.oasismedical.com
SIC: 3851 5048 Ophthalmic goods; ophthalmic goods

(P-11259)
OPHTHONIX INC
900 Glenneyre St, Laguna Beach
(92651-2707)
PHONE.................................760 842-5600
Stephen J Osbaldeston, *CEO*
Jim Bergmark, *Finance Dir*
▲ **EMP:** 21 **EST:** 2000
SQ FT: 50,000
SALES (est): 2.2MM **Privately Held**
WEB: www.ophthonix.com
SIC: 3851 Eyes, glass & plastic

(P-11260)
PRESBIBIO LLC
Also Called: Presbia
36 Plateau, Aliso Viejo (92656-8026)
PHONE.................................949 502-7010
Todd Cooper,
Richard Fogarty, *CFO*
Vladimir Feingold, *Officer*
Erentia Gillmer, *Vice Pres*
Nela Gonzales, *Vice Pres*
EMP: 45 **EST:** 2008
SALES (est): 6.2MM **Privately Held**
SIC: 3851 Frames, lenses & parts, eyeglass & spectacle

(P-11261)
RXSIGHT INC (PA)
100 Columbia Ste 120, Aliso Viejo
(92656-4114)
PHONE.................................949 521-7830
Ron Kurtz, *President*
J Andy Corley, *Ch of Bd*
Ilya Goldshleger, *COO*
Shelley Thunen, *CFO*
Eric Weinberg, *Ch Credit Ofcr*
▼ **EMP:** 168 **EST:** 1997
SQ FT: 109,822
SALES (est): 14.6MM **Publicly Held**
WEB: www.rxsight.com
SIC: 3851 Ophthalmic goods

(P-11262)
SPORTIFEYE OPTICS INC
1854 Business Center Dr, Duarte
(91010-2901)
PHONE.................................626 521-5600
Tom Pfeiffer, *CEO*
Carlos Guevara, *Regl Sales Mgr*
EMP: 20 **EST:** 2017
SALES (est): 1.2MM **Privately Held**
WEB: www.sportifeye.com
SIC: 3851 Frames, lenses & parts, eyeglass & spectacle

(P-11263)
STAAR SURGICAL COMPANY (PA)
25651 Atlantic Ocean Dr A1, Lake Forest
(92630-8835)
PHONE.................................626 303-7902
Caren Mason, *President*
Louis E Silverman, *Ch of Bd*
Deborah Andrews, *CFO*
Patrick F Williams, *CFO*
Samuel Gesten,
▲ **EMP:** 344 **EST:** 1982
SALES: 163.4MM **Publicly Held**
WEB: www.staar.com
SIC: 3851 Ophthalmic goods

(P-11264)
STAAR SURGICAL COMPANY
15102 Redhiiill Ave, Tustin (92780)
PHONE.................................626 303-7902
Keith Holiday, *Branch Mgr*
EMP: 16
SALES (corp-wide): 163.4MM **Publicly Held**
WEB: www.staar.com
SIC: 3851 Ophthalmic goods
PA: Staar Surgical Company
25651 Atlantic Ocean Dr A1
Lake Forest CA 92630
626 303-7902

PRODUCTS & SVCS

(P-11265)
TEKIA INC
17 Hammond Ste 414, Irvine (92618-1635)
PHONE.................................949 699-1300
Gene Currie, *President*
Larry Blake, *VP Engrg*
EMP: 20 EST: 1995
SQ FT: 5,000
SALES (est): 2.9MM **Privately Held**
WEB: www.tekia.com
SIC: 3851 8742 Intraocular lenses; hospital & health services consultant

(P-11266)
YOUNGER MFG CO (PA)
Also Called: Younger Optics
2925 California St, Torrance (90503-3914)
PHONE.................................310 783-1533
Joseph David Rips, *CEO*
Tom Balch, *President*
Roshan Seresinhe, *CFO*
Nancy Yamasaki, *Admin Sec*
◆ **EMP: 280 EST:** 1955
SQ FT: 130,000
SALES (est): 104.1MM **Privately Held**
WEB: www.youngeroptics.com
SIC: 3851 Lenses, ophthalmic

3861 Photographic Eqpt & Splys

(P-11267)
ANSCHUTZ FILM GROUP LLC (HQ)
1888 Century Park E # 1400, Los Angeles (90067-1718)
PHONE.................................310 887-1000
Michael Bostick, *CEO*
Szymon Lassak, *Executive Asst*
▲ **EMP: 30 EST:** 2004
SALES (est): 9.3MM **Privately Held**
WEB: www.walden.com
SIC: 3861 Motion picture film

(P-11268)
AVID TECHNOLOGY INC
14007 Runnymede St, Van Nuys (91405-2510)
PHONE.................................818 779-7860
EMP: 215
SALES (corp-wide): 677.9MM **Publicly Held**
SIC: 3861 Mfg Photographic Equipment/Supplies
PA: Avid Technology, Inc.
75 Network Dr
Burlington MA 01803
978 640-6789

(P-11269)
CDS CALIFORNIA LLC
3330 Chnga Blvd W Ste 200, Los Angeles (90068-1354)
PHONE.................................818 766-5000
Nicole Santiago, *COO*
Jed Unrot, *CTO*
EMP: 15 EST: 2012
SALES (est): 6.9MM **Privately Held**
WEB: www.epscineworks.com
SIC: 3861 Photographic equipment & supplies

(P-11270)
CHRISTIE DIGITAL SYSTEMS INC (HQ)
10550 Camden Dr, Cypress (90630-4600)
PHONE.................................714 236-8610
Rex Balz, *President*
Sean James, *Exec VP*
Lin Yu, *Vice Pres*
Clayton Brito, *General Mgr*
Dave Murison, *Software Dev*
EMP: 110 EST: 1999
SALES (est): 127.7MM **Privately Held**
WEB: www.christiedigital.com
SIC: 3861 6719 Projectors, still or motion picture, silent or sound; investment holding companies, except banks

(P-11271)
CLOVER IMAGING GROUP LLC
Also Called: Distribution Cente
315 Weakley St Bldg 3, Calexico (92231-9659)
PHONE.................................760 357-9277
EMP: 50
SALES (corp-wide): 173.6MM **Privately Held**
SIC: 3861 Printing equipment, photographic
PA: Clover Imaging Group, Llc
2700 W Higgins Rd Ste 100
Hoffman Estates IL 60169
866 734-6548

(P-11272)
COMPANY OF MOTION LLC
Also Called: Fluidstance
121 E Mason St Ste A, Santa Barbara (93101-1852)
PHONE.................................805 963-1996
Joel Heath, *Mng Member*
EMP: 15 EST: 2014
SALES (est): 2.8MM **Privately Held**
WEB: www.fluidstance.com
SIC: 3861 Motion picture film

(P-11273)
DJI TECHNOLOGY INC
17301 Edwards Rd, Cerritos (90703-2427)
PHONE.................................818 235-0789
Jie Shen, *CEO*
Ferdinand Wolf, *Creative Dir*
Siddharth Utgikar, *Software Dev*
Andre Ortega, *Technician*
Javier Caina, *Technical Staff*
EMP: 25 EST: 2015
SALES (est): 3.3MM **Privately Held**
WEB: www.dji.com
SIC: 3861 Aerial cameras; cameras & related equipment

(P-11274)
DOREMI CINEMA LLC
1020 Chestnut St, Burbank (91506-1623)
PHONE.................................818 562-1101
Camille Rizko,
Safar Ghazal,
Emil Rizko,
EMP: 18 EST: 2005
SQ FT: 20,000
SALES (est): 253.1K **Privately Held**
SIC: 3861 Motion picture apparatus & equipment

(P-11275)
ELITE SCREENS INC
12282 Knott St, Garden Grove (92841-2825)
PHONE.................................877 511-1211
Jeff Chen, *President*
Henry Yoh, *CFO*
Molly Draper, *Sales Staff*
Johnny Juarez, *Sales Staff*
Jaime Luna, *Cust Mgr*
◆ **EMP: 30 EST:** 2004
SALES (est): 7.5MM **Privately Held**
WEB: www.elitescreens.com
SIC: 3861 Photographic equipment & supplies

(P-11276)
FREESTYLE FILMWORKS LLC
1518 Talmadge St, Los Angeles (90027-1535)
PHONE.................................818 660-2888
Michael Barnett, *Mng Member*
Gregory Barnett, *Principal*
EMP: 15 EST: 2010
SALES (est): 1.2MM **Privately Held**
WEB: www.freestylephoto.biz
SIC: 3861 Photographic equipment & supplies

(P-11277)
HF GROUP INC (PA)
Also Called: Houston Fearless 76
203 W Artesia Blvd, Compton (90220-5517)
PHONE.................................310 605-0755
Myung S Lee, *Ch of Bd*
James H Lee, *President*
Virginia C Clark, *CFO*
Virginia Clark, *Officer*
Gary Colby, *Vice Pres*

EMP: 40 EST: 1929
SQ FT: 45,000
SALES (est): 16.6MM **Privately Held**
WEB: www.hf76.com
SIC: 3861 Processing equipment, photographic; cameras, still & motion picture (all types); sensitized film, cloth & paper

(P-11278)
HITI DIGITAL AMERICA INC
20803 Valley Blvd Ste 110, Walnut (91789-2532)
PHONE.................................909 594-0099
Kuo-Hua Liang, *CEO*
▲ **EMP: 22 EST:** 2008
SALES (est): 1.4MM **Privately Held**
WEB: www.hiti.com
SIC: 3861 7384 Printing equipment, photographic; photographic services

(P-11279)
HOLLYWOOD FILM COMPANY
Also Called: Hav Holdings & Subsidiaries
9265 Borden Ave, Sun Valley (91352-2034)
PHONE.................................818 683-1130
Vincent Carabello, *President*
Antonia L Carabello, *Director*
◆ **EMP: 19 EST:** 1937
SQ FT: 79,000
SALES (est): 958.5K **Privately Held**
WEB: www.tommylentsch.com
SIC: 3861 7819 Editing equipment, motion picture: viewers, splicers, etc.; services allied to motion pictures

(P-11280)
JONDO LTD (PA)
22700 Savi Ranch Pkwy, Yorba Linda (92887-4608)
PHONE.................................714 279-2300
John Stuart DOE, *CEO*
Maryann DOE, *Admin Sec*
Elayne Rogers, *Admin Asst*
Amy Barnes, *Accounting Mgr*
Amy Clark, *Accounting Mgr*
EMP: 60 EST: 1989
SQ FT: 50,000
SALES (est): 8MM **Privately Held**
WEB: www.jondo.com
SIC: 3861 Photographic equipment & supplies

(P-11281)
KALTEC ELECTRONICS INC (PA)
Also Called: Kaltec Enterprises
16220 Bloomfield Ave, Cerritos (90703-2113)
PHONE.................................813 888-9555
Hee K Lee, *CEO*
Wade Thomas, *COO*
Roy Nilsen, *General Mgr*
Raj Ramsook, *IT Specialist*
Chris Hwang, *Technical Staff*
▲ **EMP: 14 EST:** 1987
SQ FT: 13,000
SALES (est): 52MM **Privately Held**
WEB: www.digital-watchdog.com
SIC: 3861 Cameras & related equipment

(P-11282)
LUCARE CORPORATION
Also Called: Outex
1292 Journeys End Dr, La Canada Flintridge (91011-1709)
PHONE.................................818 583-7731
Desouza, *President*
EMP: 15 EST: 2010
SALES (est): 502.6K **Privately Held**
SIC: 3861 Cameras & related equipment

(P-11283)
MATTHEWS STUDIO EQUIPMENT INC
Also Called: M S E
15148 Bledsoe St, Sylmar (91342-3807)
PHONE.................................818 843-6715
Edward Phillips III, *President*
Rick Hansen, *Sales Staff*
▲ **EMP: 49 EST:** 1970
SALES (est): 1.3MM **Privately Held**
WEB: www.msegrip.com
SIC: 3861 Motion picture apparatus & equipment; stands, camera & projector; tripods, camera & projector

(P-11284)
MODERN STUDIO EQUIPMENT INC
16200 Stagg St, Van Nuys (91406-1715)
PHONE.................................818 764-8574
Seno Mousally, *President*
Rina Mousally, *Vice Pres*
Anoush Motto, *Executive*
Rosy Valencia, *Accounts Exec*
EMP: 19 EST: 1980
SALES (est): 4.1MM **Privately Held**
WEB: www.modernstudio.com
SIC: 3861 Motion picture apparatus & equipment

(P-11285)
MOVING IMAGE TECHNOLOGIES LLC
17760 Newhope St Ste B, Fountain Valley (92708-5442)
PHONE.................................714 751-7998
Glenn Sherman, *Mng Member*
Dan Hodgdon, *Technical Staff*
Brandon Shaffer, *Engineer*
Debra White, *Purchasing*
Joe Delgado,
▲ **EMP: 46 EST:** 2003
SQ FT: 18,000
SALES (est): 11MM **Privately Held**
WEB: www.movingimagetech.com
SIC: 3861 Motion picture apparatus & equipment

(P-11286)
MPO VIDEOTRONICS INC (PA)
5069 Maureen Ln, Moorpark (93021-7148)
PHONE.................................805 499-8513
Larry Kaiser, *President*
Julius Barron, *Vice Pres*
Don Gaston, *Director*
EMP: 75 EST: 1947
SALES (est): 9.6MM **Privately Held**
WEB: www.mpo-video.com
SIC: 3861 5065 7819 3823 Motion picture apparatus & equipment; video equipment, electronic; equipment rental, motion picture; industrial instrmnts msrmnt display/control process variable; household audio & video equipment

(P-11287)
MVM PRODUCTS LLC
946 Calle Amanecer Ste E, San Clemente (92673-6221)
P.O. Box 73155 (92673-0105)
PHONE.................................949 366-1470
Daniel W Loyer,
Steve L Boden,
EMP: 17 EST: 1995
SQ FT: 76,000
SALES (est): 1.1MM **Privately Held**
WEB: www.mvm-products.com
SIC: 3861 Toners, prepared photographic (not made in chemical plants)

(P-11288)
PANAVISION INTERNATIONAL LP (HQ)
6101 Variel Ave, Woodland Hills (91367-3722)
P.O. Box 4360 (91365-4360)
PHONE.................................818 316-1080
Robert Beitcher, *President*
Ross Landfbuam, *CFO*
▲ **EMP: 380 EST:** 1991
SQ FT: 150,000
SALES (est): 104.6MM **Privately Held**
WEB: www.panavision.com
SIC: 3861 Cameras & related equipment

(P-11289)
PHOTRONICS INC (DH)
Also Called: Photronics California
2428 N Ontario St, Burbank (91504-3119)
PHONE.................................203 740-5653
James Mac Donald Jr, *Ch of Bd*
Constantine Maristos, *CEO*
Deborah Marshlick, *Technician*
Steve Mahoney, *Production*
EMP: 280 EST: 1970
SQ FT: 30,000

SALES (est): 81.7MM
SALES (corp-wide): 609.6MM **Publicly Held**
WEB: www.photronics.com
SIC: 3861 Photographic equipment & supplies

(P-11290)
REDCOM LLC (HQ)
Also Called: Red Digital Cinema Camera Co
94 Icon, Foothill Ranch (92610-3000)
PHONE.....................949 404-4084
James H Jannard, *CEO*
Kent Lane, *COO*
Vince Hassel, *CFO*
Leo Lin, *CFO*
Kevin Cabrera, *Officer*
▲ **EMP:** 490 **EST:** 1999
SALES (est): 143.2MM
SALES (corp-wide): 2MM **Privately Held**
WEB: www.red.com
SIC: 3861 Motion picture apparatus & equipment
PA: Red Europe Limited
        Pinewood Road
        Iver BUCKS SL0 0
        175 378-5454

(P-11291)
RICOH ELECTRONICS INC
2310 Redhill Ave, Santa Ana (92705-5538)
PHONE.....................714 566-6079
Tino Fauatea, *Technician*
Victor Garsot, *Technician*
Eiko Risch, *Manager*
EMP: 250 **Privately Held**
WEB: www.rei.ricoh.com
SIC: 3861 3695 Photocopy machines; toners, prepared photographic (not made in chemical plants); magnetic & optical recording media
HQ: Ricoh Electronics, Inc.
        1125 Hurricane Shoals Rd
        Lawrenceville GA 30043
        714 566-2500

(P-11292)
STEWART FILMSCREEN CORP (PA)
1161 Sepulveda Blvd, Torrance (90502-2797)
PHONE.....................310 326-1422
Grant W Stewart, *CEO*
Patrick H Stewart, *CEO*
Tom Stewart, *CFO*
Simeon Petrov, *Exec VP*
Donald R Stewart, *Vice Pres*
◆ **EMP:** 160 **EST:** 1947
SQ FT: 43,000
SALES (est): 30.3MM **Privately Held**
WEB: www.stewartfilmscreen.com
SIC: 3861 Screens, projection

(P-11293)
TECHNICAL FILM SYSTEMS INC
Also Called: T F S
4725 Calle Quetzal Ste A, Camarillo (93012-8428)
PHONE.....................805 384-9470
Manfred G Michelson, *President*
Markus Michelson, *Vice Pres*
EMP: 14 **EST:** 1984
SALES (est): 1MM **Privately Held**
WEB: www.techfilmsystems.com
SIC: 3861 Printing equipment, photographic

(P-11294)
TETRACAM INC
21601 Devonshire St # 310, Chatsworth (91311-8423)
PHONE.....................818 718-2119
George Ismael, *President*
John Edling, *COO*
Dean Shen, *Vice Pres*
Steve Heinold, *Admin Sec*
Richard Barnes, *CIO*
▲ **EMP:** 16 **EST:** 2000
SQ FT: 4,200
SALES (est): 1.9MM **Privately Held**
WEB: www.tetracam.com
SIC: 3861 Microfilm equipment: cameras, projectors, readers, etc.

(P-11295)
THERMAPRINT CORP
11 Autry Ste B, Irvine (92618-2766)
PHONE.....................949 583-0800
Natalie J Hochner, *President*
Gary Larsen, *CEO*
▲ **EMP:** 25 **EST:** 1985
SQ FT: 14,500
SALES (est): 2.7MM **Privately Held**
WEB: www.thermaprint.com
SIC: 3861 3443 3585 2759 Graphic arts plates, sensitized; fabricated plate work (boiler shop); parts for heating, cooling & refrigerating equipment; screen printing

(P-11296)
UNITY SALES INTERNATIONAL INC
Also Called: Unity Digital
2950 Airway Ave Ste A12, Costa Mesa (92626-6019)
PHONE.....................714 800-1700
Timothy McCanna, *President*
EMP: 28 **EST:** 1998
SQ FT: 4,000
SALES (est): 655.9K **Privately Held**
WEB: www.unitydigital.com
SIC: 3861 Cameras & related equipment

(P-11297)
VITA-RAY PRODUCTIONS LLC
1600 Rosecrans Ave, Manhattan Beach (90266-3708)
PHONE.....................310 220-8963
EMP: 15 **EST:** 2008
SALES (est): 1.1MM
SALES (corp-wide): 65.3B **Publicly Held**
WEB: www.marvel.com
SIC: 3861 Motion picture film
HQ: Marvel Entertainment, Llc
        1290 Avenue Of The Americ
        New York NY 10104
        212 576-4000

(P-11298)
VITEK INDUS VIDEO PDTS INC
28492 Constellation Rd, Valencia (91355-5081)
PHONE.....................661 294-8043
Greg Bier, *CEO*
Vic Korhonian, *CEO*
▲ **EMP:** 20 **EST:** 1998
SQ FT: 9,200
SALES (est): 4MM **Privately Held**
WEB: www.vitekcctv.com
SIC: 3861 5099 Cameras & related equipment; video & audio equipment

(P-11299)
VONNIC INC
16610 Gale Ave, City of Industry (91745-1801)
PHONE.....................626 964-2345
Kim Por Lin, *CEO*
Kitty Lam, *CFO*
▲ **EMP:** 23 **EST:** 2010
SALES (est): 7.8MM **Privately Held**
WEB: www.vonnic.com
SIC: 3861 Cameras & related equipment

3873 Watch & Clock Devices & Parts

(P-11300)
AMG EMPLOYEE MANAGEMENT INC
Also Called: Time Masters
3235 N San Fernando Rd 1d, Los Angeles (90065-1443)
PHONE.....................323 254-7448
Tigran Galstyan, *President*
Matt Livingston, *Technical Staff*
▲ **EMP:** 17 **EST:** 1998
SALES (est): 2.9MM **Privately Held**
WEB: www.time-masters.com
SIC: 3873 7371 7372 3579 Timers for industrial use, clockwork mechanism only; computer software development; business oriented computer software; time clocks & time recording devices

(P-11301)
CHASE-DURER LTD (PA)
8455 Ftn Ave Unit 515, West Hollywood (90069)
PHONE.....................310 550-7280
Brandon Chase, *President*
Fred Goode, *Manager*
▲ **EMP:** 17 **EST:** 1997
SALES (est): 1.2MM **Privately Held**
WEB: www.chase-durer.com
SIC: 3873 Watches, clocks, watchcases & parts

(P-11302)
MOD-ELECTRONICS INC
Also Called: Ese
142 Sierra St, El Segundo (90245-4117)
PHONE.....................310 322-2136
William Kaiser, *President*
Brian Way, *Vice Pres*
Monica Trotter, *Marketing Staff*
Fernando Vallin, *Sales Staff*
▲ **EMP:** 26 **EST:** 1971
SQ FT: 7,500
SALES (est): 4.5MM **Privately Held**
WEB: www.mod-electronics.mfgpages.com
SIC: 3873 3663 3651 3625 Clocks, assembly of; radio & TV communications equipment; household audio & video equipment; relays & industrial controls

(P-11303)
SUNBURST PRODUCTS INC
Also Called: Freestyle
1570 Corporate Dr Ste F, Costa Mesa (92626-1428)
PHONE.....................949 722-0158
EMP: 40
SQ FT: 12,000
SALES (est): 3.3MM
SALES (corp-wide): 98.7K **Privately Held**
WEB: www.freestyleusa.com
SIC: 3873 3172 3845 Mfg Watches/Clocks/Parts Mfg Personal Leather Goods Mfg Electromedical Equipment
HQ: Awc Liquidating Co.
        1407 Broadway Rm 400
        New York NY 10018
        212 221-1177

(P-11304)
TAKANE USA INC (HQ)
369 Van Ness Way Ste 715, Torrance (90501-6249)
PHONE.....................310 212-1411
Kenji Hanaoka, *President*
▲ **EMP:** 101 **EST:** 1980
SQ FT: 47,000
SALES (est): 12.2MM **Privately Held**
WEB: www.takane.co.jp
SIC: 3873 Movements, watch or clock

3911 Jewelry: Precious Metal

(P-11305)
ACE HOLDINGS INC
650 S Hill St Ste 510, Los Angeles (90014-1753)
PHONE.....................213 972-2100
John Arzoian, *CEO*
Linda Fass, *President*
EMP: 14 **EST:** 1977
SQ FT: 65,000
SALES (est): 1.1MM **Privately Held**
SIC: 3911 Jewelry, precious metal

(P-11306)
ADRIENNE DESIGNS LLC
Also Called: A/D Enterprises
17150 Newhope St Ste 514, Fountain Valley (92708-4253)
PHONE.....................714 558-1209
Clifford E Johnston, *President*
Mike Carr, *Controller*
▲ **EMP:** 13 **EST:** 1976
SQ FT: 10,000
SALES (est): 549.8K **Privately Held**
WEB: www.adgoldchain.com
SIC: 3911 Jewelry, precious metal

(P-11307)
ALEX VELVET INC
3334 Eagle Rock Blvd, Los Angeles (90065-2843)
PHONE.....................323 255-6900
Krikor Alexanian, *President*
Berj Alexanian, *CFO*
▲ **EMP:** 17 **EST:** 1986
SQ FT: 15,000
SALES (est): 1MM **Privately Held**
WEB: www.alexvelvetusa.com
SIC: 3911 7319 5046 Jewelry mountings & trimmings; display advertising service; store fixtures & display equipment

(P-11308)
ALLISON-KAUFMAN CO
7640 Haskell Ave, Van Nuys (91406-2005)
PHONE.....................818 373-5100
Bart Kaufman, *CEO*
Jay A Kaufman, *Vice Pres*
Scott Kaufman, *Vice Pres*
Jeremie Rothman, *Mktg Dir*
Jeff Glassman, *Regl Sales Mgr*
▲ **EMP:** 33 **EST:** 1946
SQ FT: 21,000
SALES (est): 2.7MM **Privately Held**
WEB: www.allisonkaufman.com
SIC: 3911 Jewelry, precious metal

(P-11309)
AMERICAS GOLD INC
Also Called: Americas Gold - Amrcas Damonds
650 S Hill St Ste 224, Los Angeles (90014-1769)
PHONE.....................213 688-4904
Rafi M Siddiqui, *President*
Samina Siddiqui, *Vice Pres*
Sami Siddiqui, *Manager*
EMP: 30 **EST:** 1999
SQ FT: 4,500
SALES (est): 11.9MM **Privately Held**
WEB: www.americasgold.com
SIC: 3911 Jewelry, precious metal

(P-11310)
AMINCO INTERNATIONAL USA INC
Also Called: California Premium Incentives
20571 Crescent Bay Dr, Lake Forest (92630-8825)
PHONE.....................949 457-3261
Ann Wu, *Exec Dir*
William Wu, *President*
Jessica Fehrenbach, *Graphic Designe*
Steve Ruiz, *Sales Mgr*
John Yarmoski, *Agent*
▲ **EMP:** 62 **EST:** 1978
SQ FT: 35,000
SALES (est): 10MM **Privately Held**
WEB: www.amincousa.com
SIC: 3911 5099 Jewelry, precious metal; brass goods

(P-11311)
ARTS ELEGANCE INC
154 W Bellevue Dr, Pasadena (91105-2504)
PHONE.....................626 793-4794
Arutiun Mikaelian, *President*
EMP: 45
SALES (corp-wide): 8.5MM **Privately Held**
SIC: 3911 Jewelry, precious metal
PA: Art's Elegance, Inc.
        739 E Walnut St Ste 200
        Pasadena CA 91101
        626 405-1522

(P-11312)
ASTOURIAN JEWELRY MFG INC
635 S Hill St Ste 407, Los Angeles (90014-1819)
PHONE.....................213 683-0436
Viken Astourian, *President*
▲ **EMP:** 13 **EST:** 1978
SQ FT: 1,200
SALES (est): 938.3K **Privately Held**
WEB: www.astourian.com
SIC: 3911 Jewelry, precious metal

(P-11313)
AVE JEWELRY INC
Also Called: Ave Jewelry Design Mfg
13127 Ebell St, North Hollywood
(91605-1006)
PHONE.................................213 488-0097
EMP: 15
SQ FT: 12,300
SALES (est): 1.3MM **Privately Held**
SIC: **3911** Mfg Precious Metal Jewelry

(P-11314)
EAR CHARMS INC
Also Called: Ear Gear
1855 Laguna Canyon Rd, Laguna Beach
(92651-1121)
P.O. Box 4289 (92652-4289)
PHONE.................................949 494-4147
Sandra Callisto, *President*
Mike Callisto, *Vice Pres*
George Reynolds, *Director*
EMP: 20 EST: 1979
SALES (est): 1.2MM **Privately Held**
WEB: www.earcharms.com
SIC: **3911** **5944** Earrings, precious metal;
jewelry, precious stones & precious met-
als

(P-11315)
ELBA JEWELRY INC
Also Called: Elba Company
910 N Amelia Ave, San Dimas
(91773-1401)
PHONE.................................909 394-5803
Edouard Bachoura, *President*
Nitania Pena, *Administration*
Richard Barnes, *Opers Staff*
▼ EMP: 19 EST: 1994
SQ FT: 10,000
SALES (est): 2.2MM **Privately Held**
SIC: **3911** Jewelry, precious metal

(P-11316)
FARSI JEWELRY MFG CO INC
631 Suth Olive St Ste 565, Los Angeles
(90014)
PHONE.................................213 624-0043
Yousef Eshaghzadeh, *President*
Masoud Eshaghzadeh, *Treasurer*
Saied Eshaghzadeh, *Admin Sec*
EMP: 15 EST: 1981
SALES (est): 2.1MM **Privately Held**
WEB: www.farsijewelrymfg.com
SIC: **3911** Jewelry, precious metal

(P-11317)
GIVING KEYS INC
836 Traction Ave, Los Angeles
(90013-1816)
PHONE.................................213 935-8791
Caitlin Crosby, *CEO*
Brit Gilmore, *President*
Derek Silva, *Finance*
▲ EMP: 28 EST: 2012
SQ FT: 8,000
SALES (est): 4MM **Privately Held**
WEB: www.thegivingkeys.com
SIC: **3911** Jewelry, precious metal

(P-11318)
GOLD STORE INC
2539 E Thousand Oaks Blvd, Thousand
Oaks (91362-3286)
PHONE.................................805 495-5464
Gary Morandi, *President*
Karen Morandi, *Corp Secy*
EMP: 16 EST: 1973
SQ FT: 2,800
SALES (est): 1.1MM **Privately Held**
WEB: www.goldstore60.com
SIC: **5944** **3911** Jewelry, precious stones
& precious metals; jewelry, precious metal

(P-11319)
KESMOR ASSOCIATES
Also Called: American Designs
610 S Broadway Ste 717, Los Angeles
(90014-1814)
PHONE.................................213 629-2300
Joseph Keshoyan, *President*
Hasmik Keshoyan, *Vice Pres*
EMP: 20 EST: 1985
SQ FT: 6,000
SALES (est): 1.4MM **Privately Held**
WEB: www.kesmorassociates.com
SIC: **3911** Jewelry, precious metal

(P-11320)
KOBI KATZ INC
Also Called: Baguette World
801 S Flower St Fl 3, Los Angeles
(90017-4617)
PHONE.................................213 689-9505
Kobi Katz, *President*
Eli Sandberg, *Treasurer*
Louise Salman
Manuel Valencia, *Accounts Exec*
EMP: 13 EST: 1981
SQ FT: 14,000
SALES (est): 1.1MM **Privately Held**
WEB: www.kobelli.com
SIC: **3911** **5094** Jewelry apparel; dia-
monds (gems)

(P-11321)
**LA GEM AND JEWELRY DESIGN
(PA)**
Also Called: La Rocks
659 S Broadway Fl 7, Los Angeles
(90014-2291)
PHONE.................................213 488-1290
Ashish Arora, *CEO*
Robert Hogeboom, *District Mgr*
Elsa Behney, *Admin Sec*
▲ EMP: 99 EST: 2002
SALES (est): 10.6MM **Privately Held**
WEB: www.la-rocks.com
SIC: **3911** Jewelry, precious metal;
jewelry

(P-11322)
LEONARD CRAFT CO LLC
3501 W Segerstrom Ave, Santa Ana
(92704-6449)
PHONE.................................714 549-0678
Stephen D Leonard, *Mng Member*
EMP: 95 EST: 2017
SALES (est): 5.9MM **Privately Held**
WEB: www.lisaleonard.com
SIC: **3911** **5947** Jewelry, precious metal;
gift shop

(P-11323)
M & G JEWELERS INC
10823 Edison Ct, Rancho Cucamonga
(91730-3868)
PHONE.................................909 989-2929
Juan Guevara, *President*
Michael Insalago, *Vice Pres*
Tom Nevin, *General Mgr*
Ryan Tigner, *VP Opers*
Tuan Phan, *Manager*
EMP: 68 EST: 1991
SQ FT: 8,432
SALES (est): 9.3MM **Privately Held**
WEB: www.myjewelryrepair.com
SIC: **5944** **3911** **7631** Jewelry, precious
stones & precious metals; jewelry, pre-
cious metal; watch repair; jewelry repair
services

(P-11324)
MALCOLM DEMILLE INC
650 S Frontage Rd, Nipomo (93446-9148)
PHONE.................................805 929-4353
Malcolm Demille, *President*
Janet Demille, *Vice Pres*
Phil Scorsone, *Purchasing*
Kirstin Ineich, *Marketing Staff*
EMP: 15 EST: 1989
SALES (est): 2.1MM **Privately Held**
WEB: www.mdemille.com
SIC: **3911** Jewelry mountings & trimmings

(P-11325)
**NATIONWIDE JEWELRY MFRS
INC**
Also Called: B & B Jewelry Mfg
631 S Olive St Ste 790, Los Angeles
(90014-3607)
PHONE.................................213 489-1215
Ben Behnam, *CEO*
Behrooz Behnam, *Vice Pres*
Parviz Behnam, *Vice Pres*
▲ EMP: 15 EST: 1980
SQ FT: 4,000
SALES (est): 1.5MM **Privately Held**
SIC: **3911** **5094** Jewelry, precious metal;
jewelry

(P-11326)
**NEW GOLD MANUFACTURING
INC**
2150 N Lincoln St, Burbank (91504-3337)
PHONE.................................818 847-1020
Mesrop Samvelian, *CEO*
Jennifer Aguilar, *Purchasing*
▲ EMP: 18 EST: 1999
SALES (est): 634.1K **Privately Held**
SIC: **3911** Jewelry, precious metal

(P-11327)
OBATAKE INC
Also Called: Lucy Ann
20309 Gramercy Pl Ste A, Torrance
(90501-1531)
PHONE.................................310 782-2730
Derrick Obatake, *President*
Jennifer Seiler, *Sales Executive*
EMP: 17 EST: 1992
SALES (est): 1.3MM **Privately Held**
SIC: **3911** **5084** Jewelry, precious metal;
industrial machinery & equipment

(P-11328)
RASTACLAT LLC
100 W Broadway Ste 3000, Long Beach
(90802-4467)
PHONE.................................424 287-0902
Daniel Kasidi Nyaggah, *CEO*
Joel Shaina, *Marketing Staff*
Jillian Leeman, *Sales Staff*
Chris Long, *Sales Staff*
EMP: 36 EST: 2010
SALES (est): 2.6MM **Privately Held**
WEB: www.rastaclat.com
SIC: **3911** Bracelets, precious metal

(P-11329)
ROBERTO MARTINEZ INC
1050 Calle Cordillera # 103, San Clemente
(92673-6240)
PHONE.................................800 257-6462
Roberto Martinez, *CEO*
Elsa Martinez-Phillips, *President*
▲ EMP: 15 EST: 1976
SQ FT: 6,000
SALES (est): 1MM **Privately Held**
WEB: www.robertomartinez.com
SIC: **3911** **5094** Jewelry apparel; jewelry

(P-11330)
SAGE GODDESS INC
21010 Figueroa St, Carson (90745-1937)
PHONE.................................650 733-6639
Athena I Perrakis, *CEO*
David Maeizlik, *COO*
Hannah Maxson, *Mktg Coord*
EMP: 42
SALES (est): 2.5MM **Privately Held**
WEB: www.sagegoddess.com
SIC: **3911** **5944** **5999** Jewelry apparel;
jewelry, precious stones & precious met-
als; perfumes & colognes

(P-11331)
TK AND COMPANY WATCHES
5827 W Pico Blvd, Los Angeles
(90019-3714)
PHONE.................................213 545-1971
EMP: 15
SALES (est): 656.6K **Privately Held**
SIC: **3911** Watch And Jewelry Manufactur-
ing And Sour

(P-11332)
US GOLD TRADING INC (PA)
117 E Providencia Ave, Burbank
(91502-1922)
PHONE.................................818 558-7766
Sarkis Adamian, *CEO*
EMP: 17 EST: 1975
SQ FT: 25,000
SALES (est): 1.2MM **Privately Held**
SIC: **3911** Jewelry, precious metal

(P-11333)
**ZALEMARK HOLDING COMPANY
INC**
15260 Ventura Blvd # 120, Sherman Oaks
(91403-5307)
P.O. Box 280725, Northridge (91328-0725)
PHONE.................................888 682-6885
Xia Wu, *CEO*
Horace Bhopalsingh, *COO*

Charels Baron, *CFO*
Caren Currier, *CFO*
Steven Zale, *Corp Secy*
EMP: 14 EST: 1999
SQ FT: 1,000
SALES (est): 225.4K **Privately Held**
WEB: www.zalemark.com
SIC: **3911** **5094** Jewelry, precious metal;
jewelry

3914 Silverware, Plated &
Stainless Steel Ware

(P-11334)
CAL SIMBA INC (PA)
1283 Flynn Rd, Camarillo (93012-8013)
PHONE.................................805 240-1177
Jay Schechter, *CEO*
John Stout, *Corp Secy*
Stuart Seeler, *Vice Pres*
Alessia Sega, *Purchasing*
Nicholas Wright, *Marketing Staff*
▲ EMP: 38 EST: 1974
SALES (est): 10.3MM **Privately Held**
WEB: www.simbaline.com
SIC: **3914** **2672** **3452** **2821** Trophies,
plated (all metals); labels (unprinted),
gummed: made from purchased materi-
als; pins; polyurethane resins; silk screen
design

3915 Jewelers Findings &
Lapidary Work

(P-11335)
CGM INC
Also Called: Cgm Findings
19611 Ventura Blvd # 211, Tarzana
(91356-2907)
PHONE.................................818 609-7088
Devinder Bindra, *CEO*
Imelda Provenzano, *Accounts Mgr*
▲ EMP: 25 EST: 1984
SQ FT: 12,000
SALES (est): 3.7MM **Privately Held**
WEB: www.cgmfindings.com
SIC: **3915** **5094** Jewelers' materials & lap-
idary work; precious metals; precious
stones (gems); precious stones & metals

(P-11336)
JEWELERS TOUCH
2535 E Imperial Hwy, Brea (92821-6131)
PHONE.................................714 579-1616
Ken Rutz, *Partner*
Jana Rutz, *Partner*
EMP: 20 EST: 1992
SALES (est): 2.6MM **Privately Held**
WEB: www.jewelerstouch.com
SIC: **5944** **3915** Jewelry, precious stones
& precious metals; lapidary work & dia-
mond cutting & polishing

(P-11337)
LUCENT DIAMONDS INC
22809 Pacific Coast Hwy, Malibu
(90265-5040)
PHONE.................................424 777-2390
Alex Grizenko, *CEO*
EMP: 31 EST: 2000
SALES (est): 1.6MM **Privately Held**
WEB: www.lucentdiamonds.com
SIC: **3915** **5094** **5999** Diamond cutting &
polishing; diamonds (gems); gems & pre-
cious stones

(P-11338)
QUADRTECH CORPORATION
Also Called: Studex
521 W Rosecrans Ave, Gardena
(90248-1514)
PHONE.................................310 523-1697
Vladimir Reil, *President*
Christie Arana, *Admin Asst*
Frank Kabacic, *Purch Mgr*
John H Jessen, *Plant Mgr*
Denielle Morrow, *Accounts Mgr*
▲ EMP: 19 EST: 1999
SALES (est): 3.6MM **Privately Held**
WEB: www.earpiercing.com
SIC: **3915** **3423** Jewelers' materials & lap-
idary work; jewelers' hand tools

▲ = Import ▼=Export
◆ =Import/Export

(P-11339)
STARDUST DIAMOND CORP
Also Called: Diamonds By Design
550 S Hill St Ste 1420, Los Angeles
(90013-2415)
PHONE.................................213 239-9999
Gall Raiman, *President*
Albert Gad, *Shareholder*
Janet Guttmann, *CFO*
EMP: 34 **EST:** 1995
SQ FT: 3,600
SALES (est): 1.7MM **Privately Held**
WEB: www.stardustdiamonds.com
SIC: 3915 5094 Jewelers' findings & materials; diamond cutting & polishing; diamonds (gems)

3931 Musical Instruments

(P-11340)
BBE SOUND INC (PA)
Also Called: G & L Musical Instruments
2548 Fender Ave Ste G, Fullerton
(92831-4439)
PHONE.................................714 897-6766
David McLaren, *CEO*
Shailesh Karia, *CFO*
David C McLaren, *Exec VP*
Robert Ruzzito, *Vice Pres*
Edward Chandler, *Principal*
▲ **EMP:** 22 **EST:** 1984
SQ FT: 10,000
SALES (est): 9.3MM **Privately Held**
WEB: www.bbesound.com
SIC: 3931 3651 Guitars & parts, electric & nonelectric; amplifiers: radio, public address or musical instrument; microphones

(P-11341)
DUNCAN CARTER
CORPORATION (PA)
Also Called: Seymour Duncan
5427 Hollister Ave, Santa Barbara
(93111-2307)
PHONE.................................805 964-9749
Seymour Duncan, *Chairman*
Cathy Carter Duncan, *CEO*
▲ **EMP:** 99 **EST:** 1976
SQ FT: 20,000
SALES (est): 21MM **Privately Held**
WEB: www.seymourduncan.com
SIC: 3931 5736 3674 3651 Guitars & parts, electric & nonelectric; musical instrument stores; semiconductors & related devices; household audio & video equipment

(P-11342)
FENDER MUSICAL INSTRS
CORP
311 Cessna Cir, Corona (92878-5021)
PHONE.................................480 596-9690
Jennifer Schwartz, *Vice Pres*
Eric Spitzer, *Vice Pres*
Christina Stejskal, *Vice Pres*
Tammy Vandonk, *Vice Pres*
Rob McCrorie, *Info Tech Dir*
EMP: 800
SALES (corp-wide): 1.8B **Privately Held**
WEB: www.fender.com
SIC: 3931 3651 Musical instruments; amplifiers: radio, public address or musical instrument
HQ: Fender Musical Instruments Corporation
17600 N Perimeter Dr # 100
Scottsdale AZ 85255
480 596-9690

(P-11343)
FULLTONE MUSICAL
PRODUCTS INC
11018 Washington Blvd, Culver City
(90232-3901)
PHONE.................................310 204-0155
Michael Fuller, *President*
◆ **EMP:** 13 **EST:** 1993
SQ FT: 3,595
SALES (est): 877.7K **Privately Held**
WEB: www.fulltonecustomshop.com
SIC: 3931 5099 Musical instruments; musical instruments

(P-11344)
HARRIS ORGANS INC
Also Called: Harris' Precision Products
7047 Comstock Ave, Whittier (90602-1399)
PHONE.................................562 693-3442
David C Harris, *President*
EMP: 21 **EST:** 1971
SQ FT: 12,000
SALES (est): 1.7MM **Privately Held**
WEB: www.harrisorgans.com
SIC: 3931 3599 Pipes, organ; machine shop, jobbing & repair

(P-11345)
KANSTUL MUSICAL INSTRS INC
Also Called: K M I
23772 Perth Bay, Dana Point (92629-4203)
PHONE.................................714 563-1000
Zigmant J Kanstul, *President*
EMP: 42 **EST:** 1982
SALES (est): 4.4MM **Privately Held**
WEB: www.kanstul.com
SIC: 3931 Brass instruments & parts

(P-11346)
LR BAGGS CORPORATION
483 N Frontage Rd, Nipomo (93444-9596)
PHONE.................................805 929-3545
Lloyd R Baggs, *CEO*
Christian Tiessen, *CIO*
Caleb Elling, *Technology*
Ed Herlihy, *Technology*
Julie Conaway, *Purch Mgr*
▲ **EMP:** 24 **EST:** 1975
SALES (est): 5.2MM **Privately Held**
WEB: www.lrbaggs.com
SIC: 3931 3825 3651 Guitars & parts, electric & nonelectric; transducers for volts, amperes, watts, vars, frequency, etc.; household audio & video equipment

(P-11347)
PALADAR MFG INC
53973 Polk St, Coachella (92236-3816)
P.O. Box 4117, San Luis Obispo (93403-4117)
PHONE.................................760 775-4222
Sterling C Ball, *President*
Roland S Ball, *Vice Pres*
▲ **EMP:** 52 **EST:** 1979
SQ FT: 6,000
SALES (est): 7.4MM **Privately Held**
WEB: www.bigpoppasmokers.com
SIC: 3931 Strings, musical instrument

(P-11348)
QUILTER LABORATORIES LLC
1700 Sunflower Ave, Costa Mesa
(92626-1505)
PHONE.................................714 519-6114
Patrick H Quilter, *Principal*
Robert Becker, *COO*
Nicole Cheshire, *Office Mgr*
Peter Melton, *Sales Mgr*
Pat Quilter, *Products*
▲ **EMP:** 16 **EST:** 2011
SALES (est): 3.2MM **Privately Held**
WEB: www.quilterlabs.com
SIC: 3931 Guitars & parts, electric & nonelectric

(P-11349)
RAISE PRAISE INC
Also Called: Tom Anderson Guitar Works
845 Rnch Conejo Blvd, Newbury Park
(91320-1794)
PHONE.................................805 498-1747
Tom Anderson, *President*
Laurie Berg, *Treasurer*
EMP: 14 **EST:** 1984
SQ FT: 4,400
SALES (est): 1MM **Privately Held**
SIC: 3931 Guitars & parts, electric & nonelectric

(P-11350)
REMO INC (PA)
28101 Industry Dr, Valencia (91355-4113)
PHONE.................................661 294-5600
Remo D Belli, *President*
Yolanda Davis, *COO*
Douglas Sink, *CFO*
AMI Belli, *Vice Pres*
Fredy Shen, *Vice Pres*
◆ **EMP:** 300 **EST:** 1957
SQ FT: 216,000

SALES (est): 50.9MM **Privately Held**
WEB: www.remo.com
SIC: 3931 Heads, drum; drums, parts & accessories (musical instruments)

(P-11351)
RICO CORPORATION (HQ)
Also Called: Rico Products
8484 San Fernando Rd, Sun Valley
(91352-3227)
PHONE.................................818 394-2700
James D Addario, *CEO*
▲ **EMP:** 214 **EST:** 1928
SALES (est): 38.6MM
SALES (corp-wide): 169.1MM **Privately Held**
WEB: www.daddario.com
SIC: 3931 5099 Reeds for musical instruments; musical instruments
PA: D'addario & Company, Inc.
595 Smith St
Farmingdale NY 11735
631 439-3300

(P-11352)
RICO HOLDINGS INC
8484 San Fernando Rd, Sun Valley
(91352-3227)
PHONE.................................818 394-2700
William Carpenter, *President*
Ruth Thresher, *Purchasing*
EMP: 13 **EST:** 1996
SQ FT: 17,000
SALES (est): 488.3K **Privately Held**
SIC: 3931 5099 Reeds for musical instruments; musical instruments

(P-11353)
SCHECTER GUITAR RESEARCH INC
10953 Pendleton St, Sun Valley
(91352-1522)
PHONE.................................818 767-1029
Michael Ciravolo, *President*
David Santiago, *CFO*
Seth Miller, *Executive*
Toshi Hayakawa, *Opers Mgr*
Brad Strickland, *Natl Sales Mgr*
◆ **EMP:** 43 **EST:** 1987
SQ FT: 11,000 **Privately Held**
WEB: www.schecterguitars.com
SIC: 3931 Musical instruments

(P-11354)
TOM ANDERSON GUITARWORKS
845 Rancho Conejo Blvd, Newbury Park
(91320-1794)
PHONE.................................805 498-1747
Tom Anderson, *Owner*
Rachel Williams, *Office Mgr*
EMP: 17 **EST:** 2012
SALES (est): 1MM **Privately Held**
WEB: www.andersonguitarworks.com
SIC: 3931 Guitars & parts, electric & nonelectric

(P-11355)
YAMAHA GUITAR GROUP INC (HQ)
26580 Agoura Rd, Calabasas
(91302-1921)
PHONE.................................818 575-3600
Joe Bentivegna, *President*
Christine Hagemann, *CFO*
Andrew Hydle, *Administration*
Alan Chen, *Technician*
Jason Fagerlie, *Technician*
◆ **EMP:** 120 **EST:** 1988
SQ FT: 20,000
SALES (est): 64.3MM **Privately Held**
WEB: www.yamahaguitargroup.com
SIC: 3931 Musical instruments; guitars & parts, electric & nonelectric

(P-11356)
YAMAHA GUITAR GROUP INC
26664 Agoura Rd, Calabasas
(91302-1954)
PHONE.................................818 575-3900
Paul Foeckler, *President*
Rutger De Groot, *Vice Pres*
Mike Paganini, *Vice Pres*
Matthew Pereyra, *Administration*
John Osmand, *Engineer*

EMP: 42 **Privately Held**
WEB: www.line6.com
SIC: 3931 Musical instruments
HQ: Yamaha Guitar Group, Inc.
26580 Agoura Rd
Calabasas CA 91302
818 575-3600

3942 Dolls & Stuffed Toys

(P-11357)
BELLZI INC
5575 Daniels St, Chino (91710-9026)
PHONE.................................888 317-1502
En Chen, *CEO*
Chun Lin, *CFO*
EMP: 14 **EST:** 2013
SALES (est): 1.5MM **Privately Held**
WEB: www.bellzi.com
SIC: 3942 Stuffed toys, including animals

(P-11358)
CLOUD B INC
150 W Walnut St Ste 100, Gardena
(90248-3145)
PHONE.................................310 781-3833
Linda Suh, *CEO*
Leticia Montoya, *Creative Dir*
Eilene Cabezas, *Administration*
Veronica Vazquez, *Administration*
Jeff Johnson, *CTO*
◆ **EMP:** 22 **EST:** 2002
SQ FT: 4,100
SALES (est): 6.8MM
SALES (corp-wide): 15.7MM **Publicly Held**
WEB: www.cloudb.com
SIC: 3942 5099 Stuffed toys, including animals; baby carriages, strollers & related products
PA: Vinco Ventures, Inc.
1 W Broad St Ste 1004
Bethlehem PA 18018
484 893-0060

(P-11359)
CUDDLY TOYS
1833 N Eastern Ave, Los Angeles
(90032-4115)
P.O. Box 41281 (90041-0281)
PHONE.................................323 980-0572
Leo Ramdwar, *President*
EMP: 18 **EST:** 1980
SQ FT: 30,000
SALES (est): 772.7K **Privately Held**
SIC: 3942 Stuffed toys, including animals

(P-11360)
FAR OUT TOYS INC
300 N Pcf Cast Hwy Ste 10, El Segundo
(90245)
PHONE.................................310 480-7554
Keith Meggs, *CEO*
EMP: 20 **EST:** 2017
SQ FT: 3,700
SALES (est): 3.6MM **Privately Held**
WEB: www.farouttoysinc.com
SIC: 3942 5092 Dolls & stuffed toys; toys & games
PA: Far Out Toys (Hk) Co., Limited
Rm 805 8/F Inter-Continental Plz
Tsim Sha Tsui KLN

(P-11361)
MAHAR MANUFACTURING CORP (PA)
Also Called: Fiesta Concession
2834 E 46th St, Vernon (90058-2404)
PHONE.................................323 581-9988
Michael Lauber, *CEO*
◆ **EMP:** 39 **EST:** 1971
SQ FT: 100,000
SALES (est): 12.7MM **Privately Held**
SIC: 3942 Stuffed toys, including animals

(P-11362)
MATTEL INC (PA)
333 Continental Blvd, El Segundo
(90245-5032)
PHONE.................................310 252-2000
Ynon Kreiz, *Ch of Bd*
Richard Dickson, *President*
Anthony Disilvestro, *CFO*

PRODUCTS & SVCS

Mandana Sadigh, *Treasurer*
Steve Totzke, *Ch Credit Ofcr*
◆ **EMP:** 1700 **EST:** 1945
SQ FT: 335,000
SALES (est): 4.5B **Publicly Held**
WEB: www.mattel.com
SIC: 3942 3944 Dolls & stuffed toys; dolls, except stuffed toy animals; stuffed toys, including animals; games, toys & children's vehicles

(P-11363)
MOOSE TOYS LLC
737 Campus Sq W, El Segundo (90245-2567)
PHONE.................310 341-4642
Manny Stul, *Chairman*
Belinda Gruebner, *Mktg Dir*
Paul Solomon,
Jacqui Tobias,
Lanny Long, *Director*
EMP: 65 **EST:** 2018
SALES (est): 29.5MM **Privately Held**
WEB: www.moosetoys.com
SIC: 3942 3944 Dolls & stuffed toys; electronic games & toys
HQ: Moose Toys Pty Ltd
29 Grange Rd
Cheltenham VIC 3192

(P-11364)
RAYKORVAY INC
Also Called: Giant Teddy
1070 N Kraemer Pl, Anaheim (92806-2610)
PHONE.................714 632-8680
Reza Khosravi, *CEO*
▲ **EMP:** 16 **EST:** 2007
SQ FT: 10,000
SALES (est): 9.2MM **Privately Held**
WEB: www.giantteddy.com
SIC: 3942 5961 Stuffed toys, including animals; toys & games (including dolls & models), mail order

(P-11365)
UPD INC
Also Called: United Pacific Designs
4507 S Maywood Ave, Vernon (90058-2610)
PHONE.................323 588-8811
Shahin Dardashty, *President*
Ben Hooshim, *COO*
Kent Ross, *Officer*
Frederick Dardashti, *Vice Pres*
Fred Dardashty, *Vice Pres*
◆ **EMP:** 60 **EST:** 1990
SQ FT: 140,000
SALES (est): 15.4MM **Privately Held**
WEB: www.updinc.net
SIC: 3942 5112 3944 Dolls & stuffed toys; pens &/or pencils; puzzles

---

3944 Games, Toys & Children's Vehicles

(P-11366)
ASSOCIATED ELECTRICS INC
21062 Bake Pkwy Ste 100, Lake Forest (92630-2183)
PHONE.................949 544-7500
Gary Titus, *CEO*
Chung L Lai, *President*
Clifton Lett, *Vice Pres*
Brad Geck, *Marketing Staff*
▲ **EMP:** 46 **EST:** 1965
SALES (est): 6.3MM **Privately Held**
WEB: www.associatedelectrics.com
SIC: 3944 Automobile & truck models, toy & hobby

(P-11367)
B DAZZLE INC
Also Called: Www.b-Dazzle.com
500 Meyer Ln, Redondo Beach (90278-5208)
P.O. Box 4244 (90277-1759)
PHONE.................310 374-3000
Kathleen A Gavin, *President*
▲ **EMP:** 19 **EST:** 1993
SQ FT: 5,500

SALES (est): 1.4MM **Privately Held**
WEB: www.b-dazzle.com
SIC: 3944 5092 Board games, puzzles & models, except electronic; puzzles; toys & games; puzzles; toys

(P-11368)
BANDAI AMERICA INCORPORATED (DH)
2120 Park Pl Ste 120, El Segundo (90245-4824)
PHONE.................714 816-9751
Atsushi Takeuchi, *President*
Katsushi Murakami, *Ch of Bd*
Takeshi Nojima, *President*
Masayuki Matsuo, *CEO*
Brian Goldner, *COO*
▲ **EMP:** 53 **EST:** 1978
SQ FT: 75,000
SALES (est): 19.2MM **Privately Held**
WEB: www.tamagotchi.com
SIC: 3944 Games, toys & children's vehicles

(P-11369)
CM SCHOOL SUPPLY INC
Also Called: Educational Emporium
1025 E Orangethorpe Ave, Anaheim (92801-1135)
PHONE.................714 680-6681
Steve Rajcic, *Owner*
Geoffrey Rajcic, *President*
Jeff Rajcic, *Principal*
Ronald Rajcic, *Principal*
Stephen Rajcic, *Principal*
EMP: 14
SQ FT: 24,005
SALES (corp-wide): 6.2MM **Privately Held**
WEB: www.shopcmss.com
SIC: 5943 5941 3944 School supplies; playground equipment; games, toys & children's vehicles; board games, puzzles & models, except electronic; toy trains, airplanes & automobiles; dollhouses & furniture
PA: Cm School Supply, Inc.
940 N Central Ave
Upland CA 91786
909 982-9695

(P-11370)
CRAFTERS COMPANION
2750 E Regal Park Dr, Anaheim (92806-2417)
PHONE.................714 630-2444
▲ **EMP:** 20 **EST:** 2012
SQ FT: 8,197
SALES (est): 1.9MM **Privately Held**
SIC: 3944 Mfg Games/Toys

(P-11371)
DREAMGEAR LLC
Also Called: Isound
20001 S Western Ave, Torrance (90501-1306)
PHONE.................310 222-5522
Yahya Ahdout, *CEO*
Moris Mirzadeh, *Vice Pres*
Amir Navid, *Vice Pres*
Richard Barnes, *CIO*
Moe Soltani, *Technology*
◆ **EMP:** 49 **EST:** 2002
SQ FT: 60,000
SALES (est): 17.3MM **Privately Held**
WEB: www.dreamgear.com
SIC: 3944 5023 Electronic games & toys; electronic game machines, except coin-operated; decorative home furnishings & supplies

(P-11372)
DT MATTSON ENTERPRISES INC
Also Called: Proline Manufacturing
201 W Lincoln St, Banning (92220-4933)
P.O. Box 456, Beaumont (92223-0456)
PHONE.................951 849-9781
Todd Mattson, *CEO*
Matt Wallace, *Engineer*
Cindy Cross, *Accountant*
Belen Rodriguez,
▲ **EMP:** 40 **EST:** 1983
SQ FT: 20,000

SALES (est): 8MM **Privately Held**
SIC: 3944 5521 Games, toys & children's vehicles; trucks, tractors & trailers; used

(P-11373)
ERGO BABY CARRIER INC (HQ)
617 W 7th St Fl 10, Los Angeles (90017-3879)
PHONE.................213 283-2090
Bill Chiasson, *CEO*
Karin A Frost, *President*
Elias Sabo, *President*
Svea Frost, *Vice Pres*
Vanessa Van Bui, *Vice Pres*
▲ **EMP:** 14 **EST:** 2003
SALES (est): 11MM **Publicly Held**
WEB: www.ergobaby.com
SIC: 3944 Baby carriages & restraint seats

(P-11374)
GROW BRAINS SYSTEM INC
2324 Ocean Park Blvd D, Santa Monica (90405-5166)
PHONE.................310 428-6445
Bruce Ward, *CEO*
EMP: 50 **EST:** 2018
SALES (est): 2.4MM **Privately Held**
WEB: www.growbrainsgame.com
SIC: 3944 5092 Board games, puzzles & models, except electronic; board games, children's & adults'; board games

(P-11375)
HARDCORE RACING COMPONENTS LLC
27717 Avenue Scott, Valencia (91355-1219)
PHONE.................661 294-5032
Fax: 661 294-0770
EMP: 16 **EST:** 2000
SALES (est): 1.2MM **Privately Held**
SIC: 3944 Mfg Handheld Radio Controls For Toy Cars

(P-11376)
IMPERIAL TOY LLC (PA)
16641 Roscoe Pl, North Hills (91343-6104)
PHONE.................818 536-6500
Peter Tiger, *Mng Member*
Danny Satyapan, *Vice Pres*
Judy Tambourine, *Vice Pres*
Rene Amparo, *Controller*
Santiago Meza, *Controller*
◆ **EMP:** 115 **EST:** 1969
SQ FT: 400,000
SALES (est): 100.4MM **Privately Held**
WEB: www.jaru.com
SIC: 3944 Games, toys & children's vehicles

(P-11377)
INSOMNIAC GAMES INC (PA)
2255 N Ontario St Ste 550, Burbank (91504-3197)
PHONE.................818 729-2400
Theodore C Price, *President*
Alex Hastings, *Vice Pres*
Brian Hastings, *Admin Sec*
EMP: 255 **EST:** 1994
SALES (est): 48.1MM **Privately Held**
WEB: www.insomniac.games
SIC: 3944 Electronic games & toys

(P-11378)
JADA GROUP INC
Also Called: Jada Toys
938 Hatcher Ave, City of Industry (91748-1035)
PHONE.................626 810-8382
William Anthony Simons, *CEO*
Manfred Duschl, *CFO*
Harvey Luong, *CFO*
Wai Han Ko, *Admin Sec*
Cindy Dam, *Administration*
◆ **EMP:** 70 **EST:** 1999
SQ FT: 45,000
SALES (est): 11.4MM
SALES (corp-wide): 274K **Privately Held**
WEB: www.jadatoysinc.com
SIC: 3944 Games, toys & children's vehicles
HQ: Simba-Dickie-Group Gmbh
Werkstr. 1
Furth BY 90765
911 976-501

(P-11379)
JAKKS PACIFIC INC
Also Called: Flying Colors
21749 Baker Pkwy, Walnut (91789-5234)
PHONE.................909 594-7771
Michelle Tromp, *Branch Mgr*
Dan Westcott, *Exec VP*
Betsy Burkett, *Vice Pres*
Scott Derman, *Vice Pres*
Michael Dwyer, *Vice Pres*
EMP: 30 **Publicly Held**
WEB: www.jakks.com
SIC: 3944 5092 Games, toys & children's vehicles; toys
PA: Jakks Pacific, Inc.
2951 28th St
Santa Monica CA 90405

(P-11380)
JAKKS PACIFIC INC (PA)
2951 28th St, Santa Monica (90405-2961)
PHONE.................424 268-9444
Stephen G Berman, *Ch of Bd*
John J McGrath, *COO*
John L Kimble, *CFO*
EMP: 275 **EST:** 1995
SQ FT: 65,858
SALES (est): 515.8MM **Publicly Held**
WEB: www.jakks.com
SIC: 3944 Games, toys & children's vehicles

(P-11381)
JOY INTERNATIONAL TRADING INC
Also Called: Jit Video Game
2440 S Hcnda Blvd Ste 219, Hacienda Heights (91745)
PHONE.................626 736-5987
David Lin, *CEO*
Jenhsiu Hsieh, *President*
Tzung Sheng Lin, *President*
Chengkang Lin, *Vice Pres*
EMP: 15 **EST:** 2010
SALES: 1.6MM **Privately Held**
WEB: www.joyinternationaltrading.com
SIC: 3944 Video game machines, except coin-operated

(P-11382)
MATTEL DIRECT IMPORT INC (HQ)
333 Continental Blvd, El Segundo (90245-5032)
PHONE.................310 252-2000
Kevin Farr, *CEO*
Bryan G Stockton, *President*
Lisa Ou, *Marketing Mgr*
James Northcutt, *Marketing Staff*
Alexander Marx, *Counsel*
EMP: 32 **EST:** 2007
SALES (est): 8.5MM
SALES (corp-wide): 4.5B **Publicly Held**
WEB: www.mattel.com
SIC: 3944 3942 3949 Games, toys & children's vehicles; dolls, except stuffed toy animals; stuffed toys, including animals; sporting & athletic goods
PA: Mattel, Inc.
333 Continental Blvd
El Segundo CA 90245
310 252-2000

(P-11383)
MATTEL OPERATIONS INC
333 Continental Blvd, El Segundo (90245-5032)
PHONE.................310 252-2000
Robert Eckert, *CEO*
EMP: 19 **EST:** 1946
SALES (est): 1MM
SALES (corp-wide): 4.5B **Publicly Held**
WEB: www.mattelpartners.com
SIC: 3944 Games, toys & children's vehicles
PA: Mattel, Inc.
333 Continental Blvd
El Segundo CA 90245
310 252-2000

(P-11384)
MEGA BRANDS AMERICA INC (DH)
Also Called: Rose Art Industries
333 Continental Blvd, El Segundo (90245-5032)
PHONE..................................949 727-9009
Marc Bertrand, *CEO*
Vic Bertrand, *CFO*
Blanca Lagares, *Analyst*
◆ **EMP:** 80 **EST:** 1923
SALES (est): 179.2MM
SALES (corp-wide): 4.5B **Publicly Held**
WEB: www.megabrands.com
SIC: 3944 Blocks, toy
HQ: Mega Brands Inc
4505 Rue Hickmore
Saint-Laurent QC H4T 1
514 333-5555

(P-11385)
MOORES IDEAL PRODUCTS LLC
Also Called: M I P
830 W Golden Grove Way, Covina (91722-3257)
PHONE..................................626 339-9007
Eustace Moore Jr, *Mng Member*
Rico Tututi, *Design Engr*
Yolanda Garcia, *Manager*
Alycia Moore, *Manager*
EMP: 28 **EST:** 1978
SQ FT: 8,600
SALES (est): 6MM **Privately Held**
WEB: www.miponline.com
SIC: 3944 Automobile & truck models, toy & hobby

(P-11386)
NEUROSMITH LLC
1000 N Studebaker Rd # 3, Long Beach (90815-4957)
PHONE..................................562 296-1100
EMP: 23
SQ FT: 7,200
SALES (est): 2.6MM **Privately Held**
SIC: 3944 Mfg Educational Toys

(P-11387)
NINJA JUMP INC
3221 N San Fernando Rd, Los Angeles (90065-1414)
PHONE..................................323 255-5418
Rouben Gourchounian, *President*
Bridgette Garcia, *Accounts Exec*
Arman Muradyan, *Accounts Exec*
◆ **EMP:** 75 **EST:** 1984
SQ FT: 35,000
SALES (est): 5.2MM **Privately Held**
WEB: www.ninjajump.com
SIC: 3944 Games, toys & children's vehicles

(P-11388)
ORIGINAL WHISTLE STOP INC
Also Called: Coach Yard
2490 E Colorado Blvd, Pasadena (91107-4250)
PHONE..................................626 796-7791
T Fredrick Hill, *CEO*
Brian B Brooks, *President*
David Allen, *Vice Pres*
Judy Hill, *Admin Sec*
▲ **EMP:** 23 **EST:** 1951
SQ FT: 3,500
SALES (est): 1.3MM **Privately Held**
WEB: www.thewhistlestop.com
SIC: 5945 3944 5092 2731 Hobbies; models, toy & hobby; trains & equipment, toy: electric & mechanical; hobby goods; book publishing

(P-11389)
PLAYHUT INC
18560 San Jose Ave, City of Industry (91748-1365)
PHONE..................................909 869-8083
Yu Zheng, *CEO*
▲ **EMP:** 20 **EST:** 1992
SALES (est): 4MM **Privately Held**
WEB: www.basicfun.com
SIC: 3944 Games, toys & children's vehicles

PA: Basic Fun, Inc.
301 E Yamato Rd Ste 4200
Boca Raton FL 33431

(P-11390)
SHELCORE INC (PA)
Also Called: Shelcore Toys
7811 Lemona Ave, Van Nuys (91405-1139)
PHONE..................................818 883-2400
Arnold Rubin, *President*
▼ **EMP:** 29 **EST:** 1975
SQ FT: 20,000
SALES (est): 61.1MM **Privately Held**
WEB: www.funrise.com
SIC: 3944 Blocks, toy: structural toy sets

(P-11391)
SKULLDUGGERY INC
5433 E La Palma Ave, Anaheim (92807-2022)
PHONE..................................714 777-6425
Peter Koehl Sr, *CEO*
Steven Koehl, *President*
Emmy Koehl, *Mktg Dir*
▲ **EMP:** 14 **EST:** 1978
SQ FT: 10,000 **Privately Held**
WEB: www.skullduggery.com
SIC: 3944 5961 Science kits: microscopes, chemistry sets, etc.; mail order house

(P-11392)
SUN-MATE CORP
19730 Ventura Blvd Ste 18, Woodland Hills (91364-6304)
PHONE..................................818 700-0572
Rami Ben-Moshe, *President*
◆ **EMP:** 15 **EST:** 1985
SQ FT: 5,000
SALES (est): 1.2MM **Privately Held**
WEB: www.sun-mate.com
SIC: 3944 Electronic games & toys

(P-11393)
TORRENCE TRADING INC
21041 S Wstn Ave Ste 200, Torrance (90501)
PHONE..................................310 649-1188
EMP: 40 **EST:** 2014
SQ FT: 4,000
SALES (est): 2.1MM **Privately Held**
SIC: 3944 5092 Mfg Games/Toys Whol Toys/Hobby Goods

(P-11394)
TOYMAX INTERNATIONAL INC (HQ)
22619 Pacific Coast Hwy, Malibu (90265-5054)
PHONE..................................310 456-7799
Jack Friedman, *CEO*
Stephen G Berman, *President*
Joel M Bennett, *CFO*
◆ **EMP:** 56 **EST:** 1990
SQ FT: 30,000
SALES (est): 47.1MM **Publicly Held**
WEB: www.jakks.com
SIC: 3944 5092 Games, toys & children's vehicles; toys & games

(P-11395)
WHAT KIDS WANT INC
19428 Londelius St, Northridge (91324-3511)
PHONE..................................818 775-0375
Jordon Kort, *CEO*
Tony Najjar, *Vice Pres*
Steven Kort, *Principal*
▲ **EMP:** 14 **EST:** 1999
SQ FT: 2,000
SALES (est): 2.8MM **Privately Held**
WEB: www.whatkidswant.com
SIC: 3944 Games, toys & children's vehicles

(P-11396)
ZURU LLC
228 Nevada St, El Segundo (90245-4210)
PHONE..................................424 277-1274
Matthew Peter Mowbray, *CEO*
James Nunziati, *Vice Pres*
Michael Hinh, *Opers Staff*
Susie Martin, *Sales Staff*
EMP: 13 **EST:** 2008

SALES: 149.2MM **Privately Held**
SIC: 3944 Games, toys & children's vehicles
PA: Zuru Inc
C/O Fidelity Corporate Services Ltd.
Road Town

3949 Sporting & Athletic Goods, NEC

(P-11397)
ADDADAY INC
12304 Santa Monica Blvd # 214, Los Angeles (90025-2551)
PHONE..................................805 300-3331
Victor Yang, *CEO*
EMP: 15 **EST:** 2019
SALES (est): 5MM **Privately Held**
SIC: 3949 Sporting & athletic goods

(P-11398)
AFTCO MFG CO INC
Also Called: BLUEWATER WEAR
2400 S Garnsey St, Santa Ana (92707-3335)
PHONE..................................877 489-4278
Bill Shedd, *President*
William Shedd, *CEO*
Cody Shedd, *CFO*
Peggie Shedd, *Treasurer*
Alex Chandler, *Regional Mgr*
◆ **EMP:** 75 **EST:** 1973
SQ FT: 24,000
SALES (est): 24MM **Privately Held**
WEB: www.aftco.com
SIC: 3949 2329 2339 Fishing tackle, general; men's & boys' leather, wool & down-filled outerwear; women's & misses' outerwear

(P-11399)
ALL INTEGRATED SOLUTIONS LLC
2900 Palisades Dr, Corona (92878-9429)
P.O. Box 28941, Anaheim (92809-0164)
PHONE..................................951 817-3328
Reuben Hernandez, *Mng Member*
EMP: 17 **EST:** 2011
SALES (est): 810.2K **Privately Held**
SIC: 3812 Bags, rosin; aircraft/aerospace flight instruments & guidance systems

(P-11400)
AMERICAN MAPLE INC
14020 S Western Ave, Gardena (90249-3008)
PHONE..................................310 515-8881
Ben Hong, *President*
Steven Howie, *Sales Staff*
◆ **EMP:** 13 **EST:** 2002
SQ FT: 24,000
SALES (est): 1.7MM **Privately Held**
WEB: www.americanmaple.com
SIC: 3949 Fishing tackle, general

(P-11401)
AMERICAN PREMIER CORP
1531 S Carlos Ave, Ontario (91761-7661)
PHONE..................................909 923-7070
Michael Wu, *President*
Ric Heat, *General Mgr*
▲ **EMP:** 31 **EST:** 2001
SQ FT: 15,000
SALES (est): 1MM **Privately Held**
WEB: www.americanpremiercorp.com
SIC: 3949 Reels, fishing; rods & rod parts, fishing; fishing equipment

(P-11402)
ANDERSON BAT COMPANY LLC
236 E Orangethorpe Ave, Placentia (92870-6442)
PHONE..................................714 524-7500
▲ **EMP:** 53
SQ FT: 5,300
SALES (est): 538.7K **Privately Held**
WEB: www.andersonbat.com
SIC: 3949 Mfg Sporting/Athletic Goods

(P-11403)
ASPHALT FABRIC AND ENGRG INC
2683 Lime Ave, Signal Hill (90755-2709)
PHONE..................................562 997-4129
Bill Goldsmith, *President*
Joe Salamone, *CFO*
Doug Coulter, *Vice Pres*
Linda Morris, *Controller*
Lori Cisneros, *Production*
EMP: 90
SQ FT: 5,000
SALES (est): 16.6MM **Privately Held**
WEB: www.afsports.com
SIC: 3949 Sporting & athletic goods

(P-11404)
AVET INDUSTRIES INC
Also Called: Avet Reels
9687 Topanga Canyon Pl, Chatsworth (91311-4118)
PHONE..................................818 576-9895
Aruttyun Alajajian, *President*
Sarkis Alajajian, *Vice Pres*
▲ **EMP:** 15 **EST:** 1989
SQ FT: 19,200
SALES (est): 1.9MM **Privately Held**
WEB: www.avetreels.net
SIC: 3949 Reels, fishing

(P-11405)
BELL FOUNDRY CO (PA)
5310 Southern Ave, South Gate (90280-3690)
P.O. Box 1070 (90280-1070)
PHONE..................................323 564-5701
Cesar Capallini, *President*
Dimitry Rabyy, *CFO*
Wanda De Wald, *Treasurer*
▲ **EMP:** 59 **EST:** 1924
SQ FT: 140,000
SALES (est): 7.6MM **Privately Held**
WEB: www.bfco.com
SIC: 3949 3321 Dumbbells & other weightlifting equipment; gray & ductile iron foundries

(P-11406)
BRAVO SPORTS (HQ)
12801 Carmenita Rd, Santa Fe Springs (90670-4805)
PHONE..................................562 484-5100
Nicholas Schultz, *President*
Hung Ly, *IT/INT Sup*
Gina Corona, *Credit Staff*
Steven Finney, *Controller*
Meghan Sinnott, *Marketing Staff*
◆ **EMP:** 80 **EST:** 1987
SQ FT: 100,000
SALES (est): 23.2MM
SALES (corp-wide): 27.6MM **Privately Held**
WEB: www.bravosportscorp.com
SIC: 3949 Sporting & athletic goods
PA: Transom Bravo Holdings Corp.
12801 Carmenita Rd
Santa Fe Springs CA 90670
562 484-5100

(P-11407)
C PREME LIMITED LLC
Also Called: C-Preme
1250 E 223rd St, Carson (90745-4266)
PHONE..................................310 355-0498
Ryan Ratner, *Mng Member*
Corey Ratner, *Mng Member*
▲ **EMP:** 19 **EST:** 2010
SQ FT: 40,000
SALES (est): 1.6MM
SALES (corp-wide): 2.2B **Publicly Held**
WEB: www.c-preme.com
SIC: 3949 5091 5571 5099 Skateboards; bicycles; motor scooters; luggage
PA: Vista Outdoor Inc.
1 Vista Way
Anoka MN 55303
763 433-1000

(P-11408)
CASA DE HERMANDAD (PA)
Also Called: West Area Opportunity Center
1639 11th St, Santa Monica (90404-3727)
PHONE..................................310 477-8272
David Abelar, *President*
EMP: 25 **EST:** 1970

PRODUCTS & SVCS

SALES (est): 80K **Privately Held**
SIC: 3949 Driving ranges, golf, electronic

(P-11409)
CHAPMN-WLTERS INTRCOASTAL CORP
Also Called: Cwic
141 Via Lampara, Rcho STA Marg
(92688-2954)
PHONE......................949 448-9940
Andrew De Camara, *Receiver*
Cindi A Walters, *President*
◆ **EMP:** 17 **EST:** 1996
SQ FT: 103,000
SALES (est): 1.1MM **Privately Held**
SIC: 3949 Sporting & athletic goods

(P-11410)
CONDOR OUTDOOR PRODUCTS INC (PA)
5268 Rivergrade Rd, Baldwin Park
(91706-1336)
PHONE......................626 358-3270
Spencer Tien, *President*
Neil Chen, *COO*
Jennifer Saavedra, *Executive*
Mandy Tsai, *Office Mgr*
Henry Ko, *Accounts Exec*
◆ **EMP:** 38 **EST:** 1994
SQ FT: 11,000
SALES (est): 12.6MM **Privately Held**
WEB: www.condoroutdoor.com
SIC: 3949 Sporting & athletic goods

(P-11411)
D HAUPTMAN CO INC
Also Called: Fold-A-Goal
4856 W Jefferson Blvd, Los Angeles
(90016-3921)
PHONE......................323 734-2507
David Hauptman, *President*
Amy Schaub, *Treasurer*
Aaron Hauptman, *Vice Pres*
Diana Hauptman, *Admin Sec*
▲ **EMP:** 17 **EST:** 1965
SQ FT: 11,000
SALES (est): 1.1MM **Privately Held**
WEB: www.fold-a-goal.com
SIC: 3949 Soccer equipment & supplies

(P-11412)
DIAMOND BASEBALL COMPANY INC
Also Called: Diamond Sports
1880 E Saint Andrew Pl, Santa Ana
(92705-5043)
P.O. Box 55090, Irvine (92619-5090)
PHONE......................800 366-2999
Jay Hicks, *CEO*
Andrea Gordon, *President*
Robert W Ezell, *Vice Pres*
Janet Carlton, *Cust Mgr*
◆ **EMP:** 23 **EST:** 1977
SQ FT: 120,000
SALES (est): 3.8MM **Privately Held**
WEB: www.diamond-sports.com
SIC: 3949 5091 Baseball equipment & supplies, general; athletic goods

(P-11413)
DYNAFLEX INTERNATIONAL
Also Called: Dynabee USA
1144 N Grove St, Anaheim (92806-2109)
PHONE......................714 630-0909
▲ **EMP:** 20
SQ FT: 5,000
SALES (est): 2MM **Privately Held**
WEB: www.dynaflexpro.com
SIC: 3949 Mfg Sporting/Athletic Goods

(P-11414)
ECI WATER SKI PRODUCTS INC
224 Malbert St, Perris (92570-6279)
PHONE......................951 940-9999
Tom Hellwig, *President*
Ronna Hellwig, *Vice Pres*
EMP: 35 **EST:** 1984
SALES (est): 1.7MM **Privately Held**
WEB: www.paradisesocal.com
SIC: 5941 3949 Water sport equipment; water skiing equipment & supplies, except skis

(P-11415)
FAIRWAY IMPORT-EXPORT INC
Also Called: Lift Aviation
2130 E Gladwick St, Rancho Dominguez
(90220-6203)
PHONE......................262 788-7313
Guido Rietdyk, *President*
Kevin Hinyub, *Admin Sec*
Pearson Castner, *Software Dev*
Larry Vale, *Sales Staff*
Charlotte Rietdyk, *Manager*
◆ **EMP:** 35 **EST:** 1987
SQ FT: 17,000
SALES (est): 5.3MM **Privately Held**
WEB: www.liftsafety.com
SIC: 3949 Protective sporting equipment

(P-11416)
FASTHOUSE INC
28757 Industry Dr, Valencia (91355-5414)
PHONE......................661 775-5963
Kenneth Alexander, *CEO*
Jason Fonzy, *Principal*
Dan Worrell, *Principal*
EMP: 16 **EST:** 2013
SALES (est): 5.1MM **Privately Held**
WEB: www.fasthouse.com
SIC: 3949 Team sports equipment

(P-11417)
FLOW SPORTS INC
1011 Calle Sombra, San Clemente
(92673-4204)
PHONE......................949 361-5260
Anthony Scaturro, *CEO*
Anthony D Scaturro, *President*
◆ **EMP:** 23 **EST:** 2003
SALES (est): 2.3MM **Privately Held**
SIC: 3949 Snow skiing equipment & supplies, except skis

(P-11418)
GAMEBREAKER INC (PA)
31324 Via Colinas Ste 102, Westlake Village (91362-6750)
PHONE......................818 224-7424
Michael Juels, *CEO*
Dina Juels, *Admin Sec*
Evan Yeager, *Opers Staff*
Craig Reddinger, *Accounts Exec*
EMP: 20 **EST:** 2011
SQ FT: 5,000
SALES (est): 4.6MM **Privately Held**
WEB: www.gamebreaker.com
SIC: 3949 2329 2339 Guards: football, basketball, soccer, lacrosse, etc.; helmets, athletic; pads: football, basketball, soccer, lacrosse, etc.; men's & boys' athletic uniforms; football uniforms: men's, youths' & boys'; uniforms, athletic: women's, misses' & juniors'

(P-11419)
GENTRY GOLF MAINTENANCE
14893 Ball Rd, Anaheim (92806-5048)
PHONE......................714 630-3541
EMP: 20
SALES (est): 987.1K **Privately Held**
SIC: 3949 5941 Mfg Sporting/Athletic Goods Ret Sporting Goods/Bicycles

(P-11420)
GLOBAL BILLIARD MFG CO INC
1141 Sandhill Ave, Carson (90746-1314)
PHONE......................310 764-5000
Torben W Gramstrup, *President*
Solveig M Gramstrup, *Admin Sec*
◆ **EMP:** 19 **EST:** 1966
SQ FT: 30,000
SALES (est): 1.3MM **Privately Held**
WEB: www.globalbilliard.com
SIC: 3949 Billiard & pool equipment & supplies, general

(P-11421)
GOLF DESIGN INC
Also Called: Golf Design USA
10523 Humbolt St, Los Alamitos
(90720-5401)
PHONE......................714 899-4040
John Tate, *President*
Patricia Tate, *VP Finance*
Michael Cheek, *Sales Staff*
▲ **EMP:** 15 **EST:** 1971
SQ FT: 18,000

SALES (est): 1MM **Privately Held**
WEB: www.golfdesignproducts.com
SIC: 3949 Golf equipment

(P-11422)
GREENFIELDS OUTDOOR FITNES INC
2617 W Woodland Dr, Anaheim
(92801-2627)
PHONE......................888 315-9037
Samuel Mendelsohn, *CEO*
Aviv Avivshay, *Shareholder*
Allison Abel, *Marketing Mgr*
◆ **EMP:** 15 **EST:** 2010
SALES (est): 2.4MM **Privately Held**
WEB: www.gfoutdoorfitness.com
SIC: 3949 Gymnasium equipment

(P-11423)
HAMPTON FITNESS PRODUCTS LTD
1913 Portola Rd, Ventura (93003-8030)
PHONE......................805 339-9733
Zangnang Guo, *Ch of Bd*
Shirley Jay, *CFO*
Robert Hornbuckle, *Vice Pres*
Metchell Deguzman, *General Mgr*
Phil Lopiano, *Opers Staff*
▲ **EMP:** 14 **EST:** 1997
SQ FT: 30,000
SALES (est): 30,000 **Privately Held**
WEB: www.hamptonfit.com
SIC: 3949 Exercise equipment

(P-11424)
HEART RATE INC
Also Called: Versaclimber
1411 E Wilshire Ave, Santa Ana
(92705-4422)
PHONE......................714 850-9716
Richard D Charnitski, *President*
Redge Henn, *Vice Pres*
Dan Charnitski, *Admin Sec*
Gary Packman, *Research*
Peri Fetsch, *Controller*
▲ **EMP:** 38 **EST:** 1978
SQ FT: 18,000
SALES (est): 75K **Privately Held**
WEB: www.versaclimber.com
SIC: 3949 Exercise equipment

(P-11425)
HUPA INTERNATIONAL INC
Also Called: Body Flex Sports
21717 Ferrero, Walnut (91789-5209)
PHONE......................909 598-9876
Bob Hsiung, *President*
Frank Chang, *General Mgr*
▲ **EMP:** 21 **EST:** 1996
SQ FT: 30,000
SALES (est): 2.7MM **Privately Held**
WEB: www.bodyflexsports.com
SIC: 3949 Exercise equipment

(P-11426)
HYPER ICE INC (PA)
Also Called: Hyperice
525 Technology Dr, Irvine (92618-1388)
PHONE......................714 524-3742
Jim Huether, *CEO*
Raymond Williams, *Marketing Staff*
Ellen Chapman, *Sales Staff*
Heidi Thelen, *Sales Staff*
Cody Brazen, *Manager*
▲ **EMP:** 26 **EST:** 2010
SALES (est): 8.3MM **Privately Held**
WEB: www.hyperice.com
SIC: 3949 Sporting & athletic goods

(P-11427)
I & I SPORTS SUPPLY COMPANY (PA)
19751 Figueroa St, Carson (90745-1004)
PHONE......................310 715-6800
Alan Iba, *President*
▲ **EMP:** 20 **EST:** 1984
SALES (est): 8.6MM **Privately Held**
WEB: www.iisports.com
SIC: 3949 5091 5941 Sporting & athletic goods; sporting & recreation goods; martial arts equipment & supplies

(P-11428)
IFIT INC
2220 Almond Ave, Redlands (92374-2073)
PHONE......................909 335-2888

EMP: 1333
SALES (corp-wide): 1.8MM **Publicly Held**
WEB: www.company.ifit.com
SIC: 3949 Treadmills
HQ: Ifit Inc.
1500 S 1000 W
Logan UT 84321
435 750-5000

(P-11429)
ILLAH SPORTS INC A CORPORATION
Also Called: Belding Golf Bag Company, The
1610 Fiske Pl, Oxnard (93033-1849)
PHONE......................805 240-7790
Brien Patermo, *CEO*
Steve Perrin, *President*
Jackie Perrin, *Vice Pres*
▲ **EMP:** 50 **EST:** 2003
SALES (est): 5.4MM **Privately Held**
SIC: 3949 Sporting & athletic goods

(P-11430)
IRON GRIP BARBELL COMPANY INC
11377 Markon Dr, Garden Grove
(92841-1402)
PHONE......................714 850-6900
Scott Frasco, *CEO*
Michael Rojas, *President*
Chuck Brown, *Officer*
Irma Ramirez, *General Mgr*
Robert Lowe, *Opers Mgr*
▼ **EMP:** 85 **EST:** 1993
SALES (est): 15.8MM **Privately Held**
WEB: www.irongrip.com
SIC: 3949 Exercise equipment

(P-11431)
JR286 INC (PA)
20100 S Vermont Ave, Torrance
(90502-1361)
PHONE......................877 464-5301
Johnathan S Hirshberg, *CEO*
Kurt Hoffman, *COO*
Lee Clifford Taylor, *CFO*
Blake Fix, *Senior VP*
John Melican, *Senior VP*
▲ **EMP:** 19 **EST:** 1989
SALES (est): 8MM **Privately Held**
WEB: www.jr286.com
SIC: 3949 5091 Team sports equipment; water sports equipment; winter sports equipment; sporting & recreation goods

(P-11432)
L A STEEL CRAFT PRODUCTS (PA)
1975 Lincoln Ave, Pasadena (91103-1321)
P.O. Box 90365 (91109-0365)
PHONE......................626 798-7401
Beverly Holt, *President*
John C Gaudesi, *COO*
▲ **EMP:** 21 **EST:** 1951
SQ FT: 200,000
SALES (est): 2.8MM **Privately Held**
WEB: www.lasteelcraft.com
SIC: 3949 Playground equipment

(P-11433)
LEATT CORPORATION (PA)
26475 Summit Cir, Santa Clarita
(91350-2991)
PHONE......................661 287-9258
Sean Macdonald, *President*
Christopher J Leatt, *Ch of Bd*
Dillon Watts, *Sales Staff*
Patrick McCord, *Manager*
EMP: 30 **EST:** 2006
SQ FT: 14,101
SALES: 20.1MM **Privately Held**
WEB: www.leatt.com
SIC: 3949 Sporting & athletic goods

(P-11434)
LUCKY STRIKE ENTERTAINMENT INC (PA)
15260 Ventura Blvd # 1110, Sherman Oaks
(91403-5346)
PHONE......................818 933-3752
Steven Foster, *President*
Julie Van, *Vice Pres*
Joseph Carini, *General Mgr*
Sean Herzfeld, *General Mgr*
Bryan Reis, *General Mgr*

EMP: 50 EST: 2004
SALES (est): 279.6MM **Privately Held**
WEB: www.luckystrikeent.com
SIC: 3949 5812 5813 Bowling alleys & accessories; American restaurant; bar (drinking places)

(P-11435)
MALBON GOLF LLC
13101 W Wash Blvd Ste 426, Los Angeles (90066-5172)
PHONE.....................323 433-4028
Stephen Malbon, *President*
EMP: 23 EST: 2016
SALES (est): 798.4K **Privately Held**
WEB: www.malbongolf.com
SIC: 3949 Golf equipment

(P-11436)
MARTIN SPORTS INC (PA)
Also Called: Martin Archery
1100 Glendon Ave Ste 920, Los Angeles (90024-3513)
PHONE.....................509 529-2554
Rich Weatherford, *Principal*
Tracy Reiff, *President*
Richard Weatherford, *CEO*
Tim Larkin, *CFO*
Kevin MA, *Vice Pres*
▲ EMP: 19 EST: 2013
SQ FT: 28,000
SALES (est): 4.8MM **Privately Held**
SIC: 3949 Sporting & athletic goods

(P-11437)
MAUI TOYS
2951 28th St Ste 1000, Santa Monica (90405-2993)
PHONE.....................330 747-4333
Brian D Kessler, *President*
Cynthia Kessler, *Principal*
◆ EMP: 13 EST: 1988
SQ FT: 17,000
SALES (est): 465.2K **Privately Held**
WEB: www.mauitoys.com
SIC: 3949 3944 Exercise equipment; games, toys & children's vehicles

(P-11438)
MURREY INTERNATIONAL INC
25701 Weston Dr, Laguna Niguel (92677-1482)
PHONE.....................310 532-6091
Patrick Murrey, *President*
Ron Murrey, *Corp Secy*
Rosemary Murrey, *Corp Secy*
Larry Murrey, *Vice Pres*
Ted Murrey, *Vice Pres*
▲ EMP: 19 EST: 1938
SQ FT: 40,000
SALES (est): 1.2MM **Privately Held**
WEB: www.murrey.com
SIC: 3949 1542 Bowling alleys & accessories; custom builders, non-residential

(P-11439)
NATION SURFBOARD MFG INC
216 Avnida Fbrcnte Ste 10, San Clemente (92672)
PHONE.....................949 370-6607
Ryan Engle, *Administration*
EMP: 16 EST: 2010
SALES (est): 1MM **Privately Held**
SIC: 3949 Surfboards

(P-11440)
NORBERTS ATHLETIC PRODUCTS INC
354 W Gardena Blvd, Gardena (90248-2739)
P.O. Box 1890, San Pedro (90733-1890)
PHONE.....................310 830-6672
Loren Dill, *President*
Angela Dill, *Vice Pres*
▲ EMP: 19 EST: 1977
SQ FT: 4,000
SALES (est): 2.9MM **Privately Held**
WEB: www.norberts.net
SIC: 3949 Sporting & athletic goods

(P-11441)
RBG HOLDINGS CORP (PA)
7855 Haskell Ave Ste 350, Van Nuys (91406-1936)
PHONE.....................818 782-6445
Paul Harrington, *Principal*

Paul E Harrington, *Principal*
Scott Nickerson, *Training Spec*
Kelsey Ping, *Opers Staff*
Paul Bihlmeyer, *Sales Staff*
EMP: 1181 EST: 2003
SALES (est): 623.7MM **Privately Held**
SIC: 3949 5091 3751 Sporting & athletic goods; sporting & recreation goods; motorcycles, bicycles & parts

(P-11442)
RIP CURL INC (DH)
Also Called: Rip Curl USA
193 Avenida La Pata, San Clemente (92673-6307)
PHONE.....................714 422-3600
Kelly Gibson, *CEO*
Diem Culley, *COO*
Michael Hiebert, *CFO*
Matt Szot, *CFO*
Paul Harvey, *Vice Pres*
◆ EMP: 60 EST: 1992
SALES (est): 45.7MM **Privately Held**
WEB: www.ripcurl.com
SIC: 3949 Surfboards; shuffleboards & shuffleboard equipment

(P-11443)
ROSEN & ROSEN INDUSTRIES INC
Also Called: R & R Industries
204 Avenida Fabricante, San Clemente (92672-7538)
PHONE.....................949 361-9238
Richard Rosen, *President*
Daniel Rosen, *Vice Pres*
Jeremy Oldham, *Manager*
▲ EMP: 80 EST: 1979
SQ FT: 22,500
SALES (est): 6.3MM **Privately Held**
WEB: www.rrind.com
SIC: 3949 7389 Sporting & athletic goods; embroidering of advertising on shirts, etc.

(P-11444)
RPSZ CONSTRUCTION LLC
1201 W 5th St Ste T340, Los Angeles (90017-1489)
PHONE.....................314 677-5831
Rick Platt, *Mng Member*
EMP: 50 EST: 2008
SQ FT: 3,500
SALES (est): 914.1K
SALES (corp-wide): 27.1MM **Privately Held**
WEB: www.skyzone.com
SIC: 3949 Trampolines & equipment
HQ: Sky Zone, Llc
1201 W 5th St Ste T340
Los Angeles CA 90017
310 734-0300

(P-11445)
SAINT NINE AMERICA INC
10700 Norwalk Blvd, Santa Fe Springs (90670-3824)
PHONE.....................562 921-5300
Timothy Chae, *CEO*
Terry Kim, *Controller*
Max Kim, *Manager*
EMP: 40 EST: 2018
SALES (est): 1.7MM **Privately Held**
WEB: www.saintnineamerica.com
SIC: 3949 Team sports equipment

(P-11446)
SHOCK DOCTOR INC (PA)
Also Called: Shock Doctor Sports
11488 Slater Ave, Fountain Valley (92708-5440)
PHONE.....................800 233-6956
Anthony Armand, *CEO*
Doug Pedersen, *CFO*
Greg Houser, *Senior VP*
Bill Best, *Vice Pres*
Rizz Delazo, *Executive Asst*
▲ EMP: 79 EST: 2008
SALES (est): 20.8MM **Privately Held**
WEB: www.shockdoctor.com
SIC: 3949 Protective sporting equipment; guards: football, basketball, soccer, lacrosse, etc.

(P-11447)
SKATE ONE CORP
Also Called: Roller Bones
6860 Cortona Dr Ste B, Goleta (93117-5568)
PHONE.....................805 964-1330
George Powell, *President*
Deville Nunes, *Technology*
Tom Toboco, *Technology*
Zak Heath, *Engineer*
Leanne Turner, *Controller*
▲ EMP: 80 EST: 1976
SALES (est): 24.6MM **Privately Held**
WEB: www.skateone.com
SIC: 3949 Skateboards; skates & parts, roller

(P-11448)
SPN INVESTMENTS INC
Also Called: Einflatables
6481 Orangethorpe Ave # 12, Buena Park (90620-1376)
PHONE.....................562 777-1140
Steven P Nero, *CEO*
Steven Nero, *CEO*
Greg Wishni, *Sales Mgr*
Luis Ramirez, *Accounts Exec*
EMP: 19 EST: 2011
SALES (est): 1.6MM **Privately Held**
WEB: www.einflatables.com
SIC: 3949 Playground equipment

(P-11449)
SUBMERSIBLE SYSTEMS LLC
7413 Slater Ave, Huntington Beach (92647-6228)
PHONE.....................714 842-6566
Anthony Buban, *President*
Christine Buban, *Corp Secy*
Christeen Buban, *Vice Pres*
Larry Tram, *Executive*
Melinda Ross, *Opers Staff*
▲ EMP: 15 EST: 1973
SQ FT: 12,000
SALES (est): 1.4MM **Privately Held**
WEB: www.submersiblesystems.com
SIC: 3949 Skin diving equipment, scuba type

(P-11450)
SUREGRIP INTERNATIONAL CO
5519 Rawlings Ave, South Gate (90280-7495)
PHONE.....................562 923-0724
James Ball, *Vice Pres*
Ione L Ball, *President*
Ralph Jenney, *General Mgr*
Sharon Plewinski, *Accountant*
▲ EMP: 60 EST: 1937
SQ FT: 30,000
SALES (est): 6.6MM **Privately Held**
WEB: www.suregrip.com
SIC: 3949 Skates & parts, roller

(P-11451)
SURF TO SUMMIT INC
7234 Hollister Ave, Goleta (93117-2807)
PHONE.....................805 964-1896
Eric States, *President*
Julie States, *Vice Pres*
Karla Esparza, *Purch Agent*
▲ EMP: 18 EST: 1993
SALES (est): 1.9MM **Privately Held**
WEB: www.surftosummit.com
SIC: 3949 Sporting & athletic goods

(P-11452)
TACKLE SPECIALTIES INC
1245 W 132nd St, Gardena (90247-1505)
PHONE.....................310 538-0535
Herbert L Todd, *President*
Pat Todd, *Treasurer*
EMP: 19 EST: 1983
SQ FT: 2,100
SALES (est): 1.1MM **Privately Held**
WEB: www.calstarrods.net
SIC: 3949 Rods & rod parts, fishing

(P-11453)
TUFFSTUFF FITNESS INTL INC
13971 Norton Ave, Chino (91710-5473)
PHONE.....................909 629-1600
Cammie Grider, *President*
Monida Grider, *Vice Pres*
Donny Penado, *General Mgr*
◆ EMP: 180 EST: 1992

SQ FT: 150,000
SALES (est): 26.8MM **Privately Held**
WEB: www.tuffstuffitness.com
SIC: 3949 Exercise equipment

(P-11454)
TWIN PEAK INDUSTRIES INC
Also Called: Jungle Jumps
12420 Montague St Ste E, Pacoima (91331-2140)
PHONE.....................800 259-5906
Edmond K Keshishian, *President*
Raffi Sepanian, *Principal*
EMP: 32 EST: 2008
SALES (est): 3.4MM **Privately Held**
SIC: 3949 3069 Playground equipment; air-supported rubber structures

(P-11455)
U S BOWLING CORPORATION
5480 Schaefer Ave, Chino (91710-6901)
PHONE.....................909 548-0644
David Frewing, *President*
Dolores Frewing, *Corp Secy*
Janet Frewing, *Officer*
Michael Conejo, *Creative Dir*
Daroll L Frewing, *Principal*
◆ EMP: 15 EST: 1994
SQ FT: 50,000
SALES (est): 2.6MM **Privately Held**
WEB: www.murreybowling.com
SIC: 3949 1799 Bowling alleys & accessories; bowling alley installation

(P-11456)
VICTORIA SKIMBOARDS
2955 Laguna Canyon Rd # 1, Laguna Beach (92651-1194)
PHONE.....................949 494-0059
Charles Haines III, *President*
▲ EMP: 15 EST: 1976
SQ FT: 4,500
SALES (est): 536.8K **Privately Held**
WEB: www.ocean.victoriaskimboards.com
SIC: 3949 5941 Surfboards; surfing equipment & supplies

(P-11457)
WELCOME SKATEBOARDS INC
26792 Vista Ter, Lake Forest (92630-8112)
PHONE.....................949 305-9200
Jason R Celaya, *Administration*
Shane Cox, *Vice Pres*
EMP: 13 EST: 2014
SALES (est): 2.7MM **Privately Held**
WEB: www.welcomeskateboards.com
SIC: 3949 Skateboards

(P-11458)
WEST COAST TRENDS INC
Also Called: Train Reaction
17811 Jamestown Ln, Huntington Beach (92647-7136)
PHONE.....................714 843-9288
Jeffrey C Herold, *CEO*
Vivienne Herold, *CFO*
Amanda Williams, *Executive Asst*
Byron Slovis, *Production*
Mickey Miller, *Sales Mgr*
▲ EMP: 50 EST: 1990
SQ FT: 26,000
SALES (est): 5.7MM **Privately Held**
WEB: www.clubglove.com
SIC: 3949 Golf equipment

(P-11459)
WESTERN GOLF INC
1340 N Jefferson St, Anaheim (92807-1614)
PHONE.....................800 448-4409
Robert B Wagner Jr, *CEO*
◆ EMP: 14 EST: 1956
SQ FT: 15,500
SALES (est): 339.7K **Privately Held**
SIC: 3949 5091 Sporting & athletic goods; golf equipment

(P-11460)
WESTERN GOLF CAR MFG INC
Also Called: Western Golf Car Sales Co
69391 Dillon Rd, Desert Hot Springs (92241-8433)
PHONE.....................760 671-6691
Scott Stevens, *President*
Robert W Thomas, *Vice Pres*
Robert Evans, *Controller*

EMP: 55 EST: 1981
SQ FT: 60,000
SALES (est): 4.9MM **Privately Held**
SIC: 3949 3799 Sporting & athletic goods;
golf carts, powered

(P-11461)
WILLIAM GETZ CORP
539 W Walnut Ave, Orange (92868-2232)
PHONE........................714 516-2050
Michael Paulsen, *President*
▲ EMP: 15 EST: 1971
SQ FT: 10,000
SALES (est): 315.1K **Privately Held**
SIC: 3949 Fishing tackle, general

(P-11462)
WORLD CLASS CHEERLEADING INC
20212 Hart St, Winnetka (91306-3520)
PHONE........................877 923-2645
Akram Hemaidan, *CEO*
EMP: 33 EST: 2009
SALES (est): 1.7MM **Privately Held**
SIC: 3949 Sporting & athletic goods

(P-11463)
XS SCUBA INC (PA)
4040 W Chandler Ave, Santa Ana
(92704-5202)
PHONE........................714 424-0434
Daniel F Babcock, *President*
Mark Gibello, *General Mgr*
Marie Grecco, *Sales Mgr*
◆ EMP: 24 EST: 2002
SALES (est): 5.1MM **Privately Held**
WEB: www.xsscuba.com
SIC: 3949 5091 Skin diving equipment,
scuba type; diving equipment & supplies

3951 Pens & Mechanical Pencils

(P-11464)
HARTLEY COMPANY
Also Called: Hartley-Racon
1987 Placentia Ave, Costa Mesa
(92627-6265)
P.O. Box 10999 (92627-0999)
PHONE........................949 646-9643
Ed Kuder, *President*
Mike Quinley, *Vice Pres*
Mark Simpson, *Vice Pres*
Billy Threadgold, *Sales Staff*
▲ EMP: 22 EST: 1947
SQ FT: 75,000
SALES (est): 2.5MM **Privately Held**
WEB: www.thehartleycompany.com
SIC: 3951 Cartridges, refill: ball point pens

3952 Lead Pencils, Crayons & Artist's Mtrls

(P-11465)
AARDVARK CLAY & SUPPLIES INC (PA)
1400 E Pomona St, Santa Ana
(92705-4858)
PHONE........................714 541-4157
George Johnston, *President*
K Douglas Mac Pherson, *Corp Secy*
Daniel T Carreon, *Vice Pres*
Richard Mac Pherson, *Vice Pres*
Rick Macpherson, *Vice Pres*
▲ EMP: 30 EST: 1972
SQ FT: 25,000
SALES (est): 5.4MM **Privately Held**
WEB: www.aardvarkclay.com
SIC: 3952 5945 Modeling clay; arts &
crafts supplies

(P-11466)
ALLIED PRESSROOM PRODUCTS INC
Also Called: Allied Litho Products
3546 Emery St, Los Angeles (90023-3908)
PHONE........................323 266-6250
Mark Rios, *Manager*
EMP: 14

SALES (corp-wide): 4.1MM **Privately Held**
WEB: www.alliedpressroomproducts.com
SIC: 3952 5199 Lead pencils & art goods;
art goods & supplies
PA: Allied Pressroom Products, Inc.
4814 Persimmon Ct
Monroe NC 28110
954 920-0909

(P-11467)
AR-CE INC
Also Called: Stretch Art
141 E 162nd St, Gardena (90248-2801)
PHONE........................310 771-1960
Sarkis Cetinyan, *President*
Herman Artinian, *Vice Pres*
EMP: 15 EST: 1994
SQ FT: 6,000
SALES (est): 1.4MM **Privately Held**
SIC: 3952 Lead pencils & art goods

(P-11468)
CONVERSION TECHNOLOGY CO INC (PA)
5360 N Commerce Ave, Moorpark
(93021-1762)
PHONE........................805 378-0033
Jim Newkirk, *President*
Russell Greenhouse, *COO*
Ray Salinas, *Branch Mgr*
Terrill Newkirk, *Office Mgr*
▲ EMP: 50 EST: 1994
SQ FT: 28,000
SALES (est): 15.8MM **Privately Held**
SIC: 3952 2893 2899 Ink, drawing: black
& colored; printing ink; ink or writing fluids

(P-11469)
J F MCCAUGHIN CO
2628 River Ave, Rosemead (91770-3302)
PHONE........................626 573-3000
Jim Mallory, *Branch Mgr*
EMP: 16
SALES (corp-wide): 741.2MM **Privately Held**
WEB: www.paramelt.com
SIC: 3952 Wax, artists'
HQ: J. F. Mccaughin Co.
2817 Mccracken St
Norton Shores MI 49441
231 759-7304

(P-11470)
WESTECH PRODUCTS INC
Also Called: Westech Wax Products
1242 Enterprise Ct, Corona (92882-7125)
PHONE........................951 279-4496
Lawrence Dahlin, *President*
Barry Dahlin, *Vice Pres*
Erik Dahlin, *Vice Pres*
Larry Dahlin, *Technology*
Aaron Niay, *Technical Staff*
▲ EMP: 25 EST: 1980
SQ FT: 31,000
SALES (est): 4.6MM **Privately Held**
WEB: www.westechwax.com
SIC: 3952 5169 Crayons: chalk, gypsum,
charcoal, fusains, pastel, wax, etc.;
waxes, except petroleum

3953 Marking Devices

(P-11471)
BRANDNEW INDUSTRIES INC
375 Pine Ave Ste 22, Santa Barbara
(93117-3725)
PHONE........................805 964-8251
Sean David Clayton, *President*
Lisa Frey, *Partner*
EMP: 15 EST: 1991
SQ FT: 2,000
SALES (est): 1MM **Privately Held**
WEB: www.brandnew.net
SIC: 3953 Irons, marking or branding

(P-11472)
JOY PRODUCTS CALIFORNIA INC
Also Called: Coastal Enterprises
17281 Mount Wynne Cir, Fountain Valley
(92708-4107)
PHONE........................714 437-7250
Shayne Perkins, *President*

Jay Kollins, *Office Mgr*
Susie Erickson, *Sales Staff*
▲ EMP: 27 EST: 1981
SQ FT: 12,000
SALES (est): 2.6MM **Privately Held**
SIC: 3953 2759 Screens, textile printing;
screen printing

(P-11473)
SVEVIA USA INC
14567 Rancho Vista Dr, Fontana
(92335-4299)
PHONE........................909 559-4134
John Lucas, *President*
EMP: 15 EST: 2016
SALES (est): 1MM **Privately Held**
SIC: 3953 Stencils, painting & marking

3955 Carbon Paper & Inked Ribbons

(P-11474)
BUSHNELL RIBBON CORPORATION
300 W Brookdale Pl, Fullerton
(92832-1465)
P.O. Box 2543, Santa Fe Springs (90670-0543)
PHONE........................562 948-1410
Jim Kinmartin, *President*
Mary Alice Milward, *Treasurer*
James C Kinmartin, *Vice Pres*
Paul C Kinmartin, *Vice Pres*
EMP: 25 EST: 1903
SQ FT: 24,000
SALES (est): 1MM **Privately Held**
WEB: www.bushnellribbon.com
SIC: 3955 Ribbons, inked: typewriter;
adding machine, register, etc.

(P-11475)
CALIFORNIA RIBBON CARBN CO INC
10914 Thienes Ave, South El Monte
(91733-3404)
PHONE........................323 724-9100
Robert J Picou, *President*
Louis Titus, *Corp Secy*
Clara Picou, *Vice Pres*
▲ EMP: 100 EST: 1939
SQ FT: 12,000
SALES (est): 5.1MM **Privately Held**
SIC: 3955 Ribbons, inked: typewriter;
adding machine, register, etc.

(P-11476)
E ALKO INC
Also Called: Laser Imaging International
8201 Woodley Ave, Van Nuys
(91406-1231)
PHONE........................818 587-9700
Eyal Alkoby, *President*
Beth Alkoby, *Principal*
▲ EMP: 27 EST: 1992
SQ FT: 45,000
SALES (est): 1MM **Privately Held**
SIC: 3955 3861 Print cartridges for laser &
other computer printers; photographic
equipment & supplies

(P-11477)
ECMM SERVICES INC
1320 Valley Vista Dr # 204, Diamond Bar
(91765-3956)
PHONE........................714 988-9388
Vincent Yang, *President*
Donald Sung, *Principal*
EMP: 250
SALES (est): 27.3MM **Privately Held**
WEB: www.foxconn.com
SIC: 3955 5045 Print cartridges for laser &
other computer printers; printers, com-
puter
PA: Hon Hai Precision Industry Co., Ltd.
No. 66, Zhongshan Rd.
New Taipei City TAP 23680

(P-11478)
GENERAL RIBBON CORP
Also Called: G R C
5775 E Los Angles Ave Ste, Chatsworth
(91311)
PHONE........................818 709-1234
Stephen R Morgan, *President*
Robert W Daggs, *Ch of Bd*
▲ EMP: 500 EST: 1946
SQ FT: 110,000
SALES (est): 29.8MM **Privately Held**
WEB: www.printgrc.com
SIC: 3955 3861 Ribbons, inked: type-
writer, adding machine, register, etc.; pho-
tographic equipment & supplies

(P-11479)
LASERCARE TECHNOLOGIES INC (PA)
3375 Robertson Pl, Los Angeles
(90034-3311)
PHONE........................310 202-4200
Paul Wilhelm, *President*
Michael Arakelian, *CFO*
Luis Vela, *Technology*
EMP: 34
SQ FT: 12,000
SALES (est): 5MM **Privately Held**
WEB: www.lasercare.com
SIC: 3955 7378 5734 Print cartridges for
laser & other computer printers; computer
peripheral equipment repair & mainte-
nance; printers & plotters: computers

(P-11480)
PACIFIC COMPUTER PRODUCTS INC
2210 S Huron Dr, Santa Ana (92704-4947)
PHONE........................714 549-7535
EMP: 25
SQ FT: 12,000
SALES (est): 1.6MM **Privately Held**
SIC: 3955 5045 Mfg Computer Ribbons

(P-11481)
PLANET GREEN CARTRIDGES INC
20724 Lassen St, Chatsworth
(91311-4507)
PHONE........................818 725-2596
Sean Levi, *President*
Natalya Levi, *Treasurer*
Pattie Saso, *Controller*
Briana Aguilar, *Purchasing*
Eric Sherman, *Marketing Staff*
◆ EMP: 84
SQ FT: 29,699
SALES (est): 13MM **Privately Held**
WEB: www.pginkjets.com
SIC: 3955 5093 Print cartridges for laser &
other computer printers; plastics scrap

(P-11482)
SERCOMP LLC (PA)
5401 Tech Cir Ste 200, Moorpark
(93021-1713)
P.O. Box 92728, City of Industry (91715-2728)
PHONE........................805 299-0020
Mike Goodman,
EMP: 89 EST: 2003
SQ FT: 67,000
SALES (est): 4.7MM **Privately Held**
WEB: www.sercomp.com
SIC: 3955 3577 Print cartridges for laser &
other computer printers; computer periph-
eral equipment

(P-11483)
US PRINT & TONER INC
Also Called: National Copy Cartridge
14751 Franklin Ave Ste B, Tustin
(92780-7272)
PHONE........................619 562-6995
James Meyers, *President*
▲ EMP: 22 EST: 2011
SALES (est): 2MM **Privately Held**
WEB: www.nationalcopycartridge.com
SIC: 3955 Print cartridges for laser & other
computer printers

(P-11484)
VISION IMAGING SUPPLIES INC
9540 Cozycroft Ave, Chatsworth (91311-5101)
PHONE..................818 710-7200
Benard Khachi, *CEO*
Raymond Khachi, *Vice Pres*
▲ EMP: 50 EST: 2004
SALES (est): 4.9MM **Privately Held**
WEB: www.visionimaginginc.com
SIC: 3955 Print cartridges for laser & other computer printers

3961 Costume Jewelry & Novelties

(P-11485)
JAM DESIGN INC
5415 Cleon Ave, North Hollywood (91601-2834)
PHONE..................818 505-1680
Marie Van Demark, *President*
▲ EMP: 14 EST: 2001
SQ FT: 1,500
SALES (est): 1.8MM **Privately Held**
WEB: www.jamdesigninc.com
SIC: 3961 Jewelry apparel, non-precious metals

(P-11486)
JENNIFER MEYER INC (PA)
8491 W Sunset Blvd # 475, West Hollywood (90069-1911)
PHONE..................310 446-0057
Jennifer Meyer, *President*
Lisa Ziven, *President*
Katie Donovan, *Production*
Sterling Tadros, *Manager*
EMP: 21 EST: 2008
SALES (est): 3.1MM **Privately Held**
WEB: www.jennifermeyer.com
SIC: 3961 Costume jewelry

(P-11487)
LOUNGEFLY LLC
Also Called: Lounge Fly
108 S Mayo Ave, Walnut (91789-3090)
PHONE..................818 718-5600
Trevor Schultz, *Sales Mgr*
Stephanie Miranda, *Graphic Designe*
Carrie Sleutskaya, *Graphic Designe*
Jason Hoffman, *Opers Staff*
Alison Labbe, *Sales Staff*
▲ EMP: 25 EST: 1998
SALES (est): 5.5MM
SALES (corp-wide): 652.5MM **Publicly Held**
WEB: www.loungefly.com
SIC: 3961 Costume jewelry
PA: Funko, Inc.
2802 Wetmore Ave Ste 100
Everett WA 98201
425 783-3616

(P-11488)
NEW ORIGINS ACCESSORIES INC (PA)
Also Called: Charming Hawaii
3980 Valley Blvd Ste D, Walnut (91789-1530)
PHONE..................909 869-7559
Vinod Kumar, *President*
Manju Kumar, *Admin Sec*
▲ EMP: 14 EST: 1984
SQ FT: 2,400
SALES (est): 1MM **Privately Held**
SIC: 3961 Costume jewelry, ex. precious metal & semiprecious stones

(P-11489)
PAGLIEI COLLECTION INC
Also Called: Campagna
2363 Alamo Pintado Rd, Los Olivos (93441-4505)
P.O. Box 820 (93441-0820)
PHONE..................805 693-9101
▲ EMP: 18
SQ FT: 4,000
SALES (est): 1MM **Privately Held**
SIC: 3961 5094 Mfg Costume Jewelry Whol Jewelry/Precious Stones

(P-11490)
PINCRAFT INC
Also Called: Pin Concepts
7933 Ajay Dr, Sun Valley (91352-5315)
PHONE..................818 248-0077
Vahe Asatourian, *President*
Kellie Torio, *Assistant*
Linna Kazanchian, *Supervisor*
▲ EMP: 27 EST: 1999
SALES (est): 4.1MM **Privately Held**
WEB: www.pincraft.com
SIC: 3961 Pins (jewelry), except precious metal

(P-11491)
SPORT PINS INTERNATIONAL INC
888 Berry Ct Ste A, Upland (91786-8445)
PHONE..................909 985-4549
Connie Bivens, *President*
John Bivens, *CFO*
Michael Bivens, *Treasurer*
Jeff Bivens, *Admin Sec*
Nancy Elliott, *Bookkeeper*
▲ EMP: 14 EST: 1981
SQ FT: 2,300
SALES (est): 2.5MM **Privately Held**
WEB: www.sportpins.com
SIC: 3961 2395 3499 Pins (jewelry), except precious metal; emblems, embroidered; novelties & giftware, including trophies

(P-11492)
V & V MANUFACTURING INC
15320 Proctor Ave, City of Industry (91745-1023)
PHONE..................626 330-0641
Everett C Visk, *President*
Everett Visk, *President*
Steve Visk, *Vice Pres*
▲ EMP: 17 EST: 1980
SQ FT: 3,500
SALES (est): 800K **Privately Held**
WEB: www.vandvmfg.com
SIC: 3961 Costume jewelry, ex. precious metal & semiprecious stones

3965 Fasteners, Buttons, Needles & Pins

(P-11493)
ALCOA FASTENING SYSTEMS
11711 Arrow Rte, Rancho Cucamonga (91730-4902)
PHONE..................909 483-2333
EMP: 52 EST: 2014
SALES (est): 769.5K **Privately Held**
WEB: www.alcoa.com
SIC: 3965 Fasteners

(P-11494)
BECKMAN INDUSTRIES
701 Del Nrte Blvd Ste 205, Oxnard (93030)
P.O. Box 2307, Agoura Hills (91376-2307)
PHONE..................805 375-3003
Robert Becker, *President*
Danny Becker, *Vice Pres*
EMP: 16 EST: 1995
SQ FT: 19,248
SALES (est): 1.5MM **Privately Held**
SIC: 3965 5072 Fasteners; hardware

(P-11495)
CATAME INC (PA)
Also Called: Ucan Zippers
1930 Long Beach Ave, Los Angeles (90058-1020)
PHONE..................213 749-2610
Liz Lai, *CEO*
Malan Lai, *Partner*
Liz H Lai, *CEO*
Paul Lai, *CFO*
Floyd Lai, *Admin Sec*
▲ EMP: 20 EST: 1995
SQ FT: 50,000
SALES (est): 4.8MM **Privately Held**
WEB: www.ucanzippers.com
SIC: 3965 5131 Zipper; zippers

(P-11496)
ENGINEERING MATERIALS CO INC
2055 W Cowles St, Long Beach (90813-1087)
PHONE..................562 436-0063
Edward Rickter, *President*
Susan J Brackett, *Treasurer*
Cynthia Ann Russell, *Admin Sec*
EMP: 17 EST: 1951
SQ FT: 24,000
SALES (est): 936.1K **Privately Held**
WEB: www.engmat.co
SIC: 3965 Fasteners

(P-11497)
HENWAY INC
Also Called: Anatase Products
1314 Goodrick Dr, Tehachapi (93561-1508)
PHONE..................661 822-6873
David Benhan, *Vice Pres*
Scott Baker, *Treasurer*
Scott D Baker, *Corp Secy*
EMP: 18 EST: 1977
SQ FT: 18,500
SALES (est): 2MM **Privately Held**
WEB: www.aircraftbolts.com
SIC: 3965 3452 Fasteners; bolts, nuts, rivets & washers

(P-11498)
LABELTEX MILLS INC (PA)
6100 Wilmington Ave, Los Angeles (90001-1826)
PHONE..................323 582-0228
Torag Pourshamtobi, *CEO*
Shahrokh Shamtobi, *President*
Ben Younessi, *Vice Pres*
Abby Hakhamanesh, *General Mgr*
Glenda Ochoa, *Graphic Designe*
◆ EMP: 200 EST: 1994
SQ FT: 135,000
SALES (est): 27.1MM **Privately Held**
WEB: www.labeltexusa.com
SIC: 3965 2253 2241 Fasteners, buttons, needles & pins; collar & cuff sets, knit; labels, woven

(P-11499)
MORTON GRINDING INC
Also Called: Morton Manufacturing
201 E Avenue K15, Lancaster (93535-4572)
PHONE..................661 298-0895
Yolanda A Morton, *Ch of Bd*
Frank Morton, *President*
Wallace Morton, *President*
Dale Ray, *COO*
Ed Kowalski, *Treasurer*
EMP: 110 EST: 1967
SQ FT: 45,000
SALES (est): 16.9MM **Privately Held**
WEB: www.mortonmanufacturing.com
SIC: 3965 3769 3452 Fasteners; guided missile & space vehicle parts & auxiliary equipment; bolts, nuts, rivets & washers

(P-11500)
PAIHO NORTH AMERICA CORP
16051 El Prado Rd, Chino (91708-9144)
PHONE..................661 257-6611
Yi Ming Lin, *President*
Shu-Ching Hsieh, *CFO*
Allen Cheng, *General Mgr*
Linda Simon-Malcomb, *Director*
▲ EMP: 22 EST: 2003
SQ FT: 52,000
SALES (est): 8.3MM **Privately Held**
WEB: www.paiho-usa.com
SIC: 3965 Fasteners, hooks & eyes

(P-11501)
SPS TECHNOLOGIES LLC
Also Called: Aerospace Fasteners Group
1224 E Warner Ave, Santa Ana (92705-5414)
PHONE..................714 545-9311
Mike Kleene, *Branch Mgr*
Jack Deakins, *Sales Mgr*
EMP: 500
SQ FT: 40,000
SALES (corp-wide): 245.5B **Publicly Held**
WEB: www.pccfasteners.com
SIC: 3965 3728 3452 3714 Fasteners; aircraft parts & equipment; bolts, nuts, rivets & washers; motor vehicle parts & accessories; machine tool accessories; iron & steel forgings
HQ: Sps Technologies, Llc
301 Highland Ave
Jenkintown PA 19046
215 572-3000

(P-11502)
SPS TECHNOLOGIES LLC
Cherry Aerospace Div
1224 E Warner Ave, Santa Ana (92705-5414)
PHONE..................714 371-1925
Michael Harhen, *Branch Mgr*
EMP: 500
SALES (corp-wide): 245.5B **Publicly Held**
WEB: www.pccfasteners.com
SIC: 3965 3452 Fasteners; bolts, nuts, rivets & washers
HQ: Sps Technologies, Llc
301 Highland Ave
Jenkintown PA 19046
215 572-3000

(P-11503)
TWO LADS INC (PA)
5001 Hampton St, Vernon (90058-2133)
P.O. Box 58572, Los Angeles (90058-0572)
PHONE..................323 584-0064
Lee R Adams, *President*
David Scharf, *Corp Secy*
Linda Gold, *Sales Mgr*
▼ EMP: 30 EST: 1991
SQ FT: 6,300
SALES (est): 2.9MM **Privately Held**
WEB: www.2lads.com
SIC: 3965 5131 2241 Buttons & parts; buttons; narrow fabric mills

(P-11504)
WCBM COMPANY (PA)
Also Called: West Coast Button Mfg Co
1812 W 135th St, Gardena (90249-2520)
PHONE..................323 262-3274
Keith Tanabe, *CEO*
Grace Kadoya, *CFO*
▲ EMP: 32 EST: 1976
SQ FT: 19,000
SALES (est): 2.9MM **Privately Held**
SIC: 3965 Buttons & parts

(P-11505)
WEST COAST AEROSPACE INC (PA)
220 W E St, Wilmington (90744-5502)
PHONE..................310 518-3167
Kenneth L Wagner Jr, *President*
Thomas Lieb, *Vice Pres*
Tom Nyikos, *Engineer*
Jake Wagner, *Mktg Dir*
▲ EMP: 90
SQ FT: 7,200
SALES (est): 17.7MM **Privately Held**
WEB: www.westcoastaerospace.com
SIC: 3965 3452 Fasteners; bolts, nuts, rivets & washers

3991 Brooms & Brushes

(P-11506)
A & B BRUSH MFG CORP
1150 3 Ranch Rd, Duarte (91010-2751)
PHONE..................626 303-8856
Donn Anawalt Jr, *President*
Tom Derto, *Manager*
▲ EMP: 32 EST: 1963
SQ FT: 26,500
SALES (est): 1.9MM **Privately Held**
SIC: 3991 Brushes, household or industrial

(P-11507)
AMERICAN ROTARY BROOM CO INC
688 New York Dr, Pomona (91768-3311)
PHONE..................909 629-9117
Joe Baeskens, *Vice Pres*
Clayton Trejo, *Sales Executive*

P
R
O
D
U
C
T
S

&

S
V
C
S

EMP: 23
SALES (corp-wide): 2.4MM **Privately Held**
WEB: www.united-rotary.com
SIC: 3991 3711 4959 Brooms; motor vehicles & car bodies; sweeping service: road, airport, parking lot, etc.
PA: American Rotary Broom Co., Inc.
  181 Pawnee St Ste B
  San Marcos CA 92078
  760 591-4025

(P-11508)
BRUSH RESEARCH MFG CO
Also Called: Brm Manufacturing
4642 Floral Dr, Los Angeles (90022-1288)
PHONE..................323 261-2193
Tara L Rands, *CEO*
Grant Fowlie, *President*
Robert Fowlie, *COO*
Heather Jones, *Treasurer*
Mary Rands, *Treasurer*
▲ **EMP:** 130
SALES (est): 21.1MM **Privately Held**
WEB: www.brushresearch.com
SIC: 3991 Brushes, household or industrial

(P-11509)
BUTLER HOME PRODUCTS LLC
9409 Buffalo Ave, Rancho Cucamonga
(91730-6012)
PHONE..................909 476-3884
Paul Anton, *Branch Mgr*
EMP: 176
SALES (corp-wide): 337.5MM **Privately Held**
WEB: www.cleanerhomeliving.com
SIC: 3991 2392 Brooms; brushes, household or industrial; mops, floor & dust
HQ: Butler Home Products, Llc
  2 Cabot Rd Ste 1
  Hudson MA 01749
  508 597-8000

(P-11510)
FOAMPRO MFG INC
Also Called: Foampro Manufacturing
1781 Langley Ave, Irvine (92614-5621)
P.O. Box 18888 (92623-8888)
PHONE..................949 252-0112
Gregory Isaac, *Ch of Bd*
Chad Coil, *Vice Pres*
Marco Canela, *Warehouse Mgr*
Casey Isaac, *Manager*
▲ **EMP:** 80 **EST:** 1952
SQ FT: 25,000
SALES (est): 9.6MM **Privately Held**
WEB: www.foampromfg.com
SIC: 3991 Paint rollers; paint brushes

(P-11511)
GORDON BRUSH MFG CO INC (PA)
3737 Capitol Ave, City of Industry
(90601-1732)
PHONE..................323 724-7777
Kenneth L Rakusin, *President*
William E Loitz, *Vice Pres*
William Loitz, *Engineer*
Denis Valentine, *Engineer*
Sandra Jauregui, *Sales Staff*
▲ **EMP:** 49 **EST:** 1951
SQ FT: 51,600
SALES (est): 14.3MM **Privately Held**
WEB: www.gordonbrush.com
SIC: 3991 Brushes, household or industrial

(P-11512)
KINGSOLVER INC
Also Called: Supreme Enterprise
8417 Secura Way, Santa Fe Springs
(90670-2215)
P.O. Box 3106 (90670-0106)
PHONE..................562 945-7590
Keith Kingsolver, *President*
Christina Kingsolver, *Admin Sec*
▲ **EMP:** 19 **EST:** 1994
SQ FT: 22,000
SALES (est): 2.4MM **Privately Held**
WEB: www.supreme-enterprise.com
SIC: 3991 5199 Brooms; broom, mop & paint handles

(P-11513)
LAKIM INDUSTRIES INCORPORATED (PA)
Also Called: Quali-Tech Manufacturing
389 Rood Rd, Calexico (92231-9763)
PHONE..................310 637-8900
Song B Kim, *CEO*
Juhyun Kim, *CFO*
Hector Herrera, *Opers Staff*
Soyoung Kim, *Sales Staff*
▲ **EMP:** 29 **EST:** 1974
SALES (est): 6.4MM **Privately Held**
WEB: www.quali-tech.com
SIC: 3991 Paint rollers; paint brushes

(P-11514)
PASCO INDUSTRIES INC
2040 Redondo Pl, Fullerton (92835-3306)
PHONE..................714 992-2051
EMP: 15
SQ FT: 28,000
SALES (est): 900K **Privately Held**
SIC: 3991 5199 Mfg Paint Rollers And Brushes

(P-11515)
WESTCOAST BRUSH MFG INC
1330 Philadelphia St, Pomona
(91766-5563)
PHONE..................909 627-7170
Heriberto Guerrero, *President*
Concepcion Guerrero, *Vice Pres*
▲ **EMP:** 22 **EST:** 1979
SQ FT: 20,000
SALES (est): 2.4MM **Privately Held**
WEB: www.westcoastbrush.com
SIC: 3991 Brushes, household or industrial

(P-11516)
WORLD TREND INC (PA)
1920 W Holt Ave, Pomona (91768-3351)
PHONE..................909 620-9945
Barnabas C Chen, *President*
▲ **EMP:** 14 **EST:** 1982
SQ FT: 22,000
SALES (est): 1.4MM **Privately Held**
WEB: www.worldtrend.com
SIC: 3991 Toothbrushes, except electric; brushes, except paint & varnish

3993 Signs & Advertising Displays

(P-11517)
3S SIGN SERVICES INC
Also Called: P.S. Services
1320 N Red Gum St, Anaheim
(92806-1317)
PHONE..................714 683-1120
Michael W Schmidt, *CEO*
EMP: 25 **EST:** 2018
SALES (est): 1.4MM **Privately Held**
SIC: 3993 Signs & advertising specialties

(P-11518)
A GOOD SIGN & GRAPHICS CO
2110 S Susan St, Santa Ana (92704-4417)
PHONE..................714 444-4466
Babak Richard Abedi, *CEO*
Ted Howard, *Sales Staff*
Thang MAI, *Manager*
EMP: 16 **EST:** 2007
SALES (est): 2.5MM **Privately Held**
WEB: www.agoodsign.com
SIC: 3993 Signs, not made in custom sign painting shops

(P-11519)
AAHS ENTERPRISES INC
Also Called: Aahs Graphics Signs & Engrv
6600 Telegraph Rd, Commerce
(90040-3210)
PHONE..................323 838-9130
Gurmeet Sawhney, *CEO*
Mandeep Singh, *Info Tech Mgr*
EMP: 16 **EST:** 2005
SALES (est): 3.2MM **Privately Held**
WEB: www.aahssigns.com
SIC: 3993 Signs & advertising specialties

(P-11520)
ABSOLUTE SIGN INC
10655 Humbolt St, Los Alamitos
(90720-2447)
PHONE..................562 592-5838
Patricia Scialampo, *President*
Gregory Benedict, *Vice Pres*
EMP: 15 **EST:** 1983
SALES (est): 1.7MM **Privately Held**
WEB: www.absolutesign.com
SIC: 3993 Electric signs; neon signs

(P-11521)
AHR SIGNS INCORPORATED
Also Called: Ampersand Contract Signing Grp
3400 N San Fernando Rd, Los Angeles
(90065-1419)
PHONE..................323 255-1102
Rouben Varozian, *President*
EMP: 13 **EST:** 1978
SQ FT: 15,000
SALES (est): 1.9MM **Privately Held**
WEB: www.ampersandsigns.com
SIC: 3993 Signs, not made in custom sign painting shops

(P-11522)
AMERICAN FLEET & RET GRAPHICS
Also Called: Amgraph
2091 Del Rio Way, Ontario (91761-8038)
PHONE..................909 937-7570
Kristin Stewart, *CEO*
Brian Stewart, *President*
Dawn Miltenberger, *Department Mgr*
Jim Helm, *General Mgr*
Marlene Marrero, *Admin Asst*
EMP: 37 **EST:** 2006
SALES (est): 5.7MM **Privately Held**
WEB: www.theamgraphgroup.com
SIC: 3993 Signs & advertising specialties

(P-11523)
ARCHITECTURAL DESIGN SIGNS INC (PA)
Also Called: Ad/S Companies
1160 Railroad St, Corona (92882-1835)
PHONE..................951 278-0680
Sean L Solomon, *President*
Roberto Soltero III, *Vice Pres*
Yosimar Ramos, *Design Engr*
Yesenia Gaeta, *Project Mgr*
Robert Hudson, *Project Mgr*
EMP: 95 **EST:** 1995
SQ FT: 630,000
SALES (est): 23.5MM **Privately Held**
WEB: www.ad-s.com
SIC: 3993 Signs & advertising specialties

(P-11524)
ASTRO DISPLAY COMPANY INC
4247 E Airport Dr, Ontario (91761-1565)
PHONE..................909 605-2875
Thomas Andric, *Ch of Bd*
EMP: 20 **EST:** 1946
SQ FT: 16,000
SALES (est): 1.5MM **Privately Held**
WEB: www.astrodisplay.com
SIC: 3993 7319 3089 Displays & cutouts, window & lobby; display advertising service; plastic processing

(P-11525)
B & H SIGNS INC
926 S Primrose Ave, Monrovia
(91016-3440)
PHONE..................626 359-6643
William Henry, *President*
David Salse, *Chiropractor*
EMP: 16 **EST:** 1970
SQ FT: 7,000
SALES (est): 1.6MM **Privately Held**
WEB: www.bandhsigns.com
SIC: 3993 Signs, not made in custom sign painting shops

(P-11526)
BK SIGNS INC
1028 W Kirkwall Rd, Azusa (91702-5126)
PHONE..................626 334-5600
Brian Scott Kanner, *CEO*
EMP: 18 **EST:** 1992
SQ FT: 16,000
SALES (est): 2.9MM **Privately Held**
WEB: www.bksigns.com
SIC: 3993 1731 Signs & advertising specialties; advertising artwork; general electrical contractor

(P-11527)
BLACKCOFFEE FABRICATORS INC
Also Called: Blackcoffee Sign Fabricators
777 W Mill St, San Bernardino
(92410-3355)
PHONE..................909 974-4499
Erin Foley, *President*
Dale Foley, *Vice Pres*
Jim Foley, *Vice Pres*
Maria Foley, *Admin Sec*
EMP: 14 **EST:** 2008
SALES (est): 2.6MM **Privately Held**
WEB: www.bcfsigns.com
SIC: 3993 Signs & advertising specialties

(P-11528)
BLAKE SIGN COMPANY INC
11661 Seaboard Cir, Stanton 90680-3427)
PHONE..................714 891-5682
John A Blake, *President*
Devin Blake, *Shareholder*
Mike Blake, *Shareholder*
Dan Blake, *Vice Pres*
Joan Blake, *Vice Pres*
EMP: 23 **EST:** 1981
SQ FT: 5,400
SALES (est): 925K **Privately Held**
WEB: www.blakesigns.com
SIC: 3993 Signs, not made in custom sign painting shops

(P-11529)
BRAILLE SIGNS INC
1815 E Wilshire Ave # 901, Santa Ana
(92705-4646)
PHONE..................949 797-1570
Steve Corum, *President*
Ruth Corum, *Vice Pres*
Jason Chuang, *Supervisor*
▲ **EMP:** 22 **EST:** 1992
SQ FT: 3,000
SALES (est): 1.6MM **Privately Held**
WEB: www.braillesignsinc.com
SIC: 3993 Signs, not made in custom sign painting shops

(P-11530)
BRITE-LITE NEON CCRP
17242 Goya St, Granada Hills
(91344-1206)
PHONE..................818 763-4798
Philip Mastopietro, *President*
Mark Mastopietro, *Corp Secy*
Rick Cincis, *Vice Pres*
EMP: 14 **EST:** 1952
SALES (est): 557.9K **Privately Held**
WEB: www.briteliteneon.com
SIC: 3993 7629 Neon signs; electrical repair shops

(P-11531)
CALIFORNIA SIGNS INC
Also Called: CA Signs
10280 Glenoaks Blvd, Pacoima
(91331-1604)
PHONE..................818 899-1888
Matthew Miller, *President*
Yvette Miller, *Admin Sec*
Justin Miooer, *Opers Dir*
Daisey Navarro, *Manager*
Diego Duarte, *Consultant*
EMP: 35 **EST:** 1962
SQ FT: 21,000
SALES (est): 5.8MM **Privately Held**
WEB: www.casigns.com
SIC: 3993 Signs, not made in custom sign painting shops

(P-11532)
CANZONE AND COMPANY
Also Called: C & C Signs
1345 W Cowles St, Long Beach
(90813-2734)
PHONE..................714 537-8175
Chris Canzone, *President*
Jessica Canzone, *Treasurer*
EMP: 16 **EST:** 1985
SQ FT: 4,800

SALES (est): 636.3K **Privately Held**
WEB: www.c-csigns.com
SIC: 3993 Signs, not made in custom sign painting shops

(P-11533)
CHIEF NEON SIGN CO INC
15027 S Maple Ave, Gardena (90248-1939)
PHONE....................310 327-1317
Alan D Paulson, *President*
Alan M Paulson, *President*
Armeta Paulson, *Corp Secy*
EMP: 13 **EST:** 1948
SQ FT: 12,400
SALES (est): 730.9K **Privately Held**
SIC: 3993 Signs, not made in custom sign painting shops

(P-11534)
CLEGG INDUSTRIES INC
Also Called: Clegg Promo
19032 S Vermont Ave, Gardena (90248-4412)
PHONE....................310 225-3800
Timothy P Clegg, *CEO*
Kevin Clegg, *President*
Michael Amar, *Senior VP*
Michael Bistocchi, *Senior VP*
Los Angeles, *Vice Pres*
▲ **EMP:** 175 **EST:** 1987
SQ FT: 31,000
SALES (est): 35.6MM **Privately Held**
WEB: www.cleggpop.com
SIC: 3993 3648 2542 Advertising novelties; lighting equipment; partitions & fixtures, except wood

(P-11535)
COAST SIGN INCORPORATED
Also Called: Coast Sign Display
1500 W Embassy St, Anaheim (92802-1016)
PHONE....................714 520-9144
Afshan Alemi, *CEO*
S Charlie Alemi, *President*
Jagadish Kariyappa, *Vice Pres*
Bonnie Metz, *General Mgr*
Joanna Garcia, *Design Engr*
▲ **EMP:** 250
SQ FT: 130,000
SALES (est): 50MM **Privately Held**
WEB: www.coastsign.com
SIC: 3993 Signs, not made in custom sign painting shops

(P-11536)
CONTINENTAL SIGNS INC
7541 Santa Rita Cir Ste D, Stanton (90680-3498)
PHONE....................714 894-2011
Joseph Artinger, *President*
Edward Artinger, *Vice Pres*
Tim Shevlin, *Sales Associate*
EMP: 19 **EST:** 1971
SQ FT: 7,800
SALES (est): 985.8K **Privately Held**
WEB: www.continentalsigns.com
SIC: 3993 1731 Signs, not made in custom sign painting shops; general electrical contractor

(P-11537)
CORNERSTONE DISPLAY GROUP INC
28606 Livingston Ave, Valencia (91355-4186)
PHONE....................661 705-1700
Tom Hester, *Principal*
Kip Kirkpatrick, *Partner*
Bruce Nunn, *Info Tech Dir*
Thomas Redding, *Project Mgr*
Albert Guerra, *Sales Dir*
▲ **EMP:** 45 **EST:** 1995
SQ FT: 20,000
SALES (est): 11.3MM **Privately Held**
WEB: www.cornerstonedisplay.com
SIC: 3993 Advertising artwork; displays & cutouts, window & lobby

(P-11538)
COWBOY DIRECT RESPONSE
Also Called: Synergy Direct Response
130 E Alton Ave, Santa Ana (92707-4415)
PHONE....................714 824-3780
Cynthia Rogers, *CEO*

John T Rogers, *CEO*
Lynnette Bennett, *COO*
Kijou Morris, *Vice Pres*
Enrique Martinez, *Executive*
EMP: 35 **EST:** 2004
SQ FT: 10,000
SALES (est): 6.3MM **Privately Held**
WEB: www.synergydr.com
SIC: 3993 8999 2759 Advertising artwork; advertising copy writing; promotional printing

(P-11539)
CUMMINGS RESOURCES LLC
330 W Citrus St, Colton (92324-1417)
PHONE....................951 248-1130
Jenny Hodges, *Director*
EMP: 39
SALES (corp-wide): 574.8MM **Privately Held**
WEB: www.cummingssigns.com
SIC: 3993 Signs & advertising specialties
HQ: Cummings Resources Llc
15 Century Blvd Ste 200
Nashville TN 37214

(P-11540)
CUMMINGS RESOURCES LLC
1495 Columbia Ave, Riverside (92507-2021)
PHONE....................951 248-1130
Jim Mole, *Plant Mgr*
Ann Baker, *Vice Pres*
EMP: 39
SQ FT: 50,000
SALES (corp-wide): 574.8MM **Privately Held**
WEB: www.cummingssigns.com
SIC: 3993 Signs & advertising specialties
HQ: Cummings Resources Llc
15 Century Blvd Ste 200
Nashville TN 37214

(P-11541)
DG-DISPLAYS LLC
355 Parkside Dr, San Fernando (91340-3036)
PHONE....................877 358-5976
Robert Blumenfeld,
Zachary Blumenfeld,
EMP: 30 **EST:** 2016
SQ FT: 25,000
SALES (est): 1.2MM **Privately Held**
WEB: www.dgdisplays.com
SIC: 3993 Signs & advertising specialties

(P-11542)
DSA SIGNAGE
16961 Central Ave, Carson (90746-1302)
PHONE....................877 305-4911
EMP: 17 **EST:** 1975
SALES (est): 533K **Privately Held**
WEB: www.lightboxes.com
SIC: 3993 Signs & advertising specialties

(P-11543)
DUNBAR ELECTRIC SIGN COMPANY
Also Called: City Crane
4020 Rosedale Hwy, Bakersfield (93308-6131)
P.O. Box 10717 (93389-0717)
PHONE....................661 323-2600
Clayton Dunbar, *CEO*
EMP: 25 **EST:** 1972
SALES (est): 1.1MM **Privately Held**
SIC: 3993 7629 5999 1799 Electric signs; electrical equipment repair services; banners; sign installation & maintenance

(P-11544)
DYNAMITE SIGN GROUP INC
Also Called: TNT Electric Signs Co
3080 E 29th St, Long Beach (90806-2317)
P.O. Box 92904 (90809-2904)
PHONE....................562 595-7725
EMP: 30
SQ FT: 7,500
SALES (est): 4.8MM **Privately Held**
SIC: 3993 Signs And Advertising Specialties

(P-11545)
EAGLE SIGNS INC
1028 E Acacia St, Ontario (91761-4553)
PHONE....................909 923-3034
Robert Kneevers, *Partner*
Christopher Kneevers, *Partner*
Drew Solome, *Opers Mgr*
EMP: 15 **EST:** 1986
SQ FT: 6,700
SALES (est): 1.7MM **Privately Held**
WEB: www.eaglesigns.net
SIC: 3993 Signs & advertising specialties

(P-11546)
EDELMANN USA INC (DH)
Also Called: Bert-Co. of Ontario CA
2150 S Parco Ave, Ontario (91761-5768)
P.O. Box 4150 (91761-1068)
PHONE....................323 669-5700
Rose Van Der Zanden, *Controller*
Analia Torres, *Sales Staff*
EMP: 18 **EST:** 2016
SALES (est): 6.5MM
SALES (corp-wide): 337MM **Privately Held**
WEB: www.edelmannusa.com
SIC: 3993 Signs & advertising specialties
HQ: Edelmann Gmbh
Steinheimer Str. 45
Heidenheim An Der Brenz BW 89518
732 134-00

(P-11547)
ELITE SIGN SERVICES INC
15162 Goldenwest Cir, Westminster (92683-5234)
PHONE....................714 373-0220
Timothy Chau, *President*
EMP: 15 **EST:** 2017
SALES (est): 774.1K **Privately Held**
WEB: www.elitesignservices.com
SIC: 3993 Signs & advertising specialties

(P-11548)
ELRO MANUFACTURING COMPANY (PA)
Also Called: Elro Sign Company
400 W Walnut St, Gardena (90248-3137)
PHONE....................310 380-7444
Max R Rhodes, *CEO*
Frank J Rhodes, *Treasurer*
EMP: 20 **EST:** 1948
SQ FT: 18,000
SALES (est): 5MM **Privately Held**
WEB: www.elrosigns.com
SIC: 3993 Electric signs

(P-11549)
ENCORE IMAGE INC
303 W Main St, Ontario (91762-3843)
P.O. Box 9297 (91762-9297)
PHONE....................909 986-4632
Mark Haist, *President*
Sarah Quezada, *Human Resources*
EMP: 20 **EST:** 1945
SQ FT: 30,000
SALES (est): 3.1MM
SALES (corp-wide): 14.8MM **Privately Held**
WEB: www.encoreimage.com
SIC: 3993 1799 Electric signs; sign installation & maintenance
PA: Encore Image Group, Inc.
1445 Sepulveda Blvd
Torrance CA 90501
310 534-7500

(P-11550)
ENCORE IMAGE GROUP INC (PA)
1445 Sepulveda Blvd, Torrance (90501-5004)
PHONE....................310 534-7500
Kozell Boren, *Ch of Bd*
Tom Johnson, *President*
▲ **EMP:** 90 **EST:** 1959
SQ FT: 70,000
SALES (est): 14.8MM **Privately Held**
WEB: www.encoreimagegroup.com
SIC: 3993 Electric signs

(P-11551)
ENHANCE AMERICA INC
3463 Grapevine St, Jurupa Valley (91752-3504)
PHONE....................951 361-3000
Jackson Ling, *President*
Jeff Hasting, *Officer*
Thomas Dobmeier, *Vice Pres*
Heidi Mann, *Regl Sales Mgr*
Heather Mullen, *Regl Sales Mgr*
◆ **EMP:** 20 **EST:** 2002
SALES (est): 3.2MM **Privately Held**
WEB: www.enhanceamerica.com
SIC: 3993 Signs & advertising specialties

(P-11552)
EVANS MANUFACTURING INC (PA)
7422 Chapman Ave, Garden Grove (92841-2106)
P.O. Box 5669 (92846-0669)
PHONE....................714 379-6100
Alan Vaught, *CEO*
Tiffani Burlingame, *Manager*
Stefani Shubin, *Manager*
▲ **EMP:** 185 **EST:** 1990
SQ FT: 17,000
SALES (est): 55MM **Privately Held**
WEB: www.evans-mfg.com
SIC: 3993 3089 Signs & advertising specialties; injection molding of plastics

(P-11553)
EXPO-3 INTERNATIONAL INC
12350 Edison Way 60, Garden Grove (92841-2810)
PHONE....................714 379-8383
Daniel J Mills, *Ch of Bd*
Chris Smith, *President*
EMP: 30 **EST:** 1974
SQ FT: 60,000
SALES (est): 4.7MM **Privately Held**
WEB: www.expo3.com
SIC: 3993 Displays & cutouts, window & lobby

(P-11554)
FAN FAVE INC
Also Called: Fanfave
10329 Dorset St, Rancho Cucamonga (91730-3067)
PHONE....................909 975-4999
Gary Arnett, *CEO*
Jeff Arnett, *President*
EMP: 20 **EST:** 2012
SQ FT: 17,000
SALES (est): 800K **Privately Held**
WEB: www.fanfave.com
SIC: 3993 Advertising artwork

(P-11555)
FLYNN SIGNS AND GRAPHICS INC
Also Called: Flynn Signs and Letters
1345 Coronado Ave, Long Beach (90804-2806)
PHONE....................562 498-6655
David Flynn. *President*
EMP: 29 **EST:** 1937
SQ FT: 16,150
SALES (est): 646.8K **Privately Held**
WEB: www.signspecialists.com
SIC: 3993 Signs, not made in custom sign painting shops

(P-11556)
FOVELL ENTERPRISES INC
Also Called: Southwest Sign Company
1852 Pomona Rd, Corona (92878-3277)
PHONE....................951 734-6275
Jack Fovell, *CEO*
Karen Hendershot, *Bookkeeper*
▲ **EMP:** 26 **EST:** 1991
SQ FT: 12,500
SALES (est): 4.3MM **Privately Held**
WEB: www.southwestsign.com
SIC: 3993 Electric signs

(P-11557)
FUSION SIGN & DESIGN INC (PA)
680 Columbia Ave, Riverside (92507-2144)
PHONE....................877 477-8777
Loren Hanson, *CEO*
Mark Breininger, *Vice Pres*

P
R
O
D
U
C
T
S
&
S
V
C
S

Michael Moran, *Project Mgr*
Ric Calder, *Controller*
Chip Sigafoos, *Prdtn Mgr*
▲ **EMP:** 108 **EST:** 2006
SALES (est): 21.6MM **Privately Held**
WEB: www.fusionsign.com
SIC: 3993 Electric signs

(P-11558)
GEORGE P JOHNSON COMPANY
18500 Crenshaw Blvd, Torrance
(90504-5055)
PHONE....................310 965-4300
John Capano, *Branch Mgr*
Max Lenderman, *Officer*
Ryan Burke, *Senior VP*
David Rich, *Senior VP*
Greg Buteyn, *Vice Pres*
EMP: 38
SALES (corp-wide): 280MM **Privately Held**
WEB: www.gpj.com
SIC: 3993 Signs & advertising specialties
HQ: George P Johnson Company
　　3600 Giddings Rd
　　Auburn Hills MI 48326
　　248 475-2500

(P-11559)
GRADE A SIGN LLC
529 N La Cienega Blvd # 300, West Hollywood (90048-2001)
PHONE....................310 652-9700
EMP: 20
SALES (est): 1.3MM **Privately Held**
SIC: 3993 Mfg Signs/Advertising Specialties

(P-11560)
HOKE OUTDOOR ADVERTISING INC
1955 N Main St, Orange (92865-4101)
P.O. Box 1666, Canyon Country (91386-1666)
PHONE....................714 637-3610
Robert H Hoke, *President*
Lisa Manuz, *Manager*
EMP: 17 **EST:** 1984
SQ FT: 5,200
SALES (est): 602.4K **Privately Held**
SIC: 3993 7312 Signs, not made in custom sign painting shops; displays & cutouts, window & lobby; billboard advertising

(P-11561)
INFINITY WATCH CORPORATION
Also Called: Iwcus
21078 Commerce Point Dr, Walnut (91789-3051)
PHONE....................626 289-9878
Patrick Tam, *President*
Brenda Tam, *Vice Pres*
▲ **EMP:** 25 **EST:** 1990
SQ FT: 12,000
SALES (est): 2.8MM **Privately Held**
WEB: www.infinitywatch.com
SIC: 3993 Signs & advertising specialties

(P-11562)
INLAND SIGNS INC
Also Called: Inland Custom Manufacturing
1715 S Bon View Ave, Ontario (91761-4410)
PHONE....................909 923-0006
Nthabeleng Maxwell Monese, *CEO*
EMP: 15 **EST:** 2002
SQ FT: 15,000
SALES (est): 4MM **Privately Held**
WEB: www.inlandsigns.com
SIC: 3993 Electric signs

(P-11563)
JOHN BISHOP DESIGN INC
Also Called: J B3d
731 N Main St, Orange (92868-1105)
PHONE....................714 744-2300
John Bishop, *President*
Lisa Bishop, *Corp Secy*
EMP: 38 **EST:** 1989
SQ FT: 1,000
SALES (est): 3.3MM **Privately Held**
SIC: 3993 Signs & advertising specialties

(P-11564)
K S DESIGNS INC
Also Called: Cal West Designs
9515 Sorensen Ave, Santa Fe Springs (90670-2650)
PHONE....................562 929-3973
Robin Shelton, *President*
EMP: 32 **EST:** 1979
SQ FT: 49,000
SALES (est): 4.9MM **Privately Held**
SIC: 3993 Displays & cutouts, window & lobby

(P-11565)
KIM BONJUN INC (PA)
821 S Vermont Ave, Los Angeles (90005-1582)
PHONE....................213 385-1258
Kin Jun, *Principal*
Chris Kim, *General Mgr*
EMP: 20 **EST:** 2010
SALES (est): 125.4K **Privately Held**
SIC: 3993 Signs & advertising specialties

(P-11566)
LA6721 LLC
6721 Romaine St, Los Angeles (90038-2425)
PHONE....................323 484-4070
Maria Endoza, *President*
Julian Poon, *Administration*
EMP: 14 **EST:** 2015
SALES (est): 1MM **Privately Held**
SIC: 3993 Signs & advertising specialties

(P-11567)
LOCAL NEON CO INC
12536 Chadron Ave, Hawthorne (90250-4850)
PHONE....................310 978-2000
Scott Blakely, *President*
Cassius C Blakely, *Shareholder*
Jeanne Blakely, *Admin Sec*
EMP: 21 **EST:** 1953
SQ FT: 20,000
SALES (est): 1.5MM **Privately Held**
WEB: www.lnisigns.com
SIC: 3993 Signs & advertising specialties

(P-11568)
LOREN INDUSTRIES
Also Called: Loren Electric Sign & Lighting
12226 Coast Dr, Whittier (90601-1607)
PHONE....................562 699-1122
Daniel Marc Lorenzon, *CEO*
Michelle Lornezon, *Vice Pres*
Christopher Reiff, *Sales Staff*
EMP: 45 **EST:** 1996
SQ FT: 8,000
SALES (est): 6.7MM **Privately Held**
WEB: www.lorenindustries.com
SIC: 3993 3648 1799 Electric signs; outdoor lighting equipment; street lighting fixtures; sign installation & maintenance

(P-11569)
MANERI SIGN CO INC
1928 W 135th St, Gardena (90249-2452)
PHONE....................310 327-6261
Don Nicholas, *President*
Jamie Austin, *Sales Staff*
Samantha Norys, *Accounts Mgr*
EMP: 35
SQ FT: 20,000
SALES (est): 6MM
SALES (corp-wide): 81.9MM **Privately Held**
WEB: www.manerisign.com
SIC: 3993 Signs & advertising specialties
PA: Traffic Solutions Corporation
　　4000 Westerly Pl Ste 100
　　Newport Beach CA 92660
　　949 553-8272

(P-11570)
MANERI SIGN CO INC
1100 Main St, Irvine (92614-6737)
P.O. Box 5299 (92616-5299)
PHONE....................310 327-6261
EMP: 16 **EST:** 2018
SALES (est): 718.8K **Privately Held**
WEB: www.manerisignco.com
SIC: 3993 Signs & advertising specialties

(P-11571)
MAXWELL ALARM SCREEN MFG INC
Also Called: Maxwell Sign and Decal Div
20327 Nordhoff St, Chatsworth (91311-6128)
PHONE....................818 773-5533
Michael A Kagen, *CEO*
Patty Kagen, *Treasurer*
Rita Cortes, *Office Mgr*
EMP: 28 **EST:** 1977
SQ FT: 28,000
SALES (est): 3.7MM **Privately Held**
WEB: www.maxwellmfg.com
SIC: 3993 3442 Signs & advertising specialties; screens, window, metal

(P-11572)
MEGA SIGN INC
Also Called: Mega Led Technology
5900 S Eastrn Ave Ste 141, Commerce (90040)
PHONE....................888 315-7446
David Park, *President*
Sean Kim, *Opers Staff*
Joseph Kim, *Asst Director*
▲ **EMP:** 22 **EST:** 2007
SALES (est): 4.5MM **Privately Held**
WEB: www.megasigninc.com
SIC: 3993 Electric signs

(P-11573)
METAL ART OF CALIFORNIA INC (PA)
Also Called: Sign Mart
640 N Cypress St, Orange (92867-6604)
PHONE....................714 532-7100
Gene S Sobel, *President*
Calvin Larson, *Vice Pres*
Tori Agathakis, *General Mgr*
April Flett, *Controller*
Sergio Ruelas, *Sales Staff*
◆ **EMP:** 91
SQ FT: 22,000
SALES (est): 19MM **Privately Held**
WEB: www.sign-mart.com
SIC: 3993 Signs & advertising specialties

(P-11574)
MMXVIII HOLDINGS INC
20251 Sw Acacia St # 120, Newport Beach (92660-0768)
PHONE....................800 672-3974
John Morris,
EMP: 24 **EST:** 2016
SQ FT: 7,500
SALES (est): 3.6MM **Privately Held**
SIC: 3993 Signs & advertising specialties

(P-11575)
MYERS & SONS HI-WAY SAFETY INC (PA)
13310 5th St, Chino (91710-5125)
P.O. Box 1030 (91708-1030)
PHONE....................909 591-1781
Michael Rodgers, *CEO*
Brandon Myer, *Exec VP*
Jose Quiroz, *Sales Staff*
Jensen Carson, *Manager*
▲ **EMP:** 80 **EST:** 1970
SQ FT: 36,400
SALES (est): 24.6MM **Privately Held**
WEB: www.hiwaysafety.com
SIC: 3993 Signs, not made in custom sign painting shops

(P-11576)
NATIONAL SIGN & MARKETING CORP
13580 5th St, Chino (91710-5113)
P.O. Box 2409 (91708-2409)
PHONE....................909 591-4742
John J Kane, *President*
Jeffrey Fredrickson, *Corp Secy*
Greg Rice, *Officer*
Rhonda Robinson, *Project Mgr*
Carmen Gomez, *Human Res Dir*
EMP: 70
SQ FT: 46,000
SALES (est): 12.6MM **Privately Held**
WEB: www.nsmc.com
SIC: 3993 Neon signs

(P-11577)
NEIMAN/HOELLER INC
Also Called: Neiman & Company
6842 Valjean Ave, Van Nuys (9 406-4712)
PHONE....................8 8 781-8600
Harry J Neiman, *CEO*
Robert R Hoeller III, *President*
Will Raksin, *Sr Project Mgr*
EMP: 56
SQ FT: 17,000
SALES (est): 7.1MM **Privately Held**
WEB: www.neimanandco.com
SIC: 3993 3646 Electric signs ornamental lighting fixtures, commercial

(P-11578)
NK SIGN INDUSTRY INC
2546 S Union Ave, Bakersfield (93307-5009)
PHONE....................661 348-9580
Gurpreet S Sachdav, *Administration*
EMP: 14 **EST:** 2013
SALES (est): 494.1K **Privately Held**
WEB: www.voltechsigns.com
SIC: 3993 Signs & advertising specialties

(P-11579)
OPTEC DISPLAYS INC
1700 S De Soto Pl Ste A, Ontario (91761-8060)
PHONE....................626 369-7188
Shu Hwa Wu, *President*
Andy LI, *Prgrmr*
Mark Tangeman, *Sales Assoc-ate*
Jeff Gatzow, *Marketing Staff*
Eric Chan, *Sales Staff*
◆ **EMP:** 64 **EST:** 1996
SALES (est): 12.1MM **Privately Held**
WEB: www.optec.com
SIC: 3993 Signs & advertising specialties

(P-11580)
ORANGE CNTY NAME PLATE CO INC
13201 Arctic Cir, Santa Fe Springs (90670-5509)
P.O. Box 2764 (90670-0764
PHONE....................714 522-7693
Elias Rodriguez, *President*
Sam Rodriguez, *Corp Secy*
Ben L Rodriguez, *Vice Pres*
Mike Rogy, *Sales Mgr*
John Alfieri, *Sales Staff*
EMP: 85 **EST:** 1965
SQ FT: 31,000
SALES (est): 13.6MM **Privately Held**
WEB: www.ocnameplates.com
SIC: 3993 Name plates: except engraved, etched, etc.: metal

(P-11581)
PD GROUP
Also Called: Sign-A-Rama
41945 Boardwalk Ste L, Palm Desert (92211-9099)
PHONE....................760 674-3028
Jeff Gracy, *President*
Terrance Flannagan, *Vice Pres*
Terry Flanagan, *Info Tech Mgr*
Ed Landen, *Sales Staff*
Ashley Robbins, *Sales Staff*
EMP: 25 **EST:** 1995
SQ FT: 11,500
SALES (est): 5.5MM **Privately Held**
WEB: www.signarama.com
SIC: 3993 7389 5999 Signs & advertising specialties; sign painting & lettering shop; banners

(P-11582)
PRIMUS INC
Also Called: Western Highway Products
17901 Jamestown Ln, Huntington Beach (92647-7138)
P.O. Box 534 (92648-0534)
PHONE....................714 527-2261
Steve Ellsworth, *President*
Timothy M Riordan, *Vice Pres*
▲ **EMP:** 80 **EST:** 1926
SQ FT: 120,000
SALES (est): 9.8MM **Privately Held**
WEB: www.primus.us
SIC: 3993 Signs, not made in custom sign painting shops

(P-11583)
PRO-LITE INC
Also Called: Advanced Products
3505 Cadillac Ave Ste D, Costa Mesa
(92626-1464)
PHONE...................714 668-9988
Kuo-Fong Kaoh, *President*
Tom Yerke, *Vice Pres*
Austin Liao, *Manager*
▲ EMP: 17 EST: 1986
SQ FT: 7,200
SALES (est): 3MM **Privately Held**
WEB: www.pro-lite.com
SIC: 3993 Signs & advertising specialties

(P-11584)
QUIEL BROS ELC SIGN SVC CO INC
272 S I St, San Bernardino (92410-2408)
PHONE...................909 885-4476
Larry R Quiel, *President*
Raymond Quiel, *Chairman*
Gary Quiel, *Vice Pres*
Jerry Quiel, *Vice Pres*
David Northchutt, *Technology*
▲ EMP: 40 EST: 1962
SQ FT: 8,000
SALES (est): 4.8MM **Privately Held**
WEB: www.quielsigns.com
SIC: 3993 7353 1731 7629 Electric
signs; cranes & aerial lift equipment,
rental or leasing; general electrical con-
tractor; electrical equipment repair, high
voltage

(P-11585)
R&M DEESE INC
Also Called: Electro-Tech's
1875 Sampson Ave, Corona (92879-6009)
P.O. Box 2317 (92878-2317)
PHONE...................951 734-7342
Raymond Deese, *President*
Mary Deese, *Corp Secy*
Ray Deese, *Executive*
▲ EMP: 22 EST: 1976
SQ FT: 20,000
SALES (est): 2.3MM **Privately Held**
WEB: www.electro-techs.net
SIC: 3993 3679 Signs & advertising spe-
cialties; liquid crystal displays (LCD)

(P-11586)
RICHARDS NEON SHOP INC
Also Called: RNS Channel Letters
4375 Prado Rd Ste 102, Corona
(92878-7444)
PHONE...................951 279-6767
Richard Pando, *President*
EMP: 24 EST: 1991
SALES (est): 3.6MM **Privately Held**
WEB: www.rnsletters.com
SIC: 3993 Electric signs

(P-11587)
ROSS NAME PLATE COMPANY
2 Red Plum Cir, Monterey Park
(91755-7486)
PHONE...................323 725-6812
Michael Ross, *President*
Syndi Akopoff, *Admin Sec*
Jose Gomez, *Purchasing*
Chris Spinelli, *Sales Staff*
Letty Torres, *Receptionist*
EMP: 37 EST: 1957
SQ FT: 25,000
SALES (est): 4.8MM **Privately Held**
WEB: www.rossnameplate.com
SIC: 3993 2754 Name plates: except en-
graved, etched, etc.; metal; labels:
gravure printing

(P-11588)
RUBEN & LEON INC
Also Called: Tako Tyko Sign & Lighting
5002 Venice Blvd, Los Angeles
(90019-5308)
PHONE...................310 486-6648
Eric Cielak, *Principal*
EMP: 18 EST: 1988
SALES (est): 408.2K **Privately Held**
SIC: 3993 Electric signs

(P-11589)
RUSH BUSINESS FORMS INC
Also Called: Informs
3860 E Eagle Dr Ste A, Anaheim
(92807-1706)
PHONE...................714 630-5661
Louis John Katzman, *CEO*
David Flucht, *President*
John Katzman, *Vice Pres*
Gail Conklin, *Controller*
EMP: 22 EST: 1976
SQ FT: 10,000
SALES (est): 1.8MM **Privately Held**
WEB: www.rush-business-forms-inc-in-ana-
heim-ca.cityfos.com
SIC: 5943 3993 Office forms & supplies;
signs & advertising specialties

(P-11590)
S2K GRAPHICS INC
Also Called: S 2 K
9255 Deering Ave, Chatsworth
(91311-5804)
PHONE...................818 885-3900
Dan C Pulos, *CEO*
Jack Wilson, *Ch of Bd*
Dana Rosellini, *Corp Secy*
Jane Dretzka, *Executive*
Michelle Lindberg, *Executive*
EMP: 35 EST: 1989
SALES (est): 7.5MM
SALES (corp-wide): 2.1B **Privately Held**
WEB: www.s2kgraphics.com
SIC: 3993 7532 2759 Signs & advertising
specialties; truck painting & lettering;
screen printing
HQ: Franke Usa Holding, Inc.
1105 N Market St Ste 1300
Wilmington DE 19801

(P-11591)
SAFETY SYSTEMS HAWAII
P.O. Box 5299 (92616-5299)
PHONE...................808 847-4017
Adam Gonzalez, *Branch Mgr*
Jonathan Baijo, *Training Spec*
Romina Isimang, *Sales Staff*
Darin Fushikoshi, *Manager*
Romy Sarte, *Manager*
EMP: 22 EST: 2011
SALES (est): 2MM **Privately Held**
WEB: www.sshinc.com
SIC: 3993 Signs & advertising specialties

(P-11592)
SAFEWAY SIGN COMPANY
9875 Yucca Rd, Adelanto (92301-2282)
PHONE...................760 246-7070
Michael F Moore, *President*
Andrea M Gutierrez, *Vice Pres*
David C Moore, *Vice Pres*
Mina Alvarez, *Sales Staff*
EMP: 49 EST: 1948
SQ FT: 60,000
SALES (est): 9.4MM **Privately Held**
WEB: www.safewaysign.com
SIC: 3993 Signs, not made in custom sign
painting shops

(P-11593)
SAN PEDRO SIGN COMPANY
701 Lakme Ave, Wilmington (90744-5943)
PHONE...................310 549-4661
Gus Navarro, *President*
Margarita Bautista, *Controller*
EMP: 25 EST: 1976
SQ FT: 7,000
SALES (est): 1.4MM **Privately Held**
WEB: www.spesco.com
SIC: 3993 Electric signs

(P-11594)
SHYE WEST INC (PA)
Also Called: Imagine This
43 Corporate Park Ste 102, Irvine
(92606-5137)
PHONE...................949 486-4598
Patrick Papaccio, *President*
Craig Perkins, *President*
Shawn Keep, *Vice Pres*
Chris Tipton, *Vice Pres*
Gretchen Krebs, *Executive*
▲ EMP: 27 EST: 1999
SQ FT: 6,000

SALES (est): 11.2MM **Privately Held**
SIC: 3993 5099 Advertising novelties; novelties, durable

(P-11595)
SIGN DEVELOPMENT INC
Also Called: S D I
1366 W 9th St, Upland (91786-5721)
PHONE...................909 920-5535
Daniel P O'Hara, *President*
Fernando Baluyot, *Vice Pres*
EMP: 14 EST: 1989
SQ FT: 7,000
SALES (est): 2MM **Privately Held**
WEB: www.signs-of-development.org
SIC: 3993 Signs & advertising specialties

(P-11596)
SIGN FACTORY PRINTING & OFFIC
120 N 4th St, El Centro (92243-5105)
PHONE...................760 357-0098
Mario Rodriguez, *President*
EMP: 14 EST: 2015
SALES (est): 650.7K **Privately Held**
SIC: 3993 Signs & advertising specialties

(P-11597)
SIGN INDUSTRIES INC
2101 Carrillo Privado, Ontario
(91761-7600)
PHONE...................909 930-0303
Maria Saavedra, *President*
Enrique Saavedra, *Admin Sec*
Paul Lopez, *Director*
Mark Chavez, *Accounts Exec*
Guijarro Paul, *Accounts Exec*
▲ EMP: 30 EST: 1994
SQ FT: 4,500
SALES (est): 8.6MM **Privately Held**
WEB: www.signindustries.tv
SIC: 3993 Neon signs

(P-11598)
SIGN PIPERS INC
17451 Nichols Ln Ste C, Huntington Beach
(92647-8718)
PHONE...................657 215-3957
EMP: 16 EST: 2017
SALES (est): 417.6K **Privately Held**
WEB: www.signpipers.com
SIC: 3993 Signs & advertising specialties

(P-11599)
SIGN SPECIALISTS CORPORATION
111 W Dyer Rd Ste F, Santa Ana
(92707-3425)
PHONE...................714 641-0064
Garrick Batt, *CEO*
Tariq Shaikh, *Vice Pres*
Tony Wilbanks, *Graphic Designe*
Miguel Zavala, *Graphic Designe*
Curtis Broadway, *Sales Mgr*
EMP: 22 EST: 2001
SALES (est): 4.8MM **Privately Held**
WEB: www.signspecialists.com
SIC: 3993 Signs, not made in custom sign
painting shops

(P-11600)
SIGNAGE SOLUTIONS CORPORATION
2231 S Dupont Dr, Anaheim (92806-6105)
PHONE...................714 491-0299
Chris Deruyter, *CEO*
Jim Gledhill, *Vice Pres*
Rene Camarena, *Project Mgr*
Susanna Garcia, *Project Mgr*
Michael Morelli, *Sales Staff*
EMP: 30 EST: 1990
SQ FT: 14,000
SALES (est): 5.4MM **Privately Held**
WEB: www.signage-solutions.com
SIC: 3993 7389 Signs & advertising spe-
cialties; sign painting & lettering shop

(P-11601)
SIGNS AND SERVICES COMPANY
10980 Boatman Ave, Stanton
(90680-2602)
PHONE...................714 761-8200
Jacob Deryuyter, *CEO*
Matt De Ruyter, *President*

David Terrack, *Vice Pres*
Kelly Hunt, *Project Mgr*
Henry Hu, *Controller*
EMP: 33 EST: 1986
SQ FT: 16,000
SALES (est): 4.5MM **Privately Held**
WEB: www.signsandservicesco.com
SIC: 3993 Signs, not made in custom sign
painting shops

(P-11602)
SIGNS OF SUCCESS INC
2350 Skyway Dr Ste 10, Santa Maria
(93455-1532)
PHONE...................805 925-7545
Stephen Sheppard, *President*
Glenda Sheppard, *Treasurer*
EMP: 20 EST: 1991
SQ FT: 3,600
SALES (est): 2.6MM **Privately Held**
WEB: www.signsofsuccess.net
SIC: 3993 7389 5999 Signs & advertising
specialties; sign painting & lettering shop;
decals

(P-11603)
SIGNWORLD AMERICA INC (PA)
12023 Arrow Rte, Rancho Cucamonga
(91739-9219)
PHONE...................844 900-7446
Yangchi Chung, *CEO*
◆ EMP: 55 EST: 2013
SALES (est): 512.2K **Privately Held**
WEB: www.signworldamerica.com
SIC: 3993 5199 5999 Signs & advertising
specialties; advertising specialties; ban-
ners

(P-11604)
SIMPLY DISPLAY
12200 Los Nietos Rd, Santa Fe Springs
(90670-2910)
PHONE...................888 767-0676
Megan Barrett, *CEO*
Richard Barnes, *CIO*
Edwin Diaz, *Prdtn Mgr*
▲ EMP: 15 EST: 2013
SALES (est): 517.7K **Privately Held**
WEB: www.simplydisplays.com
SIC: 3993 Signs & advertising specialties

(P-11605)
STANDARDVISION LLC
3370 N San Fernando Rd, Los Angeles
(90065-1440)
PHONE...................323 222-3630
Adrian Velicescu, *CEO*
Brad Gwinn, *COO*
Alberto Garcia, *Officer*
Grif Palmer, *Vice Pres*
Joshua Van Blankenship, *Vice Pres*
▲ EMP: 34 EST: 2007
SQ FT: 25,000
SALES (est): 5.9MM **Privately Held**
WEB: www.standardvision.com
SIC: 3993 7336 Signs & advertising spe-
cialties; commercial art & graphic design

(P-11606)
STOP-LOOK SIGN CO INTL INC
Also Called: Stop Look Plastics Inc
401 Commercial Way, La Habra
(90631-6168)
PHONE...................562 690-7576
Larry Dobkin, *President*
Mike Dougherty, *Treasurer*
Christine Dougherty, *Vice Pres*
Janet Dobkin, *Admin Sec*
▲ EMP: 15 EST: 1960
SQ FT: 8,000
SALES (est): 1MM **Privately Held**
WEB: www.stoplooksign.com
SIC: 3993 Signs & advertising specialties

(P-11607)
SUNSET SIGNS AND PRINTING INC
Also Called: Contractor
2906 E Coronado St, Anaheim
(92806-2501)
PHONE...................714 255-9104
Tracy Eschenbrenner, *CEO*
Heather Kelperis, *Controller*
Eric Russell, *Sales Mgr*
EMP: 50 EST: 1992

SALES (est): 8.4MM Privately Held
WEB: www.sunsetsignsoc.com
SIC: 3993 Signs & advertising specialties

(P-11608)
SUPERIOR ELECTRICAL ADVG INC (PA)
1700 W Anaheim St, Long Beach (90813-1102)
PHONE...................................562 495-3808
Jim Sterk, *CEO*
Patti Skoglundadams, *President*
Stan Janocha, *COO*
Doug Tokeshi, *CFO*
Steve Feist, *Division Mgr*
▲ EMP: 85 EST: 1962
SQ FT: 100,000
SALES: 15.7MM Privately Held
WEB: www.superiorsigns.com
SIC: 3993 7629 Electric signs; electrical equipment repair services

(P-11609)
TAE GWANG INC
4922 S Figueroa St, Los Angeles (90037-3344)
PHONE...................................323 233-2882
Sammy Chu, *President*
EMP: 13 EST: 1994
SQ FT: 3,401
SALES (est): 998.5K Privately Held
WEB: www.tgsignco.com
SIC: 3993 Signs & advertising specialties

(P-11610)
TDI SIGNS
13158 Arctic Cir, Santa Fe Springs (90670-5508)
PHONE...................................562 436-5188
Arthur Rivas, *President*
Winnie Duzon, *Bookkeeper*
EMP: 25 EST: 2003
SALES (est): 3.2MM Privately Held
WEB: www.tdisigns.com
SIC: 3993 Electric signs

(P-11611)
TFN ARCHITECTURAL SIGNAGE INC (PA)
Also Called: Third Floor North Company
3411 W Lake Center Dr, Santa Ana (92704-6925)
PHONE...................................714 556-0990
Brian L Burnett, *President*
Catherine Burnett, *Shareholder*
Jeff Burnett, *Shareholder*
Teresa Burnett, *Treasurer*
Ellen Vaughn, *Admin Sec*
EMP: 44 EST: 1980
SQ FT: 8,800
SALES (est): 5.4MM Privately Held
WEB: www.thirdfloornorth.com
SIC: 3993 Signs, not made in custom sign painting shops

(P-11612)
TRADENET ENTERPRISE INC
Also Called: Vantage Led
1580 Magnolia Ave, Corona (92879-2073)
PHONE...................................888 595-3956
Chris MA, *CEO*
Yuusuke Arimura, *COO*
Ricky Chai, *Vice Pres*
Leo Mares, *Technical Staff*
Lisa Tully, *Graphic Designe*
▲ EMP: 60 EST: 1997
SALES (est): 11.4MM Privately Held
WEB: www.vantageled.com
SIC: 3993 Electric signs

(P-11613)
UNIVERSAL MERCANTILE EXCH INC
Also Called: Umx
21128 Commerce Point Dr, Walnut (91789-3053)
PHONE...................................909 839-0556
Hs Che Wang, *President*
William Huang, *Vice Pres*
▲ EMP: 14 EST: 1997
SQ FT: 8,026

SALES (est): 630.7K Privately Held
WEB: www.umei.com
SIC: 3993 5091 5099 Signs & advertising specialties; golf & skiing equipment & supplies; fire extinguishers

(P-11614)
VISIBLE GRAPHICS INC
9736 Eton Ave, Chatsworth (91311-4305)
PHONE...................................818 787-0477
Janine Kendall, *CEO*
Ken Kendall, *CFO*
Abel Barajas, *Technician*
Hugo De Leon, *Technician*
Juan Flores, *Technician*
EMP: 16 EST: 2002
SALES: 6.6MM Privately Held
WEB: www.visiblegraphics.com
SIC: 3993 Signs & advertising specialties

(P-11615)
VOGUE SIGN INC
715 Commercial Ave, Oxnard (93030-7233)
PHONE...................................805 487-7222
Jack Woodruff, *President*
Christian Muldoon, *Project Mgr*
Genaro Gomez, *Graphic Designe*
Dave Jones, *Prdtn Mgr*
Kirk Hamilton, *Sales Mgr*
EMP: 22 EST: 1955
SQ FT: 11,000
SALES (est): 1.8MM Privately Held
WEB: www.voguesigns.com
SIC: 3993 Electric signs

(P-11616)
YOUNG ELECTRIC SIGN COMPANY
Also Called: Yesco
10235 Bellegrave Ave, Jurupa Valley (91752-1919)
PHONE...................................909 923-7668
Duane Wardle, *Branch Mgr*
Megan Hornsby, *Office Mgr*
Bob Mountain, *Safety Mgr*
Dale Ingraham, *Manager*
EMP: 35
SQ FT: 8,500
SALES (corp-wide): 498.1MM Privately Held
WEB: www.yesco.com
SIC: 3993 1799 Electric signs; sign installation & maintenance
PA: Young Electric Sign Company Inc
    2401 S Foothill Dr
    Salt Lake City UT 84109
    801 464-4600

(P-11617)
ZUMAR INDUSTRIES INC
9719 Santa Fe Springs Rd, Santa Fe Springs (90670-2919)
PHONE...................................562 941-4633
Benn Limcke, *President*
Lee Young, *CFO*
Christine Alderette, *Administration*
Pamela Foster, *Accounts Mgr*
Maggie Villarreal, *Accounts Mgr*
EMP: 56 EST: 1947
SQ FT: 30,000
SALES (est): 9.9MM
SALES (corp-wide): 24.3MM Privately Held
WEB: www.zumar.com
SIC: 3993 Signs & advertising specialties
PA: Zumar Industries, Inc.
    12015 Steele St S
    Tacoma WA 98444
    253 536-7740

3996 Linoleum & Hard Surface Floor Coverings, NEC

(P-11618)
ALTRO USA INC
Also Called: Compass Flooring
12648 Clark St, Santa Fe Springs (90670-3950)
PHONE...................................562 944-8292
Al Boegh, *Principal*
Bruce Wright, *Executive*

Daniel Erickson, *Technical Staff*
EMP: 57
SALES (corp-wide): 24.2MM Privately Held
WEB: www.altrofloors.com
SIC: 3996 Hard surface floor coverings; resilient floor coverings: tile or sheet
PA: Altro Usa, Inc.
    80 Industrial Way Ste 1
    Wilmington MA 01887
    800 377-5597

(P-11619)
ARMSTRONG FLOORING INC
5037 Patata St, South Gate (90280-3549)
P.O. Box 1489 (90280-1489)
PHONE...................................323 562-7258
EMP: 83
SQ FT: 51,000
SALES (corp-wide): 584.8MM Publicly Held
WEB: www.armstrongflooring.com
SIC: 3996 Hard Surface Floor Coverings, Nec
PA: Armstrong Flooring, Inc.
    2500 Columbia Ave
    Lancaster PA 17601
    717 672-9611

(P-11620)
NEW IMAGE COMMERCIAL FLRG INC
Also Called: New Image Flooring
10444 Corporate Dr Ste B, Redlands (92374-4531)
P.O. Box 10536, San Bernardino (92423-0536)
PHONE...................................909 796-3400
Sergio Delgado Sr, *President*
Richard Delgado, *Vice Pres*
Judy Delgado, *Admin Sec*
▲ EMP: 15 EST: 1999
SQ FT: 8,697
SALES (est): 1.7MM Privately Held
SIC: 5713 3996 Floor covering stores; asphalted-felt-base floor coverings: linoleum, carpet

---
3999 Manufacturing Industries, NEC

(P-11621)
A & A JEWELRY TOOLS FINDINGS
Also Called: A&A Jewelry Tools & Supplies
319 W 6th St, Los Angeles (90014-1703)
PHONE...................................213 627-8004
Gene Adem, *Partner*
Robert Adem, *Partner*
Fouad Farah, *Partner*
Naim Farah, *Partner*
Phlip Farah, *Partner*
▲ EMP: 16 EST: 1980
SQ FT: 3,000
SALES (est): 2.3MM Privately Held
WEB: www.aajewelry.com
SIC: 3999 5944 Atomizers, toiletry; jewelry, precious stones & precious metals

(P-11622)
A S G CORPORATION
Also Called: Smith & Company
1361 Newton St, Los Angeles (90021-2723)
PHONE...................................213 748-6361
Albert Weiss, *President*
William Weiss, *Vice Pres*
Esther Weiss, *Admin Sec*
◆ EMP: 14 EST: 1947
SALES (est): 512.8K Privately Held
SIC: 3999 7929 Lamp shade frames; entertainers & entertainment groups

(P-11623)
ABOVE & BEYOND BALLOONS INC
Also Called: Above and Beyond
16661 Jamboree Rd, Irvine (92606-5118)
PHONE...................................949 586-8470
Michael Chaklos, *CEO*
Karen Chaklos, *Vice Pres*
▲ EMP: 44 EST: 2002
SQ FT: 25,000

SALES (est): 6.1MM Privately Held
WEB: www.advertisingballoons.com
SIC: 3999 Advertising display products

(P-11624)
ACCURATE STAGING MFG INC (PA)
13900 S Figueroa St, Los Angeles (90061-1028)
PHONE...................................310 324-1040
Alfredo Gomez, *CEO*
Jose Cantu, *President*
Johnny Cantu, *Sales Staff*
EMP: 13 EST: 2001
SQ FT: 18,000
SALES (est): 5.6MM Privately Held
WEB: www.accuratestaging.com
SIC: 3999 Stage hardware & equipment, except lighting

(P-11625)
ADVANCED BUILDING SYSTEMS INC
11905 Regentview Ave, Downey (90241-5515)
PHONE...................................818 652-4252
Alex Youssef, *President*
EMP: 20 EST: 2018
SALES (est): 1.4MM Privately Held
SIC: 3999 Manufacturing industries

(P-11626)
ADVANCED COSMETIC RES LABS INC
Also Called: Acrl
20550 Prairie St, Chatsworth (91311-6006)
PHONE...................................818 709-9945
Kitty Hunter, *President*
Celeste Guillen, *Research*
Alex Rapoport, *Engineer*
Fred Radvinsky, *Purchasing*
Richard Garza, *Sr Project Mgr*
▲ EMP: 50 EST: 1994
SQ FT: 48,000
SALES (est): 9.5MM Privately Held
WEB: www.acrl.com
SIC: 3999 2844 Barber & beauty shop equipment; toilet preparations

(P-11627)
ADVANCED MOBILITY INC
7720 Sepulveda Blvd, Van Nuys (91405-1018)
PHONE...................................818 780-1788
Scott Deacon, *President*
Linda V Winkle, *Treasurer*
Linda Van Winkle, *Corp Secy*
Bill Deacon, *Vice Pres*
EMP: 16 EST: 1975
SQ FT: 12,000
SALES (est): 649.5K Privately Held
WEB: www.mobilityworks.com
SIC: 3999 5531 Wool pulling; automotive accessories

(P-11628)
ALLAGASH INDUSTRIES INC
1656 Sargent Pl, Los Angeles (90026-2626)
PHONE...................................212 246-5757
Patricia O'Hearn, *Principal*
Jenny Alfrey, *Executive Asst*
Jordan Keeler, *Admin Asst*
Karl Arnberg, *Technician*
Jessica Caruso, *Project Mgr*
EMP: 13 EST: 2018
SALES (est): 321K Privately Held
WEB: www.allagash.com
SIC: 3999 Manufacturing industries

(P-11629)
AMARETTO ORCHARDS LLC
Also Called: Famoso Nut
32331 Famoso Woody Rd, Mc Farland (93250-9771)
PHONE...................................661 399-9697
Bruce Baretta,
Haydee Quevedo, *Admin Asst*
Dominique Camou, *Production*
Marisol Rodriguez, *Assistant*
◆ EMP: 20 EST: 1990
SALES (est): 2.6MM Privately Held
SIC: 3999 2068 Nut shells, grinding, from purchased nuts; salted & roasted nuts & seeds

(P-11630)
AMGEN MANUFACTURING LIMITED
1 Amgen Center Dr, Newbury Park
(91320-1799)
PHONE....................787 656-2000
Victoria H Blatter, *Principal*
Raphael Van Eemeren, *Senior Mgr*
Iris Lugo, *Manager*
EMP: 61 **EST:** 2008
SALES (est): 15.5MM
SALES (corp-wide): 25.4B **Publicly Held**
WEB: www.amgen.com
SIC: 3999 Atomizers, toiletry
PA: Amgen Inc.
  1 Amgen Center Dr
  Thousand Oaks CA 91320
  805 447-1000

(P-11631)
AR INDUSTRIES
730 E Edna Pl, Covina (91723-1408)
PHONE....................626 332-8918
Anthony Rosas, *President*
EMP: 15 **EST:** 2010
SALES (est): 720.2K **Privately Held**
WEB: www.anthonyrosaspaintingcontractor.com
SIC: 3999 Manufacturing industries

(P-11632)
ARAMARK UNIFORM MFG CO
115 N First St, Burbank (91502-1856)
PHONE....................800 999-8989
EMP: 13 **EST:** 2013
SALES (est): 3.7MM **Publicly Held**
WEB: www.aramarkuniform.com
SIC: 3999 Manufacturing industries
HQ: Aramark Services, Inc.
  2400 Market St
  Philadelphia PA 19103
  215 238-3000

(P-11633)
ARTIFICIAL GRASS LIQUIDATORS
Also Called: Agl
42505 Rio Nedo, Temecula (92590-3726)
PHONE....................951 677-3377
Dillon Georgian, *President*
EMP: 30 **EST:** 2015
SALES (est): 2.6MM **Privately Held**
WEB: www.artificialgrassliquidators.com
SIC: 3999 Grasses, artificial & preserved

(P-11634)
ATA-BOY
3171 Los Feliz Blvd # 205, Los Angeles
(90039-1536)
PHONE....................323 644-0117
Alan Cushman, *President*
Judy Albright, *CFO*
Alex Perez, *Natl Sales Mgr*
▲ **EMP:** 17 **EST:** 1986
SQ FT: 4,000
SALES (est): 967.9K **Privately Held**
WEB: www.ata-boy.com
SIC: 3999 5947 Novelties, bric-a-brac &
hobby kits; gift shop

(P-11635)
ATLAS MATCH LLC
1337 Limerick Dr, Placentia (92870-3410)
PHONE....................714 993-3328
EMP: 60
SALES (est): 2.2MM **Privately Held**
SIC: 3999 Mfg Misc Products

(P-11636)
BCD INDUSTRIES CORP
24298 Via Vargas Dr, Moreno Valley
(92553-6231)
PHONE....................760 927-8988
Juan Briseno, *Principal*
EMP: 17 **EST:** 2017
SALES (est): 1.4MM **Privately Held**
SIC: 3999 Manufacturing industries

(P-11637)
BEAUTY TENT INC
1131 N Kenmore Ave Apt 6, Los Angeles
(90029-1525)
PHONE....................323 717-7131
Naira Harutyunyan, *President*
EMP: 25 **EST:** 2019

SALES: 735.9K **Privately Held**
WEB: www.beautytent.com
SIC: 3999 Hair curlers, designed for
beauty parlors

(P-11638)
BIO-REIGNS INC
1451 Edinger Ave Ste D, Tustin
(92780-6250)
PHONE....................949 922-2032
Bryan Reed, *President*
EMP: 25 **EST:** 2018
SALES (est): 5.3MM **Privately Held**
WEB: www.bioreigns.com
SIC: 3999

(P-11639)
BLEEKER MANUFACTURING INC
2721 W Coast Hwy, Newport Beach
(92663-4720)
PHONE....................800 421-1107
EMP: 20 **EST:** 2016
SALES (est): 619K **Privately Held**
WEB: www.bleekerbros.com
SIC: 3999 Manufacturing industries

(P-11640)
BRIGHT GLOW CANDLE COMPANY INC (PA)
110 Erie St, Pomona (91768-3342)
PHONE....................909 469-4733
Richard Alcedo, *President*
◆ **EMP:** 38 **EST:** 1990
SQ FT: 64,000
SALES (est): 6.8MM **Privately Held**
WEB: www.brightglowcandle.com
SIC: 3999 Candles

(P-11641)
BROTHERS OF INDUSTRY INC
3891 N Ventura Ave Ste B1, Ventura
(93001-1271)
PHONE....................805 628-3545
Peter Hernandez, *President*
Andrew Hernandez, *President*
Kate Hernandez, *President*
Thomas Masker, *President*
EMP: 15 **EST:** 2017
SALES (est): 2MM **Privately Held**
WEB: www.brothersofindustry.com
SIC: 3999 Manufacturing industries

(P-11642)
BRYBRADAN INC
3016 N Alameda St, Compton
(90222-1471)
PHONE....................323 230-8604
Raul Gonzalez, *President*
EMP: 15 **EST:** 2007
SALES (est): 740.4K **Privately Held**
SIC: 3999 Candles

(P-11643)
C&M INDUSTRIES
4506 Maine Ave Ste D, Baldwin Park
(91706-2643)
P.O. Box 4759, La Puente (91747-4759)
PHONE....................626 391-5102
Juan Munoz, *Principal*
EMP: 14 **EST:** 2010
SALES (est): 1MM **Privately Held**
WEB: www.cmindustriesinc.com
SIC: 3999 Manufacturing industries

(P-11644)
C-GUY INDUSTRIES INC (PA)
19611 Trident Ln, Huntington Beach
(92646-3320)
PHONE....................714 587-9575
David Lee Nola, *Principal*
EMP: 15 **EST:** 2018
SALES (est): 102.6K **Privately Held**
SIC: 3999 Manufacturing industries

(P-11645)
CA937 AFJROTC
12431 Roscoe Blvd Ste 300, Sun Valley
(91352-3723)
PHONE....................818 394-3600
EMP: 99 **EST:** 2013
SALES (est): 3.1MM **Privately Held**
SIC: 3999 Manufacturing Industries, Nec,
Nsk

(P-11646)
CALIFORNIA ACRYLIC INDS INC (HQ)
Also Called: Cal Spas
1462 E 9th St, Pomona (91766-3833)
PHONE....................909 623-8781
Casey Loyd, *President*
Sheba Nobel, *CFO*
Buzz Loyd, *Admin Sec*
▲ **EMP:** 274 **EST:** 1981
SQ FT: 300,000
SALES (est): 28.3MM **Privately Held**
WEB: www.californiaacrylicindustries.com
SIC: 3999 3949 Hot tubs; billiard & pool
equipment & supplies, general

(P-11647)
CALIFORNIA EXOTIC NOVLT LLC
1455 E Francis St, Ontario (91761-8329)
P.O. Box 50400 (91761-1078)
PHONE....................909 606-1950
Susan Colvin, *CEO*
Don MA, *CFO*
Josh Leduff, *Chief Mktg Ofcr*
Jackie White, *Vice Pres*
Austin Ferdinand, *Info Tech Dir*
▲ **EMP:** 88 **EST:** 1994
SQ FT: 66,000
SALES (est): 13.6MM **Privately Held**
WEB: www.calexotics.com
SIC: 3999 5947 Novelties, bric-a-brac &
hobby kits; novelties

(P-11648)
CANNALOGIC
5404 Whitsett Ave 219, Valley Village
(91607-1615)
PHONE....................619 458-0775
Jasmine Savoy, *President*
EMP: 17 **EST:** 2017
SALES (est): 558.5K **Privately Held**
SIC: 3999 Manufacturing industries

(P-11649)
CARBERRY LLC (HQ)
Also Called: Plus Products
17130 Muskrat Ave Ste B, Adelanto
(92301-2473)
PHONE....................800 564-0842
Roy McFarland, *Director*
EMP: 24 **EST:** 2017
SQ FT: 12,000
SALES (est): 1.1MM **Privately Held**
WEB: www.alumni-friends.brown.edu
SIC: 3999 2064 ; chewing candy, not
chewing gum
PA: Plus Products Holdings Inc.
  340 S Lemon Ave Ste 9392
  Walnut CA 91789
  800 564-0842

(P-11650)
CCS INDUSTRIES INC
4125 W Noble Ave, Visalia (93277-1662)
PHONE....................559 786-8489
Jeff Orchard, *CEO*
EMP: 15 **EST:** 2016
SALES (est): 842.6K **Privately Held**
SIC: 3999 Manufacturing industries

(P-11651)
CDM COMPANY INC
12 Corporate Plaza Dr # 200, Newport
Beach (92660-7986)
PHONE....................949 644-2820
Mitchella Jankins, *President*
Mia Brown, *Vice Pres*
Wendy Diehl, *Vice Pres*
Michael Stastny, *Vice Pres*
Dana Pescrillo, *Project Mgr*
▲ **EMP:** 23 **EST:** 1990
SQ FT: 7,000
SALES (est): 2.8MM **Privately Held**
WEB: www.thecdmco.com
SIC: 3999 3944 8742 5112 Novelties,
bric-a-brac & hobby kits; games, toys &
children's vehicles; marketing consulting
services; pens &/or pencils

(P-11652)
CERTIFIX INC
Also Called: Certifix Live Scan
1950 W Corporate Way, Anaheim
(92801-5373)
PHONE....................714 496-3850
Helmy El Mangoury, *CEO*
Alexa Paredes, *Accounts Mgr*
EMP: 14 **EST:** 2007
SALES (est): 2.9MM **Privately Held**
WEB: www.certifixlivescan.com
SIC: 3999 7381 7389 Fingerprint equipment; fingerprint service; mailbox rental &
related service

(P-11653)
CJ FOODS MFG BEAUMONT CORP
415 Nicholas Rd, Beaumont (92223-2612)
PHONE....................951 916-9300
Geon IL Lee, *CEO*
EMP: 25 **EST:** 2018
SALES (est): 9MM **Privately Held**
WEB: www.cj.co.kr
SIC: 3999 Chairs, hydraulic, barber &
beauty shop
PA: Cj Cheiljedang Corporation
  330 Dongho-Ro, Jung-Gu
  Seoul 04560

(P-11654)
DARYLS PET SHOP
208 E State St, Redlands (92373-5233)
PHONE....................909 793-1788
Leslie Triplette, *President*
EMP: 15 **EST:** 1975
SALES (est): 2.3MM **Privately Held**
WEB: www.darylspetshop.com
SIC: 3999 Pet supplies; boat models, except toy; models, general, except toy; railroad models, except toy

(P-11655)
DB STUDIOS INC
17032 Murphy Ave, Irvine (92614-5914)
PHONE....................949 833-0100
Darin Rasmussen, *President*
Mark Bense, *CFO*
Mike Mikyska, *Vice Pres*
John Riley, *Vice Pres*
Ruben Sanchez, *Manager*
▲ **EMP:** 35 **EST:** 1989
SQ FT: 22,500
SALES (est): 15.9MM **Privately Held**
WEB: www.hhglobal.com
SIC: 3999 3993 7389 7319 Advertising
display products; signs & advertising specialties; advertising, promotional & trade
show services; display advertising service; commercial art & graphic design
HQ: Innerworkings, Inc.
  600 W Chicago Ave
  Chicago IL 60654
  312 642-3700

(P-11656)
DELANEY MANUFACTURING INC (PA)
6810 Downing Ave, Bakersfield
(93308-5810)
P.O. Box 21585 (93390-1585)
PHONE....................661 587-6681
Dale McBride, *President*
EMP: 30 **EST:** 2011
SALES (est): 1MM **Privately Held**
WEB: www.delaneymfg.com
SIC: 3999 Manufacturing industries

(P-11657)
DESERT SHADES INC
2928 Leonis Blvd, Vernon (90058-2916)
PHONE....................323 731-5000
Benny Nadal, *Regional Mgr*
Marlene Nadal, *Admin Sec*
▲ **EMP:** 14 **EST:** 1979
SALES (est): 644.8K **Privately Held**
SIC: 3999 Shades, lamp or candle

(P-11658)
DEVELOPLUS INC
1575 Magnolia Ave, Corona (92879-2073)
PHONE....................951 738-8595
Deorao K Agrey, *CEO*
Jeanne Nicodemus, *CFO*

PRODUCTS & SVCS

Kiran Agrey, *Info Tech Dir*
Sherry Kudren, *Sales Dir*
Scott Yoast, *Manager*
▲ **EMP:** 140 **EST:** 1990
SQ FT: 40,000
SALES (est): 32.6MM **Privately Held**
WEB: www.developlus.com
SIC: 3999 5087 Hair & hair-based products; beauty parlor equipment & supplies

(P-11659)
DKP DESIGNS INC
110 Maryland St, El Segundo (90245-4115)
PHONE....................310 322-6000
Deborah P Koppel, *President*
Brad Koppel, *Vice Pres*
Diana Rodriguez, *Vice Pres*
Trevor Koppel, *Business Dir*
Maria Defilippo, *Production*
▲ **EMP:** 15 **EST:** 1996
SQ FT: 4,000
SALES (est): 2MM **Privately Held**
WEB: www.dkpdesigns.com
SIC: 3999 Advertising display products

(P-11660)
DNG FASHION
3209 S Main St, Los Angeles (90007-4104)
PHONE....................917 747-3158
William Lee, *Principal*
EMP: 16 **EST:** 2017
SALES (est): 62.5K **Privately Held**
WEB: www.dng.com
SIC: 3999 Manufacturing industries

(P-11661)
DOLPHIN SPAS INC
701 W Foothill Blvd, Azusa (91702-2348)
PHONE....................626 334-0099
Kareem Azizeh, *President*
EMP: 17 **EST:** 1988
SQ FT: 27,000
SALES (est): 407.2K **Privately Held**
WEB: www.acc-spas.com
SIC: 3999 5999 Hot tubs; spas & hot tubs

(P-11662)
E-LIQ CUBE INC (PA)
13515 Alondra Blvd, Santa Fe Springs (90670-5602)
PHONE....................562 537-9454
▲ **EMP:** 18
SALES (est): 1MM **Privately Held**
SIC: 3999 Mfg Misc Products

(P-11663)
EARTHCORE INDUSTRIES INC
460 Calle San Pablo Ste D, Camarillo (93012-8554)
PHONE....................805 484-7350
Chad E Angle, *Principal*
EMP: 14 **EST:** 2019
SALES (est): 2.1MM **Privately Held**
SIC: 3999 Manufacturing industries

(P-11664)
EDWARDS LIFESCIENCES FING LLC
1 Edwards Way, Irvine (92614-5688)
PHONE....................949 250-3480
Mike Mussaollem, *President*
EMP: 71 **EST:** 2003
SALES (est): 8MM
SALES (corp-wide): 4.3B **Publicly Held**
WEB: www.edwards.com
SIC: 3999 Advertising curtains
PA: Edwards Lifesciences Corp
    1 Edwards Way
    Irvine CA 92614
    949 250-2500

(P-11665)
EVO MANUFACTURING INC
20420 S Susana Rd, Carson (90810-1135)
PHONE....................714 879-8913
EMP: 15 **EST:** 2010
SALES (est): 1MM **Privately Held**
WEB: www.evomfg.com
SIC: 3999 Manufacturing industries

(P-11666)
EXHART ENVMTL SYSTEMS INC (PA)
20364 Plummer St, Chatsworth (91311-5371)
PHONE....................818 576-9628
Isaac Weiser, *President*
Michael Weiser, *Exec VP*
Shari Weiser, *Exec VP*
Shawn Langton, *Vice Pres*
Margaret Weiser, *Vice Pres*
◆ **EMP:** 16 **EST:** 1989
SALES (est): 2.1MM **Privately Held**
WEB: www.exhart.com
SIC: 3999 Lawn ornaments

(P-11667)
FAMILY INDUSTRIES LLC
1700 N Spring St, Los Angeles (90012-1929)
PHONE....................619 306-1035
Alexander Barry Meiners, *Director*
Adam Calvary, *Director*
EMP: 13 **EST:** 2011
SALES (est): 1.4MM **Privately Held**
WEB: www.familyindustries.com
SIC: 3999 Barber & beauty shop equipment

(P-11668)
FLAME AND WAX INC
Also Called: Voluspa
2900 Mccabe Way, Irvine (92614-6239)
PHONE....................949 752-4000
Troy Arntsen, *President*
Danielle Dixon, *Executive*
Oanh Tran, *Accountant*
Frank Munoz, *Mfg Staff*
Gina Tomasino, *Marketing Staff*
▲ **EMP:** 31 **EST:** 2001
SALES (est): 10.4MM **Privately Held**
WEB: www.voluspa.com
SIC: 3999 2844 Candles; toilet preparations

(P-11669)
FLORA GOLD LLC
3165 Red Hill Ave, Costa Mesa (92626-3417)
PHONE....................949 252-1122
Laurie Holcomb, *Principal*
Chris Martin, *CFO*
Rhonda Delgado, *Creative Dir*
Erica Tetsworth, *Business Mgr*
Noah Holcomb, *Manager*
EMP: 14 **EST:** 2016
SALES (est): 2.6MM **Privately Held**
WEB: www.goldflora.com
SIC: 3999

(P-11670)
FORRESTER EASTLAND CORPORATION
Also Called: Versa Stage
1320 Storm Pkwy, Torrance (90501-5041)
PHONE....................310 784-2464
Clive Forrester, *CEO*
Erik Eastland, *President*
EMP: 44 **EST:** 1991
SQ FT: 17,900
SALES (est): 6.7MM **Privately Held**
SIC: 3999 7819 Stage hardware & equipment, except lighting; equipment & prop rental, motion picture production

(P-11671)
FOUNTAINHEAD INDUSTRIES
700 N San Vicente Blvd G910, West Hollywood (90069-5060)
PHONE....................310 248-2444
Hal Kline, *President*
EMP: 20 **EST:** 2005
SALES (est): 1.1MM **Privately Held**
SIC: 3999 Chairs, hydraulic, barber & beauty shop

(P-11672)
FRAGRANT JEWELS LLC
807 Mateo St, Los Angeles (90021-1711)
P.O. Box 58068 (90058-0068)
PHONE....................888 443-5049
Keyla Torres, *Vice Pres*
Claudia Guillen, *Opers Staff*
EMP: 23 **EST:** 2014

SALES (est): 8.4MM **Privately Held**
WEB: www.fragrantjewels.com
SIC: 3999 3911 Candles; jewelry, precious metal

(P-11673)
GALAXY ENTERPRISES INC
Also Called: Galaxy Medical
5411 Sheila St, Commerce (90040-2103)
PHONE....................323 728-3980
Henry Talei, *President*
Joe Bone, *Opers Mgr*
◆ **EMP:** 25 **EST:** 1949
SQ FT: 40,000
SALES (est): 3.5MM **Privately Held**
WEB: www.galaxymfg.com
SIC: 3999 3843 3841 Barber & beauty shop equipment; dental chairs; medical instruments & equipment, blood & bone work

(P-11674)
GARMON CORPORATION
Also Called: Naturvet
27461 Via Industria, Temecula (92590-3752)
PHONE....................951 296-6308
Scott J Garmon, *President*
Debra O'Brien, *Finance*
Debra O'brien, *Finance*
Laura Silva, *Human Resources*
Jodi Hoefler, *VP Mktg*
▲ **EMP:** 120 **EST:** 1979
SQ FT: 18,500
SALES (est): 25.8MM **Privately Held**
WEB: www.naturvet.com
SIC: 3999 Pet supplies

(P-11675)
GENERAL COATINGS MANUFACT
14722 Spring Ave, Santa Fe Springs (90670-5108)
PHONE....................562 802-8834
EMP: 15 **EST:** 2019
SALES (est): 807.3K **Privately Held**
WEB: www.generalcoatings.net
SIC: 3999 Manufacturing industries

(P-11676)
GENERAL WAX CO INC (PA)
Also Called: General Wax & Candle Co
6863 Beck Ave, North Hollywood (91605-6206)
P.O. Box 9398 (91609-1398)
PHONE....................818 765-5800
Carol Lazar, *CEO*
Mike Tapp, *President*
Colton Lazar, *Corp Secy*
Jerry Baker, *Executive*
Martha Smith, *Office Mgr*
◆ **EMP:** 85
SQ FT: 120,000
SALES (est): 17.3MM **Privately Held**
WEB: www.generalwax.com
SIC: 3999 Candles

(P-11677)
GENTEKK INDUSTRIES LLC (PA)
534 E Lambert Rd, Brea (92821-4116)
PHONE....................714 985-9280
Brian Jordan, *President*
EMP: 23 **EST:** 2017
SALES (est): 354.8K **Privately Held**
WEB: www.gentekk.com
SIC: 3999 Manufacturing industries

(P-11678)
GLOBAL UXE INC
Also Called: Aquiesse
405 Science Dr, Moorpark (93021-2247)
PHONE....................805 583-4600
Michael Joseph Horn, *President*
▲ **EMP:** 20 **EST:** 2011
SALES (est): 1MM **Privately Held**
SIC: 3999 Candles

(P-11679)
GLOBALUXE INC
Also Called: Candle Crafters
405 Science Dr, Moorpark (93021-2247)
PHONE....................805 583-4600
Michael Joseph Horn, *CEO*
Sam Vela, *Clerk*
▲ **EMP:** 20 **EST:** 2003

SALES (est): 3.6MM **Privately Held**
SIC: 3999 5199 5999 Candles; candles; candle shops

(P-11680)
GOLDEN SUPREME INC
12304 Mccann Dr, Santa Fe Springs (90670-3333)
PHONE....................562 903-1063
Ross Stillwagon, *President*
Ricardo J Fischbach, *Shareholder*
Fernando Fischbach, *Treasurer*
▲ **EMP:** 30 **EST:** 1990
SQ FT: 13,000
SALES (est): 4.6MM **Privately Held**
WEB: www.goldensupreme.com
SIC: 3999 5087 Hair curlers, designed for beauty parlors; beauty parlor equipment & supplies

(P-11681)
GOODNIGHT INDUSTRIES INC
15035 Califa St, Van Nuys (91411-3003)
PHONE....................318 988-2801
Beth Goodnight, *CEO*
EMP: 14 **EST:** 2014
SALES (est): 1MM **Privately Held**
WEB: www.goodnightandco.com
SIC: 3999 Manufacturing industries

(P-11682)
H & H SPECIALTIES INC
14850 Don Julian Rd Ste B, City of Industry (91746-3122)
PHONE....................626 575-0776
Reid Neslage, *Owner*
Mary Louise Higgins, *Principal*
EMP: 31 **EST:** 1967
SQ FT: 30,000
SALES (est): 5.2MM **Privately Held**
WEB: www.hhspecialties.com
SIC: 3999 3625 Stage hardware & equipment, except lighting; relays & industrial controls

(P-11683)
HEL MAR MFG LLC (PA)
3000 Paseo Mercado, Oxnard (93036-7960)
PHONE....................805 278-9099
EMP: 27 **EST:** 2017
SALES (est): 154.9K **Privately Held**
SIC: 3999 Manufacturing industries

(P-11684)
HIGH TECH PET PRODUCTS
2111 Portola Rd A, Ventura (93003-7723)
PHONE....................805 644-1797
Nicholas Donge, *President*
Bob Schilken, *Vice Pres*
Adele Bonge, *Graphic Designe*
▲ **EMP:** 60 **EST:** 1980
SALES (est): 3.4MM **Privately Held**
WEB: www.hitecpet.com
SIC: 3999 Pet supplies

(P-11685)
HIRSH INDUSTRIES-MEXICALI DIV
1778 Zinetta Rd Ste A, Calexico (92231-9511)
PHONE....................515 299-3200
◆ **EMP:** 14 **EST:** 2010
SALES (est): 309.4K **Privately Held**
SIC: 3999 Barber & beauty shop equipment

(P-11686)
HOLLYWOOD HOOKAH LOUNGE INC
6512 Hollywood Blvd, Los Angeles (90028-6210)
PHONE....................323 469-4622
Mohammad Rizvi, *President*
EMP: 15 **EST:** 2008
SQ FT: 15,000
SALES (est): 538.5K **Privately Held**
WEB: www.hollywoodhookah.com
SIC: 5812 5813 3999 Restaurant, family: chain; bars & lounges; tobacco pipes, pipestems & bits

(P-11687)
**HOOD CONTAINER
CORPORATION**
801 S Main St Ste 101, Burbank
(91506-3391)
PHONE..................818 848-1648
Craig Lutes, *General Mgr*
EMP: 15 Privately Held
WEB: www.hoodcontainer.com
SIC: 3999 Advertising display products
HQ: Hood Container Corporation
2727 Paces Ferry Rd Se 1-1850
Atlanta GA 30339
855 605-6317

(P-11688)
HOUSE OF LASHES
1565 Mcgaw Ave Ste C, Irvine
(92614-5670)
P.O. Box 9016, Fountain Valley (92728-9016)
PHONE..................714 515-4162
▲ **EMP:** 17 **EST:** 2012
SALES (est): 4.5MM Privately Held
WEB: www.houseoflashes.com
SIC: 3999 Wigs, including doll wigs, toupees or wiglets; eyelashes, artificial

(P-11689)
ICON LINE INC
Also Called: I.C.O.N. Salon
20600 Ventura Blvd Ste C, Woodland Hills
(91364-6691)
PHONE..................818 709-4266
Chiara Scudieri, *President*
Michelle Lepire, *Opers Staff*
▲ **EMP:** 15 **EST:** 2001
SQ FT: 1,800
SALES (est): 1.3MM Privately Held
WEB: www.iconproducts.com
SIC: 3999 5999 Hair, dressing of, for the trade; hair care products

(P-11690)
**INNOVATIVE CASEWORK MFG
INC**
12261 Industry St, Garden Grove
(92841-2815)
PHONE..................714 890-9100
Valerie Perez, *Principal*
EMP: 25 **EST:** 2017
SALES (est): 809K Privately Held
SIC: 3999 Manufacturing industries

(P-11691)
INTERSTATE CABINET INC
Also Called: Interstate Design Industry
1631 Pomona Rd Ste B, Corona
(92878-4327)
PHONE..................951 736-0777
James L Fago, *President*
Nancy Fago-Fleer, *Admin Sec*
▲ **EMP:** 20 **EST:** 1975
SQ FT: 56,000
SALES (est): 1.1MM Privately Held
WEB: www.interstatecabinet.openfos.com
SIC: 3999 Barber & beauty shop equipment

(P-11692)
J C INDUSTRIES INC
3977 Camino Ranchero, Camarillo
(93012-5066)
PHONE..................805 389-4040
▼ **EMP:** 15
SQ FT: 12,000
SALES (est): 980K Privately Held
WEB: www.jcind.com
SIC: 3999 Mfg & Whol Tape Measures & Other Custom Imprinted Products

(P-11693)
JACUZZI BRANDS LLC (DH)
Also Called: Jacuzzi Group Worldwide
13925 City Center Dr # 200, Chino Hills
(91709-5438)
PHONE..................909 606-1416
Robert Rowen, *CEO*
Leslie Leuschner, *President*
Alex P Marini, *President*
Peter Munk, *President*
Robert I Rowan, *President*
◆ **EMP:** 50 **EST:** 1995
SQ FT: 15,134

SALES (est): 930.8MM
SALES (corp-wide): 467.1K Privately Held
SIC: 3999 Hot tubs
HQ: Jupiter Holding I Corp.
13925 City Center Dr # 200
Chino Hills CA 91709
909 606-1416

(P-11694)
JAX AND BONES INC
345 Cloverleaf Dr, Baldwin Park
(91706-6502)
PHONE..................626 363-9350
Truong Nguyen, *CEO*
◆ **EMP:** 20 **EST:** 2009
SALES (est): 7.7MM Privately Held
WEB: www.jaxandbones.com
SIC: 5999 3999 Pet supplies; pet supplies

(P-11695)
JNJ OPERATIONS LLC
Also Called: Jackandjillkidscom
859 E Sepulveda Blvd, Carson
(90745-6130)
PHONE..................855 525-6545
EMP: 20
SALES (est): 504.6K Privately Held
SIC: 3999 Mfg Misc Products

(P-11696)
**JOE BLASCO ENTERPRISES
INC**
Also Called: Joe Blasco Cosmetics
1285 N Valdivia Way A, Palm Springs
(92262-5428)
PHONE..................323 467-4949
Joseph D Blasco, *President*
▲ **EMP:** 35 **EST:** 1986
SQ FT: 13,788
SALES (est): 585.6K
SALES (corp-wide): 3.2MM Privately Held
WEB: www.joeblasco.com
SIC: 3999 7231 2844 Barber & beauty shop equipment; cosmetology school; toilet preparations
PA: Joe Blasco Make-Up Center West, Inc.
1285 N Valdivia Way A
Palm Springs CA 92262
323 467-4949

(P-11697)
JORGE ULLOA
Also Called: Jem Unlimited Iron
3162 E La Palma Ave Ste F, Anaheim
(92806-2810)
PHONE..................714 630-0499
Martha Ulloa, *President*
Jorge Ulloa, *Vice Pres*
Isabel Huizar, *Accountant*
Martha Franco, *Opers Mgr*
EMP: 18 **EST:** 2002
SQ FT: 4,000
SALES (est): 1.1MM Privately Held
SIC: 3999 Lawn ornaments

(P-11698)
K-TOPS PLASTIC MFG INC
15051 Don Julian Rd, City of Industry
(91746-3302)
PHONE..................626 575-9679
▲ **EMP:** 22 **EST:** 2005
SALES (est): 3.1MM Privately Held
SIC: 3999 Mfg Misc Products

(P-11699)
K9 BALLISTICS INC
708 Via Alondra, Camarillo (93012-8713)
PHONE..................844 772-3125
Sean Farley, *CEO*
Jenny Chickasawah, *Human Resources*
EMP: 16 **EST:** 2010
SQ FT: 20,000
SALES (est): 1.5MM Privately Held
WEB: www.k9ballistics.com
SIC: 3999 Pet supplies

(P-11700)
KAIROS MANUFACTURING INC
201 Bridge St, San Luis Obispo
(93401-5510)
PHONE..................805 544-2216
EMP: 19 **EST:** 2017

SALES (est): 1.5MM Privately Held
WEB: www.kairosinc.net
SIC: 3999 Manufacturing industries

(P-11701)
KIMBALL NELSON INC
Also Called: Heaven or Las Vegas
7740 Lemona Ave, Van Nuys (91405-1136)
PHONE..................310 636-0081
David Kip Smith, *President*
Nina Lazutin, *Vice Pres*
EMP: 19 **EST:** 1991
SQ FT: 6,000
SALES (est): 994.1K Privately Held
SIC: 3999 Theatrical scenery

(P-11702)
KNORR-BREMSE EVAC LLC ✪
21136 S Wilmington Ave, Long Beach
(90810-1248)
PHONE..................410 875-0900
Andrew Kameen, *Mng Member*
EMP: 20 **EST:** 2021
SALES (est): 1.1MM Privately Held
SIC: 3999 Manufacturing industries

(P-11703)
**KURZ TRANSFER PRODUCTS
LP**
415 N Smith Ave, Corona (92878-4305)
PHONE..................951 738-9521
Hastings Kurz, *Principal*
EMP: 41
SALES (corp-wide): 956MM Privately Held
WEB: www.kurzusa.com
SIC: 3999 Atomizers, toiletry
HQ: Kurz Transfer Products, Lp
11836 Patterson Rd
Huntersville NC 28078
704 927-3700

(P-11704)
LA RUTAN
Also Called: Emily's Classic Beauty Salon
6284 Long Beach Blvd, Long Beach
(90805-2160)
P.O. Box 21398 (90801-4398)
PHONE..................310 940-7956
Emily Fields, *President*
Aleaha Fields, *Vice Pres*
▲ **EMP:** 18 **EST:** 1983
SQ FT: 600
SALES (est): 540.7K Privately Held
WEB: www.emilysclassicbeauty.com
SIC: 3999 2678 2676 2842 Hair, dressing of, for the trade; wigs, including doll wigs, toupees or wiglets; memorandum books, notebooks & looseleaf filler paper; sanitary paper products; specialty cleaning preparations; beauty shops

(P-11705)
LDI OPERATIONS LLC
450 N Brand Blvd Ste 900, Glendale
(91203-2397)
PHONE..................818 240-7500
Brendan McLoughlin, *Chief Mktg Ofcr*
Lon Osmond, *Vice Pres*
John Paul Uva, *Vice Pres*
Desiree Micale, *Admin Asst*
Brenda Freeman, *Technology*
▲ **EMP:** 120 **EST:** 1954
SQ FT: 35,000
SALES (est): 27.1MM
SALES (corp-wide): 5.4B Privately Held
WEB: www.healthclarity.wolterskluwer.com
SIC: 3999 Education aids, devices & supplies
HQ: Wolters Kluwer Health, Inc.
2001 Market St Ste 5
Philadelphia PA 19103
215 521-8300

(P-11706)
LEARNING RESOURCES INC
Also Called: Educational Insights
152 W Walnut St Ste 201, Gardena
(90248-3147)
PHONE..................800 995-4436
Lisa Guili, *General Mgr*
Maria Gonzalez, *Office Mgr*
Marcia Gresko, *Director*
Heather Weeks, *Director*
Janene C Russell, *Associate*
EMP: 20

SALES (corp-wide): 27.8MM Privately Held
WEB: www.learningresources.com
SIC: 3999 3944 Education aids, devices & supplies; games, toys & children's vehicles
PA: Learning Resources, Inc.
380 N Fairway Dr
Vernon Hills IL 60061
847 573-8400

(P-11707)
LEOBEN COMPANY
16692 Burke Ln, Huntington Beach
(92647-4536)
PHONE..................951 284-9653
Samir Tabikha, *President*
EMP: 16 **EST:** 2017
SALES (est): 1.7MM Privately Held
WEB: www.leobenco.com
SIC: 3999 Barber & beauty shop equipment

(P-11708)
LEXOR INC
7400 Hazard Ave, Westminster
(92683-5031)
PHONE..................714 444-4144
Marianna Magos, *CEO*
Christopher L Long, *President*
Hanson Truong, *COO*
Theo Quach, *IT/INT Sup*
▲ **EMP:** 90 **EST:** 2007
SALES (est): 15.5MM Privately Held
SIC: 3999 Chairs, hydraulic, barber & beauty shop

(P-11709)
LOLA BELLE BRANDS LLC
631 S Palm Ave, Alhambra (91803-1424)
PHONE..................855 226-3526
Arthur Maruyama,
EMP: 17 **EST:** 2017
SALES (est): 579.4K Privately Held
SIC: 5621 3999 Boutiques; candles

(P-11710)
MACS LIFT GATE INC (PA)
2801 E South St, Long Beach
(90805-3736)
PHONE..................562 529-3465
Michael Macdonald, *CEO*
Mike Macdonald, *CFO*
Richard Mac Donald, *Treasurer*
Gerald J Mac Donald, *Vice Pres*
Lawrence Mac Donald, *Vice Pres*
EMP: 24 **EST:** 1957
SALES (est): 3.6MM Privately Held
WEB: www.macsliftgate.com
SIC: 3999 5013 Wheelchair lifts; motor vehicle supplies & new parts

(P-11711)
MARCH PRODUCTS INC
Also Called: Astella
4645 Troy Ct, Jurupa Valley (92509-2003)
PHONE..................909 622-4800
Yungcheng MA, *President*
Perla Garcia, *Executive Asst*
Hibi Lin, *Controller*
Karen Hatton, *Manager*
◆ **EMP:** 72 **EST:** 2001
SQ FT: 70,000
SALES (est): 17.5MM Privately Held
WEB: www.californiaumbrella.com
SIC: 3999 2211 Garden umbrellas; umbrella cloth, cotton

(P-11712)
**MEDICAL BRKTHRUGH
MSSAGE CHIRS**
28577 Industry Dr, Valencia (91355-5424)
PHONE..................408 677-7702
Max Lun, *CEO*
Patrick O'Malley, *Manager*
Ivet Zakaryan, *Manager*
EMP: 24 **EST:** 2016
SALES (est): 12MM Privately Held
WEB: www.medicalbreakthrough.org
SIC: 3999 Massage machines, electric: barber & beauty shops

**P
R
O
D
U
C
T
S

&

S
V
C
S**

(P-11713)
MERCADO LATINO INC
Continental Candle Company
1420 W Walnut St, Compton (90220-5013)
PHONE..........................310 537-1062
Andy Sly, *Engineer*
Robert Durazo, *Buyer*
EMP: 26
SALES (corp-wide): 87MM **Privately Held**
WEB: www.mercadolatinoinc.com
SIC: 3999 3641 7699 3645 Candles; electric lamps; restaurant equipment repair; residential lighting fixtures
PA: Mercado Latino, Inc.
245 Baldwin Park Blvd
City Of Industry CA 91746
626 333-6862

(P-11714)
MFI INC
363 San Miguel Dr Ste 200, Newport Beach (92660-7891)
PHONE..........................949 887-8691
Steven Bandawat, *Principal*
Sean Bandawat, *VP Bus Dvlpt*
▲ EMP: 13 EST: 2014
SALES (est): 1.2MM **Privately Held**
WEB: www.mfiglobal.com
SIC: 3999 Manufacturing industries

(P-11715)
MGR DESIGN INTERNATIONAL INC
1950 Williams Dr, Oxnard (93036-2630)
PHONE..........................805 981-6400
Michelle Bechard, *CEO*
Rony Havive, *President*
Yolanda Valdovinos, *Vice Pres*
Amy Wagner, *General Mgr*
Leslie Hinojosa, *Opers Staff*
◆ EMP: 200
SQ FT: 80,000
SALES (est): 25.5MM **Privately Held**
WEB: www.mgrdesign.com
SIC: 3999 Potpourri; candles

(P-11716)
MICHELLE BARRIONUEVO-MAZZINI (PA)
Also Called: Casita Michi
1224 Pendio, Irvine (92620-1751)
PHONE..........................415 706-1677
Michelle B-Mazzini, *Owner*
Michelle Barrionuevo-Mazzini, *Owner*
EMP: 18 EST: 2020
SALES (est): 30K **Privately Held**
SIC: 3999 7389 Candles;

(P-11717)
MOTHER PLUCKER FEATHER CO INC
2511 W 3rd St Ste 102, Los Angeles (90057-1946)
P.O. Box 57160 (90057-0160)
PHONE..........................213 637-0411
William Zelowitz, *President*
Steven Landerth, *CEO*
Lelan Berner, *Prdtn Mgr*
EMP: 15 EST: 1974
SQ FT: 16,000
SALES (est): 1MM **Privately Held**
WEB: www.motherpluckerfeathercompany.com
SIC: 3999 5159 Trimmings, feather; feathers

(P-11718)
NANNOCARE INC
2570 Corp Pl Ste E103, Monterey Park (91754)
PHONE..........................818 823-7594
Victoria McHenry, *Vice Pres*
EMP: 14 EST: 2017
SALES (est): 1.4MM **Privately Held**
WEB: www.nannocare.com
SIC: 3999 Manufacturing industries

(P-11719)
NANO FILTER INC
22310 Bonita St, Carson (90745-4103)
PHONE..........................949 316-8866
Bennett Koo, *President*
EMP: 60 EST: 2020

SALES (est): 1.2MM **Privately Held**
WEB: www.pure-msk.com
SIC: 3999 Manufacturing industries

(P-11720)
NEWTEX INDUSTRIES INC
Also Called: Thermostatic Industries
9654 Hermosa Ave, Rancho Cucamonga (91730-5812)
PHONE..........................323 277-0900
Jerry Joliet, *Principal*
Sudhakar Dixit, *Principal*
Jerome Joliet, *Principal*
EMP: 75 EST: 2016
SALES (est): 2.5MM **Privately Held**
WEB: www.newtex.com
SIC: 3999 Manufacturing industries

(P-11721)
OLD AN INC
17651 Armstrong Ave, Irvine (92614-5727)
PHONE..........................949 263-1400
Tina Rocca-Lundstrom, *President*
Tina Rocca Lundstrom, *President*
Steven Lundstrom, *Vice Pres*
◆ EMP: 13 EST: 1993
SQ FT: 15,000
SALES (est): 296.1K **Privately Held**
SIC: 3999 Candles

(P-11722)
OLD CANDLE LLC (PA)
7630 Balasiano Ave, West Hills (91304-4570)
PHONE..........................818 436-2776
Garbis Chrikjian, *Principal*
EMP: 21 EST: 2016
SALES (est): 117.2K **Privately Held**
SIC: 3999 Candles

(P-11723)
ORTEGA MANUFACTURING INC
3960 Industrial Ave, Hemet (92545-9790)
P.O. Box 959, Wildomar (92595-0959)
PHONE..........................951 766-9363
Tony Ortega, *President*
Cindy Ortega, *Vice Pres*
EMP: 14 EST: 2001
SQ FT: 12,000
SALES (est): 267.8K **Privately Held**
WEB: www.ortegamanufacturing.com
SIC: 3999 Novelties, bric-a-brac & hobby kits

(P-11724)
OSI INDUSTRIES LLC
1155 Mt Vernon Ave, Riverside (92507-1830)
PHONE..........................951 684-4500
Holly Botos, *CIO*
Irene Ballejos, *Buyer*
▲ EMP: 67 EST: 2013
SALES (est): 19.9MM **Privately Held**
WEB: www.osigroup.com
SIC: 3999 Atomizers, toiletry

(P-11725)
PACIFIC COAST FABRICATION INC
1390 N Hundley St, Anaheim (92806-1301)
PHONE..........................714 536-8385
Kristopher L Brodowski, *President*
EMP: 14 EST: 2017
SALES (est): 694.7K **Privately Held**
SIC: 3999 Manufacturing industries

(P-11726)
PACIFIC VIAL MFG INC
2800 Supply Ave, Commerce (90040-2706)
PHONE..........................323 721-7004
EMP: 13 EST: 2017
SALES (est): 295.5K **Privately Held**
WEB: www.pacificvial.com
SIC: 3999 Manufacturing industries

(P-11727)
PACIFICA BEAUTY LLC
Also Called: Pacifica International
1090 Eugenia Pl Ste 200, Carpinteria (93013-2011)
PHONE..........................844 332-8440
Billy Taylor, *CEO*
Brook H Taylor, *President*
Adam Roelfs, *Admin Asst*
Caleb Egolf, *Engineer*
Delynn Elrod, *Plant Mgr*

▲ EMP: 100
SQ FT: 58,000
SALES (est): 8.8MM **Privately Held**
WEB: www.pacificabeauty.com
SIC: 3999 2844 Candles; toilet preparations

(P-11728)
PACMIN INCORPORATED (PA)
Also Called: Pacific Miniatures
2021 Raymer Ave, Fullerton (92833-2664)
PHONE..........................714 447-4478
Frederick Ouweleen Jr, *President*
Flora Ouweleen, *Treasurer*
Daniel Ouweleen, *Exec VP*
Tracy Campbell, *Executive*
Richard Soohoo, *Engineer*
▲ EMP: 92 EST: 1981
SQ FT: 35,400
SALES (est): 13.1MM **Privately Held**
WEB: www.pacmin.com
SIC: 3999 Models, general, except toy

(P-11729)
PARADIGM CONTRACT MFG LLC
5531 Belle Ave, Cypress (90630-4550)
PHONE..........................714 889-7074
Scott Penin, *Partner*
Faith Stancliff, *Partner*
EMP: 15 EST: 2006
SALES (est): 1.5MM **Privately Held**
SIC: 3999 Atomizers, toiletry

(P-11730)
PAUL FERRANTE INC
Also Called: Ferrante Paul Cstm Lmps & Shds
8464 Melrose Pl, West Hollywood (90069-5308)
PHONE..........................310 854-4412
Thomas Raynor, *President*
Grace Saroyan, *Office Mgr*
▲ EMP: 40 EST: 1962
SQ FT: 2,000
SALES (est): 4.7MM **Privately Held**
SIC: 3999 5099 3645 Shades, lamp or candle; antiques; residential lighting fixtures

(P-11731)
PCI INDUSTRIES INC
700 S Vail Ave, Montebello (90640-4954)
PHONE..........................323 889-6770
Jack Scilley, *Owner*
Mark Saunders, *Vice Pres*
Tim O 'hara, *Executive*
James Carlin, *Design Engr*
Brenda Duffy, *Human Res Mgr*
EMP: 37
SALES (corp-wide): 51.2MM **Privately Held**
WEB: www.pottorffcorporate.com
SIC: 3999 Atomizers, toiletry
PA: Pci Industries, Inc.
5101 Blue Mound Rd
Fort Worth TX 76106
817 509-2300

(P-11732)
PCI INDUSTRIES INC
6490 Fleet St, Commerce (90040-1710)
PHONE..........................323 728-0004
Jim Turner, *Manager*
EMP: 37
SALES (corp-wide): 51.2MM **Privately Held**
WEB: www.pottorffcorporate.com
SIC: 3999 Atomizers, toiletry
PA: Pci Industries, Inc.
5101 Blue Mound Rd
Fort Worth TX 76106
817 509-2300

(P-11733)
PENINSULA PACKAGING LLC (DH)
Also Called: Peninsula Packaging Company
1030 N Anderson Rd, Exeter (93221-9341)
PHONE..........................559 594-6813
John McKernan, *CEO*
Jamie Fife, *Technology*
▲ EMP: 70 EST: 2002

SALES (est): 66.3MM
SALES (corp-wide): 5.2B **Publicly Held**
WEB: www.sonoco.com
SIC: 3999 3085 Atomizers, toiletry; plastics bottles
HQ: Sonoco Plastics, Inc.
1 N 2nd St
Hartsville SC 29550
843 383-7000

(P-11734)
PET PARTNERS INC (PA)
Also Called: North American Pet Products
450 N Sheridan St, Corona (92878-4020)
PHONE..........................951 279-9888
Keith Bonner, *CEO*
Ronald Bonner, *President*
Gloria Bonner, *Admin Sec*
Richard Moorfoot, *Accounting Mgr*
Gordan Thulemeyer, *VP Sales*
▲ EMP: 170 EST: 1995
SQ FT: 120,000
SALES (est): 35MM **Privately Held**
WEB: www.northamericanpet.com
SIC: 3999 Pet supplies

(P-11735)
PHIARO INCORPORATED
9016 Research Dr, Irvine (92618-4215)
PHONE..........................949 727-1261
Takeichiro Iwasaki, *President*
Takuya Nishimura, *Exec Dir*
Yosuke Inoue, *Manager*
▲ EMP: 32
SQ FT: 35,000
SALES (est): 6MM **Privately Held**
WEB: www.phiaro.jp
SIC: 3999 Models, general, except toy
PA: Phiaro Corporation, Inc.
8-2-3, Nobitome
Niiza STM

(P-11736)
PIERCO INCORPORATED
680 Main St, Riverside (92501-1034)
PHONE..........................909 251-7100
Erik Flemming, *CEO*
EMP: 15 EST: 2015
SALES (est): 1.5MM **Privately Held**
WEB: www.pierco.com
SIC: 3999 3089 Beekeepers' supplies; air mattresses, plastic

(P-11737)
POMMES FRITES CANDLE CO
Also Called: Pf Candle Co
7300 E Slauson Ave, Commerce (90040-3627)
PHONE..........................213 488-2016
Kristen Pumphrey, *CEO*
Thomas Neuberger, *General Mgr*
Karen De Luca, *Marketing Staff*
Evan Dougherty, *Manager*
EMP: 30 EST: 2014
SALES (est): 4.6MM **Privately Held**
WEB: www.pfcandleco.com
SIC: 3999 5149 5199 5999 Candles; flavourings & fragrances; candles; candle shops

(P-11738)
PREVOUNCE HEALTH LLC
Also Called: Pylo Health
1426 Hidden Valley Rd, Thousand Oaks (91361-5004)
PHONE..........................800 618-7738
Daniel Tashnek, *CEO*
Gary Tashnek, *Principal*
Jim Giarratana, *Sales Mgr*
EMP: 14 EST: 2005
SALES (est): 563.7K **Privately Held**
WEB: www.prevounce.com
SIC: 3999 7371 Manufacturing industries; software programming applications

(P-11739)
QUALITY RESOURCES DIST LLC
16254 Beaver Rd, Adelanto (92301-3906)
PHONE..........................510 378-6861
Wesley Staley, *Mng Member*
EMP: 21 EST: 2018
SALES (est): 1.2MM **Privately Held**
SIC: 3999

(P-11740)
RAPID MANUFACTURING INC
9724 Eton Ave, Chatsworth (91311-4305)
PHONE..............................818 899-4377
Jorge Quiroga, *Warehouse Mgr*
Mila Beckers, *Manager*
Stephany Rangel, *Manager*
EMP: 17 EST: 2013
SALES (est): 3.8MM **Privately Held**
WEB: www.rapidprecisionsheetmetal.com
SIC: 3999 Barber & beauty shop equipment

(P-11741)
REEL EFX INC
5539 Riverton Ave, North Hollywood
(91601-2816)
PHONE..............................818 762-1710
Jim Gill, *President*
Rosy Romano, *CFO*
Susan Gill, *Vice Pres*
Susan Milliken, *Vice Pres*
Adam Forster, *Design Engr*
EMP: 25
SQ FT: 34,000
SALES: 2.7MM **Privately Held**
WEB: www.reelefx.com
SIC: 3999 Stage hardware & equipment, except lighting

(P-11742)
RELAX MEDICAL SYSTEMS INC
Also Called: RMS
3260 E Willow St, Signal Hill (90755-2309)
PHONE..............................800 405-7677
Leon Press, *CEO*
◆ EMP: 15 EST: 2000
SALES (est): 725.7K **Privately Held**
WEB: www.relaxmedsyst.com
SIC: 3999 5083 5261 Hydroponic equipment; hydroponic equipment & supplies; hydroponic equipment & supplies

(P-11743)
**REMARKABLE INDUSTRIES INC
(PA)**
6355 Topanga Canyon Blvd # 321, Woodland Hills (91367-2102)
PHONE..............................800 579-4380
Eric Mark, *Principal*
EMP: 29 EST: 2015
SALES (est): 116.9K **Privately Held**
SIC: 3999 Manufacturing industries

(P-11744)
RICON CORP (HQ)
1135 Aviation Pl, San Fernando
(91340-1460)
PHONE..............................818 267-3000
William Baldwin, *President*
Raymond T Betler, *CEO*
William Hinze, *Vice Pres*
Janice Rivera, *Vice Pres*
Stanton Saucier, *Vice Pres*
◆ EMP: 134 EST: 1971
SQ FT: 225,000
SALES (est): 25.2MM **Publicly Held**
WEB: www.riconcorp.com
SIC: 3999 Wheelchair lifts

(P-11745)
RUCCI INC
6700 11th Ave, Los Angeles (90043-4730)
PHONE..............................323 778-9000
Ramin Lavian, *President*
Elsie Lavian, *Vice Pres*
▲ EMP: 34 EST: 1990
SQ FT: 17,000
SALES (est): 1.2MM **Privately Held**
WEB: www.rucci.com
SIC: 3999 5087 Barber & beauty shop equipment; beauty parlor equipment & supplies

(P-11746)
SALEM POLYMER INDUSTRIES
5500 Owensmouth Ave # 133, Woodland Hills (91367-7086)
PHONE..............................818 331-9475
Mohammad Ali Naraghi Salem, *President*
EMP: 13 EST: 2016
SALES (est): 126.9K **Privately Held**
WEB: www.polymerindustries.com
SIC: 3999 Manufacturing industries

(P-11747)
SCHMIDT INDUSTRIES INC
91 Sequoia Dr, Pasadena (91105-1344)
PHONE..............................323 344-6400
Fred V Schmidt, *Principal*
EMP: 13 EST: 2008
SALES (est): 318.2K **Privately Held**
WEB: www.schmidtindustries.com
SIC: 3999 Manufacturing industries

(P-11748)
SCHWARZKOPF INC (DH)
600 Corporate Pointe # 1100, Culver City
(90230-7625)
PHONE..............................310 641-0990
▲ EMP: 20
SQ FT: 5,566
SALES (est): 7.5MM
SALES (corp-wide): 22.7B **Privately Held**
WEB: www.schwarzkopf-professionalusa.com
SIC: 3999 5122 Manufacturing Industries, Nec, Nsk
HQ: Henkel Us Operations Corporation
1 Henkel Way
Rocky Hill CT 06067
860 571-5100

(P-11749)
**SCRIPTO-TOKAI CORPORATION
(DH)**
2055 S Haven Ave, Ontario (91761-0736)
PHONE..............................909 930-5000
Tomoyuki Kurata, *President*
Tokiharu Murofushi, *CFO*
Fred Ashley, *Admin Sec*
▲ EMP: 80 EST: 1923
SQ FT: 120,000
SALES (est): 10.4MM **Privately Held**
WEB: www.vesta-tokai.co.jp
SIC: 3999 3951 Cigarette lighters, except precious metal; ball point pens & parts

(P-11750)
SEGA OF AMERICA INC
6430 Oak Cyn Ste 150, Irvine
(92618-5235)
PHONE..............................415 806-0169
EMP: 68 **Privately Held**
WEB: www.sega.com
SIC: 3999 5092 Coin-operated amusement machines; video games
HQ: Sega Of America, Inc.
6400 Oak Cyn Ste 100
Irvine CA 92618
949 788-0455

(P-11751)
SEGA OF AMERICA INC (DH)
6400 Oak Cyn Ste 100, Irvine
(92618-5204)
PHONE..............................949 788-0455
Tatsuyuki Miyazaki, *CEO*
Hayao Nakayama, *Ch of Bd*
Ian Curran, *President*
Howell Ivy, *President*
Yukio Aoyama, *Senior VP*
▲ EMP: 45 EST: 1985
SQ FT: 9,000
SALES (est): 144MM **Privately Held**
WEB: www.sega.com
SIC: 3999 5092 Coin-operated amusement machines; video games

(P-11752)
SENTIMENTS INC (PA)
Also Called: Best Friends By Sheri
5353 E Slauson Ave, Commerce
(90040-2916)
PHONE..............................323 843-2080
Shohreh Dadbin, *CEO*
John Dadbin, *Treasurer*
Benjamin Dadbin, *Vice Pres*
Diana Hernandez, *Executive Asst*
▲ EMP: 14 EST: 2006
SALES (est): 5.7MM **Privately Held**
WEB: www.sentimentsinc.us
SIC: 3999 Pet supplies

(P-11753)
SF TECHNOLOGY INC
16730 Gridley Rd, Cerritos (90703-1730)
PHONE..............................562 924-5763
Jitendra Patel, *Owner*
EMP: 17 EST: 2013
SALES (est): 120K **Privately Held**
WEB: www.sftech.com
SIC: 3999 3011 Education aids, devices & supplies; agricultural inner tubes

(P-11754)
SGPS INC
Also Called: Show Group Production Services
15823 S Main St, Gardena (90248-2548)
PHONE..............................310 538-4175
Barrie Owen, *CEO*
Lisa Lorenz, *Vice Pres*
Mike Estill, *General Mgr*
Katy Marx, *General Mgr*
Jesse Sugimoto, *Project Mgr*
EMP: 85 EST: 1991
SQ FT: 40,000
SALES (est): 11.5MM **Privately Held**
WEB: www.sgpsshowrig.com
SIC: 3999 Theatrical scenery

(P-11755)
SHARP INDUSTRIES LLC
1525 3rd St Ste K, Riverside (92507-3429)
PHONE..............................951 323-3677
Benjamin Sharp, *CEO*
EMP: 14 EST: 2017
SALES (est): 1MM **Privately Held**
WEB: www.sharp-industries.com
SIC: 3999 Manufacturing industries

(P-11756)
SILVESTRI STUDIO INC (PA)
Also Called: Silvester California
8125 Beach St, Los Angeles (90001-3426)
P.O. Box 512198 (90051-0198)
PHONE..............................323 277-4420
E Alain Levi, *CEO*
▲ EMP: 80
SQ FT: 130,000
SALES (est): 16.7MM **Privately Held**
WEB: www.silvestricalifornia.com
SIC: 3999 2542 3993 Mannequins; office & store showcases & display fixtures; signs & advertising specialties

(P-11757)
**SMALL WNDERS HNDCRFTED
MNTRES**
7033 Canoga Ave Ste 5, Canoga Park
(91303-3118)
PHONE..............................818 703-7450
EMP: 15
SALES (est): 908.3K **Privately Held**
SIC: 3999 Manufacturing Industries, Nec, Nsk

(P-11758)
**SNAPSHOT HAIR &
EXTENSIONS LLC ✪**
2892 N Bellflower Blvd, Long Beach
(90815-1125)
PHONE..............................877 783-5658
Jacqueline Pere,
EMP: 15 EST: 2021
SALES (est): 340K **Privately Held**
WEB: www.snapshothair.com
SIC: 3999 Hair & hair-based products

(P-11759)
SOFTUB INC (PA)
24700 Avenue Rockefeller, Valencia
(91355-3465)
PHONE..............................858 602-1920
Tom Thornbury, *Chairman*
Spencer Greer, *Info Tech Dir*
Inez Frank, *Technology*
Carol Garcia, *Technology*
Charles Fogarty, *Engineer*
▲ EMP: 85 EST: 1983
SALES (est): 23.8MM **Privately Held**
WEB: www.softub.com
SIC: 3999 Hot tubs

(P-11760)
STANG INDUSTRIES INC
Also Called: Stang Industrial Products
2616 Research Dr Ste B, Corona
(92882-6978)
PHONE..............................714 556-0222
Charles Ronie, *CEO*
Abdul Kashif, *CFO*
▲ EMP: 19 EST: 1943
SQ FT: 20,000
SALES (est): 4.6MM **Privately Held**
WEB: www.stangindustries.com
SIC: 3999 3492 3561 Fire extinguishers, portable; control valves; aircraft: hydraulic & pneumatic; pumps & pumping equipment

(P-11761)
STEELDECK INC
13147 S Western Ave, Gardena
(90249-1921)
PHONE..............................323 290-2100
Phil Parsons, *President*
Danny Razo, *COO*
Adrian Funnell, *Vice Pres*
Pete Varela, *General Mgr*
▲ EMP: 25 EST: 1993
SALES (est): 4MM **Privately Held**
WEB: www.steeldeck.com
SIC: 3999 2541 2531 Stage hardware & equipment, except lighting; partitions for floor attachment, prefabricated: wood; theater furniture

(P-11762)
STELLAR INDUSTRIES
1524 Patricia Ave, Simi Valley
(93065-3489)
PHONE..............................818 472-5432
Brian Staubach, *President*
EMP: 21 EST: 2018
SALES (est): 112.8K **Privately Held**
WEB: www.stellarindustries.com
SIC: 3999 Manufacturing industries

(P-11763)
STK
930 Hilgard Ave, Los Angeles
(90024-3009)
PHONE..............................310 659-3535
Jonathan Segal, *Principal*
Stacey Perrone, *Opers Staff*
EMP: 15 EST: 2007
SALES (est): 263.4K **Privately Held**
WEB: www.steakhousesinbeverlyhills.com
SIC: 3999 Manufacturing industries

(P-11764)
SUN BADGE CO
2248 S Baker Ave, Ontario (91761-7710)
PHONE..............................909 930-1444
Rick Hamilton, *President*
Chris Hamilton, *Vice Pres*
Benjamin Dawson, *Marketing Staff*
▲ EMP: 35 EST: 1957
SQ FT: 24,000
SALES (est): 3.5MM **Privately Held**
WEB: www.sunbadgeorders.com
SIC: 3999 Badges, metal: policemen, firemen, etc.

(P-11765)
SUNDANCE SPAS INC (DH)
13925 City Center Dr # 200, Chino Hills
(91709-5438)
PHONE..............................909 606-7733
Bob Rowan, *CEO*
Jonathan Clark, *Principal*
Paul V Slyke, *VP Finance*
Maggy Mendoza, *Buyer*
◆ EMP: 33 EST: 1998
SALES (est): 64.4MM
SALES (corp-wide): 467.1K **Privately
Held**
WEB: www.sundancespas.com
SIC: 3999 1799 5999 Hot tubs; swimming pool construction; spas & hot tubs
HQ: Jacuzzi Brands Llc
13925 City Center Dr # 200
Chino Hills CA 91709
909 606-1416

(P-11766)
SUNDERSTORM LLC
1146 N Central Ave, Glendale
(91202-2506)
PHONE..............................818 605-6682
Cameron Clark, *CEO*
Keith Cich, *President*
EMP: 17
SALES (est): 1.3MM **Privately Held**
SIC: 3999

PRODUCTS & SVCS

(P-11767)
SUNSTAR SPA COVERS INC (HQ)
26074 Avenue Hall Ste 13, Valencia (91355-3445)
PHONE.................................858 602-1950
Tom Thornbury, *Ch of Bd*
Edward McGarry, *President*
Sylvia Zaitz Sunstar, *Credit Staff*
Sue Sousa, *VP Sales*
▲ EMP: 40 EST: 2000
SALES (est): 10.9MM
SALES (corp-wide): 23.8MM **Privately Held**
WEB: www.softub.com
SIC: 3999 Hot tub & spa covers
PA: Softub, Inc.
　24700 Avenue Rockefeller
　Valencia CA 91355
　858 602-1920

(P-11768)
SUPERIOR-STUDIO SPC INC
2239 Yates Ave, Commerce (90040-1913)
PHONE.................................323 278-0100
Jean-Pierre Fournier, *President*
Lauren Ward, *Purchasing*
◆ EMP: 20 EST: 1995
SQ FT: 60,000
SALES (est): 2.9MM **Privately Held**
WEB: www.superiorstudiospecialties.com
SIC: 3999 Advertising display products

(P-11769)
SWS PANEL AND TRUSS INC
Also Called: Superior Wall Systems
4231 Liberty Blvd, South Gate (90280-2558)
PHONE.................................323 923-4900
Ronald Hudson, *CEO*
EMP: 13 EST: 2013
SALES (est): 889.7K **Privately Held**
WEB: www.swspanelinc.com
SIC: 3999 Chairs, hydraulic, barber & beauty shop

(P-11770)
T3 MICRO INC (PA)
228 Main St Ste 3, Venice (90291-5202)
PHONE.................................310 452-2888
Kent Yu, *President*
Connor Garrity, *Project Mgr*
Rami Darouiche, *Asst Controller*
Yogita Patel, *Controller*
Ming Tran, *Opers Staff*
▲ EMP: 18 EST: 2005
SALES (est): 5.2MM **Privately Held**
WEB: www.t3micro.com
SIC: 3999 Hair & hair-based products

(P-11771)
TAG TOYS INC
1810 S Acacia Ave, Compton (90220-4927)
PHONE.................................310 639-4566
Lawrence Mestyanek, *CEO*
Barbara Villafana, *CFO*
Judy Mestyanek, *Officer*
EMP: 65 EST: 1976
SQ FT: 60,000
SALES (est): 5.6MM **Privately Held**
WEB: www.tagtoys.com
SIC: 3999 8351 3944 Education aids, devices & supplies; child day care services; games, toys & children's vehicles

(P-11772)
TANDEM DESIGN INC
Also Called: Tandem Exhibit
1846 W Sequoia Ave, Orange (92868-1018)
PHONE.................................714 978-7272
Maury Bonas, *President*
Susan Bonas, *Vice Pres*
Stephen Gann, *Prdtn Mgr*
Steve Gann, *Prdtn Mgr*
Stephan Palalay, *Accounts Exec*
EMP: 23 EST: 1975
SQ FT: 20,000
SALES (est): 1.4MM **Privately Held**
WEB: www.tandemexhibits.com
SIC: 3999 Preparation of slides & exhibits

(P-11773)
TAOTAO MANUFACTURER INC (PA)
9833 Garibaldi Ave, Temple City (91780-1713)
PHONE.................................626 688-9880
J Verl Sylvester, *Principal*
EMP: 31 EST: 2010
SALES (est): 214.8K **Privately Held**
WEB: www.taotaomanufacturer.com
SIC: 3999 Manufacturing industries

(P-11774)
TAOTAO MANUFACTURER INC
9073 Arcadia Ave, San Gabriel (91775-1401)
PHONE.................................626 688-9880
Paul Tao, *Branch Mgr*
EMP: 17
SALES (corp-wide): 214.8K **Privately Held**
WEB: www.taotaomanufacturer.com
SIC: 3999 Barber & beauty shop equipment
PA: Taotao Manufacturer, Inc.
　9833 Garibaldi Ave
　Temple City CA 91780
　626 688-9880

(P-11775)
TD INDUSTRIES
3 Ironwood Cir, Trabuco Canyon (92679-4159)
PHONE.................................949 939-3685
Donald R Davis Jr, *Principal*
EMP: 21 EST: 2015
SALES (est): 109K **Privately Held**
WEB: www.tdindustries.com
SIC: 3999 Manufacturing industries

(P-11776)
TECHNICAL MANUFACTURING W LLC
24820 Avenue Tibbitts, Valencia (91355-3404)
PHONE.................................661 295-7226
Brad Topper,
Johnny Valadez,
EMP: 34 EST: 2010
SALES (est): 5.3MM **Privately Held**
WEB: www.tmwmedical.com
SIC: 3999 Barber & beauty shop equipment

(P-11777)
TECHVALVE INDUSTRIES LLC
21061 Morningside Dr, Trabuco Canyon (92679-3329)
PHONE.................................714 264-7950
Steve Smith, *Principal*
EMP: 14 EST: 2010
SALES (est): 165.3K **Privately Held**
SIC: 3999 Manufacturing industries

(P-11778)
TIBBAN MANUFACTURING INC
12593 Highline Dr, Apple Valley (92308-5047)
P.O. Box 2675 (92307-0051)
PHONE.................................760 961-1160
James A Tibban, *CEO*
Tony Tibban, *Principal*
◆ EMP: 22 EST: 2009
SALES (est): 300.8K **Privately Held**
WEB: www.tibban.com
SIC: 3999 Barber & beauty shop equipment

(P-11779)
TIS INDUSTRIES LLC (PA)
16815 E Johnson Dr, City of Industry (91745-2417)
PHONE.................................626 336-3821
Myles Kovacs, *Principal*
EMP: 43 EST: 2003
SALES (est): 955.3K **Privately Held**
SIC: 3999 Manufacturing industries

(P-11780)
TOM LEONARD INVESTMENT CO INC
Also Called: Peak Seasons
7240 Sycamore Canyon Blvd, Riverside (92508-2331)
PHONE.................................951 351-7778
Tom Leonard, *CEO*
Greg Szuba, *Vice Pres*
Sherry Morales, *Office Mgr*
Arlene Leonard, *Admin Sec*
Desiree Menjivar, *Supervisor*
▲ EMP: 21 EST: 1992
SQ FT: 35,000
SALES (est): 2.5MM **Privately Held**
WEB: www.peakseasons.com
SIC: 3999 3399 Christmas tree ornaments, except electrical & glass; paste, metal

(P-11781)
TOTAL PAPER SERVICES INC
100 S Anaheim Blvd # 250, Anaheim (92805-3848)
PHONE.................................714 780-0131
EMP: 13 EST: 2004
SALES (est): 460.7K **Privately Held**
SIC: 3999 2679 Atomizers, toiletry; book covers, paper

(P-11782)
TRANS FX INC
Also Called: T F X
2361 Eastman Ave, Oxnard (93030-8136)
PHONE.................................805 485-6110
Allen Pike, *President*
Hollis Hedrich, *CFO*
Rick Bordonaro, *Exec VP*
Annie Pike, *Manager*
EMP: 15 EST: 1993
SQ FT: 25,000
SALES (est): 2.2MM **Privately Held**
WEB: www.transfx.com
SIC: 3999 3711 7389 3812 Models, except toy; automobile assembly, including specialty automobiles; design services; acceleration indicators & systems components, aerospace

(P-11783)
TRAXX CORPORATION
1201 E Lexington Ave, Pomona (91766-5520)
PHONE.................................909 623-8032
Craig Silvers, *CEO*
Jon Hall, *Chairman*
Nico Sardo, *Technical Mgr*
CK Patel, *Engineer*
Rosie Gastelum, *Controller*
▲ EMP: 100 EST: 2007
SQ FT: 52,000
SALES (est): 19.6MM **Privately Held**
WEB: www.jastmedia.com
SIC: 3999 Carpet tackles

(P-11784)
TRE MILANO LLC
Also Called: Instyler
2730 Monterey St Ste 101, Torrance (90503-7230)
PHONE.................................310 260-8888
Mark D Friedman,
Brian Dicke, *Accountant*
Cyndy Agtarap, *Opers Staff*
Tiffany Roshanian, *Mktg Dir*
Kara Artingstall, *Sales Staff*
▲ EMP: 16 EST: 2007
SALES (est): 6.9MM **Privately Held**
WEB: www.instyler.com
SIC: 3999 Hair & hair-based products

(P-11785)
TRNLWB LLC
Also Called: Trinity Lighweight
17410 Lockwood Valley Rd, Frazier Park (93225-9318)
PHONE.................................661 245-3736
EMP: 3675
SALES (corp-wide): 115.1MM **Privately Held**
WEB: www.trinityesc.com
SIC: 3999 Barber & beauty shop equipment
PA: Trnlwb, Llc
　1112 E Cpeland Rd Ste 500
　Arlington TX 76011
　800 581-3117

(P-11786)
TTT INNOVATIONS LLC
20850 Plummer St, Chatsworth (91311-5004)
P.O. Box 86, Woodland Hills (91365-0086)
PHONE.................................818 201-8828
Thomas Bruggemann, *CEO*
Leslie Clarke,
EMP: 20 EST: 2016
SALES (est): 2.8MM **Privately Held**
WEB: www.tomstumbletrimmer.com
SIC: 3999 Barber & beauty shop equipment

(P-11787)
V AND C MANUFACTURING AND
655 E Ball Rd, Anaheim (92805-5910)
PHONE.................................615 374-2076
EMP: 13 EST: 2013
SALES (est): 621.5K **Privately Held**
SIC: 3999 Manufacturing industries

(P-11788)
VAL USA MANUFACTURER INC
1050 W Central Ave Ste A, Brea (92821-2200)
PHONE.................................526 839-8069
Lijuan Zhen, *Manager*
▲ EMP: 30 EST: 2014
SALES (est): 1.8MM **Privately Held**
WEB: www.valcosmetics.com
SIC: 3999 Manufacturing industries

(P-11789)
VENTURA FEED AND PET SUPS INC
Also Called: Wharf, The
980 E Front St, Ventura (93001-3017)
P.O. Box 1806 (93002-1806)
PHONE.................................805 648-5035
Todd Butterbaugh, *CEO*
Darren Borgstedte, *CFO*
EMP: 42
SQ FT: 13,000
SALES (est): 9MM **Privately Held**
WEB: www.store.thewharfonline.com
SIC: 5621 5661 3999 2048 Women's clothing stores; shoe stores; pet supplies; prepared feeds; apparel accessories; clothing accessories: men's & boys'

(P-11790)
VITAVET LABS INC
Also Called: Nuvet Labs
5717 Corsa Ave, Westlake Village (91362-4001)
PHONE.................................818 865-2600
Blake Kirschbaum, *President*
Matt Simpson, *COO*
Dr Raymond Kirschbaum, *CFO*
Blake G Kirschbaum, *Marketing Staff*
Pamela Okane, *Sales Staff*
▼ EMP: 20 EST: 1997
SALES (est): 2.7MM **Privately Held**
WEB: www.nuvetonline.com
SIC: 3999 Pet supplies

(P-11791)
VOLT INDUSTRIES
1831 Phillips Way, Los Angeles (90042-1038)
PHONE.................................323 982-0815
Scott R Todd, *Principal*
EMP: 14 EST: 2018
SALES (est): 78.9K **Privately Held**
WEB: www.volt.com
SIC: 3999 Manufacturing industries

(P-11792)
WALLY & PAT ENTERPRISES
Also Called: Complete Aquatic Systems
13530 S Budlong Ave, Gardena (90247-2030)
PHONE.................................310 532-2031
Shareen King, *President*
EMP: 48 EST: 2000
SALES (est): 3.8MM **Privately Held**
SIC: 3999 Barber & beauty shop equipment

(P-11793)
WBT GROUP LLC
Also Called: Wbt Industries
1401 S Shamrock Ave, Monrovia
(91016-4246)
PHONE.....................323 735-1201
Lisa Stanislawski,
▲ EMP: 40 EST: 2009
SALES (est) 4.4MM Privately Held
WEB: www.wbtindustries.com
SIC: 3999 Buttons: Red Cross, union, identification

4011 Railroads, Line-Hauling Operations

(P-11794)
BNSF RAILWAY COMPANY
Also Called: Burlington Northern
18982 Oriente Dr, Yorba Linda
(92886-2636)
PHONE.....................714 348-5810
EMP: 55
SALES (corp-wide): 245.5B Publicly Held
WEB: www.bnsf.com
SIC: 4011 Railroads, Line-Haul Operating, Nsk
HQ: Bnsf Railway Company
2650 Lou Menk Dr
Fort Worth TX 76131
800 795-2673

(P-11795)
CSX CORPORATION
14863 Clark Ave, Hacienda Heights
(91745-1308)
PHONE.....................626 336-1377
EMP: 149
SALES (corp-wide): 12.6B Publicly Held
SIC: 4011 Railroad Line-Haul Operator
PA: Csx Corporation
500 Water St Fl 15
Jacksonville FL 32202
904 359-3200

(P-11796)
LOS ANGELES JUNCTION RLWY CO
4433 Exchange Ave, Vernon (90058-2622)
PHONE.....................323 277-2004
Chuck Potempa, CEO
Rob Rellyl, President
Rm Reilly, Vice Pres
EMP: 93 EST: 1922
SALES (est): 8.5MM
SALES (corp-wide): 245.5B Publicly Held
WEB: www.bnsf.com
SIC: 4011 Railroads, line-haul operating
HQ: Bnsf Railway Company
2650 Lou Menk Dr
Fort Worth TX 76131
800 795-2673

(P-11797)
SAN JOAQUIN VALLEY RAILROAD CO
221 N F St, Exeter (93221-1119)
P.O. Box 937 (93221-0937)
PHONE.....................559 592-1857
Randy Perry, CEO
Rex Bergholm, President
Steve Coomes, Vice Pres
EMP: 63 EST: 1991
SQ FT: 1,100
SALES (est): 8.1MM
SALES (corp-wide): 2.3B Privately Held
WEB: www.gwrr.com
SIC: 4011 Railroads, line-haul operating
HQ: Railamerica, Inc.
20 West Ave
Darien CT 06820

(P-11798)
TRONA RAILWAY COMPANY
13068 Main St, Trona (93562-1911)
PHONE.....................760 372-2312
John F Tancredi,
Matthew J Dowd,
EMP: 530 EST: 1913
SQ FT: 30,000

SALES (est): 3.9MM Privately Held
WEB: www.svminerals.com
SIC: 4011 Railroads, line-haul operating
HQ: Searles Valley Minerals Inc.
9401 Indian Creek Pkwy
Overland Park KS 66210

(P-11799)
UNION PACIFIC RAILROAD COMPANY
Also Called: Union Pacific Lines
2401 E Sepulveda Blvd, Long Beach
(90810-1945)
PHONE.....................562 490-7000
Herman Madden, Superintendent
EMP: 300
SALES (corp-wide): 19.5B Publicly Held
WEB: www.up.com
SIC: 4011 Railroads, line-haul operating
HQ: Union Pacific Railroad Company Inc
1400 Douglas St
Omaha NE 68179
402 544-5000

4013 Switching & Terminal Svcs

(P-11800)
TRANSDEV NORTH AMERICA INC
1224 N San Dimas Cyn Rd, San Dimas
(91773-1223)
PHONE.....................909 394-2307
EMP: 100
SALES (corp-wide): 1.3B Privately Held
WEB: www.transdevna.com
SIC: 4013 Switching & terminal services
HQ: Transdev North America, Inc.
720 E Bttrfeld Rd Ste 300
Lombard IL 60148
630 571-7070

4111 Local & Suburban Transit

(P-11801)
ACCESS SERVICES
Also Called: ACCESS PARATRANSIT
3449 Santa Anita Ave, El Monte
(91731-2424)
P.O. Box 5728 (91734-1728)
PHONE.....................213 270-6000
Doran J Barnes, CEO
F S Jewell, COO
Shelly Verrinder, Exec Dir
William Tsuei, Info Tech Dir
Ruben Prieto, Analyst
EMP: 80 EST: 1994
SALES: 184.9MM Privately Held
WEB: www.accessla.org
SIC: 4111 Local & suburban transit

(P-11802)
AIRPORT CONNECTION INC
Also Called: Roadrunner Shuttle
95 Dawson Dr, Camarillo (93012-2001)
PHONE.....................805 389-8196
Sumaia Sandlin, CEO
Lori Rotvik, Executive Asst
Desmond P Sandlin, Admin Sec
Charles Sandlin, Technology
Jeff Brown, Manager
EMP: 180 EST: 1991
SQ FT: 3,500
SALES (est): 18.9MM Privately Held
WEB: www.smartshuttle805.com
SIC: 4111 4119 Airport transportation; airport transportation services, regular route; limousine rental, with driver

(P-11803)
CITY OF GARDENA
Also Called: Gardena Municipal Bus Lines
13999 S Western Ave, Gardena
(90249-3005)
PHONE.....................310 324-1475
Whitman Ballenger, Director
Joseph Collins, Maintence Staff
Mark E Henderson, Council Mbr
Tasha Cerda, Mayor

Ernie Crespo, Director
EMP: 54
SALES (corp-wide): 64MM Privately Held
WEB: www.cityofgardena.org
SIC: 4111 9621 Bus line operations; regulation, administration of transportation;
PA: City Of Gardena
1700 W 162nd St
Gardena CA 90247
310 217-9500

(P-11804)
CITY OF VISALIA
425 E Oak Ave Ste 301, Visalia
(93291-5035)
PHONE.....................559 713-4100
EMP: 112
SALES (corp-wide): 138.9MM Privately Held
WEB: www.ci.visalia.ca.us
SIC: 4111 Local & suburban transit
PA: Visalia, City Of (Inc)
707 W Acequia Ave
Visalia CA 93291
559 713-4565

(P-11805)
EASTERN SIERRA TRANSIT AUTH
565 Airport Rd, Bishop (93514-3610)
P.O. Box 1357 (93515-1357)
PHONE.....................760 872-1901
Brad Koehn, Principal
John Helm, Principal
Phil Moores, Exec Dir
Philip Moores, Exec Dir
Karie Bentley, Opers Spvr
EMP: 50 EST: 2010
SALES (est): 5.2MM Privately Held
WEB: www.estransit.com
SIC: 4111 Local & suburban transit

(P-11806)
FIRST STUDENT INC
Also Called: Community Transit Services
4337 Rowland Ave, El Monte
(91731-1119)
PHONE.....................626 448-9446
John Desmond, Branch Mgr
EMP: 288 Privately Held
WEB: www.firststudentinc.com
SIC: 4111 4119 Bus line operations; local passenger transportation
PA: First Student, Inc.
600 Vine St Ste 1400
Cincinnati OH 45202

(P-11807)
FIRST TRANSIT
Also Called: First Group of America
1303 Fairway Dr, Santa Maria
(93455-1407)
PHONE.....................805 925-5254
EMP: 71
SALES (est): 3.4MM Privately Held
SIC: 4111 Local/Suburban Transportation

(P-11808)
FIRST TRANSIT INC
2400 E Dominguez St, Long Beach
(90810-1012)
PHONE.....................310 515-8270
EMP: 54
SALES (corp-wide): 9.2B Privately Held
SIC: 4111 Local/Suburban Transportation
HQ: First Transit, Inc.
600 Vine St Ste 1400
Cincinnati OH 45202
513 241-2200

(P-11809)
FIRST TRANSIT INC
6671 Marine Way, Irvine (92618-1724)
PHONE.....................949 857-7211
EMP: 127
SALES (corp-wide): 903.8MM Privately Held
WEB: www.firsttransit.com
SIC: 4111 Local & suburban transit
PA: First Transit, Inc.
600 Vine St Ste 1400
Cincinnati OH 45202
513 241-2200

(P-11810)
FIRST TRANSIT INC
29 Prado Rd, San Luis Obispo
(93401-7314)
PHONE.....................805 544-2730
Kim Blakeman, Manager
EMP: 127
SALES (corp-wide): 903.8MM Privately Held
WEB: www.firsttransit.com
SIC: 4111 Bus transportation
PA: First Transit, Inc.
600 Vine St Ste 1400
Cincinnati OH 45202
513 241-2200

(P-11811)
GOLDEN EMPIRE TRANSIT DISTRICT (PA)
Also Called: Get-A-Lift Handicap Bus Trnsp
1830 Golden State Ave, Bakersfield
(93301-1012)
PHONE.....................661 869-2438
Steven Woods, CEO
Karen King, President
Jull Smith, Chief Mktg Ofcr
Jeanie Hill, Executive
Jill Smith, Administration
EMP: 232 EST: 1973
SALES (est): 34.8MM Privately Held
WEB: www.getbus.org
SIC: 4111 Bus line operations

(P-11812)
IDEAL TRANSIT INC
13404 Waco St, Baldwin Park
(91706-4734)
PHONE.....................626 448-2690
Baldo M Paseta, President
EMP: 50 EST: 1998
SALES (est): 7MM Privately Held
WEB: www.idealtransitinc.com
SIC: 4111 Local & suburban transit

(P-11813)
KEOLIS TRANSIT AMERICA INC
14663 Keswick St, Van Nuys (91405-1204)
PHONE.....................818 616-5254
Steve Shaw, President
Gavino Romero, Maintence Staff
Breana Jackson, Manager
Julia Jens, Manager
EMP: 175
SALES (corp-wide): 4.2MM Privately Held
WEB: www.keolisna.com
SIC: 4111 Local & suburban transit
HQ: Keolis Transit America, Inc.
6053 W Century Blvd # 900
Los Angeles CA 90045

(P-11814)
KEOLIS TRANSIT AMERICA INC
660 W Avenue L, Lancaster (93534-7117)
PHONE.....................661 341-3910
Steve Shaw, President
Kim Jamron, Accounting Mgr
EMP: 90
SALES (corp-wide): 4.2MM Privately Held
WEB: www.keolisna.com
SIC: 4111 Local & suburban transit
HQ: Keolis Transit America, Inc.
6053 W Century Blvd # 900
Los Angeles CA 90045

(P-11815)
LONG BEACH PUBLIC TRNSP CO (PA)
Also Called: Long Beach Transit
1963 E Anaheim St, Long Beach
(90813-3907)
PHONE.....................562 599-8571
Kenneth A McDonald, CEO
Laurence W Jackson, President
Kenneth A McDonald, CEO
Robin Gordon, COO
Rolando Cruz, Officer
EMP: 570 EST: 1963
SQ FT: 10,000
SALES (est): 57.8MM Privately Held
WEB: www.ridelbt.com
SIC: 4111 Local & suburban transit

(P-11816)
LOS ANGLES CNTY MTRO TRNSP AUT
Also Called: Green Line Rail Eqp Maint
14724 Aviation Blvd, Lawndale
(90260-1122)
PHONE..................................310 643-3804
Ed Smith, *Manager*
EMP: 683
SALES (corp-wide): 474.9MM **Privately Held**
WEB: www.metro.net
SIC: 4111 Local & suburban transit
PA: Los Angeles County Metropolitan
Transportation Authority
1 Gateway Plz Fl 25
Los Angeles CA 90012
323 466-3876

(P-11817)
LOS ANGLES CNTY MTRO TRNSP AUT
9201 Canoga Ave, Chatsworth
(91311-5839)
PHONE..................................213 922-6308
Pat Orr, *Manager*
EMP: 683
SALES (corp-wide): 474.9MM **Privately Held**
WEB: www.metro.net
SIC: 4111 Bus line operations
PA: Los Angeles County Metropolitan
Transportation Authority
1 Gateway Plz Fl 25
Los Angeles CA 90012
323 466-3876

(P-11818)
LOS ANGLES CNTY MTRO TRNSP AUT
900 Lyon St, Los Angeles (90012-2913)
PHONE..................................213 922-5887
John Drayton, *Manager*
EMP: 683
SALES (corp-wide): 474.9MM **Privately Held**
WEB: www.metro.net
SIC: 4111 Bus line operations
PA: Los Angeles County Metropolitan
Transportation Authority
1 Gateway Plz Fl 25
Los Angeles CA 90012
323 466-3876

(P-11819)
LOS ANGLES CNTY MTRO TRNSP AUT
Also Called: Division 1
1130 E 6th St, Los Angeles (90021-1108)
PHONE..................................213 922-6301
Ron Reedy, *Branch Mgr*
Aida Asuncion, *Officer*
EMP: 683
SALES (corp-wide): 474.9MM **Privately Held**
WEB: www.metro.net
SIC: 4111 Bus line operations
PA: Los Angeles County Metropolitan
Transportation Authority
1 Gateway Plz Fl 25
Los Angeles CA 90012
323 466-3876

(P-11820)
LOS ANGLES CNTY MTRO TRNSP AUT
630 W Avenue 28, Los Angeles
(90065-1502)
PHONE..................................213 922-6203
Cheryl Brown, *Manager*
EMP: 683
SALES (corp-wide): 474.9MM **Privately Held**
WEB: www.metro.net
SIC: 4111 Bus line operations
PA: Los Angeles County Metropolitan
Transportation Authority
1 Gateway Plz Fl 25
Los Angeles CA 90012
323 466-3876

(P-11821)
LOS ANGLES CNTY MTRO TRNSP AUT
Also Called: Los Angles Cnty Mtro Trnsp Aut
1 Gateway Plz, Los Angeles (90012-3745)
PHONE..................................213 922-6202
Maria Japardi, *Branch Mgr*
EMP: 683
SALES (corp-wide): 474.9MM **Privately Held**
WEB: www.metro.net
SIC: 4111 Bus line operations
PA: Los Angeles County Metropolitan
Transportation Authority
1 Gateway Plz Fl 25
Los Angeles CA 90012
323 466-3876

(P-11822)
LOS ANGLES CNTY MTRO TRNSP AUT (PA)
1 Gateway Plz Fl 25, Los Angeles
(90012-3745)
P.O. Box 512296 (90051-0296)
PHONE..................................323 466-3876
Stephanie Wiggins, *CEO*
Rick Thorpe, *CEO*
Nalini Ahuja, *CFO*
Bronwen Trice, *Officer*
Mario Del Rosario, *Project Engr*
EMP: 900 EST: 1964
SALES (est): 474.9MM **Privately Held**
WEB: www.metro.net
SIC: 4111 Local & suburban transit

(P-11823)
LOS ANGLES CNTY MTRO TRNSP AUT
8800 Santa Monica Blvd, Los Angeles
(90069-4536)
PHONE..................................213 922-6207
Grant Myers, *Manager*
EMP: 683
SALES (corp-wide): 474.9MM **Privately Held**
WEB: www.metro.net
SIC: 4111 Bus line operations; local railway passenger operation
PA: Los Angeles County Metropolitan
Transportation Authority
1 Gateway Plz Fl 25
Los Angeles CA 90012
323 466-3876

(P-11824)
LOS ANGLES CNTY MTRO TRNSP AUT
11900 Branford St, Sun Valley
(91352-1003)
PHONE..................................213 922-6215
Gary Stivack, *Manager*
EMP: 683
SALES (corp-wide): 474.9MM **Privately Held**
WEB: www.metro.net
SIC: 4111 Bus line operations
PA: Los Angeles County Metropolitan
Transportation Authority
1 Gateway Plz Fl 25
Los Angeles CA 90012
323 466-3876

(P-11825)
LOS ANGLES CNTY MTRO TRNSP AUT
720 E 15th St, Los Angeles (90021-2122)
PHONE..................................213 533-1506
Carla Aleman, *Branch Mgr*
EMP: 683
SALES (corp-wide): 474.9MM **Privately Held**
WEB: www.metro.net
SIC: 4111 Bus line operations
PA: Los Angeles County Metropolitan
Transportation Authority
1 Gateway Plz Fl 25
Los Angeles CA 90012
323 466-3876

(P-11826)
LOS ANGLES CNTY MTRO TRNSP AUT
Also Called: Lacmta
470 Bauchet St, Los Angeles (90012-2907)
PHONE..................................213 922-5012
Jim Montoya, *Branch Mgr*
EMP: 683
SALES (corp-wide): 474.9MM **Privately Held**
WEB: www.metro.net
SIC: 4111 Bus transportation
PA: Los Angeles County Metropolitan
Transportation Authority
1 Gateway Plz Fl 25
Los Angeles CA 90012
323 466-3876

(P-11827)
LOS ANGLES CNTY MTRO TRNSP AUT
Also Called: Division 7
100 Sunset Ave, Venice (90291-2517)
PHONE..................................310 392-8636
John Adams, *Manager*
EMP: 683
SALES (corp-wide): 474.9MM **Privately Held**
WEB: www.metro.net
SIC: 4111 Bus transportation
PA: Los Angeles County Metropolitan
Transportation Authority
1 Gateway Plz Fl 25
Los Angeles CA 90012
323 466-3876

(P-11828)
LOS ANGLES CNTY MTRO TRNSP AUT
Also Called: Office of Inspector General
818 W 7th St Ste 500, Los Angeles
(90017-3463)
PHONE..................................213 244-6783
Arthur Sinai, *Manager*
EMP: 683
SALES (corp-wide): 474.9MM **Privately Held**
WEB: www.metro.net
SIC: 4111 Bus line operations
PA: Los Angeles County Metropolitan
Transportation Authority
1 Gateway Plz Fl 25
Los Angeles CA 90012
323 466-3876

(P-11829)
LOS ANGLES CNTY MTRO TRNSP AUT
320 S Santa Fe Ave, Los Angeles
(90013-1812)
P.O. Box 194 (90078-0194)
PHONE..................................213 626-4455
Julian Burke, *CEO*
EMP: 683
SALES (corp-wide): 474.9MM **Privately Held**
WEB: www.metro.net
SIC: 4111 Bus line operations
PA: Los Angeles County Metropolitan
Transportation Authority
1 Gateway Plz Fl 25
Los Angeles CA 90012
323 466-3876

(P-11830)
MV TRANSPORTATION INC
7231 Rosecrans Ave, Paramount
(90723-2501)
PHONE..................................562 259-9911
EMP: 75
SALES (corp-wide): 378.4MM **Privately Held**
WEB: www.mvtransit.com
SIC: 4111 Local & suburban transit
PA: Mv Transportation, Inc.
2711 N Haskell Ave # 1500
Dallas TX 75204
972 391-4600

(P-11831)
OMNITRANS INC
4748 Arrow Hwy, Montclair (91763-1208)
PHONE..................................909 379-7100
John Steffon, *Branch Mgr*
Keith Hunt, *Maintence Staff*

EMP: 86
SALES (corp-wide): 14MM **Privately Held**
WEB: www.omnitrans.org
SIC: 4111 Bus line operations
PA: Omnitrans, Inc.
1700 W 5th St
San Bernardino CA 92411
909 379-7100

(P-11832)
ORANGE COUNTY TRNSP AUTH
11790 Cardinal Cir, Garden Grove
(92843-3839)
P.O. Box 14184, Orange (92863-1584)
PHONE..................................714 560-6282
Arthur Leahy, *CEO*
Fernando Chavarria, *Officer*
Jason Ko, *Creative Dir*
Niall Barrett, *Program Mgr*
Jay Gabrielson, *Program Mgr*
EMP: 77
SALES (corp-wide): 708.3MM **Privately Held**
WEB: www.octa.net
SIC: 4111 Bus line operations
PA: Orange County Transportation Authority
550 S Main St
Orange CA 92868
714 636-7433

(P-11833)
ORANGE COUNTY TRNSP AUTH (PA)
Also Called: ORANGE COUNTY TRANSIT DISTRICT
550 S Main St, Orange (92868-4506)
P.O. Box 14184 (92863-1584)
PHONE..................................714 636-7433
Darrell Johnson, *CEO*
Gary Jones, *Officer*
Calina North, *Officer*
Cleve Cleveland, *Program Mgr*
Ross Lew, *Program Mgr*
EMP: 350 EST: 1972
SQ FT: 77,000
SALES: 708.3MM **Privately Held**
WEB: www.octa.net
SIC: 4111 8711 Bus line operations; construction & civil engineering

(P-11834)
ORANGE COUNTY TRNSP AUTH
Also Called: Octa
600 S Main St Ste 910, Orange
(92868-4689)
PHONE..................................714 999-1726
Oscar Moreno, *Branch Mgr*
Cheryl Minion, *Admin Asst*
Louis Schmidt, *Analyst*
Marie Latino, *Maint Spvr*
Ana Ripalda, *Manager*
EMP: 600
SALES (corp-wide): 708.3MM **Privately Held**
WEB: www.octa.net
SIC: 4111 Bus line operations
PA: Orange County Transportation Authority
550 S Main St
Orange CA 92868
714 636-7433

(P-11835)
PRIVATE SUITE LAX LLC
Also Called: PS
6871 W Imperial Hwy, Los Angeles
(90045-6311)
PHONE..................................310 907-9950
Joshua Gausman, *Mng Member*
Jordi Mena, *Finance*
Amina Belouizdad, *Mng Member*
EMP: 65 EST: 2017
SQ FT: 57,590
SALES (est): 5.9MM **Privately Held**
WEB: www.reserveps.com
SIC: 4111 Airport transportation

(P-11836)
RIVERSIDE TRANSIT AGENCY (PA)
Also Called: R T A
1825 3rd St, Riverside (92507-3484)
P.O. Box 59968 (92517-1968)
PHONE..................................951 565-5000

Larry Rubio, *CEO*
Darlees Brogdon, *Administration*
Jeff Noll, *Project Mgr*
Laura Camacho, *Technology*
Tim Porterfield, *Technology*
EMP: 350 **EST:** 1977
SQ FT: 10,400
SALES (est): 9.3MM **Privately Held**
WEB: www.riversidetransit.com
SIC: 4111 Bus transportation

(P-11837)
SAN GABRIEL TRANSIT INC (PA)
Also Called: San Gabriel Valley Cab Co
3650 Rockwell Ave, El Monte (91731-2322)
PHONE....................626 258-1310
Timmy Mardirossian, *President*
Eda Aghajanian, *Treasurer*
Keshishian Petros, *Vice Pres*
Jano Baghdanian, *General Mgr*
Sedik Mardirossian, *Admin Sec*
EMP: 220 **EST:** 1953
SQ FT: 8,000
SALES (est): 47.4MM **Privately Held**
WEB: www.sgtransit.com
SIC: 4111 Local & suburban transit

(P-11838)
SAN LUIS OBSPO RGNAL TRNST AUT
Also Called: Slorta
179 Cross St Ste A, San Luis Obispo (93401-7597)
PHONE....................805 781-4465
Omar McPherson, *Principal*
Tania Arnold, *CFO*
Geoff Straw, *Director*
EMP: 90 **EST:** 1989
SALES (est): 9.9MM **Privately Held**
WEB: www.slorta.org
SIC: 4111 Local & suburban transit

(P-11839)
SANTA BARBARA METRO TRNST DST (PA)
Also Called: M T D
550 Olive St, Santa Barbara (93101-1610)
PHONE....................805 963-3364
David Davis, *Chairman*
John Britton, *Ch of Bd*
Chuck McQuary, *Vice Chairman*
Bill Shelor, *Admin Sec*
Steve Hahn, *Materials Mgr*
EMP: 204 **EST:** 1967
SQ FT: 8,500
SALES (est): 22.7MM **Privately Held**
WEB: www.sbmtd.gov
SIC: 4111 Bus line operations

(P-11840)
SHUTTLE SMART INC
6150 W 96th St, Los Angeles (90045-5218)
PHONE....................310 338-9466
Brian Clark, *Branch Mgr*
EMP: 130
SALES (corp-wide): 1.8MM **Privately Held**
WEB: www.shuttlesmart.net
SIC: 4111 Airport transportation
PA: Shuttle Smart, Inc.
25923 Washington Blvd Ne
Kingston WA 98346
303 757-4870

(P-11841)
SMS TRANSPORTATION SVCS INC
865 S Figueroa St # 2750, Los Angeles (90017-2627)
PHONE....................213 489-5367
John Harris, *CEO*
Delilah Lanoix, *President*
Jennifer Wiltz, *COO*
Danielle Wiltz, *CFO*
Jasmine Hardiman, *Business Dir*
EMP: 150 **EST:** 1994
SQ FT: 3,000
SALES (est): 14.7MM **Privately Held**
WEB: www.smstransportation.net
SIC: 4111 Airport transportation

(P-11842)
SOUTHERN CAL RGIONAL RAIL AUTH
Also Called: Metrolink Doc
2704 N Garey Ave, Pomona (91767-1810)
PHONE....................213 808-7043
Steven Holman, *Senior Mgr*
EMP: 143 **Privately Held**
WEB: www.metrolinktrains.com
SIC: 4111 Commuter rail passenger operation
PA: Southern California Regional Rail Authority
900 Wilshire Blvd # 1500
Los Angeles CA 90017

(P-11843)
SOUTHERN CAL RGIONAL RAIL AUTH (PA)
Also Called: Metrolink
900 Wilshire Blvd # 1500, Los Angeles (90017-4701)
P.O. Box 812060 (90081-0018)
PHONE....................213 452-0200
Stephanie Wiggins, *CEO*
Elissa Konove, *CEO*
Rod Bailey, *COO*
Eric Hosey, *COO*
Gary Lettengarver, *COO*
EMP: 128 **EST:** 1991
SALES (est): 111.3MM **Privately Held**
WEB: www.metrolinktrains.com
SIC: 4111 Commuter rail passenger operation

(P-11844)
SOUTHLAND TRANSIT INC (PA)
3650 Rockwell Ave, El Monte (91731-2322)
PHONE....................626 258-1310
Timmy Mardirossian, *CEO*
Dave Daley, *President*
Scott Transue, *Vice Pres*
Jaime Lopez, *General Mgr*
Esteban Rodriguez, *Opers Staff*
EMP: 149 **EST:** 2001
SALES (est): 23.1MM **Privately Held**
WEB: www.southlandtransit.com
SIC: 4111 Local & suburban transit

(P-11845)
SUNLINE TRANSIT AGENCY (PA)
Also Called: STA
32505 Harry Oliver Trl, Thousand Palms (92276-3501)
PHONE....................760 343-3456
Glenn Miller, *Chairman*
Peter Gregor, *Officer*
William Robin, *Officer*
Greg Pettis, *Principal*
Carolyn Rude, *Executive Asst*
EMP: 160 **EST:** 1977
SQ FT: 19,006
SALES (est): 53.6MM **Privately Held**
WEB: www.sunline.org
SIC: 4111 Local & suburban transit

(P-11846)
SUPERSHUTTLE ORANGE COUNTY INC
531 Van Ness Ave, Torrance (90501-6233)
PHONE....................310 222-5500
EMP: 300
SQ FT: 12,000
SALES (est): 6MM
SALES (corp-wide): 1.3B **Privately Held**
SIC: 4111 Local And Suburban Transit, Nsk
HQ: Supershuttle International, Inc.
14500 N Northsight Blvd # 329
Scottsdale AZ 85260
480 609-3000

4119 Local Passenger Transportation: NEC

(P-11847)
AEGIS AMBULANCE SERVICE INC (PA)
1907 Border Ave, Torrance (90501-3606)
PHONE....................626 685-9410
Paul Richart, *President*
Jonathan Raya, *Opers Spvr*

Nathan Goltz, *Sales Staff*
EMP: 61 **EST:** 1997
SALES (est): 3.9MM **Privately Held**
WEB: www.aegisambulance.com
SIC: 4119 Ambulance service

(P-11848)
AMBUSERVE INC
15105 S Broadway, Gardena (90248-1821)
PHONE....................310 644-0500
Melissa Harris, *CEO*
Jim Karras, *COO*
Scott Smith, *CFO*
Scott Buck, *Opers Staff*
Wendell Smith, *Director*
EMP: 71 **EST:** 2008
SALES (est): 8.6MM **Privately Held**
WEB: www.ambuserveambulance.com
SIC: 4119 Ambulance service

(P-11849)
AMERICAN MED RSPNSE AMBLNCE SV (DH)
Also Called: A M R
879 Marlborough Ave, Riverside (92507-2133)
PHONE....................303 495-1217
William A Sanger, *CEO*
Don Harvey, *President*
Randel Owen, *Vice Pres*
EMP: 692 **EST:** 1993
SALES (est): 139.3MM **Privately Held**
WEB: www.amr.net
SIC: 4119 Ambulance service

(P-11850)
AMERICAN MED RSPNSE INLAND EMP (DH)
879 Marlborough Ave, Riverside (92507-2133)
PHONE....................951 782-5200
Bill Fanger, *President*
EMP: 80 **EST:** 1993
SQ FT: 24,000
SALES (est): 110.5MM **Privately Held**
WEB: www.amr.net
SIC: 4119 Ambulance service

(P-11851)
AMERICAN MEDICAL RESPONSE INC
1111 Montalvo Way, Palm Springs (92262-5440)
PHONE....................760 883-5000
Wayne Dennis, *Principal*
EMP: 160 **Privately Held**
WEB: www.amr.net
SIC: 4119 8099 Ambulance service; medical rescue squad
HQ: American Medical Response, Inc.
6363 S Fiddlers Green Cir
Greenwood Village CO 80111

(P-11852)
AMERICAN PROF AMBULANCE CORP
16945 Sherman Way, Van Nuys (91406-3614)
P.O. Box 7263 (91409-7263)
PHONE....................818 996-2200
Lyubov Popok, *President*
EMP: 88 **EST:** 2002
SALES (est): 5.2MM **Privately Held**
WEB: www.apa-ems.com
SIC: 4119 Ambulance service

(P-11853)
AMERICARE MEDSERVICES INC
Also Called: Americare Ambulance Service
6524 Fremont Cir, Huntington Beach (92648-6637)
PHONE....................310 632-1141
Michael Summers, *President*
Harry Lee, *Technician*
Patrick Murano, *Technician*
Joseph Prestia, *Technician*
Esther Peterman, *Clerk*
EMP: 62 **EST:** 1995
SQ FT: 10,000
SALES (est): 7.6MM **Privately Held**
WEB: www.americare.org
SIC: 4119 Ambulance service

(P-11854)
BEST LIMOUSINES & TRNSP INC (PA)
2701 S Birch St, Santa Ana (92707-3403)
PHONE....................714 375-9128
John Vaughan, *Chairman*
Robert Vaughan, *President*
Todd Szilagyi, *Officer*
Sandra Vaughan, *Admin Sec*
Jill Vaughan, *Controller*
EMP: 53 **EST:** 1995
SALES (est): 17.9MM **Privately Held**
SIC: 4119 4111 Limousine rental, with driver; bus transportation

(P-11855)
BLS LMSINE SVC LOS ANGELES INC
Also Called: B L S Limousine Service
2860 Fletcher Dr, Los Angeles (90039-2452)
PHONE....................323 644-7166
Jay D Okon, *President*
Eric Okon, *COO*
Phyllis Okon, *Corp Secy*
Odette Lorenzo, *Vice Pres*
Travis Swanson, *General Mgr*
EMP: 350 **EST:** 1988
SQ FT: 20,000
SALES (est): 12MM **Privately Held**
WEB: www.blsco.com
SIC: 4119 Limousine rental, with driver

(P-11856)
CALIFORNIA MED RESPONSE INC
Also Called: Cal-Med Ambulance
1557 Santa Anita Ave, South El Monte (91733-3313)
PHONE....................562 968-1818
Ronald A Marks, *President*
Linda Marks, *Treasurer*
EMP: 70 **EST:** 2009
SALES (est): 7MM **Privately Held**
WEB: www.calmedambulance.com
SIC: 4119 Ambulance service

(P-11857)
CARECAR INC
120 Newport Center Dr, Newport Beach (92660-6916)
PHONE....................949 287-8349
EMP: 50 **EST:** 2017
SALES (est): 4.8MM **Privately Held**
SIC: 4119 8322 Local passenger transportation; individual & family services

(P-11858)
CITY OF DINUBA
Also Called: City Dinuba Ambulance Service
496 E Tulare St, Dinuba (93618-2309)
PHONE....................559 595-9999
Myles Chute, *Branch Mgr*
Chad Thompson, *Fire Chief*
EMP: 71
SALES (corp-wide): 31.5MM **Privately Held**
WEB: www.dinuba.org
SIC: 9224 4119 Fire department, not including volunteer; ambulance service
PA: City Of Dinuba
405 E El Monte Way
Dinuba CA 93618
559 591-5900

(P-11859)
CLS TRNSPRTTION LOS ANGLES LLC (HQ)
Also Called: Empire Cls Wrldwide Chffred Sv
600 S Allied Way, El Segundo (90245-4727)
PHONE....................310 414-8189
David Singler, *Mng Member*
William Minich, *CFO*
Steve Horowitz, *Vice Pres*
Michael Kushner, *Vice Pres*
Melissa Ergisi, *Executive Asst*
EMP: 150 **EST:** 1987
SALES (est): 22.2MM **Privately Held**
WEB: www.empirecls.com
SIC: 4119 Limousine rental, with driver

(PA)=Parent Co (HQ)=Headquarters (DH)=Div Headquarters
✪ = New Business established in last 2 years

2022 Southern California Business
Directory and Buyers Guide

515

P R O D U C T S & S V C S

(P-11860)
CROWN TRANSPORTATION INC
Also Called: Crown Limousine L.A.
13543 Prairie Ave, Hawthorne
(90250-6001)
PHONE....................310 737-0888
David Navon, *President*
Jackie Rizkalla, *Sales Executive*
▲ EMP: 51 EST: 1999
SALES (est): 5.1MM **Privately Held**
WEB: www.crownlimola.com
SIC: 4119 Limousine rental, with driver

(P-11861)
EASTWESTPROTO INC
Also Called: Lifeline Ambulance
1120 S Maple Ave Ste 200, Montebello
(90640-6008)
PHONE....................888 535-5728
Genady Gorin, *CEO*
Genia Gorin, *President*
Larry Cruz, *Vice Pres*
Jordan Weiss, *Vice Pres*
Daniel Santillan, *Comms Mgr*
EMP: 120 EST: 2002
SQ FT: 10,000
SALES (est): 12MM **Privately Held**
WEB: www.lifeline-ems.com
SIC: 4119 Ambulance service

(P-11862)
EMERGENCY AMBULANCE SERVICE
3200 E Birch St Ste A, Brea (92821-6287)
PHONE....................714 990-1331
Phillip E Davis, *President*
Philip Davis, *COO*
Terri Davis, *CFO*
Joe Micheels, *Officer*
Trina Adkins, *Vice Pres*
EMP: 80 EST: 1977
SALES (est): 15.3MM **Privately Held**
WEB: www.emergencyambulance.com
SIC: 4119 Ambulance service

(P-11863)
EXECUTIVE NETWORK ENTPS INC
1224 21st St Apt E, Santa Monica
(90404-1390)
PHONE....................310 457-8822
Patricia Stephenson, *Manager*
EMP: 520 **Privately Held**
SIC: 4119 Limousine rental, with driver
PA: Executive Network Enterprises, Inc.
13440 Beach Ave
Marina Del Rey CA 90292

(P-11864)
EXECUTIVE NETWORK ENTPS INC (PA)
Also Called: Malibu Limousine Service
13440 Beach Ave, Marina Del Rey
(90292-5624)
PHONE....................310 447-2759
Patricia Stephenson, *President*
Trish Rudd, *CFO*
Stori Stephenson, *Vice Pres*
EMP: 80 EST: 2003
SQ FT: 5,000
SALES (est): 20.6MM **Privately Held**
SIC: 4119 Limousine rental, with driver

(P-11865)
FALCK MOBILE HEALTH CORP
212 S Atl Blvd Ste 102, Los Angeles
(90022)
PHONE....................323 720-1578
Aric Herrera, *Technician*
Tyler Russell, *Technician*
Byron Bailey, *Marketing Staff*
Freddy Sotelo, *Emerg Med Spec*
Kristina Lentz,
EMP: 79
SALES (corp-wide): 5.3B **Privately Held**
WEB: www.careambulance.net
SIC: 4119 Ambulance service
HQ: Falck Mobile Health Corp.
1517 W Braden Ct
Orange CA 92868
714 288-3800

(P-11866)
FALCK MOBILE HEALTH CORP
8932 Katella Ave Ste 201, Anaheim
(92804-6299)
PHONE....................714 828-7750
Dan Richardson, *Principal*
EMP: 79
SALES (corp-wide): 5.3B **Privately Held**
WEB: www.careambulance.net
SIC: 4119 Ambulance service
HQ: Falck Mobile Health Corp.
1517 W Braden Ct
Orange CA 92868
714 288-3800

(P-11867)
FILYN CORPORATION
Also Called: Lynch Ambulance Service
2950 E La Jolla St, Anaheim (92806-1307)
PHONE....................714 632-0225
Walter John Lynch, *CEO*
Nancy Lynch, *CEO*
Jordan Steinbrecher, *Technician*
Robert Banuelos, *Opers Staff*
Tina Heinemann, *Director*
EMP: 200 EST: 1986
SALES (est): 19.4MM **Privately Held**
WEB: www.lynchambulance.com
SIC: 4119 Ambulance service

(P-11868)
FIRSTMED AMBULANCE SVCS INC
8630 Tamarack Ave, Sun Valley
(91352-2504)
PHONE....................818 982-8333
Kristina Bableyan, *President*
EMP: 62 EST: 2007
SALES (est): 9.3MM **Privately Held**
WEB: www.firstmedambulance.com
SIC: 4119 Ambulance service

(P-11869)
GARY CARDIFF ENTERPRISES INC
Also Called: Cardiff Transportation
75255 Sheryl Ave, Palm Desert
(92211-5129)
PHONE....................760 568-1403
Gary Cardiff, *CEO*
Sharon Cardiff, *Admin Sec*
Cathy Smith, *Human Res Dir*
Chuck Xaudaro, *Safety Dir*
Rodney Betsargon, *Manager*
EMP: 89 EST: 1990
SQ FT: 10,000
SALES (est): 7.7MM **Privately Held**
WEB: www.cardifflimo.com
SIC: 4119 Limousine rental, with driver

(P-11870)
GLOBAL EMERGENCY ROAD SVC LLC
9908 San Fernando Rd, Pacoima
(91331-2605)
PHONE....................818 518-1166
Max Krumer, *Mng Member*
EMP: 50 EST: 2016
SQ FT: 1,000
SALES (est): 2MM **Privately Held**
WEB: www.globalers.org
SIC: 4119 Local passenger transportation

(P-11871)
GLOBAL PARATRANSIT INC
400 W Compton Blvd, Gardena
(90248-1700)
PHONE....................310 715-7550
Reza Nasrollahy, *President*
Luis Garcia, *General Mgr*
Lee Habibi, *General Mgr*
Miriam Lopez, *General Mgr*
Luis Preciado,
EMP: 300 EST: 2000
SQ FT: 17,000
SALES (est): 25.4MM **Privately Held**
WEB: www.global-paratransit.com
SIC: 4119 Ambulance service

(P-11872)
HALL AMBULANCE SERVICE INC
12500 Boron Ave, Boron (93516-1647)
PHONE....................760 762-6402
EMP: 50

SALES (corp-wide): 22.6MM **Privately Held**
WEB: www.hallamb.com
SIC: 4119 Local Passenger Transportation
PA: Hall Ambulance Service, Inc.
1001 21st St
Bakersfield CA 93301
661 322-8741

(P-11873)
HALL AMBULANCE SERVICE INC
2001 O St O, Bakersfield (93301-4724)
PHONE....................661 322-8741
Harvy Hall, *President*
Anthony Saccullo, *Technician*
Rick Davis,
Armando Lazaro,
Robin Slater, *Manager*
EMP: 53
SALES (corp-wide): 32.7MM **Privately Held**
WEB: www.hallamb.com
SIC: 4119 Ambulance service
PA: Hall Ambulance Service, Inc.
1001 21st St
Bakersfield CA 93301
661 322-8741

(P-11874)
HALL AMBULANCE SERVICE INC (PA)
1001 21st St, Bakersfield (93301-4792)
PHONE....................661 322-8741
Harvey L Hall, *President*
Dewi Adams, *COO*
Johnathon Surface, *COO*
Mary Kenny, *Corp Secy*
Myron Smith, *General Mgr*
EMP: 60 EST: 1971
SQ FT: 4,000
SALES (est): 32.7MM **Privately Held**
WEB: www.hallamb.com
SIC: 4119 4729 4789 Ambulance service;
transportation ticket offices; cargo loading
& unloading services

(P-11875)
HYRECAR INC
355 S Grand Ave Ste 1650, Los Angeles
(90071-3172)
PHONE....................888 688-6769
Joseph Furnari, *CEO*
Grace Mellis, *Ch of Bd*
Henry Park, *COO*
Serge De Bock, *CFO*
Kit Tran, *Chief Mktg Ofcr*
EMP: 87 EST: 2014
SALES (est): 25.2MM **Privately Held**
WEB: www.hyrecar.com
SIC: 4119 Local rental transportation

(P-11876)
KEOLIS TRANSIT AMERICA INC (DH)
6053 W Century Blvd # 900, Los Angeles
(90045-6400)
PHONE....................310 981-9500
Steve Shaw, *President*
Joseph Cardoso, *CFO*
Kevin Adams, *Exec VP*
Michael Ake, *Senior VP*
Ryan Adams, *Vice Pres*
EMP: 50 EST: 2006
SQ FT: 17,194
SALES (est): 206.5MM
SALES (corp-wide): 4.2MM **Privately Held**
WEB: www.keolisna.com
SIC: 4119 Local passenger transportation

(P-11877)
LEADER INDUSTRIES INC
Also Called: Leader Emergency Vehicles
10941 Weaver Ave, South El Monte
(91733-2752)
PHONE....................626 575-0880
Gary Hunter, *Principal*
Sheryl Hunter, *Admin Asst*
Shila Hunter, *Marketing Staff*
Sandy Stipe, *Sales Staff*
EMP: 160 EST: 2001

SALES (est): 16.1MM **Privately Held**
WEB: www.leaderambulance.com
SIC: 4119 5046 Ambulance service;
commercial equipment; motor vehicles &
car bodies

(P-11878)
MED-LIFE AMBULANCE SERVICES
4304 Alger St, Los Angeles (90039-1206)
P.O. Box 4525, Glendale (91222-0525)
PHONE....................818 242-1785
EMP: 94
SQ FT: 3,000
SALES (est): 2.5MM **Privately Held**
SIC: 4119 Ambulance Svc

(P-11879)
MEDIC-1 AMBULANCE SERVICE INC
1305 W Arrow Hwy Ste 206, San Dimas
(91773-2338)
PHONE....................909 592-8840
Gordon Shipp, *President*
Todd Duprey, *CFO*
Gary Sylvester, *Corp Secy*
EMP: 92 EST: 2001
SALES (est): 4.5MM **Privately Held**
SIC: 4119 Ambulance service

(P-11880)
MEDRESPONSE (PA)
7040 Hayvenhurst Ave, Van Nuys
(91406-3801)
P.O. Box 8379 (91409-8379)
PHONE....................818 442-9222
Andrew Stepansky, *CEO*
EMP: 109 EST: 2002
SALES (est): 5.7MM **Privately Held**
SIC: 4119 Ambulance service

(P-11881)
MISSION AMBULANCE INC
1055 E 3rd St, Corona (92879-1606)
P.O. Box 3111 (92878-3111)
PHONE....................951 272-2300
Daniel Gold, *President*
EMP: 81 EST: 1999
SALES (est): 12.1MM **Privately Held**
WEB: www.missionambulance.com
SIC: 4119 Ambulance service

(P-11882)
MORONGO BSIN AMBLANCE ASSN INC
61828 Chollita Rd, Joshua Tree
(92252-2328)
P.O. Box 460 (92252-0460)
PHONE....................760 366-8474
Rich Middlebrough, *President*
Matthew Welsch, *Opers Staff*
Ramon Lomeli, *Manager*
EMP: 91 EST: 1948
SQ FT: 2,500
SALES (est): 3.4MM **Privately Held**
WEB: www.mbambulance.org
SIC: 4119 Ambulance service

(P-11883)
OJAI AMBULANCE NC
Also Called: Lifeline Medical Transport
632 E Thompson Blvd, Ventura
(93001-2829)
P.O. Box 1089 (93002-1089)
PHONE....................805 653-9111
Stephen Frank, *President*
Wynne Schumacher, *Exec VP*
Karen Frank, *Vice Pres*
Ryan Plum,
EMP: 110 EST: 1935
SALES (est): 3.5MM **Privately Held**
WEB: www.lifelineems.net
SIC: 4119 Ambulance service

(P-11884)
PREMIER MEDICAL TRANSPORT INC
260 N Palm St 200, Brea (92821-2870)
PHONE....................888 353-9556
David Johnson, *President*
Elizabeth Arevalo, *Chief*
EMP: 90 EST: 2007
SALES (est): 5.4MM **Privately Held**
WEB: www.premieramb.com
SIC: 4119 Ambulance service

(P-11885)
PREMIER MEDICAL TRNSP INC
575 Maple Ct Ste A, Colton (92324-3209)
P.O. Box 690 (92324-0690)
PHONE..........................909 433-3939
Antonio Myrell, *CEO*
Rick Card, *Vice Pres*
Richmond Taylor, *Vice Pres*
Rosemary Dudevoir, *Opers Staff*
Annie Myrell, *Director*
EMP: 65 **EST:** 2000
SALES (est): 9MM **Privately Held**
WEB: www.pmtpremier.com
SIC: 4119 Ambulance service

(P-11886)
PRIORITY ONE MED TRNSPT INC (PA)
9327 Fairway View Pl # 300, Rancho Cucamonga (91730-0968)
PHONE..........................909 948-4400
Michael Parker, *President*
EMP: 70 **EST:** 1996
SQ FT: 7,000
SALES (est): 11.9MM **Privately Held**
WEB: www.priorityonemedical.com
SIC: 4119 Ambulance service

(P-11887)
PRN AMBULANCE LLC
8928 Sepulveda Blvd, North Hills (91343-4306)
PHONE..........................818 810-3600
Mike Sechrist, *CEO*
Avo Avetisyan, *President*
Elena Whorton, *President*
Michael Gorman, *COO*
Kevin Gorman, *CFO*
EMP: 300 **EST:** 2001
SQ FT: 3,000
SALES (est): 58.9MM
SALES (corp-wide): 249MM **Privately Held**
WEB: www.prnambulance.com
SIC: 4119 Ambulance service
PA: Pt-1 Holdings, Llc
720 Portal St
Cotati CA 94931
707 665-4295

(P-11888)
SAN LUIS AMBULANCE SERVICE INC
3546 S Higuera St, San Luis Obispo (93401-7304)
P.O. Box 954 (93406-0954)
PHONE..........................805 543-2626
Frank I Kelton, *President*
Betsy Kelton, *Corp Secy*
EMP: 124 **EST:** 1967
SQ FT: 7,500
SALES (est): 15MM **Privately Held**
WEB: www.sanluisambulance.com
SIC: 4119 Ambulance service

(P-11889)
SECURE TRANSPORTATION COMPANY
12785 Magnolia Ave # 102, Riverside (92503-4686)
PHONE..........................951 737-7300
EMP: 71
SALES (corp-wide): 48.2MM **Privately Held**
SIC: 4119 Local Passenger Transportation
PA: Secure Transportation Company, Inc.
13111 Meyer Rd
Whittier CA 90605
562 941-0107

(P-11890)
SHORELINE AMBULANCE CORP
15105 S Broadway, Gardena (90248-1821)
PHONE..........................714 847-9107
Giovanni Chiarella, *CEO*
Brian Scott Balmer, *Vice Pres*
EMP: 59 **EST:** 2005
SQ FT: 1,300
SALES (est): 2.2MM **Privately Held**
WEB: www.shorelineambulance.com
SIC: 4119 Ambulance service

(P-11891)
SUNLINE TRANSIT AGENCY
790 Vine Ave, Coachella (92236-1736)
PHONE..........................760 972-4059
EMP: 119
SALES (corp-wide): 53.6MM **Privately Held**
WEB: www.sunline.org
SIC: 4119 Local passenger transportation
PA: Sunline Transit Agency
32505 Harry Oliver Trl
Thousand Palms CA 92276
760 343-3456

(P-11892)
TRANSDEV SERVICES INC
5640 Peck Rd, Arcadia (91006-5850)
PHONE..........................626 357-7912
Timothy Grensavitch, *Opers Staff*
Fernando Ayala, *Maintnce Staff*
Jacob Israel Ortiz, *Director*
EMP: 441
SALES (corp-wide): 1.3B **Privately Held**
WEB: www.transdevna.com
SIC: 4119 4121 Local passenger transportation; taxicabs
HQ: Transdev Services, Inc.
720 E Bttrfeld Rd Ste 300
Lombard IL 60148
630 571-7070

(P-11893)
TRIPLE R TRANSPORTATION INC
978 Rd 192, Delano (93215)
P.O. Box 38 (93216-0038)
PHONE..........................661 725-6494
Joe Rodriguez, *President*
EMP: 80 **EST:** 2008
SALES (est): 7.1MM **Privately Held**
SIC: 4119 Local rental transportation

(P-11894)
UNICO LOGISTICS USA INC
357 Van Ness Way Ste 100, Torrance (90501-1487)
PHONE..........................310 835-5656
Sang Hoon Song, *CEO*
Dookee Kim, *President*
EMP: 50 **EST:** 2008
SALES (est): 10.4MM **Privately Held**
WEB: www.unicologx.com
SIC: 4119 Local rental transportation

(P-11895)
UNITED CRBRAL PLSY ASSN SAN LU
Also Called: RIDE ON TRANSPORTATION
3620 Sacramento Dr # 201, San Luis Obispo (93401-7215)
PHONE..........................805 543-2039
Mark Shaffer, *Exec Dir*
Jason Portugal, *Opers Staff*
Elizabeth Beckett, *Manager*
EMP: 100 **EST:** 1991
SQ FT: 1,600
SALES: 6MM **Privately Held**
WEB: www.ride-on.org
SIC: 4119 Local passenger transportation

(P-11896)
VIRGIN FISH INC (PA)
Also Called: Avalon Transportation Co
1000 Corporate Pointe # 150, Culver City (90230-7690)
PHONE..........................310 391-6161
Jeff Brush, *Principal*
David Dinwiddie, *Vice Pres*
Colene Smith, *Business Dir*
Jorge Peralta, *General Mgr*
Luis Rosario, *General Mgr*
EMP: 150 **EST:** 1990
SQ FT: 3,000
SALES (est): 23.4MM **Privately Held**
WEB: www.avalontrans.com
SIC: 4119 Limousine rental, with driver

(P-11897)
WEST COAST AMBULANCE CORP
Also Called: Wca
6739 S Victoria Ave, Los Angeles (90043-4617)
P.O. Box 8721 (90008-0721)
PHONE..........................310 435-1862

Olga Binman, *President*
Teri Osato, *Prdtn Dir*
EMP: 53 **EST:** 2002
SALES (est): 1.5MM **Privately Held**
WEB: www.wcambulance.com
SIC: 4119 Ambulance service

(P-11898)
WESTMED AMBULANCE INC
3872 Las Flores Canyon Rd, Malibu (90265-5264)
PHONE..........................310 456-3830
EMP: 86 **Privately Held**
WEB: www.westmedambulance.com
SIC: 4119 Ambulance service
PA: Westmed Ambulance, Inc.
13933 Crenshaw Blvd
Hawthorne CA 90250

(P-11899)
WESTMED AMBULANCE INC (PA)
13933 Crenshaw Blvd, Hawthorne (90250-7815)
PHONE..........................510 614-1420
Richard F Roesch, *CEO*
Joe Chidley, *President*
Erik Mandler, *President*
Eric James, *Technician*
EMP: 176 **EST:** 1998
SALES (est): 14.7MM **Privately Held**
WEB: www.westmedambulance.com
SIC: 4119 Ambulance service

4121 Taxi Cabs

(P-11900)
ADMINISTRATIVE SVCS COOP INC
1515 W 190th St Ste 200, Gardena (90248-4924)
PHONE..........................310 715-1968
Martiros Manukyan, *CEO*
Raymond McGreevy, *President*
William J Rouse, *General Mgr*
EMP: 200 **EST:** 1992
SALES (est): 17.8MM **Privately Held**
SIC: 4121 Taxicabs

(P-11901)
SAN GABRIEL TRANSIT INC
Also Called: Southland Transit Co
14913 Ramona Blvd, Baldwin Park (91706-3421)
PHONE..........................626 430-3650
EMP: 78
SALES (corp-wide): 20.3MM **Privately Held**
SIC: 4121 Taxi Service & Dial-A-Ride
PA: San Gabriel Transit, Inc.
3650 Rockwell Ave
El Monte CA 91731
626 258-1310

(P-11902)
UNITED IND TAXI DRIVERS (PA)
Also Called: United Taxi San Fernando Vly
900 N Alvarado St, Los Angeles (90026-3105)
PHONE..........................323 462-1088
Andrey Primushko, *CEO*
Martin Shatakhyan, *President*
Jacob Eskin, *Treasurer*
EMP: 59 **EST:** 1977
SQ FT: 3,500
SALES (est): 6.7MM **Privately Held**
WEB: www.unitedtaxila.com
SIC: 4121 Taxicabs

4131 Intercity & Rural Bus Transportation

(P-11903)
CITY OF CULVER CITY
Also Called: Culver Cty Bus Lines Municipal
4343 Duquesne Ave, Culver City (90232-2944)
PHONE..........................310 253-6510
Steve Cunningham, *Director*
EMP: 50

SALES (corp-wide): 137.2MM **Privately Held**
WEB: www.culvercity.org
SIC: 4131 Intercity bus line
PA: City Of Culver City
9770 Culver Blvd
Culver City CA 90232
310 253-5640

(P-11904)
SANTA MONICA CITY OF
Santa Monica Big Blue Bus
1334 5th St, Santa Monica (90401-1415)
PHONE..........................310 451-5444
Edward King, *Manager*
Richard Newton, *Analyst*
Ed King, *Transptn Dir*
John Catoe, *Director*
EMP: 63
SALES (corp-wide): 455.7MM **Privately Held**
WEB: www.santamonica.gov
SIC: 4131 Intercity & rural bus transportation
PA: City Of Santa Monica
1685 Main St
Santa Monica CA 90401
310 458-8411

4141 Local Bus Charter Svc

(P-11905)
BUSWEST LLC (HQ)
Also Called: John Deere Authorized Dealer
21107 Chico St, Carson (90745-1648)
PHONE..........................310 984-3900
Jim Bernacchi, *President*
Nicole Nardiello, *Admin Asst*
Fabian Bravo, *Technician*
Scott Dehart, *Technician*
Jared Koopman, *Technician*
EMP: 55 **EST:** 2008
SALES (est): 10.3MM
SALES (corp-wide): 150.5MM **Privately Held**
WEB: www.buswest.com
SIC: 4141 5082 Local bus charter service; construction & mining machinery
PA: Los Angeles Truck Centers, Llc
2429 Peck Rd
Whittier CA 90601
562 447-1200

(P-11906)
EMPIRE TRANSPORTATION
8800 Park St, Bellflower (90706-5529)
PHONE..........................562 529-2676
Miguel Oliver, *CEO*
Bertha Aguirre, *President*
Monica Escorza Oliver, *CFO*
Mike Rios, *Program Mgr*
Jorge Espinoza, *Manager*
EMP: 425 **EST:** 2005
SQ FT: 25,000
SALES (est): 35.8MM **Privately Held**
WEB: www.emptransportation.com
SIC: 4141 7521 4111 Local bus charter service; indoor parking services; bus transportation

(P-11907)
PEGASUS TRANSIT INC
210 Beedy St, Oxnard (93036-1006)
PHONE..........................805 988-1540
Maria Paseta, *President*
Ivo Paseta, *COO*
EMP: 60 **EST:** 2004
SALES (est): 9.2MM **Privately Held**
WEB: www.pegasustransit.com
SIC: 4141 4522 8211 Local bus charter service; nonscheduled charter services; ;

4142 Bus Charter Service, Except Local

(P-11908)
AMERICAN TRNSP SYSTEMS
Also Called: Ats
3133 E South St, Long Beach (90805-3742)
PHONE..........................562 531-8000
Dan Wilson, *CEO*
Dennis Van Justice, *President*

▲ EMP: 50 EST: 2003
SALES (est): 8MM Privately Held
WEB: www.busamerican.com
SIC: 4142 4111 4141 Bus charter service, except local; bus transportation; local bus charter service

(P-11909)
CERTIFIED TRNSP SVCS INC
1038 N Custer St, Santa Ana (92701-3915)
PHONE..................714 835-8676
David Gregory, CEO
EMP: 70 EST: 1990
SQ FT: 3,000
SALES (est): 11.5MM Privately Held
WEB: www.ctsbus.com
SIC: 4142 Bus charter service, except local

(P-11910)
COACH USA INC
Also Called: Foothill Transit West Covina
5640 Peck Rd, Arcadia (91006-5850)
PHONE..................626 357-7912
Keith Whalen, Branch Mgr
EMP: 100 Privately Held
WEB: www.coachusa.com
SIC: 4142 Bus charter service, except local
HQ: Coach Usa, Inc.
160 S Route 17 N
Paramus NJ 07652

(P-11911)
FAST DEER BUS CHRTR INCRPRTION
8105 Slauson Ave, Montebello (90640-6621)
PHONE..................323 201-8988
Eddie Wong, President
Kevin Wong, General Mgr
EMP: 57 EST: 1979
SQ FT: 65,000
SALES (est): 5.5MM Privately Held
WEB: www.fastdeerbus.com
SIC: 4142 Bus charter service, except local

(P-11912)
HOT DOGGER TOURS INC
Also Called: Gold Coast Tours
105 Gemini Ave, Brea (92821-3702)
PHONE..................714 988-4088
John Hartley, President
Mark Wilkerson, Vice Pres
Willy Woneolowski, Site Mgr
Karla Salamanca, Sales Staff
Karin Shue, Sales Staff
EMP: 120
SQ FT: 955
SALES (est): 8.6MM Privately Held
WEB: www.goldcoasttours.com
SIC: 4142 4725 4141 Bus charter service, except local; tours, conducted; local bus charter service

(P-11913)
ORANGE BELT STAGES (PA)
Also Called: Orange Belt Adventures
2134 E Mineral King Ave, Visalia (93292-6905)
P.O. Box 949 (93279-0949)
PHONE..................559 733-4408
Michael Haworth, President
Bryan A Haworth Trust, Shareholder
Margaret V Haworth Trust, Shareholder
Bruce Lynn, President
EMP: 65
SQ FT: 10,000
SALES (est): 14.9MM Privately Held
WEB: www.orangebelt.com
SIC: 4142 4141 Bus charter service, except local; local bus charter service

(P-11914)
PACIFIC CCHWAYS CHRTR SVCS INC
11771 Markon Dr, Garden Grove (92841-1812)
PHONE..................714 892-5000
Tom Kevin Giddens, CEO
Jennifer Giddens, Sales Staff
Mark Richards, Director
EMP: 66 EST: 1989
SQ FT: 8,000
SALES (est): 5.6MM Privately Held
WEB: www.pacificcoachways.com
SIC: 4142 Bus charter service, except local

(P-11915)
RYANS EXPRESS TRNSP SVCS INC (PA)
19500 Mariner Ave, Torrance (90503-1644)
PHONE..................310 219-2960
John Busskohl, CEO
George Cohen, CFO
Alexander E Hansen, CFO
Chris Sanchez, Vice Pres
Jessie Alcocer, General Mgr
EMP: 80 EST: 1999
SQ FT: 20,000
SALES (est): 16.6MM Privately Held
WEB: www.ryanstransportation.com
SIC: 4142 Bus charter service, except local

(P-11916)
TRANSPORTATION CHRTR SVCS INC
1931 N Batavia St, Orange (92865-4107)
PHONE..................714 396-0346
Terry Fischer, President
Kathryn Mayer, Vice Pres
Dave Jeffers, Principal
Bailey Acosta, Admin Asst
Cerissa Riley, Admin Asst
EMP: 50 EST: 1985
SALES (est): 13.2MM Privately Held
WEB: www.tcsbus.com
SIC: 4142 Bus charter service, except local

4151 School Buses

(P-11917)
ANTELOPE VLY SCHL TRNSP AGCY
670 W Avenue L8, Lancaster (93534-7100)
PHONE..................661 952-3106
Morris Fuselier III, CEO
Kathy Phillips, Info Tech Mgr
Joanne Downen, Accountant
Tony Inglima, Director
Susan Murphy, Manager
EMP: 206 EST: 1980
SALES (est): 21MM Privately Held
WEB: www.avsta.com
SIC: 4151 School buses

(P-11918)
COUNTY OF LOS ANGELES
Also Called: Pupil Transportation
9402 Greenleaf Ave, Whittier (90605)
PHONE..................562 945-2581
Dan Ibarra, Director
Dan Gonzales, Training Super
Carina Lazcano, Opers Mgr
Monica Rodrigues, Opers Staff
EMP: 64
SALES (corp-wide): 25.2B Privately Held
WEB: www.lacounty.gov
SIC: 4151 9621 School buses; regulation, administration of transportation;
PA: County Of Los Angeles
500 W Temple St Ste 437
Los Angeles CA 90012
213 974-1101

(P-11919)
DURHAM SCHOOL SERVICES L P
723 S Alameda St, Compton (90220-3809)
PHONE..................310 767-5820
Raphael Balonos, Manager
Alma Lawrence, Human Res Dir
EMP: 157 Privately Held
WEB: www.durhamschoolservices.com
SIC: 4151 School buses
HQ: Durham School Services, L. P.
2601 Navistar Dr
Lisle IL 60532
630 836-0292

(P-11920)
DURHAM SCHOOL SERVICES L P
8555 Flower Ave, Paramount (90723-5602)
PHONE..................562 408-1206
Paul Wiggins, General Mgr
EMP: 157 Privately Held
WEB: www.durhamschoolservices.com
SIC: 4151 School buses

HQ: Durham School Services, L. P.
2601 Navistar Dr
Lisle IL 60532
630 836-0292

(P-11921)
DURHAM SCHOOL SERVICES L P
4029 Las Virgenes Rd, Calabasas (91302-3505)
PHONE..................818 880-4257
Nanette Nanzini, General Mgr
EMP: 157 Privately Held
WEB: www.durhamschoolservices.com
SIC: 4151 School buses
HQ: Durham School Services, L. P.
2601 Navistar Dr
Lisle IL 60532
630 836-0292

(P-11922)
DURHAM SCHOOL SERVICES L P
Also Called: Lidlaw Educational Services
12999 Victoria St, Rancho Cucamonga (91739-9532)
PHONE..................909 899-1809
Laura Randals, Manager
EMP: 157 Privately Held
WEB: www.durhamschoolservices.com
SIC: 4151 School buses
HQ: Durham School Services, L. P.
2601 Navistar Dr
Lisle IL 60532
630 836-0292

(P-11923)
DURHAM SCHOOL SERVICES L P
3151 W 5th St Ste A, Oxnard (93030-6415)
PHONE..................805 483-6076
Lee Philips, General Mgr
EMP: 157 Privately Held
WEB: www.durhamschoolservices.com
SIC: 4151 School buses
HQ: Durham School Services, L. P.
2601 Navistar Dr
Lisle IL 60532
630 836-0292

(P-11924)
DURHAM SCHOOL SERVICES L P
2713 River Ave, Rosemead (91770-3303)
PHONE..................626 573-3769
David Gonzales, General Mgr
EMP: 157 Privately Held
WEB: www.durhamschoolservices.com
SIC: 4151 School buses
HQ: Durham School Services, L. P.
2601 Navistar Dr
Lisle IL 60532
630 836-0292

(P-11925)
DURHAM SCHOOL SERVICES L P
2003 Laguna Canyon Rd, Laguna Beach (92651-1123)
PHONE..................949 376-0376
Kathie Lee, Manager
EMP: 157 Privately Held
WEB: www.durhamschoolservices.com
SIC: 4151 School buses
HQ: Durham School Services, L. P.
2601 Navistar Dr
Lisle IL 60532
630 836-0292

(P-11926)
FIRST STUDENT INC
5127 Heintz St, Baldwin Park (91706-1820)
PHONE..................855 870-8747
EMP: 120 Privately Held
WEB: www.firststudentinc.com
SIC: 4151 School buses
PA: First Student, Inc.
600 Vine St Ste 1400
Cincinnati OH 45202

(P-11927)
FIRST STUDENT INC
16332 Construction Cir W, Irvine (92606-4415)
PHONE..................855 870-8747
EMP: 120 Privately Held
WEB: www.firststudentinc.com
SIC: 4151 School buses
PA: First Student, Inc.
600 Vine St Ste 1400
Cincinnati OH 45202

(P-11928)
FIRST STUDENT INC
234 S I St, San Bernardino (92410-2408)
PHONE..................909 383-1640
Cheryl Seifert, Manager
EMP: 120 Privately Held
WEB: www.firststudentinc.com
SIC: 4151 School buses
PA: First Student, Inc.
600 Vine St Ste 1400
Cincinnati OH 45202

(P-11929)
FIRST STUDENT INC
Also Called: Laidlaw Educational Services
5006 E Calle San Raphael, Palm Springs (92264-3452)
PHONE..................760 320-4659
Mike Robertson, Manager
EMP: 120 Privately Held
WEB: www.firststudentinc.com
SIC: 4151 School buses
PA: First Student, Inc.
600 Vine St Ste 1400
Cincinnati OH 45202

(P-11930)
FIRST STUDENT INC
5320 Derry Ave Ste O, Agoura Hills (91301-5029)
PHONE..................818 707-2082
EMP: 79
SALES (corp-wide): 9.2B Privately Held
SIC: 4151 School Bus Service
HQ: First Student, Inc.
600 Vine St Ste 1400
Cincinnati OH 45202
513 241-2200

(P-11931)
FIRST STUDENT INC
Also Called: Laidlaw Education Services
3401 W Castor St, Santa Ana (92704-3909)
PHONE..................714 850-7578
Debi Manley, Manager
EMP: 120 Privately Held
WEB: www.firststudentinc.com
SIC: 4151 School buses
PA: First Student, Inc.
600 Vine St Ste 1400
Cincinnati OH 45202

(P-11932)
FIRST STUDENT INC
320 W Mountain View St, Barstow (92311-2790)
P.O. Box 2350 (92312-2350)
PHONE..................760 256-2333
Aliessia Morris, Manager
EMP: 120 Privately Held
WEB: www.firststudentinc.com
SIC: 4151 School buses
PA: First Student, Inc.
600 Vine St Ste 1400
Cincinnati OH 45202

(P-11933)
FIRST STUDENT INC
11233 San Fernando Rd, San Fernando (91340-3409)
PHONE..................818 896-0333
Sue Wagnon, Branch Mgr
EMP: 120 Privately Held
WEB: www.firststudentinc.com
SIC: 4151 School buses

PA: First Student, Inc.
600 Vine St Ste 1400
Cincinnati OH 45202

(P-11934)
FIRST STUDENT INC
Also Called: Cardinal Transportation
14800 S Avalon Blvd, Gardena
(90248-2012)
PHONE....................310 769-2400
Ray Borales, *President*
Roy J Weber, *President*
▲ EMP: 5104 EST: 1987
SQ FT: 18,000
SALES (est): 5.2MM
SALES (corp-wide): 6.5B Privately Held
WEB: www.firststudentinc.com
SIC: 4151 School buses
HQ: Firstgroup America, Inc.
600 Vine St Ste 1400
Cincinnati OH 45202
513 241-2200

(P-11935)
LONG BEACH UNIFIED SCHOOL DST
Also Called: Transportation Department
2700 Pine Ave, Long Beach (90806-2617)
PHONE....................562 426-6176
Paul Bailey, *Director*
Everardo Avila, *Technician*
Mickey Kim, *Technology*
Sara Slater, *Accountant*
Lorena Manzo, *Personnel Assit*
EMP: 81
SALES (corp-wide): 788.4MM Privately Held
WEB: www.lbschools.net
SIC: 4151 School buses
PA: Long Beach Unified School District
1515 Hughes Way
Long Beach CA 90810
562 997-8000

(P-11936)
RIM OF WORLD UNIFIED SCHL DST
Also Called: Transportation
27614 Hwy 18 Across Bldg, Lake Arrowhead (92352)
P.O. Box 430 (92352-0430)
PHONE....................909 336-0330
Susie Hubbard, *Director*
EMP: 55
SALES (est): 41.2MM Privately Held
WEB: www.rimsd.k12.ca.us
SIC: 4151 School buses
PA: Rim Of The World Unified School District
27315 N Bay Rd
Blue Jay CA 92317
909 336-2031

(P-11937)
SANTA BARBARA TRNSP CORP
42138 7th St W, Lancaster (93534-7145)
PHONE....................661 510-0566
EMP: 160
SALES (corp-wide): 2B Privately Held
WEB: www.gusd.us
SIC: 4151 School buses
HQ: Santa Barbara Transportation Corporation
6414 Hollister Ave
Goleta CA 93117
805 681-8355

(P-11938)
SANTA BARBARA TRNSP CORP
1131 E Houston Ave, Visalia (93292-3845)
PHONE....................559 738-5780
Ray Delegard, *Vice Pres*
EMP: 160
SALES (corp-wide): 2B Privately Held
WEB: www.gusd.us
SIC: 4151 School buses
HQ: Santa Barbara Transportation Corporation
6414 Hollister Ave
Goleta CA 93117
805 681-8355

(P-11939)
SANTA BARBARA TRNSP CORP (HQ)
6414 Hollister Ave, Goleta (93117-3145)
PHONE....................805 681-8355
Denis J Hallagher, *CEO*
Patrick Walker, *CFO*
EMP: 90 EST: 1983
SQ FT: 15,000
SALES (est): 49.3MM
SALES (corp-wide): 2B Privately Held
WEB: www.gusd.us
SIC: 4151 4141 School buses; local bus charter service
PA: Student Transportation Of America, Inc.
3349 Hwy 138
Wall Township NJ 07719
732 280-4200

(P-11940)
SANTA BARBARA TRNSP CORP
Also Called: Student Transportation America
1331 Jason Way, Santa Maria (93455-1000)
PHONE....................805 928-0402
Paula Sauvadon, *Vice Pres*
EMP: 160
SALES (corp-wide): 2B Privately Held
WEB: www.gusd.us
SIC: 4151 4121 School buses; taxicabs
HQ: Santa Barbara Transportation Corporation
6414 Hollister Ave
Goleta CA 93117
805 681-8355

(P-11941)
TEMECULA VALLEY UNIFIED SCHOOL
40516 Roripaugh Rd, Temecula (92591-4563)
PHONE....................951 695-7110
Thomas Forrest, *Branch Mgr*
Bridget Dilon-Denton, *Software Dev*
EMP: 55
SALES (corp-wide): 345.7MM Privately Held
WEB: www.tvusd.k12.ca.us
SIC: 4151 School buses
PA: Temecula Valley Unified School District
School Facilities Corporation
31350 Rancho Vista Rd
Temecula CA 92592
951 676-2661

4173 Bus Terminal & Svc Facilities

(P-11942)
DURHAM SCHOOL SERVICES L P
2818 W 5th St, Santa Ana (92703-1824)
PHONE....................714 542-8989
Debbie Williams, *Manager*
EMP: 157
SQ FT: 4,843 Privately Held
WEB: www.durhamschoolservices.com
SIC: 4173 4151 Maintenance facilities for motor vehicle passenger transport; school buses
HQ: Durham School Services, L. P.
2601 Navistar Dr
Lisle IL 60532
630 836-0292

(P-11943)
FIRST STUDENT INC
300 S Buena Vista Ave, Corona (92882-1937)
PHONE....................951 736-3234
Jackie Mansperger, *Manager*
EMP: 120 Privately Held
WEB: www.firststudentinc.com
SIC: 4173 4151 Maintenance facilities, buses; school buses
PA: First Student, Inc.
600 Vine St Ste 1400
Cincinnati OH 45202

(P-11944)
LA CANADA UNIFIED SCHOOL DST
Also Called: Maintenance Dept.
1100 Foothill Blvd, La Canada (91011-3206)
PHONE....................818 952-8320
Michael Leininger, *Director*
Danielle Newcom, *Manager*
EMP: 62
SALES (corp-wide): 61.1MM Privately Held
WEB: www.lcusd.net
SIC: 4173 Maintenance facilities, buses
PA: La Canada Unified School District
4490 Cornishon Ave Ste 1
La Canada CA 91011
818 952-8300

4212 Local Trucking Without Storage

(P-11945)
365 DELIVERY INC
440 E Huntington Dr # 300, Arcadia (91006-3775)
PHONE....................818 815-5005
Bernardo Anders, *President*
Ariana Barrera, *Office Mgr*
EMP: 100 EST: 2017
SALES (est): 8.3MM Privately Held
SIC: 4212 Delivery service, vehicular

(P-11946)
4AS TRUCKING
20604 Belshaw Ave, Carson (90746-3508)
PHONE....................424 308-9563
Alnair Tanaleon, *CEO*
EMP: 50 EST: 2017
SALES (est): 2.3MM Privately Held
WEB: www.4ashipping.com
SIC: 4212 4491 Local trucking, without storage; marine cargo handling

(P-11947)
A & S METAL RECYCLING INC (PA)
2261 E 15th St, Los Angeles (90021-2841)
PHONE....................213 623-9443
Alexander Scott, *CEO*
Cory Scott, *Vice Pres*
Corina Fernandez, *Bookkeeper*
Estela Pimentel,
▼ EMP: 95 EST: 1984
SQ FT: 18,000
SALES (est): 14.1MM Privately Held
WEB: www.aandsmetal.com
SIC: 4212 5093 Hazardous waste transport; scrap & waste materials

(P-11948)
A A A PACKING AND SHIPPING INC
2000 E 49th St, Vernon (90058-2802)
PHONE....................626 310-7787
Bruce Nebens, *President*
Frank Hallberg, *COO*
EMP: 50 EST: 1978
SQ FT: 80,000
SALES (est): 4.7MM Privately Held
WEB: www.aaapack.com
SIC: 4212 4213 4783 Local trucking, without storage; trucking, except local; packing goods for shipping

(P-11949)
A G HACIENDA INCORPORATED
32794 Sherwood Ave, Mc Farland (93250-9626)
P.O. Box 367 (93250-0367)
PHONE....................661 792-2418
Xochilht Gonzalez, *President*
EMP: 400 EST: 1997
SALES (est): 28.4MM Privately Held
SIC: 4212 0761 4214 Local trucking, without storage; farm labor contractors; local trucking with storage

(P-11950)
A J R TRUCKING INC
435 E Weber Ave, Compton (90222-1424)
PHONE....................562 989-9555
Khachatur Khudikyan, *President*

Jehan Reyes, *Shareholder*
Hakop Khudikyan, *CFO*
Angel Reyes, *Director*
EMP: 84 EST: 1989
SQ FT: 12,000
SALES (est): 3.7MM Privately Held
SIC: 4212 Mail carriers, contract

(P-11951)
A-1 DELIVERY CO
1777 S Vintage Ave, Ontario (91761-3659)
P.O. Box 4210 (91761-8910)
PHONE....................909 444-1220
Joe Romine, *President*
William Turner, *Corp Secy*
Johnny Romine, *Vice Pres*
EMP: 75
SQ FT: 10,000
SALES (est): 9.3MM Privately Held
SIC: 4212 Delivery service, vehicular

(P-11952)
ACCURATE COURIER SERVICES INC
11022 Santa Monica Blvd # 360, Los Angeles (90025-7513)
P.O. Box 252061 (90025-8977)
PHONE....................310 481-3937
EMP: 92
SALES (est): 7.7MM Privately Held
WEB: www.accuratecourierservices.com
SIC: 4212 Local Trucking, Without Storage, Nsk

(P-11953)
ACCURATE DELIVERY SYSTEMS INC
Also Called: ADS
173 Resource Dr, Bloomington (92316-3540)
P.O. Box 1620, Chino (91708-1620)
PHONE....................951 823-8870
Mahmoud Maraach, *President*
EMP: 55 EST: 1994
SQ FT: 10,000
SALES (est): 9.2MM Privately Held
WEB: www.adstransport.com
SIC: 4212 Delivery service, vehicular

(P-11954)
AJR TRUCKING INC
435 E Weber Ave, Compton (90222-1424)
P.O. Box 10129, Glendale (91209-3129)
PHONE....................562 989-9555
Jack Khudikyan, *Vice Pres*
Zachary Brys, *Business Mgr*
Erin Beemer, *Analyst*
Eddie Barragan, *Maintence Staff*
Marcus Lionetti, *Director*
EMP: 140 EST: 1990
SALES (est): 12.3MM Privately Held
WEB: www.ajrtrucking.com
SIC: 4212 Delivery service, vehicular

(P-11955)
ANCON MARINE LLC
2735 Rose Ave, Signal Hill (90755-1927)
PHONE....................562 326-5900
EMP: 96
SALES (corp-wide): 183.5MM Privately Held
WEB: www.anconservices.com
SIC: 4212 Local trucking, without storage
PA: Ancon Marine, Llc
22707 Wilmington Ave
Carson CA 90745
310 522-5110

(P-11956)
ASBURY ENVIRONMENTAL SERVICES (PA)
1300 S Santa Fe Ave, Compton (90221-4916)
PHONE....................310 886-3400
Steve Kerdoon, *CEO*
Chris Mahoney, *CFO*
Anne Asbury, *Treasurer*
Bruce De Menno, *Vice Pres*
Shad Yon, *Accounts Mgr*
EMP: 75 EST: 1936
SQ FT: 22,000
SALES (est): 41.4MM Privately Held
WEB: www.asburyenv.com
SIC: 4212 Local trucking, without storage

(P-11957)
ATCHESONS EXPRESS INC
1590 S Archibald Ave, Ontario
(91761-7629)
PHONE..................................714 808-9199
Brad Atcheson, *President*
Gail Atcheson, *CFO*
Mark Atcheson, *Vice Pres*
Jeniffer Bowles, *Info Tech Mgr*
Evelyn Abel, *Accounts Exec*
EMP: 50 EST: 1988
SQ FT: 10,000
SALES (est): 5.8MM Privately Held
WEB: www.atchesonexpress.com
SIC: 4212 4731 Local trucking, without
storage; freight transportation arrange-
ment

(P-11958)
**BOB HUBBARD HORSE TRNSP
INC (PA)**
3730 S Riverside Ave, Colton
(92324-3329)
PHONE..................................951 369-3770
Bob Hubbard, *CEO*
Tom Hubbard, *President*
Pat Hubbard, *Vice Pres*
Patricia Hubbard, *Vice Pres*
Kathy Copeland, *CIO*
EMP: 50 EST: 1976
SQ FT: 9,375
SALES (est): 11.9MM Privately Held
WEB: www.bobhubbardhorsetrans.com
SIC: 4212 4213 4789 Animal transport;
trucking, except local; cargo loading & un-
loading services

(P-11959)
C P S EXPRESS (HQ)
3401 Space Center Ct 711a, Jurupa Valley
(91752-1131)
P.O. Box 248, Mira Loma (91752-0248)
PHONE..................................951 685-1041
William Smerber, *CEO*
Kirt Allen, *Corp Secy*
James E Ford, *Vice Pres*
EMP: 100 EST: 1980
SQ FT: 7,000
SALES (est): 19.2MM Privately Held
WEB: www.haddycompanies.com
SIC: 4212 4213 4214 Local trucking, with-
out storage; trucking, except local; local
trucking with storage
PA: Haddy, J G Sales Co, Inc
3401 Space Center Ct 711a
Jurupa Valley CA 91752
951 685-4100

(P-11960)
C S TRANSPORT INC
Also Called: Southern California Carriers
425 E Heber Rd Ste 200, Heber
(92249-9660)
PHONE..................................760 666-5661
Samuel Colin, *President*
EMP: 64 EST: 2006
SQ FT: 700
SALES (est): 9MM Privately Held
SIC: 4212 4731 Local trucking, without
storage; transportation agents & brokers

(P-11961)
**CARGO SOLUTION
BROKERAGE INC**
14587 Valley Blvd, Fontana (92335-6248)
PHONE..................................909 350-1644
Yudvinder S Kang, *CEO*
EMP: 200 EST: 2004
SALES (est): 5.4MM Privately Held
WEB: www.cargosolutionexpress.com
SIC: 4212 Local trucking, without storage

(P-11962)
CJ LOGISTICS AMERICA LLC
12350 Philadelphia Ave, Eastvale
(91752-3228)
PHONE..................................909 605-7233
Adrian Potgieter, *Manager*
Chris Boughey, *Opers Mgr*
Rigo Mendoza, *Manager*
EMP: 203 Privately Held
WEB: www.america.cjlogistics.com

SIC: 4212 4213 4225 4731 Local trucking, without storage; trucking, except
local; general warehousing & storage;
freight consolidation
HQ: Cj Logistics America, Llc
1750 S Wolf Rd
Des Plaines IL 60018

(P-11963)
CNET EXPRESS
15134 Indiana Ave Apt 38, Paramount
(90723-3582)
PHONE..................................949 357-5475
Diana Diaz Vargas, *CEO*
EMP: 102 EST: 2018
SALES (est): 5.6MM Privately Held
SIC: 4212 Delivery service, vehicular

(P-11964)
**DEDICATED FLEET SYSTEMS
INC (PA)**
1350 Philadelphia St, Pomona
(91766-5563)
P.O. Box 2829 (91769-2829)
PHONE..................................909 590-8209
Anthony Osterkamp Jr, *Ch of Bd*
Gene Segrist, *Vice Pres*
Shelley Fajardo, *Admin Sec*
Susan Badgett, *Administration*
EMP: 59 EST: 1970
SALES (est): 6.3MM Privately Held
WEB: www.osterkampgrp.com
SIC: 4212 Local trucking, without storage

(P-11965)
DELUXE AUTO CARRIERS INC
Also Called: Excel Auto Transporting Towing
4788 Brookhollow Cir, Jurupa Valley
(92509-3072)
PHONE..................................909 746-0900
Jesus Holguin, *President*
Jason Evans, *Vice Pres*
Raul Silva, *Vice Pres*
EMP: 60 EST: 2004
SALES (est): 15.9MM Privately Held
SIC: 4212 Local trucking, without storage

(P-11966)
**DESMOND MAIL DELIVERY
SERVICE**
4600 Worth St, Los Angeles (90063-1623)
P.O. Box 4836, Anaheim (92803-4836)
PHONE..................................323 262-1085
Fax: 323 262-6440
EMP: 75
SQ FT: 3,000
SALES (est): 2.6MM
SALES (corp-wide): 33.1MM Privately
Held
SIC: 4212 Mail Carrier Service
PA: Norco Delivery Service, Inc.
1560 N Missile Way
Anaheim CA 92801
714 520-8600

(P-11967)
GALE/TRIANGLE INC (PA)
Also Called: Triangle West
12816 Shoemaker Ave, Santa Fe Springs
(90670-6346)
PHONE..................................562 741-1300
Michael Kaplan, *CEO*
Bob Kaplan, *President*
Craig Kaplan, *CEO*
▲ EMP: 99 EST: 1994
SQ FT: 40,000
SALES (est): 4.8MM Privately Held
SIC: 4212 4214 Local trucking, without
storage; local trucking with storage

(P-11968)
**GENERAL LGSTICS SYSTEMS
US INC**
24305 Prielipp Rd, Wildomar (92595-7425)
PHONE..................................951 677-3972
EMP: 128
SALES (corp-wide): 17.8B Privately Held
WEB: www.gls-us.com
SIC: 4212 Delivery service, vehicular
HQ: General Logistics Systems Us, Inc.
4000 Executive Pkwy # 295
San Ramon CA 94583

(P-11969)
**GENERAL LGSTICS SYSTEMS
US INC**
12300 Bell Ranch Dr, Santa Fe Springs
(90670-3356)
PHONE..................................562 577-6037
EMP: 128
SALES (corp-wide): 17.8B Privately Held
WEB: www.gls-us.com
SIC: 4212 Delivery service, vehicular;
draying, local: without storage
HQ: General Logistics Systems Us, Inc.
4000 Executive Pkwy # 295
San Ramon CA 94583

(P-11970)
HANKS INC
Also Called: Sun Express
13866 Slover Ave, Fontana (92337-7037)
PHONE..................................909 350-8365
Brian Bachar, *President*
Shirley Bachar, *Vice Pres*
Brenda Cash, *General Mgr*
▲ EMP: 68 EST: 1961
SQ FT: 24,000
SALES (est): 10MM Privately Held
WEB: www.shipsun.com
SIC: 4212 4213 Local trucking, without
storage; trucking, except local

(P-11971)
**HANSON AGGRGTES MD-
PACIFIC INC**
50 S Kellogg Ave, Goleta (93117-3417)
PHONE..................................805 967-2371
Chris Clifford, *Sales/Mktg Mgr*
EMP: 34
SALES (corp-wide): 20.8B Privately Held
SIC: 4212 3281 Local trucking, without
storage; stone, quarrying & processing of
own stone products
HQ: Hanson Aggregates Mid-Pacific, Inc.
12667 Alcosta Blvd # 400
San Ramon CA

(P-11972)
HARTWICK & HAND INC (PA)
Also Called: H & H Truck Terminal
16953 N D St, Victorville (92394-1417)
P.O. Box 1595 (92393-1595)
PHONE..................................760 245-1666
Stacy L Hand, *CEO*
Edward Perreria, *President*
EMP: 73 EST: 1961
SQ FT: 8,800
SALES (est): 9.5MM Privately Held
WEB: www.hhbulk.com
SIC: 4212 Local trucking, without storage

(P-11973)
HEAVY LOAD TRANSFER LLC
18735 S Ferris Pl, Rancho Dominguez
(90220-6405)
PHONE..................................310 816-0260
Victor Larosa,
EMP: 75 EST: 2016
SALES (est): 4.8MM Privately Held
WEB: www.ttsi.com
SIC: 4212 Local trucking, without storage

(P-11974)
HF COX INC
Also Called: Cox Petroleum Transport
8330 Atlantic Ave, Cudahy (90201-5808)
PHONE..................................323 587-2359
Diane Judge, *Branch Mgr*
Kelley Grantham, *Maintence Staff*
Dave Green, *Manager*
Lloyd Ponder, *Manager*
Kenny Saunders, *Manager*
EMP: 290
SALES (corp-wide): 683.2K Privately
Held
WEB: www.coxpetroleum.com
SIC: 4212 Petroleum haulage, local
PA: H.F. Cox, Inc.
118 Cox Transport Way
Bakersfield CA 93307
661 366-3236

(P-11975)
**HIGH PERFORMANCE
LOGISTICS LLC**
7227 Central Ave, Riverside (92504-1432)
PHONE..................................702 300-4880
Michael Waters, *Mng Member*
EMP: 75 EST: 2018
SALES (est): 3.5MM Privately Held
SIC: 4212 Local trucking, without storage

(P-11976)
HUB GROUP TRUCKING INC
13867 Valley Blvd, Fontana (92335-5230)
PHONE..................................909 770-8950
Roy Sheredon, *Branch Mgr*
EMP: 500
SALES (corp-wide): 3.5B Publicly Held
WEB: www.hubgroup.com
SIC: 4212 Local trucking, without storage
HQ: Hub Group Trucking, Inc.
2000 Clearwater Dr
Oak Brook IL 60523
630 271-3600

(P-11977)
HUB GROUP TRUCKING INC
Also Called: Hgt
3801 E Guasti Rd, Ontario (91761-1575)
PHONE..................................951 693-9813
EMP: 174
SALES (corp-wide): 4B Publicly Held
SIC: 4212 Local Trucking Operator
HQ: Hub Group Trucking, Inc.
2000 Clearwater Dr
Oak Brook IL 60523
630 271-3600

(P-11978)
JAMES B BRANCH INC (PA)
Also Called: Gemini Moving Specialists
4367 Clybourn Ave, Toluca Lake
(91602-2906)
PHONE..................................818 765-3521
Eugene W Luni, *President*
Mark A Luni, *Corp Secy*
Louise W Luni, *Vice Pres*
EMP: 50 EST: 1934
SQ FT: 35,000
SALES (est): 4.8MM Privately Held
WEB: www.unitedvanlines.com
SIC: 4212 Moving services

(P-11979)
LAC MOTOR ENTERPRISES INC
127 N Acacia St, San Dimas (91773-2585)
PHONE..................................626 329-1411
Laura Ciauri, *Branch Mgr*
EMP: 58
SALES (corp-wide): 1.2MM Privately
Held
SIC: 4212 Dump truck haulage
PA: L.A.C. Motor Enterprises, Inc.
700 E Route 66
Glendora CA
626 915-1713

(P-11980)
MADDEN CORPORATION
Also Called: Pam's Delivery Svc & Nat Msgnr
733 W Taft Ave, Orange (92865-4229)
PHONE..................................714 922-1670
Donald L Madden, *President*
EMP: 100
SQ FT: 7,000
SALES (est): 12.9MM Privately Held
WEB: www.pamsnational.com
SIC: 4212 Courier services, except by air

(P-11981)
MAMBA LOGISTICS INC
23749 Fitzgerald St, West Hills
(91304-5704)
PHONE..................................661 234-8050
Danisha Danielle Wrighster, *CEO*
EMP: 65 EST: 2020
SALES (est): 4.7MM Privately Held
WEB: www.mambalogistics.com
SIC: 4212 4215 Delivery service, vehicu-
lar; package delivery, vehicular

(P-11982)
MULECHAIN INC
2901 W Coast Hwy Ste 200, Newport
Beach (92663-4045)
PHONE..................................888 456-8881

Ralph Liu, *CEO*
EMP: 56
SALES (est): 1MM **Privately Held**
WEB: www.mulechain.com
SIC: 4212 7372 Delivery service, vehicular; application computer software

(P-11983)
NEAL TRUCKING INC
9749 Bellegrave Ave, Riverside (92509-2642)
PHONE...............................951 685-5048
Dianne Neal, *CEO*
Randy Neal, *Principal*
Corey Gouthro, *Manager*
EMP: 65 **EST:** 1976
SQ FT: 1,500
SALES (est): 8.7MM **Privately Held**
WEB: www.nealtrucking.com
SIC: 4212 Dump truck haulage

(P-11984)
NIPPON EX NEC LGSTICS AMER INC
18615 S Ferris Pl, Rancho Dominguez (90220-6452)
PHONE...............................310 604-6100
Kazuhiko Takahashi, *CEO*
Hidehito Tachikawa, *CEO*
Gerald Sabino, *Director*
▲ **EMP:** 75 **EST:** 1990
SQ FT: 353,000
SALES (est): 24.6MM **Privately Held**
WEB: www.nipponexpress-necl.co.th
SIC: 4212 4213 4225 Local trucking, without storage; trucking, except local; general warehousing & storage
HQ: Nec Corporation Of America
3929 W John Carpenter Fwy
Irving TX 75063
214 262-6000

(P-11985)
OCEAN BLUE ENVMTL SVCS INC (PA)
925 W Esther St, Long Beach (90813-1423)
PHONE...............................562 624-4120
Maria C Lee, *CEO*
Ron Dare, *President*
Moonho C Lee, *CFO*
Cherisse Patterson, *Admin Asst*
Donald Ostrand, *Project Mgr*
EMP: 63 **EST:** 1994
SQ FT: 5,000
SALES (est): 10.7MM **Privately Held**
WEB: www.ocean-blue.com
SIC: 4212 8734 Hazardous waste transport; hazardous waste testing

(P-11986)
OLDENKAMP TRUCKING INC (PA)
10303 S Enos Ln, Bakersfield (93311-8600)
PHONE...............................661 833-3400
John Oldenkamp, *CEO*
Dana L Oldenkamp, *Vice Pres*
Dana Oldenkamp, *Admin Sec*
EMP: 61 **EST:** 1993
SALES (est): 9MM **Privately Held**
WEB: www.oldenkamptrucking.com
SIC: 4212 Light haulage & cartage, local

(P-11987)
PACIFIC DRAYAGE SERVICES LLC
550 W Artesia Blvd, Compton (90220-5524)
PHONE...............................901 746-3794
Ted Showalter, *VP Finance*
Steven Wagner, *Project Mgr*
EMP: 167 **EST:** 2019
SALES (est): 30MM **Privately Held**
WEB: www.pdsusa.com
SIC: 4212 Draying, local: without storage

(P-11988)
RADFORD ALEXANDER CORPORATION
Also Called: Chemtrans
14700 S Avalon Blvd, Gardena (90248-2010)
PHONE...............................310 523-2555
Reginald Lathan, *CEO*

Nancy Lathan, *Vice Pres*
Carina Bassett, *Office Mgr*
Reid Lathan, *Manager*
EMP: 55 **EST:** 1973
SQ FT: 4,000
SALES (est): 7.7MM **Privately Held**
WEB: www.chemtrans.com
SIC: 4212 Light haulage & cartage, local

(P-11989)
RDS LOGISTICS GROUP (PA)
8600 Banana Ave, Fontana (92335-3033)
PHONE...............................909 355-4100
Judi Girard, *Ch of Bd*
Sharon Brooks, *President*
Greg Stefflre, *CEO*
EMP: 67 **EST:** 1981
SQ FT: 50,000
SALES (est): 26.4MM **Privately Held**
WEB: www.rdsrally.com
SIC: 4212 Moving services

(P-11990)
RHINO READY MIX TRUCKING INC (PA)
3701 Pegasus Dr Ste 126, Bakersfield (93308-6843)
P.O. Box 80297 (93380-0297)
PHONE...............................661 679-3643
EMP: 50
SALES (est): 8MM **Privately Held**
SIC: 4212 Local Trucking Operator

(P-11991)
ROY MILLER FREIGHT LINES LLC (PA)
3165 E Coronado St, Anaheim (92806-1915)
P.O. Box 18419 (92817-8419)
PHONE...............................714 632-5511
Danny Miller, *CEO*
Theresa Lindsay, *Accounting Mgr*
Alex Vallejo, *Sales Mgr*
Ralph Huerta, *Terminal Mgr*
Manuel Perez, *Terminal Mgr*
EMP: 100 **EST:** 1942
SALES (est): 19.1MM **Privately Held**
WEB: www.roymiller.com
SIC: 4212 Local trucking, without storage

(P-11992)
SAVAGE SERVICES CORPORATION
8636 Sorensen Ave, Santa Fe Springs (90670-2633)
PHONE...............................562 400-2044
EMP: 79
SALES (corp-wide): 1.7B **Privately Held**
WEB: www.savageservices.com
SIC: 4212 Local trucking, without storage
HQ: Savage Services Corporation
901 W Legacy Center Way
Midvale UT 84047

(P-11993)
SGI LOGISTICS
2500 Broadway Ste F125, Santa Monica (90404-3080)
PHONE...............................310 513-5339
Gregory Labe, *President*
EMP: 50 **EST:** 2020
SALES (est): 2MM **Privately Held**
SIC: 4212 Delivery service, vehicular

(P-11994)
SOUTH COAST TRNSP & DIST INC
Western Regional Delivery
1424 S Raymond Ave, Fullerton (92831-5235)
PHONE...............................310 816-0280
Elias Youkhehpaz, *President*
EMP: 73 **Privately Held**
WEB: www.wrds.com
SIC: 4212 Local trucking, without storage
PA: South Coast Transportation & Distribution, Inc.
1424 S Raymond Ave
Fullerton CA 92831

(P-11995)
SPEEDS OIL TOOL SERVICE INC
1573 E Betteravia Rd, Santa Maria (93454-9647)
P.O. Box 276 (93456-0276)
PHONE...............................805 925-1369
Sonja L Gerfen, *President*
Patricia L Kirchhof, *Corp Secy*
Kim A Kirchhof, *Vice Pres*
Cheryl Wetta, *Administration*
EMP: 77 **EST:** 1950
SQ FT: 8,400
SALES (est): 4.7MM **Privately Held**
WEB: www.speedsoil.com
SIC: 4212 7353 Petroleum haulage, local; oil field equipment, rental or leasing

(P-11996)
STANFORD TRANSPORTATION INC
10201 Alondra Dr, Bakersfield (93311-4550)
PHONE...............................661 302-3288
Gurjeet Singh, *President*
Charnhjit Badhesha, *CFO*
Navjot Singh, *Vice Pres*
EMP: 60
SALES (est): 7MM **Privately Held**
SIC: 4212 Local trucking, without storage

(P-11997)
STINSON COMMERCIAL TRNSP
1443 E Washngtn Blvd, Pasadena (91104-2650)
PHONE...............................626 807-6265
Ashley Stinson, *CEO*
EMP: 52 **EST:** 2015
SALES (est): 2.9MM **Privately Held**
SIC: 4212 Delivery service, vehicular

(P-11998)
SUN DELIVERY LLC
51 Zaca Ln Ste 120, San Luis Obispo (93401-7353)
PHONE...............................336 472-5000
Rick Phillips, *CEO*
Aimee Boozer, *Vice Pres*
EMP: 50 **EST:** 1995
SALES (est): 9.6MM **Privately Held**
WEB: www.sundeliveryllc.com
SIC: 4212 Delivery service, vehicular
PA: American West Worldwide Express, Inc.
51 Zaca Ln Ste 120
San Luis Obispo CA 93401

(P-11999)
TOPLAND TRUCKING INC (HQ)
2727 Workman Mill Rd, City of Industry (90601-1452)
PHONE...............................562 908-6988
Robert Wang, *CEO*
Andy Wang, *Vice Pres*
▲ **EMP:** 69 **EST:** 2005
SALES (est): 7.9MM **Privately Held**
WEB: www.topocean.com
SIC: 4212 Local trucking, without storage

(P-12000)
TRAIL LINES INC
9415 Sorensen Ave, Santa Fe Springs (90670-2648)
P.O. Box 3567 (90670-1567)
PHONE...............................562 758-6980
Ofer Shitrit, *CEO*
Reuven Spivak, *Vice Pres*
Adriana Ortega, *Manager*
EMP: 75 **EST:** 1994
SALES (est): 14.8MM **Privately Held**
WEB: www.traillines.com
SIC: 4212 4789 Local trucking, without storage; pipeline terminal facilities, independently operated

(P-12001)
TRANSPRTTION BRKG SPCLISTS INC
Also Called: Tbs
15170 Transistor Ln, Huntington Beach (92649-1150)
PHONE...............................714 754-4230
Ben Haeri, *CEO*
Steve Kennedy, *Managing Prtnr*

Fred Khac, *Managing Prtnr*
Mike Owens, *COO*
Lee Mayer, *Vice Pres*
EMP: 450 **EST:** 2016
SALES (est): 18MM **Privately Held**
SIC: 4212 Local trucking, without storage

(P-12002)
TRUMP CARD LLC (HQ)
23807 Aliso Creek Rd, Laguna Niguel (92677-3929)
PHONE...............................949 360-7340
Michael Xavier Hanlon, *CEO*
EMP: 60 **EST:** 1995
SALES (est): 17.3MM
SALES (corp-wide): 239.3MM **Privately Held**
WEB: www.magnateworldwide.com
SIC: 5947 4212 4731 Greeting cards; local trucking, without storage; freight forwarding
PA: Magnate Worldwide, Llc
25w186 Jane Ave
Naperville IL 60540
630 394-1030

(P-12003)
TT TRUCKING SERVICES LLC
12745 Jade Rd, Victorville (92392-6256)
PHONE...............................323 790-3408
Tiffany Taylor, *Mng Member*
Terry Taylor, *Mng Member*
EMP: 76 **EST:** 2019
SALES (est): 250.7K **Privately Held**
WEB: www.ttttrucking.com
SIC: 4212 4215 Delivery service, vehicular; courier services, except by air

(P-12004)
ULS EXPRESS INC
2850 E Del Amo Blvd, Compton (90221-6007)
P.O. Box 7547, Long Beach (90807-0547)
PHONE...............................310 631-0800
Iain Atchison, *President*
Richard Ferguson, *Exec VP*
Laura Toxqui,
EMP: 129 **EST:** 1987
SQ FT: 220,000
SALES (est): 3.5MM **Privately Held**
WEB: www.uwc-net.com
SIC: 4212 Local trucking, without storage
HQ: Universal Logistics System, Inc.
2850 Del Amo Blvd
Carson CA 90810
310 631-0800

(P-12005)
UNITED PUMPING SERVICE INC
14000 Valley Blvd, City of Industry (91746-2801)
PHONE...............................626 961-9326
Eduardo T Perry Jr, *President*
Eduardo Perry Jr, *Corp Secy*
Daniel C Perry, *Vice Pres*
Margaret Perry, *Vice Pres*
Daniel Perry, *Project Mgr*
EMP: 95 **EST:** 1970
SQ FT: 25,000
SALES (est): 25MM **Privately Held**
WEB: www.unitedpumping.com
SIC: 4212 Hazardous waste transport

(P-12006)
UNIVERSAL MAIL DELIVERY SVC (PA)
Also Called: Universal Custom Courier
501 S Brand Blvd 104, San Fernando (91340-4000)
PHONE...............................818 365-3144
Robert M Reznick, *CEO*
Barbara Reznick, *Shareholder*
Saddie Reznick, *Shareholder*
Bernard Reznick, *CEO*
Sal Hernandez, *Executive*
EMP: 95 **EST:** 1953
SQ FT: 1,000
SALES (est): 9.8MM **Privately Held**
SIC: 4212 Delivery service, vehicular

(P-12007)
VALLEY COURIERS INC
181 S Wineville Ave Ste O, Ontario (91761-7888)
PHONE...............................909 605-2999
Henry Kilantang, *Manager*

PRODUCTS & SVCS

EMP: 68
SALES (corp-wide): 7.2MM **Privately Held**
WEB: www.valleycouriers.com
SIC: **4212** Delivery service, vehicular
PA: Valley Couriers, Inc.
23955 Park Granada
Calabasas CA

(P-12008)
WASTE MANAGEMENT RECYCLING
9227 Tujunga Ave, Sun Valley (91352-1542)
P.O. Box 7400, Pasadena (91109-7400)
PHONE..............................818 767-6180
EMP: 170 EST: 1955
SALES (est): 48.1MM
SALES (corp-wide): 15.2B **Publicly Held**
WEB: www.wm.com
SIC: **4212** **4953** Garbage collection & transport, no disposal; sanitary landfill operation
PA: Waste-Management, Inc.
800 Capitol St Ste 3000
Houston TX 77002
713 512-6200

(P-12009)
YUMMY FOODS LLC
5520 San Vicente Blvd, Los Angeles (90019-2717)
PHONE..............................323 965-0600
Barnady Montgomery, *Mng Member*
EMP: 55
SALES (corp-wide): 15.5MM **Privately Held**
WEB: www.yummy.com
SIC: **5411** **4212** Grocery stores, independent; delivery service, vehicular
PA: Yummy Foods, Llc
3255 Cahuenga Blvd W # 302
Los Angeles CA 90068
323 876-1600

4213 Trucking, Except Local

(P-12010)
AMGEN DISTRIBUTION INC
1244 Valley View Rd # 119, Glendale (91202-1752)
PHONE..............................760 989-4424
EMP: 73
SQ FT: 3,900
SALES (est): 4.8MM **Privately Held**
SIC: **4213** Non-Local Trucking Company

(P-12011)
ARDWIN INC
Also Called: Ardwin Freight
2940 N Hollywood Way, Burbank (91505-1024)
P.O. Box 1609 (91507-1609)
PHONE..............................818 767-7777
Edwin Sahakian, *President*
Oscar Calderon, *Manager*
Saul Fernandez, *Manager*
Tania Orellana, *Manager*
Fernandez Saul, *Manager*
EMP: 130 EST: 1988
SQ FT: 10,000
SALES (est): 20.9MM **Privately Held**
WEB: www.ardwin.com
SIC: **4213** Contract haulers

(P-12012)
ASBURY TRANSPORTATION CO
2144 Mohawk St, Bakersfield (93308-6001)
PHONE..............................661 327-2271
Richard Boyer, *CEO*
Bruce Haupt, *Vice Pres*
EMP: 52 EST: 1991
SQ FT: 2,100
SALES (est): 9.8MM **Privately Held**
WEB: www.asburytrans.com
SIC: **4213** Contract haulers

(P-12013)
AVERITT EXPRESS INC
3133 W 131st St, Hawthorne (90250-5516)
PHONE..............................310 970-9520
EMP: 73 **Privately Held**

WEB: www.averittexpress.com
SIC: **4213** Trucking, except local
HQ: Averitt Express, Inc.
1415 Neal St
Cookeville TN 38501
931 526-3306

(P-12014)
BEST OVERNITE EXPRESS INC (PA)
Also Called: Best Overnight Express
406 Live Oak Ave, Irwindale (91706-1314)
P.O. Box 90816, City of Industry (91715-0816)
PHONE..............................626 256-6340
William K Applebee, *President*
Mike White, *CFO*
Jeff Siri, *Branch Mgr*
Mike Saucedo, *VP Opers*
Micah Applebee, *Traffic Mgr*
EMP: 100 EST: 1988
SQ FT: 25,000
SALES (est): 32.1MM **Privately Held**
WEB: www.bestovernite.com
SIC: **4213** Trucking, except local

(P-12015)
BLUE CHIP MOVING AND STOR INC
Also Called: Blue Chip Mayflower
13525 Crenshaw Blvd, Hawthorne (90250-7811)
PHONE..............................323 463-6888
Dennis Doody, *CEO*
Jack Doody, *Vice Pres*
Kyle Kilpatrick, *Agent*
EMP: 55 EST: 1963
SQ FT: 30,000
SALES (est): 9.9MM **Privately Held**
WEB: www.bluechipmoving.net
SIC: **4213** **4214** Household goods transport; contract haulers; local trucking with storage

(P-12016)
BOETHING TREELAND NURSERY CO
Also Called: Treeland Farms
23475 Long Valley Rd, Woodland Hills (91367-6006)
PHONE..............................818 883-1222
John E Boething, *President*
Marjorie Boething Arnold, *Shareholder*
Cathy Boething Pherson, *Shareholder*
Susan Boething, *Treasurer*
Richard T Anderson, *Vice Pres*
EMP: 60 EST: 1953
SQ FT: 1,500
SALES (est): 1.5MM **Privately Held**
WEB: www.boethingtreeland.com
SIC: **4213** **5261** **0782** Heavy hauling; nursery stock, seeds & bulbs; landscape contractors

(P-12017)
BUDWAY ENTERPRISES INC (PA)
Also Called: Budway Trucking & Warehousing
13600 Napa St, Fontana (92335-2944)
PHONE..............................909 463-0500
Vincent McLeod, *CEO*
Jim Barbour, *CFO*
Daniel Heykoop, *Exec VP*
Marcy McKenzie, *Vice Pres*
Alex Nicholas, *Vice Pres*
EMP: 55 EST: 1974
SQ FT: 120,000
SALES (est): 18.8MM **Privately Held**
WEB: www.budway.net
SIC: **4213** Contract haulers

(P-12018)
BULK TRANSPORTATION (PA)
415 S Lemon Ave, Walnut (91789-2911)
P.O. Box 390 (91788-0390)
PHONE..............................909 594-2855
Brett Richardson, *President*
Gary K Cross, *President*
George G Cross, *CEO*
Susan Duffield, *Admin Sec*
Jeff Machado, *Maintence Staff*
▲ EMP: 60 EST: 1961
SQ FT: 3,500

SALES (est): 23.3MM **Privately Held**
WEB: www.bulk-dti.com
SIC: **4213** **4789** Contract haulers; cargo loading & unloading services

(P-12019)
CALIFRNIA INTERMODAL ASSOC INC (PA)
6666 E Washington Blvd, Commerce (90040-1814)
PHONE..............................323 562-7788
Gabriel Chaul, *CEO*
Ron Mejia, *Division Mgr*
▲ EMP: 50 EST: 2001
SALES (est): 11.8MM **Privately Held**
WEB: www.ciatrucking.com
SIC: **4213** Trucking, except local

(P-12020)
CARGO SOLUTION EXPRESS INC (PA)
14587 Valley Blvd 89, Fontana (92335-6248)
PHONE..............................909 350-1644
Balwinder Kaur Kang, *President*
Steve Shirazi, *Vice Pres*
D Pillai, *Controller*
Priyanka Arora, *Opers Staff*
Harsimran Singh, *Marketing Mgr*
EMP: 250 EST: 2002
SQ FT: 10,000
SALES (est): 99.1MM **Privately Held**
WEB: www.cargosolutionexpress.com
SIC: **4213** Trucking, except local

(P-12021)
CERTIFIED FRT LOGISTICS INC (PA)
1344 White Ct, Santa Maria (93458-3732)
P.O. Box 5668 (93456-5668)
PHONE..............................800 592-5906
James O Nelson, *President*
Scott Cramer, *CFO*
Jon Cramer, *Vice Pres*
Tim Cramer, *Vice Pres*
Edwin F Nelson Jr, *Vice Pres*
EMP: 120 EST: 1963
SQ FT: 40,000
SALES (est): 42MM **Privately Held**
WEB: www.certifiedfreightlogistics.com
SIC: **4213** Refrigerated products transport

(P-12022)
CJ LOGISTICS AMERICA LLC
1895 Marigold Ave, Redlands (92374-5028)
PHONE..............................909 363-4354
Greg Hart, *General Ptnr*
EMP: 226 **Privately Held**
WEB: www.america.cjlogistics.com
SIC: **4213** **4212** Trucking, except local; local trucking, without storage
HQ: Cj Logistics America, Llc
1750 S Wolf Rd
Des Plaines IL 60018

(P-12023)
COAST VALLEY MOVING & STOR INC
1111 Via Callejon, San Clemente (92673-6230)
PHONE..............................949 361-7500
Ken Merrill Hite, *President*
Teresa Hite, *Vice Pres*
EMP: 52 EST: 1971
SQ FT: 21,000
SALES (est): 1.7MM **Privately Held**
WEB: www.coastvalleymoving.com
SIC: **4213** **4214** Household goods transport; local trucking with storage

(P-12024)
COMPLETE LOGISTICS COMPANY
15895 Valley Blvd 200, Fontana (92335-6430)
PHONE..............................909 427-9800
EMP: 150
SALES (corp-wide): 45MM **Privately Held**
SIC: **4213** Trucking Operator-Nonlocal

PA: The Complete Logistics Company
1670 Etiwanda Ave Ste A
Ontario CA 92335
909 544-5040

(P-12025)
CONTRACTORS CARGO COMPANY (PA)
Also Called: Contractors Rigging & Erectors
500 S Alameda St, Compton (90221-3801)
P.O. Box 5290 (90224-5290)
PHONE..............................310 609-1957
Carla Ann Wheeler, *CEO*
Gerald D Wheeler, *President*
Kimberly Dorio, *Corp Secy*
Vanessa Topete, *Analyst*
Rob Fleer, *Opers Mgr*
◆ EMP: 80 EST: 1959
SQ FT: 25,000
SALES (est): 24.2MM **Privately Held**
WEB: www.contractorscargo.com
SIC: **4213** **4731** **1623** **4741** Contract haulers; freight transportation arrangement; water, sewer & utility lines; rental of railroad cars; cargo loading & unloading services; boiler maintenance contractor

(P-12026)
COVENANT TRANSPRT INC
1300 E Franklin Ave, Pomona (91766-5416)
PHONE..............................909 469-0130
Bill Furgess, *Manager*
Richard Cribbs, *Officer*
Paul Bunn, *Sr Exec VP*
Edward Kern, *Vice Pres*
Mary B Roseman, *Vice Pres*
EMP: 549 **Publicly Held**
WEB: www.covenantlogistics.com
SIC: **4213** Contract haulers
HQ: Covenant Transport, Inc.
400 Birmingham Hwy
Chattanooga TN 37419
423 821-1212

(P-12027)
CRST INTERNATIONAL INC
10641 Calabash Ave, Fontana (92337-7011)
PHONE..............................909 829-1313
EMP: 149
SALES (corp-wide): 2B **Privately Held**
SIC: **4213** Trucking Operator-Nonlocal
PA: Crst International, Inc.
3930 16th Ave Sw
Cedar Rapids IA 52401
319 396-4400

(P-12028)
D C SHOWER DOORS INC
Also Called: Image Transfer
26121 Avenue Hall, Valencia (91355-3490)
PHONE..............................661 257-1177
Jason Shepard, *President*
EMP: 152 EST: 1996
SQ FT: 125,000
SALES (est): 1.9MM
SALES (corp-wide): 114.5MM **Privately Held**
WEB: www.cwdoors.com
SIC: **4213** Trucking, except local
PA: Contractors Wardrobe, Inc.
26121 Avenue Hall
Valencia CA 91355
661 257-1177

(P-12029)
DAYLIGHT TRANSPORT LLC (PA)
1501 Hughes Way Ste 200, Long Beach (90810-1879)
P.O. Box 93155 (90809-3155)
PHONE..............................310 507-8200
Richard S Breen, *CEO*
Jim Mc Carthy, *CFO*
Jim McCarthy, *CFO*
Edward Marsh, *Vice Pres*
Greg Steele, *Vice Pres*
▲ EMP: 88 EST: 1997
SQ FT: 3,000
SALES (est): 61.5MM **Privately Held**
WEB: www.dylt.com
SIC: **4213** Contract haulers

▲ = Import ▼=Export
◆ =Import/Export

(P-12030)
DEPENDABLE HIGHWAY EXPRESS INC
Also Called: Dhe
1351 S Campus Ave, Ontario (91761-4352)
PHONE..................909 923-0065
Bob Bianchi, *Branch Mgr*
David Marler, *Regional Mgr*
Jonathon Torres, *Clerk*
EMP: 79
SALES (corp-wide): 206.3MM **Privately Held**
WEB: www.godependable.com
SIC: **4213** Contract haulers
PA: Dependable Highway Express, Inc.
2555 E Olympic Blvd
Los Angeles CA 90023
323 526-2200

(P-12031)
DEPENDABLE HIGHWAY EXPRESS INC
800 E 230th St, Carson (90745-5002)
PHONE..................310 522-4111
Keith Norris, *Manager*
EMP: 79
SALES (corp-wide): 206.3MM **Privately Held**
WEB: www.godependable.com
SIC: **4213 4225** Contract haulers; general warehousing & storage
PA: Dependable Highway Express, Inc.
2555 E Olympic Blvd
Los Angeles CA 90023
323 526-2200

(P-12032)
DEPENDABLE HIGHWAY EXPRESS INC (PA)
Also Called: Dependable Logistics Services
2555 E Olympic Blvd, Los Angeles (90023-2605)
P.O. Box 58047 (90058-0047)
PHONE..................323 526-2200
Ronald Massman, *President*
Nancy Ordaz, *Partner*
Blanca Reyes, *Partner*
Karen Shaw, *Partner*
Joe Finney, *COO*
◆ EMP: 300 EST: 1984
SQ FT: 1,680,000
SALES (est): 206.3MM **Privately Held**
WEB: www.godependable.com
SIC: **4213 4225** Contract haulers; general warehousing & storage

(P-12033)
DESERT COASTAL TRANSPORT INC (PA)
Also Called: Dct
10686 Banana Ave, Fontana (92337-7002)
P.O. Box 8185, Rancho Cucamonga (91701-0185)
PHONE..................909 357-3395
Tim Wyant, *President*
Timothy A Wyant, *CEO*
Chuck Wyant, *Admin Sec*
EMP: 55 EST: 1972
SQ FT: 6,000
SALES (est): 14.2MM **Privately Held**
WEB: www.desertcoastal.com
SIC: **4213** Trucking, except local

(P-12034)
DIRECTLINE MOTOR EXPRESS INC
2720 E 26th St, Vernon (90058-8004)
P.O. Box 58048, Los Angeles (90058-0048)
PHONE..................213 266-2670
Phil Rogers, *President*
Paul Stover, *CFO*
EMP: 280 EST: 1991
SQ FT: 34,000
SALES (est): 5.1MM **Privately Held**
WEB: www.directlineinc.com
SIC: **4213** Trucking, except local

(P-12035)
DOUBLE EAGLE TRNSP CORP
12135 Scarbrough Ct, Oak Hills (92344-9200)
PHONE..................760 956-3770
Gerald E Butcher, *President*
EMP: 140 EST: 1992
SQ FT: 10,125

SALES (est): 21.1MM
SALES (corp-wide): 1.4B **Privately Held**
WEB: www.trimac.com
SIC: **4213 4212** Contract haulers; local trucking, without storage
PA: Trimac Transportation Ltd
3215 12 St Ne
Calgary AB T2E 7
403 298-5100

(P-12036)
ESPARZA ENTERPRISES INC
500 Workman St, Bakersfield (93307-6871)
PHONE..................661 631-0347
EMP: 568
SALES (corp-wide): 135MM **Privately Held**
WEB: www.esparzainc.com
SIC: **4213** Trucking, except local
PA: Esparza Enterprises, Inc.
3851 Fruitvale Ave
Bakersfield CA 93308
661 831-0002

(P-12037)
ESTES EXPRESS LINES
14727 Alondra Blvd, La Mirada (90638-5617)
PHONE..................714 994-3770
Benjamin J Torman, *Branch Mgr*
Tom Donahue, *Vice Pres*
Marty Whitacre, *Info Tech Mgr*
Patrick Lynch, *Manager*
Juan Rios-Orozco, *Supervisor*
EMP: 51
SALES (corp-wide): 3.5B **Privately Held**
WEB: www.estes-express.com
SIC: **4213** Contract haulers
PA: Estes Express Lines
3901 W Broad St
Richmond VA 23230
804 353-1900

(P-12038)
ESTES EXPRESS LINES
10736 Cherry Ave, Fontana (92337-7196)
PHONE..................909 427-9850
Mark Brown, *Manager*
Nancy Lefevre-Dhore, *Accounts Mgr*
Jorge Ruiz, *Accounts Mgr*
EMP: 51
SALES (corp-wide): 3.5B **Privately Held**
WEB: www.estes-express.com
SIC: **4213 4212** Less-than-truckload (LTL) transport; local trucking, without storage
PA: Estes Express Lines
3901 W Broad St
Richmond VA 23230
804 353-1900

(P-12039)
ESTES EXPRESS LINES
13327 Temple Ave, City of Industry (91746-1513)
PHONE..................626 333-9090
Kieran O'Carroll, *Manager*
EMP: 51
SQ FT: 6,156
SALES (corp-wide): 3.5B **Privately Held**
WEB: www.estes-express.com
SIC: **4213 4212** Less-than-truckload (LTL) transport; local trucking, without storage
PA: Estes Express Lines
3901 W Broad St
Richmond VA 23230
804 353-1900

(P-12040)
ESTES EXPRESS LINES
9120 San Fernando Rd, Sun Valley (91352-1413)
PHONE..................818 504-4155
Eric Reyes, *Manager*
Michael Hall, *Manager*
Chris Ronca, *Manager*
Mayanin Mendoza, *Regional*
EMP: 51
SALES (corp-wide): 3.5B **Privately Held**
WEB: www.estes-express.com
SIC: **4213** Contract haulers
PA: Estes Express Lines
3901 W Broad St
Richmond VA 23230
804 353-1900

(P-12041)
ESTES EXPRESS LINES
945 Noble Way, Santa Maria (93454-1521)
PHONE..................805 922-8206
Dan Sampson, *Branch Mgr*
EMP: 51
SALES (corp-wide): 3.5B **Privately Held**
WEB: www.estes-express.com
SIC: **4213** Contract haulers
PA: Estes Express Lines
3901 W Broad St
Richmond VA 23230
804 353-1900

(P-12042)
ESTES EXPRESS LINES
1531 Blinn Ave, Wilmington (90744-1601)
PHONE..................310 549-7306
Rob Clagg, *Manager*
EMP: 51
SALES (corp-wide): 3.5B **Privately Held**
WEB: www.estes-express.com
SIC: **4213** Contract haulers
PA: Estes Express Lines
3901 W Broad St
Richmond VA 23230
804 353-1900

(P-12043)
FAST LANE TRANSPORTATION INC (PA)
Also Called: Fast Lane Container Services
2400 E Pacific Coast Hwy, Wilmington (90744-2921)
PHONE..................562 435-3000
Patrick L Wilson, *President*
Chris Henry, *CFO*
Christine Henry, *Corp Secy*
James Henry, *Exec VP*
▲ EMP: 59 EST: 1979
SQ FT: 36,000
SALES (est): 22.8MM **Privately Held**
WEB: www.fastlanetrans.com
SIC: **4213 4214** Trailer or container on flat car (TOFC/COFC); local trucking with storage

(P-12044)
FEDEX FREIGHT CORPORATION
4500 Bandini Blvd, Vernon (90058-5409)
PHONE..................323 269-9800
EMP: 200
SQ FT: 20,000
SALES (corp-wide): 69.2B **Publicly Held**
WEB: www.fedex.com
SIC: **4213 4231** Trucking Operator-Nonlocal Truck Terminal Facility
HQ: Fedex Freight Corporation
8285 Tournament Dr # 100
Memphis TN 38125

(P-12045)
FEDEX FREIGHT WEST INC
11153 Mulberry Ave, Fontana (92337-7030)
PHONE..................909 357-3555
EMP: 355
SQ FT: 79,735
SALES (corp-wide): 47.4B **Publicly Held**
SIC: **4213 4731 4212** Trucking Operator-Nonlocal Freight Transportation Arrangement Local Trucking Operator
HQ: Fedex Freight West, Inc.
6411 Guadalupe Mines Rd
San Jose CA 95120
775 356-7600

(P-12046)
FRIENDS GROUP EXPRESS INC
14520 Village Dr Apt 1013, Fontana (92337-2501)
P.O. Box 310488 (92331-0488)
PHONE..................909 346-6814
Parmjit Singh Grewal, *Principal*
EMP: 78 EST: 2014
SQ FT: 700
SALES (est): 194K **Privately Held**
SIC: **4213 4212** Trucking, except local; local trucking, without storage

(P-12047)
GARDNER TRUCKING INC (HQ)
1219 E Elm St, Ontario (91761-4585)
P.O. Box 747, Chino (91708-0747)
PHONE..................909 563-5606

Thomas J Lanting, *President*
Cory Peters, *Vice Pres*
Joseph Florendo, *Planning*
Richard Galvan, *Info Tech Mgr*
Colin Marshall, *Software Dev*
EMP: 490 EST: 1974
SQ FT: 3,000
SALES (est): 79.2MM
SALES (corp-wide): 859.9MM **Privately Held**
WEB: www.gardnertrucking.com
SIC: **4213 4212** Trucking, except local; local trucking, without storage
PA: Crst International, Inc.
201 1st St Se Ste 400
Cedar Rapids IA 52401
319 396-4400

(P-12048)
GORES URS HOLDINGS CORP (PA)
10877 Wilshire Blvd Fl 18, Los Angeles (90024-4373)
PHONE..................310 209-3010
Alex Gores, *President*
Jennifer Kwon, *Vice Pres*
Spencer Kam, *Analyst*
EMP: 2021 EST: 2007
SALES (est): 127.3MM **Privately Held**
WEB: www.gores.com
SIC: **4213** Automobiles, transport & delivery

(P-12049)
H & H TRANSPORTATION LLC
300 El Sobrante Rd, Corona (92879-5757)
P.O. Box 77697 (92877-0123)
PHONE..................951 817-2300
Tim Hyde,
EMP: 60 EST: 1998
SALES (est): 5.2MM **Privately Held**
SIC: **4213 4212** Trucking, except local; local trucking, without storage

(P-12050)
H RAUVEL INC
Also Called: Nova Transportation Services
501 W Walnut St, Compton (90220-5221)
PHONE..................562 989-3333
Hector Velasco, *Manager*
EMP: 180
SALES (corp-wide): 32.3MM **Privately Held**
WEB: www.novafreight.net
SIC: **4213** Trucking, except local
PA: H. Rauvel, Inc.
1710 E Sepulveda Blvd
Carson CA 90745
310 604-0060

(P-12051)
HAWK TRANSPORTATION INC
15238 Arrow Blvd, Fontana (92335-3250)
PHONE..................800 709-4295
Manprit K Sandhu, *CEO*
Jagtar Sandhu, *President*
Harry Bhangu, *Manager*
EMP: 60 EST: 2002
SQ FT: 1,300
SALES (est): 10.6MM **Privately Held**
WEB: www.hawktransportationinc.com
SIC: **4213** Trucking, except local

(P-12052)
HEARTLAND EXPRESS INC IOWA
10131 Redwood Ave, Fontana (92335-6236)
PHONE..................319 626-3600
Matthew Gonzalez, *Supervisor*
Daniel Caldera, *Vice Pres*
EMP: 611
SALES (corp-wide): 645.2MM **Publicly Held**
WEB: www.heartlandexpress.com
SIC: **4213** Trucking, except local
HQ: Heartland Express, Inc. Of Iowa
901 Heartland Way
North Liberty IA 52317
319 626-3600

(P-12053)
HF COX INC (PA)
Also Called: Cox Petroleum Transport
118 Cox Transport Way, Bakersfield
(93307)
PHONE..............................661 366-3236
Dainiel L Mairs, *President*
Larry Oconnell, *COO*
Brue McKinnon, *CFO*
Gwen Mairs, *Treasurer*
Jeremy Mairs, *Exec VP*
EMP: 60 EST: 1969
SQ FT: 5,000
SALES (est): 683.2K **Privately Held**
WEB: www.coxpetroleum.com
SIC: 4213 4212 Trucking, except local; petroleum haulage, local

(P-12054)
J B HUNT TRANSPORT INC
11559 Jersey Blvd, Rancho Cucamonga
(91730-4924)
PHONE..............................909 466-5361
EMP: 167
SALES (corp-wide): 6.1B **Publicly Held**
SIC: 4213 Trucking Operator-Nonlocal
HQ: J. B. Hunt Transport, Inc.
    615 J B Hunt Corporate Dr
    Lowell AR 72745
    479 820-0000

(P-12055)
JACK JONES TRUCKING INC
1090 E Belmont St, Ontario (91761-4501)
PHONE..............................909 456-2500
Valerie Liese, *President*
Erin Craig, *Exec VP*
Mike Brooks, *Vice Pres*
Robert Liese, *Vice Pres*
Bob Liese, *General Mgr*
EMP: 100 EST: 1971
SQ FT: 3,000
SALES (est): 9.8MM **Privately Held**
WEB: www.jjtinc.com
SIC: 4213 Trucking, except local

(P-12056)
**KINGS COUNTY TRUCK LINES
(HQ)**
754 S Blackstone St, Tulare (93274-5757)
P.O. Box 1016 (93275-1016)
PHONE..............................559 686-2857
Mark Tisdale, *Vice Pres*
EMP: 162 EST: 1940
SQ FT: 45,000
SALES (est): 25.5MM
SALES (corp-wide): 1.6B **Privately Held**
WEB: www.ruan.com
SIC: 4213 Contract haulers
PA: Ruan Transportation Management Systems, Inc.
    666 Grand Ave Ste 3100
    Des Moines IA 50309
    515 245-2500

(P-12057)
KLX LLC
1351 Charles Willard St, Carson
(90746-4023)
P.O. Box 4438, Visalia (93278-4438)
PHONE..............................559 684-1037
Ron Greenberg, *President*
Jeff Peterson, *Corp Secy*
Marlene Lawrence, *Administration*
Percy Greenberg, *Director*
EMP: 65 EST: 1983
SQ FT: 12,000
SALES (est): 5.1MM **Privately Held**
WEB: www.klxllc.com
SIC: 4213 Trucking, except local

(P-12058)
LANDFORCE CORPORATION
17201 N D St, Victorville (92394-1401)
PHONE..............................760 843-7839
Rajinder Bhangu, *CEO*
EMP: 120 EST: 2000
SALES (est): 21.2MM **Privately Held**
WEB: www.landforcecorp.com
SIC: 4213 Trucking, except local

(P-12059)
**LANDSTAR GLOBAL LOGISTICS
INC**
2313 E Philadelphia St, Ontario
(91761-8047)
PHONE..............................909 266-0096
EMP: 93 **Publicly Held**
WEB: www.landstar.com
SIC: 4213 Trucking, except local
HQ: Landstar Global Logistics, Inc.
    13410 Sutton Park Dr S
    Jacksonville FL 32224

(P-12060)
**LAS VEGAS / LA EXPRESS INC
(PA)**
1000 S Cucamonga Ave, Ontario
(91761-3461)
PHONE..............................909 972-3100
Ronald Cain Jr, *CEO*
Beverly A Adley, *Vice Pres*
Michael P Adley, *Admin Sec*
Michael Adley, *Admin Sec*
EMP: 170 EST: 1988
SQ FT: 163,000
SALES (est): 18.9MM **Privately Held**
WEB: www.lvla.com
SIC: 4213 Trucking, except local

(P-12061)
LEXMAR DISTRIBUTION INC
200 Erie St, Pomona (91768-3327)
PHONE..............................909 620-7001
Alex Kole, *CEO*
Antoinette Magpily, *Officer*
Marlon Brover, *Vice Pres*
Alex Kolesnikov, *Vice Pres*
Clint Dotson, *Opers Mgr*
EMP: 50 EST: 1990
SQ FT: 10,000
SALES (est): 21.3MM **Privately Held**
WEB: www.lexmardistribution.com
SIC: 4213 Trucking, except local

(P-12062)
MARK CLEMONS
Also Called: Mtc Transportation
4584 Adobe Rd, Twentynine Palms
(92277-1671)
P.O. Box 148 (92277-0148)
PHONE..............................760 361-1531
Mark Clemons, *Owner*
Rebecca Hewson Hubbard, *Office Mgr*
Genevieve Clemons, *Manager*
EMP: 200 EST: 1978
SALES (est): 21MM **Privately Held**
SIC: 4213 4212 4513 4522 Heavy machinery transport; local trucking, without storage; air courier services; air transportation, nonscheduled

(P-12063)
MASHBURN TRNSP SVCS INC
1423 Kern St, Taft (93268-4607)
P.O. Box 66 (93268-8066)
PHONE..............................661 763-5724
Denise Mashburn, *President*
Michael Mashburn, *Vice Pres*
Courtney Dunbar, *Office Mgr*
Scott Blackwood, *Supervisor*
EMP: 120 EST: 1987
SQ FT: 2,000
SALES (est): 15.1MM **Privately Held**
WEB: www.mashburntransportation.com
SIC: 4213 4212 Contract haulers; local trucking, without storage

(P-12064)
MEATHEAD MOVERS INC (PA)
3600 S Higuera St, San Luis Obispo
(93401-7306)
PHONE..............................805 544-6328
Evan Steed, *COO*
Aaron B Steed, *CEO*
Angela Aleen, *General Mgr*
Linnea Fritch, *Accounting Mgr*
Trace Wilson, *Human Resources*
EMP: 68 EST: 2001
SQ FT: 1,700
SALES (est): 20MM **Privately Held**
WEB: www.meatheadmovers.com
SIC: 4213 Household goods transport

(P-12065)
NATIONAL RETAIL TRNSP INC
500 W Victoria St, Compton (90220-5514)
PHONE..............................310 631-8951
EMP: 67
SALES (corp-wide): 484.2MM **Privately
Held**
WEB: www.nrs3pl.com
SIC: 4213 Trucking, except local
HQ: National Retail Transportation, Inc.
    2820 16th St
    North Bergen NJ 07047
    201 866-0462

(P-12066)
NATIONAL RETAIL TRNSP INC
400 Harley Knox Blvd, Perris (92571-7566)
PHONE..............................951 243-6110
EMP: 67
SALES (corp-wide): 484.2MM **Privately
Held**
WEB: www.nrs3pl.com
SIC: 4213 Trucking, except local
HQ: National Retail Transportation, Inc.
    2820 16th St
    North Bergen NJ 07047
    201 866-0462

(P-12067)
NATIONAL RETAIL TRNSP INC
355 W Carob St, Compton (90220-5212)
PHONE..............................310 605-3777
Manuel Villasenor, *Branch Mgr*
John Tabor, *Vice Pres*
Amalia Dominguez, *Office Mgr*
Jamel Perez, *Network Enginr*
David Mehlfelder, *Prgrmr*
EMP: 67
SALES (corp-wide): 484.2MM **Privately
Held**
WEB: www.nrs3pl.com
SIC: 4213 Trucking, except local
HQ: National Retail Transportation, Inc.
    2820 16th St
    North Bergen NJ 07047
    201 866-0462

(P-12068)
NETO EXPRESS LLC
7536 Goodland Ave, North Hollywood
(91605-2036)
PHONE..............................818 625-5615
Carlos Ernesto Herrera, *Mng Member*
EMP: 51 EST: 2006
SALES (est): 1.1MM **Privately Held**
SIC: 4213 Trucking, except local

(P-12069)
NEW LEGEND INC
8613 Etiwanda Ave, Rancho Cucamonga
(91739-9611)
PHONE..............................855 210-2300
EMP: 316 **Privately Held**
SIC: 4213 4212 Trucking, except local;
local trucking, without storage
PA: New Legend, Inc.
    811 S 59th Ave
    Phoenix AZ 85043

(P-12070)
NY TRANSPORT INC
10191 Redwood Ave, Fontana
(92335-6236)
PHONE..............................909 355-9832
Nazario Yanez, *CEO*
Nazario Y Perez, *President*
EMP: 65 EST: 2005
SALES (est): 16MM **Privately Held**
WEB: www.nytransportinc.com
SIC: 4213 Trucking, except local

(P-12071)
**PAN PACIFIC PETROLEUM CO
INC (PA)**
9302 Garfield Ave, South Gate
(90280-3805)
P.O. Box 1966 (90280-1966)
PHONE..............................562 928-0100
Robert Roth, *CEO*
Dale Snyder, *Exec VP*
Steven Roth, *Vice Pres*
EMP: 100 EST: 1962
SQ FT: 600
SALES (est): 17.2MM **Privately Held**
SIC: 4213 5172 Liquid petroleum transport, non-local; petroleum brokers

(P-12072)
**PAN PACIFIC PETROLEUM CO
INC**
Also Called: Truck Terminal
1850 Coffee Rd, Bakersfield (93308-5746)
PHONE..............................661 589-3200
Dave Palmer, *Manager*
EMP: 200
SALES (corp-wide): 17.2MM **Privately
Held**
SIC: 4213 Liquid petroleum transport, non-local
PA: Pan Pacific Petroleum Company, Inc.
    9302 Garfield Ave
    South Gate CA 90280
    562 928-0100

(P-12073)
POINTDIRECT TRANSPORT INC
10858 Almond Ave, Fontana (92337-7103)
PHONE..............................909 371-0837
Adolfo De La Herran, *President*
Adolfo D La Herran, *President*
EMP: 100 EST: 2014
SQ FT: 2,500
SALES (est): 500K **Privately Held**
WEB: www.point-direct.com
SIC: 4213 Trucking, except local

(P-12074)
**PRODUCTION DELIVERY SVCS
INC**
Also Called: Production Transport
806 W Valencia Mesa Dr, Fullerton
(92835-4008)
PHONE..............................562 777-0060
James Harkins, *President*
Michelle Harkins, *Corp Secy*
Ashkan Mohkami, *Technician*
Sabrina Grewal, *Fmly & Gen Dent*
Ahmad Rojaib, *Fmly & Gen Dent*
EMP: 55 EST: 1994
SALES (est): 6.9MM **Privately Held**
WEB:
www.productiondeliveryservicesinc.com
SIC: 4213 Trucking, except local

(P-12075)
**RPM TRANSPORTATION INC
(DH)**
11660 Arroyo Ave, Santa Ana
(92705-3057)
PHONE..............................714 388-3500
Shawn Duke, *President*
Andrew Lewes, *CFO*
Robert Ogdon, *Manager*
▲ EMP: 110 EST: 1985
SQ FT: 175,000
SALES (est): 35MM
SALES (corp-wide): 1.1B **Privately Held**
WEB: www.odysseylogistics.com
SIC: 4213 4225 4214 Trailer or container on flat car (TOFC/COFC); general warehousing; local trucking with storage
HQ: Rpm Consolidated Services, Inc.
    1901 Raymer Ave
    Fullerton CA 92833
    714 388-3500

(P-12076)
**SAIA MOTOR FREIGHT LINE
LLC**
14731 Santa Ana Ave, Fontana
(92337-7233)
PHONE..............................909 356-2808
Mike Ewing, *Manager*
EMP: 55
SALES (corp-wide): 1.8B **Publicly Held**
SIC: 4213 4212 Contract haulers; local trucking, without storage
HQ: Saia Motor Freight Line, Llc
    11465 Johns Creek Pkwy # 400
    Duluth GA 30097
    770 232-5067

(P-12077)
**SAIA MOTOR FREIGHT LINE
LLC**
14719 S San Pedro St, Gardena
(90248-2029)
PHONE..............................310 217-1499

David McNichols, *Manager*
EMP: 55
SALES (corp-wide): 1.8B **Publicly Held**
SIC: 4213 Contract haulers
HQ: Saia Motor Freight Line, Llc
    11465 Johns Creek Pkwy # 400
    Duluth GA 30097
    770 232-5067

(P-12078)
SAIA MOTOR FREIGHT LINE LLC
2550 E 28th St, Vernon (90058-1430)
PHONE..................323 277-2880
Gerard Francois, *Branch Mgr*
EMP: 55
SALES (corp-wide): 1.8B **Publicly Held**
SIC: 4213 Contract haulers
HQ: Saia Motor Freight Line, Llc
    11465 Johns Creek Pkwy # 400
    Duluth GA 30097
    770 232-5067

(P-12079)
SWIFT LEASING CO LLC
14392 Valley Blvd, Fontana (92335-5240)
PHONE..................909 347-0500
EMP: 53 **Publicly Held**
WEB: www.swifttrans.com
SIC: 4213 Contract haulers
HQ: Swift Leasing Co., Llc
    2200 S 75th Ave
    Phoenix AZ 85043
    602 269-9700

(P-12080)
TCI TRANSPORTATION SERVICES (PA)
4950 Triggs St, Commerce (90022-4832)
PHONE..................323 269-3033
Gerald Flynn, *CEO*
Andrew Flynn, *President*
Ryan Flynn, *President*
Cara Swank, *CFO*
John Sappington, *Vice Pres*
EMP: 297 **EST:** 1989
SALES (est): 108.7MM **Privately Held**
WEB: www.tcitransportation.com
SIC: 4213 4231 Automobiles, transport &
    delivery; trucking terminal facilities

(P-12081)
TLN INC
6801 Ave 304, Goshen (93227)
P.O. Box 578, Marsing ID (83639-0578)
PHONE..................208 880-9935
Troy Newsome, *Branch Mgr*
EMP: 58
SALES (corp-wide): 5MM **Privately Held**
SIC: 4213 Trucking, except local
PA: Tln Inc
    600 W Main St
    Marsing ID 83639
    208 817-1667

(P-12082)
TMT INDUSTRIES INC
14774 Jurupa Ave, Fontana (92337-7263)
PHONE..................909 493-3441
Antonio Y Martinez, *CEO*
Tony Martinez Sr, *President*
Evelyn Martinez, *Corp Secy*
Tony Martinez Jr, *Vice Pres*
Debbie Rush, *Office Mgr*
EMP: 63
SALES (est): 18.1MM **Privately Held**
WEB: www.tmtindustries.com
SIC: 4213 4212 Trucking, except local;
    local trucking, without storage

(P-12083)
TOTAL TRNSP LOGISTICS INC
4325 Etiwanda Ave Ste A, Jurupa Valley
(91752-3720)
PHONE..................951 360-9521
Robert E Hicks, *President*
Mike Stadler, *CFO*
Douglas Shockley, *Exec VP*
Steve Todare, *Vice Pres*
Kai Scharnweber, *Executive*
▲ **EMP:** 75
SQ FT: 125,000
SALES (est): 22.8MM **Privately Held**
WEB: www.ttllogistics.com
SIC: 4213 Contract haulers

(P-12084)
TRIPLE-E MACHINERY MOVING INC
3301 Gilman Rd, El Monte (91732-3225)
PHONE..................626 444-1137
Steve Englebrecht, *CEO*
Joe Englbrecht, *Vice Pres*
Ed Langan, *Foreman/Supr*
EMP: 60 **EST:** 1974
SQ FT: 12,000
SALES (est): 8.7MM **Privately Held**
WEB: www.tripleemachinery.com
SIC: 4213 Heavy machinery transport

(P-12085)
TRIWAYS INC
Also Called: Warehouse and Distribution
11201 Iberia St Ste B, Jurupa Valley
(91752-3280)
P.O. Box 9342, Ontario (91762-9342)
PHONE..................951 361-4840
Juan M Jauregui, *President*
Fredy R Jimenez, *CFO*
Bob Schwenig, *Vice Pres*
Maria Paez, *Admin Asst*
Gary Arredondo, *Opers Mgr*
▲ **EMP:** 65 **EST:** 1978
SQ FT: 228,000
SALES (est): 16.8MM **Privately Held**
WEB: www.triways.net
SIC: 4213 Trucking, except local

(P-12086)
U C L INCORPORATED (PA)
Also Called: United Cargo Logistics
620 S Hacienda Blvd, City of Industry
(91745-1126)
PHONE..................323 235-0099
Byung Y Chang, *CEO*
Chris Chang, *President*
Jenny Kim, *Department Mgr*
Yong Ku, *General Mgr*
Richard Ka, *Opers Staff*
EMP: 100 **EST:** 1998
SQ FT: 16,000
SALES (est): 27.7MM **Privately Held**
WEB: www.uclinc-reviews.com
SIC: 4213 Trucking, except local

(P-12087)
U S XPRESS INC
363 Nina Lee Rd, Calexico (92231-9527)
PHONE..................760 768-6707
EMP: 508 **Publicly Held**
WEB: www.usxpress.com
SIC: 4213 Trucking, except local
HQ: U. S. Xpress, Inc.
    4080 Jenkins Rd
    Chattanooga TN 37421
    866 266-7270

(P-12088)
VALLEY BULK INC
17649 Turner Rd, Victorville (92394-8716)
P.O. Box 1100 (92393-1100)
PHONE..................760 843-0574
Jeff W Golson, *President*
EMP: 85 **EST:** 1995
SALES (est): 10.3MM **Privately Held**
WEB: www.valleybulkinc.com
SIC: 4213 Contract haulers

(P-12089)
VAN KING & STORAGE INC
Also Called: King Relocation Services
13535 Larwin Cir, Santa Fe Springs
(90670-5032)
PHONE..................562 921-0555
Steve Komorous, *President*
Edwin Nabal, *CFO*
Keith Hindsley, *Senior VP*
Martin Delaney, *Vice Pres*
Jj Krukenkamp, *Vice Pres*
EMP: 75 **EST:** 1955
SQ FT: 60,000
SALES (est): 14.9MM **Privately Held**
WEB: www.kingvanstorage.com
SIC: 4213 4225 Trucking, except local;
    general warehousing & storage

(P-12090)
VENTURA TRANSFER COMPANY (PA)
2418 E 223rd St, Long Beach
(90810-1697)
PHONE..................310 549-1660
Randall J Clifford, *CEO*
Ian Hart, *CFO*
Galen Clifford, *Vice Pres*
Greg Clifford, *Vice Pres*
Steven F Clifford, *Vice Pres*
▲ **EMP:** 75
SQ FT: 10,000
SALES (est): 15MM **Privately Held**
WEB: www.venturatransfercompany.com
SIC: 4213 4212 4214 Contract haulers;
    local trucking, without storage; local truck-
    ing with storage

(P-12091)
VIP TRANSPORT INC
2703 Wardlow Rd, Corona (92882-2869)
PHONE..................951 272-3700
Brittany Johnson, *President*
Laurie Griffiths, *Treasurer*
Laurie L Griffiths, *Treasurer*
Brittany Griffiths, *Admin Sec*
Tina McKee, *Administration*
◆ **EMP:** 50 **EST:** 1982
SQ FT: 127,000
SALES (est): 11.2MM **Privately Held**
WEB: www.viptransport.com
SIC: 4213 4214 4731 Trucking, except
    local; local trucking with storage; foreign
    freight forwarding

(P-12092)
WESTERN FREIGHT CARRIER INC (PA)
321 E Gardena Blvd, Gardena
(90248-2815)
PHONE..................310 767-1042
Yoo Joong Kim, *President*
Tony Kim, *CEO*
Patricia Yi, *Human Res Dir*
Jay Jung, *Manager*
Sean Kim, *Manager*
EMP: 73 **EST:** 2001
SALES (est): 10.9MM **Privately Held**
WEB: www.westernfreightcarrier.com
SIC: 4213 Trucking, except local

(P-12093)
XPO LOGISTICS FREIGHT INC
298 Rood Rd, Calexico (92231-9726)
PHONE..................760 768-0280
Jose Ruiz, *Branch Mgr*
Claudia Vargas, *Accounts Exec*
EMP: 70
SALES (corp-wide): 16.2B **Publicly Held**
WEB: www.xpo.com
SIC: 4213 Contract haulers
HQ: Xpo Logistics Freight, Inc.
    2211 Old Earhart Rd # 10
    Ann Arbor MI 48105
    800 755-2728

(P-12094)
XPO LOGISTICS FREIGHT INC
219a Tank Farm Rd, San Luis Obispo
(93401-7509)
PHONE..................805 541-4581
Bill Silva, *Manager*
Kevin Christie, *Sales Staff*
EMP: 70
SALES (corp-wide): 16.2B **Publicly Held**
WEB: www.xpo.com
SIC: 4213 Contract haulers
HQ: Xpo Logistics Freight, Inc.
    2211 Old Earhart Rd # 10
    Ann Arbor MI 48105
    800 755-2728

(P-12095)
XPO LOGISTICS FREIGHT INC
226 Washington St, Bakersfield
(93307-2718)
PHONE..................661 324-2947
EMP: 70
SALES (corp-wide): 16.2B **Publicly Held**
WEB: www.xpo.com
SIC: 4213 Contract haulers

(P-12096)
XPO LOGISTICS FREIGHT INC
12466 Montague St, Pacoima
(91331-2121)
PHONE..................818 890-2095
Paul Styers, *Manager*
Todd Williams, *General Mgr*
EMP: 70
SQ FT: 20,187
SALES (corp-wide): 16.2B **Publicly Held**
WEB: www.xpo.com
SIC: 4213 4214 Contract haulers; local
    trucking with storage
HQ: Xpo Logistics Freight, Inc.
    2211 Old Earhart Rd # 10
    Ann Arbor MI 48105
    800 755-2728

(P-12097)
XPO LOGISTICS FREIGHT INC
2102 N Batavia St, Orange (92865-3104)
PHONE..................714 282-7717
Tim Worner, *Manager*
Juan Melero, *Manager*
EMP: 70
SALES (corp-wide): 16.2B **Publicly Held**
WEB: www.xpo.com
SIC: 4213 Contract haulers
HQ: Xpo Logistics Freight, Inc.
    2211 Old Earhart Rd # 10
    Ann Arbor MI 48105
    800 755-2728

(P-12098)
XPO LOGISTICS FREIGHT INC
2900 Camino Del Sol, Oxnard
(93030-7255)
PHONE..................805 485-6466
David Daton, *Manager*
David Badon, *Manager*
EMP: 70
SALES (corp-wide): 16.2B **Publicly Held**
WEB: www.xpo.com
SIC: 4213 Contract haulers
HQ: Xpo Logistics Freight, Inc.
    2211 Old Earhart Rd # 10
    Ann Arbor MI 48105
    800 755-2728

(P-12099)
XPO LOGISTICS FREIGHT INC
20697 Prism Pl, Lake Forest (92630-7803)
PHONE..................949 581-9030
Joseph Tickford, *Branch Mgr*
Joseph Pickford, *General Mgr*
EMP: 70
SQ FT: 13,890
SALES (corp-wide): 16.2B **Publicly Held**
WEB: www.xpo.com
SIC: 4213 Contract haulers
HQ: Xpo Logistics Freight, Inc.
    2211 Old Earhart Rd # 10
    Ann Arbor MI 48105
    800 755-2728

(P-12100)
XPO LOGISTICS FREIGHT INC
1955 E Washington Blvd, Los Angeles
(90021-3206)
PHONE..................213 744-0664
Todd Liverman, *Branch Mgr*
EMP: 70
SQ FT: 39,842
SALES (corp-wide): 16.2B **Publicly Held**
WEB: www.xpo.com
SIC: 4213 4212 4731 Contract haulers;
    local trucking, without storage; freight for-
    warding
HQ: Xpo Logistics Freight, Inc.
    2211 Old Earhart Rd # 10
    Ann Arbor MI 48105
    800 755-2728

(P-12101)
XPO LOGISTICS FREIGHT INC
Also Called: Con-Way
12555 Mesa Dr, Blythe (92225-3363)
PHONE..................760 922-8538
Butch Russell, *Manager*
EMP: 70

SALES (corp-wide): 16.2B **Publicly Held**
WEB: www.xpo.com
SIC: **4213** Contract haulers
HQ: Xpo Logistics Freight, Inc.
　　2211 Old Earhart Rd # 10
　　Ann Arbor MI 48105
　　800 755-2728

(P-12102)
XPO LOGISTICS FREIGHT INC
13364 Marlay Ave, Fontana (92337-6919)
PHONE...................................951 685-1244
Mark Logan, *General Mgr*
John Sheriff, *Opers Mgr*
EMP: 70
SALES (corp-wide): 16.2B **Publicly Held**
WEB: www.xpo.com
SIC: **4213** Contract haulers
HQ: Xpo Logistics Freight, Inc.
　　2211 Old Earhart Rd # 10
　　Ann Arbor MI 48105
　　800 755-2728

(P-12103)
XPO LOGISTICS FREIGHT INC
12903 Lakeland Rd, Santa Fe Springs
(90670-4516)
PHONE...................................562 946-8331
Jim Lutze, *Manager*
EMP: 70
SALES (corp-wide): 16.2B **Publicly Held**
WEB: www.xpo.com
SIC: **4213** Contract haulers
HQ: Xpo Logistics Freight, Inc.
　　2211 Old Earhart Rd # 10
　　Ann Arbor MI 48105
　　800 755-2728

4214 Local Trucking With Storage

(P-12104)
17400 INC
17400 Chestnut St, City of Industry
(91748-1013)
PHONE...................................626 913-1800
John W Miller, *CEO*
James R Miller, *Treasurer*
Jim Miller, *Vice Pres*
Patrick Walsh, *Accounts Exec*
▲ EMP: 60 EST: 1933
SQ FT: 110,000
SALES (est): 7.2MM **Privately Held**
WEB: www.halbertbrothersinc.com
SIC: **4214** 1796 Local trucking with storage; machine moving & rigging

(P-12105)
ALL CARTAGE TRANSPORTATION INC (PA)
Also Called: A C T
12621 Chadron Ave, Hawthorne
(90250-4809)
P.O. Box 90521, Los Angeles (90009-0521)
PHONE...................................310 970-0600
George Aiello, *President*
Jeff De Seire, *Vice Pres*
Jeff Desirier, *Executive*
May Ng, *Office Admin*
Janet Garcia, *Representative*
EMP: 78 EST: 1979
SQ FT: 24,000
SALES (est): 14.9MM **Privately Held**
WEB: www.allcartage.com
SIC: **4214** 4449 Local trucking with storage; transportation (freight) on bays & sounds of the ocean

(P-12106)
AMERICAN WEST WORLDWIDE EX INC (PA)
51 Zaca Ln Ste 120, San Luis Obispo
(93401-7353)
PHONE...................................800 788-4534
Josh Brown, *CEO*
Cathie Brown, *President*
▲ EMP: 68 EST: 1986
SALES (est): 37.8MM **Privately Held**
WEB: www.awest.com
SIC: **4214** 4213 4225 Local trucking with storage; trucking, except local; general warehousing

(P-12107)
BEKINS MOVING SOLUTIONS INC (PA)
Also Called: Bekins Moving & Storage
12610 Shoemaker Ave, Santa Fe Springs
(90670-6344)
PHONE...................................562 356-9460
David Caruso, *President*
Jim March, *General Mgr*
Gene Douglis, *Sales Mgr*
Scott Fackrell, *Sales Staff*
Andi McPherson, *Manager*
EMP: 63 EST: 2003
SALES (est): 18.9MM **Privately Held**
SIC: **4214** 4213 Local trucking with storage; trucking, except local

(P-12108)
CADOGAN TATE FINE ART LGSTICS (PA)
5233 Alcoa Ave, Vernon (90058-3709)
PHONE...................................562 206-0191
EMP: 56 EST: 2009
SALES (est): 22.6MM **Privately Held**
WEB: www.cadogantate.com
SIC: **4214** Local trucking with storage

(P-12109)
CALKO TRANSPORT COMPANY INC
Also Called: Redman Container
720 E Watson Center Rd, Carson
(90745-4108)
PHONE...................................310 816-0602
Chong Suh, *President*
Simon Chung, *Vice Pres*
Leticia Gutierrez, *Manager*
Tim Suh, *Manager*
▲ EMP: 58
SQ FT: 24,000
SALES (est): 6MM **Privately Held**
WEB: www.calko.com
SIC: **4214** 4225 Local trucking with storage; general warehousing

(P-12110)
CITY MOVING INC
6319 Colfax Ave, North Hollywood
(91606-3409)
PHONE...................................888 794-8808
Lior Oren, *CEO*
Carolina Vela, *Assistant*
EMP: 150 EST: 2014
SALES (est): 14.1MM **Privately Held**
WEB: www.citymoving.com
SIC: **4214** Local trucking with storage

(P-12111)
CRUZ MODULAR INC (PA)
Also Called: Systechs
249 W Baywood Ave Ste B, Orange
(92865-2604)
PHONE...................................714 283-2890
Linda Galleran, *CEO*
Vince Schlachter, *President*
Malcolm Craycroft, *Vice Pres*
Kevin Collins, *Opers Mgr*
Brandy Whitaker, *Manager*
EMP: 99 EST: 1991
SALES (est): 12.9MM **Privately Held**
WEB: www.cruzmodulard.openfos.com
SIC: **4214** 7641 4226 1799 Furniture moving & storage, local; reupholstery & furniture repair; special warehousing & storage; office furniture installation

(P-12112)
FN LOGISTICS LLC
12588 Florence Ave, Santa Fe Springs
(90670-3919)
PHONE...................................213 625-5900
Richard Saghian, *President*
EMP: 73 **Privately Held**
SIC: **4214** Local trucking with storage
HQ: Fn Logistics, Llc.
　　2801 E 46th St
　　Vernon CA 90058
　　213 625-5900

(P-12113)
GREAT AMRCN LOGISTICS DIST INC
13565 Larwin Cir, Santa Fe Springs
(90670-5032)
PHONE...................................800 381-4527

Lawrence D Whittet, *CEO*
James Hooper, *President*
Robert Lechich, *CFO*
Bill Doherty,
Chris Sorgi, *Manager*
EMP: 86 EST: 1993
SQ FT: 120,000
SALES (est): 13.4MM **Privately Held**
WEB: www.greatamerican-logistics.com
SIC: **4214** 4212 4213 6719 Household goods moving & storage, local; moving services; trucking, except local; investment holding companies, except banks

(P-12114)
LINEAGE LOGISTICS HOLDINGS LLC
Also Called: Inland Cold Storage
2551 S Lilac Ave, Bloomington
(92316-3209)
PHONE...................................909 874-1200
Bill Hendricksen, *CEO*
Mandar Prabhu Gaunker, *Manager*
EMP: 209 **Privately Held**
WEB: www.lineagelogistics.com
SIC: **4214** 4222 Household goods moving & storage, local; warehousing, cold storage or refrigerated
HQ: Lineage Logistics Holdings, Llc
　　46500 Humboldt Dr
　　Novi MI 48377
　　800 678-7271

(P-12115)
MELKO LOGISTIC GROUP CORP (PA)
15000 Nelson Ave, City of Industry
(91744-4331)
PHONE...................................626 363-6300
Leonardo Fernandez, *CEO*
Michelle Nguyen, *Principal*
EMP: 74 EST: 2015
SALES (est): 10.6MM **Privately Held**
WEB: www.melko.us
SIC: **4214** Local trucking with storage

(P-12116)
NELSON MOVING & STORAGE INC
Also Called: Nelson North American
25742 Atlantic Ocean Dr, Lake Forest
(92630-8854)
PHONE...................................949 582-0380
Gust Nelson, *President*
Rosean Maricondo, *Office Mgr*
Lindsey Hileman, *Manager*
EMP: 50 EST: 1970
SQ FT: 24,000
SALES (est): 8.1MM **Privately Held**
WEB: www.nelsonmoving.com
SIC: **4214** 4731 Local trucking with storage; freight transportation arrangement

(P-12117)
SAMUEL J PIAZZA & SON INC (PA)
Also Called: Piazza Trucking
9001 Rayo Ave, South Gate (90280-3606)
PHONE...................................323 357-1999
Michael Piazza, *CEO*
Robert Piazza, *Vice Pres*
William Piazza, *Vice Pres*
Beth Elkins, *Regional Mgr*
Bob Piazza, *Regl Sales Mgr*
EMP: 70
SQ FT: 20,000
SALES (est): 18.8MM **Privately Held**
WEB: www.piazzatrucking.com
SIC: **4214** 4213 Local trucking with storage; trucking, except local

(P-12118)
SCHICK MOVING & STORAGE CO (PA)
2721 Michelle Dr, Tustin (92780-7018)
P.O. Box 3627 (92781-3627)
PHONE...................................714 731-5500
Gordon C Schick, *President*
Lynn Larson, *CFO*
Lynne M Larson, *Treasurer*
Arthur C Schick Jr, *Vice Pres*
Beverly C Schick, *Vice Pres*
EMP: 100 EST: 1956
SQ FT: 113,000

SALES: 6.9MM **Privately Held**
WEB: www.schickusa.com
SIC: **4214** Household goods moving & storage, local

(P-12119)
SPECIAL DISPATCH CAL INC (PA)
234 Loma Ave, Long Beach (90803-6016)
PHONE...................................7 4 521-8200
John Edward Dearing, *CEO*
Thomas Dearing, *Vice Pres*
Tom Dearing, *Vice Pres*
Ty Clarno, *Opers Mgr*
Matthew Garcia, *Opers Staff*
EMP: 60 EST: 1968
SALES (est): 25MM **Privately Held**
WEB: www.specialdispatch.com
SIC: **4214** 4212 Local trucking with storage; delivery service, vehicular

(P-12120)
VERNON CENTRAL WAREHOUSE INC
Also Called: Vernon Warehouse Co
2050 E 38th St, Vernon (90058-1615)
P.O. Box 58426 (90058-0426)
PHONE...................................323 234-2200
Joseph E Tack, *CEO*
Joe Tack, *President*
Jim Boltinghouse, *Corp Secy*
Tom Rodd, *Vice Pres*
Steve Shanklin, *Vice Pres*
EMP: 125 EST: 1933
SQ FT: 100,000
SALES (est): 20.6MM **Privately Held**
WEB: www.sweetenerproducs.com
SIC: **4214** 5149 Local trucking with storage; natural & organic foods

(P-12121)
W WHY W ENTERPRISES INC
Also Called: Atlas/Eastern Van Lines
2671 Pomona Blvd, Pomona (91768-3221)
PHONE...................................626 969-4292
William Coffman, *President*
Yvonne Coffman, *Vice Pres*
Noel Fernandez, *Accountant*
EMP: 60 EST: 1956
SALES (est): 5.7MM **Privately Held**
WEB: www.easternvanlines.com
SIC: **4214** 4213 Local trucking with storage; household goods transport

(P-12122)
WETZEL & SONS MVG & STOR INC
Also Called: Wetzel Trucking
12400 Osborne St, Pacoima (91331-2002)
PHONE...................................818 890-0992
Donald C Wetzel, *President*
Daniel S Wetzel, *Vice Pres*
Debbe Wetzel, *Executive*
Stacie Vereuck, *Associate*
EMP: 70 EST: 1976
SQ FT: 146,000
SALES (est): 6.5MM **Privately Held**
WEB: www.wetzelmovingandstorage.com
SIC: **4214** Furniture moving & storage, local; household goods moving & storage, local

---

4215 Courier Svcs Except Air

(P-12123)
ALL COUNTIES COURIER INC
1642 Kaiser Ave, Irvine (92614-5700)
PHONE...................................714 599-9300
Patricia Cochran, *President*
Ted Heath, *Vice Pres*
Dean Steward, *Vice Pres*
Jack Lipczynski, *General Mgr*
Scott Lajoie, *Office Mgr*
EMP: 200 EST: 1984
SALES (est): 20.2MM **Privately Held**
WEB: www.accdelivers.com
SIC: **4215** Package delivery, vehicular

(P-12124)
APOLLO COURIERS INC (PA)
1039 W Hillcrest Blvd, Inglewood
(90301-2023)
PHONE...................................310 337-0377
Frank Ghamari, *President*

Fred Ghamarifard, *President*
Payman Khosravi, *CFO*
Miguel Banda, *Human Resources*
EMP: 69 **EST:** 1988
SQ FT: 2,200
SALES (est): 10.8MM **Privately Held**
WEB: www.apollocouriers.com
SIC: 4215 Package delivery, vehicular

(P-12125)
CLASSIC COURIERS INC (PA)
Also Called: A A A Couriers
1601 N El Centro Ave, Los Angeles
(90028-6412)
P.O. Box 1069 (90078-1069)
PHONE..................................323 461-3741
Jose J Perez, *President*
Mario Alaniz, *CFO*
Eddie Perez, *Vice Pres*
Chris Karapetyan, *Technology*
EMP: 61 **EST:** 1982
SQ FT: 2,500
SALES (est): 7.4MM **Privately Held**
WEB: www.classic-couriers.com
SIC: 4215 Courier services, except by air

(P-12126)
DHB DELIVERY LLC
1134 N Chestnut Ln, Azusa (91702-6867)
PHONE..................................626 588-7562
Daniel R Bourgault, *Mng Member*
EMP: 84 **EST:** 2019
SALES (est): 2MM **Privately Held**
SIC: 4215 Package delivery, vehicular

(P-12127)
DI OVERNITE LLC
Also Called: Deliver-It
1900 S State College Blvd, Anaheim
(92806-0101)
PHONE..................................877 997-7447
Michael Paul Martin,
Michael Martin, *COO*
Cristian Mackenney, *General Mgr*
Phil Nabal,
Pablo Trigueros, *Manager*
EMP: 52 **EST:** 2013
SALES (est): 12.1MM **Privately Held**
WEB: www.deliver-it.com
SIC: 4215 Package delivery, vehicular

(P-12128)
EXPRESS GROUP INC (PA)
Also Called: Westwood Express Messenger
Svc
10801 National Blvd # 104, Los Angeles
(90064-4140)
PHONE..................................310 474-5999
David F Davoodian, *President*
Malek Neman, *Vice Pres*
Joanna Young, *Managing Dir*
EMP: 74 **EST:** 1980
SQ FT: 4,000
SALES (est): 6.3MM **Privately Held**
WEB: www.deliverla.com
SIC: 4215 Courier services, except by air

(P-12129)
EXPRESS MESSENGER SYSTEMS INC
Also Called: California Overnight
1240 S Allec St, Anaheim (92805-6301)
PHONE..................................949 235-1400
Dave Denholm, *Manager*
EMP: 71 **Privately Held**
WEB: www.ontrac.com
SIC: 4215 7389 Courier services, except
by air; courier or messenger service
PA: Express Messenger Systems, Inc.
2501 S Price Rd Ste 201
Chandler AZ 85286

(P-12130)
EXPRESS MESSENGER SYSTEMS INC
Also Called: Ontrac
914 W Boone St, Santa Maria
(93458-5450)
PHONE..................................800 488-2829
Polo Cabello, *Branch Mgr*
Raymond Haylock, *General Mgr*
Ann Chau-Bella, *Human Resources*
James Lomas, *Opers Mgr*
EMP: 71 **Privately Held**
WEB: www.ontrac.com

SIC: 4215 Courier services, except by air
PA: Express Messenger Systems, Inc.
2501 S Price Rd Ste 201
Chandler AZ 85286

(P-12131)
EXPRESS MESSENGER SYSTEMS INC
Ontrac
11085 Olinda St, Sun Valley (91352-3302)
PHONE..................................818 504-9043
Audra Ferguson, *Sales Staff*
Karly Arroyo, *Manager*
Larry Hardie, *Manager*
Mark Magill, *Manager*
EMP: 71 **Privately Held**
WEB: www.ontrac.com
SIC: 4215 Courier services, except by air
PA: Express Messenger Systems, Inc.
2501 S Price Rd Ste 201
Chandler AZ 85286
-

(P-12132)
EXPRESS MESSENGER SYSTEMS INC
Also Called: Ontrac
375 W Apra St, Compton (90220-5528)
PHONE..................................800 359-2959
Michael Kerper, *Principal*
EMP: 71 **Privately Held**
WEB: www.ontrac.com
SIC: 4215 Package delivery, vehicular
PA: Express Messenger Systems, Inc.
2501 S Price Rd Ste 201
Chandler AZ 85286
-

(P-12133)
EXPRESS MESSENGER SYSTEMS INC
Ontrac
9774 Calabash Ave, Fontana (92335-5204)
PHONE..................................804 334-5000
Deanna Jay, *Manager*
EMP: 71 **Privately Held**
WEB: www.ontrac.com
SIC: 4215 Package delivery, vehicular
PA: Express Messenger Systems, Inc.
2501 S Price Rd Ste 201
Chandler AZ 85286

(P-12134)
FEDEX OFFICE & PRINT SVCS INC
8642 Whittier Blvd, Pico Rivera
(90660-2655)
PHONE..................................562 942-1953
EMP: 100
SALES (corp-wide): 47.4B **Publicly Held**
SIC: 4215 5999 7221 7389 Courier Serv-
ice Ret Misc Merchandise Photo Portrait
Studio Business Services
HQ: Fedex Office And Print Services, Inc.
7900 Legacy Dr
Dallas TX 75024
214 550-7000

(P-12135)
FEDEX SMARTPOST INC
5560 Ferguson Dr, Commerce
(90022-5140)
PHONE..................................323 888-8879
EMP: 85
SALES (corp-wide): 47.4B **Publicly Held**
SIC: 4215 Parcel Services
HQ: Fedex Smartpost, Inc.
16555 W Rogers Dr
New Berlin WI 53151
262 796-6800

(P-12136)
GENERAL LGSTICS SYSTEMS US INC
827 N American St, Visalia (93291-9337)
PHONE..................................559 651-1850
Dave Johnson, *Manager*
EMP: 143
SALES (corp-wide): 17.8B **Privately Held**
WEB: www.gls-us.com
SIC: 4215 4513 Package delivery, vehicu-
lar; parcel delivery, private air

HQ: General Logistics Systems Us, Inc.
4000 Executive Pkwy # 295
San Ramon CA 94583

(P-12137)
HAWTHORNE DISTRIBUTION CTR INC
6099 Malburg Way, Vernon (90058-3947)
PHONE..................................213 431-6101
Abbas Rezaei, *CEO*
Jose Gomez, *Clerk*
EMP: 50 **EST:** 2014
SALES (est): 4.9MM **Privately Held**
WEB: www.hawthornedistribution.com
SIC: 4215 5963 Package delivery, vehicu-
lar; food services, direct sales

(P-12138)
INTEGRATED PARCEL NETWORK
Also Called: Pacific Couriers
4373 Santa Anita Ave, El Monte
(91731-1690)
PHONE..................................714 278-6100
Nadia Youssef, *CEO*
EMP: 275 **EST:** 1985
SALES (est): 7.1MM **Privately Held**
SIC: 4215 4214 7389 Package delivery,
vehicular; local trucking with storage;
courier or messenger service

(P-12139)
JET DELIVERY INC (PA)
2169 Wright Ave, La Verne (91750-5835)
PHONE..................................800 716-7177
Michael Barbata, *President*
Mark Sur, *Vice Pres*
Tanya Baez, *Executive*
Jason Barbata, *CIO*
Susie Alvarez, *Accounting Mgr*
EMP: 90 **EST:** 1950
SQ FT: 34,000
SALES (est): 29.6MM **Privately Held**
WEB: www.jetdelivery.com
SIC: 4215 4231 4212 4213 Package de-
livery, vehicular; trucking terminal facili-
ties; local trucking, without storage;
trucking, except local

(P-12140)
KXP CARRIER SERVICES LLC
Also Called: Expak Logistics
11777 San Vicente Blvd, Los Angeles
(90049-5011)
PHONE..................................424 320-5300
Michael S Kraus, *CEO*
EMP: 140 **EST:** 2014
SQ FT: 1,500
SALES (est): 1.1MM
SALES (corp-wide): 24MM **Privately
Held**
WEB: www.expaklogistics.com
SIC: 4215 Parcel delivery, vehicular
PA: Kxp Advantage Services, Llc
11777 San Vicente Blvd # 747
Los Angeles CA 90049
424 320-5300

(P-12141)
M & N CONSULTING INC
Also Called: A-LINE MESSENGER SERVICE
21358 Nordhoff St, Chatsworth
(91311-6921)
PHONE..................................818 349-9400
Robin Anderson, *President*
Noah Anderson, *Vice Pres*
Noah Joseph Anderson, *Marketing Staff*
Shain Hymon, *Marketing Staff*
Doug Anderson, *Supervisor*
EMP: 61 **EST:** 1990
SQ FT: 1,170
SALES (est): 3.6MM **Privately Held**
WEB: www.alinems.com
SIC: 4215 Package delivery, vehicular

(P-12142)
MESSENGER EXPRESS (PA)
5435 Cahuenga Blvd Ste C, North Holly-
wood (91601-2948)
PHONE..................................213 614-0475
Gilbert Kort, *President*
EMP: 143 **EST:** 1976

SALES (est): 8.4MM **Privately Held**
WEB:
www.lightningmessengerexpress.com
SIC: 4215 7389 4212 Package delivery,
vehicular; courier or messenger service;
delivery service, vehicular

(P-12143)
NATIONAL LOGISTICS TEAM LLC
21496 Main St, Grand Terrace
(92313-5806)
P.O. Box 75, Perris (92572-0075)
PHONE..................................951 369-5841
Eric Meza, *Mng Member*
EMP: 20 **EST:** 2013
SALES (est): 1.2MM **Privately Held**
WEB: www.nlt-llc.com
SIC: 4215 2448 Package delivery, vehicu-
lar; pallets, wood

(P-12144)
PACIFIC COURIERS INC
4373 Santa Anita Ave A, El Monte
(91731-1690)
PHONE..................................714 278-6100
EMP: 50 **EST:** 2020
SALES (est): 5.2MM **Privately Held**
WEB: www.pacificcouriers.com
SIC: 4215 Courier services, except by air

(P-12145)
PEACH INC
Also Called: Action Messenger Service
1311 N Highland Ave, Los Angeles
(90028-7608)
P.O. Box 69673 (90069-0673)
PHONE..................................323 654-2333
Arthur P Ruben, *President*
Jerry Battagliotti, *Credit Mgr*
Brian Nealy, *Opers Mgr*
Les Alter, *Sales Staff*
EMP: 125 **EST:** 1990
SQ FT: 3,500 **Privately Held**
SIC: 4215 7389 Courier services, except
by air; courier or messenger service

(P-12146)
RUSSELL SIGLER INC
14751 Meridian Pkwy, March ARB
(92518-3039)
PHONE..................................951 656-3737
Jocelyn Legaspi, *Branch Mgr*
EMP: 136
SALES (corp-wide): 174.2MM **Privately
Held**
WEB: www.siglers.com
SIC: 4215 Courier services, except by air
PA: Russell Sigler, Inc.
9702 W Tonto St
Tolleson AZ 85353
623 388-5100

(P-12147)
TOP PRIORITY COURIERS INC (PA)
1257 Columbia Ave Ste D1, Riverside
(92507-2124)
P.O. Box 20376 (92516-0376)
PHONE..................................951 781-1000
Siroos Zakikhani, *President*
EMP: 60 **EST:** 1988
SQ FT: 6,000
SALES (est): 11.3MM **Privately Held**
WEB: www.topprioritycouriers.com
SIC: 4215 Package delivery, vehicular

(P-12148)
UNITED PARCEL SERVICE INC
Also Called: UPS
160 W Main St, El Centro (92243-2513)
PHONE..................................858 541-2336
Edgar Zaragoza, *Manager*
EMP: 152
SALES (corp-wide): 84.6B **Publicly Held**
WEB: www.ups.com
SIC: 4215 4513 Parcel delivery, vehicular;
parcel delivery, private air
HQ: United Parcel Service, Inc.
55 Glenlake Pkwy
Atlanta GA 30328
404 828-6000

(P-12149)
UNITED PARCEL SERVICE INC
Also Called: UPS
650 N Commercial Rd, Palm Springs
(92262-6299)
PHONE..................760 325-1762
Doug Nelson, *Manager*
Rick Vanden Bossche, *Business Mgr*
Richard Day, *Manager*
Rick Vandenbossche, *Manager*
EMP: 152
SALES (corp-wide): 84.6B **Publicly Held**
WEB: www.ups.com
SIC: 4215 4513 Parcel delivery, vehicular;
air courier services
HQ: United Parcel Service, Inc.
55 Glenlake Pkwy
Atlanta GA 30328
404 828-6000

(P-12150)
UNITED PARCEL SERVICE INC
Also Called: UPS
2800 W 227th St, Torrance (90505-2912)
PHONE..................800 742-5877
EMP: 152
SALES (corp-wide): 84.6B **Publicly Held**
WEB: www.ups.com
SIC: 4215 Package delivery, vehicular
HQ: United Parcel Service, Inc.
55 Glenlake Pkwy
Atlanta GA 30328
404 828-6000

(P-12151)
UNITED PARCEL SERVICE INC
Also Called: UPS
711 W Ridgecrest Blvd, Ridgecrest
(93555-4020)
PHONE..................760 375-7861
Trina Williams, *General Mgr*
EMP: 152
SALES (corp-wide): 84.6B **Publicly Held**
WEB: www.ups.com
SIC: 4215 Parcel delivery, vehicular
HQ: United Parcel Service, Inc.
55 Glenlake Pkwy
Atlanta GA 30328
404 828-6000

(P-12152)
UNITED PARCEL SERVICE INC
Also Called: UPS
2915 N Sierra Hwy, Bishop (93514-7633)
PHONE..................760 872-7661
EMP: 152
SALES (corp-wide): 84.6B **Publicly Held**
WEB: www.ups.com
SIC: 4215 Parcel delivery, vehicular
HQ: United Parcel Service, Inc.
55 Glenlake Pkwy
Atlanta GA 30328
404 828-6000

(P-12153)
UNITED PARCEL SERVICE INC
Also Called: UPS
2790 E Main St, Barstow (92311-5880)
PHONE..................760 252-5766
Debbie Hamilton, *Manager*
EMP: 152
SALES (corp-wide): 84.6B **Publicly Held**
WEB: www.ups.com
SIC: 4215 Parcel delivery, vehicular
HQ: United Parcel Service, Inc.
55 Glenlake Pkwy
Atlanta GA 30328
404 828-6000

(P-12154)
UNITED PARCEL SERVICE INC
Also Called: UPS
17115 S Western Ave, Gardena
(90247-5299)
PHONE..................310 217-2646
Randy Hulhellt, *Manager*
EMP: 152
SALES (corp-wide): 84.6B **Publicly Held**
WEB: www.ups.com
SIC: 4215 4513 Parcel delivery, vehicular;
air courier services
HQ: United Parcel Service, Inc.
55 Glenlake Pkwy
Atlanta GA 30328
404 828-6000

(P-12155)
UNITED PARCEL SERVICE INC
Also Called: UPS
3140 E Jurupa Ave, Ontario (91761)
PHONE..................909 974-7212
Richard Ricardo, *Principal*
EMP: 152
SALES (corp-wide): 84.6B **Publicly Held**
WEB: www.ups.com
SIC: 4215 Parcel delivery, vehicular
HQ: United Parcel Service, Inc.
55 Glenlake Pkwy
Atlanta GA 30328
404 828-6000

(P-12156)
UNITED PARCEL SERVICE INC
Also Called: UPS
1522 Sabovich St, Mojave (93501-1681)
PHONE..................661 824-9391
Bobby Pastrole, *Manager*
EMP: 152
SALES (corp-wide): 84.6B **Publicly Held**
WEB: www.ups.com
SIC: 4215 Parcel delivery, vehicular
HQ: United Parcel Service, Inc.
55 Glenlake Pkwy
Atlanta GA 30328
404 828-6000

(P-12157)
UNITED PARCEL SERVICE INC
Also Called: UPS
10690 Santa Monica Blvd, Los Angeles
(90025-4838)
PHONE..................310 474-0019
EMP: 152
SALES (corp-wide): 84.6B **Publicly Held**
WEB: www.ups.com
SIC: 4215 Parcel delivery, vehicular
HQ: United Parcel Service, Inc.
55 Glenlake Pkwy
Atlanta GA 30328
404 828-6000

(P-12158)
UNITED PARCEL SERVICE INC
Also Called: UPS
290 W Avenue L, Lancaster (93534-7109)
PHONE..................800 828-8264
James Adams, *Principal*
EMP: 152
SALES (corp-wide): 84.6B **Publicly Held**
WEB: www.ups.com
SIC: 4215 Parcel delivery, vehicular
HQ: United Parcel Service, Inc.
55 Glenlake Pkwy
Atlanta GA 30328
404 828-6000

(P-12159)
UNITED PARCEL SERVICE INC
Also Called: UPS
16000 Arminta St, Van Nuys (91406-1895)
PHONE..................404 828-6000
EMP: 152
SALES (corp-wide): 84.6B **Publicly Held**
WEB: www.ups.com
SIC: 4215 Parcel delivery, vehicular
HQ: United Parcel Service, Inc.
55 Glenlake Pkwy
Atlanta GA 30328
404 828-6000

(P-12160)
UNITED PARCEL SERVICE INC
Also Called: UPS
13233 Moore St, Cerritos (90703-2276)
PHONE..................562 404-3236
Gary Mieredos, *Manager*
EMP: 152
SALES (corp-wide): 84.6B **Publicly Held**
WEB: www.ups.com
SIC: 4215 Parcel delivery, vehicular
HQ: United Parcel Service, Inc.
55 Glenlake Pkwy
Atlanta GA 30328
404 828-6000

(P-12161)
UNITED PARCEL SERVICE INC
Also Called: UPS
3601 Sacramento Dr, San Luis Obispo
(93401-7115)
PHONE..................801 973-3400
EMP: 152

SALES (corp-wide): 84.6B Publicly Held
WEB: www.ups.com
SIC: 4215 Parcel delivery, vehicular
HQ: United Parcel Service, Inc.
55 Glenlake Pkwy
Atlanta GA 30328
404 828-6000

(P-12162)
UNITED PARCEL SERVICE INC
Also Called: UPS
505 Pine Ave, Goleta (93117-3707)
PHONE..................805 964-7848
Jason Chang, *Manager*
EMP: 152
SALES (corp-wide): 84.6B **Publicly Held**
WEB: www.ups.com
SIC: 4215 Parcel delivery, vehicular
HQ: United Parcel Service, Inc.
55 Glenlake Pkwy
Atlanta GA 30328
404 828-6000

(P-12163)
UNITED PARCEL SERVICE INC
Also Called: UPS
309 Cooley Ln, Santa Maria (93455-1218)
PHONE..................805 922-7851
Michael King, *Manager*
EMP: 152
SALES (corp-wide): 84.6B **Publicly Held**
WEB: www.ups.com
SIC: 4215 Parcel delivery, vehicular
HQ: United Parcel Service, Inc.
55 Glenlake Pkwy
Atlanta GA 30328
404 828-6000

(P-12164)
UNITED PARCEL SERVICE INC
Also Called: UPS
56174 29th Palms Hwy, Yucca Valley
(92284)
PHONE..................760 365-3158
Rick Van Denbossche, *Branch Mgr*
EMP: 152
SALES (corp-wide): 84.6B **Publicly Held**
WEB: www.ups.com
SIC: 4215 Parcel delivery, vehicular
HQ: United Parcel Service, Inc.
55 Glenlake Pkwy
Atlanta GA 30328
404 828-6000

(P-12165)
UNITED PARCEL SERVICE INC
Also Called: UPS
1501 Rancho Conejo Blvd, Newbury Park
(91320-1410)
PHONE..................805 375-1832
Grant Nissan, *Branch Mgr*
EMP: 152
SALES (corp-wide): 84.6B **Publicly Held**
WEB: www.ups.com
SIC: 4215 Parcel delivery, vehicular
HQ: United Parcel Service, Inc.
55 Glenlake Pkwy
Atlanta GA 30328
404 828-6000

(P-12166)
UNITED PARCEL SERVICE INC
Also Called: UPS
3000 E Washington Blvd, Los Angeles
(90023-4220)
PHONE..................323 729-6762
Art Nakamoto, *Branch Mgr*
EMP: 152
SALES (corp-wide): 84.6B **Publicly Held**
WEB: www.ups.com
SIC: 4215 Parcel delivery, vehicular
HQ: United Parcel Service, Inc.
55 Glenlake Pkwy
Atlanta GA 30328
404 828-6000

(P-12167)
UNITED PARCEL SERVICE INC
Also Called: UPS
3140 Jurupa St, Ontario (91761-2902)
PHONE..................909 974-7000
Brenda Hiza, *Branch Mgr*
EMP: 152

SALES (corp-wide): 84.6B **Publicly Held**
WEB: www.ups.com
SIC: 4215 Package delivery, vehicular; par-
cel delivery, vehicular
HQ: United Parcel Service, Inc.
55 Glenlake Pkwy
Atlanta GA 30328
404 828-6000

(P-12168)
UNITED PARCEL SERVICE INC
Also Called: UPS
2559 Palma Dr, Ventura (93003-5733)
PHONE..................805 642-6784
Keith Hughes, *Manager*
EMP: 152
SALES (corp-wide): 84.6B **Publicly Held**
WEB: www.ups.com
SIC: 4215 Parcel delivery, vehicular
HQ: United Parcel Service, Inc.
55 Glenlake Pkwy
Atlanta GA 30328
404 828-6000

(P-12169)
UNITED PARCEL SERVICE INC
Also Called: UPS
1100 Baldwin Park Blvd, Baldwin Park
(91706-5895)
PHONE..................626 814-6216
Lero Stamply, *Manager*
EMP: 152
SALES (corp-wide): 84.6B **Publicly Held**
WEB: www.ups.com
SIC: 4215 4513 Parcel delivery, vehicular;
air courier services
HQ: United Parcel Service, Inc.
55 Glenlake Pkwy
Atlanta GA 30328
404 828-6000

(P-12170)
**UNITY COURIER SERVICE INC
(PA)**
3231 Fletcher Dr, Los Angeles
(90065-2919)
PHONE..................323 255-9800
Ali Sharifi, *President*
Larry Lum, *CEO*
Kyle Hamilton, *Branch Mgr*
Saran Singh, *Branch Mgr*
Manmohan Bhamra, *Info Tech Mgr*
EMP: 200
SQ FT: 11,000
SALES (est): 44.9MM **Privately Held**
WEB: www.unitycourier.com
SIC: 4215 Package delivery, vehicular

4221 Farm Product Warehousing & Storage

(P-12171)
HONEYVILLE INC
11600 Dayton Dr, Rancho Cucamonga
(91730-5525)
PHONE..................909 980-9500
Johnny Ferry, *President*
Greg Shoemaker, *Administration*
Kathy Charlton, *Purch Agent*
Craig Smith, *Opers Mgr*
Veronica Tucker, *Opers Staff*
EMP: 85
SALES (corp-wide): 188.4MM **Privately
Held**
WEB: www.honeyville.com
SIC: 4221 5153 2045 2041 Grain eleva-
tor, storage only; grains; prepared flour
mixes & doughs; flour & other grain mill
products
PA: Honeyville, Inc.
1040 W 600 N
Ogden UT 84404
435 494-4193

(P-12172)
VEG-LAND INC
Also Called: J B J Distributing
1518 E Valencia Dr, Fullerton (92831-4734)
P.O. Box 1287 (92836-8287)
PHONE..................714 871-6712
James E Matiasevich, *President*
John P Matiasevich, *Corp Secy*
Caitlin Reed, *Manager*
EMP: 50 EST: 1976

SQ FT: 70,000
SALES (est): 9.7MM
SALES (corp-wide): 25MM **Privately Held**
WEB: www.veg-land.com
SIC: **4221** Farm product warehousing & storage
PA: Veg-Land Sales, Inc.
1518 E Valencia Dr
Fullerton CA 92831
714 871-6712

4222 Refrigerated Warehousing & Storage

(P-12173)
EXETER PACKERS INC
Also Called: Sun Pacific Cold Storage
33374 Lerdo Hwy, Bakersfield (93308-9782)
PHONE..............................661 399-0416
Richard Peters, *Manager*
EMP: 137
SALES (corp-wide): 75.1MM **Privately Held**
WEB: www.sunpacific.com
SIC: **4222** 0172 Warehousing, cold storage or refrigerated; grapes
PA: Exeter Packers, Inc.
1250 E Myer Ave
Exeter CA 93221
559 592-5168

(P-12174)
KONOIKE-PACIFIC CALIFORNIA INC (HQ)
Also Called: Kpac
1420 Coil Ave, Wilmington (90744-2205)
PHONE..............................310 518-1000
Bob Smola, *President*
Ulises Sam, *CFO*
Wayne Lamb, *Vice Pres*
Yutaka Kane Urabe, *Vice Pres*
Jeffrey Waite, *Vice Pres*
◆ EMP: 78 EST: 1994
SQ FT: 784,080
SALES (est): 48.1MM **Privately Held**
WEB: www.kpaccoldstorage.com
SIC: **4222** Warehousing, cold storage or refrigerated

(P-12175)
MIKE CAMPBELL & ASSOCIATES LTD
Also Called: Mike Campbell Assoc Logictics
10907 Downey Ave Ste 203, Downey (90241-3737)
PHONE..............................626 369-3981
Vickie J Campbell, *CEO*
James Heermans, *President*
Paul Trump, *President*
EMP: 1000 EST: 1983
SALES (est): 54.3MM **Privately Held**
SIC: **4222** 4225 4214 4213 Storage, frozen or refrigerated goods; general warehousing & storage; local trucking with storage; trucking, except local

(P-12176)
PREFERRED FRZR SVCS - LBF LLC
4901 Bandini Blvd, Vernon (90058-5400)
PHONE..............................323 263-8811
Brian Beattie, *CEO*
Jerome Donaldson, *Maintence Staff*
▲ EMP: 100 EST: 2013
SALES (est): 3.7MM **Privately Held**
WEB: www.preferredfreezer.com
SIC: **4222** Warehousing, cold storage or refrigerated

(P-12177)
STANDARD-SOUTHERN CORPORATION
Also Called: Los Angeles Cold Storage Co
400 S Central Ave, Los Angeles (90013-1712)
P.O. Box 54244 (90054-0244)
PHONE..............................213 624-1831
Larry Rauch, *Manager*
Dan Nestor, *Engineer*
Renee Ross, *Teacher*
EMP: 80

SALES (corp-wide): 21.7MM **Privately Held**
WEB: www.standardsouthern.com
SIC: **4222** Warehousing, cold storage or refrigerated
PA: Standard-Southern Corporation
4635 Suthwest Fwy Ste 910
Houston TX 77027
713 627-1700

(P-12178)
STANDARD-SOUTHERN CORPORATION
Also Called: L.A. Cold Storage
440 S Central Ave, Los Angeles (90013-1712)
PHONE..............................213 624-1831
Larry Rauch, *President*
John Scherer, *Engineer*
Chuck Gunther, *Chief Engr*
Sam Reyes, *Manager*
EMP: 145
SALES (corp-wide): 21.7MM **Privately Held**
WEB: www.standardsouthern.com
SIC: **4222** Warehousing, cold storage or refrigerated
PA: Standard-Southern Corporation
4635 Suthwest Fwy Ste 910
Houston TX 77027
713 627-1700

(P-12179)
STANDARD-SOUTHERN CORPORATION
Also Called: Los Angeles Cold Storage
715 E 4th St, Los Angeles (90013-1727)
PHONE..............................213 624-1831
Thom Thomas, *Branch Mgr*
EMP: 145
SALES (corp-wide): 21.7MM **Privately Held**
WEB: www.standardsouthern.com
SIC: **4222** Warehousing, cold storage or refrigerated
PA: Standard-Southern Corporation
4635 Suthwest Fwy Ste 910
Houston TX 77027
713 627-1700

(P-12180)
WEBER DISTRIBUTION LLC (PA)
Also Called: Weber Logistics
13530 Rosecrans Ave, Santa Fe Springs (90670-5087)
PHONE..............................855 469-3237
Bob Lilja, *CEO*
Maggie Movius, *CFO*
Kevin Dixon, *Technology*
EMP: 474 EST: 2004
SALES (est): 53.9MM **Privately Held**
WEB: www.weberlogistics.com
SIC: **4222** 4225 4213 4212 Refrigerated warehousing & storage; general warehousing & storage; trucking, except local; local trucking, without storage; local trucking with storage

---

4225 General Warehousing & Storage

(P-12181)
99 CENTS ONLY STORES LLC (HQ)
4000 Union Pacific Ave, Commerce (90023-3202)
PHONE..............................323 980-8145
Barry J Feld, *CEO*
Henry Chu, *President*
Travis Hill, *President*
Mike Matteri, *President*
Steven Thagard, *President*
◆ EMP: 500 EST: 1982
SALES (est): 730MM **Privately Held**
WEB: www.99only.com
SIC: **4225** 5331 5199 General warehousing & storage; variety stores; general merchandise, non-durable
PA: Number Holdings, Inc.
4000 Union Pacific Ave
Commerce CA 90023
323 980-8145

(P-12182)
ACT FULFILLMENT INC (PA)
3155 Universe Dr, Jurupa Valley (91752-3252)
PHONE..............................909 930-9083
Randolph Cox, *CEO*
Lydiann Cox, *CFO*
Asma Malik, *Administration*
Brennan Haines, *Info Tech Mgr*
Morena Arias, *Opers Staff*
▲ EMP: 220
SALES (est): 26.4MM **Privately Held**
WEB: www.actfulfillment.com
SIC: **4225** General warehousing

(P-12183)
ADVANTAGE MEDIA SERVICES INC
Also Called: AMS Fulfillment
28220 Industry Dr, Valencia (91355-4105)
PHONE..............................661 705-7588
John Bevacqua, *Vice Pres*
EMP: 74
SALES (corp-wide): 56.1MM **Privately Held**
WEB: www.amsfulfillment.com
SIC: **4225** General warehousing
PA: Advantage Media Services, Inc.
29010 Commerce Center Dr
Valencia CA 91355
661 775-0611

(P-12184)
ALBERTSONS LLC
Also Called: Albertsons Brea Dist Ctr
200 N Puente St, Brea (92821-3841)
PHONE..............................714 990-8200
EMP: 1000
SALES (corp-wide): 62.4B **Publicly Held**
WEB: www.albertsons.com
SIC: **4225** General Warehousing And Storage, Nsk
HQ: Albertson's Llc
250 E Parkcenter Blvd
Boise ID 83706
208 395-4722

(P-12185)
ASHLEY FURNITURE INDS LLC
2250 W Lugonia Ave, Redlands (92374-5050)
PHONE..............................909 825-4900
Kurt Haines, *Manager*
Marco Sanchez,
Manny Martinez, *Director*
EMP: 392
SALES (corp-wide): 4.1B **Privately Held**
WEB: www.ashleyfurniture.com
SIC: **4225** 5021 General warehousing; furniture
PA: Ashley Furniture Industries, Llc
1 Ashley Way
Arcadia WI 54612
608 323-3377

(P-12186)
C & B DELIVERY SERVICES
Also Called: Temco
230 Diamond St, Laguna Beach (92651-3610)
PHONE..............................909 623-4708
Virginia Templeton, *President*
EMP: 85 EST: 1967
SQ FT: 91,000
SALES (est): 7.9MM **Privately Held**
SIC: **4225** General warehousing

(P-12187)
CALIFORNIA CARTAGE COMPANY INC
2902 E Val Verde Ct, Compton (90221-5702)
PHONE..............................888 537-1432
Zavel Brubaker, *Principal*
EMP: 55
SQ FT: 180,000
SALES (corp-wide): 1.2B **Privately Held**
WEB: www.calcartage.com
SIC: **4225** General warehousing
HQ: California Cartage Company, Inc.
3545 Long Beach Blvd Fl 5
Long Beach CA 90807
310 537-1432

(P-12188)
CASESTACK LLC (HQ)
Also Called: Casestack, Inc.
3000 Ocean Park Blvd, Santa Monica (90405-3020)
PHONE..............................310 473-8885
Daniel A Sanker, *President*
Ryan Casady, *Partner*
Steve Sezna, *COO*
David Isaksen, *CFO*
Colby Beland, *Vice Pres*
▲ EMP: 65 EST: 2000
SQ FT: 10,000
SALES (est): 293.9MM
SALES (corp-wide): 3.5B **Publicly Held**
WEB: www.hubgroup.com
SIC: **4225** 4731 General warehousing & storage; freight transportation arrangement
PA: Hub Group, Inc.
2000 Clearwater Dr
Oak Brook IL 60523
630 271-3600

(P-12189)
CHINO-PACIFIC WAREHOUSE CORP (PA)
Also Called: Pcwc
3601 Jurupa St, Ontario (91761-2905)
PHONE..............................909 545-8100
Jim Marcoly, *President*
David Boras, *CFO*
George Ramirez, *Vice Pres*
David Strawn, *Vice Pres*
Tony Gurrola, *Director*
▲ EMP: 66
SQ FT: 975,000
SALES (est): 17.3MM **Privately Held**
WEB: www.pcwc.com
SIC: **4225** General warehousing

(P-12190)
COSTCO WHOLESALE CORPORATION
Also Called: Costco Wholesale Depot
11600 Riverside Dr Ste A, Jurupa Valley (91752-3700)
PHONE..............................951 361-3606
Stu Bell, *Branch Mgr*
Denny Vollmar, *Manager*
EMP: 450
SALES (corp-wide): 195.9B **Publicly Held**
WEB: www.costco.com
SIC: **4225** General warehousing & storage
PA: Costco Wholesale Corporation
999 Lake Dr Ste 200
Issaquah WA 98027
425 313-8100

(P-12191)
CRYOMAX USA INC (HQ)
127 N California Ave B, City of Industry (91744-4313)
PHONE..............................626 330-3388
Yen T Liu, *President*
James Ting, *COO*
James Ho, *CFO*
EMP: 17 EST: 2006
SQ FT: 55,000
SALES (est): 10.1MM **Privately Held**
WEB: www.cryomaxusa.com
SIC: **4225** 3443 3714 General warehousing; heat exchangers: coolers (after, inter), condensers, etc.; radiators & radiator shells & cores, motor vehicle

(P-12192)
CUSTOM GOODS LLC
907 E 236th St, Carson (90745-6234)
PHONE..............................310 241-6700
Byron Mejia, *Warehouse Mgr*
EMP: 70 **Privately Held**
WEB: www.customgoodsllc.com
SIC: **4225** General warehousing
PA: Custom Goods, Llc
1035 E Watson Center Rd
Carson CA 90745

(P-12193)
CUSTOM GOODS LLC
809 E 236th St, Carson (90745-6232)
PHONE..............................310 241-6700
Byron Mejia, *Warehouse Mgr*

(PA)=Parent Co (HQ)=Headquarters (DH)=Div Headquarters
✪ = New Business established in last 2 years

EMP: 70 **Privately Held**
WEB: www.customgoodsllc.com
SIC: 4225 General warehousing
PA: Custom Goods, Llc
    1035 E Watson Center Rd
    Carson CA 90745
    -

(P-12194)
CUSTOM GOODS LLC (PA)
1035 E Watson Center Rd, Carson
(90745-4203)
PHONE.....................................310 241-6700
Tony Gregory,
Celia Miller, *Executive Asst*
Huerta Jorge, *Info Tech Dir*
Marie Olivarez, *Purch Mgr*
Cesar Alvarado, *Facilities Mgr*
EMP: 50 **EST:** 2000
SQ FT: 240,000
SALES (est): 62MM **Privately Held**
WEB: www.customgoodsllc.com
SIC: 4225 General warehousing

(P-12195)
CVS HEALTH CORPORATION
777 S Harbor Blvd E-163, La Habra
(90631-6882)
PHONE.....................................714 578-4601
Chris Preli, *Director*
Paul Stumpe, *District Mgr*
Michelle Dogey, *Supervisor*
Debra Reed, *Clerk*
EMP: 86
SALES (corp-wide): 268.7B **Publicly Held**
WEB: www.cvshealth.com
SIC: 4225 General warehousing & storage
PA: Cvs Health Corporation
    1 Cvs Dr
    Woonsocket RI 02895
    401 765-1500

(P-12196)
DALTON TRUCKING INC (PA)
13560 Whittram Ave, Fontana
(92335-2951)
P.O. Box 5025 (92334-5025)
PHONE.....................................909 823-0663
Terry Klenske, *CEO*
Mathew Klenske, *Vice Pres*
Matt Kunkel, *Executive*
Eleanor Klenske, *Admin Sec*
Roszetta Bautista, *Accounts Mgr*
EMP: 198 **EST:** 1970
SQ FT: 11,000
SALES (est): 36.1MM **Privately Held**
WEB: www.daltontrucking.com
SIC: 4225 General warehousing & storage

(P-12197)
DART INTERNATIONAL A CORP (HQ)
Also Called: Dart Entities
1430 S Eastman Ave, Commerce
(90023-4006)
P.O. Box 23944, Los Angeles (90023-0944)
PHONE.....................................323 264-8746
Terence Dedeaux, *CEO*
Paul Martin, *President*
William J Smollen, *Corp Secy*
Joseph M Medlin, *Exec VP*
Don Brown, *Vice Pres*
EMP: 110 **EST:** 1979
SQ FT: 50,000
SALES (est): 26.5MM
SALES (corp-wide): 107.1MM **Privately Held**
WEB: www.dartentities.com
SIC: 4225 General warehousing
PA: Dart Transportation Service, A Corporation
    1430 S Eastman Ave Ste 1
    Commerce CA 90023
    323 981-8205

(P-12198)
DART WAREHOUSE CORPORATION (HQ)
1430 S Eastman Ave Ste 1, Commerce
(90023-4091)
P.O. Box 23931, Los Angeles (90023-0931)
PHONE.....................................323 264-1011
Robert Anthony Santich, *CEO*
Raoul Dedeaux, *President*
Ashok Aggarwal, *CFO*

Ashok Agarwal, *Treasurer*
Steve Roskelley, *Exec VP*
▲ **EMP:** 255 **EST:** 1938
SQ FT: 1,200,000
SALES (est): 58.6MM
SALES (corp-wide): 107.1MM **Privately Held**
WEB: www.dartentities.com
SIC: 4225 General warehousing
PA: Dart Transportation Service, A Corporation
    1430 S Eastman Ave Ste 1
    Commerce CA 90023
    323 981-8205

(P-12199)
DISTRIBUTION ALTERNATIVES INC
Also Called: Scholls
1990 S Cucamonga Ave, Ontario
(91761-5605)
PHONE.....................................909 673-1000
Mark Chase, *Manager*
EMP: 70
SALES (corp-wide): 104.4MM **Privately Held**
WEB: www.daserv.com
SIC: 4225 7319 General warehousing; distribution of advertising material or sample services
PA: Distribution Alternatives, Inc.
    6870 21st Ave
    Lino Lakes MN 55038
    651 636-9167

(P-12200)
DISTRIBUTION ALTERNATIVES INC
10621 6th St, Rancho Cucamonga
(91730-5900)
PHONE.....................................909 746-5600
EMP: 70
SALES (corp-wide): 104.4MM **Privately Held**
WEB: www.daserv.com
SIC: 4225 General warehousing
PA: Distribution Alternatives, Inc.
    6870 21st Ave
    Lino Lakes MN 55038
    651 636-9167

(P-12201)
EDGE SYSTEMS LLC
Also Called: Hydrafacial Company, The
3600 E Burnett St, Long Beach
(90815-1749)
PHONE.....................................562 391-2052
Evan Hoover, *Branch Mgr*
EMP: 30
SALES (corp-wide): 74.1MM **Privately Held**
WEB: www.hydrafacial.com
SIC: 4225 2844 General warehousing & storage; toilet preparations
PA: Edge Systems Llc
    2165 E Spring St
    Long Beach CA 90806
    800 603-4996

(P-12202)
ERLANGER DISTRIBUTION CTR INC
Also Called: Erlanger Sales
797 Palmyrita Ave, Riverside (92507-1811)
PHONE.....................................951 784-5147
David Erlanger, *CEO*
Claude M Erlanger, *President*
Doris Erlanger, *Vice Pres*
Steve Erlanger, *Vice Pres*
Larry McFarland, *General Mgr*
▲ **EMP:** 50 **EST:** 1946
SQ FT: 160,000
SALES (est): 8MM **Privately Held**
WEB: www.erlangerdc.com
SIC: 4225 5192 5099 5137 General warehousing; books; luggage; handbags

(P-12203)
EXEL INC
Also Called: Dhl Supply Chain
9211 Kaiser Way, Fontana (92335-2600)
PHONE.....................................909 350-6976
Dan Dantzler, *Info Tech Dir*
Jonathon Laperchia, *Opers Mgr*
EMP: 50

SALES (corp-wide): 79B **Privately Held**
WEB: www.onestoporderform.com
SIC: 4225 General warehousing
HQ: Exel Inc.
    360 Westar Blvd
    Westerville OH 43082
    614 865-8500

(P-12204)
F R T INTERNATIONAL INC
Also Called: Frontier Logistics Services
14439 S Avalon Blvd, Gardena
(90248-2005)
PHONE.....................................310 329-5700
Daniel Park, *Branch Mgr*
EMP: 65
SALES (corp-wide): 26.2MM **Privately Held**
WEB: www.frontier-logistics.com
SIC: 4225 4731 4412 4214 General warehousing; customhouse brokers; deep sea foreign transportation of freight; local trucking with storage
PA: F. R. T. International, Inc.
    1700 N Alameda St
    Compton CA 90222
    310 604-8208

(P-12205)
F R T INTERNATIONAL INC (PA)
Also Called: Frontier Logistics Services
1700 N Alameda St, Compton
(90222-4128)
PHONE.....................................310 604-8208
Brian Chung, *CEO*
Joyce Chung, *Admin Sec*
Timothy OH, *Manager*
◆ **EMP:** 80 **EST:** 1983
SQ FT: 200,000
SALES (est): 26.2MM **Privately Held**
SIC: 4225 4731 4412 4214 General warehousing; customhouse brokers; deep sea foreign transportation of freight; local trucking with storage

(P-12206)
FOAMEX LP
19201 S Reyes Ave, Compton
(90221-5807)
PHONE.....................................323 774-5600
Dean Offerman, *Engr R&D*
Gina Codd, *Human Res Dir*
EMP: 150 **Privately Held**
WEB: www.fxi.com
SIC: 4225 General warehousing & storage
PA: Foamex L.P.
    100 W Matsonford Rd # 5
    Wayne PA 19087

(P-12207)
FTDI WEST INC
3375 Enterprise Dr, Bloomington
(92316-3539)
PHONE.....................................909 473-1111
Alan Baum, *President*
Steve Rocha, *Vice Pres*
Erica Alfaro,
Paul Kardiban,
Teresa Wisuri, *Cust Mgr*
EMP: 80 **EST:** 2008
SALES (est): 11MM **Privately Held**
WEB: www.ftdiwest.com
SIC: 4225 Warehousing, self-storage

(P-12208)
GENERAL MOTORS LLC
11900 Cabernet Dr Dr1, Fontana
(92337-7707)
PHONE.....................................951 361-6302
EMP: 80 **Publicly Held**
SIC: 4225 Distribution Center
HQ: General Motors Llc
    300 Renaissance Ctr L1
    Detroit MI 48243
    -

(P-12209)
GENERATIONAL PROPERTIES INC
3141 E 44th St, Vernon (90058-2405)
PHONE.....................................323 583-3163
Angelo V Antoci, *Principal*
Sam Perricone, *Admin Sec*
EMP: 291 **EST:** 1950
SQ FT: 4,000

SALES (est): 26.5MM **Privately Held**
SIC: 4225 General warehousing & storage

(P-12210)
GXO LOGISTICS SUPPLY CHAIN INC
3520 S Cactus Ave, Bloomington
(92316-3816)
PHONE.....................................336 309-6201
Christopher Cotto, *Manager*
EMP: 1000
SALES (corp-wide): 16.2B **Publicly Held**
SIC: 4225 General warehousing & storage
HQ: Gxo Logistics Supply Chain, Inc.
    4035 Piedmont Pkwy
    High Point NC 27265
    336 882-8159

(P-12211)
GXO LOGISTICS SUPPLY CHAIN INC
2163 S Riverside Ave, Colton (92324)
PHONE.....................................951 512-1201
Miguel Moreno, *Branch Mgr*
EMP: 100
SALES (corp-wide): 16.2B **Publicly Held**
SIC: 4225 General warehousing
HQ: Gxo Logistics Supply Chain, Inc.
    4035 Piedmont Pkwy
    High Point NC 27265
    336 882-8159

(P-12212)
H RAUVEL INC (PA)
Also Called: Nova Container Freight Station
1710 E Sepulveda Blvd, Carson
(90745-6142)
PHONE.....................................310 604-0060
Hector R Velasco, *President*
Mike Lee, *Info Tech Mgr*
Holly Magdalena, *Accounting Mgr*
Dennis Haynes, *Manager*
Vicky Ruste, *Manager*
▼ **EMP:** 70
SQ FT: 258,000
SALES (est): 32.3MM **Privately Held**
WEB: www.novafreight.net
SIC: 4225 4731 General warehousing; agents, shipping; brokers, shipping; freight consolidation; railroad freight agency

(P-12213)
HAULAWAY STORAGE CNTRS INC
11292 Western Ave, Stanton (90680-2912)
P.O. Box 125 (90680-0125)
PHONE.....................................800 826-9040
Clifford Robert Ronnenberg, *CEO*
Daniel Letto, *President*
Joyce Amato, *CFO*
Tina Stelzer, *Vice Pres*
John Boyle, *Manager*
EMP: 482 **EST:** 2000
SALES (est): 18.5MM
SALES (corp-wide): 335.2MM **Privately Held**
WEB: www.haulaway.com
SIC: 4225 General warehousing & storage
PA: Cr&R Incorporated
    11292 Western Ave
    Stanton CA 90680
    714 826-9049

(P-12214)
HOUDINI INC
6311 Knott Ave, Buena Park (90620-1021)
PHONE.....................................714 228-4406
EMP: 125
SALES (corp-wide): 71.8MM **Privately Held**
SIC: 4225 General Warehouse/Storage
PA: Houdini, Inc.
    4225 N Palm St
    Fullerton CA 92835
    714 525-0325

(P-12215)
KKW TRUCKING INC (PA)
3100 Pomona Blvd, Pomona (91768-3230)
P.O. Box 2960 (91769-2960)
PHONE.....................................909 869-1200
Dennis W Firestone, *CEO*
Steve Benninghoff, *COO*
Lynnette Brown, *CFO*

Susan Dancel, *Office Mgr*
Brandon Krueger, *Info Tech Dir*
EMP: 180 **EST:** 1962
SQ FT: 150,000
SALES (est): 72.2MM **Privately Held**
WEB: www.kkwtrucks.com
SIC: 4225 4231 4226 4214 General warehousing & storage; trucking terminal facilities; special warehousing & storage; local trucking with storage

(P-12216)
KOHLS CORPORATION
890 E Mill St, San Bernardino (92408-1614)
PHONE..................................909 382-4300
Justin Delgadillo, *Manager*
Moni Knox, *Associate*
EMP: 418 **Publicly Held**
WEB: www.corporate.kohls.com
SIC: 4225 General warehousing
PA: Kohl's Corporation
N56w17000 Ridgewood Dr
Menomonee Falls WI 53051

(P-12217)
KROGER CO
Also Called: Ralphs Logistics - Compton DC
2201 S Wilmington Ave, Compton (90220-5448)
PHONE..................................859 630-6959
Lisa Allen, *Branch Mgr*
EMP: 500
SALES (corp-wide): 132.5B **Publicly Held**
WEB: www.thekrogerco.com
SIC: 4225 General warehousing & storage
PA: The Kroger Co
1014 Vine St Ste 1000
Cincinnati OH 45202
513 762-4000

(P-12218)
LEAN SUPPLY SOLUTIONS AMER INC (PA)
26871 San Bernardino Ave, Redlands (92374-5052)
PHONE..................................844 310-5252
Tomasz Krzepkowski, *President*
Robert Rogut, *Admin Sec*
Carlos Murray, *Opers Mgr*
EMP: 72 **EST:** 2014
SALES (est): 5.3MM **Privately Held**
WEB: www.leansupplysolutions.com
SIC: 4225 4213 General warehousing; trucking, except local

(P-12219)
LMD INTGRTED LGISTICS SVCS INC (PA)
3136 E Victoria St, Compton (90221-5618)
PHONE..................................310 605-5100
Louis M Diblosi Jr, *CEO*
Marilyn Zakis, *CFO*
Carolyn Rossi, *Officer*
Martha Mendoza, *Administration*
Carlos Porras, *Accounting Mgr*
EMP: 65 **EST:** 2003
SQ FT: 120,000
SALES (est): 16.2MM **Privately Held**
WEB: www.lmdlogistics.com
SIC: 4225 General warehousing

(P-12220)
LOCKHEED MARTIN CORPORATION
Also Called: Rotary and Miission Systems
South Loop Bldg 821, Fort Irwin (92310)
PHONE..................................760 386-2572
Kurt Pinkerton, *Manager*
EMP: 142 **Publicly Held**
WEB: www.lockheedmartin.com
SIC: 4225 General warehousing & storage
PA: Lockheed Martin Corporation
6801 Rockledge Dr
Bethesda MD 20817

(P-12221)
M BLOCK & SONS INC
26875 Pioneer Ave, Redlands (92374-2026)
PHONE..................................909 335-6684
EMP: 200

SALES (corp-wide): 283MM **Privately Held**
WEB: www.mblock.com
SIC: 4225 General Warehouse/Storage
PA: M. Block & Sons, Inc.
5020 W 73rd St
Bedford Park IL 60638
708 728-8400

(P-12222)
MIDAS EXPRESS LOS ANGELES INC
11854 Alameda St, Lynwood (90262-4019)
PHONE..................................310 609-0366
Jack Wu, *President*
Jacky Strong, *Shareholder*
▲ **EMP:** 200 **EST:** 1995
SQ FT: 90,000
SALES (est): 16.2MM **Privately Held**
WEB: www.midasexpress.com
SIC: 4225 4731 4226 General warehousing & storage; freight forwarding; textile warehousing

(P-12223)
MITSUBISHI WAREHOUSE CAL CORP
3040 E Victoria St, Compton (90221-5617)
PHONE..................................310 886-5500
Soichiro Sam Orihara, *President*
▲ **EMP:** 58 **EST:** 1970
SQ FT: 750,000
SALES (est): 4.1MM **Privately Held**
WEB: www.mwc-corp.com
SIC: 4225 General warehousing
PA: Mitsubishi Logistics Corporation
1-19-1, Nihombashi
Chuo-Ku TKY 103-0

(P-12224)
MOTIVATIONAL MARKETING INC
Also Called: Motivational Fulfillmen
15785 Mountain Ave, Chino (91708-9131)
PHONE..................................909 517-2200
Hal Altman, *President*
Anthony Altman, *Principal*
Melanie Altman, *Principal*
Vanessa Saenz, *Accounts Exec*
EMP: 76
SQ FT: 50,500 **Privately Held**
WEB: www.mfals.com
SIC: 4225 General warehousing & storage
PA: Motivational Marketing, Inc.
15820 Euclid Ave
Chino CA 91708

(P-12225)
MSBLOUS LLC
11671 Dayton Dr, Rancho Cucamonga (91730-5526)
PHONE..................................909 929-9689
Jiayi CU, *Manager*
EMP: 84
SALES (corp-wide): 400K **Privately Held**
SIC: 4225 General warehousing & storage
PA: Msblous Llc
8 The Grn Ste 7360
Dover DE 19901
909 908-1889

(P-12226)
NEOVIA LOGISTICS DIST LP
5750 E Francis St, Ontario (91761-3607)
PHONE..................................909 657-4900
EMP: 87
SALES (corp-wide): 672.5MM **Privately Held**
WEB: www.neovialogistics.com
SIC: 4225 General warehousing & storage
HQ: Neovia Logistics Distribution, Lp
6363 N State Highway # 700
Irving TX 75038

(P-12227)
OSRAM SYLVANIA INC
1651 S Archibald Ave, Ontario (91761-7651)
PHONE..................................909 923-3003
Wayne Cansford, *Branch Mgr*
EMP: 143

SALES (corp-wide): 4.1B **Privately Held**
WEB: www.osram.us
SIC: 4225 Warehousing, self-storage
HQ: Osram Sylvania Inc
200 Ballardvale St # 305
Wilmington MA 01887
978 570-3000

(P-12228)
PATINA FREIGHT INC
Also Called: Dura Freight Lines
525 S Lemon Ave, Walnut (91789-2912)
PHONE..................................909 444-1025
Clint Schaffer, *Manager*
Roger Sanghavi, *Planning*
Brett Johnson, *Technical Staff*
Michael Martin, *Natl Sales Mgr*
Denise Myers, *Manager*
EMP: 63
SALES (corp-wide): 56.4MM **Privately Held**
SIC: 4225 General warehousing
PA: Patina Freight, Inc.
20405 Business Pkwy
Walnut CA 91789
909 595-8100

(P-12229)
PERFORMANCE TEAM FRT SYS INC
Also Called: PERFORMANCE TEAM FREIGHT SYSTEM, INC.
12816 Shoemaker Ave, Santa Fe Springs (90670-6346)
PHONE..................................562 741-1300
Bob Kaplan, *Branch Mgr*
Brian Briggs, *Opers Dir*
Sonya Medlin, *Opers Dir*
Gary Kendle, *Director*
EMP: 55
SALES (corp-wide): 1.2MM **Privately Held**
WEB: www.performanceteam.net
SIC: 4225 4731 4213 General warehousing; freight transportation arrangement; trucking, except local
HQ: Performance Team Llc
2240 E Maple Ave
El Segundo CA 90245
562 345-2200

(P-12230)
PERFORMANCE TEAM LLC
Also Called: Gale/Triangle
401 Westmont Dr, San Pedro (90731-1011)
PHONE..................................310 241-4100
Scott Pearigan, *Manager*
Jim Snodgrass, *VP Business*
Susan McHugh, *Executive Asst*
Linda Kaplan, *Admin Sec*
Michael Hendrie, *Technical Staff*
EMP: 91
SALES (corp-wide): 1.2MM **Privately Held**
WEB: www.performanceteam.net
SIC: 4225 General warehousing
HQ: Performance Team Llc
2240 E Maple Ave
El Segundo CA 90245
562 345-2200

(P-12231)
PHYSICAL DISTRIBUTION SVC INC (PA)
16000 Heron Ave, La Mirada (90638-5513)
P.O. Box 60622, Los Angeles (90060-0622)
PHONE..................................323 881-0886
Trygve W Lodrup Jr, *President*
▲ **EMP:** 54 **EST:** 1969
SQ FT: 120,000
SALES (est): 8.4MM **Privately Held**
WEB: www.physicaldistributionservice.com
SIC: 4225 4214 General warehousing; local trucking with storage

(P-12232)
PILOT INC (PA)
Also Called: Pilot Automotive
13000 Temple Ave, City of Industry (91746-1416)
PHONE..................................626 937-6988
Tim Lebeau, *CEO*
Jenna Jefferies, *Vice Pres*
Aaron Lyle, *Manager*
▼ **EMP:** 93 **EST:** 1994
SQ FT: 407,000

SALES (est): 27MM **Privately Held**
WEB: www.pilot.com
SIC: 4225 5015 General warehousing & storage; automotive accessories, used

(P-12233)
PRECISE DISTRIBUTION INC
12215 Holly St, Riverside (92509-2315)
PHONE..................................951 367-1037
Debra Catherine Martinez, *CEO*
Levone Myro, *Vice Pres*
Ricardo Cazessus, *Admin Sec*
Alicia Zavala, *Manager*
◆ **EMP:** 50 **EST:** 1994
SQ FT: 350,000
SALES (est): 13.2MM **Privately Held**
SIC: 4225 General warehousing & storage

(P-12234)
PREMIUM TRNSP SVCS INC (PA)
Also Called: Ttsi
18735 S Ferris Pl, Rancho Dominguez (90220-6405)
PHONE..................................310 816-0260
Victor Larosa, *CEO*
Victor La Rosa, *CEO*
Tom Franklin, *CFO*
Bill Allen, *Exec VP*
Scott Freeborn, *Vice Pres*
EMP: 149 **EST:** 1997
SQ FT: 10,000
SALES (est): 53MM **Privately Held**
WEB: www.tts-i.com
SIC: 4225 5399 4212 General warehousing & storage; warehouse club stores; local trucking, without storage

(P-12235)
PS LPT PROPERTIES INVESTORS (HQ)
701 Western Ave, Glendale (91201-2349)
PHONE..................................818 244-8080
John Reyes, *Director*
EMP: 78 **EST:** 1996
SALES (est): 38.6MM
SALES (corp-wide): 2.9B **Publicly Held**
WEB: www.psbusinessparks.com
SIC: 4225 Warehousing, self-storage
PA: Public Storage
701 Western Ave
Glendale CA 91201
818 244-8080

(P-12236)
QUAKER OATS COMPANY
2501 E Orangethorpe Ave, Fullerton (92831-5333)
PHONE..................................714 526-8800
EMP: 50
SALES (corp-wide): 66.4B **Publicly Held**
SIC: 4225 5149 General Warehouse/Storage Whol Groceries
HQ: The Quaker Oats Company
555 W Monroe St Fl 1
Chicago IL 60661
312 821-1000

(P-12237)
QUILL LLC
Also Called: Quill Distribution Center
1500 S Dupont Ave, Ontario (91761-1406)
PHONE..................................909 390-0600
Rocky Velasquez, *Manager*
Susan Kinowski, *Info Tech Mgr*
Maria Todorova, *Info Tech Mgr*
Marcelino Cruz, *Database Admin*
Lisa Erickson, *Project Mgr*
EMP: 70 **Privately Held**
WEB: www.quill.com
SIC: 4225 General warehousing & storage
HQ: Quill Llc
100 Schelter Rd
Lincolnshire IL 60069
800 982-3400

(P-12238)
RADIAL SOUTH LP
2225 Alder Ave, Rialto (92377-8513)
PHONE..................................610 491-7000
EMP: 461
SALES (corp-wide): 2.6B **Privately Held**
WEB: www.radial.com
SIC: 4225 General warehousing

HQ: Radial South, L.P.
935 1st Ave
King Of Prussia PA 19406
610 491-7000

(P-12239)
ROADEX AMERICA INC
2132 E Dominguez St Ste B, Long Beach
(90810-1026)
PHONE....................................310 878-9800
Nicholas Sim, *President*
Rob Chan, *CFO*
Russle Loh, *Vice Pres*
Johnny Kwan, *Principal*
Kamischke Chad, *Regional Mgr*
▲ EMP: 100 EST: 2001
SALES (est): 24.7MM Privately Held
WEB: www.roadexamerica.com
SIC: 4225 5113 4789 General warehous-
ing & storage; industrial & personal serv-
ice paper; cargo loading & unloading
services

(P-12240)
**RPM CONSOLIDATED SERVICES
INC (HQ)**
1901 Raymer Ave, Fullerton (92833-2512)
PHONE....................................714 388-3500
Shawn K Duke, *CEO*
Dan Laporte, *Vice Pres*
Chad Duke, *General Mgr*
Ian Smith, *Admin Asst*
Bill Mahoney, *Technician*
▲ EMP: 100 EST: 2002
SQ FT: 15,000
SALES (est): 109.8MM
SALES (corp-wide): 1.1B Privately Held
WEB: www.odysseylogistics.com
SIC: 4225 4214 General warehousing &
storage; local trucking with storage
PA: Odyssey Logistics & Technology Cor-
poration
100 Reserve Rd Ste Cc210
Danbury CT 06810
203 448-3900

(P-12241)
**SCHAFER BROS TRNSF PANO
MVERS (PA)**
Also Called: Schafer Logistics
1981 E 213th St, Carson (90810-1202)
PHONE....................................310 835-7231
Gary A Schafer, *President*
Richard W Schafer, *Vice Pres*
Rick Schafer, *Manager*
Jim Schafer, *Accounts Mgr*
▲ EMP: 55
SQ FT: 402,000
SALES (est): 10.4MM Privately Held
WEB: www.schaferlogistics.com
SIC: 4225 4214 4213 General warehous-
ing; local trucking with storage; heavy
hauling

(P-12242)
SCHNEIDER ELECTRIC USA INC
Also Called: Pelco By Schneider Electric
14725 Monte Vista Ave, Chino
(91710-5732)
PHONE....................................909 438-2295
Jessie Ortega, *Director*
EMP: 100
SALES (corp-wide): 177.9K Privately
Held
WEB: www.se.com
SIC: 4225 General warehousing & storage
HQ: Schneider Electric Usa, Inc.
201 Wshngton St Ext Ste 2
Boston MA 02108
978 975-9600

(P-12243)
**SMARTSTOP SELF STORAGE
(DH)**
Also Called: Smartstop Op
111 Corporate Dr Ste 120, Ladera Ranch
(92694-1199)
PHONE....................................949 429-6600
Spencer Kirk, *Partner*
EMP: 78 EST: 2015
SALES (est): 2.5MM
SALES (corp-wide): 1.3B Publicly Held
WEB: www.smartstopselfstorage.com
SIC: 4225 Warehousing, self-storage

(P-12244)
**SMARTSTOP SELF STORAGE
INC (HQ)**
111 Corporate Dr Ste 120, Ladera Ranch
(92694-1199)
PHONE....................................949 429-6600
Wayne Johnson, *Principal*
EMP: 78 EST: 2014
SALES (est): 2.7MM
SALES (corp-wide): 3.4MM Privately
Held
WEB: www.strategicreit.com
SIC: 4225 Warehousing, self-storage
PA: Smartstop Asset Management, Llc
10 Terrace Rd
Ladera Ranch CA 92694
949 429-6600

(P-12245)
**SOUTH BAY PUBLIC
WAREHOUSE**
490 W Manville St, Compton (90220-5618)
PHONE....................................310 637-1133
William Simonoff, *President*
Christopher Simonoff, *Vice Pres*
Helen Rittman, *Admin Sec*
Bruce Hearn, *Regl Sales Mgr*
M McAstaneda, *Director*
EMP: 61 EST: 1948
SQ FT: 80,000
SALES (est): 2MM Privately Held
WEB: www.sbwarehouse.com
SIC: 4225 General warehousing

(P-12246)
**SPROUTS FARMERS MARKET
INC**
280 De Berry St, Colton (92324-4404)
PHONE....................................888 577-7688
EMP: 190
SALES (corp-wide): 6.4B Publicly Held
WEB: www.sprouts.com
SIC: 4225 5411 General warehousing &
storage; grocery stores
PA: Sprouts Farmers Market, Inc.
5455 E High St Ste 111
Phoenix AZ 85054
480 814-8016

(P-12247)
**SST IV 8020 LAS VGAS BLVD S
LL**
10 Terrace Rd, Ladera Ranch
(92694-1182)
PHONE....................................949 429-6600
H Michael Schwartz, *Mng Member*
Wayne Johnson,
Matt Lopez,
Paula Mathews,
Michael McClure,
EMP: 99 EST: 2018
SALES (est): 2.5MM Privately Held
WEB: www.smartstopselfstorage.com
SIC: 4225 Warehousing, self-storage

(P-12248)
**STATES LOGISTICS SERVICES
INC**
7151 Cate Dr, Buena Park (90621-1881)
PHONE....................................714 523-1276
EMP: 56 Privately Held
WEB: www.stateslogistics.com
SIC: 4225 General warehousing
PA: States Logistics Services, Inc.
5650 Dolly Ave
Buena Park CA 90621

(P-12249)
**STORQUEST SELF STORAGE
(HQ)**
201 Wilshire Blvd Ste 102, Santa Monica
(90401-1220)
P.O. Box 2034 (90406-2034)
PHONE....................................310 451-2130
William Hobin, *Principal*
Storquest Torrance, *Property Mgr*
Zachary Kim, *Director*
EMP: 78 EST: 2001
SALES (est): 45.4MM
SALES (corp-wide): 63.3MM Privately
Held
WEB: www.storquest.com
SIC: 4225 Warehousing, self-storage

PA: The William Warren Group Inc
201 Wilshire Blvd Ste 102
Santa Monica CA 90401
310 451-2130

(P-12250)
**TANIMURA ANTLE FRESH
FOODS INC**
761 Commercial Ave, Oxnard
(93030-7233)
PHONE....................................805 483-2358
Sergio Romero, *Manager*
EMP: 224
SALES (corp-wide): 321.4MM Privately
Held
WEB: www.taproduce.com
SIC: 4225 Warehousing, self-storage
PA: Tanimura & Antle Fresh Foods, Inc.
1 Harris Rd
Salinas CA 93908
831 455-2950

(P-12251)
TARGET CORPORATION
Also Called: T.com Ontario Fc T-9479
1505 S Haven Ave, Ontario (91761-2928)
PHONE....................................909 937-5500
Jacqueline Yee, *Branch Mgr*
Sara Vick, *Opers Staff*
Gaetano Chiurillo, *Sales Staff*
Kevin Jackson,
Lisa Mullins, *Asst Director*
EMP: 177
SALES (corp-wide): 93.5B Publicly Held
WEB: www.target.com
SIC: 4225 General warehousing & storage
PA: Target Corporation
1000 Nicollet Mall
Minneapolis MN 55403
612 304-6073

(P-12252)
TAYLORED SERVICES LLC (DH)
1495 E Locust St, Ontario (91761-4570)
PHONE....................................909 510-4800
Jim Deveau, *CEO*
Mark Chamberlain, *Controller*
▲ EMP: 80 EST: 1992
SQ FT: 330,000
SALES (est): 100MM
SALES (corp-wide): 224MM Privately
Held
WEB: www.tayloredservices.com
SIC: 4225 4731 General warehousing &
storage; agents, shipping
HQ: Taylored Services Holdings, Llc
1495 E Locust St
Ontario CA 91761
909 510-4800

(P-12253)
**TAYLORED SERVICES
HOLDINGS LLC (HQ)**
1495 E Locust St, Ontario (91761-4570)
PHONE....................................909 510-4800
Bill Butler, *CEO*
Michael Yusko, *CFO*
Mike Yusko, *CFO*
Jesse Fernandez, *Opers Staff*
Ralph Marez, *Manager*
EMP: 80 EST: 2012
SQ FT: 330,000
SALES (est): 179.4MM
SALES (corp-wide): 224MM Privately
Held
WEB: www.tayloredservices.com
SIC: 4225 General warehousing & storage
PA: Taylored Services Parent Co. Inc.
1495 E Locust St
Ontario CA 91761
909 510-4800

(P-12254)
TONYS EXPRESS INC (PA)
10613 Jasmine St, Fontana (92337-8241)
PHONE....................................909 427-8700
George Raluy, *President*
Anthony Raluy, *Exec VP*
Ken Fasola, *Vice Pres*
Jamie Wasserman, *Terminal Mgr*
Tom Kister, *Manager*
▲ EMP: 127 EST: 1954
SQ FT: 180,000

SALES (est): 17.2MM Privately Held
WEB: www.tonysexpress.com
SIC: 4225 4214 4212 General warehousing & storage; local trucking with storage;
local trucking, without storage

(P-12255)
UNIS LLC
19914 S Via Baron, Rancho Dominguez
(90220-6104)
PHONE....................................310 747-7388
Omar Garcia, *Branch Mgr*
Carlos Morales, *Opers Staff*
EMP: 90
SALES (corp-wide): 194.5MM Privately
Held
SIC: 4225 General warehousing & storage
PA: Unis, Llc
218 Machlin Ct Ste A
Walnut CA 91789
909 839-2600

(P-12256)
**UNIVERSAL LOGISTICS SYSTEM
INC (DH)**
2850 Del Amo Blvd, Carson (90810)
P.O. Box 7547, Long Beach (90807-0547)
PHONE....................................310 631-0800
Richard A Ferguson, *Principal*
Richard Ferguson, *Exec VP*
EMP: 78 EST: 1986
SQ FT: 200,000
SALES (est): 15MM Privately Held
WEB: www.cds-net.com
SIC: 4225 4212 General warehousing;
local trucking, without storage

(P-12257)
**UNIVERSAL PACKG SYSTEMS
INC**
Also Called: Paklab
14570 Monte Vista Ave, Chino
(91710-5743)
PHONE....................................909 517-2442
EMP: 125
SALES (corp-wide): 359.7MM Privately
Held
SIC: 4225 General Warehousing And Stor-
age, Nsk
PA: Universal Packaging Systems, Inc.
380 Townline Rd Ste 130
Hauppauge NY 91710
631 543-2277

(P-12258)
**VANGUARD LGISTICS SVCS
USA INC (DH)**
2665 E Del Amo Blvd, E Rncho Dmngz
(90221-6003)
PHONE....................................310 637-3700
Jeff Alinsangan, *Treasurer*
Jenny Koh, *Executive*
Tina Hansen, *Technical Staff*
Nigel Fost, *Finance Mgr*
Sandra Lerma, *Analyst*
◆ EMP: 107 EST: 1998
SALES (est): 27MM
SALES (corp-wide): 227.7MM Privately
Held
WEB: www.vanguardlogistics.com
SIC: 4225 General warehousing & storage
HQ: Vanguard Logistics Services (Usa),
Inc.
5000 Arprt Plz Dr Ste 200
Long Beach CA 90815
310 847-3000

(P-12259)
**WEST COAST DISTRIBUTION
INC (PA)**
2602 E 37th St, Vernon (90058-1723)
PHONE....................................323 588-6508
Jilali Elbasri, *President*
Jilali El Basri, *President*
Glenn Lehrich, *CFO*
Janet Enriquez, *Office Mgr*
Martha Gatica, *Administration*
▲ EMP: 87 EST: 2005
SALES (est): 30MM Privately Held
WEB: www.montagefulfillment.com
SIC: 4225 4789 General warehousing &
storage; pipeline terminal facilities, inde-
pendently operated

▲ = Import ▼=Export
◆ =Import/Export

(P-12260)
WESTCOAST WAREHOUSING LLC
100 W Manville St, Rancho Dominguez (90220-5612)
PHONE...............................310 537-9958
Jay Patel,
Nikesh Chand, *Manager*
EMP: 50 **EST:** 2002
SQ FT: 61,440 **Privately Held**
WEB: www.westcoastwarehouse.com
SIC: 4225 General warehousing

(P-12261)
WORLD CLASS DISTRIBUTION INC
800 S Shamrock Ave, Monrovia (91016-6346)
PHONE...............................909 574-4140
Charles Pilliter, *Branch Mgr*
EMP: 68
SALES (corp-wide): 355.8K **Privately Held**
SIC: 4225 General warehousing & storage
HQ: World Class Distribution Inc.
10288 Calabash Ave
Fontana CA 92335

(P-12262)
WORLD CLASS DISTRIBUTION INC
343 S Lena Rd, San Bernardino (92408-1601)
PHONE...............................909 574-4140
EMP: 68
SALES (corp-wide): 355.8K **Privately Held**
SIC: 4225 General warehousing & storage
HQ: World Class Distribution Inc.
10288 Calabash Ave
Fontana CA 92335

(P-12263)
WORLD CLASS DISTRIBUTION INC (DH)
Also Called: Trader Joe Fontana Warehouse
10288 Calabash Ave, Fontana (92335-5272)
PHONE...............................909 574-4140
Danny Bane, *CEO*
Robert Camarena, *President*
Sharon A Drabeck, *Corp Secy*
Barry Sutliff, *Info Tech Mgr*
Ronda Walker, *Payroll Mgr*
EMP: 242 **EST:** 2009
SALES (est): 342.7MM
SALES (corp-wide): 355.8K **Privately Held**
WEB: www.livingtraderjoes.com
SIC: 4225 General warehousing
HQ: Trader Joe's Company
800 S Shamrock Ave
Monrovia CA 91016
626 599-3700

(P-12264)
WTI DISTRIBUTION INC
5491 E Francis St, Ontario (91761-3604)
PHONE...............................909 597-8410
Marcella Harpenau, *Officer*
Kyle Parisi, *Officer*
Marcy Wti, *Opers Mgr*
Tina Parisi, *Representative*
EMP: 60 **EST:** 2011
SALES (est): 6.6MM **Privately Held**
WEB: www.wtidi.com
SIC: 4225 General warehousing

4226 Special Warehousing & Storage, NEC

(P-12265)
ACCESS INFO HOLDINGS LLC
12135 Davis St, Moreno Valley (92557-6369)
PHONE...............................909 459-1417
EMP: 208

SALES (corp-wide): 107.8MM **Privately Held**
WEB: www.accesscorp.com
SIC: 4226 Document & office records storage
PA: Access Information Holdings, Llc
500 Unicorn Park Dr # 500
Woburn MA 01801
925 583-0100

(P-12266)
DOMINOS PIZZA LLC
301 S Rockefeller Ave, Ontario (91761-7865)
PHONE...............................909 390-1990
EMP: 120
SALES (corp-wide): 4.1B **Publicly Held**
WEB: www.dominos.com
SIC: 4226 4222 Special Warehouse/Storage Refrigeration Warehouse/Storage
HQ: Domino's Pizza Llc
30 Frank Lloyd Wright Dr
Ann Arbor MI 48105
734 930-3030

(P-12267)
EXPRESS IMAGING SERVICES INC
1805 W 208th St Ste 202, Torrance (90501-1808)
PHONE...............................888 846-8804
Paul Terry, *President*
Kenny Ly, *Vice Pres*
Tan Ly, *CIO*
Anni Ly, *Manager*
EMP: 100 **EST:** 2004
SQ FT: 10,000
SALES (est): 13MM **Privately Held**
WEB: www.eiscallcenter.com
SIC: 4226 Document & office records storage

(P-12268)
IMPERIAL CFS INC
1000 Francisco St, Torrance (90502-1216)
PHONE...............................310 768-8188
Tong Hsing Hsu, *CEO*
Kathy Hsu, *CFO*
Anne Su, *General Mgr*
I-Hsin Chen, *Admin Sec*
David Hsu, *Accounts Exec*
EMP: 50 **EST:** 1994
SQ FT: 200,000
SALES (est): 24.1MM **Privately Held**
WEB: www.imperialcfs.com
SIC: 4226 Document & office records storage

(P-12269)
KW INTERNATIONAL INC
18724 S Broadwick St, Rancho Dominguez (90220-6426)
PHONE...............................213 703-6914
Allen Lee, *Branch Mgr*
EMP: 52 **Privately Held**
WEB: www.kwinternational.com
SIC: 4226 8744 4731 Special warehousing & storage; facilities support services; freight forwarding
PA: Kw International, Inc.
18655 Bishop Ave
Carson CA 90746

(P-12270)
MCLANE FOODSERVICE DIST INC
Also Called: Mbm
1051 Wineville Ave # 100, Ontario (91764-6901)
PHONE...............................252 955-9547
Fred Lowrey, *Branch Mgr*
EMP: 53
SALES (corp-wide): 245.5B **Publicly Held**
WEB: www.mbmcorp.com
SIC: 5963 4226 Direct selling establishments; special warehousing & storage
HQ: Mclane Foodservice Distribution, Inc.
2641 Meadowbrook Rd
Rocky Mount NC 27801
252 985-7200

(P-12271)
PACIFIC CHEMICAL DIST CORP (HQ)
6250 Caballero Blvd, Buena Park (90620-1124)
PHONE...............................714 521-7161
James N Tausz, *President*
Rhonda Tausz, *Corp Secy*
James Banister, *Vice Pres*
◆ **EMP:** 100 **EST:** 1978
SQ FT: 144,000
SALES (est): 20MM
SALES (corp-wide): 445.5MM **Privately Held**
WEB: www.pacchem.com
SIC: 4226 Special warehousing & storage
PA: Quantix Scs, Inc.
24 Waterway Ave Ste 450
The Woodlands TX 77380
800 542-8058

(P-12272)
WOOD SPACE INDUSTRIES INC
429 W Levers Pl, Orange (92867-3620)
PHONE...............................714 996-4552
David E Reed, *President*
Gary Broyles, *Shareholder*
Jeff Horn, *Shareholder*
EMP: 15 **EST:** 1970
SALES (est): 1MM **Privately Held**
WEB: www.amexport.net
SIC: 4226 2441 4731 2449 Special warehousing & storage; nailed wood boxes & shook; freight forwarding; wood containers; packaging & labeling services

4412 Deep Sea Foreign Transportation Of Freight

(P-12273)
DAMCO USA INC
11900 Riverside Dr, Jurupa Valley (91752-1002)
PHONE...............................951 360-4940
EMP: 136
SALES (corp-wide): 1.2MM **Privately Held**
SIC: 4412 Deep sea foreign transportation of freight
HQ: Damco Usa Inc.
180 Park Ave Ste 105
Florham Park NJ 07932

(P-12274)
FOSS MARITIME CO INC
Berth 35 Pier D, Long Beach (90802)
PHONE...............................562 435-0171
Steve Scalzo, *President*
Bruno Kalmeta, *Master*
EMP: 77 **EST:** 1936
SQ FT: 50,000
SALES (est): 8.8MM
SALES (corp-wide): 2B **Privately Held**
WEB: www.foss.com
SIC: 4412 Deep sea foreign transportation of freight
HQ: Foss Maritime Company, Llc.
450 Alaskan Way S Ste 706
Seattle WA 98104
206 281-3800

(P-12275)
GOLDEN STATE HOLDG GROUP CORP (PA)
23624 Falcons View Dr, Diamond Bar (91765-3335)
PHONE...............................909 860-7668
Peter Jiang, *President*
Henry F Hsieh, *General Counsel*
EMP: 697 **EST:** 1993
SALES (est): 14MM **Privately Held**
SIC: 4412 4731 8711 Deep sea foreign transportation of freight; agents, shipping; engineering services

4424 Deep Sea Domestic Transportation Of Freight

(P-12276)
PASHA STEVEDORING TERMINALS LP
802 Suth Fries Ave La Hbr, Wilmington (90744)
PHONE...............................415 927-6353
Jeff Burgin, *Senior VP*
Jackie Bailey, *Treasurer*
Braxton Craghill, *Controller*
▲ **EMP:** 54 **EST:** 1992
SALES (est): 19.6MM
SALES (corp-wide): 632.2MM **Privately Held**
WEB: www.psterminals.com
SIC: 4424 4412 Deep sea domestic transportation of freight; deep sea foreign transportation of freight
PA: The Pasha Group
4040 Civic Center Dr # 350
San Rafael CA 94903
415 927-6400

(P-12277)
POLAR TANKERS INC
60 Berth, San Pedro (90731-7252)
PHONE...............................310 519-8260
Chris Adams, *Branch Mgr*
EMP: 210
SALES (corp-wide): 19.2B **Publicly Held**
WEB: www.polartankers.conocophillips.com
SIC: 4424 Deep sea domestic transportation of freight
HQ: Polar Tankers, Inc.
300 Oceangate
Long Beach CA 90802
562 388-1400

(P-12278)
POLAR TANKERS INC (DH)
300 Oceangate, Long Beach (90802-6801)
PHONE...............................562 388-1400
John R Hennon, *President*
George McShea, *Vice Pres*
John L Sullivan, *Vice Pres*
▲ **EMP:** 75 **EST:** 1956
SALES (est): 71.8MM
SALES (corp-wide): 19.2B **Publicly Held**
WEB: www.polartankers.conocophillips.com
SIC: 4424 4412 Deep sea domestic transportation of freight; deep sea foreign transportation of freight
HQ: Conocophillips Company
925 N Eldridge Pkwy
Houston TX 77079
281 293-1000

4481 Deep Sea Transportation Of Passengers

(P-12279)
PRINCESS CRUISE LINES LTD (HQ)
Also Called: Princess Cruises
24305 Town Center Dr, Santa Clarita (91355-1307)
PHONE...............................661 753-0000
Jan Swartz, *CEO*
Nina Kass, *President*
John Padgett, *President*
Natalya Leahy, *CFO*
Corey Aungst, *Officer*
◆ **EMP:** 2000 **EST:** 1965
SALES (est): 1.5B
SALES (corp-wide): 2.4B **Privately Held**
WEB: www.princess.com
SIC: 4481 4725 7011 Deep sea passenger transportation, except ferry; tour operators; hotels
PA: Carnival Plc
Carnival House
Southampton HANTS SO15
344 338-8650

PRODUCTS & SVCS

4489 Water Transport Of Passengers, NEC

(P-12280)
CATALINA CHANNEL EXPRESS INC (HQ)
Also Called: Catalina Express Cruises
385 E Swinford St, San Pedro (90731-1002)
PHONE.................................310 519-7971
Greg Bombard, *President*
Douglas Bombard, *Ch of Bd*
Kate Mirkovich, *Human Res Dir*
EMP: 200 **EST:** 1981
SQ FT: 20,000
SALES (est): 54.1MM **Privately Held**
WEB: www.catalinaexpress.com
SIC: 4489 Excursion boat operators
PA: Bombard Marine & Resort Management Services, Inc.
95 Berth
San Pedro CA 90731
310 519-7971

(P-12281)
CATALINA CHANNEL EXPRESS INC
Also Called: Catalina Express
95 Berth, San Pedro (90731-3384)
PHONE.................................310 510-1212
Judy Whitman, *Branch Mgr*
EMP: 58
SALES (corp-wide): 54.1MM **Privately Held**
WEB: www.catalinaexpress.com
SIC: 4489 Excursion boat operators
HQ: Catalina Channel Express, Inc.
385 E Swinford St
San Pedro CA 90731
310 519-7971

(P-12282)
HORNBLOWER YACHTS LLC
Also Called: Hornblower Dining Yachts
13755 Fiji Way, Marina Del Rey (90292-9328)
PHONE.................................310 301-6000
Kevin Lorton, *Branch Mgr*
EMP: 55
SALES (corp-wide): 536MM **Privately Held**
WEB: www.hornblower.com
SIC: 4489 7299 4499 Excursion boat operators; banquet hall facilities; chartering of commercial boats
PA: Hornblower Yachts, Llc
On The Embarcadero Pier 3 St Pier
San Francisco CA 94111
415 788-8866

(P-12283)
ISLAND PACKERS CORPORATION
1691 Spinnaker Dr 105b, Ventura (93001-4378)
PHONE.................................805 642-1393
Mark Connelly, *President*
Lillian Connelly, *Corp Secy*
Alex Brodie, *Manager*
Cheryl Connelly, *Asst Mgr*
EMP: 51 **EST:** 1968
SQ FT: 750
SALES (est): 4.1MM **Privately Held**
WEB: www.islandpackers.com
SIC: 4489 4725 Excursion boat operators; sightseeing boats; tour operators

(P-12284)
SO CAL SHIP SERVICES
971 S Seaside Ave, San Pedro (90731-7331)
PHONE.................................310 519-8411
Michael A Lanham, *President*
Doug Malin, *Executive*
Freddy Saenz, *Manager*
EMP: 85 **EST:** 1982
SQ FT: 10,000
SALES (est): 12.2MM **Privately Held**
WEB: www.ship-services.com
SIC: 4489 Water taxis

4491 Marine Cargo Handling

(P-12285)
APM TERMINALS PACIFIC LLC (DH)
2500 Navy Way, San Pedro (90731-7554)
PHONE.................................704 571-2768
Steven Trombley, *CEO*
John Loepprich, *Treasurer*
Vakhtang Kvaratskhelia, *Officer*
Michael Ahern, *General Mgr*
Sameer Kazi, *Finance Dir*
▲ **EMP:** 104 **EST:** 1978
SQ FT: 33,000
SALES (est): 103.3MM
SALES (corp-wide): 1.2MM **Privately Held**
WEB: www.apmterminals.com
SIC: 4491 Stevedoring
HQ: Apm Terminals North America, Inc.
9300 Arrowpoint Blvd
Charlotte NC 28273
704 571-2768

(P-12286)
CATALINA CHANNEL EXPRESS INC
Also Called: Catalina Express
320 Golden Shore Lbby, Long Beach (90802-4200)
PHONE.................................562 435-8686
Rachel Lane, *Branch Mgr*
EMP: 58
SALES (corp-wide): 54.1MM **Privately Held**
WEB: www.catalinaexpress.com
SIC: 4491 Docks, piers & terminals
HQ: Catalina Channel Express, Inc.
385 E Swinford St
San Pedro CA 90731
310 519-7971

(P-12287)
EVERPORT TERMINAL SERVICES INC (PA)
389 Terminal Island Way, San Pedro (90731)
PHONE.................................310 221-0220
George Lang, *CEO*
Rick Garcia, *Opers Staff*
EMP: 80 **EST:** 2010
SALES (est): 25.2MM **Privately Held**
SIC: 4491 Marine cargo handling

(P-12288)
INTERNATIONAL TRNSP SVC LLC (PA)
1281 Pier G Way, Long Beach (90802-6353)
P.O. Box 22704 (90801-5704)
PHONE.................................562 435-7781
Kim Holtermand, *CEO*
Sean Lindsay, *COO*
Richard Nicholson,
Louis Paul,
▲ **EMP:** 136 **EST:** 1971
SQ FT: 10,000
SALES (est): 55.9MM **Privately Held**
WEB: www.itslb.com
SIC: 4491 Marine loading & unloading services

(P-12289)
PASHA STEVEDORING TERMINALS LP
802 S Fries Ave, Wilmington (90744-6415)
PHONE.................................310 233-2006
EMP: 50
SALES (est): 1.6MM **Privately Held**
SIC: 4491 Marine Cargo Handler

(P-12290)
PORT OF LONG BEACH
415 W Ocean Blvd, Long Beach (90802-4511)
P.O. Box 570 (90801-0570)
PHONE.................................562 283-7000
Paula Grond, *Admin Sec*
Noel Hacegaba, *COO*
Julia Wu, *Treasurer*
Sunny Zia, *Trustee*
John Comer, *Officer*
EMP: 221 **EST:** 2014
SALES (est): 27.2MM
SALES (corp-wide): 889.7MM **Privately Held**
WEB: www.polb.com
SIC: 4491 Docks, piers & terminals
PA: City Of Long Beach
411 W Ocean Blvd
Long Beach CA 90802
562 570-6450

(P-12291)
PORT OF LOS ANGELES
425 S Palos Verdes St, San Pedro (90731-3309)
PHONE.................................310 732-3508
Gene Seroka, *Exec Dir*
David Castillo, *Officer*
Arthur Kurkowski, *Officer*
Damon Lankford, *Officer*
Theresa A Lopez, *Officer*
EMP: 65 **EST:** 2017
SALES: 467.6MM **Privately Held**
WEB: www.portoflosangeles.org
SIC: 4491 Waterfront terminal operation

(P-12292)
TOTAL INTERMODAL SERVICES INC
2757 E Del Amo Blvd, Compton (90221-6005)
PHONE.................................562 427-6300
Amador Sanchez Jr, *President*
▲ **EMP:** 57 **EST:** 1991
SALES (est): 8.8MM **Privately Held**
WEB: www.totalintermodal.com
SIC: 4491 4213 7534 4731 Marine cargo handling; trucking, except local; tire retreading & repair shops; freight forwarding

(P-12293)
TRAPAC LLC (HQ)
630 W Hrry Brdges Blvd Br 136 Berths, Wilmington (90744)
P.O. Box 1178 (90748-1178)
PHONE.................................380 830-2000
Yoshiharu Hirakawa, *CEO*
K Kurahara, *CFO*
Ron Triemstra, *CFO*
Robert Owens, *Vice Pres*
Michael Porte, *Vice Pres*
EMP: 50 **EST:** 1985
SQ FT: 50,000
SALES (est): 58.8MM **Privately Held**
WEB: www.trapac.com
SIC: 4491 Waterfront terminal operation

(P-12294)
YUSEN TERMINALS LLC (DH)
Also Called: Yti
701 New Dock St, San Pedro (90731-7535)
PHONE.................................310 548-8000
Patrick Burgoyne, *CEO*
Betsy Christie, *CFO*
Ken Fletcher, *General Mgr*
Gene Harris, *General Mgr*
Carl Kendrick, *General Mgr*
▲ **EMP:** 63 **EST:** 1991
SALES (est): 24.4MM **Privately Held**
WEB: www.yti.com
SIC: 4491 Marine terminals

4492 Towing & Tugboat Svcs

(P-12295)
BRUSCO TUG & BARGE INC
170 E Port Hueneme Rd, Port Hueneme (93041-3213)
PHONE.................................805 986-1600
David Brusco, *Branch Mgr*
EMP: 125
SALES (corp-wide): 43.2MM **Privately Held**
WEB: www.bruscotug.com
SIC: 4492 Tugboat service
PA: Brusco Tug & Barge, Inc.
548 14th Ave
Longview WA 98632
360 423-9856

(P-12296)
PACIFIC MARITIME FREIGHT INC
1512 Pier C St, Long Beach (90813-4043)
PHONE.................................562 590-8188
Kimberly Norman, *Office Mgr*
Richard Barnes, *CIO*
Corey Umstead, *Opers Mgr*
Vicky Eads, *Opers Staff*
Pat Neal, *Opers Staff*
EMP: 87
SALES (corp-wide): 41.5MM **Privately Held**
WEB: www.pacificmaritimegroup.com
SIC: 4492 Tugboat service
PA: Pacific Maritime Group, Inc.
1444 Cesar E Chavez Pkwy
San Diego CA 92113
619 533-7932

4499 Water Transportation Svcs, NEC

(P-12297)
BLUE OCEAN MARINE LLC (PA)
2060 Knoll Dr Ste 100, Ventura (93003-7391)
PHONE.................................805 658-2628
Daniel Randopoulos,
Charlotte Randopoulos,
EMP: 28 **EST:** 2010
SALES (est): 4.1MM **Privately Held**
SIC: 4499 1389 7359 Boat rental, commercial; oil field services; equipment rental & leasing

(P-12298)
C & C BOATS INC
2124 Main St Ste 145, Huntington Beach (92648-6471)
P.O. Box 1279 (92647-1279)
PHONE.................................714 969-0900
Thomas Croft, *President*
Don Croft, *Treasurer*
EMP: 26 **EST:** 1960
SALES (est): 684.6K **Privately Held**
WEB: www.cccrewboats.com
SIC: 4499 3731 Chartering of commercial boats; shipbuilding & repairing

(P-12299)
HANJIN SHIPPING CO LTD
301 Hanjin Rd, Long Beach (90802)
PHONE.................................201 291-4600
Taisoo Suk, *Exec Dir*
Jon Stegehuis, *Senior Mgr*
◆ **EMP:** 691 **EST:** 1994
SALES (est): 19.6MM **Privately Held**
SIC: 4499 Steamship leasing

4512 Air Transportation, Scheduled

(P-12300)
AEROTRANSPORTE DE CARGE UNION
Also Called: Aerounion
5625 W Imperial Hwy, Los Angeles (90045-6323)
PHONE.................................310 649-0069
Luis Ramo, *President*
Steven Connolly, *Vice Pres*
EMP: 400 **EST:** 2006
SALES (est): 14.2MM **Privately Held**
WEB: www.pcola.gulf.net
SIC: 4512 Air cargo carrier, scheduled

(P-12301)
AIR NEW ZEALAND LIMITED
222 N Pacific Coast Hwy # 90, El Segundo (90245-5648)
PHONE.................................310 648-7000
Roger Poulton, *Vice Pres*
Janet Eden, *Executive Asst*
Chrystal Peters, *Human Res Mgr*
Lupe Tavana, *Opers Staff*
Tritia Cantun, *Marketing Staff*
EMP: 100 **Privately Held**
WEB: www.airnewzealand.cn
SIC: 4512 Air passenger carrier, scheduled

PA: Air New Zealand Limited
185 Fanshawe St
Auckland 1010

(P-12302)
AMERICA WEST AIRLINES INC
18601 Airport Way Ste 238, Santa Ana
(92707-5204)
PHONE..................949 852-5471
EMP: 80
SALES (corp-wide): 42.2B **Publicly Held**
SIC: 4512 Scheduled Air Transportation
HQ: America West Airlines, Inc.
4000 E Sky Harbor Blvd
Phoenix AZ 85034
480 693-0800

(P-12303)
AMERICAN AIRLINES INC
7000 World Way W, Los Angeles
(90045-7503)
PHONE..................213 935-6045
EMP: 150
SALES (corp-wide): 42.2B **Publicly Held**
SIC: 4512 Scheduled Air Transportation
HQ: American Airlines, Inc.
4333 Amon Carter Blvd
Fort Worth TX 76155
817 963-1234

(P-12304)
CHINA AIRLINES LTD
5651 W 96th St, Los Angeles (90045-5539)
PHONE..................310 484-1818
Jeff Hu, Assistant
EMP: 79 **Privately Held**
WEB: www.china-airlines.com
SIC: 4512 Air passenger carrier, scheduled
HQ: China Airlines, Ltd.
11201 Aviation Blvd
Los Angeles CA 90045
-

(P-12305)
CHINA AIRLINES LTD (HQ)
11201 Aviation Blvd, Los Angeles
(90045-6100)
PHONE..................310 646-4233
Huang Hsiang Sun, President
Yanira Reyes, Officer
David Tang, Opers Mgr
Josephine Chiu, Marketing Mgr
Jenny Lee, Marketing Mgr
EMP: 473 EST: 1969
SALES (est): 140.6MM **Privately Held**
WEB: www.china-airlines.com
SIC: 4512 Air passenger carrier, scheduled

(P-12306)
FEDERAL EXPRESS CORPORATION
Also Called: Fedex
2601 Main St Ste 1000, Irvine
(92614-4233)
PHONE..................949 862-4500
EMP: 120
SALES (corp-wide): 47.4B **Publicly Held**
SIC: 4512 4513 Scheduled Air Transporta-
tion Air Courier Services
HQ: Federal Express Corporation
3610 Hacks Cross Rd
Memphis TN 38125
901 369-3600

(P-12307)
JETBLUE AIRWAYS INC
Also Called: Jet Blue
4100 E Donald Douglas Dr, Long Beach
(90808-1754)
PHONE..................562 394-4397
Alex Wilcox, Director
Masheea Zackery, Supervisor
EMP: 103 EST: 2004
SALES (est): 17.7MM
SALES (corp-wide): 2.9B **Publicly Held**
WEB: www.jetblue.com
SIC: 4512 Air passenger carrier, scheduled
PA: Jetblue Airways Corporation
2701 Queens Plz N
Long Island City NY 11101
718 286-7900

(P-12308)
KOREAN AIR LINES CO LTD
380 World Way Ste S4, Los Angeles
(90045-5847)
PHONE..................310 646-4866
Gunyoung Lee, General Mgr
Robert Ang, Technology
Jaewuk Lee, Accounting Mgr
Bongsoo Moon, Marketing Staff
Alan Fan, Manager
EMP: 175 **Privately Held**
WEB: www.koreanair.com
SIC: 4512 Air passenger carrier, scheduled
PA: Korean Airlines Co., Ltd.
260 Haneul-Gil, Gangseo-Gu
Seoul 07505

(P-12309)
KOREAN AIRLINES CO LTD
Also Called: Korean Arln Crgo Reservations
6101 W Imperial Hwy, Los Angeles
(90045-6305)
PHONE..................310 410-2000
Jinkul Lee, President
Jong Myung Park, Treasurer
John Jackson, Vice Pres
Soyoung Kim, General Mgr
Steven Kang, Technology
EMP: 250 **Privately Held**
WEB: www.koreanair.com
SIC: 4512 4513 Air passenger carrier,
scheduled; package delivery, private air
PA: Korean Airlines Co., Ltd.
260 Haneul-Gil, Gangseo-Gu
Seoul 07505

(P-12310)
KOREAN AIRLINES CO LTD
1813 Wilshire Blvd # 400, Los Angeles
(90057-3600)
PHONE..................213 484-1900
Kyung Kim, Branch Mgr
Ys Kang, Vice Pres
Ki Kang, General Mgr
Donovan Kim, General Mgr
Young Lee, General Mgr
EMP: 100 **Privately Held**
WEB: www.koreanair.com
SIC: 4512 4729 Air passenger carrier,
scheduled; airline ticket offices
PA: Korean Airlines Co., Ltd.
260 Haneul-Gil, Gangseo-Gu
Seoul 07505

(P-12311)
L A AIR INC
5933 W Century Blvd 500, Los Angeles
(90045-5471)
PHONE..................310 215-8245
Dennis W Altbrandt, CEO
Wayne Schoenfeld, Ch of Bd
Dennis Altbrandt, Acting CFO
Al Claseman, Exec VP
Tim Clary, Senior VP
EMP: 134 EST: 1980
SQ FT: 6,119
SALES (est): 3.7MM **Privately Held**
SIC: 4512 Air passenger carrier, sched-
uled; air cargo carrier, scheduled

(P-12312)
PIEDMONT AIRLINES INC
Also Called: American Airlines/Eagle
4100 E Donald Douglas Dr, Long Beach
(90808-1754)
PHONE..................562 421-1806
Sean Lucas, Manager
EMP: 170
SALES (corp-wide): 17.3B **Publicly Held**
WEB: www.piedmont-airlines.com
SIC: 4512 Air passenger carrier, scheduled
HQ: Piedmont Airlines, Inc.
5443 Airport Terminal Rd
Salisbury MD 21804
410 572-5100

(P-12313)
SINGAPORE AIRLINES LIMITED
222 N Pcf Cast Hwy Ste 16, El Segundo
(90245)
PHONE..................310 647-1922
Tee Hooi Teoh, Manager
Loh Meng See Meng See, Senior VP

Yau Seng Chin, Vice Pres
Kok Wah Chow, Vice Pres
Kah Kheng Goh, Vice Pres
EMP: 135 **Privately Held**
WEB: www.singaporeair.com
SIC: 4512 Air passenger carrier, scheduled
PA: Singapore Airlines Limited
25 Airline Road
Singapore 81982

(P-12314)
SKYWEST AIRLINES INC
32128 Chagall Ct, Winchester
(92596-9024)
PHONE..................951 926-9511
EMP: 75
SALES (corp-wide): 3.5B **Publicly Held**
SIC: 4512 Nonclassified Establishment
HQ: Skywest Airlines, Inc.
444 S River Rd
St George UT 84790
435 634-3000

(P-12315)
SKYWEST AIRLINES INC
26818 Bahama Way, Murrieta
(92563-2553)
PHONE..................951 600-9181
EMP: 75
SALES (corp-wide): 2.1B **Publicly Held**
WEB: www.skywest.com
SIC: 4512 7389 Scheduled Air Transporta-
tion Business Services At Non-Commer-
cial Site
HQ: Skywest Airlines, Inc.
444 S River Rd
St George UT 84790
435 634-3000

(P-12316)
SOUTHWEST AIRLINES CO
18601 Airport Way Ste 237, Santa Ana
(92707-5257)
PHONE..................949 252-5200
Larry Pits, Manager
Mike Duggan, Administration
John Pape, Project Mgr
Vincent Rose, Technology
Scott Hagan, Opers Staff
EMP: 80
SALES (corp-wide): 9B **Publicly Held**
WEB: www.southwest.com
SIC: 4512 Air passenger carrier, scheduled
PA: Southwest Airlines Co.
2702 Love Field Dr
Dallas TX 75235
214 792-4000

(P-12317)
SOUTHWEST AIRLINES CO
100 World Way Ste 328, Los Angeles
(90045-5854)
PHONE..................310 665-5700
Fax: 310 670-0723
EMP: 70
SALES (corp-wide): 21.1B **Publicly Held**
SIC: 4512 4581 Scheduled Air Transporta-
tion Airport/Airport Services
PA: Southwest Airlines Co.
2702 Love Field Dr
Dallas TX 75235
214 792-4000

(P-12318)
UNITED COURIERS INC (DH)
Also Called: U C I Distribution Plus
3280 E Foothill Blvd, Pasadena
(91107-3103)
PHONE..................213 383-3611
Stephan Cretier, CEO
Richard R Irvin, President
Robert G Irvin, Treasurer
EMP: 200 EST: 1957
SQ FT: 25,000
SALES (est): 75.6MM
SALES (corp-wide): 145.8MM **Privately Held**
WEB: www.garda.com
SIC: 4512 4215 4212 7381 Air cargo car-
rier, scheduled; courier services, except
by air; local trucking, without storage; ar-
mored car services; freight forwarding

HQ: Ati Systems International, Inc.
2000 Nw Corp Blvd Ste 101
Boca Raton FL 33431
561 939-7000

(P-12319)
UNITED PARCEL SERVICE INC
Also Called: UPS
5720 Avion Dr Bay 8, Los Angeles
(90045-5662)
PHONE..................310 670-5849
EMP: 76
SALES (corp-wide): 84.6B **Publicly Held**
WEB: www.ups.com
SIC: 4512 Air cargo carrier, scheduled
HQ: United Parcel Service, Inc.
55 Glenlake Pkwy
Atlanta GA 30328
404 828-6000

(P-12320)
UNITED PARCEL SERVICE INC
Also Called: UPS
2925 Jurupa St, Ontario (91761-2915)
PHONE..................909 906-5700
EMP: 76
SALES (corp-wide): 84.6B **Publicly Held**
WEB: www.ups.com
SIC: 4512 Air cargo carrier, scheduled
HQ: United Parcel Service, Inc.
55 Glenlake Pkwy
Atlanta GA 30328
404 828-6000

(P-12321)
UNITED PARCEL SERVICE INC
Also Called: UPS
1457 E Victoria Ave, San Bernardino
(92408-2923)
PHONE..................800 742-5877
EMP: 76
SALES (corp-wide): 84.6B **Publicly Held**
WEB: www.ups.com
SIC: 4512 Air cargo carrier, scheduled
HQ: United Parcel Service, Inc.
55 Glenlake Pkwy
Atlanta GA 30328
404 828-6000

(P-12322)
UNITED PARCEL SERVICE INC
Also Called: UPS
19440 Arenth Ave, City of Industry
(91748-1424)
PHONE..................951 757-8176
EMP: 76
SALES (corp-wide): 84.6B **Publicly Held**
WEB: www.ups.com
SIC: 4512 Air cargo carrier, scheduled
HQ: United Parcel Service, Inc.
55 Glenlake Pkwy
Atlanta GA 30328
404 828-6000

(P-12323)
UNITED PARCEL SERVICE INC
Also Called: UPS
10760 Tamarind Ave, Bloomington
(92316-2546)
PHONE..................909 349-4343
EMP: 76
SALES (corp-wide): 84.6B **Publicly Held**
WEB: www.ups.com
SIC: 4512 Air cargo carrier, scheduled
HQ: United Parcel Service, Inc.
55 Glenlake Pkwy
Atlanta GA 30328
404 828-6000

(P-12324)
UNITED PARCEL SERVICE INC
Also Called: UPS
3110 Jurupa St, Ontario (91761-2902)
PHONE..................909 605-7740
Joseph Snedeker, Manager
EMP: 76
SALES (corp-wide): 84.6B **Publicly Held**
WEB: www.ups.com
SIC: 4512 Air cargo carrier, scheduled
HQ: United Parcel Service, Inc.
55 Glenlake Pkwy
Atlanta GA 30328
404 828-6000

4513 Air Courier Svcs

(P-12325)
BINEX LINE CORP (PA)
19515 S Vermont Ave, Torrance
(90502-1121)
PHONE....................310 416-8600
David Paek, *President*
Hyun K Cho, *CFO*
Tim Park, *Vice Pres*
Sue Baek, *Sales Staff*
Andres Pulido, *Manager*
◆ EMP: 70 EST: 1995
SQ FT: 32,000
SALES: 89.4MM **Privately Held**
WEB: www.binexline.com
SIC: 4513 4731 Air courier services;
freight forwarding

(P-12326)
**FEDERAL EXPRESS
CORPORATION**
Also Called: Fedex
3333 S Grand Ave, Los Angeles
(90007-4116)
PHONE....................800 463-3339
EMP: 100
SALES (corp-wide): 83.9B **Publicly Held**
WEB: www.fedex.com
SIC: 4513 Package delivery, private air
HQ: Federal Express Corporation
3610 Hacks Cross Rd
Memphis TN 38125
901 369-3600

(P-12327)
**FEDERAL EXPRESS
CORPORATION**
Also Called: Fedex
2060 S Wineville Ave B, Ontario
(91761-3633)
PHONE....................909 390-3237
EMP: 60
SALES (corp-wide): 47.4B **Publicly Held**
SIC: 4513 Trucking Operator-Nonlocal
HQ: Federal Express Corporation
3610 Hacks Cross Rd
Memphis TN 38125
901 369-3600

(P-12328)
**FEDERAL EXPRESS
CORPORATION**
Also Called: Fedex
2451 N Palm Dr, Long Beach
(90755-4006)
PHONE....................800 463-3339
EMP: 150
SALES (corp-wide): 47.4B **Publicly Held**
SIC: 4513 Air & Surface Courier Service
HQ: Federal Express Corporation
3610 Hacks Cross Rd
Memphis TN 38125
901 369-3600

(P-12329)
**FEDERAL EXPRESS
CORPORATION**
Also Called: Fedex
1 World Trade Ctr Ste 191, Long Beach
(90831-0191)
PHONE....................562 522-4014
EMP: 150
SALES (corp-wide): 45.5B **Publicly Held**
SIC: 4513 Air Courier Service
HQ: Federal Express Corporation
3610 Hacks Cross Rd
Memphis TN 38125
901 369-3600

(P-12330)
MEJICO EXPRESS INC (PA)
Also Called: Grupoex
14849 Firestone Blvd Fl 1, La Mirada
(90638)
PHONE....................714 690-8300
Jose Leon, *President*
Raymond Butner, *Manager*
EMP: 150 EST: 1988
SALES (est): 8.9MM **Privately Held**
SIC: 4513 Letter delivery, private air

(P-12331)
UNITED PARCEL SERVICE INC
Also Called: UPS
3333 S Downey Rd, Vernon (90058-4116)
PHONE....................323 260-8957
Tony Peralta, *Sales Staff*
EMP: 76
SALES (corp-wide): 84.6B **Publicly Held**
WEB: www.ups.com
SIC: 4513 4215 Air courier services;
courier services, except by air
HQ: United Parcel Service, Inc.
55 Glenlake Pkwy
Atlanta GA 30328
404 828-6000

(P-12332)
UNITED PARCEL SERVICE INC
Also Called: UPS
25283 Sherman Rd, Sun City
(92585-9352)
PHONE....................951 928-5221
Sean Nichols, *Branch Mgr*
EMP: 76
SALES (corp-wide): 84.6B **Publicly Held**
WEB: www.ups.com
SIC: 4513 Parcel delivery, private air
HQ: United Parcel Service, Inc.
55 Glenlake Pkwy
Atlanta GA 30328
404 828-6000

(P-12333)
UNITED PARCEL SERVICE INC
Also Called: UPS
Ontario Airport, Ontario (91758)
PHONE....................909 974-7190
Steve Welsh, *Manager*
EMP: 76
SALES (corp-wide): 84.6B **Publicly Held**
WEB: www.ups.com
SIC: 4513 Parcel delivery, private air
HQ: United Parcel Service, Inc.
55 Glenlake Pkwy
Atlanta GA 30328
404 828-6000

4522 Air Transportation, Nonscheduled

(P-12334)
**AIR RUTTER INTERNATIONAL
LLC**
Also Called: Alerion Aviation
3501 N Lakewood Blvd, Long Beach
(90808-1736)
PHONE....................855 359-2576
Robert Seidel, *Mng Member*
Jeremy Meyer, *Info Tech Mgr*
Mark Gabriel, *Controller*
EMP: 50 EST: 1995
SQ FT: 2,500
SALES (est): 5.5MM **Privately Held**
WEB: www.arijets.com
SIC: 4522 Air passenger carriers, non-
scheduled

(P-12335)
JALTRANS INC (HQ)
6041 W Imperial Hwy, Los Angeles
(90045-6328)
PHONE....................310 215-7471
Toshiaki Suzuki, *Exec VP*
EMP: 169 EST: 1988
SQ FT: 42,500
SALES (est): 2.5MM **Privately Held**
WEB: www.jal.co.jp
SIC: 4522 4513 Air cargo carriers, non-
scheduled; package delivery, private air

(P-12336)
JETSUITE INC (PA)
18952 Macarthur Blvd # 200, Irvine
(92612-1401)
PHONE....................949 892-4300
Alex Wilcox, *CEO*
Stephanie Chung, *President*
Keith Rabin, *CFO*
Sunil Ramchandani, *CFO*
Jordan Lamotte, *Officer*
EMP: 147 EST: 2007
SQ FT: 7,641

SALES (est): 42.3MM **Privately Held**
WEB: www.jetsuite.com
SIC: 4522 Flying charter service

(P-12337)
NAVAJO INVESTMENTS INC (PA)
17962 Cowan, Irvine (92614-6026)
PHONE....................949 863-9200
William Langston, *President*
EMP: 82 EST: 1985
SQ FT: 17,000
SALES (est): 3.1MM **Privately Held**
SIC: 4522 Air transportation, nonscheduled

4581 Airports, Flying Fields & Terminal Svcs

(P-12338)
**AIRCRAFT REPAIR &
OVERHAUL SVC (PA)**
Also Called: A R O Service
1186 N Grove St, Anaheim (92806-2109)
PHONE....................714 630-9494
Thomas Haefele, *CEO*
Robert C Haefele, *President*
Shirley Haefele, *CFO*
Mark Haefele, *Vice Pres*
Shirley M Haefele, *Admin Sec*
EMP: 20 EST: 1975
SQ FT: 90,000
SALES (est): 7.4MM **Privately Held**
WEB: www.aroservice.com
SIC: 4581 3728 Airports, flying fields &
services; aircraft parts & equipment

(P-12339)
ALLIANCE GROUND INTL LLC
6181 W Imperial Hwy, Los Angeles
(90045-6305)
PHONE....................310 646-2446
Malia Jennings, *General Mgr*
EMP: 167
SALES (corp-wide): 213.1MM **Privately
Held**
WEB: www.allianceground.com
SIC: 4581 Airfreight loading & unloading
services
PA: Alliance Ground International, Llc
9130 S Ddland Blvd Ste 18
Miami FL 33156
305 740-3252

(P-12340)
**ATLANTIC AVIATION HOLDING
CORP**
2828 Donald Douglas Loop, Santa Monica
(90405-2978)
PHONE....................310 396-6770
Gregory Wain, *General Mgr*
Jay Hixson, *Opers Mgr*
Tracy McCollum, *Production*
Cristian Archila, *Supervisor*
EMP: 59
SALES (corp-wide): 847MM **Publicly
Held**
WEB: www.atlanticaviation.com
SIC: 4581 Aircraft maintenance & repair
services
HQ: Atlantic Aviation Holding Corporation
6652 Pinecrest Dr Ste 300
Plano TX 75024
972 905-2500

(P-12341)
AVIATION & DEFENSE INC
Also Called: ADI
255 S Leland Norton Way, San Bernardino
(92408-0103)
PHONE....................909 382-3487
Daniel M Scanlon, *CEO*
Hector Guerrero, *Ch of Bd*
Mike Scanlon, *President*
Ben Flores, *CFO*
Dan Scanlon, *Vice Pres*
EMP: 180 EST: 2011
SQ FT: 180,000
SALES (est): 24.4MM **Privately Held**
WEB: www.adi.aero
SIC: 4581 Aircraft maintenance & repair
services

(P-12342)
**AVIATION MAINTENANCE
GROUP INC**
8352 Kimball Ave Hngr 3, Chino
(91708-9267)
PHONE....................7 4 469-0515
Jeremy G Schuster, *President*
Doug Crowther, *Vice Pres*
Douglas Crowther, *Sales Staff*
Jerry Perez, *Director*
Nicole Dilullo, *Manager*
EMP: 85 EST: 1995
SALES (est): 6.6MM **Privately Held**
SIC: 4581 Aircraft maintenance & repair
services

(P-12343)
**AVIATION REPAIR SOLUTIONS
INC**
1480 Canal Ave, Long Beach 90813-1244)
PHONE....................562 437-2825
James Meyer, *President*
Walter Mroch, *COO*
Lori Stouffer, *Accountant*
Scott Kline, *Opers Mgr*
Mark Falkowski, *QC Mgr*
EMP: 15 EST: 2005
SQ FT: 12,500
SALES (est): 2.6MM **Privately Held**
WEB: www.aviation-repair.com
SIC: 4581 3471 Aircraft servicing & repair-
ing; electroplating & plating

(P-12344)
BETRIA INTERACTIVE LLC
Also Called: Flightpath3d
26170 Enterprise Way, Lake Forest
(92630-8414)
PHONE....................949 273-0920
Duncan Jackson, *President*
EMP: 50 EST: 2012
SALES (est): 2.3MM **Privately Held**
SIC: 4581 Aircraft servicing & repairing

(P-12345)
BOEING COMPANY
Slc 2 Bldg 1628, San Luis Obispo (93401)
P.O. Box 5219, Lompoc (93 37-0219)
PHONE....................805 606-6340
Rich Niederhauser, *Manager*
James B Boyle, *Mng Officer*
EMP: 18
SALES (corp-wide): 58.1B **Publicly Held**
WEB: www.boeing.com
SIC: 4581 3761 3721 Airports & flying
fields; guided missiles & space vehicles;
aircraft
PA: The Boeing Company
100 N Riverside Plz
Chicago IL 60606
312 544-2000

(P-12346)
CERTIFIED AVIATION SVCS LLC
5720 Avion Dr, Los Angeles (90045-5662)
PHONE....................310 338-1224
Henry Havash, *Manager*
EMP: 99 **Privately Held**
WEB: www.certifiedaviation.com
SIC: 4581 Aircraft maintenance & repair
services
PA: Certified Aviation Services Llc
1150 S Vineyard Ave
Ontario CA 91761

(P-12347)
CITY OF LONG BEACH
Also Called: Long Beach Airport
4100 E Don Douglas Dr Fl Flr 2, Long
Beach (90808)
PHONE....................562 570-2600
Chris Kunze, *Manager*
Juan Lopez-Rios, *Deputy Dir*
Ken Mason, *Assistant*
EMP: 65
SALES (corp-wide): 889.7MM **Privately
Held**
WEB: www.longbeach.gov
SIC: 4581 9111 Airport; mayors' offices
PA: City Of Long Beach
411 W Ocean Blvd
Long Beach CA 90802
562 570-6450

(P-12348)
CITY OF TORRANCE
Also Called: Torrance Municipal Airport
3301 Airport Dr, Torrance (90505-6152)
PHONE..................................310 784-7950
Bill Tilden, *Branch Mgr*
EMP: 57
SALES (corp-wide): 211.1MM **Privately Held**
WEB: www.torranceca.gov
SIC: 4581 9111 Airport; mayors' offices
PA: City Of Torrance
3031 Torrance Blvd
Torrance CA 90503
310 328-5310

(P-12349)
CLAY LACY AVIATION INC (PA)
Also Called: C L A
7435 Valjean Ave, Van Nuys (91406-2977)
PHONE..................................818 989-2900
Brian Kirkdoffer, *President*
Bradford Wright, *CFO*
Hershel Clay Lacy, *Founder*
Dave R Anderson, *Vice Pres*
Chris Broyhill, *Vice Pres*
EMP: 350 EST: 1969
SQ FT: 18,000
SALES (est): 157.1MM **Privately Held**
WEB: www.claylacy.com
SIC: 4581 Airport terminal services

(P-12350)
**COMAV TECHNICAL SERVICES
LLC**
Also Called: S C A
18438 Readiness St, Victorville
(92394-7945)
PHONE..................................760 530-2400
Craig Garrick, *CEO*
Jon Day, *CFO*
▲ EMP: 223 EST: 1999
SQ FT: 47,625
SALES (est): 70.9MM
SALES (corp-wide): 101.1MM **Privately
Held**
WEB: www.comav.com
SIC: 4581 Aircraft maintenance & repair
services
PA: Comav, Llc
18499 Phantom St Ste 17
Victorville CA 92394
760 523-5100

(P-12351)
COUNTY OF LOS ANGELES
12653 Osborne St Ste 8, Pacoima
(91331-2101)
PHONE..................................818 896-5271
Andrew Marino, *Branch Mgr*
EMP: 114
SALES (corp-wide): 25.2B **Privately Held**
WEB: www.americanairports.net
SIC: 4581 Airport terminal services
PA: County Of Los Angeles
500 W Temple St Ste 437
Los Angeles CA 90012
213 974-1101

(P-12352)
COUNTY OF LOS ANGELES
12605 Osborne St, Pacoima (91331-2129)
PHONE..................................818 890-5777
EMP: 114
SALES (corp-wide): 25.2B **Privately Held**
WEB: www.lacounty.gov
SIC: 4581 Aircraft maintenance & repair
services
PA: County Of Los Angeles
500 W Temple St Ste 437
Los Angeles CA 90012
213 974-1101

(P-12353)
COUNTY OF ORANGE
Also Called: John Wayne Airport
3160 Airway Ave, Costa Mesa
(92626-4608)
PHONE..................................949 252-5006
Loan Leblow, *Branch Mgr*
Ben Hamatake, *Comms Mgr*
Daniel Lopez, *Manager*
Marisa Unvert, *Manager*
EMP: 135

SALES (corp-wide): 4.3B **Privately Held**
WEB: www.ocgov.com
SIC: 4581 9621 Airport; aircraft regulating
agencies;
PA: County Of Orange
333 W Santa Ana Blvd
Santa Ana CA 92701
714 834-6200

(P-12354)
COUNTY OF VENTURA
Also Called: Airports Cmrllo Oxnard Arprt I
2889 W 5th St, Oxnard (93030-6437)
PHONE..................................805 388-4274
Jorge Rubio, *Branch Mgr*
EMP: 69
SALES (corp-wide): 1.5B **Privately Held**
WEB: www.ventura.org
SIC: 4581 9111 Airport; executive offices
PA: County Of Ventura
800 S Victoria Ave
Ventura CA 93009
805 654-2644

(P-12355)
COUNTY OF VENTURA
555 Airport Way Ste D, Camarillo
(93010-8531)
PHONE..................................805 388-4274
Don Occhiline, *Branch Mgr*
Mark Lorenzen, *Fire Chief*
Gloria Nieves, *Sheriff*
Jaclyn Smith, *Counsel*
EMP: 69
SALES (corp-wide): 1.5B **Privately Held**
WEB: www.ventura.org
SIC: 4581 Airport
PA: County Of Ventura
800 S Victoria Ave
Ventura CA 93009
805 654-2644

(P-12356)
DSD TRUCKING INC (PA)
2411 Santa Fe Ave, Redondo Beach
(90278-1125)
PHONE..................................310 338-3395
Dan Cuevas, *President*
Kalonde Gilbert, *CTO*
Wendy Silva, *Human Res Mgr*
Evelyn Wildelberg, *Opers Staff*
Danielle Martinez, *Facilities Mgr*
EMP: 99 EST: 1984
SQ FT: 300,000
SALES (est): 15.5MM **Privately Held**
WEB: www.dsdcompanies.com
SIC: 4581 Air freight handling at airports

(P-12357)
DYNAMO AVIATION INC
9601 Mason Ave A, Chatsworth
(91311-5207)
P.O. Box 14040, Van Nuys (91409-4040)
PHONE..................................818 785-9561
Masoud S Rabadi, *CEO*
Robin C Scott, *CFO*
Lary Hockens, *Officer*
Cathy Castillo, *General Mgr*
Eric Pesicka, *Info Tech Mgr*
EMP: 80 EST: 1986
SALES (est): 31.4MM **Privately Held**
WEB: www.dynamoaviation.com
SIC: 4581 3444 3679 5063 Aircraft serv-
icing & repairing; sheet metalwork; har-
ness assemblies for electronic use: wire
or cable; storage batteries, industrial

(P-12358)
**F & E ARCFT MINT LOS ANGLES
LL**
531 Main St, El Segundo (90245-3006)
PHONE..................................310 338-0063
Everett R Arinwine,
Keiney Mosley, *Manager*
EMP: 350 EST: 1992
SALES (est): 18.6MM **Privately Held**
WEB: www.feairmaintenance.com
SIC: 4581 7699 Aircraft servicing & repair-
ing; aircraft & heavy equipment repair
services

(P-12359)
**JET EDGE INTERNATIONAL LLC
(PA)**
16700 Roscoe Blvd Hngr C, Van Nuys
(91406-1102)
PHONE..................................818 442-0096
William Papariella, *CEO*
Kevin White, *Partner*
Michael Sanders, *CFO*
Mike Sanders, *CFO*
Robert Schiller, *CFO*
EMP: 66 EST: 2011
SALES (est): 36.3MM **Privately Held**
WEB: www.flyjetedge.com
SIC: 4581 Airports, flying fields & services

(P-12360)
LAWA INC
Also Called: Los Angeles World Airports
7333 World Way W, Los Angeles
(90045-5828)
P.O. Box 92216 (90009-2216)
PHONE..................................424 646-7770
Janice Guevara, *Principal*
Hugh Johnson, *Project Mgr*
Thomas Mumau, *Analyst*
Ebony Harper, *Personnel*
Henry Kachouri, *Manager*
EMP: 60 EST: 2015
SALES (est): 9.2MM **Privately Held**
WEB: www.lawa.org
SIC: 4581 Airport

(P-12361)
**LOS ANGELES WORLD
AIRPORTS (PA)**
6320 W 96th St, Los Angeles (90045-5233)
P.O. Box 92216 (90009-2216)
PHONE..................................310 646-7911
Arif Alikhan, *Director*
Robert L Gilbert, *Officer*
Kathryn Pantoja, *Officer*
Michael Strouse, *Officer*
Michael Cummings, *Principal*
EMP: 440 EST: 2010
SALES: 1.3B **Privately Held**
WEB: www.lawa.aero
SIC: 4581 Airport

(P-12362)
**MENZIES AVIATION (TEXAS)
INC**
Also Called: Asig
1049 S Vineyard Ave, Ontario
(91761-8029)
P.O. Box 4178 (91761-1011)
PHONE..................................909 937-3998
Debbie Martin, *Manager*
EMP: 92
SALES (corp-wide): 1.1B **Privately Held**
WEB: www.menziesaviation.com
SIC: 4581 Airport
HQ: Menzies Aviation (Texas), Inc.
4900 Diplomacy Rd
Fort Worth TX 76155
469 281-8200

(P-12363)
MERCURY AIR CARGO INC (HQ)
Also Called: Mercury World Cargo
2780 Skypark Dr Ste 300, Torrance
(90505-7518)
PHONE..................................310 258-6100
Joseph A Czyzyk, *CEO*
John Peery, *President*
John E Peery, *COO*
Lawrence Samuels, *CFO*
Dan K Barnard, *Treasurer*
▲ EMP: 180 EST: 1988
SQ FT: 206,000
SALES (est): 51.2MM
SALES (corp-wide): 455.2MM **Privately
Held**
WEB: www.mercuryaircargo.com
SIC: 4581 4512 4522 Airports, flying
fields & services; air cargo carrier, sched-
uled; air cargo carriers, nonscheduled
PA: Mercury Air Group, Inc.
2780 Skypark Dr Ste 300
Torrance CA 90505
310 602-3770

(P-12364)
**PACIFIC AVIATION
CORPORATION (PA)**
201 Continental Blvd # 220, El Segundo
(90245-4507)
PHONE..................................310 646-4015
Phil Shah, *Exec Dir*
Victor Mena, *Corp Secy*
Modesta Castillo, *Admin Asst*
Nileshni Devi, *Manager*
Robert Mok, *Manager*
EMP: 200 EST: 1995
SALES (est): 30.4MM **Privately Held**
WEB: www.pacificaviation.com
SIC: 4581 Airport terminal services

(P-12365)
**PACIFIC OIL COOLER SERVICE
IN**
1677 Curtiss Ct, La Verne (91750-5848)
PHONE..................................909 593-8400
Paul Saurenman Sr, *President*
Jan Saurenman, *Principal*
◆ EMP: 20 EST: 1988
SALES (est): 3.3MM **Privately Held**
WEB: www.oilcoolers.com
SIC: 4581 3443 Aircraft servicing & repair-
ing; fabricated plate work (boiler shop)

(P-12366)
**REPAIRTECH INTERNATIONAL
INC**
Also Called: Repair Tech International
7850 Gloria Ave, Van Nuys (91406-1821)
PHONE..................................818 989-2681
Stanley H Bennett, *President*
Patricia J Bennett, *Vice Pres*
Alis Ekmekchyan, *CIO*
Jose Alfaro, *Engineer*
Pantea Shokouh, *Mfg Staff*
EMP: 30 EST: 1978
SALES (est): 4MM **Privately Held**
WEB: www.repairtechinternational.com
SIC: 4581 3721 3999 Aircraft servicing &
repairing; aircraft; atomizers, toiletry

(P-12367)
ROTORCRAFT SUPPORT INC
67 D St, Fillmore (93015-1668)
PHONE..................................818 997-7667
Phillip G Difiore, *President*
Teri Neville, *Vice Pres*
Jeffrey Teubner, *Vice Pres*
Matt Roach, *Sales Staff*
Ricardo Lemus, *Maint Spvr*
▲ EMP: 63
SQ FT: 10,000
SALES (est): 24MM **Privately Held**
WEB: www.rotorcraftsupport.com
SIC: 4581 5088 5599 Aircraft mainte-
nance & repair services; helicopter parts;
aircraft instruments, equipment or parts

(P-12368)
**SANTA MARIA PUBLIC AIRPORT
DST**
3217 Terminal Dr, Santa Maria
(93455-1836)
PHONE..................................805 922-1726
Christopher Hastert, *President*
Hugh Rafferty, *Vice Pres*
Kerry Fenton, *Director*
EMP: 69 EST: 1942
SQ FT: 30,000
SALES (est): 5.5MM **Privately Held**
WEB: www.santamariaairport.com
SIC: 4581 Airport

(P-12369)
SIERRA GROUP INC
1129 N Calvert Blvd, Ridgecrest
(93555-7815)
P.O. Box 1628, Inyokern (93527-1628)
PHONE..................................760 377-1000
Tyrrell Richards-O'tyrrell, *Principal*
Mary K Jacobs, *Senior VP*
◆ EMP: 14 EST: 1957
SQ FT: 4,800
SALES (est): 569.1K **Privately Held**
SIC: 4581 7379 3429 8711 Aircraft serv-
icing & repairing; computer related main-
tenance services; parachute hardware;
consulting engineer; aircraft radio equip-
ment repair; welding on site

P
R
O
D
U
C
T
S

&

S
V
C
S

(P-12370)
SWISSPORT CARGO SERVICES LP
Also Called: Cargo Service Center
11001 Aviation Blvd, Los Angeles
(90045-6123)
PHONE..................................310 910-9541
Mark Wood, *General Mgr*
EMP: 197
SALES (corp-wide): 355.8K **Privately Held**
WEB: www.swissport.com
SIC: 4581 Airport terminal services
HQ: Swissport Cargo Services, L.P.
23723 Air Frt Ln Bldg 5
Dulles VA 20166
703 742-4300

(P-12371)
SWISSPORT USA INC
Also Called: Employment Intake Training Ctr
7025 W Imperial Hwy, Los Angeles
(90045-6313)
PHONE..................................310 345-1986
Jerry Harris, *General Mgr*
EMP: 73
SALES (corp-wide): 355.8K **Privately Held**
WEB: www.swissport.com
SIC: 4581 Air freight handling at airports
HQ: Swissport Usa, Inc.
227 Fayetteville St # 900
Raleigh NC 27601

(P-12372)
SWISSPORT USA INC
11001 Aviation Blvd, Los Angeles
(90045-6123)
PHONE..................................310 910-9560
Dion Fatafehi, *Manager*
EMP: 73
SALES (corp-wide): 355.8K **Privately Held**
WEB: www.swissport.com
SIC: 4581 Airport terminal services
HQ: Swissport Usa, Inc.
227 Fayetteville St # 900
Raleigh NC 27601

(P-12373)
VIRGIN ATLANTIC AIRWAYS LTD
Also Called: Ontario International Airport
2900 E Arprt Dr Ste 1243, Ontario (91761)
PHONE..................................888 747-7474
Craig Kreeger, *CEO*
EMP: 53 EST: 1990
SALES (est): 754.8K **Privately Held**
SIC: 4581 Airport

(P-12374)
WORLD SVC WST/LA INFLGHT SVC L
Also Called: L.A. Inflight Service Company
1812 W 135th St, Gardena (90249-2520)
PHONE..................................310 538-7000
Steven H Yoon, *Mng Member*
Byung Yoon,
Mall Yoon,
◆ EMP: 170 EST: 1988
SQ FT: 13,572
SALES (est): 6.2MM **Privately Held**
SIC: 4581 Aircraft cleaning & janitorial service

4612 Crude Petroleum Pipelines

(P-12375)
SFPP LP
2319 S Riverside Ave, Bloomington
(92316-2931)
PHONE..................................909 877-2373
T F Jensen, *Branch Mgr*
EMP: 52 **Publicly Held**
SIC: 4612 Crude petroleum pipelines
HQ: Sfpp, L.P.
1100 W Town And Country R
Orange CA 92868

4613 Refined Petroleum Pipelines

(P-12376)
SFPP LP
Also Called: Product Transportation
20410 S Wilmington Ave, Long Beach
(90810-1028)
PHONE..................................323 636-4447
Martin Vice, *Branch Mgr*
EMP: 52 **Publicly Held**
SIC: 4613 Refined petroleum pipelines
HQ: Sfpp, L.P.
1100 W Town And Country R
Orange CA 92868

(P-12377)
SFPP LP (DH)
1100 W Town And Country R, Orange
(92868-4647)
PHONE..................................714 560-4400
Park Shaper, *General Ptnr*
Richard D Kinder, *General Ptnr*
EMP: 150 EST: 1998
SQ FT: 75,000
SALES: 285.3MM **Publicly Held**
WEB: www.kindermorgan.com
SIC: 4613 Gasoline pipelines (common carriers)
HQ: Kinder Morgan Energy Partners, L.P.
1001 La St Ste 1000
Houston TX 77002
713 369-9000

4724 Travel Agencies

(P-12378)
ALTOUR INTERNATIONAL INC
21800 Burbank Blvd # 120, Woodland Hills
(91367-6470)
PHONE..................................818 464-9200
Karleen Moussa, *Manager*
Jackie Ezra, *Consultant*
Debbie Sabah, *Consultant*
EMP: 84 **Privately Held**
WEB: www.altour.com
SIC: 4724 Tourist agency arranging transport, lodging & car rental
PA: Altour International, Inc.
1270 Avenue Of The Flr 15
New York NY 10020

(P-12379)
ALTOUR INTERNATIONAL INC (PA)
12100 W Olympic Blvd # 300, Los Angeles
(90064-1051)
PHONE..................................310 571-6000
Alexander Chemla, *President*
Barry Noskeau, *Exec VP*
David Sefton, *Senior VP*
Peter Bernhardt, *Vice Pres*
Laura Mattingly, *Vice Pres*
EMP: 80 EST: 1995
SQ FT: 8,000 **Privately Held**
WEB: www.altour.com
SIC: 4724 Travel agencies

(P-12380)
ALTOUR INTERNATIONAL INC
Also Called: Altour Travel Master
10635 Santa Monica Blvd # 200, Los Angeles (90025-8307)
PHONE..................................310 571-6000
Julie Valentine, *Branch Mgr*
Barry Noskeau, *Exec VP*
Emily Zellmann, *Planning*
EMP: 84 **Privately Held**
WEB: www.altour.com
SIC: 4724 Travel agencies
PA: Altour International, Inc.
1270 Avenue Of The Flr 15
New York NY 10020

(P-12381)
AMAWATERWAYS LLC (PA)
4500 Park Granada 200, Calabasas
(91302-1663)
PHONE..................................800 626-0126

Rudi Schreiner, *Mng Member*
Ron Santangelo, *President*
Janet Bava, *Chief Mktg Ofcr*
Jerre Fuqua, *Chief Mktg Ofcr*
Jon Burrows, *Vice Pres*
EMP: 248 EST: 2008
SALES (est): 6.2MM **Privately Held**
WEB: www.amawaterways.com
SIC: 4724 Travel agencies

(P-12382)
AMERICAN TRAVEL SOLUTIONS LLC
Also Called: Amtrav
27509 Agoura Rd Ste 100, Agoura Hills
(91301-5150)
PHONE..................................818 359-6514
Jeff Klee, *CEO*
Ted Perlstein, *Vice Pres*
Wayne Hustis, *CIO*
Shane Kamine, *Sales Staff*
Lauren Johnson, *Director*
EMP: 65 EST: 1989
SALES (est): 9.7MM **Privately Held**
SIC: 4724 4729 Tourist agency arranging transport, lodging & car rental; airline ticket offices

(P-12383)
AMERICANTOURS INTL LLC (HQ)
6053 W Century Blvd # 70, Los Angeles
(90045-6430)
PHONE..................................310 641-9953
Noel Irwin-Hentschel,
Michael Fitzpatrick,
EMP: 105 EST: 2003
SQ FT: 20,000
SALES: 29.1MM
SALES (corp-wide): 32.9MM **Privately Held**
WEB: www.americantours.com
SIC: 4724 4725 Travel agencies; tour operators
PA: Americantours International Inc.
6053 W Century Blvd # 70
Los Angeles CA 90045
310 641-9953

(P-12384)
FLIGHT CENTRE USA INC
888 W 6th St Ste 110, Los Angeles
(90017-2728)
PHONE..................................310 458-3310
Robin Durham, *President*
EMP: 65 **Privately Held**
SIC: 4724 4729 Tourist agency arranging transport, lodging & car rental; airline ticket offices
HQ: Flight Centre Usa, Inc.
1000 E Dominguez St # 200
Carson CA 90746
213 346-0230

(P-12385)
HELLOWORLD TRAVEL SVCS USA INC
Also Called: Qantas Vctons Nwmans Vacations
6510 E Spring St, Long Beach
(90815-1554)
PHONE..................................310 535-1000
Ross Webster, *President*
Mark Punshon, *President*
Gary Goeldner, *CEO*
Justine Liddelow, *Vice Pres*
Brittany Alvarez, *Marketing Mgr*
EMP: 100 EST: 1985
SALES (est): 21.7MM **Privately Held**
WEB: www.helloworldlimited.com.au
SIC: 4724 Tourist agency arranging transport, lodging & car rental
PA: Helloworld Travel Limited
179 Normanby Rd
South Melbourne VIC 3205

(P-12386)
HIS INTL TOURS NY INC (DH)
404 S Figueroa St Ste 500, Los Angeles
(90071-1710)
PHONE..................................213 624-0777
Masaaki Yahata, *Ch of Bd*
Mafuaki Kipaya, *President*
Hideki Furukawa, *CEO*
Hideo Sawda, *Treasurer*

Kazumasa Namekata, *Admin Sec*
EMP: 76 EST: 1988
SQ FT: 4,000
SALES (est): 13.7MM **Privately Held**
WEB: www.flights.hisgo.com
SIC: 4724 Travel agencies

(P-12387)
HORNBLOWER YACHTS LLC
100 Aquarium Way, Long Beach
(90802-8126)
PHONE..................................562 901-3420
Stephanie Sawler, *Branch Mgr*
EMP: 92
SALES (corp-wide): 536MM **Privately Held**
WEB: www.hornblower.com
SIC: 4724 Travel agencies
PA: Hornblower Yachts, Llc
On The Embarcadero Pier 3 St Pier
San Francisco CA 94111
415 788-8866

(P-12388)
HORNBLOWER YACHTS LLC
13755 Fiji Way, Marina Del Rey
(90292-9328)
PHONE..................................310 301-9900
EMP: 92
SALES (corp-wide): 536MM **Privately Held**
WEB: www.hornblower.com
SIC: 4724 Travel agencies
PA: Hornblower Yachts, Llc
On The Embarcadero Pier 3 St Pier
San Francisco CA 94111
415 788-8866

(P-12389)
HORNBLOWER YACHTS LLC
Also Called: Hornblower Cruisers and Events
2527 W Coast Hwy, Newport Beach
(92663-4709)
PHONE..................................949 650-2412
Kevin Lorton, *Manager*
Kim Wright, *Vice Pres*
Diana Nunez, *Purchasing*
Thomas Saguin-Vuletich, *Manager*
EMP: 92
SALES (corp-wide): 536MM **Privately Held**
WEB: www.hornblower.com
SIC: 4724 Travel agencies
PA: Hornblower Yachts, Llc
On The Embarcadero Pier 3 St Pier
San Francisco CA 94111
415 788-8866

(P-12390)
IDS INC
Also Called: IDS Technology
20300 Ventura Blvd # 200, Woodland Hills
(91364-2448)
PHONE..................................866 297-5757
Nathan Morad, *CEO*
Alberto Gamez, *Chief Mktg Ofcr*
ARI Daniels, *Vice Pres*
John Ledo, *CTO*
Gary Kurtz, *Legal Staff*
EMP: 97 EST: 2009
SQ FT: 9,000
SALES (est): 65MM **Privately Held**
SIC: 4724 7372 Travel agencies; business oriented computer software

(P-12391)
JTB AMERICAS LTD (HQ)
19700 Mariner Ave, Torrance (90503-1648)
PHONE..................................310 406-3121
Tsuneo Irita, *President*
Benny Harrell, *President*
Takeshi Sato, *Branch Mgr*
Yasuhisa Fukuta, *General Mgr*
Mike Nesbihal, *General Mgr*
EMP: 100
SALES (est): 196.6MM **Privately Held**
WEB: www.jtbamericas.com
SIC: 4724 Travel agencies

(P-12392)
LUXE TRAVEL MANAGEMENT INC (HQ)
Also Called: Luxe Travel Group
18650 Macarthur Blvd # 00, Irvine
(92612-1269)
PHONE..................................949 336-1000

Craig Carter, *President*
Lili Dallal, *CFO*
Bill Kramer, *Officer*
Crystal Green, *Senior VP*
Raquel Nagy, *Vice Pres*
EMP: 70 **EST:** 2009
SALES (est): 16.7MM
SALES (corp-wide): 166.5MM **Privately Held**
WEB: www.luxetm.com
SIC: 4724 Tourist agency arranging transport, lodging & car rental
PA: Frosch International Travel, Llc
1 Greenway Plz Ste 800
Houston TX 77046
713 590-8216

(P-12393)
NIPPON TRAVEL AGENCY AMER INC
Also Called: Nta America
1411 W 190th St Ste 650, Gardena
(90248-4369)
PHONE..................................310 768-1817
Tadashi Wakayama, *President*
Julie Kawaguchi, *Purchasing*
Tsutomu Ochiai, *Senior Mgr*
Romeo Dublin, *Manager*
Pat Fujimoto, *Manager*
EMP: 70 **EST:** 1999
SQ FT: 8,000
SALES (est): 10.5MM **Privately Held**
WEB: www.ntaamerica.com
SIC: 4724 Tourist agency arranging transport, lodging & car rental
HQ: Nippon Travel Agency Co.,Ltd.
1-19-1, Nihombashi
Chuo-Ku TKY 103-0

(P-12394)
NIPPON TRAVEL AGENCY PCF INC (DH)
Also Called: Nta Pacific
1025 W 190th St Ste 300, Gardena
(90248-4332)
PHONE..................................310 768-0017
Tadashi Wakayama, *President*
Akio Tsuna, *CFO*
▲ **EMP:** 80 **EST:** 1973
SQ FT: 20,000
SALES (est): 51.1MM **Privately Held**
WEB: www.ntaamerica.com
SIC: 4724 Tourist agency arranging transport, lodging & car rental

(P-12395)
PINNACLE TRAVEL SERVICES LLC
390 N Pacific Coast Hwy, El Segundo
(90245-4475)
PHONE..................................310 414-1787
Robert G Singh, *CEO*
Chris Winchell, *Exec VP*
Kathy Underwood, *Human Res Dir*
EMP: 151 **EST:** 1999
SQ FT: 15,000
SALES (est): 10MM **Privately Held**
WEB: www.ptsla.com
SIC: 4724 Tourist agency arranging transport, lodging & car rental

(P-12396)
PLEASANT HOLIDAYS LLC (HQ)
Also Called: Pleasant Hawaiian Holiday
2404 Townsgate Rd, Westlake Village
(91361-2505)
PHONE..................................818 991-3390
Jack E Richards, *CEO*
Gary Hunn, *Partner*
Ron Krueger, *Exec VP*
Bruce Rosenberg, *Senior VP*
Czarina Gatmaitan, *Vice Pres*
EMP: 300 **EST:** 1998
SQ FT: 55,000
SALES (est): 154.3MM
SALES (corp-wide): 1B **Privately Held**
WEB: www.pleasantholidays.com
SIC: 4724 Tourist agency arranging transport, lodging & car rental
PA: Automobile Club Of Southern California
2601 S Figueroa St
Los Angeles CA 90007
213 741-3686

(P-12397)
PRINCESS CRUISE LINES LTD
Also Called: Princess Cruises
24833 Anza Dr, Santa Clarita (91355-1259)
P.O. Box 966 (91380-9066)
PHONE..................................661 753-2197
Princess Cruise, *Principal*
John Chernesky, *Vice Pres*
EMP: 1114
SALES (corp-wide): 2.4B **Privately Held**
WEB: www.princess.com
SIC: 4724 Travel agencies
HQ: Princess Cruise Lines, Ltd.
24305 Town Center Dr
Santa Clarita CA 91355
661 753-0000

(P-12398)
PRINCESS CRUISES AND TOURS INC (HQ)
24305 Town Center Dr # 200, Valencia
(91355-4999)
PHONE..................................206 336-6000
Will Wenholz, *Principal*
EMP: 70 **EST:** 1987
SALES (est): 26.1MM
SALES (corp-wide): 5.6B **Publicly Held**
WEB: www.carnivalcorp.com
SIC: 4724 Travel agencies
PA: Carnival Corporation
3655 Nw 87th Ave
Doral FL 33178
305 599-2600

(P-12399)
PROTRAVEL INTERNATIONAL LLC
9171 Wilshire Blvd # 428, Beverly Hills
(90210-5530)
PHONE..................................310 271-9566
Sara Sessa, *Branch Mgr*
Leda Alpert, *Consultant*
EMP: 100
SALES (corp-wide): 101.4MM **Privately Held**
WEB: www.protravelinc.com
SIC: 4724 Travel agencies
PA: Protravel International Llc
1633 Broadway Fl 35
New York NY 10019
212 755-4550

(P-12400)
TRAVEL STORE
633 S Brea Blvd, Brea (92821-5308)
PHONE..................................714 529-1947
Eva Bailon, *Manager*
Jerri Williams, *Master*
EMP: 77 **EST:** 2011
SALES (est): 1.9MM
SALES (corp-wide): 49.8MM **Privately Held**
WEB: www.travelstore.com
SIC: 4724 Tourist agency arranging transport, lodging & car rental
PA: Travel Store
11601 Wilshire Blvd # 30
Los Angeles CA 90025
310 575-5540

(P-12401)
TRAVEL STORE (PA)
Also Called: Travelstore
11601 Wilshire Blvd # 30, Los Angeles
(90025-0509)
P.O. Box 6576, San Pedro (90734-6576)
PHONE..................................310 575-5540
Wido Schaefer, *President*
Osvaldo Ramos, *CFO*
Trudy Flores, *Vice Pres*
Dan Ilves, *Vice Pres*
Eva B C, *General Mgr*
EMP: 70 **EST:** 1975
SQ FT: 7,000
SALES (est): 49.8MM **Privately Held**
WEB: www.travelstore.com
SIC: 4724 Tourist agency arranging transport, lodging & car rental

(P-12402)
UNIWORLD RIVER CRUISES INC (HQ)
Also Called: Uniworld Boutique River Cruise
17323 Ventura Blvd # 300, Encino
(91316-3964)
PHONE..................................818 382-2322
Guy A Young, *President*
Shirnett Fleet, *Chief Mktg Ofcr*
Chris Townson, *Managing Dir*
Silva Reyes, *Office Mgr*
Andrea Segall, *Executive Asst*
EMP: 109 **EST:** 2004
SALES (est): 48.4MM
SALES (corp-wide): 355.8K **Privately Held**
WEB: www.uniworldrivercruises.com
SIC: 4724 Travel agencies

(P-12403)
VIKING RIVER CRUISES INC (HQ)
Also Called: Viking Ocean Cruises
5700 Canoga Ave Ste 200, Woodland Hills
(91367-6569)
PHONE..................................818 227-1234
Torstein Hagen, *CEO*
Leah Talactac, *Senior VP*
Cheri Allen, *Vice Pres*
Jeffrey Dash, *Vice Pres*
Tony Hofmann, *Vice Pres*
EMP: 5877 **EST:** 2000
SALES (est): 682.3MM
SALES (corp-wide): 798.1MM **Privately Held**
WEB: www.vikingrivercruises.com
SIC: 4724 Tourist agency arranging transport, lodging & car rental
PA: Viking River Cruises Ag
Schaferweg 18
Basel BS 4057
616 386-011

4725 Tour Operators

(P-12404)
CONTIKI US HOLDINGS INC
Also Called: Contiki Holidays
5551 Katella Ave, Cypress (90630-5002)
PHONE..................................714 935-0808
Richard Launder, *Officer*
Kirsten Bain, *Vice Pres*
Abbey Ramge, *Vice Pres*
Kelly Jackson, *General Mgr*
Natasha Lawrence, *Project Dir*
EMP: 60 **EST:** 1981
SALES (est): 13.8MM **Privately Held**
WEB: www.contiki.com
SIC: 4725 Tours, conducted; tourist agency arranging transport, lodging & car rental

(P-12405)
COST SAVER TOURS
5551 Katella Ave, Anaheim (92805)
PHONE..................................714 935-2569
Christopher McConnell, *CFO*
EMP: 50 **EST:** 2020
SALES (est): 7MM **Privately Held**
SIC: 4725 Tour operators

(P-12406)
INMOMENT RESEARCH LLC
Also Called: Maritz
20285 S Wstn Ave Ste 101, Torrance
(90501)
PHONE..................................310 783-4300
Joe Sarquiz, *Principal*
Ron Steinkamp, *President*
Joel Barone, *Vice Pres*
Bill Higgins, *Vice Pres*
Tom O'Rourke, *Executive*
EMP: 51
SALES (corp-wide): 423.1MM **Privately Held**
WEB: www.inmoment.com
SIC: 4725 8748 8732 4899 Arrangement of travel tour packages, wholesale; employee programs administration; market analysis or research; data communication services; advertising consultant

HQ: Inmoment Research, Llc
10355 S Jordan Gtwy # 60
South Jordan UT 84095
800 530-4251

(P-12407)
PACIFIC COAST SIGHTSEEING TOUR
2001 S Manchester Ave, Anaheim
(92802-3803)
PHONE..................................714 507-1157
Kristin Martinez, *Vice Pres*
Luis Silva, *Controller*
EMP: 230 **EST:** 2012
SALES (est): 23MM **Privately Held**
WEB: www.visitanaheim.org
SIC: 4725 4173 Arrangement of travel tour packages, wholesale; sightseeing tour companies; bus terminal operation
HQ: Coach Usa, Inc.
160 S Route 17 N
Paramus NJ 07652

(P-12408)
PRINCESS CRUISE LINES LTD
24200 Magic Mountain Pkwy, Santa Clarita
(91355-4886)
PHONE..................................661 753-0000
Barbara Potter, *Branch Mgr*
Island Princess, *Officer*
Patricia Bothwell, *Vice Pres*
Dan Guinnip, *Vice Pres*
Brian O 'connor, *Vice Pres*
EMP: 1597
SALES (corp-wide): 2.4B **Privately Held**
WEB: www.princess.com
SIC: 4725 7011 4481 Tours, conducted; hotels; deep sea passenger transportation, except ferry
HQ: Princess Cruise Lines, Ltd.
24305 Town Center Dr
Santa Clarita CA 91355
661 753-0000

(P-12409)
SANTA BARBARA CITY OF
Also Called: Courthuse Tours-Docent Council
1100 Anacapa St Dept 3, Santa Barbara
(93101-6013)
PHONE..................................805 962-6464
Lori Bevon, *President*
EMP: 60
SALES (corp-wide): 201.4MM **Privately Held**
WEB: www.santabarbaraca.gov
SIC: 4725 Tours, conducted
PA: City Of Santa Barbara
735 Anacapa St
Santa Barbara CA 93101
805 963-0611

(P-12410)
SANTA CATALINA ISLAND COMPANY (PA)
Also Called: Scico
4 Park Plz Ste 420, Irvine (92614-5259)
P.O. Box 737, Avalon (90704-0737)
PHONE..................................310 510-2000
Randall Herrel Sr, *CEO*
Paxson H Offield, *Ch of Bd*
John T Dravinski, *COO*
Ronald C Doutt, *Treasurer*
Roberto Perico, *Vice Pres*
EMP: 132 **EST:** 1959
SALES (est): 78.1MM **Privately Held**
WEB: www.visitcatalinaisland.com
SIC: 4725 Sightseeing tour companies

(P-12411)
SCREAMLINE INVESTMENT CORP
Also Called: Tourcoach Transportation
2130 S Tubeway Ave, Commerce
(90040-1614)
PHONE..................................323 201-0114
Kamrouz Farhadi, *CEO*
Vahid Sapir, *President*
Shoeleh Sapir, *Treasurer*
Tony Cordon, *General Mgr*
Farima Akopians, *VP Sales*
▲ **EMP:** 120 **EST:** 1992
SQ FT: 8,000

SALES (est): 20.7MM **Privately Held**
WEB: www.tourcoach.com
SIC: **4725** Sightseeing tour companies;
tours, conducted

(P-12412)
VIP TOURS OF CALIFORNIA INC
1419 E Maple Ave, El Segundo
(90245-3302)
PHONE..............................310 216-7507
Marco Khorasani, *President*
Nicole J Khorasani, *Vice Pres*
Luis Aguilar, *Controller*
Fred Vardeh, *Mktg Dir*
EMP: 70 EST: 2002
SALES (est): 9.8MM **Privately Held**
WEB: www.viptoursofcalifornia.com
SIC: **4725** Tours, conducted

4729 Passenger Transportation Arrangement, NEC

(P-12413)
ELITE AIRWAYS LLC (PA)
4607 Lakeview Canyon Rd, Westlake Village (91361-4028)
PHONE..............................805 496-3334
Robert Lyle, *Exec VP*
Jackie Smock, *Accountant*
EMP: 143 EST: 2012
SQ FT: 5,000
SALES (est): 15.6MM **Privately Held**
WEB: www.res.eliteairways.net
SIC: **4729** Airline ticket offices

(P-12414)
FIVE STAR TRANSPORTATION INC
8703 La Tijera Blvd # 102, Los Angeles
(90045-3900)
PHONE..............................310 348-0820
George Reyes, *President*
Linda Reyes, *Vice Pres*
Demetri Ross, *Exec Dir*
EMP: 50 EST: 1998
SALES (est): 6.1MM **Privately Held**
SIC: **4729** Airline ticket offices

(P-12415)
GAT - ARLN GROUND SUPPORT INC
2627 N Hollywood Way, Burbank
(91505-1062)
PHONE..............................818 847-9127
Lenore Lahti, *Finance*
Jim Dayberry, *Manager*
EMP: 99 **Privately Held**
WEB: www.gatags.com
SIC: **4729** Airline ticket offices
PA: Gat - Airline Ground Support, Inc.
246 City Cir Ste 2000
Peachtree City GA 30269

(P-12416)
MATRIX AVIATION SERVICES INC
6171 W Century Blvd # 10, Los Angeles
(90045-5300)
PHONE..............................310 337-3037
Ramez Reno, *CEO*
Borseen Oushana, *Officer*
Jan Steinwald, *Business Dir*
Yama Popal, *Regional Mgr*
Rully Santosa, *Bookkeeper*
EMP: 175 EST: 2008
SQ FT: 3,000
SALES (est): 21.2MM **Privately Held**
WEB: www.matrix-aviation.com
SIC: **4729** Airline ticket offices

4731 Freight Forwarding & Arrangement

(P-12417)
AGILITY HOLDINGS INC (DH)
Also Called: Agility Logistics
310 Commerce Ste 250, Irvine
(92602-1399)
PHONE..............................714 617-6300
Essa Al-Saleh, *President*
Tarek Sultan, *Vice Chairman*
John Iacouzzi, *President*
Jamie Robertson, *President*
Mark Soubry, *CEO*
◆ EMP: 80 EST: 1996
SALES (est): 1B
SALES (corp-wide): 18.4B **Privately Held**
WEB: www.agility.com
SIC: **4731** 4213 4214 Domestic freight
forwarding; household goods transport;
household goods moving & storage, local
HQ: Agility Logistics International B.V.
Fokkerweg 300 Gebouw 2a
Oude Meer
884 360-105

(P-12418)
AIR-SEA FORWARDERS INC (PA)
9009 S La Cienega Blvd, Inglewood
(90301-4459)
P.O. Box 90637, Los Angeles (90009-0637)
PHONE..............................310 216-1616
Todd Hinkley, *CEO*
Paul Talley, *COO*
Monica Villavicencio, *CFO*
Luisa Nakamura, *Vice Pres*
Mark Kolber, *District Mgr*
EMP: 60 EST: 1950
SQ FT: 42,000
SALES (est): 32.7MM **Privately Held**
WEB: www.airseainc.com
SIC: **4731** Foreign freight forwarding

(P-12419)
ALLEN LUND COMPANY LLC (HQ)
4529 Angeles Crest Hwy, La Canada
Flintridge (91011-3247)
P.O. Box 1369, La Canada (91012-5369)
PHONE..............................818 790-8412
D Allen Lund, *Mng Member*
Tracy Lowen, *Vice Pres*
Nick Terry, *Admin Sec*
Patricia McDonald, *Admin Asst*
Rosa Ruelas, *Admin Asst*
EMP: 70 EST: 1976
SQ FT: 16,000
SALES (est): 201.7MM **Privately Held**
WEB: www.allenlund.com
SIC: **4731** Truck transportation brokers

(P-12420)
ALLEN LUND CORPORATION (PA)
4529 Angeles Crest Hwy, La Canada
Flintridge (91011-3247)
P.O. Box 1369, La Canada (91012-5369)
PHONE..............................818 790-8412
David Allen Lund, *President*
Steve Doerfler, *CFO*
David F Lund, *Vice Pres*
Edward V Lund, *Vice Pres*
Ken Lund, *Vice Pres*
EMP: 50 EST: 1990
SQ FT: 18,000
SALES (est): 423.5MM **Privately Held**
WEB: www.allenlund.com
SIC: **4731** Truck transportation brokers

(P-12421)
AMERITRANS EXPRESS INC
15130 Ventura Blvd # 313, Sherman Oaks
(91403-3301)
PHONE..............................818 201-0524
Chunlei Hou, *CEO*
EMP: 19 EST: 2014
SALES (est): 820.4K **Privately Held**
SIC: **4731** 3799 Freight transportation
arrangement; transportation equipment

(P-12422)
AP EXPRESS LLC (PA)
Also Called: A P Express Worldwide
5301a Rivergrade Rd, Irwindale
(91706-1347)
PHONE..............................562 236-2250
Jeffery D Pont, *Mng Member*
Keith Davis, *Exec VP*
Mike Lee Choi, *Vice Pres*
EMP: 71 EST: 1992
SQ FT: 170,000
SALES (est): 30.4MM **Privately Held**
WEB: www.apexpressfreight.com
SIC: **4731** Freight forwarding

(P-12423)
APEX LOGISTICS INTL INC (PA)
Also Called: Apex USA
18554 S Susana Rd, Compton
(90221-5620)
PHONE..............................310 665-0288
Elsie Qian, *CEO*
Edward Piza, *Partner*
Hui Qian, *Exec VP*
Justin Park, *Senior VP*
Sangna Kuhia, *Vice Pres*
▲ EMP: 80 EST: 2003
SALES (est): 1B **Privately Held**
WEB: www.apexglobe.com
SIC: **4731** Freight forwarding

(P-12424)
APM TERMINALS PACIFIC LLC
Also Called: Mearsk
2500 Navy Way Pier 400, San Pedro
(90731-7554)
PHONE..............................310 221-4000
Milan Do, *Branch Mgr*
Jon Poelma, *Managing Dir*
Steven Trombley, *Managing Dir*
Wendy Robertson, *General Mgr*
Eric Winterberg, *General Mgr*
EMP: 400
SALES (corp-wide): 1.2MM **Privately Held**
WEB: www.apmterminals.com
SIC: **4731** Agents, shipping
HQ: Apm Terminals Pacific Llc
2500 Navy Way
San Pedro CA 90731

(P-12425)
BYRNES W J & CO OF LOS ANGELES
Also Called: W.J. Byrnes & Co. Los Angeles
615 N Nash St, El Segundo (90245-2825)
P.O. Box 90595, Los Angeles (90009-0595)
PHONE..............................310 615-2325
Robert Thompson, *President*
Abel Iwaz, *Treasurer*
Janet Molina, *Admin Sec*
Pam Ordaz, *Sales Mgr*
▲ EMP: 70 EST: 1933
SQ FT: 10,000
SALES (est): 3.6MM **Privately Held**
WEB: www.wjbyrnes.com
SIC: **4731** 6411 Customhouse brokers;
freight forwarding; insurance brokers

(P-12426)
C-AIR INTERNATIONAL INC
9841 Arprt Blvd Ste 1400, Los Angeles
(90045)
PHONE..............................310 695-3400
Guss Antico, *President*
Eric Jones, *Executive*
EMP: 55 EST: 1988
SQ FT: 7,000
SALES (est): 8.7MM **Privately Held**
WEB: www.cairla.com
SIC: **4731** Customhouse brokers; domestic
freight forwarding

(P-12427)
CAPABLE TRANSPORT INC
3528 Torrance Blvd # 220, Torrance
(90503-4826)
PHONE..............................310 697-0198
Steven Troyer, *President*
EMP: 70 EST: 2004
SALES (est): 5.6MM **Privately Held**
WEB: www.capabletransport.com
SIC: **4731** Truck transportation brokers

(P-12428)
CARGOMATIC INC
211 E Ocean Blvd Ste 350, Long Beach
(90802-8837)
PHONE..............................866 513-2343
Richard Gerstein, *CEO*
Brett Parker, *COO*
Steve Jackson, *Officer*
Tom Finkbiner, *Vice Pres*
Andrea Martinez, *Executive*
EMP: 100 EST: 2013
SALES (est): 34.4MM **Privately Held**
WEB: www.cargomatic.com
SIC: **4731** Transportation agents & brokers

(P-12429)
CARMICHAEL INTERNATIONAL SVC (HQ)
Also Called: C I Container Line
1200 Corp Ctr Dr Ste 200, Monterey Park
(91754)
PHONE..............................213 353-0800
John Salvo, *President*
Vince Salvo, *President*
Jim Ryan, *CFO*
◆ EMP: 100 EST: 1961
SQ FT: 19,000
SALES (est): 107.6MM **Privately Held**
WEB: www.carmnet.com
SIC: **4731** Customhouse brokers

(P-12430)
CARROLL FULMER LOGISTICS CORP
13773 Algranti Ave, Sylmar (91342-2607)
PHONE..............................626 435-9940
Josh Quijano, *Branch Mgr*
EMP: 294
SALES (corp-wide): 182.1MM **Privately Held**
WEB: www.cfulmer.com
SIC: **4731** Truck transportation brokers
HQ: Carroll Fulmer Logistics Corporation
8340 American Way
Groveland FL 34736
352 429-5000

(P-12431)
CENTRA FREIGHT SERVICES INC
5140 W 104th St, Inglewood (90304-1128)
PHONE..............................310 568-8810
Johnathan Wang, *President*
Winnie Lo, *Finance*
Elsa Aguilar, *Export Mgr*
EMP: 52
SALES (corp-wide): 10.4MM **Privately Held**
WEB: www.centrafreight.com
SIC: **4731** Freight forwarding
PA: Centra Freight Services, Inc.
279 Lawrence Ave
South San Francisco CA 94080
650 873-8147

(P-12432)
CEVA LOGISTICS LLC
19600 S Western Ave, Torrance
(90501-1117)
PHONE..............................310 223-6500
Marvin O Schlanger, *Manager*
Erin Turner, *Executive*
Eli Camarillo, *Opers Spvr*
Rigoberto Estrada, *Opers Staff*
Ward Willie, *Opers Staff*
EMP: 300
SALES (corp-wide): 355.8K **Privately Held**
WEB: www.cevalogistics.com
SIC: **4731** Domestic freight forwarding; for-
eign freight forwarding
HQ: Ceva Logistics, Llc
15350 Vickery Dr
Houston TX 77032
281 618-3100

(P-12433)
CEVA LOGISTICS US INC
19600 S Western Ave, Torrance
(90501-1117)
PHONE..............................310 972-5500
Steve Shields, *Manager*
EMP: 67 EST: 1980

SALES (est): 12.9MM
SALES (corp-wide): 355.8K **Privately Held**
WEB: www.cevalogistics.com
SIC: 4731 Freight forwarding
HQ: Ceva Logistics Ag
    Suurstoffi 37
    Rotkreuz ZG 6343

(P-12434)
CFR RINKENS LLC (PA)
15501 Texaco Ave, Paramount
(90723-3921)
PHONE..................310 639-7725
Maximiliaan Hoes, *Mng Member*
Amber Daniels, *Human Res Mgr*
Lizbeth Cruz, *Purchasing*
Gino Bermeo, *Export Mgr*
Irina Krasnova, *Export Mgr*
▼ EMP: 75 EST: 2012
SALES (est): 49.6MM **Privately Held**
WEB: www.cfrrinkens.com
SIC: 4731 Freight forwarding

(P-12435)
CITY FASHION EXPRESS INC
Also Called: C F X
2888 E El Presidio St, Carson
(90810-1119)
PHONE..................310 223-1010
Walter John Malishka, *CEO*
Cammie Leroy, *Technology*
Walt Malishka, *Human Resources*
Gary Michel, *VP Opers*
EMP: 58 EST: 1986
SALES (est): 10.6MM **Privately Held**
SIC: 4731 Freight forwarding

(P-12436)
CJ LOGISTICS AMERICA LLC
5690 Industrial Pkwy, San Bernardino
(92407-1885)
PHONE..................540 377-2302
Michael Silva, *Opers Staff*
Enrique Tirado, *Manager*
EMP: 113 **Privately Held**
WEB: www.america.cjlogistics.com
SIC: 4731 Freight transportation arrangement
HQ: Cj Logistics America, Llc
    1750 S Wolf Rd
    Des Plaines IL 60018

(P-12437)
CNC WORLDWIDE INC (PA)
12217 Rosecrans Ave, Norwalk
(90650-5051)
PHONE..................310 670-7121
Henry Kim, *Ch of Bd*
▲ EMP: 98 EST: 2001
SALES (est): 9.9MM **Privately Held**
WEB: www.cncworldwide.com
SIC: 4731 Transportation agents & brokers

(P-12438)
COMMODITY FORWARDERS INC (DH)
Also Called: C F I
11101 S La Cienega Blvd, Los Angeles
(90045-6111)
P.O. Box 894925 (90189-4925)
PHONE..................310 348-8855
Alfred P Kuehlewind, *CEO*
Christopher A Connell, *President*
Brian West, *Vice Pres*
Jenny Mendez, *Accounting Mgr*
Evelyn Menjivar, *Human Res Mgr*
◆ EMP: 150 EST: 1974
SQ FT: 30,000
SALES (est): 104MM
SALES (corp-wide): 22.3B **Privately Held**
WEB: www.cfiperishables.com
SIC: 4731 Foreign freight forwarding
HQ: Kuhne + Nagel International Ag
    Dorfstrasse 50
    Schindellegi SZ 8834
    447 869-511

(P-12439)
CONTINENTAL AGENCY INC (PA)
1768 W 2nd St, Pomona (91766-1206)
PHONE..................909 595-8884
Jimmy Jaing, *CEO*

Beverly Jiang, *President*
Winnie Indaheng, *Sales Staff*
Josephine Chien, *Manager*
Jean Cai, *Supervisor*
◆ EMP: 53 EST: 1987
SQ FT: 105,000
SALES (est): 16.5MM **Privately Held**
WEB: www.unipacshipping.com
SIC: 4731 Customhouse brokers

(P-12440)
COSCO AGENCIES LOS ANGELES INC (DH)
588 Harbor Scenic Way, Long Beach
(90802-6317)
PHONE..................213 689-6700
Jin Guoqiang, *President*
Tom Somma, *Exec VP*
Zhang Xiaolan, *General Mgr*
Art Mathis, *Manager*
Arthur Mathis, *Assistant VP*
▲ EMP: 56 EST: 1992
SQ FT: 11,000
SALES (est): 10.8MM **Privately Held**
WEB: www.na.coscoshipping.com
SIC: 4731 Freight forwarding
HQ: Cosco Shipping Lines (North America)
    Inc.
    100 Lighting Way Fl 3
    Secaucus NJ 07094
    201 422-0500

(P-12441)
CROWLEY MARINE SERVICES INC
86 Berth, San Pedro (90731-3353)
PHONE..................310 732-6500
Andrew Gauphier, *Manager*
EMP: 303 **Privately Held**
WEB: www.crowley.com
SIC: 4731 Freight transportation arrangement
HQ: Crowley Marine Services, Inc.
    9487 Regency Square Blvd
    Jacksonville FL 32225

(P-12442)
CSC AUTO SALV DISMANTLING INC
12207 Branford St, Sun Valley
(91352-1010)
PHONE..................818 532-4624
Scott Sakajian, *President*
Garrett Brady, *Admin Sec*
EMP: 54 EST: 2008
SALES (est): 8MM **Privately Held**
WEB: www.autoquestdismantling.com
SIC: 4731 4953 Freight transportation arrangement; refuse systems

(P-12443)
DE WELL CONTAINER SHIPPING INC
Also Called: Logistics
5553 Bandini Blvd Unit A, Bell
(90201-6421)
PHONE..................310 735-8600
Yang Shi, *CEO*
Jamie Yen, *Executive*
Vanza Lian, *Regl Sales Mgr*
Shlomo Greenberg, *Director*
Danny Qian, *Manager*
▲ EMP: 90 EST: 2004
SALES (est): 27.4MM **Privately Held**
WEB: www.de-well.com
SIC: 4731 Freight forwarding
PA: De Well Container Shipping Corp.
    No.1568, Gangcheng Road, Pudong
    New District
    Shanghai 20012

(P-12444)
DEPENDABLE GLOBAL EXPRESS INC (PA)
Also Called: D G X
19201 S Susana Rd, E Rncho Dmngz
(90221-5710)
P.O. Box 513370, Los Angeles (90051-3370)
PHONE..................310 537-2000
Ronald Massman, *CEO*
Raquel Fonville, *Partner*
Bradley Dechter, *President*

Tim Rice, *CFO*
Verena Berger, *Officer*
EMP: 148 EST: 2004
SALES (est): 29.8MM **Privately Held**
WEB: www.dgxglobal.com
SIC: 4731 Freight forwarding

(P-12445)
DFDS INTERNATIONAL CORPORATION
Also Called: Dfds Transport US
898 N Pacific Coast Hwy # 6, El Segundo
(90245-2705)
PHONE..................310 414-1516
Tina Larsen, *General Mgr*
EMP: 80
SALES (corp-wide): 2.2B **Privately Held**
WEB: www.dfds.com
SIC: 4731 Foreign freight forwarding
HQ: Dfds International Corporation
    100 Walnut Ave Ste 405
    Clark NJ 07066

(P-12446)
DHX-DEPENDABLE HAWAIIAN EX INC (PA)
19201 S Susana Rd, Compton
(90221-5710)
PHONE..................310 537-2000
Ronald Massman, *Chairman*
Chris Johnson, *Chief Mktg Ofcr*
Cammie Laster, *Officer*
Gerard Crisostomo, *VP Bus Dvlpt*
Elaine Quantz, *Executive*
◆ EMP: 150 EST: 1980
SQ FT: 106,000
SALES (est): 108.7MM **Privately Held**
WEB: www.dhx.com
SIC: 4731 Foreign freight forwarding

(P-12447)
DISPATCH TRUCKING LLC (PA)
14032 Santa Ana Ave, Fontana
(92337-7035)
PHONE..................909 355-5531
Bruce L Degler, *CEO*
Jalayne Pugmire, *Vice Pres*
EMP: 70 EST: 1991
SQ FT: 600
SALES (est): 11MM **Privately Held**
SIC: 4731 Truck transportation brokers

(P-12448)
DSV SOLUTIONS LLC
Also Called: Corp., R.g Barry
13230 San Bernardino Ave, Fontana
(92335-5229)
PHONE..................909 349-6100
EMP: 121
SALES (corp-wide): 18.4B **Privately Held**
SIC: 4731 Freight forwarding
HQ: Dsv Solutions, Llc
    200 Wood Ave S 300
    Iselin NJ 08830
    732 850-8000

(P-12449)
DSV SOLUTIONS LLC
1670 Etiwanda Ave Ste A, Ontario
(91761-3641)
PHONE..................909 390-4563
Bob McCullough, *Manager*
EMP: 121
SQ FT: 400,000
SALES (corp-wide): 18.4B **Privately Held**
SIC: 4731 Freight transportation arrangement
HQ: Dsv Solutions, Llc
    200 Wood Ave S 300
    Iselin NJ 08830
    732 850-8000

(P-12450)
DSV SOLUTIONS LLC
3454 E Miraloma Ave, Anaheim
(92806-2101)
PHONE..................714 630-0110
EMP: 121
SALES (corp-wide): 18.4B **Privately Held**
SIC: 4731 Freight forwarding
HQ: Dsv Solutions, Llc
    200 Wood Ave S 300
    Iselin NJ 08830
    732 850-8000

(P-12451)
DYNAMIC WORLDWIDE WEST INC (PA)
14141 Alondra Blvd, Santa Fe Springs
(90670-5804)
PHONE..................562 407-1000
John J Belsito, *CEO*
Andrew D Rotondi, *COO*
Richard Morabito, *CFO*
Candace Lam, *Manager*
▲ EMP: 149 EST: 1991
SQ FT: 395,000
SALES (est): 35.1MM **Privately Held**
WEB: www.dynamiconline.com
SIC: 4731 Freight forwarding

(P-12452)
ELITE ANYWHERE CORP (PA)
82585 Showcase Pkwy A101, Indio
(92203-9692)
PHONE..................917 860-9247
Robert Sabo, *CEO*
EMP: 66 EST: 2016
SQ FT: 50,000
SALES (est): 2MM **Privately Held**
WEB: www.eliteanywhere.com
SIC: 4731 4225 Freight forwarding; general warehousing & storage

(P-12453)
EMPIRE MED TRANSPORTATIONS LLC
Also Called: Unicare Medical Transportation
1433 W Linden St Ste M, Riverside
(92507-6816)
PHONE..................951 530-8420
Jamal Abdel-Hadi,
EMP: 83 EST: 2017
SALES (est): 800K **Privately Held**
SIC: 4731 Freight forwarding

(P-12454)
ENGLEWOOD MARKETING GROUP LLC
127 W Jurupa Ave Ste 1, Bloomington
(92316-3510)
PHONE..................909 875-3649
Genie Gonzales, *Branch Mgr*
EMP: 55
SALES (corp-wide): 110.3MM **Privately Held**
WEB: www.emg-usa.com
SIC: 4731 5961 5722 Transportation agents & brokers; ; household appliance stores
HQ: Englewood Marketing Group Llc
    1471 Partnership Rd
    Green Bay WI 54304
    920 337-9800

(P-12455)
EXPEDITORS INTL WASH INC
19701 Hamilton Ave, Torrance
(90502-1352)
PHONE..................310 343-6200
Eric Mooney, *Branch Mgr*
EMP: 300
SALES (corp-wide): 10.1B **Publicly Held**
WEB: www.expeditors.com
SIC: 4731 Freight forwarding
PA: Expeditors International Of Washington, Inc.
    1015 3rd Ave
    Seattle WA 98104
    206 674-3400

(P-12456)
EXTRA EXPRESS (CERRITOS) INC
20405 Business Pkwy, Walnut
(91789-2939)
P.O. Box 5100, Cerritos (90703-5100)
PHONE..................714 985-6000
Kirk Baerwaldt, *President*
Robert Bell, *Vice Pres*
Tom Webb, *Director*
EMP: 50 EST: 2004
SALES (est): 26.9MM
SALES (corp-wide): 69.7MM **Privately Held**
WEB: www.extraexpress.com
SIC: 4731 Freight transportation arrangement

HQ: Dicom West Llc
676 N Michigan Ave # 3700
Chicago IL 60611
312 255-4800

(P-12457)
F R T INTERNATIONAL INC
Also Called: Frontier Logistics Services
2825 Jurupa St, Ontario (91761-2903)
PHONE..........................909 390-4892
Steven Hall, *Branch Mgr*
EMP: 82
SALES (corp-wide): 26.2MM **Privately Held**
SIC: 4731 Freight forwarding
PA: F. R. T. International, Inc.
1700 N Alameda St
Compton CA 90222
310 604-8208

(P-12458)
FNS INC (PA)
1545 Francisco St, Torrance (90501-1330)
PHONE..........................661 615-2300
Young Bin Kim, *CEO*
Bennet Koo, *Principal*
Myung Kim, *General Mgr*
Myung Joon Kim, *General Mgr*
Wook Jin Choi, *Admin Sec*
◆ **EMP:** 100 **EST:** 1995
SQ FT: 100,000
SALES (est): 105.1MM **Privately Held**
WEB: www.fnsusa.com
SIC: 4731 Freight forwarding

(P-12459)
FURNITURE TRNSP SYSTEMS INC
3100 Pomona Blvd, Pomona (91768-3230)
P.O. Box 2960 (91769-2960)
PHONE..........................909 869-1200
Dennis Firestone, *President*
Lynnette Genereux, *Corp Secy*
John Naughton, *Vice Pres*
EMP: 160 **EST:** 1978
SQ FT: 100,000
SALES (est): 6.6MM
SALES (corp-wide): 72.2MM **Privately Held**
WEB: www.kkwtrucks.com
SIC: 4731 4212 Freight consolidation; local trucking, without storage
PA: Kkw Trucking, Inc.
3100 Pomona Blvd
Pomona CA 91768
909 869-1200

(P-12460)
GELS LOGISTICS INC
Also Called: 360zebra
20275 Business Pkwy, City of Industry
(91789-2950)
PHONE..........................909 610-2277
Xindi Hu, *CEO*
Ling Wang, *CFO*
Liangna Zhong, *General Mgr*
EMP: 60 **EST:** 2013
SALES (est): 23.8MM **Privately Held**
SIC: 4731 Transportation agents & brokers

(P-12461)
GEODIS USA INC
Also Called: Ohl International
2255 E 220th St, Carson (90810-1639)
PHONE..........................310 518-6467
EMP: 52
SALES (corp-wide): 4.2MM **Privately Held**
WEB: www.geodis.com
SIC: 4731 8741 Freight forwarding; management services
HQ: Geodis Usa, Llc
5101 S Broad St
Philadelphia PA 19112
215 238-8600

(P-12462)
GEODIS WILSON USA INC
2155 E 220th St, Long Beach
(90810-1606)
PHONE..........................310 507-6300
P As Delachesta, *Branch Mgr*
EMP: 342
SALES (corp-wide): 4.2MM **Privately Held**
SIC: 4731 Foreign freight forwarding

HQ: Geodis Wilson Usa, Inc.
75a Northfield Ave
Edison NJ 08837

(P-12463)
GLOBAL MAIL INC
921 W Artesia Blvd, Compton
(90220-5105)
PHONE..........................310 735-0800
Eric Ricardo, *Branch Mgr*
Melanie Krips, *Vice Pres*
Craig Morris, *VP Bus Dvlpt*
Gia Motley, *General Mgr*
Mike Lawrence, *Administration*
EMP: 141
SALES (corp-wide): 79B **Privately Held**
SIC: 4731 Freight transportation arrangement
HQ: Global Mail, Inc.
2700 S Comm Pkwy Ste 300
Weston FL 33331
800 805-9306

(P-12464)
GLOVIS AMERICA INC (HQ)
17305 Von Karman Ave # 200, Irvine
(92614-6674)
PHONE..........................714 435-2960
B O N G Jeong Ko, *CEO*
Bong Jeong Ko, *CEO*
Scott Cornell, *COO*
Sandra V BSN, *Bd of Directors*
Sonia V Aprn, *Vice Pres*
◆ **EMP:** 185 **EST:** 2002
SQ FT: 34,700
SALES (est): 492.6MM **Privately Held**
WEB: www.america.glovis.net
SIC: 4731 Freight forwarding

(P-12465)
GREEN WORLDWIDE SHIPPING LLC
5777 W Century Blvd # 1285, Los Angeles
(90045-5632)
PHONE..........................310 988-1550
Edward Chambers, *Branch Mgr*
Rex Sherman, *Vice Pres*
Jenny Dykman, *Branch Mgr*
Claus Henning, *Branch Mgr*
Daniele Naldini, *Branch Mgr*
EMP: 53 **Privately Held**
WEB: www.greenworldwide.com
SIC: 4731 Freight forwarding
PA: Green Worldwide Shipping Llc
619 E College Ave Ste F
Decatur GA 30030

(P-12466)
HAM BROKERAGE
325 W Hospitality Ln # 102, San Bernardino
(92408-3243)
PHONE..........................909 659-5392
Ruben Nunez, *CEO*
EMP: 75 **EST:** 2019
SALES (est): 5.6MM **Privately Held**
SIC: 4731 Freight transportation arrangement

(P-12467)
HANJIN TRANSPORTATION CO LTD
Also Called: HANJIN GLOBAL LOGISTICS
1111 E Watson Center Rd Ua, Carson
(90745-4217)
PHONE..........................310 522-5030
Bryce Dalziel, *President*
Omer Uloomi, *Regional Mgr*
J B Park, *Admin Sec*
EMP: 90 **EST:** 1996
SQ FT: 28,000
SALES (est): 16.1MM **Privately Held**
SIC: 4731 Transportation agents & brokers

(P-12468)
HANKYU HANSHIN EXPRESS USA INC (DH)
1561 Beachey Pl, Carson (90746-4005)
PHONE..........................630 285-7100
Minorru Tanabe, *CEO*
Tamotsu Yamasaki, *President*
Tomohiro Yasuda, *CFO*
Tomomy CHI Yoshida, *Accounts Mgr*
◆ **EMP:** 50 **EST:** 1970

SQ FT: 1,362
SALES (est): 72.1MM **Privately Held**
WEB: www.hhe-global.com
SIC: 4731 Freight forwarding; customhouse brokers

(P-12469)
HAPAG-LLOYD (AMERICA) LLC
555 E Ocean Blvd Ste 300, Long Beach
(90802-5052)
PHONE..........................562 435-0771
Oli Reichol, *Branch Mgr*
Andreas Brauch, *Vice Pres*
Jennifer Jiang, *Executive*
Martin Gnass, *Managing Dir*
Alexander Martino, *General Mgr*
EMP: 75
SQ FT: 5,000
SALES (corp-wide): 15.1B **Privately Held**
WEB: www.hapag-lloyd.com
SIC: 4731 4412 4729 Agents, shipping; deep sea foreign transportation of freight; steamship ticket offices
HQ: Hapag-Lloyd (America) Llc
399 Hoes Ln Ste 101
Piscataway NJ 08854
732 562-1800

(P-12470)
HOME EXPRESS DELIVERY SVC LLC
Also Called: Temco Logistics
230 Diamond St, Laguna Beach
(92651-3610)
PHONE..........................949 715-9844
Lance Templeton, *Controller*
Charlie Sunberg, *Controller*
Virginia Templeton, *Controller*
EMP: 1000 **EST:** 2013
SQ FT: 900
SALES (est): 35MM **Privately Held**
SIC: 4731 Freight transportation arrangement

(P-12471)
INLOG INC
6765 Westminster Blvd # 4, Westminster
(92683-3769)
PHONE..........................949 212-3867
EMP: 85
SALES (corp-wide): 6.8MM **Privately Held**
SIC: 4731 Freight transportation arrangement
PA: Inlog, Inc.
4760 Preston Rd
Frisco TX 75034
949 212-5241

(P-12472)
INNOVEL SOLUTIONS INC
Also Called: Sears
5691 E Philadelphia St # 2, Ontario
(91761-2805)
PHONE..........................909 605-1446
Derrick Daniel, *Manager*
EMP: 592
SALES (corp-wide): 4.1B **Privately Held**
WEB: www.sears.com
SIC: 4731 Agents, shipping
HQ: Innovel Solutions, Inc.
3333 Beverly Rd
Hoffman Estates IL 60179
847 286-2500

(P-12473)
INTELLIGENT SCM LLC (PA)
12900 Simms Ave, Hawthorne
(90250-5533)
PHONE..........................310 775-9195
Peter Lamy, *President*
Robert Thatcher, *Branch Mgr*
Wanda Stone, *Director*
Karina Distefano, *Manager*
EMP: 56 **EST:** 2012
SQ FT: 96,000
SALES (est): 42.2MM **Privately Held**
WEB: www.intelligentscm.com
SIC: 4731 Foreign freight forwarding

(P-12474)
IRON MOUNTAIN INFO MGT LLC
441 N Oak St, Inglewood (90302-3314)
PHONE..........................818 848-9766
Jesse Ascencio, *Manager*
EMP: 94 **Publicly Held**

WEB: www.bondednj.com
SIC: 4731 Freight forwarding
HQ: Iron Mountain Information Management, Llc
3205 Burton Ave
Burbank CA 91504

(P-12475)
KW INTERNATIONAL INC
1457 Glenn Curtiss St, Carson
(90746-4036)
PHONE..........................310 354-6944
Dj Kim, *Branch Mgr*
EMP: 65 **Privately Held**
WEB: www.kwinternational.com
SIC: 4731 Freight forwarding
PA: Kw International, Inc.
18655 Bishop Ave
Carson CA 90746

(P-12476)
KW INTERNATIONAL INC
18511 S Broadwick St, Rancho Dominguez
(90220-6440)
PHONE..........................310 747-1380
Dj Kim, *Manager*
EMP: 70 **Privately Held**
WEB: www.kwinternational.com
SIC: 4731 Freight forwarding
PA: Kw International, Inc.
18655 Bishop Ave
Carson CA 90746

(P-12477)
L E COPPERSMITH INC (PA)
Also Called: Coppersmith Global Logistics
525 S Douglas St Ste 100, E Segundo
(90245-4828)
PHONE..........................310 607-8000
Jeffrey Craig Coppersmith, *President*
Douglas S Walkley, *CFO*
Lew Coppersmith Jr, *Vice Pres*
Lew E Coppersmith II, *Admin Sec*
Jim Rowley, *Controller*
◆ **EMP:** 80 **EST:** 1948
SQ FT: 40,000
SALES (est): 20MM **Privately Held**
WEB: www.coppersmith.com
SIC: 4731 4789 Customhouse brokers; cargo loading & unloading services

(P-12478)
LANDMARK GLOBAL INC (HQ)
506 Chapala St, Santa Barbara
(93101-3412)
PHONE..........................805 679-5029
James Edge, *CEO*
Gary Michael Crowe, *CFO*
Drew Evans, *Vice Pres*
Ross Steven Hurwitz, *Admin Sec*
Mario Guilin, *IT/INT Sup*
EMP: 96 **EST:** 2010
SALES (est): 82.2MM
SALES (corp-wide): 2.6B **Privately Held**
WEB: www.landmarkglobal.com
SIC: 4731 Foreign freight forwarding
PA: Bpost
Place De La Monnaie
Bruxelles 1000
220 123-45

(P-12479)
LINK LOGISTICS SOLUTIONS INC
220 W Victoria St, Compton (90220-6034)
PHONE..........................800 932-3383
Robert M Reznick, *CEO*
EMP: 58 **EST:** 2017
SALES (est): 5.3MM **Privately Held**
SIC: 4731 Freight forwarding

(P-12480)
M-7 CONSOLIDATION INC
475 W Apra St, Compton (90220-5527)
PHONE..........................310 898-3456
John J Brown, *President*
Harvey Turner, *Ch of Bd*
John Brown, *President*
Harald Niehenke, *CEO*
Kathleen Hogan, *Admin Sec*
▼ **EMP:** 140
SQ FT: 2,000

SALES (est): 24MM **Privately Held**
SIC: 4731 Foreign freight forwarding

(P-12481)
MAINFREIGHT INC (HQ)
1400 Glenn Curtiss St, Carson
(90746-4030)
PHONE................................310 900-1974
John Hepworth, *President*
Tim Williams, *CFO*
Brandon Fuller, *Executive*
Cary Chung, *Regional Mgr*
Ben Fitts, *Regional Mgr*
◆ EMP: 90
SQ FT: 100,000
SALES (est): 493.9MM **Privately Held**
WEB: www.mainfreight.com
SIC: 4731 Domestic freight forwarding

(P-12482)
MAPCARGO GLOBAL
LOGISTICS (PA)
2501 Santa Fe Ave, Redondo Beach
(90278-1117)
PHONE................................310 297-8300
Marek Adam Panasewicz, *President*
Jeffery Murphy, *Opers Mgr*
Katherine Long, *Sales Staff*
Yero Clarke, *Agent*
◆ EMP: 74 EST: 1990
SQ FT: 20,000
SALES (est): 38.5MM **Privately Held**
WEB: www.mapcargo.com
SIC: 4731 2448 Domestic freight forward-
ing; cargo containers, wood & wood with
metal

(P-12483)
MHX LLC
22707 Wilmington Ave, Carson
(90745-4321)
PHONE................................800 234-2098
Rick McLeod, *President*
Brooke Smith, *Vice Pres*
Conrad Hardin,
Vincent McLeod,
Daniel Boyd, *Manager*
EMP: 75 EST: 2016
SALES (est): 12.9MM **Privately Held**
WEB: www.mhx.solutions
SIC: 4731 Domestic freight forwarding

(P-12484)
MNX GLOBAL LOGISTICS CORP
(HQ)
5000 Arprt Plz Dr Ste 100, Long Beach
(90815)
PHONE................................310 981-0918
John Labrie, *CEO*
James Galante, *President*
Nathan Gesse, *COO*
Matt Ackerman, *CFO*
Paul Hickey, *Exec VP*
EMP: 55 EST: 1984
SALES (est): 127MM **Privately Held**
WEB: www.mnx.com
SIC: 4731 Freight forwarding

(P-12485)
MODIVCARE SOLUTIONS LLC
7441 Lincoln Way 225, Garden Grove
(92841-1452)
PHONE................................714 503-6871
Kymblyn Brown, *Principal*
Benjamin Highlander, *Manager*
EMP: 220
SALES (corp-wide): 1.3B **Publicly Held**
WEB: www.modivcare.com
SIC: 4731 Freight transportation arrange-
ment
HQ: Modivcare Solutions, Llc
6900 E Layton Ave # 1200
Denver CO 80237

(P-12486)
MOTIVATIONAL MARKETING
INC
Also Called: Motivational Fulfillment
16133 Fern Ave, Chino (91708-9001)
PHONE................................909 517-2200
EMP: 95 **Privately Held**
WEB: www.mfals.com
SIC: 4731 Freight transportation arrange-
ment

PA: Motivational Marketing, Inc.
15820 Euclid Ave
Chino CA 91708

(P-12487)
NATIONWIDE TRANS INC (PA)
1633 S Campus Ave, Ontario (91761-4335)
P.O. Box 4207 (91761-8907)
PHONE................................909 355-3211
Kong Lee, *President*
EMP: 100 EST: 2006
SALES (est): 16MM **Privately Held**
SIC: 4731 Freight transportation arrange-
ment

(P-12488)
NEOVIA LOGISTICS DIST LP
600 Live Oak Ave, Irwindale (91706-1344)
PHONE................................626 359-4500
Hector Legaspi, *Branch Mgr*
EMP: 109
SALES (corp-wide): 672.5MM **Privately
Held**
WEB: www.neovialogistics.com
SIC: 4731 Truck transportation brokers
HQ: Neovia Logistics Distribution, Lp
6363 N State Highway # 700
Irving TX 75038

(P-12489)
NEXT TRUCKING INC
2383 Utah Ave Ste 108, El Segundo
(90245-4845)
P.O. Box 7849, Torrance (90504-9249)
PHONE................................855 688-6398
Lidia Yan, *CEO*
Bryan Jolliff, *VP Bus Dvlpt*
Jackie Kembi, *Opers Staff*
Roy Rosell, *Marketing Staff*
Steven Nguyen, *Manager*
EMP: 200 EST: 2016
SALES (est): 32.2MM **Privately Held**
WEB: www.nexttrucking.com
SIC: 4731 4225 Freight forwarding; gen-
eral warehousing & storage

(P-12490)
NIPPON EXPRESS USA INC
970 Francisco St, Torrance (90502-1201)
PHONE................................310 532-6300
Yozo Komiya, *Vice Pres*
EMP: 50 **Privately Held**
WEB: www.nipponexpressusa.com
SIC: 4731 4412 4491 Freight forwarding;
deep sea foreign transportation of freight;
marine cargo handling
HQ: Nippon Express U.S.A., Inc.
800 N Il Route 83
Wood Dale IL 60191
708 304-9800

(P-12491)
NIPPON EXPRESS USA INC
2233 E Grand Ave, El Segundo
(90245-2837)
PHONE................................310 535-7200
Yozo Komiya, *Manager*
EMP: 56 **Privately Held**
WEB: www.nipponexpressusa.com
SIC: 4731 Foreign freight forwarding
HQ: Nippon Express U.S.A., Inc.
800 N Il Route 83
Wood Dale IL 60191
708 304-9800

(P-12492)
NIPPON EXPRESS USA INC
19500 S Vermont Ave, Torrance
(90502-1120)
PHONE................................310 527-4237
Masashi Hachimoto, *Principal*
EMP: 70 **Privately Held**
WEB: www.nipponexpressusa.com
SIC: 4731 Freight forwarding
HQ: Nippon Express U.S.A., Inc.
800 N Il Route 83
Wood Dale IL 60191
708 304-9800

(P-12493)
NISSIN INTL TRNSPT USA INC
(HQ)
1540 W 190th St, Torrance (90501-1121)
PHONE................................310 222-8500

Yasushi Ihara, *CEO*
Mitsugu Matsusaka, *CFO*
Melodee King, *Officer*
Hiromi Matsumoto, *Vice Pres*
Kwok Linda, *General Mgr*
◆ EMP: 50 EST: 1973
SQ FT: 98,000
SALES (est): 193.7MM **Privately Held**
WEB: www.nitusa.com
SIC: 4731 Domestic freight forwarding

(P-12494)
NRI USA LLC (PA)
Also Called: Nri Distribution
13200 S Broadway, Los Angeles
(90061-1124)
PHONE................................323 345-6456
Chris Maydaniuk,
Andres Castillo, *VP Opers*
Jennifer Alvarez, *Client Mgr*
Avelyn Warren, *Director*
Paul McNichol, *Supervisor*
▲ EMP: 100 EST: 2011
SQ FT: 65,000
SALES (est): 71MM **Privately Held**
WEB: www.nri-distribution.com
SIC: 4731 Freight forwarding

(P-12495)
O E C SHIPG LOS ANGELES INC
Also Called: Oec Group
13100 Alondra Blvd # 100, Cerritos
(90703-2278)
PHONE................................562 926-7186
Robert Han, *President*
John Su, *President*
Thomas Tae Kim, *Vice Pres*
Josh Steinberg, *Recruiter*
◆ EMP: 50 EST: 1998
SALES (est): 28.8MM **Privately Held**
WEB: www.oecgroup.com
SIC: 4731 Foreign freight forwarding
PA: Oec Freight Worldwide Co., Ltd.
7f, No. 131, Nanjing E. Rd., Sec. 3
Taipei City TAP 10410

(P-12496)
OCEAN BLUE EXPRESS INC
(PA)
255 W Victoria St, Compton (90220-6042)
PHONE................................310 719-2500
Sung Sun, *CEO*
Sung Ho Sun, *CEO*
Peter Shim, *Branch Mgr*
Sean Kim, *Export Mgr*
Jay Lee, *Manager*
◆ EMP: 55 EST: 2004
SQ FT: 79,000
SALES (est): 41.6MM **Privately Held**
WEB: www.oceanbluexp.com
SIC: 4731 4225 4214 Freight forwarding;
domestic freight forwarding; foreign
freight forwarding; customs clearance of
freight; general warehousing; local truck-
ing with storage

(P-12497)
OCONCA SHIPPING (LAX) INC
Also Called: Oconca Shipping New York
10628 Central Ave, Montclair (91763-4812)
PHONE................................909 625-5555
Scott Chen, *President*
May M Mak, *Vice Pres*
◆ EMP: 50 EST: 1998
SQ FT: 74,000
SALES (est): 5.5MM **Privately Held**
SIC: 4731 Foreign freight forwarding

(P-12498)
PACIFIC AIR CARGO LLC
6041 W Imperial Hwy, Los Angeles
(90045-6328)
PHONE................................310 645-2178
Tanja Janfruechte, *Principal*
Thomas Ingram, *Principal*
EMP: 97 EST: 2012
SALES (est): 4.8MM **Privately Held**
WEB: www.pacificaircargo.com
SIC: 4731 Freight forwarding

(P-12499)
PACIFIC LOGISTICS CORP (PA)
Also Called: Paclo
7255 Rosemead Blvd, Pico Rivera
(90660-4047)
PHONE................................562 478-4700
Douglas E Hockersmith, *President*
Timothy K Hewey, *COO*
Mark Nakamura, *CFO*
Cherise Sorbello, *Executive*
William Trodden, *Executive*
▲ EMP: 208
SQ FT: 206,000
SALES (est): 84.2MM **Privately Held**
WEB: www.pacific-logistics.com
SIC: 4731 Freight forwarding

(P-12500)
PACIFICA TRUCKS LLC
1450 Dominguez St, Carson (90810-1463)
PHONE................................310 549-1351
Aris Lazo, *President*
EMP: 55
SQ FT: 2,500 **Privately Held**
WEB: www.pacificatrucks.com
SIC: 4731 4213 4212 4214 Freight trans-
portation arrangement; trucking, except
local; local trucking, without storage; local
trucking with storage
PA: Pacifica Trucks, Llc
340 Golden Shore Ste 240
Long Beach CA 90802

(P-12501)
PACTRACK INC
4373 Santa Anita Ave A, El Monte
(91731-1690)
PHONE................................213 201-5856
Nabeil Hazu, *CEO*
Michael Vega, *President*
EMP: 75 EST: 2014
SALES (est): 9.2MM **Privately Held**
WEB: www.courierserviceslosangeles.com
SIC: 4731 7389 Freight transportation
arrangement; courier or messenger serv-
ice

(P-12502)
PANALPINA INC
19900 S Vermont Ave Ste A, Torrance
(90502-1147)
PHONE................................310 819-4060
Maurice Joseph, *Branch Mgr*
Cynthia Underwood, *Sales Staff*
EMP: 60
SALES (corp-wide): 18.4B **Privately Held**
WEB: www.ssc-solutions.com
SIC: 4731 Freight forwarding
HQ: Panalpina, Inc.
12430 Nw 25th St 100
Miami FL 33182
305 894-1300

(P-12503)
PATINA FREIGHT INC
Also Called: St George Logistics
1650 S Central Ave, Compton
(90220-5317)
PHONE................................310 764-4395
Matt Freeman CHI, *Planning*
Brandon Fibrow, *Opers Staff*
Pablo Seary Sav, *Manager*
Juan Nieto, *Supervisor*
EMP: 79
SALES (corp-wide): 56.4MM **Privately
Held**
WEB: www.stgusa.com
SIC: 4731 Shipping documents preparation
PA: Patina Freight, Inc.
20405 Business Pkwy
Walnut CA 91789
909 595-8100

(P-12504)
PATRIOT BROKERAGE INC
7840 Foothill Blvd Ste H, Sunland
(91040-2907)
PHONE................................910 227-4142
Ross Tsarukyan, *Mng Member*
Liyan Tsarukyan,
EMP: 84
SQ FT: 13,000
SALES (est): 13MM **Privately Held**
SIC: 4731 Freight forwarding

(P-12505)
PEGASUS MARITIME INC
535 N Brand Blvd Ste 400, Glendale
(91203-3907)
PHONE..................714 728-8565
Khurram Mahmood, *President*
Moazam Mahmood, *CEO*
Mookie Mahmood, *Exec VP*
Syed M Ali, *Vice Pres*
Imran Ahmed, *Opers Staff*
EMP: 75 **EST:** 2000
SQ FT: 10,000
SALES (est): 15.3MM **Privately Held**
WEB: www.pegasusmaritime.com
SIC: 4731 Freight forwarding

(P-12506)
**PERFORMANCE TEAM FRT SYS
INC**
1331 Torrance Blvd, Torrance
(90501-2351)
PHONE..................562 345-2200
Craig Kaplan, *CEO*
EMP: 113
SALES (corp-wide): 1.2MM **Privately
Held**
WEB: www.performanceteam.net
SIC: 4731 Customs clearance of freight
HQ: Performance Team Llc
2240 E Maple Ave
El Segundo CA 90245
562 345-2200

(P-12507)
**PERFORMANCE TEAM FRT SYS
INC**
1651 California St, Redlands (92374-2904)
PHONE..................424 358-6943
EMP: 113
SALES (corp-wide): 1.2MM **Privately
Held**
WEB: www.performanceteam.net
SIC: 4731 Freight forwarding
HQ: Performance Team Llc
2240 E Maple Ave
El Segundo CA 90245
562 345-2200

(P-12508)
PERFORMANCE TEAM LLC
1651 California St Ste A, Redlands
(92374-2904)
PHONE..................801 301-1732
Alberto Aguirre, *Analyst*
Tina Garcia, *Human Resources*
Grecia Mercado, *Opers Mgr*
Louis Navarro, *Opers Mgr*
Daniel Guerrero, *Opers Staff*
EMP: 113
SALES (corp-wide): 1.2MM **Privately
Held**
WEB: www.performanceteam.net
SIC: 4731 Freight forwarding
HQ: Performance Team Llc
2240 E Maple Ave
El Segundo CA 90245
562 345-2200

(P-12509)
PERFORMANCE TEAM LLC (DH)
2240 E Maple Ave, El Segundo
(90245-6507)
PHONE..................562 345-2200
Craig Kaplan, *CEO*
Jim Snodgrass, *President*
Paul Pickrell, *Senior VP*
Jason Walker, *Senior VP*
Steven Ayala, *Vice Pres*
◆ **EMP:** 200 **EST:** 1987
SQ FT: 80,000
SALES (est): 278.6MM
SALES (corp-wide): 1.2MM **Privately
Held**
WEB: www.performanceteam.net
SIC: 4731 4225 4213 Freight forwarding;
general warehousing & storage; trucking,
except local
HQ: A.P. Moller - Marsk A/S
Esplanaden 50
KObenhavn 1263
331 429-90

(P-12510)
**PRIME GLOBAL SOLUTIONS
INC (PA)**
Also Called: Pgs 360
15805 E Valley Blvd, City of Industry
(91744-3929)
P.O. Box 1669, Walnut (91788-1669)
PHONE..................800 424-7746
Michael Katyal, *CEO*
Garrett Fisher, *CFO*
Jaswant Khorana, *Vice Pres*
Jess Khorana, *Vice Pres*
Gomez Ron, *Human Res Mgr*
◆ **EMP:** 58 **EST:** 1989
SALES (est): 9.2MM **Privately Held**
WEB: www.pgs360.com
SIC: 4731 4225 Domestic freight forward-
ing; general warehousing & storage

(P-12511)
PRIME VALUE LOGISTIC INC
Also Called: Prime Value Logistics
16700 Valley View Ave # 30, La Mirada
(90638-5830)
PHONE..................213 218-3917
Luis Gomez, *CEO*
EMP: 50 **EST:** 2018
SQ FT: 5,000
SALES (est): 9.2MM **Privately Held**
WEB: www.primevaluelogistic.com
SIC: 4731 Brokers, shipping

(P-12512)
PRO LOADERS INC
14032 Santa Ana Ave, Fontana
(92337-7035)
PHONE..................909 355-5531
Bruce Degler, *President*
Chris Ebert, *CFO*
Christopher Ebert, *CFO*
Kim Pugmire, *Vice Pres*
Oscar Runyon, *General Mgr*
EMP: 200 **EST:** 1981
SQ FT: 600
SALES (est): 23.8MM **Privately Held**
SIC: 4731 1629 7359 7519 Truck trans-
portation brokers; earthmoving contractor;
equipment rental & leasing; trailer rental

(P-12513)
PRODUCTSGO LLC
14515 Alondra Blvd, La Mirada
(90638-5602)
PHONE..................714 242-4299
Marybelle Nguyen,
Belle Nguyen, *CFO*
EMP: 50 **EST:** 2015
SALES (est): 6MM **Privately Held**
WEB: www.productsgo.com
SIC: 4731 7371 5961 Freight forwarding;
computer software development & appli-
cations; catalog & mail-order houses

(P-12514)
QUARTZ LOGISTICS INC
780 Nogales St Ste D, City of Industry
(91748-1306)
PHONE..................626 606-2001
Tai Ruenn Wang, *CEO*
Jennifer Chou, *Vice Pres*
Sandy Chen, *Admin Sec*
EMP: 60 **EST:** 2010
SQ FT: 12,000
SALES (est): 106.6MM **Privately Held**
SIC: 4731 Freight forwarding

(P-12515)
QUIK PICK EXPRESS LLC
23610 Banning Blvd, Carson (90745-6220)
PHONE..................310 763-3000
Tom Boyle, *Mng Member*
Danny Boyle, *Mng Member*
EMP: 193
SALES (corp-wide): 40.6MM **Privately
Held**
WEB: www.quikpickexpress.com
SIC: 4731 Freight transportation arrange-
ment
PA: Quik Pick Express Llc
1021 E 233rd St
Carson CA 90745
310 763-3000

(P-12516)
QUIK PICK EXPRESS LLC (PA)
1021 E 233rd St, Carson (90745-6206)
P.O. Box 1129, Lakewood (90714-1129)
PHONE..................310 763-3000
George Boyle, *CEO*
Tom Boyle, *CFO*
Maria Alfassa, *Vice Pres*
Aurora Mendoza, *Executive*
Caroline Vivas, *Administration*
◆ **EMP:** 196 **EST:** 1988
SQ FT: 500,000
SALES (est): 40.6MM **Privately Held**
WEB: www.quikpickexpress.com
SIC: 4731 4214 Freight transportation
arrangement; local trucking with storage

(P-12517)
R L JONES-SAN DIEGO INC (PA)
1778 Zinetta Rd Ste A, Calexico
(92231-9511)
P.O. Box 472 (92232-0472)
PHONE..................760 357-3177
Russell L Jones, *President*
Earl Roberts, *Vice Pres*
Lucy Topete, *Administration*
Baltazar Espinoza, *Info Tech Mgr*
Jarr Baltazar, *Web Dvlpr*
EMP: 100 **EST:** 1952
SALES (est): 55.3MM **Privately Held**
SIC: 4731 4225 Customhouse brokers;
freight forwarding; general warehousing &
storage

(P-12518)
RED ROCK PALLET COMPANY
81153 Red Rock Rd, La Quinta
(92253-9334)
P.O. Box 1231, Folsom (95763-1231)
PHONE..................530 852-7744
Mark John Allen, *CEO*
EMP: 41 **EST:** 2008
SQ FT: 2,000
SALES (est): 2.1MM **Privately Held**
SIC: 4731 2448 Freight transportation
arrangement; pallets, wood

(P-12519)
**RESOURCE MANAGEMENT
GROUP INC (PA)**
Also Called: Rmg Recycling
2301 E 7th St Ste A337, Los Angeles
(90023-1043)
PHONE..................858 677-0884
Armen Derderian, *President*
Robert Garcia, *COO*
Josie Pantangco, *CFO*
Steve Joseph, *Managing Dir*
Chrissy Connerton, *Office Mgr*
▲ **EMP:** 56 **EST:** 1994
SALES (est): 23.2MM **Privately Held**
WEB: www.prezero.us
SIC: 4731 Freight transportation arrange-
ment

(P-12520)
ROCK-IT CARGO USA LLC
5343 W Imperial Hwy # 900, Los Angeles
(90045-6241)
PHONE..................310 410-0935
Raimar Schmitt, *COO*
Ed Butler, *Vice Pres*
Jordan Lenhoff, *Administration*
Anderson Maae, *Engineer*
Erin Cutri, *Accountant*
EMP: 84 **Privately Held**
WEB: www.rockitcargo.com
SIC: 4731 Freight forwarding
PA: Rock-It Cargo Usa Llc
201 Rock Lititz Blvd # 9
Lititz PA 17543

(P-12521)
SALSON LOGISTICS INC
1331 Torrance Blvd, Torrance
(90501-2351)
PHONE..................973 986-0200
Brian Howver, *Branch Mgr*
Saul Valle, *Opers Mgr*
EMP: 90
SALES (corp-wide): 174.1MM **Privately
Held**
WEB: www.salson.com
SIC: 4731 Freight forwarding

PA: Salson Logistics, Inc.
888 Doremus Ave
Newark NJ 07114
973 986-0200

(P-12522)
SAMTEX FABRICS INC
Also Called: Kamali Print Division Samtex
2424 E 28th St, Vernon (90058-1402)
PHONE..................213 742-0200
Justin Kachan, *CEO*
Sam Kachan, *President* ,
▲ **EMP:** 50 **EST:** 1986
SQ FT: 30,000
SALES (est): 2.4MM **Privately Held**
WEB: www.samtexinc.com
SIC: 5949 4731 Fabric stores piece
goods; foreign freight forwarding

(P-12523)
**SCHUMACHER CARGO
LOGISTICS INC (PA)**
Also Called: S C L
550 W 135th St, Gardena (90248-1506)
PHONE..................562 408-6677
Martin D Baker, *CEO*
Mark Novoselitsky, *General Mgr*
Ryan Nicholas, *Engineer*
Martin Kelly, *Controller*
Martha Covarrubias, *Export Mgr*
◆ **EMP:** 50 **EST:** 1974
SQ FT: 200,000
SALES (est): 23.2MM **Privately Held**
WEB: www.schumachercargo.com
SIC: 4731 Foreign freight forwarding;
freight forwarding

(P-12524)
**SEAWORLD GLOBAL
LOGISTICS**
9350 Wilshire Blvd # 203, Beverly Hills
(90212-3214)
PHONE..................310 579-9164
Dhakshitha Gabriel, *President*
EMP: 385 **EST:** 2017
SALES (est): 18.5MM **Privately Held**
SIC: 4731 Foreign freight forwarding

(P-12525)
**SHO-AIR INTERNATIONAL INC
(PA)**
5401 Argosy Ave Ste 102, Huntington
Beach (92649-1038)
PHONE..................949 476-9111
James Nicoll, *Ch of Bd*
R Scott Tedro, *President*
Eric Monroe, *COO*
Jessica Elende, *CFO*
Ryan Suavet, *General Mgr*
▲ **EMP:** 50 **EST:** 1985
SQ FT: 18,000
SALES (est): 16MM **Privately Held**
WEB: www.shoair.com
SIC: 4731 Domestic freight forwarding

(P-12526)
SMD LOGISTICS INC (PA)
101 E Main St, Heber (92249-9702)
P.O. Box 472 (92249-0472)
PHONE..................760 352-3194
Steve Scaroni, *President*
Brenda Scaroni, *Admin Sec*
Martha Camacho, *Human Res Mgr*
Liz Guillen, *Assistant*
EMP: 122 **EST:** 1999
SQ FT: 5,000
SALES (est): 20.2MM **Privately Held**
WEB: www.sfcos.com
SIC: 4731 Freight transportation arrange-
ment

(P-12527)
**SOURCE FREIGHT SYSTEM LLC
(PA)**
Also Called: Source Logistic
812 Union St, Montebello (90640-6523)
PHONE..................323 887-3884
Marcelo G Sada, *Mng Member*
Raul V Flores, *Mng Member*
Erick Luna, *Mng Member*
Fernando Ramirez-Orosco, *Mng Member*
EMP: 67 **EST:** 2005

▲ = Import ▼=Export
◆ =Import/Export

SALES (est): 7.7MM **Privately Held**
WEB: www.sourcelogistics.com
SIC: **4731** Brokers, shipping; freight forwarding

(P-12528)
SOURCE LOGISTICS CENTER CORP
812 Union St, Montebello (90640-6523)
PHONE..................323 887-3884
Marcelo Sada, *President*
Wendy Escobedo, *Vice Pres*
Raul Villarreal, *Vice Pres*
Fernando Ramirez, *Admin Sec*
EMP: 75 EST: 1999
SQ FT: 300,000
SALES (est): 7.1MM **Privately Held**
WEB: www.sourcelogistics.com
SIC: **4731** Freight transportation arrangement

(P-12529)
SOUTH BAY FREIGHT SYSTEM LLC (PA)
Also Called: South Bay Group
900 Turnbull Canyon Rd, City of Industry (91745-1404)
PHONE..................626 271-9800
James Lin, *Mng Member*
EMP: 60 EST: 2006
SALES (est): 15.2MM **Privately Held**
WEB: www.unisco.com
SIC: **4731** Freight forwarding

(P-12530)
STATES LOGISTICS SERVICES INC
7221 Cate Dr, Buena Park (90621-1883)
PHONE..................714 523-1276
Cathy J Monson, *Branch Mgr*
EMP: 69 **Privately Held**
WEB: www.stateslogistics.com
SIC: **4731** Truck transportation brokers
PA: States Logistics Services, Inc.
 5650 Dolly Ave
 Buena Park CA 90621

(P-12531)
STATES LOGISTICS SERVICES INC (PA)
5650 Dolly Ave, Buena Park (90621-1872)
PHONE..................714 521-6520
Daniel Monson, *CEO*
William Donovan, *President*
Kirk Hellofs, *Vice Pres*
Jennifer Monson, *Admin Sec*
Nancy Molina, *Human Resources*
▲ EMP: 140 EST: 1958
SQ FT: 900,000
SALES (est): 182.9MM **Privately Held**
WEB: www.stateslogistics.com
SIC: **4731** Freight transportation arrangement

(P-12532)
STEVENS GLOBAL LOGISTICS INC (PA)
Also Called: Steven Global Freight Services
3700 Redondo Beach Ave, Redondo Beach (90278-1108)
P.O. Box 729, Lawndale (90260-0729)
PHONE..................310 216-5645
Thomas J Petrizzio, *CEO*
Karl Chambers, *COO*
Gary Hooper, *CFO*
Timothy Hewey, *Officer*
John Tiseo, *Managing Dir*
◆ EMP: 95 EST: 1985
SQ FT: 48,000
SALES (est): 34.9MM **Privately Held**
WEB: www.stevensglobal.com
SIC: **4731** Freight forwarding

(P-12533)
STRAIGHT FORWARDING INC
Also Called: MEOW LOGISTICS
20275 Business Pkwy, Walnut (91789-2950)
PHONE..................909 594-3400
Yihsiang Wu, *CEO*
Jane Xu, *Accounting Mgr*
Sfi-Aven Pian, *Sales Staff*
EMP: 100 EST: 2011

SALES (est): 78.8MM **Privately Held**
WEB: www.sfi.com
SIC: **4731** Foreign freight forwarding; freight forwarding

(P-12534)
SUPRA NATIONAL EXPRESS INC
1411 E Watson Center Rd, Carson (90745-4305)
PHONE..................310 549-7105
Daniel Linares, *CEO*
Albert Martinez, *Technology*
Joe Balbuena, *Business Mgr*
Donald Aleshire, *Manager*
EMP: 125 EST: 2014
SALES (est): 28.5MM **Privately Held**
WEB: www.snecorp.com
SIC: **4731** Truck transportation brokers

(P-12535)
SYNCREON AMERICA INC
14780 Bar Harbor Rd Ste B, Fontana (92336-4254)
PHONE..................909 610-4511
EMP: 89 **Privately Held**
WEB: www.syncreon.com
SIC: **4731** Freight transportation arrangement
HQ: Syncreon America Inc.
 2851 High Meadow Cir # 25
 Auburn Hills MI 48326
 248 377-4700

(P-12536)
TAYLORED SVCS PARENT CO INC (PA)
1495 E Locust St, Ontario (91761-4570)
PHONE..................909 510-4800
Bill Butler, *CEO*
Michael Yusko, *CFO*
EMP: 80 EST: 2012
SQ FT: 330,000
SALES (est): 224MM **Privately Held**
WEB: www.tayloredservices.com
SIC: **4731** Agents, shipping

(P-12537)
TOLL GLOBAL FORWARDING USA INC (HQ)
2000 E Carson St, Carson (90810-1222)
PHONE..................626 363-2400
Myles O Brien, *Ch of Bd*
Cynthia Oliver, *President*
Neil Devine, *Treasurer*
Bill Cunningham, *Vice Pres*
Anthony Lau, *Vice Pres*
◆ EMP: 50 EST: 1983
SQ FT: 79,900
SALES (est): 73.7MM
SALES (corp-wide): 224.3MM **Privately Held**
WEB: www.tollgroup.com
SIC: **4731** Foreign freight forwarding; freight forwarding
PA: Toll Global Forwarding Holdings (Usa) Inc.
 800 Federal Blvd
 Carteret NJ 07008
 732 750-9000

(P-12538)
TOLL GLOBAL FWDG SCS USA INC
3355 Dulles Dr, Jurupa Valley (91752-3244)
PHONE..................951 360-8310
Bryan Howber, *Senior VP*
EMP: 100
SALES (corp-wide): 224MM **Privately Held**
SIC: **4731** Freight forwarding
HQ: Toll Global Forwarding Scs (Usa) Inc.
 800 Federal Blvd Ste 2
 Carteret NJ 07008
 732 750-9000

(P-12539)
TOLL GLOBAL FWDG SCS USA INC
Also Called: FMI International West 2
400-450 Westmont Dr, San Pedro (90731)
PHONE..................732 750-9000
Gary Hecht, *Manager*
EMP: 75

SALES (corp-wide): 224MM **Privately Held**
SIC: **4731** Freight forwarding
HQ: Toll Global Forwarding Scs (Usa) Inc.
 800 Federal Blvd Ste 2
 Carteret NJ 07008
 732 750-9000

(P-12540)
TOPLAND LOGISTICS INC (PA)
2727 Workman Mill Rd, City of Industry (90601-1452)
PHONE..................562 908-6988
Robert Wang, *CEO*
EMP: 94 EST: 2003
SALES (est): 9MM **Privately Held**
WEB: www.topocean.com
SIC: **4731** Freight forwarding

(P-12541)
TOPOCEAN CONSOLIDATION SERVICE (PA)
2727 Workman Mill Rd, City of Industry (90601-1452)
PHONE..................562 908-1688
Robert Wang, *President*
Jay Kong, *Partner*
Andy Wang, *Vice Pres*
Khong Goh, *General Mgr*
Gonzalo Palafox, *CIO*
◆ EMP: 134 EST: 1995
SQ FT: 350,000
SALES (est): 170.2MM **Privately Held**
WEB: www.topocean.com
SIC: **4731** Foreign freight forwarding; freight forwarding

(P-12542)
TOTAL LOGISTICS ONLINE LLC
628 N Gilbert St, Fullerton (92833-2555)
PHONE..................714 526-3559
Ed Mock, *Branch Mgr*
EMP: 56
SALES (corp-wide): 2.1B **Publicly Held**
WEB: www.totallogistic.com
SIC: **4731** Freight transportation arrangement
HQ: Total Logistics Online L.L.C.
 4432 S Buttermilk Ct # 10
 Hudsonville MI 49426

(P-12543)
TRANSIT AIR CARGO INC
2204 E 4th St, Santa Ana (92705-3868)
P.O. Box 10053 (92711-0053)
PHONE..................714 571-0393
Gulnawaz Khodayar, *CEO*
Christy Colton, *Vice Pres*
Tania Khodayar, *Vice Pres*
Michelle Nguyen, *Vice Pres*
Huethi Croteau, *Opers Staff*
◆ EMP: 185 EST: 1989
SQ FT: 10,000
SALES (est): 33MM **Privately Held**
WEB: www.transitair.com
SIC: **4731** Foreign freight forwarding

(P-12544)
TRI-TECH LOGISTICS LLC
3230 E Imperial Hwy # 140, Brea (92821-6721)
PHONE..................855 373-7049
Kuldip S Dhaliwal,
Gurdeep Singh Dhaliwal,
Jeremy Engstrom, *Manager*
EMP: 210 EST: 2014
SALES (est): 23.6MM
SALES (corp-wide): 6.5MM **Privately Held**
WEB: www.tritechlogistics.com
SIC: **4731** Freight forwarding
PA: Tri-Tech Logistics Ltd
 17660 65a Ave Unit 208
 Surrey BC V3S 5
 604 415-9898

(P-12545)
TRICAP INTERNATIONAL LLC
19067 S Reyes Ave, Compton (90221-5813)
PHONE..................509 703-8780
Puneet Bawa, *Director*
EMP: 93

SALES (corp-wide): 224MM **Privately Held**
SIC: **4731** Freight forwarding
HQ: Toll Global Forwarding Scs (Usa) Inc.
 800 Federal Blvd Ste 2
 Carteret NJ 07008
 732 750-9000

SALES (corp-wide): 5.4MM **Privately Held**
WEB: www.thetrianglegroup.com
SIC: **4731** Freight forwarding
PA: Tricap International, Llc
 9 Hackensack Ave Bldg 43
 Kearny NJ 07032
 310 605-5089

(P-12546)
TRICOR AMERICA INC
12441 Eucalyptus Ave 7, Hawthorne (90250-4208)
PHONE..................310 676-0800
Fax: 310 973-1565
EMP: 100
SALES (corp-wide): 102.7MM **Privately Held**
SIC: **4731** Courier Service
PA: Tricor America, Inc.
 717 Airport Blvd
 South San Francisco CA 94080
 650 877-3650

(P-12547)
TRIPLE B FORWARDERS INC (PA)
Also Called: Triple B Forwarders
1511 Glenn Curtiss St, Carson (90746-4035)
PHONE..................310 604-5840
Richard Beliveau, *CEO*
Connie Ladin, *Treasurer*
Frank Chung, *Export Mgr*
Bob Mathieu, *Export Mgr*
Rowena Viray, *Export Mgr*
◆ EMP: 143 EST: 1976
SQ FT: 37,800
SALES (est): 20.3MM **Privately Held**
WEB: www.tripleb.com
SIC: **4731** **4783** Domestic freight forwarding; foreign freight forwarding; packing goods for shipping

(P-12548)
UNIS LLC (PA)
Also Called: United Network Info Svcs
218 Machlin Ct Ste A, Walnut (91789-3057)
PHONE..................909 839-2600
James Lin, *President*
Gracie Leung, *CFO*
Joe Dabbs, *Vice Pres*
Nicole Gomes, *Counsel*
Angel Hernandez, *Director*
EMP: 200 EST: 2012
SALES (est): 194.5MM **Privately Held**
SIC: **4731** Freight forwarding

(P-12549)
US LINES LLC (DH)
3501 Jamboree Rd Ste 300, Newport Beach (92660-2936)
PHONE..................714 751-3333
Ed Aldridge, *President*
Dan Raia, *Regl Sales Mgr*
Fran Bagaman, *Manager*
◆ EMP: 75 EST: 2004
SALES (est): 34MM
SALES (corp-wide): 355.8K **Privately Held**
WEB: www.marcopolo-cmacgm.fr
SIC: **4731** Freight forwarding
HQ: Cma Cgm
 4 Boulevard J Saade
 Marseille 13002
 185 149-775

(P-12550)
VANGUARD LGISTICS SVCS USA INC (HQ)
5000 Arprt Plz Dr Ste 200, Long Beach (90815)
PHONE..................310 847-3000
Charles Brennan, *Chairman*
James Julian, *President*
Jeff Lee, *COO*
J Thurso Barendse, *CFO*
Scott Shellow, *Treasurer*
◆ EMP: 100 EST: 1978
SALES (est): 227.7MM **Privately Held**
WEB: www.vanguardlogistics.com
SIC: **4731** Freight consolidation

PA: Naca Holdings, Inc.
5000 Arprt Plz Dr Ste 200
Long Beach CA 90815
310 847-3000

(P-12551)
WESTERN OVERSEAS CORPORATION (PA)
10731 Walker St Ste B, Cypress (90630-4757)
P.O. Box 90099, Long Beach (90809-0099)
PHONE..................562 985-0616
Michael F Dugan, *President*
Carlo Deatougia, *Vice Pres*
Barbara Chopin, *Branch Mgr*
Andy Werner, *Branch Mgr*
Aurora Rojas, *Executive Asst*
◆ EMP: 50 EST: 1953
SQ FT: 40,000
SALES (est): 62.1MM **Privately Held**
WEB: www.westernoverseas.com
SIC: 4731 Western forwarding; foreign freight forwarding

(P-12552)
XPO STACKTRAIN LLC
2700 E Imperial Hwy, Lynwood (90262-4017)
PHONE..................310 661-4000
Donald Orris, *Branch Mgr*
EMP: 130
SALES (corp-wide): 16.2B **Publicly Held**
WEB: www.xpo.com
SIC: 4731 Freight transportation arrangement
HQ: Xpo Stacktrain, Llc
5165 Emerald Pkwy
Dublin OH 43017

(P-12553)
YUSEN LOGISTICS AMERICAS INC
2417 E Carson St Ste 100, Carson (90810-1252)
PHONE..................310 518-3008
P Smith, *Branch Mgr*
Nohemi Mederos, *Internal Med*
Lah Donovan, *Supervisor*
Osiris Galindo, *Supervisor*
Shawn Hollis, *Supervisor*
EMP: 200 **Privately Held**
WEB: www.us.yusen-logistics.com
SIC: 4731 Freight forwarding
HQ: Yusen Logistics (Americas) Inc.
300 Lighting Way Ste 600
Secaucus NJ 07094
201 553-3800

4783 Packing & Crating Svcs

(P-12554)
ADVANTAGE MEDIA SERVICES INC (PA)
Also Called: AMS Fulfillement
29010 Commerce Center Dr, Valencia (91355-4188)
PHONE..................661 775-0611
Jay Catlin, *President*
Ken Wiseman, *CEO*
Marco Pelaez, *Vice Pres*
Louise Aldrich, *Principal*
Eric Wiseman, *Opers Mgr*
▲ EMP: 212 EST: 2002
SQ FT: 142,000
SALES (est): 56.1MM **Privately Held**
WEB: www.amsfulfillment.com
SIC: 4783 4731 Packing goods for shipping; agents, shipping

(P-12555)
CALAVO GROWERS INC
Also Called: Calavo Foods
15765 W Telegraph Rd, Santa Paula (93060-3041)
P.O. Box 751 (93061-0751)
PHONE..................805 525-5511
EMP: 80
SALES (corp-wide): 1B **Publicly Held**
SIC: 4783 Packing/Crating Service
PA: Calavo Growers, Inc.
1141 Cummings Rd Ste A
Santa Paula CA 93060
805 525-1245

(P-12556)
DISNEYLAND RESORT
Also Called: Shipping Department
1020 W Ball Rd, Anaheim (92802-1804)
PHONE..................714 781-7560
Mark Steinmetz, *Branch Mgr*
EMP: 299
SALES (corp-wide): 65.3B **Publicly Held**
SIC: 4783 Containerization of goods for shipping
HQ: Disneyland Resort
1313 S Harbor Blvd
Anaheim CA 92802
714 781-4000

(P-12557)
DIVERSIFIED LOGISTIC SVCS INC
13033 Telegraph Rd, Santa Fe Springs (90670-4011)
PHONE..................562 941-3600
Anthony Dellaquila, *President*
EMP: 22 EST: 2008
SQ FT: 11,000
SALES (est): 1.2MM **Privately Held**
WEB: www.dlspro1.com
SIC: 4783 2449 1796 4214 Packing & crating; rectangular boxes & crates, wood; machine moving & rigging; household goods moving & storage, local; local trucking, without storage; vacuum packaging machinery

(P-12558)
SUNTREAT PKG SHIPG A LTD PRTNR
391 Oxford Ave, Lindsay (93247-2208)
P.O. Box 850 (93247-0850)
PHONE..................559 562-4991
Dennis A Griffith, *Managing Prtnr*
Dwight J Griffith, *Partner*
Tom Clark, *Vice Pres*
Richard Sholander, *Director*
EMP: 200 EST: 1958
SQ FT: 75,000
SALES (est): 21.2MM **Privately Held**
WEB: www.suntreat.com
SIC: 4783 8742 Packing goods for shipping; management consulting services

(P-12559)
UNIFIED AIRCRAFT SERVICES INC (PA)
1571 S Lilac Ave, Bloomington (92316-2141)
P.O. Box 401060, Las Vegas NV (89140-1060)
PHONE..................909 877-0535
Ben C Warren, *President*
Venida L Warren, *Corp Secy*
Benjamin T Warren, *Vice Pres*
EMP: 65 EST: 1972
SQ FT: 14,500
SALES (est): 15.4MM **Privately Held**
SIC: 4783 Packing goods for shipping; containerization of goods for shipping

(P-12560)
WHALING PACKAGING CO
21020 S Wilmington Ave, Carson (90810-1232)
P.O. Box 4547 (90749-4547)
PHONE..................310 518-6021
Thomas Whaling, *President*
Michelle Whaling, *Treasurer*
Chuck Whaling, *Vice Pres*
Chris Whaling, *Sales Executive*
Tom Whaling, *Sales Staff*
EMP: 27 EST: 1978
SQ FT: 12,973
SALES (est): 4.2MM **Privately Held**
WEB: www.whalingpackaging.com
SIC: 4783 2653 2441 Packing & crating; corrugated & solid fiber boxes; nailed wood boxes & shook

---

4785 Fixed Facilities, Inspection, Weighing Svcs Transptn

(P-12561)
COFIROUTE USA LLC
200 Spectrum Center Dr # 16, Irvine (92618-5003)
PHONE..................949 754-0198
Gary Hausdorfer, *CEO*
Darla Casby, *Vice Pres*
David Hartt, *Vice Pres*
Carly Lancaster, *Vice Pres*
Jill Stefanelli, *Vice Pres*
▲ EMP: 112 EST: 2002
SQ FT: 9,000
SALES: 18MM
SALES (corp-wide): 17.7MM **Privately Held**
WEB: www.cofirouteusa.com
SIC: 4785 Toll road operation
HQ: Vinci Concessions
1973 Boulevard De La Defense
Nanterre 92000

4789 Transportation Svcs, NEC

(P-12562)
ALSTOM SIGNALING OPERATION LLC
7337 Central Ave, Riverside (92504-1440)
PHONE..................951 343-9699
EMP: 192 **Privately Held**
WEB: www.wabtec.com
SIC: 4789 Transportation Services
HQ: Alstom Signaling Operation, Llc
2712 S Dillingham Rd
Grain Valley MO 64029
816 650-3112

(P-12563)
AMBIANCE TRANSPORTATION LLC
6901 San Fernando Rd, Glendale (91201-1608)
PHONE..................818 955-5757
Ryan Ferreira,
EMP: 90 EST: 2018
SALES (est): 5.4MM **Privately Held**
WEB: www.ambiancetrans.com
SIC: 4789 Transportation services

(P-12564)
AMERICAN TRANSPORTATION CO LLC
635 W Colo St Ste 108a, Glendale (91204)
PHONE..................818 660-2343
Michael Ahmed,
Isaac Albekyan, *Principal*
EMP: 88 EST: 2012
SALES (est): 1.7MM **Privately Held**
SIC: 4789 Transportation services

(P-12565)
CAPSTONE LOGISTICS LLC
12661 Aldi Pl, Moreno Valley (92555-6703)
PHONE..................770 414-1929
EMP: 525
SALES (corp-wide): 1.1B **Privately Held**
WEB: www.capstonelogistics.com
SIC: 4789 Cargo loading & unloading services
PA: Capstone Logistics, Llc
30 Technology Pkwy S # 200
Peachtree Corners GA 30092
770 414-1929

(P-12566)
COMPASS TRANSPORTATION INC
11591 Martha Ann Dr, Los Alamitos (90720-4003)
PHONE..................310 834-4530
EMP: 66
SALES (corp-wide): 66.8K **Privately Held**
WEB: www.compasstransportation.net
SIC: 4789 Cargo loading & unloading services

PA: Compass Transportation, Inc.
3749 Stonemont Dr
Hemet CA

(P-12567)
COMPREHENSIVE DIST SVCS INC
18726 S Wstn Ave Ste 300, Gardena (90248)
PHONE..................310 523-1546
Sam Lee, *President*
EMP: 150 EST: 2010
SALES (est): 5.3MM **Privately Held**
WEB: www.cdsintro.com
SIC: 4789 Freight car loading & unloading

(P-12568)
COUNTY OF LOS ANGELES
Also Called: Transportation Bureau
441 Bauchet St, Los Angeles (90012-2906)
PHONE..................213 974-4561
EMP: 250 **Privately Held**
SIC: 4789 9621 Transportation Services Regulation/Administrative Transportation
PA: County Of Los Angeles
500 W Temple St Ste 375
Los Angeles CA 90012
213 974-1101

(P-12569)
DSI LOGISTICS LLC (FA)
675 Placentia Ave Ste 325, Brea (92821-6172)
PHONE..................800 335-6557
Dave Thompson, *President*
David Whitley, *Chief Mktg Ofcr*
Jonathan Arrendale, *Vice Pres*
EMP: 96 EST: 2015
SALES (est): 17.7MM **Privately Held**
WEB: www.dsicompanies.org
SIC: 4789 Pipeline terminal facilities, independently operated

(P-12570)
EAC INTRNATIONAL LOGISTICS INC
18945 San Jose Ave, City of Industry (91748-1328)
P.O. Box 1184, Mansfield MA (02048-5184)
PHONE..................877 668-7837
Chaojin Ye, *Vice Pres*
EMP: 50 EST: 2018
SALES (est): 1.8MM **Privately Held**
WEB: www.eacinternationallogisticsinc.com
SIC: 4789 Transportation services

(P-12571)
FLUOR FLTRON BLFOUR BTTY DRGDO
5901 W Century Blvd, Los Angeles (90045-5411)
PHONE..................949 420-5000
Kenneth Isett, *Principal*
Terry Gohde, *Principal*
EMP: 99 EST: 2018
SALES (est): 2.4MM **Privately Held**
WEB: www.lalinxs.com
SIC: 4789 Transportation services

(P-12572)
GUNDERSON RAIL SERVICES LLC
Also Called: Greenbrier Rail Services
1475 Cooley Ct, San Bernardino (92408-2830)
P.O. Box 1715 (92402-1715)
PHONE..................909 478-0541
Kevin Johnson, *Controller*
EMP: 93
SQ FT: 64,248
SALES (corp-wide): 1.7B **Publicly Held**
WEB: www.gbrx.com
SIC: 4789 Railroad car repair
HQ: Gunderson Rail Services Llc
1 Centerpointe Dr Ste 200
Lake Oswego OR 97035
503 684-7000

(P-12573)
HYPERLOOP TECHNOLOGIES INC (PA)
Also Called: Hyperloop One
2159 Bay St, Los Angeles (90021-1707)
PHONE..................213 800-3270

▲ = Import ▼=Export
◆ =Import/Export

Sultan Ahmed Bin Sulayem, *Ch of Bd*
Jay Walder, *CEO*
Brent Callinicos, *COO*
William Mulholland, *Exec VP*
Desmond Atkins, *Vice Pres*
EMP: 199 **EST:** 2014
SALES (est): 103MM **Privately Held**
WEB: www.virginhyperloop.com
SIC: 4789 Pipeline terminal facilities, independently operated

(P-12574)
JESSE ALEXANDER TRANSPORT
9338 Azurite Ave, Hesperia (92344-4611)
PHONE.................................760 669-0379
Jesus Gomez, *Mng Member*
EMP: 60 **EST:** 2014
SALES (est): 1.6MM **Privately Held**
SIC: 4789 Transportation services

(P-12575)
JP MOTORSPORTS INC
11582 Sheldon St, Sun Valley (91352-1501)
PHONE.................................818 381-8313
George Sukunyan, *President*
Ovsep Sukunyan, *CEO*
Arman Sukunyan, *General Mgr*
EMP: 54 **EST:** 2009
SQ FT: 18,000
SALES (est): 5.9MM **Privately Held**
WEB: www.jplogistics.net
SIC: 4789 Cargo loading & unloading services

(P-12576)
KAYDAN LOGISTICS LLC
45562 Ponderosa Ct, Temecula (92592-2829)
PHONE.................................951 961-9000
Kirk Morrison, *CEO*
EMP: 91 **EST:** 2020
SALES (est): 4.2MM **Privately Held**
SIC: 4789 Transportation services

(P-12577)
LA INSTALLS CORPORATION (PA)
2949 S Vineyard Ave, Ontario (91761-6475)
PHONE.................................909 923-7076
Jaime Ricardo Melero, *Principal*
EMP: 24 **EST:** 2015
SALES (est): 241.4K **Privately Held**
SIC: 4789 4212 2431 Transportation services; local trucking, without storage; millwork

(P-12578)
LINEAGE LOGISTICS HOLDINGS LLC
2344 Fleetwood Dr, Riverside (92509-2409)
PHONE.................................951 369-0230
Sean Vanderelzen, *Officer*
Dominic Dicarlo, *Vice Pres*
Todd Drass, *Vice Pres*
Jt Marcum, *VP Bus Dvlpt*
Bruce Hirz, *Executive*
EMP: 111 **Privately Held**
WEB: www.lineagelogistics.com
SIC: 4789 Pipeline terminal facilities, independently operated
HQ: Lineage Logistics Holdings, Llc
46500 Humboldt Dr
Novi MI 48377
800 678-7271

(P-12579)
MERIDIAN RAIL ACQUISITION
Also Called: Greenbrier Rail
1475 Cooley Ct, San Bernardino (92408-2830)
P.O. Box 1715 (92402-1715)
PHONE.................................909 478-0541
EMP: 150
SALES (corp-wide): 1.7B **Publicly Held**
WEB: www.gbrx.com
SIC: 4789 Railroad car repair
HQ: Meridian Rail Acquisition Corp
1 Centerpointe Dr Ste 400
Lake Oswego OR 97035
503 684-7000

(P-12580)
MERIT LOGISTICS LLC
Also Called: Drop Lot Services
33332 Valle Rd Ste 100, San Juan Capistrano (92675-4856)
PHONE.................................949 481-0685
Cesar Raul Scolari, *Mng Member*
Vern Malpass, *COO*
Jason Giuliany, *Vice Pres*
Andy Nguyen, *Info Tech Mgr*
Robert Gunderson, *VP Finance*
EMP: 1100 **EST:** 2012
SALES (est): 77.8MM **Privately Held**
WEB: www.meritlogistics.com
SIC: 4789 4225 Cargo loading & unloading services; general warehousing & storage

(P-12581)
PRIME TRANSPORT INC (PA)
14726 Ramona Ave Ste 104, Chino (91710-5730)
PHONE.................................909 972-1300
Angad Singh Pasricha, *CEO*
Joe Verrill, *Maintence Staff*
EMP: 79 **EST:** 2015
SALES (est): 2.6MM **Privately Held**
WEB: www.primetransport.com
SIC: 4789 Transportation services

(P-12582)
PROPAK LOGISTICS INC
11555 Iberia St, Jurupa Valley (91752-3288)
PHONE.................................951 934-7160
Brian Harris, *Branch Mgr*
EMP: 98 **Privately Held**
WEB: www.propak.com
SIC: 4789 Cargo loading & unloading services
PA: Propak Logistics, Inc.
1100 Garrison Ave
Fort Smith AR 72901

(P-12583)
TURN KEY LOGISTICS INC
14939 Summit Dr, Eastvale (92880-3099)
PHONE.................................714 931-1625
EMP: 145
SQ FT: 60,000
SALES: 165.5MM **Privately Held**
SIC: 4789 4225 Transportation Services General Warehouse/Storage

(P-12584)
TW SERVICES INC
2751 E Chapman Ave # 204, Fullerton (92831-3758)
PHONE.................................714 441-2400
Charles An, *President*
Thomas Hwang, *Controller*
EMP: 300 **EST:** 2009
SALES (est): 28.8MM **Privately Held**
WEB: www.twserviceinc.com
SIC: 4789 Freight car loading & unloading

(P-12585)
WHALE LOGISTICS (USA) INC (PA)
6320 Caballero Blvd, Buena Park (90620-1126)
PHONE.................................714 891-8265
Jason Hsu, *CEO*
EMP: 70 **EST:** 2014
SALES (est): 1.5MM **Privately Held**
WEB: www.whalelogistics.com
SIC: 4789 Pipeline terminal facilities, independently operated

(P-12586)
WHITE HORSE LOGISTICS INC
12400 Philadelphia Ave, Eastvale (91752-3230)
PHONE.................................909 947-7822
Hassan Farid, *Principal*
EMP: 50 **EST:** 2019
SALES (est): 3.8MM **Privately Held**
WEB: www.whitehorselogistics.com
SIC: 4789 Transportation services

(P-12587)
WHO DAT NATION TRNSP LLC
13186 Rincon Rd, Apple Valley (92308-6214)
PHONE.................................760 403-7237
Ricky D Jones, *Mng Member*
EMP: 73 **EST:** 2017
SALES (est): 1.1MM **Privately Held**
SIC: 4789 Cargo loading & unloading services

4812 Radiotelephone Communications

(P-12588)
20/20 MOBILE CORP (PA)
10050 Magnolia Ave, Riverside (92503-3530)
PHONE.................................951 354-8100
Enam Alghunaim, *Director*
EMP: 82 **EST:** 2013
SALES (est): 619.2K **Privately Held**
SIC: 4812 Cellular telephone services

(P-12589)
4G WIRELESS INC (PA)
Also Called: Verizon Wireless
8871 Research Dr, Irvine (92618-4236)
PHONE.................................949 748-6100
Mohammad Honarkar, *President*
Regan Barnes, *Store Mgr*
Linda Ibarra, *Store Mgr*
Cassandra Sosa, *Site Mgr*
Earl Odell, *Sales Staff*
EMP: 212 **EST:** 2005
SQ FT: 5,000
SALES (est): 334.3MM **Privately Held**
WEB: www.verizon.com
SIC: 4812 Cellular telephone services

(P-12590)
ARCH TELECOM INC (PA)
Also Called: Sprint
1940 W Corporate Way, Anaheim (92801-5373)
PHONE.................................714 312-2724
Vijayant Ghai, *CEO*
Suresh Sachdeva, *President*
Trevor Speir, *Regional Mgr*
Ashley Furillo, *District Mgr*
Tonika Burns, *Executive Asst*
EMP: 288 **EST:** 2010
SALES (est): 90.5MM **Privately Held**
WEB: www.archtelecom.net
SIC: 4812 Cellular telephone services

(P-12591)
AT&T CORP
Rm 620, Anaheim (92805)
PHONE.................................714 284-2878
Brian Robertson, *Area Mgr*
Jim Barker, *Sales Staff*
EMP: 311
SALES (corp-wide): 171.7B **Publicly Held**
WEB: www.att.com
SIC: 4812 Cellular telephone services
HQ: At&T Corp.
1 At&T Way
Bedminster NJ 07921
800 403-3302

(P-12592)
AT&T CORP
17675 Harvard Ave Ste B, Irvine (92614-3527)
PHONE.................................949 622-8240
EMP: 69
SALES (corp-wide): 171.7B **Publicly Held**
WEB: www.att.com
SIC: 4812 Radiotelephone Communication
HQ: At&T Corp.
1 At&T Way
Bedminster NJ 07921
800 403-3302

(P-12593)
AT&T CORP
998 S Robertson Blvd # 103, Los Angeles (90035-1637)
PHONE.................................310 659-7600
EMP: 94

SALES (corp-wide): 160.5B **Publicly Held**
SIC: 4812 Radiotelephone Communication
HQ: At&T Corp.
1 At&T Way
Bedminster NJ 07921
800 403-3302

(P-12594)
AXXCELERA BRDBAND WIRELESS INC (DH)
82 Coromar Dr, Santa Barbara (93117-3024)
PHONE.................................805 968-9621
Jamal Hamdani, *CEO*
Bruce Tarr, *CFO*
Tony Masters, *Senior VP*
Philip Rushton, *Senior VP*
Alex Clamann, *Sr Software Eng*
▲ **EMP:** 80 **EST:** 2001
SQ FT: 56,000
SALES (est): 10.1MM
SALES (corp-wide): 92.2MM **Privately Held**
WEB: www.axxcelera.com
SIC: 4812 Cellular telephone services
HQ: Moseley Associates, Inc.
82 Coromar Dr
Goleta CA 93117
805 968-9621

(P-12595)
BLACK DOT WIRELESS LLC
23456 Madero Ste 210, Mission Viejo (92691-2783)
PHONE.................................949 502-3800
Marc Anthony, *Mng Member*
Howard Forgey, *Vice Pres*
Joseph Winkler, *Vice Pres*
Sergey Varlitskiy, *Software Dev*
Doug Getty, *Marketing Staff*
EMP: 85 **EST:** 2004
SALES (est): 24.1MM **Privately Held**
WEB: www.blackdotwireless.com
SIC: 4812 Cellular telephone services

(P-12596)
BRAVO TECH INC
Also Called: Bti Wireless
14600 Industry Cir, La Mirada (90638-5815)
PHONE.................................714 230-8333
Bailey Zheng, *CEO*
Tammy Metzger, *Marketing Mgr*
▲ **EMP:** 50 **EST:** 1999
SALES (est): 9.5MM **Privately Held**
SIC: 4812 Cellular telephone services

(P-12597)
CELLCO PARTNERSHIP
Also Called: Verizon Wireless
18471 Ventura Blvd, Tarzana (91356-4201)
PHONE.................................818 344-3366
EMP: 71
SALES (corp-wide): 128.2B **Publicly Held**
SIC: 4812 Cellular telephone services
HQ: Cellco Partnership
1 Verizon Way
Basking Ridge NJ 07920

(P-12598)
CELLCO PARTNERSHIP
Also Called: Verizon Wireless
237 E Compton Blvd, Compton (90220-2412)
PHONE.................................310 603-0101
EMP: 71
SALES (corp-wide): 128.2B **Publicly Held**
WEB: www.verizonwireless.com
SIC: 4812 Cellular telephone services
HQ: Cellco Partnership
1 Verizon Way
Basking Ridge NJ 07920

(P-12599)
CELLCO PARTNERSHIP
1023 E Colorado St, Glendale (91205-4542)
PHONE.................................818 500-7779
EMP: 71
SALES (corp-wide): 126B **Publicly Held**
SIC: 4812 Radiotelephone Communication

PRODUCTS & SVCS

HQ: Cellco Partnership
1 Verizon Way
Basking Ridge NJ 07920

(P-12600)
CELLCO PARTNERSHIP
Also Called: Verizon Wireless
407 Kern St, Taft (93268-2812)
PHONE...................................661 765-5397
EMP: 71
SALES (corp-wide): 128.2B **Publicly Held**
WEB: www.verizonwireless.com
SIC: 4812 Cellular telephone services
HQ: Cellco Partnership
1 Verizon Way
Basking Ridge NJ 07920

(P-12601)
CELLCO PARTNERSHIP
Also Called: Verizon Wireless
20 City Blvd W, Orange (92868-3100)
PHONE...................................951 205-4170
Cvc Cellular, *Principal*
EMP: 71
SALES (corp-wide): 128.2B **Publicly Held**
WEB: www.verizonwireless.com
SIC: 4812 Cellular telephone services
HQ: Cellco Partnership
1 Verizon Way
Basking Ridge NJ 07920

(P-12602)
CELLCO PARTNERSHIP
2921 Los Feliz Blvd, Los Angeles
(90039-1539)
PHONE...................................323 662-0009
Fernando Lara, *Principal*
EMP: 71
SALES (corp-wide): 128.2B **Publicly Held**
WEB: www.verizonwireless.com
SIC: 4812 Cellular telephone services
HQ: Cellco Partnership
1 Verizon Way
Basking Ridge NJ 07920

(P-12603)
CELLCO PARTNERSHIP
Also Called: Verizon Wireless
11902 Gem St, Norwalk (90650-2448)
PHONE...................................562 244-8814
Jorge A Molina, *Principal*
EMP: 74
SALES (corp-wide): 128.2B **Publicly Held**
WEB: www.verizonwireless.com
SIC: 4812 Cellular telephone services
HQ: Cellco Partnership
1 Verizon Way
Basking Ridge NJ 07920

(P-12604)
CELLCO PARTNERSHIP
Also Called: Verizon Wireless
638 Cmino De Los Mres Ste, San Clemente
(92673)
PHONE...................................949 488-9990
EMP: 71
SALES (corp-wide): 128.2B **Publicly Held**
WEB: www.verizonwireless.com
SIC: 4812 Radiotelephone Communication
HQ: Cellco Partnership
1 Verizon Way
Basking Ridge NJ 07920

(P-12605)
DIGITAL COMMUNICATIONS NETWORK (PA)
Also Called: D C N Wireless
6300 Canoga Ave Ste 1625, Woodland Hills
(91367-8045)
PHONE...................................818 227-3333
Robert H Mogadam, *President*
Margrit Dorgelo, *Vice Pres*
Terry Gilson, *Info Tech Mgr*
Robert Mogadam, *CPA*
Maryann Roan, *Supervisor*

EMP: 54
SALES (est): 6.3MM **Privately Held**
WEB: www.cssimpact.com
SIC: 4812 5999 Cellular telephone services; telephone & communication equipment

(P-12606)
DIRECTV GROUP HOLDINGS LLC (HQ)
2260 E Imperial Hwy, El Segundo
(90245-3501)
PHONE...................................310 964-5000
Michael White, *President*
Douglas Dillon, *President*
Jim Worley, *President*
Patrick Doyle, *CFO*
Fazal Merchant, *Treasurer*
▲ EMP: 170 EST: 1977
SALES (est): 2.6B
SALES (corp-wide): 171.7B **Publicly Held**
WEB: www.att.com
SIC: 4812 Cellular telephone services
PA: At&T Inc.
208 S Akard St
Dallas TX 75202
210 821-4105

(P-12607)
EA MOBILE INC
5510 Lincoln Blvd, Los Angeles
(90094-2034)
PHONE...................................310 754-7125
Mitch Lasky, *Ch of Bd*
Scott Lahman, *President*
Craig Gatarz, *COO*
Michael Marchetti, *CFO*
Minard Hamilton, *Exec VP*
EMP: 75 EST: 2000
SQ FT: 23,000
SALES (est): 6.4MM
SALES (corp-wide): 5.5B **Publicly Held**
WEB: www.ea.com
SIC: 4812 Cellular telephone services
PA: Electronic Arts Inc.
209 Redwood Shores Pkwy
Redwood City CA 94065
650 628-1500

(P-12608)
J5 INFRASTRUCTURE PARTNERS LLC
23 Mauchly Ste 110, Irvine (92618-2330)
PHONE...................................949 299-5258
Jerry Elliott, *CEO*
Ken Czosnowski, *Exec VP*
Brian Kennell, *Exec VP*
Dan Davis, *Vice Pres*
James Lemons, *Vice Pres*
EMP: 58 EST: 2016
SALES (est): 10.2MM **Privately Held**
WEB: www.j5infrastructurepartners.com
SIC: 4812 Cellular telephone services

(P-12609)
MBIT WIRELESS INC (PA)
4340 Von Karman Ave # 140, Newport
Beach (92660-1201)
PHONE...................................949 205-4559
Bhasker Patel, *President*
Ajay Rane, *President*
Mw Sohn, *Vice Pres*
EMP: 209 EST: 2005
SALES (est): 9.7MM **Privately Held**
WEB: www.mbitwireless.com
SIC: 4812 Cellular telephone services

(P-12610)
PACIFIC BELL TELEPHONE COMPANY
3847 Cardiff Ave, Culver City (90232-2613)
PHONE...................................310 515-2898
EMP: 4444
SALES (corp-wide): 171.7B **Publicly Held**
WEB: www.att.com
SIC: 4812 Cellular telephone services
HQ: Pacific Bell Telephone Company
430 Bush St Fl 3
San Francisco CA 94108
415 542-9000

(P-12611)
SPRINT COMMUNICATIONS CO LP
15582 Whittwood Ln, Whittier
(90603-2355)
PHONE...................................562 943-8907
EMP: 177
SALES (corp-wide): 68.4B **Publicly Held**
SIC: 4812 Cellular telephone services
HQ: Sprint Communications Company L.P.
6391 Sprint Pkwy
Overland Park KS 66251
800 829-0965

(P-12612)
SPRINT COMMUNICATIONS CO LP
23865 Clinton Keith Rd, Wildomar
(92595-9829)
PHONE...................................951 461-9786
EMP: 177
SALES (corp-wide): 68.4B **Publicly Held**
SIC: 4812 Cellular telephone services
HQ: Sprint Communications Company L.P.
6391 Sprint Pkwy
Overland Park KS 66251
800 829-0965

(P-12613)
SPRINT COMMUNICATIONS CO LP
44416 Valley Central Way, Lancaster
(93536-6528)
PHONE...................................661 951-8927
EMP: 177
SALES (corp-wide): 68.4B **Publicly Held**
SIC: 4812 Cellular telephone services
HQ: Sprint Communications Company L.P.
6391 Sprint Pkwy
Overland Park KS 66251
800 829-0965

(P-12614)
SPRINT INTL CMMUNICATIONS CORP
9 Lakewood Center Mall, Lakewood
(90712-2417)
PHONE...................................562 408-6978
EMP: 160
SALES (corp-wide): 1.3B **Privately Held**
SIC: 4812 Cellular telephone services
PA: Sprint International Communications
Corporation
6200 Sprint Pkwy
Overland Park KS 66251
800 259-3755

(P-12615)
UNITED WIRELESS INC (DH)
Also Called: Cingular Wireless
31915 Mission Trl, Lake Elsinore
(92530-4583)
PHONE...................................951 471-5999
Tom Sagten, *President*
James Sweasy, *President*
Craig Thomas, *Treasurer*
Kenneth Wayne, *Vice Pres*
EMP: 80 EST: 2001
SQ FT: 1,000
SALES (est): 3.5MM
SALES (corp-wide): 171.7B **Publicly Held**
WEB: www.att.com
SIC: 4812 Cellular telephone services
HQ: At&T Mobility Llc
1025 Lenox Park Blvd Ne A
Brookhaven GA 30319
800 331-0500

(P-12616)
VERIZON COMMUNICATIONS INC
176 E Badillo St, Covina (91723-2113)
PHONE...................................626 858-1739
Mark Clark, *Director*
EMP: 60
SALES (corp-wide): 128.2B **Publicly Held**
WEB: www.verizon.com
SIC: 4812 4813 Cellular telephone services; telephone communication, except radio

PA: Verizon Communications Inc.
1095 Ave Of The Americas
New York NY 10036
212 395-1000

(P-12617)
VERIZON MEDIA INC (HQ)
11995 Bluff Creek Dr, Los Angeles
(90094-2929)
PHONE...................................310 907-3016
Guru Gowrappan, *CEO*
EMP: 1009 EST: 2020
SALES (est): 143.2MM **Publicly Held**
WEB: www.apollo.com
SIC: 4812 Cellular telephone services

(P-12618)
VERIZON SERVICES CORP
2530 Wilshire Blvd Fl 1, Santa Monica
(90403-4664)
PHONE...................................310 315-1100
EMP: 319
SALES (corp-wide): 128.2B **Publicly Held**
WEB: www.verizonwireless.com
SIC: 4812 Cellular telephone services
HQ: Verizon Services Corp.
22001 Loudoun County Pkwy 125-100
Ashburn VA 20147
703 729-5931

(P-12619)
VERIZON SOUTH INC
424 S Patterson Ave, Goleta 93111-2404)
PHONE...................................805 681-8527
Dennis Candini, *Manager*
EMP: 291
SALES (corp-wide): 128.2B **Publicly Held**
SIC: 4812 Cellular telephone services
HQ: Verizon South Inc
600 Hidden Rdg
Irving TX 75038
972 718-5600

(P-12620)
VERIZON WIRELESS (PA)
15505 Sand Canyon Ave, Irvine
(92618-3114)
PHONE...................................949 286-7000
Dana Z Keefer, *Exec Dir*
Rima Qureshi, *Exec VP*
Jason Allen, *Engineer*
Chris Nguyen, *Engineer*
Sarah Bohannon, *Sales Staff*
EMP: 158 EST: 2012
SALES (est): 63.6MM **Privately Held**
WEB: www.verizonwireless.com
SIC: 4812 Cellular telephone services

4813 Telephone Communications, Except Radio

(P-12621)
3H COMMUNICATION SYSTEMS INC
3 Winterbranch, Irvine (92604-4604)
PHONE...................................949 529-1583
Purna Subedi, *CEO*
Michael Giarratano, *President*
Luis Wong, *Principal*
EMP: 47 EST: 2014
SALES (est): 3.8MM **Privately Held**
WEB: www.3hcommunicationsystems.com
SIC: 4813 4812 3663 3731 Voice telephone communications; radio telephone communication; radio & TV communications equipment; rockets, space & military, complete; search & navigation equipment; radar systems & equipment

(P-12622)
AAMCOM LLC
800 N Pacific Coast Hwy, Redondo Beach
(90277-2148)
PHONE...................................310 318-8100
Steve Diels, *Mng Member*
Linda Paxton, *Prgrmr*
Elisabeth Diels,
Xochil Flores, *Manager*
EMP: 50 EST: 2009
SQ FT: 4,000

SALES (est): 2.6MM **Privately Held**
WEB: www.aamcom.com
SIC: **4813** Telephone communication, except radio

(P-12623)
AFRIX TELECOM LLC
722 N Lucia Ave B, Redondo Beach (90277-2231)
PHONE.....................323 359-8683
Norman Albi, *Principal*
Todd Loewenstein, *Principal*
EMP: 80 EST: 2020
SALES (est): 4.8MM **Privately Held**
WEB: www.afr-ix.com
SIC: **4813** Telephone communication, except radio

(P-12624)
AIRESPRING INC
7800 Woodley Ave, Van Nuys (91406-1722)
PHONE.....................818 786-8990
AVI Lonstein, *CEO*
Daniel Lonstein, *COO*
Arno Vigen, *CFO*
Tony Lonstein, *Exec VP*
Betty Ramirez, *Exec VP*
▲ EMP: 100 EST: 2001
SQ FT: 12,500
SALES (est): 54MM **Privately Held**
WEB: www.airespring.com
SIC: **4813**

(P-12625)
ALLSTATE TECHNOLOGIES INC (PA)
Also Called: Allstate Communications
5699 Kanan Rd Ste 455, Agoura Hills (91301-3358)
P.O. Box 332 (91376-0332)
PHONE.....................818 889-7600
Gail S Ramas, *President*
Jodie L Gardener, *Vice Pres*
Milton Ramas, *General Mgr*
T Ciancimino, *Manager*
EMP: 55 EST: 1990
SQ FT: 2,400
SALES (est): 4MM **Privately Held**
SIC: **4813** Telephone communication, except radio

(P-12626)
AT&T CORP
2260 E Imperial Hwy, El Segundo (90245-3501)
PHONE.....................303 596-8431
Anne Chow, *CEO*
EMP: 206
SALES (corp-wide): 4.7MM **Privately Held**
SIC: **4813** Telephone communication, except radio
PA: At&T Corp.
28 Liberty St
New York NY

(P-12627)
AXAIO INDUSTRIES LLC
538 S Oxford Ave Apt 302, Los Angeles (90020-4288)
PHONE.....................323 504-1074
An Arafat Abir,
EMP: 50 EST: 2016
SALES (est): 1.4MM **Privately Held**
SIC: **4813**

(P-12628)
BP COMMUNICATIONS INC (PA)
Also Called: My Wireless
1600 N Broadway Ste 900, Santa Ana (92706-3931)
PHONE.....................626 912-0600
Shawn Yeh, *President*
Alfred Antonio, *Managing Prtnr*
Scott Chen, *Vice Pres*
Kyndra Dennis, *Branch Mgr*
Eric Brown, *Info Tech Mgr*
EMP: 201 EST: 2008
SALES (est): 16.4MM **Privately Held**
SIC: **4813** Voice telephone communications

(P-12629)
BROADSPIRE INC
19425 Soledad Canyon Rd # 34, Santa Clarita (91351-2632)
PHONE.....................213 785-8043
Suresh Srinivasan, *CEO*
Arun Srinivasan, *COO*
Terry Turon, *Vice Pres*
Doris Ross, *Executive*
Kelly Dickens, *Analyst*
EMP: 52 EST: 2000
SALES (est): 2.6MM **Privately Held**
WEB: www.choosebroadspire.com
SIC: **4813**
PA: Platinum Equity, Llc
360 N Crescent Dr Bldg S
Beverly Hills CA 90210

(P-12630)
CALIFORNIA INTERNET LP (PA)
Also Called: Geolinks
251 Camarillo Ranch Rd, Camarillo (93012-5082)
PHONE.....................805 225-4638
Skyler Ditchfield, *Partner*
Ryan Adams, *Partner*
Ryan Hauf, *Partner*
Phil Oseas, *Partner*
Vito Adamo, *COO*
EMP: 54 EST: 2011
SALES (est): 52.2MM **Privately Held**
WEB: www.geolinks.com
SIC: **4813**

(P-12631)
CDNETWORKS INC (DH)
1550 Valley Vista Dr # 110, Diamond Bar (91765-3961)
PHONE.....................408 228-3379
Jongchan Kim, *CEO*
John J Kang, *President*
Samuyeol Ko, *President*
Jerry Miller, *Vice Pres*
Chanhee Nam, *Vice Pres*
EMP: 99 EST: 2006
SALES (est): 32.4MM **Privately Held**
WEB: www.cdnetworks.com
SIC: **4813**

(P-12632)
CONNEXITY INC (HQ)
Also Called: Shopzilla.com
2120 Colorado Ave Ste 400, Santa Monica (90404-3563)
PHONE.....................310 571-1235
William Glass, *CEO*
Aaron Young, *CFO*
Craig Teich, *Officer*
Blythe Holden, *Senior VP*
Lonna Bell Rimestad, *Senior VP*
EMP: 203 EST: 2012
SALES (est): 109.1MM
SALES (corp-wide): 191.2MM **Privately Held**
WEB: www.connexity.com
SIC: **4813** 7383 7331 ; news syndicates; direct mail advertising services
PA: Symphony Technology Group, L.L.C.
428 University Ave
Palo Alto CA 94301
650 935-9500

(P-12633)
DIVERSFIED CMMNCTIONS SVCS INC
Also Called: D C S
1260 Pioneer St, Brea (92821-3725)
PHONE.....................714 888-2284
Steve Hurley, *CEO*
Steven Hurley, *Vice Pres*
Bill Shields, *Vice Pres*
Leo Gonzalez, *CIO*
Elizabeth Brezden, *Payroll Mgr*
▲ EMP: 63 EST: 1972
SQ FT: 19,000
SALES (est): 14.2MM **Privately Held**
WEB: www.diversified.net
SIC: **4813** Telephone communications broker

(P-12634)
DOCIRCLE INC
Also Called: Trumpia
2544 W Woodland Dr, Anaheim (92801-2636)
PHONE.....................415 484-4221
Kyung Hoon Rhie, *CEO*
Kobbe Taylor, *Executive*
Jihoon Koo, *CTO*
Raphael Malabanan, *Technical Staff*
Andrew Su, *Technical Staff*
EMP: 50 EST: 2006
SALES (est): 8MM **Privately Held**
SIC: **4813**

(P-12635)
FILANITY CORPORATION
Also Called: Vietnumber
17011 Beach Blvd Ste 1440, Huntington Beach (92647)
PHONE.....................714 475-3521
Frank Kim, *President*
Luan Kim, *Shareholder*
Tina Le, *Accountant*
Jessica Doan, *Manager*
EMP: 60 EST: 2007
SQ FT: 2,800
SALES (est): 2MM **Privately Held**
SIC: **4813** Local & long distance telephone communications

(P-12636)
FREE CONFERENCING CORPORATION
Also Called: Freeconferencecall.com
4300 E Pacific Coast Hwy, Long Beach (90804-2114)
P.O. Box 41069 (90853-1069)
PHONE.....................562 437-1411
David Erickson, *CEO*
Josh Lowenthal, *COO*
Scott Southron, *CFO*
Robert Wise, *Exec VP*
Jeff Erickson, *Vice Pres*
EMP: 116 EST: 2004
SQ FT: 10,000
SALES (est): 65MM **Privately Held**
WEB: www.freeconferencecall.com
SIC: **4813** 7389 Voice telephone communications;

(P-12637)
FRONTIER CALIFORNIA INC
Also Called: Verizon
83793 Dr Carreon Blvd, Indio (92201-7035)
PHONE.....................760 342-0500
EMP: 305
SALES (corp-wide): 7.1B **Privately Held**
WEB: www.frontier.sale
SIC: **4813** Local & long distance telephone communications
HQ: Frontier California Inc.
401 Merritt 7
Norwalk CT 06851

(P-12638)
FRONTIER CALIFORNIA INC
Also Called: Verizon
200 W Church St, Santa Maria (93458-5005)
PHONE.....................805 925-0000
Carrie Ramsey, *Manager*
EMP: 305
SALES (corp-wide): 7.1B **Privately Held**
WEB: www.frontier.sale
SIC: **4813** Long distance telephone communications
HQ: Frontier California Inc.
401 Merritt 7
Norwalk CT 06851

(P-12639)
FRONTIER CALIFORNIA INC
Also Called: Verizon
510 Park Ave, San Fernando (91340-2527)
PHONE.....................818 365-0542
Gloria Caudill, *Branch Mgr*
EMP: 305
SALES (corp-wide): 7.1B **Privately Held**
WEB: www.frontier.sale
SIC: **4813** Telephone communication, except radio

HQ: Frontier California Inc.
401 Merritt 7
Norwalk CT 06851

(P-12640)
FRONTIER CALIFORNIA INC
Also Called: Verizon
350 Lagoon St, Bishop (93514-3406)
PHONE.....................760 872-0812
EMP: 305
SALES (corp-wide): 7.1B **Privately Held**
WEB: www.frontier.sale
SIC: **4813** Local telephone communications
HQ: Frontier California Inc.
401 Merritt 7
Norwalk CT 06851

(P-12641)
FRONTIER CALIFORNIA INC
Also Called: Verizon
7352 Slater Ave, Huntington Beach (92647-6227)
PHONE.....................714 375-6713
Patrick Dillon, *Manager*
EMP: 305
SALES (corp-wide): 7.1B **Privately Held**
WEB: www.frontier.sale
SIC: **4813** 8721 5065 8711 Local & long distance telephone communications; local telephone communications; billing & bookkeeping service; telephone & telegraphic equipment; electrical or electronic engineering
HQ: Frontier California Inc.
401 Merritt 7
Norwalk CT 06851

(P-12642)
FRONTIER CALIFORNIA INC
Also Called: Verizon
1 Wellpoint Way, Westlake Village (91362-3893)
PHONE.....................805 372-6000
Alex Stadler, *Principal*
John Dixon,
EMP: 305
SALES (corp-wide): 7.1B **Privately Held**
WEB: www.frontier.sale
SIC: **4813** Telephone communication, except radio
HQ: Frontier California Inc.
401 Merritt 7
Norwalk CT 06851

(P-12643)
GOOGLE FIBER INC (DH)
35018 Avenue D, Yucaipa (92399-4407)
PHONE.....................650 253-0000
Milo Medin, *Vice Pres*
EMP: 74 EST: 2010
SALES (est): 128.5MM
SALES (corp-wide): 182.5B **Publicly Held**
WEB: www.fiber.google.com
SIC: **4813**
HQ: Google Llc
1600 Amphitheatre Pkwy
Mountain View CA 94043
650 253-0000

(P-12644)
GOOGLE INTERNATIONAL LLC (DH)
35018 Avenue D, Yucaipa (92399-4407)
PHONE.....................650 253-0000
Eric Schmidt, *Ch of Bd*
Larry Page, *CEO*
David C Drummond, *Senior VP*
▼ EMP: 1859 EST: 2014
SALES (est): 19.2MM
SALES (corp-wide): 182.5B **Publicly Held**
WEB: www.google.com
SIC: **4813** 7375 ; ; information retrieval services
HQ: Google Llc
1600 Amphitheatre Pkwy
Mountain View CA 94043
650 253-0000

P R O D U C T S & S V C S

(P-12645)
HUF WORLDWIDE LLC
420 Boyd St Ste 400, Los Angeles
(90013-1614)
PHONE..................323 264-8656
Keith Hufnagel, *Ch Credit Ofcr*
Neal Berniker, *Controller*
Velasco Erika, *Human Resources*
Dolly Carrillo, *Prdtn Mgr*
Monique Patterson, *Prdtn Mgr*
▲ EMP: 150 EST: 2013
SQ FT: 60,000
SALES (est): 19.7MM **Privately Held**
WEB: www.hufworldwide.com
SIC: 5961 4813 Clothing, mail order (except women's);

(P-12646)
HULU LLC
12312 W Olympic Boulev, Los Angeles
(90064)
PHONE..................888 631-4858
Mike Hopkins, *CEO*
Brian Henderson, *Vice Pres*
Jason Kim, *Vice Pres*
Vanessa Ansoorian, *Executive Asst*
Stephanie Daniels, *Executive Asst*
EMP: 55
SALES (corp-wide): 65.3B **Publicly Held**
WEB: www.hulu.com
SIC: 4813 4833 ; television translator station
HQ: Hulu, Llc
2500 Broadway Ste 200
Santa Monica CA 90404

(P-12647)
HULU LLC (HQ)
2500 Broadway Ste 200, Santa Monica
(90404-3071)
PHONE..................310 571-4700
Randy Freer, *CEO*
Reagan Feeney, *Partner*
James Galley, *Partner*
Kailin Ryan, *Partner*
Chadwick Ho, *Senior VP*
EMP: 2152 EST: 2007
SALES (est): 405MM
SALES (corp-wide): 65.3B **Publicly Held**
WEB: www.hulu.com
SIC: 4813 4833 ; television translator station
PA: The Walt Disney Company
500 S Buena Vista St
Burbank CA 91521
818 560-1000

(P-12648)
IFNCOM INC (PA)
Also Called: Tollfreeforwarding.com
13005 Artesia Blvd A10, Cerritos
(90703-1356)
PHONE..................213 452-1505
Travis May, *CEO*
Jason O'Brien, *COO*
Jason Obrien, *COO*
Matt Hemingway, *Vice Pres*
Mitch May, *Vice Pres*
▲ EMP: 58 EST: 2009
SALES (est): 22.7MM **Privately Held**
SIC: 4813 Local & long distance telephone communications; voice telephone communications

(P-12649)
IMPULSE INTERNET SERVICES LLC
6144 Calle Real Ste 200, Goleta
(93117-2012)
P.O. Box 1450 (93116-1450)
PHONE..................805 456-5800
Anthony Papa, *Mng Member*
Andrew Alker, *Vice Pres*
Lee Carlander, *Business Dir*
Lindsay Garris, *Administration*
Justin Maness, *Administration*
EMP: 55 EST: 1994
SQ FT: 20,000
SALES (est): 8.8MM **Privately Held**
WEB: www.impulse.net
SIC: 4813

(P-12650)
INCOMNET COMMUNICATIONS CORP
2801 Main St, Irvine (92614-5027)
PHONE..................949 251-8000
George P Blanco, *President*
John Hill, *Ch of Bd*
Stephen A Garcia, *CFO*
Robert D Cron, *CTO*
Andrew Kalinowski, *VP Mktg*
EMP: 80 EST: 1983
SQ FT: 68,000
SALES (est): 7.7MM **Privately Held**
SIC: 4813 Long distance telephone communications

(P-12651)
INFONET SERVICES CORPORATION (DH)
Also Called: BT Infonet
2160 E Grand Ave, El Segundo
(90245-5024)
PHONE..................310 335-2600
David Andrew, *CEO*
Jose A Collazo, *President*
Pete Sweers, *COO*
Akbar H Firdosy, *CFO*
John C Hoffman, *Exec VP*
▲ EMP: 600 EST: 1988
SQ FT: 150,000
SALES (est): 202.8MM
SALES (corp-wide): 30B **Privately Held**
WEB: www.infonet.com
SIC: 4813 7373 7375 Data telephone communications; computer integrated systems design; information retrieval services
HQ: British Telecommunications Public Limited Company
Bt Centre
London EC1A
207 356-5000

(P-12652)
JYNORMUS LLC
19800 Macarthur Blvd 3, Irvine
(92612-2421)
PHONE..................949 436-2112
Edward Longoria,
EMP: 17 EST: 2006
SQ FT: 5,000
SALES (est): 1.1MM **Privately Held**
SIC: 4813 2741 ; ; racing forms & programs; publishing & printing

(P-12653)
MEDIA TEMPLE INC
12655 W Jefferson Blvd # 40, Los Angeles
(90066-7008)
PHONE..................877 578-4000
Russell P Reeder, *CEO*
Marc Dumont, *Ch of Bd*
Rod Stoddard, *President*
John Carey, *COO*
Lou Kikos, *Vice Pres*
EMP: 203 EST: 1998
SALES (est): 56.9MM
SALES (corp-wide): 3.3B **Publicly Held**
WEB: www.mediatemple.net
SIC: 4813 7371 ; computer software development & applications
HQ: Godaddy.Com, Llc
2150 E Warner Rd
Tempe AZ 85284

(P-12654)
MIS SCIENCES CORP
2550 N Hollywood Way # 4, Burbank
(91505-1055)
PHONE..................818 847-0213
Lauren Ross, *President*
Jeff Willis, *Exec VP*
Sharon Greathouse, *Program Mgr*
Ricky Torre, *General Mgr*
Christopher Voisey, *CTO*
EMP: 125 EST: 1996
SQ FT: 7,500
SALES (est): 11.8MM **Privately Held**
WEB: www.mis-sciences.com
SIC: 4813 8748 7376 8742 ; ; systems engineering consultant, ex. computer or professional; computer facilities management; management information systems consultant; custom computer programming services

(P-12655)
MOBILITIE SERVICES LLC
660 Nwport Ctr Dr Ste 200, Newport Beach
(92660)
PHONE..................877 999-7070
Gary Jabara, *Chairman*
Christos Karmis, *CEO*
Dana Tardelli, *COO*
Dissy Sarabosing, *CFO*
EMP: 350 EST: 2015
SALES (est): 350MM
SALES (corp-wide): 223.4B **Privately Held**
WEB: www.mobilitie.com
SIC: 4813 Local telephone communications
HQ: Mobilitie Management, Llc
660 Nwport Ctr Dr Ste 200
Newport Beach CA 92660
877 999-7070

(P-12656)
MPOWER HOLDING CORPORATION (HQ)
Also Called: Tpx Communications
515 S Flower St Fl 36, Los Angeles
(90071-2221)
PHONE..................866 699-8242
Richard A Jalkut, *CEO*
James E Ferguson, *President*
Timothy J Medina, *CFO*
Richard Finkelson, *Vice Pres*
Mukesh Tikarya, *Vice Pres*
EMP: 693 EST: 1996
SALES (est): 131.9MM **Privately Held**
SIC: 4813

(P-12657)
MPULSE MOBILE INC (PA)
16530 Ventura Blvd # 500, Encino
(91436-4554)
PHONE..................888 678-5735
Chris Nicholson, *CEO*
Brian Chudleigh, *CFO*
Allison Gage, *Officer*
Akshay Agrawal, *Vice Pres*
Kevin White, *Vice Pres*
EMP: 368 EST: 2014
SQ FT: 2,000
SALES (est): 36.6MM **Privately Held**
WEB: www.mpulsemobile.com
SIC: 4813 Data telephone communications

(P-12658)
NEW DREAM NETWORK LLC
Also Called: Dreamhost.com
707 Wilshire Blvd # 5050, Los Angeles
(90017-3607)
PHONE..................323 375-3842
Art Elivarov, *Manager*
Art Elizarov, *VP Human Res*
EMP: 74
SALES (corp-wide): 38.4MM **Privately Held**
WEB: www.dreamhost.com
SIC: 4813
PA: New Dream Network, Llc
417 Assod Rd Pmb 257 257 Pmb
Brea CA 92821
626 644-9466

(P-12659)
NEXTPOINT INC (PA)
Also Called: Break Media
8750 Wilshire Blvd 300e, Beverly Hills
(90211-2700)
PHONE..................310 360-5904
Keith Richman, *President*
Andrew Doyle, *CFO*
David Subar, *CTO*
EMP: 80 EST: 2005
SALES (est): 22.6MM **Privately Held**
WEB: www.breakmedia.com
SIC: 4813

(P-12660)
OPEX COMMUNICATIONS INC
1677 E 28th St, Signal Hill (90755-1922)
P.O. Box 9270, Uniondale NY (11555-9270)
PHONE..................562 968-5420
Mark Leafstedt, *CEO*
Sean Trepeta, *President*
John Wonak, *CFO*
Lucy Sung, *Principal*
Robert Yap, *Admin Sec*

EMP: 50 EST: 1998
SALES (est): 14.7MM **Privately Held**
WEB: www.opexld.com
SIC: 4813 Local telephone communications
PA: Premiercom Management Company
6 Jacqueline Ln
Fox River Grove IL

(P-12661)
ORANGE COUNTY INTERNET XCHANGE
2001 E Dyer Rd Ste 102, Santa Ana
(92705-5709)
PHONE..................714 450-7109
EMP: 86 EST: 2010
SALES (est): 1MM **Privately Held**
WEB: www.tpx.com
SIC: 4813 Local & long distance telephone communications
HQ: U.S. Telepacific Corp.
515 S Flower St Ste 4500
Los Angeles CA 90071
877 487-8722

(P-12662)
PACKETFABRIC INC
9920 Jefferson Blvd, Culver City
(90232-3506)
PHONE..................844 475-8322
Dave Ward, *CEO*
Chad Milam, *President*
Nida Hasan, *Sr Software Eng*
Elisa Jasinska, *Sr Software Eng*
Nalin Kuachusr, *Sr Software Eng*
EMP: 100 EST: 2015
SALES (est): 19.2MM **Privately Held**
WEB: www.packetfabric.com
SIC: 4813

(P-12663)
PARADIGM COMMUNICATIONS CORP
Also Called: Global Communications Network
401 Wilshire Blvd Ste 900, Santa Monica
(90401-1449)
PHONE..................310 395-5757
Nils Shapiro, *President*
Steven Kalish, *COO*
EMP: 50 EST: 1975
SQ FT: 2,200
SALES (est): 6MM **Privately Held**
SIC: 4813 Long distance telephone communications

(P-12664)
PCS MOBILE SOLUTIONS LLC
3534 Tweedy Blvd, South Gate
(90280-6026)
PHONE..................323 567-2490
EMP: 71
SALES (corp-wide): 86MM **Privately Held**
WEB: www.sprint.com
SIC: 4813 4812 Local & long distance telephone communications; cellular telephone services
PA: Pcs Mobile Solutions, Llc
32000 Northwestern Hwy # 279
Farmington Hills MI 43334
248 539-2221

(P-12665)
PUBLIC COMMUNICATIONS SVCS INC
11859 Wilshire Blvd # 60, Los Angeles
(90025-6616)
P.O. Box 2868, Mobile AL (36652-2868)
PHONE..................310 231-1000
Paul Jennings, *CEO*
Tommie Joe, *President*
Dennis Komai, *CFO*
EMP: 150 EST: 1987
SQ FT: 15,000
SALES (est): 38.8MM **Privately Held**
SIC: 4813 Local & long distance telephone communications

(P-12666)
QUALITY SPEAKS LLC (PA)
Also Called: Phonepower
9221 Corbin Ave Ste 260, Northridge
(91324-1625)
PHONE..................818 264-4400

▲ = Import ▼=Export
◆ =Import/Export

Jim Murphy, *CEO*
Liz Baker, *Partner*
Alan Kaplan, *Partner*
Sam Ghahremanpour, *President*
Kevin Connor, *CFO*
EMP: 172 **EST:** 2010
SALES (est): 33.6MM **Privately Held**
SIC: 4813 Local & long distance telephone
communications

(P-12667)
RED POCKET INC
Also Called: Red Pocket Mobile
2060d E Avnida De Los Arb, Thousand
Oaks (91362)
PHONE................................888 993-3888
Joshua Gordon, *President*
Steve Bowman, *CFO*
Wong Dean, *VP Bus Dvlpt*
Sergey Filippov, *Software Engr*
Kaisha Barela, *Opers Staff*
EMP: 75 **EST:** 2005
SALES (est): 8.4MM **Privately Held**
WEB: www.redpocket.com
SIC: 4813 Telephone communication, ex-
cept radio

(P-12668)
SEARCH123
30699 Russell Ranch Rd # 2, Westlake Vil-
lage (91362-7315)
PHONE................................818 575-4600
James Beriker, *CEO*
EMP: 79 **EST:** 2005
SALES (est): 1MM
SALES (corp-wide): 29.1MM **Privately
Held**
SIC: 4813 Telephone communication, ex-
cept radio
HQ: Conversant, Llc
101 N Wacker Dr
Chicago IL 60606

(P-12669)
SOLVERE INC
Also Called: PEC HI FI
15560 Rckfeld Blvd Ste B1, Irvine (92618)
PHONE................................949 707-0035
Alexander Truong, *President*
Nhuan Vu, *Vice Pres*
EMP: 50 **EST:** 1997
SQ FT: 3,200 **Privately Held**
WEB: www.solvere.com
SIC: 4813

(P-12670)
**SOUTHERN CALIFORNIA TELE
CO (PA)**
Also Called: Southern Cal Tele & Enrgy
27515 Enterprise Cir W, Temecula
(92590-4864)
PHONE................................951 693-1880
Greg Michaels, *President*
Kristine Michaels, *CFO*
Bill Short, *Officer*
Kevin Reno, *Vice Pres*
Ryan McGuire, *Executive Asst*
EMP: 59 **EST:** 2005
SQ FT: 10,000
SALES (est): 14.5MM **Privately Held**
WEB: www.socaltelephone.com
SIC: 4813 Local telephone communica-
tions

(P-12671)
**SPRINT COMMUNICATIONS CO
LP**
111 Unversal Hollywood Dr, Universal City
(91608-1054)
PHONE................................818 755-7100
Bill Henry, *Manager*
EMP: 177
SALES (corp-wide): 68.4B **Publicly Held**
SIC: 4813 4812 Long distance telephone
communications; radio telephone commu-
nication
HQ: Sprint Communications Company L.P.
6391 Sprint Pkwy
Overland Park KS 66251
800 829-0965

(P-12672)
**SPRINT COMMUNICATIONS CO
LP**
1505 E Enterprise Dr, San Bernardino
(92408-0159)
PHONE................................909 382-6030
Bill Neece, *Manager*
EMP: 177
SALES (corp-wide): 68.4B **Publicly Held**
SIC: 4813 4812 Long distance telephone
communications; radio telephone commu-
nication
HQ: Sprint Communications Company L.P.
6391 Sprint Pkwy
Overland Park KS 66251
800 829-0965

(P-12673)
TEKWORKS INC
12742 Knott St, Garden Grove
(92841-3904)
PHONE................................877 835-9675
William E Bourgeois, *CEO*
EMP: 70
SALES (corp-wide): 13.1MM **Privately
Held**
WEB: www.paladintechnologies.com
SIC: 4813 1731 Telephone communica-
tion, except radio; communications spe-
cialization
PA: Paladin Technologies Inc
1350-355 Burrard St
Vancouver BC V6C 2
604 676-0136

(P-12674)
TEUTONIC HOLDINGS LLC (PA)
9221 Corbin Ave Ste 260, Northridge
(91324-1625)
PHONE................................818 264-4400
James Murphy, *CEO*
Sam Ghahremanpour, *President*
Doreen Paisano, *Human Resources*
EMP: 71 **EST:** 2012
SALES (est): 1.8MM **Privately Held**
SIC: 4813

(P-12675)
**TRUCONNECT
COMMUNICATIONS INC (PA)**
Also Called: Telescape
1149 S Hill St Ste 400, Los Angeles
(90015-2894)
PHONE................................512 919-2641
Mathew Johnson, *CEO*
Robert A Yap, *President*
Nathan Johnson, *CEO*
Jeff Misthal, *CFO*
Juan Carlos Davila, *Senior VP*
EMP: 201 **EST:** 2001
SALES (est): 22.9MM **Privately Held**
WEB: www.wefi.com
SIC: 4813

(P-12676)
US TELEPACIFIC CORP (HQ)
Also Called: Tpx Communications
515 S Flower St Ste 4500, Los Angeles
(90071-2237)
PHONE................................877 487-8722
Richard A Jalkut, *President*
David Glickman, *Ch of Bd*
Timothy Medina, *CFO*
Ken Bisnoff, *Senior VP*
Erich Everbach, *Senior VP*
◆ **EMP:** 50 **EST:** 1998
SQ FT: 75,000
SALES (est): 878.3MM **Privately Held**
WEB: www.tpx.com
SIC: 4813 Local & long distance telephone
communications

(P-12677)
UVNV INC (PA)
Also Called: Ultra Mobile
1550 Scenic Ave Ste 100, Costa Mesa
(92626-1420)
PHONE................................888 777-0446
David Glickman, *CEO*
Tyler R Leshney, *President*
John Janes, *COO*
Dave Schofield, *COO*
Sherrie Simmons, *COO*
EMP: 112 **EST:** 2012
SQ FT: 8,600

SALES (est): 58.2MM **Privately Held**
SIC: 4813 Telephone communication, except radio

(P-12678)
**VINCENT HUANG &
ASSOCIATES LLC (PA)**
1550 Valley Vista Dr, Diamond Bar
(91765-3957)
PHONE................................909 861-9600
Vincent WEI Cheng Huang, *CEO*
Cyndia Lin, *CFO*
Joe Dunkle, *Administration*
Ryan Emerick, *Business Anlyst*
Dave Gartner, *Opers Staff*
▲ **EMP:** 86 **EST:** 2001
SQ FT: 9,500
SALES (est): 69.3MM **Privately Held**
WEB: www.vhacorp.com
SIC: 4813 Telephone communications bro-
ker

(P-12679)
VPLS INC
1744 W Katella Ave # 200, Orange
(92867-3479)
PHONE................................213 406-9000
Arman Khalili, *CEO*
Timothy Mektrakarn, *COO*
Minnix John, *Vice Pres*
Takahiro Masuda, *Vice Pres*
John Minnix, *Vice Pres*
EMP: 50 **EST:** 2005
SQ FT: 15,000
SALES (est): 31.6MM
SALES (corp-wide): 45.6MM **Privately
Held**
WEB: www.vpls.com
SIC: 4813
PA: Evodc, Llc
600 W 7th St Ste 510
Los Angeles CA 90017
888 365-2656

(P-12680)
ZENLAYER INC
21680 Gateway Center Dr # 350, Diamond
Bar (91765-2456)
P.O. Box 5709 (91765-7709)
PHONE................................909 718-3558
Joe Zhu, *CEO*
Nikhil Vasa, *CFO*
Sophie Chen, *Vice Pres*
Lawrence Lee, *Vice Pres*
Anthony Zapanta, *Executive*
EMP: 408 **EST:** 2016
SALES (est): 62.2MM **Privately Held**
WEB: www.zenlayer.com
SIC: 4813

(P-12681)
ZYXEL COMMUNICATIONS INC
1130 N Miller St, Anaheim (92806-2001)
PHONE................................714 632-0882
Howie Chu, *President*
Art Ramirez, *IT/INT Sup*
Shawn Rogers, *Manager*
◆ **EMP:** 80
SQ FT: 32,000
SALES (est): 100MM **Privately Held**
WEB: www.zyxel.com
SIC: 4813
HQ: Zyxel Communications Corporation
No. 2, Gongye E. 9th Rd.,
Paoshan Hsiang HSI 30075

4822 Telegraph & Other
Message Communications

(P-12682)
J2 CLOUD SERVICES LLC (HQ)
Also Called: Efax Corporate
700 S Flower St Fl 15, Los Angeles
(90017-4101)
PHONE................................323 860-9200
Nehemia Zucker, *CEO*
Laura Hinson, *President*
Vince Niedzielski, *President*
Ken Truesdale, *President*
R Scott Turicchi, *President*
EMP: 80 **EST:** 1995
SQ FT: 40,000

SALES (est): 646MM
SALES (corp-wide): 1.4B **Publicly Held**
WEB: www.j2global.com
SIC: 4822 Telegraph & other communica-
tions
PA: Davis Ziff Inc
114 5th Ave Fl 15
New York NY 10011
212 503-3500

4832 Radio Broadcasting
Stations

(P-12683)
939 HOLDINGS INC
2600 W Olive Ave Ste 800, Burbank
(91505-4553)
PHONE................................818 525-5000
Francisco Aguirre Cranz, *President*
EMP: 86 **EST:** 2012
SALES (est): 248.4K
SALES (corp-wide): 537.8K **Privately
Held**
SIC: 4832 Radio broadcasting stations
PA: 93.9 Investment, Llc
2600 W Olive Ave
Burbank CA 91505
818 525-5000

(P-12684)
939 INVESTMENT LLC (PA)
2600 W Olive Ave, Burbank (91505-4549)
PHONE................................818 525-5000
Francisco Aguirre Cranz, *President*
Cindy Melgar, *Executive*
Gabrielle Bernstein, *Natl Sales Mgr*
EMP: 107 **EST:** 2012
SALES (est): 537.8K **Privately Held**
SIC: 4832 Radio broadcasting stations

(P-12685)
**ABC CABLE NETWORKS
GROUP (HQ)**
500 S Buena Vista St, Burbank
(91521-0007)
PHONE................................818 460-7477
Gary K Marsh, *CEO*
Anne M Sweeney, *President*
Patrick Lopker, *Senior VP*
Sonia Coleman, *Vice Pres*
Kristin McClamroch, *Vice Pres*
▲ **EMP:** 200 **EST:** 1969
SALES (est): 147.7MM
SALES (corp-wide): 65.3B **Publicly Held**
WEB: www.thewaltdisneycompany.com
SIC: 4832 4833 Radio broadcasting sta-
tions; television broadcasting stations
PA: The Walt Disney Company
500 S Buena Vista St
Burbank CA 91521
818 560-1000

(P-12686)
ADELMAN BROADCASTING INC
Also Called: Kraj Radio
731 Balsam St, Ridgecrest (93555-3510)
PHONE................................760 371-1700
Robert Adelman, *President*
Bill Corbin, *COO*
Vince Garcia, *Mfg Dir*
Bc Corbin, *Opers Staff*
Nelson Rasse, *Opers Staff*
EMP: 58 **EST:** 1956
SQ FT: 2,100
SALES (est): 5.7MM **Privately Held**
WEB: www.adelmanbroadcasting.com
SIC: 4832 Radio broadcasting stations,
music format

(P-12687)
DISNEY ENTERPRISES INC (DH)
500 S Buena Vista St, Burbank
(91521-0001)
P.O. Box 3232, Anaheim (92803-3232)
PHONE................................818 560-1000
Zenia Mucha, *Sr Exec VP*
Nick Franklin, *Vice Pres*
Kevin Mayer, *Vice Pres*
Stacy Heard, *Finance*
Cate Cranston, *Opers Staff*
◆ **EMP:** 2427 **EST:** 1986

P R O D U C T S   &   S V C S

SALES (est): 40.6B
SALES (corp-wide): 65.3B Publicly Held
WEB: www.disney.com
SIC: 4832 6794 5331 7996 Radio broadcasting stations; copyright buying & licensing; variety stores; theme park, amusement; ice hockey club

(P-12688)
ENTERCOM MEDIA CORP
Also Called: CBS
5670 Wilshire Blvd # 200, Los Angeles (90036-5679)
PHONE..............................323 930-7317
Sials Marshall, Branch Mgr
Morgan Wilkins, Sales Staff
Julie Chin, Director
Brian Ludmer, Manager
EMP: 82
SALES (corp-wide): 1B Publicly Held
SIC: 4832 Radio broadcasting stations, music format
HQ: Entercom Media Corp.
345 Hudson St
New York NY 10014
212 314-9200

(P-12689)
ENTERCOM MEDIA CORP
Also Called: CBS
900 E Washington St # 315, Colton (92324-7111)
PHONE..............................909 825-9525
Kevin Murphy, General Mgr
EMP: 82
SALES (corp-wide): 1B Publicly Held
SIC: 4832 Radio broadcasting stations
HQ: Entercom Media Corp.
345 Hudson St
New York NY 10014
212 314-9200

(P-12690)
ESTRELLA MEDIA INC
1845 W Empire Ave, Burbank (91504-3402)
PHONE..............................818 729-5316
Peter Markham, CEO
Brian Kei, COO
Arya Towfighi, Senior VP
Mike Todd, Chief Engr
Eli Kamionski, Controller
EMP: 96 EST: 2014
SALES (est): 38.2MM
SALES (corp-wide): 283.6MM Privately Held
WEB: www.estrellamedia.com
SIC: 4832 Radio broadcasting stations
HQ: Lbi Media Holdings, Inc.
1845 W Empire Ave
Burbank CA 91504

(P-12691)
FAR EAST BROADCASTING CO INC
Also Called: Radio Station Kfbs
15700 Imperial Hwy, La Mirada (90638-2598)
P.O. Box 1 (90637-0001)
PHONE..............................562 947-4651
Gregg Harris, President
Charles Blake, CFO
Robert Bartz, Exec VP
Nancy Bates, Vice Pres
James Hwang, Vice Pres
▲ EMP: 52
SQ FT: 20,000
SALES: 12.1MM Privately Held
WEB: www.febc.org
SIC: 4832 Radio broadcasting stations

(P-12692)
GRACE TO YOU (PA)
Also Called: Grace To You Radio Ministries
28001 Harrison Pkwy, Valencia (91355-4190)
P.O. Box 4000, Van Nuys (91412-4000)
PHONE..............................661 295-5777
John Mac Arthur, President
Ted Ng, Administration
Rufus Harvey, Finance Mgr
Connie Bishop, Accountant
Darrell Harrison, Dean
▲ EMP: 54 EST: 1969
SQ FT: 40,000

SALES: 25MM Privately Held
WEB: www.gty.org
SIC: 4832 5942 Radio broadcasting stations; book stores

(P-12693)
IHEARTCOMMUNICATIONS INC
352 E Avenue K4, Lancaster (93535-4505)
PHONE..............................661 942-1268
EMP: 61
SALES (corp-wide): 6.2B Publicly Held
SIC: 4832 Radio Broadcast Station
HQ: Iheartcommunications, Inc.
200 E Basse Rd
San Antonio TX 78258
210 822-2828

(P-12694)
INFINITY BROADCASTING CORP CAL
Also Called: Krth Radio 101 FM
5670 Wilshire Blvd # 200, Los Angeles (90036-5679)
PHONE..............................323 936-5784
John Sykes, President
Maureen Lesourd, Vice Pres
EMP: 57 EST: 2001
SALES (est): 5.5MM
SALES (corp-wide): 25.3B Publicly Held
WEB: www.viacomcbs.com
SIC: 4832 Radio broadcasting stations
HQ: Viacomcbs Inc.
1515 Broadway
New York NY 10036
212 258-6000

(P-12695)
JACOR COMMUNICATIONS COMPANY
Also Called: Kqsb Radio 990
414 E Cota St, Santa Barbara (93101-1624)
PHONE..............................805 879-8300
Jim Votaw, Branch Mgr
Jennifer Van Donge, Advt Staff
EMP: 53 Publicly Held
WEB: www.klite.com
SIC: 4832 Radio broadcasting stations
HQ: Jacor Communications Company
200 E Basse Rd
San Antonio TX 78209
210 822-2828

(P-12696)
K WAVE 1079
3000 W Macarthur Blvd # 50, Santa Ana (92704-6916)
PHONE..............................714 918-6207
Lance Emma, General Mgr
EMP: 54 EST: 1985
SALES (est): 2.2MM
SALES (corp-wide): 31.1MM Privately Held
WEB: www.kwve.com
SIC: 4832 Radio broadcasting stations
PA: Calvary Chapel Of Costa Mesa
3800 S Fairview St
Santa Ana CA 92704
714 979-4422

(P-12697)
KKZZ 1590
Also Called: Gold Coast Broadcasting
2284 S Victoria Ave 2g, Ventura (93003-6641)
PHONE..............................805 289-1400
EMP: 50
SALES (est): 1.3MM Privately Held
SIC: 4832 Radio Broadcasting Stations

(P-12698)
LBI MEDIA HOLDINGS INC (HQ)
1845 W Empire Ave, Burbank (91504-3402)
PHONE..............................818 563-5722
Brian Kei, Principal
Lenard Liberman, President
Winter Horton, COO
Blima Tuller, CFO
EMP: 80 EST: 2003
SALES (est): 130.4MM
SALES (corp-wide): 283.6MM Privately Held
WEB: www.estrellamedia.com
SIC: 4832 Radio broadcasting stations

PA: Liberman Broadcasting, Inc.
1845 W Empire Ave
Burbank CA 91504
818 729-5300

(P-12699)
LEARFIELD COMMUNICATIONS LLC
5291 California Ave # 100, Irvine (92617-3220)
PHONE..............................949 823-1729
Spencer Christiansen, General Mgr
EMP: 74 Privately Held
WEB: www.learfield.com
SIC: 4832 Radio broadcasting stations
HQ: Learfield Communications, Llc
2400 Dallas Pkwy Ste 510
Plano TX 75093
336 464-0224

(P-12700)
LIBERMAN BROADCASTING INC (PA)
1845 W Empire Ave, Burbank (91504-3402)
PHONE..............................818 729-5300
Lenard D Liberman, CEO
Jose Liberman, President
Frederic T Boyer, CFO
Jason Hall, Exec VP
Michael Sheron, Senior VP
EMP: 83
SALES (est): 283.6MM Privately Held
WEB: www.estrellamedia.com
SIC: 4832 Radio broadcasting stations

(P-12701)
LOTUS COMMUNICATIONS CORP (PA)
3301 Barham Blvd Ste 200, Los Angeles (90068-1358)
PHONE..............................323 512-2225
Howard Kalmenson, President
William H Shriftman, Treasurer
Jim Kalmenson, Senior VP
Jerry Roy, Senior VP
Jasmin Dorismond, Vice Pres
EMP: 60 EST: 1959
SQ FT: 25,848
SALES (est): 114.1MM Privately Held
WEB: www.lotuscorp.com
SIC: 4832 Radio broadcasting stations

(P-12702)
MULTICULTURAL RDO BRDCSTG INC
747 E Green St, Pasadena (91101-2145)
PHONE..............................626 844-8882
Hon Vu, Program Dir
EMP: 85
SALES (corp-wide): 42.6MM Privately Held
WEB: www.wkdm1380am.com
SIC: 4832 Radio broadcasting stations, music format
PA: Multicultural Radio Broadcasting, Inc.
207 William St Fl 11 Flr 11
New York NY 10005
212 966-1059

(P-12703)
NEW INSPIRATION BRDCSTG CO INC (HQ)
4880 Santa Rosa Rd, Camarillo (93012-5190)
PHONE..............................805 987-0400
Edward G Atsinger III, CEO
Stuart Epperson, Ch of Bd
David Evans, President
Evan Masyr, CFO
Christopher Henderson, Vice Pres
EMP: 872 EST: 1982
SQ FT: 40,000
SALES (est): 48.4MM
SALES (corp-wide): 236.2MM Publicly Held
WEB: www.salemmedia.com
SIC: 4832 2731 Radio broadcasting stations; book publishing
PA: Salem Media Group, Inc.
6400 N Belt Line Rd
Irving TX 75063
805 987-0400

(P-12704)
RADIO DISNEY GROUP LLC
3800 W Alameda Ave # 115, Burbank (91505-4300)
PHONE..............................818 569-5000
Natalie Eig, Sales Staff
Jody Weissman, Sales Staff
EMP: 70 EST: 2003
SALES (est): 13.6MM
SALES (corp-wide): 65.3B Publicly Held
WEB: www.radio.disney.com
SIC: 4832 Radio broadcasting stations
HQ: Abc Cable Networks Group
500 S Buena Vista St
Burbank CA 91521
818 460-7477

(P-12705)
SAN BRNRDINO CMNTY COLLEGE DST
Also Called: Kvcr, TV & FM
701 S Mount Vernon Ave, San Bernardino (92410-2705)
PHONE..............................909 384-4444
Larry Ciecalone, President
Lillian Vasquez, Marketing Staff
EMP: 239
SALES (corp-wide): 46.5MM Privately Held
WEB: www.sbccd.org
SIC: 4832 4833 Radio broadcasting stations; television broadcasting stations
PA: San Bernardino Community College District
550 E Hospitality Ln # 200
San Bernardino CA 92408
909 382-4000

(P-12706)
SPANISH BRDCSTG SYS OF CAL
Also Called: Klax Radio Station
7007 Nw 77th Ave, Los Angeles (90064)
PHONE..............................310 203-0900
Raul Alarcon Sr, Ch of Bd
Joseph Garcia, CFO
Rafael Navarro, Managing Dir
EMP: 70 EST: 1984
SALES (est): 15.1MM
SALES (corp-wide): 156.6MM Publicly Held
WEB: www.spanishbroadcasting.com
SIC: 4832 7313 Radio broadcasting stations; radio advertising representative
HQ: Spanish Broadcasting System Of Greater Miami, Inc.
7007 Nw 77th Ave
Medley FL 33166
305 644-4800

(P-12707)
TRITON MEDIA GROUP LLC
Also Called: Dial Global Digital
8935 Lindblade St, Culver City (90232-2438)
PHONE..............................661 294-9000
Phil Barry, Branch Mgr
EMP: 199 Privately Held
WEB: www.tritonmedia.com
SIC: 4832 Radio broadcasting stations, music format
PA: Triton Media Group, Llc
15303 Ventura Blvd # 1500
Sherman Oaks CA 91403

4833 Television Broadcasting Stations

(P-12708)
ABC SIGNATURE STUDIOS INC
500 S Buena Vista St, Burbank (91521-0001)
PHONE..............................818 569-7500
Linda A Bagley, CEO
EMP: 86 EST: 1989
SALES (est): 14.8MM
SALES (corp-wide): 65.3B Publicly Held
WEB: www.thewaltdisneycompany.com
SIC: 4833 Television broadcasting stations

PA: The Walt Disney Company
500 S Buena Vista St
Burbank CA 91521
818 560-1000

(P-12709)
ACME COMMUNICATIONS INC (PA)
4790 Irvine Blvd Ste 105, Irvine
(92620-1998)
PHONE................714 245-9499
Jamie Kellner, *Ch of Bd*
Douglas Gealy, *President*
Thomas Allen, *CFO*
EMP: 65 **EST:** 1997
SALES (est): 19MM **Privately Held**
WEB: www.acmecommunications.com
SIC: 4833 Television broadcasting stations

(P-12710)
AMERICAN MULTIMEDIA TV USA
Also Called: Amtv USA
530 S Lake Ave Unit 368, Pasadena
(91101-3515)
PHONE................626 466-1038
Jason Quin, *President*
EMP: 67 **EST:** 2004
SALES (est): 357K **Privately Held**
SIC: 4833 7372 Television broadcasting stations; application computer software

(P-12711)
CHANNEL 9 AUSTRALIA INC (DH)
Also Called: Nine Network Australia
6255 W Sunset Blvd # 1500, Los Angeles
(90028-7416)
PHONE................323 461-3853
Noel Masson, *Vice Pres*
EMP: 80 **EST:** 1980
SQ FT: 7,544
SALES (est): 6MM **Privately Held**
WEB: www.nineforbrands.com.au
SIC: 4833 Television broadcasting stations

(P-12712)
CROWN MEDIA UNITED STATES LLC (DH)
Also Called: Hallmark Channel
12700 Ventura Blvd # 100, Studio City
(91604-2469)
PHONE................818 755-2400
David Evans,
Susanne McAvoy, *President*
Barroso Lisa, *Senior VP*
Chris Ward, *Senior VP*
Lisa Barroso, *Vice Pres*
EMP: 95 **EST:** 1995
SALES (est): 60.8MM
SALES (corp-wide): 2.7B **Privately Held**
WEB: www.hallmarkchannel.com
SIC: 4833 Television broadcasting stations
HQ: Crown Media Holdings, Inc.
12700 Ventura Blvd # 100
Studio City CA 91604
888 390-7474

(P-12713)
CW NETWORK LLC (PA)
Also Called: Cwtv
3300 W Olive Ave Fl 3, Burbank
(91505-4640)
PHONE................818 977-2500
Mark Pedowitz, *CEO*
John Maatta, *COO*
Dana Abel, *Senior VP*
Caty Burgess, *Senior VP*
Betty Ellen Berlamino, *Vice Pres*
EMP: 199 **EST:** 2006
SALES (est): 62.6MM **Privately Held**
WEB: www.cwtv.com
SIC: 4833 Television broadcasting stations

(P-12714)
DISNEY ONLINE
500 S Buena Vista St, Burbank
(91521-0001)
PHONE................818 553-7200
Justin G Warbrooke, *CEO*
EMP: 78 **EST:** 2001
SALES (est): 13.4MM
SALES (corp-wide): 65.3B **Publicly Held**
WEB: www.thewaltdisneycompany.com
SIC: 4833 Television broadcasting stations

PA: The Walt Disney Company
500 S Buena Vista St
Burbank CA 91521
818 560-1000

(P-12715)
ENCOMPASS DGTAL MDIA GROUP INC (PA)
15260 Ventura Blvd # 680, Sherman Oaks
(91403-5307)
PHONE................323 344-4500
Kenneth Sexton, *President*
Brian Stewart, *CFO*
Steve Cooper, *Vice Pres*
Lou Dimauro, *Vice Pres*
Joe Garzillo, *Vice Pres*
EMP: 240 **EST:** 2008
SALES (est): 3MM **Privately Held**
WEB: www.encompass.tv
SIC: 4833 Television broadcasting stations

(P-12716)
ENTRAVSION COMMUNICATIONS CORP
Also Called: K S S C - F M
5700 Wilshire Blvd # 250, Los Angeles
(90036-3659)
PHONE................323 900-6100
Jeff Liberman, *President*
Marty Avila, *Executive*
Sergio Delatorre, *Chief Engr*
Ian Bradley, *Marketing Staff*
Xochil Velez, *Sales Staff*
EMP: 100 **Publicly Held**
WEB: www.entravision.com
SIC: 4833 4832 Television broadcasting stations; radio broadcasting stations
PA: Entravision Communications Corporation
2425 Olympic Blvd Ste 600
Santa Monica CA 90404

(P-12717)
ENTRAVSION COMMUNICATIONS CORP
Also Called: Kyue TV
72920 Parkview Dr, Palm Desert
(92260-9357)
P.O. Box 13750 (92255-3750)
PHONE................760 836-0466
Mario Carrera, *Exec Officer*
Walter Ulloa, *Exec Officer*
EMP: 53 **EST:** 1989
SQ FT: 3,000
SALES (est): 6.2MM **Publicly Held**
WEB: www.nbcpalmsprings.com
SIC: 4833 Television broadcasting stations
PA: Entravision Communications Corporation
2425 Olympic Blvd Ste 600
Santa Monica CA 90404

(P-12718)
ENTRAVSION COMMUNICATIONS CORP (PA)
2425 Olympic Blvd Ste 600, Santa Monica
(90404-4030)
PHONE................310 447-3870
Walter F Ulloa, *Ch of Bd*
Jeffery A Liberman, *President*
Christopher T Young, *CFO*
Lilly Gonzalez, *Exec VP*
Rich Ripley, *Vice Pres*
EMP: 493 **EST:** 1996
SQ FT: 16,000
SALES (est): 344MM **Publicly Held**
WEB: www.entravision.com
SIC: 4833 4832 Television broadcasting stations; radio broadcasting stations

(P-12719)
ESTRELLA COMMUNICATIONS INC
Also Called: Kvea-Tv-Channel 52
3000 W Alameda Ave, Burbank
(91523-0001)
PHONE................818 260-5700
EMP: 90
SALES (est): 3.7MM
SALES (corp-wide): 68.7B **Publicly Held**
SIC: 4833 Television Station

HQ: Telemundo Communications Group, Inc.
2290 W 8th Ave
Hialeah FL 33010
305 884-8200

(P-12720)
FOX INC (DH)
Also Called: Home Entertainment Div
2121 Avenue Of The Stars, Los Angeles
(90067-5010)
P.O. Box 900, Beverly Hills (90213-0900)
PHONE................310 369-1000
K Rupert Murdoch, *Ch of Bd*
Mike Dunn, *President*
Robert Fusco, *President*
Jay Itzkowitz, *President*
Naya Resnick, *Vice Pres*
▲ **EMP:** 2000 **EST:** 1984
SQ FT: 25,000
SALES (est): 881.2MM
SALES (corp-wide): 65.3B **Publicly Held**
WEB: www.fox.com
SIC: 4833 7812 Television broadcasting stations; motion picture production & distribution
HQ: 21st Century Fox America, Inc.
1211 Ave Of The Americas
New York NY 10036
212 852-7000

(P-12721)
FOX BROADCASTING COMPANY LLC (HQ)
10201 W Pico Blvd Bldg 10, Los Angeles
(90064-2606)
P.O. Box 900, Beverly Hills (90213-0900)
PHONE................310 369-1000
David F Devoe Jr, *CEO*
Michael Thorn, *President*
Nancy Utley, *President*
Charlie Collier, *CEO*
Joe Earley, *COO*
EMP: 200 **EST:** 1986
SQ FT: 41,000
SALES (est): 115.5MM
SALES (corp-wide): 12.9B **Publicly Held**
WEB: www.fox.com
SIC: 4833 Television broadcasting stations
PA: Fox Corporation
1211 Ave Of The Americas
New York NY 10036
212 852-7000

(P-12722)
FOX INTRNTONAL CHANNELS US INC (DH)
10201 W Pico Blvd, Los Angeles
(90064-2606)
PHONE................310 369-8759
William Mechanic, *President*
Emiliano Saccone, *President*
EMP: 80 **EST:** 2002
SALES (est): 111.6MM
SALES (corp-wide): 65.3B **Publicly Held**
WEB: www.thewaltdisneycompany.com
SIC: 4833 Television broadcasting stations
HQ: Fox Entertainment Group, Llc
1211 Ave Of The Americas
New York NY 10036
212 852-7000

(P-12723)
FOX NETWORKS GROUP INC (DH)
Also Called: Fox Network Center
10201 W Pico Blvd Bldg 10, Los Angeles
(90064-2606)
P.O. Box 900, Beverly Hills (90213-0900)
PHONE................310 369-1000
Brian Sullivan, *President*
Raul De Quesada, *Info Tech Dir*
Sanchez Christine, *Technology*
Ryan Tomlin, *Senior Mgr*
Christopher Park, *Manager*
EMP: 148 **EST:** 1996
SALES (est): 92.1MM
SALES (corp-wide): 65.3B **Publicly Held**
WEB: www.fox.com
SIC: 4833 Television broadcasting stations
HQ: Fox Entertainment Group, Llc
1211 Ave Of The Americas
New York NY 10036
212 852-7000

(P-12724)
FOX SPORTS INC (DH)
Also Called: F O X
10201 W Pico Blvd, Los Angeles
(90064-2606)
PHONE................310 369-1000
Randy Freer, *CEO*
Tara Bridges, *Partner*
Dan Donnelly, *Exec VP*
Robert Gottlieb, *Exec VP*
Haigaz Farajian, *Senior VP*
EMP: 115 **EST:** 1995
SALES (est): 192.6MM
SALES (corp-wide): 65.3B **Publicly Held**
WEB: www.foxsports.com
SIC: 4833 Television broadcasting stations
HQ: Fox Entertainment Group, Llc
1211 Ave Of The Americas
New York NY 10036
212 852-7000

(P-12725)
FOX SPORTS PRODUCTIONS INC
10201 W Pico Blvd, Los Angeles
(90064-2606)
P.O. Box 900, Beverly Hills (90213-0900)
PHONE................310 369-1000
David Hill, *Ch of Bd*
EMP: 60 **EST:** 1994
SALES (est): 6.4MM
SALES (corp-wide): 12.9B **Publicly Held**
WEB: www.fox.com
SIC: 4833 Television broadcasting stations
PA: Fox Corporation
1211 Ave Of The Americas
New York NY 10036
212 852-7000

(P-12726)
FOX TELEVISION STATIONS INC (HQ)
Also Called: Fox Entertainment Television
1999 S Bundy Dr, Los Angeles
(90025-5203)
PHONE................310 584-2000
Jim Burke, *President*
Roger Ailes, *Ch of Bd*
Jim Burke, *President*
Tom Herwitz, *President*
Dennis Swanson, *President*
▲ **EMP:** 300 **EST:** 1998
SALES (est): 871MM
SALES (corp-wide): 12.9B **Publicly Held**
WEB: www.foxla.com
SIC: 4833 7313 Television broadcasting stations; radio, television, publisher representatives
PA: Fox Corporation
1211 Ave Of The Americas
New York NY 10036
212 852-7000

(P-12727)
FOX US PRODUCTIONS 27 INC
1600 Rosecrans Ave 5a, Manhattan Beach
(90266-3708)
PHONE................310 727-2550
EMP: 174
SALES (est): 4.7MM
SALES (corp-wide): 65.3B **Publicly Held**
WEB: www.fox.com
SIC: 4833 Television broadcasting stations
HQ: Fox Entertainment Group, Llc
1211 Ave Of The Americas
New York NY 10036
212 852-7000

(P-12728)
GULF- CALIFORNIA BROADCAST CO
Also Called: Kesq Tv
31276 Dunham Way, Thousand Palms
(92276-3310)
PHONE................760 773-0342
John Kuenuke, *President*
Gus Ibarra, *Producer*
Sarah-Jayne Simon, *Producer*
Chip Shenkan, *Sales Staff*
Daniel Bell, *Director*
EMP: 68 **EST:** 1984

PRODUCTS & SVCS

SALES (est): 6.4MM
SALES (corp-wide): 181MM **Privately Held**
WEB: www.kesq.com
SIC: 4833 7922 Television broadcasting stations; theatrical producers & services
PA: News-Press & Gazette Company Inc
825 Edmond St
Saint Joseph MO 64501
816 271-8500

(P-12729)
KABC-TV
500 Circle Seven Dr, Glendale
(91201-2331)
PHONE..............................818 863-7171
Arnold Kleiner, *Principal*
EMP: 58 **EST:** 2013
SALES (est): 28.5MM
SALES (corp-wide): 65.3B **Publicly Held**
WEB: www.thewaltdisneycompany.com
SIC: 4833 Television broadcasting stations
HQ: Twdc Enterprises 18 Corp.
500 S Buena Vista St
Burbank CA 91521

(P-12730)
KOREAN TELEVISION ENTERPRISES
625 S Kingsley Dr, Los Angeles
(90005-2319)
PHONE..............................213 382-6700
Bong He Lee, *President*
Choon Keun Han, *Controller*
EMP: 64 **EST:** 1983
SQ FT: 20,100
SALES (est): 2MM **Privately Held**
WEB: www.kbs.co.kr
SIC: 4833 Television broadcasting stations
HQ: Korean Broadcasting System
13 Yeouigongwon-Ro, Yeongdeungpo-Gu
Seoul 07235

(P-12731)
KRCA TELEVISION LLC (DH)
Also Called: Krca Tv-62
1845 W Empire Ave, Burbank
(91504-3402)
PHONE..............................818 563-5722
Jose Liberman,
Wisdom W Lu, *CFO*
Leonard Liberman, *Exec VP*
Ozzie Mendoza, *Sales Mgr*
EMP: 99 **EST:** 2007
SQ FT: 50,000
SALES (est): 33.5MM
SALES (corp-wide): 283.6MM **Privately Held**
SIC: 4833 Television broadcasting stations

(P-12732)
KSBY COMMUNICATIONS LLC
1772 Calle Joaquin, San Luis Obispo
(93405-7210)
PHONE..............................805 541-6666
Kathleen Choal, *President*
Lisa Moore, *Director*
EMP: 99 **EST:** 2005
SALES (est): 6.4MM
SALES (corp-wide): 1.8B **Publicly Held**
WEB: www.ksby.com
SIC: 4833 Television broadcasting stations
PA: The E W Scripps Company
312 Walnut St Ste 2800
Cincinnati OH 45202
513 977-3000

(P-12733)
LIFETIME ENTRMT SVCS LLC
Also Called: Lifetime TV Network
2049 Century Park E # 840, Los Angeles
(90067-3101)
PHONE..............................310 556-7500
Maryann Harris, *General Mgr*
Michelle Shack, *Administration*
EMP: 300
SALES (corp-wide): 694.4MM **Privately Held**
WEB: www.mylifetime.com
SIC: 4833 5942 Television broadcasting stations; book stores

HQ: Lifetime Entertainment Services, Llc
235 E 45th St
New York NY 10017
212 424-7000

(P-12734)
NBC SUBSIDIARY (KNBC-TV) LLC
100 Unvrsal Cy Plz Bldg 2, Universal City
(91608)
P.O. Box 66132, Los Angeles (90066-0132)
PHONE..............................818 684-5746
Steve Carlston, *President*
Joann Alfano, *Exec VP*
Pauline Bohm, *Vice Pres*
Phil Perry, *Vice Pres*
Christopher Williams, *Vice Pres*
EMP: 250 **EST:** 2009
SALES (est): 76.1MM
SALES (corp-wide): 103.5B **Publicly Held**
WEB: www.nbcuniversal.com
SIC: 4833 Television broadcasting stations
PA: Comcast Corporation
1701 John F Kennedy Blvd
Philadelphia PA 19103
215 286-1700

(P-12735)
NEWPORT TELEVISION LLC
Kget-Tv
2120 L St, Bakersfield (93301-2331)
PHONE..............................661 283-1700
Sandy Dipasquale, *President*
Raphael Stroud, *Producer*
EMP: 288
SALES (corp-wide): 26.5MM **Privately Held**
WEB: www.newporttv.com
SIC: 4833 Television translator station
PA: Newport Television Llc
460 Nichols Rd Ste 250
Kansas City MO 64112
816 751-0200

(P-12736)
ODS TECHNOLOGIES LP (DH)
Also Called: Television Games Network
6701 Center Dr W Ste 160, Los Angeles
(90045-1558)
PHONE..............................310 242-9400
David Nathanson, *General Ptnr*
Karen Fox, *Executive Asst*
Jeffrey Grayson, *Admin Sec*
John Shepphird, *Director*
Neil Halstead, *Manager*
EMP: 132 **EST:** 1994
SQ FT: 20,000
SALES (est): 62.5MM **Privately Held**
WEB: www.betfair.com
SIC: 4833 7948 Television broadcasting stations; horses, racing
HQ: Betfair Group Limited
Waterfront
London W6 9H
208 834-8000

(P-12737)
OVATION LLC
12910 Culver Blvd Ste J, Los Angeles
(90066-6709)
PHONE..............................310 430-7575
Charles Segars, *CEO*
Philip Gilligan, *CFO*
Ken Solomon, *Chairman*
Liz Jannemann, *Exec VP*
John Malkin, *Exec VP*
EMP: 55 **EST:** 2006
SALES (est): 5.4MM **Privately Held**
WEB: www.ovationtv.com
SIC: 4833 Television broadcasting stations

(P-12738)
PUBLIC MDIA GROUP SOUTHERN CAL (PA)
2900 W Alameda Ave # 600, Burbank
(91505-4220)
PHONE..............................714 241-4100
Andrew Russell, *President*
Jamie Myers, *COO*
Paul Nelson, *CFO*
Corbett Barklie, *Vice Pres*
Alexis Stringfellow, *Vice Pres*
EMP: 134 **EST:** 1960
SQ FT: 50,000

SALES: 38MM **Privately Held**
WEB: www.kcet.org
SIC: 4833 Television broadcasting stations

(P-12739)
REVOLT MEDIA AND TV LLC
1800 N Highland Ave Fl 7, Los Angeles
(90028-4522)
PHONE..............................323 645-3000
Detavio Samuels, *CEO*
Vincent Lambino, *Vice Pres*
Adina Smith, *Vice Pres*
Kia Riley, *Accountant*
Ryan Peterson, *Production*
EMP: 120 **EST:** 2010
SALES (est): 46.8MM **Privately Held**
WEB: www.revolt.tv
SIC: 4833 Television broadcasting stations

(P-12740)
S F BROADCASTING OF WISCONSIN
2425 Olympic Blvd, Santa Monica
(90404-4030)
PHONE..............................310 586-2410
EMP: 151
SALES (est): 2.9MM
SALES (corp-wide): 3.2B **Publicly Held**
SIC: 4833 Holding Company
PA: Iac/Interactivecorp
555 W 18th St
New York NY 75231
212 314-7300

(P-12741)
SMITH BROADCASTING GROUP INC
Also Called: Keyt Television
730 Miramonte Dr, Santa Barbara
(93109-1417)
P.O. Box 729 (93102-0729)
PHONE..............................805 882-3933
Michael Granados, *General Mgr*
Yizel Medrano, *Producer*
Mark Keenan, *Manager*
EMP: 332
SALES (corp-wide): 15.2MM **Privately Held**
WEB: www.keyt.com
SIC: 4833 7313 Television broadcasting stations; television & radio time sales
PA: Smith Broadcasting Group, Inc
2315 Red Rose Way
Santa Barbara CA 93109
805 965-0400

(P-12742)
SMWD INC (PA)
3800 Barham Blvd Ste 410, Los Angeles
(90068-1042)
PHONE..............................323 904-4680
Nick Powell, *President*
EMP: 64 **EST:** 2010
SALES (est): 141.5K **Privately Held**
SIC: 4833 Television broadcasting stations

(P-12743)
SUBTRACTIVE INC (PA)
Santa Monica Airport N 28, Santa Monica
(90405)
PHONE..............................310 664-0540
Kyle Alan Schember, *CEO*
Luke Bechthold, *Engineer*
Joe Lombardi, *Editor*
Lauren Walsh, *Editor*
EMP: 54 **EST:** 2005
SALES (est): 3.3MM **Privately Held**
WEB: www.subtractive.net
SIC: 4833 Television broadcasting stations

(P-12744)
TRINITY BRDCSTG NETWRK INC
Also Called: Trinity Christn Ctr Santa Ana
2442 Michelle Dr, Tustin (92780-7015)
PHONE..............................714 665-3619
Paul F Crouch, *President*
Daniel Digello, *Info Tech Dir*
Obed Sandoval, *IT/INT Sup*
Felecia Ligon, *Producer*
EMP: 150 **EST:** 1987
SALES (est): 5MM
SALES (corp-wide): 129.4MM **Privately Held**
WEB: www.tbn.org
SIC: 4833 Television broadcasting stations

PA: Trinity Christian Center Of Santa Ana, Inc.
2442 Michelle Dr
Tustin CA 92780
714 665-3619

(P-12745)
TRINITY CHRISTIAN CENTER OF SA (PA)
Also Called: Trinity Broadcasting Network
2442 Michelle Dr, Tustin (92780-7015)
P.O. Box A, Santa Ana (92711-2101)
PHONE..............................714 665-3619
Janice W Crouch, *Principal*
Paul F Crouch, *President*
Colby May, *Bd of Directors*
Bob Fopma, *Vice Pres*
Rosa Marin, *Vice Pres*
▲ **EMP:** 200 **EST:** 1973
SQ FT: 20,000
SALES (est): 129.4MM **Privately Held**
WEB: www.tbn.org
SIC: 4833 7922 Television broadcasting stations; television program, including commercial producers

(P-12746)
TVB (USA) INC (DH)
15411 Blackburn Ave, Norwalk
(90650-6844)
PHONE..............................562 345-9871
Philip Tam, *President*
Melissa Wang, *Vice Pres*
Vivian Keung, *Sales Staff*
▲ **EMP:** 50 **EST:** 1984
SQ FT: 25,000
SALES (est): 10.2MM **Privately Held**
WEB: www.tvbusa.com
SIC: 4833 Television broadcasting stations
HQ: Tvb Holdings (Usa) Inc.
15411 Blackburn Ave
Norwalk CA 90650
562 802-8868

(P-12747)
TWDC ENTERPRISES 18 CORP (HQ)
Also Called: Disney Financial Services
500 S Buena Vista St, Burbank
(91521-0001)
PHONE..............................818 560-1000
Christine M McCarthy, *Executive*
Dorothy Attwood, *Vice Pres*
Christine Cadena, *Vice Pres*
Tami Garcia, *Vice Pres*
Jill Hotchkiss, *Vice Pres*
◆ **EMP:** 464 **EST:** 1925
SALES (est): 46.3B
SALES (corp-wide): 65.3B **Publicly Held**
WEB: www.thewaltdisneycompany.com
SIC: 4833 4841 7011 7996 Television broadcasting stations; cable television services; resort hotel; amusement parks; motion picture & video production; books; publishing only
PA: The Walt Disney Company
500 S Buena Vista St
Burbank CA 91521
818 560-1000

(P-12748)
TWENTETH CNTURY FOX INTL TV IN (DH)
10201 W Pico Blvd, Los Angeles
(90064-2606)
PHONE..............................310 369-1000
Peter Chernin, *Ch of Ed*
EMP: 80 **EST:** 1996
SALES (est): 25.6MM
SALES (corp-wide): 65.3B **Publicly Held**
WEB: www.fox.com
SIC: 4833 Television broadcasting stations
HQ: Fox Entertainment Group, Llc
1211 Ave Of The Americas
New York NY 10036
212 852-7000

(P-12749)
TWENTIETH TELEVISION INC
1999 S Bundy Dr, Los Angeles
(90025-5203)
PHONE..............................310 584-2000
Kevin Hael, *Branch Mgr*
EMP: 97

SALES (corp-wide): 65.3B **Publicly Held**
WEB: www.mynetworktv.com
SIC: **4833** Television broadcasting stations
HQ: Twentieth Television, Inc.
  10201 W Pico Blvd
  Los Angeles CA 90064

(P-12750)
VALLEYCREST PRODUCTIONS LTD
500 S Buena Vista St, Burbank (91521-0001)
PHONE..................818 560-5391
Joseph Santaniello, *CEO*
EMP: 100 EST: 1999
SALES (est): 37MM
SALES (corp-wide): 65.3B **Publicly Held**
WEB: www.thewaltdisneycompany.com
SIC: **4833** Television broadcasting stations
HQ: Twdc Enterprises 18 Corp.
  500 S Buena Vista St
  Burbank CA 91521

4841 Cable & Other Pay TV Svcs

(P-12751)
BDR INDUSTRIES INC (PA)
Also Called: R N D Enterprises
820 E Avenue L12, Lancaster (93535-5403)
PHONE..................661 940-8554
Scott Riddle, *President*
Edward Donovan, *Vice Pres*
▲ EMP: 95 EST: 1984
SQ FT: 30,000
SALES (est): 25.8MM **Privately Held**
SIC: **4841** Cable television services

(P-12752)
CALIFORNIA BROADCAST CTR LLC
3800 Via Oro Ave, Long Beach (90810-1866)
PHONE..................310 233-2425
Bruce Churchill, *CEO*
EMP: 118 EST: 1955
SALES (est): 11.5MM
SALES (corp-wide): 171.7B **Publicly Held**
SIC: **4841** Cable & other pay television services
HQ: Directv Latin America, Llc
  1 Rockefeller Plz
  New York NY 10020
  212 205-0500

(P-12753)
COMCAST CORPORATION
1205 S Dupont Ave, Ontario (91761-1536)
PHONE..................909 890-0886
Mike Shanter, *Branch Mgr*
Steve Burke, *Coordinator*
Bao Dao, *Coordinator*
EMP: 100
SQ FT: 23,318
SALES (corp-wide): 103.5B **Publicly Held**
WEB: www.corporate.comcast.com
SIC: **4841** Cable television services
PA: Comcast Corporation
  1701 John F Kennedy Blvd
  Philadelphia PA 19103
  215 286-1700

(P-12754)
CROWN MEDIA HOLDINGS INC (HQ)
12700 Ventura Blvd # 100, Studio City (91604-2469)
PHONE..................888 390-7474
William J Abbott, *President*
Kristen Roberts, *President*
Michelle Vicary, *President*
Andrew Rooke, *CFO*
Stedem Deanne, *Exec VP*
EMP: 105 EST: 1999
SQ FT: 41,423

SALES (est): 478.7MM
SALES (corp-wide): 2.7B **Privately Held**
WEB: www.hallmarkchannel.com
SIC: **4841** Cable television services
PA: Hallmark Cards, Incorporated
  2501 Mcgee St
  Kansas City MO 64108
  816 274-5111

(P-12755)
DIRECTV INC
2230 E Imperial Hwy, El Segundo (90245-3504)
P.O. Box 105249, Atlanta GA (30348-5249)
PHONE..................888 388-4249
Todd Mathers, *Vice Pres*
Rene Weaver, *Vice Pres*
Dan Gibson, *Executive*
William Becker, *Principal*
Fabiana Vaz, *Program Mgr*
EMP: 476 EST: 2015
SALES (est): 45.3MM **Privately Held**
WEB: www.directv.com
SIC: **4841** Cable & other pay television services

(P-12756)
DIRECTV ENTERPRISES LLC
2230 E Imperial Hwy, El Segundo (90245-3504)
P.O. Box 956 (90245-0956)
PHONE..................310 535-5000
Michael D White, *Site Mgr*
Eddy W Hartenstein, *Ch of Bd*
Odie C Donald, *President*
R L Myers, *CFO*
Edward Aleman, *VP Accounting*
EMP: 14699 EST: 1995
SQ FT: 75,000
SALES (est): 10MM
SALES (corp-wide): 171.7B **Publicly Held**
SIC: **4841** Direct broadcast satellite services (DBS)
HQ: Directv Holdings Llc
  2230 E Imperial Hwy
  El Segundo CA 90245
  310 964-5000

(P-12757)
DIRECTV GROUP HOLDINGS LLC
140 Station Ave, Ridgecrest (93555-3838)
PHONE..................760 375-8300
EMP: 114
SALES (corp-wide): 171.7B **Publicly Held**
SIC: **4841** Cable & other pay television services
HQ: Directv Group Holdings, Llc
  2260 E Imperial Hwy
  El Segundo CA 90245

(P-12758)
DIRECTV GROUP HOLDINGS LLC
360 Cortez Cir, Camarillo (93012-8630)
PHONE..................805 207-6675
EMP: 114
SALES (corp-wide): 171.7B **Publicly Held**
SIC: **4841** Cable television services
HQ: Directv Group Holdings, Llc
  2260 E Imperial Hwy
  El Segundo CA 90245

(P-12759)
DIRECTV GROUP HOLDINGS LLC
715 E Avenue L8 Ste 101, Lancaster (93535-5405)
PHONE..................661 632-6562
EMP: 114
SALES (corp-wide): 171.7B **Publicly Held**
SIC: **4841** Direct broadcast satellite services (DBS)
HQ: Directv Group Holdings, Llc
  2260 E Imperial Hwy
  El Segundo CA 90245

(P-12760)
DIRECTV GROUP INC (DH)
2260 E Imperial Hwy, El Segundo (90245-3501)
PHONE..................310 964-5000
Michael White, *CEO*
Patrick T Doyle, *CFO*
J William Little, *Treasurer*
Romulo Pontual, *Exec VP*
John F Murphy, *Senior VP*
▲ EMP: 128 EST: 1977
SALES (est): 1.8B
SALES (corp-wide): 171.7B **Publicly Held**
SIC: **4841** 6794 Direct broadcast satellite services (DBS); franchises, selling or licensing

(P-12761)
DIRECTV HOLDINGS LLC (DH)
2230 E Imperial Hwy, El Segundo (90245-3504)
PHONE..................310 964-5000
Michael D White, *President*
Patrick T Doyle, *CFO*
Larry D Hunter, *Exec VP*
John F Murphy, *Senior VP*
Art Casas, *Engineer*
◆ EMP: 1601 EST: 2002
SALES (est): 1.2B
SALES (corp-wide): 171.7B **Publicly Held**
SIC: **4841** Direct broadcast satellite services (DBS)
HQ: The Directv Group Inc
  2260 E Imperial Hwy
  El Segundo CA 90245
  310 964-5000

(P-12762)
DIRECTV INTERNATIONAL INC (DH)
2230 E Imperial Hwy Fl 10, El Segundo (90245-3504)
PHONE..................310 964-6460
Michael D White, *Site Mgr*
Kevin McGrath, *President*
Celso Azevedo, *Senior VP*
EMP: 150 EST: 1996
SALES (est): 115.2MM
SALES (corp-wide): 171.7B **Publicly Held**
SIC: **4841** Cable & other pay television services
HQ: The Directv Group Inc
  2260 E Imperial Hwy
  El Segundo CA 90245
  310 964-5000

(P-12763)
DIRECTV SPORTS NETWORK LLC (DH)
2230 E Imperial Hwy, El Segundo (90245-3504)
PHONE..................310 964-5000
Patrick W Crumb,
EMP: 80 EST: 2010
SALES (est): 10.1MM
SALES (corp-wide): 171.7B **Publicly Held**
SIC: **4841** Direct broadcast satellite services (DBS)

(P-12764)
DISH NETWORK CORPORATION
396 Orange Show Ln, San Bernardino (92408-2012)
PHONE..................909 381-4767
EMP: 55 **Publicly Held**
WEB: www.dish.com
SIC: **4841** Direct broadcast satellite services (DBS)
PA: Dish Network Corporation
  9601 S Meridian Blvd
  Englewood CO 80112

(P-12765)
DISH NETWORK CORPORATION
1297 N Verdugo Rd, Glendale (91206-1508)
PHONE..................818 334-8740
EMP: 55 **Publicly Held**
WEB: www.dish.com

SIC: **4841** Direct broadcast satellite services (DBS)
PA: Dish Network Corporation
  9601 S Meridian Blvd
  Englewood CO 80112

(P-12766)
DISH NETWORK CORPORATION
2602 Halladay St, Santa Ana (92705-5601)
PHONE..................714 424-0503
Raul Guidi, *General Mgr*
Laura Lewis, *Natl Sales Mgr*
Lindsey Thiel, *Sales Staff*
EMP: 55 **Publicly Held**
WEB: www.dish.com
SIC: **4841** Direct broadcast satellite services (DBS)
PA: Dish Network Corporation
  9601 S Meridian Blvd
  Englewood CO 80112

(P-12767)
DTV NETWORK SYSTEMS INC (PA)
2230 E Imperial Hwy, El Segundo (90245-3504)
PHONE..................800 531-5000
Chase Carey, *President*
Jeff Knight, *Administration*
Lynn Forcier, *Database Admin*
Robert Mercer, *Pub Rel Dir*
Dan Ferguson, *Marketing Staff*
EMP: 111 EST: 2001
SALES (est): 1.5MM **Privately Held**
WEB: www.ceodirectv.com
SIC: **4841** Cable television services

(P-12768)
FX NETWORKS LLC
10201 W Pico Blvd Bldg 10, Los Angeles (90064-2606)
P.O. Box 900, Beverly Hills (90213-0900)
PHONE..................310 369-1000
John Landgraf, *President*
Stephanie Gibbons, *Partner*
Gina Balian, *President*
Eric Schrier, *President*
Rob Evanko, *Vice Pres*
EMP: 150 EST: 1997
SALES (est): 63.2MM
SALES (corp-wide): 65.3B **Publicly Held**
WEB: www.fxnetworks.com
SIC: **4841** Cable television services
HQ: Fox Entertainment Group, Llc
  1211 Ave Of The Americas
  New York NY 10036
  212 852-7000

(P-12769)
GAME SHOW NETWORK MUSIC LLC (DH)
Also Called: G S N
2150 Colorado Ave Ste 100, Santa Monica (90404-5514)
PHONE..................310 255-6800
Mark Seldman, *Mng Member*
Peter Blacklow, *Exec VP*
Jeffrey Anderson, *Vice Pres*
Ann Boreing, *Vice Pres*
Marcelo Guerra, *Vice Pres*
EMP: 336 EST: 1992
SALES (est): 66.7MM **Privately Held**
WEB: www.gsn.com
SIC: **4841** Cable television services
HQ: Sony Pictures Entertainment, Inc.
  10202 Washington Blvd
  Culver City CA 90232
  310 244-4000

(P-12770)
GLOBECAST AMERICA INCORPORATED (DH)
10525 Washington Blvd, Culver City (90232-3311)
PHONE..................310 845-3900
Michele Gosetti, *CEO*
Lisa Coelho, *President*
Batrice De Lagrevol, *Vice Pres*
Tim Jackson, *Vice Pres*
Didier Mainard, *Vice Pres*
▲ EMP: 303 EST: 1993

P R O D U C T S & S V C S

SALES (est): 105.4MM
SALES (corp-wide): 26.7B **Privately Held**
WEB: www.globecast.com
SIC: **4841** Satellite master antenna systems services (SMATV)

(P-12771)
HOME BOX OFFICE INC
Also Called: HBO
2500 Broadway Ste 400, Santa Monica
(90404-3176)
PHONE..................................310 382-3000
EMP: 95
SALES (corp-wide): 171.7B **Publicly Held**
WEB: www.hbo.com
SIC: **4841** 7812 Cable And Other Pay Television Services
HQ: Home Box Office, Inc.
1100 Avenue Of The Americ
New York NY 10036
212 512-1000

(P-12772)
INTERNATIONAL FMLY ENTRMT INC (DH)
Also Called: Fox Family Channel
3800 W Alameda Ave, Burbank
(91505-4300)
PHONE..................................818 560-1000
Mel Woods, *President*
EMP: 144 EST: 1990
SALES (est): 102.3MM
SALES (corp-wide): 65.3B **Publicly Held**
SIC: **4841** 7812 7922 7999 Cable television services; television film production; theatrical producers; recreation services
HQ: Abc Family Worldwide, Inc.
500 S Buena Vista St
Burbank CA 91521
818 560-1000

(P-12773)
LIBERTY ENTERTAINMENT INC (DH)
2230 E Imperial Hwy, El Segundo
(90245-3504)
PHONE..................................310 964-5000
EMP: 268 EST: 2007
SALES (est): 17.5MM
SALES (corp-wide): 171.7B **Publicly Held**
SIC: **4841** Cable & other pay television services

(P-12774)
NDS AMERICAS INC (DH)
3500 Hyland Ave, Costa Mesa
(92626-1459)
PHONE..................................714 434-2100
Abe Peled, *President*
Peter Lynskey, *Vice Pres*
Dov Rubin, *Vice Pres*
Alex Gersh, *Admin Sec*
Donna Matos, *Manager*
EMP: 90 EST: 1992
SALES (est): 60.3MM
SALES (corp-wide): 49.8B **Publicly Held**
WEB: www.cisco.com
SIC: **4841** Cable television services

(P-12775)
OWN LLC
Also Called: Oprah Winfrey Network
1041 N Formosa Ave, West Hollywood
(90046-6703)
PHONE..................................323 602-5500
Oprah Winfrey, *CEO*
Sylva Zakian, *President*
Erik Logan, *Co-President*
Sheri Salata, *Co-President*
Liz Dolan, *Chief Mktg Ofcr*
EMP: 140 EST: 2008
SQ FT: 50,000
SALES (est): 64.8MM
SALES (corp-wide): 108.1MM **Privately Held**
WEB: www.oprah.com
SIC: **4841** Cable television services
PA: Discovery Communications, Inc.
10100 Santa Monica Blvd
Los Angeles CA 90067
310 975-5906

(P-12776)
PHOENIX SATELLITE TV US INC
3810 Durbin St, Baldwin Park
(91706-6800)
PHONE..................................626 388-1188
Xiaoyong Wu, *CEO*
Shing Ping, *CEO*
Yan Lu, *Finance Mgr*
Daisy Deng, *Producer*
Victor Liang, *Marketing Mgr*
▲ EMP: 50 EST: 2000
SQ FT: 18,000
SALES (est): 22MM **Privately Held**
WEB: www.ifengus.com
SIC: **4841** Cable television services
HQ: Phoenix Media Investment (Holdings) Limited
Tai Po Indl Est
Tai Po NT

(P-12777)
SPECTRUM MGT HOLDG CO LLC
Also Called: Time Warner
3550 Wilshire Blvd, Los Angeles
(90010-2401)
PHONE..................................323 657-0899
EMP: 84
SALES (corp-wide): 48.1B **Publicly Held**
WEB: www.spectrum.com
SIC: **4841** Cable television services
HQ: Spectrum Management Holding Company, Llc
400 Atlantic St
Stamford CT 06901
203 905-7801

(P-12778)
SPECTRUM MGT HOLDG CO LLC
Also Called: Time Warner
6021 Katella Ave Ste 100, Cypress
(90630-5250)
PHONE..................................714 657-1060
EMP: 120
SALES (corp-wide): 29B **Publicly Held**
SIC: **4841** Cable & Pay Television Services
HQ: Spectrum Management Holding Company, Llc
400 Atlantic St
Stamford CT 06901
203 905-7801

(P-12779)
TIME WARNER CABLE INC
313 N 8th St, El Centro (92243-2303)
PHONE..................................760 335-4800
EMP: 83
SALES (corp-wide): 41.5B **Publicly Held**
HQ: Spectrum Management Holding Company, Llc
400 Atlantic St
Stamford CT 06901
203 905-7801

(P-12780)
VUBIQUITY HOLDINGS INC (DH)
15301 Ventura Blvd # 3000, Sherman Oaks
(91403-3102)
PHONE..................................818 526-5000
Darcy Antonellis, *CEO*
Doug Sylvester, *President*
William G Arendt, *CFO*
James P Riley, *Officer*
Pete Bryant, *Exec VP*
EMP: 185 EST: 2006
SALES (est): 177.1MM
SALES (corp-wide): 3.5B **Privately Held**
WEB: www.vubiquity.com
SIC: **4841** Cable & other pay television services
HQ: Amdocs, Inc.
1390 Tmberlake Manor Pkwy
Chesterfield MO 63017
314 212-7000

4899 Communication Svcs, NEC

(P-12781)
COMMUNICATIONS SUPPLY CORP
6251 Knott Ave, Buena Park (90620-1010)
PHONE..................................714 670-7711
Michael Davis, *General Mgr*
Miryam Lopez, *Sales Associate*
Diana Sobol, *Sales Staff*
EMP: 70 **Publicly Held**
WEB: www.wesco.com
SIC: **4899** 1731 3577 3357 Data communication services; communications specialization; computer peripheral equipment; nonferrous wiredrawing & insulating
HQ: Communications Supply Corp
200 E Lies Rd
Carol Stream IL 60188
630 221-6400

(P-12782)
CTEK INC
2425 Golden Hill Rd # 106, Paso Robles
(93446-7038)
PHONE..................................310 241-2973
Phil Sutter, *President*
EMP: 25 EST: 2003
SALES (est): 2.5MM
SALES (corp-wide): 279.2MM **Publicly Held**
WEB: www.ctekproducts.com
SIC: **4899** 3661 Communication signal enhancement network system; fiber optics communications equipment
PA: Digi International Inc.
9350 Excelsior Blvd # 70
Hopkins MN 55343
952 912-3444

(P-12783)
DIGITAL MAP PRODUCTS INC
Also Called: Lightbox
5201 California Ave # 200, Irvine
(92617-3098)
PHONE..................................949 333-5111
James Skurzynski, *President*
Thomas R Patterson Jr, *Officer*
Colleen Ellison, *Vice Pres*
Eade Hopkinson, *Administration*
Jeff Wilson, *Software Engr*
EMP: 51 EST: 1996
SQ FT: 8,000
SALES (est): 17.7MM **Privately Held**
WEB: www.digmap.com
SIC: **4899** Data communication services

(P-12784)
DISCOVERY COMMUNICATIONS INC (PA)
10100 Santa Monica Blvd, Los Angeles
(90067-4003)
PHONE..................................310 975-5906
David Zazlov, *CEO*
Lauren Tuck, *Admin Asst*
Jojo Jalapit, *Technician*
Michelle Fernando, *Research*
Jeff Monarch, *Prdtn Mgr*
EMP: 107 EST: 2014
SALES (est): 108.1MM **Privately Held**
SIC: **4899** Data communication services

(P-12785)
GODIGITAL MEDIA GROUP LLC
3103 S La Cienega Blvd, Los Angeles
(90016-3110)
PHONE..................................310 853-7940
Jason Peterson, *Mng Member*
Jay Winship, *COO*
Hunter Paletsas, *CFO*
Manfred Van Ursel, *CTO*
Michael Sorenson, *Opers Staff*
EMP: 60 EST: 2005
SALES (est): 4.8MM **Privately Held**
WEB: www.godigitalvod.com
SIC: **4899** 8741 7389 Data communication services; business management; copyright protection service

(P-12786)
HORIZON COMMUNICATION TECH INC (PA)
16441 Scientific Ste 200, Irvine
(92618-4367)
PHONE..................................714 982-3900
Micheal Degraw, *CEO*
Anthony Turrentine, *President*
Kyle Moody, *COO*
Larry J Beebe, *Vice Pres*
Liz Carlisle, *Vice Pres*
EMP: 79 EST: 1998
SALES (est): 19.5MM **Privately Held**
WEB: www.horizon-com.com
SIC: **4899** Data communication services

(P-12787)
NEXSAN CORPORATION (HQ)
325 E Hillcrest Dr # 150, Thousand Oaks
(91360-7799)
PHONE..................................408 724-9809
Mihir Shah, *CEO*
James Bellaby, *Engineer*
Mike Veal, *Engineer*
EMP: 80 EST: 1999
SALES (est): 36.2MM
SALES (corp-wide): 41MM **Privately Held**
WEB: www.nexsan.com
SIC: **4899** 7374 Data communication services; data processing & preparation
PA: Storcentric, Inc.
1289 Anvilwood Ave
Sunnyvale CA 94089
408 454-4200

(P-12788)
ON TARGET SOLUTIONS LLC (PA)
Also Called: Ots
17691 Mitchell N Ste A, Irvine
(92614-6828)
PHONE..................................949 543-3200
Aaron Egdahl, *President*
Sean Sloan, *CFO*
Sean Smith, *Exec VP*
Brian Watts, *Vice Pres*
Mark Travers, *General Mgr*
EMP: 51 EST: 2000
SALES (est): 17.6MM **Privately Held**
WEB: www.teamontarget.com
SIC: **4899** Data communication services

(P-12789)
PROSOFT TECHNOLOGY INC (HQ)
9201 Camino Media Ste 200, Bakersfield
(93311-1362)
PHONE..................................661 716-5100
Thomas Crone, *President*
Chris Fisher, *Vice Pres*
Carla Nelson, *Executive Asst*
Jose Carrillo, *Engineer*
Josh Machado, *Engineer*
EMP: 141 EST: 1990
SALES (est): 36.6MM
SALES (corp-wide): 1.8B **Publicly Held**
WEB: www.prosoft-technology.com
SIC: **4899** Data communication services
PA: Belden Inc.
1 N Brentwood Blvd Fl 15
Saint Louis MO 63105
314 854-8000

(P-12790)
TELETRAC INC (HQ)
Also Called: Fleet Mangement Solutions
310 Commerce Ste 100, Irvine
(92602-1360)
PHONE..................................714 897-0877
Tj Chung, *President*
Tim Van Cleve, *COO*
Julie Hildreth, *Vice Pres*
Jonathan Miller, *Vice Pres*
Rachel Trindade, *Vice Pres*
▲ EMP: 325 EST: 1995
SALES (est): 104.1MM
SALES (corp-wide): 4.6B **Publicly Held**
WEB: www.teletracnavman.com
SIC: **4899** Data communication services
PA: Fortive Corporation
6920 Seaway Blvd
Everett WA 98203
425 446-5000

▲ = Import ▼ =Export
◆ =Import/Export

(P-12791)
THINKOM SOLUTIONS INC
4881 W 145th St, Hawthorne (90250-6701)
PHONE..................................310 371-5486
Mark Silk, *CEO*
Michael Burke, *President*
Stuart Coppedge, *CFO*
Matthew Turk, *CFO*
William W Milroy, *Principal*
EMP: 116 **EST:** 2000
SQ FT: 74,000
SALES (est): 30MM **Privately Held**
WEB: www.thinkom.com
SIC: 4899 Satellite earth stations; television antenna construction & rental

(P-12792)
TRUEX INC
11925 Wilshire Blvd Fl 2, Los Angeles (90025-6625)
PHONE..................................310 657-9900
Joe Marchese, *CEO*
EMP: 50 **EST:** 2014
SALES (est): 17MM
SALES (corp-wide): 65.3B **Publicly Held**
WEB: www.truex.com
SIC: 4899 8742 7311 Data communication services; marketing consulting services; advertising agencies
HQ: Tfcf Corporation
1211 Ave Of The Americas
New York NY 10036
212 852-7000

(P-12793)
VIDEO VICE DATA COMMUNICATIONS
Also Called: Vvd Comuunications
12681 Pala Dr, Garden Grove (92841-3926)
P.O. Box 91421, Long Beach (90809-1421)
PHONE..................................714 897-6300
Bantofin Montoya, *President*
EMP: 396 **EST:** 2002
SALES (est): 28.4MM **Privately Held**
WEB: www.vvdservices.com
SIC: 4899 1731 Data communication services; electrical work; cable television installation; fiber optic cable installation; voice, data & video wiring contractor

(P-12794)
WOVEXX HOLDINGS INC (DH)
Also Called: Redwood
10381 Jefferson Blvd, Culver City (90232-3511)
PHONE..................................310 424-2080
Benjamin Blank, *CEO*
David Barko, *Partner*
James Huffman, *Partner*
Ben Blank, *Officer*
Jarret Myer, *Officer*
EMP: 90 **EST:** 2010
SQ FT: 12,000
SALES (est): 22.4MM **Publicly Held**
WEB: www.uproxx.com
SIC: 4899 7929 Data communication services; entertainment service
HQ: Warner Music Group Corp.
1633 Broadway
New York NY 10019
212 275-2000

4911 Electric Svcs

(P-12795)
AES ALAMITOS LLC
690 N Studebaker Rd, Long Beach (90803-2221)
PHONE..................................562 493-7891
Weikko Wirta, *Mng Member*
John Sanchez, *Manager*
EMP: 90 **EST:** 1997
SALES (est): 47.3MM
SALES (corp-wide): 9.6B **Publicly Held**
WEB: www.aes.com
SIC: 4911 Generation, electric power
PA: The Aes Corporation
4300 Wilson Blvd Ste 1100
Arlington VA 22203
703 522-1315

(P-12796)
AES HUNTINGTON BEACH LLC
21730 Newland St, Huntington Beach (92646-7612)
PHONE..................................714 374-1476
Eric Pendergraft,
Weikko Wirta, *Opers Staff*
Minh Hoang,
Stephen O'Kane, *Mng Member*
EMP: 50 **EST:** 1997
SALES (est): 33MM
SALES (corp-wide): 9.6B **Publicly Held**
WEB: www.aes.com
SIC: 4911 Generation, electric power
PA: The Aes Corporation
4300 Wilson Blvd Ste 1100
Arlington VA 22203
703 522-1315

(P-12797)
COMBUSTION ASSOCIATES INC
Also Called: Cai
555 Monica Cir, Corona (92878-5447)
PHONE..................................951 272-6999
Mukund Kavia, *President*
Pooya Kabiri, *Vice Pres*
Kusum Kavia, *Vice Pres*
Bharat Kavia, *Executive*
Prajesh Kavia, *Admin Sec*
▼ **EMP:** 50 **EST:** 1991
SQ FT: 40,000
SALES (est): 48.7MM **Privately Held**
WEB: www.cai3.com
SIC: 4911 3443 ; boiler & boiler shop work

(P-12798)
COSO OPERATING COMPANY LLC
2 Gill Station Coso Rd, Little Lake (93542)
P.O. Box 1690, Inyokern (93527-1690)
PHONE..................................760 764-1300
Jim Pagano, *CEO*
Joseph Greco, *Senior VP*
▲ **EMP:** 90 **EST:** 1999
SALES (est): 50.5MM **Privately Held**
WEB: www.cosoenergy.com
SIC: 4911 Generation, electric power

(P-12799)
CYPRESS CREEK HOLDINGS LLC
3250 Ocean Park Blvd # 355, Santa Monica (90405-3206)
PHONE..................................310 581-6299
Ben Van De Bunt, *Chairman*
Michael Cohen, *President*
Matthew McGovern, *CEO*
EMP: 100 **EST:** 2014
SALES (est): 13.6MM **Privately Held**
WEB: www.ccrenew.com
SIC: 4911

(P-12800)
CYPRESS CREEK RENEWABLES LLC (PA)
3250 Ocean Park Blvd # 355, Santa Monica (90405-3206)
PHONE..................................310 581-6299
Sarah Slusser, *CEO*
Ned Hall, *Ch of Bd*
Rebecca Cranna, *COO*
Bryan Ellis, *CFO*
Peter Farlekas, *Exec VP*
EMP: 123 **EST:** 2014
SALES (est): 419MM **Privately Held**
WEB: www.ccrenew.com
SIC: 4911

(P-12801)
DUKE ENERGY CORPORATION
8001 Irvine Center Dr, Irvine (92618-2938)
PHONE..................................949 727-7434
EMP: 170
SALES (corp-wide): 23.4B **Publicly Held**
SIC: 4911 4924 Electric Utility Natural Gas & Natural Gas Liquids
PA: Duke Energy Corporation
550 S Tryon St
Charlotte NC 28202
704 382-3853

(P-12802)
EDISON CAPITAL
18101 Von Karman Ave, Irvine (92612-1012)
PHONE..................................909 594-3789
Thomas Mc Daniel, *President*
Oded Rhone, *President*
Phillip Dandridge, *CFO*
Steve Dandridge, *CFO*
Jim Phillipsen, *Treasurer*
EMP: 103 **EST:** 1987
SQ FT: 12,000
SALES (est): 59.7MM
SALES (corp-wide): 13.5B **Publicly Held**
WEB: www.sce.com
SIC: 4911 Electric services
HQ: Edison Mission Group Inc.
2244 Walnut Grove Ave
Rosemead CA 91770
626 302-2222

(P-12803)
EDISON INTERNATIONAL (PA)
2244 Walnut Grove Ave, Rosemead (91770-3714)
P.O. Box 976 (91770-0976)
PHONE..................................626 302-2222
Pedro J Pizarro, *President*
William P Sullivan, *Ch of Bd*
Maria Rigatti, *CFO*
Didier Dorga, *Officer*
Adam S Umanoff, *Exec VP*
EMP: 2249 **EST:** 1987
SALES (est): 13.5B **Publicly Held**
WEB: www.edison.com
SIC: 4911 Electric services; distribution, electric power; generation, electric power; transmission, electric power

(P-12804)
EDISON MISSION ENERGY (DH)
2244 Walnut Grove Ave, Rosemead (91770-3714)
PHONE..................................626 302-5778
Pedro J Pizarro, *President*
Andrew J Hertneky, *Senior VP*
Paul Jacob, *Senior VP*
John C Kennedy, *Senior VP*
S Daniel Melita, *Senior VP*
▲ **EMP:** 426 **EST:** 1986
SQ FT: 71,000
SALES (est): 807.9MM **Publicly Held**
WEB: www.edison.com
SIC: 4911 Electric services
HQ: Nrg Energy Holdings Inc.
849 Eastwood Dr
Golden CO 80401
609 524-4500

(P-12805)
EDISON MSSION MIDWEST HOLDINGS
2244 Walnut Grove Ave, Rosemead (91770-3714)
PHONE..................................626 302-2222
Guy F Gorney, *President*
Lindsay Lawrence, *Exec VP*
EMP: 2378 **EST:** 1999
SALES (est): 8.6MM
SALES (corp-wide): 13.5B **Publicly Held**
WEB: www.edison.com
SIC: 4911 Electric services
HQ: Edison Mission Group Inc.
2244 Walnut Grove Ave
Rosemead CA 91770
626 302-2222

(P-12806)
IMPERIAL IRRIGATION DISTRICT (PA)
Also Called: I ID
333 E Barioni Blvd, Imperial (92251-1773)
P.O. Box 937 (92251-0937)
PHONE..................................800 303-7756
Stephen Benson, *President*
Anthony Sanchez, *President*
Keven Kelly, *CEO*
Steve Burch, *Bd of Directors*
Carl Stills, *Officer*
▲ **EMP:** 700 **EST:** 1911
SQ FT: 10,000
SALES: 705.4MM **Privately Held**
WEB: www.iid.com
SIC: 4911 4971 4931 ; water distribution or supply systems for irrigation; electric & other services combined

(P-12807)
INSPIRE ENERGY HOLDINGS LLC
3402 Pico Blvd Ste 300, Santa Monica (90405-2091)
PHONE..................................866 403-2620
Patrick Maloney, *CEO*
Zac Lowder, *Vice Pres*
Charity Miller, *Vice Pres*
Mike Durst, *CTO*
Matt Anderson, *Software Dev*
EMP: 138 **EST:** 2013
SALES (est): 44.5MM **Privately Held**
WEB: www.inspirecleanenergy.com
SIC: 4911 Distribution, electric power

(P-12808)
LOS ANGELES DEPT WTR & PWR
Also Called: Ladwp
111 N Hope St, Los Angeles (90012-2607)
P.O. Box 51111 (90051-5700)
PHONE..................................213 367-4211
Ronald Nichols, *Branch Mgr*
Silvia Denis, *Executive Asst*
Adrian Cruz, *Planning*
Jimmy Lin, *Planning*
Minh Le, *Info Tech Mgr*
EMP: 99 **Privately Held**
WEB: www.ladwp.com
SIC: 4911 4941 Generation, electric power; water supply
HQ: Los Angeles Department Of Water And Power
111 N Hope St
Los Angeles CA 90012
213 367-1320

(P-12809)
NRG CALIFORNIA SOUTH LP
Also Called: Mandalay Generating Station
393 Harbor Blvd, Oxnard (93035-1108)
PHONE..................................805 984-5241
Thomas Di Ciolli, *Manager*
EMP: 56 **Publicly Held**
SIC: 4911 ; generation, electric power
HQ: Nrg California South Lp
804 Carnegie Ctr
Princeton NJ 08540

(P-12810)
NRG CALIFORNIA SOUTH LP
Also Called: Etiwanda Power Plant
8996 Etiwanda Ave, Rancho Cucamonga (91739-9662)
PHONE..................................909 899-7241
Lee Moore, *Branch Mgr*
Gary Ackerman, *Exec Dir*
Vince Munoz, *Analyst*
EMP: 56 **Publicly Held**
SIC: 4911 Generation, electric power
HQ: Nrg California South Lp
804 Carnegie Ctr
Princeton NJ 08540

(P-12811)
NRG CALIFORNIA SOUTH LP
Also Called: Coolwater Generating Station
37000 E Santa Fe St, Daggett (92327)
PHONE..................................760 254-5241
Bob Ott, *Manager*
EMP: 56 **Publicly Held**
SIC: 4911 Generation, electric power
HQ: Nrg California South Lp
804 Carnegie Ctr
Princeton NJ 08540

(P-12812)
NRG CLEAN POWER INC
7012 Owensmouth Ave, Canoga Park (91303-2005)
PHONE..................................818 444-2020
Oren Tamir, *CEO*
Ryan Kidder, *Sales Staff*
Charstan Mussman, *Sales Staff*
EMP: 50 **EST:** 2016
SALES (est): 5.5MM **Privately Held**
WEB: www.nrgcleanpower.com
SIC: 4911

(P-12813)
**NRG EL SEGUNDO
OPERATIONS INC**
301 Vista Del Mar, El Segundo
(90245-3650)
PHONE...................310 615-6344
John Ragan, *President*
▲ EMP: 65 EST: 1998
SALES (est): 144MM **Publicly Held**
WEB: www.elsegundo.org
SIC: 4911 Generation, electric power
PA: Nrg Energy, Inc.
910 Louisiana St
Houston TX 77002

(P-12814)
**OUTSOURCE UTILITY CONTR
CORP**
8015 E Crystal Dr, Anaheim (92807-2523)
PHONE...................714 238-9263
Heather Morgan, *President*
Matthew Bates, *Vice Pres*
Jack Crabbs, *Vice Pres*
Frank Farwell, *Vice Pres*
Joe Morgan, *Vice Pres*
EMP: 200 EST: 2010
SALES (est): 50.2MM **Privately Held**
WEB: www.outsourceucc.com
SIC: 4911 Distribution, electric power

(P-12815)
PACIFIC GAS AND ELECTRIC CO
Also Called: PG&e
34453 Pleymouth, Avenal (93204)
PHONE...................559 386-2052
George Ringlestetter, *Manager*
EMP: 120 **Publicly Held**
WEB: www.pge.com
SIC: 4911 4924 Generation, electric
power; natural gas distribution
HQ: Pacific Gas And Electric Company
77 Beale St
San Francisco CA 94105
415 973-7000

(P-12816)
PACIFIC GAS AND ELECTRIC CO
Also Called: PG&e
4340 Old Santa Fe Rd, San Luis Obispo
(93401-8160)
PHONE...................805 545-4562
Del Richie, *Manager*
Chris Foster, *Vice Pres*
Jessica Hogle, *Vice Pres*
EMP: 120 **Publicly Held**
WEB: www.pge.com
SIC: 4911 Generation, electric power;
transmission, electric power
HQ: Pacific Gas And Electric Company
77 Beale St
San Francisco CA 94105
415 973-7000

(P-12817)
PACIFIC GAS AND ELECTRIC CO
Also Called: PG&e
9 Mi Nw Of Avila Bch, Avila Beach (93424)
P.O. Box 56 (93424-0056)
PHONE...................805 506-5280
David Oatley, *Branch Mgr*
Chad Sorensen, *Engineer*
Guy Vaughan, *Regl Sales Mgr*
Richard Van Der Linden, *Sr Project Mgr*
Vanessa Masters, *Manager*
EMP: 1400 **Publicly Held**
WEB: www.pge.com
SIC: 4911 Transmission, electric power
HQ: Pacific Gas And Electric Company
77 Beale St
San Francisco CA 94105
415 973-7000

(P-12818)
PACIFIC GAS AND ELECTRIC CO
Also Called: PG&e
35863 Fairview Rd, Hinkley (92347-9710)
PHONE...................760 253-2925
Dan Lytle, *Manager*
EMP: 120 **Publicly Held**
WEB: www.pge.com
SIC: 4911 Transmission, electric power

HQ: Pacific Gas And Electric Company
77 Beale St
San Francisco CA 94105
415 973-7000

(P-12819)
PACIFIC GAS AND ELECTRIC CO
Also Called: PG&e
800 Price Canyon Rd, Pismo Beach
(93449-2722)
PHONE...................805 546-5267
Don Boatman, *Branch Mgr*
EMP: 120 **Publicly Held**
WEB: www.pge.com
SIC: 4911 Transmission, electric power
HQ: Pacific Gas And Electric Company
77 Beale St
San Francisco CA 94105
415 973-7000

(P-12820)
PACIFIC GAS AND ELECTRIC CO
Also Called: PG&e
145453 Nat Trails Hwy, Needles (92363)
P.O. Box 337 (92363-0337)
PHONE...................760 326-2615
Felix Vasquez, *Manager*
EMP: 120 **Publicly Held**
WEB: www.pge.com
SIC: 4911 Transmission, electric power
HQ: Pacific Gas And Electric Company
77 Beale St
San Francisco CA 94105
415 973-7000

(P-12821)
PACIFIC GAS AND ELECTRIC CO
Also Called: PG&e
4201 Arrow St, Bakersfield (93308-4938)
PHONE...................661 398-5918
Don Hacks, *Manager*
EMP: 120 **Publicly Held**
WEB: www.pge.com
SIC: 4911 Transmission, electric power
HQ: Pacific Gas And Electric Company
77 Beale St
San Francisco CA 94105
415 973-7000

(P-12822)
PACIFIC GAS AND ELECTRIC CO
Also Called: PG&e
160 Cow Meadow Pl, Templeton (93465)
PHONE...................805 434-4418
Bob Burroughs, *Branch Mgr*
EMP: 120 **Publicly Held**
WEB: www.pge.com
SIC: 4911 Transmission, electric power
HQ: Pacific Gas And Electric Company
77 Beale St
San Francisco CA 94105
415 973-7000

(P-12823)
RIDGETOP ENERGY LLC
7021 Oak Creek Rd, Mojave (93501-7723)
PHONE...................661 822-2400
Dale L Smith, *Manager*
EMP: 50 EST: 1998
SALES (est): 17.8MM **Privately Held**
WEB: www.ceoflatransco.com
SIC: 4911 Generation, electric power

(P-12824)
RRI ENERGY COOLWATER INC
37000 E Santa Fe St, Daggett (92327)
PHONE...................760 254-5290
Mark Jacobs, *President*
EMP: 508 EST: 1997
SALES (est): 11.2MM **Publicly Held**
WEB: www.reliant.com
SIC: 4911 Generation, electric power
HQ: Reliant Energy Retail Holdings, Llc
1000 Main St
Houston TX 77002
713 497-3000

(P-12825)
SILVERADO ENERGY COMPANY
18101 Von Karman Ave # 9, Irvine
(92612-1012)
PHONE...................949 752-5588
Thomas McDaniel, *Principal*
Alan Fohrer, *President*
EMP: 73 EST: 1988

SALES (est): 32.5MM **Publicly Held**
WEB: www.edison.com
SIC: 4911 Generation, electric power
HQ: Edison Mission Energy
2244 Walnut Grove Ave
Rosemead CA 91770
626 302-5778

(P-12826)
SOLARRESERVE INC
520 Broadway Fl 6, Santa Monica
(90401-2420)
PHONE...................310 315-2200
Kevin B Smith, *CEO*
Kevin Smith, *COO*
Stephen Mullennix, *CFO*
Tim Rosenzweig, *CFO*
Pauline Doohan, *Senior VP*
EMP: 99
SQ FT: 20,000
SALES (est): 18.1MM **Privately Held**
SIC: 4911 Distribution, electric power

(P-12827)
**SOUTHERN CALIFORNIA
EDISON CO (HQ)**
Also Called: SCE
2244 Walnut Grove Ave, Rosemead
(91770-3714)
P.O. Box 976 (91770-0976)
PHONE...................626 302-1212
Kevin M Payne, *President*
William M Petmecky III, *CFO*
Steven D Powell, *Exec VP*
Caroline Choi, *Senior VP*
Jacqueline Trapp, *Senior VP*
▲ EMP: 1200 EST: 1909
SALES (est): 13.5B
SALES (corp-wide): 13.5B **Publicly Held**
WEB: www.sce.com
SIC: 4911 Generation, electric power;
transmission, electric power; distribution,
electric power
PA: Edison International
2244 Walnut Grove Ave
Rosemead CA 91770
626 302-2222

(P-12828)
**SOUTHERN CALIFORNIA
EDISON CO**
4900 Rivergrade Rd 2b1, Irwindale
(91706-1401)
PHONE...................626 543-8081
Peter Quon, *Branch Mgr*
EMP: 151
SALES (corp-wide): 13.5B **Publicly Held**
WEB: www.sce.com
SIC: 4911 Generation, electric power
HQ: Southern California Edison Company
2244 Walnut Grove Ave
Rosemead CA 91770
626 302-1212

(P-12829)
**SOUTHERN CALIFORNIA
EDISON CO**
Also Called: Monrovia Service Center
1440 S California Ave, Monrovia
(91016-4211)
PHONE...................626 303-8480
Robert Robinson, *Principal*
EMP: 151
SQ FT: 31,603
SALES (corp-wide): 13.5B **Publicly Held**
WEB: www.sce.com
SIC: 4911 Electric services
HQ: Southern California Edison Company
2244 Walnut Grove Ave
Rosemead CA 91770
626 302-1212

(P-12830)
**SOUTHERN CALIFORNIA
EDISON CO**
4000 Bishop Creek Rd, Bishop
(93514-7026)
PHONE...................760 873-0715
EMP: 151
SALES (corp-wide): 13.5B **Publicly Held**
WEB: www.sce.com
SIC: 4911 Generation, electric power

HQ: Southern California Edison Company
2244 Walnut Grove Ave
Rosemead CA 91770
626 302-1212

(P-12831)
**SOUTHERN CALIFORNIA
EDISON CO**
14799 Chestnut St, Westminster
(92683-5240)
PHONE...................714 934-0838
EMP: 176
SALES (corp-wide): 13.5B **Publicly Held**
WEB: www.sce.com
SIC: 4911 Electric Services
HQ: Southern California Edison Company
2244 Walnut Grove Ave
Rosemead CA 91770
626 302-1212

(P-12832)
**SOUTHERN CALIFORNIA
EDISON CO**
8380 Klingerman St, Rosemead
(91770-3609)
PHONE...................626 302-5101
Arthur Guerra, *Principal*
EMP: 151
SALES (corp-wide): 13.5B **Publicly Held**
WEB: www.sce.com
SIC: 4911 Generation, electric power
HQ: Southern California Edison Company
2244 Walnut Grove Ave
Rosemead CA 91770
626 302-1212

(P-12833)
**SOUTHERN CALIFORNIA
EDISON CO**
4900 Rivergrade Rd, Baldwin Park
(91706-1401)
PHONE...................626 543-6093
Linda Gilleland, *Principal*
Rahab Mahfud, *Analyst*
EMP: 151
SALES (corp-wide): 13.5B **Publicly Held**
WEB: www.sce.com
SIC: 4911 Generation, electric power
HQ: Southern California Edison Company
2244 Walnut Grove Ave
Rosemead CA 91770
626 302-1212

(P-12834)
**SOUTHERN CALIFORNIA
EDISON CO**
Also Called: Valley Substation
26125 Menifee Rd, Romoland
(92585-9441)
PHONE...................800 336-2822
Henry Herrea, *Branch Mgr*
EMP: 151
SALES (corp-wide): 13.5B **Publicly Held**
WEB: www.sce.com
SIC: 4911 Generation, electric power
HQ: Southern California Edison Company
2244 Walnut Grove Ave
Rosemead CA 91770
626 302-1212

(P-12835)
**SOUTHERN CALIFORNIA
EDISON CO**
Also Called: North Orange County Svc Ctr
1851 W Valencia Dr, Fullerton
(92833-3215)
PHONE...................714 870-3225
David Kama, *District Mgr*
EMP: 151
SALES (corp-wide): 13.5B **Publicly Held**
WEB: www.sce.com
SIC: 4911 Distribution, electric power
HQ: Southern California Edison Company
2244 Walnut Grove Ave
Rosemead CA 91770
626 302-1212

(P-12836)
**SOUTHERN CALIFORNIA
EDISON CO**
3589 Foothill Dr, Westlake Village
(91361-2475)
PHONE...................805 496-3406
EMP: 151

SALES (corp-wide): 13.5B **Publicly Held**
WEB: www.sce.com
SIC: **4911** Electric services
HQ: Southern California Edison Company
2244 Walnut Grove Ave
Rosemead CA 91770
626 302-1212

(P-12837)
SOUTHERN CALIFORNIA EDISON CO
Also Called: Southern Cal Edson - Prvate Ch
2131 Walnut Grove Ave, Rosemead
(91770-3769)
PHONE...........................626 302-1212
Grant Thomas, *Branch Mgr*
Brenda Torres, *Executive Asst*
Kristie Mathis, *Business Anlyst*
Albert Melikian, *Design Engr*
Paul Kasick, *Project Mgr*
EMP: 151
SALES (corp-wide): 13.5B **Publicly Held**
WEB: www.sce.com
SIC: **4911** Distribution, electric power; generation, electric power; transmission, electric power
HQ: Southern California Edison Company
2244 Walnut Grove Ave
Rosemead CA 91770
626 302-1212

(P-12838)
SOUTHERN CALIFORNIA EDISON CO
2 Innovation Way Fl 1, Pomona
(91768-2560)
PHONE...........................909 274-1925
Gonzalez Ronald, *Program Mgr*
Gregory Dennis, *Project Mgr*
Sarah Key, *Project Mgr*
EMP: 151
SALES (corp-wide): 13.5B **Publicly Held**
WEB: www.sce.com
SIC: **4911** Electric services
HQ: Southern California Edison Company
2244 Walnut Grove Ave
Rosemead CA 91770
626 302-1212

(P-12839)
SOUTHERN CALIFORNIA EDISON CO
Also Called: Central Orange County Svc Ctr
1241 S Grand Ave, Santa Ana
(92705-4404)
PHONE...........................714 973-5481
Percy Haralson, *Principal*
Blake Miller, *Supervisor*
EMP: 151
SALES (corp-wide): 13.5B **Publicly Held**
WEB: www.sce.com
SIC: **4911** Electric services
HQ: Southern California Edison Company
2244 Walnut Grove Ave
Rosemead CA 91770
626 302-1212

(P-12840)
SOUTHERN CALIFORNIA EDISON CO
4175 S Laspina St, Tulare (93274-9142)
PHONE...........................559 625-7126
Robert Juskalian, *Technical Staff*
EMP: 151
SALES (corp-wide): 13.5B **Publicly Held**
WEB: www.sce.com
SIC: **4911** Generation, electric power
HQ: Southern California Edison Company
2244 Walnut Grove Ave
Rosemead CA 91770
626 302-1212

(P-12841)
SOUTHERN CALIFORNIA EDISON CO
Also Called: Thousand Oaks Service Center
3589 Foothill Dr, Thousand Oaks
(91361-2475)
PHONE...........................818 999-1880
Jerry Willaferd, *Branch Mgr*
EMP: 151
SALES (corp-wide): 13.5B **Publicly Held**
WEB: www.sce.com
SIC: **4911 8741** Electric services; business management

HQ: Southern California Edison Company
2244 Walnut Grove Ave
Rosemead CA 91770
626 302-1212

(P-12842)
SOUTHERN CALIFORNIA EDISON CO
Also Called: Irwindale 6000
6000 N Irwindale Ave A, Irwindale
(91702-3200)
PHONE...........................626 815-7296
Ray Maese, *Branch Mgr*
Raul Martinez, *General Mgr*
EMP: 151
SALES (corp-wide): 13.5B **Publicly Held**
WEB: www.sce.com
SIC: **4911** Electric services
HQ: Southern California Edison Company
2244 Walnut Grove Ave
Rosemead CA 91770
626 302-1212

(P-12843)
SOUTHERN CALIFORNIA EDISON CO
265 N East End Ave, Pomona
(91767-5803)
PHONE...........................909 469-0251
John Risen, *Branch Mgr*
Annette Candelaria, *Executive Asst*
Kathie Conaway, *Project Mgr*
Wilfredo Alas, *Engineer*
Diego Hinojosa, *Engineer*
EMP: 151
SALES (corp-wide): 13.5B **Publicly Held**
WEB: www.sce.com
SIC: **4911** Electric services
HQ: Southern California Edison Company
2244 Walnut Grove Ave
Rosemead CA 91770
626 302-1212

(P-12844)
SOUTHERN CALIFORNIA EDISON CO
Also Called: Compton Service Center
1924 E Cashdan St, Compton
(90220-6403)
PHONE...........................310 608-5029
Floyd Rich, *Branch Mgr*
Nelson Herrera, *Engineer*
Richard Richard Clarke, *Manager*
Kevin Schmeichel, *Supervisor*
EMP: 151
SALES (corp-wide): 13.5B **Publicly Held**
WEB: www.sce.com
SIC: **4911** Electric services
HQ: Southern California Edison Company
2244 Walnut Grove Ave
Rosemead CA 91770
626 302-1212

(P-12845)
SOUTHERN CALIFORNIA EDISON CO
Also Called: Santa Barbara Service Center
103 Love Pl, Goleta (93117-3200)
PHONE...........................805 683-5291
Brian Adair, *Manager*
EMP: 151
SALES (corp-wide): 13.5B **Publicly Held**
WEB: www.sce.com
SIC: **4911** Generation, electric power
HQ: Southern California Edison Company
2244 Walnut Grove Ave
Rosemead CA 91770
626 302-1212

(P-12846)
SOUTHERN CALIFORNIA EDISON CO
Also Called: Southeastern Westminster
7300 Fenwick Ln, Westminster
(92683-5238)
PHONE...........................714 895-0420
Dee Pak Nanda, *Vice Pres*
John Davies, *Vice Pres*
Paul Grigaux, *Vice Pres*
Michael Montoya, *Vice Pres*
Marc Ulrich, *Vice Pres*
EMP: 151
SALES (corp-wide): 13.5B **Publicly Held**
WEB: www.sce.com
SIC: **4911** Electric services

(P-12847)
SOUTHERN CALIFORNIA EDISON CO
Also Called: Saddleback Valley Service Ctr
14155 Bake Pkwy, Irvine (92618-1818)
PHONE...........................949 587-5416
Robert Torres, *Manager*
Jim Ouyeung, *Project Mgr*
Antony Liwanag, *Analyst*
Edgardo Cruz, *Supervisor*
EMP: 151
SALES (corp-wide): 13.5B **Publicly Held**
WEB: www.sce.com
SIC: **4911** Electric services
HQ: Southern California Edison Company
2244 Walnut Grove Ave
Rosemead CA 91770
626 302-1212

(P-12848)
SOUTHERN CALIFORNIA EDISON CO
6042 N Irwindale Ave A, Irwindale
(91702-3250)
PHONE...........................626 633-3070
Jami McDonald, *Branch Mgr*
Maria Becca, *Executive Asst*
Yun Han, *Engineer*
Niraj Shah, *Senior Mgr*
Terry Dunn, *Manager*
EMP: 151
SALES (corp-wide): 13.5B **Publicly Held**
WEB: www.sce.com
SIC: **4911** Generation, electric power
HQ: Southern California Edison Company
2244 Walnut Grove Ave
Rosemead CA 91770
626 302-1212

(P-12849)
SOUTHERN CALIFORNIA EDISON CO
Also Called: Lighthipe Substation
6900 Orange Ave, Long Beach
(90805-1599)
PHONE...........................562 529-7301
Jim Hill, *Manager*
Bidisha Kar, *Technical Staff*
Cassandra Burch, *Maintence Staff*
EMP: 151
SQ FT: 38,928
SALES (corp-wide): 13.5B **Publicly Held**
WEB: www.sce.com
SIC: **4911** Electric services
HQ: Southern California Edison Company
2244 Walnut Grove Ave
Rosemead CA 91770
626 302-1212

(P-12850)
SOUTHERN CALIFORNIA EDISON CO
Also Called: Orange Coast Service Center
7333 Bolsa Ave, Westminster
(92683-5210)
PHONE...........................714 895-0163
Jeff Lebow, *Branch Mgr*
Maria Avila, *Engineer*
Carlos Barrios, *Supervisor*
EMP: 151
SALES (corp-wide): 13.5B **Publicly Held**
WEB: www.sce.com
SIC: **4911** Electric services
HQ: Southern California Edison Company
2244 Walnut Grove Ave
Rosemead CA 91770
626 302-1212

(P-12851)
SOUTHERN CALIFORNIA EDISON CO
13025 Los Angeles St, Irwindale
(91706-2241)
PHONE...........................626 814-4212
Ed Entillon, *Branch Mgr*
EMP: 151
SQ FT: 21,000
SALES (corp-wide): 13.5B **Publicly Held**
WEB: www.sce.com
SIC: **4911** Electric services

HQ: Southern California Edison Company
2244 Walnut Grove Ave
Rosemead CA 91770
626 302-1212

(P-12852)
SOUTHERN CALIFORNIA EDISON CO
Also Called: Covina Service Center
800 W Cienega Ave, San Dimas
(91773-2490)
PHONE...........................909 592-3757
Gary Martinez, *Branch Mgr*
Travis Parks, *Senior Mgr*
EMP: 151
SALES (corp-wide): 13.5B **Publicly Held**
WEB: www.sce.com
SIC: **4911** Electric services
HQ: Southern California Edison Company
2244 Walnut Grove Ave
Rosemead CA 91770
626 302-1212

(P-12853)
SOUTHERN CALIFORNIA EDISON CO
Also Called: Whittier Service Center
9901 Geary Ave, Santa Fe Springs
(90670-3251)
PHONE...........................562 903-3191
Fred Swearingen, *Principal*
Maria Gonzales, *Human Resources*
Inkyoo Chang, *Supervisor*
EMP: 151
SALES (corp-wide): 13.5B **Publicly Held**
WEB: www.sce.com
SIC: **4911** Electric services
HQ: Southern California Edison Company
2244 Walnut Grove Ave
Rosemead CA 91770
626 302-1212

(P-12854)
SOUTHERN CALIFORNIA EDISON CO
Also Called: Western Division Regional Off
125 Elm Ave, Long Beach (90802-4918)
PHONE...........................562 491-3803
Lorene Miller, *Manager*
Troy Wilson, *Technician*
EMP: 151
SALES (corp-wide): 13.5B **Publicly Held**
WEB: www.sce.com
SIC: **4911** Generation, electric power
HQ: Southern California Edison Company
2244 Walnut Grove Ave
Rosemead CA 91770
626 302-1212

(P-12855)
SOUTHERN CALIFORNIA EDISON CO
Also Called: High Desert
12353 Hesperia Rd, Victorville
(92395-4797)
PHONE...........................760 951-3172
Sheila Luna, *Branch Mgr*
Jill Carlisle, *Manager*
Patrick Nandy, *Manager*
Paul Millan, *Supervisor*
EMP: 151
SALES (corp-wide): 13.5B **Publicly Held**
WEB: www.sce.com
SIC: **4911** Electric services
HQ: Southern California Edison Company
2244 Walnut Grove Ave
Rosemead CA 91770
626 302-1212

(P-12856)
SOUTHERN CALIFORNIA EDISON CO
Also Called: Ctac Research 60901
6090 N Irwindale Ave, Irwindale
(91702-3207)
PHONE...........................626 812-7380
Diane Ronewko, *Manager*
Gonzalo Heredia, *Training Spec*
Raymond Maese, *Manager*
EMP: 151
SALES (corp-wide): 13.5B **Publicly Held**
WEB: www.sce.com
SIC: **4911** Electric services

HQ: Southern California Edison Company
2244 Walnut Grove Ave
Rosemead CA 91770
626 302-1212

(P-12857)
SOUTHERN CALIFORNIA EDISON CO
Also Called: Ridgecrest Service Center
510 S China Lake Blvd, Ridgecrest
(93555-5006)
PHONE.................................760 375-1821
Howell Applegrath, *Manager*
EMP: 151
SALES (corp-wide): 13.5B **Publicly Held**
WEB: www.sce.com
SIC: 4911 Electric services
HQ: Southern California Edison Company
2244 Walnut Grove Ave
Rosemead CA 91770
626 302-1212

(P-12858)
SOUTHERN CALIFORNIA EDISON CO
7400 Fenwick Ln, Westminster
(92683-5243)
PHONE.................................714 895-0119
EMP: 151
SALES (corp-wide): 13.5B **Publicly Held**
WEB: www.sce.com
SIC: 4911 Electric services
HQ: Southern California Edison Company
2244 Walnut Grove Ave
Rosemead CA 91770
626 302-1212

(P-12859)
SOUTHERN CALIFORNIA EDISON CO
Also Called: Villa Park Substation
1900 E Taft Ave, Orange (92865-4702)
PHONE.................................714 283-8568
Mary Finn, *Program Mgr*
Tiffany Vuong, *Analyst*
Reed Reisner, *Manager*
EMP: 151
SALES (corp-wide): 13.5B **Publicly Held**
WEB: www.sce.com
SIC: 4911 Generation, electric power
HQ: Southern California Edison Company
2244 Walnut Grove Ave
Rosemead CA 91770
626 302-1212

(P-12860)
SOUTHERN CALIFORNIA EDISON CO
Alhambra Combined Facility
501 S Marengo Ave, Alhambra
(91803-1640)
P.O. Box 700, Rosemead (91770-0700)
PHONE.................................626 308-6193
Kevin M Payne, *CEO*
Victor Pimentel, *IT/INT Sup*
Minh Ly, *Technology*
Charles Reilly, *Technology*
Gilbert Lemos, *Technical Staff*
EMP: 151
SALES (corp-wide): 13.5B **Publicly Held**
WEB: www.sce.com
SIC: 4911 Generation, electric power
HQ: Southern California Edison Company
2244 Walnut Grove Ave
Rosemead CA 91770
626 302-1212

(P-12861)
SOUTHERN SIERRA ENERGY COMPANY
18101 Von Karman Ave # 9, Irvine
(92612-1012)
PHONE.................................949 752-5588
Maria Rigatti, *Principal*
Willie Heller, *President*
▲ EMP: 120 EST: 1983
SALES (est): 10.2MM **Publicly Held**
WEB: www.edison.com
SIC: 4911 Generation, electric power
HQ: Edison Mission Energy
2244 Walnut Grove Ave
Rosemead CA 91770
626 302-5778

(P-12862)
SYCAMORE COGENERATION CO (PA)
1546 China Grade Loop, Bakersfield
(93308-9700)
P.O. Box 81438 (93380-1438)
PHONE.................................661 615-4630
Neal Burgess, *Exec Dir*
▲ EMP: 56 EST: 1988
SQ FT: 10,000
SALES (est): 41MM **Privately Held**
SIC: 4911 4961 Distribution, electric
power; steam supply systems, including
geothermal

(P-12863)
WATSON COGENERATION CO INC
22850 Wilmington Ave, Carson
(90745-5021)
P.O. Box 6203 (90749-6203)
PHONE.................................310 816-8100
Paul L Foster, *Ch of Bd*
EMP: 63 EST: 1986
SQ FT: 1,000
SALES (est): 47.2MM **Publicly Held**
WEB: www.wnr.com
SIC: 4911 Generation, electric power
HQ: Western Refining, Inc.
212 N Clark Dr
El Paso TX 79905

(P-12864)
WEST COAST ELECTRIC & PWR INC
741 E Ball Rd Ste 206, Anaheim
(92805-5952)
PHONE.................................562 447-3254
Sergio Zorio, *CEO*
EMP: 60 EST: 2017
SALES (est): 32.6MM **Privately Held**
WEB: www.wcepinc.com
SIC: 4911 7389 8711 Electric services;
mapmaking or drafting, including aerial;
design services; engineering services

4924 Natural Gas Distribution

(P-12865)
CLEAN ENERGY
4675 Macarthur Ct Ste 800, Newport Beach
(92660-1895)
PHONE.................................949 437-1000
Andrew Littlefair, *President*
Mitchell Pratt, *COO*
Robert Vreeland, *CFO*
Gary Foster, *Vice Pres*
Marc Klein, *Vice Pres*
EMP: 832 EST: 1996
SALES (est): 563.1MM
SALES (corp-wide): 291.7MM **Publicly Held**
WEB: www.cleanenergyfuels.com
SIC: 4924 Natural gas distribution
PA: Clean Energy Fuels Corp.
4675 Macarthur Ct Ste 800
Newport Beach CA 92660
949 437-1000

(P-12866)
SOUTHERN CALIFORNIA GAS CO (DH)
Also Called: GAS COMPANY, THE
555 W 5th St, Los Angeles (90013-1010)
PHONE.................................213 244-1200
Scott D Drury, *CEO*
Maryam Sabbaghian Brown, *President*
Jimmie I Cho, *COO*
Debra L Reed, *Chairman*
Steven D Davis, *Exec VP*
EMP: 4772 EST: 1910
SALES (est): 4.7B
SALES (corp-wide): 11.3B **Publicly Held**
WEB: www.sempra.com
SIC: 4924 4922 4932 Natural gas distri-
bution; natural gas transmission; gas &
other services combined
HQ: Pacific Enterprises
101 Ash St
San Diego CA 92101
619 696-2020

(P-12867)
SOUTHERN CALIFORNIA GAS CO
1600 Corporate Center Dr, Monterey Park
(91754-7626)
P.O. Box C (91756-0001)
PHONE.................................213 244-1200
Joe M Rivera, *Regional Mgr*
Kelly Porras, *Executive*
Sonja Carroll, *IT Executive*
David Andri, *Advisor*
EMP: 223
SALES (corp-wide): 11.3B **Publicly Held**
SIC: 4924 Natural gas distribution
HQ: Southern California Gas Company
555 W 5th St
Los Angeles CA 90013
213 244-1200

(P-12868)
SOUTHERN CALIFORNIA GAS TOWER
555 W 5th St, Los Angeles (90013-1010)
PHONE.................................213 244-1200
Ed Guiles, *President*
EMP: 1000 EST: 1987
SALES (est): 133.1MM
SALES (corp-wide): 11.3B **Publicly Held**
SIC: 4924 Natural gas distribution
HQ: Southern California Gas Company
555 W 5th St
Los Angeles CA 90013
213 244-1200

4931 Electric & Other Svcs Combined

(P-12869)
CITY OF BURBANK
Also Called: Burbank Water & Power
164 W Magnolia Blvd, Burbank
(91502-1772)
PHONE.................................818 238-3550
Ronald E Davis, *Branch Mgr*
Joyce Thompson, *Executive Asst*
Sherry Kristoff, *Admin Sec*
Evilia Waloejo, *Planning*
Jeanne Keeler, *Analyst*
EMP: 315
SALES (corp-wide): 242.8MM **Privately Held**
WEB: www.burbankca.gov
SIC: 4931 4941 4911 7389 Electric &
other services combined; water supply;
electric services; interior design services
PA: City Of Burbank
275 E Olive Ave
Burbank CA 91502
818 238-5800

(P-12870)
EDISON MISSION OPER & MAINT (DH)
3 Macarthur Pl Ste 100, Santa Ana
(92707-6068)
PHONE.................................626 302-5151
Thomas R McDaniel, *President*
Brian Sorensen, *President*
Guy Gorney, *Vice Pres*
Georgia R Nelson, *Vice Pres*
Kevin M Smith, *Vice Pres*
EMP: 120 EST: 1986
SALES (est): 20.6MM **Publicly Held**
WEB: www.edison.com
SIC: 4931 Electric & other services com-
bined
HQ: Edison Mission Energy
2244 Walnut Grove Ave
Rosemead CA 91770
626 302-5778

(P-12871)
IMPERIAL IRRIGATION DISTRICT
Also Called: Purchasing Department
Bell Bldg, El Centro (92243)
PHONE.................................760 339-9253
Donna Gray, *Branch Mgr*
EMP: 50

SALES (corp-wide): 705.4MM **Privately Held**
WEB: www.iid.com
SIC: 4931 4971 7389 Electric & other
services combined; irrigation systems;
purchasing service
PA: Imperial Irrigation District
333 E Barioni Blvd
Imperial CA 92251
800 303-7756

(P-12872)
IMPERIAL IRRIGATION DISTRICT
2151 W Adams Ave, El Centro
(92243-9457)
P.O. Box 937, Imperial (92251-0937)
PHONE.................................760 339-9800
Frank Montoya, *Branch Mgr*
Efren Garcia, *Engineer*
EMP: 50
SALES (corp-wide): 705.4MM **Privately Held**
WEB: www.iid.com
SIC: 4931 Electric & other services com-
bined
PA: Imperial Irrigation District
333 E Barioni Blvd
Imperial CA 92251
800 303-7756

(P-12873)
SAN DIEGO GAS & ELECTRIC CO
Also Called: Orange County Service Center
662 Camino De Los Mares, San Clemente
(92673-2827)
PHONE.................................949 361-8090
James Valentine, *Branch Mgr*
Phil Sheridan, *Supervisor*
EMP: 53
SALES (corp-wide): 11.3B **Publicly Held**
WEB: www.sdge.com
SIC: 4931 4911 Electric & other services
combined; electric services
HQ: San Diego Gas & Electric Company
8326 Century Park Ct
San Diego CA 92123
619 696-2000

4932 Gas & Other Svcs Combined

(P-12874)
CLEAN ENERGY FUELS CORP (PA)
4675 Macarthur Ct Ste 800 Newport Beach
(92660-1895)
PHONE.................................949 437-1000
Warren I Mitchell, *Ch of Bd*
Stephen A Scully, *Ch of Bd*
Andrew J Littlefair, *President*
Mitchell W Pratt, *COO*
Robert M Vreeland, *CFO*
▲ EMP: 120 EST: 2001
SQ FT: 48,000
SALES (est): 291.7MM **Publicly Held**
WEB: www.cleanenergyfuels.com
SIC: 4932 4924 4922 Gas & other serv-
ices combined; natural gas distribution;
natural gas transmission

(P-12875)
MAXGEN ENERGY SERVICES LLC (DH)
1222 Vine St Ste 301, Paso Robles
(93446-2333)
PHONE.................................714 908-5266
Mark McLanahan, *CEO*
Kristin Osborne, *CFO*
Robert Forster, *Vice Pres*
Tony Padgett, *Vice Pres*
James Tillman, *Business Dir*
EMP: 64 EST: 2008
SALES (est): 4MM
SALES (corp-wide): 488.1MM **Privately Held**
WEB: www.maxgen.com
SIC: 4932 Gas & other services combined
HQ: Pearce Services, Llc
1222 Vine St Ste 301
Paso Robles CA 93446
805 467-2528

4939 Combination Utilities, NEC

(P-12876)
AGILE SOURCING PARTNERS INC
2385 Railroad St, Corona (92878-5411)
PHONE 951 279-4154
Luis Ramirez, *CEO*
Mitchell Diehl, *President*
Mark Cascio, *Vice Pres*
Courtney Gaik, *Vice Pres*
Sean Dempsey, *Business Anlyst*
EMP: 225 **EST:** 2006
SQ FT: 2,300
SALES (est): 222.5MM **Privately Held**
WEB: www.agilesourcingpartners.com
SIC: 4939 Combination utilities

(P-12877)
IMPERIAL IRRIGATION DISTRICT
81600 58th Ave, La Quinta (92253-7663)
P.O. Box 1080 (92247-1080)
PHONE 760 398-5811
Charles Haskin, *General Mgr*
Raquel Buenrostro, *Principal*
Michael A Pacheco, *Department Mgr*
Tina A Shields, *Department Mgr*
Henry Martinez, *General Mgr*
EMP: 50
SALES (corp-wide): 705.4MM **Privately Held**
WEB: www.iid.com
SIC: 4939 4911 Combination utilities; electric services
PA: Imperial Irrigation District
333 E Barioni Blvd
Imperial CA 92251
800 303-7756

(P-12878)
LOS ANGELES DEPT WTR & PWR
Also Called: Scattergood Generation Plant
12700 Vista Del Mar, Playa Del Rey (90293-8502)
PHONE 310 524-8500
Nazih Batarseh, *Branch Mgr*
EMP: 366 **Privately Held**
WEB: www.ladwp.com
SIC: 4939 Combination utilities
HQ: Los Angeles Department Of Water And Power
111 N Hope St
Los Angeles CA 90012
213 367-1320

4941 Water Sply

(P-12879)
AMERICAN STATES WATER COMPANY (PA)
Also Called: Awr
630 E Foothill Blvd, San Dimas (91773-1207)
PHONE 909 394-3600
Robert J Sprowls, *President*
Anne M Holloway, *Ch of Bd*
Eva G Tang, *CFO*
Kerwin Fujikam, *Project Mgr*
Rebecca Hooper, *Manager*
EMP: 568 **EST:** 1929
SALES (est): 488.2MM **Publicly Held**
WEB: www.americanstateswatercompany.gcs-web.com
SIC: 4941 4911 Water supply; electric services; distribution, electric power; generation, electric power

(P-12880)
ARVIN-EDISON WATER STORAGE DST (PA)
20401 E Bear Mtn Blvd, Arvin (93203-9475)
P.O. Box 175 (93203-0175)
PHONE 661 854-5573
Howard Frick, *President*
John C Moore, *Corp Secy*
Salvadore Giumarra, *Vice Pres*
EMP: 50
SQ FT: 5,000

SALES (est): 17.7MM **Privately Held**
WEB: www.aewsd.org
SIC: 4941 Water supply

(P-12881)
CALLEGUAS MUNICIPAL WATER DICT
2100 E Olsen Rd, Thousand Oaks (91360-6800)
PHONE 805 526-9323
Thomas Slosson, *President*
Jeff Mocalis, *Officer*
Henry Graumlich, *General Mgr*
Andy Waters, *Admin Sec*
Fernando Baez, *Project Mgr*
EMP: 62 **EST:** 1953
SQ FT: 8,000
SALES (est): 120MM **Privately Held**
WEB: www.calleguas.com
SIC: 4941 Water supply

(P-12882)
CENTRAL BSIN MNCPL WTR DST FIN
6252 Telegraph Rd, Commerce (90040-2512)
PHONE 323 201-5500
Gary A Morse, *President*
Alex Rojas, *General Mgr*
Jacque Koontz, *Engineer*
Dorrett Lambey, *Accounting Mgr*
Chris Alvarez, *Analyst*
EMP: 75 **EST:** 1947
SQ FT: 29,790
SALES (est): 11.6MM **Privately Held**
WEB: www.centralbasin.org
SIC: 4941 Water supply

(P-12883)
COACHLLA VLY WTR DST PUB FCLTI (PA)
Also Called: Coachella Valley Water Dst
75515 Hovley Ln E, Palm Desert (92211-5104)
P.O. Box 1058, Coachella (92236-1058)
PHONE 760 398-2651
Toll Free: .... 888 -
James M Barrett, *General Mgr*
Jim Barrett, *General Mgr*
Robert Cheng, *General Mgr*
Steve Robbins, *General Mgr*
Isabel Luna, *Executive Asst*
▲ **EMP:** 225 **EST:** 1918
SALES: 177.9MM **Privately Held**
WEB: www.cvwd.org
SIC: 4941 4971 4952 7389 Water supply; water distribution or supply systems for irrigation; sewerage systems; water softener service

(P-12884)
COACHLLA VLY WTR DST PUB FCLTI
75 525 Hovley Ln, Palm Desert (92260)
PHONE 760 398-2651
Steve Robins, *Branch Mgr*
EMP: 172
SALES (corp-wide): 177.9MM **Privately Held**
WEB: www.cvwd.org
SIC: 4941 4952 4971 Water supply; sewerage systems; irrigation systems
PA: Coachella Valley Water District Public Facilities Corporation
75515 Hovley Ln E
Palm Desert CA 92211
760 398-2651

(P-12885)
COUNTY OF LOS ANGELES
Also Called: Department of Public Works
900 S Fremont Ave, Alhambra (91803-1331)
P.O. Box 1460 (91802-2460)
PHONE 626 458-4000
Gail Farber, *Director*
Salve Ores, *Database Admin*
Hector Bordas, *IT/INT Sup*
Jeff Orlin, *IT/INT Sup*
Ken Farris, *Technology*
EMP: 300

SALES (corp-wide): 25.2B **Privately Held**
WEB: www.lacounty.gov
SIC: 4941 9511 4971 Water supply; air, water & solid waste management; irrigation systems
PA: County Of Los Angeles
500 W Temple St Ste 437
Los Angeles CA 90012
213 974-1101

(P-12886)
CUCAMONGA VALLEY WATER DST
10440 Ashford St, Rancho Cucamonga (91730-3057)
P.O. Box 638 (91729-0638)
PHONE 909 987-2591
Martin Zvirbulis, *CEO*
Diane Schumacher, *Senior Partner*
Kathleen Tiegs, *President*
Braden Yu, *CFO*
Chad Brantley, *Officer*
EMP: 100
SQ FT: 15,000
SALES: 103.4MM **Privately Held**
WEB: www.cvwdwater.com
SIC: 4941 Water supply

(P-12887)
DESERT WATER AGENCY FING CORP
Also Called: DWA
1200 S Gene Autry Trl, Palm Springs (92264-3533)
P.O. Box 1710 (92263-1710)
PHONE 760 323-4971
Patricia G Oyga, *CEO*
Martin Krieger, *CFO*
James Cioffi, *Vice Pres*
Joseph Stuart, *Vice Pres*
Mark S Krause, *General Mgr*
EMP: 88
SQ FT: 38,000
SALES (est): 41.8MM **Privately Held**
WEB: www.dwa.org
SIC: 4941 Water supply

(P-12888)
EAST VALLEY WATER DISTRICT
31111 Greenspot Rd, Highland (92346-4427)
P.O. Box 3427, San Bernardino (92413-3427)
PHONE 909 889-9501
John Mura, *CEO*
Matt Levesque, *President*
Brian W Tompkins, *CFO*
Kip E Sturgeon, *Vice Pres*
Shayla Gerber, *Admin Asst*
EMP: 61
SALES: 39.8MM **Privately Held**
WEB: www.eastvalley.org
SIC: 4941 8734 Water supply; water testing laboratory

(P-12889)
EASTERN MUNICIPAL WATER DST (PA)
2270 Trumble Rd, Perris (92572)
P.O. Box 8300 (92572-8300)
PHONE 951 928-3777
Paul D Jones II, *CEO*
Laura Nomura, *General Mgr*
Lisa Esparza, *Executive Asst*
Allan Freetage, *Executive Asst*
Terri Guerrero, *Executive Asst*
▲ **EMP:** 420
SQ FT: 160,000
SALES: 256.9MM **Privately Held**
WEB: www.emwd.org
SIC: 4941 4952 Water supply; sewerage systems

(P-12890)
EASTERN MUNICIPAL WATER DST
19750 Evans Rd, Perris (92571-7469)
PHONE 951 657-7469
Paul D Jones II, *Branch Mgr*
Susan Barnes, *Officer*
Rosemarie Howard, *General Mgr*
Lisa Esparza, *Executive Asst*
Monica McGrath, *Executive Asst*
EMP: 200

SALES (corp-wide): 256.9MM **Privately Held**
WEB: www.emwd.org
SIC: 4941 Water supply
PA: Eastern Municipal Water District
2270 Trumble Rd
Perris CA 92572
951 928-3777

(P-12891)
ELSINORE VLY MUNICPL WTR DST (PA)
31315 Chaney St, Lake Elsinore (92530-2743)
P.O. Box 3000 (92531-3000)
PHONE 951 674-3146
Andy Morris, *President*
Sarah Meyer, *Officer*
Phil Williams, *Vice Pres*
Ronald Young, *Vice Pres*
Greg Thomas, *General Mgr*
EMP: 65 **EST:** 1950
SQ FT: 4,000
SALES: 78.1MM **Privately Held**
WEB: www.evmwd.com
SIC: 4941 4971 4952 Water supply; water distribution or supply systems for irrigation; sewerage systems

(P-12892)
GOLDEN STATE WATER COMPANY (HQ)
Also Called: AWR
630 E Foothill Blvd, San Dimas (91773-1212)
PHONE 909 394-3600
Robert J Sprowls, *President*
Anne M Holloway, *Ch of Bd*
Eva G Tang, *CFO*
Gladys M Farrow, *Treasurer*
Randy Miller, *Vice Pres*
EMP: 243 **EST:** 1929
SALES (est): 349.2MM
SALES (corp-wide): 488.2MM **Publicly Held**
WEB: www.gswater.com
SIC: 4941 4911 Water supply; distribution, electric power
PA: American States Water Company
630 E Foothill Blvd
San Dimas CA 91773
909 394-3600

(P-12893)
INLAND EMPIRE UTLTIES AGCY A M (PA)
6075 Kimball Ave, Chino (91708-9174)
P.O. Box 9020, Chino Hills (91709-0902)
PHONE 909 993-1600
Kati Parker, *President*
John Anderson, *President*
Ging Cookman, *Corp Secy*
Steve Elie, *Corp Secy*
Michael Camacho, *Vice Pres*
EMP: 92 **EST:** 1950
SQ FT: 60,000
SALES: 144.1MM **Privately Held**
WEB: www.ieua.org
SIC: 4941 Water supply

(P-12894)
IRVINE RANCH WATER DISTRICT (PA)
15600 Sand Canyon Ave, Irvine (92618-3102)
P.O. Box 57000 (92619-7000)
PHONE 949 453-5300
Paul Jones, *General Mgr*
Robert Jacobson, *Treasurer*
Thomas Bonkowski, *Project Mgr*
Nang Mwe, *Engineer*
Lisa Srader, *Analyst*
EMP: 110 **EST:** 1961
SQ FT: 52,000
SALES (est): 88.9MM **Privately Held**
WEB: www.irwd.com
SIC: 4941 4952 Water supply; sewerage systems

(P-12895)
IRVINE RANCH WATER DISTRICT
3512 Michelson Dr, Irvine (92612-1757)
P.O. Box 14128 (92623-4128)
PHONE 949 453-5300

Carl Ballard, *Director*
John Fabris, *Manager*
Lisa Haney, *Manager*
EMP: 205
SALES (corp-wide): 88.9MM **Privately Held**
WEB: www.irwd.com
SIC: 4941 4952 Water supply; sewerage systems
PA: Irvine Ranch Water District Inc
15600 Sand Canyon Ave
Irvine CA 92618
949 453-5300

(P-12896)
JURUPA COMMUNITY SERVICES DST
11201 Harrel St, Riverside (92509)
PHONE..................................951 685-7073
Carol McGreevy, *Manager*
Julie Saba, *Executive*
Frank Temple, *Technician*
Steven Popelar, *Finance*
Benjamin Armel, *Opers Staff*
EMP: 89
SALES (corp-wide): 16MM **Privately Held**
WEB: www.jcsd.us
SIC: 4941 4952 Water supply; sewerage systems
PA: Jurupa Community Services District
11201 Harrel St
Jurupa Valley CA 91752
951 360-5770

(P-12897)
LAKE HEMET MUNICIPAL WATER DST (PA)
26385 Fairview Ave, Hemet (92544-6607)
P.O. Box 5039 (92544-0039)
PHONE..................................951 658-3241
Michael A Gow, *General Mgr*
Tom Wagoner, *General Mgr*
Jason Venable, *Technician*
Mike Gow, *Government*
Mitchell Freeman, *Manager*
EMP: 53 EST: 1955
SQ FT: 4,900
SALES: 19.3MM **Privately Held**
SIC: 4941 4971 Water supply; water distribution or supply systems for irrigation

(P-12898)
LAS VIRGENES MUNICIPAL WTR DST
4232 Las Virgenes Rd Lbby, Calabasas (91302-3594)
PHONE..................................818 251-2100
Glen Peterson, *President*
Jay Lewitt, *Treasurer*
Lee Renger, *Vice Pres*
David Pedersen, *General Mgr*
Harold Matthews, *MIS Dir*
EMP: 125
SQ FT: 10,000
SALES: 67MM **Privately Held**
WEB: www.lvmwd.com
SIC: 4941 Water supply

(P-12899)
LIBERTY UTILITIES PK WTR CORP (DH)
9750 Washburn Rd, Downey (90241-5625)
PHONE..................................562 923-0711
Greg Sorensen, *President*
Chris Alario, *CFO*
Jeanne Marie Bruno, *Senior VP*
Dave Warner, *Risk Mgmt Dir*
Jeanne Bruno, *General Mgr*
EMP: 68
SQ FT: 15,000
SALES (est): 81.8MM
SALES (corp-wide): 1.6B **Privately Held**
WEB: www.libertyutilities.com
SIC: 4941 Water supply
HQ: Liberty Utilities (Canada) Corp
2845 Bristol Cir
Oakville ON L6H 7
905 465-4500

(P-12900)
LINDA YORBA WATER DISTRICT (PA)
1717 E Miraloma Ave, Placentia (92870-6785)
P.O. Box 309, Yorba Linda (92885-0309)
PHONE..................................714 701-3000
Ken Vecchiarelli, *General Mgr*
Andrew J Hall, *Vice Pres*
Gina Knight, *Executive*
Brett Barbre, *General Mgr*
Art Vega, *Info Tech Mgr*
▲ EMP: 59 EST: 1959
SQ FT: 7,900
SALES: 35.8MM **Privately Held**
WEB: www.ylwd.com
SIC: 4941 4952 Water supply; sewerage systems

(P-12901)
LOS ANGELES DEPT WTR & PWR
4030 Crenshaw Blvd, Los Angeles (90008-2533)
P.O. Box 51211 (90051-5511)
PHONE..................................323 256-8079
Jeffrey McCann, *IT/INT Sup*
Faranak Sarbaz, *Electrical Engi*
Alexander Santos, *Engineer*
Diego Calvera, *Analyst*
Dave Christensen, *Manager*
EMP: 366 **Privately Held**
WEB: www.ladwp.com
SIC: 4941 4911 Water supply; electric services
HQ: Los Angeles Department Of Water And Power
111 N Hope St
Los Angeles CA 90012
213 367-1320

(P-12902)
LOS ANGELES DEPT WTR & PWR
11801 Sheldon St, Sun Valley (91352-1508)
PHONE..................................213 367-1342
Kirk Bergland, *Branch Mgr*
Thieu Doan, *Electrical Engi*
Olivia Morales, *Security Mgr*
Walter Zeisl, *Advt Staff*
EMP: 366 **Privately Held**
WEB: www.ladwp.com
SIC: 4941 Water supply
HQ: Los Angeles Department Of Water And Power
111 N Hope St
Los Angeles CA 90012
213 367-1320

(P-12903)
LOS ANGELES DEPT WTR & PWR
Also Called: Ladwp
201 S Webster St, Independence (93526-1769)
PHONE..................................760 878-2156
Steve Howe, *Supervisor*
EMP: 366 **Privately Held**
WEB: www.ladwp.com
SIC: 4941 Water supply
HQ: Los Angeles Department Of Water And Power
111 N Hope St
Los Angeles CA 90012
213 367-1320

(P-12904)
LOS ANGELES DEPT WTR & PWR (HQ)
Also Called: Ladwp
111 N Hope St, Los Angeles (90012-2607)
P.O. Box 51111 (90051-5700)
PHONE..................................213 367-1320
Martin Adams, *General Mgr*
Martin L Adams, *COO*
Ann M Santilli, *CFO*
Donna I Stevener, *Officer*
Nancy Sutley, *Officer*
▲ EMP: 7180 EST: 1902
SALES (est): 1B **Privately Held**
WEB: www.ladwp.com
SIC: 4941 4911 Water supply; electric services

PA: City Of Los Angeles
200 N Spring St Ste 303
Los Angeles CA 90012
213 978-0600

(P-12905)
LOS ANGELES DEPT WTR & PWR
1141 W 2nd St Bldg D, Los Angeles (90012-2007)
PHONE..................................213 367-5706
Carol Tharp, *Branch Mgr*
Kianiwai Spangler, *Engineer*
Heather Yegiazaryan, *Engineer*
John Cox, *Manager*
Niko Houston, *Representative*
EMP: 366 **Privately Held**
WEB: www.ladwp.com
SIC: 4941 Water supply
HQ: Los Angeles Department Of Water And Power
111 N Hope St
Los Angeles CA 90012
213 367-1320

(P-12906)
MESA CNSLD WTR DST IMPRV CORP (PA)
Also Called: MESA WATER DISTRICT
1965 Placentia Ave, Costa Mesa (92627-3420)
PHONE..................................949 631-1200
Lee Pearl, *Director*
James R Fisler, *President*
Shawn Dewane, *Vice Pres*
Coleen L Monteleone, *Admin Sec*
Carrie Fesili, *Technology*
EMP: 66 EST: 1960
SQ FT: 26,000
SALES: 36.7MM **Privately Held**
WEB: www.mesawater.org
SIC: 4941 Water supply

(P-12907)
METROPOLITAN WATER DISTRICT
Also Called: Metropolitan Water Lavern
700 Moreno Ave, La Verne (91750-3399)
P.O. Box 54153, Los Angeles (90054-0153)
PHONE..................................909 593-7474
Wendell Williams, *Branch Mgr*
Adam Again, *Counsel*
EMP: 370
SALES (corp-wide): 1.4B **Privately Held**
WEB: www.mwdh2o.com
SIC: 4941 Water supply
PA: The Metropolitan Water District Of Southern California
700 N Alameda St
Los Angeles CA 90012
213 217-6000

(P-12908)
MOULTON NGUEL WTR DST PUB FCLT (PA)
27500 La Paz Rd, Laguna Niguel (92677-3402)
P.O. Box 30203 (92607-0203)
PHONE..................................949 831-2500
Richard Fiore, *President*
David Cain, *Treasurer*
Matthew Brown, *Officer*
Jose Solorio, *Officer*
Duane Cave, *Vice Pres*
EMP: 82 EST: 1960
SQ FT: 9,000
SALES: 65.2MM **Privately Held**
WEB: www.mnwd.com
SIC: 4941 4959 Water supply; sanitary services

(P-12909)
MUNICPAL WTR DST ORNGE CNTY WT
18700 Ward St, Fountain Valley (92708-6930)
P.O. Box 20895 (92728-0895)
PHONE..................................714 963-3058
Joan Finnegan, *President*
Wayne Clark, *President*
Kevin Hunt, *CEO*
Philip Letrong, *CFO*
Satoru Tamaribuchi, *Bd of Directors*
EMP: 78 EST: 1951
SQ FT: 30,000

SALES (est): 9.4MM **Privately Held**
WEB: www.mwdoc.com
SIC: 4941 Water supply

(P-12910)
ORANGE COUNTY WATER DISTRICT
Also Called: Facilty
14980 River Rd, Eastvale (92830-9607)
PHONE..................................714 378-3200
Stephanie Dosier, *Human Res Dir*
EMP: 53
SALES (corp-wide): 146.7MM **Privately Held**
WEB: www.ocwd.com
SIC: 4941 Water supply
PA: Orange County Water District
18700 Ward St
Fountain Valley CA 92708
714 378-3200

(P-12911)
ORANGE COUNTY WATER DISTRICT
Also Called: Accounts Payable Dept
18700 Ward St, Fountain Valley (92708-6930)
P.O. Box 20845 (92728-0845)
PHONE..................................714 378-3200
Dina L Nguyen, *Branch Mgr*
EMP: 53
SALES (corp-wide): 146.7MM **Privately Held**
WEB: www.ocwd.com
SIC: 4941 Water supply
PA: Orange County Water District
18700 Ward St
Fountain Valley CA 92708
714 378-3200

(P-12912)
ORANGE COUNTY WATER DISTRICT
4060 E La Palma Ave, Anaheim (92807-1754)
PHONE..................................714 378-3320
Kevin McGillicuddy, *Manager*
Lee Yoo, *Lab Dir*
John Kennedy, *Exec Dir*
Adam Hutchinson, *Manager*
EMP: 53
SALES (corp-wide): 146.7MM **Privately Held**
WEB: www.ocwd.com
SIC: 4941 Water supply
PA: Orange County Water District
18700 Ward St
Fountain Valley CA 92708
714 378-3200

(P-12913)
PALMDALE WATER DISTRICT
2029 E Avenue Q, Palmdale (93550-4050)
PHONE..................................661 947-4111
Michael Williams, *CFO*
Randy Hill, *General Mgr*
Kathy Laren, *Admin Sec*
Jennifer Emery, *Human Res Mgr*
Ryan Oates, *Buyer*
EMP: 93 EST: 1991
SALES: 27.5MM **Privately Held**
WEB: www.palmdalewater.org
SIC: 4941 Water supply

(P-12914)
RANCHO CALIFORNIA WATER DST (PA)
Also Called: RCWD
42135 Winchester Rd, Temecula (92590-4800)
P.O. Box 9017 (92589-9017)
PHONE..................................951 296-6900
William E Plummer, *Principal*
Stephen J Corona, *President*
Ralph Daily, *President*
Bennet Drake, *President*
Jeff Armstrong, *CFO*
EMP: 143 EST: 1965
SQ FT: 71,000
SALES: 72MM **Privately Held**
WEB: www.ranchowater.com
SIC: 4941 Water supply

(P-12915)
SAN GABRIEL VALLEY WATER CO (PA)
Also Called: Fontana Water Company
11142 Garvey Ave, El Monte (91733-2498)
P.O. Box 6010 (91734-2010)
PHONE..........................626 448-6183
R H Nicholson Jr, *Ch of Bd*
Michael L Whitehead, *President*
David Batt, *Treasurer*
Frank A Lo Guidice, *Vice Pres*
Josh Swift, *General Mgr*
EMP: 125 **EST:** 1936
SQ FT: 30,000
SALES (est): 57.8MM **Privately Held**
WEB: www.sgvwater.com
SIC: 4941 Water supply

(P-12916)
SAN GABRIEL VALLEY WATER CO
8440 Nuevo Ave, Fontana (92335-3824)
P.O. Box 987 (92334-0987)
PHONE..........................909 822-2201
Mike McGraw, *Manager*
Matt Yucelen, *Engineer*
EMP: 116
SQ FT: 2,727
SALES (corp-wide): 57.8MM **Privately Held**
WEB: www.sgvwater.com
SIC: 4941 Water supply
PA: San Gabriel Valley Water Co.
11142 Garvey Ave
El Monte CA 91733
626 448-6183

(P-12917)
SANTA ANA WATERSHED PRJ AUTH
Also Called: Sawpa
11615 Sterling Ave, Riverside (92503-4979)
PHONE..........................951 354-4220
Celeste Cantu, *General Mgr*
David Ruhl, *Planning Mgr*
Kelly Berry, *Manager*
EMP: 51 **EST:** 1977
SQ FT: 2,500
SALES (est): 18.9MM **Privately Held**
WEB: www.sawpa.org
SIC: 4941 Water supply

(P-12918)
SANTA CLARITA VALLEY WTR AGCY
Also Called: Santa Clarita Water Division
26521 Summit Cir, Santa Clarita (91350-3049)
PHONE..........................661 259-2737
Mauricio E Guardado Jr, *Principal*
Matt Stone, *General Mgr*
Estella Valderrama, *Engineer*
EMP: 160
SALES (corp-wide): 90.9MM **Privately Held**
WEB: www.yourscvwater.com
SIC: 4941 Water supply
PA: Santa Clarita Valley Water Agency
27234 Bouquet Canyon Rd
Santa Clarita CA 91350
661 297-1600

(P-12919)
SANTA CLRITA VLY WTR AGCY FING
27234 Bouquet Canyon Rd, Santa Clarita (91350-2173)
PHONE..........................661 259-2737
Tom Campbell, *CEO*
Matt Stone, *Ch of Bd*
Ronald J Kelly, *President*
Dan Masnada, *Treasurer*
William Cooper, *Vice Pres*
EMP: 120 **EST:** 1962
SQ FT: 1,000
SALES (est): 30.9MM **Privately Held**
WEB: www.yourscvwater.com
SIC: 4941 Water supply

(P-12920)
SANTA MARGARITA WATER DISTRICT (PA)
26111 Antonio Pkwy, Rcho STA Marg (92688-5596)
PHONE..........................949 459-6400
Daniel R Ferons, *Manager*
Justin McCusker, *Bd of Directors*
Jennifer Wilt, *Executive Asst*
Laurel Haberchak, *Admin Sec*
Kelly Radvansky, *Admin Sec*
EMP: 70 **EST:** 1964
SQ FT: 5,600
SALES (est): 59.4MM **Privately Held**
WEB: www.smwd.com
SIC: 4941 4952 Water supply; sewerage systems

(P-12921)
TEMPLETON COMMUNITY SVC DST
420 Crocker St, Templeton (93465-5303)
P.O. Box 780 (93465-0780)
PHONE..........................805 434-4900
William Van Orden, *General Mgr*
Robert Bergman, *President*
Judith Dietch, *Bd of Directors*
Navid Fardanesh, *Bd of Directors*
Natalie Klock, *Officer*
EMP: 54 **EST:** 1976
SQ FT: 2,000
SALES (est): 14MM **Privately Held**
WEB: www.templetoncsd.org
SIC: 4941 4952 4911 Water supply; sewerage systems; distribution, electric power

(P-12922)
WALNUT VALLEY WATER DISTRICT
271 Brea Canyon Rd, Walnut (91789-3002)
P.O. Box 508 (91788-0508)
PHONE..........................909 595-7554
Theodore Ebenkamp, *President*
Scarlet Kwong, *Vice Pres*
Edwin Hilden, *Principal*
Michael Holmes, *General Mgr*
Sherry Shaw, *Engineer*
EMP: 55 **EST:** 1952
SQ FT: 7,900
SALES (est): 40.4MM **Privately Held**
WEB: www.wvwd.com
SIC: 4941 Water supply

(P-12923)
YUCAIPA VALLEY WATER DISTRICT (PA)
12770 2nd St, Yucaipa (92399-5670)
P.O. Box 730 (92399-0730)
PHONE..........................909 797-5117
Bruce Granlund, *President*
James Cansler, *Supervisor*
Matt Flordelis, *Supervisor*
Steven Molina, *Supervisor*
EMP: 56 **EST:** 1971
SQ FT: 2,500
SALES (est): 26.4MM **Privately Held**
WEB: www.yvwd.us
SIC: 4941 Water supply

4952 Sewerage Systems

(P-12924)
ELSINORE VLY MUNICPL WTR DST
1800 E Lakeshore Dr, Lake Elsinore (92530-4469)
PHONE..........................951 245-0276
Ronald Young, *General Mgr*
EMP: 58
SALES (corp-wide): 78.1MM **Privately Held**
WEB: www.evmwd.com
SIC: 4952 Sewerage systems
PA: Elsinore Valley Municipal Water District
31315 Chaney St
Lake Elsinore CA 92530
951 674-3146

4953 Refuse Systems

(P-12925)
ANTELOPE VLY RCYCL DSPSAL FCLT
Also Called: Arklin Brothers Hauling
1200 W City Ranch Rd, Palmdale (93551-4456)
PHONE..........................661 945-5944
Lee Hicks, *Principal*
EMP: 54 **EST:** 1978
SALES (est): 15.2MM
SALES (corp-wide): 15.2B **Publicly Held**
WEB: www.wm.com
SIC: 4953 Recycling, waste materials
PA: Waste Management, Inc.
800 Capitol St Ste 3000
Houston TX 77002
713 512-6200

(P-12926)
ARACO ENTERPRISES LLC
Also Called: Athens Environmental Services
9189 De Garmo Ave, Sun Valley (91352-2609)
PHONE..........................818 767-0675
Ronald Krall,
Michael R Arakelian,
EMP: 400 **EST:** 2017
SALES (est): 30.7MM **Privately Held**
SIC: 4953 Garbage: collecting, destroying & processing

(P-12927)
ARAKELIAN ENTERPRISES INC (PA)
Also Called: Athens Services
14048 Valley Blvd, City of Industry (91746-2801)
P.O. Box 60009 (91716-0009)
PHONE..........................626 336-3636
Ron Arakelian Jr, *CEO*
Michael Arakelian, *CEO*
Gary Clifford, *COO*
Kevin Hanifin, *CFO*
Dennis Chiappetta, *Exec VP*
EMP: 972 **EST:** 1958
SQ FT: 10,000
SALES (est): 199.6MM **Privately Held**
WEB: www.athensservices.com
SIC: 4953 Recycling, waste materials; street refuse systems

(P-12928)
ARROW DISPOSAL SERVICES INC
14332 Valley Blvd, La Puente (91746-2931)
P.O. Box 2917 (91746-0917)
PHONE..........................626 336-2255
Kirk Tahmizian, *President*
EMP: 50 **EST:** 1984
SQ FT: 40,000
SALES (est): 21.9MM **Privately Held**
WEB: www.arrowdisposalservices.com
SIC: 4953 Garbage: collecting, destroying & processing

(P-12929)
ATHENS DISPOSAL COMPANY INC (PA)
14048 Valley Blvd, La Puente (91746-2801)
P.O. Box 60009, City of Industry (91716-0009)
PHONE..........................626 336-3636
Ron Arakelian Sr, *President*
Lindsay Jones, *Ch Invest Ofcr*
Ron Arakelian Jr, *Vice Pres*
EMP: 350 **EST:** 1958
SALES (est): 261.2MM **Privately Held**
WEB: www.athensservices.com
SIC: 4953 Recycling, waste materials

(P-12930)
BEST WAY DISPOSAL CO INC
Also Called: Advance Disposal Company
17105 Mesa St, Hesperia (92345-5155)
P.O. Box 400997 (92340-0997)
PHONE..........................760 244-9773
Robert Bath, *Ch of Bd*
Sheila Bath, *President*
EMP: 75 **EST:** 1965

SALES (est): 8.4MM **Privately Held**
WEB: www.advancedisposal.com
SIC: 4953 Garbage: collecting, destroying & processing

(P-12931)
BESTWAY RECYCLING COMPANY INC (PA)
1032 Industrial St, Pomona (91766-3809)
P.O. Box 109, South Gate (90280-0109)
PHONE..........................323 588-8157
Edward Young Kim, *President*
David Cho, *CFO*
Nam Sook Kim, *Corp Secy*
Dong Kim, *Opers Mgr*
▼ **EMP:** 52 **EST:** 1963
SALES (est): 19MM **Privately Held**
WEB: www.bestwayrecyclingla.com
SIC: 4953 Recycling, waste materials

(P-12932)
BKK CORPORATION (PA)
2210 S Azusa Ave, West Covina (91792-1510)
PHONE..........................626 965-0911
Fax: 626 965-9569
EMP: 57
SALES (est): 22.2MM **Privately Held**
SIC: 4953 Refuse System

(P-12933)
BURRTEC WASTE INDUSTRIES INC (HQ)
9890 Cherry Ave, Fontana (92335-5298)
PHONE..........................909 429-4200
Cole Burr, *President*
Michael Arreguin, *Vice Pres*
Trevor Scrogins, *Vice Pres*
Nick Burciaga, *Division Mgr*
Octavio Camacho, *Division Mgr*
▲ **EMP:** 150 **EST:** 1978
SQ FT: 10,000
SALES (est): 307.4MM
SALES (corp-wide): 320.1MM **Privately Held**
WEB: www.burrtec.com
SIC: 4953 4212 Rubbish collection & disposal; recycling, waste materials; local trucking, without storage
PA: Burrtec Waste Group, Inc.
9890 Cherry Ave
Fontana CA 92335
909 429-4200

(P-12934)
CALIFORNIA WASTE SERVICES LLC
621 W 152nd St, Gardena (90247-2732)
PHONE..........................310 538-5998
Eric Casper, *President*
Sophie Zaldi, *Cust Mgr*
Giovanni Lopez, *Manager*
EMP: 120 **EST:** 1999
SQ FT: 20,000
SALES (est): 21.2MM **Privately Held**
WEB: www.californiawasteservices.com
SIC: 4953 Refuse collection & disposal services

(P-12935)
CALMET INC (PA)
Also Called: Metropolitan Waste Disposal
7202 Petterson Ln, Paramount (90723-2022)
PHONE..........................323 721-8120
Thomas K Blackman, *President*
Gary Kazarian, *Treasurer*
William Kalpakoff, *Vice Pres*
Kris Kazarian, *Admin Sec*
EMP: 180 **EST:** 1953
SQ FT: 38,000
SALES (est): 14.6MM **Privately Held**
SIC: 4953 4212 Rubbish collection & disposal; recycling, waste materials; local trucking, without storage

(P-12936)
CALMET SERVICES INC
7202 Petterson Ln, Paramount (90723-2022)
PHONE..........................562 259-1239
Bill Kalpakoff, *President*
EMP: 57 **EST:** 1966

SALES (est): 9.4MM **Privately Held**
WEB: www.calmetservices.com
SIC: **4953** Rubbish collection & disposal

(P-12937)
CEDARWOOD-YOUNG COMPANY (PA)
Also Called: Allan Company
14620 Joanbridge St, Baldwin Park
(91706-1750)
PHONE...................................626 962-4047
Jason Young, *President*
Michael Ochniak, *CFO*
Stephen Young, *Chairman*
Francisco Del Rincon, *Vice Pres*
Yun Koo, *Vice Pres*
◆ EMP: 175 EST: 1963
SQ FT: 4,350
SALES (est): 252.1MM **Privately Held**
WEB: www.allancompany.com
SIC: **4953** Recycling, waste materials

(P-12938)
CHEMICAL WASTE MANAGEMENT INC
35251 Old Skyline Rd, Kettleman City
(93239-4534)
P.O. Box 471 (93239-0471)
PHONE...................................559 386-9711
Robert Henry, *Manager*
EMP: 64
SQ FT: 5,000
SALES (corp-wide): 15.2B **Publicly Held**
SIC: **4953** Non-hazardous waste disposal
　sites
HQ: Chemical Waste Management, Inc.
　1001 Fannin St Ste 4000
　Houston TX 77002
　713 512-6200

(P-12939)
CITY OF LEMOORE
Also Called: Refuse Department
711 W Cinnamon Dr, Lemoore
(93245-9142)
PHONE...................................559 924-6744
David Wlaschin, *Director*
Steven McPherson, *Officer*
Valerie Cazares, *Executive Asst*
Jenarae Benavente, *Accountant*
EMP: 50
SALES (corp-wide): 14.2MM **Privately Held**
WEB: www.lemoore.com
SIC: **4953** Refuse systems
PA: City Of Lemoore
　711 W Cinnamon Dr
　Lemoore CA 93245
　559 924-6700

(P-12940)
CLEAN HARBORS BUTTONWILLOW LLC
2500 W Lokern Rd, Buttonwillow (93206)
P.O. Box 787 (93206-0787)
PHONE...................................661 762-6200
Marianna Boni, *General Mgr*
Victoria McDertt Luwis, *Manager*
EMP: 79 EST: 2002
SALES (est): 17.7MM
SALES (corp-wide): 3.1B **Publicly Held**
WEB: www.cleanharbors.com
SIC: **4953** Sanitary landfill operation
PA: Clean Harbors, Inc.
　42 Longwater Dr
　Norwell MA 02061
　781 792-5000

(P-12941)
COLD CANYON LAND FILL INC
2268 Carpenter Canyon Rd, San Luis
Obispo (93401-8241)
PHONE...................................805 549-8332
Rick King, *Manager*
EMP: 50
SALES (corp-wide): 5.4B **Privately Held**
WEB: www.coldcanyonlandfill.com
SIC: **4953** Sanitary landfill operation
HQ: Cold Canyon Land Fill, Inc.
　970 Monterey St Unit B
　San Luis Obispo CA 93401
　805 549-8332

(P-12942)
CORRIDOR RECYCLING INC
22500 S Alameda St, Long Beach
(90810-1905)
PHONE...................................310 835-3849
Gilbert Dodson, *President*
Steve Young, *Vice Pres*
Mark Tranckino, *CPA*
Kenneth J Kim, *Manager*
▲ EMP: 52 EST: 1996
SQ FT: 13,594
SALES (est): 12.4MM **Privately Held**
WEB: www.corridorrecycling.com
SIC: **4953** 5941 5093 Recycling, waste
　materials; sporting goods & bicycle
　shops; metal scrap & waste materials

(P-12943)
COVANTA LONG BCH RNWBLE ENRGY
118 Pier S Ave, Long Beach (90802-1039)
PHONE...................................562 436-0636
▲ EMP: 240 EST: 2013
SALES (est): 15.7MM
SALES (corp-wide): 1.9B **Publicly Held**
SIC: **4953** Recycling, waste materials
HQ: Covanta Energy, Llc
　445 South St
　Morristown NJ 07960
　862 345-5000

(P-12944)
DELNORTE RGNAL RCYCL TRNSF STN (PA)
111 S Del Norte Blvd, Oxnard
(93030-7915)
PHONE...................................805 278-8200
Bill Corral, *Manager*
EMP: 63 EST: 1995
SALES (est): 7.1MM **Privately Held**
SIC: **4953** 4212 Refuse collection & dis-
　posal services; recycling, waste materials;
　local trucking, without storage

(P-12945)
E J HARRISON & SONS INC
Also Called: Harrison, E J & Sons Recycling
1589 Lirio Ave, Ventura (93004-3227)
PHONE...................................805 647-1414
Ken Keys, *General Mgr*
Myron Harrison, *General Mgr*
David Tripp, *Telecom Exec*
Donnie Harrison, *Opers Staff*
EMP: 173
SALES (corp-wide): 29.8MM **Privately Held**
WEB: www.ejharrison.com
SIC: **4953** 2611 Rubbish collection & dis-
　posal; pulp mills
PA: E. J. Harrison & Sons, Inc.
　5275 Colt St
　Ventura CA 93003
　805 647-1414

(P-12946)
EARTH TECHNOLOGY CORP USA
300 S Grand Ave Ste 900, Los Angeles
(90071-3135)
PHONE...................................213 593-8000
Keenan Driscoll, *President*
Thomas Walsh, *Project Engr*
EMP: 112 EST: 1987
SALES (est): 6.2MM
SALES (corp-wide): 13.2B **Publicly Held**
WEB: www.aecom.com
SIC: **4953** 8748 8742 8711 Refuse sys-
　tems; environmental consultant; manage-
　ment consulting services; engineering
　services
PA: Aecom
　13355 Noel Rd Ste 400
　Dallas TX 75240
　972 788-1000

(P-12947)
ECOLOGY RECYCLING SERVICES LLC (PA)
13750 Imperial Hwy, Santa Fe Springs
(90670-4823)
PHONE...................................562 921-9975
Aaron R Siroonian, *Mng Member*
Charles B Siroonian,
James Rajacich, *Manager*
EMP: 139 EST: 2017

SALES (est): 107.8MM **Privately Held**
SIC: **4953** Recycling, waste materials

(P-12948)
ECOLOGY RECYCLING SERVICES LLC
785 E M St, Colton (92324-3911)
PHONE...................................909 370-1318
EMP: 61
SALES (corp-wide): 107.8MM **Privately Held**
SIC: **4953** Recycling, waste materials
PA: Ecology Recycling Services, Llc
　13750 Imperial Hwy
　Santa Fe Springs CA 90670
　562 921-9975

(P-12949)
EDCO DISPOSAL CORPORATION (PA)
Also Called: La Mesa Disposal
2755 California Ave, Signal Hill
(90755-3304)
PHONE...................................619 287-7555
Steve South, *CEO*
Edward Burr, *President*
Dimas Cisneros, *Officer*
Sandra Burr, *Vice Pres*
Yvette Snyder, *Comms Dir*
EMP: 250 EST: 1967
SQ FT: 8,000
SALES (est): 134.3MM **Privately Held**
WEB: www.edcodisposal.com
SIC: **4953** Rubbish collection & disposal

(P-12950)
EMERALD TRANS LOS ANGELES LLC
5756 Alba St, Los Angeles (90058-3808)
PHONE...................................323 277-2500
Al Harrell, *Manager*
Eric Zimmer, *Senior VP*
Mark Zimmerman, *Senior VP*
Clyde Phillips, *Vice Pres*
Alex Richard, *Vice Pres*
EMP: 50
SQ FT: 23,350
SALES (est): 573.8MM **Privately Held**
WEB: www.emeraldtransformer.com
SIC: **4953** Recycling, waste materials
HQ: Emerald Transformer Los Angeles Llc
　9820 Westpoint Dr Ste 300
　Indianapolis IN 46256
　800 908-8800

(P-12951)
FLAT WHITE ECONOMY INV USA LLC
5151 Cal Ave Ste 100, Costa Mesa
(92626)
PHONE...................................949 344-5013
Ionut Georgescu, *CEO*
EMP: 165 EST: 2016
SALES (est): 1MM **Privately Held**
SIC: **4953** Recycling, waste materials

(P-12952)
GI INDUSTRIES
195 W Los Angeles Ave, Simi Valley
(93065-1651)
P.O. Box 940430 (93094-0430)
PHONE...................................805 522-2150
Michael Smith, *Senior VP*
EMP: 98 EST: 1985
SQ FT: 7,000
SALES (est): 27.7MM
SALES (corp-wide): 15.2B **Publicly Held**
WEB: www.wm.com
SIC: **4953** 4212 Garbage: collecting, de-
　stroying & processing; recycling, waste
　materials; local trucking, without storage
PA: Waste Management, Inc.
　800 Capitol St Ste 3000
　Houston TX 77002
　713 512-6200

(P-12953)
HAZMAT TSDF INC (PA)
180 W Monte Ave, Rialto (92376)
PHONE...................................909 873-4141
Jon L Bennett Jr, *President*
Jim Arnold, *Treasurer*
Jim Goyich, *Vice Pres*
Dianna Vepeda, *Admin Sec*

▲ EMP: 63 EST: 1988
SQ FT: 33,000
SALES (est): 19.1MM **Privately Held**
WEB: www.usahazmat.com
SIC: **4953** Hazardous waste collection &
　disposal

(P-12954)
JOES SWEEPING INC
Also Called: Nationwide Environmental Svcs
11914 Front St, Norwalk (90650-2911)
PHONE...................................562 929-4344
Never Samuelian, *President*
Joe Samuelian, *Vice Pres*
Ani Samuelian, *Admin Sec*
EMP: 65 EST: 1989
SQ FT: 10,500
SALES (est): 32.7MM **Privately Held**
WEB: www.nes-sweeping.com
SIC: **4953** Street refuse systems

(P-12955)
LIGHTING RESOURCES LLC
805 E Francis St, Ontario (91761-5516)
PHONE...................................909 923-7252
EMP: 62 **Privately Held**
WEB: www.lightingresourcesinc.com
SIC: **4953** 5093 Recycling, waste materi-
　als; scrap & waste materials
PA: Lighting Resources, Llc
　1919 Williams St Ste 350
　Simi Valley CA 93065

(P-12956)
LOONEY BINS INC (HQ)
12153 Montague St, Pacoima
(91331-2210)
PHONE...................................818 485-8200
Myan Spaccarelli, *President*
Jerry Lucera, *CFO*
Phyllis Shukiar, *Admin Sec*
EMP: 70 EST: 1995
SQ FT: 1,000
SALES (est): 22.6MM
SALES (corp-wide): 15.2B **Publicly Held**
WEB: www.wm.com
SIC: **4953** Garbage: collecting, destroying
　& processing
PA: Waste Management, Inc.
　800 Capitol St Ste 3000
　Houston TX 77002
　713 512-6200

(P-12957)
MAIN STREET FIBERS INC
608 E Main St, Ontario (91761-1711)
P.O. Box 51491 (91761-0091)
PHONE...................................909 986-6310
Gregory S Young, *CEO*
Wayne Young, *President*
Ernie Alvarez, *CFO*
Steve Young, *Corp Secy*
Mary Gomez, *Human Resources*
EMP: 60
SQ FT: 25,000
SALES (est): 46MM **Privately Held**
WEB: www.mainstreetfibers.com
SIC: **4953** Recycling, waste materials

(P-12958)
MARBORG INDUSTRIES (PA)
728 E Yanonali St, Santa Barbara
(93103-3233)
P.O. Box 4127 (93140-4127)
PHONE...................................805 963-1852
Mario Borgatello Jr, *President*
David Borgatello, *CFO*
Peter Tierney, *Department Mgr*
Anthony Borgatello, *General Mgr*
Richard Barnes, *CIO*
EMP: 250 EST: 1974
SALES (est): 52.3MM **Privately Held**
WEB: www.marborg.com
SIC: **4953** 7359 7699 4212 Rubbish col-
　lection & disposal; portable toilet rental;
　septic tank cleaning service; local truck-
　ing, without storage

(P-12959)
MARBORG RECOVERY LP
14470 Calle Real, Goleta (93117-9732)
PHONE...................................805 963-1852
Brian Borgatello, *Partner*
EMP: 250 EST: 2016

SALES (est): 25.9MM
SALES (corp-wide): 52.3MM **Privately
Held**
WEB: www.marborg.com
SIC: **4953** Recycling, waste materials
PA: Marborg Industries
728 E Yanonali St
Santa Barbara CA 93103
805 963-1852

(P-12960)
MISSION COUNTRY DISPOSAL
4388 Old Santa Fe Rd, San Luis Obispo
(93401-8160)
PHONE....................805 543-0875
Ron Middlestaff, *President*
EMP: 67 EST: 1978
SQ FT: 1,200
SALES (est): 7MM
SALES (corp-wide): 5.4B **Privately Held**
WEB: www.sanluisgarbage.com
SIC: **4953** Garbage: collecting, destroying
& processing
HQ: Waste Connections Us, Inc.
3 Waterway Square Pl # 110
The Woodlands TX 77380

(P-12961)
MP ENVIRONMENTAL SVCS INC
(PA)
Also Called: M P Vacuum Truck Service
3400 Manor St, Bakersfield (93308-1451)
P.O. Box 80358 (93380-0358)
PHONE....................800 458-3036
Dawn Calderwood, *President*
Shawn Calderwood, *Vice Pres*
Jamie Robinson, *Office Mgr*
Laren Kaufman, *Project Mgr*
Jesse Soltero, *Project Mgr*
▲ EMP: 117 EST: 1991
SQ FT: 8,000
SALES (est): 71MM **Privately Held**
WEB: www.mpenviro.com
SIC: **4953** 4213 8748 7699 Hazardous
waste collection & disposal; radioactive
waste materials, disposal; trucking, ex-
cept local; environmental consultant; tank
repair & cleaning services

(P-12962)
ORANGE COUNTY SANITATION
(PA)
10844 Ellis Ave, Fountain Valley
(92708-7018)
P.O. Box 8127 (92728-8127)
PHONE....................714 962-2411
James Herberg, *General Mgr*
Raju Patel, *Vice Pres*
Jim Herberg, *General Mgr*
James Ruth, *General Mgr*
Isabel Arango, *Technician*
▲ EMP: 300 EST: 1954
SALES (est): 315.4MM **Privately Held**
WEB: www.ocsan.gov
SIC: **4953** Waste materials, disposal at sea

(P-12963)
PALM SPRINGS DISPOSAL
SERVICES
4690 E Mesquite Ave, Palm Springs
(92264-3510)
P.O. Box 2711 (92263-2711)
PHONE....................760 327-1351
Frederic Wade, *CEO*
James Cunningham, *President*
Mike Jaycox, *Treasurer*
Ray Wade, *Vice Pres*
Rick Wade, *General Mgr*
EMP: 82
SQ FT: 2,000
SALES (est): 14MM **Privately Held**
WEB: www.palmspringsdisposal.com
SIC: **4953** Recycling, waste materials

(P-12964)
PENAS DISPOSAL INC
Also Called: Pena's Recycling Center
12094 Avenue 408, Cutler (93615-2055)
PHONE....................559 528-3909
Gabriel Pena, *President*
Maria Pena, *COO*
Art Pena, *Vice Pres*
Arthur Pena, *Vice Pres*
Lupe Felix, *Office Spvr*
EMP: 91

SQ FT: 1,000
SALES (est): 17.8MM **Privately Held**
WEB: www.penasdisposal.com
SIC: **4953** Recycling, waste materials

(P-12965)
PJBS HOLDINGS INC (PA)
Also Called: Benz - One Complete Operation
1401 Goodrick Dr, Tehachapi (93561-1532)
P.O. Box 1750 (93581-1750)
PHONE....................661 822-5273
Paul Benz, *CEO*
Louis Visco, *COO*
Joan Benz, *Corp Secy*
Julie Sanchez, *Human Resources*
Alison Ledwidge, *Director*
EMP: 75 EST: 1975
SQ FT: 4,500
SALES (est): 23.3MM **Privately Held**
WEB: www.benz.blue
SIC: **4953** 4212 Refuse collection & dis-
posal services; petroleum haulage, local

(P-12966)
PORTA - KAN SANITATION INC
(PA)
4320 San Gbriel Rver Pkwy, Pico Rivera
(90660-1837)
P.O. Box 2042, Glendale (91209-2042)
PHONE....................562 463-8282
Gevik Hovsepian, *CEO*
▲ EMP: 146 EST: 2005
SALES (est): 503.7K **Privately Held**
SIC: **4953** Rubbish collection & disposal

(P-12967)
POTENTIAL INDUSTRIES INC
(PA)
922 E E St, Wilmington (90744-6145)
P.O. Box 293 (90748-0293)
PHONE....................310 807-4466
Anthony J Fan, *President*
Tony Fan, *President*
Henry J Chen, *CEO*
Jessica Chen, *Treasurer*
Jessie Chen, *Corp Secy*
◆ EMP: 149 EST: 1975
SQ FT: 45,000
SALES (est): 48.1MM **Privately Held**
WEB: www.potentialindustries.com
SIC: **4953** 5093 Recycling, waste materi-
als; scrap & waste materials

(P-12968)
R PLANET EARTH LLC
3200 Fruitland Ave, Vernon (90058-3718)
PHONE....................213 320-0601
Robert Daviduk, *President*
Alan Cherry, *Human Res Dir*
Mario Lozano, *Human Resources*
Phil Barhouse, *Director*
EMP: 135 EST: 2013
SALES (est): 11.7MM **Privately Held**
WEB: www.rplanetearth.com
SIC: **4953** 2611 Recycling, waste materi-
als; pulp mills, mechanical & recycling
processing; pulp manufactured from
waste or recycled paper

(P-12969)
RAINBOW DISPOSAL CO INC
(HQ)
Also Called: Rainbow Refuse Recycling
17121 Nichols Ln, Huntington Beach
(92647-5719)
P.O. Box 1026 (92647-1026)
PHONE....................714 847-3581
Jerry Moffatt, *CEO*
Stan Tkaczyck, *President*
Cynthia Covarrubias, *Opers Staff*
Francisco Espinoza, *Opers Staff*
Octavio Camacho, *Asst Mgr*
EMP: 115 EST: 1956
SQ FT: 6,000
SALES (est): 48.2MM
SALES (corp-wide): 10.1B **Publicly Held**
WEB: www.republicservices.com
SIC: **4953** Garbage: collecting, destroying
& processing; recycling, waste materials
PA: Republic Services, Inc.
18500 N Allied Way # 100
Phoenix AZ 85054
480 627-2700

(P-12970)
RECYCLER CORE COMPANY
INC
Also Called: Northwest Recycler Core
2727 Kansas Ave, Riverside (92507-2638)
PHONE....................951 276-1687
Kenneth Meier, *President*
Gisela Meier, *Corp Secy*
Robert Palmer, *Executive*
Greg Meier, *General Mgr*
Simona Johnson, *Office Mgr*
▲ EMP: 100 EST: 1984
SQ FT: 280,000
SALES (est): 16MM **Privately Held**
WEB: www.rccauto.com
SIC: **4953** Recycling, waste materials

(P-12971)
RERUBBER LLC
115 N Del Rosa Dr Ste C, San Bernardino
(92408-0192)
PHONE....................909 786-2811
J D Wang, *CEO*
Kc Tarn, *COO*
Ken Winters, *Vice Pres*
Oscar Lopez, *Engineer*
Enertech Solutions LLC, *Mng Member*
▲ EMP: 19 EST: 2007
SALES (est): 14.4MM **Privately Held**
WEB: www.rerubber.com
SIC: **4953** 3069 Recycling, waste materi-
als; type, rubber
PA: Enertech Solutions, Llc
30515 7th Ave
Redlands CA 92374

(P-12972)
RUUHWA DANN AND
ASSOCIATES INC (PA)
Also Called: Cal Micro
1541 Brooks St, Ontario (91762-3619)
PHONE....................909 467-4800
Ruuhwa Dann, *CEO*
Harry Saliba, *President*
Al Cortez, *Manager*
▲ EMP: 76 EST: 2002
SQ FT: 88,000
SALES (est): 22.3MM **Privately Held**
WEB: www.calmicrousa.com
SIC: **4953** Recycling, waste materials

(P-12973)
SA RECYCLING LLC
11614 Eastend Ave, Chino (91710-1557)
PHONE....................909 622-3337
EMP: 68
SALES (corp-wide): 49.7MM **Privately
Held**
SIC: **4953** 5093 Refuse Systems Whol
Scrap/Waste Mat
PA: Sa Recycling Llc
2411 N Glassell St
Orange CA 92865
714 632-2000

(P-12974)
SA RECYCLING LLC (PA)
2411 N Glassell St, Orange (92865-2717)
PHONE....................714 632-2000
George Adams, *Mng Member*
Mark Sweetman, *CFO*
Steve Weiner, *Vice Pres*
Kyle Hardenburg, *Executive*
Abigail Delangel, *General Mgr*
◆ EMP: 160 EST: 2007
SQ FT: 40,000
SALES (est): 742.7MM **Privately Held**
WEB: www.sarecycling.com
SIC: **4953** Recycling, waste materials

(P-12975)
SA RECYCLING LLC
42353 8th St E, Lancaster (93535-5439)
PHONE....................661 723-1383
EMP: 68
SALES (corp-wide): 49.7MM **Privately
Held**
SIC: **4953** Refuse System
PA: Sa Recycling Llc
2411 N Glassell St
Orange CA 92865
714 632-2000

(P-12976)
SANITEC INDUSTRIES INC
10700 Sherman Way, Burbank
(91505-1042)
PHONE....................818 523-1942
James Harkess, *President*
▲ EMP: 75 EST: 2003
SQ FT: 200,000
SALES (est): 8.3MM **Privately Held**
WEB: www.sanitecind.com
SIC: **4953** 5047 Medical waste disposal;
medical & hospital equipment

(P-12977)
SANITTION DSTRCTS LOS
ANGLES C
1955 Workman Mill Rd, Whittier
(90601-1415)
P.O. Box 4998 (90607-4998)
PHONE....................562 908-4288
Steve McGuin, *Manager*
John Boyd, *Vice Chairman*
Cari Johnson, *Executive*
Grace Robinson Chan, *General Mgr*
Sam Perdoza, *General Mgr*
EMP: 1698 EST: 2007
SALES (est): 467.6MM
SALES (corp-wide): 627MM **Privately
Held**
WEB: www.lacsd.org
SIC: **4953** Sanitary landfill operation
PA: County Sanitation District No. 2 Of Los
Angeles County
1955 Workman Mill Rd
Whittier CA 90601
562 699-7411

(P-12978)
SEA/SUE INC (HQ)
Also Called: Anderson Rubbish Disposal
195 W Los Angeles Ave, Simi Valley
(93065-1651)
PHONE....................805 526-1919
Chuck Anderson, *President*
Susan Anderson, *CEO*
James Safechuck, *Vice Pres*
Lorenn Kouri, *Admin Sec*
EMP: 184 EST: 1972
SQ FT: 3,000
SALES (est): 52.3MM
SALES (corp-wide): 15.2B **Publicly Held**
WEB: www.wm.com
SIC: **4953** Garbage: collecting, destroying
& processing
PA: Waste Management, Inc.
800 Capitol St Ste 3000
Houston TX 77002
713 512-6200

(P-12979)
SELF SERVE AUTO
DISMANTLERS (PA)
Also Called: Adams Steel
3200 E Frontera St, Anaheim (92806-2822)
P.O. Box 6258 (92816-0258)
PHONE....................714 630-8901
George Adams Jr, *President*
Wendy Adams, *CFO*
Mike Adams, *Vice Pres*
Thomas Knippel, *Vice Pres*
David Cassele, *General Mgr*
◆ EMP: 120 EST: 1987
SQ FT: 41,000
SALES (est): 47.1MM **Privately Held**
SIC: **4953** Recycling, waste materials

(P-12980)
SMC GREASE SPECIALIST INC
1600 W Pellisier Rd, Colton (92324-3301)
P.O. Box 79200, Corona (92877-0173)
PHONE....................951 788-6042
Salvatore Coco, *President*
EMP: 27 EST: 2003
SQ FT: 2,500
SALES (est): 5.9MM **Privately Held**
WEB: www.smcgrease.com
SIC: **4953** 2992 Recycling, waste materi-
als; oils & greases, blending & com-
pounding

(PA)=Parent Co (HQ)=Headquarters (DH)=Div Headquarters

✪ = New Business established in last 2 years

(P-12981)
SOLAG INCORPORATED
Also Called: Solag Disposal Co
31641 Ortege Hwy, San Juan Capistrano (92675)
PHONE..................................949 728-1206
Clifford Ronnenberg, *Ch of Bd*
Patricia Leyes, *Vice Pres*
EMP: 476 **EST:** 1958
SALES (est): 3.6MM
SALES (corp-wide): 335.2MM **Privately Held**
WEB: www.crrwasteservices.com
SIC: 4953 4212 Rubbish collection & disposal; local trucking, without storage
PA: Cr&R Incorporated
   11292 Western Ave
   Stanton CA 90680
   714 826-9049

(P-12982)
SOUTH COUNTY SANITARY SVC INC
Also Called: Nopomo Garbage
4388 Old Santa Fe Rd, San Luis Obispo (93401-8160)
PHONE..................................805 489-4246
Alvizio Rizzoli, *President*
Dorothy Pasco, *Corp Secy*
EMP: 94 **EST:** 1963
SALES (est): 6.5MM
SALES (corp-wide): 5.4B **Privately Held**
WEB: www.sanluisgarbage.com
SIC: 4953 Garbage: collecting, destroying & processing
HQ: Waste Connections Us, Inc.
   3 Waterway Square Pl # 110
   The Woodlands TX 77380

(P-12983)
STAR SCRAP METAL COMPANY INC
1509 S Bluff Rd, Montebello (90640-6601)
PHONE..................................562 921-5045
Rose Starow Stein, *President*
Allen Stein, *Vice Pres*
Zack Stein, *Vice Pres*
Veronica Mummert, *Human Resources*
David Stein, *Marketing Mgr*
▼ **EMP:** 70 **EST:** 1974
SQ FT: 600
SALES (est): 12.3MM **Privately Held**
WEB: www.sarecycling.com
SIC: 4953 Recycling, waste materials

(P-12984)
STRATEGIC MATERIALS INC
7000 Bandini Blvd, Commerce (90040-3303)
PHONE..................................323 887-6831
Sal Ramirez, *Manager*
EMP: 65
SALES (corp-wide): 474MM **Privately Held**
WEB: www.smi.com
SIC: 4953 Recycling, waste materials
HQ: Strategic Materials, Inc.
   17220 Katy Fwy Ste 150
   Houston TX 77094

(P-12985)
TALCO PLASTICS INC (PA)
1000 W Rincon St, Corona (92878-9228)
PHONE..................................951 531-2000
John L Shedd Sr, *Chairman*
John L Shedd Jr, *President*
Bill O 'grady, *Vice Pres*
William O'Grady, *Vice Pres*
Ajit Perera, *Vice Pres*
EMP: 85 **EST:** 1972
SQ FT: 110,000
SALES (est): 36.8MM **Privately Held**
WEB: www.talcoplastics.com
SIC: 4953 2821 Recycling, waste materials; plastics materials & resins

(P-12986)
UNITED PACIFIC WASTE
4334 San Gbriel Rver Pkwy, Pico Rivera (90660-1837)
P.O. Box 908 (90660-0908)
PHONE..................................562 699-7600
Michael Kandilian, *President*

Mike Kandilian, *Exec VP*
Shawna Kandilian, *Admin Sec*
EMP: 70 **EST:** 2001
SQ FT: 3,500
SALES (est): 12MM **Privately Held**
WEB: www.crrwasteservices.com
SIC: 4953 4213 Garbage: collecting, destroying & processing; rubbish collection & disposal; contract haulers

(P-12987)
USA WASTE OF CALIFORNIA INC
Also Called: Los Angeles City Hauling
9081 Tujunga Ave, Sun Valley (91352-1516)
P.O. Box 541, Los Angeles (90078-0541)
PHONE..................................818 252-3112
Jim Fish, *CEO*
EMP: 100
SALES (corp-wide): 15.2B **Publicly Held**
SIC: 4953 Recycling, waste materials
HQ: Usa Waste Of California, Inc.
   11931 Foundation Pl # 200
   Gold River CA 95670
   916 387-1400

(P-12988)
VALLEY GARBAGE RUBBISH CO INC
Also Called: Heallth Sanitation Services
1850 W Betteravia Rd, Santa Maria (93455-1065)
PHONE..................................805 614-1131
Keith Ramsey, *Principal*
EMP: 146 **EST:** 1957
SQ FT: 3,000
SALES (est): 41.3MM
SALES (corp-wide): 15.2B **Publicly Held**
WEB: www.wmhss.wm.com
SIC: 4953 Garbage: collecting, destroying & processing
PA: Waste Management, Inc.
   800 Capitol St Ste 3000
   Houston TX 77002
   713 512-6200

(P-12989)
VARNER BROS INC
1808 Roberts Ln, Bakersfield (93308-2228)
P.O. Box 80427 (93380-0427)
PHONE..................................661 399-2944
Vernon Varner, *CEO*
Elvey L Varner, *President*
EMP: 96 **EST:** 1959
SQ FT: 12,000
SALES (est): 9.4MM **Privately Held**
WEB: www.varnerbros.com
SIC: 4953 Garbage: collecting, destroying & processing

(P-12990)
VENTURA RGIONAL SANITATION DST
3500 Toland Rd, Santa Paula (93060-9639)
PHONE..................................805 525-8217
Gary Haden, *Branch Mgr*
EMP: 51
SQ FT: 840
SALES (corp-wide): 20.2MM **Privately Held**
WEB: www.vrsd.com
SIC: 4953 Sanitary landfill operation
PA: Ventura Regional Sanitation District
   1001 Partridge Dr Ste 150
   Ventura CA
   805 658-4600

(P-12991)
VICTORVILLE DISPOSAL INC
9890 Cherry Ave, Fontana (92335-5202)
PHONE..................................909 429-4200
Edward G Burr, *Chairman*
Cole Burr, *President*
David Marriner, *CFO*
Tracy A Burr, *Vice Pres*
Eric D Herbert, *Vice Pres*
EMP: 60 **EST:** 1952
SQ FT: 1,900
SALES (est): 3.6MM
SALES (corp-wide): 320.1MM **Privately Held**
WEB: www.burrtec.com
SIC: 4953 Rubbish collection & disposal

HQ: Burrtec Waste Industries, Inc.
   9890 Cherry Ave
   Fontana CA 92335
   909 429-4200

(P-12992)
WARE DISPOSAL INC
1451 Manhattan Ave, Fullerton (92831-5221)
PHONE..................................714 834-0234
Judith Helaine Ware, *CEO*
Ben Ware, *Vice Pres*
Jay Ware, *General Mgr*
Lucy Aguilar, *Office Mgr*
Jason Rush, *Technology*
EMP: 120 **EST:** 1970
SQ FT: 48,900
SALES (est): 30.3MM **Privately Held**
WEB: www.waredisposal.com
SIC: 4953 Refuse collection & disposal services

(P-12993)
WASTE MANAGEMENT CAL INC (HQ)
9081 Tujunga Ave, Sun Valley (91352-1516)
PHONE..................................877 836-6526
Ken Maxey, *General Mgr*
Rebecca Zayatz, *Engineer*
Mary Nordin, *Clerk*
EMP: 230 **EST:** 1953
SQ FT: 35,000
SALES (est): 340.5MM
SALES (corp-wide): 15.2B **Publicly Held**
WEB: www.wm.com
SIC: 4953 Garbage: collecting, destroying & processing; recycling, waste materials
PA: Waste Management, Inc.
   800 Capitol St Ste 3000
   Houston TX 77002
   713 512-6200

(P-12994)
WASTE MANAGEMENT CAL INC
1200 W City Ranch Rd, Palmdale (93551-4456)
PHONE..................................661 947-7197
Carl McCarthy, *Manager*
EMP: 117
SALES (corp-wide): 15.2B **Publicly Held**
SIC: 4953 Rubbish collection & disposal
HQ: Waste Management Of California, Inc.
   9081 Tujunga Ave
   Sun Valley CA 91352
   877 836-6526

(P-12995)
WASTE MANAGEMENT CAL INC
2801 N Madera Rd, Simi Valley (93065-6208)
PHONE..................................805 522-7023
Scott Tignac, *Manager*
EMP: 117
SALES (corp-wide): 15.2B **Publicly Held**
SIC: 4953 Recycling, waste materials
HQ: Waste Management Of California, Inc.
   9081 Tujunga Ave
   Sun Valley CA 91352
   877 836-6526

(P-12996)
WASTE MANAGEMENT CAL INC
10910 Dawson Canyon Rd, Corona (92883-5020)
PHONE..................................951 277-1740
Damon De Frates, *Branch Mgr*
EMP: 117
SALES (corp-wide): 15.2B **Publicly Held**
SIC: 4953 Garbage: collecting, destroying & processing
HQ: Waste Management Of California, Inc.
   9081 Tujunga Ave
   Sun Valley CA 91352
   877 836-6526

(P-12997)
WASTE MGT COLLECTN RECYCL INC
17700 Indian St, Moreno Valley (92551-9511)
PHONE..................................951 242-0421
Scott Jenkins, *Manager*
Carson Brown, *Manager*
EMP: 88

SALES (corp-wide): 15.2B **Publicly Held**
SIC: 4953 Recycling, waste materials
HQ: Waste Management Collection And Recycling, Inc.
   1001 Fannin St Ste 4000
   Houston TX 77002

(P-12998)
WASTE MGT COLLECTN RECYCL INC
13940 Live Oak Ave, Baldwin Park (91706-1321)
PHONE..................................626 960-7551
Rick Decaiva, *Manager*
EMP: 88
SALES (corp-wide): 15.2B **Publicly Held**
SIC: 4953 4212 Rubbish collection & disposal; local trucking, without storage
HQ: Waste Management Collection And Recycling, Inc.
   1001 Fannin St Ste 4000
   Houston TX 77002

(P-12999)
WASTE MGT COLLECTN RECYCL INC
1449 W Rosecrans Ave, Gardena (90249-2639)
P.O. Box 1428 (90249-0428)
PHONE..................................310 532-6511
Dave Hauser, *Principal*
EMP: 88
SALES (corp-wide): 15.2B **Publicly Held**
SIC: 4953 5064 Garbage: collecting, destroying & processing; garbage disposals
HQ: Waste Management Collection And Recycling, Inc.
   1001 Fannin St Ste 4000
   Houston TX 77002

(P-13000)
WASTE MGT COLLECTN RECYCL INC
16122 Construction Cir E, Irvine (92606-4498)
PHONE..................................949 451-2600
Fidel Gutierrez, *Branch Mgr*
David Steiner, *CEO*
EMP: 88
SALES (corp-wide): 15.2B **Publicly Held**
SIC: 4953 4212 Recycling, waste materials; garbage collection & transport, no disposal
HQ: Waste Management Collection And Recycling, Inc.
   1001 Fannin St Ste 4000
   Houston TX 77002

(P-13001)
WASTE MGT COLLECTN RECYCL INC
17700 Indian St, Moreno Valley (92551-9511)
PHONE..................................909 242-0421
EMP: 88
SALES (corp-wide): 15.23 **Publicly Held**
SIC: 4953 Recycling, waste materials
HQ: Waste Management Collection And Recycling, Inc.
   1001 Fannin St Ste 4000
   Houston TX 77002

(P-13002)
YUCAIPA DISPOSAL INC
9890 Cherry Ave, Fontana (92335-5202)
PHONE..................................909 429-4200
Cole Burr, *President*
David R Marriner, *CFO*
EMP: 104 **EST:** 1959
SQ FT: 1,500
SALES (est): 4.1MM
SALES (corp-wide): 320.1MM **Privately Held**
WEB: www.burrtec.com
SIC: 4953 4212 Rubbish collection & disposal; local trucking, without storage
PA: Burrtec Waste Group, Inc.
   9890 Cherry Ave
   Fontana CA 92335
   909 429-4200

(P-13003)
ZEREP MANAGEMENT CORPORATION (PA)
17445 Railroad St, City of Industry (91748-1026)
PHONE..................626 968-1796
Manuel Perez, *CEO*
Jesse Quintana, *CFO*
Min Kim, *Accountant*
Jose Low, *Human Res Mgr*
Andrew Palomares, *Opers Mgr*
EMP: 59 EST: 1970
SQ FT: 4,000
SALES (est): 47MM **Privately Held**
SIC: 4953 4212 Refuse collection & disposal services; local trucking, without storage

---

4959 Sanitary Svcs, NEC

(P-13004)
AMPCO CONTRACTING INC
1420 S Allec St, Anaheim (92805-6305)
PHONE..................949 955-2255
Andrew Pennor, *President*
Michael King, *Vice Chairman*
Matthew Suiter, *President*
Benjamin Reynolds, *CFO*
Reggie Kama, *Officer*
EMP: 220 EST: 2004
SALES (est): 53.1MM **Privately Held**
WEB: www.ampcocontracting.com
SIC: 4959 1795 1794 Environmental cleanup services; wrecking & demolition work; excavation & grading, building construction

(P-13005)
CLEANSTREET LLC
1937 W 169th St, Gardena (90247-5253)
PHONE..................800 225-7316
Christopher Valerian, *President*
Claudia Cervantes, *Executive*
Debby Garnica, *Admin Asst*
Angie Cruz, *Administration*
Mayra Peralta, *Administration*
EMP: 194 EST: 1965
SQ FT: 15,000
SALES (est): 25.5MM
SALES (corp-wide): 352.1MM **Privately Held**
WEB: www.cleanstreet.com
SIC: 4959 Sweeping service: road, airport, parking lot, etc.
HQ: Sweeping Corporation Of America, Inc.
4141 Rockside Rd Ste 100
Seven Hills OH 44131

(P-13006)
COUNTY SNTTION DST NO 2 LOS AN (PA)
Also Called: L.A.cO.
1955 Workman Mill Rd, Whittier (90601-1415)
P.O. Box 4998 (90607-4998)
PHONE..................562 699-7411
Stephen Maguin, *General Mgr*
Amy Smet, *Bd of Directors*
Dan Sanchez,
Sam Perdoza, *General Mgr*
Rechelle Asperin, *Admin Sec*
EMP: 850 EST: 1924
SALES (est): 627MM **Privately Held**
SIC: 4959 Sanitary services

(P-13007)
JONSET CORPORATION
Also Called: Sunset Property Services
16251 Construction Cir W, Irvine (92606-4412)
PHONE..................949 551-5151
John Howhannesian, *President*
Andrea Howhannesian, *General Mgr*
Carmen Howhannesian, *Admin Sec*
Andrea E Howhannesian, *Opers Staff*
Angie Ramos, *Manager*
EMP: 96 EST: 1968
SQ FT: 6,000
SALES (est): 9.4MM **Privately Held**
SIC: 4959 7349 Sweeping service: road, airport, parking lot, etc.; janitorial service, contract basis

(P-13008)
RHO CHEM LLC (DH)
425 Isis Ave, Inglewood (90301-2076)
PHONE..................323 776-6234
Ramon Robles, *CEO*
▲ EMP: 50 EST: 2008
SALES (est): 17.3MM
SALES (corp-wide): 2.6B **Publicly Held**
SIC: 4959 Sanitary services
HQ: Nortru, Llc
515 Lycaste St
Detroit MI 48214
313 824-5840

4961 Steam & Air Conditioning Sply

(P-13009)
CGP HOLDINGS LLC
2 Gill Station Coastal Rd, Little Lake (93542)
PHONE..................760 764-1300
Joe Greco, *CEO*
EMP: 82 EST: 2007
SALES (est): 5.5MM **Privately Held**
SIC: 4961 Steam supply systems, including geothermal

4971 Irrigation Systems

(P-13010)
CORCORAN IRRIGATION DISTRICT
1150 6 1/2 Ave, Corcoran (93212-9656)
P.O. Box 566 (93212-0566)
PHONE..................559 992-5165
Peter Rietkerk, *President*
Jean Kilgore, *General Mgr*
EMP: 58 EST: 1920
SQ FT: 1,000
SALES (est): 14.5MM **Privately Held**
WEB: www.cityofcorcoran.com
SIC: 4971 Water distribution or supply systems for irrigation

(P-13011)
IMPERIAL IRRIGATION DISTRICT
Also Called: Imperial Irrgtion Dst Wtr Dept
333 E Barioni Blvd, Imperial (92251-1773)
P.O. Box 937 (92251-0937)
PHONE..................760 339-9220
Robert McCullough, *Branch Mgr*
EMP: 50
SQ FT: 10,000
SALES (corp-wide): 705.4MM **Privately Held**
WEB: www.iid.com
SIC: 4971 Water distribution or supply systems for irrigation
PA: Imperial Irrigation District
333 E Barioni Blvd
Imperial CA 92251
800 303-7756

(P-13012)
IMPERIAL IRRIGATION DISTRICT
Also Called: Imperial Dam
2400 Imperial Rd, Winterhaven (92283-9797)
PHONE..................760 572-0392
Bobby L Moore, *Branch Mgr*
EMP: 50
SALES (corp-wide): 705.4MM **Privately Held**
WEB: www.iid.com
SIC: 4971 Water distribution or supply systems for irrigation
PA: Imperial Irrigation District
333 E Barioni Blvd
Imperial CA 92251
800 303-7756

(P-13013)
OAK SPRINGS NURSERY INC
13761 Eldridge Ave, Sylmar (91342-1764)
P.O. Box 922906 (91392-2906)
PHONE..................818 367-5832
Manuel Cacho, *President*
EMP: 90 EST: 1993
SALES (est): 11.6MM **Privately Held**
SIC: 4971 0781 Irrigation systems; landscape services

(P-13014)
PALO VERDE IRRIGATION DISTRICT
180 W 14th Ave, Blythe (92225-2714)
PHONE..................760 922-3144
Ed Smith, *General Mgr*
Janice Love, *Treasurer*
Charlie Defreese, *Superintendent*
EMP: 85 EST: 1923
SQ FT: 8,125
SALES (est): 14MM **Privately Held**
WEB: www.pvid.org
SIC: 4971 Water distribution or supply systems for irrigation

(P-13015)
UNITED IRRIGATION INC
44907 Golf Center Pkwy # 3, Indio (92201-7303)
PHONE..................760 347-6161
Anthony Cunzio, *President*
Samantha Chisholm, *Admin Sec*
Mark Avon, *Controller*
EMP: 60 EST: 2002
SQ FT: 1,300
SALES (est): 26.9MM **Privately Held**
WEB: www.unitedgli.com
SIC: 4971 Irrigation systems

5012 Automobiles & Other Motor Vehicles Wholesale

(P-13016)
A-Z BUS SALES INC (PA)
Also Called: John Deere Authorized Dealer
1900 S Riverside Ave, Colton (92324-3344)
PHONE..................951 781-7188
Edwin John Landherr, *CEO*
James Reynolds, *President*
Clay Hartman, *Treasurer*
Tessa Sebeni, *Administration*
Ashley Villalpando, *Administration*
▼ EMP: 90 EST: 1984
SQ FT: 20,000
SALES: 3.9MM **Privately Held**
WEB: www.a-zbus.com
SIC: 5012 5082 Buses; construction & mining machinery

(P-13017)
ABC BUS INC
1485 Dale Way, Costa Mesa (92626-3918)
PHONE..................714 444-5888
Dane Cornell, *CEO*
Kathy Henderson, *Business Anlyst*
Lance Martin, *Sales Associate*
Jake Benson, *Accounts Mgr*
EMP: 85
SALES (corp-wide): 182.4MM **Privately Held**
WEB: www.abc-companies.com
SIC: 5012 4173 Buses; bus terminal & service facilities
HQ: Abc Bus, Inc.
1506 30th St Nw
Faribault MN 55021
507 334-1871

(P-13018)
AMERICAN HONDA MOTOR CO INC (HQ)
1919 Torrance Blvd, Torrance (90501-2722)
P.O. Box 2200 (90509-2200)
PHONE..................310 783-2000
Noriya Kaihara, *CEO*
Desmond Tamaki, *Partner*
Martin Varela, *Partner*
Ed Maurer, *Managing Prtnr*
Takanobu Ito, *President*
◆ EMP: 2375 EST: 1959
SALES (est): 12.8B **Privately Held**
WEB: www.hondacertified.com
SIC: 5012 3732 Automobiles; jet skis

(P-13019)
AQUIRECORPS NORWALK AUTO AUCTN
12405 Rosecrans Ave, Norwalk (90650-5056)
PHONE..................562 864-7464
Rj Romero, *Ch of Bd*
Lou Rudich, *COO*

Steve Fleurant, *CFO*
Chuck Doskow, *Admin Sec*
David Aker, *Controller*
EMP: 125 EST: 1979
SQ FT: 55,000
SALES (est): 34MM **Privately Held**
WEB: www.norwalkautoauction.com
SIC: 5012 Automobile auction

(P-13020)
AUTO BUYLINE SYSTEMS INC (PA)
Also Called: A B S Auto Auctions
341 Corporate Terrace Cir, Corona (92879-6028)
P.O. Box 78086 (92877-0136)
PHONE..................951 271-8999
Thomas Harmon, *President*
Richard Stankiewicz, *Business Dir*
John Addington, *District Mgr*
Larry Champagne, *District Mgr*
Carl Loizzi, *District Mgr*
EMP: 50 EST: 1992
SQ FT: 23,000
SALES (est): 26.9MM **Privately Held**
WEB: www.absautoauctions.com
SIC: 5012 Automobile auction

(P-13021)
BARGAIN RENT-A-CAR
Also Called: Lexus of Cerritos
18800 Studebaker Rd, Cerritos (90703-5339)
PHONE..................562 865-7447
Afshin Kahensohayegh, *Manager*
Lewis M Webb, *President*
Sarah Ventresca, *Asst Mgr*
EMP: 130 EST: 1960
SALES (est): 44.4MM
SALES (corp-wide): 20.3B **Publicly Held**
WEB: www.cerritoslexus.com
SIC: 5511 5521 5012 Automobiles, new & used; used car dealers; automobiles & other motor vehicles
HQ: Webb Automotive Group, Inc.
200 Sw 1st Ave
Fort Lauderdale FL 33301
954 769-7000

(P-13022)
CALIFRNIA AUTO DALERS EXCH LLC
Also Called: Riverside Auto Auction
1320 N Tustin Ave, Anaheim (92807-1619)
PHONE..................714 996-2400
Tim Van Dam, *General Mgr*
Karen Gage-Ellsworth, *Office Mgr*
Kory Serrajian, *Controller*
Mark Emigh, *Opers Mgr*
Joe Coniglione, *Security Mgr*
EMP: 400 EST: 1985
SALES (est): 70.7MM
SALES (corp-wide): 1.6MM **Privately Held**
WEB: www.manheim.com
SIC: 5012 Automobile auction
HQ: Manheim Investments, Inc.
6205 Pachtree Dunwoody Rd
Atlanta GA 30328
866 626-4346

(P-13023)
CENTER AUTOMOTIVE INC
Also Called: Center B M W
5201 Van Nuys Blvd, Sherman Oaks (91401-5618)
PHONE..................818 907-9995
David Farguson, *President*
Donna Banaka, *Admin Sec*
Poun Gefrerer, *Administration*
Nathan Litt, *Finance Mgr*
Frank Castanon, *Plant Mgr*
EMP: 85 EST: 1968
SQ FT: 50,000
SALES (est): 27.9MM **Privately Held**
WEB: www.bmwshermanoaks.com
SIC: 5511 5012 Automobiles, new & used; automobiles & other motor vehicles

(P-13024)
E M THARP INC (PA)
Also Called: Golden Peterbilt
15243 Road 192, Porterville (93257-8967)
PHONE..................559 782-5800
Morris Tharp, *President*
Morris A Tharp, *President*

Ursula Ybarra, *Executive*
Randy Ray, *Marketing Staff*
Pat Cornaggia, *Sales Staff*
EMP: 55 **EST:** 1952
SALES (est): 46.2MM **Privately Held**
WEB: www.emtharp.com
SIC: 5012 5013 5511 5531 Trucks, commercial; truck parts & accessories; trucks, tractors & trailers: new & used; truck equipment & parts; recreational vehicle repairs

(P-13025)
EMERGENCY VEHICLE GROUP INC
Also Called: E V G
2883 E Coronado St Ste A, Anaheim (92806-2552)
PHONE................714 238-0110
Travis Grinstead, *President*
Sherry Grinstead, *Admin Asst*
Ali Mahmoudi, *Opers Mgr*
Stephen Carleton, *Sales Dir*
Adam Halliwell,
EMP: 25 **EST:** 2005
SQ FT: 15,000
SALES (est): 8.4MM **Privately Held**
WEB: www.evginc.net
SIC: 5511 5012 3569 5013 Trucks, tractors & trailers: new & used; ambulances; firefighting apparatus; motor vehicle supplies & new parts

(P-13026)
FORD OF SANTA MONICA INC
1230 Santa Monica Blvd, Santa Monica (90404-1706)
PHONE................310 451-1588
Ron Davis, *Owner*
Abigail Colcol, *Admin Asst*
Simon Kerendian, *Finance Mgr*
Larry Rosen, *Controller*
Dan Pulido, *Foreman/Supr*
EMP: 92 **EST:** 1948
SQ FT: 15,500
SALES (est): 36.4MM **Privately Held**
WEB: www.smford.com
SIC: 5511 5012 Automobiles, new & used; ambulances

(P-13027)
HAAKER EQUIPMENT COMPANY (PA)
Also Called: Total Clean
2070 N White Ave, La Verne (91750-5679)
PHONE................909 598-2706
Edward R Blackman, *CEO*
Randy Blackman, *President*
Edward C Haaker, *CFO*
Nick Tomas, *Area Mgr*
Wilson Shyu, *General Mgr*
▼ **EMP:** 60
SQ FT: 50,000
SALES (est): 56.2MM **Privately Held**
WEB: www.haaker.com
SIC: 5012 5087 5999 Ambulances; cleaning & maintenance equipment & supplies; cleaning equipment & supplies

(P-13028)
HARBILL INC
Also Called: Crest Chevrolet
909 W 21st St, San Bernardino (92405-3201)
P.O. Box 501 (92402-0501)
PHONE................909 883-8833
D William Bader, *CEO*
Robert Bader, *President*
Douglas Bader, *Vice Pres*
Patty Bader, *Admin Sec*
Stephanie Rudd, *Controller*
EMP: 93 **EST:** 1958
SQ FT: 20,000
SALES (est): 38.4MM **Privately Held**
WEB: www.chevrolet.com
SIC: 5511 5012 5531 5521 Automobiles, new & used; automobiles & other motor vehicles; automotive & home supply stores; used car dealers

(P-13029)
HYUNDAI MOTOR AMERICA (HQ)
10550 Talbert Ave, Fountain Valley (92708-6032)
P.O. Box 20850 (92728-0850)
PHONE................714 965-3000

Kyung SOO Lee, *President*
Brian Smith, *COO*
Youngil Ko, *CFO*
Angela Zepeda, *Chief Mktg Ofcr*
Jerry Flannery, *Exec VP*
◆ **EMP:** 454 **EST:** 1985
SQ FT: 469,000
SALES (est): 1.1B **Privately Held**
WEB: www.hyundaiusa.com
SIC: 5012 5511 Automobiles & other motor vehicles; automobiles, new & used

(P-13030)
INDIEV INC
Also Called: Independent Electric Vehicles
5001 S Soto St, Vernon (90058-3612)
PHONE................323 703-5720
Shi Hai, *CEO*
Esther Kimm, *Principal*
Jim Tsai, *Principal*
Ying Zhou, *Principal*
Diego Furtado, *Engineer*
EMP: 55
SALES (est): 22.5MM **Privately Held**
WEB: www.driveindi.com
SIC: 5012 Automobiles & other motor vehicles

(P-13031)
INLAND KENWORTH INC (HQ)
9730 Cherry Ave, Fontana (92335-5257)
PHONE................909 823-9955
Leigh Parker, *Chairman*
Jim Beidrwieden, *President*
William Currie, *CEO*
Les Ziegler, *CFO*
Howard Ross, *General Mgr*
▼ **EMP:** 105 **EST:** 1934
SQ FT: 60,000
SALES (est): 104.2MM
SALES (corp-wide): 1.1MM **Privately Held**
WEB: www.inland-group.com
SIC: 5012 7538 5013 7513 Trucks, commercial; diesel engine repair: automotive; truck parts & accessories; truck rental & leasing, no drivers
PA: Inland Industries Ltd
2482 Douglas Rd
Burnaby BC V5C 6
604 291-6021

(P-13032)
LOS ANGELES TRUCK CENTERS LLC
Also Called: Los Angeles Freightliner
13800 Valley Blvd, Fontana (92335-5216)
PHONE................909 510-4000
Ricardo Flores, *Manager*
Scott Zeppenfeldt, *Vice Pres*
Sal Maldonado, *General Mgr*
Bryan Crawford, *Administration*
Alma Mariscal, *Administration*
EMP: 200
SALES (corp-wide): 150.5MM **Privately Held**
WEB: www.velocitytruckcenters.com
SIC: 5012 7538 5531 5511 Trucks, commercial; general automotive repair shops; automotive & home supply stores; new & used car dealers
PA: Los Angeles Truck Centers, Llc
2429 Peck Rd
Whittier CA 90601
562 447-1200

(P-13033)
MARATHON INDUSTRIES INC
Also Called: Marathon Truck Bodies
25597 Springbrook Ave, Santa Clarita (91350-2427)
P.O. Box 800279 (91380-0279)
PHONE................661 286-1520
Chad Hess, *President*
Roger K Hess, *Chairman*
Tom Garcia, *Vice Pres*
Stacy Sabine, *Sales Staff*
EMP: 145 **EST:** 1993
SQ FT: 75,000
SALES (est): 27.5MM **Privately Held**
WEB: www.marathontruckbody.com
SIC: 5012 3713 Automobiles & other motor vehicles; truck & bus bodies

(P-13034)
ONTARIO AUTOMOTIVE LLC
Also Called: Penske Honda Ontario
1401 Auto Center Dr, Ontario (91761-2221)
PHONE................909 974-3800
Roger Penske, *Ch of Bd*
Greg Penske, *President*
Brian Kobus, *Corp Secy*
Kris Kratky, *General Mgr*
Jasmine Ascencio, *Business Mgr*
EMP: 125 **EST:** 1990
SALES (est): 36.1MM
SALES (corp-wide): 5.1B **Privately Held**
WEB: www.penskehondaontario.com
SIC: 5511 5521 5012 Automobiles, new & used; used car dealers; automobiles & other motor vehicles
PA: Penske Corporation
2555 S Telegraph Rd
Bloomfield Hills MI 48302
248 648-2000

(P-13035)
SUNRISE FORD
Also Called: Quick Lane
16005 Valley Blvd, Fontana (92335-6419)
P.O. Box 2469 (92334-2469)
PHONE................909 822-4401
Robert Bruncati, *CEO*
Maureen Bruncati, *Corp Secy*
Al Tanner, *Executive*
Daemeth Rooney, *General Mgr*
Stephen Miarecki, *Office Mgr*
EMP: 200 **EST:** 1944
SQ FT: 100,000
SALES (est): 59.6MM **Privately Held**
WEB: www.sunriseford.com
SIC: 5511 5012 7538 Automobiles, new & used; automobiles & other motor vehicles; general automotive repair shops

(P-13036)
THEODORE ROBINS INC
Also Called: Theodore Robins Ford
2060 Harbor Blvd, Costa Mesa (92627-2673)
P.O. Box 5055 (92628-5055)
PHONE................949 642-0010
James M Robins, *President*
Denise Gla, *President*
David Robins, *Corp Secy*
Pablo Cozzani, *Finance Mgr*
Pete Alborzfar, *Sales Mgr*
EMP: 94 **EST:** 1921
SQ FT: 65,000
SALES (est): 21.7MM **Privately Held**
WEB: www.robinsford.com
SIC: 5511 5012 Automobiles, new & used; pickups, new & used; vans, new & used; automobiles & other motor vehicles

(P-13037)
TOMS TRUCK CENTER INC
Also Called: Isuzu Truck Services
1008 E 4th St, Santa Ana (92701-4751)
P.O. Box 88 (92702-0088)
PHONE................714 835-1978
Kc Heidler, *Manager*
Lisa Metcalf, *CFO*
Chris Kaiser, *Administration*
Tim Bui, *Info Tech Mgr*
Natalie Lawrence, *Human Res Dir*
EMP: 177
SALES (corp-wide): 84.8MM **Privately Held**
WEB: www.ttruck.com
SIC: 5511 5012 Automobiles, new & used; automobiles & other motor vehicles
PA: Tom's Truck Center, Inc.
909 N Grand Ave
Santa Ana CA 92701
800 238-9308

(P-13038)
TOYOTA OF ORANGE INC
1400 N Tustin St, Orange (92867-3995)
PHONE................714 639-6750
David Wilson, *President*
Kevin Cutts, *Vice Pres*
Aron Parra, *Vice Pres*
Mac McGee, *Portfolio Mgr*
Art Campos, *Finance Mgr*
EMP: 135 **EST:** 1972
SQ FT: 38,000

SALES (est): 60.8MM **Privately Held**
WEB: www.toyotaoforange.com
SIC: 5511 5012 5012 Automobiles, new & used; used car dealers; automobiles & other motor vehicles
PA: D W W Co., Inc.
1400 N Tustin St
Orange CA 92867
714 516-3111

(P-13039)
UTILITY TRLR SLS STHERN CAL LL (PA)
15567 Valley Blvd, Fontana (92335-6351)
PHONE................877 275-4887
Paul F Bennett,
Bobby Garcia, *Marketing Staff*
Stephen F Bennet,
Craig M Bennett,
Harold C Bennett,
EMP: 100 **EST:** 2007
SALES (est): 20.9MM **Privately Held**
WEB: www.utilitytrailersales.com
SIC: 5012 5013 5531 5561 Trailers for passenger vehicles; automotive supplies & parts; automobile & truck equipment & parts; travel trailers: automobile, new & used

---

5013 Motor Vehicle Splys & New Parts Wholesale

(P-13040)
AGILITY POWERTRAIN SYSTEMS LLC (DH)
3335 Susan St Ste 100, Costa Mesa (92626-1647)
PHONE................949 236-5520
Kathleen Ligocki, *CEO*
Brad Garner, *President*
William Nowicki, *COO*
EMP: 313 **EST:** 2017
SQ FT: 10,000
SALES (est): 90.6MM
SALES (corp-wide): 339.9MM **Privately Held**
WEB: www.hexagonagility.com
SIC: 5013 5172 Motor vehicle supplies & new parts; petroleum products
HQ: Agility Fuel Solutions Llc
3335 Susan St Ste 100
Costa Mesa CA 92626
949 236-5520

(P-13041)
APU INC (PA)
14939 Oxnard St, Van Nuys (91411-2611)
PHONE................661 948-2880
John Christy Jr, *President*
EMP: 60 **EST:** 1978
SQ FT: 20,000
SALES (est): 8.2MM **Privately Held**
SIC: 5013 5531 Automotive supplies & parts; automotive parts

(P-13042)
APU INC
Also Called: Auto Parts Unlimited
10452 Magnolia Blvd, North Hollywood (91601-4110)
PHONE................818 508-7211
John Christy, *President*
EMP: 54
SALES (corp-wide): 8.2MM **Privately Held**
SIC: 5013 5531 7539 Automotive supplies & parts; automotive parts; carburetor repair
PA: Apu, Inc.
14939 Oxnard St
Van Nuys CA 91411
661 948-2880

(P-13043)
APW KNOX-SEEMAN WAREHOUSE INC (HQ)
1073 E Artesia Blvd, Carson (90746-1601)
PHONE................310 604-4373
Tong Y Suhr, *CEO*
Susan Suhr, *Admin Sec*
Sonia Barahona, *Sales Staff*
Luis Estrada, *Manager*
▲ **EMP:** 98 **EST:** 1972

SQ FT: 32,000
SALES (est): 47.9MM
SALES (corp-wide): 49.2MM **Privately Held**
WEB: www.apwks.com
SIC: **5013** 5531 Automotive supplies & parts; automotive parts
PA: Auto Parts Warehouse, Inc.
　16941 Keegan Ave
　Carson CA 90746
　800 913-6119

(P-13044)
AUTO PARTS WAREHOUSE INC (PA)
16941 Keegan Ave, Carson (90746-1307)
PHONE...................................800 913-6119
Tong Young Suhr, *Principal*
Jim Hastie, *President*
Houman Akhavan, *Vice Pres*
Sleung Ja Suhr, *Vice Pres*
Byung Joon Lee, *Admin Sec*
▼ EMP: 50 EST: 1972
SQ FT: 40,000
SALES (est): 49.2MM **Privately Held**
WEB: www.apwks.com
SIC: **5013** Automotive supplies & parts

(P-13045)
AUTOMOTIVE AFTERMARKET INC
Also Called: Completes Plus
15912 Hawthorne Blvd, Lawndale (90260-2644)
PHONE...................................310 793-0046
Guy Cooper, *Branch Mgr*
EMP: 72
SALES (corp-wide): 20.9MM **Privately Held**
WEB: www.completesplus.com
SIC: **5013** Truck parts & accessories
PA: Automotive Aftermarket, Inc.
　10425 S La Cienega Blvd
　Los Angeles CA 90045
　310 703-5700

(P-13046)
AUTOZONE INC
1361 W 190th St, Gardena (90248-4306)
PHONE...................................310 525-2333
Raul Luna, *Branch Mgr*
EMP: 60
SALES (corp-wide): 12.6B **Publicly Held**
WEB: www.autozonepro.com
SIC: **5531** 5013 Automotive parts; automotive supplies & parts
PA: Autozone, Inc.
　123 S Front St
　Memphis TN 38103
　901 495-6500

(P-13047)
AZIMC INVESTMENTS INC
8901 Canoga Ave, Canoga Park (91304-1512)
PHONE...................................818 678-1200
Kristen Wright, *Admin Sec*
William Giles, *CFO*
Thomas Kliman, *Vice Pres*
◆ EMP: 250 EST: 1962
SALES (est): 87.5MM
SALES (corp-wide): 505MM **Privately Held**
WEB: www.imcparts.net
SIC: **5013** Automotive supplies & parts
HQ: Interamerican Motor, Llc
　8901 Canoga Ave
　Canoga Park CA 91304
　800 874-8925

(P-13048)
BBK PERFORMANCE INC
Also Called: Gripp
27427 Bostik Ct, Temecula (92590-3698)
PHONE...................................951 296-1771
Brian Murphy, *President*
Ken Murphy, *Treasurer*
EMP: 75 EST: 1988
SALES (est): 13.3MM **Privately Held**
WEB: www.bbkperformance.com
SIC: **5013** 5531 Automotive supplies & parts; automotive parts

(P-13049)
CAL-STATE AUTO PARTS INC (PA)
Also Called: Auto Pride
1361 N Red Gum St, Anaheim (92806-1318)
PHONE...................................714 630-5950
Richard J Deblasi, *CEO*
John McMillin, *CFO*
Steven Brooker, *Vice Pres*
Steve Brooker, *Executive*
Chuck Killen, *Info Tech Dir*
▲ EMP: 105 EST: 1971
SQ FT: 76,000
SALES (est): 58.8MM **Privately Held**
WEB: www.autopride.com
SIC: **5013** Automotive supplies & parts

(P-13050)
CH MORRIS CO INC
Also Called: Morris Automotive Supply
8539 Nuevo Ave, Fontana (92335-3825)
PHONE...................................909 829-4481
Randall Swedlove, *President*
Hershel M Swedlove, *President*
Caroldyne Swedlove, *Corp Secy*
EMP: 20 EST: 1952
SQ FT: 9,000
SALES (est): 9.9MM **Privately Held**
SIC: **5013** 7539 5531 3714 Automotive supplies & parts; machine shop, automotive; automotive parts; motor vehicle parts & accessories

(P-13051)
CLASSIC CAMARO INC
Also Called: Classic Firebird
18460 Gothard St, Huntington Beach (92648-1229)
PHONE...................................714 847-6887
Jeffrey M Leonard, *CEO*
Bret Dethlefsen, *Creative Dir*
Mark Vogt, *General Mgr*
Jeff Berg, *Administration*
Nick Dang, *Administration*
▲ EMP: 115 EST: 1977
SQ FT: 30,000
SALES (est): 30.8MM **Privately Held**
WEB: www.classicindustries.com
SIC: **5531** 5013 Automotive accessories; automotive supplies & parts

(P-13052)
CLAUDES BUGGIES INC
Also Called: CB Performance Products
1715 N Farmersville Blvd, Farmersville (93223-2302)
PHONE...................................559 733-8222
Richard A Tomlinson, *CEO*
Loretta Tomlinson, *Corp Secy*
Marcus Jump, *Webmaster*
Patrick Downs, *Sales Staff*
Mark Lawless, *Sales Staff*
▲ EMP: 30 EST: 1959
SQ FT: 50,000
SALES (est): 7.9MM **Privately Held**
WEB: www.cbperformance.com
SIC: **5013** 3714 Automotive supplies & parts; motor vehicle engines & parts

(P-13053)
CLUB ASSIST NORTH AMERICA INC (DH)
888 W 6th St Ste 300, Los Angeles (90017-2729)
PHONE...................................213 388-4333
Brett Davies, *CEO*
Scott Davies, *COO*
Alex Leombruni, *CFO*
Darshan Parikh, *CFO*
Candace Enman, *Treasurer*
▲ EMP: 64 EST: 2001
SALES (est): 139.2MM **Privately Held**
WEB: www.clubassist.com
SIC: **5013** Automotive batteries

(P-13054)
DENSO PDTS & SVCS AMERICAS INC (DH)
Also Called: Dsca
3900 Via Oro Ave, Long Beach (90810-1868)
PHONE...................................310 834-6352
Yoshihiko Yamada, *CEO*

Takefumi Momose, *President*
Hirokatsu Yamashita, *President*
Roy Nakaue, *Exec VP*
Peter Clotz, *Vice Pres*
◆ EMP: 447 EST: 1971
SQ FT: 235,000
SALES (est): 221.8MM **Privately Held**
WEB: www.denso.com
SIC: **5013** 7361 5075 3714 Automotive supplies & parts; employment agencies; warm air heating & air conditioning; motor vehicle parts & accessories
HQ: Denso International America, Inc.
　24777 Denso Dr
　Southfield MI 48033
　248 350-7500

(P-13055)
DNA SPECIALTY INC
200 W Artesia Blvd, Compton (90220-5500)
PHONE...................................310 767-4070
James Choi, *President*
Sun Choi, *Admin Sec*
Aileen Zhang, *Manager*
▲ EMP: 90 EST: 1984
SQ FT: 80,000
SALES (est): 24.1MM **Privately Held**
WEB: www.dnaspecialty.com
SIC: **5013** 3714 Wheels, motor vehicle; wheels, motor vehicle

(P-13056)
ED TUCKER DISTRIBUTOR INC
Also Called: Tucker Rocky Distribution
8505 W Doe Ave, Visalia (93291-9286)
PHONE...................................800 347-1010
Ronnie Haun, *Manager*
EMP: 50 **Privately Held**
WEB: www.tucker.com
SIC: **5013** Motorcycle parts
HQ: Ed Tucker Distributor, Inc.
　4900 Alliance Gateway Fwy
　Fort Worth TX 76177
　817 258-9000

(P-13057)
EGGE MACHINE COMPANY INC (PA)
8403 Allport Ave, Santa Fe Springs (90670-2109)
PHONE...................................562 945-3419
Robert Egge, *President*
Kathy Weaver, *Treasurer*
Judy Egge, *Admin Sec*
Caleb Weaver, *Production*
Jim Ketchum, *Director*
▲ EMP: 28 EST: 1915
SQ FT: 10,000
SALES (est): 8.1MM **Privately Held**
WEB: www.egge.com
SIC: **5013** 3592 5531 Automotive supplies & parts; valves; pistons & piston rings; automotive parts

(P-13058)
ELLSWORTH TRCK AUTO MACHINING
1167 N Knollwood Cir, Anaheim (92801-1363)
PHONE...................................714 761-2500
Fran Ellsworth, *President*
Allen Ellsworth, *Treasurer*
EMP: 16 EST: 1961
SQ FT: 14,000
SALES (est): 1.8MM **Privately Held**
SIC: **5013** 3599 Motor vehicle supplies & new parts; machine shop, jobbing & repair

(P-13059)
EMPI INC
301 E Orangethorpe Ave, Anaheim (92801-1032)
PHONE...................................714 446-9606
Peter Guile, *CEO*
Todd Tyler, *CFO*
Erica Cooper, *Vice Pres*
Patrick Duke, *Info Tech Mgr*
Henry Wu, *Info Tech Mgr*
EMP: 89 EST: 2018
SQ FT: 127,000
SALES (est): 28.7MM **Privately Held**
WEB: www.empius.com
SIC: **5013** 3713 Automotive supplies & parts; specialty motor vehicle bodies

(P-13060)
GLOBAL TRADE ALLIANCE INC
Also Called: Action Crash Parts
13642 Orden Dr, Santa Fe Springs (90670-6353)
PHONE...................................562 944-6422
Todd Hanson, *Manager*
EMP: 114
SALES (corp-wide): 11.6B **Publicly Held**
SIC: **5531** 5013 Automotive parts; automotive supplies & parts
HQ: Global Trade Alliance, Inc.
　2040 S Hamilton Rd
　Columbus OH
　614 751-3100

(P-13061)
GOODRIDGE USA INC (DH)
529 Van Ness Ave, Torrance (90501-1424)
PHONE...................................310 533-1924
Celso Pierre, *CEO*
Lori Giovenco, *General Mgr*
Perla Alcaraz, *Administration*
Roger Day, *Engineer*
Daniel Phan, *Engineer*
▲ EMP: 55 EST: 1984
SQ FT: 15,000
SALES (est): 25.6MM
SALES (corp-wide): 3.8MM **Privately Held**
WEB: www.goodridge.com
SIC: **5013** Automotive supplies
HQ: Goodridge Limited
　Dart Building
　Exeter EX1 3
　139 236-9090

(P-13062)
HANSON DISTRIBUTING COMPANY (PA)
975 W 8th St, Azusa (91702-2246)
PHONE...................................626 224-9800
Daniel Hanson, *CEO*
Dan Hanson, *Vice Pres*
Adam Holloway, *IT/INT Sup*
Laurie Hanson, *Buyer*
Juan Chavez, *Opers Staff*
EMP: 115 EST: 1954
SQ FT: 160,000
SALES (est): 64.2MM **Privately Held**
WEB: www.hansondistributing.com
SIC: **5013** Automotive supplies & parts

(P-13063)
HANSON DISTRIBUTING COMPANY
7940 W Doe Ave, Visalia (93291-9703)
PHONE...................................559 802-1198
EMP: 98
SALES (corp-wide): 64.2MM **Privately Held**
WEB: www.hansondistributing.com
SIC: **5013** Automotive supplies & parts
PA: Hanson Distributing Company
　975 W 8th St
　Azusa CA 91702
　626 224-9800

(P-13064)
HINO MOTORS MFG USA INC
4550 Wineville Ave, Jurupa Valley (91752-3723)
PHONE...................................951 727-0286
Debra Martinas, *Branch Mgr*
Yasuhiko Shibazaki, *Treasurer*
Shinichi Takemasa, *Exec VP*
Lisa Bastian, *Vice Pres*
Tsutomu Hara, *Vice Pres*
EMP: 62 **Privately Held**
WEB: www.hmmusa.com
SIC: **5013** Truck parts & accessories
HQ: Hino Motors Manufacturing U.S.A., Inc.
　45501 W 12 Mile Rd
　Novi MI 48377

(P-13065)
IAP WEST INC
20036 S Via Baron, Rancho Dominguez (90220-6105)
PHONE...................................310 667-9720
Michel Berg, *CEO*
Louis Berg, *President*
John Kelley, *CFO*
Sharon Berg, *Admin Sec*

PRODUCTS & SVCS

Tom Urbaniak, *VP Mktg*
◆ **EMP:** 71
SQ FT: 80,000
SALES (est): 13.6MM **Privately Held**
WEB: www.iapperformance.com
SIC: 5013 Automotive engines & engine parts

(P-13066)
INNOVATIVE METAL DESIGNS INC
12691 Monarch St, Garden Grove (92841-3918)
PHONE....................714 799-6700
Carlos Danze, *CEO*
Marcelo Danze, *President*
▲ **EMP:** 20 **EST:** 1983
SQ FT: 6,000
SALES (est): 5.2MM **Privately Held**
WEB: www.innovativemetals.com
SIC: 5013 3841 3827 Motorcycle parts; surgical & medical instruments; optical instruments & lenses

(P-13067)
INTERAMERICAN MOTOR LLC (HQ)
8901 Canoga Ave, Canoga Park (91304-1512)
PHONE....................800 874-8925
Randy Buller, *CEO*
David Wotman, *CFO*
Kevin McCloskey, *Vice Pres*
Brian Lonergan, *Administration*
Roger Guedikian, *Technology*
EMP: 147 **EST:** 2018
SALES (est): 87.5MM
SALES (corp-wide): 505MM **Privately Held**
WEB: www.imcparts.net
SIC: 5013 5599 Automotive supplies & parts; dunebuggies
PA: Parts Authority, Llc
3 Dakota Dr Ste 110
New Hyde Park NY 11042
833 380-8511

(P-13068)
KATANA RACING INC (PA)
Also Called: Katana Racing Whl & Tire Distr
4490 Ayers Ave, Vernon (90058-4317)
PHONE....................562 340-6252
ARA Tchaghlassian, *President*
Craig Anderson, *CFO*
▲ **EMP:** 101 **EST:** 1998
SALES (est): 70.1MM **Privately Held**
WEB: www.katanawheels.com
SIC: 5013 5014 Wheels, motor vehicle; automobile tires & tubes

(P-13069)
KAWASAKI MOTORS CORP USA (HQ)
26972 Burbank, Foothill Ranch (92610-2506)
P.O. Box 25252, Santa Ana (92799-5252)
PHONE....................949 837-4683
Eigo Konya, *President*
Ryan Collins, *COO*
Richard N Beattie, *Officer*
Terunori Kitajima, *Executive*
Tom Leimkuhler, *Exec Dir*
◆ **EMP:** 400
SQ FT: 40,000
SALES (est): 267.7MM **Privately Held**
WEB: www.kawasaki.com
SIC: 5571 5013 5084 5091 Motorcycle dealers; motorcycle parts; engines, gasoline; boats, canoes, watercrafts & equipment

(P-13070)
KAY AUTOMOTIVE DISTRS INC (PA)
14650 Calvert St, Van Nuys (91411-2807)
PHONE....................818 781-6850
Jona Kardish, *President*
Jona Karadish, *President*
Annette Karadish, *Admin Sec*
EMP: 50 **EST:** 1964
SALES (est): 9.8MM **Privately Held**
WEB: www.kayauto.com
SIC: 5013 Automotive supplies & parts

(P-13071)
KEYSTONE AUTOMOTIVE WAREHOUSE
15640 Cntu Gllano Rnch Rd, Eastvale (91752-1404)
PHONE....................951 277-5237
Michael Decicco, *Principal*
John Grier, *Regional Mgr*
EMP: 100
SALES (corp-wide): 11.6B **Publicly Held**
WEB: www.keystoneautomotive.com
SIC: 5013 Radiators; automotive supplies & parts
HQ: Keystone Automotive Warehouse, Inc.
44 Tunkhannock Ave
Exeter PA 18643
570 655-4514

(P-13072)
MAXZONE VEHICLE LIGHTING CORP (HQ)
Also Called: Depo Auto Parts
15889 Slover Ave Unit A, Fontana (92337-7299)
PHONE....................909 822-3288
Polo Hsu, *President*
Judy Hsu, *CFO*
Tony Lin, *Info Tech Mgr*
◆ **EMP:** 50 **EST:** 1997
SQ FT: 32,000
SALES (est): 32.2MM **Privately Held**
WEB: www.maxzone.com
SIC: 5013 3714 Automotive supplies & parts; motor vehicle electrical equipment

(P-13073)
MIKUNI AMERICAN CORPORATION (HQ)
Also Called: M A C
8910 Mikuni Ave, Northridge (91324-3403)
PHONE....................310 676-0522
Jun Iida, *CEO*
Masashi Seike, *CFO*
Hiroyuki Ono, *Vice Pres*
Yutaka Fujita, *Admin Sec*
Robert Sein, *Human Res Mgr*
▲ **EMP:** 64 **EST:** 1968
SQ FT: 50,000
SALES (est): 80.2MM **Privately Held**
WEB: www.mikuni.com
SIC: 5013 5088 Automotive hardware; aircraft engines & engine parts; aircraft parts

(P-13074)
MOBIS PARTS AMERICA LLC (HQ)
10550 Talbert Ave Fl 4, Fountain Valley (92708-6031)
PHONE....................786 515-1101
Yun Dong Park, *Mng Member*
Lena Gray, *Admin Asst*
Michael Wilson, *Administration*
Claudio Barrera, *Engineer*
Francis Camacho, *Engineer*
◆ **EMP:** 90 **EST:** 2003
SALES (est): 224.3MM **Privately Held**
WEB: www.mobisusa.com
SIC: 5013 Automotive supplies & parts

(P-13075)
NSV INTERNATIONAL CORP
1250 E 29th St, Signal Hill (90755-1800)
P.O. Box 14660, Long Beach (90853-4660)
PHONE....................562 438-3836
Victor Harris, *CEO*
Stephan Humphries, *CEO*
Isabel Palafox, *COO*
EMP: 100 **EST:** 2011
SQ FT: 1,200
SALES (est): 7.4MM **Privately Held**
WEB: www.nsvauto.com
SIC: 5013 Automotive supplies

(P-13076)
OCELOT ENGINEERING INC
Also Called: Chaparral Motorsports
555 S H St, San Bernardino (92410-3415)
PHONE....................800 841-2960
David S Damron, *President*
Linda J Damron, *Treasurer*
James E Damron, *Vice Pres*
Melissa A Damron, *Vice Pres*
Crystal Ashby, *Mktg Dir*
◆ **EMP:** 160

SALES (est): 9.5MM **Privately Held**
WEB: www.chapmoto.com
SIC: 5571 5551 5013 3751 Motorcycles; all-terrain vehicles; motorcycle parts & accessories; jet skis; motorcycle parts; motorcycle accessories

(P-13077)
ONE STOP PARTS SOURCE LLC (DH)
2610 S Birch St, Santa Ana (92707-3449)
PHONE....................949 955-2600
Mike Thompson, *CEO*
Bill Shaver, *Director*
EMP: 69 **EST:** 1989
SQ FT: 2,500
SALES (est): 25.5MM **Privately Held**
SIC: 5013 Automotive brakes
HQ: Uriman Inc.
650 N Puente St
Brea CA 92821
714 257-2080

(P-13078)
PARTS AUTHORITY LLC
Also Called: Fast Undercar
4277 Transport St, Ventura (93003-5657)
PHONE....................805 676-3410
Randy Buller, *President*
EMP: 110
SALES (corp-wide): 505MM **Privately Held**
WEB: www.partsauthority.com
SIC: 5013 Automotive supplies & parts
PA: Parts Authority, Llc
3 Dakota Dr Ste 110
New Hyde Park NY 11042
833 380-8511

(P-13079)
PERFORMANCE AUTOMOTIVE WHL INC (PA)
Also Called: Paw
20235 Nordhoff St, Chatsworth (91311-6213)
P.O. Box 829, Newbury Park (91319-0829)
PHONE....................805 499-8973
Keith E Harvie, *CEO*
Brian McElroy, *President*
EMP: 100 **EST:** 1978
SALES (est): 2.4MM **Privately Held**
WEB: www.pawinc.com
SIC: 5961 5013 Automotive supplies & equipment, mail order; automotive supplies & parts

(P-13080)
PREVOST CAR (US) INC
3384 Deforest Cir, Mira Loma (91752)
PHONE....................951 360-2550
Tim Willmuth, *Branch Mgr*
Gerardo Cerda, *Manager*
Raymond Auclair, *Parts Mgr*
EMP: 28
SALES (corp-wide): 39.1B **Privately Held**
WEB: www.prevostcar.com
SIC: 5013 4173 5012 3711 Automotive supplies & parts; maintenance facilities, buses; buses; buses, all types, assembly of
HQ: Prevost Car (Us) Inc.
7817 National Service Rd
Greensboro NC 27409
908 222-7211

(P-13081)
R1 CONCEPTS INC
Also Called: Zion Automotive Group
13140 Midway Pl, Cerritos (90703-2233)
PHONE....................714 777-2323
Phouc Martin Trinh, *President*
Danh Nguyen, *Vice Pres*
Cynthia Trinh, *Creative Dir*
Thang Trinh, *Admin Sec*
Nafi Sedaghat, *Controller*
◆ **EMP:** 52 **EST:** 2004
SALES (est): 22.8MM **Privately Held**
WEB: www.r1concepts.com
SIC: 5013 3714 Automotive engines & engine parts; motor vehicle brake systems & parts

(P-13082)
RALCO HOLDINGS INC (DH)
13861 Rosecrans Ave, Santa Fe Springs (90670-5207)
PHONE....................949 440-5500
Michael Moore, *CEO*
EMP: 799 **EST:** 2009
SALES (est): 305.5MM **Privately Held**
SIC: 5013 3751 Motorcycle parts; motorcycle accessories

(P-13083)
RALLY HOLDINGS LLC
17771 Mitchell N, Irvine (92614-6028)
PHONE....................817 919-6833
Andrew Graves,
EMP: 1151 **EST:** 2006
SALES (est): 305.5MM **Privately Held**
SIC: 5013 3751 Motorcycle parts; motorcycle accessories
HQ: Ralco Holdings, Inc.
13861 Rosecrans Ave
Santa Fe Springs CA 90670
949 440-5500

(P-13084)
RAMCAR BATTERIES INC
2700 Carrier Ave, Commerce (90040-2572)
PHONE....................323 726-1212
Clifford J Crowe, *President*
◆ **EMP:** 50 **EST:** 1990
SQ FT: 90,000
SALES (est): 12.3MM **Privately Held**
WEB: www.ramcarbattery.com
SIC: 5013 3691 Automotive batteries; lead acid batteries (storage batteries)

(P-13085)
RICHARD HUETTER INC
Also Called: Pacific Parts International
21050 Osborne St, Canoga Park (91304-1744)
PHONE....................818 700-8001
Richard Huetter, *CEO*
Maria L Huetter, *Treasurer*
▲ **EMP:** 70 **EST:** 1982
SQ FT: 30,000
SALES (est): 12.7MM **Privately Held**
WEB: www.pacificparts.net
SIC: 5013 Automotive supplies & parts

(P-13086)
SADDLEMEN CORPORATION
17801 S Susana Rd, Compton (90221-5411)
PHONE....................310 638-1222
David Echert, *CEO*
John Baricevic, *Vice Pres*
Kelly Rowe, *Accounting Dir*
Samuel Rodriguez, *QC Mgr*
Alex Fox, *Sales Staff*
▲ **EMP:** 90 **EST:** 1987
SQ FT: 20,000
SALES (est): 12.7MM **Privately Held**
WEB: www.saddlemen.com
SIC: 5013 3751 Motorcycle parts; motorcycle accessories

(P-13087)
SCAT ENTERPRISES INC
1400 Kingsdale Ave, Redondo Beach (90278-3983)
PHONE....................310 370-5501
Philip T Lieb, *President*
Craig Schenasi, *CFO*
Thomas Mendoza, *Asst Controller*
Toby Raine, *Analyst*
Marty Blanc, *Prdtn Mgr*
◆ **EMP:** 65
SQ FT: 42,000
SALES (est): 20.8MM **Privately Held**
WEB: www.scatenterprises.com
SIC: 5013 3714 Automotive supplies & parts; automotive supplies; motor vehicle parts & accessories

(P-13088)
SHANK KRETZ MCH AUTO PARTS INC
Also Called: Carquest Auto Parts
375 N 8th St, Brawley (92227-1903)
PHONE....................760 344-4541
Donald Shank, *President*
Don Shank, *President*
Robert Shank, *Vice Pres*
EMP: 14 **EST:** 1934

SALES (est): 350K Privately Held
WEB: www.carquest.com
SIC: 5013 5531 3599 Automotive supplies & parts; automotive parts; column clamps & shores

(P-13089)
SHRIN LLC
Also Called: Coverking
900 E Arlee Pl, Anaheim (92805-5645)
P.O. Box 9860 (92812-7860)
PHONE.................................714 850-0303
Narendra Gupta, *Mng Member*
Ramin Edalat, *Engineer*
Bansari Shah, *Accounting Mgr*
James Yu, *Analyst*
Anita Gupta, *Director*
◆ **EMP:** 100 **EST:** 1988
SQ FT: 90,000
SALES (est): 34.2MM Privately Held
SIC: 5013 3714 Automotive supplies & parts; motor vehicle parts & accessories

(P-13090)
SILLA AUTOMOTIVE LLC
1901 Mineral Ct Ste C, Bakersfield (93308-6819)
PHONE.................................661 392-8880
EMP: 52
SALES (corp-wide): 73.4MM Privately Held
SIC: 5013 Whol Auto Parts/Supplies
PA: Silla Automotive, Llc
1217 W Artesia Blvd
Compton CA 90220
310 323-0001

(P-13091)
SOUND INVESTMENT GROUP
Also Called: Frsport.com
16402 Gothard St Ste E, Huntington Beach (92647-3647)
PHONE.................................714 515-4001
Dung T Nguyen, *CEO*
Donny Ton, *Vice Pres*
Lien Truong, *Admin Sec*
Alex Chang, *Director*
EMP: 15 **EST:** 2004
SALES (est): 5MM Privately Held
WEB: www.frsport.com
SIC: 5013 3465 Automotive supplies & parts; body parts, automobile: stamped metal

(P-13092)
SOUTHERN CAL DISC TIRE CO INC
600 W Florida Ave, Hemet (92543-4009)
PHONE.................................951 929-2130
Josh McCartner, *Manager*
EMP: 106
SALES (corp-wide): 3.6B Privately Held
WEB: www.discounttire.com
SIC: 5531 5013 Automotive tires; wheels, motor vehicle
HQ: Southern California Discount Tire Co., Inc.
16100 N Grnway Hyden Loop
Scottsdale AZ 85260
602 996-0201

(P-13093)
SOUTHERN CAL DISC TIRE CO INC
15672 Springdale St, Huntington Beach (92649-1315)
PHONE.................................714 901-8226
Joe Ortiz, *Manager*
EMP: 106
SALES (corp-wide): 3.6B Privately Held
WEB: www.discounttire.com
SIC: 5531 5013 Automotive tires; wheels, motor vehicle
HQ: Southern California Discount Tire Co., Inc.
16100 N Grnway Hyden Loop
Scottsdale AZ 85260
602 996-0201

(P-13094)
SOUTHERN CAL DISC TIRE CO INC
705 S Grand Ave, Glendora (91740-4141)
PHONE.................................626 335-2883
Abel Ariola, *Manager*

EMP: 106
SALES (corp-wide): 3.6B Privately Held
WEB: www.discounttire.com
SIC: 5531 5013 Automotive tires; wheels, motor vehicle
HQ: Southern California Discount Tire Co., Inc.
16100 N Grnway Hyden Loop
Scottsdale AZ 85260
602 996-0201

(P-13095)
SPECIALTY INTERIOR MFG INC
Also Called: Sim Ideation
16751 Millikan Ave, Irvine (92606-5009)
PHONE.................................714 296-8618
Courtney Tassie, *CEO*
EMP: 35 **EST:** 2012
SQ FT: 4,500
SALES (est): 4MM Privately Held
SIC: 5013 2531 Automotive supplies & parts; seats, aircraft

(P-13096)
SPECTRA PREMIUM (USA) CORP
2220 Almond Ave, Redlands (92374-2073)
PHONE.................................951 653-0640
Sergio Zapata, *Branch Mgr*
EMP: 62
SALES (corp-wide): 251.5MM Privately Held
WEB: www.spectrapremium.com
SIC: 5013 Automotive supplies & parts
HQ: Spectra Premium (Usa) Corp.
3052 N Distribution Way
Greenfield IN 46140
317 891-1700

(P-13097)
STANLEY M SCHER INC (PA)
Also Called: Auto Supply Company
2716 S Main St, Los Angeles (90007-3332)
PHONE.................................213 746-1922
Steven J Scher, *CEO*
David Scher, *CFO*
EMP: 58 **EST:** 1932
SQ FT: 17,000
SALES (est): 8.1MM Privately Held
WEB: www.partsplus.com
SIC: 5013 5531 Truck parts & accessories; automotive parts

(P-13098)
TAP WORLDWIDE LLC (DH)
Also Called: 4 Wheel Parts Performance Ctrs
400 W Artesia Blvd, Compton (90220-5501)
PHONE.................................310 900-5500
Greg Adler, *President*
Tim Mongi, *COO*
Greg Gardiner, *CTO*
Mike Ahmad, *Info Tech Mgr*
Tim Hamner, *Buyer*
◆ **EMP:** 699 **EST:** 2009
SALES (est): 413.1MM
SALES (corp-wide): 7B Publicly Held
WEB: www.4wheelparts.com
SIC: 5013 Motor vehicle supplies & new parts
HQ: Tap Automotive Holdings, Llc
400 W Artesia Blvd
Compton CA 90220
310 900-5500

(P-13099)
TOTAL IMPORT SOLUTIONS INC
Also Called: Nanoskin Car Care Products
14700 Radburn Ave, Santa Fe Springs (90670-5318)
PHONE.................................562 691-6818
Jerry Heilian, *CEO*
Shengi Chang, *CFO*
▲ **EMP:** 15 **EST:** 2008
SQ FT: 31,000
SALES (est): 3.3MM Privately Held
WEB: www.nanoskinusa.com
SIC: 5013 3089 Automotive supplies; automotive parts, plastic

(P-13100)
TRANS-WEST FORD TRUCK SLS INC (PA)
10150 Cherry Ave, Fontana (92335-5282)
PHONE.................................909 770-5127
Richard E Textor, *President*

Tom Textor, *Treasurer*
Lee Leabman, *Vice Pres*
Vicki Bixby, *Administration*
Mike Moyer, *Sales Staff*
▲ **EMP:** 64 **EST:** 1975
SQ FT: 4,000
SALES (est): 15.9MM Privately Held
WEB: www.trans-west.com
SIC: 5511 5531 5013 Automobiles, new & used; truck equipment & parts; automotive supplies & parts

(P-13101)
TRANSAMERICAN DISSOLUTION LLC (PA)
Also Called: Four Wheel Parts Wholesalers
400 W Artesia Blvd, Compton (90220-5501)
PHONE.................................310 900-5500
Greg Adler, *Mng Member*
Craig Scanlon, *President*
Paul Rizo, *Software Dev*
Nestor Reyes, *Export Mgr*
Amanda Huskey, *Sales Staff*
◆ **EMP:** 200 **EST:** 1959
SQ FT: 120,000
SALES (est): 466.5MM Privately Held
WEB: www.transamericanautoparts.com
SIC: 5531 5013 Automotive parts; automotive supplies & parts

(P-13102)
TRANSWEST TRUCK CENTER LLC
10150 Cherry Ave, Fontana (92335-5222)
PHONE.................................909 770-5170
Bradley Fauvre,
Douglas Ahn, *Sales Mgr*
Blozis Bill, *Sales Associate*
Dave Gilmer, *Sales Staff*
James Barker,
EMP: 75 **EST:** 1975
SQ FT: 4,000
SALES (est): 25.8MM
SALES (corp-wide): 150.5MM Privately Held
WEB: www.trans-west.com
SIC: 5511 5531 5013 Automobiles, new & used; automotive parts; motor vehicle supplies & new parts
PA: Los Angeles Truck Centers, Llc
2429 Peck Rd
Whittier CA 90601
562 447-1200

(P-13103)
UNITED SYATT AMERICA CORP (PA)
Also Called: Broadway Auto Parts
920 E 1st St, Santa Ana (92701-5365)
PHONE.................................714 568-1938
Ron Hanson, *Ch of Bd*
Donna Hanson, *Corp Secy*
Tom Bettis, *Sales Staff*
Jeff Spaulding, *Sales Staff*
Tina Jackson, *Supervisor*
EMP: 109 **EST:** 1955
SQ FT: 27,000
SALES (est): 5.8MM Privately Held
SIC: 5531 5013 Automotive parts; automotive supplies & parts

(P-13104)
VALLEY FRICTION MATERIALS
12036 Carson St, Hawaiian Gardens (90716-1143)
PHONE.................................323 875-1783
Thomas Hanamuni, *President*
Nina Hanamuni, *Corp Secy*
EMP: 13 **EST:** 1957
SQ FT: 10,000
SALES (est): 867.7K Privately Held
SIC: 5013 3714 Automotive brakes; motor vehicle brake systems & parts

(P-13105)
VEHICLE ACCESSORY CENTER LLC
10863 Jersey Blvd Ste 101, Rancho Cucamonga (91730-5151)
PHONE.................................909 987-8237
Russell Hoyt, *Mng Member*
Ana McDonald, *Office Mgr*
Wallace Diangelo, *Opers Mgr*
Justin Roberts, *Opers Staff*

Cory Mitchem, *Sales Staff*
EMP: 53 **EST:** 2002
SQ FT: 100,000
SALES (est): 17.8MM
SALES (corp-wide): 76.5MM Privately Held
WEB: www.vehicleaccessorycenter.com
SIC: 5013 Automotive supplies & parts
PA: Mark Christopher Chevrolet, Inc.
2131 E Convention Ctr Way
Ontario CA 91764
909 321-5860

(P-13106)
WABASH NATIONAL TRLR CTRS INC
16025 Slover Ave, Fontana (92337-7368)
PHONE.................................765 771-5300
Joe Newfield, *Manager*
William Bottomley, *Partner*
EMP: 43
SALES (corp-wide): 1.4B Publicly Held
WEB: www.wabashnational.com
SIC: 5013 5012 7539 3715 Motor vehicle supplies & new parts; automobiles & other motor vehicles; automotive repair shops; truck trailers; industrial trucks & tractors
HQ: Wabash National Trailer Centers, Inc.
1000 Sagamore Pkwy S
Lafayette IN 47905
765 771-5300

(P-13107)
WARREN DISTRIBUTING INC (PA)
Also Called: Wdi
3435 Wilshire Blvd # 990, Los Angeles (90010-1998)
PHONE.................................562 789-3360
Brian Weiss, *President*
Linnea Herndon, *CFO*
Jake Boggs, *Vice Pres*
Dave Erlenbach, *Vice Pres*
Gary Jacobson, *Vice Pres*
◆ **EMP:** 55 **EST:** 1963
SALES (est): 49.7MM Privately Held
WEB: www.warrendist.com
SIC: 5013 Automotive supplies

(P-13108)
WEBASTO CHARGING SYSTEMS INC (DH)
1333 S Mayflower Ave # 100, Monrovia (91016-5265)
PHONE.................................626 415-4000
John Thomas, *CEO*
Doug McElroy, *CFO*
Brian Izumida, *Technician*
EMP: 85 **EST:** 2018
SALES (est): 26.4MM
SALES (corp-wide): 3.9B Privately Held
WEB: www.evtestsystems.com
SIC: 5013 Automobile service station equipment
HQ: Webasto Roof Systems Inc.
2500 Executive Hills Dr
Auburn Hills MI 48326
248 997-5100

(P-13109)
YAMAHA MOTOR CORPORATION USA (HQ)
6555 Katella Ave, Cypress (90630-5101)
PHONE.................................714 761-7300
Toshi Kato, *CEO*
Phil Dyskow, *President*
Jeff Young, *President*
Takuwy Watanabe, *Corp Secy*
Sean Bice, *Officer*
◆ **EMP:** 400 **EST:** 1955
SQ FT: 200,000
SALES (est): 1.4B Privately Held
WEB: www.yamaha-motor.com
SIC: 5571 5013 5091 5012 Motorcycle dealers; motor vehicle supplies & new parts; boats, canoes, watercrafts & equipment; motorcycles

(P-13110)
YOSHIMURA RES & DEV AMER INC
5420 Daniels St Ste A, Chino (91710-9012)
PHONE.................................909 628-4722
Fujio Yoshimura, *President*

Suehiro Watanabe, *CFO*
Rich Doan, *Officer*
Don Sakakura, *Senior VP*
Yusaku Yoshimura, *Administration*
▲ **EMP:** 100 **EST:** 1975
SQ FT: 12,000
SALES (est): 27.9MM **Privately Held**
WEB: www.yoshimura-rd.com
SIC: 5013 Motorcycle parts

5014 Tires & Tubes Wholesale

(P-13111)
AKH COMPANY INC
Also Called: Discount Tire Center 077
23316 Sunnymead Blvd, Moreno Valley
(92553-5227)
PHONE....................951 924-5356
Juan Valdes, *Manager*
EMP: 88
SALES (corp-wide): 31MM **Privately
Held**
WEB: www.discounttires.com
SIC: 5531 5014 7539 Automotive tires;
automobile tires & tubes; wheel align-
ment, automotive
PA: Akh Company, Inc.
1160 N Anaheim Blvd
Anaheim CA 92801
800 999-2878

(P-13112)
ATD CORPORATION
5100 Ontario Mills Pkwy, Ontario
(91764-5103)
PHONE....................909 481-6210
Joe Garcia, *Administration*
EMP: 158
SALES (corp-wide): 1.8B **Privately Held**
WEB: www.atd-us.com
SIC: 5014 3011 Tires & tubes; inner tubes,
all types
PA: Atd Corporation
12200 Herbert Wayne Ct # 1
Huntersville NC 28078
704 992-2000

(P-13113)
CANYON TIRE SALES INC (PA)
10064 Dawson Canyon Rd A, Corona
(92883-2113)
PHONE....................951 603-0615
Mitchell Leinen, *President*
Nick Leinen, *Vice Pres*
Allison Leinen, *Executive*
Steve Paul, *Sales Staff*
▲ **EMP:** 90 **EST:** 1990
SQ FT: 7,000
SALES (est): 33.6MM **Privately Held**
WEB: www.border-tire.com
SIC: 5531 5014 Automotive tires; automo-
bile tires & tubes

(P-13114)
COSTCO WHOLESALE CORPORATION
1345 N Montebello Blvd, Montebello
(90640-2585)
PHONE....................323 890-1904
EMP: 205 **Privately Held**
SIC: 5399 5014 Misc. General Merchandise Stores,Nsk

(P-13115)
FALKEN TIRE HOLDINGS INC
Also Called: Falken Tires
8656 Haven Ave, Rancho Cucamonga
(91730-9103)
PHONE....................800 723-2553
Richard Smallwood, *President*
Anthony Paparone, *Analyst*
Jim Hale, *Sales Staff*
Ron Papcun, *Director*
Nick Fousekis, *Manager*
▲ **EMP:** 80 **EST:** 2006
SALES (est): 23.4MM **Privately Held**
WEB: www.srigroup.co.jp
SIC: 5014 Automotive tires & tubes
PA: Sumitomo Rubber Industries, Ltd.
3-6-9, Wakinohamacho, Chuo-Ku
Kobe HYO 651-0

(P-13116)
GLOBE TIRE & MOTORSPORTS CORP
Also Called: Globe Tire & Motor Sports
2450 S La Cienega Blvd, Los Angeles
(90034-2216)
PHONE....................310 836-0804
Arnold Sperling, *CEO*
Miguel Gomez, *Sales Staff*
▲ **EMP:** 51 **EST:** 1959
SALES (est): 9.6MM **Privately Held**
WEB: www.globemotorsports.com
SIC: 5014 5531 Automobile tires & tubes;
automotive tires

(P-13117)
GREENBALL CORP (PA)
Also Called: Towmaster Tire & Wheel
222 S Harbor Blvd Ste 700, Anaheim
(92805-3730)
PHONE....................714 782-3060
Chris S H Tsai, *CEO*
Jenny Tsai, *Treasurer*
Cathy Tsai, *Executive Asst*
Alex Latios, *Administration*
Edmund Adams, *Sales Staff*
◆ **EMP:** 50 **EST:** 1976
SQ FT: 80,000
SALES (est): 50MM **Privately Held**
WEB: www.greenballtires.com
SIC: 5014 5013 3999 Automobile tires &
tubes; wheels, motor vehicle; atomizers,
toiletry

(P-13118)
LAKIN TIRE WEST INCORPORATED (PA)
Also Called: Lakin Tire of Calif
15305 Spring Ave, Santa Fe Springs
(90670-5645)
PHONE....................562 802-2752
Robert Lakin, *CEO*
Marco Jimenez, *Vice Pres*
David Lakin, *Vice Pres*
Sean Lakin, *Vice Pres*
Michael Bertrand, *Business Dir*
◆ **EMP:** 167 **EST:** 1973
SQ FT: 50,000
SALES (est): 63.8MM **Privately Held**
WEB: www.lakintire.com
SIC: 5531 5014 Tires, used; automotive &
home supply stores

(P-13119)
SOUTHERN CAL DISC TIRE CO INC
20741 Avalon Blvd, Carson (90746-3313)
PHONE....................310 324-2569
Arnel Ramos, *Manager*
EMP: 106
SALES (corp-wide): 3.6B **Privately Held**
WEB: www.discounttire.com
SIC: 5531 5014 5013 Automotive tires;
automobile tires & tubes; wheels, motor
vehicle
HQ: Southern California Discount Tire Co.,
Inc.
16100 N Grnway Hyden Loop
Scottsdale AZ 85260
602 996-0201

(P-13120)
SUMITOMO RUBBER NORTH AMER INC (HQ)
Also Called: Falken Tire
8656 Haven Ave, Rancho Cucamonga
(91730-9103)
PHONE....................909 466-1116
Richard Smallwood, *CEO*
Rick Brennan, *Exec Dir*
Sam Williams, *Division Mgr*
Rosa Borjas, *Administration*
Jeremy Templeman, *Administration*
◆ **EMP:** 120
SQ FT: 190,000
SALES (est): 101.5MM **Privately Held**
WEB: www.falkentire.com
SIC: 5014 Automobile tires & tubes

(P-13121)
TIRECO INC (PA)
500 W 190th St Ste 600, Gardena
(90248-4269)
PHONE....................310 767-7990
Robert W Liu, *CEO*

Justin Liu, *COO*
Mimi Liu, *CFO*
Andrew Hoit, *Vice Pres*
Chris Holbert, *Vice Pres*
◆ **EMP:** 150 **EST:** 2000
SALES (est): 112.5MM **Privately Held**
WEB: www.tireco.com
SIC: 5014 5013 5051 Tires, used; wheels,
motor vehicle; tubing, metal

(P-13122)
TIRES WAREHOUSE LLC
18203 Mount Baldy Cir, Fountain Valley
(92708-6117)
PHONE....................714 432-8851
Terry Ahlstrom, *Branch Mgr*
EMP: 194
SALES (corp-wide): 957.5MM **Privately
Held**
WEB: www.tireswarehouse.com
SIC: 5531 5014 Automotive tires; tires &
tubes
HQ: Tire's Warehouse, Llc
1820 Fullerton Ave # 300
Corona CA 92881
951 808-0111

5015 Motor Vehicle Parts, Used Wholesale

(P-13123)
CADNCHEV INC
Also Called: Lakenor Auto Salvage
13603 Foster Rd, Santa Fe Springs
(90670-4834)
PHONE....................562 944-6422
Donald Flynn, *Ch of Bd*
Thomas Raterman, *CFO*
Frank Erlain, *Vice Pres*
EMP: 54 **EST:** 1952
SQ FT: 10,000
SALES (est): 5.9MM
SALES (corp-wide): 11.6B **Publicly Held**
WEB: www.lkqcorp.com
SIC: 5015 5531 Automotive parts & sup-
plies, used; automotive parts
PA: Lkq Corporation
500 W Madison St Ste 2800
Chicago IL 60661
312 621-1950

(P-13124)
RVSHILFY LLC
1515 E 15th St, Los Angeles (90021-2711)
PHONE....................313 329-0146
Yanfeng Wu,
EMP: 50 **EST:** 2019
SALES (est): 2MM **Privately Held**
SIC: 5015 Automotive supplies, used

5021 Furniture Wholesale

(P-13125)
ALTON IRVINE INC
Also Called: Millwork Holdings
2052 Alton Pkwy, Irvine (92606-4905)
PHONE....................949 428-4141
Alan True, *CEO*
Dan Tacheny, *President*
Don Smith, *Exec VP*
Tom Pierce, *Info Tech Dir*
Marcelo Mezzera, *Research*
▲ **EMP:** 53 **EST:** 2001
SQ FT: 45,000
SALES (est): 18.8MM **Privately Held**
WEB: www.trueinnovations.com
SIC: 5021 Office furniture

(P-13126)
ASHLEY FURNITURE INDS LLC
Also Called: Ashley Furniture Homestore
2250 W Lugonia Ave, Redlands
(92374-5050)
PHONE....................800 240-3440
Marco Sanchez, *Manager*
EMP: 294
SALES (corp-wide): 4.1B **Privately Held**
WEB: www.ashleyfurniture.com
SIC: 5021 5712 Furniture; furniture stores
PA: Ashley Furniture Industries, Llc
1 Ashley Way
Arcadia WI 54612
608 323-3377

(P-13127)
BENETTIS ITALIA INC
3037 E Maria St, Compton (90221-5803)
PHONE....................310 537-8036
Mohammad A Ahmadinia, *CEO*
Sarah Ahmadinia, *CFO*
◆ **EMP:** 21 **EST:** 1991
SQ FT: 120,000
SALES (est): 3.9MM **Privately Held**
WEB: www.benettisitalia.com
SIC: 5021 2426 Office furniture; furniture
stock & parts, hardwood

(P-13128)
BEST QUALITY FURNITURE MFG INC
5400 E Francis St, Ontario (91761-3603)
P.O. Box 310795, Fontana (92331-0795)
PHONE....................909 230-6440
Khoa Van Ta, *President*
Craig Alford, *Vice Pres*
◆ **EMP:** 14 **EST:** 1996
SALES (est): 2.1MM **Privately Held**
SIC: 5021 2512 2511 Household furni-
ture; upholstered household furniture;
wood household furniture

(P-13129)
BLUMENTHAL DISTRIBUTING INC (PA)
Also Called: Office Star Products
1901 S Archibald Ave, Ontario
(91761-8548)
P.O. Box 3520 (91761-0952)
PHONE....................909 930-2000
Richard Blumenthal, *President*
Rose Blumenthal, *Shareholder*
Jennifer Blumenthal, *Corp Secy*
Lili Avimi, *Vice Pres*
Doug Freeman, *Vice Pres*
◆ **EMP:** 150 **EST:** 1983
SQ FT: 200,000
SALES (est): 54.5MM **Privately Held**
SIC: 5021 2522 Office furniture; chairs, of-
fice: padded or plain, except wood

(P-13130)
CAMBIUM BUSINESS GROUP INC (PA)
Also Called: Fairmont Designs
6950 Noritsu Ave, Buena Park
(90620-1311)
PHONE....................714 670-1171
George Tsai, *Chairman*
Kevin Fitzgerald, *President*
Jason Liu, *CEO*
Mark Klingensmith, *Vice Pres*
Scott Mesel, *Vice Pres*
◆ **EMP:** 120 **EST:** 1984
SQ FT: 200,000
SALES (est): 39.4MM **Privately Held**
WEB: www.fairmontdesigns.com
SIC: 5021 2511 Household furniture; din-
ing room furniture; tables, occasional;
beds; wood household furniture

(P-13131)
COMPLETE OFFICE CALIFORNIA INC
12724 Moore St, Cerritos (90703-2121)
PHONE....................714 880-1222
Edward B Walter, *CEO*
Rick Israel, *Principal*
EMP: 62 **EST:** 1961
SQ FT: 28,000
SALES (est): 42.8MM
SALES (corp-wide): 9.73 **Publicly Held**
WEB: www.officedepot.com
SIC: 5021 5112 Office furniture; office sup-
plies
HQ: Office Depot, Llc
6600 N Military Trl
Boca Raton FL 33436
561 438-4800

(P-13132)
COPPEL CORPORATION
503 Scaroni Ave, Calexico (92231-9791)
PHONE....................760 357-3707
David Coppel Calvo, *CEO*
Joaquin Aguirre Ruiz, *Vice Pres*
Angel Olguin, *Principal*
Allan Lewis, *Controller*
▲ **EMP:** 78 **EST:** 1991
SQ FT: 70,000

SALES: 522.4MM **Privately Held**
WEB: www.coppel.com
SIC: 5021 5137 5136 Household furniture; women's & children's clothing; men's & boys' clothing
HQ: Coppel, S.A. De C.V.
Republica Poniente No. 2855
Culiacan SIN. 80105

(P-13133)
DESIGNER IMPORTS INTL INC
6931 Stanford Ave, Los Angeles
(90001-1543)
PHONE..................................323 753-5448
Joubin Torkan, *President*
▲ **EMP:** 21 **EST:** 1952
SQ FT: 60,000
SALES (est): 1.8MM **Privately Held**
SIC: 5021 2511 Office & public building furniture; household furniture; wood household furniture

(P-13134)
EC GROUP INC (PA)
Also Called: Dennis & Leen
5960 Bowcroft St, Los Angeles
(90016-4302)
PHONE..................................310 815-2700
Richard Hallberg, *President*
Daniel Cuevas, *Vice Pres*
Barbara Wiseley, *Admin Sec*
▲ **EMP:** 80 **EST:** 1985
SQ FT: 18,000
SALES (est): 29.3MM **Privately Held**
WEB: www.dennisandleen.com
SIC: 5021 Furniture

(P-13135)
EMPIRE ENTERPRISES INC (PA)
4264 Fulton Ave Ste 1, Studio City
(91604-1802)
P.O. Box 1344 (91614-0344)
PHONE..................................818 784-8918
William Landes, *President*
Margie Clapper, *Vice Pres*
Wendy Landes, *Vice Pres*
EMP: 15
SQ FT: 2,200
SALES (est): 2.8MM **Privately Held**
SIC: 5021 2731 Furniture; books: publishing only

(P-13136)
ERGOMOTION INC
6790 Navigator Way, Goleta (93117-3656)
P.O. Box 8330 (93118-8330)
PHONE..................................805 979-9400
Wenbiao Hou, *CEO*
Guohai Tang, *CEO*
Johnny Griggs, *COO*
Harry Hou, *CFO*
Paris Fealy, *Vice Pres*
▲ **EMP:** 70 **EST:** 2006
SALES (est): 24.6MM **Privately Held**
WEB: www.ergomotion.com
SIC: 5021 Beds & bedding

(P-13137)
FURNITURE AMERICA CAL INC (PA)
Also Called: Furniture America California
19605 E Walnut Dr N, City of Industry
(91789-2815)
PHONE..................................909 718-7276
George Wells, *CEO*
Rocky Yang, *Vice Pres*
Chen Jean, *Accountant*
Aki Furutani, *Superintendent*
◆ **EMP:** 68 **EST:** 2005
SQ FT: 200,000
SALES (est): 25MM **Privately Held**
WEB: www.foagroup.com
SIC: 5021 2512 Furniture; upholstered household furniture

(P-13138)
HUMAN TOUCH LLC
4600 E Conant St, Long Beach
(90808-1874)
PHONE..................................562 426-8700
Andrew Cohen, *President*
David Wood, *CEO*
Chang Han, *Principal*
Karen Bush, *Administration*
Ralph Obregon, *Technical Mgr*

◆ **EMP:** 80 **EST:** 1999
SQ FT: 98,500
SALES (est): 15.5MM **Privately Held**
WEB: www.humantouch.com
SIC: 5021 Chairs

(P-13139)
JANUS ET CIE (PA)
12310 Greenstone Ave, Santa Fe Springs
(90670-4737)
PHONE..................................310 601-2958
Janice K Feldman, *CEO*
Paul Warren, *COO*
Greg Buscher, *CFO*
Danya Lane, *Vice Pres*
Cindy Wolf, *VP Bus Dvlpt*
◆ **EMP:** 110 **EST:** 1977
SQ FT: 154,000
SALES (est): 53.4MM **Privately Held**
WEB: www.janusetcie.com
SIC: 5021 5712 Outdoor & lawn furniture; furniture stores

(P-13140)
LIMA TRADING LLC
Also Called: Vig Furniture
3251 E Slauson Ave, Vernon (90058-3918)
PHONE..................................323 588-7434
Irina Reznik, *Mng Member*
EMP: 50 **EST:** 1998
SQ FT: 200,000
SALES (est): 9.6MM **Privately Held**
WEB: www.vigfurniture.com
SIC: 5021 Furniture

(P-13141)
LIVING SPACES FURNITURE LLC (PA)
14501 Artesia Blvd, La Mirada
(90638-5805)
P.O. Box 2309, Buena Park (90621-0809)
PHONE..................................714 523-2000
Grover Geiselman,
Jay Martinez, *COO*
Chris Lynch, *CFO*
Luke Parker, *Exec VP*
Heriberto De La Torre, *Department Mgr*
▲ **EMP:** 112 **EST:** 2003
SQ FT: 136,000
SALES (est): 302.5MM **Privately Held**
WEB: www.livingspaces.com
SIC: 5712 5021 Mattresses; furniture

(P-13142)
LOGISTAR LLC
3030 S Atl Blvd Unit B, Vernon (90058)
PHONE..................................323 274-9651
Jessyca Nahmani, *President*
EMP: 60 **EST:** 2018
SALES (est): 5.2MM **Privately Held**
SIC: 5021 Furniture

(P-13143)
MACHINEHOME INC
8960 Toronto Ave, Rancho Cucamonga
(91730-5411)
PHONE..................................858 336-9471
Jianxin Chen, *CEO*
EMP: 50 **EST:** 2019
SALES (est): 3MM **Privately Held**
SIC: 5021 Outdoor & lawn furniture

(P-13144)
MODERN IMAGING SOLUTIONS INC
22122 Sherman Way Ste 209, Canoga Park
(91303-1138)
PHONE..................................800 511-7585
Carol Paula Greenhut, *President*
Ivan Greenhut, *Vice Pres*
Briones April, *Human Res Mgr*
David Dilao, *Accounts Mgr*
Irwin Apid, *Accounts Exec*
◆ **EMP:** 50 **EST:** 2005
SALES (est): 6.6MM **Privately Held**
SIC: 5734 5021 5112 Printers & plotters: computers; office furniture; stationery & office supplies

(P-13145)
MODWAY INC
Also Called: Modway Furniture
15816 Santa Ana Ave, Fontana
(92337-7358)
PHONE..................................323 729-3299

Moshe Gitlin, *Executive*
Hershy Ives, *Accountant*
Meir Brash, *Manager*
Ashley Logan, *Accounts Mgr*
EMP: 65
SALES (corp-wide): 87.8MM **Privately Held**
WEB: www.modway.com
SIC: 5021 Furniture
PA: Modway Inc.
329 Wyckoff Mills Rd
Hightstown NJ 08520
609 256-9000

(P-13146)
OMNIA ITALIAN DESIGN LLC
4900 Edison Ave, Chino (91710-5713)
PHONE..................................909 393-4400
Peter Zolferino, *Mng Member*
Luie Nastri,
◆ **EMP:** 200 **EST:** 1989
SQ FT: 110,000
SALES (est): 37.7MM **Privately Held**
WEB: www.omnialeather.com
SIC: 5021 Household furniture

(P-13147)
PHYLLIS MORRIS ORIGINALS (PA)
Also Called: Morris, Phyllis
8772 Beverly Blvd, West Hollywood
(90048-1804)
PHONE..................................310 289-6868
Jamie Goller Adler, *President*
Nathan Goller, *Corp Secy*
John Adler, *Vice Pres*
EMP: 16 **EST:** 1954
SQ FT: 27,000
SALES (est): 5.5MM **Privately Held**
WEB: www.phyllismorris.com
SIC: 5021 2519 2511 Furniture; fiberglass & plastic furniture; wood household furniture

(P-13148)
PHYLLIS MORRIS ORIGINALS
655 N Robertson Blvd, Los Angeles
(90069-5016)
PHONE..................................310 289-4800
EMP: 28
SALES (corp-wide): 5.5MM **Privately Held**
WEB: www.phyllismorris.com
SIC: 5021 2519 Mfg & Whol Furniture
PA: Phyllis Morris Originals
8772 Beverly Blvd
West Hollywood CA 90048
310 289-6868

(P-13149)
POUNDEX ASSOCIATES CORPORATION
21490 Baker Pkwy, City of Industry
(91789-5239)
PHONE..................................909 444-5878
Lionel Chen, *President*
◆ **EMP:** 100 **EST:** 1988
SQ FT: 55,000
SALES (est): 18.9MM **Privately Held**
WEB: www.poundex.com
SIC: 5021 Household furniture; dining room furniture; tables, occasional

(P-13150)
PRIVILEGE INTERNATIONAL INC
2323 Firestone Blvd, South Gate
(90280-2684)
PHONE..................................323 585-0777
Eddy Sarraf, *President*
Mark Darwish, *Senior VP*
Richard Darwish, *Vice Pres*
Elizabeth Alvarado, *Office Mgr*
◆ **EMP:** 75 **EST:** 1999
SQ FT: 350,000
SALES (est): 18MM **Privately Held**
WEB: www.privilegeinc.com
SIC: 5021 Furniture

(P-13151)
RESIDENT HOME LLC (PA)
Also Called: Nectar Sleep
340 S Lemon Ave 9599, Walnut
(91789-2706)
PHONE..................................888 863-2827

Eric Hutchinson,
EMP: 120 **EST:** 2016
SALES (est): 74.6MM **Privately Held**
SIC: 5021 5023 Mattresses; rugs

(P-13152)
SITONIT SEATING INC
6415 Katella Ave, Cypress (90630-5245)
PHONE..................................714 995-4800
Paul Devries, *CEO*
EMP: 561 **EST:** 2008
SALES (est): 8.4MM **Privately Held**
WEB: www.sitonit.net
SIC: 5021 Office furniture
PA: Exemplis Llc
6415 Katella Ave
Cypress CA 90630

(P-13153)
UNISOURCE SOLUTIONS INC (PA)
8350 Rex Rd, Pico Rivera (90660-3785)
PHONE..................................562 654-3500
James Kastner, *CEO*
Marc Flax, *President*
Ken Kastner, *President*
Clem Nieto, *CFO*
Jim Kastner, *Chairman*
▲ **EMP:** 105 **EST:** 1987
SQ FT: 186,000
SALES (est): 54.4MM **Privately Held**
WEB: www.unisourceit.com
SIC: 5021 Office furniture

(P-13154)
VIRCO INC (HQ)
2027 Harpers Way, Torrance (90501-1524)
PHONE..................................310 533-0474
Robert Virtue, *CEO*
Scotty Bell, *Vice Pres*
Robert Dose, *Vice Pres*
Patricia Quinones, *Vice Pres*
Larry Maddox, *Admin Sec*
▼ **EMP:** 227 **EST:** 1998
SQ FT: 560,000
SALES (est): 65.2MM
SALES (corp-wide): 152.8MM **Publicly Held**
WEB: www.virco.com
SIC: 5021 Furniture
PA: Virco Mfg. Corporation
2027 Harpers Way
Torrance CA 90501
310 533-0474

5023 Home Furnishings Wholesale

(P-13155)
AL FAKHORY TRADING LLC (PA)
13047 Lakeland Rd, Santa Fe Springs
(90670-4518)
PHONE..................................323 728-8840
Emil Girgis,
Edmon Girgis, *Finance Mgr*
▲ **EMP:** 14 **EST:** 2011
SQ FT: 11,712
SALES (est): 2.9MM **Privately Held**
WEB: www.alfakhory.com
SIC: 5023 2515 Sheets, textile; mattresses, innerspring or box spring

(P-13156)
ALPINE INTERIORS CORPORATION (PA)
Also Called: Alpine Carpets
3961 Sepulveda Blvd # 205, Culver City
(90230-4600)
PHONE..................................310 390-7639
Johannes Van Ierland, *CEO*
Klaus Friederic, *President*
EMP: 50 **EST:** 1966
SQ FT: 21,000
SALES (est): 17.6MM **Privately Held**
WEB: www.alpinecarpetoneculvercity.com
SIC: 5023 5713 Floor coverings; carpets

(P-13157)
AMERDALE INDUSTRIES INC
Also Called: Dale Tiffany
14750 Northam St, La Mirada
(90638-5620)
PHONE..............714 521-3800
Don Lucas, *Manager*
EMP: 51
SALES (corp-wide): 11.8MM **Privately Held**
SIC: 5023 Lamps: floor, boudoir, desk
PA: Amerdale Industries, Inc.
14765 Industry Cir
La Mirada CA
-

(P-13158)
ARCHITECTURAL WINDOW SHADES
9900 Gidley St, El Monte (91731-1112)
PHONE..............626 578-1936
Tom Robertson, *General Mgr*
Maria Juarez, *Executive Asst*
Cindy Justice, *Sales Staff*
Larry Taylor, *Sr Project Mgr*
Calyn Lim, *Manager*
EMP: 60 EST: 2016
SALES (est): 10.1MM **Privately Held**
WEB: www.awshades.com
SIC: 5719 5023 Window shades; window covering parts & accessories; window shades
PA: Hunter Douglas N.V.
Dokweg 19
Willemstad

(P-13159)
BECKER INTERIORS LTD
Also Called: Alexander Becker Carpets
5552 Hollywood Blvd, Los Angeles (90028-6808)
PHONE..............323 469-1938
Theodore Fox, *President*
EMP: 13 EST: 1949
SQ FT: 10,000
SALES (est): 1.2MM **Privately Held**
SIC: 5023 5713 2273 Carpets; carpets; carpets & rugs

(P-13160)
BP INDUSTRIES INCORPORATED
5300 E Concours St, Ontario (91764)
PHONE..............909 481-0227
Dong Koo Kim, *President*
Wayne Craparo, *Exec VP*
Maria Hon, *Controller*
Charles Wang, *Controller*
Allisha Merrill, *Sales Staff*
◆ EMP: 57 EST: 1989
SQ FT: 140,000
SALES (est): 10.7MM **Privately Held**
WEB: www.bpindustries.com
SIC: 5023 Mirrors & pictures, framed & unframed

(P-13161)
BRADSHAW INTERNATIONAL INC (HQ)
Also Called: Bradshaw Home
9409 Buffalo Ave, Rancho Cucamonga (91730-6012)
PHONE..............909 476-3884
Arthur Zambelli, *CEO*
Robert Michelson, *President*
Jeff Megorden, *COO*
Sandip Grewal, *CFO*
Scott Bradshaw, *Vice Pres*
◆ EMP: 280 EST: 2010
SQ FT: 750,000
SALES (est): 355.4MM
SALES (corp-wide): 337.5MM **Privately Held**
WEB: www.bradshawhome.com
SIC: 5023 Kitchenware
PA: Oncap Ii L.P.
161 Bay St
Toronto ON M5J 2
416 214-4300

(P-13162)
BREVILLE USA INC
19400 S Western Ave, Torrance (90501-1119)
PHONE..............310 755-3000
Damian Baden Court, *CEO*
Simon Schober, *CFO*
Jennifer Crasta, *Planning*
Henry Hsu, *Technical Mgr*
Brett Schwab, *Technology*
◆ EMP: 50 EST: 1989
SQ FT: 135,000
SALES (est): 56.7MM **Privately Held**
WEB: www.support.breville.com
SIC: 5023 5064 Home furnishings; appliance parts, household
HQ: Breville Holdings Pty Limited
G Se 2 170 Bourke Rd
Alexandria NSW 2015

(P-13163)
BUSTER AND PUNCH INC
10844 Burbank Blvd, North Hollywood (91601-2519)
PHONE..............818 392-3827
David Schlocker, *President*
EMP: 25 EST: 2020
SALES (est): 1.2MM **Privately Held**
WEB: www.busterandpunch.com
SIC: 5023 5063 5719 3429 Home furnishings; decorative home furnishings & supplies; lighting fixtures, residential; lighting fixtures; cabinet hardware

(P-13164)
CARPET USA LTD (PA)
9310 S La Cienega Blvd, Inglewood (90301-4410)
PHONE..............310 390-8570
Giora Agam, *CEO*
Jerry Agam, *President*
Nathan Agam, *COO*
Lien Tien, *Controller*
Yosi Drori, *Marketing Staff*
EMP: 65 EST: 1974
SQ FT: 25,000
SALES (est): 19.5MM **Privately Held**
WEB: www.carpetusafloors.com
SIC: 5713 5023 Carpets; carpets

(P-13165)
CLASSIC CONCEPTS INC (PA)
Also Called: Classic Home
4505 Bandini Blvd, Vernon (90058-5408)
PHONE..............323 266-8993
Harpal Singh, *President*
Zaidi Bilgees, *Treasurer*
John Moody, *Vice Pres*
Gita Singh, *Vice Pres*
Renuka Gujral, *VP Bus Dvlpt*
◆ EMP: 15 EST: 1990
SQ FT: 2,500
SALES (est): 29.3MM **Privately Held**
WEB: www.classichome.com
SIC: 5023 2511 2512 Decorative home furnishings & supplies; rugs; wood household furniture; living room furniture: upholstered on wood frames

(P-13166)
CONTRACTORS FLRG SVC CAL INC
300 E Dyer Rd, Santa Ana (92707-3740)
P.O. Box 15106 (92735-0106)
PHONE..............714 556-6100
Joseph J Ott, *President*
EMP: 110 EST: 1996
SQ FT: 10,000
SALES (est): 16.6MM **Privately Held**
WEB: www.cfsofca.com
SIC: 5023 Floor coverings

(P-13167)
ELDER STATESMAN LLC (PA)
2416 Hunter St, Los Angeles (90021-2504)
PHONE..............310 920-4659
Gregory Chait,
Sarai Hernandez, *Production*
Jhonnattan Perez, *Production*
▲ EMP: 13 EST: 2007
SALES (est): 4.2MM **Privately Held**
WEB: www.elder-statesman.com
SIC: 5023 7221 2399 Blankets; photographic studios, portrait; hand woven apparel

(P-13168)
ELIJAH TEXTILES INC
Also Called: Sharp Fabric
1251 E Olympic Blvd, Los Angeles (90021-1859)
PHONE..............310 666-3443
Kourosh Amirianfar, *President*
EMP: 82 EST: 2001
SQ FT: 100,000
SALES (est): 34MM **Privately Held**
SIC: 5023 5949 Sheets, textile; fabric stores piece goods

(P-13169)
EV RAY INC
6400 Variel Ave, Woodland Hills (91367-2577)
PHONE..............818 346-5381
Lee Brown, *President*
Helen Kim, *Finance Mgr*
Diana Villa, *Purchasing*
Beatrice Gomes, *Manager*
EMP: 50 EST: 1962
SQ FT: 22,000
SALES (est): 6.9MM **Privately Held**
WEB: www.rayev.com
SIC: 5023 2211 2591 2391 Draperies; draperies & drapery fabrics, cotton; drapery hardware & blinds & shades; curtains & draperies

(P-13170)
GALLEHER LLC (PA)
9303 Greenleaf Ave, Santa Fe Springs (90670-3029)
PHONE..............562 944-8885
Ted Kozikowski, *President*
Rick Coates, *COO*
Jeff Hamar, *Chairman*
Todd Hamar, *Senior VP*
Jim Harrington, *Vice Pres*
▲ EMP: 110 EST: 2018
SQ FT: 100,000
SALES (est): 83.4MM **Privately Held**
WEB: www.galleher.com
SIC: 5023 Wood flooring

(P-13171)
GIBSON OVERSEAS INC
2410 Yates Ave, Commerce (90040-1918)
PHONE..............323 832-8900
Sol Gabbay, *CEO*
Sal Gabbay, *CEO*
Darioush Gabbay, *COO*
Soloman Gabbay, *CFO*
Laura Fischer, *Senior VP*
◆ EMP: 510 EST: 1979
SQ FT: 850,000
SALES (est): 221.8MM **Privately Held**
WEB: www.gibsonusa.com
SIC: 5023 Glassware; china; kitchen tools & utensils

(P-13172)
GINA B LTD
Also Called: Gina B Showroom
1601 W 134th St, Gardena (90249-2013)
PHONE..............310 366-7926
Rolf Berschneider, *President*
Gina Berschneider, *Vice Pres*
EMP: 14 EST: 1968
SALES (est): 2MM **Privately Held**
WEB: www.gbfurniture.net
SIC: 5023 2599 2542 2273 Home furnishings; factory furniture & fixtures; partitions & fixtures, except wood; carpets & rugs

(P-13173)
GTT INTERNATIONAL INC
1615 Eastridge Ave, Riverside (92507-7111)
PHONE..............951 788-8729
Mohammed Arshad, *President*
Hafiz Ur Rahaman, *Vice Pres*
▲ EMP: 35 EST: 1991
SALES (est): 2.5MM **Privately Held**
SIC: 5023 2258 Bedspreads; curtains; draperies; pillowcases; lace & warp knit fabric mills

(P-13174)
INNOVATIVE BEDG SOLUTIONS INC
6560 Caballero Blvd, Buena Park (90620-1130)
PHONE..............714 994-2223
Cesar A Chavez, *CEO*
EMP: 17 EST: 2012
SALES (est): 7.8MM **Privately Held**
WEB: www.ibscomfort.com
SIC: 5023 5021 2392 Decorative home furnishings & supplies; beds & bedding; blankets, comforters & beddings

(P-13175)
KATZIRS FLOOR & HM DESIGN INC (PA)
Also Called: National Hrdwood Flrg Moulding
14959 Delano St, Van Nuys (91411-2123)
PHONE..............818 988-9663
Omer Katzir, *CEO*
Jeannette Katzir, *Treasurer*
Anatoliy Katzir, *Sales Executive*
Rolando Tejeda, *Sales Mgr*
▲ EMP: 20 EST: 1982
SQ FT: 19,270
SALES (est): 10.8MM **Privately Held**
WEB: www.nationalhardwood.com
SIC: 5023 2435 Wood flooring; hardwood veneer & plywood

(P-13176)
LEDRA BRANDS INC
Also Called: Bruck Lighting Systems
88 Maxwell, Irvine (92618-4641)
PHONE..............714 259-9959
Alex Ladjevardi, *President*
Farah Emami, *COO*
John Oveisi, *CFO*
Jade Turney, *Vice Pres*
Lawrence Cagatin, *Engineer*
▲ EMP: 112 EST: 1993
SALES (est): 26.5MM **Privately Held**
WEB: www.ledrabrands.com
SIC: 5023 Lamps: floor, boudoir, desk

(P-13177)
MARIAK INDUSTRIES INC
Also Called: Mariak Window Fashion
575 W Manville St, Rancho Dominguez (90220-5509)
PHONE..............310 661-4400
Leo Elinson, *CEO*
▲ EMP: 269 EST: 1986
SQ FT: 80,000
SALES (est): 48.9MM
SALES (corp-wide): 4.4B **Privately Held**
WEB: www.mariak.com
SIC: 5023 2591 Vertical blinds; blinds vertical
HQ: Springs Window Fashions, Llc
7549 Graber Rd
Middleton WI 53562
608 836-1011

(P-13178)
NEW CLASSIC HM FURNISHING INC (PA)
Also Called: New Classic Furniture
7351 Mcguire Ave, Fontana (92336-1668)
PHONE..............909 484-7676
Jean Tong, *CEO*
Vicky Wang, *Principal*
Hogen Quiel, *Info Tech Mgr*
Lan Tong, *IT/INT Sup*
Beth Schreck, *Broker*
◆ EMP: 73 EST: 2001
SALES (est): 104MM **Privately Held**
SIC: 5023 2512 Home furnishings; upholstered household furniture

(P-13179)
NEXGRILL INDUSTRIES INC (PA)
14050 Laurelwood Pl, Chino (91710-5454)
PHONE..............909 598-8799
Sherman Lin, *CEO*
Coleman Caldwell, *Exec VP*
Jeff Tsai, *Vice Pres*
Pak LI, *IT/INT Sup*
Annette Ho, *Opers Mgr*
◆ EMP: 97 EST: 1993
SQ FT: 50,000

SALES (est): 27.2MM **Privately Held**
WEB: www.nexgrill.com
SIC: 5023 3631 Grills, barbecue; barbe-
cues, grills & braziers (outdoor cooking)

(P-13180)
NORCAL POTTERY PRODUCTS INC
5700 E Airport Dr, Ontario (91761-8620)
PHONE................................909 390-3745
Carrie Roberts, *Manager*
EMP: 135
SALES (corp-wide): 2.7B **Publicly Held**
SIC: 5023 Pottery
HQ: Norcal Pottery Products, Inc.
1000 Washington St
Foxboro MA 02035
510 895-5966

(P-13181)
NORMAN INTERNATIONAL INC
Also Called: Norman Charter
28 Centerpointe Dr # 120, La Palma
(90623-2500)
PHONE................................562 946-0420
Ranjan Mada, *CEO*
Paul Shih, *Vice Pres*
Jeffrey Zagorski, *Regional Mgr*
Jackie Yu, *MIS Mgr*
Susan Huang, *Business Mgr*
◆ **EMP:** 70 **EST:** 2001
SALES (est): 46.4MM **Privately Held**
WEB: www.normanusa.com
SIC: 5023 Home furnishings

(P-13182)
OMEGA MOULDING WEST LLC
5500 Lindbergh Ln, Bell (90201-6410)
PHONE................................323 261-3510
Bernard Portnoy, *Mng Member*
Ken Brodsky, *CFO*
Anastasia Portnoy, *Vice Pres*
Terry Essig, *Purchasing*
David Ratinov, *Sales Staff*
◆ **EMP:** 130 **EST:** 1998
SQ FT: 130,000
SALES (est): 18.2MM **Privately Held**
WEB: www.omegamoulding.com
SIC: 5023 Frames & framing, picture &
mirror

(P-13183)
PACIFIC HERITG HM FASHION INC
Also Called: Home Decor Wholesaler
901 Lawson St, City of Industry
(91748-1121)
PHONE................................909 598-5200
Meng Lan Liu, *President*
Frank Hsu, *Vice Pres*
Brenda Wilson, *Sales Staff*
▲ **EMP:** 25 **EST:** 2002
SALES (est): 5.5MM **Privately Held**
SIC: 5023 2392 Window shades; blankets;
comforters & beddings; tablecloths &
table settings

(P-13184)
RSI HOME PRODUCTS SALES INC
400 E Orangethorpe Ave, Anaheim
(92801-1046)
PHONE................................714 449-2200
Alex Calabrese, *President*
EMP: 51 **EST:** 2000
SALES (est): 11.1MM
SALES (corp-wide): 1.7B **Publicly Held**
WEB: www.americanwoodmark.com
SIC: 5023 Home furnishings
HQ: Rsi Home Products, Inc.
400 E Orangethorpe Ave
Anaheim CA 92801
714 449-2200

(P-13185)
SIMPLEHUMAN LLC (PA)
19850 Magellan Dr, Torrance (90502-1106)
PHONE................................310 436-2250
Frank Yang, *Mng Member*
Jenni Lain, *Executive*
Richard Huang, *Technology*
Chris Colagiovanni, *Engineer*
David Harper, *Business Mgr*
◆ **EMP:** 97 **EST:** 2001
SQ FT: 55,000

SALES (est): 113.1MM **Privately Held**
WEB: www.simplehuman.com
SIC: 5023 Kitchenware

(P-13186)
SOTO PROVISION INC
Also Called: Soto Food Service
488 Parriott Pl W, City of Industry
(91745-1015)
PHONE................................626 458-4600
John R Renna Sr, *President*
Russ Fischer, *CFO*
Bonnie Lea, *Officer*
John R Renna Jr, *Vice Pres*
EMP: 70 **EST:** 1974
SQ FT: 35,000
SALES (est): 34.9MM **Privately Held**
WEB: www.sotofoodservice.com
SIC: 5023 5046 Kitchen tools & utensils;
kitchenware; commercial cooking & food
service equipment

(P-13187)
TABLETOPS UNLIMITED INC (PA)
23000 Avalon Blvd, Carson (90745-5017)
PHONE................................310 549-6000
Javad Asgari, *CEO*
Mohsen Asgari, *President*
Hamid Ebrahimi, *President*
Mosen Asgari, *CFO*
Fred Rabizadeh, *Officer*
◆ **EMP:** 67 **EST:** 1983
SQ FT: 350,000
SALES (est): 32.5MM **Privately Held**
WEB: www.ttustore.com
SIC: 5023 Kitchenware

(P-13188)
TEST-RITE PRODUCTS CORP (DH)
1900 Burgundy Pl, Ontario (91761-2308)
PHONE................................909 605-9899
Kelly Ho, *President*
Jack Ho, *Treasurer*
Johnny Lin, *Network Enginr*
Katherine Chang, *Manager*
Vivian Huang, *Accounts Mgr*
◆ **EMP:** 80 **EST:** 1975
SQ FT: 400,000
SALES (est): 243.7MM **Privately Held**
SIC: 5023 Home furnishings

(P-13189)
TIFFANY DALE INC (PA)
14765 Industry Cir, La Mirada
(90638-5818)
PHONE................................714 739-2700
Ye H Chung, *CEO*
Garbiel Chung, *Vice Pres*
Connie Chung, *Admin Sec*
Griselda Ceballos, *Administration*
Serina Chung, *Administration*
▲ **EMP:** 83 **EST:** 1979
SQ FT: 88,480
SALES (est): 12.3MM **Privately Held**
WEB: www.daletiffany.com
SIC: 5023 Lamps: floor, boudoir, desk

(P-13190)
TRI - STAR WIN COVERINGS INC
Also Called: Carpet Care By Tri-Star
19555 Prairie St, Northridge (91324-2424)
PHONE................................818 718-3188
Bernard Warshauer, *CEO*
Deborah Newhouse, *Executive*
Saul Motola, *Sales Staff*
Craig Briggs, *Manager*
EMP: 50 **EST:** 1995
SQ FT: 22,000
SALES (est): 23.5MM **Privately Held**
WEB: www.tristarfwc.com
SIC: 5023 5719 Floor coverings; window
furnishings; window furnishings

(P-13191)
TRI-WEST LTD (PA)
12005 Pike St, Santa Fe Springs
(90670-6100)
PHONE................................562 692-9166
Allen Gage, *Partner*
John Lubinxki, *Partner*
Randy Sims, *Partner*
John Lubinski, *COO*
Laura Robledo, *Administration*
▲ **EMP:** 200 **EST:** 1976

SQ FT: 300,000
SALES (est): 93.8MM **Privately Held**
WEB: www.triwestltd.com
SIC: 5023 Floor coverings; resilient floor
coverings: tile or sheet; wood flooring

(P-13192)
UMA ENTERPRISES INC (PA)
Also Called: Uma Home Decor
350 W Apra St, Compton (90220-5529)
PHONE................................310 631-1166
James Buch, *CEO*
Larry Woods, *CFO*
Melissa Dench, *Vice Pres*
Robert Rich, *Vice Pres*
Bill Moylan, *Planning*
◆ **EMP:** 60 **EST:** 1986
SQ FT: 460,000
SALES (est): 48.1MM **Privately Held**
WEB: www.umainc.com
SIC: 5023 Decorative home furnishings &
supplies

(P-13193)
UNIQUE CARPETS LTD
7360 Jurupa Ave, Riverside (92504-1025)
PHONE................................951 352-8125
Bill D Graves, *President*
Robert L Binford, *Exec VP*
Robert Binford, *Exec VP*
Martin Lopez, *Vice Pres*
Andrea Bergman, *Office Admin*
▲ **EMP:** 55 **EST:** 1985
SALES (est): 15.7MM **Privately Held**
WEB: www.uniquecarpetsltd.com
SIC: 5023 2273 Carpets; carpets & rugs

(P-13194)
UNIVERSAL WOOD MOULDING INC (PA)
Also Called: Universal Framing Products
21139 Centre Pointe Pkwy, Santa Clarita
(91350-2994)
PHONE................................661 362-6262
Jon M Bromberg, *CEO*
AVI Feibenlatt, *Ch of Bd*
Mark Gottlieb, *President*
Bill Conn, *Sales Staff*
Amy Lorenz, *Sales Staff*
▲ **EMP:** 50 **EST:** 1995
SALES (est): 15.6MM **Privately Held**
WEB: www.universalarquati.com
SIC: 5023 3999 Frames & framing, picture
& mirror; atomizers; toiletry; advertising
curtains

(P-13195)
VALLEY WHOLESALE SUPPLY CORP (PA)
Also Called: Valley Molding & Frame
10708 Vanowen St, North Hollywood
(91605-6401)
PHONE................................818 769-5656
Charles Aaron, *Ch of Bd*
Michelle Merritt, *Shareholder*
David A Labowitz, *President*
Suzanne Ehrmann, *Vice Pres*
▲ **EMP:** 57 **EST:** 1974
SQ FT: 30,000
SALES (est): 7MM **Privately Held**
WEB: www.internationalmoulding.com
SIC: 5023 5031 Frames & framing, picture
& mirror; decorating supplies; molding, all
materials

(P-13196)
VENUS GROUP INC
Also Called: Venus Textiles
25861 Wright, Foothill Ranch (92610-3504)
PHONE................................949 609-1299
Kirit D Patel, *CEO*
Rajni D Patel, *Vice Pres*
Rita Epperson, *Executive Asst*
Dennis Jackson, *VP Prdtn*
Karan Madhrani, *Marketing Mgr*
◆ **EMP:** 103 **EST:** 1971
SALES (est): 72MM **Privately Held**
WEB: www.venusgroup.com
SIC: 5023 2392 5719 Towels; towels, fab-
ric & nonwoven: made from purchased
materials; towels

(P-13197)
VOGUE ENTERPRISE INC
Also Called: Vogue Developement
1801 Kettering, Irvine (92614-5617)
PHONE................................949 833-9787
Douglas Wong, *President*
Jenny Wong, *Vice Pres*
▲ **EMP:** 15 **EST:** 1981
SQ FT: 24,000
SALES (est): 2.6MM **Privately Held**
WEB: www.voguewindows.com
SIC: 5023 2591 Venetian blinds; venetian
blinds

(P-13198)
W DIAMOND SUPPLY CO (DH)
Also Called: Diamond W Floorcovering
19321 E Walnut Dr N, City of Industry
(91748-1436)
PHONE................................909 859-8939
Louis J Bettitta, *CEO*
Mike Klingele, *President*
Kandi Anderson, *COO*
Daniel Erickson, *CFO*
Eric Erman, *Purchasing*
▲ **EMP:** 60 **EST:** 1948
SQ FT: 106,000
SALES (est): 31.8MM
SALES (corp-wide): 167.1K **Privately Held**
WEB: www.diamondw.com
SIC: 5023 Floor coverings
HQ: Tarkett, Inc.
30000 Aurora Rd
Solon OH 44139
800 899-8916

5031 Lumber, Plywood & Millwork Wholesale

(P-13199)
AMERICAN BUILDING SUPPLY INC
120 S Cedar Ave, Rialto (92376-9010)
PHONE................................909 879-8700
Carlos Duran, *Branch Mgr*
EMP: 99 **Publicly Held**
WEB: www.abs-abs.com
SIC: 5031 Doors
HQ: American Building Supply, Inc.
8360 Elder Creek Rd
Sacramento CA 95828
916 503-4100

(P-13200)
ANEMOSTAT INC
1220 E Watson Center Rd, Carson
(90745-4206)
PHONE................................310 835-7500
Mark M Cassidy, *CEO*
Bobby Banaban, *Vice Pres*
David Chipman, *Vice Pres*
EMP: 50 **EST:** 1984
SALES (est): 12.5MM **Privately Held**
WEB: www.anemostat-hvac.com
SIC: 5031 Doors & windows

(P-13201)
ANFINSON LUMBER SALES INC (PA)
13041 Union Ave, Fontana (92337-6952)
PHONE................................951 681-4707
Richard Anfinson, *President*
Patricia J Anfinson, *Admin Sec*
EMP: 60 **EST:** 1957
SQ FT: 48,000
SALES (est): 6.5MM **Privately Held**
WEB: www.anfinson.com
SIC: 5031 Lumber: rough, dressed & fin-
ished

(P-13202)
ARCHITECTURAL DOORS INC (PA)
17102 Newhope St, Fountain Valley
(92708-8223)
PHONE................................714 898-3667
Robert R Crane, *President*
Robert W Crane, *CEO*
Dorothy Crane, *Corp Secy*
EMP: 59 **EST:** 1982
SQ FT: 96,000 **Privately Held**
SIC: 5031 Doors

(P-13203)
ATRIUM DOOR & WIN CO ARIZ INC
5455 E La Palma Ave Ste A, Anaheim (92807-2006)
PHONE..................714 693-0601
Gregory T Faherty, *President*
Randall S Fojtasek, *President*
Jeff Hull, *CEO*
EMP: 144 EST: 1960
SQ FT: 220,000
SALES (est): 26.3MM
SALES (corp-wide): 4.6B **Publicly Held**
WEB: www.atrium.com
SIC: 5031 Windows
HQ: Atrium Windows And Doors, Inc.
    9001 Ambassador Row
    Dallas TX 75247
    214 583-1840

(P-13204)
BLACK EGLE PLLET LOGISTICS INC (PA)
9651 Bellegrave Ave, Riverside (92509-2646)
P.O. Box 310919, Fontana (92331-0919)
PHONE..................951 332-6315
Norberto Alvarado, *President*
EMP: 50 EST: 2017
SALES (est): 2MM **Privately Held**
WEB: www.blackeaglepalletsinc.com
SIC: 5031 Pallets, wood

(P-13205)
BOISE CASCADE COMPANY
7145 Arlington Ave, Riverside (92503-1508)
PHONE..................951 343-3000
Mike Bland, *Manager*
Frank Elfering, *Vice Pres*
Jackie Pierce, *Administration*
Lance Devol, *Sales Staff*
Joe Lozano, *Sales Staff*
EMP: 167
SALES (corp-wide): 5.4B **Publicly Held**
WEB: www.bc.com
SIC: 5211 5031 Lumber products; lumber: rough, dressed & finished
PA: Boise Cascade Company
    1111 W Jefferson St # 100
    Boise ID 83702
    208 384-6161

(P-13206)
BUILDERS FENCE COMPANY INC (PA)
8937 San Fernando Rd, Sun Valley (91352-1410)
P.O. Box 125 (91353-0125)
PHONE..................818 768-5500
Marshall K Frankel, *President*
▲ EMP: 35 EST: 1959
SQ FT: 6,400
SALES (est): 46.4MM **Privately Held**
WEB: www.buildersfence.com
SIC: 5031 1799 3446 Fencing, wood; or-namental metal work; architectural metal-work

(P-13207)
DECWOOD INC
Also Called: Decorative Woods Lbr & Molding
3 Oldfield, Irvine (92618-2800)
PHONE..................949 588-9663
Peter Juteau, *CEO*
Elise Juteau, *CFO*
Steve Spencer, *Exec VP*
EMP: 24 EST: 1979
SQ FT: 22,200
SALES (est): 3.8MM **Privately Held**
WEB: www.decorativewoods.com
SIC: 5031 5211 2431 Building materials, exterior; building materials, interior; mill-work & lumber; doors & door parts & trim, wood

(P-13208)
FOUNDATION BUILDING MTLS INC (HQ)
2520 Redhill Ave, Santa Ana (92705-5542)
PHONE..................714 380-3127
Ruben Mendoza, *President*
Pete Welly, *COO*
John Gorey, *CFO*
Kirby Thompson, *Senior VP*

Jim Carpenter, *Vice Pres*
EMP: 1064 EST: 2011
SALES: 2.1B **Privately Held**
WEB: www.fbmsales.com
SIC: 5031 5033 5039 Building materials, interior; wallboard; roofing, siding & insu-lation; insulation materials; ceiling sys-tems & products

(P-13209)
GANAHL LUMBER COMPANY
Also Called: Benjamin Moore Authorized Ret
6586 Beach Blvd, Buena Park (90621-2903)
PHONE..................714 522-2864
Chad Kidder, *Manager*
Diane Tanner, *Credit Mgr*
Chad Barclay, *Sales Staff*
Andree Primrose, *Sales Staff*
EMP: 52
SALES (corp-wide): 502.3MM **Privately Held**
WEB: www.ganahllumber.com
SIC: 5251 5031 5231 Hardware; builders' hardware; lumber: rough, dressed & fin-ished; paint, glass & wallpaper
PA: Ganahl Lumber Company
    1220 E Ball Rd
    Anaheim CA 92805
    714 772-5444

(P-13210)
GANAHL LUMBER COMPANY
Also Called: Benjamin Moore Authorized Ret
10742 Los Alamitos Blvd, Los Alamitos (90720-2331)
PHONE..................562 346-2100
Tom Barkley, *Branch Mgr*
Brandon Petersen, *Sales Mgr*
Gerardo Leal, *Sales Staff*
Ron Souto, *Manager*
EMP: 52
SALES (corp-wide): 502.3MM **Privately Held**
WEB: www.ganahllumber.com
SIC: 5251 5231 5031 1751 Hardware; paint; lumber: rough, dressed & finished; window & door (prefabricated) installation
PA: Ganahl Lumber Company
    1220 E Ball Rd
    Anaheim CA 92805
    714 772-5444

(P-13211)
GANAHL LUMBER COMPANY
Also Called: Benjamin Moore Authorized Ret
23132 Orange Ave, Lake Forest (92630-4881)
PHONE..................949 830-3600
John Ganahl, *CFO*
Tom Barclay, *General Mgr*
Paul Lee, *Technology*
Omar Diaz, *Sales Staff*
Amy Hertzler, *Sales Staff*
EMP: 52
SALES (corp-wide): 502.3MM **Privately Held**
WEB: www.ganahllumber.com
SIC: 5251 5231 5031 Hardware; paint; lumber products; lumber: rough, dressed & finished; window & door (pre-fabricated) installation
PA: Ganahl Lumber Company
    1220 E Ball Rd
    Anaheim CA 92805
    714 772-5444

(P-13212)
GROVE LUMBER & BLDG SUPS INC (PA)
1300 S Campus Ave, Ontario (91761-4378)
PHONE..................909 947-0277
Raymond G Croll Jr, *CEO*
EMP: 190 EST: 1979
SQ FT: 3,000
SALES (est): 50.7MM **Privately Held**
WEB: www.grovelumber.com
SIC: 5031 5211 Lumber: rough, dressed & finished; lumber products

(P-13213)
HARDY WINDOW COMPANY (PA)
1639 E Miraloma Ave, Placentia (92870-6623)
PHONE..................714 996-1807
Chance P Hardy, *President*

Vanessa Castrejon, *Office Mgr*
Mark Britten, *Sales Staff*
Darin Edmonds, *Sales Staff*
Holly Hanson, *Sales Staff*
EMP: 141
SQ FT: 14,000
SALES (est): 33.5MM **Privately Held**
WEB: www.orangecountywindowanddoor.com
SIC: 5031 Windows

(P-13214)
HEPPNER HARDWOODS INC
555 W Danlee St, Azusa (91702-2342)
PHONE..................626 969-7983
Lorraine Heppner, *President*
▲ EMP: 60 EST: 1972
SQ FT: 217,800
SALES (est): 11.7MM **Privately Held**
WEB: www.heppnerhardwoods.com
SIC: 5031 Lumber: rough, dressed & fin-ished

(P-13215)
HIGHLAND LUMBER SALES INC
300 E Santa Ana St, Anaheim (92805-3953)
PHONE..................714 778-2293
Ken Lobue, *President*
Richard Phillips, *President*
Richard J Phillips, *CEO*
▲ EMP: 60 EST: 1991
SQ FT: 2,000
SALES (est): 21.9MM **Privately Held**
WEB: www.highlandlumber.com
SIC: 5031 2493 2431 5211 Lumber: rough, dressed & finished; reconstituted wood products; millwork; lumber products

(P-13216)
HOME DECO CORP (PA)
11116 Tuxford St, Sun Valley (91352-2631)
PHONE..................818 669-5287
Arman Chichyan, *CEO*
Artur Muradyan, *Principal*
EMP: 60 EST: 2015
SALES (est): 525.7K **Privately Held**
SIC: 5031 2541 2434 2431 Doors; panel-ing, wood; wallboard; cabinets, lockers & shelving; wood kitchen cabinets; doors & door parts & trim, wood

(P-13217)
INLAND BUILDERS SUPPLY INC
Also Called: Ace Hardware
1224 W Hobsonway, Blythe (92225-1424)
PHONE..................760 922-0361
David Burton Bayles, *CEO*
Art Bayles, *President*
Linda Bayles, *Corp Secy*
EMP: 50 EST: 1965
SQ FT: 40,000
SALES (est): 15.2MM **Privately Held**
WEB: www.store.inlandbuilderssupply.com
SIC: 5211 5031 Lumber & other building materials; lumber, plywood & millwork

(P-13218)
KELLY-WRIGHT HARDWOODS INC
450 Delta Ave, Brea (92821-2935)
P.O. Box 728, La Mirada (90637-0728)
PHONE..................714 632-9930
Harold J Wright, *CEO*
EMP: 19 EST: 1982
SQ FT: 60,000
SALES (est): 553.6K **Privately Held**
WEB: www.kelly-wright.com
SIC: 5031 2431 2426 Hardboard; lumber: rough, dressed & finished; plywood; mill-work; hardwood dimension & flooring mills

(P-13219)
LOWES HOME CENTERS LLC
2840 N Bellflower Blvd, Long Beach (90815-1125)
PHONE..................562 496-8120
John Bowman, *Manager*
EMP: 119

SALES (corp-wide): 89.6B **Publicly Held**
WEB: www.lowes.com
SIC: 5211 5031 5722 5064 Home cen-ters; building materials, exterior; building materials, interior; household appliance stores; electrical appliances, television & radio
HQ: Lowe's Home Centers, Llc
    1000 Lowes Blvd
    Mooresville NC 28117
    336 658-4000

(P-13220)
LOWES HOME CENTERS LLC
11399 Foothill Blvd, Rancho Cucamonga (91730-7626)
PHONE..................909 476-9697
Jeniffer Lang, *Manager*
EMP: 119
SALES (corp-wide): 89.6B **Publicly Held**
WEB: www.lowes.com
SIC: 5211 5031 5722 5064 Home cen-ters; building materials, exterior; building materials, interior; household appliance stores; electrical appliances, television & radio
HQ: Lowe's Home Centers, Llc
    1000 Lowes Blvd
    Mooresville NC 28117
    336 658-4000

(P-13221)
LOWES HOME CENTERS LLC
30481 Avnida De Las Flres, Rancho Santa Margari (92688)
PHONE..................949 589-5005
Pete Bradley, *Branch Mgr*
EMP: 119
SALES (corp-wide): 89.6B **Publicly Held**
WEB: www.lowes.com
SIC: 5211 5031 5722 5064 Home cen-ters; building materials, exterior; building materials, interior; household appliance stores; electrical appliances, television & radio
HQ: Lowe's Home Centers, Llc
    1000 Lowes Blvd
    Mooresville NC 28117
    336 658-4000

(P-13222)
LOWES HOME CENTERS LLC
14333 Bear Valley Rd, Victorville (92392-5403)
PHONE..................760 949-9565
Shawn Pierson, *Manager*
EMP: 119
SALES (corp-wide): 89.6B **Publicly Held**
WEB: www.lowes.com
SIC: 5211 5031 5722 5064 Home cen-ters; building materials, exterior; building materials, interior; household appliance stores; electrical appliances, television & radio
HQ: Lowe's Home Centers, Llc
    1000 Lowes Blvd
    Mooresville NC 28117
    336 658-4000

(P-13223)
LOWES HOME CENTERS LLC
13500 Paxton St, Pacoima (91331-2352)
PHONE..................818 686-4300
Mario Garza, *Branch Mgr*
EMP: 119
SALES (corp-wide): 89.6B **Publicly Held**
WEB: www.lowes.com
SIC: 5211 5031 5722 5064 Home cen-ters; building materials, exterior; building materials, interior; household appliance stores; electrical appliances, television & radio
HQ: Lowe's Home Centers, Llc
    1000 Lowes Blvd
    Mooresville NC 28117
    336 658-4000

(P-13224)
LOWES HOME CENTERS LLC
30472 Haun Rd, Menifee (92584-6810)
PHONE..................951 723-1930
Dave Jenkins, *Branch Mgr*
EMP: 119

▲ = Import ▼=Export
◆ =Import/Export

SALES (corp-wide): 89.6B **Publicly Held**
WEB: www.lowes.com
SIC: **5211** 5031 5722 5064 Home centers; building materials, exterior; building materials, interior; household appliance stores; electrical appliances, television & radio
HQ: Lowe's Home Centers, Llc
    1000 Lowes Blvd
    Wilkesboro NC 28117
    336 658-4000

(P-13225)
LOWES HOME CENTERS LLC
2445 Golden Hill Rd, Paso Robles (93446-6385)
PHONE..................................805 602-9051
EMP: 119
SALES (corp-wide): 89.6B **Publicly Held**
WEB: www.lowes.com
SIC: **5211** 5031 5722 5064 Home centers; building materials, exterior; building materials, interior; household appliance stores; electrical appliances, television & radio
HQ: Lowe's Home Centers, Llc
    1000 Lowes Blvd
    Wilkesboro NC 28117
    336 658-4000

(P-13226)
LOWES HOME CENTERS LLC
907 Avenida Pico, San Clemente (92673-3908)
PHONE..................................949 369-4644
Sonya Olmedo, *Manager*
EMP: 119
SALES (corp-wide): 89.6B **Publicly Held**
WEB: www.lowes.com
SIC: **5211** 5031 5722 5064 Home centers; building materials, exterior; building materials, interior; household appliance stores; electrical appliances, television & radio
HQ: Lowe's Home Centers, Llc
    1000 Lowes Blvd
    Wilkesboro NC 28117
    336 658-4000

(P-13227)
LOWES HOME CENTERS LLC
9851 Magnolia Ave, Riverside (92503-3528)
PHONE..................................951 509-5500
Daniel Mergio, *Branch Mgr*
Hanh Pham, *District Mgr*
Jennifer Goatcher, *Human Resources*
Renee McMichael, *Sales Mgr*
EMP: 119
SALES (corp-wide): 89.6B **Publicly Held**
WEB: www.lowes.com
SIC: **5211** 5031 5722 5064 Home centers; building materials, exterior; building materials, interior; household appliance stores; electrical appliances, television & radio
HQ: Lowe's Home Centers, Llc
    1000 Lowes Blvd
    Wilkesboro NC 28117
    336 658-4000

(P-13228)
LOWES HOME CENTERS LLC
78865 Highway 111, La Quinta (92253-2003)
PHONE..................................760 771-5566
Ron Stewart, *Manager*
EMP: 119
SALES (corp-wide): 89.6B **Publicly Held**
WEB: www.lowes.com
SIC: **5211** 5031 5722 5064 Home centers; building materials, exterior; building materials, interior; household appliance stores; electrical appliances, television & radio
HQ: Lowe's Home Centers, Llc
    1000 Lowes Blvd
    Wilkesboro NC 28117
    336 658-4000

(P-13229)
LOWES HOME CENTERS LLC
14873 Carmenita Rd, Norwalk (90650-5232)
PHONE..................................562 926-0826
Patrick Cosley, *Manager*

EMP: 119
SALES (corp-wide): 89.6B **Publicly Held**
WEB: www.lowes.com
SIC: **5211** 5031 5722 5064 Home centers; building materials, exterior; building materials, interior; household appliance stores; electrical appliances, television & radio
HQ: Lowe's Home Centers, Llc
    1000 Lowes Blvd
    Mooresville NC 28117
    336 658-4000

(P-13230)
LOWES HOME CENTERS LLC
13251 Peyton Dr, Chino Hills (91709-6003)
PHONE..................................909 627-6039
Joseph Gallardo, *Branch Mgr*
EMP: 119
SALES (corp-wide): 89.6B **Publicly Held**
WEB: www.lowes
SIC: **5211** 5031 5722 5064 Home centers; building materials, exterior; building materials, interior; household appliance stores; electrical appliances, television & radio
HQ: Lowe's Home Centers, Llc
    1000 Lowes Blvd
    Mooresville NC 28117
    336 658-4000

(P-13231)
LOWES HOME CENTERS LLC
8383 Topanga Canyon Blvd, West Hills (91304-2343)
PHONE..................................818 610-1960
Pete Reed, *Branch Mgr*
Jeff Storm, *Store Mgr*
EMP: 119
SALES (corp-wide): 89.6B **Publicly Held**
WEB: www.lowes.com
SIC: **5211** 5031 5722 5064 Home centers; building materials, exterior; building materials, interior; household appliance stores; electrical appliances, television & radio
HQ: Lowe's Home Centers, Llc
    1000 Lowes Blvd
    Mooresville NC 28117
    336 658-4000

(P-13232)
LOWES HOME CENTERS LLC
1659 W Foothill Blvd, Upland (91786-3533)
PHONE..................................909 982-4795
Dan Caganap, *Manager*
EMP: 119
SALES (corp-wide): 89.6B **Publicly Held**
WEB: www.lowes.com
SIC: **5211** 5031 5722 5064 Home centers; building materials, exterior; building materials, interior; household appliance stores; electrical appliances, television & radio
HQ: Lowe's Home Centers, Llc
    1000 Lowes Blvd
    Mooresville NC 28117
    336 658-4000

(P-13233)
LOWES HOME CENTERS LLC
26415 Bouquet Canyon Rd, Santa Clarita (91350-2396)
PHONE..................................661 297-1400
Jeff Starnes, *Branch Mgr*
EMP: 119
SALES (corp-wide): 89.6B **Publicly Held**
WEB: www.lowes.com
SIC: **5211** 5031 5722 5064 Home centers; building materials, exterior; building materials, interior; household appliance stores; electrical appliances, television & radio
HQ: Lowe's Home Centers, Llc
    1000 Lowes Blvd
    Mooresville NC 28117
    336 658-4000

(P-13234)
LOWES HOME CENTERS LLC
5201 E Ramon Rd, Palm Springs (92264-3600)
PHONE..................................760 866-1901
Robert Richmond, *Branch Mgr*
EMP: 119

SALES (corp-wide): 89.6B **Publicly Held**
WEB: www.lowes.com
SIC: **5211** 5031 5722 5064 Home centers; building materials, exterior; building materials, interior; household appliance stores; electrical appliances, television & radio
HQ: Lowe's Home Centers, Llc
    1000 Lowes Blvd
    Mooresville NC 28117
    336 658-4000

(P-13235)
LOWES HOME CENTERS LLC
2000 W Empire Ave, Burbank (91504-3434)
PHONE..................................818 557-2300
Chris McGilroy, *Manager*
EMP: 119
SALES (corp-wide): 89.6B **Publicly Held**
WEB: www.lowes.com
SIC: **5211** 5031 5722 5064 Home centers; building materials, exterior; building materials, interior; household appliance stores; electrical appliances, television & radio
HQ: Lowe's Home Centers, Llc
    1000 Lowes Blvd
    Mooresville NC 28117
    336 658-4000

(P-13236)
LOWES HOME CENTERS LLC
1500 N Lemon St, Anaheim (92801-1204)
PHONE..................................714 447-6140
Brian Hefel, *Branch Mgr*
EMP: 119
SALES (corp-wide): 89.6B **Publicly Held**
WEB: www.lowes.com
SIC: **5211** 5031 5722 5064 Home centers; building materials, exterior; building materials, interior; household appliance stores; electrical appliances, television & radio
HQ: Lowe's Home Centers, Llc
    1000 Lowes Blvd
    Mooresville NC 28117
    336 658-4000

(P-13237)
LOWES HOME CENTERS LLC
24701 Madison Ave, Murrieta (92562-9763)
PHONE..................................951 461-8916
Scott Holland, *Manager*
Analisa Lechuga, *Merchandising*
EMP: 119
SALES (corp-wide): 89.6B **Publicly Held**
WEB: www.lowes.com
SIC: **5211** 5031 5722 5064 Home centers; building materials, exterior; building materials, interior; household appliance stores; electrical appliances, television & radio
HQ: Lowe's Home Centers, Llc
    1000 Lowes Blvd
    Mooresville NC 28117
    336 658-4000

(P-13238)
LOWES HOME CENTERS LLC
Also Called: Hawthorne Lowe's
2800 W 120th St, Hawthorne (90250-3338)
PHONE..................................323 327-4000
Mike Bryant, *Manager*
Alex Arteaga, *Manager*
EMP: 119
SALES (corp-wide): 89.6B **Publicly Held**
WEB: www.lowes.com
SIC: **5211** 5031 5722 5064 Home centers; building materials, exterior; building materials, interior; household appliance stores; electrical appliances, television & radio
HQ: Lowe's Home Centers, Llc
    1000 Lowes Blvd
    Mooresville NC 28117
    336 658-4000

(P-13239)
LOWES HOME CENTERS LLC
8600 Washington Blvd, Pico Rivera (90660-3790)
PHONE..................................562 942-9909
Jose Rodriquez, *Branch Mgr*
EMP: 119

SALES (corp-wide): 89.6B **Publicly Held**
WEB: www.lowes.com
SIC: **5211** 5031 5722 5064 Home centers; building materials, exterior; building materials, interior; household appliance stores; electrical appliances, television & radio
HQ: Lowe's Home Centers, Llc
    1000 Lowes Blvd
    Mooresville NC 28117
    336 658-4000

(P-13240)
LOWES HOME CENTERS LLC
12400 Day St, Moreno Valley (92553-7501)
PHONE..................................951 656-1859
David Jenkins, *Manager*
EMP: 119
SALES (corp-wide): 89.6B **Publicly Held**
WEB: www.lowes.com
SIC: **5211** 5031 5722 5064 Home centers; building materials, exterior; building materials, interior; household appliance stores; electrical appliances, television & radio
HQ: Lowe's Home Centers, Llc
    1000 Lowes Blvd
    Mooresville NC 28117
    336 658-4000

(P-13241)
LOWES HOME CENTERS LLC
633 W Bonita Ave, San Dimas (91773-2512)
PHONE..................................909 305-2960
Gary Norman, *Manager*
EMP: 119
SALES (corp-wide): 89.6B **Publicly Held**
WEB: www.lowes.com
SIC: **5211** 5031 5722 5064 Home centers; building materials, exterior; building materials, interior; household appliance stores; electrical appliances, television & radio
HQ: Lowe's Home Centers, Llc
    1000 Lowes Blvd
    Mooresville NC 28117
    336 658-4000

(P-13242)
LOWES HOME CENTERS LLC
1380 S Beach Blvd, La Habra (90631-6374)
PHONE..................................562 690-5122
Ken Konkel, *Manager*
EMP: 119
SALES (corp-wide): 89.6B **Publicly Held**
WEB: www.lowes.com
SIC: **5211** 5031 5722 5064 Home centers; building materials, exterior; building materials, interior; household appliance stores; electrical appliances, television & radio
HQ: Lowe's Home Centers, Llc
    1000 Lowes Blvd
    Wilkesboro NC 28117
    336 658-4000

(P-13243)
LOWES HOME CENTERS LLC
7825 Rosedale Hwy, Bakersfield (93308-5730)
PHONE..................................661 588-6420
Lennie Hill, *Manager*
Richard Barnes, *CIO*
EMP: 119
SALES (corp-wide): 89.6B **Publicly Held**
WEB: www.lowes.com
SIC: **5211** 5031 5722 5064 Home centers; building materials, exterior; building materials, interior; household appliance stores; electrical appliances, television & radio
HQ: Lowe's Home Centers, Llc
    1000 Lowes Blvd
    Wilkesboro NC 28117
    336 658-4000

(P-13244)
LOWES HOME CENTERS LLC
7300 E Carson St, Long Beach (90808)
PHONE..................................562 421-9996
Ronnie Hunneycutt, *Manager*
EMP: 119

SALES (corp-wide): 89.6B **Publicly Held**
WEB: www.lowes.com
SIC: **5211** 5031 5722 5064 Home centers; building materials, exterior; building materials, interior; household appliance stores; electrical appliances, television & radio
HQ: Lowe's Home Centers, Llc
    1000 Lowes Blvd
    Wilkesboro NC 28117
    336 658-4000

(P-13245)
LOWES HOME CENTERS LLC
39500 Lowes Dr, Palmdale (93551-3754)
PHONE......................................661 267-9888
Veronica Pinkui, *Manager*
EMP: 119
SQ FT: 133,410
SALES (corp-wide): 89.6B **Publicly Held**
WEB: www.lowes.com
SIC: **5211** 5031 5722 5064 Home centers; building materials, exterior; building materials, interior; household appliance stores; electrical appliances, television & radio
HQ: Lowe's Home Centers, Llc
    1000 Lowes Blvd
    Wilkesboro NC 28117
    336 658-4000

(P-13246)
LOWES HOME CENTERS LLC
40390 Winchester Rd, Temecula (92591-5519)
PHONE......................................951 296-1618
Rose Burns, *Manager*
EMP: 119
SALES (corp-wide): 89.6B **Publicly Held**
WEB: www.lowes.com
SIC: **5211** 5031 5722 5064 Home centers; building materials, exterior; building materials, interior; household appliance stores; electrical appliances, television & radio
HQ: Lowe's Home Centers, Llc
    1000 Lowes Blvd
    Mooresville NC 28117
    336 658-4000

(P-13247)
LOWES HOME CENTERS LLC
22255 S Western Ave, Torrance (90501-4106)
PHONE......................................310 787-1469
Ricky Garcia, *Manager*
EMP: 119
SALES (corp-wide): 89.6B **Publicly Held**
WEB: www.lowes.com
SIC: **5211** 5031 5722 5064 Home centers; building materials, exterior; building materials, interior; household appliance stores; electrical appliances, television & radio
HQ: Lowe's Home Centers, Llc
    1000 Lowes Blvd
    Wilkesboro NC 28117
    336 658-4000

(P-13248)
LOWES HOME CENTERS LLC
4144 S Mooney Blvd, Visalia (93277-9144)
PHONE......................................559 624-4300
Scott Roy, *Manager*
Lyle Hale, *Sales Staff*
EMP: 119
SQ FT: 134,561
SALES (corp-wide): 89.6B **Publicly Held**
WEB: www.lowes.com
SIC: **5211** 5031 5722 5064 Home centers; building materials, exterior; building materials, interior; household appliance stores; electrical appliances, television & radio
HQ: Lowe's Home Centers, Llc
    1000 Lowes Blvd
    Wilkesboro NC 28117
    336 658-4000

(P-13249)
LOWES HOME CENTERS LLC
500 S Mills Rd, Ventura (93003-3459)
PHONE......................................805 675-8800
Glen Sueishi, *Manager*
EMP: 119

SALES (corp-wide): 89.6B **Publicly Held**
WEB: www.lowes.com
SIC: **5211** 5031 5722 5064 Home centers; building materials, exterior; building materials, interior; household appliance stores; electrical appliances, television & radio
HQ: Lowe's Home Centers, Llc
    1000 Lowes Blvd
    Mooresville NC 28117
    336 658-4000

(P-13250)
LOWES HOME CENTERS LLC
16851 Sierra Lakes Pkwy, Fontana (92336-1226)
PHONE......................................909 350-7900
Jan Hardy, *Manager*
EMP: 119
SALES (corp-wide): 89.6B **Publicly Held**
WEB: www.lowes.com
SIC: **5211** 5031 5722 5064 Home centers; building materials, exterior; building materials, interior; household appliance stores; electrical appliances, television & radio
HQ: Lowe's Home Centers, Llc
    1000 Lowes Blvd
    Wilkesboro NC 28117
    336 658-4000

(P-13251)
LOWES HOME CENTERS LLC
1285 Magnolia Ave, Corona (92879-2092)
PHONE......................................951 256-9004
Jeff Fowler, *Branch Mgr*
EMP: 119
SALES (corp-wide): 89.6B **Publicly Held**
WEB: www.lowes.com
SIC: **5211** 5031 5722 5064 Home centers; building materials, exterior; building materials, interior; household appliance stores; electrical appliances, television & radio
HQ: Lowe's Home Centers, Llc
    1000 Lowes Blvd
    Mooresville NC 28117
    336 658-4000

(P-13252)
LOWES HOME CENTERS LLC
350 S Sanderson Ave, Hemet (92545-9014)
PHONE......................................951 492-7000
Randy Scott, *Manager*
EMP: 119
SALES (corp-wide): 89.6B **Publicly Held**
WEB: www.lowes.com
SIC: **5211** 5031 5722 5064 Home centers; building materials, exterior; building materials, interior; household appliance stores; electrical appliances, television & radio
HQ: Lowe's Home Centers, Llc
    1000 Lowes Blvd
    Mooresville NC 28117
    336 658-4000

(P-13253)
LOWES HOME CENTERS LLC
6200 Colony St, Bakersfield (93307-6535)
PHONE......................................661 699-1000
Phil Cardins, *Manager*
Mike Salazar, *Manager*
EMP: 119
SALES (corp-wide): 89.6B **Publicly Held**
WEB: www.lowes.com
SIC: **5211** 5031 5722 5064 Home centers; building materials, exterior; building materials, interior; household appliance stores; electrical appliances, television & radio
HQ: Lowe's Home Centers, Llc
    1000 Lowes Blvd
    Mooresville NC 28117
    336 658-4000

(P-13254)
LOWES HOME CENTERS LLC
1725 W Redlands Blvd, Redlands (92373-8012)
PHONE......................................909 307-8883
Jim Riley, *Manager*
Lynne Yingst, *Sales Staff*
EMP: 119

SALES (corp-wide): 89.6B **Publicly Held**
WEB: www.lowes.com
SIC: **5211** 5031 5722 5064 Home centers; building materials, exterior; building materials, interior; household appliance stores; electrical appliances, television & radio
HQ: Lowe's Home Centers, Llc
    1000 Lowes Blvd
    Wilkesboro NC 28117
    336 658-4000

(P-13255)
LOWES HOME CENTERS LLC
730 W Avenue K, Lancaster (93534-6001)
PHONE......................................661 341-9000
Pete Reed, *General Mgr*
EMP: 119
SALES (corp-wide): 89.6B **Publicly Held**
WEB: www.lowes.com
SIC: **5211** 5031 5722 5064 Home centers; building materials, exterior; building materials, interior; household appliance stores; electrical appliances, television & radio
HQ: Lowe's Home Centers, Llc
    1000 Lowes Blvd
    Wilkesboro NC 28117
    336 658-4000

(P-13256)
LOWES HOME CENTERS LLC
2053 N Imperial Ave, El Centro (92243-1324)
PHONE......................................760 337-6700
Chad Manley, *Manager*
Patty Rivera, *Executive*
EMP: 119
SALES (corp-wide): 89.6B **Publicly Held**
WEB: www.lowes.com
SIC: **5211** 5031 5722 5064 Home centers; building materials, exterior; building materials, interior; household appliance stores; electrical appliances, television & radio
HQ: Lowe's Home Centers, Llc
    1000 Lowes Blvd
    Wilkesboro NC 28117
    336 658-4000

(P-13257)
LOWES HOME CENTERS LLC
8175 Warner Ave, Huntington Beach (92647-8251)
PHONE......................................714 907-9006
Jose Rodriquez, *Manager*
Caleb Blacksher, *Receiver*
EMP: 119
SALES (corp-wide): 89.6B **Publicly Held**
WEB: www.lowes.com
SIC: **5211** 5031 5722 5064 Home centers; building materials, exterior; building materials, interior; household appliance stores; electrical appliances, television & radio
HQ: Lowe's Home Centers, Llc
    1000 Lowes Blvd
    Mooresville NC 28117
    336 658-4000

(P-13258)
LOWES HOME CENTERS LLC
37080 47th St E, Palmdale (93552-4449)
PHONE......................................661 533-9900
Greg Mitchell, *Manager*
EMP: 119
SALES (corp-wide): 89.6B **Publicly Held**
WEB: www.lowes.com
SIC: **5211** 5031 5722 5064 Home centers; building materials, exterior; building materials, interior; household appliance stores; electrical appliances, television & radio
HQ: Lowe's Home Centers, Llc
    1000 Lowes Blvd
    Mooresville NC 28117
    336 658-4000

(P-13259)
LOWES HOME CENTERS LLC
12189 Apple Valley Rd, Apple Valley (92308-6702)
PHONE......................................760 961-3000
Chris Horan, *Manager*
EMP: 119

SALES (corp-wide): 89.6B **Publicly Held**
WEB: www.lowes.com
SIC: **5211** 5031 5722 5064 Home centers; building materials, exterior; building materials, interior; household appliance stores; electrical appliances, television & radio
HQ: Lowe's Home Centers, Llc
    1000 Lowes Blvd
    Wilkesboro NC 28117
    336 658-4000

(P-13260)
LOWES HOME CENTERS LLC
29335 Central Ave, Lake Elsinore (92532-2212)
PHONE......................................951 253-6000
A Nuseibtel, *Principal*
Arturo Conchas, *Sales Mgr*
EMP: 119
SALES (corp-wide): 89.6B **Publicly Held**
WEB: www.lowes.com
SIC: **5211** 5031 5722 5064 Home centers; building materials, exterior; building materials, interior; household appliance stores; electrical appliances, television & radio
HQ: Lowe's Home Centers, Llc
    1000 Lowes Blvd
    Wilkesboro NC 28117
    336 658-4000

(P-13261)
LOWES HOME CENTERS LLC
1275 Simi Town Center Way, Simi Valley (93065-0513)
PHONE......................................805 426-2780
Bob Derr, *Manager*
EMP: 119
SALES (corp-wide): 89.6B **Publicly Held**
WEB: www.lowes.com
SIC: **5211** 5031 5722 5064 Home centers; building materials, exterior; building materials, interior; household appliance stores; electrical appliances, television & radio
HQ: Lowe's Home Centers, Llc
    1000 Lowes Blvd
    Wilkesboro NC 28117
    336 658-4000

(P-13262)
LOWES HOME CENTERS LLC
19601 Nordhoff St, Northridge (91324-2422)
PHONE......................................818 477-9022
Mark Harrison, *Store Mgr*
EMP: 119
SALES (corp-wide): 89.6E **Publicly Held**
WEB: www.lowes.com
SIC: **5211** 5031 5722 5064 Home centers; building materials, exterior; building materials, interior; household appliance stores; electrical appliances, television & radio
HQ: Lowe's Home Centers, Llc
    1000 Lowes Blvd
    Mooresville NC 28117
    336 658-4000

(P-13263)
LOWES HOME CENTERS LLC
2390 S Grove Ave, Ontario (91761-4808)
PHONE......................................909 969-9053
Myarna Zega, *Manager*
EMP: 119
SALES (corp-wide): 89.6B **Publicly Held**
WEB: www.lowes.com
SIC: **5211** 5031 5722 5064 Home centers; building materials, exterior; building materials, interior; household appliance stores; electrical appliances, television & radio
HQ: Lowe's Home Centers, Llc
    1000 Lowes Blvd
    Mooresville NC 28117
    336 658-4000

(P-13264)
LOWES HOME CENTERS LLC
1145 E Prosperity Ave, Tulare (93274-8030)
PHONE......................................559 366-5000
Eric Locke, *Manager*
Ob Leong, *Project Mgr*
Crystal Wilkins, *Assistant*

▲ = Import ▼=Export
◆ =Import/Export

EMP: 119
SALES (corp-wide): 89.6B Publicly Held
WEB: www.lowes.com
SIC: 5211 5031 5722 5064 Home centers; building materials, exterior; building materials, interior; household appliance stores; electrical appliances, television & radio
HQ: Lowe's Home Centers, Llc
1000 Lowes Blvd
Mooresville NC 28117
336 658-4000

(P-13265)
LOWES HOME CENTERS LLC
2700 Skypark Dr, Torrance (90505-5315)
PHONE..................................310 602-2090
Desiree Poro, Branch Mgr
EMP: 119
SALES (corp-wide): 89.6B Publicly Held
WEB: www.lowes.com
SIC: 5211 5031 5722 5064 Home centers; building materials, exterior; building materials, interior; household appliance stores; electrical appliances, television & radio
HQ: Lowe's Home Centers, Llc
1000 Lowes Blvd
Mooresville NC 28117
336 658-4000

(P-13266)
LOWES HOME CENTERS LLC
1601 Columbus St, Bakersfield (93305-2133)
PHONE..................................661 889-9000
Francisco Dubon, Branch Mgr
Andrew Robinson, District Mgr
EMP: 119
SALES (corp-wide): 89.6B Publicly Held
WEB: www.lowes.com
SIC: 5211 5031 5722 5064 Home centers; building materials, exterior; building materials, interior; household appliance stores; electrical appliances, television & radio
HQ: Lowe's Home Centers, Llc
1000 Lowes Blvd
Mooresville NC 28117
336 658-4000

(P-13267)
LOWES HOME CENTERS LLC
17789 Castleton St, City of Industry (91748-1706)
PHONE..................................626 217-1133
Robert Dominguez, Branch Mgr
EMP: 119
SALES (corp-wide): 89.6B Publicly Held
WEB: www.lowes.com
SIC: 5211 5031 5722 5064 Home centers; building materials, exterior; building materials, interior; household appliance stores; electrical appliances, television & radio
HQ: Lowe's Home Centers, Llc
1000 Lowes Blvd
Wilkesboro NC 28117
336 658-4000

(P-13268)
LOWES HOME CENTERS LLC
6413 Pats Ranch Rd, Jurupa Valley (91752-4430)
PHONE..................................951 256-9034
Jon Kennard, Manager
EMP: 119
SALES (corp-wide): 89.6B Publicly Held
WEB: www.lowes.com
SIC: 5211 5031 5722 5064 Home centers; building materials, exterior; building materials, interior; household appliance stores; electrical appliances, television & radio
HQ: Lowe's Home Centers, Llc
1000 Lowes Blvd
Wilkesboro NC 28117
336 658-4000

(P-13269)
LOWES HOME CENTERS LLC
2500 Park Ave, Tustin (92782-2712)
PHONE..................................714 913-2663
Nico Zavala, Manager
EMP: 119

SALES (corp-wide): 89.6B Publicly Held
WEB: www.lowes.com
SIC: 5211 5031 5722 5064 Home centers; building materials, exterior; building materials, interior; household appliance stores; electrical appliances, television & radio
HQ: Lowe's Home Centers, Llc
1000 Lowes Blvd
Mooresville NC 28117
336 658-4000

(P-13270)
LOWES HOME CENTERS LLC
3020 N Demaree St, Visalia (93291-7147)
PHONE..................................559 802-9055
Tandy Karri, Branch Mgr
Karri Tandy, Human Res Mgr
EMP: 119
SALES (corp-wide): 89.6B Publicly Held
WEB: www.lowes.com
SIC: 5211 5031 5722 5064 Home centers; building materials, exterior; building materials, interior; household appliance stores; electrical appliances, television & radio
HQ: Lowe's Home Centers, Llc
1000 Lowes Blvd
Mooresville NC 28117
336 658-4000

(P-13271)
LOWES HOME CENTERS LLC
500 W Vandalia Ave, Porterville (93257-5912)
PHONE..................................559 306-5000
Bryan Bernard, Manager
EMP: 119
SALES (corp-wide): 89.6B Publicly Held
WEB: www.lowes.com
SIC: 5211 5031 5722 5064 Home centers; building materials, exterior; building materials, interior; household appliance stores; electrical appliances, television & radio
HQ: Lowe's Home Centers, Llc
1000 Lowes Blvd
Mooresville NC 28117
336 658-4000

(P-13272)
LOWES HOME CENTERS LLC
4777 Chino Hills Pkwy, Chino Hills (91709-5849)
PHONE..................................909 438-9000
EMP: 119
SALES (corp-wide): 89.6B Publicly Held
WEB: www.lowes.com
SIC: 5211 5031 5722 5064 Home centers; building materials, exterior; building materials, interior; household appliance stores; electrical appliances, television & radio
HQ: Lowe's Home Centers, Llc
1000 Lowes Blvd
Wilkesboro NC 28117
336 658-4000

(P-13273)
LOWES HOME CENTERS LLC
19001 Golden Valley Rd, Santa Clarita (91387-1471)
PHONE..................................661 678-4430
Veronica January, Branch Mgr
EMP: 119
SALES (corp-wide): 89.6B Publicly Held
WEB: www.lowes.com
SIC: 5211 5031 5722 5064 Home centers; building materials, exterior; building materials, interior; household appliance stores; electrical appliances, television & radio
HQ: Lowe's Home Centers, Llc
1000 Lowes Blvd
Wilkesboro NC 28117
336 658-4000

(P-13274)
LOWES HOME CENTERS LLC
1955 W Lacey Blvd, Hanford (93230-7439)
PHONE..................................559 410-9000
Garrett Barth, Branch Mgr
EMP: 119

SALES (corp-wide): 89.6B Publicly Held
WEB: www.lowes.com
SIC: 5211 5031 5722 5064 Home centers; building materials, exterior; building materials, interior; household appliance stores; electrical appliances, television & radio
HQ: Lowe's Home Centers, Llc
1000 Lowes Blvd
Mooresville NC 28117
336 658-4000

(P-13275)
LOWES HOME CENTERS LLC
27847 Greenspot Rd, Highland (92346-4381)
PHONE..................................909 557-9010
Veronica Archuletta, Manager
EMP: 119
SALES (corp-wide): 89.6B Publicly Held
WEB: www.lowes.com
SIC: 5211 5031 5722 5064 Home centers; building materials, exterior; building materials, interior; household appliance stores; electrical appliances, television & radio
HQ: Lowe's Home Centers, Llc
1000 Lowes Blvd
Mooresville NC 28117
336 658-4000

(P-13276)
LUMBER CITY CORP
Also Called: Do It Center
3775 E Thousand Oaks Blvd, Westlake Village (91362-3607)
PHONE..................................805 497-2753
Tony Capitelli, Branch Mgr
EMP: 55
SALES (corp-wide): 72.8MM Privately Held
WEB: www.doitbest.com
SIC: 5251 5211 5999 5261 Hardware; lumber & other building materials; electrical construction materials; plumbing & heating supplies; nurseries; outdoor & garden furniture; lumber, plywood & millwork; building materials, exterior; building materials, interior
PA: Lumber City Corp.
20525 Nordhoff St Ste 210
Chatsworth CA 91311
818 407-3888

(P-13277)
MEGABRAND KITCHEN & BATH INC
15600 Blackburn Ave, Norwalk (90650-6847)
PHONE..................................562 229-0088
Weijiang Huang, Principal
EMP: 22
SALES (corp-wide): 1.1MM Privately Held
WEB: www.megabrandkitchen.com
SIC: 5031 2499 Kitchen cabinets; seats, toilet
PA: Megabrand Kitchen & Bath Inc.
44 Hillcrest Ave
Edison NJ 08817
201 417-5960

(P-13278)
NICHOLS LUMBER & HARDWARE CO
Also Called: Ace Hardware
13470 Dalewood St, Baldwin Park (91706-5883)
PHONE..................................626 960-4802
Judith A Nichols, President
Rick Dean, Vice Pres
Charles Nichols, Admin Sec
Frank Wright, Opers Staff
EMP: 75 EST: 1958
SALES (est): 24.8MM Privately Held
WEB: www.nicholslumber.com
SIC: 5031 5251 2421 Lumber: rough, dressed & finished; hardware; sawmills & planing mills, general

(P-13279)
NOVO DISTRIBUTION LLC
31 Heron Ln, Riverside (92507-1243)
PHONE..................................951 742-5273
Scott Price, Branch Mgr
EMP: 155

SALES (corp-wide): 950.6MM Privately Held
WEB: www.empireco.com
SIC: 5031 Lumber, plywood & millwork
HQ: Novo Distribution Llc
8181 Logistics Dr
Zeeland MI 49464
616 772-7272

(P-13280)
OREGON PCF BLDG PDTS MAPLE INC
Also Called: Orepac Millwork Products
2401 E Philadelphia St, Ontario (91761-7743)
PHONE..................................909 627-4043
Douglas Hart, President
Kristopher Schroeder, General Mgr
Mark Calhoun, Opers Staff
▲ EMP: 125 EST: 1992
SALES (est): 25.8MM
SALES (corp-wide): 322.9MM Privately Held
WEB: www.orepac.com
SIC: 5031 5032 Building materials, exterior; brick, stone & related material
PA: Orepac Holding Company
30170 Sw Ore Pac Ave
Wilsonville OR 97070
503 685-5499

(P-13281)
PHILLIPS PLYWOOD CO INC
Also Called: Quality Laminating
13599 Desmond St, Pacoima (91331-2300)
P.O. Box 51396, Los Angeles (90051-5696)
PHONE..................................818 897-7736
Douglas F Madsen, CEO
Shawn Carlisle, President
Lynne Corwin, VP Finance
Belen Ibarra, Human Resources
Jeanne Wilson, Personnel
EMP: 55 EST: 1986
SQ FT: 100,000
SALES (est): 22.6MM Privately Held
WEB: www.phillipsplywood.com
SIC: 5031 Plywood

(P-13282)
POTTER ROEMER LLC (HQ)
17451 Hurley St, City of Industry (91744-5106)
P.O. Box 3527 (91744-0527)
PHONE..................................626 855-4890
Donald E Morris, Mng Member
Monique Chavez, CFO
Jeff Herne, Regional Mgr
Ray Revels, Branch Mgr
Eva Ramirez, Credit Mgr
▲ EMP: 85 EST: 1937
SQ FT: 110,000
SALES: 27MM
SALES (corp-wide): 90MM Privately Held
WEB: www.potterroemer.com
SIC: 5031 3569 2542 Skylights, all materials; firefighting apparatus & related equipment; partitions & fixtures, except wood
PA: Acorn Engineering Company
15125 Proctor Ave
City Of Industry CA 91746
800 488-8999

(P-13283)
RELIABLE WHOLESALE LUMBER INC (PA)
7600 Redondo Cir, Huntington Beach (92648-1303)
P.O. Box 191 (92648-0191)
PHONE..................................714 848-8222
Jerome M Higman, President
Will Higman, COO
David Higman, CFO
Bogie Nicols, Exec VP
Randall Richards, Exec VP
EMP: 90 EST: 1970
SQ FT: 4,500
SALES (est): 119.3MM Privately Held
WEB: www.rwli.net
SIC: 5031 2421 Lumber: rough, dressed & finished; sawmills & planing mills, general

(P-13284)
ROBERTS LUMBER SALES INC
Also Called: Robert's Lumber
2661 S Lilac Ave, Bloomington
(92316-3211)
PHONE..................909 350-9164
Robert Cantero Jr, *CEO*
Lori Cantero, *Principal*
EMP: 57 EST: 1997
SALES (est): 18.3MM **Privately Held**
WEB: www.robertslumbersales.com
SIC: 5031 2448 Lumber: rough, dressed & finished; wood pallets & skids

(P-13285)
ROYAL PLYWOOD COMPANY LLC (PA)
14171 Park Pl, Cerritos (90703-2463)
P.O. Box 728, La Mirada (90637-0728)
PHONE..................562 404-2989
Gabriel N Marshi,
Brian McMaster, *Info Tech Mgr*
Maria Bautista-Hamson, *Buyer*
Steve Healy, *Opers Mgr*
Stephen Fuller,
▲ EMP: 78 EST: 1999
SQ FT: 120,000
SALES (est): 62.2MM **Privately Held**
WEB: www.royalplywood.com
SIC: 5031 Lumber: rough, dressed & finished

(P-13286)
SAROYAN LUMBER COMPANY INC (PA)
Also Called: Saroyan Lumber and Moulding Co
6230 S Alameda St, Huntington Park (90255-3503)
PHONE..................800 624-9309
Richard Saroyan, *President*
Dorothy A Robinson, *Shareholder*
Marylne Nahery, *CFO*
John Saroyan, *Corp Secy*
Robert Lemke, *Vice Pres*
▲ EMP: 75 EST: 1958
SQ FT: 144,000
SALES (est): 25.7MM **Privately Held**
WEB: www.saroyanhardwoods.com
SIC: 5031 Lumber: rough, dressed & finished

(P-13287)
SHAPP INTERNATIONAL TRDG INC
Also Called: Shapp Internatioonal
6000 Reseda Blvd Ste J, Tarzana (91356-1571)
P.O. Box 893, Woodland Hills (91365-0893)
PHONE..................818 348-3000
Allan Shapiro, *President*
Louis Justin, *Treasurer*
EMP: 118 EST: 1991
SQ FT: 8,000
SALES (est): 10.2MM **Privately Held**
SIC: 5031 5064 5112 5021 Lumber, plywood & millwork; electrical appliances, major; stationery & office supplies; furniture

(P-13288)
SIERRA FOREST PRODUCTS
9000 Road 234, Terra Bella (93270-9560)
P.O. Box 10060 (93270-0060)
PHONE..................559 535-4893
Kent Duysen, *CEO*
Glenn Duysen, *Treasurer*
EMP: 110 EST: 1964
SQ FT: 3,000
SALES (est): 26.1MM **Privately Held**
WEB: www.ucfp.com
SIC: 5031 Lumber, plywood & millwork

(P-13289)
STATES DRAWER BOX SPC LLC
1482 N Batavia St, Orange (92867-3505)
PHONE..................714 744-4247
Cathy Blankenship, *President*
Kris Smith, *Engineer*
Scott Luehring, *Business Mgr*
Doug Johnson, *Purch Agent*
Tommy Hargett, *Production*
EMP: 60

SALES (est): 14.7MM **Privately Held**
WEB: www.dbsdrawers.com
SIC: 5031 Lumber: rough, dressed & finished
PA: States Industries, Llc
29545 E Enid Rd
Eugene OR 97402
-

(P-13290)
TOWNSTEEL INC
17901 Railroad St, City of Industry (91748-1113)
PHONE..................626 965-8917
Lydia Meng, *President*
Teresa Jenisch, *Vice Pres*
Michael Johnson, *Vice Pres*
Shien Cheng Meng, *Vice Pres*
Ernie Mitchell, *Vice Pres*
◆ EMP: 100 EST: 2001
SQ FT: 10,000
SALES (est): 11.9MM **Privately Held**
WEB: www.townsteel.com
SIC: 5031 Lumber, plywood & millwork

(P-13291)
WEST WOOD PRODUCTS INC
2943 E Las Hermanas St, Compton (90221-5508)
PHONE..................310 631-8978
Golan Levy, *President*
Shrone Levy, *Vice Pres*
Orly Levy, *Admin Sec*
Maynor Juarez, *Plant Mgr*
▲ EMP: 25 EST: 1988
SQ FT: 91,000
SALES (est): 15.6MM **Privately Held**
WEB: www.west-wood.net
SIC: 5031 2499 Lumber, plywood & millwork; decorative wood & woodwork

---

5032 Brick, Stone & Related Construction Mtrls Wholesale

(P-13292)
ARIZONA TILE LLC
1620 S Lewis St, Anaheim (92805-6436)
PHONE..................714 978-6403
EMP: 100
SALES (corp-wide): 322.1MM **Privately Held**
SIC: 5032 Whol Brick/Stone Material
PA: Arizona Tile, L.L.C.
8829 S Priest Dr
Tempe AZ 85284
480 893-9393

(P-13293)
ATLAS CONSTRUCTION SUPPLY INC
7550 Stage Rd, Buena Park (90621-1253)
PHONE..................714 441-9500
Pat Kelley, *Manager*
Robert Wiegman, *General Mgr*
EMP: 30
SALES (corp-wide): 47.3MM **Privately Held**
WEB: www.atlasform.com
SIC: 5032 5211 5082 3444 Concrete building products; masonry materials & supplies; contractors' materials; concrete forms, sheet metal
PA: Atlas Construction Supply, Inc.
4640 Brinnell St
San Diego CA 92111
858 277-2100

(P-13294)
BEST CHEER STONE INC (PA)
3190 E Miraloma Ave, Anaheim (92806-1906)
PHONE..................714 399-1588
Chung Lun Ko, *CEO*
Yanlin K Xu, *CFO*
Yanlin Xu, *CFO*
Yanlin Kathy Xu, *Vice Pres*
Fola Linebarger, *Human Res Mgr*
▲ EMP: 22 EST: 2005
SALES (est): 29.3MM **Privately Held**
WEB: www.bestcheerstone.com
SIC: 5032 3281 Granite building stone; stone, quarrying & processing of own stone products

(P-13295)
CARRARA MARBLE CO AMER INC (PA)
15939 Phoenix Dr, City of Industry (91745-1624)
PHONE..................626 961-6010
William Cordova, *President*
James Hogan, *Senior VP*
Dirk Wietstock, *Vice Pres*
Eloise Paz, *Controller*
Gael Keating-Clay, *Opers Staff*
▲ EMP: 70 EST: 1953
SQ FT: 30,000
SALES (est): 16.1MM **Privately Held**
WEB: www.carrara.com
SIC: 5032 1743 1741 Ceramic wall & floor tile; marble installation, interior; masonry & other stonework

(P-13296)
CEMEX CEMENT INC
1201 W Gladstone St, Azusa (91702-5142)
P.O. Box 575 (91702-0575)
PHONE..................626 969-1747
Steve Hayes, *Manager*
Valora Engels, *Planning*
EMP: 21 **Privately Held**
WEB: www.cemexusa.com
SIC: 5032 3273 3251 1411 Concrete mixtures; ready-mixed concrete; brick & structural clay tile; dimension stone
HQ: Cemex Cement, Inc.
10100 Katy Fwy Ste 300
Houston TX 77043
713 650-6200

(P-13297)
CEMEX CONSTRUCTION MTLS INC (DH)
3990 Concourse Ste 200, Ontario (91764)
PHONE..................909 974-5500
Deborah Sue Politte, *President*
Gilberto Perez, *President*
Thomas Edgeller, *Corp Secy*
◆ EMP: 35 EST: 1990
SQ FT: 20,419
SALES (est): 50.7MM **Privately Held**
WEB: www.cemex.com
SIC: 5032 1423 Cement; crushed & broken granite
HQ: Cemex, Inc.
10100 Katy Fwy Ste 300
Houston TX 77043
713 650-6200

(P-13298)
CLASSIC TILE & MOSAIC INC (PA)
Also Called: Ctm
14463 S Broadway, Gardena (90248-1807)
PHONE..................310 538-9605
Vincent Cullinan, *CEO*
Bonnie Daland, *Vice Pres*
Shannon Thomas, *Vice Pres*
Carolina Rios, *Project Mgr*
▲ EMP: 56 EST: 2001
SALES (est): 22.3MM **Privately Held**
WEB: www.ctandm.com
SIC: 5032 5211 Tile, clay or other ceramic, excluding refractory; tile, ceramic

(P-13299)
COAST ROCK PRODUCTS INC
1625 E Donovan Rd, Santa Maria (93454-2500)
P.O. Box 1280 (93456-1280)
PHONE..................805 925-2505
Ron Root, *President*
Steve Will, *President*
George Hamel, *Corp Secy*
John Will, *Vice Pres*
EMP: 45 EST: 1955
SQ FT: 5,000
SALES (est): 4.1MM **Privately Held**
SIC: 5032 3273 3241 2951 Cement; ready-mixed concrete; cement, hydraulic; asphalt paving mixtures & blocks; construction sand & gravel

(P-13300)
CONCRETE TIE INDUSTRIES INC (PA)
130 E Oris St, Compton (90222-2714)
P.O. Box 5406 (90224-5406)
PHONE..................310 628-2328

Paul J Schoendienst, *President*
Steve Sim, *Admin Sec*
Steve Sims, *Controller*
EMP: 70 EST: 1981
SQ FT: 280,000
SALES (est): 12.6MM **Privately Held**
SIC: 5032 3452 Concrete & cinder building products; bolts, nuts, rivets & washers

(P-13301)
DAL-TILE CORPORATION
Also Called: Daltile
16300 Stagg St, Van Nuys (91406-1717)
PHONE..................818 780-1301
EMP: 17 **Publicly Held**
WEB: www.daltile.com
SIC: 5211 5032 3253 Tile, ceramic; ceramic wall & floor tile; ceramic wall & floor tile
HQ: Dal-Tile Corporation
7834 C F Hawn Fwy
Dallas TX 75217
214 398-1411

(P-13302)
DOUGLAS MAXIM INC
Also Called: D G Associates
1726 N Ventura Ave Ste A, Ventura (93001-1549)
PHONE..................805 648-7761
EMP: 20
SQ FT: 20,000
SALES (est): 1.7MM **Privately Held**
WEB: www.maximdouglas.com
SIC: 5032 3272 2599 Whol Brick/Stone Material Mfg Concrete Products Mfg Furniture/Fixtures

(P-13303)
ELDORADO STONE LLC
24100 Orange Ave, Perris (92570-8791)
PHONE..................951 601-3838
EMP: 555 **Privately Held**
WEB: www.eldoradostone.com
SIC: 5032 Brick, stone & related material
HQ: Eldorado Stone Llc
1370 Grand Ave Bldg E
San Marcos CA 92078
800 925-1491

(P-13304)
EMSER INTERNATIONAL LLC (PA)
8431 Santa Monica Blvd, Los Angeles (90069-4294)
PHONE..................323 650-2000
Sam Ghodsian, *Mng Member*
Mark Comstock, *Vice Pres*
Cindy Dalessio, *Branch Mgr*
David Hille, *Branch Mgr*
Barry Dambrowsk, *General Mgr*
▲ EMP: 70 EST: 1967
SQ FT: 50,000
SALES (est): 45.9MM **Privately Held**
WEB: www.emser.com
SIC: 5032 Ceramic wall & floor tile

(P-13305)
FST SAND & GRAVEL INC
21780 Temescal Canyon Rd, Corona (92883-5669)
P.O. Box 2798 (92878-2798)
PHONE..................951 277-8440
Frank Smith, *President*
Pattie Peck,
EMP: 50 EST: 1982
SQ FT: 1,078
SALES (est): 10.4MM **Privately Held**
WEB: www.fstsand.com
SIC: 5032 Sand, construction; gravel

(P-13306)
KRETUS GROUP INC (PA)
1129 N Patt St, Anaheim (92801-2568)
PHONE..................714 738-6640
Ron Webber, *President*
Thomas Caltabiano, *Business Mgr*
EMP: 21 EST: 2005
SQ FT: 8,800 **Privately Held**
SIC: 5032 3569 Concrete building products; concrete mixtures; assembly machines, non-metalworking

(P-13307)
M S INTERNATIONAL INC (PA)
Also Called: MSI Orange Showroom & Dist Ctr
2095 N Batavia St, Orange (92865-3101)
PHONE................................714 685-7500
Manahar Shah, *CEO*
Rajesh Shah, *President*
Rutesh Shah, *President*
Chandrika Shah, *Corp Secy*
Sam Kim, *Senior VP*
◆ **EMP:** 300 **EST:** 1983
SQ FT: 500,000
SALES (est): 427.8MM **Privately Held**
WEB: www.msisurfaces.com
SIC: 5032 5023 Granite building stone; floor coverings; wood flooring; resilient floor coverings: tile or sheet

(P-13308)
NEW GENERATION ENGRG CNSTR INC
22815 Frampton Ave, Torrance (90501-5034)
PHONE................................424 329-3950
Raul Ocegueda, *President*
EMP: 25 **EST:** 2016
SALES (est): 8.2MM **Privately Held**
WEB: www.tngec.com
SIC: 5032 1459 3317 3531 Brick, stone & related material; clays (common) quarrying; steel pipe & tubes; construction machinery; refractory or acid brick masonry; welding on site

(P-13309)
PABCO CLAY PRODUCTS LLC
Also Called: Gladding, McBean
4301 Firestone Blvd, South Gate (90280-3318)
PHONE................................323 568-1860
Dennis Osborne,
Michael Amaral, *Marketing Staff*
EMP: 69
SALES (corp-wide): 1.1B **Privately Held**
WEB: www.paccoast.com
SIC: 5032 Clay construction materials, except refractory
HQ: Pabco Clay Products, Llc
605 Industrial Way
Dixon CA 95620

(P-13310)
PACIFIC CLAY PRODUCTS INC
14741 Lake St, Lake Elsinore (92530-1610)
PHONE................................661 857-1401
Barry Coley, *President*
Kai Chin, *Vice Pres*
Dale Kline, *Vice Pres*
Brenna De Paris, *Administration*
Brenna Deparis, *Administration*
▲ **EMP:** 160 **EST:** 1930
SQ FT: 200,000
SALES (est): 62.8MM **Privately Held**
WEB: www.pacificclay.com
SIC: 5032 3251 Tile & clay products; paving brick, clay

(P-13311)
PARAGON INDUSTRIES INC
Also Called: Bedrosian's Tile & Marble
4301 Ashe Rd, Bakersfield (93313-2032)
PHONE................................661 396-0555
Luz Acosta, *Branch Mgr*
EMP: 75
SALES (corp-wide): 251.5MM **Privately Held**
SIC: 5211 5032 Tile, ceramic; ceramic wall & floor tile; granite building stone
PA: Paragon Industries, Inc.
4285 N Golden State Blvd
Fresno CA 93722
559 275-5000

(P-13312)
PARAGON INDUSTRIES INC
Also Called: Bedrosian Tile & Stone
1515 E Winston Rd, Anaheim (92805-6445)
PHONE................................714 778-1800
Diana Kelly, *President*
Courtney Nicholas, *Creative Dir*
Scott Giesecke, *Regional Mgr*
Shawnette Blank, *Branch Mgr*

Mignon Ferguson, *Branch Mgr*
EMP: 100
SALES (corp-wide): 251.5MM **Privately Held**
WEB: www.bedrosians.com
SIC: 5211 5032 Tile, ceramic; brick, stone & related material
PA: Paragon Industries, Inc.
4285 N Golden State Blvd
Fresno CA 93722
559 275-5000

(P-13313)
RCP BLOCK & BRICK INC
25725 Jefferson Ave, Murrieta (92562-6903)
PHONE................................951 677-1489
Mark Degrave, *Manager*
EMP: 51
SALES (corp-wide): 43.4MM **Privately Held**
WEB: www.rcpblock.com
SIC: 5032 Brick, stone & related material
PA: Rcp Block & Brick, Inc.
8240 Broadway
Lemon Grove CA 91945
619 460-9101

(P-13314)
ROBERTSONS READY MIX LTD
16952 S D St, Victorville (92395-3302)
PHONE................................702 798-0568
EMP: 110 **Privately Held**
WEB: www.rrmca.com
SIC: 5032 Gravel
HQ: Robertson's Ready Mix, Ltd., A California Limited Partnership
200 S Main St Ste 200 # 200
Corona CA 92882
951 493-6500

(P-13315)
TILE KING
949 N Cataract Ave Ste C, San Dimas (91773-1464)
PHONE................................909 599-7300
Elie Sfeir, *Owner*
EMP: 16 **EST:** 2010
SALES (est): 3.4MM **Privately Held**
WEB: www.tileking.net
SIC: 5211 5032 3253 Tile, ceramic; ceramic wall & floor tile; ceramic wall & floor tile

(P-13316)
UGM CITATAH INC (PA)
Also Called: Ugmc
13220 Cambridge St, Santa Fe Springs (90670-4902)
PHONE................................562 921-9549
Viken Dave Yaghjian, *President*
Bruce Feaster, *Exec VP*
Irmen Yaghjian, *Admin Sec*
▲ **EMP:** 125 **EST:** 1987
SQ FT: 46,000
SALES (est): 26.5MM **Privately Held**
WEB: www.ugmcstone.com
SIC: 5032 1741 1743 Marble building stone; stone masonry; terrazzo, tile, marble, mosaic work

(P-13317)
VALORI SAND & GRAVEL COMPANY
Also Called: Thompson Building Materials
11027 Cherry Ave, Fontana (92337-7118)
P.O. Box 950 (92334-0950)
PHONE................................909 350-3000
Tom Rievley, *Branch Mgr*
EMP: 250
SALES (corp-wide): 16MM **Privately Held**
WEB: www.thompsonbldg.com
SIC: 5032 5211 Brick, stone & related material; cement
PA: Valori Sand & Gravel Company Inc
141 W Taft Ave
Orange CA 92865
714 637-0104

(P-13318)
VERONA QUARTZ INC
9415 Telfair Ave, Sun Valley (91352-1332)
PHONE................................818 962-3668
Sarkis Grigoryan, *CEO*
▲ **EMP:** 17 **EST:** 2016

SALES (est): 4.8MM **Privately Held**
WEB: www.veronaquartz.com
SIC: 5032 3281 Granite building stone; architectural sculptures: gypsum, clay, papier mache, etc.; cut stone & stone products

(P-13319)
WALKER & ZANGER LLC (HQ)
16719 Schoenborn St A, North Hills (91343-6115)
PHONE................................818 280-8300
Jonathan Zanger, *CEO*
Pat Petrocelli, *COO*
Kim Bernard, *Exec Dir*
Daniel Clark, *Branch Mgr*
Bing Sulistijowadi, *Technology*
◆ **EMP:** 60 **EST:** 1958
SQ FT: 30,000
SALES (est): 105.8MM
SALES (corp-wide): 118.7MM **Privately Held**
WEB: www.walkerzanger.com
SIC: 5032 Marble building stone; ceramic wall & floor tile
PA: Mosaic Companies, Llc
1530 Nw 98th Ct Ste 101
Doral FL 33172
305 372-9787

(P-13320)
WEST COAST SAND AND GRAVEL INC (PA)
Also Called: West Coast Materials
7282 Orangethorpe Ave, Buena Park (90621-3331)
P.O. Box 5067 (90622-5067)
PHONE................................714 522-0282
Daniel C Reyneveld, *CEO*
Marvin J Struiksma, *President*
Jeff Struiksma, *COO*
John Struiksma, *Vice Pres*
James Slater, *General Mgr*
EMP: 71 **EST:** 1968
SQ FT: 4,200
SALES (est): 55.1MM **Privately Held**
WEB: www.wcsg.com
SIC: 5032 Sand, construction; gravel

(P-13321)
WESTERN PACIFIC DISTRG LLC
Also Called: Westpac Materials
341 W Meats Ave, Orange (92865-2623)
PHONE................................714 974-6837
Mark Hamilton, *Mng Member*
Carol Tomura, *Branch Mgr*
Leslie Dixon, *Credit Mgr*
Paul Rosenge, *Accountant*
John Demott, *Purch Mgr*
EMP: 157 **EST:** 2001
SALES (est): 50.4MM **Privately Held**
WEB: www.westpacmaterials.com
SIC: 5032 Drywall materials

(P-13322)
WHITEWATER ROCK & SUP CO INC
58645 Old Highway 60, Whitewater (92282-7600)
PHONE................................760 325-2747
Allan E Bankus Jr, *President*
Irene Bankus, *Treasurer*
Linda Jo Bankus, *Executive Asst*
▲ **EMP:** 36 **EST:** 1962
SQ FT: 4,500
SALES (est): 3.6MM **Privately Held**
WEB: www.whitewater-rock.com
SIC: 5032 3281 Building stone; gravel; stone, crushed or broken; stone, quarrying & processing of own stone products

---

5033 Roofing, Siding & Insulation Mtrls Wholesale

(P-13323)
ALL ROOFG MTLS LONG BCH INC
1435 Walter St, Ventura (93003-5669)
PHONE................................805 656-6319
Allen Hopper, *Manager*
EMP: 69

SALES (corp-wide): 6.9B **Publicly Held**
WEB: www.onlongbeach.com
SIC: 5033 Roofing, asphalt & sheet metal
HQ: A.L.L. Roofing Materials Of Long Beach, Inc.
3645 Long Beach Blvd
Long Beach CA 90807
562 595-7531

(P-13324)
ALL ROOFG MTLS LONG BCH INC
3100 Orange Ave, Long Beach (90755-5220)
PHONE................................562 595-7377
Greg Bynum, *Manager*
EMP: 69
SALES (corp-wide): 6.9B **Publicly Held**
WEB: www.onlongbeach.com
SIC: 5033 Roofing, asphalt & sheet metal
HQ: A.L.L. Roofing Materials Of Long Beach, Inc.
3645 Long Beach Blvd
Long Beach CA 90807
562 595-7531

(P-13325)
J B WHL ROOFG BLDG SUPS INC (DH)
Also Called: J B
21524 Nordhoff St, Chatsworth (91311-5822)
P.O. Box 5289 (91313-5289)
PHONE................................818 998-0440
W Keith Jones, *President*
Brian Jones, *Admin Sec*
EMP: 70 **EST:** 1981
SQ FT: 2,000
SALES (est): 48.8MM **Privately Held**
WEB: www.jbwholesale.com
SIC: 5211 5033 Roofing material; shingles, except wood

(P-13326)
PACIFIC AWARD METALS INC
Also Called: Gibraltar
10302 Birtcher Dr, Jurupa Valley (91752-1829)
PHONE................................909 390-9880
Brian Lipke, *Branch Mgr*
EMP: 55
SALES (corp-wide): 1B **Publicly Held**
SIC: 5033 2952 3444 Roofing & siding materials; roofing materials; sheet metalwork
HQ: Pacific Award Metals, Inc.
1450 Virginia Ave
Baldwin Park CA 91706
626 814-4410

(P-13327)
REVCHEM COMPOSITES INC (PA)
Also Called: Revchem Plastics
2720 S Willow Ave B, Bloomington (92316-3259)
P.O. Box 333 (92316-0333)
PHONE................................909 877-8477
Douglas L Dennis, *CEO*
Gina L Dennis, *Principal*
◆ **EMP:** 71 **EST:** 1975
SALES (est): 31.4MM **Privately Held**
WEB: www.revchem.com
SIC: 5033 Fiberglass building materials

(P-13328)
ROOFLINE SUPPLY SRS DIST
2016 S Reservoir St, Pomona (91766-5545)
PHONE................................909 623-8191
EMP: 92 **Privately Held**
WEB: www.rooflinesupply.com
SIC: 5033 Roofing & siding materials
HQ: Roofline Supply Srs Dist
5900 S Lake Forest Dr # 400
Mckinney TX 75070
214 491-4149

(P-13329)
STANDARD INDUSTRIES INC
Also Called: GAF Materials
6505 Zerker Rd, Shafter (93263-9614)
PHONE................................661 387-1110
Phil Halpin, *General Mgr*
EMP: 100

PRODUCTS & SVCS

SALES (corp-wide): 4.4B **Privately Held**
WEB: www.gaf.com
SIC: 5033 Roofing & siding materials
HQ: Standard Industries Inc.
　1 Campus Dr
　Parsippany NJ 07054

(P-13330)
VALLEY METAL SUPPLY INC
12950 Bradley Ave, Sylmar (91342-3829)
PHONE.................................818 837-6566
Douglas Kowalski, *President*
Alice Kowalski, *Vice Pres*
Coaudi Venegas, *Admin Sec*
EMP: 15 EST: 1996
SQ FT: 12,000
SALES (est): 4.6MM **Privately Held**
WEB: www.valleygutter.com
SIC: 5033 3444 1761 Roofing & siding materials; metal roofing & roof drainage equipment; roofing, siding & sheet metal work

---

5039 Construction Materials, NEC Wholesale

(P-13331)
CHARMSHIN GROUP INC (PA)
9039 Bolsa Ave Ste 309, Westminster (92683-5596)
PHONE.................................949 331-0301
Michael Shim, *CEO*
Chris Kim, *CFO*
Hyun Seok Kim, *Admin Sec*
EMP: 19 EST: 2019
SALES (est): 1.1MM **Privately Held**
WEB: www.charmshingroup.com
SIC: 5039 2835 5122 5047 Prefabricated structures; in vitro diagnostics; cosmetics; medical & hospital equipment; medical equipment & supplies; medical laboratory equipment; trade binding services

(P-13332)
LARRY MTHVIN INSTALLATIONS INC
Also Called: All Counties
210 S Center St, Santa Ana (92703-4302)
PHONE.................................714 547-8021
Dave Forker, *Manager*
Mary Duran, *Manager*
EMP: 73
SALES (corp-wide): 2.4B **Publicly Held**
WEB: www.larrymethvin.com
SIC: 5039 5023 Glass construction materials; glassware
HQ: Larry Methvin Installations, Inc.
　501 Kettering Dr
　Ontario CA 91761
　909 563-1700

(P-13333)
LSF9 CYPRESS LP (PA)
2741 Walnut Ave Ste 200, Tustin (92780-7063)
PHONE.................................714 380-3127
Ruben Mendoza, *President*
Lsf9 Genpar LLC, *General Ptnr*
EMP: 1472 EST: 2015
SALES (est): 153.9MM **Privately Held**
SIC: 5039 5031 5033 Ceiling systems & products; wallboard; insulation materials

(P-13334)
LSF9 CYPRESS PARENT LLC (DH)
2741 Walnut Ave Ste 200, Tustin (92780-7063)
PHONE.................................714 380-3127
Ruben Mendoza, *President*
Samuel D Loughlin, *Ch of Bd*
Pete Welly, *COO*
John Gorey, *CFO*
Ray Sears, *Senior VP*
EMP: 741 EST: 2015
SALES (est): 112MM **Privately Held**
WEB: www.fbmsales.com
SIC: 5039 5031 5033 Ceiling systems & products; wallboard; insulation materials
HQ: Foundation Building Materials, Inc.
　2520 Redhill Ave
　Santa Ana CA 92705
　714 380-3127

(P-13335)
LSF9 CYPRESS PARENT 2 LLC
2741 Walnut Ave Ste 200, Tustin (92780-7063)
PHONE.................................714 380-3127
EMP: 3500 EST: 2016
SALES (est): 153.9MM **Privately Held**
SIC: 5039 5031 5033 Ceiling systems & products; wallboard; insulation materials
PA: Lsf9 Cypress L.P.
　2741 Walnut Ave Ste 200
　Tustin CA 92780
　714 380-3127

(P-13336)
MID COAST SUPPLIERS INC
Also Called: Contractors Glass Company
60 Prado Rd, San Luis Obispo (93401-7313)
PHONE.................................805 543-0871
Paul Sverchek, *President*
Donald Sverchek, *President*
Carl Burrier, *Vice Pres*
EMP: 14 EST: 1971
SQ FT: 6,000
SALES (est): 2.5MM **Privately Held**
WEB: www.replacementwindowssanluisobispo.com
SIC: 5211 5719 5231 5039 Windows, storm: wood or metal; mirrors; glass; air ducts, sheet metal; glass & glazing work; doors, glass: made from purchased glass

(P-13337)
ULTRAGLAS INC
9200 Gazette Ave, Chatsworth (91311-5930)
PHONE.................................818 772-7744
Jane Skeeter, *President*
Victoria Ocampo, *Finance*
▼ EMP: 23 EST: 1972
SQ FT: 25,000
SALES (est): 9.5MM **Privately Held**
WEB: www.ultraglas.com
SIC: 5039 3231 3211 5231 Glass construction materials; products of purchased glass; flat glass; glass, leaded or stained

(P-13338)
VOPAK TERMINAL LONG BEACH INC
3601 Dock St, San Pedro (90731-7540)
PHONE.................................310 521-7969
Tom Burke, *President*
EMP: 54 EST: 2003
SQ FT: 23,563
SALES (est): 24.4MM
SALES (corp-wide): 1.4B **Privately Held**
WEB: www.vopak.com
SIC: 5039 Septic tanks
PA: Koninklijke Vopak N.V.
　Westerlaan 10
　Rotterdam 3016
　104 002-911

(P-13339)
WHITE CAP SUPPLY GROUP INC
Also Called: White Cap 301
28255 Kelly Johnson Pkwy, Santa Clarita (91355-5080)
PHONE.................................661 294-7737
Julia Laguardia, *Branch Mgr*
EMP: 546
SALES (corp-wide): 6.7B **Privately Held**
SIC: 5039 5072 Air ducts, sheet metal; hardware
HQ: White Cap Supply Group, Inc.
　6250 Brook Hllow Pkwy Ste
　Norcross GA 30071

5043 Photographic Eqpt & Splys Wholesale

(P-13340)
AAA IMAGING & SUPPLIES INC
Also Called: AAA Imaging Solutions
2313 S Susan St, Santa Ana (92704-4420)
PHONE.................................714 431-0570
Robert G Noterman, *CEO*
Lou Burgess, *Vice Pres*
Michael Wodushek, *VP Bus Dvlpt*

John Burnasky, *Prdtn Mgr*
Tony Lee, *VP Sales*
◆ EMP: 25 EST: 1998
SALES (est): 8.9MM **Privately Held**
WEB: www.aaaimaging.com
SIC: 5043 3861 7699 Photographic processing equipment; processing equipment, photographic; photographic equipment repair

(P-13341)
CANON USA INC
15955 Alton Pkwy, Irvine (92618-3731)
PHONE.................................949 753-4000
Glen Takahashi, *Manager*
Seymour E Liebman, *Exec VP*
Chuck Arnold, *Executive*
Jennifer Mathews, *Executive*
Alissa Simpson, *Executive*
EMP: 350 **Privately Held**
WEB: www.usa.canon.com
SIC: 5043 5044 5045 8741 Photographic cameras, projectors, equipment & supplies; office equipment; computers; management services
HQ: Canon U.S.A., Inc.
　1 Canon Park
　Melville NY 11747
　516 328-5000

(P-13342)
CHRISTIE DGTAL SYSTEMS USA INC (DH)
10550 Camden Dr, Cypress (90630-4600)
PHONE.................................714 236-8610
Kazuhisa Kamiyama, *Ch of Bd*
Zoran Veselic, *President*
Greg Shepherd, *Vice Pres*
Terry Breland, *Technician*
Jan Miller, *Senior Mgr*
◆ EMP: 188 EST: 1992
SQ FT: 85,000
SALES (est): 76.6MM **Privately Held**
WEB: www.christiedigital.com
SIC: 5043 Projection apparatus, motion picture & slide
HQ: Christie Digital Systems, Inc.
　10550 Camden Dr
　Cypress CA 90630
　714 236-8610

(P-13343)
CHRISTYS EDTORIAL FILM SUP INC
3625 W Pacific Ave, Burbank (91505-1451)
PHONE.................................818 845-1755
Craig Christy, *President*
Sheli Christy, *Corp Secy*
Bob Campos, *Vice Pres*
Alice Christy, *Principal*
Dominic Zerpoli, *Technician*
EMP: 89 EST: 1969
SQ FT: 12,500
SALES (est): 8.2MM **Privately Held**
WEB: www.christys.net
SIC: 5946 5043 Camera & photographic supply stores; motion picture cameras, equipment & supplies

(P-13344)
FILMTOOLS INC (PA)
Also Called: Moviola Digital
1015 N Hollywood Way, Burbank (91505-2546)
PHONE.................................323 467-1116
Joseph Paskal, *President*
Randy Paskal, *Exec VP*
Carl Nelson, *Vice Pres*
Jerry Pierucci, *Vice Pres*
Dana Newman, *Admin Sec*
EMP: 50 EST: 1923
SQ FT: 30,000
SALES (est): 48MM **Privately Held**
WEB: www.moviola.com
SIC: 5946 5043 7819 3861 Photographic supplies; motion picture equipment; editing services, motion picture production; photographic equipment & supplies

(P-13345)
FREESTYLE SALES CO LTD PARTNR
12231 Florence Ave, Santa Fe Springs (90670-3805)
P.O. Box 27924, Los Angeles (90027-0924)
PHONE.................................323 660-3460

Ronald M Resch, *Partner*
Leonore King, *Partner*
Patrick White, *CIO*
Emmalee Garcia, *Senior Buyer*
Amy Mendoza, *Buyer*
▲ EMP: 90
SALES (est): 12.1MM **Privately Held**
WEB: www.freestylephoto.biz
SIC: 5946 5043 Photographic supplies; photographic equipment & supplies

(P-13346)
JK IMAGING LTD
17239 S Main St, Gardena (90248-3129)
PHONE.................................310 755-6848
Joe Atick, *CEO*
Shu-Ping Wu, *CFO*
Mike Feng, *Admin Sec*
▲ EMP: 100 EST: 2012
SQ FT: 6,000
SALES (est): 24MM **Privately Held**
SIC: 5043 Cameras & photographic equipment

(P-13347)
NORITSU-AMERICA CORPORATION (HQ)
6900 Noritsu Ave, Buena Park (90620-1372)
P.O. Box 5039 (90622-5039)
PHONE.................................714 521-9040
Michiro Niikura, *CEO*
Kanichi Nishimoto, *Ch of Bd*
Kathy Cryer, *Vice Pres*
Frank Morrow, *Vice Pres*
Patrick Todd, *Vice Pres*
◆ EMP: 115
SQ FT: 27,500
SALES (est): 69.1MM **Privately Held**
WEB: www.noritsu.com
SIC: 5043 Photographic processing equipment

(P-13348)
PILGRIM OPERATIONS LLC
Also Called: Tailroom Media Grop
12020 Chanl Blvd Ste 200, North Hollywood (91607)
PHONE.................................818 478-4500
Douglas Liechty, *Mng Member*
Rebecka Biejo, *Vice Pres*
Rebecca Forde, *Producer*
Luke Wanagel, *Producer*
Steve Durgin, *Editor*
EMP: 400 EST: 2012
SALES (est): 44.6MM **Privately Held**
WEB: www.pilgrimediagroup.com
SIC: 5043 Motion picture studio & theater equipment

(P-13349)
UNINET IMAGING INC (PA)
3232 W El Segundo Blvd, Hawthorne (90250-4823)
PHONE.................................424 675-3300
Nestor Saporiti, *CEO*
Claudia Saporiti, *CFO*
Joseph Jean, *Business Mgr*
Karen Hughes, *Sales Staff*
Richard Soto, *Manager*
◆ EMP: 42 EST: 1997
SQ FT: 50,000
SALES (est): 14.6MM **Privately Held**
WEB: www.uninetcolombia.com
SIC: 5043 3955 5084 Photographic equipment & supplies; print cartridges for laser & other computer printers; printing trades machinery, equipment & supplies

---

5044 Office Eqpt Wholesale

(P-13350)
ACM TECHNOLOGIES INC (PA)
Also Called: Allstate
2535 Research Dr, Corona (92882-7607)
PHONE.................................951 738-9898
Stan Shue Lin, *CEO*
Sharon Lee, *COO*
Monica Lin, *Corp Secy*
Clarence Perera, *Business Anlyst*
Carolyne Chu, *Marketing Mgr*
◆ EMP: 52 EST: 1995

SALES (est): 28.4MM **Privately Held**
WEB: www.acmtech.com
SIC: 5044 Copying equipment; photocopy machines

(P-13351)
ALLSTATE IMAGING INC (PA)
21621 Nordhoff St, Chatsworth (91311-5828)
PHONE..................................818 678-4550
Alan Jurick, *President*
Russel Leventhal, *CEO*
Richard Shapiro, *CFO*
EMP: 80 **EST:** 1990
SALES (est): 14.9MM **Privately Held**
SIC: 5044 Office equipment

(P-13352)
CANON SOLUTIONS AMERICA INC
6435 Ventura Blvd Ste C00, Ventura (93003-7228)
PHONE..................................844 443-4636
Suzanne Alpizar, *Manager*
Scott Markell, *Executive*
Gregory Boyce, *Manager*
EMP: 31 **Privately Held**
WEB: www.csa.canon.com
SIC: 5044 7699 3861 Copying equipment; photocopy machine repair; photographic equipment & supplies
HQ: Canon Solutions America, Inc.
1 Canon Park
Melville NY 11747
631 330-5000

(P-13353)
COAST TO COAST BUS EQP INC (PA)
8 Vanderbilt Ste 200, Irvine (92618-2080)
PHONE..................................949 457-7300
Paul M Faus, *President*
Julie Davis, *Treasurer*
Manny Torres, *Officer*
Christian Smith, *IT/INT Sup*
Marla Gastelum, *Human Resources*
EMP: 52 **EST:** 1981
SQ FT: 20,100
SALES (est): 12.1MM **Privately Held**
WEB: www.ctcbe.com
SIC: 5044 5065 Photocopy machines; teletype equipment

(P-13354)
COPIER SOURCE INC
Also Called: Image Source
650 E Hospitality Ln # 500, San Bernardino (92408-3535)
PHONE..................................909 890-4040
David Bradley Craft, *CEO*
Jill Craft, *Corp Secy*
Sonia Rodriguez, *Accounts Exec*
EMP: 135 **EST:** 1989
SALES (est): 49MM **Privately Held**
WEB: www.imagesourceusa.com
SIC: 5044 Office equipment

(P-13355)
CUSTOM BUSINESS SOLUTIONS INC (PA)
Also Called: Northstar
1 Studebaker, Irvine (92618-2013)
PHONE..................................949 380-7674
Art Julian, *CEO*
Colleen Julian, *President*
Rom Krupp, *President*
Mike Bloch, *President*
Michael Block, *CFO*
▼ **EMP:** 68 **EST:** 1995
SALES (est): 27.7MM **Privately Held**
WEB: www.cbsnorthstar.com
SIC: 5044 Cash registers

(P-13356)
DUPLO USA CORPORATION (PA)
3050 Daimler St, Santa Ana (92705-5813)
PHONE..................................949 752-8222
Peter Tu, *President*
Jim Peffer, *COO*
Eric Von Schimpf, *Info Tech Dir*
Armando Olivares, *Technical Mgr*
Eric Schimpf, *Data Proc Staff*
◆ **EMP:** 71 **EST:** 1979
SQ FT: 30,000

SALES (est): 23.4MM **Privately Held**
WEB: www.duplousa.com
SIC: 5044 Duplicating machines

(P-13357)
IMAGE IV SYSTEMS INC (PA)
512 S Varney St, Burbank (91502-2196)
PHONE..................................323 849-3049
Ronald Warren, *President*
Sue Warren, *Vice Pres*
Kevin Nguyen, *Technician*
Rickie Miyake, *Controller*
Tammy Kolb, *Marketing Staff*
EMP: 79 **EST:** 1984
SQ FT: 4,000
SALES (est): 18.1MM **Privately Held**
WEB: www.imageiv.com
SIC: 5044 Photocopy machines; copying equipment

(P-13358)
INTEGRATED OFFICE TECH LLC (PA)
Also Called: Iotec
12150 Mora Dr U2, Santa Fe Springs (90670-3700)
PHONE..................................562 236-9200
Robert Zieman,
Dane Figliola, *Sales Staff*
Matt Zieman, *Sales Staff*
Doug Lu,
Dana Ruf,
EMP: 70
SQ FT: 30,000
SALES (est): 20MM **Privately Held**
WEB: www.iotecdigital.com
SIC: 5044 7371 7379 Copying equipment; computer software systems analysis & design, custom; computer related maintenance services

(P-13359)
INTEGRUS LLC
Also Called: Advanced Office
14370 Myford Rd Ste 100, Irvine (92606-1015)
PHONE..................................714 547-9500
Mike Dixon, *CEO*
Richard Van Dyke, *President*
Tim Wickers, *Vice Pres*
Steven Fox, *Executive*
Christine Billones, *Administration*
EMP: 100 **EST:** 2011
SALES (est): 18MM **Privately Held**
SIC: 5044 Office equipment

(P-13360)
INTERNTNAL LITIGATION SVCS INC
65 Enterprise, Aliso Viejo (92656-2705)
PHONE..................................888 313-4457
Joseph Thorpe, *CEO*
Mark Liekkio, *Senior VP*
Tony Chu, *Litigation*
Elizabeth Koenig, *Litigation*
Douglas Forrest,
EMP: 57 **EST:** 1988
SQ FT: 7,000
SALES (est): 5.6MM **Privately Held**
WEB: www.ilsteam.com
SIC: 5044 Office equipment

(P-13361)
KYOCERA DCMENT SOLUTIONS W LLC
14101 Alton Pkwy, Irvine (92618-1815)
PHONE..................................800 996-9591
Norihiko INA, *Mng Member*
Andy Kabir, *Technology*
Mike Graves,
EMP: 150 **EST:** 2008
SALES (est): 25.1MM **Privately Held**
WEB: www.copystar.com
SIC: 5044 Office equipment
HQ: Kyocera Document Solutions America, Inc.
225 Sand Rd
Fairfield NJ 07004
973 808-8444

(P-13362)
MICROTEK LAB INC (HQ)
13337 South St, Cerritos (90703-7308)
PHONE..................................310 687-5823
Clark Hsu, *President*

Stewart Chow, *President*
▲ **EMP:** 110 **EST:** 1980
SQ FT: 126,000
SALES (est): 61MM **Privately Held**
WEB: www.microtekusa.com
SIC: 5044 Copying equipment

(P-13363)
MWB COPY PRODUCTS INC (DH)
Also Called: Socal Office Technologies
5700 Warland Dr, Cypress (90630-5030)
PHONE..................................800 736-7979
David Riener, *CEO*
Joseph Payne, *President*
Juan Salcedo, *CFO*
Jeff Mason, *Vice Pres*
Brenda Merrill, *Vice Pres*
EMP: 50 **EST:** 1985
SQ FT: 8,000
SALES (est): 44.1MM
SALES (corp-wide): 7B **Publicly Held**
WEB: www.socal-office.com
SIC: 5999 5044 Photocopy machines; typewriters; photocopy machines; duplicating machines; typewriters

(P-13364)
NATIONAL LINK INCORPORATED
2235 Auto Centre Dr, Glendora (91740-6721)
PHONE..................................909 670-1900
Sam Kandah, *President*
Jim Scott, *CFO*
Carol Kandah, *Admin Sec*
Rami Kassar, *Project Mgr*
Michael Joyner, *Technical Staff*
EMP: 68 **EST:** 1992
SQ FT: 5,000
SALES (est): 16.3MM **Privately Held**
WEB: www.nationallinkatm.com
SIC: 5044 7389 7359 Bank automatic teller machines; credit card service; electronic equipment rental, except computers

(P-13365)
OFFISERVE INC
Also Called: Advanced Office Services
14370 Myford Rd Ste 100, Irvine (92606-1015)
PHONE..................................714 547-9500
Patricia Dixon, *CEO*
Doug Sillasen, *CFO*
Haydee Duchene, *Executive Asst*
Randi Hein, *Controller*
EMP: 57 **EST:** 1980
SQ FT: 20,000
SALES (est): 7.1MM **Privately Held**
SIC: 5044 5045 7699 7378 Typewriters; computers, peripherals & software; typewriter repair, including electric; computer maintenance & repair; typewriters; personal computers

(P-13366)
TOPAC USA INC (DH)
Also Called: Toshiba Business Solutions
25530 Commercentre Dr, Lake Forest (92630-8855)
PHONE..................................949 462-6000
Rick Taylor, *CEO*
Fred C Berger, *President*
Mark Downing, *President*
Kimihiro Yoshino, *Assoc VP*
Jim Hawkins, *Vice Pres*
▼ **EMP:** 808 **EST:** 1994
SQ FT: 789,000
SALES (est): 105MM **Privately Held**
WEB: www.business.toshiba.com
SIC: 5044 Office equipment
HQ: Toshiba America Business Solutions, Inc.
25530 Commercentre Dr
Lake Forest CA 92630
949 462-6000

(P-13367)
TOSHIBA AMER BUS SOLUTIONS INC (DH)
25530 Commercentre Dr, Lake Forest (92630-8855)
PHONE..................................949 462-6000
Scott Maccabe, *CEO*
Matt Barnes, *President*
Mark Mathews, *President*

Desmond Allen, *CFO*
Larry White, *Officer*
◆ **EMP:** 350 **EST:** 1999
SQ FT: 90,000
SALES (est): 1.3B **Privately Held**
WEB: www.toshibatec.co.jp
SIC: 5044 Copying equipment

(P-13368)
UNITED MERCHANT SVCS CAL INC
Also Called: Ums Banking
750 Fairmont Ave Ste 201, Glendale (91203-1074)
PHONE..................................818 246-6767
Joyce Gaines, *President*
Lynda Neuman, *CFO*
Bruce Ferguson, *Exec VP*
Chris Lake, *Exec VP*
James Cantlen, *Vice Pres*
EMP: 72 **EST:** 1987
SQ FT: 8,580
SALES (est): 17.2MM **Privately Held**
WEB: www.umsbanking.com
SIC: 5044 5065 7629 Office equipment; electronic parts & equipment; electronic equipment repair

(P-13369)
UNITED RIBBON COMPANY INC
Also Called: United Imaging
21201 Oxnard St, Woodland Hills (91367-5015)
PHONE..................................818 716-1515
Michael Cohen, *President*
Yigal Avrahamy, *Vice Pres*
Skye Stilson, *Vice Pres*
Arturo Jimenez, *Executive*
Evelyn Placencia, *Info Tech Mgr*
EMP: 85 **EST:** 1973
SQ FT: 22,000
SALES (est): 53.6MM **Privately Held**
WEB: www.unitedimaging.com
SIC: 5044 5943 5021 7699 Office equipment; office forms & supplies; office & public building furniture; office equipment & accessory customizing; computer & photocopying supplies

(P-13370)
XEROX EDUCATION SERVICES LLC (DH)
2277 E 220th St, Long Beach (90810-1639)
PHONE..................................310 830-9847
J M Peffer, *Mng Member*
Adriel Ewell, *Program Mgr*
Keri Vasquez,
Mike R Festa, *Mng Member*
Norwin Espiritu, *Director*
EMP: 90 **EST:** 1970
SALES (est): 247MM
SALES (corp-wide): 4.1B **Publicly Held**
WEB: www.conduenteducation.com
SIC: 5044 Office equipment
HQ: Conduent Business Services, Llc
100 Campus Dr Ste 200
Florham Park NJ 07932
973 261-7100

5045 Computers & Peripheral Eqpt & Software Wholesale

(P-13371)
ADESSO INC
Also Called: ADS Techonlogy
20659 Valley Blvd, Walnut (91789-2731)
PHONE..................................909 839-2929
Allen Ku, *President*
▲ **EMP:** 200 **EST:** 1994
SALES (est): 21.7MM **Privately Held**
WEB: www.adesso.com
SIC: 5045 Computer peripheral equipment

(P-13372)
ADVANCED INDUSTRIAL CMPT INC (PA)
Also Called: Aic Inc USA
21808 Garcia Ln, City of Industry (91789-0941)
PHONE..................................909 895-8989
Michael Liang, *Ch of Bd*
Shun Ying Liang, *CEO*

Belle Wang, *CFO*
Roxanna Lee, *Project Mgr*
Kathryn Chen, *Purchasing*
▲ **EMP:** 57 **EST:** 1998
SQ FT: 65,000
SALES (est): 19.8MM **Privately Held**
WEB: www.aicipc.com
SIC: 5045 Mainframe computers

(P-13373)
ALTAMETRICS HOSTING LLC
3191 Red Hill Ave Ste 100, Costa Mesa
(92626-3451)
PHONE..........................800 676-1281
Mitesh Gala, *President*
Anand Gala, *CFO*
Jay Scime, *Vice Pres*
Tim Yost, *Vice Pres*
Kimberly Lebish, *Administration*
EMP: 140 **EST:** 2001
SQ FT: 6,000
SALES (est): 34.9MM **Privately Held**
WEB: www.altametrics.com
SIC: 5045 Computer software

(P-13374)
AMERICAN FUTURE TECH CORP
Also Called: Ibuypower
529 Baldwin Park Blvd, City of Industry
(91746-1419)
PHONE..........................888 462-3899
Alex Hou, *CEO*
Darren Su, *Vice Pres*
▲ **EMP:** 120 **EST:** 1997
SQ FT: 25,000
SALES (est): 133.7MM **Privately Held**
SIC: 5045 Computer peripheral equipment

(P-13375)
AMERICAN SCALE CO INC
Also Called: Scales
21326 E Arrow Hwy, Covina (91724-1442)
P.O. Box 158, San Dimas (91773-0158)
PHONE..........................800 773-7225
David William Eccles III, *CEO*
EMP: 24 **EST:** 1946
SQ FT: 4,150
SALES (est): 9.5MM **Privately Held**
WEB: www.americanscale.com
SIC: 5045 3596 7699 Computers, periph-
erals & software; scales & balances, ex-
cept laboratory; counting scales; railroad
track scales; truck (motor vehicle) scales;
scale repair service

(P-13376)
ARBITECH LLC
64 Fairbanks, Irvine (92618-1602)
PHONE..........................949 376-6650
Jimmy Whalen, *President*
David Walker, *CFO*
Stuart Jeffries, *Vice Pres*
Don Shafer, *Vice Pres*
Doug Kari, *Principal*
▲ **EMP:** 74 **EST:** 2000
SQ FT: 40,000
SALES (est): 119.8MM **Privately Held**
WEB: www.arbitech.com
SIC: 5045 Computer peripheral equipment

(P-13377)
AVATAR TECHNOLOGY INC
339 Cheryl Ln, City of Industry
(91789-3003)
PHONE..........................909 598-7696
Juanito Pangalilingan, *CEO*
Toresa Lou, *CEO*
Vicky LI, *Manager*
Dorrie Tan, *Manager*
▲ **EMP:** 30 **EST:** 1999
SQ FT: 48,000
SALES (est): 10MM **Privately Held**
WEB: www.v4me.com
SIC: 5045 3571 Computers; electronic
computers

(P-13378)
AXIOM MEMORY SOLUTIONS INC
16 Goodyear Ste 120, Irvine (92618-3757)
PHONE..........................949 581-1450
Keith Carpenter, *President*
Jason Major, *Vice Pres*
Chris McClave, *CTO*
Danielle Mueller, *Project Mgr*

Dave Sutherland, *Technical Staff*
EMP: 75 **EST:** 1995
SALES (est): 21.8MM **Privately Held**
WEB: www.axiomupgrades.com
SIC: 5045 Computer peripheral equipment

(P-13379)
BELL TECHNOLOGIES INC
Also Called: Bell Computer
187 Pacific St, Pomona (91768-3215)
PHONE..........................909 598-1006
William Chen, *President*
Tony Huang, *Exec VP*
▲ **EMP:** 14 **EST:** 1996
SQ FT: 11,000
SALES (est): 4.9MM **Privately Held**
WEB: www.bellcomputer.com
SIC: 5045 3571 Computers; electronic
computers

(P-13380)
BENQ AMERICA CORP (HQ)
3200 Park Center Dr # 150, Costa Mesa
(92626-7163)
PHONE..........................714 559-4900
KY Lee, *Chairman*
Jaime Garcia, *Partner*
Lars Yoder, *President*
Ellin Lee, *CFO*
Robert Wudeck, *Assoc VP*
◆ **EMP:** 65 **EST:** 1997
SALES (est): 78.3MM **Privately Held**
WEB: www.info.benq.us
SIC: 5045 Computer peripheral equipment

(P-13381)
CASEWISE SYSTEMS INC (DH)
9465 Wilshire Blvd # 300, Beverly Hills
(90212-2612)
PHONE..........................424 284-4101
EMP: 85
SQ FT: 5,000
SALES (est): 9.7MM **Privately Held**
SIC: 5045 8742 7372 Computers, Periph-
erals, And Software, Nsk

(P-13382)
COMMERCIAL INDUS DESIGN CO INC
Also Called: C I Design
20372 N Sea Cir, Lake Forest
(92630-8806)
PHONE..........................949 273-6199
Jeff Wu, *CEO*
Kae J Lee, *President*
Cupid Chiu, *Technology*
Matthew Martel, *Sales Staff*
▲ **EMP:** 60 **EST:** 1983
SALES (est): 10.6MM **Privately Held**
WEB: www.cidesign.com
SIC: 5045 Computer peripheral equipment

(P-13383)
CONTEC MICROELECTRONICS USA
Also Called: Contec USA
17811 Gillette Ave Fl 1, Irvine
(92614-6501)
PHONE..........................949 250-4025
Fax: 408 400-9115
▲ **EMP:** 52
SQ FT: 4,500
SALES (est): 3.2MM **Privately Held**
SIC: 5045 Whol Computers/Peripherals

(P-13384)
CREDIBLE LABS INC
2121 Avenue Of The Stars # 25, Los Ange-
les (90067-5010)
PHONE..........................650 866-5861
Steven Dash, *Manager*
Kyle Dougherty, *Partner*
Jereme Albin, *COO*
Alex Wechsler, *Sr Software Eng*
Jaideep Vijan, *CTO*
EMP: 71 **EST:** 2012
SALES (est): 16.9MM
SALES (corp-wide): 12.9B **Publicly Held**
WEB: www.credible.com
SIC: 5045 Computer software
PA: Fox Corporation
1211 Ave Of The Americas
New York NY 10036
212 852-7000

(P-13385)
CURVATURE LLC (DH)
859 Ward Dr 200, Santa Barbara
(93111-2920)
PHONE..........................800 230-6638
Sachi Thompson, *Exec VP*
Stephen Kimura, *Partner*
Sanford Tassel, *CFO*
Wayne Scalf, *Vice Pres*
Mark Kelly, *Vice Pres*
◆ **EMP:** 300 **EST:** 2001
SALES (est): 251MM **Privately Held**
WEB: www.curvature.com
SIC: 5045 7379 Computer peripheral
equipment; computer related mainte-
nance services
HQ: Nhr Newco Holdings Llc
6500 Hollister Ave # 210
Santa Barbara CA 93117
805 964-9975

(P-13386)
D-LINK SYSTEMS INCORPORATED
Also Called: D - Link
14420 Myford Rd Ste 100, Irvine
(92606-1019)
PHONE..........................714 885-6000
William Brown, *President*
Carlos Casassus Fontecilla, *President*
Raman Bridwell, *Assoc VP*
Reyes Oscar, *Assoc VP*
Kathy Villasenor, *Vice Pres*
▲ **EMP:** 164 **EST:** 1986
SQ FT: 120,000
SALES (est): 47.9MM **Privately Held**
WEB: www.d-linksystems.com
SIC: 5045 3577 Computers; computer pe-
ripheral equipment
PA: D-Link Corporation
289, Sinhu 3rd Rd.,
Taipei City TAP 11494

(P-13387)
DANE ELEC CORP USA (HQ)
Also Called: Gigastone America
17520 Von Karman Ave, Irvine
(92614-6208)
PHONE..........................949 450-2900
Michael Wang, *CEO*
◆ **EMP:** 32 **EST:** 1985
SQ FT: 25,000
SALES (est): 1MM **Privately Held**
WEB: www.gigastone.com
SIC: 5045 3577 8731 Computer software;
computer peripheral equipment; computer
(hardware) development

(P-13388)
DATA EXCHANGE CORPORATION (PA)
Also Called: D E X
3600 Via Pescador, Camarillo
(93012-5035)
PHONE..........................805 388-1711
Sheldon Malchicoff, *CEO*
Alan Kheel, *COO*
Burcak Sungur, *CFO*
Bob Jacques, *Manager*
▲ **EMP:** 300 **EST:** 1980
SQ FT: 100,000
SALES (est): 70.9MM **Privately Held**
WEB: www.dex.com
SIC: 5045 7378 Computers, peripherals &
software; computer & data processing
equipment repair/maintenance; computer
peripheral equipment repair & mainte-
nance

(P-13389)
DATALLEGRO INC
85 Enterprise Ste 200, Aliso Viejo
(92656-2614)
PHONE..........................949 680-3000
Stuart Frost, *Ch of Bd*
Mark Theissen, *Vice Pres*
EMP: 100 **EST:** 2003
SQ FT: 16,000
SALES (est): 26.3MM
SALES (corp-wide): 168B **Publicly Held**
WEB: www.datallegro.com
SIC: 5045 Computer software

PA: Microsoft Corporation
1 Microsoft Way
Redmond WA 98052
425 882-8080

(P-13390)
ELOTEK SYSTEMS INC (PA)
216 Avnida Fbrcnte Ste 11, San Clemente
(92672)
PHONE..........................949 366-4404
Michael Elovitz, *President*
Herbert H Dwyer, *Officer*
Adam Elovitz, *Vice Pres*
David Elovitz, *Vice Pres*
Judith Elovitz, *Vice Pres*
EMP: 20 **EST:** 1981
SQ FT: 4,500
SALES (est): 8MM **Privately Held**
WEB: www.elotek.com
SIC: 5045 3825 Computers; computer pe-
ripheral equipment; instruments to meas-
ure electricity

(P-13391)
EN POINTE TECHNOLOGIES SLS LLC
200 N Pacific Coast Hwy, El Segundo
(90245-4340)
PHONE..........................310 337-6151
Frank Khulusi, *CEO*
Robert Miley, *President*
Brandon Laverne, *CFO*
EMP: 200 **EST:** 2015
SALES (est): 182.5MM **Publicly Held**
WEB: www.pcm.com
SIC: 5045 Computer peripheral equipment;
computers
HQ: Pcm, Inc.
200 N Pacific Coast Hwy
El Segundo CA 90245
310 354-5600

(P-13392)
EON REALITY INC (PA)
18 Technology Dr Ste 110, Irvine
(92618-2309)
PHONE..........................949 460-2000
Mats Johansson, *President*
Jan Kjallstrom, *Exec VP*
Sridhar Sunkad, *Business Dir*
Yeunchul Choi, *Senior Engr*
Nancy Johansson, *Purch Mgr*
EMP: 119 **EST:** 2002
SQ FT: 16,000
SALES (est): 33.9MM **Privately Held**
WEB: www.eonreality.com
SIC: 5045 5734 Computer software; com-
puter software & accessories

(P-13393)
EPHESOFT INC (PA)
8707 Research Dr, Irvine (92618-4217)
PHONE..........................949 335-5335
Ike Kavas, *CEO*
Chris Macwilliams, *Partner*
Naren Goel, *CFO*
Stephen Boals, *Vice Pres*
Scott Whitlock, *Vice Pres*
▼ **EMP:** 68 **EST:** 2010
SQ FT: 3,600
SALES (est): 13.3MM **Privately Held**
WEB: www.ephesoft.com
SIC: 5045 Computer software

(P-13394)
EPSON ACCESSORIES INC
3840 Kilroy Airport Way, Long Beach
(90806-2452)
P.O. Box 93107 (90809-3107)
PHONE..........................562 981-3840
John Lang, *President*
Alan Tound, *CEO*
Susie Moir, *Corp Secy*
Sandra Tea, *Executive*
EMP: 60 **EST:** 1974
SALES (est): 2.1MM **Privately Held**
WEB: www.epson.com
SIC: 5734 5045 5812 Personal comput-
ers; computers; eating places
HQ: Epson America Inc
3131 Katella Ave
Los Alamitos CA 90720
800 463-7766

(P-13395)
ESRI INTERNATIONAL LLC
380 New York St, Redlands (92373-8118)
PHONE.....................................909 793-2853
Jack Dangermond, *President*
EMP: 29 **EST:** 2002
SALES (est): 2.2MM
SALES (corp-wide): 1B **Privately Held**
WEB: www.esri.com
SIC: 5045 7371 7372 7373 Computer
software; custom computer programming
services; prepackaged software; com-
puter integrated systems design; com-
puter related maintenance services
PA: Environmental Systems Research Insti-
tute, Inc.
380 New York St
Redlands CA 92373
909 793-2853

(P-13396)
EVGA CORPORATION (PA)
408 Saturn St, Brea (92821-1710)
PHONE.....................................714 528-4500
Taisheng Han, *President*
Marnie Sutton, *COO*
Matthew Gilleland, *Officer*
Bob Klase, *Vice Pres*
Berman Rivera, *Managing Dir*
▲ **EMP:** 50 **EST:** 1999
SALES (est): 48.5MM **Privately Held**
WEB: www.evga.com
SIC: 5045 Computers & accessories, per-
sonal & home entertainment

(P-13397)
**EWORKPLACE
MANUFACTURING INC**
Also Called: Batchmaster Software
9861 Irvine Center Dr, Irvine (92618-4307)
PHONE.....................................949 583-1646
Sahib Dudani, *President*
Jitendra Verma, *Vice Pres*
Maria Figueroa, *Office Mgr*
Deepesh Bagtharia, *Software Engr*
Shashank Awasthi, *Applctn Conslt*
EMP: 200
SQ FT: 5,000
SALES (est): 52.9MM **Privately Held**
WEB: www.batchmaster.com
SIC: 5045 Computer software

(P-13398)
GAR ENTERPRISES (PA)
Also Called: K G S Electronics
418 E Live Oak Ave, Arcadia (91006-5619)
PHONE.....................................626 574-1175
Nathan Sugimoto, *CEO*
Phillip Dao, *General Mgr*
Rebecca Feinstein, *Technical Staff*
Khanh Truong, *Production*
Cory Soto, *Sales Mgr*
EMP: 70 **EST:** 1960
SQ FT: 17,000
SALES (est): 23MM **Privately Held**
WEB: www.kgselectronics.com
SIC: 5045 3728 Anti-static equipment &
devices; aircraft assemblies, subassem-
blies & parts

(P-13399)
GBT INC
Also Called: GIGABYTE TECHNOLOGY CO
17358 Railroad St, City of Industry
(91748-1023)
PHONE.....................................626 854-9338
Eric C Lu, *President*
Richard MA, *Sr Exec VP*
Tony Liao, *Vice Pres*
James Liao, *Principal*
Oscar Wang, *Sales Dir*
▲ **EMP:** 130 **EST:** 1990
SQ FT: 35,000
SALES: 634.4MM **Privately Held**
WEB: www.gigabyte.com
SIC: 5045 Computers & accessories, per-
sonal & home entertainment
PA: Gigabyte Technology Co., Ltd.
5f, 6, Baoqiang Rd.,
New Taipei City TAP 23144

(P-13400)
GEMTEK TECHNOLOGY INC
Also Called: Connectpro
20525 Paseo Del Prado, Walnut
(91789-2793)
PHONE.....................................909 444-9288
Rex Wu, *President*
Edward Lin, *Sales Staff*
▲ **EMP:** 17 **EST:** 1992
SQ FT: 5,000
SALES (est): 1.5MM **Privately Held**
WEB: www.connectpro.com
SIC: 5045 3663 Computer peripheral
equipment; radio & TV communications
equipment

(P-13401)
**GENERAL MICRO SYSTEMS INC
(PA)**
Also Called: G M S
8358 Maple Pl, Rancho Cucamonga
(91730-3839)
P.O. Box 3689 (91729-3689)
PHONE.....................................909 980-4863
Benjamin K Sharfi, *President*
Susan Moorhead, *Administration*
Melinda Mejia, *Info Tech Mgr*
Linda Mendoza, *Bookkeeper*
Amalia Villarreal, *Director*
EMP: 75 **EST:** 1979
SQ FT: 20,000
SALES (est): 44.6MM **Privately Held**
WEB: www.gms4sbc.com
SIC: 5045 Computers, peripherals & soft-
ware

(P-13402)
**GENERAL PROCUREMENT INC
(PA)**
Also Called: Connect Computers
1964 W Corporate Way, Anaheim
(92801-5373)
PHONE.....................................949 679-7960
Imad Boukai, *President*
Sam Boukai, *Vice Pres*
Jesus Aguilar, *Buyer*
Mohammed Kalbouneh, *Sales Dir*
Juan Carbajal, *Sales Staff*
▲ **EMP:** 228 **EST:** 1996
SALES (est): 80.4MM **Privately Held**
WEB: www.generalprocurement.com
SIC: 5045 5065 Computers, peripherals &
software; electronic parts

(P-13403)
**GENESIS COMPUTER SYSTEMS
INC**
4055 E La Palma Ave Ste C, Anaheim
(92807-1750)
PHONE.....................................714 632-3648
Awaiz Akram, *President*
Shawn Dewan, *Vice Pres*
Gary Stockburger, *Technical Mgr*
Sam Patel, *Purch Agent*
▼ **EMP:** 20 **EST:** 1994
SQ FT: 3,500
SALES (est): 7MM **Privately Held**
WEB: www.usgenesis.com
SIC: 5045 3571 Computers, peripherals &
software; electronic computers

(P-13404)
GETAC INC
15495 Sand Canyon Ave # 300, Irvine
(92618-3153)
PHONE.....................................949 681-2900
Ming-Hang Hwang, *CEO*
Jim Rimay, *President*
James Rimay, *Vice Pres*
Joseph Huang, *General Mgr*
Elysha Thomas, *Executive Asst*
▲ **EMP:** 90
SQ FT: 12,000
SALES (est): 26.8MM **Privately Held**
WEB: www.getac.com
SIC: 5045 Mainframe computers
HQ: Mitac International Corporation
No. 1, Yanfa 2nd Rd., Hsinchu Sci-
ence Industrial Park Science Ba
Paoshan Hsiang HSI 30076

(P-13405)
**HITACHI SOLUTIONS AMERICA
LTD (DH)**
100 Spectrum Center Dr # 350, Irvine
(92618-4967)
PHONE.....................................949 242-1300
Keiho Akiyama, *CEO*
David Bishop, *Vice Pres*
Craig Burbidge, *Vice Pres*
Paul Gomez, *Vice Pres*
Brad Koontz, *Vice Pres*
▲ **EMP:** 30 **EST:** 1990
SQ FT: 12,000
SALES (est): 266.4MM **Privately Held**
WEB: www.hitachi-solutions.co.jp
SIC: 5045 7372 Computer software;
prepackaged software

(P-13406)
IMS FLIGHTDECK LLC
2929 E Imperial Hwy # 170, Brea
(92821-6716)
PHONE.....................................714 854-8600
Joseph Renton, *CEO*
Keith L Lockwood, *President*
Chris Miller, *CFO*
EMP: 164 **EST:** 2003
SALES (est): 6.4MM
SALES (corp-wide): 639.8MM **Privately
Held**
WEB: www.imsco-us.com
SIC: 5045 Computer software
HQ: Safran Passenger Innovations, Llc
3151 E Imperial Hwy
Brea CA 92821

(P-13407)
INGRAM MICRO INC (HQ)
3351 Michelson Dr Ste 100, Irvine
(92612-0697)
PHONE.....................................714 566-1000
Alain Monie, *CEO*
Jeff McHenry, *Partner*
Mike Ziliz, *CFO*
Augusto Aragone, *Exec VP*
Paul Bay, *Exec VP*
◆ **EMP:** 4000 **EST:** 1979
SALES (est): 47.2B **Privately Held**
WEB: www.ingrammicro.com
SIC: 5045 Computer software

(P-13408)
**INGRAM MICRO MANAGEMENT
CO (DH)**
3351 Michelson Dr Ste 100, Irvine
(92612-0697)
PHONE.....................................714 566-1000
EMP: 170 **EST:** 1995
SALES (est): 598.4K **Privately Held**
WEB: www.ingrammicro.com
SIC: 5045 Computers, peripherals & soft-
ware
HQ: Ingram Micro Inc.
3351 Michelson Dr Ste 100
Irvine CA 92612
714 566-1000

(P-13409)
IXOS SOFTWARE INC (PA)
8717 Research Dr, Irvine (92618-4200)
PHONE.....................................949 784-8000
Mark Smith, *CFO*
EMP: 100 **EST:** 1994
SQ FT: 30,000
SALES (est): 72.3MM **Privately Held**
SIC: 5045 Computer software

(P-13410)
JAL AVIONET USA (HQ)
300 Continental Blvd # 190, El Segundo
(90245-5045)
PHONE.....................................310 606-1000
Koichiro Aratake, *President*
Mayumi Laubscher, *Treasurer*
◆ **EMP:** 30 **EST:** 1985
SQ FT: 13,375
SALES (est): 9.8MM **Privately Held**
WEB: www.jalavionet.com
SIC: 5045 7372 5065 7377 Computer
software; prepackaged software; commu-
nication equipment; computer rental &
leasing

(P-13411)
K-MICRO INC
Also Called: Corpinfo Services
1618 Stanford St, Santa Monica
(90404-4114)
PHONE.....................................310 442-3200
Michael Sabourian, *President*
Ahmad Gramian, *Vice Pres*
EMP: 96 **EST:** 1984
SQ FT: 25,000
SALES (est): 16.6MM **Privately Held**
WEB: www.corpinfo.com
SIC: 5045 7378 7373 7371 Computers &
accessories, personal & home entertain-
ment; computer maintenance & repair;
computer integrated systems design; cus-
tom computer programming services

(P-13412)
M86 AMERICAS INC (DH)
Also Called: M 86 Security
8845 Irvine Center Dr # 101, Irvine
(92618-4247)
PHONE.....................................714 282-6111
John Vigouroux, *CEO*
Rodney S Miller, *CFO*
Gal Mizrachi, *CIO*
Sunny Chakravarty, *Info Tech Dir*
Dean Curlew, *Sales Engr*
EMP: 61 **EST:** 2007
SALES (est): 3.5MM **Privately Held**
SIC: 5045 Computer software

(P-13413)
MAGNELL ASSOCIATE INC (DH)
Also Called: A B S
17560 Rowland St, City of Industry
(91748-1114)
PHONE.....................................626 271-9700
James Wu, *CEO*
Albert Chong, *Officer*
Craig Hayes, *Vice Pres*
Howard Tong, *Vice Pres*
William Slusher, *Info Tech Dir*
◆ **EMP:** 130 **EST:** 1990
SALES (est): 490.3MM
SALES (corp-wide): 2.2B **Privately Held**
WEB: www.abs.com
SIC: 5045 Computers & accessories, per-
sonal & home entertainment
HQ: Newegg Inc.
17560 Rowland St
City Of Industry CA 91748
626 271-9700

(P-13414)
**MAX GROUP CORPORATION
(PA)**
17011 Green Dr, City of Industry
(91745-1800)
PHONE.....................................626 935-0050
Su-Tzu Tsai, *CEO*
Chung-Jen Tsai, *President*
Jonathan Min, *Finance Mgr*
Dan Wagner, *Sales Mgr*
Monica Duong, *Director*
▲ **EMP:** 63 **EST:** 1985
SQ FT: 120,000
SALES (est): 50.9MM **Privately Held**
WEB: www.maxgroup.com
SIC: 5045 Computer peripheral equipment;
disk drives; keying equipment; printers,
computer

(P-13415)
**MICRO-TECHNOLOGY
CONCEPTS INC**
Also Called: M T C
17837 Rowland St, City of Industry
(91748-1122)
PHONE.....................................626 839-6800
Roy Han, *President*
Richard Shyu, *Vice Pres*
▲ **EMP:** 85 **EST:** 1989
SQ FT: 42,500
SALES (est): 38.6MM
SALES (corp-wide): 56.3MM **Privately
Held**
WEB: www.mtcusa.com
SIC: 5045 Computer peripheral equipment
PA: Mtc Direct, Inc.
17837 Rowland St
City Of Industry CA 91748
626 839-6800

PRODUCTS & SVCS

(P-13416)
MOTOR VEHICLE SOFTWARE CORP (PA)
Also Called: Vitu
29901 Agoura Rd, Agoura Hills
(91301-2513)
PHONE..................818 706-1949
Donald Armstrong, *CEO*
Marcy Roth, *Vice Pres*
Jon Reyes, *VP Bus Dvlpt*
Jamison Kingfield, *Regional Mgr*
Don McNamara, *General Mgr*
EMP: 118 **EST:** 2005
SALES (est): 25.3MM **Privately Held**
WEB: www.mvscusa.com
SIC: 5045 Computers, peripherals & software

(P-13417)
MSI COMPUTER CORP (HQ)
901 Canada Ct, City of Industry
(91748-1136)
PHONE..................626 913-0828
Andy Tung, *CEO*
Connie Chang, *CFO*
Tom Carney, *Vice Pres*
David Wu, *Vice Pres*
Renee Gastellum, *Office Mgr*
◆ **EMP:** 90 **EST:** 1998
SQ FT: 77,500
SALES (est): 70.2MM **Privately Held**
WEB: www.us.msi.com
SIC: 5045 Computer peripheral equipment

(P-13418)
MTC WORLDWIDE CORP
17837 Rowland St, City of Industry
(91748-1122)
PHONE..................626 839-6800
Roy Han, *Principal*
▲ **EMP:** 79 **EST:** 1989
SQ FT: 42,500
SALES (est): 17.7MM
SALES (corp-wide): 56.3MM **Privately Held**
WEB: www.mtcusa.com
SIC: 5045 3577 Computer peripheral equipment; computer peripheral equipment
PA: Mtc Direct, Inc.
17837 Rowland St
City Of Industry CA 91748
626 839-6800

(P-13419)
NEXINFO SOLUTIONS INC
8502 E Chapman Ave # 364, Orange
(92869-2461)
PHONE..................714 368-1452
Arun Cavale, *President*
Sahil Gupta, *Technical Staff*
Melody Benabou, *Regl Sales Mgr*
Moises Oropeza, *Sales Staff*
Arun Sharma, *Manager*
EMP: 50 **EST:** 1999
SALES (est): 5.5MM **Privately Held**
WEB: www.nexinfo.com
SIC: 5045 8742 Computer software; management consulting services

(P-13420)
NGUYEN MINH
300 Old Newport Blvd, Newport Beach
(92663-4121)
PHONE..................949 646-2584
Minh Nguyen, *Principal*
EMP: 13 **EST:** 2007
SALES (est): 172.9K **Privately Held**
WEB: www.keckmedicine.org
SIC: 5045 3571 Computers, peripherals & software; electronic computers

(P-13421)
NHR NEWCO HOLDINGS LLC (DH)
6500 Hollister Ave # 210, Santa Barbara
(93117-3011)
PHONE..................805 964-9975
Sachi Thompson, *COO*
Misty Helms, *Partner*
Sanford Tassel, *CFO*
Emily Khashoggi, *Officer*
Ryan Harrigan, *Executive*
EMP: 122 **EST:** 2001

SALES (est): 251MM **Privately Held**
WEB: www.sysmaint.com
SIC: 5045 Computers, peripherals & software
HQ: Curvature Technologies Llc
2810 Coliseum Centre Dr
Charlotte NC 28217
704 921-1620

(P-13422)
NORTH ORNGE CNTY CMNTY CLLEGE
Also Called: Fullerton College Bookstore
330 E Chapman Ave, Fullerton
(92832-2087)
PHONE..................714 992-7008
Nick Karvia, *Branch Mgr*
Jami Josifek, *Instructor*
Corey Neyland, *Instructor*
EMP: 169
SALES (corp-wide): 79.7MM **Privately Held**
WEB: www.nocccd.edu
SIC: 5942 5045 College book stores; computers, peripherals & software
PA: North Orange County Community College District
1830 W Romneya Dr
Anaheim CA 92801
714 808-4500

(P-13423)
PARASOFT CORPORATION (PA)
101 E Huntington Dr Fl 2, Monrovia
(91016-3496)
PHONE..................626 256-3680
Elzbieta Kolawa, *President*
Adam Sontag, *CFO*
Daniel Hamilton, *Administration*
Mateusz Orczykowski, *Info Tech Dir*
Nicole Marsh, *Info Tech Mgr*
EMP: 50 **EST:** 1987
SALES (est): 39.6MM **Privately Held**
WEB: www.parasoft.com
SIC: 5045 7371 8748 Computers; computer software development; systems engineering consultant, ex. computer or professional

(P-13424)
PAYDARFAR INDUSTRIES INC
Also Called: Saratech
26054 Acero, Mission Viejo (92691-2768)
PHONE..................949 481-3267
Saeed Paydarfar PHD, *CEO*
Robert McLoughlin, *Vice Pres*
Tim Rothenberg, *Executive*
Sara Paydarfar, *Admin Asst*
Saeed Imani, *IT/INT Sup*
EMP: 60 **EST:** 2002
SQ FT: 5,930
SALES (est): 21MM **Privately Held**
WEB: www.saratech.com
SIC: 5045 8711 7372 7373 Computer software; engineering services; prepackaged software; value-added resellers; computer systems; computer-aided design (CAD) systems service; computer-aided engineering (CAE) systems service

(P-13425)
PC CLUB INC (HQ)
Also Called: Enpower Innovation
18537 Gale Ave, City of Industry
(91748-1338)
PHONE..................626 839-8080
Jackson Lan, *President*
Shirley Sheum, *Admin Mgr*
Rudy Velasquez, *Manager*
▲ **EMP:** 60 **EST:** 1991
SQ FT: 30,000
SALES (est): 9MM **Privately Held**
WEB: www.pcclub.com
SIC: 5734 5045 Computer & software stores; computers, peripherals & software

(P-13426)
PCM INC (HQ)
200 N Pacific Coast Hwy, El Segundo
(90245-4340)
PHONE..................310 354-5600
Glynis A Bryan, *CFO*
Simon Durocher, *CFO*
Karen Montenegro, *CFO*
Rachael A Bertrandt, *Officer*
James Mayer, *Exec VP*

EMP: 1217 **EST:** 1987
SALES: 2.1B **Publicly Held**
WEB: www.pcm.com
SIC: 5961 5731 5045 5734 Computer equipment & electronics, mail order; computers & peripheral equipment, mail order; computer software, mail order; radio, television & electronic stores; computers, peripherals & software; computers; computer peripheral equipment; computer software; personal computers

(P-13427)
PHELPS UNITED LLC
Also Called: Sourcing Solutions
3183 Red Hill Ave, Costa Mesa
(92626-3401)
PHONE..................657 212-8050
Larry Weng, *CEO*
Kent Kerbs, *CFO*
Jack Einwechter, *Vice Pres*
Greg Dalby, *General Mgr*
Chris Raub, *General Mgr*
EMP: 55 **EST:** 2018
SQ FT: 31,000
SALES (est): 50MM **Privately Held**
WEB: www.sourcingsolutions.com
SIC: 5045 Computers, peripherals & software

(P-13428)
PREMIER SYSTEMS USA INC (PA)
Also Called: Olloclip
16291 Gothard St, Huntington Beach
(92647-3612)
PHONE..................657 204-9861
Patrick O'Neill, *CEO*
Norman Alexander, *CFO*
Steven Muttram, *Vice Pres*
Janine Booth, *Business Mgr*
Anne O'Neill, *Opers Mgr*
▲ **EMP:** 15 **EST:** 2010
SQ FT: 6,000
SALES (est): 4.4MM **Privately Held**
SIC: 5045 3841 Computer peripheral equipment; surgical & medical instruments

(P-13429)
PRIVATE LABEL PC LLC
748 Epperson Dr, City of Industry
(91748-1336)
PHONE..................626 965-8686
Rachel Luke, *Mng Member*
Chris Luke, *Treasurer*
Jonathan Wang, *Vice Pres*
Mary Ting, *Purch Mgr*
Caroline Lin, *Sales Staff*
▲ **EMP:** 120 **EST:** 1987
SALES (est): 26.2MM **Privately Held**
WEB: www.plpc.com
SIC: 5045 Computer peripheral equipment

(P-13430)
QUANMAX USA INC
25 Delamesa E, Irvine (92620-1838)
PHONE..................949 272-2930
Chunchen Hsu, *CEO*
Tony Hsu, *General Mgr*
▲ **EMP:** 68 **EST:** 2000
SALES (est): 2.4MM **Privately Held**
SIC: 5045 Accounting machines using machine readable programs
PA: Quadnamix, Inc.
1818 S State College Blvd
Anaheim CA

(P-13431)
RAISE 3D INC
43 Tesla, Irvine (92618-4603)
PHONE..................888 963-9028
Hua Feng, *CEO*
Marc Franz, *Exec VP*
John Yu, *Vice Pres*
Vanessa Wilbur, *Marketing Mgr*
EMP: 15 **EST:** 2014
SQ FT: 12,000
SALES (est): 2.9MM **Privately Held**
WEB: www.raise3d.com
SIC: 5045 5734 3999 8742 Printers, computer; printers & plotters: computers; advertising display products; marketing consulting services

PA: Shanghai Fusion Tech Co., Ltd.
4/F, Block B5, No.1600 North Guoquan Rd., Yangpu Dist.
Shanghai 20008

(P-13432)
REGAL TECHNOLOGY PARTNERS INC
2921 Daimler St, Santa Ana (92705-5810)
PHONE..................714 835-1162
Allen Ronk, *President*
Paul Sorrentino, *Senior VP*
Jeff Ronk, *Vice Pres*
Ken Nelson, *Program Mgr*
Apichaya Gail Tanapong, *Analyst*
◆ **EMP:** 65 **EST:** 1988
SQ FT: 26,000
SALES (est): 46.3MM **Privately Held**
WEB: www.regaltechnology.com
SIC: 5045 7379 Computers; computer related consulting services

(P-13433)
RESECURITY INC
445 S Figueroa St # 3100, Los Angeles
(90071-1635)
PHONE..................388 273-8276
EMP: 50
SALES (est): 3.1MM **Privately Held**
WEB: www.resecurity.com
SIC: 5045 8748 7382 Computers, Peripherals, And Software, Nsk

(P-13434)
ROLAND DGA CORPORATION (HQ)
15363 Barranca Pkwy, Irvine (92618-2216)
PHONE..................949 727-2100
Andrew Oransky, *CEO*
Bruce Lauper, *CFO*
David Goward, *Exec VP*
Connie Caigoy, *Executive*
Dan Wilson, *Creative Dir*
◆ **EMP:** 103 **EST:** 1974
SQ FT: 53,000
SALES: 119.4MM **Privately Held**
WEB: www.rolanddga.com
SIC: 5045 8741 Computer peripheral equipment; management services

(P-13435)
SANYO DENKI AMERICA INC (HQ)
468 Amapola Ave, Torrance (90501-1474)
PHONE..................310 783-5400
Stan Kato, *CEO*
Tin Tran, *CFO*
Daisuke Kanamatsu, *Engineer*
Rieko Suzuki, *Human Resources*
Wilson LI, *Sales Associate*
▲ **EMP:** 52
SQ FT: 45,000
SALES (est): 30MM **Privately Held**
WEB: www.sanyodenki.us
SIC: 5045 7373 Computers & accessories, personal & home entertainment; computer-aided system services

(P-13436)
SERVERS DIRECT LLC
20480 Business Pkwy, Walnut
(91789-2938)
PHONE..................800 576-7931
Andy Juang, *CEO*
Howard Gilles, *CFO*
EMP: 93 **EST:** 2003
SALES (est): 2.5MM **Privately Held**
WEB: www.serversdirect.com
SIC: 5045 Computers, peripherals & software
PA: Equus Computer Systems, Inc.
201 General Mills Blvd
Minneapolis MN 55426

(P-13437)
SIGMANET INC (HQ)
4290 E Brickell St, Ontario (91761-1524)
PHONE..................909 230-7500
Ahmed Al Khatib, *CEO*
Neil Wada, *President*
Apo Hagopian, *Senior VP*
Stephen Monteros, *Vice Pres*
Bryan Buno, *Technology*

EMP: 203 EST: 1986
SQ FT: 100,000
SALES (est): 51MM Privately Held
WEB: www.convergeone.com
SIC: 5045 7373 Computer software; computer integrated systems design

(P-13438)
SMC NETWORKS INC (HQ)
20 Mason, Irvine (92618-2706)
PHONE..................................949 679-8029
Alex Kim, CEO
Inho Kim, President
Frank Kuo, President
Lane Ruoff, CFO
Ashley Chung, Manager
▲ EMP: 80 EST: 1971
SQ FT: 22,650
SALES (est): 25.3MM Privately Held
WEB: www.smc.com
SIC: 5045 Computer peripheral equipment

(P-13439)
SOLID OAK SOFTWARE INC (PA)
319 W Mission St, Santa Barbara
(93101-2822)
P.O. Box 6826 (93160-6826)
PHONE..................................805 568-5415
Brian P Milburn Sr, President
Brian Milburn, President
Mark Kanter, Vice Pres
EMP: 25 EST: 1990
SALES (est): 9.2MM Privately Held
WEB: www.27labs.com
SIC: 5045 7372 Computer software; prepackaged software

(P-13440)
SOLVER INC
10780 Santa Monica Blvd # 370, Los Angeles (90025-4779)
PHONE..................................310 691-5300
Nils Rasmussen, President
Corey Barak, COO
Hadrian Knotz, CIO
Michael Applegate, CTO
Mike Buhlert, Sr Consultant
EMP: 50 EST: 1996
SQ FT: 5,000
SALES (est): 10.5MM Privately Held
WEB: www.solverglobal.com
SIC: 5045 7379 7374 Computer software; computer related consulting services; data processing & preparation

(P-13441)
SPIRENT COMMUNICATIONS INC (HQ)
Also Called: Spirent Calabasas
27349 Agoura Rd, Calabasas
(91301-2413)
PHONE..................................818 676-2300
Eric G Hutchinson, CEO
Derek Newbern, Partner
Bill Burns, President
Pamela Mallette, Vice Pres
Chris O 'loughlin, Vice Pres
▲ EMP: 350 EST: 1988
SALES (est): 598.5MM
SALES (corp-wide): 522.4MM Privately Held
WEB: www.spirent.com
SIC: 5045 3663 3829 3825 Computers, peripherals & software; radio & TV communications equipment; measuring & controlling devices; instruments to measure electricity
PA: Spirent Communications Plc
Origin One
Crawley W SUSSEX RH10
129 376-7676

(P-13442)
SQUARE ENIX INC
999 N Pcf Cast Hwy Fl 3 Flr 3, El Segundo (90245)
PHONE..................................310 846-0400
Mike Fischer, President
Clinton Foy, COO
Michihiro Sasaki, Officer
Jim Burley, Vice Pres
Jon Grant, Associate Dir
▲ EMP: 110 EST: 1998

SALES (est): 52.5MM Privately Held
WEB: www.square-enix.com
SIC: 5045 7372 Computer software; publishers' computer software
HQ: Square Enix Of America Holdings, Inc.
999 N Pacific Coast Hwy # 3
El Segundo CA 90245

(P-13443)
SQUARE ENIX AMER HOLDINGS INC (HQ)
999 N Pacific Coast Hwy # 3, El Segundo (90245-2731)
PHONE..................................310 321-6979
Yoichi Wada, CEO
Jim Burley, Vice Pres
Doug Bone, General Mgr
Dustin Brower, Marketing Staff
Kaori Takasue, Marketing Staff
▲ EMP: 50 EST: 2006
SALES (est): 59MM Privately Held
WEB: www.square-enix-games.com
SIC: 5045 Computer software

(P-13444)
SYSPRO IMPACT SOFTWARE INC
1775 Flight Way Ste 150, Tustin
(92782-1844)
PHONE..................................714 437-1000
Brian Stein, CEO
Jeremy Clinton, Partner
Ralph Kubek, Partner
Joey Benadretti, President
Piero Broccardo, CFO
EMP: 200 EST: 1991
SALES (est): 48.9MM Privately Held
WEB: www.us.syspro.com
SIC: 5045 7372 7371 Computer software; prepackaged software; custom computer programming services

(P-13445)
TEAC AMERICA INC (HQ)
10410 Pioneer Blvd Ste 1, Santa Fe Springs (90670-8269)
PHONE..................................323 726-0303
Koichiro Nakamura, President
H Derek Davis, COO
Derek Davis, Exec VP
David Husted, Vice Pres
Joe Stopka, Business Dir
▲ EMP: 30 EST: 1967
SALES (est): 17.6MM Privately Held
WEB: www.teac.com
SIC: 5045 5064 5065 3651 Computer peripheral equipment; electrical entertainment equipment; magnetic recording tape; household audio & video equipment

(P-13446)
TONER SUPPLY USA INC
Also Called: Tsu Corporate Services
8055 Lankershim Blvd # 11, North Hollywood (91605-1628)
PHONE..................................818 504-6540
Omar Bian, President
Gus Obregon, Vice Pres
▲ EMP: 50 EST: 2005
SQ FT: 120,000
SALES (est): 7.6MM Privately Held
WEB: www.tsucorporateservices.com
SIC: 5045 7378 Computer peripheral equipment; computer peripheral equipment repair & maintenance

(P-13447)
TP-LINK USA CORPORATION (DH)
10 Mauchly, Irvine (92618-2306)
PHONE..................................626 333-0234
Louis Liu, CEO
Zheng Wu, Exec VP
Andy Chen, Vice Pres
Bijoy Alaylo, General Mgr
Steven Kunze, Admin Sec
▲ EMP: 108 EST: 2008
SALES (est): 94.2MM Privately Held
WEB: www.tp-link.com
SIC: 5045 Computer peripheral equipment
HQ: Tp-Link Uk Limited
Unit 2
Reading BERKS RG1 8
118 327-1135

(P-13448)
TRENDNET INC (PA)
20675 Manhattan Pl, Torrance
(90501-1827)
PHONE..................................310 961-5500
Pei Cheng Huang, President
Peggy Huang, CFO
Thea Lee, Treasurer
Jaime Castro, General Mgr
Cristina Baba, Graphic Designe
◆ EMP: 71 EST: 1990
SQ FT: 90,000
SALES (est): 23MM Privately Held
WEB: www.trendnet.com
SIC: 5045 Computer peripheral equipment

(P-13449)
TREY ARCH LLC
3420 Ocean Park Blvd # 2000, Santa Monica (90405-3304)
PHONE..................................310 581-4700
Don Likemess,
John Bojorquez, Vice Pres
John Rafacz, Comms Dir
John Herman, Principal
Pravin Babar, Sr Software Eng
EMP: 63 EST: 1996
SALES (est): 20MM
SALES (corp-wide): 8B Publicly Held
WEB: www.activisionblizzard.com
SIC: 5045 5092 Computer software; video games
PA: Activision Blizzard, Inc.
3100 Ocean Park Blvd
Santa Monica CA 90405
310 255-2000

(P-13450)
TW SECURITY CORP (DH)
5 Park Plz Ste 400, Irvine (92614-8524)
PHONE..................................949 932-1000
John Vigouroux, CEO
Bruce Green, COO
Rodney S Miller, CFO
William Kilmer, Chief Mktg Ofcr
Paul D Myer, Senior VP
EMP: 120 EST: 2008
SQ FT: 28,000
SALES (est): 98.2MM Privately Held
WEB: www.trustwave.com
SIC: 5045 Computer software
HQ: Trustwave Holdings, Inc.
70 W Madison St Ste 600
Chicago IL 60602
312 750-0950

(P-13451)
VIRTIUM LLC
30052 Tomas, Rcho STA Marg
(92688-2127)
PHONE..................................949 888-2444
Robert P Healy, Mng Member
Shane Mortazavi, Vice Pres
Michael Nilsson, Vice Pres
Scott Phillips, Vice Pres
Jonathan Pyon, Regional Mgr
EMP: 100 EST: 2015
SALES (est): 18.3MM Privately Held
WEB: www.virtium.com
SIC: 5045 Computers, peripherals & software

(P-13452)
WHI SOLUTIONS INC
Also Called: D S T Macdonald
28470 Ave Stnford Ste 200, Valencia
(91355)
PHONE..................................661 257-2120
Bruce Adamson, Branch Mgr
EMP: 140 Publicly Held
WEB: www.whisolutions.com
SIC: 5045 7371 Computers; computer software development
HQ: Whi Solutions, Inc.
5 International Dr # 210
Rye Brook NY 10573
914 697-9301

5046 Commercial Eqpt, NEC Wholesale

(P-13453)
CHEFS TOYS LLC (HQ)
18430 Pacific St, Fountain Valley
(92708-7005)
PHONE..................................508 399-2400
Chris Homewood,
Doug Schonfeld, Store Mgr
Joe Zirretta, Project Mgr
Dwight Thomas, Purchasing
Toyo Tsujino, Opers Staff
EMP: 164 EST: 2018
SALES (est): 65.2MM Privately Held
WEB: www.chefstoys.com
SIC: 5046 Restaurant equipment & supplies

(P-13454)
COOKINGCOM INC
1960 E Grand Ave Ste 60, El Segundo
(90245-5000)
PHONE..................................310 664-1283
Tracy Randall, President
Bryan Handlen, COO
Sarah Cohen, Vice Pres
Laura Shaff, VP Finance
Larry Sales, VP Mktg
EMP: 150 EST: 1998
SQ FT: 8,000
SALES (est): 22.2MM Privately Held
WEB: www.cooking.com
SIC: 5719 5046 Cookware, except aluminum; commercial cooking & food service equipment

(P-13455)
CROSSROADS EQP LEASE & FIN LLC
9385 Haven Ave, Rancho Cucamonga
(91730-5338)
PHONE..................................909 291-6400
Howard Shiebler, Mng Member
Mike Cohen, Officer
Brent Stout, Vice Pres
Pat Clemens, Business Dir
Joe Cunningham, Administration
EMP: 54 EST: 2006
SALES (est): 10.4MM
SALES (corp-wide): 150.5MM Privately Held
WEB: www.crlease.com
SIC: 5046 6159 7515 7513 Commercial equipment; equipment & vehicle finance leasing companies; passenger car leasing; truck rental & leasing, no drivers; equipment rental & leasing
PA: Los Angeles Truck Centers, Llc
2429 Peck Rd
Whittier CA 90601
562 447-1200

(P-13456)
GEMCO DISPLAY AND STR'FIXS LLC (PA)
Also Called: Victory Display & Store Fixs
2640 E Del Amo Blvd, Compton
(90221-6004)
PHONE..................................800 262-1126
David Nutel, President
Fred Berman, Ch of Bd
Marcel Neutel, Exec Dir
Mandy Hurwitz, Graphic Designe
Debbie Anderson, Personnel Exec
▲ EMP: 20 EST: 1999
SALES (est): 5.8MM Privately Held
WEB: www.victorydisplay.com
SIC: 5046 3089 Store fixtures; plastic processing

(P-13457)
HANNAM CHAIN USA INC (PA)
Also Called: Hannam Chain Super 1 Market
2740 W Olympic Blvd, Los Angeles
(90006-2633)
PHONE..................................213 382-2922
Kee W Ha, CEO
▲ EMP: 105 EST: 1987
SQ FT: 22,000
SALES (est): 34.1MM Privately Held
WEB: www.hannamchain.com
SIC: 5046 5411 Restaurant equipment & supplies; supermarkets, independent

(P-13458)
HERITAGE EQUIPMENT COMPANY
29341 Kimberlina Rd, Wasco (93280-7617)
P.O. Box 1200 (93280-8100)
PHONE..................661 587-2250
Keith B Gardiner, *CEO*
EMP: 100 EST: 2011
SALES (est): 13.6MM **Privately Held**
SIC: 5046 Commercial equipment

(P-13459)
INNOVATIVE DISPLAYWORKS INC
Also Called: I D W
8825 Boston Pl Ste 100, Rancho Cucamonga (91730-4922)
PHONE..................909 447-8254
Leo Wills, *CEO*
Nathan W Linder, *Vice Pres*
Nathan Linder, *Vice Pres*
John Cote, *Sales Staff*
Jenni Vences,
◆ EMP: 40 EST: 2001
SQ FT: 5,000
SALES (est): 23MM **Privately Held**
WEB: www.idw.global
SIC: 5046 3441 2541 Display equipment, except refrigerated; fabricated structural metal; display fixtures, wood

(P-13460)
INTERSTATE ELECTRIC CO INC (PA)
Also Called: IEC
2240 Yates Ave, Commerce (90040-1914)
PHONE..................323 724-0420
Edward Urlik, *President*
Arnie Binter, *Branch Mgr*
Ed Brent, *Branch Mgr*
George Haberstroh, *General Mgr*
James Earhart, *Technician*
▲ EMP: 94 EST: 1966
SQ FT: 72,000
SALES (est): 37.8MM **Privately Held**
WEB: www.iecdelivers.com
SIC: 5046 Signs, electrical

(P-13461)
JC FOODSERVICE INC (PA)
Also Called: Action Sales
415 S Atlantic Blvd, Monterey Park (91754-3209)
PHONE..................626 299-3800
Joel Chang, *President*
Rita Huang, *Officer*
Tony Yeung, *Officer*
Jack Chang, *Vice Pres*
Stephen Yeung, *Sales Associate*
◆ EMP: 55 EST: 1997
SQ FT: 25,000
SALES (est): 25.3MM **Privately Held**
WEB: www.actionsales.com
SIC: 5046 Restaurant equipment & supplies

(P-13462)
JETRO HOLDINGS LLC
1611 E Washington Blvd, Los Angeles (90021-3133)
PHONE..................213 516-0301
Javier Gomez, *Principal*
EMP: 183
SALES (corp-wide): 533.7K **Privately Held**
WEB: www.restaurantdepot.com
SIC: 5046 Restaurant equipment & supplies
HQ: Jetro Holdings, Llc
1710 Whitestone Expy
Whitestone NY 11357

(P-13463)
JUSTMAN PACKAGING & DISPLAY
5819 Telegraph Rd, Commerce (90040-1515)
PHONE..................323 728-8888
Morley Justman, *President*
Barbara Cabaret, *CFO*
Russell Justman, *Vice Pres*
Howard Mallen, *Executive*
▲ EMP: 70 EST: 1989
SQ FT: 125,000

SALES (est): 51MM **Privately Held**
SIC: 5046 5113 2752 Display equipment, except refrigerated; corrugated & solid fiber boxes; commercial printing, lithographic

(P-13464)
KUBOTA INDUSTRIAL EQUIPMENT
3401 Del Amo Blvd, Torrance (90503-1636)
PHONE..................817 756-1171
Brian Arnold, *Officer*
Dan Jones, *Vice Pres*
Diego Ayala, *Managing Dir*
Chris Nielsen, *General Mgr*
Ryota Tanimura, *General Mgr*
EMP: 72 EST: 2017
SALES (est): 22.2MM **Privately Held**
WEB: www.kubota.com
SIC: 5046 Commercial equipment

(P-13465)
PBI-BIRKENWALD MARKET EQP INC (PA)
Also Called: P B I
2667 Gundry Ave, Long Beach (90755-1808)
P.O. Box 6097 (90806-0097)
PHONE..................562 595-4785
Thomas L Everson, *President*
Kim Everson, *COO*
Jim Ennis, *CFO*
Laurie Stone, *Senior VP*
Erik Everson, *Vice Pres*
▲ EMP: 50
SQ FT: 85,000
SALES (est): 24.1MM **Privately Held**
WEB: www.pbimarketing.com
SIC: 5046 Store equipment; scales, except laboratory; shelving, commercial & industrial; cooking equipment, commercial

(P-13466)
SHOPPER INC
3987 Heritage Oak Ct, Simi Valley (93063-6711)
PHONE..................805 527-6700
Bill Bieda, *CEO*
Sally Quioan, *CFO*
Elliot Bieda, *Vice Pres*
Jon Benson, *Executive*
Brock Helvie, *Executive*
◆ EMP: 300 EST: 1992
SQ FT: 80,000
SALES (est): 31.7MM **Privately Held**
WEB: www.tsisupplies.com
SIC: 5046 Store fixtures

(P-13467)
TRIMARK RAYGAL LLC
Also Called: Trimark Orange County
210 Commerce, Irvine (92602-1318)
PHONE..................949 474-1000
Michael Anthony Costanzo, *President*
Dirk Hallett, *Treasurer*
Eric Smith, *Vice Pres*
Kelly Mabry, *Executive Asst*
Agatha Aguila, *Administration*
EMP: 220
SQ FT: 62,850
SALES (est): 153MM **Privately Held**
WEB: www.trimarkusa.com
SIC: 5046 Restaurant equipment & supplies
PA: Trimark Usa, Llc
9 Hampshire St
Mansfield MA 02048

(P-13468)
TRINITY EQUIPMENT INC
2650 S La Cadena Dr, Colton (92324-3708)
PHONE..................951 790-1905
Irene Cuevas, *Manager*
EMP: 75 EST: 2016
SALES (est): 10.4MM **Privately Held**
SIC: 5046 Commercial equipment

5047 Medical, Dental & Hospital Eqpt & Splys Wholesale

(P-13469)
A PLUS INTERNATIONAL INC (PA)
5138 Eucalyptus Ave, Chino (91710-9254)
PHONE..................909 591-5168
Wayne Lin, *President*
Maggie Lin, *CFO*
David Lee, *Vice Pres*
James Su, *Vice Pres*
Olivia Tavares, *Human Res Mgr*
◆ EMP: 93 EST: 1988
SQ FT: 150,000
SALES (est): 22.6MM **Privately Held**
WEB: www.aplusgroup.net
SIC: 5047 3842 Medical equipment & supplies; surgical appliances & supplies

(P-13470)
ALPHA IMAGING TECHNOLOGY
16453 Old Valley Blvd, City of Industry (91744-5541)
PHONE..................626 330-0808
◆ EMP: 15
SQ FT: 25,000
SALES: 4MM **Privately Held**
SIC: 5047 3579 Medical And Hospital Equipment, Nsk

(P-13471)
ALPHAEON CORPORATION (HQ)
17901 Von Karman Ave # 150, Irvine (92614-5245)
PHONE..................949 284-4555
Murthy Simhambhatla, *CEO*
Clint Carnell, *President*
Jeff Castillo, *President*
Kuntal Joshi, *President*
Bob Rhatigan, *COO*
EMP: 52 EST: 2012
SALES (est): 55.6MM
SALES (corp-wide): 58.4MM **Publicly Held**
WEB: www.alphaeon.com
SIC: 5047 Hospital equipment & furniture
PA: Strathspey Crown Holdings Llc
4040 Macarthur Blvd # 210
Newport Beach CA 92660
949 260-1700

(P-13472)
AMERICAN MED & HOSP SUP CO INC
Also Called: Am-Touch Dental
28703 Industry Dr, Valencia (91355-5414)
PHONE..................661 294-1213
Harish Khetarpal, *CEO*
Roma Khetarpal, *President*
Nitasha Khetarpal, *Pharmacy Dir*
Tracy De Rivel, *Manager*
Michael Lopez, *Manager*
▲ EMP: 32 EST: 1987
SQ FT: 25,000
SALES (est): 16.1MM **Privately Held**
WEB: www.amtouch.com
SIC: 5047 3843 3842 Medical equipment & supplies; dental equipment & supplies; surgical appliances & supplies

(P-13473)
AMERICAN MEDICAL TECH INC
17595 Cartwright Rd, Irvine (92614-5847)
PHONE..................949 553-0359
Jean Signore, *President*
Richard Barnes, *Vice Pres*
Bryan Kelly, *Vice Pres*
Jerry Signore, *Vice Pres*
Julia Zhou, *Vice Pres*
EMP: 100 EST: 1989
SALES (est): 21.7MM **Privately Held**
WEB: www.amtwoundcare.com
SIC: 5047 Medical equipment & supplies

(P-13474)
AMERICAN TOOTH INDUSTRIES
1200 Stellar Dr, Oxnard (93033-2404)
PHONE..................805 487-9868
Emilio Pozzi, *CEO*
Angela Fontenot, *President*
Bruno Pozzi, *President*

Kathleen Norton, *Officer*
Victoria Pozzi, *Exec VP*
▲ EMP: 98 EST: 1985
SQ FT: 28,000
SALES (est): 20.5MM **Privately Held**
WEB: www.americantooth.com
SIC: 5047 Dental equipment & supplies

(P-13475)
AMPRONIX INC
15 Whatney, Irvine (92618-2808)
PHONE..................949 273-8000
Aladdin Douroudi, *CEO*
Brian Yamada, *Vice Pres*
Aladdin Doroudi, *CFO*
Gennie Bui, *Admin Asst*
Nausser Fathollahi, *CIO*
◆ EMP: 78
SQ FT: 58,000
SALES (est): 20MM **Privately Held**
WEB: www.ampronix.com
SIC: 5047 3845 Diagnostic equipment, medical; electrotherapeutic apparatus

(P-13476)
ARJO INC
17502 Fabrica Way, Cerritos 90703-7014)
PHONE..................714 412-1170
Harald Stock, *Branch Mgr*
Brad Hall, *Vice Pres*
Gary Holder, *Vice Pres*
EMP: 227
SALES (corp-wide): 7.3B **Privately Held**
WEB: www.arjo.com
SIC: 5047 Medical equipment & supplies
HQ: Arjo, Inc.
2349 W Lake St Ste 250
Addison IL 60101
630 785-4490

(P-13477)
ATG - DESIGNING MOBILITY INC (DH)
Also Called: Numotion
11075 Knott Ave Ste B, Cypress (90630-5150)
PHONE..................562 921-0258
Mike Swinford, *CEO*
Jennie Hanson, *Officer*
EMP: 35 EST: 1996
SQ FT: 10,500
SALES: 8.3MM
SALES (corp-wide): 491.3MM **Privately Held**
SIC: 5047 5999 3842 Medical equipment & supplies; medical apparatus & supplies; wheelchairs

(P-13478)
AVITA MEDICAL AMERICAS LLC
28159 Ave Stnford Ste 220, Valencia (91355)
PHONE..................661 367-9170
Michael S Perry, *Exec Dir*
David Fencil, *Vice Pres*
Rob Hall, *Vice Pres*
Lorraine Glover, *General Mgr*
Suzette Gerzina, *Admin Asst*
▲ EMP: 71 EST: 2008
SQ FT: 23,000
SALES: 29.2MM **Privately Held**
WEB: www.avitamedical.com
SIC: 5047 Medical & hospital equipment
HQ: Avita Medical Pty Limited
L 7 330 Collins St
Melbourne VIC 3000

(P-13479)
BALT USA LLC
Also Called: Blockade Mecical
29 Parker Ste 100, Irvine (92618-1667)
PHONE..................949 788-1443
David A Ferrera, *President*
Fred Gunderman, *Vice Pres*
Donna Hyle, *Vice Pres*
Ryan Solomon, *Vice Pres*
Dave Portillo, *Controller*
EMP: 90 EST: 2011
SQ FT: 47,000
SALES (est): 5.2MM
SALES (corp-wide): 1.1MM **Privately Held**
WEB: www.balt-usa.com
SIC: 5047 3841 Medical equipment & supplies; surgical & medical instruments

HQ: Balt International
10 Rue De La Croix Vigneron
Montmorency 95160
139 894-641

(P-13480)
BIONIME USA CORPORATION
1450 E Spruce St Ste B, Ontario
(91761-8313)
PHONE..................909 781-6969
Chun-Mu Huang, *Principal*
Alex Wang, *CFO*
▲ EMP: 25 EST: 2008
SALES (est): 10MM **Privately Held**
WEB: www.bionimeusa.com
SIC: 5047 2835 Diagnostic equipment,
medical; in vitro diagnostics

(P-13481)
BRENTWOOD MEDICAL TECH CORP
Also Called: Midmark Diagnostics Group
1125 W.190th St, Gardena (90248-4303)
PHONE..................800 624-8950
Rebecca Mabry, *President*
Max Geittmann, *Planning*
David Klosterman, *CIO*
Earl Kiamzon, *Technical Staff*
Kurt Blythe, *Sales Staff*
EMP: 77 EST: 2000
SQ FT: 27,000
SALES (est): 7.3MM
SALES (corp-wide): 565.9MM **Privately Held**
WEB: www.midmark.com
SIC: 5047 Medical equipment & supplies
PA: Midmark Corporation
10170 Penny Ln Ste 300
Miamisburg OH 45342
937 528-7500

(P-13482)
CANON MEDICAL SYSTEMS USA INC (DH)
Also Called: Video Sensing Division
2441 Michelle Dr, Tustin (92780-7047)
P.O. Box 2068 (92781-2068)
PHONE..................714 730-5000
Shuzo Yamamoto, *President*
John Patterson, *CFO*
Peter N S Annand, *Senior VP*
Calum G Cunningham, *Vice Pres*
Scott Goodwin, *Vice Pres*
◆ EMP: 300 EST: 1989
SQ FT: 135,000
SALES (est): 506.7MM **Privately Held**
WEB: www.us.medical.canon
SIC: 5047 X-ray machines & tubes

(P-13483)
CARDINAL HEALTH INC
1100 Bird Center Dr, Palm Springs
(92262-8000)
PHONE..................951 360-2199
EMP: 52
SALES (corp-wide): 102.5B **Publicly Held**
SIC: 5047 Whol Medical/Hospital Equipment
PA: Cardinal Health, Inc.
7000 Cardinal Pl
Dublin OH 43017
614 757-5000

(P-13484)
CONVAID PRODUCTS LLC
2830 California St, Torrance (90503-3908)
P.O. Box 4209, Pls Vrds Pnsl (90274-9571)
PHONE..................310 618-0111
Chris Braun, *CEO*
Mervyn M Watkins, *CEO*
Henry Velazquez, *Prdtn Mgr*
Donald Griggs, *QC Mgr*
Kathleen Cook, *Opers Staff*
◆ EMP: 89 EST: 1976
SALES (est): 30.7MM **Privately Held**
WEB: www.convaid.com
SIC: 5047 Medical equipment & supplies

(P-13485)
ELERS MEDICAL USA INC
21707 Hawthorne Blvd # 20, Torrance
(90503-7009)
PHONE..................858 336-4900
Donald McCormick, *President*
EMP: 20 EST: 2020

SALES (est): 100K
SALES (corp-wide): 27.1MM **Privately Held**
WEB: www.elersmedical.com
SIC: 5047 5999 3841 Medical equipment
& supplies; medical apparatus & supplies;
surgical & medical instruments
PA: Elers Medical Finland Oy
Niittytaival 13
Espoo 02200
207 305-010

(P-13486)
EXPEREA HEALTHCARE LLC
27 Spectrum Pointe Dr # 30, Lake Forest
(92630-2273)
PHONE..................949 716-3071
Donald Woods, *Mng Member*
Wendy Toohey, *Sales Mgr*
EMP: 59 EST: 1999
SQ FT: 4,000
SALES (est): 5.2MM **Privately Held**
WEB: www.abc-med.com
SIC: 5047 Medical equipment & supplies

(P-13487)
FISHER & PAYKEL HEALTHCARE INC
173 Technology Dr Ste 100, Irvine
(92618-2489)
PHONE..................949 453-4000
Justin Callahan, *President*
Tony Barclay, *CFO*
Sarah Mannion, *Officer*
Bryan Goudzwaard, *Vice Pres*
Ben Normoyle, *General Mgr*
▲ EMP: 150 EST: 1995
SQ FT: 5,000
SALES (est): 106.7MM **Privately Held**
WEB: www.fphcare.com
SIC: 5047 Medical equipment & supplies
HQ: Fisher & Paykel Healthcare Corporation Limited
15 Maurice Paykel Place
Auckland 2013

(P-13488)
FLEXICARE INCORPORATED
15281 Barranca Pkwy Ste D, Irvine
(92618-2202)
PHONE..................949 450-9999
Ghassem Poormand, *CEO*
Hash Poormand, *Managing Dir*
Gabriela Arita, *Marketing Staff*
Patrick Kaiser, *Sales Staff*
EMP: 53 EST: 2011
SALES (est): 8.8MM **Privately Held**
WEB: www.myflexicare.com
SIC: 5047 Medical equipment & supplies

(P-13489)
GOLDEN STATE MEDICAL SUP INC
5187 Camino Ruiz, Camarillo
(93012-8601)
PHONE..................805 477-9866
Benjamin Hall, *CEO*
Shiela Curran, *COO*
Thomas S Weaver, *CFO*
Dave Arnold, *Senior VP*
Jim McManimie, *Senior VP*
EMP: 150 EST: 1989
SQ FT: 95,500
SALES (est): 61MM **Privately Held**
WEB: www.gsms.us
SIC: 5047 Medical equipment & supplies
PA: Gsms, Inc.
5187 Camino Ruiz
Camarillo CA 93012
805 477-9866

(P-13490)
GORDIAN MEDICAL INC
Also Called: American Medical Technologies
17595 Cartwright Rd, Irvine (92614-5847)
PHONE..................714 556-0200
Joseph Del Signore, *President*
Gerald Del Signore, *CEO*
David Simon, *Vice Pres*
John Presson, *Personnel Assit*
Bruce Bickford, *Materials Mgr*
EMP: 290 EST: 2007
SALES (est): 51.2MM **Privately Held**
WEB: www.amtwoundcare.com
SIC: 5047 Medical equipment & supplies

(P-13491)
GRIFOLS USA LLC
13111 Temple Ave, City of Industry
(91746-1500)
PHONE..................626 435-2600
EMP: 283
SALES (corp-wide): 657.6MM **Privately Held**
WEB: www.grifols.jobs
SIC: 5047 Diagnostic equipment, medical
HQ: Grifols Usa, Llc
2410 Lillyvale Ave
Los Angeles CA 90032
323 225-2221

(P-13492)
H AND H DRUG STORES INC (PA)
Also Called: Western Drug
3604 San Fernando Rd, Glendale
(91204-2917)
PHONE..................818 956-6691
Hagop Youredjian, *Ch of Bd*
Haig Youredjian, *President*
Zarig Youredjian, *Vice Pres*
Marina Mukelyan, *Office Mgr*
Selin Madadian, *Admin Asst*
EMP: 70 EST: 1977
SQ FT: 19,000
SALES (est): 52.8MM **Privately Held**
WEB: www.westerndrug.com
SIC: 5047 Medical equipment & supplies

(P-13493)
H AND H DRUG STORES INC
Also Called: Western Drug Medical Supply
114 E Airport Dr, San Bernardino
(92408-3473)
PHONE..................909 890-9700
EMP: 77
SALES (corp-wide): 52.8MM **Privately Held**
WEB: www.westerndrug.com
SIC: 5047 Medical equipment & supplies
PA: H And H Drug Stores, Inc.
3604 San Fernando Rd
Glendale CA 91204
818 956-6691

(P-13494)
HARDY DIAGNOSTICS (PA)
1430 W Mccoy Ln, Santa Maria
(93455-1005)
P.O. Box 645240, Cincinnati OH (45264-5264)
PHONE..................805 346-2766
Jay R Hardy, *President*
Jeff Schroder, *CFO*
Susan Pruett, *QA Dir*
Kerry D Pierce, *Technical Mgr*
Khaleel Rahman, *Research*
◆ EMP: 300 EST: 1980
SQ FT: 75,000
SALES (est): 45MM **Privately Held**
WEB: www.hardydiagnostics.com
SIC: 5047 2836 Medical equipment & supplies; agar culture media

(P-13495)
HEMOCUE INC
Also Called: Hemocue America
250 S Kraemer Blvd # 250, Brea
(92821-6232)
PHONE..................800 881-1611
Peter Troija, *Exec Dir*
Greg Libudziewski, *Business Mgr*
Murray Masterson, *Finance*
Mark Bellwood, *Natl Sales Mgr*
Steve Ohman, *Senior Mgr*
EMP: 82 EST: 1999
SQ FT: 23,000
SALES (est): 27.5MM
SALES (corp-wide): 22.2B **Publicly Held**
WEB: www.hemocue.us
SIC: 5999 5047 Medical apparatus & supplies; diagnostic equipment, medical
HQ: Radiometer Medical Aps
Akandevej 21
BrOnshOj 2700
382 738-27

(P-13496)
JB DENTAL SUPPLY CO INC (PA)
17000 Kingsview Ave, Carson
(90746-1230)
PHONE..................310 202-8855
Joseph Berman, *President*
Manny Chada, *Vice Pres*
Kimberly A Arana, *Director*
EMP: 120 EST: 1973
SQ FT: 26,000
SALES (est): 21.7MM **Privately Held**
SIC: 5047 Dental equipment & supplies

(P-13497)
JOERNS LLC (HQ)
19748 Dearborn St, Chatsworth
(91311-6509)
PHONE..................800 966-6662
Mark Ludwig, *Mng Member*
Mark Urbania, *CFO*
Juan Jimenez, *Opers Staff*
EMP: 150 EST: 1998
SQ FT: 28,000
SALES (est): 54.3MM
SALES (corp-wide): 238.2MM **Privately Held**
WEB: www.joerns.com
SIC: 5047 Hospital equipment & furniture
PA: Quad-C Jh Holdings Inc.
2430 Whthall Pk Dr Ste 10
Charlotte NC 28273
800 826-0270

(P-13498)
KLM LABORATORIES INC
Also Called: Klm Orthotic
28280 Alta Vista Ave, Valencia
(91355-0958)
PHONE..................661 295-2600
Kirk Marshall, *President*
Scott Marshall, *Corp Secy*
Kent Marshall, *Vice Pres*
Melinda Dawson, *Supervisor*
EMP: 100 EST: 1974
SQ FT: 35,000
SALES (est): 24.3MM **Privately Held**
WEB: www.klmlabstore.com
SIC: 5047 3842 Medical laboratory equipment; foot appliances, orthopedic

(P-13499)
MEDLINE INDUSTRIES INC
1455 Research Dr, Redlands (92374-4584)
PHONE..................909 799-8983
EMP: 34
SALES (corp-wide): 8B **Privately Held**
SIC: 5047 3999 Whol Medical/Hospital Equipment Mfg Misc Products
PA: Medline Industries, Inc.
3 Lakes Dr
Northfield IL 60093
847 949-5500

(P-13500)
MENTOR WORLDWIDE LLC
5425 Hollister Ave, Santa Barbara
(93111-3341)
PHONE..................805 681-6000
Diane Becker, *Manager*
Troy Hinshaw, *IT/INT Sup*
Greg Lynch, *Sales Staff*
Grenham William, *Director*
EMP: 500
SALES (corp-wide): 82.5B **Publicly Held**
WEB: www.mentordirect.com
SIC: 5047 Medical & hospital equipment
HQ: Mentor Worldwide Llc
31 Technology Dr Ste 200
Irvine CA 92618
800 636-8678

(P-13501)
MKR MEDICAL SUPPLY INC
Also Called: Concordance Healthcare
1950 E 220th St Ste 203, Long Beach
(90810-1651)
P.O. Box 5507, Carson (90749-5507)
PHONE..................310 830-3980
Jack Rockwell, *President*
EMP: 189 EST: 1979
SQ FT: 6,000

(PA)=Parent Co (HQ)=Headquarters (DH)=Div Headquarters
✪ = New Business established in last 2 years

SALES (est): 8.2MM
SALES (corp-wide): 496.7MM **Privately Held**
WEB: www.concordancehealthcare.com
SIC: **5047** Medical equipment & supplies
PA: Concordance Healthcare Solutions Llc
85 Shaffer Park Dr
Tiffin OH 44883
419 447-0222

(P-13502)
MORIGON TECHNOLOGIES LLC
Also Called: Medstop Medical
7615 Fulton Ave, North Hollywood
(91605-1805)
PHONE..................818 764-8880
Amaury J Agoncillo, *CEO*
Cyron Ng, *COO*
Mark Aquino, *Opers Mgr*
EMP: 50 EST: 2006
SQ FT: 8,000
SALES (est): 2.6MM **Privately Held**
WEB: www.morigontech.com
SIC: **5047** Medical equipment & supplies

(P-13503)
NANTBIOSCIENCE INC
9920 Jefferson Blvd, Culver City
(90232-3506)
PHONE..................310 883-1300
Patrick Soon-Shiong, *CEO*
Kyle White, *Sales Staff*
Mollie Meyer, *Manager*
Rudy Vazquez, *Manager*
EMP: 63 EST: 2013
SALES (est): 14.6MM
SALES (corp-wide): 158.2K **Publicly Held**
WEB: www.nantworks.com
SIC: **5047** 8099 Medical laboratory equipment; blood related health services
PA: Nantworks, Llc
9920 Jefferson Blvd
Culver City CA 90232
310 883-1300

(P-13504)
NEOTECH PRODUCTS LLC
28430 Witherspoon Pkwy, Valencia
(91355-4167)
PHONE..................661 775-7466
Craig McCrary, *President*
Judy McCrary, *Exec Dir*
Crystal De Leon, *Engineer*
Neil Ceniza, *Opers Staff*
Juan Torres, *Manager*
EMP: 54 EST: 1987
SQ FT: 4,000
SALES (est): 10.2MM **Privately Held**
WEB: www.neotechproducts.com
SIC: **5999** 5047 Medical apparatus & supplies; medical equipment & supplies

(P-13505)
NIHON KOHDEN AMERICA INC (HQ)
15353 Barranca Pkwy, Irvine (92618-2216)
PHONE..................949 580-1555
Eiichi Tanaka, *CEO*
Barry Klegerman, *President*
Josh Lewis, *President*
Ken Kanzler, *CFO*
Shinya Hama, *Officer*
▲ EMP: 130
SQ FT: 35,000
SALES (est): 179MM **Privately Held**
WEB: www.us.nihonkohden.com
SIC: **5047** Electro-medical equipment

(P-13506)
NOVA ORTHO-MED INC (PA)
Also Called: Nova Medical Products
1470 Beachey Pl, Carson (90746-4002)
PHONE..................310 352-3600
Sue Chen, *CEO*
Ronald Gaudiano, *Vice Pres*
Annette Aoyama, *General Mgr*
Vitou Sam, *Accountant*
Amy Klose, *Controller*
▲ EMP: 53 EST: 1993
SQ FT: 5,500
SALES (est): 26.1MM **Privately Held**
WEB: www.novajoy.com
SIC: **5047** Medical equipment & supplies

(P-13507)
PACIFIC MEDICAL GROUP INC
Also Called: Avante Health Solutions
212 Avenida Fabricante, San Clemente
(92672-7538)
PHONE..................949 493-1030
Sterling Peloso, *President*
Andrew S Bonin, *Principal*
Ricky Camargo, *Technician*
Fernando Sanchez, *Purch Agent*
Sean Armstrong, *Director*
EMP: 100 EST: 2006
SALES (est): 21.1MM **Privately Held**
WEB: www.pacificmedicalsupply.com
SIC: **5047** Medical equipment & supplies

(P-13508)
PARTER MEDICAL PRODUCTS INC
17015 Kingsview Ave, Carson
(90746-1220)
PHONE..................310 327-4417
Hormonz Foroughi, *President*
Parviz Hassanzadeh, *Shareholder*
Rene Paradis, *Exec VP*
Ali Iravani, *Consultant*
Roberto Anaya, *Supervisor*
▲ EMP: 160 EST: 1984
SQ FT: 40,000
SALES (est): 38.9MM **Privately Held**
WEB: www.partermedical.com
SIC: **5047** Medical equipment & supplies

(P-13509)
PEARSON DENTAL SUPPLIES INC (PA)
Also Called: Pearson Surgical Supply Co
13161 Telfair Ave, Sylmar (91342-3574)
PHONE..................818 362-2600
Keyhan Kashfian, *President*
Nader Kashfian, *Corp Secy*
David Kashfian, *Vice Pres*
Parviz Kashfian, *Vice Pres*
Richard Cintron, *Executive*
▲ EMP: 105 EST: 1983
SQ FT: 88,000
SALES (est): 71.9MM **Privately Held**
WEB: www.pearsondental.com
SIC: **5047** Dental equipment & supplies

(P-13510)
PETER BRASSELER HOLDINGS LLC
Also Called: Comet Medical
4837 Mcgrath St Ste J, Ventura
(93003-8077)
PHONE..................805 650-5209
Orlando Deleon, *Manager*
Lisa Larue, *General Mgr*
EMP: 88
SALES (corp-wide): 50.2MM **Privately Held**
WEB: www.brasselerusa.com
SIC: **5047** 3841 3843 Dental equipment & supplies; medical equipment & supplies; surgical & medical instruments; dental equipment
PA: Peter Brasseler Holdings, Llc
1 Brasseler Blvd
Savannah GA 31419
912 925-8525

(P-13511)
PHILIPS MED SYSTEMS CLVLAND IN
1 Marconi, Irvine (92618-2520)
PHONE..................949 699-2300
David Carter, *Branch Mgr*
EMP: 61
SALES (corp-wide): 133.6MM **Privately Held**
SIC: **5047** X-ray machines & tubes
HQ: Philips Medical Systems (Cleveland), Inc.
595 Miner Rd
Cleveland OH 44143
440 483-3000

(P-13512)
POM MEDICAL LLC
5456 Endeavour Ct, Moorpark
(93021-1705)
PHONE..................805 306-2105
Jeff Voss,
EMP: 99 EST: 2012

SALES (est): 5.2MM **Privately Held**
WEB: www.proceduraloxygenmask.com
SIC: **5047** Oxygen therapy equipment

(P-13513)
PORTERVILLE SHELTERED WORKSHOP
1853 E Cross Ave, Tulare (93274-7388)
PHONE..................559 684-9168
EMP: 59
SALES (corp-wide): 10.4MM **Privately Held**
SIC: **5047** Whol Medical/Hospital Equipment
PA: Porterville Sheltered Workshop
194 W Poplar Ave
Porterville CA 93257
559 784-7187

(P-13514)
POSEY PRODUCTS LLC (HQ)
Also Called: Posey Co
2530 Lndsay Prvado Dr Uni, Ontario
(91761)
PHONE..................626 443-3143
Kevin McNamara, *President*
Bonnie Bishop, *Vice Pres*
Paul Carter, *Vice Pres*
Stacey McGuire, *Vice Pres*
Carol Lucas, *Office Mgr*
▲ EMP: 143 EST: 1937
SALES (est): 100MM
SALES (corp-wide): 264.6MM **Privately Held**
WEB: www.posey.com
SIC: **5047** 3842 Medical equipment & supplies; belts: surgical, sanitary & corrective
PA: Tidi Products, Llc
570 Enterprise Dr
Neenah WI 54956
920 751-4300

(P-13515)
RADIOMETER AMERICA INC (HQ)
250 S Kraemer Blvd Msb1sw, Brea
(92821-6232)
PHONE..................800 736-0600
Torben Neilson, *President*
Frank T McFaden, *Treasurer*
Cathy Yang, *Vice Pres*
Joseph Morgan, *Technician*
Gabriella Gagliani, *Human Resources*
▲ EMP: 50 EST: 1962
SQ FT: 35,000
SALES (est): 50.4MM
SALES (corp-wide): 22.2B **Publicly Held**
WEB: www.radiometeramerica.com
SIC: **5047** Medical equipment & supplies
PA: Danaher Corporation
2200 Penn Ave Nw Ste 800w
Washington DC 20037
202 828-0850

(P-13516)
RASHMAN CORPORATION
Also Called: Uniform Accessories
8600 Wilbur Ave, Northridge (91324-4438)
PHONE..................818 993-3030
Richard Rashman, *CEO*
Roger Rashman, *Vice Pres*
▲ EMP: 65 EST: 1969
SQ FT: 50,000
SALES (est): 21.3MM **Privately Held**
WEB: www.prestigemedical.com
SIC: **5047** Medical equipment & supplies

(P-13517)
SAKURA FINETEK USA INC (HQ)
1750 W 214th St, Torrance (90501-2857)
PHONE..................310 972-7800
Takashi Tsuzuki, *Ch of Bd*
Anthony C Marotti, *President*
Kam Patel, *Corp Secy*
Peter Luu, *Vice Pres*
Raphael Cuevas, *Area Mgr*
▲ EMP: 109 EST: 1986
SQ FT: 68,000
SALES (est): 202.8MM **Privately Held**
WEB: www.sakuraus.com
SIC: **5047** Medical laboratory equipment; diagnostic equipment, medical

(P-13518)
SHIELD-DENVER HEALTH CARE CTR (HQ)
Also Called: Shield Healthcare
27911 Franklin Pkwy, Valencia
(91355-4110)
PHONE..................661 294-4200
Jim Snell, *President*
Jeffery Thompson, *Corp Secy*
Cheryl Hornberger, *VP Sales*
EMP: 200 EST: 1983
SQ FT: 95,000
SALES (est): 43MM **Privately Held**
WEB: www.shieldhealthcare.com
SIC: **5047** Medical equipment & supplies

(P-13519)
SHIMADZU PRECISION INSTRS INC
Shimadzu Medical Systems
20101 S Vermont Ave, Torrance
(90502-1328)
PHONE..................310 217-8855
Akinori Yamaguchi, *President*
Tetsuo Imanishi, *General Mgr*
Annette Carlisle, *Administration*
Eri Kubo, *Administration*
Brandon Harvey, *Engineer*
EMP: 80 **Privately Held**
WEB: www.spi-inc.com
SIC: **5047** Medical equipment & supplies
HQ: Shimadzu Precision Instruments, Inc.
3645 N Lakewood Blvd
Long Beach CA 90808
562 420-6226

(P-13520)
SIGMA SUPPLY & DIST INC
701 W Harvard St, Glendale (91204-1142)
PHONE..................818 246-4624
Arthur Keshishyan, *CEO*
Armen Keshishyan, *VP Sales*
▲ EMP: 18 EST: 1998
SQ FT: 6,500
SALES (est): 7.5MM **Privately Held**
SIC: **5047** 3841 Medical equipment & supplies; surgical & medical instruments

(P-13521)
STARZ INC
Also Called: Starz Tipz
23016 Lk Frest Dr Ste D30, Laguna Hills
(92653)
PHONE..................877 595-6789
Donovan Berkely, *CEO*
Jamila Daniel, *Vice Pres*
David Nebel, *Analyst*
Jessica Tafur, *Analyst*
Daniel Germanov, *Production*
EMP: 16 EST: 2008
SQ FT: 6,000
SALES (est): 1.7MM **Privately Held**
WEB: www.starztipz.com
SIC: **5047** 3843 Dental equipment & supplies; dental equipment & supplies

(P-13522)
STRUERS INC
1724 Gramercy Ave, Torrance
(90501-3535)
PHONE..................310 320-6288
Christopher Sopko, *CEO*
Cory Hamilton, *Engineer*
Beth A Bunevich,
Nancy J Kacius, *Manager*
EMP: 50
SALES (corp-wide): 2.6MM **Privately Held**
WEB: www.struers.com
SIC: **5047** Medical & hospital equipment
HQ: Struers, Inc
24766 Detroit Rd
Westlake OH 44145
440 871-0071

(P-13523)
TEAM MAKENA LLC (PA)
Also Called: Restore Motion
27051 Towne Centre Dr # 180, Foothill
Ranch (92610-2819)
PHONE..................949 474-1753
Mark Tymchenko, *Sales Staff*
Kristin Golden, *Area Mgr*
Jason Fortman, *Sales Staff*
Mark Krumholtz, *Sales Staff*

Jim Schuerger,
EMP: 53 **EST:** 2007 **Privately Held**
WEB: www.restoremotiondme.com
SIC: 5047 Hospital equipment & supplies

(P-13524)
TEAM POST-OP INC
17256 Red Hill Ave, Irvine (92614-5628)
P.O. Box 650846, Dallas TX (75265-0846)
PHONE..................................949 253-5500
Jeffrey Salamon, *President*
Lisa Salamon, *Admin Sec*
EMP: 105 **EST:** 1988
SQ FT: 1,400
SALES (est): 14MM
SALES (corp-wide): 1B **Publicly Held**
WEB: www.orthokinetix.net
SIC: 5047 Orthopedic equipment & supplies
HQ: Hanger Prosthetics & Orthotics, Inc.
  10910 Domain Dr Ste 300
  Austin TX 78758
  512 777-3800

(P-13525)
THERAPAK LLC (DH)
651 Wharton Dr, Claremont (91711-4819)
PHONE..................................909 267-2000
Todd Gates, *President*
Frank Brandauer, *Vice Pres*
Arbi Harootoonian, *Vice Pres*
Fanie Bernardo, *General Mgr*
Christina Wellington, *Project Mgr*
◆ **EMP:** 70 **EST:** 2000
SQ FT: 24,000
SALES (est): 296.1MM
SALES (corp-wide): 6.3B **Publicly Held**
WEB: www.therapak.com
SIC: 5047 Medical equipment & supplies;
  diagnostic equipment, medical
HQ: Vwr Corporation
  100 W Matsonford Rd Ste 1
  Radnor PA 19087
  610 386-1700

(P-13526)
TOTAL HEALTH ENVIRONMENT LLC
743 W Taft Ave, Orange (92865-4229)
PHONE..................................714 637-1010
Kennette Peck,
EMP: 30 **EST:** 2014
SALES (est): 3.7MM **Privately Held**
SIC: 5047 3843 5021 Medical & hospital
  equipment; dental equipment; office furniture

(P-13527)
ULTRA SOLUTIONS LLC
1137 E Philadelphia St, Ontario
(91761-5611)
PHONE..................................909 628-1778
Sterling Peloso, *CEO*
Tommy Ly, *Vice Pres*
Alice Stewart, *Vice Pres*
Ricardo Armenta, *Engineer*
Felix Hoang, *Engineer*
▲ **EMP:** 50 **EST:** 1998
SQ FT: 7,500
SALES (est): 23.8MM **Privately Held**
WEB: www.ultrasolutions.com
SIC: 5047 Diagnostic equipment, medical;
  medical equipment & supplies

(P-13528)
VCA INC (DH)
12401 W Olympic Blvd, Los Angeles
(90064-1022)
PHONE..................................310 571-6500
Doug Drew, *CEO*
Arthur J Antin, *COO*
Bob Doak, *Vice Pres*
Elizabeth Facey, *Vice Pres*
Steve Mehringer, *Vice Pres*
EMP: 6205 **EST:** 1987
SQ FT: 81,000
SALES: 2.5B
SALES (corp-wide): 42.8B **Privately Held**
WEB: www.vcahospitals.com
SIC: 5999 5047 0742 Pets & pet supplies;
  pet food; pet supplies; veterinarians'
  equipment & supplies; animal hospital
  services, pets & other animal specialties

HQ: Mmi Holdings, Inc.
  18101 Se 6th Way
  Vancouver WA 98683
  360 784-5422

(P-13529)
VETERINARY SERVICE INC
935 Palmyrita Ave, Riverside (92507-1819)
PHONE..................................951 328-4900
Colin Anderson, *Branch Mgr*
EMP: 50
SALES (corp-wide): 70.6MM **Privately Held**
WEB: www.vsi.cc
SIC: 5047 5199 5083 Veterinarians'
  equipment & supplies; pet supplies; poultry equipment
PA: Veterinary Service, Inc.
  4100 Bangs Ave
  Modesto CA 95356
  209 545-5100

(P-13530)
VETERINARY SERVICE INC
1607 N Plaza Dr, Visalia (93291-8887)
PHONE..................................559 651-1633
Tom Babb, *Branch Mgr*
EMP: 50
SALES (corp-wide): 70.6MM **Privately Held**
WEB: www.vsi.cc
SIC: 5047 Veterinarians' equipment & supplies
PA: Veterinary Service, Inc.
  4100 Bangs Ave
  Modesto CA 95356
  209 545-5100

(P-13531)
VIDENT
Also Called: Vita North America
22705 Savi Ranch Pkwy, Yorba Linda
(92887-4604)
PHONE..................................714 221-6700
Emanuel Rauter, *CEO*
Janet Siwinski, *Business Dir*
Janette Gorman, *Administration*
Aj Papez, *Business Mgr*
Tim Thompson, *VP Opers*
▲ **EMP:** 70 **EST:** 1984
SQ FT: 43,000
SALES (est): 49.1MM
SALES (corp-wide): 108.1MM **Privately Held**
WEB: www.vita-zahnfabrik.com
SIC: 5047 Dental equipment & supplies
PA: Vita - Zahnfabrik H. Rauter
  Gesellschaft Mit Beschrankter Haftung
  & Co Kg
  Spitalgasse 3
  Bad Sackingen BW 79713
  776 156-20

5049 Professional Eqpt & Splys, NEC Wholesale

(P-13532)
ABC SCHOOL EQUIPMENT INC
Also Called: Platinum Visual Systems
1451 E 6th St, Corona (92879-1715)
PHONE..................................951 817-2200
Gary P Stell Jr, *CEO*
Thomas Mendez, *CFO*
Timothy R Brantley, *Vice Pres*
Tom Mendez, *Controller*
EMP: 70 **EST:** 1964
SQ FT: 35,000
SALES (est): 20.5MM **Privately Held**
WEB: www.abcse.com
SIC: 5049 3861 2531 School supplies;
  photographic equipment & supplies; public building & related furniture

(P-13533)
EXCEL SCIENTIFIC LLC
18350 George Blvd, Victorville
(92394-7930)
PHONE..................................760 246-4545
Julie Cameron, *CEO*
Gene Platter, *VP Bus Dvlpt*
Steve Kerkstra, *Controller*
Paul Chadwick, *Marketing Staff*
Mindy Rowley, *Marketing Staff*
▲ **EMP:** 32 **EST:** 2001

SQ FT: 27,000
SALES (est): 41.7MM **Privately Held**
WEB: www.excelscientific.com
SIC: 5049 3821 Scientific & engineering
  equipment & supplies; laboratory apparatus, except heating & measuring
PA: Vance Street Capital Llc
  11150 Santa Monica Blvd # 750
  Los Angeles CA 90025

(P-13534)
LEXICON MARKETING (USA) INC (PA)
640 S San Vicente Blvd, Los Angeles
(90048-4654)
PHONE..................................323 782-8282
Valeria Rico, *President*
EMP: 499 **EST:** 1979
SALES (est): 62MM **Privately Held**
SIC: 5049 5999 School supplies; education aids, devices & supplies

(P-13535)
MCBAIN SYSTEMS A CAL LTD PRTNR
756 Lakefield Rd Ste G, Westlake Village
(91361-2669)
PHONE..................................805 581-6800
Michael Crump, *President*
Pete Walker, *Supervisor*
▲ **EMP:** 20 **EST:** 1965
SQ FT: 20,400
SALES (est): 7.9MM **Privately Held**
WEB: www.mcbainsystems.com
SIC: 5049 3827 7699 Scientific & engineering equipment & supplies; optical instruments & apparatus; optical instrument repair

(P-13536)
RADIABEAM TECHNOLOGIES LLC (PA)
1717 Stewart St, Santa Monica
(90404-4021)
PHONE..................................310 822-5845
Salime Boucher,
Finn O'Shea, *Research*
Pedro Frigola, *Engineer*
Josiah Hartzell, *Engineer*
Jacob McNevin, *Engineer*
EMP: 14 **EST:** 2004
SQ FT: 8,600
SALES (est): 6.4MM **Privately Held**
WEB: www.radiabeam.com
SIC: 5049 3829 5731 Laboratory equipment, except medical or dental; accelerators, rubber processing: cyclic or acyclic; metal detectors

(P-13537)
REAGENT WORLD INC
2100 Main St Ste 106, Irvine (92614-6238)
PHONE..................................909 947-7779
Daniel Shen, *President*
Frank Tsai, *Project Mgr*
Ron Tash, *Sales Staff*
Kyros Le, *Manager*
EMP: 15 **EST:** 2007
SALES (est): 5.6MM **Privately Held**
WEB: www.reagentworld.com
SIC: 5049 5169 2869 2899 Laboratory equipment, except medical or dental; industrial chemicals; industrial organic chemicals; laboratory chemicals, organic; fire retardant chemicals; medicinal chemicals

(P-13538)
REM OPTICAL COMPANY INC
Also Called: REM Eye Wear
10941 La Tuna Canyon Rd, Sun Valley
(91352-2012)
PHONE..................................818 504-3950
Alessandro Baronti, *President*
Steve Horowitz, *President*
Donna Gindy, *COO*
Donna Nakawaki, *Senior VP*
David Esperanza, *Vice Pres*
◆ **EMP:** 100 **EST:** 1977
SQ FT: 42,000
SALES (est): 41.4MM **Privately Held**
WEB: www.derigo.us
SIC: 5049 Optical goods

HQ: De Rigo Vision Spa
  Zona Industriale Villanova 12
  Longarone BL 32013

(P-13539)
RINCON TECHNOLOGY INC (PA)
810 E Montecito St, Santa Barbara
(93103-3221)
P.O. Box 123081, Dallas TX (75312-3081)
PHONE..................................805 684-8100
Jason Kelly, *President*
Rhet Hedrick, *Exec VP*
Michael J Bartling, *Vice Pres*
Tony Prince, *Vice Pres*
Heidi Heidger, *VP Finance*
EMP: 31 **EST:** 2005
SQ FT: 15,000
SALES (est): 93.4MM **Privately Held**
WEB: www.rincontechnology.com
SIC: 5049 3825 Scientific & engineering equipment & supplies; network analyzers

(P-13540)
SAPPHIRE CLEAN ROOMS LLC (PA)
505 Porter Way, Placentia (92870-6454)
PHONE..................................714 316-5036
Hector Garibay, *President*
EMP: 140 **EST:** 2016
SALES (est): 8.9MM **Privately Held**
SIC: 5049 Laboratory equipment, except medical or dental

(P-13541)
SOCIAL STUDIES SCHOOL SERVICE
Also Called: Writing Company
10200 Jefferson Blvd, Culver City
(90232-3524)
P.O. Box 802 (90232-0802)
PHONE..................................310 839-2436
David M Weigner, *CEO*
Irwin Ledin, *President*
Sanford Weiner, *President*
Kristine Hofve, *Executive*
Luis Castro, *Opers Staff*
▲ **EMP:** 65 **EST:** 1967
SALES (est): 20.5MM **Privately Held**
WEB: www.socialstudies.com
SIC: 5049 School supplies

(P-13542)
TECAN SP INC
14180 Live Oak Ave, Baldwin Park
(91706-1350)
P.O. Box 1608 (91706-7608)
PHONE..................................626 962-0010
Philip A Dimson, *CEO*
Christian Herr, *CFO*
Nancy Dimson, *Train & Dev Mgr*
▲ **EMP:** 84 **EST:** 1997
SALES (est): 41.6MM
SALES (corp-wide): 641.7MM **Privately Held**
WEB: www.tecan.com
SIC: 5049 Laboratory equipment, except medical or dental
PA: Tecan Group Ag
  Seestrasse 103
  MAnnedorf ZH 8708
  449 228-111

5051 Metals Service Centers

(P-13543)
101 VERTICAL FABRICATION INC
10255 Beech Ave, Fontana (92335-6356)
PHONE..................................909 428-6000
Dustin J Nabor, *President*
Fidel J Nabor, *Ch of Bd*
Paul Kwon, *CFO*
Dusty J Nabor, *Exec VP*
Richard Berg, *Vice Pres*
EMP: 58 **EST:** 1990
SQ FT: 48,000
SALES (est): 13.9MM
SALES (corp-wide): 17.9MM **Privately Held**
WEB: www.101pipe.com
SIC: 5051 Pipe & tubing, steel

PA: 101 Pipe & Casing, Inc.
30300 Agoura Rd Ste 240
Agoura Hills CA 91301
818 707-9101

(P-13544)
ALUMINUM PRECISION PDTS INC (PA)
3333 W Warner Ave, Santa Ana (92704-5898)
PHONE...................714 546-8125
Gregory S Keeler, *President*
Rafael Ramirez, *COO*
Simona Manoiu, *CFO*
Roark Keeler, *Vice Pres*
David P Silva, *Vice Pres*
◆ **EMP:** 550 **EST:** 1965
SALES (est): 106.7MM **Privately Held**
WEB: www.aluminumprecision.com
SIC: 5051 Steel

(P-13545)
ALUMINUM PRECISION PDTS INC
1001 Mcwane Blvd, Oxnard (93033-9016)
PHONE...................805 488-4401
Richard Hayes, *Branch Mgr*
Gerald Bornman, *Vice Pres*
Vanessa Ramirez, *Executive*
Jennifer Meyers, *General Mgr*
Debabrata Mishra, *General Mgr*
EMP: 125
SQ FT: 15,000
SALES (corp-wide): 106.7MM **Privately Held**
WEB: www.aluminumprecision.com
SIC: 5051 Steel
PA: Aluminum Precision Products, Inc.
3333 W Warner Ave
Santa Ana CA 92704
714 546-8125

(P-13546)
AURORA CASTING & ENGRG INC
1790 E Lemonwood Dr, Santa Paula (93060-9510)
PHONE...................805 933-2761
John Carlos Penrose, *CEO*
John Penrose, *Sales Staff*
Patty Hostetler, *Accounts Mgr*
David Williams, *Accounts Mgr*
EMP: 65
SQ FT: 25,000
SALES (est): 21.6MM **Privately Held**
WEB: www.auroracasting.com
SIC: 5051 Steel

(P-13547)
B & B SURPLUS INC (PA)
Also Called: B & B Specialty Metals
7020 Rosedale Hwy, Bakersfield (93308-5842)
PHONE...................661 589-0381
Donice Boylan, *President*
Michelle Boylan-Pisano, *CFO*
Bill Scrivner, *Chief Mktg Ofcr*
Michael Georgino, *Vice Pres*
Katherine Johansen, *Credit Mgr*
▲ **EMP:** 65 **EST:** 1963
SQ FT: 20,000
SALES (est): 67.4MM **Privately Held**
WEB: www.bbsurplus.com
SIC: 5051 Steel

(P-13548)
BERGSEN INC
12241 Florence Ave, Santa Fe Springs (90670-3805)
PHONE...................562 236-9787
Thomas Sharpe, *President*
Kathy Peck, *General Mgr*
Stan Reed, *Sales Staff*
◆ **EMP:** 23 **EST:** 1971
SQ FT: 27,000
SALES (est): 11MM **Privately Held**
WEB: www.bergsen.com
SIC: 5051 3317 Steel; boiler tubes (wrought)

(P-13549)
BLUE CHIP STAMPS INC
301 E Colo Blvd Ste 300, Pasadena (91101)
PHONE...................626 585-6700
Robert H Bird, *CEO*
Charles T Munger, *CEO*
Jeffrey L Jacobson, *CFO*
Kenneth E Wittmeyer, *Vice Pres*
EMP: 3074 **EST:** 1956
SQ FT: 123,732
SALES (est): 221.8MM
SALES (corp-wide): 245.5B **Publicly Held**
WEB: www.berkshirehathaway.com
SIC: 5051 Steel
PA: Berkshire Hathaway Inc.
3555 Farnam St Ste 1140
Omaha NE 68131
402 346-1400

(P-13550)
BOBCO METALS LLC
Also Called: Sion & Shamoneil Fmly Partner
2000 S Alameda St, Vernon (90058-1016)
PHONE...................213 748-5171
Sion Shooshani, *Mng Member*
Omar Zuniga, *Technology*
Fred Shooshani, *Human Res Mgr*
James Duran, *Sales Staff*
Phil Pelayre, *Sales Staff*
▲ **EMP:** 69 **EST:** 1979
SQ FT: 100,000
SALES (est): 12.5MM **Privately Held**
WEB: www.bobcometal.com
SIC: 5051 5251 5072 Aluminum bars, rods, ingots, sheets, pipes, plates, etc.; hardware; hardware

(P-13551)
BORRMANN METAL CENTER (DH)
110 W Olive Ave, Burbank (91502-1822)
PHONE...................818 846-7171
Jane Borrmann, *CEO*
Robert Wedeen, *President*
William L Todd, *Corp Secy*
Bob Persson, *Vice Pres*
David Carbajal, *Administration*
▲ **EMP:** 59 **EST:** 1946
SQ FT: 75,000
SALES (est): 43.9MM
SALES (corp-wide): 575.6MM **Privately Held**
WEB: www.borrmannmetals.com
SIC: 5051 Steel
HQ: Contractors Steel Company
36555 Amrhein Rd
Livonia MI 48150
734 464-4000

(P-13552)
BPS SUPPLY GROUP (PA)
Also Called: Imperial Pipe & Supply
3301 Zachary Ave, Shafter (93263-9424)
P.O. Box 639, Bakersfield (93302-0639)
PHONE...................661 589-9141
Dwight Byrum, *CEO*
Dan Byrum, *President*
John Byrum, *COO*
Cary Evans, *CFO*
Dwight Byrumm, *Chairman*
◆ **EMP:** 60
SQ FT: 60,000
SALES (est): 115.3MM **Privately Held**
WEB: www.bpssg.com
SIC: 5051 5085 Pipe & tubing, steel; valves & fittings

(P-13553)
CALIFORNIA STEEL AND TUBE
16049 Stephens St, City of Industry (91745-1786)
PHONE...................626 968-5511
Rick Hirsch, *President*
Ron Prichard, *Vice Pres*
James Udell, *Info Tech Mgr*
Kent Lulewich, *Opers Staff*
EMP: 108 **EST:** 1952
SQ FT: 108,000
SALES (est): 25.9MM
SALES (corp-wide): 6B **Privately Held**
WEB: www.californiasteelandtube.com
SIC: 5051 Steel
HQ: Kloeckner Metals Corporation
500 Colonial Center Pkwy # 500
Roswell GA 30076

(P-13554)
CALIFORNIA STEEL SERVICES INC
1212 S Mountain View Ave, San Bernardino (92408-3001)
PHONE...................909 796-2222
Parviz Razavian, *CEO*
Saman Didban, *Production*
Nicole Shandoan, *Sales Staff*
Parvin Rezainia, *General Counsel*
Behrouz Razavian, *Manager*
EMP: 49 **EST:** 1983
SQ FT: 78,000
SALES (est): 42.2MM **Privately Held**
WEB: www.calsteel.com
SIC: 5051 3444 3443 Steel; sheet metalwork; fabricated plate work (boiler shop)

(P-13555)
CALPIPE INDUSTRIES LLC (HQ)
Also Called: Calbond
12160 Woodruff Ave, Downey (90241-5606)
PHONE...................562 803-4388
Daniel J Markus, *CEO*
Fred Arjani, *CFO*
Sheri Caine-Markus, *Admin Sec*
▲ **EMP:** 75 **EST:** 1995
SALES (est): 51.4MM **Publicly Held**
WEB: www.atkore.com
SIC: 5051 3498 Pipe & tubing, steel; fabricated pipe & fittings; tube fabricating (contract bending & shaping)

(P-13556)
CASTER TECHNOLOGY CORP (PA)
11552 Markon Dr, Garden Grove (92841-1828)
PHONE...................714 893-6886
Karl Elles, *President*
Gregg Gaston, *Acting CFO*
David Elles, *Vice Pres*
Dean Clark, *Administration*
Bob Pettingill, *Sales Staff*
EMP: 17 **EST:** 1984
SQ FT: 17,100
SALES (est): 14.9MM **Privately Held**
WEB: www.bakerycasters.com
SIC: 5051 3562 Metals service centers & offices; casters

(P-13557)
CKKM INC (PA)
Also Called: Nova Steel Company
265 Radio Rd, Corona (92879-1725)
PHONE...................951 371-8484
Bernard Smokowski, *President*
Mary Jo Thometz, *CFO*
Jacqueline Lowery, *Admin Sec*
EMP: 29 **EST:** 1991
SQ FT: 50,000
SALES (est): 25.6MM **Privately Held**
SIC: 5051 3444 Steel; pipe, sheet metal

(P-13558)
CMC REBAR WEST
5425 Industrial Pkwy, San Bernardino (92407-1803)
PHONE...................909 713-1130
Lee Albright, *Manager*
Chris Speelman, *Manager*
Dave McCannell, *Regional*
EMP: 56 **Privately Held**
SIC: 5051 Steel
HQ: Cmc Rebar West
3880 Murphy Canyon Rd # 100
San Diego CA 92123

(P-13559)
COAST ALUMINUM INC (PA)
10628 Fulton Wells Ave, Santa Fe Springs (90670-3740)
P.O. Box 2144 (90670-0440)
PHONE...................562 946-6061
Thomas C Clark, *President*
Bonnie Clark, *Shareholder*
Charley Holton, *Branch Mgr*
Karen Smith, *General Mgr*
Erica Cantal, *Technology*
▲ **EMP:** 125 **EST:** 1982
SQ FT: 112,000

SALES (est): 162.4MM **Privately Held**
WEB: www.coastaluminum.com
SIC: 5051 Miscellaneous nonferrous products

(P-13560)
COONER SALES COMPANY LLC (PA)
Also Called: Cooner Wire Company
9265 Owensmouth Ave, Chatsworth (91311-5854)
PHONE...................818 882-8311
Patrick G Weir, *President*
Steve Wynn, *Sales Staff*
Steve W Smith,
Joe Steinberger,
Isabel Bitarian, *Assistant*
▲ **EMP:** 19 **EST:** 1957
SQ FT: 17,825
SALES (est): 12.6MM **Privately Held**
WEB: www.coonerwire.com
SIC: 5051 3679 Wire; harness assemblies for electronic use; wire or cable

(P-13561)
CREST STEEL CORPORATION
6580 General Rd, Riverside (92509-0103)
PHONE...................310 830-2651
James Hoffman, *CEO*
Kris Farris, *President*
Paul Worden, *CFO*
Dave Zertuche, *CFO*
David Hannah, *Bd of Directors*
▲ **EMP:** 90 **EST:** 1964
SQ FT: 12,000
SALES (est): 60.9MM
SALES (corp-wide): 8.8B **Publicly Held**
WEB: www.creststeel.com
SIC: 5051 Steel
PA: Reliance Steel & Aluminum Co.
350 S Grand Ave Ste 5100
Los Angeles CA 90071
213 687-7700

(P-13562)
DANIEL GERARD WORLDWIDE INC
Also Called: City Wire Cloth
13055 Jurupa Ave, Fontana (92337-6982)
PHONE...................951 361-1111
Todd Snelbaker, *Manager*
Lori Hahn, *Info Tech Mgr*
Fernando Morales, *Prdtn Mgr*
Tom Alexander, *Sales Staff*
EMP: 71
SQ FT: 50,000
SALES (corp-wide): 52.4MM **Privately Held**
WEB: www.gerarddaniel.com
SIC: 5051 3496 3356 3315 Wire; mesh, made from purchased wire; nonferrous rolling & drawing; steel wire & related products
PA: Gerard Daniel Worldwide, Inc.
34 Barnhart Dr
Hanover PA 17331
800 232-3332

(P-13563)
DIX METALS INC
14801 Able Ln Ste 101, Huntington Beach (92647-2059)
PHONE...................714 677-0777
Donald Carr, *Vice Pres*
Stefanie Salazar, *COO*
Bob Dix Sr, *Vice Pres*
Jon-David Nutter, *General Mgr*
Kimberly Schear, *Human Resources*
▲ **EMP:** 59 **EST:** 1972
SQ FT: 111,000
SALES (est): 30.4MM **Privately Held**
WEB: www.dixmetals.com
SIC: 5051 Steel; nonferrous metal sheets, bars, rods, etc.

(P-13564)
DOUGLAS STEEL SUPPLY INC (PA)
Also Called: DOUGLAS STEEL SUPPLY CO.
4804 Laurel Canyon Blvd, Valley Village (91607-3717)
PHONE...................323 587-7676
Douglas Stein, *CEO*
Don Hecht, *Vice Pres*
Donal Hecht, *Vice Pres*
Donald Miller, *Executive*

Leonel Cardiel, *Sales Staff*
EMP: 87 **EST:** 1972
SQ FT: 100,000
SALES: 88.5K **Privately Held**
SIC: 5051 Steel

(P-13565)
ENDURA STEEL INC (HQ)
Also Called: Smith Ironworks
17671 Bear Valley Rd, Hesperia
(92345-4902)
PHONE..........................760 244-9325
Jonathan D Hove, *President*
Robert E Hove, *Ch of Bd*
Lori A Clifton, *Corp Secy*
Dan Such, *Vice Pres*
AMI Hill, *Accounts Mgr*
EMP: 18 **EST:** 1972
SQ FT: 6,500
SALES (est): 34MM
SALES (corp-wide): 63.9MM **Privately
Held**
WEB: www.robar.com
SIC: 5051 3441 Steel; fabricated structural
metal
PA: Robar Enterprises, Inc.
17671 Bear Valley Rd
Hesperia CA 92345
760 244-5456

(P-13566)
GEORG FISCHER LLC (DH)
Also Called: Georg Fischer Piping
9271 Jeronimo Rd, Irvine (92618-1906)
PHONE..........................714 731-8800
James Jackson, *Vice Pres*
Daniel Vaterlaus, *Officer*
Max Holloway, *Vice Pres*
Thomas Sixsmith, *Vice Pres*
Becky Tseng, *Managing Dir*
◆ **EMP:** 70 **EST:** 1967
SQ FT: 55,000
SALES (est): 75.3MM
SALES (corp-wide): 3.5B **Privately Held**
WEB: www.gfps.com
SIC: 5051 5085 Pipe & tubing, steel;
valves & fittings
HQ: George Fischer, Inc.
5462 Irwindale Ave Ste A
Baldwin Park CA 91706
626 571-2770

(P-13567)
GVS ITALY
8616 La Tijera Blvd, Los Angeles
(90045-3944)
PHONE..........................424 382-4343
Bruno Montesano, *Manager*
EMP: 100
SALES (est): 30MM **Privately Held**
SIC: 5051 Aluminum bars, rods, ingots,
sheets, pipes, plates, etc.

(P-13568)
HARBOR PIPE AND STEEL INC
Also Called: James Metals
1495 Columbia Ave Bldg 10, Riverside
(92507-2074)
PHONE..........................951 369-3990
Joseph W Beattie, *President*
Martha Fournier, *Corp Secy*
Joe Beattie, *Principal*
Tom Liljegren, *Principal*
P Jay Peterson, *Principal*
▲ **EMP:** 150 **EST:** 1962
SALES (est): 44.2MM **Privately Held**
WEB: www.harborpipe.com
SIC: 5051 Steel

(P-13569)
HARTMAN INDUSTRIES
Also Called: Commercial Casting Co
14933 Whittram Ave, Fontana
(92335-3186)
PHONE..........................909 428-0114
Brad J Hartman, *CEO*
Brett Hartman, *Vice Pres*
Sean Hartman, *Vice Pres*
Anthony Alba, *Director*
▲ **EMP:** 60 **EST:** 1991
SQ FT: 73,000
SALES (est): 8MM **Privately Held**
WEB: www.sandcast-parts.com
SIC: 5051 Steel

(P-13570)
JACK RUBIN & SONS INC (PA)
13103 S Alameda St, Compton
(90222-2898)
P.O. Box 3005 (90223-3005)
PHONE..........................310 635-5407
Bruce Rubin, *CEO*
Michael Rubin, *Vice Pres*
Phillip Mandel, *Admin Sec*
◆ **EMP:** 25 **EST:** 1945
SQ FT: 30,000
SALES (est): 27.7MM **Privately Held**
WEB: www.wirerope.net
SIC: 5051 3496 3999 Rope, wire (not in-
sulated); woven wire products; atomizers,
toiletry

(P-13571)
JAYEM ENTERPRISES INC
Also Called: Acme Metals
14930 S San Pedro St, Gardena
(90248-2036)
PHONE..........................310 329-2263
Jack Goldberg, *Chairman*
Avelino Garcia, *General Mgr*
Cristina Martinez, *Controller*
◆ **EMP:** 60 **EST:** 1988
SQ FT: 265,000
SALES (est): 22MM **Privately Held**
WEB: www.acmemetalsonline.com
SIC: 5051 Steel

(P-13572)
JFE SHOJI AMERICA HOLDINGS INC (DH)
301 E Ocean Blvd Ste 1750, Long Beach
(90802-4879)
PHONE..........................562 637-3500
Toshihiro Kabasawa, *Exec VP*
Hidehiko Ogawa, *Exec VP*
Tad Takahashi, *Vice Pres*
◆ **EMP:** 85 **EST:** 1965
SQ FT: 7,500
SALES (est): 185.1MM **Privately Held**
WEB: www.jfe-shoji-steel-america.com
SIC: 5051 Steel

(P-13573)
JIMS SUPPLY CO INC (PA)
3500 Buck Owens Blvd, Bakersfield
(93308-4920)
P.O. Box 668 (93302-0668)
PHONE..........................661 616-6977
Doreen M Boylan, *CEO*
Bryan Boylan, *CFO*
Jonathan Thomas, *CFO*
Jennifer Drake, *Treasurer*
Jennice Boylan, *Vice Pres*
▲ **EMP:** 82 **EST:** 1959
SQ FT: 25,300
SALES (est): 39.1MM **Privately Held**
WEB: www.commercial.jscagsupply.com
SIC: 5051 Steel

(P-13574)
JOOR BROS WELDING INC
Also Called: Joor Bros Metal Supply
2818 Garretson Ave, Corona (92881-3509)
PHONE..........................951 737-3950
William Joor, *CEO*
Garrett Joor, *Corp Secy*
EMP: 18 **EST:** 1949
SQ FT: 20,000
SALES (est): 9.8MM **Privately Held**
WEB:
www.joorsweldingandmetalservice.com
SIC: 5051 3443 Steel; tanks, standard or
custom fabricated: metal plate

(P-13575)
KLOECKNER METALS CORPORATION
Also Called: Gary Steel Division
9804 Norwalk Blvd Ste A, Santa Fe Springs
(90670-2901)
PHONE..........................562 906-2020
John Ganem, *CEO*
Bob Tripp, *Vice Pres*
Sergio Torres, *General Mgr*
Frankie Puente, *Project Mgr*
Scott Britt, *Opers Staff*
EMP: 75
SALES (corp-wide): 6B **Privately Held**
WEB: www.kloecknermetals.com
SIC: 5051 Steel

HQ: Kloeckner Metals Corporation
500 Colonial Center Pkwy # 500
Roswell GA 30076

(P-13576)
KLOECKNER METALS CORPORATION
2000 S O St, Tulare (93274-6852)
PHONE..........................559 688-7980
John Ganem, *CEO*
Phil Hill, *Opers Staff*
Jim Walser, *Production*
Linda Duarte, *Sales Staff*
Stella Trujillo, *Sales Staff*
EMP: 52
SALES (corp-wide): 6B **Privately Held**
WEB: www.kloecknermetals.com
SIC: 5051 Steel
HQ: Kloeckner Metals Corporation
500 Colonial Center Pkwy # 500
Roswell GA 30076

(P-13577)
MCNICHOLS COMPANY
14108 Arbor Pl, Cerritos (90703-2404)
PHONE..........................562 921-3344
Pat Roche, *Manager*
Jennifer McNichols, *Vice Pres*
Dan Taylor, *General Mgr*
Daniel Taylor, *General Mgr*
Oneill Taylor, *Business Mgr*
EMP: 22
SQ FT: 20,000
SALES (corp-wide): 191.3MM **Privately
Held**
WEB: www.mcnichols.com
SIC: 5051 3496 3446 Steel; wire cloth &
woven wire products; open flooring &
grating for construction
PA: Mcnichols Company
2502 N Rocky Point Dr # 750
Tampa FL 33607
877 884-4653

(P-13578)
MWS PRECISION WIRE INDS INC
Also Called: Mws Wire Industries
31200 Cedar Valley Dr, Westlake Village
(91362-4035)
PHONE..........................818 991-8553
Toll Free:..........................888
Darrell H Friedman, *President*
Alan Friedman, *President*
Lois J Friedman, *Admin Sec*
Tom Carlson, *Info Tech Mgr*
Tomm Carlson, *Info Tech Mgr*
EMP: 52 **EST:** 1968
SQ FT: 32,000
SALES (est): 29.9MM **Privately Held**
WEB: www.mwswire.com
SIC: 5051 3351 3357 Copper sheets,
plates, bars, rods, pipes, etc.; wire, cop-
per & copper alloy; nonferrous wiredraw-
ing & insulating

(P-13579)
NEIGHBORHOOD STEEL LLC (HQ)
Also Called: Maas-Hansen Steel
5555 Garden Grove Blvd, Westminster
(92683-1886)
P.O. Box 58307, Vernon (90058-0307)
PHONE..........................714 236-8700
Gary Stein, *Mng Member*
Chris Loscalzo, *Credit Staff*
Sylvia Wong, *Sales Staff*
EMP: 30 **EST:** 2015
SALES (est): 52.7MM
SALES (corp-wide): 541.8MM **Privately
Held**
WEB: www.sss-steel.com
SIC: 5051 3312 Steel; blast furnaces &
steel mills
PA: Triple-S Steel Holdings, Inc.
6000 Jensen Dr
Houston TX 77026
713 697-7105

(P-13580)
NORMAN INDUSTRIAL MTLS INC (PA)
Also Called: Industrial Metal Supply Co
8300 San Fernando Rd, Sun Valley
(91352-3222)
PHONE..........................818 729-3333
Eric Steinhauer, *CEO*
David Pace, *President*
Dave Cohen, *COO*
David Berkey, *CFO*
Ram Shenoy, *Officer*
▲ **EMP:** 125 **EST:** 1945
SQ FT: 70,000
SALES (est): 150MM **Privately Held**
SIC: 5051 3441 3449 Metals service cen-
ters & offices; fabricated structural metal;
miscellaneous metalwork

(P-13581)
NORMAN INDUSTRIAL MTLS INC
Also Called: Industrial Metal Supply Co
2481 Alton Pkwy, Irvine (92606-5030)
PHONE..........................949 250-3343
Jerry Entin, *Vice Pres*
Carl Dembek, *Vice Pres*
Jerald D Entin, *Vice Pres*
Carla Borbolla, *HR Admin*
EMP: 46
SQ FT: 40,000
SALES (corp-wide): 150MM **Privately
Held**
SIC: 5051 5099 3366 Steel; brass goods;
bronze foundry
PA: Norman Industrial Materials, Inc.
8300 San Fernando Rd
Sun Valley CA 91352
818 729-3333

(P-13582)
NU-STEEL TRADE LLC
15005 S Avalon Blvd, Gardena
(90248-2039)
PHONE..........................310 329-2263
Lawrence Dobos, *Mng Member*
◆ **EMP:** 50 **EST:** 2017
SQ FT: 1,500
SALES (est): 19.1MM **Privately Held**
WEB: www.nu-trade.com
SIC: 5051 Steel

(P-13583)
PACIFIC METALS GROUP LLC
Also Called: Pacmet Aerospace
787 S Wanamaker Ave, Ontario
(91761-8116)
PHONE..........................909 218-8889
David Janes, *CEO*
David A Janes Jr,
Marco Vissuet, *Consultant*
◆ **EMP:** 50 **EST:** 2005
SQ FT: 45,000
SALES (est): 14.8MM **Privately Held**
WEB: www.pacmetaerospace.com
SIC: 5051 3519 Steel; jet propulsion en-
gines

(P-13584)
PACIFIC REBAR INC
501 S Oaks Ave, Ontario (91762-4020)
PHONE..........................909 984-7199
Tim Herwehe, *President*
EMP: 60 **EST:** 1986
SQ FT: 3,000
SALES (est): 11.5MM **Privately Held**
WEB: www.pacificrebarinc.com
SIC: 5051 Steel

(P-13585)
PIERCE-SPAFFORD METALS CO INC
Also Called: Rti Pierce-Spafford
7373 Hunt Ave, Garden Grove
(92841-2109)
PHONE..........................714 895-7756
John W Spafford, *CEO*
Michelle Benda, *Accounts Mgr*
▲ **EMP:** 129 **EST:** 1976
SQ FT: 37,000
SALES (est): 4.7MM **Privately Held**
WEB: www.titanium.com
SIC: 5051 Steel

P R O D U C T S & S V C S

PA: Titanium Industries, Inc.
18 Green Pond Rd Ste 1
Rockaway NJ 07866

(P-13586)
RAMCAST ORNAMENTAL SUP CO INC
Also Called: Ramcast Steel
1450 E Mission Blvd, Pomona
(91766-2229)
PHONE....................909 469-4767
Ismael Ramirez, *Branch Mgr*
Hector Ramirez, *Treasurer*
Jose Luis Ramirez, *Manager*
EMP: 26
SQ FT: 5,478
SALES (corp-wide): 47.9MM **Privately Held**
WEB: www.ramcaststeel.net
SIC: 5051 3312 Steel; stainless steel
PA: Ramcast Ornamental Supply Company, Inc.
2201 Firestone Blvd
Los Angeles CA 90002
323 585-1625

(P-13587)
RAPID CONN INC
25172 Arctic Ocean Dr # 106, Lake Forest
(92630-8851)
PHONE....................949 951-3722
Chuang Juay Ang, *CEO*
Balaji Raghunathan, *Vice Pres*
Francois Lindsay, *Engineer*
Andy Hoang, *Manager*
◆ **EMP:** 20 **EST:** 2000
SALES (est): 8.3MM **Privately Held**
SIC: 5051 3643 5085 Wire; cable, wire; connectors & terminals for electrical devices; twine

(P-13588)
RELIANCE STEEL & ALUMINUM CO (PA)
350 S Grand Ave Ste 5100, Los Angeles
(90071-3421)
PHONE....................213 687-7700
James D Hoffman, *CEO*
Mark V Kaminski, *Ch of Bd*
Karla R Lewis, *President*
Lisa Baldwin, *Bd of Directors*
Karen W Colonias, *Bd of Directors*
◆ **EMP:** 82 **EST:** 1939
SALES (est): 8.8B **Publicly Held**
WEB: www.rsac.com
SIC: 5051 Metals service centers & offices; structural shapes, iron or steel

(P-13589)
RELIANCE STEEL & ALUMINUM CO
Tube Service
9351 Norwalk Blvd, Santa Fe Springs
(90670-2925)
P.O. Box 2728 (90670-0728)
PHONE....................562 695-0467
Jan Hollar, *Branch Mgr*
Stephen Koch, *Senior VP*
Ginger McIntyre, *Office Mgr*
Kari Parnell, *Office Mgr*
Dorothy Kinsey, *Human Res Dir*
EMP: 58
SQ FT: 40,000
SALES (corp-wide): 8.8B **Publicly Held**
WEB: www.rsac.com
SIC: 5051 Steel
PA: Reliance Steel & Aluminum Co.
350 S Grand Ave Ste 5100
Los Angeles CA 90071
213 687-7700

(P-13590)
RELIANCE STEEL & ALUMINUM CO
Bralco Metals
15090 Northam St, La Mirada
(90638-5757)
PHONE....................714 736-4800
Michael Hubbart, *Branch Mgr*
Heather Ashton, *Office Mgr*
Tracie Ichikawa, *Credit Staff*
Laureano Gomez, *Production*
Henry Szeto, *Sales Associate*
EMP: 118

SALES (corp-wide): 8.8B **Publicly Held**
WEB: www.rsac.com
SIC: 5051 Steel; ferrous metals
PA: Reliance Steel & Aluminum Co.
350 S Grand Ave Ste 5100
Los Angeles CA 90071
213 687-7700

(P-13591)
RELIANCE STEEL & ALUMINUM CO
Also Called: Reliance Steel Company
2537 E 27th St, Vernon (90058-1284)
PHONE....................323 583-6111
John Becknell, *Branch Mgr*
Dave S McCarrell, *General Mgr*
Gisela Magani, *Office Mgr*
Robyn Lill, *CIO*
Hector Galvan, *QC Mgr*
EMP: 200
SALES (corp-wide): 8.8B **Publicly Held**
WEB: www.rsac.com
SIC: 5051 Steel
PA: Reliance Steel & Aluminum Co.
350 S Grand Ave Ste 5100
Los Angeles CA 90071
213 687-7700

(P-13592)
RELIANCE STEEL & ALUMINUM CO
Metal Center
12034 Greenstone Ave, Santa Fe Springs
(90670-4727)
P.O. Box 2101 (90670-0013)
PHONE....................562 944-3322
Jay Rose, *Branch Mgr*
Al Cawley, *Opers Mgr*
Al Cawly, *Opers Mgr*
EMP: 80
SQ FT: 142,000
SALES (corp-wide): 8.8B **Publicly Held**
WEB: www.rsac.com
SIC: 5051 Steel
PA: Reliance Steel & Aluminum Co.
350 S Grand Ave Ste 5100
Los Angeles CA 90071
213 687-7700

(P-13593)
SAC INTERNATIONAL STEEL INC (PA)
6130 Avalon Blvd, Los Angeles
(90003-1633)
PHONE....................323 232-2467
Shaukat A Chohan, *President*
Shaukaj Ali Chohan, *President*
Omar Chohan, *Vice Pres*
Mahmooda Chohan, *Admin Sec*
◆ **EMP:** 74 **EST:** 1979
SQ FT: 100,000
SALES (est): 22.4MM **Privately Held**
WEB: www.sacsteel.com
SIC: 5051 Sheets, metal

(P-13594)
SAMUEL SON & CO (USA) INC
12389 Lower Azusa Rd, Arcadia
(91006-5889)
PHONE....................323 722-0300
David Olivia, *Branch Mgr*
Kurt Perine, *Sales Staff*
Rick Silva, *Sales Staff*
Judith Betancourt, *Receptionist*
EMP: 50
SALES (corp-wide): 1.8B **Privately Held**
WEB: www.samuel.com
SIC: 5051 Ferroalloys; steel
HQ: Samuel, Son & Co. (Usa) Inc.
1401 Davey Rd Ste 300
Woodridge IL 60517
630 783-8900

(P-13595)
SHAPCO INC (PA)
1666 20th St Ste 100, Santa Monica
(90404-3828)
PHONE....................310 264-1666
Leonard Shapiro, *President*
Bernard J Shapiro, *Ch of Bd*
Jaime Gesundheidt, *Vice Pres*
Steve Teller, *Vice Pres*
◆ **EMP:** 15 **EST:** 1984
SQ FT: 7,598

SALES: 98.4MM **Privately Held**
SIC: 5051 3317 6799 Iron & steel (ferrous) products; pipe & tubing, steel; steel pipe & tubes; real estate investors, except property operators

(P-13596)
STATE PIPE & SUPPLY INC (DH)
183 S Cedar Ave, Rialto (92376-9011)
PHONE....................909 877-9999
Byung Joon Lee, *CEO*
Honggie Kim, *President*
Gary Knoroski, *Vice Pres*
Howard W Lee, *Admin Sec*
Blanche Goforth, *Credit Staff*
EMP: 55 **EST:** 1990
SQ FT: 20,000
SALES (est): 94MM **Privately Held**
WEB: www.statepipe.com
SIC: 5051 5085 Pipe & tubing, steel; industrial supplies
HQ: Seah Steel California, Llc
2100 Main St Ste 100
Irvine CA 92614
949 655-8000

(P-13597)
STEEL UNLIMITED INC
Also Called: Sui Companies
3200 Myers St, Riverside (92503-5530)
PHONE....................909 873-1222
Mike Frabotta, *President*
Mike Johnston, *Officer*
David Sunde, *Vice Pres*
Sheridan Sunde, *CIO*
Mark Hubbard, *Engineer*
▲ **EMP:** 75 **EST:** 1996
SQ FT: 142,000
SALES (est): 36.3MM **Privately Held**
WEB: www.steelunlimited.com
SIC: 5051 Steel

(P-13598)
STREUTER TECHNOLOGIES
Also Called: Streuter Fastel Timtel
208 Avnida Fbrcnte Ste 20, San Clemente
(92672)
PHONE....................949 369-7676
Bart Streuter, *President*
Bart S Streuter, *President*
Brad Streuter, *Vice Pres*
▲ **EMP:** 50 **EST:** 2005
SQ FT: 13,000
SALES (est): 9.8MM **Privately Held**
WEB: www.streuter.com
SIC: 5051 2891 Ferrous metals; adhesives & sealants; adhesives

(P-13599)
TA CHEN INTERNATIONAL INC (HQ)
Also Called: Sunland Shutters
5855 Obispo Ave, Long Beach
(90805-3715)
PHONE....................562 808-8000
Johnny Hsieh, *CEO*
Andrew Chang, *CFO*
Rahul Mehta, *Officer*
James Chang, *Vice Pres*
John Hellighausen, *Vice Pres*
◆ **EMP:** 172 **EST:** 1989
SQ FT: 200,000
SALES (est): 917MM **Privately Held**
WEB: www.tachen.com
SIC: 5051 Steel

(P-13600)
TELL STEEL INC
2345 W 17th St, Long Beach (90813-1097)
PHONE....................562 435-4826
Greg More, *President*
Pete V Trigt, *Admin Sec*
Donna Hanson, *Human Res Dir*
Greg Moore, *VP Opers*
Kevin McClister, *Sales Executive*
▲ **EMP:** 60 **EST:** 1958
SQ FT: 100,000
SALES (est): 47.5MM
SALES (corp-wide): 50.8MM **Privately Held**
WEB: www.tellsteel.com
SIC: 5051 Steel; aluminum bars, rods, ingots, sheets, pipes, plates, etc.

PA: Tuffli Company Incorporated
2245 W 190th St
Torrance CA 90504
310 326-4747

(P-13601)
TMX AEROSPACE
12821 Carmenita Rd Unit F, Santa Fe Springs (90670-4805)
PHONE....................562 215-4410
EMP: 120 **EST:** 2006
SALES (est): 7.6MM **Privately Held**
WEB: www.thyssenkrupp-aerospace.com
SIC: 5051 Steel

(P-13602)
TOTTEN TUBES INC (PA)
500 W Danlee St, Azusa (91702-2341)
PHONE....................626 812-0220
Tracy N Totten, *CEO*
Linda Furse, *Owner*
Paul Totten, *COO*
David Totten, *Chairman*
Jeffrey Totten, *Treasurer*
EMP: 60 **EST:** 1955
SQ FT: 73,000
SALES (est): 50.3MM **Privately Held**
WEB: www.tottentubes.com
SIC: 5051 3498 Pipe & tubing, steel; coils, pipe: fabricated from purchased pipe

(P-13603)
TRI-TECH METALS INC
9039 Charles Smith Ave, Rancho Cucamonga (91730-5566)
PHONE....................909 948-1401
Sam Allen, *President*
Richard Lee Hiromoto, *CEO*
Margo Beltran, *Treasurer*
Rock Hargus, *Vice Pres*
EMP: 18 **EST:** 1998
SQ FT: 10,000
SALES (est): 7.8MM **Privately Held**
WEB: www.tri-techmetals.com
SIC: 5051 3499 3291 Steel; iron & steel (ferrous) products; aluminum bars, rods, ingots, sheets, pipes, plates, etc.; aerosol valves, metal; steel wool

(P-13604)
VER SALES INC (PA)
2509 N Naomi St, Burbank (91504-3236)
PHONE....................818 567-3000
Gloria Ryan, *CEO*
James J Ryan, *CEO*
Craig Ryan, *Vice Pres*
Patrick Ryan, *Vice Pres*
Paul Ryan, *Vice Pres*
▲ **EMP:** 53 **EST:** 1972
SQ FT: 30,000
SALES (est): 32.9MM **Privately Held**
WEB: www.versales.com
SIC: 5051 5099 3357 Metal wires, ties, cables & screening; safety equipment & supplies; nonferrous wiredrawing & insulating

(P-13605)
WIELAND METAL SERVICES LLC
Also Called: Wieland Brookes
10634 Shoemaker Ave, Santa Fe Springs
(90670-4038)
PHONE....................562 968-2100
EMP: 69 **Privately Held**
SIC: 5051 Metals service centers & offices
HQ: Wieland Metal Services, Llc
301 Metro Center Blvd # 204
Warwick RI 02886
401 736-2600

(P-13606)
WIELAND METAL SERVICES W LLC (DH)
5100 S Archibald Ave, Ontario
(91762-7414)
PHONE....................714 692-1000
Aaron Baldridge,
Marc R Bacon,
Robert M James,
Joseph T Woo,
Donna V Diggelen, *Manager*
▲ **EMP:** 56 **EST:** 1892

SALES (est): 27.3MM Privately Held
WEB: www.gbcmetals.com
SIC: 5051 Metals service centers & offices

5063 Electrl Apparatus, Eqpt, Wiring Splys Wholesale

(P-13607)
AAA ELECTRIC MOTOR SALES & SVC (PA)
1346 Venice Blvd, Los Angeles (90006-5595)
PHONE..................................213 749-2367
Brian A Maloney, *President*
Robert A Maloney, *President*
Nancy Maloney, *Treasurer*
Al Ramirez, *Foreman/Supr*
Juven Alan, *Sales Staff*
EMP: 19 EST: 1971
SQ FT: 3,500
SALES (est): 10.3MM Privately Held
WEB: www.aaa-electric.net
SIC: 5063 7694 Motors, electric; electric motor repair

(P-13608)
ADJ PRODUCTS LLC (PA)
6122 S Eastern Ave, Commerce (90040-3402)
PHONE..................................323 582-2650
Charles J Davies, *CEO*
Toby Velasquez, *President*
Chuck Green, *Sales Staff*
Shenor Sakadjian, *Sales Staff*
Jake Rhodes, *Manager*
EMP: 120 EST: 2012
SALES (est): 15.4MM Privately Held
WEB: www.adj.com
SIC: 5063 Lighting fixtures

(P-13609)
ADVANTAGE MANUFACTURING INC
Also Called: Electric Motors
616 S Santa Fe St, Santa Ana (92705-4109)
PHONE..................................714 505-1166
Michael Collins, *President*
Lyann Courant, *CFO*
Eben Collins, *Sales Associate*
◆ EMP: 30 EST: 1997
SQ FT: 25,000
SALES (est): 11.9MM Privately Held
WEB: www.advantageman.com
SIC: 5063 5091 3621 5999 Motors, electric; swimming pools, equipment & supplies; motors, electric; swimming pools, hot tubs & sauna equipment & supplies

(P-13610)
AEE SOLAR INC (DH)
775 Fiero Ln Ste 200, San Luis Obispo (93401-7904)
PHONE..................................800 777-6609
Lynn Jurich, *CEO*
Robert Komin, *CFO*
Antonio Cintra, *Vice Pres*
Jeanna Steele, *Admin Sec*
Brad Bassett, *Engineer*
◆ EMP: 21
SQ FT: 10,000
SALES (est): 74.1MM Publicly Held
WEB: www.aeesolar.com
SIC: 5063 3645 Generators; residential lighting fixtures
HQ: Sunrun South Llc
595 Market St Fl 29
San Francisco CA 94105
415 580-6900

(P-13611)
ALLSALE ELECTRIC INC
9261 Jordan Ave, Chatsworth (91311-5739)
PHONE..................................818 715-0181
Evan Joel Regenstreif, *President*
Cory Devine, *Branch Mgr*
Hannah Devos, *Office Mgr*
Doug Fasching, *Info Tech Mgr*
Cynara Solorio, *Comp Spec*
EMP: 56 EST: 1985
SALES (est): 30.9MM Privately Held
WEB: www.allsale.com
SIC: 5063 Electrical supplies

(P-13612)
AMERICAN ELECTRIC SUPPLY INC (PA)
361 S Maple St, Corona (92878-4307)
P.O. Box 2710 (92878-2710)
PHONE..................................951 734-7910
Michael Pratt, *CEO*
Jerry Empson, *Treasurer*
Kevin Klinzing, *Admin Sec*
Rachel Duron, *Human Res Dir*
Shannon Winans, *Marketing Mgr*
▲ EMP: 97 EST: 1984
SQ FT: 13,086
SALES (est): 63MM Privately Held
WEB: www.amelect.com
SIC: 5063 Electrical supplies

(P-13613)
AQ LIGHTING GROUP TEXAS INC
28486 Wstnghuse Pl Ste 12, Santa Clarita (91355)
PHONE..................................818 534-5300
Cynthia Piana, *President*
Tom Piana, *Vice Pres*
EMP: 25 EST: 2017
SQ FT: 16,000
SALES (est): 21MM Privately Held
SIC: 5063 3645 3612 2599 Light bulbs & related supplies; light shades, metal; distribution transformers, electric; factory furniture & fixtures

(P-13614)
ARCHIPELAGO LIGHTING INC
4615 State St, Montclair (91763-6130)
PHONE..................................909 627-5333
Jia H Deng, *President*
Malinda Redman, *Vice Pres*
Phil Garcia, *Manager*
EMP: 70 EST: 2005
SQ FT: 120,000
SALES (est): 12.1MM Privately Held
WEB: www.archipelagolighting.com
SIC: 5063 Electrical apparatus & equipment

(P-13615)
AT BATTERY COMPANY INC
Also Called: Atbatt.com
28381 Constellation Rd, Valencia (91355-5048)
PHONE..................................661 775-2020
Young Lee, *CEO*
Roger Lim, *General Mgr*
Yong Lee, *Purch Mgr*
Brandy Lee, *Marketing Staff*
◆ EMP: 20 EST: 2000
SALES (est): 4.2MM Privately Held
WEB: www.atbatt.com
SIC: 5999 5063 3691 Electronic parts & equipment; batteries; alkaline cell storage batteries

(P-13616)
BARTCO LIGHTING INC
5761 Research Dr, Huntington Beach (92649-1616)
PHONE..................................714 230-3200
Robert Barton, *CEO*
Brad Barton, *Exec VP*
Dana B McKe, *Exec VP*
Brian Labbe, *Vice Pres*
Frank Hollenkamp, *Regional Mgr*
▲ EMP: 70 EST: 1998
SALES (est): 20MM Privately Held
WEB: www.bartcolighting.com
SIC: 5063 3648 Lighting fixtures, commercial & industrial; lighting fixtures; airport lighting fixtures: runway approach, taxi or ramp

(P-13617)
BRITHINEE ELECTRIC
620 S Rancho Ave, Colton (92324-3296)
PHONE..................................909 825-7971
Wallace P Brithinee, *President*
Donald P Brithinee, *Vice Pres*
Donald Brithinee, *Vice Pres*
Craig Slape, *Department Mgr*
Carlos Mazariegos, *Design Engr*
EMP: 57 EST: 1963

SALES (est): 17.3MM Privately Held
WEB: www.brithinee.com
SIC: 5063 7694 Motors, electric; electric motor repair

(P-13618)
BURNABY INTL TECH CORP
20955 Pathfinder Rd # 100, Diamond Bar (91765-4028)
PHONE..................................888 930-2090
Tony Liu, *Managing Dir*
EMP: 53
SQ FT: 1,200
SALES (est): 5MM Privately Held
SIC: 5063 Batteries

(P-13619)
COMMERCIAL LIGHTING INDS INC
Also Called: Cli
81161 Indio Blvd, Indio (92201-1931)
PHONE..................................800 755-0155
Frank Halcovich, *CEO*
Greg Read, *Vice Pres*
Natasha Taormina, *Vice Pres*
Jennifer Johnson, *General Mgr*
Gregory Fusco, *Project Mgr*
▼ EMP: 74 EST: 1991
SQ FT: 81,000
SALES (est): 30.9MM Privately Held
WEB: www.commercial-lighting.net
SIC: 5063 Light bulbs & related supplies; lighting fixtures

(P-13620)
CORDELIA LIGHTING INC
20101 S Santa Fe Ave, Compton (90221-5917)
PHONE..................................310 886-3490
James Keng, *President*
Tim Norton, *Vice Pres*
Jay Spowart, *Vice Pres*
Li-WEI Wang, *Vice Pres*
Edmond Daniels, *Engineer*
▲ EMP: 106 EST: 1985
SQ FT: 200,000
SALES (est): 23.8MM Privately Held
WEB: www.cordelia.com
SIC: 5063 Lighting fixtures

(P-13621)
COUNTY WHL ELC CO LOS ANGELES
Also Called: C E D
560 N Main St, Orange (92868-1102)
PHONE..................................714 633-3801
Joe Mihelich, *Principal*
Craig Peters, *Branch Mgr*
Don Ulery, *Purchasing*
Fernando Yazon, *Purchasing*
Norma Galdamez, *Opers Staff*
EMP: 76 EST: 1986
SALES (est): 24.8MM
SALES (corp-wide): 1.4B Privately Held
WEB: www.countywholesale.com
SIC: 5063 Electrical supplies
PA: Consolidated Electrical Distributors, Inc.
1920 Westridge Dr
Irving TX 75038
972 582-5300

(P-13622)
DARDANELLA ELECTRIC CORP
Also Called: Deco
150 N Santa Anita Ave # 220, Arcadia (91006-3113)
PHONE..................................818 445-5009
William Hoban, *Ch of Bd*
EMP: 80 EST: 1972
SQ FT: 2,500
SALES (est): 8.4MM Privately Held
SIC: 5063 Electrical apparatus & equipment

(P-13623)
EATON AEROSPACE LLC
4690 Colorado Blvd, Los Angeles (90039-1106)
PHONE..................................818 409-0200
Stephanie Stewart, *Branch Mgr*
Gary Peters, *Program Mgr*
Diana Hollenbeck, *Info Tech Mgr*
Frank Loi, *Software Dev*
Sokuntheatony Ung, *Software Dev*
EMP: 256

SQ FT: 41,117
SALES (corp-wide): 385.8MM Privately Held
WEB: www.eaton.com
SIC: 5063 Electrical apparatus & equipment
PA: Eaton Aerospace Llc
1000 Eaton Blvd
Cleveland OH 44122
216 523-5000

(P-13624)
ECOSENSE LIGHTING INC (PA)
837 N Spring St Ste 103, Los Angeles (90012-2594)
PHONE..................................855 632-6736
Mark Reynoso, *CEO*
Luetrell Toler, *Partner*
Ray Letasi, *President*
Christina Loh, *COO*
George Mueller, *Chairman*
▲ EMP: 95 EST: 2008
SALES (est): 101.4MM Privately Held
WEB: www.ecosenselighting.com
SIC: 5063 Lighting fixtures

(P-13625)
ELECTRIC SALES UNLIMITED
9023 Norwalk Blvd, Santa Fe Springs (90670-2531)
PHONE..................................562 463-8300
John J Defazio Jr, *President*
Chuck Beadle, *Vice Pres*
Teresa D Fackiner, *Vice Pres*
Debbie D Fagan, *Vice Pres*
Bill Wilkins, *Area Mgr*
▲ EMP: 50 EST: 1976
SQ FT: 75,000
SALES (est): 17.5MM Privately Held
WEB: www.esu.com
SIC: 5063 Electrical supplies

(P-13626)
ELESCO
170 Mccormick Ave, Costa Mesa (92626-3307)
PHONE..................................714 673-6600
Richard Morris, *Principal*
Becky Very, *Sales Mgr*
Wade Allemand, *Manager*
EMP: 20 EST: 2007
SALES (est): 1MM Privately Held
WEB: www.lightinginverters.com
SIC: 5999 5731 5063 3691 Safety supplies & equipment; radio, television & electronic stores; storage batteries, industrial; storage batteries

(P-13627)
ERS SEC ALARM SYSTEMS INC
Also Called: Emergency Reporting Systems
4538 Santa Anita Ave, El Monte (91731-1318)
PHONE..................................626 579-2525
David Chao, *President*
EMP: 53
SQ FT: 15,000
SALES (est): 16.9MM Privately Held
SIC: 5063 1731 Burglar alarm systems; fire detection & burglar alarm systems specialization

(P-13628)
EXPO POWER SYSTEMS INC
Also Called: Enviroguard
5534 Olive St, Montclair (91763-1649)
PHONE..................................800 506-9884
Doug Frazier, *President*
Tanya Bradford, *Vice Pres*
Morgan Arzola, *Finance*
Lily Zepeda, *Sales Staff*
EMP: 34 EST: 1993
SQ FT: 15,000
SALES (est): 18.7MM Privately Held
WEB: www.enviroguard.com
SIC: 5063 3444 Batteries; sheet metalwork

(P-13629)
FACILITY SHIELD INTL INC
Also Called: FSI Energy Services
2950 E Philadelphia St, Ontario (91761-8545)
PHONE..................................909 923-1800
Donna Cotton, *President*
Zenaida Ilanan, *Controller*

P R O D U C T S & S V C S

▲ **EMP:** 23 **EST:** 2006
SALES (est): 2MM **Privately Held**
WEB: www.fsienergyservices.com
SIC: 5063 3822 7373 Storage batteries, industrial; auto controls regulating residntl & coml environmt & applncs; systems integration services

(P-13630)
FACILITY SOLUTIONS GROUP INC
801 Richfield Rd, Placentia (92870-6731)
PHONE..........................714 993-3966
Jeff Johnson, *District Mgr*
Rick Brown, *Sales Staff*
EMP: 64
SALES (corp-wide): 787.7MM **Privately Held**
WEB: www.fsg.com
SIC: 5063 1731 Lighting fixtures, commercial & industrial; light bulbs & related supplies; electrical work; lighting contractor
PA: Facility Solutions Group, Inc.
4401 West Gate Blvd # 310
Austin TX 78745
512 440-7985

(P-13631)
GRAYBAR ELECTRIC COMPANY INC
1370 Valley Vista Dr # 100, Diamond Bar (91765-3921)
PHONE..........................909 451-4300
Bruce Spencer, *Engr R&D*
Scott S Clifford, *CFO*
David Meyer, *Vice Pres*
Franco Sabalones, *Business Mgr*
Jennifer Caldera, *Finance Mgr*
EMP: 153
SALES (corp-wide): 7.5B **Privately Held**
WEB: www.graybar.com
SIC: 5063 5065 Electrical supplies; telephone equipment
PA: Graybar Electric Company, Inc.
34 N Meramec Ave
Saint Louis MO 63105
314 573-9200

(P-13632)
HAMMOND POWER SOLUTIONS INC
17715 S Susana Rd, Compton (90221-5409)
PHONE..........................310 537-4690
Raymundo Regalado, *Manager*
Steve D 'avanzo, *Technical Staff*
Jay Tucker, *Business Mgr*
Karen Witzel, *Marketing Staff*
Kelly Okapal, *Sales Staff*
EMP: 51
SALES (corp-wide): 269.4MM **Privately Held**
WEB: www.hammondpowersolutions.com
SIC: 5063 Electrical apparatus & equipment
HQ: Hammond Power Solutions, Inc.
1100 Lake St
Baraboo WI 53913
608 356-3921

(P-13633)
HOCHIKI AMERICA CORPORATION
7051 Village Dr Ste 100, Buena Park (90621-2268)
P.O. Box 514689, Los Angeles (90051-4689)
PHONE..........................714 522-2246
Hisham Harake, *CEO*
Hiroshi Kamei, *CFO*
Rick Boisclair, *Vice Pres*
Sunichi Shoji, *Vice Pres*
Steven Bailey, *Regional Mgr*
◆ **EMP:** 104 **EST:** 1972
SQ FT: 30,000
SALES (est): 37.8MM **Privately Held**
WEB: www.hochikiamerica.com
SIC: 5063 3669 Fire alarm systems; fire detection systems, electric
PA: Hochiki Corporation
2-10-43, Kamiosaki
Shinagawa-Ku TKY 141-0

(P-13634)
HUBBELL POWER SYSTEMS INC
Also Called: Greenjacket
27151 Burbank, Foothill Ranch (92610-2501)
PHONE..........................949 305-3311
Billy Huard, *Manager*
EMP: 61
SALES (corp-wide): 4.1B **Publicly Held**
WEB: www.hubbell.com
SIC: 5063 Electrical apparatus & equipment
HQ: Hubbell Power Systems, Inc.
200 Center Point Cir # 200
Columbia SC 29210
803 216-2600

(P-13635)
ICONN INC
Also Called: Iconn Technologies
8909 Irvine Center Dr, Irvine (92618-4249)
PHONE..........................800 286-6742
Turker Hidirlar, *CEO*
Shirley Wong, *Controller*
Anna Chan, *Purchasing*
Emre Harputluoglu, *Sales Executive*
▲ **EMP:** 45 **EST:** 2007
SQ FT: 9,920
SALES (est): 21.7MM **Privately Held**
WEB: www.iconn-ems.com
SIC: 5063 3613 3714 3678 Lugs & connectors, electrical; power connectors, electric; booster (jump-start) cables, automotive; electronic connectors; wire, copper & copper alloy; connectors & terminals for electrical devices

(P-13636)
IMPRESSIONS VANITY COMPANY (PA)
1402 Morgan Cir, Tustin (92780-6423)
PHONE..........................844 881-0790
Kevin Choi, *President*
Michael Lien, *Director*
EMP: 64 **EST:** 2015
SALES (est): 11MM **Privately Held**
WEB: www.impressionsvanity.com
SIC: 5719 5063 2531 Mirrors; lighting fixtures; chairs, table & arm

(P-13637)
JELIGHT COMPANY INC (PA)
2 Mason, Irvine (92618-2513)
PHONE..........................949 380-8774
Marinko Jelic, *President*
Renata Jelic, *Admin Sec*
Hao Nguyen, *Design Engr*
Dick Amen, *Engineer*
▲ **EMP:** 64 **EST:** 1978
SQ FT: 27,000
SALES (est): 22.5MM **Privately Held**
WEB: www.jelight.com
SIC: 5063 Lighting fixtures

(P-13638)
JME INC (PA)
Also Called: T M B
527 Park Ave, San Fernando (91340-2557)
PHONE..........................201 896-8600
Colin R Waters, *CEO*
Thomas M Bissett, *President*
Luis V De Dios, *Administration*
◆ **EMP:** 80 **EST:** 1982
SQ FT: 34,000
SALES (est): 38.1MM **Privately Held**
WEB: www.tmb.com
SIC: 5063 Lighting fittings & accessories

(P-13639)
JUSTICE DESIGN GROUP LLC (PA)
500 S Grand Ave Ste 1100, Los Angeles (90071-2606)
PHONE..........................213 437-0102
Bruce Levin, *President*
Adrianna Arambula, *Creative Dir*
Susan Levin, *Admin Sec*
Nigel Heals, *Accounting Mgr*
David S Brenneman, *Sales Mgr*
◆ **EMP:** 45
SQ FT: 12,500

SALES (est): 17.4MM **Privately Held**
WEB: www.jdg.com
SIC: 5063 3645 Lighting fixtures; residential lighting fixtures; boudoir lamps

(P-13640)
LIGHTING TECHNOLOGIES INTL LLC
13700 Live Oak Ave, Baldwin Park (91706-1319)
PHONE..........................626 480-0755
Ken Luttio,
Allan Wu, *Engineer*
Anthony Dominguez, *Controller*
Thomas Hardenburger, *Mktg Dir*
Jana Daberkow, *Sales Staff*
▲ **EMP:** 190 **EST:** 2016
SALES (est): 25.2MM **Privately Held**
WEB: www.ltilighting.com
SIC: 5063 3648 Lighting fixtures; lighting equipment

(P-13641)
LOS ANGELES LTG MFG CO INC
Also Called: L A Lighting
10141 Olney St, El Monte (91731-2311)
PHONE..........................626 454-8300
William D Shapiro, *President*
Mieko Shapiro, *Treasurer*
Angie Carra, *Administration*
Eric Crute, *Buyer*
Rick O 'neil, *Natl Sales Mgr*
◆ **EMP:** 75 **EST:** 1988
SQ FT: 50,000
SALES (est): 30.4MM **Privately Held**
WEB: www.lalighting.com
SIC: 5063 Lighting fixtures

(P-13642)
MAGNETICS TEST LAB INC
Also Called: Mtl Distribution
23167 Temescal Canyon Rd, Corona (92883-6001)
P.O. Box 78117 (92877-0137)
PHONE..........................951 270-0215
Thuy Thi Tran, *President*
Ricardo Esquer, *Treasurer*
Jacob Hughes, *Engineer*
Vicki Esquer, *Marketing Staff*
Seak L Tan, *Sales Staff*
▲ **EMP:** 13 **EST:** 1989
SQ FT: 10,000
SALES (est): 5.1MM **Privately Held**
SIC: 5063 3612 Transformers & transmission equipment; specialty transformers

(P-13643)
MAGNETIKA INC (PA)
2041 W 139th St, Gardena (90249-2409)
PHONE..........................310 527-8100
Francis Ishida, *President*
Basil P Caloyeras, *CEO*
Nagui Guirgis, *COO*
Ameet Butala, *Exec VP*
Patricia Perez, *Marketing Staff*
EMP: 80 **EST:** 1960
SQ FT: 40,000
SALES (est): 31.9MM **Privately Held**
WEB: www.magnetika.com
SIC: 5063 3612 Transformers, electric; power transmission equipment, electric; ballasts for lighting fixtures; power transformers, electric

(P-13644)
MAIN ELECTRIC SUPPLY CO LLC (PA)
3600 W Segerstrom Ave, Santa Ana (92704-6408)
P.O. Box 25750 (92799-5750)
PHONE..........................949 833-3052
Scott R Germann, *President*
Paul Vowels, *COO*
Karen Morris, *CFO*
Carlos Valencia, *Vice Pres*
Mike Willhide, *Vice Pres*
▲ **EMP:** 69
SQ FT: 35,000
SALES (est): 385.7MM **Privately Held**
WEB: www.mainelectricsupply.com
SIC: 5063 Electrical supplies

(P-13645)
MAIN ELECTRIC SUPPLY CO LLC
8146 Byron Rd, Whittier (90606-2616)
PHONE..........................323 753-5131
Aubrey Gullo, *Project Mgr*
Morgan Browning, *Analyst*
Gregg Schiewe, *Opers Staff*
April Akagi, *Sales Staff*
Rudy Pena, *Sales Staff*
EMP: 20
SALES (corp-wide): 385.7MM **Privately Held**
WEB: www.mainelectricsupply.com
SIC: 5063 3699 Electrical supplies; electrical equipment & supplies
PA: Main Electric Supply Company Llc
3600 W Segerstrom Ave
Santa Ana CA 92704
949 833-3052

(P-13646)
MAIN ELECTRIC SUPPLY CO LLC
1700 Morse Ave, Ventura (93003-5116)
PHONE..........................805 654-8600
Patrick Osullivan, *Manager*
Angelina Kays, *Project Mgr*
EMP: 21
SALES (corp-wide): 385.7MM **Privately Held**
WEB: www.mainelectricsupply.com
SIC: 5063 3699 Electrical supplies; electrical equipment & supplies
PA: Main Electric Supply Company Llc
3600 W Segerstrom Ave
Santa Ana CA 92704
949 833-3052

(P-13647)
MAXIM LIGHTING INTL INC (PA)
253 Vineland Ave, City of Industry (91746-2319)
PHONE..........................626 956-4200
Jacob Sperling, *CEO*
Michael S Andrews, *CFO*
Mike Andrews, *CFO*
Zvi Sperling, *Corp Secy*
Tim Green, *Sales Staff*
▲ **EMP:** 200 **EST:** 1999
SQ FT: 26,000
SALES (est): 52.1MM **Privately Held**
WEB: www.maximlighting.com
SIC: 5063 Lighting fixtures

(P-13648)
MINKA LIGHTING INC (PA)
Also Called: Minka Group
1151 Bradford Cir, Corona (92882-7166)
PHONE..........................951 735-9220
Marian Tang, *CEO*
Kurt Schulzman, *Principal*
Cynthia Sutton, *Office Admin*
Pao Yang, *Administration*
Carlos Gonzalez, *Graphic Designe*
◆ **EMP:** 70 **EST:** 1982
SQ FT: 350,000
SALES (est): 54.8MM **Privately Held**
WEB: www.minkagroup.net
SIC: 5063 Lighting fixtures

(P-13649)
MOTIVE ENERGY INC (PA)
125 E Coml St Bldg B, Anaheim (92801)
PHONE..........................714 888-2525
Robert J Istwan, *Presiden*
Justin Moores, *Department Mgr*
Marina Lopez, *Administration*
Kenneth Sandman, *Opers Mgr*
Max Krause, *Foreman/Supr*
▼ **EMP:** 80 **EST:** 1979
SQ FT: 35,000
SALES (est): 33.8MM **Privately Held**
WEB: www.motive-energy.com
SIC: 5063 Storage batteries, industrial

(P-13650)
MULTIQUIP INC (DH)
Also Called: Mq Power
6141 Katella Ave Ste 200, Cypress (90630-5202)
PHONE..........................310 537-3700
Robert J Graydon, *CEO*
James Henehan, *Senior VP*
Mike Schick, *District Mgr*

William Wallwin, *District Mgr*
Mary Perez, *Manager*
◆ **EMP:** 300 **EST:** 1973
SALES (est): 214.3MM **Privately Held**
WEB: www.multiquip.com
SIC: 5063 5082 3645 Generators; general construction machinery & equipment; garden, patio, walkway & yard lighting fixtures: electric
HQ: Itochu International Inc.
1251 Ave Of The Amrcas 51
New York NY 10020
212 818-8000

(P-13651)
MURCAL INC
41343 12th St W, Palmdale (93551-1442)
PHONE......................661 272-4700
Robert J Murphy, *President*
Essie Murphy, *Shareholder*
Lauren Stoner, *Info Tech Mgr*
Jacob Billeter, *Engineer*
Barbara Murphy, *Purchasing*
EMP: 26 **EST:** 1958
SQ FT: 20,000
SALES (est): 7.1MM **Privately Held**
WEB: www.murcal.com
SIC: 5063 3621 3694 Motor controls, starters & relays: electric; storage battery chargers, motor & engine generator type; ignition apparatus, internal combustion engines; spark plugs for internal combustion engines

(P-13652)
NELSON & ASSOCIATES INC
12816 Leffingwell Ave, Santa Fe Springs (90670-6343)
PHONE......................562 921-4423
Brian Haupt, *President*
Todd James Nelson, *CEO*
Kurt Nelson, *Principal*
Andy Meier, *Manager*
Corey Schramm, *Sales Staff*
▲ **EMP:** 65 **EST:** 1977
SQ FT: 120,000
SALES (est): 16.8MM **Privately Held**
WEB: www.nelsonreps.com
SIC: 5063 Electrical supplies

(P-13653)
NORA LIGHTING INC
6505 Gayhart St, Commerce (90040-2507)
PHONE......................800 686-6672
Fred Farzan, *CEO*
Jill Farzan, *Exec VP*
Jilla Farzan, *Exec VP*
Neda Farzan, *Admin Sec*
Jhenmar Carino, *Technology*
◆ **EMP:** 159 **EST:** 1989
SQ FT: 150,000
SALES (est): 46.5MM **Privately Held**
WEB: www.noralighting.com
SIC: 5063 3648 5719 Lighting fixtures; lighting fixtures, except electric: residential; lighting fixtures

(P-13654)
ONESOLUTION LIGHT AND CONTROL
Also Called: Nsi Architectural
225 S Loara St, Anaheim (92802-1019)
PHONE......................714 490-5540
John C Ortiz, *President*
EMP: 55 **EST:** 1986
SQ FT: 14,000
SALES (est): 5MM **Privately Held**
WEB: www.nsi-inc.com
SIC: 5063 Lighting fixtures, commercial & industrial

(P-13655)
ONESOURCE DISTRIBUTORS LLC
Also Called: One Source Supply Solutions
6530 Altura Blvd, Buena Park (90620-1040)
PHONE......................562 401-1264
William Mourtinzen, *Mng Member*
Jeremy Ruiz, *Sales Associate*
Jim Frankenfield, *Manager*
EMP: 59
SALES (corp-wide): 13.2MM **Privately Held**
SIC: 5063 5065 Electrical supplies; electronic parts & equipment

HQ: Onesource Distributors, Llc
3951 Oceanic Dr
Oceanside CA 92056
760 966-4500

(P-13656)
ORIENTAL MOTOR USA CORPORATION (DH)
570 Alaska Ave, Torrance (90503-3904)
PHONE......................310 715-3300
Ryan Kanemura, *President*
Greg Johnston, *Exec VP*
Pete Derose, *Vice Pres*
Todd Walker, *Vice Pres*
Jake Kitayama, *Principal*
◆ **EMP:** 60 **EST:** 1978
SQ FT: 31,600
SALES: 62.7MM **Privately Held**
WEB: www.orientalmotor.com
SIC: 5063 Motors, electric

(P-13657)
PACIFIC LIGHTING MFR INC
Also Called: Utopia Lighting
2329 E Pacifica Pl, Compton (90220-6210)
PHONE......................310 327-7711
▲ **EMP:** 62
SQ FT: 100,000
SALES: 12.5MM **Privately Held**
SIC: 5063 Whol Electrical Equipment

(P-13658)
PACIFIC LIGHTING MFR INC
Also Called: Utopia Lighting
2661 E Del Amo Blvd, Compton (90221-6003)
PHONE......................310 327-7711
Soon Goo Hong, *CEO*
David Kim, *President*
Bohi Hong, *Admin Sec*
Johan Kim, *Regl Sales Mgr*
EMP: 56 **EST:** 2005
SALES (est): 14.1MM **Privately Held**
WEB: www.utopialightingus.com
SIC: 5063 Lighting fixtures

(P-13659)
PH CORPORATION
Also Called: Hank's Electrical Supplies
1718 Placentia Ave, Costa Mesa (92627-4417)
PHONE......................949 646-7775
Betty Willemsen, *President*
Paul Willemsen, *Vice Pres*
EMP: 13 **EST:** 1972
SQ FT: 17,000
SALES (est): 5.1MM **Privately Held**
WEB: www.hankselectric.supply
SIC: 5063 7694 Electrical supplies; electric motor repair

(P-13660)
PLC IMPORTS INC
Also Called: P L C Lighting
9667 Owensmouth Ave # 201, Chatsworth (91311-4819)
PHONE......................818 349-1600
Daniel Gilardi, *President*
Robert Gilardi, *Vice Pres*
▲ **EMP:** 25 **EST:** 1992
SALES (est): 7.3MM **Privately Held**
WEB: www.plclighting.com
SIC: 5063 3646 Light bulbs & related supplies; commercial indusl & institutional electric lighting fixtures

(P-13661)
POWER PLUS INTERNATIONAL INC (PA)
5500 E La Palma Ave, Anaheim (92807-2108)
PHONE......................714 507-1881
Steven R Bray, *President*
Steve Nameroff, *Director*
EMP: 96 **EST:** 2010
SALES (est): 17.1MM **Privately Held**
WEB: www.powerplus.com
SIC: 5063 7629 Generators; generator repair

(P-13662)
PRECISION FLUORESCENT WEST INC (DH)
Also Called: Precision Energy Efficient Ltg
23281 La Palma Ave, Yorba Linda (92887-4768)
PHONE......................352 692-5900
Raymond Pustinger, *President*
Dan Rodriguez, *Vice Pres*
▲ **EMP:** 67 **EST:** 1995
SQ FT: 31,000
SALES (est): 54.7MM
SALES (corp-wide): 4.1B **Publicly Held**
WEB: www.hubbell.com
SIC: 5063 Electrical apparatus & equipment

(P-13663)
QUANTUM AUTOMATION
4400 E La Palma Ave, Anaheim (92807-1807)
P.O. Box 18687 (92817-8687)
PHONE......................714 854-0800
Brian Gallogly, *President*
Mike Kavanagh, *Vice Pres*
Michael Kavanagh. *Regional Mgr*
Maryam Afshar, *Software Engr*
Chris Doan, *Software Engr*
EMP: 35 **EST:** 1991
SQ FT: 11,000
SALES (est): 13.1MM **Privately Held**
WEB: www.quantumautomation.com
SIC: 5063 3825 3613 Electrical apparatus & equipment; electrical power measuring equipment; control panels, electric

(P-13664)
REGAL BELOIT AMERICA INC
Also Called: Morse Industrial
3505 E Francis St, Ontario (91761-2926)
PHONE......................909 591-9561
Cathy Costa, *Branch Mgr*
EMP: 13
SALES (corp-wide): 2.9B **Publicly Held**
SIC: 5063 3568 Power transmission equipment, electric; power transmission equipment
HQ: Regal Beloit America, Inc.
200 State St
Beloit WI 53511
608 364-8800

(P-13665)
REGENCY ENTERPRISES INC (PA)
Also Called: Regency Lighting
9261 Jordan Ave, Chatsworth (91311-5739)
PHONE......................818 901-0255
Ron Regenstreif, *CEO*
Scott Anderson, *President*
Isaac Regenstreif, *President*
Judah Regenstreif, *President*
Michael Goldstone, *COO*
◆ **EMP:** 272 **EST:** 1981
SALES (est): 150MM **Privately Held**
WEB: www.regencylighting.com
SIC: 5063 Light bulbs & related supplies

(P-13666)
ROS ELECTRICAL SUP EQP CO LLC
9529 Slauson Ave, Pico Rivera (90660-4749)
PHONE......................562 695-9000
John A Jauregui,
John Jauregui, *Sales Staff*
EMP: 20 **EST:** 2008
SALES (est): 1.9MM **Privately Held**
WEB: www.rps-powersystems.com
SIC: 5063 3699 Electrical supplies; electrical equipment & supplies

(P-13667)
SELECTA PRODUCTS INC (PA)
Also Called: Selecta Switch
1200 E Tehachapi Blvd, Tehachapi (93561-8129)
P.O. Box 888 (93581-0888)
PHONE......................661 823-7050
John Kenyon, *President*
Charles Kenyon, *Ch of Bd*
James Kenyon, *President*
Dorothy Kenyon, *Vice Pres*
Charlotte Tathwell, *Vice Pres*

▼ **EMP:** 60 **EST:** 1978
SQ FT: 20,000
SALES (est): 33MM **Privately Held**
WEB: www.selectainc.com
SIC: 5063 5065 Electrical supplies; electronic parts

(P-13668)
SOURCERY LLC
Also Called: Sourcery Wire
27051 Burbank, Foothill Ranch (92610-2505)
PHONE......................949 380-0466
Debbi Sullivan, *President*
Bre Sullivan, *Vice Pres*
Michael Johnston, *Sales Dir*
Jacob Brooks, *Sales Staff*
▲ **EMP:** 14 **EST:** 1983
SQ FT: 11,000
SALES (est): 16.2MM **Privately Held**
WEB: www.sourcery-llc.com
SIC: 5063 3357 Wire & cable; nonferrous wiredrawing & insulating

(P-13669)
SUNCO LIGHTING INC
27811 Hancock Pkwy Ste A, Valencia (91355-4187)
PHONE......................844 334-9938
Sorush Tahour, *CEO*
Salar Tahour, *Opers Staff*
Cyrus Talaiefar, *Cust Mgr*
Blake Farrell, *Director*
EMP: 46 **EST:** 2014
SALES (est): 60MM **Privately Held**
WEB: www.sunco.com
SIC: 5063 3699 Electrical supplies; electrical equipment & supplies

(P-13670)
THE SLOAN COMPANY INC (PA)
Also Called: Sloanled
5725 Olivas Park Dr, Ventura (93003-7697)
PHONE......................805 676-3200
Tom Beyer, *President*
Angela Davanzo, *CFO*
Jo Lamoreaux, *CFO*
Pete Todd, *Vice Pres*
John Wadsworth, *Executive*
◆ **EMP:** 118 **EST:** 1957
SQ FT: 25,545
SALES (est): 45.5MM **Privately Held**
WEB: www.sloanled.com
SIC: 5063 Lighting fixtures

(P-13671)
UNS ELECTRIC INC
6565 Valley View St, La Palma (90623-1060)
PHONE......................714 690-3660
Irene Mitchell, *Principal*
EMP: 24
SALES (corp-wide): 6.6B **Privately Held**
WEB: www.uesaz.com
SIC: 5063 3691 Storage batteries, industrial; storage batteries
HQ: Uns Electric, Inc.
88 E Broadway Blvd 901
Tucson AZ 85701
928 681-8966

(P-13672)
USHIO AMERICA INC (HQ)
5440 Cerritos Ave, Cypress (90630-4567)
PHONE......................714 236-8600
William Mackenzie, *CEO*
Shinji Kameda, *CFO*
Yuichi Asaka, *Principal*
AKO Williams, *Admin Sec*
Rez Motamed, *Info Tech Mgr*
◆ **EMP:** 90 **EST:** 1967
SQ FT: 70,000
SALES (est): 57.8MM **Privately Held**
WEB: www.ushio.com
SIC: 5063 Lighting fixtures, commercial & industrial

(P-13673)
VET NATIONAL INC
Also Called: Vet National Mail
3621 State St, Santa Barbara (93105-2521)
PHONE......................805 692-8487
Kevin Teel, *President*
Christopher Elsass, *Principal*
EMP: 20 **EST:** 1996

PRODUCTS & SVCS

SALES (est): 4.1MM **Privately Held**
WEB: www.vetnational.com
SIC: 5063 3088 3541 7331 Electrical apparatus & equipment; plastics plumbing fixtures; machine tools, metal cutting type; mailing service

(P-13674)
WALTERS WHOLESALE ELECTRIC CO (HQ)
18626 S Susana Rd, Compton (90221-5621)
PHONE...................................562 988-3100
John L Walter, *CEO*
Bill Durkee, *President*
Roland Wood, *CFO*
Andy Salz, *Vice Pres*
Cindy Lombardo, *Executive*
▼ EMP: 50 EST: 1953
SALES (est): 374.7MM
SALES (corp-wide): 1.4B **Privately Held**
WEB: www.walterswholesale.com
SIC: 5063 3699 1731 Wire & cable; electrical equipment & supplies; lighting contractor
PA: Consolidated Electrical Distributors, Inc.
1920 Westridge Dr
Irving TX 75038
972 582-5300

(P-13675)
WALTERS WHOLESALE ELECTRIC CO
425 W Rider St Ste C1, Perris (92571-3230)
PHONE...................................951 943-7708
EMP: 16
SALES (corp-wide): 1.4B **Privately Held**
WEB: www.walterswholesale.com
SIC: 5063 3699 1731 Wire & cable; electrical equipment & supplies; lighting contractor
HQ: Walters Wholesale Electric Co.
18626 S Susana Rd
Compton CA 90221
562 988-3100

(P-13676)
WALTON MOTORS & CONTROLS INC
1843 Floradale Ave, South El Monte (91733-3605)
PHONE...................................626 442-4610
Ray A Garcia, *President*
Andranik Avanesian, *Admin Sec*
EMP: 15 EST: 1977
SQ FT: 10,000
SALES (est): 5.7MM **Privately Held**
WEB: www.waltonmotors.com
SIC: 5063 7694 Motors, electric; rewinding stators

(P-13677)
WAMCO INC (PA)
17752 Fitch, Irvine (92614-6033)
PHONE...................................714 545-5560
Michael Matthews, *CEO*
Chris Matthews, *President*
Steve Dunkerken, *CFO*
Jean-Marc Lemaitre, *Vice Pres*
Eric Lemay, *Vice Pres*
▲ EMP: 19 EST: 1968
SQ FT: 30,000
SALES (est): 12.9MM **Privately Held**
WEB: www.wamcoinc.com
SIC: 5063 3647 5088 Electrical supplies; vehicular lighting equipment; transportation equipment & supplies

(P-13678)
WESTERN LIGHTING INDS INC
Also Called: Orgatech Omegalux
205 W Blueridge Ave, Orange (92865-4226)
PHONE...................................626 969-6820
Lawrence St Ives, *CEO*
Victor Ortiz, *Production*
Asha Narayan, *Accounts Mgr*
▲ EMP: 22 EST: 1983
SQ FT: 16,000
SALES (est): 5.2MM **Privately Held**
SIC: 5063 3646 Lighting fixtures; fluorescent lighting fixtures, commercial

(P-13679)
ZIPPY USA INC
Also Called: Kpower Sup McRswitch Inverters
1 Morgan, Irvine (92618-1917)
PHONE...................................949 366-9525
Chin W Chou, *President*
Chin S Tsai, *Treasurer*
Frank Lee, *Admin Mgr*
Jonathan Wang, *Project Mgr*
Stephanie Shih, *Sales Staff*
▲ EMP: 54 EST: 1996
SQ FT: 19,000
SALES (est): 11MM **Privately Held**
WEB: www.zippy.com
SIC: 5063 Motor controls, starters & relays: electric
PA: Zippy Technology Corp.
10f, No. 50, Minquan Rd.,
New Taipei City TAP 23141

5064 Electrical Appliances, TV & Radios Wholesale

(P-13680)
ALPINE ELECTRONICS AMERICA INC (HQ)
2150 195th St, Torrance (90501-1162)
PHONE...................................310 326-8000
Toshinori Kobayashi, *CEO*
Kanya Aoki, *President*
Isao Nagasako, *President*
Masanobu Takagi, *CFO*
Ed Moriarty, *Vice Pres*
◆ EMP: 200 EST: 1978
SALES (est): 278.2MM **Privately Held**
WEB: www.alpine-usa.com
SIC: 5064 3651 3679 Radios, motor vehicle; household audio & video equipment; harness assemblies for electronic use: wire or cable

(P-13681)
AUTOMATIC LEASING INC (PA)
Also Called: Alco Service
445 S Figueroa St, Los Angeles (90071-1602)
PHONE...................................213 746-4117
Peter Pierre III, *President*
Peter Pierre Sr, *Vice Pres*
Lorena Garcia, *Bookkeeper*
Regina Vasquez, *Consultant*
EMP: 439 EST: 1959
SQ FT: 13,000
SALES (est): 34.5MM **Privately Held**
SIC: 5064 7359 Electrical appliances, major; appliance rental

(P-13682)
AVA ENTERPRISES INC
Also Called: Boss Audio Systems
3451 Lunar Ct, Oxnard (93030-8976)
PHONE...................................805 988-0192
Soheil Rabbani, *President*
Kam Mobini, *Shareholder*
Sheila Rabbani, *Sales Pres*
◆ EMP: 50 EST: 1988
SQ FT: 70,000
SALES (est): 13MM **Privately Held**
WEB: www.bossaudio.com
SIC: 5064 Radios, motor vehicle

(P-13683)
DATABYTE TECHNOLOGY INC (PA)
2300 Peck Rd, City of Industry (90601-1601)
PHONE...................................626 305-0500
Lawrence Ho, *President*
Brian Yang, *Products*
▲ EMP: 20 EST: 1980
SQ FT: 32,000
SALES (est): 3.5MM **Privately Held**
SIC: 5064 3651 Electrical entertainment equipment; household audio equipment; household video equipment

(P-13684)
E & S INTERNATIONAL ENTPS INC (PA)
Also Called: Import Direct
7801 Hayvenhurst Ave, Van Nuys (91406-1712)
PHONE...................................818 887-0700
Philip Asherian, *CEO*
Farshad Asherian, *President*
Michael RAD, *COO*
Mike RAD, *COO*
Mark Barron, *CFO*
◆ EMP: 136 EST: 1983
SQ FT: 60,000
SALES (est): 80.2MM **Privately Held**
WEB: www.esintl.com
SIC: 5064 Electrical appliances, television & radio

(P-13685)
EPSILON ELECTRONICS INC (PA)
Also Called: Power Acoustik Electronics
1550 S Maple Ave, Montebello (90640-6508)
PHONE...................................323 722-3333
Jack Rochel, *President*
Mossa Rochel, *Vice Pres*
Hugo Sapetas, *Mktg Dir*
◆ EMP: 78 EST: 1983
SQ FT: 69,000
SALES (est): 21.6MM **Privately Held**
WEB: www.epsilonelectronicsinc.com
SIC: 5064 Electrical entertainment equipment

(P-13686)
FLW INC
5672 Bolsa Ave, Huntington Beach (92649-1113)
PHONE...................................714 751-7512
Andrew Peek, *President*
Dave Horacek, *Vice Pres*
Dave Washburn, *Vice Pres*
Jesse Toledo, *Engineer*
Brian Velt, *Sales Engr*
EMP: 55 EST: 2012
SALES (est): 13.9MM **Privately Held**
WEB: www.flw.com
SIC: 5064 Electrical appliances, major

(P-13687)
HARMAN-KARDON INCORPORATED
8500 Balboa Blvd, Northridge (91329-0003)
P.O. Box 2200 (91328-2200)
PHONE...................................818 841-4600
Tom McLoughlin, *President*
Chet Simon, *Senior VP*
John Schoeffler, *General Mgr*
Sydney Harman, *Director*
Bob Kilker, *Manager*
▲ EMP: 275 EST: 1949
SALES (est): 72.9K **Privately Held**
WEB: www.harman.com
SIC: 5064 3651 High fidelity equipment; household audio & video equipment
HQ: Harman International Industries Incorporated
400 Atlantic St
Stamford CT 06901
203 328-3500

(P-13688)
KING AUDIO INC
Also Called: Concept
152 S Brent Cir, Walnut (91789-3050)
PHONE...................................626 968-8827
Edward Liu, *President*
Calvin Liu, *Exec VP*
▲ EMP: 15 EST: 1994
SQ FT: 45,000
SALES (est): 2.5MM **Privately Held**
WEB: www.conceptbuy.com
SIC: 5064 3651 High fidelity equipment; speaker systems

(P-13689)
MEMOREX PRODUCTS INC
17777 Center Court Dr N # 80, Cerritos (90703-9320)
PHONE...................................562 653-2800
Michael Golacinski, *President*
Allan Yap, *Ch of Bd*

Kevin McDonnell, *CFO*
Mae Higa, *Admin Sec*
▲ EMP: 159 EST: 1993
SQ FT: 212,000
SALES (est): 4.6MM **Publicly Held**
WEB: www.glassbridge.com
SIC: 5064 5065 5045 3652 Electrical entertainment equipment; radio & television equipment & parts; computer peripheral equipment; pre-recorded records & tapes; household audio & video equipment
PA: Glassbridge Enterprises, Inc.
411 E 57th St Apt 1a
New York NY 10022

(P-13690)
NEW AIR LLC
Also Called: Newair
6600 Katella Ave, Cypress (90630-5104)
PHONE...................................657 257-4349
Luke Peters, *Mng Member*
Jen Danks, *Human Res Dir*
Mariella L Peters, *Manager*
Latoya Diamond, *Manager*
Leo KAO, *Manager*
EMP: 50 EST: 2016
SQ FT: 130,000
SALES (est): 31.5MM **Privately Held**
SIC: 5064 Air conditioning appliances

(P-13691)
PIONEER NORTH AMERICA INC (DH)
2050 W 190th St Ste 100, Torrance (90504-6229)
P.O. Box 1720, Long Beach (90801-1720)
PHONE...................................310 952-2000
Masao Kawabata, *CEO*
Kazunori Yamamoto, *President*
◆ EMP: 19 EST: 1978
SQ FT: 4,855
SALES (est): 450.8MM
SALES (corp-wide): 2.6MM **Privately Held**
WEB: www.pioneerelectronics.com
SIC: 5064 3651 High fidelity equipment; household audio & video equipment

(P-13692)
R & B WHOLESALE DISTRS INC (PA)
2350 S Milliken Ave, Ontario (91761-2332)
PHONE...................................909 230-5400
Robert O Burggraf, *President*
Shamsul Hyder, *CFO*
Masako Burggraf, *Vice Pres*
Sam Snyder, *Controller*
Doug Hebler, *Regl Sales Mgr*
◆ EMP: 75 EST: 1968
SQ FT: 72,000
SALES (est): 83.9MM **Privately Held**
WEB: www.rbdist.com
SIC: 5064 Electrical appliances, major; electrical entertainment equipment

(P-13693)
SAMSUNG ELECTRONICS AMER INC
5601 E Slauson Ave # 200, Commerce (90040-2953)
PHONE...................................323 374-6300
EMP: 274 **Privately Held**
WEB: www.samsung.com
SIC: 5064 Electrical appliances, television & radio
HQ: Samsung Electronics America, Inc.
85 Challenger Rd
Ridgefield Park NJ 07660
201 229-4000

(P-13694)
SAMSUNG ELECTRONICS AMER INC
18600 S Broadwick St, Rancho Dominguez (90220-6434)
PHONE...................................310 537-7000
K Hilm, *Manager*
Hasan Kazerani, *Regional Mgr*
Alexander Arnette, *Regl Sales Mgr*
James MO, *Sales Staff*
Michelle Quinn, *Manager*
EMP: 100 **Privately Held**
WEB: www.samsung.com

SIC: 5064 5065 Electrical appliances, television & radio; communication equipment
HQ: Samsung Electronics America, Inc.
85 Challenger Rd
Ridgefield Park NJ 07660
201 229-4000

(P-13695)
SONANCE
212 Avenida Fabricante, San Clemente (92672-7538)
PHONE..................................949 492-7777
James D Boswell, *CEO*
Tommy Rucci, *President*
Rob Roland, *General Mgr*
Erin Foote, *Executive Asst*
Janet Francis, *Executive Asst*
▲ EMP: 51 EST: 2007
SALES (est): 7.2MM **Privately Held**
WEB: www.sonance.com
SIC: 5064 Electrical entertainment equipment

(P-13696)
TV GUIDE ENTRMT GROUP LLC
2700 Colorado Ave Ste 200, Santa Monica (90404-5502)
PHONE..................................310 360-1441
EMP: 439 EST: 1998
SALES (est): 28.7MM
SALES (corp-wide): 25.3B **Publicly Held**
WEB: www.cbsinteractive.com
SIC: 5064 Electrical entertainment equipment
HQ: Cbs Interactive Inc.
235 2nd St
San Francisco CA 94105

5065 Electronic Parts & Eqpt Wholesale

(P-13697)
ADVANCED MNLYTHIC CERAMICS INC
Also Called: AMC
15191 Bledsoe St, Sylmar (91342-2710)
PHONE..................................818 364-9800
N Eric Johanson, *Ch of Bd*
Phu Luu, *President*
Steve Makl, *Principal*
Dan Jordan, *Project Mgr*
Richard Donovan, *Controller*
▲ EMP: 53 EST: 1994
SQ FT: 35,000
SALES (est): 10.4MM **Privately Held**
WEB: www.johansondielectrics.com
SIC: 5065 Electronic parts & equipment
HQ: Johanson Dielectrics, Inc.
4001 Calle Tecate
Camarillo CA 93012
805 389-1166

(P-13698)
ADVANCED MP TECHNOLOGY LLC (DH)
27271 Las Ramblas Ste 300, Mission Viejo (92691-8042)
PHONE..................................800 492-3113
Homayoun Shorooghi, *President*
Michele Anderson, *Vice Pres*
Stephanie Han, *Vice Pres*
Kelly Bessette, *Executive*
Alexander Romaniolis, *Executive*
◆ EMP: 126 EST: 1978
SALES (est): 101.4MM
SALES (corp-wide): 410.2MM **Privately Held**
WEB: www.a2globalelectronics.com
SIC: 5065 Electronic parts
HQ: America Ii Electronics, Llc
2600 118th Ave N
Saint Petersburg FL 33716
727 573-0900

(P-13699)
ALTURA COMM SOLUTIONS LLC (DH)
1540 S Lewis St, Anaheim (92805-6423)
PHONE..................................714 948-8400
Robert Blazek, *CEO*
David Key, *CFO*
John Herold, *Engineer*

Terry Sullivan, *Sales Executive*
Katherine Guarino, *Manager*
EMP: 55 EST: 2001
SQ FT: 25,000
SALES (est): 79.2MM **Privately Held**
WEB: www.alturacs.com
SIC: 5065 Electronic parts & equipment

(P-13700)
AMERICAN ZETTLER INC (HQ)
75 Columbia, Aliso Viejo (92656-4115)
PHONE..................................949 831-5000
Michael P Morgan, *President*
Rainer Moegling, *CFO*
Ricardo Anaya, *General Mgr*
Edward Edsinga, *Engineer*
▲ EMP: 50 EST: 1964
SQ FT: 63,000
SALES (est): 32.4MM **Privately Held**
WEB: www.azettler.com
SIC: 5065 Communication equipment

(P-13701)
AP GLOBAL INC
Also Called: Accessory Power
2326 Townsgate Rd, Westlake Village (91361-2501)
PHONE..................................818 707-3167
Robert Breines, *President*
Gail Breines, *Vice Pres*
Michael Fetchet, *Administration*
EMP: 60 EST: 2013
SALES (est): 9.8MM **Privately Held**
WEB: www.accessorypower.com
SIC: 5065 Electronic parts & equipment

(P-13702)
BAIT INC (PA)
2753 S Dmnd Bar Blvd B, Diamond Bar (91765-3542)
PHONE..................................909 595-1712
Eric Cheng, *CEO*
Chloe Lu, *Sales Associate*
Andrew Arcaina, *Marketing Staff*
EMP: 25 EST: 2011
SALES (est): 5.2MM **Privately Held**
WEB: www.baitme.com
SIC: 5065 2323 Mobile telephone equipment; telephone equipment; men's & boys' neckties & bow ties

(P-13703)
BRANDYWINE COMMUNICATIONS
1609 E Mcfadden Ave Ste B, Santa Ana (92705-4316)
PHONE..................................714 755-1050
Gary Smith, *President*
Tin MAI, *Engineer*
Kevin Garrod, *VP Mfg*
Steve Travis, *Sales Staff*
EMP: 57 **Privately Held**
WEB: www.brandywinecomm.com
SIC: 5065 5049 Telephone & telegraphic equipment; communication equipment; laboratory equipment, except medical or dental
PA: Brandywine Communications
1153 Warner Ave
Tustin CA 92780

(P-13704)
BRANDYWINE COMMUNICATIONS (PA)
1153 Warner Ave, Tustin (92780-6458)
PHONE..................................714 755-1050
Gareth H Smith, *Principal*
Kevin Garrod, *Vice Pres*
Alyona Diachenko, *Sales Staff*
◆ EMP: 13 EST: 1995
SQ FT: 7,200
SALES (est): 27.1MM **Privately Held**
WEB: www.brandywinecomm.com
SIC: 5065 3825 Telephone & telegraphic equipment; communication equipment; elapsed time meters, electronic

(P-13705)
BT AMERICAS INC
2160 E Grand Ave, El Segundo (90245-5024)
PHONE..................................646 487-7400
EMP: 100

SALES (corp-wide): 33.2B **Privately Held**
SIC: 5065 Whol Electronic Parts/Equipment
HQ: Bt Americas Inc.
8951 Cypress Waters Blvd # 200
Coppell TX 75019
877 272-0832

(P-13706)
BUYERS CONSULTATION SVC INC (PA)
Also Called: B C S
8735 Remmet Ave, Canoga Park (91304-1519)
P.O. Box 8427, Calabasas (91372-8427)
PHONE..................................818 341-4820
Jo Manhan, *President*
Mike Baker, *Vice Pres*
Steve Pazmany, *Vice Pres*
Jill Oldenburg, *Marketing Mgr*
Larry Manhan, *Manager*
▲ EMP: 75 EST: 1988
SQ FT: 40,000
SALES (est): 56.8MM **Privately Held**
WEB: www.scrapdr.com
SIC: 5065 7389 5093 4953 Electronic parts & equipment; auctioneers, fee basis; metal scrap & waste materials; recycling, waste materials

(P-13707)
CALRAD ELECTRONICS INC
819 N Highland Ave, Los Angeles (90038-3416)
PHONE..................................323 465-2131
Robert Shupper, *President*
Ana Garcia, *Sales Associate*
▲ EMP: 20 EST: 1939
SALES (est): 5.1MM **Privately Held**
WEB: www.calrad.com
SIC: 5065 5678 3663 3661 Electronic parts; electronic connectors; radio & TV communications equipment; telephone & telegraph apparatus

(P-13708)
CBOL CORPORATION
19850 Plummer St, Chatsworth (91311-5652)
PHONE..................................818 704-8200
Howard Nam, *COO*
Spencer H Kim, *CEO*
Kenneth Cheung, *CFO*
Lynn Turk, *Admin Sec*
Elizabeth Ahn, *Project Mgr*
◆ EMP: 131 EST: 1987
SQ FT: 69,820
SALES (est): 62.6MM **Privately Held**
WEB: www.cbol.com
SIC: 5065 5072 5013 5088 Electronic parts & equipment; hardware; staples; motor vehicle supplies & new parts; transportation equipment & supplies; industrial machinery & equipment; plastics materials & basic shapes

(P-13709)
CICOIL LLC
24960 Avenue Tibbitts, Valencia (91355-3426)
PHONE..................................661 295-1295
Howard Lind, *Mng Member*
Robert Newbrey, *Engineer*
Shelley Mears,
Johnathan Hinkley, *Director*
Giulie Styles, *Manager*
EMP: 90 EST: 1956
SQ FT: 16,000
SALES (est): 16.9MM **Privately Held**
WEB: www.cicoil.com
SIC: 5065 Electronic parts & equipment

(P-13710)
COMPART ENGINEERING INC (DH)
1730 E Philadelphia St, Ontario (91761-7705)
P.O. Box 4664, El Dorado Hills (95762-0022)
PHONE..................................909 947-6688
Sheung Sze Wong, *Chairman*
Rob Starr, *Exec VP*
◆ EMP: 84 EST: 1980
SALES (est): 20.5MM **Privately Held**
WEB: www.compartgroup.com
SIC: 5065 Electronic parts & equipment

(P-13711)
CONESYS INC (PA)
2280 W 208th St, Torrance (90501-1452)
PHONE..................................310 618-3737
Walter Neubauer Jr, *CEO*
John Vinke, *CFO*
Andres Murillo, *General Mgr*
Laurent Gonin, *Technology*
Odin Becerra, *Engineer*
EMP: 328 EST: 1993
SQ FT: 95,000
SALES (est): 106.7MM **Privately Held**
WEB: www.conesys.com
SIC: 5065 Electronic parts

(P-13712)
CORNER PRODUCTS COMPANY
Also Called: CP Technologies
15774 Gateway Cir, Tustin (92780-6469)
PHONE..................................949 231-5000
Rick Hsu, *CEO*
Carlos Tovar, *Production*
▲ EMP: 55 EST: 1984
SQ FT: 17,000
SALES (est): 22.7MM **Privately Held**
SIC: 5065 5045 Telephone equipment; computer peripheral equipment

(P-13713)
CYNERGY PROF SYSTEMS LLC
23187 La Cadena Dr # 102, Laguna Hills (92653-1481)
PHONE..................................800 776-7978
Cynthia Mason, *Mng Member*
Denton Browning, *Vice Pres*
Peter Durkin, *Executive*
Mark Perzi, *Executive*
Kevin McGann, *Opers Staff*
EMP: 30 EST: 2009
SALES (est): 75MM **Privately Held**
WEB: www.cynergy.pro
SIC: 5065 7379 3663 3661 Communication equipment; computer related maintenance services; computer related consulting services; radio & TV communications equipment; communication headgear, telephone

(P-13714)
DAVID LEVY CO INC
Also Called: Dlc
12753 Moore St, Cerritos (90703-2136)
PHONE..................................562 404-9998
David Levy, *CEO*
John Latino, *Vice Pres*
Gordon Schaer, *Admin Sec*
Raul Gomez, *Sales Staff*
▲ EMP: 50
SQ FT: 25,000
SALES (est): 14.7MM **Privately Held**
WEB: www.dlcparts.com
SIC: 5065 Electronic parts

(P-13715)
EACO CORPORATION (PA)
5065 E Hunter Ave, Anaheim (92807-6001)
PHONE..................................714 876-2490
Glen F Ceiley, *Ch of Bd*
Michael Narikawa,
Brian Stover, *Info Tech Dir*
Mason Milner, *Sales Staff*
EMP: 92 EST: 1973
SALES: 225.2MM **Publicly Held**
WEB: www.eacocorp.com
SIC: 5065 Electronic parts & equipment

(P-13716)
ELECTRONIC HARDWARE LIMITED (PA)
13257 Saticoy St, North Hollywood (91605-3486)
PHONE..................................818 982-6100
R E Vudrogivic, *CEO*
Richard Degn, *President*
EMP: 33 EST: 1973
SQ FT: 10,000
SALES (est): 9.2MM **Privately Held**
WEB: www.electronichardware.cloudflareaccess.com
SIC: 5065 5072 3541 Electronic parts; hardware; machine tools, metal cutting type

P R O D U C T S & S V C S

(P-13717)
ELROB INC
Also Called: El-Com Systems
12691 Monarch St, Garden Grove
(92841-3918)
PHONE..................714 230-6122
Elie Vrobel, *CEO*
Arik Vrobel, *President*
Dan Balentine, *Vice Pres*
Kevin Melstrom, *MIS Mgr*
Ken Chau, *Purch Agent*
▲ **EMP:** 54 **EST:** 1960
SQ FT: 38,500
SALES (est): 52.3MM **Privately Held**
WEB: www.el-comsystems.com
SIC: 5065 3679 3613 3643 Electronic
parts; harness assemblies for electronic
use: wire or cable; switchgear & switch-
board apparatus; current-carrying wiring
devices

(P-13718)
ENERPRO INC
99 Aero Camino, Goleta (93117-3822)
PHONE..................805 683-2114
Thomas Bourbeau, *President*
Frank J Bourbeau, *President*
Ilse Bourbeau, *Admin Sec*
Dana Ireland, *Enginr/R&D Asst*
Celina Gonzales, *Purch Agent*
◆ **EMP:** 25 **EST:** 1983
SQ FT: 27,000
SALES (est): 10MM **Privately Held**
WEB: www.enerpro-inc.com
SIC: 5065 3699 Electronic parts & equip-
ment; accelerating waveguide structures

(P-13719)
EURASIA POWER LLC
4022 Cmino Ranchero Ste D, Camarillo
(93012)
PHONE..................805 383-1234
Marilou Erb,
Bill Glynn, *Vice Pres*
Dan Erb,
▲ **EMP:** 50 **EST:** 2002
SALES (est): 14.7MM **Privately Held**
WEB: www.eurasiapower.com
SIC: 5065 Electronic parts & equipment

(P-13720)
**EVER WIN INTERNATIONAL
CORP**
17579 Railroad St, City of Industry
(91748-1125)
PHONE..................626 810-8218
Henry Chen, *President*
Christine Cheng, *CFO*
Jackson Chan, *Vice Pres*
Shyen Wang, *Vice Pres*
Bernard Chan, *Project Mgr*
▲ **EMP:** 50 **EST:** 1980
SQ FT: 90,000
SALES (est): 11.2MM **Privately Held**
WEB: www.everwin.com
SIC: 5065 Telephone & telegraphic equip-
ment

(P-13721)
**EVERFOCUS ELECTRONICS
CORP (HQ)**
324 W Blueridge Ave, Orange
(92865-4202)
PHONE..................626 844-8888
John Lee, *Ch of Bd*
Alan Ying, *President*
James Weng, *CEO*
Brian Chiu, *Info Tech Mgr*
Miguel Romero, *Technical Staff*
◆ **EMP:** 35 **EST:** 1996
SALES (est): 12.2MM **Privately Held**
WEB: www.everfocus.com
SIC: 5065 3699 Security control equip-
ment & systems; security control equip-
ment & systems

(P-13722)
FEDERAL CUSTOM CABLE LLC
1891 Alton Pkwy Ste A, Irvine
(92606-4985)
PHONE..................949 851-3114
Juliette Khamis,
Violet Kamis, *Human Res Mgr*
Jan Deckert, *Purch Agent*
ISA Kamis, *VP Sales*

Jabra Khamis, *Sales Mgr*
EMP: 50 **EST:** 1999
SALES (est): 9.8MM **Privately Held**
WEB: www.fccable.com
SIC: 5065 Electronic parts & equipment

(P-13723)
FRONTIER CALIFORNIA INC
112 S Lakeview Canyon Rd, Westlake Vil-
lage (91362-3925)
PHONE..................805 372-6000
Deb Anders, *President*
EMP: 381
SALES (corp-wide): 7.1B **Privately Held**
WEB: www.frontier.sale
SIC: 5065 4813 4812 Telephone equip-
ment; telephone communication, except
radio; radio telephone communication
HQ: Frontier California Inc.
401 Merritt 7
Norwalk CT 06851

(P-13724)
**GENERAL TRANSISTOR
CORPORATION (PA)**
Also Called: G T C
12449 Putnam St, Whittier (90602-1023)
PHONE..................310 578-7344
Albert A Barrios, *President*
Ilan Israely, *Vice Pres*
Jack Hobb, *Human Res Mgr*
EMP: 30 **EST:** 1976
SALES (est): 21.5MM **Privately Held**
WEB: www.gtcelectronics.com
SIC: 5065 3674 Semiconductor devices;
semiconductor circuit networks

(P-13725)
HEC INC
Also Called: Total Garments
30961 Agoura Rd Ste 311, Westlake Village
(91361-5607)
PHONE..................818 879-7414
Shaukat H Zaidi, *CEO*
Shamim Zaidi, *Vice Pres*
Mona Zaidi Simmons, *Marketing Staff*
EMP: 338 **EST:** 1996
SQ FT: 4,500
SALES (est): 23.5MM **Privately Held**
WEB: www.hoorayusa.com
SIC: 5065 Electronic parts

(P-13726)
HIRSCH ELECTRONICS LLC
1900 Carnegie Ave Ste B, Santa Ana
(92705-5557)
PHONE..................949 250-8888
John Picc, *Mng Member*
Manfred Mueller, *COO*
Robinr Braun, *Bd of Directors*
Ninab Shapiro, *Bd of Directors*
Diana Midland, *Info Tech Mgr*
EMP: 85 **EST:** 1981
SQ FT: 34,600
SALES (est): 17.4MM **Publicly Held**
WEB: www.identiv.com
SIC: 5065 Security control equipment &
systems
PA: Identiv, Inc.
2201 Walnut Ave Ste 100
Fremont CA 94538

(P-13727)
HYPERCEL CORPORATION
Also Called: Naztech
28385 Constellation Rd, Valencia
(91355-5048)
PHONE..................661 310-1000
David Nazar, *President*
Charles Rosenbach, *CFO*
Steve Legato, *Vice Pres*
Paula Nazar, *Vice Pres*
Sam Onda, *Vice Pres*
▲ **EMP:** 60 **EST:** 1995
SQ FT: 16,800
SALES (est): 13.7MM **Privately Held**
WEB: www.hypercel.com
SIC: 5999 5065 Mobile telephones &
equipment; mobile telephone equipment

(P-13728)
**I C CLASS COMPONENTS CORP
(PA)**
Also Called: Classic
23605 Telo Ave, Torrance (90505-4028)
PHONE..................310 539-5500
Jeffrey Klein, *President*
Chris Klein, *COO*
Kris Klein, *COO*
Emma Klein, *Treasurer*
Perry Klein, *Vice Pres*
▲ **EMP:** 100 **EST:** 1985
SQ FT: 53,000
SALES (est): 66.9MM **Privately Held**
WEB: www.class-ic.com
SIC: 5065 Electronic parts

(P-13729)
INDUCTORS INC
1740 W Collins Ave, Orange (92867-5423)
PHONE..................949 623-2460
Judy Macdonald, *CEO*
Albert Valentin, *Sales Staff*
▲ **EMP:** 50 **EST:** 1991
SALES (est): 16.3MM **Privately Held**
WEB: www.ctparts.com
SIC: 5065 Electronic parts

(P-13730)
INSULECTRO (PA)
20362 Windrow Dr Ste 100, Lake Forest
(92630-8140)
PHONE..................949 587-3200
Patrick Redfern, *CEO*
Brad Biddle, *CFO*
Chris Hunrath, *Vice Pres*
Kevin M Miller, *Vice Pres*
Kenneth Parent, *Vice Pres*
▲ **EMP:** 70 **EST:** 1991
SQ FT: 40,000
SALES (est): 121.2MM **Privately Held**
WEB: www.insulectro.com
SIC: 5065 Electronic parts

(P-13731)
INTELLIPOWER INC
Also Called: Ametek Intellipower
1746 N Saint Thomas Cir, Orange
(92865-4247)
PHONE..................714 921-1580
G W Bill Shipman, *CEO*
Dan Johnson, *CFO*
Rameshchandra Kathiriya, *Technician*
Paul Newman, *Project Mgr*
Thuy Tran, *Senior Buyer*
EMP: 100 **EST:** 1988
SQ FT: 22,000
SALES (est): 44MM
SALES (corp-wide): 4.5B **Publicly Held**
WEB: www.intellipower.com
SIC: 5065 Electronic parts & equipment
PA: Ametek, Inc.
1100 Cassatt Rd
Berwyn PA 19312
610 647-2121

(P-13732)
**INTERNTIONAL TECH SYSTEMS
CORP**
Also Called: Itsco
10721 Walker St, Cypress (90630-4720)
PHONE..................714 761-8886
Stanley Ning, *President*
Eric Lecesne, *Vice Pres*
Justin Ning, *Vice Pres*
Bill Rorick, *Vice Pres*
Jimmy MO, *Software Dev*
▲ **EMP:** 48 **EST:** 1985
SQ FT: 40,000
SALES (est): 21.6MM **Privately Held**
WEB: www.itsco.net
SIC: 5065 3578 Electronic parts & equip-
ment; point-of-sale devices

(P-13733)
**INTERSTATE ELECTRONICS
CORP**
707a E Vermont Ave, Anaheim
(92805-5612)
PHONE..................714 758-0500
Richard Paul, *Branch Mgr*
EMP: 71
SALES (corp-wide): 18.1B **Publicly Held**
SIC: 5065 Electronic parts

HQ: Interstate Electronics Corporation
602 E Vermont Ave
Anaheim CA 92805
714 758-0500

(P-13734)
JAE ELECTRONICS INC (HQ)
142 Technology Dr Ste 100, Irvine
(92618-2430)
PHONE..................949 753-2600
Noriyuki Konishi, *President*
Glen Griffin, *COO*
Shinjiro Ando, *Treasurer*
Nina Duong, *Officer*
Yasutoshi Ogino, *Senior VP*
◆ **EMP:** 36
SQ FT: 20,000
SALES: 154.5MM **Privately Held**
WEB: www.jaeusa.com
SIC: 5065 3679 3829 3678 Connectors,
electronic; electronic circuits; measuring
& controlling devices; electronic connec-
tors

(P-13735)
JEB HOLDINGS CORP (PA)
54125 Maranatha Dr, Idyllwild (92549)
P.O. Box 67 (92549-0067)
PHONE..................951 659-2183
Gordon Brown Sr, *CEO*
Joyce Brown, *Corp Secy*
Oscar Lehuede, *Engineer*
EMP: 75 **EST:** 1957
SQ FT: 80,000
SALES (est): 19.1MM **Privately Held**
WEB: www.southbaycable.com
SIC: 5065 Electronic parts

(P-13736)
JIT CORPORATION
Also Called: J I T Supply
2790 Valley View Ave, Norco (92860-2349)
PHONE..................805 238-5000
Brent Smith, *President*
Sharon Smith, *CFO*
Sheryl Knott, *Representative*
EMP: 60 **EST:** 1986
SQ FT: 30,000
SALES (est): 11MM **Privately Held**
WEB: www.jitmfg.com
SIC: 5065 Electronic parts

(P-13737)
JRI INC
Also Called: J R Industries
31280 La Baya Dr, Westlake Village
(91362-4005)
PHONE..................818 706-2424
Craig Pfefferman, *CEO*
Gary Becker, *Treasurer*
Mirian Handal, *Production*
▲ **EMP:** 50
SQ FT: 20,000
SALES (est): 20.8MM **Privately Held**
WEB: www.jri.com
SIC: 5065 3679 Electronic parts; harness
assemblies for electronic use: wire or
cable

(P-13738)
**JVCKENWOOD USA
CORPORATION (HQ)**
2201 E Dominguez St, Long Beach
(90810-1009)
P.O. Box 22745 (90801-5745)
PHONE..................310 639-9000
Kuhiro Aigami, *President*
Kazuhiro Aigami, *President*
Joseph Glassett, *CEO*
Dilip Patki, *CFO*
Craig Geiger, *Exec VP*
▲ **EMP:** 160 **EST:** 1961
SQ FT: 238,000
SALES (est): 152.5MM **Privately Held**
WEB: www.kenwood.com
SIC: 5065 Electronic parts & equipment

(P-13739)
JXP TECH INC
6950 Aragon Cir Ste 6, Buena Park
(90620-1163)
PHONE..................714 723-0696
Won Kun Kim, *President*
Moses Chae, *Manager*
EMP: 13 **EST:** 2016

SALES (est): 1.6MM Privately Held
WEB: www.jxptech.com
SIC: 5065 3612 Electronic parts; voltage regulators, transmission & distribution

(P-13740)
KOA ELECTRONICS DISTRIBUTION (PA)
Also Called: KOA Cctv
7306 Coldwater Canyon Ave, North Hollywood (91605-4220)
PHONE....................818 255-6666
Anton Tomassian, CEO
◆ EMP: 75 EST: 2010
SALES (est): 27.5MM Privately Held
WEB: www.koacctv.com
SIC: 5065 Security control equipment & systems

(P-13741)
LEGACY FRAMES
11220 Wright Rd, Lynwood (90262-3124)
PHONE....................310 537-4210
Angelica Serrano, CEO
EMP: 54 EST: 2013 Privately Held
SIC: 5065 Mobile telephone equipment

(P-13742)
LINKSYS LLC
120 Theory, Irvine (92617-3210)
PHONE....................408 526-4000
Ned Hooper, Branch Mgr
EMP: 175 Privately Held
WEB: www.linksys.com
SIC: 5065 Electronic parts & equipment
HQ: Linksys Llc
121 Theory
Irvine CA 92617
949 270-8500

(P-13743)
LINKSYS LLC
12045 Waterfront Dr, Playa Vista (90094-2999)
PHONE....................310 751-5100
Dang Nguyen, Manager
EMP: 175 Privately Held
WEB: www.linksys.com
SIC: 5065 Electronic parts & equipment
HQ: Linksys Llc
121 Theory
Irvine CA 92617
949 270-8500

(P-13744)
LINKSYS LLC (DH)
121 Theory, Irvine (92617-3209)
P.O. Box 91830, Los Angeles (90009-1830)
PHONE....................949 270-8500
Chet Pipkin, Mng Member
Gutti Fulij, Technology
Eric Lin, Engineer
Jin Choe, Finance
CHI-De Huang, Finance
◆ EMP: 275 EST: 1988
SQ FT: 20,000
SALES (est): 104.6MM Privately Held
WEB: www.linksys.com
SIC: 5065 Communication equipment
HQ: Belkin International, Inc.
12045 Waterfront Dr
Playa Vista CA 90094
310 751-5100

(P-13745)
LINKSYS USA INC
12045 Waterfront Dr, Playa Vista (90094-2999)
PHONE....................310 751-5100
Harry Dewhirst, CEO
EMP: 100 EST: 2018
SALES (est): 43.1MM Privately Held
WEB: www.belkin.com
SIC: 5065 Communication equipment
HQ: Belkin International, Inc.
12045 Waterfront Dr
Playa Vista CA 90094
310 751-5100

(P-13746)
LT SECURITY INC (PA)
Also Called: L T S
17333 Freedom Way, City of Industry (91748-1001)
PHONE....................626 435-2838
Grant Long, CEO

Carlo Yu, Vice Pres
Hector Chow, Executive
Tzu Ping Ho, Principal
Robert Lu, Branch Mgr
▲ EMP: 152 EST: 2008
SALES (est): 129.7MM Privately Held
WEB: www.ltsecurityinc.com
SIC: 5065 Security control equipment & systems

(P-13747)
LTS ASSOCIATE INC (PA)
17333 Freedom Way, City of Industry (91748-1001)
PHONE....................626 435-2838
Grant Long, CEO
Kai Yang, Co-CEO
Carlo Yu, Admin Sec
EMP: 50 EST: 2019
SALES (est): 12.5MM Privately Held
WEB: www.ltsecurityinc.com
SIC: 5065 Security control equipment & systems

(P-13748)
LYNX INNOVATION INC (PA)
500 Wald, Irvine (92618-4637)
P.O. Box 25406, Anaheim (92825-5406)
PHONE....................949 345-1847
Christopher Kurt McNall, CEO
Allen Auchenpaugh, President
Todd Black, Vice Pres
Vannin Gale, Vice Pres
Dan Breunig, Executive
▲ EMP: 127 EST: 2007
SALES (est): 33.4MM Privately Held
WEB: www.lynxinnovation.com
SIC: 5065 Electronic parts

(P-13749)
M WAVE DESIGN CORPORATION
82 W Cochran St Ste B, Simi Valley (93065-6214)
PHONE....................805 499-8825
Ken Boswell, CEO
Bonnie Murray, Admin Sec
EMP: 13 EST: 1989
SQ FT: 6,600
SALES (est): 2.7MM Privately Held
WEB: www.mwavedesign.com
SIC: 5065 3679 Electronic parts & equipment; microwave components

(P-13750)
MAURY MICROWAVE INC
2900 Inland Empire Blvd, Ontario (91764-4804)
PHONE....................909 987-4715
Michael Howo, CEO
Steve Dudkiewicz, Vice Pres
Jane Cary, General Mgr
Monica Amos, Admin Asst
Mark Posjena, Planning
▲ EMP: 115 EST: 1957
SQ FT: 6,000
SALES (est): 31.8MM Privately Held
WEB: www.maurymw.com
SIC: 5065 Electronic parts & equipment

(P-13751)
MITSUBISHI ELECTRIC US INC
7345 Orangewood Ave, Garden Grove (92841-1411)
PHONE....................714 934-5300
EMP: 60
SALES (corp-wide): 36.3B Privately Held
SIC: 5065 5045 Whol Industrial Electronic Equipment Semiconductors & Peripheral Equipment
HQ: Mitsubishi Electric Us, Inc.
5900 Katella Ave Ste A
Cypress CA 90630
714 220-2500

(P-13752)
MOTORS & CONTROLS WHSE INC
Also Called: Sabina Motors & Controls
1440 N Burton Pl, Anaheim (92806-1204)
PHONE....................714 956-0480
Vincent Tjelmeland, President
Andy Aragon, Sales Staff
◆ EMP: 29 EST: 1969
SQ FT: 35,000

SALES (est): 11.8MM Privately Held
WEB: www.sabinadrives.com
SIC: 5065 3621 Electronic parts; motors, electric

(P-13753)
MTROIZ INTERNATIONAL
150 S Kenmore Ave, Los Angeles (90004-5603)
PHONE....................661 998-8013
Eun H Chae, CEO
Stephen Banks, Vice Pres
Hong Chae, Vice Pres
EMP: 32 EST: 2011
SALES (est): 4.2MM Privately Held
WEB: www.mtroiz.com
SIC: 5065 2844 5023 5047 Communication equipment; toilet preparations; home furnishings; medical & hospital equipment; plastic containers, except foam; hobby, toy & game shops

(P-13754)
NALLATECH INC
741 Flynn Rd, Camarillo (93012-8056)
PHONE....................805 383-8997
Colin Rutherford, Chairman
Allan Cantle, President
William P Miller, CEO
Ed Hennessy, Vice Pres
EMP: 64 EST: 2008
SALES (est): 23.6MM
SALES (corp-wide): 36.9B Privately Held
WEB: www.bittware.com
SIC: 5065 Electronic parts & equipment
HQ: Interconnect Systems International, Llc
741 Flynn Rd
Camarillo CA 93012
805 482-2870

(P-13755)
NETSOURCE TECHNOLOGY INC
951 Calle Negocio Ste B, San Clemente (92673-6283)
PHONE....................949 713-0800
Gary B Munoz, President
Lisa Quijada, Office Mgr
Lisa Faria, Opers Mgr
Adrian Stapfer, Sales Staff
Kristin Wels, Director
▲ EMP: 15 EST: 1997
SQ FT: 6,300
SALES (est): 7.6MM Privately Held
WEB: www.nstechnology.com
SIC: 5065 3674 Electronic parts; capacitors, electronic; resistors, electronic; integrated circuits, semiconductor networks, etc.; computer logic modules; microcircuits, integrated (semiconductor)

(P-13756)
NORTH AMERICAN VIDEO CORP (PA)
Also Called: Navco Security Systems
1335 S Acacia Ave, Fullerton (92831-5315)
PHONE....................714 779-7499
Jason Oakley, CEO
Margaret Groves, Ch of Bd
William Groves, President
Debra L Berge, Treasurer
Debra Laberge, Treasurer
◆ EMP: 45 EST: 1975
SALES (est): 81.6MM Privately Held
WEB: www.navco.com
SIC: 5065 3812 Video equipment, electronic; security control equipment & systems; acceleration indicators & systems components, aerospace

(P-13757)
NOVACAP LLC
25111 Anza Dr, Valencia (91355-3478)
PHONE....................661 295-5920
Mark Skoog, CEO
Shelley Mears, Info Tech Mgr
Bob Nelson, Technician
Teri Servera, Human Res Dir
Rene Mendez, Production
▲ EMP: 280 EST: 1980
SQ FT: 38,000
SALES (est): 55.8MM
SALES (corp-wide): 764.3MM Publicly Held
WEB: www.knowlescapacitors.com
SIC: 5065 Electronic parts & equipment

PA: Knowles Corporation
1151 Maplewood Dr
Itasca IL 60143
630 250-5100

(P-13758)
NUCOURSE DISTRIBUTION INC
22342 Avenida Empresa # 200, Rcho STA Marg (92688-2140)
PHONE....................866 655-4366
Nicholas Troy Seedorf, CEO
Brandon Seedorf, Vice Pres
Ian Shiry, Finance
EMP: 55 EST: 2008
SALES (est): 89MM Privately Held
WEB: www.nucourse.com
SIC: 5065 Electronic parts & equipment

(P-13759)
ODU-USA INC (HQ)
300 Camarillo Ranch Rd A, Camarillo (93012-5208)
PHONE....................805 484-0540
Michael Savage, CEO
Joseph Cisi, President
Kurt Woefl, CEO
Joe Vigil, Business Mgr
▲ EMP: 58 EST: 1985
SQ FT: 20,000
SALES (est): 40MM
SALES (corp-wide): 139.8MM Privately Held
WEB: www.odu-usa.com
SIC: 5065 Connectors, electronic
PA: Odu Gmbh & Co. Kg
Pregelstr. 11
Muhldorf A. Inn BY 84453
863 161-560

(P-13760)
OMNITRON SYSTEMS TECH INC
38 Tesla, Irvine (92618-4603)
PHONE....................949 250-6510
Arie Goldberg, CEO
Heidi Cairns, Vice Pres
Paul Boettcher, Prdtn Mgr
Juan Castro, Sales Engr
Jake Edler, Marketing Staff
EMP: 75 EST: 1985
SQ FT: 15,000
SALES (est): 22.6MM Privately Held
WEB: www.omnitron-systems.com
SIC: 5065 Electronic parts & equipment

(P-13761)
P C A ELECTRONICS INC
16799 Schoenborn St, North Hills (91343-6194)
PHONE....................818 892-0761
Morris Weinberg, President
Benjamin Weinberg, Vice Pres
Ira Goldstein, Technology
Greg Barajas, Manager
Leticia Romo, Manager
EMP: 44 EST: 1949
SQ FT: 30,000
SALES (est): 9.4MM Privately Held
WEB: www.pca.com
SIC: 5065 3674 Electronic parts; semiconductors & related devices

(P-13762)
PERILLO INDUSTRIES INC
Also Called: Century Electronics
2150 Anchor Ct Ste A, Newbury Park (91320-1609)
PHONE....................805 498-9838
Mary Perillo, President
Nick Hayworth, Info Tech Mgr
Clint Wilder, Research
EMP: 50
SQ FT: 20,000
SALES (est): 23.4MM Privately Held
WEB: www.centuryelectronics.us
SIC: 5065 Electronic parts & equipment

(P-13763)
Q-TECH CORPORATION
6161 Chip Ave, Cypress (90630-5213)
PHONE....................310 836-7900
Sally Phillips, President
Rosa Menendez, Vice Pres
Richard Taylor, Executive
Minh Dao, Program Mgr
Basheer Remtulla, Program Mgr
EMP: 200 EST: 1972

PRODUCTS & SVCS

SALES (est): 57.1MM Privately Held
WEB: www.q-tech.com
SIC: 5065 Electronic parts & equipment

(P-13764)
QMADIX INC
9321 Eton Ave, Chatsworth (91311-5810)
PHONE..................818 988-4300
Ezra Soumekh, *CEO*
David Khalepari, *CEO*
Richard Mertz, *COO*
Heidi Dianaty, *CFO*
Joey Lasko, *Vice Pres*
◆ EMP: 51 EST: 2003
SALES (est): 14.5MM Privately Held
WEB: www.qmadix.com
SIC: 5065 Mobile telephone equipment

(P-13765)
QUEST COMPONENTS INC
14711 Clark Ave, City of Industry
(91745-1307)
PHONE..................626 333-5858
Dave A Hozen, *CEO*
Elaine Bowker, *CFO*
Andre A Hozen, *Treasurer*
Rich Harn, *CIO*
Alva Wurtz, *Sales Executive*
▲ EMP: 50 EST: 1995
SQ FT: 32,000
SALES (est): 27MM Privately Held
WEB: www.questcomp.com
SIC: 5065 Electronic parts

(P-13766)
QUINSTAR TECHNOLOGY INC
24085 Garnier St, Torrance (90505-5319)
PHONE..................310 320-1111
Leo Fong, *President*
John Kuno, *Exec VP*
Hj Kuno, *Vice Pres*
Naresh Deo, *VP Bus Dvlpt*
Tracy Lee, *Program Mgr*
▲ EMP: 72 EST: 1993
SALES (est): 37.8MM Privately Held
WEB: www.quinstar.com
SIC: 5065 Electronic parts & equipment

(P-13767)
RAND TECHNOLOGY LLC (PA)
15225 Alton Pkwy Unit 100, Irvine
(92618-2351)
PHONE..................949 255-5700
Andrea Klein, *CEO*
Paul Bockstedt, *President*
Tawnie Bassett-Parkin, *CFO*
Tawnie Bassett-Parkins, *Officer*
Andy Murphy, *Vice Pres*
EMP: 64 EST: 1992
SQ FT: 25,000
SALES (est): 147.5MM Privately Held
WEB: www.randtech.com
SIC: 5065 Semiconductor devices

(P-13768)
RANTEC POWER SYSTEMS INC (HQ)
1173 Los Olivos Ave, Los Osos
(93402-3230)
PHONE..................805 596-6000
Michael C Bickel, *President*
Frank Janku, *CFO*
Sean Odell, *Administration*
Sam Poland, *Technician*
Kevin Aban, *Engineer*
EMP: 97 EST: 1963
SQ FT: 40,000
SALES: 58MM
SALES (corp-wide): 62.3MM Privately Held
WEB: www.rantec.com
SIC: 5065 Electronic parts & equipment
PA: Rps Holdings, Inc.
1173 Los Olivos Ave
Los Osos CA 93402
805 596-6000

(P-13769)
RAYTHEON CMMAND CTRL SLTONS LL
2000 E El Segundo Blvd, El Segundo
(90245-4501)
PHONE..................714 446-3232
Ron Levesque, *Branch Mgr*
EMP: 50

SALES (corp-wide): 56.5B Publicly Held
SIC: 5065 Security control equipment & systems
HQ: Raytheon Command And Control Solutions Llc
1801 Hughes Dr
Fullerton CA 92833

(P-13770)
RAYTHEON CMMAND CTRL SLTONS LL (DH)
1801 Hughes Dr, Fullerton (92833-2200)
P.O. Box 34055 (92834-9455)
PHONE..................714 446-3118
Peter W Chiarelli,
Alex Cresswell,
Don Johnson,
▲ EMP: 700 EST: 2001
SALES (est): 281.8MM
SALES (corp-wide): 56.5B Publicly Held
WEB: www.rtx.com
SIC: 5065 Security control equipment & systems
HQ: Raytheon Company
870 Winter St
Waltham MA 02451
781 522-3000

(P-13771)
RECOM GROUP
449 Borrego Ct, San Dimas (91773-2971)
PHONE..................909 599-1370
Robert Norden, *CEO*
Jess Haro, *Office Mgr*
Lady R Norden, *Technical Staff*
◆ EMP: 28 EST: 1997
SALES (est): 9.8MM Privately Held
WEB: www.recomgroup.com
SIC: 5065 3679 5046 Electronic parts; liquid crystal displays (LCD); passive repeaters; store fixtures & display equipment

(P-13772)
SARCO INC
Also Called: 123ewireless
30412 Esperanza, Rcho STA Marg
(92688-2144)
PHONE..................949 888-5548
Ali Sar, *President*
Derren Versoza, *Engineer*
Claudia Hernandez, *Accounting Mgr*
Eleanor Jackson, *Human Res Mgr*
Mike Vela, *Production*
◆ EMP: 50 EST: 1998
SQ FT: 30,000
SALES (est): 15.7MM Privately Held
WEB: www.sarco.org
SIC: 5065 Electronic parts & equipment

(P-13773)
SDI LLC
Also Called: Systems Division
21 Morgan Ste 150, Irvine (92618-2086)
PHONE..................949 583-1001
John W Korbonski, *Mng Member*
Vic Klashorst, *Sales Staff*
John A Korbonski,
▲ EMP: 13 EST: 1981
SQ FT: 20,000
SALES (est): 4.3MM Privately Held
WEB: www.sdinetwork.com
SIC: 5065 3699 Electronic parts; electrical equipment & supplies

(P-13774)
SL POWER ELECTRONICS CORP (DH)
6050 King Dr Ste A, Ventura (93003-7176)
PHONE..................800 235-5929
Jim Taylor, *President*
Ken Owens, *CEO*
Adam J Fisk, *Vice Pres*
Steven Miller, *Vice Pres*
Tammy Matteson, *Executive Asst*
◆ EMP: 65 EST: 1978
SQ FT: 36,480
SALES (est): 162.8MM
SALES (corp-wide): 1.3B Publicly Held
WEB: www.slpower.com
SIC: 5065 Electronic parts & equipment
HQ: Handy & Harman
C/O Steel Partners
New York NY 10022
212 520-2300

(P-13775)
SPRINT COMMUNICATIONS CO LP
5381 W Centinela Ave, Los Angeles
(90045-2003)
PHONE..................310 216-9093
EMP: 222
SALES (corp-wide): 68.4B Publicly Held
SIC: 5065 4813 4812 Telephone & telegraphic equipment; local & long distance telephone communications; cellular telephone services
HQ: Sprint Communications Company L.P.
6391 Sprint Pkwy
Overland Park KS 66251
800 829-0965

(P-13776)
SPRINT COMMUNICATIONS CO LP
3580 Grand Oaks, Corona (92881-4656)
PHONE..................951 340-1924
EMP: 222
SALES (corp-wide): 68.4B Publicly Held
SIC: 5065 4813 4812 Telephone & telegraphic equipment; local & long distance telephone communications; cellular telephone services
HQ: Sprint Communications Company L.P.
6391 Sprint Pkwy
Overland Park KS 66251
800 829-0965

(P-13777)
SUPERIOR COMMUNICATIONS INC (PA)
Also Called: Puregear
5027 Irwindale Ave # 900, Irwindale
(91706-2187)
PHONE..................877 522-4727
Solomon Chen, *Ch of Bd*
Michael Cavanah, *Shareholder*
Jeffrey Banks, *President*
Mike Cavah, *President*
Mike Cost, *COO*
▲ EMP: 248 EST: 1991
SQ FT: 11,000
SALES: 746.4MM Privately Held
WEB: www.superiorcommunications.com
SIC: 5065 Communication equipment

(P-13778)
SWANN COMMUNICATIONS USA INC
12636 Clark St, Santa Fe Springs
(90670-3950)
PHONE..................562 777-2551
Michael Lucas, *CEO*
Jason Carrington, *CFO*
Ann Cook, *Human Res Dir*
Richard Villa, *Train & Dev Mgr*
Kane Chan, *Manager*
▲ EMP: 87 EST: 2000
SQ FT: 45,000
SALES (est): 30MM Privately Held
SIC: 5065 Video equipment, electronic

(P-13779)
TALLEY INC (PA)
Also Called: Talley & Associates
12976 Sandoval St, Santa Fe Springs
(90670-4061)
P.O. Box 3123 (90670-0123)
PHONE..................562 906-8000
John R Talley, *CEO*
Mark D Talley, *President*
Karen Frankenberg, *CFO*
George R Hulbert, *CFO*
Elizabeth J Talley, *Exec VP*
◆ EMP: 110 EST: 1968
SQ FT: 80,000
SALES (est): 93.1MM Privately Held
WEB: www.talleycom.com
SIC: 5065 Communication equipment

(P-13780)
TAPE SPECIALTY INC
Also Called: T S I
24831 Avenue Tibbitts, Valencia
(91355-3405)
PHONE..................661 702-9030
Steve Feldman, *President*
Irma Hernandez, *President*
Stu Feldman, *Vice Pres*
Peggy James, *Controller*

John Ancell, *Production*
▲ EMP: 28 EST: 1976
SQ FT: 19,000
SALES (est): 11.1MM Privately Held
WEB: www.tsidm.com
SIC: 5065 3652 7389 Magnetic recording tape; magnetic tape (audio): prerecorded; music & broadcasting services

(P-13781)
TECH SYSTEMS INC
7372 Walnut Ave Ste J, Buena Park
(90620-1718)
PHONE..................714 523-5404
Raymond Downs, *Manager*
Jerry Hayden, *Technician*
EMP: 356
SALES (corp-wide): 88.5MM Privately Held
WEB: www.techsystemsinc.com
SIC: 5065 Closed circuit television
PA: Tech Systems, Inc.
4942 Summer Oak Dr
Buford GA 30518
770 495-8700

(P-13782)
TINNOVATE LLC
6255 Providence Way, Eastvale
(92880-9635)
PHONE..................909 860-6900
Russel Johnston, *President*
Tara Dake, *Manager*
EMP: 50 EST: 2013
SALES (est): 4.2MM Privately Held
SIC: 5065 Electronic parts & equipment

(P-13783)
TRI-STAR ELECTRONICS INTL INC (HQ)
Also Called: Carlisle Interconnect
2201 Rosecrans Ave, El Segundo
(90245-4910)
PHONE..................310 536-0444
John Berlin, *President*
Amelia Murillo, *Vice Pres*
Shawn McLean, *Engineer*
Ken Raihala, *Engineer*
Victoria Harris, *Human Resources*
◆ EMP: 270 EST: 1975
SQ FT: 80,000
SALES (est): 89.7MM
SALES (est): 4.2B Publicly Held
WEB: www.carlisle.com
SIC: 5065 Electronic parts & equipment
PA: Carlisle Companies Incorporated
16430 N Scottsdale Rd
Scottsdale AZ 85254
480 781-5000

(P-13784)
UNION TECHNOLOGY CORP
718 Monterey Pass Rd, Monterey Park
(91754-3607)
PHONE..................323 266-6871
David I Chu, *CEO*
Lori Chu, *CFO*
Robert Boughrum, *Vice Pres*
John Yang, *Principal*
Robert H Boughrum, *VP Sls/Mktg*
◆ EMP: 50 EST: 1991
SQ FT: 21,800
SALES (est): 15MM Privately Held
WEB: www.uniontechcorp.com
SIC: 5065 3675 Electronic parts; electronic capacitors

(P-13785)
WENZLAU ENGINEERING INC
2950 E Harcourt St, Compton
(90221-5502)
PHONE..................310 604-3400
William D Wenzlau Jr, *CEO*
Theodore Amberman, *Engineer*
Henry Delgado, *Engineer*
Spencer Watson, *Financial Analy*
William Dellinger, *Prdtn Mgr*
◆ EMP: 64
SQ FT: 40,000
SALES (est): 24.2MM Privately Held
WEB: www.wenzlau.com
SIC: 5065 8711 5511 Electronic parts; consulting engineer; trucks, tractors & trailers: new & used

(P-13786)
XP POWER LLC
15641 Red Hill Ave # 100, Tustin
(92780-7323)
PHONE.............................714 597-7100
Martin Brabham, *Director*
TAC Pham, *Manager*
EMP: 56 **Privately Held**
WEB: www.xppower.com
SIC: 5065 Electronic parts & equipment
HQ: Xp Power Llc
990 Benecia Ave
Sunnyvale CA 94085

(P-13787)
YUNEEC USA INC
9227 Haven Ave Ste 210, Rancho Cuca-
monga (91730-5473)
P.O. Box 970, Pleasanton (94566-0970)
PHONE.............................855 284-8888
Mike Kahn, *CEO*
Ryan Borders, *COO*
Larry Liu, *CFO*
Min Fu, *Controller*
▲ **EMP:** 70 **EST:** 2013
SALES (est): 54MM **Privately Held**
WEB: www.us.yuneec.com
SIC: 5065 7629 Video equipment, elec-
tronic; electrical equipment repair serv-
ices
PA: Yuneec International Co., Limited
Rm D 10/F Billion Ctr Twr A
Kowloon Bay KLN

(P-13788)
ZETTLER COMPONENTS INC
(PA)
75 Columbia, Orange (92868)
PHONE.............................949 831-5000
Kurt Rexius, *General Mgr*
Scott Peavey, *Vice Pres*
▲ **EMP:** 250 **EST:** 1996
SQ FT: 27,000
SALES (est): 65.7MM **Privately Held**
WEB: www.zettler-group.com
SIC: 5065 3669 5087 Intercommunication
equipment, electronic; intercommunica-
tion systems, electric; firefighting equip-
ment

5072 Hardware Wholesale

(P-13789)
ADEPT FASTENERS INC (PA)
27949 Hancock Pkwy, Valencia
(91355-4116)
P.O. Box 579, Castaic (91310-0579)
PHONE.............................661 257-6600
Gary Young, *President*
Don List, *Vice Pres*
Martha Bermudez, *Business Dir*
Cheryl Odermatt, *Program Mgr*
Rose Gaona, *Administration*
EMP: 118 **EST:** 2001
SQ FT: 40,000
SALES (est): 65MM **Privately Held**
WEB: www.adeptfasteners.com
SIC: 5072 Miscellaneous fasteners

(P-13790)
ALLFAST FASTENING SYSTEMS
LLC
15200 Don Julian Rd, City of Industry
(91745-1098)
P.O. Box 3166 (91744-0166)
PHONE.............................626 968-9388
Thomas A Amato,
Jody Schoolcraft, *General Mgr*
Bradley Johnson, *Project Engr*
Paul Keller, *Engineer*
Regina Lewis, *Sales Staff*
◆ **EMP:** 58 **EST:** 1971
SALES (est): 40.7MM
SALES (corp-wide): 769.9MM **Publicly
Held**
WEB: www.trimascorp.com
SIC: 5072 Miscellaneous fasteners
PA: Trimas Corporation
38505 Woodward Ave # 200
Bloomfield Hills MI 48304
248 631-5450

(P-13791)
ALLIED INTERNATIONAL LLC
(PA)
28955 Avenue Sherman, Valencia
(91355-5446)
PHONE.............................818 364-2333
Timothy Florian, *CEO*
Melissa Berninger, *CFO*
Robert Esguerra, *Sales Mgr*
Geraldine Becker, *Sales Staff*
Nina Da Costa, *Manager*
▲ **EMP:** 49 **EST:** 1962
SQ FT: 106,000
SALES (est): 14.8MM **Privately Held**
WEB: www.alliedtools.com
SIC: 5072 3499 Hand tools; stabilizing
bars (cargo), metal

(P-13792)
ALLTRADE TOOLS LLC
6122 Katella Ave, Cypress (90630-5203)
PHONE.............................310 522-9008
Greg Livingston, *Mng Member*
Robert Ellis, *CFO*
Golden Huang, *Info Tech Dir*
Annie Fung, *Asst Treas*
Sue McNeese, *Human Res Mgr*
◆ **EMP:** 50
SQ FT: 140,000
SALES (est): 21.4MM **Privately Held**
WEB: www.alltradetools.com
SIC: 5072 Hand tools

(P-13793)
ALS GROUP INC
Also Called: Capri Tools
1788 W 2nd St, Pomona (91766-1206)
PHONE.............................909 622-7555
Anderson Cheung, *CEO*
▲ **EMP:** 25 **EST:** 2005
SALES (est): 10.3MM **Privately Held**
SIC: 5072 5084 3545 3546 Hand tools;
power tools & accessories; pneumatic
tools & equipment; precision measuring
tools; sockets (machine tool accessories);
power-driven handtools; wrenches, hand
tools

(P-13794)
AMERICAN KAL ENTERPRISES
INC (PA)
Also Called: Pro America Premium Tools
4265 Puente Ave, Baldwin Park
(91706-3420)
PHONE.............................626 338-7308
John Toshima, *President*
Mila Bierotte, *Admin Sec*
▲ **EMP:** 90 **EST:** 1966
SQ FT: 32,000
SALES (est): 24.3MM **Privately Held**
WEB: www.americankal.com
SIC: 5072 3546 3463 3462 Hand tools;
power-driven handtools; nonferrous forg-
ings; iron & steel forgings; hand & edge
tools

(P-13795)
ASSA ABLOY RSDENTIAL
GROUP INC (HQ)
Also Called: Emtek Products
12801 Schabarum Ave, Baldwin Park
(91706-6808)
PHONE.............................626 961-0413
Thomas Millar, *President*
Lucas Boselli, *CEO*
Brian Jackson, *Engineer*
Benjamin Sultze, *Director*
◆ **EMP:** 200 **EST:** 1979
SALES (est): 157.7MM
SALES (corp-wide): 10.1B **Privately Held**
WEB: www.emtek.com
SIC: 5072 Hardware
PA: Assa Abloy Ab
Klarabergsviadukten 90
Stockholm 111 6
850 648-500

(P-13796)
ASSA ABLOY RSDENTIAL
GROUP INC
600 Balwin Park Blvd, City of Industry
(91746)
PHONE.............................626 369-4718
Birk Sorennsen, *Manager*
Maty Expediter, *Admin Sec*

Birk Sorensen, *VP Mfg*
Jeremy Stoll, *Sales Staff*
EMP: 597
SALES (corp-wide): 10.1B **Privately Held**
WEB: www.emtek.com
SIC: 5072 Hardware
HQ: Assa Abloy Residential Group, Inc.
12801 Schabarum Ave
Baldwin Park CA 91706
626 961-0413

(P-13797)
B & B SPECIALTIES INC
G S Aerospace Division
4321 E La Palma Ave, Anaheim
(92807-1887)
PHONE.............................714 985-3075
Tom Rutan, *Manager*
EMP: 100
SALES (corp-wide): 22.6MM **Privately
Held**
WEB: www.bbspecialties.com
SIC: 5072 3429 Miscellaneous fasteners;
manufactured hardware (general)
PA: B & B Specialties, Inc.
4321 E La Palma Ave
Anaheim CA 92807
714 985-3000

(P-13798)
CAMSTAR INTERNATIONAL INC
939 W 9th St, Upland (91786-4543)
PHONE.............................909 931-2540
Bingqing LI, *President*
Monica Wise, *General Mgr*
Jason Jaime, *Sales Staff*
Bill Vigil, *Property Mgr*
▲ **EMP:** 75 **EST:** 2007
SQ FT: 1,500
SALES (est): 9.1MM **Privately Held**
WEB: www.camstarusa.com
SIC: 5072 Security devices, locks
PA: Yuxin Technology Company
Dayao Village
Weifang

(P-13799)
CHUAOLSON ENTERPRISES
INC
1274 N Grove St, Anaheim (92806-2113)
P.O. Box 1240, Placentia (92871-1240)
PHONE.............................714 630-4751
Terry Olson, *CEO*
John Chua, *CFO*
William Juan, *Project Mgr*
Anthony Flanigan, *Sales Mgr*
EMP: 22 **EST:** 1984
SQ FT: 11,785
SALES (est): 7MM **Privately Held**
SIC: 5072 3429 Builders' hardware; manu-
factured hardware (general)

(P-13800)
CLARENDON SPECIALTY FAS
INC
16761 Burke Ln, Huntington Beach
(92647-4560)
PHONE.............................714 842-2603
Michael Lang, *President*
Jeff Heywood, *Executive*
Matthew Blackburn, *Controller*
Larry Pointer, *Purchasing*
Simon Martin, *Opers Dir*
▲ **EMP:** 90 **EST:** 1985
SQ FT: 4,000
SALES (est): 23MM **Privately Held**
WEB: www.clarendonsf.com
SIC: 5072 3444 Miscellaneous fasteners;
sheet metalwork

(P-13801)
CORONA CLIPPER INC
Also Called: Corona Tools
22 West Temescal Canyon Rd # 102, Corona
(92883-4200)
PHONE.............................951 737-6515
Stephen J Erickson, *CEO*
Al Schulten, *CFO*
John Reisveck, *Exec VP*
Kevin Howe, *Info Tech Dir*
Armando Del Valle, *Marketing Staff*
◆ **EMP:** 70 **EST:** 1927
SQ FT: 85,000

SALES (est): 33.1MM
SALES (corp-wide): 26.9MM **Privately
Held**
WEB: www.coronatoolsusa.com
SIC: 5072 3524 Hand tools; lawn & gar-
den equipment
PA: Natt Tools Group Inc
460 Sherman Ave N
Hamilton ON L8L 8
905 549-7433

(P-13802)
CPO COMMERCE LLC
251 S Lake Ave Ste 400, Pasadena
(91101-3051)
PHONE.............................626 585-3600
Robert H Tolleson, *President*
Girisha Chandraraj, *COO*
Todd A Shelton, *CFO*
Robert J Kelderhouse, *Treasurer*
Eric A Blanchard, *Senior VP*
▼ **EMP:** 81 **EST:** 2003
SALES (est): 24.8MM **Privately Held**
WEB: www.cpooutlets.com
SIC: 5072 Power tools & accessories
HQ: Essendant Co.
1 Parkway North Blvd # 100
Deerfield IL 60015
847 627-7000

(P-13803)
DH CASTER INTERNATIONAL
INC
2260 S Haven Ave Ste C, Ontario
(91761-0740)
PHONE.............................909 930-6400
Mary Lyn Baker, *CEO*
Richard J Baker, *President*
Drissro Dominguez, *Bookkeeper*
Tony Garcia, *Manager*
Jim Sonsalla, *Manager*
▲ **EMP:** 18 **EST:** 1996
SQ FT: 10,000
SALES (est): 3.6MM **Privately Held**
WEB: www.dhcasters.com
SIC: 5072 3999 Hardware; atomizers; toi-
letry

(P-13804)
DONALD O SMITH COMPANY
Also Called: All American Fabricators
5420 S Santa Fe Ave, Vernon
(90058-3522)
PHONE.............................323 685-5011
John Landis, *President*
Scott Landis, *Corp Secy*
Hal Landis, *Vice Pres*
Alice Landis, *Director*
EMP: 14 **EST:** 1943
SQ FT: 10,000
SALES (est): 2.5MM **Privately Held**
SIC: 5072 3423 Hand tools; plumbers'
hand tools

(P-13805)
E B BRADLEY CO (PA)
5602 Bickett St, Vernon (90058-2826)
P.O. Box 58548, Los Angeles (90058-0548)
PHONE.............................323 585-9917
Don Lorey, *President*
Chris Burns, *CFO*
Scott Simons, *CFO*
Kathy Hernandez, *Credit Staff*
Ingrid Smith, *Analyst*
▲ **EMP:** 48 **EST:** 1946
SQ FT: 45,000
SALES (est): 85MM **Privately Held**
WEB: www.ebbradley.com
SIC: 5072 2452 Hardware; panels & sec-
tions, prefabricated, wood

(P-13806)
E B BRADLEY CO
10903 Vanowen St, North Hollywood
(91605-6408)
PHONE.............................800 533-3030
Earl Bertrand Bradley, *Branch Mgr*
Junaid Ahmed, *Analyst*
EMP: 20
SALES (corp-wide): 85MM **Privately
Held**
WEB: www.ebbradley.com
SIC: 5072 2452 Hardware; panels & sec-
tions, prefabricated, wood

PA: E. B. Bradley Co.
5602 Bickett St
Vernon CA 90058
323 585-9917

(P-13807)
G K TOOL CORP
Also Called: Kal Tool Co
4265 Puente Ave, Baldwin Park
(91706-3420)
PHONE............................626 338-7300
EMP: 90
SQ FT: 32,000
SALES (est): 8.6MM
SALES (corp-wide): 24.9MM **Privately Held**
SIC: 5072 Whol Hand Tools
PA: American Kal Enterprises, Inc.
4265 Puente Ave
Baldwin Park CA 91706
626 338-7308

(P-13808)
HAMPTON PRODUCTS INTL CORP (PA)
50 Icon, Foothill Ranch (92610-3000)
PHONE............................949 472-4256
Gregory Gluchowski Jr, President
Brian Millsap, Officer
Ted Arnold, Vice Pres
Jon Quan, Vice Pres
Caroline Gray, Executive
▲ EMP: 100 EST: 1971
SQ FT: 160,000
SALES (est): 105.8MM **Privately Held**
WEB: www.hamptonproducts.com
SIC: 5072 Hardware

(P-13809)
LEIGHT SALES CO INC
1611 S Catalina Ave L45, Redondo Beach
(90277-5255)
PHONE............................310 223-1000
Bryan Moskowitz, CEO
Helene Moskowitz, Corp Secy
Alan Moskowitz, Principal
▲ EMP: 60 EST: 1943
SQ FT: 60,000
SALES (est): 5.3MM **Privately Held**
SIC: 5072 Miscellaneous fasteners; hand tools

(P-13810)
LIBERTY HARDWARE MFG CORP
5555 Jurupa St, Ontario (91761-3606)
PHONE............................909 605-2300
Kevin Buckner, Branch Mgr
EMP: 51
SALES (corp-wide): 7.1B **Publicly Held**
WEB: www.libertyhardware.com
SIC: 5072 Hardware
HQ: Liberty Hardware Mfg. Corp.
140 Business Park Dr
Winston Salem NC 27107
336 769-4077

(P-13811)
MAKITA USA INC (HQ)
14930 Northam St, La Mirada
(90638-5753)
PHONE............................714 522-8088
Toru Nazawa, CEO
Yuhei Iwanaga, CFO
Richard Chapman, Exec VP
Eunice Han, Senior VP
Joe Blackwell, Vice Pres
◆ EMP: 250 EST: 1970
SQ FT: 130,000
SALES (est): 468.5MM **Privately Held**
WEB: www.makitatools.com
SIC: 5072 Power handtools; power tools & accessories

(P-13812)
MONROE MAGNUS LLC (PA)
Also Called: Magnus Caster-Pro
2805 Barranca Pkwy, Irvine (92606-5114)
PHONE............................714 771-2630
Richard Edward Verwayne, CEO
Christa Verwayne, Chief Mktg Ofcr
Johnathan Kuiler, Vice Pres
Paula Harrisberger, Engineer
Tony Alfano, Purch Mgr
▲ EMP: 16 EST: 1978
SQ FT: 10,000

SALES (est): 12.1MM **Privately Held**
WEB: www.monroeengineering.com
SIC: 5072 3562 Casters & glides; casters

(P-13813)
PBB INC
1311 E Philadelphia St, Ontario
(91761-5719)
PHONE............................909 923-6250
Jeff Wood, President
R C Kung, Vice Pres
▲ EMP: 20 EST: 1987
SQ FT: 30,000
SALES (est): 5.2MM **Privately Held**
WEB: www.pbbinc.com
SIC: 5072 3429 Builders' hardware; builders' hardware

(P-13814)
PENN ELCOM INC (HQ)
Also Called: Penn Elcom Hardware
7465 Lampson Ave, Garden Grove
(92841-2903)
PHONE............................714 230-6200
Philip John Stratford, CEO
Roger Willems, Chairman
Rasha Nivot, Executive Asst
Frank McCourt, VP Sales
Gerardo Fandino, Warehouse Mgr
◆ EMP: 35 EST: 1993
SQ FT: 28,000
SALES (est): 27MM **Privately Held**
SIC: 5072 3429 Hardware; manufactured hardware (general)

(P-13815)
PENN ENGINEERING COMPONENTS
29045 Avenue Penn, Valencia
(91355-5426)
PHONE............................818 503-1511
Robert Washburn, President
Jane Washburn, Corp Secy
Bill Down, Vice Pres
EMP: 20 EST: 1971
SQ FT: 10,500
SALES (est): 4MM **Privately Held**
WEB: www.pennengineering.com
SIC: 5072 3679 Hardware; microwave components

(P-13816)
PRIME-LINE PRODUCTS LLC (DH)
Also Called: Slide Go
26950 San Bernardino Ave, Redlands
(92374-5022)
PHONE............................909 887-8118
Ronald F Turk, President
Bryan Aernan, Vice Pres
Paul Entwisele, Vice Pres
Jeff Grande, Vice Pres
Howard Kauffman, Vice Pres
◆ EMP: 325 EST: 1978
SQ FT: 100,000
SALES (est): 90.7MM **Privately Held**
WEB: www.primeline.net
SIC: 5072 Builders' hardware
HQ: Great Star Tools Usa, Inc.
271 Mayhill St
Saddle Brook NJ 07663
201 562-1232

(P-13817)
SHAMROCK SUPPLY COMPANY INC (PA)
Also Called: Shamrock Companies, The
3366 E La Palma Ave, Anaheim
(92806-2814)
PHONE............................714 575-1800
John J O'Connor, Ch of Bd
Michael O'Connor, President
Christopher Navarro, General Mgr
Juan Ossa, Info Tech Dir
Tim Parus, Engineer
▲ EMP: 52 EST: 1975
SQ FT: 45,000
SALES (est): 51MM **Privately Held**
WEB: www.shamrocksupply.com
SIC: 5072 5084 3842 Hand tools; industrial machinery & equipment; personal safety equipment

(P-13818)
SOFFIETTI CO
236 W Orange Show, San Bernardino
(92408)
PHONE............................909 907-2277
EMP: 65 EST: 2009
SQ FT: 2,700
SALES (est): 200K **Privately Held**
SIC: 5072 5084 5511 Wholesales Hardware Wholesales Industrial Equipment Ret New/Used Automobiles

(P-13819)
TOMARCO CONTRACTOR SPC INC (PA)
Also Called: Tomarco Fastening Systems
14848 Northam St, La Mirada
(90638-5747)
PHONE............................714 523-1771
William Thompson, CEO
Keith Watkins, President
Dave Lewis, COO
Sterling Higdon, Vice Pres
Jennifer Ferguson, Admin Mgr
▲ EMP: 60 EST: 1977
SQ FT: 33,000
SALES (est): 50MM **Privately Held**
WEB: www.tomarco.com
SIC: 5072 Hand tools; power handtools; builders' hardware

(P-13820)
UNBRAKO LLC
11939 Woodruff Ave, Downey
(90241-5601)
PHONE............................310 817-2400
Gary Bains, CEO
Alvin Cacabelos, Principal
Sanjeev Kalra, Principal
Dinesh Kurl, Business Mgr
▲ EMP: 15 EST: 2012
SQ FT: 25,000 **Privately Held**
WEB: www.unbrako.com
SIC: 5072 3399 3429 Bolts, nuts & screws; miscellaneous fasteners; metal fasteners; metal fasteners

(P-13821)
WURTH LOUIS AND COMPANY (DH)
895 Columbia St, Brea (92821-2917)
P.O. Box 2253 (92822-2253)
PHONE............................714 529-1771
Vito Mancini, President
Tom Mauss, President
Ed McGraw, CFO
Steven Branham, Regional Mgr
Jeremy Mitchell, Branch Mgr
▲ EMP: 90 EST: 1975
SQ FT: 116,000
SALES (est): 87.7MM
SALES (corp-wide): 17B **Privately Held**
SIC: 5072 5198 Furniture hardware; stain

5074 Plumbing & Heating Splys Wholesale

(P-13822)
ANGELUS SHTMTL & PLBG SUP INC
1355 Carroll Ave, Los Angeles
(90026-5109)
PHONE............................323 221-4191
Leonard Coutin, President
Ronald S Coutin, Vice Pres
EMP: 13 EST: 1929
SALES (est): 2MM **Privately Held**
SIC: 5074 3444 Plumbing fittings & supplies; sheet metalwork

(P-13823)
ELMCO SALES INC (PA)
15070 Proctor Ave, City of Industry
(91746-3305)
P.O. Box 3787 (91744-0787)
PHONE............................626 855-4831
Donald E Morris, Ch of Bd
Kristin E Kahle, Corp Secy
Joe Joyce, Sales Associate
Ron Samuelson, Products
Jazmin Pelayo, Sales Staff
EMP: 90 EST: 1944
SQ FT: 49,650

SALES (est): 23.2MM **Privately Held**
WEB: www.elmcostewart.com
SIC: 5074 Plumbing fittings & supplies

(P-13824)
ELMCO/DUDDY INC (HQ)
Also Called: Elmco Stewart
15070 Proctor Ave, City of Industry
(91746-3305)
P.O. Box 3787 (91744-0787)
PHONE............................626 333-9942
Donald E Morris, CEO
Rondall Stewart, President
Randall Morris, Vice Pres
John Plowman, Controller
Mike Barry, Purch Agent
EMP: 50 EST: 1990
SQ FT: 49,650
SALES (est): 17MM
SALES (corp-wide): 23.2MM **Privately Held**
WEB: www.elmcostewart.com
SIC: 5074 Plumbers' brass goods & fittings
PA: Elmco Sales Inc.
15070 Proctor Ave
City Of Industry CA 91746
626 855-4831

(P-13825)
EPS CORPORATE HOLDINGS INC
1235 S Lewis St, Anaheim (92805-6429)
PHONE............................714 635-3131
Greg Boiko, Manager
David Naranjo, IT/INT Sup
Mark Rose, Manager
EMP: 60 **Privately Held**
SIC: 5074 1711 Plumbing fittings & supplies; plumbing contractors
HQ: Eps Corporate Holdings, Inc.
3100 Dnald Dglas Loop Hng
Santa Monica CA 90405

(P-13826)
EZ-FLO INTERNATIONAL INC (PA)
Also Called: Contractor Access
2750 E Mission Blvd, Ontario (91761-2909)
P.O. Box 51485 (91761-0085)
PHONE............................909 947-5256
Paul Wilson, President
Saleem A Lahlouh, Ch of Bd
Candace Barnard, COO
Kevin Wheeler, CFO
Armando Cesare, Exec VP
◆ EMP: 30 EST: 1980
SQ FT: 70,000
SALES (est): 103MM **Privately Held**
WEB: www.ez-flo.net
SIC: 5074 3432 Plumbing & hydronic heating supplies; plumbing fixture fittings & trim

(P-13827)
FERGUSON FIRE FABRICATION INC (DH)
Also Called: Pacific Fire Safety
2750 S Towne Ave, Pomona (91766-6205)
PHONE............................909 517-3085
Leo J Klein, President
Leo J Klein, President
Dave Keltner, CFO
Mike Karanovich, Oper Mgr
Ted Nelson, Manager
▲ EMP: 100 EST: 1987
SQ FT: 120,000
SALES (est): 232.9MM
SALES (corp-wide): 21.8B **Privately Held**
WEB: www.ferguson.com
SIC: 5074 5099 Plumbing fittings & supplies; safety equipment & supplies
HQ: Ferguson Enterprises, Llc
12500 Jefferson Ave
Newport News VA 23602
757 874-7795

(P-13828)
GEARY PACIFIC CORPORATION
Also Called: Geary Pacific Supply
16037 E Foothill Blvd, Irwindale
(91702-2813)
PHONE............................626 513-0273
EMP: 23

SALES (corp-wide): 130.7MM **Privately Held**
WEB: www.gearypacific.com
SIC: 5722 5074 3432 Gas household appliances; plumbing & hydronic heating supplies; plumbing fixture fittings & trim
PA: Geary Pacific Corporation
   1360 N Hancock St
   Anaheim CA 92807
   714 279-2950

(P-13829)
GREEN CONVERGENCE (PA)
Also Called: Sunpower By Green Convergence
28476 Westinghouse Pl, Valencia
(91355-0929)
PHONE..............................661 294-9495
Mark Clinton Figearo, *CEO*
Donald Schramm, *President*
Stacy Hitt, *CFO*
Pablo Padilla, *Department Mgr*
Susan Marks, *Admin Asst*
EMP: 56 **EST:** 2008
SQ FT: 6,000
SALES (est): 20MM **Privately Held**
WEB: www.greenconvergence.com
SIC: 5074 1711 2493 2621 Heating equipment & panels, solar; solar energy contractor; roofing board, unsaturated; roofing felt stock; building & roofing paper, felts & insulation siding; roofing & gutter work; roofing contractor; battery service & repair

(P-13830)
HARRINGTON INDUSTRIAL PLAS LLC (PA)
14480 Yorba Ave, Chino (91710-5766)
P.O. Box 5128 (91708-5128)
PHONE..............................909 597-8641
Eben Lenderking, *CEO*
Dave Abercrombie, *President*
Mike Tourtelot, *CFO*
James Kasprick, *Regional Mgr*
Bill Reilly, *Branch Mgr*
▼ **EMP:** 85 **EST:** 1959
SQ FT: 50,000
SALES (est): 600.6MM **Privately Held**
WEB: www.hipco.com
SIC: 5074 Pipes & fittings, plastic

(P-13831)
J HARRIS INDUS WTR TRTMNT INC (PA)
Also Called: Puretec Industrial Water
3151 Sturgis Rd, Oxnard (93030-8931)
PHONE..............................805 656-4411
James A Harris, *CEO*
Mike Coniglio, *Partner*
Ben Desantis, *CFO*
Rachel Eppenger, *Officer*
Cody George, *Engineer*
▲ **EMP:** 76 **EST:** 1986
SALES (est): 28.5MM **Privately Held**
WEB: www.puretecwater.com
SIC: 5999 5074 Water purification equipment; water purification equipment

(P-13832)
KEYLINE SALES INC
9768 Firestone Blvd, Downey
(90241-5510)
PHONE..............................562 904-3910
Richard Banner, *President*
Mike Powers, *Treasurer*
Alan Racal, *Division Mgr*
Alan Racalbuto, *Division Mgr*
Mike Fisk, *General Mgr*
EMP: 42 **EST:** 1974
SQ FT: 3,500
SALES (est): 9.7MM **Privately Held**
WEB: www.keylinesales.com
SIC: 5074 3822 Plumbing fittings & supplies; auto controls regulating residntl & coml environmt & applncs

(P-13833)
LARSEN SUPPLY CO (PA)
Also Called: Lasco
12055 Slauson Ave, Santa Fe Springs
(90670-2601)
PHONE..............................562 698-0731
John Palumbo, *CEO*
Ruth Larsen, *Shareholder*
Alan Holderness, *CFO*

Rella Bodinus, *Vice Pres*
Danny Pro, *Technology*
◆ **EMP:** 100 **EST:** 1930
SQ FT: 60,000
SALES (est): 33.5MM **Privately Held**
WEB: www.lasco.net
SIC: 5074 5075 Plumbing fittings & supplies; warm air heating & air conditioning

(P-13834)
MITTAL RAM
100 E Hillcrest Blvd, Inglewood
(90301-2415)
PHONE..............................310 769-6669
Ram Mittal, *Owner*
Lillian Mittal, *Principal*
EMP: 95 **EST:** 1989
SALES (est): 4.4MM **Privately Held**
SIC: 5074 Heating equipment & panels, solar

(P-13835)
PLUMBINGANDFIRE INC
Also Called: Allied Plumbing & Fire Supply
11120 Sherman Way, Sun Valley
(91352-4949)
PHONE..............................818 764-9800
Sevada Sarkisyan, *CEO*
EMP: 50 **EST:** 2018
SALES (est): 10.3MM **Privately Held**
SIC: 5074 Plumbing fittings & supplies

(P-13836)
RYAN HERCO PRODUCTS CORP (HQ)
Also Called: Ryan Herco Flow Solutions
3010 N San Fernando Blvd, Burbank
(91504-2524)
PHONE..............................818 841-1141
Randy Beckwith, *CEO*
David Guardia, *Vice Pres*
Ryan Briggs, *Administration*
Merlin Landaverde, *Administration*
Nestor Sosa, *Info Tech Dir*
◆ **EMP:** 60
SQ FT: 48,000
SALES (est): 165.4MM **Privately Held**
WEB: www.rhfs.com
SIC: 5074 5162 Pipes & fittings, plastic; plastics materials & basic shapes

(P-13837)
TA INDUSTRIES INC (HQ)
Also Called: Truaire
11130 Bloomfield Ave, Santa Fe Springs
(90670-4603)
P.O. Box 4448 (90670-1460)
PHONE..............................562 466-1000
Yongki Yi, *Principal*
Janice Kim, *CFO*
Elizabeth Yi, *Vice Pres*
Jamie Kwon, *Accounting Mgr*
▲ **EMP:** 63 **EST:** 1996
SQ FT: 86,000
SALES (est): 31.6MM
SALES (corp-wide): 419.2MM **Publicly Held**
WEB: www.truaire.com
SIC: 5074 5075 3567 Heating equipment (hydronic); air conditioning & ventilation equipment & supplies; heating units & devices, industrial: electric
PA: Csw Industrials, Inc.
   5420 Lyndon B Johnson Fwy
   Dallas TX 75240
   214 884-3777

(P-13838)
WATERSTONE LLC
Also Called: Waterstone Faucets
41180 Raintree Ct, Murrieta (92562-7020)
P.O. Box 1240, Temecula (92593-1240)
PHONE..............................951 304-0520
Christopher G Kuran, *Mng Member*
Steve Kliewer, *Vice Pres*
Debbie Culver, *Technical Staff*
Pam Donnelly, *Purchasing*
Paul Yandell, *VP Opers*
▲ **EMP:** 134
SQ FT: 42,000
SALES (est): 19MM **Privately Held**
WEB: www.waterstoneco.com
SIC: 5074 3432 Plumbing fittings & supplies; faucets & spigots, metal & plastic

---

5075 Heating & Air Conditioning Eqpt & Splys Wholesale

(P-13839)
AIR TREATMENT CORPORATION (PA)
640 N Puente St, Brea (92821-2830)
PHONE..............................909 869-7975
Mark Hartman, *Ch of Bd*
Craig Domagala, *President*
Deborah Hudson, *CFO*
Greg Blackfelner, *Vice Pres*
Dayna Jones, *Executive Asst*
▲ **EMP:** 65 **EST:** 1990
SQ FT: 45,000
SALES (est): 95.3MM **Privately Held**
WEB: www.airtreatment.com
SIC: 5075 Electrical heating equipment; air conditioning equipment, except room units

(P-13840)
ALLIED REFRIGERATION INC (PA)
2300 E 28th St, Signal Hill (90755-2180)
PHONE..............................562 595-5301
Robert Nichols, *Chairman*
Michael R Luther, *President*
Robert Nichols Jr, *CEO*
Michael Luther, *COO*
Navi Lyman, *CFO*
▲ **EMP:** 86 **EST:** 1934
SQ FT: 30,000
SALES (est): 69.7MM **Privately Held**
WEB: www.allied-refrig.com
SIC: 5075 5078 Air conditioning & ventilation equipment & supplies; refrigeration equipment & supplies

(P-13841)
ECO-AIR PRODUCTS INC
Also Called: Air Pure
17122 Marquardt Ave, Cerritos
(90703-1021)
PHONE..............................562 801-0133
Rick Casados, *President*
EMP: 14 **EST:** 1971
SALES (est): 7.9MM **Privately Held**
WEB: www.aafintl.com
SIC: 5075 3564 Air filters; filters, air: furnaces, air conditioning equipment, etc.
HQ: Flanders Corporation
   531 Flanders Filter Rd
   Washington NC 27889

(P-13842)
ESPECIAL T HVAC SHTMTL FTTNGS
1239 E Franklin Ave, Pomona
(91766-5450)
PHONE..............................909 869-9150
Gerardo Tavarez, *President*
Maria Tavarez, *Corp Secy*
Elizabeth Hernandez, *Accounts Exec*
▲ **EMP:** 30 **EST:** 2001
SQ FT: 12,000
SALES (est): 10.9MM **Privately Held**
WEB: www.especialt.com
SIC: 5075 3444 Air conditioning & ventilation equipment & supplies; sheet metalwork

(P-13843)
FLORENCE FILTER CORPORATION
530 W Manville St, Compton (90220-5587)
PHONE..............................310 637-1137
Adrian M Anhood, *CEO*
Erika A Anhood, *President*
Floriana A Anhood, *CEO*
Michael Kimmitt, *Senior Buyer*
Ryan Toso, *Buyer*
▲ **EMP:** 60 **EST:** 1971
SQ FT: 55,000
SALES (est): 21.9MM **Privately Held**
WEB: www.florencefilter.com
SIC: 5075 3564 5211 Air filters; filters, air: furnaces, air conditioning equipment, etc.; lumber & other building materials

(P-13844)
GEORGE T HALL CO INC (PA)
1605 E Gene Autry Way, Anaheim
(92805-6730)
P.O. Box 25269 (92825-5269)
PHONE..............................909 825-9751
Charles Niemann, *President*
Mike Howard, *Vice Pres*
Dina Johnson, *Vice Pres*
James Martin, *Vice Pres*
Paul Summerlin, *Branch Mgr*
▲ **EMP:** 30 **EST:** 1932
SQ FT: 15,000
SALES (est): 27.4MM **Privately Held**
WEB: www.georgethall.com
SIC: 5075 5085 3613 Warm air heating & air conditioning; industrial supplies; control panels, electric

(P-13845)
HEAT TRANSFER PDTS GROUP LLC
Also Called: Htpghnl
1933 S Vineyard Ave, Ontario
(91761-7747)
PHONE..............................909 786-3669
EMP: 121 **Privately Held**
WEB: www.htpg.com
SIC: 5075 Warm air heating & air conditioning
HQ: Heat Transfer Products Group, Llc
   3885 Crestwood Pkwy Nw # 50
   Duluth GA 30096

(P-13846)
HKF INC (PA)
Also Called: Therm Pacific
5983 Smithway St, Commerce
(90040-1607)
PHONE..............................323 225-1318
James P Hartfield, *President*
▲ **EMP:** 57 **EST:** 1990
SALES (est): 62.2MM **Privately Held**
SIC: 5075 3873 5064 3567 Warm air heating & air conditioning; watches, clocks, watchcases & parts; electrical appliances, television & radio; industrial furnaces & ovens; current-carrying wiring devices

(P-13847)
INJEN TECHNOLOGY COMPANY LTD
244 Pioneer Pl, Pomona (91768-3275)
PHONE..............................909 839-0706
Ron Delgado, *CEO*
Justin Oltz, *Exec VP*
Virginia Cardenas,
▲ **EMP:** 30 **EST:** 1998
SALES (est): 15.6MM **Privately Held**
WEB: www.injen.com
SIC: 5075 3714 Air filters; filters: oil, fuel & air, motor vehicle

(P-13848)
NORITZ AMERICA CORPORATION (HQ)
11160 Grace Ave, Fountain Valley
(92708-5436)
PHONE..............................714 433-2905
Hisashi Uryu, *CEO*
Toshiyuki Otaki, *CEO*
Chloe Zhan, *Administration*
Akie Kurakata, *Planning*
Bart Evans, *Sales Staff*
▲ **EMP:** 56 **EST:** 2001
SALES (est): 28MM **Privately Held**
WEB: www.noritz.com
SIC: 5075 Warm air heating equipment & supplies

(P-13849)
SNOW BALL TRADING COMPANY (PA)
Also Called: Snowball Trading
1352 S Diamond Bar Blvd B, Diamond Bar
(91765-5459)
PHONE..............................626 893-9415
Zhongping Yang, *CEO*
EMP: 51 **EST:** 2015
SALES (est): 297.1K **Privately Held**
SIC: 5075 Air conditioning & ventilation equipment & supplies

---

(PA)=Parent Co (HQ)=Headquarters (DH)=Div Headquarters
✪ = New Business established in last 2 years
   2022 Southern California Business
   Directory and Buyers Guide
   605

(P-13850)
ULTRAVIOLET DEVICES INC
26145 Technology Dr, Valencia
(91355-1138)
PHONE..................661 295-8140
Peter Veloz, *CEO*
David Veloz, *Shareholder*
Richard Hayes, *Vice Pres*
Ashish Mathur, *Vice Pres*
Lev Rotkop, *Vice Pres*
▲ EMP: 53 EST: 1992
SQ FT: 45,000
SALES (est): 20.2MM **Privately Held**
WEB: www.uvdi.com
SIC: 5075 5074 Air filters; water purification equipment

5078 Refrigeration Eqpt & Splys Wholesale

(P-13851)
BRIO WATER TECHNOLOGY INC
Also Called: Dtwusa
768 Turnbull Canyon Rd, Hacienda Heights
(91745-1401)
PHONE..................800 781-1680
Frank Melkonian, *CEO*
Arman Melkonian, *Vice Pres*
Harry Dtw, *Manager*
Michael Fructuoso, *Manager*
Harry Mesak, *Manager*
▲ EMP: 30 EST: 2013
SALES (est): 9.8MM **Privately Held**
WEB: www.briowt.com
SIC: 5078 3589 Drinking water coolers, mechanical; water filters & softeners, household type

(P-13852)
CUSTOM COOLER INC (HQ)
420 E Arrow Hwy, San Dimas
(91773-3340)
PHONE..................909 592-1111
Sangyup Steve Lee, *President*
Young G Kim, *Vice Pres*
Ray Tolcher, *Vice Pres*
▲ EMP: 79 EST: 2006
SALES (est): 25.1MM
SALES (corp-wide): 276.7MM **Privately Held**
WEB: www.customcooler.com
SIC: 5078 Refrigeration equipment & supplies
PA: Kps Global Llc
4201 N Beach St
Fort Worth TX 76137
817 281-5121

(P-13853)
MARKET FIXTURES UNLIMITED INC (PA)
13235 Woodruff Ave, Downey
(90242-5096)
PHONE..................562 803-5553
Randall Fitzpatrick, *President*
Eunice Fitzpatrick, *Corp Secy*
Gail Fitzpatrick, *Vice Pres*
EMP: 15 EST: 1959
SQ FT: 14,000
SALES (est): 7.6MM **Privately Held**
WEB: www.marketfixturesunlimited.net
SIC: 5078 3231 5046 Refrigeration equipment & supplies; doors, glass: made from purchased glass; restaurant equipment & supplies

(P-13854)
MYCOM NORTH AMERICA INC (PA)
19475 Gramercy Pl, Torrance
(90501-1134)
PHONE..................310 328-1362
Sumihiko Kaneko, *CEO*
Kenji Ohki, *President*
Toshiyuki Takanami, *Admin Sec*
◆ EMP: 20 EST: 1995
SQ FT: 35,000
SALES (est): 10.3MM **Privately Held**
SIC: 5078 3585 3563 Refrigeration equipment & supplies; refrigeration equipment, complete; air & gas compressors

(P-13855)
OMNITEAM INC
9300 Hall Rd, Downey (90241-5309)
PHONE..................562 923-9660
Kans Haasis Jr, *CEO*
Robert Davis, *Vice Pres*
Don Hyatt Sr, *Vice Pres*
Bob Davis, *General Mgr*
Karen Winder, *Cust Mgr*
EMP: 125 EST: 1999
SQ FT: 100,000
SALES (est): 40.4MM **Privately Held**
WEB: www.omniteaminc.com
SIC: 5078 Commercial refrigeration equipment

(P-13856)
REFRIGERATION HDWR SUP CORP
9021 Norris Ave, Sun Valley (91352-2618)
PHONE..................818 768-3636
EMP: 50
SALES (corp-wide): 24.7MM **Privately Held**
SIC: 5078 5722 3585 7699 Whol Refrig Equip/Supply Ret Household Appliances Mfg Refrig/Heat Equip Repair Services
PA: Refrigeration Hardware Supply Corporation
632 Foresight Cir
Grand Junction CO 81505
970 241-2800

5082 Construction & Mining Mach & Eqpt Wholesale

(P-13857)
CAMERON WEST COAST INC
Also Called: Cameron Surface Systems
4315 Yeager Way, Bakersfield
(93313-2018)
PHONE..................661 837-4980
Stefan Radwanski, *Principal*
▲ EMP: 90 EST: 1992
SQ FT: 48,000
SALES (est): 37.9MM **Publicly Held**
WEB: www.slb.com
SIC: 5082 1389 7353 Oil field equipment; oil field services; oil field equipment, rental or leasing
HQ: Cameron International Corporation
4646 W Sam Houston Pkwy N
Houston TX 77041

(P-13858)
EVERPAC
1499 Palmyrita Ave, Riverside
(92507-1600)
PHONE..................951 774-3274
William R Johnson Jr, *President*
EMP: 117 EST: 2002
SALES (est): 2.9MM
SALES (corp-wide): 47.3MM **Privately Held**
WEB: www.quinncompany.com
SIC: 5082 General construction machinery & equipment
PA: Johnson Machinery Co.
800 E La Cadena Dr
Riverside CA 92507
951 686-4560

(P-13859)
GAMA CONTRACTING SERVICES INC
1835 Floradale Ave, South El Monte
(91733-3605)
PHONE..................626 442-7200
Jose Sergio Duenas, *President*
Jose Duenas, *Exec Dir*
Fernando Pureco, *Project Mgr*
Juan Garcia, *Manager*
Mike Schatz, *Manager*
EMP: 140 EST: 2008
SALES (est): 19.3MM **Privately Held**
WEB: www.gamacsi.com
SIC: 5082 1795 8744 General construction machinery & equipment; wrecking & demolition work;

(P-13860)
GOTTSTEIN CONTRACTING CORP
4114 Armour Ave, Bakersfield
(93308-4509)
PHONE..................661 322-8934
Scott Gottstein, *Branch Mgr*
EMP: 60
SALES (corp-wide): 24.2MM **Privately Held**
WEB: www.gottsteincorporation.com
SIC: 5082 General construction machinery & equipment
PA: Gottstein Corporation
39 Elm Rd
Hazle Township PA 18202
570 454-7162

(P-13861)
HERCA TELECOMM SERVICES INC
Also Called: Herca Construction Services
18610 Beck St, Perris (92570-9185)
PHONE..................951 940-5941
Hector R Castellon, *President*
Tracy Hertel, *CFO*
Raul Castellon, *Opers Staff*
Alfredo Castellon, *Director*
Alfonso Catellon, *Director*
EMP: 56 EST: 2005
SQ FT: 67,900
SALES (est): 16.2MM **Privately Held**
WEB: www.hercatelecomm.com
SIC: 5082 1623 1731 3663 General construction machinery & equipment; communication line & transmission tower construction; general electrical contractor; antennas, transmitting & communications

(P-13862)
HULSEY CONTRACTING INC
1740 Howard Pl, Redlands (92373-8090)
PHONE..................951 549-3665
Roberto Hulsey, *CEO*
Manuel Hulsey,
EMP: 20 EST: 2012
SALES (est): 5.4MM **Privately Held**
WEB: www.hulseycontracting.com
SIC: 5082 2493 2851 General construction machinery & equipment; insulation & roofing material, reconstituted wood; polyurethane coatings

(P-13863)
JOHNSON MACHINERY CO (PA)
Also Called: Caterpillar Authorized Dealer
800 E La Cadena Dr, Riverside
(92507-8715)
P.O. Box 351 (92502-0351)
PHONE..................951 686-4560
William Johnson Jr, *President*
Kevin Kelly, *Exec VP*
Matt Merickel, *Exec VP*
Rebecca Palmer, *Accountant*
◆ EMP: 175 EST: 1940
SQ FT: 70,000
SALES (est): 47.3MM **Privately Held**
WEB: www.johnson-machinery.com
SIC: 5082 General construction machinery & equipment

(P-13864)
MALOOF NAMAN BUILDERS INC
Also Called: Heavy Civil - Gen Engrg Cnstr
9614 Cozycroft Ave, Chatsworth
(91311-5116)
PHONE..................818 775-0040
Omar G Maloof, *President*
EMP: 52 EST: 2009
SALES (est): 6MM **Privately Held**
SIC: 5082 3531 1629 8711 Road construction equipment; road construction & maintenance machinery; dams, waterways, docks & other marine construction; building construction consultant; general contractor, highway & street construction

(P-13865)
OAKCROFT ASSOCIATES INC (PA)
Also Called: American Roof Tools
750 Monterey Pass Rd, Monterey Park
(91754-3607)
P.O. Box 63309, Los Angeles (90063-0309)
PHONE..................323 261-5122
James D Yundt, *President*
Joellen Yundt, *Treasurer*
Julia Hannah, *Vice Pres*
James S Yundt, *Vice Pres*
Jonathan Yundt, *Vice Pres*
▲ EMP: 31 EST: 1950
SQ FT: 14,500
SALES (est): 13.8MM **Privately Held**
WEB: www.roofmaster.com
SIC: 5082 3531 5199 General construction machinery & equipment; roofing equipment; broom, mop & paint handles

(P-13866)
QUINN COMPANY
Also Called: Caterpillar Authorized Dealer
510 Pickerell Ave, Corcoran (93212)
P.O. Box 578 (93212-0578)
PHONE..................559 992-2193
Greg Thomas, *Manager*
Monte Baker, *Vice Pres*
Dennis Madden, *Sales Staff*
EMP: 70
SQ FT: 10,000
SALES (corp-wide): 378.6MM **Privately Held**
WEB: www.quinncompany.com
SIC: 5082 5083 5084 7353 General construction machinery & equipment; farm & garden machinery; industrial machinery & equipment; heavy construction equipment rental
HQ: Quinn Company
10006 Rose Hills Rd
City Of Industry CA 90601
562 463-4000

(P-13867)
QUINN COMPANY
13275 Golden State Rd, Sylmar
(91342-1129)
PHONE..................818 767-7171
EMP: 70
SALES (corp-wide): 378.6MM **Privately Held**
WEB: www.quinncompany.com
SIC: 5082 General construction machinery & equipment
HQ: Quinn Company
10006 Rose Hills Rd
City Of Industry CA 90601
562 463-4000

(P-13868)
QUINN COMPANY
Also Called: Caterpillar Authorized Dealer
2200 Pegasus Dr, Bakersfield
(93308-6801)
PHONE..................661 393-5800
Steve Eucce, *Branch Mgr*
Eliseo Contreras, *Branch Mgr*
Bill Craft, *Branch Mgr*
Mike Ford, *Branch Mgr*
Jane Stanley, *Administration*
EMP: 70
SALES (corp-wide): 378.6MM **Privately Held**
WEB: www.quinncompany.com
SIC: 5082 5083 5084 7353 General construction machinery & equipment; farm & garden machinery; industrial machinery & equipment; heavy construction equipment rental
HQ: Quinn Company
10006 Rose Hills Rd
City Of Industry CA 90601
562 463-4000

(P-13869)
QUINN COMPANY
Also Called: Caterpillar Authorized Dealer
801 Del Norte Blvd, Oxnard (93030-8966)
PHONE..................805 485-2171
Jay Ervine, *Branch Mgr*
William Buchanan, *Branch Mgr*
Jim Champany, *Branch Mgr*
Dave Vangrouw, *Technical Staff*
Coco McWade, *Marketing Staff*

EMP: 70
SALES (corp-wide): 378.6MM Privately Held
WEB: www.quinncompany.com
SIC: 5082 5083 5084 7353 General construction machinery & equipment; farm & garden machinery; industrial machinery & equipment; heavy construction equipment rental
HQ: Quinn Company
10006 Rose Hills Rd
City Of Industry CA 90601
562 463-4000

(P-13870)
QUINN COMPANY
Also Called: Caterpillar Authorized Dealer
1655 Carlotti Dr, Santa Maria (93454-1503)
PHONE...................................805 925-8611
Dan Hunt, Manager
Monty Baker, General Mgr
EMP: 70
SALES (corp-wide): 378.6MM Privately Held
WEB: www.quinncompany.com
SIC: 5082 5083 5084 7353 General construction machinery & equipment; farm & garden machinery; industrial machinery & equipment; heavy construction equipment rental
HQ: Quinn Company
10006 Rose Hills Rd
City Of Industry CA 90601
562 463-4000

(P-13871)
QUINN SHEPHERD MACHINERY
Also Called: Caterpillar Authorized Dealer
10006 Rose Hills Rd, City of Industry (90601-1702)
P.O. Box 226789, Los Angeles (90022-6789)
PHONE...................................562 463-6000
Blake Quinn, President
Jay Ervine, Vice Pres
Jake Lewis, Sales Staff
Jim Lorenzen, Master
Chris Erving, Manager
▲ EMP: 287 EST: 1924
SQ FT: 163,000
SALES (est): 99MM
SALES (corp-wide): 378.6MM Privately Held
WEB: www.quinncompany.com
SIC: 5082 5084 General construction machinery & equipment; excavating machinery & equipment; mining machinery & equipment, except petroleum; industrial machinery & equipment
PA: Quinn Group, Inc.
10006 Rose Hills Rd
City Of Industry CA 90601
562 463-4000

(P-13872)
THOMPCO INC
899 Mission Rock Rd, Santa Paula (93060-9800)
PHONE...................................805 933-8048
Dori Thompson, Principal
EMP: 27 EST: 2008
SALES (est): 3.2MM Privately Held
SIC: 5082 1389 Oil field equipment; oil & gas field services

(P-13873)
TOM MALLOY CORPORATION (PA)
Also Called: Trench Shoring Company
206 N Central Ave, Compton (90220-1463)
PHONE...................................310 327-5554
Thomas E Malloy, CEO
Kevin Malloy, President
Randy Payette, Branch Mgr
Sandy Leslie, Asst Controller
Al Scatpaticci, Sales Executive
▲ EMP: 50 EST: 1973
SALES (est): 45.9MM Privately Held
WEB: www.trenchshoring.com
SIC: 5082 7353 Construction & mining machinery; heavy construction equipment rental

(P-13874)
WHITE CAP CONSTRUCTION SUPPLY
1815 Ritchey St, Santa Ana (92705-5127)
PHONE...................................949 794-5300
Jack Karg, Principal
Kevin Burns, Branch Mgr
Michelle Debay, Credit Staff
Janet Deal, Human Res Mgr
Cathy Collier, Purchasing
EMP: 702 EST: 2013
SALES (est): 36.6MM
SALES (corp-wide): 6.7B Privately Held
WEB: www.whitecap.com
SIC: 5082 General construction machinery & equipment
HQ: White Cap Construction Supply, Inc.
3100 Cumberland Blvd Se # 1700
Atlanta GA 30339
404 879-7740

5083 Farm & Garden Mach & Eqpt Wholesale

(P-13875)
BECO DAIRY AUTOMATION INC
9955 9 1/4 Ave, Hanford (93230-4241)
PHONE...................................559 582-2566
Stan Brown, CEO
Pam Rego, Technology
Colby Bown, Human Resources
Jason Legassick, Sales Staff
◆ EMP: 14 EST: 1958
SQ FT: 22,000
SALES (est): 5.2MM Privately Held
WEB: www.becoknows.com
SIC: 5083 3556 Dairy machinery & equipment; food products machinery

(P-13876)
I BRANDS LLC
2617 N Sepulveda Blvd, Manhattan Beach (90266-2737)
PHONE...................................424 336-5216
Quentine Beningfield,
EMP: 140 EST: 2010
SALES (est): 8.7MM Privately Held
SIC: 5083 Agricultural machinery & equipment

(P-13877)
PARADISE GARDEN CENTER INC
7109 Dufferin Ave, Riverside (92504-5402)
PHONE...................................951 789-0386
Stephen Fessler, President
Patrick Sawhill, Admin Sec
EMP: 14 EST: 1990
SQ FT: 8,500
SALES (est): 7.2MM Privately Held
WEB: www.paradisegardencenterriverside.com
SIC: 5083 5992 5261 2879 Irrigation equipment; flowers, fresh; plants, potted; nurseries; soil conditioners; sodding contractor

(P-13878)
S A CAMP COMPANIES (PA)
17876 Zerker Rd, Bakersfield (93308-9221)
PHONE...................................661 399-4451
James S Camp, President
D M Hart, Vice Pres
Kurt Eilers, Sales Engr
Warren Richardson, Superintendent
EMP: 50 EST: 1932
SQ FT: 10,000
SALES (est): 21.8MM Privately Held
WEB: www.sacampcompanies.com
SIC: 5083 0191 6552 Agricultural machinery; general farms, primarily crop; subdividers & developers

(P-13879)
SPEARS MANUFACTURING CO (PA)
15853 Olden St, Sylmar (91342-1293)
P.O. Box 9203 (91392-9203)
PHONE...................................818 364-1611
Robert W Spears, CEO
Wayne Spears, President
Ken Ruggles, Treasurer

Michael Valasquez, Vice Pres
Mike Velasquez, Vice Pres
◆ EMP: 134 EST: 1970
SQ FT: 119,088
SALES (est): 1.3B Privately Held
WEB: www.spearsmanufacturing.com
SIC: 5083 3494 Irrigation equipment; valves & pipe fittings

5084 Industrial Mach & Eqpt Wholesale

(P-13880)
ACE HYDRAULIC SALES & SVC INC
2901 Gibson St, Bakersfield (93308-6107)
P.O. Box 5097 (93388-5097)
PHONE...................................661 327-0571
Gary Chambers, CEO
Claus Bjorneboe, Vice Pres
Pete Briones, Sales Mgr
EMP: 18 EST: 1976
SQ FT: 20,000
SALES (est): 6.3MM Privately Held
WEB: www.hydraulic-controls.com
SIC: 5084 7699 3561 Hydraulic systems equipment & supplies; hydraulic equipment repair; cylinders, pump

(P-13881)
AGGRESSIVE ENGINEERING CORP
1235 N Knollwood Cir, Anaheim (92801-1382)
PHONE...................................714 995-8313
John L Bridges, CEO
Daniel M Bridges, President
Rich Gilbert, IT Executive
Kathy Carter, Controller
EMP: 16
SQ FT: 23,000
SALES (est): 3.3MM Privately Held
WEB: www.aggrengr.com
SIC: 5084 3544 Industrial machine parts; special dies & tools

(P-13882)
AIRGAS SAFETY INC
2355 Workman Mill Rd, City of Industry (90601-1459)
PHONE...................................562 699-5239
Olaya Rivera, Branch Mgr
Arlene Fleenor,
EMP: 15
SALES (corp-wide): 102.6MM Privately Held
WEB: www.airgas.com
SIC: 5084 5085 3561 3841 Safety equipment; welding supplies; cylinders, pump; surgical & medical instruments
HQ: Airgas Safety, Inc.
2501 Green Ln
Levittown PA 19057

(P-13883)
ALLTEK COMPANY U S A INC
18281 Gothard St Ste 102, Huntington Beach (92648-1205)
PHONE...................................714 375-9785
Weishui W Zhang, President
Joline Yin, Vice Pres
John Zhang, Vice Pres
Linda Zhu, Vice Pres
Sean Wang, Analyst
EMP: 50 EST: 1990
SQ FT: 2,000
SALES (est): 16.9MM Privately Held
WEB: www.alltekusa.com
SIC: 5084 5065 Industrial machinery & equipment; semiconductor devices

(P-13884)
AMADA AMERICA INC (HQ)
7025 Firestone Blvd, Buena Park (90621-1869)
PHONE...................................714 739-2111
Mike Guarin, CEO
KOA Nakata, CFO
Pablo Cervantes, Vice Pres
Mike Guerin, Principal
Charles Wittig, Exec Dir
▲ EMP: 75 EST: 1971
SQ FT: 103,000

SALES (est): 185.2MM Privately Held
WEB: www.amada.com
SIC: 5084 6159 Metalworking machinery; machinery & equipment finance leasing

(P-13885)
AMADA NORTH AMERICA INC (HQ)
7025 Firestone Blvd, Buena Park (90621-1869)
PHONE...................................714 739-2111
Michael Guerin, Principal
◆ EMP: 269 EST: 1990
SALES (est): 16.7MM Privately Held
WEB: www.amada.com
SIC: 5084 Metalworking machinery

(P-13886)
AMPHENOL NELSON-DUNN TECH INC (HQ)
Also Called: Nelson Dunn
17707 Valley View Ave, Cerritos (90703-7004)
PHONE...................................714 249-7700
R Adam Norwitt, CEO
Kevin Dunn, President
Ron Evans, Sr Corp Ofcr
David Dodwell, Vice Pres
Chantani Nandwana, Accounts Mgr
EMP: 50 EST: 1959
SQ FT: 25,000
SALES (est): 20.6MM
SALES (corp-wide): 8.6B Publicly Held
WEB: www.amphenol-energy.com
SIC: 5084 Hydraulic systems equipment & supplies
PA: Amphenol Corporation
358 Hall Ave
Wallingford CT 06492
203 265-8900

(P-13887)
ANA TRADING CORP USA (DH)
3625 Del Amo Blvd Ste 300, Torrance (90503-1693)
PHONE...................................310 542-2500
Hideto Osada, President
Makoto Kajiwara, CFO
Brent Johnson, Treasurer
Boo Noriyuki Shibat, Vice Pres
Yasuhiro Ueno, General Mgr
◆ EMP: 55 EST: 1971
SQ FT: 11,000
SALES: 27.5MM Privately Held
WEB: www.anatu.com
SIC: 5084 5088 0173 0175 Industrial machine parts; aircraft & parts; walnut grove; prune orchard

(P-13888)
BARDEX CORPORATION (PA)
6338 Lindmar Dr, Goleta (93117-3112)
PHONE...................................805 964-7747
Thomas Miller, CEO
Kusnadhi Sidikpramana, CFO
Anita Elovitz, Admin Asst
Krystin Calvin, Administration
Corazon Salvador, Administration
◆ EMP: 61 EST: 1963
SQ FT: 80,000
SALES (est): 22.1MM Privately Held
WEB: www.bardex.com
SIC: 5084 Hydraulic systems equipment & supplies

(P-13889)
BC RENTALS LLC (HQ)
Also Called: Bc Traffic Specialist
638 W Southern Ave, Orange (92865-3219)
PHONE...................................714 974-1190
Robert Carson, President
Tom Harden, CFO
Rick Webb, General Mgr
Sally Carson, Admin Sec
Danny Ely, Project Mgr
▲ EMP: 78 EST: 1995
SQ FT: 3,000
SALES (est): 25.8MM Privately Held
WEB: www.bctraffic.com
SIC: 5084 5999 7359 Safety equipment; safety supplies & equipment; equipment rental & leasing

PRODUCTS & SVCS

PA: Infrastripe, Llc
11121 Carmel Commons Blvd
Charlotte NC 28226
704 936-0125

(P-13890)
BEJAC CORPORATION (PA)
569 S Van Buren St, Placentia
(92870-6613)
PHONE................714 528-6224
Ron Barlet, *President*
Kim Smith-Grime, *CFO*
Peggy Barlet, *Corp Secy*
Enrique Serrano, *Info Tech Mgr*
Nicki Potrykus, *Human Res Mgr*
▼ **EMP:** 66 **EST:** 1953
SQ FT: 2,000
SALES (est): 48.1MM **Privately Held**
WEB: www.bejac.com
SIC: 5084 7353 Industrial machinery &
equipment; heavy construction equipment
rental

(P-13891)
BLAKE H BROWN INC (DH)
Also Called: John Tillman Company
1300 W Artesia Blvd, Compton
(90220-5307)
P.O. Box 6257 (90224-6257)
PHONE................310 764-0110
Blake H Brown, *CEO*
Ella Taylor, *VP Admin*
▲ **EMP:** 100 **EST:** 1928
SQ FT: 25,000
SALES (est): 37.9MM
SALES (corp-wide): 13.4B **Privately Held**
WEB: www.jtillman.com
SIC: 5084 3842 3548 Safety equipment;
personal safety equipment; welding appa-
ratus

(P-13892)
BRILLIANT IMAGING GROUP INC
Also Called: Envision Computer Design
1206 John Reed Ct, City of Industry
(91745-2404)
P.O. Box 91053 (91715-1053)
PHONE................626 333-1868
Benjamin Chan, *President*
EMP: 13 **EST:** 1995
SALES (est): 599.2K **Privately Held**
SIC: 5084 2759 7389 Printing trades ma-
chinery, equipment & supplies; advertis-
ing literature: printing; trade show
arrangement

(P-13893)
CAL LIFT INC
13027 Crossroads Pkwy S, La Puente
(91746-3406)
PHONE................562 566-1400
Mark T Maechling, *CEO*
Michele Suire, *Executive*
Robert Bey, *VP Sales*
Brett Millette, *Manager*
EMP: 55 **EST:** 1964
SQ FT: 40,000
SALES: 208.7K **Privately Held**
WEB: www.cal-lift.com
SIC: 5084 7699 7359 Materials handling
machinery; industrial equipment services;
equipment rental & leasing

(P-13894)
CAL SOUTHERN PACKG EQP INC
Also Called: Scpe
4102 Valley Blvd, Walnut (91789-1404)
PHONE................909 598-3198
David Byrne, *President*
David Pagkalinawan, *Vice Pres*
Jose Rodela, *Technician*
EMP: 15 **EST:** 1994
SQ FT: 10,000
SALES (est): 5.9MM **Privately Held**
WEB: www.scpe.com
SIC: 5084 3565 Packaging machinery &
equipment; packaging machinery

(P-13895)
CALMATION INCORPORATED
2222 Shasta Way, Simi Valley
(93065-1831)
PHONE................805 520-2515
Dieter Reese, *President*

Andre Reese, *CFO*
Anita Reese, *Admin Sec*
Michael Moore, *Manager*
EMP: 23 **EST:** 1987
SQ FT: 11,000
SALES (est): 5.6MM **Privately Held**
WEB: www.calmation.com
SIC: 5084 3559 Conveyor systems; auto-
motive related machinery

(P-13896)
CDS MOVING EQUIPMENT INC (PA)
375 W Manville St, Rancho Dominguez
(90220-5617)
PHONE................310 631-1100
Allen J Sidor, *President*
Hector Buendia, *VP Bus Dvlpt*
Eric Paul, *Sales Staff*
Mike Dellenbach, *Manager*
Jerry Serrata, *Accounts Exec*
▲ **EMP:** 80 **EST:** 1981
SQ FT: 100,000
SALES (est): 47.8MM **Privately Held**
WEB: www.cds-usa.com
SIC: 5084 Materials handling machinery

(P-13897)
CUMMINS PACIFIC LLC
1105 S Greenwood Ave, Montebello
(90640-6003)
PHONE................323 728-8111
Susan Morales, *Manager*
EMP: 15
SALES (corp-wide): 19.8B **Publicly Held**
WEB: www.cummins.com
SIC: 5084 3519 Engines & parts, diesel;
internal combustion engines
HQ: Cummins Pacific, Llc
1939 Deere Ave
Irvine CA 92606

(P-13898)
DRILL COOL SYSTEMS INC (PA)
627 Williams St, Bakersfield (93305-5437)
PHONE................661 633-2665
Al Tom Champness, *CEO*
Tom Champness, *President*
▲ **EMP:** 19 **EST:** 1974
SQ FT: 10,000
SALES (est): 5.8MM **Privately Held**
WEB: www.drillcool.com
SIC: 5084 1389 3533 Industrial machin-
ery & equipment; oil field services; oil &
gas drilling rigs & equipment

(P-13899)
ELEVATOR EQUIPMENT CORPORATION (PA)
Also Called: Eeco
4035 Goodwin Ave, Los Angeles
(90039-1190)
P.O. Box 39714 (90039-0714)
PHONE................323 245-0147
Abe Salehpour, *CEO*
Abdul Mozayeni, *CFO*
Charlie Schisler, *Info Tech Mgr*
Don Brown, *Engineer*
Bill Payton, *Manager*
◆ **EMP:** 75 **EST:** 1944
SQ FT: 20,000
SALES (est): 35.9MM **Privately Held**
WEB: www.elevatorequipment.com
SIC: 5084 Elevators

(P-13900)
EQUIPMENT DEPOT INC
Also Called: Southern California Mtl Hdlg
12393 Slauson Ave, Whittier (90606-2824)
PHONE................562 949-1000
David Turner, *President*
Neil Jones, *Executive*
Jermaine Ratcliffe, *Technology*
Jim Nolan, *Manager*
EMP: 150 **Privately Held**
WEB: www.eqdepot.theonlinecatalog.com
SIC: 5084 Conveyor systems; materials
handling machinery
HQ: Equipment Depot, Inc.
16330 Air Center Blvd
Houston TX 77032
713 365-2530

(P-13901)
FARM PUMP & IRRIGATION CO INC (PA)
Also Called: F P I
535 N Shafter Ave, Shafter (93263-1900)
P.O. Box 1477 (93263-1477)
PHONE................661 589-6901
John Gargan, *CEO*
Kathy Gargan, *Corp Secy*
EMP: 60 **EST:** 1983
SQ FT: 4,000
SALES (est): 16.6MM **Privately Held**
WEB: www.farmpump.com
SIC: 5084 5083 Pumps & pumping equip-
ment; irrigation equipment

(P-13902)
FUELING AND SERVICE TECH INC
Also Called: Fastech
7050 Village Dr Ste D, Buena Park
(90621-2281)
PHONE................714 523-0194
M Dan McGill, *CEO*
Christine Hawley, *Vice Pres*
Glen Ragle, *Program Mgr*
Christine Awbrey, *General Mgr*
Stephen Thai, *Technician*
EMP: 75 **EST:** 1994
SQ FT: 15,000
SALES (est): 36.8MM **Privately Held**
WEB: www.fastechus.com
SIC: 5084 Petroleum industry machinery

(P-13903)
HARBOR DIESEL AND EQP INC
Also Called: Hd Industries
537 W Anaheim St, Long Beach
(90813-2895)
P.O. Box 21399 (90801-4399)
PHONE................562 591-5665
James V Zupanovich, *Ch of Bd*
Mike Zupanovich, *President*
David Hiveley, *CFO*
Thomas Weersing, *Vice Pres*
▲ **EMP:** 51 **EST:** 1971
SALES (est): 24.6MM **Privately Held**
WEB: www.gohdi.com
SIC: 5084 5531 7538 Engines & parts,
diesel; truck equipment & parts; diesel en-
gine repair: automotive

(P-13904)
IMPAX AUTOMATION LLC
2131 Saturn Ct, Bakersfield (93308-6828)
PHONE................661 391-8210
Tim McCorkle, *President*
Jerry Scarola, *Technician*
Casey Skidgel, *Analyst*
Anton Holty, *Mng Member*
EMP: 50 **EST:** 2008
SALES (est): 11.6MM **Privately Held**
WEB: www.impaxautomation.com
SIC: 5084 Industrial machinery & equip-
ment

(P-13905)
INDUSTRIAL DATA COMMUNICATIONS
Also Called: I D C
4000 Fruitvale Ave Ste 16, Bakersfield
(93308-5176)
P.O. Box 13155 (93389-3155)
PHONE................661 589-4477
Lisa Sanli, *CEO*
EMP: 22 **EST:** 1989
SALES (est): 1.8MM **Privately Held**
WEB: www.ese-corp.com
SIC: 5084 7371 3663 Measuring & testing
equipment, electrical; custom computer
programming services; digital encoders

(P-13906)
INDUSTRIAL PARTS DEPOT LLC (HQ)
Also Called: Ipd
23231 Normandie Ave, Torrance
(90501-5096)
PHONE................310 530-1900
Michael Badar, *President*
Richard Grishaber, *COO*
Brian Steffens, *Business Dir*
Janice Urmanita, *Area Spvr*
Mark Tu, *Data Proc Dir*
◆ **EMP:** 70 **EST:** 1955

SQ FT: 40,000
SALES (est): 21MM
SALES (corp-wide): 77.2MM **Privately Held**
WEB: www.ipdparts.com
SIC: 5084 3519 Engines & parts, diesel;
parts & accessories, internal combustion
engines
PA: Storm Industries, Inc.
23223 Normandie Ave
Torrance CA 90501
310 534-5232

(P-13907)
ISUZU NORTH AMERICA CORP (HQ)
1400 S Douglass Rd # 100, Anaheim
(92806-6906)
PHONE................714 935-9300
Masanori Katayama, *President*
Masatoshi Ito, *Principal*
Shinichi Takahashi, *Principal*
Richard Golding, *Technical Staff*
Sandy Holman, *Supervisor*
◆ **EMP:** 150 **EST:** 1975
SQ FT: 64,000
SALES (est): 560.5MM **Privately Held**
WEB: www.isuzutechcenter.com
SIC: 5511 5084 5013 5015 Automobiles,
new & used; engines & parts, diesel; au-
tomotive supplies & parts; motor vehicle
parts, used

(P-13908)
JWC ENVIRONMENTAL INC (DH)
Also Called: Windjmmer Capitl Investors III
2850 Redhill Ave Ste 125, Santa Ana
(92705-5541)
PHONE................949 833-3888
Ken Biele, *CEO*
Adriaan Van Der Beek, *President*
Joe Ruiz, *CFO*
Joseph Chambers, *Bd of Directors*
Norma Raistrick, *Executive Asst*
◆ **EMP:** 30 **EST:** 1989
SALES (est): 66.1MM
SALES (corp-wide): 3.6B **Privately Held**
WEB: www.jwce.com
SIC: 5084 3589 Industrial machinery &
equipment; commercial cleaning equip-
ment
HQ: Sulzer Management Ag
Neuwiesenstrasse 15
Winterthur ZH 8401
522 623-000

(P-13909)
KAFCO SALES COMPANY
2300 E 37th St, Vernon (90058-1405)
P.O. Box 58563, Los Angeles (90058-0563)
PHONE................323 588-7141
Akira Urakawa, *CEO*
▲ **EMP:** 26 **EST:** 1978
SQ FT: 15,500
SALES (est): 5.2MM **Privately Held**
WEB: www.kafcodemexico.com
SIC: 5084 3842 Safety equipment; surgi-
cal appliances & supplies

(P-13910)
KENTMASTER MFG CO INC (PA)
1801 S Mountain Ave, Monrovia
(91016-4270)
PHONE................626 359-8888
Ralph Karubian, *CEO*
▲ **EMP:** 50 **EST:** 1948
SQ FT: 50,000
SALES (est): 25MM **Privately Held**
WEB: www.kentmaster.com
SIC: 5084 Industrial machinery & equip-
ment

(P-13911)
KWL INDUSTRIAL COMPANY
Also Called: Microtronix Systems Co
17925 Metzler Ln, Huntington Beach
(92647-6258)
PHONE................714 847-3268
Yih-Shung Lee, *President*
MEI-Kuei Lee, *Vice Pres*
EMP: 23 **EST:** 1979
SQ FT: 10,000
SALES (est): 1.8MM **Privately Held**
SIC: 5084 3827 Industrial machinery &
equipment; optical instruments & lenses

(P-13912)
MACHINING TIME SAVERS INC
Also Called: Haas Factory Outlet
1338 S State College Pkwy, Anaheim
(92806-5241)
PHONE..............................714 635-7373
Donald Martin, *President*
EMP: 53 **EST:** 1985
SQ FT: 10,000
SALES (est): 18.2MM **Privately Held**
WEB: www.mtscnc.com
SIC: 5084 7699 Machine tools & accessories; industrial machinery & equipment repair

(P-13913)
MANUFACTURERS SERVICE INC
Also Called: M S I
9715 Klingerman St, South El Monte
(91733-1728)
PHONE..............................323 283-1013
Hiram W Allstun, *President*
Douglas Alston, *Vice Pres*
EMP: 26 **EST:** 1957
SQ FT: 8,000
SALES (est): 2.4MM **Privately Held**
WEB: www.manufacturersserviceinc.com
SIC: 5251 5084 3599 Tools; metal refining machinery & equipment; machine shop, jobbing & repair

(P-13914)
MATERIAL HANDLING SUPPLY INC (HQ)
12900 Firestone Blvd, Santa Fe Springs
(90670-5405)
PHONE..............................562 921-7715
Alexander Stephen Lynn, *CEO*
Donn C Lynn Jr, *Ch of Bd*
John Hanson, *Corp Secy*
Ben Miller, *Warehouse Mgr*
Steve Birdsall, *Director*
EMP: 80 **EST:** 1962
SQ FT: 85,000
SALES (est): 19MM **Privately Held**
WEB: www.mhs-ca.com
SIC: 5084 7629 5046 Food industry machinery; engines & transportation equipment; materials handling machinery; electrical repair shops; commercial equipment
PA: Envicor
12900 Firestone Blvd
Santa Fe Springs CA 90670
562 921-7715

(P-13915)
MAXON LIFT CORPORATION
11921 Slauson Ave, Santa Fe Springs
(90670-2221)
PHONE..............................562 464-0099
Casey Lugash, *President*
Brenda Leung, *CFO*
Anton Griessner, *Vice Pres*
Hakan Peterson, *Vice Pres*
Ted Raquet, *Vice Pres*
▲ **EMP:** 110 **EST:** 1957
SQ FT: 30,000
SALES (est): 62.7MM **Privately Held**
WEB: www.maxonlift.com
SIC: 5084 3537 3534 Lift trucks & parts; industrial trucks & tractors; elevators & moving stairways

(P-13916)
MCKINLEY EQUIPMENT CORPORATION (PA)
17611 Armstrong Ave, Irvine (92614-5760)
PHONE..............................800 770-6094
W Michael Mc Kinley, *President*
Kevin Rusin, *CFO*
William White Mc Kinley, *Vice Pres*
McKinley Mark, *General Mgr*
Marcus Crockett, *VP Sales*
▲ **EMP:** 50 **EST:** 1948
SQ FT: 12,000
SALES (est): 25.7MM **Privately Held**
WEB: www.mckinleyequipment.com
SIC: 5084 Materials handling machinery

(P-13917)
MENKE MARKING DEVICES INC
Also Called: Menke Marking Devices
10440 Pioneer Blvd Ste 4, Santa Fe
Springs (90670-5574)
P.O. Box 2986 (90670-0986)
PHONE..............................562 921-1380
Stephen Menke, *President*
David Powell, *Sales Staff*
EMP: 29 **EST:** 1943
SALES (est): 5.6MM **Privately Held**
WEB: www.menkemarking.com
SIC: 5084 3953 Industrial machinery & equipment; marking devices

(P-13918)
MIC
Also Called: Electrcal Instrmnttion Cntrls
2960 Pacini St, Bakersfield (93314-8796)
PHONE..............................661 401-0070
Robert Smith, *President*
EMP: 29 **EST:** 2012
SALES (est): 5.8MM **Privately Held**
SIC: 5084 1623 3825 3823 Industrial machinery & equipment; electric power line construction; instruments for measuring electrical quantities; industrial process measurement equipment; electric power systems contractors

(P-13919)
MIGHTY ENTERPRISES INC
Also Called: Mighty USA
19706 Normandie Ave, Torrance
(90502-1111)
PHONE..............................310 516-7478
Peter Th Tsai, *President*
Daniel Huang, *Vice Pres*
Gloria Zuniga, *Admin Sec*
Kelly Lee, *Accountant*
Alana Tsai, *Human Res Mgr*
▲ **EMP:** 55
SQ FT: 18,000
SALES (est): 23.4MM **Privately Held**
WEB: www.mightyviper.com
SIC: 5084 Machine tools & accessories

(P-13920)
MITSUBISHI MATERIALS USA CORP (HQ)
3535 Hyland Ave Ste 200, Costa Mesa
(92626-1456)
PHONE..............................714 352-6100
Motoharu Yamamoto, *CEO*
Niro Odani, *Treasurer*
Chris Brandt, *District Mgr*
Kevin Caldwell, *District Mgr*
Bruce Carter, *District Mgr*
◆ **EMP:** 50 **EST:** 1984
SQ FT: 55,000
SALES (est): 143.1MM **Privately Held**
WEB: www.mmus.com
SIC: 5511 5084 Automobiles, new & used; machine tools & accessories

(P-13921)
MURPHY-RODGERS INCORPORATED
1340 Valwood St, La Habra (90631-7252)
PHONE..............................714 525-2952
Otto E Seeman, *President*
Bill Hearne, *Vice Pres*
Norman R Murphy, *Vice Pres*
John Arellano, *Purchasing*
Deborah Hearne, *Manager*
EMP: 14 **EST:** 1972
SQ FT: 45,000
SALES (est): 1.3MM **Privately Held**
WEB: www.murphy-rodgers.com
SIC: 5084 3564 Industrial machinery & equipment; dust or fume collecting equipment, industrial

(P-13922)
MUTUAL LIQUID GAS & EQP CO INC (PA)
Also Called: Mutual Propane
17117 S Broadway, Gardena (90248-3191)
PHONE..............................310 515-0553
Melvin Moore, *CEO*
Steve Moore, *CEO*
Tom Boerum, *Info Tech Mgr*
Roger Wheeler, *Technical Mgr*
Mark Medina, *Programmer Anys*
EMP: 30

SQ FT: 3,100
SALES (est): 18.6MM **Privately Held**
WEB: www.mutualpropane.com
SIC: 5084 3549 Propane conversion equipment; metalworking machinery

(P-13923)
NORMONT HYDRAULIC SLS SVC INC
Also Called: International Fluid Power Amer
43123 Business Park Dr, Temecula
(92590-3628)
PHONE..............................951 676-2155
Denis Grierson, *CEO*
Patricia Turitz, *Bookkeeper*
Cassandra Grierson, *Marketing Staff*
▲ **EMP:** 15 **EST:** 1979
SALES (est): 4.2MM **Privately Held**
SIC: 5084 3594 Pumps & pumping equipment; pumps, hydraulic power transfer

(P-13924)
OLIVER HEALTHCARE PACKAGING CO
Also Called: Clean Cut Technologies
1145 N Ocean Cir, Anaheim (92806-1939)
PHONE..............................714 864-3500
Mike Benevento, *President*
EMP: 100
SALES (corp-wide): 1.8B **Privately Held**
WEB: www.oliverhcp.com
SIC: 5084 5199 3053 Processing & packaging equipment; packaging materials; packing materials
HQ: Oliver Healthcare Packaging Company
445 6th St Nw
Grand Rapids MI 49504
616 456-7711

(P-13925)
OTIS ELEVATOR COMPANY
2701 Media Center Dr # 2, Los Angeles
(90065-1700)
PHONE..............................323 342-4500
Marcus Burten, *Manager*
Gary Shandalov, *Regl Sales Mgr*
Aaron Harju, *Supervisor*
EMP: 50
SALES (corp-wide): 12.7B **Publicly Held**
WEB: www.otis.com
SIC: 5084 Elevators
HQ: Otis Elevator Company
341 Southport Cir Ste B
Virginia Beach VA 23452
860 676-6000

(P-13926)
OTIS ELEVATOR COMPANY
512 Paula Ave Ste A, Glendale
(91201-2363)
PHONE..............................818 241-2828
Sam Goe, *Branch Mgr*
EMP: 250
SQ FT: 15,000
SALES (corp-wide): 12.7B **Publicly Held**
WEB: www.otis.com
SIC: 5084 7699 Elevators; elevators: inspection, service & repair
HQ: Otis Elevator Company
341 Southport Cir Ste B
Virginia Beach VA 23452
860 676-6000

(P-13927)
PAPE MATERIAL HANDLING INC
2615 Pellissier Pl, City of Industry
(90601-1508)
PHONE..............................562 463-8000
Jordan Pape, *Branch Mgr*
EMP: 200 **Privately Held**
WEB: www.papemh.com
SIC: 5084 7699 7359 Lift trucks & parts; industrial machinery & equipment repair; industrial truck rental
HQ: Pape' Material Handling, Inc.
355 Goodpasture Island Rd
Eugene OR 97401

(P-13928)
POWELL WORKS INC
17807 Maclaren St Ste B, La Puente
(91744-5700)
PHONE..............................909 861-6699
Jerry Wang, *President*
▲ **EMP:** 256 **EST:** 2015

SQ FT: 2,500
SALES (est): 18.5MM **Privately Held**
SIC: 5084 Compressors, except air conditioning

(P-13929)
POWER GENERATION ENTPS INC
11411 Cumpston St Ste 104, North Hollywood (91601-2674)
PHONE..............................818 484-8550
Vartan Seropian, *CEO*
Victor Seropian, *Sales Staff*
EMP: 110 **EST:** 2014
SALES (est): 11.2MM **Privately Held**
WEB: www.powergenenterprises.com
SIC: 5084 Industrial machinery & equipment

(P-13930)
PRO SAFETY INC
20503 Belshaw Ave, Carson (90746-3505)
PHONE..............................562 364-7450
Catherina Zember, *President*
Jon Santa, *Opers Staff*
EMP: 148 **EST:** 2015
SQ FT: 88,000
SALES (est): 22.8MM **Privately Held**
WEB: www.airprotarservices.com
SIC: 5084 8331 Industrial machinery & equipment; job training & vocational rehabilitation services

(P-13931)
QUALLS STUD WELDING PDTS INC
9459 Washburn Rd, Downey (90242-2912)
PHONE..............................562 923-7883
Robert Butcher, *Branch Mgr*
EMP: 15
SALES (corp-wide): 8.7MM **Privately Held**
WEB: www.studweldprod.com
SIC: 5084 7692 1799 Welding machinery & equipment; welding repair; welding on site
PA: Quall's Stud Welding Products, Inc.
7820 S 210th St Ste C103
Kent WA 98032
425 656-9787

(P-13932)
R & J MATERIAL HANDLING INC
345 Adams Cir, Corona (92882-1896)
PHONE..............................951 735-0000
John Lessing Jr, *President*
Jason Lessing, *CFO*
Marie Johnson, *Office Admin*
Johnny Lessing, *Manager*
Nathan Flower, *Supervisor*
EMP: 19 **EST:** 2006
SQ FT: 14,100
SALES (est): 7.7MM **Privately Held**
WEB: www.rjforklift.com
SIC: 5084 7692 Materials handling machinery; welding repair

(P-13933)
RACK DEPOT INC
10226 Greenleaf Ave, Santa Fe Springs
(90670-3418)
PHONE..............................562 777-9809
Pedro Alvarez, *President*
EMP: 23 **EST:** 2006
SALES (est): 4.4MM **Privately Held**
WEB: www.rack-depot.com
SIC: 5084 2542 5046 5021 Materials handling machinery; pallet racks: except wood; shelving, commercial & industrial; shelving

(P-13934)
RAJYSAN INCORPORATED (PA)
Also Called: Mmd Equipment
4175 Guardian St, Simi Valley
(93063-3382)
P.O. Box 1360 (93062-1360)
PHONE..............................661 775-4920
Gurpreet Sahani, *President*
Amarjit S Sahani, *Ch of Bd*
Rajinder Sahani, *Admin Sec*
▲ **EMP:** 20 **EST:** 1984
SQ FT: 127,000

PRODUCTS & SVCS

SALES (est): 19.8MM **Privately Held**
WEB: www.rajysan.com
SIC: 5084 3715 Lift trucks & parts; truck trailers

(P-13935)
RAYMOND HANDLING SOLUTIONS INC (DH)
9939 Norwalk Blvd, Santa Fe Springs (90670-3321)
P.O. Box 3683 (90670-1683)
PHONE.................................562 944-8067
James Wilcox, *CEO*
Scott Stowers, *Exec VP*
James Thomas, *District Mgr*
Jessica Figueroa, *Administration*
Mike Bausley, *Info Tech Dir*
EMP: 190 EST: 2002
SQ FT: 5,000
SALES (est): 118.8MM **Privately Held**
WEB: www.raymondwest.com
SIC: 5084 7699 7359 Materials handling machinery; industrial machinery & equipment repair; industrial truck rental
HQ: The Raymond Corporation
22 S Canal St
Greene NY 13778
607 656-2311

(P-13936)
REBAS INC
Also Called: Toyota Material Hdlg Solutions
12907 Imperial Hwy, Santa Fe Springs (90670-4715)
PHONE.................................562 941-4155
Shankar Basu, *Ch of Bd*
Simon Walker, *COO*
Mark Clark, *Vice Pres*
Bo Hansson Holmquist, *Technology*
Chris Myers, *VP Finance*
▲ EMP: 104 EST: 1990
SQ FT: 103,000
SALES (est): 37.9MM **Privately Held**
WEB: www.toyotamhs.com
SIC: 5084 Materials handling machinery

(P-13937)
SAN JOAQUIN BIT SERVICE INC
2543 S Union Ave, Bakersfield (93307-5008)
P.O. Box 40186 (93384-0186)
PHONE.................................661 834-3233
Brad Peters, *Owner*
Todd Barksdale, *Manager*
Jason Mundorf, *Accounts Mgr*
EMP: 105 EST: 1979
SQ FT: 1,000
SALES (est): 10.4MM **Privately Held**
WEB: www.sanjoaquinbit.com
SIC: 5084 Drilling bits

(P-13938)
SHIP & SHORE ENVIRONMENTAL INC
2474 N Palm Dr, Signal Hill (90755-4007)
PHONE.................................562 997-0233
Anoosheh Mostafaei, *President*
Anu D Vij, *COO*
Joshua Obispo, *Admin Asst*
Mike Pawlowski, *Technical Staff*
Khosrow Shafiayane, *Project Engr*
▲ EMP: 38 EST: 2000
SQ FT: 4,000
SALES (est): 15MM **Privately Held**
WEB: www.shipandshore.com
SIC: 5084 3444 Pollution control equipment, air (environmental); awnings & canopies

(P-13939)
SOUTHERN CAL HYDRLIC ENGRG COR
Also Called: S C Hydraulic Engineering
1130 Columbia St, Brea (92821-2921)
PHONE.................................714 257-4800
Donna Perez, *President*
Manuel Perez, *Corp Secy*
David Vedder, *Vice Pres*
Gary Fisk, *Info Tech Mgr*
Christina Verbeek, *Controller*
EMP: 40 EST: 1953
SQ FT: 65,000
SALES (est): 11.3MM **Privately Held**
WEB: www.schydraulic.com
SIC: 5084 3594 Pumps & pumping equipment; pumps, hydraulic power transfer

(P-13940)
SPARLING INSTRUMENTS LLC
4097 Temple City Blvd, El Monte (91731-1046)
PHONE.................................626 444-0571
Yosufi Tyebkhan, *Mng Member*
Craig Hutcher, *Natl Sales Mgr*
Justine Harder, *Sales Staff*
▲ EMP: 25 EST: 1996
SQ FT: 56,000
SALES (est): 9.7MM **Privately Held**
WEB: www.sparlinginstruments.com
SIC: 5084 3824 3823 Industrial machinery & equipment; fluid meters & counting devices; industrial instrmnts msrmnt display/control process variable

(P-13941)
SPECIALIZED ELEVATOR SVCS LLC (PA)
14320 Iseli Rd, Santa Fe Springs (90670-5204)
PHONE.................................562 407-1200
Don Webster, *Mng Member*
Jeff Feltch, *CFO*
Barry Meacham, *Treasurer*
Robert Baehr, *Admin Sec*
Amanda Rubio, *Administration*
EMP: 97 EST: 2003
SQ FT: 6,000
SALES (est): 31.1MM **Privately Held**
WEB: www.specializedelevator.com
SIC: 5084 Elevators

(P-13942)
SSTMAS Y ARANDA EQPOS HDRLICOS
280 Campillo St Ste L, Calexico (92231-3200)
PHONE.................................619 245-4502
Armando Aranda, *President*
Carlos Verdugo, *Principal*
Roberto Pena, *Director*
EMP: 50
SALES (est): 15MM **Privately Held**
WEB: www.aranda.com.mx
SIC: 5084 Hydraulic systems equipment & supplies
PA: Aranda Sistemas Y Equipos Hidraulicos, S. De R.L. De C.V.
Jose Del Barco No. 3574, Int B
Mexicali B.C.

(P-13943)
STAINLESS STL FABRICATORS INC
Also Called: Cook King
15120 Desman Rd, La Mirada (90638-5737)
PHONE.................................714 739-9904
Craig Miller, *President*
Glenna Miller, *CFO*
Dave Hart, *Vice Pres*
Jim Schoff, *Sales Engr*
EMP: 60
SQ FT: 11,204
SALES (est): 23.4MM **Privately Held**
WEB: www.ssfab.net
SIC: 5084 3444 Industrial machinery & equipment; restaurant sheet metalwork

(P-13944)
STATCO ENGRG & FABRICATORS INC (PA)
Also Called: Interstate Mnroe McHy Sups Div
7595 Reynolds Cir, Huntington Beach (92647-6752)
PHONE.................................714 375-6300
Eric Perkins, *CEO*
Jack Jordan, *Vice Pres*
Gabriela Letendre, *Office Admin*
Tom Fletcher, *Info Tech Dir*
George Stumm, *Technical Staff*
EMP: 20 EST: 1982
SQ FT: 11,000
SALES (est): 98.4MM **Privately Held**
WEB: www.statco-dsi.com
SIC: 5084 3556 Processing & packaging equipment; food products machinery; meat, poultry & seafood processing machinery

(P-13945)
SUN RICH FOODS
1240 N Barsten Way, Anaheim (92806-1822)
PHONE.................................714 632-7577
Wally Barakat, *Owner*
CAM Haygarth, *Principal*
EMP: 13 EST: 2004
SQ FT: 10,635
SALES (est): 1.6MM **Privately Held**
WEB: www.sunrichfoods.com
SIC: 5084 3556 5149 Food product manufacturing machinery; dehydrating equipment, food processing; fruit peel

(P-13946)
SURFACE PUMPS INC (PA)
3301 Unicorn Rd, Bakersfield (93308-6852)
P.O. Box 5757 (93388-5757)
PHONE.................................661 393-1545
Steven J Durrett, *President*
Marty Rushing, *Corp Secy*
David Cook, *Vice Pres*
Steve Durrett, *Executive*
Carly Collins, *Human Resources*
EMP: 51 EST: 1970
SQ FT: 14,000
SALES (est): 22.5MM **Privately Held**
WEB: www.surfacepumps.com
SIC: 5084 7699 8711 3519 Pumps & pumping equipment; pumps & pumping equipment repair; engineering services; parts & accessories, internal combustion engines

(P-13947)
SVF FLOW CONTROLS INC
5595 Fresca Dr, La Palma (90623-1006)
PHONE.................................562 802-2255
Wayne Ulanski, *President*
Russell Stern, *Shareholder*
David Steel, *Ch of Bd*
Eduardo Garcia, *Admin Asst*
Erik Perez, *Engineer*
▲ EMP: 40 EST: 1993
SQ FT: 20,000 **Privately Held**
WEB: www.svf.net
SIC: 5084 3491 3494 5085 Instruments & control equipment; industrial valves; valves & pipe fittings; valves & fittings

(P-13948)
THIRKETTLE CORPORATION (PA)
Also Called: Utiliuse
4050 Flat Rock Dr, Riverside (92505-5858)
PHONE.................................951 637-1400
Chris Thirkettle, *President*
Lea Thirkettle, *Vice Pres*
Michael Wood, *Technology*
Todd Madrid, *Sales Mgr*
Steve Kamiyama, *Sales Staff*
EMP: 64 EST: 1993
SQ FT: 9,000
SALES (est): 10.2MM **Privately Held**
WEB: www.aqua-metric.com
SIC: 5084 Meters, consumption registering

(P-13949)
TK ELEVATOR CORPORATION
10955 Matthews Dr, Tustin (92782-3304)
PHONE.................................714 423-6340
Ashleigh Hauer, *Branch Mgr*
EMP: 53
SALES (corp-wide): 1B **Privately Held**
WEB: www.tkelevator.com
SIC: 5084 Elevators
HQ: Tk Elevator Corporation
11605 Haynes Bridge Rd
Alpharetta GA 30009
678 319-3240

(P-13950)
TK ELEVATOR CORPORATION
6048 Triangle Dr, Commerce (90040-3641)
PHONE.................................323 278-2801
Scott Silitsky, *Principal*
EMP: 53
SALES (corp-wide): 1B **Privately Held**
WEB: www.tkelevator.com
SIC: 5084 Elevators
HQ: Tk Elevator Corporation
11605 Haynes Bridge Rd
Alpharetta GA 30009
678 319-3240

(P-13951)
TK ELEVATOR CORPORATION
2850 N California St, Burbank (91504-2560)
PHONE.................................8 8 847-2568
Christina Siebold, *Manager*
Bob Saylor, *Superintendent*
EMP: 53
SALES (corp-wide): 1B **Privately Held**
WEB: www.tkelevator.com
SIC: 5084 Elevators
HQ: Tk Elevator Corporation
11605 Haynes Bridge Rd
Alpharetta GA 30009
678 319-3240

(P-13952)
TK ELEVATOR CORPORATION
1601 S Sunkist St Ste A, Anaheim (92806-5812)
PHONE.................................714 939-0888
Drew Joosten, *Branch Mgr*
EMP: 53
SALES (corp-wide): 1B **Privately Held**
WEB: www.tkelevator.com
SIC: 5084 Elevators
HQ: Tk Elevator Corporation
11605 Haynes Bridge Rd
Alpharetta GA 30009
678 319-3240

(P-13953)
TOYOTA INDUSTRIES N AMER INC ◆
Also Called: Toyota-Lift of Los Angeles
12907 Imperial Hwy, Santa Fe Springs (90670-4715)
PHONE.................................562 941-4155
EMP: 50 EST: 2021
SALES (est): 1.2MM **Privately Held**
WEB: www.toyota.com
SIC: 5084 Lift trucks & parts
HQ: Toyota Industries North America, Inc.
3030 Barker Dr
Columbus IN 47201
812 341-3810

(P-13954)
TRAFFIC CONTROL & SAFETY CORP (PA)
Also Called: Tcsc
1100 Main St, Irvine (92614-6737)
PHONE.................................949 553-8272
Keith Costello, *CEO*
Gregory Edward Grosch, *President*
Greg Andrews, *CFO*
Michael Flormann, *Technology*
Juzie Torres, *Accountant*
EMP: 68 EST: 2007
SALES (est): 40.3MM **Privately Held**
WEB: www.statewidess.com
SIC: 5084 Safety equipment

(P-13955)
UNITED MATERIAL HANDLING INC
23900 Brodiaea Ave, Moreno Valley (92553-8841)
PHONE.................................951 657-4900
Ryan Bartlett, *President*
Brook Bartlett, *Vice Pres*
Frida Anguiano, *Manager*
Raul Perez, *Manager*
▲ EMP: 61 EST: 2011
SALES (est): 18.6MM **Privately Held**
WEB: www.unitedmh.com
SIC: 5084 Materials handling machinery

(P-13956)
VALLEY INSTRUMENT SERVICE INC (PA)
3536 Brian Way, Bakersfield (93308-6202)
P.O. Box 9278 (93389-9278)
PHONE.................................661 327-8681
Fernando Angelini, *President*
Carlos A Angelini Jr, *Treasurer*
Virginia Angelini, *Admin Sec*
Kimberly Kemp, *Sales Staff*
EMP: 145 EST: 1971
SQ FT: 1,100

SALES (est): 10.1MM Privately Held
WEB: www.valleyinstrument.com
SIC: **5084** 3829 7629 Measuring & testing equipment, electrical; thermometers & temperature sensors; electrical measuring instrument repair & calibration

(P-13957)
VALLEY POWER SYSTEMS INC (PA)
Also Called: John Deere Authorized Dealer
425 S Hacienda Blvd, City of Industry (91745-1123)
PHONE....................626 333-1243
Hampton Clark Lee, *Ch of Bd*
Michael Barnett, *President*
Robert K Humphryes, *CFO*
Richard Kickliter, *Vice Pres*
Bruce Noble, *Vice Pres*
◆ **EMP:** 100 **EST:** 1949
SQ FT: 49,000
SALES (est): 178.7MM Privately Held
WEB: www.valleypowersystems.com
SIC: **5084** Engines & parts, diesel

(P-13958)
VALTRA INC (PA)
Also Called: Strong Hand Tools
8750 Pioneer Blvd, Santa Fe Springs (90670-2006)
PHONE....................562 949-8625
Harry Hon Wong, *CEO*
Josephine Lai, *Office Mgr*
Carin Huang, *Business Anlyst*
▲ **EMP:** 30 **EST:** 1983
SQ FT: 24,000
SALES (est): 14.2MM Privately Held
WEB: www.valtrainc.com
SIC: **5084** 5085 3452 3429 Industrial machine parts; machine tools & accessories; industrial supplies; bolts, nuts, rivets & washers; manufactured hardware (general)

(P-13959)
VAUGHANS INDUSTRIAL REPAIR INC
16224 Garfield Ave, Paramount (90723-4804)
P.O. Box 1898 (90723-1898)
PHONE....................562 633-2660
Thomas Vaughan, *President*
David Newton, *Treasurer*
Keven Vaughan, *Vice Pres*
Patricia Vaughan, *Vice Pres*
John L Smith, *Admin Sec*
EMP: 35 **EST:** 1978
SQ FT: 20,000
SALES (est): 9.5MM Privately Held
WEB: www.virc1.com
SIC: **5084** 1711 3599 Oil refining machinery, equipment & supplies; mechanical contractor; machine & other job shop work
PA: Vss Sales, Inc.
16220 Garfield Ave
Paramount CA 90723
562 630-0606

(P-13960)
VESCIO ENTERPRISES INC (PA)
Also Called: All Racks Solutions
4915 E Olympic Blvd, Los Angeles (90022-3831)
PHONE....................323 263-7225
Peter Eliso, *President*
EMP: 69 **EST:** 2007
SQ FT: 4,000
SALES (est): 1.7MM Privately Held
WEB: www.allracksolutions.com
SIC: **5084** Materials handling machinery

(P-13961)
WASTECH CONTROLS & ENGRG INC
20600 Nordhoff St, Chatsworth (91311-6114)
PHONE....................818 998-3500
Paul Nicolas, *President*
▲ **EMP:** 45 **EST:** 1987
SQ FT: 30,000

SALES (est): 15MM Privately Held
WEB: www.wastechengineering.com
SIC: **5084** 3561 3823 3559 Waste compactors; pumps, domestic: water or sump; industrial flow & liquid measuring instruments; anodizing equipment

(P-13962)
WCS DISTRIBUTING INC
Also Called: Pro Spray Equipment
268 W Orange Show Ln, San Bernardino (92408-2037)
PHONE....................909 888-2015
Steve Sykes, *President*
◆ **EMP:** 21 **EST:** 1990
SQ FT: 20,000
SALES (est): 11.4MM Privately Held
WEB: www.wcsdistributinginc.com
SIC: **5084** 3499 5083 Engines & transportation equipment; nozzles, spray: aerosol, paint or insecticide; lawn machinery & equipment

(P-13963)
WESTAIR GASES & EQUIPMENT INC
3901 Buck Owens Blvd, Bakersfield (93308-4927)
PHONE....................661 387-6800
Steve Castiglione, *Manager*
EMP: 160
SALES (corp-wide): 60MM Privately Held
WEB: www.westairgases.com
SIC: **5084** Welding machinery & equipment
PA: Westair Gases & Equipment, Inc.
2506 Market St
San Diego CA 92102
866 937-8247

(P-13964)
WESTCOAST ROTOR INC
119 W 154th St, Gardena (90248-2201)
PHONE....................310 327-5050
Vehan Mahdessian, *President*
Krikor Mahdessian, *CFO*
▲ **EMP:** 21 **EST:** 1982
SQ FT: 15,625
SALES (est): 4.8MM Privately Held
WEB: www.westcoastrotor.com
SIC: **5084** 3561 Pumps & pumping equipment; pumps & pumping equipment

(P-13965)
WIGGINS LIFT CO INC
2571 Cortez St, Oxnard (93036-1642)
P.O. Box 5187 (93031-5187)
PHONE....................805 485-7821
Hattie Wiggins, *Ch of Bd*
Michael M Wiggins, *President*
Michelle Mc Dowell, *Treasurer*
Paul Hurbace, *Vice Pres*
Jack Mc Dowell, *Vice Pres*
◆ **EMP:** 50 **EST:** 1951
SQ FT: 55,000
SALES (est): 30.4MM Privately Held
WEB: www.wigginslift.com
SIC: **5084** Materials handling machinery

(P-13966)
ZEMARC CORPORATION (PA)
6431 Flotilla St, Commerce (90040-1597)
PHONE....................323 721-5598
Abduz Zahid, *CEO*
Viren Patel, *Vice Pres*
Igor Turov, *Vice Pres*
Irma Zahid, *Vice Pres*
Ron Richards, *Branch Mgr*
EMP: 50 **EST:** 1976
SQ FT: 50,000
SALES (est): 33.8MM Privately Held
WEB: www.zemarc.com
SIC: **5084** Hydraulic systems equipment & supplies; pneumatic tools & equipment

---
5085 Industrial Splys Wholesale

(P-13967)
A ROYAL WOLF PORTABLE STOR INC
400 E Compton Blvd, Gardena (90248-2017)
PHONE....................310 719-1048
Sherry Nocachuma, *Branch Mgr*
EMP: 25
SALES (corp-wide): 1.3B Publicly Held
WEB: www.ksend.com
SIC: **5085** 7359 2448 Commercial containers; shipping container leasing; cargo containers, wood & wood with metal
HQ: A Royal Wolf Portable Storage, Inc.
23422 Clawiter Rd
Hayward CA 94545
510 264-3321

(P-13968)
ACHEM INDUSTRY AMERICA INC (PA)
4250 N Harbor Blvd, Fullerton (92835-1017)
PHONE....................562 802-0998
Joseph Lin, *CEO*
Shin Pai Kuei, *President*
Bob Kuminski, *Natl Sales Mgr*
Brian Lin, *Sales Mgr*
Contreras Edgar, *Sales Staff*
◆ **EMP:** 50 **EST:** 1960
SALES (est): 18.1MM Privately Held
WEB: www.achem.com
SIC: **5085** Industrial supplies

(P-13969)
ADCO CONTAINER COMPANY
9959 Canoga Ave, Chatsworth (91311-3090)
PHONE....................818 998-2565
Fax: 818 998-3648
EMP: 50
SQ FT: 24,000
SALES (est): 12.2MM Privately Held
WEB: www.adcocontainer.com
SIC: **5085** 7336 Whol Industrial Supplies Commercial Art/Graphic Design

(P-13970)
ALLIED HIGH TECH PRODUCTS INC
2376 E Pacifica Pl, Rancho Dominguez (90220-6214)
P.O. Box 4608, Compton (90224-4608)
PHONE....................310 635-2466
Clayton A Smith, *President*
Shirley A Smith, *Corp Secy*
Eddie Padilla, *General Mgr*
Betsy O'Connell, *Technology*
Betsy O 'connell, *Technology*
▲ **EMP:** 70 **EST:** 1983
SQ FT: 34,000
SALES (est): 43MM Privately Held
WEB: www.alliedhightech.com
SIC: **5085** Abrasives

(P-13971)
AMERICAN BOLT & SCREW MFG CORP (PA)
600 S Wanamaker Ave, Ontario (91761-8118)
P.O. Box 4300 (91761-8800)
PHONE....................909 390-0522
Jimmie W Hooper, *President*
Cynthia Alvarez, *Vice Pres*
Josh Hutton, *Vice Pres*
Jerry Alvarez, *Technician*
David Klesser, *Analyst*
▲ **EMP:** 52 **EST:** 1970
SQ FT: 110,000
SALES (est): 38.4MM Privately Held
WEB: www.absfasteners.com
SIC: **5085** Fasteners, industrial: nuts, bolts, screws, etc.

(P-13972)
BEACON ROOFING SUPPLY INC
8501 Telfair Ave, Sun Valley (91352-3928)
PHONE....................818 768-4661
EMP: 60

SALES (corp-wide): 6.9B Publicly Held
WEB: www.becn.com
SIC: **5085** 5169 Industrial supplies; sealants
PA: Beacon Roofing Supply, Inc.
505 Huntmar Park Dr # 300
Herndon VA 20170
571 323-3939

(P-13973)
BEARING ENGINEERS INC (PA)
Also Called: Motion Solutions
27 Argonaut, Aliso Viejo (92656-1423)
PHONE....................949 586-7442
Scott Depenbrok, *President*
Elizabeth Gordon, *CFO*
Peter Hoffman, *Vice Pres*
Henry Kim, *Vice Pres*
Wallis Logan, *Vice Pres*
▲ **EMP:** 57 **EST:** 1956
SQ FT: 22,000
SALES (est): 51.5MM Privately Held
WEB: www.motionsolutions.com
SIC: **5085** Bearings

(P-13974)
BEARING INSPECTION INC (DH)
4422 Corp Ctr Dr, Los Alamitos (90720)
PHONE....................714 484-9373
James R Menning, *CEO*
Drew F Baker, *President*
Douglas B Howland, *Vice Pres*
Scott F Radcliffe, *Vice Pres*
▲ **EMP:** 141 **EST:** 1955
SQ FT: 74,000
SALES (est): 37MM
SALES (corp-wide): 3.5B Publicly Held
WEB: www.bearinginspectioninc.com
SIC: **5085** Bearings
HQ: Mpb Corporation
7 Optical Ave
Keene NH 03431
603 352-0310

(P-13975)
BELL PIPE & SUPPLY CO
215 E Ball Rd, Anaheim (92805-6394)
P.O. Box 151 (92815-0151)
PHONE....................714 772-3200
Franklin M Bell III, *CEO*
Kristin C Bell, *Corp Secy*
Larry Harper, *Sales Associate*
Mark Arndt, *Sales Staff*
Robert Fagan, *Manager*
▲ **EMP:** 50 **EST:** 1956
SQ FT: 35,000
SALES (est): 18.9MM Privately Held
WEB: www.bpssg.com
SIC: **5085** Valves & fittings

(P-13976)
BOURGET BROS BUILDING MTLS INC (PA)
Also Called: Bourget Flagstone Co
1636 11th St, Santa Monica (90404-3708)
PHONE....................310 450-6556
John J Bourget, *President*
Leonard J Bourget, *CFO*
▲ **EMP:** 50
SALES (est): 22MM Privately Held
WEB: www.bourgetbros.com
SIC: **5211** 5251 5085 Masonry materials & supplies; tools, hand; tools

(P-13977)
BRIDGESTONE HOSEPOWER LLC
Also Called: Hose Power USA
2865 Pellissier Pl, City of Industry (90601-1512)
PHONE....................562 699-9500
Alfonso Sanchez, *General Mgr*
Manuel Cuellar, *Branch Mgr*
EMP: 13 **Privately Held**
WEB: www.hosepower.com
SIC: **5085** 3492 Hose, belting & packing; hose & tube fittings & assemblies, hydraulic/pneumatic
HQ: Bridgestone Hosepower, Llc
50 Industrial Loop N
Orange Park FL 32073

PRODUCTS & SVCS

(P-13978)
CENTRAL PURCHASING LLC (HQ)
Also Called: Harbor Freight Tools
3491 Mission Oaks Blvd, Camarillo (93012-5034)
P.O. Box 6010 (93011-6010)
PHONE.............................800 444-3353
Eric Smidt, *President*
Roger Sheaves, *Vice Pres*
Jason Sprong, *Vice Pres*
Trey Feiler, *VP Bus Dvlpt*
Chris Calvert, *District Mgr*
◆ **EMP:** 500 **EST:** 1968
SQ FT: 277,000
SALES (est): 1.8B
SALES (corp-wide): 1.9B **Privately Held**
WEB: www.harborfreight.com
SIC: 5085 5961 5251 Tools; tools & hardware, mail order; tools
PA: Harbor Freight Tools Usa, Inc.
26677 Agoura Rd
Calabasas CA 91302
818 836-5001

(P-13979)
CLOVER IMAGING GROUP LLC
Also Called: Color Laser R&D
9414 Eton Ave, Chatsworth (91311-5862)
PHONE.............................815 431-8100
Baltazar Marquez, *Engineer*
Tim Cahill, *Sales Staff*
Mario Linares, *Manager*
EMP: 450
SALES (corp-wide): 173.6MM **Privately Held**
SIC: 5085 Ink, printers'
PA: Clover Imaging Group, Llc
2700 W Higgins Rd Ste 100
Hoffman Estates IL 60169
866 734-6548

(P-13980)
DARLY FILTRATION INC (PA)
14225 Telephone Ave, Chino (91710-5781)
PHONE.............................909 591-7999
Xiaoteng He,
Jessica Hamilton, *Sales Staff*
Alicia Barela,
▲ **EMP:** 29 **EST:** 2014
SALES (est): 3.3MM **Privately Held**
WEB: www.darllyfilter.com
SIC: 5085 3569 Filters, industrial; filters, general line: industrial

(P-13981)
DHV INDUSTRIES INC
3451 Pegasus Dr, Bakersfield (93308-6827)
PHONE.............................661 392-8948
Tingchun Huang, *President*
Sonny Simmons, *Vice Pres*
◆ **EMP:** 52 **EST:** 1996
SQ FT: 180,000
SALES (est): 8MM **Privately Held**
WEB: www.dhvindustries.com
SIC: 5085 3491 Valves & fittings; industrial valves

(P-13982)
EDWARDS VACUUM LLC
15326 Valley Blvd, City of Industry (91746-3324)
PHONE.............................626 532-5585
EMP: 53
SALES (corp-wide): 1.9MM **Privately Held**
WEB: www.edwardsvacuum.com
SIC: 5085 Industrial supplies
PA: Edwards Vacuum Llc
2041 Mission College Blvd
Santa Clara CA 95054
978 658-5410

(P-13983)
FASTENER TECHNOLOGY CORP
7415 Fulton Ave, North Hollywood (91605-4116)
PHONE.............................818 764-6467
Dennis Suedkamp, *CEO*
Thomas Boat, *CFO*
Saul Bautista, *Engineer*
Victoria Ocampo, *Accountant*
Tom Boat, *Controller*
EMP: 125 **EST:** 1979
SQ FT: 24,000

SALES (est): 23MM
SALES (corp-wide): 140.1MM **Privately Held**
WEB: www.ftc-usa.com
SIC: 5085 3812 5251 Fasteners, industrial: nuts, bolts, screws, etc.; aircraft/aerospace flight instruments & guidance systems; tools
HQ: Avantus Aerospace, Inc.
29101 The Old Rd
Valencia CA 91355
661 295-8620

(P-13984)
G W MAINTENANCE INC (PA)
Also Called: Petroquip
1101 E 6th St, Santa Ana (92701-4912)
P.O. Box 10696 (92711-0696)
PHONE.............................714 541-2211
Kami Keshmiri, *President*
Barry F Branin, *Ch of Bd*
Vivian Branin, *Treasurer*
EMP: 59 **EST:** 1962
SQ FT: 24,000
SALES (est): 7.3MM **Privately Held**
SIC: 5085 5084 Valves & fittings; gas equipment, parts & supplies; instruments & control equipment; hoists; pumps & pumping equipment

(P-13985)
GENERAL TOOL INC
Also Called: Gt Diamond
2025 Alton Pkwy, Irvine (92606-4904)
PHONE.............................949 261-2322
Jae Woo Kim, *CEO*
Jinsik Shin, *CFO*
Jay Kim, *Admin Sec*
Eric Tak, *Engineer*
Sarah Yun, *Hum Res Coord*
▲ **EMP:** 90 **EST:** 1984
SQ FT: 40,000
SALES (est): 22MM **Privately Held**
WEB: www.gtdiamond.com
SIC: 5085 Diamonds, industrial: natural, crude

(P-13986)
HK AERSPACE KRKHILL ARCFT PRTS
3098 N California St, Burbank (91504-2004)
PHONE.............................818 559-9783
Sherman D Chinn, *General Mgr*
Dennis Mc Kinney, *Controller*
EMP: 64 **EST:** 1999
SQ FT: 10,000
SALES (est): 5.2MM
SALES (corp-wide): 109.2MM **Privately Held**
WEB: www.proponent.com
SIC: 5085 5063 Fasteners & fastening equipment; electrical fittings & construction materials
PA: Kirkhill Aircraft Parts Co.
3120 Enterprise St
Brea CA 92821
714 223-5400

(P-13987)
HOWMET GLOBL FSTNING SYSTEMS I
3000 Lomita Blvd, Torrance (90505-5103)
PHONE.............................310 784-0700
Kenneth Paine, *Sales Staff*
Andrew Valmocena, *Engineer*
James Warner, *Engineer*
Greg Lamb, *Buyer*
Muhammad Jaseem, *Opers Mgr*
EMP: 60
SALES (corp-wide): 5.2B **Publicly Held**
SIC: 5085 Fasteners & fastening equipment
HQ: Howmet Global Fastening Systems Inc.
3990a Heritage Oak Ct
Simi Valley CA 93063
805 426-2270

(P-13988)
HOWMET GLOBL FSTNING SYSTEMS I (HQ)
Also Called: Howmet Fastening Systems
3990a Heritage Oak Ct, Simi Valley (93063-6711)
PHONE.............................805 426-2270

Olivier Jarrault, *President*
Greg Lamb, *Buyer*
Scott Ryan, *Manager*
▲ **EMP:** 120 **EST:** 1977
SQ FT: 37,000
SALES (est): 1.1B
SALES (corp-wide): 5.2B **Publicly Held**
WEB: www.arconic.com
SIC: 5085 5072 5065 Fasteners & fastening equipment; hardware; electronic parts & equipment
PA: Howmet Aerospace Inc.
201 Isabella St Ste 200
Pittsburgh PA 15212
412 553-1950

(P-13989)
HUNTINGTON VALLEY INDS INC
Also Called: H V I
16752 Burke Ln, Huntington Beach (92647-4559)
PHONE.............................714 892-0256
Gary Fisher, *President*
Nancy Fisher, *Vice Pres*
Sam Wallace, *Vice Pres*
Kelli Cash, *Sales Mgr*
Rick Mattson, *Sales Staff*
EMP: 13 **EST:** 1980
SQ FT: 8,350
SALES (est): 9.9MM **Privately Held**
WEB: www.hvi.aero
SIC: 5085 3452 Fasteners, industrial: nuts, bolts, screws, etc.; bolts, metal; screws, metal

(P-13990)
IDEAL FASTENERS INC
3850 E Miraloma Ave, Anaheim (92806-2127)
PHONE.............................714 630-7840
George Hennes, *President*
Lawrence McBride, *Treasurer*
David Boehm, *Vice Pres*
Christine Sumner, *Controller*
Dave Aguilera, *Foreman/Supr*
EMP: 50 **EST:** 1969
SQ FT: 35,500
SALES (est): 11.4MM **Privately Held**
WEB: www.idealfasteners.com
SIC: 5085 Fasteners, industrial: nuts, bolts, screws, etc.

(P-13991)
INDEX FASTENERS INC (PA)
Also Called: Distribution
945 E Grevillea Ct, Ontario (91761-5612)
PHONE.............................909 923-5002
Shane Bearly, *CEO*
Jaimie Barraco, *Office Mgr*
Richard Peterson, *Admin Sec*
Steve Fernandez, *Sales Staff*
Greg Graham, *Manager*
▲ **EMP:** 28 **EST:** 1977
SQ FT: 30,000
SALES (est): 14.5MM **Privately Held**
WEB: www.indexthermoplastics.com
SIC: 5085 2821 3081 Fasteners, industrial: nuts, bolts, screws, etc.; plastics materials & resins; plastic film & sheet

(P-13992)
INDUSTRIAL CONT SVCS - CA LLC (DH)
1540 S Greenwood Ave, Montebello (90640-6536)
PHONE.............................323 724-8507
David O'Bryan, *Controller*
Jeff Pettigrew, *Division Mgr*
Paul Belfer, *Facilities Mgr*
Bart Kaminsky, *Manager*
Jeff Jones, *Accounts Mgr*
EMP: 121 **EST:** 2002
SALES (est): 50.3MM
SALES (corp-wide): 1.1B **Privately Held**
WEB: www.mauserpackaging.com
SIC: 5085 Industrial supplies
HQ: Industrial Container Services Llc
375 Northridge Rd Ste 600
Atlanta GA 30350
407 930-4182

(P-13993)
INDUSTRIAL VALCO INC (PA)
3135 E Ana St, Compton (90221-5606)
PHONE.............................310 635-0711
Rob C Raban, *President*

Lisa Preston, *Accounting Mgr*
Vernon Preston, *Buyer*
John Tatum, *Regl Sales Mgr*
Cheryl McClanahan, *Sales Staff*
▲ **EMP:** 20 **EST:** 1983
SQ FT: 62,000
SALES (est): 18.2MM **Privately Held**
WEB: www.ivalco.com
SIC: 5085 3498 Valves & fittings; pipe fittings, fabricated from purchased pipe

(P-13994)
JEWELERS SECURITY PRODUCTS (PA)
Also Called: Jsp
939 E 31st St, Los Angeles (90011-2501)
PHONE.............................323 231-0600
Leo Esch, *President*
Rosylin Esch, *Treasurer*
▲ **EMP:** 14 **EST:** 1978
SALES (est): 2.1MM **Privately Held**
WEB: www.jsp.cc
SIC: 5085 5065 3423 Tools; security control equipment & systems; hand & edge tools

(P-13995)
LINEAR INDUSTRIES LTD (PA)
1850 Enterprise Way, Monrovia (91016-4271)
PHONE.............................626 303-1130
Anthony Dell Angelica, *President*
Jean Cade, *CFO*
Savonia Angelica, *Vice Pres*
▲ **EMP:** 60 **EST:** 1960
SQ FT: 45,000
SALES (est): 22MM **Privately Held**
WEB: www.linearindustries.com
SIC: 5085 3625 5065 5072 Bearings; positioning controls, electric; electronic parts; hardware; power transmission equipment; machine tool accessories

(P-13996)
LONESTAR SIERRA L.L.C
1820 W Orangewood Ave, Orange (92868-2043)
PHONE.............................866 575-5680
David Wood,
EMP: 225 **EST:** 2016
SALES (est): 15MM **Privately Held**
WEB: www.lonestarsierra.com
SIC: 5085 Refractory material

(P-13997)
LONG BCH HOSE COUPLING CO INC
1265 W 16th St, Long Beach (90813-1305)
PHONE.............................562 901-2970
Raul Alcala, *President*
EMP: 13 **EST:** 1988
SQ FT: 22,000
SALES (est): 2.5MM **Privately Held**
WEB: www.lbhose.com
SIC: 5531 5085 3492 Automotive & home supply stores; hose, belting & packing; hose & tube fittings & assemblies, hydraulic/pneumatic

(P-13998)
LONG-LOK FASTENERS CORPORATION
20501 Belshaw Ave, Carson (90746-3505)
PHONE.............................310 667-4200
Robert M Bennett, *CEO*
Tyler Cox, *Cust Mgr*
EMP: 50 **EST:** 1971
SALES (est): 6MM **Privately Held**
WEB: www.longlok.com
SIC: 5085 Fasteners, industrial: nuts, bolts, screws, etc.

(P-13999)
LOS ANGELES RUBBER COMPANY (PA)
Also Called: Mechanical Drives and Belting
2915 E Washington Blvd, Los Angeles (90023-4218)
PHONE.............................323 263-4131
Carol A Durst, *CEO*
David Durst, *Vice Pres*
Michael Durst, *Vice Pres*
Wayne Roberts, *Vice Pres*
Matthew Menashe, *General Mgr*
▲ **EMP:** 51 **EST:** 1898

SQ FT: 31,000
SALES (est): 24.9MM **Privately Held**
WEB: www.mrosupply.com
SIC: 5085 Industrial supplies

(P-14000)
MCMASTER-CARR SUPPLY COMPANY
9630 Norwalk Blvd, Santa Fe Springs (90670-2954)
P.O. Box 54960, Los Angeles (90054-0960)
PHONE..................562 692-5911
Luis Vasquez,
Erin Laxamana, *Executive*
Matthew Tilley, *Regional Mgr*
Steve Gryczynski, *Info Tech Dir*
Emily Rapport, *Info Tech Dir*
EMP: 375
SALES (corp-wide): 621MM **Privately Held**
WEB: www.mcmaster.com
SIC: 5085 Industrial supplies
PA: Mcmaster-Carr Supply Company
600 N County Line Rd
Elmhurst IL 60126
630 834-9600

(P-14001)
MIDLAND INDUSTRIES
659 E Ball Rd, Anaheim (92805-5910)
PHONE..................800 821-5725
Vince Hodes, *Owner*
EMP: 100 EST: 2020
SALES (est): 4.7MM **Privately Held**
SIC: 5085 Valves, pistons & fittings

(P-14002)
MILLENNIA STAINLESS INC
10016 Romandel Ave, Santa Fe Springs (90670-3424)
PHONE..................562 946-3545
Ching-PO LI, *CEO*
Lisa Chen, *Accounting Mgr*
▲ EMP: 75 EST: 1996
SQ FT: 10,500
SALES (est): 23.6MM **Privately Held**
WEB: www.millenniastainless.com
SIC: 5085 5065 5051 Industrial supplies; coils, electronic; steel
PA: Chain Chon Industrial Co., Ltd.
No.178, Ta Guan Rd.,
Taoyuan City TAY 33753

(P-14003)
MILLS IRON WORKS
14834 S Maple Ave, Gardena (90248-1936)
PHONE..................323 321-6520
Jeffrey Griffith, *CEO*
Kenneth E Berger, *President*
EMP: 75 EST: 1905
SQ FT: 48,000
SALES (est): 19.5MM **Privately Held**
WEB: www.millsiron.com
SIC: 5085 Valves & fittings

(P-14004)
MILWAUKEE ELECTRIC TOOL CORP
1130 N Magnolia Ave, Anaheim (92801-2605)
PHONE..................714 827-1301
Mike Parslow, *Manager*
Derek Flores, *Regional Mgr*
Jason Warschauer, *Sales Staff*
Jared Jackson, *Manager*
EMP: 71 **Privately Held**
WEB: www.milwaukeetool.com
SIC: 5085 7699 Industrial tools; power tool repair
HQ: Milwaukee Electric Tool Corporation
13135 W Lisbon Rd
Brookfield WI 53005
800 729-3878

(P-14005)
MISSION RUBBER COMPANY LLC (HQ)
1660 Leeson Ln, Corona (92879-2061)
P.O. Box 2349 (92878-2349)
PHONE..................951 736-1313
David Vansell,
Chris Vansell, *Vice Pres*
Jay Clark, *Plant Mgr*

▲ EMP: 199 EST: 1950
SQ FT: 100,000
SALES (est): 40.5MM
SALES (corp-wide): 91.1MM **Privately Held**
WEB: www.missionrubber.com
SIC: 5085 Industrial supplies
PA: Mcp Industries, Inc.
708 S Temescal St Ste 101
Corona CA 92879
951 736-1881

(P-14006)
MT SUPPLY INC (DH)
Also Called: Machine Tools Supply
2752 Walnut Ave, Tustin (92780-7025)
PHONE..................800 938-6658
George H Ponce Jr, *CEO*
Joseph Custer, *Principal*
Steve Pixley, *Principal*
George Ponce, *General Mgr*
David Ramos, *Admin Asst*
EMP: 162 EST: 1987
SALES (est): 65.3MM
SALES (corp-wide): 1.6B **Publicly Held**
WEB: www.dnow.com
SIC: 5085 5084 Industrial supplies; materials handling machinery
HQ: Dnow L.P.
7402 N Eldridge Pkwy
Houston TX 77041
281 823-4700

(P-14007)
ND INDUSTRIES INC
Also Called: N D Industries
13929 Dinard Ave, Santa Fe Springs (90670-4920)
PHONE..................562 926-3321
David Palmquist, *Opers-Prdtn-Mfg*
Scot Wickham, *Vice Pres*
Richard Cook, *Sales Staff*
EMP: 58
SALES (corp-wide): 59.9MM **Privately Held**
WEB: www.ndindustries.com
SIC: 5085 Fasteners, industrial: nuts, bolts, screws, etc.
PA: Nd Industries Inc
1000 N Crooks Rd
Clawson MI 48017
248 288-0000

(P-14008)
NMC GROUP INC
Also Called: Nylon Molding
300 E Cypress St, Brea (92821-4007)
PHONE..................714 223-3525
Michael Johnson, *President*
Wolfgang Hombrecher, *VP Finance*
Gabriel Lerma, *Buyer*
▲ EMP: 24 EST: 1972
SALES (est): 21.1MM
SALES (corp-wide): 4.8B **Publicly Held**
WEB: www.transdigm.com
SIC: 5085 3089 Fasteners & fastening equipment; injection molding of plastics
HQ: Ta Aerospace Co.
28065 Franklin Pkwy
Valencia CA 91355
661 775-1100

(P-14009)
NSK PRECISION AMERICA INC
Also Called: NSK Prcsion Amer Snta Fe Sprng
13921 Bettencourt St, Cerritos (90703-1011)
PHONE..................562 968-1000
Philip Jennings, *Manager*
EMP: 104 **Privately Held**
SIC: 5085 Bearings
HQ: Nsk Precision America, Inc.
3450 Bearing Dr
Franklin IN 46131
317 738-5000

(P-14010)
PACIFIC COAST BOLT CORPORATION
12748 Florence Ave, Santa Fe Springs (90670-3906)
PHONE..................562 944-9549
Robert Gardner, *President*
Joe Santa Maria, *Vice Pres*
▲ EMP: 35 EST: 1989

SQ FT: 47,000
SALES (est): 12MM **Privately Held**
WEB: www.pacificcoastbolt.com
SIC: 5085 3965 3452 5072 Fasteners, industrial: nuts, bolts, screws, etc.; fasteners; bolts, nuts, rivets & washers; bolts, nuts & screws

(P-14011)
PACIFIC ECHO INC
23540 Telo Ave, Torrance (90505-4098)
PHONE..................310 539-1822
Yasuo Ogami, *CEO*
▲ EMP: 90
SQ FT: 110,000
SALES (est): 40.1MM **Privately Held**
WEB: www.pacificecho.com
SIC: 5085 Hose, belting & packing
HQ: Kakuichi Co., Ltd.
1415, Midoricho, Tsuruga
Nagano NAG 380-0

(P-14012)
RBC SOUTHWEST PRODUCTS INC
Also Called: U S Bearings
5001b Commerce Dr, Baldwin Park (91706-1424)
PHONE..................626 358-0181
Michael Harnett, *President*
Daniel Molnar, *Counsel*
EMP: 65 EST: 1953
SALES (est): 2.7MM
SALES (corp-wide): 608.9MM **Publicly Held**
WEB: www.rbcbearings.com
SIC: 5085 Bearings
HQ: Roller Bearing Company Of America, Inc.
102 Willenbrock Rd
Oxford CT 06478
203 267-7001

(P-14013)
RBC TRANSPORT DYNAMICS CORP
3131 W Segerstrom Ave, Santa Ana (92704-5811)
PHONE..................203 267-7001
Michael Harnett, *President*
Charles Bliss, *General Mgr*
Daniela Gigliotti, *Business Anlyst*
Ryan Gregson, *Engineer*
Don Marcia, *Engineer*
▲ EMP: 185 EST: 1992
SQ FT: 75,000
SALES (est): 36.9MM
SALES (corp-wide): 608.9MM **Publicly Held**
WEB: www.rbcbearings.com
SIC: 5085 Bearings
HQ: Roller Bearing Company Of America, Inc.
102 Willenbrock Rd
Oxford CT 06478
203 267-7001

(P-14014)
REVCO INDUSTRIES INC (PA)
10747 Norwalk Blvd, Santa Fe Springs (90670-3823)
PHONE..................562 777-1588
C Edward Chu, *Ch of Bd*
Steve Hwang, *President*
Thomas Han, *CFO*
Hong Brian Choi, *Vice Pres*
Charles Hwang, *Vice Pres*
◆ EMP: 28 EST: 1974
SQ FT: 24,000
SALES (est): 10.3MM **Privately Held**
WEB: www.blackstallion.com
SIC: 5085 5136 3842 Valves & fittings; work clothing, men's & boys'; personal safety equipment

(P-14015)
RUBY INDUSTRIAL TECH LLC
910 S Wanamaker Ave, Ontario (91761-8151)
PHONE..................909 390-7919
EMP: 50
SALES (corp-wide): 748.1MM **Privately Held**
WEB: www.kaman.com
SIC: 5085 Whol Industrial Supplies

PA: Ruby Industrial Technologies, Llc
1 Vision Way
Bloomfield CT 06002
860 687-5000

(P-14016)
RUTLAND TOOL & SUPPLY CO (HQ)
Also Called: MSC Metalworking
2225 Workman Mill Rd, City of Industry (90601-1437)
PHONE..................562 566-5000
Thomas J Neri, *CEO*
Andrew Verey, *President*
◆ EMP: 140 EST: 2005
SALES (est): 27.6MM **Publicly Held**
WEB: www.mscdirect.com
SIC: 5085 5251 Industrial supplies; tools

(P-14017)
SHAR-CRAFT INC (PA)
Also Called: Seal & Packing Supply
1103 33rd St, Bakersfield (93301-2121)
PHONE..................661 324-4985
James L Craft, *President*
Sharon Craft, *CFO*
Chris Craft, *Vice Pres*
Ron Paul, *Sales Mgr*
Tim Poulin, *Sales Staff*
EMP: 22 EST: 1966
SQ FT: 14,000
SALES (est): 9.7MM **Privately Held**
WEB: www.sharcraftinc.com
SIC: 5085 3599 3479 Packing, industrial; seals, industrial; machine shop, jobbing & repair; coating of metals & formed products

(P-14018)
SO CAL SANDBAGS INC
12620 Bosley Ln, Corona (92883-6358)
PHONE..................951 277-3404
Peter Rasinski, *President*
Wanda Chavez, *Controller*
Dennis Feidner, *Opers Mgr*
Tracy Pensko,
Lynn Hamblin, *Manager*
EMP: 100 EST: 1986
SALES (est): 29.1MM **Privately Held**
WEB: www.socalsandbags.com
SIC: 5085 5999 Industrial supplies; safety supplies & equipment

(P-14019)
SOLAR LINK INTERNATIONAL INC
4652 E Brickell St Ste A, Ontario (91761-1593)
P.O. Box 56, San Dimas (91773-0056)
PHONE..................909 605-7789
Johnny Tsai, *Vice Pres*
▲ EMP: 218 EST: 1998
SALES (est): 22.4MM **Privately Held**
WEB: www.linkinternationalinc.com
SIC: 5085 Industrial supplies

(P-14020)
SPS TECHNOLOGIES LLC
Also Called: Pb Fasteners
1700 W 132nd St, Gardena (90249-2008)
PHONE..................310 323-6222
EMP: 260
SALES (corp-wide): 245.5B **Publicly Held**
WEB: www.pccfasteners.com
SIC: 5085 Fasteners, industrial: nuts, bolts, screws, etc.
HQ: Sps Technologies, Llc
301 Highland Ave
Jenkintown PA 19046
215 572-3000

(P-14021)
SPS TECHNOLOGIES LLC
Airdrome Precision Components
14800 S Figueroa St, Gardena (90248-1719)
P.O. Box 1867, Long Beach (90801-1867)
PHONE..................562 426-9411
EMP: 65
SALES (corp-wide): 245.5B **Publicly Held**
WEB: www.pccfasteners.com
SIC: 5085 Whol Industrial Supplies

HQ: Sps Technologies, Llc
301 Highland Ave
Jenkintown PA 19046
215 572-3000

(P-14022)
TCT CIRCUIT SUPPLY INC
560 S Melrose St, Placentia (92870-6327)
PHONE.....................714 644-9700
Ian Hemmings, *President*
Kathy Chen, *Principal*
Amie Chien Chien, *Principal*
Chalachew Ejigu, *Branch Mgr*
Amy Fan, *Accounting Mgr*
EMP: 55 **EST:** 2015
SALES (est): 9.6MM **Privately Held**
WEB: www.tctcircuitsupply.com
SIC: 5085 Tools

(P-14023)
TEN DAYS MANUFACTURING
Also Called: Daily Manufacturing
458 Commercial Rd, San Bernardino
(92408-3706)
PHONE.....................888 222-1575
Mohammed Shabeer Humkar, *CEO*
EMP: 103 **EST:** 2020
SALES (est): 9.4MM **Privately Held**
SIC: 5085 Plastic bottles

(P-14024)
THALASINOS ENTERPRISES INC
Also Called: T & T Enterprises
1220 Railroad St, Corona (92882-1837)
PHONE.....................951 340-0911
Brent Thalasinos, *CEO*
John Thalasinos, *Ch of Bd*
Alison Siedler, *Vice Pres*
Alison S Siedler, *Manager*
▲ **EMP:** 28 **EST:** 1993
SQ FT: 54,000
SALES (est): 11MM **Privately Held**
WEB: www.ttenterprises.com
SIC: 5085 3452 Fasteners, industrial:
nuts, bolts, screws, etc.; nuts, metal;
bolts, metal

(P-14025)
THOMPSON INDUS SUP A LTD LBLTY
3945 E La Palma Ave, Anaheim
(92807-1714)
PHONE.....................714 632-8895
David Phitts, *Manager*
Jeff Carpenter, *Sales Staff*
Ron Noriega, *Sales Staff*
Scott Peterson, *Sales Staff*
Ryan Phipps, *Sales Staff*
EMP: 13
SALES (corp-wide): 30MM **Privately Held**
WEB: www.tismc.com
SIC: 5251 5085 5063 3568 Hardware;
bearings; power transmission equipment,
electric; bearings, plain
PA: Thompson Industrial Supply, A Limited
Liability Company
10222 6th St
Rancho Cucamonga CA 91730
909 941-8881

(P-14026)
TONNAGE INDUSTRIAL LLC
2130 W Cowles St, Long Beach
(90813-1022)
PHONE.....................800 893-9681
Todd Phillips,
Greg Phillips,
EMP: 24 **EST:** 2018
SALES (est): 12.8MM **Privately Held**
WEB: www.tonnageindustrial.com
SIC: 5085 3312 5051 Industrial supplies;
bars & bar shapes, steel, hot-rolled;
pipes, iron & steel; plate, steel; structural
shapes, iron or steel

(P-14027)
TRICO LEASING COMPANY LLC
30154 Rhone Dr, Rancho Palos Verdes
(90275-5736)
PHONE.....................877 259-9997
Julian Kim,
EMP: 33

SALES (corp-wide): 2.2MM **Privately Held**
WEB: www.tricoleasing.com
SIC: 5085 3792 Commercial containers;
travel trailer chassis
PA: Trico Leasing Company, Llc
30154 Rhone Dr
Rancho Palos Verdes CA 90275
877 259-9997

(P-14028)
TRISTAR INDUSTRIAL LLC
Also Called: Columbia Spclty A Trstar Indus
5875 Obispo Ave, Long Beach
(90805-3715)
PHONE.....................562 634-6425
Michael Taylor, *Branch Mgr*
EMP: 78 **Privately Held**
WEB: www.tristaraz.com
SIC: 5085 Valves & fittings
PA: Tristar Industrial, Llc
1645 W Buckeye Rd
Phoenix AZ 85007

(P-14029)
TSC AUTO ID TECHNOLOGY AMERICA (HQ)
3040 Saturn St Ste 200, Brea
(92821-6231)
PHONE.....................909 468-0100
Hank Wang, *President*
Jaime Changllio, *Engineer*
Jiunn-Chyi Lee, *Production*
Matt Botts, *Sales Staff*
▲ **EMP:** 124 **EST:** 2008
SALES (est): 27.7MM **Privately Held**
WEB: www.tscprinters.com
SIC: 5085 Ink, printers'

(P-14030)
UFP RIVERSIDE LLC
Also Called: Universal Forest Products
2100 Avalon St, Riverside (92509-2000)
PHONE.....................951 826-3000
Art Vega, *Manager*
Jared Hillier, *Sales Staff*
Carl Suderman, *Accounts Mgr*
Jesus Magana, *Supervisor*
EMP: 50 **EST:** 2014
SALES (est): 32.3MM
SALES (corp-wide): 5.1B **Publicly Held**
WEB: www.ufpi.com
SIC: 5085 5031 Crates, except paper;
lumber, plywood & millwork
PA: Ufp Industries, Inc.
2801 E Beltline Ave Ne
Grand Rapids MI 49525
616 364-6161

(P-14031)
WEST COAST AEROSPACE INC
24224 Broad St, Carson (90745-6006)
PHONE.....................310 518-0633
Ken Wagner, *President*
David Arnado, *Supervisor*
EMP: 18
SQ FT: 26,456
SALES (corp-wide): 17.7MM **Privately Held**
WEB: www.westcoastaerospace.com
SIC: 5085 3545 3541 3452 Fasteners,
industrial: nuts, bolts, screws, etc.; ma-
chine tool accessories; machine tools,
metal cutting type; bolts, nuts, rivets &
washers
PA: West Coast Aerospace, Inc.
220 W E St
Wilmington CA 90744
310 518-3167

5087 Service Establishment Eqpt & Splys Wholesale

(P-14032)
AMERICAN SANITARY SUPPLY INC
3800 E Miraloma Ave, Anaheim
(92806-2108)
P.O. Box 6436 (92816-0436)
PHONE.....................714 632-3010
Luis Salazar, *CEO*
Tammy Zingmark, *CFO*
Silvia Salazar, *Vice Pres*

Sylvia Salazar, *Office Mgr*
▲ **EMP:** 75 **EST:** 1983
SQ FT: 20,000
SALES (est): 21.7MM **Privately Held**
WEB: www.amersan.com
SIC: 5087 Janitors' supplies

(P-14033)
CARTER FIRE PROTECTION INC
Also Called: Integrated Fire and Safety
1229 N Ventura Ave, Ventura (93001-1707)
PHONE.....................805 648-5906
Shelley Merrell, *President*
Christine Goetz, *Admin Asst*
EMP: 50 **EST:** 1980
SQ FT: 1,300
SALES (est): 11.5MM **Privately Held**
WEB: www.integratedfireandsafety.com
SIC: 5087 Firefighting equipment

(P-14034)
CHIRO INC (PA)
Also Called: Mr Clean Maintenance Systems
2260 S Vista Ave, Bloomington
(92316-2908)
P.O. Box 31, Colton (92324-0031)
PHONE.....................909 879-1160
Arthur Rose, *President*
Timothy Russell, *Vice Pres*
Douglas Black, *Technology*
Jack Sedgwick, *QC Mgr*
Duane Chandler, *Sales Mgr*
EMP: 430 **EST:** 1980
SQ FT: 10,000
SALES (est): 47.9MM **Privately Held**
WEB: www.mrccompanies.us
SIC: 5087 7349 5169 Cleaning & mainte-
nance equipment & supplies; cleaning
service, industrial or commercial; chemi-
cals & allied products

(P-14035)
EXTENSIONS PLUS INC
5428 Reseda Blvd, Tarzana (91356-2606)
PHONE.....................818 881-5611
Helene Stahl, *President*
Rosalia Gallo, *Accounting Mgr*
Patricia Wernke, *Purch Mgr*
EMP: 30 **EST:** 1994
SALES (est): 10.3MM **Privately Held**
WEB: www.extensions-plus.com
SIC: 5087 3999 Beauty parlor equipment
& supplies; hair & hair-based products

(P-14036)
FLORA BEAUTY INC
1608 Nogales St D02, Rowland Heights
(91748-2257)
PHONE.....................213 374-0448
EMP: 80
SALES (est): 900K **Privately Held**
SIC: 5087 Whol Service Establishment
Equipment

(P-14037)
GLAMOUR INDUSTRIES CO
100 Wilshire Blvd Ste 700, Santa Monica
(90401-3602)
PHONE.....................213 687-8600
EMP: 100
SALES (corp-wide): 110.3MM **Privately Held**
WEB: www.aiibeauty.com
SIC: 5087 Beauty parlor equipment & sup-
plies; barber shop equipment & supplies
PA: Glamour Industries, Co.
2220 Gaspar Ave
Commerce CA 90040
323 728-2999

(P-14038)
HYDRO TEK SYSTEMS INC
2353 Almond Ave, Redlands (92374-2035)
PHONE.....................909 799-9222
John S Koen, *President*
Andrea S Koen, *Admin Sec*
◆ **EMP:** 63 **EST:** 1985
SQ FT: 45,000
SALES (est): 20.6MM
SALES (corp-wide): 983.9MM **Privately Held**
WEB: www.hydrotek.us
SIC: 5087 3589 5084 Service establish-
ment equipment; commercial cleaning
equipment; industrial machinery & equip-
ment

HQ: Nilfisk A/S
Kornmarksvej 1
BrOndby 2605
432 381-00

(P-14039)
JWDANGELO COMPANY INC
601 S Harbor Blvd, La Habra (90631-6187)
P.O. Box 3744 (90632-3744)
PHONE.....................562 690-1000
John W D Angelo, *CEO*
Jack Giguere, *Vice Pres*
Grady Smith, *Vice Pres*
Rodney Gifford, *Info Tech Mgr*
Julie Stegelvik, *Credit Mgr*
EMP: 50 **EST:** 1987
SQ FT: 35,000
SALES (est): 35.8MM **Privately Held**
WEB: www.jwdco.com
SIC: 5087 Firefighting equipment

(P-14040)
M & M FLORISTS INC
Also Called: Conroy's Florist
27592 Sierra Hwy, Canyon Country
(91351-3091)
PHONE.....................661 298-7088
Thomas Morrison, *President*
Annette Morrison, *Treasurer*
Michael Morrison, *Vice Pres*
EMP: 60 **EST:** 1987
SQ FT: 1,800
SALES (est): 1.9MM **Privately Held**
SIC: 5992 5087 Flowers, fresh; funeral di-
rectors' equipment & supplies

(P-14041)
NIKKEN GLOBAL INC (HQ)
18301 Von Karman Ave # 1, Irvine
(92612-1009)
PHONE.....................949 789-2000
Tom Toshizo Watanabe, *Ch of Bd*
Kendall Cho, *President*
Ruth Ann Bellino, *Accountant*
▲ **EMP:** 155 **EST:** 1996
SALES (est): 92MM **Privately Held**
SIC: 5087 5023 5013 5122 Stress reduc-
ing equipment, electric; bedspreads; seat
covers; vitamins & minerals; long distance
telephone communications

(P-14042)
O P I PRODUCTS INC (HQ)
13034 Saticoy St, North Hollywood
(91605-3510)
PHONE.....................818 759-8688
Jules Kaufman, *CEO*
John Heffner, *President*
Eric Schwartz, *COO*
William Halface, *Exec VP*
Susan Weiss-Fischmann, *Exec VP*
◆ **EMP:** 500 **EST:** 1981
SQ FT: 250,000
SALES (est): 104.6MM **Publicly Held**
WEB: www.opi.com
SIC: 5087 2844 Beauty parlor equipment
& supplies; toilet preparations

(P-14043)
PWS INC (PA)
12020 Garfield Ave, South Gate
(90280-7823)
PHONE.....................323 721-8832
Brad Pollack, *CEO*
Ella Taylor, *CFO*
Brad Steinberg, *Admin Sec*
Yumi Ryoo, *Sales Staff*
▲ **EMP:** 51 **EST:** 1966
SQ FT: 50,000
SALES (est): 35.2MM **Privately Held**
WEB: www.pwslaundry.com
SIC: 5087 Laundry equipment & supplies

(P-14044)
SPILO WORLDWIDE INC
100 Wilshire Blvd Ste 700, Santa Monica
(90401-3602)
PHONE.....................213 687-8600
Marc Spilo, *CEO*
◆ **EMP:** 100 **EST:** 1977
SALES (est): 44MM
SALES (corp-wide): 3B **Publicly Held**
WEB: www.colfaxcorp.com
SIC: 5087 Beauty parlor equipment & sup-
plies

PA: Colfax Corporation
420 Natl Bus Pkwy Ste 500
Annapolis Junction MD 20701
301 323-9000

(P-14045)
SWEIS INC (PA)
23760 Hawthorne Blvd, Torrance
(90505-5906)
PHONE....................310 375-0558
Karl Sweis, *President*
Theresa Sweis, *Vice Pres*
Randi Katz, *Area Mgr*
Caprise Hewes, *Office Mgr*
Sophie Dupart, *CIO*
EMP: 70 **EST:** 2000
SQ FT: 4,200
SALES (est): 24.2MM **Privately Held**
WEB: www.sweisinc.com
SIC: 5087 2844 Beauty parlor equipment
& supplies; hair preparations, including
shampoos

(P-14046)
**UNITED FABRICARE SUPPLY
INC (PA)**
1237 W Walnut St, Compton (90220-5009)
P.O. Box 1796, Los Angeles (90001-0796)
PHONE....................310 886-3790
Steve S Hong, *CEO*
Hae S Hong, *Corp Secy*
Mike Fahar, *Exec VP*
Kirby Schnebly, *Exec VP*
W David Weimer, *Exec VP*
▲ **EMP:** 75
SQ FT: 50,000
SALES (est): 33.6MM **Privately Held**
WEB: www.unitedfabricaresupply.com
SIC: 5087 Janitors' supplies

(P-14047)
**WORLDWIDE INTGRTED
RSURCES INC**
7171 Telegraph Rd, Montebello
(90640-6511)
PHONE....................323 838-8938
Fred Morad, *President*
Sina Salamat, *CFO*
Ana Marquez, *Office Mgr*
Susan Morad, *Admin Sec*
◆ **EMP:** 60 **EST:** 1991
SQ FT: 20,000
SALES (est): 13.5MM **Privately Held**
WEB: www.wwir.com
SIC: 5087 Janitors' supplies

**5088 Transportation Eqpt &
Splys, Except Motor Vehicles
Wholesale**

(P-14048)
**AIR FRAME MFG & SUPPLY CO
INC**
26135 Technology Dr, Valencia
(91355-1138)
PHONE....................661 257-7728
Yoshinobu Kawamura, *CEO*
Yoshimi Sussan, *CFO*
Ignacio Estrada, *Executive*
Daiki Yamaguchi, *Business Dir*
Yuki Nakagiri, *Department Mgr*
▼ **EMP:** 35 **EST:** 1964
SQ FT: 30,000
SALES (est): 13.1MM **Privately Held**
WEB: www.afmsupply.com
SIC: 5088 3999 3728 Aircraft & parts; at-
omizers, toiletry; accumulators, aircraft
propeller

(P-14049)
AIRCRAFT HARDWARE WEST
Also Called: Ahw
2180 Temple Ave, Long Beach
(90804-1020)
PHONE....................562 961-9324
Frank Ioffrida, *CEO*
Nicole Faulkner, *CFO*
Ashley Miller, *Administration*
Brenda Husman, *Controller*
Krista Wildermuth, *Opers Dir*
▲ **EMP:** 30 **EST:** 2002
SQ FT: 15,000

SALES: 14.3MM **Privately Held**
WEB: www.ahw-global.com
SIC: 5088 3993 5072 Aircraft & parts;
name plates: except engraved, etched,
etc.: metal; hardware

(P-14050)
AIREY ENTERPRISES LLC
Also Called: A Transportation
5530 Corbin Ave Ste 325, Tarzana
(91356-6037)
P.O. Box 17328, Encino (91416-7328)
PHONE....................818 530-3362
Latasha George,
EMP: 160 **EST:** 2015
SALES (est): 9.7MM **Privately Held**
SIC: 5088 Transportation equipment &
supplies

(P-14051)
AM MACHINING INC
Also Called: APV Manufacturing & Engrg Co
7422 Walnut Ave, Buena Park
(90620-1762)
PHONE....................714 367-0830
Frank T Amador Jr, *President*
Stella Mermingez, *CFO*
F Michael Amador III, *Vice Pres*
Jay Conlon, *General Mgr*
Brett Grace, *Purch Mgr*
EMP: 34 **EST:** 1993
SQ FT: 24,000
SALES (est): 11.2MM **Privately Held**
WEB: www.apvmfg.com
SIC: 5088 3541 Aeronautical equipment &
supplies; machine tool replacement & re-
pair parts, metal cutting types

(P-14052)
**ANSETT ARCFT SPARES &
SVCS INC (PA)**
12675 Encinitas Ave, Sylmar (91342-3635)
P.O. Box Dept La, Pasadena (91185-0001)
PHONE....................818 362-1100
Gregory Quinlan, *President*
Brad Barton, *CFO*
John Boyce, *CFO*
Tessie Cue, *Treasurer*
Luis Mora, *Vice Pres*
▲ **EMP:** 55 **EST:** 1958
SQ FT: 50,000
SALES (est): 21MM **Privately Held**
SIC: 5088 Aircraft & parts

(P-14053)
**BOEING STLLITE SYSTEMS INTL
IN (HQ)**
Also Called: Boeing Company, The
2260 E Imperial Hwy, El Segundo
(90245-3501)
P.O. Box 92919, Los Angeles (90009-2919)
PHONE....................310 364-4000
Randy Brinkley, *President*
David Lillington, *President*
Craig R Cooning, *CEO*
Anu Garg, *Executive*
David Staley, *Program Mgr*
▲ **EMP:** 40 **EST:** 1967
SALES (est): 201.7MM
SALES (corp-wide): 58.1B **Publicly Held**
WEB: www.boeing.com
SIC: 5088 4899 3663 Aircraft & space ve-
hicle supplies & parts; satellite earth sta-
tions; radio & TV communications
equipment
PA: The Boeing Company
100 N Riverside Plz
Chicago IL 60606
312 544-2000

(P-14054)
COMAV LLC (PA)
18499 Phantom St Ste 17, Victorville
(92394-7967)
PHONE....................760 523-5100
Craig Garrick, *President*
Jon Day, *CFO*
William Tollison, *Exec VP*
Cory Cloward, *Vice Pres*
Eugene Corey, *Opers Staff*
EMP: 155 **EST:** 2012
SQ FT: 58,732

SALES (est): 101.1MM **Privately Held**
WEB: www.comav.com
SIC: 5088 4581 Aircraft & parts; aircraft
maintenance & repair services; aircraft
servicing & repairing

(P-14055)
**DESSER TIRE & RUBBER CO
LLC**
Also Called: Cee Baileys Aircraft Plastics
6900 W Acco St, Montebello (90640-5435)
PHONE....................323 837-1497
Brian Elliott, *Controller*
EMP: 30 **Privately Held**
WEB: www.desser.com
SIC: 5088 3728 Aircraft & space vehicle
supplies & parts; aircraft parts & equip-
ment
HQ: Desser Tire & Rubber Co., Llc
6900 W Acco St
Montebello CA 90640
323 721-4900

(P-14056)
**FALCON AEROSPACE
HOLDINGS LLC**
Also Called: Wesco Aircraft
27727 Avenue Scott, Valencia
(91355-1219)
PHONE....................661 775-7200
Randy J Snyder, *Ch of Bd*
Gregory A Hann, *Exec VP*
Tommy Lee, *Exec VP*
Alex Murray, *Exec VP*
Kerry Shiba, *Exec VP*
EMP: 1250 **EST:** 2006
SALES (est): 221.8MM **Privately Held**
WEB: www.incora.com
SIC: 5088 Aircraft & parts

(P-14057)
IRWIN INTERNATIONAL INC (PA)
Also Called: Aircraft Spruce Speciality Co
225 Airport Cir, Corona (92878-5027)
P.O. Box 4000 (92878-4000)
PHONE....................951 372-9555
James J Irwin, *President*
Elizabeth Irwin, *Vice Pres*
Nanci Irwin, *Vice Pres*
Rob Irwin, *Vice Pres*
Debbie Moss, *Vice Pres*
▼ **EMP:** 95 **EST:** 1965
SQ FT: 5,000
SALES (est): 146.7MM **Privately Held**
WEB: www.aircraftspruce.com
SIC: 5599 5088 Aircraft instruments,
equipment or parts; aircraft & parts

(P-14058)
ITOCHU AVIATION INC (DH)
222 N Pcf Cast Hwy Ste 22, El Segundo
(90245)
P.O. Box 997 (90245-0997)
PHONE....................310 640-2770
Naoya Osaki, *CEO*
Takehiko Yamada, *President*
▲ **EMP:** 25 **EST:** 1973
SALES (est): 46.6MM **Privately Held**
WEB: www.itochu.com
SIC: 5088 3728 Aircraft & parts; aircraft
parts & equipment
HQ: Itochu International Inc.
1251 Ave Of The Amrcas 51
New York NY 10020
212 818-8000

(P-14059)
JCM ENGINEERING CORP
2690 E Cedar St, Ontario (91761-8533)
PHONE....................909 923-3730
Robert Schenkkan, *President*
Myrna Lamar, *COO*
Jay Gross, *CFO*
Ken Safford, *CFO*
Greg Marsella, *Vice Pres*
EMP: 85 **EST:** 1979
SQ FT: 140,000
SALES (est): 23.6MM **Privately Held**
WEB: www.jcmcorp.com
SIC: 5088 Aeronautical equipment & sup-
plies

(P-14060)
**KELLSTROM HOLDING
CORPORATION (PA)**
Also Called: Merex Group
100 N Pcf Cast Hwy Ste 19, El Segundo
(90245)
PHONE....................561 222-7455
Christopher R Celtruda, *President*
Michael P Hompesch, *Partner*
Frank J Pados Jr, *Partner*
Thomas J Caracciolo, *Managing Prtnr*
Richard Drinkward, *CFO*
EMP: 54 **EST:** 2011
SQ FT: 25,821
SALES (est): 178.4MM **Privately Held**
WEB: www.goallclear.com
SIC: 5088 Aircraft engines & engine parts

(P-14061)
**KIRKHILL AIRCRAFT PARTS CO
(PA)**
Also Called: Proponent Main Whse
3120 Enterprise St, Brea (92821-6236)
PHONE....................714 223-5400
Andrew Todhunter, *CEO*
Scott Joynt, *President*
Steven Frields, *CFO*
Ron Basbas, *Vice Pres*
Michael Berecz, *Vice Pres*
▲ **EMP:** 175 **EST:** 1972
SQ FT: 177,000
SALES (est): 109.2MM **Privately Held**
WEB: www.proponent.com
SIC: 5088 3728 Aircraft & parts; aircraft
parts & equipment

(P-14062)
LOGISTICAL SUPPORT LLC
20409 Prairie St, Chatsworth (91311-6029)
PHONE....................818 341-3344
Brad Hart,
William Hart, *Vice Pres*
Jerry Hill, *Vice Pres*
Joseph Lucan, *Vice Pres*
EMP: 120 **EST:** 1997
SQ FT: 14,600
SALES (est): 24.8MM
SALES (corp-wide): 39.6MM **Privately
Held**
WEB: www.rtcaerospace.com
SIC: 5088 Aircraft & parts
PA: Rtc Aerospace Llc
7215 4th Street Ct E
Fife WA 98424
918 407-0291

(P-14063)
**ONTIC ENGINEERING AND MFG
INC (PA)**
20400 Plummer St, Chatsworth
(91311-5372)
P.O. Box 2424 (91313-2424)
PHONE....................818 678-6555
Gareth Hall, *CEO*
Peg Billson, *President*
Greth Hall, *CEO*
Terry Streb, *Program Mgr*
Diana Bevacqua, *Division Mgr*
EMP: 124 **EST:** 1986
SQ FT: 54,000
SALES (est): 193.1MM **Privately Held**
WEB: www.ontic.com
SIC: 5088 3728 3812 Aircraft equipment
& supplies; aircraft parts & equipment;
search & navigation equipment

(P-14064)
**SHIMADZU PRECISION INSTRS
INC (DH)**
Also Called: Shimadzu Medical Systems USA
3645 N Lakewood Blvd, Long Beach
(90808-1797)
PHONE....................562 420-6226
Takashi Ishii, *CEO*
Tina Kang, *CFO*
Tsuyosh Hirai, *Admin Sec*
▲ **EMP:** 70 **EST:** 1979
SQ FT: 60,000
SALES (est): 153.8MM **Privately Held**
WEB: www.spi-inc.com
SIC: 5088 5047 5084 Aircraft equipment
& supplies; medical equipment & sup-
plies; industrial machinery & equipment

P R O D U C T S   &   S V C S

(P-14065)
STRECH PLASTICS INCORPORATED
900 John St Ste J, Banning (92220-6204)
PHONE.....................951 922-2224
James M Strech, *CEO*
Jim Underwood, *Info Tech Dir*
Aron Tacchia, *Sales Staff*
▲ **EMP:** 50 **EST:** 1974
SQ FT: 52,000
SALES (est): 20.5MM **Privately Held**
WEB: www.strechplastics.com
SIC: 5088 3949 Golf carts; sporting & athletic goods

(P-14066)
TELEDYNE RESON INC
5212 Verdugo Way, Camarillo
(93012-8662)
PHONE.....................805 964-6260
Robert Mehrabian, *CEO*
Doug Lockhart, *Vice Pres*
Efren Castro, *Technology*
Dewi Hertzberg, *Accountant*
Steve Rook, *Controller*
EMP: 33 **EST:** 1985
SALES (est): 2.8MM
SALES (corp-wide): 3B **Publicly Held**
WEB: www.teledynemarine.com
SIC: 5088 3812 Navigation equipment & supplies; sonar systems & equipment
PA: Teledyne Technologies Inc
1049 Camino Dos Rios
Thousand Oaks CA 91360
805 373-4545

(P-14067)
UNICAL AVIATION INC (PA)
680 S Lemon Ave, City of Industry
(91789-2934)
PHONE.....................909 348-1700
Han Tan, *President*
Mercy Tan, *CFO*
Roger Lew, *Officer*
Phil Arroyo, *Vice Pres*
Lucy Dewi, *Vice Pres*
◆ **EMP:** 190 **EST:** 1986
SQ FT: 480,000
SALES (est): 127.8MM **Privately Held**
WEB: www.unical.com
SIC: 5088 Aircraft & parts

(P-14068)
UNICAL DEFENSE INC
680 S Lemon Ave Ste A, City of Industry
(91789-2934)
PHONE.....................909 348-1500
Mercy Tan, *CEO*
Roger Lew, *CFO*
Eddie Chen, *Vice Pres*
Suna Widjaja, *Executive*
Yenty Lie, *General Mgr*
EMP: 50 **EST:** 2015
SALES (est): 11.3MM **Privately Held**
WEB: www.unical.com
SIC: 5088 Aircraft & parts

(P-14069)
UNITED AERONAUTICAL CORP
7360 Laurel Canyon Blvd, North Hollywood
(91605-3710)
P.O. Box 7102 (91615-0102)
PHONE.....................818 764-2102
Lawrence P Holt, *CEO*
Bradford T Beck, *CFO*
June Fitzgerald, *CFO*
Jessica Bautista, *Admin Sec*
Jon Eliot, *Manager*
◆ **EMP:** 32 **EST:** 1988
SQ FT: 200,000
SALES (est): 16.3MM **Privately Held**
WEB: www.unitedaero.com
SIC: 5088 3812 Aeronautical equipment & supplies; search & navigation equipment

(P-14070)
UNITED VLVE DIV OF FDERAL INDS
645 Hawaii St, El Segundo (90245-4814)
PHONE.....................310 297-4000
AVI Wacht, *President*
Asher Bartov, *Vice Pres*
Alvin James, *QC Mgr*
▲ **EMP:** 15 **EST:** 1981
SQ FT: 30,000

SALES (est): 3.6MM **Privately Held**
WEB: www.fedindustries.com
SIC: 5088 3728 3444 Aircraft equipment & supplies; aircraft parts & equipment; sheet metalwork

(P-14071)
WESCO AIRCRAFT HARDWARE CORP
Also Called: Incora
27727 Avenue Scott, Valencia
(91355-3909)
PHONE.....................661 775-7200
Steve Halford, *Opers Mgr*
Jim Taylor, *Vice Pres*
Bruce Weinstein, *Director*
Brett Pickin, *Manager*
Joshua Finesilver, *Regional*
EMP: 400
SALES (corp-wide): 1.7B **Privately Held**
WEB: www.incora.com
SIC: 5088 Aircraft & parts
HQ: Wesco Aircraft Hardware Corp.
2601 Meacham Blvd Ste 400
Fort Worth TX 76137
817 284-4449

(P-14072)
WILLIAMS AEROSPACE & MFG INC (HQ)
999 Avenida Acaso, Camarillo
(93012-8700)
PHONE.....................805 446-2700
Greg Beason, *CEO*
Kevin Cofer, *CTO*
Robert B Codol, *Director*
Bradley J Morton, *Director*
Bob Shettle, *Director*
▲ **EMP:** 23 **EST:** 1982
SQ FT: 9,910
SALES (est): 9.5MM
SALES (corp-wide): 178.4MM **Privately Held**
WEB: www.goallclear.com
SIC: 5088 3728 3724 Aircraft equipment & supplies; aircraft parts & equipment; airframe assemblies, except for guided missiles; aircraft engines & engine parts
PA: Kellstrom Holding Corporation
100 N Pcf Cast Hwy Ste 19
El Segundo CA 90245
561 222-7455

5091 Sporting & Recreational Goods & Splys Wholesale

(P-14073)
AQUA PERFORMANCE INC
Also Called: A.J. Metal Manufacturing
425 N Smith Ave, Corona (92878-4305)
P.O. Box 370 (92878-0370)
PHONE.....................951 340-2056
Sue Curi, *Vice Pres*
EMP: 34 **EST:** 1990
SQ FT: 20,000
SALES (est): 9.1MM **Privately Held**
WEB: www.aquaperformance.com
SIC: 5091 3339 3444 Watersports equipment & supplies; primary nonferrous metals; silicon & chromium; sheet metalwork

(P-14074)
BARRYS BOOTCAMP HOLDINGS LLC
7373 Beverly Blvd, Los Angeles
(90036-2502)
PHONE.....................270 535-5005
Joseph Gonzalez,
John Mumford,
Rachelle Mumford,
Barry Stitch,
EMP: 500 **EST:** 1998
SALES (est): 30MM **Privately Held**
SIC: 5091 7999 Fitness equipment & supplies; physical fitness instruction

(P-14075)
DAIWA CORPORATION
Also Called: Daiwa Golf Company Division
11137 Warland Dr, Cypress (90630-5034)
P.O. Box 6600 (90630-0066)
PHONE.....................562 375-6800
Tomoaki Komatsu, *CEO*

Tad Suzuki, *President*
Carey Graves, *Vice Pres*
William Steiner, *Vice Pres*
Cynthia Young, *Vice Pres*
◆ **EMP:** 58 **EST:** 1966
SALES (est): 25.5MM **Privately Held**
WEB: www.daiwa.com
SIC: 5091 3949 Fishing tackle; golf equipment
PA: Globeride, Inc.
3-14-16, Maesawa
Higashi Kurume TKY 203-0

(P-14076)
EASTON BASEBALL / SOFTBALL INC
3500 Willow Ln, Thousand Oaks
(91361-4921)
PHONE.....................800 632-7866
Maria Easton, *Principal*
Dewey Chauvin, *Vice Pres*
Dolores Ambriz-Monje, *Analyst*
Brittany Selsky, *Manager*
▲ **EMP:** 18 **EST:** 2014
SALES (est): 4.5MM **Privately Held**
WEB: www.easton.rawlings.com
SIC: 5091 3949 Sporting & recreation goods; sporting & athletic goods

(P-14077)
EASTON DIAMOND SPORTS LLC
3500 Willow Ln, Thousand Oaks
(91361-4921)
PHONE.....................800 632-7866
Ed Kinnaly, *CEO*
Duke Stump, *Senior VP*
Dewey Chauvin, *Vice Pres*
Ron Thomas, *Office Admin*
Robert Wagstaff, *Technician*
EMP: 100 **EST:** 2017
SALES (est): 26.6MM
SALES (corp-wide): 73.2MM **Privately Held**
SIC: 5091 Sporting & recreation goods
PA: Bce Acquisition Us, Inc.
100 Domain Dr
Exeter NH 03833
603 430-2111

(P-14078)
FORME LIFE RETAIL LLC
942 N Laurel Ave, Los Angeles
(90046-6922)
PHONE.....................703 577-9585
Trent Ward, *CEO*
EMP: 50 **EST:** 2020
SALES (est): 2MM **Privately Held**
WEB: www.formelife.com
SIC: 5091 Fitness equipment & supplies

(P-14079)
GOLFSMITH INTL HOLDINGS
72700 Dinah Shore Dr # 200, Palm Desert
(92211-0818)
PHONE.....................760 202-1023
EMP: 24
SALES (corp-wide): 7.9B **Publicly Held**
SIC: 5941 5091 3949 Ret Sporting Goods/Bicycles Whol Sporting/Recreational Goods Mfg Sporting/Athletic Goods
HQ: Golfsmith International Holdings, Inc.
11000 N Interstate 35
Austin TX 75201
512 837-8810

(P-14080)
INTER VALLEY POOL SUPPLY INC
Also Called: Intervalley Pools
1415 E 3rd St, Pomona (91766-2241)
PHONE.....................626 969-5657
John A Fry, *President*
EMP: 60 **EST:** 1985
SQ FT: 23,000
SALES (est): 10.7MM
SALES (corp-wide): 149MM **Privately Held**
WEB: www.hasapool.com
SIC: 5091 5963 Swimming pools, equipment & supplies; bottled water delivery
PA: Hasa, Inc.
23119 Drayton St
Saugus CA 91350
661 259-5848

(P-14081)
INTEX RECREATION CORP (PA)
4001 Via Oro Ave Ste 210, Long Beach
(90810-1400)
PHONE.....................310 549-5400
Tien P Zee, *President*
Wayne Farmer, *Info Tech Dir*
Rosevilla Tan, *Credit Staff*
Liz Botek, *Analyst*
Norm Gold, *Controller*
◆ **EMP:** 413 **EST:** 1970
SQ FT: 80,000
SALES (est): 165.2MM **Privately Held**
WEB: www.intexcorp.com
SIC: 5091 5092 5021 3081 Watersports equipment & supplies; toys; waterbeds; vinyl film & sheet; polyethylene film

(P-14082)
JUPITER HOLDING I CCRP (HQ)
13925 City Center Dr # 200, Chino Hills
(91709-5437)
PHONE.....................909 606-1416
Charles Huebner, *CEO*
EMP: 50 **EST:** 2007
SALES (est): 1.2B
SALES (corp-wide): 467.1K **Privately Held**
SIC: 5091 7991 5719 Spa equipment & supplies; spas; bath accessories

(P-14083)
KUBIC MARKETING INC (HQ)
225 S Aviation Blvd, El Segundo
(90245-4604)
PHONE.....................310 297-1600
Bob Sayre, *President*
Rodney Mullen, *Vice Pres*
▲ **EMP:** 135 **EST:** 1986
SALES (est): 7.6MM **Privately Held**
WEB: www.globecorporate.com
SIC: 5091 5136 5139 Sporting & recreation goods; sportswear, men's & boys'; footwear, athletic

(P-14084)
MADRID PRO DESIGNS INC
Also Called: Full Circle Distribution
5271 Business Dr, Huntington Beach
(92649-1221)
PHONE.....................714 897-5656
Jerry Madrid, *President*
Chuck Demoss, *Manager*
▲ **EMP:** 14 **EST:** 1988
SQ FT: 7,000
SALES (est): 2.2MM **Privately Held**
WEB: www.madridskateboards.com
SIC: 5091 3949 5941 Sporting & recreation goods; skateboards; skateboarding equipment

(P-14085)
POOL WATER PRODUCTS (PA)
17872 Mitchell N Ste 250, Irvine
(92614-6034)
P.O. Box 17359 (92623-7359)
PHONE.....................949 756-1666
Dean C Allred, *President*
Zelma Mabel Allred, *Ch of Bd*
James R Bledsoe, *Exec VF*
Juan Ly, *Branch Mgr*
Charles Schadowsky, *Branch Mgr*
◆ **EMP:** 15 **EST:** 1964
SQ FT: 12,000
SALES (est): 89.8MM **Privately Held**
WEB: www.poolwaterproducts.com
SIC: 5091 2899 2812 Swimming pools, equipment & supplies; chemical preparations; alkalies & chlorine

(P-14086)
RAZOR USA LLC (PA)
12723 166th St, Cerritos (90703-2102)
P.O. Box 3610 (90703-3610)
PHONE.....................562 345-6000
Carlton Calvin, *Mng Member*
Maribel Espinoza, *Officer*
Erin Bitar, *Vice Pres*
Ian Desberg, *Vice Pres*
David Kim, *Planning*
◆ **EMP:** 60 **EST:** 2000
SQ FT: 50,000
SALES (est): 38.6MM **Privately Held**
WEB: www.razor.com
SIC: 5091 Sporting & recreation goods

(P-14087)
SHIMANO NORTH AMER HOLDG INC (HQ)
1 Holland, Irvine (92618-2506)
PHONE...................................949 951-5003
David Pfeiffer, *President*
Jim Lafrance, *CFO*
Taizo Shimano, *Sr Exec VP*
Yoshihiro Hirata, *Exec VP*
Kiyoshi Tarutani, *Senior VP*
▲ EMP: 150 EST: 1986
SQ FT: 122,000
SALES (est): 117.1MM **Privately Held**
WEB: www.shimanofish.com.au
SIC: 5091 Bicycle parts & accessories

(P-14088)
SPORT CHALET LLC
25560 The Old Rd, Stevenson Ranch
(91381-1705)
PHONE...................................661 253-3883
EMP: 100
SALES (corp-wide): 443.9MM **Privately Held**
SIC: 5941 5699 5091 Ret Sporting Goods/Bicycles Ret Misc Apparel/Accessories Whol Sporting/Recreational Goods
HQ: Sport Chalet Llc
160 Corporate Ct
Meriden CT 06450
818 790-2717

(P-14089)
TROY LEE DESIGNS LLC (PA)
155 E Rincon St, Corona (92879-1328)
PHONE...................................951 371-5219
Troy Lee, *President*
Ryan Vance, *CFO*
Shane Will, *CFO*
Ricardo Gonzalez, *Vice Pres*
Prissy Rodriguez, *Vice Pres*
▲ EMP: 79 EST: 1985
SQ FT: 6,000
SALES (est): 32.1MM **Privately Held**
WEB: www.troyleedesigns.ca
SIC: 5091 7336 Sporting & recreation goods; graphic arts & related design

5092 Toys & Hobby Goods & Splys Wholesale

(P-14090)
A L S INDUSTRIES INC
1942 Artesia Blvd, Torrance (90504-3599)
PHONE...................................310 532-9262
Richard D Smith, *President*
David Albert, *Vice Pres*
▲ EMP: 51 EST: 1970
SQ FT: 70,000
SALES (est): 4.1MM **Privately Held**
WEB: www.alsindustries.com
SIC: 5092 Video games

(P-14091)
ANATEX ENTERPRISES INC
15929 Arminta St, Van Nuys (91406-1803)
PHONE...................................818 908-1888
Fleur Chesler, *President*
Mark Chesler, *Vice Pres*
▲ EMP: 25 EST: 1982
SQ FT: 25,000
SALES (est): 3.9MM **Privately Held**
WEB: www.anatex.com
SIC: 5092 3944 Toys; games, toys & children's vehicles

(P-14092)
AURORA WORLD INC
8820 Mercury Ln, Pico Rivera
(90660-6706)
PHONE...................................562 205-1222
Heui-Yul Noh, *CEO*
Kee Sun Hong, *Exec VP*
K S Hong, *MIS Dir*
Ellie Kim, *Purchasing*
Ellie S Kim, *Purch Agent*
◆ EMP: 110 EST: 1991
SQ FT: 100,000
SALES (est): 51.3MM **Privately Held**
WEB: www.auroragift.com
SIC: 5092 Toys

PA: Aurora World Corporation
624 Teheran-Ro, Gangnam-Gu
Seoul 06175

(P-14093)
BANZAI
2229 Barry Ave, Los Angeles (90064-1401)
PHONE...................................310 231-7292
Brian Dubinsky, *CEO*
EMP: 15 EST: 2005
SALES (est): 852.4K **Privately Held**
SIC: 5092 3949 Toys; water sports equipment

(P-14094)
BEVERLY HILLS TEDDY BEAR CO (PA)
Also Called: Bhtb
12725 Encinitas Ave, Sylmar (91342-3517)
PHONE...................................661 257-0750
David Socha, *CEO*
Randy Clark, *President*
Perriann Ennis, *Accountant*
Kelle Rich, *Opers Staff*
Mindi Hardesty, *Natl Sales Mgr*
▲ EMP: 63 EST: 2003
SALES (est): 17.2MM **Privately Held**
WEB: www.bhteddybear.com
SIC: 5945 5092 3942 Toys & games; toys & hobby goods & supplies; stuffed toys, including animals

(P-14095)
BIG TREE SALES INC
10401 Rush St, South El Monte
(91733-3343)
PHONE...................................626 672-0048
Haibo Zheng, *President*
EMP: 15 EST: 2015
SALES (est): 1MM **Privately Held**
WEB: www.bigtree-sales.com
SIC: 5092 3949 5199 Toys & games; bags, rosin; gifts & novelties

(P-14096)
DELTA CREATIVE INC
2690 Pellissier Pl, City of Industry
(90601-1507)
PHONE...................................800 423-4135
William B George, *President*
Martina Mueller, *CEO*
Alexander Ritchie, *Vice Pres*
▲ EMP: 105 EST: 1974
SQ FT: 112,000
SALES (est): 29.2MM
SALES (corp-wide): 412.7MM **Privately Held**
WEB: www.plaidonline.com
SIC: 5092 5198 Arts & crafts equipment & supplies; paints
HQ: Dk Household Brands Holding Ag
Muhlebachstrasse 20
ZUrich ZH 8008

(P-14097)
ME & MY BIG IDEAS LLC
Also Called: Happy Planner, The
17777 Newhope St, Fountain Valley
(92708-5434)
PHONE...................................877 462-6241
Kevin Fleming, *Officer*
Stephanie Rahmatulla, *Admin Sec*
Alisa Brainard, *Graphic Designe*
Tawni Coakley, *Graphic Designe*
Amadeus Rodriguez, *Production*
▲ EMP: 75 EST: 1998
SALES (est): 17.1MM **Privately Held**
WEB: www.meandmybigideas.com
SIC: 5092 Arts & crafts equipment & supplies

(P-14098)
MGA ENTERTAINMENT INC (PA)
9220 Winnetka Ave, Chatsworth
(91311-8172)
PHONE...................................818 894-2525
Isaac Larian, *President*
Susan Cole Hill, *Senior VP*
Leon Djiguerian, *Vice Pres*
Martin Elliott, *Vice Pres*
Becky Harris, *Vice Pres*
◆ EMP: 300 EST: 1980
SALES (est): 642.6MM **Privately Held**
SIC: 5092 Toys; toys & games

(P-14099)
PERFORMANCE DESIGNED PDTS LLC (PA)
2300 W Empire Ave Ste 600, Burbank
(91504-3399)
PHONE...................................323 248-9236
Tom Roberts, *CEO*
Dave Mason, *COO*
Ryan O'Desky, *CFO*
Navin Kumar, *Chief Mktg Ofcr*
Shawn Kinninger, *Vice Pres*
◆ EMP: 64 EST: 1990
SQ FT: 18,000
SALES (est): 54.4MM **Privately Held**
WEB: www.pdp.com
SIC: 5092 Video games

(P-14100)
RADICA ENTERPRISES LTD (DH)
Also Called: Radica USA
333 Continental Blvd, El Segundo
(90245-5032)
PHONE...................................310 252-2000
Patrick Feely, *CEO*
◆ EMP: 55 EST: 1992
SQ FT: 24,000
SALES (est): 31.6MM
SALES (corp-wide): 4.5B **Publicly Held**
SIC: 5092 Toy novelties & amusements

(P-14101)
SANRIO INC (HQ)
2050 W 190th St Ste 205, Torrance
(90504-6251)
PHONE...................................650 952-2880
Kunihiko Tsuji, *Ch of Bd*
Katsumi Murakami, *President*
Janet Hsu, *COO*
Craig Takiguchi, *COO*
Daphnie Carrillo, *Business Dir*
◆ EMP: 95 EST: 1976
SALES (est): 57.2MM **Privately Held**
WEB: www.sanrio.com
SIC: 5945 5092 5137 Toys & games; toys & hobby goods & supplies; women's & children's clothing

(P-14102)
TALL MOUSE ARTS & CRAFTS INC
13233 South St, Cerritos (90703-7307)
PHONE...................................714 693-4900
Kevin Brooks, *Branch Mgr*
EMP: 51
SALES (corp-wide): 4.9MM **Privately Held**
SIC: 5945 5947 5092 7699 Arts & crafts supplies; hobbies; gift, novelty & souvenir shop; arts & crafts equipment & supplies; hobby goods; picture framing, custom; fabric stores piece goods
PA: Tall Mouse Arts & Crafts, Inc.
5437 E La Palma Ave
Anaheim CA
714 693-4900

(P-14103)
TORNANTE-MDP JOE HOLDING LLC (PA)
233 S Beverly Dr, Beverly Hills
(90212-3886)
PHONE...................................310 228-6800
EMP: 13 EST: 2007
SALES (est): 194.1MM **Privately Held**
SIC: 5092 5112 2064 5145 Toys & games; social stationery & greeting cards; candy & other confectionery products; candy

(P-14104)
VICTORY INTL GROUP LLC
14748 Pipeline Ave Ste B, Chino Hills
(91709-6024)
PHONE...................................949 407-5888
Dawson Fan, *CEO*
Amanda Meng, *Vice Pres*
Marc Itow, *Managing Dir*
Kelly Lu, *Prdt Dvlpt Mgr*
Cory Knuteson, *Director*
▲ EMP: 230 EST: 2001
SQ FT: 4,960

SALES (est): 896MM **Privately Held**
WEB: www.victoryintlgroup.com
SIC: 5092 3843 2389 3842 Toys & hobby goods & supplies; dental equipment & supplies; hospital gowns; respiratory protection equipment, personal; surgical & medical instruments; kitchenware, plastic

(P-14105)
WHAM-O INC
6301 Owensmouth Ave # 700, Woodland Hills (91367-2265)
PHONE...................................818 963-4200
Raylin Hsieh, *CEO*
Blake Wong, *CFO*
Jeff Hsieh, *Chairman*
Darren Pike, *Vice Pres*
David Huang, *Director*
◆ EMP: 59 EST: 1997
SALES (est): 15.7MM **Privately Held**
WEB: www.wham-o.com
SIC: 5092 5091 3944 3949 Toys & games; surfing equipment & supplies; toy trains, airplanes & automobiles; sporting & athletic goods

5093 Scrap & Waste Materials Wholesale

(P-14106)
75S CORP
Also Called: FMC Metals
800 E 62nd St, Los Angeles (90001-1506)
PHONE...................................323 234-7708
Kevin Armstrong, *CEO*
Octavio Cabrerra, *President*
Octavio Cabrera, *Vice Pres*
Brad Efune, *Buyer*
◆ EMP: 42 EST: 1959
SALES (est): 33.4MM **Privately Held**
WEB: www.fmcmet.com
SIC: 5093 3341 Nonferrous metals scrap; recovery & refining of nonferrous metals

(P-14107)
AADLEN BROS AUTO WRECKING INC (PA)
11590 Tuxford St, Sun Valley (91352-3186)
PHONE...................................323 875-1400
Sam Adlen, *President*
Samuel Lewinstein, *Corp Secy*
Jorge Trujillo, *Opers Mgr*
EMP: 79 EST: 1951
SALES (est): 8.8MM **Privately Held**
WEB: www.aadlenbros.com
SIC: 5093 Metal scrap & waste materials

(P-14108)
AMERICA CHUNG NAM LLC (HQ)
Also Called: A C N
1163 Fairway Dr Fl 3, City of Industry
(91789-2851)
PHONE...................................909 839-8383
Teresa Cheung, *CEO*
Sam Liu, *COO*
Xue Bai, *CFO*
Kevin Zhao, *CFO*
Scott Taylor, *Vice Pres*
◆ EMP: 198 EST: 2008
SALES (est): 83.4MM **Privately Held**
WEB: www.acni.net
SIC: 5093 Waste paper

(P-14109)
ANGELUS WESTERN PPR FIBERS INC
2474 Porter St, Los Angeles (90021-2511)
PHONE...................................213 623-9221
Greg Rouchon, *President*
Steve Young, *Treasurer*
Tom Rouchon, *Vice Pres*
David Jones, *Admin Sec*
EMP: 51 EST: 1977
SQ FT: 10,000
SALES (est): 7.3MM **Privately Held**
WEB:
www.angeluswesternpaperfibers.com
SIC: 5093 Waste paper

(P-14110)
ATLAS PACIFIC CORPORATION (PA)
2803 Industrial Dr, Bloomington (92316-3249)
P.O. Box 726, Colton (92324-0726)
PHONE..............................909 421-1200
Gregory Woolfson, *President*
Holly Michael, *Buyer*
Ronald Reich, *Manager*
▼ **EMP:** 25 **EST:** 1980
SQ FT: 10,000
SALES (est): 14.6MM **Privately Held**
WEB: www.atlaspacific.net
SIC: 5093 3341 3339 Nonferrous metals scrap; brass smelting & refining (secondary); zinc refining (primary), including slabs & dust

(P-14111)
B & B PLASTICS RECYCLERS INC (PA)
3040 N Locust Ave, Rialto (92377-3706)
PHONE..............................909 829-3606
Baltasar Mejia, *President*
Bacilio Mejia, *Vice Pres*
Christy Dawson, *Executive*
Sofia Crespo, *Assistant*
EMP: 133 **EST:** 1998
SQ FT: 100,000
SALES (est): 40.9MM **Privately Held**
WEB: www.bbplasticsinc.com
SIC: 5093 2673 Plastics scrap; bags: plastic, laminated & coated

(P-14112)
CEDARWOOD-YOUNG COMPANY
Also Called: Allan Company
14618 Arrow Hwy, Baldwin Park (91706-1733)
PHONE..............................626 962-4047
Brett Weigand, *Branch Mgr*
EMP: 55
SQ FT: 10,664
SALES (corp-wide): 252.1MM **Privately Held**
WEB: www.allancompany.com
SIC: 5093 2611 Waste paper; pulp mills
PA: Cedarwood-Young Company
14620 Joanbridge St
Baldwin Park CA 91706
626 962-4047

(P-14113)
CITY FIBERS INC (PA)
2500 S Santa Fe Ave, Vernon (90058-1116)
P.O. Box 58646, Los Angeles (90058-0646)
PHONE..............................323 583-1013
David T Jones, *President*
Kipp Jones, *Vice Pres*
Vanessa Acosta, *Purch Agent*
Brett Jones, *Marketing Staff*
EMP: 60 **EST:** 1984
SQ FT: 55,000
SALES (est): 15.2MM **Privately Held**
WEB: www.cityfibers.com
SIC: 5093 4953 Waste paper; recycling, waste materials

(P-14114)
FIRMA PLASTIC CO INC
9309 Rayo Ave, South Gate (90280-3612)
PHONE..............................323 567-7767
David A Carpenter, *Vice Pres*
EMP: 318 **EST:** 1990
SALES (est): 2.6MM **Privately Held**
WEB: www.simsmm.com
SIC: 5093 Metal scrap & waste materials
HQ: Metal Management, Inc.
200 W Madison St Ste 3950
Chicago IL 60606
312 645-0700

(P-14115)
GLOBAL PLASTICS INC
145 Malbert St, Perris (92570-8624)
PHONE..............................951 657-5466
Nadim Salim Bahou, *President*
Patti Gilmour, *CFO*
Michael Aquino, *Vice Pres*
▲ **EMP:** 120 **EST:** 1996
SQ FT: 55,000

SALES (est): 32.2MM **Privately Held**
WEB: www.globalpetinc.com
SIC: 5093 4953 3053 Plastics scrap; recycling, waste materials; packing materials

(P-14116)
GREENPATH RECOVERY WEST INC
Also Called: Greenpath Recovery Recycl Svcs
330 W Citrus St Ste 250, Colton (92324-1422)
PHONE..............................909 954-0686
Joe Castro, *President*
Rebecca Somerville, *Opers Staff*
Ed Inferrere, *Manager*
EMP: 60
SQ FT: 90,000
SALES (est): 28MM **Privately Held**
WEB: www.greenpathrecovery.com
SIC: 5093 3089 2821 Scrap & waste materials; plastic processing; injection molding of plastics; plastics materials & resins; molding compounds, plastics

(P-14117)
JACK ENGLE & CO (PA)
10556 Ilona Ave, Los Angeles (90064-2313)
P.O. Box 1705 (90001-0705)
PHONE..............................323 589-8111
Alan M Engle, *CEO*
Jack Engle, *CEO*
Jason Engle, *Vice Pres*
Andrew Hyde, *Vice Pres*
Julius Miller, *General Mgr*
◆ **EMP:** 54 **EST:** 1965
SALES (est): 22MM **Privately Held**
WEB: www.alpertandalpert.com
SIC: 5093 Ferrous metal scrap & waste

(P-14118)
KINSBURSKY BROS SUPPLY INC (PA)
Also Called: K B I
125 E Commercial St Ste A, Anaheim (92801-1214)
PHONE..............................714 738-8516
Steven Kinsbursky, *President*
Aaron Zisman, *CFO*
Scott Kinsbursky, *Vice Pres*
Todd Coy, *Admin Sec*
Trevor Henderson, *Software Dev*
▲ **EMP:** 68 **EST:** 1958
SQ FT: 35,000
SALES (est): 25MM **Privately Held**
WEB: www.kbirecycling.com
SIC: 5093 Metal scrap & waste materials

(P-14119)
PAVEMENT RECYCLING SYSTEMS INC (PA)
Also Called: Prsi
10240 San Sevaine Way, Jurupa Valley (91752-1100)
PHONE..............................951 682-1091
Richard W Gove, *President*
Stephen Concannon, *President*
Debbie Whitson, *COO*
Nathan Beyler, *Officer*
Spencer Skipworth, *Executive*
▲ **EMP:** 125 **EST:** 1989
SQ FT: 40,000
SALES (est): 72.5MM **Privately Held**
WEB: www.pavementrecycling.com
SIC: 5093 1611 Scrap & waste materials; surfacing & paving; concrete construction: roads, highways, sidewalks, etc.; resurfacing contractor

(P-14120)
RALISON INTERNATIONAL INC
15328 Central Ave, Chino (91710-7658)
PHONE..............................909 393-0008
Jihong Luo, *President*
Eric Lao, *Vice Pres*
Byron Luo, *Vice Pres*
Albert Chiu, *Manager*
Eddie Lam, *Manager*
▼ **EMP:** 50 **EST:** 2000
SQ FT: 6,000
SALES (est): 11MM **Privately Held**
SIC: 5093 Waste paper

(P-14121)
RIVERSIDE SCRAP IR & MET CORP (PA)
Also Called: Redlands Recycling
2993 6th St, Riverside (92507-4131)
P.O. Box 5288 (92517-5288)
PHONE..............................951 686-2120
Samuel Frankel, *Ch of Bd*
Daniel Jay Frankel, *President*
Raj Gandhi, *Exec VP*
Muriel K Frankel, *Vice Pres*
EMP: 50 **EST:** 1954
SQ FT: 22,275
SALES (est): 9.3MM **Privately Held**
WEB: www.riversidemetalrecycling.com
SIC: 5093 Nonferrous metals scrap; waste paper; bottles, waste; plastics scrap

(P-14122)
SIERRA INTERNATIONAL MCHY LLC
1620 E Brundage Ln Frnt, Bakersfield (93307-2756)
P.O. Box 1340 (93302-1340)
PHONE..............................661 327-7073
Phillip Sacco, *Mng Member*
Dean Carpenter, *CFO*
Felipe Guerra, *Officer*
Wendy Adams, *Admin Asst*
Adrian Bernal, *Technical Staff*
◆ **EMP:** 65 **EST:** 1946
SQ FT: 15,000
SALES (est): 45.9MM **Privately Held**
WEB: www.sierraintl.com
SIC: 5093 5084 Nonferrous metals scrap; industrial machinery & equipment

(P-14123)
SOS METALS INC (DH)
201 E Gardena Blvd, Gardena (90248-2813)
PHONE..............................310 217-8848
Kenneth Buck, *CEO*
◆ **EMP:** 165 **EST:** 1972
SQ FT: 115,000
SALES (est): 46.1MM
SALES (corp-wide): 245.5B **Publicly Held**
WEB: www.precast.com
SIC: 5093 5051 Ferrous metal scrap & waste; ferroalloys
HQ: Precision Castparts Corp.
4650 Sw Mcdam Ave Ste 300
Portland OR 97239
503 946-4800

(P-14124)
USA-SRDC CORPORATION (DH)
500 W 140th St, Gardena (90248-1510)
PHONE..............................310 418-7064
Joseph Hyunmo, *CEO*
EMP: 50 **EST:** 2011
SALES (est): 3.6MM **Privately Held**
WEB: www.poscointl.com
SIC: 5093 Metal scrap & waste materials

5094 Jewelry, Watches, Precious Stones Wholesale

(P-14125)
A-MARK PRECIOUS METALS INC (PA)
2121 Rosecrans Ave # 6300, El Segundo (90245-4743)
PHONE..............................310 587-1477
Gregory N Roberts, *CEO*
Jeffrey D Benjamin, *Ch of Bd*
Thor G Gjerdrum, *President*
Brian Aquilino, *COO*
Kathleen Simpson Taylor, *CFO*
▲ **EMP:** 117 **EST:** 1965
SQ FT: 9,000
SALES: 7.6B **Publicly Held**
WEB: www.amark.com
SIC: 5094 Jewelry; precious metals

(P-14126)
BUNGALOW 16 ENTERTAINMENT LLC
8113 Melrose Ave, Los Angeles (90046-7011)
PHONE..............................310 226-7870
▲ **EMP:** 50

SQ FT: 2,000
SALES (est): 4.2MM **Privately Held**
SIC: 5094 Whol Jewelry/Precious Stones

(P-14127)
C&C JEWELRY MFG INC
323 W 8th St Fl 4, Los Angeles (90014-3109)
PHONE..............................213 623-6800
Mikhail Chekhman, *President*
Robert Connolly, *Vice Pres*
▲ **EMP:** 56
SQ FT: 3,000
SALES: 28.3MM **Privately Held**
SIC: 5094 3911 Jewelry; jewelry, precious metal

(P-14128)
CPI LUXURY GROUP
Also Called: China Pearl
10220 Norris Ave, Pacoima (91331-2217)
PHONE..............................818 249-9888
Harold Jabarian, *CEO*
Kevork Hasbanian, *Vice Pres*
▲ **EMP:** 54 **EST:** 1994
SQ FT: 15,000
SALES (est): 23MM **Privately Held**
WEB: www.cpilg.com
SIC: 5094 Pearls

(P-14129)
CW INDUSTRIES INC
761 Majors Ct, Bakersfield (93308-9436)
PHONE..............................661 399-5422
Ellis Firatt, *Branch Mgr*
Rocky Marquez, *General Mgr*
Jason Rodriguez, *Project Mgr*
Branden Wildvank, *Project Mgr*
EMP: 51 **Privately Held**
WEB: www.cwindustries.us
SIC: 5094 5051 1761 Precious stones & metals; metals service centers & offices; sheet metalwork
PA: Cw Industries, Inc.
1735 Santa Fe Ave
Long Beach CA 90813

(P-14130)
DIAMOND GOLDENWEST CORPORATION (PA)
Also Called: Jewelry Exchange, The
15732 Tustin Village Way, Tustin (92780-4924)
PHONE..............................714 542-9000
William S Doddridge, *President*
Sylvia Trujillo, *CFO*
Nancy Tahvildaran, *Vice Pres*
Michael Gordon, *Sales Staff*
Ashkan Tahvildaran, *Manager*
EMP: 150 **EST:** 1977
SQ FT: 25,000
SALES (est): 32.7MM **Privately Held**
WEB: www.jewelryexchange.com
SIC: 5944 5094 Jewelry; precious stones & precious metals; jewelry

(P-14131)
GOLD/GOLD/GOLD INC
4605 Lankershim Blvd, North Hollywood (91602-1818)
PHONE..............................323 845-9746
Boris Bystritsky,
Boris Bystrisky,
EMP: 20 **EST:** 2003
SALES (est): 6.3MM **Privately Held**
SIC: 5094 3911 Jewelry; jewelry, precious metal

(P-14132)
LUCAS DESIGN INTERNATIONAL INC (PA)
Also Called: Playboy Jewelry
606 S Hill St Ste 1001, Los Angeles (90014-1766)
PHONE..............................213 387-4444
Daniel Landver, *CEO*
Jason Landver, *President*
◆ **EMP:** 58
SQ FT: 100,000
SALES: 9MM **Privately Held**
SIC: 5094 Jewelry

(P-14133)
MALANIS INC
Also Called: Sona Chaandi Jewelry
18307 Pioneer Blvd, Artesia (90701-5532)
PHONE.................................562 924-7274
Manorma Malani, *President*
Pradip Malani, *Director*
▲ EMP: 17 EST: 1981
SQ FT: 11,000
SALES (est): 2.4MM Privately Held
SIC: 5094 2329 Jewelry; riding clothes:,
men's, youths' & boys'

(P-14134)
MAURICE KRAIEM & COMPANY
Also Called: Mk Diamonds & Jewelry
228 S Beverly Dr, Beverly Hills
(90212-3805)
PHONE.................................213 629-0038
Moshe Kraiem, *CEO*
Sylvia Arias, *COO*
Gina Renteria, *Consultant*
▲ EMP: 24 EST: 1978
SALES (est): 6.4MM Privately Held
WEB: www.mkdiamonds.com
SIC: 5094 3911 Jewelry; jewelry, precious
metal

(P-14135)
MEL BERNIE AND COMPANY INC (PA)
Also Called: 1928 Jewelry Company
3000 W Empire Ave, Burbank
(91504-3109)
PHONE.................................818 841-1928
Melvyn Bernie, *CEO*
▲ EMP: 250 EST: 1968
SQ FT: 65,000
SALES (est): 37.2MM Privately Held
WEB: www.1928.com
SIC: 5094 Jewelry

(P-14136)
NER PRECIOUS METALS INC
640 St Hill St Ste 450, Los Angeles
(90014)
PHONE.................................310 367-3179
Pedram Shamekh, *CEO*
▲ EMP: 60 EST: 2017
SQ FT: 900
SALES (est): 4.8MM Privately Held
SIC: 5094 5131 5085 Precious metals;
piece goods & other fabrics; industrial
supplies

(P-14137)
PARADE DESIGNS INC
1327 S Myrtle Ave, Monrovia (91016-4150)
PHONE.................................213 627-4019
Allen Pung, *President*
Nelson Fortier, *VP Sales*
Lyndsay Hirsch, *Mktg Coord*
▲ EMP: 14 EST: 2001
SALES (est): 2.9MM Privately Held
WEB: www.paradedesign.com
SIC: 5094 3961 Jewelers' findings;
bracelets, except precious metal

(P-14138)
SA KITSINIAN INC
Also Called: Kitsinian Jewellers
27101 Mcbean Pkwy, Valencia
(91355-5146)
PHONE.................................818 988-9961
Sarkis A Kitsinian, *President*
Susan Kitsinian, *Vice Pres*
Archi Kitsinian, *Admin Sec*
▲ EMP: 19 EST: 1978
SALES (est): 3MM Privately Held
WEB: www.kitsinianjewelers.com
SIC: 5094 3911 Jewelry; jewelry apparel

(P-14139)
SIMON G JEWELRY INC
Also Called: Zeghani
528 State St, Glendale (91203-1524)
PHONE.................................818 500-8595
Zaven Ghanimian, *CEO*
Simon Ghanimian, *President*
Hratch Shahbazian, *Vice Pres*
▲ EMP: 48 EST: 1994
SQ FT: 10,000
SALES (est): 14.7MM Privately Held
WEB:
SIC: 5094 3911 Jewelry; jewelry, precious
metal

(P-14140)
SUPERIOR GALLERIES INC (HQ)
20011 Ventura Blvd, Woodland Hills
(91364-2573)
PHONE.................................818 444-8699
Don Ketterling, *President*
EMP: 50 EST: 1983
SQ FT: 7,000
SALES (est): 6.1MM
SALES (corp-wide): 113.9MM Publicly
Held
WEB: www.dgse.com
SIC: 5094 5999 Coins; coins, medals &
trophies; coins
PA: Envela Corporation
1901 Gateway Dr Ste 100
Irving TX 75038
972 587-4049

(P-14141)
SWEDA COMPANY LLC
17411 E Valley Blvd, City of Industry
(91744-5159)
PHONE.................................626 357-9999
Jim Hagan, *CEO*
Kellie Claudio, *Vice Pres*
Scott Pearson, *Vice Pres*
Scott McDonald, *Administration*
Paul Beck,
◆ EMP: 200 EST: 1976
SQ FT: 350,000
SALES (est): 56.5MM Privately Held
WEB: www.swedausa.com
SIC: 5094 5044 Watches & parts; clocks;
calcvlators, electronic

(P-14142)
TACORI ENTERPRISES
Also Called: Tacori By B & T Jewelers
1736 Gardena Ave, Glendale (91204-2907)
PHONE.................................818 863-1536
Haig Tacorian, *CEO*
Alred Margousian, *CFO*
Christine Altimore, *Vice Pres*
Gilda Tacorian, *Vice Pres*
Alfred Margousian, *Controller*
▲ EMP: 58 EST: 1975
SQ FT: 16,000
SALES (est): 12.1MM Privately Held
WEB: www.tacori.com
SIC: 5094 Jewelry

(P-14143)
ZINA STERLING SILVER INC
Also Called: Zina Sterling Silver & Gifts
3268 Motor Ave, Los Angeles
(90034-3710)
PHONE.................................310 286-2206
Zina Sherman, *President*
Deborah Hecht, *Natl Sales Mgr*
Andrew Goldstein, *Marketing Staff*
Dorian Goldstein, *Manager*
EMP: 14 EST: 1983
SALES (est): 2.6MM Privately Held
WEB: www.zinabeverlyhills.com
SIC: 5094 5944 3911 Jewelry; jewelry,
precious stones & precious metals; jew-
elry, precious metal

5099 Durable Goods: NEC Wholesale

(P-14144)
ACTION GYPSUM SUPPLY WEST LP (PA)
13940 Magnolia Ave, Chino (91710-7029)
PHONE.................................909 993-5655
Cathy Wielt, *Manager*
EMP: 57 EST: 2018
SALES (est): 4.4MM Privately Held
WEB: www.actiongypsum.com
SIC: 5099 Durable goods

(P-14145)
AGRITEC INTERNATIONAL LTD
Also Called: Cleantech Environmental
5820 Martin Rd, Irwindale (91706-6213)
PHONE.................................626 812-7200
Robert Eldon Brown III, *President*
EMP: 50 EST: 1987
SQ FT: 5,000
SALES (est): 44.3MM Privately Held
WEB: www.cleantechenv.com
SIC: 5099 Safety equipment & supplies

(P-14146)
AUSTIN PANG GLV MFG USA CORP (HQ)
Also Called: Johnson Wilshire
17343 Freedom Way, City of Industry
(91748-1001)
P.O. Box 928, Downey (90241-0928)
PHONE.................................562 777-0088
David Pang, *CEO*
Michael Pang, *CFO*
Valerie Pang, *Admin Sec*
Danny Orosco, *Accounts Mgr*
▲ EMP: 50 EST: 1979
SQ FT: 54,000
SALES (est): 95MM Privately Held
WEB: www.johnsonwilshire.com
SIC: 5099 Safety equipment & supplies

(P-14147)
BRETHREN INC
Also Called: Fire Safety First
1170 E Fruit St, Santa Ana (92701-4205)
PHONE.................................714 836-4800
Al Saia, *CEO*
Mike Saia, *Vice Pres*
Peggy Saia, *Admin Sec*
EMP: 50 EST: 1984
SQ FT: 4,000
SALES (est): 20.9MM Privately Held
WEB: www.firesafetyfirst.com
SIC: 5099 7389 Fire extinguishers; fire ex-
tinguishing servicing

(P-14148)
CENTERLINE WOOD PRODUCTS
10007 Yucca Rd, Adelanto (92301-2242)
PHONE.................................760 246-4530
Michael Rodriguez, *President*
EMP: 99 EST: 2017
SALES (est): 6.1MM Privately Held
WEB: www.cwp.cab
SIC: 5099 Wood & wood by-products

(P-14149)
CMC RESCUE INC
6740 Cortona Dr, Goleta (93117-5574)
PHONE.................................805 562-9120
James A Frank, *Chairman*
Richard M Phillips, *President*
Beth Henry, *CFO*
Elizabeth Henry, *CFO*
Mike Crook, *Vice Pres*
▲ EMP: 65 EST: 1978
SQ FT: 23,000
SALES (est): 16.6MM Privately Held
WEB: www.cmcpro.com
SIC: 5099 5099 3842 8299 Safety sup-
plies & equipment; safety equipment &
supplies; lifesaving & survival equipment
(non-medical); personal safety equip-
ment; educational services

(P-14150)
D J AMERICAN SUPPLY INC
Also Called: American Dj Group of Compa-
nies
6122 S Eastern Ave, Commerce
(90040-3402)
PHONE.................................323 582-2650
Charles Davies, *President*
Alfred Gonzales, *President*
Toby Velazquez, *President*
Brian Dowdle, *Telecom Exec*
Ernie Velazquez, *Sales Mgr*
◆ EMP: 126 EST: 1985
SQ FT: 100,000
SALES (est): 26.3MM Privately Held
WEB: www.americandj.eu
SIC: 5099 5719 5999 Firearms & ammu-
nition, except sporting; lighting fixtures;
theatrical equipment & supplies

(P-14151)
DAMAO LUGGAGE INTL INC
Also Called: Chariot Travelware
1909 S Vineyard Ave, Ontario
(91761-7747)
PHONE.................................909 923-6531
Moon Woo, *President*
Wendy Fan, *CFO*
Austin Alvano, *Sales Staff*
Abby Kee, *Director*

Jian Kee, *Director*
▲ EMP: 3014 EST: 2014
SQ FT: 60,000
SALES (est): 92.2MM Privately Held
SIC: 5099 3161 Luggage; luggage

(P-14152)
DENNIS FOLAND INC (PA)
Also Called: Logo Expressions
1500 S Hellman Ave, Ontario (91761-7634)
PHONE.................................909 930-9900
Dennis Foland, *CEO*
Beverly Foland, *Corp Secy*
Miguel Tugas, *Info Tech Mgr*
Jennifer Foland, *Human Resources*
Darren Foland, *VP Opers*
▲ EMP: 79 EST: 1979
SQ FT: 140,000
SALES (est): 38.9MM Privately Held
WEB: www.folandgroup.com
SIC: 5099 3944 Souvenirs; games, toys &
children's vehicles

(P-14153)
DZ TRADING LTD
12492 Feather Dr, Eastvale (91752-1483)
PHONE.................................951 479-5700
Berenice Monay, *Manager*
Berenice Trading, *Manager*
EMP: 57 Privately Held
SIC: 5099 Brass goods
PA: Dz Trading, Ltd.
58 W 40th St Fl 8
New York NY 10018

(P-14154)
EASTMAN MUSIC COMPANY (PA)
Also Called: Eastmans Guitars
2158 Pomona Blvd, Pomona (91768-3332)
PHONE.................................909 868-1777
Saul Friedgood, *CEO*
Qian Ni, *CEO*
Saul N Friedgood, *Exec VP*
Julie Liu, *Purchasing*
Steve Bernstein, *Regl Sales Mgr*
▲ EMP: 63 EST: 2001
SALES (est): 38.5MM Privately Held
WEB: www.eastmanmusiccompany.com
SIC: 5099 3931 Musical instruments; ac-
cordions & parts

(P-14155)
FAM PPE LLC
5553-B Bandini Blvd B, Bell (90201)
PHONE.................................323 888-7755
Frank M Zarabi, *Mng Member*
EMP: 109 EST: 2020
SALES (est): 459.6K Privately Held
WEB: www.fambrands.com
SIC: 5099 Safety equipment & supplies
PA: Fam, Llc
5553-B Bandini Blvd
Bell CA 90201

(P-14156)
FOX LUGGAGE INC
221 N Orange Ave, City of Industry
(91744-3433)
PHONE.................................323 588-1688
Wayne Wang, *CEO*
Sherrishan H Lee, *President*
▲ EMP: 65 EST: 1987
SALES (est): 10.7MM Privately Held
WEB: www.foxluggage.com
SIC: 5099 Luggage

(P-14157)
FR-INDUSTRIES INC (DH)
1701 Lombard St Ste 200, Oxnard
(93030-8235)
PHONE.................................817 645-4366
Jerry Meyer, *CEO*
Jeffrey Cordes, *COO*
William Aisenberg, *Vice Pres*
Roy Whitehead, *Vice Pres*
▲ EMP: 50 EST: 2005
SQ FT: 50,000
SALES (est): 983K
SALES (corp-wide): 9.2B Publicly Held
WEB: www.walls.com
SIC: 5099 Fireproof clothing

PRODUCTS & SVCS

HQ: Walls Industries Llc
125 S Jennings Ave
Fort Worth TX 76104
844 259-2557

(P-14158)
GENIUS PRODUCTS INC
3301 Expo Blvd Ste 100, Santa Monica
(90404)
PHONE...................310 453-1222
Trevor Drinkwater, *President*
Stephen K Bannon, *Ch of Bd*
Edward J Byrnes, *CFO*
▲ EMP: 222 EST: 2005
SQ FT: 40,520
SALES (est): 46.4MM **Privately Held**
WEB: www.greenfo.rest
SIC: 5099 3652 7819 Video & audio
equipment; pre-recorded records & tapes;
video tape or disk reproduction

(P-14159)
**GOLDEN STATE MEDICAL
SUPPLY**
5247 Camino Ruiz, Camarillo
(93012-8602)
PHONE...................805 477-8966
Benjamin Hall, *CEO*
Thomas Weaver, *CFO*
EMP: 99 EST: 2017
SALES (est): 2.5MM **Privately Held**
WEB: www.gsms.us
SIC: 5099 Durable goods

(P-14160)
**GOLDEN WEST CUSTOM WD
SHUTTERS**
20561 Pascal Way, Lake Forest
(92630-8119)
PHONE...................949 951-0600
Fax: 949 595-0363
EMP: 50
SALES (est): 3.4MM **Privately Held**
SIC: 5099 Whol Durable Goods

(P-14161)
GUTHY-RENKER LLC
Also Called: Guthy-Renker Direct
3340 Ocean Park Blvd Fl 2, Santa Monica
(90405-3204)
PHONE...................310 581-6250
Bill Guthy, *President*
Keith Manning, *Exec VP*
MAI Farrag, *Vice Pres*
John Grazal, *Vice Pres*
Felipe Jimenez, *Vice Pres*
EMP: 80 **Privately Held**
WEB: www.guthy-renker.com
SIC: 5099 7812 5999 Tapes & cassettes,
prerecorded; commercials, television:
tape or film; cosmetics
PA: Guthy-Renker Llc
100 N Pcf Cast Hwy Ste 16
El Segundo CA 90245

(P-14162)
H2W
Also Called: Iced Out Gear
20630 Superior St, Chatsworth
(91311-4414)
PHONE...................800 578-3088
Dan Gershon, *CEO*
David Levich, *CFO*
Annette Barder, *Vice Pres*
Eric Liberman, *Admin Sec*
Debbie Silva, *Accounts Exec*
▲ EMP: 17 EST: 2002
SQ FT: 8,000
SALES: 6.3MM **Privately Held**
WEB: www.noveltysunglasses.com
SIC: 5099 3052 Sunglasses; air line or air
brake hose, rubber or rubberized fabric

(P-14163)
**HANSON DISTRIBUTING
COMPANY**
19154 San Jose Ave, Rowland Heights
(91748-1415)
PHONE...................626 839-4026
EMP: 65

SALES (corp-wide): 64.2MM **Privately
Held**
WEB: www.hansondistributing.com
SIC: 5531 5099 Automotive & home sup-
ply stores; brass goods
PA: Hanson Distributing Company
975 W 8th St
Azusa CA 91702
626 224-9800

(P-14164)
**IRIDIUM TECHNOLOGY GROUP
(PA)**
Also Called: Itg
17578 Rowland St, City of Industry
(91748-1114)
PHONE...................626 839-7488
John C Chu, *President*
Mandy F Niu, *CFO*
▲ EMP: 59 EST: 1999
SQ FT: 6,000
SALES (est): 1MM **Privately Held**
SIC: 5099 Compact discs

(P-14165)
JOHNSON SAFETY INC
Also Called: Myron & Davis
3404 De Forest Cir, Jurupa Valley
(91752-1165)
PHONE...................909 796-3385
Chung L Chang, *President*
Melody Chang, *Admin Sec*
Arthur Chang, *Project Mgr*
Tonette N Bombase, *VP Sales*
Luis Bojorquez, *Manager*
▲ EMP: 16 EST: 1984
SALES (est): 4.1MM **Privately Held**
WEB: www.myronanddavis.com
SIC: 5099 2531 2211 Video & audio
equipment; seats, automobile; seat cover
cloth, automobile: cotton

(P-14166)
**KAWAI AMERICA CORPORATION
(HQ)**
2055 E University Dr, Compton
(90220-6411)
PHONE...................310 631-1771
Hirotaka Kawai, *President*
Naoki Mori, *President*
Yoshiro Kataoka, *Admin Sec*
Tom Love, *VP Sales*
Don Mannino, *Master*
◆ EMP: 50 EST: 1963
SQ FT: 73,000
SALES (est): 26.7MM **Privately Held**
WEB: www.kawaius.com
SIC: 5099 Pianos

(P-14167)
LA SIERRA RECORDS INC
Also Called: La Sierra Promotions
8628 Van Nuys Blvd, Panorama City
(91402-2913)
PHONE...................818 830-1919
Matias R Meza, *President*
Guicila Meza, *CFO*
EMP: 23 EST: 1991
SQ FT: 12,000
SALES (est): 1.5MM **Privately Held**
WEB: www.lasierrarecords.com
SIC: 5099 2782 5813 5812 Phonograph
records; record albums; night clubs; Mexi-
can restaurant

(P-14168)
**MADACO SAFETY PRODUCTS
INC**
1313 N Grand Ave 249, Walnut
(91789-1317)
PHONE...................909 614-1756
Frank Hsu, *President*
Ryan Marquette, *Accounts Exec*
▲ EMP: 15 EST: 1997
SQ FT: 2,000
SALES (est): 3MM **Privately Held**
WEB: www.madaco.com
SIC: 5099 3841 Safety equipment & sup-
plies; surgical & medical instruments

(P-14169)
MERIDIAN MOULDING INC
330 Cessna Cir, Corona (92878-5009)
PHONE...................951 279-5220
George Noor, *CEO*

Najil Azzi, *CFO*
Mary Jo Elkareh, *Admin Sec*
▲ EMP: 15 EST: 2001
SQ FT: 34,000
SALES (est): 2.7MM **Privately Held**
SIC: 5099 3089 Wood & wood by-prod-
ucts; prefabricated plastic buildings

(P-14170)
MONOPRICE INC (HQ)
Also Called: Monoprice.com
1 Pointe Dr Ste 400, Brea (92821-7634)
PHONE...................909 989-6887
Bernard Luthi, *CEO*
Leila Cheung, *Vice Pres*
Thomas Nutty, *Vice Pres*
Michelle Macias, *Program Mgr*
Lance Aldas, *Planning*
◆ EMP: 164 EST: 2002
SQ FT: 30,000
SALES (est): 147.7MM **Privately Held**
WEB: www.monoprice.com
SIC: 5099 Video & audio equipment

(P-14171)
NEW CENTURY MEDIA CORP
2727 Pellissier Pl, City of Industry
(90601-1510)
PHONE...................562 695-1000
Carson Yu, *President*
Jennifer Yu, *Vice Pres*
Eva Gonzalez, *Office Mgr*
Andy Forman, *VP Sales*
▲ EMP: 50 EST: 1989
SQ FT: 21,000
SALES (est): 16MM **Privately Held**
WEB: www.newcenturymediausa.com
SIC: 5099 Video cassettes, accessories &
supplies

(P-14172)
**OLIVET INTERNATIONAL INC
(PA)**
11015 Hopkins St, Jurupa Valley
(91752-3248)
PHONE...................951 681-8888
Sean Lin, *Mng Member*
Andrew Bomes, *President*
Lydia Hsu, *President*
David Yu, *CFO*
Lin Jason, *Exec Dir*
▲ EMP: 89 EST: 1984
SQ FT: 456,000
SALES (est): 172.9MM **Privately Held**
WEB: www.olivetintl.com
SIC: 5099 3161 Luggage; luggage

(P-14173)
**OWENS & MINOR DISTRIBUTION
INC**
452 Sespe Ave, Fillmore (93015-2042)
PHONE...................805 524-0243
Michael Guelzow, *Branch Mgr*
Sara Rosendale, *Accountant*
C J Leggett, *Sales Staff*
EMP: 989 **Publicly Held**
WEB: www.owens-minor.com
SIC: 5099 Firearms & ammunition, except
sporting
HQ: Owens & Minor Distribution, Inc.
9120 Lockwood Blvd
Mechanicsville VA 23116
804 723-7000

(P-14174)
PLATINUM DISC LLC
Also Called: Echo Bridge Home Entertain-
ment
10203 Santa Monica Blvd # 5, Los Angeles
(90067-6416)
PHONE...................608 784-6620
Nate Hart, *President*
Nathan Hart, *President*
▼ EMP: 91 EST: 1995
SALES (est): 13MM **Privately Held**
SIC: 5099 Compact discs
PA: Echo Bridge Entertainment, Llc
75 2nd Ave Ste 500
Needham MA 02494
781 444-6767

(P-14175)
**PRAJIN 1 STOP DISTRIBUTORS
INC (PA)**
Also Called: Prajin Discount Distributors
5701 Pacific Blvd 5711, Huntington Park
(90255-2615)
PHONE...................323 395-5302
Antonio Prajin, *President*
Maria Gina Prajin, *Shareholder*
George Prajin, *Corp Secy*
Anthony Prajin Jr, *Vice Pres*
Peter Prajin, *General Mgr*
EMP: 50 EST: 1975
SQ FT: 1,000
SALES (est): 8MM **Privately Held**
SIC: 5099 5735 Compact discs; compact
discs

(P-14176)
QUEST GROUP (PA)
Also Called: Audioquest
2621 White Rd, Irvine (92614-6247)
PHONE...................949 585-0111
William E Low, *CEO*
Mike McConnell, *CFO*
Joe Anzenberger, *Vice Pres*
Jessica Carr, *Vice Pres*
David Nichols, *Vice Pres*
◆ EMP: 58 EST: 1980
SQ FT: 45,000
SALES (est): 25.3MM **Privately Held**
WEB: www.audioquest.com
SIC: 5099 Video & audio equipment

(P-14177)
RGGD INC (PA)
Also Called: Crystal Art of Florida
4950 S Santa Fe Ave, Vernon
(90058-2106)
PHONE...................323 581-6617
Randy Greenberg, *CEO*
Douglas Song, *President*
Glenn Knecht, *Admin Sec*
◆ EMP: 79 EST: 1994
SQ FT: 120,000
SALES (est): 26.7MM **Privately Held**
WEB: www.crystalartgallery.com
SIC: 5099 3441 Wood & wood by-prod-
ucts; fabricated structural metal

(P-14178)
**ROLAND CORPORATION US
(HQ)**
5100 S Eastern Ave, Los Angeles
(90040-2950)
P.O. Box 910921 (90091-0921)
PHONE...................323 890-3700
Christopher Bristol, *CEO*
Dennis M Houlihan, *Vice Pres*
Mark S Malbon, *Vice Pres*
Charles L Wright, *Vice Pres*
Jun Yamato, *Vice Pres*
◆ EMP: 165 EST: 1953
SQ FT: 50,000
SALES (est): 70.9MM **Privately Held**
WEB: www.roland.com
SIC: 5099 5045 3931 Musical instru-
ments; computer peripheral equipment;
organs, all types: pipe, reed, hand, elec-
tronic, etc.

(P-14179)
**ROSE K TARLOW ANTIQUES
LTD (PA)**
Also Called: Tarlow R Antiques
425 N Robertson Blvd, West Hollywood
(90048-1735)
PHONE...................323 651-2202
Rose K Tarlow, *President*
Barry Tarlow, *Treasurer*
Angie Cooper, *Production*
▲ EMP: 61 EST: 1974
SQ FT: 2,000
SALES (est): 1.5MM **Privately Held**
WEB: www.rosetarlow.com
SIC: 5099 Antiques

(P-14180)
ROSEN ELECTRONICS LLC
2500 E Francis St, Ontario (91761-7730)
PHONE...................951 898-9808
W Thomas Clements, *President*
▲ EMP: 75 EST: 2003

SALES (est): 21.5MM
SALES (corp-wide): 52.3MM **Privately Held**
WEB: www.rosenelectronics.com
SIC: 5099 3679 Video & audio equipment; liquid crystal displays (LCD)
PA: Aamp Of Florida, Inc.
15500 Lightwave Dr # 202
Clearwater FL 33760
727 572-9255

(P-14181)
RWP TRANSFER INC
Also Called: Recycled Wood Products
1313 E Phillips Blvd, Pomona (91766-5431)
PHONE..............................909 868-6882
Chris Kiralla, *President*
EMP: 50 **EST:** 1983
SQ FT: 1,100
SALES (est): 13.9MM **Privately Held**
WEB: www.rwpmulch.com
SIC: 5099 5083 Wood & wood by-products; landscaping equipment

(P-14182)
SUN COAST MERCHANDISE CORP
6600 Bandini Blvd, Commerce (90040-3302)
PHONE..............................323 720-9700
Kumar C Bhavnani, *President*
Dilip Bhavnani, *Vice Pres*
Vidya Bhavnani, *Admin Sec*
Venkat Ganapathy, *Controller*
Bob Fallon, *Natl Sales Mgr*
◆ **EMP:** 250 **EST:** 1943
SQ FT: 120,000
SALES (est): 31MM **Privately Held**
WEB: www.sunscopeusa.com
SIC: 5099 Brass goods

(P-14183)
SUNBELT USA INC (PA)
Also Called: Sunbelt of California
1941 Yeager Ave, La Verne (91750-5833)
P.O. Box 760 (91750-0760)
PHONE..............................909 593-0500
Roy Burchett, *President*
Rebecca Burchett, *Treasurer*
▲ **EMP:** 19 **EST:** 1983
SQ FT: 6,000
SALES (est): 6.4MM **Privately Held**
WEB: www.sunbeltoptic.com
SIC: 5099 3851 Sunglasses; glasses, sun or glare; goggles: sun, safety, industrial, underwater, etc.

(P-14184)
SUNSCAPE EYEWEAR INC
17526 Von Karman Ave A, Irvine (92614-4258)
PHONE..............................949 553-0590
Ali Adam Rizza, *President*
Adam Rizza, *CFO*
Wally Rizza, *Vice Pres*
▲ **EMP:** 78 **EST:** 1999
SQ FT: 10,500
SALES (est): 6.1MM **Privately Held**
WEB: www.isunscape.com
SIC: 5099 Sunglasses

(P-14185)
TRAVELERS CLUB LUGGAGE INC
5911 Fresca Dr, La Palma (90623-1056)
PHONE..............................714 523-8808
Peter Yu, *CEO*
Martin Jolie, *Vice Pres*
Nick Johnson, *Sales Staff*
Danny Cho, *Manager*
◆ **EMP:** 54
SQ FT: 120,000
SALES (est): 16.7MM **Privately Held**
WEB: www.travelersclub.com
SIC: 5099 Luggage

(P-14186)
YAMAHA CORPORATION OF AMERICA (HQ)
Also Called: Yamaha Music Corporation U S A
6600 Orangethorpe Ave, Buena Park (90620-1396)
PHONE..............................714 522-9011

Hitoshi Fukutome, *CEO*
Terry Lewis, *Senior VP*
Randy Beck, *Vice Pres*
Garth Gilman, *Vice Pres*
Douglas Penstone-Smith, *Vice Pres*
◆ **EMP:** 300 **EST:** 1958
SALES (est): 584.7MM **Privately Held**
WEB: www.usa.yamaha.com
SIC: 5099 5065 5091 3931 Musical instruments; pianos; sound equipment, electronic; sporting & recreation goods; golf equipment; musical instruments

5111 Printing & Writing Paper Wholesale

(P-14187)
KELLY PAPER COMPANY (HQ)
12310 Slauson Ave, Santa Fe Springs (90670-2629)
PHONE..............................909 859-8200
Janice Gottesman, *President*
Danny Hernandez, *Branch Mgr*
Fernando Pinal, *Branch Mgr*
John Echavarria, *District Mgr*
Larry Armanino, *Store Mgr*
▲ **EMP:** 50 **EST:** 1936
SALES (est): 240.7MM
SALES (corp-wide): 1.3B **Privately Held**
WEB: www.kellypaper.com
SIC: 5111 5943 Printing paper; office forms & supplies
PA: Central National Gottesman Inc.
3 Manhattanville Rd # 301
Purchase NY 10577
914 696-9000

(P-14188)
KELLY SPICERS INC (HQ)
Also Called: Kelly Spicers Packaging
12310 Slauson Ave, Santa Fe Springs (90670-2629)
PHONE..............................562 698-1199
Janice Gottesman, *CEO*
Jimmy Vo, *Treasurer*
Ozgur Aydin, *Officer*
Rick Anderson, *Vice Pres*
Jeff Jarvis, *Regional Mgr*
▲ **EMP:** 180 **EST:** 1965
SQ FT: 365,000
SALES (est): 672.9MM
SALES (corp-wide): 1.3B **Privately Held**
WEB: www.spicers.com
SIC: 5111 5199 5087 Fine paper; printing paper; writing paper; packaging materials; janitors' supplies
PA: Central National Gottesman Inc.
3 Manhattanville Rd # 301
Purchase NY 10577
914 696-9000

5112 Stationery & Office Splys Wholesale

(P-14189)
5 DAY BUSINESS FORMS MFG INC (PA)
2910 E La Cresta Ave, Anaheim (92806-1818)
P.O. Box 6269 (92816-0269)
PHONE..............................213 623-3577
Leslie Messick, *President*
Walter Messick, *Shareholder*
Robert Bemmer, *Purchasing*
Gaby Atonio, *Receptionist*
EMP: 54 **EST:** 1976
SQ FT: 22,500
SALES (est): 20.5MM **Privately Held**
WEB: www.5daybf.com
SIC: 5112 Business forms

(P-14190)
5 DAY BUSINESS FORMS MFG INC
2921 E La Cresta Ave, Anaheim (92806-1873)
PHONE..............................714 632-8674
Lesley Messick, *Branch Mgr*
Norman Hamamoto, *Chief Mktg Ofcr*
Wendy Schul, *Human Res Dir*
Scott Kirschner, *Prdtn Mgr*

Norm Hamamoto, *Sales Associate*
EMP: 62
SALES (corp-wide): 20.5MM **Privately Held**
WEB: www.5daybf.com
SIC: 5112 Business forms
PA: 5 Day Business Forms Mfg., Inc.
2910 E La Cresta Ave
Anaheim CA 92806
213 623-3577

(P-14191)
A YAFA PEN COMPANY
21306 Gault St, Canoga Park (91303-2123)
PHONE..............................818 704-8888
Yair Greenberg, *CEO*
Niv Avidan, *Exec VP*
Eddie Olague, *Webmaster*
Isela Leon, *Export Mgr*
Ross Cameron, *Natl Sales Mgr*
▲ **EMP:** 50 **EST:** 1978
SQ FT: 25,000
SALES (est): 20.4MM **Privately Held**
WEB: www.yafa.com
SIC: 5112 5199 Office supplies; advertising specialties

(P-14192)
BANGKIT (USA) INC
Also Called: Bazic Product
10511 Valley Blvd, El Monte (91731-2403)
PHONE..............................626 672-0888
Handy Hioe, *CEO*
Eric Concepcion, *Vice Pres*
Daniel Graham, *Vice Pres*
Anita Handojo, *Vice Pres*
Lanny Sanjaya, *Executive*
◆ **EMP:** 76 **EST:** 1998
SQ FT: 195,000
SALES (est): 39MM **Privately Held**
WEB: www.bazicproducts.com
SIC: 5112 Office supplies

(P-14193)
CENVEO WORLDWIDE LIMITED
705 Baldwin Park Blvd, City of Industry (91746-1504)
PHONE..............................626 369-4921
Timothy Hollywood, *Branch Mgr*
Peter Popovich, *Representative*
EMP: 253
SALES (corp-wide): 1B **Privately Held**
WEB: www.cenveo.com
SIC: 5112 Stationery & office supplies
HQ: Cenveo Worldwide Limited
200 First Stamford Pl
Stamford CT 06902
203 595-3000

(P-14194)
ESSENDANT CO
Also Called: United Stationers
918 S Stimson Ave, City of Industry (91745-1640)
PHONE..............................626 961-0011
Terry Deines, *Manager*
Bill Sutter, *MIS Dir*
Kurt Standen, *Opers Staff*
EMP: 78 **Privately Held**
WEB: www.essendant.com
SIC: 5112 5044 5021 5943 Office supplies; office equipment; furniture; office forms & supplies
HQ: Essendant Co.
1 Parkway North Blvd # 100
Deerfield IL 60015
847 627-7000

(P-14195)
OFFICE XPRESS INC
Also Called: Oxpros
7705 Alabama Ave, Canoga Park (91304-4904)
P.O. Box 11110 (91309-2110)
PHONE..............................818 884-5737
Mike Bushman, *President*
Michael Helou, *General Mgr*
EMP: 24 **EST:** 2003
SQ FT: 20,000

SALES (est): 3.5MM **Privately Held**
WEB: www.jthayer.com
SIC: 5943 5112 3955 7389 Office forms & supplies; laserjet supplies; print cartridges for laser & other computer printers; advertising, promotional & trade show services; customized clothing & apparel; office furniture

(P-14196)
PENTEL OF AMERICA LTD (HQ)
2715 Columbia St, Torrance (90503-3861)
PHONE..............................310 320-3831
Chotaro Koumi, *President*
Norikazu Hasegama, *CFO*
Gozo Kiknchi, *Treasurer*
Nobuo Aihara, *Chief Mktg Ofcr*
Minoru Mike Osada, *Exec VP*
◆ **EMP:** 132
SQ FT: 46,000
SALES (est): 97.6MM **Privately Held**
WEB: www.pentel.com
SIC: 5112 3951 5199 3952 Pens &/or pencils; pens & mechanical pencils; artists' materials; artists' materials, except pencils & leads

(P-14197)
PUNCH STUDIO LLC (PA)
6025 W Slauson Ave, Culver City (90230-6507)
P.O. Box 3663 (90231-3663)
PHONE..............................310 390-9900
Todd Kirshner, *Mng Member*
Nathalie Carrer, *CFO*
◆ **EMP:** 230 **EST:** 2001
SQ FT: 106,000
SALES (est): 55MM **Privately Held**
WEB: www.punchstudio.com
SIC: 5112 Greeting cards

(P-14198)
SYSTEM SUPPLY STATIONERY CORP
1251 E Walnut St, Carson (90746-1383)
PHONE..............................310 223-0880
Enrico Ventura, *President*
Amber Ventura, *Vice Pres*
Lorena Cisneros, *Administration*
▲ **EMP:** 18 **EST:** 1949
SQ FT: 30,000
SALES (est): 4MM **Privately Held**
WEB: www.3scorp.com
SIC: 5112 5021 2752 Office supplies; office furniture; billheads, lithographed

(P-14199)
TAYLOR PRINT VSUAL IMPRSSONS I
Also Called: Curtis 1000 Los Angeles
4100 E Jurupa Ave Ste 106, Ontario (91761)
PHONE..............................909 357-0661
Chris Fortunato, *Branch Mgr*
Roy Moose, *Executive*
EMP: 50
SALES (corp-wide): 3.6B **Privately Held**
WEB: www.curtis1000.com
SIC: 5112 Envelopes; business forms
HQ: Taylor Print & Visual Impressions, Inc.
1725 Brecknrdg Pkwy Ste 5
Duluth GA 30096
770 925-4500

(P-14200)
VIKING OFFICE PRODUCTS INC (DH)
3366 E Willow St, Signal Hill (90755-2311)
PHONE..............................562 490-1000
M Bruce Nelson, *President*
Ronald W Weissman, *Senior VP*
Mark R Brown, *Vice Pres*
▲ **EMP:** 292 **EST:** 1960
SQ FT: 187,000
SALES (est): 349.4MM
SALES (corp-wide): 9.7B **Publicly Held**
WEB: www.officedepot.com
SIC: 5112 5021 5045 5087 Office supplies; business forms; stationery; office furniture; computers, peripherals & software; janitors' supplies; photographic equipment & supplies; catalog & mail-order houses

HQ: Office Depot, Llc
6600 N Military Trl
Boca Raton FL 33496
561 438-4800

(P-14201)
WRIGHT BUS GRAPHICS CAL INC
13602 12th St Ste A, Chino (91710-5200)
PHONE..............................800 310-3676
Gene Snitker, *President*
Rose Marie Phipps, *Purch Agent*
EMP: 19 EST: 1965
SQ FT: 34,000
SALES (est): 904.7K **Privately Held**
WEB: www.wrightbg.com
SIC: 5112 2761 2671 Business forms; manifold business forms; packaging paper & plastics film, coated & laminated

(P-14202)
XSE GROUP INC
92 Argonaut Ste 235, Aliso Viejo (92656-4112)
PHONE..............................888 272-8340
EMP: 199
SALES (corp-wide): 120.3MM **Privately Held**
WEB: www.xsegroup.com
SIC: 5112 Office supplies
PA: Xse Group, Inc.
35 Phil Mack Dr
Middletown CT 06457
888 272-8340

5113 Indl & Personal Svc Paper Wholesale

(P-14203)
ANDWIN CORPORATION (PA)
Also Called: Andwin Scientific
167 W Cochran St, Simi Valley (93065-6217)
P.O. Box 689, Woodland Hills (91365-0689)
PHONE..............................818 999-2828
Natalie Sarraf, *CEO*
Abner Levy, *President*
Stacey Katz, *Executive*
Teresa Cisneros, *Purchasing*
Sandy Rosenblum, *Purchasing*
▲ EMP: 94 EST: 1950
SALES (est): 59.7MM **Privately Held**
WEB: www.andwincorp.com
SIC: 5113 5199 5087 5047 Shipping supplies; art goods & supplies; packaging materials; janitors' supplies; hospital equipment & furniture; barium diagnostic agents

(P-14204)
BUNZL DISTRIBUTION CAL LLC (DH)
3310 E Miraloma Ave, Anaheim (92806-1911)
PHONE..............................714 688-1900
Patrick L Larmon, *President*
Michael Bohannon, *Senior VP*
Frank Terry, *Senior VP*
Scot Gregory, *General Mgr*
Stephen Cousins, *Administration*
◆ EMP: 98 EST: 1989
SQ FT: 150,000
SALES (est): 87.3MM
SALES (corp-wide): 13.4B **Privately Held**
WEB: www.bunzldistribution.com
SIC: 5113 Paper & products, wrapping or coarse
HQ: Bunzl Distribution Usa, Llc
1 Cityplace Dr Ste 200
Saint Louis MO 63141
314 997-5959

(P-14205)
BUNZL RETAIL SERVICES LLC
8449 Milliken Ave Ste 102, Rancho Cucamonga (91730-5540)
PHONE..............................909 476-2457
EMP: 78
SALES (corp-wide): 13.4B **Privately Held**
WEB: www.bunzldistribution.com
SIC: 5113 Paper & products, wrapping or coarse

HQ: Bunzl Retail Services, Llc
8338 Austin Ave
Morton Grove IL 60053
847 733-1469

(P-14206)
CALIFORNIA SUPPLY INC (PA)
491 E Compton Blvd, Gardena (90248-2078)
P.O. Box 3906 (90247-7598)
PHONE..............................310 532-2500
Mark Weinstein, *CEO*
Art Gaford, *CFO*
Michael Rosson, *Exec VP*
Mike McMillen, *Vice Pres*
Michel Rosson, *Vice Pres*
◆ EMP: 69
SQ FT: 75,000
SALES (est): 36.3MM **Privately Held**
WEB: www.calsupply.com
SIC: 5113 5087 Industrial & personal service paper; janitors' supplies

(P-14207)
CASE PAPER COMPANY
9168 Hermosa Ave Unit 100, Rancho Cucamonga (91730-5307)
PHONE..............................626 358-8450
Marty Rosebaum, *Principal*
Jacque Mullen, *Admin Mgr*
Tim Resser, *General Mgr*
Lisa Bailey, *Sales Staff*
Sandy Barraza, *Sales Staff*
EMP: 17 EST: 2015
SALES (est): 5MM **Privately Held**
WEB: www.casepaper.com
SIC: 5113 2621 Patterns, paper; paper mills

(P-14208)
E & S PAPER CO
Also Called: Delta Packaging Products
14110 S Broadway, Los Angeles (90061-1019)
PHONE..............................310 538-8700
Spencer Pritkin, *President*
Richard Hemmer, *Treasurer*
Rosalind Pritikin, *Treasurer*
EMP: 28 EST: 1964
SQ FT: 21,000
SALES (est): 5.3MM **Privately Held**
SIC: 5113 5085 2679 3086 Paperboard & products; packing, industrial; paperboard products, converted; packaging & shipping materials, foamed plastic

(P-14209)
FRICK PAPER COMPANY
Also Called: Paper Mart Indus & Ret Packg
2164 N Batavia St, Orange (92865-3104)
PHONE..............................323 726-8200
John Frick, *Partner*
Thomas Frick, *Partner*
Tom Frick, *Partner*
Julia Felde, *Vice Pres*
Gary Zhang, *Sr Software Eng*
◆ EMP: 106 EST: 1921
SQ FT: 210,000
SALES (est): 126.5MM **Privately Held**
WEB: www.papermart.com
SIC: 5113 Paper & products, wrapping or coarse

(P-14210)
GEORGIA-PACIFIC LLC
9206 Santa Fe Springs Rd, Santa Fe Springs (90670-2618)
PHONE..............................562 861-6226
EMP: 275
SALES (corp-wide): 36.9B **Privately Held**
WEB: www.gp.com
SIC: 5113 2653 Corrugated & solid fiber boxes; bags, paper & disposable plastic; boxes, corrugated: made from purchased materials; display items, corrugated: made from purchased materials
HQ: Georgia-Pacific Llc
133 Peachtree St Nw
Atlanta GA 30303
404 652-4000

(P-14211)
IMPERIAL BAG & PAPER CO LLC
Also Called: Paper Company, The
2825 Warner Ave, Irvine (92606-4443)
PHONE..............................800 834-6248
Julie Scheibe, *Vice Pres*
EMP: 98
SALES (corp-wide): 1.4B **Privately Held**
WEB: www.imperialbag.com
SIC: 5113 5199 Containers, paper & disposable plastic; sanitary food containers; packaging materials
PA: Imperial Bag & Paper Co. Llc
255 Us Highway 1 And 9
Jersey City NJ 07306
201 437-7440

(P-14212)
MAXCO SUPPLY INC
8419 Di Giorgio Rd, Lamont (93241-2547)
PHONE..............................559 646-6700
Steve Grote, *Principal*
EMP: 78
SALES (corp-wide): 72.1MM **Privately Held**
WEB: www.maxcopackaging.com
SIC: 5113 Bags, paper & disposable plastic
PA: Maxco Supply, Inc.
605 S Zediker Ave
Parlier CA 93648
559 646-8449

(P-14213)
MICHAEL MADDEN CO INC
Also Called: Paper Company, The
2825 Warner Ave, Irvine (92606-4443)
P.O. Box 17807 (92623-7807)
PHONE..............................800 834-6248
◆ EMP: 70
SQ FT: 75,000
SALES (est): 62.2MM
SALES (corp-wide): 1.4B **Privately Held**
WEB: www.thepapercompany.net
SIC: 5113 Whol Industrial/Service Paper
PA: Imperial Bag & Paper Co. Llc
255 Route 1 And 9
Jersey City NJ 07306
201 437-7440

(P-14214)
NEWAY PACKAGING CORP (PA)
1973 E Via Arado, Rancho Dominguez (90220-6102)
PHONE..............................602 454-9000
Russell E Freebury, *President*
Sarah D Giles-Bell, *Vice Pres*
Carole Freebury, *Controller*
Robert Hayward, *Sales Executive*
Kathleen Menning, *Sales Staff*
◆ EMP: 60 EST: 1977
SQ FT: 36,000
SALES (est): 50.1MM **Privately Held**
WEB: www.newaypkgshop.com
SIC: 5113 5084 Shipping supplies; packaging machinery & equipment

(P-14215)
NORTHCROSS PAPER CO INC
9667 Canoga Ave, Chatsworth (91311-4115)
PHONE..............................818 998-3774
Charles R Northcross, *President*
Bryan Romero, *Sales Associate*
EMP: 22 EST: 1955
SQ FT: 3,000
SALES (est): 646.1K **Privately Held**
SIC: 5113 3497 2672 Cardboard & products; corrugated & solid fiber boxes; metal foil & leaf; coated & laminated paper

(P-14216)
NOVIPAX INC
Also Called: Paper-Pak Industries
1941 N White Ave, La Verne (91750-5663)
PHONE..............................909 392-1750
Ron Leach, *CEO*
Jeffrey Williams, *CFO*
Sophia Smeragliuolo, *Research*
Bob Schindel, *Plant Mgr*
Bob Bova, *Marketing Staff*
◆ EMP: 100 EST: 2001
SQ FT: 100,000

SALES (est): 46.6MM
SALES (corp-wide): 2.9B **Privately Held**
WEB: www.novipax.com
SIC: 5113 Industrial & personal service paper
HQ: Npx One Llc
4275 Reading Crest Ave
Reading PA 19605
866 764-8338

(P-14217)
OAK PAPER PRODUCTS CO INC (PA)
Also Called: Acorn Paper Products Co.
3686 E Olympic Blvd, Los Angeles (90023-3146)
P.O. Box 23965 (90023-0965)
PHONE..............................323 268-0507
David Weissberg, *CEO*
Max Weissberg, *President*
Renee Duncan, *Sales Staff*
▲ EMP: 174 EST: 1959
SQ FT: 250,000
SALES (est): 91.8MM **Privately Held**
WEB: www.acorn-paper.com
SIC: 5113 5199 5087 2653 Shipping supplies; packaging materials; janitors' supplies; corrugated & solid fiber boxes

(P-14218)
OASIS BRANDS INC
100 S Anaheim Blvd # 280, Anaheim (92805-3807)
PHONE..............................540 658-2830
Lee Shuchun, *Director*
Michelle Wu, *Accountant*
John Bartow, *Sales Staff*
▲ EMP: 75 EST: 2009
SALES (est): 156MM **Privately Held**
WEB: www.solarispaper.com
SIC: 5113 Napkins, paper

(P-14219)
ORORA NORTH AMERICA
Also Called: Landsberg La Valey Div 1027
12708 Branford St, Pacoima (91331-4203)
P.O. Box Dept 2583, Los Angeles (90084-0001)
PHONE..............................818 896-3449
EMP: 45
SALES (corp-wide): 3B **Privately Held**
SIC: 5113 2653 Whol Industrial/Service Paper Mfg Corrugated/Solid Fiber Boxes
HQ: Orora Packaging Solutions
6600 Valley View St
Buena Park CA 90620
714 562-6000

(P-14220)
ORORA NORTH AMERICA
Also Called: Corru Kraft Buena Pk Div 5058
6200 Caballero Blvd, Buena Park (90620-1124)
PHONE..............................714 562-6002
Jim Wilczek, *Vice Pres*
Geoff O 'shannassy, *Opers Staff*
Frank Hernandez, *Maint Spvr*
Michael Jonsson, *Manager*
EMP: 149 **Privately Held**
WEB: www.ororapackagingsolutions.com
SIC: 5113 2653 Paper & products, wrapping or coarse; boxes, corrugated: made from purchased materials
HQ: Orora Packaging Solutions
6600 Valley View St
Buena Park CA 90620
714 562-6000

(P-14221)
ORORA PACKAGING SOLUTIONS (HQ)
Also Called: Landsberg Orora
6600 Valley View St, Buena Park (90620-1145)
PHONE..............................714 562-6000
Bernardino Salvatore, *President*
Bernardino Salvatorre, *President*
David Conley, *CFO*
Greg Hummel, *Vice Pres*
Matt Jones, *Vice Pres*
◆ EMP: 100
SQ FT: 300,000

SALES (est): 1.8B Privately Held
WEB: www.ororapackagingsolutions.com
SIC: 5113 2653 Paper & products, wrapping or coarse; sanitary food containers; boxes, corrugated: made from purchased materials

(P-14222)
ORORA PACKAGING SOLUTIONS
Also Called: Landsberg Los Angeles Div 1001
1640 S Greenwood Ave, Montebello
(90640-6538)
P.O. Box 800 (90640-0800)
PHONE....................323 832-2000
Jed Wockenfuss, *Manager*
David Conley, *Finance Mgr*
David Graney, *Finance*
Rudy Robles, *Foreman/Supr*
EMP: 168 **Privately Held**
WEB: www.ororapackagingsolutions.com
SIC: 5113 2653 Paper & products, wrapping or coarse; boxes, corrugated: made from purchased materials
HQ: Orora Packaging Solutions
6600 Valley View St
Buena Park CA 90620
714 562-6000

(P-14223)
P & R PAPER SUPPLY CO INC (HQ)
1898 E Colton Ave, Redlands
(92374-9798)
P.O. Box 590 (92373-0201)
PHONE....................909 389-1807
Mark S Maiberger, *CEO*
Joe Maiberger, *President*
Luke Maiberger, *Vice Pres*
Brian Leftwich, *Branch Mgr*
Sam Mackie, *Branch Mgr*
▼ **EMP:** 223 **EST:** 1965
SQ FT: 75,000
SALES (est): 81.6MM
SALES (corp-wide): 1.4B **Privately Held**
WEB: www.prpaper.com
SIC: 5113 5169 5149 5072 Paper & products, wrapping or coarse; chemicals & allied products; groceries & related products; hardware; commercial equipment
PA: Imperial Bag & Paper Co. Llc
255 Us Highway 1 And 9
Jersey City NJ 07306
201 437-7440

(P-14224)
PERRIN BERNARD SUPOWITZ LLC (HQ)
Also Called: Fergadis Enterprises
5496 Lindbergh Ln, Bell (90201-6409)
PHONE....................323 981-2800
Jeremy Shapiro, *CEO*
Ron Margolis, *CFO*
Heidi Palikan, *CFO*
David Graham, *Executive*
James Borillo, *IT/INT Sup*
EMP: 73 **EST:** 1926
SQ FT: 175,000
SALES (est): 276.8MM
SALES (corp-wide): 870.7MM **Privately Held**
WEB: www.kelso.com
SIC: 5113 Industrial & personal service paper
PA: Kelso & Company, L.P.
320 Park Ave Fl 24
New York NY 10022
212 350-7700

(P-14225)
PIONEER PACKING INC (PA)
2430 S Grand Ave, Santa Ana
(92705-5211)
PHONE....................714 540-9751
Michael S Blower, *President*
Ronald Scagliotti, *Vice Pres*
Cindy Davidson,
▲ **EMP:** 21 **EST:** 1976
SQ FT: 170,000
SALES (est): 94.6MM **Privately Held**
WEB: www.pioneerpackinginc.com
SIC: 5113 2653 Shipping supplies; boxes, corrugated: made from purchased materials

(P-14226)
PLASTICBAGSONSALECOM INC
Also Called: Aplasticbag.com
4023 Trail Creek Rd, Riverside
(92505-5863)
PHONE....................951 710-1340
Mahendra Babaria, *President*
Mash Barbaria, *Marketing Staff*
▲ **EMP:** 15 **EST:** 2000
SQ FT: 10,000
SALES (est): 2MM **Privately Held**
WEB: www.aplasticbag.com
SIC: 5113 2821 Bags, paper & disposable plastic; molding compounds, plastics

(P-14227)
ROYAL PAPER CORP (PA)
Also Called: Royal Supply Midwest
10232 Palm Dr, Santa Fe Springs
(90670-3368)
PHONE....................562 903-9030
Michael Rashtchi, *CEO*
George ABI-Aad, *President*
Sunil Kanuga, *COO*
Anessa McKinzie, *COO*
Jonathan Soon, *CFO*
▲ **EMP:** 60 **EST:** 1985
SQ FT: 65,000
SALES (est): 46.5MM **Privately Held**
WEB: www.royalcorporation.com
SIC: 5113 5087 Containers, paper & disposable plastic; paper & products, wrapping or coarse; cleaning & maintenance equipment & supplies

(P-14228)
SOLARIS PAPER INC (DH)
100 S Anaheim Blvd # 280, Anaheim
(92805-3807)
PHONE....................562 653-1680
Stephen Maher, *CEO*
Andre Soetjahja, *COO*
Peter Brown, *Vice Pres*
Ronald Iswono, *Vice Pres*
Corey Rodriguez, *Vice Pres*
▲ **EMP:** 203 **EST:** 2005
SQ FT: 200,000
SALES (est): 198.2MM **Privately Held**
WEB: www.solarispaper.com
SIC: 5113 Industrial & personal service paper

(P-14229)
T & W CONVERTERS INC
15020 Marquardt Ave, Santa Fe Springs
(90670-5704)
PHONE....................818 241-1707
Toni Hibbard, *President*
EMP: 16 **EST:** 1983
SQ FT: 12,500
SALES (est): 1.9MM **Privately Held**
WEB: www.qspac.com
SIC: 5113 2759 2675 2672 Pressure sensitive tape; corrugated & solid fiber boxes; commercial printing; die-cut paper & board; coated & laminated paper

(P-14230)
USED CARDBOARD BOXES INC
4032 Wilshire Blvd # 402, Los Angeles
(90010-3413)
PHONE....................323 724-2500
Marty Metro, *CEO*
David Krasnow, *Officer*
Martin Metro, *Exec Dir*
Jonathan Arias, *Purchasing*
Bob Windsor, *Production*
▲ **EMP:** 71 **EST:** 2006
SALES (est): 17.9MM **Privately Held**
WEB: www.usedcardboardboxes.com
SIC: 5113 Corrugated & solid fiber boxes

5122 Drugs, Drug Proprietaries & Sundries Wholesale

(P-14231)
ADVANCED PHRM SVCS INC
11555 Monarch St Ste B, Garden Grove
(92841-1814)
PHONE....................714 903-1006
Tracy Nguyen, *CEO*

Dennis Ngo, *CEO*
▲ **EMP:** 19 **EST:** 2005
SALES (est): 2.2MM **Privately Held**
SIC: 5122 2833 Pharmaceuticals; medicinals & botanicals

(P-14232)
AGOURA HEALTH PRODUCTS LLC (PA)
Also Called: Gundry MD
9465 Wilshire Blvd # 300, Beverly Hills
(90212-2612)
PHONE....................800 852-0477
Steven Gundry MD,
EMP: 93 **EST:** 2014
SALES (est): 2.1MM **Privately Held**
SIC: 5122 Vitamins & minerals

(P-14233)
AMERISOURCEBERGEN DRUG CORP
Also Called: ABC Valencia
1851 California Ave, Corona (92881-6477)
PHONE....................951 371-2000
Ron Green, *Manager*
Albert G Morales, *Officer*
Rich Tremonte, *Exec VP*
Mike Quick, *Vice Pres*
Tina Peterson, *Program Mgr*
EMP: 150
SALES (corp-wide): 189.8B **Publicly Held**
WEB: www.amerisourcebergen.com
SIC: 5122 4225 Pharmaceuticals; general warehousing & storage
HQ: Amerisourcebergen Drug Corporation
1 W 1st Ave
Conshohocken PA 19428
610 727-7000

(P-14234)
BEAUTY 21 COSMETICS INC
Also Called: L A Girl
2021 S Archibald Ave, Ontario
(91761-8535)
PHONE....................909 945-2220
Lan Jack Yu, *CEO*
Chafe Trinh, *Exec Dir*
Charles Yu, *Analyst*
Jessica Tondre, *Mktg Dir*
Kim Hamilton, *Marketing Staff*
◆ **EMP:** 105 **EST:** 1997
SQ FT: 250,000
SALES (est): 80.1MM **Privately Held**
WEB: www.lagirlusa.com
SIC: 5122 2844 Cosmetics; toilet preparations

(P-14235)
BRYANT RANCH PREPACK
1919 N Victory Pl, Burbank (91504-3425)
PHONE....................818 764-7225
Sanjay Anand, *President*
Edmond Deravanessian, *CFO*
Edrick Atacador, *Technology*
Bryant Prepack, *Marketing Staff*
Bryan Spann, *Director*
EMP: 50 **EST:** 2004
SALES (est): 11.2MM **Privately Held**
WEB: www.brppharma.com
SIC: 5122 Pharmaceuticals

(P-14236)
CC WELLNESS LLC (PA)
29000 Hancock Pkwy, Valencia
(91355-1007)
PHONE....................661 714-0841
Joe Walls, *COO*
Ryan McCrobie, *Marketing Staff*
Anthony Jimenez, *Manager*
EMP: 55 **EST:** 2015
SQ FT: 38,000
SALES (est): 41MM **Privately Held**
WEB: www.ccwellness.com
SIC: 5122 Pharmaceuticals

(P-14237)
COPAN DIAGNOSTICS INC
26055 Jefferson Ave, Murrieta
(92562-6983)
PHONE....................951 696-6957
Norman Sharples, *CEO*
Stefania Triva, *Ch of Bd*
Bob Cooper, *President*
Angelo Messa, *CFO*
Jaimie Augustine, *Marketing Staff*

◆ **EMP:** 148 **EST:** 1994
SQ FT: 28,000
SALES: 62.8MM
SALES (corp-wide): 177.9K **Privately Held**
WEB: www.copanusa.com
SIC: 5122 5049 Biologicals & allied products; laboratory equipment, except medical or dental
HQ: Copan Italia Spa
Via Francesco Perotti 10
Brescia BS 25125
030 268-7211

(P-14238)
COUNTER BRANDS LLC (PA)
Also Called: Beautycounter
1733 Ocean Ave, Santa Monica
(90401-3223)
PHONE....................888 988-9108
Gregg Renfrew, *CEO*
Ana Badell, *COO*
Patty Wu, *Ch Credit Ofcr*
Don Florence, *Officer*
Linda Simon, *Officer*
▲ **EMP:** 54 **EST:** 2012
SALES (est): 38.9MM **Privately Held**
WEB: www.beautycounter.com
SIC: 5122 Cosmetics

(P-14239)
DANNE MONTAGUE-KING CO (PA)
Also Called: Dmk
10420 Pioneer Blvd, Santa Fe Springs
(90670-3734)
PHONE....................562 944-0230
Danne King, *President*
Randy Larsen, *Corp Secy*
Lynn Gregory, *Accounts Mgr*
▲ **EMP:** 33 **EST:** 1996
SQ FT: 30,000
SALES (est): 14.8MM **Privately Held**
WEB: www.dannemking.com
SIC: 5122 5999 2844 Cosmetics; toiletries, cosmetics & perfumes; cosmetic preparations

(P-14240)
DERM COSMETIC LABS INC (PA)
6370 Altura Blvd, Buena Park
(90620-1001)
PHONE....................714 562-8873
Loksarang D Hardas, *President*
▲ **EMP:** 21 **EST:** 1988
SQ FT: 60,000
SALES (est): 9.6MM **Privately Held**
WEB: www.lastotallyawesome.com
SIC: 5122 2844 Cosmetics, perfumes & hair products; cosmetic preparations

(P-14241)
DEVERAUX SPECIALTIES LLC (PA)
12835 Arroyo St, Sylmar (91342-5303)
PHONE....................818 837-3700
Andrea Jones, *Mng Member*
John Luna, *Partner*
Stella Martinez, *Sales Staff*
▲ **EMP:** 13 **EST:** 1998
SQ FT: 13,000
SALES (est): 6MM **Privately Held**
WEB: www.deverauxspecialties.com
SIC: 5122 2833 5169 Cosmetics; organic medicinal chemicals: bulk, uncompounded; industrial chemicals

(P-14242)
DISTRIBUTION ALTERNATIVES INC
1979 Renaissance Pkwy, Rialto
(92376-2403)
PHONE....................909 770-8900
Kevin Scholl, *Analyst*
Ruth Gonzales, *Regional*
EMP: 105
SALES (corp-wide): 104.4MM **Privately Held**
WEB: www.daserv.com
SIC: 5122 Cosmetics
PA: Distribution Alternatives, Inc.
6870 21st Ave
Lino Lakes MN 55038
651 636-9167

(P-14243)
FFF ENTERPRISES INC (PA)
44000 Winchester Rd, Temecula
(92590-2578)
PHONE..............................951 296-2500
Patrick M Schmidt, *CEO*
Chris Ground, *COO*
Wayne Talleur, *CFO*
Richard Bagley, *Vice Pres*
Nancy Creadon, *Vice Pres*
EMP: 300 **EST:** 1988
SQ FT: 162,000
SALES (est): 230.5MM **Privately Held**
WEB: www.fffenterprises.com
SIC: 5122 Pharmaceuticals

(P-14244)
GLAMOUR INDUSTRIES CO (PA)
Also Called: American International Inds
2220 Gaspar Ave, Commerce
(90040-1516)
PHONE..............................323 728-2999
Zvi Ryzman, *President*
Theresa Cooper, *Exec VP*
Charlie Loveless, *Vice Pres*
Marwan Zreik, *Vice Pres*
Gabriela Strong, *Executive*
EMP: 497 **EST:** 1971
SQ FT: 224,000
SALES (est): 110.3MM **Privately Held**
WEB: www.aiibeauty.com
SIC: 5122 2844 Cosmetics; cosmetic
   preparations

(P-14245)
GLOVES IN A BOTTLE INC
3720 Park Pl, Montrose (91020-1623)
P.O. Box 615 (91021-0615)
PHONE..............................818 248-9980
Dan Mueller, *President*
Katya Mueller, *General Mgr*
Olesja Mueller, *Admin Sec*
Klaus Hilgers, *Director*
Wayne Weber, *Director*
▲ **EMP:** 20 **EST:** 1994
SQ FT: 4,000
SALES (est): 5.2MM **Privately Held**
WEB: www.glovesinabottle.com
SIC: 5122 2844 5999 Cosmetics; toilet
   preparations; toiletries, cosmetics & per-
   fumes

(P-14246)
GRIFOLS SHARED SVCS N AMER INC (HQ)
2410 Lillyvale Ave, Los Angeles
(90032-3514)
PHONE..............................323 225-2221
Gregory Rich, *CEO*
Max Debrouwer, *CFO*
Thomas Glanzmann, *Chairman*
Reza Anayat, *Vice Pres*
David Bell, *Vice Pres*
▲ **EMP:** 2404 **EST:** 2010
SALES (est): 3.4B
SALES (corp-wide): 657.6MM **Privately Held**
WEB: www.grifols.jobs
SIC: 5122 2834 Drugs, proprietaries &
   sundries; druggists' preparations (phar-
   maceuticals)
PA: Grifols Sa
   Calle Jesus I Maria 6
   Barcelona 08022
   935 710-000

(P-14247)
H & H NAIL PRODUCTS INC
7011 Hayvenhurst Ave D, Van Nuys
(91406-3822)
PHONE..............................818 902-9995
Houshang Rastegar, *President*
▲ **EMP:** 13 **EST:** 1983
SQ FT: 6,000
SALES (est): 8.6MM **Privately Held**
SIC: 5122 2844 Cosmetics; manicure
   preparations

(P-14248)
HARD CANDY LLC
833 W 16th St, Newport Beach
(92663-2801)
PHONE..............................949 515-3923
Anna Hes Levin,
Bruce Ingram,
EMP: 30 **EST:** 1995

SQ FT: 12,200
SALES (est): 2.5MM **Privately Held**
SIC: 5122 2844 Cosmetics; toilet prepara-
   tions

(P-14249)
HATCHBEAUTY PRODUCTS LLC (PA)
10951 W Pico Blvd Ste 300, Los Angeles
(90064-2188)
P.O. Box 641415 (90064-6415)
PHONE..............................310 396-7070
Ben Bennett, *Mng Member*
Anais Green, *Marketing Staff*
Lori Sinanyan, *General Counsel*
Benjamin Bennett,
Tracy Holland, *Mng Member*
◆ **EMP:** 83 **EST:** 2009
SQ FT: 1,500
SALES (est): 38.7MM **Privately Held**
WEB: www.hatchbeautybrands.com
SIC: 5122 Cosmetics, perfumes & hair
   products

(P-14250)
HOYU AMERICA CO
Also Called: Samy Co
6265 Phyllis Dr, Cypress (90630-5240)
PHONE..............................714 230-3000
Yoshihiro Sasaki, *President*
Minoru Tsuda, *Senior VP*
Jeanette De La Luz, *Marketing Staff*
Joshua Thompson, *Marketing Staff*
▲ **EMP:** 58 **EST:** 2004
SALES (est): 19.5MM **Privately Held**
WEB: www.hoyu-usa.com
SIC: 5122 5999 Cosmetics; hair care
   products
HQ: Hoyu Co.,Ltd.
   1-501, Tokugawa, Higashi-Ku
   Nagoya AIC 461-0

(P-14251)
IHERB LLC (PA)
Also Called: Iherb House Brands
22780 Hrley Knox Blvd Uni, Perris (92570)
PHONE..............................951 616-3600
Reza Faraee, *Mng Member*
Arcelia Nava, *Receiver*
Steve Cho, *Chief Mktg Ofcr*
Brenden Tkach, *Surgery Dir*
John Cowell, *Department Mgr*
◆ **EMP:** 672 **EST:** 2001
SQ FT: 336,000
SALES (est): 1.6B **Privately Held**
WEB: www.iherb.com
SIC: 5499 5122 Vitamin food stores;
   drugs, proprietaries & sundries

(P-14252)
JARROW FORMULAS INC (PA)
1824 S Robertson Blvd, Los Angeles
(90035-4317)
PHONE..............................310 204-6936
Ojesh Bhalla, *CEO*
Jarrow L Rogovin, *President*
Wayne Grubbs, *CFO*
Clayton Dubose, *Treasurer*
Michael Jacobs, *Vice Pres*
◆ **EMP:** 80 **EST:** 1977
SQ FT: 37,000
SALES (est): 74.5MM **Privately Held**
WEB: www.jarrow.com
SIC: 5122 Vitamins & minerals

(P-14253)
JESSICA COSMETICS INTL INC
Also Called: Jessica's Cosmetics
13209 Saticoy St, North Hollywood
(91605-3405)
PHONE..............................818 759-1050
Jessica Vartoughian, *President*
Valerie Celia, *Chief Mktg Ofcr*
Victor Recinos, *Opers Mgr*
Iris Bostanian, *Sales Staff*
▲ **EMP:** 60 **EST:** 1968
SALES (est): 11.9MM **Privately Held**
WEB: www.jessicacosmetics.com
SIC: 5122 7231 Cosmetics; beauty shops

(P-14254)
JORDANA COSMETICS LLC
2035 E 49th St, Vernon (90058-2801)
P.O. Box 8382, Los Angeles (90008-0382)
PHONE..............................310 730-4400

Laurie Minc, *President*
Gina Hagen, *CFO*
Rhonda Baron, *VP Business*
Ralph Bijou, *Principal*
Olga Arzola, *General Mgr*
◆ **EMP:** 65 **EST:** 1986
SQ FT: 30,000
SALES (est): 22.2MM **Privately Held**
WEB: www.jordanacosmetics.com
SIC: 5122 5961 Cosmetics; catalog &
   mail-order houses

(P-14255)
KATE SOMERVILLE SKINCARE LLC
5959 Randolph St, Commerce
(90040-3416)
PHONE..............................310 623-6822
EMP: 51 **Privately Held**
WEB: www.katesomerville.com
SIC: 5122 Toiletries
PA: Kate Somerville Skincare, Llc
   144 S Beverly Dr Ste 500
   Beverly Hills CA 90212

(P-14256)
LIFETECH RESOURCES LLC
Also Called: International Research Labs
700 Science Dr, Moorpark (93021-2012)
PHONE..............................805 944-1199
Richard Carieri, *Ch of Bd*
Susan McCarthy, *President*
Anna Carieri, *CFO*
Joseph Carieri, *Vice Pres*
Twee Le-Roth, *Vice Pres*
▲ **EMP:** 85 **EST:** 1990
SQ FT: 152,000
SALES (est): 46MM **Privately Held**
WEB: www.lifetechresources.com
SIC: 5122 5149 Cosmetics; health foods;
   natural & organic foods; specialty food
   items

(P-14257)
LINA GALE (USA) INC
Also Called: Markwins Beauty Brands
22067 Ferrero, Walnut (91789-5214)
PHONE..............................909 595-8898
John Chen, *CEO*
Lina Chen, *CFO*
▲ **EMP:** 100 **EST:** 1991
SALES (est): 22.1MM **Privately Held**
SIC: 5122 Cosmetics

(P-14258)
LIP INK INTERNATIONAL
225 Arena St, El Segundo (90245-3806)
PHONE..............................310 414-9246
Rosemarie Nichols, *CEO*
EMP: 14 **EST:** 1995
SQ FT: 6,000
SALES (est): 3.9MM **Privately Held**
WEB: www.lipink.com
SIC: 5122 2844 Cosmetics; bath salts

(P-14259)
MARKWINS BEAUTY BRANDS INC (PA)
22067 Ferrero, Walnut (91789-5214)
PHONE..............................909 595-8898
Sung-Tsei Eric Chen, *President*
Jeff Rogers, *President*
Leslie H Hernandez, *CFO*
Lina Chen,
Eric Wu, *Software Dev*
◆ **EMP:** 150 **EST:** 1983
SQ FT: 320,000
SALES (est): 283.8MM **Privately Held**
WEB: www.markwinsbeauty.com
SIC: 5122 Cosmetics

(P-14260)
MARKWINS BEAUTY PRODUCTS INC
Also Called: Wet N Wild Los Angeles
22067 Ferrero, City of Industry
(91789-5214)
PHONE..............................909 595-8898
Eric Chen, *President*
Stefano Curti, *President*
Michael Shaw, *COO*
Shawn Haynes, *Senior VP*
James Koeppl, *Senior VP*
◆ **EMP:** 66 **EST:** 2003

SQ FT: 200,000
SALES (est): 55.1MM
SALES (corp-wide): 283.8MM **Privately Held**
WEB: www.wetnwildbeauty.com
SIC: 5122 Cosmetics
PA: Markwins Beauty Brands, Inc.
   22067 Ferrero
   Walnut CA 91789
   909 595-8898

(P-14261)
MCKESSON MDCL-SRGCAL MDMART IN
2800 E Philadelphia St, Ontario
(91761-8523)
PHONE..............................800 755-2090
Tom Cummings, *Principal*
EMP: 60
SALES (corp-wide): 238.2B **Publicly Held**
SIC: 5122 Pharmaceuticals
HQ: Mckesson Medical-Surgical Medimart
   Inc.
   8121 10th Ave N
   Minneapolis MN 55427
   763 595-6000

(P-14262)
MCKESSON MEDICAL-SURGICAL INC
1525 Rnch Conejo Blvd # 104, Newbury
Park (91320-1441)
PHONE..............................805 375-8800
Mike Douglas, *Branch Mgr*
Garrett Muramoto, *Senior Mgr*
EMP: 54
SALES (corp-wide): 238.2B **Publicly Held**
WEB: www.mckgenmed.com
SIC: 5122 Pharmaceuticals
HQ: Mckesson Medical-Surgical Inc.
   9954 Mayland Dr Ste 4000
   Richmond VA 23233
   855 571-2100

(P-14263)
METAGENICS INC (DH)
25 Enterprise Ste 200, Aliso Viejo
(92656-2713)
PHONE..............................949 366-0818
Brent Eck, *President*
Jean M Bellin, *President*
Dave Tuit, *CFO*
Sara Gottfried, *Chief Mktg Ofcr*
John Troup, *Officer*
◆ **EMP:** 150 **EST:** 1983
SQ FT: 88,000
SALES (est): 188.5MM **Privately Held**
WEB: www.metagenics.com
SIC: 5122 Vitamins & minerals
HQ: Alticor Inc.
   7575 Fulton St E
   Ada MI 49355
   616 787-1000

(P-14264)
MISSION SERIES INC
Also Called: Prestige Beauty Care
1585 W Mission Blvd, Pomona
(91766-1233)
PHONE..............................714 736-1000
Robert Friedland, *President*
EMP: 50 **EST:** 2018
SALES (est): 2.3MM **Privately Held**
SIC: 5122 Cosmetics

(P-14265)
MOROCCANOIL INC (PA)
16311 Ventura Blvd # 120, Encino
(91436-2124)
PHONE..............................888 700-1817
Jay Elarar, *CEO*
Ofer Tal, *President*
Allan Weizmann, *CFO*
Brian Nagle, *Executive*
Crystal Civil, *Office Mgr*
◆ **EMP:** 75 **EST:** 2010
SQ FT: 25,000
SALES (est): 26.8MM **Privately Held**
WEB: www.moroccanoil.com
SIC: 5122 Cosmetics

(P-14266)
N QIAGEN AMERCN HOLDINGS INC (HQ)
27220 Turnberry Ln # 200, Valencia (91355-1018)
PHONE............................800 426-8157
Peer Schatz, *President*
Elise Stephens, *Officer*
John Gilardi, *Vice Pres*
Barthold Piening, *Vice Pres*
Jonathan Sheldon, *Vice Pres*
EMP: 250 **EST:** 2000
SALES (est): 310MM
SALES (corp-wide): 1.8B **Privately Held**
WEB: www.qiagen.com
SIC: 5122 Biologicals & allied products
PA: Qiagen N.V.
  Hulsterweg 82
  Venlo 5912
  773 556-600

(P-14267)
NAPOLEON PERDIS COSMETICS INC
16825 Saticoy St, Van Nuys (91406-2728)
PHONE............................323 817-3611
Napoleon Perdis, *President*
Jennifer Seeder, *President*
Taylor Gooley, *Vice Pres*
Kelly Hughes, *Executive*
Ana Vu Tapson, *Executive Asst*
EMP: 93 **EST:** 2005
SALES (est): 13.7MM **Privately Held**
WEB: www.napoleonperdis.com
SIC: 5999 5122 Cosmetics; cosmetics

(P-14268)
NATUREWARE INC
6590 Darin Way, Cypress (90630-5121)
PHONE............................714 251-4510
Eun Ah Shin, *CEO*
Han C Shin, *President*
EMP: 96
SALES (est): 5.9MM **Privately Held**
SIC: 5122 Vitamins & minerals

(P-14269)
NEW MILANI GROUP LLC
Also Called: Milani Cosmetics
10000 Wash Blvd Ste 210, Culver City (90232-2782)
P.O. Box 58585, Los Angeles (90058-0585)
PHONE............................323 582-9404
Mary Van Praag, *CEO*
Lindsay Shumlas, *COO*
Evelyn Wang, *Chief Mktg Ofcr*
Tim Kaiser, *Senior VP*
Ellen Markus, *Marketing Staff*
▲ **EMP:** 93 **EST:** 2018
SQ FT: 11,893
SALES (est): 19.7MM **Privately Held**
WEB: www.milanicosmetics.com
SIC: 5122 Cosmetics

(P-14270)
NHT GLOBAL INC
609 Deep Valley Dr # 395, Rllng HLS Est (90274-9900)
PHONE............................972 241-6525
Chris Sharng, *President*
Scott Davidson, *CEO*
Karen Simmons, *Vice Pres*
Jung Chen, *Opers Mgr*
▲ **EMP:** 65 **EST:** 2001
SALES (est): 5.7MM **Publicly Held**
WEB: www.naturalhealthtrendscorp.com
SIC: 5122 Cosmetics
PA: Natural Health Trends Corp.
  609 Deep Valley Dr # 395
  Rllng Hls Est CA 90274

(P-14271)
NOEVIR HOLDING AMERICA INC (DH)
1095 Main St, Irvine (92614-6788)
PHONE............................949 660-1111
Michael Moritani, *President*
Hami Wadbam, *Vice Pres*
◆ **EMP:** 50 **EST:** 2001
SQ FT: 30,000
SALES (est): 24.6MM **Privately Held**
WEB: www.noevirusa.com
SIC: 5122 5088 Cosmetics; aircraft & parts

(P-14272)
OLAPLEX INTERMEDIATE INC (HQ) ✪
1187 Coast Village Rd 1-52, Santa Barbara (93108-2737)
PHONE............................805 452-8110
Jue Wong, *CEO*
EMP: 50 **EST:** 2021
SALES (est): 22.4MM **Publicly Held**
SIC: 5122 Drugs, proprietaries & sundries
PA: Olaplex Holdings, Inc.
  1187 Coast Village Rd 1-52
  Santa Barbara CA 93108
  310 691-0776

(P-14273)
OLAPLEX INTERMEDIATE II INC (DH) ✪
1187 Coast Village Rd 1-52, Santa Barbara (93108-2737)
PHONE............................805 452-8110
Jue Wong, *CEO*
EMP: 50 **EST:** 2021
SALES (est): 22.4MM **Publicly Held**
SIC: 5122 Drugs, proprietaries & sundries
HQ: Olaplex Intermediate, Inc.
  1187 Coast Village Rd 1-52
  Santa Barbara CA 93108
  805 452-8110

(P-14274)
OMP INC (HQ)
3760 Kilroy Arprt Way, Long Beach (90806-2443)
PHONE............................562 628-1007
Al Hummel, *President*
Preston Romm, *CFO*
David Goldstein, *Exec VP*
Albert F Hummel, *Principal*
Alex Daza, *Technical Staff*
EMP: 154 **EST:** 1983
SQ FT: 16,000
SALES (est): 23.7MM **Privately Held**
WEB: www.obagi.com
SIC: 5122 Cosmetics

(P-14275)
PACIFIC PHARMA INC
18600 Von Karman Ave, Irvine (92612-1513)
PHONE............................714 246-4600
Roger Maffia, *Director*
EMP: 2000 **EST:** 1997
SALES (est): 82.1MM **Privately Held**
WEB: www.allergan.com
SIC: 5122 Pharmaceuticals
HQ: Allergan, Inc.
  5 Giralda Farms
  Madison NJ 07940
  862 261-7000

(P-14276)
PAUL MITCHELL JOHN SYSTEMS (PA)
20705 Centre Pointe Pkwy, Santa Clarita (91350-2967)
P.O. Box 10597, Beverly Hills (90213-3597)
PHONE............................800 793-8790
Michaeline Dejoria, *CEO*
Rick Battaglini, *Officer*
Dana Baumgart, *Vice Pres*
Julie Solwold, *Vice Pres*
John Paul Dejoria, *Co-Founder*
◆ **EMP:** 80 **EST:** 1980
SQ FT: 90,000
SALES (est): 76.4MM **Privately Held**
WEB: www.paulmitchell.com
SIC: 5122 Hair preparations

(P-14277)
PENELOPE HOLDINGS CORP (DH)
1187 Coast Village Rd 1-52, Santa Barbara (93108-2737)
PHONE............................805 452-8110
Jue Wong, *CEO*
EMP: 50 **EST:** 2019
SALES (est): 17.6MM
SALES (corp-wide): 22.4MM **Publicly Held**
SIC: 5122 Drugs, proprietaries & sundries

HQ: Olaplex Intermediate Ii, Inc.
  1187 Coast Village Rd 1-52
  Santa Barbara CA 93108
  805 452-8110

(P-14278)
PENELOPE INTERMEDIATE CORP (DH)
1187 Coast Village Rd 1-52, Santa Barbara (93108-2737)
PHONE............................805 452-8110
Jue Wong, *CEO*
EMP: 50 **EST:** 2019
SALES (est): 17.6MM
SALES (corp-wide): 22.4MM **Publicly Held**
SIC: 5122 Drugs, proprietaries & sundries
HQ: Penelope Holdings Corp.
  1187 Coast Village Rd 1-52
  Santa Barbara CA 93108
  805 452-8110

(P-14279)
PIXI INC
Also Called: Pixi Beauty
10351 Santa Monica Blvd # 410, Los Angeles (90025-6908)
PHONE............................310 670-7767
Felix Strand, *President*
Anthony Oppe, *CEO*
Marc Serrio, *CFO*
Petra Strand Oppe, *Founder*
Andres Sosa, *Chief Mktg Ofcr*
EMP: 64 **EST:** 2007
SQ FT: 8,400
SALES (est): 20.6MM **Privately Held**
WEB: www.pixibeauty.com
SIC: 5122 Cosmetics

(P-14280)
PLASMA BIOLIFE SERVICES L P
23727 Sunnymead Blvd, Moreno Valley (92553-3021)
PHONE............................951 497-4407
Aimee Ford, *Manager*
EMP: 50 **Privately Held**
SIC: 5122 Drugs, proprietaries & sundries
HQ: Biolife Plasma Services L.P.
  1200 Lakeside Dr
  Bannockburn IL 60015
  224 940-2000

(P-14281)
PLATINUM PERFORMANCE INC (HQ)
90 Thomas Rd, Buellton (93427-9657)
P.O. Box 990 (93427-0990)
PHONE............................800 553-2400
Mark J Herthel, *President*
Lucca Rockhold, *CIO*
Heather Elliott, *Sales Staff*
Jessie Condit, *Director*
Schembri Beth, *Manager*
EMP: 27 **EST:** 1996
SQ FT: 7,000
SALES (est): 35MM
SALES (corp-wide): 6.6B **Publicly Held**
WEB: www.platinumperformance.com
SIC: 5122 2023 Vitamins & minerals; dietary supplements, dairy & non-dairy based
PA: Zoetis Inc.
  10 Sylvan Way
  Parsippany NJ 07054
  973 822-7000

(P-14282)
PRIMAL ELEMENTS INC
18062 Redondo Cir, Huntington Beach (92648-1326)
PHONE............................714 899-0757
Faith Freeman, *CEO*
Scott Freeman, *President*
Curtis Allen, *Vice Pres*
Mitchell Freeman, *Sales Staff*
Frank Asbury, *Director*
▲ **EMP:** 99 **EST:** 1993
SQ FT: 56,500
SALES (est): 34.1MM **Privately Held**
WEB: www.primalelements.com
SIC: 5122 2841 Cosmetics; detergents, synthetic organic or inorganic alkaline

(P-14283)
PRIMAL NUTRITION LLC
Also Called: Primal Blueprint
1101 Maulhardt Ave, Oxnard (93030-7995)
P.O. Box 145, Malibu (90265-0145)
PHONE............................310 317-4414
Mark Sisson, *CEO*
Morgan Zanoti, *President*
Adrian Vasquez, *Opers Staff*
EMP: 50 **EST:** 1997
SQ FT: 3,500
SALES (est): 37.8MM
SALES (corp-wide): 26.1B **Publicly Held**
WEB: www.primalblueprint.com
SIC: 5122 5149 Vitamins & minerals; health foods
PA: The Kraft Heinz Company
  1 Ppg Pl Ste 3400
  Pittsburgh PA 15222
  412 456-5700

(P-14284)
QYK BRANDS LLC
12101 Western Ave, Garden Grove (92841-2914)
PHONE............................949 312-7119
Rakesh Tammabattula, *CEO*
Alexandra Aldana, *Executive Asst*
EMP: 189 **EST:** 2017
SQ FT: 2,000
SALES (est): 27MM **Privately Held**
WEB: www.qyksonic.com
SIC: 5122 2842 3842 2023 Pharmaceuticals; disinfectants, household or industrial plant; respiratory protection equipment, personal; dietary supplements, dairy & non-dairy based; pharmaceuticals, mail order; surgical & medical instruments

(P-14285)
RARE BEAUTY LLC
222 N Pacific Coast Hwy, El Segundo (90245-5648)
PHONE............................424 502-1900
Scott Friedman, *CEO*
Marcel Lopez, *Vice Pres*
EMP: 55 **EST:** 2019
SALES (est): 26.4MM **Privately Held**
SIC: 5122 Cosmetics, perfumes & hair products

(P-14286)
RUGBY LABORATORIES INC (DH)
311 Bonnie Cir, Corona (92878-5182)
PHONE............................951 270-1400
David C Hsia PHD, *President*
Michael E Boser, *CFO*
Michel J Feldman, *Officer*
Frederick Wilkinson, *Vice Pres*
Chato Abad, *VP Finance*
EMP: 90 **EST:** 1961
SALES (est): 148.9MM
SALES (corp-wide): 152.9B **Publicly Held**
WEB: www.theharvarddruggroup.com
SIC: 5122 2834 Pharmaceuticals; pharmaceutical preparations
HQ: The Harvard Drug Group L L C
  17177 N Laurel Park Dr # 233
  Livonia MI 48152
  734 525-8700

(P-14287)
SCIENCE OF SKINCARE LLC
Also Called: Innovative Skin Care
3333 N San Fernando Blvd, Burbank (91504-2531)
PHONE............................818 254-7961
C B Johns, *Mng Member*
Rachel Wiest, *Executive Asst*
Kimberly Johnson, *Business Mgr*
Katherine Medina, *Business Mgr*
Alison Sudfeld, *Business Mgr*
◆ **EMP:** 66 **EST:** 2003
SQ FT: 36,000
SALES (est): 23MM **Privately Held**
WEB: www.isclinical.com
SIC: 5122 Cosmetics

(P-14288)
SGII INC (PA)
Also Called: Senegence International
19651 Alter, Foothill Ranch (92610-2507)
PHONE............................949 521-6161
Joni Rogers Kante, *CEO*

Philippe Guerreau, *President*
Ben Kante, *COO*
Jerome Kaiser, *CFO*
James Roh, *Officer*
▲ **EMP:** 247 **EST:** 1997
SQ FT: 49,415
SALES (est): 97.7MM **Privately Held**
WEB: www.seneweb.senegence.com
SIC: 5122 Cosmetics; vitamins & minerals

(P-14289)
SKINFOOD USA INC
9301 Tampa Ave Unit 59, Northridge
(91324-5653)
PHONE...................................818 998-1142
EMP: 59
SALES (corp-wide): 1.3MM **Privately
Held**
SIC: 5999 5122 Ret Misc Merchandise
Whol Drugs/Sundries
PA: Skinfood Usa, Inc.
6 Centerpointe Dr Ste 375
La Palma CA 90701
714 523-5551

(P-14290)
SOS BEAUTY INC
700 N San Vicnte Blvd G460, West Holly-
wood (90069-5078)
PHONE...................................424 285-1405
Dustin Cash, *CEO*
Joshua Jones, *Vice Pres*
EMP: 14 **EST:** 2017
SALES (est): 5.2MM **Privately Held**
WEB: www.sosbty.com
SIC: 5122 3221 7389 3172 Cosmetics,
perfumes & hair products; cosmetics; cos-
metic jars, glass; cosmetic kits, assem-
bling & packaging; cosmetic bags;
cosmetic preparations

(P-14291)
SPA DE SOLEIL INC
Also Called: Pharmaskincare
10443 Arminta St, Sun Valley (91352-4109)
PHONE...................................818 504-3200
Rena Revivo, *CEO*
Andrea Revivo, *Director*
Aziz Quadri, *Manager*
▲ **EMP:** 20 **EST:** 1994
SALES (est): 6MM **Privately Held**
WEB: www.spadesoleil.com
SIC: 5122 2844 Cosmetics; cosmetic
preparations

(P-14292)
STAR NAIL PRODUCTS INC
Also Called: Star Nail International
29120 Avenue Paine, Valencia
(91355-5402)
PHONE...................................661 257-3376
Tony Cuccio, *CEO*
Anthony Cuccio, *President*
Roberta Cuccio, *Vice Pres*
Elaine Watson, *Vice Pres*
Marilyn Garcia, *Education*
◆ **EMP:** 55 **EST:** 1982
SQ FT: 14,000
SALES (est): 11.6MM **Privately Held**
WEB: www.starnail.com
SIC: 5122 2844 7231 Cosmetics; toilet
preparations; beauty shops

(P-14293)
**SUNRIDER EASTERN EUROPE
INC (PA)**
1625 Abalone Ave, Torrance (90501-2860)
PHONE...................................310 781-3808
Tei Fu Chen,
EMP: 166 **EST:** 1993
SALES (est): 558.9K **Privately Held**
WEB: www.home.sunrider.com
SIC: 5122 Drugs, proprietaries & sundries

(P-14294)
**VALLEY OF SUN COSMETICS
LLC**
Also Called: Valley of The Sun Labs
535 Patrice Pl, Gardena (90248-4232)
PHONE...................................310 327-9062
Jimmy Ajmal,
Ajmal Shehzad,
◆ **EMP:** 156 **EST:** 1994
SQ FT: 10,000

SALES (est): 24.8MM **Privately Held**
WEB: www.hollywoodstyle.vscosmo.com
SIC: 5122 Cosmetics

(P-14295)
**VETERINARY
PHARMACEUTICALS INC**
13159 Hanford Armona Rd, Hanford
(93230-9395)
PHONE...................................559 582-6800
Harold Des Jardins, *CEO*
Alice Des Jardins, *Vice Pres*
◆ **EMP:** 52 **EST:** 1972
SALES (est): 21.7MM **Privately Held**
SIC: 5122 Pharmaceuticals

(P-14296)
VIVA LIFE SCIENCE INC
350 Paularino Ave, Costa Mesa
(92626-4616)
PHONE...................................949 645-6100
David Fan, *President*
EMP: 220 **EST:** 1987
SQ FT: 60,000
SALES (est): 1.8MM
SALES (corp-wide): 29.1MM **Privately
Held**
WEB: www.westarnutrition.com
SIC: 5122 2833 Vitamins & minerals; cos-
metics; medicinals & botanicals
PA: Westar Nutrition Corp.
350 Paularino Ave
Costa Mesa CA 92626
949 645-6100

(P-14297)
**WECKERLE COSMETICS USA
INC**
Also Called: Weckerle Sales Corporation
525 Maple Ave, Torrance (90503-3905)
PHONE...................................310 328-7000
Thomas Weckerle, *President*
Petra Webersberger, *CEO*
Stefan Lohaus, *General Mgr*
Gabriela Cruz-Aedo, *Project Mgr*
Nadia Siddiqah, *Research*
▲ **EMP:** 35 **EST:** 1979
SQ FT: 20,000
SALES (est): 24.5MM
SALES (corp-wide): 121.9MM **Privately
Held**
WEB: www.weckerle.com
SIC: 5122 5084 2844 Cosmetics; packag-
ing machinery & equipment; lipsticks
PA: Weckerle Holding Gmbh
Holzhofstr. 26
Weilheim I. Ob BY 82362
881 929-30

(P-14298)
WELLA OPERATIONS US LLC
4500 Park Granada Ste 100, Calabasas
(91302-1665)
PHONE...................................818 999-5112
Sennen Pamich, *Senior VP*
Chartrice Carter, *Manager*
EMP: 500 **EST:** 2020
SALES (est): 45.9MM **Privately Held**
WEB: www.wella.com
SIC: 5122 Cosmetics, perfumes & hair
products

(P-14299)
WHOLE HEALTH PHARMACY
1415 N Broadway, Santa Ana
(92706-3904)
PHONE...................................949 305-0788
Eileen Andreasyan, *President*
EMP: 50 **EST:** 2018
SALES (est): 5.9MM **Privately Held**
SIC: 5122 Drugs, proprietaries & sundries

5131 Piece Goods, Notions & Dry Goods Wholesale

(P-14300)
A W CHANG CORPORATION (PA)
Also Called: Excalibur International
6945 Atlantic Ave, Long Beach
(90805-1415)
PHONE...................................310 764-2000
William Chang, *CEO*
Abraham K Chang, *CEO*

Young Chu, *Finance*
Leanna Camacho, *Marketing Staff*
▲ **EMP:** 27 **EST:** 1989
SQ FT: 12,000
SALES (est): 27.2MM **Privately Held**
SIC: 5131 5632 2211 Silk piece goods,
woven; apparel accessories; apparel &
outerwear fabrics, cotton

(P-14301)
**ADERANS HAIR GOODS INC
(HQ)**
9135 Independence Ave, Chatsworth
(91311-5903)
PHONE...................................818 428-1626
Nobuo Nemoto, *President*
Kuniyuki Sasaki, *COO*
Mariam Yegoyan, *Sales Staff*
John Eenigenburg, *General Counsel*
Olha Kisil, *Manager*
◆ **EMP:** 50 **EST:** 2009
SALES (est): 19.9MM **Privately Held**
WEB: www.reneofparis.com
SIC: 5131 5999 Hair accessories; hair
care products

(P-14302)
**ALEXANDER HENRY FABRICS
INC**
1550 Flower St, Glendale (91201-2356)
PHONE...................................818 562-8200
Marcus De Leon, *President*
Kim Dunn, *CFO*
EMP: 40 **EST:** 1992
SALES (est): 5.2MM **Privately Held**
WEB: www.ahfabrics.com
SIC: 5131 2211 Cotton goods; broadwo-
ven fabric mills, cotton

(P-14303)
DESIGN COLLECTION INC
Also Called: Global Garments
2209 S Santa Fe Ave, Los Angeles
(90058-1109)
PHONE...................................323 277-9200
Simon Barlava, *CEO*
Sohail Hussain, *CFO*
Morris Barlava, *Vice Pres*
John Lee, *General Mgr*
Nasser Barlava, *Admin Sec*
◆ **EMP:** 60 **EST:** 1987
SQ FT: 67,000
SALES (est): 18.5MM **Privately Held**
WEB: www.designcollection.com
SIC: 5131 5023 Trimmings, apparel;
sheets, textile

(P-14304)
I S W INC
Also Called: International Silk
8347 Beverly Blvd, Los Angeles
(90048-2634)
PHONE...................................323 653-6453
Salim Y Israwi, *CEO*
Salim Israwi, *CEO*
Paul H Mandel, *Chairman*
Souhail Israwi, *Vice Pres*
Safwat Israwi, *Admin Sec*
▲ **EMP:** 50 **EST:** 1969
SQ FT: 30,000
SALES (est): 5.7MM **Privately Held**
SIC: 5949 5131 Fabric stores piece
goods; piece goods & other fabrics

(P-14305)
KOMAR ALLIANCE LLC (PA)
6900 Washington Blvd, Montebello
(90640-5424)
PHONE...................................323 890-3000
Michael Feldman, *Mng Member*
Mary Chown, *Controller*
Greg Colbern, *VP Sales*
Phil Glauben, *Sales Staff*
Chris Smith, *Sales Staff*
▲ **EMP:** 73 **EST:** 2000
SQ FT: 70,000
SALES (est): 40.2MM **Privately Held**
WEB: www.komar.com
SIC: 5131 Sewing accessories

(P-14306)
M M FAB INC
Also Called: South Seas Imports
2300 E Gladwick St, Compton
(90220-6208)
PHONE...................................310 763-3800

Richard Friedman, *Principal*
Albert Mass, *VP Finance*
Gloria Yit, *Plant Mgr*
Sergio Garcia, *Sales Mgr*
Renshaw Justin, *Sales Staff*
▲ **EMP:** 85
SQ FT: 110,000
SALES (est): 25.3MM **Privately Held**
WEB: www.southimports.com
SIC: 5131 Textiles, woven

(P-14307)
**MATRIX INTERNATIONAL TEX
INC**
1363 S Bonnie Beach Pl, Commerce
(90023-4001)
P.O. Box 23484, Los Angeles (90023-0409)
PHONE...................................323 582-9100
Kourosh Neman, *CEO*
Chris Neman, *President*
Simin Neman, *Treasurer*
Kevin Neman, *Vice Pres*
Adrian Leyva, *Sales Staff*
◆ **EMP:** 28 **EST:** 1997
SQ FT: 60,000
SALES (est): 16.4MM **Privately Held**
WEB: www.matrixtextiles.com
SIC: 5131 2299 Broadwoven fabrics; ap-
parel filling: cotton waste, kapok & related
material

(P-14308)
MERIDIAN TEXTILES INC (PA)
6415 Canning St, Commerce (90040-3121)
PHONE...................................323 869-5700
Howard Deutchman, *President*
Ron Shapiro, *Accounts Exec*
▲ **EMP:** 74 **EST:** 1981
SQ FT: 36,000
SALES (est): 18MM **Privately Held**
WEB: www.meridiantex.com
SIC: 5131 Textiles, woven

(P-14309)
MICHAEL LEVINE INC (PA)
920 Maple Ave, Los Angeles (90015-1812)
PHONE...................................213 622-6259
Laurence A Freidin, *Principal*
Laurence Freidin, *President*
▲ **EMP:** 60 **EST:** 2011
SQ FT: 60,000
SALES (est): 10.1MM **Privately Held**
WEB: www.lowpricefabric.com
SIC: 5949 5131 Fabric, remnants; uphol-
stery fabrics, woven

(P-14310)
MOMENTUM TEXTILES LLC (PA)
17811 Fitch, Irvine (92614-6001)
PHONE...................................949 833-8886
David Krakoff, *CEO*
Joanne Corrao, *CFO*
Kathy Gowdy, *Vice Pres*
Carl Patrick, *Technology*
Tammy Markle, *Sales Executive*
◆ **EMP:** 40 **EST:** 1987
SQ FT: 20,000
SALES (est): 99.6MM **Privately Held**
WEB: www.memosamples.com
SIC: 5131 2221 Upholstery fabrics,
woven; broadwoven fabric mills, man-
made

(P-14311)
**MORGAN FABRICS
CORPORATION (PA)**
4265 Exchange Ave, Vernon (90058-2604)
P.O. Box 58523, Los Angeles (90058-0523)
PHONE...................................323 583-9981
Arnold Gittelson, *Chairman*
Michael Gittelson, *President*
Ken Yang, *CFO*
Bob Gittelson, *Vice Pres*
Robert Gittelson, *Vice Pres*
◆ **EMP:** 60 **EST:** 1956
SQ FT: 50,000
SALES (est): 34.2MM **Privately Held**
WEB: www.morganfabrics.com
SIC: 5131 2759 Textiles, woven; uphol-
stery fabrics, woven; commercial printing

(P-14312)
NORTHWEST GROUP LLC
1535 W 139th St, Gardena (90249-2603)
PHONE...................................310 327-4670
Jack Burns, *CEO*

▲ = Import ▼=Export
◆ =Import/Export

Allan Guo, *Mng Member*
EMP: 50 **EST:** 2020
SALES (est) 25MM **Privately Held**
SIC: 5131 Cotton goods

(P-14313)
PHOENIX TEXTILE INC (PA)
Also Called: Level 99
14600 S Broadway, Gardena (90248-1812)
PHONE..................................310 715-7090
Dominic Poon, *President*
Joseph TSE, *Treasurer*
Cindy Chang, *Opers Staff*
Cathy Scileny, *Sales Staff*
Bernadette Topjian, *Sales Staff*
◆ **EMP:** 89 **EST:** 1984
SQ FT: 39,000
SALES (est): 29.1MM **Privately Held**
WEB: www.level99jeans.com
SIC: 5131 7389 Textiles, woven; sewing contractor; textile designers

(P-14314)
PIECEMAKERS LLC
Also Called: Piecemaker's Country Store
1720 Adams Ave, Costa Mesa (92626-4890)
PHONE..................................714 641-3112
Doug Follette, *Mng Member*
Marie Kolasinski
▲ **EMP:** 30 **EST:** 1978
SQ FT: 11,467
SALES (est): 2MM **Privately Held**
WEB: www.piecemakers.com
SIC: 5947 8299 5131 5949 Gift shop; arts & crafts schools; piece goods & other fabrics; quilting materials & supplies; fabric stores piece goods; needlework goods & supplies; book publishing

(P-14315)
PINDLER & PINDLER INC (PA)
11910 Poindexter Ave, Moorpark (93021-1748)
P.O. Box 8007 (93020-8007)
PHONE..................................805 531-9090
Curt R Pindler, *President*
Sean Quinn, *CFO*
S L Crawford Jr, *Exec VP*
Barbara Bick, *Admin Sec*
Bill Crawford, *Info Tech Mgr*
▲ **EMP:** 95 **EST:** 1939
SQ FT: 75,000
SALES (est): 58.5MM **Privately Held**
WEB: www.pindler.com
SIC: 5131 Drapery material, woven; upholstery fabrics, woven

(P-14316)
RADIX TEXTILE INC
600 E Wash Blvd Ste C2, Los Angeles (90015-3739)
PHONE..................................323 234-1667
Arad Shemirani, *CEO*
▲ **EMP:** 99 **EST:** 2007
SALES (est): 6MM **Privately Held**
SIC: 5131 2211 Piece goods & other fabrics; textiles, woven; broadwoven fabric mills, cotton

(P-14317)
ROMEX TEXTILES INC (PA)
1430 Griffith Ave, Los Angeles (90021-2127)
PHONE..................................213 749-9090
Shawn Binafard, *CEO*
Soleyman Binafard, *Admin Sec*
Grethelle Simon, *Opers Mgr*
Shahab Binafard, *Director*
▲ **EMP:** 39 **EST:** 1993
SALES (est): 17.3MM **Privately Held**
WEB: www.romextex.com
SIC: 5131 2211 Textiles, woven; apparel & outerwear fabrics, cotton

(P-14318)
ROSHAN TRADING INC
Also Called: Laguna Fabrics
2734 E 46th St, Vernon (90058-2303)
PHONE..................................213 622-9904
David Roshan, *CEO*
Mansoor Roshan, *President*
Andre Roshan, *Principal*
◆ **EMP:** 22 **EST:** 1986
SQ FT: 18,000

SALES (est): 8.5MM **Privately Held**
WEB: www.envirofabrics.la
SIC: 5131 2231 Textiles, woven; broadwoven fabric mills, wool

(P-14319)
SHASON INC (PA)
Also Called: Dream River
5525 S Soto St, Vernon (90058-3622)
PHONE..................................323 269-6666
Barok Shahery, *President*
Henry Shahery, *Vice Pres*
Vic Japson, *Manager*
▲ **EMP:** 52 **EST:** 1981
SALES (est): 18.6MM **Privately Held**
WEB: www.shasoninc.com
SIC: 5131 Textiles, woven

(P-14320)
SO TECH/SPCL OP TECH INC (PA)
206 Star Of India Ln, Carson (90746-1418)
PHONE..................................310 202-9007
James W V Cragg, *President*
▲ **EMP:** 33 **EST:** 1997
SQ FT: 12,000
SALES (est): 13MM **Privately Held**
WEB: www.sotechtactical.com
SIC: 5131 2396 Nylon piece goods, woven; apparel findings & trimmings

(P-14321)
SOFTLINE HOME FASHIONS INC
13130 S Normandie Ave, Gardena (90249-2128)
PHONE..................................310 630-4848
Jason Carr, *President*
Rodney Carr, *President*
Gene Ober, *Natl Sales Mgr*
Pierre Mathieu, *Sales Dir*
Nohemi Ramirez, *Marketing Staff*
◆ **EMP:** 20 **EST:** 2000
SALES (est): 8.3MM **Privately Held**
WEB: www.softlinehome.com
SIC: 5131 2391 Piece goods & other fabrics; curtains & draperies

(P-14322)
TALON INTERNATIONAL INC (PA)
21900 Burbank Blvd # 101, Woodland Hills (91367-6469)
PHONE..................................818 444-4100
Mark Dyne, *Ch of Bd*
Larry Dyne, *CEO*
James Reeder, *COO*
Daniel Ryu, *Officer*
Gary Dyne, *Exec VP*
EMP: 186 **EST:** 1997
SALES: 48.2MM **Privately Held**
WEB: www.taloninternational.com
SIC: 5131 3965 Sewing supplies & notions; zipper

(P-14323)
UNITED FABRICS INTL INC
Also Called: U F I
1723 S Central Ave, Los Angeles (90021-3030)
PHONE..................................213 749-8200
Shahariar S Simantob, *President*
Ramin Simantob, *Vice Pres*
▲ **EMP:** 51
SQ FT: 35,000
SALES (est): 16.5MM **Privately Held**
WEB: www.unitedfabric.com
SIC: 5131 5949 Textiles, woven; fabric stores piece goods

(P-14324)
ZABIN INDUSTRIES INC (PA)
3957 S Hill St Ste A, Los Angeles (90037-1343)
P.O. Box 15218 (90015-0218)
PHONE..................................213 749-1215
Alan Faiola, *President*
Eric Sebso, *Exec VP*
Virginia Acosta, *Vice Pres*
Zabin Kong, *Managing Dir*
Fernando F Garcia, *Manager*
▲ **EMP:** 70 **EST:** 1940
SQ FT: 43,000
SALES (est): 12.4MM **Privately Held**
WEB: www.zabin.com
SIC: 5131 Zippers; textile converters; buttons; net goods

5136 Men's & Boys' Clothing & Furnishings Wholesale

(P-14325)
2253 APPAREL LLC (PA)
Also Called: Celebrity Pink
1708 Aeros Way, Montebello (90640-6504)
PHONE..................................323 837-9800
Doron Kadosh, *CEO*
Benny Goldstein, *Admin Sec*
Ivan Dal Pont, *Planning*
Mary Noland, *Sales Staff*
David Kadosh,
▲ **EMP:** 55 **EST:** 2004
SQ FT: 50,000
SALES (est): 44.2MM **Privately Held**
WEB: www.celebpink.com
SIC: 5136 5137 Men's & boys' clothing; women's & children's dresses, suits, skirts & blouses

(P-14326)
ARTICOUTURE INC
1265 S Johnson Dr, City of Industry (91745-2409)
PHONE..................................626 336-7299
Kuei-Lin Hsieh, *CEO*
EMP: 50 **EST:** 2011
SALES (est): 4.5MM **Privately Held**
SIC: 5136 5137 Men's & boys' clothing; women's & children's clothing

(P-14327)
ARTWEAR INC
13621 S Main St, Los Angeles (90061-2163)
PHONE..................................310 217-1393
Ora Ketpongsuda, *President*
Paul Ketpongsuda, *Vice Pres*
Janchay Bhongjan, *Controller*
▲ **EMP:** 21 **EST:** 1991
SQ FT: 48,000
SALES (est): 2.3MM **Privately Held**
SIC: 5136 5137 2396 2331 Shirts, men's & boys'; women's & children's sportswear & swimsuits; automotive & apparel trimmings; women's & misses' blouses & shirts; men's & boys' furnishings; finishing plants, cotton

(P-14328)
BRAD RAMBO & ASSOCIATES INC (PA)
Also Called: Independent Trading Company
1341 Calle Avanzado, San Clemente (92673-6351)
PHONE..................................949 366-9911
Brad Rambo, *President*
Brandon Rambo, *Principal*
Wendy Rambo, *CIO*
Dena Marques, *Info Tech Dir*
Jen Francisco, *Controller*
▲ **EMP:** 54 **EST:** 1995
SQ FT: 20,500
SALES (est): 23.7MM **Privately Held**
WEB: www.independenttradingco.com
SIC: 5136 Shirts, men's & boys'

(P-14329)
CALIFORNIA SHIRT PRINTER INC
12221 Monarch St, Garden Grove (92841-2906)
P.O. Box 801, La Jolla (92038-0801)
PHONE..................................714 898-9946
Suresh Khemlani, *President*
Sylvia Johnson, *Corp Secy*
▲ **EMP:** 60 **EST:** 1980
SQ FT: 47,000
SALES (est): 9.8MM **Privately Held**
WEB: www.calshirtprinter.com
SIC: 5136 7336 Shirts, men's & boys'; silk screen design

(P-14330)
COLOSSEUM ATHLETICS CORP
2400 S Wilmington Ave, Compton (90220-5403)
PHONE..................................310 667-8341
Stuart Whang, *CEO*
Sean Lee, *CFO*
Alphan Tsoi, *Exec VP*

Maria Donoghue, *Vice Pres*
Jeff Jung, *General Mgr*
◆ **EMP:** 85 **EST:** 1992
SQ FT: 64,227
SALES (est): 36.1MM **Privately Held**
WEB: www.colosseumusa.com
SIC: 5136 5137 Sportswear, men's & boys'; sportswear, women's & children's

(P-14331)
EISENBERG INTERNATIONAL CORP (PA)
9128 Jordan Ave, Chatsworth (91311-5707)
PHONE..................................818 365-8161
Joel Eisenberg, *President*
Lynn Eisenberg, *Corp Secy*
Richard Eisenberg, *Vice Pres*
◆ **EMP:** 55 **EST:** 1967
SQ FT: 36,000
SALES (est): 9.3MM **Privately Held**
SIC: 5136 Coats, men's & boys'; sportswear, men's & boys'; suits, men's & boys'; trousers, men's & boys'

(P-14332)
FASHION WORLD INCORPORATED
Also Called: Bijan
420 N Rodeo Dr, Beverly Hills (90210-4502)
PHONE..................................310 273-6544
Manigeh Messa, *Sales/Mktg Mgr*
EMP: 128
SALES (corp-wide): 8.6MM **Privately Held**
SIC: 5136 Men's & boys' clothing
PA: Fashion World, Incorporated
   421 N Rodeo Dr Ph
   Beverly Hills CA 90210
   310 273-6544

(P-14333)
FOX HEAD INC (PA)
Also Called: Fox Racing
16752 Armstrong Ave, Irvine (92606-4912)
PHONE..................................408 776-8800
Jeffrey McGuane, *CEO*
Pete Fox, *President*
Tanya Fischesser, *CFO*
Peter Fox, *Chairman*
Geoffrey Fox, *Vice Pres*
◆ **EMP:** 200 **EST:** 1975
SALES (est): 211.3MM **Privately Held**
WEB: www.foxracing.com
SIC: 5136 5137 5961 5699 Sportswear, men's & boys'; sportswear, women's & children's; mail order house; sports apparel

(P-14334)
GERALD MICHAEL LTD
Also Called: Mgl
1852 Carnegie Ave, Santa Ana (92705-5545)
PHONE..................................562 921-9611
Gerald D Barnes, *CEO*
Gloria Santa Cruz, *Office Mgr*
▲ **EMP:** 35 **EST:** 1983
SALES (est): 7.2MM **Privately Held**
SIC: 5136 2329 3999 Sweaters, men's & boys'; men's & boys' sportswear & athletic clothing; atomizers, toiletry

(P-14335)
H & C HEADWEAR INC (PA)
Also Called: King's Caps
17145 Margay Ave, Carson (90746-1209)
PHONE..................................310 324-5263
Shun On Ngan, *CEO*
John Lee, *President*
Chuck Schoonover, *Executive*
Ken Feldman, *Principal*
Buddy Cheng, *Technology*
◆ **EMP:** 72 **EST:** 1991
SQ FT: 143,000
SALES (est): 20MM **Privately Held**
WEB: www.eastwestemb.com
SIC: 5136 6794 Caps, men's & boys'; copyright buying & licensing

---

(P-14336)
HELMET HOUSE LLC (PA)
Also Called: Tour Master
26855 Malibu Hills Rd, Calabasas Hills
(91301-5100)
PHONE..................800 421-7247
Robert M Miller, *CEO*
Randy Hutchings, *CFO*
Philip Bellomy, *Vice Pres*
Mark Gandy, *Vice Pres*
Lauren Markling, *Admin Asst*
◆ **EMP:** 121 **EST:** 1969
SQ FT: 80,000
SALES (est): 40.3MM **Privately Held**
WEB: www.helmethouse.com
SIC: 5136 3949 3751 Men's & boys'
clothing; helmets, athletic; motorcycle ac-
cessories

(P-14337)
HWMM (HQ)
Also Called: Lifted Research Group
7 Studebaker, Irvine (92618-2013)
P.O. Box 4743, Laguna Beach (92652-
4743)
PHONE..................949 581-1144
Robert D Wright, *President*
Zach Wright, *Vice Pres*
Ryan Horne, *Software Dev*
◆ **EMP:** 92 **EST:** 1999
SALES (est): 30.8MM
SALES (corp-wide): 195.4MM **Privately
Held**
WEB: www.madengine.com
SIC: 5136 Sportswear, men's & boys'
PA: Mad Engine, Llc
6740 Cobra Way Ste 100
San Diego CA 92121
858 558-5270

(P-14338)
HYBRID PROMOTIONS LLC (PA)
10711 Walker St, Cypress (90630-4720)
PHONE..................714 952-3866
Bill Hutchison, *CEO*
David Lederman, *COO*
Christine Sana, *CFO*
Brad Shapiro, *CFO*
Dori Stratton, *Officer*
◆ **EMP:** 474 **EST:** 1999
SQ FT: 100,000
SALES (est): 252.1MM **Privately Held**
WEB: www.hybridapparel.com
SIC: 5136 5137 5611 Sportswear, men's
& boys'; women's & children's clothing;
men's & boys' clothing stores

(P-14339)
LA BRANDS LLC
Also Called: US Blanks
4726 Loma Vista Ave, Vernon
(90058-3215)
PHONE..................323 234-5070
Greg Baxter, *Manager*
EMP: 50
SALES (corp-wide): 51.4MM **Privately
Held**
SIC: 5136 5137 Men's & boys' sportswear
& work clothing; women's & children's
clothing
PA: L.A. Brands Llc
1717 N Naper Blvd Ste 203
Naperville IL

(P-14340)
LA JOLLA SPORT USA INC (PA)
Also Called: O'Neill Sportswear
14350 Myford Rd, Irvine (92606-1002)
PHONE..................949 428-2800
Daniel Neukomm, *CEO*
Jim White, *President*
Josh Wellington, *COO*
Cristy Abella, *CFO*
Garth Tarlow, *Chief Mktg Ofcr*
◆ **EMP:** 58 **EST:** 1987
SQ FT: 1,500,000
SALES (est): 58.7MM **Privately Held**
WEB: www.lajollagroup.com
SIC: 5136 Men's & boys' clothing

(P-14341)
M & S TRADING INC
Also Called: 7 Diamonds Clothing
15778 Gateway Cir, Tustin (92780-6469)
PHONE..................714 241-7190

Sami Khalil, *CEO*
Loli Samia, *CFO*
Shawn Stolfus, *Marketing Staff*
Mohammad Harake, *Sales Staff*
Mario Pasillas, *Sales Staff*
▲ **EMP:** 71 **EST:** 1991
SQ FT: 36,000
SALES (est): 7.3MM **Privately Held**
SIC: 5136 5137 Sportswear, men's &
boys'; women's & children's clothing

(P-14342)
**MOUNTAIN GEAR
CORPORATION**
Also Called: Tri-Mountain
4889 4th St, Irwindale (91706-2194)
PHONE..................626 851-2488
Daniel Tsai, *CEO*
Sandy Treagus, *CFO*
Rosie Tsai, *Vice Pres*
Olga Duran, *CTO*
Niem Thai, *Info Tech Mgr*
▲ **EMP:** 125 **EST:** 1994
SQ FT: 300,000
SALES (est): 29MM **Privately Held**
WEB: www.trimountain.com
SIC: 5136 Sportswear, men's & boys'

(P-14343)
NEW MODE SPORTSWEAR
12762 Monarch St, Garden Grove
(92841-3928)
PHONE..................714 899-7800
Jung Duk Kim, *Co-Owner*
Jin O Kim, *Co-Owner*
▲ **EMP:** 17 **EST:** 1984
SQ FT: 22,888
SALES (est): 730.3K **Privately Held**
WEB: www.21prousa.com
SIC: 5136 7336 2261 Shirts, men's &
boys'; silk screen design; printing of cot-
ton broadwoven fabrics

(P-14344)
OTTO INTERNATIONAL INC (PA)
Also Called: Otto Cap
3550 Jurupa St Ste A, Ontario
(91761-2946)
PHONE..................909 937-1998
Razgo Lee, *President*
Frank Jou, *CFO*
Percy Vasunia, *General Mgr*
Yvette Dominguez, *Marketing Mgr*
Heidi Soria, *Sales Associate*
◆ **EMP:** 50 **EST:** 1983
SQ FT: 136,000
SALES (est): 36.3MM **Privately Held**
WEB: www.ottocap.com
SIC: 5136 Caps, men's & boys'

(P-14345)
PIEGE CO (PA)
Also Called: Gh Bass
20120 Plummer St, Chatsworth
(91311-5448)
PHONE..................818 727-9100
Kambiz Zarabi, *President*
Morad Zarabi, *Ch of Bd*
Michael Zarabi, *Exec VP*
Sherry Kamali, *Executive*
Kass Delany, *Info Tech Mgr*
▲ **EMP:** 95 **EST:** 1981
SQ FT: 48,000
SALES (est): 46.2MM **Privately Held**
WEB: www.felina.com
SIC: 5136 5137 Men's & boys' suits &
trousers; lingerie

(P-14346)
QUAKE CITY CASUALS INC
Also Called: Quake City Caps
1800 S Flower St, Los Angeles
(90015-3424)
PHONE..................213 746-0540
John Glucksman, *CEO*
Steve De Mars, *President*
Soledad Wong, *Chief Mktg Ofcr*
Priscilla Hill, *Vice Pres*
Nathan Munoz, *Accountant*
▲ **EMP:** 125 **EST:** 1977
SQ FT: 11,500
SALES (est): 20.3MM **Privately Held**
WEB: www.capstoneheadwear.com
SIC: 5136 Men's & boys' clothing

(P-14347)
**RICK SOLOMON ENTERPRISES
INC (PA)**
Also Called: Axis
8460 Higuera St, Culver City (90232-2520)
P.O. Box 266, Los Angeles (90078-0266)
PHONE..................310 280-3700
Richard Solomon, *President*
Barbara Baskin, *CFO*
◆ **EMP:** 64 **EST:** 1983
SQ FT: 14,058
SALES (est): 17.6MM **Privately Held**
WEB: www.resmechanical.com
SIC: 5136 Sportswear, men's & boys'

(P-14348)
RRZ ENTERPRISES INC
Also Called: Spectra Apparel
5521 Schaefer Ave, Chino (91710-9070)
PHONE..................714 683-2820
Rauf Gajiani, *President*
Mohammad Joorabchi, *COO*
Jeannette Yeon, *Production*
Brad Eisman, *Sales Mgr*
EMP: 14 **EST:** 2011
SQ FT: 40,000
SALES (est): 1MM **Privately Held**
SIC: 5136 5137 2253 2321 Men's &
boys' clothing; women's & children's
clothing; T-shirts & tops, knit; sport shirts,
men's & boys'; from purchased materials;
T-shirts & tops, women's: made from pur-
chased materials

(P-14349)
SAYARI SHAHRZAD
Also Called: Blue Bay Industries
4822 Aqueduct Ave, Encino (91436-1621)
PHONE..................310 903-6368
Shahrzad Sayari, *Owner*
EMP: 25 **EST:** 2017
SALES (est): 1.6MM **Privately Held**
SIC: 5136 2339 2329 5651 Men's &
boys' sportswear & work clothing;
women's & misses' athletic clothing &
sportswear; athletic clothing: women's,
misses' & juniors'; ski & snow clothing:
men's & boys'; unisex clothing stores

(P-14350)
SOEX WEST USA LLC (PA)
Also Called: Soex Group
3294 E 26th St, Vernon (90058-8008)
PHONE..................323 264-8300
Roubik Aftandilians,
Anne Guevara, *Controller*
Nursis Ohanian,
◆ **EMP:** 299 **EST:** 1981
SQ FT: 120,000
SALES (est): 41MM **Privately Held**
SIC: 5136 Men's & boys' clothing

(P-14351)
SPORTEK INTERNATIONAL INC
Also Called: Sport Tek
2425 S Eastern Ave, Commerce
(90040-1414)
PHONE..................213 239-6700
Joseph Hanasabzadeh, *President*
Ben Hanasabzadeh, *CEO*
Manouchehr Satirian, *Vice Pres*
Lorna Maynigo, *Sales Staff*
◆ **EMP:** 18 **EST:** 2003
SQ FT: 50,000
SALES (est): 11.4MM **Privately Held**
WEB: www.sportek.com
SIC: 5136 5137 2254 Sportswear, men's
& boys'; sportswear, women's & chil-
dren's; underwear, knit

(P-14352)
STR WORLDWIDE INC
Also Called: Silver Star Distribution
17462 Von Karman Ave, Irvine
(92614-6206)
PHONE..................949 276-5990
Luke Burrett, *President*
▲ **EMP:** 5036 **EST:** 1991
SQ FT: 2,000
SALES (est): 8.4MM **Privately Held**
WEB: www.authenticbrands.com
SIC: 5136 Sportswear, men's & boys'
PA: Authentic Brands Group Llc
1411 Broadway Fl 4
New York NY 10018

(P-14353)
STUSSY INC
17426 Daimler St, Irvine (92614-5514)
PHONE..................949 474-9255
Frank Sinatra, *CEO*
Andy Tirpstra, *General Mgr*
Cameron Deeds, *Administration*
Aj Danan, *Software Dev*
Jim Amia, *Purch Mgr*
▲ **EMP:** 90 **EST:** 1980
SQ FT: 30,000
SALES (est): 35MM **Privately Held**
WEB: www.stussy.com
SIC: 5136 Men's & boys' clothing

(P-14354)
**TEE TOP OF CALIFORNIA INC
(PA)**
Also Called: Procelebrity
11801 Goldring Rd, Arcadia (91006-5880)
PHONE..................626 303-1868
Herbert Huang, *CEO*
Frances Huang, *Treasurer*
Balentina Huang, *Vice Pres*
▲ **EMP:** 20 **EST:** 1977
SQ FT: 2,000
SALES (est): 9.9MM **Privately Held**
WEB: www.goprocelebrity.com
SIC: 5136 2396 2395 Shirts, men's &
boys'; automotive & apparel trimmings;
pleating & stitching

(P-14355)
**TOPSON DOWNS CALIFORNIA
INC (PA)**
3840 Watseka Ave, Culver City
(90232-2633)
PHONE..................310 558-0300
John Poyer, *President*
Kelly Gordon, *COO*
Kristopher Scott, *CFO*
Benji Hein, *Vice Pres*
Joe Wirht, *Admin Sec*
▲ **EMP:** 250 **EST:** 1971
SQ FT: 42,000
SALES: 450.1MM **Privately Held**
WEB: www.topsondowns.com
SIC: 5621 5136 Women's clothing stores;
shirts, men's & boys'

(P-14356)
TOPWIN CORPORATION (PA)
Also Called: People's Place
1808 Abalone Ave, Torrance (90501-3703)
PHONE..................310 325-2255
Tomokazu Yoshimura, *CEO*
Chris Park, *Controller*
Kacey Abe, *Prdtn Mgr*
Gil Vizconde, *Opers Staff*
Takeshi Yogi, *Manager*
◆ **EMP:** 60 **EST:** 1984
SQ FT: 22,000
SALES (est): 22.3MM **Privately Held**
WEB: www.topwin.com
SIC: 5136 5137 5611 5621 Men's &
boys' clothing; women's & children's
clothing; men's & boys' clothing stores;
women's clothing stores; mannequins

(P-14357)
UNI HOSIERY CO INC (PA)
1911 E Olympic Blvd, Los Angeles
(90021-2421)
PHONE..................213 228-0100
Harry Chung, *CEO*
Kenny Chung, *Vice Pres*
Byong Lee, *Branch Mgr*
Gene Kim, *Accountant*
Eric Park, *Accountant*
◆ **EMP:** 120
SQ FT: 500,000
SALES (est): 40.1MM **Privately Held**
WEB: www.unihosiery.com
SIC: 5136 5137 Hosiery, men's & boys';
hosiery: women's, children's & infants';
lingerie

(P-14358)
**VANTAGE CUSTOM CLASSICS
INC**
Also Called: Vantage Apparel
3321 S Susan St, Santa Ana (92704-6858)
PHONE..................714 755-1133
Patty Venny, *Manager*
EMP: 26

SALES (corp-wide): 45.2MM **Privately Held**
WEB: www.vantageapparel.com
SIC: 5136 2397 2395 Sportswear, men's & boys'; schiffli machine embroideries; pleating & stitching
PA: Vantage Custom Classics, Inc.
100 Vantage Dr
Avenel NJ 07001
732 340-3000

(P-14359)
WALKING COMPANY HOLDINGS INC (PA)
Also Called: Big Dog Sportswear
1800 Avenue Of The Stars # 300, Los Angeles (90067-4204)
PHONE...................................805 963-8727
Andrew D Feshbach, *CEO*
Fred Kayne, *Ch of Bd*
Mike Grenley, *COO*
Roberta J Morris, *CFO*
Anthony J Wall, *Exec VP*
▲ EMP: 160 EST: 1993
SQ FT: 24,000
SALES (est): 307.7MM **Privately Held**
WEB: www.thewalkingcompany.com
SIC: 5651 5961 5136 5137 Family clothing stores; clothing, mail order (except women's); sportswear, men's & boys'; sportswear, women's & children's; sports apparel

(P-14360)
WEEKENDZ-OFF INC
Also Called: Weekendz Off, The
6838 E Acco St, Commerce (90040-1902)
PHONE...................................323 888-9966
Winston Gu, *CEO*
Kc Huang, *President*
Carmen Trujillo, *Accounts Exec*
▲ EMP: 22 EST: 1994
SQ FT: 10,500
SALES (est): 3.1MM **Privately Held**
WEB: www.weekendzoff.com
SIC: 5136 5621 2339 2326 Sportswear, men's & boys'; women's sportswear; athletic clothing: women's, misses' & juniors'; men's & boys' work clothing

---

5137 Women's, Children's & Infants Clothing Wholesale

(P-14361)
ALSTYLE AP & ACTIVEWEAR MGT CO (HQ)
1501 E Cerritos Ave, Anaheim (92805-6400)
PHONE...................................714 765-0400
Rauf Gajiani, *CEO*
Amin Amdani, *Vice Pres*
Mohammad Meah, *Purchasing*
Ian Macleod, *Sales Staff*
John Cook, *Manager*
◆ EMP: 1800 EST: 2001
SQ FT: 715,000
SALES (est): 555.1MM
SALES (corp-wide): 1.9B **Privately Held**
WEB: www.mygildan.com
SIC: 5137 Women's & children's clothing
PA: Les Vetements De Sport Gildan Inc
600 Boul De Maisonneuve O 33eme etage
Montreal QC H3A 3
514 735-2023

(P-14362)
B BOSTON & ASSOCIATES INC (PA)
Also Called: Western Connection, Carol Rose
4871 S Santa Fe Ave, Vernon (90058-2103)
PHONE...................................323 264-3915
Benjamin Boston, *CEO*
Ram Kundani, *President*
Anthony Farmer, *Vice Pres*
▲ EMP: 126 EST: 1981
SQ FT: 100,000

WEB: www.bboston.com
SIC: 5137 7389 Sweaters, women's & children's; women's & children's outerwear; personal service agents, brokers & bureaus

(P-14363)
BABY TREND INC (HQ)
1607 S Campus Ave, Ontario (91761-4335)
PHONE...................................909 773-0018
Jiangfeng Su, *CEO*
Shuyi Ll, *CFO*
Yong Kim, *Executive Asst*
Kim Yong, *Executive Asst*
Jenny Wang, *Business Anlyst*
◆ EMP: 78 EST: 1988
SQ FT: 67,000
SALES (est): 43.8MM **Privately Held**
WEB: www.babytrend.com
SIC: 5137 Baby goods

(P-14364)
BCBG MAX AZRIA GROUP LLC
2761 Fruitland Ave, Vernon (90058-3607)
PHONE...................................323 589-2224
EMP: 69 EST: 2014
SALES (est): 1.1MM
SALES (corp-wide): 1.5B **Privately Held**
SIC: 5137 5621 2335 Whol Women's/Child's Clothing Ret Women's Clothing Mfg Women's/Misses' Dresses
PA: Guggenheim Partners, Llc
330 Madison Ave Rm 201
New York NY 10017
212 739-0700

(P-14365)
BIZZ INC (PA)
Also Called: Ark & Co
170 E Jefferson Blvd, Los Angeles (90011-2331)
PHONE...................................323 235-5450
Sung T Kim, *CEO*
▲ EMP: 53 EST: 2002
SALES (est): 8.3MM **Privately Held**
SIC: 5137 5136 Women's & children's clothing; men's & boys' clothing

(P-14366)
BLUE PLANET INTERNATIONAL INC
Also Called: Boom-Boom Jeans
1526 E Washington Blvd, Los Angeles (90021-3122)
PHONE...................................323 526-9999
Simon Parsakar, *President*
Ezra Parsakar, *Vice Pres*
◆ EMP: 50 EST: 1985
SQ FT: 30,000
SALES (est): 22MM **Privately Held**
WEB: www.shopbbj.com
SIC: 5137 Women's & children's clothing

(P-14367)
CALIFORNIA RAIN COMPANY INC
1213 E 14th St, Los Angeles (90021-2215)
PHONE...................................213 623-6061
Jack Jhy C Jang, *President*
Ling Wang,
◆ EMP: 90 EST: 1986
SQ FT: 8,600
SALES (est): 15.8MM **Privately Held**
WEB: www.californiarainla.com
SIC: 5137 5136 5699 Sportswear, women's & children's; sportswear, men's & boys'; customized clothing & apparel

(P-14368)
COMAK TRADING INC A CAL CORP
2550 S Soto St, Vernon (90058-8013)
PHONE...................................323 261-3404
EMP: 100
SALES (est): 12.6MM **Privately Held**
SIC: 5137 5136 5139 Whol Women's/Child's Clothing Whol Men's/Boy's Clothing Whol Footwear

(P-14369)
DAMO TEXTILE INC
Also Called: Damo Clothing Company
12121 Wilshire Blvd # 1120, Los Angeles (90025-1164)
PHONE...................................213 741-1323
James Min, *CEO*
Paul Eeahn, *Vice Pres*
Edwin Min, *Managing Dir*
CJ Kim, *General Mgr*
Grace Park, *Technology*
▲ EMP: 40 EST: 1999
SALES (est): 21MM **Privately Held**
WEB: www.damoclothing.com
SIC: 5137 3999 Women's & children's clothing; atomizers, toiletry

(P-14370)
DELTA GALIL USA INC
Also Called: Loomworks Apparel
16912 Von Karman Ave, Irvine (92606-4972)
PHONE...................................949 296-0380
EMP: 73 **Privately Held**
WEB: www.deltagalil.com
SIC: 5137 Women's & children's lingerie & undergarments
HQ: Delta Galil Usa Inc.
1 Harmon Plz Fl 5
Secaucus NJ 07094
201 902-0055

(P-14371)
DOUBLE ZERO INC (PA)
Also Called: Double Zero Aougenoire
2011 E 49th St, Vernon (90058-2801)
PHONE...................................323 846-1400
Hellen Lee, *President*
Bill Kim, *CFO*
Denny Choi, *Vice Pres*
Smith Kang, *Account Dir*
▲ EMP: 28 EST: 2001
SALES (est): 6.8MM **Privately Held**
WEB: www.doublezerousa.com
SIC: 5137 5699 2339 Apparel belts, women's & children's; designers, apparel; service apparel, washable: women's

(P-14372)
EDGEMINE INC
Also Called: Mine Fashion
1801 E 50th St, Los Angeles (90058-1940)
PHONE...................................323 267-8222
Kevin Chang Kang, *President*
Kristen Han, *Exec VP*
Jimmy Shin, *Technology*
Joon Wang, *Human Resources*
Sarah King, *Sales Mgr*
▲ EMP: 120 EST: 1994
SQ FT: 45,000
SALES (est): 23.1MM **Privately Held**
WEB: www.edgemine.com
SIC: 5137 Women's & children's clothing

(P-14373)
EIGHTY ONE ENTERPRISE INC
9401 Whitmore St, El Monte (91731-2821)
PHONE...................................626 371-1980
May Sayphraraj, *President*
Darren Sayphraraj, *Treasurer*
◆ EMP: 50 EST: 2012
SQ FT: 60,000
SALES (est): 12.5MM **Privately Held**
WEB: www.carrieamber.com
SIC: 5137 Lingerie

(P-14374)
ESP GROUP LTD
2397 Bateman Ave, Duarte (91010-3313)
PHONE...................................626 301-0280
◆ EMP: 68
SQ FT: 150,000
SALES (est): 25.8MM **Privately Held**
WEB: www.espgroupltd.net
SIC: 5137 Clothing: Womens, Childrens, And Infants

(P-14375)
FIESTA FASHION CO INC (PA)
1100 Wall St Ste 106, Los Angeles (90015-2326)
PHONE...................................213 748-5775
Edward Kim, *President*
Peter Choi, *Vice Pres*
▲ EMP: 20 EST: 1996
SQ FT: 1,000

SALES (est): 10MM **Privately Held**
WEB: www.fiestafashionla.com
SIC: 5137 2339 Women's & children's clothing; athletic clothing: women's, misses' & juniors'

(P-14376)
FINAL TOUCH APPAREL INC
4801 Pacific Blvd, Vernon (90058-2211)
PHONE...................................323 484-9621
Mark Min Hyuk Kim, *CEO*
June Lim, *Admin Sec*
EMP: 19 EST: 2017
SQ FT: 16,000
SALES (est): 8MM **Privately Held**
WEB: www.finaltouchapparel.com
SIC: 5632 5137 2331 Apparel accessories; women's & children's clothing; women's & misses' blouses & shirts

(P-14377)
FUTURE HEALTH COMPANY
4404 Chaumont Rd, Woodland Hills (91364-5617)
PHONE...................................424 244-2221
Deborah Farnoush, *CEO*
EMP: 20 EST: 2020
SALES (est): 2MM **Privately Held**
SIC: 5137 5047 2326 5122 Hospital gowns, women's & children's; hospital equipment & furniture; hospital furniture; medical equipment & supplies; medical & hospital uniforms, men's; medical rubber goods

(P-14378)
GURU DENIM LLC (DH)
Also Called: True Religion Apparel
500 W 190th St Ste 300, Gardena (90248-4269)
PHONE...................................323 266-3072
John Ermatinger,
Alan Weiss, *Controller*
▲ EMP: 150 EST: 2002
SALES (est): 145.3MM
SALES (corp-wide): 350MM **Privately Held**
WEB: www.truereligion.com
SIC: 5611 5137 Clothing accessories: men's & boys'; women's & children's clothing
HQ: True Religion Apparel, Inc.
500 W 190th St Ste 300
Gardena CA 90248
323 266-3072

(P-14379)
HARVEYS INDUSTRIES INC
Also Called: Original Seatbeltbag , The
724 N Poinsettia St, Santa Ana (92701-3941)
PHONE...................................714 277-4700
Dana Harvey, *CEO*
Melanie Harvey, *Admin Sec*
Montes Sabrina, *Bookkeeper*
Jessica McNew, *Human Res Mgr*
Jessica Rice, *Human Res Mgr*
▲ EMP: 55
SQ FT: 12,000
SALES (est): 20.5MM **Privately Held**
WEB: www.shopharveys.com
SIC: 5137 5632 Handbags; women's accessory & specialty stores

(P-14380)
HUB DISTRIBUTING INC (HQ)
Also Called: Anchor Blue
1260 Corona Pointe Ct, Corona (92879-5013)
PHONE...................................951 340-3149
Thomas Sands, *CEO*
Thomas Shaw, *Treasurer*
Elaine Gregg, *Admin Sec*
▲ EMP: 300 EST: 1947
SQ FT: 500,000
SALES (est): 50.7MM
SALES (corp-wide): 3.4B **Privately Held**
WEB: www.suncappart.com
SIC: 5611 5621 5632 5137 Men's & boys' clothing stores; women's clothing stores; apparel accessories; women's & children's clothing; men's & boys' clothing; jewelry & precious stones

---

PA: Sun Capital Partners, Inc.
5200 Town Center Cir # 600
Boca Raton FL 33486
561 962-3400

(P-14381)
IMG WORLDWIDE LLC (PA)
9601 Wilshire Blvd, Beverly Hills
(90210-5213)
PHONE...............424 653-1900
Heath Trentham, *Partner*
Gary Krakower, *Vice Pres*
James Leitz, *Vice Pres*
Scott Mackenzie, *Vice Pres*
Justin Delille, *Executive*
EMP: 111 EST: 2015
SALES (est): 33.7MM Privately Held
WEB: www.img.com
SIC: 5137 Skirts

(P-14382)
INCREMENTO INC (PA)
Also Called: Fantastic Fawn
2670 Leonis Blvd, Vernon (90058-2204)
PHONE...............213 624-7777
Su Hee Choi, *CEO*
EMP: 59 EST: 2011
SQ FT: 50,000
SALES (est): 9.7MM Privately Held
WEB: www.peachloveca.com
SIC: 5137 Women's & children's clothing

(P-14383)
ISABEL GARRETON INC (PA)
770 Miraflores, San Pedro (90731-1437)
PHONE...............310 833-7768
Isabel Garreton, *President*
Alexandra Garreton, *Vice Pres*
Michael Juneau, *Data Proc Dir*
Erika Whitham, *Software Dev*
EMP: 123 EST: 1986
SALES (est): 22.2MM Privately Held
WEB: www.isabelgarreton.com
SIC: 5137 Women's & children's clothing

(P-14384)
JOHNNY WAS
395 Santa Monica Pl # 124, Santa Monica
(90401-3477)
PHONE...............310 656-0600
Eli Levite, *Branch Mgr*
Johnny Was, *Officer*
EMP: 15
SALES (corp-wide): 2.8MM Privately
Held
WEB: www.johnnywas.com
SIC: 5137 2339 Women's & children's
clothing; women's & misses' accessories
PA: Johnny Was
903 Newport Center Dr
Newport Beach CA 92660
949 219-0557

(P-14385)
JOHNNY WAS (PA)
903 Newport Center Dr, Newport Beach
(92660-6903)
PHONE...............949 219-0557
Eli Levite, *Principal*
Maggee Villanueva, *Area Mgr*
Roselle Agles, *Store Mgr*
Stephanie Charest, *Store Mgr*
Gail Cope, *Store Mgr*
EMP: 27 EST: 2011
SALES (est): 2.8MM Privately Held
WEB: www.johnnywas.com
SIC: 5137 2389 Women's & children's
clothing; apparel & accessories

(P-14386)
JOHNNY WAS LLC (PA)
2423 E 23rd St, Los Angeles (90058-1201)
PHONE...............323 582-1005
Rob Trauber, *CEO*
Meg Newman, *Vice Pres*
Chelsey Lovell, *Executive*
Santos Dominique, *Project Mgr*
Karin Smith, *Prdtn Mgr*
EMP: 220 EST: 2015
SQ FT: 85,370
SALES (est): 38.7MM Privately Held
WEB: www.johnnywas.com
SIC: 5137 Women's & children's clothing

(P-14387)
KAREN KANE STORES INC (PA)
2275 E 37th St, Vernon (90058-1427)
PHONE...............323 588-0000
Lonnie Kane, *President*
Cecelia Jenkins, *Treasurer*
Karen Kane, *Vice Pres*
Duane Putnam, *Info Tech Dir*
Myung Hong, *Design Engr*
▲ EMP: 130 EST: 1979
SQ FT: 96,000
SALES (est): 96.7MM Privately Held
WEB: www.karenkane.com
SIC: 5137 Women's & children's clothing;
women's & children's accessories

(P-14388)
**KBL GROUP INTERNATIONAL
LTD**
Also Called: Kbl International
9142 9150 Norwalk Blvd, Santa Fe Springs
(90670)
PHONE...............562 699-9995
Thomas Ko, *Branch Mgr*
EMP: 50
SALES (corp-wide): 24.5MM Privately
Held
WEB: www.kblgroupintl.com
SIC: 5137 Sportswear, women's & chil-
dren's
PA: Kbl Group International Ltd.
1441 Broadway Fl 17th
New York NY 10018
212 391-1551

(P-14389)
KC EXCLUSIVE INC (PA)
Also Called: Zenana
1100 S San Pedro St M06, Los Angeles
(90015-2328)
PHONE...............213 749-0088
Seok Jun Choi, *President*
◆ EMP: 89 EST: 2003
SALES (est): 22.4MM Privately Held
WEB: www.ezenana.com
SIC: 5137 Women's & children's clothing

(P-14390)
LA DYE & PRINT INC
13416 Estrella Ave, Gardena (90248-1513)
PHONE...............310 327-3200
George Chaghouri, *CEO*
EMP: 35 EST: 2011
SQ FT: 1,800
SALES (est): 5,000 Privately Held
WEB: www.ladyeandprint.com
SIC: 5137 2269 Women's & children's
dresses, suits, skirts & blouses; linen fab-
rics: dyeing, finishing & printing

(P-14391)
**LEIGH JERRY CALIFORNIA INC
(PA)**
Also Called: Jerry Leigh Entertainment AP
7860 Nelson Rd, Panorama City
(91402-6044)
PHONE...............818 909-6200
Andrew Leigh, *President*
Tamar Aba, *CFO*
Jonathan Hirsh, *Exec VP*
Michael Eichberg, *Vice Pres*
Pamela Wong, *Vice Pres*
◆ EMP: 490 EST: 1977
SQ FT: 40,000
SALES (est): 302.7MM Privately Held
WEB: www.jerryleigh.com
SIC: 5137 2361 Sportswear, women's &
children's; girls' & children's dresses,
blouses & shirts

(P-14392)
LENOVATI INC (PA)
Also Called: Ena Intouch, Three
3251 E 26th St, Vernon (90058-8007)
PHONE...............323 307-9878
Jin Young Suh, *CEO*
Nader Pavirandeh, *CFO*
EMP: 21 EST: 2009
SQ FT: 5,000
SALES (est): 9.2MM Privately Held
WEB: www.lenovati.com
SIC: 5137 3999 Women's & children's
clothing; atomizers, toiletry

(P-14393)
LILY BLEU INC
Also Called: Jessie & Jenna
1406 W 178th St, Gardena (90248-3202)
PHONE...............310 225-2522
Michael Weis, *CEO*
Barbara Cambilargiu, *Vice Pres*
▲ EMP: 20 EST: 2002
SQ FT: 8,700
SALES (est): 5.5MM Privately Held
WEB: www.leahzawadzki.com
SIC: 5137 2339 Women's & children's
clothing; sportswear, women's

(P-14394)
LOVE TREE FASHION INC
Also Called: Love Style
2154 E 51st St, Vernon (90058-2817)
PHONE...............213 747-3755
Dong Sheng Ning, *CEO*
Jin Kim, *Manager*
◆ EMP: 50 EST: 2009
SQ FT: 1,800
SALES (est): 32.9MM Privately Held
WEB: www.lovetreefashion.com
SIC: 5137 Women's & children's clothing

(P-14395)
LYMI INC (PA)
Also Called: Reformation, The
2263 E Vernon Ave, Vernon (90058-1631)
PHONE...............855 756-0560
Yael Aflalo, *CEO*
Jennifer Loo, *CFO*
Hali Borenstein, *Vice Pres*
Sarah Logan, *Vice Pres*
Sarah Budhiman, *Business Dir*
▲ EMP: 100 EST: 2013
SQ FT: 120,000
SALES (est): 272.4MM Privately Held
WEB: www.thereformation.com
SIC: 5137 Women's & children's clothing

(P-14396)
**MAD DOGG ATHLETICS INC
(PA)**
Also Called: Spinning
2111 Narcissus Ct, Venice (90291-4818)
PHONE...............310 823-7008
John R Baudhuin, *President*
Aerin Shaw, *COO*
Michele McDonnell, *Vice Pres*
Rhona Attwater, *Executive Asst*
Jonathan Goldberg, *Admin Sec*
◆ EMP: 95 EST: 1991
SALES (est): 41.9MM Privately Held
WEB: www.maddogg.com
SIC: 5137 5122 7812 Sportswear,
women's & children's; vitamins & miner-
als; video tape production

(P-14397)
MADALUXE GROUP LLC (PA)
Also Called: Madaluxe Eyewear
1760 Apollo Ct, Seal Beach (90740-5617)
PHONE...............562 296-1055
Sandra Sholl, *Mng Member*
Carly Arrasmith, *Vice Pres*
Adam Freede, *Vice Pres*
Steven Barbery, *CIO*
Tad Bright, *Info Tech Mgr*
◆ EMP: 50 EST: 2010
SQ FT: 64,000
SALES (est): 60.6MM Privately Held
WEB: www.madaluxegroup.com
SIC: 5137 5136 Women's & children's
clothing; men's & boys' clothing

(P-14398)
MALIBU DESIGN GROUP
Also Called: Ocean Dream
1748 Camino Lindo, South Pasadena
(91030-4132)
PHONE...............323 271-1700
Mollie Cha, *CEO*
Mary Chung, *Admin Sec*
◆ EMP: 50 EST: 1982
SALES (est): 17MM Privately Held
WEB: www.malibuswim.com
SIC: 5137 Swimsuits: women's, children's
& infants'

(P-14399)
MATESTA CORPORATION
5620 Knott Ave, Buena Park (90621-1808)
P.O. Box 5395 (90622-5395)
PHONE...............949 874-6052
Salim Saeed, *CEO*
Robert Abraham, *CFO*
EMP: 106
SALES (est): 62MM Privately Held
WEB: www.matesta.com
SIC: 5137 5136 Women's & children's
clothing; men's & boys' clothing

(P-14400)
MIAS FASHION MFG CO INC
Also Called: California Basic
12623 Cisneros Ln, Santa Fe Springs
(90670-3373)
PHONE...............562 906-1060
Peter D Anh, *President*
Brian Song, *CFO*
Cindy Kim, *Managing Dir*
Lee Alice, *Legal Staff*
Kj Cho, *Manager*
◆ EMP: 252 EST: 1999
SALES: 83MM Privately Held
WEB: www.miasfashion.com
SIC: 5137 Women's & children's clothing

(P-14401)
MIKEN SALES INC (PA)
Also Called: Miken Clothing
7230 Oxford Way, Commerce
(90040-3643)
PHONE...............323 266-2560
Michael Bobbitt, *CEO*
Kenny Landy, *Vice Pres*
Juan Zepeda, *Prdtn Mgr*
Jordan Maroko, *Sales Staff*
◆ EMP: 53 EST: 1996
SQ FT: 23,000
SALES (est): 19MM Privately Held
WEB: www.mikenclothing.com
SIC: 5137 Women's & children's clothing

(P-14402)
MOLA INC
2957 E 46th St, Vernon (90058-2423)
PHONE...............323 582-0088
▲ EMP: 150
SALES (est): 45.2MM Privately Held
SIC: 5137 Whol Women's/Child's Clothing

(P-14403)
MS BUBBLES INC (PA)
Also Called: Eighty Eight
2731 S Alameda St, Los Angeles
(90058-1311)
PHONE...............323 544-0300
Aneeta Chopra, *CEO*
Sanjiv Chopra, *Treasurer*
Renu Chopra, *Vice Pres*
Rajeshwar Chopra, *Admin Sec*
Dale Dischner, *Cust Svc Dir*
▲ EMP: 75 EST: 1993
SQ FT: 50,000
SALES (est): 31.9MM Privately Held
WEB: www.msbubbles.com
SIC: 5137 Women's & children's clothing

(P-14404)
NEW PRIDE CORPORATION
Also Called: Belinda
5101 Pacific Blvd, Vernon (90058-2217)
PHONE...............323 584-6608
Miran Byun, *CEO*
Ho Lee, *President*
EMP: 55 EST: 2007
SQ FT: 5,000
SALES (est): 5.6MM Privately Held
SIC: 5137 2331 Women's & children's
clothing; women's & misses' blouses &
shirts

(P-14405)
**NEWPORT APPAREL
CORPORATION (PA)**
Also Called: I N G
1215 W Walnut St, Compton (90220-5009)
PHONE...............310 605-1900
James Kim, *President*
Kimberly Kim, *CFO*
Susie Ahn, *General Mgr*
Yong Chung, *General Mgr*
Lisa Yoon, *General Mgr*
▲ EMP: 62 EST: 1988

SQ FT: 38,500
SALES (est): 21.3MM **Privately Held**
WEB: www.newportapparel.com
SIC: 5137 Sportswear, women's & children's

(P-14406)
NHN GLOBAL INC (PA)
Also Called: Fashiongo.com
3530 Wilshire Blvd # 160, Los Angeles (90010-2328)
PHONE......................424 672-1177
Daniel Lee, *CEO*
Soohyun Lee, *Engineer*
Jennifer Cho, *Business Mgr*
Kyle Jang, *Controller*
Kevin Lee, *Senior Mgr*
EMP: 57 **EST:** 2005
SALES (est): 44.8MM **Privately Held**
WEB: www.nhn.com
SIC: 5137 7389 Women's & children's clothing

(P-14407)
NYDJ APPAREL LLC
Also Called: Not Your Daughters Jeans
5401 S Soto St, Vernon (90058-3618)
PHONE......................323 581-9040
Lisa Collier, *President*
Steve Brink, *CFO*
Jennifer Adams, *Officer*
Rosella Giuliani, *Vice Pres*
Demetra Mazria, *Creative Dir*
▲ **EMP:** 200 **EST:** 2003
SQ FT: 6,000
SALES (est): 67.8MM **Privately Held**
WEB: www.nydj.com
SIC: 5137 Women's & children's clothing

(P-14408)
O & K INC (PA)
Also Called: One Clothing
2121 E 37th St, Vernon (90058-1416)
PHONE......................323 846-5700
Chang Ho OK, *CEO*
Seongeun Kim, *President*
Chang Ho, *Admin Sec*
▲ **EMP:** 134 **EST:** 1989
SQ FT: 55,000
SALES (est): 44.2MM **Privately Held**
WEB: www.oneclothing.com
SIC: 5137 Women's & children's clothing

(P-14409)
PARAGON TEXTILES INC
Also Called: Samiyatex
13003 S Figueroa St, Los Angeles (90061-1136)
PHONE......................310 323-7500
Murtaza Haji, *CEO*
Farhana Haji, *Treasurer*
Jasmin Cervantes, *Opers Staff*
▼ **EMP:** 65 **EST:** 1992
SQ FT: 42,500
SALES (est): 23.4MM **Privately Held**
SIC: 5137 Women's & children's clothing

(P-14410)
POSH PEANUT INC (PA)
Also Called: Poshpeanut
2279 Ward Ave, Simi Valley (93065-1863)
PHONE......................805 335-1960
Fiona Sahakian, *CEO*
EMP: 70 **EST:** 2011
SALES (est): 15.7MM **Privately Held**
WEB: www.poshpeanut.com
SIC: 5137 5136 Women's & children's clothing; men's & boys' robes, nightwear & undergarments

(P-14411)
PRINCESS CRUISE LINES LTD
1242 E 25th St, Los Angeles (90011-1708)
PHONE......................213 745-0314
Delcino Fernandez, *Branch Mgr*
EMP: 3514
SALES (corp-wide): 2.4B **Privately Held**
WEB: www.princess.com
SIC: 5137 Infants' wear
HQ: Princess Cruise Lines, Ltd.
24305 Town Center Dr
Santa Clarita CA 91355
661 753-0000

(P-14412)
RCRV INC (PA)
Also Called: ROCK REVIVAL
4715 S Alameda St, Vernon (90058-2014)
PHONE......................323 235-7300
Eric S Choi, *President*
SOO Han Kim, *CFO*
Kheim Nguyen, *Vice Pres*
Young S Cho, *Admin Sec*
Andy Kim, *Sales Staff*
◆ **EMP:** 23 **EST:** 2008
SQ FT: 70,000
SALES (est): 51.1MM **Privately Held**
WEB: www.rockrevival.com
SIC: 5137 2673 Women's & children's clothing; garment & wardrobe bags, (plastic film)

(P-14413)
RICHARD CANTRELL (PA)
Also Called: Hard Tail
1661 9th St, Santa Monica (90404-3703)
PHONE......................310 399-5511
Richard R Cantrell, *Owner*
Dana Franklin, *VP Prdtn*
EMP: 85 **EST:** 1992
SQ FT: 18,000
SALES (est): 15.5MM **Privately Held**
SIC: 5137 5136 Women's & children's clothing; men's & boys' clothing

(P-14414)
RUNWAY LIQUIDATION LLC (HQ)
2761 Fruitland Ave, Vernon (90058-3607)
PHONE......................323 589-2224
Max Azria,
Brian Fleming, *CFO*
Bernd Kroeber, *Exec VP*
Martine Melloul, *Exec VP*
Cynthia Rash, *Branch Mgr*
◆ **EMP:** 1261 **EST:** 1989
SQ FT: 500,000
SALES (est): 630MM
SALES (corp-wide): 729.1MM **Privately Held**
WEB: www.marqueebrands.com
SIC: 5137 5621 2335 Women's & children's clothing; women's clothing stores; women's, juniors' & misses' dresses
PA: Marquee Brands Llc
330 W 34th St Fl 15
New York NY 10001
212 203-8135

(P-14415)
SAME SWIM LLC
2333 E 49th St, Vernon (90058-2820)
PHONE......................323 582-2588
Shea Petranovic,
Ryan Horne,
EMP: 90 **EST:** 2015
SALES (est): 10.1MM **Privately Held**
SIC: 5137 Women's & children's sportswear & swimsuits

(P-14416)
SEVEN LICENSING COMPANY LLC
Also Called: Seven7 Brands
5401 S Soto St, Vernon (90058-3618)
PHONE......................323 881-0308
Jacqueline Rose Guez, *Mng Member*
Gerald Guez,
▲ **EMP:** 80 **EST:** 2002
SALES (est): 38.7MM **Privately Held**
WEB: www.sunrisebrands.com
SIC: 5137 Women's & children's accessories
PA: Sunrise Brands, Llc
5401 S Soto St
Vernon CA 90058

(P-14417)
SNOWMASS APPAREL INC (PA)
Also Called: County Clothing Company
15225 Alton Pkwy, Irvine (92618-2354)
PHONE......................949 788-0617
George Wong, *CEO*
Edmond Wong, *President*
Harry Yip, *Admin Sec*
▲ **EMP:** 45 **EST:** 1984

SALES (est): 7.7MM **Privately Held**
SIC: 5137 5136 2339 Women's & children's outerwear; men's & boys' outerwear; women's & misses' outerwear

(P-14418)
STANCE INC (PA)
197 Avenida La Pata, San Clemente (92673-6307)
PHONE......................949 391-9030
John Wilson, *CEO*
Brian Shea, *CFO*
Tran Khang, *General Mgr*
Jeremy Cannon, *Store Mgr*
Amy Vong, *Store Mgr*
▲ **EMP:** 242 **EST:** 2009
SALES (est): 101.2MM **Privately Held**
WEB: www.stance.com
SIC: 5137 Women's & children's clothing

(P-14419)
SUNRISE BRANDS LLC (PA)
5401 S Soto St, Vernon (90058-3618)
PHONE......................323 780-8250
Gerard Guez, *CEO*
Donald Waldman, *CFO*
Linda Cohen, *Vice Pres*
Griffin Guez, *Vice Pres*
Oana Taylor, *Vice Pres*
EMP: 50 **EST:** 2008
SALES (est): 97MM **Privately Held**
WEB: www.sunrisebrands.com
SIC: 5137 5136 Women's & children's clothing; men's & boys' clothing

(P-14420)
SWATFAME INC (PA)
Also Called: Kut From The Kloth
16425 Gale Ave, City of Industry (91745-1722)
PHONE......................626 961-7928
Bruce Stern, *Ch of Bd*
Jonathan Greenberg, *President*
Mitchell Quaranta, *CEO*
Brian Min, *CFO*
J P Wolk, *CFO*
▲ **EMP:** 290 **EST:** 1978
SQ FT: 233,000
SALES (est): 88MM **Privately Held**
WEB: www.swatfame.com
SIC: 5137 2211 2339 Dresses; sportswear, women's & children's; denims; women's & misses' outerwear

(P-14421)
THE TIMING INC (PA)
Also Called: Timing Fashion
2809 S Santa Fe Ave, Vernon (90058-1408)
PHONE......................323 589-5577
Bowhan Kim, *President*
Kevin Kim, *Vice Pres*
Young Kim, *Admin Sec*
Diane Lee, *Accountant*
◆ **EMP:** 39 **EST:** 1989
SQ FT: 2,000
SALES (est): 9.7MM **Privately Held**
WEB: www.timingfashion.com
SIC: 5137 2331 2335 2339 Women's & children's clothing; women's & misses' blouses & shirts; women's, juniors' & misses' dresses; women's & misses' outerwear

(P-14422)
TLC SPORTSWEAR INC
5049 Jacobs Ct, Oak Park (91377-4716)
PHONE......................805 375-2494
Steve Primack, *President*
Mark Le Duc, *Vice Pres*
EMP: 14 **EST:** 1981
SALES (est): 2.2MM **Privately Held**
WEB: www.tlcsportswear.com
SIC: 5137 5136 2759 Sportswear, women's & children's; sportswear, men's & boys'; screen printing

(P-14423)
TRUE RELIGION SALES LLC (DH)
Also Called: True Religion Jeans
1888 Rosecrans Ave # 1000, Manhattan Beach (90266-3795)
PHONE......................323 266-3072
Michael Buckley,
Allen Weiss, *Vice Pres*

Vanessa Gamboa, *Executive*
Boris Blazevic, *Area Mgr*
Maral Mattosin, *General Mgr*
EMP: 296 **EST:** 2008
SALES (est): 145.3MM
SALES (corp-wide): 350MM **Privately Held**
WEB: www.truereligionbrandjeans.com
SIC: 5137 5136 Women's & children's dresses, suits, skirts & blouses; work clothing, men's & boys'
HQ: Guru Denim Llc
500 W 190th St Ste 300
Gardena CA 90248
323 266-3072

(P-14424)
TYR SPORT INC
Also Called: T Y R
1790 Apollo Ct, Seal Beach (90740-5617)
P.O. Box 1930, Huntington Beach (92647-1930)
PHONE......................562 430-1380
Matthew Dilorenzo, *CEO*
Joe Roehrig, *CFO*
David Melendez, *Info Tech Mgr*
Cy Bledman, *Graphic Designe*
Jennifer McCaughey, *Human Res Mgr*
◆ **EMP:** 60 **EST:** 1984
SQ FT: 80,000
SALES (est): 25.9MM
SALES (corp-wide): 39.8MM **Privately Held**
WEB: www.tyr.com
SIC: 5137 5136 5091 2329 Sportswear, women's & children's; swimsuits: women's, children's & infants'; women's & children's accessories; beachwear, men's & boys'; sporting & recreation goods; bathing suits & swimwear: men's & boys'; basketball uniforms: men's, youths' & boys'
PA: Swimwear Anywhere, Inc.
85 Sherwood Ave
Farmingdale NY 11735
631 420-1400

(P-14425)
UNCONDITIONAL LOVE INC
Also Called: Hello Bello
17383 W Sunset Blvd 200b, Pacific Palisades (90272-4181)
PHONE......................888 860-6888
Sean Kane, *CEO*
Jay McGraw, *President*
Jennifer Pullen, *COO*
EMP: 100 **EST:** 2018
SQ FT: 4,000
SALES (est): 200MM **Privately Held**
SIC: 5137 5999 Baby goods; toiletries, cosmetics & perfumes; infant furnishings & equipment

(P-14426)
WALL STREET ALLEY T-SHIRT CO
4125 E Brundage Ln, Bakersfield (93307-2387)
PHONE......................661 324-6207
Dominic S Webby, *Partner*
Stella Webby, *Partner*
EMP: 28 **EST:** 1980
SQ FT: 4,400
SALES (est): 2.1MM **Privately Held**
WEB: www.wsimp.com
SIC: 5137 5136 2395 2331 Sportswear, women's & children's; women's & children's dresses, suits, skirts & blouses; women's & children's outerwear; hats: women's, children's & infants'; sportswear, men's & boys'; shirts, men's & boys'; men's & boys' outerwear; hats, men's & boys'; emblems, embroidered; women's & misses' blouses & shirts; men's & boys' furnishings

5139 Footwear Wholesale

(P-14427)
412280 INC (DH)
Also Called: Hi-TEC Sports Usa, Inc.
5990 Sepulvda Blvd # 600, Van Nuys (91411-2500)
PHONE......................209 545-1111
Simon Bonham, *CEO*

Ed Van Wezel, *CEO*
William Berta, *CFO*
Frank Van Wezel, *Chairman*
Brad Gebhard, *Principal*
▲ **EMP:** 57 **EST:** 1978
SQ FT: 120,000
SALES (est): 19.6MM
SALES (corp-wide): 21MM **Publicly Held**
WEB: www.hi-tec.com
SIC: 5139 Footwear, athletic; boots
HQ: Hi-Tec Sports Limited
Aviation Way
Southend-On-Sea SS2 6
170 254-1741

(P-14428)
ACI INTERNATIONAL (PA)
844 Moraga Dr, Los Angeles (90049-1632)
PHONE..................310 889-3400
Steve Jackson, *CEO*
Jay Jackson, *President*
David Mankowitz, *CFO*
Scott Coble, *Exec VP*
Scott Cameron, *Vice Pres*
▲ **EMP:** 81 **EST:** 1952
SQ FT: 40,000
SALES (est): 54.1MM **Privately Held**
WEB: www.acifootwear.com
SIC: 5139 Shoes; slippers, house

(P-14429)
ASICS AMERICA CORPORATION (HQ)
Also Called: Asics Tiger
7755 Irvine Center Dr # 400, Irvine (92618-2904)
PHONE..................949 453-8888
Kevin Wulff, *CEO*
Seiho Gohashi, *Ch of Bd*
Richard Bourne, *President*
Kenji Sakai, *CFO*
Ron Pietersen, *Officer*
◆ **EMP:** 109 **EST:** 1973
SALES (est): 222.8MM **Privately Held**
WEB: www.asics.com
SIC: 5139 5136 5137 2369 Footwear, athletic; sportswear, men's & boys'; men's & boys' furnishings; sportswear, women's & children's; women's & children's accessories; girls' & children's outerwear; women's & misses' outerwear; men's & boys' furnishings

(P-14430)
AYLESVA INC
14537 Garfield Ave, Paramount (90723-3425)
PHONE..................562 688-0592
Jose Luis Solorcano, *President*
EMP: 120
SALES (est): 24MM **Privately Held**
WEB: www.aylesva-com-inc.hub.biz
SIC: 5139 5661 5651 5137 Shoes; shoe stores; family clothing stores; coordinate sets: women's, children's & infants'

(P-14431)
CAPE ROBBIN INC
1943 W Mission Blvd, Pomona (91766-1037)
PHONE..................626 810-8080
Michael Chen, *CEO*
Cindy Chang, *Sales Mgr*
Sandy Mancuso, *Sales Staff*
▲ **EMP:** 50 **EST:** 2011
SQ FT: 20,000
SALES (est): 6.7MM **Privately Held**
WEB: www.caperobbin.com
SIC: 5139 3171 Shoes; handbags, women's

(P-14432)
CHARLES DAVID OF CALIFORNIA (PA)
Also Called: CD
5731 Buckingham Pkwy, Culver City (90230-6985)
PHONE..................310 348-5050
Charles Malka, *President*
David Lann, *Vice Pres*
▲ **EMP:** 62 **EST:** 1987
SQ FT: 33,000
SALES (est): 24.9MM **Privately Held**
WEB: www.charlesdavid.com
SIC: 5661 5139 Women's shoes; shoes

(P-14433)
CHINESE LAUNDRY INC
Also Called: Chinese Laundry Shoes
3485 S La Cienega Blvd, Los Angeles (90016-4497)
PHONE..................310 945-3299
Robert Goldman, *President*
Derek Bordeaux, *Vice Pres*
Sam Chagzoetsang, *Executive*
Donald Leong, *Prgrmr*
Sean Corpuz, *Programmer Anys*
EMP: 50 **EST:** 1985
SQ FT: 72,000
SALES (est): 13.5MM **Privately Held**
WEB: www.chineselaundry.com
SIC: 5139 Shoes

(P-14434)
CONVERSE INC
1437-39 3rd St Promenade, Santa Monica (90401)
PHONE..................310 451-0314
Lisa Isham, *Store Mgr*
EMP: 89
SALES (corp-wide): 44.5B **Publicly Held**
WEB: www.ru.converse.com
SIC: 5139 5661 Footwear, athletic; footwear, athletic
HQ: Converse Inc.
1 Lovejoy Wharf
Boston MA 02114
978 983-3300

(P-14435)
E M S TRADING INC
Also Called: Michael-Antonio Studio
5161 Richton St, Montclair (91763-1310)
PHONE..................909 581-7800
Michael C Su, *CEO*
Ruby Su, *CFO*
Jack Su, *Admin Sec*
◆ **EMP:** 50 **EST:** 1985
SQ FT: 150,000
SALES (est): 13.1MM **Privately Held**
WEB: www.iheartmashoes.com
SIC: 5139 Shoes

(P-14436)
EAST LION CORPORATION
Also Called: Qupid Shoe
318 Brea Canyon Rd, Walnut (91789-3093)
PHONE..................626 912-1818
Ben Yi Kuo, *CEO*
Julie Kuo, *Vice Pres*
Connie Kuo, *Creative Dir*
Alexander Arreaga, *Sales Staff*
Jessica Lepe, *Sales Staff*
◆ **EMP:** 50 **EST:** 1982
SALES (est): 23.5MM **Privately Held**
WEB: www.eastlioncorp.com
SIC: 5139 Shoes

(P-14437)
ESQUIVEL DESIGNS LLC (PA)
7372 Walnut Ave Ste U, Buena Park (90620-1749)
PHONE..................714 670-2200
George Esquivel, *Mng Member*
Oscar Arreola, *Prdtn Mgr*
EMP: 58 **EST:** 2003
SALES (est): 2MM **Privately Held**
SIC: 5139 5661 5699 Shoes; custom & orthopedic shoes; customized clothing & apparel

(P-14438)
FOREVER LINK INTERNATIONAL INC
888 S Azusa Ave, City of Industry (91748-1028)
PHONE..................877 839-9899
Charles Hailongcui, *CEO*
Nicole Chen, *Purchasing*
Jason Lee, *Sales Associate*
Ivy Yang, *Manager*
◆ **EMP:** 50 **EST:** 2008
SALES (est): 15.3MM **Privately Held**
WEB: www.foreverlinkshoes.com
SIC: 5139 Shoes

(P-14439)
FORTUNE DYNAMIC INC
21923 Ferrero, City of Industry (91789-5210)
PHONE..................909 979-8318

Carol Lee, *President*
James Lee, *Vice Pres*
Sherry Yang, *Vice Pres*
Joan Lee, *Controller*
◆ **EMP:** 90 **EST:** 1986
SQ FT: 150,000
SALES (est): 28.2MM **Privately Held**
WEB: www.fortunedynamic.com
SIC: 5139 Shoes

(P-14440)
J P ORIGINAL CORP (PA)
Also Called: Doll House Footwear
19101 E Walnut Dr N, City of Industry (91748-1429)
PHONE..................626 839-4300
C H Hsueh, *Ch of Bd*
Si-Tuo Hsu, *President*
Christen Ho, *Human Resources*
Tom Chiang, *Sales Staff*
Greg Grace, *Director*
◆ **EMP:** 55
SQ FT: 67,000
SALES (est): 23.1MM **Privately Held**
WEB: www.jpo.com
SIC: 5139 Shoes

(P-14441)
MITSUWA CORPORATION
665 Paularino Ave, Costa Mesa (92626-3033)
PHONE..................714 557-6699
Nobukazu Suzuki, *Manager*
EMP: 63 **Privately Held**
WEB: www.mitsuwa.com
SIC: 5411 5311 5139 Grocery stores, independent; department stores, non-discount; footwear
HQ: Mitsuwa Corporation
3525 W Carson St Ste 164
Torrance CA 90503
310 782-6800

(P-14442)
NASTY GAL INC (HQ)
2049 Century Park E # 3400, Los Angeles (90067-3101)
PHONE..................213 542-3436
Sheree Waterson, *CEO*
Bob Ross, *CFO*
Spencer Niemetz, *Producer*
Courtney Maglaras, *Merchandising*
Sophia Klamt, *Marketing Staff*
◆ **EMP:** 23 **EST:** 2008
SALES (est): 29.8MM
SALES (corp-wide): 2.3B **Privately Held**
WEB: www.nastygal.com
SIC: 5621 5139 2389 Ready-to-wear apparel, women's; shoes; academic vestments (caps & gowns)
PA: Boohoo Group Plc
49-51 Dale Street
Manchester M1 2H
161 237-7700

(P-14443)
OSATA ENTERPRISES INC
Also Called: Globe Shoes
225 S Aviation Blvd, El Segundo (90245-4604)
PHONE..................888 445-6237
Matthew Hill, *President*
Gary Valentine, *Vice Pres*
▲ **EMP:** 100 **EST:** 1997
SQ FT: 30,000
SALES (est): 54.7MM **Privately Held**
WEB: www.us.globebrand.com
SIC: 5139 Shoes
PA: Globe International Limited
1 Fennell St
Port Melbourne VIC 3207

(P-14444)
PENTLAND USA INC (DH)
35 W Haley St, Santa Barbara (93101-3428)
PHONE..................516 365-1333
Dave Grange, *President*
▲ **EMP:** 50 **EST:** 1992
SALES (est): 55.7MM **Privately Held**
WEB: www.pentlandbrands.com
SIC: 5139 5137 Shoes; women's & children's clothing

HQ: Pentland Holdings B.V.
Onbekend Nederlands Adres
Amsterdam
205 222-555

(P-14445)
PRIMA ROYALE ENTERPRISES LTD
Also Called: Prima Royale
150 S Los Robles Ave # 100, Pasadena (91101-2456)
PHONE..................626 960-8388
Ing Nan Yu, *CEO*
Harry K T Chow, *President*
Judy Chow, *COO*
Bobby Bruce Levy, *Vice Pres*
Prima Royale, *Vice Pres*
◆ **EMP:** 28 **EST:** 1988
SQ FT: 55,000
SALES (est): 3MM **Privately Held**
SIC: 5139 3143 Shoes; men's footwear, except athletic

(P-14446)
STONE AGE EQUIPMENT INC (PA)
Also Called: Five Ten
1411 W State St, Redlands (92373-8164)
P.O. Box 7039 (92375-0039)
PHONE..................909 798-4222
Charles David Cole III, *President*
Mary E Cole, *Treasurer*
Iris Liao, *Director*
▲ **EMP:** 23 **EST:** 1985
SALES (est): 7MM **Privately Held**
WEB: www.v-shoes.com
SIC: 5139 2329 5136 Shoes; men's & boys' athletic uniforms; sportswear, men's & boys'

5141 Groceries, General Line Wholesale

(P-14447)
ABACUS BUSINESS CAPITAL INC
Also Called: Island Pacific Supermarket
738 Epperson Dr, City of Industry (91748-1336)
PHONE..................909 594-8080
Chengbiao Xue, *CEO*
Mina Hong, *General Mgr*
EMP: 50 **EST:** 2018
SALES (est): 11.8MM **Privately Held**
SIC: 5141 Groceries, general line

(P-14448)
ACOSTA INC
Also Called: Acosta Sales & Marketing
480 Apollo St Ste C, Brea (92821-3121)
PHONE..................714 988-1500
Rick Nist, *Branch Mgr*
Derick Hebert, *Vice Pres*
Pam Coale, *Business Mgr*
Michael Welter, *Business Mgr*
Cheryl Cena, *Manager*
EMP: 150
SALES (corp-wide): 1.7B **Privately Held**
WEB: www.acosta.com
SIC: 5141 Food brokers
HQ: Acosta, Inc.
6600 Corporate Ctr Pkwy
Jacksonville FL 32216
904 281-9800

(P-14449)
ADVANTAGE-CROWN SLS & MKTG LLC (DH)
1400 S Douglass Rd # 200, Anaheim (92806-6904)
P.O. Box 66010 (92816-6010)
PHONE..................714 780-3000
Sonny King, *CEO*
Bob Vesley, *CFO*
Mona Szumlas, *Business Dir*
Ruth Orris, *Regional Mgr*
Joel Miller, *District Mgr*
▲ **EMP:** 1100 **EST:** 1995
SALES (est): 340.5MM
SALES (corp-wide): 4.73 **Publicly Held**
WEB: www.advantagesolutions.net
SIC: 5141 Food brokers

▲ = Import ▼ = Export
◆ = Import/Export

HQ: Advantage Sales & Marketing Llc
560 Benigno Blvd # 10010
Bellmawr NJ 08031
949 797-2900

(P-14450)
AFC DISTRIBUTION CORP
19205 S Laurel Park Rd, Rancho
Dominguez (90220-6032)
PHONE.................................310 604-3630
Sadamu Taniguch, *CEO*
EMP: 250 **EST:** 2016
SALES (est): 73.2MM **Privately Held**
WEB: www.afcsushi.com
SIC: 5141 Groceries, general line
PA: Zensho Holdings Co., Ltd.
2-18-1, Konan
Minato-Ku TKY 108-0

(P-14451)
AFC TRADING & WHOLESALE INC
4738 Valley Blvd, Los Angeles
(90032-3834)
PHONE.................................323 223-7738
Jackson K H Wu, *President*
Leo Wu, *Exec VP*
Leonard Wu, *Vice Pres*
Alejandro TSE, *QC Mgr*
◆ **EMP:** 20 **EST:** 1985
SQ FT: 20,000
SALES (est): 5.6MM **Privately Held**
WEB: www.afcsoyfoods.com
SIC: 5141 2099 Food brokers; tofu, except frozen desserts

(P-14452)
ALBERTS ORGANICS INC
Also Called: Albert's Organics - West
3268 E Vernon Ave, Vernon (90058-1821)
PHONE.................................323 587-6367
Don Hessl, *Branch Mgr*
Keith Israel, *Accountant*
Curtis Steinback, *Merchandising*
Kevin Quinteros, *Sales Staff*
Erica Stewart, *Sales Staff*
EMP: 56
SQ FT: 13,000 **Publicly Held**
WEB: www.albertsorganics.com
SIC: 5141 Food brokers
HQ: Albert's Organics, Inc
1155 Commerce Blvd
Logan Township NJ 08085
856 241-9090

(P-14453)
AMERIFOODS TRADING COMPANY LLC (DH)
600 Citadel Dr, Commerce (90040-1562)
PHONE.................................323 869-7500
Ross E Roeder, *Ch of Bd*
Richard Phegley, *CFO*
Donald G Alvarado, *Senior VP*
Robert Bishoff, *Vice Pres*
◆ **EMP:** 672 **EST:** 1990
SALES (est): 123.9MM
SALES (corp-wide): 4.7B **Privately Held**
SIC: 5141 Food brokers
HQ: Smart & Final Stores Llc
600 Citadel Dr
Commerce CA 90040
323 869-7500

(P-14454)
AMK FOODSERVICES INC
Also Called: Kaney Foods
830 Capitolio Way, San Luis Obispo
(93401-7122)
P.O. Box 1188 (93406-1188)
PHONE.................................805 544-7600
John P Kaney, *CEO*
EMP: 130 **EST:** 1988
SQ FT: 35,000
SALES (est): 25.3MM **Privately Held**
SIC: 5141 Food brokers

(P-14455)
ANSAR GALLERY INC
2505 El Camino Rd, Tustin (92782)
PHONE.................................949 220-0000
Ali Akbar Feroozesh, *Principal*
Hussein Saadat, *President*
▲ **EMP:** 200 **EST:** 2013
SQ FT: 120,000

SALES (est): 36.4MM **Privately Held**
WEB: www.ansargallery.us
SIC: 5141 Food brokers
PA: Ansar Mall
P.O. Box 38880
Sharjah

(P-14456)
B & S FOOD PRODUCTS
20268 Pase Del Prado, Walnut (91789)
PHONE.................................323 263-6728
Peter Barrett, *President*
Gladys Herring, *Corp Secy*
Gloria Nejia, *Manager*
Eduardo Barrett, *Agent*
EMP: 13 **EST:** 1955
SQ FT: 8,000
SALES (est): 3.7MM **Privately Held**
SIC: 5141 5147 2013 Food brokers; meats, fresh; sausages from purchased meat

(P-14457)
CALIFORNIA RESTAURANT SUP CO
4665 E 49th St, Vernon (90058-3225)
PHONE.................................213 581-5100
Ruth Ross, *Ch of Bd*
Alan Ross, *President*
Hank Friedman, *Vice Pres*
Ann Ross, *Vice Pres*
EMP: 50 **EST:** 1967
SQ FT: 50,000
SALES (est): 8.1MM **Privately Held**
SIC: 5141 5113 5046 Groceries, general line; containers, paper & disposable plastic; dishes, disposable plastic & paper; cups, disposable plastic & paper; napkins, paper; restaurant equipment & supplies

(P-14458)
CANTON FOOD CO INC
750 S Alameda St, Los Angeles
(90021-1624)
PHONE.................................213 688-7707
Shiu Lit Kwan, *CEO*
Cho W Kwan, *President*
Shui Lit Kwan, *CEO*
Cho Kwan, *Vice Pres*
Wai Kam Kwan, *Vice Pres*
▲ **EMP:** 106 **EST:** 1979
SQ FT: 96,000
SALES (est): 29.6MM **Privately Held**
WEB: www.cantonfoodco.com
SIC: 5141 5146 5411 5421 Food brokers; seafoods; grocery stores; seafood markets; groceries & related products; refrigerated warehousing & storage

(P-14459)
CERENZIA FOODS INC
8585 White Oak Ave, Rancho Cucamonga
(91730-5146)
P.O. Box 3719 (91729-3719)
PHONE.................................909 989-4000
Joseph F Annunziato, *CEO*
Erik Zamora, *Buyer*
Armando Curiel, *Sales Staff*
▲ **EMP:** 60 **EST:** 1984
SQ FT: 75,000
SALES (est): 45MM **Privately Held**
WEB: www.cerenziafoods.com
SIC: 5141 Food brokers

(P-14460)
CHEFS WAREHOUSE WEST COAST LLC (HQ)
16633 Gale Ave, City of Industry
(91745-1802)
PHONE.................................626 465-4200
Chris Pappas, *President*
Tom Burghardt, *Finance*
Mark Espinoza, *Senior Buyer*
Marcia Little, *Sales Staff*
Ken Clark, *Mng Member*
▲ **EMP:** 59 **EST:** 2005
SALES (est): 40.7MM **Publicly Held**
WEB: www.chefswarehouse.com
SIC: 5141 Food brokers

(P-14461)
CONCORD FOODS INC (PA)
4601 E Guasti Rd, Ontario (91761-8105)
PHONE.................................909 975-2000
Nick J Sciortino Jr, *President*

Roy Sciortino, *CFO*
John Sciortino, *Vice Pres*
Emily Patten, *Research*
John Bernieri, *Purchasing*
EMP: 88 **EST:** 1985
SQ FT: 67,000
SALES (est): 47.3MM **Privately Held**
WEB: www.concordfoodsinc.com
SIC: 5141 Food brokers

(P-14462)
DAVID OPPENHEIMER AND CO I LLC
Also Called: Oppenheimer Group
15345 Frfeld Rnch Rd Ste, Chino Hills
(91709)
PHONE.................................909 631-2600
Staci Burke, *Opers Staff*
EMP: 51 **Privately Held**
WEB: www.oppy.com
SIC: 5141 Food brokers
HQ: David Oppenheimer And Company I, L.L.C.
180 Nickerson St Ste 211
Seattle WA 98109
206 284-1705

(P-14463)
DAVID OPPENHEIMER AND CO I LLC
317 W Main St, Visalia (93291-6242)
PHONE.................................559 636-7700
Barbara Marquez, *Manager*
Karin Gardner, *Exec Dir*
Debbie Anderson, *Executive Asst*
EMP: 51 **Privately Held**
WEB: www.oppy.com
SIC: 5141 5148 Food brokers; fresh fruits & vegetables
HQ: David Oppenheimer And Company I, L.L.C.
180 Nickerson St Ste 211
Seattle WA 98109
206 284-1705

(P-14464)
DAVID OPPENHEIMER AND CO I LLC
Also Called: Oppenheimer Group
1071 E 233rd St 2, Carson (90745-6206)
PHONE.................................310 900-7140
Fernando Caudillo, *Manager*
EMP: 51 **Privately Held**
WEB: www.oppy.com
SIC: 5141 Food brokers
HQ: David Oppenheimer And Company I, L.L.C.
180 Nickerson St Ste 211
Seattle WA 98109
206 284-1705

(P-14465)
DPI SPECIALTY FOODS WEST INC (DH)
601 S Rockefeller Ave, Ontario
(91761-7871)
PHONE.................................909 975-1019
John Jordan, *CEO*
James De Keyser, *President*
Donna Robbins, *President*
Francis Haren, *COO*
Conor Crowley, *CFO*
◆ **EMP:** 566 **EST:** 1951
SQ FT: 250,000
SALES (est): 477.2MM
SALES (corp-wide): 936.3MM **Privately Held**
WEB: www.dpispecialtyfoods.com
SIC: 5141 Food brokers

(P-14466)
FOOD SALES WEST INC (PA)
235 Baker St, Costa Mesa (92626-4521)
P.O. Box 19738, Irvine (92623-9738)
PHONE.................................714 966-2900
David Lyons, *CEO*
Carl Scharffenberger, *President*
Mary Ellen Scharffenberger, *Corp Secy*
Michael Berkson, *Vice Pres*
Robert Watkins, *Vice Pres*
EMP: 60 **EST:** 1973
SQ FT: 12,000
SALES (est): 18.8MM **Privately Held**
WEB: www.asmwaypoint.com
SIC: 5141 Food brokers

(P-14467)
FOOTHILL PACKING INC
2255 S Broadway, Santa Maria
(93454-7871)
PHONE.................................805 925-7900
Jorge Rivera, *President*
EMP: 489
SALES (corp-wide): 46.8MM **Privately Held**
WEB: www.foothillpacking.com
SIC: 5141 Food brokers
PA: Foothill Packing, Inc.
1582 Moffett St
Salinas CA 93905
831 784-1453

(P-14468)
FORTUNE AVENUE FOODS INC
2117 Pointe Ave, Ontario (91761-8529)
PHONE.................................909 930-5989
Daniel C Yang, *CEO*
Fula Yang, *Vice Pres*
Brian Bou, *Plant Mgr*
Harrison Chu, *Marketing Staff*
▲ **EMP:** 55 **EST:** 1990
SQ FT: 27,000
SALES (est): 25.1MM **Privately Held**
WEB: www.fortuneavenuefoods.com
SIC: 5141 Food brokers

(P-14469)
GOURMET FOODS INC (PA)
2910 E Harcourt St, Compton
(90221-5502)
PHONE.................................310 632-3300
Heinz Naef, *President*
Gary David, *CFO*
Ursina Naef, *Corp Secy*
Robbie Golzalez, *IT/INT Sup*
Markus Schaedler, *Research*
◆ **EMP:** 140 **EST:** 1986
SQ FT: 35,000
SALES (est): 70.7MM **Privately Held**
WEB: www.gourmetfoodsinc.com
SIC: 5141 5812 2099 Food brokers; eating places; food preparations

(P-14470)
GROCERS SPECIALTY COMPANY (DH)
Also Called: G S C Ball
5200 Sheila St, Commerce (90040-3906)
P.O. Box 513396, Los Angeles (90051-1396)
PHONE.................................323 264-5200
Joe Falvey, *President*
Rich Martin, *CFO*
Christine Neal, *Treasurer*
Bob Ling, *Admin Sec*
▲ **EMP:** 50 **EST:** 1981
SQ FT: 106,000
SALES (est): 52MM **Publicly Held**
WEB: www.unifiedgrocers.com
SIC: 5141 Groceries, general line
HQ: Unified Grocers, Inc.
2500 S Atlantic Blvd
Commerce CA 90040
323 264-5200

(P-14471)
HOUWELING NURSERIES OXNARD INC
Also Called: Houweling's Tomatoes
645 Laguna Rd, Camarillo (93012-8523)
P.O. Box 7027, Westlake Village (91359-7027)
PHONE.................................805 271-5105
Casey Houweling, *Chairman*
Kevin Doran, *President*
Chris Brocklesby, *CFO*
Christopher Brocklesby, *CFO*
Linton Clarke, *Info Tech Dir*
▲ **EMP:** 450 **EST:** 1995
SALES (est): 87.9MM **Privately Held**
WEB: www.houwelings.com
SIC: 5141 Groceries, general line

(P-14472)
IBITTA ENTERPRISES INC
Also Called: Natural and Healthy Products
4593 Firestone Blvd, South Gate
(90280-3343)
PHONE.................................323 588-6300
David Figueroa, *CEO*
Elvia Jacobo, *Vice Pres*

PRODUCTS & SVCS

Diane McKay, *Human Resources*
Abraham Reyes, *Sales Staff*
▲ **EMP:** 14 **EST:** 2002
SQ FT: 5,858
SALES (est): 6MM **Privately Held**
WEB: www.ibitta.com
SIC: 5141 2099 Food brokers; food preparations

(P-14473)
ICPK CORPORATION
Also Called: Hpp Food Services
1130 W C St, Wilmington (90744-5102)
PHONE..................310 830-8020
EMP: 70
SALES (corp-wide): 4MM **Privately Held**
SIC: 5141 2035 Groceries, general line; dressings, salad: raw & cooked (except dry mixes)
PA: Icpk Corporation
4380 Cerritos Ave
Los Alamitos CA 90720
714 321-7025

(P-14474)
LAX-C INC
1100 N Main St, Los Angeles (90012-1832)
PHONE..................323 343-9000
Suprata Bovornsivamon, *President*
Kittiphan Saengsri, *Info Tech Mgr*
Chatwadee Sangsri, *Buyer*
▲ **EMP:** 50 **EST:** 1983
SALES (est): 10.8MM **Privately Held**
WEB: www.rajprasongla.com
SIC: 5141 Groceries, general line

(P-14475)
MARQUEZ BROTHERS ENTPS INC
15480 Valley Blvd, City of Industry (91746-3325)
PHONE..................626 330-3310
Gustavo Marquez, *President*
Jaime Marquez, *Vice Pres*
Juan Marquez, *Vice Pres*
Francisco Lara, *VP Opers*
◆ **EMP:** 200 **EST:** 1993
SQ FT: 200,000
SALES (est): 36.5MM **Privately Held**
SIC: 5141 Food brokers

(P-14476)
MCLANE FOODSERVICE INC
14813 Meridian Pkwy, Riverside (92518-3004)
PHONE..................951 867-3555
Richard Arzinger, *General Mgr*
EMP: 240
SALES (corp-wide): 245.5B **Publicly Held**
WEB: www.mclaneco.com
SIC: 5141 Groceries, general line
HQ: Mclane Foodservice, Inc.
2085 Midway Rd
Carrollton TX 75006
972 364-2000

(P-14477)
MEGAMEX FOODS LLC (PA)
333 S Anita Dr Ste 1000, Orange (92868-3318)
PHONE..................714 385-4500
Scott D Aakre, *Mng Member*
Cindy Williams, *Administration*
Kathy Schnee, *Analyst*
Ronald W Fielding, *Mng Member*
Lorenzo Jimenez Garza, *Director*
EMP: 63 **EST:** 2009
SQ FT: 285,000
SALES (est): 454.4MM **Privately Held**
WEB: www.megamexfoods.com
SIC: 5141 Food brokers

(P-14478)
MERCADO LATINO INC (PA)
245 Baldwin Park Blvd, City of Industry (91746-1404)
P.O. Box 6168, El Monte (91734-6168)
PHONE..................626 333-6862
Graciliano Rodriguez, *President*
George Rodriguez, *CFO*
Richard Rodriguez, *Senior VP*
Roberto Rodriguez, *Vice Pres*
Kirk Zehnder, *VP Bus Dvlpt*
◆ **EMP:** 100 **EST:** 1963
SQ FT: 105,000

SALES (est): 87MM **Privately Held**
WEB: www.mercadolatinoinc.com
SIC: 5141 5148 Food brokers; fresh fruits & vegetables

(P-14479)
MISHIMA FOODS USA INC (PA)
3812 Sepulveda Blvd # 505, Torrance (90505-2462)
PHONE..................310 787-1533
Yutaka Mishima, *President*
Tsukasa Hatsukade, *Vice Pres*
Harumi Ishikawa, *Accountant*
Yuho Quintero, *Marketing Staff*
▲ **EMP:** 55 **EST:** 1988
SALES (est): 18.1MM **Privately Held**
WEB: www.mishima.com
SIC: 5141 Food brokers

(P-14480)
NAFTA DISTRIBUTORS
5120 Santa Ana St, Ontario (91761-8632)
PHONE..................800 956-2382
Samuel Madikians, *CEO*
Cary Puerta, *Buyer*
Jesse Gaxiola, *Sales Staff*
Alfredo Zatarain, *Sales Staff*
Alfredo Zataray, *Sales Staff*
▲ **EMP:** 75 **EST:** 1994
SQ FT: 12,000
SALES (est): 28.2MM **Privately Held**
WEB: www.naftadistributors.com
SIC: 5141 Food brokers

(P-14481)
NASSER COMPANY INC (PA)
Also Called: Nasser Company of Arizona
22720 Savi Ranch Pkwy, Yorba Linda (92887-4614)
PHONE..................714 279-2100
Burhan Nasser, *President*
Bill Arink, *President*
Mary Beth Nasser, *Corp Secy*
Nevart Majarian, *Vice Pres*
Becky Salazar, *VP Admin*
EMP: 60 **EST:** 1984
SQ FT: 17,445
SALES (est): 44.5MM **Privately Held**
WEB: www.nasserco.com
SIC: 5141 Food brokers

(P-14482)
NONGSHIM AMERICA INC (HQ)
12155 6th St, Rancho Cucamonga (91730-6115)
PHONE..................909 481-3698
Dong Y Shin, *CEO*
Chris Gepford, *Principal*
Krith Roth, *General Mgr*
Lorena Aguirre, *Administration*
Jae Yoon, *Administration*
◆ **EMP:** 250 **EST:** 1994
SALES (est): 107.8MM **Privately Held**
WEB: www.nongshimusa.com
SIC: 5141 2098 Food brokers; noodles (e.g. egg, plain & water), dry

(P-14483)
NZG SPECIALTIES INC (PA)
Also Called: Gourmet Trading Company
2580 Santa Fe Ave, Redondo Beach (90278-1116)
P.O. Box 88432, Los Angeles (90009-8432)
PHONE..................310 216-7575
Peter Lineen, *President*
Trent Grose, *CFO*
Marisala Morlett, *Admin Sec*
German Gomez, *Administration*
Chris Capelton, *Info Tech Mgr*
◆ **EMP:** 57 **EST:** 1988
SQ FT: 55,000
SALES (est): 77MM **Privately Held**
WEB: www.gourmettrading.net
SIC: 5141 Food brokers

(P-14484)
OTASTY FOODS INC
160 S Hacienda Blvd, City of Industry (91745-1101)
PHONE..................626 330-1229
Ming Chao Huang, *President*
Ken Chen, *Vice Pres*
◆ **EMP:** 91 **EST:** 1994
SQ FT: 58,000

SALES (est): 27.8MM **Privately Held**
WEB: www.otastyfoods.com
SIC: 5141 Food brokers

(P-14485)
PALISADES RANCH INC
Also Called: Goldberg and Solovy Foods Inc
5925 Alcoa Ave, Vernon (90058-3920)
PHONE..................323 581-6161
Paul Paget, *CEO*
Earl Goldberg, *President*
EMP: 285 **EST:** 1974
SQ FT: 70,000
SALES (est): 93.6MM
SALES (corp-wide): 52.8B **Publicly Held**
WEB: www.gsfoods.com
SIC: 5141 5149 5046 5169 Food brokers; groceries & related products; restaurant equipment & supplies; chemicals & allied products
PA: Sysco Corporation
1390 Enclave Pkwy
Houston TX 77077
281 584-1390

(P-14486)
PREMIER FOOD SERVICES INC
14359 Amargosa Rd Ste F, Victorville (92392-2334)
PHONE..................760 843-8000
David Lopez, *Branch Mgr*
EMP: 468
SALES (corp-wide): 1.1B **Privately Held**
WEB: www.premierfoodservices.com
SIC: 5141 Groceries, general line
HQ: Premier Food Services, Inc.
9500 Gilman Dr
La Jolla CA

(P-14487)
ROBERT KINSELLA INC
15375 Barranca Pkwy G107, Irvine (92618-2217)
PHONE..................949 453-9533
Robert Kinsella, *Owner*
Justin Clark, *Sales Mgr*
EMP: 77
SALES (corp-wide): 4.8MM **Privately Held**
SIC: 5141 Food brokers
PA: Robert Kinsella, Inc.
535 S Nolen Dr Ste 100
Southlake TX 76092
214 260-8670

(P-14488)
SMART & FINAL STORES INC
3049 E Coast Hwy, Corona Del Mar (92625-2234)
PHONE..................949 675-2396
EMP: 226
SALES (corp-wide): 5.1B **Privately Held**
SIC: 5141 Groceries, General Line, Nsk
PA: Smart & Final Stores Llc
600 Citadel Dr
Commerce CA 90040
323 869-7500

(P-14489)
SMART & FINAL STORES INC
4550 W Pico Blvd, Los Angeles (90019-4257)
PHONE..................323 549-9586
Sheena Bellinger, *Analyst*
EMP: 243
SALES (corp-wide): 4.7B **Privately Held**
SIC: 5141 Groceries, general line
HQ: Smart & Final Stores Llc
600 Citadel Dr
Commerce CA 90040
323 869-7500

(P-14490)
SMART & FINAL STORES INC
1005 W Arrow Hwy, San Dimas (91773-2422)
PHONE..................909 592-2190
EMP: 243
SALES (corp-wide): 4.7B **Privately Held**
SIC: 5141 Groceries, general line
HQ: Smart & Final Stores Llc
600 Citadel Dr
Commerce CA 90040
323 869-7500

(P-14491)
SMART & FINAL STORES INC
13346 Limonite Ave, Eastvale (92880-3360)
PHONE..................909 773-1813
EMP: 243
SALES (corp-wide): 4.7B **Privately Held**
SIC: 5141 Groceries, general line
HQ: Smart & Final Stores Llc
600 Citadel Dr
Commerce CA 90040
323 869-7500

(P-14492)
SMART & FINAL STORES INC
850 Linden Ave, Carpinteria (93013-2043)
PHONE..................805 566-2174
EMP: 243
SALES (corp-wide): 4.7B **Privately Held**
SIC: 5141 Groceries, general line
HQ: Smart & Final Stores Llc
600 Citadel Dr
Commerce CA 90040
323 869-7500

(P-14493)
SMART & FINAL STORES INC
1308 W Edinger Ave, Santa Ana (92704-4306)
PHONE..................714 549-2362
EMP: 243
SALES (corp-wide): 4.7B **Privately Held**
SIC: 5141 Groceries, general line
HQ: Smart & Final Stores Llc
600 Citadel Dr
Commerce CA 90040
323 869-7500

(P-14494)
SMART & FINAL STORES INC
15427 Amar Rd, La Puente (91744-2803)
PHONE..................626 330-2495
Robert Terry, *Branch Mgr*
EMP: 243
SALES (corp-wide): 4.7B **Privately Held**
SIC: 5141 Groceries, general line
HQ: Smart & Final Stores Llc
600 Citadel Dr
Commerce CA 90040
323 869-7500

(P-14495)
SMART & FINAL STORES INC
18555 Devonshire St, Northridge (91324-1308)
PHONE..................818 368-6409
Marie Teolis, *Branch Mgr*
EMP: 243
SALES (corp-wide): 4.7B **Privately Held**
SIC: 5141 Groceries, general line
HQ: Smart & Final Stores Llc
600 Citadel Dr
Commerce CA 90040
323 869-7500

(P-14496)
SMART & FINAL STORES INC
644 Redondo Ave, Long Beach (90814-1453)
PHONE..................562 438-0450
EMP: 243
SALES (corp-wide): 4.7B **Privately Held**
SIC: 5141 Groceries, general line
HQ: Smart & Final Stores Llc
600 Citadel Dr
Commerce CA 90040
323 869-7500

(P-14497)
SMART & FINAL STORES INC
2121 Spring St, Paso Robles (93446-1455)
PHONE..................805 237-0323
EMP: 243
SALES (corp-wide): 4.7B **Privately Held**
SIC: 5141 Groceries, general line
HQ: Smart & Final Stores Llc
600 Citadel Dr
Commerce CA 90040
323 869-7500

(P-14498)
SMART & FINAL STORES INC
26911 Trabuco Rd, Mission Viejo (92691-3506)
PHONE..................949 581-1212
EMP: 243

SALES (corp-wide): 4.7B **Privately Held**
SIC: **5141** Groceries, general line
HQ: Smart & Final Stores Llc
600 Citadel Dr
Commerce CA 90040
323 869-7500

(P-14499)
SMART & FINAL STORES INC
615 N Pacific Coast Hwy, Redondo Beach
(90277-2107)
PHONE..................323 497-8528
EMP: 243
SALES (corp-wide): 4.7B **Privately Held**
SIC: **5141** Groceries, general line
HQ: Smart & Final Stores Llc
600 Citadel Dr
Commerce CA 90040
323 869-7500

(P-14500)
SMART & FINAL STORES INC
240 S Diamond Bar Blvd, Diamond Bar
(91765-1605)
PHONE..................323 855-8434
EMP: 243
SALES (corp-wide): 4.7B **Privately Held**
SIC: **5141** Groceries, general line
HQ: Smart & Final Stores Llc
600 Citadel Dr
Commerce CA 90040
323 869-7500

(P-14501)
SMART & FINAL STORES INC
3830 W Verdugo Ave, Burbank
(91505-3441)
PHONE..................818 954-8631
EMP: 243
SALES (corp-wide): 4.7B **Privately Held**
SIC: **5141** Groceries, general line
HQ: Smart & Final Stores Llc
600 Citadel Dr
Commerce CA 90040
323 869-7500

(P-14502)
SMART & FINAL STORES INC
5038 W Avenue N, Palmdale (93551-5729)
PHONE..................661 722-6210
Danny Omada, *Branch Mgr*
EMP: 243
SALES (corp-wide): 4.7B **Privately Held**
SIC: **5141** Groceries, general line
HQ: Smart & Final Stores Llc
600 Citadel Dr
Commerce CA 90040
323 869-7500

(P-14503)
SMART & FINAL STORES INC
5770 Lindero Canyon Rd, Westlake Village
(91362-4088)
PHONE..................818 889-8253
EMP: 243
SALES (corp-wide): 4.7B **Privately Held**
SIC: **5141** Groceries, general line
HQ: Smart & Final Stores Llc
600 Citadel Dr
Commerce CA 90040
323 869-7500

(P-14504)
SMART & FINAL STORES INC
7800 Telegraph Rd, Ventura (93004-1503)
PHONE..................805 647-4276
Brian Gillman, *Branch Mgr*
EMP: 243
SALES (corp-wide): 4.7B **Privately Held**
SIC: **5141** Groceries, general line
HQ: Smart & Final Stores Llc
600 Citadel Dr
Commerce CA 90040
323 869-7500

(P-14505)
SMART & FINAL STORES INC
13003 Whittier Blvd, Whittier (90602-3046)
PHONE..................562 907-7037
David Hirs, *Branch Mgr*
EMP: 243
SALES (corp-wide): 4.7B **Privately Held**
SIC: **5141** Groceries, general line

HQ: Smart & Final Stores Llc
600 Citadel Dr
Commerce CA 90040
323 869-7500

(P-14506)
SMART & FINAL STORES INC
303 E Foothill Blvd, Azusa (91702-2516)
PHONE..................626 334-5189
EMP: 243
SALES (corp-wide): 4.7B **Privately Held**
SIC: **5141** Groceries, general line
HQ: Smart & Final Stores Llc
600 Citadel Dr
Commerce CA 90040
323 869-7500

(P-14507)
SMART & FINAL STORES INC
5135 E Los Angeles Ave, Simi Valley
(93063-3431)
PHONE..................805 520-6035
EMP: 243
SALES (corp-wide): 4.7B **Privately Held**
SIC: **5141** Groceries, general line
HQ: Smart & Final Stores Llc
600 Citadel Dr
Commerce CA 90040
323 869-7500

(P-14508)
SMART & FINAL STORES LLC
(HQ)
600 Citadel Dr, Commerce (90040-1562)
PHONE..................323 869-7500
David B Kaplan, *Ch of Bd*
David G Hirz, *President*
Scott Drew, *COO*
Richard N Phegley, *CFO*
Eugene M Smith, *Treasurer*
EMP: 447 **EST:** 1900
SQ FT: 81,000
SALES: 4.7B **Privately Held**
SIC: **5141** Groceries, general line
PA: Smart & Final Holdings, Inc.
600 Citadel Dr
Commerce CA 90040
800 894-0511

(P-14509)
SMART & FINAL STORES LLC
(DH)
600 Citadel Dr, Commerce (90040-1562)
PHONE..................323 869-7500
Etienne P Snollaerts, *CEO*
Ross E Roeder, *Ch of Bd*
Diane Godfrey, *President*
Martin Lynch, *CFO*
Dennis L Chiavelli, *Exec VP*
EMP: 366 **EST:** 1991
SALES (est): 461.8MM
SALES (corp-wide): 4.7B **Privately Held**
WEB: www.shop.smartandfinal.com
SIC: **5141** Groceries, general line
HQ: Smart & Final Llc
600 Citadel Dr
Commerce CA 90040
323 869-7500

(P-14510)
SOUTHWEST TRADERS INCORPORATED (PA)
Also Called: Swt Stockton
27565 Diaz Rd, Temecula (92590-3411)
PHONE..................951 699-7800
Ken Smith, *CEO*
Lynne Bredemeier, *CFO*
Ambrose Earle, *CIO*
Stephanie Eisenhower, *Human Res Mgr*
Jennifer Landrigan, *Buyer*
▲ **EMP:** 180
SQ FT: 130,000
SALES (est): 398.7MM **Privately Held**
WEB: www.southwesttraders.com
SIC: **5141** Food brokers

(P-14511)
SYGMA NETWORK INC
46905 47th St W, Lancaster (93536-8527)
PHONE..................661 723-0405
Mike Wren, *Branch Mgr*
Randi Valenzuela,
Christopher Angst, *Director*
EMP: 162

SALES (corp-wide): 52.8B **Publicly Held**
WEB: www.sygmanetwork.com
SIC: **5141** Food brokers
HQ: The Sygma Network Inc
5550 Blazer Pkwy Ste 300
Dublin OH 43017

(P-14512)
SYSCO LOS ANGELES INC
20701 Currier Rd, Walnut (91789-2904)
PHONE..................909 595-9595
Daniel S Haag, *CEO*
John Hinshaw, *Bd of Directors*
Sal Adelberg, *Exec VP*
John KAO, *Senior VP*
Janice Puket, *Comp Tech*
◆ **EMP:** 1000 **EST:** 1988
SALES (est): 221.8MM
SALES (corp-wide): 52.8B **Publicly Held**
WEB: www.syscola.com
SIC: **5141 5084** Groceries, general line;
food industry machinery
PA: Sysco Corporation
1390 Enclave Pkwy
Houston TX 77077
281 584-1390

(P-14513)
SYSCO RIVERSIDE INC
15750 Meridian Pkwy, Riverside
(92518-3001)
PHONE..................951 601-5300
Saul Adelsberg, *CEO*
EMP: 375 **EST:** 2009
SALES (est): 198.2MM
SALES (corp-wide): 52.8B **Publicly Held**
WEB: www.sysco-riverside.com
SIC: **5141 5142 5143 5144** Food bro-
kers; packaged frozen goods; dairy prod-
ucts, except dried or canned; poultry &
poultry products; confectionery; fish &
seafoods
PA: Sysco Corporation
1390 Enclave Pkwy
Houston TX 77077
281 584-1390

(P-14514)
SYSCO VENTURA INC
3100 Sturgis Rd, Oxnard (93030-7276)
PHONE..................805 205-7000
Jerry L Barash, *President*
Manny Fernandez, *Ch of Bd*
Bill Delaney, *President*
William Mastrosimone, *CFO*
Brian Beach, *Vice Pres*
EMP: 300 **EST:** 2003
SQ FT: 370,000
SALES (est): 118.3MM
SALES (corp-wide): 52.8B **Publicly Held**
WEB: www.sysco.com
SIC: **5141** Food brokers
PA: Sysco Corporation
1390 Enclave Pkwy
Houston TX 77077
281 584-1390

(P-14515)
TAPIA ENTERPRISES INC (PA)
Also Called: Tapia Brothers Co
6067 District Blvd, Maywood (90270-3560)
PHONE..................323 560-7415
Raul Tapia, *CEO*
Francisco Tapia, *Treasurer*
Ramon Tapia, *Admin Sec*
Sergio Vasquez, *Purchasing*
Ramiro Rubalcava, *Marketing Staff*
▲ **EMP:** 95 **EST:** 1985
SQ FT: 40,000
SALES (est): 95.1MM **Privately Held**
WEB: www.tapiabrothers.com
SIC: **5141** Groceries, general line

(P-14516)
UNION SUP COMSY SOLUTIONS INC
2301 E Pacifica Pl, Rancho Dominguez
(90220-6210)
PHONE..................785 357-5005
Guy Steele, *COO*
Nayeli Medina, *Executive*
Ashley Lear, *Program Mgr*
Cesar Rosas, *IT/INT Sup*
Staci Morrow, *Human Res Mgr*
EMP: 119 **EST:** 2012

SALES (est): 50MM **Privately Held**
WEB: www.unionsupply.com
SIC: **5141 5661 2252** Food brokers;
footwear, athletic; men's, boys' & girls'
hosiery
PA: Union Supply Group, Inc.
2500 Regent Blvd
Dallas TX 75261

(P-14517)
US FOODS INC
15155 Northam St, La Mirada
(90638-5754)
P.O. Box 29283, Phoenix AZ (85038-9283)
PHONE..................714 670-3500
David Patterson, *Branch Mgr*
Michael Ell, *Business Mgr*
Jenny Jenike, *Business Mgr*
Marlene Grove, *Human Resources*
Marybel Orozco, *Inv Control Mgr*
EMP: 172 **Publicly Held**
WEB: www.usfoods.com
SIC: **5141 5046 3556 2099** Food bro-
kers; commercial equipment; food prod-
ucts machinery; food preparations;
restaurant equipment repair
HQ: Us Foods, Inc.
9399 W Higgins Rd # 100
Rosemont IL 60018

(P-14518)
USFI INC
110 W Walnut St 221, Gardena
(90248-3100)
PHONE..................310 768-1937
Gary Place, *President*
William Baek, *CFO*
Chris Lee, *Exec VP*
Steven Choi, *Vice Pres*
Byung Hak Erick Yoo, *Director*
▲ **EMP:** 75 **EST:** 1998
SQ FT: 4,000
SALES (est): 26MM **Privately Held**
WEB: www.usfifoods.com
SIC: **5141 5149** Food brokers; groceries &
related products

(P-14519)
VIELE & SONS INC
Also Called: Viele & Sons Instnl Groc
1820 E Valencia Dr, Fullerton (92831-4847)
PHONE..................714 447-3663
Anthony J Viele, *President*
Jim Viele, *Shareholder*
Nancy Montez Viele, *Shareholder*
Joseph Viele, *Treasurer*
Anthony Viele Jr, *Vice Pres*
EMP: 90 **EST:** 1958
SQ FT: 95,000
SALES (est): 57.4MM **Privately Held**
WEB: www.vieleandsons.com
SIC: **5141** Food brokers

(P-14520)
VITCO DISTRIBUTORS INC
Also Called: Vitco Food Service
715 E California St, Ontario (91761-1814)
PHONE..................909 355-1300
Kostas Vitakis, *President*
Dean Vitakis, *CFO*
Emmanuel Vitakis, *Treasurer*
Terry Morvan, *Vice Pres*
Stellios Samaradellis, *Buyer*
EMP: 60 **EST:** 2001
SQ FT: 20,000
SALES (est): 59.5MM **Privately Held**
WEB: www.vitcofoods.com
SIC: **5141** Food brokers

(P-14521)
WEST PICO DISTRIBUTORS LLC
5201 S Downey Rd, Vernon (90058-3703)
P.O. Box 58107 (90058-0107)
PHONE..................323 586-9050
Mordy Herzog,
David Kagan,
EMP: 55 **EST:** 2016
SALES (est): 18.6MM **Privately Held**
SIC: **5141** Food brokers

(P-14522)
WISMETTAC ASIAN FOODS INC (HQ)
Also Called: Wismettac Fresh Fish
13409 Orden Dr, Santa Fe Springs (90670-6336)
PHONE..............................562 802-1900
Takayuki Kanai, *CEO*
Tom Kawaguchi, *CFO*
La Guardado Senlla, *Chief Mktg Ofcr*
Teijiro Sho, *Officer*
Raul Amado, *Vice Pres*
◆ **EMP:** 200 **EST:** 1960
SQ FT: 225,000
SALES (est): 540.7MM **Privately Held**
WEB: www.wismettac.com
SIC: 5141 Groceries, general line

5142 Packaged Frozen Foods Wholesale

(P-14523)
DARING FOODS INC (PA)
3505 Helms Ave, Culver City (90232-2414)
PHONE..............................855 862-5825
Andrew Ross Mackay, *CEO*
Jim Gellas, *Principal*
EMP: 165 **EST:** 2019
SALES (est): 16.2MM **Privately Held**
WEB: www.daring.com
SIC: 5142 7389 Frozen vegetables & fruit products;

(P-14524)
JON-LIN FROZEN FOODS (PA)
Also Called: Jon-Lin Foods
1620 N 8th St, Colton (92324-1302)
PHONE..............................909 825-8542
Russell H Burch, *President*
Jan Burch, *Treasurer*
Joseph Burch, *Vice Pres*
Mary Kate Burch, *Admin Sec*
EMP: 137 **EST:** 1962
SALES (est): 20.2MM **Privately Held**
SIC: 5142 Packaged frozen goods

(P-14525)
KINGS HAWAIIAN BAKERY W INC (HQ)
Also Called: Kings Hawaiian Bakery
1411 W 190th St, Gardena (90248-4324)
PHONE..............................310 533-3250
Mark Taira, *President*
Leatrice Taira, *Corp Secy*
Curtis Taira, *Vice Pres*
Laurene Taira, *Vice Pres*
Stella Taira, *Vice Pres*
▲ **EMP:** 25 **EST:** 1950
SALES (est): 142.5MM **Privately Held**
WEB: www.kingshawaiian.com
SIC: 5812 5142 2051 Restaurant, family: independent; bakery products, frozen; bread, cake & related products
PA: King's Hawaiian Holding Company, Inc.
19161 Harborgate Way
Torrance CA 90501
310 533-3250

(P-14526)
LAMONICAS PIZZA DOUGH INTL
3706 E 26th St, Vernon (90058-4106)
PHONE..............................323 263-0644
John Lamonica, *Branch Mgr*
EMP: 50
SALES (corp-wide): 34.4MM **Privately Held**
WEB: www.lamonicaspizzadough.com
SIC: 5142 Packaged frozen goods
PA: Lamonica's Pizza Dough International, Inc.
1066 Gayley Ave
Los Angeles CA 90024
310 208-5535

(P-14527)
LAMONICAS PIZZA DOUGH INTL INC (PA)
1066 Gayley Ave, Los Angeles (90024-3402)
PHONE..............................310 208-5535
John Lamonica, *CEO*
Helen Toledo, *Admin Sec*
EMP: 57 **EST:** 2012

SALES (est): 34.4MM **Privately Held**
WEB: www.lamonicaspizzadough.com
SIC: 5142 Packaged frozen goods

(P-14528)
MARIE CLLENDER WHOLESALERS INC
170 E Rincon St, Corona (92879-1327)
PHONE..............................951 737-6760
Phillip Ratner, *President*
Gerald Tanaka, *Senior VP*
Kurt Schweickhart, *Vice Pres*
EMP: 4944 **EST:** 1968
SQ FT: 28,000
SALES (est): 38.6MM
SALES (corp-wide): 421.8MM **Privately Held**
WEB: www.castleharlan.com
SIC: 5142 Bakery products, frozen
HQ: Castle Harlan Partners Iii Lp
150 E 58th St Fl 38
New York NY 10155
212 644-8600

(P-14529)
MCLANE FOODSERVICE DIST INC
Also Called: Mbm
17872 Cartwright Rd, Irvine (92614-6217)
PHONE..............................714 863-0163
Ken McDonald, *Branch Mgr*
EMP: 70
SALES (corp-wide): 245.5B **Publicly Held**
WEB: www.mbmcorp.com
SIC: 5142 5141 5144 Packaged frozen goods; groceries, general line; poultry & poultry products
HQ: Mclane Foodservice Distribution, Inc.
2641 Meadowbrook Rd
Rocky Mount NC 27801
252 985-7200

(P-14530)
S J S LINK INTERNATIONAL INC (PA)
468 N Camden Dr Ste 311, Beverly Hills (90210-4507)
PHONE..............................310 860-7666
Shiraz Mamedov, *CEO*
Olga Sedova, *CFO*
Alex Zimmer, *Treasurer*
▼ **EMP:** 50
SALES (est): 8.5MM **Privately Held**
SIC: 5142 Frozen fish, meat & poultry

(P-14531)
SJ DISTRIBUTORS INC
6116 Walker Ave, Maywood (90270-3447)
PHONE..............................888 988-2328
Steven Guang, *Branch Mgr*
Jerry Yeung, *CFO*
EMP: 52 **Privately Held**
WEB: www.sjfood.com
SIC: 5142 5149 5148 Meat, frozen: packaged; canned goods: fruit, vegetables, seafood, meats, etc.; fresh fruits & vegetables
PA: S.J. Distributors Inc.
625 Vista Way
Milpitas CA 95035

(P-14532)
WEI-CHUAN USA INC
13031 Temple Ave, La Puente (91746-1418)
PHONE..............................323 838-0088
Anthony Liu, *Branch Mgr*
Kenny Ye, *Accounts Exec*
EMP: 25
SALES (corp-wide): 97.2MM **Privately Held**
WEB: www.weichuanusa.com
SIC: 5142 2038 Packaged frozen goods; dinners, frozen & packaged; ethnic foods, frozen
PA: Wei-Chuan U.S.A., Inc.
13031 Temple Ave
City Of Industry CA 91746
626 225-7168

(P-14533)
WEI-CHUAN USA INC (PA)
13031 Temple Ave, City of Industry (91746-1418)
PHONE..............................626 225-7168
Steve Lin, *President*
William Huang, *Treasurer*
Benny Chang, *Admin Sec*
Tony Lee, *Technical Staff*
Robert Hsu, *Purch Mgr*
◆ **EMP:** 120 **EST:** 1972
SQ FT: 38,000
SALES (est): 97.2MM **Privately Held**
WEB: www.weichuanusa.com
SIC: 5142 2038 Packaged frozen goods; dinners, frozen & packaged; ethnic foods, frozen

(P-14534)
WEST PICO FOODS INC
5201 S Downey Rd, Vernon (90058-3703)
P.O. Box 58107 (90058-0107)
PHONE..............................323 586-9050
Elias Naghi, *President*
Don Lubitz, *Treasurer*
Jason Schultz, *Buyer*
▲ **EMP:** 125 **EST:** 1969
SQ FT: 42,000
SALES (est): 34.7MM **Privately Held**
WEB: www.westpicofoods.com
SIC: 5142 5144 Packaged frozen goods; poultry: live, dressed or frozen (unpackaged)

5143 Dairy Prdts, Except Dried Or Canned Wholesale

(P-14535)
ARYA ICE CREAM DISTRG CO INC
914 E 31st St, Los Angeles (90011-2502)
P.O. Box 456, Harbor City (90710-0456)
PHONE..............................323 234-2994
Ali Pakravan, *CEO*
Mansour Azizian, *Shareholder*
Farhad Karamati, *Shareholder*
Mansour Sahabi, *Shareholder*
Hossein Sahabi, *Vice Pres*
▲ **EMP:** 60 **EST:** 1990
SQ FT: 46,000
SALES (est): 25MM **Privately Held**
WEB: www.aryaicecream.com
SIC: 5143 Ice cream & ices

(P-14536)
CACIQUE INC
14923 Proctor Ave, La Puente (91746-3206)
P.O. Box 1047, Monrovia (91017-1047)
PHONE..............................626 961-3399
Christopher Iglesias, *President*
Timothy Campbell, *Analyst*
Michael Schmidt, *Regional*
EMP: 240
SALES (corp-wide): 129MM **Privately Held**
WEB: www.caciqueinc.com
SIC: 5143 Cheese
PA: Cacique Foods Llc
800 Royal Oaks Dr Ste 200
Monrovia CA 91016
626 961-3399

(P-14537)
CALIFIA FARMS LLC (PA)
1321 Palmetto St, Los Angeles (90013-2228)
PHONE..............................213 694-4667
Greg Stelpenpoho, *CEO*
Demir Vangelov, *CFO*
Karen Gifford, *Officer*
Halee Patel, *Vice Pres*
Vance Luc, *Surgery Dir*
▼ **EMP:** 50 **EST:** 2010
SALES (est): 97.6MM **Privately Held**
WEB: www.califiafarms.com
SIC: 5143 5149 Milk & cream, fluid; coffee, green or roasted

(P-14538)
CALIFORNIA DAIRIES INC
11894 Avenue 120, Pixley (93256-9748)
P.O. Box 837, Tipton (93272-0837)
PHONE..............................559 752-5200
Steve Cooper, *Branch Mgr*
James Anderson, *Controller*
Michael Morrissey, *Sales Staff*
EMP: 108
SALES (corp-wide): 3.3B **Privately Held**
WEB: www.californiadairies.com
SIC: 5143 Dairy products, except dried or canned
PA: California Dairies, Inc.
2000 N Plaza Dr
Visalia CA 93291
559 625-2200

(P-14539)
CALIFORNIA DAIRY DISTRIBUTORS (PA)
43861 Sierra Hwy, Lancaster (93534-5034)
PHONE..............................661 948-0829
John Ciufo, *President*
Linda Ciufo, *Admin Sec*
EMP: 66 **EST:** 1969
SQ FT: 1,000
SALES (est): 22.3MM **Privately Held**
SIC: 5143 Dairy products, except dried or canned

(P-14540)
CLEMSON DISTRIBUTION INC (PA)
20722 Currier Rd, City of Industry (91789-2903)
PHONE..............................909 595-2770
Rolando T Santos, *President*
Fernando Mancera, *General Mgr*
Emeline Santos, *Admin Sec*
Jose Valencia, *VP Opers*
▲ **EMP:** 39 **EST:** 1994
SQ FT: 32,000
SALES (est): 77.3MM **Privately Held**
WEB: www.clemsondistribution.com
SIC: 5143 2013 Ice cream & ices; cheese; milk; butter; prepared beef products from purchased beef

(P-14541)
DFA DAIRY BRANDS FLUID LLC
17851 Railroad St, City of Industry (91748-1118)
PHONE..............................800 395-7004
Michael Greenwald, *Manager*
EMP: 326
SALES (corp-wide): 17.8B **Privately Held**
SIC: 5143 Dairy products, except dried or canned
HQ: Dfa Dairy Brands Fluid, Llc
1405 N 98th St
Kansas City KS 66111
816 801-6455

(P-14542)
KLM MANAGEMENT COMPANY
Also Called: Amcom Food Service
14120 Valley Blvd, City of Industry (91746-2802)
PHONE..............................626 330-3479
Ted Degroot, *President*
VA Mechelen David, *Vice Pres*
Curtis Degroot, *Admin Sec*
▼ **EMP:** 56 **EST:** 1993
SQ FT: 91,000
SALES (est): 12.8MM **Privately Held**
WEB: www.am-com.net
SIC: 5143 Dairy products, except dried or canned

(P-14543)
LOS ALTOS FOOD PRODUCTS LLC
450 Baldwin Park Blvd, City of Industry (91746-1407)
PHONE..............................626 330-6555
Raul Andrade, *President*
Gloria Andrade, *Vice Pres*
Cesar Barajas, *District Mgr*
Patricia Valera, *Executive Asst*
Gaby Medina, *Purchasing*
EMP: 105 **EST:** 1988
SQ FT: 38,000

SALES (est): 91.8MM **Privately Held**
WEB: www.losaltosfoods.com
SIC: **5143** Cheese

(P-14544)
MCCONNELLS FINE ICE CREAMS LLC
800 Del Norte Blvd, Oxnard (93030-8971)
PHONE...................................805 963-8813
Briana Gray, *Mng Member*
Tom Stanley, *Creative Dir*
Olivia Alvarado, *Sales Staff*
Matt Lara, *Sales Staff*
Lily Moffett, *Sales Staff*
EMP: 38 EST: 2011
SQ FT: 184,000
SALES (est): 20.2MM **Privately Held**
SIC: **5143** 2024 Ice cream & ices; ice cream, bulk

(P-14545)
NESTLE ICE CREAM COMPANY LLC
7301 District Blvd, Bakersfield (93313-2042)
PHONE...................................661 398-3500
James L Dintaman, *CEO*
▲ EMP: 1920 EST: 1993
SALES (est): 221.8MM
SALES (corp-wide): 177.9K **Privately Held**
WEB: www.nestleusa.com
SIC: **5143** Ice cream & ices; ice cream (packaged)
HQ: Dreyer's Grand Ice Cream Holdings, Inc.
5929 College Ave
Oakland CA 94618
510 652-8187

(P-14546)
SVD INC
Also Called: Sun Valley Dairy
8088 San Fernando Rd, Sun Valley (91352-4001)
PHONE...................................818 504-1775
Jack Galadjian, *CEO*
ARA Kozanian, *President*
Moses Posheian, *CIO*
▲ EMP: 55 EST: 2002
SQ FT: 40,000
SALES (est): 17.2MM **Privately Held**
SIC: **5143** Yogurt

5144 Poultry & Poultry Prdts Wholesale

(P-14547)
HIDDEN VILLA RANCH PRODUCE INC
310 N Harbor Blvd Ste 205, Fullerton (92832-1954)
P.O. Box 34001 (92834-9411)
PHONE...................................714 680-3447
Tim E Luberski, *President*
Don Lawson, *CFO*
Robert J Kelly, *Exec VP*
Greg Schneider, *Exec VP*
Michael Sencer, *Exec VP*
◆ EMP: 270 EST: 1995
SQ FT: 21,619
SALES (est): 410MM
SALES (corp-wide): 350MM **Privately Held**
WEB: www.hiddenvilla.com
SIC: **5144** Eggs
PA: Luberski, Inc.
310 N Harbor Blvd Ste 205
Fullerton CA 92832
714 680-3447

(P-14548)
INTERSTATE FOODS INC
310 S Long Beach Blvd, Compton (90221-3400)
PHONE...................................310 635-0426
Carlos Velasco, *CEO*
EMP: 145
SQ FT: 13,000
SALES (est): 42.5MM **Privately Held**
SIC: **5144** Poultry products

(P-14549)
ROGERS POULTRY CO (PA)
5050 S Santa Fe Ave, Vernon (90058-2124)
PHONE...................................323 585-0802
George V Saffarrans, *CEO*
John C Butler, *COO*
Koen Hennon, *Officer*
Ralph Schemel, *Administration*
Laura Perez, *Accounting Mgr*
EMP: 100 EST: 1979
SQ FT: 15,000
SALES (est): 56.7MM **Privately Held**
WEB: www.rogerspoultry.com
SIC: **5144** Poultry products

(P-14550)
ROGERS POULTRY CO
2020 E 67th St, Los Angeles (90001-2169)
PHONE...................................800 585-0802
John C Butler, *COO*
Doria Macshane, *Purchasing*
Raquel Navarro, *Manager*
EMP: 80
SALES (corp-wide): 56.7MM **Privately Held**
WEB: www.rogerspoultry.com
SIC: **5144** Poultry products
PA: Roger's Poultry Co.
5050 S Santa Fe Ave
Vernon CA 90058
323 585-0802

(P-14551)
SOUTHERN NENG EGGS ACQSTION LL (DH)
12005 Capperney Dr, Fontana (92337)
PHONE...................................951 332-3300
Jerry Kil,
▼ EMP: 50 EST: 1970
SALES (est): 1.9MM
SALES (corp-wide): 2.8B **Privately Held**
SIC: **5144** Eggs
HQ: Moark, Llc
28 Under The Mountain Rd
North Franklin CT 06254
951 332-3300

5145 Confectionery Wholesale

(P-14552)
8TH STREET ENTERPRISE INC
Also Called: Jack's Candy
777 S Central Ave, Los Angeles (90021-1507)
PHONE...................................213 622-9287
Minaz Ahamed, *CEO*
Shafiq Ahamed, *Vice Pres*
EMP: 52 EST: 2006
SALES (est): 20MM **Privately Held**
WEB: www.jackscandy.com
SIC: **5145** 5441 Candy; candy, nut & confectionery stores

(P-14553)
A & R WHOLESALE DISTRS INC
1765 W Penhall Way, Anaheim (92801-6728)
PHONE...................................714 777-7742
Martin R Alsobrooks, *CEO*
Ron Paz, *President*
Jeff Kuriel, *CEO*
EMP: 60 EST: 1986
SALES (est): 24.1MM
SALES (corp-wide): 519.5MM **Privately Held**
WEB: www.anrwholesale.com
SIC: **5145** Snack foods
HQ: Gold Star Foods, Inc.
3781 E Airport Dr
Ontario CA 91761
909 843-9600

(P-14554)
ALL NUTS AND SNACKS INC
12910 San Fernando Rd, Sylmar (91342-3601)
PHONE...................................818 367-5902
Gary Eshgian, *CEO*
Mehdi Vosogh, *COO*
EMP: 15 EST: 2011
SQ FT: 38,000

SALES (est): 2.1MM **Privately Held**
WEB: www.americannuts.com
SIC: **5145** 2096 Nuts, salted or roasted; cheese curls & puffs

(P-14555)
AMERICAN NUTS IMPRT-EXPORT INC
12950 San Fernando Rd, Sylmar (91342-3601)
PHONE...................................818 364-8855
Gary Eshgian, *CEO*
Souren Gara, *Vice Pres*
Soffy Eshgian, *Admin Sec*
Alenjandra Martinez, *Admin Sec*
Tamar Gara, *Sales Mgr*
◆ EMP: 30 EST: 1993
SQ FT: 42,000
SALES (est): 14.7MM **Privately Held**
WEB: www.americannuts.com
SIC: **5145** 2068 Nuts, salted or roasted; salted & roasted nuts & seeds

(P-14556)
AMERICAN TRADING INTL INC
3415 S Sepulveda Blvd # 6, Los Angeles (90034-6060)
PHONE...................................310 445-2000
Seth Merrick Wilen, *CEO*
Emily Stewart, *CFO*
Teresa Ko, *Regional*
◆ EMP: 60 EST: 1995
SQ FT: 9,000
SALES (est): 74.8MM **Privately Held**
WEB: www.american-trading.com
SIC: **5145** 5141 Confectionery; food brokers

(P-14557)
AWESOME OFFICE INC
Also Called: Snacknation
3415 S Sepulveda Blvd # 1100, Los Angeles (90034-7090)
PHONE...................................310 845-7733
Sean Kelly, *CEO*
Jordan Narducci, *CFO*
Jordan Cohen, *Vice Pres*
Kevin Dorsey, *Vice Pres*
Chelsie Lee, *Vice Pres*
EMP: 91 EST: 2015
SALES (est): 62.3MM **Privately Held**
WEB: www.snacknation.com
SIC: **5145** Snack foods

(P-14558)
B B G MANAGEMENT GROUP (PA)
Also Called: Granlund Candies
12164 California St, Yucaipa (92399-4333)
PHONE...................................909 797-9581
R Scott Burkle, *President*
Margie Rogan, *Vice Pres*
EMP: 50 EST: 1961
SQ FT: 10,000
SALES (est): 8.4MM **Privately Held**
SIC: **5145** 2064 Candy; candy & other confectionery products

(P-14559)
BALANCE FOODS INC
5743 Smithway St Ste 103, Commerce (90040-1548)
PHONE...................................323 838-5555
Florencia Cuetara, *CEO*
Nasim Kheshti, *Director*
Jose Zavala, *Manager*
EMP: 38 EST: 2014
SALES (est): 9.5MM **Privately Held**
WEB: www.balancefoods.net
SIC: **5145** 2096 Snack foods; potato chips & similar snacks

(P-14560)
CENTURY SNACKS LLC
5560 E Slauson Ave, Commerce (90040-2921)
PHONE...................................323 278-9578
Valerie Oswalt, *CEO*
Stephen Famolaro, *CFO*
David Lowe, *Chairman*
Tiffany Obenchain, *Vice Pres*
Sharon Siliezar, *Engineer*
EMP: 330 EST: 1999
SQ FT: 280,000

SALES (est): 118.3MM
SALES (corp-wide): 177.6MM **Privately Held**
WEB: www.centurysnacks.com
SIC: **5145** 2064 Nuts, salted or roasted; nuts, candy covered; nuts, glace
HQ: Scncs, Llc
5560 E Slauson Ave
Commerce CA 90040
323 278-9578

(P-14561)
CONSOLIDATED SVC DISTRS INC
Also Called: Jacks Candy
777 S Central Ave, Los Angeles (90021-1507)
PHONE...................................908 687-5800
Steven Simon, *President*
Bill German, *CFO*
Herbert Lefkowitz, *Chairman*
Mark Leskowitz, *Corp Secy*
Steve Simon, *Administration*
▲ EMP: 85 EST: 1937
SALES (est): 42.8MM **Privately Held**
WEB: www.candycentral.com
SIC: **5145** 5194 Candy; tobacco & tobacco products

(P-14562)
FRITO-LAY NORTH AMERICA INC
9535 Archibald Ave, Rancho Cucamonga (91730-5737)
PHONE...................................909 941-6214
Brian Birrell, *Manager*
EMP: 500
SALES (corp-wide): 70.3B **Publicly Held**
WEB: www.fritolay.com
SIC: **5145** Snack foods
HQ: Frito-Lay North America, Inc.
7701 Legacy Dr
Plano TX 75024

(P-14563)
JOS CANDIES LLC
2530 W 237th St, Torrance (90505-5217)
PHONE...................................800 770-1946
Thomas King, *CEO*
Alex Schneider, *President*
David Choe, *CFO*
Andy Chiu, *Vice Pres*
Grant Childers, *Controller*
▲ EMP: 16 EST: 2012
SALES (est): 10.4MM **Privately Held**
WEB: www.joscandies.com
SIC: **5145** 2064 Candy; candy & other confectionery products

(P-14564)
LAYMON CANDY CO INC
276 Commercial Rd, San Bernardino (92408-4149)
PHONE...................................909 825-4408
Kenneth Laymon, *President*
Paul T Applen, *Vice Pres*
Linda Applen, *Manager*
▲ EMP: 27 EST: 1927
SQ FT: 43,000
SALES (est): 8.2MM **Privately Held**
WEB: www.laymoncandy.com
SIC: **5145** 2064 Candy; candy & other confectionery products

(P-14565)
S&E GOURMET CUTS INC
Also Called: Country Archer Jerky
1055 E Cooley Ave, San Bernardino (92408-2819)
PHONE...................................909 370-0155
Eugene Kang, *CEO*
Susan Kang, *Vice Pres*
Jeff Wong, *Vice Pres*
Daniel Palacios, *Graphic Designe*
Eric Kim, *Accounting Mgr*
EMP: 150 EST: 2011
SALES (est): 66.2MM **Privately Held**
WEB: www.countryarcher.com
SIC: **5145** 2013 Snack foods; cured meats from purchased meat

(P-14566)
SUPERIOR NUT CO INC
5200 Valley Blvd, Los Angeles
(90032-3929)
PHONE..................323 223-2431
Laura Rosen, *CEO*
Jacqueline Rosen, *Shareholder*
Debbie Rosen, *Treasurer*
EMP: 18 EST: 1964
SQ FT: 22,000
SALES (est): 11.3MM **Privately Held**
WEB: www.superiornutla.com
SIC: 5145 2068 Nuts, salted or roasted;
  nuts: dried, dehydrated, salted or roasted

(P-14567)
YOUBAR INC
445 Wilson Way, City of Industry
(91744-3935)
PHONE..................626 537-1851
Anthony M Flynn, *CEO*
Dennis Flynn, *COO*
Joel E Lipman, *Info Tech Mgr*
Emily Flynn, *Director*
David Miller, *Manager*
EMP: 75 EST: 2007
SALES (est): 31.3MM **Privately Held**
WEB: www.youbars.com
SIC: 5145 5812 2064 Snack foods; food
  bars; contract food services; granola &
  muesli, bars & clusters

5146 Fish & Seafood
Wholesale

(P-14568)
CENTRAL COAST SEAFOODS
5495 Traffic Way, Atascadero (93422-4246)
PHONE..................805 462-3474
Giovanni Comin, *President*
Molly Comin, *Vice Pres*
EMP: 214 EST: 1973
SQ FT: 10,000
SALES (est): 1MM
SALES (corp-wide): 121.9MM **Privately
Held**
WEB: www.santamonicaseafood.com
SIC: 5146 Fish, fresh; fish, frozen, unpack-
  aged; seafoods
PA: Santa Monica Seafood Company
  18531 S Broadwick St
  Rancho Dominguez CA 90220
  310 886-7900

(P-14569)
DEL MAR SEAFOODS INC
1449 Spinnaker Dr, Ventura (93001-4355)
PHONE..................805 850-0421
EMP: 185 **Privately Held**
WEB: www.delmarseafoods.com
SIC: 5146 Seafoods
PA: Del Mar Seafoods, Inc.
  331 Ford St
  Watsonville CA 95076

(P-14570)
**H & N FOODS INTERNATIONAL
INC (HQ)**
Also Called: H & N Fish Co.
5580 S Alameda St, Vernon (90058-3426)
PHONE..................323 586-9300
Hua Thanh Ngo, *President*
Bobby Ngo, *Vice Pres*
Christine Ngo, *Vice Pres*
Dat Trieu, *Vice Pres*
Nancy Yang, *Vice Pres*
◆ EMP: 125 EST: 1981
SQ FT: 45,000
SALES (est): 48.3MM
SALES (corp-wide): 68.9MM **Privately
Held**
WEB: www.hngroup.com
SIC: 5146 Seafoods; fish, frozen, unpack-
  aged
PA: H & N Group, Inc.
  5580 S Alameda St
  Vernon CA 90058
  323 586-9388

(P-14571)
**INTERNATIONAL MARINE PDTS
INC (HQ)**
3020 E Washington Blvd, Los Angeles
(90023-4220)
PHONE..................213 893-6123
Yuji Masunaga, *CEO*
Yuichiro Tanaka, *Planning*
Lawrence Pai, *Finance*
Hector Esparza, *Opers Staff*
Shota Tanaka, *Supervisor*
▲ EMP: 50 EST: 1965
SQ FT: 10,000
SALES (est): 35MM **Privately Held**
WEB: www.intmarine.com
SIC: 5146 Seafoods; fish, frozen, unpack-
  aged

(P-14572)
M & J SEAFOOD COMPANY INC
6859 Walthall Way, Paramount
(90723-2028)
PHONE..................562 529-2786
J Jesus Rodriguez, *CEO*
Wendy McDonalds, *COO*
EMP: 55 EST: 2001
SALES (est): 75MM **Privately Held**
WEB: www.mjseafoodcompany.com
SIC: 5146 5147 Seafoods; meats & meat
  products

(P-14573)
**MARUHIDE MARINE PRODUCTS
INC**
Also Called: M M P
2145 W 17th St, Long Beach (90813-1013)
PHONE..................562 435-6509
Hideo Kawamura, *President*
EMP: 60 EST: 1975
SQ FT: 14,352
SALES (est): 7.9MM **Privately Held**
WEB: www.maruhide.us
SIC: 5146 Seafoods

(P-14574)
OCEAN DUKE CORPORATION
21250 Hawthorne Blvd # 500, Torrance
(90503-5514)
PHONE..................310 326-3198
Duke Lin, *President*
Alice Lin, *CFO*
◆ EMP: 50 EST: 1984
SQ FT: 8,000
SALES (est): 4.5MM **Privately Held**
WEB: www.oceanduke.com
SIC: 5146 Seafoods

(P-14575)
OCEAN GROUP INC (PA)
Also Called: Ocean Fresh Fish Seafood Mktg
1100 S Santa Fe Ave, Los Angeles
(90021-1743)
PHONE..................213 622-3677
Young Won Kim, *President*
Katie Chung Yeh, *CFO*
Hyojin Ahn, *Vice Pres*
Jason Young Kim, *Admin Sec*
Kurt Kim, *Human Resources*
◆ EMP: 60 EST: 1983
SQ FT: 20,000
SALES (est): 40MM **Privately Held**
WEB: www.oceanfreshinc.com
SIC: 5146 Seafoods

(P-14576)
OCEAN QUEEN 87 INC
4511 Everett Ave, Vernon (90058-2621)
PHONE..................323 585-1200
Yuho Nagata, *President*
Justin Genochio, *Opers Mgr*
EMP: 50 EST: 1973
SQ FT: 3,700
SALES (est): 5.4MM **Privately Held**
WEB: www.oceanqueenusa.com
SIC: 5146 Seafoods

(P-14577)
**PACIFIC AMERICAN FISH CO
INC (PA)**
Also Called: Pafco
5525 S Santa Fe Ave, Vernon
(90058-3523)
PHONE..................323 319-1551
Peter Huh, *CEO*
Paul Huh, *Exec VP*

Tim Chu, *Program Mgr*
Sonny Sy, *Division Mgr*
Giang Cao, *Financial Analy*
◆ EMP: 150 EST: 1977
SQ FT: 100,000
SALES (est): 67.3MM **Privately Held**
WEB: www.pafco.net
SIC: 5146 2091 Fish, fresh; fish, filleted
  (boneless)

(P-14578)
PLD ENTERPRISES INC
Also Called: Superior Seafood Co
440 Stanford Ave, Los Angeles
(90013-2121)
PHONE..................213 626-4444
Chip Mezin, *General Mgr*
EMP: 70 **Privately Held**
SIC: 5146 Fish & seafoods
PA: P.L.D. Enterprises, Inc.
  1621 W 25th St Ste 228
  San Pedro CA 90732

(P-14579)
**PROSPECT ENTERPRISES INC
(PA)**
Also Called: American Fish and Seafood
625 Kohler St, Los Angeles (90021-1023)
PHONE..................213 599-5700
Ernest Y Doizaki, *Ch of Bd*
Jack King, *President*
Paula Eberhardt, *CFO*
Peter Alvino, *General Mgr*
Reyna Novelo, *Controller*
◆ EMP: 160 EST: 1947
SQ FT: 20,000
SALES (est): 97.7MM **Privately Held**
SIC: 5146 2092 Fish, fresh; fish, frozen,
  unpackaged; seafoods; fresh or frozen
  packaged fish

(P-14580)
RED CHAMBER CO (PA)
1912 E Vernon Ave, Vernon (90058-1611)
PHONE..................323 234-9000
Shan Chun Kou, *Ch of Bd*
Shu Chin Kou, *Ch of Bd*
Ming Bin Kou, *CEO*
Mingbin Kou, *COO*
Rick Martin, *Exec Dir*
◆ EMP: 341 EST: 1974
SQ FT: 15,000
SALES (est): 132.5MM **Privately Held**
WEB: www.redchamber.com
SIC: 5146 4222 Seafoods; warehousing,
  cold storage or refrigerated

(P-14581)
SAN PEDRO FISH MARKET LLC
1190 Nagoya Way 78, San Pedro
(90731-4408)
PHONE..................323 775-2921
Tommy Amalfitano, *Mng Member*
Nicole Edwards, *Human Res Dir*
Henry Ungaro,
EMP: 65 EST: 1961
SQ FT: 9,600
SALES (est): 6.6MM **Privately Held**
WEB: www.sanpedrofish.com
SIC: 5421 5812 5146 Fish markets;
  seafood markets; seafood restaurants;
  fish, fresh; seafoods

(P-14582)
SEA SNACK FOODS INC (PA)
914 E 11th St, Los Angeles (90021-2091)
P.O. Box 21467 (90021-0467)
PHONE..................213 622-2204
Fred W Ockrim, *CEO*
Barbara Kahn, *Treasurer*
Jeffrey Kahn, *Vice Pres*
Sheri Ockrim, *Admin Sec*
◆ EMP: 50 EST: 1954
SQ FT: 2,000
SALES (est): 9.6MM **Privately Held**
WEB: www.seasnack.com
SIC: 5146 Seafoods

(P-14583)
SEA WIN INC
526 Stanford Ave, Los Angeles
(90013-2123)
PHONE..................213 688-2899
Nam Tran, *CEO*
Frances Tran, *Admin Sec*

Hubert Tran, *Opers Staff*
▲ EMP: 50 EST: 1983
SQ FT: 29,000
SALES (est): 27.7MM **Privately Held**
WEB: www.seawin.com
SIC: 5146 Seafoods; fish, frozen, unpack-
  aged

(P-14584)
SLADE GORTON & CO INC
1 Centerpointe Dr Ste 311, La Palma
(90623-2512)
PHONE..................714 676-4200
Holly Hunt, *Manager*
Dana Bartholomew, *Vice Pres*
EMP: 66 **Privately Held**
WEB: www.sladegorton.com
SIC: 5146 Fish & seafoods
HQ: Slade Gorton & Co Inc
  255 Bear Hill Rd Ste 4
  Waltham MA 02451
  800 225-1573

(P-14585)
SOUTHWIND FOODS LLC (PA)
Also Called: Great American Seafood Import
Co
20644 S Fordyce Ave, Carson
(90810-1018)
P.O. Box 86021, Los Angeles (90086-0021)
PHONE..................323 262-8222
Sebastiano Buddy Galletti, *CEO*
Jim Lee, *CFO*
Don Sutherland, *CFO*
Maria Tovar-Davila, *Officer*
Paul Galletti, *Senior VP*
▲ EMP: 125 EST: 1999
SQ FT: 80,000
SALES (est): 100.1MM **Privately Held**
WEB: www.southwindfoods.com
SIC: 5146 5147 Seafoods; meats & meat
  products

(P-14586)
TRADEWIND SEAFOOD INC
1505 Mountain View Ave, Oxnard
(93030-5107)
PHONE..................805 483-8555
Mack Demachi, *President*
Gene Demachi, *Officer*
Hiromi Demachi, *Vice Pres*
EMP: 50 EST: 1981
SQ FT: 5,000
SALES (est): 9.5MM **Privately Held**
WEB: www.twseafood.com
SIC: 5146 Seafoods

(P-14587)
**TRI-MARINE FISH COMPANY
LLC**
220 Cannery St, San Pedro (90731-7308)
PHONE..................310 547-1144
Vince Torre, *Regional Mgr*
Walt Hadlow, *Plant Engr*
◆ EMP: 75 EST: 2001
SQ FT: 30,000
SALES (est): 27.2MM **Privately Held**
SIC: 5146 Seafoods

(P-14588)
**TRI-UNION SEAFOODS LLC
(DH)**
Also Called: Chicken of Sea International
2150 E Grand Ave, El Segundo
(90245-5024)
P.O. Box 85568, San Diego (92186-5568)
PHONE..................858 558-9662
Shue Wing Chan, *President*
David E Roszmann, *COO*
Jim Cox, *Senior VP*
Christie Fleming, *Senior VP*
Brenden Beck, *Vice Pres*
◆ EMP: 69 EST: 1996
SQ FT: 24,000
SALES (est): 101.3MM **Privately Held**
WEB: www.thaiunion.com
SIC: 5146 2091 Seafoods; tuna fish: pack-
  aged in cans, jars, etc.; salmon: pack-
  aged in cans, jars, etc.
HQ: Thai Union North America, Inc.
  2150 E Grand Ave
  El Segundo CA 90245
  424 397-8556

▲ = Import ▼=Export
◆ =Import/Export

(P-14589)
TRUE WRLD FODS LOS ANGELES LLC
4200 S Alameda St, Vernon (90058-1602)
PHONE 323 846-3300
Jang Hoee Kim, *President*
Yasuko Fujita, *Principal*
Scott Howard, *General Mgr*
Jun Okamoto, *IT/INT Sup*
Teiji Kawasaki, *Sales Mgr*
◆ EMP: 55 EST: 1983
SQ FT: 55,000
SALES (est): 30.1MM
SALES (corp-wide): 1.2B **Privately Held**
WEB: www.trueworldfoods.com
SIC: 5146 Fish, frozen, unpackaged; fish, fresh
HQ: True World Foods New York Llc
32-34 Papetti Plz
Elizabeth NJ 07206
908 351-9090

5147 Meats & Meat Prdts Wholesale

(P-14590)
AI FOODS CORPORATION
1700 N Soto St, Los Angeles (90033-1127)
PHONE 323 222-0827
Clarissa Takakawa, *CEO*
▲ EMP: 25 EST: 1983
SALES (est): 9.2MM **Privately Held**
WEB: www.aifoodscorp.com
SIC: 5147 2013 Meats, fresh; cured meats from purchased meat

(P-14591)
BICARA LTD
318 Avenue I Ste 65, Redondo Beach (90277-5601)
PHONE 310 316-6222
William Jeffrey Hughes, *CEO*
William D Hughes, *President*
Raymond Rosenthal, *Vice Pres*
◆ EMP: 300 EST: 1948
SQ FT: 105,000
SALES (est): 22.7MM **Privately Held**
SIC: 5147 5146 5141 Meats & meat products; seafoods; groceries, general line

(P-14592)
BRIDGFORD MARKETING COMPANY (DH)
1308 N Patt St, Anaheim (92801-2551)
P.O. Box 3773 (92803-3773)
PHONE 714 526-5533
John Simmons, *President*
Ray Lancey, *CFO*
William L Bridgford, *Chairman*
EMP: 89 EST: 1957
SQ FT: 100,000
SALES (corp-wide): 197.9MM **Publicly Held**
WEB: www.bridgford.com
SIC: 5147 5149 Meats & meat products; bakery products
HQ: Bridgford Foods Corporation
1308 N Patt St
Anaheim CA 92801
714 526-5533

(P-14593)
EASTLAND CORPORATION
Also Called: C & H Meat Company
3017 Bandini Blvd, Vernon (90058-4109)
PHONE 323 261-5388
Young Yoo, *President*
Young Won, *Vice Pres*
EMP: 23 EST: 1973
SQ FT: 10,000
SALES (est): 13.4MM **Privately Held**
WEB: www.candhmeatco.com
SIC: 5147 2013 Meats, fresh; cooked meats from purchased meat

(P-14594)
GOLDEN WEST TRADING INC
Also Called: Royal Poultry
4401 S Downey Rd, Vernon (90058-2518)
P.O. Box 58161 (90058-0161)
PHONE 323 581-3663
Erik Litmanovich, *CEO*

Levi Litmanovich, *Ch of Bd*
Tony Cimolino, *President*
Josh Solovy, *President*
Richard Lunsford, *CFO*
▲ EMP: 180 EST: 1992
SQ FT: 40,000
SALES (est): 205.1MM
SALES (corp-wide): 256.8MM **Privately Held**
WEB: www.gwfg.com
SIC: 5147 5142 Meats & meat products; meat, frozen; packaged
PA: Golden West Food Group, Inc.
4401 S Downey Rd
Vernon CA 90058
888 807-3663

(P-14595)
L & T MEAT CO
3050 E 11th St, Los Angeles (90023-3606)
PHONE 323 262-2815
Chak Por Tea, *President*
Bobby Lu, *Vice Pres*
EMP: 80 EST: 1995
SQ FT: 20,000
SALES (est): 23MM **Privately Held**
WEB: www.ltmeat.com
SIC: 5147 Meats, fresh

(P-14596)
LEYEN FOOD LLC (PA)
14328 Lomitas Ave, City of Industry (91746-3016)
PHONE 626 333-8812
Huo You Liang,
Jacob Liang, *General Mgr*
Richard Andrade, *Buyer*
◆ EMP: 59 EST: 1992
SALES (est): 41MM **Privately Held**
WEB: www.leyenfood.com
SIC: 5147 5144 Meats, fresh; poultry & poultry products

(P-14597)
MCLANE FOODSERVICE DIST INC
Also Called: Mbm Distribution
1051 Wineville Ave # 100, Ontario (91764-6901)
PHONE 909 912-3700
EMP: 62
SALES (corp-wide): 245.5B **Publicly Held**
WEB: www.mbmcorp.com
SIC: 5147 Meats & meat products
HQ: Mclane Foodservice Distribution, Inc.
2641 Meadowbrook Rd
Rocky Mount NC 27801
252 985-7200

(P-14598)
MCLANE FOODSERVICE DIST INC
6800 Artesia Blvd, Buena Park (90620-1015)
PHONE 714 562-6893
EMP: 62
SALES (corp-wide): 245.5B **Publicly Held**
WEB: www.mbmcorp.com
SIC: 5147 Meats & meat products
HQ: Mclane Foodservice Distribution, Inc.
2641 Meadowbrook Rd
Rocky Mount NC 27801
252 985-7200

(P-14599)
MCLANE FOODSERVICE DIST INC
3051 N Church St, Rancho Cucamonga (91730)
PHONE 909 484-6100
EMP: 62
SALES (corp-wide): 245.5B **Publicly Held**
WEB: www.mbmcorp.com
SIC: 5147 5113 5149 5142 Lard; cardboard & products; breakfast cereals; bakery products, frozen
HQ: Mclane Foodservice Distribution, Inc.
2641 Meadowbrook Rd
Rocky Mount NC 27801
252 985-7200

(P-14600)
NEWPORT MEAT SOUTHERN CAL INC
Also Called: Newport Meat Company
16691 Hale Ave, Irvine (92606-5025)
PHONE 949 399-4200
Timothy K Hussman, *CEO*
Denise Van Voorhis, *CFO*
Chad Hattery, *Transptn Dir*
EMP: 227 EST: 1976
SQ FT: 92,000
SALES (est): 114.1MM
SALES (corp-wide): 52.8B **Publicly Held**
WEB: www.newportmeat.com
SIC: 5147 5142 Meats, fresh; packaged frozen goods
PA: Sysco Corporation
1390 Enclave Pkwy
Houston TX 77077
281 584-1390

(P-14601)
PONTRELLI & LARRICCHIA LTD
Also Called: Pontrlli-Laricchia Sausage Mfg
6080 Malburg Way, Vernon (90058-3946)
PHONE 323 583-6690
Dominic T Pontrelli, *Partner*
Vito Pontrelli, *Partner*
EMP: 21 EST: 1925
SQ FT: 20,000
SALES (est): 13.2MM **Privately Held**
WEB: www.maestrosausage.com
SIC: 5147 2013 Meats & meat products; sausages & other prepared meats

(P-14602)
R W ZANT CO (PA)
1470 E 4th St, Los Angeles (90033-4288)
PHONE 323 980-5457
Robert W Zant, *President*
William Zant, *Principal*
Mary Zant, *Admin Sec*
Lupe Rincon, *Administration*
Richard Barnes, *CIO*
▲ EMP: 90
SQ FT: 42,000
SALES (est): 301MM **Privately Held**
WEB: www.rwzant.com
SIC: 5147 5146 5144 4222 Meats, fresh; fish & seafoods; poultry & poultry products; cheese warehouse

(P-14603)
RANCHO FOODS INC
2528 E 37th St, Vernon (90058-1725)
P.O. Box 58504, Los Angeles (90058-0504)
PHONE 323 585-0503
Annette Mac Donald, *President*
John Mac Donald, *Vice Pres*
Frank Celano, *Executive*
Martin Vigil, *Credit Mgr*
Scott Dean, *Sales Executive*
EMP: 100 EST: 1972
SQ FT: 26,000
SALES (est): 29.1MM **Privately Held**
WEB: www.ranchofoods.com
SIC: 5147 2013 Meats, fresh; sausages & other prepared meats

(P-14604)
RANDALL HV FOODS LLC
2905 E 50th St, Vernon (90058-2919)
P.O. Box 2669, Huntington Park (90255-8069)
PHONE 323 261-6565
M Scott Dineen, *CEO*
Alan Cutler, *CFO*
EMP: 140 EST: 2020
SALES (est): 9.1MM **Privately Held**
SIC: 5147 Meats & meat products

(P-14605)
RITE-WAY MEAT PACKERS INC
5151 Alcoa Ave, Vernon (90058-3715)
PHONE 323 826-2144
Irwin Miller, *President*
Carol Miller, *Corp Secy*
▲ EMP: 69 EST: 1961
SQ FT: 64,000
SALES (est): 28.8MM **Privately Held**
WEB: www.roseandshore.com
SIC: 5147 Meats, fresh

(P-14606)
RONGCHENG TRADING LLC
Also Called: Always Best
19319 Arenth Ave, City of Industry (91748-1401)
PHONE 626 338-1090
MEI Lan Liang, *Mng Member*
Angie Lee, *CFO*
Sha Zhang, *CFO*
Xiao Mou Zhang, *Mng Member*
Yi Tuan Zhang, *Mng Member*
▲ EMP: 50 EST: 2006
SQ FT: 80,000
SALES (est): 86.4MM
SALES (corp-wide): 566.8MM **Publicly Held**
WEB: www.hffoodsgroup.com
SIC: 5147 Meats, fresh
PA: Hf Foods Group Inc.
19319 Arenth Ave
City Of Industry CA 91748
626 338-1090

(P-14607)
STROUK GROUP LLC
Also Called: MONSIEUR MARCEL
6333 W 3rd St Ste 150, Los Angeles (90036-3191)
PHONE 323 939-7792
Stephane Strouk, *President*
Katrin Strouk, *Corp Secy*
Manuel De Freitas, *Admin Asst*
EMP: 85 EST: 1998
SALES (est): 13.9MM **Privately Held**
WEB: www.mrmarcel.com
SIC: 5147 5143 5812 Meats & meat products; cheese; French restaurant

(P-14608)
THREE SONS INC
Also Called: American Companies
5201 Industry Ave, Pico Rivera (90660-2505)
P.O. Box 6 (90660-0006)
PHONE 562 801-4100
Michael Shannon Day, *CEO*
David Day, *Shareholder*
Mariellen Day, *Shareholder*
Michael Day, *Shareholder*
John Brenan, *Vice Pres*
▲ EMP: 87 EST: 1975
SQ FT: 40,000
SALES (est): 31.9MM **Privately Held**
WEB: www.americanmeatcompanies.com
SIC: 5147 2013 2011 Meats, cured or smoked; sausages & other prepared meats; meat packing plants

(P-14609)
WAYNE PROVISION CO INC (PA)
Also Called: Premier Meat Company
5030 Gifford Ave, Vernon (90058-2726)
P.O. Box 58183, Los Angeles (90058-0183)
PHONE 323 277-5888
Naftali Greenberg, *CEO*
Terry Hanks, *Shareholder*
Eldad Hadar, *Vice Pres*
Andy Rocker, *Sales Mgr*
Adriana Espinoza, *Cust Mgr*
▼ EMP: 88 EST: 1975
SQ FT: 7,822
SALES (est): 42.4MM **Privately Held**
WEB: www.premiermeatcompany.com
SIC: 5147 5144 Meats, fresh; poultry & poultry products

5148 Fresh Fruits & Vegetables Wholesale

(P-14610)
4 EARTH FARMS LLC (PA)
Also Called: McL Fresh
5555 E Olympic Blvd, Commerce (90022-5129)
PHONE 323 201-5800
David Lake, *CEO*
Robert Lake, *COO*
Anthony Innocenti, *Vice Pres*
Mark Munger, *Vice Pres*
Kevin Whiteman, *Executive*
◆ EMP: 329 EST: 1993
SQ FT: 165,000

PRODUCTS & SVCS

SALES: 230.3MM **Privately Held**
WEB: www.4earthfarms.com
SIC: **5148** Fresh fruits & vegetables

(P-14611)
ADVANTAGE PRODUCE INC
1511 Bay St, Los Angeles (90021-1634)
P.O. Box 86388 (90086-0388)
PHONE..........................213 627-2777
Steven A Beck, *President*
Don Beck, *Vice Pres*
EMP: 50 **EST:** 1996
SQ FT: 27,000
SALES (est): 16.3MM **Privately Held**
SIC: **5148** Fruits, fresh; vegetables

(P-14612)
AGRI-EMPIRE
630 W 7th St, San Jacinto (92583-4015)
P.O. Box 490 (92581-0490)
PHONE..........................951 654-7311
Larry J Minor, *President*
EMP: 120 **EST:** 1943
SQ FT: 5,000
SALES (est): 47.7MM **Privately Held**
WEB: www.agri-empire.com
SIC: **5148** Potatoes, fresh

(P-14613)
ALL ABOUT PRODUCE INC
712 Fiero Ln Ste 30, San Luis Obispo (93401-8705)
PHONE..........................805 543-9000
Guy Demangeon, *President*
EMP: 108 **EST:** 1993
SALES (est): 4.3MM **Privately Held**
WEB: www.theberryman.com
SIC: **5148** Fruits, fresh
PA: The Berry Man Inc
205 W Montecito St
Santa Barbara CA 93101

(P-14614)
AMS - EXOTIC LLC
720 S Alameda St, Los Angeles (90021-1616)
PHONE..........................213 612-5888
Sinera Chau-Pech, *Mng Member*
Donna Hazelton, *Regional Mgr*
Scott Lehmann, *Marketing Staff*
Thierry Delappe,
Martin Seymour,
◆ **EMP:** 55
SQ FT: 14,000
SALES (est): 20MM **Privately Held**
WEB: www.ams-exotic.com
SIC: **5148** Fruits, fresh

(P-14615)
BOSKOVICH FRESH CUT LLC
711 Diaz Ave, Oxnard (93030-7247)
P.O. Box 1272 (93032-1272)
PHONE..........................805 487-2299
George Boskovich, *CEO*
Lina Perez, *Controller*
EMP: 250 **EST:** 2018
SALES (est): 34.2MM **Privately Held**
WEB: www.boskovichfarms.com
SIC: **5148** Vegetables, fresh; fruits, fresh

(P-14616)
BUY FRESH PRODUCE INC
6636 E 26th St, Commerce (90040-3216)
PHONE..........................323 796-0127
Ted Kasnetsis, *President*
Traci Kasnetsis, *CFO*
Ashley Kasnetsis, *Sales Associate*
EMP: 80 **EST:** 2005
SQ FT: 23,500
SALES (est): 22.6MM **Privately Held**
WEB: www.buyfreshproduceinc.com
SIC: **5148** Fruits, fresh

(P-14617)
CIRCLE PRODUCE CO INC
2420 M L King St Ste A, Calexico (92231-3214)
P.O. Box 2240 (92232-2240)
PHONE..........................760 357-5454
Terry Poiriez, *President*
Susan Solis, *Treasurer*
Julio Muro, *QC Mgr*
▲ **EMP:** 50 **EST:** 1985
SQ FT: 25,000

SALES: (est): 6.6MM
SALES (corp-wide): 10.1MM **Privately Held**
WEB: www.circleproduce.com
SIC: **5148** 0161 Vegetables; lettuce farm
PA: Poiriez Properties, Inc.
2420 M L King St Ste A
Calexico CA 92231
760 357-5454

(P-14618)
COAST PRODUCE COMPANY (PA)
1791 Bay St, Los Angeles (90021-1655)
P.O. Box 86468 (90086-0468)
PHONE..........................213 955-4900
Mike Ito, *CEO*
Rick Uyeno, *CFO*
Vincent Calvillo, *Vice Pres*
Steve Janedis, *Vice Pres*
John K Dunn, *Principal*
▲ **EMP:** 165 **EST:** 1955
SQ FT: 80,000
SALES (est): 44.9MM **Privately Held**
WEB: www.coastproduce.com
SIC: **5148** Fruits, fresh

(P-14619)
D & D WHOLESALE DISTRS INC
777 Baldwin Park Blvd, City of Industry (91746-1504)
PHONE..........................626 333-2111
Joe Dupree, *President*
Pamela Dupree, *Corp Secy*
Pam Dupre, *Comptroller*
Omar Oceguera, *Supervisor*
EMP: 90 **EST:** 1979
SQ FT: 20,000
SALES (est): 31MM **Privately Held**
WEB: www.ddwholesale.com
SIC: **5148** 5143 Fruits, fresh; dairy products, except dried or canned

(P-14620)
DAVALAN SALES INC
Also Called: Davalan Fresh
1601 E Olympic Blvd # 325, Los Angeles (90021-1957)
PHONE..........................213 623-2500
Alan Frick, *President*
Dave Bouton, *CEO*
Jimmy Kha, *Sales Mgr*
Bob Morse, *Sales Staff*
Miguel Sanchez, *Sales Staff*
▲ **EMP:** 200 **EST:** 1983
SQ FT: 15,000
SALES (est): 24.5MM **Privately Held**
WEB: www.davalanfresh.com
SIC: **5148** Fruits, fresh; vegetables

(P-14621)
DEARDORFF-JACKSON CO
Also Called: Deardorff Family Farm
400 Lombard St, Oxnard (93030-5100)
P.O. Box 1188 (93032-1188)
PHONE..........................805 487-7801
Tom Deardorff Jr, *President*
Scott Deardorff, *Admin Sec*
Juana Gonzalez, *Personnel*
Steve Steve Donovan, *Prdtn Mgr*
Geremy Olsen, *Director*
EMP: 50 **EST:** 1954
SQ FT: 115,000
SALES (est): 18MM **Privately Held**
WEB: www.deardofffamilyfarms.com
SIC: **5148** Fresh fruits & vegetables

(P-14622)
DOLE CITRUS
1 Dole Dr, Westlake Village (91362-7300)
P.O. Box 5132 (91359-5132)
PHONE..........................818 879-6600
C Michael Carter, *President*
EMP: 129 **EST:** 1979
SALES (est): 144.7MM **Privately Held**
WEB: www.dole.com
SIC: **5148** Fruits, fresh
HQ: Dole Food Company, Inc.
1 Dole Dr
Westlake Village CA 91362
818 874-4000

(P-14623)
ECO FARMS AVOCADOS INC (PA)
28790 Las Haciendas St, Temecula (92590-2614)
PHONE..........................951 694-3013
Steve Taft, *CEO*
Norman Traner, *Corp Secy*
Gahl Crane, *Sales Staff*
▲ **EMP:** 55 **EST:** 1976
SQ FT: 20,000
SALES (est): 22.6MM **Privately Held**
WEB: www.ecofarmsusa.com
SIC: **5148** Fresh fruits & vegetables

(P-14624)
ECO FARMS SALES INC (PA)
28790 Las Haciendas St, Temecula (92590-2614)
PHONE..........................951 694-3013
Steve Taft, *President*
Norman Traner, *Corp Secy*
Steve Quinn, *Controller*
Marisa Buckles, *Human Res Mgr*
Jeff Davis, *Manager*
▲ **EMP:** 50 **EST:** 1989
SQ FT: 20,000
SALES (est): 11.6MM **Privately Held**
WEB: www.ecofarmsusa.com
SIC: **5148** Fresh fruits & vegetables

(P-14625)
ECO FARMS TRDG OPERATIONS LLC
28790 Las Haciendas St, Temecula (92590-2614)
PHONE..........................951 676-4047
Steve Taft, *CEO*
◆ **EMP:** 51 **EST:** 2014
SALES (est): 41.5MM **Privately Held**
WEB: www.ecofarmsusa.com
SIC: **5148** Fresh fruits & vegetables
PA: Total Produce Limited
29 North Anne Street
Dublin D07 P

(P-14626)
EVOLUTION FRESH INC
Also Called: Evolution Juice
11655 Jersey Blvd Ste A, Rancho Cucamonga (91730-4903)
PHONE..........................800 794-9986
Chris Bruzzo, *CEO*
James Rosenberg, *Ch of Bd*
Ricki Reves, *CFO*
Kelli Lesiuk, *Accountant*
▲ **EMP:** 180 **EST:** 2010
SQ FT: 70,000
SALES (est): 72.2MM
SALES (corp-wide): 23.5B **Publicly Held**
WEB: www.evolutionfresh.com
SIC: **5148** 2037 Fruits, fresh; vegetables, fresh; frozen fruits & vegetables
PA: Starbucks Corporation
2401 Utah Ave S
Seattle WA 98134
206 447-1575

(P-14627)
FAMILY TREE PRODUCE INC
5510 E La Palma Ave, Anaheim (92807-2108)
PHONE..........................714 693-5688
Fidel Guzman, *President*
Christy Guzman, *Corp Secy*
Michael Selberis, *Sales Executive*
EMP: 115
SQ FT: 33,000
SALES (est): 37.4MM **Privately Held**
WEB: www.familytreeproduce.com
SIC: **5148** Fruits, fresh; potatoes, fresh; vegetables, fresh

(P-14628)
FAMOUS VINEYARDS LLC
20715 Ave 8, Richgrove (93261)
PHONE..........................661 392-5000
Joe Butkiewicz, *Mng Member*
EMP: 100 **EST:** 2019
SALES (est): 18MM **Privately Held**
SIC: **5148** Fruits, fresh

(P-14629)
FOREMOST FRESH DIRECT LLC (PA)
4747 S Mooney Blvd, Visalia (93277-9450)
PHONE..........................559 735-3100
Allan Dodge,
Jessica Lopez, *Accountant*
Jacquie Ediger,
EMP: 50 **EST:** 2014
SALES (est): 5.9MM **Privately Held**
WEB: www.foremostfreshdirect.com
SIC: **5148** Fresh fruits & vegetables

(P-14630)
FRESHPOINT SOUTHERN CAL INC
Also Called: Freshpoint Southern California
155 N Orange Ave, City of Industry (91744-3432)
PHONE..........................626 855-1400
Verne L Lusby, *CEO*
Jeff Ronk, *Exec VP*
Jon Greco, *Vice Pres*
Joel Barker, *Director*
Rich Dachman, *Director*
EMP: 208 **EST:** 1921
SQ FT: 97,000
SALES: 67.5MM
SALES (corp-wide): 52.8B **Publicly Held**
WEB: www.freshpoint.com
SIC: **5148** 5142 Fruits, fresh; vegetables, fresh; packaged frozen goods
PA: Sysco Corporation
1390 Enclave Pkwy
Houston TX 77077
281 584-1390

(P-14631)
FRIEDAS INC
Also Called: Friedas Specialty Produce
4465 Corporate Center Dr, Los Alamitos (90720-2561)
PHONE..........................714 826-6100
Karen Caplan, *President*
Jackie Caplan, *COO*
Jackie Caplan-Wiggins, *COO*
Karen Rosolowski, *CFO*
Patricia Gil, *Executive Asst*
▲ **EMP:** 75 **EST:** 1962
SQ FT: 81,306
SALES (est): 34.6MM **Privately Held**
WEB: www.friedas.com
SIC: **5148** 5499 7389 Vegetables, fresh; fruits, fresh; dried fruit; labeling bottles, cans, cartons, etc.

(P-14632)
GILLS ONIONS LLC
1051 Pacific Ave, Oxnard (93030-7254)
PHONE..........................805 240-1983
Steve Gill, *Mng Member*
Cesar Flores, *MIS Mgr*
Jaime Cota, *Purchasing*
Arturo Coronado, *Plant Mgr*
Ronald Perry, *Opers Staff*
▲ **EMP:** 55 **EST:** 1983
SALES (est): 42.1MM **Privately Held**
WEB: www.gillsonions.com
SIC: **5148** Fresh fruits & vegetables

(P-14633)
GIUMARRA BROS FRUIT CO INC (PA)
Also Called: Giumarra International Berry
1601 E Olympic Blvd # 40B, Los Angeles (90021-1943)
P.O. Box 861449 (90086-1449)
PHONE..........................213 627-2900
Donald Corsaro, *CEO*
John Corsaro, *President*
John Giumarra Jr, *Treasurer*
Gil Munguia, *Division Mgr*
Kevin Kehoe, *General Mgr*
◆ **EMP:** 74 **EST:** 1950
SQ FT: 8,000
SALES (est): 59.3MM **Privately Held**
WEB: www.giumarra.com
SIC: **5148** Fresh fruits & vegetables

(P-14634)
GOURMET SPECIALTIES INC
2120 E 25th St, Vernon (90058-1126)
PHONE..........................323 587-1734
Abundio Ruiz, *CEO*
Michelle Medina, *Office Mgr*

EMP: 75 EST: 2010
SALES (est): 12.3MM **Privately Held**
SIC: 5148 Fresh fruits & vegetables

(P-14635)
GREEN FARMS CALIFORNIA LLC (PA)
Also Called: Worldwide Produce
2652 Long Beach Ave Ste 2, Los Angeles (90058-1323)
P.O. Box 54399 (90054-0399)
PHONE..................213 747-4411
Jeri Powers, *Administration*
Ghulam Abbas, *President*
Stuart Weisfeld, *CEO*
Ron Warenkiewicz, *CFO*
Leo Curiel, *Vice Pres*
▼ EMP: 104 EST: 1995
SQ FT: 150
SALES (est): 79.5MM **Privately Held**
SIC: 5148 Fresh fruits & vegetables

(P-14636)
GREEN THUMB PRODUCE INC
2648 W Ramsey St, Banning (92220-3716)
P.O. Box 1357 (92220-0010)
PHONE..................951 849-4711
Lonnie Saverino, *President*
Jeff Young, *Buyer*
EMP: 250 EST: 1996
SALES (est): 47.9MM **Privately Held**
WEB: www.greenthumbproduce.com
SIC: 5148 Fresh fruits & vegetables

(P-14637)
GRIMMWAY ENTERPRISES INC
Also Called: Cal-Organic Farms
12000 Main St, Lamont (93241-2836)
P.O. Box 81498, Bakersfield (93380-1498)
PHONE..................661 845-3758
Roodzant Steve, *General Mgr*
Joanne Ford, *Sales Staff*
Rhonda Perez, *Sales Staff*
EMP: 194
SALES (corp-wide): 1.8B **Privately Held**
WEB: www.grimmway.com
SIC: 5148 Vegetables, fresh
PA: Grimmway Enterprises, Inc.
14141 Di Giorgio Rd
Arvin CA 93203
800 301-3101

(P-14638)
HARVEST SENSATIONS LLC
3030 E Washington Blvd, Los Angeles (90023-4220)
PHONE..................305 591-8173
Jose Ruano, *Branch Mgr*
Dilia Marval, *Officer*
Walter Hoffmann, *Business Dir*
Diana Rios, *Administration*
Tony Sambrano, *Buyer*
EMP: 50 **Privately Held**
WEB: www.harvestsensations.com
SIC: 5148 Vegetables
PA: Harvest Sensations, Llc
8303 Nw 27th St Ste 11
Doral FL 33122

(P-14639)
INDEX FRESH INC (PA)
1250 Corona Pointe Ct # 40, Corona (92879-2099)
PHONE..................909 877-0999
Dana L Thomas, *President*
Giovanni Cavaletto, *COO*
Merrill Causey, *CFO*
Lorena Dominguez, *Vice Pres*
Ana Pelaez, *Vice Pres*
◆ EMP: 52 EST: 1914
SQ FT: 40,000
SALES (est): 50.9MM **Privately Held**
WEB: www.indexfresh.com
SIC: 5148 2099 Fruits, fresh; vegetables, peeled for the trade

(P-14640)
JHP PRODUCE INC
1601 E Olympic Blvd Ste 2, Los Angeles (90021-1936)
PHONE..................213 627-1093
Chuck Johnson, *President*
Breccia Hellman, *Shareholder*
James Johnson, *Treasurer*
Daniel Rodriguez, *Vice Pres*

Dena Murphy, *Admin Sec*
EMP: 55 EST: 1941
SQ FT: 21,000
SALES (est): 11MM **Privately Held**
WEB:
SIC: 5148 Vegetables; potatoes, fresh; vegetables, fresh; fruits, fresh

(P-14641)
LA SPECIALTY PRODUCE CO (PA)
Also Called: Vesta Foodservice
13527 Orden Dr, Santa Fe Springs (90670-6338)
P.O. Box 2293 (90670-0293)
PHONE..................562 741-2200
Michael Glick, *President*
Richard Fisher, *Vice Pres*
Kathleen Glick, *Vice Pres*
Joycee Del Toro, *Executive*
Jennifer Romero, *Administration*
EMP: 375 EST: 1985
SQ FT: 188,000
SALES (est): 3.6MM **Privately Held**
WEB: www.vestafoodservice.com
SIC: 5148 Fruits, fresh

(P-14642)
LEGACY FARMS LLC
1765 W Penhall Way, Anaheim (92801-6728)
PHONE..................714 736-1800
Nick Cancellieri,
Richard Tansley, *CFO*
Rick Baxter, *Principal*
Vince Mendoza, *Principal*
Michael Sanders, *Principal*
▲ EMP: 120 EST: 1991
SQ FT: 95,000
SALES (est): 52.2MM **Privately Held**
WEB: www.legacyproduce.com
SIC: 5148 Fruits, fresh

(P-14643)
LOS ANGELES PRODUCE DISTRS LLC (HQ)
1601 E Olympic Blvd, Los Angeles (90021-1936)
P.O. Box 86307 (90086-0307)
PHONE..................562 448-5555
Matthew Clark, *President*
Paul Ross, *Sales Staff*
Jesse Garcia,
EMP: 50 EST: 2016
SQ FT: 20,000
SALES (est): 49.6MM
SALES (corp-wide): 20MM **Privately Held**
WEB: www.laproducedistributors.com
SIC: 5148 Fruits, fresh
PA: Sierra Nevada Produce Llc
1601 E Olympic Blvd
Los Angeles CA 90021
949 903-8459

(P-14644)
NATURES PRODUCE
3305 Bandini Blvd, Vernon (90058-4130)
P.O. Box 58366 (90058-0366)
PHONE..................323 235-4343
Rick Polisky, *CEO*
Luis Orendain, *Opers Spvr*
Michael Feuerstein, *Sales Dir*
▲ EMP: 110 EST: 2000
SALES (est): 26.6MM **Privately Held**
WEB: www.naturesproduce.com
SIC: 5148 Fruits, fresh; vegetables, fresh

(P-14645)
PACIFIC COAST PRODUCE INC
950 Mountain View Ave # 1, Oxnard (93030-6201)
PHONE..................805 240-3385
Carlos Marez, *CEO*
Uvence Cortez, *Treasurer*
Maribelle Cortez, *Vice Pres*
Cesar Garcia, *Manager*
EMP: 50 EST: 1999
SQ FT: 16,000
SALES (est): 18.1MM **Privately Held**
WEB: www.pacificcoastproduce.com
SIC: 5148 5149 5812 5142 Fruits, fresh; canned goods: fruit, vegetables, seafood, meats, etc.; contract food services; frozen fish, meat & poultry; frozen dairy desserts

(P-14646)
PACIFIC TRELLIS FRUIT LLC (PA)
Also Called: Dulcinea Farms
2301 E 7th St Ste C200, Los Angeles (90023-1041)
PHONE..................323 859-9600
Linda Chen,
Jason Okabayashi, *CFO*
Camille Lombardo, *Opers Staff*
Patty Denson, *Sales Staff*
Angie Eastham, *Sales Staff*
▲ EMP: 130
SQ FT: 10,000
SALES (est): 187.8MM **Privately Held**
WEB: www.pacifictrellisfruit.com
SIC: 5148 Fruits, fresh

(P-14647)
PRIMETIME INTERNATIONAL INC
86705 Avenue 54 Ste A, Coachella (92236-3814)
PHONE..................760 399-4166
Carl Sam Maggio, *CEO*
Mark Nickerson, *Mng Member*
Jeff Taylor, *Mng Member*
Mike Way, *Mng Member*
▲ EMP: 95 EST: 1994
SQ FT: 4,000
SALES (est): 200MM **Privately Held**
WEB: www.primetimeproduce.com
SIC: 5148 4783 Vegetables, fresh; packing goods for shipping
PA: Sun And Sands Enterprises, Llc
86705 Avenue 54 Ste A
Coachella CA 92236

(P-14648)
PRODUCE AVAILABLE INC (PA)
Also Called: Valley Spuds of Oxnard
910 Commercial Ave, Oxnard (93030-7232)
PHONE..................805 483-5292
Evelyn Gardiner, *President*
Helmut Brinkmann, *President*
Marlene C Kaiser, *Vice Pres*
Travis Dergan, *Comp Spec*
Eva Rico, *Director*
EMP: 59 EST: 1984
SQ FT: 20,000
SALES (est): 23.6MM **Privately Held**
WEB: www.produceavailable.com
SIC: 5148 Fresh fruits & vegetables

(P-14649)
PROFESSIONAL PRODUCE
2570 E 25th St, Los Angeles (90058-1211)
P.O. Box 58308 (90058-0308)
PHONE..................323 277-1550
Ted Kaplan, *CEO*
Maribel Reyes, *CFO*
Michael Gaskins, *Vice Pres*
Richard Jimenez, *Sales Staff*
Debbie Ponce, *Sales Staff*
◆ EMP: 99 EST: 1994
SQ FT: 5,000
SALES (est): 40.3MM **Privately Held**
WEB: www.profproduce.com
SIC: 5148 Fruits, fresh

(P-14650)
PROGRESSIVE PRODUCE LLC (HQ)
Also Called: Progressive Marketing Group
5790 Peachtree St, Commerce (90040-4000)
PHONE..................323 890-8100
James K Leimkuhler, *President*
Jeannie Berger, *President*
Howard Nager, *Vice Pres*
Donna Sabatasso, *Vice Pres*
Janet Echols, *Administration*
▲ EMP: 84 EST: 1967
SQ FT: 106,000
SALES (est): 76.9MM **Privately Held**
WEB: www.progressiveproduce.com
SIC: 5148 4213 7389 Fruits, fresh; refrigerated products transport; packaging & labeling services

(P-14651)
SAMBAZON INC (PA)
209 Avnida Fbrcnte Ste 20, San Clemente (92672)
PHONE..................877 726-2296
Ryan Black, *CEO*
Ricardo Perdigao, *COO*
Bruce Peasland, *CFO*
Jeremy Black, *Vice Pres*
Shereen Elsammaa, *Vice Pres*
◆ EMP: 60 EST: 2000
SQ FT: 10,000
SALES (est): 57.5MM **Privately Held**
WEB: www.sambazon.com
SIC: 5148 5499 Fruits; juices, fruit or vegetable

(P-14652)
SEASON PRODUCE CO INC
1601 E Olympic Blvd # 315, Los Angeles (90021-1942)
PHONE..................213 689-0008
Patrick R Horwath, *President*
Daniel Horwath, *President*
Timothy R Horwath, *Vice Pres*
EMP: 353 EST: 1958
SQ FT: 20,000
SALES (est): 57.3MM **Privately Held**
SIC: 5148 Fresh fruits & vegetables
PA: S & H Packing & Sales Co., Inc.
2590 Harriet St
Vernon CA 90058
323 581-7172

(P-14653)
SGF PRODUCE HOLDING CORP
701 W Kimberly Ave # 210, Placentia (92870-6342)
PHONE..................714 630-6292
Ed Haft, *CEO*
Joe McCarthy, *CFO*
EMP: 14 EST: 2008
SALES (est): 846.4K **Privately Held**
SIC: 5148 2037 1711 Fruits; vegetables; frozen fruits & vegetables; general farms, primarily crop

(P-14654)
SHAPIRO-GILMAN-SHANDLER CO (HQ)
Also Called: S G S Produce
739 Decatur St, Los Angeles (90021-1649)
PHONE..................213 593-1200
Minyi Xu, *CEO*
Carol C Shandler, *President*
Muriel Shandler, *Vice Pres*
Morris Shander, *Principal*
David Roman, *Sales Associate*
▲ EMP: 100 EST: 1907
SQ FT: 50,000
SALES (est): 26.3MM
SALES (corp-wide): 116.6MM **Privately Held**
WEB: www.sgsproduce.com
SIC: 5148 Fruits, fresh; vegetables
PA: Grubmarket, Inc.
1925 Jerrold Ave
San Francisco CA 94124
510 556-4786

(P-14655)
SUN AND SANDS ENTERPRISES LLC (PA)
Also Called: Prime Time International
86705 Avenue 54 Ste A, Coachella (92236-3814)
PHONE..................760 399-4278
Carl Sam Maggio, *Mng Member*
James Wisener, *CFO*
Rena Agoot, *Administration*
Carl Maggio, *Data Proc Staff*
Andrea Thomas, *Controller*
▲ EMP: 64 EST: 1986
SQ FT: 7,500
SALES (est): 204.1MM **Privately Held**
WEB: www.primetimeproduce.com
SIC: 5148 Fresh fruits & vegetables

(P-14656)
SUN PACIFIC MARKETING COOP INC
20715 Ave 8, Richgrove (93261)
PHONE..................559 784-6845
EMP: 395

SALES (corp-wide): 336MM **Privately Held**
WEB: www.sunpacific.com
SIC: 5148 Fresh fruits & vegetables
PA: Sun Pacific Marketing Cooperative, Inc.
　　1095 E Green St
　　Pasadena CA 91106
　　213 612-9957

(P-14657)
SUN PACIFIC MARKETING COOP INC
Also Called: Sun Pacific Farming
31452 Old River Rd, Bakersfield
(93311-9621)
PHONE............................661 847-1015
Bob Dipiazza, *Branch Mgr*
EMP: 395
SALES (corp-wide): 336MM **Privately Held**
WEB: www.sunpacific.com
SIC: 5148 Fresh fruits & vegetables
PA: Sun Pacific Marketing Cooperative, Inc.
　　1095 E Green St
　　Pasadena CA 91106
　　213 612-9957

(P-14658)
SUNKIST GROWERS INC (PA)
27770 Entertainment Dr, Valencia
(91355-1092)
PHONE............................661 290-8900
Russell Hanlin II, *President*
Christian Harris, *COO*
Richard G French, *CFO*
Terra Jacobs, *CFO*
Kevin Fiori, *Exec VP*
◆ **EMP:** 223 **EST:** 1893
SQ FT: 50,000
SALES: 1.1B **Privately Held**
WEB: www.sunkist.com
SIC: 5148 2033 2037 2899 Fruits, fresh;
　　fruit juices: packaged in cans, jars, etc.;
　　fruit juice concentrates, frozen; lemon oil
　　(edible); orange oil; grapefruit oil; copy-
　　right buying & licensing; display equip-
　　ment, except refrigerated

(P-14659)
UMINA BROTHERS INC (PA)
1601 E Olympic Blvd # 403, Los Angeles
(90021-1943)
P.O. Box 861146 (90086-1146)
PHONE............................213 622-9206
Richard Flamminio, *President*
Mark Golden, *Vice Pres*
Matt Beltran, *General Mgr*
Nelson Tran, *General Mgr*
Eden A Hernandez, *Administration*
◆ **EMP:** 82 **EST:** 1933
SQ FT: 24,800
SALES (est): 39.8MM **Privately Held**
WEB: www.umina.com
SIC: 5148 Fruits, fresh

(P-14660)
V & L PRODUCE INC
Also Called: General Produce
2550 E 25th St, Vernon (90058-1211)
PHONE............................323 589-3125
Victor Mendoza, *President*
Denice Mendoza, *Office Mgr*
▲ **EMP:** 140 **EST:** 1984
SQ FT: 12,000
SALES (est): 25.1MM **Privately Held**
SIC: 5148 Fresh fruits & vegetables

(P-14661)
VAL-PRO INC
Also Called: Continental Sales Co.
1661 Mcgarry St, Los Angeles
(90021-3116)
PHONE............................213 689-0844
Joe Vidal, *Branch Mgr*
David Kunisaki, *Division Mgr*
EMP: 60
SALES (corp-wide): 35.4MM **Privately Held**
WEB: www.valleyproduce.com
SIC: 5148 Fruits, fresh
PA: Val-Pro, Inc.
　　1601 E Olympic Blvd # 300
　　Los Angeles CA 90021
　　213 627-8736

(P-14662)
VEG-FRESH FARMS LLC
1400 W Rincon St, Corona (92878-9205)
PHONE............................800 422-5535
Lawrence Cancellieri Jr,
Dino Cancellieri Sr, *General Ptnr*
Bob Wright, *Officer*
Juan Palacio, *Technology*
Tiffany Topor, *Controller*
EMP: 220 **EST:** 1989
SQ FT: 94,000
SALES (est): 51.2MM **Privately Held**
WEB: www.vegfresh.com
SIC: 5148 Vegetables, fresh; fruits

(P-14663)
VENTURA COUNTY LEMON COOPS
Also Called: Ventura Pacific Co
245 E Colonia Rd, Oxnard (93030-3618)
P.O. Box 6986 (93031-6986)
PHONE............................805 385-3345
Donald Dames, *President*
Milton Daily, *Ch of Bd*
Jim Waters, *Treasurer*
James H Gill, *Admin Sec*
EMP: 80 **EST:** 1943
SQ FT: 87,000
SALES (est): 12.2MM **Privately Held**
WEB: www.venturapacific.com
SIC: 5148 Fruits, fresh

(P-14664)
VISION PRODUCE ACQUISITION LLC ✪
1651 Bay St, Los Angeles (90021-1635)
PHONE............................213 622-4435
Bill Vogel,
EMP: 50 **EST:** 2021
SALES (est): 1.6MM **Privately Held**
SIC: 5148 Fresh fruits & vegetables

(P-14665)
WAWONA PACKING CO LLC (PA)
12133 Avenue 408, Cutler (93615-2056)
PHONE............................559 528-4000
Brent Smittcamp, *Mng Member*
Georgia Griffin, *Office Mgr*
Tara Sondergaard, *Controller*
Chris Deleon, *QC Mgr*
Mark Burlinger, *Sales Mgr*
▼ **EMP:** 990 **EST:** 1999
SQ FT: 16,000
SALES (est): 455.3MM **Privately Held**
WEB: www.prima.com
SIC: 5148 Fresh fruits & vegetables

(P-14666)
WEST CENTRAL PRODUCE INC
Also Called: West Central Food Service
12840 Leyva St, Norwalk (90650-6852)
PHONE............................213 629-3600
Michael Dodo, *CEO*
Lance Shiring, *COO*
Jamie Purcell, *CFO*
Blanca Gonzalez, *Payroll Mgr*
Alex Dobosi, *Sales Staff*
▲ **EMP:** 400 **EST:** 1970
SQ FT: 34,000
SALES: 155.9MM **Privately Held**
WEB: www.westcentralfoodservice.com
SIC: 5148 5147 5149 5146 Fruits, fresh;
　　meats & meat products; dairy products;
　　dried or canned; seafoods

(P-14667)
WIEMAR DISTRIBUTORS INC
Also Called: M & M Distributors
1953 S Alameda St, Los Angeles
(90058-1013)
PHONE............................213 747-7036
Marco Moreno, *President*
Rosa Moreno, *Vice Pres*
Margarita Orduno, *Controller*
▲ **EMP:** 65 **EST:** 1992
SQ FT: 31,000
SALES (est): 1.2MM **Privately Held**
WEB: www.mm-farms.com
SIC: 5148 Fruits, fresh

(P-14668)
WORLD VARIETY PRODUCE INC
Also Called: Melissas World Variety Produce
5325 S Soto St, Vernon (90058-3624)
P.O. Box 514599, Los Angeles (90051-2599)
PHONE............................800 588-0151
Anna Raya, *Principal*
Joe V Hernandez, *President*
Lee Zellner, *CFO*
Sharon Hernandez, *Corp Secy*
Janene Allen, *Executive*
◆ **EMP:** 325 **EST:** 1983
SQ FT: 244,000
SALES (est): 109.6MM **Privately Held**
WEB: www.melissas.com
SIC: 5148 Fruits, fresh

5149 Groceries & Related Prdts, NEC Wholesale

(P-14669)
APP WHOLESALE LLC
3686 E Olympic Blvd, Los Angeles
(90023-3146)
PHONE............................323 980-8315
David Weissberg,
EMP: 500 **EST:** 2013
SQ FT: 220,000
SALES (est): 91.4MM **Privately Held**
WEB: www.app-wholesale.com
SIC: 5149 2741 Specialty food items;
　　business service newsletters: publishing
　　& printing

(P-14670)
ASPIRE BAKERIES LLC
Also Called: Fresh Start Bakeries
1220 S Baker Ave, Ontario (91761-7739)
P.O. Box 1283, Alhambra (91802-1283)
PHONE............................909 472-3500
Rob Crawford, *General Mgr*
Bob Mitchell, *Manager*
EMP: 197
SALES (corp-wide): 1.7B **Privately Held**
WEB: www.aryzta.com
SIC: 5149 Bakery products
HQ: Aspire Bakeries Llc
　　350 N Orleans St 3001n
　　Chicago IL 60654
　　855 427-9982

(P-14671)
ASPIRE BAKERIES LLC
2350 Pullman St, Santa Ana (92705-5507)
PHONE............................949 261-7400
Zac Morris, *Branch Mgr*
Nancy Kirksey, *Vice Pres*
EMP: 51
SALES (corp-wide): 1.7B **Privately Held**
WEB: www.aryzta.com
SIC: 5149 Bakery products
HQ: Aspire Bakeries Llc
　　350 N Orleans St 3001n
　　Chicago IL 60654
　　855 427-9982

(P-14672)
AZ GEMS INC (PA)
405 Missouri Ct, Redlands (92373-8083)
PHONE............................909 206-3384
Jhansi L Kunam, *President*
Syam P Kunam, *Vice Pres*
Chowdary Kunam, *Exec Dir*
◆ **EMP:** 13 **EST:** 1998
SQ FT: 6,000
SALES (est): 430.9MM **Privately Held**
WEB: www.azgems.com
SIC: 5149 2091 2092 Coffee, green or
　　roasted; caviar, preserved; seafood prod-
　　ucts: packaged in cans, jars, etc.; shrimp,
　　frozen: prepared

(P-14673)
BAKERY EX SOUTHERN CAL LLC
1910 W Malvern Ave, Fullerton
(92833-2105)
PHONE............................714 446-9470
Charles Burman,
Ronald Currie, *General Mgr*
EMP: 100 **EST:** 2001
SQ FT: 28,000

SALES (est): 40.9MM **Privately Held**
SIC: 5149 Bakery products

(P-14674)
BAKKAVOR FOODS USA INC (DH)
18201 Central Ave, Carson (90746-4007)
PHONE............................704 522-1977
Ivan Clingan, *CEO*
Jolyon Punnett, *CFO*
Ron Pearson, *General Mgr*
Joe Alonso, *CIO*
Alexandra Carpenter, *Technical Staff*
▲ **EMP:** 300 **EST:** 1985
SQ FT: 100,000
SALES (est): 313.8MM
SALES (corp-wide): 2.3B **Privately Held**
WEB: www.bakkavor.com
SIC: 5149 2051 Bakery products; bread,
　　cake & related products

(P-14675)
BAR BAKERS LLC
10711 Bloomfield St, Los Alamitos
(90720-2503)
PHONE............................562 719-0300
Harold Rothman, *Mng Member*
John Gutteridge, *Vice Pres*
Duane Rose, *Vice Pres*
Alvaro Bolanos, *QA Dir*
Singh Shawn, *Engineer*
EMP: 68 **EST:** 1970
SALES (est): 35.4MM **Privately Held**
WEB: www.barbakers.com
SIC: 5149 Bakery products; cookies;
　　crackers

(P-14676)
BREEDERS CHOICE PET FOODS LLC
16321 Arrow Hwy, Irwindale (91706-2084)
PHONE............................626 334-9301
Joseph A Herrick, *President*
EMP: 50 **EST:** 2020
SALES (est): 14.8MM **Privately Held**
WEB: www.breederschoice.com
SIC: 5149 Pet foods

(P-14677)
BUENA VISTA FOOD PRODUCTS INC (DH)
823 W 8th St, Azusa (91702-2247)
PHONE............................626 815-8859
Laura Trujillo, *President*
Norma Flores, *CFO*
Philippe Francoz, *Vice Pres*
Lucy Santos, *Controller*
Linda Naranjo, *Human Res Mgr*
EMP: 115 **EST:** 1991
SALES (est): 50.5MM **Privately Held**
WEB: www.bvfoods.com
SIC: 5149 Bakery products
HQ: Sterling Foods, Llc
　　1075 Arion Pkwy
　　San Antonio TX 78213
　　210 490-1669

(P-14678)
CAKE COLLECTION LLC
2221 Barry Ave Fl 1, Los Angeles
(90064-1414)
PHONE............................310 479-7783
EMP: 30 **EST:** 1987
SALES (est): 1.2MM **Privately Held**
SIC: 5461 5149 2051 Retail Bakery Whol
　　Groceries Mfg Bread/Related Products

(P-14679)
CAPITAL BRANDS LLC (DH)
11601 Wilshire Blvd # 360, Los Angeles
(90025-1700)
P.O. Box 4564, Pacoima (91333-4564)
PHONE............................310 996-7200
Rich Krause, *CEO*
Nick Sternberg, *COO*
Jeff Klausner, *CFO*
Mark Suzumoto,
Jay N Corson, *Officer*
EMP: 50 **EST:** 2009
SALES (est): 65.1MM **Privately Held**
WEB: www.capitalbrands.com
SIC: 5149 Groceries & related products

▲ = Import ▼ =Export
◆ =Import/Export

HQ: Capital Brands Holdings Inc.
11601 Wilshire Blvd # 360
Los Angeles CA 90025
310 996-7200

(P-14680)

CIBARIA INTERNATIONAL INC
705 Columbia Ave, Riverside (92507-2141)
PHONE..................................951 823-8490
Kathy Griset, *President*
Karen Moore, *Vice Pres*
Bryan Siegel, *Director*
▲ EMP: 30
SQ FT: 55,000
SALES (est): 4MM **Privately Held**
WEB: www.cibaria-intl.com
SIC: 5149 2899 Cooking oils; essential oils

(P-14681)

CITY BEAN INC
5051 W Jefferson Blvd, Los Angeles (90016-3940)
PHONE..................................323 734-0828
Gary Salzer, *President*
EMP: 15 EST: 1991
SQ FT: 2,000
SALES (est): 1MM **Privately Held**
WEB: www.citybean.com
SIC: 5499 5149 2095 Coffee; coffee, green or roasted; coffee roasting (except by wholesale grocers)

(P-14682)

CJ AMERICA INC (HQ)
Also Called: C J Foods
5700 Wilshire Blvd # 540, Los Angeles (90036-3819)
PHONE..................................213 427-5566
Hyunsoo Shin, *CEO*
Angela Killoren, *COO*
Jae Kyung Jeon, *CFO*
Soohee Lee, *CFO*
Justin Lee, *Officer*
◆ EMP: 54 EST: 1984
SQ FT: 6,000
SALES (est): 495.8MM **Privately Held**
WEB: www.cjamerica.com
SIC: 5149 1541 3556 5169 Groceries & related products; food products manufacturing or packing plant construction; food products machinery; food additives & preservatives

(P-14683)

COMPLETE FOOD SERVICE INC
3815 Wabash Dr, Jurupa Valley (91752-1143)
PHONE..................................951 685-8490
Keith Kahn, *President*
Mitchell Kahn, *Vice Pres*
Mark Kahn, *Admin Sec*
EMP: 52 EST: 1948
SQ FT: 40,000
SALES (est): 5.6MM **Privately Held**
WEB: www.completefoodservice.com
SIC: 5149 5722 Groceries & related products; sewing machines

(P-14684)

COMPLETELY FRESH FOODS INC
4401 S Downey Rd, Vernon (90058-2518)
P.O. Box 58667, Los Angeles (90058-0667)
PHONE..................................323 722-9136
Josh Solovy, *President*
Eric Litmanovich, *Vice Pres*
Levi Litmanovich, *Vice Pres*
EMP: 200 EST: 2006
SQ FT: 15,000
SALES (est): 36.5MM
SALES (corp-wide): 256.8MM **Privately Held**
WEB: www.gwfg.com
SIC: 5149 5046 Specialty food items; commercial equipment; commercial cooking & food service equipment
PA: Golden West Food Group, Inc.
4401 S Downey Rd
Vernon CA 90058
888 807-3663

(P-14685)

CORE NUTRITION LLC
1222 E Grand Ave Ste 102, El Segundo (90245-4219)
PHONE..................................310 640-0500
EMP: 50 EST: 2014
SALES (est): 4MM **Privately Held**
SIC: 5149 2834 Whol Groceries Mfg Pharmaceutical Preparations

(P-14686)

DESERT VALLEY DATE LLC
86740 Industrial Way, Coachella (92236-2718)
PHONE..................................760 398-0999
Greg Willsey, *Mng Member*
Lesli Pence, *Principal*
EMP: 85 EST: 2020
SALES (est): 33MM **Privately Held**
WEB: www.desertvalleydate.com
SIC: 5149 5148 Organic & diet foods; fruits

(P-14687)

EL GUAPO SPICES INC (PA)
Also Called: El Guapo Spices and Herbs Pkg
6200 E Slauson Ave, Commerce (90040-3012)
PHONE..................................213 312-1300
Dan Terrazas, *President*
EMP: 100
SALES (est): 11.8MM **Privately Held**
SIC: 5149 Spices & seasonings

(P-14688)

GALASSOS BAKERY (PA)
10820 San Sevaine Way, Jurupa Valley (91752-1116)
PHONE..................................951 360-1211
Jeannette Galasso, *President*
Mark Bailey, *Treasurer*
Rick Vargas, *Vice Pres*
Elias Neri, *Technician*
Pearl Denault, *Project Mgr*
EMP: 180 EST: 1923
SQ FT: 110,000
SALES (est): 95.3MM **Privately Held**
WEB: www.galassos.com
SIC: 5149 Bakery products

(P-14689)

GANO EXCEL (USA) INC
15439 Dupont Ave, Chino (91710-7605)
P.O. Box 9275, Glendale (91226-0275)
PHONE..................................626 338-8081
Matthew Nguyen, *President*
Ruben Cardenas, *President*
Soon Seng Leow, *President*
Chin Iakooi, *CEO*
Chang Ching Lew, *Treasurer*
▲ EMP: 67 EST: 2002
SALES (est): 18MM **Privately Held**
WEB: www.goganoexcel.com
SIC: 5149 Coffee, green or roasted; coffee & tea

(P-14690)

GOGLANIAN BAKERIES INC (HQ)
3401 W Segerstrom Ave, Santa Ana (92704-6404)
PHONE..................................714 338-1145
◆ EMP: 300 EST: 1978
SQ FT: 71,500
SALES (est): 47.3MM
SALES (corp-wide): 4B **Privately Held**
WEB: www.richsusa.com
SIC: 5149 Bakery products
PA: Rich Products Corporation
1 Robert Rich Way
Buffalo NY 14213
716 878-8000

(P-14691)

GOLDA & I CHOCOLATIERS INC
23052 Alicia Pkwy Ste H, Mission Viejo (92692-1661)
PHONE..................................949 660-9581
Stephen Y S Lee,
EMP: 55
SQ FT: 3,000
SALES (est): 6.5MM **Privately Held**
WEB: www.crowncityconfections.com
SIC: 5149 Whol Groceries

(P-14692)

GOURMET INDIA FOOD COMPANY LLC
12220 Rivera Rd Ste A, Whittier (90606-6206)
PHONE..................................562 698-9763
Sam Jeevan,
Saleem Hai,
▲ EMP: 75 EST: 2000
SALES (est): 6.9MM **Privately Held**
WEB: www.gourmetindiafood.com
SIC: 5149 Bakery products

(P-14693)

HANDELS HOMEMADE ICE CREAM
6403 Haven Ave, Rancho Cucamonga (91737-3860)
PHONE..................................909 989-7065
EMP: 20 EST: 2012
SALES (est): 167.6K **Privately Held**
WEB: www.handelsicecream.com
SIC: 5812 5149 2052 Ice cream stands or dairy bars; bakery products; cones, ice cream

(P-14694)

HARRIS FREEMAN & CO INC (PA)
Also Called: Harris Tea Company
3110 E Miraloma Ave, Anaheim (92806-1906)
PHONE..................................714 765-7525
Anil J Shah, *CEO*
Kevin Shah, *President*
Meena Shah, *Treasurer*
Al Paruthi, *Vice Pres*
Jay Shah, *Vice Pres*
◆ EMP: 500 EST: 1981
SQ FT: 58,000
SALES (est): 236.6MM **Privately Held**
WEB: www.harrisfreeman.com
SIC: 5149 2099 Tea; spices, including grinding

(P-14695)

IL FORNAIO (AMERICA) LLC
16932 Valley View Ave A, La Mirada (90638-5826)
PHONE..................................714 752-7052
Luis Espinoza, *Branch Mgr*
EMP: 160
SALES (corp-wide): 7.3B **Privately Held**
WEB: www.ilfornaio.com
SIC: 5812 5813 5149 2051 Italian restaurant; drinking places; bakery products; bread, cake & related products
HQ: Il Fornaio (America) Llc
770 Tamalpais Dr Ste 208
Corte Madera CA 94925
415 945-0500

(P-14696)

JANS ENTERPRISES CORPORATION
Also Called: Wira Co
4181 Temple City Blvd A, El Monte (91731-1029)
PHONE..................................626 575-2000
Anthony Kartawinata, *President*
Nila Prawirawidjaja, *Admin Sec*
Firlhi Tissa, *Accounts Exec*
◆ EMP: 25 EST: 1998
SQ FT: 50,000
SALES (est): 6.4MM **Privately Held**
WEB: www.jansfood.com
SIC: 5149 2026 2096 Specialty food items; milk, ultra-high temperature (longlife); milk drinks, flavored; potato chips & similar snacks

(P-14697)

JESSIE LORD BAKERY LLC
21100 S Western Ave, Torrance (90501-1705)
PHONE..................................310 533-6010
Stephen Y S Lee,
Deborah Marcotte, *Controller*
John Vandriel, *Controller*
Hratch Doctorian, *Purch Mgr*
Christine Valley, *Marketing Staff*
▲ EMP: 50 EST: 2003
SQ FT: 130,000
SALES (est): 62.5MM **Privately Held**
WEB: www.jessielordpies.com
SIC: 5149 Bakery products

(P-14698)

JFC INTERNATIONAL INC (HQ)
7101 E Slauson Ave, Commerce (90040-3622)
P.O. Box 875349, Los Angeles (90087-0449)
PHONE..................................323 721-6100
Yoshiyuki Ishigaki, *CEO*
Hiroyuki Enomoto, *President*
Taka N Tsuematsu, *Vice Pres*
Ichiro Komatsubara, *Branch Mgr*
Derek Kaneko, *General Mgr*
◆ EMP: 203 EST: 1948
SALES (est): 604.9MM **Privately Held**
WEB: www.jfc.com
SIC: 5149 7389 Specialty food items; labeling bottles, cans, cartons, etc.

(P-14699)

JFC INTERNATIONAL INC
Also Called: Los Angeles Branch
7101 E Slauson Ave, Commerce (90040-3622)
PHONE..................................323 721-6900
Tamaki Saijo, *Branch Mgr*
EMP: 165 **Privately Held**
WEB: www.jfc.com
SIC: 5149 Specialty food items
HQ: Jfc International Inc.
7101 E Slauson Ave
Commerce CA 90040
323 721-6100

(P-14700)

K T LUCKY CO INC
10925 Schmidt Rd, El Monte (91733-2707)
PHONE..................................626 579-7272
Hang Huynh, *President*
▲ EMP: 70 EST: 1986
SQ FT: 12,000
SALES (est): 9.2MM **Privately Held**
SIC: 5149 Macaroni; rice, polished

(P-14701)

KAYLAS CAKE CORPORATION
1311 S Gilbert St, Fullerton (92833-4302)
PHONE..................................714 869-1522
Kayla Lee, *CEO*
EMP: 30 EST: 2014
SALES (est): 1.1MM **Privately Held**
WEB: www.thekaylascake.com
SIC: 5461 5149 2024 Cakes; bakery products; ice cream & frozen desserts

(P-14702)

KIDS HEALTHY FOODS LLC
2030 Main St Ste 1300, Irvine (92614-7220)
PHONE..................................949 260-4950
Jeff McClelland, *CEO*
Diane Lee McClelland,
Jeffrey Scott McClelland,
Lance Robert McClelland,
EMP: 25 EST: 2010
SALES (est): 10.8MM **Privately Held**
WEB: www.kidshealthyfoods.com
SIC: 5149 2099 Beverages, except coffee & tea; tea blending

(P-14703)

KRADJIAN IMPORTING COMPANY INC (PA)
5018 San Fernando Rd, Glendale (91204-1114)
PHONE..................................818 502-1313
Raffi Kradjian, *President*
Viken Kradjian, *Vice Pres*
Raffi Krakjian, *Info Tech Mgr*
Ram Sethuram, *Controller*
Sahag Arabian, *Marketing Staff*
◆ EMP: 60 EST: 1987
SQ FT: 50,000
SALES (est): 29.5MM **Privately Held**
WEB: www.kraimpco.com
SIC: 5149 Specialty food items

(P-14704)

LEE KUM KEE (USA) INC (DH)
Also Called: Lee's Kitchen
14841 Don Julian Rd, City of Industry (91746-3110)
PHONE..................................626 709-1888

Simon Wu, *CEO*
Gary Cheung, *President*
David H W Lee, *President*
Victor Fan, *COO*
Alan Lui, *CFO*
◆ **EMP:** 44 **EST:** 1983
SQ FT: 50,000
SALES (est): 177.3MM **Privately Held**
WEB: www.usa.lkk.com
SIC: 5149 2099 2035 Sauces; food preparations; pickles, sauces & salad dressings

(P-14705)
LONGSTAR HEALTHPRO INC
Also Called: J&P Nutriceutical Services
4010 Valley Blvd Ste 101, Walnut (91789-0935)
PHONE....................909 468-9215
Joy Pingwwi Pan, *CEO*
Jian MEI Wang, *President*
Ping WEI Pan, *Principal*
▲ **EMP:** 13 **EST:** 1999
SQ FT: 9,500
SALES (est): 3.5MM **Privately Held**
SIC: 5149 2833 Organic & diet foods; vitamins, natural or synthetic: bulk, uncompounded

(P-14706)
MAMOLOS CNTNTL BAILEY BAKERIES
Also Called: Viktor Benes Bakeries
2734 Townsgate Rd, Westlake Village (91361-2906)
PHONE....................805 496-0045
Manigeh Tabataba, *Manager*
EMP: 141
SALES (corp-wide): 23.6MM **Privately Held**
WEB: www.viktorbenesbakery.com
SIC: 5461 5149 Cakes; bread; bakery products
PA: Mamolo's Continental & Bailey Bakeries Inc
703 S Main St
Burbank CA 91506
818 841-9347

(P-14707)
MHH HOLDINGS INC
5653 Alton Pkwy, Irvine (92618-4058)
PHONE....................949 651-9903
Cynthia Espere, *Branch Mgr*
EMP: 130
SALES (corp-wide): 30.5MM **Privately Held**
SIC: 5149 Tea
PA: Mhh Holdings, Inc.
4580 Calle Alto
Camarillo CA 93012
805 484-7924

(P-14708)
MHH HOLDINGS INC
415 S Lake Ave Ste 108, Pasadena (91101-5047)
PHONE....................626 744-9370
Xiomara Bellido, *Principal*
EMP: 130
SALES (corp-wide): 30.5MM **Privately Held**
SIC: 5149 Tea
PA: Mhh Holdings, Inc.
4580 Calle Alto
Camarillo CA 93012
805 484-7924

(P-14709)
MOJAVE GOLD LLC
74100 Fillmore St, Thermal (92274)
P.O. Box 70, Coachella (92236-0070)
PHONE....................760 397-0408
Donald J Kizirian, *Mng Member*
EMP: 14 **EST:** 2011
SALES (est): 13.7MM **Privately Held**
WEB: www.mojavegoldllc.com
SIC: 5149 2034 Fruits, dried; raisins

(P-14710)
MONSTER ENERGY COMPANY (HQ)
1 Monster Way, Corona (92879-7101)
PHONE....................951 739-6200
Rodney C Sacks, *CEO*
Thomas J Kelly, *CFO*

Hilton H Scholsberg, *Vice Ch Bd*
Dan McHugh, *Chief Mktg Ofcr*
Mitch Covington, *Vice Pres*
◆ **EMP:** 942 **EST:** 1992
SQ FT: 300,000
SALES (est): 1.1B
SALES (corp-wide): 4.6B **Publicly Held**
WEB: www.monsterbevcorp.com
SIC: 5149 Juices; soft drinks
PA: Monster Beverage Corporation
1 Monster Way
Corona CA 92879
951 739-6200

(P-14711)
MORRIS NATIONAL INC (HQ)
Also Called: McGrever Dnlee Very Spcial Chc
760 N Mckeever Ave, Azusa (91702-2349)
PHONE....................626 385-2000
Gerry Morris Zubatoff, *CEO*
Gerald Morris, *President*
David Kiel, *CFO*
Bram Zubatoff, *Admin Sec*
◆ **EMP:** 56 **EST:** 1974
SQ FT: 125,000
SALES (est): 98.8MM
SALES (corp-wide): 179.1MM **Privately Held**
WEB: www.morrisnational.com
SIC: 5149 5145 Chocolate; confectionery
PA: Morris National Inc
2235 Rue Lapierre
Lasalle QC H8N 1
514 368-1000

(P-14712)
MUTUAL TRADING CO INC (DH)
Also Called: M T C
4200 Shirley Ave, El Monte (91731-1130)
PHONE....................213 626-9458
Kosei Yamamoto, *CEO*
Noritoshi Kanai, *President*
Seicho Fujikawa, *Vice Pres*
Atsuko Kanai, *Executive*
Kotaro Hoshizaki, *Principal*
◆ **EMP:** 105 **EST:** 1926
SALES (est): 191.5MM **Privately Held**
WEB: www.lamtc.com
SIC: 5149 5141 5023 Groceries & related products; groceries, general line; home furnishings

(P-14713)
NEUROBRANDS LLC
Also Called: Neuro Drinks
15303 Ventura Blvd # 675, Sherman Oaks (91403-6608)
P.O. Box 55245 (91413-0245)
PHONE....................310 393-6444
Diana Jenkins, *CEO*
Scott Laporta, *President*
Greg Buscher, *Principal*
Rigo De Leon, *Area Mgr*
Armando Lassale, *Area Mgr*
▲ **EMP:** 125 **EST:** 2009
SALES (est): 34.5MM **Privately Held**
WEB: www.drinkneuro.com
SIC: 5149 Soft drinks

(P-14714)
NIITAKAYA USA INC (PA)
1801 Aeros Way, Montebello (90640-6505)
PHONE....................323 720-5050
Katsutoshi Suda, *President*
Hideo Nakagawa, *President*
Ajith Ganewatte, *Asst Mgr*
▲ **EMP:** 47 **EST:** 1981
SQ FT: 17,000
SALES (est): 27.5MM **Privately Held**
WEB: www.niitakaya.com
SIC: 5149 2099 Pickles, preserves, jellies & jams; food preparations

(P-14715)
PASTA PICCININI INC
950 N Fair Oaks Ave, Pasadena (91103-3009)
PHONE....................626 798-0841
Stefano Piccinini, *Principal*
William Coulvane, *Admin Mgr*
Alex Branchi, *Technician*
Sandra Bane, *VP Finance*
Peggy Flores, *Human Resources*
▲ **EMP:** 65
SQ FT: 30,000

SALES (est): 21.5MM **Privately Held**
WEB: www.gourmetpasta.com
SIC: 5149 5812 Pasta & rice; eating places

(P-14716)
PEETS COFFEE & TEA LLC
1151 Glendale Galleria, Glendale (91210-1301)
PHONE....................818 546-1030
Kea Lewis, *Branch Mgr*
EMP: 54
SALES (corp-wide): 177.9K **Privately Held**
WEB: www.peets.com
SIC: 5812 5499 5149 Coffee shop; beverage stores; coffee & tea
HQ: Peet's Coffee & Tea, Llc
1400 Park Ave
Emeryville CA 94608
510 594-2100

(P-14717)
PIE PLACE
Also Called: Marie Callender's Pie Shops
1175 E Alosta Ave, Azusa (91702-2740)
PHONE....................626 963-9475
Bob Hall, *President*
EMP: 53 **EST:** 1988
SALES (est): 2.3MM **Privately Held**
WEB: www.mariecallenders.com
SIC: 5812 5149 Restaurant, family: chain; bakery products

(P-14718)
PIONEER TRADING INC
Also Called: Omni Foods Manufacturing
6305 Alondra Blvd, Paramount (90723-3750)
PHONE....................562 531-3842
Fax: 562 531-2625
▲ **EMP:** 30
SQ FT: 4,000
SALES (est): 3.7MM **Privately Held**
SIC: 5149 2099 Whol Groceries Mfg Food Preparations

(P-14719)
POLLYS PIES INC
Also Called: Pollys 208
9791 Adams Ave, Huntington Beach (92646-4804)
PHONE....................714 964-4424
Susan Rushton, *Branch Mgr*
EMP: 65
SALES (corp-wide): 39.3MM **Privately Held**
WEB: www.pollyspies.com
SIC: 5812 5149 Cafe; bakery products
HQ: Polly's Pies, Inc.
14325 Iseli Rd
Santa Fe Springs CA 90670
714 773-9588

(P-14720)
POMWONDERFUL LLC (DH)
11444 W Olympic Blvd, Los Angeles (90064-1549)
PHONE....................310 966-5800
Richard Cottrell, *CEO*
Matt Tupper, *President*
Kurt Vetter, *Vice Pres*
Andy Pennebaker, *Analyst*
Leon Tin Change, *Controller*
◆ **EMP:** 223 **EST:** 2000
SALES (est): 280.8MM
SALES (corp-wide): 2B **Privately Held**
WEB: www.wonderful.com
SIC: 5149 5148 5085 Beverage concentrates; juices; tea; fruits, fresh; plastic bottles
HQ: Pom Wonderful Holdings Llc
11444 W Olympic Blvd # 210
Los Angeles CA 90064
310 966-5800

(P-14721)
PORTOS BAKERY WEST COVINA INC
584 S Sunset Ave, West Covina (91790-2813)
PHONE....................626 214-3490
Raul Porto, *CEO*
EMP: 300 **EST:** 2018

SALES (est): 26MM **Privately Held**
WEB: www.portosbakery.com
SIC: 5149 Bakery products

(P-14722)
PRESSED JUICERY INC
21540 Hawthorne Blvd, Torrance (90503-5707)
PHONE....................310 214-2144
EMP: 14
SALES (corp-wide): 124.2MM **Privately Held**
WEB: www.pressed.com
SIC: 5499 5149 2033 Health & dietetic food stores; water, distilled; fruit juices: packaged in cans, jars, etc.
PA: Pressed Juicery, Inc.
4016 Wilshire Blvd
Los Angeles CA 90010
310 477-7171

(P-14723)
PRESSED JUICERY INC
23500 Park Sorrento, Calabasas (91302-4116)
PHONE....................318 225-8985
EMP: 14
SALES (corp-wide): 124.2MM **Privately Held**
WEB: www.pressed.com
SIC: 5499 5149 2033 Health & dietetic food stores; water, distilled; fruit juices: packaged in cans, jars, etc.
PA: Pressed Juicery, Inc.
4016 Wilshire Blvd
Los Angeles CA 90010
310 477-7171

(P-14724)
PRESSED JUICERY INC
651 Paseo Nuevo, Santa Barbara (93101-3391)
PHONE....................805 966-0099
EMP: 14
SALES (corp-wide): 124.2MM **Privately Held**
WEB: www.pressed.com
SIC: 5499 5149 2033 Dried fruit; water, distilled; fruit juices: packaged in cans, jars, etc.
PA: Pressed Juicery, Inc.
4016 Wilshire Blvd
Los Angeles CA 90010
310 477-7171

(P-14725)
PRESSED JUICERY INC
1116 Irvine Ave, Newport Beach (92660-4603)
PHONE....................949 650-0661
Pressed Juicery, *Principal*
EMP: 14
SALES (corp-wide): 124.2MM **Privately Held**
WEB: www.pressed.com
SIC: 5499 5149 2033 Health & dietetic food stores; water, distilled; fruit juices: packaged in cans, jars, etc.
PA: Pressed Juicery, Inc.
4016 Wilshire Blvd
Los Angeles CA 90010
310 477-7171

(P-14726)
PRESSED JUICERY INC
7922 E Coast Hwy, Newport Beach (92657-2139)
PHONE....................949 715-7006
EMP: 17
SALES (corp-wide): 124.2MM **Privately Held**
WEB: www.pressed.com
SIC: 5149 2086 2033 Water, distilled; bottled & canned soft drinks; fruit juices: packaged in cans, jars. etc.
PA: Pressed Juicery, Inc.
4016 Wilshire Blvd
Los Angeles CA 90010
310 477-7171

(P-14727)
QUEST NUTRITION LLC
777 S Avi Blvd Ste 100, El Segundo (90245)
PHONE....................562 272-0180
Michael Osborn, *Mng Member*

Michael Mauze, *Bd of Directors*
Kara Roell, *Bd of Directors*
Steve Galinski, *Exec VP*
Reza Mazloumi, *Vice Pres*
▲ **EMP:** 85 **EST:** 2010
SQ FT: 43,728
SALES (est): 62.2MM
SALES (corp-wide): 1B **Publicly Held**
WEB: www.questnutrition.com
SIC: 5149 Beverages, except coffee & tea;
health foods; cookies
HQ: Simply Good Foods Usa, Inc.
1225 17th St Ste 1000
Denver CO 80202

(P-14728)
QUOC VIET FOODS
Also Called: Cafvina Coffee & Tea
1967 N Glassell St, Orange (92865-4320)
PHONE..............................714 283-3131
Tuan Nguyen, *President*
Alan Khoa Nguyen, *Shareholder*
Khanh Nguyen, *Shareholder*
Kim Vu, *Shareholder*
Theresa Nguyen, *Exec VP*
▲ **EMP:** 30 **EST:** 2002
SQ FT: 2,000
SALES (est): 18MM **Privately Held**
WEB: www.quocviet.com
SIC: 5149 2099 Seasonings, sauces & ex-
tracts; seasonings & spices

(P-14729)
REAL GOOD FOOD COMPANY
LLC
444 E Santa Clara St, Ventura
(93001-2749)
PHONE..............................818 299-4179
Gerard Law, *CEO*
Ron Ashley, *Vice Pres*
Mista Asbury,
Josh Schreider,
Albert Antonyants, *Manager*
EMP: 200 **EST:** 2016
SALES (est): 22.9MM **Privately Held**
WEB: www.realgoodfoods.com
SIC: 5149 Specialty food items

(P-14730)
RED BULL DISTRIBUTION CO
INC (HQ)
Also Called: Redbull Distribution Co Colo
1740 Stewart St, Santa Monica
(90404-4022)
PHONE..............................916 515-3501
Selin Chidiak, *CEO*
Tiffany Arrington, *Division Mgr*
Peter Kwon, *Admin Sec*
Amanda Kamen, *Planning*
Ross Harmony, *Production*
EMP: 127 **EST:** 2008
SALES (est): 140.9MM
SALES (corp-wide): 6.7B **Privately Held**
WEB: www.redbulldistributioncompany.com
SIC: 5149 Beverage concentrates
PA: Red Bull Gmbh
Am Brunnen 1
Fuschl Am See 5330
662 658-20

(P-14731)
RED BULL MEDIA HSE N AMER
INC (HQ)
1740 Stewart St, Santa Monica
(90404-4022)
PHONE..............................310 393-4647
Stefan Kozak, *CEO*
Scott Bradfield, *Vice Pres*
EMP: 248 **EST:** 2011
SALES (est): 193.4MM
SALES (corp-wide): 6.7B **Privately Held**
WEB: www.redbull.com
SIC: 5149 Beverage concentrates
PA: Red Bull Gmbh
Am Brunnen 1
Fuschl Am See 5330
662 658-20

(P-14732)
REYES COCA-COLA BOTTLING
LLC
12925 Bradley Ave, Sylmar (91342-3830)
PHONE..............................818 362-4307
Larry Campbell, *Branch Mgr*

EMP: 48
SALES (corp-wide): 850.1MM **Privately**
Held
WEB: www.coca-cola.com
SIC: 5149 4225 2086 Soft drinks; general
warehousing; bottled & canned soft drinks
PA: Reyes Coca-Cola Bottling, L.L.C.
3 Park Plz Ste 600
Irvine CA 92614
213 744-8616

(P-14733)
ROCKVIEW DAIRIES INC (PA)
Also Called: Motive Nation
7011 Stewart And Gray Rd, Downey
(90241-4347)
P.O. Box 668 (90241-0668)
PHONE..............................562 927-5511
Egbert Jim Degroot, *CEO*
Valarie Cooke, *President*
Edgar Del Rio, *CFO*
Joe Valadez, *CFO*
Ted De Groot, *Admin Sec*
◆ **EMP:** 168 **EST:** 1966
SALES (est): 70.7MM **Privately Held**
WEB: www.rockviewfarms.com
SIC: 5149 5143 2026 Dried or canned
foods; milk; fluid milk

(P-14734)
RTR BAKERY INC
2640 Walnut Ave Ste C, Tustin
(92780-7035)
PHONE..............................714 415-2233
Raffi O Sepetjian, *CEO*
EMP: 50 **EST:** 2010
SALES (est): 2.5MM **Privately Held**
WEB: www.rtrbakery.com
SIC: 5461 5149 Bakeries; bakery products

(P-14735)
SETTON PSTCHIO TERRA
BELLA INC (HQ)
9370 Road 234, Terra Bella (93270-9226)
P.O. Box 11089 (93270-1089)
PHONE..............................559 535-6050
Joshua Setton, *President*
Morris Setton, *Vice Pres*
Matt Changala, *Engineer*
Patrick Braddock, *Manager*
▲ **EMP:** 64 **EST:** 1986
SQ FT: 133,000
SALES (est): 45.6MM
SALES (corp-wide): 48.6MM **Privately**
Held
WEB: www.settonfarms.com
SIC: 5149 5145 0173 2068 Fruits, dried;
nuts, salted or roasted; pistachio grove;
salted & roasted nuts & seeds
PA: Setton's International Foods, Inc.
85 Austin Blvd
Commack NY 11725
631 543-8090

(P-14736)
SHAMROCK FOODS COMPANY
12400 Riverside Dr, Eastvale (91752-1004)
PHONE..............................951 685-6314
Kent Mullison, *Branch Mgr*
Debra Myers, *Human Res Mgr*
Andie Covarrubias, *Human Resources*
Edgar Pineda, *Manager*
Paul Provost, *Transportation*
EMP: 360
SALES (corp-wide): 3.8B **Privately Held**
WEB: www.shamrockfoods.com
SIC: 5149 Groceries & related products
PA: Shamrock Foods Company
3900 E Camelback Rd # 300
Phoenix AZ 85018
602 477-2500

(P-14737)
SOOFER CO INC
Also Called: Sadaf Foods
2828 S Alameda St, Vernon (90058-1347)
PHONE..............................323 234-6666
Dariush Soofer, *CEO*
Jamshid Soofer, *President*
Behrooz David Soofer, *COO*
George Melikian, *Principal*
Ramon Sentimental, *Principal*
◆ **EMP:** 75 **EST:** 1981
SQ FT: 70,000

SALES (est): 38.8MM **Privately Held**
WEB: www.sadaffoods.com
SIC: 5149 Spices & seasonings

(P-14738)
SUN CHLORELLA USA CORP
3305 Kashiwa St, Torrance (90505-4022)
PHONE..............................310 891-0600
Futoshi Nakayama, *CEO*
Yoshihito Nishimaki, *President*
Rose Straub, *COO*
Ellen Kubijanto, *CFO*
Allen Harold, *Sales Staff*
▲ **EMP:** 54 **EST:** 1982
SQ FT: 20,000
SALES (est): 24.3MM **Privately Held**
WEB: www.sunchlorellausa.com
SIC: 5149 Health foods
PA: Sun Chlorella Corp.
369, Osakacho, Karasumadori-Go-
josagaru, Shimogyo-Ku
Kyoto KYO 600-8

(P-14739)
SUN TEN LABS LIQUIDATION
CO
9250 Jeronimo Rd, Irvine (92618-1905)
PHONE..............................949 587-0509
Charleson C Hsu, *CEO*
▲ **EMP:** 20 **EST:** 1986
SALES (est): 947K **Privately Held**
WEB: www.sunten.com
SIC: 5149 2834 2833 Spices & season-
ings; pharmaceutical preparations; medic-
inals & botanicals

(P-14740)
SURGE GLOBL BKRIES
HLDINGS LLC (PA)
13336 Paxton St, Pacoima (91331-2339)
PHONE..............................818 896-0525
Chris Botticella, *CEO*
Ash Aghasi, *COO*
Nora Rodriguez, *Office Mgr*
EMP: 122 **EST:** 2018
SQ FT: 44,000
SALES (est): 22.6MM **Privately Held**
WEB: www.globalbakeriesinc.com
SIC: 5149 Bakery products

(P-14741)
SWEETENER PRODUCTS INC
Also Called: Sweetener Products Company
2050 E 38th St, Vernon (90058-1615)
P.O. Box 58426 (90058-0426)
PHONE..............................323 234-2200
Joseph E Tack, *CEO*
Tom Rodd, *Vice Pres*
Charlie Hengsathorn, *MIS Dir*
Lewis Ennist, *QA Dir*
David Culp, *Engineer*
EMP: 78 **EST:** 1923
SALES (est): 47.6MM **Privately Held**
WEB: www.sweetenerproducts.com
SIC: 5149 2062 Groceries & related prod-
ucts; cane sugar refining

(P-14742)
TAMA TRADING COMPANY
1920 E 20th St, Vernon (90058-1076)
PHONE..............................213 748-8262
William A Sauro, *CEO*
Sandra Sauro, *Corp Secy*
◆ **EMP:** 61 **EST:** 1926
SQ FT: 60,000
SALES (est): 22.7MM **Privately Held**
WEB: www.tamatrading.com
SIC: 5149 5143 5147 5145 Specialty
food items; seasonings, sauces & ex-
tracts; pasta & rice; cheese; meats &
meat products; candy

(P-14743)
TANAKA FARMS
5380 University Dr, Irvine (92612-2944)
PHONE..............................949 653-2100
Glenn Tannaka, *Owner*
Kenny Tanaka, *Manager*
EMP: 60 **EST:** 1975
SALES (est): 10.1MM **Privately Held**
WEB: www.tanakafarms.com
SIC: 5149 Groceries & related products

(P-14744)
TASTEFUL SELECTIONS LLC
13003 Di Giorgio Rd, Arvin (93203-9529)
PHONE..............................661 588-1053
Robert Bender, *Mng Member*
Celeste Porter, *CFO*
Charles Daniels, *Vice Pres*
Aimee Rabanal, *Accountant*
Eric Ranney, *Maintence Staff*
EMP: 109 **EST:** 2010
SALES (est): 50.2MM **Privately Held**
WEB: www.tastefulselections.com
SIC: 5149 5812 Condiments; eating
places

(P-14745)
TAWA SERVICES INC (PA)
6338 Regio Ave, Buena Park (90620-1026)
PHONE..............................714 521-8899
Jonson Chen, *CEO*
Young You, *Principal*
▼ **EMP:** 220 **EST:** 2012
SALES (est): 60.9MM **Privately Held**
SIC: 5149 5411 Groceries & related prod-
ucts; grocery stores

(P-14746)
UMEKEN USA INC (PA)
13012 Moore St, Cerritos (90703-2226)
PHONE..............................888 941-3311
Brian Han, *CEO*
Shu Lu, *Sales Staff*
Taejoo Kim, *Art Dir*
Marilyn Han, *Manager*
June Lee, *Manager*
▲ **EMP:** 78 **EST:** 2002
SALES (est): 21.1MM **Privately Held**
WEB: www.umeken.com
SIC: 5149 Health foods

(P-14747)
WALONG MARKETING INC (PA)
Also Called: Foods and Produce
6281 Regio Ave, Buena Park (90620-1023)
PHONE..............................714 670-8899
Chang Hua Chen, *CEO*
Roger Chen, *Ch of Bd*
Chen James, *COO*
Alice Chen, *CFO*
Danny Wong, *Sales Associate*
◆ **EMP:** 100 **EST:** 1999
SALES (est): 65.2MM **Privately Held**
WEB: www.asianfoodsonline.com
SIC: 5149 5411 Groceries & related prod-
ucts; grocery stores

(P-14748)
WILDFLOUR BAKERY & CAFE
LLC
21160 Califa St, Woodland Hills
(91367-5002)
PHONE..............................818 575-7280
Gregory M Yulish, *CEO*
Lisa Yulish,
EMP: 62 **EST:** 2012
SQ FT: 30,000
SALES (est): 10.2MM **Privately Held**
WEB: www.wfbakery.com
SIC: 5149 5461 2051 5812 Bakery prod-
ucts; bakeries; breads, rolls & buns;
bread, all types (white, wheat, rye, etc):
fresh or frozen; bakery: wholesale or
wholesale/retail combined; restaurant,
family: independent; contract food serv-
ices; bakery products, frozen

5153 Grain & Field Beans Wholesale

(P-14749)
COILWSCOM INC
Also Called: Cws International
353 W Grove Ave, Orange (92865-3205)
PHONE..............................714 279-9010
James Lau, *CEO*
Lee Emanuel, *Sales Mgr*
▲ **EMP:** 27 **EST:** 1978
SQ FT: 8,500
SALES (est): 2.7MM **Privately Held**
SIC: 5153 3679 Wild rice; microwave
components

P
R
O
D
U
C
T
S
&
S
V
C
S

5159 Farm-Prdt Raw Mtrls, NEC Wholesale

(P-14750)
FLUIDS MANUFACTURING INC
11941 Vose St, North Hollywood
(91605-5750)
P.O. Box 16297 (91615-6297)
PHONE...............818 264-4657
Stephan Sutton, *CEO*
EMP: 150 **EST:** 2015
SALES (est): 11.1MM **Privately Held**
SIC: 5159

(P-14751)
IMPERIAL WESTERN PRODUCTS INC
4085 Bain St, Jurupa Valley (91752-1268)
PHONE...............951 727-8950
Ana Olaya, *Branch Mgr*
Dustin Duarte, *Manager*
EMP: 69
SALES (corp-wide): 100.4MM **Privately Held**
WEB: www.imperialwesternproducts.com
SIC: 5159 Cotton merchants & products
PA: Imperial Western Products, Inc., A California Corporation
86600 Avenue 54
Coachella CA 92236
760 398-0815

(P-14752)
SOUTH VALLEY ALMOND CO LLC
Also Called: South Valley Farms
15443 Beech Ave, Wasco (93280-7604)
PHONE...............661 391-9000
Paul C Genho, *Mng Member*
Lorin Clark, *Controller*
Kevin Philley, *Sales Staff*
Daryl Wilkendorf,
Merrill Dibble, *Mng Member*
◆ **EMP:** 200 **EST:** 2007
SQ FT: 4,000
SALES (est): 33.3MM **Privately Held**
SIC: 5159 Nuts & nut by-products

5162 Plastics Materials & Basic Shapes Wholesale

(P-14753)
CIRRUS ENTERPRISES LLC
Also Called: E.V. Roberts
18027 Bishop Ave, Carson (90746-4019)
PHONE...............310 204-6159
Ron Cloud, *CEO*
Seth Arnold, *Technical Staff*
Michelle Cummings, *Technical Staff*
Kevin Hart, *Technical Staff*
Josh Rhee, *Controller*
▲ **EMP:** 52 **EST:** 1938
SQ FT: 26,000
SALES (est): 22.8MM **Privately Held**
SIC: 5162 2821 2891 5198 Plastics products; epoxy resins; adhesives & sealants; paints, varnishes & supplies; chemicals & allied products

(P-14754)
COAST PLASTICS INC (PA)
936 E Francis St, Ontario (91761-5683)
PHONE...............626 812-9174
Matt Humphries, *President*
EMP: 17 **EST:** 1979
SQ FT: 7,000
SALES (est): 5.8MM **Privately Held**
WEB: www.coastplasticsinc.com
SIC: 5162 3089 Plastics materials; plastic processing

(P-14755)
COATED FABRICS COMPANY (HQ)
Also Called: Crystal Form
12658 Cisneros Ln, Santa Fe Springs (90670-3372)
P.O. Box 2222 (90670-0008)
PHONE...............562 298-1300
Jindas B Shah, *Ch of Bd*
Eric Shah, *CEO*
Neil Shah, *CFO*
Logan Meuth, *Mktg Dir*
◆ **EMP:** 15 **EST:** 1966
SQ FT: 50,000
SALES (est): 34.2MM **Privately Held**
WEB: www.coatedfabrics.com
SIC: 5162 2339 5131 Plastics materials; plastics products; women's & misses' athletic clothing & sportswear; coated fabrics
PA: Symbex Corporation
12658 Cisneros Ln
Santa Fe Springs CA 90670
310 945-5043

(P-14756)
COMPOSITES ONE LLC
11917 Altamar Pl, Santa Fe Springs (90670-2543)
PHONE...............562 906-0173
Paul Colonna, *Branch Mgr*
Andy Flad, *Vice Pres*
Don Hairhoger, *Vice Pres*
Mary Bravo, *General Mgr*
Barry Wilsonsmith, *Technical Mgr*
EMP: 13
SALES (corp-wide): 543.4MM **Privately Held**
WEB: www.compositesone.com
SIC: 5162 3229 5999 Plastics products; pressed & blown glass; fiberglass materials, except insulation
HQ: Composites One Llc
955 National Pkwy # 95560
Schaumburg IL 60173
847 437-0200

(P-14757)
CONSOLIDATED PLASTICS CORP (PA)
Also Called: Paragon Plastics Co Div
14954 La Palma Dr, Chino (91710-9695)
PHONE...............909 393-8222
Jean Bouris, *President*
Gloria Jean Bouris, *CEO*
Cesar Nunez, *CIO*
EMP: 50 **EST:** 1973
SQ FT: 45,000
SALES (est): 18.9MM **Privately Held**
WEB: www.planetplastics.com
SIC: 5162 3599 Plastics sheets & rods; machine shop, jobbing & repair

(P-14758)
ELKAY PLASTICS CO INC (PA)
6000 Sheila St, Commerce (90040-2405)
PHONE...............323 722-7073
Louis Chertkow, *President*
Percy Thompson, *Receiver*
Geoffrey Pankau, *CFO*
Vicki Gosnell, *Info Tech Mgr*
Anjelica Mayorga, *Technology*
▲ **EMP:** 100 **EST:** 1966
SQ FT: 175,000
SALES (est): 96.3MM **Privately Held**
WEB: www.lkpkg.com
SIC: 5162 Plastics products

(P-14759)
ORANGE COUNTY INDUS PLAS INC (PA)
Also Called: Ocip
4811 E La Palma Ave, Anaheim (92807-1954)
PHONE...............714 632-9450
Robert Robinson, *President*
Richard Weeks, *Accounts Mgr*
▲ **EMP:** 25 **EST:** 1985
SQ FT: 70,198
SALES (est): 41.9MM **Privately Held**
WEB: www.ocip.com
SIC: 5162 2821 Plastics products; plastics materials & resins

(P-14760)
PLASTIC SALES SOUTHERN INC
425 Havana Ave, Long Beach (90814-1928)
PHONE...............714 375-7900
James Quinn, *President*
EMP: 23 **EST:** 1980
SALES (est): 1MM **Privately Held**
SIC: 5162 3089 Plastics sheets & rods; injection molding of plastics

(P-14761)
RDM INDUSTRIES
14310 Gannet St, La Mirada (90638-5221)
PHONE...............714 690-0380
Jaz Manak, *President*
Dan Gilmore, *Shareholder*
▲ **EMP:** 17 **EST:** 2011
SALES (est): 8.1MM **Privately Held**
WEB: www.rdmindustriesla.com
SIC: 5162 5084 3565 Plastics materials; industrial machinery & equipment; aerating machines, for beverages

(P-14762)
REGAL-PIEDMONT PLASTICS LLC
17000 Valley View Ave, La Mirada (90638-5827)
P.O. Box 1274, Inglewood (90308-1274)
PHONE...............562 404-4014
Carlos Bennett, *Sales & Mktg St*
Janet Jones, *Marketing Mgr*
EMP: 20
SALES (corp-wide): 201.6MM **Privately Held**
WEB: www.regalpiedmontplastics.com
SIC: 5162 2396 5169 Plastics sheets & rods; furniture trimmings, fabric; silicon lubricants
HQ: Regal-Piedmont Plastics, Llc
5010 W W T Harris Blvd
Charlotte NC 28269
-

(P-14763)
S & W PLASTIC STORES INC (PA)
Also Called: S & W Plastics Supply
14270 Albers Way, Chino (91710-6940)
PHONE...............909 390-0090
William B Goldstein, *CEO*
David Goldstein, *Vice Pres*
▲ **EMP:** 35 **EST:** 1964
SQ FT: 25,000
SALES (est): 19.5MM **Privately Held**
WEB: www.sandwplastics.com
SIC: 5162 5719 3089 Plastics products; housewares; plastic kitchenware, tableware & houseware

(P-14764)
SOL-PAK THERMOFORMING INC
3388 Fruitland Ave, Vernon (90058-3714)
PHONE...............323 582-3333
Moussa Soleimani, *President*
Joubin Soleimani, *CFO*
Al Meshkati, *Vice Pres*
Joseph Soleimani, *Vice Pres*
▲ **EMP:** 23 **EST:** 2004
SALES (est): 15MM **Privately Held**
WEB: www.solpak.com
SIC: 5162 2821 Plastics products; plastics materials & resins

(P-14765)
SPIGEN INC
Also Called: Spigen Sgp
9975 Toledo Way Ste 100, Irvine (92618-1826)
PHONE...............949 502-5121
Dae Young Kim, *CEO*
Jayden Song, *Business Mgr*
Sang Hoon Jun, *Human Res Mgr*
Sang Jun, *Human Res Mgr*
Sang H Jun, *Human Res Mgr*
▲ **EMP:** 91
SQ FT: 9,000
SALES (est): 11.7MM **Privately Held**
WEB: www.spigen.com
SIC: 5271 5162 Mobile home parts & accessories; plastics products
PA: Spigen Korea Co., Ltd.
Spigen Hq A Bldg.
Seoul 06153
-

5169 Chemicals & Allied Prdts, NEC Wholesale

(P-14766)
ABIANCA KHANNA LLC
Also Called: California Plastics
8504 Firestone Blvd, Downey (90241-4926)
PHONE...............833 225-7527
Abhimanyu Khanna, *Mng Member*
Bianca Khanna,
EMP: 13 **EST:** 2019
SALES (est): 5MM **Privately Held**
SIC: 5169 2326 Synthetic resins, rubber & plastic materials; medical & hospital uniforms, men's

(P-14767)
ACCESS BUSINESS GROUP LLC
Also Called: Access Logistics
12825 Leffingwell Ave, Santa Fe Springs (90670-6339)
PHONE...............308 422-9482
Hee Douglas, *Branch Mgr*
EMP: 109 **Privately Held**
WEB: www.accessbusinessgroup.com
SIC: 5169 Chemicals & allied products
HQ: Access Business Group Llc
7575 Fulton St E
Ada MI 49355

(P-14768)
ACCESS BUSINESS GROUP LLC
5600 Beach Blvd, Buena Park (90621-2007)
P.O. Box 5940 (90622-5940)
PHONE...............714 562-6200
Steve Vanandel, *Ch of Bd*
Jamie Francis, *Manager*
EMP: 109 **Privately Held**
WEB: www.accessbusinessgroup.com
SIC: 5169 Chemicals & allied products
HQ: Access Business Group Llc
7575 Fulton St E
Ada MI 49355
-

(P-14769)
ACCESS BUSINESS GROUP LLC
Also Called: Nutrilite
5609 River Way, Buena Park (90621-1709)
PHONE...............714 562-7914
EMP: 109 **Privately Held**
WEB: www.accessbusinessgroup.com
SIC: 5169 Chemicals & allied products
HQ: Access Business Group Llc
7575 Fulton St E
Ada MI 49355
-

(P-14770)
ADVANTAGE CHEMICAL LLC
27375 Via Industria, Temecula (92590-3699)
PHONE...............951 225-4631
Mark Hottinger, *Officer*
Ben Olk III, *CEO*
EMP: 22 **EST:** 2010
SQ FT: 20,000
WEB: www.advantagechemical.com
SIC: 5169 2842 Specialty cleaning & sanitation preparations; sanitation preparations

(P-14771)
AIRGAS SPECIALTY PRODUCTS INC
6270 Wilderness Ave, Riverside (92504-1055)
PHONE...............951 353-2390
Joe Ennes, *Branch Mgr*
EMP: 55
SALES (corp-wide): 102.6MM **Privately Held**
WEB: www.airgasspecialtyproducts.com
SIC: 5169 Ammonia
HQ: Airgas Specialty Products, Inc.
2530 Sever Rd Ste 300
Lawrenceville GA 30043

(P-14772)
AQUA-SERV ENGINEERS INC (HQ)
13560 Colombard Ct, Fontana (92337-7702)
PHONE...................951 681-9696
Earl L Harper, *CEO*
Garland Rachels, *President*
Buck Long, *Senior VP*
Kent Duncan, *Technical Staff*
Christy Brown, *Manager*
EMP: 111 **EST:** 1958
SQ FT: 63,000
SALES (est): 25.4MM **Privately Held**
WEB: www.aqua-serv.com
SIC: 5169 Chemicals & allied products

(P-14773)
BRENNTAG PACIFIC INC (DH)
10747 Patterson Pl, Santa Fe Springs (90670-4043)
PHONE...................562 903-9626
William A Fidler, *CEO*
Steven Pozzi, *President*
H Edward Boyadjian, *CFO*
Viktor Alvarado, *Vice Pres*
Julia Tu, *Controller*
▲ **EMP:** 194 **EST:** 2003
SALES (est): 543.8MM
SALES (corp-wide): 13.9B **Privately Held**
WEB: www.brenntag.com
SIC: 5169 Chemicals, industrial & heavy; industrial chemicals
HQ: Brenntag North America, Inc.
5083 Pottsville Pike
Reading PA 19605
610 926-6100

(P-14774)
CALWAX LLC (DH)
16511 Knott Ave, La Mirada (90638-6011)
PHONE...................626 969-4334
John Paraszczak, *Mng Member*
Robert L Weil, *Principal*
Paul Morris, *Technician*
▲ **EMP:** 37 **EST:** 1955
SQ FT: 40,000
SALES (est): 21.7MM **Privately Held**
WEB: www.calwax.com
SIC: 5120 2842 Waxes, except petroleum; waxes for wood, leather & other materials
HQ: Remet Corporation
210 Commons Rd
Utica NY 13502
315 797-8700

(P-14775)
CHAMPION CHEMICAL CO CAL INC
8319 Greenleaf Ave, Whittier (90602-2998)
P.O. Box 5429 (90607-5429)
PHONE...................562 945-1456
Andrew L Ellis, *President*
Dennis C Hall, *Vice Pres*
David C Ellis, *Consultant*
David Ellis, *Consultant*
EMP: 31 **EST:** 1960
SQ FT: 8,000
SALES (est): 9.9MM **Privately Held**
SIC: 5169 2841 2842 2843 Specialty cleaning & sanitation preparations; soap & other detergents; specialty cleaning, polishes & sanitation goods; surface active agents

(P-14776)
CHEMSIL SILICONES INC
21900 Marilla St, Chatsworth (91311-4129)
PHONE...................818 700-0302
Williams S Patrick, *CEO*
Patrick S Williams, *President*
Ian Cleminson, *CFO*
Tom Martin, *Treasurer*
Bruce McDonald, *Vice Pres*
◆ **EMP:** 26 **EST:** 2000
SQ FT: 32,789
SALES (est): 21MM
SALES (corp-wide): 1.1B **Publicly Held**
WEB: www.chemsil.com
SIC: 5169 2869 Chemicals & allied products; silicones
PA: Innospec Inc.
8310 S Valley Hwy Ste 350
Englewood CO 80112
303 792-5554

(P-14777)
CHEROKEE CHEMICAL CO INC (PA)
Also Called: CCI
3540 E 26th St, Vernon (90058-4103)
PHONE...................323 265-1112
D A Criswell, *CEO*
Cindy Kilgore, *Office Mgr*
Brock Naquin, *Administration*
Butch Vanzant, *Technical Staff*
Dan Walker, *Technical Staff*
EMP: 47
SQ FT: 30,000
SALES (est): 28.7MM **Privately Held**
WEB: www.ccichemical.com
SIC: 5169 2842 2819 Specialty cleaning & sanitation preparations; specialty cleaning, polishes & sanitation goods; industrial inorganic chemicals

(P-14778)
DURRANI INVESTMENTS CORP
Also Called: California Chemical
555 Anton Blvd Ste 150, Costa Mesa (92626-7036)
PHONE...................424 292-3424
Sirdar D Durrani, *CEO*
EMP: 50 **EST:** 2016
SALES (est): 22.4MM **Privately Held**
SIC: 5169 Chemical bulk station & terminal

(P-14779)
E T HORN COMPANY (PA)
16050 Canary Ave, La Mirada (90638-5585)
P.O. Box 1238 (90637-1238)
PHONE...................714 523-8050
Jeffrey Martin, *CEO*
Kevin Salerno, *President*
Julie Wubbena, *CFO*
Roger Clemens, *Officer*
Vince Anderson, *Vice Pres*
▲ **EMP:** 70 **EST:** 1961
SQ FT: 1,200
SALES (est): 100.4MM **Privately Held**
WEB: www.imcdus.com
SIC: 5169 Industrial chemicals

(P-14780)
EMBEE PERFORMANCE LLC
Also Called: Embee Powder Coating
2100 Ritchey St, Santa Ana (92705-5134)
PHONE...................714 540-1354
David Dahlberg, *Mng Member*
John Dahlberg,
EMP: 20 **EST:** 2000
SALES (est): 3.3MM **Privately Held**
WEB: www.embeeperformance.com
SIC: 5169 3471 Polishes; plating of metals or formed products

(P-14781)
ESE ELECTRONICS INC
Also Called: Ese
1111 S Central Ave, Los Angeles (90021-2041)
PHONE...................213 614-0102
David Kazemi, *CEO*
▲ **EMP:** 25 **EST:** 1993
SALES (est): 9.7MM **Privately Held**
WEB: www.eseelectronics.com
SIC: 5169 2841 5065 Alcohols & anti-freeze compounds; soap & other detergents; electronic parts & equipment

(P-14782)
GEO DRILLING FLUIDS INC (PA)
1431 Union Ave, Bakersfield (93305-5732)
P.O. Box 1478 (93302-1478)
PHONE...................661 325-5919
Jim Clifford, *President*
Don Boulet, *Treasurer*
Tom Needham, *Vice Pres*
Dan Bauman, *Admin Sec*
Matt Monroe, *Engineer*
▲ **EMP:** 30 **EST:** 1950
SQ FT: 7,500
SALES (est): 51.3MM **Privately Held**
WEB: www.geodf.com
SIC: 5169 1389 7389 Chemicals & allied products; servicing oil & gas wells; grinding, precision: commercial or industrial

(P-14783)
HILL BROTHERS CHEMICAL COMPANY (PA)
3000 E Birch St Ste 108, Brea (92821-6261)
PHONE...................714 998-8800
Adam Hill, *President*
Thomas F James, *CFO*
Tom James, *CFO*
Kathryn J Waters, *Corp Secy*
Matthew Thorne, *Exec VP*
▲ **EMP:** 150 **EST:** 1935
SALES (est): 125.4MM **Privately Held**
WEB: www.hillbrothers.com
SIC: 5169 2819 Acids; calcium chloride & hypochlorite; magnesium compounds or salts, inorganic

(P-14784)
HYDRITE CHEMICAL CO
1603 Clancy Ct, Visalia (93291-9253)
PHONE...................559 651-3450
Steve Reid, *Manager*
Matt Cholakian, *Business Mgr*
Dawn Benere, *Accounts Mgr*
EMP: 68
SALES (corp-wide): 686.3MM **Privately Held**
WEB: www.hydrite.com
SIC: 5169 Industrial chemicals
PA: Hydrite Chemical Co.
300 N Patrick Blvd Fl 2
Brookfield WI 53045
262 792-1450

(P-14785)
INEOS COMPOSITES US LLC
6608 E 26th St, Commerce (90040-3216)
P.O. Box 22118, Los Angeles (90022-0118)
PHONE...................323 767-1300
Reid Mork, *Branch Mgr*
Grant Needham, *Plant Mgr*
Fernando Celaya, *Maintence Staff*
EMP: 60
SQ FT: 45,845
SALES (corp-wide): 1.1MM **Privately Held**
SIC: 5169 Alkalines & chlorine
HQ: Ineos Composites Us, Llc
5220 Blazer Pkwy
Dublin OH 43017
614 790-9299

(P-14786)
LUCAS OIL PRODUCTS INC (PA)
302 N Sheridan St, Corona (92878-4067)
PHONE...................951 270-0154
Forrest Lucas, *CEO*
Matthew Kimmick, *CFO*
Shane Burns, *Vice Pres*
Charlotte Lucas, *Vice Pres*
Josh Hunter, *Executive*
◆ **EMP:** 150 **EST:** 1989
SQ FT: 80,000
SALES (est): 182.3MM **Privately Held**
WEB: www.lucasoil.com
SIC: 5169 2992 Oil additives; lubricating oils & greases

(P-14787)
MCHEM INC (PA)
2425 Golden Hill Rd, Paso Robles (93446-7038)
PHONE...................541 913-7892
Chad Walrod, *CEO*
EMP: 93 **EST:** 2013
SALES (est): 6.6MM **Privately Held**
WEB: www.mcheminc.com
SIC: 5169 Chemicals & allied products

(P-14788)
NORAC ADDITIVES LLC
100 W Fthill Blvd Ste 101, San Dimas (91773)
PHONE...................909 321-5952
Mike Connor, *Mng Member*
EMP: 55 **EST:** 2017
SALES (est): 12.2MM **Privately Held**
WEB: www.noracadditives.com
SIC: 5169 Chemical additives

(P-14789)
NORMAN FOX & CO
5511 S Boyle Ave, Vernon (90058-3932)
P.O. Box 58727, Los Angeles (90058-0727)
PHONE...................323 973-4900

Alex Kirby, *Branch Mgr*
Chuck Hulsey, *Technical Staff*
Gary Ray, *Purch Mgr*
Michael Perez, *Opers Staff*
Don Oshea, *Sales Mgr*
EMP: 23
SALES (corp-wide): 44.8MM **Privately Held**
WEB: www.norfoxchem.com
SIC: 5169 2841 Industrial chemicals; soap: granulated, liquid, cake, flaked or chip; detergents, synthetic organic or inorganic alkaline
PA: Norman, Fox & Co.
14970 Don Julian Rd
City Of Industry CA 91746
800 632-1777

(P-14790)
NORMAN FOX & CO (PA)
Also Called: Norfox
14970 Don Julian Rd, City of Industry (91746-3111)
PHONE...................800 632-1777
Stephen Halpin, *CEO*
Bob Code, *CFO*
Daniel Baumgartner, *Controller*
Vickie Madore, *Purch Mgr*
Lori Williams, *Cust Mgr*
◆ **EMP:** 40 **EST:** 1971
SQ FT: 5,000
SALES (est): 44.8MM **Privately Held**
WEB: www.norfoxchem.com
SIC: 5169 2841 Chemicals & allied products; soap: granulated, liquid, cake, flaked or chip; detergents, synthetic organic or inorganic alkaline

(P-14791)
SPECTRUM LABORATORY PDTS INC
Also Called: Spectrum Lab & Phrm Pdts
14422 S San Pedro St, Gardena (90248-2027)
PHONE...................520 292-3103
Elizabeth Brown, *CEO*
EMP: 49
SALES (corp-wide): 126.9MM **Privately Held**
SIC: 5169 2869 2819 Organic chemicals, synthetic; laboratory chemicals, organic; industrial inorganic chemicals
PA: Spectrum Laboratory Products, Inc.
769 Jersey Ave
New Brunswick NJ 08901
732 214-1300

(P-14792)
UNIVAR SOLUTIONS USA INC
2600 Garfield Ave, Commerce (90040-2608)
P.O. Box 512062 (90040)
PHONE...................323 727-7005
Gary Cramer, *Branch Mgr*
Jim Foley, *Train & Dev Mgr*
Vee Olivarez, *Sales Staff*
Robert Rojas, *Sales Staff*
Rick Spraul, *Sales Staff*
EMP: 175
SALES (corp-wide): 8.2B **Publicly Held**
WEB: www.univarsolutions.com
SIC: 5169 Industrial chemicals
HQ: Univar Solutions Usa Inc.
3075 Highland Pkwy # 200
Downers Grove IL 60515
331 777-6000

(P-14793)
VALEANT BIOMEDICALS INC (DH)
1 Enterprise, Aliso Viejo (92656-2606)
PHONE...................949 461-6000
Tim Tyson, *President*
Jocelyne Lachapelle, *President*
Jerry Janeczko, *Vice Pres*
Denise Raimondo, *Associate Dir*
Yana Amani, *Executive Asst*
EMP: 100 **EST:** 1983
SQ FT: 55,000

SALES (est): 104.7MM
SALES (corp-wide): 8.6B **Privately Held**
WEB: www.bauschhealth.com
SIC: **5169** 2835 8731 3826 Chemicals & allied products; in vitro & in vivo diagnostic substances; blood derivative diagnostic agents; biotechnical research, commercial; analytical instruments; liquid testing apparatus; medical equipment & supplies
HQ: Bausch Health Americas, Inc.
　　400 Somerset Corp Blvd
　　Bridgewater NJ 08807
　　908 927-1400

(P-14794)
VIJALL INC
Also Called: Chemtec Chemical Company
21900 Marilla St, Chatsworth (91311-4129)
PHONE..........................818 700-0071
Patrick S Williams, *President*
Bruce McDonald, *President*
Tom Martin, *Treasurer*
David E Williams, *Vice Pres*
Ian Cleminson, *VP Finance*
▲ EMP: 26 EST: 1987
SQ FT: 32,789
SALES (est): 10.5MM
SALES (corp-wide): 1.1B **Publicly Held**
WEB: www.chemteccc.com
SIC: **5169** 2819 Industrial chemicals; industrial inorganic chemicals
HQ: Innospec Active Chemicals Llc
　　510 W Grimes Ave
　　High Point NC 27260
　　336 882-3308

5171 Petroleum Bulk Stations & Terminals

(P-14795)
DAL CHEM INC
Also Called: Alexis Oil Company
219 Glider Cir, Corona (92878-5034)
PHONE..........................951 279-9830
Angelo Leara, *CEO*
Diana Wilson, *CFO*
Dan Leara, *Treasurer*
Denise Leara, *Vice Pres*
Mark Leara, *Admin Sec*
▼ EMP: 53 EST: 1987
SQ FT: 13,500
SALES (est): 35.8MM **Privately Held**
WEB: www.reladyne.com
SIC: **5171** 5172 Petroleum bulk stations; lubricating oils & greases
PA: Reladyne, Inc.
　　8280 Montgomery Rd # 101
　　Cincinnati OH 45236

(P-14796)
JANKOVICH COMPANY (PA)
Also Called: Tjc CA
307 W 22nd St, San Pedro (90731)
P.O. Box 670 (90733-0670)
PHONE..........................310 547-3305
Thomas J Jankovich, *CEO*
Maryann Jankovich, *Corp Secy*
John Kenner, *Vice Pres*
Bill Pratley, *Vice Pres*
Shelley Imhoff, *Controller*
▲ EMP: 60 EST: 1983
SQ FT: 2,000
SALES (est): 20.4MM **Privately Held**
WEB: www.jankovichcompany.com
SIC: **5984** 5171 2911 5172 Liquefied petroleum gas dealers; petroleum bulk stations & terminals; diesel fuels; diesel fuel

(P-14797)
SOUTHERN COUNTIES OIL CO (PA)
Also Called: SC Fuels
1800 W Katella Ave # 400, Orange (92867-3449)
P.O. Box 4159 (92863-4159)
PHONE..........................714 744-7140
Frank P Greinke, *CEO*
Michael Baldwin,
Steve Greinke, *President*
David Larimer, *COO*
Mimi Taylor, *CFO*
EMP: 95

SALES (est): 960.5MM **Privately Held**
WEB: www.scfuels.com
SIC: **5171** 5541 5172 Petroleum bulk stations; gasoline service stations; petroleum products

(P-14798)
ZECO SYSTEMS INC
Also Called: Greenlots
767 S Alameda St Ste 200, Los Angeles (90021-1664)
PHONE..........................888 751-8560
Andreas Lips, *CEO*
Brett Hauser, *CEO*
Mark Steffler, *CFO*
Matthew Kline, *Officer*
Jeff Tolnar, *Officer*
EMP: 95 EST: 2012
SQ FT: 10,000
SALES (est): 53.3MM
SALES (corp-wide): 180.5B **Privately Held**
SIC: **5171** Petroleum bulk stations & terminals
HQ: Shell New Energies Us Llc
　　767 S Alameda St Ste 200
　　Los Angeles CA 90021
　　888 751-8560

5172 Petroleum & Petroleum Prdts Wholesale

(P-14799)
AERA ENERGY LLC
1800 School Canyon Rd, Ventura (93001-4459)
PHONE..........................661 427-9717
Nicole Kennedy, *Engineer*
Rich Jacoby, *Sales Staff*
EMP: 71
SALES (corp-wide): 180.5B **Privately Held**
WEB: www.aeraenergy.com
SIC: **5172** Crude oil
HQ: Aera Energy Services Company
　　10000 Ming Ave
　　Bakersfield CA 93311
　　661 665-5000

(P-14800)
APEX HOLDING CO
23901 Calabasas Rd # 2090, Calabasas (91302-1542)
PHONE..........................818 876-0161
Louis Silvers, *Branch Mgr*
EMP: 67
SALES (corp-wide): 871.2MM **Privately Held**
WEB: www.apexoil.com
SIC: **5172** Petroleum products
PA: Apex Holding Co.
　　8235 Forsyth Blvd Ste 400
　　Saint Louis MO 63105
　　314 889-9600

(P-14801)
CASEY COMPANY (PA)
180 E Ocean Blvd Ste 1010, Long Beach (90802-4711)
PHONE..........................562 436-9685
Larry Delpit Sr, *Chairman*
Steven Christovich, *CFO*
Barbara Odom, *Treasurer*
Betty Jane Blanchette, *Admin Sec*
EMP: 129 EST: 1982
SQ FT: 4,000
SALES (est): 160.3MM **Privately Held**
SIC: **5172** Petroleum products

(P-14802)
EFUEL LLC
Also Called: Easy Fuel
65 Enterprise Fl 3, Aliso Viejo (92656-2705)
PHONE..........................949 330-7145
Donald Harper, *CEO*
Mario Cole, *Info Tech Mgr*
EMP: 90 EST: 2016
SALES (est): 37.6MM **Privately Held**
WEB: www.efuelco.com
SIC: **5172** Petroleum products

(P-14803)
EMPIRE OIL CO
2756 S Riverside Ave, Bloomington (92316-3500)
PHONE..........................909 877-0226
Richard Alden Sr, *CEO*
Richard Scott Alden Jr, *President*
Donald Welker, *CFO*
EMP: 2183 EST: 1961
SQ FT: 2,300
SALES (est): 6.9MM **Publicly Held**
WEB: www.empireoil.info
SIC: **5172** Diesel fuel; lubricating oils & greases
HQ: Northern Tier Energy Lp
　　1250 W Washington St # 300
　　Tempe AZ 85281
　　602 302-5450

(P-14804)
GENERAL PETROLEUM CORPORATION (HQ)
Also Called: G P Resources
19501 S Santa Fe Ave, Compton (90221-5913)
PHONE..........................562 983-7300
James A Halsam III, *CEO*
Michael Ruehring, *President*
Sean Kha, *Vice Pres*
Charles McDaniels, *Vice Pres*
Tracy Mausser, *Human Res Mgr*
▲ EMP: 150 EST: 1946
SQ FT: 5,000
SALES (est): 67.5MM
SALES (corp-wide): 89MM **Privately Held**
SIC: **5172** Crude oil
PA: Pecos, Inc.
　　19501 S Santa Fe Ave
　　Compton CA 90221
　　310 356-2300

(P-14805)
M O DION & SONS INC (PA)
1543 W 16th St, Long Beach (90813-1210)
PHONE..........................562 432-3946
Toll Free:..........................888　-
Pat Cullen, *CEO*
Matt Cullen, *President*
Patrick B Cullen, *CEO*
Bill Frank, *CFO*
Mark Hein, *Director*
EMP: 60 EST: 1930
SQ FT: 85,000
SALES (est): 201.9MM **Privately Held**
WEB: www.amberresources.com
SIC: **5172** Gasoline; diesel fuel; lubricating oils & greases

(P-14806)
RPP PRODUCTS INC (PA)
Also Called: Race Pro Products
2756 S Riverside Ave, Bloomington (92316-3248)
PHONE..........................800 657-4811
Eric Zwigart, *CEO*
Scot Lamb, *President*
Karen Dobschutz, *CFO*
Shane Francis, *Vice Pres*
Bob Oberg, *Vice Pres*
▲ EMP: 17 EST: 2006
SALES (est): 97.4MM **Privately Held**
SIC: **5172** 3069 Lubricating oils & greases; acid bottles, rubber

(P-14807)
SOCO GROUP INC
Also Called: Soco Petroleum Group
240 E 1st St, Perris (92570-2215)
PHONE..........................951 657-2350
Ron Lamb, *Manager*
Greg Barnicle, *General Mgr*
Ron Overacker, *Manager*
EMP: 56
SALES (corp-wide): 300K **Privately Held**
WEB: www.texaco.com
SIC: **5172** Gasoline
PA: The Soco Group Inc
　　5962 Priestly Dr
　　Carlsbad CA 92008
　　760 804-8460

(P-14808)
SOCO GROUP INC
Also Called: Soco Petroleum
350 E Main St, El Centro (92243-2618)
P.O. Box 1905 (92244-1905)
PHONE..........................760 352-4683
Mark Schultz, *Branch Mgr*
EMP: 56
SALES (corp-wide): 300K **Privately Held**
WEB: www.texaco.com
SIC: **5172** Petroleum products
PA: The Soco Group Inc
　　5962 Priestly Dr
　　Carlsbad CA 92008
　　760 804-8460

(P-14809)
TESORO REFINING & MKTG CO LLC
39224 Winchester Rd, Murrieta (92563-3506)
PHONE..........................951 461-3063
EMP: 78 **Publicly Held**
SIC: **5172** Petroleum products
HQ: Tesoro Refining & Marketing Company Llc
　　19100 Ridgewood Pkwy
　　San Antonio TX 78259
　　210 828-8484

(P-14810)
TESORO REFINING & MKTG CO LLC
2101 E Pacific Coast Hwy, Wilmington (90744-2914)
PHONE..........................877 837-6762
James Nichols, *Branch Mgr*
Jimmy Griego, *Technician*
Jason Williams, *Opers Mgr*
EMP: 78 **Publicly Held**
SIC: **5172** Service station supplies, petroleum
HQ: Tesoro Refining & Marketing Company Llc
　　19100 Ridgewood Pkwy
　　San Antonio TX 78259
　　210 828-8484

(P-14811)
TESORO REFINING & MKTG CO LLC
Also Called: Am/PM Mini Market
3907 E Telegraph Rd, Piru (93040)
PHONE..........................805 521-0615
Charipha Eragoda, *General Mgr*
EMP: 78 **Publicly Held**
SIC: **5172** Petroleum products
HQ: Tesoro Refining & Marketing Company Llc
　　19100 Ridgewood Pkwy
　　San Antonio TX 78259
　　210 828-8484

(P-14812)
TIODIZE CO INC
15701 Industry Ln, Huntington Beach (92649-1569)
PHONE..........................714 898-4377
Thomas Adams, *President*
Patty Enna, *Controller*
EMP: 38
SALES (corp-wide): 9.1MM **Privately Held**
WEB: www.tiodize.com
SIC: **5172** 3471 Lubricating oils & greases; anodizing (plating) of metals or formed products
PA: Tiodize Co., Inc.
　　5858 Engineer Dr
　　Huntington Beach CA 92649
　　714 898-4377

(P-14813)
TOMLIN SCIENTIFIC INC
6780 8th St, Buena Park (90620-1097)
PHONE..........................714 523-7971
Ryan J Willey, *CEO*
Tom Willey, *Vice Pres*
▲ EMP: 14 EST: 1991
SQ FT: 6,000
SALES (est): 20.8MM **Privately Held**
WEB: www.tomlinscientific.com
SIC: **5172** 2992 Lubricating oils & greases; lubricating oils & greases

(P-14814)

TOTAL PETROLEUM SERVICES INC

7071 Warner Ave Ste F-397, Huntington Beach (92647-5495)
PHONE....................714 907-0117
Josh Ritter, *Administration*
EMP: 65
SALES (corp-wide): 19.9MM **Privately Held**
SIC: 5172 Petroleum products
PA: Total Petroleum Services Inc.
1623 N Odonnell Way Ste B
Orange CA 92867
714 907-0117

(P-14815)

TOWER ENERGY GROUP (PA)

1983 W 190th St Ste 100, Torrance (90504-6240)
PHONE....................310 538-8000
John Rogers, *Principal*
Twanna Rogers, *Vice Pres*
Denise Kyles, *Manager*
Adam Zolezzi, *Clerk*
EMP: 132 EST: 1989
SQ FT: 22,702
SALES (est): 124MM **Privately Held**
WEB: www.towerenergy.com
SIC: 5172 Gasoline

(P-14816)

WHOLESALE FUELS INC

2200 E Brundage Ln, Bakersfield (93307-3066)
P.O. Box 82277 (93380-2277)
PHONE....................661 327-4900
Charles McCan, *Officer*
Brian Bucassa, *CFO*
Tom Jamieson, *CFO*
EMP: 63 EST: 1982
SQ FT: 5,000
SALES: 69.9MM **Privately Held**
WEB: www.wholesalefuels.com
SIC: 5172 Gasoline

5181 Beer & Ale Wholesale

(P-14817)

ACE BEVERAGE CO

550 S Mission Rd, Los Angeles (90033-4234)
P.O. Box 33256 (90033-0256)
PHONE....................323 266-6238
Dan Holland, *Principal*
Beatrez Quemada, *Manager*
EMP: 138
SALES (corp-wide): 446.1MM **Privately Held**
SIC: 5181 Beer & other fermented malt liquors
HQ: Ace Beverage Co.
401 S Anderson St
Los Angeles CA 90033
323 264-6001

(P-14818)

ADVANCE BEVERAGE CO INC

5200 District Blvd, Bakersfield (93313-2330)
P.O. Box 9517 (93389-9517)
PHONE....................661 833-3783
William K Lazzerini Sr, *Ch of Bd*
William K Lazzerini Jr, *President*
Anthony Lazzerini, *Vice Pres*
Darrell Grace, *Division Mgr*
Terrie Brewer, *Human Res Mgr*
◆ EMP: 90 EST: 1952
SQ FT: 93,000
SALES (est): 41.5MM **Privately Held**
WEB: www.advancebeverage.com
SIC: 5181 5182 Beer & other fermented malt liquors; wine

(P-14819)

ALLIED COMPANY HOLDINGS INC (PA)

Also Called: Best-Way Distributing Co
13235 Golden State Rd, Sylmar (91342-1129)
PHONE....................818 493-6400
Kevin Williams, *CEO*
Erin S Gabler, *CFO*
William L Larson, *Vice Pres*

Earl J Whitehead, *Admin Sec*
Terry Parco, *Human Resources*
◆ EMP: 385 EST: 1953
SQ FT: 240,000
SALES (est): 48.4MM **Privately Held**
SIC: 5181 Beer & other fermented malt liquors

(P-14820)

ANHEUSER-BUSCH LLC

18952 Macarthur Blvd, Irvine (92612-1432)
PHONE....................949 263-9270
EMP: 111
SALES (corp-wide): 1.9B **Privately Held**
SIC: 5181 Sales Office
HQ: Anheuser-Busch, Llc
1 Busch Pl
Saint Louis MO 63118
314 632-6777

(P-14821)

BASSO DISTRIBUTING COINC

2505 Pleasant Valley Rd, Camarillo (93012-8505)
P.O. Box 1019 (93011-1019)
PHONE....................805 656-1946
James L Basso, *President*
Steve Basso, *Vice Pres*
▲ EMP: 65 EST: 1940
SQ FT: 68,000
SALES (est): 9.5MM **Privately Held**
WEB: www.bassodist.com
SIC: 5181 5812 5182 Beer & other fermented malt liquors; soda fountain; wine

(P-14822)

BEAUCHAMP DISTRIBUTING COMPANY

1911 S Santa Fe Ave, Compton (90221-5306)
PHONE....................310 639-5320
Patrick L Beauchamp, *President*
Peter J Gumpert, *CFO*
Mary S Beauchamp, *Corp Secy*
Stacee L Beauchamp, *Vice Pres*
David Schreiber, *Sales Staff*
▲ EMP: 100 EST: 1971
SQ FT: 100,000
SALES (est): 55.2MM **Privately Held**
WEB: www.beauchampdist.com
SIC: 5181 5149 Beer & other fermented malt liquors; groceries & related products

(P-14823)

CENTRAL COAST DISTRIBUTING LLC

815 S Blosser Rd, Santa Maria (93458-4915)
PHONE....................805 922-2108
Michael Larrabee Jr,
Gil Fierros, *Sales Mgr*
▲ EMP: 90 EST: 2001
SQ FT: 51,651
SALES (est): 26.7MM **Privately Held**
WEB: www.greatbeer.us
SIC: 5181 Beer & other fermented malt liquors

(P-14824)

CLASSIC DISTRG & BEV GROUP INC

120 Puente Ave, City of Industry (91746-2301)
PHONE....................626 934-3700
Carlos Joseph Sanchez, *President*
John Thomas, *CFO*
Michael Blumfield, *Vice Pres*
Dan Chilson, *Opers Staff*
Mike Gutierrez, *Sales Staff*
▲ EMP: 261 EST: 1978
SQ FT: 102,000
SALES (est): 69.6MM **Privately Held**
WEB: www.cdbginc.com
SIC: 5181 Beer & other fermented malt liquors

(P-14825)

GATE CITY BEVERAGE DISTRS (PA)

2505 Steele Rd, San Bernardino (92408-3913)
PHONE....................909 799-0281
Leona Aronoff, *President*
Barry Aronoff, *CFO*
▲ EMP: 294 EST: 1940

SQ FT: 280,000
SALES (est): 29.5MM **Privately Held**
WEB: www.gatecitybeverage.com
SIC: 5181 5149 5145 Beer & other fermented malt liquors; soft drinks; mineral or spring water bottling; confectionery

(P-14826)

HARALAMBOS BEVERAGE CO

26717 Palmetto Ave, Redlands (92374-1513)
PHONE....................562 347-4300
H T Haralambos, *CEO*
Anthony Haralambos, *President*
Thomas Haralambos, *Vice Pres*
Sally Haralambos, *Admin Sec*
Sophia Kokoris, *Credit Mgr*
▲ EMP: 300 EST: 1933
SALES (est): 59MM **Privately Held**
WEB: www.haralambos.com
SIC: 5181 5149 Beer & other fermented malt liquors; beverages, except coffee & tea

(P-14827)

HARBOR DISTRIBUTING LLC (HQ)

Also Called: Golden Brands
5901 Bolsa Ave, Huntington Beach (92647-2053)
PHONE....................714 933-2400
David K Reyes,
Tom Cressman, *Sales Staff*
Tim McGuire,
Chris Reyes,
Jude Reyes,
▲ EMP: 200 EST: 1989
SQ FT: 150,000
SALES (est): 634.6MM **Privately Held**
WEB: www.harbordistributingllc.com
SIC: 5181 Beer & other fermented malt liquors

(P-14828)

HARBOR DISTRIBUTING LLC

Also Called: Harbor Distributing Co
16407 S Main St, Gardena (90248-2823)
PHONE....................310 538-5483
David Reyes, *Branch Mgr*
Tom Cressman, *Sales Staff*
EMP: 70 **Privately Held**
WEB: www.harbordistributingllc.com
SIC: 5181 Beer & other fermented malt liquors
HQ: Harbor Distributing, Llc
5901 Bolsa Ave
Huntington Beach CA 92647
714 933-2400

(P-14829)

JORDANOS INC (PA)

Also Called: Jordano's Food Service
550 S Patterson Ave, Santa Barbara (93111-2498)
P.O. Box 6803 (93160-6803)
PHONE....................805 964-0611
Peter Jordano, *CEO*
Michael F Sieckowski, *CFO*
Jeffrey S Jordano, *Exec VP*
Jim Scoville, *Sales Executive*
▲ EMP: 250
SQ FT: 80,000
SALES (est): 315.6MM **Privately Held**
WEB: www.jordanos.com
SIC: 5181 5182 5149 5141 Beer & other fermented malt liquors; wine; soft drinks; groceries, general line; packaged frozen goods; fresh fruits & vegetables

(P-14830)

LE VECKE CORPORATION (PA)

Also Called: Le Vecke Group
10810 Inland Ave, Jurupa Valley (91752-3235)
PHONE....................951 681-8600
Neil Levecke, *President*
Jimmy Sarenana, *Opers Staff*
Martin Rezac, *Production*
Michael Karich, *Natl Sales Mgr*
Jennifer Leyva, *Marketing Mgr*
◆ EMP: 62 EST: 1949
SALES (est): 72.2MM **Privately Held**
WEB: www.levecke.com
SIC: 5181 Beer & other fermented malt liquors

(P-14831)

MISSION BEVERAGE CO (HQ)

550 S Mission Rd, Los Angeles (90033-4256)
P.O. Box 33256 (90033-0256)
PHONE....................323 266-6238
John E Anderson Sr, *Ch of Bd*
Don Holland, *President*
Therese D Curtis, *Corp Secy*
◆ EMP: 210 EST: 1952
SALES (est): 41.9MM
SALES (corp-wide): 446.1MM **Privately Held**
WEB: www.misbev.com
SIC: 5181 5149 Beer & other fermented malt liquors; soft drinks
PA: Topa Equities, Ltd.
1800 Avenue Of The Stars # 1400
Los Angeles CA 90067
310 203-9199

(P-14832)

PACIFIC BEVERAGE CO

900 Fairway Dr, Santa Maria (93455-1535)
P.O. Box 5834 (93456-5834)
PHONE....................805 922-7901
Jerry English, *Manager*
EMP: 52
SALES (corp-wide): 315.6MM **Privately Held**
WEB: www.jordanos.com
SIC: 5181 Beer & other fermented malt liquors
HQ: Pacific Beverage Co.
550 S Patterson Ave
Santa Barbara CA 93111
805 964-0611

(P-14833)

PACIFIC BEVERAGE CO

Also Called: Pacific Beverage Company
401 Del Norte Blvd, Oxnard (93030-7256)
P.O. Box 392 (93032-0392)
PHONE....................805 278-5600
Burt Von Bieberstein, *Manager*
EMP: 52
SALES (corp-wide): 315.6MM **Privately Held**
WEB: www.jordanos.com
SIC: 5181 Beer & other fermented malt liquors
HQ: Pacific Beverage Co.
550 S Patterson Ave
Santa Barbara CA 93111
805 964-0611

(P-14834)

PACIFIC BEVERAGE CO

22255 El Camino Real, Santa Margarita (93453-8678)
P.O. Box 850 (93453-0850)
PHONE....................805 438-5766
Bob Cochran, *Manager*
EMP: 52
SALES (corp-wide): 315.6MM **Privately Held**
WEB: www.jordanos.com
SIC: 5181 Beer & other fermented malt liquors
HQ: Pacific Beverage Co.
550 S Patterson Ave
Santa Barbara CA 93111
805 964-0611

(P-14835)

SEQUOIA BEVERAGE COMPANY LP

2122 N Plaza Dr, Visalia (93291-9358)
P.O. Box 5025 (93278-5025)
PHONE....................559 651-2444
Dan Bueno, *Partner*
Rose Bueno, *Partner*
Joan Carpenter, *Partner*
Bill McAlister, *Administration*
Laurie Zuniga, *Administration*
EMP: 101 EST: 1939
SQ FT: 100,000
SALES (est): 22MM **Privately Held**
WEB: www.sequoiabeverage.com
SIC: 5181 Beer & other fermented malt liquors

P
R
O
D
U
C
T
S

&

S
V
C
S

(P-14836)
STRAUB DISTRIBUTING CO LTD (PA)
4633 E La Palma Ave, Anaheim (92807-1909)
PHONE...............714 779-4000
Michael L Cooper, *General Ptnr*
Robert K Adams, *Partner*
Don Beightol, *Partner*
Gil Barajas, *Accounting Mgr*
Kim Lambert, *Human Res Mgr*
▲ EMP: 150 EST: 1948
SQ FT: 32,000
SALES (est): 64MM **Privately Held**
WEB: www.straubdistributing.com
SIC: 5181 Beer & other fermented malt liquors

(P-14837)
W A THOMPSON INC (PA)
5101 District Blvd, Bakersfield (93313-2329)
P.O. Box 40310 (93384-0310)
PHONE...............661 832-5101
Mary G Trichell, *President*
Robert N Lee, *Sales Mgr*
▲ EMP: 60 EST: 1936
SQ FT: 68,000
SALES (est): 23MM **Privately Held**
SIC: 5181 Beer & other fermented malt liquors

5182 Wine & Distilled Alcoholic Beverages Wholesale

(P-14838)
BEN MYERSON CANDY CO INC (PA)
Also Called: Wine Warehouse
6550 E Washington Blvd, Commerce (90040-1822)
P.O. Box 910900, Los Angeles (90091-0900)
PHONE...............800 331-2829
James P Myerson, *President*
Linda Perez, *President*
James Myerson, *Corp Secy*
Kelly Bruckart, *Officer*
Scott Rankin, *Exec VP*
◆ EMP: 350 EST: 1966
SQ FT: 135,000
SALES (est): 363.7MM **Privately Held**
WEB: www.winewarehouse.com
SIC: 5182 5023 Wine; glassware

(P-14839)
CUSHMAN WINERY CORPORATION
Also Called: Zaca Mesa Winery
6905 Foxen Canyon Rd, Los Olivos (93441-4530)
P.O. Box 899 (93441-0899)
PHONE...............805 688-9339
Brook Williams, *President*
Susan English, *CFO*
Taylor Powell, *Marketing Staff*
▲ EMP: 29 EST: 1972
SALES (est): 11.9MM **Privately Held**
SIC: 5182 2084 0172 Wine; wines; grapes

(P-14840)
DRINKS HOLDINGS INC (PA)
10900 Wilshire Blvd # 1600, Los Angeles (90024-6538)
PHONE...............310 441-8400
Zac Brandenberg, *President*
Kelly Martin, *Officer*
Hans Holmer, *Vice Pres*
Tha Leang, *Sr Software Eng*
Barry Collier, *Research*
EMP: 86 EST: 2013
SALES (est): 22.2MM **Privately Held**
WEB: www.drinks.com
SIC: 5182 Wine

(P-14841)
FARM STREET DESIGNS INC
Also Called: Van's Gifts
2520 Mira Mar Ave, Long Beach (90815-1758)
PHONE...............562 985-0026
Howard Colover, *Ch of Bd*
Reva Colover, *President*
▲ EMP: 34 EST: 1984
SQ FT: 39,000
SALES (est): 10MM **Privately Held**
SIC: 5182 2033 2035 5023 Wine; tomato sauce: packaged in cans, jars, etc.; dressings, salad: raw & cooked (except dry mixes); kitchenware; kitchen & bathroom remodeling; food gift baskets

(P-14842)
FLYING EMBERS BREWING CO
3200 Golf Course Dr, Ventura (93003-7696)
PHONE...............781 856-3648
Cameron Block, *Principal*
Max Steinberg, *Sales Staff*
EMP: 55 EST: 2018
SALES (est): 5MM **Privately Held**
SIC: 5813 5182 Bars & lounges; wine & distilled beverages

(P-14843)
GUARACHI WINE PARTNERS INC
Also Called: Parker Station
22837 Ventura Blvd # 300, Woodland Hills (91364-1224)
PHONE...............818 225-5100
Alejandro Guarachi, *CEO*
Daniel Lyons, *President*
Marilyn Vogel, *Vice Pres*
Jim Demartino, *Regional Mgr*
James Eder, *Area Mgr*
▲ EMP: 80 EST: 1988
SQ FT: 5,000
SALES (est): 31.7MM **Privately Held**
WEB: www.guarachiwinepartners.com
SIC: 5182 Wine

(P-14844)
LUCAS & LEWELLEN VINEYARDS INC (PA)
Also Called: Lucas Lwllen Vnyrds Tasting Rm
1645 Copenhagen Dr, Solvang (93463-3742)
P.O. Box 648, Los Alamos (93440-0648)
PHONE...............805 686-9336
Royce R Lewellen, *President*
Louis A Lucas, *Principal*
Matt Brown, *Regl Sales Mgr*
Jill Armijo,
Megan McGrath Gates, *Director*
EMP: 27 EST: 1996
SALES (est): 10MM **Privately Held**
WEB: www.llwine.com
SIC: 5182 2084 Wine; wines

(P-14845)
PACIFIC EDGE MKTG GROUP INC (PA)
Also Called: Pacific Edge Wine and Spirits
5155 Clareton Dr Ste 100, Agoura Hills (91301-6308)
PHONE...............818 879-0946
Joel Beth, *CEO*
Richard Trachtenberg, *President*
Bill Haskin, *Sales Staff*
Ken Dayton, *Real Est Agnt*
◆ EMP: 51 EST: 2002
SQ FT: 72,000
SALES (est): 23.2MM **Privately Held**
WEB: www.pacificedgesales.com
SIC: 5182 Liquor

(P-14846)
SOUTHERN GLZERS WINE SPRITS WA
Also Called: Southern Glazer's of CA
17101 Valley View Ave, Cerritos (90703-2413)
PHONE...............562 926-2000
Wayne Chaplin, *CEO*
Joe Fortson, *Area Mgr*
Dane Meza, *Area Mgr*
Tony Miller, *Branch Mgr*
Courtney Sanders, *Office Mgr*
EMP: 500

SALES (corp-wide): 7.2B **Privately Held**
WEB: www.southernglazers.com
SIC: 5182 5181 Wine; liquor; beer & ale
PA: Southern Glazer's Wine And Spirits, Llc
2400 Sw 145th Ave Ste 200
Miramar FL 33027
866 375-5555

(P-14847)
YOUNGS HOLDINGS INC (PA)
15 Enterprise Ste 100, Aliso Viejo (92656-2654)
PHONE...............714 368-4615
Chris Underwood, *CEO*
Vernon Underwood Jr, *Ch of Bd*
Melody Badgley, *Vice Pres*
John Barton, *Vice Pres*
Scott Blackburn, *Vice Pres*
EMP: 100 EST: 1973
SALES (est): 1.3B **Privately Held**
WEB: www.rndc-usa.com
SIC: 5182 Wine

(P-14848)
YOUNGS MARKET COMPANY LLC (HQ)
14402 Franklin Ave, Tustin (92780-7013)
PHONE...............800 317-6150
Chris Underwood, *CEO*
Dennis Hamann, *CFO*
Kevin Manion, *CFO*
Vern Underwood, *Chairman*
Brian O'Neill, *Exec VP*
◆ EMP: 350 EST: 1888
SQ FT: 250,000
SALES (est): 1B
SALES (corp-wide): 1.3B **Privately Held**
WEB: www.rndc-usa.com
SIC: 5182 Wine
PA: Young's Holdings, Inc.
15 Enterprise Ste 100
Aliso Viejo CA 92656
714 368-4615

(P-14849)
YOUNGS MARKET COMPANY LLC
Also Called: Wine Dept
500 S Central Ave, Los Angeles (90013-1715)
PHONE...............213 629-3929
Mark Sneed, *Branch Mgr*
Mark Poynter, *Officer*
Hugh Duncan, *Exec VP*
Christa Wittmier, *Senior VP*
Nick Claitman, *Vice Pres*
EMP: 70
SALES (corp-wide): 1.3B **Privately Held**
WEB: www.rndc-usa.com
SIC: 5182 Wine
HQ: Young's Market Company, Llc
14402 Franklin Ave
Tustin CA 92780
800 317-6150

(P-14850)
YOUNGS MARKET COMPANY LLC
6711 Bickmore Ave, Chino (91708-9103)
PHONE...............909 393-4540
Terrie Young, *Branch Mgr*
EMP: 70
SALES (corp-wide): 1.3B **Privately Held**
WEB: www.rndc-usa.com
SIC: 5182 Wine
HQ: Young's Market Company, Llc
14402 Franklin Ave
Tustin CA 92780
800 317-6150

5191 Farm Splys Wholesale

(P-14851)
ACX INTERMODAL INC
920 E Pacific Coast Hwy, Wilmington (90744-2725)
PHONE...............310 241-6229
John Gombos, *President*
▼ EMP: 125 EST: 1983
SALES (est): 9.3MM **Privately Held**
WEB: www.acxintermodal.com
SIC: 5191 Animal feeds

HQ: Al Dahra Acx, Inc.
920 E Pacific Coast Hwy
Wilmington CA 90744

(P-14852)
AG RX (PA)
751 S Rose Ave, Oxnard (93030-5146)
P.O. Box 2008 (93034-2008)
PHONE...............805 487-0696
Ken Burdullis, *President*
Troy Schlundt, *Sales Dir*
Kirk Ellis, *Sales Staff*
Susan Macdonald, *Consultant*
EMP: 92 EST: 1993
SQ FT: 45,000
SALES (est): 51.8MM **Privately Held**
WEB: www.agrx.com
SIC: 5191 Fertilizer & fertilizer materials

(P-14853)
ANDERSON HAY & GRAIN CO INC
915 E Colon St, Wilmington (90744-2101)
PHONE...............509 925-9818
EMP: 78
SALES (corp-wide): 110MM **Privately Held**
WEB: www.anderson-hay.com
SIC: 5191 Feed
PA: Anderson Hay & Grain Co., Inc.
910 Anderson Rd
Ellensburg WA 98926
509 925-9818

(P-14854)
BORDER VALLEY TRADING LTD
604 Mead Rd, Brawley (92227-9748)
P.O. Box 62 (92227-0062)
PHONE...............760 344-6700
EMP: 56 **Privately Held**
SIC: 5191 Whol Farm Supplies
PA: Border Valley Trading, Ltd.
14503 W Harding Rd
Turlock CA 92227

(P-14855)
BORDER VALLEY TRADING LTD
604 Mead Rd, Brawley (92227-9748)
P.O. Box 62 (92227-0062)
PHONE...............760 344-6700
Greg Braun, *President*
Paul Cameron, *Corp Secy*
Robert Presley, *Vice Pres*
Joe Favela, *Manager*
◆ EMP: 68 EST: 1990
SQ FT: 1,200
SALES (est): 13.4MM **Privately Held**
WEB: www.bordervalley.com
SIC: 5191 Hay

(P-14856)
BROMA APPLICATORS LLC
322 W J St, Brawley (92227-3116)
PHONE...............760 351-0101
Fred P Mamer,
Cristi Mamer,
EMP: 20 EST: 1997
SQ FT: 1,200
SALES (est): 5MM **Privately Held**
SIC: 5191 2879 Pesticides; fungicides, herbicides

(P-14857)
BUTTONWILLOW WAREHOUSE CO INC (HQ)
3430 Unicorn Rd, Bakersfield (93308-6829)
P.O. Box 98, Buttonwillow (93206-0098)
PHONE...............661 695-6500
Donald Houchin, *President*
Brad Crowder, *COO*
Scott Stanley, *CFO*
Wallace Houchin, *Vice Pres*
Rob Poznoff, *Opers Mgr*
EMP: 69 EST: 1948
SALES: 111.3MM
SALES (corp-wide): 113.4MM **Privately Held**
WEB: www.techag.com
SIC: 5191 Fertilizer & fertilizer materials
PA: Tech Agricultural, Inc.
125 Front St
Buttonwillow CA 93206
661 764-5234

(P-14858)
EXCEL GARDEN PRODUCTS (HQ)
Also Called: Central Garden Distribution
10708 Norwalk Blvd, Santa Fe Springs (90670-3824)
PHONE..................................562 567-2000
Charlie Naush, *Principal*
Brett Kresin, *General Mgr*
China Young, *Admin Asst*
▲ EMP: 443 EST: 2007
SALES (est): 76MM
SALES (corp-wide): 2.7B **Publicly Held**
WEB: www.centralgarden.com
SIC: 5191 Garden supplies
PA: Central Garden & Pet Company
1340 Treat Blvd Ste 600
Walnut Creek CA 94597
925 948-4000

(P-14859)
FOSTER POULTRY FARMS
4107 Ave 360, Traver (93673)
PHONE..................................559 457-6509
Larry Ficken, *Plant Mgr*
EMP: 232
SALES (corp-wide): 1.2B **Privately Held**
WEB: www.fosterfarms.com
SIC: 5191 Farm supplies
PA: Foster Poultry Farms
1000 Davis St
Livingston CA 95334
209 394-7901

(P-14860)
H & M NURSERY SUPPLY CORP
Also Called: Arthur Enterprises
5181 Argosy Ave, Huntington Beach (92649-1058)
PHONE..................................714 898-1311
William Helzer, *President*
Gail Helzer, *Corp Secy*
EMP: 13 EST: 1962
SQ FT: 25,000
SALES (est): 1.1MM **Privately Held**
WEB: www.harrisind.com
SIC: 5191 1542 5162 0811 Greenhouse equipment & supplies; greenhouse construction; plastics film; tree farm; products of purchased glass

(P-14861)
HEMME HAY & FEED INC
Also Called: Hemme Hay Feed
43719 Sierra Hwy, Lancaster (93534-5032)
PHONE..................................661 942-7880
John E Hemme, *President*
John W Hemme, *Vice Pres*
EMP: 54 EST: 1965
SQ FT: 32,000
SALES (est): 3.7MM **Privately Held**
WEB: www.hemme-hay-feed-inc.sbcontract.com
SIC: 5191 Feed; hay

(P-14862)
L & L NURSERY SUPPLY INC (DH)
Also Called: Unigro
2552 Shenandoah Way, San Bernardino (92407-1845)
PHONE..................................909 591-0461
Lloyd Swindell, *Ch of Bd*
Tom Medhurst, *President*
Harvey Luth, *Exec VP*
Hillary Welton, *Program Mgr*
Orlando Neri, *CIO*
▲ EMP: 150 EST: 1953
SQ FT: 107,000
SALES (est): 111.1MM
SALES (corp-wide): 3.6MM **Privately Held**
WEB: www.llsupply.net
SIC: 5191 2875 2449 5193 Insecticides; fertilizer & fertilizer materials; soil, potting & planting; potting soil, mixed; wood containers; flowers & florists' supplies
HQ: Bfg Supply Co., Llc
14500 Kinsman Rd
Burton OH 44021
800 883-0234

(P-14863)
L J T FLOWERS INC (PA)
Also Called: Skyline Flwr Growers Shippers
2425 Bonita School Rd, Nipomo (93444-9728)
P.O. Box 120 (93444-0120)
PHONE..................................877 929-2476
Joe Goldberg, *President*
Tom Goldberg, *Vice Pres*
Carma Pollard, *Controller*
Katrina Carrasco, *Sales Staff*
EMP: 104 EST: 1954
SQ FT: 8,000
SALES (est): 14.7MM **Privately Held**
WEB: www.skylineflowers.com
SIC: 5191 0181 Flower & field bulbs; flowers grown in field nurseries

(P-14864)
LEACH GRAIN & MILLING CO INC
8131 Pivot St, Downey (90241-4853)
PHONE..................................562 869-4451
Willis R Leach Sr, *President*
Bruce Leach, *Shareholder*
Willis R Leach Jr, *Corp Secy*
Roy Leach, *Vice Pres*
Jeff Leach, *Plant Mgr*
EMP: 26 EST: 1934
SQ FT: 20,000
SALES (est): 7.8MM **Privately Held**
WEB: www.leachgrain.com
SIC: 5191 2047 2048 Farm supplies; dog & cat food; bird food, prepared

(P-14865)
NEWCO DISTRIBUTORS INC
9060 Rochester Ave, Rancho Cucamonga (91730-5522)
P.O. Box 1449 (91729-1449)
PHONE..................................909 291-2240
Randall Barb, *CEO*
Rob Chell, *Officer*
Scott O'brien, *Vice Pres*
Jodi Barb, *Technology*
Carlos Elgueta, *Technology*
EMP: 60 EST: 1959
SQ FT: 60,000
SALES (est): 43.1MM **Privately Held**
WEB: www.newcopet.com
SIC: 5191 5149 Animal feeds; pet foods

(P-14866)
PLANTERS HAY INC
1295 E St 78, Brawley (92227-2119)
PHONE..................................760 344-0620
Stephen Benson, *CEO*
Marivel Melesio, *Bookkeeper*
◆ EMP: 52 EST: 2010
SALES (est): 9.4MM **Privately Held**
SIC: 5191 7389 Hay; styling of fashions, apparel, furniture, textiles, etc.

(P-14867)
RENTOKIL NORTH AMERICA INC
Also Called: Target Specialty Products
15415 Marquardt Ave, Santa Fe Springs (90670-5711)
PHONE..................................562 802-2238
Bonnie Fallon, *Manager*
Todd McMackin, *Executive*
Andrew Wade, *Executive*
Doug Bennett, *Sales Staff*
Eric Carlson, *Sales Staff*
EMP: 100
SALES (corp-wide): 3.7B **Privately Held**
SIC: 5191 Chemicals, agricultural
HQ: Rentokil North America, Inc.
1125 Berkshire Blvd # 15
Wyomissing PA 19610
610 372-9700

(P-14868)
SEEDS OF CHANGE INC
Also Called: Sustainable Agriculture
2555 S Dominguez Hills Dr, Rancho Dominguez (90220-6402)
P.O. Box 4908 (90224-4908)
PHONE..................................310 764-7700
Will Righeimer, *CEO*
◆ EMP: 120 EST: 1997
SQ FT: 25,411
SALES (est): 47MM
SALES (corp-wide): 42.8B **Privately Held**
WEB: www.seedsofchange.com
SIC: 5191 0723 Seeds: field, garden & flower; crop preparation services for market
HQ: Mars Food Us, Llc
2001 E Cashdan St Ste 201
Rancho Dominguez CA 90220
310 933-0670

(P-14869)
SEMINIS VEGETABLE SEEDS INC (DH)
2700 Camino Del Sol, Oxnard (93030-7967)
PHONE..................................855 733-3834
Michael J Frank, *CEO*
Kerry Preete, *President*
◆ EMP: 600 EST: 1962
SQ FT: 370,000
SALES (est): 463.7MM
SALES (corp-wide): 48.9B **Privately Held**
WEB: www.vegetables.bayer.com
SIC: 5191 0723 Seeds: field, garden & flower; crop preparation services for market
HQ: Monsanto Company
800 N Lindbergh Blvd
Saint Louis MO 63167
314 694-1000

5192 Books, Periodicals & Newspapers Wholesale

(P-14870)
DEVORSS & CO
Also Called: Devorss Publications
553 Constitution Ave, Camarillo (93012-8510)
PHONE..................................805 322-9010
Gary R Peattie, *President*
Arthur Vergara, *Corp Secy*
Melinda Grubbauer, *Vice Pres*
Debbie Krovitz, *Marketing Staff*
Donald Peattie, *Director*
▲ EMP: 14 EST: 1929
SQ FT: 35,000
SALES (est): 5MM **Privately Held**
WEB: www.devorss.com
SIC: 5192 2731 Books; books: publishing only

(P-14871)
EL AVISO MAGAZINE
4850 Gage Ave, Bell (90201-1409)
P.O. Box 3360 (90202-3360)
PHONE..................................323 586-9199
Jose Zepeda, *CEO*
Martha Ramirez, *Office Admin*
Yazmin Gonzalez, *Opers Mgr*
Mynor Duque, *Advt Staff*
Miguel Gabrielli, *Advt Staff*
EMP: 36 EST: 1988
SALES (est): 3.4MM **Privately Held**
WEB: www.elaviso.com
SIC: 5192 2721 Magazines; magazines: publishing & printing

(P-14872)
EMMIS PUBLISHING CORPORATION
Also Called: Los Angeles Magazine
5900 Wilshire Blvd # 1000, Los Angeles (90036-5024)
PHONE..................................323 801-0100
Jean Greene, *Advt Staff*
Kristy Day, *Sales Staff*
Brian Baker, *Director*
Rose Demaria, *Director*
Bonnie Magid, *Manager*
EMP: 55
SALES (corp-wide): 39.7MM **Privately Held**
WEB: www.emmis.com
SIC: 5192 Magazines
HQ: Emmis Publishing Corporation
40 Monument Cir Ste 700
Indianapolis IN 46204
317 266-0100

(P-14873)
GREAT ATLANTIC NEWS LLC
Also Called: News Group, The
1575 N Main St, Orange (92867-3439)
PHONE..................................770 863-9000
John Seebach, *Branch Mgr*
Jeff Bean, *Exec VP*
Monte Ahlemeyer, *Vice Pres*
Jim Deighan, *Vice Pres*
Colin Foley, *Vice Pres*
EMP: 109
SALES (corp-wide): 19B **Privately Held**
SIC: 5192 5994 Periodicals; magazine stand
HQ: Great Atlantic News L.L.C.
1962 Highway 160 W # 102
Fort Mill SC 29708

(P-14874)
HITS MAGAZINE INC (PA)
Also Called: Music Market Update
6906 Hollywood Blvd Fl 2, Los Angeles (90028-6104)
PHONE..................................323 946-7600
Dennis Lavinthal, *President*
Lenny Beer, *Principal*
Robin Gerber, *Assoc Editor*
Tim Carney, *Director*
EMP: 54 EST: 1986
SALES (est): 10.3MM **Privately Held**
WEB: www.hitsdailydouble.com
SIC: 5192 Magazines

(P-14875)
MADER NEWS INC
913 Ruberta Ave, Glendale (91201-2346)
PHONE..................................818 551-5000
Avan Mader, *President*
Steven Chia, *Executive*
Rafael Sotomayor, *Opers Mgr*
EMP: 100 EST: 1972
SQ FT: 2,400
SALES (est): 19MM **Privately Held**
WEB: www.madernews.com
SIC: 5192 Newspapers

5193 Flowers, Nursery Stock & Florists' Splys Wholesale

(P-14876)
B & B NURSERIES INC
Also Called: Landscape Center
9505 Cleveland Ave, Riverside (92503-6241)
P.O. Box 7399 (92513-7399)
PHONE..................................951 352-8383
Mark Barrett, *CEO*
EMP: 109 EST: 1985
SALES (est): 13.1MM **Privately Held**
WEB: www.tlcnurseries.com
SIC: 5193 0781 Flowers & nursery stock; landscape counseling services

(P-14877)
BOUQS COMPANY
Also Called: Thebouqs.com
4094 Glencoe Ave, Marina Del Rey (90292-5608)
PHONE..................................888 320-2687
Alejandro Bethlen, *CEO*
John Tabis, *Ch of Bd*
Darcy Cozzetto, *COO*
JP Montfar, *COO*
Ryan Yocum, *Web Dvlpr*
EMP: 64 EST: 2012
SALES (est): 25.9MM **Privately Held**
WEB: www.bouqs.com
SIC: 5193 Flowers, fresh

(P-14878)
BRAND FLOWER FARMS INC (PA)
Also Called: Farmers W Flowers & Bouquets
5300 Foothill Rd, Carpinteria (93013-3017)
P.O. Box 600 (93014-0600)
PHONE..................................805 684-5531
Wilja Happ, *CEO*
Maximino Santillon, *President*
Tom Lemus, *COO*
Monica Preciado, *CFO*
Will Stewart, *Vice Pres*
▲ EMP: 194 EST: 1990

SQ FT: 500,000
SALES (est): 16.2MM **Privately Held**
WEB: www.farmerswest.com
SIC: 5193 Flowers, fresh

(P-14879)
COLOR SPOT NURSERIES INC
321 W Sepulveda Blvd, Carson
(90745-6313)
PHONE...................................310 549-7470
Fax: 310 549-7312
EMP: 98
SALES (corp-wide): 3.2B **Privately Held**
SIC: 5193 Whol Flowers/Florist Supplies
HQ: Color Spot Nurseries, Inc.
27368 Via
Temecula CA 92590

(P-14880)
COREY NURSERY CO INC (PA)
1650 Monte Vista Ave, Claremont
(91711-2999)
P.O. Box 609 (91711-0609)
PHONE...................................909 621-6886
Jeffrey E Corey, *CEO*
Brian Corey, *Shareholder*
Ken Corey, *Shareholder*
Gene Corey, *Ch of Bd*
Eugene K Corey, *President*
▲ EMP: 60 EST: 1978
SQ FT: 170,000
SALES (est): 24.7MM **Privately Held**
WEB: www.claremontchamber.org
SIC: 5193 Nursery stock

(P-14881)
COUNTRY FLORAL SUPPLY INC (PA)
Also Called: Country Furnishings
3802 Weatherly Cir, Westlake Village
(91361-3821)
PHONE...................................805 520-8026
Mark Reese, *President*
Debbie Reese, *Vice Pres*
▲ EMP: 80 EST: 1982
SQ FT: 60,000
SALES (est): 15.2MM **Privately Held**
SIC: 5193 5999 Artificial flowers; artificial
flowers

(P-14882)
DELTA FLORAL DISTRIBUTORS INC
6810 West Blvd, Los Angeles
(90043-4668)
PHONE...................................323 751-8116
Foti Defterios, *President*
Heidi Hansen, *Controller*
Colleen McGowan, *Sales Staff*
Joseph Nieves, *Clerk*
▲ EMP: 200 EST: 1984
SQ FT: 30,000
SALES (est): 23.1MM **Privately Held**
WEB: www.deltafloral.com
SIC: 5193 Flowers, fresh

(P-14883)
GALLUP & STRIBLING ORCHIDS LLC
Also Called: Gallup and Stribling Holdings
3450 Via Real, Carpinteria (93013-3047)
PHONE...................................805 684-1998
Alexander L Stribling, *CEO*
Steve Dodge, *Vice Pres*
Liz Noriega, *Office Mgr*
Michael E Pfau, *Admin Sec*
▲ EMP: 50 EST: 1956
SQ FT: 1,400,000 **Privately Held**
WEB: www.gallup-stribling.com
SIC: 5193 Flowers, fresh

(P-14884)
GREEN THUMB INTERNATIONAL INC
Also Called: Green Thumb Nurseries
23734 Newhall Ave, Newhall (91321-3125)
PHONE...................................661 259-1071
Bryan Payne, *Manager*
EMP: 108

SALES (corp-wide): 23.3MM **Privately Held**
WEB: www.greenthumb.com
SIC: 5261 5712 5193 0782 Nursery
stock, seeds & bulbs; outdoor & garden
furniture; nursery stock; sodding contractor
PA: Green Thumb International Inc
7105 Jordan Ave
Canoga Park CA 91303
818 340-6400

(P-14885)
GREEN THUMB INTERNATIONAL INC
21812 Sherman Way, Canoga Park
(91303-1940)
PHONE...................................818 340-6400
Del Berquist, *Principal*
EMP: 87
SALES (corp-wide): 23.3MM **Privately Held**
WEB: www.greenthumb.com
SIC: 5193 5261 0782 0181 Nursery
stock; nurseries & garden centers; lawn &
garden services; ornamental nursery
products
PA: Green Thumb International Inc
7105 Jordan Ave
Canoga Park CA 91303
818 340-6400

(P-14886)
GROLINK PLANT COMPANY INC (PA)
4107 W Gonzales Rd, Oxnard
(93036-7783)
P.O. Box 5506 (93031-5506)
PHONE...................................805 984-7958
Anthony Vollering, *CEO*
Harry Van Wingerden, *Shareholder*
Jerry Van Wingerden, *Corp Secy*
Art Gordijin, *Principal*
Ton Vallering, *Principal*
▲ EMP: 149 EST: 1985
SQ FT: 400,000
SALES (est): 17.8MM **Privately Held**
WEB: www.grolink.com
SIC: 5193 0181 Nursery stock; ornamental nursery products

(P-14887)
MAYESH WHOLESALE FLORIST INC (PA)
5401 W 104th St, Los Angeles
(90045-6011)
PHONE...................................310 342-0980
Patrick Dahlson, *CEO*
Cindie Boer, *COO*
Ben Henderson, *Branch Mgr*
Tracy Olmedo, *Personnel Assit*
Katherine Clifford, *Buyer*
▲ EMP: 50 EST: 1947
SQ FT: 20,000
SALES (est): 89MM **Privately Held**
WEB: www.mayesh.com
SIC: 5193 5992 Flowers, fresh; florists

(P-14888)
MELLANO & CO (PA)
Also Called: Mellano Enterprises
766 Wall St, Los Angeles (90014-2316)
P.O. Box 100, San Luis Rey (92068-0100)
PHONE...................................213 622-0796
John Mellano, *President*
Michael Matthew Mellano, *President*
Battista Castellano, *Corp Secy*
Michelle Castellano, *Vice Pres*
Bob Mellano, *Vice Pres*
EMP: 75 EST: 1975
SALES (est): 76.7MM **Privately Held**
WEB: www.mellano.com
SIC: 5193 Flowers, fresh

(P-14889)
NAKASE BROTHERS WHOLESALE NURS (PA)
9441 Krepp Dr, Huntington Beach
(92646-2799)
PHONE...................................949 855-4388
Shigeo Gary Nakase, *Principal*
Jun Turalba, *Executive Asst*
▲ EMP: 100 EST: 1965

SALES (est): 31.5MM **Privately Held**
WEB: www.nakasebros.com
SIC: 5193 Nursery stock

(P-14890)
NAKASE BROTHERS WHOLESALE NURS
20621 Lake Forest Dr, Lake Forest
(92630-7743)
PHONE...................................949 855-4388
Joann Shurlock, *Manager*
EMP: 180
SALES (corp-wide): 31.5MM **Privately Held**
WEB: www.nakasebros.com
SIC: 5193 Nursery stock
PA: Nakase Brothers Wholesale Nursery
9441 Krepp Dr
Huntington Beach CA 92646
949 855-4388

(P-14891)
NORMANS NURSERY INC (PA)
8665 Duarte Rd, San Gabriel (91775-1139)
PHONE...................................626 285-9795
Charles Norman, *President*
Caroline Norman, *Treasurer*
Andrew Dam, *Technology*
Michelle Brown, *Sales Staff*
Kevin Chesshir, *Sales Staff*
▼ EMP: 50 EST: 1949
SQ FT: 4,000
SALES (est): 95.8MM **Privately Held**
WEB: www.normansnursery.com
SIC: 5193 0181 Nursery stock; nursery
stock, growing of

(P-14892)
NORMANS NURSERY INC
5800 Via Real, Carpinteria (93013-2610)
PHONE...................................805 684-5442
EMP: 120
SALES (corp-wide): 95.8MM **Privately Held**
WEB: www.normansnursery.com
SIC: 5193 Nursery stock
PA: Norman's Nursery, Inc.
8665 Duarte Rd
San Gabriel CA 91775
626 285-9795

(P-14893)
NORMANS NURSERY INC
20500 Ramona Blvd, Baldwin Park (91706)
PHONE...................................626 285-9795
Ricardo Goodman, *Manager*
EMP: 120
SALES (corp-wide): 95.8MM **Privately Held**
WEB: www.normansnursery.com
SIC: 5193 Nursery stock
PA: Norman's Nursery, Inc.
8665 Duarte Rd
San Gabriel CA 91775
626 285-9795

(P-14894)
PLANTEL NURSERIES INC
2775 E Clark Ave, Santa Maria
(93455-5813)
PHONE...................................805 349-8952
EMP: 98
SALES (corp-wide): 19.3MM **Privately Held**
WEB: www.plantelnurseries.com
SIC: 5193 Nursery stock
PA: Plantel Nurseries Inc
2775 E Clark Ave
Santa Maria CA 93455
805 349-8952

(P-14895)
SUNSHINE FLORAL INC
4595 Foothill Rd, Carpinteria (93013-3096)
PHONE...................................805 684-1177
Henry Vanwingerden, *President*
Anthony Vollering, *Vice Pres*
▲ EMP: 70 EST: 1972
SALES (est): 5.1MM **Privately Held**
WEB: www.sunshinefloral.com
SIC: 5193 Flowers, fresh

(P-14896)
SUNSHINE FLORAL LLC
1070 S Rice Ave Ste 1, Oxnard
(93033-2110)
P.O. Box 728, Carpinteria (93014-0728)
PHONE...................................805 982-8822
Anthony Vollering, *Mng Member*
Adri Durieux, *Prdtn Mgr*
Betty Alvarez, *Sales Staff*
Henry Van Wingerden, *Mng Member*
Ton Vollering, *Mng Member*
▲ EMP: 60 EST: 1985
SQ FT: 10,000
SALES (est): 9.6MM **Privately Held**
WEB: www.sunshinefloral.com
SIC: 5193 Flowers, fresh

(P-14897)
VICTORIA NURSERY INC (PA)
Also Called: Milgro
1085 Victoria Ave, Oxnard (93030-4710)
P.O. Box 6069 (93031-6069)
PHONE...................................805 985-0855
Gary F Miller, *President*
▲ EMP: 99 EST: 1980
SALES (est): 10.8MM **Privately Held**
SIC: 5193 Flowers & florists' supplies

(P-14898)
VILLAGE NURSERIES WHL LLC (PA)
1589 N Main St, Orange (92867-3439)
PHONE...................................714 279-3100
David House, *Mng Member*
Rick Rehm, *CFO*
Terri Cook, *Vice Pres*
Brett Krey, *Sales Staff*
Rick Stiles, *Sales Staff*
EMP: 50 EST: 2001
SQ FT: 12,321
SALES (est): 61.2MM **Privately Held**
WEB: www.everde.com
SIC: 5193 Nursery stock

(P-14899)
VILLAGE NURSERIES WHL LLC
20099 Santa Rosa Mine Rd, Perris
(92570-7774)
PHONE...................................951 657-3940
Joseph Jensen, *Branch Mgr*
Jesse Cruz, *Sales Staff*
Julianna Martinez, *Sales Staff*
Luis Verdoza, *Supervisor*
EMP: 272
SALES (corp-wide): 61.2MM **Privately Held**
WEB: www.everde.com
SIC: 5193 Nursery stock
PA: Village Nurseries Wholesale, Llc
1589 N Main St
Orange CA 92867
714 279-3100

(P-14900)
WESTLAND FLRAL CARPINTERIA INC
1400 Cravens Ln, Carpinteria
(93013-3166)
P.O. Box 1323 (93014-1323)
PHONE...................................805 684-4011
Case Van Wingerden, *CEO*
EMP: 50 EST: 2013
SALES (est): 11.2MM **Privately Held**
WEB: www.westlandfloral.com
SIC: 5193 Flowers, fresh

(P-14901)
WESTLAND ORCHIDS INC
Also Called: Westland Flora
1400 Cravens Ln, Carpinteria
(93013-3166)
P.O. Box 1323 (93014-1323)
PHONE...................................805 684-1436
David Van Wingerden, *CEO*
Jerry Vanwingerden, *Vice Pres*
John Riddle, *CIO*
Ellie Ramirez, *Human Resources*
Patricia Henmi, *Sales Staff*
▲ EMP: 50 EST: 2013
SALES (est): 14.3MM **Privately Held**
WEB: www.westlandorchids.com
SIC: 5193 Flowers, fresh

5194 Tobacco & Tobacco Prdts Wholesale

(P-14902)
FLAWLESS VAPE WHL & DIST INC
1021 E Orangethorpe Ave, Anaheim (92801-1135)
PHONE...................714 406-2933
Jason Grace, *President*
EMP: 60 EST: 2015
SALES (est): 30MM **Privately Held**
WEB: www.flawlessvapeshop.com
SIC: 5194 Cigarettes

(P-14903)
KRETEK INTERNATIONAL INC (DH)
5449 Endeavour Ct, Moorpark (93021-1712)
PHONE...................805 531-8888
Hugh R Cassar, *CEO*
Sean Cassar, *COO*
Donald Gormley, *CFO*
Lynn K Cassar, *Corp Secy*
Heather Shaner, *Purch Agent*
◆ EMP: 90 EST: 1983
SQ FT: 80,000
SALES (est): 76.3MM **Privately Held**
WEB: www.kretek.com
SIC: 5194 Cigarettes; smoking tobacco; cigars

(P-14904)
LA EJUICE LLC (PA)
Also Called: Five Star Juice
22873 Lockness Ave, Torrance (90501-5103)
PHONE...................310 257-1198
Robert Hummer, *Mng Member*
Dan Cordei,
Gus Makridis,
Fili Moala,
Kansley Mallari, *Director*
EMP: 50 EST: 2014
SQ FT: 10,000
SALES (est): 19.4MM **Privately Held**
WEB: www.fivestarjuice.com
SIC: 5194 Smoking tobacco

5198 Paints, Varnishes & Splys Wholesale

(P-14905)
BERG LACQUER CO (PA)
Also Called: Pacific Coast Lacquer
3150 E Pico Blvd, Los Angeles (90023-3632)
PHONE...................323 261-8114
Sandra Berg, *President*
Robert O Berg, *Ch of Bd*
Donna Berg, *Treasurer*
▲ EMP: 65 EST: 1934
SQ FT: 85,000
SALES (est): 23.8MM **Privately Held**
WEB: www.ellispaint.com
SIC: 5198 2851 Paints; paints & paint additives

(P-14906)
SHILPARK PAINT CORPORATION (PA)
1640 S Vermont Ave, Los Angeles (90006-4522)
PHONE...................323 732-7093
Shil Kyoung Park, *CEO*
Mina Park, *Treasurer*
Jose Huaracha, *Sales Associate*
Andres Ruiz, *Sales Staff*
Corman Park, *Manager*
EMP: 50 EST: 1991
SALES (est): 27.6MM **Privately Held**
WEB: www.shilpark.com
SIC: 5198 5231 5013 Paints; paint & painting supplies; body repair or paint shop supplies, automotive

5199 Nondurable Goods, NEC Wholesale

(P-14907)
A B P INC
Also Called: Scb Distributors
15608 New Century Dr, Gardena (90248-2129)
PHONE...................310 532-9400
Aaron Silverman, *President*
▲ EMP: 15 EST: 1989
SQ FT: 12,000
SALES (est): 3.3MM **Privately Held**
WEB: www.scbdistributors.com
SIC: 5199 2731 5192 Foil, aluminum: household; book publishing; books

(P-14908)
AHI INVESTMENT INC (DH)
Also Called: Linzer Products
675 Glenoaks Blvd, San Fernando (91340-1471)
P.O. Box 310 (91341-0310)
PHONE...................818 979-0030
Hisatoshi Ohtsuka, *Principal*
Mark Saji, *Exec VP*
Yuko Waki, *Principal*
Anne Matechi,
▲ EMP: 50 EST: 1989
SQ FT: 75,000
SALES (est): 120MM **Privately Held**
WEB: www.linzerproducts.com
SIC: 5199 3991 Broom, mop & paint handles; paint brushes

(P-14909)
ALLAQUARIA LLC
Also Called: Quality Marine
5420 W 104th St, Los Angeles (90045-6012)
P.O. Box 2439 (90051-0439)
PHONE...................310 645-1107
G Christopher Bverner, *Mng Member*
Fabiola Duarte, *Purchasing*
Oscar Velazquez, *Opers Mgr*
Thomas Troy, *Production*
Jo Gries, *Sales Staff*
▲ EMP: 60 EST: 2003
SQ FT: 45,000
SALES (est): 20.1MM **Privately Held**
WEB: www.qualitymarine.com
SIC: 5199 Tropical fish

(P-14910)
AMERICAN PAPER & PLASTICS LLC
Also Called: American Paper & Provisions
550 S 7th Ave, City of Industry (91746-3120)
PHONE...................626 444-0000
Daniel Emrani, *CEO*
Rhonda Smith, *President*
Dennis Tye, *Vice Pres*
Angel Herandez, *Admin Sec*
Fred Moaven, *Info Tech Dir*
EMP: 119 EST: 1982
SQ FT: 300,000
SALES (est): 57MM **Privately Held**
WEB: www.appinc.com
SIC: 5199 Packaging materials

(P-14911)
ANNS TRADING COMPANY INC
Also Called: Urban Concepts
5333 S Downey Rd, Vernon (90058-3725)
PHONE...................323 585-4702
Hyung Don Kim, *CEO*
Daniel Im, *Vice Pres*
MI H Kim, *Admin Sec*
◆ EMP: 30 EST: 1981
SALES (est): 11.6MM **Privately Held**
WEB: www.annstrading.com
SIC: 5199 2335 Gifts & novelties; general merchandise, non-durable; women's, juniors' & misses' dresses

(P-14912)
ARMINAK & ASSOCIATES LLC
4832 Azusa Canyon Rd A, Irwindale (91706-1904)
P.O. Box 2245, Baldwin Park (91706-1141)
PHONE...................626 358-4804
Thomas A Amanto, *President*
▲ EMP: 55 EST: 1999
SQ FT: 50,000
SALES (est): 22.3MM
SALES (corp-wide): 769.9MM **Publicly Held**
WEB: www.arminak-associates.com
SIC: 5199 Packaging materials
PA: Trimas Corporation
38505 Woodward Ave # 200
Bloomfield Hills MI 48304
248 631-5450

(P-14913)
ATLANTIS ENTERPRISES INC
8100 Remmet Ave Ste 1, Canoga Park (91304-6413)
PHONE...................818 712-0572
Vartan Schaljian, *President*
Valentine Gorski, *Treasurer*
▲ EMP: 24 EST: 1998
SALES (est): 2.1MM **Privately Held**
WEB: www.atlantistime.com
SIC: 5199 3993 Advertising specialties; advertising novelties

(P-14914)
BLOWER-DEMPSAY CORPORATION (PA)
Also Called: Pak West Paper & Packaging
4042 W Garry Ave, Santa Ana (92704-6300)
PHONE...................714 481-3800
James Blower, *President*
Serge Poirier, *CFO*
Linda Dempsay, *Admin Sec*
Don Tuleja, *Info Tech Mgr*
Ally Tomkinson, *Project Mgr*
▲ EMP: 217 EST: 1973
SQ FT: 190,000
SALES (est): 83.3MM **Privately Held**
WEB: www.pakwest.com
SIC: 5199 Packaging materials

(P-14915)
BLUEMARK INC
27909 Hancock Pkwy, Valencia (91355-4116)
PHONE...................323 230-0770
Joseph Shusterman, *CEO*
Yosef Shusterman, *CFO*
Donart Young, *Managing Dir*
Isaac Smith, *Sales Mgr*
EMP: 112 EST: 2009
SALES (est): 28.2MM **Privately Held**
WEB: www.bluemark.com
SIC: 5199 Advertising specialties

(P-14916)
BRICA INC (HQ)
7835 Gloria Ave, Van Nuys (91406-1822)
PHONE...................818 893-5000
Robert E Capps, *Ch of Bd*
Joseph Gantz, *Ch of Bd*
Bryan T Miller, *President*
Lee Johnson, *Vice Pres*
Brett S Nover, *Vice Pres*
◆ EMP: 58 EST: 1997
SQ FT: 60,000
SALES (est): 6MM **Privately Held**
WEB: www.munchkin.com
SIC: 5199 5099 Gifts & novelties; safety equipment & supplies

(P-14917)
C SANDERS EMBLEMS LP
26370 Diamond Pl Unit 506, Santa Clarita (91350-2986)
PHONE...................800 336-7467
Penelope Ledbetter, *Partner*
Aileen Ibarzabal, *Executive*
Jay Ewing, *Sales Mgr*
Susanne Dennett, *Manager*
Yvonne Livingston, *Asst Mgr*
▲ EMP: 15 EST: 1959
SALES (est): 3MM **Privately Held**
WEB: www.csanders.net
SIC: 5199 2395 Badges; emblems, embroidered

(P-14918)
CALICO BRANDS INC
Also Called: Scripto
2055 S Haven Ave, Ontario (91761-0736)
PHONE...................909 930-5000
Felix M Hon, *CEO*
Mark Deasy, *Vice Pres*
Moon Fung, *Purch Mgr*
Laurie Hon, *Director*
▲ EMP: 50 EST: 1993
SQ FT: 125,000
SALES (est): 48.5MM **Privately Held**
WEB: www.calicobrands.com
SIC: 5199 Lighters, cigarette & cigar
PA: Tokai International Holdings, Inc.
2055 S Haven Ave
Ontario CA 91761

(P-14919)
CELMOL INC
Also Called: Mark Roberts
1611 E Saint Andrew Pl, Santa Ana (92705-4932)
PHONE...................714 259-1000
Mark Rees, *President*
Norine Anson, *Analyst*
▲ EMP: 60 EST: 1983
SQ FT: 36,000
SALES (est): 12MM **Privately Held**
WEB: www.markrobertswholesale.com
SIC: 5199 5193 Christmas novelties; gifts & novelties; flowers, fresh

(P-14920)
CHUS PACKAGING SUPPLIES INC
10011 Santa Fe Springs Rd, Santa Fe Springs (90670-2921)
PHONE...................562 944-6411
Pao Chang Chu, *CEO*
Julie Chieh Yu Chu, *President*
▲ EMP: 22 EST: 1985
SQ FT: 30,000
SALES (est): 25.9MM **Privately Held**
WEB: www.chuspkg.com
SIC: 5199 2653 Packaging materials; boxes, corrugated: made from purchased materials

(P-14921)
CLOUDRADIANT CORP (PA)
Also Called: Enbiz International
12 Fuchsia, Lake Forest (92630-1431)
PHONE...................408 256-1527
Anil RAO, *President*
◆ EMP: 128 EST: 2010
SALES (est): 42.9MM **Privately Held**
SIC: 5199 8748 7371 8711 General merchandise, non-durable; business consulting; computer software systems analysis & design, custom; consulting engineer; general management consultant

(P-14922)
COMMAND PACKAGING LLC (HQ)
3840 E 26th St, Vernon (90058-4107)
PHONE...................323 980-0918
Dhu Thompson,
Dede Mack, *Executive*
Vickie Niesley, *Executive*
Ben Escobar, *Department Mgr*
Linda Marmolejo, *Office Mgr*
◆ EMP: 188 EST: 1989
SQ FT: 170,000
SALES (est): 56.6MM **Privately Held**
WEB: www.commandpackaging.com
SIC: 5199 Packaging materials

(P-14923)
CORE-MARK INTRRLTED CMPNIES IN (DH)
Also Called: Allied Merchandising Industry
311 Reed Cir, Corona (92879-1349)
PHONE...................951 272-4790
Thomas Perkins, *CEO*
Mike Dunn, *President*
J Michael Walsh, *CEO*
Jennifer Hulett, *Senior VP*
EMP: 50 EST: 1975
SQ FT: 70,000
SALES (est): 100.8MM
SALES (corp-wide): 30.4B **Publicly Held**
WEB: www.core-mark.com
SIC: 5199 5122 5087 General merchandise, non-durable; druggists' sundries; service establishment equipment
HQ: Core-Mark International, Inc.
1500 Solana Blvd Ste 3400
Westlake TX 76262
650 589-9445

PRODUCTS & SVCS

(P-14924)
COSTCO WHOLESALE CORPORATION
16505 Sierra Lakes Pkwy, Fontana (92336-1256)
PHONE..............................909 823-8270
EMP: 196
SALES (corp-wide): 116.2B **Publicly Held**
SIC: 5199 Whol Nondurable Goods
PA: Costco Wholesale Corporation
999 Lake Dr Ste 200
Issaquah WA 98027
425 313-8100

(P-14925)
DOLPHIN HKG LTD (PA)
Also Called: Dolphin International
1125 W Hillcrest Blvd, Inglewood (90301-2021)
P.O. Box 91081, Los Angeles (90009-1081)
PHONE..............................310 215-3356
Steven Lundblad, *President*
Helen Lundblad, *Executive*
◆ EMP: 70 EST: 1970
SQ FT: 12,000
SALES (est): 21MM **Privately Held**
WEB: www.dolphin-int.com
SIC: 5199 Tropical fish

(P-14926)
EPSILON PLASTICS INC
3100 E Harcourt St, Compton (90221-5506)
PHONE..............................310 609-1320
Jim Gifford, *Manager*
Brian Fraser, *Vice Pres*
Michael Reiger, *Vice Pres*
Luz Franco, *Office Mgr*
Elaine Lafratta, *Executive Asst*
EMP: 75
SQ FT: 39,963 **Privately Held**
WEB: www.sigmaplasticsgroup.com
SIC: 5199 Packaging materials
HQ: Epsilon Plastics Inc.
Page & Schuyler Ave 8
Lyndhurst NJ 07071
201 933-6000

(P-14927)
ERNEST PACKAGING (PA)
Also Called: Ernest Paper
5777 Smithway St, Commerce (90040-1507)
PHONE..............................800 233-7788
Charles Wilson, *Ch of Bd*
Timothy Wilson, *President*
Richard Barnes, *CIO*
Dan Weisbach, *CIO*
Naomi Chavez, *Credit Staff*
▲ EMP: 130 EST: 1947
SQ FT: 300,000
SALES (est): 189.3MM **Privately Held**
WEB: www.ernestpackaging.com
SIC: 5199 7389 5113 Packaging materials; cosmetic kits, assembling & packaging; shipping supplies

(P-14928)
EVE HAIR INC (PA)
3935 Paramount Blvd, Lakewood (90712-4100)
PHONE..............................562 377-1020
Young SOO Cho, *President*
◆ EMP: 37 EST: 1990
SQ FT: 44,000
SALES (est): 15MM **Privately Held**
WEB: www.evehairinc.com
SIC: 5199 3999 Wigs; hair & hair-based products

(P-14929)
GAJU MARKET CORPORATION
450 S Western Ave, Los Angeles (90020-4120)
PHONE..............................213 382-9444
David Rhee, *CEO*
EMP: 135 EST: 2015
SQ FT: 2,000
SALES (est): 2MM **Privately Held**
WEB: www.gajumarketplace.com
SIC: 5199 General merchandise, non-durable

(P-14930)
GANZ USA LLC
307 S Sadler Ave 1d, Los Angeles (90022-2324)
PHONE..............................323 629-9871
Gustavo A Nunez, *Branch Mgr*
EMP: 74 **Privately Held**
WEB: www.ganz.com
SIC: 5199 Gifts & novelties
HQ: Ganz U.S.A., Llc
3855 Shallowford Rd # 220
Marietta GA 30062

(P-14931)
GIFTING GROUP LLC
42210 Zevo Dr, Temecula (92590-3732)
PHONE..............................951 296-0310
Andrea Stringer, *President*
▲ EMP: 75 EST: 2011
SQ FT: 24,575
SALES (est): 4.2MM **Privately Held**
WEB: www.aldercreekgiftbaskets.com
SIC: 5199 5149 5145 5947 Gifts & novelties; food gift baskets; candy; gift baskets; gift items, mail order

(P-14932)
GRAPHIC PACKAGING INTL LLC
Also Called: International Paper
1600 Kelsey Rd, Visalia (93291)
P.O. Box 4349 (93278-4349)
PHONE..............................559 651-3535
Robert E Eades, *Opers-Prdtn-Mfg*
EMP: 150 **Publicly Held**
WEB: www.graphicpkg.com
SIC: 5199 Packaging materials
HQ: Graphic Packaging International, Llc
1500 Riveredge Pkwy # 100
Atlanta GA 30328

(P-14933)
GRHT INC
Also Called: Foam Co, The
14818 Raymer St, Van Nuys (91405-1219)
PHONE..............................323 873-6393
Gil Rosky, *President*
Hossein Tehrani, *Vice Pres*
EMP: 60 EST: 1978
SQ FT: 11,000
SALES (est): 10.1MM **Privately Held**
SIC: 5199 Foam rubber

(P-14934)
GUARDIAN SAFETY AND SUPPLY LLC
Also Called: Enviro Safety Products
8248 W Doe Ave, Visalia (93291-9263)
PHONE..............................559 651-0919
John Maly, *Mng Member*
Matt Ridenour, *CEO*
Jennifer Barbee, *Vice Pres*
Austin Maly, *General Mgr*
Daniel Fields, *Info Tech Dir*
◆ EMP: 65 EST: 1996
SQ FT: 20,000
SALES (corp-wide): 15MM **Privately Held**
WEB: www.guardiansafety.com
SIC: 5999 5199 Safety supplies & equipment; first aid supplies
PA: Guardian Safety And Supply Holdings Company, Llc
25763 Calle Ct
Valencia CA 91355
559 651-0919

(P-14935)
HAY KUHN INC
1880 Jeffrey Rd, El Centro (92243-9532)
P.O. Box 338 (92244-0338)
PHONE..............................760 353-0124
Felipe Irigoyen, *President*
Jim Ohland, *General Mgr*
Terry Allegranza, *Controller*
◆ EMP: 50 EST: 1974
SQ FT: 1,500
SALES (est): 11MM **Privately Held**
WEB: www.kuhnhay.com
SIC: 5199 4789 Packaging materials; car loading

(P-14936)
HIPPO CORPORATION
Also Called: Displays & Holders
2535 W Via Palma, Anaheim (92801-2624)
PHONE..............................714 229-9152
Aloysius Aaron, *President*
Dawnna Aaron, *Treasurer*
Maureen Aaron, *Vice Pres*
EMP: 19 EST: 1986
SQ FT: 1,800
SALES (est): 2.6MM **Privately Held**
WEB: www.hippodisplays.com
SIC: 5199 2754 2396 7319 Advertising specialties; imprinting; gravure; screen printing on fabric articles; display advertising service; plastic processing

(P-14937)
HOOD PACKAGING CORPORATION
Also Called: Coveris
10801 Iona Ave, Hanford (93230-9415)
PHONE..............................559 585-2040
Walter Gerst, *Branch Mgr*
EMP: 140 **Privately Held**
WEB: www.hoodpkg.com
SIC: 5199 Packaging materials
HQ: Hood Packaging Corporation
25 Woodgreen Pl
Madison MS 39110
601 853-7260

(P-14938)
HOUDINI INC (PA)
Also Called: Wine Country Gift Baskets
4225 N Palm St, Fullerton (92835-1045)
PHONE..............................714 525-0325
Timothy J Dean, *President*
Margaret McIntyre, *COO*
Daniel Maguire, *CFO*
Dan Maguire, *Officer*
Richard Germann, *Exec VP*
◆ EMP: 60 EST: 1984
SQ FT: 300,000
SALES (est): 101MM **Privately Held**
WEB: www.winecountrygiftbaskets.com
SIC: 5947 5199 Gift baskets; gift baskets

(P-14939)
IMPORT COLLECTION (PA)
Also Called: Tic
7885 Nelson Rd, Panorama City (91402-6829)
PHONE..............................818 782-3060
David Mehdyzadeh, *CEO*
Sina Mehdyzadeh, *Corp Secy*
Sammy Mehdizadeh, *Vice Pres*
Jennifer McMorris, *Clerk*
◆ EMP: 65 EST: 1971
SQ FT: 160,000
SALES (est): 17.9MM **Privately Held**
WEB: www.importcollection.com
SIC: 5199 5023 Gifts & novelties; decorative home furnishings & supplies

(P-14940)
JEALOUS DEVIL LLC
2629 Manhattan Ave # 214, Hermosa Beach (90254-2411)
PHONE..............................800 446-0135
Rahmeen P Farudi, *CEO*
EMP: 52 EST: 2016
SALES (est): 7.5MM **Privately Held**
WEB: www.jealousdevil.com
SIC: 5199 Gifts & novelties

(P-14941)
JOAN BAKER DESIGNS INC
1130 Via Callejon, San Clemente (92673-6230)
PHONE..............................949 498-1983
Joan Baker, *President*
Michael Daley, *COO*
Doug Ormerod, *Controller*
Ted Blaylock, *Sales Dir*
Andrew Coward, *Manager*
▲ EMP: 50 EST: 1977
SQ FT: 23,000
SALES (est): 7.5MM **Privately Held**
WEB: www.joanbaker.com
SIC: 5199 Gifts & novelties

(P-14942)
JOBAR INTERNATIONAL INC
Also Called: Bibi Products Co
21022 Figueroa St, Carson (90745-1937)
PHONE..............................310 222-8682
Mitch Sussman, *President*
Simon Schober, *CFO*
Al Wiseman, *Exec VP*
Nicole Julius, *Project Mgr*
Lakisha Holley, *Bookkeeper*
◆ EMP: 59
SQ FT: 60,000
SALES (est): 11.8MM **Privately Held**
WEB: www.jobar.com
SIC: 5961 5199 ; general merchandise, non-durable

(P-14943)
KATZKIN LEATHER INC (PA)
6868 W Acco St, Montebello (90640-5441)
PHONE..............................323 725-1243
Brook Mayberry, *President*
Jim Roberson, *Vice Pres*
Bill North, *Regional Mgr*
Alan Pittle, *Sales Mgr*
Justin Harbold, *Manager*
▲ EMP: 200 EST: 1998
SQ FT: 50,000
SALES (est): 91.8MM **Privately Held**
WEB: www.katzkin.com
SIC: 5199 2531 Leather & cut stock; seats, automobile

(P-14944)
KOLE IMPORTS
Also Called: Basket Basics
24600 Main St, Carson (90745-6332)
PHONE..............................310 834-0004
Robert Kole, *CEO*
Fernando Garcia, *Exec VP*
Dan Kole, *Vice Pres*
Andy Kole, *VP Bus Dvlpt*
Kevin Kole, *VP Business*
◆ EMP: 84 EST: 1985
SQ FT: 150,000
SALES (est): 30.8MM **Privately Held**
WEB: www.koleimports.com
SIC: 5199 General merchandise, non-durable

(P-14945)
LANE WINPAK INC (HQ)
1365 N Ayala Dr, Rialto (92376-3101)
PHONE..............................909 386-1762
Bruce J Berry, *CEO*
Ted Torrens, *President*
M G Johnston, *CFO*
Sue liams, *Executive*
William A Lane Jr, *Admin Sec*
▲ EMP: 69 EST: 1996
SALES (est): 53.4MM
SALES (corp-wide): 852.4MM **Privately Held**
WEB: www.winpak.com
SIC: 5199 Packaging materials
PA: Winpak Ltd
100 Saulteaux Cres
Winnipeg MB R3J 3
204 889-1015

(P-14946)
LATITUDES INTL FRAGRANCE INC
Also Called: Maesa Home
10940 Wilshire Blvd # 23, Los Angeles (90024-3915)
PHONE..............................866 639-3999
Jil Belasco, *President*
George Cashman, *CFO*
▲ EMP: 52 EST: 1994
SALES (est): 2.8MM **Privately Held**
SIC: 5199 Candles

(P-14947)
LEATHER IN CHICAGO
11808 Turtle Springs Ln, Porter Ranch (91326-4026)
PHONE..............................818 349-3456
Camarali Shah, *CEO*
Cyndi Boyd, *General Mgr*
▲ EMP: 17 EST: 1993

SALES (est): 1.5MM **Privately Held**
WEB: www.leatherinchicago.mypinnacle-cart.com
SIC: **5948** 5199 2389 Leather goods, except luggage & shoes; leather, leather goods & furs; apparel for handicapped

(P-14948)
LOGOMARK INC
1201 Bell Ave, Tustin (92780-6420)
PHONE..................................714 675-6100
Trevor Gnesin, *President*
Romy Beaty, *Vice Pres*
Lori Bolton, *Vice Pres*
Maggie Wheeler, *Vice Pres*
Steve Morse, *Division Mgr*
▲ **EMP:** 250 **EST:** 1992
SQ FT: 200,000
SALES (est): 106.2MM **Privately Held**
WEB: www.logomark.com
SIC: **5199** Advertising specialties

(P-14949)
LUNGSAL INTERNATIONAL INC
Also Called: Lungsal USA
360 Thor Pl, Brea (92821-4117)
PHONE..................................714 671-9788
Janus Chen, *President*
Aileen Chen, *Vice Pres*
Annie Tsang, *Accounts Exec*
▲ **EMP:** 18 **EST:** 1989
SALES (est): 2.8MM **Privately Held**
SIC: **5199** 5112 4731 3951 Gifts & novelties; pens &/or pencils; freight forwarding; pens & mechanical pencils

(P-14950)
M M S TRADING INC
5390 Rickenbacker Rd, Bell (90201-6435)
PHONE..................................323 587-1082
Sumir Kaytee, *CEO*
◆ **EMP:** 13 **EST:** 2005
SALES (est): 6.1MM **Privately Held**
WEB: www.mmstradinginc.com
SIC: **5199** 3171 Yarns; women's handbags & purses

(P-14951)
MELTON INTL TACKLE INC
1375 S State College Blvd, Anaheim (92806-5728)
PHONE..................................714 978-9192
Tracy M Melton, *President*
Sonja Leonard, *Buyer*
Will Melton, *Sales Staff*
◆ **EMP:** 28 **EST:** 1993
SALES (est): 5.4MM **Privately Held**
WEB: www.meltontackle.com
SIC: **5961** 5199 3949 5091 Fishing, hunting & camping equipment & supplies: mail order; advertising specialties; lures, fishing: artificial; boat accessories & parts

(P-14952)
MIDWAY INTERNATIONAL INC
Also Called: Bobbi Boss
13131 166th St, Cerritos (90703-2202)
PHONE..................................562 921-2255
Ha Chung, *President*
Ha Suk Chung, *President*
◆ **EMP:** 50 **EST:** 1985
SQ FT: 32,700
SALES (est): 20.2MM **Privately Held**
SIC: **5199** 5047 Wigs; medical equipment & supplies; industrial safety devices: first aid kits & masks

(P-14953)
MODERN CANDLE CO INC
Also Called: Modern Candles
12884 Bradley Ave, Sylmar (91342-3827)
PHONE..................................323 441-0104
Armik Pirijanian, *CEO*
Nora Pirijanian, *Treasurer*
Lynette Reed, *Project Mgr*
▲ **EMP:** 45 **EST:** 1995
SALES (est): 17.5MM **Privately Held**
WEB: www.modern-candle.com
SIC: **5199** 3999 Candles; candles

(P-14954)
MUTUAL TRADING CO INC
843 E 4th St, Los Angeles (90013-1801)
PHONE..................................213 229-9393
EMP: 71 **Privately Held**
WEB: www.lamtc.com

SIC: **5199** Advertising specialties
HQ: Mutual Trading Co., Inc.
4200 Shirley Ave
El Monte CA 91731
213 626-9458

(P-14955)
NATIONAL SALES CORP
7250 Oxford Way, Commerce (90040-3643)
PHONE..................................323 586-0200
Karmel Nazarian, *President*
Ehsanollah Eshaghian, *Treasurer*
▲ **EMP:** 52 **EST:** 1980
SQ FT: 55,000
SALES: 25MM **Privately Held**
WEB: www.e-nsc.com
SIC: **5199** General merchandise, nondurable

(P-14956)
NIKKEN INTERNATIONAL INC (PA)
18301 Von Karman Ave, Irvine (92612-1009)
PHONE..................................949 789-2000
Kurt H Fulle, *Administration*
Luis Kasuga, *President*
Toshizo Watanabe, *Bd of Directors*
Ata Sharif, *Officer*
Gabriel Button, *Bookkeeper*
◆ **EMP:** 103 **EST:** 1989
SQ FT: 5,000
SALES (est): 55.4MM **Privately Held**
SIC: **5199** General merchandise, nondurable

(P-14957)
NUMBER HOLDINGS INC (PA)
4000 Union Pacific Ave, Commerce (90023-3202)
PHONE..................................323 980-8145
Frank J Schools, *CFO*
David Vega, *Store Mgr*
Elizabeth Chavez, *Administration*
Stella Kim, *Analyst*
Desiree Anderson, *Marketing Staff*
▲ **EMP:** 148 **EST:** 2011
SALES (est): 730MM **Privately Held**
WEB: www.99only.com
SIC: **5331** 5199 Variety stores; general merchandise, non-durable

(P-14958)
NW PACKAGING LLC (PA)
1201 E Lexington Ave, Pomona (91766-5520)
P.O. Box 357, Placentia (92871-0357)
PHONE..................................909 706-3627
Robert E Sliter, *Administration*
Geoffory Eide, *Sales Staff*
EMP: 100 **EST:** 2012
SALES (est): 19.3MM **Privately Held**
WEB: www.nwpackagingonline.com
SIC: **5199** Packaging materials

(P-14959)
P C P INC
Also Called: Pacific Packaging Components
13462 Brooks Dr, Baldwin Park (91706-2292)
PHONE..................................626 813-6166
Claryce M Palmer, *Ch of Bd*
Brandon Frank, *President*
Candace M Palmer Frank, *CEO*
Norm Frank, *Vice Pres*
Frank Nolan, *Vice Pres*
▲ **EMP:** 19 **EST:** 1970
SQ FT: 18,000
SALES (est): 6.2MM **Privately Held**
WEB: www.ppcpackaging.com
SIC: **5199** 3221 Packaging materials; bottles for packing, bottling & canning: glass

(P-14960)
PACIFIC PAPER CONVERTING INC (PA)
Also Called: Paper Cutters
6023 Bandini Blvd, Los Angeles (90040-2904)
PHONE..................................323 888-1330
Susan Feinstein, *President*
Beth Feinstein Thurber, *Vice Pres*
Beth Thurber, *Vice Pres*
EMP: 66 **EST:** 1996
SQ FT: 150,000

SALES (est): 10MM **Privately Held**
SIC: **5199** Packaging materials

(P-14961)
PACIFIC WESTERN SALES (PA)
Also Called: Pbfy Flexible Packaging
2980 Enterprise St Ste A, Brea (92821-6283)
PHONE..................................714 572-6730
Lyndsey William Tidwell, *President*
Jimmy Hou, *President*
Lorraine Clements, *Treasurer*
Andrea Pennington, *Vice Pres*
Deagle Soon, *Info Tech Mgr*
▲ **EMP:** 53 **EST:** 1979
SQ FT: 49,000
SALES (est): 16MM **Privately Held**
WEB: www.gopwsproducts.com
SIC: **5199** 7336 Packaging materials; package design

(P-14962)
PACTIV PACKAGING INC (DH)
Also Called: Pwp
3751 Seville Ave, Vernon (90058-1741)
PHONE..................................323 513-9000
Ira Maroofion, *President*
Peter J Lazaredes, *President*
Michele Kramer, *Executive Asst*
Weng Teng, *IT/INT Sup*
Aisha McClinton, *Technology*
◆ **EMP:** 541 **EST:** 2006
SALES (est): 162.4MM **Publicly Held**
WEB: www.pactiv.com
SIC: **5199** Packaging materials
HQ: Pactiv Llc
1900 W Field Ct
Lake Forest IL 60045
847 482-2000

(P-14963)
PD LIQUIDATION INC
Also Called: Pipe Dream Products
21350 Lassen St, Chatsworth (91311-4254)
PHONE..................................818 772-0100
David Feldman, *CEO*
Robert Feldman, *President*
Tami Aguilar, *Vice Pres*
Steve Sav, *Vice Pres*
Hernan Zegarra, *Accountant*
◆ **EMP:** 150 **EST:** 1979
SALES (est): 59.1MM
SALES (corp-wide): 63.6MM **Privately Held**
WEB: www.diamondproductsllc.com
SIC: **5199** Gifts & novelties
PA: Diamond Products, Llc
8501 Fllbrook Ave Ste 370
West Hills CA 91304
818 772-0100

(P-14964)
PETCO ANIMAL SUPS STORES INC
8161 Beverly Blvd, Los Angeles (90048-4514)
PHONE..................................323 852-1370
EMP: 17
SALES (corp-wide): 68.7MM **Privately Held**
WEB: www.petco.com
SIC: **5999** 5199 2048 Pets & pet supplies; pet supplies; prepared feeds
HQ: Petco Animal Supplies Stores, Inc.
10850 Via Frontera
San Diego CA 92127

(P-14965)
PHD MARKETING INC
1373 Ridgeway St, Pomona (91768-2701)
PHONE..................................909 620-1000
Thaer Ahmad, *President*
John Kamar, *Treasurer*
▲ **EMP:** 60 **EST:** 2010
SQ FT: 20,000
SALES (est): 12.2MM **Privately Held**
SIC: **5199** 5399 General merchandise, non-durable; Army-Navy goods

(P-14966)
PICNIC TIME INC
5131 Maureen Ln, Moorpark (93021-1783)
PHONE..................................805 529-7400
Mario W Tagliati, *Principal*

Gustavo Cosaro, *Vice Pres*
Jaime Whitt, *Buyer*
Holly Escobedo, *Sales Mgr*
Tesh Hatharasinghe, *Sales Staff*
◆ **EMP:** 30 **EST:** 1996
SQ FT: 20,000
SALES (est): 23.1MM **Privately Held**
WEB: www.picnictime.com
SIC: **5199** 3999 Bags, baskets & cases; handles, handbag & luggage

(P-14967)
POLYCELL PACKAGING CORPORATION
12851 Midway Pl, Cerritos (90703-2141)
PHONE..................................562 483-6000
Chin Ching Hsu, *President*
▲ **EMP:** 35 **EST:** 1995
SALES (est): 13.9MM **Privately Held**
WEB: www.polycell.com.au
SIC: **5199** 3089 Packaging materials; blister or bubble formed packaging, plastic

(P-14968)
PREMIERE PACKAGING INDS INC
Also Called: P P I
6530 Altura Blvd, Buena Park (90620-1040)
PHONE..................................562 799-9200
John Luyben, *CEO*
Christi Luyben, *President*
EMP: 77 **EST:** 1999
SALES (est): 21.7MM
SALES (corp-wide): 1.3B **Privately Held**
www.socalpackaging.kellyspicers.com
SIC: **5199** Packaging materials
HQ: Kelly Spicers Inc.
12310 Slauson Ave
Santa Fe Springs CA 90670

(P-14969)
PROACTIVE PACKG & DISPLAY LLC (DH)
602 S Rockefeller Ave, Ontario (91761-8190)
PHONE..................................909 390-5624
Richard Hartman, *CEO*
Tarek Saduddin, *Executive*
▲ **EMP:** 71 **EST:** 1994
SQ FT: 164,000
SALES (est): 75K
SALES (corp-wide): 679.2MM **Privately Held**
WEB: www.proactivepkg.com
SIC: **5199** Packaging materials
HQ: New-Indy Containerboard Llc
3500 Porsche Way Ste 150
Ontario CA 91764
909 296-3400

(P-14970)
QUETICO LLC (PA)
5610 Daniels St, Chino (91710-9024)
PHONE..................................909 628-6200
Thomas Fenchel, *Mng Member*
Maria Cantero, *Finance*
Janet Guerrero, *Personnel Assit*
Rindala Duaybis, *Opers Mgr*
Nick Aghakhanian,
▲ **EMP:** 144 **EST:** 1995
SALES (est): 193.5MM **Privately Held**
WEB: www.queticollc.com
SIC: **5199** 7389 General merchandise, non-durable; packaging & labeling services

(P-14971)
REDBARN PET PRODUCTS INC (PA)
Also Called: Redbarn Premium Pet Products
3229 E Spring St Ste 310, Long Beach (90806-2478)
PHONE..................................562 495-7315
Jeff Baikie, *CEO*
Howard Bloxam, *President*
Joe Martinez, *Principal*
Javier Solorzano, *Graphic Designe*
Lucy Salermo, *Human Res Mgr*
◆ **EMP:** 159 **EST:** 1994
SQ FT: 50,000

PRODUCTS & SVCS

SALES (est): 54.6MM **Privately Held**
WEB: www.redbarn.com
SIC: **5199** 2047 Pet supplies; dog & cat food

(P-14972)
ROCKWELL ENTERPRISES INC
15194 Prairie Ave, Lawndale (90260-2209)
PHONE..................................626 796-1511
Frank Giovinazzo, *President*
Akemi Giovinazzo, *Treasurer*
EMP: 20 **EST:** 1967
SALES (est): 2.5MM **Privately Held**
WEB: www.rockwellenterprises.com
SIC: **5199** 3581 Maps & charts; automatic vending machines

(P-14973)
ROYAL PAPER BOX CO CALIFORNIA (PA)
1105 S Maple Ave, Montebello (90640-6007)
P.O. Box 458 (90640-0458)
PHONE..................................323 728-7041
Jim Hodges, *CEO*
Darryl Carlson, *Vice Pres*
Scott Larson, *Vice Pres*
Steve Perez, *Vice Pres*
Andy Polanco, *Vice Pres*
▲ **EMP:** 198 **EST:** 1940
SQ FT: 172,500
SALES (est): 70MM **Privately Held**
WEB: www.royalpaperbox.com
SIC: **5199** Packaging materials

(P-14974)
SEA DWELLING CREATURES INC
5515 W 104th St, Los Angeles (90045-6013)
PHONE..................................310 676-9697
Bradford Remmer, *President*
Eric Cohen, *Treasurer*
Jeremy Cabot, *Executive*
Jason Hackett, *Executive*
Scott Lapham, *Executive*
◆ **EMP:** 70 **EST:** 1993
SQ FT: 24,000
SALES (est): 11.9MM **Privately Held**
WEB: www.seadwelling.com
SIC: **5999** 5199 Tropical fish; pets & pet supplies; tropical fish

(P-14975)
SHIMS BARGAIN INC (PA)
Also Called: J C Sales
2600 S Soto St, Vernon (90058-8015)
PHONE..................................323 881-0099
Kenneth Suh, *President*
BJ Chang, *CFO*
James Shim, *Chairman*
Sena OH, *Bookkeeper*
Ben Cho, *Human Resources*
◆ **EMP:** 100 **EST:** 1993
SQ FT: 420,000
SALES (est): 90.4MM **Privately Held**
WEB: www.jcsalesweb.com
SIC: **5199** General merchandise, nondurable

(P-14976)
SPECIALTY MERCHANDISE CORP (PA)
Also Called: Smart Living Company
4100 Guardian St Ste 112, Simi Valley (93063-6727)
P.O. Box 6704, Greenville SC (29606-6704)
PHONE..................................805 578-5500
Mark Schelbert, *CEO*
Scott Palladino, *CFO*
Tom Krutilek, *Marketing Staff*
Bernice Reyes, *Manager*
Fairelynn Villa, *Manager*
◆ **EMP:** 50 **EST:** 1955
SALES (est): 83.9MM **Privately Held**
SIC: **5199** Gifts & novelties

(P-14977)
TARGUS INTERNATIONAL LLC (PA)
1211 N Miller St, Anaheim (92806-1933)
PHONE..................................714 765-5555
Mikel H Williams, *CEO*
Bill Oppenlander, *President*

Victor C Streufert, *CFO*
Andrew Corkill, *Vice Pres*
Ronald Decamp, *Vice Pres*
◆ **EMP:** 175 **EST:** 1995
SQ FT: 200,656
SALES (est): 125.5MM **Privately Held**
WEB: www.us.targus.com
SIC: **5199** 5065 Bags, baskets & cases; electronic parts & equipment

(P-14978)
TECHFLEX PACKAGING LLC
Also Called: Xsential
13771 Gramercy Pl, Gardena (90249-2470)
PHONE..................................424 266-9400
Burt Siegelman,
Lucas Van Winkle, *Engineer*
Neil Kinney,
David Lopex, *Manager*
▲ **EMP:** 52 **EST:** 1995
SALES (est): 19.8MM **Privately Held**
WEB: www.tfpack.com
SIC: **5199** Packaging materials

(P-14979)
THORO—PACKAGING (DH)
1467 Davril Cir, Corona (92878-4357)
PHONE..................................951 278-2100
Janet Dabek Steiner, *President*
EMP: 129 **EST:** 1967
SQ FT: 56,000
SALES (est): 52.3MM
SALES (corp-wide): 6.9MM **Privately Held**
WEB: www.thoropackaging.com
SIC: **5199** Packaging materials
HQ: Autajon Cs
    Autajon Packaging Montelimar Cs
    Petit Pelican
    Montelimar 26200
    475 002-000

(P-14980)
ULINE INC
2950 Jurupa St, Ontario (91761-2936)
PHONE..................................909 605-7090
Toll Free:..................................877 -
Israel Baluja, *Branch Mgr*
Claudia Navarro, *Recruiter*
Christian Underwood, *Opers Mgr*
Andrew Atakpo, *Sales Staff*
Eric Chen, *Sales Staff*
EMP: 57
SALES (corp-wide): 2.1B **Privately Held**
WEB: www.uline.com
SIC: **5199** Packaging materials
PA: Uline, Inc.
    12575 Uline Dr
    Pleasant Prairie WI 53158
    262 612-4200

(P-14981)
VENIDA PACKING COMPANY
19823 Avenue 300, Exeter (93221-9771)
P.O. Box 212 (93221-0212)
PHONE..................................559 592-2816
Verne Crookshanks, *CEO*
Michael Murray, *Treasurer*
Myra Crookshanks, *Office Mgr*
George Tantua, *Admin Sec*
Tammy Rodgers, *Controller*
EMP: 125 **EST:** 1977
SQ FT: 50,000
SALES (est): 19.8MM **Privately Held**
WEB: www.venidapacking.com
SIC: **5199** Packaging materials

(P-14982)
VIA TRADING CORPORATION
2520 Industry Way, Lynwood (90262-4015)
PHONE..................................877 202-3616
Jacques Stambouli, *CEO*
Alain Stambouli, *President*
Alex Antypas, *COO*
Luis Nunez, *Executive*
Edwin Cortez, *Administration*
◆ **EMP:** 57 **EST:** 2002
SQ FT: 240,000
SALES (est): 41.2MM **Privately Held**
WEB: www.viatrading.com
SIC: **5199** General merchandise, nondurable

(P-14983)
VICTORY FOAM INC (PA)
3 Holland, Irvine (92618-2506)
PHONE..................................949 474-0690
Frank M Comerford, *CEO*
Helen Comerford, *Corp Secy*
Myles Comerford, *Vice Pres*
Nate Munshower, *Materials Mgr*
Virginia Valdez, *QC Mgr*
▲ **EMP:** 94 **EST:** 1982
SQ FT: 53,000
SALES (est): 37.5MM **Privately Held**
WEB: www.victoryfoam.com
SIC: **5199** 3086 Packaging materials; cups & plates, foamed plastic

(P-14984)
VICTORY SPORTSWEAR INC
2381 Buena Vista St, Duarte (91010-3301)
PHONE..................................626 359-5400
Victor Ju, *CEO*
Xiao Can Zhang, *CFO*
▲ **EMP:** 22 **EST:** 1999
SQ FT: 22,000
SALES (est): 5.6MM **Privately Held**
WEB: www.victorysportswearinc.com
SIC: **5199** 5949 2321 2326 Automobile fabrics; cotton yarns; leather goods, except footwear, gloves, luggage, belting; knitting goods & supplies; men's & boys' dress shirts; men's & boys' sports & polo shirts; men's & boys' work clothing; men's & boys' suits & coats; women's & misses' blouses & shirts

(P-14985)
VIPSTORE USA CO
13674 Star Ruby Ave, Eastvale (92880-5557)
PHONE..................................626 934-7880
EMP: 400
SALES (est): 12MM **Privately Held**
SIC: **5199** Whol Nondurable Goods

(P-14986)
WEST BAY IMPORTS INC
7245 Oxford Way, Commerce (90040-3644)
PHONE..................................323 720-5777
Jae Hee Kang, *CEO*
Yong K Yi, *President*
Paul Jang, *Sales Executive*
Sonia Carrillo, *Manager*
◆ **EMP:** 30 **EST:** 1981
SALES (est): 7MM **Privately Held**
WEB: www.westbayinc.com
SIC: **5199** 2389 Wigs; masquerade costumes

(P-14987)
WYLAND INTERNATIONAL LLC (PA)
Also Called: Wyland Galleries
30265 Tomas, Rcho STA Marg (92688-2123)
PHONE..................................949 643-7070
Ron Bass, *Treasurer*
Joe Carruth, *Admin Sec*
Robin Norde, *Credit Staff*
Robin Norde-Davis, *Finance*
Plata Christy, *Mktg Dir*
▲ **EMP:** 50 **EST:** 1978
SQ FT: 3,500
SALES (est): 21.3MM **Privately Held**
WEB: www.wyland.com
SIC: **5999** 5199 Art dealers; art goods

6011 Federal Reserve Banks

(P-14988)
FEDERAL RSRVE BNK SAN FRNCISCO
Also Called: Los Angeles Branch
950 S Grand Ave, Los Angeles (90015-4202)
P.O. Box 512077 (90051-0077)
PHONE..................................213 683-2300
Mark Mullinix, *Manager*
Henry Aguilar, *Officer*
Edward Hodges, *Officer*
Doyle Roberts, *Officer*
Doug Conover, *Vice Pres*
EMP: 640 **Privately Held**
WEB: www.frbsf.org

SIC: **6011** Federal reserve branches
HQ: Federal Reserve Bank Of San Francisco
    101 Market St
    San Francisco CA 94105
    415 974-2000

6021 National Commercial Banks

(P-14989)
BANA HOME LOAN SERVICING
31303 Agoura Rd, Westlake Village (91361-4635)
PHONE..................................213 345-7975
Rachel Fiorillo, *Senior VP*
EMP: 900 **EST:** 2016
SALES (est): 28.3MM **Privately Held**
SIC: **6021** National commercial banks

(P-14990)
BANC CALIFORNIA NATIONAL ASSN (HQ)
3 Macarthur Pl, Santa Ana (92707-6067)
PHONE..................................877 770-2262
Robert Franko, *President*
Denise Chambliss, *President*
Hamid Hussain, *President*
Tigran Karavardanyan, *President*
Romeo Blackburn, *Officer*
EMP: 73 **EST:** 1967
SALES: 303.6MM
SALES (corp-wide): 309.1MM **Publicly Held**
WEB: www.bancofcal.com
SIC: **6021** National commercial banks
PA: Banc Of California, Inc.
    3 Macarthur Pl Ste 100
    Santa Ana CA 92707
    855 361-2262

(P-14991)
BANC CALIFORNIA NATIONAL ASSN
10100 Santa Monica Blvd, Los Angeles (90067-4003)
PHONE..................................310 286-0710
EMP: 50
SALES (corp-wide): 309.1MM **Publicly Held**
WEB: www.bancofcal.com
SIC: **6021** National Commercial Banks, Nsk
HQ: Banc Of California, National Association
    3 Macarthur Pl
    Santa Ana CA 92707
    877 770-2262

(P-14992)
BANC OF CALIFORNIA INC (PA)
3 Macarthur Pl Ste 100, Santa Ana (92707-6068)
P.O. Box 61452, Irvine (92602-6048)
PHONE..................................855 361-2262
Douglas H Bowers, *President*
Robert D Sznewajs, *Ch of Bd*
Joyce Jicka, *President*
John A Bogler, *CFO*
Kris A Gagnon, *Ch Credit Ofcr*
EMP: 120 **EST:** 2002
SALES (est): 309.1MM **Publicly Held**
WEB: www.bancofcal.com
SIC: **6021** National commercial banks

(P-14993)
BANK OF HOPE (HQ)
3200 Wilshire Blvd # 1400, Los Angeles (90010-1325)
PHONE..................................213 639-1700
Kevin S Kim, *CEO*
Scott Yoon-Suk Whang, *Ch of Bd*
Camelia Easmin, *President*
Min J Kim, *President*
Stacy Kim, *President*
▲ **EMP:** 108 **EST:** 1985
SALES (est): 638.8MM
SALES (corp-wide): 652.3MM **Publicly Held**
WEB: www.bankofhope.com
SIC: **6021** National commercial banks

PA: Hope Bancorp, Inc.
3200 Wilshire Blvd # 1400
Los Angeles CA 90010
213 639-1700

(P-14994)
BBVA USA
Also Called: Compass Bank
27851 Bradley Rd Ste 125, Sun City
(92586-2282)
PHONE......................951 672-4829
EMP: 123
SALES (corp-wide): 18.2B **Publicly Held**
WEB: www.bbvausa.com
SIC: 6021 National commercial banks
HQ: Bbva Usa
15 20th St S Ste 100
Birmingham AL 35233
205 297-1986

(P-14995)
CIT BANK NA (HQ)
75 N Fair Oaks Ave Ste C, Pasadena
(91103-3647)
P.O. Box 7056 (91109-7056)
PHONE......................626 859-5400
Ellen R Alemany, *Ch of Bd*
James P Broom, *President*
James L Hudak, *President*
C Jeffrey Knittel, *President*
Joseph Otting, *President*
EMP: 62 **EST:** 2009
SALES: 2.4B
SALES (corp-wide): 3.1B **Publicly Held**
WEB: www.owb.com
SIC: 6021 National commercial banks
PA: Cit Group Inc.
11 W 42nd St
New York NY 10036
212 461-5200

(P-14996)
CITIBANK FSB
1 World Trade Ctr Ste 100, Long Beach
(90831-0100)
PHONE......................562 999-3453
Jim Drake, *Branch Mgr*
EMP: 122
SALES (corp-wide): 88.8B **Publicly Held**
WEB: www.citigroup.com
SIC: 6021 National commercial banks
HQ: Citibank, F.S.B.
1 Sansome St
San Francisco CA 94104
415 627-6000

(P-14997)
CITIGROUP INC
3996 Barranca Pkwy # 130, Irvine
(92606-8239)
PHONE......................949 726-5124
EMP: 65
SALES (corp-wide): 90.7B **Publicly Held**
SIC: 6021 Financial Services
PA: Citigroup Inc.
399 Park Ave
New York NY 10013
212 559-1000

(P-14998)
CITY NATIONAL BANK (DH)
555 S Flower St Ste 2500, Los Angeles
(90071-2326)
PHONE......................310 888-6000
Kelly Coffey, *CEO*
Brett Altman, *President*
Gina Calipes, *President*
Marilou Escobedo, *President*
Iris Pyun, *President*
▲ **EMP:** 300 **EST:** 1968
SQ FT: 80,000
SALES: 2.3B
SALES (corp-wide): 31.1B **Privately Held**
WEB: www.cnb.com
SIC: 6021 6022 National commercial banks; state commercial banks
HQ: Rbc Usa Holdco Corporation
3 World Financial Ctr
New York NY 10281
212 858-7200

(P-14999)
CITY NATIONAL SECURITIES INC
400 N Roxbury Dr Ste 400 # 400, Beverly Hills (90210-5021)
PHONE......................310 888-6393
Michael Nunnelee, *President*
EMP: 165 **EST:** 2005
SALES (est): 16.1MM
SALES (corp-wide): 31.1B **Privately Held**
WEB: www.cnb.com
SIC: 6021 National commercial banks
HQ: City National Bank
555 S Flower St Ste 2500
Los Angeles CA 90071
310 888-6000

(P-15000)
FIRST BANK AND TRUST
4040 Atlantic Ave, Long Beach
(90807-2908)
PHONE......................562 595-8775
Kennith P Maness, *Ch of Bd*
David Goren, *Vice Ch Bd*
Ronald F Clark, *Vice Pres*
Clement W Morin, *Admin Sec*
EMP: 76 **EST:** 1982
SQ FT: 2,880
SALES (est): 4.7MM **Privately Held**
SIC: 6021 National trust companies with deposits, commercial

(P-15001)
FOOTHILL GROUP INC (HQ)
Also Called: West Fargo Capital Finance
1800 Century Park E # 1100, Los Angeles
(90067-1501)
PHONE......................310 453-7300
John F Nickoll, *Ch of Bd*
Kevin Gary, *CFO*
David C Hilton, *General Mgr*
Peter Schwab, *General Mgr*
EMP: 117 **EST:** 1970
SALES (est): 92.8MM
SALES (corp-wide): 80.3B **Publicly Held**
WEB: www.wellsfargo.com
SIC: 6021 6159 6282 National commercial banks; loan institutions, general & industrial; investment advice
PA: Wells Fargo & Company
420 Montgomery St
San Francisco CA 94104
866 249-3302

(P-15002)
HOPE BANCORP INC (PA)
3200 Wilshire Blvd # 1400, Los Angeles
(90010-1333)
PHONE......................213 639-1700
Kevin S Kim, *Ch of Bd*
Christine Chun, *President*
Jason K Kim, *President*
Kyu S Kim, *President*
David P Malone, *President*
EMP: 54 **EST:** 2000
SALES (est): 652.3MM **Publicly Held**
WEB: www.ir-hopebancorp.com
SIC: 6021 National commercial banks

(P-15003)
MUFG UNION BANK FOUNDATION
445 S Figueroa St Ste 710, Los Angeles
(90071-1615)
PHONE......................213 236-5000
Masashi Oka, *President*
John F Harrigan, *Ch of Bd*
Carol Brewer, *President*
W H Wofford, *Exec VP*
David Anderson, *Vice Pres*
EMP: 4200 **EST:** 1967
SALES (est): 135.4MM **Privately Held**
WEB: www.mufgamericas.com
SIC: 6021 National commercial banks

(P-15004)
NORTHERN TRUST COMPANY
2049 Century Park E # 3600, Los Angeles
(90067-3210)
PHONE......................310 282-3800
James Dryden, *Branch Mgr*
Donna Coffey, *Trust Officer*
Richard Blackman, *Vice Pres*
Judd Eberhart, *Vice Pres*
Lynn Knox, *Vice Pres*

EMP: 50
SALES (corp-wide): 6.3B **Publicly Held**
WEB: www.northerntrust.com
SIC: 6021 National commercial banks
HQ: The Northern Trust Company
50 S La Salle St
Chicago IL 60603
312 630-6000

(P-15005)
NOVARE NAT SETTLEMENT SVC LLC
320 Commerce Ste 150, Irvine
(92602-1364)
PHONE......................714 352-4088
Cathy McIndoo, *President*
Lea Romo, *President*
Alex Morgan, *Vice Pres*
EMP: 50 **EST:** 2014
SALES (est): 7.7MM **Privately Held**
WEB: www.novarenss.com
SIC: 6021 National commercial banks

(P-15006)
PACWEST BANCORP (PA)
9701 Wilshire Blvd # 700, Beverly Hills
(90212-2020)
PHONE......................310 887-8500
Matthew P Wagner, *President*
John M Eggemeyer III, *Ch of Bd*
James J Pieczynski, *Vice Chairman*
Mark T Yung, *COO*
Bart R Olson, *CFO*
EMP: 103 **EST:** 1999
SALES (est): 1.2B **Publicly Held**
WEB: www.pacwestbancorp.com
SIC: 6021 National commercial banks

(P-15007)
UNION BANK OF CALIFORNIA (PA)
11551 Foothill Blvd, Rancho Cucamonga
(91730-3943)
PHONE......................909 350-7176
EMP: 54 **EST:** 2013
SALES (est): 695K **Privately Held**
WEB: www.unionbank.com
SIC: 6021 National commercial banks

(P-15008)
WELLS FARGO BANK LTD
333 S Grand Ave Ste 500, Los Angeles
(90071-1569)
PHONE......................213 253-6227
Randy Reyes, *Branch Mgr*
Theodore Craver, *Bd of Directors*
Vince Avelar, *Vice Pres*
Courtney Cassidy, *Vice Pres*
Daniel MAI, *Vice Pres*
EMP: 56 **EST:** 2013
SALES: 444.7MM
SALES (corp-wide): 80.3B **Publicly Held**
WEB: www.wellsfargo.com
SIC: 6021 National commercial banks
HQ: Wfc Holdings, Llc
420 Montgomery St
San Francisco CA 94104
415 396-7392

6022 State Commercial Banks

(P-15009)
AMERICAN BUSINESS BANK
3633 Inland Empire Blvd, Ontario
(91764-4922)
PHONE......................909 919-2040
Elaine Lopez, *Vice Pres*
Larry Pyle, *Manager*
EMP: 89
SALES (corp-wide): 98.9MM **Publicly Held**
WEB: www.americanbb.bank
SIC: 6022 State commercial banks
PA: American Business Bank
400 S Hope St Ste 300
Los Angeles CA 90071
213 430-4000

(P-15010)
AMERICAN BUSINESS BANK
970 W 190th St Ste 301, Torrance
(90502-1045)
PHONE......................310 808-1200
Debbie Dm, *Manager*

EMP: 89
SALES (corp-wide): 98.9MM **Publicly Held**
WEB: www.cbbank.com
SIC: 6022 State trust companies accepting deposits, commercial
PA: American Business Bank
400 S Hope St Ste 300
Los Angeles CA 90071
213 430-4000

(P-15011)
BANK OF SIERRA (HQ)
90 N Main St, Porterville (93257-3712)
P.O. Box 1930 (93258-1930)
PHONE......................559 782-4300
Kevin McPhaill, *President*
Morris Tharp, *Ch of Bd*
Jennie Andrade, *President*
Kelli Blackburn, *President*
Dustin Oliver, *President*
EMP: 105 **EST:** 1977
SQ FT: 37,000
SALES: 135.8MM
SALES (corp-wide): 136.3MM **Publicly Held**
WEB: www.bankofthesierra.com
SIC: 6022 State commercial banks
PA: Sierra Bancorp
86 N Main St
Porterville CA 93257
559 782-4900

(P-15012)
BBVA USA
Also Called: Compass Bank
195 W Ontario Ave, Corona (92882-5276)
PHONE......................951 279-7071
Eileen Blaga, *Branch Mgr*
Natalie Corente, *VP Bus Dvlpt*
EMP: 123
SALES (corp-wide): 18.2B **Publicly Held**
WEB: www.bbvausa.com
SIC: 6022 State commercial banks
HQ: Bbva Usa
15 20th St S Ste 100
Birmingham AL 35233
205 297-1986

(P-15013)
BNY MELLON NATIONAL ASSN
1600 Nwport Ctr Dr Ste 20, Newport Beach
(92660)
PHONE......................877 420-6377
Carrie Gibson, *Principal*
Megan Van Buskirk, *Sales Associate*
Andrew Low, *Director*
EMP: 115
SALES (corp-wide): 15.8B **Publicly Held**
WEB: www.bnymellon.com
SIC: 6022 State commercial banks
HQ: Bny Mellon, National Association
1 Mellon Center Ste 3831
Pittsburgh PA 15258
412 234-5000

(P-15014)
BUSA SERVICING INC (DH)
787 W 5th St, Los Angeles (90071-2003)
PHONE......................310 203-3400
Manuel Sanchez Lugo, *Ch of Bd*
Rebecca Macieira-Kaufmann, *CEO*
Roger Johnston, *Ch Credit Ofcr*
Gabriel De La Peza, *Exec VP*
Theodore Michaels, *Exec VP*
▲ **EMP:** 200 **EST:** 1963
SALES: 33.7MM
SALES (corp-wide): 88.8B **Publicly Held**
WEB: www.citigroup.com
SIC: 6022 State commercial banks

(P-15015)
CATHAY BANK (HQ)
777 N Broadway, Los Angeles
(90012-2819)
PHONE......................626 279-3698
Dunson K Cheng, *Ch of Bd*
Melissa Fung, *President*
Kitty Hu, *President*
Heng W Chen, *CFO*
Heng Chen, *Treasurer*
▲ **EMP:** 125 **EST:** 1962
SALES (est): 748MM **Publicly Held**
WEB: www.cathaybank.com
SIC: 6022 State trust companies accepting deposits, commercial

---

(P-15016)
CATHAY GENERAL BANCORP (PA)
777 N Broadway, Los Angeles
(90012-2819)
PHONE..............213 625-4700
Chang M Liu, *President*
Dunson K Cheng, *Ch of Bd*
Tigran Karavardanyan, *President*
Heng W Chen, *CFO*
Anthony M Tang, *Vice Ch Bd*
EMP: 66 EST: 1990
SALES (est) 743.3MM **Publicly Held**
WEB: www.cathaybank.com
SIC: 6022 State commercial banks

(P-15017)
CITIZENS BUSINESS BANK (HQ)
701 N Haven Ave Ste 280, Ontario
(91764-4920)
P.O. Box 51000 (91761-1087)
PHONE..............909 980-4030
Toll Free:..............877 -
Christopher D Myers, *President*
Barbara Lowry, *President*
David C Harvey, *COO*
E Allen Nicholson, *CFO*
David F Farnsworth, *Ch Credit Ofcr*
▲ EMP: 150 EST: 1973
SQ FT: 23,000
SALES (est): 479.2MM **Publicly Held**
WEB: www.cbbank.com
SIC: 6022 State trust companies accepting
deposits, commercial

(P-15018)
CVB FINANCIAL CORP (PA)
701 N Haven Ave Ste 350, Ontario
(91764-4920)
PHONE..............909 980-4030
David A Brager, *CEO*
Raymond V O'Brien III, *Ch of Bd*
Charla Gomez, *President*
Karen Vaage, *President*
E Allen Nicholson, *CFO*
EMP: 59 EST: 1981
SALES (est): 480.2MM **Publicly Held**
WEB: www.cbbank.com
SIC: 6022 State commercial banks

(P-15019)
EAST WEST BANCORP INC (PA)
135 N Los Robles Ave Fl 7, Pasadena
(91101-4525)
PHONE..............626 768-6000
Dominic Ng, *Ch of Bd*
Joanna Kha, *President*
Candy Lei, *President*
Jack Liu, *President*
Judy Wong, *President*
◆ EMP: 257 EST: 1998
SALES (est): 1.8B **Publicly Held**
WEB: www.investor.eastwestbank.com
SIC: 6022 State commercial banks

(P-15020)
EAST WEST BANK (HQ)
135 N Los Robles Ave # 100, Pasadena
(91101-4526)
PHONE..............626 768-6000
Dominic Ng, *Ch of Bd*
Ling Chen, *President*
Donald S Chow, *President*
Betty Liu, *President*
Belsazar Uriarte, *President*
◆ EMP: 300 EST: 1973
SQ FT: 18,000
SALES: 1.8B
SALES (corp-wide): 1.8B **Publicly Held**
WEB: www.eastwestbank.com
SIC: 6022 State commercial banks
PA: East West Bancorp, Inc.
135 N Los Robles Ave Fl 7
Pasadena CA 91101
626 768-6000

(P-15021)
ENTERPRISE BANK & TRUST
17785 Center Court Dr N # 750, Cerritos
(90703-9310)
PHONE..............562 345-9092
EMP: 184 **Publicly Held**
WEB: www.enterprisebank.com
SIC: 6022 State trust companies accepting
deposits, commercial

HQ: Enterprise Bank & Trust
150 N Meramec Ave Ste 300
Saint Louis MO 63105
314 725-5500

(P-15022)
FARMERS MERCHANTS BNK LONG BCH (HQ)
Also Called: F&M Bank
302 Pine Ave, Long Beach (90802-2326)
P.O. Box 1370 (90801-1370)
PHONE..............562 437-0011
W Henry Walker, *CEO*
Lamonte Lee, *President*
Sandra Marquez, *President*
Larry Prible, *President*
Kenneth G Walker, *President*
▲ EMP: 130 EST: 1907
SQ FT: 150,000
SALES (est): 303.5MM **Privately Held**
WEB: www.fmb.com
SIC: 6022 6029 State trust companies ac-
cepting deposits, commercial; commercial
banks

(P-15023)
FIRST CHOICE BANK
888 W 6th St Ste 550, Los Angeles
(90017-2731)
PHONE..............213 617-0082
EMP: 65
SALES (corp-wide): 100.2MM **Publicly Held**
WEB: www.firstchoicebankca.com
SIC: 6022 State Commercial Banks
HQ: First Choice Bank
17785 Center Court Dr N # 750
Cerritos CA 90703

(P-15024)
FIRST FOUNDATION INC (PA)
Also Called: FFI
18101 Von Karman Ave # 7, Irvine
(92612-1012)
PHONE..............949 202-4160
Scott F Kavanaugh, *CEO*
Ulrich E Keller Jr, *Ch of Bd*
David S Depillo, *President*
John Knak, *President*
Ann Small, *President*
EMP: 170 EST: 2006
SALES (est): 298.5MM **Publicly Held**
WEB: www.firstfoundationinc.com
SIC: 6022 State commercial banks

(P-15025)
FIRST REPUBLIC BANK
888 S Figueroa St Ste 100, Los Angeles
(90017-5325)
PHONE..............213 239-8883
Sev Araradian, *Branch Mgr*
Lourdes Ochoa, *Officer*
Dan Sokol, *Officer*
Jonathan Fox, *Vice Pres*
Matthew Babrick, *Managing Dir*
EMP: 87
SALES (corp-wide): 4.5B **Publicly Held**
WEB: www.firstrepublic.com
SIC: 6022 State commercial banks
PA: First Republic Bank
111 Pine St Fl 2
San Francisco CA 94111
415 392-1400

(P-15026)
FIRST REPUBLIC BANK
16300 Ventura Blvd Fl 1, Encino
(91436-2143)
PHONE..............818 263-8798
EMP: 87
SALES (corp-wide): 4.5B **Publicly Held**
WEB: www.firstrepublic.com
SIC: 6022 State commercial banks
PA: First Republic Bank
111 Pine St Fl 2
San Francisco CA 94111
415 392-1400

(P-15027)
FIRST REPUBLIC BANK
12070 Ventura Blvd, Studio City
(91604-2608)
PHONE..............818 752-4777
Chere Castle, *Branch Mgr*
EMP: 87

SALES (corp-wide): 4.5B **Publicly Held**
WEB: www.firstrepublic.com
SIC: 6022 State commercial banks
PA: First Republic Bank
111 Pine St Fl 2
San Francisco CA 94111
415 392-1400

(P-15028)
FIRST REPUBLIC BANK
601 N Sepulveda Blvd, Manhattan Beach
(90266-5920)
PHONE..............424 408-6088
EMP: 87
SALES (corp-wide): 4.5B **Publicly Held**
WEB: www.firstrepublic.com
SIC: 6022 State commercial banks
PA: First Republic Bank
111 Pine St Fl 2
San Francisco CA 94111
415 392-1400

(P-15029)
HANMI BANK (HQ)
3660 Wilshire Blvd Ph A, Los Angeles
(90010-2387)
PHONE..............213 382-2200
Joon H Lee, *Ch of Bd*
Michael Choi, *President*
Susan Kim, *President*
Chong Guk Kum, *President*
Jenny Park, *President*
▲ EMP: 350 EST: 1981
SQ FT: 35,000
SALES: 251.8MM
SALES (corp-wide): 266.9MM **Publicly Held**
WEB: www.hanmi.com
SIC: 6022 State commercial banks
PA: Hanmi Financial Corporation
3660 Wlshire Blvd Pnthuse
Los Angeles CA 90010
213 382-2200

(P-15030)
LOS ROBLES BANK
33 W Thousand Oaks Blvd, Thousand Oaks
(91360-4416)
P.O. Box 1438 (91358-0438)
PHONE..............805 373-6763
Fax: 805 379-2857
EMP: 52
SQ FT: 11,000
SALES (est): 5.3MM
SALES (corp-wide): 5.2B **Privately Held**
SIC: 6022 State Commercial Bank
HQ: Mufg Americas Holdings Corporation
1251 Ave Of The Americas
New York NY 10020
212 782-6800

(P-15031)
MANUFACTURERS BANK (DH)
515 S Figueroa St Fl 4, Los Angeles
(90071-3301)
PHONE..............213 489-6200
Mitsugu Serizawa, *CEO*
Jeffrey Lee, *President*
Koichi Miyata, *President*
Naresh Sheth, *President*
Adrian Danescu, *Exec VP*
▲ EMP: 164
SQ FT: 69,206
SALES: 106.8MM **Privately Held**
WEB: www.manufacturersbank.com
SIC: 6022 State commercial banks

(P-15032)
MERCHANTS BANK CALIFORNIA N A
1 Civic Plaza Dr Ste 100, Carson
(90745-7958)
P.O. Box 6008, Long Beach (90806-0008)
PHONE..............310 549-4350
Joyce Yamasaki, *CEO*
Daniel K Roberts, *Principal*
EMP: 75
SQ FT: 5,551
SALES (est): 6.9MM **Privately Held**
WEB: www.merchantsbankca.com
SIC: 6022 State commercial banks

(P-15033)
MORGAN STNLEY SMITH BARNEY LLC
74199 El Paseo Ste 201, Palm Desert
(92260-4151)
PHONE..............760 568-3500
Anthony Maddlina, *Manager*
EMP: 158
SALES (corp-wide): 52B **Publicly Held**
WEB: www.morganstanley.com
SIC: 6022 State commercial banks
HQ: Morgan Stanley Smith Barney, Llc
1585 Broadway
New York NY 10036

(P-15034)
MORGAN STNLEY SMITH BARNEY LLC
28202 Cabot Rd Ste 150, Laguna Niguel
(92677-1250)
PHONE..............300 490-5412
EMP: 158
SALES (corp-wide): 52B **Publicly Held**
WEB: www.morganstanley.com
SIC: 6022 State commercial banks
HQ: Morgan Stanley Smith Barney, Llc
1585 Broadway
New York NY 10036

(P-15035)
PACIFIC MERCANTILE BANK (HQ)
Also Called: PMBC
949 S Coast Dr Ste 300, Costa Mesa
(92626-7733)
PHONE..............714 438-2500
Brad R Dinsmore, *President*
Denis P Kalscheur, *Ch of Bd*
Steven Buster, *President*
Neil B Kornswiet, *President*
Thomas M Vertin, *President*
EMP: 50 EST: 1999
SALES: 66.6MM
SALES (corp-wide): 66.9MM **Privately Held**
WEB: www.pmbank.com
SIC: 6022 6712 State trust companies ac-
cepting deposits, commercial; bank hold-
ing companies
PA: Pacific Mercantile Bancorp
949 S Coast Dr Ste 300
Costa Mesa CA 92626
714 438-2500

(P-15036)
PACIFIC PREMIER BANCORP INC (PA)
17901 Von Karman Ave # 1, Irvine
(92614-6297)
PHONE..............949 864-8000
Steven R Gardner, *Ch of Ed*
Brian Fitzmaurice, *Vice Chairman*
Edward Padilla, *Vice Chairman*
Marina Bennett, *President*
Tauqir Rathor, *President*
EMP: 72 EST: 1996
SALES (est): 702MM **Publicly Held**
WEB: www.ppbi.com
SIC: 6022 State commercial banks

(P-15037)
PACIFIC PREMIER BANK (HQ)
17901 Von Karman Ave # 1, Irvine
(92614-6297)
PHONE..............714 431-4000
Steven R Gardner, *President*
Jeff C Jones, *Ch of Bd*
Ronald J Nicolas Jr, *CFC*
Kent Smith, *CFO*
Donn Jakosky, *Ch Credit Ofcr*
EMP: 62 EST: 1983
SQ FT: 36,159
SALES (est): 687.6MM **Publicly Held**
WEB: www.ppbi.com
SIC: 6022 State commercial banks

(P-15038)
PACIFIC PREMIER BANK
333 S Grand Ave Ste 3550, Los Angeles
(90071-3477)
PHONE..............213 626-0085
Arlet Hur, *Vice Pres*
EMP: 78 **Publicly Held**

WEB: www.ppbi.com
SIC: 6022 State trust companies accepting deposits, commercial
HQ: Pacific Premier Bank
17901 Von Karman Ave # 1
Irvine CA 92614
714 431-4000

(P-15039)
PREMIER COMMERCIAL BANCORP
2400 E Katella Ave # 125, Anaheim (92806-5920)
PHONE..................714 978-2400
Kenneth J Cosgrove, *Ch of Bd*
Ashokkumar Patel, *President*
Viktor R Uehlinger, *CFO*
Stephen W Pihl, *Exec VP*
Jane Weblemoe, *Vice Pres*
EMP: 64 EST: 2004 Privately Held
WEB: www.ppbi.com
SIC: 6022 State commercial banks

(P-15040)
PROVIDENT FINCL HOLDINGS INC (PA)
3756 Central Ave, Riverside (92506-2421)
PHONE..................951 686-6060
Craig G Blunden, *Ch of Bd*
Donavon P Ternes, *President*
Rscott Ritter, *Senior VP*
Chris Martin, *Vice Pres*
Bruce Bennett, *Director*
EMP: 57 EST: 1996
SALES: 39.7MM Publicly Held
WEB: www.myprovident.com
SIC: 6022 State commercial banks

(P-15041)
PROVIDENT SAVINGS BANK (HQ)
Also Called: Provident Bank
6570 Magnolia Ave, Riverside (92506-2410)
P.O. Box 59998 (92517-1998)
PHONE..................951 782-6177
Craig G Blunden, *Ch of Bd*
Lee Sunarto, *Treasurer*
David S Weiant,
Donavon Ternes, *Officer*
Richard L Gale, *Senior VP*
EMP: 128 EST: 1956
SALES: 62.6MM Publicly Held
WEB: www.myprovident.com
SIC: 6022 State commercial banks

(P-15042)
SAEHAN BANK (PA)
3200 Wilshire Blvd # 700, Los Angeles (90010-1333)
PHONE..................213 368-7700
Dong IL Kim, *President*
Dong II Kim, *President*
▲ EMP: 50 EST: 1991
SQ FT: 12,000
SALES (est): 19.2MM Privately Held
SIC: 6022 State commercial banks

(P-15043)
SOUTHERN CALIFORNIA BANCORP
22342 Avnida Empresa Ste, Rancho Santa Margari (92688)
PHONE..................949 766-3015
Mike Conte, *Vice Pres*
Rosa Yomtoubian, *Loan*
Cate Riggs, *Marketing Staff*
EMP: 55
SALES (corp-wide): 3.1MM Privately Held
SIC: 6022 State commercial banks
PA: Southern California Bancorp
2600 E Coast Hwy Ste K
Corona Del Mar CA
949 644-6074

(P-15044)
SUNWEST BANK (DH)
2050 Main St Ste 300, Irvine (92614-8279)
PHONE..................714 730-4441
Glenn Gray, *President*
Lillian Higuera, *President*
Carson Lappetito, *President*
Wesley Thomas, *President*
Chris Walsh, *President*

EMP: 50 EST: 1969
SALES: 80MM Privately Held
WEB: www.sunwestbank.com
SIC: 6022 State commercial banks

(P-15045)
VALLEY REPUBLIC BANK
5000 California Ave # 110, Bakersfield (93309-0711)
PHONE..................661 371-2000
Geraud Smith, *President*
Jeff Pace, *President*
Nathan Wilkerson, *President*
Michele Jasso, *COO*
Garth A Corrigan, *CFO*
EMP: 85
SQ FT: 8,000
SALES: 36MM Privately Held
WEB: www.valleyrepublic.bank
SIC: 6022 State commercial banks

6029 Commercial Banks, NEC

(P-15046)
BARCLAYS USA INC
1620 26th St Ste 2000n, Santa Monica (90404-4045)
PHONE..................310 829-9539
Antony Jenkins, *Branch Mgr*
Steve Song, *Technology*
Ted Iantuono, *Director*
EMP: 64
SALES (corp-wide): 36.7B Privately Held
WEB: www.home.barclays
SIC: 6029 Commercial banks
HQ: Barclays Usa Inc.
200 Park Ave W Fl 3 Flr 3
New York NY 10038
212 412-4000

(P-15047)
FIRST REPUBLIC BANK
1888 Century Park E # 200, Los Angeles (90067-1706)
PHONE..................310 712-1888
Simon Clark, *Branch Mgr*
Cate Hollenbeck, *Trust Officer*
Ryan Pile, *Trust Officer*
Jim Felton, *Credit Staff*
Alexander Rodriguez, *Accountant*
EMP: 87
SALES (corp-wide): 4.5B Publicly Held
WEB: www.firstrepublic.com
SIC: 6029 Commercial banks
PA: First Republic Bank
111 Pine St Fl 2
San Francisco CA 94111
415 392-1400

(P-15048)
N A TOMATOBANK
901 S Baldwin Ave, Arcadia (91007-6704)
PHONE..................626 759-9200
Charles Fenton, *CEO*
Lichen Herman, *President*
EMP: 57 EST: 2000
SALES (est): 4.2MM Privately Held
SIC: 6029 Commercial banks
PA: Tfc Holding Company
18605 Gale Ave Ste 238
City Of Industry CA 91748

(P-15049)
PACIFIC CITY BANK
13140 Yale Ave, Irvine (92620-2661)
PHONE..................714 263-1800
Haeyoung Cho, *Owner*
EMP: 80
SALES (corp-wide): 91.5MM Publicly Held
WEB: www.paccity.net
SIC: 6029 6021 Commercial banks; national commercial banks
HQ: Pacific City Bank
3701 Wilshire Blvd # 100
Los Angeles CA 90010
626 363-6730

6035 Federal Savings Institutions

(P-15050)
BBVA USA
420 S Palm Canyon Dr, Palm Springs (92262-7304)
PHONE..................760 325-2021
Janet Cook, *Branch Mgr*
EMP: 123
SALES (corp-wide): 18.2B Publicly Held
WEB: www.bbvausa.com
SIC: 6035 6211 Federal savings banks; security brokers & dealers
HQ: Bbva Usa
15 20th St S Ste 100
Birmingham AL 35233
205 297-1986

(P-15051)
ONEWEST BANK NA
3500 E 7th St, Long Beach (90804-5137)
PHONE..................562 433-0971
Fax: 562 433-0975
EMP: 56
SALES (corp-wide): 876.3MM Privately Held
SIC: 6035 Federal Savings Institution
HQ: Onewest Bank N.A.
888 E Walnut St
Pasadena CA 91103
626 535-4300

(P-15052)
PAN AMERICAN BANK FSB
18191 Von Karman Ave # 300, Irvine (92612-7106)
PHONE..................949 224-1917
Jim Vagim, *President*
EMP: 350 EST: 1994
SQ FT: 20,000
SALES (corp-wide): 84.6MM Privately Held
SIC: 6035 Federal savings & loan associations
PA: United Panam Financial Corp.
1071 Camelback St Ste 100
Newport Beach CA 92660
949 224-1226

(P-15053)
PFF BANCORP INC (PA)
2058 N Mills Ave Ste 139, Claremont (91711-2812)
PHONE..................213 683-6393
Kevin McCarthy, *President*
Robert W Burwell, *Ch of Bd*
Gregory C Talbott, *COO*
EMP: 718 EST: 1995 Privately Held
SIC: 6035 Federal savings & loan associations

(P-15054)
UNIVERSAL BANK (PA)
3455 S Nogales St Fl 2, West Covina (91792-5106)
PHONE..................626 854-2818
Frank Chang, *President*
Dwayne Matsuda, *President*
Edgar Gatchlian, *Vice Pres*
Richard Lopez, *Analyst*
Veronica Lopez, *Analyst*
EMP: 53
SQ FT: 28,223
SALES: 16.3MM Privately Held
WEB: www.universalbank.com
SIC: 6035 Federal savings banks

6036 Savings Institutions, Except Federal

(P-15055)
MALAGA FINANCIAL CORPORATION (PA)
2514 Via Tejon, Palos Verdes Estates (90274-1311)
PHONE..................310 375-9000
Randy C Bowers, *President*
Jerry Donahue, *Ch of Bd*
Jasna Penich, *CFO*
Gayle Cdebaca, *Assoc VP*
Mark S Smith, *Senior VP*

EMP: 55 EST: 2002
SALES (est): 49MM Privately Held
WEB: www.malagabank.com
SIC: 6036 State savings banks, not federally chartered

6061 Federal Credit Unions

(P-15056)
ALTAONE FEDERAL CREDIT UNION (PA)
Also Called: ALTA ONE FCU
701 S China Lake Blvd, Ridgecrest (93555-5027)
P.O. Box 1209 (93556-1209)
PHONE..................760 371-7000
Stephanie Sievers, *President*
Beverly Wagner, *President*
Denise Mattice, *COO*
Bill Christensen, *Officer*
Shannen Foreman, *Executive Asst*
EMP: 114
SQ FT: 33,000
SALES: 28.4MM Privately Held
WEB: www.altaone.org
SIC: 6061 Federal credit unions

(P-15057)
AMERICAN FIRST CREDIT UNION (PA)
6 Pointe Dr Ste 400, Brea (92821-6322)
PHONE..................562 691-1112
Julie Glance, *CFO*
Brian Thompson,
EMP: 96
SALES: 27.3MM Privately Held
WEB: www.amerfirst.org
SIC: 6061 Federal credit unions

(P-15058)
AMERICAS CHRISTIAN CREDIT UN (PA)
Also Called: ACCU
2100 E Route 66 Ste 100, Glendora (91740-4623)
PHONE..................626 208-5400
Mendell Thompson, *President*
Lucinda Garcia, *Officer*
Richard H Mathews, *Officer*
Naomi Paris, *Officer*
Natalie Turman, *Assoc VP*
EMP: 61 EST: 1958
SQ FT: 22,000
SALES: 16.3MM Privately Held
WEB: www.americaschristiancu.com
SIC: 6061 Federal credit unions

(P-15059)
ARROWHEAD CENTRAL CREDIT UNION (PA)
8686 Haven Ave, Rancho Cucamonga (91730-9109)
P.O. Box 4100 (91729-4100)
PHONE..................866 212-4333
Darin Woinarowicz, *CEO*
Raymond Mesler, *CFO*
Marie A Alonzo, *Chairman*
Doug Hallen, *Treasurer*
Susan Conjurski, *Exec VP*
EMP: 301 EST: 1949
SQ FT: 40,000
SALES: 47.3MM Privately Held
WEB: www.arrowheadcu.org
SIC: 6061 Federal credit unions

(P-15060)
CAL TECH EMPLYEES FDERAL CR UN (PA)
Also Called: CALTECH EFCU
528 Foothill Blvd, La Canada Flintridge (91011-3506)
P.O. Box 11001 (91012-6001)
PHONE..................818 952-4444
Richard Harris, *Principal*
Stephen L Proia, *Ch of Bd*
Richard L Harris, *President*
Willis Chapman, *Vice Ch Bd*
Yuling LI, *Officer*
EMP: 64 EST: 1955
SALES: 43.7MM Privately Held
WEB: www.caltechefcu.org
SIC: 6061 Federal credit unions

(P-15061)
CREDIT UNION SOUTHERN CAL (PA)
8028 Greenleaf Ave, Whittier (90602-2109)
P.O. Box 200 (90608-0200)
PHONE......................................562 698-8326
Dave Gunderson, *President*
Patty Dickason, *President*
Ed Fost, *COO*
Peter Putnam, *CFO*
Debbie Childs, *Exec VP*
▲ EMP: 163 EST: 1954
SQ FT: 12,000
SALES: 62.2MM **Privately Held**
WEB: www.cusocal.org
SIC: **6061** Federal credit unions

(P-15062)
F & A FEDERAL CREDIT UNION
2625 Corporate Pl, Monterey Park
(91754-7645)
P.O. Box 30831, Los Angeles (90030-0831)
PHONE......................................213 268-1226
Richard Andrews, *President*
Brendan Flannery, *Officer*
Rene McLean, *Officer*
Ralph Ramirez, *Officer*
Tanya Ruiz, *Officer*
EMP: 70
SQ FT: 43,000
SALES: 46.3MM **Privately Held**
WEB: www.fafcu.org
SIC: **6061** Federal credit unions

(P-15063)
FARMERS INSUR GROUP FDRAL CR U (PA)
2255 N Ontario St Ste 320, Burbank
(91504-3191)
P.O. Box 2723, Torrance (90509-2723)
PHONE......................................323 209-6000
Mark Herter, *CEO*
Sandy Medeiros, *President*
Laszlo Haredy, *Chairman*
Micah Bouloy, *Officer*
Sylvia Diaz, *Officer*
EMP: 70 EST: 1936
SQ FT: 12,000
SALES: 57.1MM **Privately Held**
WEB: www.figfcu.org
SIC: **6061** Federal credit unions

(P-15064)
FINANCIAL PARTNERS CREDIT UN (PA)
7800 Imperial Hwy, Downey (90242-3457)
P.O. Box 7005 (90241-7005)
PHONE......................................562 904-3000
John Crites, *Ch of Bd*
Barbara A Smith, *Vice Chairman*
Nader Moghaddam, *President*
Alan Bergman, *Treasurer*
Pam Ellens, *Officer*
EMP: 73
SQ FT: 32,000
SALES: 21.1MM **Privately Held**
WEB: www.fpcu.org
SIC: **6061** Federal credit unions

(P-15065)
FIREFIGHTERS FIRST CREDIT UN (PA)
815 Colorado Blvd, Los Angeles
(90041-1720)
PHONE......................................323 254-1700
Dixie Abramian, *CEO*
Richard Dillon, *CFO*
Ron Jackson, *Bd of Directors*
Ceasar Del Toro, *Officer*
Carrie Espinoza, *Officer*
EMP: 138
SQ FT: 25,000
SALES: 36.4MM **Privately Held**
WEB: www.firefightersfirstcu.org
SIC: **6061** Federal credit unions

(P-15066)
FIRST CITY CREDIT UNION (PA)
717 W Temple St Ste 400, Los Angeles
(90012-2632)
P.O. Box 93727, Pasadena (91109-3727)
PHONE......................................213 482-3477
James D Likens, *Ch of Bd*
Steve Punch, *CEO*
Terry O'Steen, *COO*

James Miller, *CFO*
Richard Reese, *CFO*
EMP: 50
SQ FT: 24,896
SALES: 22.9MM **Privately Held**
WEB: www.firstcitycu.org
SIC: **6061** Federal credit unions

(P-15067)
FIRST ENTERTAINMENT CREDIT UN (PA)
6735 Forest Lawn Dr # 100, Los Angeles
(90068-1055)
P.O. Box 100 (90078-0100)
PHONE......................................323 851-3673
Charles A Bruen, *President*
Matthew Vandegrift, *Partner*
Mitch Nedick, *Ch of Bd*
Lucy Wander-Perna, *Ch of Bd*
Gari Douglass, *Vice Chairman*
EMP: 80
SQ FT: 57,000
SALES: 56.9MM **Privately Held**
WEB: www.firstent.org
SIC: **6061** Federal credit unions

(P-15068)
HANIN FEDERAL CREDIT UNION (PA)
3700 Wilshire Blvd # 104, Los Angeles
(90010-2902)
PHONE......................................213 368-9000
James Lee, *President*
EMP: 50
SQ FT: 2,190
SALES: 2MM **Privately Held**
WEB: www.haninfcu.org
SIC: **6061** Federal credit unions

(P-15069)
ILWU FEDERAL CREDIT UNION
3447 Atlantic Ave, Long Beach
(90807-4513)
P.O. Box 7629 (90807-0629)
PHONE......................................310 834-6411
Ralph Ruiz, *President*
Kimberly Mathis, *COO*
Kim Mathis, *Vice Pres*
Devric Thomas, *Vice Pres*
Shannon White, *Technology*
EMP: 61 EST: 1954
SQ FT: 10,000
SALES: 12.5MM **Privately Held**
WEB: www.ilwucu.org
SIC: **6061** Federal credit unions

(P-15070)
KERN FEDERAL CREDIT UNION
1717 Truxtun Ave, Bakersfield
(93301-5102)
PHONE......................................661 327-9461
Brandon Ivie, *CEO*
Brenda O'Doherty, *President*
Jennifer Brucker, *Branch Mgr*
George Fuentes, *Loan Officer*
Ashley Morrison,
EMP: 66 EST: 1949
SQ FT: 17,000
SALES: 10.4MM **Privately Held**
WEB: www.stratacu.org
SIC: **6061** 6163 Federal credit unions;
loan brokers

(P-15071)
KINECTA FEDERAL CREDIT UNION (PA)
1440 Rosecrans Ave, Manhattan Beach
(90266-3702)
P.O. Box 10003 (90267-7503)
PHONE......................................310 643-5400
Keith Sultemeier, *CEO*
Teresa Freeborn, *President*
Douglas C Wicks, *President*
Joseph E Whitaker, *COO*
Gregory C Talbott, *CFO*
EMP: 250 EST: 1940
SQ FT: 80,000
SALES: (est) 169.1MM **Privately Held**
WEB: www.kinecta.org
SIC: **6061** Federal credit unions

(P-15072)
LOGIX FEDERAL CREDIT UNION (PA)
2340 N Hollywood Way, Burbank
(91505-1124)
P.O. Box 10249 (91510-0249)
PHONE......................................888 718-5328
Ana Fonseca, *CEO*
Dave Styler, *COO*
Julie Kim, *CFO*
Jesse Burk, *Officer*
Ana M Cortez, *Officer*
EMP: 210
SQ FT: 75,000
SALES: 240.8MM **Privately Held**
WEB: www.logixbanking.com
SIC: **6061** Federal credit unions

(P-15073)
LOS ANGELES FEDERAL CREDIT UN (PA)
300 S Glendale Ave # 100, Glendale
(91205-1752)
PHONE......................................818 242-8640
John T DEA, *CEO*
Richard Lie, *CFO*
Anthony Cuevas, *Senior VP*
Leta Cook, *Vice Pres*
Antonio Robinson, *Technology*
EMP: 100
SQ FT: 40,000
SALES: 37.2MM **Privately Held**
WEB: www.lafcu.org
SIC: **6061** Federal credit unions

(P-15074)
NORTHROP GRUMMAN FEDERAL CR UN (PA)
879 W 190th St Ste 800, Gardena
(90248-4205)
PHONE......................................310 808-4000
Stanley R Swenson Jr, *President*
Stephen Considine, *Vice Chairman*
Kathi Harper, *Chairman*
Jim Barnfather, *Vice Pres*
Harry Lee, *Vice Pres*
EMP: 60 EST: 1946
SALES: 44.3MM **Privately Held**
WEB: www.ngfcu.us
SIC: **6061** Federal credit unions

(P-15075)
NUVISION FINCL FEDERAL CR UN (PA)
7812 Edinger Ave Ste 100, Huntington
Beach (92647-3727)
P.O. Box 1220 (92647-1220)
PHONE......................................714 375-8000
Roger Ballard, *CEO*
John Afdem, *CFO*
Robert Geraci, *Treasurer*
Cathy Dominguez, *Officer*
Tami Ortega, *Officer*
EMP: 137 EST: 1935
SALES: 98.7MM **Privately Held**
WEB: www.nuvisionfederal.com
SIC: **6061** Federal credit unions

(P-15076)
ORANGE COUNTYS CREDIT UNION (PA)
1721 E Saint Andrew Pl, Santa Ana
(92705-4934)
P.O. Box 11777 (92711-1777)
PHONE......................................714 755-5900
Shruti S Miyashiro, *Principal*
Connie Peregretti, *President*
Amanda Verive, *President*
Dan Dillon, *Chairman*
Walt Krause, *Treasurer*
EMP: 157
SALES: 58.8MM **Privately Held**
WEB: www.orangecountyscu.org
SIC: **6061** Federal credit unions

(P-15077)
PARTNERS FEDERAL CREDIT UNION (PA)
100 N First St Ste 400, Burbank
(91502-1818)
PHONE......................................800 948-6677
Ricky Otey, *President*
Jerad Broaddus, *President*
Rick Wise, *CFO*

Idania Colon, *Officer*
Brian Kairnes, *Vice Pres*
EMP: 73 EST: 1968
SQ FT: 26,000
SALES: (est) 74.3MM **Privately Held**
WEB: www.partnersfcu.org
SIC: **6061** 6163 Federal credit unions;
loan brokers

(P-15078)
PASADENA SERVICE FEDERAL CR UN
670 N Rosemead Blvd, Pasadena
(91107-2101)
P.O. Box 70789 (91117-7789)
PHONE......................................626 351-9651
Charlene Bowman, *President*
Courtney Higuchi, *Exec VP*
Kenneth Landis, *Vice Pres*
Rhonda Newborg, *Vice Pres*
Andy Tien, *Vice Pres*
EMP: 75 EST: 1936
SQ FT: 13,600
SALES: 4.7MM **Privately Held**
WEB: www.mypsfcu.org
SIC: **6061** Federal credit unions

(P-15079)
SAG- AFTRA FEDERAL CREDIT UN
134 N Kenwood St, Burbank (91505-4201)
P.O. Box 11419 (91510-1419)
PHONE......................................818 562-3400
Randy Kahn, *Chairman*
Roger Runyan, *CEO*
Samuel Ketsoyan, *Officer*
Phillip Weiss, *Vice Pres*
James Pimentel, *Technology*
EMP: 52
SQ FT: 5,500
SALES: 10.7MM **Privately Held**
WEB: www.sagaftrafcu.org
SIC: **6061** Federal credit unions

(P-15080)
SCE FEDERAL CREDIT UNION (PA)
Also Called: SCE FCU
12701 Schabarum Ave, Baldwin Park
(91706-6807)
P.O. Box 8017, El Monte (91734-2317)
PHONE......................................626 960-6888
Dennis Huber, *CEO*
George Poitou, *COO*
Garland Koch, *CFO*
Daniel Rader, *CFO*
Kitty L Hunter,
EMP: 90 EST: 1952
SQ FT: 30,000
SALES: 30.5MM **Privately Held**
WEB: www.scefcu.org
SIC: **6061** Federal credit unions

(P-15081)
SCHOOLSFIRST FEDERAL CREDIT UN
5305 Alton Pkwy, Irvine (92604-8609)
PHONE......................................800 462-8328
Irene Long, *Planning*
Edward Rocha, *Technology*
Gianfranco Piccollo, *Manager*
Terry Thiel, *Manager*
EMP: 51
SALES: (corp-wide): 653.6MM **Privately Held**
WEB: www.orangecountyscu.org
SIC: **6061** Federal credit unions
PA: Schoolsfirst Federal Credit Union
2115 N Broadway
Santa Ana CA 92706
714 258-4000

(P-15082)
SCHOOLSFIRST FEDERAL CREDIT UN
161 E 40th St, San Bernardino
(92404-1301)
PHONE......................................800 462-8328
EMP: 51
SALES: (corp-wide): 653.6MM **Privately Held**
WEB: www.schoolsfirstfcu.org
SIC: **6061** Federal credit unions

PA: Schoolsfirst Federal Credit Union
2115 N Broadway
Santa Ana CA 92706
714 258-4000

(P-15083)
SCHOOLSFIRST FEDERAL CREDIT UN
12831 Moreno Beach Dr, Moreno Valley (92555-4558)
PHONE..................................800 462-8328
EMP: 51
SALES (corp-wide): 653.6MM **Privately Held**
WEB: www.schoolsfirstfcu.org
SIC: 6061 Federal credit unions
PA: Schoolsfirst Federal Credit Union
2115 N Broadway
Santa Ana CA 92706
714 258-4000

(P-15084)
SCHOOLSFIRST FEDERAL CREDIT UN
26892 La Paz Rd, Aliso Viejo (92656-3038)
PHONE..................................800 462-8328
EMP: 51
SALES (corp-wide): 653.6MM **Privately Held**
WEB: www.schoolsfirstfcu.org
SIC: 6061 Federal credit unions
PA: Schoolsfirst Federal Credit Union
2115 N Broadway
Santa Ana CA 92706
714 258-4000

(P-15085)
SCHOOLSFIRST FEDERAL CREDIT UN (PA)
2115 N Broadway, Santa Ana (92706-2613)
P.O. Box 11547 (92711-1547)
PHONE..................................714 258-4000
Bill Cheney, *President*
Francisco Nebot, *CFO*
Adam Jacoby, *Officer*
Jasmine Rivas, *Officer*
Andrea Whedbee, *Officer*
EMP: 270
SALES: 584.8MM **Privately Held**
WEB: www.schoolsfirstfcu.org
SIC: 6061 Federal credit unions

(P-15086)
SCHOOLSFIRST FEDERAL CREDIT UN
9125 Imperial Hwy Ste A, Downey (90242-2843)
PHONE..................................714 258-4000
EMP: 51
SALES (corp-wide): 653.6MM **Privately Held**
WEB: www.schoolsfirstfcu.org
SIC: 6061 Federal credit unions
PA: Schoolsfirst Federal Credit Union
2115 N Broadway
Santa Ana CA 92706
714 258-4000

(P-15087)
SCHOOLSFIRST FEDERAL CREDIT UN
Also Called: Consumer Loan Dept
15442 Del Amo Ave, Tustin (92780-6445)
P.O. Box 11547, Santa Ana (92711-1547)
PHONE..................................480 777-5995
Rudy Tafoya, *Director*
Brian Bargy, *Vice Pres*
Nubia Carrillo, *Vice Pres*
Shaelin Martinez, *Vice Pres*
Brenda Zimmerman, *Vice Pres*
EMP: 51
SQ FT: 61,058
SALES (corp-wide): 653.6MM **Privately Held**
WEB: www.orangecountyscu.org
SIC: 6061 Federal credit unions
PA: Schoolsfirst Federal Credit Union
2115 N Broadway
Santa Ana CA 92706
714 258-4000

(P-15088)
SESLOC FEDERAL CREDIT UNION (PA)
3855 Broad St, San Luis Obispo (93401-7109)
P.O. Box 5360 (93403-5360)
PHONE..................................805 543-1816
Bertha Foxford, *President*
Andy Bechinsky, *Senior VP*
Micki Myall, *Vice Pres*
Liz Summer, *Vice Pres*
Regina Ojeda, *Branch Mgr*
EMP: 77 **EST:** 1942
SQ FT: 19,700
SALES: 30.4MM **Privately Held**
WEB: www.sesloc.org
SIC: 6061 Federal credit unions

(P-15089)
SKYONE FEDERAL CREDIT UNION (PA)
14600 Aviation Blvd, Hawthorne (90250-6656)
PHONE..................................310 491-7500
Eileen C Rivera, *CEO*
Amy Chambers, *COO*
Shannon Doiron, *Chief Mktg Ofcr*
Adriana Gonzalez, *Officer*
Monique Luca, *Officer*
EMP: 58
SQ FT: 40,000
SALES: 20.4MM **Privately Held**
WEB: www.skyone.org
SIC: 6061 Federal credit unions

(P-15090)
SOUTHLAND CREDIT UNION (PA)
10701 Los Alamitos Blvd, Los Alamitos (90720-2353)
P.O. Box 7022, Downey (90241-7022)
PHONE..................................562 862-6831
Ferris R Foster, *CEO*
Jose L Manzano, *Vice Chairman*
Rene Lejay, *COO*
Tom Lent, *CFO*
Bradley P Silcox, *Treasurer*
EMP: 60 **EST:** 1999
SALES: 26.7MM **Privately Held**
WEB: www.southlandcu.org
SIC: 6061 Federal credit unions

(P-15091)
SUN COMMUNITY FEDERAL CR UN
1001 E Us Highway 98, Calexico (92231-9759)
PHONE..................................760 337-4200
Lolie Escalante, *Branch Mgr*
EMP: 67
SALES (corp-wide): 18.3MM **Privately Held**
WEB: www.suncommunityfcu.org
SIC: 6061 Federal credit unions
PA: Sun Community Federal Credit Union
1068 Broadway Ave
El Centro CA 92243
760 336-8622

(P-15092)
TELESIS COMMUNITY CREDIT UNION (PA)
9301 Winnetka Ave, Chatsworth (91311-6069)
PHONE..................................818 885-1226
Grace Mayo, *President*
Jean Faenza, *Exec VP*
EMP: 90 **EST:** 1993
SQ FT: 17,000 **Privately Held**
WEB: www.telesiscu.com
SIC: 6061 6163 Federal credit unions; loan brokers

(P-15093)
UNIFY FINANCIAL FEDERAL CR UN (PA)
1899 Western Way Ste 100, Torrance (90501-1146)
P.O. Box 10018, Manhattan Beach (90267-7518)
PHONE..................................310 536-5000
Gordon M Howe, *CEO*
Nathan Montgomery, *CFO*
Jenny Bell, *Officer*

Tracey Ewert, *Officer*
Lorena Tarin, *Officer*
EMP: 80
SALES: 137.6MM **Privately Held**
WEB: www.unifyfcu.com
SIC: 6061 Federal credit unions

(P-15094)
UNITED METHODIST FEDERAL CR UN (PA)
9040 Benson Ave, Montclair (91763-1615)
PHONE..................................909 946-4096
Ramon Noperi, *Principal*
EMP: 118 **EST:** 1948
SALES: 3.2MM **Privately Held**
WEB: www.interfaithfcu.org
SIC: 6061 Federal credit unions

(P-15095)
UNIVERSITY CREDIT UNION
1500 S Sepulveda Blvd, Los Angeles (90025-3312)
PHONE..................................310 477-6628
Charles Bumbarger, *President*
Carole D Zaima, *Bd of Directors*
Tristan Dion Chen, *Chief Mktg Ofcr*
Jose Ascencio, *Officer*
Evany Perkins, *Officer*
EMP: 104 **EST:** 1945
SALES: 22.8MM **Privately Held**
WEB: www.ucu.org
SIC: 6061 Federal credit unions

(P-15096)
USC CREDIT UNION
3720 S Flower St, Los Angeles (90089-4303)
PHONE..................................213 821-7100
Gary J Perez, *President*
Sandra Gonzalez, *Officer*
Alex Johnson, *Officer*
Peter Tom, *Vice Pres*
Valerie Ives, *Branch Mgr*
EMP: 56
SQ FT: 4,000
SALES: 24.1MM
SALES (corp-wide): 4.9B **Privately Held**
WEB: www.usccreditunion.org
SIC: 6061 Federal credit unions
PA: University Of Southern California
3720 S Flower St Fl 3
Los Angeles CA 90089
213 740-7762

(P-15097)
V A DESERT PCF FEDERAL CR UN
5901 E 7th St, Long Beach (90822-5201)
PHONE..................................562 498-1250
Cindy Glessner, *CEO*
Charles Feistman, *Ch of Bd*
Christine Wood, *COO*
Craig Kasper, *Admin Sec*
Marion G Smith, *Admin Sec*
EMP: 70 **EST:** 1947
SQ FT: 2,500
SALES: 3.6MM **Privately Held**
WEB: www.vadpfcu.org
SIC: 6061 Federal credit unions

(P-15098)
VALLEY STRONG CREDIT UNION
Also Called: Kern Schools Federal Credit Un
1828 Cecil Ave, Delano (93215-1520)
PHONE..................................661 725-1014
EMP: 58
SALES (corp-wide): 61.7MM **Privately Held**
WEB: www.valleystrong.com
SIC: 8299 6061 Airline training; federal credit unions
PA: Valley Strong Credit Union
11500 Bolthouse Dr
Bakersfield CA 93311
661 833-7900

(P-15099)
VALLEY STRONG CREDIT UNION (PA)
Also Called: Ksfcu
11500 Bolthouse Dr, Bakersfield (93311-8822)
P.O. Box 9506 (93389-9506)
PHONE..................................661 833-7900

Stephen P Renock IV, *CEO*
Joseph Drew, *Vice Chairman*
Mike Killen, *Vice Chairman*
Neil Marshall, *CFO*
Scott Begin, *Bd of Directors*
EMP: 60
SQ FT: 18,000
SALES: 59.5MM **Privately Held**
WEB: www.valleystrong.com
SIC: 6061 Federal credit unions

(P-15100)
VALLEY STRONG CREDIT UNION
3901 Mount Vernon Ave, Bakersfield (93306-1444)
P.O. Box 9506 (93389-9506)
PHONE..................................661 833-7920
Linda Boleschka, *Manager*
EMP: 58
SALES (corp-wide): 61.7MM **Privately Held**
WEB: www.valleystrong.com
SIC: 6061 Federal credit unions
PA: Valley Strong Credit Union
11500 Bolthouse Dr
Bakersfield CA 93311
661 833-7900

(P-15101)
VALLEY STRONG CREDIT UNION
8200 Stockdale Hwy Ste P, Bakersfield (93311-1029)
P.O. Box 9506 (93389-9506)
PHONE..................................661 833-7940
Diane Pinson, *Manager*
EMP: 58
SALES (corp-wide): 61.7MM **Privately Held**
WEB: www.valleystrong.com
SIC: 6061 Federal credit unions
PA: Valley Strong Credit Union
11500 Bolthouse Dr
Bakersfield CA 93311
661 833-7900

(P-15102)
VALLEY STRONG CREDIT UNION
6101 Coffee Rd, Bakersfield (93308-9415)
P.O. Box 9506 (93389-9506)
PHONE..................................661 833-7900
Ruth Rubbo, *Manager*
Micaela Venegas, *Opers Staff*
EMP: 58
SALES (corp-wide): 61.7MM **Privately Held**
WEB: www.valleystrong.com
SIC: 6061 Federal credit unions
PA: Valley Strong Credit Union
11500 Bolthouse Dr
Bakersfield CA 93311
661 833-7900

(P-15103)
VENTURA COUNTY CREDIT UNION (PA)
2575 Vista Del Mar Dr, Ventura (93001-3900)
PHONE..................................805 477-4000
Joseph Schroeder, *President*
Natalie Yanez, *Partner*
Sean McCulloch, *President*
Linda Sim, *CFO*
Gavin Bradley, *Senior VP*
EMP: 84
SQ FT: 22,500
SALES: 49.9MM **Privately Held**
WEB: www.vccuonline.net
SIC: 6061 Federal credit unions

(P-15104)
XCEED FINANCIAL CREDIT UNION (PA)
888 N Nash St, El Segundo (90245-2826)
PHONE..................................800 932-8222
EMP: 96
SQ FT: 30,000
SALES: 33.6MM **Privately Held**
WEB: www.xfcu.org
SIC: 6061 Federal Credit Union

P R O D U C T S & S V C S

6062 State Credit Unions

(P-15105)
ALTA VISTA CREDIT UNION
2025 N Riverside Ave, Rialto (92377-4601)
PHONE.....................................909 809-3838
Larry Palochik, *Branch Mgr*
James Dawson, *Marketing Mgr*
Taylor Carroll,
Leslie Hall, *Clerk*
EMP: 59
SALES (corp-wide): 6.7MM **Privately Held**
WEB: www.altavistacu.org
SIC: 6062 State credit unions, not federally chartered
PA: Vista Alta Credit Union
　　1425 W Lugonia Ave # 101
　　Redlands CA 92374
　　909 809-3838

(P-15106)
ALTURA CREDIT UNION (PA)
2847 Campus Pkwy, Riverside
(92507-0906)
PHONE.................................888 883-7228
Toll Free:.....................................888　-
Mark Hawkins, *President*
Tom Shryock, *CFO*
Diana Wilcox, *CFO*
Blanca Sanchez, *Officer*
Ron Woodbury, *Exec VP*
EMP: 59
SQ FT: 60,000
SALES: 57.6MM **Privately Held**
WEB: www.alturacu.com
SIC: 6062 State credit unions, not federally chartered

(P-15107)
CALIFORNIA CREDIT UNION (PA)
701 N Brand Blvd Fl 7, Glendale
(91203-1218)
P.O. Box 29100 (91209-9100)
PHONE.................................818 291-6700
Steve O'Connell, *CEO*
Mark Los Cobos, *President*
Albert Gomez, *President*
Jason Pugh, *President*
Hudson Lee, *CFO*
EMP: 120 **EST:** 1933
SALES: 113.1MM **Privately Held**
WEB: www.ccu.com
SIC: 6062 6061 State credit unions, not federally chartered; federal credit unions

(P-15108)
CHRISTIAN COMMUNITY CREDIT UN (PA)
255 N Lone Hill Ave, San Dimas
(91773-2308)
P.O. Box 3012, Covina (91722-9012)
PHONE.................................626 915-7551
Marji Hughes, *CEO*
John T Walling, *President*
Aaron Caid, *Chief Mktg Ofcr*
David Estridge, *Exec VP*
Mike Poirier, *Senior VP*
EMP: 70 **EST:** 1957
SQ FT: 24,000
SALES: 26.7MM **Privately Held**
WEB: www.mycccu.com
SIC: 6062 State credit unions, not federally chartered

(P-15109)
COASTHILLS CREDIT UNION (PA)
Also Called: Cscu
1075 E Betteravia Rd, Santa Maria
(93454-7023)
P.O. Box 8000 (93456-8000)
PHONE.................................805 733-7600
Jeff York, *President*
Cathy Cachu, *President*
Barbara Hartsfield, *CFO*
Chuck Scheithauer, *Treasurer*
Daniel Walls, *Ch Credit Ofcr*
EMP: 80 **EST:** 1958
SQ FT: 30,000

SALES: 50.2MM **Privately Held**
WEB: www.coasthills.coop
SIC: 6062 State credit unions, not federally chartered

(P-15110)
CU COOPERATIVE SYSTEMS INC (PA)
Also Called: Co-Op Network
9692 Haven Ave, Rancho Cucamonga
(91730-5891)
PHONE.................................909 948-2500
Todd Clark, *President*
Tom Sargent, *Ch of Bd*
John Bommarito, *Treasurer*
Shaun Gehman, *Senior VP*
Amber Danford, *Vice Pres*
▲ **EMP:** 285 **EST:** 1981
SALES (est): 399.9MM **Privately Held**
WEB: www.co-opfs.org
SIC: 6062 State credit unions, not federally chartered

(P-15111)
EDUCATIONAL EMPLOYEES CR UN
1460 W 7th St, Hanford (93230-4938)
PHONE.................................559 587-4460
Dianne Mitchell, *Owner*
EMP: 64
SALES (corp-wide): 99.7MM **Privately Held**
WEB: www.myeecu.com
SIC: 6062 6061 State credit unions, not federally chartered; federal credit unions
PA: Educational Employees Credit Union
　　2222 W Shaw Ave
　　Fresno CA 93711
　　559 437-7700

(P-15112)
EVANGELICAL CHRISTIAN CR UN
955 W Imperial Hwy # 100, Brea
(92821-3814)
PHONE.................................714 671-5700
EMP: 157
SALES (corp-wide): 37.2MM **Privately Held**
SIC: 6062 6061 State Credit Union Federal Credit Union
PA: Evangelical Christian Credit Union
　　955 W Imperial Hwy # 100
　　Brea CA 92821
　　714 671-5700

(P-15113)
EVANGELICAL CHRISTIAN CR UN (PA)
Also Called: ECCU
955 W Imperial Hwy # 100, Brea
(92821-3812)
P.O. Box 2400 (92822-2400)
PHONE.................................714 671-5700
Abel Pomar, *CEO*
Susan Rushing, *COO*
Gregory Talbott, *CFO*
Joseph Graham, *Officer*
Tom Honan, *Senior VP*
EMP: 146 **EST:** 1964
SQ FT: 125,000
SALES: 19.5MM **Privately Held**
WEB: www.eccu.org
SIC: 6062 State credit unions, not federally chartered

(P-15114)
LOS ANGELES POLICE CREDIT UN (PA)
Also Called: L A P F C U
16150 Sherman Way, Van Nuys
(91406-3938)
P.O. Box 10188 (91410-0188)
PHONE.................................818 787-6520
Tyler E Izen, *Ch of Bd*
G Michael Padgett, *President*
Angelino Cayanan, *CFO*
Warren D Spayth, *Treasurer*
Joseph MA, *Officer*
EMP: 100 **EST:** 1936
SQ FT: 30,000
SALES: 41MM **Privately Held**
WEB: www.lapfcu.org
SIC: 6062 6061 State credit unions, not federally chartered; federal credit unions

(P-15115)
PREMIER AMERICA CREDIT UNION (PA)
19867 Prairie St Lbby, Chatsworth
(91311-6532)
P.O. Box 2178 (91313-2178)
PHONE.................................818 772-4000
John M Merlo, *President*
Nancy Wheeler-Chandler, *Vice Chairman*
Brad Cunningham, *CFO*
James Anderson, *Chairman*
Richard Ziebell, *Corp Secy*
EMP: 135 **EST:** 1957
SQ FT: 80,000
SALES: 101.4MM **Privately Held**
WEB: www.premieramerica.com
SIC: 6062 6163 State credit unions, not federally chartered; loan brokers

(P-15116)
WESCOM CENTRAL CREDIT UNION (PA)
123 S Marengo Ave, Pasadena
(91101-2428)
P.O. Box 7058 (91109-7058)
PHONE.................................888 493-7266
Toll Free:.....................................888　-
Darren Williams, *Principal*
Renee Boyce, *Officer*
Jeanne Brown, *Officer*
Whitney Bullock, *Officer*
Bryan Tinoco, *Officer*
EMP: 425 **EST:** 1934
SQ FT: 90,000
SALES: 126.2MM **Privately Held**
WEB: www.wescom.org
SIC: 6062 State credit unions, not federally chartered

6081 Foreign Banks, Branches & Agencies

(P-15117)
HONG KONG & SHANGHAI BANKING
Also Called: Hong Kong Bank
770 Wilshire Blvd Ste 800, Los Angeles
(90017-3719)
PHONE.................................213 626-2460
EMP: 60
SALES (corp-wide): 79.8B **Privately Held**
SIC: 6081 Non-Depository Banking Agency
HQ: Hongkong And Shanghai Banking Corporation Limited, The
　　Hsbc Main Bldg
　　Central District HK
　　282 211-11

6091 Nondeposit Trust Facilities

(P-15118)
BANK OF NEW YORK TRUST OF CAL (HQ)
700 S Flower St Ste 340, Los Angeles
(90017-4102)
PHONE.................................213 630-6327
Mike Klugman, *President*
William J Winklemann, *Vice Pres*
EMP: 138 **EST:** 1980
SQ FT: 4,750
SALES (est): 14.8MM
SALES (corp-wide): 15.8B **Publicly Held**
WEB: www.bnymellon.com
SIC: 6091 6022 Nondeposit trust facilities; state trust companies accepting deposits, commercial
PA: The Bank Of New York Mellon Corporation
　　240 E Greenwich St
　　New York NY 10007
　　212 495-1784

(P-15119)
DEUTSCHE BANK NATIONAL TR CO
1761 E Saint Andrew Pl, Santa Ana
(92705-4934)
PHONE.................................714 247-6054
F Jim Della Sala, *Principal*

David West, *Managing Dir*
Joseph Campbell, *Sales Staff*
EMP: 75 **EST:** 2007
SALES (est): 53.7MM
SALES (corp-wide): 15.4B **Privately Held**
WEB: www.db.com
SIC: 6091 6021 Nondeposit trust facilities; national commercial banks
HQ: Deutsche Bank Trust Company Americas
　　60 Wall St Bsmt 1
　　New York NY 10005
　　212 250-2500

(P-15120)
SUNAMERICA INC (HQ)
1 Sun America Ctr Fl 38, Los Angeles
(90067-6100)
PHONE.................................310 772-6000
Eli Broad, *Chairman*
Jay S Wintrob, *CEO*
James R Belardi, *Exec VP*
Jana Waring Greer, *Exec VP*
Michael J Akers, *Senior VP*
EMP: 1000 **EST:** 1957
SQ FT: 95,845
SALES (est): 459.8MM
SALES (corp-wide): 43.7B **Publicly Held**
WEB: www.lifeandretirement.aig.com
SIC: 6091 6311 6211 6282 Nondeposit trust facilities; life insurance carriers; mutual funds, selling by independent salesperson; brokers, security; dealers, security; manager of mutual funds, contract or fee basis; pension & retirement plan consultants; pension, health & welfare funds
PA: American International Group, Inc.
　　175 Water St Rm 1800
　　New York NY 10038
　　212 770-7000

6099 Functions Related To Deposit Banking, NEC

(P-15121)
ASSOCIATED FOREIGN EXCH INC (HQ)
Also Called: Afex
21045 Califa St, Woodland Hills
(91367-5104)
PHONE.................................888 307-2339
Jan Vlietstra, *CEO*
Irving Barr, *Ch of Bd*
Fred Kunik, *President*
Richard Verasamy, *CFO*
Michael Smith, *Treasurer*
EMP: 57 **EST:** 1979
SALES (est): 49.7MM **Publicly Held**
WEB: www.afex.com
SIC: 6099 Foreign currency exchange

(P-15122)
ASSOCTED FGN EXCH HOLDINGS INC (PA)
21045 Califa St, Woodland Hills
(91367-5104)
PHONE.................................818 386-2702
Irving Barr, *Chairman*
Fred Kunik, *President*
Jan Vliestra, *CEO*
Richard Verasamy, *CFO*
Michael Downing, *CIO*
EMP: 89
SALES (est): 58MM **Privately Held**
WEB: www.afex.com
SIC: 6099 Foreign currency exchange

(P-15123)
BUCKEYE CHECK CASHING INC
1615 W Redlands Blvd, Redlands
(92373-8085)
PHONE.................................909 792-8816
EMP: 73 **Privately Held**
WEB: www.ccfi.com
SIC: 6099 Check cashing agencies
HQ: Buckeye Check Cashing, Inc.
　　5165 Emerald Pkwy Ste 100
　　Dublin OH 43017
　　614 798-5900

(P-15124)
CONTINENTAL CURRENCY SVCS INC (HQ)
1108 E 17th St, Santa Ana (92701-2600)
PHONE..............................714 569-0300
Irving Barr, *Ch of Bd*
Fred Kunik, *President*
Silvia Posada, *Officer*
Frank Ochoa, *Sales Staff*
EMP: 50 **EST:** 1940
SQ FT: 10,000
SALES (est): 11.7MM
SALES (corp-wide): 244.7MM **Privately Held**
WEB: www.ccurr.com
SIC: 6099 Check cashing agencies
PA: Continental Currency Services, Inc.
     1108 E 17th St
     Santa Ana CA 92701
     714 569-0300

(P-15125)
CONTINENTAL CURRENCY SVCS INC (PA)
Also Called: Cash It Here
1108 E 17th St, Santa Ana (92701-2600)
P.O. Box 10970 (92711-0970)
PHONE..............................714 569-0300
Fred Kunik, *President*
Irving Barr, *Ch of Bd*
Bradley Hauser, *COO*
David Wilder, *COO*
Dave Atwater, *Security Dir*
EMP: 80 **EST:** 1977
SQ FT: 12,500
SALES (est): 244.7MM **Privately Held**
WEB: www.ccurr.com
SIC: 6099 Check cashing agencies; electronic funds transfer network, including switching; money order issuance

(P-15126)
CONTINENTAL EXCH SOLUTIONS INC (HQ)
Also Called: Ria Financial Service
6565 Knott Ave, Buena Park (90620-1139)
PHONE..............................714 522-7044
Juan C Bianchi, *CEO*
Timothy A Fanning, *COO*
Shawn D Fielder, *CFO*
Chris Hirth, *Officer*
Enric Balcells, *Vice Pres*
EMP: 1461 **EST:** 1987
SALES (est): 493.4MM **Publicly Held**
WEB: www.us.riafinancial.com
SIC: 6099 Electronic funds transfer network, including switching

(P-15127)
DEBISYS INC (PA)
Also Called: Emida Technologies
27442 Portola Pkwy # 150, Foothill Ranch (92610-2823)
PHONE..............................949 699-1401
Dennis Andrews, *CEO*
Jim Wodach, *CFO*
Ang L Pelaez, *Vice Pres*
Oscar Cortes, *Opers Mgr*
Traci Rall, *Accounts Mgr*
EMP: 80 **EST:** 1977
SQ FT: 10,000
SALES (est): 46.5MM **Privately Held**
WEB: www.emida.net
SIC: 6099 Automated teller machine (ATM) network

(P-15128)
FCTI INC (PA)
11766 Wilshire Blvd # 30, Los Angeles (90025-6538)
PHONE..............................310 405-0022
Jeff Wernecke, *President*
Robel Gugsa, *CEO*
Brian Sickles, *COO*
Joni Gaudes, *Vice Pres*
Patrick Harnisch, *Vice Pres*
EMP: 87 **EST:** 1993
SALES (est): 36.7MM **Privately Held**
WEB: www.fcti.com
SIC: 6099 Automated teller machine (ATM) network

(P-15129)
LENLYN LTD WHICH WILL DO BUS I (HQ)
6151 W Century Blvd # 11, Los Angeles (90045-5310)
P.O. Box 92192 (90009-2192)
PHONE..............................310 417-3432
Bharat Shah, *CEO*
Dan Northam, *Vice Pres*
Mark Garrett, *IT/INT Sup*
EMP: 75 **EST:** 1984
SQ FT: 1,000
SALES (est): 25.2MM **Privately Held**
WEB: www.iceplc.com
SIC: 6099 Foreign currency exchange

(P-15130)
MOBILE MONEY INC (HQ)
7633 Industry Ave, Pico Rivera (90660-4301)
PHONE..............................562 948-3916
Irving Barr, *President*
Fred Kunik, *Treasurer*
EMP: 62 **EST:** 1981
SALES (est): 555.9K
SALES (corp-wide): 244.7MM **Privately Held**
WEB: www.mobilmoney.ru
SIC: 6099 Money order issuance; check cashing agencies
PA: Continental Currency Services, Inc.
     1108 E 17th St
     Santa Ana CA 92701
     714 569-0300

(P-15131)
POPULUS FINANCIAL GROUP INC
Also Called: Ace Cash Express
6302 Van Buren Blvd, Riverside (92503-2051)
PHONE..............................951 509-3506
Michael Mc Knight, *Branch Mgr*
EMP: 105 **Privately Held**
WEB: www.acecashexpress.com
SIC: 6099 Check cashing agencies
HQ: Populus Financial Group, Inc
     300 E John Carpenter Fwy # 900
     Irving TX 75062
     972 550-5000

(P-15132)
SERFIN FUNDS TRANSFER (PA)
1000 S Fremont Ave A-O, Alhambra (91803-8800)
PHONE..............................626 457-3070
Richard Stevenson, *President*
EMP: 100
SALES (est): 8.4MM **Privately Held**
SIC: 6099 Electronic funds transfer network, including switching

6111 Federal Credit Agencies

(P-15133)
DEUTSCHE BANK NATIONAL TR CO (DH)
1999 Avenue Of The Stars, Los Angeles (90067-6022)
PHONE..............................310 788-6200
EMP: 90 **EST:** 1983
SALES: 161.9MM
SALES (corp-wide): 15.4B **Privately Held**
WEB: www.db.com
SIC: 6111 National Consumer Cooperative Bank
HQ: Deutsche Bank Trust Company Americas
     60 Wall St Bsmt 1
     New York NY 10005
     212 250-2500

(P-15134)
LAW SCHOOL FINANCIAL INC
Also Called: Law School Loans
175 S Lake Ave Unit 200, Pasadena (91101-2629)
PHONE..............................626 243-1800
EMP: 190
SQ FT: 25,000
SALES (est): 15.5MM **Privately Held**
WEB: www.lawschoolloans.com
SIC: 6111 Federal & Federally Sponsored Credit,Nsk

(P-15135)
LBS FINANCIAL CREDIT UNION (PA)
5505 Garden Grove Blvd # 500, Westminster (92683-1894)
PHONE..............................562 598-9007
Jeffrey A Napper, *President*
Gene Allen, *Ch of Bd*
Heather Summers, *COO*
Sue White, *CFO*
Dug Woog, *Treasurer*
EMP: 120 **EST:** 1935
SQ FT: 63,000
SALES: 50MM **Privately Held**
WEB: www.lbsfcu.org
SIC: 6111 6163 Federal & federally sponsored credit agencies; loan brokers

6141 Personal Credit Institutions

(P-15136)
AICCO INC (HQ)
Also Called: Imperial Credit
3 Hutton Cntre Dr Ste 630, Santa Ana (92707)
PHONE..............................714 481-3215
Paul Zarookian, *President*
EMP: 70 **EST:** 1974
SALES (est): 2.8MM
SALES (corp-wide): 43.7B **Publicly Held**
WEB: www.aig.com
SIC: 6141 Personal credit institutions
PA: American International Group, Inc.
     175 Water St Rm 1800
     New York NY 10038
     212 770-7000

(P-15137)
AMERICAN HONDA FINANCE CORP (DH)
1919 Torrance Blvd, Torrance (90501-2722)
P.O. Box 2200 (90509-2200)
PHONE..............................310 972-2239
Hideo Tamaka, *CEO*
John Weisickle, *CFO*
Stephan Smith, *Senior VP*
Dean Hardesty, *Regional Mgr*
Katy Parato, *Admin Mgr*
EMP: 200 **EST:** 1980
SALES: 3.1B **Privately Held**
WEB: www.hondafinancialservices.com
SIC: 6141 Financing: automobiles, furniture, etc., not a deposit bank; automobile & consumer finance companies
HQ: American Honda Motor Co., Inc.
     1919 Torrance Blvd
     Torrance CA 90501
     310 783-2000

(P-15138)
ASSOCIATES FIRST CAPITAL CORP
Also Called: Avco Financial
3634 5th Ave, Glendale (91214-2444)
PHONE..............................818 248-7055
EMP: 106
SALES (corp-wide): 88.8B **Publicly Held**
SIC: 6141 Consumer finance companies
HQ: Associates First Capital Corporation
     4000 Regent Blvd
     Irving TX 75063
     800 922-6235

(P-15139)
ASSOCIATES FIRST CAPITAL CORP
Also Called: Avco Financial
519 S C St, Oxnard (93030-7001)
PHONE..............................805 487-9825
Warren R Lyons, *Ch of Bd*
EMP: 106
SALES (corp-wide): 88.8B **Publicly Held**
SIC: 6141 Personal credit institutions
HQ: Associates First Capital Corporation
     4000 Regent Blvd
     Irving TX 75063
     800 922-6235

(P-15140)
AUTOGRAVITY CORPORATION
15495 Sand Canyon Ave # 100, Irvine (92618-3152)
PHONE..............................949 392-8777
Alex Mallmann, *President*
Jason Bonifay, *CFO*
Serge Vartanov, *Chief Mktg Ofcr*
Jennifer Y Ishiguro, *Exec VP*
Aleks Bogoeski, *Vice Pres*
EMP: 60 **EST:** 2015
SALES (est): 17.8MM **Privately Held**
WEB: www.autogravity.com
SIC: 6141 Automobile & consumer finance companies

(P-15141)
CASHCALL INC
1 City Blvd W Ste 102, Orange (92868-3621)
P.O. Box 66007, Anaheim (92816-6007)
PHONE..............................949 752-4600
John Paul Reddam, *CEO*
Ethan Taub, *Chief Mktg Ofcr*
Hilary Holland, *Senior VP*
Steve Klopstock, *Vice Pres*
Derrick Wheatley, *Branch Mgr*
EMP: 1400
SALES (est): 323.4MM **Privately Held**
WEB: www.cashcall.com
SIC: 6141 Personal finance licensed loan companies, small

(P-15142)
CITIFINANCIAL CREDIT COMPANY
2655 Del Vista Dr, City of Industry (91745-5244)
PHONE..............................626 712-8780
EMP: 135
SALES (corp-wide): 88.8B **Publicly Held**
SIC: 6141 Consumer finance companies
HQ: Citifinancial Credit Company
     300 Saint Paul Pl Fl 3
     Baltimore MD 21202
     410 332-3000

(P-15143)
GREEN DOT CORPORATION (PA)
3465 E Foothill Blvd, Pasadena (91107-6071)
P.O. Box 5100 (91117-0100)
PHONE..............................626 765-2000
Dan Henry, *CEO*
Konrad Alt, *Partner*
Jimmy Ngor, *Partner*
William I Jacobs, *Ch of Bd*
Steven W Streit, *President*
EMP: 759 **EST:** 1999
SQ FT: 140,000
SALES (est): 1.1B **Publicly Held**
WEB: www.greendot.com
SIC: 6141 7389 Personal credit institutions; credit card service

(P-15144)
HYUNDAI CAPITAL AMERICA (DH)
Also Called: Hyundai Finance
3161 Michelson Dr # 1900, Irvine (92612-4418)
PHONE..............................714 965-3000
Sam Sanghyuk Suh, *CEO*
Sukjoon Won, *President*
Jwa Jin Cho, *CEO*
Minsok Randy Park, *CFO*
Marcelo Brutti, *Vice Pres*
EMP: 495 **EST:** 1989
SQ FT: 60,000
SALES (est): 473.8MM **Privately Held**
WEB: www.hyundaicapitalamerica.com
SIC: 6141 Automobile loans, including insurance
HQ: Hyundai Motor America
     10550 Talbert Ave
     Fountain Valley CA 92708
     714 965-3000

PRODUCTS & SVCS

(P-15145)
LOBEL FINANCIAL CORPORATION (PA)
1150 N Magnolia Ave, Anaheim
(92801-2605)
P.O. Box 3000 (92803-3000)
PHONE..............................714 995-3333
Harvey Lobel, *CEO*
Gary Lobel, *Corp Secy*
Maggie Lawson, *Officer*
David Lobel, *Vice Pres*
Murray Lobel, *Vice Pres*
EMP: 58 **EST:** 1979
SQ FT: 11,000
SALES (est): 27.4MM **Privately Held**
WEB: www.lobelfinancial.com
SIC: 6141 Automobile loans, including in-
surance

(P-15146)
MITSUBISHI MOTORS CR AMER INC (DH)
6400 Katella Ave, Cypress (90630-5208)
P.O. Box 689040, Franklin TN (37068-
9040)
PHONE..............................714 799-4730
Dan Booth, *President*
Hideyuki Kitamura, *Treasurer*
Charles Tredway, *Exec VP*
Ellen Gleberman, *Admin Sec*
Angie O 'leary, *Director*
EMP: 394 **EST:** 1990
SQ FT: 32,256
SALES (est): 151.8MM **Privately Held**
WEB: www.mitsubishicars.com
SIC: 6141 6159 Automobile loans, includ-
ing insurance; truck finance leasing
HQ: Mitsubishi Motors North America, Inc.
4031 Aspen Grove Dr
Franklin TN 37067
714 799-4730

(P-15147)
NORTH AMERICAN ACCEPTANCE CORP
Also Called: An Open Check
3191 Red Hill Ave Ste 100, Costa Mesa
(92626-3451)
PHONE..............................714 868-3195
Marco J Rasic, *CEO*
Mary Clancey Rasic, *Vice Pres*
EMP: 123 **EST:** 2002
SQ FT: 24,000
SALES (est): 11.1MM **Privately Held**
SIC: 6141 6719 Automobile & consumer
finance companies; personal holding
companies, except banks

(P-15148)
PAYOFF INC
Also Called: Happy Money
3200 Park Center Dr # 800, Costa Mesa
(92626-7163)
PHONE..............................949 430-0630
Scott Saunders, *CEO*
Jessie Hennen, *Partner*
Christopher Hilliard, *Ch Credit Ofcr*
Adam Zarlengo,
Chris Hilliard, *Officer*
EMP: 89 **EST:** 2012
SQ FT: 19,500
SALES (est): 20.3MM **Privately Held**
WEB: www.payoff.com
SIC: 6141 Personal credit institutions

6153 Credit Institutions, Short-Term Business

(P-15149)
AMWEST FUNDING CORP
6 Pointe Dr Ste 300, Brea (92821-6323)
PHONE..............................714 831-3333
Ryan Kim, *President*
Mark Yoon, *CFO*
Wayne Liu, *Exec VP*
Benjie Alvidera, *Vice Pres*
Rebecca Bruggeman, *Vice Pres*
EMP: 58 **EST:** 2017
SALES (est): 17.2MM **Privately Held**
SIC: 6153 Working capital financing

(P-15150)
BALBOA CAPITAL CORPORATION (PA)
575 Anton Blvd Ste 1200, Costa Mesa
(92626-7685)
PHONE..............................949 756-0800
Patrick Byrne, *CEO*
Phil Silva, *President*
Robert Rasmussen, *COO*
Mark Hendrickson, *CFO*
Heather Parker, *CFO*
EMP: 200 **EST:** 1988
SQ FT: 24,000
SALES (est): 144.3MM **Privately Held**
WEB: www.balboacapital.com
SIC: 6153 Working capital financing

(P-15151)
BROKER SOLUTIONS INC
Also Called: New American Funding
19300 Rinaldi St Ste M, Porter Ranch
(91326-3785)
PHONE..............................818 235-0640
Harry Zakarian, *Branch Mgr*
EMP: 86 **Privately Held**
WEB: www.newamericanfunding.com
SIC: 6153 Working capital financing
PA: Broker Solutions, Inc.
14511 Myford Rd Ste 100
Tustin CA 92780

(P-15152)
EAST LOS ANGELES COMMUNITY UN (PA)
Also Called: Telacu
5400 E Olympic Blvd Fl 3, Commerce
(90022-5147)
PHONE..............................323 721-1655
David C Lizarraga, *Ch of Bd*
Michael D Lizarraga, *Exec VP*
Jay Bell, *Senior VP*
Paul Samuel, *Senior VP*
Gerald Barham, *Vice Pres*
EMP: 50 **EST:** 1968
SQ FT: 60,000
SALES (est): 16.4MM **Privately Held**
WEB: www.telacu.com
SIC: 6153 8322 6512 6514 Short-term
business credit; multi-service center; non-
residential building operators; dwelling
operators, except apartments

(P-15153)
HANA COMMERCIAL FINANCE INC
1000 Wilshire Blvd # 2000, Los Angeles
(90017-5645)
PHONE..............................213 240-1234
Suyong Kim, *CFO*
Sunnie Kim, *CEO*
Young Shim, *COO*
Suyoung Kim, *CFO*
EMP: 85 **EST:** 2016
SALES (est): 6.5MM **Privately Held**
WEB: www.hanafinancial.com
SIC: 6153 Factoring services

(P-15154)
INPUT 1 LLC
6200 Canoga Ave Ste 400, Woodland Hills
(91367-2459)
PHONE..............................818 340-0030
Todd Greenbaum, *Mng Member*
Ken Henrie, *Info Tech Dir*
Erika Gnacadja, *Software Engr*
Mark Joseph, *Analyst*
Daniel Cervantes, *Broker*
EMP: 110 **EST:** 1984
SQ FT: 24,000
SALES: 18.9MM **Privately Held**
WEB: www.input1.com
SIC: 6153 7371 Short-term business
credit; computer software development &
applications; computer software develop-
ment

(P-15155)
MORGAN STNLEY SMITH BARNEY LLC
9665 Wilshire Blvd # 600, Beverly Hills
(90212-2340)
PHONE..............................310 285-4800
Joel Davidman, *Principal*
EMP: 113

SALES (corp-wide): 52B **Publicly Held**
WEB: www.morganstanley.com
SIC: 6153 Working capital financing
HQ: Morgan Stanley Smith Barney, Llc
1585 Broadway
New York NY 10036

(P-15156)
NATIONS CAPITAL GROUP LLC
Also Called: Nations Surgery Center
5353 Balboa Blvd Ste 300, Encino
(91316-2863)
PHONE..............................818 793-2050
Fax: 818 793-2059
EMP: 50
SALES (corp-wide): 5.1MM **Privately
Held**
SIC: 6153 Business Credit Intstitutions
PA: Nations Capital Group, Llc
5370 S Durango Dr
Las Vegas NV

(P-15157)
PACIFIC LIFE GLOBAL FUNDING
700 Newport Center Dr, Newport Beach
(92660-6307)
PHONE..............................949 219-3011
William Gross, *Principal*
EMP: 66 **EST:** 2007
SALES (est): 3.1MM
SALES (corp-wide): 12.8B **Privately Held**
WEB: www.pacificfunds.com
SIC: 6153 Short-term business credit
HQ: Pacific Life Insurance Company
700 Newport Center Dr
Newport Beach CA 92660
949 219-3011

(P-15158)
RIVIERA FINANCE OF TEXAS INC
10430 Pioneer Blvd Ste 1, Santa Fe
Springs (90670-8245)
PHONE..............................562 777-1300
Sandy Newman, *Branch Mgr*
EMP: 88 **Privately Held**
WEB: www.rivierafinance.com
SIC: 6153 Factors of commercial paper
PA: Riviera Finance Of Texas, Inc
220 Avenue I
Redondo Beach CA 90277

(P-15159)
SKYVIEW CAPITAL LLC
2000 Avenue Of The Stars # 810, Los An-
geles (90067-4709)
PHONE..............................310 273-6000
Alex Soltani, *CEO*
Dean Estrada, *Vice Pres*
Carin Morris, *Executive Asst*
Jason Stewart, *Analyst*
Baudy Bueno, *Associate*
EMP: 99 **EST:** 2002
SALES (est): 16.3MM **Privately Held**
WEB: www.skyviewcapital.com
SIC: 6153 Direct working capital financing

6159 Credit Institutions, Misc Business

(P-15160)
AMERICAN CAPITAL GROUP INC
Also Called: A C G
23382 Mill Creek Dr # 115, Laguna Hills
(92653-1682)
PHONE..............................949 271-5800
Carl Heaton, *President*
Carl J Heaton, *President*
Burke Wiedel, *Controller*
David Salas, *Opers Staff*
Stefanie Viada, *Sales Mgr*
EMP: 64 **EST:** 1995
SALES (est): 20.9MM **Privately Held**
WEB: www.acgcapital.com
SIC: 6159 Equipment & vehicle finance
leasing companies
PA: Nationwide Capital Holdings, Inc.
31726 Rncho Viejo Ste 111
San Juan Capistrano CA
949 271-5816

(P-15161)
CAPNET FINANCIAL SERVICES INC (PA)
Also Called: Capital Network Funding Svcs
11901 Santa Monica Blvd, Los Angeles
(90025-2767)
PHONE..............................877 980-0558
John Armstron, *CEO*
Blake Johnson, *President*
Michael Kromnick, *CFO*
Armita Dalal, *Controller*
EMP: 90 **EST:** 2001
SQ FT: 23,000
SALES (est): 12MM **Privately Held**
SIC: 6159 Equipment & vehicle finance
leasing companies

(P-15162)
CENTRALIZE LEASING CORP
18301 Von Karman Ave # 1, Irvine
(92612-1009)
PHONE..............................949 252-2000
Mark Wetterau, *Ch of Bd*
Mike Waitukaitis, *CFO*
Richard W Gochnauer, *Vice Ch Bd*
EMP: 96 **EST:** 2000
SALES: 32.6MM
SALES (corp-wide): 821K **Privately Held**
WEB: www.goldenstatefoods.com
SIC: 6159 Machinery & equipment finance
leasing
PA: Golden State Foods Corp.
18301 Von Karman Ave # 1
Irvine CA 92612
949 247-8000

(P-15163)
ELECTRONIC COMMERCE LLC
4100 Nwport Pl Dr Ste 500, Newport Beach
(92660)
PHONE..............................800 770-5520
Darnell Ponder, *Managing Ptnr*
Khaazra Maaranu, *Managing Prtnr*
Amanda Padilla, *Marketing Staff*
Nichole Ray, *Manager*
EMP: 85 **EST:** 2013
SALES (est): 8.6MM **Privately Held**
SIC: 6159 Intermediate investment banks

(P-15164)
FARM CREDIT WEST
19628 Industry Parkway Dr, Bakersfield
(93308-9588)
PHONE..............................661 399-7360
Paul Nugent, *Branch Mgr*
Larry Bowser, *Vice Pres*
EMP: 56
SALES (corp-wide): 50.9MM **Privately
Held**
WEB: www.farmcreditwest.com
SIC: 6159 6162 Farm mortgage compa-
nies; mortgage bankers & correspondents
PA: Farm Credit West
3755 Atherton Rd
Rocklin CA 95765
916 724-4800

(P-15165)
MOTOLEASE FUNDING LLC
5200 W Century Blvd # 75, Los Angeles
(90045-5928)
PHONE..............................310 601-4779
Maurice M Salter, *Ch of Bd*
Emre Ucer, *President*
EMP: 70 **EST:** 2018
SALES (est): 3.9MM **Privately Held**
WEB: www.motolease-llc.business.site
SIC: 6159 Automobile finance leasing

(P-15166)
NISSAN OF TUSTIN
Also Called: Tustin Saab
30 Auto Center Dr, Tustin (92782-8401)
PHONE..............................714 669-8282
James H Parkinson, *President*
Mark Parkinson, *Vice Pres*
Greg Anderson, *General Mgr*
Adolfo Mejia, *Technician*
Ronnie Eljaouhari, *Finance Mgr*
EMP: 149 **EST:** 1972
SQ FT: 30,000
SALES (est): 45MM **Privately Held**
WEB: www.nissanoftustin.com
SIC: 5511 6159 Automobiles, new & used;
automobile finance leasing

▲ = Import ▼=Export
◆ =Import/Export

(P-15167)
WELLS FARGO CAPITAL FIN LLC (DH)
2450 Colo Ave Ste 3000w, Santa Monica (90404)
PHONE..................310 453-7300
Peter E Schwab, *Vice Pres*
Michael Ackad, *Vice Pres*
David Meier, *Vice Pres*
Osbaldo Nieves, *Vice Pres*
Nichol Shuart, *Vice Pres*
EMP: 99 **EST:** 2002
SALES (est): 129.3MM
SALES (corp-wide): 80.3B **Publicly Held**
WEB: www.wellsfargocapitalfinance.com
SIC: 6159 Loan institutions, general & industrial
HQ: Wells Fargo Bank, National Association
1301 N Cliff Ave
Sioux Falls SD 57103
605 575-6900

(P-15168)
WESTLAKE SERVICES LLC (HQ)
Also Called: Westlake Financial Services
4751 Wilshire Blvd # 100, Los Angeles (90010-3847)
P.O. Box 76809 (90076-0809)
PHONE..................323 692-8800
Don Hankey, *Ch of Bd*
Bret Hankey, *Vice Chairman*
Ian Anderson, *President*
David Goff, *President*
Ralph Ontiveros, *President*
EMP: 128 **EST:** 1988
SQ FT: 22,000
SALES (est): 286.8MM
SALES (corp-wide): 352.6MM **Privately Held**
WEB: www.westlakefinancial.com
SIC: 6159 6141 Automobile finance leasing; personal credit institutions
PA: Hankey Investment Company, Lp
4751 Wilshire Blvd # 110
Los Angeles CA
323 692-4008

6162 Mortgage Bankers & Loan Correspondents

(P-15169)
A-A MORTGAGE OPPORTUNITIES LP (PA)
1 Baxter Way, Westlake Village (91362-3889)
PHONE..................888 469-0810
James S Furash, *CEO*
EMP: 324 **EST:** 2013
SALES (est): 81.2MM **Privately Held**
SIC: 6162 Mortgage bankers & correspondents

(P-15170)
AMERICAN FINANCIAL NETWORK INC (PA)
Also Called: Gateway Home Realty
10 Pointe Dr Ste 330, Brea (92821-7620)
PHONE..................909 606-3905
John B Sherman, *President*
Jacob Emmel, *Managing Prtnr*
Andy Kalyviaris, *Ch Credit Ofcr*
Thomas Andrews, *Officer*
Shelbi Baugh, *Officer*
EMP: 200
SQ FT: 8,000
SALES (est): 201.9MM **Privately Held**
WEB: www.afncorp.com
SIC: 6162 Mortgage bankers

(P-15171)
AMERIHOME INC
1 Baxter Way Ste 300, Westlake Village (91362-3888)
PHONE..................888 469-0810
James S Furash, *CEO*
John Hedlund, *COO*
Garrett Galati, *CFO*
Josh Adler, *Ch Invest Ofcr*
Mark Miller, *Risk Mgmt Dir*
EMP: 738 **EST:** 2020

SALES (est): 81.2MM **Privately Held**
WEB: www.amerihome.com
SIC: 6162 Mortgage bankers & correspondents
PA: A-A Mortgage Opportunities, L.P.
1 Baxter Way
Westlake Village CA 91362
888 469-0810

(P-15172)
ANCHOR LOANS LP
Also Called: Anchor Nationwide Loans
1 Baxter Way 220, Westlake Village (91362-3889)
PHONE..................310 395-0010
Stephen Pollack, *CEO*
Tracey Williams, *CEO*
Bryan Thompson, *CFO*
Matt Ediger, *Vice Pres*
Lance Spencer, *Vice Pres*
EMP: 200 **EST:** 2015
SALES (est): 41.4MM **Privately Held**
WEB: www.anchorloans.com
SIC: 6162 Mortgage bankers & correspondents

(P-15173)
ARCS COMMERCIAL MORTGAGE CO LP (DH)
26901 Agoura Rd Ste 200, Calabasas (91301-5109)
PHONE..................818 676-3274
Timothy White, *CEO*
Kathryn Solis, *President*
▲ **EMP:** 110 **EST:** 1995
SQ FT: 15,000
SALES (est): 29MM
SALES (corp-wide): 18.2B **Publicly Held**
SIC: 6162 Mortgage bankers
HQ: Pnc Bank, National Association
300 5th Ave
Pittsburgh PA 15222
877 762-2000

(P-15174)
ATHAS CAPITAL GROUP INC
27001 Agoura Rd Ste 200, Agoura Hills (91301-5357)
PHONE..................877 877-1477
Brian O'Shaughnessy, *CEO*
Jeffery Gray, *Officer*
Jon Nierengarten, *Vice Pres*
Carlettia Ellis, *Executive*
Jose Gonzalez, *Executive*
EMP: 56 **EST:** 2007
SALES (est): 15.3MM **Privately Held**
WEB: www.athascapital.com
SIC: 6162 Mortgage bankers & correspondents

(P-15175)
BANKERS INVESTMENT GROUP INC
12341 Lewis St Apt 26, Garden Grove (92840-4629)
PHONE..................714 618-1736
Ana Lidia Reyes, *Branch Mgr*
EMP: 122
SALES (corp-wide): 901.7K **Privately Held**
SIC: 6162 Mortgage bankers
PA: Bankers Investment Group, Inc.
22792 Centre Dr Ste 109
Lake Forest CA 92630
949 699-2999

(P-15176)
BLEND INC
415 Kearny St, Los Angeles (90041)
P.O. Box 41063 (90041-0063)
PHONE..................650 550-4810
Danny J Roman, *CEO*
Ladell Stapp, *Principal*
Emily Barry, *Executive Asst*
Alen Lukic, *Sr Software Eng*
Alex Lew, *Software Engr*
EMP: 54 **EST:** 1972
SALES (est): 5.5MM **Privately Held**
WEB: www.blend.com
SIC: 6162 Mortgage bankers & correspondents

(P-15177)
BROKER SOLUTIONS INC
233 Milford Dr, Corona Del Mar (92625-3118)
PHONE..................800 450-2010
EMP: 86 **Privately Held**
WEB: www.newamericanfunding.com
SIC: 6162 Mortgage bankers & correspondents
PA: Broker Solutions, Inc.
14511 Myford Rd Ste 100
Tustin CA 92780

(P-15178)
BROOKSAMERICA MORTGAGE CORP
2 Ada Ste 100, Irvine (92618-5324)
PHONE..................714 429-4500
Michael W Brooks, *CEO*
Tricia Bailey, *President*
Hobb Tom, *Accounts Mgr*
EMP: 50 **EST:** 1981
SQ FT: 19,000
SALES (est): 5MM **Privately Held**
SIC: 6162 Mortgage bankers

(P-15179)
BSNAP LLC
4 Hutton Centre Dr Fl 10, Santa Ana (92707-8713)
PHONE..................657 269-4410
EMP: 99
SALES (est): 2.4MM **Privately Held**
SIC: 6162 Mortgage Bankers And Correspondents, Nsk

(P-15180)
CAL MUTUAL INC
34077 Temecula Creek Rd, Temecula (92592-5646)
PHONE..................888 700-4650
Dennis Shane Dailey, *President*
Cesar Garcia, *Vice Pres*
Ted Glavas, *Vice Pres*
EMP: 87 **EST:** 2013
SALES (est): 5.5MM **Privately Held**
WEB: www.calmutualmortgage.com
SIC: 6162 6531 Mortgage bankers & correspondents; real estate agent, residential

(P-15181)
CARRINGTON MRTG HOLDINGS LLC
1600 S Douglass Rd # 110, Anaheim (92806-5951)
PHONE..................888 267-0584
Phil Grassbaugh, *Principal*
Lori Grigg, *Exec VP*
Steve Patton, *Exec VP*
Rick Sharga, *Exec VP*
Rob Petruska, *Senior VP*
EMP: 123 **EST:** 2001
SQ FT: 192,000
SALES (est): 66.9MM
SALES (corp-wide): 98.2MM **Privately Held**
WEB: www.carringtonmortgage.com
SIC: 6162 Mortgage bankers & correspondents
PA: Carrington Capital Management Llc
1700 E Putnam Ave Ste 501
Old Greenwich CT 06870
203 661-6186

(P-15182)
CHANGE LENDING LLC (PA)
Also Called: Change Home Mortgage
16845 Von Karman Ave # 2, Irvine (92606-4959)
PHONE..................949 423-6814
Mario De Tomasi, *CEO*
Theodore Ray, *President*
Scott Simonich, *President*
Kari Hallowell, *CFO*
Tracy Belle, *Officer*
EMP: 60 **EST:** 1994
SQ FT: 1,400
SALES (est): 101.3MM **Privately Held**
WEB: www.changemtg.com
SIC: 6162 Mortgage bankers & correspondents

(P-15183)
CLOSINGMARK FINCL GROUP LLC (DH)
4695 Macarthur Ct Fl 8, Newport Beach (92660-1882)
PHONE..................949 833-3600
Matthew Zaist, *CEO*
EMP: 62 **EST:** 2018
SALES (est): 138.8MM
SALES (corp-wide): 6.1B **Publicly Held**
WEB: www.taylormorrison.com
SIC: 6162 6163 Mortgage bankers; loan brokers

(P-15184)
COMMERCE HOME MORTGAGE LLC
32 Discovery Ste 160, Irvine (92618-3156)
PHONE..................949 769-3526
EMP: 97 **Privately Held**
WEB: www.changemtg.com
SIC: 6162 Mortgage bankers & correspondents
PA: Change Lending, Llc
16845 Von Karman Ave # 2
Irvine CA 92606

(P-15185)
COUNTRYWIDE HOME LOANS INC
801 N Brand Blvd Ste 750, Glendale (91203-3218)
PHONE..................818 550-8700
Lynda Martinlawley, *Manager*
EMP: 1755
SALES (corp-wide): 93.7B **Publicly Held**
WEB: www.bankofamerica.com
SIC: 6162 Mortgage bankers
HQ: Countrywide Home Loans, Inc.
225 W Hillcrest Dr
Thousand Oaks CA 91360

(P-15186)
DECISION READY SOLUTIONS INC
400 Spectrum Center Dr # 2050, Irvine (92618-5024)
PHONE..................949 400-1126
Ravi Ramanathan, *President*
Claudia Sanchez, *COO*
Tom Schmidt, *CFO*
Michael Graves, *Exec VP*
Dan Mahler, *Security Dir*
EMP: 50 **EST:** 2011
SALES (est): 6MM **Privately Held**
WEB: www.decisionreadysolutions.com
SIC: 6162 7371 7372 Mortgage bankers; computer software systems analysis & design, custom; business oriented computer software

(P-15187)
DOMINION CORPORATION
Also Called: Dominion Mortgage
11355 W Olympic Blvd # 210, Los Angeles (90064-1665)
PHONE..................310 477-3041
Paul Horvitz, *President*
Deloris Kitchin, *President*
Keith Allen Olson, *Vice Pres*
EMP: 56 **EST:** 1976
SQ FT: 3,500
SALES (est): 5.7MM **Privately Held**
WEB: www.dominfin.com
SIC: 6162 6282 Mortgage bankers; investment advice

(P-15188)
ECC CAPITAL CORPORATION (PA)
2600 E Coast Hwy Ste 250, Corona Del Mar (92625-2144)
PHONE..................949 954-7060
Steven G Holder, *Ch of Bd*
Roque A Santi, *President*
Joe McKnight, *Officer*
Larry Moretti, *Officer*
Brian Heitmeier, *General Mgr*
EMP: 673 **EST:** 2004
SALES (est): 35.5MM **Privately Held**
WEB: www.ecccapital.com
SIC: 6162 Mortgage bankers & correspondents

(P-15189)
EMET LENDING GROUP INC
2601 Saturn St Ste 200, Brea
(92821-6702)
PHONE...............................714 933-9800
Julie Ahn, CEO
EMP: 80 **EST:** 2015
SALES (est): 6.3MM **Privately Held**
WEB: www.emetlending.com
SIC: 6162 Mortgage bankers

(P-15190)
FEDERAL HOME LOAN MRTG CORP
Also Called: Freddie Mac
444 S Flower St Fl 44, Los Angeles
(90071-2944)
PHONE...............................213 337-4200
Steve Griffin, Enginr/R&D Mgr
Henry Judy, Exec VP
Richard Lichvar, Surgery Dir
John Toye, Administration
Anh Nguyen, Technical Staff
EMP: 117
SALES (corp-wide): 66.2B **Publicly Held**
WEB: www.freddiemac.com
SIC: 6162 Mortgage bankers & correspondents
PA: Federal Home Loan Mortgage Corporation
8200 Jones Branch Dr
Mc Lean VA 22102
703 903-2000

(P-15191)
FINANCE AMERICA LLC (HQ)
1901 Main St Ste 150, Irvine (92614-0516)
PHONE...............................949 440-1000
Brian Libman,
Karen H Cornell,
Graham Fleming,
Arthur K Rice,
EMP: 227 **EST:** 1999
SQ FT: 60,000
SALES (est): 101.3MM
SALES (corp-wide): 28.1MM **Privately Held**
WEB: www.nb.com
SIC: 6162 6163 Mortgage bankers; loan brokers
PA: Lehman Brothers Holdings Inc.
110 E 42nd St Rm 820
New York NY 10017
646 285-9000

(P-15192)
FINANCE AMERICA MORTGAGE LLC
13200 Crssrads Pkwy N Ste, City of Industry (91746)
PHONE...............................562 478-4664
Gabriel Garza, Manager
EMP: 73 **Privately Held**
WEB: www.financeofamerica.com
SIC: 6162 Mortgage bankers
PA: Finance Of America Mortgage Llc
1 W Elm St Ste 100
Conshohocken PA 19428

(P-15193)
FINANCE AMERICA MORTGAGE LLC
23734 Valencia Blvd, Valencia
(91355-2100)
PHONE...............................661 775-6253
Steve OH, Senior VP
EMP: 73 **Privately Held**
WEB: www.financeofamerica.com
SIC: 6162 Mortgage bankers & correspondents
PA: Finance Of America Mortgage Llc
1 W Elm St Ste 100
Conshohocken PA 19428

(P-15194)
FINANCE AMERICA MORTGAGE LLC
680 E Colo Blvd Ste 230, Pasadena
(91101)
PHONE...............................215 591-0222
EMP: 73 **Privately Held**
WEB: www.financeofamerica.com

SIC: 6162 Mortgage bankers & correspondents
PA: Finance Of America Mortgage Llc
1 W Elm St Ste 100
Conshohocken PA 19428

(P-15195)
GENPACT MORTGAGE SERVICES INC (HQ)
Also Called: Moneyline Lending Services
15420 Laguna Canyon Rd, Irvine
(92618-2119)
PHONE...............................949 417-5131
Gregory Gentek, CEO
Evan Gentry, President
Richard Belliston, CFO
Bradley J Barber, Exec VP
Taylor Woods, Exec VP
EMP: 70 **EST:** 1996
SQ FT: 17,000
SALES (est): 55.1MM **Privately Held**
WEB: www.genpactmortgage.com
SIC: 6163 Mortgage brokers, using own money; loan brokers

(P-15196)
GOLDEN EMPIRE MORTGAGE INC (PA)
1200 Discovery Dr Ste 300, Bakersfield
(93309-7036)
PHONE...............................661 328-1600
John Copeland, Manager
David Chesney, CFO
Frank Cerney, Officer
Ray Escano, Officer
Virginia Lara, Officer
EMP: 80 **EST:** 2006
SALES (est): 61.1MM **Privately Held**
WEB: www.gemcorp.com
SIC: 6162 Mortgage bankers

(P-15197)
GOLDEN EMPIRE MORTGAGE INC (PA)
2130 Chester Ave, Bakersfield
(93301-4471)
PHONE...............................661 328-1600
Howard Kootstra, CEO
Joe Ewens, Exec VP
Robert Satnick, Exec VP
Rebecca Wegman, Exec VP
Mike Simpfenderfer, Branch Mgr
EMP: 100 **EST:** 1987
SQ FT: 25,000
SALES (est): 46.6MM **Privately Held**
WEB: www.gemcorp.com
SIC: 6162 Mortgage bankers

(P-15198)
GOLDEN EMPIRE MORTGAGE INC
Also Called: Gem
41331 12th St W Ste 102, Palmdale
(93551-1423)
PHONE...............................661 949-3388
Jane Lawrence, Branch Mgr
EMP: 254 **Privately Held**
WEB: www.gemcorp.com
SIC: 6162 Mortgage bankers
PA: Golden Empire Mortgage, Inc.
2130 Chester Ave
Bakersfield CA 93301

(P-15199)
GUARANTEED RATE INC
230 Commerce Ste 200, Irvine
(92602-1337)
PHONE...............................424 354-5344
Glenn Bushmire, Vice Pres
Mary L Yoch, Vice Pres
Mykal Vailuu, Opers-Prdtn-Mfg
EMP: 205 **Privately Held**
WEB: www.rate.com
SIC: 6162 Mortgage bankers & correspondents
PA: Guaranteed Rate, Inc.
3940 N Ravenswood Ave
Chicago IL 60613

(P-15200)
GUARANTEED RATE INC
1065 Higuera St 100, San Luis Obispo
(93401-3786)
PHONE...............................805 550-6933
EMP: 205 **Privately Held**
WEB: www.rate.com
SIC: 6162 Mortgage bankers & correspondents
PA: Guaranteed Rate, Inc.
3940 N Ravenswood Ave
Chicago IL 60613

(P-15201)
HARVEST SMALL BUSINESS FIN LLC
24422 Avnida De Crlota St, Laguna Hills
(92653)
PHONE...............................949 446-8683
David Scherer, Mng Member
Brian Crawford, President
Evan Mitnick, CFO
Kyle Nagato, Officer
Elizabeth Cortez, Exec VP
EMP: 51 **EST:** 2015
SALES (est): 3.4MM **Privately Held**
WEB: www.harvestsbf.com
SIC: 6162 Mortgage bankers & correspondents

(P-15202)
IMPAC FUNDING CORPORATION (HQ)
19500 Jamboree Rd, Irvine (92612-2411)
PHONE...............................949 475-3600
Joseph R Tomkinson, CEO
William Ashmore, President
Richard Johnson, CFO
Kathy Hancock, Treasurer
EMP: 112 **EST:** 1995
SQ FT: 10,000
SALES (est): 33.3MM **Publicly Held**
WEB: www.impaccompanies.com
SIC: 6162 Mortgage bankers & correspondents

(P-15203)
IMPAC MORTGAGE CORP
19500 Jamboree Rd Ste 100, Irvine
(92612-2426)
PHONE...............................949 475-3600
Joseph R Tomkinson, President
Natasha Gilmore, President
Irma Ventura, President
Lisa Thomas, Vice Pres
John Woodruff, Vice Pres
EMP: 298 **EST:** 2008
SALES (est): 82.8MM **Publicly Held**
WEB: www.cashcallmortgage.com
SIC: 6162 Mortgage bankers
PA: Impac Mortgage Holdings, Inc.
19500 Jamboree Rd Ste 100
Irvine CA 92612

(P-15204)
IMPAC MORTGAGE HOLDINGS INC (PA)
19500 Jamboree Rd Ste 100, Irvine
(92612-2426)
PHONE...............................949 475-3600
George A Mangiaracina, Ch of Bd
Tiffany M Entsminger, COO
Justin R Moisio, Officer
Justin Moisio, Officer
Jon Gloeckner, Senior VP
EMP: 216 **EST:** 1995
SQ FT: 119,600
SALES (est): 90.6MM **Publicly Held**
WEB: www.impaccompanies.com
SIC: 6162 Mortgage bankers & correspondents

(P-15205)
JMAC LENDING INC
2510 Redhill Ave, Santa Ana (92705-5542)
PHONE...............................949 390-2688
MAI Christina Pham, President
Alan Vidal, Vice Pres
Ginger Fields, Executive
Michael Johnson, Executive
Bridgette Klein, Executive
EMP: 60 **EST:** 2007 **Privately Held**
WEB: www.jmaclending.com

SIC: 6162 Mortgage bankers & correspondents

(P-15206)
JMJ FINANCIAL GROUP (PA)
26800 Aliso Viejo Pkwy # 200, Aliso Viejo
(92656-2625)
PHONE...............................949 340-6336
Virgil Kyle, President
Devin Langager, Partner
Thomas Kish, COO
Ryan Robertson, CFO
Margaret Wilder, Admin Asst
EMP: 50 **EST:** 2010
SQ FT: 10,000
SALES (est): 500MM **Privately Held**
WEB: www.web.jmj.me
SIC: 6162 Mortgage bankers

(P-15207)
LENDERS INVESTMENT CORP
18101 Von Karman Ave # 400, Irvine
(92612-1012)
PHONE...............................714 540-4747
Kerry M Smith, President
Marisela Amezquita, Officer
Bill Ammerman, Vice Pres
EMP: 86 **EST:** 2003
SQ FT: 14,000
SALES (est): 5.3MM **Privately Held**
SIC: 6162 Mortgage bankers

(P-15208)
LENOX FINANCIAL MORTGAGE CORP
Also Called: Weslend Financial
200 Sandpointe Ave # 800, Santa Ana
(92707-5751)
PHONE...............................949 428-5100
Wesley C Hoaglund, CEO
Trinh Bui, Business Mgr
Brian Levy, Sales Staff
Brian Head, Accounts Exec
Yolanda Fierro, Supervisor
EMP: 251 **EST:** 1999
SALES (est): 77MM **Privately Held**
WEB: www.lenoxhomeloans.com
SIC: 6162 Mortgage bankers

(P-15209)
LMB MORTGAGE SERVICES INC (HQ)
Also Called: Lowermybills
4859 W Slauson Ave # 405 Los Angeles
(90056-1290)
PHONE...............................310 348-6800
Steve Krenzer, CEO
Pat Gregory, CFO
Jeff Hughes, Vice Pres
Mitch Viner, Admin Sec
Ashley Gonzalez, Human Res Mgr
EMP: 149 **EST:** 2010
SALES (est): 51.8MM
SALES (corp-wide): 16.5B **Publicly Held**
WEB: www.lowermybills.com
SIC: 6162 Mortgage bankers
PA: Rock Holdings Inc.
1090 Woodward Ave
Detroit MI 48226
313 373-7700

(P-15210)
LOANDEPOT INC (PA)
26642 Towne Centre Dr, Foothill Ranch
(92610-2808)
PHONE...............................888 337-6888
Anthony Hsieh, Ch of Bd
Patrick Flanagan, CFO
Jeff Dergurahian, Exec VP
Jeff Walsh, Executive
EMP: 2709 **EST:** 2010
SQ FT: 144,398
SALES (est): 4.4B **Publicly Held**
WEB: www.loandepot.com
SIC: 6162 Mortgage bankers & correspondents

(P-15211)
LOANDEPOTCOM LLC
42455 10th St W Ste 109, Lancaster
(93534-7060)
PHONE...............................661 202-1700
EMP: 639
SALES (corp-wide): 4.4B **Publicly Held**
WEB: www.loandepot.com
SIC: 6162 Loan correspondents

HQ: Loandepot.Com, Llc
26642 Towne Centre Dr
Foothill Ranch CA 92610

(P-15212)
LOANDEPOTCOM LLC
901 N Palm Canyon Dr # 107, Palm
Springs (92262-4449)
PHONE..............................760 797-6000
Anthony Hsieh, *Branch Mgr*
EMP: 639
SALES (corp-wide): 4.4B **Publicly Held**
WEB: www.loandepot.com
SIC: 6162 Mortgage bankers
HQ: Loandepot.Com, Llc
26642 Towne Centre Dr
Foothill Ranch CA 92610

(P-15213)
LOANDEPOTCOM LLC (DH)
Also Called: Customer Loan Depot
26642 Towne Centre Dr, Foothill Ranch
(92610-2808)
PHONE..............................888 337-6888
Anthony Hsieh, *CEO*
Andrew Dodson, *President*
David Norris, *President*
Jon Frojen, *CFO*
David King, *Chief Mktg Ofcr*
EMP: 963 **EST:** 2009
SALES (est): 986.9MM
SALES (corp-wide): 4.4B **Publicly Held**
WEB: www.loandepot.com
SIC: 6162 Mortgage bankers
HQ: Ld Holdings Group Llc
26642 Towne Centre Dr
Foothill Ranch CA 92610
888 337-6888

(P-15214)
METROPOLITAN HOME
MORTGAGE INC
3090 Bristol St Ste 600, Costa Mesa
(92626-7318)
PHONE..............................949 428-0161
Daryl Preedge, *President*
Robin Clayton, *Vice Pres*
Rosie Herrera, *Vice Pres*
Neecole Bell, *Loan*
Timothy Takeshita, *Training Dir*
EMP: 100 **EST:** 1993
SQ FT: 5,000
SALES (est): 20.7MM **Privately Held**
WEB: www.metrohmc.com
SIC: 6162 Mortgage bankers & correspon-
dents

(P-15215)
MILLENNIAL HOME LENDING
INC
9200 Oakdale Ave Ste 501, Chatsworth
(91311-6562)
PHONE..............................818 812-5150
David Arshak Abelyan, *CEO*
EMP: 70 **EST:** 2019
SALES (est): 5.9MM **Privately Held**
WEB: www.mhlending.us
SIC: 6162 Mortgage bankers & correspon-
dents

(P-15216)
MISSION HILLS MORTGAGE
CORP (HQ)
Also Called: Mission Hills Mortgage Bankers
18500 Von Karman Ave # 1100, Irvine
(92612-0546)
PHONE..............................714 972-3832
Jay Ledbetter, *President*
Faith Aldstadt, *Loan Officer*
Keri Arnsparger, *Loan Officer*
Yolanda Contreras, *Loan Officer*
Allen Ensign, *Loan Officer*
EMP: 140 **EST:** 1969
SQ FT: 27,000
SALES (est): 86.1MM
SALES (corp-wide): 145.1MM **Privately**
Held
WEB: www.mhmb.com
SIC: 6162 Mortgage bankers & correspon-
dents
PA: Tarbell Financial Corporation
1403 N Tustin Ave Ste 380
Santa Ana CA 92705
714 972-0988

(P-15217)
MORTGAGE CAPITAL
PARTNERS INC (PA)
12400 Wilshire Blvd # 900, Los Angeles
(90025-1030)
PHONE..............................310 295-2900
Carolyn W Chang, *President*
David Anthony, *President*
Thomas Bayles, *Vice Pres*
Steven Constantino, *Vice Pres*
Jordan Donolow, *Vice Pres*
EMP: 72 **EST:** 2008
SALES (est): 11.6MM **Privately Held**
WEB: www.mortgagecapitalpartners.com
SIC: 6162 Mortgage bankers

(P-15218)
MORTGAGE GUY INC (PA)
8721 W Sunset Blvd Ph 10, West Holly-
wood (90069-2273)
PHONE..............................310 625-8809
Alberto Preciado, *Principal*
Crystal Aguilar, *Loan*
Betsy Salas, *Loan*
John Delgado, *Production*
Eli Delgado, *Sales Mgr*
EMP: 53 **EST:** 2016
SALES (est): 3.4MM **Privately Held**
WEB: www.themortgageguys.com
SIC: 6162 Mortgage bankers & correspon-
dents

(P-15219)
MOUNTAIN WEST FINANCIAL
INC (PA)
Also Called: Mortgage Works Financial
1209 Nevada St Ste 200, Redlands
(92374-4581)
PHONE..............................909 793-1500
Gary H Martell Jr, *President*
Michael W Douglas, *CFO*
Courtney Crosley, *Officer*
Lisa Marth, *Officer*
Wendy Wright, *Senior VP*
EMP: 391 **EST:** 1990
SQ FT: 4,729
SALES (est): 116.4MM **Privately Held**
WEB: www.mwfinc.com
SIC: 6162 Mortgage bankers

(P-15220)
NETWORK CAPITAL FUNDING
CORP (PA)
7700 Irvine Center Dr # 3, Irvine
(92618-2923)
PHONE..............................949 442-0060
Tri Nguyen, *President*
▲ **EMP:** 345 **EST:** 2002
SALES (est): 116.7MM **Privately Held**
SIC: 6162 Mortgage bankers

(P-15221)
NEW CENTURY MORTGAGE
CORP
18400 Von Karman Ave # 1000, Irvine
(92612-1514)
PHONE..............................949 440-7030
Brad A Morrice, *President*
Edward Gotschall, *Vice Chairman*
Joseph F Eckroth, *COO*
Edward F Gotschall, *COO*
Patti M Dodge, *CFO*
EMP: 3261 **EST:** 1995
SALES (est): 58.2MM **Privately Held**
SIC: 6162 Mortgage bankers & correspon-
dents

(P-15222)
OCMBC INC
Also Called: Ocmban
19000 Macarthur Blvd # 200, Irvine
(92612-1420)
PHONE..............................714 479-0999
Rabi H Aziz, *CEO*
Madelina L Colon, *President*
Jon Castle, *CFO*
Rebecca Bruggeman, *Officer*
Rick Holguin, *Exec VP*
EMP: 132 **EST:** 2001
SQ FT: 12,500
SALES (est): 32.5MM **Privately Held**
WEB: www.lsmortgage.com
SIC: 6162 Mortgage bankers

(P-15223)
PENNYMAC FINANCIAL SVCS
INC (PA)
3043 Townsgate Rd, Westlake Village
(91361-3027)
PHONE..............................818 224-7442
David A Spector, *Ch of Bd*
Doug Jones, *President*
Andrew S Chang, *COO*
Daniel S Perotti, *CFO*
Derek W Stark,
EMP: 471 **EST:** 2008
SQ FT: 66,000
SALES (est): 3.7B **Publicly Held**
SIC: 6162 **6282** Mortgage bankers & cor-
respondents; investment advice

(P-15224)
PENNYMAC MORTGAGE INV TR
(PA)
6101 Condor Dr, Moorpark (93021-2602)
PHONE..............................818 224-7442
David A Spector, *Ch of Bd*
Steve Bailey, *COO*
Anne D McCallion, *CFO*
Scott Carnahan, *Trustee*
Preston Dufauchard, *Trustee*
EMP: 1326 **EST:** 2009
SALES (est): 469.3MM **Privately Held**
WEB: www.pennymac.com
SIC: 6162 Mortgage bankers & correspon-
dents

(P-15225)
PEOPLES CHICE HM LN
SCRTIES CO (PA)
7515 Irvine Center Dr, Irvine (92618-2930)
PHONE..............................949 494-6167
Neil B Kornswiet, *CEO*
EMP: 55 **EST:** 1999
SQ FT: 20,000
SALES (est): 25MM **Privately Held**
WEB: www.peopleschoicehomeloan.com
SIC: 6162 Mortgage companies, urban

(P-15226)
PMAC LENDING SERVICES INC
(PA)
6 Pointe Dr Ste 150, Brea (92821-6324)
PHONE..............................909 614-2000
Brian Witham, *CEO*
John Randall, *CFO*
Larry Davis, *Officer*
EMP: 100 **EST:** 1995
SALES (est): 14.6MM **Privately Held**
WEB: www.amwestfunding.com
SIC: 6162 Mortgage bankers

(P-15227)
PNMAC HOLDINGS INC (HQ)
3043 Townsgate Rd, Westlake Village
(91361-3027)
PHONE..............................818 224-7442
David A Spector, *President*
Stanford L Kurland, *Ch of Bd*
Andrew S Chang, *CFO*
Grant Mills, *Finance*
EMP: 369 **EST:** 2008
SQ FT: 60,000
SALES (est): 1.1B
SALES (corp-wide): 3.7B **Publicly Held**
WEB: www.ir.pennymacfinancial.com
SIC: 6162 **6282** Mortgage bankers & cor-
respondents; investment advice
PA: Pennymac Financial Services, Inc.
3043 Townsgate Rd
Westlake Village CA 91361
818 224-7442

(P-15228)
PRIVATE NAT MRTG
ACCPTANCE LLC (DH)
Also Called: Pennymac
6101 Condor Dr, Agoura Hills (91301)
PHONE..............................818 224-7401
Jeff Grogin,
Dan Perotti, *CFO*
Scott Muldowney, *Assoc VP*
Nickolas Akl, *Exec VP*
Kevin Chamberlain, *Exec VP*
EMP: 800 **EST:** 2008
SALES (est): 417.7MM
SALES (corp-wide): 3.7B **Publicly Held**
WEB: www.ir.pennymacfinancial.com
SIC: 6162 Mortgage bankers

HQ: Pnmac Holdings, Inc.
3043 Townsgate Rd
Westlake Village CA 91361
818 224-7442

(P-15229)
RESIDENTIAL BANCORP (PA)
22632 Goln Spgs Dr Ste 20, Diamond Bar
(91765)
PHONE..............................330 499-8333
Corey A Wood, *CEO*
William H James III, *President*
Michael J Luu, *CFO*
Tobias Hoy, *Exec VP*
Tom Wong, *Exec VP*
EMP: 54 **EST:** 1989
SQ FT: 10,000
SALES (est): 10.5MM **Privately Held**
WEB: www.bancorp.com
SIC: 6162 Mortgage bankers

(P-15230)
RUSHMORE LOAN MGT SVCS
LLC (PA)
15480 Laguna Canyon Rd, Irvine
(92618-2132)
P.O. Box 514707, Los Angeles (90051-
4707)
PHONE..............................949 727-4798
Terry Smith, *CEO*
Michael Barry, *Vice Pres*
Linda Chapa, *Vice Pres*
Jeffrey Lisinicchia, *Vice Pres*
Brian Martin, *Vice Pres*
EMP: 793 **EST:** 2008
SQ FT: 3,000
SALES (est): 165.7MM **Privately Held**
WEB: www.rushmorelm.com
SIC: 6162 Mortgage bankers & correspon-
dents

(P-15231)
SEA BREEZE FINANCIAL SVCS
INC
Also Called: Sea Breeze Mortgage Services
18191 Von Karman Ave # 1, Irvine
(92612-7102)
P.O. Box 19079, Anaheim (92817-9079)
PHONE..............................949 223-9700
Leonard Hamilton, *President*
Curtis Green, *Executive*
Jeff Whiteman, *Manager*
EMP: 150 **EST:** 1985
SQ FT: 50,000
SALES (est): 17.6MM **Privately Held**
SIC: 6162 Mortgage bankers & correspon-
dents

(P-15232)
SUN WEST MORTGAGE
COMPANY INC (PA)
Also Called: Lowratscom 1st Lbrty Cal State
6131 Orangethorpe Ave # 500, Buena Park
(90620-4903)
PHONE..............................800 453-7884
Pavan Agarwal, *CEO*
Hari S Agarwal, *President*
Sharda Agarwal, *Corp Secy*
Jim Trapinski, *Exec VP*
Peter Schwartz, *Senior VP*
EMP: 69 **EST:** 1980
SQ FT: 9,800
SALES (est): 33.7MM **Privately Held**
WEB: www.swmc.com
SIC: 6162 **6163** Mortgage bankers; loan
brokers

(P-15233)
WALKER & DUNLOP INC
12100 Wilshire Blvd # 1500, Los Angeles
(90025-7129)
PHONE..............................301 215-5500
Willy Walker, *Manager*
Cliff Carnes, *Senior VP*
Riley Manke, *Assistant VP*
EMP: 63 **Publicly Held**
WEB: www.walkerdunlop.com
SIC: 6162 **6411** **6531** Mortgage bankers;
insurance agents, brokers & service; real
estate agents & managers
PA: Walker & Dunlop, Inc.
7501 Wscnsin Ave Ste 1200
Bethesda MD 20814

6163 Loan Brokers

(P-15234)
5 ARCHES LLC
19800 Macarthur Blvd, Irvine (92612-2421)
PHONE..................................949 387-8092
Shawn Miller, *CEO*
Gene Clark, *President*
Steven Davis, *CFO*
EMP: 95 EST: 2012
SALES (est): 19.3MM **Publicly Held**
WEB: www.redwoodtrust.com
SIC: 6163 Mortgage brokers arranging for loans, using money of others
PA: Redwood Trust, Inc.
1 Belvedere Pl Ste 300
Mill Valley CA 94941

(P-15235)
AMERICAN LIBERTY CAPITAL CORP
Also Called: American Liberty Funding
19000 Macarthur Blvd # 400, Irvine (92612-1438)
P.O. Box 10059, Newport Beach (92658-0059)
PHONE..................................949 623-0288
Christopher Chase, *President*
Mike R Chase, *Shareholder*
Chris Bull, *Admin Sec*
EMP: 105 EST: 1996
SALES (est): 10.1MM **Privately Held**
SIC: 6163 Mortgage brokers arranging for loans, using money of others

(P-15236)
AMERICAS MONEYLINE INC
27081 Aliso Creek Rd # 20, Aliso Viejo (92656-5365)
PHONE..................................800 247-6663
Dean Lob, *COO*
EMP: 50 EST: 2019
SALES (est): 3.1MM **Privately Held**
WEB: www.americasmoneyline.com
SIC: 6163 Mortgage brokers arranging for loans, using money of others

(P-15237)
CARNEGIE MORTGAGE LLC
Also Called: Ovation Home Loans
15480 Laguna Canyon Rd # 100, Irvine (92618-2132)
PHONE..................................949 379-7000
Graham Fleming, *Mng Member*
EMP: 300 **Privately Held**
WEB: www.carnegiemtg.com
SIC: 6163 Mortgage brokers arranging for loans, using money of others
PA: Carnegie Mortgage Llc
2297 Highway 33
Trenton NJ 08690

(P-15238)
CLEARPATH LENDING
15635 Alton Pkwy Ste 300, Irvine (92618-7332)
PHONE..................................949 502-3577
Amir Ali Omid, *CEO*
Lily Ali, *Officer*
Mark Hoagland, *Officer*
Dave Wilson, *Officer*
Maria Zamora, *Managing Dir*
EMP: 130 EST: 2012
SALES (est): 36.8MM **Privately Held**
WEB: www.clearpathlending.com
SIC: 6163 Mortgage brokers arranging for loans, using money of others

(P-15239)
DANA CAPITAL GROUP INC (PA)
8001 Irvine Center Dr, Irvine (92618-2938)
PHONE..................................949 789-0200
Dana H Smith, *President*
Matthew Klahorst, *Consultant*
EMP: 65 EST: 1995
SQ FT: 12,259
SALES (est): 14MM **Privately Held**
SIC: 6163 Mortgage brokers arranging for loans, using money of others

(P-15240)
E&S FINANCIAL GROUP INC
Also Called: Capital Mortgage Services
3140 Telegraph Rd Ste A, Ventura (93003-3238)
PHONE..................................805 644-1621
Jordan Eller, *President*
Frank Doud, *Technology*
Jerry Avila, *Loan Officer*
Ginger Doud, *Loan Officer*
Chris Dritz, *Loan Officer*
EMP: 70 EST: 2008
SALES (est): 10.2MM **Privately Held**
SIC: 6163 Mortgage brokers arranging for loans, using money of others

(P-15241)
EMERY FINANCIAL INC (PA)
Also Called: Wjbradley Mortgage Capital
625 Kings Rd, Newport Beach (92663-5711)
PHONE..................................949 219-0640
Bradford Sarvak, *President*
Ty Kern, *COO*
Alan Godfrey, *Officer*
Mike Henderson, *Officer*
John Wlcek, *Loan Officer*
EMP: 60 EST: 1993
SALES (est): 10.2MM **Privately Held**
WEB: www.emeryfinancial.com
SIC: 6163 Mortgage brokers arranging for loans, using money of others

(P-15242)
FIRST AMRCN MRTG SOLUTIONS LLC (HQ)
3 First American Way, Santa Ana (92707-5913)
PHONE..................................800 333-4510
Jeff Moyer, *President*
Tony Anderson, *Bd of Directors*
Constance Wilson, *Exec VP*
Paul Harris, *Senior VP*
David G Kittle, *Senior VP*
EMP: 225 EST: 1998
SQ FT: 12,000
SALES (est): 200.5MM **Publicly Held**
WEB: www.firstam.com
SIC: 6163 Mortgage brokers arranging for loans, using money of others

(P-15243)
FLEXPOINT FUNDING CORPORATION (PA)
30 Executive Park Ste 200, Irvine (92614-4725)
PHONE..................................949 250-4466
Stan Gordon, *Chairman*
Ryan Knott, *President*
EMP: 133 EST: 1998
SQ FT: 7,200
SALES (est): 12.7MM **Privately Held**
SIC: 6163 Mortgage brokers arranging for loans, using money of others

(P-15244)
HOMEBRIDGE FINANCIAL SVCS INC
15301 Ventura Blvd, Sherman Oaks (91403-3102)
PHONE..................................818 981-0606
Douglas Rotella, *President*
EMP: 1700 **Privately Held**
WEB: www.homebridge.com
SIC: 6163 Mortgage brokers arranging for loans, using money of others
PA: Homebridge Financial Services, Inc.
194 Wood Ave S Fl 9
Iselin NJ 08830

(P-15245)
LMB OPCO LLC
Also Called: Lowermybills.com
12181 Bluff Creek Dr, Playa Vista (90094-2992)
PHONE..................................310 348-6800
Jeff Hughes, *CEO*
Scott Edwards, *Vice Pres*
James Washington, *Sr Software Eng*
Nathan Buskirk, *Software Dev*
Narorm Mayoeurn, *Software Engr*
EMP: 320 EST: 2016

SALES (est): 65.1MM **Privately Held**
WEB: www.policypilot.com
SIC: 6163 7389 Mortgage brokers arranging for loans, using money of others; financial services

(P-15246)
MARK 1 MORTGAGE CORPORATION (PA)
1342 E Chapman Ave, Orange (92866-2219)
PHONE..................................714 752-5700
Mark D Prather, *President*
Bernadine Wiggins, *Officer*
Kim Rangell, *Exec VP*
Don Cherry, *Broker*
Letty Verde, *VP Opers*
EMP: 50 EST: 1994
SQ FT: 8,000
SALES (est): 31.3MM **Privately Held**
WEB: www.m1m.com
SIC: 6163 Mortgage brokers arranging for loans, using money of others

(P-15247)
PACIFIC BAY LENDING GROUP
Also Called: Bay Valley Mortgage
7390 Lincoln Way, Garden Grove (92841-1427)
PHONE..................................714 367-5125
John Nelson, *CEO*
Christine Kim, *Officer*
Steve Gogolab, *Branch Mgr*
Jennifer Song, *Administration*
James Lee, *CTO*
EMP: 100 EST: 2011
SALES (est): 13.8MM **Privately Held**
WEB: www.pacbaylending.com
SIC: 6163 Mortgage brokers arranging for loans, using money of others

(P-15248)
PENNYMAC CORP
27001 Agoura Rd, Agoura Hills (91301-5339)
PHONE..................................818 878-8416
Stanford L Kurland, *President*
EMP: 81 EST: 2010
SALES (est): 8.7MM **Privately Held**
WEB: www.pennymac.com
SIC: 6163 Loan brokers
PA: Pennymac Mortgage Investment Trust
6101 Condor Dr
Moorpark CA 93021

(P-15249)
POPE MORTGAGE & ASSOCIATES INC
2980 Inland Empire Blvd, Ontario (91764-6531)
PHONE..................................909 466-5380
Paul Pope, *President*
Benedict Gallardo, *Finance Dir*
EMP: 72 EST: 2003
SQ FT: 14,000
SALES (est): 6.3MM **Privately Held**
SIC: 6163 Mortgage brokers arranging for loans, using money of others

(P-15250)
RMR FINANCIAL LLC (DH)
Also Called: Online Capital
610 Newport Center Dr, Newport Beach (92660-6419)
PHONE..................................408 355-2000
Rob Reid,
EMP: 84 EST: 2000
SQ FT: 11,300
SALES (est): 28.4MM
SALES (corp-wide): 960.9MM **Publicly Held**
WEB: www.phh.com
SIC: 6163 6162 Mortgage brokers arranging for loans, using money of others; mortgage bankers
HQ: Phh Corporation
3000 Leadenhall Rd
Mount Laurel NJ 08054
856 917-1744

(P-15251)
SAND CANYON CORPORATION (HQ)
7595 Irvine Center Dr # 12, Irvine (92618-2957)
P.O. Box 57080 (92619-7080)
PHONE..................................949 727-9425
Robert Dubrish, *President*
Dale M Sugimoto, *CEO*
Steve Nadon, *COO*
William O'Neill, *CFO*
EMP: 100 EST: 1992
SALES (est): 106.9MM
SALES (corp-wide): 466.1MM **Publicly Held**
WEB: www.sandcanyondentistry.com
SIC: 6163 6162 Loan brokers; mortgage bankers & correspondents
PA: H & R Block, Inc.
1 H And R Block Way
Kansas City MO 64105
816 854-3000

(P-15252)
SECURED FUNDING CORPORATION
2955 Red Hill Ave, Costa Mesa (92626-5907)
PHONE..................................714 689-6749
Lorne Lahodny, *President*
Phil Dandrige, *CFO*
John R Lynch Jr, *Vice Pres*
Joe Lindsay, *CIO*
EMP: 800 EST: 1993
SQ FT: 60,000
SALES (est): 37MM **Privately Held**
SIC: 6163 Mortgage brokers arranging for loans, using money of others

(P-15253)
SERVIS ONE INC
Also Called: BSI Financial Services
7505 Irvine Center Dr, Irvine (92618-2991)
PHONE..................................888 738-5873
Gagan Sharma, *Branch Mgr*
EMP: 81 **Privately Held**
WEB: www.bsifinancial.com
SIC: 6163 Mortgage brokers arranging for loans, using money of others
PA: Servis One, Inc.
1425 Greenway Dr
Irving TX 75038

(P-15254)
STRATUS REAL ESTATE INC
Also Called: Stratus Realestate
435 Garfield Ave, South Pasadena (91030-2249)
PHONE..................................626 441-5549
Steve Heighmler, *President*
EMP: 82
SALES (corp-wide): 631.4MM **Privately Held**
WEB: www.stratusrealestate.com
SIC: 6163 Loan brokers
HQ: Stratus Real Estate, Inc.
5311 Topanga Canyon Blvd # 3
Woodland Hills CA 91364

(P-15255)
STRATUS REAL ESTATE INC
Banning Villa Apartments
1100 N Banning Blvd # 11, Wilmington (90744-3530)
PHONE..................................310 549-7028
Bernadette Saunder, *Manager*
EMP: 82
SALES (corp-wide): 631.4MM **Privately Held**
WEB: www.stratusrealestate.com
SIC: 6163 6513 Loan brokers; apartment building operators
HQ: Stratus Real Estate, Inc.
5311 Topanga Canyon Blvd # 3
Woodland Hills CA 91364

(P-15256)
TARBELL FINANCIAL CORPORATION (PA)
1403 N Tustin Ave Ste 380, Santa Ana (92705-8691)
PHONE..................................714 972-0988

Donald Tarbell, *CEO*
Tina Jimov, *President*
Jin Lee, *COO*
Ronald Tarbell, *CFO*
Elizabeth Tarbell, *Admin Sec*
EMP: 100 **EST:** 1982
SQ FT: 60,000
SALES (est): 145.1MM **Privately Held**
WEB: www.tarbellcareers.com
SIC: 6163 6531 6099 Mortgage brokers arranging for loans, using money of others; real estate brokers & agents; escrow institutions other than real estate

(P-15257)
UNITED VISION FINANCIAL INC
16027 Ventura Blvd # 200, Encino
(91436-2728)
PHONE....................818 285-0211
Dan Michaels, *President*
Richard Levy, *Manager*
EMP: 180 **EST:** 2003
SQ FT: 3,000
SALES (est): 6.4MM **Privately Held**
SIC: 6163 Mortgage brokers arranging for loans, using money of others

(P-15258)
VELOCITY COMMERCIAL CAPITL LLC
30699 Russell Ranch Rd, Westlake Village
(91362-7315)
PHONE....................818 532-3700
Christopher D Farrar, *CFO*
Mark Szczepaniak, *CFO*
Kathy Rodriguez, *Ch Credit Ofcr*
Christopher Oltmann, *Officer*
David Ryan, *Officer*
EMP: 50 **EST:** 2004
SQ FT: 15,000
SALES (est): 44.3MM
SALES (corp-wide): 173.6MM **Publicly Held**
WEB: www.velocitymortgage.com
SIC: 6163 Loan brokers
PA: Velocity Financial, Llc
30699 Russell Ranch Rd
Westlake Village CA 91362
818 532-3700

(P-15259)
VELOCITY FINANCIAL LLC (PA)
30699 Russell Ranch Rd, Westlake Village
(91362-7315)
PHONE....................818 532-3700
Christopher D Farrar, *CEO*
Alan H Mantel, *Ch of Bd*
Joseph A Cowell, *COO*
Mark R Szczepaniak, *CFO*
Jeffrey T Taylor, *Exec VP*
EMP: 58 **EST:** 2012
SALES (est): 173.6MM **Publicly Held**
WEB: www.velocitymortgage.com
SIC: 6163 Loan brokers

(P-15260)
VILLA VENETIA
2775 Mesa Verde Dr E, Costa Mesa
(92626-4957)
PHONE....................714 540-1800
United Dominion, *President*
EMP: 329 **EST:** 2001
SALES (est): 6.8MM
SALES (corp-wide): 631.4MM **Privately Held**
WEB: www.stratusrealestate.com
SIC: 6163 Loan brokers
HQ: Stratus Real Estate, Inc.
5311 Topanga Canyon Blvd # 3
Woodland Hills CA 91364

6211 Security Brokers & Dealers

(P-15261)
ADVENT SECURITIES INVESTMENTS (PA)
Also Called: Olympic Security
9631 Alondra Blvd Ste 202, Bellflower
(90706-3674)
PHONE....................562 920-5467
Cynthia Jocson, *President*
Eric Sera, *Treasurer*

EMP: 50 **EST:** 1992
SQ FT: 5,000
SALES (est): 12.9MM **Privately Held**
SIC: 6211 5699 Security brokers & dealers; uniforms

(P-15262)
AMERIHOME MORTGAGE COMPANY LLC
1 Baxter Way Ste 300, Westlake Village
(91362-3888)
PHONE....................888 469-0810
James Furash, *CEO*
Rashmi Gulrajani, *President*
Thomas Smith, *President*
Todd Taylor, *CFO*
Josh Adler, *Ch Invest Ofcr*
EMP: 704 **EST:** 2014
SALES (est): 2.9MM
SALES (corp-wide): 1.3B **Publicly Held**
WEB: www.amerihome.com
SIC: 6211 Mortgages, buying & selling
PA: Western Alliance Bancorporation
1 E Wshington St Ste 1400
Phoenix AZ 85004
602 389-3500

(P-15263)
CANYON PARTNERS INCORPORATED (HQ)
2000 Ave Of The Sts Fl 11, Los Angeles
(90067)
PHONE....................310 272-1000
Joshua S Friedman, *CEO*
Mitchell R Julis, *CEO*
John Simpson, *COO*
Natalie Park, *CFO*
John Plaga, *CFO*
EMP: 62 **EST:** 1990
SQ FT: 5,500
SALES (est): 97.1MM **Privately Held**
WEB: www.canyonpartners.com
SIC: 6211 Investment firm, general brokerage
PA: Canyon Partners, Llc
2000 Avenue Of The Stars # 11
Los Angeles CA 90067
310 272-1000

(P-15264)
GEHR HOSPITALITY LLC (HQ)
1999 Avenue Of The Stars, Los Angeles
(90067-6022)
PHONE....................323 728-5558
David Lifschitz, *President*
Thuong Luong, *CIO*
EMP: 62 **EST:** 2016
SALES (est): 54.7MM
SALES (corp-wide): 166.1MM **Privately Held**
WEB: www.gehrhospitality.com
SIC: 6211 Investment firm, general brokerage
PA: The Gehr Group Inc
7400 E Slauson Ave
Commerce CA 90040
323 728-5558

(P-15265)
GENEQUITY MORTGAGE INC
3848 W Carson St, Torrance (90503-6717)
PHONE....................310 540-1550
EMP: 69 **Privately Held**
WEB: www.paragonhomeresources.com
SIC: 6211 Mortgages, buying & selling
HQ: Genequity Mortgage, Inc.
405 State Highway 121 Byp A250
Lewisville TX 75067

(P-15266)
GOLD PARENT LP
11111 Santa Monica Blvd, Los Angeles
(90025-3333)
PHONE....................310 954-0444
Jonathan D Sokoloff, *Principal*
EMP: 3400 **EST:** 2016
SALES (est): 104.2MM **Privately Held**
SIC: 6211 Investment bankers

(P-15267)
GOLDMAN SACHS & CO LLC
2121 Avenue Of The Stars # 2600, Los Angeles (90067-5050)
PHONE....................310 407-5700
John Mallory, *Branch Mgr*

Eddie Arhagba, *Vice Pres*
Michelle Capecelatro, *Vice Pres*
Melanie Fennimore, *Vice Pres*
Rajkumar Ganesan, *Vice Pres*
EMP: 120
SALES (corp-wide): 53.5B **Publicly Held**
WEB: www.goldmansachs.com
SIC: 6211 Investment bankers
HQ: Goldman Sachs & Co. Llc
200 West St Bldg 200 # 200
New York NY 10282
212 346-5440

(P-15268)
GORES GROUP LLC (PA)
9800 Wilshire Blvd, Beverly Hills
(90212-1804)
PHONE....................310 209-3010
Alec Gores, *CEO*
Eileen Moore, *CEO*
Joseph Page, *COO*
Jay Delatte, *Officer*
Niklas Fallgren, *Exec VP*
EMP: 60 **EST:** 2003
SALES (est): 1.8B **Privately Held**
WEB: www.gores.com
SIC: 6211 7372 5734 Investment firm, general brokerage; prepackaged software; computer software & accessories

(P-15269)
HFF SECURITIES LP (PA)
1999 Avenue Of The Stars # 1200, Los Angeles (90067-6022)
PHONE....................310 407-2100
Daniel Cashdan, *Principal*
EMP: 85 **EST:** 2006
SALES (est): 631.5K **Privately Held**
WEB: www.us.jll.com
SIC: 6211 Security brokers & dealers

(P-15270)
IMPERIAL CAPITAL LLC (PA)
10100 Santa Monica Blvd # 2400, Los Angeles (90067-4136)
PHONE....................310 246-3700
Randall Wooster, *CEO*
Timothy Sullivan, *President*
Randall E Wooster, *CEO*
Mark Martis, *COO*
Jason W Reese, *Chairman*
EMP: 85 **EST:** 1997
SALES (est): 66.9MM **Privately Held**
SIC: 6211 Investment bankers

(P-15271)
INTERLINK SECURITIES CORP
20750 Ventura Blvd # 300, Woodland Hills
(91364-2338)
P.O. Box 4323 (91365-4323)
PHONE....................818 992-6700
Barry Wolfe, *President*
Karen Perry, *Officer*
EMP: 100 **EST:** 1992
SALES (est): 7MM **Privately Held**
SIC: 6211 6722 Security brokers & dealers; management investment, open-end

(P-15272)
INVESTMENT TECH GROUP INC
400 Crprate Pinte Ste 855, Culver City
(90230)
PHONE....................310 216-6777
EMP: 150
SALES (corp-wide): 634.8MM **Publicly Held**
SIC: 6211 7371 Security Broker/Dealer Custom Computer Programing
PA: Investment Technology Group, Inc.
1 Liberty Plz
New York NY 10282
212 588-4000

(P-15273)
LEAR CAPITAL INC
1990 S Bundy Dr Ste 600, Los Angeles
(90025-5256)
PHONE....................310 571-0190
John Ohanesian, *President*
Kevin Demeritt, *Chairman*
Jason Liyanage, *Opers Staff*
Cher Cusumano, *Marketing Staff*
Terrence Moloney, *Manager*
EMP: 72 **EST:** 1997
SQ FT: 4,500

SALES (est): 30.8MM **Privately Held**
WEB: www.learcapital.com
SIC: 6211 Mineral, oil & gas leasing & royalty dealers

(P-15274)
LERETA LLC (PA)
901 Corporate Center Dr, Pomona
(91768-2642)
PHONE....................626 543-1765
John Walsh, *CEO*
John Permejo, *President*
James V Micali, *COO*
Tyler Page, *CFO*
Jonathan Willen, *Officer*
EMP: 350 **EST:** 2009
SALES (est): 272MM **Privately Held**
WEB: www.lereta.com
SIC: 6211 6541 6361 Tax certificate dealers; title search companies; real estate title insurance

(P-15275)
M L STERN & CO LLC (DH)
8350 Wilshire Blvd # 300, Beverly Hills
(90211-2327)
PHONE....................323 658-4400
Milford L Stern,
Richard Dimino, *Vice Pres*
Bill Pinkerton, *Branch Mgr*
Corey Falikoff, *Info Tech Mgr*
Gary Frazeur, *Marketing Staff*
EMP: 117 **EST:** 1980
SQ FT: 8,100
SALES (est): 40.2MM
SALES (corp-wide): 2.2B **Publicly Held**
WEB: www.mlstern.com
SIC: 6211 Brokers, security
HQ: Hilltop Securities Holdings Llc
200 Crescent Ct Ste 1330
Dallas TX 75201
214 855-2177

(P-15276)
MERRILL LYNCH PIERCE FENNER
9560 Wilshire Blvd Fl 3, Beverly Hills
(90212-2430)
PHONE....................310 858-1500
Brad Dykes, *Branch-Mgr*
John Mulcahy, *Advisor*
Brian Sixt, *Advisor*
Joe Wingard, *Advisor*
Camelia Barsoum, *Agent*
EMP: 50
SALES (corp-wide): 93.7B **Publicly Held**
WEB: www.ml.com
SIC: 6211 6282 Security brokers & dealers; investment advisory service
HQ: Merrill Lynch, Pierce, Fenner & Smith Incorporated
111 8th Ave
New York NY 10011
800 637-7455

(P-15277)
MERRILL LYNCH PRCE FNNER SMITH
21215 Burbank Blvd # 600, Woodland Hills
(91367-7090)
PHONE....................818 340-9500
EMP: 85
SALES (corp-wide): 93.7B **Publicly Held**
WEB: www.ml.com
SIC: 6211 Security brokers & dealers
HQ: Merrill Lynch, Pierce, Fenner & Smith Incorporated
111 8th Ave
New York NY 10011
800 637-7455

(P-15278)
MERRILL LYNCH PRCE FNNER SMITH
650 Town Center Dr # 500, Costa Mesa
(92626-1989)
PHONE....................714 429-2800
Joseph Volz, *Branch Mgr*
William Wheatley, *Consultant*
EMP: 85
SALES (corp-wide): 93.7B **Publicly Held**
WEB: www.ml.com
SIC: 6211 8742 Security brokers & dealers; financial consultant

---

HQ: Merrill Lynch, Pierce, Fenner & Smith
Incorporated
111 8th Ave
New York NY 10011
800 637-7455

(P-15279)
MERRILL LYNCH PRCE FNNER SMITH
730 W Lancaster Blvd, Lancaster
(93534-3177)
PHONE.....................661 802-0764
Ann Johnson, *Branch Mgr*
EMP: 85
SALES (corp-wide): 93.7B **Publicly Held**
WEB: www.ml.com
SIC: 6211 Security brokers & dealers
HQ: Merrill Lynch, Pierce, Fenner & Smith
Incorporated
111 8th Ave
New York NY 10011
800 637-7455

(P-15280)
MERRILL LYNCH PRCE FNNER SMITH
74800 Us Highway 111, Indian Wells
(92210-7116)
PHONE.....................760 862-1400
Robert O Braun, *Branch Mgr*
EMP: 85
SALES (corp-wide): 93.7B **Publicly Held**
WEB: www.ml.com
SIC: 6211 Security brokers & dealers
HQ: Merrill Lynch, Pierce, Fenner & Smith
Incorporated
111 8th Ave
New York NY 10011
800 637-7455

(P-15281)
MERRILL LYNCH PRCE FNNER SMITH
520 Nwport Ctr Dr Ste 190, Newport Beach
(92660)
PHONE.....................949 467-3760
David Gunta, *Branch Mgr*
Anthony Morillo, *Vice Pres*
MEI Chan, *Advisor*
Ronald Roach, *Advisor*
Linda Rusmisel, *Advisor*
EMP: 85
SALES (corp-wide): 93.7B **Publicly Held**
WEB: www.ml.com
SIC: 6211 Security brokers & dealers
HQ: Merrill Lynch, Pierce, Fenner & Smith
Incorporated
111 8th Ave
New York NY 10011
800 637-7455

(P-15282)
MERRILL LYNCH PRCE FNNER SMITH
300 E Esplanade Dr # 215, Oxnard
(93036-1238)
PHONE.....................800 964-5182
James Hardy, *Branch Mgr*
EMP: 85
SALES (corp-wide): 93.7B **Publicly Held**
WEB: www.ml.com
SIC: 6211 Security brokers & dealers
HQ: Merrill Lynch, Pierce, Fenner & Smith
Incorporated
111 8th Ave
New York NY 10011
800 637-7455

(P-15283)
MERRILL LYNCH PRCE FNNER SMITH
28202 Cabot Rd, Laguna Niguel
(92677-1222)
PHONE.....................949 456-8082
Michael Sussman, *Vice Pres*
EMP: 85
SALES (corp-wide): 93.7B **Publicly Held**
WEB: www.ml.com
SIC: 6211 Security brokers & dealers
HQ: Merrill Lynch, Pierce, Fenner & Smith
Incorporated
111 8th Ave
New York NY 10011
800 637-7455

(P-15284)
MERRILL LYNCH PRCE FNNER SMITH
100 Wilshire Blvd Ste 300, Santa Monica
(90401-1110)
PHONE.....................310 477-3400
Baldwin Chin, *Manager*
Lucian Vincent, *Advisor*
EMP: 85
SALES (corp-wide): 93.7B **Publicly Held**
WEB: www.ml.com
SIC: 6211 Security brokers & dealers
HQ: Merrill Lynch, Pierce, Fenner & Smith
Incorporated
111 8th Ave
New York NY 10011
800 637-7455

(P-15285)
MERRILL LYNCH PRCE FNNER SMITH
100 Spectrum Center Dr, Irvine
(92618-4962)
PHONE.....................949 235-5050
C De Lorm, *Branch Mgr*
EMP: 85
SALES (corp-wide): 93.7B **Publicly Held**
WEB: www.ml.com
SIC: 6211 Stock brokers & dealers
HQ: Merrill Lynch, Pierce, Fenner & Smith
Incorporated
111 8th Ave
New York NY 10011
800 637-7455

(P-15286)
MERRILL LYNCH PRCE FNNER SMITH
901 Via Piemonte Ste 503, Ontario
(91764-8507)
PHONE.....................909 476-5100
Chris Barney, *Manager*
Rosemary Wendorf, *Vice Pres*
EMP: 85
SALES (corp-wide): 93.7B **Publicly Held**
WEB: www.ml.com
SIC: 6211 Security brokers & dealers
HQ: Merrill Lynch, Pierce, Fenner & Smith
Incorporated
111 8th Ave
New York NY 10011
800 637-7455

(P-15287)
MERRILL LYNCH PRCE FNNER SMITH
1424 State St, Santa Barbara
(93101-2512)
PHONE.....................805 963-0333
Frederick Burrows, *Branch Mgr*
Kyle Feighner, *Consultant*
EMP: 85
SALES (corp-wide): 93.7B **Publicly Held**
WEB: www.ml.com
SIC: 6211 Security brokers & dealers; mutual funds, selling by independent salesperson
HQ: Merrill Lynch, Pierce, Fenner & Smith
Incorporated
111 8th Ave
New York NY 10011
800 637-7455

(P-15288)
MERRILL LYNCH PRCE FNNER SMITH
5080 California Ave # 102, Bakersfield
(93309-1698)
P.O. Box 9788 (93389-9788)
PHONE.....................661 326-7700
Gary Sampson, *Manager*
Greg Meister, *Advisor*
EMP: 85
SALES (corp-wide): 93.7B **Publicly Held**
WEB: www.ml.com
SIC: 6211 Security brokers & dealers
HQ: Merrill Lynch, Pierce, Fenner & Smith
Incorporated
111 8th Ave
New York NY 10011
800 637-7455

(P-15289)
MERRILL LYNCH PRCE FNNER SMITH
145 S State College Blvd, Brea
(92821-5818)
PHONE.....................714 257-4400
Robert Max, *Manager*
Stephanie Sheeks, *Director*
Joshua Murty, *Advisor*
Joseph B Yu, *Agent*
Ryan Taleghani, *Associate*
EMP: 85
SALES (corp-wide): 93.7B **Publicly Held**
WEB: www.ml.com
SIC: 6211 Security brokers & dealers; mutual funds, selling by independent salesperson
HQ: Merrill Lynch, Pierce, Fenner & Smith
Incorporated
111 8th Ave
New York NY 10011
800 637-7455

(P-15290)
MERRILL LYNCH PRCE FNNER SMITH
2049 Century Park E # 1100, Los Angeles
(90067-3101)
PHONE.....................310 407-3900
Michael Rogers, *Branch Mgr*
Ban Hong, *Manager*
Carmen Portnoy, *Assistant VP*
EMP: 85
SALES (corp-wide): 93.7B **Publicly Held**
WEB: www.ml.com
SIC: 6211 Security brokers & dealers
HQ: Merrill Lynch, Pierce, Fenner & Smith
Incorporated
111 8th Ave
New York NY 10011
800 637-7455

(P-15291)
MERRILL LYNCH PRCE FNNER SMITH
2301 Rosecrans Ave # 3150, El Segundo
(90245-4967)
PHONE.....................310 536-1600
Shawn Soroush, *Manager*
Joseph Dallape, *Advisor*
EMP: 85
SALES (corp-wide): 93.7B **Publicly Held**
WEB: www.ml.com
SIC: 6211 Security brokers & dealers
HQ: Merrill Lynch, Pierce, Fenner & Smith
Incorporated
111 8th Ave
New York NY 10011
800 637-7455

(P-15292)
MERRILL LYNCH PRCE FNNER SMITH
800 E Colo Blvd Ste 400, Pasadena
(91101)
PHONE.....................800 637-7455
Mark Mixon, *Manager*
Lawrence De Santis, *Advisor*
Sarah Flick, *Advisor*
Pan Katie, *Advisor*
Lance Marcus, *Advisor*
EMP: 85
SALES (corp-wide): 93.7B **Publicly Held**
WEB: www.ml.com
SIC: 6211 Security brokers & dealers; mutual funds, selling by independent salesperson
HQ: Merrill Lynch, Pierce, Fenner & Smith
Incorporated
111 8th Ave
New York NY 10011
800 637-7455

(P-15293)
MERRILL LYNCH PRCE FNNER SMITH
3010 Old Ranch Pkwy # 15, Seal Beach
(90740-2764)
PHONE.....................562 493-1300
Julie Danaho, *Manager*
Kenneth Paul, *Marketing Staff*
EMP: 85
SALES (corp-wide): 93.7B **Publicly Held**
WEB: www.ml.com
SIC: 6211 Security brokers & dealers

(P-15294)
MERRILL LYNCH PRCE FNNER SMITH
2815 Townsgate Rd Ste 300, Westlake Village (91361-3094)
PHONE.....................805 381-2600
Brian Riley, *Manager*
Brandon Asher, *Vice Pres*
Eyal Yaffe, *Manager*
Joshua Cummins, *Advisor*
EMP: 85
SALES (corp-wide): 93.7B **Publicly Held**
WEB: www.ml.com
SIC: 6211 Security brokers & dealers
HQ: Merrill Lynch, Pierce, Fenner & Smith
Incorporated
111 8th Ave
New York NY 10011
800 637-7455

(P-15295)
MERRILL LYNCH PRCE FNNER SMITH
1020 Marsh St, San Luis Obispo
(93401-3630)
PHONE.....................805 596-2222
M Barry Epperson, *Director*
Michael Stenvall, *Vice Pres*
Valerie Fishel, *Purchasing*
Tommy Lopez, *Advisor*
Cheryl Millard, *Agent*
EMP: 85
SALES (corp-wide): 93.7B **Publicly Held**
WEB: www.ml.com
SIC: 6211 Security brokers & dealers
HQ: Merrill Lynch, Pierce, Fenner & Smith
Incorporated
111 8th Ave
New York NY 10011
800 637-7455

(P-15296)
METROPOLITAN W ASSET MGT LLC (HQ)
865 S Figueroa St, Los Angeles
(90017-2543)
PHONE.....................213 244-0000
Scott Dubchansky, *
Sumie Branch, *Assoc VP*
Ruben Hovhannisyan, *Senior VP*
Richard Kim, *Senior VP*
Melinda Newman, *Senior VP*
EMP: 78 EST: 1996
SALES (est): 52.4MM **Privately Held**
SIC: 6211 Security brokers & dealers

(P-15297)
MORGAN STNLEY SMITH BARNEY LLC
21650 Oxnard St Ste 1800, Woodland Hills
(91367-4944)
PHONE.....................818 715-1800
Fred Rucker Esq, *Branch Mgr*
EMP: 68
SALES (corp-wide): 52B **Publicly Held**
WEB: www.morganstanley.com
SIC: 6211 Stock brokers & dealers
HQ: Morgan Stanley Smith Barney, Llc
1585 Broadway
New York NY 10036

(P-15298)
MORGAN STNLEY SMITH BARNEY LLC
10 Pointe Dr Ste 400, Brea (92821-7620)
PHONE.....................714 674-4100
Vincent Daigneault, *Principal*
EMP: 68
SALES (corp-wide): 52B **Publicly Held**
WEB: www.morganstanley.com
SIC: 6211 Stock brokers & dealers
HQ: Morgan Stanley Smith Barney, Llc
1585 Broadway
New York NY 10036

▲ = Import ▼=Export
◆ =Import/Export

(P-15299)
MORGAN STNLEY SMITH BARNEY LLC
1111 Coast Village Rd, Santa Barbara (93108-2716)
PHONE..................................805 565-4447
Timothy Gandy, *Manager*
EMP: 68
SALES (corp-wide): 52B **Publicly Held**
WEB: www.morganstanley.com
SIC: 6211 Stock brokers & dealers
HQ: Morgan Stanley Smith Barney, Llc
    1585 Broadway
    New York NY 10036

(P-15300)
MORGAN STNLEY SMITH BARNEY LLC
3750 University Ave # 600, Riverside (92501-3323)
PHONE..................................951 682-1181
James Gibson, *Manager*
EMP: 68
SALES (corp-wide): 52B **Publicly Held**
WEB: www.morganstanley.com
SIC: 6211 Security brokers & dealers
HQ: Morgan Stanley Smith Barney, Llc
    1585 Broadway
    New York NY 10036

(P-15301)
MORGAN STNLEY SMITH BARNEY LLC
1014 Santa Barbara St, Santa Barbara (93101-2126)
PHONE..................................805 963-3381
Walter Harris, *President*
EMP: 68
SALES (corp-wide): 52B **Publicly Held**
WEB: www.morganstanley.com
SIC: 6211 Stock brokers & dealers
HQ: Morgan Stanley Smith Barney, Llc
    1585 Broadway
    New York NY 10036

(P-15302)
NATIONAL FINANCIAL SVCS LLC
19200 Von Karman Ave, Irvine (92612-8553)
PHONE..................................949 476-0157
Lawrence Goodkind, *Branch Mgr*
EMP: 688
SALES (corp-wide): 4.3B **Privately Held**
WEB: www.mybrokerageinfo.com
SIC: 6211 Investment firm, general brokerage
HQ: National Financial Services Llc
    200 Seaport Blvd Ste 630
    Boston MA 02210
    800 471-0382

(P-15303)
PACIFIC SELECT DISTRIBUTORS
Also Called: Pacific Mutual Distributors
700 Newport Center Dr # 4, Newport Beach (92660-6307)
PHONE..................................949 219-3011
Gerald W Robinson, *President*
Edward R Byrd, *CFO*
Kathy R Gough, *Assoc VP*
Audrey L Milfs, *Admin Sec*
Thomas C Sutton, *Director*
EMP: 96 EST: 1969
SQ FT: 300,000
SALES (est): 16.3MM
SALES (corp-wide): 12.8B **Privately Held**
WEB: www.pacificlife.com
SIC: 6211 Brokers, security; dealers, security
HQ: Pacific Life Insurance Company
    700 Newport Center Dr
    Newport Beach CA 92660
    949 219-3011

(P-15304)
PALISADES GROUP LLC
11755 Wilshire Blvd # 1700, Los Angeles (90025-1500)
PHONE..................................424 280-7560
Stephen Kirch, *CEO*

Justin Bodiya, *COO*
Sally Kawana, *CFO*
Haseeb Rahman, *Managing Dir*
Jack Macdowell Jr, *CIO*
EMP: 95 EST: 2012
SALES (est): 4.8MM **Privately Held**
WEB: www.palisades.us.com
SIC: 6211 Investment firm, general brokerage
PA: The Palisades Holdings I Llc
    11755 Wilshire Blvd # 17
    Los Angeles CA 90025
    424 280-7560

(P-15305)
ROTH CAPITAL PARTNERS LLC (PA)
888 San Clemente Dr # 400, Newport Beach (92660-6369)
PHONE..................................800 678-9147
Byron Roth, *CEO*
Gordon Roth, *COO*
John Chambers, *Vice Ch Bd*
Kristin Lamarche, *Officer*
Dustin F Cabrera, *Vice Pres*
EMP: 100 EST: 1984
SQ FT: 52,000
SALES (est): 60.7MM **Privately Held**
WEB: www.roth.com
SIC: 6211 Investment bankers

(P-15306)
STERNOCANDLELAMP HOLDINGS INC
1880 Compton Ave Ste 101, Corona (92881-2780)
PHONE..................................951 682-9600
Patrick A Maciariello, *President*
C Sean Day, *Ch of Bd*
Ryan J Faulkingham, *CFO*
EMP: 2727 EST: 2014
SALES (est): 234.6MM **Publicly Held**
WEB: www.sternopro.com
SIC: 6211 Investment firm, general brokerage
PA: Compass Diversified Holdings
    301 Riverside Ave Fl 2
    Westport CT 06880

(P-15307)
STOCKCROSS FINANCIAL SVCS INC (DH)
9464 Wilshire Blvd, Beverly Hills (90212-2707)
PHONE..................................800 993-2015
Richard S Gebbia, *President*
Michael Jonathan Colombino, *CFO*
George H Kupper, *Admin Sec*
Ed Shaughnessy, *Cust Mgr*
EMP: 50 EST: 1971
SQ FT: 8,000
SALES (est): 25.3MM
SALES (corp-wide): 54.8MM **Publicly Held**
WEB: www.siebert.com
SIC: 6211 Brokers, security
HQ: Muriel Siebert & Co., Inc.
    15 Exchange Pl Ste 615
    Jersey City NJ 07302
    212 644-2400

(P-15308)
SUTTER SECURITIES INCORPORATED
6 Venture Ste 395, Irvine (92618-7315)
PHONE..................................415 352-6300
Robert Muh, *CEO*
Frank Soriano, *President*
H D Kavrell, *Managing Dir*
Ea Sachs, *Managing Dir*
Mitchell Miller, *Opers Staff*
EMP: 67 EST: 1992
SALES (est): 7.9MM **Privately Held**
WEB: www.suttersecurities.com
SIC: 6211 Investment bankers
PA: Sutter Securities Group, Inc.
    6 Venture Ste 395
    Irvine CA 92618
    310 504-3706

(P-15309)
VERSITY INVESTMENTS LLC
20 Enterprise Ste 400, Aliso Viejo (92656-7118)
PHONE..................................877 827-6272
Brian Nelson, *President*
Blake Wettengel, *CEO*
Tanya Muro, *COO*
Jennifer Welker, *CFO*
James Hogen, *Exec VP*
EMP: 55 EST: 2018
SALES (est): 7.5MM **Privately Held**
WEB: www.versityinvest.com
SIC: 6211 Investment firm, general brokerage

(P-15310)
WEDBUSH SECURITIES INC (HQ)
1000 Wilshire Blvd # 800, Los Angeles (90017-2466)
P.O. Box 30014 (90030-0014)
PHONE..................................213 688-8000
Edward W Wedbush, *President*
Robert Limmer, *Owner*
Peter Allman-Ward, *CFO*
Dan Billings, *CFO*
David Weaver, *CFO*
EMP: 300 EST: 1955
SQ FT: 100,000
SALES (est): 224.6MM
SALES (corp-wide): 272.5MM **Privately Held**
WEB: www.wedbush.com
SIC: 6211 Brokers, security; stock brokers & dealers; bond dealers & brokers
PA: Wedbush, Inc.,
    1000 Wilshire Blvd # 900
    Los Angeles CA 90017
    213 688-8080

(P-15311)
WELLS FARGO CLEARING SVCS LLC
Also Called: Wells Fargo Advisors
3020 Old Ranch Pkwy # 190, Seal Beach (90740-2765)
PHONE..................................562 594-1220
EMP: 50
SALES (corp-wide): 97.7B **Publicly Held**
SIC: 6211 Security Brokerage Firm
HQ: Wells Fargo Clearing Services, Llc
    1 N Jefferson Ave
    Saint Louis MO 63103
    314 955-3000

(P-15312)
WILLIAM ONEIL & CO INC (PA)
12655 Beatrice St, Los Angeles (90066-7302)
PHONE..................................310 448-6800
Willaim J Oneil, *CEO*
Don Drake, *Officer*
Randy Watts, *Exec VP*
Patricia Arevalo, *Vice Pres*
Brian Lawlor, *Vice Pres*
EMP: 245 EST: 2010
SQ FT: 5,000
SALES (est): 113.3MM **Privately Held**
WEB: www.williamoneil.com
SIC: 6211 6282 Brokers, security; investment advisory service

---

6221 Commodity Contracts Brokers & Dealers

(P-15313)
CABALLERO & SONS INC
Also Called: Beyond Meat and Company
5753 E Snta Ana Cyn Rd St, Anaheim (92807-3230)
PHONE..................................562 368-1644
Perpetua Duque-Hata, *President*
Nathaniel Caballero, *Ch of Bd*
Marivet Caballero, *CEO*
EMP: 25 EST: 2017
SQ FT: 500
SALES (est): 7MM **Privately Held**
WEB: www.caballero-sons.com
SIC: 6221 2392 5141 5149 Commodity traders, contracts; cushions & pillows; blankets, comforters & beddings; food brokers; beverages, except coffee & tea

(P-15314)
CT COMMODITIES INC
217 W Terra Bella Ave, Pixley (93256-9631)
P.O. Box 44 (93256-0044)
PHONE..................................559 757-3996
Randal Lee Terrel, *President*
EMP: 61 EST: 2012
SALES (est): 10.3MM **Privately Held**
SIC: 6221 Commodity contracts brokers, dealers

(P-15315)
INVAPHARM INC
1320 W Mission Blvd, Ontario (91762-4786)
PHONE..................................909 757-1818
Manu Patolia, *President*
Kalpesh Bodar, *Vice Pres*
EMP: 40 EST: 2015
SQ FT: 60,000
SALES (est): 12MM **Privately Held**
WEB: www.invapharm.com
SIC: 6221 2023 Commodity brokers, contracts; dietary supplements, dairy & non-dairy based

---

6282 Investment Advice

(P-15316)
ANDERSON KAYNE CAPITAL
1800 Avenue Of The, Los Angeles (90067)
PHONE..................................800 231-7414
Richard Kayne, *Chairman*
Edward Cerny, *Managing Prtnr*
Robert Sinnott, *CEO*
Curt Biren, *Vice Pres*
Meegan T Motisi, *Vice Pres*
EMP: 300 EST: 1994
SALES: 977.4K **Privately Held**
WEB: www.kaynecapitalfoundation.org
SIC: 6282 Investment advisory service

(P-15317)
BALMORAL FUNDS LLC (PA)
11150 Santa Monica Blvd, Los Angeles (90025-3380)
PHONE..................................310 473-3065
Jonathan Victor,
David Shainberg, *Vice Pres*
Skip Victor, *Managing Dir*
Steven Barnett, *Business Anlyst*
Samuel Kandel, *Accountant*
EMP: 712 EST: 2011
SALES (est): 96.2MM **Privately Held**
WEB: www.balmoralfunds.com
SIC: 6282 Investment advisory service

(P-15318)
BDO CAPITAL ADVISORS LLC
1888 Century Park E, Los Angeles (90067-1702)
PHONE..................................310 557-0300
Daniel Shea, *Managing Dir*
Onicka Oxford, *Manager*
EMP: 203
SALES (corp-wide): 1.8B **Privately Held**
WEB: www.bdocap.com
SIC: 6282 6726 Investment advice; investment offices
HQ: Bdo Capital Advisors Llc
    2 International Pl Lbby 4
    Boston MA 02110
    617 422-7576

(P-15319)
BEL AIR INV ADVISORS LLC (DH)
1999 Avenue Of The Stars # 3200, Los Angeles (90067-6041)
PHONE..................................310 229-1500
David Sadkin, *President*
Todd Morgan, *Partner*
Saher Hamideh, *Officer*
Supriya Batra, *Vice Pres*
Dillon Christensen, *Vice Pres*
EMP: 65 EST: 1997
SALES (est): 7.8MM
SALES (corp-wide): 51MM **Privately Held**
WEB: www.belair-llc.com
SIC: 6282 Investment advisory service

(P-15320)
BLX GROUP LLC
777 S Figueroa St # 3200, Los Angeles
(90017-5800)
PHONE..................213 612-2400
EMP: 60 **EST:** 2010
SQ FT: 13,000
SALES (est): 6.3MM **Privately Held**
SIC: 6282 Investment Advisory Service

(P-15321)
CAPITAL GROUP COMPANIES INC (PA)
Also Called: Capital Group, The
333 S Hope St Fl 55, Los Angeles
(90071-3061)
PHONE..................213 486-9200
Tim Armour, *CEO*
Ray Stein, *Shareholder*
Rob Lovelace, *Vice Chairman*
Phil De Toledo, *President*
Dale Worrell, *President*
EMP: 800 **EST:** 1931
SQ FT: 106,000
SALES (est): 5.4B **Privately Held**
WEB: www.capitalgroup.com
SIC: 6282 6091 6722 8741 Investment advice; nondeposit trust facilities; mutual fund sales, on own account; management services

(P-15322)
CAPITAL RESEARCH AND MGT CO (HQ)
333 S Hope St Fl 55, Los Angeles
(90071-3061)
PHONE..................213 486-9200
R Michael Shanahan, *Ch of Bd*
James F Rothenberg, *Ch of Bd*
Timothy Armour, *CEO*
Jonathan Knowles, *Exec VP*
Gordon Crawford, *Senior VP*
EMP: 500 **EST:** 1944
SALES (est): 1.5B
SALES (corp-wide): 5.4B **Privately Held**
WEB: www.capitalgroup.com
SIC: 6282 Investment research
PA: The Capital Group Companies Inc
333 S Hope St Fl 55
Los Angeles CA 90071
213 486-9200

(P-15323)
CDK GLOBAL INC
Also Called: Cvr
1100 W Town And Country R, Orange
(92868-4600)
PHONE..................714 426-4800
EMP: 97
SALES (corp-wide): 1.6B **Publicly Held**
WEB: www.cdkglobal.com
SIC: 6282 Investment advice
PA: Cdk Global, Inc.
1950 Hassell Rd
Hoffman Estates IL 60169
847 397-1700

(P-15324)
CHURCHILL MANAGEMENT CORP
5900 Wilshire Blvd # 400, Los Angeles
(90036-5003)
PHONE..................877 937-7110
Fred A Fern, *President*
Brad Rodgers, *Assoc VP*
David TSE, *Exec VP*
Matthew Arber, *Vice Pres*
Bill Condon, *Vice Pres*
EMP: 50 **EST:** 1995
SALES (est): 24.1MM **Privately Held**
WEB: www.churchillmanagement.com
SIC: 6282 Investment counselors

(P-15325)
CRESCENT CAPITAL GROUP LP (HQ)
11100 Santa Monica Blvd, Los Angeles
(90025-3384)
PHONE..................310 235-5900
Joeseph Keenan, *CFO*
Ceci Tam, *President*
Anna M Lopez, *COO*
Raymond Barrios, *Vice Pres*
Kimberly Grant, *Vice Pres*
EMP: 115 **EST:** 2010

SALES (est): 170.1MM
SALES (corp-wide): 29.8B **Privately Held**
WEB: www.crescentcap.com
SIC: 6282 Investment advisory service
PA: Sun Life Financial Inc.
1 York St
Toronto ON M5J 0
416 979-9966

(P-15326)
FIRST AMERICAN TRUST COMPANY (HQ)
5 First American Way, Santa Ana
(92707-5913)
P.O. Box 267 (92702-0267)
PHONE..................714 560-7856
Toll Free:..................877 -
Thomas M Kelley, *CEO*
Kelly Dudley, *COO*
Teri Pierce, *CFO*
Eric R McMullen, *Officer*
Darliene Evans, *Trust Officer*
EMP: 54
SQ FT: 34,625
SALES: 82MM **Publicly Held**
WEB: www.firstamtrust.com
SIC: 6282 Investment advisory service

(P-15327)
FIRST FOUNDATION ADVISORS (HQ)
Also Called: First Foundation Consulting
18101 Von Karman Ave # 700, Irvine
(92612-0145)
PHONE..................949 202-4100
David Rahn, *President*
Scott Kavanaugh, *CEO*
Louis Abel, *Ch Invest Ofcr*
Robert Noble, *Exec VP*
John M Michel, *Vice Pres*
EMP: 69 **EST:** 2008
SALES (est): 42.7MM **Publicly Held**
WEB: www.firstfoundationinc.com
SIC: 6282 Investment advice

(P-15328)
GENTER CAPITAL LLC (PA)
11601 Wilshire Blvd Ph, Los Angeles
(90025-0509)
PHONE..................310 477-6543
Daniel Genter, *Mng Member*
Peter Walker, *Vice Pres*
Jacob Wood, *Vice Pres*
Andrew Robb, *Administration*
Manny Gutierrez,
EMP: 56 **EST:** 1976
SQ FT: 19,358
SALES (est): 7.9MM **Privately Held**
WEB: www.rncgenter.com
SIC: 6282 Investment counselors

(P-15329)
GROUPEX FINANCIAL CORPORATION (DH)
Also Called: Aguila Financial
14849 Firestone Blvd Fl 1 Flr 1, La Mirada
(90638)
PHONE..................714 690-8321
Raymond D Butner, *President*
Guillermo De La Vina, *CEO*
EMP: 295 **EST:** 1998
SALES (est): 13.2MM
SALES (corp-wide): 300.6MM **Privately Held**
WEB: www.coinstar.com
SIC: 6282 Investment advice

(P-15330)
HOULIHAN LOKEY INC (PA)
10250 Constellation Blvd, Los Angeles
(90067-6200)
PHONE..................310 788-5200
Scott L Beiser, *CEO*
Irwin N Gold, *Ch of Bd*
Robert Hotz, *Vice Chairman*
Scott J Adelson, *President*
David A Preiser, *President*
EMP: 300 **EST:** 1972
SALES (est): 1.5B **Publicly Held**
WEB: www.hl.com
SIC: 6282 6211 Investment advice; security brokers & dealers; investment bankers

(P-15331)
MARLIN EQUITY PARTNERS LLC (PA)
338 Pier Ave, Hermosa Beach
(90254-3617)
PHONE..................310 364-0100
David McGovern, *Mng Member*
Kelly Salisbury, *Executive Asst*
Kevin Hatch, *Finance Dir*
Joselyn Choi, *Accounting Mgr*
Joshua Portillo, *Accountant*
EMP: 80 **EST:** 2005
SQ FT: 16,000
SALES (est): 2.1B **Privately Held**
WEB: www.marlinequity.com
SIC: 6282 3661 Investment advisory service; telephones & telephone apparatus; multiplex equipment, telephone & telegraph

(P-15332)
MERCER GLOBAL SECURITIES LLC
1801 E Cabrillo Blvd A, Santa Barbara
(93108-2897)
PHONE..................805 565-1681
Gene Dongieux Jr, *Mng Member*
Steve Shelvey, *Vice Pres*
Doug Suhr, *Vice Pres*
Deb Atwater, *Executive*
Kevin Jack, *Managing Dir*
EMP: 63 **EST:** 1995
SALES (est): 3.1MM **Privately Held**
WEB: www.merceradvisors.com
SIC: 6282 Investment advisory service

(P-15333)
MIG CAPITAL LLC (PA)
660 Newport Center Dr # 450, Newport Beach (92660-6499)
PHONE..................949 474-5800
Richard Merage,
Yishay Aizik, *General Mgr*
Antonia Enriquez, *Admin Asst*
Aaron Chan, *Analyst*
Allen Cashion, *Director*
EMP: 103 **EST:** 2004
SALES (est): 38.6MM **Privately Held**
WEB: www.migcap.com
SIC: 6282 Investment advisory service

(P-15334)
OAKTREE CAPITAL MANAGEMENT LP (PA)
333 S Grand Ave Fl 28, Los Angeles
(90071-1530)
PHONE..................213 830-6300
Bruce Karsh, *CIO*
Randi Becker, *Partner*
David Kirchheimer, *Partner*
John Frank, *Vice Chairman*
Andrea Hendrick, *President*
EMP: 120 **EST:** 2007
SALES (est): 2B **Privately Held**
WEB: www.oaktreecapital.com
SIC: 6282 6722 6211 Investment advisory service; management investment, open-end; security brokers & dealers

(P-15335)
OAKTREE INTL HOLDINGS LLC (DH)
333 S Grand Ave Fl 28, Los Angeles
(90071-1504)
PHONE..................213 830-6300
Jay Wintrob, *CEO*
EMP: 62 **EST:** 1998
SALES (est): 221.1MM
SALES (corp-wide): 47.9B **Publicly Held**
WEB: www.oaktreecapital.com
SIC: 6282 6722 6211 Investment advisory service; management investment, open-end; security brokers & dealers

(P-15336)
PACIFIC ALTRNTIVE ASSET MGT LL (HQ)
Also Called: Paamco
660 Nwport Ctr Dr Ste 930, Newport Beach (92660)
PHONE..................949 261-4900
Jane Buchan, *CEO*
Max Santanaya, *Assoc Mgr*
Adair Alexander, *Vice Pres*
Ryan Rosen, *Associate Dir*

Anne Carlton, *Managing Dir*
EMP: 111 **EST:** 2000
SALES (est): 31.6MM
SALES (corp-wide): 55.8MM **Privately Held**
WEB: www.paamcoprisma.com
SIC: 6282 Investment advisory service
PA: Paamco Prisma Holdings, Llc
660 Nwport Ctr Dr Ste 930
Newport Beach CA 92660
949 261-4900

(P-15337)
PACIFIC INCOME ADVISERS INC (PA)
1299 Ocean Ave Ste 210, Santa Monica
(90401-1036)
PHONE..................310 393-1424
Heather U Baines, *President*
Isabella Aslan, *COO*
Lloyd Mc Adams, *Chairman*
Tim Tarpening, *Exec VP*
Joe McAdams, *Vice Pres*
EMP: 50 **EST:** 1986
SQ FT: 13,000
SALES (est): 10.1MM **Privately Held**
WEB: www.pacificincome.com
SIC: 6282 Investment advisory service

(P-15338)
PACIFIC LIFE FUND ADVISORS LLC (DH)
700 Newport Center Dr, Newport Beach
(92660-6307)
P.O. Box 9000 (92658-9030)
PHONE..................800 800-7646
Sharon Pacheco,
Darrell Dellandrea, *President*
Gail McIntosh, *President*
Cade Cherry, *Assoc VP*
Brian Cope, *Assoc VP*
EMP: 62 **EST:** 2007
SALES (est): 10.2MM
SALES (corp-wide): 12.8B **Privately Held**
WEB: www.pacificlife.com
SIC: 6282 Investment advisory service
HQ: Pacific Life Insurance Company
700 Newport Center Dr
Newport Beach CA 92660
949 219-3011

(P-15339)
PAYDEN & RYGEL (PA)
333 S Grand Ave Ste 4000, Los Angeles
(90071-1518)
PHONE..................213 625-1900
Joan Payden, *CEO*
Greg Morrison, *President*
Brian Matthews, *CFO*
Brad Hersh, *Treasurer*
Jared Boneno, *Vice Pres*
EMP: 140 **EST:** 1983
SALES (est): 67MM **Privately Held**
WEB: www.payden.com
SIC: 6282 6211 Investment counselors; security brokers & dealers

(P-15340)
PLAN MEMBER FINANCIAL CORP
Also Called: Planmember Services
6187 Carpinteria Ave, Carpinteria
(93013-2805)
PHONE..................800 874-6910
Jon Ziehl, *CEO*
Terry Janeway, *COO*
Bill Kemble, *CFO*
Trish Stone-Damon, *Admin Sec*
Ron Culverson, *Marketing Staff*
EMP: 100 **EST:** 1990
SQ FT: 6,000
SALES (est): 34MM **Privately Held**
WEB: www.planmember.com
SIC: 6282 Investment counselors

(P-15341)
QUADION LLC
Also Called: Mar-Kell Sea
17651 Armstrong Ave, Irvine (92614-5727)
PHONE..................714 546-0994
EMP: 1100 **EST:** 1945
SQ FT: 30,000
SALES (est): 110.7MM
SALES (corp-wide): 91.2B **Publicly Held**
SIC: 6282 Business Services At Non-Commercial Site

HQ: Norwest Venture Capital Management, Inc.
80 S 8th St Ste 3600
Minneapolis MN 55402
612 215-1600

(P-15342)
RESEARCH AFFILIATES CAPITAL LP
620 Nwport Ctr Dr Ste 900, Newport Beach (92660)
PHONE.....................949 325-8700
Rob Arnott, *CEO*
Feifei LI, *Partner*
Katrina F Sherrerd, *COO*
Chris Brightman, *Ch Invest Ofcr*
Adam Willis, *Senior VP*
EMP: 82 **EST:** 2002
SALES (est): 21.7MM **Privately Held**
WEB: www.researchaffiliates.com
SIC: 6282 Investment advisory service

(P-15343)
RESEARCH AFFILIATES MGT LLC
620 Nwport Ctr Dr Ste 900, Newport Beach (92660)
PHONE.....................949 325-8700
Rob Arnott, *Partner*
Campbell Harvey, *Partner*
ARI Polychronopoulo, *Partner*
Jonathan Treussard, *Partner*
Katrina Sherrerd, *COO*
EMP: 80 **EST:** 2002
SALES (est): 23.6MM **Privately Held**
WEB: www.researchaffiliates.com
SIC: 6282 Investment counselors

(P-15344)
RNC CAPITAL MANAGEMENT LLC
Also Called: Rnc Genter Capital Management
11601 Wilshire Blvd Ph 25, Los Angeles (90025-0509)
PHONE.....................310 477-6543
Dan Genter,
Manny Gutierrez, *CFO*
Alexander Tran, *Assoc VP*
Rocky Barber, *Vice Pres*
Kaelynn Garcia, *Vice Pres*
EMP: 65 **EST:** 1968
SQ FT: 20,000
SALES (est): 17MM **Privately Held**
WEB: www.rncgenter.com
SIC: 6282 Investment counselors

(P-15345)
SAGEPOINT FINANCIAL INC
3723 Birch St Ste 9, Newport Beach (92660-2614)
PHONE.....................949 756-1462
Rayna Elmendorf, *Manager*
Michael Coffman, *Advisor*
Charles Curtin, *Advisor*
Patrick McCormick, *Agent*
EMP: 298 **EST:** 2010
SALES (est): 6.5MM
SALES (corp-wide): 651.5MM **Privately Held**
WEB: www.sagepointfinancial.com
SIC: 6282 Investment advisory service
HQ: Sagepoint Financial, Inc.
20 E Thomas Rd Ste 2000
Phoenix AZ 85012

(P-15346)
SAGEPOINT FINANCIAL INC
3655 Torrance Blvd # 480, Torrance (90503-4862)
PHONE.....................310 792-0801
Gregory Fong, *Branch Mgr*
EMP: 54
SALES (corp-wide): 651.5MM **Privately Held**
WEB: www.sagepointfinancial.com
SIC: 6282 Investment advice
HQ: Sagepoint Financial, Inc.
20 E Thomas Rd Ste 2000
Phoenix AZ 85012

(P-15347)
SAGEVIEW ADVISORY GROUP LLC (PA)
4000 Macarthur Blvd # 1050, Newport Beach (92660-2538)
PHONE.....................949 955-1395
Randall C Long, *CEO*
Jon Upham, *President*
Mark Hendrickson, *CFO*
Mark H Kordonsky, *Officer*
Jonathan St Clair, *Officer*
EMP: 76 **EST:** 1998
SALES (est): 48.2MM **Privately Held**
WEB: www.sageviewadvisory.com
SIC: 6282 Investment advisory service

(P-15348)
SHAMROCK HOLDINGS INC (PA)
Also Called: Shamrock Holdings California
4444 W Lkeside Dr Ste 150, Burbank (91505)
P.O. Box 7774 (91510-7774)
PHONE.....................818 845-4444
Stanley P Gold, *President*
Roy E Disney, *Ch of Bd*
Gregory Martin, *CFO*
George Buchler, *Treasurer*
Robert Moskowitz, *Exec VP*
▲ **EMP:** 60 **EST:** 1966
SQ FT: 12,000
SALES (est): 14.7MM **Privately Held**
WEB: www.shamrock.com
SIC: 6282 Manager of mutual funds, contract or fee basis

(P-15349)
SUN LIFE CNADA US HOLDINGS INC
4675 Macarthur Ct Ste 770, Newport Beach (92660-1847)
PHONE.....................949 930-1570
Danae Netto, *Principal*
EMP: 133
SALES (corp-wide): 29.8B **Privately Held**
WEB: www.sunlife.com
SIC: 6282 Investment advice
HQ: Sun Life Of Canada (U.S.) Holdings, Inc.
1 Sun Life Park
Wellesley MA 02481
781 237-6030

(P-15350)
TCW GROUP INC (PA)
865 S Figueroa St # 1800, Los Angeles (90017-2543)
PHONE.....................213 244-0000
David Lippman, *President*
Anthony Hermosillo, *President*
David S Devito, *COO*
Richard M Villa, *CFO*
Samuel Bell, *Bd of Directors*
EMP: 450 **EST:** 1971
SALES (est): 212.9MM **Privately Held**
SIC: 6282 6211 Investment advisory service; security brokers & dealers

(P-15351)
THOMAS JAMES CAPITAL INC
26940 Aliso Viejo Pkwy # 100, Aliso Viejo (92656-2650)
PHONE.....................949 481-7026
Thomas L Beadel, *President*
Taylor Carlson, *Exec VP*
James Quandt, *Vice Pres*
Sergio Garay, *Project Mgr*
Anthony Spano, *Project Mgr*
EMP: 150 **EST:** 2006
SQ FT: 1,400
SALES (est): 400K **Privately Held**
WEB: www.tjh.com
SIC: 6282 6798 Investment advisory service; real estate investment trusts

(P-15352)
U S TRUST COMPANY NA
Also Called: US Trust
515 S Flower St Ste 2700, Los Angeles (90071-2216)
PHONE.....................213 861-5000
Tim Leach, *CEO*
Charlotte G Philips, *Senior VP*
David Litvack, *Managing Dir*
Rosemary Ringwald, *Managing Dir*

Erika Ron, *Sales Staff*
EMP: 350 **EST:** 1982
SQ FT: 65,000
SALES (est): 105.3MM
SALES (corp-wide): 93.7B **Publicly Held**
WEB:
www.privatebank.bankofamerica.com
SIC: 6282 6022 Investment advice; state commercial banks
HQ: Bank Of America Pvt Wealth Management
114 W 47th St Ste C-1
New York NY 10036
800 878-7878

(P-15353)
UNITED CPITL FNCL ADVISERS LLC
620 Nwport Ctr Dr Ste 500, Newport Beach (92660)
PHONE.....................949 999-8500
EMP: 77 **EST:** 2009
SALES (est): 17.2MM **Privately Held**
SIC: 6282 8742 Investment Advisory Service Management Consulting Services

(P-15354)
VMG PARTNERS LLC
2000 Avenue Of The Stars, Los Angeles (90067-4700)
PHONE.....................310 775-8603
David Baram, *Exec Dir*
EMP: 85
SALES (corp-wide): 15.3MM **Privately Held**
WEB: www.vmgpartners.com
SIC: 6282 Investment advice
PA: Vmg Partners, Llc
39 Mesa St Ste 310
San Francisco CA 94129
415 632-4200

6289 Security & Commodity Svcs, NEC

(P-15355)
COMPUTERSHARE INC
2335 Alaska Ave, El Segundo (90245-4808)
PHONE.....................800 522-6645
Rachel Hamilton-Wilkes, *Pub Rel Staff*
Matt Neylon, *Manager*
EMP: 587 **Privately Held**
WEB: www.computershare.com
SIC: 6289 Stock transfer agents
HQ: Computershare Inc.
150 Royall St
Canton MA 02021

6311 Life Insurance Carriers

(P-15356)
AETNA DENTAL OF CALIFORNIA
21215 Burbank Blvd Fl 6, Woodland Hills (91367-7090)
PHONE.....................860 273-5677
EMP: 214 **EST:** 2018
SALES (est): 1.1MM
SALES (corp-wide): 268.7B **Publicly Held**
WEB: www.cvshealth.com
SIC: 6311 Life insurance
PA: Cvs Health Corporation
1 Cvs Dr
Woonsocket RI 02895
401 765-1500

(P-15357)
BEST LIFE AND HEALTH INSUR CO
17701 Mitchell N, Irvine (92614-6028)
P.O. Box 19721 (92623-9721)
PHONE.....................949 253-4080
Donald R Lawrenz, *Ch of Bd*
Alfred Stoefell, *Shareholder*
Salvador Curiel, *Analyst*
Shawn Kaye, *Regl Sales Mgr*
Stephanie Ratliff, *Marketing Staff*
EMP: 60 **EST:** 1972
SQ FT: 22,000

SALES (est): 24.8MM **Privately Held**
WEB: www.bestlife.com
SIC: 6311 6324 Life insurance carriers; hospital & medical service plans
PA: Pension Administrators Inc
17701 Mitchell N
Irvine CA 92614
949 253-4080

(P-15358)
CATHOLIC FAMILY LIFE INSURANCE
Also Called:.Catholic Family Life Ins 991
27001 La Paz Rd Ste 412, Mission Viejo (92691-5526)
PHONE.....................949 472-2284
Frank Chirat, *Principal*
EMP: 50
SALES (corp-wide): 17.3MM **Privately Held**
WEB: www.catholicfinanciallife.org
SIC: 6311 6411 Life insurance carriers; insurance agents, brokers & service
PA: Catholic Family Life Insurance
1572 E Capitol Dr Ste 2
Milwaukee WI 53211
414 477-5120

(P-15359)
CENTURY-NATIONAL INSURANCE CO (DH)
16650 Sherman Way, Van Nuys (91406-3782)
PHONE.....................818 760-0880
Weldon Wilson, *CEO*
Michael Mahoney, *President*
Judy Osborn, *CFO*
Marie Balicki, *Admin Sec*
EMP: 260 **EST:** 1955
SQ FT: 41,000
SALES (est): 109.4MM **Publicly Held**
WEB: www.cnico.com
SIC: 6311 Life insurance carriers

(P-15360)
GOLDEN STATE MUTL LF INSUR CO (PA)
1999 W Adams Blvd, Los Angeles (90018-3514)
P.O. Box 26894, San Francisco (94126-6894)
PHONE.....................713 526-4361
Larkin Teasley, *President*
EMP: 100 **EST:** 1925
SQ FT: 57,000
SALES (est): 34.3MM **Privately Held**
SIC: 6311 Mutual association life insurance

(P-15361)
GUARDIAN LIFE INSUR CO OF AMER
975 San Pasqual St, Pasadena (91106-3368)
PHONE.....................626 792-1935
Bob Daignault, *Branch Mgr*
EMP: 67
SALES (corp-wide): 4.2B **Privately Held**
WEB: www.guardianlife.com
SIC: 6311 Life insurance
PA: The Guardian Life Insurance Company Of America
10 Hudson Yards Fl 22
New York NY 10001
212 598-8000

(P-15362)
GUARDIAN LIFE INSUR CO OF AMER
510 W 6th St Ste 815, Los Angeles (90014-1309)
PHONE.....................213 624-2002
Charles Bogue, *Branch Mgr*
EMP: 67
SALES (corp-wide): 4.2B **Privately Held**
WEB: www.guardianlife.com
SIC: 6311 Life insurance
PA: The Guardian Life Insurance Company Of America
10 Hudson Yards Fl 22
New York NY 10001
212 598-8000

PRODUCTS & SVCS

(P-15363)
JOHN HANCOCK LIFE INSUR CO USA
5000 Birch St Ste 120, Newport Beach (92660-8117)
PHONE.....................949 254-1440
EMP: 609
SALES (corp-wide): 31.6B **Privately Held**
WEB: www.johnhancock.com
SIC: 6311 Life insurance
HQ: John Hancock Life Insurance Company (U.S.A.).
865 S Figueroa St # 3320
Los Angeles CA 90017
213 689-0813

(P-15364)
MASSACHUSETTS MUTL LF INSUR CO
Also Called: Massmutual
8383 Wilshire Blvd # 600, Beverly Hills (90211-2425)
PHONE.....................323 965-6339
Grant D Fraser, *Branch Mgr*
David Streit, *Sales Staff*
Harvey Warren, *Author*
Kaleem Ansari, *Associate*
EMP: 60
SALES (corp-wide): 32.6B **Privately Held**
WEB: www.massmutual.com
SIC: 6311 Life insurance
PA: Massachusetts Mutual Life Insurance Company
1295 State St
Springfield MA 01111
413 744-8411

(P-15365)
NEW FIRST FINCL RESOURCES LLC
100 Spectrum Center Dr # 400, Irvine (92618-4966)
PHONE.....................949 223-2160
Richard Roberts,
Karl Beer, *Analyst*
EMP: 212 EST: 1987
SALES (est): 23.6MM **Privately Held**
WEB: www.ffrmembers.com
SIC: 6311 Life insurance

(P-15366)
PACIFIC ASSET HOLDING LLC
700 Newport Center Dr, Newport Beach (92660-6307)
PHONE.....................949 219-3011
EMP: 216 EST: 1997
SALES (est): 5.4MM
SALES (corp-wide): 12.8B **Privately Held**
WEB: www.pacificlife.com
SIC: 6311 6371 6321 Life insurance carriers; pension funds; accident insurance carriers
HQ: Pacific Life Insurance Company
700 Newport Center Dr
Newport Beach CA 92660
949 219-3011

(P-15367)
PACIFIC LIFE & ANNUITY COMPANY
700 Newport Center Dr, Newport Beach (92660-6307)
P.O. Box 9000 (92658-9030)
PHONE.....................949 219-3011
James Morris, *President*
Khanh T Tran, *CFO*
Audrey L Milfs, *Vice Pres*
Brian Klemens, *Controller*
Christina Q He, *Assistant VP*
EMP: 650 EST: 1982
SQ FT: 125,000
SALES (est): 203.9MM
SALES (corp-wide): 12.8B **Privately Held**
WEB: www.pacificlife.com
SIC: 6311 6411 Life insurance carriers; insurance agents, brokers & service
HQ: Pacific Life Insurance Company
700 Newport Center Dr
Newport Beach CA 92660
949 219-3011

(P-15368)
PACIFIC LIFE INSURANCE COMPANY
45 Enterprise 4, Aliso Viejo (92656-2601)
PHONE.....................949 219-5200
Evelyn Grant, *Branch Mgr*
Michael Coviello, *Vice Pres*
Anita Karanjia, *Training Super*
EMP: 94
SALES (corp-wide): 12.8B **Privately Held**
WEB: www.pacificlife.com
SIC: 6311 Life insurance carriers
HQ: Pacific Life Insurance Company
700 Newport Center Dr
Newport Beach CA 92660
949 219-3011

(P-15369)
STANDARD INSURANCE COMPANY
500 N State College Blvd # 1000, Orange (92868-1626)
PHONE.....................714 634-8200
Joy Giblin, *Manager*
Dave Friesen, *Controller*
Brandon Stokes, *Consultant*
EMP: 95 **Privately Held**
WEB: www.standard.com
SIC: 6311 Life insurance carriers
HQ: Standard Insurance Company
920 Sw 6th Ave Ste 1100
Portland OR 97204
971 321-7000

(P-15370)
TRANSMRICA RTIREMENT SVCS CORP (PA)
1150 S Olive St Ste T-91, Los Angeles (90015-2211)
PHONE.....................866 498-4557
Mark W Mullin, *CEO*
Ben Eno, *President*
Stig Nybo, *President*
Sean Rapp, *President*
Bill Tai, *President*
EMP: 121 EST: 1989
SALES (est): 7.1MM **Privately Held**
WEB: www.trsretire.com
SIC: 6311 Life insurance

(P-15371)
TRUCK UNDERWRITERS ASSOCIATION
Farmers Insurance
6303 Owensmouth Ave Fl 1, Woodland Hills (91367-2200)
PHONE.....................323 932-3200
Jane Franklin, *Vice Pres*
EMP: 1078
SQ FT: 275,000
SALES (corp-wide): 59.9B **Privately Held**
WEB: www.farmers.com
SIC: 6311 6331 6321 Life insurance; fire, marine & casualty insurance; accident & health insurance
HQ: Truck Underwriters Association
4680 Wilshire Blvd
Los Angeles CA 90010
323 932-3200

(P-15372)
WELLPOINT INC
319 N San Dimas Ave Ste F, San Dimas (91773-2658)
PHONE.....................805 375-1605
Clara Hua Wang, *Administration*
Sue Berding, *Admin Asst*
Cody Stutz, *Analyst*
Renee Fung, *Director*
Lonnee Martin, *Manager*
EMP: 200 EST: 2015
SALES (est): 11.4MM **Privately Held**
SIC: 6311 6321 6324 6331 Life insurance; accident & health insurance; hospital & medical service plans; fire, marine & casualty insurance; surety insurance; insurance agents, brokers & service

---

6321 Accident & Health Insurance

(P-15373)
21ST CENTURY LF & HLTH CO INC (PA)
Also Called: Lifecare Assurance Company
21600 Oxnard St Ste 1500, Woodland Hills (91367-4972)
P.O. Box 4243 (91365-4243)
PHONE.....................818 887-4436
James M Glickman, *President*
Iris Breeze, *President*
Pamela Corbally, *President*
Paul Weber, *President*
Alan S Hughes, *CEO*
▲ EMP: 241 EST: 1980
SQ FT: 50,000
SALES (est): 326.9MM **Privately Held**
WEB: www.lifecareassurance.com
SIC: 6321 Health insurance carriers

(P-15374)
AGENT FRANCHISE LLC
9518 9th St Ste C2, Rancho Cucamonga (91730-4568)
PHONE.....................949 930-5025
David Jackson,
EMP: 101
SQ FT: 14,980
SALES (est): 22.4MM **Privately Held**
WEB: www.agentfranchise.com
SIC: 6321 Accident & health insurance

(P-15375)
ALTAMED HEALTH SERVICES CORP
535 S 2nd Ave, Covina (91723-3013)
PHONE.....................626 214-1480
Robert Young, *Owner*
EMP: 50
SALES (corp-wide): 702MM **Privately Held**
WEB: www.altamed.org
SIC: 6321 Accident & health insurance carriers
PA: Altamed Health Services Corporation
2040 Camfield Ave
Commerce CA 90040
323 725-8751

(P-15376)
AMERICAN IMAGING MGT INC
505 N Brand Blvd Ste 900, Glendale (91203-3396)
PHONE.....................847 310-0366
Joel Cesario, *Vice Pres*
Lisa Hu, *Vice Pres*
Fred Karutz, *Vice Pres*
Nick Lecker, *Vice Pres*
Mark Mansell, *Vice Pres*
EMP: 586
SALES (corp-wide): 121.8B **Publicly Held**
SIC: 6321 Health insurance carriers
HQ: American Imaging Management, Inc.
8600 W Bryn Mawr Ave 800s
Chicago IL 60631

(P-15377)
AUTO CLUB ENTERPRISES (PA)
3333 Fairview Rd Msa451, Costa Mesa (92626-1610)
P.O. Box 25001, Santa Ana (92799-5001)
PHONE.....................714 850-5111
Robert T Bouttier, *CEO*
Thomas Mc Kernon, *President*
John F Boyle, *Treasurer*
Filomena Andre, *Vice Pres*
Avery Brown, *Vice Pres*
EMP: 1200 EST: 1912
SQ FT: 700,000
SALES (est): 1.3B **Privately Held**
WEB: www.aaa.com
SIC: 6321 Accident & health insurance

(P-15378)
AUTO CLUB ENTERPRISES
8761 Santa Monica Blvd, West Hollywood (90069-4538)
PHONE.....................310 914-8500
Bob Szhwab, *Manager*
EMP: 235

SALES (corp-wide): 1.3B **Privately Held**
WEB: www.aaa.com
SIC: 6321 Accident & health insurance
PA: Auto Club Enterprises
3333 Fairview Rd Msa451
Costa Mesa CA 92626
714 850-5111

(P-15379)
EASY CHOICE HEALTH PLAN INC (DH)
10803 Hope St, Cypress (90630-5229)
PHONE.....................856 999-3945
Eric E Spencer, *President*
EMP: 62 EST: 2006
SALES (est): 51.3MM **Publicly Held**
WEB: www.easychoicehealthplan.com
SIC: 6321 Accident & health insurance
HQ: Wellcare Health Plans, Inc.
8735 Henderson Rd
Tampa FL 33634
813 290-6200

(P-15380)
INLAND EMPIRE HEALTH PLAN (PA)
Also Called: Iehp
10801 6th St Ste 120, Rancho Cucamonga (91730-5987)
P.O. Box 1400 (91729-1400)
PHONE.....................909 890-2000
Jarrod McNaughton, *CEO*
Chet Uma, *CFO*
Bob Buster, *Chairman*
Randee Roberts, *Finance Dir*
EMP: 850 EST: 1994
SQ FT: 72,000
SALES (est): 715.8MM **Privately Held**
WEB: www.iehp.org
SIC: 6321 6324 Health insurance carriers; health maintenance organization (HMO), insurance only

(P-15381)
LIFECARE ASSURANCE COMPANY
21600 Oxnard St Fl 16, Woodland Hills (91367-4976)
PHONE.....................818 887-4436
James Glickman, *President*
Alan S Hughes, *COO*
Daniel J Disipio, *CFO*
Peter Diffley, *Vice Pres*
Gwen D Franklin, *Vice Pres*
EMP: 246 EST: 1988
SQ FT: 35,000
SALES: 326.9MM **Privately Held**
WEB: www.lifecareassurance.com
SIC: 6321 6411 Accident & health insurance; insurance agents, brokers & service; life insurance
PA: 21st Century Life And Health Company, Inc.
21600 Oxnard St Ste 1500
Woodland Hills CA 91367

(P-15382)
MOLINA HLTHCARE CAL PRTNER PLA
200 Oceangate Ste 100, Long Beach (90802-4317)
PHONE.....................562 435-3666
Richard Chambers, *CEO*
J Mario Molina, *Ch of Bd*
John Kotal, *President*
Terry Bayer, *COO*
Dr James Howatt, *Officer*
EMP: 532 EST: 1980
SALES (est): 6.1MM
SALES (corp-wide): 19.43 **Publicly Held**
WEB: www.molinahealthcare.com
SIC: 6321 8011 Health insurance carriers; clinic, operated by physicians
PA: Molina Healthcare, Inc.
200 Oceangate Ste 100
Long Beach CA 90802
562 435-3666

(P-15383)
SANTA BARBARA SAN LUIS OBISPO
Also Called: Cencal Health
4050 Calle Real, Santa Barbara (93110-3413)
PHONE...................800 421-2560
Robert Freeman, *CEO*
Kashina Bishop, *CFO*
Danica Chappell, *Comp Spec*
Keith Holt, *Comp Spec*
Diane Sheffield, *Project Mgr*
EMP: 140 **EST:** 2009
SALES (est): 66.1MM **Privately Held**
WEB: www.cencalhealth.org
SIC: 6321 Accident & health insurance

(P-15384)
STATE COMPENSATION INSUR FUND
2901 N Ventura Rd Ste 100, Oxnard (93036-1126)
PHONE...................888 782-8338
Martin Goldman, *Manager*
EMP: 92
SALES (corp-wide): 2.7B **Privately Held**
WEB: www.statefundca.com
SIC: 6321 9651 Disability health insurance; insurance commission, government;
PA: State Compensation Insurance Fund
333 Bush St Fl 8
San Francisco CA 94104
888 782-8338

(P-15385)
SWISS RE UNDERWRITERS AGENCY (DH)
26050 Mureau Rd, Calabasas (91302-3127)
PHONE...................818 226-0028
Russell T John, *COO*
Stuart De Haaf, *Admin Sec*
EMP: 139 **EST:** 1987
SALES (est): 37.8MM
SALES (corp-wide): 43.3B **Privately Held**
WEB: www.ericnishimoto-re.com
SIC: 6321 Reinsurance carriers, accident & health
HQ: Swiss Reinsurance America Corporation
175 King St
Armonk NY 10504
914 828-8000

6324 Hospital & Medical Svc Plans Carriers

(P-15386)
ALIGNMENT HEALTH PLAN
Also Called: Citizens Choice Health Plan
1100 W Town & Country, Orange (92868-4600)
PHONE...................323 728-7232
Chuck Weber, *President*
Elizabeth Tejada, *COO*
Charlotte Leblanc,
EMP: 90 **EST:** 2003
SALES (est): 49.6MM **Privately Held**
WEB: www.alignmenthealthplan.com
SIC: 6324 Health maintenance organization (HMO), insurance only
PA: Alignment Healthcare, Usa Llc
1100 W Twn Cntry Rd
Orange CA 92868
844 310-2247

(P-15387)
ALIGNMENT HEALTHCARE INC
1100 W Twn Cntry Rd, Orange (92868-4600)
PHONE...................844 310-2247
John KAO, *CEO*
Joseph Konowiecki, *Ch of Bd*
Dawn Maroney, *President*
Thomas Freeman, *CFO*
Donald Furman, *Ch Credit Ofcr*
EMP: 775 **EST:** 2013
SALES (est): 959.2MM **Privately Held**
SIC: 6324 7372 Hospital & medical service plans; prepackaged software; application computer software

(P-15388)
BLUE CROSS OF CALIFORNIA (DH)
21215 Burbank Blvd, Woodland Hills (91367-7090)
PHONE...................805 557-6050
Mark Morgan, *President*
Kenneth C Zurek, *CFO*
Thomas C Geiser, *Admin Sec*
EMP: 72 **EST:** 1992
SQ FT: 427,104
SALES (est): 177.7MM
SALES (corp-wide): 121.8B **Publicly Held**
SIC: 6324 6411 Health maintenance organization (HMO), insurance only; insurance agents, brokers & service

(P-15389)
CALIFORNIA PHYSICIANS SERVICE
2020 17th St, Bakersfield (93301-4252)
PHONE...................661 631-2277
Ricard Maiatico, *Owner*
EMP: 98
SALES (corp-wide): 17.6B **Privately Held**
WEB: www.blueshieldca.com
SIC: 6324 6321 Hospital & medical service plans; accident & health insurance
PA: California Physicians' Service
601 12th St
Oakland CA 94607
510 607-2000

(P-15390)
CALIFORNIA PHYSICIANS SERVICE
Also Called: Blue Shield of California
100 N Pacific Coast Hwy # 20, El Segundo (90245-4359)
PHONE...................310 744-2668
Aubrey Chernick, *Branch Mgr*
Mitchell Danita, *Executive*
Janet Blackwell, *Manager*
EMP: 98
SALES (corp-wide): 17.6B **Privately Held**
WEB: www.blueshieldca.com
SIC: 6324 Hospital & medical service plans
PA: California Physicians' Service
601 12th St
Oakland CA 94607
510 607-2000

(P-15391)
CALIFORNIA PHYSICIANS SERVICE
Also Called: Blue Shield of California
3401 Centre Lake Dr # 400, Ontario (91761-1201)
PHONE...................909 974-5201
Sue Britton, *Manager*
EMP: 98
SALES (corp-wide): 17.6B **Privately Held**
WEB: www.blueshieldca.com
SIC: 6324 Hospital & medical service plans
PA: California Physicians' Service
601 12th St
Oakland CA 94607
510 607-2000

(P-15392)
CALIFORNIA PHYSICIANS SERVICE
Also Called: Blue Shield of California
6300 Canoga Ave Ste A, Woodland Hills (91367-8000)
PHONE...................818 598-8000
John Headberg, *Branch Mgr*
Carol Soltero, *District Mgr*
Jamie Holzhauer, *Manager*
Wendy Ladin, *Manager*
Cheryl Mack, *Consultant*
EMP: 98
SALES (corp-wide): 17.6B **Privately Held**
WEB: www.blueshieldca.com
SIC: 6324 Hospital & medical service plans
PA: California Physicians' Service
601 12th St
Oakland CA 94607
510 607-2000

(P-15393)
CENTENE CHWP
1699 W Main St, El Centro (92243-5421)
PHONE...................760 482-5593

EMP: 139 **EST:** 2015
SALES (est): 5.1MM **Publicly Held**
WEB: www.cahealthwellness.com
SIC: 6324 Health maintenance organization (HMO), insurance only
PA: Centene Corporation
7700 Forsyth Blvd Ste 800
Saint Louis MO 63105

(P-15394)
CIGNA BEHAVIORAL HEALTH OF CAL
450 N Brand Blvd Ste 500, Glendale (91203-4414)
PHONE...................800 753-0540
Timothy Pierzina, *Manager*
EMP: 335 **EST:** 2014
SALES (est): 1.9MM
SALES (corp-wide): 160.4B **Publicly Held**
SIC: 6324 Health maintenance organization (HMO), insurance only
HQ: Evernorth Behavioral Health, Inc.
11095 Viking Dr Ste 350
Eden Prairie MN 55344

(P-15395)
CIGNA HEALTHCARE CAL INC (DH)
400 N Brand Blvd Ste 400 # 400, Glendale (91203-2357)
P.O. Box 188045, Chattanooga TN (37422-8045)
PHONE...................818 500-6262
Leroy Volberding, *President*
Michelle Demonteverde, *Vice Pres*
Barry Ford, *Vice Pres*
David Yeager, *Controller*
Siroun Pakdaman, *Manager*
EMP: 400 **EST:** 1968
SQ FT: 110,000
SALES (est): 259MM
SALES (corp-wide): 160.4B **Publicly Held**
WEB: www.cigna.com
SIC: 6324 Health maintenance organization (HMO), insurance only
HQ: Healthsource, Inc.
1750 Elm St Ste 800
Manchester NH 03104
603 268-7000

(P-15396)
EBA & M CORPORATION (PA)
Also Called: Employees Benefit ADM & MGT
3505 Cadillac Ave O201, Costa Mesa (92626-1429)
PHONE...................714 668-8920
Bradl Gossen, *President*
Vernon Gossen, *President*
Mary Ann Wessel, *Senior VP*
Elizabeth Ciaccio, *Vice Pres*
Bob Desoto, *Vice Pres*
EMP: 69 **EST:** 1972
SQ FT: 12,000
SALES (est): 17.8MM **Privately Held**
WEB: www.ebam.com
SIC: 6324 Hospital & medical service plans

(P-15397)
HEALTH NET LLC (HQ)
21650 Oxnard St Fl 25, Woodland Hills (91367-7829)
PHONE...................818 676-6000
Jay M Gellert, *President*
James E Woys, *COO*
Rich Hall, *Officer*
Juanell Hefner, *Officer*
Gary Neiman, *Officer*
EMP: 250 **EST:** 2015
SQ FT: 115,488
SALES (est): 1.1B **Publicly Held**
WEB: www.healthnet.com
SIC: 6324 6311 Hospital & medical service plans; life insurance carriers

(P-15398)
HEALTH NET LLC
6013 Niles St, Bakersfield (93306-4696)
PHONE...................661 321-3904
Beth Johnson, *Executive Asst*
Tina Smithhart, *Executive Asst*
Alison King, *Administration*
Joy Yamamoto, *Sales Associate*

Aloke Mandal, *Director*
EMP: 103 **Publicly Held**
WEB: www.healthnet.com
SIC: 6324 Hospital & medical service plans
HQ: Health Net, Llc
21650 Oxnard St Fl 25
Woodland Hills CA 91367
818 676-6000

(P-15399)
HEALTH NET LLC
21281 Burbank Blvd, Woodland Hills (91367-7073)
PHONE...................818 676-5000
Jay Gellert, *Branch Mgr*
Dan Tyler, *President*
John R Roberts, *Bd of Directors*
Marshall Bentley, *Vice Pres*
Maryam Kazemi, *Vice Pres*
EMP: 103 **Publicly Held**
WEB: www.healthnet.com
SIC: 6324 Hospital & medical service plans
HQ: Health Net, Llc
21650 Oxnard St Fl 25
Woodland Hills CA 91367
818 676-6000

(P-15400)
INTER VALLEY HEALTH PLAN INC
300 S Park Ave Ste 300 # 300, Pomona (91766-1546)
P.O. Box 6002 (91769-6002)
PHONE...................909 623-6333
Ronald Bolding, *CEO*
Paul Biberkraut, *CFO*
Michael Nelson, *CFO*
Robin Davis, *Vice Pres*
Patricia Jacobson, *Vice Pres*
EMP: 70
SQ FT: 54,700
SALES: 271.1MM **Privately Held**
WEB: www.ivhp.com
SIC: 6324 8011 Hospital & medical service plans; offices & clinics of medical doctors

(P-15401)
KAISER FNDTION HLTH PLAN GA IN
1850 California Ave, Corona (92881-3378)
PHONE...................951 270-1200
Anita Ward, *Manager*
Darryl Duncan, *Technician*
Jason Twyman, *Production*
Sassan Salimpour, *Manager*
EMP: 233
SALES (corp-wide): 30.5B **Privately Held**
WEB: www.healthy.kaiserpermanente.org
SIC: 6324 Hospital & medical service plans
HQ: Kaiser Foundation Health Plan Of Georgia, Inc.
3495 Piedmont Rd Ne # 9
Atlanta GA 30305
404 364-7000

(P-15402)
KAISER FOUNDATION HOSPITALS
Also Called: Alton/Sand Canyon Medical Offs
6670 Alton Pkwy, Irvine (92618-3734)
PHONE...................949 932-5000
George Disalvo, *Branch Mgr*
Shahed Ghanimati, *Obstetrician*
Ann Ullrich, *Emerg Med Spec*
EMP: 104
SALES (corp-wide): 30.5B **Privately Held**
WEB: www.kaisercenter.com
SIC: 6324 Hospital & medical service plans
HQ: Kaiser Foundation Hospitals Inc
1 Kaiser Plz
Oakland CA 94612
510 271-6611

(P-15403)
KAISER FOUNDATION HOSPITALS
Also Called: Kaiser Permanente
3750 Grand Ave, Chino (91710-5478)
PHONE...................888 750-0036
Jonathan Rothchild, *Manager*
EMP: 104
SALES (corp-wide): 30.5B **Privately Held**
WEB: www.kaisercenter.com
SIC: 6324 Hospital & medical service plans

P
R
O
D
U
C
T
S

&

S
V
C
S

HQ: Kaiser Foundation Hospitals Inc
1 Kaiser Plz
Oakland CA 94612
510 271-6611

(P-15404)
KAISER FOUNDATION HOSPITALS
Also Called: Kaiser Permanente
1011 Baldwin Park Blvd, Baldwin Park
(91706-5806)
PHONE................................626 851-1011
Linda Margarita Gutierrez, *Principal*
Yi-Wen Chang, *Database Admin*
Martha Acero, *Project Mgr*
Giselle Fernandez, *Project Mgr*
Shirley Lac, *Project Mgr*
EMP: 793
SALES (corp-wide): 30.5B **Privately Held**
WEB: www.kaisercenter.com
SIC: 6324 Hospital & medical service plans
HQ: Kaiser Foundation Hospitals Inc
1 Kaiser Plz
Oakland CA 94612
510 271-6611

(P-15405)
KAISER FOUNDATION HOSPITALS
Also Called: Kaiser Prmnente Downey Med Ctr
9333 Imperial Hwy, Downey (90242-2812)
PHONE................................562 657-9000
Gemma Abad, *Branch Mgr*
Liza Arabian, *Telecomm Dir*
Victoria Sarreal, *Department Mgr*
Roger Preciado, *Technician*
Connie Pinkerton, *Project Mgr*
EMP: 410
SALES (corp-wide): 30.5B **Privately Held**
WEB: www.kaisercenter.com
SIC: 6324 Hospital & medical service plans
HQ: Kaiser Foundation Hospitals Inc
1 Kaiser Plz
Oakland CA 94612
510 271-6611

(P-15406)
KAISER FOUNDATION HOSPITALS
Also Called: Kaiser Foundation Health Plan
393 E Walnut St, Pasadena (91188-0002)
PHONE................................626 405-5000
David Lamm, *Branch Mgr*
Sierra Griffin, *Corp Comm Staff*
Elita Adjei, *Director*
EMP: 50
SALES (corp-wide): 30.5B **Privately Held**
WEB: www.healthy.kaiserpermanente.org
SIC: 6324 Hospital & medical service plans
HQ: Kaiser Foundation Hospitals Inc
1 Kaiser Plz
Oakland CA 94612
510 271-6611

(P-15407)
KAISER FOUNDATION HOSPITALS
Also Called: Kaiser Foundation Health Plan
1550 W Manchester Ave, Los Angeles
(90047-5424)
PHONE................................800 954-8000
EMP: 104
SALES (corp-wide): 30.5B **Privately Held**
WEB: www.healthy.kaiserpermanente.org
SIC: 6324 Hospital & medical service plans
HQ: Kaiser Foundation Hospitals Inc
1 Kaiser Plz
Oakland CA 94612
510 271-6611

(P-15408)
KAISER FOUNDATION HOSPITALS
Also Called: Kaiser Foundation Health Plan
14011 Park Ave, Victorville (92392-2413)
PHONE................................888 750-0036
EMP: 104
SALES (corp-wide): 30.5B **Privately Held**
WEB: www.healthy.kaiserpermanente.org
SIC: 6324 Hospital & medical service plans
HQ: Kaiser Foundation Hospitals Inc
1 Kaiser Plz
Oakland CA 94612
510 271-6611

(P-15409)
KAISER FOUNDATION HOSPITALS
Also Called: Kaiser Foundation Health Plan
27309 Madison Ave, Temecula
(92590-5685)
PHONE................................866 984-7483
David Kvancz, *Vice Pres*
Elizabeth Farnum, *Finance Dir*
Yana Durmashkin, *Pediatrics*
Cindy German, *Clerk*
EMP: 104
SALES (corp-wide): 30.5B **Privately Held**
WEB: www.healthy.kaiserpermanente.org
SIC: 6324 Hospital & medical service plans
HQ: Kaiser Foundation Hospitals Inc
1 Kaiser Plz
Oakland CA 94612
510 271-6611

(P-15410)
KAISER FOUNDATION HOSPITALS
Also Called: Kaiser Foundation Health Plan
11001 Sepulveda Blvd, Mission Hills
(91345-1413)
PHONE................................888 778-5000
EMP: 104
SALES (corp-wide): 30.5B **Privately Held**
WEB: www.healthy.kaiserpermanente.org
SIC: 6324 Hospital & medical service plans
HQ: Kaiser Foundation Hospitals Inc
1 Kaiser Plz
Oakland CA 94612
510 271-6611

(P-15411)
KAISER FOUNDATION HOSPITALS
Also Called: Kaiser Foundation Health Plan
8001 Ventura Canyon Ave, Panorama City
(91402-6312)
PHONE................................818 375-2028
Teresa Park, *Branch Mgr*
EMP: 104
SALES (corp-wide): 30.5B **Privately Held**
WEB: www.healthy.kaiserpermanente.org
SIC: 6324 Hospital & medical service plans
HQ: Kaiser Foundation Hospitals Inc
1 Kaiser Plz
Oakland CA 94612
510 271-6611

(P-15412)
KAISER FOUNDATION HOSPITALS
Also Called: Kaiser Foundation Health Plan
5620 Mesmer Ave, Los Angeles
(90230-6315)
PHONE................................800 954-8000
EMP: 104
SALES (corp-wide): 30.5B **Privately Held**
WEB: www.healthy.kaiserpermanente.org
SIC: 6324 Hospital & medical service plans
HQ: Kaiser Foundation Hospitals Inc
1 Kaiser Plz
Oakland CA 94612
510 271-6611

(P-15413)
KAISER FOUNDATION HOSPITALS
Also Called: Kaiser Permanente Med Library
4733 W Sunset Blvd, Los Angeles
(90027-6021)
PHONE................................323 783-8568
Anne Fraser, *Branch Mgr*
Karine Tagmazyan, *Gnrl Med Prac*
Alexander Miric, *Med Doctor*
EMP: 104
SALES (corp-wide): 30.5B **Privately Held**
WEB: www.kaisercenter.com
SIC: 6324 Hospital & medical service plans
HQ: Kaiser Foundation Hospitals Inc
1 Kaiser Plz
Oakland CA 94612
510 271-6611

(P-15414)
KAISER FOUNDATION HOSPITALS
Also Called: Kaiser Permanente
1249 S Sunset Ave, West Covina
(91790-3960)
PHONE................................866 319-4269
Jane Lau, *Manager*
Amir Goharbin, *Family Practiti*
Eli Tsou, *Family Practiti*
Chan Kiet Wong, *Pharmacist*
EMP: 104
SALES (corp-wide): 30.5B **Privately Held**
WEB: www.kaisercenter.com
SIC: 6324 Hospital & medical service plans
HQ: Kaiser Foundation Hospitals Inc
1 Kaiser Plz
Oakland CA 94612
510 271-6611

(P-15415)
KAISER FOUNDATION HOSPITALS
Also Called: Kaiser Foundation Health Plan
1011 S East St Fl 1, Anaheim
(92805-5749)
PHONE................................714 284-6634
Ruth Ann Ferreria, *Manager*
Lorraine Goodwin, *Supervisor*
EMP: 104
SQ FT: 63,920
SALES (corp-wide): 30.5B **Privately Held**
WEB: www.healthy.kaiserpermanente.org
SIC: 6324 Hospital & medical service plans
HQ: Kaiser Foundation Hospitals Inc
1 Kaiser Plz
Oakland CA 94612
510 271-6611

(P-15416)
KAISER FOUNDATION HOSPITALS
Also Called: Kaiser Permanente
5055 California Ave # 110, Bakersfield
(93309-0701)
P.O. Box 12099 (93389-2099)
PHONE................................661 334-2020
Angelica Zambrano, *Cert Phar Tech*
EMP: 104
SALES (corp-wide): 30.5B **Privately Held**
WEB: www.kaisercenter.com
SIC: 6324 Hospital & medical service plans
HQ: Kaiser Foundation Hospitals Inc
1 Kaiser Plz
Oakland CA 94612
510 271-6611

(P-15417)
KAISER FOUNDATION HOSPITALS
Also Called: Kaiser Permanente
12470 Whittier Blvd, Whittier (90602-1017)
PHONE................................866 340-5974
Beth Lopez, *Principal*
Maria Acosta, *Pharmacist*
EMP: 104
SALES (corp-wide): 30.5B **Privately Held**
WEB: www.kaisercenter.com
SIC: 6324 Hospital & medical service plans
HQ: Kaiser Foundation Hospitals Inc
1 Kaiser Plz
Oakland CA 94612
510 271-6611

(P-15418)
KAISER FOUNDATION HOSPITALS
Also Called: Kaiser Foundation Health Plan
21263 Erwin St, Woodland Hills
(91367-3715)
PHONE................................888 515-3500
EMP: 104
SALES (corp-wide): 30.5B **Privately Held**
WEB: www.healthy.kaiserpermanente.org
SIC: 6324 Hospital & medical service plans
HQ: Kaiser Foundation Hospitals Inc
1 Kaiser Plz
Oakland CA 94612
510 271-6611

(P-15419)
KAISER FOUNDATION HOSPITALS
Also Called: Kaiser Foundation Health Plan
2295 S Vineyard Ave, Ontario
(91761-7925)
PHONE................................888 750-0036
Arlene Freeman, *Manager*
Suniel Khemlani, *Family Practit*
EMP: 104
SALES (corp-wide): 30.5B **Privately Held**
WEB: www.healthy.kaiserpermanente.org
SIC: 6324 Hospital & medical service plans
HQ: Kaiser Foundation Hospitals Inc
1 Kaiser Plz
Oakland CA 94612
510 271-6611

(P-15420)
KAISER FOUNDATION HOSPITALS
Also Called: Kaiser Foundation Health Plan
3330 Centre Lake Dr, Ontario
(91761-1211)
PHONE................................866 205-3595
David Rodriguez, *Administration*
EMP: 104
SALES (corp-wide): 30.5B **Privately Held**
WEB: www.healthy.kaiserpermanente.org
SIC: 6324 Hospital & medical service plans
HQ: Kaiser Foundation Hospitals Inc
1 Kaiser Plz
Oakland CA 94612
510 271-6611

(P-15421)
KAISER FOUNDATION HOSPITALS
Also Called: Kaiser Foundation Health Plan
888 S Hill Rd, Ventura (93003-8400)
PHONE................................888 515-3500
Michael Steinbaum, *Manager*
EMP: 104
SALES (corp-wide): 30.5B **Privately Held**
WEB: www.healthy.kaiserpermanente.org
SIC: 6324 Hospital & medical service plans
HQ: Kaiser Foundation Hospitals Inc
1 Kaiser Plz
Oakland CA 94612
510 271-6611

(P-15422)
KAISER FOUNDATION HOSPITALS
Also Called: Kaiser Foundation Health Plan
3401 S Harbor Blvd, Santa Ana
(92704-7933)
PHONE................................888 988-2800
Linh Kamikawa, *Principal*
EMP: 104
SALES (corp-wide): 30.5B **Privately Held**
WEB: www.healthy.kaiserpermanente.org
SIC: 6324 Hospital & medical service plans
HQ: Kaiser Foundation Hospitals Inc
1 Kaiser Plz
Oakland CA 94612
510 271-6611

(P-15423)
KAISER FOUNDATION HOSPITALS
Also Called: Kaiser Foundation Health Plan
23701 Main St, Carson (90745-5745)
PHONE................................310 816-5440
Donna Menecola, *Branch Mgr*
EMP: 104
SALES (corp-wide): 30.5B **Privately Held**
WEB: www.healthy.kaiserpermanente.org
SIC: 6324 Hospital & medical service plans
HQ: Kaiser Foundation Hospitals Inc
1 Kaiser Plz
Oakland CA 94612
510 271-6611

(P-15424)
KAISER FOUNDATION HOSPITALS
Also Called: Kaiser Foundation Health Plan
11911 Central Ave, Chino (91710-1906)
PHONE................................888 750-0036
Ken Lee, *Principal*
EMP: 104

SALES (corp-wide): 30.5B **Privately Held**
WEB: www.healthy.kaiserpermanente.org
SIC: 6324 Hospital & medical service plans
HQ: Kaiser Foundation Hospitals Inc
   1 Kaiser Plz
   Oakland CA 94612
   510 271-6611

(P-15425)
KAISER FOUNDATION HOSPITALS
Also Called: Kaiser Foundation Health Plan
1539 W Garvey Ave N, West Covina
(91790-2139)
PHONE..................626 856-3045
Kwame Okoreeh, *Manager*
EMP: 104
SQ FT: 10,403
SALES (corp-wide): 30.5B **Privately Held**
WEB: www.healthy.kaiserpermanente.org
SIC: 6324 Hospital & medical service plans
HQ: Kaiser Foundation Hospitals Inc
   1 Kaiser Plz
   Oakland CA 94612
   510 271-6611

(P-15426)
KAISER FOUNDATION HOSPITALS
Also Called: Kaiser Foundation Health Plan
9333 Rosecrans Ave, Bellflower
(90706-2141)
PHONE..................562 461-3084
Arlene M Dolorico MD, *Manager*
EMP: 104
SALES (corp-wide): 30.5B **Privately Held**
WEB: www.healthy.kaiserpermanente.org
SIC: 6324 Hospital & medical service plans
HQ: Kaiser Foundation Hospitals Inc
   1 Kaiser Plz
   Oakland CA 94612
   510 271-6611

(P-15427)
KAISER FOUNDATION HOSPITALS
Also Called: Kaiser Foundation Health Plan
1717 E Vista Chino Ste B2, Palm Springs
(92262-3569)
PHONE..................866 370-1942
Ed McMahon, *Principal*
EMP: 104
SALES (corp-wide): 30.5B **Privately Held**
WEB: www.healthy.kaiserpermanente.org
SIC: 6324 Hospital & medical service plans
HQ: Kaiser Foundation Hospitals Inc
   1 Kaiser Plz
   Oakland CA 94612
   510 271-6611

(P-15428)
KAISER FOUNDATION HOSPITALS
Also Called: Kaiser Foundation Health Plan
20790 Madrona Ave, Torrance
(90503-3777)
PHONE..................800 780-1230
Shirley Oka, *Principal*
EMP: 104
SALES (corp-wide): 30.5B **Privately Held**
WEB: www.healthy.kaiserpermanente.org
SIC: 6324 Hospital & medical service plans
HQ: Kaiser Foundation Hospitals Inc
   1 Kaiser Plz
   Oakland CA 94612
   510 271-6611

(P-15429)
KAISER FOUNDATION HOSPITALS
Also Called: Kaiser Foundation Health Plan
365 E Hillcrest Dr, Thousand Oaks
(91360-5820)
PHONE..................888 515-3500
Beverly Torres, *Branch Mgr*
Joni Jordan, *Internal Med*
EMP: 104
SALES (corp-wide): 30.5B **Privately Held**
WEB: www.healthy.kaiserpermanente.org
SIC: 6324 Hospital & medical service plans
HQ: Kaiser Foundation Hospitals Inc
   1 Kaiser Plz
   Oakland CA 94612
   510 271-6611

(P-15430)
KAISER FOUNDATION HOSPITALS
Also Called: Kaiser Foundation Health Plan
3900 Alamo St, Simi Valley (93063-2111)
PHONE..................888 515-3500
Nami Kim, *Principal*
EMP: 104
SALES (corp-wide): 30.5B **Privately Held**
WEB: www.healthy.kaiserpermanente.org
SIC: 6324 Hospital & medical service plans
HQ: Kaiser Foundation Hospitals Inc
   1 Kaiser Plz
   Oakland CA 94612
   510 271-6611

(P-15431)
KAISER FOUNDATION HOSPITALS
Also Called: Kaiser Foundation Health Plan
30400 Camino Capistrano, San Juan
Capistrano (92675-1300)
PHONE..................888 988-2800
Patrick Roth, *Branch Mgr*
Debra Gierut, *Obstetrician*
EMP: 104
SALES (corp-wide): 30.5B **Privately Held**
WEB: www.healthy.kaiserpermanente.org
SIC: 6324 Hospital & medical service plans
HQ: Kaiser Foundation Hospitals Inc
   1 Kaiser Plz
   Oakland CA 94612
   510 271-6611

(P-15432)
KAISER FOUNDATION HOSPITALS
Also Called: Kaiser Foundation Health Plan
9961 Sierra Ave, Fontana (92335-6720)
P.O. Box None (92335)
PHONE..................909 427-3910
Gerald Mc Call, *Branch Mgr*
Jan Herrman, *Med Doctor*
Vikas Mehta, *Med Doctor*
EMP: 104
SALES (corp-wide): 30.5B **Privately Held**
WEB: www.healthy.kaiserpermanente.org
SIC: 6324 Hospital & medical service plans
HQ: Kaiser Foundation Hospitals Inc
   1 Kaiser Plz
   Oakland CA 94612
   510 271-6611

(P-15433)
KAISER FOUNDATION HOSPITALS
Also Called: Kaiser Foundation Health Plan
12200 Bellflower Blvd, Downey
(90242-2804)
PHONE..................562 622-4190
Jim Harrington, *Branch Mgr*
EMP: 104
SALES (corp-wide): 30.5B **Privately Held**
WEB: www.healthy.kaiserpermanente.org
SIC: 6324 Hospital & medical service plans
HQ: Kaiser Foundation Hospitals Inc
   1 Kaiser Plz
   Oakland CA 94612
   510 271-6611

(P-15434)
KAISER FOUNDATION HOSPITALS
Also Called: Kaiser Foundation Health Plan
110 N La Brea Ave, Inglewood
(90301-1708)
PHONE..................800 954-8000
Jim Selsa, *Branch Mgr*
EMP: 104
SALES (corp-wide): 30.5B **Privately Held**
WEB: www.healthy.kaiserpermanente.org
SIC: 6324 Hospital & medical service plans
HQ: Kaiser Foundation Hospitals Inc
   1 Kaiser Plz
   Oakland CA 94612
   510 271-6611

(P-15435)
KAISER FOUNDATION HOSPITALS
Also Called: Kaiser Foundation Health Plan
11666 Sherman Way, North Hollywood
(91605-5831)
PHONE..................818 503-7082

Charles Ford, *Manager*
Alfonso Aragon, *Vice Pres*
Vincent Dizon, *Lab Dir*
Ronald Nicholson, *Engineer*
Halimah Nakakawa, *Nurse*
EMP: 104
SALES (corp-wide): 30.5B **Privately Held**
WEB: www.healthy.kaiserpermanente.org
SIC: 6324 Hospital & medical service plans
HQ: Kaiser Foundation Hospitals Inc
   1 Kaiser Plz
   Oakland CA 94612
   510 271-6611

(P-15436)
KAISER FOUNDATION HOSPITALS
Also Called: Kaiser Foundation Health Plan
73733 Fred Waring Dr # 1, Palm Desert
(92260-2589)
PHONE..................303 404-4700
Virginia McLain, *Branch Mgr*
EMP: 104
SALES (corp-wide): 30.5B **Privately Held**
WEB: www.healthy.kaiserpermanente.org
SIC: 6324 Hospital & medical service plans
HQ: Kaiser Foundation Hospitals Inc
   1 Kaiser Plz
   Oakland CA 94612
   510 271-6611

(P-15437)
KAISER FOUNDATION HOSPITALS
Also Called: Kaiser Foundation Health Plan
1707 Barcelona Cir, Placentia
(92870-6630)
PHONE..................714 572-5700
Dennis Baker, *General Mgr*
EMP: 104
SQ FT: 46,243
SALES (corp-wide): 30.5B **Privately Held**
WEB: www.healthy.kaiserpermanente.org
SIC: 6324 Hospital & medical service plans
HQ: Kaiser Foundation Hospitals Inc
   1 Kaiser Plz
   Oakland CA 94612
   510 271-6611

(P-15438)
KAISER FOUNDATION HOSPITALS
Also Called: Kaiser Foundation Health Plan
200 N Lewis St Fl 1, Orange (92868-1538)
PHONE..................888 988-2800
Harriet Brown, *Director*
James De Fontes III, *Anesthesiology*
Judie Vandalsem, *Nurse*
Joanna Ramey, *Director*
EMP: 104
SALES (corp-wide): 30.5B **Privately Held**
WEB: www.healthy.kaiserpermanente.org
SIC: 6324 8011 Hospital & medical service
plans; clinic, operated by physicians
HQ: Kaiser Foundation Hospitals Inc
   1 Kaiser Plz
   Oakland CA 94612
   510 271-6611

(P-15439)
KAISER FOUNDATION HOSPITALS
Also Called: Kaiser Permanente
1900 E 4th St, Santa Ana (92705-3910)
PHONE..................714 967-4700
Martha Bieser, *Principal*
Vicki Ewing, *Family Practiti*
Melissa Toffel, *Family Practiti*
Massoud Mehdizadeh, *Pediatrics*
Vincent Valenzuela III, *Pediatrics*
EMP: 104
SALES (corp-wide): 30.5B **Privately Held**
WEB: www.kaisercenter.com
SIC: 6324 Hospital & medical service plans
HQ: Kaiser Foundation Hospitals Inc
   1 Kaiser Plz
   Oakland CA 94612
   510 271-6611

(P-15440)
LIBERTY DENTAL PLAN CAL INC
340 Commerce Ste 100, Irvine
(92602-1358)
PHONE..................949 223-0007
Amir Hossein Neshat, *Principal*

Maja Kapic, *CFO*
Richard Goren, *Officer*
John Carvelli, *Exec VP*
Randy Brecher, *Senior VP*
EMP: 300 EST: 2001
SALES (est): 64.6MM **Privately Held**
WEB: www.libertydentalplan.com
SIC: 6324 Dental insurance

(P-15441)
LIBERTY DENTAL PLAN CORP (PA)
340 Commerce Ste 100, Irvine
(92602-1358)
PHONE..................888 703-6999
Amir Neshat, *CEO*
Janet Cardillo, *President*
Anne Weeks, *President*
Eugene Miao, *COO*
Rohan C Reid, *COO*
EMP: 119 EST: 2007
SALES (est): 121.2MM **Privately Held**
WEB: www.libertydentalplan.com
SIC: 6324 Dental insurance

(P-15442)
LIBERTY DENTAL PLAN NEVADA INC
340 Commerce, Irvine (92602-1334)
PHONE..................888 703-6999
Amir Neshat, *President*
EMP: 54
SALES (est): 7.1MM **Privately Held**
WEB: www.libertydentalplan.com
SIC: 6324 Dental insurance

(P-15443)
LOCAL INTTIVE HLTH AUTH FOR LO (PA)
Also Called: L.A. Care Health Plan
1055 W 7th St Fl 10, Los Angeles
(90017-2750)
PHONE..................213 694-1250
John Baackes, *CEO*
Cindy Doorn, *Partner*
Dino Kasdagly, *COO*
Marie Montgomery, *CFO*
Andrea Van Hook, *Bd of Directors*
EMP: 890 EST: 1995
SALES (est): 701.7MM **Privately Held**
WEB: www.lacare.org
SIC: 6324 Health maintenance organization (HMO), insurance only

(P-15444)
MANAGED DENTAL CARE
Also Called: Managed Dental Care California
6200 Canoga Ave Ste 100, Woodland Hills
(91367-2426)
PHONE..................818 598-6599
Michael Gould, *President*
EMP: 154 EST: 1990
SALES (est): 3.4MM
SALES (corp-wide): 4.2B **Privately Held**
WEB: www.manageddentalcare.net
SIC: 6324 Dental insurance
PA: The Guardian Life Insurance Company
   Of America
   10 Hudson Yards Fl 22
   New York NY 10001
   212 598-8000

(P-15445)
MANAGED HEALTH NETWORK
7755 Center Ave Ste 700, Huntington
Beach (92647-9126)
PHONE..................714 934-5519
Carol McLean, *Branch Mgr*
Stefan Doren, *Sales Mgr*
EMP: 142 **Publicly Held**
WEB: www.mhn.com
SIC: 6324 Hospital & medical service plans
HQ: Managed Health Network
   2370 Kerner Blvd
   San Rafael CA 94901

(P-15446)
OPTUMRX INC (DH)
2300 Main St, Irvine (92614-6223)
P.O. Box 509075, San Diego (92150-9075)
PHONE..................714 825-3600
John Michael Prince, *CEO*
Timothy Wicks, *President*
Jeff Park, *COO*

(PA)=Parent Co (HQ)=Headquarters (DH)=Div Headquarters
✪ = New Business established in last 2 years

Jeffrey Grosklags, *CFO*
Christine Draskovich, *Vice Pres*
EMP: 300 **EST:** 1990
SALES (est): 22.2B
SALES (corp-wide): 257.1B **Publicly Held**
WEB: www.optumrx.com
SIC: 6324 6321 Hospital & medical service plans; accident & health insurance
HQ: Optum, Inc.
11000 Optum Cir
Eden Prairie MN 55344
952 936-1300

(P-15447)
PACIFCARE HLTH PLAN ADMNSTRTOR (DH)
3120 W Lake Center Dr, Santa Ana (92704-6917)
P.O. Box 25186 (92799-5186)
PHONE..............................714 825-5200
David Reed, *Ch of Bd*
Coy F Baugh, *Treasurer*
Debra Lord, *Project Mgr*
EMP: 400 **EST:** 1975
SQ FT: 220,000
SALES (est): 1B
SALES (corp-wide): 257.1B **Publicly Held**
WEB: www.unitedhealthgroup.com
SIC: 6324 Group hospitalization plans

(P-15448)
PRIVATE MEDICAL-CARE INC
12898 Towne Center Dr, Cerritos (90703-8546)
PHONE..............................562 924-8311
Robert Elliott, *President*
EMP: 1682 **EST:** 1970
SALES (est): 6.1MM
SALES (corp-wide): 5.8B **Privately Held**
WEB: www.deltadentalins.com
SIC: 6324 Dental insurance
PA: Delta Dental Of California
560 Mission St Ste 1300
San Francisco CA 94105
415 972-8300

(P-15449)
SAFEGUARD HEALTH ENTPS INC (HQ)
95 Enterprise Ste 100, Aliso Viejo (92656-2605)
PHONE..............................800 880-1800
Steven J Baileys DDS, *Ch of Bd*
James E Buncher, *President*
Stephen J Baker, *COO*
Dennis L Gates, *CFO*
Ronald I Brendzel, *Senior VP*
EMP: 355 **EST:** 1974
SQ FT: 68,000
SALES (est): 249.5MM
SALES (corp-wide): 67.8B **Publicly Held**
WEB: www.metlife.com
SIC: 6324 Dental insurance
PA: Metlife, Inc.
200 Park Ave Fl 1200
New York NY 10166
212 578-9500

(P-15450)
SAFEGUARD HEALTH PLANS INC (DH)
Also Called: Safeguard Dental Plan
95 Enterprise Ste 100, Aliso Viejo (92656-2605)
PHONE..............................800 880-1800
Steven J Baileys DDS, *Ch of Bd*
Stephen J Baker, *President*
Ronald Brendzel, *Senior VP*
EMP: 64 **EST:** 1974
SQ FT: 65,000
SALES (est): 57.8MM
SALES (corp-wide): 67.8B **Publicly Held**
WEB: www.metlife.com
SIC: 6324 Dental insurance
HQ: Safeguard Health Enterprises, Inc.
95 Enterprise Ste 100
Aliso Viejo CA 92656
800 880-1800

(P-15451)
SCAN GROUP (PA)
3800 Kilroy Arprt Way, Long Beach (90806-2494)
PHONE..............................562 308-2733

Sachin H Jain, *President*
Linda Rosenstock, *Ch of Bd*
Michael Plumb, *CFO*
Holly Ackman, *Vice Pres*
Lisa Davis, *Vice Pres*
EMP: 306 **EST:** 1983
SALES (est): 6.1MM **Privately Held**
WEB: www.scanhealthplan.com
SIC: 6324 Health maintenance organization (HMO), insurance only

(P-15452)
SENIOR CARE (PA)
Also Called: Scan Health Plan
3800 Kilroy Airport Way, Long Beach (90806-2494)
P.O. Box 22616 (90801-5616)
PHONE..............................562 989-5100
David Schmidt, *CEO*
Susan Cameron, *COO*
Dennis Eder, *CFO*
Sharon Jhawar, *Officer*
Moon Leung, *Officer*
EMP: 650 **EST:** 1978
SQ FT: 119,219
SALES (est): 113.8MM **Privately Held**
WEB: www.scanhealthplan.com
SIC: 6324 Health maintenance organization (HMO), insurance only

(P-15453)
SENIOR CARE ACTION NTWRK FNDTI
Also Called: Independence At Home Iah
2501 Cherry Ave Ste 380, Long Beach (90755-2050)
PHONE..............................562 492-9878
Kit Donaldson, *Branch Mgr*
Eve Gelb, *Senior VP*
Chris Bond, *Vice Pres*
Sophie Howlett, *Research*
Cindy Canela, *Auditor*
EMP: 93
SALES (corp-wide): 113.8MM **Privately Held**
SIC: 6324 Health maintenance organization (HMO), insurance only
PA: Senior Care Action Network Foundation
3800 Kilroy Airport Way
Long Beach CA 90806
562 989-5100

(P-15454)
SOUTHERN CAL PRMNNTE MED GROUP
13652 Cantara St, Panorama City (91402-5423)
PHONE..............................800 272-3500
Arthur Phelps, *Branch Mgr*
Jarrel Phillips, *Regional Mgr*
Clinton Anderson, *Technician*
Mel Ramos, *Project Mgr*
Issakhanian Marika, *Neurology*
EMP: 104
SALES (corp-wide): 30.5B **Privately Held**
SIC: 6324 Hospital & medical service plans
HQ: Southern California Permanente Medical Group
393 Walnut Dr
Pasadena CA 91107
626 405-5704

(P-15455)
SOUTHERN CAL PRMNNTE MED GROUP
10800 Magnolia Ave, Riverside (92505-3043)
PHONE..............................866 984-7483
Jeffrey A Weisz, *Principal*
EMP: 104
SALES (corp-wide): 30.5B **Privately Held**
SIC: 6324 Hospital & medical service plans
HQ: Southern California Permanente Medical Group
393 Walnut Dr
Pasadena CA 91107
626 405-5704

(P-15456)
SOUTHERN CAL PRMNNTE MED GROUP
1511 W Garvey Ave N, West Covina (91790-2138)
PHONE..............................626 960-4844
Helen Serimian, *Auditor*

Mihai Chituc, *Psychiatry*
Jarvis Ngati, *Psychiatry*
Rachel Taruc, *Psychiatry*
EMP: 104
SALES (corp-wide): 30.5B **Privately Held**
SIC: 6324 Hospital & medical service plans
HQ: Southern California Permanente Medical Group
393 Walnut Dr
Pasadena CA 91107
626 405-5704

(P-15457)
SOUTHERN CAL PRMNNTE MED GROUP
Also Called: Tustin Executive Center
17542 17th St Ste 300, Tustin (92780-1960)
PHONE..............................714 734-4500
Adamma Agufoh, *Director*
Deepa Savani, *Med Doctor*
EMP: 104
SALES (corp-wide): 30.5B **Privately Held**
SIC: 6324 Hospital & medical service plans
HQ: Southern California Permanente Medical Group
393 Walnut Dr
Pasadena CA 91107
626 405-5704

(P-15458)
SOUTHERN CAL PRMNNTE MED GROUP (HQ)
Also Called: Kaiser Permanente
393 Walnut Dr, Pasadena (91107-4922)
PHONE..............................626 405-5704
Gregory Adams, *CEO*
Ramin Davidoff, *Ch of Bd*
Gregory A Adams, *Exec VP*
Janet A Liang, *Exec VP*
Kathryn Beiser, *Vice Pres*
EMP: 60 **EST:** 1981
SQ FT: 600,000
SALES (est): 1.7B
SALES (corp-wide): 30.5B **Privately Held**
WEB: www.healthy.kaiserpermanente.org
SIC: 6324 8741 Health maintenance organization (HMO), insurance only; management services
PA: Kaiser Foundation Health Plan, Inc.
1 Kaiser Plz
Oakland CA 94612
510 271-5800

(P-15459)
SOUTHERN CAL PRMNNTE MED GROUP
1465 E 103rd St, Los Angeles (90002-3306)
PHONE..............................323 564-7911
Joanne Robinson, *Director*
Alice Holt, *Admin Asst*
EMP: 182
SALES (corp-wide): 30.5B **Privately Held**
SIC: 8299 6324 8351 Educational services; group hospitalization plans; preschool center
HQ: Southern California Permanente Medical Group
393 Walnut Dr
Pasadena CA 91107
626 405-5704

(P-15460)
SOUTHERN CAL PRMNNTE MED GROUP
Also Called: S C P M G
1255 W Arrow Hwy, San Dimas (91773-2340)
PHONE..............................909 394-2505
EMP: 104
SALES (corp-wide): 30.5B **Privately Held**
SIC: 6324 Hospital & medical service plans
HQ: Southern California Permanente Medical Group
393 Walnut Dr
Pasadena CA 91107
626 405-5704

(P-15461)
SOUTHERN CAL PRMNNTE MED GROUP
Also Called: Kaiser Permanente
9353 Imprl Hwy Grdn Med, Downey (90242)
PHONE..............................562 657-2200
Kirt Patel, *Research*
Connie Pinkerton, *Technology*
Tsuneo Takasugi, *Surgeon*
Audrey Briscoe, *Endocrinology*
Marvin Tan, *Pediatrics*
EMP: 104
SALES (corp-wide): 30.5B **Privately Held**
SIC: 6324 Hospital & medical service plans
HQ: Southern California Permanente Medical Group
393 Walnut Dr
Pasadena CA 91107
626 405-5704

(P-15462)
UHC OF CALIFORNIA (DH)
Also Called: Pacificare Health Systems
5995 Plaza Dr, Cypress (90630-5028)
PHONE..............................714 952-1121
Brad A Bowlus, *Principal*
Michael Montevideo, *Treasurer*
Lisa Espinosa, *Branch Mgr*
Joseph S Konowiecki, *Admin-Sec*
Melanie Zierer, *Technology*
EMP: 800 **EST:** 1975
SALES (est): 257.3MM
SALES (corp-wide): 257.1B **Publicly Held**
WEB: www.unitedhealthgroup.com
SIC: 6324 8732 Health maintenance organization (HMO), insurance only; commercial nonphysical research

6331 Fire, Marine & Casualty Insurance

(P-15463)
ALLIANZ GLOBL RISKS US INSUR (DH)
Also Called: Allianz Insurance Company
2350 W Empire Ave, Burbank (91504-3431)
P.O. Box 7780 (91510-7780)
PHONE..............................818 260-7500
Hugh Burgess, *CEO*
Paul Yun, *President*
Randy Renn, *CFO*
Mike Brandriet, *Senior VP*
Peter Lefkin, *Vice Pres*
EMP: 175 **EST:** 1938
SQ FT: 20,000
SALES (est): 243MM
SALES (corp-wide): 26.4B **Privately Held**
SIC: 6331 Property damage insurance; fire, marine & casualty insurance & carriers; workers' compensation insurance
HQ: Fireman's Fund Insurance Company
1 Progress Point Pkwy # 200
O Fallon MO 63368
415 899-2000

(P-15464)
ALLIANZ UNDERWRITERS INSUR CO
Also Called: Allianz Globl Corp & Specialty
2350 W Empire Ave Ste 200, Burbank (91504-3439)
PHONE..............................818 260-7500
Paul Yun, *Vice Pres*
Paul Davis, *CFO*
Kurt Miner, *Managing Dir*
Ryan Lee, *Finance Mgr*
James Marchese, *Human Resources*
EMP: 86 **EST:** 1978
SALES (est): 42.1MM
SALES (corp-wide): 26.4B **Privately Held**
WEB: www.allianz.com
SIC: 6331 Fire, marine & casualty insurance
PA: Allianz Se
Koniginstr. 28
Munchen BY 80802
893 800-0

(P-15465)
CALIFORNIA AUTOMOBILE INSUR CO (HQ)
Also Called: Cai Company
555 W Imperial Hwy, Brea (92821-4802)
P.O. Box 1150 (92822-1150)
PHONE.....................................714 232-8669
George Joseph, *President*
Leo Lam, *CFO*
EMP: 62 **EST:** 1962
SQ FT: 80,000
SALES (est): 35.8MM
SALES (corp-wide): 3.7B **Publicly Held**
WEB: www.mercuryinsurance.com
SIC: 6331 Automobile insurance
PA: Mercury General Corporation
4484 Wilshire Blvd
Los Angeles CA 90010
323 937-1060

(P-15466)
CRUSADER INSURANCE COMPANY
26050 Mureau Rd, Calabasas
(91302-3127)
PHONE.....................................818 591-9800
Cary Cheldin, *President*
Lester Aaron, *Principal*
Michael Budnitsky, *Principal*
Erik Schoeneborn, *Production*
Jackie Cornelius, *Manager*
EMP: 79 **EST:** 1976
SQ FT: 46,000
SALES (est): 9.4MM
SALES (corp-wide): 32.5MM **Publicly Held**
WEB: www.crusaderinsurance.com
SIC: 6331 Fire, marine & casualty insurance
PA: Unico American Corporation
26050 Mureau Rd
Calabasas CA 91302
818 591-9800

(P-15467)
FIRST AMERCN SPECIALTY INSUR (HQ)
4 First American Way, Santa Ana
(92707-5913)
PHONE.....................................949 474-7500
George McNamee, *Ch of Bd*
Dirk McNamee, *President*
Kelly Dunn, *COO*
George Grupp, *CFO*
Barbara Betts, *Business Anlyst*
EMP: 182 **EST:** 1987
SALES (est): 24.5MM **Publicly Held**
WEB: www.fapcig.com
SIC: 6331 6163 Automobile insurance; loan brokers

(P-15468)
KRAMER-WILSON COMPANY INC (PA)
Also Called: Century National
340 N Westlake Blvd # 210, Westlake Village (91362-7034)
P.O. Box 3999, North Hollywood (91609-0599)
PHONE.....................................818 760-0880
Weldon Wilson, *CEO*
Kevin Wilson, *President*
Daniel Sherrin, *CFO*
Mary Ann Wagner, *Admin Sec*
◆ **EMP:** 240 **EST:** 1969
SALES (est): 79.9MM **Privately Held**
SIC: 6331 Fire, marine & casualty insurance & carriers

(P-15469)
MERCURY CASUALTY COMPANY (HQ)
Also Called: M C C
555 W Imperial Hwy, Brea (92821-4802)
P.O. Box 54600, Los Angeles (90054-0600)
PHONE.....................................323 937-1060
Gabriel Tirador, *CEO*
George Joseph, *CEO*
Ricardo Valdivia, *Technology*
EMP: 600
SALES (est): 3.5B
SALES (corp-wide): 3.7B **Publicly Held**
WEB: www.mercuryinsurance.com
SIC: 6331 6351 Automobile insurance; warranty insurance, home

PA: Mercury General Corporation
4484 Wilshire Blvd
Los Angeles CA 90010
323 937-1060

(P-15470)
MERCURY GENERAL CORPORATION (PA)
4484 Wilshire Blvd, Los Angeles
(90010-3710)
P.O. Box 36662 (90036-0662)
PHONE.....................................323 937-1060
Gabriel Tirador, *President*
George Joseph, *Ch of Bd*
Theodore R Stalick, *CFO*
Brandt N Minnich, *Chief Mktg Ofcr*
Victor G Joseph, *Officer*
EMP: 1565 **EST:** 1961
SQ FT: 41,000
SALES (est): 3.7B **Publicly Held**
WEB: www.mercuryinsurance.com
SIC: 6331 6411 Automobile insurance; property damage insurance; fire, marine & casualty insurance & carriers; insurance agents, brokers & service

(P-15471)
MERCURY INSURANCE COMPANY
555 W Imperial Hwy, Brea (92821-4839)
P.O. Box 1150 (92822-1150)
PHONE.....................................714 671-6700
Gave Tirador, *President*
Brian Hudson, *Branch Mgr*
Dawne Baker, *Manager*
Kim Burton, *Manager*
Kim Tran, *Underwriter*
EMP: 89
SALES (corp-wide): 3.7B **Publicly Held**
WEB: www.mercuryinsurance.com
SIC: 6331 6411 Fire, marine & casualty insurance; insurance agents, brokers & service
HQ: Mercury Insurance Company
4484 Wilshire Blvd
Los Angeles CA 90010
323 937-1060

(P-15472)
MERCURY INSURANCE COMPANY
Also Called: Mercury Insurance Broker
1433 Santa Monica Blvd, Santa Monica
(90404-1709)
PHONE.....................................310 451-4943
Ken Donaldson, *Owner*
EMP: 354
SALES (corp-wide): 3.7B **Publicly Held**
WEB: www.mercuryinsurance.com
SIC: 6331 6411 Fire, marine & casualty insurance; insurance agents, brokers & service
HQ: Mercury Insurance Company
4484 Wilshire Blvd
Los Angeles CA 90010
323 937-1060

(P-15473)
MERCURY INSURANCE COMPANY
1700 Greenbriar Ln, Brea (92821-5971)
PHONE.....................................714 255-5000
Ken Kitzmiller, *Branch Mgr*
Bill Snead, *Branch Mgr*
Emily Reza, *Opers Staff*
Melba Militante, *Sr Project Mgr*
Kim M Casas, *Manager*
EMP: 354
SALES (corp-wide): 3.7B **Publicly Held**
WEB: www.mercuryinsurance.com
SIC: 6331 Fire, marine & casualty insurance
HQ: Mercury Insurance Company
4484 Wilshire Blvd
Los Angeles CA 90010
323 937-1060

(P-15474)
MERCURY INSURANCE COMPANY (HQ)
4484 Wilshire Blvd, Los Angeles
(90010-3710)
P.O. Box 54600 (90054-0600)
PHONE.....................................323 937-1060
Gabe Tirador, *CEO*

Ted Stalick, *CFO*
George Joseph, *Chairman*
Jeffrey Schroeder, *Vice Pres*
Judith Walters, *Vice Pres*
EMP: 160 **EST:** 1972
SQ FT: 40,809
SALES (est): 1.2B
SALES (corp-wide): 3.7B **Publicly Held**
WEB: www.mercuryinsurance.com
SIC: 6331 Fire, marine & casualty insurance
PA: Mercury General Corporation
4484 Wilshire Blvd
Los Angeles CA 90010
323 937-1060

(P-15475)
MERCURY INSURANCE COMPANY
27200 Tourney Rd Ste 400, Valencia
(91355-4997)
PHONE.....................................661 291-6470
David Levy, *Manager*
Kevin Quinn, *Vice Pres*
Judy Walters, *Vice Pres*
Rob Pierce, *Regional Mgr*
Bill Snead, *Branch Mgr*
EMP: 354
SALES (corp-wide): 3.7B **Publicly Held**
WEB: www.mercuryinsurance.com
SIC: 6331 Fire, marine & casualty insurance
HQ: Mercury Insurance Company
4484 Wilshire Blvd
Los Angeles CA 90010
323 937-1060

(P-15476)
MERCURY INSURANCE SERVICES LLC
4484 Wilshire Blvd, Los Angeles
(90010-3710)
PHONE.....................................323 937-1060
Gabriel Tirador, *CEO*
EMP: 2977 **EST:** 2000
SALES (est): 45.1MM
SALES (corp-wide): 3.7B **Publicly Held**
WEB: www.mercuryinsurance.com
SIC: 6331 Property damage insurance
HQ: Mercury Casualty Company
555 W Imperial Hwy
Brea CA 92821
323 937-1060

(P-15477)
MID-CENTURY INSURANCE COMPANY (DH)
6303 Owensmouth Ave, Woodland Hills
(91367-2264)
PHONE.....................................323 932-7116
Ron Coble, *Senior VP*
Bob Woodstra, *President*
EMP: 210 **EST:** 1953
SALES (est): 246.8MM
SALES (corp-wide): 59.9B **Privately Held**
WEB: www.farmers.com
SIC: 6331 6351 Automobile insurance; fidelity insurance
HQ: Farmers Insurance Exchange
6301 Owensmouth Ave # 750
Woodland Hills CA 91367
888 327-6335

(P-15478)
REPUBLIC INDEMNITY CO AMER (DH)
4500 Park Granada Ste 300, Calabasas
(91302-1667)
P.O. Box 20036, Encino (91416-0036)
PHONE.....................................818 990-9860
Dwayne Marioni, *CEO*
Marion Chappel, *Senior VP*
Vazrik Tarverdi, *Admin Asst*
Anu Ponto, *Analyst*
Rita Sarmiento, *Analyst*
EMP: 129 **EST:** 1973
SQ FT: 70,000
SALES (est): 703.4MM **Publicly Held**
WEB: www.republicindemnity.com
SIC: 6331 Workers' compensation insurance
HQ: Pennsylvania Company Inc
1 E 4th St
Cincinnati OH 45202
513 579-2121

(P-15479)
ROYAL SPECIALTY UNDWRT INC
Also Called: Rsui Group
15303 Ventura Blvd # 500, Sherman Oaks
(91403-3110)
PHONE.....................................818 922-6700
Christine Chinen, *Administration*
Kim Gleeson, *President*
Phil Allison, *Vice Pres*
Cynthia Castro, *Vice Pres*
Tony Demaria, *Vice Pres*
EMP: 103
SALES (corp-wide): 8.9B **Publicly Held**
WEB: www.rsui.com
SIC: 6331 6411 Fire, marine & casualty insurance; insurance agents, brokers & service
HQ: Royal Specialty Underwriting, Inc.
945 E Paces Ferry Rd Ne
Atlanta GA 30326

(P-15480)
STATE COMPENSATION INSUR FUND
Also Called: Santa Ana District Office
1750 E 4th St Fl 3, Santa Ana
(92705-3929)
PHONE.....................................714 565-5000
Liz Glidden, *Manager*
Matthew Day, *Legal Staff*
Dina Camiolo, *Manager*
Lizeth Mercado, *Manager*
EMP: 92
SALES (corp-wide): 2.7B **Privately Held**
WEB: www.statefundca.com
SIC: 6331 9651 Workers' compensation insurance; insurance commission, government;
PA: State Compensation Insurance Fund
333 Bush St Fl 8
San Francisco CA 94104
888 782-8338

(P-15481)
STATE COMPENSATION INSUR FUND
Also Called: Bakersfield District Office
9801 Camino Media Ste 101, Bakersfield
(93311-1312)
P.O. Box 21810 (93390-1810)
PHONE.....................................661 664-4000
Robert Kean, *Manager*
Mike La Deaux, *Executive*
EMP: 92
SALES (corp-wide): 2.7B **Privately Held**
WEB: www.statefundca.com
SIC: 6331 9651 Workers' compensation insurance; insurance commission, government;
PA: State Compensation Insurance Fund
333 Bush St Fl 8
San Francisco CA 94104
888 782-8338

(P-15482)
STATE COMPENSATION INSUR FUND
Also Called: Claims Management Service
1750 E 4th St Ste 260, Santa Ana
(92705-3932)
P.O. Box 11828 (92711-1828)
PHONE.....................................714 565-7000
Dennis Sheey, *Manager*
EMP: 92
SALES (corp-wide): 2.7B **Privately Held**
WEB: www.statefundca.com
SIC: 6331 9651 Workers' compensation insurance; insurance commission, government
PA: State Compensation Insurance Fund
333 Bush St Fl 8
San Francisco CA 94104
888 782-8338

(P-15483)
STATE COMPENSATION INSUR FUND
Also Called: Los Angeles District Office
655 N Central Ave Ste 200, Glendale
(91203-1424)
P.O. Box 65005, Fresno (93650-5005)
PHONE.....................................888 782-8338
Linda Hoban, *Manager*

Michael Banks, *Information Mgr*
William Poncelet, *Auditor*
Colleen Hunt, *Marketing Staff*
EMP: 92
SALES (corp-wide): 2.7B **Privately Held**
WEB: www.statefundca.com
SIC: 6331 9651 6321 Workers' compensation insurance; insurance commission, government; ; accident & health insurance
PA: State Compensation Insurance Fund
333 Bush St Fl 8
San Francisco CA 94104
888 782-8338

(P-15484)
STATE COMPENSATION INSUR FUND
Also Called: Riverside District Office
6301 Day St, Riverside (92507-0902)
PHONE..............................888 782-8338
Barbara Katzka, *Manager*
Beverly Rosas, *Counsel*
Laurie Coughenour, *Manager*
EMP: 92
SALES (corp-wide): 2.7B **Privately Held**
WEB: www.statefundca.com
SIC: 6331 9651 Workers' compensation insurance; insurance commission, government;
PA: State Compensation Insurance Fund
333 Bush St Fl 8
San Francisco CA 94104
888 782-8338

(P-15485)
STATE COMPENSATION INSUR FUND
Also Called: Los Angles Dst Off Policy Svcs
900 Corporate Center Dr, Monterey Park
(91754-7620)
P.O. Box 65005, Fresno (93650-5005)
PHONE..............................323 266-5000
Joe Codron, *Officer*
Jerri Shaul, *Broker*
Richard Whiting, *Manager*
Jenny Siu, *Consultant*
Denice Hebb, *Underwriter*
EMP: 92
SALES (corp-wide): 2.7B **Privately Held**
WEB: www.statefundca.com
SIC: 6331 9651 Workers' compensation insurance; insurance commission, government;
PA: State Compensation Insurance Fund
333 Bush St Fl 8
San Francisco CA 94104
888 782-8338

(P-15486)
TRISTAR INSURANCE GROUP INC (PA)
Also Called: Tristart Risk Management
100 Oceangate Ste 700, Long Beach
(90802-4368)
PHONE..............................562 495-6600
Thomas J Veale, *President*
Denise J Cotter, *CFO*
Joseph McLaughlin, *Senior VP*
Curt Crockett, *Vice Pres*
Vickie Gonzales, *Vice Pres*
EMP: 700 **EST:** 1982
SQ FT: 9,000
SALES (est): 544.4MM **Privately Held**
WEB: www.tristargroup.net
SIC: 6331 8741 Workers' compensation insurance; management services

(P-15487)
UNICO AMERICAN CORPORATION (PA)
26050 Mureau Rd, Calabasas
(91302-3127)
PHONE..............................818 591-9800
Ron Closser, *Ch of Bd*
Michael Budnitsky, *CFO*
David Russell, *Bd of Directors*
Adam Lapierre, *Officer*
Kristen Lewis, *Manager*
EMP: 79 **EST:** 1969

SALES (est): 32.5MM **Publicly Held**
WEB: www.crusaderinsurance.com
SIC: 6331 6321 6311 6411 Property damage insurance; accident & health insurance; life insurance; insurance agents, brokers & service

(P-15488)
WESTERN GENERAL HOLDING CO (PA)
5230 Las Virgenes Rd # 100, Calabasas
(91302-3448)
PHONE..............................818 880-9070
Robert M Ehrlich, *Ch of Bd*
Daniel Mallut, *President*
Marlene Kushner, *Admin Sec*
EMP: 240 **EST:** 1999
SQ FT: 51,000
SALES (est): 52.9MM **Privately Held**
WEB: www.westerngeneral.com
SIC: 6331 Fire, marine & casualty insurance

(P-15489)
WESTERN GENERAL INSURANCE CO
5230 Las Virgenes Rd # 10, Calabasas
(91302-3448)
PHONE..............................818 880-9070
Robert M Ehrlich, *Ch of Bd*
Denise M Tyson, *COO*
John Albanese, *CFO*
Daniel Mallut, *Exec VP*
Marleen Kushner, *Admin Sec*
EMP: 165
SQ FT: 51,000
SALES (est): 47.6MM
SALES (corp-wide): 52.9MM **Privately Held**
WEB: www.westerngeneral.com
SIC: 6331 Automobile insurance
PA: Western General Holding Co
5230 Las Virgenes Rd # 100
Calabasas CA 91302
818 880-9070

(P-15490)
WESTERN MUTUAL INSURANCE CO
27489 Agoura Rd, Agoura Hills
(91301-2419)
PHONE..............................818 879-2142
Joe Crail, *President*
Cathy Crail, *Sales Executive*
EMP: 70 **EST:** 1942
SALES (est): 4.7MM **Privately Held**
SIC: 6331 Fire, marine & casualty insurance: mutual

(P-15491)
WORKMENS AUTO INSURANCE CO
714 W Olympic Blvd # 800, Los Angeles
(90015-1440)
PHONE..............................213 742-8700
Jeanette Shammas, *Ch of Bd*
Nicholas J Lannotti, *President*
Denise M Tyson, *President*
Lisa Campbell, *VP Sales*
EMP: 100 **EST:** 1949
SALES (est): 36.8MM
SALES (corp-wide): 3.7B **Publicly Held**
WEB: www.waic.com
SIC: 6331 Fire, marine & casualty insurance
PA: Mercury General Corporation
4484 Wilshire Blvd
Los Angeles CA 90010
323 937-1060

(P-15492)
ZENITH INSURANCE COMPANY (DH)
Also Called: Zenith A Fairfax Company, The
21255 Califa St, Woodland Hills
(91367-5021)
P.O. Box 9055, Van Nuys (91409-9055)
PHONE..............................818 713-1000
Stanley R Zax, *Ch of Bd*
Kenneth Hildebrand, *President*
Jack D Miller, *President*
Kari Van Gundy, *CFO*
Anne Searcy, *Officer*
EMP: 400 **EST:** 1950
SQ FT: 120,000

SALES (est): 1B
SALES (corp-wide): 19.7B **Privately Held**
WEB: www.thezenith.com
SIC: 6331 Workers' compensation insurance; automobile insurance; agricultural insurance; property damage insurance
HQ: Zenith National Insurance Corp.
21255 Califa St
Woodland Hills CA 91367
818 713-1000

(P-15493)
ZENITH NATIONAL INSURANCE CORP (HQ)
Also Called: Zenith Insurance Company
21255 Califa St, Woodland Hills
(91367-5005)
PHONE..............................818 713-1000
Andrew A Barnard, *President*
Stanley R Zax, *Ch of Bd*
Ramona Garcia, *President*
Jack D Miller, *President*
Kari L Van Gundy, *CFO*
EMP: 77 **EST:** 1971
SQ FT: 130,000
SALES (est): 1B
SALES (corp-wide): 19.7B **Privately Held**
WEB: www.thezenith.com
SIC: 6331 Workers' compensation insurance
PA: Fairfax Financial Holdings Limited
95 Wellington St W Suite 800
Toronto ON M5J 2
416 367-4941

6351 Surety Insurance Carriers

(P-15494)
AMERICAN CONTRS INDEMNITY CO (DH)
Also Called: HCC Surety Group
801 S Figueroa St Ste 700, Los Angeles
(90017-2523)
PHONE..............................213 330-1309
Adam S Pessin, *President*
Michael Budnitsky, *Vice Pres*
Rico Cruz, *Vice Pres*
Paul A Yasilli, *Vice Pres*
William White, *Manager*
EMP: 150 **EST:** 1990
SALES (est): 87.4MM **Privately Held**
WEB: www.tmhcc.com
SIC: 6351 Surety insurance bonding

(P-15495)
CAP-MPT (PA)
333 S Hope St Fl 8, Los Angeles
(90071-3001)
PHONE..............................213 473-8600
Jim Weidner, *CEO*
Michael Wormley MD, *Ch of Bd*
John Donaldson, *CFO*
Nancy Brusegaard John, *Senior VP*
Nancy Brusegaard Johnson, *Senior VP*
EMP: 140 **EST:** 1977
SALES (est): 20.1MM **Privately Held**
WEB: www.capphysicians.com
SIC: 6351 Liability insurance

(P-15496)
DEVELOPERS SURETY INDEMNITY CO (DH)
Also Called: Insco Dico Group , The
17771 Cowan Ste 100, Irvine (92614-6044)
P.O. Box 19725 (92623-9725)
PHONE..............................949 263-3300
Walter Crowell, *President*
Harry C Crowell, *Ch of Bd*
David Rhodes, *Exec VP*
Rahat Faghfoor, *Manager*
EMP: 70 **EST:** 1936
SQ FT: 25,000
SALES (est): 56.5MM
SALES (corp-wide): 5.9B **Privately Held**
WEB: www.inscodico.com
SIC: 6351 Fidelity or surety bonding
HQ: Insco Insurance Services, Inc.
17771 Cowan Ste 100
Irvine CA 92614
949 263-3415

6361 Title Insurance

(P-15497)
CHICAGO TITLE COMPANY (DH)
725 S Figueroa St Ste 200, Los Angeles
(90017-5403)
PHONE..............................2 3 488-4375
Cheryl Yanez, *President*
Chris MA, *Vice Pres*
Madeline Lovejoy, *Assistant VP*
Gabriela Delgado, *Assistant*
Maria Leal, *Supervisor*
EMP: 62 **EST:** 1984
SALES (est): 30.7MM **Publicly Held**
WEB: www.ctic.com
SIC: 6361 Title insurance
HQ: Chicago Title Insurance Company
10 S Lasalle St Ste 2850
Chicago IL 60603
312 223-2402

(P-15498)
CHICAGO TITLE INSURANCE CO (HQ)
4050 Calle Real, Santa Barbara
(93110-3413)
PHONE..............................305 565-6900
William Halvorsen, *President*
A Larry Sisk, *Treasurer*
Peter G Leemputte, *Vice Pres*
EMP: 150 **EST:** 1984
SQ FT: 44,637
SALES (est): 955.4MM **Publicly Held**
WEB: www.ctt.com
SIC: 6361 Real estate title insurance

(P-15499)
COMMONWEALTH LAND TITLE INSUR
4100 Nwport Pl Dr Ste 120, Newport Beach
(92660)
PHONE..............................800 432-0706
Griffin Wayne, *Vice Pres*
EMP: 188 **Publicly Held**
WEB: www.cwtitle.net
SIC: 6361 Real estate title insurance
HQ: Commonwealth Land Title Insurance Company
201 Cncourse Blvd Ste 200
Glen Allen VA 23059
904 854-8100

(P-15500)
COMMONWEALTH LAND TITLE INSUR
6 Executive Cir Ste 100, Irvine
(92614-6732)
PHONE..............................949 460-4500
Carl Brown, *CEO*
EMP: 188 **Publicly Held**
WEB: www.cwtitle.net
SIC: 6361 Title insurance
HQ: Commonwealth Land Title Insurance Company
201 Cncourse Blvd Ste 200
Glen Allen VA 23059
904 854-8100

(P-15501)
COMMONWEALTH LAND TITLE INSUR
41637 Margarita Rd # 101 Temecula
(92591-2990)
PHONE..............................951 296-6289
Linda Delaney, *Manager*
EMP: 188 **Publicly Held**
WEB: www.cwtitle.net
SIC: 6361 Real estate title insurance
HQ: Commonwealth Land Title Insurance Company
201 Cncourse Blvd Ste 200
Glen Allen VA 23059
904 854-8100

(P-15502)
EXPERIENCE 1 INC (DH)
5000 Birch St Ste 300, Newport Beach
(92660-2147)
PHONE..............................949 475-3752
Michael Tafoya, *CEO*
EMP: 62 **EST:** 2009

SALES (est): 192MM Publicly Held
WEB: www.xome.com
SIC: **6361** 6531 Title insurance; real estate agents & managers
HQ: Xome Holdings Llc
    750 Hwy 121 Byp Ste 100
    Lewisville TX 75067
    888 321-2192

(P-15503)

FIRST AMERICAN FINANCIAL CORP (PA)

1 First American Way, Santa Ana (92707-5913)
PHONE....................714 250-3000
Dennis J Gilmore, *CEO*
Parker S Kennedy, *Ch of Bd*
Kenneth D Degiorgio, *President*
Mark E Seaton, *CFO*
Matthew F Wajner, *Treasurer*
EMP: **4319** EST: 1889
SQ FT: 490,000
SALES (est): 7B Publicly Held
WEB: www.firstam.com
SIC: **6361** 6351 Title insurance; surety insurance

(P-15504)

FIRST AMERICAN MORTGAGE SVCS

3 First American Way, Santa Ana (92707-5913)
PHONE....................714 250-4210
Wes Mee, *President*
Jeanie Matten, *Senior VP*
Margarita Mejia, *Supervisor*
EMP: **350** EST: 2009
SALES (est): 28.1MM Privately Held
WEB: www.firstam.com
SIC: **6361** Title insurance

(P-15505)

FIRST AMERICAN TITLE INSUR CO (HQ)

1 First American Way, Santa Ana (92707-5913)
P.O. Box 267 (92702-0267)
PHONE....................800 854-3643
Dennis J Gilmore, *CEO*
Kurt Pfotenhauer, *Vice Chairman*
Kevin Wall, *President*
Jacqueline Winter, *President*
Curt Caspersen, *COO*
EMP: **62** EST: 1889
SALES (est): 3.6B Publicly Held
WEB: www.firstam.com
SIC: **6361** Real estate title insurance

(P-15506)

LAWYERS TITLE COMPANY (HQ)

7530 N Glenoaks Blvd, Burbank (91504-1052)
PHONE....................818 767-0425
Edward Zerwekh, *CEO*
Lewis AZ, *Officer*
Amit Patel, *Officer*
Cindy Taggart, *Officer*
Edward Beierle, *Senior VP*
EMP: **50** EST: 1961
SQ FT: 20,000
SALES (est): 312.9MM Publicly Held
WEB: www.laltic.com
SIC: **6361** 6531 Real estate title insurance; escrow agent, real estate

(P-15507)

LAWYERS TITLE INSURANCE CORP

Also Called: Lawyers Title Escrow
16755 Von Karman Ave # 100, Irvine (92606-4930)
PHONE....................949 223-5575
Dan Williams, *Owner*
Leslie Shrimplin, *Vice Pres*
Timothy Wright, *Executive*
EMP: **174** Publicly Held
WEB: www.ltic.com
SIC: **6361** Real estate title insurance
HQ: Lawyers Title Insurance Corporation
    601 Riverside Ave
    Jacksonville FL 32204
    888 866-3684

(P-15508)

LAWYERS TITLE INSURANCE CORP

2751 Park View Ct, Oxnard (93036-5452)
PHONE....................805 484-2701
John Arnold, *Manager*
Noel Palacio, *Officer*
Mark Quandt, *Vice Pres*
Margaret Kelley, *Banking Exec*
Sylvia Wallis, *Assistant*
EMP: **174** Publicly Held
WEB: www.ltic.com
SIC: **6361** Guarantee of titles; real estate title insurance
HQ: Lawyers Title Insurance Corporation
    601 Riverside Ave
    Jacksonville FL 32204
    888 866-3684

(P-15509)

LAWYERS TITLE INSURANCE CORP

18551 Von Karman Ave # 100, Irvine (92612-1552)
PHONE....................949 223-5575
Dan Williams, *Branch Mgr*
David Cook,
EMP: **174** Publicly Held
WEB: www.ltic.com
SIC: **6361** 6541 Real estate title insurance; title & trust companies
HQ: Lawyers Title Insurance Corporation
    601 Riverside Ave
    Jacksonville FL 32204
    888 866-3684

(P-15510)

NORTH AMERICAN TITLE CO INC

505 S Main St Ste 101, Orange (92868-4509)
PHONE....................714 550-6400
EMP: **150**
SALES (corp-wide): 22.4B Publicly Held
WEB: www.natic.com
SIC: **6361** Title Insurance Carrier
HQ: North American Title Company, Inc.
    1981 N Broadway Ste 100
    Walnut Creek CA 94596
    925 935-5599

(P-15511)

OLD REPUBLIC TITLE COMPANY

101 N Brand Blvd Ste 1400, Glendale (91203-2691)
PHONE....................818 240-1936
Merv Morris, *President*
Lisa Connally, *Officer*
Wendy McLaughlin, *Officer*
Amanda Raner, *Officer*
Chris Ritter, *Officer*
EMP: **231** EST: 1967
SQ FT: 25,000
SALES (est): 30.5MM
SALES (corp-wide): 7.1B Publicly Held
WEB: www.ortconline.com
SIC: **6361** Real estate title insurance
HQ: Old Republic Title Holding Company, Inc.
    275 Battery St Ste 1500
    San Francisco CA 94111
    415 421-3500

(P-15512)

TICOR TITLE INSURANCE COMPANY (DH)

131 N El Molino Ave # 13, Pasadena (91101-1873)
PHONE....................616 302-3121
John Rau, *Ch of Bd*
Gust Totlis, *CFO*
Peter Leemputte, *Treasurer*
Debbie Miller, *Officer*
Paul T Sands Jr, *Exec VP*
EMP: **62** EST: 1965
SQ FT: 44,637
SALES (est): 227.5MM Publicly Held
WEB: www.ctic.com
SIC: **6361** Real estate title insurance
HQ: Chicago Title And Trust Company
    10 S La Salle St Ste 3100
    Chicago IL 60603
    312 223-2000

(P-15513)

WFG NATIONAL TITLE INSUR CO (PA)

Also Called: Alliance Title
700 N Brand Blvd Ste 1100, Glendale (91203-1208)
PHONE....................818 476-4000
Jeffrey Fox, *CEO*
Brandon Baker, *President*
Brian Hughes, *President*
Roberto Olivera, *President*
Chris White, *President*
EMP: **75** EST: 1980
SQ FT: 15,000
SALES (est): 102.5MM Privately Held
WEB: www.wfgtitle.com
SIC: **6361** Title insurance

6371 Pension, Health & Welfare Funds

(P-15514)

CAL SOUTHERN UNITED FOOD

Also Called: U F C Pension Trust Fund
6425 Katella Ave, Cypress (90630-5246)
P.O. Box 6010 (90630-0010)
PHONE....................714 220-2297
P Thompson, *Administration*
Luisa Estes, *Trust Officer*
William Smith, *Analyst*
Patricia Mathieu, *Director*
George Gamil, *Manager*
EMP: **240** EST: 1957
SQ FT: 36,000
SALES (est): 42.8MM Privately Held
WEB: www.scufcwfunds.com
SIC: **6371** Pension funds

(P-15515)

EMPLOYEE BENEFITS SECURITY ADM

Also Called: Los Angeles Regional Office
1055 E Colo Blvd Ste 200, Pasadena (91106)
PHONE....................626 229-1000
EMP: **55** Publicly Held
SIC: **6371** Pension/Health/Welfare Fund
HQ: Employee Benefits Security Administration
    200 Constitution Ave Nw
    Washington DC 20210
    202 219-8233

(P-15516)

LOS ANGLES CNTY EMPLYEES RTRME (PA)

Also Called: Lacera
300 N Lake Ave Ste 720, Pasadena (91101-5674)
P.O. Box 7060 (91109-7060)
PHONE....................626 564-6000
Gregg Rademather, *CEO*
Jonathan Grabel, *Ch Invest Ofcr*
Robert Santos, *Officer*
Christopher J Wagner, *Sr Invest Ofcr*
Ana Chang, *Vice Pres*
EMP: **200**
SQ FT: 85,000
SALES (est): 2B Privately Held
WEB: www.lacera.com
SIC: **6371** Pension funds

(P-15517)

MOTION PCTURE INDUST PNSION HL

11365 Ventura Blvd # 300, Studio City (91604-3148)
PHONE....................818 769-0007
David Wescoe, *CEO*
Chuck Killian, *CFO*
Thomas Zimmerman, *Executive*
Angie McCormick, *Admin Asst*
Austin Anderson, *Administration*
EMP: **150** EST: 1954
SQ FT: 12,500
SALES (est): 90.6MM Privately Held
SIC: **6371** Pension, health & welfare funds

(P-15518)

PRODUCER -WRITERS GUILD

2900 W Alameda Ave # 1100, Burbank (91505-4220)
PHONE....................818 846-1015

Jim Hedges, *Administration*
Rocco Calabrese, *Administration*
Alan Weidlich, *CIO*
Ed Zix, *Info Tech Dir*
Sero Eskandaryan, *Web Dvlpr*
EMP: **70** EST: 1960
SQ FT: 30,000
SALES (est): 18.4MM Privately Held
WEB: www.wgaplans.org
SIC: **6371** Pension funds; pensions

(P-15519)

SCREEN ACTORS GUILD - AMERICAN

Also Called: Screen Actors Guild-Producers
3601 W Olive Ave Fl 2, Burbank (91505-4662)
P.O. Box 7830 (91510-7830)
PHONE....................818 954-9400
Victoria Ballesteros, *Comms Dir*
Gene Kalpakian, *Controller*
Sara Bennett, *Director*
David Besbris, *Director*
Paul Schoeman, *Director*
EMP: **109**
SALES (corp-wide): 79.3MM Privately Held
SIC: **6371** 6411 Pensions; pension & retirement plan consultants
PA: Screen Actors Guild - American Federation Of Television And Radio Artists
    5757 Wilshire Blvd Fl 7
    Los Angeles CA 90036
    415 391-7510

(P-15520)

SELF-INSURED SCHOOLS CAL (PA)

Also Called: Sisc
1300 17th St 5, Bakersfield (93301-4504)
P.O. Box 1847 (93303-1847)
PHONE....................661 636-4000
Russell E Bigler, *President*
Laurie Swan, *Office Mgr*
Cindy Sproles, *Finance Dir*
EMP: **142** EST: 2002
SALES (est): 302.7MM Privately Held
WEB: www.kern.org
SIC: **6371** Pension, health & welfare funds

(P-15521)

SOUTHERN CAL IBW-NECA ADM CORP (PA)

100 Corson St Ste 200, Pasadena (91103-3841)
PHONE....................323 221-5861
Allen Sloan, *Principal*
Brandon Schwebs, *Database Admin*
Celso Perez, *Technology*
Alrick Mansen, *Accountant*
Dolly Jackson, *Human Res Mgr*
EMP: **96** EST: 2014
SALES (est): 3.8MM Privately Held
WEB: www.scibew-neca.org
SIC: **6371** Pension, health & welfare funds

(P-15522)

VALLEY MANAGEMENT ASSOCIATES (PA)

Also Called: McDonald's
18747 Sherman Way Frnt, Reseda (91335-4055)
PHONE....................818 881-6801
Kenneth Lopaty, *President*
Ronald Lopaty, *Vice Pres*
Leroy Ratliff, *Vice Pres*
Fred Tillman, *Vice Pres*
EMP: **60** EST: 1968
SQ FT: 10,000
SALES (est): 10.1MM Privately Held
WEB: www.corporate.mcdonalds.com
SIC: **5812** 6371 Fast-food restaurant, chain; union welfare, benefit & health funds

---

6399 Insurance Carriers, NEC

(P-15523)

AMWINS CONNECT INSUR SVCS LLC

2677 N Main St Ste 800, Santa Ana (92705-6687)
PHONE....................714 460-5153

Philip Lebherz, *Branch Mgr*
Kimberly Siemone, *Broker*
Tyler Shepard, *Sales Staff*
EMP: 71
SALES (corp-wide): 57MM **Privately Held**
WEB: www.amwinsconnect.com
SIC: 6399 Deposit insurance
PA: Amwins Connect Insurance Services, Llc
1600 W Hillsdale Blvd
San Mateo CA 94402
650 348-4131

6411 Insurance Agents, Brokers & Svc

(P-15524)
21ST CENTURY LIFE INSURANCE CO (DH)
Also Called: 21st Century Insurance
6301 Owensmouth Ave # 700, Woodland Hills (91367-2265)
PHONE..............................877 310-5687
Glenn A Pfeil, *CEO*
Richard R Andre, *Senior VP*
Michael J Cassanego, *Senior VP*
Dean E Stark, *Senior VP*
Barbary Baer, *Principal*
EMP: 1800 **EST:** 1955
SQ FT: 412,000
SALES (est): 583.6MM
SALES (corp-wide): 59.9B **Privately Held**
WEB: www.21st.com
SIC: 6411 Fire insurance underwriters' laboratories
HQ: 21st Century North America Insurance Company
3 Beaver Valley Rd
Wilmington DE 19803
877 310-5687

(P-15525)
9200 DATA DEVICES CORPORATION
9200 W Sunset Blvd, West Hollywood (90069-3502)
PHONE..............................310 494-1794
Anthony Dacquisto, *CEO*
EMP: 50 **EST:** 2019
SALES (est): 2.1MM **Privately Held**
SIC: 6411 Loss prevention services, insurance

(P-15526)
ADMINSURE INC
3380 Shelby St, Ontario (91764-5566)
PHONE..............................909 718-1200
Alithia Vargas-Flores, *President*
David Vargas, *Business Dir*
Joel Meza, *Administration*
Diana Sullivan, *Manager*
Ashley Sells, *Assistant*
EMP: 130 **EST:** 1982
SQ FT: 30,000
SALES (est): 19.6MM **Privately Held**
WEB: www.adminsure.com
SIC: 6411 Insurance agents

(P-15527)
ADRIANAS INSURANCE LLC
9445 Charles Smith Ave, Rancho Cucamonga (91730-5546)
PHONE..............................909 291-4040
Adriana Fregoso, *President*
Claudia Campos, *Department Mgr*
Priscilla Abundis, *Accounting Dir*
Paola Lomelin, *Sales Mgr*
Karina Cano, *Manager*
EMP: 52 **EST:** 2006
SALES (est): 3.5K **Privately Held**
WEB: www.adrianasinsurance.com
SIC: 6411 Insurance agents

(P-15528)
ADRIANAS INSURANCE SVCS INC (PA)
9445 Charles Smith Ave, Rancho Cucamonga (91730-5546)
PHONE..............................909 291-4040
Leon Fregoso, *President*
EMP: 113 **EST:** 2000

SALES (est): 26.3MM **Privately Held**
WEB: www.adrianasinsurance.com
SIC: 6411 Insurance agents

(P-15529)
AGIA INC (PA)
Also Called: Agia Affinity
1155 Eugenia Pl, Carpinteria (93013-2062)
PHONE..............................805 566-9191
J Christopher Burke, *President*
Marlis Kerby, *President*
Julie L Capritto, *COO*
Andrew Dowen, *CFO*
Carl A Adamek, *Senior VP*
EMP: 237 **EST:** 1965
SQ FT: 18,000
SALES (est): 141.5MM **Privately Held**
WEB: www.agia.com
SIC: 6411 Medical insurance claim processing, contract or fee basis

(P-15530)
ALLSTATE FLORAL INC
15928 Commerce Way, Cerritos (90703-2319)
PHONE..............................562 926-2989
EMP: 224
SALES (corp-wide): 54.3MM **Privately Held**
WEB: www.allstatefloral.com
SIC: 6411 Insurance agents & brokers
PA: Allstate Floral, Inc.
14101 Park Pl
Cerritos CA 90703
562 926-2302

(P-15531)
AMWINS ACCESS INSUR SVCS LLC (HQ)
435 N Pcf Cst Hwy Ste 2, Redondo Beach (90277)
PHONE..............................310 683-0469
Michael Steven Decarlo, *CEO*
W H Skip Cooper, *President*
Scott Purviance, *COO*
Linda Huynh, *Admin Asst*
Todd Atwood, *CIO*
EMP: 62 **EST:** 2004
SALES (est): 7.7MM
SALES (corp-wide): 797.1MM **Privately Held**
WEB: www.amwins.com
SIC: 6411 Insurance brokers
PA: Amwins Group, Inc.
4725 Piedmont Row Dr # 600
Charlotte NC 28210
704 749-2700

(P-15532)
AMWINS INSURANCE BRKG CAL LLC (HQ)
21550 Oxnard St Ste 1100, Woodland Hills (91367-7106)
PHONE..............................818 772-1774
Michael Steven Decarlo,
George Maggay, *President*
Marissa McGinnis, *Vice Pres*
Elizabeth Goldie, *Executive*
Luis Marquez, *Administration*
EMP: 60 **EST:** 1981
SQ FT: 16,000
SALES (est): 21.7MM
SALES (corp-wide): 797.1MM **Privately Held**
WEB: www.amwins.com
SIC: 6411 Insurance brokers
PA: Amwins Group, Inc.
4725 Piedmont Row Dr # 600
Charlotte NC 28210
704 749-2700

(P-15533)
AON/ALBERT G RUBEN INSUR SVCS (DH)
10880 Wilshire Blvd # 700, Los Angeles (90024-4101)
PHONE..............................310 234-6800
Paul Jones, *Director*
Mark Oshima, *Exec VP*
Linda Pace, *Finance*
EMP: 62 **EST:** 1960
SALES (est): 12.6MM
SALES (corp-wide): 45.4B **Privately Held**
WEB: www.aon.com
SIC: 6411 Insurance brokers

(P-15534)
APPLIED GENERAL AGENCY INC (PA)
1040 N Tustin Ave, Anaheim (92807-1724)
PHONE..............................800 498-6880
Felipe Virgilio, *Principal*
Bryan Birchard, *COO*
Yessica Castanon, *Administration*
Joan Kulifay, *VP Finance*
Brie Lopez, *Broker*
EMP: 99 **EST:** 2009
SALES (est): 14.7MM **Privately Held**
WEB: www.appliedga.com
SIC: 6411 Insurance agents

(P-15535)
ARROYO INSURANCE SERVICES INC (PA)
440 E Huntington Dr # 100, Arcadia (91006-3750)
P.O. Box 661840 (91066-1840)
PHONE..............................626 799-9532
Robert J Knauf, *President*
Richard Beedle, *Corp Secy*
James Armitage, *Vice Pres*
Vera Gale, *Vice Pres*
Jim Simands, *Vice Pres*
EMP: 52 **EST:** 1987
SQ FT: 3,500
SALES (est): 20.8MM **Privately Held**
WEB: www.williamsandcompanyins.com
SIC: 6411 Insurance brokers

(P-15536)
ARTHUR J GALLAGHER & CO
Also Called: Nationwide
500 N Santa Fe St, Visalia (93292-5065)
PHONE..............................559 733-1181
Kelly Ventura, *Accounts Exec*
Thomas Tackett, *Supervisor*
Diana Velasquez, *Supervisor*
EMP: 90
SALES (corp-wide): 7B **Publicly Held**
WEB: www.ajg.com
SIC: 6411 Insurance brokers
PA: Arthur J. Gallagher & Co.
2850 Golf Rd Ste 600
Rolling Meadows IL 60008
630 773-3800

(P-15537)
ARTHUR J GALLAGHER & CO
1825 Chicago Ave Ste 240, Riverside (92507-2374)
PHONE..............................800 217-9800
EMP: 55
SALES (corp-wide): 7B **Publicly Held**
WEB: www.ajg.com
SIC: 6411 Insurance brokers
PA: Arthur J. Gallagher & Co.
2850 Golf Rd Ste 600
Rolling Meadows IL 60008
630 773-3800

(P-15538)
ARTHUR J GALLAGHER RISK MGMT
Also Called: Nationwide
505 N Brand Blvd Ste 600, Glendale (91203-3944)
PHONE..............................818 539-2300
Gregory S Chapman, *President*
Paulette Chapman, *Treasurer*
Gerald S Chapman, *Vice Pres*
Nelson Debasa, *Vice Pres*
Susan Patelson, *Vice Pres*
EMP: 71 **EST:** 1973
SALES (est): 11.9MM
SALES (corp-wide): 7B **Publicly Held**
WEB: www.ajg.com
SIC: 6411 Insurance brokers
PA: Arthur J. Gallagher & Co.
2850 Golf Rd Ste 600
Rolling Meadows IL 60008
630 773-3800

(P-15539)
AUTO INSURANCE SPECIALISTS LLC (DH)
Also Called: Nationwide
17785 Center Court Dr N # 110, Cerritos (90703-8573)
PHONE..............................562 345-6247
Mark Ribisi, *CEO*
Chris Bremer, *CFO*

Jerry Baker, *Vice Pres*
Mark Casas, *Vice Pres*
Lani Elkin, *Vice Pres*
EMP: 210 **EST:** 1968
SQ FT: 45,000
SALES (est): 56.9MM
SALES (corp-wide): 3.7B **Publicly Held**
WEB: www.aisinsurance.com
SIC: 6411 Insurance brokers

(P-15540)
AUTOMOBILE CLUB SOUTHERN CAL (PA)
Also Called: A A A Automobile Club So Cal
2601 S Figueroa St, Los Angeles (90007-3294)
P.O. Box 25001, Santa Ana (92799-5001)
PHONE..............................213 741-3686
John F Boyle, *CEO*
Zoo Babies, *President*
Peter R McDonald, *Senior VP*
Jennifer Schnittjer, *Vice Pres*
Braddley Arruda, *Administration*
EMP: 150 **EST:** 1900
SQ FT: 425,000
SALES (est): 1B **Privately Held**
WEB: www.ace.aaa.com
SIC: 6411 8699 Insurance agents; automobile owners' association

(P-15541)
AUTOMOBILE CLUB SOUTHERN CAL
33323 Fairview R Ste Msa, Costa Mesa (92626)
PHONE..............................213 741-3686
EMP: 93
SALES (corp-wide): 1B **Privately Held**
WEB: www.ace.aaa.com
SIC: 6411 Insurance agents
PA: Automobile Club Of Southern California
2601 S Figueroa St
Los Angeles CA 90007
213 741-3686

(P-15542)
AUTOMOBILE CLUB SOUTHERN CAL
3534 Peck Rd, El Monte (91731-3526)
PHONE..............................626 442-0944
Roger S Penske, *Branch Mgr*
EMP: 93
SALES (corp-wide): 1B **Privately Held**
WEB: www.ace.aaa.com
SIC: 6411 Insurance agents
PA: Automobile Club Of Southern California
2601 S Figueroa St
Los Angeles CA 90007
213 741-3686

(P-15543)
AUTOMOBILE CLUB SOUTHERN CAL
Also Called: AAA Auto Club
3333 Fairview Rd, Costa Mesa (92626-1698)
PHONE..............................714 885-1343
Becky Martinez, *Branch Mgr*
Ryan Sharkey, *Analyst*
Carmel Urquhart, *Recruiter*
Valerie Granados, *Sales Staff*
Henry Lee, *Sales Staff*
EMP: 200
SALES (corp-wide): 1B **Privately Held**
WEB: www.ace.aaa.com
SIC: 6411 Insurance agents, brokers & service
PA: Automobile Club Of Southern California
2601 S Figueroa St
Los Angeles CA 90007
213 741-3686

(P-15544)
AUTOMOBILE CLUB SOUTHERN CAL
10540 Fthill Blvd Ste 100, Rancho Cucamonga (91730)
PHONE..............................909 980-0233
Alice Holguin, *Branch Mgr*
EMP: 93
SALES (corp-wide): 1B **Privately Held**
WEB: www.ace.aaa.com
SIC: 6411 Insurance agents, brokers & service

PA: Automobile Club Of Southern California
2601 S Figueroa St
Los Angeles CA 90007
213 741-3686

(P-15545)

CAESAR AND SEIDER INSUR SVCS (PA)

Also Called: Talbot Insurance & Fincl Svcs
40 E Alamar Ave Ste 4, Santa Barbara
(93105-3400)
P.O. Box 3310 (93130-3310)
PHONE...........................805 682-2571
Thomas Caesar, *President*
Ray Seider, *Vice Pres*
EMP: 52 **EST:** 1954
SQ FT: 2,400
SALES (est): 7.3MM **Privately Held**
WEB: www.rivierains.com
SIC: 6411 Insurance brokers

(P-15546)

CALIFORNIA FAIR PLAN ASSN

725 S Figueroa St # 3900, Los Angeles
(90017-5439)
PHONE...........................213 487-0111
Stuart M Wilkinson, *President*
John Boeder, *Vice Pres*
Estee Natalie, *Vice Pres*
Victoria Roach, *Vice Pres*
Tammy Schwartz, *Vice Pres*
EMP: 80 **EST:** 1968
SALES (est): 16.6MM **Privately Held**
WEB: www.cfpnet.com
SIC: 6411 Insurance agents

(P-15547)

CALIFRNIA INSUR GUARANTEE ASSN

Also Called: C I G A
101 N Brand Blvd Ste 600, Glendale
(91203-2653)
P.O. Box 29066 (91209-9066)
PHONE...........................818 844-4300
Lawrence E Mulryan, *Director*
Elizabeth Hunter, *Treasurer*
Wayne Wilson, *Exec Dir*
Devo Heller, *Info Tech Dir*
Jonathan Antonio, *Software Dev*
EMP: 110 **EST:** 1969
SALES (est): 24.8MM **Privately Held**
WEB: www.ciga.org
SIC: 6411 Insurance agents, brokers & service

(P-15548)

CANNON COCHRAN MGT SVCS INC

Also Called: Ccmsi
18881 Von Karman Ave # 380, Irvine
(92612-6580)
PHONE...........................949 474-6500
William Hougland, *Manager*
Andy Hougland, *Branch Mgr*
EMP: 59 **Privately Held**
WEB: www.ccmsi.com
SIC: 6411 Insurance agents
HQ: Cannon Cochran Management Services, Inc.
2 E Main St Twne Ctr Bldg Towne
Danville IL 61832
217 446-1089

(P-15549)

CARTEL MARKETING INC

Also Called: Insure Express Insurance Svc
5230 Las Virgenes Rd # 25, Calabasas
(91302-3448)
PHONE...........................818 483-1130
Robert M Humphreys, *Ch of Bd*
Jack Edelstein, *President*
Brian Murphy, *COO*
William Russell, *CFO*
Sean Willis, *Officer*
EMP: 101 **EST:** 1984
SQ FT: 14,000
SALES (est): 11.4MM
SALES (corp-wide): 57.2MM **Privately Held**
WEB: www.cartel.net
SIC: 6411 Insurance agents
HQ: Expresslink, Inc.
16501 Ventura Blvd # 300
Encino CA 91436
818 788-5555

(P-15550)

CHOIC ADMINI INSUR SERVI

Also Called: California Choice
721 S Parker St Ste 200, Orange
(92868-4772)
PHONE...........................714 542-4200
Michael Close, *President*
Kevin J Counihan, *President*
Brenda Scott, *Senior VP*
Raymond D Godeke, *Vice Pres*
Macpherson Ta Reis, *Vice Pres*
EMP: 500 **EST:** 1984
SALES (est): 50.2MM **Privately Held**
WEB: www.choicebuilder.com
SIC: 6411 Insurance agents

(P-15551)

CIBA INSURANCE SVCS CAL INC (PA)

655 N Central Ave # 2100, Glendale
(91203-1422)
PHONE...........................818 638-8525
Michael Marino, *President*
Julie Sharp, *Vice Pres*
Tracey Ajani, *Controller*
Julie Kim, *Opers Staff*
Craig Morton, *Director*
EMP: 61 **EST:** 2004
SALES (est): 12.6MM **Privately Held**
WEB: www.cibaservices.com
SIC: 6411 Insurance agents

(P-15552)

COMMERCIAL CRRERS INSUR AGCY I

4 Centerpointe Dr Ste 300, La Palma
(90623-1074)
PHONE...........................562 404-4900
Charles J Escalante, *President*
Henry H Escalante, *Ch of Bd*
Shannon S Walker, *Treasurer*
Helen M Escalante, *Admin Sec*
EMP: 147 **EST:** 1979
SQ FT: 16,000
SALES (est): 6MM **Privately Held**
WEB: www.cciainsurance.com
SIC: 6411 Insurance agents
HQ: Meadowbrook, Inc.
26255 American Dr
Southfield MI 48034
248 358-1100

(P-15553)

CONEXIS BNFITS ADMNSTRATORS LP (HQ)

721 S Parker St Ste 300, Orange
(92868-4732)
PHONE...........................714 835-5006
Michael Close, *President*
Tamra L Macpherson, *Vice Pres*
Bill Mason, *Vice Pres*
Marc McGinnis, *Vice Pres*
Avery Anton, *Sales Staff*
EMP: 120 **EST:** 1988
SQ FT: 57,000
SALES (est): 51.2MM
SALES (corp-wide): 383.5MM **Privately Held**
WEB: www.wordandbrown.com
SIC: 6411 Insurance information & consulting services
PA: Word & Brown, Insurance Administrators, Inc.
721 S Parker St Ste 300
Orange CA 92868
714 835-5006

(P-15554)

CONFIE SEGUROS INC (DH)

Also Called: Freeway Insurance
7711 Center Ave Ste 200, Huntington
Beach (92647-9124)
PHONE...........................714 252-2500
Cesar Soriano, *CEO*
Michael Kaplan, *CFO*
Darrin Silveria, *Officer*
Kyle Garst, *Senior VP*
Jose Guardado, *Vice Pres*
EMP: 148 **EST:** 2005
SALES (est): 409.1MM
SALES (corp-wide): 1.1B **Privately Held**
WEB: www.confie.com
SIC: 6411 Insurance agents

HQ: Confie Seguros California, Inc.
7711 Center Ave Ste 200
Huntington Beach CA 92647
714 252-2649

(P-15555)

CONFIE SEGUROS HOLDINGS II CO (PA)

7711 Center Ave Ste 200, Huntington
Beach (92647-9124)
PHONE...........................714 252-2500
Cesar Soriano, *CEO*
Michael Kaplan, *CFO*
Joshua Marder, *Chief Mktg Ofcr*
Tim Clark, *Officer*
Andrew Shrout, *Exec VP*
EMP: 160 **EST:** 2007
SALES (est): 121.1MM **Privately Held**
WEB: www.confie.com
SIC: 6411 Insurance agents

(P-15556)

CONFIE SEGUROS TEXAS INC (HQ)

7711 Center Ave Ste 200, Huntington
Beach (92647-9124)
PHONE...........................714 252-2649
Mordy Rothberg, *President*
Robert Trebing, *CFO*
Liz Fallucca, *Vice Pres*
Barry Shook, *Vice Pres*
Latoi Brown, *Finance*
EMP: 62 **EST:** 2008
SALES (est): 120MM
SALES (corp-wide): 121.1MM **Privately Held**
WEB: www.confie.com
SIC: 6411 Insurance agents
PA: Confie Seguros Holdings Ii Co.
7711 Center Ave Ste 200
Huntington Beach CA 92647
714 252-2500

(P-15557)

COVERANCE INSUR SOLUTIONS INC (PA)

100 W Broadway Ste 3000, Long Beach
(90802-4467)
PHONE...........................231 218-6100
Christopher Mullins, *CEO*
Teague McGrath, *Senior Mgr*
EMP: 98 **EST:** 2017
SALES (est): 16.4MM **Privately Held**
WEB: www.coveranceis.com
SIC: 6411 Insurance agents, brokers & service

(P-15558)

CREST FINANCIAL CORPORATION (DH)

12641 166th St, Cerritos (90703-2101)
P.O. Box 3190 (90703-3190)
PHONE...........................562 733-6500
Susan Scurti, *President*
Shannon S Walker, *CFO*
Michael Costello, *Senior VP*
Walter E Erker, *Vice Pres*
EMP: 62 **EST:** 1983
SQ FT: 15,000
SALES (est): 24.5MM **Privately Held**
WEB: www.ameritrustgroup.com
SIC: 6411 7311 Insurance agents; insurance information & consulting services; insurance adjusters; insurance agents & brokers; advertising agencies

(P-15559)

CYBERPOLICY INC

19584 Pine Valley Ave, Porter Ranch
(91326-1408)
PHONE...........................877 626-9991
Keith Moore, *CEO*
Dana Maxman, *COO*
Katherine Moura, *Senior VP*
Catherine Pallivathuckal, *General Mgr*
EMP: 103 **EST:** 2016
SALES (est): 11.7MM **Privately Held**
WEB: www.cyberpolicy.com
SIC: 6411 Insurance agents, brokers & service

(P-15560)

DEWITT STERN GROUP INC

5990 Sepulvda Blvd # 550, Van Nuys
(91411-2536)
PHONE...........................818 933-2700
Jolyon F Stern, *Branch Mgr*
EMP: 137
SALES (corp-wide): 772.2MM **Privately Held**
WEB: www.dewittstern.com
SIC: 6411 Insurance brokers
HQ: Dewitt Stern Group, Inc.
420 Lexington Ave Rm 2700
New York NY 10170
212 867-3550

(P-15561)

DMA CLAIMS MANAGEMENT INC (PA)

Also Called: Dma Claims Services
330 N Brand Blvd Ste 230, Glendale
(91203-2380)
P.O. Box 26004 (91222-6004)
PHONE...........................323 342-6800
Thomas J Reitze, *President*
Henning Heldt, *Vice Pres*
Diane Cook, *Executive*
K WA, *Admin Asst*
Debbie Cavallerano, *Administration*
EMP: 233 **EST:** 1980
SQ FT: 20,000
SALES (est): 56.2MM **Privately Held**
WEB: www.dmaclaims.com
SIC: 6411 Insurance claim adjusters, not employed by insurance company

(P-15562)

EMPLOYERS COMPENSATION INSUR (DH)

500 N Brand Blvd Ste 800, Glendale
(91203-4707)
PHONE...........................818 549-4600
Stephen V Festa, *President*
Michael S Paquette, *Treasurer*
Nathan Kotchou, *Technology*
Eddie Trapps, *Sales Executive*
Monica Tobin, *Underwriter*
EMP: 137 **EST:** 1970
SALES (est): 12.1MM **Publicly Held**
WEB: www.employers.com
SIC: 6411 Insurance agents

(P-15563)

FARMERS FINCL SOLUTIONS LLC (PA)

Also Called: Farmers Insurance
30801 Agoura Rd, Agoura Hills
(91301-2054)
PHONE...........................818 584-0200
Barbara Huppert, *COO*
Sharon Fernandez, *President*
Eric Kappler, *President*
Jason Crawshaw, *CFO*
Rob Howard, *Ch Credit Ofcr*
EMP: 64 **EST:** 1999
SALES (est): 25.4MM **Privately Held**
WEB: www.farmers.com
SIC: 6411 Insurance agents, brokers & service

(P-15564)

FARMERS GROUP INC (HQ)

Also Called: Farmers Insurance
6301 Owensmouth Ave, Woodland Hills
(91367-2216)
P.O. Box 2450, Grand Rapids MI (49501-2450)
PHONE...........................323 932-3200
Jeff Dailey, *CEO*
Tony Desantis, *President*
Steve McAnena, *President*
Jarow Myers, *President*
Mhayse Samalya, *President*
▲ **EMP:** 2100 **EST:** 1927
SALES (est): 4B
SALES (corp-wide): 59.9B **Privately Held**
WEB: www.farmers.com
SIC: 6411 Insurance agents, brokers & service
PA: Zurich Insurance Group Ag
C/O Zurich Versicherungs-Gesellschaft Ag
ZUrich ZH 8002
446 252-525

PRODUCTS & SVCS

(P-15565)
FARMERS GROUP INC
Also Called: Farmers Insurance
6303 Owensmouth Ave Fl 1, Woodland Hills
(91367-2200)
PHONE....................805 583-7400
EMP: 900
SALES (corp-wide): 74.2B **Privately Held**
SIC: 6411 Ins Agnts And Brkrs
HQ: Farmers Group, Inc.
6301 Owensmouth Ave
Woodland Hills CA 91367
323 932-3200

(P-15566)
FARMERS INSURANCE
EXCHANGE (DH)
6301 Owensmouth Ave # 750, Woodland
Hills (91367-2212)
PHONE....................888 327-6335
Jeff Pailey, *CEO*
Scott Lindquist, *CFO*
Ron Myhan, *CFO*
Thomas Noh, *CFO*
Eric Kappler,
EMP: 3000 **EST:** 1928
SQ FT: 210,000
SALES (est): 1.7B
SALES (corp-wide): 59.9B **Privately Held**
WEB: www.farmers.com
SIC: 6411 Insurance agents, brokers &
service
HQ: Farmers Group, Inc.
6301 Owensmouth Ave
Woodland Hills CA 91367
323 932-3200

(P-15567)
FARMERS INSURANCE
EXCHANGE
411 E Pine St Ste A, Exeter (93221-1800)
PHONE....................559 594-4149
Sammy Harrell, *Branch Mgr*
EMP: 288
SALES (corp-wide): 59.9B **Privately Held**
WEB: www.farmers.com
SIC: 6411 Insurance agents, brokers &
service
HQ: Farmers Insurance Exchange
6301 Owensmouth Ave # 750
Woodland Hills CA 91367
888 327-6335

(P-15568)
FINANCIAL GROUP INC
Also Called: Finan Group
12432 Oxnard St, North Hollywood
(91606-4510)
PHONE....................818 308-8527
Andres Saavedra, *Principal*
EMP: 136
SALES (corp-wide): 1.3B **Publicly Held**
WEB: www.securian.com
SIC: 6411 Insurance agents, brokers &
service
HQ: The Financial Group Inc
2555 Severn Ave Ste 100
Metairie LA 70002
504 456-0101

(P-15569)
FIRE INSURANCE EXCHANGE
(PA)
6301 Owensmouth Ave, Woodland Hills
(91367-2216)
PHONE....................323 932-3200
Martin Feinstein, *President*
John Harrington, *President*
Scott Lindquist, *CFO*
Ron Myhan, *Treasurer*
Rob Howard, *Officer*
EMP: 2300 **EST:** 1942 **Privately Held**
WEB: www.farmers.com
SIC: 6411 Insurance agents, brokers &
service

(P-15570)
FIRST AMRCN PRPRTY INSUR
CSLTY
114 E 5th St, Santa Ana (92701-4642)
PHONE....................949 474-7500
Dirk McNamee, *President*
EMP: 52 **EST:** 1930

SALES (est): 6MM **Publicly Held**
WEB: www.fapcia.com
SIC: 6411 Insurance agents
HQ: First American Specialty Insurance
Company
4 First American Way
Santa Ana CA 92707
949 474-7500

(P-15571)
FMC FINANCIAL GROUP (PA)
4675 Macarthur Ct # 1250, Newport Beach
(92660-1875)
PHONE....................949 225-9369
James Chapel, *Owner*
David Krouse, *COO*
Jordan Ceraso, *Vice Pres*
Nick McLaughlin, *Vice Pres*
Max Pashman, *Vice Pres*
▲ **EMP:** 75 **EST:** 1981
SALES (est): 8.3MM **Privately Held**
WEB: www.fmcfg.com
SIC: 6411 Insurance agents & brokers

(P-15572)
FREEWAY INSURANCE (PA)
Also Called: South Coast Auto Insurance
7711 Center Ave Ste 200, Huntington
Beach (92647-9124)
P.O. Box 669, Cypress (90630-0669)
PHONE....................714 252-2500
Elias Assaf, *President*
Norm Hudson, *COO*
Chad Maxwell, *Senior VP*
John Klaeb, *Vice Pres*
EMP: 120 **EST:** 1988
SQ FT: 20,000
SALES (est): 56.6MM **Privately Held**
WEB: www.freewayinsurance.com
SIC: 6411 Insurance agents

(P-15573)
GGIS INSURANCE SERVICES
INC
Also Called: Guardian General Insur Svcs
600 N Brand Blvd Ste 300, Glendale
(91203-4207)
PHONE....................818 553-2110
EMP: 135
SALES (est): 12.7MM **Privately Held**
WEB: www.guardiangeneral.com
SIC: 6411 Insurance Agent/Broker

(P-15574)
GROSSLIGHT INSURANCE INC
Also Called: Nationwide
6200 Canoga Ave Ste 325, Woodland Hills
(91367-7475)
PHONE....................310 473-9611
Joan Schiewe, *CEO*
Steven Schiewe, *President*
Linda Flanagan, *General Mgr*
Colleen Malfitano, *Human Res Dir*
Susan Haro, *Accounts Mgr*
EMP: 60 **EST:** 1950
SALES (est): 16.2MM
SALES (corp-wide): 26.8MM **Privately**
Held
WEB: www.grosslight.com
SIC: 6411 Insurance agents
PA: Pcf Insurance Services Of The West,
Llc
6200 Canoga Ave Ste 325
Woodland Hills CA 91367
818 703-8057

(P-15575)
GROSVENOR INV MGT US INC
2308 Chelsea Rd, Palos Verdes Estates
(90274-2606)
PHONE....................310 265-0297
Stephen Waddell, *Branch Mgr*
EMP: 80
SALES (corp-wide): 5.5B **Publicly Held**
SIC: 6411 Pension & retirement plan con-
sultants
HQ: Grosvenor Investment Management
Us Inc.
10 New King St Ste 214
White Plains NY 10604
914 683-3710

(P-15576)
H & H AGENCY INC (PA)
1403 N Tustin Ave Ste 280, Santa Ana
(92705-8691)
PHONE....................949 260-8840
Michael Weinstein, *CEO*
EMP: 114 **EST:** 1969
SQ FT: 25,000
SALES (est): 14.1MM **Privately Held**
WEB: www.hhagency.com
SIC: 6411 Insurance agents

(P-15577)
HAMILTON BRWART INSUR
AGCY LLC
1282 W Arrow Hwy, Upland (91786-5040)
P.O. Box 1949 (91785-1949)
PHONE....................909 920-3250
Hamilton Brewart,
Derek Brewart,
EMP: 67 **EST:** 1976
SQ FT: 12,000
SALES (est): 7.7MM **Privately Held**
WEB: www.dailybulletin.com
SIC: 6411 Insurance agents; insurance
brokers

(P-15578)
HAZELRIGG CLAIMS MGT SVCS
INC (HQ)
15345 Frfeld Rnch Rd Ste, Chino (91710)
P.O. Box 669 (91708-0669)
PHONE....................909 606-6373
Arlene Hazelrigg, *President*
EMP: 60 **EST:** 1991
SQ FT: 5,000
SALES (est): 17.2MM
SALES (corp-wide): 544.4MM **Privately**
Held
WEB: www.hazelriggclaims.com
SIC: 6411 Insurance claim adjusters, not
employed by insurance company
PA: Tristar Insurance Group, Inc.
100 Oceangate Ste 700
Long Beach CA 90802
562 495-6600

(P-15579)
HEALTHCOMPARE INSUR SVCS
INC (DH)
721 S Parker St, Orange (92868-4763)
PHONE....................714 542-4200
John M Word III, *CEO*
Edward J Brown Jr, *President*
Clinton Gee, *Treasurer*
Michael Close, *Admin Sec*
Melissa Gomez, *Manager*
EMP: 62 **EST:** 2009
SALES (est): 10.1MM **Publicly Held**
WEB: www.healthcompare.com
SIC: 6411 Insurance agents, brokers &
service

(P-15580)
HEALTHSMART MANAGEMENT
SERVICE
10855 Bus Ctr Dr Ste C, Cypress (90630)
P.O. Box 6300 (90630-0063)
PHONE....................714 947-8600
Carol Houchins, *President*
Dennis Valero, *Sales Staff*
EMP: 90 **EST:** 1996
SALES (est): 8.5MM **Privately Held**
WEB: www.healthsmartmso.com
SIC: 6411 8741 8721 Medical insurance
claim processing, contract or fee basis;
hospital management; business manage-
ment; billing & bookkeeping service

(P-15581)
HEIGHTS INSURANCE GROUP
INC (PA)
Also Called: Kcal Insurance
2048 S Hacienda Blvd, Hacienda Heights
(91745-4240)
PHONE....................626 333-1111
Chung Chang, *Principal*
Steve MA, *Info Tech Dir*
David Dang, *Technology*
Annie Chou, *Director*
Angel LI, *Agent*
EMP: 51 **EST:** 2010
SALES (est): 1.8MM **Privately Held**
WEB: www.kcal.net
SIC: 6411 Insurance agents

(P-15582)
INDEMNITY COMPANY
CALIFORNIA (DH)
17771 Cowan Ste 100, Irvine (92614-6044)
P.O. Box 19725 (92623-9725)
PHONE....................949 263-3300
Harry C Crowell, *Chairman*
Fern Haberman, *CFO*
Sam Zaza, *CFO*
Walter A Crowell, *Admin Sec*
EMP: 71 **EST:** 1967
SQ FT: 50,000
SALES (est): 47MM
SALES (corp-wide): 5.9B **Privately Held**
WEB: www.inscodico.com
SIC: 6411 Insurance agents
HQ: Insco Insurance Services, Inc.
17771 Cowan Ste 100
Irvine CA 92614
949 263-3415

(P-15583)
INSCO INSURANCE SERVICES
INC (DH)
Also Called: Developers Surety Indemnity Co
17771 Cowan Ste 100, Irvine (92614-6044)
P.O. Box 19725 (92623-9725)
PHONE....................949 263-3415
Harry Crowell, *Ch of Bd*
Steve Rauch, *Branch Mgr*
Dan Schoen, *Accounting Mgr*
Todd Nelson, *Manager*
Peggy Roy, *Underwriter*
EMP: 70 **EST:** 1970
SQ FT: 50,000
SALES (est): 103.6MM
SALES (corp-wide): 5.9B **Privately Held**
WEB: www.inscodico.com
SIC: 6411 6351 Property & casualty insur-
ance agent; surety insurance bonding; lia-
bility insurance

(P-15584)
INSURANCE INC SOUTHERN
CAL
Also Called: Nationwide
3400 Central Ave Ste 220, Riverside
(92506-2180)
PHONE....................951 300-9333
Timothy Dean, *President*
Nowel Milik, *Vice Pres*
Mark Olivarez, *Sales Associate*
Tom Thomas, *Marketing Staff*
Cynthia Brown, *Manager*
◆ **EMP:** 51 **EST:** 1958
SALES (est): 3.7MM **Privately Held**
WEB: www.insuranceinc.com
SIC: 6411 Insurance agents; life insurance
agents; property & casualty insurance
agent

(P-15585)
JOHN HANCOCK LIFE INSUR CO
USA (DH)
865 S Figueroa St # 3320, Los Angeles
(90017-2543)
PHONE....................213 689-0813
Emeritus D'Alessandro, *CEO*
Cecile Butler, *President*
David F D'Alessandro, *President*
Ross Fryer, *President*
Gregory P Winn, *Treasurer*
▲ **EMP:** 2000 **EST:** 1862
SQ FT: 3,600,000
SALES (est): 653.3MM
SALES (corp-wide): 31.63 **Privately Held**
WEB: www.johnhancock.com
SIC: 6411 6351 6371 6321 Insurance
agents & brokers; mortgage guarantee in-
surance; pensions; accident insurance
carriers; health insurance carriers
HQ: John Hancock Financial Services, Inc.
200 Clarendon St
Boston MA 02116
617 572-6000

(P-15586)
KEENAN & ASSOCIATES (HQ)
2355 Crenshaw Blvd # 200, Torrance
(90501-3395)
P.O. Box 4328 (90510-4328)
PHONE....................310 212-3344
John Keenan, *Ch of Bd*
Sean Smith, *CEO*
Davis Seres, *COO*

Henry Loubet, *Senior VP*
Danielle Keenan, *Vice Pres*
EMP: 339
SQ FT: 80,000
SALES (est): 432.5MM **Privately Held**
WEB: www.keenan.com
SIC: 6411 Insurance brokers

(P-15587)
KORAM INSURANCE CENTER INC
Also Called: Nationwide
3807 Wilshire Blvd # 400, Los Angeles
(90010-3104)
PHONE....................323 660-1000
Edward Haan, *CEO*
James D Hahn, *Ch of Bd*
Edward M Hahn, *President*
Kyung W Jo, *Sales Associate*
EMP: 58 **EST:** 1974
SQ FT: 3,300
SALES (est): 6.9MM **Privately Held**
WEB: www.koraminsurance.com
SIC: 6411 Insurance agents

(P-15588)
LEXISNEXIS RISK ASSETS INC
Also Called: Choicepoint
2112 Bus Ctr Dr Ste 150, Irvine (92614)
PHONE....................949 222-0028
Tim Coon, *Owner*
EMP: 112
SALES (corp-wide): 9.4B **Privately Held**
SIC: 6411 Information bureaus, insurance
HQ: Lexisnexis Risk Assets Inc.
1105 N Market St Ste 501
Wilmington DE 19801
800 458-9410

(P-15589)
LOCKTON COMPANIES LLC-PACIFI (HQ)
Also Called: Lockton Insurance Brokers
777 S Figueroa St # 5200, Los Angeles
(90017-5800)
PHONE....................213 689-0500
Timothy J Noonan, *President*
Philip Hurrle, *Partner*
Matthew Sweeney, *Partner*
Lenny Fodemski, *Managing Prtnr*
Nate Lindstrom, *President*
EMP: 294 **EST:** 2006
SQ FT: 72,300
SALES (est): 213.8MM
SALES (corp-wide): 1.6B **Privately Held**
WEB: www.global.lockton.com
SIC: 6411 Insurance brokers
PA: Lockton, Inc.
444 W 47th St Ste 900
Kansas City MO 64112
816 960-9000

(P-15590)
MANIACI GROUP INC
500 Silver Spur Rd # 121, Rllng HLS Est
(90275-3637)
PHONE....................310 541-4824
Daniel V Maniaci, *President*
Terisa Price, *President*
Karina Flores, *Vice Pres*
Stacy Johnson, *Office Mgr*
Don Imel, *Administration*
EMP: 54 **EST:** 1975
SQ FT: 1,300
SALES (est): 6MM **Privately Held**
WEB: www.maniaciinsurance.com
SIC: 6411 Insurance brokers

(P-15591)
MARKEL CORP
Also Called: Associated Intl Insur Co
21600 Oxnard St Ste 900, Woodland Hills
(91367-7834)
PHONE....................818 595-0600
Anthony Markel, *President*
Alan Kirshner, *Ch of Bd*
Andrew Barnard, *CEO*
Steven Markel, *Vice Ch Bd*
Kathleen Weldon, *Vice Pres*
EMP: 268 **EST:** 1972
SQ FT: 32,000
SALES (est): 9.5MM
SALES (corp-wide): 9.7B **Publicly Held**
WEB: www.markel.com
SIC: 6411 Insurance agents, brokers & service

HQ: Markel North America, Inc
4521 Highwoods Pkwy
Glen Allen VA 23060
804 747-0136

(P-15592)
MARSH RISK & INSURANCE SVCS
Also Called: MMC
633 W 5th St Ste 1200, Los Angeles
(90071-2095)
PHONE....................213 624-5555
Paul Gibbs, *Managing Dir*
Robert Finkelstein, *Senior VP*
Melody Schwartz, *Senior VP*
Susan Hedges, *Vice Pres*
Chris Hoshimiya, *Vice Pres*
EMP: 687 **EST:** 1883
SALES (est): 93.3MM
SALES (corp-wide): 17.2B **Publicly Held**
WEB: www.marshmclennan.com
SIC: 6411 Insurance brokers
PA: Marsh & Mclennan Companies, Inc.
1166 Ave Of The Americas
New York NY 10036
212 345-5000

(P-15593)
MC GRAW COMMERCIAL INSUR SVC
Also Called: McGraw Insurance Services
8185 E Kaiser Blvd, Anaheim
(92808-2214)
PHONE....................714 939-9875
Vivian Tafolla, *Principal*
EMP: 51
SALES (corp-wide): 7.9MM **Privately Held**
WEB: www.mcgrawpowersports.com
SIC: 6411 Insurance agents
PA: Mc Graw Commercial Insurance Service, Inc
3601 Haven Ave
Menlo Park CA 94025
650 780-4800

(P-15594)
MEDICAL EYE SERVICES INC
345 Baker St, Costa Mesa (92626-4518)
P.O. Box 25209, Santa Ana (92799-5209)
PHONE....................714 619-4660
Aspasia Shappet, *President*
Chuck Kupfer, *CFO*
Ric Piecuch, *Vice Pres*
Arvin Vinas, *Administration*
Libi Granda,
EMP: 91 **EST:** 1976
SQ FT: 12,000
SALES (est): 23.2MM **Privately Held**
WEB: www.mesvision.com
SIC: 6411 Insurance claim processing, except medical
PA: The Eye Care Network Of California Inc
345 Baker St
Costa Mesa CA 92626
714 619-4660

(P-15595)
MITCHELL BUCKMAN INC (PA)
Also Called: Kemper Insurance
500 N Santa Fe St, Visalia (93292-5065)
P.O. Box 629 (93279-0629)
PHONE....................559 733-1181
EMP: 80
SQ FT: 16,000
SALES (est): 50.1MM **Privately Held**
WEB: www.bminc.com
SIC: 6411 General Insurance Agency

(P-15596)
MOMENTOUS INSURANCE BRKG INC
5990 Sepulvda Blvd # 550, Van Nuys
(91411-2536)
PHONE....................818 933-2700
Diane Brinson Schiele, *President*
Erin Gaston, *Senior VP*
David Oliver, *Senior VP*
Susan Borders, *Vice Pres*
Susan Brien, *Vice Pres*
EMP: 72 **EST:** 2008
SALES (est): 18.7MM
SALES (corp-wide): 17.2B **Publicly Held**
WEB: www.momentousins.com
SIC: 6411 Insurance agents; insurance brokers

PA: Marsh & Mclennan Companies, Inc.
1166 Ave Of The Americas
New York NY 10036
212 345-5000

(P-15597)
MONY LIFE INSURANCE COMPANY
333 S Anita Dr Ste 750, Orange
(92868-3322)
PHONE....................714 939-6669
Joseph Moore, *Manager*
EMP: 51 **Privately Held**
WEB: www.protective.com
SIC: 6411 Insurance agents, brokers & service
HQ: Mony Life Insurance Company
1740 Broadway
New York NY 10019
800 487-6669

(P-15598)
MORGAN KLEPPE AND NASH LLC
Also Called: Mkni
501 N Church St, Visalia (93291-5004)
P.O. Box 1390 (93279-1390)
PHONE....................559 732-3436
Keith Kleppe, *Partner*
Gerry Folmer, *Partner*
EMP: 58 **EST:** 1943
SQ FT: 2,500
SALES (est): 22MM **Privately Held**
WEB: www.kemperhsc.com
SIC: 6411 Insurance agents

(P-15599)
MORRIS GRRITANO INSUR AGCY INC
Also Called: Nationwide
1122 Laurel Ln, San Luis Obispo
(93401-5895)
P.O. Box 1189 (93406-1189)
PHONE....................805 543-6887
Brendan Morris, *CEO*
David Morgan, *Shareholder*
Kelly Morgan, *Shareholder*
Kerry Pollock, *Shareholder*
John Pullock, *Shareholder*
EMP: 85 **EST:** 1916
SQ FT: 14,000
SALES (est): 22.7MM **Privately Held**
WEB: www.morrisgarritano.com
SIC: 6411 Insurance agents; insurance brokers

(P-15600)
NATIONAL INSURANCE CRIME BUR
15545 Devonshire St # 309, Mission Hills
(91345-2655)
PHONE....................818 895-2867
Bob Jones, *Director*
Fred Lohmann, *Opers Staff*
Fred Langley, *Agent*
EMP: 73
SALES (corp-wide): 59.5MM **Privately Held**
WEB: www.nicb.org
SIC: 6411 Insurance agents, brokers & service
PA: National Insurance Crime Bureau, Inc
1111 E Touhy Ave Ste 400
Des Plaines IL 60018
847 544-7000

(P-15601)
NDI (PA)
17106 Devonshire St, Northridge
(91325-1619)
PHONE....................818 368-5650
Nick Diamenti, *Owner*
Ande Villegas, *Instructor*
EMP: 62 **EST:** 2008
SALES (est): 1.1MM **Privately Held**
SIC: 6411 Insurance brokers

(P-15602)
NEW ALLIANCE INSURANCE BROKERS
3700 Santa Fe Ave Ste 300, Long Beach
(90810-2171)
PHONE....................424 205-6700
Marcello Povolo, *President*
Monica De La Cruz, *Office Mgr*

Jorge De La Cruz, *Agent*
EMP: 50 **EST:** 2004
SALES (est): 25MM **Privately Held**
WEB: www.newallianceins.com
SIC: 6411 Insurance agents

(P-15603)
NNA INSURANCE SERVICES LLC
9350 De Soto Ave, Chatsworth
(91311-4926)
P.O. Box 2402 (91313-2402)
PHONE....................818 739-4071
Milton G Valera, *Ch of Bd*
Thomas A Heymann, *CEO*
Robert A Clarke, *CFO*
Deborah M Thaw, *Exec VP*
Phillip Browne, *Vice Pres*
▲ **EMP:** 204 **EST:** 1957
SQ FT: 55,000
SALES (est): 8.1MM **Privately Held**
WEB: www.nationalnotary.org
SIC: 6411 Insurance agents, brokers & service

(P-15604)
OMEGA INSURANCE SERVICES
Also Called: Word and Brown
721 S Parker St Ste 300, Orange
(92868-4732)
PHONE....................714 973-0311
D P Thomas, *CEO*
Michael Close, *COO*
Paula Serios, *Chief Mktg Ofcr*
Polly Neves, *Exec VP*
David Duker, *Vice Pres*
EMP: 50 **EST:** 1971
SQ FT: 2,500
SALES (est): 17.3MM **Privately Held**
SIC: 6411 Insurance brokers

(P-15605)
PACIFIC COMPENSATION CORP (DH)
3011 Townsgate Rd Ste 120, Westlake Village (91361-5876)
PHONE....................602 631-2300
Marc E Schmittlein, *President*
Mark L Joos, *CFO*
Chris Closser, *Officer*
Denise K Richardson, *Finance*
Wayne Phillips, *Controller*
EMP: 69 **EST:** 2002
SALES (est): 170MM
SALES (corp-wide): 808.7MM **Privately Held**
WEB: www.copperpoint.com
SIC: 6411 Insurance agents

(P-15606)
PACIFIC COMPENSATION INSUR CO
3011 Townsgate Rd Ste 120, Westlake Village (91361-5876)
P.O. Box 5034, Thousand Oaks (91359-5034)
PHONE....................818 575-8500
Marc E Schmittlein, *President*
David Kuhn, *President*
Denise Richardson, *Vice Pres*
David Skaggs, *Vice Pres*
Teresa Smiley, *Vice Pres*
EMP: 150 **EST:** 2002
SALES (est): 48.2MM
SALES (corp-wide): 808.7MM **Privately Held**
WEB: www.copperpoint.com
SIC: 6411 Insurance agents
HQ: Pacific Compensation Corporation
3011 Townsgate Rd Ste 120
Westlake Village CA 91361

(P-15607)
PACIFIC INDEMNITY COMPANY
Also Called: Chubb
555 S Flower St Ste 300, Los Angeles
(90071-2427)
PHONE....................213 622-2334
John Fennigan, *President*
Chris Ford, *Assoc VP*
Mary Marshall, *Nurse*
Lenea Sawyer, *Nurse*
Alison Wooden, *Director*
EMP: 300 **EST:** 1926

SALES (est): 61.8MM
SALES (corp-wide): 34.1B **Privately Held**
WEB: www.chubb.com
SIC: **6411** 6331 6351 Property & casualty insurance agent; fire, marine & casualty insurance: mutual; surety insurance
HQ: Ina Chubb Holdings Inc
436 Walnut St
Philadelphia PA 19106
215 640-1000

(P-15608)
PACIFIC PIONEER INSUR GROUP (PA)
Also Called: Nationwide
6363 Katella Ave, Cypress (90630-5205)
PHONE...................714 228-7888
Lin W Lan, *Founder*
Frank Stipati, *Vice Pres*
Sherri Carlson, *Branch Mgr*
Lori Carlberg, *Executive Asst*
Sonia Morris, *Assistant*
EMP: 80 EST: 1989
SQ FT: 32,000
SALES (est): 8.7MM **Privately Held**
WEB: www.pacificexcess.com
SIC: **6411** Insurance agents

(P-15609)
PACIFIC SPECIALTY INSURANCE CO
5515 E La Palma Ave # 150, Anaheim (92807-2130)
P.O. Box 40 (92815-0040)
PHONE...................800 303-5000
Timothy Summers, *CEO*
John Mc Graw, *Shareholder*
Ann Mc Graw-Morrical, *Shareholder*
John Chu, *President*
Mike Graw, *President*
EMP: 50 EST: 1990
SQ FT: 20,000
SALES (est): 33.9MM **Privately Held**
WEB: www.pacificspecialty.com
SIC: **6411** Insurance agents
PA: Western Service Contract Corp.
2200 Geng Rd Ste 200
Palo Alto CA 94303

(P-15610)
PARADIGM 360 INC ✪
Also Called: Paradigm 360 Insur Fincl Svcs
41593 Winchester Rd # 200, Temecula (92590-4860)
PHONE...................951 638-9917
Juan Gonzalez, *CEO*
Lorena Rodriguez, *Principal*
Demeytric Weathersby, *Principal*
EMP: 50 EST: 2021
SALES (est): 1.7MM **Privately Held**
SIC: **6411** Insurance agents, brokers & service

(P-15611)
PENSION GROUP INC
23046 Avnida De La Crltlo Carlotalota, Laguna Hills (92653)
P.O. Box 2024 W 48t, Los Angeles (90062)
PHONE...................949 768-4015
Peter R Stephan, *President*
James R Norman Jr, *Vice Pres*
EMP: 54 EST: 1984
SQ FT: 4,600
SALES (est): 1MM
SALES (corp-wide): 547.9MM **Privately Held**
WEB: www.futureplan.com
SIC: **6411** Pension & retirement plan consultants
HQ: United Retirement Plan Consultants, Inc.
545 Metro Pl S Ste 240
Dublin OH 43017

(P-15612)
PERR & KNIGHT INC (PA)
401 Wilshire Blvd Ste 300, Santa Monica (90401-1454)
PHONE...................310 230-9339
Timothy B Perr, *CEO*
Neresa Torres, *Analyst*
EMP: 72 EST: 1995
SQ FT: 10,098

SALES (est): 15.1MM **Privately Held**
WEB: www.perrknight.com
SIC: **6411** Loss prevention services, insurance

(P-15613)
PETRA RISK SOLUTIONS (PA)
Also Called: Nationwide
13950 Cerritos Corprt Dr A, Cerritos (90703-2468)
PHONE...................800 466-8951
Doug Douthit, *Principal*
Darren Richardson, *Vice Pres*
Veronique Collin, *Executive*
Amie Patel, *Executive*
Ron Derrico, *Broker*
EMP: 56 EST: 2007
SALES (est): 11.2MM **Privately Held**
WEB: www.petrarisksolutions.com
SIC: **6411** Insurance brokers

(P-15614)
POLISEEK AIS INSUR SLTIONS INC
Also Called: Nationwide
17785 Center Court Dr N # 25, Cerritos (90703-8573)
PHONE...................866 480-7335
Mark Ribisi, *President*
Chris Bremer, *CFO*
Lani Elkin, *VP Opers*
Romayne Levee, *VP Mktg*
Mark Casas, *VP Sales*
EMP: 85 EST: 2008
SALES (est): 2.5MM
SALES (corp-wide): 3.7B **Publicly Held**
WEB: www.nationwide.com
SIC: **6411** Insurance agents, brokers & service
HQ: Ais Management, Llc
17785 Center Court Dr N # 250
Cerritos CA 90703

(P-15615)
PRECEPT INC (DH)
Also Called: Precept Group The
130 Theory Ste 200, Irvine (92617-3065)
PHONE...................949 955-1430
Wade R Olson, *President*
Steve Williams, *President*
Steve Zarate, *COO*
Christopher H Coulter, *Chief Mktg Ofcr*
Karen Reid, *Officer*
EMP: 90 EST: 1987
SQ FT: 32,000
SALES (est): 52.2MM
SALES (corp-wide): 24.4B **Publicly Held**
WEB: www.bbt.com
SIC: **6411** Insurance brokers
HQ: Mcgriff Insurance Services, Inc.
3201 Beechleaf Ct Ste 200
Raleigh NC 27604
919 716-9907

(P-15616)
PRESTIGE INTERNATIONAL USA INC (HQ)
Also Called: Premio
19800 Macarthur Blvd # 400, Irvine (92612-2431)
PHONE...................949 870-1640
Mikako Nitsumnso, *President*
Tuan Vu, *Technology*
Yuri Imamura, *Marketing Mgr*
Shinichi Tamagami, *Director*
EMP: 61 EST: 1989
SALES (est): 20.3MM **Privately Held**
WEB: www.premio.com
SIC: **6411** Insurance agents, brokers & service

(P-15617)
PROPERTYPLUS INSUR AGCY INC
21820 Burbank Blvd # 130, Woodland Hills (91367-6443)
PHONE...................818 432-2640
EMP: 283 EST: 2015
SALES (est): 3.9MM
SALES (corp-wide): 42.6B **Publicly Held**
WEB: www.propertyplusins.com
SIC: **6411** Real estate insurance agents

HQ: Arx Holding Corp.
1 Asi Way N
Saint Petersburg FL 33702
727 821-8765

(P-15618)
PROSIGHT SPECLTY INSUR GRP INC
101 N Brand Blvd Ste 1900, Glendale (91203-2634)
PHONE...................818 230-8200
Andrea Godoy, *Assistant*
Joel Judson, *Assistant*
Sofia Mejia, *Assistant*
EMP: 59
SALES (corp-wide): 816.1MM **Privately Held**
WEB: www.prosightspecialty.com
SIC: **6411** Insurance brokers
HQ: Prosight Specialty Insurance Group, Inc.
412 Mount Kemble Ave 300c
Morristown NJ 07960

(P-15619)
PRUDENTIAL INSUR CO OF AMER
5990 Sepulvda Blvd # 300, Van Nuys (91411-2500)
PHONE...................818 901-0028
EMP: 60
SALES (corp-wide): 41.4B **Publicly Held**
SIC: **6411** Insurance Agent
HQ: The Prudential Insurance Company Of America
751 Broad St
Newark NJ 07102
973 802-6000

(P-15620)
R MC CLOSKEY INSURANCE AGENCY
Also Called: Tax and Financial Group
4001 Macarthur Blvd # 300, Newport Beach (92660-2505)
PHONE...................949 223-8100
Richard Mc Closkey, *President*
Brian McNulty, *Managing Prtnr*
Brian Freeman, *Vice Pres*
Christine Bond, *Executive*
Paul Salerno, *CTO*
EMP: 120 EST: 1969
SQ FT: 15,000
SALES (est): 19.9MM **Privately Held**
SIC: **6411** Insurance agents; life insurance agents

(P-15621)
RAMKADE INSURANCE SERVICES
Also Called: Time Financial Services
21550 Oxnard St Ste 500, Woodland Hills (91367-7111)
PHONE...................818 444-1340
Kate Kinkade, *President*
Patrick Ramsey, *Vice Pres*
EMP: 2007 EST: 1978
SALES (est): 28.7MM
SALES (corp-wide): 88.8B **Publicly Held**
WEB: www.citigroup.com
SIC: **6411** Insurance agents
HQ: Citi Investor Services, Inc.
105 Eisenhower Pkwy Ste 2
Roseland NJ 07068

(P-15622)
ROBERT MORENO INSURANCE SVCS
3110 E Guasti Rd Ste 500, Ontario (91761-1228)
PHONE...................714 578-3318
Robert B Moreno, *Owner*
Laura Moreno, *COO*
Robert Moreno, *Executive*
Oscar Baeza, *Manager*
Bobby Moreno, *Manager*
EMP: 140 EST: 1978
SALES (est): 20.4MM **Privately Held**
WEB: www.rmis.informins.com
SIC: **6411** Insurance agents

(P-15623)
RSI INSURANCE BROKERS INC (DH)
4000 Westerly Pl Ste 110, Newport Beach (92660-2347)
PHONE...................714 546-6616
Barry Rabune, *President*
Ben Thomas, *Vice Pres*
Linda Miller, *Manager*
Aaron Fawcett, *Agent*
EMP: 50 EST: 1989
SALES (est): 22.4MM
SALES (corp-wide): 524MM **Privately Held**
WEB: www.rsiinsurancebrokers.com
SIC: **6411** Insurance brokers
HQ: Acrisure, Llc
100 Ottawa Ave Sw
Grand Rapids MI 49503
800 748-0351

(P-15624)
SAFECO INSURANCE COMPANY AMER
330 N Brand Blvd Ste 680, Glendale (91203-2385)
PHONE...................818 956-4250
Don Chambers, *Manager*
EMP: 108
SALES (corp-wide): 20.6B **Privately Held**
WEB: www.safeco.com
SIC: **6411** Insurance agents
HQ: Safeco Insurance Company Of America
1001 4th Ave Ste 800
Seattle WA 98185
206 545-5000

(P-15625)
SCOTTISH AMERICAN INSURANCE (PA)
Also Called: Yates & Associates
2002 E Mcfadden Ave # 100, Santa Ana (92705-4766)
PHONE...................714 550-5050
Paul A Thomson, *CEO*
Carl Ledbetter, *President*
James M Yates, *President*
Justin Clayton, *Asst Broker*
Delia Ponce, *Opers Spvr*
EMP: 57 EST: 1986
SQ FT: 14,300
SALES (est): 24.6MM **Privately Held**
WEB: www.scottishamerican.com
SIC: **6411** Insurance brokers

(P-15626)
SEDGWICK CLAIMS MGT SVCS INC
3230 E Imperial Hwy, Brea (92821-6721)
PHONE...................714 572-1207
EMP: 66 **Privately Held**
WEB: www.sedgwick.com
SIC: **6411** Insurance claim adjusters, not employed by insurance company
HQ: Sedgwick Claims Management Services, Inc.
8125 Sedgwick Way
Memphis TN 38125
901 415-7400

(P-15627)
SEDGWICK CLAIMS MGT SVCS INC
24025 Park Sorrento # 200, Calabasas (91302-4018)
P.O. Box 9830 (91372-0830)
PHONE...................818 591-9444
John Gernert, *Manager*
Shawn Johnson, *Vice Pres*
Cheryl Powers, *Vice Pres*
Jeff Loeffelman, *Business Dir*
Jenni Stange, *Administration*
EMP: 66 **Privately Held**
WEB: www.sedgwick.com
SIC: **6411** Insurance claim adjusters, not employed by insurance company
HQ: Sedgwick Claims Management Services, Inc.
8125 Sedgwick Way
Memphis TN 38125
901 415-7400

(P-15628)

SIGNATURE RSRCES INSUR FNCL SV

Also Called: John Hancock
19900 Macarthur Blvd, Irvine (92612-2445)
PHONE....................949 930-2400
Gary Kaltenbach, *Owner*
Jeff Kaltenbach, *Managing Prtnr*
Nick Ewen, *Managing Dir*
Nina Manning, *Office Mgr*
Elaine Hallman, *Admin Asst*
EMP: 86 **EST:** 1983
SQ FT: 1,800
SALES (est): 6.4MM **Privately Held**
WEB: www.srcmadvisors.com
SIC: 6411 Insurance agents & brokers

(P-15629)

SPECIALTY RISK SERVICES INC

1 Pointe Dr Ste 220, Brea (92821-7631)
P.O. Box 7007, La Habra (90632-7007)
PHONE....................714 674-1000
Sharon Bartholomew, *Principal*
EMP: 97 **Privately Held**
SIC: 6411 Insurance agents, brokers & service
HQ: Specialty Risk Services, Inc.
100 Corporate Dr Ste 211
Windsor CT 06095

(P-15630)

STATE FARM MUTL AUTO INSUR CO

Also Called: State Farm Insurance
900 Old River Rd 400, Bakersfield (93311-9501)
PHONE....................309 766-2311
EMP: 72
SALES (corp-wide): 39.5B **Privately Held**
SIC: 6411 Ins Agnts And Brkrs
PA: State Farm Mutual Automobile Insurance Company
1 State Farm Plz
Bloomington IL 61710
309 766-2311

(P-15631)

SURECO HLTH LF INSUR AGCY INC

201 Sandpointe Ave # 600, Santa Ana (92707-5778)
PHONE....................949 333-0263
Marc Steven Bablot, *CEO*
Donald Nosek, *Chief Mktg Ofcr*
Raymond Lin, *Business Anlyst*
Harrison Kim, *Broker*
Julianne Towle, *Broker*
EMP: 75 **EST:** 2016
SALES (est): 9.4MM **Privately Held**
WEB: www.sureco.com
SIC: 6411 7379 7311 Insurance agents, brokers & service; insurance agents; ; advertising agencies

(P-15632)

SYNCIS INSURANCE SOLUTIONS INC (PA)

301 E Ocean Blvd Ste 1170, Long Beach (90802-8818)
PHONE....................424 233-1764
Les B Schlais, *CEO*
Susan Kim, *Vice Pres*
John Kim, *Principal*
Nadia Habibi, *Director*
Farah Hashemi, *Director*
EMP: 109 **EST:** 2009
SALES (est): 11.8MM **Privately Held**
WEB: www.syncis.com
SIC: 6411 7389 Insurance agents, brokers & service; financial services

(P-15633)

TBG INSURANCE SERVICES CORP

100 N Pacific Coast Hwy # 500, El Segundo (90245-5658)
PHONE....................310 203-8770
Michael R Shute, *CEO*
Michael Glickman, *CFO*
EMP: 102 **EST:** 1983

SALES (est): 10.8MM
SALES (corp-wide): 57B **Publicly Held**
WEB: www.prudential.com
SIC: 6411 8111 Insurance agents, brokers & service; legal services
PA: Prudential Financial, Inc.
751 Broad St
Newark NJ 07102
973 802-6000

(P-15634)

THI HOLDINGS (DELAWARE) INC

2140 E Palmdale Blvd O, Palmdale (93550-1202)
PHONE....................661 266-7423
Lewis Pelser, *Manager*
EMP: 401
SALES (corp-wide): 17.6B **Privately Held**
SIC: 6411 Insurance agents
HQ: Thi Holdings (Delaware), Inc.
5915 Landerbrook Dr
Cleveland OH 44124

(P-15635)

TM CLAIMS SERVICE INC

Also Called: Tokio Marine Michido
800 E Colorado Blvd, Pasadena (91101-2103)
P.O. Box 7216 (91109-7316)
PHONE....................626 568-7800
Tommy Hasegawa, *Manager*
EMP: 96 **Privately Held**
WEB: www.tmamerica.com
SIC: 6411 Insurance brokers
HQ: Tm Claims Service, Inc.
499 Wshngton Blvd Ste 150
Jersey City NJ 07310

(P-15636)

TOPA INSURANCE COMPANY (HQ)

1800 Avenue Of The Stars # 1200, Los Angeles (90067-4200)
PHONE....................310 201-0451
John E Anderson, *Ch of Bd*
Noshirwan Marfatia, *President*
Dan Sherrin, *CFO*
Harry W Degner, *Vice Ch Bd*
Olive Chang, *Vice Pres*
EMP: 79 **EST:** 1979
SALES (est): 24.3MM
SALES (corp-wide): 446.1MM **Privately Held**
WEB: www.topains.com
SIC: 6411 Insurance agents
PA: Topa Equities, Ltd.
1800 Avenue Of The Stars # 1400
Los Angeles CA 90067
310 203-9199

(P-15637)

TOTAL FINCL & INSUR SVCS INC

300 Crprate Pinte Ste 250, Culver City (90230)
PHONE....................310 477-7500
Diana Greenberg, *President*
Kimberly Fleming, *Vice Pres*
Lisa Greenberg, *Vice Pres*
Mark Bugli, *CIO*
Joseph Tanner, *IT/INT Sup*
EMP: 67 **EST:** 1974
SALES (est): 14.3MM **Privately Held**
WEB: www.totalfinancial.com
SIC: 6411 Life insurance agents

(P-15638)

TRG INSURANCE SERVICES

Also Called: The Rule Group
3620 Birch St Ste 100, Newport Beach (92660-2653)
PHONE....................949 474-1550
Kent Crawford, *President*
EMP: 82 **EST:** 1983
SALES (est): 1.4MM **Privately Held**
WEB: www.tysers.com
SIC: 6411 Insurance brokers
HQ: Integro Usa Inc.
1 State St Fl 9
New York NY 10004
212 295-8000

(P-15639)

UNITED AGENCIES INC (PA)

Also Called: Nationwide
301 E Colo Blvd Ste 200, Pasadena (91101)
P.O. Box 7139 (91109-7139)
PHONE....................818 952-8818
Thomas Hays, *Ch of Bd*
Gary Conkey, *President*
Karen Bader, *CFO*
Robert W Bader, *Vice Pres*
James Behtash, *Vice Pres*
EMP: 66 **EST:** 1962
SQ FT: 5,900
SALES (est): 24.3MM **Privately Held**
WEB: www.unitedagencies.com
SIC: 6411 Insurance agents; insurance brokers

(P-15640)

UNITED CHINESE AMERICAN GENERA (PA)

Also Called: Uca General Insurance
6363 Katella Ave, Cypress (90630-5205)
PHONE....................714 228-7800
Robert Lan, *President*
Lin Lan, *Shareholder*
Ping Chen, *Corp Secy*
EMP: 50 **EST:** 1984
SQ FT: 20,000
SALES (est): 5.6MM **Privately Held**
SIC: 6411 Insurance agents

(P-15641)

UNITED STATES FIRE INSUR CO

Also Called: Crum & Forster
777 S Figueroa St # 1500, Los Angeles (90017-5800)
PHONE....................213 797-3100
Mark Owens, *Manager*
Amy Nicholl, *Credit Staff*
Jeannie Ballman, *Manager*
Mark Orlow, *Manager*
Julie Kelpien, *Assistant VP*
EMP: 60
SALES (corp-wide): 19.7B **Privately Held**
WEB: www.cfins.com
SIC: 6411 Insurance agents
HQ: United States Fire Insurance Company
305 Madison Ave
Morristown NJ 07960
973 490-6600

(P-15642)

VALLEY INSURANCE SERVICE INC (HQ)

4695 Macarthur Ct Ste 600, Newport Beach (92660-1861)
PHONE....................626 966-3664
Chris Utterback, *CEO*
Dennis Monahan, *Vice Pres*
EMP: 62 **EST:** 1940
SALES (est): 19.1MM
SALES (corp-wide): 306.1MM **Privately Held**
WEB: www.leavitt.com
SIC: 6411 Insurance agents
PA: Leavitt Group Enterprises Inc
216 S 200 W
Cedar City UT 84720
435 586-6553

(P-15643)

VALLEY INSURANCE SERVICE INC

Also Called: Brower Hale
23181 Verdugo Dr Ste 100b, Laguna Hills (92653-1313)
PHONE....................949 707-4080
Debbie Hale, *Manager*
EMP: 454
SALES (corp-wide): 306.1MM **Privately Held**
SIC: 6411 Insurance agents, brokers & service
HQ: Valley Insurance Service, Inc.
4695 Macarthur Ct Ste 600
Newport Beach CA 92660
626 966-3664

(P-15644)

VALUEOPTIONS OF CALIFORNIA

Also Called: Value Options-V B H
5665 Plaza Dr Ste 400, Cypress (90630-5037)
PHONE....................800 228-1286
Juan Molina, *VP Opers*
Steve Rockowitz, *Ch of Bd*
Jolene Myrter, *CFO*
EMP: 225 **EST:** 1989
SALES (est): 464.1K
SALES (corp-wide): 482.1MM **Privately Held**
WEB: www.s18637.p536.sites.pressdns.com
SIC: 6411 6321 Insurance agents; accident & health insurance
PA: Fhc Health Systems, Inc
240 Corporate Blvd # 212
Norfolk VA 23502
757 459-5100

(P-15645)

VERN FONK INSURANCE SVCS INC (DH)

7711 Center Ave Ste 200, Huntington Beach (92647-9124)
PHONE....................714 252-2500
Robert Thielke, *President*
Craig Rexroat, *COO*
EMP: 62 **EST:** 1952
SQ FT: 3,000
SALES (est): 14.1MM
SALES (corp-wide): 1.1B **Privately Held**
WEB: www.vernfonk.com
SIC: 6411 Insurance agents

(P-15646)

VERONICAS AUTO INSUR SVCS INC (PA)

290 W Orange Show Rd # 1, San Bernardino (92408-3349)
PHONE....................909 723-1910
Veronica Gallardo, *President*
EMP: 78 **EST:** 2007
SALES (est): 15.2MM **Privately Held**
WEB: www.gmacinsurance.com
SIC: 6411 Insurance brokers

(P-15647)

WARNER PACIFIC INSUR SVCS INC (PA)

32110 Agoura Rd, Westlake Village (91361-4026)
PHONE....................408 298-4049
John H Nelson, *CEO*
Debbie Adrian, *Vice Pres*
David Nelson, *Vice Pres*
David Aragon, *Graphic Designe*
Marybeth Hernandez, *Analyst*
EMP: 125 **EST:** 1984
SQ FT: 10,000
SALES (est): 65.9MM **Privately Held**
WEB: www.warnerpacific.com
SIC: 6411 Insurance agents

(P-15648)

WEST COVINA FOSTER FAMILY AGCY

Also Called: HOMES OF HOPE
1107 S Glendora Ave, West Covina (91790-4923)
PHONE....................626 814-9085
Sukhwinder Singh, *Exec Dir*
Emmanuel Azariah, *President*
EMP: 70 **EST:** 1994
SALES (est): 3.5MM **Privately Held**
WEB: www.westcovina.org
SIC: 6411 Insurance agents, brokers & service

(P-15649)

WESTWOOD INSURANCE AGENCY (DH)

8407 Fllbrook Ave Ste 200, Canoga Park (91304)
PHONE....................818 990-9715
John Flynn, *President*
Tom Kriby, *Vice Pres*
Mark Nettleton, *Vice Pres*
Ben Sokoll, *Vice Pres*
EMP: 89 **EST:** 1952
SQ FT: 17,765

(PA)=Parent Co (HQ)=Headquarters (DH)=Div Headquarters
✪ = New Business established in last 2 years

SALES (est): 9.2MM **Publicly Held**
WEB: www.westwoodinsurance.com
SIC: 6411 Insurance agents

(P-15650)
WINDSOR INSURANCE ASSOC INC
21820 Burbank Blvd # 100, Woodland Hills (91367-6476)
PHONE...................818 710-9890
Mark Schwartz, *President*
Hal Brooks, *CEO*
Terry Ertl, *CFO*
Paula Knighten, *Vice Pres*
Lisa Koonce, *CIO*
EMP: 50 EST: 1976
SQ FT: 3,300
SALES (est): 7.7MM **Privately Held**
WEB: www.windsorinsurance.com
SIC: 6411 Insurance brokers

(P-15651)
WOOD GUTMANN BOGART INSUR BRKG
Also Called: Nationwide
15901 Red Hill Ave # 100, Tustin (92780-7318)
PHONE...................714 505-7000
Kevin S Bogart, *CEO*
Lupe Erwin, *Exec VP*
Bill Holdren, *Exec VP*
Eric Schroeder, *Exec VP*
John Balian, *Vice Pres*
EMP: 93 EST: 1984
SALES (est): 28.7MM **Privately Held**
WEB: www.wgbib.com
SIC: 6411 Insurance agents

(P-15652)
WORLDWIDE HOLDINGS INC (PA)
725 S Figueroa St # 1900, Los Angeles (90017-5496)
PHONE...................213 236-4500
Donald R Davis, *Chairman*
Davis D Moore, *President*
Daniel Colacurcio, *Exec VP*
Todd Pollock, *Senior VP*
Paula Cobbett, *Vice Pres*
EMP: 85 EST: 1970
SQ FT: 23,000
SALES (est): 45.2MM **Privately Held**
WEB: www.marketing.wwfi.com
SIC: 6411 Insurance brokers

(P-15653)
WORXSITEHR INSUR SOLUTIONS INC
5000 Parkway Calabasas # 302, Calabasas (91302-1400)
PHONE...................877 479-3591
EMP: 60
SQ FT: 2,500
SALES (est): 4.7MM **Privately Held**
SIC: 6411 7371 Insurance Agent/Broker Custom Computer Programing

(P-15654)
ZNAT INSURANCE COMPANY
21255 Califa St, Woodland Hills (91367-5021)
PHONE...................818 713-1000
Stanley Zax, *President*
EMP: 199 EST: 1990
SALES (est): 4.9MM
SALES (corp-wide): 19.7B **Privately Held**
WEB: www.thezenith.com
SIC: 6411 Insurance agents & brokers
HQ: Zenith Insurance Company
21255 Califa St
Woodland Hills CA 91367
818 713-1000

6512 Operators Of Nonresidential Bldgs

(P-15655)
6500 HLLISTER AVE PARTNERS LLC
6500 Hollister Ave, Goleta (93117-3011)
PHONE...................805 722-1362
Rob Ramirez, *Manager*
EMP: 100 EST: 2014

SALES (est): 5.2MM **Privately Held**
SIC: 6512 Commercial & industrial building operation

(P-15656)
ABBEY-PROPERTIES LLC (PA)
12447 Lewis St Ste 203, Garden Grove (92840-6601)
PHONE...................562 435-2100
Donald G Abbey,
Wendelyn Walker, *Property Mgr*
Sean Murray, *Manager*
▲ EMP: 75 EST: 1989
SQ FT: 276,000
SALES (est): 14.4MM **Privately Held**
SIC: 6512 Commercial & industrial building operation

(P-15657)
ALLIANCE RESIDENTIAL LLC
Also Called: Royal Equestrian Apartments
1200 W Riverside Dr Ofc, Burbank (91506-3113)
PHONE...................818 841-2441
David Page, *Branch Mgr*
Christon Greene, *Business Mgr*
Aaron Rose, *Business Mgr*
Natasha Vargas, *Opers Staff*
Marco Vakili, *Director*
EMP: 111
SALES (corp-wide): 192.7MM **Privately Held**
WEB: www.allresco.com
SIC: 6512 Commercial & industrial building operation
PA: Alliance Residential, Llc
2525 E Camelback Rd # 500
Phoenix AZ 85016
602 778-2800

(P-15658)
ALPINE VILLAGE
Also Called: Alpine Inn Restaurant
833 Torrance Blvd Ste 1a, Torrance (90502-1733)
PHONE...................310 327-4384
Ursula Wilson, *CEO*
EMP: 250 EST: 1968
SALES (est): 14.8MM **Privately Held**
WEB: www.alpinevillagecenter.com
SIC: 6512 Commercial & industrial building operation

(P-15659)
ANTON PAAR USA INC
2824 Columbia St, Torrance (90503-3808)
PHONE...................310 775-2196
EMP: 50
SALES (corp-wide): 452.3MM **Privately Held**
WEB: www.anton-paar.com
SIC: 6512 Commercial & industrial building operation
HQ: Anton Paar Usa, Inc.
10215 Timber Ridge Dr
Ashland VA 23005
804 550-1051

(P-15660)
APPLIED COMPANIES RE LLC
28020 Avenue Stanford, Valencia (91355-1105)
P.O. Box 802078, Santa Clarita (91380-2078)
PHONE...................661 257-0090
Mary Elizabeth Klinger, *CEO*
Joseph Klinger, *Vice Pres*
EMP: 50 EST: 1998
SALES (est): 3.4MM **Privately Held**
WEB: www.appliedcompanies.net
SIC: 6512 Nonresidential building operators

(P-15661)
BH CENTRO INTERNACIONAL LLC
11111 Santa Monica Blvd, Los Angeles (90025-3333)
P.O. Box 49993 (90049-0993)
PHONE...................310 820-8888
Luz Marquez,
Elahe Pezeshki,
EMP: 53 EST: 2017
SALES (est): 1.9MM **Privately Held**
SIC: 6512 Nonresidential building operators

(P-15662)
CB RICHARD ELLIS STRGC PRTNERS
515 S Flower St, Los Angeles (90071-2201)
PHONE...................213 683-4200
Richard Ellis,
EMP: 100 EST: 2000
SALES (est): 15.4MM **Publicly Held**
WEB: www.cbre.us
SIC: 6512 Nonresidential building operators
PA: Cbre Group, Inc.
2100 Mckinney Ave Fl 12
Dallas TX 75201

(P-15663)
CRMLS INC
15325 Frfeld Rnch Rd Ste, Chino Hills (91709)
PHONE...................909 859-2040
Art Carter, *CEO*
Adrese Roundree, *COO*
Ray Ewing, *Officer*
Edward Zorn, *Vice Pres*
Mark Bessett, *CTO*
EMP: 106 EST: 2019
SALES (est): 6.5MM **Privately Held**
WEB: www.go.crmls.org
SIC: 6512 Nonresidential building operators

(P-15664)
DESERT HOT SPRNG REAL PRPTS IN
Also Called: Desert Hot Springs Spa Hotel
10805 Palm Dr, Desert Hot Springs (92240-2511)
PHONE...................760 329-6000
Lynn Byrnes, *CEO*
Abel Silva, *Purch Agent*
EMP: 85 EST: 1988
SQ FT: 44,070
SALES (est): 4.6MM **Privately Held**
WEB: www.dhsspa.com
SIC: 6512 Nonresidential building operators

(P-15665)
DONAHUE SCHRIBER RLTY GROUP LP (PA)
Also Called: Ds Lakeshore LP
200 Baker St Ste 100, Costa Mesa (92626-4551)
PHONE...................714 545-1400
Patrick S Donahue, *CEO*
Lawrence P Casey, *President*
Lisa L Hirose, *Exec VP*
Mark L Whitfield, *Exec VP*
Kathryn Yoshimura, *Info Tech Mgr*
EMP: 100 EST: 1969
SQ FT: 44,805
SALES (est): 32.1MM **Privately Held**
WEB: www.donahueschriber.com
SIC: 6512 Shopping center, property operation only

(P-15666)
ENTREPRENEURIAL CAPITAL CORP
4100 Nwport Pl Dr Ste 400, Newport Beach (92660)
PHONE...................949 809-3900
John K Abel, *Principal*
EMP: 240
SALES (corp-wide): 33.2MM **Privately Held**
WEB: www.missionpacific.com
SIC: 6512 Commercial & industrial building operation
PA: Entrepreneurial Capital Corporation
4100 Newport Place Dr # 400
Newport Beach CA 92660
949 809-3900

(P-15667)
FORD MOTOR LAND DEV CORP
3 Glen Bell Way Ste 100, Irvine (92618-3390)
PHONE...................949 242-6606
Dan Werbin, *Exec Dir*
Tony Varlesi, *Technology*
EMP: 345

SALES (corp-wide): 127.1B **Publicly Held**
WEB: www.fordland.com
SIC: 6512 Commercial & industrial building operation
HQ: Ford Motor Land Development Corporation
330 Town Center Dr # 1100
Dearborn MI 48126
313 323-3100

(P-15668)
FREEDOM PROPERTIES-HEMET LLC
Also Called: Village The
27122 Paseo Espada Ste 1b, San Juan Capistrano (92675-5706)
PHONE...................949 489-0430
Cheryl L Roskamp, *Mng Member*
Ms Cheryl L Roskamp, *Mng Member*
EMP: 250 EST: 1999
SALES (est): 6.9MM **Privately Held**
SIC: 6512 Nonresidential building operators

(P-15669)
GEHR HOSPITALITY NEW YORK LLC (DH)
Also Called: Gehr Development New York LLC
7400 E Slauson Ave, Commerce (90040-3308)
PHONE...................323 728-5558
David Lifschitz, *President*
Mark Goldman, *COO*
EMP: 62 EST: 2006
SALES (est): 32.4MM
SALES (corp-wide): 166.1MM **Privately Held**
WEB: www.gehr.com
SIC: 6512 6513 Nonresidential building operators; apartment building operators
HQ: Gehr Hospitality Llc
1999 Avenue Of The Stars
Los Angeles CA 90067
323 728-5558

(P-15670)
GLENDALE ASSOCIATES LTD
Also Called: Apple Store Glendale Galleria
100 W Broadway Ste 100 # 100, Glendale (91210-1230)
PHONE...................818 246-6737
Knickerbocker Properties, *Partner*
EMP: 100 EST: 1976
SALES (est): 7.9MM **Privately Held**
WEB: www.glendalegalleria.com
SIC: 6512 Shopping center, property operation only

(P-15671)
GUMBINER SAVETT NC
Also Called: Gumbiner Svett Finkel Fnglson R
1723 Cloverfield Blvd, Santa Monica (90404-4017)
PHONE...................310 828-9798
Louis Savett, *Ch of Bd*
Charles Gumbiner, *President*
Gary Finkel, *Exec VP*
Rodney Fingleson, *Vice Pres*
David Rose, *Vice Pres*
EMP: 90
SQ FT: 25,000
SALES (est): 10.4MM **Privately Held**
WEB: www.gscpa.com
SIC: 6512 Nonresidential building operators

(P-15672)
HAILWOOD INC
Also Called: Chase Bros Dairy
5755 Valentine Rd Ste 2C3, Ventura (93003-7460)
P.O. Box 1272, Oxnard (93032-1272)
PHONE...................805 487-4981
Glywn S Chase Jr, *President*
Miriam Wille, *Corp Secy*
H M Chase, *Vice Pres*
EMP: 14 EST: 1927
SQ FT: 1,600,000
SALES (est): 1.2MM **Privately Held**
WEB: www.chasebrosdairy.com
SIC: 6512 5143 5451 2024 Commercial & industrial building operation; dairy products, except dried or canned; dairy products stores; ice cream & frozen desserts

▲ = Import ▼=Export
◆ =Import/Export

(P-15673)
INSIGNIA/ESG HT PARTNERS INC (DH)
11150 Santa Monica Blvd # 220, Los Angeles (90025-3380)
PHONE.................................310 765-2600
Mary Ann Tighe, *CEO*
John Powers, *President*
EMP: 325 EST: 1993
SALES (est): 211.5MM **Publicly Held**
SIC: 6512 Property operation, retail establishment
HQ: Cb Richard Ellis Real Estate Services, Llc
200 Park Ave Fl 19
New York NY 10166
212 984-8000

(P-15674)
INTERNTNL CH OF FRSQARE GOSPL (PA)
Also Called: Foursquare International
1910 W Sunset Blvd, Los Angeles (90026-3275)
P.O. Box 26902 (90026-0176)
PHONE.................................213 989-4234
Glenn C Burris Jr, *President*
Ron Thigpenn, *CFO*
Brent Morgan, *Treasurer*
Sterling Brackett, *Vice Pres*
Tammy Dunahoo, *Vice Pres*
▲ EMP: 100
SQ FT: 110,000
SALES (est): 175.9MM **Privately Held**
WEB: www.foursquare.org
SIC: 8661 6512 7032 8211 Miscellaneous denomination church; nonresidential building operators; sporting & recreational camps; elementary & secondary schools; colleges universities & professional schools; business associations

(P-15675)
INVITATION HOMES INC
465 N Halstead St Ste 150, Pasadena (91107-6017)
PHONE.................................805 372-2900
Luke Kochniuk, *Branch Mgr*
Eddie Quezada, *Maintence Staff*
EMP: 80
SALES (corp-wide): 1.8B **Publicly Held**
WEB: www.invitationhomes.com
SIC: 6512 Nonresidential building operators
PA: Invitation Homes Inc.
1717 Main St Ste 2000
Dallas TX 75201
972 421-3600

(P-15676)
LOS ANGELES CONVEN AND EXH
Also Called: Los Angeles Dept Convetion Tou
1201 S Figueroa St, Los Angeles (90015-1308)
PHONE.................................213 741-1151
Brad Gessner, *General Mgr*
Annie Bebber, *President*
Ben Zarhoud, *Vice Pres*
Thomas Drew, *Manager*
Richard Serna, *Manager*
EMP: 288 EST: 1968
SQ FT: 867,000
SALES (est): 21.5MM **Privately Held**
WEB: www.lacclink.com
SIC: 6512 Commercial & industrial building operation; property operation, auditoriums & theaters

(P-15677)
MALIBU CONFERENCE CENTER INC
327 Latigo Canyon Rd, Malibu (90265-2708)
PHONE.................................818 889-6440
Glen Gerson, *President*
EMP: 500 EST: 1985
SALES (est): 29.6MM **Privately Held**
WEB: www.calamigos.com
SIC: 6512 Commercial & industrial building operation

(P-15678)
MILLS CORPORATION
Also Called: Ontario Mills Shopping Center
1 Mills Cir Ste 1 # 1, Ontario (91764-5215)
PHONE.................................909 484-8300
Laurence Siegel, *Branch Mgr*
EMP: 57 **Privately Held**
WEB: www.themill.com
SIC: 6512 Shopping center, property operation only
HQ: The Mills Corporation
5425 Wisconsin Ave # 300
Chevy Chase MD 20815
301 968-6000

(P-15679)
MILWOOD HEALTHCARE INC
Also Called: MAYWOOD ACRES HEALTHCARE
2641 S C St, Oxnard (93033-4502)
PHONE.................................626 274-4345
Alger Brion, *CEO*
Girlie Yatco, *Office Mgr*
Ida Cantor, *Nursing Dir*
Carla Oleta, *Director*
Gloria Olguin, *Director*
EMP: 97 EST: 2007
SQ FT: 10,000
SALES (est): 7.6MM **Privately Held**
SIC: 6512 Nonresidential building operators

(P-15680)
MJW INVESTMENTS (PA)
1640 5th St Ste 112, Santa Monica (90401-3325)
PHONE.................................310 395-3430
Mark Weinstein, *President*
Karen Spill, *Controller*
Sean Murray, *Director*
▲ EMP: 74 EST: 1985
SQ FT: 1,800
SALES (est): 11MM **Privately Held**
WEB: www.mjwinvestments.com
SIC: 6512 Nonresidential building operators

(P-15681)
MSG FORUM LLC
3900 W Manchester Blvd, Inglewood (90305-2200)
PHONE.................................310 330-7339
EMP: 52 EST: 2018
SALES (est): 1.6MM
SALES (corp-wide): 415.7MM **Publicly Held**
WEB: www.msg.com
SIC: 6512 Nonresidential building operators
PA: Madison Square Garden Sports Corp.
2 Penn Plz Fl 15
New York NY 10121
212 465-4111

(P-15682)
NEVINS/ADAMS PROPERTIES INC (PA)
Also Called: Nevins Adams Properties
920 Garden St Ste A, Santa Barbara (93101-7465)
PHONE.................................805 963-2884
Henry Nevins, *President*
David Adams, *Chairman*
EMP: 250 EST: 1992
SALES (est): 10.7MM **Privately Held**
SIC: 6512 Commercial & industrial building operation

(P-15683)
OLEN COMMERCIAL REALTY CORP
Also Called: Olen Residential Realty
7 Corporate Plaza Dr, Newport Beach (92660-7904)
PHONE.................................949 644-6536
Igor M Olenicoff, *President*
Andrei Olenicoff, *Corp Secy*
Linda Davis, *Executive*
Bret Vannortwick, *Broker*
Patricia Stone, *Manager*
EMP: 400 EST: 1974
SQ FT: 44,000

(P-15684)
OLTMANS INVESTMENT COMPANY LLC
Also Called: Oltmans Property Management
10005 Mission Mill Rd, Whittier (90601-1739)
P.O. Box 985 (90608-0985)
PHONE.................................562 948-4242
J O Oltmans II, *President*
Basil C Johnson, *Managing Prtnr*
Robert Roy, *Managing Prtnr*
Chris Bell, *Vice Pres*
Thanh Nguyen, *Admin Sec*
EMP: 53 EST: 1981
SQ FT: 56,000
SALES (est): 5MM **Privately Held**
SIC: 6512 6552 Commercial & industrial building operation; subdividers & developers

(P-15685)
ONE TOWN CENTER ASSOCIATES LLC
3315 Fairview Rd, Costa Mesa (92626-1610)
PHONE.................................714 435-2100
Stan Taeder, *Director*
Debbie Alcock, *Treasurer*
Karen Graham, *Associate Dir*
EMP: 50 EST: 2017
SALES (est): 2.2MM **Privately Held**
SIC: 6512 Commercial & industrial building operation

(P-15686)
ORANGE BAKERY INC
75 Parker, Irvine (92618-1605)
PHONE.................................949 454-1247
Patti Wallace, *Production*
EMP: 56 **Privately Held**
WEB: www.orangebakery.com
SIC: 6512 Commercial & industrial building operation
HQ: Orange Bakery, Inc.
17751 Cowan
Irvine CA 92614
949 863-1377

(P-15687)
ORANGE CITY MILLS LTD PARTNR
Also Called: Block At Orange, The
20 City Blvd W Ste C5, Orange (92868-3127)
P.O. Box 7033, Indianapolis IN (46207-7033)
PHONE.................................317 636-1600
Rashid Salman, *Branch Mgr*
EMP: 84 **Publicly Held**
SIC: 6512 Nonresidential building operators
HQ: Orange City Mills Limited Partnership
225 W Washington St
Indianapolis IN 46204

(P-15688)
ORMOND BEACH LP
1259 E Thousand Oaks Blvd, Thousand Oaks (91362-2818)
PHONE.................................805 496-4948
Derrick Wada, *Partner*
Rick Schroeder, *Partner*
EMP: 80 EST: 2016
SALES (est): 4.1MM **Privately Held**
SIC: 6512 Nonresidential building operators

(P-15689)
PAN AMERICAN PROPERTIES INC
17491 Irvine Blvd Ste 100, Tustin (92780-3060)
PHONE.................................714 505-5544
Richard J Hoegler, *President*
Desiree Anderson, *Office Mgr*
Rick Hoegler, *CIO*
Brittany Martell, *Accountant*
Crystal Maroshek, *Human Resources*
EMP: 50 EST: 1983

SALES (est): 26.7MM **Privately Held**
WEB: www.olenproperties.com
SIC: 6512 Commercial & industrial building operation

(P-15690)
PM REALTY GROUP LP
3 Park Plz Ste 450, Irvine (92614-2572)
PHONE.................................949 390-5500
Jim Proehl, *Vice Pres*
Leslie Nguyen, *Manager*
Leslie Carroll, *Assistant*
EMP: 56 **Privately Held**
WEB: www.madisonmarquette.com
SIC: 6512 7349 Nonresidential building operators; building maintenance services
HQ: Pm Realty Group, L.P.
1000 Main St Ste 2400
Houston TX 77002
713 209-5800

(P-15691)
PREMIUM OUTLET PARTNERS LP
Camarillo Premium Outlets
740 Ventura Blvd, Camarillo (93010-5842)
PHONE.................................805 445-8520
Brian Hassett, *General Mgr*
EMP: 94 **Publicly Held**
WEB: www.simon.com
SIC: 6512 Shopping center, property operation only
HQ: Premium Outlet Partners, L.P.
225 W Washington St
Indianapolis IN 46204

(P-15692)
PREMIUM OUTLET PARTNERS LP
Desert Hills Premium Outlets
48400 Seminole Dr, Cabazon (92230-2125)
PHONE.................................951 849-6641
Kathy Frederiksen, *Branch Mgr*
EMP: 94
SQ FT: 430,000 **Publicly Held**
WEB: www.simon.com
SIC: 6512 Shopping center, property operation only
HQ: Premium Outlet Partners, L.P.
225 W Washington St
Indianapolis IN 46204

(P-15693)
RMBB PROPERTIES LLC (PA)
9190 W Olympic Blvd, Beverly Hills (90212-3540)
PHONE.................................310 473-5562
Brenda Brams, *Principal*
EMP: 51 EST: 2011
SALES (est): 224.5K **Privately Held**
SIC: 6512 Nonresidential building operators

(P-15694)
RP REALTY PARTNERS LLC
990 W 8th St Ste 600, Los Angeles (90017-2831)
PHONE.................................310 207-6990
Stuart Ruben, *Vice Pres*
Richard Costanzo, *Exec VP*
Annie Lippman, *Executive Asst*
Gabriel Nash, *Administration*
Michael Chase, *Manager*
EMP: 50 EST: 1999
SALES (est): 5.1MM **Privately Held**
SIC: 6512 Commercial & industrial building operation

(P-15695)
SDMV HOTEL PARTNERS LP
520 Newport Center Dr # 2, Newport Beach (92660-7020)
PHONE.................................949 516-0088
Marshall Young, *Partner*
Peiing Lee, *Partner*
Li Hui Lo, *Partner*
EMP: 71 EST: 2019
SALES (est): 1.6MM **Privately Held**
SIC: 6512 Nonresidential building operators

SALES (est): 9.1MM **Privately Held**
WEB: www.papinc.com
SIC: 6512 6514 6552 6531 Commercial & industrial building operation; dwelling operators, except apartments; subdividers & developers; real estate managers

(P-15696)
SHEA LA QUINTA LLC
Also Called: Shea Homes
655 Brea Canyon Rd, Walnut
(91789-3078)
PHONE..................................909 594-9500
John F Shea, *CEO*
Leann Dang, *Finance Mgr*
Drew Owens, *Sales Mgr*
Cassidy Nicholls, *Marketing Staff*
Darren Molles, *Superintendent*
EMP: 78 EST: 2013
SALES (est): 2.7MM
SALES (corp-wide): 2.1B **Privately Held**
SIC: 6512 Nonresidential building operators
HQ: Shea Homes Limited Partnership, A
California Limited Partnership
655 Brea Canyon Rd
Walnut CA 91789

(P-15697)
SHEA PROPERTIES MGT CO INC
130 Vantis Dr Ste 200, Aliso Viejo
(92656-2691)
P.O. Box 62814, Irvine (92602-6093)
PHONE..................................949 389-7000
Colm Macken, *CEO*
Julie Ball, *CEO*
Lori Klasner, *Senior VP*
Kelly Adkins, *Vice Pres*
Deanna Bembry, *Vice Pres*
EMP: 347 EST: 2003
SQ FT: 48,000
SALES (est): 51.1MM
SALES (corp-wide): 2.1B **Privately Held**
WEB: www.sheaproperties.com
SIC: 6512 Nonresidential building operators
PA: J. F. Shea Co., Inc.
655 Brea Canyon Rd
Walnut CA 91789
909 594-9500

(P-15698)
SMG HOLDINGS LLC
Also Called: Long Beach Convention Center
300 E Ocean Blvd, Long Beach
(90802-4825)
PHONE..................................562 499-7611
Charles Beirne, *General Mgr*
Veronica Quintero, *General Mgr*
Cindy Robbins, *Controller*
Nancy Garvey, *Sales Staff*
Jennifer Gonzalez, *Sales Staff*
EMP: 69
SALES (corp-wide): 1.1B **Privately Held**
WEB: www.asmglobal.com
SIC: 6512 Nonresidential building operators
HQ: Smg Holdings, Llc
300 Cnshohckn State Rd # 450
Conshohocken PA 19428

(P-15699)
SOLARI ENTERPRISES INC
1507 W Yale Ave, Orange (92867-3447)
PHONE..................................714 282-2520
Johrita Solari, *President*
Bruce Solari, *Vice Pres*
Mary Oliver, *Regional Mgr*
Shivahn Petty, *Regional Mgr*
Sean Theile, *Regional Mgr*
EMP: 140 EST: 1986
SQ FT: 8,400
SALES (est): 17.5MM **Privately Held**
WEB: www.solari-ent.com
SIC: 6512 Property operation, retail establishment

(P-15700)
SOUTH COAST PLAZA LLC (PA)
Also Called: South Coast Plaza Village
3333 Bristol St Ofc, Costa Mesa
(92626-1811)
PHONE..................................714 546-0110
N R Segerstrom, *Mng Member*
Mark Heim, *CFO*
Marilyn Mocilnikar, *Vice Pres*
Ignacio Garcia, *Executive*
Constance Harrison, *Executive*
EMP: 55 EST: 1965
SQ FT: 8,000

SALES (est): 76MM **Privately Held**
WEB: www.southcoastplaza.com
SIC: 6512 Shopping center, property operation only

(P-15701)
SOUTH COAST PLAZA LLC
Also Called: South Coast Plaza Mall
3333 Bristol St Ofc, Costa Mesa
(92626-1811)
PHONE..................................714 435-2000
David Grant, *Manager*
EMP: 73
SALES (corp-wide): 76MM **Privately Held**
WEB: www.southcoastplaza.com
SIC: 6512 Shopping center, property operation only
PA: South Coast Plaza, Llc
3333 Bristol St Ofc
Costa Mesa CA 92626
714 546-0110

(P-15702)
THRIFTY OIL CO (PA)
13116 Imperial Hwy, Santa Fe Springs
(90670-4817)
PHONE..................................562 921-3581
Ted Orden, *President*
Stephane Wandel, *Vice Chairman*
Sean Tabor, *COO*
Perry Freidrich, *CFO*
Dori Barber, *Admin Sec*
EMP: 37 EST: 1959
SQ FT: 1,624
SALES (est): 17.8MM **Privately Held**
SIC: 6512 2911 6552 Nonresidential
building operators; petroleum refining;
subdividers & developers

(P-15703)
TOPA PROPERTY GROUP INC (HQ)
1800 Avenue Of The Stars # 1200, Los Angeles (90067-4200)
PHONE..................................310 203-9199
James Brooks, *CEO*
Jim Brooks, *President*
Jeanne Gettemy-Lazar, *CFO*
Darren Bell, *Vice Pres*
Paul Gienger, *Vice Pres*
EMP: 158 EST: 1981
SALES (est): 47.1MM
SALES (corp-wide): 446.1MM **Privately Held**
WEB: www.topapropertygroup.com
SIC: 6512 Commercial & industrial building operation
PA: Topa Equities, Ltd.
1800 Avenue Of The Stars # 1400
Los Angeles CA 90067
310 203-9199

(P-15704)
TRIAD PROPERTIES
995 Riverside St, Ventura (93001-1636)
PHONE..................................805 648-5008
Denise Wise, *Principal*
John Polanskey, *Ch of Bd*
Jim White, *Ch of Bd*
Joe Nocella, *CFO*
Edward L Moses, *Principal*
EMP: 60
SALES: 451.8K **Privately Held**
SIC: 6512 Nonresidential building operators

(P-15705)
UNIVERSAL SHOPPING PLAZA A CA
6281 Regio Ave, Buena Park (90620-1023)
PHONE..................................714 521-8899
Ho Yuan Chen, *General Ptnr*
Ms Nini Golden Pacific Realty, *Property Mgr*
EMP: 200 EST: 1987
SALES (est): 5MM **Privately Held**
SIC: 6512 Shopping center, property operation only

(P-15706)
UNIVERSITY BUSINESS CTR ASSOC
5425 Hollister Ave # 160, Santa Barbara
(93111-3341)
PHONE..................................601 354-3555

David H Hoster II, *CEO*
EMP: 80 EST: 1996
SALES (est): 3.4MM
SALES (corp-wide): 363MM **Publicly Held**
WEB: www.eastgroup.net
SIC: 6512 Commercial & industrial building operation
PA: Eastgroup Properties, Inc.
400 W Parkway Pl Ste 100
Ridgeland MS 39157
601 354-3555

(P-15707)
WEST ANGELES CH GOD IN CHRST
Also Called: West Angeles Christian Academy
3010 Crenshaw Blvd, Los Angeles
(90016-4263)
PHONE..................................323 731-2567
Deloris A Dumbar, *Principal*
Earl Jordan, *Exec Dir*
Jonni Crear, *Admin Asst*
Evan Farmer, *Info Tech Dir*
Paula Litt, *Relg Ldr*
EMP: 152
SALES (corp-wide): 25MM **Privately Held**
WEB: www.westa.org
SIC: 8211 6512 Private elementary
school; theater building, ownership & operation
PA: West Angeles Church Of God In Christ
3045 Crenshaw Blvd
Los Angeles CA 90016
323 733-8300

(P-15708)
WEST SIDE REHAB CORPORATION
1755 Kings Way, Los Angeles
(90069-1512)
PHONE..................................323 231-4174
Dean Foley, *President*
EMP: 200 EST: 1973
SQ FT: 1,500
SALES (est): 3.2MM **Privately Held**
SIC: 6512 Commercial & industrial building operation

(P-15709)
WESTFIELD LLC (DH)
2049 Century Park E # 4100, Los Angeles
(90067-3101)
PHONE..................................813 926-4600
Peter Lowy, *CEO*
Gregory Miles, *COO*
Mark Stefanel, *CFO*
Eileen Hanson, *Senior VP*
Mark Barrios, *Vice Pres*
EMP: 400 EST: 1978
SQ FT: 120,000
SALES (est): 404.9MM
SALES (corp-wide): 195MM **Privately Held**
WEB: www.westfield.com
SIC: 6512 Shopping center, property operation only
HQ: Westfield America, Inc.
2049 Century Park E Fl 41
Los Angeles CA 90067
310 478-4456

(P-15710)
WESTFIELD AMERICA INC (HQ)
2049 Century Park E Fl 41, Los Angeles
(90067-3101)
PHONE..................................310 478-4456
Peter S Lowy, *CEO*
Mark A Stefanek, *CFO*
Elizabeth Westman, *Senior VP*
John Fleming, *Vice Pres*
Dominic Lowe, *Vice Pres*
EMP: 200 EST: 1924
SALES (est): 791.4MM
SALES (corp-wide): 195MM **Privately Held**
WEB: www.urw.com
SIC: 6512 Shopping center, property operation only
PA: Unibail-Rodamco-Westfield Se
Unibail Rodamco
Paris 75116
145 051-082

(P-15711)
WESTFIELD AMERICA LTD PARTNR
2049 Century Park E # 4100, Los Angeles
(90067-3101)
PHONE..................................310 277-3898
John Widdup, *CEO*
Peter Lowy, *Partner*
Amy Alyeshmerni, *Vice Pres*
Kevin Burton, *Vice Pres*
Zach Eichman, *Vice Pres*
EMP: 500 EST: 1998
SALES (est): 97.4MM
SALES (corp-wide): 195MM **Privately Held**
WEB: www.westfield.com
SIC: 6512 Shopping center, property operation only
HQ: Westfield, Llc
2049 Century Park E # 4100
Los Angeles CA 90067

(P-15712)
WILLIAM MORRIS RODEO INC (HQ)
151 El Camino Dr, Beverly Hills
(90212-2704)
PHONE..................................310 859-4000
Norman Brokaw, *Chairman*
Jerome F Katzman, *President*
Walter Zifkin, *COO*
Irving J Weintraub, *CFO*
Mary Harding, *Vice Pres*
EMP: 62 EST: 1989
SALES (est): 2.5MM **Privately Held**
SIC: 6512 Commercial & industrial building operation

(P-15713)
WILSHIRE KINGSLEY INC
Also Called: Bcd Tofu House
3575 Wilshire Blvd, Los Angeles
(90010-2303)
PHONE..................................213 382-6677
Edward S Lee, *President*
Hee Sook Lee, *President*
EMP: 100 EST: 2001
SALES (est): 2.6MM **Privately Held**
WEB: www.wilshirecenter.com
SIC: 6512 Commercial & industrial building operation

(P-15714)
YAMAMOTO OF ORIENT INC (HQ)
Also Called: YAMAMOTOYAMA OF AMERICA
122 Voyager St, Pomona (91768-3252)
PHONE..................................909 594-7356
Nami Yamamoto, *CEO*
Kahei Yamamoto, *Ch of Bd*
Hisayuki Nakagawa, *President*
Daniel Goldstein, *COO*
Kazumi Ikeda, *Treasurer*
◆ EMP: 130 EST: 1975
SQ FT: 60,000
SALES (est): 62.6MM **Privately Held**
WEB: www.yamamotoyama.com
SIC: 6512 5812 5149 Shopping center,
property operation only; eating places; tea

6513 Operators Of Apartment Buildings

(P-15715)
10632 BOLSA AVENUE LP
Also Called: SYCAMORE COURT APT
500 Nwport Ctr Dr Ste 200, Newport Beach
(92660)
P.O. Box 13326 (92658-5093)
PHONE..................................949 673-1221
Shawn Boyd, *Principal*
EMP: 62
SALES: 1.4MM **Privately Held**
SIC: 6513 Apartment building operators

(P-15716)
A COMMUNITY OF FRIENDS
3701 Wilshire Blvd # 700, Los Angeles
(90010-2813)
PHONE..................................213 480-0809
Dora Leong Gallo, *CEO*

Cathy Viloria, *CEO*
Dinde Patrick, *Office Mgr*
Maggie Ip, *Accounting Mgr*
Jose Torres, *Sr Project Mgr*
EMP: 60 **EST:** 1988
SQ FT: 5,800
SALES: 10MM **Privately Held**
WEB: www.acof.org
SIC: 6513 Apartment building operators

(P-15717)
ADEPT BUILDER LLC
285 Imperial Hwy Ste 201, Fullerton
(92835-1048)
P.O. Box 2325, La Habra (90632-2325)
PHONE....................949 933-2785
Laura Preciado, *CEO*
EMP: 50 **EST:** 2017
SALES (est): 2.9MM **Privately Held**
WEB: www.adeptbuilder.com
SIC: 6513 8742 Apartment building operators; management consulting services

(P-15718)
APERTO PROPERTY MANAGEMENT INC
17351 Main St, La Puente (91744-5155)
PHONE....................626 965-1961
EMP: 186
SALES (corp-wide): 15.8MM **Privately Held**
WEB: www.apertoliving.com
SIC: 6513 Apartment building operators
PA: Aperto Property Management, Inc.
2 Venture Ste 525
Irvine CA 92618
949 873-4200

(P-15719)
ARNEL COMMERCIAL PROPERTIES (PA)
949 S Coast Dr Ste 600, Costa Mesa
(92626-7734)
PHONE....................714 481-5023
Terry Petersen, *Principal*
George L Argyros, *President*
Allyson D 'affronte, *Director*
Joe Murray, *Director*
EMP: 109 **EST:** 2004
SALES (est): 8.3MM **Privately Held**
WEB: www.arneloffice.com
SIC: 6513 Apartment building operators

(P-15720)
BROWNING APARTMENTS
1104 Browning Blvd, Los Angeles
(90037-1662)
PHONE....................213 252-8847
Tina Booth, *Manager*
EMP: 50
SALES (est): 55.4K **Privately Held**
SIC: 6513 Apartment building operators

(P-15721)
CAL SOUTHERN PRESBT HOMES
Also Called: Park Paseo
516 Burchett St, Glendale (91203-1014)
PHONE....................818 247-0420
Gerald W Dingivan, *President*
Greg Bearce, *Vice Pres*
Dewayne McMullin, *Principal*
EMP: 55 **EST:** 1981
SALES (est): 100.4K **Privately Held**
WEB: www.humangood.org
SIC: 6513 Retirement hotel operation

(P-15722)
CHARLES & CYNTHIA EBERLY INC
Also Called: The Eberly Company
8383 Wilshire Blvd # 906, Beverly Hills
(90211-2425)
PHONE....................323 937-6468
Charles Eberly, *President*
Cynthia Eberly, *Vice Pres*
Cynthia A Eberly, *Vice Pres*
Dayana Bonilla, *Admin Asst*
Laura Olvera, *Comp Spec*
EMP: 90 **EST:** 1986
SALES (est): 8.1MM **Privately Held**
WEB: www.eberlyco.com
SIC: 6513 Apartment building operators

(P-15723)
DOMINO REALTY MANAGEMENT CO
Also Called: Versailles On The Lake
3700 S Plaza Dr Ofc, Santa Ana
(92704-7465)
PHONE....................714 556-0466
Phil Noden, *Principal*
EMP: 68
SALES (corp-wide): 23.3MM **Privately Held**
WEB: www.dominorealty.com
SIC: 6513 Apartment hotel operation
PA: Domino Realty Management Company
9990 Santa Monica Blvd
Beverly Hills CA 90212
310 712-1700

(P-15724)
ESSEX PROPERTY TRUST INC
Also Called: Huxley Apartments, The
1234 Larrabee St, West Hollywood
(90069-2004)
PHONE....................323 461-9346
Mike Shall, *CEO*
EMP: 50
SALES (corp-wide): 1.5B **Publicly Held**
WEB: www.essexapartmenthomes.com
SIC: 6513 Apartment hotel operation
PA: Essex Property Trust, Inc.
1100 Park Pl Ste 200
San Mateo CA 94403
650 655-7800

(P-15725)
HARVEST MANAGEMENT SUB LLC
Also Called: Las Brisas
1299 Briarwood Dr, San Luis Obispo
(93401-5965)
PHONE....................805 543-0187
David Dolan, *Branch Mgr*
EMP: 1055
SALES (corp-wide): 352.3MM **Privately Held**
WEB: www.holidayseniorliving.com
SIC: 6513 Retirement hotel operation
PA: Harvest Management Sub Llc
631 W Morse Blvd Ste 100
Winter Park FL 32789
503 370-7070

(P-15726)
HUMANGOOD SOCAL (HQ)
Also Called: Southern Cal Presbt Homes
516 Burchett St, Glendale (91203-1014)
PHONE....................818 247-0420
John H Cochrane, *CEO*
Gerald W Dingivan, *CEO*
Ruben Grigorians, *Treasurer*
Jill Troedson, *Sales Dir*
EMP: 55 **EST:** 1955
SQ FT: 11,000
SALES (est): 101.5MM
SALES (corp-wide): 25.9MM **Privately Held**
WEB: www.humangood.org
SIC: 6513 Retirement hotel operation
PA: Humangood
6120 Stoneridge Mall Rd
Pleasanton CA 94588
602 906-4024

(P-15727)
HUNTINGTON BCH SENIOR HSING LP
Also Called: Huntington Gardens
18765 Florida St, Huntington Beach
(92648-1999)
PHONE....................714 842-4006
Don Jones, *Partner*
EMP: 193 **EST:** 2008
SALES (est): 476.6K
SALES (corp-wide): 17.7MM **Privately Held**
SIC: 6513 Apartment building operators
PA: Living Opportunities Management Company, Llc
3787 Worsham Ave
Long Beach CA 90808
562 595-7567

(P-15728)
INTERVEST PROPERTY MGT INC
Also Called: Southwood Garden Apartments
5601 N Paramount Blvd, Long Beach
(90805-5124)
PHONE....................562 634-5672
Debbie Ward, *Branch Mgr*
EMP: 50
SALES (corp-wide): 8.6MM **Privately Held**
SIC: 6513 Apartment building operators
PA: Intervest Property Management, Inc.
2201 Dupont Dr Ste 300
Irvine CA 92612
949 833-1554

(P-15729)
INVESTORS MGT TR RE GROUP INC (PA)
Also Called: I M T
15303 Ventura Blvd # 200, Sherman Oaks
(91403-3110)
PHONE....................818 784-4700
John M Tesoriero, *President*
Steve Shin, *Assoc VP*
Scott Burns, *Vice Pres*
Christopher Hill, *Vice Pres*
Bryan Scherr, *Vice Pres*
EMP: 50 **EST:** 1995
SQ FT: 8,000
SALES (est): 34.6MM **Privately Held**
SIC: 6513 Apartment building operators

(P-15730)
IRVINE APT COMMUNITIES LP
299 N State College Blvd, Orange
(92868-1703)
PHONE....................714 937-8900
EMP: 211
SALES (corp-wide): 1.4B **Privately Held**
WEB: www.irvinecompanyapartments.com
SIC: 6513 Apartment building operators
HQ: Irvine Apartment Communities, Lp
110 Innovation Dr
Irvine CA 92617

(P-15731)
IRVINE APT COMMUNITIES LP
Also Called: 1221 Ocean Ave Apartments
1221 Ocean Ave, Santa Monica
(90401-1034)
PHONE....................310 255-1221
Stephanie Van Dermotter, *Manager*
EMP: 211
SALES (corp-wide): 1.4B **Privately Held**
WEB: www.irvinecompanyapartments.com
SIC: 6513 6531 Apartment building operators; rental agent, real estate
HQ: Irvine Apartment Communities, Lp
110 Innovation Dr
Irvine CA 92617

(P-15732)
IRVINE APT COMMUNITIES LP
146 Berkeley, Irvine (92612-4618)
PHONE....................949 854-4942
Kevin Baldridge, *Branch Mgr*
EMP: 211
SALES (corp-wide): 1.4B **Privately Held**
WEB: www.irvinecompanyapartments.com
SIC: 6513 Apartment building operators
HQ: Irvine Apartment Communities, Lp
110 Innovation Dr
Irvine CA 92617

(P-15733)
IRVINE APT COMMUNITIES LP
13212 Magnolia St Ofc, Garden Grove
(92844-1368)
PHONE....................714 537-8500
Mike Conway, *Branch Mgr*
EMP: 211
SALES (corp-wide): 1.4B **Privately Held**
WEB: www.irvinecompanyapartments.com
SIC: 6513 Apartment building operators
HQ: Irvine Apartment Communities, Lp
110 Innovation Dr
Irvine CA 92617

(P-15734)
IRVINE APT COMMUNITIES LP (HQ)
Also Called: I A C
110 Innovation Dr, Irvine (92617-3040)
PHONE....................949 720-5600
Raymond Watson, *Vice Chairman*
Mike Ellis, *Exec VP*
EMP: 200 **EST:** 1993
SQ FT: 8,316
SALES (est): 166.9MM
SALES (corp-wide): 1.4B **Privately Held**
WEB: www.irvinecompanyapartments.com
SIC: 6513 6552 6798 Apartment building operators; subdividers & developers; real estate investment trusts
PA: The Irvine Company Llc
550 Newport Center Dr
Newport Beach CA 92660
949 720-2000

(P-15735)
IRVINE APT COMMUNITIES LP
Also Called: Rancho Monterey Apartments
100 Robinson Dr, Tustin (92782-1095)
PHONE....................714 505-7181
Brooks Foy, *Manager*
EMP: 211
SALES (corp-wide): 1.4B **Privately Held**
WEB: www.irvinecompanyapartments.com
SIC: 6513 Apartment building operators
HQ: Irvine Apartment Communities, Lp
110 Innovation Dr
Irvine CA 92617

(P-15736)
KISCO SENIOR LIVING LLC
1731 W Medical Center Dr, Anaheim
(92801-1837)
PHONE....................714 872-9785
Carol Bush, *Director*
EMP: 62
SALES (corp-wide): 138.2MM **Privately Held**
WEB: www.kiscoseniorliving.com
SIC: 6513 Retirement hotel operation
PA: Senior Kisco Living Llc
5790 Fleet St Ste 300
Carlsbad CA 92008
760 804-5900

(P-15737)
KISCO SENIOR LIVING LLC
Also Called: KRC Santa Margarita
21952 Buena Suerte, Rcho STA Marg
(92688-3903)
PHONE....................949 888-2250
Rick Lansford, *Branch Mgr*
Jerry Church, *Exec Dir*
EMP: 62
SALES (corp-wide): 138.2MM **Privately Held**
WEB: www.kiscoseniorliving.com
SIC: 6513 Retirement hotel operation
PA: Senior Kisco Living Llc
5790 Fleet St Ste 300
Carlsbad CA 92008
760 804-5900

(P-15738)
KISCO SENIOR LIVING LLC
Also Called: KRC Orange
620 S Glassell St, Orange (92866-3000)
PHONE....................714 997-5355
Bruce Hoggan, *Exec Dir*
Susan Parker, *Marketing Staff*
EMP: 62
SALES (corp-wide): 138.2MM **Privately Held**
WEB: www.kiscoseniorliving.com
SIC: 6513 Retirement hotel operation
PA: Senior Kisco Living Llc
5790 Fleet St Ste 300
Carlsbad CA 92008
760 804-5900

(P-15739)
MARINA CITY CLUB LP A CALI
4333 Admiralty Way, Marina Del Rey
(90292-5469)
PHONE....................310 822-0611
J H Snyder, *Partner*
Lewis Geyser, *Partner*
Lon Snyder, *Partner*
Milton Swimmer, *Partner*

PRODUCTS & SVCS

Eileen Mc Carthy, *Sales Dir*
EMP: 125 **EST:** 1969
SQ FT: 10,000
SALES (est): 23.5MM **Privately Held**
WEB: www.marinacityclub.net
SIC: 6513 7997 4493 Apartment building operators; membership sports & recreation clubs; marinas

(P-15740)
MBK SENIOR LIVING LLC (PA)
4 Park Plz Ste 1700, Irvine (92614-2559)
PHONE..........................949 242-1400
Terry Howard, *President*
Jeff Fischer, *President*
Brittany Andrews, *Exec Dir*
Nicole Tucker,
Roger Green, *Director*
EMP: 706 **EST:** 2004
SALES (est): 72.1MM **Privately Held**
WEB: www.mbkseniorliving.com
SIC: 6513 Retirement hotel operation

(P-15741)
MONARK LP
2804 W El Segundo Blvd, Gardena (90249-1551)
PHONE..........................310 769-6669
EMP: 99
SALES (est): 1.9MM **Privately Held**
SIC: 6513 Apartment Building Operators, Nsk

(P-15742)
NORTH PK APARTMENTS HSING CORP (PA)
601 Douglas St, Bakersfield (93308-2362)
PHONE..........................661 399-3084
Tina Williams,
EMP: 50 **EST:** 2000
SALES (est): 610K **Privately Held**
SIC: 6513 Apartment building operators

(P-15743)
PARK NEWPORT LTD (PA)
Also Called: Park Newport Apartments
1 Park Newport, Newport Beach (92660-5004)
PHONE..........................949 644-1900
Gerson Bakar, *Owner*
EMP: 75 **EST:** 1970
SQ FT: 10,000
SALES (est): 4.8MM **Privately Held**
WEB: www.parknewportapts.com
SIC: 6513 Apartment hotel operation

(P-15744)
PARSONS GROUP INC (PA)
Also Called: Urban Group, The
1921 State St Ste A, Santa Barbara (93101-2559)
PHONE..........................805 564-3341
Robert Parsons, *President*
Alyce Parsons, *COO*
Mary McDougal, *Accountant*
EMP: 54 **EST:** 1984
SALES (est): 8.8MM **Privately Held**
WEB: www.parsonsgroupinc.com
SIC: 6513 Apartment building operators

(P-15745)
PRC MULTI-FAMILY LLC
Also Called: Park Regency Club Apts
10000 Imperial Hwy, Downey (90242-3243)
PHONE..........................562 803-5000
David Lifschitz, *CEO*
Alfred Somekh, *President*
EMP: 72 **EST:** 1984
SALES (est): 2.5MM
SALES (corp-wide): 166.1MM **Privately Held**
WEB: www.gehrdevelopment.com
SIC: 6513 Apartment building operators
HQ: Gehr Development Corporation
7400 E Slauson Ave
Commerce CA 90040

(P-15746)
RANCE KING PROPERTIES INC (PA)
Also Called: R K Properties
3737 E Broadway, Long Beach (90803-6104)
PHONE..........................562 240-1000
William Rance King Jr, *President*

Steven King, *Vice Pres*
Marilyn P Munson, *Vice Pres*
Denise Warren, *Broker*
Heather Fitzgerald, *Property Mgr*
EMP: 104
SQ FT: 5,000
SALES (est): 17.9MM **Privately Held**
WEB: www.rkprop.com
SIC: 6513 Apartment building operators

(P-15747)
RUCHEL ENTERPRISES
Also Called: Pasadena Manor Retirement Ht
4032 Wilshire Blvd, Los Angeles (90010-3405)
PHONE..........................213 389-6900
Jacob Friedman, *President*
EMP: 137 **EST:** 1977
SALES (est): 945.7K
SALES (corp-wide): 179.6MM **Privately Held**
WEB: www.longwoodmgmt.com
SIC: 6513 Retirement hotel operation
PA: Longwood Management Corp.
4032 Wilshire Blvd Fl 6
Los Angeles CA 90010
213 389-6900

(P-15748)
SAN DIMAS RETIREMENT CENTER (PA)
Also Called: Longwood Management
834 W Arrow Hwy, San Dimas (91773-2418)
PHONE..........................909 599-8441
Frankie Ramirez, *Administration*
EMP: 70 **EST:** 1965
SALES (est): 4.8MM **Privately Held**
SIC: 6513 8059 Retirement hotel operation; personal care home, with health care

(P-15749)
SELTZER-DOREN MANAGEMENT CO
Also Called: Seltzer-Doren Company
20201 Sherman Way Ste 209, Canoga Park (91306-3269)
PHONE..........................818 709-5210
Sheldon Seltzer, *Corp Secy*
Gerald Doren, *President*
EMP: 65 **EST:** 1970
SQ FT: 3,275
SALES (est): 5.9MM **Privately Held**
SIC: 6513 6552 Apartment building operators; subdividers & developers

(P-15750)
STEVENS POND APT PROPTY OWNR (PA)
Also Called: Residences At Stevens Pond
11766 Wilshire Blvd # 1500, Los Angeles (90025-6538)
PHONE..........................310 268-8344
Christine Goshorn, *Regional Mgr*
EMP: 54 **EST:** 2014
SALES (est): 726.3K **Privately Held**
SIC: 6513 Apartment building operators

(P-15751)
VINTAGE SENIOR HOUSING LLC
Also Called: Vintage Simi Hills
5300 E Los Angeles Ave, Simi Valley (93063-4136)
PHONE..........................805 583-3500
EMP: 317
SALES (corp-wide): 23.3MM **Privately Held**
WEB: www.vintagehousing.com
SIC: 6513 Apartment Building Operators, Nsk
PA: Senior Vintage Housing Llc
23 Corporate Plaza Dr # 190
Newport Beach CA 92660
949 719-4080

(P-15752)
VINTAGE SENIOR MANAGEMENT INC (PA)
Also Called: Vintage Senior Living
23 Corporate Plaza Dr # 190, Newport Beach (92660-7943)
PHONE..........................949 719-4080
Brian Flornes, *CEO*
Vicki Clark, *President*

Mark Schulz, *CFO*
Eric Davidson, *Vice Pres*
EMP: 1429 **EST:** 2002
SALES (est): 36MM **Privately Held**
WEB: www.vintagehousing.com
SIC: 6513 Retirement hotel operation

(P-15753)
WILLIAM WARREN PROPERTIES INC
201 Wilshire Blvd Ste 102, Santa Monica (90401-1220)
PHONE..........................310 454-1500
William Hobin, *President*
Keith Haberstroh, *District Mgr*
EMP: 100 **EST:** 2000
SALES (est): 17.8MM
SALES (corp-wide): 63.3MM **Privately Held**
WEB: www.williamwarren.com
SIC: 6513 Apartment building operators
PA: The William Warren Group Inc
201 Wilshire Blvd Ste 102
Santa Monica CA 90401
310 451-2130

6514 Operators Of Dwellings, Except Apartments

(P-15754)
ACTION PROPERTY MANAGEMENT INC (PA)
2603 Main St Ste 500, Irvine (92614-4261)
PHONE..........................949 450-0202
Matthew Holbrook, *CEO*
Dalilah Bernardo, *Regional Mgr*
Candace Caldana-Walk, *Regional Mgr*
Dean Driscoll, *Regional Mgr*
Eve Lopez, *Regional Mgr*
EMP: 90 **EST:** 1980
SQ FT: 18,000
SALES (est): 107.1MM **Privately Held**
WEB: www.actionlife.com
SIC: 6514 8641 Residential building, four or fewer units: operation; homeowners' association

(P-15755)
PROFESSIONAL CMNTY MGT CAL INC
Also Called: Pcm
27051 Towne Centre Dr, Foothill Ranch (92610-2819)
PHONE..........................949 768-7261
Jeffrey Olson, *CEO*
EMP: 80
SALES (corp-wide): 51.5MM **Privately Held**
WEB: www.pcminternet.com
SIC: 6514 Dwelling operators, except apartments
PA: Professional Community Management Of California, Inc.
27051 Twne Cntre Dr Ste 2
Foothill Ranch CA 92610
800 369-7260

6515 Operators of Residential Mobile Home Sites

(P-15756)
CAREFREE COMMUNITIES INC
1251 Old Conejo Rd, Newbury Park (91320-1031)
PHONE..........................805 498-2612
EMP: 167
SALES (corp-wide): 1.4B **Publicly Held**
WEB: www.protofuse.com
SIC: 6515 Mobile home site operators
HQ: Carefree Communities Inc.
6991 E Camelback Rd B310
Scottsdale AZ 85251
480 423-5700

(P-15757)
TRAVEL AMERICA INC (HQ)
17672 Cowan Bldg B, Irvine (92614-6027)
PHONE..........................949 474-0404
Raymond Novelli, *President*
Marlies Novelli, *Corp Secy*
EMP: 50 **EST:** 1997

SALES (est): 6MM
SALES (corp-wide): 10.1MM **Privately Held**
WEB: www.gorms.com
SIC: 6515 Mobile home site operators
PA: Rennhack Marketing Services, Llc
752 Port America Pl # 300
Grapevine TX 76051
817 481-6516

(P-15758)
WATT CONSTRUCTION COMPANY (PA)
Also Called: Rive Gauche Cafe
14106 Ventura Blvd # 200, Sherman Oaks (91423-2778)
PHONE..........................818 905-6601
Brady Watt, *President*
Charles E Watt, *President*
Wende Watt, *Corp Secy*
EMP: 53 **EST:** 1946
SQ FT: 3,500
SALES (est): 1.4MM **Privately Held**
SIC: 5812 6515 Cafe; mobile home site operators

6519 Lessors Of Real Estate, NEC

(P-15759)
APERTO PROPERTY MANAGEMENT INC (PA)
2 Venture Ste 525, Irvine (92618-7453)
PHONE..........................949 873-4200
Ed Quigley, *CEO*
Terry Liddard, *Controller*
Jeff Peach, *Controller*
Malia Mendiola, *Human Res Mgr*
Nissa Zunba, *Property Mgr*
EMP: 214 **EST:** 2017
SALES (est): 15.8MM **Privately Held**
WEB: www.apertoliving.com
SIC: 6519 8741 Real property lessors; management services

(P-15760)
LAACO LTD (PA)
Also Called: Storage West
431 W 7th St, Los Angeles (90014-1601)
PHONE..........................213 622-1254
Karen L Hathaway, *President*
Bryan J Cusworth, *CFO*
John K Hathaway, *Vice Pres*
Steven K Hathaway, *Vice Pres*
Charles Michaels, *Vice Pres*
EMP: 125 **EST:** 1986
SQ FT: 100,000
SALES (est): 96.2MM **Privately Held**
WEB: www.laac.com
SIC: 6519 7997 7011 5812 Real property lessors; yacht club, membership; hotels; resort hotel; eating places

(P-15761)
OLYMPUS PROPERTY
3411 State Rd, Bakersfield (93308-4537)
PHONE..........................661 393-1700
Chandler Wonderly, *Owner*
Nehal Patel, *Vice Pres*
Jimmy Henry, *Business Mgr*
Angelica Velasco, *Business Mgr*
Canania Perry, *Recruiter*
EMP: 56
SALES (corp-wide): 78.5MM **Privately Held**
WEB: www.olympusproperty.com
SIC: 6519 1741 Real property lessors; foundation building
PA: Olympus Property
500 Throckmorton St # 300
Fort Worth TX 76102
817 795-4900

6531 Real Estate Agents & Managers

(P-15762)
1370 REALTY CORP
14545 Friar St Shrmanc, Van Nuys (91411-2397)
PHONE..........................818 817-0092

▲ = Import ▼=Export
◆ =Import/Export

Kambiz Merabi, *President*
EMP: 25 **EST:** 1995
SQ FT: 16,400
SALES (est): 2.6MM **Privately Held**
WEB: www.1370realty.com
SIC: 6531 2451 Real estate agents & managers; mobile buildings; for commercial use

(P-15763)
ABODE COMMUNITIES LLC
1149 S Hill St Fl 7, Los Angeles (90015-2219)
PHONE....................213 629-2702
Robin Hughes, *President*
Rick Saperstein, *CFO*
Kenneth Krug, *Chairman*
Sandra Kulli, *Chairman*
Holly Benson, *Exec VP*
▲ **EMP:** 150 **EST:** 1968
SQ FT: 10,094
SALES (est): 14.1MM **Privately Held**
WEB: www.abodecommunities.org
SIC: 6531 8712 8711 Housing authority operator; architectural services; engineering services

(P-15764)
ADAMS AND BARNES INC
Also Called: Century 21
433 W Foothill Blvd, Monrovia (91016-2025)
PHONE....................626 358-1858
Lou Jean Barnes, *President*
Andrew Barnes, *Treasurer*
Thomas E Adams, *Vice Pres*
Stone Bradley, *Sales Staff*
EMP: 60 **EST:** 1956
SALES (est): 6.1MM **Privately Held**
WEB: www.century21.com
SIC: 6531 Real estate agent, residential

(P-15765)
AGUA CALIENTE DEVELOPMENT AUTH
5401 Dinah Shore Dr, Palm Springs (92264-5970)
PHONE....................760 699-6800
Richard M Milanovich, *Chairman*
Mary Silverman, *Manager*
EMP: 93 **EST:** 2008
SALES (est): 2.4MM
SALES (corp-wide): 194.2MM **Privately Held**
WEB: www.aguacaliente.org
SIC: 6531 Real estate leasing & rentals
PA: Agua Caliente Band Of Cahuilla Indians
5401 Dinah Shore Dr
Palm Springs CA 92264
760 699-6800

(P-15766)
ALLIANT ASSET MGT CO LLC (PA)
21600 Oxnard St Ste 1200, Woodland Hills (91367-4949)
PHONE....................818 668-2805
Shawn Horwitz, *Mng Member*
Drew Foster, *Senior VP*
Hammad Graham, *Vice Pres*
Macy Kisilinsky, *Vice Pres*
D Livingston, *Vice Pres*
EMP: 81 **EST:** 1997
SQ FT: 19,816
SALES (est): 22.3MM **Privately Held**
WEB: www.alliantcapital.com
SIC: 6531 Real estate managers

(P-15767)
ALLMARK INC (PA)
10070 Arrow Rte, Rancho Cucamonga (91730-4194)
PHONE....................909 989-7556
Wayne Slavitt, *CEO*
Michael Krcelic, *President*
Pat Price, *CFO*
Steve Strebel, *CFO*
Michael Payne, *Treasurer*
EMP: 65 **EST:** 1971
SQ FT: 3,167
SALES (est): 11.3MM **Privately Held**
WEB: www.allmarkproperties.com
SIC: 6531 Real estate managers

(P-15768)
AMERICAN DEVELOPMENT CORP (PA)
3605 Long Beach Blvd # 41, Long Beach (90807-4013)
PHONE....................562 989-3730
Marco Gomez, *President*
EMP: 87 **EST:** 1994
SQ FT: 8,000
SALES (est): 7.9MM **Privately Held**
SIC: 6531 Real estate agents & managers

(P-15769)
ANGELES PARK COMMUNITIES LTD
10301 W Pico Blvd, Los Angeles (90064-2607)
PHONE....................310 277-4900
William Elliott, *CEO*
EMP: 250
SALES (est): 5.6MM **Privately Held**
SIC: 6531 Real estate agents & managers

(P-15770)
ANZA MANAGEMENT COMPANY (PA)
2280 University Dr, Newport Beach (92660-3300)
PHONE....................949 645-1422
Donald P Johnson, *Ch of Bd*
Kenneth M Teske, *President*
Devon L Syme, *Vice Pres*
Kathleen Dover, *Regional Mgr*
Lucy Gaxiola, *District Mgr*
EMP: 195 **EST:** 1975
SQ FT: 11,000
SALES (est): 14.4MM **Privately Held**
WEB: www.anzamanagement.com
SIC: 6531 Real estate managers

(P-15771)
AREA HSING AUTH OF THE CNTY VN (PA)
1400 W Hillcrest Dr, Newbury Park (91320-2721)
PHONE....................805 480-9991
Douglas A Tapking, *Exec Dir*
Douglas Tapking, *Exec Dir*
George McGehee, *General Mgr*
Alexandria Banks, *Executive Asst*
Denise Howells, *Accounting Mgr*
EMP: 50 **EST:** 1972
SQ FT: 24,000
SALES (est): 41.2MM **Privately Held**
WEB: www.ahacv.org
SIC: 6531 Housing authority operator

(P-15772)
ARGENT MANAGEMENT LLC (PA)
Also Called: Suncal
4131 S Main St, Santa Ana (92707-5758)
PHONE....................949 777-4000
Bruce Elieff, *Principal*
Marc Magstadt, *COO*
Robert Starkman, *Senior VP*
Tom Rollins, *Vice Pres*
Tara Sheehan, *Vice Pres*
EMP: 315 **EST:** 2003
SALES (est): 22.9MM **Privately Held**
WEB: www.argentmanagementllc.com
SIC: 6531 Real estate agents & managers

(P-15773)
ARGENT MANAGEMENT LLC
4131 S Main St, Santa Ana (92707-5758)
PHONE....................949 777-4070
Rosemarie Dyvig, *Mng Member*
Frank Faye, *CFO*
Joe Garcia, *Vice Pres*
Stephan Elieff,
Steve Elieff,
EMP: 72 **EST:** 2000
SALES (est): 3.2MM **Privately Held**
WEB: www.argentmanagementllc.com
SIC: 6531 Rental agent, real estate

(P-15774)
ATLAS HOSPITALITY GROUP
1901 Main St Ste 175, Irvine (92614-0517)
PHONE....................949 622-3400
Alan Reay, *President*
S Shah, *Vice Pres*
Kyle Ensign, *Associate*

EMP: 90 **EST:** 1991
SALES (est): 5.5MM **Privately Held**
WEB: www.atlashospitality.com
SIC: 6531 Real estate agent, commercial

(P-15775)
ATTOM DATA SOLUTIONS LLC (PA)
505 Technology Dr Ste 100, Irvine (92618-1387)
PHONE....................949 502-8300
Rob Barber, *CEO*
Richard Lombardi, *COO*
David Dam, *CFO*
Richard Sawicky, *Officer*
Rick Sharga, *Exec VP*
EMP: 73 **EST:** 2011
SALES (est): 17.2MM **Privately Held**
WEB: www.attomdata.com
SIC: 6531 Real estate brokers & agents

(P-15776)
AUCTIONCOM INC
1 Mauchly Ste 27, Irvine (92618-2305)
PHONE....................800 499-6199
Jeffrey Frieden, *CEO*
Jake Seid, *President*
James Corum, *COO*
Tim Morse, *CFO*
Virginia Pierce, *CFO*
EMP: 200 **EST:** 1990
SQ FT: 18,000
SALES (est): 5.1MM **Privately Held**
SIC: 6531 Auction, real estate

(P-15777)
AUCTIONCOM LLC (PA)
1 Mauchly, Irvine (92618-2305)
PHONE....................949 859-2777
Monte J M Koch, *CEO*
Jeff Friesen, *President*
Keith McLane, *President*
Jeffrey Frieden, *CEO*
Min Alexander, *CFO*
EMP: 760 **EST:** 2008
SALES (est): 162.8MM **Privately Held**
SIC: 6531 Real estate agents & managers

(P-15778)
AUTHORITY OF HOUSING (PA)
Also Called: Hacsb
815 W Ocean Ave, Lompoc (93436-6526)
P.O. Box 397 (93438-0397)
PHONE....................805 736-3423
Frederick C Lamont, *Exec Dir*
Robert Havlicek, *CFO*
Fran Clow, *Principal*
Robert Dickerson, *Principal*
Mickey Flacks, *Principal*
EMP: 68 **EST:** 1941
SQ FT: 3,500
SALES (est): 41.7MM **Privately Held**
WEB: www.hasbarco.org
SIC: 6531 Housing authority operator

(P-15779)
AVALONBAY COMMUNITIES INC
Also Called: Avalon At Penasquitos Hills
2050 Main St Ste 1200, Irvine (92614-8280)
PHONE....................949 955-6200
Chris Payne, *Vice Pres*
Joshua Spalasso, *Manager*
EMP: 50
SALES (corp-wide): 2.3B **Publicly Held**
WEB: www.avaloncommunities.com
SIC: 6531 Real estate managers
PA: Avalonbay Communities, Inc.
4040 Wilson Blvd Ste 1000
Arlington VA 22203
703 329-6300

(P-15780)
AVANTRA REAL ESTATE SERVICES
Also Called: Avantra Financial
148 E Fthill Blvd Ste 100, Arcadia (91006)
PHONE....................626 357-7028
Robert B Doeppel, *CEO*
Vicky Hansen, *President*
Debbie Bello, *Treasurer*
Gina Olivares, *Admin Sec*
EMP: 50 **EST:** 1998
SQ FT: 1,800
SALES (est): 35MM **Privately Held**
SIC: 6531 Real estate brokers & agents

(P-15781)
AVISON YUNG - SOUTHERN CAL LTD (DH)
10940 Wilshire Blvd # 2100, Los Angeles (90024-3915)
PHONE....................424 265-9200
Jonathan J Larsen, *Managing Dir*
Wendy Bell, *Owner*
Neil Resnick, *President*
Mark E Rose, *CEO*
Kevin Clarke, *Senior VP*
EMP: 98 **EST:** 2011
SALES (est): 18.6MM
SALES (corp-wide): 1.8B **Privately Held**
WEB: www.avisonyoung.us
SIC: 6531 Real estate agent, commercial
HQ: Avison Young (Canada) Inc
18 York St Suite 400
Toronto ON M5J 2
416 955-0000

(P-15782)
BAKERSFIELD WESTWIND CORP
Also Called: Coldwell Banker
1810 Westwind Dr, Bakersfield (93301-3027)
PHONE....................661 327-2121
John Garone, *President*
Adam Belter, *Managing Dir*
Roland Simpson, *CTO*
Wendy Fausett, *Sales Staff*
Tishana Debenham, *Director*
EMP: 145 **EST:** 1972
SALES (est): 12.2MM **Privately Held**
WEB: www.cbbakersfield.com
SIC: 6531 Real estate agent, residential

(P-15783)
BAYCO FINANCIAL CORPORATION (PA)
24050 Madison St Ste 101, Torrance (90505-6016)
PHONE....................310 378-8181
Brenda McKenneth, *President*
Robert Cohen, *Ch of Bd*
Sheri Pfau, *Treasurer*
Mary Colin, *Vice Pres*
EMP: 53 **EST:** 1964
SALES (est): 8.8MM **Privately Held**
WEB: www.baycocorp.com
SIC: 6531 Real estate managers

(P-15784)
BEACH FRONT PROPERTY MGT INC (PA)
Also Called: Beachfront Properties
1212 Long Beach Blvd, Long Beach (90813-3225)
PHONE....................562 981-7777
Kyle Kazan, *President*
Kris Hulgreen, *Officer*
Carolyn Easley, *Regional Mgr*
Hannah Santy, *Office Mgr*
Sharon Alo, *Executive Asst*
EMP: 62 **EST:** 1999
SALES (est): 9.5MM **Privately Held**
WEB: www.bfpminc.com
SIC: 6531 Real estate managers

(P-15785)
BEITLER & ASSOCIATES INC (PA)
Also Called: Beitler Commercial Realty Svcs
825 S Barrington Ave, Los Angeles (90049-6759)
PHONE....................310 820-2955
Barry Beitler, *CEO*
Robert H Sargent, *CFO*
Tony Dorn, *Exec VP*
Willa McNamara, *Exec VP*
Doug Green, *Senior VP*
EMP: 50 **EST:** 1980
SQ FT: 13,000
SALES (est): 12.9MM **Privately Held**
SIC: 6531 Real estate agent, commercial

(P-15786)
BENNION DEVILLE FINE HOMES INC
Also Called: Windermere RE Coachella Vly
74850 Us Highway 111, Indian Wells (92210-7116)
PHONE....................760 674-3452

Rick Fisk, *Branch Mgr*
Martin Duggan, *Marketing Staff*
EMP: 378
SALES (corp-wide): 42.6MM **Privately Held**
WEB: www.bdhomes.com
SIC: 6531 Real estate brokers & agents
PA: Bennion & Deville Fine Homes, Inc.
71691 Highway 111
Rancho Mirage CA 92270
760 770-6801

(P-15787)
BERKSHIRE HTHWAY HM SVCS CA RP (PA)
18000 Studebaker Rd # 600, Cerritos (90703-2679)
PHONE................562 860-2625
Bruce Mulhearn, *President*
Sue Peralta, *Admin Asst*
EMP: 65 **EST:** 2017
SALES (est): 4.2MM **Privately Held**
WEB: www.brucemulhearn.com
SIC: 6531 Real estate agent, residential

(P-15788)
BERRO MANAGEMENT
3950 Parmnt Blvd Ste 115, Lakewood (90712)
PHONE................562 432-3444
Jack Berro, *President*
Angelica Medina, *Supervisor*
EMP: 52 **EST:** 1977
SQ FT: 2,000
SALES (est): 5.8MM **Privately Held**
WEB: www.berromgmt.com
SIC: 6531 Real estate managers

(P-15789)
BEVERLY HILLS ESCROW A CAL
Also Called: Transition Team, The
118 S Beverly Dr Ste 222, Beverly Hills (90212-3016)
PHONE................310 273-9850
Lola Levoy, *President*
Natuasha Braddock, *Assistant*
Sandra Crisanto, *Assistant*
Alejandra Garcia, *Assistant*
EMP: 68 **EST:** 1950
SQ FT: 2,100
SALES (est): 5.4MM **Privately Held**
WEB: www.bhescrow.com
SIC: 6531 Escrow agent, real estate

(P-15790)
BGK EQUITIES INC (HQ)
2000 Avenue Of The Stars, Los Angeles (90067-4700)
PHONE................505 982-2184
Michael Mahony, *COO*
Ian Brownlow, *CFO*
EMP: 70 **EST:** 1995
SALES (est): 22.7MM **Privately Held**
WEB: www.geminirosemont.com
SIC: 6531 Real estate agent, commercial

(P-15791)
BKM DIABLO 227 LLC
1701 Quail St Ste 100, Newport Beach (92660-2796)
PHONE................602 688-6409
Brian K Malliet, *Principal*
Rene Velasquez, *Principal*
Melissa Boyle, *General Mgr*
EMP: 85
SALES (est): 1.7MM **Privately Held**
WEB: www.bkmmanagementco.com
SIC: 6531 Real estate managers

(P-15792)
BLACK KNGHT RE DATA SLTONS LLC (DH)
Also Called: Black Knight Data & Analytics
121 Theory Ste 100, Irvine (92617-3209)
PHONE................626 808-9000
Anthony Jabbour, *CEO*
Justin Romano, *Business Anlyst*
Deborah Bell, *Manager*
Gary Grojean, *Manager*
EMP: 3081 **EST:** 2010
SALES (est): 102.4MM
SALES (corp-wide): 1.2B **Publicly Held**
WEB: www.blackknightinc.com
SIC: 6531 Real estate listing services

HQ: Black Knight Financial Services, Inc.
601 Riverside Ave
Jacksonville FL 32204
904 854-5100

(P-15793)
BUCHANAN STREET PARTNERS LP
3501 Jamboree Rd Ste 4200, Newport Beach (92660-2958)
PHONE................949 721-1414
Robert Brunswick, *CEO*
Timothy Ballard, *COO*
Chris Cervisi, *Vice Pres*
James Gill, *Vice Pres*
Kimberly Kanen, *Vice Pres*
EMP: 85 **EST:** 2000
SALES (est): 6.4MM **Privately Held**
WEB: www.buchananstreet.com
SIC: 6531 Real estate agents & managers

(P-15794)
C B COAST NEWPORT PROPERTIES
Also Called: Coldwell Bnkr Rsdntial Rfrrl
840 Nwport Ctr Dr Ste 100, Newport Beach (92660)
PHONE................949 644-1600
Daniel F Bibb, *President*
Tom Queen, *Senior VP*
Gary Legrand, *VP Finance*
Edgar Reynoso, *Broker*
Cristi Ulrich, *Associate*
EMP: 5044 **EST:** 1990
SQ FT: 7,300
SALES (est): 14.3MM **Publicly Held**
WEB: www.oc-coastalproperties.com
SIC: 6531 Real estate agent, residential; selling agent, real estate
HQ: Coldwell Banker Residential Referral Network
27271 Las Ramblas
Mission Viejo CA 92691
949 367-1800

(P-15795)
CAMDEN DEVELOPMENT INC
27261 Las Ramblas, Mission Viejo (92691-6441)
PHONE................949 427-4674
EMP: 239 **Privately Held**
WEB: www.camdenbuildersinc.com
SIC: 6531 Real estate agent, commercial
HQ: Camden Development, Inc.
11 Greenway Plz Ste 2400
Houston TX 77046

(P-15796)
CAPITAL KINGZ LLC
3415 S Sepulveda Blvd # 1, Los Angeles (90034-6060)
PHONE................888 470-4114
Jonte B King, *CEO*
EMP: 50 **EST:** 2019
SALES (est): 1.5MM **Privately Held**
SIC: 6531 Real estate agents & managers

(P-15797)
CARLYLE GROUP INC (PA)
9073 Nemo St Ste 100, West Hollywood (90069-5511)
PHONE................310 550-8656
Ronald Singer, *CEO*
Karen Burcombe-Vogogel, *Vice Pres*
David Lam, *Vice Pres*
Charles Moore, *Principal*
David Maldonado, *CTO*
▲ **EMP:** 375 **EST:** 1975
SQ FT: 3,000
SALES (est): 42.1MM **Privately Held**
WEB: www.carlyle.com
SIC: 6799 Buying agent, real estate; investors

(P-15798)
CARUSO MGT LTD A CAL LTD PRTNR (PA)
Also Called: Commons At Calabasas, The
101 The Grove Dr, Los Angeles (90036-6221)
PHONE................323 900-8100
Rick Caruso, *Partner*
Peter Hayden, *President*
Carol Pacheco, *President*

Denise Ware, *CEO*
Matt Middlebrook, *Exec VP*
EMP: 98 **EST:** 1991
SALES (est): 30.6MM **Privately Held**
WEB: www.caruso.com
SIC: 6531 Rental agent, real estate

(P-15799)
CBABR INC (PA)
Also Called: Coldwell Banker
31620 Rr Cyn Rd Ste A, Canyon Lake (92587-9476)
PHONE................951 640-7056
Budge Huskey, *CEO*
Dennis M McCoy, *President*
Margaret McCoy, *Treasurer*
Mike Duffy, *Officer*
Jody Regus, *Vice Pres*
EMP: 73 **EST:** 1983
SQ FT: 4,000
SALES (est): 9.9MM **Privately Held**
WEB: www.coldwellbanker.com
SIC: 6531 Real estate agent, residential

(P-15800)
CBRE INC (HQ)
Also Called: CB Richard Ellis
400 S Hope St Ste 2500, Los Angeles (90071-1993)
PHONE................213 613-3333
Bob Sulentic, *President*
Andrew Behrens, *Vice Chairman*
Camille Julmy, *Vice Chairman*
Thomas Monahan, *Vice Chairman*
Aron Will, *Vice Chairman*
▲ **EMP:** 150 **EST:** 1906
SALES (est): 1.4B **Publicly Held**
WEB: www.cbre.com
SIC: 6531 6726 Real estate agent, commercial; real estate managers; appraiser, real estate; investment offices

(P-15801)
CBRE GLOBAL INVESTORS INC (DH)
601 S Figueroa St Ste 49, Los Angeles (90017-5253)
PHONE................213 683-4200
T Ritson Ferguson, *CEO*
Dave Witham, *Partner*
Emily Dovey, *CFO*
Maurice Voskuilen, *Officer*
Roxanne Cruz, *Executive Asst*
EMP: 173 **EST:** 2011
SALES (est): 16.6MM **Publicly Held**
WEB: www.cbreim.com
SIC: 6531 Real estate agents & managers
HQ: Cbre, Inc.
400 S Hope St Ste 2500
Los Angeles CA 90071
213 613-3333

(P-15802)
CBRE GLOBL VALUE INVESTORS LLC (DH)
Also Called: Global Innovation Partner
601 S Figueroa St Ste 49, Los Angeles (90017-5253)
PHONE................213 683-4200
Ritson Ferguson, *CEO*
Charles Leitner, *CEO*
Maurice Voskuilen, *CFO*
Edwin Fung, *Technical Staff*
Joe Meza, *Finance*
EMP: 150 **EST:** 1972
SALES (est): 328.6MM **Publicly Held**
WEB: www.cbreim.com
SIC: 6531 Real estate agent, commercial
HQ: Cbre, Inc.
400 S Hope St Ste 2500
Los Angeles CA 90071
213 613-3333

(P-15803)
CBRE HOLDINGS LLC (HQ)
400 S Hope St Ste 2500, Los Angeles (90071-1993)
PHONE................213 613-3333
EMP: 62 **EST:** 2019
SALES (est): 5.1MM **Publicly Held**
WEB: www.cbre.us
SIC: 6531 6162 8742 Real estate agents & managers; mortgage bankers & correspondents; management consulting services

(P-15804)
CENTURY 21 A BETTER SVC RLTY
5831 Firestone Blvd Ste J, South Gate (90280-3718)
PHONE................562 806-1000
EMP: 97
SQ FT: 4,000
SALES (est): 3.7MM **Privately Held**
WEB: www.c21abetterservice.com
SIC: 6531 Real Estate Agents And Managers

(P-15805)
CENTURY 21 CREST
4005 Foothill Blvd, La Crescenta (91214-1623)
PHONE................818 248-9100
Ray Mirzakhanian, *Owner*
EMP: 80 **EST:** 2004
SALES (est): 1.3MM **Privately Held**
WEB: www.century21.com
SIC: 6531 Real estate agent, residential
PA: E.A.M. Enterprises Inc.
4005 Foothill Blvd
La Crescenta CA 91214

(P-15806)
CENTURY 21 EXCLUSIVE REALTORS
22831 Hawthorne Blvd, Torrance (90505-3615)
PHONE................310 373-5252
EMP: 130 **EST:** 1998
SALES (est): 2.6MM **Privately Held**
SIC: 6531 Rl Este Agntresidntl

(P-15807)
CENTURY 21 LANDMARK PROPERTIES
1650 Ximeno Ave Ste 120, Long Beach (90804-2179)
PHONE................562 422-0911
Fax: 562 428-1842
EMP: 50 **EST:** 1960
SALES (est): 2.3MM **Privately Held**
SIC: 6531 Rl Este Agntresidntl

(P-15808)
CENTURY 21 LUDECKE INC (PA)
34 E Foothill Blvd, Arcadia (91006-2305)
PHONE................626 445-0123
Michael W Ludecke, *President*
Clinton Ludecke, *Manager*
EMP: 55 **EST:** 1983
SALES (est): 5.9MM **Privately Held**
WEB: www.c21ludecke.com
SIC: 6531 Real estate agent, residential

(P-15809)
CENTURY 21 MASTERS (PA)
1169 Fairway Dr Ste 100, Walnut (91789-2847)
PHONE................909 595-6697
Neil Schwartz, *Owner*
Eric Feigenbaum, *COO*
Esther Berg, *Info Tech Mgr*
Javier Guerrero, *Asst Broker*
Dinorah Carmenate, *Broker*
EMP: 69 **EST:** 1989
SALES (est): 9.8MM **Privately Held**
WEB: www.century21masters.com
SIC: 6531 Real estate agent, residential

(P-15810)
CENTURY 21 SUPERSTARS (PA)
22342 Avend Emprs S 155, Rancho Santa Margari (92688)
PHONE................949 888-1950
Phil Romero, *President*
Panky Romero, *Sales Mgr*
EMP: 74 **EST:** 1993
SQ FT: 3,800
SALES (est): 10.2MM **Privately Held**
WEB: www.century21.com
SIC: 6531 Real estate agent, residential

(P-15811)
CENTURY PROPERTIES OWNERS ASSN
Also Called: Century, The
1 W Century Dr, Los Angeles (90067-3401)
PHONE................310 272-8580
EMP: 50 **EST:** 2014

SALES (est): 4.7MM **Privately Held**
WEB: www.related.com
SIC: 6531 Real estate agent, residential

(P-15812)
CHARLES DUNN RE SVCS INC (PA)
800 W 6th St Ste 600, Los Angeles (90017-2709)
PHONE....................213 270-6200
Walter Conn, *CEO*
Patrick Conn, *President*
Charles Dunn, *Vice Pres*
Romy Miura, *Vice Pres*
Kyle Gulock, *Director*
EMP: 86 EST: 1995
SQ FT: 30,000
SALES (est): 10.5MM **Privately Held**
SIC: 6531 Real estate brokers & agents; real estate managers

(P-15813)
CHILD DEVELOPMENT INCORPORATED
17341 Jacquelyn Ln, Huntington Beach (92647-5713)
PHONE....................714 842-4064
EMP: 232
SALES (corp-wide): 28MM **Privately Held**
WEB: www.catalystkids.org
SIC: 6531 Real estate agents & managers
PA: Child Development Incorporated
350 Woodview Ave
Morgan Hill CA 95037
408 556-7300

(P-15814)
CIRRUS ASSET MANAGEMENT INC (PA)
20720 Ventura Blvd # 300, Woodland Hills (91364-6266)
PHONE....................818 222-4840
Steve Heimler, *CEO*
Deek Kapadia, *COO*
Carrie E Roth, *CFO*
Kelli Baldwin, *District Mgr*
Hansa Shamsudeen, *Office Mgr*
EMP: 336 EST: 2007
SALES (est): 35.9MM **Privately Held**
WEB: www.cirrusami.com
SIC: 6531 Real estate managers

(P-15815)
CITIVEST INC
4340 Von Karman Ave # 110, Newport Beach (92660-1201)
PHONE....................949 474-0440
Dana Haynes, *President*
Gerry Martin, *Managing Prtnr*
Johnathan Loevenguth, *CFO*
Larry Weese, *Exec VP*
McCullough Brooke, *Loan*
EMP: 90 EST: 1987
SQ FT: 4,000
SALES (est): 12.5MM **Privately Held**
WEB: www.citivestinc.com
SIC: 6531 Real estate managers

(P-15816)
CITY VENTURES LLC (PA)
3121 Michelson Dr Ste 150, Irvine (92612-5679)
PHONE....................949 258-7555
Mark R Buckland,
Natasha LI, *Bd of Directors*
Ben Besley, *Vice Pres*
Kerry Choppin, *Vice Pres*
Phil Kerr, *Vice Pres*
EMP: 328 EST: 2009
SALES (est): 24.4MM **Privately Held**
WEB: www.cityventures.com
SIC: 6531 Real estate agent, residential

(P-15817)
COASTAL ALLIANCE HOLDINGS INC
Also Called: Coldwell Banker Coastl Aliance
1650 Ximeno Ave Ste 120, Long Beach (90804-2179)
PHONE....................562 370-1000
Jack Irvin, *President*
EMP: 140 EST: 2003

SALES (est): 6.5MM **Privately Held**
WEB: www.cbcoastalalliance.com
SIC: 6531 Real estate agent, residential

(P-15818)
COLDWELL BANKER HOME SOURCE
15500 W Sand St Ste 2, Victorville (92392-2931)
PHONE....................760 684-8100
Jason Lamoreaux, *Owner*
Chris Lamoreaux, *Owner*
Fran Fox, *Broker*
Garrett Dobbs, *Manager*
EMP: 60 EST: 2012
SALES (est): 5.2MM **Privately Held**
WEB: www.coldwellbanker.com
SIC: 6531 Real estate agent, residential

(P-15819)
COLDWELL BANKER RESIDENTIAL (DH)
27742 Vista Del Lago # 1, Mission Viejo (92692-1119)
PHONE....................949 837-5700
Robert M Becker, *President*
Jeffrey Bogert, *President*
Beverly Fairchild, *President*
Gregory S Campbell, *Exec VP*
Robert J Arrigoni, *Senior VP*
EMP: 75 EST: 1987
SALES (est): 98.6MM **Publicly Held**
WEB: www.stacieandrella1.com
SIC: 6531 Real estate agent, residential

(P-15820)
COLDWELL BANKERS RESIDENTIAL (PA)
604 Lindero Canyon Rd, Agoura Hills (91377-5455)
PHONE....................818 575-2660
Irma Haldane, *Manager*
Randy Paller, *Admin Sec*
Anthony Garoosi, *Broker*
James Tess, *Broker*
Pavleta Alexander, *Sales Associate*
EMP: 52 EST: 1978
SALES (est): 13.6MM **Privately Held**
WEB: www.coldwellbanker.com
SIC: 6531 Real estate agent, residential

(P-15821)
COLDWELL BNKR RSDNTIAL RFRRAL (DH)
27271 Las Ramblas, Mission Viejo (92691-8041)
PHONE....................949 367-1800
Robert Becker, *President*
Laura Rittenberg, *Vice Pres*
Millicent Good, *Asst Broker*
Gaye Barnett, *Sales Associate*
Nancy Gunderman, *Sales Associate*
EMP: 410 EST: 1984
SQ FT: 6,000
SALES (est): 210.1MM **Publicly Held**
WEB: www.coldwellbanker.com
SIC: 6531 Real estate agent, residential

(P-15822)
COLDWELL BNKR RSDNTIAL RFRRAL
201 Marine Ave, Newport Beach (92662-1203)
P.O. Box 68 (92662-0068)
PHONE....................949 673-8700
Steve Sutherland, *Manager*
EMP: 504 **Publicly Held**
WEB: www.coldwellbanker.com
SIC: 6531 Real estate agent, residential
HQ: Coldwell Banker Residential Referral Network
27271 Las Ramblas
Mission Viejo CA 92691
949 367-1800

(P-15823)
COLLEGE PARK REALTY INC (PA)
Also Called: Re/Max
10791 Los Alamitos Blvd, Los Alamitos (90720-2309)
PHONE....................562 594-6753
Barry Binder, *President*
Betty Binder, *Treasurer*
Carol Treadway, *Vice Pres*

Brian Binder, *Office Mgr*
Tiffany M Banks, *Admin Asst*
EMP: 80 EST: 1974
SQ FT: 5,000
SALES (est): 11.9MM **Privately Held**
WEB: www.remaxcollegepark.com
SIC: 6531 Real estate agent, residential

(P-15824)
COMMERCIAL PROPERTY MANAGEMENT (PA)
3251 W 6th St Ste 109, Los Angeles (90020-5018)
PHONE....................213 739-2000
David Soufer, *President*
Daniel Azadegan, *Analyst*
EMP: 64 EST: 1990
SQ FT: 4,500
SALES (est): 5.9MM **Privately Held**
WEB: www.cpmusa.com
SIC: 6531 Real estate managers

(P-15825)
CORE REALTY HOLDINGS MGT INC
Also Called: Crh Management
1600 Dove St Ste 450, Newport Beach (92660-2447)
PHONE....................949 863-1031
Dougless Morehead, *CEO*
Justin Morehead, *COO*
Nels Billsten, *Vice Pres*
Donna Grant, *Vice Pres*
David Kish, *Regional Mgr*
EMP: 99 EST: 2010
SALES (est): 7.2MM **Privately Held**
WEB: www.crhmi.com
SIC: 6531 Real estate agent, commercial

(P-15826)
CORELOGIC INC
40 Pacifica Ste 900, Irvine (92618-7487)
PHONE....................714 250-6400
EMP: 50
SALES (corp-wide): 1.8B **Publicly Held**
SIC: 6531 Real Estate Agent/Manager
PA: Corelogic, Inc.
40 Pacifica Ste 900
Irvine CA 92618
949 214-1000

(P-15827)
CRESA PARTNERS LOS ANGELES INC
11726 San Vicente Blvd, Los Angeles (90049-5044)
PHONE....................310 207-1700
Matthew Miller, *President*
Gerald A Porter, *Vice Chairman*
Chris Aitken, *Vice Pres*
Anthony Balbona, *Vice Pres*
Donna Banks, *Vice Pres*
EMP: 50 EST: 1981
SQ FT: 8,500
SALES (est): 1.7MM **Privately Held**
WEB: www.cresa.com
SIC: 6531 Real estate agent, commercial

(P-15828)
CUSHMAN & WAKEFIELD CAL INC
Also Called: Cushman & Wakefield California
7281 Garden Grove Blvd G, Garden Grove (92841-4212)
PHONE....................714 591-0451
EMP: 546
SALES (corp-wide): 7.8B **Privately Held**
WEB: www.cushmanwakefield.com
SIC: 6531 Real estate agent, commercial
HQ: Cushman & Wakefield Of California, Inc.
1 Maritime Plz Ste 900
San Francisco CA 94111
408 275-6730

(P-15829)
CUSHMAN & WAKEFIELD CAL INC
770 Paseo Camarillo 315, Camarillo (93010-6095)
PHONE....................805 322-7244
Robin Fox, *Portfolio Mgr*
EMP: 546

SALES (corp-wide): 7.8B **Privately Held**
WEB: www.cushmanwakefield.com
SIC: 6531 Real estate agent, commercial
HQ: Cushman & Wakefield Of California, Inc.
1 Maritime Plz Ste 900
San Francisco CA 94111
408 275-6730

(P-15830)
CUSHMAN & WAKEFIELD CAL INC
901 Via Piemonte Ste 200, Ontario (91764-6597)
PHONE....................909 980-3781
Luanne Alleman, *Sales/Mktg Mgr*
Scott Evans, *Broker*
Charles Belden, *Director*
EMP: 546
SALES (corp-wide): 7.8B **Privately Held**
WEB: www.cushmanwakefield.com
SIC: 6531 Real estate agent, commercial
HQ: Cushman & Wakefield Of California, Inc.
1 Maritime Plz Ste 900
San Francisco CA 94111
408 275-6730

(P-15831)
CUSHMAN & WAKEFIELD CAL INC
10250 Constellation Blvd # 2200, Los Angeles (90067-6255)
PHONE....................310 556-1805
Eric Olosson, *Manager*
Eric Olofson, *Exec VP*
EMP: 546
SALES (corp-wide): 7.8B **Privately Held**
WEB: www.cushmanwakefield.com
SIC: 6531 Real estate agent, commercial
HQ: Cushman & Wakefield Of California, Inc.
1 Maritime Plz Ste 900
San Francisco CA 94111
408 275-6730

(P-15832)
CUSHMAN & WAKEFIELD CAL INC
3780 Kilroy Arprt Way, Long Beach (90806-2457)
PHONE....................562 276-1400
Joe Vargus, *Manager*
Howard Daschbach, *Director*
Tom Sheets, *Director*
EMP: 546
SALES (corp-wide): 7.8B **Privately Held**
WEB: www.cushmanwakefield.com
SIC: 6531 Real estate agent, commercial
HQ: Cushman & Wakefield Of California, Inc.
1 Maritime Plz Ste 900
San Francisco CA 94111
408 275-6730

(P-15833)
CUSHMAN & WAKEFIELD CAL INC
18111 Von Karman Ave # 1000, Irvine (92612-7101)
PHONE....................949 474-4004
Dee Shipley, *Sales/Mktg Mgr*
John Griffin, *Director*
EMP: 546
SALES (corp-wide): 7.8B **Privately Held**
WEB: www.cushmanwakefield.com
SIC: 6531 Real estate agent, commercial
HQ: Cushman & Wakefield Of California, Inc.
1 Maritime Plz Ste 900
San Francisco CA 94111
408 275-6730

(P-15834)
DEAN GOODMAN INC
10833 Valley View St # 240, Cypress (90630-5051)
PHONE....................714 229-8999
Candice H Miller, *President*
Amber Henson, *Admin Mgr*
Ray Pelaez, *Dean*
Jennifer Haider, *Manager*
Stacy McCombs, *Manager*
EMP: 55 EST: 1993

P R O D U C T S & S V C S

SALES (est): 3.7MM Privately Held
WEB: www.goodmandean.com
SIC: 6531 Appraiser, real estate

(P-15835)
**DECRON PROPERTIES CORP
(PA)**
6222 Wilshire Blvd # 400, Los Angeles
(90048-5100)
PHONE..........................323 556-6600
Jack M Nagel, *Ch of Bd*
David J Nagel, *President*
Elias E Danho, *CFO*
Elias Danho, *Officer*
Zev Nagel, *Exec VP*
EMP: 135 EST: 1988
SQ FT: 14,089
SALES (est): 34.2MM Privately Held
WEB: www.decron.com
SIC: 6531 6552 1542 Real estate man-
agers; land subdividers & developers;
commercial; commercial & office building
contractors

(P-15836)
**DESERT RESORT
MANAGEMENT**
42635 Melanie Pl Ste 103, Palm Desert
(92211-9113)
PHONE..........................760 831-0172
Mark Dodge, *President*
Walter KAO, *Accountant*
Julie Harris, *HR Admin*
EMP: 52 EST: 1987
SQ FT: 11,000
SALES (est): 5.3MM Privately Held
WEB: www.drminternet.com
SIC: 6531 Condominium manager; real es-
tate managers

(P-15837)
**DIAMOND RIDGE
CORPORATION**
Also Called: Re/Max
121 S Mountain Ave, Upland (91786-6257)
PHONE..........................909 949-0605
Jennifer Lynn Puglisi, *CEO*
Catherine Garza, *Associate*
EMP: 165 EST: 2001
SALES (est): 12MM Privately Held
WEB: www.remaxchampions.com
SIC: 6531 Real estate agent, residential

(P-15838)
DILBECK INC (PA)
Also Called: Dilbeck Realtors
1030 Foothill Blvd, La Canada
(91011-3285)
PHONE..........................818 790-6774
Mark Dilbeck, *Ch of Bd*
Lynn Kornmann, *CFO*
Sean Baroni, *Vice Pres*
Bruce Dilbeck, *Admin Sec*
Edgar De Alba, *Graphic Designe*
EMP: 70 EST: 1963
SQ FT: 9,000
SALES (est): 15.7MM Privately Held
WEB: www.dilbeck.com
SIC: 6531 Real estate agent, commercial;
real estate managers

(P-15839)
DILBECK INC
Also Called: Dilbeck Realtors
850 Hampshire Rd Ste A, Westlake Village
(91361-2800)
PHONE..........................805 379-1880
Chuck Lech, *Branch Mgr*
Millie Gordon, *Manager*
EMP: 50
SALES (corp-wide): 15.7MM Privately
Held
WEB: www.dilbeck.com
SIC: 6531 Real estate agent, commercial;
real estate managers
PA: Dilbeck Inc.
1030 Foothill Blvd
La Canada CA 91011
818 790-6774

(P-15840)
**DONAHUE SCHRBER RLTY
GROUP INC (PA)**
200 Baker St Ste 100, Costa Mesa
(92626-4551)
PHONE..........................714 545-1400
Thomas Schriber, *Ch of Bd*
Patrick S Donahue, *President*
Larry Casey, *CFO*
EMP: 80 EST: 1954
SQ FT: 20,000
SALES (est): 57.3MM Privately Held
WEB: www.donahueschriber.com
SIC: 6531 Real estate agent, commercial

(P-15841)
**E & S RING MANAGEMENT
CORP**
Also Called: Mariner's Village
4600 Via Marina Apt 209, Marina Del Rey
(90292-7231)
PHONE..........................310 821-4916
Christine Valentino, *Manager*
Kandi Wolf-Brown, *Manager*
EMP: 63
SALES (corp-wide): 52.5MM Privately
Held
WEB: www.esring.com
SIC: 6531 6513 Real estate managers;
apartment building operators
PA: E & S Ring Management Corp.
6601 Center Dr W Ste 600
Culver City CA 90230
310 337-5400

(P-15842)
**E & S RING MANAGEMENT
CORP**
Also Called: Bar Hrbor Apartments Anchorage
11050 Santa Monica Blvd # 2, Los Angeles
(90025-7571)
PHONE..........................310 337-5444
Katie Bailey, *Manager*
Jesse Hill, *Manager*
Alicia Miranda, *Manager*
EMP: 63
SALES (corp-wide): 52.5MM Privately
Held
WEB: www.esring.com
SIC: 6531 Real estate managers
PA: E & S Ring Management Corp.
6601 Center Dr W Ste 600
Culver City CA 90230
310 337-5400

(P-15843)
**E & S RING MANAGEMENT
CORP**
Also Called: Meadows, The
6300 Green Valley Cir, Culver City
(90230-7009)
PHONE..........................310 670-5983
Kelly Donavan, *Manager*
EMP: 63
SALES (corp-wide): 52.5MM Privately
Held
WEB: www.esring.com
SIC: 6531 6513 Real estate managers;
apartment hotel operation
PA: E & S Ring Management Corp.
6601 Center Dr W Ste 600
Culver City CA 90230
310 337-5400

(P-15844)
EAM ENTERPRISES INC (PA)
Also Called: Crest R E O & Relocation
4005 Foothill Blvd, La Crescenta
(91214-1623)
PHONE..........................818 248-9100
Razmik Mirzakhanian, *CEO*
EMP: 100 EST: 1991
SQ FT: 5,000
SALES (est): 11.5MM Privately Held
WEB: www.crestreo.com
SIC: 6531 Real estate agent, residential

(P-15845)
ELMER F KARPE INC
Also Called: Karpe Real Estate Center
8501 Camino Media Ste 400, Bakersfield
(93311-1358)
P.O. Box 1968 (93303-1968)
PHONE..........................661 847-4800
Raymond Karpe, *President*

Craig Lindsay, *CFO*
Scott Berry, *Vice Pres*
Jerrold Fisher, *Vice Pres*
Randy Merriman, *Vice Pres*
EMP: 50 EST: 1925
SQ FT: 7,200
SALES (est): 5.9MM Privately Held
WEB: www.karpe.com
SIC: 6531 6163 Real estate brokers &
agents; mortgage brokers arranging for
loans, using money of others

(P-15846)
ESSEX PROPERTIES LLC
18012 Sky Park Cir # 200, Irvine
(92614-6671)
PHONE..........................949 798-8100
Jim Niger, *President*
Burrel D Magnusson, *Chairman*
Linda Webber, *Vice Pres*
Peggy Saylor, *Info Tech Dir*
Susan Longshore, *Marketing Staff*
EMP: 75 EST: 1987
SALES (est): 2.2MM Privately Held
WEB: www.essexrealty.com
SIC: 6531 Real estate agent, commercial

(P-15847)
EVOQ PROPERTIES INC
1318 E 7th St Ste 200, Los Angeles
(90021-1128)
PHONE..........................213 988-8890
Martin Caveroy, *CEO*
John Charles Maddux, *President*
Andrew Murray, *CFO*
Miguel Enrique Echemendia, *Officer*
Lynn Beckemeyer, *Exec VP*
EMP: 82 EST: 2006
SALES (est): 5.8MM Privately Held
WEB: www.evoqproperties.com
SIC: 6531 Real estate agent, commercial;
real estate agent, residential

(P-15848)
EVR LENDING INC (PA)
Also Called: Evergreen Realty
9901 Irvine Center Dr, Irvine (92618-4308)
PHONE..........................949 753-7888
Valentina Rector, *CEO*
Randy Rector, *President*
Damara Gray, *Officer*
Lorraine Zuschlag, *CTO*
Vimpi Pawra, *Loan Officer*
EMP: 74 EST: 2004
SALES (est): 15.8MM Privately Held
WEB: www.homeloansandequity.com
SIC: 6531 Real estate brokers & agents

(P-15849)
**EXCELSIOR CAPITAL
PARTNERS LLC (PA)**
4695 Macarthur Ct Ste 370, Newport Beach
(92660-8868)
P.O. Box 2385 (92659-1385)
PHONE..........................949 566-8110
Ravi Bhagavatula, *Mng Member*
Andrew Young, *Associate*
EMP: 110 EST: 2011
SALES (est): 79.3MM Privately Held
WEB: www.excelcp.com
SIC: 6531 Real estate agent, commercial

(P-15850)
F M TARBELL CO
Also Called: Tarbell Realtors
321 S State College Blvd, Anaheim
(92806-4118)
PHONE..........................714 772-8990
Fax: 714 772-3801
EMP: 55
SALES (corp-wide): 134.2MM Privately
Held
SIC: 6531 Real Estate Agents And Brokers
HQ: F. M. Tarbell Co
1403 N Tustin Ave Ste 380
Santa Ana CA 92705
714 972-0988

(P-15851)
F M TARBELL CO (HQ)
Also Called: Tarbell Realtors
1403 N Tustin Ave Ste 380, Santa Ana
(92705-8691)
PHONE..........................714 972-0988
Tina Jimov, *President*
Donald M Tarbell, *CEO*

Urrea Gilbert, *Info Tech Dir*
Eva De Fuente, *Real Est Agnt*
EMP: 110 EST: 1956
SQ FT: 60,000
SALES (est): 53.8MM
SALES (corp-wide): 145.1MM Privately
Held
WEB: www.jen4homes.com
SIC: 6531 Real estate agent, residential
PA: Tarbell Financial Corporation
1403 N Tustin Ave Ste 380
Santa Ana CA 92705
714 972-0988

(P-15852)
F M TARBELL CO
Also Called: Tarbell Realtors
73700 El Paseo, Palm Desert
(92260-4380)
PHONE..........................760 346-7405
Dan Trevino, *Branch Mgr*
Carol Rounsley, *Broker*
Alonso Umanzor, *Real Est Agnt*
EMP: 50
SALES (corp-wide): 145.1MM Privately
Held
WEB: www.jen4homes.com
SIC: 6531 Real estate brokers & agents
HQ: F. M. Tarbell Co.
1403 N Tustin Ave Ste 380
Santa Ana CA 92705
714 972-0988

(P-15853)
FAIRWAY REALTY INC (PA)
Also Called: Century 21
14281 Seventh St, Victorville (92395-4207)
PHONE..........................760 245-3471
James Phillips, *President*
Joe Rinchiuso, *Broker*
Lauren Decker, *Real Est Agnt*
Steve Hess, *Real Est Agnt*
Myrna Scorza, *Real Est Agn*
EMP: 53 EST: 1972
SQ FT: 3,000
SALES (est): 7.1MM Privately Held
WEB: www.century21fairway.com
SIC: 6531 Real estate agent, residential

(P-15854)
FIRST & LA REALTY CORP (PA)
Also Called: Century 21 Hill Top Realtors
1301 E Los Angeles Ave, Simi Valley
(93065-2882)
PHONE..........................805 581-0021
Robert Connlee, *President*
Pat Connlee, *Treasurer*
Susan Hill, *Admin Sec*
EMP: 67 EST: 1983
SQ FT: 2,600
SALES (est): 5.2MM Privately Held
WEB: www.century21.com
SIC: 6531 Real estate agent, residential

(P-15855)
**FIRST AMERCN PRCF RE SVCS
INC (HQ)**
200 Commerce, Irvine (92602-5000)
PHONE..........................714 250-1400
Larry Davidson, *President*
Jones Eric, *President*
Jerry Bumbaugh, *CFO*
Mickey Allee, *Exec VP*
Scott Klein, *Vice Pres*
EMP: 240 EST: 1997
SQ FT: 28,000
SALES (est): 26.7MM Publicly Held
WEB: www.firstamsms.com
SIC: 6531 Real estate agents & managers

(P-15856)
**FIRST AMERICAN TEAM REALTY
INC (PA)**
Also Called: Best Financial, The
2501 Cherry Ave Ste 100, Signal Hill
(90755-2039)
PHONE..........................562 427-7765
Steve S Vong, *President*
Ron Jimenez, *Manager*
Raymond Ramirez, *Rea Est Agnt*
EMP: 150 EST: 1995
SQ FT: 3,300
SALES (est): 9.5MM Privately Held
WEB: www.firstamericanteam.com
SIC: 6531 Real estate agent, residential

(P-15857)
FIRST TEAM RE - ORANGE CNTY
18180 Yorba Linda Blvd # 501, Yorba Linda (92886-3901)
PHONE..............714 223-2143
EMP: 100
SALES (corp-wide): 63.6MM Privately Held
SIC: 6531 Real Estate Agent/Manager
PA: First Team Real Estate - Orange County
108 Pacifica Ste 300
Irvine CA 92618
888 236-1943

(P-15858)
FIRST TEAM RE - ORANGE CNTY
12501 Seal Beach Blvd # 1, Seal Beach (90740-2763)
PHONE..............562 596-9911
Judy Sharp, Manager
Carole Campbell, Real Est Agnt
Celeste Haybittle, Real Est Agnt
Simone Moore, Real Est Agnt
Nancy Nam, Real Est Agnt
EMP: 119
SALES (corp-wide): 263.9MM Privately Held
WEB: www.firstteam.com
SIC: 6531 Real estate agent, residential; real estate brokers & agents
PA: First Team Real Estate - Orange County
108 Pacifica Ste 300
Irvine CA 92618
888 236-1943

(P-15859)
FIRST TEAM RE - ORANGE CNTY
4 Corporate Plaza Dr # 100, Newport Beach (92660-7906)
PHONE..............949 759-5747
Jennifer Berman, Office Mgr
Daniel Pirz, Agent
Kristin Ajer, Real Est Agnt
Ilene Aldrich, Real Est Agnt
Margaret Brien, Real Est Agnt
EMP: 119
SALES (corp-wide): 263.9MM Privately Held
WEB: www.firstteam.com
SIC: 6531 Real estate brokers & agents
PA: First Team Real Estate - Orange County
108 Pacifica Ste 300
Irvine CA 92618
888 236-1943

(P-15860)
FIRST TEAM RE - ORANGE CNTY (PA)
Also Called: First Team Walk-In Realty
108 Pacifica Ste 300, Irvine (92618-7435)
PHONE..............888 236-1943
Cameron Merage, CEO
Michele Harrington, COO
Gary Fabian, CFO
Michelle Williams Harringto, Vice Pres
Jeana Sander, Branch Mgr
EMP: 160 EST: 1976
SQ FT: 8,000
SALES (est): 263.9MM Privately Held
WEB: www.firstteam.com
SIC: 6531 Real estate agent, residential

(P-15861)
FIRST TEAM RE - ORANGE CNTY
200 S Main St Ste 100, Corona (92882-2213)
PHONE..............951 270-2800
Linda Rocha, Principal
Kathleen Rapoza, Real Est Agnt
Norma Rodriguez, Real Est Agnt
EMP: 119
SALES (corp-wide): 263.9MM Privately Held
WEB: www.firstteam.com
SIC: 6531 Real estate brokers & agents

PA: First Team Real Estate - Orange County
108 Pacifica Ste 300
Irvine CA 92618
888 236-1943

(P-15862)
FIRST TEAM RE - ORANGE CNTY
42 64th Pl, Long Beach (90803-5676)
PHONE..............562 346-5088
EMP: 119
SALES (corp-wide): 263.9MM Privately Held
WEB: www.firstteam.com
SIC: 6531 Real estate agent, residential
PA: First Team Real Estate - Orange County
108 Pacifica Ste 300
Irvine CA 92618
888 236-1943

(P-15863)
FIRST TEAM RE - ORANGE CNTY
32451 Golden Lantern # 21, Laguna Niguel (92677-5344)
PHONE..............949 240-7979
Mark Kojac, General Mgr
Debbie Quechenberger, Agent
Beau Beardslee, Real Est Agnt
Jacqueline Chase, Real Est Agnt
Colin Farris, Real Est Agnt
EMP: 119
SALES (corp-wide): 263.9MM Privately Held
WEB: www.firstteam.com
SIC: 6531 Real estate agent, residential
PA: First Team Real Estate - Orange County
108 Pacifica Ste 300
Irvine CA 92618
888 236-1943

(P-15864)
FIRST TEAM RE - ORANGE CNTY
Also Called: 1st Team Real Estate
17240 17th St, Tustin (92780-1945)
PHONE..............714 544-5456
Michael Hampton, Manager
Scott Gruszczynski, Controller
Howard Poulton, Broker
Loriann Andreotti, Sales Associate
Chizuko Higuchi, Sales Associate
EMP: 119
SALES (corp-wide): 263.9MM Privately Held
WEB: www.firstteam.com
SIC: 6531 Real estate agent, residential
PA: First Team Real Estate - Orange County
108 Pacifica Ste 300
Irvine CA 92618
888 236-1943

(P-15865)
FIRST TEAM RE - ORANGE CNTY
8028 E Santa Ana Cyn Rd, Anaheim (92808-1108)
PHONE..............714 974-9191
Anna Bennet, Manager
Sandra Meucci, Office Admin
Sharon Campa, Real Est Agnt
Tauna Crippen, Real Est Agnt
Andy Lam, Real Est Agnt
EMP: 119
SALES (corp-wide): 263.9MM Privately Held
WEB: www.firstteam.com
SIC: 6531 Real estate brokers & agents
PA: First Team Real Estate - Orange County
108 Pacifica Ste 300
Irvine CA 92618
888 236-1943

(P-15866)
FIRST TEAM RE - ORANGE CNTY
26711 Aliso Creek Rd, Aliso Viejo (92656-4820)
PHONE..............949 389-0004
Michele Williams, Branch Mgr

Peggy Salazar, Director
EMP: 150
SALES (corp-wide): 263.9MM Privately Held
WEB: www.firstteam.com
SIC: 6531 Real estate brokers & agents
PA: First Team Real Estate - Orange County
108 Pacifica Ste 300
Irvine CA 92618
888 236-1943

(P-15867)
FIRSTSERVICE RESIDENTIAL (HQ)
Also Called: Merit Companies The
15241 Laguna Canyon Rd, Irvine (92618-3146)
PHONE..............949 448-6000
Bob Cardoza, President
Robbin Brown, Exec VP
Shane Gillaspie, Exec VP
John Santoro, Exec VP
Roy Almeida, Vice Pres
EMP: 200 EST: 1980
SQ FT: 21,000
SALES (est): 239.6MM
SALES (corp-wide): 2.4B Privately Held
WEB: www.fsresidential.com
SIC: 6531 Real estate managers
PA: Firstservice Corporation
1255 Bay St Suite 600
Toronto ON M5R 2
416 960-9566

(P-15868)
FIRSTSRVICE RSIDENTIAL CAL INC (DH)
9130 Anaheim Pl Ste 110, Rancho Cucamonga (91730-8540)
P.O. Box 1510, Upland (91785-1510)
PHONE..............909 981-4131
Glennon Gray, President
James Gray, Vice Pres
Tad Creasey, Property Mgr
Deborah Maglasang, Property Mgr
Lorena Vasquez,
EMP: 69 EST: 1986
SALES (est): 20.4MM
SALES (corp-wide): 2.4B Privately Held
WEB: www.fsresidential.com
SIC: 6531 Real estate managers

(P-15869)
FIVE POINT HOLDINGS LLC (PA)
15131 Alton Pkwy Ste 400, Irvine (92618-2386)
PHONE..............949 349-1000
Emile Haddad, Ch of Bd
Lynn Jochim, COO
Erik R Higgins, CFO
Michael Alvarado,
Greg McWilliams,
EMP: 107 EST: 2009
SALES (est): 153.6MM Publicly Held
WEB: www.fivepoint.com
SIC: 6531 Real estate brokers & agents; real estate agent, commercial; real estate agent, residential

(P-15870)
FOREST HLLS INVSTORS MMBER LLC (HQ)
15301 Ventura Blvd B570, Sherman Oaks (91403-3102)
PHONE..............818 808-0600
Gregory Pearlman,
Clarice Silva,
EMP: 62 EST: 2010
SALES (est): 477.9K Privately Held
SIC: 6531 Real estate agent, commercial

(P-15871)
FRED LEEDS PROPERTIES
3860 Crenshaw Blvd # 201, Los Angeles (90008-1851)
PHONE..............310 826-2466
Fred Leeds, President
Serenity Pelayo, Property Mgr
EMP: 50 EST: 1976
SQ FT: 3,000
SALES (est): 5.7MM Privately Held
WEB: www.fredleedsproperties.com
SIC: 6531 Real estate agents & managers

(P-15872)
GEMDALE USA CORPORATION (HQ)
680 E Colo Blvd Ste 300, Pasadena (91101)
PHONE..............626 381-9709
Jason Zhu, CEO
Stephen D Hutto, Ch Invest Ofcr
Dongbo Wang, Exec VP
Allen Huang, Exec Dir
Tim Nguyen, Exec Dir
EMP: 62 EST: 2016
SALES (est): 11.1MM Privately Held
WEB: www.gemdaleusa.com
SIC: 6531 Real estate managers

(P-15873)
GEMMM CORP (PA)
Also Called: Prudential
2860 E Thousand Oaks Blvd, Thousand Oaks (91362-3201)
PHONE..............805 496-0555
Robert L Majorino, President
Anthony Principe, CFO
Robert Hamilton, Vice Pres
Lynn Gilbert, Admin Sec
Kimberly Chan, Broker
EMP: 100 EST: 1990
SQ FT: 12,500
SALES (est): 20.6MM Privately Held
WEB: www.juliechavannes.com
SIC: 6531 Real estate agent, residential

(P-15874)
GK MANAGEMENT CO INC (PA)
5150 Overland Ave, Culver City (90230-4914)
PHONE..............310 204-2050
Carole Glodney, CEO
Jona Goldrich, Vice Pres
Lori Horn, Vice Pres
Paul Dubord, Managing Dir
Cecy Avilla, Regional Mgr
EMP: 150 EST: 1972
SALES (est): 99.8MM Privately Held
WEB: www.goldrichkest.com
SIC: 6531 Real estate managers

(P-15875)
GOODMAN NORTH AMERICA LLC (PA)
18201 Von Karman Ave # 1, Irvine (92612-1000)
PHONE..............949 407-0100
Brandon Birtcher, CEO
Dan Grable, COO
Shannon Hondl, Officer
Charles Crossland, Managing Dir
Ben McGilp, General Mgr
EMP: 53 EST: 1939
SALES (est): 20.3MM Privately Held
SIC: 6531 6552 1542 Real estate managers; land subdividers & developers, commercial; commercial & office building, new construction

(P-15876)
GREYSTAR MANAGEMENT SVCS LP
6320 Canoga Ave Ste 1512, Woodland Hills (91367-2526)
PHONE..............818 596-2180
Grace White, Owner
Janelle Yule, Manager
EMP: 278 Privately Held
WEB: www.greystar.com
SIC: 6531 Real estate brokers & agents
PA: Greystar Management Services, L.P.
750 Bering Dr Ste 300
Houston TX 77057

(P-15877)
GREYSTAR MANAGEMENT SVCS LP
620 Nwport Ctr Dr Fl 15 Flr 15, Newport Beach (92660)
PHONE..............949 705-0010
Kevin Kaverna, Director
Ezequiel Del Rio Jr, Regional Mgr
Richard Barnes, CIO
Catherine Tang, Marketing Staff
Holly Jones, Manager
EMP: 278 Privately Held
WEB: www.greystar.com

PRODUCTS & SVCS

SIC: 6531 Real estate managers
PA: Greystar Management Services, L.P.
750 Bering Dr Ste 300
Houston TX 77057

(P-15878)
GSF PROPERTIES INC
Also Called: Casa Serena Apts
5051 Ming Ave Apt 69, Bakersfield
(93309-4761)
PHONE..........................661 834-1498
Haresh Singh, *Manager*
Michael Salles, *Controller*
Joedavid Sanchez, *Asst Mgr*
EMP: 57 Privately Held
WEB: www.gsfpi.com
SIC: 6531 Real estate brokers & agents
PA: Gsf Properties Inc.
6485 N Palm Ave Ste 101
Fresno CA 93704

(P-15879)
HANNAKNAPP REALTY INC
Also Called: Century 21
15311 Bear Valley Rd # 1, Hesperia
(92345-0833)
PHONE..........................760 244-8557
Hannelore Hannaknapp, *President*
Charles Knapp, *Owner*
EMP: 50 EST: 1989
SALES (est): 2.9MM Privately Held
WEB: www.century21.com
SIC: 6531 Real estate agent, residential

(P-15880)
HARTWIG REALTY INC (PA)
Also Called: Coldwell Banker Hartwig Co
43912 20th St W, Lancaster (93534-5221)
PHONE..........................661 948-8424
Burl W Patterson, *President*
Conrad Engelhardt, *Vice Pres*
Dennis McCollam, *Sales Staff*
EMP: 53 EST: 1957
SQ FT: 20,000
SALES (est): 7.2MM Privately Held
WEB: www.coldwellbanker.com
SIC: 6531 Real estate agent, residential

(P-15881)
HERTZ INVESTMENT GROUP LLC (PA)
21860 Burbank Blvd # 300, Woodland Hills
(91367-6477)
PHONE..........................310 584-8000
Gary Horwitz, *President*
William Brown, *Vice Pres*
Don Dvorin, *Vice Pres*
Alex Faguet, *Vice Pres*
Donald Fishoff, *Vice Pres*
EMP: 127 EST: 2007
SALES (est): 71.6MM Privately Held
WEB: www.hertzgroup.com
SIC: 6531 Real estate managers

(P-15882)
HOUSE SEVEN GABLES RE INC
19440 Goldenwest St, Huntington Beach
(92648-2116)
PHONE..........................714 500-3300
Terry Reay, *Manager*
Lisa Dowell, *Real Est Agnt*
EMP: 68
SALES (corp-wide): 33.4MM Privately
Held
WEB: www.sevengables.com
SIC: 6531 Real estate agent, residential
PA: House Of Seven Gables Real Estate,
Inc.
12651 Newport Ave
Tustin CA 92780
714 731-3777

(P-15883)
HOUSE SEVEN GABLES RE INC
5481 E Santa Ana Cyn Dr, Anaheim
(92807-3100)
PHONE..........................714 974-7000
Mike Hickman, *Branch Mgr*
EMP: 68
SALES (corp-wide): 33.4MM Privately
Held
WEB: www.sevengables.com
SIC: 6531 Real estate agent, residential

PA: House Of Seven Gables Real Estate,
Inc.
12651 Newport Ave
Tustin CA 92780
714 731-3777

(P-15884)
HOUSE SEVEN GABLES RE INC
Also Called: AMC
16872 Bolsa Chica St # 1, Huntington
Beach (92649-3509)
PHONE..........................714 754-6262
Kelli Ludden, *CFO*
EMP: 68
SALES (corp-wide): 33.4MM Privately
Held
WEB: www.sevengables.com
SIC: 6531 Real estate brokers & agents
PA: House Of Seven Gables Real Estate,
Inc.
12651 Newport Ave
Tustin CA 92780
714 731-3777

(P-15885)
HOUSE SEVEN GABLES RE INC
Also Called: Cole, Norman Anne
5753 E Santa Ana Canyon P, Anaheim
(92807-3230)
PHONE..........................714 282-0306
Kelli Ludden, *CFO*
EMP: 68
SALES (corp-wide): 33.4MM Privately
Held
WEB: www.sevengables.com
SIC: 6531 Real estate brokers & agents
PA: House Of Seven Gables Real Estate,
Inc.
12651 Newport Ave
Tustin CA 92780
714 731-3777

(P-15886)
HUNT ENTERPRISES INC
Also Called: Shibui Apartments
2270 Sepulveda Blvd # 50, Torrance
(90501-5304)
PHONE..........................310 325-1496
EMP: 106
SQ FT: 53,813
SALES (corp-wide): 13.1MM Privately
Held
WEB: www.shibuiaptstorrance.com
SIC: 6531 Real estate leasing & rentals
PA: Hunt Enterprises, Inc.
4416 W 154th St
Lawndale CA 90260
310 675-3555

(P-15887)
I D PROPERTY CORPORATION
Also Called: Property I D
1001 Wilshire Blvd # 100, Los Angeles
(90017-2820)
PHONE..........................213 625-0100
Carlos Siderman, *President*
John Cote, *President*
Victor Marquez, *Executive*
Cynthia Marquez, *Managing Dir*
Janet Martinez, *Admin Asst*
▲ EMP: 120 EST: 1983
SALES (est): 10.2MM Privately Held
WEB: www.propertyid.com
SIC: 6531 8742 Real estate listing serv-
ices; real estate consultant

(P-15888)
IDS REAL ESTATE GROUP (PA)
Also Called: I S D
515 S Figueroa St # 1600, Los Angeles
(90071-3301)
PHONE..........................213 627-9937
Murad M Siam, *CEO*
David G Mgrubllan, *President*
Mickey Siam, *COO*
Jeff Newman, *CFO*
Lauren Cain, *Officer*
EMP: 60 EST: 1986
SQ FT: 20,000
SALES (est): 17.5MM Privately Held
WEB: www.idsrealestate.com
SIC: 6531 Real estate agent, commercial;
real estate managers

(P-15889)
IMPACT REALTY INC (PA)
Also Called: Century 21
3110 E Garvey Ave S, West Covina
(91791-2344)
PHONE..........................626 331-4868
Taffy Bishara, *President*
EMP: 123 EST: 1980
SQ FT: 4,600
SALES (est): 5.1MM Privately Held
WEB: www.rmoly.com
SIC: 6531 6162 Real estate brokers &
agents; escrow agent, real estate; mort-
gage bankers & correspondents

(P-15890)
INLAND EMPIRE RE SOLUTIONS
Also Called: Remax Legends
8794 19th St, Alta Loma (91701-4608)
P.O. Box 129, Rancho Cucamonga (91739-
0129)
PHONE..........................909 476-1000
EMP: 76
SQ FT: 5,600
SALES: 4MM Privately Held
SIC: 6531 Real Estate Agent/Manager

(P-15891)
INTERCOASTAL PROPERTY SVCS LLC (PA)
Also Called: Intercoastal Group
1755 E Martin Lu, Los Angeles (90058)
PHONE..........................310 277-0057
Sheldon P Berger, *President*
Charles Dethloff, *Exec Dir*
Pearl Gray, *Regional Mgr*
Sue Rager, *Regional Mgr*
Alec Frank, *Marketing Staff*
EMP: 111 EST: 1999
SALES (est): 9.6MM Privately Held
SIC: 6531 Real estate managers

(P-15892)
INVESERVE CORPORATION
123 S Chapel Ave, Alhambra (91801-3951)
PHONE..........................626 458-3435
Norman Chang, *President*
Amy Chang, *Vice Pres*
Michael Fang, *Advisor*
EMP: 80 EST: 1987
SQ FT: 1,000
SALES (est): 7.2MM Privately Held
WEB: www.inveserve.com
SIC: 6531 Real estate agent, commercial;
real estate managers

(P-15893)
J & M REALTY COMPANY (PA)
41 Corporate Park Ste 240, Irvine
(92606-3125)
PHONE..........................949 261-2727
John Woolley, *President*
Michael Aimola, *General Mgr*
EMP: 78 EST: 1988
SQ FT: 4,000
SALES (est): 6.5MM Privately Held
SIC: 6531 8641 6798 6519 Real estate
managers; homeowners' association; real
estate investment trusts; real property
lessors; apartment building operators;
nonresidential building operators

(P-15894)
J H SYNDER CO LLC
5757 Wilshire Blvd Ph 30, Los Angeles
(90036-3690)
PHONE..........................323 857-5546
Jerome Snyder, *Managing Prtnr*
Joseph Irvine, *Vice Pres*
Patrick Irvine, *Vice Pres*
Dan Schneider, *Vice Pres*
Jose Anaya, *Info Tech Mgr*
EMP: 60 EST: 1997
SALES (est): 5.5MM Privately Held
WEB: www.jhsnyder.net
SIC: 6531 Buying agent, real estate

(P-15895)
JAMBOREE REALTY CORP (PA)
Also Called: Jamboree Management
22982 Mill Creek Dr, Laguna Hills
(92653-1214)
PHONE..........................949 380-0300
Fred G Sparks, *President*
Richard M Tucker, *CEO*
Kathleen Tucker, *Treasurer*

Jeremy Metz, *Vice Pres*
Ed Rash, *Vice Pres*
EMP: 120 EST: 1982
SALES (est): 23.4MM Privately Held
WEB: www.jamboreemanagement.com
SIC: 6531 Real estate managers

(P-15896)
JC MAJESTIC REAL ESTATE LLC ✪
6750 Clybourn Ave Apt 218, North Holly-
wood (91606-2248)
PHONE..........................800 398-6879
Jojo Crown, *CEO*
EMP: 50 EST: 2021
SALES (est): 1.2MM Privately Held
SIC: 6531 Real estate agent, residential

(P-15897)
JOHN STEWART COMPANY
888 S Figueroa St Ste 700, Los Angeles
(90017-5320)
PHONE..........................213 787-2700
Monica Salirdano, *Branch Mgr*
Daphne Oakley, *Accounting Mgr*
Peter Purtell, *Director*
EMP: 50
SALES (corp-wide): 118MM Privately
Held
WEB: www.jsco.net
SIC: 6531 6513 Real estate managers;
apartment building operators
PA: John Stewart Company
1388 Sutter St Ste 1100
San Francisco CA 94109
415 345-4400

(P-15898)
JORDAN - LINK & COMPANY (PA)
Also Called: Century 21
2009 W Feemster Ave, Visalia
(93277-2111)
PHONE..........................559 733-9696
Bill Jordan, *President*
Steve McFadden, *Vice Pres*
Curt Link, *Admin Sec*
Raquel Galaviz, *Admin Asst*
Lana Fahoum, *Manager*
EMP: 95 EST: 1976
SQ FT: 11,200
SALES (est): 14.6MM Privately Held
WEB: www.jordanlink.com
SIC: 6531 Real estate agent, residential

(P-15899)
KELLER WLLAMS RLTY BVRLY HILLS
Also Called: Keller Williams Realtors
439 N Canon Dr Ste 300, Beverly Hills
(90210-3909)
PHONE..........................310 432-6400
Paul Morris, *Principal*
EMP: 90 EST: 2005
SALES (est): 10.7MM Privately Held
WEB: www.kwbeverlyhills.com
SIC: 6531 Real estate agent, residential

(P-15900)
KENNEDY-WILSON INC (PA)
151 El Camino Dr, Beverly Hills
(90212-2704)
PHONE..........................310 887-6400
William McMorrow, *Ch of Bd*
Justin Enbody, *CFO*
Fraser Kennedy, *CFO*
Matt Windisch, *Exec VP*
Scott Gordon, *Senior VP*
EMP: 103 EST: 1977
SALES (est): 109.7MM Privately Held
WEB: www.kennedywilson.com
SIC: 6531 6799 Auction, real estate; real
estate investors, except property opera-
tors

(P-15901)
KEYSTONE PCF PROPERTY MGT INC (PA)
Also Called: Reflections and Enclave Hoa
16775 Von Karman Ave # 100, Irvine
(92606-4966)
PHONE..........................949 833-2600
Cary Treff, *President*
Denise Bergstrom, *COO*
Lonnie Hardin, *COO*

Jared Jones, *CFO*
Gerry Kay, *CFO*
EMP: 55 **EST:** 1982
SALES (est): 20.3MM **Privately Held**
WEB: www.kppm.com
SIC: 6531 Real estate managers

(P-15902)
KILROY REALTY LP (PA)
12200 W Olympic Blvd # 200, Los Angeles
(90064-1044)
PHONE....................310 481-8400
John B Kilroy Jr, *President*
Kilroy Realty Corporation, *General Ptnr*
Michelle Ngo, *CFO*
EMP: 192 **EST:** 1996
SALES (est): 898.4MM **Privately Held**
WEB: www.kilroyrealty.com
SIC: 6531 6798 Real estate agent, commercial; real estate investment trusts

(P-15903)
KINGZ & KOMPANY LLC
3415 S Sepulveda Blvd # 1, Los Angeles
(90034-6060)
PHONE....................888 274-8882
Jonte B King,
EMP: 50 **EST:** 2020
SALES (est): 1MM **Privately Held**
SIC: 6531 Real estate leasing & rentals

(P-15904)
KOR REALTY GROUP LLC (PA)
1212 S Flower St Fl 5, Los Angeles
(90015-2123)
PHONE....................323 930-3700
Bradford Korzen,
Jeffrey Smith,
EMP: 71 **EST:** 2001
SQ FT: 6,500
SALES (est): 5MM **Privately Held**
SIC: 6531 Real estate managers

(P-15905)
LA CIENEGA ASSOCIATES
Also Called: Beverly Center
8500 Beverly Blvd Ste 501, Los Angeles
(90048-6277)
PHONE....................310 854-0071
Laurel Crary-Globus, *General Mgr*
Sheldon Gordon, *Partner*
A Alfred Taubman, *Partner*
EMP: 75 **EST:** 1982
SQ FT: 2,500
SALES (est): 6.4MM **Privately Held**
WEB: www.beverlycenter.com
SIC: 6531 6512 Real estate brokers & agents; auditorium & hall operation

(P-15906)
LAGUNA WOODS VILLAGE
24351 El Toro Rd, Laguna Woods
(92637-4901)
P.O. Box 2220, Laguna Hills (92654-2220)
PHONE....................949 597-4267
Milton John, *Director*
Russ Disbro, *Director*
EMP: 1000 **EST:** 1964
SALES (est): 18.7K **Privately Held**
WEB: www.lagunawoodsvillage.com
SIC: 6531 Real estate agents & managers

(P-15907)
LANDMARK DIVIDEND LLC (PA)
400 Continental Blvd # 500, El Segundo
(90245-5078)
PHONE....................323 306-2683
Karen Delarosa, *Manager*
Jeff Knyal, *CEO*
George Doyle, *CFO*
Dan R Parsons, *Officer*
Graeme Kavanagh, *Exec VP*
EMP: 161 **EST:** 2010
SQ FT: 7,500
SALES (est): 85.6MM **Privately Held**
WEB: www.landmarkdividend.com
SIC: 6531 Real estate agent, commercial

(P-15908)
LBA REALTY LLC (PA)
3347 Michelson Dr Ste 200, Irvine
(92612-0687)
PHONE....................949 833-0400
Philip A Belling, *Mng Member*
Stephen Silla, *COO*
Tom Rutherford, *CFO*

Tim Brosnan, *Vice Pres*
Michael Coppola, *Vice Pres*
EMP: 50 **EST:** 2004
SALES (est): 89.5MM **Privately Held**
WEB: www.lbacorp.net
SIC: 6531 Real estate agent, commercial

(P-15909)
LEE & ASSOC COML RE SVCS INC - (PA)
7700 Irvine Center Dr # 60, Irvine
(92618-2923)
PHONE....................949 727-1200
John Matus, *Vice Pres*
Russ Johnson, *President*
Irma Rios, *COO*
Guy La Ferrara, *Corp Secy*
Greg Tannor, *Exec VP*
EMP: 50 **EST:** 1979
SQ FT: 8,500
SALES (est): 7.5MM **Privately Held**
SIC: 6531 Real estate agent, commercial

(P-15910)
LEE & ASSOC COMM REAL EST SVCS
Also Called: Lee & Associates Coml RE Svcs
3535 Inland Empire Blvd, Ontario
(91764-4908)
PHONE....................909 989-7771
Donald Kazanjian, *President*
Vincent Anthony, *Vice Pres*
Michael Chavez, *Vice Pres*
Douglas Earnhart, *Vice Pres*
Paul Earnhart, *Vice Pres*
EMP: 50 **EST:** 1987
SALES (est): 13MM **Privately Held**
WEB: www.lee-ie.com
SIC: 6531 8742 Real estate agent, commercial; real estate consultant

(P-15911)
LEE & ASSOC RLTY GROUP NWPORT
Also Called: LEE& Associates
100 Bayview Cir Ste 600, Newport Beach
(92660-2982)
PHONE....................949 724-1000
Steve Jehorek, *President*
EMP: 50 **EST:** 1983
SQ FT: 8,600
SALES (est): 5.1MM **Privately Held**
WEB:
www.leeandassociatesaccountancy.com
SIC: 6531 Real estate agent, commercial

(P-15912)
LOIS LAUER REALTY (PA)
Also Called: Century 21
1998 Orange Tree Ln, Redlands
(92374-2841)
P.O. Box 524 (92373-0161)
PHONE....................909 748-7000
David Coy, *President*
Lawn Brian, *CEO*
Ann Bryan, *Treasurer*
Paul Dimarino, *Bd of Directors*
Shirley Harrington, *Vice Pres*
EMP: 250 **EST:** 1976
SQ FT: 17,000
SALES (est): 20.4MM **Privately Held**
WEB: www.loislauer.com
SIC: 6531 Real estate agent, residential

(P-15913)
LONG BEACH UNIFIED SCHOOL DST
Also Called: Muir Elementary School
3038 Delta Ave, Long Beach (90810-2843)
PHONE....................562 426-5571
Sophia Griffieth, *Principal*
Sue Lagerborg, *Principal*
Carrie Barrios, *Teacher*
Nora Campion, *Teacher*
Darren Junier, *Teacher*
EMP: 121
SALES (corp-wide): 788.4MM **Privately Held**
WEB: www.lbschools.net
SIC: 8211 6531 Public junior high school; public elementary school; rental agent, real estate

PA: Long Beach Unified School District
1515 Hughes Way
Long Beach CA 90810
562 997-8000

(P-15914)
LOWE ENTERPRISES RLTY SVCS INC
Also Called: Encino Financial Center
16133 Ventura Blvd # 535, Encino
(91436-2403)
PHONE....................818 990-9555
Karla Akins, *Branch Mgr*
EMP: 2303
SALES (corp-wide): 935.4MM **Privately Held**
WEB: www.lowe-re.com
SIC: 6531 Real estate managers
HQ: Lowe Enterprises Realty Services, Inc.
11777 San Vicente Blvd
Los Angeles CA 90049
310 820-6661

(P-15915)
LRES CORPORATION (PA)
765 The City Dr S Ste 300, Orange
(92868-6916)
PHONE....................714 520-5737
Roger Beane, *President*
Mark R Johnson, *President*
Paul Abbamonto, *COO*
Susheel Mantha, *CFO*
Todd Taylor, *CFO*
EMP: 91 **EST:** 2001
SQ FT: 11,000
SALES (est): 19.1MM **Privately Held**
WEB: www.lres.com
SIC: 6531 Real estate managers

(P-15916)
LUXRE REALTY INC
222 Avenida Del Mar, San Clemente
(92672-4005)
PHONE....................949 498-3702
Deborah Gietter, *CEO*
Mikey Bente, *Senior Mgr*
EMP: 71 **EST:** 2011
SALES (est): 5.7MM **Privately Held**
WEB: www.luxrerealty.com
SIC: 6531 Real estate agent, residential

(P-15917)
LYONSGATE REALTY INC
6317 Simpson Ave, North Hollywood
(91606-3417)
PHONE....................561 961-4934
Karen Gary Khachatrian, *President*
EMP: 50 **EST:** 2010
SALES (est): 1.9MM **Privately Held**
WEB: www.lyonsgaterealty.com
SIC: 6531 Real estate brokers & agents

(P-15918)
M & S ACQUISITION CORPORATION (PA)
707 Wilshire Blvd # 5200, Los Angeles
(90017-3501)
PHONE....................213 385-1515
Mark Santarsiero, *CFO*
Robert Kerslake, *Ch of Bd*
Paul Craig, *CFO*
Merle Atkins, *Exec VP*
John Spude, *Exec VP*
EMP: 115 **EST:** 1993
SALES (est): 12.9MM **Privately Held**
SIC: 6531 8742 Appraiser, real estate; management consulting services

(P-15919)
MAIN STREET MANAGEMENT LLC (PA)
2015 Manhattan Beach Blvd # 1, Redondo
Beach (90278-1226)
PHONE....................310 640-3100
Grace O'Brien,
Darin Puhl, *COO*
David Wehrly, *COO*
Jamie Bedner, *Vice Pres*
Gregory Geiser, *Vice Pres*
EMP: 68 **EST:** 1998
SQ FT: 3,550
SALES (est): 7.6MM **Privately Held**
SIC: 6531 Rental agent, real estate

(P-15920)
MARCUS & MILLCHAP REAL ESTATE (DH)
23975 Park Sorrento # 400, Calabasas
(91302-4015)
PHONE....................818 212-2250
George M Marcus, *President*
EMP: 62 **EST:** 2014
SALES (est): 1.5MM
SALES (corp-wide): 716.9MM **Publicly Held**
WEB:
www.institutionalpropertyadvisors.com
SIC: 6531 Real estate agent, commercial

(P-15921)
MARCUS & MILLICHAP INC (PA)
23975 Park Sorrento # 400, Calabasas
(91302-4014)
PHONE....................818 212-2250
Hessam Nadji, *President*
Gary Cohen, *Partner*
Mitchell R Labar, *COO*
Matthew Luchs, *COO*
Richard Matricaria, *COO*
EMP: 308 **EST:** 1971
SQ FT: 24,028
SALES (est): 716.9MM **Publicly Held**
WEB: www.marcusmillichap.com
SIC: 6531 Real estate agent, commercial

(P-15922)
MARCUS MLLCHAP RE INV SVCS ATL (DH)
23975 Park Sorrento # 400, Calabasas
(91302-4015)
PHONE....................818 212-2250
George M Marcus, *Owner*
EMP: 62 **EST:** 2016
SALES (est): 2.5MM
SALES (corp-wide): 716.9MM **Publicly Held**
WEB:
www.institutionalpropertyadvisors.com
SIC: 6531 Real estate agent, commercial

(P-15923)
MATTHEWS RE INV SVCS INC (PA)
841 Apollo St Ste 150, El Segundo
(90245-4724)
PHONE....................866 889-0550
Kyle B Matthews, *CEO*
Chad Kurz, *Managing Prtnr*
Radoslav Zlatkov, *CFO*
Redoslav Zlatkov, *CFO*
Zack Bates, *Assoc VP*
EMP: 54 **EST:** 2014
SALES (est): 6.5MM **Privately Held**
WEB: www.matthews.com
SIC: 6531 7389 Real estate agent, commercial; financial services

(P-15924)
MEMCO HOLDINGS INC
10390 Santa Monica Blvd # 210, Los Angeles (90025-5058)
PHONE....................310 277-0057
Mitchell Stein, *President*
EMP: 130 **EST:** 1987
SALES (est): 3.1MM **Privately Held**
SIC: 6531 Real estate managers

(P-15925)
MESA MANAGEMENT INC
1451 Quail St Ste 201, Newport Beach
(92660-2741)
P.O. Box 2990 (92658-9018)
PHONE....................949 851-0995
Steve Mensinger, *President*
Robert Lucas, *Vice Pres*
George Grant, *Info Tech Mgr*
Delmy Cortez, *Business Mgr*
Jim Davis, *Asst Controller*
EMP: 70 **EST:** 1977
SQ FT: 5,000
SALES (est): 9.5MM **Privately Held**
WEB: www.mesamanagement.net
SIC: 6531 Real estate managers

PRODUCTS & SVCS

(P-15926)
MOONSTONE MANAGEMENT CORP (PA)
Also Called: Moonstone Hotel Properties
2905 Burton Dr, Cambria (93428-4001)
PHONE..................805 927-4200
Dirk Winter, *President*
Jacob Aura, *General Mgr*
Matthew Holder, *CIO*
Griffin Moore, *Asst Controller*
John Hughes, *Financial Analy*
EMP: 175 **EST:** 1995
SQ FT: 5,000
SALES (est): 12.7MM **Privately Held**
WEB: www.moonstonehotels.com
SIC: 6531 Real estate managers

(P-15927)
MOSS & COMPANY INC (PA)
15300 Ventura Blvd # 418, Sherman Oaks
(91403-3140)
PHONE..................310 453-0911
Cindy Gray, *President*
Don Shields, *COO*
Henriette Saffron, *CFO*
Chris Gray, *Exec VP*
Jackie Feinberg, *Vice Pres*
EMP: 70 **EST:** 1957
SQ FT: 10,000
SALES (est): 13.2MM **Privately Held**
WEB: www.mosscompany.com
SIC: 6531 Real estate managers

(P-15928)
MOUNTAIN HIGH RESORT ASSOC LLC
24512 Highway 2, Wrightwood (92397)
P.O. Box 3010 (92397-3010)
PHONE..................760 249-5808
Karl Kapuscinski,
John McColly, *VP Sales*
George Dynes, *Instructor*
Zac Greenlee, *Instructor*
Michelle Roy,
EMP: 57 **EST:** 2005
SALES (est): 5.5MM **Privately Held**
SIC: 6531 Real estate managers

(P-15929)
MSE ENTERPRISES INC (PA)
Also Called: Marshall S Ezralow & Assoc
23622 Calabasas Rd # 200, Calabasas
(91302-1549)
PHONE..................818 223-3500
Marshall S Ezralow, *President*
EMP: 90 **EST:** 1974
SALES (est): 5.8MM **Privately Held**
SIC: 6531 Real estate managers

(P-15930)
MURCOR INC
Also Called: Pcv Murcor Real Estate Svcs
740 Corp Ctr Dr, Pomona (91768)
PHONE..................909 623-4001
Keith D Murray, *President*
Cindy Nasser, *COO*
Tim Scherf, *COO*
Richard J Barkley, *Exec VP*
Jon D Van Deuren, *Exec VP*
EMP: 225 **EST:** 1981
SALES (est): 26MM **Privately Held**
WEB: www.pcvmurcor.com
SIC: 6531 Appraiser, real estate

(P-15931)
NIJJAR REALTY INC (PA)
4900 Santa Anita Ave 2b, El Monte
(91731-1498)
P.O. Box 6085 (91734-2085)
PHONE..................626 575-0062
Daljit Kler, *Principal*
Mike Nijjar, *President*
Swaranjit S Nijjar, *CEO*
Peter Nijjar, *Treasurer*
EMP: 70 **EST:** 1949
SQ FT: 2,000
SALES (est): 7.5MM **Privately Held**
SIC: 6531 Real estate brokers & agents;
real estate agent, commercial; real estate
agent, residential

(P-15932)
NMS PROPERTIES INC
10960 Wilshire Blvd, Los Angeles
(90024-3702)
PHONE..................310 656-2700
Naum Shekhter, *CEO*
Margot Shekhter, *President*
Dino Ciarmoli, *Exec VP*
Scott Walter, *Exec VP*
Maria Constantin, *Area Mgr*
EMP: 95 **EST:** 1997
SALES (est): 11.2MM **Privately Held**
WEB: www.nmsproperties.com
SIC: 6531 Real estate managers

(P-15933)
NNN REALTY ADVISORS INC
1551 N Tustin Ave Ste 300, Santa Ana
(92705-8638)
PHONE..................714 667-8252
Scott D Peters, *President*
Francene Lapoint, *CFO*
Kenneth Cave, *Officer*
Brian Coleman, *Assoc VP*
Richard Arnitz, *Exec VP*
EMP: 469 **EST:** 2007
SALES (est): 16.9MM
SALES (corp-wide): 2B **Publicly Held**
WEB: www.bgcpartners.com
SIC: 6531 Real estate agents & managers
PA: Bgc Partners, Inc.
499 Park Ave
New York NY 10022
212 610-2200

(P-15934)
NOURMAND & ASSOCIATES
421 N Beverly Dr Ste 200, Beverly Hills
(90210-4643)
PHONE..................310 274-4000
Saeed Nourmand, *President*
Katie Everds, *Mktg Dir*
Andrea Kang, *Mktg Dir*
Myra Nourmand, *Agent*
Brendan Brown, *Real Est Agnt*
EMP: 50 **EST:** 1975
SALES (est): 5MM **Privately Held**
WEB: www.nourmand.com
SIC: 6531 Real estate agent, residential

(P-15935)
ON CENTRAL REALTY INC (PA)
Also Called: Prudential
1625 W Glenoaks Blvd, Glendale
(91201-1826)
PHONE..................818 476-3000
Vazrik Bonyadi, *President*
EMP: 347 **EST:** 1988
SQ FT: 7,000
SALES (est): 17.7MM **Privately Held**
WEB: www.pgim.com
SIC: 6531 Real estate agent, residential

(P-15936)
ORCHARD HOLDINGS GROUP INC
1 Venture Ste 300, Irvine (92618-7416)
PHONE..................949 502-8300
James Saccacio, *President*
Jim Merriweather, *General Ptnr*
Brian Mushaney, *Exec VP*
Michael Sawtell, *Exec VP*
Larry Spencer, *Vice Pres*
EMP: 76 **EST:** 2001
SQ FT: 1,300
SALES (est): 6.5MM **Privately Held**
SIC: 6531 Real estate brokers & agents

(P-15937)
OWNING CORPORATION
1 City Blvd W Ste 1000, Orange
(92868-3611)
PHONE..................949 269-3300
Ronald Radziminsky, *President*
Thomas Morgan, *Vice Pres*
Jay Marx, *Business Dir*
Jason Goliver, *Project Mgr*
Christopher Barton, *Production*
EMP: 275 **EST:** 2018
SALES (est): 25.5MM **Privately Held**
WEB: www.owning.com
SIC: 6531 Real estate agents & managers
PA: Guaranteed Rate, Inc.
3940 N Ravenswood Ave
Chicago IL 60613

(P-15938)
PACIFIC HOUSING MANAGEMENT (PA)
945 Katella St, Laguna Beach
(92651-3705)
PHONE..................714 508-1777
Richard Hall, *President*
EMP: 60
SALES (est): 3.6MM **Privately Held**
SIC: 6531 Real estate managers

(P-15939)
PACIFIC MONARCH RESORTS INC (PA)
Also Called: Vacation Interval Realty
4000 Macarthur Blvd # 600, Newport Beach
(92660-2558)
PHONE..................949 609-2400
Mark D Post, *CEO*
Richard Muller, *President*
Nick Baldwin, *Vice Pres*
Pete Mitchell, *Vice Pres*
Carlton Post, *Director*
EMP: 100 **EST:** 1987
SQ FT: 20,000
SALES (est): 79.1MM **Privately Held**
WEB: www.monarchgrandvacations.com
SIC: 6531 7011 Time-sharing real estate
sales, leasing & rentals; vacation lodges

(P-15940)
PACIFIC RIM REALTY GROUP
740 Lucille Ct, Moorpark (93021-1241)
P.O. Box 364 (93020-0364)
PHONE..................805 553-9562
Stuart Groten, *President*
EMP: 50
SALES (est): 950K **Privately Held**
SIC: 6531 Real estate brokers & agents

(P-15941)
PACIFIC VALUATION
15615 Alton Pkwy Ste 450, Irvine
(92618-3308)
PHONE..................949 271-6377
Michael Yates, *Owner*
EMP: 50
SALES (est): 250K **Privately Held**
WEB: www.pacificvaluation.org
SIC: 6531 Appraiser, real estate

(P-15942)
PACIFICA HOTEL COMPANY (HQ)
39 Argonaut, Aliso Viejo (92656-1423)
PHONE..................805 957-0095
Matthew D Marquis, *CEO*
Mike Barnard, *President*
Dale J Marquis, *CEO*
Stephen Medel, *Vice Pres*
Todd Moreau, *Vice Pres*
EMP: 50 **EST:** 1993
SQ FT: 12,500
SALES (est): 56.7MM
SALES (corp-wide): 61.3MM **Privately Held**
WEB: www.pacificahotels.com
SIC: 6531 7011 Real estate brokers &
agents; real estate managers; hotels &
motels
PA: Invest West Financial Corp
1933 Cliff Dr Ste 1
Santa Barbara CA 93109
805 957-0095

(P-15943)
PANGO GROUP INC
6100 San Fernando Rd, Glendale
(91201-2247)
PHONE..................818 502-0400
Scott Akerley, *CEO*
Brett Yates, *CFO*
Kari Bodine, *Vice Pres*
Liz Nunez, *Executive Asst*
Vahram Hopalian, *Project Mgr*
EMP: 62 **EST:** 2009
SQ FT: 6,500
SALES (est): 4.9MM **Privately Held**
WEB: www.pangogroup.com
SIC: 6531 Real estate brokers & agents

(P-15944)
PARAMUNT CONTRS DEVELOPERS INC
Also Called: Tops Auto Parks
6464 W Sunset Blvd # 700, Los Angeles
(90028-8001)
PHONE..................323 464-7050
Brad Folb, *President*
Brian Folb, *Exec VP*
Aaron Folb, *Research*
EMP: 50 **EST:** 1949
SQ FT: 102,000
SALES (est): 5.2MM **Privately Held**
WEB: www.hollywoodoffices.com
SIC: 6531 1541 1521 Real estate man-
agers; industrial buildings & warehouses;
single-family housing construction

(P-15945)
PARK REGENCY INC
10146 Balboa Blvd, Granada Hills
(91344-7408)
PHONE..................318 363-6116
Joseph Alexander, *President*
Patrick Pace, *CFO*
Ken Engeron, *Vice Pres*
Kenneth Engeron, *Vice Pres*
Melody Cutler, *Info Tech Mgr*
EMP: 70 **EST:** 1980
SQ FT: 4,500
SALES (est): 18.9MM **Privately Held**
WEB: www.parkregency.com
SIC: 6531 Real estate agent, residential;
real estate agent, commercial

(P-15946)
PASSCO COMPANIES LLC (PA)
2050 Main St Ste 650, Irvine (92614-8265)
PHONE..................949 442-1000
William O Passo,
William H Winn, *President*
Thomas B Jahncke, *Senior VP*
Tom Jahncke, *Senior VP*
Nika Dufour, *Vice Pres*
EMP: 65 **EST:** 1975
SALES (est): 26.3MM **Privately Held**
WEB: www.passco.com
SIC: 6531 Real estate brokers & agents

(P-15947)
PAUL CALVO AND COMPANY
1619 W Garvey Ave N # 201, West Covina
(91790-2144)
PHONE..................626 814-8000
Paul Calvo, *Owner*
Lillian Tijerna, *Administration*
Nelson Chavez, *Maintence Staff*
Loretta Chavez, *Superviso*
EMP: 50 **EST:** 1996
SALES (est): 5MM **Privately Held**
WEB: www.calvogroup.com
SIC: 6531 Real estate agent, commercial;
real estate managers

(P-15948)
PCS PROPERTY MANAGEMENT LLC
11859 Wilshire Blvd # 60, Los Angeles
(90025-6616)
PHONE..................310 231-1000
Michael Ross, *Branch Mgr*
Elizabeth Goldman, *Exec VP*
EMP: 141 **Privately Held**
WEB: www.pcsnorthvalley.com
SIC: 6531 Real estate managers
PA: Pcs Property Managment Llc
4500 Woodman Ave Ofc
Sherman Oaks CA 91423

(P-15949)
PINNACLE ESTATE PROPERTIES INC
Also Called: Pinnacle Escrow Company
9137 Reseda Blvd, Northridge
(91324-3039)
PHONE..................818 993-4707
Dana Potter, *President*
Jeff Black, *CFO*
Danny Ross, *Exec VP*
Kris Carr, *Technical Staf*
Leila Terwilliger, *Controller*
EMP: 120 **EST:** 1985
SQ FT: 13,000

SALES (est): 27.1MM **Privately Held**
WEB: www.pinnacleestate.com
SIC: 6531 Real estate agent, residential; escrow agent, real estate

(P-15950)
PINNACLE IRWIN LLC (PA)
Also Called: Pinnacle Housing
4553 Tippecanoe St, Fort Irwin
(92310-1501)
P.O. Box 10034 (92310-0034)
PHONE..................................760 386-4663
Stan Harrelson, *Mng Member*
EMP: 53 **EST:** 2002
SALES (est): 5MM **Privately Held**
WEB: www.villagesatfortirwin.com
SIC: 6531 Real estate agents & managers

(P-15951)
PITTS & BACHMANN REALTORS INC
1482 E Valley Rd Ste 44, Santa Barbara
(93108-1200)
P.O. Box 50816 (93150-0816)
PHONE..................................805 969-5005
Dennis Walsh, *Owner*
EMP: 78
SALES (corp-wide): 12.8MM **Privately Held**
SIC: 6531 Real estate brokers & agents
PA: Pitts & Bachmann Realtors Inc
1165 Coast Village Rd K
Santa Barbara CA 93108
805 682-6415

(P-15952)
PITTS & BACHMANN REALTORS INC
1436 State St, Santa Barbara
(93101-2512)
PHONE..................................805 963-1391
Patty Tunnicliffe, *Manager*
EMP: 78
SALES (corp-wide): 12.8MM **Privately Held**
SIC: 6531 Real estate brokers & agents
PA: Pitts & Bachmann Realtors Inc
1165 Coast Village Rd K
Santa Barbara CA 93108
805 682-6415

(P-15953)
PM REALTY GROUP LP
4680 Macarthur Ct, Newport Beach
(92660-1870)
PHONE..................................949 553-8246
EMP: 56 **Privately Held**
WEB: www.madisonmarquette.com
SIC: 6531 Real estate agent, commercial
HQ: Pm Realty Group, L.P.
1000 Main St Ste 2400
Houston TX 77002
713 209-5800

(P-15954)
PREFERRED BROKERS INC (PA)
Also Called: Coldwell Banker
9100 Ming Ave Ste 100, Bakersfield
(93311-1329)
PHONE..................................661 836-2345
John Mackessey, *President*
Gary Belter, *Vice Pres*
Sandy Garone, *Vice Pres*
Tishana Debenham, *Admin Asst*
Stephanie Parish, *Sales Associate*
EMP: 70 **EST:** 1990
SQ FT: 8,000
SALES (est): 10MM **Privately Held**
WEB: www.coldwellbanker.com
SIC: 6531 Real estate agent, residential

(P-15955)
PRO GROUP INC
Also Called: Keller Williams Realtors
4160 Temescal Canyon Rd # 500, Corona
(92883-4625)
PHONE..................................951 271-3000
James Brown, *President*
Jim Brown, *President*
Joseph Regan, *CFO*
David Clark, *Vice Pres*
EMP: 195 **EST:** 2003
SQ FT: 18,000

SALES (est): 6MM **Privately Held**
WEB: www.pgescrow.com
SIC: 6531 Real estate agent, residential

(P-15956)
PROFESSIONAL CMNTY MGT CAL INC (PA)
Also Called: P C M
27051 Twne Cntre Dr Ste 2, Foothill Ranch
(92610)
PHONE..................................800 369-7260
Donny Disbro, *CEO*
Russ Disbro, *Senior VP*
Markus Ashley, *Vice Pres*
Susan Finley, *Vice Pres*
Ed Thira, *Info Tech Mgr*
EMP: 50 **EST:** 1972
SQ FT: 12,000
SALES (est): 51.5MM **Privately Held**
WEB: www.pcminternet.com
SIC: 6531 Real estate managers

(P-15957)
PROFESSIONAL CMNTY MGT CAL INC
Also Called: Sun Lakes Country Club
850 Country Club Dr, Banning
(92220-5306)
PHONE..................................951 845-2191
Mike Bennett, *Manager*
Colleen Jacob, *Asst Controller*
Deborah Serrano, *Manager*
EMP: 159
SALES (corp-wide): 51.5MM **Privately Held**
WEB: www.pcminternet.com
SIC: 6531 Real estate managers
PA: Professional Community Management Of California, Inc.
27051 Twne Cntre Dr Ste 2
Foothill Ranch CA 92610
800 369-7260

(P-15958)
PROFESSIONAL CMNTY MGT CAL INC
Also Called: Pcm
24351 El Toro Rd, Laguna Woods
(92637-4901)
PHONE..................................949 206-0580
Milt Johns, *Manager*
EMP: 159
SALES (corp-wide): 51.5MM **Privately Held**
WEB: www.pcminternet.com
SIC: 6531 Real estate managers
PA: Professional Community Management Of California, Inc.
27051 Twne Cntre Dr Ste 2
Foothill Ranch CA 92610
800 369-7260

(P-15959)
PROFESSIONAL CMNTY MGT CAL INC
Also Called: Leisure World Resales
23522 Paseo De Valencia, Laguna Hills
(92653)
P.O. Box 2220 (92654-2220)
PHONE..................................949 597-4200
Gabrielle Velten, *Manager*
EMP: 159
SALES (corp-wide): 51.5MM **Privately Held**
WEB: www.pcminternet.com
SIC: 6531 Real estate managers
PA: Professional Community Management Of California, Inc.
27051 Twne Cntre Dr Ste 2
Foothill Ranch CA 92610
800 369-7260

(P-15960)
PROLAND PROPERTY MANAGMENT LLC (PA)
Also Called: Hollingshead Management
2510 W 7th St Fl 2, Los Angeles
(90057-3802)
PHONE..................................213 738-8175
Ronald Gregg,
James Harris,
EMP: 80 **EST:** 1998
SQ FT: 5,000
SALES (est): 6.3MM **Privately Held**
SIC: 6531 Real estate managers

(P-15961)
PROPERTY MANAGEMENT ASSOC INC (PA)
Also Called: Capital Commercial Property
6011 Bristol Pkwy, Culver City
(90230-6601)
PHONE..................................323 295-2000
Thomas Spear, *President*
Joshua Fein, *CFO*
Patrick Lacey, *Officer*
Cheryl McDonald, *Vice Pres*
Helena Cueto, *Info Tech Mgr*
EMP: 130
SQ FT: 6,500
SALES (est): 12.1MM **Privately Held**
WEB: www.wemanageproperties.com
SIC: 6531 Real estate managers

(P-15962)
R & B REALTY GROUP LP
Also Called: Oakwood Worldwide
1 World Trade Ctr # 2400, Long Beach
(90831-0002)
PHONE..................................310 478-1021
EMP: 1500
SALES (est): 52.4MM **Privately Held**
WEB: www.oakwood.com
SIC: 6531 Real Estate Agents And Managers

(P-15963)
RAJ MANUFACTURING INC (PA)
Also Called: Athena Pick Your Fit
2692 Dow Ave, Tustin (92780-7208)
PHONE..................................714 838-3110
Raj S Bhathal,
Rick Kuhn, *Exec VP*
Gurmeet Pandori, *Vice Pres*
Jeniffer Renish, *Controller*
Deanne Turner, *Human Resources*
◆ **EMP:** 18 **EST:** 1967
SQ FT: 100,000
SALES (est): 5MM **Privately Held**
WEB: www.rajswim.com
SIC: 6531 4581 2339 Real estate agents & managers; airports, flying fields & services; athletic clothing: women's, misses' & juniors'

(P-15964)
RANCHO MISSION VIEJO LLC
28811 Ortega Hwy, San Juan Capistrano
(92675-2023)
PHONE..................................949 240-3363
EMP: 60 **EST:** 1996
SALES (est): 2.6MM **Privately Held**
WEB: www.ranchomissionviejo.com
SIC: 6531 Real estate agents & managers

(P-15965)
RANCON REAL ESTATE CORPORATION
41391 Kalmia St Ste 100, Murrieta
(92562-9766)
PHONE..................................951 677-1800
Mike Diaz, *Branch Mgr*
Wil Cucuta, *Broker*
Elena Vineyard, *Sales Staff*
Chase Lytle, *Agent*
Susan Loomis, *Real Est Agnt*
EMP: 54
SALES (corp-wide): 11.3MM **Privately Held**
WEB: www.corcorangl.com
SIC: 6531 Real estate agent, residential
PA: Rancon Real Estate Corporation
27740 Jefferson Ave # 100
Temecula CA
951 677-1800

(P-15966)
RBABS INVESTMENTS 1 LLC
5967 W 3rd St Ste 102, Los Angeles
(90036-2835)
PHONE..................................818 577-7171
Briar Dror, *Principal*
EMP: 50 **EST:** 2010
SALES (est): 2.1MM **Privately Held**
SIC: 6531 Real estate leasing & rentals

(P-15967)
RE/MAX
201 New Stine Rd Ste 300, Bakersfield
(93309-2680)
PHONE..................................661 616-4040

EMP: 50
SALES (est): 1.3MM **Privately Held**
SIC: 6531 Real Estate Agents And Managers

(P-15968)
RE/MAX BCH CTIES RLTY MRQUEE P
400 S Sepulveda Blvd # 100, Manhattan Beach (90266-6814)
PHONE..................................310 376-2225
Robert Kenneth Todd, *Owner*
Patricia Hedstrom, *Executive*
Nicole Pagan, *CIO*
Terry Ballentine, *Broker*
Sheri Kapust, *Real Est Agnt*
EMP: 53 **EST:** 1982
SQ FT: 15,000
SALES (est): 2.9MM **Privately Held**
WEB: www.remax.com
SIC: 6531 Real estate agent, residential

(P-15969)
RE/MAX OF VALENCIA INC (PA)
25101 The Old Rd, Santa Clarita
(91381-2206)
PHONE..................................661 255-2650
John O'Hare, *President*
John Ohare, *President*
Alice O'Hare, *Vice Pres*
Rocky Coennen, *Associate*
Vartaz Minassian, *Associate*
EMP: 118 **EST:** 1985
SQ FT: 10,000
SALES (est): 17.2MM **Privately Held**
WEB: www.remax-valencia-ca.com
SIC: 6531 8742 Real estate agent, residential; real estate consultant

(P-15970)
REALSELECT INC
3063 W Chapman Ave # 620, Orange
(92868-1738)
PHONE..................................661 803-5188
Ashley Ivey, *Branch Mgr*
EMP: 151
SALES (corp-wide): 9.3B **Publicly Held**
WEB: www.realtor.com
SIC: 6531 Real estate brokers & agents
HQ: Realselect, Inc.
30700 Russell Ranch Rd
Westlake Village CA 91362

(P-15971)
REALTY ONE GROUP INC
19322 Jesse Ln, Riverside (92508-5072)
PHONE..................................951 565-8105
EMP: 60
SALES (corp-wide): 62.2MM **Privately Held**
WEB: www.realtyonegroup.com
SIC: 6531 Real estate agent, residential
PA: Realty One Group, Inc.
25 S Arizona Pl Ste 320
Chandler AZ 85225
949 596-4300

(P-15972)
REGENCY PARK SENIOR LIVING INC
Also Called: Regency Park El Molino
245 S El Molino Ave, Pasadena
(91101-2996)
PHONE..................................626 578-0460
Emil Fish, *President*
EMP: 101
SALES (corp-wide): 10.7MM **Privately Held**
SIC: 6531 Real estate agents & managers
PA: Regency Park Senior Living, Inc.
350 Cordova St
Pasadena CA 91101
626 773-8800

(P-15973)
REGISTRY MNTRING INSUR SVCS IN
Also Called: Rmis
5388 Sterling Center Dr, Westlake Village
(91361-4688)
PHONE..................................800 400-4924
Marvin Landon, *Chairman*
Hayden Landon, *President*
David Kolchins, *COO*

Emily Lyons, *Vice Pres*
Matthew Mandery, *Software Dev*
EMP: 66 **EST:** 1996
SALES (est): 11.8MM **Privately Held**
WEB: www.rmis.com
SIC: 6531 6411 Real estate agents &
managers; insurance information & con-
sulting services
PA: Internet Truckstop, Llc
222 N Plymouth Ave
New Plymouth ID 83655

(P-15974)
REMAX OLSON & ASSOCIATES
INC
Also Called: Re/Max
11141 Tampa Ave, Northridge
(91326-2254)
PHONE.................818 366-3300
Todd C Olson, *CEO*
Keith Myers, *Exec VP*
Daniella Duliere, *Administration*
Stacy McKinley, *Data Proc Exec*
Cindy Pelter, *Broker*
EMP: 74 **EST:** 1987
SQ FT: 30,000
SALES (est): 10MM **Privately Held**
WEB: www.remax.com
SIC: 6531 Real estate agent, residential

(P-15975)
RETIREMENT HOUSING
FOUNDATION (PA)
911 N Studebaker Rd # 100, Long Beach
(90815-4980)
PHONE.................562 257-5100
Laverne R Joseph, *CEO*
Stacie Doebler, *Records Dir*
Raymond East, *Ch of Bd*
Christina E Potter, *Vice Chairman*
Darryl M Sexton, *Vice Chairman*
EMP: 65 **EST:** 1961
SALES: 38.7MM **Privately Held**
WEB: www.rhf.org
SIC: 6531 Real estate agents & managers

(P-15976)
RGC SERVICES INC (PA)
Also Called: Re/Max
5720 Ralston St Ste 100, Ventura
(93003-7845)
PHONE.................805 644-1242
Glenn Sipes, *President*
Jerry Beebe, *CFO*
Michael Sipes, *Vice Pres*
Lilamani Perera, *Administration*
Maria Abundis, *Broker*
EMP: 110 **EST:** 1994
SQ FT: 35,000
SALES (est): 25.2MM **Privately Held**
WEB: www.fredevans.com
SIC: 6531 Real estate agent, residential

(P-15977)
RGC SERVICES INC
Also Called: Re/Max
601 E Daily Dr Ste 102, Camarillo
(93010-5838)
PHONE.................805 484-1600
Teresa Toomey, *Manager*
Jose Luiz, *Manager*
Marisol Mendoza, *Agent*
Susan Stuart, *Associate*
EMP: 89 **Privately Held**
WEB: www.remax.com
SIC: 6531 Real estate agent, residential
PA: Rgc Services, Inc.
5720 Ralston St Ste 100
Ventura CA 93003

(P-15978)
RIPHAGEN & BULLERDICK INC
Also Called: Re/Max
5925 Ball Rd, Cypress (90630-3245)
PHONE.................714 763-2100
Gary Riphagen, *President*
Gerry Bullerdick, *Treasurer*
Kerry Louis, *Manager*
Heather Schultz, *Associate*
EMP: 50 **EST:** 1989
SQ FT: 2,600
SALES (est): 5.8MM **Privately Held**
WEB: www.socalsuperagent.com
SIC: 6531 Real estate agent, residential

(P-15979)
RODEO REALTY INC
15300 Ventura Blvd # 500, Sherman Oaks
(91403-3144)
PHONE.................818 986-7300
Jason Katzman, *Branch Mgr*
Nicole Vivian, *Office Admin*
Chiara M Mott, *Graphic Designe*
Ana Yes, *Graphic Designe*
Karolina Nunez, *Human Res Mgr*
EMP: 54 **Privately Held**
WEB: www.rodeore.com
SIC: 6531 Real estate brokers & agents
PA: Rodeo Realty, Inc.
9171 Wilshire Blvd # 321
Beverly Hills CA 90210

(P-15980)
RODEO REALTY INC
11940 San Vicente Blvd, Los Angeles
(90049-5004)
PHONE.................310 873-0100
Simon Pozi, *Manager*
Peter Maurice, *Director*
Allison Gold, *Real Est Agnt*
Felix Fooks, *Associate*
EMP: 54 **Privately Held**
WEB: www.rodeore.com
SIC: 6531 Real estate agent, residential
PA: Rodeo Realty, Inc.
9171 Wilshire Blvd # 321
Beverly Hills CA 90210

(P-15981)
RODEO REALTY INC
Also Called: Paramount Properties Encino BR
17501 Ventura Blvd, Encino (91316-3836)
PHONE.................818 285-3700
Syd Leibovitch, *President*
EMP: 54 **Privately Held**
WEB: www.rodeore.com
SIC: 6531 Real estate brokers & agents
PA: Rodeo Realty, Inc.
9171 Wilshire Blvd # 321
Beverly Hills CA 90210

(P-15982)
RODEO REALTY INC
12345 Ventura Blvd Ste A, Studio City
(91604-2511)
PHONE.................818 308-8273
Sib Leibovitch, *President*
Todd Jones, *Broker*
EMP: 54 **Privately Held**
WEB: www.rodeore.com
SIC: 6531 Real estate brokers & agents
PA: Rodeo Realty, Inc.
9171 Wilshire Blvd # 321
Beverly Hills CA 90210

(P-15983)
RODEO REALTY INC
Also Called: Paramount Properties
100 N Wstlke Blvd 100 # 100, Westlake Vil-
lage (91362)
PHONE.................805 494-0449
Sid Leibovitch, *Branch Mgr*
Demetra Kalivas-Rees, *Real Est Agnt*
EMP: 54 **Privately Held**
WEB: www.rodeore.com
SIC: 6531 Real estate brokers & agents
PA: Rodeo Realty, Inc.
9171 Wilshire Blvd # 321
Beverly Hills CA 90210

(P-15984)
RODEO REALTY INC (PA)
Also Called: Paramount Properties
9171 Wilshire Blvd # 321, Beverly Hills
(90210-5562)
PHONE.................818 349-9997
Sydney Leibovitch, *CEO*
Linda Leibovitch, *Vice Pres*
Randy Vanlandingham, *Vice Pres*
Karim Shiraz Ghelani, *Executive*
Brent Barker, *Principal*
EMP: 76 **EST:** 1986
SQ FT: 5,000
SALES (est): 57MM **Privately Held**
WEB: www.rodeore.com
SIC: 6531 Real estate agent, residential

(P-15985)
RODEO REALTY INC
9338 Reseda Blvd Ste 102, Northridge
(91324-2986)
PHONE.................818 349-9997
Teresa Todd, *Branch Mgr*
EMP: 54 **Privately Held**
WEB: www.rodeo.com
SIC: 6531 Real estate brokers & agents
PA: Rodeo Realty, Inc.
9171 Wilshire Blvd # 321
Beverly Hills CA 90210

(P-15986)
RODEO REALTY INC
2424 Erringer Rd, Northridge (91324)
PHONE.................805 582-8700
Syd Leibovitch, *President*
EMP: 54 **Privately Held**
WEB: www.rodeo.com
SIC: 6531 Real estate brokers & agents
PA: Rodeo Realty, Inc.
9171 Wilshire Blvd # 321
Beverly Hills CA 90210

(P-15987)
RODEO REALTY INC
23901 Calabasas Rd # 1050, Calabasas
(91302-3379)
PHONE.................818 657-4609
Lu Duffy, *Branch Mgr*
Paul Stafford, *Office Mgr*
Michelle Cohan, *Broker*
Eva Horland, *Agent*
Behnaz Tavakoli, *Real Est Agnt*
EMP: 54 **Privately Held**
WEB: www.rodeo.com
SIC: 6531 6519 6162 6141 Real estate
brokers & agents; real property lessors;
loan correspondents; personal credit insti-
tutions
PA: Rodeo Realty, Inc.
9171 Wilshire Blvd # 321
Beverly Hills CA 90210

(P-15988)
RODEO REALTY INC
Also Called: Paramount Properties
21031 Ventura Blvd # 100, Woodland Hills
(91364-2208)
PHONE.................818 999-2030
Demetra Kalizki, *Manager*
Jason Katzman, *Exec VP*
Ruzanna Bella, *Agent*
Alison De Caussin, *Real Est Agnt*
Rahuman Hamza, *Real Est Agnt*
EMP: 54 **Privately Held**
WEB: www.rodeo.com
SIC: 6531 Real estate brokers & agents
PA: Rodeo Realty, Inc.
9171 Wilshire Blvd # 321
Beverly Hills CA 90210

(P-15989)
RONALD L WOLFE & ASSOC INC
Also Called: Wolfe & Associates
173 Chapel St, Santa Barbara
(93111-2333)
PHONE.................805 964-6770
Ronald L Wolfe, *President*
Valerie McDonald, *Executive Asst*
Scott Marrison, *Maintence Staff*
Mark Figueroa, *Manager*
Tom Donnelly, *Supervisor*
EMP: 50 **EST:** 1971
SQ FT: 5,000
SALES (est): 8.9MM **Privately Held**
WEB: www.rlwa.com
SIC: 6531 Real estate managers

(P-15990)
ROSANO PARTNERS
3530 Wilshire Blvd # 1700, Los Angeles
(90010-2341)
PHONE.................213 802-0300
Sagiv Rosano, *CEO*
EMP: 50 **EST:** 2006
SALES (est): 6MM **Privately Held**
WEB: www.rosanopartners.com
SIC: 6531 Real estate agent, commercial

(P-15991)
ROSEMONT REALTY LLC (PA)
2000 Avenue Of The Stars # 55C, Los An-
geles (90067-4713)
PHONE.................505 992-5100
Michael Mahony, *CEO*
Devon Archer, *General Ptnr*
Jeffrey V Langdon, *President*
Ian Pbrownlow, *CFO*
Paul Gerwin, *Exec VP*
EMP: 107 **EST:** 2006
SALES (est): 34.4MM **Privately Held**
WEB: www.geminirosemont.com
SIC: 6531 Real estate agent, commercial

(P-15992)
ROW MANAGEMENT LTD INC
499 N Canon Dr, Beverly Hills
(90210-4887)
PHONE.................310 887-3671
Kevin Shahin, *Branch Mgr*
EMP: 305
SALES (corp-wide): 38MM **Privately
Held**
WEB: www.aboardtheworld.com
SIC: 6531 Real estate agents & managers
PA: Row Management Ltd. Inc.
1551 Sawgrs Corp Pkwy
Sunrise FL 33323
954 538-8400

(P-15993)
RVTLZATION ANAHEIM II
PARTNERS
1515 S Calle Del Mar, Anaheim
(92802-2607)
PHONE.................714 520-4041
EMP: 75 **EST:** 2014
SALES (est): 1.7MM **Privately Held**
SIC: 6531 Real Estate Agent/Manager

(P-15994)
SATELLITE MANAGEMENT CO
(PA)
Also Called: Ccts
1010 E Chestnut Ave, Santa Ana
(92701-6497)
PHONE.................714 558-2411
Ronald Jensen, *CEO*
Mary E Conzelman, *Vice Pres*
Helen M Jensen, *Vice Pres*
EMP: 121 **EST:** 1963
SQ FT: 800
SALES (est): 24.2MM **Privately Held**
WEB: www.satellitemanagement.com
SIC: 6531 Real estate managers

(P-15995)
SELF HELP ENTERPRISES (PA)
8445 W Elowin Ct, Visalia (93291-9262)
P.O. Box 6520 (93290-6520)
PHONE.................559 651-1000
Thomas Collishaw, *CEO*
Julie Scaife, *Executive Asst*
Carlos Bravo, *CIO*
Loren Ayarzagoitia, *Technician*
Victor Echeveste, *Technician*
EMP: 86 **EST:** 1998
SALES (est): 23.6MM **Privately Held**
WEB: www.selfhelpenterprises.org
SIC: 6531 6411 Real estate agent, resi-
dential; insurance agents, brokers & serv-
ice

(P-15996)
SFT REALTY GALWAY DOWNS
LLC
Also Called: Kentina
38801 Los Porralitos, Temecula (92592)
P.O. Box 4404 Jeremie Dr
PHONE.................951 232-1880
Kenneth C Smith, *Mng Member*
EMP: 70 **EST:** 2013
SQ FT: 2,000
SALES (est): 400K **Privately Held**
WEB: www.galwaydowns.com
SIC: 6531 Real estate agents & managers

(P-15997)
SHAMROCK HOLDINGS CAL INC
(HQ)
4444 W Lakeside Dr Lbby, Burbank
(91505-4069)
P.O. Box 7774 (91510-7774)
PHONE.................818 845-4444

Stanley Gold, *CEO*
Roy E Disney, *Ch of Bd*
Stanley P Gold, *President*
David Robbins, *Exec VP*
EMP: 62 **EST:** 1978
SQ FT: 12,000
SALES (est): 1.4MM
SALES (corp-wide): 14.7MM **Privately Held**
WEB: www.shamrock.com
SIC: 6531 Real estate managers
PA: Shamrock Holdings, Inc.
  4444 W Lkeside Dr Ste 150
  Burbank CA 91505
  818 845-4444

(P-15998)
SHII LLC
Also Called: Frontier Communities
2151 E Cnvntn Ctr Way # 222, Ontario (91764-5429)
PHONE..................909 354-8000
James Previti, *Mng Member*
Marie Alcantar, *Purch Agent*
Ed Hunter, *Sales Staff*
Juliann Armendariz, *Manager*
Rodrigo Rodriguez, *Representative*
EMP: 50 **EST:** 2007
SALES (est): 8.3MM **Privately Held**
SIC: 6531 Real estate brokers & agents

(P-15999)
SKYHILL FINANCIAL INC
5762 Bolsa Ave Ste 110, Huntington Beach (92649-1172)
PHONE..................714 657-3938
Rosanne Covy, *President*
Angela Hess, *COO*
Michelle Meier, *Officer*
Bryan Palomares, *General Mgr*
Tyrone Helton, *Technology*
EMP: 60 **EST:** 2008
SALES (est): 5.3MM **Privately Held**
WEB: www.skyhillfinancial.com
SIC: 6531 8741 Real estate managers; administrative management

(P-16000)
SOLA IMPACT FUND II LP
9221 Kalmia St, Los Angeles (90002-2600)
PHONE..................323 306-4648
Martin Muoto, *Partner*
EMP: 50
SALES (corp-wide): 23.8MM **Privately Held**
WEB: www.solaimpact.com
SIC: 6531 Housing authority operator
PA: Sola Impact Fund Ii, Lp
  8629 S Vermont Ave
  Los Angeles CA 90044
  323 306-4648

(P-16001)
SOLA IMPACT FUND II LP
1401 E 52nd St, Los Angeles (90011-4964)
PHONE..................323 306-4648
Martin Muoto, *General Ptnr*
EMP: 50
SALES (corp-wide): 23.8MM **Privately Held**
WEB: www.solaimpact.com
SIC: 6531 Housing authority operator
PA: Sola Impact Fund Ii, Lp
  8629 S Vermont Ave
  Los Angeles CA 90044
  323 306-4648

(P-16002)
SOLA IMPACT FUND II LP
1639 E 92nd St, Los Angeles (90002-2373)
PHONE..................323 306-4648
Martin Muoto, *General Ptnr*
EMP: 50
SALES (corp-wide): 23.8MM **Privately Held**
WEB: www.solaimpact.com
SIC: 6531 Housing authority operator
PA: Sola Impact Fund Ii, Lp
  8629 S Vermont Ave
  Los Angeles CA 90044
  323 306-4648

(P-16003)
SOLA IMPACT FUND II LP
629 E 48th St, Los Angeles (90011-4049)
PHONE..................323 306-4648

Martin A Muoto, *General Ptnr*
EMP: 50
SALES (corp-wide): 23.8MM **Privately Held**
WEB: www.solaimpact.com
SIC: 6531 Housing authority operator
PA: Sola Impact Fund Ii, Lp
  8629 S Vermont Ave
  Los Angeles CA 90044
  323 306-4648

(P-16004)
SOLA IMPACT FUND II LP
11809 Robin St, Los Angeles (90059-2840)
PHONE..................323 306-4648
Martin A Muoto, *General Ptnr*
EMP: 50
SALES (corp-wide): 23.8MM **Privately Held**
WEB: www.solaimpact.com
SIC: 6531 Real estate leasing & rentals
PA: Sola Impact Fund Ii, Lp
  8629 S Vermont Ave
  Los Angeles CA 90044
  323 306-4648

(P-16005)
SOLA IMPACT FUND II LP
6415 Makee Ave, Los Angeles (90001-1768)
PHONE..................323 306-4648
EMP: 50
SALES (corp-wide): 23.8MM **Privately Held**
WEB: www.solaimpact.com
SIC: 6531 Housing authority operator
PA: Sola Impact Fund Ii, Lp
  8629 S Vermont Ave
  Los Angeles CA 90044
  323 306-4648

(P-16006)
SOUTHERN STATES REALTY
2244 Walnut Grove Ave, Rosemead (91770-3714)
PHONE..................626 302-1212
Emiko Banfield, *President*
Georgia R Nelson, *President*
John Ferdinando, *Vice Pres*
EMP: 634 **EST:** 1973
SALES (est): 1MM
SALES (corp-wide): 13.5B **Publicly Held**
WEB: www.sce.com
SIC: 6531 Real estate brokers & agents
HQ: Southern California Edison Company
  2244 Walnut Grove Ave
  Rosemead CA 91770
  626 302-1212

(P-16007)
SPUS7 125 CAMBRIDGEPARK LP
515 S Flower St Ste 3100, Los Angeles (90071-2233)
PHONE..................213 683-4200
EMP: 94 **EST:** 2014
SALES (est): 3.3MM **Publicly Held**
WEB: www.cbreim.com
SIC: 6531 Real estate agent, commercial
HQ: Cbre Global Value Investors, Llc
  601 S Figueroa St Ste 49
  Los Angeles CA 90017
  213 683-4200

(P-16008)
SPUS7 150 CAMBRIDGEPARK LP
515 S Flower St Ste 3100, Los Angeles (90071-2233)
PHONE..................213 683-4200
EMP: 113 **EST:** 2014
SALES (est): 3.4MM **Publicly Held**
WEB: www.cbreim.com
SIC: 6531 Real estate agent, commercial
HQ: Cbre Global Value Investors, Llc
  601 S Figueroa St Ste 49
  Los Angeles CA 90017
  213 683-4200

(P-16009)
SRHT PROPERTY HOLDING LLC
Also Called: Skid Row Housing Trust
1317 E 7th St, Los Angeles (90021-1101)
PHONE..................213 683-0522
Jerrick Holloway, *Director*
EMP: 150 **EST:** 2005

SALES (est): 9.6MM **Privately Held**
SIC: 6531 Real estate managers

(P-16010)
STARPINT 1031 PROPERTY MGT LLC
Also Called: Vision Realty Managements
450 N Roxbury Dr Ste 1050, Beverly Hills (90210-4235)
PHONE..................310 247-0550
Paul Daneshrad,
Jon Suematsu, *Regional Mgr*
Sheila Daneshrad, *Human Res Dir*
Jenni Lauri, *Marketing Staff*
Sheila Dameshrad,
EMP: 110 **EST:** 1997
SALES (est): 8.7MM **Privately Held**
WEB: www.starpointproperties.com
SIC: 6531 Real estate agent, commercial

(P-16011)
STEADFAST COML MGT CO INC (HQ)
4343 Von Karman Ave # 30, Newport Beach (92660-2099)
PHONE..................949 852-0700
Rodney F Emery, *President*
Lisa Vincent, *Owner*
Dinesh Davar, *CFO*
Dean Curci, *Vice Pres*
Ana Marie Del Rio, *Vice Pres*
EMP: 67 **EST:** 2002
SQ FT: 8,000
SALES (est): 1.6MM
SALES (corp-wide): 43.4MM **Privately Held**
WEB: www.steadfastcompanies.com
SIC: 6531 Real estate managers
PA: Steadfast Management Company, Inc.
  18100 Von Karman Ave # 500
  Irvine CA 92612
  949 748-3000

(P-16012)
STEADFAST MANAGEMENT CO INC (PA)
Also Called: Steadfast Companies
18100 Von Karman Ave # 500, Irvine (92612-0196)
PHONE..................949 748-3000
Rodney F Emery, *CEO*
Cindy White, *Partner*
Michael Brown, *President*
Rick Burdick, *President*
Chris Collins, *President*
EMP: 274 **EST:** 2000
SALES (est): 43.4MM **Privately Held**
WEB: www.steadfastliving.com
SIC: 6531 Real estate managers

(P-16013)
SURTERRE PROPERTIES INC (PA)
1400 Nwport Ctr Dr Ste 10, Newport Beach (92660)
PHONE..................949 717-7100
Gary E Legrand, *CEO*
Gary Le Grand, *Sales Executive*
EMP: 104 **EST:** 2006
SALES (est): 15.3MM **Privately Held**
WEB: www.surterreproperties.com
SIC: 6531 Real estate agent, residential

(P-16014)
TELES PROPERTIES INC (PA)
9470 Wilshire Blvd # 120, Beverly Hills (90212-2707)
PHONE..................424 202-3200
Peter Loewy, *Ch of Bd*
Lou Piatt, *President*
Sharran Srivatsaa, *COO*
EMP: 66 **EST:** 2007
SALES (est): 6.1MM **Privately Held**
WEB: www.elliman.com
SIC: 6531 Real estate agent, residential

(P-16015)
TEN-X FINANCE INC
15295 Alton Pkwy, Irvine (92618-2315)
PHONE..................949 465-8523
Steve Jacobs, *CEO*
EMP: 111 **EST:** 2013
SALES (est): 550.9K
SALES (corp-wide): 1.6B **Publicly Held**
SIC: 6531 Real estate agents & managers

HQ: Ten-X, Inc.
  15295 Alton Pkwy
  Irvine CA 92618
  949 465-8523

(P-16016)
TOP DECK INVESTMENTS INC
731 E Ball Rd Ste 102, Anaheim (92805-5951)
P.O. Box 25465 (92825-5465)
PHONE..................714 956-7712
Ray Johnston, *President*
EMP: 50 **EST:** 2011
SALES (est): 1.3MM **Privately Held**
SIC: 6531 Real estate agents & managers

(P-16017)
TRAMMELL CROW CENTL TEXAS LTD
2221 Rosecrans Ave, El Segundo (90245-4931)
PHONE..................310 765-2600
Robert Ruth, *Principal*
EMP: 73 **Publicly Held**
WEB: www.trammellcrow.com
SIC: 6531 Real estate agent, commercial
HQ: Trammell Crow Central Texas, Ltd.
  2001 Ross Ave Ste 325
  Dallas TX 75201

(P-16018)
TRG INC
Also Called: Rosenthal Group, The
1350 Abbot Kinney Blvd # 101, Venice (90291-3893)
P.O. Box 837 (90294-0837)
PHONE..................310 396-6750
EMP: 100
SALES (est): 3.3MM **Privately Held**
WEB: www.trgnational.com
SIC: 6531 Real Estate Agents And Managers

(P-16019)
TRIYAR SV LLC (PA)
10850 Wilshire Blvd, Los Angeles (90024-4305)
PHONE..................310 234-2888
Steven Yari,
Sharod Yari,
Ashkan Farr, *Director*
EMP: 251 **EST:** 2012
SALES (est): 27.2MM **Privately Held**
WEB: www.triyar.com
SIC: 6531 Buying agent, real estate

(P-16020)
TROOP REAL ESTATE INC
2365 E Vineyard Ave, Oxnard (93036-2102)
PHONE..................805 487-2892
Danielle McGrath, *Vice Pres*
EMP: 98
SALES (corp-wide): 22.9MM **Privately Held**
WEB: www.karentroop.com
SIC: 6531 Real estate agent, residential
PA: Troop Real Estate, Inc.
  1308 Madera Rd Ste 8
  Simi Valley CA 93065
  805 581-3200

(P-16021)
TROOP REAL ESTATE INC
4165 E Thsand Oaks Ste 10, Westlake Village (91362)
PHONE..................805 402-3028
Jeff Rosenblum, *Branch Mgr*
Carol Thornton, *Office Admin*
Jan Roth, *Analyst*
Samantha Kirkpatrick, *Broker*
Kelly Estes, *Sales Staff*
EMP: 98
SALES (corp-wide): 22.9MM **Privately Held**
WEB: www.karentroop.com
SIC: 6531 Real estate agent, residential; real estate brokers & agents
PA: Troop Real Estate, Inc.
  1308 Madera Rd Ste 8
  Simi Valley CA 93065
  805 581-3200

PRODUCTS & SVCS

(P-16022)
TROOP REAL ESTATE INC (PA)
1308 Madera Rd Ste 8, Simi Valley
(93065-4044)
PHONE..................805 581-3200
Brian C Troop, *CEO*
Laura Lee Anthony, *President*
Deborah McCarthy, *COO*
Ray De Silva, *Exec VP*
Paul Gonzales, *General Mgr*
EMP: 95 **EST:** 1987
SALES (est): 22.9MM **Privately Held**
WEB: www.karentroop.com
SIC: 6531 Real estate agent, residential;
real estate brokers & agents

(P-16023)
TROOP REAL ESTATE INC
586 W Main St, Santa Paula (93060-3209)
PHONE..................805 921-0030
Brian Troop, *Owner*
Laura L Anthony, *President*
Linda M Gonzalez, *Real Est Agnt*
Alan J Hollaar, *Real Est Agnt*
Alexis E King, *Real Est Agnt*
EMP: 98
SALES (corp-wide): 22.9MM **Privately
Held**
WEB: www.karentroop.com
SIC: 6531 Real estate agent, residential
PA: Troop Real Estate, Inc.
1308 Madera Rd Ste 8
Simi Valley CA 93065
805 581-3200

(P-16024)
TROOP REAL ESTATE INC
236 W Ojai Ave Ste 100, Ojai (93023-3274)
PHONE..................805 640-1440
Barry Snyder, *Branch Mgr*
Troop Estate, *Office Admin*
Debi Chmielewski, *Administration*
Thelma Concepcion, *Sales Staff*
Chris Loveall, *Director*
EMP: 98
SALES (corp-wide): 22.9MM **Privately
Held**
WEB: www.karentroop.com
SIC: 6531 Real estate agent, residential
PA: Troop Real Estate, Inc.
1308 Madera Rd Ste 8
Simi Valley CA 93065
805 581-3200

(P-16025)
UNITED EL SEGUNDO INC (PA)
Also Called: United Oil
4130 Cover St, Long Beach (90808-1885)
PHONE..................310 323-3992
Ronald Appel, *President*
Marv Toland, *CFO*
Jeff Appel, *Corp Secy*
Nancy Riggs, *Division VP*
Ken Green, *Vice Pres*
EMP: 60 **EST:** 1954
SQ FT: 3,500
SALES (est): 102MM **Privately Held**
WEB: www.chevron.com
SIC: 5541 6531 Filling stations, gasoline;
real estate leasing & rentals

(P-16026)
US REAL ESTATE SERVICES INC
Also Called: Res.net
25520 Commercentre Dr # 1, Lake Forest
(92630-8884)
PHONE..................949 598-9920
Keith Guenther, *CEO*
Michael Bull, *CFO*
Gregory Metz, *Treasurer*
Garrett Mays, *Vice Pres*
Rob Pajon, *Vice Pres*
EMP: 90 **EST:** 1994
SQ FT: 37,000
SALES (est): 22.1MM **Privately Held**
WEB: www.usres.com
SIC: 6531 Real estate brokers & agents

(P-16027)
V TROTH INC
Also Called: Berkshire Hthway Hmsrvces Trot
1801 W Avenue K Ste 101, Lancaster
(93534-5999)
P.O. Box 2024 (93539-2024)
PHONE..................661 948-4646
Debra K Anderson, *President*

Donald L Anderson, *Vice Pres*
Mark A Troth, *Admin Sec*
Tessa Bresnahan, *Sales Associate*
Natasha Coleman, *Sales Associate*
EMP: 75 **EST:** 1965
SALES (est): 8.6MM **Privately Held**
WEB: www.bhhstroth.com
SIC: 6531 8742 Real estate agent, resi-
dential; real estate consultant

(P-16028)
VACATION PALM SPRINGS RE INC
901 E Tahquitz Canyon Way B200, Palm
Springs (92262-6757)
PHONE..................760 778-7832
Mary Lyn Clark, *President*
Bill Brennan, *General Mgr*
EMP: 221 **EST:** 2004
SALES (est): 9.4MM
SALES (corp-wide): 1.3B **Publicly Held**
WEB: www.vacationpalmsprings.com
SIC: 6531 Rental agent, real estate; real
estate leasing & rentals
HQ: Wyndham Vacation Resorts, Inc.
6277 Sea Harbor Dr
Orlando FL 32821
407 370-5200

(P-16029)
VILLA TOSCANA PROPERTIES LLC
633 W 5th St Ste 2600, Los Angeles
(90071-2053)
PHONE..................213 223-2261
David A Capablanca, *Mng Member*
EMP: 52 **EST:** 2019
SALES (est): 1.5MM **Privately Held**
SIC: 6531 Real estate agents & managers

(P-16030)
WATT COMPANIES INC (PA)
2716 Ocean Park Blvd # 20, Santa Monica
(90405-5207)
PHONE..................310 314-2430
J Scott Watt, *CEO*
Brian Burdzinski, *CFO*
Audra Arbini, *Bd of Directors*
Kellie Anderson, *Vice Pres*
Tony Dolim, *Vice Pres*
EMP: 143 **EST:** 1953
SALES (est): 12.4MM **Privately Held**
WEB: www.wattcompanies.com
SIC: 6531 8742 Real estate agent, com-
mercial; general management consultant

(P-16031)
WESTCOE REALTORS INC
Also Called: Westcoe Escrow Division
7191 Magnolia Ave, Riverside
(92504-3805)
PHONE..................951 784-2500
Rich Simonin, *Manager*
Susan Simonin, *President*
Liz Freiling, *Officer*
Richard Simonin, *Vice Pres*
Wally Drake, *Broker*
EMP: 65 **EST:** 1985
SQ FT: 11,200
SALES (est): 7.3MM **Privately Held**
WEB: www.westcoerealtors.com
SIC: 6531 Real estate agent, residential

(P-16032)
WESTERN NATIONAL GROUP LP
Also Called: Wng
8 Executive Cir, Irvine (92614-6746)
PHONE..................949 862-6200
Michael Hayde, *Partner*
Laura Khouri, *President*
Chris Kennedy, *Vice Pres*
Scott Wickman, *Vice Pres*
Kyle Crimi, *Executive*
EMP: 82 **EST:** 1994
SALES (est): 11.5MM **Privately Held**
WEB: www.wng.com
SIC: 6531 Real estate managers

(P-16033)
WESTERN NATIONAL SECURITIES (PA)
Also Called: Ramada By Wyndham
8 Executive Cir, Irvine (92614-6746)
P.O. Box 19528 (92623-9528)
PHONE..................949 862-6200

Michael K Hayde, *CEO*
James Gilly, *President*
Jerry Lapointe, *Principal*
Brian Gilchrist, *Managing Dir*
Charlotte Alvarado, *Admin Asst*
EMP: 120 **EST:** 1981
SQ FT: 35,000
SALES (est): 223MM **Privately Held**
WEB: www.wng.com
SIC: 6531 7011 Real estate managers;
hotels & motels

(P-16034)
WOODMAN REALTY INC
Also Called: Sierra Springs Apartments
26030 Base Line St Apt 97, San Bernardino
(92410-7066)
PHONE..................909 425-5324
Kelly Fox, *Manager*
EMP: 216 **Privately Held**
SIC: 6531 Real estate agent, commercial
HQ: Woodman Realty Inc.
2016 Riverside Dr
Los Angeles CA 90039

(P-16035)
WORLDWIDE INC
9601 Wilshire Blvd, Beverly Hills
(90210-5213)
PHONE..................310 276-7171
Steve Lewis, *President*
Emory Donelson, *Mktg Dir*
EMP: 60 **EST:** 2006
SQ FT: 9,800
SALES (est): 1.6MM **Privately Held**
WEB: www.mlslimo.com
SIC: 6531 Real estate brokers & agents

(P-16036)
YOUNG REALTORS
Also Called: Joan Young Co Realtors
971 S Westlake Blvd # 100, Westlake Vil-
lage (91361-3115)
PHONE..................805 497-0947
Fax: 805 494-8986
EMP: 53
SALES (est): 1.5MM **Privately Held**
SIC: 6531 Real Estate Agents Managers

6541 Title Abstract Offices

(P-16037)
CALIFORNIA TITLE COMPANY (PA)
28202 Cabot Rd Ste 625, Laguna Niguel
(92677-1261)
PHONE..................949 582-8709
Dave Erb, *President*
Jim Waterman, *President*
Christina Hattem, *CFO*
Geoffrey Allen, *Officer*
CAM Hunter, *Officer*
EMP: 52 **EST:** 2001
SALES (est): 11.2MM **Privately Held**
WEB: www.caltitle.com
SIC: 6541 Title & trust companies

(P-16038)
EQUITY TITLE COMPANY (DH)
801 N Brand Blvd Ste 400, Glendale
(91203-3261)
PHONE..................818 291-4400
Jim Cossell, *President*
Jeremy Thompson, *Officer*
Neil Gulley, *Senior VP*
John Chadbourne, *Vice Pres*
Dindo De, *Vice Pres*
EMP: 80 **EST:** 1979
SALES (est): 11.4MM **Publicly Held**
WEB: www.equitytitle.com
SIC: 6541 Title & trust companies

(P-16039)
FIDELITY NAT TITLE INSUR CO NY
950 Hampshire Rd, Westlake Village
(91361-2805)
PHONE..................805 370-1400
EMP: 1078 **Publicly Held**
WEB: www.newyork.fntic.com
SIC: 6541 Title & trust companies

HQ: Fidelity National Title Insurance Co Of
New York
1 Pak Ave Ste 1402
New York NY 10016
904 854-8100

(P-16040)
FIRST AMERICAN TITLE COMPANY
1 First American Way, Santa Ana
(92707-5913)
PHONE..................714 250-3109
James Boxdell, *Vice Pres*
Marie Cruz, *Sr Corp Ofcr*
Steve Degrandis, *Sr Corp Ofcr*
Joyce Avila, *Officer*
Brace Berg, *Officer*
EMP: 6000 **EST:** 1964
SALES (est): 31.9MM **Privately Held**
WEB: www.firstam.com
SIC: 6541 Title & trust companies

(P-16041)
PROPERTY INSIGHT LLC
2510 Redhill Ave, Santa Ana (92705-5542)
PHONE..................377 747-2537
John Walsh, *Mng Member*
Ron Sree,
EMP: 1119 **EST:** 2004
SALES (est): 1.1MM
SALES (corp-wide): 1.2B **Publicly Held**
WEB: www.propertyinsight.biz
SIC: 6541 Title search companies
HQ: Black Knight Real Estate Data Solu-
tions, Llc
121 Theory Ste 100
Irvine CA 92617
626 808-9000

(P-16042)
STEWART TITLE CALIFORNIA INC
525 N Brand Blvd Ste 200, Glendale
(91203-3993)
PHONE..................818 502-2700
Steve Lessack, *President*
Tamara Ortiz, *Vice Pres*
Farrer Cameron, *Executive*
Liz Nardi, *Opers Staff*
Marcia Packota, *Marketing Staff*
EMP: 125
SALES (corp-wide): 2.2B **Publicly Held**
SIC: 6541 Title & trust companies
HQ: Stewart Title Of California, Inc.
7676 Hazard Center Dr # 1400
San Diego CA 92108
619 692-1600

(P-16043)
TITLE365 COMPANY (DH)
5000 Birch St Ste 300, Newport Beach
(92660-2147)
PHONE..................877 365-9365
Michael J Tafoya, *CEO*
Vickie Crestani, *President*
Peter Derbonne, *President*
Ingrid Baysinger, *Officer*
Lorissa Berkheimer, *Officer*
EMP: 339 **EST:** 2009
SALES (est): 28.7MM **Publicly Held**
SIC: 6541 Title & trust companies
HQ: Experience 1 Inc.
5000 Birch St Ste 300
Newport Beach CA 92660
949 475-3752

(P-16044)
WFG LENDERS SERVICES LLC (HQ)
2625 Townsgate Rd Ste 101, Westlake Vil-
lage (91361-5729)
PHONE..................503 387-3636
James W Moody, *Exec VP*
Kristin Hutchinson, *Trust Officer*
David Wilson, *Senior VP*
Janet Godby, *Vice Pres*
Lisa Johnston, *Vice Pres*
EMP: 62 **EST:** 2011
SALES (est): 30.4MM **Privately Held**
WEB: www.wfgls.com
SIC: 6541 Title & trust companies

▲ = Import ▼ =Export
◆ =Import/Export

6552 Land Subdividers & Developers

(P-16045)
A M S PARTNERSHIP (PA)
Also Called: La Mancha Development
1517 S Sepulveda Blvd, Los Angeles (90025-3311)
PHONE..................................310 312-6698
Marvin B Levine, *Partner*
Samuel Bachner, *Partner*
EMP: 60 EST: 1981
SQ FT: 2,500
SALES (est): 3.2MM **Privately Held**
SIC: 6552 6512 Subdividers & developers; commercial & industrial building operation

(P-16046)
ALLEN DEVELOPMENT PARTNERS LLC (PA)
125 Sbridge 100, Visalia (93291)
PHONE..................................559 732-5425
Richard S Allen,
Kevin Noell,
EMP: 60 EST: 1993
SALES (est): 3.5MM **Privately Held**
SIC: 6552 Subdividers & developers

(P-16047)
CAREER DEV INST FOR EXCPTNAL I
1470 Marsh Way, Riverside (92501-1962)
PHONE..................................951 337-3678
Alan Schwerdt, *Principal*
EMP: 50 EST: 2015
SALES (est): 943.5K **Privately Held**
SIC: 6552 Subdividers & developers

(P-16048)
CENTURY PACIFIC REALTY CORP
9401 Wilshire Blvd # 1250, Beverly Hills (90212-2945)
PHONE..................................310 729-9922
Irwin J Deutch, *President*
Charles L Schwennessen, *Exec VP*
Eric Maman, *Vice Pres*
John Deutch, *Research*
EMP: 250 EST: 1987
SQ FT: 3,500
SALES (est): 9.1MM **Privately Held**
SIC: 6552 Subdividers & developers

(P-16049)
CHATHAM RIGG LLC
Also Called: Residnce Inn Anheim Rsort Ar/G
11931 Harbor Blvd, Garden Grove (92840-2703)
PHONE..................................714 591-4000
Gregg Forde, *Principal*
EMP: 50 EST: 2011
SALES (est): 2.6MM **Privately Held**
SIC: 6552 Subdividers & developers

(P-16050)
COMSTOCK CROSSER ASSOC DEV INC
Also Called: Comstock Homes
321 12th St Ste 200, Manhattan Beach (90266-5354)
PHONE..................................310 546-5781
David Lauletta, *CEO*
Nicholas Long, *CFO*
Gary L Lyter, *CFO*
Dan Crosser, *Vice Pres*
Peggy Miccio, *Accountant*
EMP: 50 EST: 1981
SQ FT: 7,000
SALES (est): 14.2MM **Privately Held**
WEB: www.comstockco.com
SIC: 6552 Land subdividers & developers, residential

(P-16051)
GOLDRICH & KEST INDUSTRIES LLC (PA)
5150 Overland Ave, Culver City (90230-4914)
P.O. Box 3623 (90231-3623)
PHONE..................................310 204-2050
Warren Breslow,
Paul Dubord, *Exec VP*
Sarah Furchtenicht, *Exec VP*

Angel Herrera, *Vice Pres*
Rowena Bangsil, *Regional Mgr*
EMP: 750 EST: 1957
SQ FT: 5,000
SALES (est): 51.9MM **Privately Held**
WEB: www.goldrichkest.com
SIC: 6552 Subdividers & developers

(P-16052)
GOLDRICHKEST (PA)
5150 Overland Ave, Culver City (90230-4914)
P.O. Box 3623 (90231-3623)
PHONE..................................310 204-2050
Jona Goldrich, *President*
Sol Kest, *Vice Pres*
Elsa Laufer, *Regional Mgr*
Daniel Lopez, *Regional Mgr*
Julie Williams, *Technician*
EMP: 250 EST: 1963
SQ FT: 5,000
SALES (est): 30.3MM **Privately Held**
WEB: www.goldrichkest.com
SIC: 6552 Land subdividers & developers, commercial

(P-16053)
JH SNYDER COMPANY
5757 Wilshire Blvd Ph 30, Los Angeles (90036-3690)
P.O. Box 48440 (90048-0440)
PHONE..................................323 857-5546
Jerome H Snyder, *CEO*
Michael Wise, *Senior Partner*
Dan Schneider, *Vice Pres*
Mary Schwei, *Executive*
Richard Barnes, *VP Opers*
EMP: 50 EST: 2013
SALES (est): 6.5MM **Privately Held**
WEB: www.jhsnyder.net
SIC: 6552 Subdividers & developers

(P-16054)
KING VENTURES
285 Bridge St, San Luis Obispo (93401-5510)
PHONE..................................805 544-4444
John E King, *Owner*
EMP: 126 EST: 1977
SQ FT: 10,000
SALES (est): 7.2MM **Privately Held**
WEB: www.kingventures.net
SIC: 6552 6512 Land subdividers & developers, commercial; land subdividers & developers, residential; commercial & industrial building operation

(P-16055)
L AND W DEVELOPERS LLC
Also Called: Contractor
1635 Centinela Ave, Inglewood (90302-1056)
PHONE..................................310 654-8428
Terry Williams, *Mng Member*
EMP: 25 EST: 2017
SALES (est): 1MM **Privately Held**
SIC: 6552 0782 1389 Subdividers & developers; landscape contractors; construction, repair & dismantling services

(P-16056)
LANDSEA HOMES US CORPORATION (DH)
660 Nwport Ctr Dr Ste 300, Newport Beach (92660)
PHONE..................................949 345-8080
John Ho, *CEO*
Mike Forsum, *CFO*
Franco Tenerelli,
Peter Beucke, *Vice Pres*
Karen Dresher, *Vice Pres*
EMP: 76 EST: 2017
SALES (est): 41.4MM
SALES (corp-wide): 136.5MM **Publicly Held**
WEB: www.landseahomes.com
SIC: 6552 Land subdividers & developers, residential
HQ: Landsea Homes Corporation
660 Nwport Ctr Dr Ste 300
Newport Beach CA 92660
949 345-8080

(P-16057)
LOWE ENTERPRISES INC
11777 San Vicente Blvd # 900, Los Angeles (90049-5084)
PHONE..................................310 820-6661
Bob Lowe, *President*
Bill Wethe, *CFO*
Peter S Morgan, *Senior VP*
EMP: 70 EST: 1971
SQ FT: 15,000
SALES (est): 821.5K
SALES (corp-wide): 935.4MM **Privately Held**
WEB: www.lowe-re.com
SIC: 6552 Land subdividers & developers, commercial
HQ: Lowe Development Corporation-Reserve Manager
11777 San Vicente Blvd
Los Angeles CA 90049
310 820-6661

(P-16058)
LOWE ENTERPRISES RE GROUP
11777 San Vicente Blvd, Los Angeles (90049-5011)
PHONE..................................310 820-6661
Bob Lowe, *President*
Mark Rivers, *Exec VP*
Tom Wulf, *Vice Pres*
EMP: 257 EST: 1994
SQ FT: 10,000
SALES (est): 23.5MM
SALES (corp-wide): 935.4MM **Privately Held**
WEB: www.lowe-re.com
SIC: 6552 6531 Land subdividers & developers, commercial; real estate managers
PA: Lowe Enterprises, Inc.
11777 San Vicente Blvd # 900
Los Angeles CA 90049
310 820-6661

(P-16059)
LPC COMMERCIAL SERVICES INC
915 Wilshire Blvd Ste 250, Los Angeles (90017-3409)
PHONE..................................213 362-9080
David Binswangar, *Branch Mgr*
EMP: 241
SALES (corp-wide): 1.3B **Privately Held**
WEB: www.lpcretail.com
SIC: 6552 6531 Land subdividers & developers, commercial; real estate brokers & agents
HQ: Lpc Commercial Services, Inc.
2000 Mckinney Ave # 1000
Dallas TX 75201

(P-16060)
MAKAR PROPERTIES LLC (PA)
Also Called: Makallon La Jolla Properties
4100 Macarthur Blvd # 150, Newport Beach (92660-2063)
P.O. Box 7080 (92658-7080)
PHONE..................................949 255-1100
Paul P Makarechian, *CEO*
Peter Ciaccia, *President*
Douglas Kiel, *COO*
Trilby Clifford, *Executive Asst*
Jill Turner, *Executive Asst*
EMP: 1059 EST: 2001
SALES (est): 61.1MM **Privately Held**
WEB: www.makarproperties.com
SIC: 6552 1542 Land subdividers & developers, commercial; commercial & office building, new construction

(P-16061)
MBK REAL ESTATE COMPANIES
Also Called: MBK Laguna
4 Park Plz Ste 1700, Irvine (92614-2559)
PHONE..................................949 789-8300
Kain Matsumoto, *Chairman*
Kent Crandall, *CFO*
Edward Stokx, *CFO*
David Kurian, *Vice Pres*
Vijay Pandurangadu, *Vice Pres*
EMP: 50 EST: 1990
SALES (est): 17.1MM **Privately Held**
WEB: www.mbk.com
SIC: 6552 Subdividers & developers

PA: Mitsui & Co., Ltd.
1-2-1, Otemachi
Chiyoda-Ku TKY 100-0

(P-16062)
MBK REAL ESTATE LTD A CAL LTD (HQ)
4 Park Plz Ste 1700, Irvine (92614-2559)
PHONE..................................949 789-8300
Stefan Markowitz, *President*
Kent Crandall, *CFO*
Yoshitaka Suzuki, *CFO*
Jonathan Evans, *Analyst*
Michael Phan, *Accountant*
EMP: 58 EST: 1989
SALES (est): 29MM **Privately Held**
WEB: www.mbk.com
SIC: 6552 Subdividers & developers; land subdividers & developers, residential

(P-16063)
NATIONAL CMNTY RENAISSANCE CAL (PA)
9421 Haven Ave, Rancho Cucamonga (91730-5886)
PHONE..................................909 483-2444
Steven J Pontell, *CEO*
Orlando Cabrera, *President*
Tracy Thomas, *COO*
Richard Whittingham, *CFO*
Sebastiano Sterpa, *Chairman*
EMP: 100 EST: 1992
SALES (est): 53.3K **Privately Held**
WEB: www.nationalcore.org
SIC: 6552 Subdividers & developers

(P-16064)
NATIONAL COMMUNITY RENAISSANCE (PA)
9421 Haven Ave, Rancho Cucamonga (91730-5886)
PHONE..................................909 483-2444
Steve Pontell, *CEO*
Angela Lindsey, *Vice Pres*
Tony Mize, *Vice Pres*
Julie Mungai, *Vice Pres*
John Taylor, *Vice Pres*
EMP: 72 EST: 2007
SALES (est): 0 **Privately Held**
WEB: www.nationalcore.org
SIC: 6552 Subdividers & developers

(P-16065)
OLSON COMPANY LLC (PA)
Also Called: Olson Homes
3010 Old Ranch Pkwy # 100, Seal Beach (90740-2750)
PHONE..................................562 596-4770
Steve Olson,
Karen Hoover, *President*
Mario Urzua, *CFO*
Anjelina Barraza, *Vice Pres*
Annita Goldy, *Vice Pres*
EMP: 99 EST: 2014
SALES (est): 26.2MM **Privately Held**
WEB: www.olsonhomes.com
SIC: 6552 Subdividers & developers

(P-16066)
OLSON URBAN HOUSING LLC
Also Called: Olson Company, The
3010 Old Ranch Pkwy # 100, Seal Beach (90740-2750)
PHONE..................................562 596-4770
Steve Olson,
William E Holford, *President*
Todd J Olson, *President*
Stephen E Olson, *CEO*
Scott Laurie, *COO*
EMP: 60 EST: 1988
SALES (est): 7.5MM **Privately Held**
WEB: www.olsonhomes.com
SIC: 6552 Subdividers & developers

(P-16067)
PANATTONI DEVELOPMENT CO INC (PA)
2442 Dupont Dr, Irvine (92612-1523)
PHONE..................................916 381-1561
Carl Panattoni, *Chairman*
Rob Riner, *Partner*
Fredm Bohne, *Managing Prtnr*
Dudley Mitchell, *President*
Greg Thurman, *President*

PRODUCTS & SVCS

EMP: 90 **EST:** 1986
SALES (est): 39.7MM **Privately Held**
WEB: www.panattoni.com
SIC: 6552 Subdividers & developers

(P-16068)
PDC CAPITAL GROUP LLC
250 Fischer Ave, Costa Mesa
(92626-4515)
PHONE....................866 500-8550
Emilio Francisco, *CEO*
Joseph N Fransciso, *Admin Sec*
Wilkin Acedera, *CTO*
EMP: 52 **EST:** 2012
SQ FT: 25,000
SALES (est): 8.6MM **Privately Held**
SIC: 6552 Subdividers & developers

(P-16069)
PUBLIC INVESTMENT CORPORATION
4340 Eucalyptus Ave, Chino (91710-9705)
PHONE....................310 451-5227
EMP: 199
SALES (corp-wide): 17.5MM **Privately Held**
SIC: 6552 Subdividers & developers
PA: Public Investment Corporation
1207 W Magnolia Blvd C
Burbank CA 91506
310 451-5227

(P-16070)
RELATED/NORMONT DEV CO LLC
18201 Von Karman Ave # 900, Irvine (92612-1097)
PHONE....................949 660-7272
William Witte,
Jorge Perez,
Stephen Ross,
EMP: 63 **EST:** 1989
SALES (est): 13.1MM
SALES (corp-wide): 104MM **Privately Held**
WEB: www.related.com
SIC: 6552 8742 Land subdividers & developers, residential; real estate consultant
PA: The Related Companies Inc
450 W 42nd St Apt 7a
New York NY 10036
212 801-1000

(P-16071)
ROCKEFELLER GROUP DEV CORP
4 Park Plz Ste 840, Irvine (92614-3504)
PHONE....................949 468-1800
Kevin Hackett, *President*
Tom McCormick, *Vice Pres*
EMP: 141 **EST:** 2001
SALES (est): 3.6MM **Privately Held**
WEB: www.rockefellergroup.com
SIC: 6552 Land subdividers & developers, commercial
HQ: Rockefeller Group Development Corporation
1221 Ave Of Americas Fl 17 Flr 17
New York NY 10020
212 282-2000

(P-16072)
SHAPELL INDUSTRIES LLC (HQ)
Also Called: S & S Construction Co
8383 Wilshire Blvd # 700, Beverly Hills
(90211-2425)
PHONE....................323 655-7330
Nathan Shapell, *CEO*
Margaret F Leong, *CFO*
David Shapell, *Exec VP*
Max Webb, *Senior VP*
Brett Smith, *Project Mgr*
EMP: 100 **EST:** 1955
SQ FT: 25,000
SALES (est): 56.3MM
SALES (corp-wide): 7B **Publicly Held**
WEB: www.tollbrothers.com
SIC: 6552 6514 1522 Land subdividers & developers, residential; residential building, four or fewer units: operation; residential construction

PA: Toll Brothers, Inc.
1140 Virginia Dr
Fort Washington PA 19034
215 938-8000

(P-16073)
SILVER SADDLE RANCH & CLUB INC
20751 Aristotle Dr, California City (93505)
PHONE....................760 373-8617
Debra Nicastro, *Principal*
EMP: 93
SALES (corp-wide): 8MM **Privately Held**
SIC: 6552 7011 Subdividers & developers; hotels & motels
PA: Silver Saddle Ranch & Club, Inc.
7635 N San Fernando Rd
Burbank CA 91505
818 768-8808

(P-16074)
SM 10000 PROPERTY LLC
Also Called: Michelle Pasternak
10000 Santa Monica Blvd, Los Angeles
(90067-7000)
PHONE....................305 374-5700
Roman Speron, *CEO*
Aaron Gutierrez, *Manager*
EMP: 55 **EST:** 2010
SALES (est): 2.7MM **Privately Held**
SIC: 6552 Subdividers & developers

(P-16075)
TAYLOR MORRISON CALIFORNIA LLC
100 Spectrum Center Dr # 1450, Irvine
(92618-4984)
PHONE....................949 341-1200
Stephen J Wethor, *Mng Member*
Jyll Fuhler, *Consultant*
EMP: 84 **EST:** 2008
SALES (est): 17.1MM
SALES (corp-wide): 6.1B **Publicly Held**
SIC: 6552 Land subdividers & developers, residential
HQ: Taylor Morrison Home Ii Corporation
4900 N Scottsdale Rd # 2
Scottsdale AZ 85251
480 840-8100

(P-16076)
TELACU INDUSTRIES INC (HQ)
5400 E Olympic Blvd # 300, Commerce
(90022-5187)
PHONE....................323 721-1655
David Lizarraga, *CEO*
Michael D Lizarraga, *President*
Jose Lozano, *Advisor*
EMP: 50 **EST:** 1975
SQ FT: 17,000
SALES (est): 195.4K
SALES (corp-wide): 16.4MM **Privately Held**
WEB: www.telacu.com
SIC: 6552 6162 Subdividers & developers; loan correspondents
PA: East Los Angeles Community Union Inc
5400 E Olympic Blvd Fl 3
Commerce CA 90022
323 721-1655

(P-16077)
TOWBES GROUP INC (PA)
33 E Carrillo St Ste 200, Santa Barbara
(93101-2706)
P.O. Box 20130 (93120-0130)
PHONE....................805 962-2121
Michael Towbes, *CEO*
Craig Zimmerman, *President*
R D R Deaver, *CFO*
Michelle Konoske, *CFO*
Derek Hansen, *Exec VP*
EMP: 97 **EST:** 1973
SQ FT: 7,250
SALES (est): 24.7MM **Privately Held**
WEB: www.towbes.com
SIC: 6552 6512 1542 Subdividers & developers; nonresidential building operators; nonresidential construction

(P-16078)
VOIT DEVELOPMENT MANAGER INC
Also Called: Voit Commercial Brokerage
2020 Main St Ste 100, Irvine (92614-8218)
PHONE....................949 851-5110
Fax: 949 261-9092
EMP: 57
SALES (corp-wide): 25.4MM **Privately Held**
SIC: 6552 6531 Subdivider/Developer Real Estate Agent/Manager
PA: Voit Development Manager, Inc.
101 Shipyard Way Ste M
Newport Beach CA 92663
949 644-8648

(P-16079)
VOIT REAL ESTATE SERVICES LLC
2020 Main St, Irvine (92614-8200)
PHONE....................949 851-5100
Robert D Voit, *Mng Member*
Robert Voit, *Partner*
Vance McNeilly, *COO*
Mike Bench, *Vice Pres*
Kimberly Clark, *Vice Pres*
EMP: 61 **EST:** 2007
SALES (est): 13MM **Privately Held**
WEB: www.voitco.com
SIC: 6552 6519 6531 Subdividers & developers; real property lessors; real estate agents & managers

(P-16080)
WATT PROPERTIES INC (PA)
Also Called: Watt Commercial Properties
2716 Ocean Park Blvd # 2025, Santa Monica (90405-5207)
PHONE....................310 314-2430
Janet Watt Van Huisen, *Ch of Bd*
Jim Maginn, *Managing Prtnr*
Susan Rorison, *President*
James Maginn, *CEO*
Audra Arbini, *Bd of Directors*
EMP: 78 **EST:** 1973
SQ FT: 8,700
SALES (est): 26.9MM **Privately Held**
WEB: www.wattcompanies.com
SIC: 6552 6512 6531 Land subdividers & developers, commercial; shopping center, property operation only; real estate managers

(P-16081)
WEBB DEL CALIFORNIA CORP (DH)
39755 Berkey Dr, Palm Desert
(92211-1106)
PHONE....................760 772-5300
Nancy E Abbott, *Principal*
EMP: 300 **EST:** 1965
SQ FT: 14,000
SALES (est): 23.8MM
SALES (corp-wide): 11B **Publicly Held**
WEB: www.scpdca.com
SIC: 6552 Subdividers & developers
HQ: Pulte Home Company, Llc
3350 Peachtree Rd Ne # 150
Atlanta GA 30326
248 647-2750

6553 Cemetery Subdividers & Developers

(P-16082)
FOREST LAWN CO
1712 S Glendale Ave, Glendale
(91205-3320)
PHONE....................818 241-4151
John Llewellyn, *President*
Nick Scinocca, *Security Dir*
Mark Rosenblum, *Office Mgr*
Ricardo Rojas, *Supervisor*
EMP: 150 **EST:** 1906
SQ FT: 50,000
SALES (est): 17.3MM **Privately Held**
WEB: www.forestlawn.com
SIC: 6553 Real property subdividers & developers, cemetery lots only

(P-16083)
FOREST LAWN MEMORIAL-PARK ASSN (PA)
Also Called: Forest Lawn Mem Parks Mortuary
1712 S Glendale Ave, Glendale
(91205-3320)
PHONE....................323 254-3131
Darin B Drabing, *CEO*
Thomas McKernan, *Ch of Bd*
John Llewellyn, *CEO*
Russel Whittenberg, *CFO*
Susan R Sandler, *Senior VP*
▲ **EMP:** 300
SQ FT: 450,000
SALES (est): 129.4MM **Privately Held**
WEB: www.forestlawn.com
SIC: 5992 6553 7261 Flowers, fresh; cemetery association; funeral service & crematories

(P-16084)
HANIL DEVELOPMENT INC
Also Called: Aroma Wilshire Center
3680 Wilshire Blvd B01, Los Angeles
(90010-2708)
PHONE....................213 387-0111
Yeong Ik Kweon, *CEO*
Kee June Huh, *Vice Pres*
Jae Whang, *Executive*
Joung Ki Kim, *Exec Dir*
Joung Kim, *Exec Dir*
EMP: 50 **EST:** 1997
SALES (est): 3.1MM **Privately Held**
SIC: 6553 Real property subdividers & developers, cemetery lots only

(P-16085)
INGLEWOOD PARK CEMETERY (PA)
720 E Florence Ave, Inglewood
(90301-1482)
P.O. Box 6042 (90312-6042)
PHONE....................310 412-6500
Daniel Villa, *President*
Chris Winners, *CFO*
Kevin Brown, *Vice Pres*
Cheryl Lewis, *Vice Pres*
David Wharmby, *Vice Pres*
EMP: 149 **EST:** 1905
SQ FT: 14,000
SALES (est): 19.1MM **Privately Held**
WEB: www.inglewoodparkcemetery.com
SIC: 6553 Cemeteries, real estate operation

(P-16086)
JOSHUA TREE MEMORIAL PARK
6021 Twentynine Palms Hwy, Joshua Tree
(92252)
PHONE....................760 366-9210
EMP: 50 **EST:** 1968
SALES (est): 1.6MM **Privately Held**
WEB: www.joshuatreememorialpark.com
SIC: 6553 Cemetery association

(P-16087)
OAKDALE MEMORIAL PARK (PA)
1401 S Grand Ave, Glendora (91740-5406)
PHONE....................626 335-0281
Genny Delgado, *Manager*
EMP: 75 **EST:** 1890
SQ FT: 10,000
SALES (est): 3.6MM **Privately Held**
WEB: www.oakdalemortuaryglendora.com
SIC: 6553 Cemeteries, real estate operation

(P-16088)
ROSE HILLS COMPANY (DH)
Also Called: Rose Hills Mem Pk & Mortuary
3888 Workman Mill Rd, Whittier
(90601-1626)
PHONE....................562 699-0921
Dennis Poulsen, *Ch of Bd*
Kenton Woods, *President*
Mary Guzman, *CFO*
Ellen Uzialko, *Treasure*
Ophelia Camero, *Vice Pres*
EMP: 595 **EST:** 1996
SQ FT: 143,950

SALES (est): 77.9MM
SALES (corp-wide): 3.5B **Publicly Held**
WEB: www.rosehills.com
SIC: **6553** Real property subdividers & developers, cemetery lots only
HQ: Rose Hills Holdings Corp.
3888 Workman Mill Rd
Whittier CA 90601
562 699-0921

(P-16089)
ROSE HILLS HOLDINGS CORP (HQ)
Also Called: Rose Hills Mem Pk & Mortuary
3888 Workman Mill Rd, Whittier (90601-1626)
PHONE........................562 699-0921
Pat Monroe, *CEO*
Gregory Bradley, *Vice Pres*
Julie Lin, *Exec Dir*
Joe Menchaca, *Security Mgr*
Nick Clark, *Marketing Staff*
EMP: 500 EST: 1996
SQ FT: 143,950
SALES (est): 87.1MM
SALES (corp-wide): 3.5B **Publicly Held**
WEB: www.rosehills.com
SIC: **6553** Cemeteries, real estate operation
PA: Service Corporation International
1929 Allen Pkwy
Houston TX 77019
713 522-5141

(P-16090)
WILSHIRE BOULEVARD TEMPLE
4334 Whittier Blvd, Los Angeles (90023-2019)
PHONE........................323 261-6135
Carol J Bova, *Manager*
EMP: 112
SALES (corp-wide): 36.2MM **Privately Held**
WEB: www.wbtla.org
SIC: **8661 6553 7261** Temples; cemetery subdividers & developers; funeral service & crematories
PA: Wilshire Boulevard Temple
3663 Wilshire Blvd
Los Angeles CA 90010
213 388-2401

6712 Offices Of Bank Holding Co's

(P-16091)
BANAMEX USA BANCORP (DH)
787 W 5th St, Los Angeles (90071-2003)
PHONE........................310 203-3440
Salvador Villar Jr, *President*
Francisco Moreno Sr, *Vice Pres*
▲ EMP: 210 EST: 1977
SALES (est): 94.9MM
SALES (corp-wide): 88.8B **Publicly Held**
WEB: www.citigroup.com
SIC: **6712 6029 6022** Bank holding companies; commercial banks; state commercial banks

6719 Offices Of Holding Co's, NEC

(P-16092)
AMBULNZ CO LLC
1907 Border Ave, Torrance (90501-3606)
PHONE........................877 311-5555
Michael Witkowski, *Principal*
Stan Vashovsky, *Principal*
EMP: 99 EST: 2018 **Privately Held**
WEB: www.ambulnz.com
SIC: **6719** Holding companies

(P-16093)
AME-GYU CO LTD
20000 Mariner Ave Ste 500, Torrance (90503-1670)
PHONE........................310 214-9572
Ryo Tozu, *CEO*
Hidekazu Seo, *CFO*
Hiratsugu Aiba, *Treasurer*
EMP: 1100 EST: 2016 **Privately Held**

SIC: **6719** 5812 Investment holding companies, except banks; Japanese restaurant

(P-16094)
ARCH BAY HOLDINGS LLC
327 W Maple Ave, Monrovia (91016-3331)
PHONE........................949 679-2400
EMP: 60 EST: 2008 **Privately Held**
SIC: **6719** Holding Company

(P-16095)
ASP HENRY HOLDINGS INC
999 N Pcf Cast Hwy Ste 80, El Segundo (90245)
PHONE........................310 955-9200
Frank Ready, *CEO*
EMP: 600 EST: 2016
SALES (corp-wide): 4.2B **Publicly Held**
WEB: www.carlisle.com
SIC: **6719** 2952 Investment holding companies, except banks; roof cement: asphalt, fibrous or plastic
PA: Carlisle Companies Incorporated
16430 N Scottsdale Rd
Scottsdale AZ 85254
480 781-5000

(P-16096)
CCC PROPERTY HOLDINGS LLC
Also Called: Contractors Cargo Company
500 S Alameda St, Compton (90221-3801)
P.O. Box 5290 (90224-5290)
PHONE........................310 609-1957
Gerald Wheeler, *Ch of Bd*
Carla Ann Wheeler, *CFO*
Jerry Wheeler, *Chairman*
Kim Dorio, *Admin Sec*
EMP: 121 EST: 2009
SQ FT: 18,000
SALES (est): 4.5MM **Privately Held**
SIC: **6719** Investment holding companies, except banks

(P-16097)
CPL HOLDINGS LLC
12181 Bluff Creek Dr 25, Playa Vista (90094-2992)
PHONE........................310 348-6800
Patrick Gregory, *CFO*
Stephen Krenzer, *CEO*
Jonathan Ripper, *Vice Pres*
Sooraj Akkammadam, *Info Tech Mgr*
Garron MA, *Software Engr*
EMP: 200 EST: 2012
SQ FT: 40,000
SALES (est): 200MM **Privately Held**
WEB: www.coredigital.com
SIC: **5331 6719 5961** Variety stores; investment holding companies, except banks;

(P-16098)
DESSER HOLDING COMPANY LLC (HQ)
Also Called: Desser Tire & Rubber Co.
6900 W Acco St, Montebello (90640-5435)
P.O. Box 1028 (90640-1028)
PHONE........................323 721-4900
Christopher Lawler, *Chairman*
Steven D Chlavin, *CEO*
Joseph Heinmiller, *Vice Pres*
EMP: 30 EST: 2014
SALES (est): 69.8MM **Privately Held**
WEB: www.desser.com
SIC: **6719** 3011 3691 Investment holding companies, except banks; airplane tires, pneumatic; batteries, rechargeable

(P-16099)
DHARMA VENTURES GROUP INC (PA)
24700 Ave Rockefeller, Valencia (91355-3465)
PHONE........................661 294-4200
Jim Snell, *President*
Tina Borella, *Admin Asst*
Benjamin Stroba, *Technology*
Cheryl Horn Berger, *VP Sales*
Jeff Daetweiler, *Sales Staff*
EMP: 280 EST: 2006
SQ FT: 75,000

SALES (est): 43MM **Privately Held**
WEB: www.shieldhealthcare.com
SIC: **5999 6719** Medical apparatus & supplies; personal holding companies, except banks

(P-16100)
FORTRESS HOLDING GROUP LLC
5500 E Snta Ana Cyn Rd St, Anaheim (92807-3154)
PHONE........................714 202-8710
Luis Perez, *Chairman*
Adam Forbs, *President*
EMP: 90 EST: 2009 **Privately Held**
SIC: **6719** Investment holding companies, except banks

(P-16101)
GH GROUP INC
Also Called: Glass House Group
3645 Long Beach Blvd, Long Beach (90807-4018)
PHONE........................562 264-5078
Kyle Kazan, *CEO*
Graham Farrar, *President*
Daryl Kato, *COO*
Derrek Higgins, *CFO*
EMP: 250 EST: 2006 **Privately Held**
WEB: www.gh-group.com
SIC: **6719** Investment holding companies, except banks

(P-16102)
HCO HOLDING I CORPORATION (HQ)
999 N Pacific Coast Hwy # 80, El Segundo (90245-2714)
PHONE........................323 583-5000
Brian C Strauss, *CEO*
Jason Peel, *CFO*
Dori M Reap, *CFO*
Robert D Armstrong, *Senior VP*
James F Barry, *Senior VP*
◆ EMP: 100 EST: 2005
SALES (est): 249.7MM
SALES (corp-wide): 254.1MM **Privately Held**
SIC: **6719** Investment holding companies, except banks
PA: Hnc Parent, Inc.
999 N Pacific Coast Hwy # 80
El Segundo CA 90245
310 955-9200

(P-16103)
KELLY TOYS HOLDINGS LLC
4811 S Alameda St, Vernon (90058-2805)
PHONE........................323 923-1300
Jonathan Kelly, *President*
David Neustein, *COO*
Matthew Siesel, *CFO*
EMP: 100 EST: 2020
SALES (corp-wide): 8.9B **Publicly Held**
WEB: www.jazwares.com
SIC: **6719** 5092 Investment holding companies, except banks; toys & hobby goods & supplies
HQ: Jazwares, Llc
1067 Shotgun Rd
Sunrise FL 33326
-

(P-16104)
MAFAB INC (PA)
1925 Century Park E # 650, Los Angeles (90067-2752)
PHONE........................714 893-0551
Ronald B Grey, *President*
Ronald Grey, *President*
EMP: 60 EST: 1972
SQ FT: 3,600
SALES (est): 15.8MM **Privately Held**
SIC: **6719** Personal holding companies, except banks

(P-16105)
N2 ACQUISITION COMPANY INC
Also Called: N2 Imaging Systems
14440 Myford Rd, Irvine (92606-1001)
PHONE........................714 942-3563
Tony Bacarella, *CEO*
Timothy Boyle, *CFO*
EMP: 92 EST: 2019 **Privately Held**
WEB: www.n2imaging.com

SIC: **6719** Investment holding companies, except banks

(P-16106)
NRP HOLDING CO INC (PA)
1 Mauchly, Irvine (92618-2305)
PHONE........................949 583-1000
Jeffrey P Frieden, *President*
Ali Haralson, *Officer*
Ken Rivkin, *Exec VP*
Robert Friedman, *Vice Pres*
Robert D Friedman, *Vice Pres*
EMP: 200 EST: 2003
SQ FT: 40,000
SALES (est): 80.7MM **Privately Held**
SIC: **6719** Investment holding companies, except banks

(P-16107)
PLATINUM GROUP COMPANIES INC (PA)
Also Called: Top Finance Company
22560 La Quilla Dr, Chatsworth (91311-1221)
P.O. Box 280518, Northridge (91328-0518)
PHONE........................818 721-3800
David Mandel, *CEO*
Sandy To, *Treasurer*
Sandy Mandel, *Officer*
Cristina Valdovinos, *Administration*
Robert Netzel, *Info Tech Mgr*
EMP: 125 EST: 2005
SQ FT: 20,000
SALES (est): 39.6MM **Privately Held**
SIC: **6719** Personal holding companies, except banks

(P-16108)
PROJECT SKYLINE INTERMEDIATE H
360 N Crescent Dr Bldg S, Beverly Hills (90210-2529)
PHONE........................310 712-1850
Tom Gores, *President*
EMP: 2020 EST: 2009 **Privately Held**
SIC: **6719** Investment holding companies, except banks

(P-16109)
R AND I HOLDINGS INC
2145 Dashwood St Lakewood, Lakewood (90712)
PHONE........................562 483-0577
Susan Gerros, *President*
Jason Gerros, *CFO*
EMP: 47
SALES (est): 6.5MM **Privately Held**
SIC: **6719** 5084 3799 Investment holding companies, except banks; pneumatic tools & equipment; trailers & trailer equipment

(P-16110)
RSG GROUP USA INC
Also Called: Gold's Gym
7000 Romaine St Ste 201, West Hollywood (90038-2304)
PHONE........................214 574-4653
Sebastian Schoepe, *CEO*
EMP: 2000 EST: 2020
SALES (corp-wide): 395.6MM **Privately Held**
WEB: www.goldsgym.com
SIC: **6719** 7991 Investment holding companies, except banks; physical fitness facilities
PA: Rsg Group Gmbh
Tannenberg 4
Schlusselfeld BY 96132
955 293-190

(P-16111)
SKEFFINGTON ENTERPRISES INC
2200 S Yale St, Santa Ana (92704-4404)
PHONE........................714 540-1700
William J Skeffington, *President*
John Skeffington, *CFO*
EMP: 100
SQ FT: 180,000
SALES (est): 32.1MM **Privately Held**
SIC: **6719** Personal holding companies, except banks

PRODUCTS & SVCS

(P-16112)
SOLARIANT CAPITAL LLC
301 N Lake Ave Ste 950, Pasadena
(91101-5105)
PHONE...................................626 544-0279
Daniel Kim, *Mng Member*
EMP: 102 EST: 2012
SALES (est): 23.4MM **Privately Held**
WEB: www.solariantcapital.com
SIC: 6719 1629 6722 Investment holding
companies, except banks; power plant
construction; management investment,
open-end

(P-16113)
STANTEC HOLDINGS DEL III INC
Also Called: Stantec Oil and Gas
5500 Ming Ave Ste 300, Bakersfield
(93309-4627)
PHONE...................................661 396-3770
Robert Gomes, *President*
Ysmael Suarez, *Engineer*
EMP: 460 EST: 2005
SALES (corp-wide): 3.6B **Privately Held**
WEB: www.stantec.com
SIC: 6719 Investment holding companies,
except banks
PA: Stantec Inc
10220 103 Ave Nw Suite 400
Edmonton AB T5J 0
780 917-7000

(P-16114)
TOKAI INTL HOLDINGS INC (PA)
2055 S Haven Ave, Ontario (91761-0736)
PHONE...................................909 930-5000
Felix M Hon, *CEO*
EMP: 50 EST: 2005
SALES (est): 48.5MM **Privately Held**
WEB: www.calicobrands.com
SIC: 6719 Investment holding companies,
except banks

(P-16115)
WILBUR CURTIS CO INC
6913 W Acco St, Montebello (90640-5403)
PHONE...................................800 421-6150
Kevin Curtis, *President*
Joe Laws, *COO*
Norman Fujitaki, *CFO*
Michael A Curtis, *Exec VP*
Steve Bradley, *Vice Pres*
◆ EMP: 280 EST: 1941
SQ FT: 175,000 **Privately Held**
WEB: www.wilburcurtis.com
SIC: 6719 3589 Investment holding com-
panies, except banks; coffee brewing
equipment

(P-16116)
**WOLVERINE TOP HOLDING
CORP**
360 N Crescent Dr Bldg S, Beverly Hills
(90210-2529)
PHONE...................................661 772-7500
Mary Ann Sigler, *President*
Dawn Walloch, *Treasurer*
Eva Kalawski, *Vice Pres*
Joe Kaczorowski, *Admin Sec*
Barbara Velasco, *Asst Sec*
EMP: 99 EST: 2019 **Privately Held**
SIC: 6719 Holding companies

(P-16117)
**XENEL INTERNATIONAL USA
(HQ)**
Also Called: Aeromovel
2637 Townsgate Rd Ste 300, Westlake Vil-
lage (91361-2720)
PHONE...................................805 496-2227
James W Thomas, *President*
Pauline Jackson, *Vice Pres*
Diego Ceballos, *Principal*
RE Mabus, *Governor*
Albert Hummel, *Director*
EMP: 14 EST: 1979
SALES (est): 9.6MM **Privately Held**
SIC: 6719 3822 Investment holding com-
panies, except banks; auto controls regu-
lating residntl & coml environmt & applncs

(P-16118)
YF ART HOLDINGS GP LLC
9130 W Sunset Blvd, Los Angeles
(90069-3110)
PHONE...................................678 441-1400
Fred Boehler, *President*
EMP: 10600 EST: 2014 **Privately Held**
SIC: 6719 Investment holding companies,
except banks

6722 Management Investment
Offices

(P-16119)
**ALLIANZ ASSET MGT AMER LLC
(DH)**
650 Newport Center Dr, Newport Beach
(92660-6310)
PHONE...................................949 219-2200
Summer Zhang, *Vice Pres*
Kari Furry, *Vice Pres*
Sara Oudin, *Vice Pres*
Mike Puntoriero, *Managing Dir*
Irene Hill, *Executive Asst*
EMP: 62 EST: 2014
SALES (est): 1.9B
SALES (corp-wide): 26.4B **Privately Held**
WEB: www.allianz.com
SIC: 6722 Money market mutual funds
HQ: Allianz Of America, Inc.
55 Greens Farms Rd Ste 1
Westport CT 06880
203 221-8500

(P-16120)
**ALLIANZ GLOBL INVSTORS
CPITL L**
680 Nwport Ctr Dr Ste 250, Newport Beach
(92660)
PHONE...................................949 219-2200
David Flattum,
Kerry Murphy, *Executive*
Steve Ricci, *Human Res Dir*
Wesley Edens,
EMP: 70 EST: 2001
SALES (est): 17.2MM
SALES (corp-wide): 26.4B **Privately Held**
WEB: www.allianz.com
SIC: 6722 Money market mutual funds
PA: Allianz Se
Koniginstr. 28
Munchen BY 80802
893 800-0

(P-16121)
ALTURA HOLDINGS LLC (HQ)
1335 S Acacia Ave, Fullerton (92831-5315)
PHONE...................................714 948-8400
Robert Blazek, *CEO*
Karen Frankenberg, *CFO*
EMP: 62 EST: 2011
SALES (est): 84MM **Privately Held**
WEB: www.alturacs.com
SIC: 6722 Management investment, open-
end

(P-16122)
**AMERICAN FUNDS DISTRS INC
(DH)**
333 S Hope St Ste Levb, Los Angeles
(90071-3003)
PHONE...................................213 486-9200
Michael Johnston, *Ch of Bd*
Larry Clemmensen, *Ch of Bd*
J Kelly Webb, *Treasurer*
Ryan Doyle, *Vice Pres*
Robert Hartig, *Vice Pres*
EMP: 116 EST: 1972
SQ FT: 6,000
SALES (est): 97.3MM
SALES (corp-wide): 5.4B **Privately Held**
WEB: www.capitalgroup.com
SIC: 6722 Mutual fund sales, on own ac-
count; money market mutual funds
HQ: Capital Research And Management
Company
333 S Hope St Fl 55
Los Angeles CA 90071
213 486-9200

(P-16123)
AMERICAN MUTUAL FUND
333 S Hope St Fl 51, Los Angeles
(90071-1420)
PHONE...................................213 486-9200
Jonathan B Lovelace Jr, *Ch of Bd*
James K Dunton, *Ch of Bd*
Robert G O'Donnell, *President*
Mary C Hall, *Treasurer*
Mary Hall, *Treasurer*
EMP: 200 EST: 1949
SQ FT: 5,000
SALES: 1.6B **Privately Held**
WEB: www.capitalgroup.com
SIC: 6722 Money market mutual funds

(P-16124)
**ARES MANAGEMENT
CORPORATION (PA)**
2000 Avenue Of The Stars # 12, Los Ange-
les (90067-4733)
PHONE...................................310 201-4100
Michael J Arougheti, *President*
Tony Ressler, *Senior Partner*
R Kipp Deveer, *Partner*
Antony P Ressler, *Ch of Bd*
Michael R McFerran, *COO*
EMP: 287 EST: 1997
SALES (est): 1.7B **Publicly Held**
WEB: www.aresmgmt.com
SIC: 6722 Management investment, open-
end

(P-16125)
ARES MANAGEMENT LLC (HQ)
2000 Avenue Of The Stars # 12, Los Ange-
les (90067-4733)
PHONE...................................310 201-4100
Antony Ressler, *President*
Jamie Dufauchard, *President*
John Kissick, *Bd of Directors*
Don Haisch, *Officer*
Alexander Morgan, *Assoc VP*
EMP: 60 EST: 2001
SALES (est): 840.5MM
SALES (corp-wide): 1.7B **Publicly Held**
WEB: www.aresmgmt.com
SIC: 6722 Management investment, open-
end
PA: Ares Management Corporation
2000 Avenue Of The Stars # 12
Los Angeles CA 90067
310 201-4100

(P-16126)
**CAPITAL PRVATE CLENT SVCS
FNDS**
6455 Irvine Center Dr, Irvine (92618-4518)
PHONE...................................949 975-5000
EMP: 80 EST: 2010
SALES (est): 1MM
SALES (corp-wide): 5.4B **Privately Held**
SIC: 6722 Money market mutual funds
HQ: Capital Guardian Trust Company
333 S Hope St Fl 52
Los Angeles CA 90071
213 486-9200

(P-16127)
CAUSEWAY CAPITAL MGT LLC
11111 Santa Monica Blvd # 1500, Los Ange-
les (90025-3349)
PHONE...................................310 231-6100
Gracie Fermelia, *Officer*
Daniel Pham, *Officer*
Kumar Mahadeva, *Vice Pres*
Trent Ashby, *Administration*
Taline Hagopian, *Business Anlyst*
EMP: 109 EST: 2001
SALES (est): 34.3MM **Privately Held**
WEB: www.causewaycap.com
SIC: 6722 Money market mutual funds

(P-16128)
**CLEARLAKE CAPITAL GROUP
LP (PA)**
233 Wilshire Blvd Ste 800, Santa Monica
(90401-1207)
PHONE...................................310 400-8800
Behdad Eghbali, *Partner*
Jose Feliciano, *Partner*
Paul Huber, *Partner*
Fred Ebrahemi, *COO*
John Cannon, *Managing Dir*
EMP: 258 EST: 2006

SALES (est): 3.8B **Privately Held**
WEB: www.clearlake.com
SIC: 6722 Management investment, open-
end

(P-16129)
FIRST QUADRANT LP (PA)
800 E Colo Blvd Ste 900, Pasadena
(91101)
PHONE...................................626 795-8220
Max Darnell, *Partner*
Joel Brouwer, *Partner*
Ghene Faulcon, *Partner*
Dori Levanoni, *Partner*
Edgar Peters, *Partner*
EMP: 79 EST: 1985
SQ FT: 22,000
SALES (est): 22.6MM **Privately Held**
WEB: www.firstquadrant.com
SIC: 6722 Management investment, open-
end

(P-16130)
**GUGGENHEIM PRTNERS INV
MGT LLC**
100 Wilshire Blvd Fl 5, Santa Monica
(90401-1110)
PHONE...................................310 576-1270
Robert Daviduk, *Director*
Robert Khuzami, *Partner*
Ana Zador, *Vice Pres*
Becky Bowler, *Managing Dir*
Steve Lee, *Managing Dir*
EMP: 73
SALES (est): 15MM
SALES (corp-wide): 1.8B **Privately Held**
WEB: www.guggenheimpartners.com
SIC: 6722 Money market mutual funds
PA: Guggenheim Partners, Llc
330 Madison Ave Rm 201
New York NY 10017
212 739-0700

(P-16131)
**KAYNE ANDERSON RDNICK INV
MGT L**
1800 Avenue Of The Stars, Los Angeles
(90067-4201)
PHONE...................................310 229-9260
Stephen Rigali, *Chief Mktg Ofcr*
Sheryl Sadis, *CFO*
Spuds Powell, *Vice Pres*
Michael Heinz, *Managing Dir*
Sandeep Mishra, *Managing Dir*
EMP: 60 EST: 1995
SQ FT: 20,000
SALES (est): 48.1MM **Publicly Held**
WEB: www.kayne.com
SIC: 6722 Management investment, open-
end
HQ: Virtus Partners, Inc.
755 Main St
Hartford CT 06103

(P-16132)
**LOS ANGELES CAPITAL MGT
LLC (PA)**
Also Called: LA CAPITAL
11150 Santa Monica Blvd # 200, Los Ange-
les (90025-0418)
PHONE...................................310 479-9998
Thomas Stevens, *Ch of Bd*
Thomas D Stevens, *President*
Jennifer Reynolds, *CFO*
Hal Reynolds, *Treasurer*
Hal W Reynolds, *Ch Invest Ofcr*
EMP: 87 EST: 2002
SQ FT: 10,192
SALES: 105.6K **Privately Held**
WEB: www.lacapm.com
SIC: 6722 8741 8211 8282 Management
investment, open-end; management serv-
ices; elementary & secondary schools; in-
vestment advice

(P-16133)
**MONEX DEPOSIT A CAL LTD
PARTNR**
4910 Birch St, Newport Beach
(92660-8100)
PHONE...................................949 752-1400
Mike Carabini, *Managing Prtnr*
Louis E Carabini, *Partner*
Pat Caparelli, *Executive Asst*

Darrel Hamilton, *Technology*
Kathleen Krogius, *VP Adv*
EMP: 100 **EST:** 1987
SALES (est): 11.3MM **Privately Held**
WEB: www.monex.com
SIC: 5944 6722 3324 Jewelry, precious stones & precious metals; management investment, open-end; steel investment foundries

(P-16134)
NOGALES INVESTORS MGT LLC (PA)
9229 W Sunset Blvd # 900, Los Angeles (90069-3410)
PHONE......................310 276-7439
Erika Marroquin, *Executive Asst*
EMP: 240 **EST:** 2001
SALES (est): 16.6MM **Privately Held**
WEB: www.nogalesinvestors.com
SIC: 6722 Management investment, open-end

(P-16135)
OAKTREE CAPITAL GROUP LLC (HQ)
333 S Grand Ave Fl 28, Los Angeles (90071-1530)
PHONE......................213 830-6300
Jay S Wintrob, *CEO*
Bruce A Karsh, *Ch of Bd*
Howard S Marks, *Ch of Bd*
Daniel D Levin, *CFO*
John B Frank, *Vice Ch Bd*
EMP: 62 **EST:** 1995
SALES (est): 429MM
SALES (corp-wide): 47.9B **Publicly Held**
WEB: www.oaktreecapital.com
SIC: 6722 Management investment, open-end
PA: Brookfield Asset Management Inc
181 Bay St Suite 300
Toronto ON M5J 2
416 363-9491

(P-16136)
OAKTREE CPITL GROUP HLDINGS LP (PA)
333 S Grand Ave Fl 28, Los Angeles (90071-1530)
PHONE......................213 830-6300
Howard S Marks, *Chairman*
Bruce Allen Karsh, *Ch Invest Ofcr*
Sumanta Chakravarty, *Vice Pres*
Jenny Kim, *Vice Pres*
Allison Lee, *Vice Pres*
EMP: 889 **EST:** 2007
SALES (est): 898MM **Privately Held**
WEB: www.oaktreecapital.com
SIC: 6722 Management investment, open-end

(P-16137)
OAKTREE HOLDINGS INC
333 Suth Grnd Ave Fl 28 Flr 28, Los Angeles (90071)
PHONE......................213 830-6300
EMP: 737 **EST:** 2014
SALES (est): 6.1MM **Privately Held**
WEB: www.oaktreecapital.com
SIC: 6722 Management investment, open-end
PA: Oaktree Capital Group Holdings, L.P.
333 S Grand Ave Fl 28
Los Angeles CA 90071

(P-16138)
OAKTREE REAL ESTATE OPPRTNTIES (DH)
333 S Grand Ave Fl 28, Los Angeles (90071-1504)
PHONE......................213 830-6300
EMP: 66 **EST:** 2012
SALES (est): 115.6MM
SALES (corp-wide): 47.9B **Publicly Held**
WEB: www.oaktreecapital.com
SIC: 6722 Money market mutual funds

(P-16139)
OAKTREE REAL ESTATE OPPRTNTIES
333 S Grand Ave Fl 28, Los Angeles (90071-1530)
PHONE......................213 830-6300

EMP: 442 **EST:** 2014
SALES (est): 3.9MM **Privately Held**
WEB: www.oaktreecapital.com
SIC: 6722 Money market mutual funds
PA: Oaktree Capital Group Holdings, L.P.
333 S Grand Ave Fl 28
Los Angeles CA 90071

(P-16140)
OAKTREE STRATEGIC INCOME LLC
333 S Grand Ave Fl 28, Los Angeles (90071-1530)
PHONE......................213 830-6300
EMP: 786 **EST:** 2015
SALES (est): 7.2MM **Privately Held**
WEB: www.oaktreecapital.com
SIC: 6722 Money market mutual funds
PA: Oaktree Capital Group Holdings, L.P.
333 S Grand Ave Fl 28
Los Angeles CA 90071

(P-16141)
OCM REAL ESTATE OPPRTNTIES FUN
333 S Grand Ave Fl 28, Los Angeles (90071-1504)
PHONE......................213 830-6300
EMP: 393 **EST:** 2014
SALES (est): 2.2MM **Privately Held**
WEB: www.oaktreecapital.com
SIC: 6722 Money market mutual funds
PA: Oaktree Capital Group Holdings, L.P.
333 S Grand Ave Fl 28
Los Angeles CA 90071

(P-16142)
ORANGE CNTY EMPLYEES RTRMENT S
2223 S Wellington Ave, Santa Ana (92701)
PHONE......................714 558-6200
Raymond Fleming, *CEO*
Molly Murphy, *Ch Invest Ofcr*
David Beeson, *Analyst*
Stina Walander-Sarkin, *Analyst*
Cynthia Hockless, *Human Res Dir*
EMP: 51 **EST:** 1945
SALES (est): 12.1MM **Privately Held**
WEB: www.ocers.org
SIC: 6722 8111 Management investment, open-end; legal services

(P-16143)
PACIFIC INVESTMENT MGT CO LLC (DH)
Also Called: Pimco
650 Newport Center Dr, Newport Beach (92660-6392)
P.O. Box 6430 (92658-6430)
PHONE......................949 720-6000
Emmanuel Roman, *CEO*
John Studzinski, *Vice Chairman*
Jay Jacobs, *President*
Robin Shanahan, *COO*
Peter Strelow, *COO*
EMP: 240 **EST:** 1969
SQ FT: 25,000
SALES (est): 596.7MM
SALES (corp-wide): 26.4B **Privately Held**
SIC: 6722 Money market mutual funds
HQ: Allianz Asset Management Of America Llc
650 Newport Center Dr
Newport Beach CA 92660
949 219-2200

(P-16144)
PIMCO GLOBAL ADVISORS LLC (DH)
840 Nwport Ctr Dr Ste 100, Newport Beach (92660)
P.O. Box 6430 (92658-6430)
PHONE......................949 219-2200
John Maney,
Geraldine Sundstrom, *Portfolio Mgr*
Rick Lebrun, *General Counsel*
EMP: 62 **EST:** 1998
SALES (est): 35.5MM
SALES (corp-wide): 26.4B **Privately Held**
WEB: www.pimco.com
SIC: 6722 Money market mutual funds

HQ: Allianz Global Investors Of America Lp
104 E 213th St
Carson CA 90745
310 549-0729

(P-16145)
SUNAMERICA INVESTMENTS INC
1 Sun America Ctr Fl 38, Los Angeles (90067-6101)
PHONE......................310 772-6000
EMP: 200
SALES (est): 7.2MM
SALES (corp-wide): 52.3B **Publicly Held**
SIC: 6722 Investment Company
HQ: Sunamerica Inc.
1 Sun America Ctr Fl 38
Los Angeles CA 90067
310 772-6000

(P-16146)
TCW ABSOLUTE RETURN CREDIT LLC
865 S Figueroa St # 2100, Los Angeles (90017-2543)
PHONE......................213 244-0000
Richard Clotfelter, *CEO*
EMP: 70 **EST:** 2007
SALES (est): 6MM **Privately Held**
SIC: 6722 Money market mutual funds
HQ: Tcw Asset Management Company
865 S Figueroa St # 2100
Los Angeles CA 90017
213 244-0000

(P-16147)
VANGUARD HOSPICE CARE INC (PA)
1450 W 6th St Ste 215, Corona (92882-6502)
PHONE......................951 371-5681
Xinke Chen, *Principal*
EMP: 56 **EST:** 2013
SALES (est): 667.6K **Privately Held**
SIC: 6722 Money market mutual funds

(P-16148)
WESTERN ASSET CORE PLUS BOND P
385 E Colorado Blvd, Pasadena (91101-1923)
PHONE......................626 844-9400
Larry Clark, *Principal*
EMP: 150 **EST:** 2012
SALES (est): 15.3MM
SALES (corp-wide): 5.5B **Publicly Held**
WEB: www.westernasset.com
SIC: 6722 Money market mutual funds
HQ: Western Asset Management Company
385 E Colorado Blvd # 250
Pasadena CA 91101
626 844-9265

(P-16149)
WESTERN ASSET MANAGEMENT CO (DH)
385 E Colorado Blvd # 250, Pasadena (91101-1929)
PHONE......................626 844-9265
James W Hirschmann III, *CEO*
Travis M Carr, *COO*
Cynthia Bui, *Officer*
Dena J Ebinger, *Officer*
Kevin Ehrlich, *Officer*
▲ **EMP:** 50 **EST:** 1971
SQ FT: 55,000
SALES (est): 267.5MM
SALES (corp-wide): 5.5B **Publicly Held**
WEB: www.westernasset.com
SIC: 6722 Money market mutual funds
HQ: Legg Mason Inc
100 International Dr
Baltimore MD 21202
410 539-0000

(P-16150)
WESTERN ASSET MANAGEMENT CO
385 E Colorado Blvd # 250, Pasadena (91101-1929)
PHONE......................626 844-9400
EMP: 50
SALES (corp-wide): 5.5B **Publicly Held**
WEB: www.westernasset.com
SIC: 6722 Money market mutual funds

HQ: Western Asset Management Company
385 E Colorado Blvd # 250
Pasadena CA 91101
626 844-9265

(P-16151)
ZILLIONAIRE EMPRESS DANIELLE B
8549 Wilshire Blvd # 817, Beverly Hills (90211-3104)
PHONE......................310 461-9923
EMP: 1000
SQ FT: 300
SALES (est): 44.6MM **Privately Held**
SIC: 6722 Open-End Management Investment

6726 Unit Investment Trusts, Face-Amount Certificate Offices

(P-16152)
3L CAPITAL I LP (PA)
1100 Glendon Ave Ph 1, Los Angeles (90024-3526)
PHONE......................310 801-3789
EMP: 75 **EST:** 2018
SALES (est): 1.8MM **Privately Held**
WEB: www.3lcap.com
SIC: 6726 Investment offices

(P-16153)
CENTURY PK CAPITL PARTNERS LLC (PA)
2101 Rosecrans Ave # 4275, El Segundo (90245-4749)
PHONE......................310 867-2210
Martin A Sarafa,
Guy Zaczepinski, *Partner*
Charles W Roellig, *Managing Prtnr*
Paul J Wolf, *Managing Prtnr*
Matt Reilly, *Analyst*
EMP: 160 **EST:** 2005
SALES (est): 120.4MM **Privately Held**
WEB: www.centuryparkcapital.com
SIC: 6726 3569 3086 3448 Management investment funds, closed-end; firefighting apparatus & related equipment; carpet & rug cushions, foamed plastic; ramps: prefabricated metal

(P-16154)
GLOBAL REACH 18 INC (PA)
10100 Santa Monica Blvd # 900, Los Angeles (90067-4003)
PHONE......................310 203-5850
Haim Saban, *CEO*
Adam Chesnoff, *President*
Fred Gluckman, *CFO*
Joel Andryc, *Ch Credit Ofcr*
Philip Han, *Exec VP*
EMP: 51 **EST:** 1994
SALES (est): 42.9MM **Privately Held**
SIC: 6726 6531 6799 Investment offices; real estate agents & managers; investors

(P-16155)
IDEALAB (HQ)
130 W Union St, Pasadena (91103-3628)
PHONE......................626 356-3654
Bill Gross, *Ch of Bd*
Larry Gross, *Vice Chairman*
Marcia Goodstein, *President*
Craig Chrisney, *CFO*
Teresa Bridwell, *Vice Pres*
▲ **EMP:** 82 **EST:** 1996
SQ FT: 30,000
SALES (est): 138.9MM
SALES (corp-wide): 148.2MM **Privately Held**
WEB: www.idealab.com
SIC: 5511 6726 New & used car dealers; investment offices
PA: Idealab Holdings, L.L.C.
130 W Union St
Pasadena CA 91103
626 585-6900

PRODUCTS & SVCS

(P-16156)
J ALEXANDER INVESTMENTS INC (PA)
Also Called: Investment Banking
922 S Barrington Ave A, Los Angeles (90049-5554)
PHONE..............................213 687-8400
James Alexander, *President*
EMP: 50 **EST:** 1978
SQ FT: 4,500
SALES (est): 4.4MM **Privately Held**
SIC: 6726 Investment offices

(P-16157)
KINGSWOOD CAPITAL MGT LP
11111 Santa Monica Blvd # 1700, Los Angeles (90025-0449)
PHONE..............................424 744-8238
Alexander Wolf, *Partner*
EMP: 200 **EST:** 2019
SALES (est): 12.7MM **Privately Held**
WEB: www.kingswood-capital.com
SIC: 6726 Investment offices

(P-16158)
LOWE ENTERPRISES INV MGT (HQ)
11777 San Vicente Blvd, Los Angeles (90049-5011)
PHONE..............................310 820-6661
Bleecker P Seaman III, *President*
Dick Poladian, *CFO*
William Cockrum, *Vice Pres*
EMP: 62 **EST:** 1991
SQ FT: 12,000
SALES (est): 16.8MM
SALES (corp-wide): 935.4MM **Privately Held**
WEB: www.lowe-re.com
SIC: 6726 Investment offices
PA: Lowe Enterprises, Inc.
11777 San Vicente Blvd # 900
Los Angeles CA 90049
310 820-6661

(P-16159)
OASIS WEST REALTY LLC (PA)
1800 Century Park E # 500, Los Angeles (90067-1508)
PHONE..............................310 274-8066
Beny Alagem,
Samuel Surloff,
David Levin, *Director*
Jesus Salcedo, *Director*
EMP: 379 **EST:** 2003
SALES (est): 60.6MM **Privately Held**
SIC: 6726 5947 5813 5812 Investment offices; gift shop; drinking places; eating places; hotels

(P-16160)
PACIFIC AVE CPITL PARTNERS LLC
2321 Rosecrans Ave # 3255, El Segundo (90245-4903)
PHONE..............................424 254-9774
Christopher R Sznewajs, *Mng Member*
Jonathan Sinnott, *Vice Pres*
Doug Brookman, *VP Bus Dvlpt*
Jason Leach, *Managing Dir*
EMP: 587 **EST:** 2018
SALES (est): 55.9MM **Privately Held**
WEB: www.pacificavenuecapital.com
SIC: 6726 Investment offices

(P-16161)
PLATINUM EQUITY PARTNERS LLC
360 N Crescent Dr South, Beverly Hills (90210-2529)
PHONE..............................310 712-1850
Tom Gores, *Ch of Bd*
Mary Ann Sigler, *CFO*
Eva Kalawski, *Admin Sec*
EMP: 51 **EST:** 2003
SALES (est): 6.6MM **Privately Held**
WEB: www.platinumequity.com
SIC: 6726 Investment offices
PA: Platinum Equity, Llc
360 N Crescent Dr Bldg S
Beverly Hills CA 90210

(P-16162)
SABRA HEALTH CARE LTD PARTNR (HQ)
18500 Von Karman Ave # 5, Irvine (92612-0504)
PHONE..............................949 255-7100
Harold W Andrews, *CFO*
EMP: 62 **EST:** 2010
SALES (est): 1B **Privately Held**
WEB: www.sabrahealth.com
SIC: 6726 Investment offices

(P-16163)
SCHAUMBOND GROUP INC (PA)
225 S Lake Ave Ste 300, Pasadena (91101-3009)
PHONE..............................626 215-4998
Baohua Zheng, *President*
EMP: 319 **EST:** 1996
SQ FT: 8,000 **Privately Held**
SIC: 6726 Investment offices

(P-16164)
TRUE FAMILY ENTERPRISES (PA)
27156 Burbank, Foothill Ranch (92610-2503)
PHONE..............................888 665-8638
Robert T Jones, *Principal*
Douglas Urbanski, *CFO*
Barbara Fogg, *Vice Pres*
Gwendolyn Wilson, *Vice Pres*
Torrey Beard, *Project Mgr*
EMP: 59 **EST:** 2016
SALES (est): 30MM **Privately Held**
WEB: www.truefamilyenterprises.com
SIC: 6726 Management investment funds, closed-end

6732 Education, Religious & Charitable Trusts

(P-16165)
CALIFORNIA CMNTY FOUNDATION (PA)
221 S Figueroa St Ste 400, Los Angeles (90012-3760)
PHONE..............................213 413-4130
Antonia Hernandez, *President*
Tom Unterman, *Ch of Bd*
Steve Cobb, *CFO*
Peter Dunn, *Vice Pres*
Margaret Jones, *Office Admin*
EMP: 58 **EST:** 1915
SQ FT: 16,000
SALES (est): 725.1K **Privately Held**
WEB: www.calfund.org
SIC: 6732 Charitable trust management

(P-16166)
EMPOWER OUR YOUTH
Also Called: Eoy
6767 W Sunset Blvd 8-188, Los Angeles (90028-7177)
PHONE..............................323 203-5436
Ihkisha Levell, *Principal*
EMP: 99 **EST:** 2008
SALES (est): 950K **Privately Held**
SIC: 6732 Trusts: educational, religious, etc.

(P-16167)
GREATER LOS ANGLES VTRANS RES
11301 Wilshire Blvd # 1, Los Angeles (90073-1003)
PHONE..............................310 312-1554
Jane Cheung, *Exec Dir*
Thoyd Ellis, *CFO*
Bonita Krall,
Leila Ghayouri, *Director*
Ron Waldorf, *Director*
EMP: 90 **EST:** 2018
SALES (est): 8.5MM **Privately Held**
SIC: 6732 Trusts: educational, religious, etc.

(P-16168)
KASH ORGANIZATION
81964 Camino Cantos, Indio (92203-7814)
PHONE..............................702 330-9215
Bahram Kashan, *CEO*

Borna Kashan, *President*
EMP: 55 **EST:** 2020
SALES (est): 1.8MM **Privately Held**
SIC: 6732 7389 Trusts: educational, religious, etc.;

(P-16169)
KRISHNAMURTI FOUNDATION AMER (PA)
134 Besant Rd, Ojai (93023-2305)
P.O. Box 1560 (93024-1560)
PHONE..............................805 646-2726
Jaap Sluijter, *Exec Dir*
Holly Johnson, *Program Mgr*
Michael Krohnen, *Librarian*
Julien Griffault, *Director*
Denny Gottschalk, *Manager*
EMP: 50 **EST:** 1969
SQ FT: 10,000
SALES (est): 8.8MM **Privately Held**
WEB: www.kfa.org
SIC: 6732 Educational trust management; charitable trust management

(P-16170)
UCLA FOUNDATION
10889 Wilshire Blvd # 11, Los Angeles (90024-4201)
PHONE..............................310 794-3193
Craig Ehrlich, *Ch of Bd*
Peter L Evans, *COO*
Neal Axelrod, *Treasurer*
Yael APT, *Associate Dir*
Jennifer Wheelock, *Associate Dir*
EMP: 317 **EST:** 1945
SALES (est): 41.2MM **Privately Held**
WEB: www.uclafoundation.org
SIC: 6732 Educational trust management

6733 Trusts Except Educational, Religious & Charitable

(P-16171)
2100 TRUST LLC (PA)
625 N Grand Ave, Santa Ana (92701-4347)
PHONE..............................877 469-7344
Erek J Delorenzi, *Principal*
Thomas Halligan, *Director*
Linda Knudtson, *Manager*
Josh Moore, *Manager*
Joshua Cain, *Editor*
EMP: 200 **EST:** 2010
SALES (est): 371.7MM **Privately Held**
WEB: www.socalnewsgroup.com
SIC: 6733 Trusts

(P-16172)
ANNENBERG FNDTION TR AT SNNYLN (PA)
37977 Bob Hope Dr, Rancho Mirage (92270-2008)
PHONE..............................760 202-2222
Wallis Anneberg, *CEO*
Geoffrey Cowan, *President*
Wallis Annenberg, *CEO*
Debbi Hinton, *CFO*
Lauren Bon, *Trustee*
EMP: 108 **EST:** 2006
SALES (est): 33.8MM **Privately Held**
WEB: www.sunnylands.org
SIC: 6733 Trusts

(P-16173)
ATHLETIC SCHLARSHIP CONNECTION
3920 Cinnamon Ct, Bakersfield (93309-6254)
PHONE..............................909 705-5875
EMP: 33 **EST:** 2016
SALES (est): 1.2MM **Privately Held**
SIC: 6733 3161 3949 6111 Trusts; clothing & apparel carrying cases; sporting & athletic goods; Export/Import Bank

(P-16174)
CAPITAL GUARDIAN TRUST COMPANY (HQ)
333 S Hope St Fl 52, Los Angeles (90071-3061)
PHONE..............................213 486-9200
Richard C Barker, *Ch of Bd*

Robert Ronus, *President*
Teri Valenzuela, *President*
William Flumenbaum, *Vice Pres*
Ralph Heckert, *Vice Pres*
EMP: 100 **EST:** 1968
SQ FT: 6,000
SALES (est): 68.5MM
SALES (corp-wide): 5.4B **Privately Held**
WEB: www.capitalgroup.com
SIC: 6733 Trusts, except educational, religious, charity: management
PA: The Capital Group Companies Inc
333 S Hope St Fl 55
Los Angeles CA 90071
213 486-9200

(P-16175)
CHRISTMAS BONUS FUND OF THE PL
501 Shatto Pl Fl 5, Los Angeles (90020-1730)
PHONE..............................213 385-6161
Milton D Johnson, *Administration*
Mike Ayre, *Ch of Bd*
E A Norris, *Ch of Bd*
Allen Jones Jr, *Co-COB*
Raymond Forman, *Trustee*
EMP: 60
SQ FT: 70,000
SALES (est): 4.7MM **Privately Held**
WEB: www.scptac.org
SIC: 6733 Trusts, except educational, religious, charity: management

(P-16176)
DEFINED CNTRBTION TR FUND FOR
Also Called: Southern Cal Pipe Trades
501 Shatto Pl Ste 500, Los Angeles (90020-1730)
PHONE..............................213 385-6161
Milton D Johnson, *CEO*
Mike Ayre, *Ch of Bd*
Raymond Forman, *Trustee*
Charles La Bouff, *Admin Sec*
EMP: 96 **EST:** 1991
SQ FT: 70,000
SALES (est): 4.2MM **Privately Held**
WEB: www.scptac.org
SIC: 6733 Trusts, except educational, religious, charity: management

(P-16177)
EPIDAURUS
Also Called: Amity Foundation
3745 S Grand Ave, Los Angeles (90007-4332)
PHONE..............................213 743-9075
Mark Schettenger, *President*
Barry Warne, *Comms Dir*
EMP: 272 **Privately Held**
SIC: 6733 Trusts
PA: Epidaurus
721 N 4th Ave
Tucson AZ 85705

(P-16178)
IRON WORKERS LOCAL 433
Also Called: California Field Ironwrkrs
252 Hillcrest Ave, San Bernardino (92408-2120)
PHONE..............................909 884-5500
Fax: 909 885-0047
EMP: 50
SALES (est): 1.5MM **Privately Held**
SIC: 6733 Trust Management

(P-16179)
IRONWRKER EMPLYEES BENEFT CORP
Also Called: IRONWORKERS UNION
131 N El Molino Ave # 330, Pasadena (91101-1873)
PHONE..............................626 792-7337
Dick Zampa, *President*
John Stonehouse, *Vice Pres*
Rise Spiegel, *Exec Dir*
Jessica Lozano, *Admin Sec*
Paul Aragon, *Controller*
EMP: 65 **EST:** 1977
SQ FT: 19,000

SALES: 2MM **Privately Held**
WEB: www.ironworkerbenny.com
SIC: 6733 Trusts, except educational, religious, charity: management; vacation funds for employees

(P-16180)
KAISER FOUNDATION HOSPITALS
Also Called: Huntington Beach Medical Offs
18081 Beach Blvd, Huntington Beach (92648-1304)
PHONE.....................714 841-7293
Linda Sawasaki, *Branch Mgr*
EMP: 52
SALES (corp-wide): 30.5B **Privately Held**
WEB: www.kaisercenter.com
SIC: 6733 Trusts
HQ: Kaiser Foundation Hospitals Inc
1 Kaiser Plz
Oakland CA 94612
510 271-6611

(P-16181)
KAISER FOUNDATION HOSPITALS
Also Called: Kaiser Permanente
5119 Pomona Blvd, Los Angeles (90022-1711)
PHONE.....................323 881-5516
Judy Nantes, *Manager*
Benjamin Clyde, *Marketing Staff*
Michelle Ramirez,
Linda Tom,
Michael Mathess, *Assistant*
EMP: 52
SALES (corp-wide): 30.5B **Privately Held**
WEB: www.kaisercenter.com
SIC: 6733 Trusts
HQ: Kaiser Foundation Hospitals Inc
1 Kaiser Plz
Oakland CA 94612
510 271-6611

(P-16182)
KAISER FOUNDATION HOSPITALS
Also Called: Moreno Valley Heacock Med Offs
12815 Heacock St, Moreno Valley (92553-2836)
PHONE.....................951 601-6174
Mark Ituah, *Principal*
Rhoda Blum, *Pediatrics*
EMP: 52
SALES (corp-wide): 30.5B **Privately Held**
WEB: www.kaisercenter.com
SIC: 6733 Trusts
HQ: Kaiser Foundation Hospitals Inc
1 Kaiser Plz
Oakland CA 94612
510 271-6611

(P-16183)
KAISER FOUNDATION HOSPITALS
Also Called: Kaiser Permanente
789 E Cooley Dr, Colton (92324-4007)
PHONE.....................909 427-5521
Barry A Wolfman, *Principal*
Vinod Dasika, *Family Practiti*
Almira Karpenko, *Family Practiti*
Leland Okubo, *Family Practiti*
Donald Harlan, *Med Doctor*
EMP: 52
SQ FT: 23,088
SALES (corp-wide): 30.5B **Privately Held**
WEB: www.kaisercenter.com
SIC: 6733 Trusts
HQ: Kaiser Foundation Hospitals Inc
1 Kaiser Plz
Oakland CA 94612
510 271-6611

(P-16184)
KAISER FOUNDATION HOSPITALS
Also Called: Palmdale Medical Offices
4502 E Avenue S, Palmdale (93552-4480)
PHONE.....................661 533-7500
Adam Guo, *Manager*
EMP: 52
SALES (corp-wide): 30.5B **Privately Held**
WEB: www.kaisercenter.com
SIC: 6733 Trusts

(P-16185)
KAISER FOUNDATION HOSPITALS
Also Called: Corona Medical Offices
182 Granite St, Corona (92879-1288)
PHONE.....................866 984-7483
Randy Florence, *Branch Mgr*
EMP: 52
SALES (corp-wide): 30.5B **Privately Held**
WEB: www.kaisercenter.com
SIC: 6733 8011 Trusts; internal medicine practitioners; general & family practice, physician/surgeon
HQ: Kaiser Foundation Hospitals Inc
1 Kaiser Plz
Oakland CA 94612
510 271-6611

(P-16186)
KAISER FOUNDATION HOSPITALS
Also Called: Orange County-Irvine Med Ctr
6640 Alton Pkwy, Irvine (92618-3734)
PHONE.....................949 932-5000
George Disalvo, *Branch Mgr*
Jaci Block, *Admin Asst*
Christine Luu, *Administration*
Lorna Manapat, *Info Tech Mgr*
Brent R Davis, *Surgeon*
EMP: 52
SALES (corp-wide): 30.5B **Privately Held**
WEB: www.kaisercenter.com
SIC: 6733 Trusts
HQ: Kaiser Foundation Hospitals Inc
1 Kaiser Plz
Oakland CA 94612
510 271-6611

(P-16187)
MANAGEMENT TRUST ASSN INC
100 E Thousand Oaks Blvd, Thousand Oaks (91360-5713)
PHONE.....................805 496-5514
EMP: 93 **Privately Held**
WEB: www.managementtrust.com
SIC: 6733 Trusts
PA: The Management Trust Association Inc
15661 Red Hill Ave # 201
Tustin CA 92780

(P-16188)
MANAGEMENT TRUST ASSN INC
4160 Temescal Canyon Rd # 202, Corona (92883-4625)
PHONE.....................951 694-1758
EMP: 93 **Privately Held**
WEB: www.managementtrust.com
SIC: 6733 Trusts
PA: The Management Trust Association Inc
15661 Red Hill Ave # 201
Tustin CA 92780

(P-16189)
MANAGEMENT TRUST ASSN INC (PA)
Also Called: Management Trust, The
15661 Red Hill Ave # 201, Tustin (92780-7300)
PHONE.....................714 285-2626
William B Sasser, *CEO*
Mindy Dent, *General Mgr*
Tracy Robinson, *General Mgr*
Josie Mendolia, *Admin Asst*
Tiffany Wright, *Asst Controller*
EMP: 58 EST: 2011
SALES (est): 89.3MM **Privately Held**
WEB: www.managementtrust.com
SIC: 6733 Trusts

(P-16190)
MOELIS & COMPANY LLC
1999 Avenue Of The Stars, Los Angeles (90067-6022)
PHONE.....................310 443-2300
Stella Hoe, *Branch Mgr*
Carlo De Girolamo, *Vice Pres*

Will Mroz, *Vice Pres*
Liljana Xheka, *Vice Pres*
J R Leaman, *Managing Dir*
EMP: 70
SALES (corp-wide): 943.2MM **Publicly Held**
WEB: www.moelis.com
SIC: 6733 6282 Private estate, personal investment & vacation fund trusts; investment advisory service
HQ: Moelis & Company Llc
399 Park Ave Fl 5
New York NY 10022

(P-16191)
MTC FINANCIAL INC
Also Called: Trustee Corps
17100 Gillette Ave, Irvine (92614-5603)
PHONE.....................949 252-8300
Fax: 949 634-1011
EMP: 50 EST: 1992
SALES (est): 4.7MM **Privately Held**
SIC: 6733 Trust Management

(P-16192)
OPERATING ENGINEERS FUNDS INC (PA)
100 Corson St Ste 222, Pasadena (91103-3892)
P.O. Box 7063 (91109-7063)
PHONE.....................866 400-5200
Mike Roddy, *CEO*
Matt Erieg, *COO*
Chuck Killian, *CFO*
Klairissa Sikorski, *Admin Asst*
Enrique Cabanas, *Administration*
EMP: 135
SQ FT: 84,600
SALES: 314.2K **Privately Held**
WEB: www.oefi.org
SIC: 6733 Trusts, except educational, religious, charity: management

(P-16193)
PIMCO MORTGAGE INCOME TR INC
650 Newport Center Dr, Newport Beach (92660-6310)
PHONE.....................949 720-6000
Casey Newell, *CEO*
Jason Mandinach, *President*
John Lane, *CFO*
EMP: 284 EST: 2018
SALES (est): 68.1MM
SALES (corp-wide): 26.4B **Privately Held**
SIC: 6733 Trusts
HQ: Pacific Investment Management Company Llc
650 Newport Center Dr
Newport Beach CA 92660
949 720-6000

(P-16194)
PMT CRDIT RISK TRNSF TR 2015-2
3043 Townsgate Rd, Westlake Village (91361-3027)
PHONE.....................818 224-7442
EMP: 54 EST: 2017
SALES (est): 2.6MM **Privately Held**
WEB: www.ir.pennymacfinancial.com
SIC: 6733 Trusts
PA: Pennymac Mortgage Investment Trust
6101 Condor Dr
Moorpark CA 93021

(P-16195)
PNMAC GMSR ISSUER TRUST
3043 Townsgate Rd, Westlake Village (91361-3027)
PHONE.....................818 746-2271
EMP: 2431 EST: 2017
SALES (est): 5.3MM
SALES (corp-wide): 3.7B **Publicly Held**
WEB: www.ir.pennymacfinancial.com
SIC: 6733 Trusts
HQ: Pnmac Holdings, Inc.
3043 Townsgate Rd
Westlake Village CA 91361
818 224-7442

(P-16196)
PROVIDENCE HEALTH SYSTEM
3551 Voyager St Ste 201, Torrance (90503-1674)
PHONE.....................310 370-5895
EMP: 200
SALES (corp-wide): 17.6B **Privately Held**
SIC: 6733 Trust Management
HQ: Providence Health System-Southern California
1801 Lind Ave Sw
Renton WA 98057
425 525-3355

(P-16197)
SOUTHERN CAL PIPE TRADES ADM (PA)
Also Called: Southern Cal Pipe Trades ADM
501 Shatto Pl Ste 500, Los Angeles (90020-1730)
PHONE.....................213 385-6161
Milton D Johnson, *President*
Raquel Gallardo, *Human Resources*
Nahuel Costilla, *Cust Mgr*
John Ferruccio, *Director*
Sylvea Allington, *Manager*
EMP: 70 EST: 1956
SQ FT: 70,000
SALES (est): 13.3MM **Privately Held**
WEB: www.scptac.org
SIC: 6733 6513 Trusts, except educational, religious, charity: management; retirement hotel operation

(P-16198)
VARNER FAMILY LTD PARTNERSHIP (PA)
5900 E Lerdo Hwy, Shafter (93263-4023)
PHONE.....................661 399-1163
James Varner, *General Ptnr*
James R Varner, *Partner*
EMP: 80 EST: 2000
SALES (est): 116.5MM **Privately Held**
SIC: 6733 Private estate, personal investment & vacation fund trusts

---

6794 Patent Owners & Lessors

(P-16199)
ACACIA TECHNOLOGIES INC (HQ)
520 Nwport Cntr Dr 12th F Flr 12, Newport Beach (92660)
PHONE.....................949 480-8300
Paul R Ryan, *CEO*
Robert L Harris II, *President*
Clayton J Haynes, *Treasurer*
Dooyong Lee, *Exec VP*
Eric Lucas, *Vice Pres*
EMP: 62 EST: 1996
SALES (est): 245.7MM **Publicly Held**
WEB: www.acaciaresearch.com
SIC: 6794 Patent buying, licensing, leasing

(P-16200)
ADIR RESTAURANTS CORP (PA)
Also Called: Pollo Campero
1625 W Olympic Blvd # 1020, Los Angeles (90015-3853)
PHONE.....................213 201-2990
Tim Pulido, *Principal*
Jerry Azarkman, *Co-Owner*
Admir Siddigi, *COO*
Carlo Divita, *CFO*
Andrew Hatzsis, *Vice Pres*
▲ EMP: 289 EST: 2001
SQ FT: 1,500
SALES (est): 18.7MM **Privately Held**
WEB: www.us.campero.com
SIC: 5812 6794 Chicken restaurant; franchises, selling or licensing

(P-16201)
ADVANCED FRESH CONCEPTS CORP (PA)
Also Called: A F C
19205 S Laurel Park Rd, Rancho Dominguez (90220-6032)
PHONE.....................310 604-3630
Jeffery Seiler, *CEO*
Jeff Seiler, *Vice Pres*
Jeffrey Asido, *Research*

PRODUCTS & SVCS

Sophie Lee, *Recruiter*
Masahiko Tajima, *Director*
◆ **EMP:** 61 **EST:** 1986
SQ FT: 60,000
SALES (est): 28.2MM **Privately Held**
WEB: www.afcsushi.com
SIC: 6794 2032 2092 5141 Patent owners & lessors; Chinese foods: packaged in cans, jars, etc.; fresh or frozen packaged fish; food brokers

(P-16202)
BLAZE PIZZA LLC (PA)
Also Called: Blaze Fast Fire'd Pizza
35 N Lake Ave Ste 710, Pasadena
(91101-4185)
PHONE...................626 584-5880
Amanda Shaw, *President*
Edward Hitner, *Partner*
Carolyne Canady, *President*
Brad Reynolds, *CFO*
Vince Szwajkowski, *Chief Mktg Ofcr*
EMP: 56 **EST:** 2011
SALES (est): 88.4MM **Privately Held**
WEB: www.blazepizza.com
SIC: 5812 6794 Pizzeria, chain; franchises, selling or licensing

(P-16203)
BRER AFFILIATES LLC (DH)
Also Called: Prudential
18500 Von Karman Ave # 4, Irvine
(92612-0504)
PHONE...................949 794-7900
John Vanderwall, *Ch of Bd*
Patti Ray, *Senior VP*
Anthony Harrell, *Software Dev*
Gary Kooba, *Broker*
EMP: 208
SQ FT: 55,500
SALES (est): 120.3MM
SALES (corp-wide): 57B **Publicly Held**
WEB: www.prudential.com
SIC: 6794 6531 Franchises, selling or licensing; real estate agents & managers
HQ: The Prudential Insurance Company Of America
751 Broad St
Newark NJ 07102
973 802-6000

(P-16204)
DEL TACO RESTAURANTS INC (PA)
25521 Commercentre Dr # 200, Lake Forest (92630-8872)
PHONE...................949 462-9300
John D Cappasola, *President*
Lawrence F Levy, *Ch of Bd*
Chad Gretzema, *COO*
ARI Levy, *Bd of Directors*
Joseph Stein, *Bd of Directors*
EMP: 169 **EST:** 1964
SQ FT: 37,500
SALES (est): 491.8MM **Publicly Held**
WEB: www.deltaco.com
SIC: 5812 6794 Fast-food restaurant, chain; American restaurant; Mexican restaurant; franchises, selling or licensing

(P-16205)
DINE BRANDS GLOBAL INC (PA)
450 N Brand Blvd, Glendale (91203-2347)
PHONE...................818 240-6055
Stephen P Joyce, *CEO*
Richard J Dahl, *Ch of Bd*
John C Cywinski, *President*
Tony Moralejo, *President*
Darren M Rebelez, *President*
EMP: 500 **EST:** 1958
SALES (est): 689.2MM **Publicly Held**
WEB: www.applebees.com
SIC: 5812 6794 Restaurant, family: chain; franchises, selling or licensing

(P-16206)
EL POLLO LOCO HOLDINGS INC (PA)
3535 Harbor Blvd Ste 100, Costa Mesa (92626-1494)
PHONE...................714 599-5000
Laurance Roberts, *CEO*
Michael G Maselli, *Ch of Bd*
Bernard Acoca, *President*
Miguel Lozano, *COO*

Sophia Stratton, *Personnel Assit*
EMP: 164 **EST:** 1980
SQ FT: 29,880
SALES (est): 426MM **Publicly Held**
WEB: www.elpolloloco.com
SIC: 6794 5812 Franchises, selling or licensing; Mexican restaurant

(P-16207)
FLAME BROILER INC (PA)
1538 E Warner Ave Ste E, Santa Ana (92705-5476)
PHONE...................714 549-2870
Young Lee, *President*
Mike Sweet, *Vice Pres*
Selene Padilla, *Admin Asst*
Daniel Lee, *Technology*
EMP: 234 **EST:** 2007
SALES (est): 33.6MM **Privately Held**
WEB: www.flamebroilerusa.com
SIC: 5812 6794 Steak & barbecue restaurants; franchises, selling or licensing

(P-16208)
HIGH RISE GDIES REST GROUP INC (PA)
Also Called: Trimana
1875 Century Park E Ste A, Los Angeles (90067-2535)
PHONE...................310 772-0726
Bijan Yadegar, *President*
EMP: 164 **EST:** 1996
SQ FT: 5,000
SALES (est): 5.7MM **Privately Held**
SIC: 5812 6794 Eating places; franchises, selling or licensing

(P-16209)
INTERNATIONAL COFFEE & TEA LLC (HQ)
Also Called: Coffee Bean & Tea Leaf, The
5700 Wilshire Blvd # 120, Los Angeles (90036-3644)
PHONE...................310 237-2326
John Fuller, *President*
Sanjiv Razdan, *President*
Jeff Harris, *CFO*
Gregg Benvenuto, *Vice Pres*
Paul Diver, *Vice Pres*
▲ **EMP:** 75 **EST:** 1963
SQ FT: 20,000
SALES (est): 150.8MM **Privately Held**
WEB: www.coffeebean.com
SIC: 5812 5499 6794 Coffee shop; coffee; tea; franchises, selling or licensing

(P-16210)
KOTT KOATINGS INC (PA)
27161 Burbank, El Toro (92610-2501)
PHONE...................949 770-5055
John T Kott, *President*
Dorothy Kott, *Treasurer*
EMP: 14 **EST:** 1953
SQ FT: 14,000
SALES (est): 11MM **Privately Held**
WEB: www.kottkoating.com
SIC: 6794 1743 3996 Franchises, selling or licensing; tile installation, ceramic; tile, floor: supported plastic

(P-16211)
LEVINE LEICHTMAN CAPITAL
345 N Maple Dr Ste 300, Beverly Hills (90210-5183)
PHONE...................310 275-5335
Lauren Leichtman,
EMP: 60 **EST:** 2010
SALES (est): 45.7MM
SALES (corp-wide): 148.4MM **Privately Held**
WEB: www.llcp.com
SIC: 6794 Franchises, selling or licensing
PA: Levine Leichtman Capital Partners, Llc
345 N Maple Dr Ste 300
Beverly Hills CA 90210
310 275-5335

(P-16212)
NEKTER JUICE BAR INC (PA)
1844 Carnegie Ave, Santa Ana (92705-5545)
PHONE...................949 660-0071
Steve Schulze, *CEO*
Natalie Laclair, *President*
Maya Fox, *District Mgr*
Denette Williams, *District Mgr*

Anne Cynn, *General Mgr*
EMP: 87 **EST:** 2010
SALES (est): 3.2MM **Privately Held**
WEB: www.nekterjuicebar.com
SIC: 5499 6794 Juices, fruit or vegetable; franchises, selling or licensing

(P-16213)
PANDA SYSTEMS INC
Also Called: Panda Express
1683 Walnut Grove Ave, Rosemead (91770-3711)
P.O. Box 1159 (91770-1011)
PHONE...................626 799-9898
Andrew J Cherng, *Ch of Bd*
Peggy T Cherng, *President*
EMP: 130 **EST:** 1988
SQ FT: 10,000
SALES (est): 10.2MM
SALES (corp-wide): 1.6B **Privately Held**
WEB: www.pandarg.com
SIC: 5812 6794 Chinese restaurant; franchises, selling or licensing
PA: Panda Restaurant Group, Inc.
1683 Walnut Grove Ave
Rosemead CA 91770
626 799-9898

(P-16214)
PARABLE GROUP INC (PA)
Also Called: Parable Christian Store
102 Cross St Ste 210, San Luis Obispo (93401-7579)
PHONE...................805 543-2644
Steven O Potratz, *President*
Tim Blair, *CFO*
Jeff Bruenning, *Merchandising*
Laura Clark, *Marketing Staff*
Nancy Randise, *Sales Staff*
EMP: 62 **EST:** 1991
SQ FT: 18,000
SALES (est): 12.4MM **Privately Held**
WEB: www.ag.parable.com
SIC: 6794 5942 5999 Franchises, selling or licensing; books, religious; religious goods

(P-16215)
PARAMOUNT LICENSING INC
Also Called: Viacom Consumer Products Inc
5555 Melrose Ave, Los Angeles (90038-3989)
PHONE...................323 956-5634
Andrea Hein, *President*
Charles Phillips, *Vice Chairman*
William Schwartz, *Bd of Directors*
Mike Goldman, *Senior VP*
Terry Helton, *Senior VP*
EMP: 50 **EST:** 1991
SALES (est): 51.7MM
SALES (corp-wide): 25.3B **Publicly Held**
WEB: www.paramountstudiotour.com
SIC: 6794 Patent buying, licensing, leasing
HQ: Paramount Pictures Corporation
5555 Melrose Ave
Los Angeles CA 90038
323 956-5000

(P-16216)
PIEOLOGY FRANCHISE LLC
Also Called: Pieology Pizzeria
2642 Michelle Dr Ste 100, Tustin (92780-7019)
PHONE...................949 774-2380
EMP: 62 **EST:** 2019
SALES (est): 3.8MM **Privately Held**
WEB: www.pieology.com
SIC: 5812 6794 Pizzeria, chain; franchises, selling or licensing

(P-16217)
SIZZLER USA RESTAURANTS INC (HQ)
25910 Acero Ste 350, Mission Viejo (92691-7908)
PHONE...................949 273-4497
Christopher Perkins, *Security Dir*
Mike Branigan, *Vice Pres*
Todd Peterson, *Vice Pres*
EMP: 202 **EST:** 1967
SALES (est): 236.1MM
SALES (corp-wide): 238.8MM **Privately Held**
WEB: www.sizzler.com
SIC: 6794 5812 Franchises, selling or licensing; steak restaurant

(P-16218)
SLATERS 50/50 INC (PA)
5801 E Camino Pinzon, Anaheim (92807-3910)
PHONE...................714 685-1103
Scott Slater, *Principal*
Dustin Frye, *General Mgr*
Tsuha Jorge, *Accounting Mgr*
Shane Johnson, *Manager*
Jordan Scott, *Manager*
EMP: 111 **EST:** 2009
SALES (est): 10.8MM **Privately Held**
WEB: www.slaters5050.com
SIC: 5812 5813 6794 American restaurant; drinking places; patent owners & lessors

(P-16219)
TACO BELL CORP (HQ)
1 Glen Bell Way, Irvine (92618-3344)
PHONE...................949 863-4500
Mark King, *CEO*
Nikki Lawson, *Officer*
▲ **EMP:** 1025 **EST:** 1962
SQ FT: 278,000
SALES (est): 999.9MM
SALES (corp-wide): 5.6B **Publicly Held**
WEB: www.tacobell.com
SIC: 5812 6794 Fast-food restaurant, chain; franchises, selling or licensing
PA: Yum Brands, Inc.
1900 Colonel Sanders Ln
Louisville KY 40213
502 874-8300

(P-16220)
TODAI SSB INC
19481 San Jose Ave, City of Industry (91748-1435)
PHONE...................909 869-7727
Ralph Kim, *President*
EMP: 69 **EST:** 2005
SALES (est): 366.4K **Privately Held**
WEB: www.todai.com
SIC: 5812 6794 Eating places; patent owners & lessors

(P-16221)
UNIVERSAL STDIOS LICENSING LLC
100 Universal City Plz, Universal City (91608-1002)
PHONE...................818 695-1273
Sheetal Madadi, *Manager*
Gabriela Kornzweig, *Admin Sec*
Evan Langweiler, *Corp Comm Staff*
EMP: 150 **EST:** 2010
SALES (est): 93.6MM
SALES (corp-wide): 103.5B **Publicly Held**
WEB: www.nbcuniversal.com
SIC: 6794 Copyright buying & licensing
HQ: Nbcuniversal Media, Llc
30 Rockefeller Plz Fl 2
New York NY 10112

(P-16222)
WKS FROSTY CORPORATION (HQ)
Also Called: Wendy's
5856 Corp Ave Ste 200, Cypress (90630)
P.O. Box 39, Lakewood (90714-0039)
PHONE...................562 425-1402
Roland Spongberg, *President*
Leslie Pettey, *Executive Asst*
Sergio Porras, *Technology*
EMP: 62 **EST:** 2017
SALES (est): 155.1MM
SALES (corp-wide): 200.5MM **Privately Held**
WEB: www.wksusa.com
SIC: 6794 5812 Franchises, selling or licensing; fast-food restaurant, chain
PA: W.K.S. Restaurant Corporation
5856 Corp Ave Ste 200
Cypress CA 90630
562 425-1402

(P-16223)
WKS RESTAURANT CORPORATION (PA)
Also Called: El Pollo Loco
5856 Corp Ave Ste 200, Cypress (90630)
P.O. Box 39, Lakewood (90714-0039)
PHONE...............................562 425-1402
Roland Spongberg, *President*
Matt McGuinness, *Exec VP*
Joanna Blake, *Vice Pres*
Paul E Tanner, *Vice Pres*
Minerva Del Villar, *District Mgr*
EMP: 2796 EST: 1987
SQ FT: 1,200
SALES (est): 200.5MM **Privately Held**
WEB: www.wksusa.com
SIC: 5812 6794 Mexican restaurant; franchises, selling or licensing

(P-16224)
WSM INVESTMENTS LLC
Also Called: Topco Sales
3990b Heritage Oak Ct, Simi Valley
(93063-6716)
PHONE...............................818 332-4600
Scott Tucker, *CEO*
Martin Tucker, *Ch of Bd*
Michael Siegel, *COO*
Gabriel Scally, *Controller*
Nancy Cosimini, *Sales Staff*
▲ EMP: 145 EST: 2009
SQ FT: 150,000
SALES (est): 39.7MM **Privately Held**
WEB: www.eailv.cn
SIC: 6794 5122 5099 4731 Performance rights, publishing & licensing; cosmetics; novelties, durable; freight forwarding
PA: Lover Health Science And Technology Incorporated Co., Ltd
No.1208, Taihu Ave., Changxing Economic Development Zone, Changx
Huzhou 31310

(P-16225)
YOGURTLAND FRANCHISING INC (PA)
17801 Cartwright Rd, Irvine (92614-6216)
PHONE...............................949 265-8000
Phillip Chang, *President*
John Wayne Carlson, *Vice Pres*
Samantha Baz, *Executive*
Sunida Tee, *Accounting Mgr*
Kimberly Bryant, *Contract Mgr*
EMP: 74 EST: 2006
SALES (est): 48.4MM **Privately Held**
WEB: www.yogurt-land.com
SIC: 6794 5812 Franchises, selling or licensing; frozen yogurt stand

---

6798 Real Estate Investment Trusts

(P-16226)
5525 E PACIFIC COAST HWY INC
2016 Riverside Dr, Los Angeles
(90039-3707)
PHONE...............................323 669-9090
Anil Mehta, *President*
EMP: 60
SALES (est): 3.4MM **Privately Held**
SIC: 6798 Real estate investment trusts

(P-16227)
AMERICAN HEALTHCARE REIT INC (PA)
18191 Von Karman Ave # 300, Irvine
(92612-7106)
PHONE...............................949 270-9200
Jeffrey Hanson, *President*
EMP: 61 EST: 2015
SALES (est): 155.1MM **Privately Held**
SIC: 6798 Real estate investment trusts

(P-16228)
AMERICAN HMES 4 RENT MGT HLDNG
23975 Park Sorrento # 300, Calabasas
(91302-4015)
PHONE...............................805 413-5300
David P Singelyn, *CEO*
EMP: 57 EST: 2012

SALES (est): 9.3MM
SALES (corp-wide): 1.1B **Publicly Held**
WEB: www.ah4r.com
SIC: 6798 Mortgage investment trusts
HQ: American Homes 4 Rent, L.P.
23975 Park Sorrento # 300
Calabasas CA 91302
805 413-5300

(P-16229)
AMERICAN HOMES 4 RENT (PA)
23975 Park Sorrento # 300, Calabasas
(91302-4012)
PHONE...............................805 413-5300
David P Singelyn, *CEO*
Bryan Smith, *COO*
Diana M Laing, *CFO*
Christopher Lau, *CFO*
David Goldberg, *Trustee*
EMP: 179 EST: 2012
SALES (est): 1.1B **Publicly Held**
WEB: www.ah4r.com
SIC: 6798 Real estate investment trusts

(P-16230)
AMERICAN REALTY ADVISORS
515 S Flower St Ste 4900, Los Angeles
(90071-2220)
PHONE...............................818 545-1152
Stanley Iezman, *President*
Austin Maddux, *Exec VP*
Bill M Pantazopoulos, *Vice Pres*
Brian Sheffron, *Vice Pres*
Gregory A Blomstrand, *Principal*
EMP: 58 EST: 1988
SALES (est): 4.8MM **Privately Held**
WEB: www.aracapital.com
SIC: 6798 Real estate investment trusts

(P-16231)
CORE REALTY HOLDINGS LLC (PA)
1600 Dove St Ste 450, Newport Beach
(92660-2447)
PHONE...............................949 863-1031
Doug Morehead, *Mng Member*
Henry Fitzpatrick, *CFO*
Jonathan Harmer, *CFO*
William Russ Colvin, *Chm Emeritus*
John Saunders, *Bd of Directors*
EMP: 53 EST: 2005
SALES (est): 23.1MM **Privately Held**
WEB: www.corerealtyholdings.com
SIC: 6798 Realty investment trusts

(P-16232)
CORESITE LLC
624 S Grand Ave Ste 1800, Los Angeles
(90017-3336)
PHONE...............................213 327-1231
Thomas Ray, *President*
Jordan Orsolini, *Sales Dir*
Evan Ducker, *Manager*
EMP: 55 **Publicly Held**
WEB: www.coresite.com
SIC: 6798 Real estate investment trusts
HQ: Coresite, L.L.C.
1001 17th St Ste 500
Denver CO 80202
866 777-2673

(P-16233)
DOUGLAS EMMETT BUILDERS
1299 Ocean Ave Ste 1000, Santa Monica
(90401-1063)
PHONE...............................310 255-7800
Kenneth Panzer, *President*
Jordan Kaplan, *Vice Pres*
Sanaz Bacon, *Project Mgr*
Sue Kim, *Director*
EMP: 76 EST: 1991
SALES (est): 9.9MM
SALES (corp-wide): 891.5MM **Publicly Held**
WEB: www.douglasemmett.com
SIC: 6798 Real estate investment trusts
PA: Douglas Emmett, Inc.
1299 Ocean Ave Ste 1000
Santa Monica CA 90401
310 255-7700

(P-16234)
HUDSON PACIFIC PROPERTIES INC (PA)
11601 Wilshire Blvd # 600, Los Angeles
(90025-1797)
PHONE...............................310 445-5700
Victor J Coleman, *Ch of Bd*
Mark T Lammas, *President*
Harout Diramerian, *CFO*
Dale Shimoda, *Exec VP*
Kay L Tidwell, *Exec VP*
EMP: 147 EST: 2009
SALES (est): 804.9MM **Publicly Held**
WEB: www.hudsonpacificproperties.com
SIC: 6798 Real estate investment trusts

(P-16235)
HUDSON PACIFIC PROPERTIES LP (HQ)
11601 Wilshire Blvd # 600, Los Angeles
(90025-1797)
PHONE...............................310 445-5700
Victor J Coleman, *Ch of Bd*
Hudson Pacific Properties, *General Ptnr*
Harout K Diramerian, *CFO*
Manuel Campos, *IT/INT Sup*
Caroline Grafft, *Manager*
EMP: 345 EST: 2010
SQ FT: 500,475
SALES (est): 804.9MM **Publicly Held**
WEB: www.hudsonpacificproperties.com
SIC: 6798 Real estate investment trusts

(P-16236)
IMT CAPITAL LLC (PA)
15303 Ventura Blvd # 200, Sherman Oaks
(91403-3110)
PHONE...............................818 784-4700
Michael H Browne, *Managing Dir*
Bryan A Scher, *Managing Dir*
Bryan Scher, *Managing Dir*
John M Tesoriero, *Managing Dir*
Cory S Thabit, *Managing Dir*
EMP: 111 EST: 2006
SALES (est): 21.9MM **Privately Held**
WEB: www.imtcapital.com
SIC: 6798 Real estate investment trusts

(P-16237)
IRVINE EASTGATE OFFICE II LLC
Also Called: Irvine Company Office Property
550 Newport Center Dr, Newport Beach
(92660-7010)
P.O. Box 2460 (92658-8960)
PHONE...............................949 720-2000
Pam Van Nort, *Vice Pres*
Gino Bianchini, *Senior VP*
Leah Matthew, *Opers Staff*
Neil Deramos, *Property Mgr*
Kandace Kopensky, *Sr Associate*
EMP: 3000 EST: 2013
SQ FT: 3,000
SALES (est): 302.8MM **Privately Held**
WEB: www.irvinecompany.com
SIC: 6798 Real estate investment trusts

(P-16238)
KILROY REALTY CORPORATION (PA)
12200 W Olympic Blvd # 200, Los Angeles
(90064-1044)
PHONE...............................310 481-8400
John Kilroy, *Ch of Bd*
Tyler Rose, *President*
Michelle Ngo, *CFO*
Heidi Roth, *Officer*
A Robert Paratte, *Exec VP*
EMP: 144 EST: 1996
SQ FT: 150,832
SALES (est): 898.4MM **Publicly Held**
WEB: www.kilroyrealty.com
SIC: 6798 Real estate investment trusts

(P-16239)
MACERICH COMPANY (PA)
401 Wilshire Blvd Ste 700, Santa Monica
(90401-1452)
PHONE...............................310 394-6000
Thomas E O'Hern, *CEO*
Steven R Hash, *Ch of Bd*
Edward C Coppola, *President*
Allan Gee, *President*
Mace Siegel, *COO*
EMP: 80 EST: 1965

SALES (est): 786MM **Publicly Held**
WEB: www.macerich.com
SIC: 6798 Real estate investment trusts

(P-16240)
PRIME ADMINISTRATION LLC
Also Called: Prime Group
357 S Curson Ave, Los Angeles
(90036-5201)
P.O. Box 360859 (90036-1359)
PHONE...............................323 549-7155
Daniel H James, *Chairman*
John C Atwater, *CEO*
David Godin, *Vice Pres*
Karen James, *Vice Pres*
Justin Pan, *Vice Pres*
EMP: 522 EST: 2004
SALES (est): 104.6MM **Privately Held**
SIC: 6798 Real estate investment trusts

(P-16241)
PS BUSINESS PARKS INC (PA)
701 Western Ave, Glendale (91201-2349)
PHONE...............................818 244-8080
Dan Chandler, *President*
Ronald L Havner Jr, *Ch of Bd*
Elena Lee, *CEO*
John W Petersen, *COO*
John Petersen, *COO*
◆ EMP: 63 EST: 1990
SALES (est): 415.6MM **Publicly Held**
WEB: www.psbusinessparks.com
SIC: 6798 Real estate investment trusts

(P-16242)
PUBLIC STORAGE (PA)
701 Western Ave, Glendale (91201-2349)
PHONE...............................818 244-8080
Joseph D Russell Jr, *President*
Ronald L Havner Jr, *Ch of Bd*
David Lee, *COO*
Steven Lentin, *COO*
John Reyes, *CFO*
EMP: 200 EST: 1980
SALES (est): 2.9B **Publicly Held**
WEB: www.publicstorage.com
SIC: 6798 Real estate investment trusts

(P-16243)
REXFORD INDUSTRIAL REALTY INC (PA)
11620 Wilshire Blvd Fl 10, Los Angeles
(90025-6821)
PHONE...............................310 966-1680
Howard Schwimmer, *Co-CEO*
Richard Ziman, *Ch of Bd*
Laura Clark, *CFO*
Michael S Frankel, *Co-CEO*
Alexander Dehaven, *Vice Pres*
EMP: 121 EST: 2013
SALES (est): 330.1MM **Privately Held**
WEB: www.rexfordindustrial.com
SIC: 6798 Real estate investment trusts

(P-16244)
STEADFAST INCOME REIT INC (HQ)
18100 Von Karman Ave # 500, Irvine
(92612-0196)
PHONE...............................949 852-0700
Rodney F Emery, *CEO*
Phillip Meserve, *President*
Ana Marie Del Rio, *COO*
Dinesh K Davar, *CFO*
Christopher M Hilbert, *Exec VP*
EMP: 184 EST: 2009
SALES (est): 141.9MM **Privately Held**
WEB: www.steadfastcompanies.com
SIC: 6798 Real estate investment trusts

(P-16245)
WESTERN ASSET MRTG CAPITL CORP
385 E Colorado Blvd, Pasadena
(91101-1923)
PHONE...............................626 844-9400
Jennifer W Murphy, *President*
John Riddle, *Managing Prtnr*
James W Hirschmann III, *Ch of Bd*
Elliott Neumayer, *COO*
Lisa Meyer, *CFO*
EMP: 804 EST: 2012
SALES (est): 100.5MM **Privately Held**
WEB: www.westernassetmcc.com
SIC: 6798 Real estate investment trusts

(PA)=Parent Co (HQ)=Headquarters (DH)=Div Headquarters
✪ = New Business established in last 2 years

6799 Investors, NEC

(P-16246)
ALLIANZ GLOBL INVSTORS AMER LP (HQ)
104 E 213th St, Carson (90745-1525)
PHONE.................310 549-0729
Michael Matute,
EMP: 62 **EST:** 2010
SALES (est): 35.5MM
SALES (corp-wide): 26.4B **Privately Held**
WEB: www.dresdnerrcm.com
SIC: 6799 Investors
PA: Allianz Se
　　Koniginstr. 28
　　Munchen BY 80802
　　893 800-0

(P-16247)
ARES INVESTMENTS HOLDINGS LLC (HQ)
2000 Avenue Of The Stars # 12, Los Angeles (90067-4733)
PHONE.................310 201-4100
EMP: 62 **EST:** 2012
SALES (est): 36.4MM
SALES (corp-wide): 1.7B **Publicly Held**
WEB: www.aresmgmt.com
SIC: 6799 Investors
PA: Ares Management Corporation
　　2000 Avenue Of The Stars # 12
　　Los Angeles CA 90067
　　310 201-4100

(P-16248)
BDEEBZ INVESTMENT INC (PA)
Also Called: Prestige Fuels
16414 Foothill Blvd, Fontana (92335-3367)
PHONE.................909 646-9498
Sameer I Deeb, *CEO*
EMP: 81 **EST:** 2017
SALES (est): 843.3K **Privately Held**
SIC: 6799 Investors

(P-16249)
BROADREACH CAPITL PARTNERS LLC
6430 W Sunset Blvd # 504, Los Angeles (90028-7901)
PHONE.................310 691-5760
Andre Ramillon, *Branch Mgr*
EMP: 1161
SALES (corp-wide): 46.7MM **Privately Held**
WEB: www.broadreachcp.com
SIC: 6799 Investors
PA: Broadreach Capital Partners Llc
　　855 El Cmino Real Bldg 5
　　Palo Alto CA 94301
　　650 331-2500

(P-16250)
C B RICHARD ELLIS INC (DH)
8521 Fallbrook Ave # 150, West Hills (91304-3240)
PHONE.................818 737-1200
Robert Ruth, *President*
EMP: 212 **EST:** 1991
SALES (est): 18.7MM **Publicly Held**
WEB: www.trammellcrow.com
SIC: 6799 6512 Real estate investors, except property operators; nonresidential building operators

(P-16251)
CALL TO ACTION PARTNERS LLC
11601 Wilshire Blvd Fl 23, Los Angeles (90025-0509)
PHONE.................310 996-7200
Colin Sapire, *Mng Member*
Jeff Klausner, *CFO*
Richard Kam, *Marketing Mgr*
Lenny Sands,
▲ **EMP:** 190 **EST:** 2009
SQ FT: 9,500
SALES (est): 19.6MM **Privately Held**
SIC: 6799 Investors

(P-16252)
CCCC GROWTH FUND LLC
899 El Centro St, South Pasadena (91030-3101)
PHONE.................626 441-8770

Carl L Herrmann Jr, *Mng Member*
EMP: 61 **EST:** 2001
SQ FT: 10,000
SALES (est): 3.3MM **Privately Held**
WEB: www.ccccgrowthfund.com
SIC: 6799 6411 Investors; insurance agents, brokers & service

(P-16253)
CENTERLINE MORTGAGE CAPITL INC
18300 Von Karman Ave # 6, Irvine (92612-1057)
PHONE.................949 221-6685
Andy Mackay, *Branch Mgr*
Yogesh Joshi, *Vice Pres*
EMP: 79
SALES (corp-wide): 661.2MM **Privately Held**
WEB: www.lument.com
SIC: 6799 Investors
HQ: Centerline Mortgage Capital, Inc.
　　100 Church St Fl 15
　　New York NY 10007
　　212 317-5700

(P-16254)
CLEARVIEW CAPITAL LLC
12100 Wilshire Blvd # 800, Los Angeles (90025-7140)
PHONE.................310 806-9555
Larry Simon, *Branch Mgr*
EMP: 862
SALES (corp-wide): 244.6MM **Privately Held**
WEB: www.clearviewcap.com
SIC: 6799 Venture capital companies
PA: Clearview Capital, Llc
　　1010 Washington Blvd 2-9
　　Stamford CT 06901
　　203 698-2777

(P-16255)
COLONY CAPITAL LLC (PA)
Also Called: Colony Management
2450 Broadway Ste 600, Santa Monica (90404-3591)
PHONE.................310 282-8820
Thomas J Barrack Jr, *Chairman*
David Palame, *Officer*
Rebel Blackwell, *Assoc VP*
Brendan McCarthy, *Assoc VP*
David Sibley, *Assoc VP*
EMP: 899 **EST:** 1992
SALES (est): 429.9MM **Privately Held**
WEB: www.clny.com
SIC: 6799 7999 7011 5813 Real estate investors, except property operators; gambling & lottery services; hotels & motels; drinking places; eating places

(P-16256)
CORRIDOR CAPITAL LLC (PA)
12400 Wilshire Blvd # 645, Los Angeles (90025-1260)
PHONE.................310 442-7000
Craig L Enenstein, *CEO*
Craig Enenstein, *Managing Prtnr*
Jessamyn Davis, *CFO*
Erich Sorger, *Vice Pres*
Rohit Bassi, *Managing Dir*
EMP: 126 **EST:** 2005
SALES (est): 136.5MM **Privately Held**
WEB: www.corridor-capital.com
SIC: 6799 Venture capital companies

(P-16257)
CRESCENT CAPITAL BDC INC (PA)
11100 Santa Monica Blvd # 2000, Los Angeles (90025-3335)
PHONE.................310 235-5971
Jason A Breaux, *CEO*
Gerhard Lombard, *CFO*
Joe Hanlon, *Officer*
Mark Devincentis, *Director*
EMP: 215 **EST:** 2015
SALES (est): 77.1MM **Publicly Held**
WEB: www.crescentcap.com
SIC: 6799 Investors

(P-16258)
CRESTMONT CAPITAL LLC
1422 Edinger Ave Ste 210, Tustin (92780-6298)
PHONE.................949 537-3882

Gregory Keleshian, *CEO*
Rick Hughes, *Chief Mktg Ofcr*
Allan Garfinkle, *Portfolio Mgr*
Aren Kamberian, *Manager*
Travis Gerlach, *Advisor*
EMP: 250 **EST:** 2015
SALES (est): 22.5MM **Privately Held**
WEB: www.crestmontcapital.com
SIC: 6799 Investors

(P-16259)
EMP III INC
Also Called: Duarte Manor
1755 Mrtn Lthr Kng Jr Blv, Los Angeles (90058-1522)
PHONE.................323 231-4174
Ernie Piltil, *President*
Tim English, *CEO*
Scott Mason, *Vice Pres*
EMP: 80 **EST:** 2010
SALES (est): 3.5MM **Privately Held**
SIC: 6799 Real estate investors, except property operators

(P-16260)
EXCHANGRGHT NLP 3 MSTR LSSEE L (PA)
1055 E Colo Blvd Ste 310, Pasadena (91106)
PHONE.................855 317-4448
Joshua Ungerecht, *Mng Member*
Dave Van, *CFO*
William Prather, *Administration*
Kori Kurtz, *Opers Staff*
Jennifer Chase, *Director*
EMP: 65 **EST:** 2013
SALES (est): 7MM **Privately Held**
WEB: www.exchangeright.com
SIC: 6799 Real estate investors, except property operators

(P-16261)
FIRST GROUP HOLDINGS INC
700 N Brand Blvd Ste 200, Glendale (91203-3234)
PHONE.................855 910-5626
EMP: 99 **EST:** 2017
SALES (est): 3MM **Privately Held**
WEB: www.firstgroupholdings.com
SIC: 6799 Investors

(P-16262)
FISH HOUSE PARTNERS ONE LLC
Also Called: Restaurants Bars & Food Svcs
5955 Melrose Ave, Los Angeles (90038-3623)
PHONE.................323 460-4170
Michael Cimarusti, *Mng Member*
Cristina Echiverri,
EMP: 96 **EST:** 2015
SALES (est): 1.5MM **Privately Held**
SIC: 5812 6799 Seafood restaurants; investors

(P-16263)
GOLDEN INTERNATIONAL
424 S Los Angeles St # 2, Los Angeles (90013-1470)
PHONE.................213 628-1388
GI Hanbae, *Branch Mgr*
EMP: 2968
SALES (corp-wide): 15.4MM **Privately Held**
SIC: 6799 Investors
PA: Golden International
　　36720 Palmdale Rd
　　Rancho Mirage CA 92270
　　760 568-1912

(P-16264)
GREEN EQUITY INVESTORS IV LP (PA)
11111 Santa Monica Blvd, Los Angeles (90025-3333)
PHONE.................310 954-0444
Jonathan D Sokoloff, *Mng Member*
Cody Franklin, *CFO*
Reginald Holden, *Officer*
Anna Batko, *Vice Pres*
Nick Okano, *Vice Pres*
EMP: 7657 **EST:** 2002
SALES (est): 271.1MM **Privately Held**
WEB: www.leonardgreen.com
SIC: 6799 Investors

(P-16265)
GRIFFIN CAPITAL HOLDINGS CORP
1520 E Grand Ave, El Segundo (90245-4341)
PHONE.................3 0 469-6100
Kevin Shields, *CEO*
Jeffrey S Schwaber, *President*
Charles Huang, *COO*
Javier Bitar, *CFO*
Joseph E Miller, *CFO*
EMP: 95 **EST:** 1996
SALES (est): 38.3MM **Privately Held**
WEB: www.griffincapital.com
SIC: 6799 Investors

(P-16266)
GSA DES PLAINES LLC
10100 Santa Monica Blvd # 2600, Los Angeles (90067-4003)
PHONE.................310 557-5100
Daniel Goldstone, *Mng Member*
Adam Chesnoff,
EMP: 70 **EST:** 2012
SQ FT: 100
SALES (est): 2.6MM **Privately Held**
SIC: 6799 Real estate investors, except property operators

(P-16267)
HARVARD GRAND INV INC A CAL
2 Civic Plaza Dr, Carson (90745-2231)
PHONE.................310 513-7560
Chang Hun Lee, *President*
Kathy Choy, *Controller*
EMP: 99
SALES (est): 950K **Privately Held**
SIC: 6799 Investors

(P-16268)
IDEALAB HOLDINGS LLC (PA)
130 W Union St, Pasadena (91103-3628)
PHONE.................626 585-6900
Bill Gross, *CEO*
Marcia Goodstein, *President*
Craig Chrisney, *CFO*
Allen Morgan, *Bd of Directors*
Kristen Ding, *Vice Pres*
EMP: 626 **EST:** 1996
SALES (est): 148.2MM **Privately Held**
WEB: www.idealab.com
SIC: 6799 5045 5734 Venture capital companies; computer software; computer software & accessories

(P-16269)
IMPERIAL CAPITAL GROUP LLC (PA)
2000 Avenue Of The Stars 900s, Los Angeles (90067-4700)
PHONE.................310 246-3700
Randall Wooster,
Lenny Bianco, *Senior VP*
Gregg Poillucci, *Vice Pres*
James P Kenney, *Managing Dir*
Peter Lapina, *Managing Dir*
EMP: 70 **EST:** 1989
SQ FT: 14,909
SALES (est): 10.5MM **Privately Held**
SIC: 6799 Investors

(P-16270)
INTREPID INV BANKERS LLC
11755 Wilshire Blvd # 2200, Los Angeles (90025-1567)
PHONE.................310 478-9000
Ed Bagdasarian, *CEO*
Steve Davis, *Managing Dir*
Gary Rabishaw, *Managing Dir*
Chris Park, *Director*
Kyle Berkman, *Associate*
EMP: 492 **EST:** 2010
SALES (est): 14.8MM **Privately Held**
WEB: www.intrepidib.com
SIC: 6799 Investors
HQ: Mufg Americas Holdings Corporation
　　1251 Ave Of The Americas
　　New York NY 10020
　　212 782-6800

▲ = Import ▼ =Export
◆ =Import/Export

(P-16271)
JMG INVESTMENTS INC
23041 Hatteras St, Woodland Hills
(91367-4236)
PHONE..................818 519-0670
Justin Helfert, *Marketing Staff*
EMP: 60 EST: 2017
SALES (est): 3.5MM **Privately Held**
SIC: 6799 Investors

(P-16272)
KONDAUR CAPITAL CORPORATION (PA)
333 S Anita Dr Ste 400, Orange
(92868-3314)
PHONE..................714 352-2038
John Kontouis, *President*
Lorenzo Marin, *Vice Pres*
Mike Perry, *Portfolio Mgr*
Dustin Standridge, *Portfolio Mgr*
Shantha Ramesh, *Analyst*
EMP: 141 EST: 2007
SALES (est): 71.2MM **Privately Held**
WEB: www.kondaur.com
SIC: 6799 Investors

(P-16273)
LD ACQUISITION COMPANY 16 LLC
400 Continental Blvd # 500, El Segundo
(90245-5078)
PHONE..................310 294-8160
Tim Brazy, *CEO*
Dan Parsons, *COO*
George Doyle, *CFO*
Josef Bobek, *Principal*
EMP: 99 EST: 2017
SALES (est): 3.7MM **Privately Held**
SIC: 6799 Investors

(P-16274)
LIGHTHOUSE CAPITAL FUNDING
Also Called: Light House Group, The
15332 Antioch St Ste 540, Pacific Palisades
(90272-3603)
PHONE..................310 230-8335
Gary Leshgold, *President*
Gina Newsome, *General Mgr*
Meghan Hartnett, *Executive Asst*
Laurie Dennis, *Accountant*
Jennifer Napier, *VP Mktg*
EMP: 50 EST: 2003
SALES (est): 5.6MM **Privately Held**
WEB: www.thelighthousegroup.net
SIC: 6799 Venture capital companies

(P-16275)
MARINE HOLDING US CORP
6000 Condor Dr, Moorpark (93021-2601)
PHONE..................805 529-2000
Francois Mirallie, *President*
Joel Silva, *CFO*
Mark Cortell, *Vice Pres*
Anita Cox, *Asst Treas*
Elisa Mojica, *Asst Sec*
EMP: 650 EST: 2004
SALES (est): 156.3MM
SALES (corp-wide): 888.7MM **Privately Held**
WEB: www.zodiacpoolsystems.ca
SIC: 6799 Investors
HQ: Zodiac Pool Solutions Llc
2882 Whiptail Loop # 100
Carlsbad CA 92010
760 599-9600

(P-16276)
MARLIN OPERATIONS GROUP INC (PA)
338 Pier Ave, Hermosa Beach
(90254-3617)
PHONE..................310 364-0100
David McGovern, *CEO*
EMP: 54 EST: 2012
SALES (est): 912.4K **Privately Held**
WEB: www.marlinequity.com
SIC: 6799 Investors

(P-16277)
MATSUSHITA INTERNATIONAL CORP (PA)
1141 Via Callejon, San Clemente
(92673-6230)
PHONE..................949 498-1000
Hiroyuki Matsushita, *President*
EMP: 80 EST: 1990
SALES (est): 20.3MM **Privately Held**
SIC: 6799 3711 3714 Real estate investors, except property operators; automobile assembly, including specialty automobiles; motor vehicle parts & accessories

(P-16278)
MSR HOTELS & RESORTS INC
Also Called: Sheraton Inn Bakersfield
5101 California Ave # 204, Bakersfield
(93309-1623)
PHONE..................661 325-9700
Kole Siefken, *Manager*
EMP: 98
SALES (corp-wide): 52B **Publicly Held**
WEB: www.cnl.com
SIC: 6799 Investors
HQ: Msr Hotels & Resorts, Inc.
450 S Orange Ave
Orlando FL 32801
407 650-1000

(P-16279)
NNN REALTY INVESTORS LLC
19700 Fairchild Ste 300, Irvine
(92612-2515)
PHONE..................714 667-8252
Jeffrey T Hanson, *President*
Michael Van Dusen, *Senior VP*
Fred D Cochran, *Vice Pres*
Todd A Mikles,
EMP: 458 EST: 1998
SQ FT: 18,800
SALES (est): 13.3MM **Privately Held**
SIC: 6799 6531 Investors; real estate managers

(P-16280)
NOGALES INVESTORS LLC
9229 W Sunset Blvd # 900, Los Angeles
(90069-3410)
PHONE..................310 276-7439
Luis Nogales, *Mng Member*
Mark Nicholson,
EMP: 60 EST: 2001
SQ FT: 2,500
SALES (est): 245.2K **Privately Held**
WEB: www.nogalesinvestors.com
SIC: 6799 Investors
PA: Nogales Investors Management, Llc
9229 W Sunset Blvd # 900
Los Angeles CA 90069

(P-16281)
NRLL LLC
Also Called: Land Disposition Company
1 Mauchly, Irvine (92618-2305)
P.O. Box 15534 (92623-5534)
PHONE..................949 768-7777
Robert D Friedman,
Jeffrey Friedman,
EMP: 360 EST: 1995
SQ FT: 18,000
SALES (est): 710.4K **Privately Held**
WEB: www.landauction.com
SIC: 6799 Real estate investors, except property operators
PA: Nrp Holding Co., Inc.
1 Mauchly
Irvine CA 92618

(P-16282)
OTTS ASIA MOORER DEVON
Also Called: Newshire Investment
10015 Baring Cross St, Los Angeles
(90044-4511)
PHONE..................323 603-6959
Asia Otts, *Owner*
Devon Moorer, *Owner*
EMP: 105 EST: 2016
SALES (est): 2.5MM **Privately Held**
SIC: 6799 Investors

(P-16283)
PEDESTAL CAPITAL II LLC
13111 Sycamore Dr, Norwalk (90650-8339)
PHONE..................562 863-5555
Rui Zhao, *Principal*
Adam Stanchina, *Principal*
EMP: 80 EST: 2016
SALES (est): 6.5MM **Privately Held**
SIC: 6799 Investors

(P-16284)
PMC CAPITAL PARTNERS LLC
12243 Branford St, Sun Valley
(91352-1010)
PHONE..................818 896-1101
Michel Tamer, *Managing Prtnr*
EMP: 1000 EST: 2019
SALES (est): 34.5MM **Privately Held**
WEB: www.pmccapital.com
SIC: 6799 Venture capital companies

(P-16285)
PROVIDENCE REST PARTNERS LLC
Also Called: Restaurant Investment
5955 Melrose Ave, Los Angeles
(90038-3623)
PHONE..................323 460-4170
Michael Cimarusti, *Mng Member*
EMP: 88 EST: 2004
SALES (est): 2.5MM **Privately Held**
SIC: 6799 5963 Investors; food services, direct sales

(P-16286)
PYRAMID PEAK CORPORATION
450 Nwport Ctr Dr Ste 650, Newport Beach
(92660)
PHONE..................949 769-8600
Cindy Ragsdale, *President*
Cindy Brown, *COO*
Debbie Hanratty, *Human Res Mgr*
EMP: 70 EST: 2002
SALES (est): 5.9MM **Privately Held**
SIC: 6799 Investors

(P-16287)
RAPISCAN HOLDINGS INC (HQ)
12525 Chadron Ave, Hawthorne
(90250-4807)
PHONE..................310 978-0516
Deepak Chopra, *Principal*
Ghazi Kashmolah, *Vice Pres*
Shehul Parikh, *Vice Pres*
Sunil Shah, *Engineer*
Jack Shirley, *Engineer*
EMP: 75 EST: 2014
SALES (est): 2.9MM
SALES (corp-wide): 1.1B **Publicly Held**
WEB: www.osi-systems.com
SIC: 6799 Investors
PA: Osi Systems, Inc.
12525 Chadron Ave
Hawthorne CA 90250
310 978-0516

(P-16288)
REGENT LP (PA)
9720 Wilshire Blvd, Beverly Hills
(90212-2021)
PHONE..................310 299-4100
Michael A Reinstein, *CEO*
Roxanna Sassanian, *CFO*
Louise Meyers, *Vice Pres*
Pamela Coffey, *Manager*
Chantal Lamers, *Editor*
EMP: 85 EST: 2017
SALES (est): 206.5MM **Privately Held**
WEB: www.regentlp.com
SIC: 6799 Investors

(P-16289)
ROLL PROPERTIES INTL INC
Also Called: Paramout Farms
13646 Highway 33, Lost Hills (93249-9719)
PHONE..................661 797-6500
Bill Bowers, *Manager*
Alycia Morris, *Executive Asst*
Janet Flanagan, *Manager*
EMP: 121
SALES (corp-wide): 27.2MM **Privately Held**
SIC: 6799 Real estate investors, except property operators
PA: Roll Properties International, Inc.
11444 W Olympic Blvd # 10
Los Angeles CA 90064
310 966-5700

(P-16290)
RUSTIC CANYON GROUP LLC
Also Called: Rustic Canyon Partners
1025 Westwood Blvd, Los Angeles
(90024-2902)
PHONE..................310 998-8000
Nate Redmond, *Managing Prtnr*
Mike Shundoff, *Administration*
John Babcock,
Lee Bailey,
Michael Kim,
EMP: 75 EST: 2000
SALES (est): 9.5MM **Privately Held**
WEB: www.rusticcanyon.com
SIC: 6799 Venture capital companies

(P-16291)
SABAL CAPITAL PARTNERS LLC
465 N Halstead St Ste 105, Pasadena
(91107-6075)
PHONE..................949 255-1007
Pat Jackson, *CEO*
Sarah Suther, *Ch Credit Ofcr*
Boyega Adelekan, *Vice Pres*
Juan C Aragon, *Managing Dir*
James Barry, *Managing Dir*
EMP: 73 EST: 2018
SALES (est): 9.4MM **Privately Held**
WEB: www.sabal.com
SIC: 6799 Investors

(P-16292)
SABAN CAPITAL GROUP INC (PA)
10100 Santa Monica Blvd, Los Angeles
(90067-4003)
PHONE..................310 557-5100
Adam Chesnoss, *COO*
Greg Ivancich, *CFO*
Bernie Leypold, *Vice Pres*
Richard Yen, *Managing Dir*
Natalie Toliver, *Accountant*
EMP: 55 EST: 2016
SALES (est): 15.1MM **Privately Held**
WEB: www.saban.com
SIC: 6799 Investors

(P-16293)
STONECALIBRE LLC (PA)
2049 Century Park E # 2550, Los Angeles
(90067-3110)
PHONE..................310 774-0014
Brian Wall, *President*
Brian Anderson, *Vice Pres*
Usman Shakeel, *Vice Pres*
Danyel O 'dea, *Office Mgr*
Brice Geoffrion, *Associate*
EMP: 100 EST: 2012
SALES (est): 228.3MM **Privately Held**
WEB: www.stonecalibre.com
SIC: 6799 Investors

(P-16294)
SUMMIT COMMERCIAL PRPTS INC (HQ)
400 Continental Blvd # 160, El Segundo
(90245-5076)
PHONE..................310 648-7500
Jack Mahoney, *President*
EMP: 106 EST: 1982
SALES (est): 1.6MM
SALES (corp-wide): 2.2MM **Privately Held**
WEB: www.summitcommercialprop.com
SIC: 6799 Real estate investors, except property operators
PA: Highridge Partners, Inc.
400 Continental Blvd # 160
El Segundo CA 90245
310 648-7600

(P-16295)
TCG CAPITAL MANAGEMENT LP
12180 Millennium Ste 500, Playa Vista
(90094-2948)
PHONE..................310 633-2900
Peter Chernin, *CEO*
EMP: 135 EST: 2018

P R O D U C T S & S V C S

SALES (est): 13.2MM **Privately Held**
SIC: 6799 Investors

(P-16296)
TENNENBAUM CAPITL PARTNERS LLC (HQ)
Also Called: T C P
2951 28th St Ste 1000, Santa Monica
(90405-2993)
PHONE.....................310 566-1000
Lee Landrum, *Managing Prtnr*
Mark Holdsworth, *Managing Prtnr*
Michael Leitner, *Managing Prtnr*
Howard Levkowitz, *Managing Prtnr*
Philip Tseng, *Managing Prtnr*
EMP: 68 EST: 1999
SQ FT: 15,850
SALES (est): 87.9MM **Publicly Held**
WEB: www.tennenbaumcapital.com
SIC: 6799 Venture capital companies

(P-16297)
TRANSOM CAPITAL GROUP LLC (PA)
10990 Wilshire Blvd # 44, Los Angeles
(90024-3913)
PHONE.....................424 293-2818
Ken Firtel, *Mng Member*
Nathan Dastic, *CFO*
Jaime Crawford, *Vice Pres*
Justin Gilson, *Vice Pres*
Colin Sullivan, *Software Dev*
EMP: 55 EST: 2007
SALES (est): 1.3B **Privately Held**
WEB: www.transomcap.com
SIC: 6799 5112 5943 3951 Investors;
pens &/or pencils; writing supplies; foun-
tain pens & fountain pen desk sets

(P-16298)
TRUE INVESTMENTS LLC (PA)
2260 University Dr, Newport Beach
(92660-3319)
PHONE.....................949 258-9720
Alan True, *CEO*
Peter Nelson, *Executive*
EMP: 49 EST: 2012
SALES (est): 16MM **Privately Held**
WEB: www.truelanehomes.com
SIC: 6799 7372 Investors; application
computer software

(P-16299)
TRV INVESTMENTS LLC (HQ)
3001 Calloway Dr, Bakersfield
(93312-2666)
PHONE.....................661 378-3846
Tonya Vadnais,
EMP: 79 EST: 2014
SALES (est): 1.7MM
SALES (corp-wide): 88.8B **Publicly Held**
WEB: www.citigroup.com
SIC: 6799 Investors
PA: Citigroup Inc.
388 Greenwich St Fl 38
New York NY 10013
212 559-1000

(P-16300)
WEDGEWOOD INC (PA)
2015 Manhattan Beach Blvd, Redondo
Beach (90278-1226)
PHONE.....................310 640-3070
Gregory L Geiser, *CEO*
Eric Borgeson, *Owner*
Bruce H McLain, *Partner*
Kim Mellman, *CEO*
Lisa Wehrly, *COO*
EMP: 351 EST: 1985
SQ FT: 3,200
SALES (est): 251.2MM **Privately Held**
WEB: www.wedgewood-inc.com
SIC: 6799 Real estate investors, except
property operators

(P-16301)
WELKIN WELKIN CAPITL GROUP LLC (PA)
7190 W Sunset Blvd, Los Angeles
(90046-4415)
PHONE.....................323 312-3200
Jonathan Marquez, *Mng Member*
Carol Shaw,
EMP: 75 EST: 2020

SALES (est): 10.9MM **Privately Held**
WEB: www.welkincapital.com
SIC: 6799 Investors

(P-16302)
WESTERN MILLING LLC (HQ)
Also Called: O.H. Kruse Grain and Milling
31120 W St, Goshen (93227)
P.O. Box 1029 (93227-1029)
PHONE.....................559 302-1000
Kevin Kruse, *CEO*
Paul Schmidt, *Managing Prtnr*
Mike Rosa, *Vice Pres*
Joseph Bridgwater-Rowe, *Technology*
Chris Christensen, *Senior Engr*
▼ EMP: 243 EST: 2000
SALES (est): 587.3MM **Privately Held**
WEB: www.westernmilling.com
SIC: 6799 5191 6221 Real estate in-
vestors, except property operators; secu-
rity speculators for own account; animal
feeds; commodity dealers, contracts
PA: Kruse Investment Company, Inc.
31120 W St
Goshen CA 93227
559 302-1000

(P-16303)
WINDJMMER CAPITL INVESTORS LLC
610 Newport Center Dr, Newport Beach
(92660-6419)
PHONE.....................949 706-9989
Robert Bartholomew, *Mng Member*
Jeff Dunnigan, *CFO*
Matt Anderson, *Vice Pres*
Ryan Pertz, *Vice Pres*
Kerry Muse, *Business Dir*
EMP: 51 EST: 1990
SALES (est): 10.4MM **Privately Held**
WEB: www.windjammercapital.com
SIC: 6799 Investors

(P-16304)
WINDJMMER CPITL INVSTORS III L
Also Called: Westwind Equity Investors
610 Nwport Ctr Dr Ste 110, Newport Beach
(92660)
PHONE.....................949 706-9989
Robert Bartholomew, *Chairman*
Matt Anderson, *Vice Pres*
Jeffery Dunnigan, *Vice Pres*
J Derek Watson, *Principal*
Ryan Pertz, *Managing Dir*
EMP: 724 EST: 1990
SALES (est): 13.8MM **Privately Held**
WEB: www.windjammercapital.com
SIC: 6799 Investors

7011 Hotels, Motels & Tourist Courts

(P-16305)
1260 BB PROPERTY LLC
Also Called: Four Ssons Rsort Santa Barbara
1260 Channel Dr, Santa Barbara
(93108-2805)
PHONE.....................805 969-2261
H Ty Warner, *CEO*
Diane Kildun, *Human Res Dir*
Tina A Franco, *Hum Res Coord*
Miles Blum, *Sales Staff*
Sue McLain, *Sales Staff*
▲ EMP: 500 EST: 1986
SALES (est): 58.5MM
SALES (corp-wide): 103.8MM **Privately Held**
SIC: 7011 Resort hotel
HQ: Fsb Cal Corp.
280 Chestnut Ave
Westmont IL 60559
630 920-1515

(P-16306)
1855 S HBR BLVD DRV HLDNGS LLC
Also Called: Sheraton Pk Ht At Anheim Rsort
1855 S Harbor Blvd, Anaheim
(92802-3509)
PHONE.....................714 750-1811
Kunthea Hang, *Principal*
Tony Bruno, *General Mgr*

Ian Gee, *Manager*
EMP: 250 EST: 2012
SALES (est): 4.7MM **Privately Held**
WEB: www.four-points.marriott.com
SIC: 7011 Hotels & motels

(P-16307)
23627 CALABASAS ROAD LLC
Also Called: Anza A Calabasas Hotel, The
23627 Calabasas Rd, Calabasas
(91302-1502)
PHONE.....................818 222-5300
Mona Rigdon, *Principal*
James McCrimmon, *Principal*
EMP: 65 EST: 2016
SALES (est): 3.5MM **Privately Held**
WEB: www.theanzahotel.com
SIC: 7011 Hotels

(P-16308)
29 PALMS INN
73950 Inn Ave, Twentynine Palms
(92277-3418)
PHONE.....................760 367-3505
Jane Grunt-Smith, *Owner*
Aden Grunt, *Facilities Mgr*
Heidi Grunt, *Manager*
EMP: 67 EST: 1928
SQ FT: 6,000
SALES (est): 1.2MM **Privately Held**
WEB: www.29palmsinn.com
SIC: 5813 7011 Bar (drinking places); mo-
tels; hotels

(P-16309)
417 STOCKTON ST LLC
1180 S Beverly Dr Ste 508, Los Angeles
(90035-1157)
PHONE.....................323 327-9656
Jim Ciki, *Finance*
EMP: 60 EST: 2018
SALES (est): 1.7MM **Privately Held**
SIC: 7011 Hotels & motels

(P-16310)
550 FLOWER ST OPERATIONS LLC
Also Called: Standard Hotel, The
550 S Flower St, Los Angeles
(90071-2501)
PHONE.....................213 892-8080
EMP: 200
SQ FT: 172,197
SALES (est): 5.6MM **Privately Held**
WEB: www.standardhotels.com
SIC: 7011 5813 5812 Hotel/Motel Opera-
tion Drinking Place Eating Place

(P-16311)
6417 SELMA HOTEL LLC
Also Called: Dream Hollywood
6417 Selma Ave, Los Angeles
(90028-7310)
PHONE.....................323 844-6417
Richard Heyman, *Mng Member*
Ashok Advani, *Senior VP*
German Inguanzo, *Chief Engr*
Lynn Griffith, *VP Human Res*
Yasmin Liang, *Opers Staff*
EMP: 250 EST: 2017
SALES (est): 6.8MM **Privately Held**
SIC: 7011 Hotels

(P-16312)
901 WEST OLYMPIC BLVD LTD PRTN
Also Called: Courtyard & Residence Inn La
901 W Olympic Blvd, Los Angeles
(90015-1327)
PHONE.....................347 992-5707
Greg Steinhauer, *Partner*
Homer Williams, *Partner*
EMP: 110 EST: 2011
SQ FT: 286,000
SALES (est): 9.1MM **Privately Held**
SIC: 7011 Hotels

(P-16313)
ACCOR CORP
Also Called: Sofitel Los Angeles
8555 Beverly Blvd, Los Angeles
(90048-3303)
PHONE.....................310 278-5444
Gunter Zweimuller, *President*
Eric McCauley, *Receiver*
Philippe Bone, *Vice Pres*

Stephane Lombard, *Vice Pres*
Daria Shearer, *Vice Pres*
EMP: 200 EST: 1986
SQ FT: 380,000
SALES (est): 30.9MM
SALES (corp-wide): 627.9MM **Privately Held**
WEB: www.sofitel-los-angeles.com
SIC: 5812 7011 Eating places; hotels
PA: Accor
82 Rue Henry Farman
Issy Les Moulineaux 92130
146 429-193

(P-16314)
ACE HOTEL & SWIM CLUB
701 E Palm Canyon Dr, Palm Springs
(92264-8811)
PHONE.....................760 325-9900
Jeanette Collins, *Executive Asst*
Ryan Buckstein, *Info Tech Dir*
Miller Ben, *Project Mgr*
Denise Nizza, *Asst Controller*
Ian Rabinek, *Controller*
EMP: 52 EST: 2008
SALES (est): 18.3MM **Privately Held**
WEB: www.acehotel.com
SIC: 7011 Resort hotel; hotels

(P-16315)
AGRE DCP PALM SPRNG TENANT LLC (PA)
Also Called: Riviera Palm Sprng A Trbute Pr
1600 N Palm Spgs, Palm Springs (92262)
PHONE.....................760 327-8311
EMP: 119 EST: 2015
SALES (est): 1.2MM **Privately Held**
WEB: www.margaritavilleresorts.com
SIC: 7011 Resort hotel

(P-16316)
AGUA CLNTE BAND CHILLA INDIANS
Also Called: Agua Caliente Casino & Resort
32250 Bob Hope Dr, Rancho Mirage
(92270-2704)
PHONE.....................760 321-2000
Ken Kettler, *Branch Mgr*
Frank Charolla, *CFO*
Tom Bonanne, *Vice Pres*
Laura Fregozo, *Executive Asst*
David McCarthy, *Business Anlyst*
EMP: 1000
SALES (corp-wide): 194.2MM **Privately Held**
WEB: www.dwa.org
SIC: 7011 Casino hotel
PA: Agua Caliente Band Of Cahuilla Indi-
ans
5401 Dinah Shore Dr
Palm Springs CA 92254
760 699-6800

(P-16317)
ALOFT ONTARIO-RANCHO CUCAMONGA
Also Called: Ihr Grnbuck Rncho Ccmnga Ventr
10480 4th St, Rancho Cucamonga
(91730-5893)
PHONE.....................909 484-2018
Cristina Riveroll, *Owner*
Yani Duran, *Director*
EMP: 54 EST: 2008
SALES (est): 1MM **Privately Held**
WEB: www.marriott.com
SIC: 7011 Hotels

(P-16318)
ANABELLE HOTEL INC
2011 W Olive Ave, Burbank (91506-2641)
PHONE.....................818 845-7800
Tony Garibian, *Owner*
EMP: 81 EST: 2000
SALES (est): 447.3K **Privately Held**
WEB: www.coasthotels.com
SIC: 7011 Hotels

(P-16319)
ANAHEIM - 1855 S HBR BLVD OWNE
Also Called: Sheraton Pk Ht At Anheim Rsort
1855 S Harbor Blvd, Anaheim
(92802-3509)
PHONE.....................714 750-1811

Ian Gee, *Principal*
EMP: 99 **EST:** 2019
SALES (est): 1.2MM **Privately Held**
WEB: www.four-points.marriott.com
SIC: 7011 Hotels & motels

(P-16320)
ANAHEIM CA LLC
Also Called: Doubltree Ht Anhim-Orange Cnty
100 The City Dr S, Orange (92868-3204)
PHONE...................................714 634-4500
Denise Pflum, *Manager*
EMP: 65 **EST:** 2011
SALES (est): 6.1MM **Privately Held**
WEB: www.hilton.com
SIC: 7011 Hotels & motels

(P-16321)
ANAHEIM HOTEL LLC
Also Called: Sheraton Pk Ht At Anheim Rsort
1855 S Harbor Blvd, Anaheim
(92802-3509)
PHONE...................................714 750-1811
Russ Cox, *Manager*
Delfin Acquiat, *Chief Engr*
Roxane Cornell, *Sales Staff*
Tony Monarez, *Facilities Mgr*
EMP: 104 **Privately Held**
WEB: www.theanaheimhotel.com
SIC: 7011 Hotels
PA: Anaheim Hotel, Llc
575 E Prkcnter Blvd Ste 5
Boise ID 83706

(P-16322)
ANAHEIM MARRIOTT SUITES
12015 Harbor Blvd, Garden Grove
(92840-4001)
PHONE...................................714 750-1000
Pat Seminario, *Principal*
Jane Dominowski, *Info Tech Mgr*
EMP: 64 **EST:** 2007
SALES (est): 6.7MM **Privately Held**
WEB: www.marriott.com
SIC: 7011 Hotels & motels

(P-16323)
ANAHEIM PARK HOTEL
Also Called: Wyndham Hotels & Resorts
222 W Houston Ave, Fullerton
(92832-3453)
PHONE...................................714 992-1700
Fred Menoufi, *Partner*
Abdul El Mekligiange, *General Mgr*
EMP: 116 **EST:** 1989
SQ FT: 174,123
SALES (est): 3.1MM **Privately Held**
WEB: www.hfullerton.com
SIC: 7011 YWCA/YWHA hotel; hotels

(P-16324)
ANAHEIM PLAZA HOTEL INC
Also Called: Anaheim Hotel, The
1700 S Harbor Blvd, Anaheim
(92802-2316)
PHONE...................................714 772-5900
Saroj Patel, *CEO*
Rajni Patel, *Vice Pres*
EMP: 170 **EST:** 1961
SQ FT: 5,600
SALES (est): 9.7MM **Privately Held**
WEB: www.dev.anaheimplazahotel.com
SIC: 7011 5812 5813 Motels; eating
places; drinking places

(P-16325)
ANDAZ WEST HOLLYWOOD
8401 W Sunset Blvd, Los Angeles
(90069-1909)
PHONE...................................323 656-1234
Sulynn Jew, *Principal*
Ashley Taylor, *Planning Mgr*
Dennis Blair, *Info Tech Mgr*
Jeff Fose, *Finance*
Tommasi Moccia, *Opers Staff*
EMP: 67 **EST:** 2010
SALES (est): 49.4MM **Publicly Held**
WEB: www.westhollywood.andaz.com
SIC: 7011 Resort hotel; hotels
HQ: Hyatt Corporation
150 N Riverside Plz
Chicago IL 60606
312 750-1234

(P-16326)
ANUP INC
Also Called: Quality Inn
600 W Donlon St, Blythe (92225-2706)
PHONE...................................760 921-2300
Vijay Amin, *CEO*
Patrick Byas, *General Mgr*
EMP: 53 **EST:** 1995
SALES (est): 1.2MM **Privately Held**
WEB: www.qualityinnblythe.com
SIC: 7011 Hotels & motels

(P-16327)
APPLE FARM COLLECTIONS-SLO INC (PA)
2015 Monterey St, San Luis Obispo
(93401-2617)
PHONE...................................805 544-2040
John E King, *President*
Carole D King, *Vice Pres*
Sergio Bernal, *IT/INT Sup*
Kim Wykoff, *Sales Staff*
Lauren Somppi, *Warehouse Mgr*
▼ **EMP:** 290 **EST:** 1977
SQ FT: 51,000
SALES (est): 11.7MM **Privately Held**
WEB: www.applefarm.com
SIC: 5812 7011 5947 Restaurant, family:
independent; motor inn; gift shop

(P-16328)
ARCADIA HOTEL VENTURE LP
Also Called: Embassy Suites Arcadia
211 E Huntington Dr, Arcadia (91006-3745)
PHONE...................................626 445-8525
Alma Teasley, *Principal*
Debbie Saunders, *Controller*
EMP: 62 **EST:** 2002
SQ FT: 131,527
SALES (est): 7.8MM **Privately Held**
WEB: www.embassysuitesarcadia.com
SIC: 7011 Hotels & motels

(P-16329)
ASCOT HOTEL LP
Also Called: Hotel Angeleno
170 N Church Ln, Los Angeles
(90049-2044)
PHONE...................................310 476-6411
Mark Beccaria, *Partner*
Jackie Vargas, *Sales Mgr*
Rick Gluth, *Manager*
Scott Gordon, *Manager*
Zulema Perez, *Manager*
EMP: 125 **EST:** 2008
SALES (est): 16.5MM **Privately Held**
WEB: www.hotelangeleno.com
SIC: 7011 Hotels

(P-16330)
ASHFORD TRS SEVEN LLC (PA)
Also Called: Courtyard By Marriott
74895 Frank Sinatra Dr, Palm Desert
(92211-2055)
PHONE...................................760 776-4150
EMP: 128 **EST:** 2014
SALES (est): 599.5K **Privately Held**
WEB: www.courtyard.marriott.com
SIC: 7011 Hotels & motels

(P-16331)
AWH BURBANK HOTEL LLC
Also Called: Marriott Burbank
2500 N Hollywood Way, Burbank
(91505-1019)
PHONE...................................813 843-6000
William Deforrest, *CEO*
Chad Cooley, *Vice Pres*
Russell Flicker, *Vice Pres*
Bernard Michael, *Vice Pres*
Jonathan Rosenfeld, *Vice Pres*
EMP: 59 **EST:** 2014
SALES (est): 5.2MM **Privately Held**
SIC: 7011 Hotels

(P-16332)
AYRES - PASO ROBLES LP
Also Called: Allegretto Vineyard Resort
2700 Buena Vista Dr, Paso Robles
(93446-9530)
PHONE...................................714 850-0409
Richard Verruni, *General Mgr*
Marcelle Moje, *Natl Sales Mgr*
Lee McGregor, *Marketing Staff*
Stacey Humphrey, *Manager*
Jeffrey Lemus, *Manager*

EMP: 120 **EST:** 2015
SALES (est): 4.2MM **Privately Held**
WEB: www.allegrettovineyardresort.com
SIC: 7011 Hotels

(P-16333)
AYRES GROUP (PA)
355 Bristol St, Costa Mesa (92626-7922)
PHONE...................................714 540-6060
Bruce F Ayres, *CEO*
EMP: 388 **EST:** 1975
SALES (est): 53.8MM **Privately Held**
WEB: www.ayreshotels.com
SIC: 7011 8741 1531 Hotels; manage-
ment services; operative builders

(P-16334)
B S A PARTNERS
Also Called: Residence Inn By Marriott
14419 Firestone Blvd, La Mirada
(90638-5912)
PHONE...................................714 523-2800
Jim Gilbert, *General Mgr*
William Swank, *General Ptnr*
William E Swank Jr, *General Ptnr*
EMP: 53 **EST:** 1988
SQ FT: 102,943
SALES (est): 1.2MM **Privately Held**
WEB: www.residence-inn.marriott.com
SIC: 7011 Hotels & motels

(P-16335)
BADALIAN ENTERPRISES INC
Also Called: Park Inn
1540 S Harbor Blvd, Anaheim
(92802-2312)
PHONE...................................714 635-4082
Ernest Badalian, *President*
Bonny Harutunian, *Treasurer*
Greg Badalian, *Vice Pres*
Suren Badalian, *Vice Pres*
Patricia Coomb, *Sales Staff*
EMP: 80 **EST:** 1958
SQ FT: 55,000
SALES (est): 2.2MM **Privately Held**
WEB: www.radissonhotels.com
SIC: 7011 Hotels & motels

(P-16336)
BAKERSFIELD INN INC
Also Called: Marriott
801 Truxtun Ave, Bakersfield (93301-4726)
PHONE...................................661 323-1900
Bernard E Cooke, *President*
Vanessa Emo, *Director*
EMP: 110 **EST:** 1979
SALES (est): 2.9MM **Privately Held**
WEB: www.marriott.com
SIC: 7011 Hotels & motels

(P-16337)
BALDWIN HOSPITALITY LLC
Also Called: Courtyard By Marriott
14635 Bldwin Pk Towne Ctr, Baldwin Park
(91706-5548)
PHONE...................................626 446-2988
Lina Mita, *Mng Member*
EMP: 80 **EST:** 1997
SALES (est): 4MM **Privately Held**
WEB: www.courtyard.marriott.com
SIC: 7011 Hotels & motels

(P-16338)
BALDWIN HOSPITALITY LLC
Also Called: Courtyard By Marriott
14635 Baldwin Ave, Baldwin Park
(91706-1739)
PHONE...................................626 962-6000
EMP: 80
SQ FT: 148,187
SALES (corp-wide): 4.4MM **Privately
Held**
WEB: www.sgvrad.com
SIC: 7011 Hotels And Motels, Nsk
PA: Baldwin Hospitality Llc
411 E Huntington Dr # 305
Arcadia CA 91706
626 446-2988

(P-16339)
BALLARD INN INC
2436 Baseline Ave, Solvang (93463-9711)
PHONE...................................805 688-7770
Budi Kazali, *President*
EMP: 52 **EST:** 1984
SQ FT: 9,062

SALES (est): 750.8K **Privately Held**
WEB: www.ballardinn.com
SIC: 7011 5812 Inns; eating places

(P-16340)
BEACH MTL PRTNERS A CAL LTD PR
Also Called: Harbor View Inn
28 W Cabrillo Blvd, Santa Barbara
(93101-3504)
PHONE...................................800 755-0222
Antonio R Romasanta, *Partner*
Birgit Romasanta, *Partner*
Irma Singer, *Accounting Mgr*
Martin Lopez, *Manager*
EMP: 75 **EST:** 1983
SQ FT: 40,000
SALES (est): 6.4MM **Privately Held**
WEB: www.harborviewinnsb.com
SIC: 7011 Motels

(P-16341)
BEHRINGER HARVARD WILSHIRE BLV
Also Called: Hotel Palomar
10740 Wilshire Blvd, Los Angeles
(90024-4493)
PHONE...................................310 475-8711
Ravi Sikand, *Partner*
Marco Scherer, *Manager*
EMP: 99 **EST:** 2006
SALES (est): 10MM **Privately Held**
WEB: www.kimptonhotels.com
SIC: 7011 6531 Hotels; real estate agents
& managers

(P-16342)
BELVEDERE HOTEL PARTNERSHIP
Also Called: Peninsula Beverly Hill's
9882 Santa Monica Blvd, Beverly Hills
(90212-1605)
PHONE...................................310 551-2888
Ali Kasikci, *Manager*
EMP: 442 **Privately Held**
SIC: 7011 6512 5813 5812 Hotels; non-
residential building operators; drinking
places; eating places
PA: The Belvedere Hotel Partnership
421 N Beverly Dr Ste 350
Beverly Hills CA 90210

(P-16343)
BELVEDERE PARTNERSHIP
Also Called: Peninsula Beverly Hills, The
9882 Santa Monica Blvd, Beverly Hills
(90212-1605)
PHONE...................................310 551-2888
Robert Zarnegan, *President*
Eric Linderman, *Technology*
Rossana Magat, *Credit Mgr*
Nancy Kupka, *Human Res Mgr*
Brad Miller, *Purchasing*
▲ **EMP:** 400 **EST:** 2005
SALES (est): 25.4MM **Privately Held**
SIC: 7011 Bed & breakfast inn

(P-16344)
BEST WESTERN PORTERVILLE INN
350 Montgomery Ave, Porterville
(93257-5965)
PHONE...................................559 781-7411
Larry Catalina, *Partner*
Robert Polish, *Partner*
EMP: 57 **EST:** 1992
SQ FT: 50,000
SALES (est): 1.2MM **Privately Held**
WEB: www.bestwestern.com
SIC: 7011 Hotels & motels

(P-16345)
BEST WESTERN STOVALLS INN (PA)
1110 W Katella Ave, Anaheim
(92802-2805)
PHONE...................................714 956-4430
James Stovall, *Partner*
Bill O'Connell, *Partner*
Minta Pettis-Stovall, *Partner*
Robert Stovall, *Partner*
EMP: 90 **EST:** 1966
SQ FT: 4,800

P R O D U C T S & S V C S

SALES (est): 22.4MM **Privately Held**
WEB: www.bestwestern.com
SIC: 7011 Hotels & motels

(P-16346)
BEST WSTN BSHP HLDAY SPA LODGE
1025 N Main St, Bishop (93514-2407)
PHONE......................760 873-3543
Pravin Ladd, *Partner*
Mohan Enterprises, *Partner*
EMP: 55 **EST:** 1973
SQ FT: 20,000
SALES (est): 974.5K **Privately Held**
WEB: www.bestwesternbishop.com
SIC: 7011 Hotels & motels

(P-16347)
BEST WSTN CAPISTRANO INN LLC
27174 Ortega Hwy, San Juan Capistrano (92675-2702)
PHONE......................949 493-5661
Ernest F Grether, *Partner*
EMP: 59 **EST:** 1973
SQ FT: 45,000
SALES (est): 1.5MM **Privately Held**
WEB: www.bestwestern.com
SIC: 7011 Hotels & motels

(P-16348)
BEVERLY HILLS LUXURY HOTEL LLC
1801 Century Park E # 1200, Los Angeles (90067-2334)
PHONE......................310 274-9999
Kenneth Bordewick, *Mng Member*
Ana Martinez, *Credit Mgr*
Bharath Bangalore, *Finance*
Mercedes Lucero, *Director*
EMP: 450 **EST:** 2002
SALES (est): 33MM **Privately Held**
SIC: 7011 Resort hotel; hotels

(P-16349)
BEVERLY HOLDINGS INC
9876 Wilshire Blvd, Beverly Hills (90210-3115)
PHONE......................310 274-7777
Beny Alagem, *Ch of Bd*
EMP: 123 **EST:** 1997
SALES (est): 1.1MM
SALES (corp-wide): 60.6MM **Privately Held**
WEB: www.beverlyhilton.com
SIC: 5947 5813 5812 7011 Gift shop; drinking places; eating places; hotels
PA: Oasis West Realty Llc
1800 Century Park E # 500
Los Angeles CA 90067
310 274-8066

(P-16350)
BEVERLY SUNSTONE HILLS LLC
Also Called: Residence Inn By Marriott
1177 S Beverly Dr, Los Angeles (90035-1119)
PHONE......................310 228-4100
Robert Alter, *CEO*
EMP: 55 **EST:** 2009
SALES (est): 786.3K **Privately Held**
WEB: www.beverlyhillsresidenceinn.com
SIC: 7011 Hotels & motels

(P-16351)
BICYCLE CASINO LP
Also Called: Bicycle Hotel and Casino
888 Bicycle Casino Dr, Bell Gardens (90201-7617)
PHONE......................562 806-4646
Hashem Minaiy, *General Ptnr*
Michelle Hackett, *COO*
Qian Wang, *IT/INT Sup*
Claire Markham, *Personnel Assit*
Kimberly Torres, *Marketing Mgr*
EMP: 1500 **EST:** 1984
SALES (est): 98.5MM **Privately Held**
WEB: www.thebike.com
SIC: 7011 Casino hotel

(P-16352)
BIG BEAR LAKE RESORT ASSN INC
630 Bartlett Rd, Big Bear Lake (92315)
P.O. Box 1936 (92315-1936)
PHONE......................909 866-6190
Ken Brengle, *CEO*
Ken Brengle Cce, *CEO*
EMP: 50 **EST:** 1994
SALES (est): 3MM **Privately Held**
WEB: www.bigbear.com
SIC: 7011 Resort hotel

(P-16353)
BISHOP PAIUTE GAMING CORP
Also Called: Paiute Palace Casino
2742 N Sierra Hwy, Bishop (93514-2218)
P.O. Box 1325 (93515-1325)
PHONE......................760 872-6005
Gloriana Bailey, *President*
Arlene Stone, *Agent*
EMP: 135 **EST:** 1995
SALES (est): 9.8MM **Privately Held**
WEB: www.paiutegaming.com
SIC: 7011 Casino hotel

(P-16354)
BLACK OAKS INC
Also Called: Best Wstn Black Oak Mtr Lodge
1135 24th St, Paso Robles (93446-1309)
P.O. Box 486 (93447-0486)
PHONE......................805 238-2392
Shirley Masia, *President*
Mat Masia, *Vice Pres*
Angela McKee, *General Mgr*
Linda Pacheco, *Admin Sec*
EMP: 60 **EST:** 1961
SALES (est): 2.3MM **Privately Held**
WEB: www.bestwesternblackoak.com
SIC: 7011 Motel, franchised

(P-16355)
BRISAM LAX (DE) LLC
Also Called: Holiday Inn
9901 S La Cienega Blvd, Los Angeles (90045-5915)
PHONE......................310 649-5151
Steve Hostetter, *General Mgr*
David Romero, *Sales Mgr*
Joyce Camou, *Sales Staff*
Joann Endow, *Sales Staff*
Rodolfo Gutierrez, *Director*
EMP: 95 **EST:** 2007
SALES (est): 4.7MM **Privately Held**
WEB: www.holidayinn.com
SIC: 7011 Hotels & motels

(P-16356)
BURBANK PARTNERS LLC
Also Called: Courtyard By Marriott
15433 Ventura Blvd, Sherman Oaks (91403-3003)
PHONE......................818 263-8704
Keith Wolff,
Adam Keller,
EMP: 93 **EST:** 1968
SALES (est): 2.3MM **Privately Held**
WEB: www.courtyard.marriott.com
SIC: 7011 5813 5812 7299 Hotels & motels; cocktail lounge; eating places; banquet hall facilities

(P-16357)
BURTON WAY HOTELS LLC
Also Called: Four Seasons Hotels Limited
300 S Doheny Dr, Los Angeles (90048-3704)
PHONE......................310 273-2222
Isadore Sharp, *Chairman*
Rosemar Christopher, *Vice Pres*
Mohamed Elbanna, *Vice Pres*
Sean Dunlevy, *Security Dir*
Laura Castonguay, *General Mgr*
EMP: 80 **EST:** 2015
SALES (est): 16.5MM **Privately Held**
SIC: 7011 Hotels

(P-16358)
BURTON WAY HTELS LTD A CAL LTD (PA)
Also Called: Four Seasons Hotel
2029 Century Park E # 2200, Los Angeles (90067-2901)
PHONE......................310 552-6623
Susan Cohen, *General Ptnr*

Ernest Cohen, *General Ptnr*
▲ **EMP:** 50 **EST:** 1985
SALES (est): 26.6MM **Privately Held**
SIC: 7011 Hotels

(P-16359)
BURTON-WAY HOUSE LTD A CA
Also Called: Four Seasons Hotel
2 Dole Dr, Westlake Village (91362-7300)
PHONE......................805 214-8075
Robert Cohen, *Branch Mgr*
Christine Oliver, *Executive Asst*
Julius Santos, *Marketing Staff*
Edgar Bautista, *Director*
Brian Leighton, *Manager*
EMP: 215
SALES (corp-wide): 26.6MM **Privately Held**
SIC: 7011 Hotels
PA: Burton Way Hotels, Ltd., A California
Limited Partnership
2029 Century Park E # 2200
Los Angeles CA 90067
310 552-6623

(P-16360)
BURTON-WAY HOUSE LTD A CA
Also Called: Four Seasons Hotel
300 S Doheny Dr, Los Angeles (90048-3704)
PHONE......................310 273-2222
Mehdi Efpekari, *General Mgr*
EMP: 215
SALES (corp-wide): 26.6MM **Privately Held**
SIC: 7011 5812 Hotels; eating places
PA: Burton Way Hotels, Ltd., A California
Limited Partnership
2029 Century Park E # 2200
Los Angeles CA 90067
310 552-6623

(P-16361)
BW HOTEL LLC
Also Called: Buffalo Wild Wings
9500 Wilshire Blvd, Beverly Hills (90212-2405)
PHONE......................310 275-5200
Kathleen Taylor, *CEO*
▲ **EMP:** 820 **EST:** 1928
SALES (est): 82.5MM **Privately Held**
WEB: www.buffalowildwings.com
SIC: 5812 7011 Grills (eating places); hotels & motels

(P-16362)
BY THE BLUE SEA LLC
Also Called: Shutters On The Beach
1 Pico Blvd, Santa Monica (90405-1063)
PHONE......................310 458-0030
Tim Dubois, *President*
Klaus Mennekes, *Vice Pres*
Levar SAI, *Asst Director*
Ruben Hernandez, *Manager*
Beatrice Lamhene, *Manager*
EMP: 350 **EST:** 2001
SALES (est): 28MM **Privately Held**
WEB: www.shuttersonthebeach.com
SIC: 7011 Hotels

(P-16363)
C W HOTELS LTD
Also Called: JW Marriott Le Merigot
1740 Ocean Ave, Santa Monica (90401-3214)
PHONE......................310 395-9700
Damien Hirsch, *General Mgr*
Paul Hortobagyi, *Manager*
EMP: 150
SALES (corp-wide): 12.3MM **Privately Held**
WEB: www.marriott.com
SIC: 7011 Hotels & motels
PA: C W Hotels Ltd
740 Centre View Blvd
Crestview Hills KY 41017
859 578-1100

(P-16364)
CABAZON BAND MISSION INDIANS
Fantasy Spring Resort Casino
84245 Indio Springs Dr, Indio (92203-3405)
PHONE......................760 342-5000
Jim McCannon, *Manager*
EMP: 520 **Privately Held**
WEB: www.fantasyspringsresort.com
SIC: 7011 Casino hotel
PA: Cabazon Band Of Mission Indians
84245 Indio Springs Dr
Indio CA 92203

(P-16365)
CALIFORNIA COMMERCE CLUB INC
Also Called: Commerce Casino
6131 Telegraph Rd, Commerce (90040-2501)
PHONE......................323 721-2100
Haig Papaian, *CEO*
Dante Oliveto, *CFO*
Harvey Ross, *Vice Pres*
Andrew Schneiderman, *Vice Pres*
Ralph Wong, *Vice Pres*
▲ **EMP:** 2600
SQ FT: 350,000
SALES (est): 126.3MM **Privately Held**
WEB: www.commercecasino.com
SIC: 7011 5812 Casino hotel; eating places

(P-16366)
CANDLEBERRY PROPERTIES LP
Also Called: AC Hotel Beverly Hills
6399 Wilshire Blvd, Los Angeles (90048-5703)
PHONE......................323 852-7000
Jack Nourafshan, *Managing Prtnr*
EMP: 50 **EST:** 1994
SQ FT: 100,000
SALES (est): 31.2K **Privately Held**
WEB: www.ac-hotels.marriott.com
SIC: 7011 Hotels

(P-16367)
CARPENTERS SOUTHWEST ADM CORP (PA)
533 S Fremont Ave, Los Angeles (90071-1712)
P.O. Box 17969 (90017-0969)
PHONE......................213 386-8590
Douglas McCarron, *CEO*
Eddy Navarro, *Info Tech Mer*
Sandra Maloney, *Project Mgr*
Anthony Nickell, *Technology*
Kristin Tingley, *Manager*
EMP: 70 **EST:** 1982
SQ FT: 25,000
SALES (est): 45.9MM **Privately Held**
WEB: www.carpenterssw.org
SIC: 7011 Hotels & motels

(P-16368)
CARPINTERIA MOTOR INN INC
Also Called: Best Western
4558 Carpinteria Ave, Carpinteria (93013-1863)
PHONE......................805 684-0473
Kevin Sweniak, *General Mgr*
EMP: 50 **EST:** 1986
SALES (est): 1.9MM **Privately Held**
WEB: www.carpinteriainnow.com
SIC: 7011 Hotels & motels

(P-16369)
CARSON OPERATING COMPANY LLC
Also Called: Doubletree By Hilton Carson
2 Civic Plaza Dr, Carson (90745-2231)
PHONE......................310 830-9200
Greg Guthrie, *General Mgr*
Leroy Russell, *Controller*
EMP: 90 **EST:** 2015
SALES (est): 2.7MM **Privately Held**
WEB: www.hilton.com
SIC: 7011 Hotels

(P-16370)
CASTLE INN INC
1734 S Harbor Blvd, Anaheim
(92802-2316)
PHONE....................855 214-3079
Bharat Patel, *President*
Purushottam R Patel, *Shareholder*
Donna Hill, *General Mgr*
Ashik Patel, *Info Tech Mgr*
Jarett Rodriguez, *Facilities Mgr*
EMP: 77 EST: 1987
SQ FT: 120,000
SALES (est): 6.9MM **Privately Held**
WEB: www.castleinn.com
SIC: 7011 Motels

(P-16371)
CAVALIER INN INCORPORATED
Also Called: Best Western
250 San Simeon Ave Ste 4c, San Simeon
(93452-9715)
PHONE....................805 927-6444
Michael R Hanchett, *President*
Barbara J Hanchett, *CFO*
Barbara Hanchett, *CFO*
EMP: 89 EST: 1968
SALES (est): 775.6K **Privately Held**
WEB: www.cavalierresort.com
SIC: 7011 Hotels & motels

(P-16372)
CAVALIER INN INC
Also Called: Cavalier Oceanfront Resort
9415 Hearst Dr, San Simeon (93452-9724)
PHONE....................805 927-4688
Mona Rigdon, *Principal*
Barb Hanchett, *CFO*
Michael Hanchett, *Principal*
Lu Fletcher, *Exec Dir*
EMP: 80 EST: 2016
SALES (est): 2.4MM **Privately Held**
WEB: www.cavalierresort.com
SIC: 7011 Motels

(P-16373)
CELEBRITY CASINOS INC
Also Called: Crystal Casino & Hotel
123 E Artesia Blvd, Compton (90220-4921)
PHONE....................310 631-3838
Mark A Kelegian, *President*
Haig Kelegian Jr, *CEO*
Joyce Sun, *Controller*
Emily Irving, *Legal Staff*
EMP: 400 EST: 2005
SQ FT: 190,000
SALES (est): 19.4MM **Privately Held**
WEB: www.thecrystalcasino.com
SIC: 7011 Casino hotel

(P-16374)
CENTURY NATIONAL PROPERTIES (PA)
Also Called: Daytona Surfise
12200 Sylvan St Ste 250, North Hollywood
(91606-3229)
PHONE....................818 760-0880
Weldon Wilson, *President*
Judith Osborne, *Treasurer*
Marie Balicki, *Admin Sec*
EMP: 61 EST: 1983
SQ FT: 92,000
SALES (est): 5.2MM **Privately Held**
WEB: www.crowneplaza.com
SIC: 7011 Hotels & motels

(P-16375)
CENTURY WILSHIRE INC
Also Called: Century Wilshire Hotel
9400 Culver Blvd, Culver City
(90232-2617)
PHONE....................310 558-9400
Theodora Mallick, *President*
Monika Mallick, *Corp Secy*
Maya Mallick, *Vice Pres*
Virginie Rogers, *Controller*
London Doby, *Human Resources*
EMP: 60 EST: 1970
SQ FT: 38,000
SALES (est): 8.8MM **Privately Held**
WEB: www.theculverhotel.com
SIC: 7011 Resort hotel; hotels

(P-16376)
CHA LA MIRADA LLC
Also Called: Holiday Inn La Mirada
14299 Firestone Blvd, La Mirada
(90638-5523)
PHONE....................714 739-8500
Regina Stryker, *Principal*
Jay Macaluso, *Principal*
Richard Choi, *General Mgr*
Ahmed Quintana, *Finance*
Marissa Ojeda, *Human Res Mgr*
EMP: 120 EST: 1984 **Privately Held**
WEB: www.holidayinn.com
SIC: 7011 Hotels & motels

(P-16377)
CHAMSON MANAGEMENT INC
Also Called: Doubletree Hotel
7 Hutton Centre Dr, Santa Ana
(92707-5753)
PHONE....................714 751-2400
Jung-Hsiung Chiu, *President*
Magaly Marquez, *Accounting Mgr*
Michelle Van Winkle, *Sales Mgr*
EMP: 54 EST: 1994
SALES (est): 1.6MM **Privately Held**
WEB: www.hilton.com
SIC: 7011 Hotels & motels

(P-16378)
CHARLES TING
Also Called: Comfort Inn
2815 Santa Monica Blvd, Santa Monica
(90404-2409)
PHONE....................310 828-5517
Charles Ting, *Partner*
TAC Nahn, *Controller*
Lois Sajarder, *Manager*
EMP: 134 EST: 1977
SQ FT: 15,200
SALES (est): 1.2MM **Privately Held**
WEB: www.comfortinnsantamonica.com
SIC: 7011 Hotels & motels

(P-16379)
CHATHAM MDR LLC
Also Called: Hilton Grdn Inn Marina Del Rey
4200 Admiralty Way, Marina Del Rey
(90292-5422)
PHONE....................310 301-2000
Gregg Forde, *Principal*
Triin Botero, *Principal*
EMP: 50 EST: 2015
SALES (est): 994.9K **Privately Held**
WEB: www.hilton.com
SIC: 7011 Hotels & motels

(P-16380)
CHEN & HUANG PARTNERS LP
Also Called: Travelodge
1400 S Bristol St, Santa Ana (92704-3426)
PHONE....................714 557-8700
James Chen, *Partner*
Yi-Ho Huang, *Partner*
EMP: 58 EST: 1978
SQ FT: 50,000
SALES (est): 927.4K **Privately Held**
WEB: www.wyndhamhotels.com
SIC: 7011 Hotels & motels

(P-16381)
CIM GROUP LP (PA)
Also Called: Commercial Inv MGT Group
4700 Wilshire Blvd Ste 1, Los Angeles
(90010-3854)
PHONE....................323 860-4900
Avraham Shemesch, *Partner*
Eric P Rubenfeld, *Partner*
Matthew Courtney, *Assoc VP*
Victoria Entine, *Assoc VP*
Justin Evans, *Assoc VP*
EMP: 248 EST: 2000
SALES (est): 217.8MM **Privately Held**
WEB: www.cimgroup.com
SIC: 7011 6798 6552 Hotels & motels;
real estate investment trusts; land subdi-
viders & developers, commercial

(P-16382)
CINDERELLA MOTEL
Also Called: Candy Cane Inn
1747 S Harbor Blvd, Anaheim
(92802-2315)
PHONE....................559 432-0118
Ralph Kazarian, *President*
Rigo Hernandez, *Office Mgr*

EMP: 81
SQ FT: 65,542
SALES (corp-wide): 7.5MM **Privately Held**
SIC: 7011 Motels
PA: Cinderella Motel
2416 W Shaw Ave Ste 109
Fresno CA 93711
559 432-0118

(P-16383)
CITRUS NORTH VENTURE LLC
6591 Collins Dr Ste E11, Moorpark
(93021-1493)
PHONE....................256 428-2000
Marc Pierguidi, *Admin Sec*
EMP: 99 EST: 2017
SALES (est): 1.3MM **Privately Held**
SIC: 7011 Hotel, franchised

(P-16384)
CLEAR GROUP INC
408 N Avalon Blvd, Los Angeles
(90074-0001)
PHONE....................603 325-5600
Chris Barone, *Branch Mgr*
EMP: 71
SALES (corp-wide): 487.7K **Privately Held**
SIC: 7011 Resort hotel
PA: The Clear Group Inc
1069 E Wardlow Rd
Long Beach CA

(P-16385)
CNI THL PROPCO FE LLC
Also Called: Four Points Bakersfield
5101 California Ave, Bakersfield
(93309-1623)
PHONE....................661 325-9700
Keon Marvasti,
Lori La Bare, *Director*
EMP: 80 EST: 2017
SALES (est): 3.6MM **Privately Held**
SIC: 7011 Hotels & motels

(P-16386)
COLONY PALMS HOTEL LLC
572 N Indian Canyon Dr, Palm Springs
(92262-6030)
PHONE....................760 969-1800
Al Wertheimer, *Principal*
Arturo Ramirez, *Facilities Dir*
EMP: 70 EST: 2011
SALES (est): 6.4MM **Privately Held**
WEB: www.colonypalmshotel.com
SIC: 7011 Resort hotel; hotels

(P-16387)
COMFORT CALIFORNIA INC
Also Called: Clarion Hotel
616 W Convention Way, Anaheim
(92802-3401)
PHONE....................714 750-3131
Mike Thomas, *Branch Mgr*
Kenny Scoby, *General Mgr*
Cathy Dutton, *Sales Dir*
EMP: 149
SALES (corp-wide): 91.4MM **Privately Held**
WEB: www.choicehotels.com
SIC: 7011 Hotels & motels
HQ: Comfort California, Inc.
8171 Maple Lawn Blvd # 380
Fulton MD 20759

(P-16388)
CONESTOGA HOTEL
Also Called: Holiday Inn
1240 S Walnut St, Anaheim (92802-2241)
PHONE....................714 535-0300
Kevin Clayton, *General Mgr*
Mark Nunneley, *CFO*
Tom Van Winkle, *General Mgr*
▲ EMP: 51 EST: 1980
SQ FT: 150,000
SALES (est): 1.9MM **Privately Held**
WEB: www.holidayinn.com
SIC: 7011 5812 5813 Hotels & motels;
American restaurant; drinking places

(P-16389)
CORE MONROVIA LLC
Also Called: Courtyard By Marriott
700 W Huntington Dr, Monrovia
(91016-3104)
PHONE....................626 357-5211
Steven Smith, *Mng Member*
Norma Castaneda, *Controller*
EMP: 127 EST: 2004
SQ FT: 100,000
SALES (est): 2.6MM **Privately Held**
WEB: www.courtyard.marriott.com
SIC: 7011 Hotels & motels

(P-16390)
COUNTRY SIDE INN ONTARIO LP
Also Called: Ayres Hotel Barstow
2812 Lenwood Rd, Barstow (92311-9589)
PHONE....................909 390-7778
Don Ayres Jr,
Mathew Hildebrant,
Gregg Kleminsky,
EMP: 51 EST: 1994
SALES (est): 317.3K **Privately Held**
WEB: www.ayreshotels.com
SIC: 7011 Hotels

(P-16391)
COURTYARD BY MARRIOTT
500 E 1st St, Long Beach (90802-5024)
PHONE....................562 435-8511
Doug Smith, *Principal*
Rudy Arroyo, *Chief Engr*
EMP: 64 EST: 1994
SALES (est): 2.4MM **Privately Held**
WEB: www.courtyard.marriott.com
SIC: 7011 Hotels & motels

(P-16392)
COURTYARD BY MARRIOTT/LAX
6161 W Century Blvd, Los Angeles
(90045-5310)
PHONE....................310 981-2350
Patricia Marks, *Finance*
Jacob Reed, *Agent*
EMP: 63 EST: 2010
SALES (est): 2.6MM **Privately Held**
WEB: www.courtyard.marriott.com
SIC: 7011 Hotels & motels

(P-16393)
COURTYARD MANAGEMENT CORP
Also Called: Courtyard By Marriott Irvine
7955 Irvine Center Dr, Irvine (92618-3207)
PHONE....................949 453-1033
Audun Poulsen, *General Mgr*
EMP: 70
SALES (corp-wide): 10.5B **Publicly Held**
WEB: www.courtyard.marriott.com
SIC: 7011 Hotels & motels
HQ: Courtyard Management Corporation
10400 Fernwood Rd
Bethesda MD 20817

(P-16394)
COURTYARD MANAGEMENT CORP
Also Called: Courtyard By Marriott
2633 Sepulveda Blvd, Torrance
(90505-2963)
PHONE....................310 533-8000
David Zimmerman, *Principal*
Sandy Tanaka, *Planning*
EMP: 51 EST: 2007
SALES (est): 1.4MM **Privately Held**
WEB: www.courtyard.marriott.com
SIC: 7011 Hotels & motels

(P-16395)
COURTYARD MANAGEMENT CORP
Also Called: Courtyard By Marriott
1905 S Azusa Ave, Hacienda Heights
(91745-6850)
PHONE....................626 965-1700
Michael Sweany, *Principal*
EMP: 70 EST: 2007
SALES (est): 4.6MM **Privately Held**
WEB: www.courtyard.marriott.com
SIC: 7011 Hotels & motels

(P-16396)
COURTYARD OXNARD
600 E Esplanade Dr, Oxnard (93036-2480)
PHONE..................................805 988-3600
Patricia Tewes, General Mgr
EMP: 80 **EST:** 2009
SALES (est): 1.7MM **Privately Held**
SIC: 7011 Hotels & motels

(P-16397)
CPH MONARCH HOTEL LLC
Also Called: Waldorf Astria Mnrc Bch Rsort
1 Monarch Beach Resort, Dana Point
(92629-4085)
PHONE..................................949 234-3200
Paul Makarechian, President
Nicole Sutter, Chairman
▲ **EMP:** 1100 **EST:** 2001
SQ FT: 300,000
SALES (est): 60.8MM
SALES (corp-wide): 102.1MM **Privately Held**
WEB:
www.waldorfastoriamonarchbeach.com
SIC: 7011 Resort hotel
PA: Waldorf Astoria Management Llc
7930 Jones Branch Dr # 1100
Mc Lean VA 22102
703 883-1000

(P-16398)
CRESCENT HOTEL
403 N Crescent Dr, Beverly Hills
(90210-4889)
PHONE..................................310 247-0505
Gregg Teck, President
Emily Meyers, Marketing Staff
Winston Johnson, Sales Staff
EMP: 67 **EST:** 1940
SALES (est): 2.3MM **Privately Held**
WEB: www.crescentbh.com
SIC: 7011 8741 Hotels; management services

(P-16399)
CRESTLINE HOTELS & RESORTS INC (HQ)
Also Called: Kyoto Grand Hotel and Gardens
120 S Los Angeles St 11, Los Angeles
(90012-3724)
PHONE..................................213 629-1200
Richard Gaines, General Mgr
Joe Kuhn, General Mgr
Samuel Reece, Opers Staff
EMP: 130 **EST:** 1974
SALES (est): 9.4MM
SALES (corp-wide): 570.1MM **Privately Held**
WEB: www.kyotograndhotel.com
SIC: 7011 5812 5813 Hotels; restaurant, family: independent; drinking places
PA: Crestline Hotels & Resorts, Llc
3950 University Dr # 301
Fairfax VA 22030
571 529-6100

(P-16400)
CROWN PLZ HT AT CMMERCE CASINO
Also Called: Crowne Plz Ht Commerce Casino
6121 Telegraph Rd, Commerce
(90040-2501)
PHONE..................................323 728-3600
Joseph Zarrahy, Manager
Ingrid DOE, Opers Staff
Susan Hanson, Marketing Staff
EMP: 51 **EST:** 1999
SALES (est): 5.5MM **Privately Held**
WEB: www.crowneplaza.com
SIC: 7011 7999 Casino hotel; card rooms

(P-16401)
CRP CENTINELA LP
Also Called: Doubltree Los Angeles Westside
6161 W Centinela Ave, Culver City
(90230-6306)
PHONE..................................901 821-4117
Larry M Mills, Partner
EMP: 64 **EST:** 2008
SALES (est): 77.4MM
SALES (corp-wide): 2.9B **Publicly Held**
WEB: www.carlyle.com
SIC: 7011 Hotels & motels

HQ: The Carlyle Group Inc
1001 Pennsylvania Ave Nw 220s
Washington DC 20004
202 729-5626

(P-16402)
CTC GROUP INC (DH)
Also Called: Doubletree Hotel
21333 Hawthorne Blvd, Torrance
(90503-5602)
PHONE..................................310 540-0500
John Huang, CEO
EMP: 145 **EST:** 1989
SALES (est): 39.6MM
SALES (corp-wide): 852MM **Publicly Held**
WEB: www.hilton.com
SIC: 7011 Hotels & motels

(P-16403)
CUSTOM HOTEL LLC
Also Called: Hotel June, The
8639 Lincoln Blvd, Los Angeles
(90045-3503)
PHONE..................................310 645-0400
Thomas Gottlieb,
Alisa Matthews, General Mgr
Jerry Peck, Controller
EMP: 899 **EST:** 2005
SALES (est): 3.3MM
SALES (corp-wide): 138.4MM **Privately Held**
WEB: www.thehoteljune.com
SIC: 7011 Hotels
PA: Joie De Vivre Hospitality, Llc
1750 Geary Blvd
San Francisco CA 94115
415 922-6000

(P-16404)
DAVIDSON HOTEL PARTNERS LP
Also Called: Agoura Hills Renaissance Hotel
30100 Agoura Rd, Agoura Hills
(91301-2004)
PHONE..................................818 707-1220
Larry Mills, Partner
EMP: 1477 **Privately Held**
WEB: www.davidsonhospitality.com
SIC: 7011 Hotels & motels
PA: Davidson Hotel Partners, L.P
1 Ravinia Dr Ste 1600
Atlanta GA 30346

(P-16405)
DESTINATION RESIDENCES LLC
Also Called: Shadow Mtn Rsort Rcquet CLB Tn
45750 San Luis Rey Ave, Palm Desert
(92260-4728)
PHONE..................................760 346-4647
Sindy Calhoun, Manager
EMP: 224
SALES (corp-wide): 935.4MM **Privately Held**
WEB: www.destinationhotels.com
SIC: 7011 5699 6531 Resort hotel; sports apparel; condominium manager
HQ: Destination Residences Llc
10333 E Dry Creek Rd
Englewood CO 80112
303 799-3830

(P-16406)
DIAMOND RESORTS LLC
Also Called: Palm Canyon Resort & Spa
2800 S Palm Canyon Dr, Palm Springs
(92264-9337)
PHONE..................................760 866-1800
Allison Wickerham, Mng Member
Lila Carrabus, Chief Mktg Ofcr
Carl Ellis, Principal
Carlos Botello, Engineer
Kate Anderson, Pub Rel Dir
EMP: 100 **EST:** 2004
SALES (est): 300K **Privately Held**
WEB: www.thepalmcanyonresort.com
SIC: 7011 5812 7991 Resort hotel; American restaurant; spas

(P-16407)
DISNEY ENTERPRISES INC
1150 W Magic Way, Anaheim (92802-2247)
PHONE..................................714 778-6600
Michael D Eisner, President

Kelli Bazen, Executive
Weita Jimmy, Executive
Lorea Powell, Admin Asst
Deborah Emerick, Sales Staff
EMP: 3500
SALES (corp-wide): 65.3B **Publicly Held**
WEB: www.en.disneyme.com
SIC: 7011 Resort hotel
HQ: Disney Enterprises, Inc.
500 S Buena Vista St
Burbank CA 91521
818 560-1000

(P-16408)
DISNEYLAND INTERNATIONAL
1580 S Disneyland Dr, Anaheim
(92802-2294)
PHONE..................................714 956-6746
EMP: 6842
SALES (corp-wide): 65.3B **Publicly Held**
WEB: www.disneyland.disney.go.com
SIC: 7011 Resort hotel
HQ: Disneyland International
1313 S Harbor Blvd
Anaheim CA 92802
714 781-4565

(P-16409)
DISNEYLAND RESORT (DH)
1313 S Harbor Blvd, Anaheim
(92802-2309)
P.O. Box 4708 (92803-4708)
PHONE..................................714 781-4000
Micheal Colglazier, President
Ken Potrock, President
Rudy Arellanes, Officer
Cheryl Pangborn, Officer
Candice Evans, Vice Pres
▲ **EMP:** 148 **EST:** 2011
SALES (est): 44.5MM
SALES (corp-wide): 65.3B **Publicly Held**
WEB: www.thewaltdisneycompany.com
SIC: 7011 Resort hotel

(P-16410)
DJONT OPERATIONS LLC
Also Called: Embassy Suites - Lax Airport S
1440 E Imperial Ave, El Segundo
(90245-2623)
PHONE..................................310 640-3600
Shar Franklin, General Mgr
EMP: 120
SALES (corp-wide): 473MM **Privately Held**
WEB: www.hilton.com
SIC: 7011 Hotels & motels
HQ: Djont Operations, L.L.C.
125 E Houston St
San Antonio TX 78205

(P-16411)
DJONT/JPM HSPTLITY LSG SPE LLC
Also Called: Embassy Stes - Mndlay Bch Rsor
2101 Mandalay Beach Rd, Oxnard
(93035-3638)
PHONE..................................805 984-2500
Colleen Huther, General Mgr
EMP: 51
SALES (corp-wide): 473MM **Privately Held**
WEB: www.hilton.com
SIC: 7011 Hotels
HQ: Djont/Jpm Hospitality Leasing (Spe), L.L.C.
400 Arch St
Philadelphia PA 19106

(P-16412)
DJONT/JPM HSPTLITY LSG SPE LLC
Also Called: Wyndham - Santa Monica
120 Colorado Ave, Santa Monica
(90401-2316)
PHONE..................................310 451-0676
Rebecca Kirisits, General Mgr
EMP: 51
SQ FT: 64,780
SALES (corp-wide): 473MM **Privately Held**
WEB: www.phillydowntownhotel.com
SIC: 7011 Hotels

HQ: Djont/Jpm Hospitality Leasing (Spe), L.L.C.
400 Arch St
Philadelphia PA 19106

(P-16413)
DKN HOTEL LLC (PA)
42 Corporate Park Ste 200, Irvine
(92606-3104)
PHONE..................................714 427-4320
Kiran Patel, CEO
Nilesh Patel, Co-Owner
John Jorgensen, Vice Pres
Bhalesh Gandhi, Controller
Brian Benavidez, Sales Mgr
EMP: 290 **EST:** 2002
SQ FT: 4,000
SALES (est): 38.6MM **Privately Held**
WEB: www.dknhotels.com
SIC: 7011 Hotels & motels

(P-16414)
DNC PRKS RSORTS AT SEQUOIA INC
Also Called: Sequoia National Park
64740 Wuksachi Way, Seq Natl Pk
(93262-9604)
PHONE..................................559 565-4070
Joe St Laurent, CEO
James W Houser, President
Dennis J Szefel, President
Andy Grinsfelder, CEO
Janice R Trybus, Admin Sec
EMP: 71 **EST:** 1998
SALES (est): 24.5MM
SALES (corp-wide): 2.9B **Privately Held**
WEB: www.visitsequoia.com
SIC: 7011 Resort hotel
HQ: Delaware North Companies Parks & Resorts, Inc.
250 Delaware Ave Ste 3
Buffalo NY 14202

(P-16415)
DOLPHIN BAY HT & RESIDENCE INC
Also Called: Dolphin Bay Hotel & Residences
2727 Shell Beach Rd, Shell Beach
(93449-1602)
PHONE..................................805 773-4300
Richard J Loughead Jr, CEO
Christina Stieb, Marketing Staff
Krysta Faulkner, Manager
EMP: 90 **EST:** 2005
SALES (est): 5.3MM **Privately Held**
WEB: www.thedolphinbay.com
SIC: 7011 Hostels; hotels

(P-16416)
DONALD T STERLING CORPORATION
Also Called: Beverly Hills Plaza Hotel
10300 Wilshire Blvd, Los Angeles
(90024-4772)
PHONE..................................310 275-5575
Zair Caceres, Branch Mgr
EMP: 80
SALES (corp-wide): 28MM **Privately Held**
SIC: 7011 Hotels
PA: Donald T. Sterling Corporation
9441 Wilshire Blvd Prthuse Penthouse
Beverly Hills CA 90212
310 278-8000

(P-16417)
DOUBLETREE HOTEL
888 Montebello Blvd, Rosemead
(91770-4303)
PHONE..................................323 722-8800
Ying Ming Huang, Partner
Katy Huang, Executive
EMP: 58 **EST:** 1992
SQ FT: 110,000
SALES (est): 5MM **Privately Held**
WEB: www.doubletreewoodalehotel.com
SIC: 7011 Hotels & motels

(P-16418)
DOUBLTREE BY HLTON HT MONROVIA
924 W Huntington Dr, Monrovia
(91016-3112)
PHONE..................................626 357-1900
Jessi Willis, *Principal*
EMP: 114 **EST:** 2010
SALES (est): 2.1MM **Privately Held**
WEB: www.hilton.com
SIC: 7011 Hotels

(P-16419)
DOUBLTREE SUITES BY HILTON LLC
Also Called: Doubletree Hotel
2085 S Harbor Blvd, Anaheim
(92802-3513)
PHONE..................................714 750-3000
Amrit K Patel,
Subhabrata Roy, *General Mgr*
Christopher Neilson, *Technology*
Frank Aguilar, *Chief Engr*
William R O'Connell,
EMP: 175 **EST:** 2000
SALES (est): 8.8MM **Privately Held**
WEB: www.doubletreeanaheim.com
SIC: 7011 5812 Hotels & motels; American restaurant

(P-16420)
DT ONTRIO HT PRTNERS LSSEE LLC
Also Called: Doubltree By Hlton Ontrio Arpr
222 N Vineyard Ave, Ontario (91764-4428)
PHONE..................................909 937-0900
Bassam Shahin, *President*
EMP: 255 **EST:** 2016
SALES (est): 10.4MM **Privately Held**
WEB: www.hilton.com
SIC: 7011 Hotels & motels

(P-16421)
DTRS SANTA MONICA LLC
Also Called: Loews Santa Monica Beach Hotel
1700 Ocean Ave, Santa Monica
(90401-3214)
PHONE..................................310 458-6700
Younes Atolah, *General Mgr*
Kerri Metcalf, *Exec Dir*
Serene Kuramarohit, *Research*
Julio Ruiz, *Engineer*
Dunia Blanco, *Finance*
EMP: 300 **EST:** 1989
SQ FT: 300,000
SALES (est): 15MM **Privately Held**
WEB: www.loewshotels.com
SIC: 7011 Resort hotel; hotels

(P-16422)
DUTT HOSPITALITY GROUP INC
Also Called: Hampton Inn
74900 Gerald Ford Dr, Palm Desert
(92211-2081)
PHONE..................................760 340-1001
Poornima C Bhakta, *President*
Pinank Bhakta, *Manager*
EMP: 58 **EST:** 2000
SALES (est): 2MM **Privately Held**
WEB: www.hilton.com
SIC: 7011 Hotels & motels

(P-16423)
E H SUMMIT INC (PA)
Also Called: Luxe Sunset Boulevard Hotel
11461 W Sunset Blvd, Los Angeles
(90049-2031)
PHONE..................................310 476-6571
Efrem Harkhan, *CEO*
Bianca Barga, *Vice Pres*
Houssem Tasco, *Managing Dir*
Julie Sevilla, *Marketing Staff*
Israel Hernandez,
EMP: 60 **EST:** 1945
SALES (est): 20.6MM **Privately Held**
SIC: 7011 Hotels

(P-16424)
EAGLE MOUNTAIN CASINO
681 Suth Tule Rsrvtion Rd, Porterville
(93258)
P.O. Box 1659 (93258-1659)
PHONE..................................559 788-6220
Tom Stewart, *Principal*

Daniel Ledesma, *Info Tech Mgr*
Jeff Thett, *Database Admin*
Brandi Clark, *Training Spec*
Tiffani Sahagun, *Opers Staff*
EMP: 164 **EST:** 2007
SALES (est): 11.3MM **Privately Held**
WEB: www.eaglemtncasino.com
SIC: 7011 Casino hotel

(P-16425)
EAGLE TRS 1 LLC ✪
3100 E Frontera St, Anaheim (92806-2820)
PHONE..................................657 439-0060
Naveen Kakarla,
EMP: 55 **EST:** 2021
SALES (est): 713.9K **Privately Held**
SIC: 7011 Hotel, franchised

(P-16426)
EDWARD THOMAS COMPANIES
Also Called: Jolly Roger Inn
640 W Katella Ave, Anaheim (92802-3411)
PHONE..................................714 782-7500
Fred Kokash, *Branch Mgr*
EMP: 110
SALES (corp-wide): 9.6MM **Privately Held**
WEB: www.edwardthomasco.com
SIC: 7011 5812 Hotels & motels; eating places
PA: The Edward Thomas Companies
9950 Santa Monica Blvd
Beverly Hills CA 90212
310 859-9366

(P-16427)
EDWARD THOMAS HOSPITALITY CORP
Also Called: Shutters On The Beach
1 Pico Blvd, Santa Monica (90405-1063)
PHONE..................................310 458-0030
Klaus Mennekes, *Vice Pres*
Cyndi Enriquez, *Executive Asst*
Janet English, *Sales Staff*
Melissa Perez, *Director*
Alessa Kim, *Manager*
EMP: 349
SALES (corp-wide): 15.3MM **Privately Held**
WEB: www.edwardthomasco.com
SIC: 7011 5812 7991 5813 Hotels; eating places; physical fitness facilities; drinking places
PA: The Edward Thomas Hospitality Corp
9950 Santa Monica Blvd
Beverly Hills CA 90212
310 859-9366

(P-16428)
EL CENTRO HOSPITALITY LLC
Also Called: Fairfield Inn
503 E Danenberg Dr, El Centro
(92243-8507)
PHONE..................................760 353-2600
Clarissa Clark, *Principal*
EMP: 168
SALES (corp-wide): 590.1K **Privately Held**
WEB: www.fairfield.marriott.com
SIC: 7011 Hotels & motels
PA: El Centro Hospitality, L.L.C.
2300 Tower Dr
Monroe LA 71201
318 325-5561

(P-16429)
EL CENTRO HOSPITALITY 2 LLC
Also Called: TownePlace Suites El Centro
3003 S Dogwood Rd, El Centro
(92243-9160)
PHONE..................................760 370-3800
Dewey F Weaver Jr, *Branch Mgr*
EMP: 226
SALES (corp-wide): 912.4K **Privately Held**
WEB: www.marriott.com
SIC: 7011 Hotel, franchised
PA: El Centro Hospitality 2, L.L.C.
2390 Tower Dr
Monroe LA 71201
318 325-5561

(P-16430)
EL DORADO ENTERPRISES INC
Also Called: Hustler Casino
1000 W Redondo Beach Blvd, Gardena
(90247-4192)
PHONE..................................310 719-9800
Larry C Flynt, *CEO*
Tom Candy, *General Mgr*
Alyona Konova, *Info Tech Dir*
John Villarama, *Graphic Designe*
Lydell Hall MBA, *Controller*
EMP: 760 **EST:** 2000
SALES (est): 47.6MM **Privately Held**
WEB: www.hustlercasino.com
SIC: 7011 Casino hotel

(P-16431)
EL ENCANTO INC
Also Called: Belmond El Encanto
800 Alvarado Pl, Santa Barbara
(93103-2176)
PHONE..................................805 845-5800
Richard M Levine, *CEO*
Martin O'Grady, *CFO*
Jose Leonard, *Security Dir*
Victoria Loeffler, *Sales Mgr*
Shane Arrold, *Sales Staff*
EMP: 69 **EST:** 2013
SALES (est): 29.5MM
SALES (corp-wide): 419.1MM **Privately Held**
WEB: www.belmond.com
SIC: 7011 Resort hotel
HQ: Belmond Usa Inc.
205 Meeting St
Charleston SC 29401
212 302-5055

(P-16432)
EMERIK HOTEL CORP
Also Called: Luxe City Center
1020 S Figueroa St, Los Angeles
(90015-1305)
PHONE..................................213 748-1291
Emerson Glazer, *President*
Art Malmgren, *CFO*
John Kelly, *Vice Pres*
James Jones, *Admin Sec*
Brenda Walsh, *Sales Mgr*
EMP: 111 **EST:** 1987
SALES (est): 6.6MM **Privately Held**
WEB: www.ecentralhotel.com
SIC: 7011 5813 5812 Hotels; bar (drinking places); American restaurant

(P-16433)
ENCINA PEPPER TREE JOINT VENTR (PA)
Also Called: Best Western
3850 State St, Santa Barbara
(93105-3112)
PHONE..................................805 687-5511
Jeanette Webber, *Managing Prtnr*
David Potter, *Partner*
Camille Shaar, *Partner*
Pamela Webber, *Partner*
Lynn Glenn, *Executive*
EMP: 70 **EST:** 1951
SQ FT: 100,000
SALES (est): 12.9MM **Privately Held**
WEB: www.bestwestern.com
SIC: 7011 Hotels & motels

(P-16434)
ENCINA PEPPER TREE JOINT VENTR
Also Called: Best Western
2220 Bath St, Santa Barbara (93105-4322)
PHONE..................................805 682-7277
Pam Webber, *Owner*
EMP: 80
SALES (corp-wide): 12.9MM **Privately Held**
WEB: www.sbhotels.com
SIC: 7011 Hotels & motels
PA: Pepper Encina Tree Joint Venture
3850 State St
Santa Barbara CA 93105
805 687-5511

(P-16435)
EQUITABLE HOTELS
Also Called: Comfort Suites Sequoia Area
210 E Acequia Ave, Visalia (93291-6319)
PHONE..................................559 738-1700

Anil Chagan, *President*
EMP: 54 **EST:** 2001
SQ FT: 50,000
SALES (est): 1.9MM **Privately Held**
WEB: www.comfortsuitesvisalia.com
SIC: 7011 Hotels & motels

(P-16436)
ERGS AIM HOTEL REALTY LLC
Also Called: Doubletree Suites Doheny
34402 Pacific Coast Hwy, Dana Point
(92624-1211)
PHONE..................................949 661-1100
Brian Nordahl,
Louisa Yeung, *Administration*
EMP: 54 **EST:** 2017
SALES (est): 2.6MM **Privately Held**
SIC: 7011 Hotels & motels

(P-16437)
ET WHITEHALL SEASCAPE LLC
Also Called: Hotel Casa Del Mar
1910 Ocean Way, Santa Monica
(90405-1083)
PHONE..................................310 581-5533
Edward Slatkin,
Janet Jacobs, *Vice Pres*
Klaus Mennekes, *Vice Pres*
Robert Bargas, *General Mgr*
Jey Dutertre, *Sales Mgr*
◆ **EMP:** 202 **EST:** 1998
SQ FT: 200,000
SALES (est): 11.2MM **Privately Held**
WEB: www.hotelcasadelmar.com
SIC: 7011 5812 Hotels; eating places

(P-16438)
EUROPEAN HT INVSTORS I I A CAL (PA)
Also Called: O H I
2532 Dupont Dr, Irvine (92612-1524)
PHONE..................................949 474-7368
Timothy R Busch, *General Ptnr*
T R Busch Realty Corp, *Partner*
Genevieve Villanueva, *Marketing Staff*
EMP: 50 **EST:** 1987
SQ FT: 9,000
SALES (est): 5.6MM **Privately Held**
WEB: www.thebuschfirm.com
SIC: 7011 Hotels

(P-16439)
EVEREST SONOMA MANAGEMENT LLC
520 Newport Center Dr # 2, Newport Beach
(92660-7020)
PHONE..................................213 272-0088
Marshall Young, *Mng Member*
LI Hui Lo,
EMP: 60
SQ FT: 10,000
SALES (est): 14MM
SALES (corp-wide): 1.2MM **Privately Held**
SIC: 7011 Hotels
PA: Everest Hotel Group, Llc
2140 S Dupont Hwy
Camden DE 19934
213 272-0088

(P-16440)
FAIRFELD INN BY MRROTT LTD PRT
1460 S Harbor Blvd, Anaheim
(92802-2311)
PHONE..................................714 772-6777
Helen Forbs, *Manager*
Reiji Kodama, *Asst Director*
Gina Elsass, *Manager*
Daniel Garcia, *Manager*
Kristen Kennedy, *Manager*
EMP: 78 **EST:** 1989
SALES (est): 5MM **Privately Held**
WEB: www.marriott.com
SIC: 7011 Hotels & motels

(P-16441)
FELCOR LAX LESSEE LLC
1440 E Imperial Ave, El Segundo
(90245-2623)
PHONE..................................310 640-3600
Michael C Hughes,
Jonathan H Yellen,
EMP: 50 **EST:** 2015

SALES (est): 5MM
SALES (corp-wide): 473MM **Privately Held**
SIC: 7011 Hotels & motels
HQ: Rangers Sub I, Llc
　3 Bethesda Metro Ctr # 1000
　Bethesda MD 20814

(P-16442)
FESS PRKER-RED LION GEN PARTNR
Also Called: Doubletree Hotel
633 E Cabrillo Blvd, Santa Barbara
(93103-3611)
PHONE..................805 564-4333
Fess Parker, *Partner*
Scott Reams, *Exec Dir*
Raymond Montoya, *Controller*
Darrin Williams, *Security Mgr*
Beth Olsen, *Mktg Dir*
EMP: 116 EST: 1981
SALES (est): 5.5MM **Privately Held**
WEB: www.hilton.com
SIC: 7011 Hotels & motels

(P-16443)
FIRST HOTELS INTERNATIONAL INC
Also Called: Radisson Inn
295 N E St, San Bernardino (92401-1507)
P.O. Box 1805 (92402-1805)
PHONE..................909 884-9364
James Deskus, *General Mgr*
Cindy Gardner, *Treasurer*
Choqchet Koski, *Controller*
Ivan Verheijen, *Manager*
EMP: 67 EST: 1994
SALES (est): 574.6K **Privately Held**
WEB: www.radissonhotelgroup.com
SIC: 7011 Hotels & motels

(P-16444)
FITNESS RIDGE MALIBU LLC
Also Called: Biggest Lser Ftnes Rdge Malibu
277 Latigo Canyon Rd, Malibu
(90265-2707)
PHONE..................818 874-1300
EMP: 56
SALES (est): 1.2MM **Privately Held**
SIC: 7011 7991 Hotel/Motel Physical Fitness Facility

(P-16445)
FJS INC
Also Called: Anabella Hotel The
888 S Disneyland Dr # 400, Anaheim
(92802-1847)
PHONE..................714 905-1050
Francis J Sparolini, *CEO*
C Y Chan, *President*
Rachel Moorhead, *Admin Sec*
EMP: 118 EST: 1989
SALES (est): 12.3MM **Privately Held**
SIC: 7011 Resort hotel

(P-16446)
FORTUNA ENTERPRISES LP
Also Called: Hilton
5711 W Century Blvd, Los Angeles
(90045-5672)
PHONE..................310 410-4000
Henry H Hsu, *Partner*
Christine Hsu, *Partner*
David Hsu, *Partner*
Sue Trobaugh, *Human Res Dir*
Myra Hayes, *Asst Sec*
EMP: 450 EST: 1992
SQ FT: 2,700
SALES (est): 34.5MM **Privately Held**
WEB: www.airportparkinglax.net
SIC: 7011 5812 5813 Hotels & motels; eating places; bar (drinking places)
HQ: Universal Fortuna Investment, Inc.
　5711 W Century Blvd # 16
　Los Angeles CA 90045

(P-16447)
FOUR POINTS BY SHERATON
9750 Airport Blvd, Los Angeles
(90045-5404)
PHONE..................310 645-4600
Jonh Vickers, *President*
EMP: 62 EST: 2001

SALES (est): 5MM **Privately Held**
WEB: www.four-points.marriott.com
SIC: 7011 Hotels & motels

(P-16448)
FOUR SEASONS WESTLAKE
2 Dole Dr, Westlake Village (91362-7300)
PHONE..................818 575-3000
Thomas Gurtner, *Manager*
Ruby Cheema, *Research*
Justin Weaver, *Research*
Alexis Peraino, *Internal Med*
EMP: 52 EST: 2006
SALES (est): 10.2MM **Privately Held**
WEB: www.fourseasons.com
SIC: 7011 Resort hotel; hotels

(P-16449)
FPL LLC
Also Called: Wyndham Garden Pierpont Inn
550 San Jon Rd, Ventura (93001-3745)
PHONE..................805 643-6144
EMP: 55
SALES (est): 968.1K **Privately Held**
SIC: 7011 Hotel/Motel Operation

(P-16450)
FRONTIER MOTEL INC
Also Called: Best Western
1008 S Main St, Lone Pine (93545-3010)
PHONE..................760 876-5571
Martin Powell, *President*
EMP: 52 EST: 1948
SQ FT: 43,680
SALES (est): 1.1MM **Privately Held**
WEB: www.bestwestern.com
SIC: 7011 Hotels & motels

(P-16451)
GAC BROKERAGE INC (PA)
4792 Tiara Dr Apt 101, Huntington Beach
(92649-4382)
PHONE..................714 846-2732
Michael S Gargan, *CEO*
EMP: 67 EST: 2014
SALES (est): 56.1K **Privately Held**
SIC: 7011 Hotels & motels

(P-16452)
GEHR GROUP INC (PA)
7400 E Slauson Ave, Commerce
(90040-3308)
PHONE..................323 728-5558
David Lifschitz, *President*
Mark Goldman, *COO*
Ed Duess, *Vice Pres*
Richard Garcia, *Administration*
Larry Brooks, *Accounts Exec*
EMP: 131 EST: 2012
SALES (est): 166.1MM **Privately Held**
WEB: www.gehr.com
SIC: 7011 5063 6531 Hotels & motels; wire & cable; real estate agent, commercial

(P-16453)
GEORGE DRUMHELLER PROPERTIES
Also Called: Best Western
5710 E La Palma Ave, Anaheim
(92807-2230)
PHONE..................714 779-0252
Kevin Bak, *Manager*
EMP: 51
SALES (corp-wide): 1.6MM **Privately Held**
WEB: www.anaheimhillsinnsuites.com
SIC: 7011 Hotels & motels
PA: George Drumheller Properties Inc
　244 Marcus St
　Walla Walla WA 99362
　509 529-1674

(P-16454)
GEORGIAN HOTEL
1415 Ocean Ave, Santa Monica
(90401-2101)
PHONE..................310 395-9945
Richard Dodrill, *Manager*
EMP: 55 EST: 1933
SQ FT: 40,000
SALES (est): 3.9MM **Privately Held**
WEB: www.georgianhotel.com
SIC: 7011 5812 Hotels; American restaurant

(P-16455)
GGWH LLC
Also Called: Holiday Inn
9440 Santa Monica Blvd, Beverly Hills
(90210-4653)
PHONE..................310 786-1700
Emerson Glazer,
Art Malmgren, *CFO*
Ericka Glazer,
EMP: 50 EST: 1994
SALES (est): 2MM **Privately Held**
WEB: www.holidayinn.com
SIC: 7011 5812 5813 Hotels & motels; eating places; drinking places

(P-16456)
GOLDEN HOTELS LTD PARTNERSHIP
Also Called: Atrium Hotel
18700 Macarthur Blvd, Irvine (92612-1409)
PHONE..................949 833-2770
Mike Wang, *Partner*
Pacific Coast Realty Services, *General Ptnr*
John Wang, *Partner*
Maritza Ceja, *Office Mgr*
Roshni Patel, *Sales Mgr*
EMP: 140 EST: 1960
SQ FT: 120,000
SALES (est): 10.9MM **Privately Held**
SIC: 7011 Resort hotel; hotels

(P-16457)
GREENS GROUP INC
8815 Research Dr Ste 100, Irvine
(92618-4296)
PHONE..................949 829-4902
Ashutosh Kadakia, *CFO*
Ajay Raman, *Vice Pres*
EMP: 145 EST: 2004
SALES (est): 6.4MM **Privately Held**
WEB: www.greens.com
SIC: 7011 Resort hotel, franchised

(P-16458)
GROSVENOR VISALIA ASSOCIATES
Also Called: Holiday Inn
9000 W Airport Dr, Visalia (93277-9511)
PHONE..................559 651-5000
Robert K Werbe, *General Ptnr*
EMP: 50 EST: 1985
SQ FT: 163,415
SALES (est): 768.8K **Privately Held**
WEB: www.holidayinn.com
SIC: 7011 Hotels & motels

(P-16459)
GUESTY INC
340 S Lemon Ave, Walnut (91789-2706)
PHONE..................415 244-0277
Amiad Soto, *CEO*
Omer Rabin, *Director*
EMP: 109
SALES (est): 665.5K **Privately Held**
WEB: www.guesty.com
SIC: 7011 7371 Vacation lodges; computer software development & applications

(P-16460)
H D G ASSOCIATES
Also Called: Hotel Marmonte
1111 E Cabrillo Blvd, Santa Barbara
(93103-3701)
PHONE..................805 963-0744
Ruth Grande, *President*
EMP: 277 EST: 1979
SQ FT: 150,000
SALES (est): 3.4MM **Publicly Held**
WEB: www.hyatt.com
SIC: 7011 Hotels
HQ: Hyatt Corporation
　150 N Riverside Plz
　Chicago IL 60606
　312 750-1234

(P-16461)
HAMPTON INN (PA)
4747 W Noble Ave, Visalia (93277-1594)
PHONE..................559 732-3900
Anil Chagan, *Principal*
EMP: 94 EST: 2008
SALES (est): 1.2MM **Privately Held**
WEB: www.hilton.com
SIC: 7011 Hotels & motels

(P-16462)
HANFORD HOTELS INC
Also Called: Hotel Hanford, The
3131 Bristol St, Costa Mesa (92626-3037)
PHONE..................714 557-3000
Tony Eccher, *Exec Dir*
Tom Van Winkle, *General Mgr*
EMP: 239
SQ FT: 65,311 **Privately Held**
WEB: www.hanfordhotels.com
SIC: 7011 Hotels
PA: Hanford Hotels, Inc.
　17542 17th St Ste 450
　Tustin CA 92780

(P-16463)
HARBOR SUITES LLC
Also Called: Hampton Inn
11747 Harbor Blvd, Garden Grove
(92840-2701)
PHONE..................714 703-8800
David Womack, *Principal*
Navin Dimond, *Principal*
Amy Kotal, *Principal*
EMP: 50 EST: 2019
SALES (est): 1.1MM **Privately Held**
WEB: www.hilton.com
SIC: 7011 Hotels & motels

(P-16464)
HARTFORD GREAT HEALTH CORP (PA)
8832 Glendon Way, Rosemead
(91770-1806)
PHONE..................626 321-1915
Lianyue Song, *President*
Sheng-Yih Chang, *CFO*
EMP: 77 EST: 2008
SALES: 553.4K **Publicly Held**
SIC: 7011 4724 Hotels & motels; travel agencies

(P-16465)
HAVASU LANDING CASINO (PA)
1 Main St, Needles (92363-9216)
PHONE..................760 858-5380
David Nye, *General Mgr*
Dave Bartlett, *Info Tech Dir*
EMP: 71 EST: 2010
SALES (est): 3.9MM **Privately Held**
WEB: www.havasulanding.com
SIC: 7011 Casino hotel

(P-16466)
HAWAIIAN GARDENS CASINO
11871 Carson St, Hawaiian Gardens
(90716-1127)
PHONE..................562 860-5887
David Moskowitz, *CEO*
Irving Moskowitz, *President*
▲ EMP: 1000 EST: 1998
SALES (est): 47.2MM **Privately Held**
WEB: www.thegardenscasino.com
SIC: 7011 Casino hotel

(P-16467)
HAWAIIAN HOTELS & RESORTS INC
2830 Borchard Rd, Newbury Park
(91320-3810)
PHONE..................805 480-0052
Edward J Hogan, *President*
EMP: 223 EST: 2001
SALES (est): 3.8MM
SALES (corp-wide): 1B **Privately Held**
WEB: www.hawaiihotels.com
SIC: 7011 Resort hotel; hotels
HQ: Pleasant Holidays, Llc
　2404 Townsgate Rd
　Westlake Village CA 91361

(P-16468)
HAZENS INVESTMENT LLC
Also Called: Sheraton
6101 W Century Blvd, Los Angeles
(90045-5310)
PHONE..................310 642-1111
Curtiss Allen, *COO*
Mario Mora, *Exec VP*
Juana Padilla, *Vice Pres*
Greg Yanez, *Business Mgr*
Reshana Johnson, *Controller*
EMP: 395 EST: 2002

▲ = Import ▼=Export
◆ =Import/Export

SALES (est): 44.1MM **Privately Held**
WEB: www.sheraton.marriott.com
SIC: **7011** Hotels

(P-16469)
HEI HOSPITALITY LLC
Also Called: Marriott
21850 Oxnard St, Woodland Hills
(91367-3631)
PHONE....................818 887-4800
Clay Andrews, *Manager*
Lauren Close, *Finance*
Yvonne Espinoza, *Finance*
Dee Gaubert, *Sales Staff*
Marie Johnson, *Facilities Dir*
EMP: 167
SALES (corp-wide): 204.2MM **Privately Held**
WEB: www.heihotels.com
SIC: **7011** Hotels & motels
PA: Hei Hospitality, Llc
101 Merritt 7
Norwalk CT 06851
203 849-8844

(P-16470)
HEI LONG BEACH LLC
Also Called: Hilton Hotels
701 W Ocean Blvd, Long Beach
(90831-3100)
PHONE....................562 983-3400
Clark Christopher, *Principal*
HEI Hospitality Fund Holdings,
EMP: 125 EST: 2004
SALES (est): 29.4MM
SALES (corp-wide): 204.2MM **Privately Held**
WEB: www.hilton.com
SIC: **7011** Hotels
PA: Hei Hospitality, Llc
101 Merritt 7
Norwalk CT 06851
203 849-8844

(P-16471)
HEPRAND HOSPITALITY INC
Also Called: Hampton Inn
311 E Huntington Dr, Arcadia (91006-3747)
PHONE....................626 574-5600
Peter Bhakta, *President*
▲ EMP: 61 EST: 1999
SQ FT: 61,473
SALES (est): 2.8MM **Privately Held**
WEB: www.hilton.com
SIC: **7011** Hotels & motels

(P-16472)
HHC HA TRS INC
Also Called: Hilton Anaheim
777 W Convention Way, Anaheim
(92802-3425)
PHONE....................714 750-4321
Helal Suhail Hilal Rashid, *CEO*
Salem K S Aldarmaki, *CEO*
Helal Suhail Hilal Rashid Alma, *CEO*
EMP: 50 EST: 2012
SALES (est): 6.9MM **Privately Held**
SIC: **7011** Hotels & motels

(P-16473)
HHC TRS PORTSMOUTH LLC
Also Called: Renaissance Palm Springs
888 E Tahquitz Canyon Way, Palm Springs
(92262-6708)
PHONE....................760 322-6000
David Kimichik,
EMP: 52 EST: 2003
SALES (est): 2.1MM **Privately Held**
SIC: **7011** Hotels & motels

(P-16474)
HI ANAHEIM LLC
100 W Katella Ave, Anaheim (92802-3602)
PHONE....................714 533-1500
Ajesh Patel,
EMP: 60 EST: 2018
SALES (est): 1.1MM **Privately Held**
SIC: **7011** Hotels

(P-16475)
HILTON GARDEN INN
2005 N Highland Ave, Los Angeles
(90068-3238)
PHONE....................323 876-8600
Khaled Kaawar, *Principal*
EMP: 65 EST: 2012

SALES (est): 6.1MM **Privately Held**
WEB: www.hilton.com
SIC: **7011** Hotels & motels

(P-16476)
HILTON INNS INC (HQ)
9336 Civic Center Dr, Beverly Hills
(90210-3604)
PHONE....................310 278-4321
Stephen F Bollenbach, *Ch of Bd*
Dieter H Huckestein, *President*
Matthew J Hart, *CFO*
Thomas L Keltner, *Exec VP*
Gillian Nevin, *Exec VP*
EMP: 1872 EST: 1965
SQ FT: 6,250
SALES (est): 8.9B
SALES (corp-wide): 852MM **Publicly Held**
WEB: www.hiltonhyland.com
SIC: **7011** Hotels & motels
PA: Park Hotels & Resorts Inc.
1775 Tysons Blvd Fl 7
Tysons VA 22102
571 302-5757

(P-16477)
HILTON LOS ANGLES UNIVERSAL CY
555 Universal Hollywood Dr, Universal City
(91608-1001)
PHONE....................818 506-2500
Juan Aquinde, *General Mgr*
Matthew La Vine, *Managing Dir*
Yessenia Fabian, *Marketing Staff*
Chelsea Camire, *Sales Staff*
▲ EMP: 121 EST: 2003
SALES (est): 9MM **Privately Held**
WEB: www.hiltonuniversal.com
SIC: **7011** Hotels

(P-16478)
HILTON RESORT PALM SPRINGS
400 E Tahquitz Canyon Way, Palm Springs
(92262-6605)
PHONE....................760 320-6868
Aftab Dada, *General Mgr*
EMP: 200 EST: 1989
SALES (est): 10.3MM **Privately Held**
WEB: www.palmsprings.hilton.com
SIC: **7011** Resort hotel

(P-16479)
HILTON UNIVERSAL HOTEL
555 Universal Hollywood Dr, Universal City
(91608-1001)
PHONE....................818 506-2500
Michelle Szeto, *Principal*
Suzanne Casey, *Sales Dir*
EMP: 99 EST: 2007
SALES (est): 14.9MM **Privately Held**
WEB: www.hilton.com
SIC: **7011** Hotels & motels
HQ: Sun Hill Properties, Inc.
555 Unvarsal Hollywood Dr
Universal City CA 91608

(P-16480)
HILTON WOODLAND HILLS & TOWERS
6360 Canoga Ave, Woodland Hills
(91367-2501)
PHONE....................818 595-1000
Ed Debries, *General Mgr*
Conoga Hotel Corporation, *Partner*
▲ EMP: 111 EST: 1989
SALES (est): 10.7MM **Privately Held**
WEB: www.woodlandhillshotel.com
SIC: **7011** **5813** **5812** Hotels & motels; drinking places; eating places

(P-16481)
HISTORIC MISSION INN CORP
Also Called: Mission Inn Hotel and Spa, The
3649 Mission Inn Ave, Riverside
(92501-3364)
P.O. Box 1433 (92502-1433)
PHONE....................951 784-0300
Duane R Roberts, *President*
Cliff Day, *CFO*
Diana Rosure, *Vice Pres*
Richard Shippee, *Admin Sec*
Heidi Heath, *Human Res Dir*

EMP: 460 EST: 1992
SALES (est): 33.2MM **Privately Held**
WEB: www.missioninn.com
SIC: **7011** **7991** Resort hotel; spas
PA: Entrepreneurial Capital Corporation
4100 Newport Place Dr # 400
Newport Beach CA 92660
949 809-3900

(P-16482)
HIT PORTFOLIO II TRS LLC
Also Called: Hilton
400 N State College Blvd, Orange
(92868-1708)
PHONE....................714 938-1111
John Ault, *Manager*
EMP: 59
SALES (corp-wide): 852MM **Publicly Held**
WEB: www.hiltongrandvacations.com
SIC: **7011** **5812** Hotels & motels; eating places
HQ: Hit Portfolio Ii Trs, Llc
7930 Jones Branch Dr
Mc Lean VA 22102
703 883-1000

(P-16483)
HOLIDAY GARDEN SF CORP
Also Called: Clementine Ht & Suites Anaheim
1700 S Clementine St, Anaheim
(92802-2902)
PHONE....................714 533-3555
Hai-Ni Chen, *President*
EMP: 95 EST: 1997
SALES (est): 5.9MM **Privately Held**
SIC: **7011** Hotels & motels

(P-16484)
HOLIDAY INN
Also Called: Holiday Inn Anheim - Rsort Are
1915 S Manchester Ave, Anaheim
(92802-3802)
PHONE....................714 748-7777
Kym Bixler, *Mng Member*
Kim Bixler, *Manager*
Sharon Kwart, *Manager*
EMP: 50 EST: 2002
SALES (est): 1.6MM **Privately Held**
WEB: www.holidayinn.com
SIC: **7011** Hotels

(P-16485)
HOLIDAY INN EX ANHEIM MAIN GAT
435 W Katella Ave, Anaheim (92802-3607)
PHONE....................714 772-7755
Stephen C Hsu, *Partner*
Kuo-Chin Yang, *Partner*
EMP: 58 EST: 1989
SQ FT: 24,000
SALES (est): 1.3MM **Privately Held**
WEB: www.holidayinn.com
SIC: **7011** Hotels & motels

(P-16486)
HOLIDAY INN EX HT & SUITES LLC
2700 Lenwood Rd, Barstow (92311-9591)
PHONE....................760 253-9200
Peter Roberts, *Mng Member*
Marsha Bonds,
EMP: 91 EST: 2002
SQ FT: 69,900
SALES (est): 1.8MM **Privately Held**
WEB: www.holidayinn.com
SIC: **7011** Hotels & motels

(P-16487)
HOLIDAY INN EXPRESS
2550 Erringer Rd, Simi Valley
(93065-2353)
PHONE....................805 584-6006
Ashok Israni, *President*
EMP: 227 EST: 1987
SALES (est): 1.4MM
SALES (corp-wide): 112.8MM **Privately Held**
WEB: www.holidayinn.com
SIC: **7011** Hotels & motels
PA: Pacifica Hosts, Inc.
1775 Hancock St Ste 200
San Diego CA 92110
619 296-9000

(P-16488)
HOLIDAY INN EXPRESS
705 San Gabriel Blvd, Rosemead
(91770-4335)
PHONE....................323 726-1111
Tom Wu, *Partner*
Benson Wu, *Partner*
EMP: 75 EST: 1988
SQ FT: 27,000
SALES (est): 1MM **Privately Held**
WEB: www.holidayinnexpress.com
SIC: **7011** Hotels & motels

(P-16489)
HOLLYWOOD PARTNERSHIP
Also Called: Days Inn
5410 Hollywood Blvd, Los Angeles
(90027-3406)
PHONE....................323 463-7171
Mohan Patel, *Partner*
Ratilal Patel, *Partner*
Matthew Solis, *General Mgr*
EMP: 55 EST: 1989
SQ FT: 20,000
SALES (est): 1.1MM **Privately Held**
WEB: www.wyndhamhotels.com
SIC: **7011** Hotels & motels

(P-16490)
HONEYMOON REAL ESTATE LP
Also Called: Avalon Hotel
9400 W Olympic Blvd, Beverly Hills
(90212-4552)
PHONE....................310 277-5221
Brad Korzen, *Partner*
Max Aigner, *Sales Mgr*
Rosie Coats, *Sales Staff*
Yvonne Gonzalez, *Sales Staff*
Kristin Culotta, *Director*
EMP: 90 EST: 1997
SQ FT: 400,000
SALES (est): 8MM **Privately Held**
WEB: www.avalon-hotel.com
SIC: **7011** Resort hotel

(P-16491)
HOST HOTELS & RESORTS LP
Also Called: JW Marriott Dsert Sprng Rsort S
74855 Country Club Dr, Palm Desert
(92260-1961)
PHONE....................760 341-2211
Ken Forths, *Manager*
Joy Smith, *Purch Mgr*
Stacey Crawford, *Manager*
EMP: 64
SALES (corp-wide): 1.6B **Publicly Held**
WEB: www.hosthotels.com
SIC: **7011** Hotels & motels
HQ: Host Hotels & Resorts, L.P.
6903 Rockledge Dr # 1500
Bethesda MD 20817
240 744-1000

(P-16492)
HOTEL BEL-AIR
701 Stone Canyon Rd, Los Angeles
(90077-2909)
PHONE....................310 472-1211
Carlos Lopes, *Managing Dir*
Leslie Miller, *Administration*
Warren Martinez, *Finance*
Ed Anonas, *Controller*
Henry Dominguez, *Sales Staff*
EMP: 265 EST: 1994
SQ FT: 30,000
SALES (est): 13.6MM
SALES (corp-wide): 541MM **Privately Held**
WEB: www.dorchestercollection.com
SIC: **7011** Hotels
HQ: Kava Holdings, Inc.
701 Stone Canyon Rd
Los Angeles CA 90077
310 472-1211

(P-16493)
HOTEL PACIFIC GARDEN
1625 W Redondo Beach Blvd, Gardena
(90247-3241)
PHONE....................310 532-5200
Etsuko Fautt, *Manager*
EMP: 63 EST: 1993
SALES (est): 222.9K **Privately Held**
WEB: www.hotelpg.com
SIC: **7011** **7389** Hotels; hotel & motel reservation service

PRODUCTS & SVCS

(P-16494)
HST LESSEE SOUTH COAST LP
686 Anton Blvd, Costa Mesa (92626-1920)
PHONE..............................714 540-2500
Jeffrey Clark, *Principal*
EMP: 84 **EST:** 2008
SALES (est): 2MM
SALES (corp-wide): 1.6B **Publicly Held**
WEB: www.marriott.com
SIC: 7011 Resort hotel
PA: Host Hotels & Resorts, Inc.
　　4747 Bethesda Ave # 1300
　　Bethesda MD 20814
　　240 744-1000

(P-16495)
HUMNIT HOTEL AT LAX LLC
Also Called: Concorse Ht At Los Angles Arpr
6225 W Century Blvd, Los Angeles
(90045-5311)
PHONE..............................424 702-1234
Jina Luman, *Principal*
EMP: 99 **EST:** 2013
SQ FT: 49,500
SALES (est): 11.6MM
SALES (corp-wide): 231.1MM **Privately Held**
WEB: www.ihg.com
SIC: 7011 Hotels
PA: Amalgamated Financial Corp.
　　275 7th Ave
　　New York NY 10001
　　212 255-6200

(P-16496)
HUOYEN INTERNATIONAL INC
Also Called: Hotel Fullerton Anaheim, The
1500 S Raymond Ave, Fullerton
(92831-5236)
PHONE..............................714 635-9000
Hsi Jung Yang, *President*
EMP: 90 **EST:** 1995
SQ FT: 144,698
SALES (est): 5.3MM **Privately Held**
WEB: www.hfullerton.com
SIC: 7011 Hotel, franchised

(P-16497)
HYATT CORPORATION
Also Called: Hyatt Los Angeles Airport
6225 W Century Blvd, Los Angeles
(90045-5311)
PHONE..............................312 750-1234
Donald J Henderson, *Manager*
Jerri Johnson, *Sales Mgr*
EMP: 500 **Publicly Held**
WEB: www.hyatt.com
SIC: 7011 5812 5813 Hotels; restaurant,
　family; chain; bar (drinking places)
HQ: Hyatt Corporation
　　150 N Riverside Plz
　　Chicago IL 60606
　　312 750-1234

(P-16498)
HYATT CORPORATION
Also Called: Hyatt Hotel
200 S Pine Ave, Long Beach (90802-4537)
PHONE..............................562 432-0161
Steve Smith, *Manager*
Susan Ruvalcaba, *Human Resources*
EMP: 463 **Publicly Held**
WEB: www.hyatt.com
SIC: 7011 7299 Hotels & motels; banquet
　hall facilities
HQ: Hyatt Corporation
　　150 N Riverside Plz
　　Chicago IL 60606
　　312 750-1234

(P-16499)
HYATT CORPORATION
Also Called: Hyatt Hotel
1107 Jamboree Rd, Newport Beach
(92660-6219)
PHONE..............................949 729-1234
Ruth Benjamin, *General Mgr*
Craig Buckley, *Manager*
EMP: 300 **Publicly Held**
WEB: www.hyatt.com
SIC: 7011 5813 5812 Hotels & motels;
　drinking places; eating places
HQ: Hyatt Corporation
　　150 N Riverside Plz
　　Chicago IL 60606
　　312 750-1234

(P-16500)
HYATT REGENCY CENTURY PLAZA
2025 Avenue Of The Stars, Los Angeles
(90067-4741)
PHONE..............................310 228-1234
Rakesh Sarna, *CEO*
Ken Cruse, *President*
Karina Valencia, *Hum Res Coord*
EMP: 650 **EST:** 2005
SALES (est): 25.5MM **Privately Held**
WEB: www.hyatt.com
SIC: 7011 Hotels

(P-16501)
IHG MANAGEMENT (MARYLAND) LLC
Also Called: Crown Plaza Los Angeles
5985 W Century Blvd, Los Angeles
(90045-5477)
PHONE..............................310 642-7500
William Block, *Finance Dir*
EMP: 50 **EST:** 2004
SQ FT: 14,000
SALES (est): 1.4MM **Privately Held**
WEB: www.ihg.com
SIC: 7011 Hotels

(P-16502)
INDIAN WELLS PROPERTY LLC ✿
45000 Indian Wells Ln, Indian Wells
(92210-8790)
PHONE..............................442 305-4500
Chris Currie, *Mng Member*
EMP: 65 **EST:** 2021
SALES (est): 1MM **Privately Held**
SIC: 7011 Hotels

(P-16503)
INDIAN WELLS RESORT HOTEL
76661 Us Highway 111, Indian Wells
(92210-8972)
PHONE..............................760 345-6466
Brad Weimer, *President*
EMP: 60 **EST:** 1994
SQ FT: 240,000
SALES (est): 2.9MM **Privately Held**
WEB: www.indianwellsresort.com
SIC: 7011 5812 Resort hotel; eating
　places

(P-16504)
INGLESIDE INVESTORS SPE LLC
Also Called: Ingleside & Melvyn's
200 W Ramon Rd, Palm Springs
(92264-7333)
PHONE..............................760 325-0046
Graham Culp,
EMP: 51 **EST:** 1987
SALES (est): 8MM **Privately Held**
WEB: www.inglesideinn.com
SIC: 5812 7011 American restaurant; ho-
　tels

(P-16505)
INTER-CONTINENTAL HOTELS CORP (DH)
Also Called: Ihg
35016 Avenue D, Yucaipa (92399-4407)
PHONE..............................770 604-5000
Kirk Kinsell, *CEO*
Robert J Chitty, *CFO*
Robert Gunkel, *CFO*
Jo Harlow, *Bd of Directors*
Jamie Cole, *Senior VP*
EMP: 366 **EST:** 1946
SALES (est): 227MM **Privately Held**
WEB: www.ihg.com
SIC: 7011 Hotels

(P-16506)
INTERSTATE HOTELS RESORTS INC
Also Called: Santa Barbara Inn
901 E Cabrillo Blvd, Santa Barbara
(93103-3642)
P.O. Box 5634 (93150-5634)
PHONE..............................805 966-2285
Clark Sarchet, *Branch Mgr*
Mary Gregg, *General Mgr*
Marilou Deang, *Manager*
EMP: 75 **Privately Held**
WEB: www.interstatehotels.com
SIC: 7011 Hotels
HQ: Interstate Hotels & Resorts, Inc.
　　5301 Headquarters Dr
　　Plano TX 75024
　　703 387-3100

(P-16507)
INTERSTATE-RIM MGT CO LLC
3990 Westerly Pl Ste 120, Newport Beach
(92660-2310)
PHONE..............................949 783-2500
Carrie McIntyre,
Erica Hageman,
EMP: 111 **EST:** 2014
SALES (est): 384.7K **Privately Held**
WEB: www.interstatehotels.com
SIC: 7011 Hotels
HQ: Interstate Hotels & Resorts, Inc.
　　5301 Headquarters Dr
　　Plano TX 75024
　　703 387-3100

(P-16508)
IRP LAX HOTEL LLC
Also Called: Four Pnts By Shrton La Intl Ar
9750 Airport Blvd, Los Angeles
(90045-5404)
PHONE..............................310 645-4600
Phil Baxter,
EMP: 240 **EST:** 1994
SQ FT: 337,720
SALES (est): 43.2MM
SALES (corp-wide): 13.2B **Publicly Held**
WEB: www.sheraton.marriott.com
SIC: 7011 Resort hotel
HQ: Tishman Hotel Corporation
　　666 5th Ave Fl 38
　　New York NY 10103

(P-16509)
J W MRROTT LOS ANGLES L A LIVE
900 W Olympic Blvd, Los Angeles
(90015-1338)
PHONE..............................213 765-8600
Martha Saucedo, *Vice Pres*
Lourdes Ruano, *Human Res Mgr*
Zee Ali, *Manager*
Travis Case, *Manager*
EMP: 115 **EST:** 2008
SALES (est): 5.4MM **Privately Held**
WEB: www.marriott.com
SIC: 7011 Hotels

(P-16510)
JACK PARKER CORP
Also Called: Le Parker Meridien Palm Sprng
4200 E Palm Canyon Dr, Palm Springs
(92264-5230)
PHONE..............................760 770-5000
Adam Glick, *President*
Brandon McCurley, *General Mgr*
▲ **EMP:** 53 **EST:** 2003
SALES (est): 539.9K **Privately Held**
WEB: www.parkerpalmsprings.com
SIC: 7011 Resort hotel

(P-16511)
JAYBEE HUNTINGTON LLC
44 Skyward, Irvine (92620-3549)
PHONE..............................562 756-3124
Kiran Patel, *Branch Mgr*
EMP: 62
SALES (corp-wide): 552.2K **Privately Held**
SIC: 7011 Hotels & motels
PA: Jaybee Huntington, Llc
　　17251 Beach Blvd
　　Huntington Beach CA

(P-16512)
JDS HOSPITALITY GROUP
Also Called: Holiday Inn
2070 Newport Blvd, Costa Mesa
(92627-2164)
PHONE..............................949 631-6000
Narendra Patel, *President*
Sam Bhakta, *Shareholder*
Dan Bhakta, *Vice Pres*
EMP: 63 **EST:** 1999
SALES (est): 909.2K **Privately Held**
WEB: www.holidayinn.com
SIC: 7011 Hotels & motels

(P-16513)
JHC INVESTMENT INC
Also Called: Dt Club Hotel Santa Ana
7 Hutton Centre Dr, Santa Ana
(92707-5753)
PHONE..............................714 751-2400
Jung-Hsiung Chiu, *President*
EMP: 70 **EST:** 1993
SQ FT: 85,000
SALES (est): 3MM **Privately Held**
SIC: 7011 Hotels

(P-16514)
JP ALLEN INC
150 E Angeleno Ave, Burbank
(91502-1911)
PHONE..............................818 841-4770
Mark Crigler, *President*
Rich Reid, *Finance Dir*
EMP: 300 **EST:** 2015
SQ FT: 100,000
SALES (est): 11.3MM **Privately Held**
WEB: www.jpalleninc.com
SIC: 7011 6513 8741 Hotel, franchised;
　apartment building operators; hotel or
　motel management

(P-16515)
JP ALLEN EXTENDED STAY
Also Called: Holiday Inn
150 E Angeleno Ave, Burbank
(91502-1911)
PHONE..............................818 841-4770
Chris Haven, *Manager*
Craig Bilski, *Chief Engr*
EMP: 50
SALES (corp-wide): 17.9MM **Privately Held**
WEB: www.holidayinn.com
SIC: 7011 Hotels & motels
PA: Jp Allen Extended Stay
　　450 Pioneer Dr
　　Glendale CA 91203
　　818 956-0202

(P-16516)
JP ALLEN EXTENDED STAY (PA)
Also Called: Days Inn
450 Pioneer Dr, Glendale (91203-1713)
PHONE..............................818 956-0202
Joe Perry, *Owner*
EMP: 76 **EST:** 1945
SQ FT: 4,000
SALES (est): 17.9MM **Privately Held**
WEB: www.la-vintage-paperback-show.com
SIC: 7011 Hotels & motels

(P-16517)
JWMCC LIMITED PARTNERSHIP
Also Called: Hyatt Hotel
2151 Avenue Of The Stars, Los Angeles
(90067-5001)
PHONE..............................310 277-1234
Ulrich Samietz, *General Mgr*
▲ **EMP:** 75 **EST:** 1987
SQ FT: 4,600
SALES (est): 1MM **Privately Held**
WEB: www.hyatt.com
SIC: 7011 5812 Hotels & motels; eating
　places

(P-16518)
KALPANA LLC
535 S Grand Ave, Los Angeles
(90071-2601)
PHONE..............................213 624-0000
EMP: 110
SALES (est): 2.1MM **Privately Held**
WEB: www.hiltoncheckers.com
SIC: 5812 7011 Eating Place Hotel/Motel
　Operation

(P-16519)
KAM SANG COMPANY INC
Also Called: New Age Lamirada Inn
14419 Firestone Blvd, La Mirada
(90638-5912)
PHONE..............................714 523-2800
Grace Tanji, *General Mgr*
EMP: 70
SALES (corp-wide): 34.5MM **Privately Held**
WEB: www.kamsangcompany.com
SIC: 7011 Hotel, franchised

▲ = Import ▼=Export
◆ =Import/Export

PA: Kam Sang Company, Inc.
411 E Huntington Dr # 305
Arcadia CA 91006
626 446-2988

(P-16520)
KANG FAMILY PARTNERS LLC
Also Called: Santa Ynez Valley Marriott
555 Mcmurray Rd, Buellton (93427-9559)
PHONE..................................805 688-1000
Daphne Kang, *Mng Member*
Karla Azahar, *General Mgr*
German Custodio, *Engineer*
Kathleen Martinez, *Human Resources*
Deborah Holmes, *Sales Mgr*
EMP: 110 **EST:** 1995 **Privately Held**
WEB: www.marriott.com
SIC: 7011 Hotel, franchised; hotels

(P-16521)
KAVA HOLDINGS INC (DH)
Also Called: Hotel Bel-Air
701 Stone Canyon Rd, Los Angeles
(90077-2909)
PHONE..................................310 472-1211
Hj Suharafadzil, *President*
Helen Smith, *President*
Christopher Cowdary, *CEO*
Franois Delahaye, *COO*
Eugenio Pirri, *Vice Pres*
EMP: 200 **EST:** 1994
SQ FT: 30,000
SALES (est): 66.5MM
SALES (corp-wide): 541MM **Privately
Held**
WEB: www.dorchestercollection.com
SIC: 7011 Resort hotel; hotels
HQ: Dorchester Group Limited
57 Berkeley Square
London W1J 6
207 629-4848

(P-16522)
KEN REAL ESTATE LEASE LTD
Also Called: Anaheim Majestic Garden Hotel
900 S Disneyland Dr, Anaheim
(92802-1844)
PHONE..................................714 778-1700
Shigeru Sato, *President*
Kim Painter, *General Mgr*
Bruno Nocco, *Chief Engr*
Andrew Dang, *Controller*
Vicky Garcia, *Human Res Dir*
EMP: 99 **EST:** 2005
SALES (est): 9.3MM **Privately Held**
WEB: www.ken-realestate.jp
SIC: 7011 Resort hotel

(P-16523)
**KIMPTON HOTEL & REST
GROUP LLC**
6317 Wilshire Blvd, Los Angeles
(90048-5600)
PHONE..................................323 852-6000
Ashley Gochnauer, *Manager*
EMP: 206 **Privately Held**
WEB: www.kimptonhotels.com
SIC: 7011 Hotels
HQ: Kimpton Hotel & Restaurant Group Llc
222 Kearny St Ste 200
San Francisco CA 94108
415 397-5572

(P-16524)
**KINTETSU ENTERPRISES CO
AMER (HQ)**
Also Called: Kintetsu Enterprises Co Amer
21241 S Wstn Ave Ste 100, Torrance
(90501)
PHONE..................................310 782-9300
Hisao Hiro, *President*
EMP: 200 **EST:** 1961
SALES (est): 28.9MM **Privately Held**
WEB: www.kintetsu-enterprises.com
SIC: 7011 6512 Hotel, franchised; nonresidential building operators

(P-16525)
**KINTETSU ENTERPRISES CO
AMER**
328 E 1st St, Los Angeles (90012-3902)
PHONE..................................213 617-2000
Akimasa Yoneda, *Branch Mgr*
Hatano Jin, *Manager*
Kyoko Smith, *Manager*

EMP: 50 **Privately Held**
WEB: www.kintetsu-enterprises.com
SIC: 7011 Hotels
HQ: Kintetsu Enterprises Company Of
America
21241 S Wstn Ave Ste 100
Torrance CA 90501
310 782-9300

(P-16526)
**KITTRIDGE HOTELS & RESORTS
LLC**
Also Called: Hard Rock Hotel Palm Springs
150 S Indian Canyon Dr, Palm Springs
(92262-6604)
PHONE..................................760 325-9676
Stan Kantowski,
Tim Alexander, *Human Resources*
Heidi Walker, *Sales Staff*
Andre Carpiac,
EMP: 64 **EST:** 2004
SALES (est): 11MM **Privately Held**
WEB: www.hardrockhotels.com
SIC: 7011 Resort hotel

(P-16527)
KNOTTS BERRY FARM LLC
Also Called: Knott's Berry Farm Hotel
7675 Crescent Ave, Buena Park
(90620-3947)
PHONE..................................714 995-1111
Stan Dlander, *Manager*
Jose Lopez, *Purchasing*
EMP: 100
SALES (corp-wide): 181.5MM **Publicly
Held**
WEB: www.knotts.com
SIC: 7011 Resort hotel
HQ: Berry Knott's Farm Llc
8039 Beach Blvd
Buena Park CA 90620
714 827-1776

(P-16528)
KNR DEVCO
Also Called: Holiday Inn
14814 Hawthorne Blvd, Lawndale
(90260-1525)
PHONE..................................310 676-1111
Ken Bhakta, *Manager*
EMP: 64 **EST:** 1987
SALES (est): 400K **Privately Held**
WEB: www.holidayinn.com
SIC: 7011 Hotels

(P-16529)
**KSL II MNGEMENT OPERATIONS
LLC**
18575 Jamboree Rd Ste 500, Irvine
(92612-2545)
PHONE..................................760 564-8000
Scott Dalecio, *President*
Ed Eynon, *Exec VP*
Gretchen Holm, *Director*
EMP: 68 **EST:** 2004
SALES (est): 3.3MM **Privately Held**
WEB: www.kslresorts.com
SIC: 7011 Resort hotel

(P-16530)
L & O ALISO VIEJO LLC
Also Called: Renaissance Hotel Clubsport
50 Enterprise, Aliso Viejo (92656-6026)
PHONE..................................949 643-6700
Ed Tomlin, *General Mgr*
Marnie Harvey, *Opers Dir*
Dillon Johnson, *Sales Staff*
Jed Dalton, *Manager*
EMP: 76 **EST:** 2008
SALES (est): 16.5MM **Privately Held**
WEB: www.clubsports.com
SIC: 7011 Hotels & motels

(P-16531)
L & S INVESTMENT CO INC
Also Called: Best Western
14173 Green Tree Blvd, Victorville
(92395-4360)
PHONE..................................760 245-3461
Walter Schroeder, *Ch of Bd*
EMP: 53 **EST:** 1956
SQ FT: 120,000
SALES (est): 572.5K **Privately Held**
WEB: www.choicehotels.com
SIC: 7011 Hotels & motels

(P-16532)
**LAGUNA HILLS HOTEL DEV
VENTR**
Also Called: Holiday Inn
25205 La Paz Rd, Laguna Hills
(92653-5105)
PHONE..................................949 586-5000
June Chen, *Partner*
Clement Chen, *President*
Ronnie Torres, *General Mgr*
Tessa Fattahi, *Sales Mgr*
Laura Gutierrez, *Sales Staff*
EMP: 51 **EST:** 1978
SQ FT: 102,241
SALES (est): 1.5MM **Privately Held**
WEB: www.thelagunahillshotel.com
SIC: 7011 5812 7299 Hotels; eating
places; banquet hall facilities

(P-16533)
**LAKE ARRWHEAD RSORT
OPRTOR INC (HQ)**
Also Called: Marriott
27984 Hwy 189, Lake Arrowhead (92352)
PHONE..................................909 336-1511
Carmen Rodriguez, *CEO*
Veronique Williams, *Administration*
EMP: 115 **EST:** 1982
SALES (est): 13.5MM
SALES (corp-wide): 10.5B **Publicly Held**
WEB: www.lakearrowheadresort.com
SIC: 7011 5813 5812 Resort hotel; drink-
ing places; eating places
PA: Marriott International, Inc.
10400 Fernwood Rd
Bethesda MD 20817
301 380-3000

(P-16534)
LANDWIN HOSPITALITY LLC
Also Called: Hilton Hotel
225 W Valley Blvd, San Gabriel
(91776-3743)
PHONE..................................626 270-2700
Sunny Chen, *Mng Member*
Medeline Yu, *Sales Staff*
Fu-Shun Chen,
Sheue-Shiang Lin Chen,
Alfonso Mansubre, *Manager*
EMP: 58 **EST:** 2004
SQ FT: 21,755
SALES (est): 3MM **Privately Held**
WEB: www.hilton.com
SIC: 7011 Hotels & motels

(P-16535)
**LANGHAM HOTELS PACIFIC
CORP**
Also Called: Langham Hotels International
1401 S Oak Knoll Ave, Pasadena
(91106-4508)
PHONE..................................617 451-1900
Ka Shui Lo, *President*
Brett Butcher, *Vice Pres*
Evonne Kang, *Credit Staff*
Monterey Larson, *Train & Dev Mgr*
Greg Louie, *Sales Staff*
EMP: 72 **EST:** 2007
SALES (est): 8.5MM **Privately Held**
WEB: www.langhamhotels.com
SIC: 7011 Hotels; resort hotel

(P-16536)
**LAX HOTEL INVESTMENT CO
INC**
Also Called: Wingate By Wyndham
10300 S La Cienega Blvd, Inglewood
(90304-1118)
PHONE..................................310 846-3200
Linda OH, *President*
Dr George OH, *Owner*
EMP: 55 **EST:** 1995
SALES (est): 2.6MM **Privately Held**
WEB: www.wyndhamhotels.com
SIC: 7011 Hotels

(P-16537)
LAX HOTEL VENTURES LLC
Also Called: Four Points Sheraton Lax
9750 Airport Blvd, Los Angeles
(90045-5404)
PHONE..................................310 645-4600
EMP: 50
SALES: 950K **Privately Held**
SIC: 7011 Hotel/Motel Operation

(P-16538)
LE MONTROSE HOTEL
Also Called: Le Montrose Suite Hotel
900 Hammond St Apt 434, West Hollywood
(90069-4443)
PHONE..................................310 855-1115
John Douponce, *Managing Prtnr*
Andrew Maffei, *General Mgr*
EMP: 69 **EST:** 1987
SQ FT: 1,000
SALES (est): 3.9MM **Privately Held**
WEB: www.montrosewesthollywood.com
SIC: 7011 Hotels

(P-16539)
LEADER HOSPITALITY LP
Also Called: Fairfield Inn
26328 Oso Pkwy, Mission Viejo
(92691-5641)
PHONE..................................949 582-7100
Hsuehjen Kuo, *Partner*
EMP: 97 **EST:** 1987
SQ FT: 60,573
SALES (est): 1.4MM **Privately Held**
WEB: www.marriott.com
SIC: 7011 Hotels & motels

(P-16540)
**LH INDIAN WELLS OPERATING
LLC**
4500 Indian Wells Ln, Indian Wells (92210)
PHONE..................................760 341-2200
Bob Low, *Principal*
EMP: 220 **EST:** 2004
SALES (est): 644.9K **Privately Held**
SIC: 7011 7991 Resort hotel; spas
PA: Lh Indian Wells Holding, Llc
11777 San Vicente Blvd
Los Angeles CA 90049

(P-16541)
**LH UNIVERSAL OPERATING
LLC**
Also Called: Sheraton
333 Unversal Hollywood Dr, Universal City
(91608-1001)
PHONE..................................818 980-1212
Robert Lowe,
Virginia Clark, *General Mgr*
Jose Escandon, *Finance Mgr*
Rita Noriega, *Controller*
Sherry Samanon, *Director*
EMP: 280 **EST:** 1969 **Privately Held**
WEB: www.marriott.com
SIC: 7011 Hotels

(P-16542)
LINCOLN PLAZA HOTEL INC
123 S Lincoln Ave, Monterey Park
(91755-2914)
PHONE..................................626 571-8818
Thira Ratanapreuksul, *President*
William H Roach, *Corp Secy*
▲ **EMP:** 59 **EST:** 1984
SQ FT: 95,600
SALES (est): 1MM **Privately Held**
WEB: www.lincolnplazahotel.net
SIC: 7011 Hotels

(P-16543)
**LOEWS HOLLYWOOD HOTEL
LLC**
1755 N Highland Ave, Hollywood
(90028-4403)
PHONE..................................323 450-2235
Jonathan Tisch, *Ch of Bd*
Michael Hu, *Treasurer*
Gary Belvedere, *Vice Pres*
Reggie Dominique, *Managing Dir*
Younes Atallah, *General Mgr*
EMP: 375 **EST:** 2012
SALES (est): 32MM
SALES (corp-wide): 12.5B **Publicly Held**
WEB: www.loewshotels.com
SIC: 7011 Hotels
PA: Loews Corporation
667 Madison Ave Fl 7
New York NY 10065
212 521-2000

PRODUCTS & SVCS

(P-16544)
LONG BEACH GOLDEN SAILS INC
Also Called: Best Western Golden Sails Ht
23545 Crenshaw Blvd # 100, Torrance
(90505-5218)
PHONE.................................562 596-1631
Luis Vasquez, *President*
Ruben Garza, *Vice Pres*
Vicki Arreguin, *Sales Staff*
▲ EMP: 100 EST: 1964
SQ FT: 150,000
SALES (est): 19.2MM **Privately Held**
WEB: www.goldensailshotel.com
SIC: 7011 5812 5813 Hotels & motels;
   restaurant, family: independent; bar
   (drinking places)
PA: Abp Hotel, Llc
   2200 W Valley Blvd
   Alhambra CA 91803
   562 596-1631

(P-16545)
LONG POINT DEVELOPMENT LLC
Also Called: Terranea Resort
100 Terranea Way, Rancho Palos Verdes
(90275-1013)
PHONE.................................310 265-2800
Terri Haack, *Mng Member*
Mitch Mehr, *Senior VP*
Agnelo Fernandes, *Vice Pres*
Verenise Celaya, *Executive*
Hilary Feutz, *Associate Dir*
EMP: 1000
SALES (est): 65.4MM **Privately Held**
WEB: www.terranea.com
SIC: 7011 Resort hotel

(P-16546)
LOWE ENTERPRISES INC (PA)
Also Called: Lei AG Seattle
11777 San Vicente Blvd # 900, Los Angeles
(90049-5084)
PHONE.................................310 820-6661
Robert J Lowe, *President*
Sara Bravo, *President*
James Sabatier, *President*
Rick Swagerty, *President*
Michael Heiken, *CFO*
EMP: 125 EST: 1972
SQ FT: 20,000
SALES (est): 935.4MM **Privately Held**
WEB: www.lowe-re.com
SIC: 7011 6552 Hotels & motels; subdi-
   viders & developers

(P-16547)
LQR PROPERTY LLC
Also Called: La Quinta Resort & Club
49499 Eisenhower Dr, La Quinta
(92253-2722)
PHONE.................................760 564-4111
Nancy Byrne, *Executive Asst*
Veronica Alvarez, *Admin Asst*
Lynette Alarcon, *Accounting Mgr*
Katherine Stoker, *Opers Staff*
Joe Alegre, *Sales Staff*
EMP: 337 EST: 2012
SALES (est): 29.7MM **Privately Held**
WEB: www.laquintaresort.com
SIC: 7011 7999 Resort hotel; golf driving
   range

(P-16548)
LVP CY PASO ROBLES LLC
Also Called: Courtyard Paso Robles
120 S Vine St, Paso Robles (93446-3736)
PHONE.................................805 239-9700
Gregg Forde, *Principal*
EMP: 50 EST: 2017
SALES (est): 2.6MM
SALES (corp-wide): 30.9MM **Privately Held**
WEB: www.lightstonecapitalmarkets.com
SIC: 7011 Hotels & motels
PA: Lightstone Value Plus Real Estate In-
   vestment Trust Ii, Inc
   460 Park Ave Fl 13
   New York NY 10022
   800 304-0210

(P-16549)
M&C HOTEL INTERESTS INC
530 Pico Blvd, Santa Monica (90405-1223)
PHONE.................................310 399-9344
Lisa Nagahori, *Branch Mgr*
Sarah Gardina, *Executive*
Mario Leal, *Associate Dir*
Jose Pascay, *Engineer*
Gregory McIntosh, *Business Mgr*
EMP: 189 **Privately Held**
WEB: www.millenniumhotels.com
SIC: 7011 Hotels
HQ: M&C Hotel Interests, Inc.
   6560 Greenwood Plaza Blvd
   Greenwood Village CO 80111

(P-16550)
M6 DEV LLC
Also Called: Springhill Suites
1801 S Harbor Blvd, Anaheim
(92802-3509)
PHONE.................................714 533-2101
Mona Rigdon, *Principal*
Mayur Patel, *Principal*
EMP: 50 EST: 2016
SALES (est): 2.9MM **Privately Held**
WEB: www.springhillsuites.marriott.com
SIC: 7011 Hotels & motels

(P-16551)
M8 DEV LLC
Also Called: Residence Inn Anaheim
640 W Katella Ave, Anaheim (92802-3411)
PHONE.................................714 782-7500
Mayur Patel,
EMP: 99 EST: 2016
SALES (est): 3.3MM **Privately Held**
SIC: 7011 Hotels & motels

(P-16552)
MAHAVIR HOSPITALITY LLC
Also Called: Clarion Hotel
1455 Ocotillo Dr, El Centro (92243-4212)
PHONE.................................760 352-5152
Mitesh Kalthia,
Neil Patel, *Info Tech Mgr*
Rajnikant Mehta,
Kirti Shah,
EMP: 91 EST: 1980
SQ FT: 50,000
SALES (est): 699.4K **Privately Held**
WEB: www.choicehotels.com
SIC: 7011 Hotels & motels

(P-16553)
MAJESTIC INDUSTRY HILLS LLC
Also Called: Pacific Plms Conference Resort
1 Industry Hills Pkwy, City of Industry
(91744-5160)
PHONE.................................626 810-4455
Scott Huntsman, *Branch Mgr*
John Semcken, *Principal*
EMP: 547
SALES (corp-wide): 42.1MM **Privately Held**
WEB: www.pacificpalmsresort.com
SIC: 7011 7999 7389 7299 Resort hotel;
   tennis courts, outdoor/indoor: non-mem-
   bership; convention & show services;
   banquet hall facilities
PA: Majestic Industry Hills, Llc
   1 Industry Hills Pkwy
   City Of Industry CA 91744
   562 692-9581

(P-16554)
MAKAR ANAHEIM LLC
Also Called: Hilton
777 W Convention Way, Anaheim
(92802-3425)
PHONE.................................714 740-4431
Paul Makarechian,
Dawn Bartone, *Accountant*
Karl Sherman, *Purchasing*
Megan Beck, *Manager*
EMP: 1200 EST: 1984
SQ FT: 1,000,000
SALES (est): 49.7MM **Privately Held**
WEB: www.hiltongrandvacations.com
SIC: 7011 Hotels & motels

(P-16555)
MARCUS HOTELS INC
Also Called: Holiday Inn
4222 Vineland Ave, North Hollywood
(91602-3318)
PHONE.................................818 980-8000
Kroy Walter, *Director*
EMP: 231
SALES (corp-wide): 237.6MM **Publicly Held**
WEB: www.marcushotels.com
SIC: 7011 Hotels & motels
HQ: Marcus Hotels Inc
   100 E Wscnsin Ave Ste 195
   Milwaukee WI 53202

(P-16556)
MARRIOTT INTERNATIONAL INC
5855 W Century Blvd, Los Angeles
(90045-5614)
PHONE.................................310 641-5700
Jim Burns, *General Mgr*
Diane Drucker, *Executive*
Dawn Frederick, *Executive*
Shannon Montoya, *Executive*
Melanie Rodi, *Executive*
EMP: 900
SALES (corp-wide): 10.5B **Publicly Held**
WEB: www.marriott.com
SIC: 7011 7389 6513 Hotels & motels; of-
   fice facilities & secretarial service rental;
   residential hotel operation
PA: Marriott International, Inc.
   10400 Fernwood Rd
   Bethesda MD 20817
   301 380-3000

(P-16557)
MARRIOTT INTERNATIONAL INC
18000 Von Karman Ave, Irvine
(92612-1004)
PHONE.................................949 724-3606
Satinder Palpa, *Branch Mgr*
Jennifer Lindstrom, *Executive*
Stephanie Macias, *Executive*
Parker Passman, *Executive*
Alexandria Huggett, *Admin Asst*
EMP: 258
SALES (corp-wide): 10.5B **Publicly Held**
WEB: www.marriott.com
SIC: 7011 7389 Hotels & motels; office fa-
   cilities & secretarial service rental
PA: Marriott International, Inc.
   10400 Fernwood Rd
   Bethesda MD 20817
   301 380-3000

(P-16558)
MARRIOTT INTERNATIONAL INC
Also Called: Inn At Mssion San Juan Cpstran
31692 El Camino Real, San Juan Capis-
trano (92675-2657)
PHONE.................................949 503-5700
Arne Sorenson, *CEO*
Kristi Kaib, *Principal*
EMP: 90 EST: 1997
SALES (est): 2.9MM **Privately Held**
WEB: www.marriott.com
SIC: 7011 Hotels & motels

(P-16559)
MARRIOTT INTERNATIONAL INC
900 W Olympic Blvd, Los Angeles
(90015-1338)
PHONE.................................213 284-3862
EMP: 167
SALES (corp-wide): 10.5B **Publicly Held**
WEB: www.marriott.com
SIC: 7011 Hotels And Motels
PA: Marriott International, Inc.
   10400 Fernwood Rd
   Bethesda MD 20817
   301 380-3000

(P-16560)
MARRIOTT RSRTS HSPITALITY CORP
1091 Pinehurst Ln, Palm Desert
(92260-1636)
PHONE.................................760 779-1200

Timothy Hamilton, *Sales Staff*
EMP: 413 **Publicly Held**
WEB: www.marriott.com
SIC: 7011 Hotels & motels
HQ: Marriott Resorts Hospitality Corpora-
   tion
   6649 W Wood Blvd Ste 500
   Orlando FL 32821
   407 206-6000

(P-16561)
MARRIOTTS SHADOW RIDGE
9003 Shadow Ridge Rd, Palm Desert
(92211-2057)
PHONE.................................760 674-2600
John Faulk, *Owner*
EMP: 107 EST: 2006
SALES (est): 2.5MM **Privately Held**
WEB: www.marriott.com
SIC: 7011 Resort hotel

(P-16562)
MAVERICK HOSPITALITY INC
17662 Irvine Blvd Ste 4, Tustin
(92780-3132)
PHONE.................................714 730-7717
Brad Perrin, *Principal*
EMP: 96 EST: 2004
SALES (est): 519.9K **Privately Held**
SIC: 7011 Hotels & motels

(P-16563)
MERISTAR SAN PEDRO HILTON LLC
Also Called: Hilton Port Los Angls-San Pdro
2800 Via Cabrillo Marina, San Pedro
(90731-7223)
PHONE.................................310 514-3344
Paul Whetsell, *Mng Member*
Jeff Milnes, *CEO*
John Emery, *CFO*
EMP: 105 EST: 1986
SALES (est): 1.5MM **Privately Held**
WEB: www.portoflosangeles.org
SIC: 7011 Hotels & motels
HQ: Interstate Hotels & Resorts, Inc.
   5301 Headquarters Dr
   Plano TX 75024
   703 387-3100

(P-16564)
MERRITT HOSPITALITY LLC
Also Called: Hilton
701 W Ocean Blvd, Long Beach
(90831-3100)
PHONE.................................562 983-3400
Grace Sun, *Sales Mgr*
EMP: 164
SALES (corp-wide): 204.2MM **Privately Held**
WEB: www.hiltongrandvacations.com
SIC: 7011 7991 5813 5812 Resort hotel;
   physical fitness facilities; drinking places;
   eating places
HQ: Merritt Hospitality, Llc
   101 Merritt 7 Ste 14
   Norwalk CT 06851
   203 849-8844

(P-16565)
MERRITT HOSPITALITY LLC
Also Called: Marriott
2701 Nutwood Ave, Fullerton (92831-5400)
PHONE.................................714 738-7800
Tom Beebon, *Manager*
EMP: 164
SALES (corp-wide): 204.2MM **Privately Held**
WEB: www.marriott.com
SIC: 7011 7991 5813 5812 Resort hotel;
   physical fitness facilities; drinking places;
   eating places
HQ: Merritt Hospitality, Llc
   101 Merritt 7 Ste 14
   Norwalk CT 06851
   203 849-8844

(P-16566)
METROPOLE HOTEL
205 Crescent Ave, Avalon (90704-2958)
P.O. Box 1900 (90704-1900)
PHONE.................................310 510-1884
Roger F Swallow, *President*
EMP: 65 EST: 1990

SALES (est): 1MM **Privately Held**
WEB: www.hotel-metropole.com
SIC: 7011 Hotel, franchised

(P-16567)
METROPOLIS HOTEL MGT LLC
Also Called: Hotel Indigo Los Angles Dwntwn
899 Francisco St, Los Angeles
(90017-2534)
PHONE..................................213 683-4855
Raymond Vermolen, *General Mgr*
EMP: 120 EST: 2016
SALES (est): 25MM **Privately Held**
WEB: www.downtownlosangeleshotel.com
SIC: 7011 Hotels
HQ: Inter-Continental Hotels Corporation
35016 Avenue D
Yucaipa CA 92399
770 604-5000

(P-16568)
MHRP RESORT INC
Also Called: Mountain High Ski Resort
24510 Highway 2, Wrightwood (92397)
P.O. Box 3010 (92397-3010)
PHONE..................................760 249-5808
Russel S Bernard, *President*
W Gregory Geiger, *Vice Pres*
Kenneth Liang, *Vice Pres*
John McColly, *Vice Pres*
Marc Porosoff, *Vice Pres*
EMP: 100 EST: 1997
SALES (est): 5.5MM **Privately Held**
SIC: 7011 Resort hotel

(P-16569)
MIKADO HOTELS INC
Also Called: Best Western
12600 Riverside Dr, North Hollywood
(91607-3411)
PHONE..................................818 763-9141
Jerome Frick, *CEO*
Edmond Petrossian, *President*
Diran Yahyayan, *Vice Pres*
EMP: 50 EST: 1963
SQ FT: 71,500
SALES (est): 1.1MM **Privately Held**
WEB: www.bestwestern.com
SIC: 7011 5812 5813 Hotel, franchised;
restaurant, lunch counter; cocktail lounge

(P-16570)
MONDRIAN HOLDINGS LLC
8440 W Sunset Blvd, West Hollywood
(90069-1912)
PHONE..................................323 848-6004
Mathew Pargament, *General Mgr*
Daniel Espino, *Principal*
Steve Del Rosario, *Controller*
Marc Kaplan, *Controller*
Jay Thorson, *Controller*
EMP: 400 EST: 1999
SQ FT: 500,000
SALES (est): 11.7MM
SALES (corp-wide): 627.9MM **Privately Held**
WEB: www.sbe.com
SIC: 7011 Hotels
HQ: Morgans Hotel Group Co.
475 10th Ave
New York NY 10018

(P-16571)
MONTAGE HOTELS & RESORTS LLC
Also Called: Montage Beverly Hills
225 N Canon Dr, Beverly Hills
(90210-5301)
PHONE..................................310 499-4199
Alan Fuerstman, *Branch Mgr*
EMP: 83
SALES (corp-wide): 110.6MM **Privately Held**
WEB: www.montagehotels.com
SIC: 7011 7991 Resort hotel; spas
PA: Montage Hotels & Resorts, Llc
3 Ada Ste 100
Irvine CA 92618
949 715-5002

(P-16572)
MONTAGE HOTELS & RESORTS LLC (PA)
Also Called: Montage Laguna Beach
3 Ada Ste 100, Irvine (92618-2322)
P.O. Box 52031, Phoenix AZ (85072-2031)
PHONE..................................949 715-5002
Alan Fuerstman, *Mng Member*
Jason Herthel, *President*
Lindsey Sagnella, *Exec VP*
Iqbal Bashir, *Vice Pres*
James D Bermingham, *Vice Pres*
EMP: 640 EST: 2002
SQ FT: 586,000
SALES (est): 110.6MM **Privately Held**
WEB: www.montagehotels.com
SIC: 7011 Resort hotel

(P-16573)
MORGANS HOTEL GROUP MGT LLC
Also Called: Mondrian Hotel
8440 W Sunset Blvd, Los Angeles
(90069-1912)
PHONE..................................323 650-8999
David Weidlich, *General Mgr*
Benito Canche, *Purch Agent*
Kristina Puma, *Sales Staff*
Robert Gregson, *Director*
Kate Northrop, *Director*
EMP: 200
SALES (corp-wide): 627.9MM **Privately Held**
WEB: www.sbe.com
SIC: 7011 5813 5812 Hotels; drinking
places; eating places
HQ: Morgans Hotel Group Management Llc
475 10th Ave Fl 11
New York NY 10018

(P-16574)
MSR DESERT RESORT LP
Also Called: Hotel Associates Palm Springs
49499 Eisenhower Dr, La Quinta
(92253-2722)
P.O. Box 659 (92247-0659)
PHONE..................................760 564-5730
Michael Shannon, *Partner*
Tim Hansen, *CFO*
John Saer, *Treasurer*
Larry Lichliter, *Exec VP*
Nola Dyal, *Vice Pres*
▲ EMP: 1500 EST: 1926
SALES (est): 69.2MM **Privately Held**
WEB: www.kslresorts.com
SIC: 5812 7011 7997 5813 Eating
places; motel, franchised; tennis club,
membership; golf club, membership;
drinking places

(P-16575)
MSR HOTELS & RESORTS INC
Also Called: Residence Inn By Marriott
3701 Torrance Blvd, Torrance
(90503-4805)
PHONE..................................310 543-4566
David Zimmerman, *Manager*
EMP: 256
SALES (corp-wide): 52B **Publicly Held**
WEB: www.residence-inn.marriott.com
SIC: 7011 Hotels & motels
HQ: Msr Hotels & Resorts, Inc.
450 S Orange Ave
Orlando FL 32801
407 650-1000

(P-16576)
NBC SUITE HOTEL
Also Called: Embassy Suites
1440 E Imperial Ave, El Segundo
(90245-2623)
PHONE..................................310 640-3600
Shar Franklin, *President*
EMP: 57 EST: 2001
SALES (est): 1.9MM **Privately Held**
WEB: www.hilton.com
SIC: 7011 Hotels & motels

(P-16577)
NEG282 LLC
51880 Highway 190, Death Valley (92328)
PHONE..................................760 786-2387
Armand P Ortega, *CEO*
Shane P Ortega, *President*

James Hernandez, *COO*
Thomas A Williamson, *Principal*
Frank Hutton, *General Mgr*
EMP: 295 EST: 2014
SALES (est): 430K
SALES (corp-wide): 42.6MM **Privately Held**
WEB: www.deathvalleyhotels.com
SIC: 7011 Motels
PA: Ortega National Parks, Llc
54 1/2 E San Francisco St
Santa Fe NM 87501
505 988-1866

(P-16578)
NESBITT PRTNERS SAN LUIS OBSPO
333 Madonna Rd, San Luis Obispo
(93405-6506)
PHONE..................................805 549-0800
Tim Billing, *Partner*
EMP: 51 EST: 2008
SALES (est): 1.8MM **Privately Held**
WEB:
www.embassysuitessanluisobispo.com
SIC: 7011 Hotels

(P-16579)
NEW FIGUEROA HOTEL INC
1000 S Hope St Apt 201, Los Angeles
(90015-1492)
PHONE..................................213 627-8971
Uno Thimansson, *President*
Elyse Omori, *Vice Pres*
EMP: 70 EST: 1977
SQ FT: 200,000
SALES (est): 4.4MM **Privately Held**
WEB: www.hotelfigueroa.com
SIC: 7011 5812 5813 Resort hotel; eating
places; bars & lounges

(P-16580)
NEWPORT HOSPITALITY GROUP INC
Also Called: Holiday Inn
801 Truxtun Ave, Bakersfield (93301-4726)
PHONE..................................661 323-1900
Eric Iokal, *Manager*
EMP: 200 **Privately Held**
WEB: www.holidayinn.com
SIC: 7011 Hotels & motels
PA: Newport Hospitality Group Inc
1048 Irvine Ave Ste 365
Newport Beach CA
949 706-7002

(P-16581)
NEWPORT HOTEL CAPITAL LLC
Also Called: Hotel Menage
1221 S Harbor Blvd, Anaheim
(92805-6004)
PHONE..................................714 758-0900
Rob Kaulfonic, *Vice Pres*
EMP: 192 EST: 1989
SALES (est): 1MM **Privately Held**
SIC: 7011 5813 5812 Hotels; drinking
places; eating places

(P-16582)
NEWPORT MESA INN LLC
Also Called: Best Western
2642 Newport Blvd, Costa Mesa
(92627-4626)
PHONE..................................949 650-3020
James Hsuan, *Mng Member*
S P Lee, *Partner*
EMP: 83 EST: 1984
SQ FT: 60,000
SALES (est): 2.6MM **Privately Held**
WEB: www.bwnewport.com
SIC: 7011 Hotels & motels

(P-16583)
NOBLE INVESTMENT GROUP LLC
Also Called: Westin Long Beach Hotel, The
333 E Ocean Blvd, Long Beach
(90802-4827)
PHONE..................................562 436-3000
Bharat Shah, *Mng Member*
EMP: 153 EST: 2003
SQ FT: 60,000
SALES (est): 1.1MM **Privately Held**
WEB: www.westin.marriott.com
SIC: 7011 Hotels

(P-16584)
NOBLE/UTAH LONG BEACH LLC
Also Called: Westin Long Beach Hotel, The
333 E Ocean Blvd, Long Beach
(90802-4827)
PHONE..................................562 436-3000
Mitesh B Shah, *Mng Member*
Ashley Conway, *Receptionist*
EMP: 250 EST: 2005
SQ FT: 51,000
SALES (est): 25.9MM **Privately Held**
WEB: www.westin.marriott.com
SIC: 7011 Hotels & motels
PA: Noble Investment Group, Llc
3424 Peachtree Rd Ne
Atlanta GA 30326

(P-16585)
NORTHWEST HOTEL CORPORATION (PA)
Also Called: Howard Johnson
1380 S Harbor Blvd, Anaheim
(92802-2310)
PHONE..................................714 776-6120
James P Edmondson, *President*
Jonathan Whitehead, *General Mgr*
Heather Brodersen, *Marketing Staff*
EMP: 119 EST: 1965
SQ FT: 50,000
SALES (est): 6.3MM **Privately Held**
WEB: www.hojoanaheim.com
SIC: 7011 Hotels & motels

(P-16586)
NREA-TRC 711 LLC
Also Called: Sheraton
711 S Hope St, Los Angeles (90017-3803)
PHONE..................................213 488-3500
EMP: 200 EST: 2013
SQ FT: 470,000
SALES (est): 24.4MM **Privately Held**
WEB: www.marriott.com
SIC: 7011 Hotels & motels

(P-16587)
OAK CREEK LP
Also Called: Holiday Inn
21725 Gateway Center Dr, Diamond Bar
(91765-2400)
PHONE..................................909 860-5440
Billy Mendez, *Partner*
James Hsu, *Vice Pres*
Sammi Wang, *Principal*
Marie Astorga, *Admin Sec*
EMP: 53 EST: 2009
SALES (est): 5.2MM **Privately Held**
WEB: www.brightonmgtllc.com
SIC: 7011 Hotels & motels

(P-16588)
OAK PARKS INNS INC
Also Called: Holiday Inn
775 N Oak Park Blvd, Grover Beach
(93433-1417)
PHONE..................................805 481-4448
Ryan Hong, *President*
Deborah King, *President*
Lynda Backman, *Principal*
Steve Hong, *General Mgr*
Sam Miller, *Manager*
EMP: 73 EST: 1987
SALES (est): 742.1K **Privately Held**
WEB: www.holidayinn.com
SIC: 7011 Hotels & motels

(P-16589)
OASIS WEST REALTY LLC
Also Called: Waldorf Astoria Beverly Hills
9850 Wilshire Blvd, Beverly Hills
(90210-3115)
PHONE..................................310 860-6666
Damian Cabotaje, *Mng Member*
Marissa Menzer, *Executive Asst*
Kaicy Sweeney, *Finance*
Valerie Cannon, *Sales Staff*
Theodore Kahan, *Principal*
EMP: 100 EST: 2017
SALES (est): 5.1MM **Privately Held**
WEB: www.waldorfastoriabeverlyhills.com
SIC: 7011 Hotels

PRODUCTS & SVCS

(P-16590)
OCEAN AVENUE LLC
Also Called: Fairmont Miramar Hotel
101 Wilshire Blvd, Santa Monica
(90401-1106)
PHONE...............................310 576-7777
Ellis O'Connor, *Mng Member*
Matthew Lehman, *General Mgr*
Andres Fernandez, *Administration*
Zully Ruiz, *Project Mgr*
Alfredo Amaya, *Auditor*
EMP: 275 EST: 1973
SQ FT: 209,000
SALES (est): 23.6MM
SALES (corp-wide): 627.9MM **Privately Held**
WEB: www.oceanaveliving.com
SIC: 7011 Hotels
HQ: Accor Services Us Llc
950 Mason St
San Francisco CA 94108
415 772-5000

(P-16591)
OHI RESORT HOTELS LLC
Also Called: Wyndham Anaheim Garden Grove
12021 Harbor Blvd, Garden Grove
(92840-4001)
PHONE...............................714 867-5555
Jeremy Yujuico, *Principal*
Donna Coins, *Sales Staff*
EMP: 98 EST: 1998
SALES (est): 6.2MM **Privately Held**
WEB: www.anaheim.crowneplaza.com
SIC: 7011 Hotels

(P-16592)
OJAI VALLEY INN GOLF COURSE
Also Called: Ojai Valley Spa
905 Country Club Rd, Ojai (93023-3789)
PHONE...............................805 646-2420
Thad Hyland, *Director*
Vanessa Jimenez, *Human Res Mgr*
Hannah Hathaway, *Marketing Mgr*
Megan Kitagawa, *Marketing Staff*
Phil Nelson, *Director*
EMP: 71 EST: 1923
SALES (est): 3.3MM **Privately Held**
WEB: www.ojaivalleyinn.com
SIC: 7011 7992 5941 Resort hotel; public golf courses; sporting goods & bicycle shops

(P-16593)
OLS HOTELS & RESORTS LLC
Also Called: Le Parc Suite Hotel
733 W Knoll Dr, West Hollywood
(90069-5207)
PHONE...............................310 855-1115
Sam Ebeid, *CEO*
Martti Mannoja, *Exec VP*
Kealii Alexander, *Vice Pres*
Ira Kleinrock, *Vice Pres*
Bert Seneca, *General Mgr*
EMP: 509
SALES (corp-wide): 87.6MM **Privately Held**
WEB: www.springboardhospitality.com
SIC: 7011 8741 Hotels; hotel or motel management
PA: Ols Hotels & Resorts, Llc
16000 Ventura Blvd # 101
Encino CA 91436
818 905-8280

(P-16594)
OLS HOTELS & RESORTS LLC
Also Called: Marriott
14635 Bldwin Pk Towne Ctr, Baldwin Park
(91706-5548)
PHONE...............................626 962-6000
Peter Ehienberg, *Manager*
Jiyu Liang, *Human Res Dir*
Vecario Kathy, *Marketing Staff*
EMP: 509
SALES (corp-wide): 87.6MM **Privately Held**
WEB: www.springboardhospitality.com
SIC: 7011 Hotels & motels
PA: Ols Hotels & Resorts, Llc
16000 Ventura Blvd # 101
Encino CA 91436
818 905-8280

(P-16595)
OLY-REMINGTON VENTURA LLC
Also Called: Marriott Ventura Beach
2055 Harbor Blvd, Ventura (93001-3707)
PHONE...............................805 643-6000
David A Brooks,
Dave Brooks, *Executive*
EMP: 60 EST: 2001
SALES (est): 1.6MM **Privately Held**
WEB: www.marriottventurabeach.com
SIC: 7011 Hotels

(P-16596)
OMNI HOTELS CORPORATION
41000 Bob Hope Dr, Rancho Mirage
(92270-4416)
PHONE...............................760 568-2727
Ashlee Wilson, *CIO*
Stephanie Torres, *Natl Sales Mgr*
EMP: 53 **Privately Held**
WEB: www.omnihotels.com
SIC: 7011 Hotels & motels
HQ: Omni Hotels Corporation
4001 Maple Ave Ste 500
Dallas TX 75219
972 871-5600

(P-16597)
ONTARIO HOSPITALITY PROPERTIES
Also Called: Holiday Inn
3400 Shelby St, Ontario (91764-4873)
PHONE...............................909 946-9600
Larry Ferguson, *General Mgr*
EMP: 62 EST: 1986
SQ FT: 70,000
SALES (est): 437.8K **Privately Held**
WEB: www.holidayinn.com
SIC: 7011 Hotels & motels

(P-16598)
ORLANDO WILSHIRE INVESTMENTS
Also Called: Orlando, The
8384 W 3rd St, Los Angeles (90048-4311)
PHONE...............................323 658-6600
Kenneth Pressberg, *Partner*
Sidney Pressberg, *Partner*
EMP: 147 EST: 1981
SQ FT: 45,000
SALES (est): 3.1MM **Privately Held**
SIC: 7011 Hotels

(P-16599)
OSF INTERNATIONAL INC
Also Called: Newport Beach Spaghetti
2110 Newport Blvd, Newport Beach
(92663-4322)
PHONE...............................949 675-8654
Dean Rakr, *Manager*
EMP: 66
SALES (corp-wide): 145.4MM **Privately Held**
WEB: www.osf.com
SIC: 5812 7011 Italian restaurant; hotels & motels
PA: Osf International, Inc.
0715 Sw Bancroft St
Portland OR 97239
503 222-5375

(P-16600)
OTB ACQUISITION LLC
Also Called: Sierra Vista Extended Stay
770 S Brea Blvd Ste 227, Brea
(92821-5399)
PHONE...............................520 458-0540
EMP: 77 **Privately Held**
WEB: www.ontheborder.com
SIC: 7011 Hotels & motels
PA: Otb Acquisition Llc
2201 W Royal Ln Ste 240
Irving TX 75063

(P-16601)
OUTRIGGER HOTELS HAWAII
Also Called: Marina International Hotel
4200 Admiralty Way, Venice (90292-5422)
PHONE...............................310 301-2000
Mohammed Khan, *General Mgr*
EMP: 57

SALES (corp-wide): 93.8MM **Privately Held**
WEB: www.outrigger.com
SIC: 7011 6531 Resort hotel; real estate managers
PA: Outrigger Hotels Hawaii
2375 Kuhio Ave
Honolulu HI 96815
808 921-6600

(P-16602)
OUTRIGGER HOTELS HAWAII
Grafton On Sunset, The
8462 W Sunset Blvd, West Hollywood
(90069-1912)
PHONE...............................323 491-9015
Kevin Briggs, *Branch Mgr*
Jason Jackson, *Manager*
EMP: 57
SALES (corp-wide): 93.8MM **Privately Held**
WEB: www.outrigger.com
SIC: 7011 Resort hotel
PA: Outrigger Hotels Hawaii
2375 Kuhio Ave
Honolulu HI 96815
808 921-6600

(P-16603)
OVIS LLC
Also Called: Ojai Valley Inn & Spa
905 Country Club Rd, Ojai (93023-3734)
PHONE...............................805 646-5511
Toll Free:...........................888
Stephen Crown, *Mng Member*
Magdalena Morin, *CFO*
Scott Michael, *Executive*
Dan Cooper, *Info Tech Mgr*
Claire Flores, *IT/INT Sup*
EMP: 600 EST: 1923
SALES (est): 50.6MM **Privately Held**
WEB: www.ojaivalleyinn.com
SIC: 7011 5813 5812 Resort hotel; drinking places; eating places

(P-16604)
OXFORD PALACE HOTEL
745 S Oxford Ave, Los Angeles
(90005-2909)
PHONE...............................213 382-7756
Bowhan Kim, *Principal*
Don W Chang, *Principal*
Bora Park, *Sales Dir*
EMP: 96 EST: 1992
SALES (est): 6.2MM **Privately Held**
WEB: www.oxfordhotel.com
SIC: 7011 5812 Resort hotel; Korean restaurant

(P-16605)
PACIFIC CAMBRIA INC
Also Called: Cambria Pines Lodge
2905 Burton Dr, Cambria (93428-4001)
PHONE...............................805 927-6114
Dirk Winter, *President*
Rebecca Ramos, *Sales Staff*
Bram Winter, *Manager*
EMP: 90 EST: 1975
SQ FT: 70,000
SALES (est): 10MM **Privately Held**
WEB: www.cambriapineslodge.com
SIC: 7011 5812 5813 Hotels; resort hotel; restaurant, family; independent; bar (drinking places)

(P-16606)
PACIFIC CATALINA HOTEL INC
Also Called: Catalina Canyon Resort
888 Country Club Dr, Avalon (90704-2956)
P.O. Box 736 (90704-0736)
PHONE...............................310 510-9255
Gonzalo Rodriguez, *General Mgr*
EMP: 414 EST: 1977
SALES (est): 1.6MM
SALES (corp-wide): 112.8MM **Privately Held**
WEB: www.lovecatalina.com
SIC: 7011 7389 Hotels; hotel & motel reservation service
PA: Pacifica Hosts, Inc.
1775 Hancock St Ste 200
San Diego CA 92110
619 296-9000

(P-16607)
PACIFIC CITY HOTEL LLC
Also Called: Pasea Hotel & Spa
21080 Pacific Coast Hwy, Huntington Beach (92648-5305)
PHONE...............................7 4 698-6100
Joe Leinacker, *General Mgr*
Cecille-Lou Jones, *Executive Asst*
Roy Rios, *Chief Engr*
Lynette Dodd, *Finance*
David Newkirk, *Purch Mgr*
EMP: 300 EST: 2015
SALES (est): 2.8MM **Privately Held**
WEB: www.meritagecollection.com
SIC: 7011 Resort hotel

(P-16608)
PACIFIC HOTEL MANAGEMENT INC
Also Called: Radison Hotel Newport Beach
4545 Macarthur Blvd, Newport Beach
(92660-2022)
PHONE...............................949 608-1091
Ron Mavaddat, *President*
EMP: 140 EST: 2003
SALES (est): 15MM **Privately Held**
WEB: www.radissonhotelgroup.com
SIC: 7011 Hotels

(P-16609)
PACIFIC HUNTINGTON HOTEL CORP
Also Called: Langham Huntington Hotel & Spa
1401 S Oak Knoll Ave, Pasadena
(91106-4508)
PHONE...............................626 568-3900
Ying Shek Lo, *President*
Fe Bernardo, *Accounting Mgr*
EMP: 600 EST: 2000
SQ FT: 21,193
SALES (est): 95.5MM **Privately Held**
WEB: www.langhamhotels.com
SIC: 7011 Resort hotel
PA: Langham Hotels International Limited
27 & 33/F Great Eagle Ctr
Wan Chai HK

(P-16610)
PACIFIC MONARCH RESORTS INC
7 Grenada St, Laguna Niguel
(92677-4825)
PHONE...............................949 228-1396
EMP: 68
SALES (corp-wide): 79.1MM **Privately Held**
WEB: www.monarchgrandvacations.com
SIC: 7011 Resort hotel
PA: Pacific Monarch Resorts, Inc.
4000 Macarthur Blvd # 600
Newport Beach CA 92660
949 609-2400

(P-16611)
PACIFIC MONARCH RESORTS INC
Also Called: Vacation Marketing Group
981 Iowa Ave Ste C, Riverside
(92507-1615)
PHONE...............................951 342-7970
Ken Otto, *Manager*
EMP: 68
SALES (corp-wide): 79.1MM **Privately Held**
WEB: www.monarchgrandvacations.com
SIC: 7011 Resort hotel
PA: Pacific Monarch Resorts, Inc.
4000 Macarthur Blvd # 600
Newport Beach CA 92660
949 609-2400

(P-16612)
PACIFIC MONARCH RESORTS INC
Also Called: Riviera Shores
34630 Pacific Coast Hwy, Capistrano Beach (92624-1301)
PHONE...............................949 248-2944
Michael Murray, *Co-Owner*
EMP: 68

▲ = Import ▼ =Export
◆ =Import/Export

SALES (corp-wide): 79.1MM **Privately Held**
WEB: www.monarchgrandvacations.com
SIC: **7011** 6531 Resort hotel; time-sharing real estate sales, leasing & rentals
PA: Pacific Monarch Resorts, Inc.
4000 Macarthur Blvd # 600
Newport Beach CA 92660
949 609-2400

(P-16613)
PACIFIC SNOW VALLEY RESORT LLC
Also Called: Holiday Inn Resort At Lodge
40650 Village Dr, Big Bear Lake (92315-2164)
PHONE..................................909 866-3121
Dennis Montes, *General Mgr*
EMP: 60 **Privately Held**
WEB: www.holidayinnresorts.com
SIC: **7011** 7299 5812 5813 Vacation lodges; banquet hall facilities; eating places; drinking places
PA: Pacific Snow Valley Resort Llc
812 W Las Tunas Dr
San Gabriel CA 91776

(P-16614)
PACIFICA HT CNFRNCE CTR A CAL
Also Called: Radisson Hotel La Westside
6161 W Centinela Ave, Culver City (90230-6306)
PHONE..................................310 649-1776
Jim Collins, *General Ptnr*
Robert Leonard, *Partner*
EMP: 63 EST: 1994
SALES (est): 1MM **Privately Held**
WEB: www.radissonhotelgroup.com
SIC: **7011** 6512 5812 7389 Hotels & motels; commercial & industrial building operation; eating places; convention & show services

(P-16615)
PACKARD REALTY INC
Also Called: Holiday Inn
9901 S La Cienega Blvd, Los Angeles (90045-5915)
PHONE..................................310 649-5151
Tommy Spencer, *General Mgr*
EMP: 114 **Privately Held**
WEB: www.packard-1.com
SIC: **7011** Hotels & motels
PA: Packard Realty Inc.
9555 Chesapeake Dr # 202
San Diego CA 92123

(P-16616)
PALM DESERT HOSPITALITY LLC
Also Called: Homewood Suites
36999 Cook St, Palm Desert (92211-6066)
PHONE..................................760 568-1600
Maria Banning, *Branch Mgr*
EMP: 222
SALES (corp-wide): 3.6MM **Privately Held**
WEB: www.hospitalitydental.com
SIC: **7011** Hotels & motels
PA: Palm Desert Hospitality, L.L.C.
2390 Tower Dr
Monroe LA 71201
760 568-1600

(P-16617)
PALM MOUNTAIN RESORT & SPA
155 S Belardo Rd, Palm Springs (92262-6327)
PHONE..................................760 325-1301
William McWethy, *Owner*
Hector Becerra, *General Mgr*
EMP: 54 EST: 1986
SALES (est): 16.4MM **Privately Held**
WEB: www.palmmountainresort.com
SIC: **7011** Resort hotel

(P-16618)
PALM SPRINGS RENTAL AGENCY INC
Also Called: La Quinta Vacation Rental
225 S Civic Dr Ste 1-7, Palm Springs (92262-7228)
PHONE..................................760 320-7451
Peter Brooks, *President*
Kenny Cassady, *VP Business*
EMP: 50 EST: 1972
SQ FT: 2,500
SALES (est): 2.5MM **Privately Held**
WEB: www.palmspringsrentals.com
SIC: **7011** 6531 Resort hotel; rental agent, real estate

(P-16619)
PALMDALE RESORT INC
Also Called: Holiday Inn
38630 5th St W, Palmdale (93551-4208)
PHONE..................................661 947-8055
Toni Vilopas, *Owner*
EMP: 77 EST: 1991
SQ FT: 71,394
SALES (est): 2.6MM **Privately Held**
WEB: www.holidayinn.com
SIC: **7011** Hotels & motels

(P-16620)
PARK HOTELS & RESORTS INC
Also Called: Embassy Suites Brea
900 E Birch St, Brea (92821-5812)
PHONE..................................714 990-6000
Jay Badillo, *Branch Mgr*
Emily Walkner, *Director*
Zulima Mesa, *Manager*
EMP: 60
SALES (corp-wide): 852MM **Publicly Held**
WEB: www.hilton.com
SIC: **7011** Hotels & motels
PA: Park Hotels & Resorts Inc.
1775 Tysons Blvd Fl 7
Tysons VA 22102
571 302-5757

(P-16621)
PARK HOTELS & RESORTS INC
Also Called: Hilton
9876 Wilshire Blvd, Beverly Hills (90210-3115)
PHONE..................................310 415-3340
Beverly Hilton, *Principal*
James Harvey, *Vice Pres*
John Whitlam, *Technology*
Teresa Espinosa, *Chief Acct*
Luis Munoz, *Opers Dir*
EMP: 113
SALES (corp-wide): 852MM **Publicly Held**
WEB: www.hiltongrandvacations.com
SIC: **7011** Hotels & motels
PA: Park Hotels & Resorts Inc.
1775 Tysons Blvd Fl 7
Tysons VA 22102
571 302-5757

(P-16622)
PARKER PALM SPRINGS LLC
4200 E Palm Canyon Dr, Palm Springs (92264-5230)
PHONE..................................760 770-5000
Adam Glick, *Principal*
Christel Arias, *Director*
Alex Faldon, *Manager*
Yagmur Gursoy, *Manager*
EMP: 81 EST: 2003
SALES (est): 7.7MM **Privately Held**
WEB: www.parkerpalmsprings.com
SIC: **7011** Resort hotel

(P-16623)
PASADENA HOTEL DEV VENTR LP
Also Called: Sheraton Pasadena
303 Cordova St, Pasadena (91101-2426)
PHONE..................................626 449-4000
Ray Serafin, *Principal*
Howard Haberman, *Chief Mktg Ofcr*
David Iwane, *Principal*
Kathleen Blackman, *Sales Mgr*
EMP: 99 EST: 2008
SALES (est): 5.1MM **Privately Held**
WEB: www.marriott.com
SIC: **7011** Resort hotel

(P-16624)
PASO ROBLES INN LLC
Also Called: Paso Robles Hotel
1103 Spring St, Paso Robles (93446-2598)
PHONE..................................805 238-2660
Paul Wallace, *General Mgr*
Tom Martin, *Owner*
Kim Eady, *Partner*
Andrew Litton, *Partner*
Ken Litton, *Partner*
EMP: 57 EST: 1963
SALES (est): 3.4MM **Privately Held**
WEB: www.pasoroblesinn.com
SIC: **7011** 5812 5813 Hotels; restaurant, family; independent; cocktail lounge

(P-16625)
PEACOCK STES RESORT LTD PARTNR
1745 S Anaheim Blvd, Anaheim (92805-6518)
PHONE..................................714 535-8255
Sheldon Ginsburg, *General Ptnr*
Shell Development Corporation-, *General Ptnr*
Perry Snyderman, *General Ptnr*
EMP: 55 EST: 1993
SQ FT: 75,000
SALES (est): 2.1MM **Privately Held**
WEB: www.shellvacationsclub.com
SIC: **7011** 6531 Resort hotel; hotels; time-sharing real estate sales, leasing & rentals

(P-16626)
PECHANGA DEVELOPMENT CORP
Also Called: Pechanga Resort & Casino
45000 Pechanga Pkwy, Temecula (92592-5810)
P.O. Box 9041 (92589-9041)
PHONE..................................951 695-4655
Patrick Murphy, *CEO*
Jerry Konchar, *CFO*
Christina McMenamin, *Treasurer*
Shirlene Orr, *Officer*
Edith Atwood, *Vice Pres*
◆ EMP: 4000 EST: 1995
SALES (est): 206.1MM **Privately Held**
WEB: www.pechanga.com
SIC: **7011** 7929 7999 Casino hotel; entertainment service; gambling establishment

(P-16627)
PECHANGA RESORTS INCORPORATED
45000 Pechanga Pkwy, Temecula (92592-5810)
P.O. Box 1477 (92593-1477)
PHONE..................................888 732-4264
Edith Atwood, *CEO*
Miusette Garcia, *Bd of Directors*
John Durment, *Officer*
Bill Anderson, *Vice Pres*
Michelle Green, *Executive Asst*
EMP: 63 EST: 2018
SALES (est): 5.6MM **Privately Held**
WEB: www.pechanga.com
SIC: **7011** Casino hotel

(P-16628)
PHF II BURBANK LLC
Also Called: Burbank Airport Mariott Hotel
2500 N Hollywood Way, Burbank (91505-1019)
PHONE..................................818 843-6000
Linda Davey, *Mng Member*
Harry Greenblatt, *Vice Pres*
EMP: 220 EST: 2006
SALES (est): 7.5MM **Privately Held**
WEB: www.ctnanimationexpo.com
SIC: **7011** Hotels & motels

(P-16629)
PIER PONT HOTEL LP
550 San Jon Rd, Ventura (93001-3745)
PHONE..................................805 643-6144
EMP: 50
SALES (est): 692.9K **Privately Held**
SIC: **7011** Hotel/Motel Operation

(P-16630)
PIERPONT INN INC
Also Called: Central Coast Management
550 San Jon Rd, Ventura (93001-3754)
P.O. Box 335, Grover Beach (93483-0335)
PHONE..................................805 643-0245
Subhash Patel, *President*
Mauline Patel, *Vice Pres*
EMP: 60 EST: 1956
SALES (est): 556.4K **Privately Held**
WEB: www.pierpontinn.com
SIC: **7011** 5812 Bed & breakfast inn; drive-in restaurant

(P-16631)
PINNACLE RVRSIDE HSPITALITY LP
Also Called: Riverside Marriott
3400 Market St, Riverside (92501-2826)
PHONE..................................951 784-8000
Dr Bharat Lall, *General Ptnr*
EMP: 190 EST: 2007
SALES (est): 10.4MM **Privately Held**
WEB: www.marriott.com
SIC: **7011** Hotels

(P-16632)
PISMO BEACH HT INVESTMENTS LLC
Also Called: Autograph Vespera On Ocean
147 Stimson Ave, Pismo Beach (93449-2643)
PHONE..................................805 773-1011
Matthew Kaufman, *Principal*
Loisa Young, *Principal*
EMP: 50 EST: 2014
SALES (est): 1.4MM **Privately Held**
WEB: www.vesperapismobeach.com
SIC: **7011** Hotels

(P-16633)
PISMO COAST VILLAGE INC
165 S Dolliver St, Pismo Beach (93449-2999)
PHONE..................................805 773-1811
Jay Jamison, *General Mgr*
Ronald Nunlist, *President*
Wayne Hardesty, *CFO*
Terris Hughes, *Exec VP*
Dwight Plumley, *Vice Pres*
EMP: 60 EST: 1975
SALES (est): 7.4MM **Privately Held**
WEB: www.pismocoastvillage.com
SIC: **7011** Resort hotel

(P-16634)
PLAYA PROPER JV LLC
Also Called: Custom Hotel
8639 Lincoln Blvd, Los Angeles (90045-3503)
PHONE..................................310 645-0400
Brad Korzen, *CEO*
Bryan De Lowe, *President*
Jeffrey Cruz, *Finance*
EMP: 80 EST: 2017
SALES (est): 10.1MM **Privately Held**
WEB: www.thehoteljune.com
SIC: **7011** Hotels

(P-16635)
PONDEROSA YORBA LINDA LLC
Also Called: Residnce Inn Anheim Hlls Yrba
125 S Festival Dr, Anaheim (92808-1115)
PHONE..................................714 974-8880
Chelsea Roberts, *Principal*
Jillian Jackson, *Principal*
EMP: 50 EST: 2018
SALES (est): 1MM **Privately Held**
SIC: **7011** Inns

(P-16636)
PORTOFINO HOTEL PARTNERS LP
Also Called: Hotel Portofino
260 Portofino Way, Redondo Beach (90277-2033)
PHONE..................................310 379-8481
Glenn Bishop, *Principal*
Archana Olsen, *Associate Dir*
Aurora Cruz, *Exec Dir*
Jeff Perkins, *General Mgr*
Mary Dino, *Finance Dir*
EMP: 151 EST: 1980

P
R
O
D
U
C
T
S

&

S
V
C
S

SALES (est): 10MM **Privately Held**
WEB: www.hotelportofino.com
SIC: 7011 Resort hotel

(P-16637)
PORTOFINO INN & SUITES ANAHEIM
1831 S Harbor Blvd, Anaheim
(92802-3509)
PHONE..................................714 782-7600
Jennifer Reihl, *Director*
Heather Ryan, *Accounts Mgr*
EMP: 989 EST: 2008
SALES (est): 927.8K **Privately Held**
WEB: www.portofinoinnanaheim.com
SIC: 7011 Inns
PA: Tarsadia Hotels
620 Newport Center Dr # 1400
Newport Beach CA 92660

(P-16638)
POSADA ROYALE HOTEL & SUITES
1775 Madera Rd, Simi Valley (93065-3049)
PHONE..................................805 584-6300
Larry Rogers, *Partner*
Peter Zegers, *Partner*
EMP: 94 EST: 1986
SQ FT: 55,000
SALES (est): 634.9K **Privately Held**
SIC: 7011 5812 7389 7299 Hotels; American restaurant; convention & show services; banquet hall facilities

(P-16639)
POSADAS USA INC
Also Called: Hampton Inn
7828 Orangethorpe Ave, Buena Park
(90621-3435)
PHONE..................................714 522-2122
Evelyn Whalen, *Manager*
EMP: 106
SALES (corp-wide): 21.9MM **Privately Held**
WEB: www.posadas.com
SIC: 7011 Hotels & motels
PA: Posadas Usa, Inc.
1700 Pacific Ave Ste 270
Dallas TX 75201
214 891-3130

(P-16640)
PRIME HOSPITALITY LLC (PA)
Also Called: Holiday Inn
2155 E Convention Ctr Way, Ontario
(91764-4452)
PHONE..................................909 212-8000
Madan Reddy,
Gary Franklin, *Purchasing*
Steve Leeper, *Opers Staff*
EMP: 139 EST: 2006
SALES (est): 1.4MM **Privately Held**
WEB: www.holidayinn.com
SIC: 7011 Hotels & motels

(P-16641)
PRIME HOSPITALITY SERVICES LLC (PA)
Also Called: Hampton Inn
8300 Granite Falls Dr, Bakersfield
(93312-6598)
PHONE..................................661 321-9424
Raju Verma, *Principal*
EMP: 73 EST: 2009
SALES (est): 5.2MM **Privately Held**
WEB: www.hilton.com
SIC: 7011 Hotels & motels

(P-16642)
PRUTEL JOINT VENTURE
Also Called: Ritz-Carlton Laguna Niguel
1 Ritz Carlton Dr, Dana Point (92629-4205)
PHONE..................................949 240-2000
W B Johnson, *Partner*
Prudential Realty, *Partner*
Paul Patterson, *CFO*
Madelyn Abbot, *Vice Pres*
Nathalie Rader, *General Mgr*
EMP: 700 EST: 1984
SALES (est): 31MM **Privately Held**
WEB: www.ritzcarlton.com
SIC: 7011 Hotels

(P-16643)
PT GAMING LLC
235 Oregon St, El Segundo (90245-4215)
PHONE..................................323 260-5060
Patrick Tierney, *Mng Member*
David Shindle, *COO*
Kamal Rahi, *Senior Mgr*
James Razon, *Senior Mgr*
Jodi Simons, *Manager*
EMP: 700 EST: 2012
SQ FT: 7,000
SALES (est): 35.8MM **Privately Held**
WEB: www.patrickgaming.com
SIC: 7011 Casino hotel

(P-16644)
Q S H PROPERTIES INC
Also Called: Quality Inn
2701 Hotel Ter, Santa Ana (92705-5603)
PHONE..................................714 957-9200
Vahi M Melkonian, *President*
Cheng Wu, *Manager*
EMP: 199 EST: 1986
SALES (est): 1.6MM **Privately Held**
WEB: www.choicehotels.com
SIC: 7011 Hotels & motels

(P-16645)
Q S SAN LUIS OBISPO LP
Also Called: Quality Inn
1631 Monterey St, San Luis Obispo
(93401-2929)
PHONE..................................805 541-5001
George Newland, *Partner*
Harold Parker, *General Ptnr*
Robert Warmington, *General Ptnr*
Winston Newland, *General Mgr*
Christopher Houston, *Payroll Mgr*
EMP: 80 EST: 1986
SALES (est): 5.3MM **Privately Held**
WEB: www.qualitysuitesslo.com
SIC: 7011 Hotels & motels

(P-16646)
QUEENSBAY HOTEL LLC
Also Called: Hotel Maya
700 Queensway Dr, Long Beach
(90802-6343)
PHONE..................................562 481-3910
Cherie Davis, *Manager*
Michael Cox, *Finance*
EMP: 100
SALES (corp-wide): 14.5MM **Privately Held**
WEB: www.hotelmayalongbeach.com
SIC: 7011 Hotels
PA: Queensbay Hotel, Llc
444 W Ocean Blvd
Long Beach CA 90802
562 628-0625

(P-16647)
R C HOTELS INC
Also Called: Hotel On Huntington Beach
7667 Center Ave, Huntington Beach
(92647-3073)
PHONE..................................714 891-0123
Toll Free:....................................877
Shu Chin Kou, *President*
Joe Tsai, *Executive*
Christopher Deguzman, *Sales Staff*
EMP: 86 EST: 1993
SQ FT: 114,012
SALES (est): 1.2MM **Privately Held**
WEB: www.hotelhb.com
SIC: 7011 Resort hotel; hotels

(P-16648)
R C L LODGING SYSTEMS INC
Also Called: Holiday Inn
1045 E Valley Blvd A205, San Gabriel
(91776-3658)
PHONE..................................661 833-3000
Robert Lu, *President*
Julia Lu, *Admin Sec*
EMP: 64 EST: 1994
SALES (est): 711.3K **Privately Held**
WEB: www.holidayinn.com
SIC: 7011 Hotels & motels

(P-16649)
R P S RESORT CORP
1600 N Indian Canyon Dr, Palm Springs
(92262-4602)
PHONE..................................760 327-8311
Douglas McCarron, *President*

EMP: 215 EST: 1990
SALES (est): 2.1MM
SALES (corp-wide): 45.9MM **Privately Held**
WEB: www.hilton.com
SIC: 7011 Resort hotel
HQ: The San Bernardino Hilton
285 E Hospitality Ln
San Bernardino CA 92408

(P-16650)
RADISSON HOTEL AT USC
Also Called: Radisson Inn
3540 S Figueroa St, Los Angeles
(90007-4313)
PHONE..................................213 748-4141
EMP: 120 EST: 1977
SALES (est): 587.4K **Privately Held**
SIC: 7011 Hotels And Motels

(P-16651)
RADISSON HOTEL SANTA MARIA
Also Called: Radisson Inn
3455 Skyway Dr, Santa Maria
(93455-2501)
PHONE..................................805 928-8000
Ryan Swack, *Principal*
EMP: 67 EST: 1989
SQ FT: 60,000
SALES (est): 1.3MM **Privately Held**
WEB: www.santamariaairport.com
SIC: 7011 5812 Hotels & motels; eating places

(P-16652)
RADLAX GATEWAY HOTEL LLC
Also Called: Radisson Inn
6225 W Century Blvd, Los Angeles
(90045-5311)
PHONE..................................310 670-9000
Peter Dumon, *Mng Member*
EMP: 1342 EST: 2007
SALES (est): 2.5MM **Privately Held**
WEB: www.radissonhotelgroup.com
SIC: 7011 Hotels & motels
PA: Portfolio Hotels & Resorts, Llc
1211 W 22nd St Ste 1002
Oak Brook IL 60523

(P-16653)
RAFFLES LRMITAGE BEVERLY HILLS
Also Called: L'Ermitage Hotel
9291 Burton Way, Beverly Hills
(90210-3709)
PHONE..................................310 278-3344
Jack Naderkhani, *General Mgr*
Alba Gonzalez, *Facilities Dir*
EMP: 249 EST: 1993
SALES (est): 11.7MM
SALES (corp-wide): 627.9MM **Privately Held**
WEB: www.viceroyhotelsandresorts.com
SIC: 7011 5813 5812 Hotels; drinking places; eating places
HQ: Raffles International Limited
1 Wallich Street
Singapore 07888

(P-16654)
RALEIGH ENTERPRISES INC (PA)
Also Called: Raleigh Holdings
5300 Melrose Ave Fl 4, Los Angeles
(90038-5114)
PHONE..................................310 899-8900
Kristen J Raleigh, *CEO*
George I Rosenthal, *Ch of Bd*
Mark Rosenthal, *President*
Josie Lewis, *COO*
Jane Jentzsch, *Executive Asst*
EMP: 130 EST: 1955
SQ FT: 20,000
SALES (est): 53.8MM **Privately Held**
WEB: www.raleighenterprises.com
SIC: 7011 Hotels

(P-16655)
RALEIGH SUNSET MARQUIS HO
1200 Alta Loma Rd, Los Angeles
(90069-2404)
PHONE..................................3 0 358-3759
Rod Gruendyke, *General Mgr*
Christopher Nealy, *Engrg Dir*
Klaus Messner, *Sales Staff*
Jakub Skyvara, *Food Svc Dir*
Nima Javaherpour, *Manager*
EMP: 52 EST: 2007
SALES (est): 6.3MM **Privately Held**
WEB: www.sunsetmarquis.com
SIC: 7011 Hotels

(P-16656)
RBD HOTEL PALM SPRINGS LLC
Also Called: Hyatt Rgency Suites Palm Sprng
285 N Palm Canyon Dr, Palm Springs
(92262-5525)
PHONE..................................760 322-9000
Larry Mills, *Senior VP*
Grant Doheny, *Engineer*
Sargon Somo, *Sales Mgr*
Jim Lopez, *Sales Staff*
EMP: 75 EST: 2009
SALES (est): 950K **Privately Held**
WEB: www.hyatt.com
SIC: 7011 Resort hotel

(P-16657)
RED EARTH CASINO
3089 Norm Niver Rd, Thermal
(92274-6550)
PHONE..................................760 395-1200
Larry Drouse, *General Mgr*
Nicki Joukovsky, *Accounting Mgr*
Paul Marcus, *Manager*
EMP: 150 EST: 2007
SQ FT: 15,000
SALES (est): 16.2MM **Privately Held**
WEB: www.redearthcasino.com
SIC: 7011 7993 Casino hotel; gambling establishments operating coin-operated machines

(P-16658)
REMINGTON HOTEL CORPORATION
Also Called: Palm Springs Renaissance
888 E Tahquitz Canyon Way, Palm Springs
(92262-6708)
PHONE..................................760 322-6000
EMP: 80 **Privately Held**
WEB: www.remingtonhotels.com
SIC: 7011 Hotels
PA: Remington Hotel Corporation
14185 Dallas Pkwy # 1150
Dallas TX 75254

(P-16659)
REMINGTON HOTEL CORPORATION
Also Called: Holiday Inn
1150 S Beverly Dr, Los Angeles
(90035-1120)
PHONE..................................310 553-6561
Jack Jones, *Branch Mgr*
EMP: 80 **Privately Held**
WEB: www.remingtonhotels.com
SIC: 7011 Hotels & motels
PA: Remington Hotel Corporation
14185 Dallas Pkwy # 1150
Dallas TX 75254

(P-16660)
RENAISSANCE HOTEL OPERATING CO
Also Called: Marriott
9620 Airport Blvd, Los Angeles
(90045-5402)
PHONE..................................310 337-2800
Gregory Lehman, *Manager*
Susan Preston, *COO*
Jenny Ulch, *Finance*
Joanne Wildenhain, *Sales Staff*
Geovanni Arriaga, *Director*
EMP: 300

SALES (corp-wide): 10.5B **Publicly Held**
WEB: www.renaissance-hotels.marriott.com
SIC: 7011 5813 5812 7389 Hotels & motels; drinking places; eating places; office facilities & secretarial service rental
HQ: Renaissance Hotel Operating Company
10400 Fernwood Rd
Bethesda MD 20817
-

(P-16661)
RENAISSANCE HOTEL OPERATING CO
Also Called: Renaissance Indian Wells
44400 Indian Wells Ln, Indian Wells
(92210-8708)
PHONE......................760 773-4444
Tom Tabler, *Principal*
EMP: 600
SALES (corp-wide): 10.5B **Publicly Held**
WEB: www.renaissance-hotels.marriott.com
SIC: 7011 Hotels & motels
HQ: Renaissance Hotel Operating Company
10400 Fernwood Rd
Bethesda MD 20817

(P-16662)
RESORT AT PELICAN HILL LLC
22701 Pelican Hill Rd S, Newport Coast
(92657-2008)
PHONE......................949 467-6800
Elia Gutierrez, *Director*
Tim La Duke, *Executive*
Thomas Donovan, *Managing Dir*
Kelsey Lovelady, *Security Dir*
Jon Martin, *General Mgr*
EMP: 142 **EST:** 2006
SALES (est): 14MM **Privately Held**
WEB: www.pelicanhill.com
SIC: 7011 Resort hotel

(P-16663)
RIO VISTA DEVELOPMENT CO INC (PA)
Also Called: Holiday Inn
4222 Vineland Ave, North Hollywood
(91602-3318)
PHONE......................818 980-8000
Scott A Mills, *Principal*
Scott Mills, *General Ptnr*
Khondaker Bashar, *Executive*
Rhocelli Pascual, *Marketing Mgr*
Rachel Kaye, *Marketing Staff*
EMP: 133 **EST:** 1971
SQ FT: 100,000
SALES (est): 12.3MM **Privately Held**
WEB: www.thegarland.com
SIC: 7011 Hotels & motels

(P-16664)
RITZ-CARLTON HOTEL COMPANY LLC
1 Ritz Carlton Dr, Dana Point (92629-4206)
PHONE......................949 240-5020
Janinie Vanderoy, *Branch Mgr*
Lisa Holladay, *Vice Pres*
Samantha Boone, *Executive*
Mike Kass, *General Mgr*
Natalie Wise, *Executive Asst*
EMP: 348
SALES (corp-wide): 10.5B **Publicly Held**
WEB: www.ritzcarlton.com
SIC: 7011 Hotels
HQ: The Ritz-Carlton Hotel Company Llc
10400 Fernwood Rd
Bethesda MD 20817
301 380-3000

(P-16665)
RITZ-CARLTON HOTEL COMPANY LLC
8301 Hollister Ave, Santa Barbara
(93117-2474)
PHONE......................805 968-0100
Kelly Josephson, *Sales Staff*
Diana Morro,
EMP: 650
SALES (corp-wide): 10.5B **Publicly Held**
WEB: www.ritzcarlton.com
SIC: 7011 Hotels

HQ: The Ritz-Carlton Hotel Company Llc
10400 Fernwood Rd
Bethesda MD 20817
301 380-3000

(P-16666)
RITZ-CARLTON HOTEL COMPANY LLC
Also Called: Ritz Carlton Rancho Mirage
68900 Frank Sinatra Dr, Rancho Mirage
(92270-5300)
PHONE......................760 321-8282
James H Palllin Jr, *Manager*
Terrilyn Bruggemans, *General Mgr*
Steven Demeglio, *Purchasing*
Scott Lewis, *Opers Staff*
Daniel Garcia, *Manager*
EMP: 313
SALES (corp-wide): 10.5B **Publicly Held**
WEB: www.ritzcarlton.com
SIC: 7011 Hotels
HQ: The Ritz-Carlton Hotel Company Llc
10400 Fernwood Rd
Bethesda MD 20817
301 380-3000

(P-16667)
RIVIERA REINCARNATE LLC
Also Called: Palm Sprng Riviera Resorts Spa
1600 N Indian Canyon Dr, Palm Springs
(92262-4602)
PHONE......................760 327-8311
Jim Manion,
EMP: 61 **EST:** 2007
SALES (est): 1.6MM **Privately Held**
SIC: 7011 Resort hotel

(P-16668)
RMS FOUNDATION INC
Also Called: Queen Mary Hotel
1126 Queens Hwy, Long Beach
(90802-6331)
PHONE......................562 435-3511
Joseph F Prevratil, *President*
Rebecca Simmons, *Executive Asst*
Pamela Conner, *Analyst*
Christopher Wilmoth, *Marketing Staff*
Lea Quiambao, *Sales Staff*
EMP: 650 **EST:** 1993
SQ FT: 750,000
SALES (est): 51.2MM
SALES (corp-wide): 889.7MM **Privately Held**
WEB: www.queenmary.com
SIC: 7011 Hotels & motels
PA: City Of Long Beach
411 W Ocean Blvd
Long Beach CA 90802
562 570-6450

(P-16669)
ROBRAY HOTEL PARTNERSHIP LLP
Also Called: Las Brisas Hotel
222 S Indian Canyon Dr, Palm Springs
(92262-6618)
PHONE......................760 325-4372
Raymond Johnston, *President*
Las Brisas New Century, *General Ptnr*
Robby Loh,
EMP: 72 **EST:** 1988
SALES (est): 2MM **Privately Held**
SIC: 7011 Resort hotel

(P-16670)
ROOSEVELT HOTEL LLC
Also Called: Hollywood Roosevelt Hotel
7000 Hollywood Blvd, Los Angeles
(90028-6003)
PHONE......................323 466-7000
Goodwin Gaw, *Mng Member*
Gevork Keshishian, *Officer*
Jeff Hanlon, *Security Dir*
Amir Awad, *Info Tech Mgr*
Michelle Soliman, *Asst Controller*
EMP: 200 **EST:** 1995
SALES (est): 34MM **Privately Held**
WEB: www.thehollywoodroosevelt.com
SIC: 7011 5813 5812 Hotels; drinking places; eating places

(P-16671)
ROSANNA INC
Also Called: Avenue of Arts Wyndham Hotel
3350 Avenue Of The Arts, Costa Mesa
(92626-1913)
PHONE......................714 751-5100
Nick Price, *General Mgr*
Rachael Moorhead, *President*
Paul Sanford, *CEO*
Rosanna Chan, *Principal*
Kenneth Chouinard, *Marketing Mgr*
EMP: 151 **EST:** 2009
SALES (est): 19MM **Privately Held**
WEB: www.avenueoftheartshotel.com
SIC: 7011 5812 Hotels; food bars; caterers

(P-16672)
ROSCOE REAL ESTATE LTD PARTNR
Also Called: Elkor Properties
1819 Ocean Ave, Santa Monica
(90401-3215)
PHONE......................310 260-7500
Vincent Piro, *General Mgr*
Elkor Trio LL LLC, *General Ptnr*
Annie King, *Sales Mgr*
Stacy Davis, *Sales Staff*
Karen Giordano, *Sales Staff*
EMP: 113 **EST:** 2000
SALES (est): 6.3MM **Privately Held**
WEB: www.viceroyhotelsandresorts.com
SIC: 7011 7389 Hotels; hotel & motel reservation service

(P-16673)
ROYAL OAK MOTOR HOTEL
Also Called: Best Western
214 Madonna Rd, San Luis Obispo
(93405-5409)
PHONE......................805 544-4410
Loreta Gingg, *Principal*
Diane Church, *Principal*
Naomi Henn, *Manager*
EMP: 65
SQ FT: 100,000
SALES (est): 2.3MM **Privately Held**
WEB: www.royaloakhotel.com
SIC: 7011 5813 Hotels; cocktail lounge

(P-16674)
RPD HOTELS 18 LLC (PA)
Also Called: Vagabond Inns
1801 S La Cnega Blvd # 301, Los Angeles
(90035-4641)
PHONE......................213 746-1531
Juan Sanchez Llaca,
Don Johnson,
Stewart Rubin,
EMP: 800 **EST:** 1998
SALES (est): 23.1MM **Privately Held**
WEB: www.vagabondinn.com
SIC: 7011 Motels

(P-16675)
RT PASAD HOTEL PARTNERS LP
Also Called: Courtyard By Marriott
180 N Fair Oaks Ave, Pasadena
(91103-3614)
PHONE......................626 403-7600
Timothy Bristol, *General Mgr*
Luis Guzman, *Plant Mgr*
April Ponce, *Sales Staff*
EMP: 94 **EST:** 2004
SQ FT: 165,342
SALES (est): 3.8MM **Privately Held**
WEB: www.courtyard.marriott.com
SIC: 7011 Hotels & motels

(P-16676)
RUBICON B HACIENDA LLC
Also Called: Fairfield Inn
525 N Pacific Coast Hwy, El Segundo
(90245-4448)
PHONE......................424 290-5000
Marc Gordon,
EMP: 56 **EST:** 2016
SALES (est): 1.8MM **Privately Held**
WEB: www.fairfield.marriott.com
SIC: 7011 Hotels & motels

(P-16677)
RUFFIN HOTEL CORP OF CAL
Also Called: Long Beach Marriott
4700 Airport Plaza Dr, Long Beach
(90815-1252)
PHONE......................562 425-5210
Phillip G Ruffin, *President*
Jennifer Robinson, *Director*
EMP: 260 **EST:** 1993
SALES (est): 16MM **Privately Held**
SIC: 7011 5812 5813 Hotels; eating places; coffee shop; drinking places

(P-16678)
S B H HOTEL CORPORATION
285 E Hospitality Ln, San Bernardino
(92408-3411)
PHONE......................909 889-0133
Douglas McCarron, *Branch Mgr*
EMP: 745
SALES (corp-wide): 45.9MM **Privately Held**
SIC: 7011 Hotels
HQ: S B H-Hotel Corporation
520 S Virgil Ave Fl 4
Los Angeles CA

(P-16679)
S B HOTEL PARTNERS
Also Called: Holiday Inn
17 W Haley St, Santa Barbara
(93101-3428)
PHONE......................805 963-9757
Kay Morter, *Manager*
EMP: 76 **EST:** 1998
SALES (est): 1.1MM **Privately Held**
WEB: www.hiexpress.com
SIC: 7011 Hotels & motels

(P-16680)
S W K PROPERTIES LLC
Also Called: Holiday Inn
2726 S Grand Ave Lbby, Santa Ana
(92705-5404)
PHONE......................714 481-6300
Rod Hurt, *Manager*
Annette Anderson, *Sales Mgr*
EMP: 129
SALES (corp-wide): 7.1MM **Privately Held**
WEB: www.holidayinn.com
SIC: 7011 Hotels & motels
PA: S W K Properties Llc
3807 Wilshire Blvd # 122
Los Angeles CA 90010
213 383-9204

(P-16681)
S W K PROPERTIES LLC (PA)
Also Called: Sheraton
3807 Wilshire Blvd # 122, Los Angeles
(90010-3101)
PHONE......................213 383-9204
Eric Cha,
EMP: 70 **EST:** 1998
SQ FT: 3,000
SALES (est): 7.1MM **Privately Held**
WEB: www.four-points.marriott.com
SIC: 7011 Hotels & motels

(P-16682)
SAGE HOSPITALITY RESOURCES LLC
Also Called: Courtyard By Mrrott Los Angles
700 W Huntington Dr, Monrovia
(91016-3104)
PHONE......................626 357-5211
Dennis Hollingdrake, *Manager*
EMP: 159
SALES (corp-wide): 286.2MM **Privately Held**
WEB: www.sagehospitalitygroup.com
SIC: 7011 Hotels & motels
PA: Sage Hospitality Resources L.L.C.
1575 Welton St Ste 300
Denver CO 80202
303 595-7200

(P-16683)
SAHARAN MOTOR HOTEL INC
Also Called: Surestay
7212 W Sunset Blvd, Los Angeles
(90046-3406)
PHONE......................323 874-6700
Raj Patel, *Owner*

EMP: 62 EST: 1991
SQ FT: 29,000
SALES (est): 713.9K **Privately Held**
WEB: www.sunsetwesthotel.com
SIC: 7011 Motels

(P-16684)
SAI MANAGEMENT CO INC
Also Called: Desert Inn & Suites
1600 S Harbor Blvd, Anaheim
(92802-2314)
PHONE.....................................714 772-5050
Priti Hansji, *Manager*
EMP: 80
SALES (corp-wide): 8MM **Privately Held**
WEB: www.desertpalmshotel.com
SIC: 7011 Resort hotel
PA: Sai Management Co., Inc.
631 W Katella Ave
Anaheim CA
714 776-8604

(P-16685)
SAJAHTERA INC
Also Called: Beverly Hills Hotel
9641 Sunset Blvd, Beverly Hills
(90210-2938)
PHONE.....................................310 276-2251
Junaidi Masri, *President*
Edward Mady, *General Mgr*
Porfirio Caamal, *Accounting Mgr*
Ana Martinez, *Credit Staff*
Bibi Bedoya, *Payroll Mgr*
EMP: 600 EST: 1912
SQ FT: 10,758
SALES (est): 81.5MM
SALES (corp-wide): 541MM **Privately Held**
WEB: www.dorchestercollection.com
SIC: 7011 Resort hotel; hotels
HQ: Dorchester Group Limited
57 Berkeley Square
London W1J 6
207 629-4848

(P-16686)
SALIMAR INC
Also Called: Best Western
2842 Summit Cir, Bakersfield (93306-1062)
PHONE.....................................661 327-9651
Ratansha Parabia, *President*
Sam Parabia, *President*
Ray Parabia, *General Mgr*
EMP: 59 EST: 1998
SALES (est): 736.7K **Privately Held**
WEB: www.bestwestern.com
SIC: 7011 Hotels & motels

(P-16687)
SAN BERNARDINO HILTON (HQ)
285 E Hospitality Ln, San Bernardino
(92408-3411)
PHONE.....................................909 889-0133
Douglas McCarron, *President*
Morgan McPherson, *Exec Dir*
Ronald Schoen, *Admin Sec*
EMP: 152 EST: 1984
SALES (est): 27.6MM
SALES (corp-wide): 45.9MM **Privately Held**
WEB: www.hilton.com
SIC: 7011 6512 5812 Hotels & motels; commercial & industrial building operation; eating places
PA: Carpenters Southwest Administrative Corporation
533 S Fremont Ave
Los Angeles CA 90071
213 386-8590

(P-16688)
SAN PEDRO OWNERSHIP INC
Also Called: Doubletree Hotel
2800 Via Cabrillo Marina, San Pedro
(90731-7223)
PHONE.....................................310 514-3344
John Parker, *President*
EMP: 57 EST: 2005
SALES (est): 3.9MM **Privately Held**
WEB: www.sanpedro.com
SIC: 7011 Hotels & motels

(P-16689)
SAN YI US INVESTMENT CO INC
Also Called: Sheraton Los Angles San Gbriel
303 E Valley Blvd, San Gabriel
(91776-3522)
PHONE.....................................626 607-2006
Fred Kokash, *President*
EMP: 50 EST: 2018
SALES (est): 3.3MM **Privately Held**
SIC: 7011 Hotels & motels

(P-16690)
SANTA MARIA HOTEL CORP
Also Called: Holiday Inn
2100 N Broadway, Santa Maria
(93454-1140)
PHONE.....................................805 928-6000
Lawrence Lui, *President*
Susan Garcia, *General Mgr*
Tiffany Borjas, *Finance Mgr*
EMP: 84 EST: 1996
SALES (est): 3MM **Privately Held**
WEB: www.hisantamariahotel.com
SIC: 7011 5812 7389 Hotels; eating places; convention & show services

(P-16691)
SANTA MONICA DAYS INN
3007 Santa Monica Blvd, Santa Monica
(90404-2505)
PHONE.....................................310 829-6333
King Chai, *Managing Prtnr*
EMP: 59 EST: 1996
SALES (est): 813.7K **Privately Held**
WEB: www.wyndhamhotels.com
SIC: 7011 Hotels & motels

(P-16692)
SANTA MONICA HOTEL OWNER LLC
Also Called: Doubltree Stes By Hlton Snta M
1707 4th St, Santa Monica (90401-3301)
PHONE.....................................310 395-3332
EMP: 135 EST: 2005
SALES (est): 11.5MM **Privately Held**
SIC: 7011 Hotels

(P-16693)
SANTA MONICA PROPER JV LLC
Also Called: Santa Monica Proper Hotel
700 Wilshire Blvd, Santa Monica
(90401-1708)
PHONE.....................................310 620-9990
Brad Korzen, *CEO*
Julien Laracine, *Managing Dir*
Tony Diaz, *Purchasing*
Karina Nazarian, *Sales Mgr*
Molly Kinneberg, *Manager*
EMP: 250 EST: 2016
SALES (est): 14.3MM **Privately Held**
WEB: www.properhotel.com
SIC: 7011 Hotels

(P-16694)
SANWA JUTAKU CO LTD
Also Called: Embassy Suites
8425 Firestone Blvd, Downey
(90241-3843)
PHONE.....................................562 861-1900
Yoko Maeda, *President*
EMP: 64 EST: 1990
SALES (est): 1.6MM **Privately Held**
WEB: www.hilton.com
SIC: 7011 Hotels & motels

(P-16695)
SAVE QUEEN LLC
429 Shoreline Village Dr I, Long Beach
(90802-8136)
PHONE.....................................562 435-3511
Sean Meddock, *Mng Member*
Sam Rithy, *Purchasing*
EMP: 59 EST: 2007
SALES (est): 4.6MM **Privately Held**
SIC: 7011 Hotels

(P-16696)
SBE ENTERTAINMENT GROUP LLC (HQ)
2535 Las Vegas Blvd S, Los Angeles
(90036)
PHONE.....................................323 655-8000
Sam Nazarian, *Mng Member*
Bradford Reynolds, *COO*

Brad Hayden, *Vice Pres*
Sam Bakhshandehpour,
Nikki Mark,
EMP: 75 EST: 2002
SQ FT: 11,000
SALES (est): 213.5MM
SALES (corp-wide): 627.9MM **Privately Held**
WEB: www.sbe.com
SIC: 5813 7011 5812 Night clubs; hotels; American restaurant
PA: Accor
82 Rue Henry Farman
Issy Les Moulineaux 92130
146 429-193

(P-16697)
SBE HOTEL GROUP LLC
8000 Beverly Blvd, Los Angeles
(90048-4547)
PHONE.....................................323 655-8000
Sam Nazarian,
EMP: 65 EST: 2004
SQ FT: 11,000
SALES (est): 10.4MM
SALES (corp-wide): 627.9MM **Privately Held**
WEB: www.sbe.com
SIC: 7011 Hotels
HQ: Sbe Entertainment Group, Llc
2535 Las Vegas Blvd S
Los Angeles CA 90036
323 655-8000

(P-16698)
SCALZO HOSPITALITY INC
Also Called: Park Vue Inn
1570 S Harbor Blvd, Anaheim
(92802-2312)
PHONE.....................................714 772-3691
Marie Baird, *Branch Mgr*
EMP: 55 **Privately Held**
WEB: www.scalzohospitality.com
SIC: 7011 Hotels & motels
PA: Scalzo Hospitality Inc.
1330 Industrial Blvd Ne
Minneapolis MN 55413

(P-16699)
SEACREST OCEANFRONT HOTEL
Also Called: Seacrest Beach Resort
2241 Price St, Pismo Beach (93449-2108)
PHONE.....................................805 773-4608
Mike Wamboldp, *Owner*
Nancy Northcote, *Principal*
Nicole Moore, *Sales Staff*
Heather Dichirico, *Mktg Coord*
EMP: 51 EST: 1971
SQ FT: 77,000
SALES (est): 7.3MM **Privately Held**
WEB: www.seacrestpismo.com
SIC: 7011 Hotels

(P-16700)
SEATTLE ARPRT HOSPITALITY LLC
Also Called: Holiday Inn
170 N Church Ln, Los Angeles
(90049-2044)
PHONE.....................................310 476-6411
Robert Buescher, *General Mgr*
EMP: 99 **Privately Held**
WEB: www.holidayinn.com
SIC: 7011 5813 5812 Hotels & motels; drinking places; eating places
PA: Seattle Airport Hospitality, Llc
5847 San Felipe St # 4650
Houston TX 77057

(P-16701)
SECOND STREET CORPORATION
Also Called: Huntley Hotel Santa Monica Bch
1111 2nd St, Santa Monica (90403-5003)
PHONE.....................................310 394-5454
Sohrab Sassounian, *President*
Dora Levy, *Shareholder*
Marschinda Felix, *COO*
Helal M El-Sherif, *CFO*
Shiva Aghaipour, *Vice Pres*
EMP: 250 EST: 1964
SQ FT: 185,000

SALES (est): 21.6MM **Privately Held**
WEB: www.thehuntleyhotel.com
SIC: 7011 5812 Hotels; eating places

(P-16702)
SEVEN RESORTS INC (PA)
9771 Irvine Center Dr, Irvine (92618-4343)
PHONE.....................................949 588-7100
David A Ohanesian, *President*
Jacqueline S Anderson, *Treasurer*
Lynda L Ohanesian-Druan, *Admin Sec*
EMP: 59 EST: 1964
SALES (est): 13.1MM **Privately Held**
SIC: 7011 Resort hotel

(P-16703)
SHC BURBANK II LLC
Also Called: Marriott
2500 N Hollywood Way, Burbank
(91505-1019)
PHONE.....................................318 843-6000
EMP: 210
SALES (est): 10.7MM **Privately Held**
SIC: 7011 Hotels And Motels

(P-16704)
SHEN ZHEN NEW WORLD II LLC
Also Called: Sheraton
333 Unversal Hollywood Dr, Universal City
(91608-1001)
PHONE.....................................818 980-1212
Ming Yu,
EMP: 99 EST: 2011
SALES (est): 3.2MM **Privately Held**
WEB: www.sheraton.marriot.com
SIC: 7011 Hotels

(P-16705)
SHERATON LLC
6101 W Century Blvd, Los Angeles
(90045-5310)
PHONE.....................................310 642-1111
Michael Washington, *General Mgr*
EMP: 58
SALES (corp-wide): 10.5B **Publicly Held**
WEB: www.sheraton.marrictt.com
SIC: 7011 5813 5812 Hotels; drinking places; eating places
HQ: The Sheraton Llc
1111 Westchester Ave
White Plains NY 10604
800 328-6242

(P-16706)
SHERATON LLC
11960 Foothill Blvd, Rancho Cucamonga
(91739-9370)
PHONE.....................................909 204-6100
EMP: 58
SALES (corp-wide): 10.5B **Publicly Held**
WEB: www.sheraton.marriott.com
SIC: 7011 Hotels & motels
HQ: The Sheraton Llc
1111 Westchester Ave
White Plains NY 10604
800 328-6242

(P-16707)
SHERTON GRDN GROVE ANHEIM S HT
12221 Harbor Blvd, Garden Grove
(92840-4005)
PHONE.....................................714 703-8400
Ronnie Lam, *Owner*
EMP: 50 EST: 2008
SALES (est): 2.7MM **Privately Held**
WEB: www.marriott.com
SIC: 7011 Resort hotel

(P-16708)
SHIVAY HOSPITAL TY INC
1738 N Las Palmas Ave, Los Angeles
(90028-4805)
PHONE.....................................323 702-7103
Pankaj Naik, *Branch Mgr*
EMP: 53
SALES (corp-wide): 412.8K **Privately Held**
SIC: 7011 Hotels & motels
PA: Shivay Hospitality Inc
1427 Wilcox Ave
Hollywood CA

(P-16709)
SIERRA HOTEL GROUP LLC
Also Called: Hilton Garden Inn Fontana
10543 Sierra Ave, Fontana (92337-7670)
PHONE..................................909 822-7300
Rhonda Gharib, *General Mgr*
Teresa Pegorari, *Director*
EMP: 81
SALES (corp-wide): 1.5MM **Privately Held**
WEB: www.hiltongrandvacations.com
SIC: 7011 Hotels
PA: Sierra Hotel Group Llc
      1905 Park Ave Ste 220
      San Jose CA 95126
      909 822-7300

(P-16710)
SILENT VALLEY CLUB INC
46305 Poppet Flats Rd, Banning
(92220-9636)
PHONE..................................951 849-4501
Patrick Buhrer, *Director*
Jane Bryant, *Relations*
EMP: 70 **EST:** 1973
SQ FT: 2,200
SALES (est): 3.2MM **Privately Held**
WEB: www.silentvalleyclub.com
SIC: 7011 Resort hotel

(P-16711)
SIMI WEST INC
Also Called: Grand Vista Hotel
999 Enchanted Way, Simi Valley
(93065-1998)
PHONE..................................760 346-5502
Leo Cook, *Ch of Bd*
Tim Lasure, *General Mgr*
Paul Gale, *Chief Engr*
Lea Foulks, *Sales Staff*
Tawny Byron, *Manager*
EMP: 120 **EST:** 1993
SALES (est): 7.1MM **Privately Held**
WEB: www.grandvistasimi.com
SIC: 7011 Hotels & motels

(P-16712)
SIMPSON HOUSE INN INC
121 E Arrellaga St, Santa Barbara
(93101-1903)
PHONE..................................805 963-7067
Linda Davies, *President*
Tony Pace, *General Mgr*
EMP: 64 **EST:** 1985
SALES (est): 828.9K **Privately Held**
WEB: www.simpsonhouseinn.com
SIC: 7011 Bed & breakfast inn

(P-16713)
SIX CONTINENTS HOTELS INC
Also Called: Holiday Inn
612 Wainwight Ct, Lebec (93243)
PHONE..................................661 343-3316
EMP: 122 **Privately Held**
WEB: www.hiexpress.com
SIC: 7011 Hotels & motels
HQ: Six Continents Hotels, Inc
      35016 Avenue D
      Yucaipa CA 92399
      770 604-5000

(P-16714)
SKY COURT USA INC
Also Called: Hyatt Hotel
880 S Westlake Blvd, Westlake Village
(91361-2905)
PHONE..................................805 497-9991
Tetsuo Nishida, *President*
EMP: 260 **EST:** 1990
SALES (est): 1.4MM **Privately Held**
WEB: www.hyatt.com
SIC: 7011 Hotels & motels

(P-16715)
SLS HOTEL AT BEVERLY HILLS
465 S La Cienega Blvd, Los Angeles
(90048-4001)
PHONE..................................310 247-0400
Robert Leck, *General Mgr*
Scott Kreeger, *COO*
Mark Napoli, *Security Dir*
Sinem Kaya, *Opers Staff*
Kendall Wallace, *Opers Staff*
EMP: 68 **EST:** 2015

SALES (est): 9.7MM
SALES (corp-wide): 76.9MM **Privately Held**
WEB: www.sbe.com
SIC: 7011 Hotels
PA: The Sunrider Corporation
      1625 Abalone Ave
      Torrance CA 90501
      310 781-3808

(P-16716)
SMOKE TREE INC
Also Called: Smoke Tree Ranch
1850 Smoke Tree Ln, Palm Springs
(92264-1602)
PHONE..................................760 327-1221
Lisa Bell, *Manager*
Dana Fosberg, *Controller*
Brad Poncher, *Manager*
EMP: 85
SALES (est): 5.5MM **Privately Held**
WEB: www.smoketreeranch.com
SIC: 7011 Resort hotel

(P-16717)
SNK LODGING INC
Also Called: Holliday Inn Express
636 N Main St, Bishop (93514-2426)
PHONE..................................760 872-2423
Dipakchandra Bhakta, *President*
EMP: 61 **EST:** 1995
SQ FT: 35,000
SALES (est): 1.1MM **Privately Held**
WEB: www.hiexpress.com
SIC: 7011 Hotels & motels

(P-16718)
SNOW SUMMIT SKI CORPORATION (PA)
880 Summit Blvd, Big Bear Lake (92315)
P.O. Box 77 (92315-0077)
PHONE..................................909 866-5766
Richard C Kun, *President*
Wade Reeser, *COO*
Bob Tarras, *CFO*
Robert Tarras, *CFO*
Alan Macquoid, *Treasurer*
EMP: 150 **EST:** 1960
SQ FT: 10,000
SALES (est): 59.8MM **Privately Held**
WEB: www.bigbearmountainresort.com
SIC: 7011 5812 Ski lodge; American
      restaurant

(P-16719)
SONESTA LOS ANGLES ARPRT LAX L
Also Called: Crowne Plaza
5985 W Century Blvd, Los Angeles
(90045-5477)
PHONE..................................310 642-7500
Paul Gibbs, *General Mgr*
EMP: 113 **EST:** 1999
SALES (est): 18.1MM **Privately Held**
WEB: www.crowneplaza.com
SIC: 7011 Hotels
HQ: Six Continents Hotels, Inc
      35016 Avenue D
      Yucaipa CA 92399
      770 604-5000

(P-16720)
SOUTH COAST WESTIN HOTEL CO
Also Called: Starwood Hotels & Resorts
686 Anton Blvd, Costa Mesa (92626-1920)
PHONE..................................714 540-2500
Steve Heyer, *CEO*
Bob Jenness, *Vice Pres*
Mike Hall, *Managing Dir*
EMP: 99 **EST:** 1970
SALES (est): 20.3MM
SALES (corp-wide): 10.5B **Publicly Held**
WEB: www.marriott.com
SIC: 7011 5812 Hotels; eating places
HQ: Starwood Hotels & Resorts Worldwide,
      Llc
      1 Star Pt
      Stamford CT 06902
      203 964-6000

(P-16721)
SPA RESORT CASINO (PA)
401 E Amado Rd, Palm Springs
(92262-6403)
PHONE..................................888 999-1995
Kato Moy, *Exec Dir*
Agvahgue Eahilla Indian, *Owner*
Bill Caronna, *Opers Staff*
Daniel Spencer, *Director*
Duke Stacy, *Director*
EMP: 817 **EST:** 2004
SALES (est): 24.4MM **Privately Held**
WEB: www.sparesortcasino.com
SIC: 7011 Resort hotel

(P-16722)
SPA RESORT CASINO
100 N Indian Canyon Dr, Palm Springs
(92262-6414)
PHONE..................................760 883-1034
Max Ross, *CFO*
Daniel Spencer, *Manager*
EMP: 183
SALES (corp-wide): 24.4MM **Privately Held**
WEB: www.sparesortcasino.com
SIC: 7011 Casino hotel
PA: Spa Resort Casino
      401 E Amado Rd
      Palm Springs CA 92262
      888 999-1995

(P-16723)
SPECTRUM HOTEL GROUP LLC
Also Called: Doubletree Hotel
90 Pacifica, Irvine (92618-3312)
PHONE..................................949 471-8888
EMP: 69 **EST:** 1997
SALES (est): 1.5MM **Privately Held**
WEB: www.hilton.com
SIC: 7011 7991 5812 Hotels & motels;
      physical fitness facilities; eating places

(P-16724)
SPF CAPITAL REAL ESTATE LLC
Also Called: Crown Plaza La Harbor Hotel
601 S Palos Verdes St, San Pedro
(90731-3329)
PHONE..................................310 519-8200
Tiegang Yin, *Principal*
Tim Yin, *Principal*
EMP: 99 **EST:** 2017
SALES (est): 6.6MM **Privately Held**
WEB: www.ihgplc.com
SIC: 7011 Hotels

(P-16725)
SPORTSMENS LODGE HOTEL LLC
12825 Ventura Blvd, Studio City
(91604-2397)
PHONE..................................818 769-4700
Mark Harlig,
Carmen Ruiz, *Technology*
Dagmara Pawelczyk, *Accounting Mgr*
Michael Dunkel, *Controller*
Tiffany Flowers, *Controller*
EMP: 75 **EST:** 1962
SQ FT: 100,000
SALES (est): 17.3MM **Privately Held**
WEB: www.sportsmenslodge.com
SIC: 7011 5812 5813 Hotels; American
      restaurant; cocktail lounge

(P-16726)
SPRINGHILL SMC LLC
Also Called: Springhill Suites
14620 Aviation Blvd, Hawthorne
(90250-6656)
PHONE..................................310 727-9595
Benisa Woolford, *Mng Member*
Zachrias Morris, *General Mgr*
EMP: 57 **EST:** 2001
SALES (est): 821.7K **Privately Held**
WEB: www.springhillsuites.marriott.com
SIC: 7011 Hotels & motels

(P-16727)
SPRINGHILL SUITES LLC
Also Called: Arcadia Suites
99 N 2nd Ave, Arcadia (91006-7080)
PHONE..................................626 821-5400
Navin Dimond, *Principal*
EMP: 55 **EST:** 1998

SALES (est): 1.1MM **Privately Held**
WEB: www.springhillsuites.marriott.com
SIC: 7011 Hotels & motels

(P-16728)
SS HERITAGE INN ONTARIO LLC
3595 E Guasti Rd, Ontario (91761-3705)
PHONE..................................909 937-5000
Aimee Fyke, *Mng Member*
EMP: 99 **EST:** 2018
SALES (est): 1.6MM **Privately Held**
SIC: 7011 Inns

(P-16729)
STARWOOD HOSPITALITY LLC
Also Called: Springhill Suites
28220 Jefferson Ave, Temecula
(92590-6612)
PHONE..................................951 699-4477
Marie Pranger, *General Mgr*
EMP: 62 **EST:** 2009 **Privately Held**
WEB: www.springhillsuites.marriott.com
SIC: 7011 Hotels & motels

(P-16730)
STARWOOD HOTEL
Also Called: Starwood Hotels & Resorts
5990 Green Valley Cir, Culver City
(90230-6907)
PHONE..................................310 641-7740
Ian Gee, *Mng Member*
EMP: 145 **EST:** 1999
SALES (est): 7.1MM
SALES (corp-wide): 10.5B **Publicly Held**
WEB: www.marriott.com
SIC: 7011 Hotels & motels
HQ: Starwood Hotels & Resorts Worldwide,
      Llc
      1 Star Pt
      Stamford CT 06902
      203 964-6000

(P-16731)
STARWOOD HTLS & RSRTS WRLDWDE
601 W Mckinley Ave, Pomona
(91768-1635)
PHONE..................................909 622-2220
John Gilbert, *General Mgr*
Kimberly Tweedt, *Supervisor*
EMP: 195
SALES (corp-wide): 10.5B **Publicly Held**
WEB: www.marriott.com
SIC: 7011 Hotels & motels
HQ: Starwood Hotels & Resorts Worldwide,
      Llc
      1 Star Pt
      Stamford CT 06902
      203 964-6000

(P-16732)
STOCKBRIDGE/SBE HOLDINGS LLC
5900 Wilshire Blvd # 3100, Los Angeles
(90036-5013)
PHONE..................................323 655-8000
Sam Nazarian, *CEO*
Michael Brubaker, *CTO*
EMP: 3000 **EST:** 2007
SALES (est): 347.3MM **Privately Held**
SIC: 7011 Hotels; casino hotel

(P-16733)
STONEBRIDGE RLTY ADVISORS INC
Also Called: Hampton Inn
27102 Towne Centre Dr, Foothill Ranch
(92610-2801)
PHONE..................................949 597-8700
John Matthews, *Manager*
EMP: 419 **Privately Held**
WEB: www.hilton.com
SIC: 7011 Hotels & motels
PA: Stonebridge Realty Advisors, Inc.
      9100 E Panorama Dr # 300
      Englewood CO 80112

(P-16734)
STOVALL STOVALL & OCONNELL
Also Called: Park Place Inn
1544 S Harbor Blvd, Anaheim
(92802-2312)
PHONE..........................714 776-4800
Robert Stovall, *Partner*
William O'Connell, *Partner*
James Stovall, *Partner*
Terri Price, *VP Finance*
Christopher Noell, *Psychiatry*
EMP: 62 **EST:** 1987
SQ FT: 3,600
SALES (est): 432.9K **Privately Held**
SIC: 7011 Resort hotel

(P-16735)
SUMMERWOOD WINERY & INN INC
2175 Arbor Rd, Paso Robles (93446-8620)
PHONE..........................805 227-1365
Mark Uhalley, *President*
Celeste Graebner, *Controller*
Shane Cline, *Manager*
▲ **EMP:** 34 **EST:** 2002
SALES (est): 2.1MM **Privately Held**
WEB: www.summerwoodwine.com
SIC: 7011 2084 Bed & breakfast inn; wines

(P-16736)
SUMMIT HOTEL TRS 111 LLC (PA)
Also Called: Hampton Inn
50 W Daily Dr, Camarillo (93010-5707)
PHONE..........................805 389-9898
EMP: 52 **EST:** 2017
SALES (est): 1MM **Privately Held**
WEB: www.visitcamarillo.com
SIC: 7011 Hotels & motels

(P-16737)
SUMMIT HOTEL TRS 129 LLC (PA)
Also Called: Homewood Stes By Hilton Aliso V
110 Vantis Dr, Aliso Viejo (92656-2675)
PHONE..........................949 425-9500
Chris Eng, *Admin Sec*
Tracy Sauers, *Administration*
EMP: 72 **EST:** 2017
SALES (est): 1.1MM **Privately Held**
WEB: www.homewoodsuites3.hilton.com
SIC: 7011 Hotels

(P-16738)
SUN HILL PROPERTIES INC (HQ)
Also Called: Hilton Los Angls/Nversal Cy Ht
555 Unversal Hollywood Dr, Universal City
(91608-1001)
PHONE..........................818 506-2500
Denn Hu, *Ch of Bd*
Vicente Jaramillo, *VP Human Res*
▲ **EMP:** 152 **EST:** 1989
SALES (est): 41.4MM **Privately Held**
WEB: www.bdisf.com
SIC: 7011 Hotels & motels

(P-16739)
SUNSET PLAZA HOTEL
Also Called: Best Western Sunset Plaza Ht
8400 W Sunset Blvd Ste 3a, West Hollywood (90069-1934)
PHONE..........................323 656-8090
David Rose, *Partner*
Edward Brown, *Partner*
Joel Leebove, *Partner*
EMP: 59 **EST:** 1980
SQ FT: 10,000
SALES (est): 949.2K **Privately Held**
WEB: www.sunsetplazahotel.com
SIC: 7011 Motels

(P-16740)
SUNSET TOWER HOTEL LLC
8358 W Sunset Blvd, Los Angeles
(90069-1516)
PHONE..........................323 654-7100
E Peter Krulewitch, *Mng Member*
Natalie Grebe, *Facilities Dir*
Alfonso Vega, *Facilities Dir*
Jeffrey Klein, *Mng Member*
Barbara Cameron, *Asst Director*

EMP: 53 **EST:** 2004
SALES (est): 17.9MM **Privately Held**
WEB: www.sunsettowerhotel.com
SIC: 7011 Resort hotel; hotels

(P-16741)
SUNSTONE HOTEL PROPERTIES INC
Also Called: Residence Inn By Marriott
1177 S Beverly Dr, Los Angeles
(90035-1119)
PHONE..........................310 228-4100
Tom Beedon, *General Mgr*
EMP: 109 **Privately Held**
WEB: www.sunstonehotels.com
SIC: 7011 Hotels & motels
HQ: Sunstone Hotel Properties Inc
120 Vantis Dr Ste 350
Aliso Viejo CA 92656

(P-16742)
SUNSTONE HOTEL PROPERTIES INC
Also Called: Residence Inn By Marriott
1700 N Sepulveda Blvd, Manhattan Beach
(90266-5015)
PHONE..........................310 546-7627
Sandi Rae Kraft, *Branch Mgr*
Yvonne Fierro, *Info Tech Dir*
Jacqueline Delacruz, *Business Mgr*
Christine Hood, *Sales Dir*
Christos Pablico, *Sales Mgr*
EMP: 109 **Privately Held**
WEB: www.sunstonehotels.com
SIC: 7011 Hotels & motels
HQ: Sunstone Hotel Properties Inc
120 Vantis Dr Ste 350
Aliso Viejo CA 92656

(P-16743)
SUNSTONE HOTEL PROPERTIES INC (DH)
Also Called: Residence Inn By Marriott
120 Vantis Dr Ste 350, Aliso Viejo
(92656-2686)
PHONE..........................949 330-4000
Arthur Buser, *President*
Brian Hilde, *Director*
EMP: 120 **EST:** 1994
SALES (est): 45.3MM **Privately Held**
WEB: www.sunstonehotels.com
SIC: 7011 Hotels & motels
HQ: Interstate Hotels & Resorts, Inc.
5301 Headquarters Dr
Plano TX 75024
703 387-3100

(P-16744)
SUPER 8 MOTEL GOLETA
6021 Hollister Ave, Goleta (93117-3217)
PHONE..........................805 967-5591
Oliver Dixon, *Owner*
Van Bivans, *Systems Mgr*
EMP: 109 **EST:** 1960
SQ FT: 12,000
SALES (est): 966.8K **Privately Held**
WEB: www.wyndhamhotels.com
SIC: 7011 Hotels & motels

(P-16745)
SVI LAX LLC
Also Called: Residnce Inn By Mrriot Lx/Cntu
5933 W Century Blvd, Los Angeles
(90045-5471)
PHONE..........................310 281-0300
Robert A Alter,
EMP: 60 **EST:** 2013
SQ FT: 213,000 **Privately Held**
WEB: www.residenceinnlax.com
SIC: 7011 Hotels

(P-16746)
SWVP WESTLAKE LLC
Also Called: Hyatt Westlake
880 S Westlake Blvd, Westlake Village
(91361-2905)
PHONE..........................805 557-1234
David Coonan, *General Mgr*
EMP: 250
SALES (corp-wide): 9.6MM **Privately Held**
WEB: www.swvp.com
SIC: 7011 Motels

PA: Swvp Westlake Llc
12790 El Camino Real
San Diego CA 92130
858 480-2900

(P-16747)
SYCAMORE MINERAL SPRING RESORT
1215 Avila Beach Dr, San Luis Obispo
(93405-8048)
PHONE..........................805 595-7302
Russell Kiessig, *President*
John King, *President*
Steve Gregory, *Vice Pres*
Charles Yates, *Vice Pres*
EMP: 65 **EST:** 1975
SQ FT: 36,150
SALES (est): 5.1MM **Privately Held**
WEB: www.sycamoresprings.com
SIC: 7011 7991 Resort hotel; spas

(P-16748)
SYDELL HOTELS LLC
Also Called: Line Hotel, The
3515 Wilshire Blvd, Los Angeles
(90010-2301)
PHONE..........................213 381-7411
Doug Elpern,
Leo Robitschek, *Vice Pres*
Bruno Vergeynst, *Managing Dir*
Deborah Gutierrez, *General Mgr*
Sierra Pontak, *Office Mgr*
EMP: 130 **EST:** 2011
SALES (est): 29MM **Privately Held**
WEB: www.thelinehotel.com
SIC: 7011 Resort hotel
PA: Sydell Group Llc
276 5th Ave Rm 704
New York NY 10001
646 810-0208

(P-16749)
T M MIAN & ASSOCIATES INC
Also Called: Hilton Garden Inn Calabasas
24150 Park Sorrento, Calabasas
(91302-4101)
PHONE..........................818 591-2300
Shawn Nicoles, *General Mgr*
EMP: 63
SALES (corp-wide): 14.9MM **Privately Held**
WEB: www.themiancompanies.com
SIC: 7011 Hotels & motels
PA: T. M. Mian & Associates, Inc.
1055 Regal Row
Dallas TX 75247
972 960-2024

(P-16750)
T M MIAN & ASSOCIATES INC
Also Called: Hilton
2000 Solar Dr, Oxnard (93036-2694)
PHONE..........................805 983-8600
T M Mian, *Partner*
EMP: 63
SALES (corp-wide): 14.9MM **Privately Held**
WEB: www.themiancompanies.com
SIC: 7011 Hotels & motels
PA: T. M. Mian & Associates, Inc.
1055 Regal Row
Dallas TX 75247
972 960-2024

(P-16751)
TACHI PALACE CASINO RESORT
17225 Jersey Ave, Lemoore (93245-9760)
PHONE..........................559 924-7751
Tachi Yokut, *Principal*
Santa Yokut, *Principal*
Gail Mercurio, *Purch Mgr*
Deanna Patterson, *Opers Staff*
Abby Hernandez, *Sales Staff*
◆ **EMP:** 1500 **EST:** 2006
SALES (est): 113.1MM **Privately Held**
WEB: www.tachipalace.com
SIC: 7011 Casino hotel

(P-16752)
TEMECULA HHG HOTEL DEV LP
Also Called: Home2 Sites By Hilton Temecula
28400 Rancho Cal Rd, Temecula
(92590-3617)
PHONE..........................951 331-3622
EMP: 111

SALES (corp-wide): 1.7MM **Privately Held**
WEB: www.home2suites3.hilton.com
SIC: 7011 Hotels
PA: Temecula Hhg Hotel Development, Lp
105 Decker Ct Ste 500
Irving TX 75062
972 510-1200

(P-16753)
TIBURON HOSPITALITY LLC
Also Called: Super 8 Motel
901 Real Rd, Bakersfield (93309-1003)
PHONE..........................661 322-1012
Mark Grotewohl, *Partner*
Tiburon Capital LLC, *Partner*
▲ **EMP:** 150 **EST:** 1980
SQ FT: 1,600
SALES (est): 3.6MM **Privately Held**
WEB: www.wyndhamhotels.com
SIC: 7011 Hotels & motels

(P-16754)
TIC HOTELS INC
Also Called: Shorecliff Properties
2555 Price St, Pismo Beach (93449-2111)
PHONE..........................805 773-4671
Edward Brown, *Systems Mgr*
Barbara Parra, *Branch Mgr*
Karen Fyfe, *Human Res Dir*
Tammy Porter, *Sales Mgr*
Matt Classen, *Manager*
EMP: 78 **Privately Held**
WEB: www.shorecliff.com
SIC: 7011 5812 5813 Motels; eating places; bar (drinking places)
HQ: Tic Hotels, Inc.
1811 State St Ste C
Santa Barbara CA 93101
805 898-0855

(P-16755)
TORRES-MRTNEZ DSERT CHLLA INDA
Also Called: Red Earth Casino
3089 Norm Niver Rd, Thermal
(92274-6550)
PHONE..........................760 395-1200
David Seufert, *Branch Mgr*
EMP: 93 **Privately Held**
WEB: www.tmdci.org
SIC: 7011 Casino hotel
PA: Torres-Martinez Desert Cahuilla Indians
66725 Martinez Rd
Thermal CA 92274

(P-16756)
TP HERITG INN LK FOREST LLC
Also Called: TownePlace Stes Irvine Lk Fres
23150 Lake Center Dr, Lake Forest
(92630-2837)
PHONE..........................949 461-0470
Gary Tharaldson, *CEO*
Evan Ekholm, *General Mgr*
Richard Garcia, *Director*
EMP: 50 **EST:** 2016
SALES (est): 1MM **Privately Held**
WEB: www.marriott.com
SIC: 7011 Inns

(P-16757)
TRIGILD INTERNATIONAL INC
Also Called: Ramada Inn
1680 Superior Ave, Costa Mesa
(92627-3652)
PHONE..........................949 645-2221
Vince Andres, *Branch Mgr*
EMP: 68
SALES (corp-wide): 20.3MM **Privately Held**
WEB: www.trigild.com
SIC: 7011 Hotels & motels
PA: Trigild International, Inc.
3323 Carmel Mountain Rd # 2
San Diego CA 92121
858 720-6700

(P-16758)
TRIPADVISOR LLC
Also Called: Best Western
6141 Franklin Ave, Los Angeles
(90028-5205)
PHONE..........................323 464-5181
Mel Adler, *Partner*
Bernie Adler, *Partner*

▲ = Import ▼=Export
◆ =Import/Export

Herman Adler, *Partner*
EMP: 70 **EST:** 1950
SQ FT: 50,000
SALES (est): 7.4MM **Privately Held**
WEB: www.bestwestern.com
SIC: 7011 5921 5812 Hotels & motels; liquor stores; American restaurant

(P-16759)
TWO BUNCH PALMS LLC (PA)
67425 Two Bunch Palms Trl, Desert Hot Springs (92240-6034)
PHONE...................760 329-8791
John King, *Mng Member*
Annelle Kapp, *General Mgr*
Ankit Sekhri, *General Mgr*
Scott Hartford-Magana, *Human Resources*
Robert Seibel, *Director*
EMP: 110 **EST:** 2005
SALES (est): 15.7MM **Privately Held**
WEB: www.twobunchpalms.com
SIC: 7011 7991 Resort hotel; spas

(P-16760)
UHG LAX PROP LLC
Also Called: Hotel Company
1985 E Grand Ave, El Segundo (90245-5015)
PHONE...................310 322-0999
Charu Goyal, *Mng Member*
Mark Lewis, *Vice Pres*
Jordan Austin, *General Mgr*
EMP: 125 **EST:** 2017
SALES (est): 8.4MM **Privately Held**
SIC: 7011 5812 Hotels; restaurant; family; independent

(P-16761)
UKA LLC
Also Called: Tarsadia Hotels
620 Nwport Ctr Dr Ste 140, Newport Beach (92660)
PHONE...................949 610-8000
B U Patel, *Mng Member*
Nayiri Madenlian, *CFO*
Rashik Patel, *Vice Pres*
Richard Barnes, *CIO*
Pushpa Patel,
EMP: 53 **EST:** 1997
SQ FT: 12,000
SALES (est): 265.8K **Privately Held**
SIC: 7011 Hotels

(P-16762)
UNIWELL CORPORATION
Also Called: Holiday Inn
7000 Beach Blvd, Buena Park (90620-1832)
PHONE...................714 522-7000
Tracy Myer, *Branch Mgr*
Sidney Chan, *President*
Elaine Chan, *Principal*
Teddy Katuari, *Principal*
Evans Cody, *Hum Res Coord*
EMP: 150
SALES (corp-wide): 28.3MM **Privately Held**
WEB: www.holidayinn.com
SIC: 7011 5813 5812 Hotels & motels; drinking places; eating places
PA: Uniwell Corporation
21172 Figueroa St
Carson CA 90745
310 782-8888

(P-16763)
URBAN COMMONS QUEENSWAY LLC
Also Called: Queen Mary, The
1126 Queens Hwy, Long Beach (90802-6331)
PHONE...................562 499-1611
Christopher Otamias,
EMP: 900 **EST:** 2016
SALES (est): 24.2MM **Privately Held**
SIC: 7011 Hotels

(P-16764)
URBAN COMMONS QUEENSWAY LLC (PA)
1126 Qeens Hwy Queen Mary, Long Beach (90802)
PHONE...................562 499-1750
Alan Tantleff, *President*
EMP: 52

SALES (est): 157K **Privately Held**
SIC: 7011 Hotels & motels

(P-16765)
US HOTEL AND RESORT MGT INC
Also Called: Regency Inn
2544 Newport Blvd, Costa Mesa (92627-1331)
PHONE...................949 650-2988
Peggy Chen, *Manager*
EMP: 155
SALES (corp-wide): 17.9MM **Privately Held**
WEB: www.ushotels-resorts.com
SIC: 7011 Resort hotel
HQ: U.S. Hotel And Resort Management, Inc.
3211 W Sencore Dr
Sioux Falls SD 57107
605 334-2371

(P-16766)
V TODAYS INC
Also Called: Holiday Inn
19800 S Vermont Ave, Torrance (90502-1126)
PHONE...................310 781-9100
Belinda Zen, *CEO*
David Britton, *General Mgr*
Teresa Ou-Young, *Director*
EMP: 110 **EST:** 1986
SQ FT: 95,000
SALES (est): 7MM **Privately Held**
WEB: www.holidayinn.com
SIC: 7011 Hotels & motels

(P-16767)
VACATION BAY HOTEL PRPTS INC
Also Called: Vacation Village Hotel
647 S Coast Hwy, Laguna Beach (92651-2415)
PHONE...................949 494-8566
Loren W Haneline, *President*
Linda K Haneline, *Corp Secy*
Christine Haneline, *Vice Pres*
Jeff Haneline, *Vice Pres*
Russell Haneline, *Vice Pres*
EMP: 135 **EST:** 1960
SQ FT: 74,000
SALES (est): 1MM **Privately Held**
WEB: www.pacificedgehotel.com
SIC: 7011 Resort hotel

(P-16768)
VALADON HOTEL LLC
Also Called: Petit Ermitage
8822 Cynthia St, West Hollywood (90069-4502)
PHONE...................310 854-1114
Stefan Ashkenazy,
Nicolas Black, *General Mgr*
Ann Kleinhenz, *General Mgr*
Irma Martin, *Finance Dir*
Renee Gonzales, *Controller*
EMP: 80 **EST:** 1997
SQ FT: 40,000
SALES (est): 15.1MM **Privately Held**
WEB: www.petitermitage.com
SIC: 7011 Hotels

(P-16769)
VALENCIA HOTEL LTD PARTNERSHIP
Also Called: Hampton Inn
25259 The Old Rd, Santa Clarita (91381-2246)
PHONE...................661 253-2400
Timothy Bristol, *Manager*
Gary Carr, *Partner*
Jack Mc Cormick, *Partner*
EMP: 54 **EST:** 1988
SQ FT: 500,000
SALES (est): 1.1MM **Privately Held**
WEB: www.hilton.com
SIC: 7011 Hotels & motels

(P-16770)
VENTU PARK LLC
Also Called: Palm Garden Hotel
495 N Ventu Park Rd, Thousand Oaks (91320-2707)
PHONE...................805 716-4200
Bob Zonitch, *Principal*

Michael Garik, *Principal*
Dave Warner, *Principal*
EMP: 90 **EST:** 1998
SALES (est): 4MM **Privately Held**
WEB: www.palmgardenhotel.com
SIC: 7011 Resort hotel

(P-16771)
VENTURA HSPTALITY PARTNERS LLC
Also Called: Crowne Plaza Ventura Beach
450 Harbor Blvd, Ventura (93001-2708)
PHONE...................805 648-2100
David Storm,
Akemi Shapiro, *Sales Staff*
Jodi Wagner, *Director*
Dylan Dupont, *Manager*
EMP: 140 **EST:** 2006
SQ FT: 143,000 **Privately Held**
WEB: www.cpventura.com
SIC: 7011 Hotels

(P-16772)
VICTORVLLE TRSURE HOLDINGS LLC
Also Called: Holiday Inn
15494 Palmdale Rd, Victorville (92392-2408)
PHONE...................760 245-6565
Benjamin Gonzales, *General Mgr*
Daniel Cordova, *Sales Staff*
EMP: 75 **EST:** 2011
SALES (est): 5.2MM **Privately Held**
WEB: www.hivictorville.com
SIC: 7011 5812 Hotels & motels; American restaurant

(P-16773)
VISTA INVESTMENTS LLC (PA)
2225 Campus Dr, El Segundo (90245-0001)
PHONE...................310 725-8200
Juan Sanchez-Ilaca,
Les Biggins, *CFO*
Mar Ortiz, *Officer*
Dean Chapman, *Vice Pres*
Mari Estrada, *General Mgr*
EMP: 144 **EST:** 1999
SALES (est): 12.5MM **Privately Held**
WEB: www.vistainvestments.com
SIC: 7011 6726 Motels; management investment funds, closed-end

(P-16774)
W LOS ANGELES
Also Called: Westwood Marquis Hotel & Grdns
930 Hilgard Ave, Los Angeles (90024-3009)
P.O. Box 14029, Scottsdale AZ (85267-4029)
PHONE...................310 208-8765
George I Rosenthal, *President*
Mark Rosenthal, *COO*
Anil Sharma, *CFO*
Damien Hirsch, *General Mgr*
EMP: 330 **EST:** 1977
SALES (est): 39.2MM
SALES (corp-wide): 53.8MM **Privately Held**
WEB: www.marriott.com
SIC: 7011 Resort hotel; hotels
PA: Raleigh Enterprises, Inc.
5300 Melrose Ave Fl 4
Los Angeles CA 90038
310 899-8900

(P-16775)
W&J BUSINESS VENTURES LLC
Also Called: Holiday Inn
8620 Airport Blvd, Los Angeles (90045-4246)
PHONE...................310 645-7700
WEI Cheng Lee,
Hsiu Lan Lee,
WEI Hung Lee,
EMP: 130 **EST:** 1960
SQ FT: 700,000
SALES (est): 6.9MM **Privately Held**
WEB: www.hiexpress.com
SIC: 7011 Hotels & motels

(P-16776)
W2005 WYN HOTELS LP
Also Called: Doubletree Hotel
5757 Telegraph Rd, Commerce (90040-1513)
PHONE...................323 887-8100
Steve Barick, *COO*
EMP: 52 **EST:** 1991
SALES (est): 524.5K **Privately Held**
WEB: www.hilton.com
SIC: 7011 Hotels & motels

(P-16777)
WALTERS FAMILY PARTNERSHIP
Also Called: Hilton Resort In Palm Spring
400 E Tahquitz Canyon Way, Palm Springs (92262-6605)
PHONE...................760 320-6868
Lance Walters, *Partner*
EMP: 150 **EST:** 1981
SQ FT: 200,000
SALES (est): 13.6MM **Privately Held**
SIC: 7011 5813 5812 Hotels & motels; drinking places; eating places

(P-16778)
WATERFRONT HOTEL LLC
Also Called: Hilton
21100 Pacific Coast Hwy, Huntington Beach (92648-5307)
PHONE...................714 845-8000
John Gilbert, *Manager*
Esmerelda Szymanski, *Partner*
Rachel Russell, *Senior VP*
Stephen Arnold, *Vice Pres*
Donna Kelley, *Executive*
EMP: 298 **Privately Held**
WEB: www.hilton.com
SIC: 7011 5813 5812 7299 Hotels & motels; drinking places; eating places; banquet hall facilities
PA: The Waterfront Hotel Llc
660 Newport Center Dr
Newport Beach CA

(P-16779)
WCO HOTELS INC (DH)
Also Called: Disneyland Hotel
1150 W Magic Way, Anaheim (92802-2247)
PHONE...................323 636-3251
Tony Bruno, *President*
Cynthia Harriss, *Principal*
James Towning, *General Mgr*
Hidel Amemiya, *VP Opers*
EMP: 96 **EST:** 1955
SALES (est): 66.6MM
SALES (corp-wide): 65.3B **Publicly Held**
WEB: www.thewaltdisneycompany.com
SIC: 7011 5812 Resort hotel; eating places

(P-16780)
WCO HOTELS INC
Also Called: Disneys Grnd Clifornian Ht Spa
1600 S Disneyland Dr, Anaheim (92802-2317)
PHONE...................714 635-2300
Dorothy Stratton, *Branch Mgr*
EMP: 745
SALES (corp-wide): 65.3B **Publicly Held**
SIC: 7011 Resort hotel
HQ: Wco Hotels, Inc.
1150 W Magic Way
Anaheim CA 92802
323 636-3251

(P-16781)
WELCOME GROUP INC (PA)
222 N Pacific Coast Hwy # 2222, El Segundo (90245-5648)
PHONE...................860 741-2211
Amar Shokeen, *CEO*
Susan Daley, *General Mgr*
Pauls Elich, *Opers Mgr*
EMP: 255 **EST:** 2000
SALES (est): 4.3MM **Privately Held**
WEB: www.welcomegroupinc.com
SIC: 7011 Hotels & motels

PRODUCTS & SVCS

(P-16782)
**WELCOME GROUP
MANAGEMENT LLC**
Also Called: Marriott
300 S Court St, Visalia (93291-6214)
PHONE................310 378-6666
Amarjit Shokeen,
Sheri A O'Hara, *Executive*
Doug Warren, *Director*
Natalie Hobbs, *Supervisor*
EMP: 97 **EST:** 2011
SQ FT: 3,224
SALES (est): 9.6MM **Privately Held**
WEB: www.marriott.com
SIC: 7011 Hotels & motels

(P-16783)
WELK RESORT GROUP INC
Also Called: Lawrence Welk Desert Oasis
34567 Cathedral Canyon Dr, Cathedral City
(92234-6637)
PHONE................760 770-9755
Bill Palmer, *Manager*
EMP: 105 **Publicly Held**
WEB: www.welkresorts.com
SIC: 7011 Resort hotel
HQ: Welk Resort Group, Inc.
300 Rancheros Dr Ste 450
San Marcos CA 92069
760 652-4913

(P-16784)
WESTERN INN UPLAND CO INC
1191 E Foothill Blvd, Upland (91786-4049)
PHONE................909 949-4800
Frank Yang, *President*
Ahad Vahab, *Manager*
EMP: 63 **EST:** 1988
SQ FT: 35,000
SALES (est): 1.1MM **Privately Held**
WEB: www.westerninnhotel.com
SIC: 7011 Hotels & motels

(P-16785)
WESTLAKE PROPERTIES INC
Also Called: Westlake Village Inn
31943 Agoura Rd, Westlake Village
(91361-4427)
PHONE................818 889-0230
John Notter, *Principal*
Maria H Solorzano, *Sales Dir*
David Schmidt, *Sales Mgr*
Kelly Burnett, *Asst Director*
Leydi Orellana, *Manager*
EMP: 150 **EST:** 1974
SALES (est): 14.2MM **Privately Held**
WEB: www.westlakevillageinn.com
SIC: 7011 Resort hotel

(P-16786)
WHATEVER IT TAKES INC
Also Called: Desert Hot Springs Spa Hotel
10805 Palm Dr, Desert Hot Springs
(92240-2511)
PHONE................760 329-6000
Michael Bickford, *President*
EMP: 78 **EST:** 1970
SQ FT: 50,000
SALES (est): 923.2K **Privately Held**
WEB: www.dhsspa.com
SIC: 7011 5812 Resort hotel; eating places

(P-16787)
WHB CORPORATION
Also Called: Millennium Biltmore Hotel
506 S Grand Ave, Los Angeles
(90071-2602)
PHONE................213 624-1011
John Demola, *Branch Mgr*
Janlyn Mahlman, *Vice Pres*
Maselina Hansen, *Executive*
Jamal Zoukari, *Executive*
Federico Boveda, *Technology*
EMP: 630 **Privately Held**
SIC: 7011 5812 5813 Hotels; eating places; drinking places
HQ: Whb Corporation
7600 E Orchard Rd 230s
Greenwood Village CO 80111
303 779-2000

(P-16788)
**WHITMAN PTRSON CAPITL
PARTNERS (PA)**
3075 Townsgate Rd Ste 210, Westlake Village (91361-3223)
PHONE................818 483-1060
Daniel Peterson, *Partner*
Paul Novak, *Managing Dir*
Gina Lewis, *Executive Asst*
Alyssa Kennedy, *Analyst*
Lucas Liu, *Analyst*
EMP: 71 **EST:** 2011
SALES (est): 5.4MM **Privately Held**
WEB: www.whitmanpeterson.com
SIC: 7011 Hotels & motels

(P-16789)
WINDSOR CAPITAL GROUP INC
Also Called: Residence Inn By Marriott
2101 W Vineyard Ave, Oxnard
(93036-2268)
PHONE................805 988-0627
Doug Pflaumer, *Branch Mgr*
EMP: 77
SALES (corp-wide): 149.1MM **Privately Held**
WEB: www.residence-inn.marriott.com
SIC: 7011 Hotels & motels
PA: Windsor Capital Group, Inc.
3250 Ocean Park Blvd # 35
Santa Monica CA 90405
310 566-1100

(P-16790)
WINDSOR CAPITAL GROUP INC
Also Called: Embassy Suites
1117 N H St, Lompoc (93436-8115)
PHONE................805 735-8311
Toby Simmons, *Manager*
Reyna Uribe, *Supervisor*
EMP: 77
SALES (corp-wide): 149.1MM **Privately Held**
WEB: www.hilton.com
SIC: 7011 Hotels & motels
PA: Windsor Capital Group, Inc.
3250 Ocean Park Blvd # 35
Santa Monica CA 90405
310 566-1100

(P-16791)
WINDSOR CAPITAL GROUP INC
Also Called: Pacific Suites Hotel
3250 Ocean Park Blvd # 35, Santa Monica
(90405-3208)
PHONE................310 566-1100
Michael D Cryan, *Manager*
EMP: 77
SALES (corp-wide): 149.1MM **Privately Held**
WEB: www.marriott.com
SIC: 7011 Hotels
PA: Windsor Capital Group, Inc.
3250 Ocean Park Blvd # 35
Santa Monica CA 90405
310 566-1100

(P-16792)
WINDSOR CAPITAL GROUP INC
Also Called: Embassy Suites Arcadia
3250 Ocean Park Blvd # 35, Santa Monica
(90405-3208)
PHONE................310 566-1100
EMP: 77
SALES (corp-wide): 149.1MM **Privately Held**
WEB: www.hilton.com
SIC: 7011 Hotels & motels
PA: Windsor Capital Group, Inc.
3250 Ocean Park Blvd # 35
Santa Monica CA 90405
310 566-1100

(P-16793)
WINDSOR CAPITAL GROUP INC
Also Called: Embassy Suites Lompoc
3250 Ocean Park Blvd # 35, Santa Monica
(90405-3208)
PHONE................209 577-3825
EMP: 77
SALES (corp-wide): 149.1MM **Privately Held**
WEB: www.hilton.com
SIC: 7011 Hotels & motels

PA: Windsor Capital Group, Inc.
3250 Ocean Park Blvd # 35
Santa Monica CA 90405
310 566-1100

(P-16794)
WINDSOR CAPITAL GROUP INC
Also Called: Marriott
3250 Ocean Park Blvd # 35, Santa Monica
(90405-3208)
PHONE................209 577-3825
Shawn Williams, *Manager*
EMP: 77
SALES (corp-wide): 149.1MM **Privately Held**
WEB: www.marriott.com
SIC: 7011 Hotels & motels
PA: Windsor Capital Group, Inc.
3250 Ocean Park Blvd # 35
Santa Monica CA 90405
310 566-1100

(P-16795)
WINDSOR CAPITAL GROUP INC
Also Called: Embassy Suites
900 E Birch St, Brea (92821-5812)
PHONE................714 990-6000
Regina Samy, *Manager*
EMP: 77
SQ FT: 48,164
SALES (corp-wide): 149.1MM **Privately Held**
WEB: www.hilton.com
SIC: 7011 Hotels & motels
PA: Windsor Capital Group, Inc.
3250 Ocean Park Blvd # 35
Santa Monica CA 90405
310 566-1100

(P-16796)
WINDSOR CAPITAL GROUP INC
Also Called: Embassy Suites
29345 Rancho California, Temecula
(92591-5201)
PHONE................951 676-5656
Tom Demott, *General Mgr*
Mitchell Lucas, *Vice Pres*
Naomi Briones, *General Mgr*
Golda Escalante, *General Mgr*
Victor Morgenroth, *General Mgr*
EMP: 77
SALES (corp-wide): 149.1MM **Privately Held**
WEB: www.hilton.com
SIC: 7011 Hotels & motels
PA: Windsor Capital Group, Inc.
3250 Ocean Park Blvd # 35
Santa Monica CA 90405
310 566-1100

(P-16797)
WINDSOR CAPITAL GROUP INC
3250 Ocean Park Blvd # 35, Santa Monica
(90405-3208)
PHONE................310 566-1100
EMP: 77
SALES (corp-wide): 149.1MM **Privately Held**
WEB: www.marriott.com
SIC: 7011 Hotels
PA: Windsor Capital Group, Inc.
3250 Ocean Park Blvd # 35
Santa Monica CA 90405
310 566-1100

(P-16798)
WINDSOR CAPITAL GROUP INC
Also Called: Embassy Suites El Paso
3250 Ocean Park Blvd # 35, Santa Monica
(90405-3208)
PHONE................310 566-1100
EMP: 77
SALES (corp-wide): 149.1MM **Privately Held**
WEB: www.hilton.com
SIC: 7011 Hotels & motels
PA: Windsor Capital Group, Inc.
3250 Ocean Park Blvd # 35
Santa Monica CA 90405
310 566-1100

(P-16799)
WINDSOR CAPITAL GROUP INC
Also Called: Recp/Wndsor Port Hueneme
Ventr
350 E Hueneme Rd, Port Hueneme
(93041-3209)
PHONE................805 986-5353
Silvia Bernard, *Branch Mgr*
EMP: 77
SALES (corp-wide): 149.1MM **Privately Held**
WEB: www.marriott.com
SIC: 7011 Hotel, franchised
PA: Windsor Capital Group, Inc.
3250 Ocean Park Blvd # 35
Santa Monica CA 90405
310 566-1100

(P-16800)
WINDSOR CAPITAL GROUP INC
Also Called: Embassy Suites
1325 E Dyer Rd, Santa Ana (92705-5615)
PHONE................714 241-3800
Samuel Sansone, *Manager*
Chuck Leblanc, *Chief Engr*
EMP: 77
SALES (corp-wide): 149.1MM **Privately Held**
WEB: www.hilton.com
SIC: 7011 5813 5812 Hotels & motels; drinking places; eating places
PA: Windsor Capital Group, Inc.
3250 Ocean Park Blvd # 35
Santa Monica CA 90405
310 566-1100

(P-16801)
WINDSOR CAPITAL GROUP INC
Also Called: Marriott
1510 University Ave, Riverside
(92507-4468)
PHONE................951 276-1200
Jim Larson, *General Mgr*
EMP: 77
SALES (corp-wide): 149.1MM **Privately Held**
WEB: www.marriott.com
SIC: 7011 Hotels & motels
PA: Windsor Capital Group, Inc.
3250 Ocean Park Blvd # 35
Santa Monica CA 90405
310 566-1100

(P-16802)
WJ NEWPORT LLC
Also Called: Marriott
4500 Macarthur Blvd, Newport Beach
(92660-2010)
PHONE................949 476-2001
Wenjing Yang,
Elizabeth Sheldon, *Sales Staff*
EMP: 190 **EST:** 2016
SALES (est): 27.5MM **Privately Held**
WEB: www.t2hospitality.com
SIC: 7011 5812 7389 Resort hotel; family restaurants;

(P-16803)
**WOODBINE LGACY/PLAYA
OWNER LLC**
Also Called: Hilton Los Angeles Culver City
6161 W Centinela Ave, Culver City
(90230-6306)
PHONE................678 292-4962
Lakeisha Walker, *Principal*
Shelli Catron, *Manager*
EMP: 75 **EST:** 2018
SALES (est): 4.5MM **Privately Held**
SIC: 7011 Hotels & motels

(P-16804)
**WORLD TRADE CTR HT ASSOC
LTD**
Also Called: Long Beach Hilton, The
701 W Ocean Blvd, Long Beach
(90831-3100)
PHONE................562 983-3400
Steve Holloway, *Controller*
Greater Los Angeles Trade Cent, *General Ptnr*
Matsushita International Corpo, *Ltd Ptnr*
EMP: 66 **EST:** 1990

SALES (est): 1.1MM **Privately Held**
SIC: **7011** 7991 5813 5812 Hotels & motels; physical fitness facilities; drinking places; eating places

(P-16805)
WORLDMARK CLUB
Also Called: Worldmark At Palm Springs
1177 N Palm Canyon Dr, Palm Springs
(92262-4401)
PHONE.................................760 416-4428
Al Hippe, *Manager*
EMP: 66
SALES (corp-wide): 1.3B **Publicly Held**
WEB: www.worldmark.wyndhamdestinations.com
SIC: **7011** 6531 Resort hotel; time-sharing real estate sales, leasing & rentals
HQ: Worldmark, The Club
9805 Willows Rd Ne
Redmond WA 98052

(P-16806)
WYNDHAM INTERNATIONAL INC
222 W Houston Ave, Fullerton
(92832-3453)
PHONE.................................714 992-1700
EMP: 102 **Publicly Held**
WEB: www.wyndhamhotels.com
SIC: **7011** Hotel
HQ: Wyndham International, Inc
22 Sylvan Way
Parsippany NJ 07054
973 753-6000

(P-16807)
XANTERRA PARKS & RESORTS INC
Also Called: Furnace Creek Ranch & Inn
Hwy 190, Death Valley (92328)
P.O. Box 187 (92328-0187)
PHONE.................................760 786-2345
Dominie Lenz, *Branch Mgr*
Christopher Hamrick, *Engineer*
Armando Rodriguez, *Engineer*
Melissa Doherty, *Asst Controller*
EMP: 215
SALES (corp-wide): 388MM **Privately Held**
WEB: www.xanterra.com
SIC: **7011** Resort hotel
HQ: Parks Xanterra & Resorts Inc
6312 S Fiddlers Green Cir
Greenwood Village CO 80111
303 600-3400

(P-16808)
XLD GROUP LLC
Also Called: Torrance Marriott Hotel
3635 Fashion Way, Torrance (90503-4809)
PHONE.................................310 316-3636
Pam Ryan, *General Mgr*
Francis Martin, *MIS Mgr*
EMP: 66
SALES (corp-wide): 12.1MM **Privately Held**
SIC: **7011** 7389 Hotels; office facilities & secretarial service rental
PA: Xld Group, Llc
500 Sansome St Ste 502
San Francisco CA

(P-16809)
YHB LONG BEACH LLC
Also Called: Holiday Inn
2640 N Lakewood Blvd, Long Beach
(90815-1715)
PHONE.................................562 597-4401
Traycee Mayer, *Principal*
Kim Mooyon, *General Mgr*
Jorge Perez, *Chief Engr*
EMP: 90 **EST**: 2003
SALES (est): 6.6MM **Privately Held**
WEB: www.holidayinn.com
SIC: **7011** Hotels & motels

7021 Rooming & Boarding Houses

(P-16810)
AMERICAN CMPUS COMMUNITIES INC
Also Called: Vista Del Campo
62600 Arroyo Dr, Irvine (92617-4387)
PHONE.................................949 854-0900
Heather Jarzyna, *Area Mgr*
Lauren Misak, *General Mgr*
EMP: 56
SALES (corp-wide): 870.5MM **Publicly Held**
WEB: www.americancampus.com
SIC: **7021** Rooming & boarding houses
PA: American Campus Communities, Inc.
12700 Hill Country Blvd T
Austin TX 78738
512 732-1000

(P-16811)
FORTY-NINER SHOPS INC
Also Called: UNIVERSITY BOOKSTORE
6049 E 7th St, Long Beach (90840-0007)
PHONE.................................562 985-5093
Don Penrod, *CEO*
Dr Mary Ann Takemoto, *Chairman*
Ms Mary Stephens, *Treasurer*
Jason Eisenmann, *Manager*
EMP: 550 **EST**: 1949
SQ FT: 36,000
SALES (est): 17.5MM **Privately Held**
WEB: www.fortyninershops.net
SIC: **5942** 5943 5812 7021 College book stores; school supplies; cafeteria; dormitory, commercially operated

(P-16812)
OAKWOOD CORPORATE HOUSING INC (PA)
1 World Trade Ctr # 2400, Long Beach
(90831-2400)
PHONE.................................877 902-0832
Howard F Ruby, *President*
Ricardo Villarreal, *President*
Chris Brenk, *CFO*
Jill Chapman, *Senior VP*
Marina Lubinsky, *Senior VP*
EMP: 459 **EST**: 1994
SALES (est): 11.3MM **Privately Held**
WEB: www.oakwood.com
SIC: **7021** Furnished room rental

(P-16813)
PACIFIC LABOR SERVICES INC
5690 Cypress Rd, Oxnard (93033-8509)
P.O. Box 824, Buellton (93427-0824)
PHONE.................................805 488-4625
EMP: 50
SQ FT: 62,000
SALES: 1.1MM **Privately Held**
WEB: www.pacificlaborsourceinc.com
SIC: **7021** 7363 7361 Rooming/Boarding House Help Supply Services Employment Agency

(P-16814)
WORLDWIDE CORPORATE HOUSING LP
Also Called: Oakwood Temporary Housing
1 World Trade Ctr # 2400, Long Beach
(90831-2400)
PHONE.................................972 392-4747
Howard Ruby, *Partner*
Scott Jones, *Branch Mgr*
EMP: 119
SALES (corp-wide): 75.7MM **Privately Held**
WEB: www.oakwood.com
SIC: **7021** Furnished room rental
HQ: Worldwide Corporate Housing, Lp
1 World Trade Ctr # 2400
Long Beach CA 90831
562 473-7371

(P-16815)
WORLDWIDE CORPORATE HOUSING LP (HQ)
Also Called: Oakwood Worldwide
1 World Trade Ctr # 2400, Long Beach
(90831-2400)
PHONE.................................562 473-7371

Dean R Schreiber, *CEO*
EMP: 1144 **EST**: 2004
SALES (est): 60.2MM
SALES (corp-wide): 75.7MM **Privately Held**
WEB: www.oakwood.com
SIC: **7021** Furnished room rental
PA: Oakwood Worldwide (Us) Lp
2222 Corinth Ave
Los Angeles CA 90064
800 888-0808

7032 Sporting & Recreational Camps

(P-16816)
ALISAL PROPERTIES (PA)
Also Called: Alisal Guest Ranch
1054 Alisal Rd, Solvang (93463-3033)
PHONE.................................805 688-6411
Palmer Jackson, *President*
Mark Weitz, *Treasurer*
Susanne Powell, *Corp Secy*
Joan Y Jackson, *Vice Pres*
Jessica Solorio, *Executive Asst*
EMP: 242 **EST**: 1946
SQ FT: 10,000
SALES (est): 29.4MM **Privately Held**
WEB: www.alisal.com
SIC: **7032** 7997 Sporting camps; golf club, membership

(P-16817)
BIG LGUE DREAMS CONSULTING LLC
33700 Date Palm Dr, Cathedral City
(92234-4731)
PHONE.................................760 324-5600
Steve Navarro, *Vice Pres*
EMP: 59
SALES (corp-wide): 52.4MM **Privately Held**
WEB: www.bigleaguedreams.com
SIC: **7032** Recreational camps
PA: Big League Dreams Consulting, Llc
16333 Fairfield Ranch Rd
Chino Hills CA 91709
909 287-1700

(P-16818)
CAMP FRANCHISE SYSTEMS LLC (PA)
Also Called: Camp Transformation Center
14738 Pipeline Ave Ste A, Chino Hills
(91709-6022)
PHONE.................................909 325-6011
Saman Bakhtiar, *CEO*
Alejandra Font, *CFO*
EMP: 98 **EST**: 2010
SQ FT: 5,000
SALES (est): 15MM **Privately Held**
WEB: www.thecamptc.com
SIC: **7032** 6794 Sporting & recreational camps; franchises, selling or licensing

(P-16819)
CHRISTIAN HARTLAND ASSOCIATION
Also Called: Hartland Christian Camp
57611 Eshom Valley Dr # 1, Badger
(93603-9711)
PHONE.................................559 337-2349
Robert Nunziato, *Exec Pres*
Joshua Embry, *CFO*
Joseph McMurphy, *CFO*
Bryan Case, *Program Mgr*
Jeff Morris, *Business Mgr*
EMP: 52 **EST**: 1946
SQ FT: 17,000
SALES: 2MM **Privately Held**
WEB: www.hartlandcamp.com
SIC: **7032** Sporting & recreational camps

(P-16820)
FUNDAMNTAL CHRSTN ENDEAVORS INC
Also Called: Ironwood
49191 Cherokee Rd, Newberry Springs
(92365-9318)
PHONE.................................760 257-3503
Samuel Brock, *President*
Betty Brock, *Treasurer*
W C Chastain, *Exec VP*

Mark Asay, *Teacher*
Karen Daniels, *Teacher*
EMP: 81 **EST**: 1973
SQ FT: 2,500
SALES: 2.2MM **Privately Held**
WEB: www.ironwood.org
SIC: **7032** 8211 Bible camp; private combined elementary & secondary school

(P-16821)
GUIDED DISCOVERIES INC
Also Called: Desert Sun Science Center, The
26800 Saunders Meadows Rd, Idyllwild
(92549)
P.O. Box 3399 (92549-3399)
PHONE.................................951 659-6062
Allen Tiso, *Director*
EMP: 62
SALES (corp-wide): 10.1MM **Privately Held**
WEB: www.guideddiscoveries.org
SIC: **7032** 8299 Sporting & recreational camps; educational services
PA: Guided Discoveries, Inc.
27282 Calle Arroyo
San Juan Capistrano CA 92675
800 645-1423

(P-16822)
GUIDED DISCOVERIES INC
Also Called: Fox Landing
1 Toyon Bay Rd, Avalon (90704)
P.O. Box 1920 (90704-1920)
PHONE.................................310 510-1622
Erica Felins, *Manager*
EMP: 62
SALES (corp-wide): 10.1MM **Privately Held**
WEB: www.guideddiscoveries.org
SIC: **7032** Sporting & recreational camps
PA: Guided Discoveries, Inc.
27282 Calle Arroyo
San Juan Capistrano CA 92675
800 645-1423

(P-16823)
INTERVRSITY CHRSTN FLLWSHP/USA
Also Called: Campus By The Sea
Gallager&Apos S Cv, Avalon (90704)
P.O. Box 466 (90704-0466)
PHONE.................................310 510-0015
Susan Veon, *Director*
EMP: 404
SALES (corp-wide): 119.4MM **Privately Held**
WEB: www.intervarsity.org
SIC: **7032** 5942 Bible camp; book stores; books, religious
PA: Intervarsity Christian Fellowship/Usa
635 Science Dr
Madison WI 53711
608 274-9001

(P-16824)
LLC WOODWARD WEST
28400 Stallion Springs Dr, Tehachapi
(93561-5266)
PHONE.................................661 822-7900
Debbie Williams,
Darlene Olson, *Office Mgr*
Sharon Breedlove, *Human Res Mgr*
Richie Velasquez, *Mktg Dir*
Jake Kinney, *Director*
EMP: 143 **EST**: 2002
SALES (est): 10.1MM **Privately Held**
WEB: www.woodwardwest.com
SIC: **7032** Sporting & recreational camps

(P-16825)
ROMAN CATHOLIC BISHP OF FRESNO
Also Called: Saint Anthony Retreat
43816 Sierra Dr, Three Rivers
(93271-9708)
P.O. Box 249 (93271-0249)
PHONE.................................559 561-4499
John Griesbach, *Branch Mgr*
EMP: 70 **Privately Held**
WEB: www.dioceseoffresno.org
SIC: **7032** Bible camp
PA: The Roman Catholic Bishop Of Fresno
1550 N Fresno St
Fresno CA 93703

(PA)=Parent Co (HQ)=Headquarters (DH)=Div Headquarters
✪ = New Business established in last 2 years

2022 Southern California Business
Directory and Buyers Guide

737

PRODUCTS & SVCS

(P-16826)
ROYAL FAMILY KIDS CAMPS INC
3000 W Macarthur Blvd # 412, Santa Ana
(92704-7920)
PHONE..................714 438-2494
Paul Martin, *CEO*
Tony Choi, *CFO*
Jeff Juhala, *Vice Pres*
Robyn Freeman, *Administration*
Scott Murrish,
EMP: 130 **EST:** 1989
SALES: 1.6MM **Privately Held**
WEB: www.forthechildren.org
SIC: 7032 Summer camp, except day &
sports instructional

(P-16827)
**SNOW VALLEY MTN RESORT
LLC**
Also Called: Snow Valley Mountain Sports Pk
Hwy 18, Running Springs (92382)
P.O. Box 2337 (92382-2337)
PHONE..................909 867-2751
William R Sauey,
Ronald Erler, *Manager*
EMP: 64 **EST:** 1948
SQ FT: 81,000
SALES (est): 7.5MM **Privately Held**
WEB: www.snow-valley.com
SIC: 7032 7999 Sporting & recre-
ational camps; ski rental concession; ski
instruction; eating places

(P-16828)
TOM SAWYER CAMPS INC
Also Called: T.S.c
707 W Woodbury Rd Ste F, Altadena
(91001-5386)
PHONE..................626 794-1156
Sarah Horner Fish, *CEO*
Michael H Horner, *President*
Candace Toogood, *Bd of Directors*
Sally Horner, *Vice Pres*
Guy Fish, *Exec Dir*
EMP: 56 **EST:** 1970
SQ FT: 4,000
SALES (est): 4.8MM **Privately Held**
WEB: www.tomsawyercamps.com
SIC: 7032 Sporting & recreational camps

7033 Trailer Parks & Camp
Sites

(P-16829)
**BURLINGAME INDUSTRIES INC
(PA)**
Also Called: Eagle Roofing Products
3546 N Riverside Ave, Rialto (92377-3878)
PHONE..................909 355-7000
Robert C Burlingame, *Ch of Bd*
Kevin C Burlingame, *President*
Rich Jones, *CFO*
Seamus P Burlingame, *Exec VP*
William L Robinson, *Admin Sec*
▲ **EMP:** 100 **EST:** 1969
SQ FT: 100,000
SALES (est): 120.4MM **Privately Held**
WEB: www.eagleroofing.com
SIC: 7033 0971 3559 3259 Camp-
grounds; hunting preserve; tile making
machines; roofing tile, clay; asphalt felts &
coatings

(P-16830)
BURLINGAME INDUSTRIES INC
Also Called: Resort Campground Intl
277 Lytle Creek Rd, Lytle Creek
(92358-9751)
PHONE..................909 887-7038
Bob Boyter, *Manager*
Jo Torres, *Marketing Mgr*
EMP: 64
SALES (corp-wide): 120.4MM **Privately
Held**
WEB: www.eagleroofing.com
SIC: 7033 Campgrounds; campsite
PA: Burlingame Industries, Incorporated
3546 N Riverside Ave
Rialto CA 92377
909 355-7000

(P-16831)
**COLORADO RIVER
ADVENTURES INC (PA)**
Also Called: Yuma Lakes Resort
2715 Parker Dam Rd, Earp (92242-9712)
P.O. Box 1088, Parker AZ (85344-1088)
PHONE..................760 663-3737
Phil Younis, *President*
Debbie Crook, *Office Mgr*
Jeff Pierson, *Sales Mgr*
Guy Olson, *Manager*
EMP: 112 **EST:** 1982
SQ FT: 6,500
SALES (est): 8.3MM **Privately Held**
WEB: www.coloradoriveradventures.com
SIC: 7033 8641 7032 Campgrounds; so-
cial club, membership; recreational
camps

(P-16832)
EL CAPITAN CANYON LLC
11560 Calle Real, Santa Barbara
(93117-9789)
PHONE..................805 685-3887
Roger Himovitz, *Mng Member*
Diane Forman, *Controller*
Kendra Summers, *Sales Dir*
Sarah Powell, *Sales Mgr*
Terri Bowman, *Sales Staff*
EMP: 62 **EST:** 1998
SALES (est): 9.4MM **Privately Held**
WEB: www.elcapitancanyon.com
SIC: 7033 Campgrounds

7041 Membership-Basis
Hotels

(P-16833)
HIDEAWAY
80440 Hideaway Club Ct, La Quinta
(92253-7867)
PHONE..................760 777-7400
Shawn Ygnatowiz, *General Mgr*
Mike Finnell, *Principal*
Whitney Jones,
EMP: 150 **EST:** 2006
SALES (est): 4.3MM **Privately Held**
WEB: www.hideawaygolfclub.com
SIC: 5812 7041 Grills (eating places); resi-
dence club, organization

(P-16834)
**NATIONAL CMNTY RNSSNCE
DEV COR (PA)**
9421 Haven Ave, Rancho Cucamonga
(91730-5886)
PHONE..................909 483-2444
Steve Pontell, *President*
Tracy Thomas, *CFO*
Ciriaco Pinedo, *Exec VP*
Michael M Ruane, *Exec VP*
Gregory Bradbard, *Vice Pres*
EMP: 51 **EST:** 1997
SALES: 5.8MM **Privately Held**
WEB: www.nationalcore.org
SIC: 7041 Lodging house, organization

7211 Power Laundries, Family
& Commercial

(P-16835)
ANITSA INC
Also Called: Valet Services
6032 Shull St, Bell Gardens (90201-6237)
PHONE..................213 237-0533
Margo Minisiam, *President*
Gary Von, *Executive*
Joe Brancatelli, *Chief Engr*
Marilyn Enriquez, *Accounting Mgr*
Daniel Soussa, *Opers Staff*
EMP: 135 **EST:** 1988
SQ FT: 65,000
SALES (est): 7.7MM **Privately Held**
SIC: 7211 8742 Power laundries, family &
commercial; industry specialist consult-
ants

(P-16836)
BRAUN LINEN SERVICE
A-1 Pomona Linen
396 La Mesa St, Pomona (91766-2129)
P.O. Box 317 (91769-0317)
PHONE..................909 623-2678
Jim Moore, *Manager*
EMP: 50
SALES (corp-wide): 10.6MM **Privately
Held**
WEB: www.braunlinen.com
SIC: 7211 7213 5947 Power laundries,
family & commercial; linen supply; gifts &
novelties
PA: Braun Linen Service
16514 Garfield Ave
Paramount CA 90723
909 623-2678

(P-16837)
MISSION LINEN SUPPLY
520 E Mineral King Ave, Visalia
(93292-6921)
PHONE..................559 625-5423
Paul Romer, *Manager*
EMP: 74
SALES (corp-wide): 161.2MM **Privately
Held**
WEB: www.missionlinen.com
SIC: 7211 7213 Power laundries, family &
commercial; uniform supply
PA: Mission Linen Supply
717 E Yanonali St
Santa Barbara CA 93103
805 730-3620

(P-16838)
RADIANT SERVICES CORP (PA)
651 W Knox St, Gardena (90248-4409)
PHONE..................310 327-6300
Mina Keywanfar, *CEO*
Shahrokh Keywanfar, *President*
Jamshid Beroukhim, *Vice Pres*
Cyrus Shahbaz, *Opers Mgr*
Hal Nabavi, *Marketing Staff*
EMP: 235 **EST:** 1994
SALES (est): 12.4MM **Privately Held**
WEB: www.radiantservices.com
SIC: 7211 7216 Power laundries, family &
commercial; drycleaning plants, except
rugs

(P-16839)
ROYAL AIRLINE LINEN INC
125 N Ash Ave, Inglewood (90301-1648)
PHONE..................310 677-9885
Kathleen Cunningham, *CEO*
EMP: 100 **EST:** 1984
SQ FT: 12,800
SALES (est): 4.2MM **Privately Held**
SIC: 7211 Laundry collecting & distributing
outlet

7213 Linen Sply

(P-16840)
AMERICAN TEXTILE MAINT CO
Also Called: Medico Professional Linen Svc
1705 Hooper Ave, Los Angeles
(90021-3111)
P.O. Box 516564 (90051-0596)
PHONE..................213 749-4433
Kenny Immazumi, *Manager*
Erika Snipp, *Manager*
Ozzy Jaime, *Asst Mgr*
EMP: 79
SALES (corp-wide): 88.2MM **Privately
Held**
WEB: www.republicmasterchefs.com
SIC: 7213 Uniform supply
PA: American Textile Maintenance Com-
pany
1667 W Washington Blvd
Los Angeles CA 90007
323 731-3132

(P-16841)
AMERICAN TEXTILE MAINT CO
Also Called: Republic Uniform
3001 E Anaheim St, Long Beach
(90804-3810)
PHONE..................562 438-7656
Lawrence Pallan, *Manager*
EMP: 79

SALES (corp-wide): 88.2MM **Privately
Held**
WEB: www.republicmasterchefs.com
SIC: 7213 Linen supply
PA: American Textile Maintenance Com-
pany
1667 W Washington Blvd
Los Angeles CA 90007
323 731-3132

(P-16842)
AMERICAN TEXTILE MAINT CO
Also Called: Republic Master Chefs Textile
3001 E Anaheim St, Long Beach
(90804-3810)
PHONE..................562 438-1126
Lawrence Pallan, *Branch Mgr*
EMP: 79
SALES (corp-wide): 88.2MM **Privately
Held**
WEB: www.republicmasterchefs.com
SIC: 7213 Linen supply
PA: American Textile Maintenance Com-
pany
1667 W Washington Blvd
Los Angeles CA 90007
323 731-3132

(P-16843)
AMERICAN TEXTILE MAINT CO
4459 Brockton Ave, Riverside
(92501-4004)
PHONE..................951 684-4940
EMP: 79
SALES (corp-wide): 88.2MM **Privately
Held**
WEB: www.republicmasterchefs.com
SIC: 7213 Linen supply
PA: American Textile Maintenance Com-
pany
1667 W Washington Blvd
Los Angeles CA 90007
323 731-3132

(P-16844)
AMERICAN TEXTILE MAINT CO
Also Called: Master-Chef's Linen Rental
1664 W Washington Blvd, Los Angeles
(90007-1115)
PHONE..................323 735-1661
Bob Brill, *Branch Mgr*
Peter Marsalis, *Vice Pres*
Edward Sherr, *Credit Staff*
Ryan Savage, *Analyst*
Juan Amador, *Supervisor*
EMP: 79
SALES (corp-wide): 88.2MM **Privately
Held**
WEB: www.republicmasterchefs.com
SIC: 7213 Towel supply; uniform supply
PA: American Textile Maintenance Com-
pany
1667 W Washington Blvd
Los Angeles CA 90007
323 731-3132

(P-16845)
AMERIPRIDE SERVICES INC
Also Called: Ameripride Uniform Svcs
335 Washington St, Bakersfield
(93307-2719)
PHONE..................661 324-7941
EMP: 110
SQ FT: 34,000 **Publicly Held**
SIC: 7213 7218 Linen Supply Services In-
dustrial Launderer
HQ: Ameripride Services, Inc.
10801 Wayzata Blvd # 100
Minnetonka MN 55305
800 750-4628

(P-16846)
**ARAMARK UNF & CAREER AP
LLC**
115 N First St, Burbank (91502-1856)
P.O. Box 7891 (91510-7891)
PHONE..................818 973-3700
Ed Ferguson, *Administration*
Daniel Cannan, *Planning*
Josh Whitehead, *Analyst*
David Michaelson, *Controller*
Andy Bortz, *Prdtn Mgr*
EMP: 62 **Publicly Held**
WEB: www.aramarkuniform.com
SIC: 7213 Uniform supply

HQ: Aramark Uniform & Career Apparel, Llc
115 N First St Ste 203
Burbank CA 91502
818 973-3700

(P-16847)
BRAUN LINEN SERVICE (PA)
Also Called: A-1 Pomona Linen
16514 Garfield Ave, Paramount
(90723-5304)
P.O. Box 348 (90723-0348)
PHONE..............................909 623-2678
Richard A Cornwell, *CEO*
William S Cornwell, *Vice Pres*
Brandon Cornwell, *Sales Staff*
Rome Gagliano, *Sales Staff*
Bill Garcia, *Sales Staff*
▲ EMP: 125 EST: 1985
SQ FT: 28,000
SALES (est): 10.6MM Privately Held
WEB: www.braunlinen.com
SIC: 7213 Towel supply; table cover supply

(P-16848)
BRAUN LINEN SERVICE INC
738 E Turmont St, Carson (90746-3808)
PHONE..............................310 719-8661
Richard A Cornwell, *Branch Mgr*
EMP: 50
SALES (corp-wide): 10.6MM Privately
Held
WEB: www.braunlinen.com
SIC: 7213 Towel supply
PA: Braun Linen Service
16514 Garfield Ave
Paramount CA 90723
909 623-2678

(P-16849)
BUDGET INDUSTRIAL UNF SUP INC
1702 W 134th St, Gardena (90249-2016)
P.O. Box 1368 (90249-0368)
PHONE..............................310 532-7550
Saul Shrager, *President*
Stephen Shrager, *Treasurer*
Nelson Shrager, *Admin Sec*
Norma Garcia, *Admin Asst*
Ryan Ruetz, *Sales Mgr*
EMP: 56 EST: 1957
SQ FT: 40,000
SALES (est): 5.8MM Privately Held
WEB: www.budget-uniform.com
SIC: 7213 Uniform supply

(P-16850)
CAL SOUTHERN SERVICES
Also Called: Socal Uniform Rental
419 Mcgroarty St, San Gabriel
(91776-2302)
PHONE..............................626 281-5942
EMP: 99
SALES (est): 3.1MM Privately Held
SIC: 7213 Linen Supply Services

(P-16851)
CINTAS SALES CORPORATION
2618 Oak St, Santa Ana (92707-3720)
PHONE..............................714 957-2852
EMP: 75
SALES (corp-wide): 7.1B Publicly Held
WEB: www.cintas.com
SIC: 7213 5999 5912 5699 Uniform sup-
ply; alarm & safety equipment stores;
drug stores & proprietary stores; uniforms
& work clothing
HQ: Cintas Sales Corporation
6800 Cintas Blvd
Cincinnati OH 45262

(P-16852)
FOASBERG LAUNDRY AND CLRS INC (PA)
Also Called: Crdn of Southern La County
640 E Wardlow Rd, Long Beach
(90807-4624)
P.O. Box 17965 (90807-7965)
PHONE..............................562 426-7345
James W Foasberg, *CEO*
Richard Foasberg, *Vice Pres*
EMP: 70 EST: 1937
SQ FT: 40,000

SALES (est): 4.6MM Privately Held
WEB: www.foasberg.com
SIC: 7213 7216 7211 7218 Uniform supply; drycleaning collecting & distributing
agency; laundry collecting & distributing
outlet; industrial launderers

(P-16853)
GBS LINENS INC (PA)
Also Called: GBS Party Linens
305 N Muller St, Anaheim (92801-5445)
PHONE..............................714 778-6448
Pravin Mody, *President*
Ameer P Mody, *Vice Pres*
Sudha Mody, *Vice Pres*
Sujata Mody, *Admin Sec*
Mike Sung, *Info Tech Dir*
▲ EMP: 100 EST: 1962
SQ FT: 57,000
SALES (est): 13MM Privately Held
WEB: www.gbslinens.com
SIC: 7213 2392 7211 5023 Linen supply;
household furnishings; power laundries,
family & commercial; home furnishings;
textile mill waste & remnant processing

(P-16854)
MALCOLM SMITH MOTORCYCLES INC
Also Called: Smith, Malcolm Motorsports
7599 Indiana Ave, Riverside (92504-4145)
PHONE..............................951 687-1300
Malcolm A Smith, *Owner*
Abe Hernandez, *Creative Dir*
Alexander Smith, *General Mgr*
Brooke Balmer, *Admin Asst*
Linda Bates, *Controller*
EMP: 53 EST: 1984
SQ FT: 12,000
SALES (est): 12.5MM Privately Held
WEB: www.malcolmsmith.com
SIC: 5571 7213 Motorcycles; all-terrain
vehicles; shirt supply

(P-16855)
MISSION LINEN SUPPLY
Also Called: Mission Linen & Uniform Svc
619 W Avenue I, Lancaster (93534-2585)
PHONE..............................661 948-5052
Dick Grever, *Manager*
EMP: 74
SALES (corp-wide): 161.2MM Privately
Held
WEB: www.missionlinen.com
SIC: 7213 Uniform supply
PA: Mission Linen Supply
717 E Yanonali St
Santa Barbara CA 93103
805 730-3620

(P-16856)
MISSION LINEN SUPPLY
Mission Linen & Uniform Svc
399 Errol St, Morro Bay (93442-1896)
PHONE..............................805 772-4451
Josh Offil, *General Mgr*
EMP: 74
SALES (corp-wide): 161.2MM Privately
Held
WEB: www.missionlinen.com
SIC: 7213 Uniform supply
PA: Mission Linen Supply
717 E Yanonali St
Santa Barbara CA 93103
805 730-3620

(P-16857)
MISSION LINEN SUPPLY
Also Called: Mission Linen & Unf Svc 178
1260 N Jefferson St, Anaheim
(92807-1612)
PHONE..............................909 364-8752
Jake Kungl, *General Mgr*
EMP: 74
SQ FT: 3,500
SALES (corp-wide): 161.2MM Privately
Held
WEB: www.missionlinen.com
SIC: 7213 7218 Towel supply; industrial
launderers
PA: Mission Linen Supply
717 E Yanonali St
Santa Barbara CA 93103
805 730-3620

(P-16858)
MISSION LINEN SUPPLY
Also Called: Mission Linen & Uniform Svc
505 Maulhardt Ave, Oxnard (93030-7925)
PHONE..............................805 485-6794
Matthew Aguelli, *Manager*
EMP: 74
SALES (corp-wide): 161.2MM Privately
Held
WEB: www.missionlinen.com
SIC: 7213 Uniform supply
PA: Mission Linen Supply
717 E Yanonali St
Santa Barbara CA 93103
805 730-3620

(P-16859)
MISSION LINEN SUPPLY
Also Called: Mission Linen & Uniform Svc
5400 Alton Way, Chino (91710-7601)
PHONE..............................909 393-6857
Louis Filveria, *Manager*
Chris Cantrell, *Representative*
Jason Geer, *Representative*
EMP: 74
SALES (corp-wide): 161.2MM Privately
Held
WEB: www.missionlinen.com
SIC: 7213 Uniform supply
PA: Mission Linen Supply
717 E Yanonali St
Santa Barbara CA 93103
805 730-3620

(P-16860)
MISSION LINEN SUPPLY
Also Called: Mission Linen & Uniform Svc 4
725 E Montecito St, Santa Barbara
(93103-3237)
PHONE..............................805 963-0414
Paul Nicholson, *Branch Mgr*
EMP: 74
SALES (corp-wide): 161.2MM Privately
Held
WEB: www.missionlinen.com
SIC: 7213 Uniform supply
PA: Mission Linen Supply
717 E Yanonali St
Santa Barbara CA 93103
805 730-3620

(P-16861)
MISSION LINEN SUPPLY
12629 Saticoy St S, North Hollywood
(91605-4381)
PHONE..............................818 764-0720
Alex Smith, *Branch Mgr*
Lisette Rivera, *Office Mgr*
EMP: 74
SQ FT: 8,670
SALES (corp-wide): 161.2MM Privately
Held
WEB: www.missionlinen.com
SIC: 7213 7218 Uniform supply; industrial
uniform supply
PA: Mission Linen Supply
717 E Yanonali St
Santa Barbara CA 93103
805 730-3620

(P-16862)
MISSION LINEN SUPPLY
Also Called: Mission Linen & Uniform Svc
712 E Montecito St, Santa Barbara
(93103-3295)
PHONE..............................805 962-7687
Curtos Lopez, *Manager*
Shawn Swingholm, *General Mgr*
Maria Curiel, *Office Mgr*
Lori Lindgren, *Technician*
Viet Pham, *Chief Engr*
EMP: 74
SALES (corp-wide): 161.2MM Privately
Held
WEB: www.missionlinen.com
SIC: 7213 Uniform supply
PA: Mission Linen Supply
717 E Yanonali St
Santa Barbara CA 93103
805 730-3620

(P-16863)
MISSION LINEN SUPPLY
Also Called: Mission Linen & Uniform Svc
721 Washington Blvd, Montebello
(90640-6222)
PHONE..............................323 888-8971
George Hernandez, *Office Mgr*
Sean Briscoe, *Prdtn Mgr*
EMP: 74
SQ FT: 49,424
SALES (corp-wide): 161.2MM Privately
Held
WEB: www.missionlinen.com
SIC: 7213 Uniform supply
PA: Mission Linen Supply
717 E Yanonali St
Santa Barbara CA 93103
805 730-3620

(P-16864)
MISSION LINEN SUPPLY
Also Called: Mission Linen & Uniform Svc
1275 Montalvo Way, Palm Springs
(92262-5440)
PHONE..............................760 778-5288
Mike Marrian, *Manager*
EMP: 74
SALES (corp-wide): 161.2MM Privately
Held
WEB: www.missionlinen.com
SIC: 7213 Uniform supply
PA: Mission Linen Supply
717 E Yanonali St
Santa Barbara CA 93103
805 730-3620

(P-16865)
MISSION LINEN SUPPLY
Also Called: Mission Linen & Uniform Svc
602 S Western Ave, Santa Maria
(93458-5496)
PHONE..............................805 922-3579
Bill Bently, *General Mgr*
EMP: 74
SALES (corp-wide): 161.2MM Privately
Held
WEB: www.missionlinen.com
SIC: 7213 Uniform supply
PA: Mission Linen Supply
717 E Yanonali St
Santa Barbara CA 93103
805 730-3620

(P-16866)
MISSION LINEN SUPPLY
Also Called: Mission Linen & Uniform Svc
520 E Mineral King Ave, Visalia
(93292-6921)
PHONE..............................559 291-7181
Mike Toste, *Branch Mgr*
EMP: 74
SALES (corp-wide): 161.2MM Privately
Held
WEB: www.missionlinen.com
SIC: 7213 7218 Linen supply, non-cloth-
ing; linen supply, clothing; industrial laun-
derers
PA: Mission Linen Supply
717 E Yanonali St
Santa Barbara CA 93103
805 730-3620

(P-16867)
MORGAN SERVICES INC
Also Called: Morgan Linen Service
905 Yale St, Los Angeles (90012-1724)
PHONE..............................213 485-9666
Mark Smith, *Branch Mgr*
Michelle Valenzuela, *Admin Asst*
Richard Barnes, *CIO*
EMP: 91
SQ FT: 51,339
SALES (corp-wide): 74.2MM Privately
Held
WEB: www.morganservices.com
SIC: 7213 7218 Linen supply; industrial
launderers
PA: Morgan Services, Inc.
323 N Michigan Ave
Chicago IL 60601
312 346-3181

(P-16868)
PARK CLEANERS INC (PA)
Also Called: Park Uniform Rentals
419 Mcgroarty St, San Gabriel
(91776-2302)
PHONE..............................626 281-5942
James L Brittain, *President*
Ted Doll, *Vice Pres*
Theodore W Doll, *Vice Pres*
EMP: 75 **EST:** 1946
SQ FT: 7,000
SALES (est): 3.6MM **Privately Held**
SIC: 7213 7216 Uniform supply; cleaning
& dyeing, except rugs

(P-16869)
**RICHARD K NEWMAN AND
ASSOC INC (PA)**
Also Called: Sparkle Uniform & Linen Svc
121 Monterey St, Bakersfield (93305-3406)
PHONE..............................661 634-1130
Jeffrey C Newman Sr, *Ch of Bd*
Jeffrey C Newman Jr, *President*
Mike Daniel, *COO*
Jeff Newman Jr, *Executive*
Alison Daniel, *Office Mgr*
EMP: 50 **EST:** 1950
SQ FT: 26,000
SALES (est): 9.8MM **Privately Held**
WEB: www.sparklerental.com
SIC: 7213 7216 Linen supply, non-cloth-
ing; drycleaning collecting & distributing
agency

(P-16870)
**YEE YUEN LAUNDRY AND CLRS
INC**
Also Called: Yee Yuen Linen Service
2575 S Normandie Ave, Los Angeles
(90007-1598)
PHONE..............................323 734-7205
Deborah Morikawa, *President*
Luis Lee, *Corp Secy*
Cynthia Louie, *Vice Pres*
EMP: 80 **EST:** 1928
SQ FT: 20,000
SALES (est): 4.7MM **Privately Held**
WEB: www.yeeyuenlinen.com
SIC: 7213 Linen supply

7215 Coin Operated
Laundries & Cleaning

(P-16871)
**ALL VALLEY WASHER SERVICE
INC**
15008 Delano St, Van Nuys (91411-2016)
PHONE..............................818 787-1100
Ron Feinstein, *President*
Billy Feinstein, *Treasurer*
Robert Feinstein, *Vice Pres*
Trini Valenzuela, *Sales Staff*
EMP: 70 **EST:** 1961
SQ FT: 11,000
SALES (est): 12.9MM **Privately Held**
WEB: www.allvalleywasher.com
SIC: 7215 6531 7359 5087 Laundry,
coin-operated; real estate agents & man-
agers; appliance rental; laundry equip-
ment & supplies

(P-16872)
COINMACH CORPORATION (PA)
Also Called: Reliable Co
3628 San Fernando Rd, Glendale
(91204-2944)
PHONE..............................818 637-4300
EMP: 80
SQ FT: 22,000
SALES (est): 4.6MM **Privately Held**
SIC: 7215 7211 5087 Coin-Operated
Laundry Power Laundry Whol Service Es-
tablishment Equipment

(P-16873)
PRO-WASH INC
9117 S Main St, Los Angeles (90003-3722)
PHONE..............................323 756-6000
Steve Koo, *President*
EMP: 70 **EST:** 1991
SQ FT: 20,000
SALES (est): 3.2MM **Privately Held**
SIC: 7215 Laundry, coin-operated

(P-16874)
**WASH MLTFMILY LDRY
SYSTEMS LLC (PA)**
100 N Pacific Coast Hwy, El Segundo
(90245-4359)
PHONE..............................310 643-8491
Jim Gimeson, *CEO*
Arthur J Long, *CFO*
Vivian Hung, *Exec VP*
Craig Levine, *Exec VP*
Tommy Gates, *Vice Pres*
EMP: 150 **EST:** 2007
SQ FT: 130,000
SALES (est): 115.1MM **Privately Held**
WEB: www.wash.com
SIC: 7215 Laundry, coin-operated

7216 Dry Cleaning Plants,
Except Rug Cleaning

(P-16875)
**AMERICAN WINDOW COVERING
INC**
825 Williamson Ave, Fullerton
(92832-2133)
P.O. Box 3518 (92834-3518)
PHONE..............................714 879-3880
Leland B Daniels, *President*
Lisa R Wozab, *CFO*
Larry Mazawey, *Representative*
EMP: 18 **EST:** 1963
SQ FT: 2,400
SALES (est): 1.7MM **Privately Held**
WEB: www.awc-cwc.com
SIC: 7216 2391 5023 Curtain cleaning &
repair; draperies, plastic & textile; from
purchased materials; draperies

(P-16876)
PICO CLEANER INC (PA)
9150 W Pico Blvd, Los Angeles
(90035-1320)
PHONE..............................310 274-2431
Sharam Jahanbani, *CEO*
Simon Djahanbani, *President*
EMP: 80 **EST:** 1963
SQ FT: 10,000
SALES (est): 9MM **Privately Held**
WEB: www.picocleaners.com
SIC: 7216 Cleaning & dyeing, except rugs

(P-16877)
**RICHARD K NEWMAN AND
ASSOC INC**
Also Called: Today Cleaners
5600 Auburn St Ste V, Bakersfield
(93306-2891)
PHONE..............................661 634-1218
Autumn Thompson, *Branch Mgr*
EMP: 59
SALES (corp-wide): 9.8MM **Privately
Held**
WEB: www.sparklerental.com
SIC: 7216 Cleaning & dyeing, except rugs
PA: K Newman Richard And Associates Inc
121 Monterey St
Bakersfield CA 93305
661 634-1130

(P-16878)
STERLING WESTWOOD INC
Also Called: Sterling Dry Cleaners
3405 Overland Ave, Los Angeles
(90034-5405)
PHONE..............................310 287-2431
EMP: 55
SALES (corp-wide): 1.8MM **Privately
Held**
WEB: www.sterlingcleaners.com
SIC: 7216 Drycleaning Plants, Except
Rugs
PA: Sterling Westwood, Inc.
1600 Westwood Blvd
Los Angeles CA 90024
310 474-8525

7217 Carpet & Upholstery
Cleaning

(P-16879)
CHROMA SYSTEMS
Also Called: Southcoast Dyeing & Finishing
3201 S Susan St, Santa Ana (92704-6838)
PHONE..............................714 557-8480
Peer Vinther, *Partner*
Monterey Carpets, *Partner*
Camelot Carpet Mills, *Partner*
Jonathan McCallie, *Regional Mgr*
Tom Embree, *Engineer*
EMP: 55 **EST:** 1993
SQ FT: 200,000
SALES (est): 1.5MM **Privately Held**
SIC: 7217 2273 Carpet & rug dyeing plant;
carpets & rugs

(P-16880)
EXPRESS CONTRACTORS INC
11625 Industry Ave, Fontana (92337-6931)
P.O. Box 310279 (92331-0279)
PHONE..............................951 360-6500
Amaer Alhamwi, *President*
Dennis Rosales, *Project Mgr*
EMP: 100 **EST:** 1992
SQ FT: 10,000
SALES (est): 10.6MM **Privately Held**
WEB: www.expresscontractorsinc.com
SIC: 7217 1752 1721 1743 Carpet & rug
cleaning & repairing plant; carpet laying;
painting & paper hanging; terrazzo, tile,
marble, mosaic work

(P-16881)
**STANLEY STEEMER OF LOS
ANGLES (PA)**
841 W Foothill Blvd, Azusa (91702-2815)
PHONE..............................626 791-9400
Kevin Pucci, *President*
Jeff Pucci, *Vice Pres*
EMP: 103 **EST:** 1947
SQ FT: 100,000
SALES (est): 15.2MM **Privately Held**
WEB: www.stanleysteemer.com
SIC: 7217 1799 Carpet & furniture clean-
ing on location; post-disaster renovations

7218 Industrial Launderers

(P-16882)
AMERICAN TEXTILE MAINT CO
2201 E Carson St, Long Beach
(90807-3043)
PHONE..............................562 424-1607
EMP: 180
SALES (corp-wide): 197.6MM **Privately
Held**
WEB: www.republicmasterchefs.com
SIC: 7218 7213 Industrial Launderer Linen
Supply Services
PA: American Textile Maintenance Com-
pany
1667 W Washington Blvd
Los Angeles CA 90007
323 731-3132

(P-16883)
**ARAMARK UNF & CAREER AP
LLC (DH)**
115 N First St Ste 203, Burbank
(91502-1857)
P.O. Box 101179, Pasadena (91189-0005)
PHONE..............................818 973-3700
Mike Fadden, *Mng Member*
Caralee Brown, *Vice Pres*
Dan Craig, *Vice Pres*
Adam Feirstein, *Vice Pres*
Mike Neal, *Regional Mgr*
EMP: 250 **EST:** 1976
SQ FT: 63,000
SALES (est): 546.1MM **Publicly Held**
WEB: www.aramarkuniform.com
SIC: 7218 Industrial uniform supply;
treated equipment supply: mats, rugs,
mops, cloths, etc.; wiping towel supply
HQ: Aramark Uniform & Career Apparel
Group, Inc.
1101 Market St Ste 45
Philadelphia PA 19107
215 238-3000

(P-16884)
BOWSMITH INC (PA)
131 2nd St, Exeter (93221-194?)
P.O. Box 428 (93221-0428)
PHONE..............................559 592-9485
Allan L Smith, *CEO*
Kenneth Berg, *Vice Pres*
Victor Gonzalez, *Mfg Mgr*
Richard Phillips, *Mfg Mgr*
Shannon Peacock, *Plant Mgr*
▲ **EMP:** 55 **EST:** 1974
SQ FT: 14,400
SALES (est): 11.1MM **Privately Held**
WEB: www.bowsmith.com
SIC: 7218 4971 Industrial equipment laun-
derers; irrigation systems

(P-16885)
**PRUDENTIAL OVERALL SUPPLY
(PA)**
1661 Alton Pkwy, Irvine (92606-4877)
P.O. Box 11210, Santa Ana (92711-1210)
PHONE..............................949 250-4855
Dan Clark, *CEO*
Thomas C Watts, *President*
Donald C Lahn, *Vice Ch Bd*
Mark Keller, *Executive*
Nate King, *Executive*
▲ **EMP:** 95 **EST:** 1947
SQ FT: 20,000
SALES (est): 158.2MM **Privately Held**
WEB: www.prudentialuniforms.com
SIC: 7218 Wiping towel supply

(P-16886)
UNIFIRST CORPORATION
700 Etiwanda Ave Ste C, Ontario
(91761-8608)
PHONE..............................909 390-8670
Jeff Martin, *Manager*
Jorge Mendoza, *District Mgr*
Brook Taylor, *Sales Staff*
Richard Rooney, *Manager*
EMP: 130
SALES (corp-wide): 1.8B **Publicly Held**
WEB: www.unifirst.com
SIC: 7218 7213 Industrial uniform supply;
work clothing supply; radiation protective
garment supply; uniform supply
PA: Unifirst Corporation
68 Jonspin Rd
Wilmington MA 01887
978 658-8888

(P-16887)
**WORKRITE UNIFORM COMPANY
INC (DH)**
1701 Lombard St Ste 200, Oxnard
(93030-8235)
PHONE..............................805 483-0175
Philip C Williamson, *CEO*
Keith Suddaby, *President*
Mark Adler, *Vice Pres*
EMP: 385 **EST:** 1968
SALES: 32MM
SALES (corp-wide): 9.2B **Publicly Held**
SIC: 7218 Flame & heat resistant clothing
supply
HQ: Vf Outdoor, Llc
2701 Harbor Bay Pkwy
Alameda CA 94502
855 500-8639

7219 Laundry & Garment
Svcs, NEC

(P-16888)
CM LAUNDRY LLC
14919 S Figueroa St, Gardena
(90248-1720)
PHONE..............................310 436-6170
Luis Rodriguez,
Anthony Millar,
Ernesto Munoz, *Mng Member*
EMP: 100 **EST:** 2007
SQ FT: 26,500
SALES (est): 2.8MM **Privately Held**
WEB: www.cmlaundry.com
SIC: 7219 Laundry, except power & coin-
operated

(P-16889)
DY-DEE SERVICE PASADENA INC
Also Called: California Linen Service
40 E California Blvd, Pasadena
(91105-3203)
PHONE..................626 792-6183
Brian O'Neil, *President*
Andrew Oneil, *General Mgr*
Kelly Huizinga, *Office Mgr*
Mario Balderrama, *Sales Mgr*
Linda Harman, *Manager*
EMP: 60 **EST:** 1938
SQ FT: 15,000
SALES (est): 3.3MM **Privately Held**
WEB: www.calinen.com
SIC: 7219 7213 Diaper service; linen supply, non-clothing

(P-16890)
FAMA HOLDINGS LLC
4510 Loma Vista Ave, Vernon
(90058-2602)
PHONE..................323 581-5888
EMP: 13 **EST:** 2003
SALES (est): 147.5K **Privately Held**
WEB:
SIC: 7219 2299 Garment making, alteration & repair; batting, wadding, padding & fillings

(P-16891)
JOB OPTIONS INCORPORATED
1110 S Washington Ave, San Bernardino
(92408-2244)
PHONE..................909 890-4612
Susan Arsenault, *Office Mgr*
Troy Pace, *Engineer*
EMP: 820
SQ FT: 35,800 **Privately Held**
WEB: www.joboptionsinc.org
SIC: 7219 Fur garment cleaning, repairing & storage
PA: Job Options, Incorporated
3465 Cmino Del Rio S Ste
San Diego CA 92108

(P-16892)
T POINTS INC
350 W Mrtn Lthr King Jr, Los Angeles
(90037-4529)
PHONE..................323 846-9176
EMP: 50
SALES (est): 695.8K **Privately Held**
SIC: 7219 Laundry/Garment Services

7221 Photographic Studios, Portrait

(P-16893)
CORBIS IMAGES LLC (PA)
6060 Center Dr Ste 1000, Los Angeles
(90045-8842)
PHONE..................323 602-5700
Steve Davis, *CEO*
Steve Tavis, *CEO*
Corbis Corporation,
EMP: 16 **EST:** 2005
SALES (est): 9.2MM **Privately Held**
WEB: www.bengroup.com
SIC: 7221 7372 Photographic studios, portrait; prepackaged software

(P-16894)
MARVEL STUDIOS LLC (HQ)
500 S Buena Vista St, Burbank
(91521-0001)
PHONE..................310 727-2700
David Maisel, *President*
Tim Connors, *COO*
Kevin Feige, *Ch Credit Ofcr*
Alexandra Hale, *Production*
Mary Livanos, *Production*
EMP: 241 **EST:** 1998
SALES (est): 48.2MM
SALES (corp-wide): 65.3B **Publicly Held**
WEB: www.marvel.com
SIC: 7221 Photographic studios, portrait
PA: The Walt Disney Company
500 S Buena Vista St
Burbank CA 91521
818 560-1000

7231 Beauty Shops

(P-16895)
ALEXANDERS GRAND SALON
Also Called: Alexander's Grand Salon & Spa
5579 E Santa Ana Cyn Rd, Anaheim
(92807-3143)
PHONE..................714 282-6438
Fax: 714 282-6446
EMP: 65
SALES (est): 1.3MM **Privately Held**
SIC: 7231 Beauty Shop

(P-16896)
BEAUTIFUL GROUP LLC (PA)
9720 Wilshire Blvd Fl 6, Beverly Hills
(90212-2025)
PHONE..................310 299-4100
Michael A Reinstein,
Mario Prego, *Manager*
EMP: 104 **EST:** 2017
SALES (est): 5MM **Privately Held**
WEB: www.regiscorp.com
SIC: 7231 Unisex hair salons

(P-16897)
BEAUTY BARRAGE LLC
4340 Von Karman Ave # 200, Newport
Beach (92660-2084)
PHONE..................949 771-3399
Sonia Summers, *CEO*
Kirk Summers, *Officer*
Heather Forcari, *Vice Pres*
Rebekah Von Der Hellen, *Vice Pres*
Brady Heyborne, *Vice Pres*
EMP: 220 **EST:** 2015
SALES (est): 14.4MM **Privately Held**
WEB: www.beautybarrage.com
SIC: 7231 8742 Beauty shops; marketing consulting services

(P-16898)
BEAUTY COUNTER LLC
Also Called: Beautycounter
1733 Ocean Ave Ste 400, Santa Monica
(90401-3270)
PHONE..................310 828-0111
Hedieh E Revelez, *Mng Member*
Gina Murphy, *Vice Pres*
Dan Morel, *CTO*
Luis Figueroa, *Accounts Exec*
EMP: 51 **EST:** 2013
SALES (est): 12.2MM
SALES (corp-wide): 38.9MM **Privately Held**
WEB: www.beautycounter.com
SIC: 5961 7231 ; beauty shops
PA: Counter Brands, Llc
1733 Ocean Ave
Santa Monica CA 90401
888 988-9108

(P-16899)
BELLAMI HAIR LLC
21123 Nordhoff St, Chatsworth
(91311-5816)
PHONE..................844 235-5264
Julius Salerno, *Mng Member*
Anton Ranchin, *Vice Pres*
Ravi Sundaram, *IT/INT Sup*
Summer Adams, *Human Res Dir*
Caitlin Meehan, *Education*
EMP: 126 **EST:** 2013
SALES (est): 24.7MM **Privately Held**
WEB: www.bellamihair.com
SIC: 7231 Hairdressers

(P-16900)
BURKSHINE ENTERPRISES INC (PA)
Also Called: Great Clips
6404 Sierra Hills Ct, Bakersfield
(93308-6507)
PHONE..................661 399-4321
Stephen Robert Shine, *President*
EMP: 80 **EST:** 2001
SALES (est): 810.4K **Privately Held**
WEB: www.greatclips.com
SIC: 7231 Unisex hair salons

(P-16901)
DRYBAR HOLDINGS LLC (PA)
125 Technology Dr Ste 150, Irvine
(92618-2477)
PHONE..................310 776-6330

Liz Williams, *CEO*
Shannon Williams, *Partner*
Karen Kelley, *COO*
Mitch Reback, *CFO*
Diego Vidal, *CFO*
EMP: 352 **EST:** 2010
SALES (est): 53.1MM **Privately Held**
WEB: www.drybar.com
SIC: 7231 6794 Hairdressers; franchises, selling or licensing

(P-16902)
ESALONCOM LLC
1910 E Maple Ave, El Segundo
(90245-3411)
PHONE..................866 550-2424
Francisco Gimenec,
Aaron Chan, *President*
Vera Koch, *Vice Pres*
Lani Kuramoto, *Vice Pres*
Luiza Edinchikyan, *CIO*
EMP: 102 **EST:** 2008
SALES (est): 27.2MM **Privately Held**
WEB: www.esalon.com
SIC: 7231 Hairdressers

(P-16903)
FABULOUS & COMPANY LLC
19553 Enadia Way, Reseda (91335-3620)
PHONE..................818 261-7242
Maya Riley,
EMP: 50 **EST:** 2018
SALES (est): 295.4K **Privately Held**
SIC: 7231 Beauty shops

(P-16904)
GEORGE OLIVERI HAIR DESIGN (PA)
Also Called: George Oliveri Salon
3019 N Los Cytes Diagonal, Long Beach
(90808-3750)
PHONE..................562 421-4744
George Oliveri, *Owner*
EMP: 54 **EST:** 1957
SQ FT: 3,500
SALES (est): 1MM **Privately Held**
WEB: www.georgeoliverisalon.com
SIC: 7231 Hairdressers

(P-16905)
HAIR PERFECT INTERNATIONAL
135 W California Blvd, Pasadena
(91105-3005)
PHONE..................626 304-9286
Ali Movasaghi, *Manager*
EMP: 63
SALES (corp-wide): 2.6MM **Privately Held**
SIC: 7231 Hairdressers
PA: Hair Perfect International Inc
1405 San Marino Ave # 117
San Marino CA

(P-16906)
JLM & MAG ASSOCIATES INC
Also Called: Supercuts
9204 Lakewood Blvd, Downey
(90240-2909)
PHONE..................562 869-3343
James Miller, *President*
EMP: 71
SALES (corp-wide): 3MM **Privately Held**
WEB: www.supercuts.com
SIC: 7231 Unisex hair salons
PA: Jlm & Mag Associates, Inc.
22311 Ventura Blvd # 111
Woodland Hills CA 91364
818 346-2667

(P-16907)
KORA US LLC (PA)
Also Called: Kora Organics
1990 S Bundy Dr Ste 375, Los Angeles
(90025-5249)
PHONE..................424 744-8903
Richard Feldstein, *Mng Member*
Amy Hall, *Director*
Natalie Hwang, *Manager*
EMP: 55 **EST:** 2016
SALES (est): 1.4MM **Privately Held**
SIC: 7231 Beauty shops

(P-16908)
MINILUXE INC
11965 San Vicente Blvd, Los Angeles
(90049-5003)
PHONE..................424 442-1630
Emily Sinclair, *Director*
EMP: 97
SALES (corp-wide): 15MM **Privately Held**
WEB: www.miniluxe.com
SIC: 7231 Manicurist, pedicurist
PA: Miniluxe, Inc.
1 Faneuil Hall Sq Fl 7
Boston MA 02109
617 684-2731

(P-16909)
NAIL ALLIANCE - NORTH AMER INC (PA)
Also Called: Hand and Nail Harmony
1545 Moonstone, Brea (92821-2876)
PHONE..................714 773-9758
Danny Haile, *CEO*
David Daniel, *President*
Gari-Dawn Tingler, *Vice Pres*
Napoleon Espinoza, *General Mgr*
Fabian Nino, *Administration*
◆ **EMP:** 259 **EST:** 2009
SALES (est): 21.3MM **Privately Held**
WEB: www.gelish.com
SIC: 7231 Manicurist, pedicurist

(P-16910)
PENNEY OPCO LLC
Also Called: JCP
2115 S Mooney Blvd, Visalia (93277-6242)
PHONE..................559 732-4171
Tommy Ramirez, *General Mgr*
EMP: 80
SALES (corp-wide): 1.9B **Privately Held**
SIC: 5311 7231 7221 Department stores, non-discount; beauty shops; photographic studios, portrait
HQ: Penney Opco Llc
6501 Legacy Dr
Plano TX 75024
972 431-4746

(P-16911)
PENNEY OPCO LLC
Also Called: JC Penney
400 S Baldwin Ave Lowr, Arcadia
(91007-1909)
PHONE..................626 445-6454
Jeff Paige, *Manager*
EMP: 80
SALES (corp-wide): 1.9B **Privately Held**
SIC: 5311 7231 Department stores, non-discount; beauty shops
HQ: Penney Opco Llc
6501 Legacy Dr
Plano TX 75024
972 431-4746

(P-16912)
PENNEY OPCO LLC
Also Called: JC Penney
280 W Hillcrest Dr, Thousand Oaks
(91360-4210)
PHONE..................805 497-6811
M Kline, *Branch Mgr*
EMP: 80
SALES (corp-wide): 1.9B **Privately Held**
SIC: 5311 7231 5995 Department stores, non-discount; beauty shops; optical goods stores
HQ: Penney Opco Llc
6501 Legacy Dr
Plano TX 75024
972 431-4746

(P-16913)
PENNEY OPCO LLC
Also Called: JC Penney 1505
1203 Plaza Dr, West Covina (91790-2885)
PHONE..................626 960-3711
Bob Watanabe, *Branch Mgr*
EMP: 80
SALES (corp-wide): 1.9B **Privately Held**
SIC: 5311 7231 5995 Department stores, non-discount; beauty shops; optical goods stores
HQ: Penney Opco Llc
6501 Legacy Dr
Plano TX 75024
972 431-4746

PRODUCTS & SVCS

(P-16914)
PERFECTVISION MFG INC
Also Called: Perfect 10 Satellite
10837 Commerce Way Ste A, Fontana
(92337-8202)
PHONE..................................909 355-0478
EMP: 108 **Privately Held**
WEB: www.perfect-vision.com
SIC: 7231 Beauty shops
PA: Perfectvision Manufacturing, Inc.
16101 La Grande Dr
Little Rock AR 72223

(P-16915)
PHITEN USA INC (HQ)
Also Called: Yuko Systems
22301 S Wstn Ave Ste 103, Torrance
(90501)
PHONE.............310 225-4300
Yoshihiro Hirata, *President*
▲ EMP: 50 EST: 1998
SQ FT: 35,000
SALES (est): 9.5MM **Privately Held**
WEB: www.phitenusa.com
SIC: 5941 7231 Sporting goods & bicycle
shops; beauty shops

(P-16916)
REGIS CORPORATION
Also Called: Vidal Sassoon Salon
9403 Santa Monica Blvd, Beverly Hills
(90210-4604)
PHONE.............310 274-8791
EMP: 50
SALES (corp-wide): 1.7B **Publicly Held**
SIC: 7231 Hair Salon
PA: Regis Corporation
7201 Metro Blvd
Edina MN 55416
952 947-7777

(P-16917)
**SANTA BRBARA CMNTY
COLLEGE DST**
Also Called: Academy of Cosmetology
525 Anacapa St, Santa Barbara
(93101-1603)
PHONE.............805 683-4191
Ben Partee, *Manager*
Raquel Alvarado, *Admin Asst*
Grace Twedt, *Admin Asst*
Stephanie Dotson, *Dept Chairman*
Nancy Morales, *Technician*
EMP: 497
SALES (corp-wide): 68.1MM **Privately
Held**
WEB: www.sbcc.edu
SIC: 8222 7231 Community college; cos-
metology school
PA: Santa Barbara Community College Dis-
trict
721 Cliff Dr
Santa Barbara CA 93109
805 965-0581

(P-16918)
**TONI & GUY HAIRDRESSING
(PA)**
1177 Newport Center Dr, Newport Beach
(92660-6950)
PHONE.............949 721-1666
Frank Chirico, *Partner*
Jerry Watkins, *Executive*
Pavlos Kyriakidis, *Technician*
Kirstie Yallop, *Technician*
Danielle Heneghan, *Technical Staff*
EMP: 50 EST: 1985
SALES (est): 2.5MM **Privately Held**
WEB: www.toniguy.com
SIC: 7231 Unisex hair salons

(P-16919)
TRILOGY SQUAW SPA LLC
Also Called: Trilogy Day Spa
451 Manhattan Beach Blvd, Manhattan
Beach (90266-5345)
PHONE.............310 760-0044
Shandra Shaw,
Ratna Goravani, *Director*
EMP: 50 EST: 2004
SALES (est): 1.3MM **Privately Held**
WEB: www.trilogyspa.com
SIC: 7231 Facial salons

(P-16920)
**WELCH MANAGEMENT
CORPORATION**
Also Called: Fantastic Sams
1233 W Foothill Blvd, Upland (91786-3681)
PHONE.............909 981-4302
Louisa Corales, *Manager*
EMP: 68
SALES (corp-wide): 1MM **Privately Held**
WEB: www.fantasticsams.com
SIC: 7231 Unisex hair salons
PA: Welch Management Corporation
10261 Trademark St Ste D
Rancho Cucamonga CA
909 980-9961

7241 Barber Shops

(P-16921)
HAIRCUTTERS
1230 W Imperial Hwy Ste A, La Habra
(90631-6961)
PHONE.............562 690-2217
EMP: 92
SALES (corp-wide): 14.9MM **Privately
Held**
SIC: 7241 7231 Barber Shop Beauty Shop
PA: The Haircutters
5160 Van Nuys Blvd
Sherman Oaks CA
818 716-5319

7261 Funeral Svcs &
Crematories

(P-16922)
FOREST LAWN MORTUARY (HQ)
1712 S Glendale Ave, Glendale
(91205-3320)
PHONE.............323 254-3131
John Llewellyn, *President*
EMP: 479 EST: 1933
SQ FT: 432,000
SALES (est): 22MM
SALES (corp-wide): 129.4MM **Privately
Held**
WEB: www.forestlawn.com
SIC: 7261 Funeral home
PA: Forest Lawn Memorial-Park Associa-
tion
1712 S Glendale Ave
Glendale CA 91205
323 254-3131

(P-16923)
**GRUPO DECO CALIFORNIA
CORP (HQ)**
8545 Rosecrans Ave, Paramount
(90723-3645)
PHONE.............562 634-8990
Salvador Canales Pahissa, *President*
Leon M Cooper, *CEO*
EMP: 52 EST: 1998
SALES (est): 3.1MM **Privately Held**
WEB: www.grupodeco.com
SIC: 7261 Funeral home

(P-16924)
**INGLEWOOD CMTRY
MORTUARY INC**
3801 W Manchester Blvd, Inglewood
(90305-2106)
PHONE.............310 412-6811
William J Mc Kinley, *President*
EMP: 62 EST: 1962
SQ FT: 10,000
SALES (est): 5.9MM
SALES (corp-wide): 20MM **Privately
Held**
WEB: www.inglewoodparkcemetery.com
SIC: 7261 6553 Funeral director; cemeter-
ies, real estate operation
PA: The Lafayette Corporation
1525 State St Ste 203
Santa Barbara CA 93101
805 965-2009

(P-16925)
PIERCE BROTHERS (DH)
Also Called: SCI
10621 Victory Blvd, North Hollywood
(91606-3918)
PHONE.............818 763-9121
Oliver Yeo, *Manager*
R L Waltrip, *Ch of Bd*
David Anderson, *President*
Curtis Briggs, *Vice Pres*
Ray Gipson, *Vice Pres*
EMP: 80 EST: 1902
SQ FT: 10,000
SALES (est): 20.8MM
SALES (corp-wide): 3.5B **Publicly Held**
WEB: www.sci-corp.com
SIC: 7261 6553 Crematory; cemeteries,
real estate operation

(P-16926)
R A F LP (PA)
Also Called: Fairhaven Mem Pk & Mortuary
1702 Fairhaven Ave, Santa Ana
(92705-6821)
PHONE.............714 633-1442
Marla Noel, *Partner*
Charity Gallardo, *IT/INT Sup*
Jon Searfoss, *Accounting Mgr*
Richard Landuyt, *Director*
Sandy Luevanos, *Director*
EMP: 76 EST: 1986
SQ FT: 11,000
SALES (est): 7.9MM **Privately Held**
WEB: www.fairhavenmemorial.com
SIC: 7261 5992 5999 6512 Funeral
home; flowers, fresh; gravestones, fin-
ished; commercial & industrial building
operation; mausoleum operation

(P-16927)
ROSE HILLS MORTUARY INC
Also Called: Rose Hills Co
3888 Workman Mill Rd, Whittier
(90601-1626)
P.O. Box 110 (90608-0110)
PHONE.............562 699-0921
Dennis Poulsen, *Ch of Bd*
John Short, *Senior VP*
Monique Lopez, *Vice Pres*
Nick Clark, *Executive*
Bruce Lazenby, *Exec Dir*
EMP: 67 EST: 1976
SQ FT: 230,000
SALES (est): 2.5MM **Privately Held**
WEB: www.rosehills.com
SIC: 7261 6553 Funeral home; cemetery
subdividers & developers

(P-16928)
SCI WESTERN REGION INC
10621 Victory Blvd, North Hollywood
(91606-3918)
P.O. Box 3 (91603-0003)
PHONE.............818 286-0640
Thomas E Weaver Jr, *President*
EMP: 51 EST: 1994
SALES (est): 1.2MM
SALES (corp-wide): 3.5B **Publicly Held**
WEB: www.sci-corp.com
SIC: 7261 Funeral home
PA: Service Corporation International
1929 Allen Pkwy
Houston TX 77019
713 522-5141

(P-16929)
**SE ACQSTION LNCASTER CAL
INC (DH)**
Also Called: Halley Olsen Murphy Mem
Chapel
44831 Cedar Ave, Lancaster (93534-3212)
PHONE.............661 942-1139
Elaine Heitman, *Office Mgr*
EMP: 52 EST: 1996
SQ FT: 3,500
SALES (est): 1.6MM
SALES (corp-wide): 3.5B **Publicly Held**
WEB: www.cityoflancasterca.org
SIC: 7261 Funeral home
HQ: Stewart Enterprises, Inc.
1333 S Clearview Pkwy
New Orleans LA 70121
504 729-1400

(P-16930)
SINAI TEMPLE
Also Called: Mt Sinai Mem Pk & Mortuary
5950 Forest Lawn Dr, Los Angeles
(90068-1010)
PHONE.............323 469-6000
Len Lawrence, *Manager*
Josie Gonzales, *Admin Sec*
Gloria Garcia, *Admin Asst*
Doreen Kayne, *Planning*
Karen Maurise, *Planning*
EMP: 125
SQ FT: 22,633
SALES (corp-wide): 43.3MM **Privately
Held**
WEB: www.sinaiakiba.org
SIC: 7261 6553 Funeral home; cemeter-
ies, real estate operation
PA: Temple Sinai
10400 Wilshire Blvd
Los Angeles CA 90024
310 474-1518

(P-16931)
SINAI TEMPLE (PA)
Also Called: Mt Sinai Mem Pk & Mortuary
10400 Wilshire Blvd, Los Angeles
(90024-4600)
PHONE.............310 474-1518
Howard Lesner, *COO*
Joel Weinstein, *President*
Marcella Berga, *Principal*
Marcus Feldman, *Exec Dir*
Rachel Polansky, *Program Mgr*
EMP: 300 EST: 1908
SQ FT: 100,000
SALES (est): 43.3MM **Privately Held**
WEB: www.sinaiakiba.org
SIC: 8661 7261 5947 Synagogue; funeral
service & crematories; gift shop

(P-16932)
**TEMPLE ISRAEL OF
HOLLYWOOD (PA)**
Also Called: Hillside Mem Pk & Mortuary
7300 Hollywood Blvd, Los Angeles
(90046-2999)
PHONE.............323 876-8330
Steve Sloan, *President*
David Cremin, *Treasurer*
Renee Mochkatel, *Vice Pres*
Jane Zuckerman, *Exec Dir*
Nancy Ortenberg, *Admin Sec*
EMP: 83 EST: 1926
SQ FT: 15,000
SALES (est): 17.5MM **Privately Held**
WEB: www.tioh.org
SIC: 7261 8299 Funeral service & crema-
tories; religious school

7291 Tax Return Preparation
Svcs

(P-16933)
AHG INC
340 S Lemon Ave 6633, Walnut
(91789-2706)
PHONE.............703 596-0111
Sanzar Kakar, *Officer*
EMP: 300 EST: 2018
SALES (est): 7.5MM **Privately Held**
SIC: 7291 8721 Tax return preparation
services; accounting, auditing & book-
keeping; payroll accounting service

(P-16934)
ANDERSEN TAX LLC
3200 Park Center Dr # 1200, Costa Mesa
(92626-7108)
PHONE.............949 885-4550
Dave Kapnick, *Owner*
EMP: 53
SALES (corp-wide): 83.3MM **Privately
Held**
WEB: www.andersen.com
SIC: 7291 Tax return preparation services
PA: Andersen Tax Llc
333 Bush St Ste 1700
San Francisco CA 94104
415 764-2700

(P-16935)
ANDERSEN TAX LLC
400 Suth Hope St Ste 2000, Los Angeles (90071)
PHONE.................................213 593-2300
Kurt Brune, *Managing Dir*
Margie Lopez, *Risk Mgmt Dir*
Vena Prasatarporn, *Associate*
EMP: 53
SALES (corp-wide): 83.3MM **Privately Held**
WEB: www.andersen.com
SIC: 7291 Tax return preparation services
PA: Andersen Tax Llc
　　333 Bush St Ste 1700
　　San Francisco CA 94104
　　415 764-2700

(P-16936)
EXACTAX INC (PA)
1100 E Orngthrp Ave # 100, Anaheim (92801-5168)
PHONE.................................714 284-4802
Kevin Love, *President*
Franklin Pang, *Shareholder*
Richard Johnson, *Treasurer*
Michael Leonetti, *Vice Pres*
Bob Lynch, *Vice Pres*
EMP: 74 **EST:** 1989
SALES (est): 2.6MM **Privately Held**
WEB: www.exactax.com
SIC: 7291 7371 Tax return preparation services; computer software development

(P-16937)
H G GROUP INC
4225 Saviers Rd, Oxnard (93033-7158)
PHONE.................................805 486-6463
EMP: 382
SALES (corp-wide): 185.2MM **Privately Held**
WEB: www.hyatt.com
SIC: 7291 Tax return preparation services
HQ: H G Group Inc
　　71 S Wacker Dr Ste 1000
　　Chicago IL

(P-16938)
INTERNAL REVENUE SERVICE
2400 E Katella Ave # 800, Anaheim (92806-5945)
PHONE.................................714 512-2818
EMP: 56 **Publicly Held**
WEB: www.irs.gov
SIC: 7291 Tax return preparation services
HQ: Internal Revenue Service
　　1973 N Rulon White Blvd
　　Ogden UT 84404
　　202 803-9000

(P-16939)
OPTIMA TAX RELIEF LLC
3100 S Harbor Blvd # 250, Santa Ana (92704-6823)
PHONE.................................714 361-4636
Jesse Torres,
Amanda Gorrin, *Partner*
Harry Langenberg, *Partner*
Venkata Pottululla, *Exec VP*
Christine Bui, *Vice Pres*
EMP: 180 **EST:** 2010
SQ FT: 30,000
SALES (est): 26.2MM **Privately Held**
WEB: www.optimataxrelief.com
SIC: 7291 Tax return preparation services

(P-16940)
TAX CREDIT CO LLC (PA)
6121 W Sunset Blvd Fl 2, Los Angeles (90028-6449)
PHONE.................................323 927-0752
Brandon Edwards, *CEO*
Larae Pieroni, *Senior VP*
Elizabeth May, *Vice Pres*
Quintessa Lane, *Office Mgr*
Ali Shahzad, *Info Tech Dir*
EMP: 86 **EST:** 2014
SALES (est): 10.1MM **Privately Held**
WEB: www.taxcreditco.com
SIC: 7291 Tax return preparation services

7299 Miscellaneous Personal Svcs, NEC

(P-16941)
A-1 EVENT & PARTY RENTALS
Also Called: A1 Event & Party Rentals
251 E Front St, Covina (91723-1613)
PHONE.................................626 967-0500
Chet Fortney, *President*
Rene Martinez, *Vice Pres*
EMP: 55 **EST:** 1999
SQ FT: 40,000
SALES (est): 3.4MM **Privately Held**
WEB: www.a1partyrental.com
SIC: 7299 7359 Party planning service; party supplies rental services

(P-16942)
ACAPULCO RESTAURANTS INC
Also Called: Acapulco Mxican Rest Y Cantina
12625 Frederick St Ste T, Moreno Valley (92553-5236)
PHONE.................................951 653-8809
Fernando Correa, *Manager*
EMP: 77
SALES (corp-wide): 1.2B **Privately Held**
WEB: www.acapulcorestaurants.com
SIC: 5812 7299 Mexican restaurant; banquet hall facilities
HQ: Acapulco Restaurants, Inc.
　　4001 Via Oro Ave Ste 200
　　Long Beach CA 90810
　　310 513-7538

(P-16943)
AMERICAN STREAM SOLAR INC
1149 W 190th St, Gardena (90248-4321)
PHONE.................................888 919-6636
Muhammad Masood, *CEO*
EMP: 50 **EST:** 2016
SALES (est): 2.9MM **Privately Held**
WEB: www.americanstreamsolar.com
SIC: 7299 1711 Home improvement & renovation contractor agency; solar energy contractor

(P-16944)
AMERICOR FUNDING INC
18200 Von Karman Ave # 600, Irvine (92612-1023)
PHONE.................................866 333-8686
Banir Ganatra, *CEO*
EMP: 170 **EST:** 2008
SALES (est): 11MM **Privately Held**
WEB: www.americor.com
SIC: 7299 Debt counseling or adjustment service, individuals

(P-16945)
CARPENTERS SOUTHWEST ADM CORP
Also Called: Pea Soup Andersen's Restaurant
376 Ave Of The Flags, Buellton (93427-9704)
P.O. Box 195 (93427-0195)
PHONE.................................805 688-5581
Ed Sarbinie, *Manager*
EMP: 239
SALES (corp-wide): 45.9MM **Privately Held**
WEB: www.carpenterssw.org
SIC: 5812 7299 Eating places; banquet hall facilities
PA: Carpenters Southwest Administrative Corporation
　　533 S Fremont Ave
　　Los Angeles CA 90071
　　213 386-8590

(P-16946)
CHEVYS RESTAURANTS LLC
Also Called: Chevys Fresh Mex Restaurant
701 N San Fernando Blvd, Burbank (91502-1024)
PHONE.................................818 846-6999
Fax: 818 846-9237
EMP: 62
SALES (corp-wide): 453.2MM **Privately Held**
SIC: 5812 7299 Eating Place Misc Personal Services

HQ: Chevys Restaurants Llc
　　2000 Powell St Ste 200
　　Emeryville CA 94608
　　510 768-1400

(P-16947)
CHOURA VENUE SERVICES
Also Called: Choura Vnue Svcs At Carson Ctr
4101 E Willow St, Long Beach (90815-1740)
PHONE.................................562 426-0555
James Choura, *CEO*
Tammy Weir, *General Mgr*
Dan DSA, *Director*
Devin Wright, *Director*
Jeff Pye, *Manager*
EMP: 99 **EST:** 2012
SALES (est): 11.4MM **Privately Held**
WEB: www.thegrandlb.com
SIC: 7299 5812 Information services, consumer; caterers

(P-16948)
CIRI - STROUP INC
Also Called: Mile High Valet
25135 Park Lantern, Dana Point (92629-2878)
PHONE.................................949 488-3104
Rob Stroup, *Owner*
EMP: 290 **Privately Held**
SIC: 7299 7521 Valet parking; automobile parking
PA: Ciri - Stroup, Inc.
　　1 Park Pl Ste 200
　　Annapolis MD

(P-16949)
CLIFFS RESORT LLC
Also Called: Sea Cliffs Restaurant & Lounge
2757 Shell Beach Rd, Pismo Beach (93449-1602)
PHONE.................................805 773-5000
John King,
Lauren Hock, *Executive*
Ruthann Hernandez, *Accountant*
Hali Sandschulte, *Human Res Mgr*
Mike Casola, *Opers Staff*
▲ **EMP:** 50 **EST:** 1999
SALES (est): 9.9MM **Privately Held**
WEB: www.cliffshotelandspa.com
SIC: 5812 7299 5813 7011 Eating places; banquet hall facilities; cocktail lounge; hotels & motels

(P-16950)
CLOUDSTAFF LLC
26895 Aliso Creek Rd B-2, Aliso Viejo (92656-5301)
PHONE.................................888 551-5339
Patrick Allen,
EMP: 107
SALES (corp-wide): 19.9MM **Privately Held**
WEB: www.cloudstaffllc.com
SIC: 7299 Personal appearance services
PA: Cloudstaff Llc
　　1165 E San Antonio Dr
　　Long Beach CA 90807
　　888 551-5339

(P-16951)
CLUTTER INC (PA)
3526 Hayden Ave, Culver City (90232-2413)
PHONE.................................800 805-4023
ARI Mir, *CEO*
Rony Kort, *Vice Pres*
Edward Bramanti, *Sr Software Eng*
Matt Agra, *Software Engr*
Ben Warner, *VP Finance*
EMP: 244 **EST:** 2013
SALES (est): 44.7MM **Privately Held**
WEB: www.clutter.com
SIC: 7299 4212 Personal item care & storage services; moving services

(P-16952)
CP OPCO LLC (HQ)
Also Called: Classic Party Rentals
901 W Hillcrest Blvd A, Inglewood (90301-2101)
PHONE.................................310 966-4900
EMP: 2300

SALES (est): 154.7MM
SALES (corp-wide): 1.9MM **Privately Held**
SIC: 7299 Misc Personal Services

(P-16953)
DEBTMERICA LLC
Also Called: Debtmerica Relief
3100 S Harbor Blvd # 250, Santa Ana (92704-6823)
PHONE.................................714 389-4200
Jesse Torres,
Prem Jayaraman, *Software Engr*
Anthony Doan, *Technology*
Nancy Khader, *Sales Dir*
Lindsay Dage, *Sales Staff*
EMP: 65 **EST:** 2006
SQ FT: 15,000
SALES (est): 4.9MM **Privately Held**
WEB: www.debtmerica.com
SIC: 7299 Debt counseling or adjustment service, individuals

(P-16954)
EHARMONY INC (HQ)
Also Called: Eharmony.com
10900 Wilshire Blvd Fl 17, Los Angeles (90024-6522)
P.O. Box 241810 (90024-9610)
PHONE.................................424 258-1199
Grant Langston, *CEO*
Ashley Chisholm, *Vice Pres*
Jesamine Tapia, *Planning*
Carlos Robles, *Info Tech Mgr*
Jeffrey Thompson, *Software Dev*
EMP: 119 **EST:** 2000
SQ FT: 6,000
SALES (est): 38.9MM
SALES (corp-wide): 4.7B **Privately Held**
WEB: www.eharmony.com
SIC: 7299 Dating service
PA: Prosiebensat.1 Media Se
　　Medienallee 7
　　Unterfohring BY 85774
　　899 507-10

(P-16955)
EMI-JAY INC
16060 Ventura Blvd # 110, Encino (91436-2761)
PHONE.................................888 779-9733
Soomi Goldmark, *CEO*
Jill Greenbaum, *Co-Owner*
EMP: 16 **EST:** 2009
SQ FT: 10,000
SALES (est): 1MM **Privately Held**
WEB: www.emijay.com
SIC: 7299 3999 Personal shopping service; hair & hair-based products

(P-16956)
GALKOS CONSTRUCTION INC (PA)
15262 Pipeline Ln, Huntington Beach (92649-1136)
PHONE.................................714 373-8545
Frank E Gialketsis, *President*
Lonnie Gialketsis, *President*
Lonnie Gailketsis, *Vice Pres*
EMP: 211 **EST:** 1986
SALES (est): 18MM **Privately Held**
WEB: www.safesteptubcalifornia.com
SIC: 7299 Home improvement & renovation contractor agency

(P-16957)
GLEN IVY HOT SPRINGS
1001 Brea Mall, Brea (92821-5721)
PHONE.................................714 990-2090
Jen Breakey, *Manager*
Lori Edgell, *Marketing Staff*
Nicole Evans, *Marketing Staff*
Patty Rook, *Director*
EMP: 190
SALES (corp-wide): 12.1MM **Privately Held**
WEB: www.glenivy.com
SIC: 7299 7991 5812 5699 Massage parlor; spas; cafe; bathing suits; toiletries, cosmetics & perfumes
PA: Glen Ivy Hot Springs
　　25000 Glen Ivy Rd
　　Temescal Valley CA 92883
　　951 277-3529

P R O D U C T S & S V C S

(P-16958)
IDEAL PRODUCTS LLC
14724 Ventura Blvd Fl 200, Sherman Oaks
(91403-3514)
PHONE..............................818 217-2574
Mark Bess, *Mng Member*
Gabriela Hinojoza, *Project Mgr*
Vivian Medina, *Opers Staff*
Amanda Sol, *Sales Mgr*
Nicole Flessati, *Marketing Staff*
EMP: 50 EST: 2003
SALES (est): 2MM **Privately Held**
SIC: 7299 Information services, consumer

(P-16959)
INFORMTION RFRRAL FDRTION OF L
Also Called: 211 LA COUNTY
526 W Las Tunas Dr, San Gabriel
(91776-1111)
P.O. Box 726 (91778-0726)
PHONE..............................626 350-1841
Maribel Marin, *CEO*
Amy Latzer, *COO*
Laura Nelson, *CFO*
Juan Chavez, *Admin Mgr*
Alana Hitchcock, *Executive Asst*
EMP: 100 EST: 1980
SQ FT: 23,000
SALES (est): 11.8MM **Privately Held**
WEB: www.211la.org
SIC: 7299 Information services, consumer

(P-16960)
JET FLEET INTERNATIONAL CORP
Also Called: J F I
2370 Westwood Blvd Ste K, Los Angeles
(90064-2150)
PHONE..............................310 440-3820
Finn Moller, *President*
Arcy Lariz, *Admin Sec*
EMP: 28 EST: 2003
SALES (est): 2.2MM **Privately Held**
WEB: www.jetfleetinternational.com
SIC: 7299 7363 2911 6361 Buyers' club;
pilot service, aviation; jet fuels; title insurance

(P-16961)
JMJ ENTERPRISES INC
Also Called: Someone's In The Kitchen
5973 Reseda Blvd, Tarzana (91356-1505)
PHONE..............................818 343-5151
Joann R Oseary, *President*
Jason Perel, *Vice Pres*
Karlee Gates, *Manager*
EMP: 120 EST: 1981
SQ FT: 6,000
SALES (est): 5.3MM **Privately Held**
WEB: www.sitk.com
SIC: 5812 7299 7359 Caterers; party
planning service; sound & lighting equipment rental

(P-16962)
LAWRYS RESTAURANTS II INC
Also Called: Tam O'Shanter Inn
2980 Los Feliz Blvd, Los Angeles
(90039-1524)
PHONE..............................323 664-0228
Bryan Lytle, *Manager*
Karen Castellana, *Human Res Mgr*
Vanessa Silvera, *Human Res Mgr*
Robert Nevera, *Manager*
EMP: 131
SALES (corp-wide): 25.9MM **Privately Held**
WEB: www.lawrysonline.com
SIC: 5812 7299 Steak restaurant; banquet
hall facilities
PA: Lawry's Restaurants Ii, Inc.
100 N La Cienega Blvd
Beverly Hills CA 90211
626 440-5234

(P-16963)
LIBERTY DEBT RELIEF LLC
333 City Blvd W Fl 17, Orange
(92868-5905)
PHONE..............................800 756-8447
Omar Chouche, *CEO*
Aaron Bauer, *Mng Member*
EMP: 65 EST: 2017

SALES (est): 1.3MM **Privately Held**
WEB: www.libertydebtrelief.com
SIC: 7299 Debt counseling or adjustment
service, individuals

(P-16964)
LOVE AT FIRST BITE CATERING
Also Called: Premere Event Services
18281 Gothard St Ste 108, Huntington
Beach (92648-1205)
PHONE..............................714 369-0561
John Labrake, *President*
Vanessa Gerrie, *Manager*
EMP: 70 EST: 1982
SQ FT: 2,600
SALES (est): 4.4MM **Privately Held**
WEB: www.lafbcatering.com
SIC: 5812 7299 Caterers; party planning
service

(P-16965)
MASTROIANNI FAMILY ENTPS LTD
Also Called: Jay's Catering
10581 Garden Grove Blvd, Garden Grove
(92843-1128)
PHONE..............................310 952-1700
Jay Mastroiannis, *President*
EMP: 360
SALES (corp-wide): 24.3MM **Privately Held**
WEB: www.jayscatering.com
SIC: 7299 Banquet hall facilities
PA: Mastroianni Family Enterprises Ltd.
10581 Garden Grove Blvd
Garden Grove CA 92843
714 636-6045

(P-16966)
MEXICALI INC
Also Called: Mexicali Restaurant
631 18th St, Bakersfield (93301-4934)
PHONE..............................661 327-3861
Sunny Crews, *Manager*
EMP: 115
SALES (corp-wide): 4.5MM **Privately Held**
WEB: www.mexicalifood.com
SIC: 5812 5813 7299 Mexican restaurant;
bar (drinking places); banquet hall facilities
PA: Mexicali, Inc.
419 Baker St
Bakersfield CA 93305
661 327-4218

(P-16967)
MOUNTASIA OF SANTA CLARITA
Also Called: Mountasia Family Fun Center
21516 Golden Triangle Rd, Santa Clarita
(91350-2612)
PHONE..............................661 253-4386
EMP: 60
SALES (est): 1.7MM **Privately Held**
WEB: www.mountasiafuncenter.com
SIC: 7299 7999 Misc Personal Services
Amusement/Recreation Services

(P-16968)
ONE CALL PLUMBER GOLETA
140 Nectarine Ave Apt 4, Goleta
(93117-3359)
PHONE..............................805 284-0441
One Call Plumber Goleta, *Owner*
EMP: 99 EST: 2001
SALES (est): 0 **Privately Held**
WEB: www.plumbersgoleta.com
SIC: 7299 Handyman service

(P-16969)
ONE EVENTS INC
8581 Santa Monica Blvd, West Hollywood
(90069-4120)
PHONE..............................310 498-5471
Nickolas William Potocic, *CEO*
EMP: 90 EST: 2012
SALES (est): 734.9K **Privately Held**
WEB: www.oneevents.biz
SIC: 7299 Banquet hall facilities

(P-16970)
OSF INTERNATIONAL INC
Also Called: Old Spaghetti Factory-Duarte
1431 Buena Vista St, Duarte (91010-2458)
PHONE..............................626 358-2115
Jennifer Smith, *Manager*

Jim Devenpeck, *Office Mgr*
EMP: 66
SALES (corp-wide): 145.4MM **Privately Held**
WEB: www.osf.com
SIC: 5812 7299 5813 Restaurant, lunch
counter; banquet hall facilities; drinking
places
PA: Osf International, Inc.
0715 Sw Bancroft St
Portland OR 97239
503 222-5375

(P-16971)
PARKING VETERANS LLC
18282 Gramercy Dr, North Tustin
(92705-2020)
PHONE..............................714 699-3541
John Sparks, *CEO*
David Graham, *Principal*
EMP: 50 EST: 2014
SALES (est): 3MM **Privately Held**
WEB: www.parkingveterans.com
SIC: 7299 4119 7521 Valet parking; local
passenger transportation; parking lots;
parking garage

(P-16972)
PPS PARKING INC
1800 E Garry Ave Ste 107, Santa Ana
(92705-5803)
P.O. Box 16635, Irvine (92623-6635)
PHONE..............................949 223-8707
Steve Paliska, *President*
Stephen Paliska, *COO*
Paul Paliska, *Exec VP*
Karen Such, *Vice Pres*
Gabriel Shubin, *Transportation*
EMP: 506 EST: 1982
SQ FT: 5,000
SALES (est): 14.1MM **Privately Held**
WEB: www.ppsparkingandtrans.com
SIC: 7299 8748 Valet parking; business
consulting

(P-16973)
PREMIER RESIDENTIAL SVCS LLC
43100 Cook St Ste 101, Palm Desert
(92211-3124)
P.O. Box 13250 (92255-3250)
PHONE..............................760 773-4081
Daniel Loera, *Mng Member*
Stephen Ezer, *Vice Pres*
Ed Connolly, *Associate*
EMP: 60 EST: 1999
SALES (est): 1MM **Privately Held**
WEB: www.premier-residential-services.com
SIC: 7299 Miscellaneous personal service

(P-16974)
QUIET CANNON MONTEBELLO INC
Also Called: The Quiet Cannon
901 Via San Clemente, Montebello
(90640-1610)
PHONE..............................323 724-4500
MO Dianat, *General Mgr*
Marbella Ortega, *Sales Staff*
Savannah Yslas, *Sales Staff*
Marbella Garcia, *Director*
EMP: 84
SALES (corp-wide): 2.5MM **Privately Held**
WEB: www.quietcannon.com
SIC: 5812 5813 7299 6512 Eating
places; bars & lounges; ; nonresidential
building operators
PA: Quiet Cannon Montebello Inc.
1913 E 17th St Ste 118
Santa Ana CA 92705
714 648-0880

(P-16975)
REUNIFY LLC
12121 Wilshire Blvd # 505, Los Angeles
(90025-1176)
PHONE..............................310 893-1736
Jafar Adibi, *CTO*
Mahdi Shafiee, *Business Anlyst*
EMP: 68 EST: 2011
SALES (est): 536.7K **Privately Held**
WEB: www.reunify.com
SIC: 7299 Information services, consumer

PA: Njk Holding Corporation
411 S County Rd Ste 200
Palm Beach FL 33480

(P-16976)
SERVIZ INC
15303 Ventura Blvd # 1600, Sherman Oaks
(91403-3133)
PHONE..............................818 381-4826
Zorik Gordon, *CEO*
Michael Klien, *President*
Jeremy Burgess, *Software Engr*
Darrel Held, *Training Spec*
Richard Repich, *Sales Staff*
EMP: 70 EST: 2014
SQ FT: 8,000
SALES (est): 8.4MM **Privately Held**
WEB: www.ahs.com
SIC: 7299 Home improvement & renovation contractor agency

(P-16977)
SPECIALTY RESTAURANTS CORP
Also Called: Castaway Restaurant, The
1250 E Harvard Rd, Burbank (91501-1002)
PHONE..............................818 843-5013
Saeed Fazeli, *General Mgr*
Nicole Ellis, *Sales Mgr*
Arianna Garibo, *Sales Mgr*
Susana Montes, *Director*
EMP: 115
SALES (corp-wide): 201.1MM **Privately Held**
WEB: www.specialtyrestaurants.com
SIC: 5812 7299 American restaurant; banquet hall facilities
PA: Specialty Restaurants Corporation
8191 E Kaiser Blvd
Anaheim CA 92808
714 279-6100

(P-16978)
SPECTRUM HHI
Also Called: Spectrum Brands Hardware and H
19701 Da Vinci, Foothill Ranch
(92610-2622)
PHONE..............................949 672-4000
Eric Kenney, *Division VP*
Kendra Williams, *Division VP*
David Prichard, *Vice Pres*
Shawn Simmons, *Vice Pres*
Phil Szuba, *Vice Pres*
EMP: 72 EST: 2015
SALES (est): 25.8MM **Privately Held**
SIC: 7299 Home improvement & renovation contractor agency

(P-16979)
SPORTSMENS LODGE RESTAURANT
Also Called: Sportsmens Lodge Rest Spcial Ev
12833 Ventura Blvd, Studio City
(91604-2396)
PHONE..............................818 755-5000
Patrick Holleran, *CEO*
EMP: 53 EST: 1946
SQ FT: 60,000
SALES (est): 701.7K **Privately Held**
WEB: www.sportsmenslodge.com
SIC: 5812 7299 5813 Restaurant, family;
independent; banquet hall facilities; cocktail lounge

(P-16980)
SUGARED + BRONZED LLC (PA)
34241 E Pcf Cast Hwy Ste, Dana Point
(92629)
PHONE..............................410 493-3467
Sam Offit, *CEO*
Rachel Solomon, *COO*
Andrea Berberian, *Vice Pres*
Colleen Maria Ryan, *Administration*
Marty Moore, *Director*
EMP: 83 EST: 2011
SALES (est): 5.5MM **Privately Held**
WEB: www.sugaredandbronzed.com
SIC: 7299 Tanning salon

(P-16981)
TRE VENEZIE INC
Also Called: Ca'del Sole
4100 Cahuenga Blvd, Toluca Lake
(91602-2831)
PHONE...............................818 985-4669
Rodolfo Costela, *President*
Jean Louis De Mori, *President*
Rodolfo Costello, *Vice Pres*
EMP: 73 **EST:** 1994
SQ FT: 7,000
SALES (est): 4.8MM **Privately Held**
WEB: www.cadelsole.com
SIC: 5812 7299 Italian restaurant;

(P-16982)
U C L A CONFERENCE & CATERING
330 De Neve Dr Ste L16, Los Angeles
(90024-8301)
PHONE...............................310 825-5305
Jason Walley, *Director*
Georgina Babcock, *Office Mgr*
Mary Raffety, *Executive Asst*
Robert J Kitay, *Admin Sec*
Edward Kon, *Project Mgr*
EMP: 80 **EST:** 1969
SALES (est): 3.9MM **Privately Held**
SIC: 5812 7299 Caterers; facility rental & party planning services

(P-16983)
UNITED ONLINE INC (HQ)
30870 Russell Ranch Rd # 250, Westlake
Village (91362-7372)
PHONE...............................818 287-3000
Jeff Goldstein, *CEO*
Edward Zinser, *CFO*
Mark Harrington, *Exec VP*
Mv Krishnamurthty, *Senior VP*
Mark Brown, *Vice Pres*
EMP: 100 **EST:** 2001
SALES (est): 128.6MM **Publicly Held**
WEB: www.unitedonline.net
SIC: 5961 7299 Mail order house; consumer buying service

(P-16984)
US HARDSHIP GROUP LLC
260 Newport Center Dr # 100, Newport
Beach (92660-7522)
PHONE...............................877 777-0174
Kevin Miller, *CEO*
EMP: 50 **EST:** 2012
SALES (est): 436.9K **Privately Held**
WEB: www.ushardship.com
SIC: 7299 Personal financial services

(P-16985)
VIBIANA EVENTS LLC
214 S Main St, Los Angeles (90012-3708)
PHONE...............................213 626-1507
Amy Knoll Fraser, *Mng Member*
Nina Smadja, *Mktg Dir*
Denise Decker, *Director*
EMP: 88 **EST:** 2011
SALES (est): 2.3MM **Privately Held**
WEB: www.vibiana.com
SIC: 7299 Facility rental & party planning services

(P-16986)
WEDGEWOOD HSPITALITY GROUP INC
43385 Business Park Dr, Temecula
(92590-3688)
PHONE...............................951 491-8110
Daniel Bylund, *CFO*
EMP: 50 **EST:** 2013
SQ FT: 5,000
SALES (est): 1.9MM **Privately Held**
WEB: www.wedgewoodweddings.com
SIC: 7299 Banquet hall facilities

(P-16987)
WESTERN COSTUME CO (HQ)
11041 Vanowen St, North Hollywood
(91605-6314)
PHONE...............................818 760-0900
Eddie Marks, *President*
Bobbi Constantine, *COO*
Jeff Marks, *General Mgr*
Kristin Holbak, *Executive Asst*
Xz Lim, *Controller*
EMP: 48 **EST:** 1912

SQ FT: 150,000
SALES (est): 10.2MM **Privately Held**
WEB: www.westerncostume.com
SIC: 7299 2389 Costume rental; costumes

7311 Advertising Agencies

(P-16988)
180LA LLC
12555 W Jefferson Blvd # 200, Los Angeles
(90066-7032)
PHONE...............................310 382-1400
Michael Allen, *Mng Member*
Jillian Nalty, *Business Dir*
Erin Bremmer, *Project Mgr*
Jason Lau, *Buyer*
Brian Jarmon, *Production*
EMP: 110 **EST:** 2006
SQ FT: 13,000
SALES (est): 18.2MM
SALES (corp-wide): 13.1B **Publicly Held**
WEB: www.180la.com
SIC: 7311 Advertising consultant
HQ: Tbwa Worldwide Inc.
488 Madison Ave
New York NY 10022

(P-16989)
72ANDSUNNY MIDCO LLC
12101 Bluff Creek Dr, Playa Vista
(90094-2627)
PHONE...............................310 215-9009
EMP: 3679 **EST:** 2013
SALES (est): 266.4K
SALES (corp-wide): 1.2B **Publicly Held**
SIC: 7311 Advertising agencies
PA: Mdc Stagwell Holdings Inc.
1 World Trade Ctr Fl 65
New York NY 10007
646 429-1800

(P-16990)
ADCONION MEDIA INC (PA)
Also Called: Adconion Media Group
3301 Exposition Blvd Fl 1, Santa Monica
(90404-5082)
PHONE...............................310 382-5521
Kristian Wilson, *President*
Amanda Currie, *Vice Pres*
James Malins, *Vice Pres*
Scott Sullivan, *CTO*
Patrick Morris, *Technology*
EMP: 129 **EST:** 2007
SALES (est): 10.4MM **Privately Held**
WEB: www.amobee.com
SIC: 7311 Advertising consultant

(P-16991)
ADVANTAGE SOLUTIONS INC (HQ)
18100 Von Karman Ave # 1, Irvine
(92612-0169)
PHONE...............................949 797-2900
Tanya Domier, *CEO*
Jill Griffin, *President*
Brian Stevens, *COO*
EMP: 20187 **EST:** 2014
SQ FT: 22,000
SALES (est): 3.1B
SALES (corp-wide): 4.7B **Publicly Held**
WEB: www.advantagesolutions.net
SIC: 7311 Advertising agencies
PA: Karman Topco L.P.
18100 Von Karman Ave # 1000
Irvine CA 92612
949 797-2900

(P-16992)
ALCONE MARKETING GROUP INC (HQ)
Also Called: Jeep Gear
4 Studebaker, Irvine (92618-2012)
PHONE...............................949 595-5322
William Hahn, *CEO*
Sean Conciatore, *Ch Credit Ofcr*
Bill Hahn, *Principal*
▲ **EMP:** 100 **EST:** 1975
SQ FT: 90,000
SALES (est): 29.7MM
SALES (corp-wide): 13.1B **Publicly Held**
WEB: www.alcone.com
SIC: 7311 Advertising consultant

PA: Omnicom Group Inc.
280 Park Ave Fl 31w
New York NY 10017
212 415-3600

(P-16993)
AYZENBERG GROUP INC
49 E Walnut St, Pasadena (91103-3832)
PHONE...............................626 584-4070
Eric Ayzenberg, *President*
Chris Younger, *Partner*
Scott Cookson, *Exec VP*
Bill Buckley, *Vice Pres*
Heather Cohen, *Vice Pres*
▲ **EMP:** 65 **EST:** 1993
SQ FT: 10,000
SALES (est): 48.8MM **Privately Held**
WEB: www.ayzenberg.com
SIC: 7311 7336 Advertising consultant; commercial art & graphic design

(P-16994)
BASIS WORLDWIDE
1557 7th St, Santa Monica (90401-2605)
PHONE...............................424 261-2354
Joe Dipietro, *CEO*
EMP: 50
SALES (est): 1.1MM **Privately Held**
WEB: www.basisworldwide.com
SIC: 7311 Advertising consultant

(P-16995)
BATTERY MARKETING INC
Also Called: Battery Agency
6515 W Sunset Blvd # 200, Hollywood
(90028-7251)
PHONE...............................323 467-7267
Anson Sowby, *CEO*
Philip Khosid, *Ch Credit Ofcr*
Maximilian Kislevitz, *Director*
EMP: 52 **EST:** 2014
SALES (est): 5.8MM **Privately Held**
WEB: www.batteryagency.com
SIC: 7311 Advertising consultant

(P-16996)
BDS MARKETING LLC (DH)
9750 Irvine Blvd Ste 101, Irvine
(92618-1676)
PHONE...............................949 472-6700
Sean Ludick, *President*
Kat Nejdl, *Partner*
Ken Kress, *Managing Prtnr*
Scott McDaniel, *President*
Mike Britton, *Officer*
EMP: 491 **EST:** 1985
SALES (est): 99.9MM
SALES (corp-wide): 255.7MM **Privately Held**
WEB: www.bdsmktg.com
SIC: 7311 8743 Advertising consultant; promotion service
HQ: Bds Solutions Group, Llc
10 Holland
Irvine CA 92618
949 472-6700

(P-16997)
BDS SOLUTIONS GROUP LLC (DH)
10 Holland, Irvine (92618-2504)
PHONE...............................949 472-6700
Mike Sunderland, *CEO*
Bob Salem, *CFO*
EMP: 50 **EST:** 2016
SALES (est): 107MM
SALES (corp-wide): 255.7MM **Privately Held**
WEB: www.bdssolutionsgroup.com
SIC: 7311 Advertising consultant

(P-16998)
CASANOVA PNDRILL PBLICIDAD INC (PA)
275 Mccormick Ave Ste 1a, Costa Mesa
(92626-3325)
PHONE...............................949 474-5001
Daniel Nance, *President*
Laura Marella, *Vice Pres*
Jacqueline Garcia, *Executive*
Julia Hernandez, *Executive*
Patricia Hernandez, *Executive*
EMP: 55 **EST:** 1984
SQ FT: 12,000

SALES (est): 12.5MM **Privately Held**
WEB: www.casanova.com
SIC: 7311 Advertising agencies

(P-16999)
COLLAB INC
155 W Wash Blvd Ste 417, Los Angeles
(90015-3581)
PHONE...............................310 991-0062
Tyler McFadden, *CEO*
Cassie Banaszek, *Partner*
James McFadden, *CEO*
Song Kang, *COO*
Dave Rosner, *Exec VP*
EMP: 60 **EST:** 2011
SALES (est): 50MM **Privately Held**
WEB: www.collab.inc
SIC: 7311 Advertising agencies

(P-17000)
COLOR AD INC
18601 S Santa Fe Ave, Compton
(90221-5901)
PHONE...............................310 632-5500
Daryl Oldencamp, *President*
Tanya Kravtsova, *Project Mgr*
Nina Lopez, *Project Mgr*
Caroline Woodford, *Project Mgr*
Merle Palumbo, *Production*
EMP: 20 **EST:** 1994
SQ FT: 33,000
SALES (est): 4.1MM **Privately Held**
WEB: www.gocolorad.com
SIC: 7311 2752 Advertising agencies; commercial printing, lithographic

(P-17001)
CONSUMER ATTRNEY MKTG GROUP LL (PA)
21051 Warner Center Ln # 25, Woodland
Hills (91367-6551)
PHONE...............................800 200-2264
Stephen Nober, *CEO*
Adam Brown, *Vice Pres*
Christopher Princis, *Vice Pres*
Jenn Robertson, *Vice Pres*
Joseph Wahl, *Business Dir*
EMP: 66 **EST:** 2012
SALES (est): 11.9MM **Privately Held**
WEB: www.camginc.com
SIC: 7311 8742 Advertising consultant; marketing consulting services

(P-17002)
DAILEY & ASSOCIATES
8687 Melrose Ave Ste 100, West Hollywood
(90069-5076)
P.O. Box 931629, Los Angeles (90093-1629)
PHONE...............................323 490-3847
Jean Grabow, *CEO*
Michelle Wong, *President*
William Waldner, *Treasurer*
Michael Perdigao, *Exec VP*
Bradley Johnson, *Vice Pres*
EMP: 82 **EST:** 1964
SALES (est): 7.2MM **Privately Held**
WEB: www.daileyla.com
SIC: 7311 Advertising consultant

(P-17003)
DAVID & GOLIATH LLC
909 N Pacific Coast Hwy # 700, El Segundo (90245-2724)
PHONE...............................310 445-5200
Yumi Prentice, *President*
Wells Davis, *Officer*
Bobby Pearce, *Officer*
Sean Hong, *Vice Pres*
Lilit Chaparyan, *Administration*
EMP: 200
SQ FT: 1,000
SALES (est): 33.5MM **Privately Held**
WEB: www.dng.com
SIC: 7311 Advertising consultant
PA: Innocean Worldwide Inc.
308 Gangnam-Daero, Gangnam-Gu
Seoul 06253

(P-17004)
DAVISELEN ADVERTISING INC (PA)
865 S Figueroa St # 1200, Los Angeles
(90017-2543)
PHONE...............................213 688-7000

Mark Davis, *CEO*
Stan Kaplan, *Partner*
Jim Kelly, *Partner*
Malu Santamaria, *Partner*
Robert Elen, *President*
EMP: 172 **EST:** 1915
SQ FT: 32,000
SALES (est): 35.5MM **Privately Held**
WEB: www.daviselen.com
SIC: 7311 Advertising consultant

(P-17005)
DEDICATED MEDIA INC (PA)
1221 Hermosa Ave Ste 210, Hermosa
Beach (90254-5252)
PHONE..............................310 524-9400
Scott Yamano, *CEO*
Chris Berman, *COO*
Ryan Becker, *Vice Pres*
Brian Malone, *Vice Pres*
EMP: 68 **EST:** 2004
SALES (est): 10MM **Privately Held**
WEB: www.dedicatednetworks.com
SIC: 7311 Advertising consultant

(P-17006)
DEUTSCH LA INC
12901 W Jefferson Blvd, Los Angeles
(90066-7023)
PHONE..............................310 862-3000
Mike Sheldon, *CEO*
Pete Favat, *Officer*
Nancy Alley, *Exec VP*
Dana Commandatore, *Exec VP*
Heide Peper Hays, *Exec VP*
EMP: 100 **EST:** 1995
SALES (est): 26.4MM
SALES (corp-wide): 9B **Publicly Held**
WEB: www.deutsch.com
SIC: 7311 Advertising agencies
PA: The Interpublic Group Of Companies
　Inc
　909 3rd Ave
　New York NY 10022
　212 704-1200

(P-17007)
DG2 WORLDWIDE GROUP LLC
12655 W Jefferson Blvd, Los Angeles
(90066-7008)
PHONE..............................310 809-0899
Michael Lay, *Mng Member*
Mike Laraway, *Officer*
Celeste Fiorenza, *CTO*
EMP: 22 **EST:** 2017
SQ FT: 10,000
SALES (est): 4.3MM **Privately Held**
WEB: www.dg2ww.com
SIC: 7311 3577 8748 Advertising consult-
　ant; data conversion equipment, media-
　to-media: computer; agricultural
　consultant

(P-17008)
DGWB INC
Also Called: Dgwb Advg & Communications
217 N Main St Ste 200, Santa Ana
(92701-4843)
PHONE..............................714 881-2300
Mike Wiseman, *CEO*
Jon Gothold, *Partner*
Mike Weisman, *Partner*
Michael Shudak, *CFO*
Ed Collins, *Chief Mktg Ofcr*
EMP: 70
SALES (est): 21.2MM **Privately Held**
SIC: 7311 Advertising consultant

(P-17009)
DIRECT PARTNERS INC (HQ)
12777 W Jefferson Blvd, Los Angeles
(90066-7048)
PHONE..............................310 482-4200
Tom Harrison, *President*
Tom Parr, *CFO*
Barry Wagner, *Admin Sec*
EMP: 52 **EST:** 1994
SQ FT: 31,000
SALES (est): 22MM
SALES (corp-wide): 13.1B **Publicly Held**
WEB: www.directpartners.com
SIC: 7311 Advertising consultant
PA: Omnicom Group Inc.
　280 Park Ave Fl 31w
　New York NY 10017
　212 415-3600

(P-17010)
EMAK WORLDWIDE INC (PA)
Also Called: Equity Marketing
1727 Berkeley St, Santa Monica
(90404-4104)
PHONE..............................310 633-9311
Teresa L Tormey, *Admin Sec*
Jon Kramer, *President*
Peter Boutros, *CEO*
James L Holbrook Jr, *CEO*
Brian Kristofek, *CEO*
EMP: 90 **EST:** 1986
SQ FT: 42,000
SALES (est): 39MM **Privately Held**
SIC: 7311 8743 8742 Advertising agen-
　cies; promotion service; marketing con-
　sulting services

(P-17011)
EVANS HARDY & YOUNG INC
Also Called: Ehy
829 De La Vina St Ste 100, Santa Barbara
(93101-3285)
PHONE..............................805 963-5841
Jim L Evans, *President*
Sue Andrews, *CFO*
Dennis Hardy, *Exec VP*
Donald De Luccio, *Vice Pres*
Donald Deluccio, *Vice Pres*
EMP: 50 **EST:** 1986
SQ FT: 5,000
SALES (est): 11.6MM **Privately Held**
WEB: www.ehy.com
SIC: 7311 Advertising consultant

(P-17012)
**EVOLVE MEDIA HOLDINGS LLC
(PA)**
Also Called: Springboard
11390 W Olympic Blvd # 450, Los Angeles
(90064-1684)
PHONE..............................310 449-1890
Aaron Broder, *CEO*
Brian Fitzgerald, *President*
Michael Kumin, *CEO*
Geoff Schiller, *Officer*
Walder Amaya, *Senior VP*
EMP: 110 **EST:** 2006
SALES (est): 23MM **Privately Held**
SIC: 7311 8742 Advertising agencies;
　management consulting services; market-
　ing consulting services

(P-17013)
FULLSCREEN INC (DH)
12180 Millennium, Playa Vista
(90094-2947)
PHONE..............................310 202-3333
George Strompolos, *CEO*
Mike Wann, *Officer*
Jasmine Andrews, *Vice Pres*
Khudor Annous, *Vice Pres*
Rhiannon Apple, *Vice Pres*
EMP: 149 **EST:** 2011
SALES (est): 77.1MM
SALES (corp-wide): 171.7B **Publicly
Held**
WEB: www.fullscreen.com
SIC: 7311 6719 Advertising agencies; in-
　vestment holding companies, except
　banks
HQ: Otter Media Holdings, Llc
　12180 Millennium Ste 200
　Playa Vista CA 90094
　310 202-3333

(P-17014)
GIDDYUP GROUP INC
20 N Oak St Ste B, Ventura (93001-2631)
PHONE..............................800 828-2785
Christopher Grant, *CEO*
Jordan Carter, *Partner*
Michelle Paquette, *Business Mgr*
Glenn Anderson, *Opers Staff*
Darren Engle, *Opers Staff*
EMP: 60 **EST:** 2013
SALES (est): 6.9MM **Privately Held**
WEB: www.giddyup.io
SIC: 7311 Advertising agencies

(P-17015)
GL NEMIROW INC
Also Called: Terry Hines & Assoc
2550 N Hollywood Way # 5, Burbank
(91505-1055)
PHONE..............................818 562-9433

Grant W Nemirow, *President*
Ralph Terraciano, *CFO*
Kevin Kerr, *Art Dir*
EMP: 97 **EST:** 1989
SALES (est): 9MM **Privately Held**
SIC: 7311 Advertising agencies

(P-17016)
GLOBAL WIDE MEDIA INC (PA)
Also Called: Casual Iq
11766 Wilshire Blvd # 1400, Los Angeles
(90025-6562)
PHONE..............................805 267-7000
Farshad Fardad, *CEO*
Patrick Finn, *Exec VP*
Bjorn Hougaard, *Vice Pres*
Sara Menashe, *Vice Pres*
Tim Kwan, *Technician*
EMP: 63 **EST:** 2009
SQ FT: 10,000
SALES (est): 10.7MM **Privately Held**
WEB: www.globalwidemedia.com
SIC: 7311 Advertising agencies

(P-17017)
HORIZON MEDIA INC
1888 Century Park E # 700, Los Angeles
(90067-1702)
PHONE..............................310 282-0909
Zach Rosenberg, *Branch Mgr*
Wanda Kato, *Managing Prtnr*
Serena Duff, *Exec VP*
Stan Fields, *Exec VP*
Mia Cosgrove, *Senior VP*
EMP: 300 **Privately Held**
WEB: www.horizonmedia.com
SIC: 7311 Advertising agencies
PA: Horizon Media, Inc.
　75 Varick St Ste 1404
　New York NY 10013

(P-17018)
ICON MEDIA DIRECT INC (PA)
5910 Lemona Ave, Van Nuys (91411-3006)
P.O. Box 55818, Sherman Oaks (91413-
0818)
PHONE..............................818 995-6400
Nancy Lazkani, *CEO*
Seth Klein, *COO*
Jeff Bailes, *Exec VP*
Minnie Dimesa, *Vice Pres*
Stacy Karabuykov, *Vice Pres*
EMP: 81 **EST:** 1999
SQ FT: 16,445
SALES (est): 24.8MM **Privately Held**
WEB: www.iconmediadirect.com
SIC: 7311 Advertising consultant

(P-17019)
IGNITE HEALTH LLC (PA)
7535 Irvine Center Dr # 200, Irvine
(92618-2962)
PHONE..............................949 861-3200
Matt Brown, *President*
Brian Lefkowitz, *Officer*
Alison Ward, *Accounting Mgr*
Richard E Fair,
Fabio Gratton,
EMP: 99 **EST:** 2000
SQ FT: 15,000
SALES (est): 7.7MM **Privately Held**
SIC: 7311 Advertising consultant

(P-17020)
IGNITED LLC (PA)
2150 Park Pl Ste 100, El Segundo
(90245-4714)
PHONE..............................310 773-3100
Eric Johnson, *CEO*
Bill Rosenthal, *COO*
William Rosenthal, *COO*
Whitney Stephenson, *CFO*
Chalita Dasnanjali, *Vice Pres*
EMP: 115 **EST:** 1999
SQ FT: 55,000
SALES (est): 24.1MM **Privately Held**
WEB: www.ignitedusa.com
SIC: 7311 Advertising consultant

(P-17021)
**INNOCEAN WRLDWIDE
AMERICAS LLC (HQ)**
180 5th St Ste 200, Huntington Beach
(92648-7107)
PHONE..............................714 861-5200

Yun Jong Beak, *CFO*
Tim Murphy, *COO*
Nicolette Spencer, *Senior VP*
Eddie Austin, *Vice Pres*
Jeff Bossin, *Vice Pres*
EMP: 439 **EST:** 2002
SALES (est): 78.3MM **Privately Held**
WEB: www.innoceanusa.com
SIC: 7311 Advertising consultant

(P-17022)
**INTER/MEDIA TIME BUYING
CORP (PA)**
Also Called: Inter/Media Advertising
22120 Clarendon St # 300, Woodland Hills
(91367-6315)
PHONE..............................818 995-1455
Robert B Yallen, *President*
James Christensen, *Vice Pres*
Malena Cruz, *Vice Pres*
Grant Rosenquist, *Vice Pres*
Hunington Sachs, *Vice Pres*
EMP: 50 **EST:** 1974
SQ FT: 12,000
SALES (est): 17.2MM **Privately Held**
WEB: www.intermedia-advertising.com
SIC: 7311 Advertising consultant

(P-17023)
**INTERACTIVE MEDIA HOLDINGS
INC (DH)**
Also Called: Viant
2722 Michelson Dr Ste 100, Irvine
(92612-8905)
PHONE..............................949 861-8888
Timothy C Vanderhook, *President*
Chris Vanderhook, *COO*
Roy E Luna, *CFO*
Larry Madden, *CFO*
Bill Schild, *Exec VP*
EMP: 50 **EST:** 2004
SALES (est): 41MM
SALES (corp-wide): 165.2MM **Publicly
Held**
WEB: www.viantinc.com
SIC: 7311 7313 Advertising consultant;
　newspaper advertising representative
HQ: Viant Technology Llc
　2722 Michelson Dr Ste 100
　Irvine CA 92612
　949 861-8888

(P-17024)
**INTERTREND
COMMUNICATIONS INC**
228 E Broadway, Long Beach
(90802-4840)
PHONE..............................562 733-1888
Julia Huang, *CEO*
Susanna Jue, *General Mgr*
Stacy Liu, *Executive Asst*
Flo Kuraoka, *Administration*
Tate Allen, *Info Tech Mgr*
▲ **EMP:** 70 **EST:** 1991
SQ FT: 10,000
SALES (est): 18.3MM **Privately Held**
WEB: www.intertrend.com
SIC: 7311 Advertising consultant

(P-17025)
IW GROUP (PA)
6300 Wilshire Blvd # 215 Los Angeles
(90048-5204)
PHONE..............................213 262-6978
Bill Imada, *CEO*
Sally Choi, *Partner*
Isabelle Chu, *Partner*
Jennifer Kim, *Partner*
Vanessa Ordonez, *Partner*
EMP: 54 **EST:** 1990
SQ FT: 7,500
SALES (est): 14.3MM **Privately Held**
WEB: www.iwgroup.agency
SIC: 7311 8743 Advertising consultant;
　public relations services

(P-17026)
KERN ORGANIZATION INC
Also Called: Kern Direct Marketing
20955 Warner Center Ln, Woodland Hills
(91367-6511)
PHONE..............................818 703-8775
Russell Kern, *President*
Zeke Ibarbia, *CFO*
Steven Orenstein, *CFO*
David Azulay, *Senior VP*

Tom Mackendrick, *Vice Pres*
EMP: 80 **EST:** 1991
SQ FT: 11,350
SALES (est): 42.7MM
SALES (corp-wide): 13.1B **Publicly Held**
WEB: www.kernagency.com
SIC: 7311 Advertising consultant
PA: Omnicom Group Inc.
   280 Park Ave Fl 31w
   New York NY 10017
   212 415-3600

(P-17027)
KITARA MEDIA CORP (HQ)
2010 Main St Ste 900, Irvine (92614-7215)
PHONE...................................201 539-2200
Robert Regular, *CEO*
Joshua Silberstein, *President*
Limor Regular, *COO*
Lisa Vanpatten, *CFO*
EMP: 50 **EST:** 2005
SQ FT: 12,235
SALES (est): 2.1MM
SALES (corp-wide): 88.6MM **Publicly Held**
WEB: www.propelmedia.com
SIC: 7311 7372 Advertising agencies; prepackaged software
PA: Propel Media, Inc.
   18565 Jamboree Rd Ste 200
   Irvine CA 92612
   949 251-0640

(P-17028)
KOVEL/FULLER LLC
9925 Jefferson Blvd, Culver City (90232-3505)
PHONE...................................310 841-4444
John Fuller, *President*
J Reilly, *Vice Pres*
James Reilly, *Vice Pres*
Devin Green, *Project Mgr*
Lee Kovel,
EMP: 55 **EST:** 1989
SQ FT: 40,000
SALES (est): 11.5MM **Privately Held**
WEB: www.kovelfuller.com
SIC: 7311 Advertising consultant

(P-17029)
LIQUID ADVERTISING INC
138 Eucalyptus Dr, El Segundo (90245-3819)
PHONE...................................310 450-2653
William Akerlof, *CEO*
Shuly Millstein, *CFO*
Patrick Runco, *Officer*
Marlo Huang, *Vice Pres*
Alison Hamon, *Executive*
EMP: 91 **EST:** 2000
SQ FT: 2,000
SALES (est): 3.9MM **Privately Held**
WEB: www.liquidarcade.com
SIC: 7311 Advertising consultant

(P-17030)
LOCAL CORPORATION (PA)
Also Called: Local.com
7555 Irvine Center Dr, Irvine (92618-2912)
P.O. Box 50700 (92619-0700)
PHONE...................................949 784-0800
Frederick G Thiel, *Ch of Bd*
Kenneth S Cragun, *CFO*
Scott Reinke, *Officer*
Erick Herring, *Senior VP*
Randy Sesser, *Engineer*
EMP: 92 **EST:** 1999
SQ FT: 34,612 **Publicly Held**
WEB: www.localcorporation.com
SIC: 7311 Advertising agencies

(P-17031)
MAGNITE INC (PA)
6080 Center Dr Ste 400, Los Angeles (90045-1591)
PHONE...................................310 207-0272
Michael G Barrett, *President*
Paul Caine, *Ch of Bd*
Katie Evans, *COO*
David L Day, *CFO*
Shawna Hughes,
EMP: 174 **EST:** 2007
SQ FT: 47,000

SALES (est): 221.6MM **Publicly Held**
WEB: www.rubiconproject.com
SIC: 7311 7313 Advertising agencies; radio, television, publisher representatives

(P-17032)
MANY LLC
17575 Pacific Coast Hwy, Pacific Palisades (90272-4148)
PHONE...................................310 399-1515
Jens Stoelken, *Partner*
EMP: 71 **EST:** 2009
SALES (est): 5.5MM **Privately Held**
WEB: www.themany.com
SIC: 7311 Advertising agencies

(P-17033)
MEDIABRANDS WORLDWIDE INC
Also Called: Initiative Media North America
5700 Wilshire Blvd # 400, Los Angeles (90036-3659)
PHONE...................................323 370-8000
Samantha Gilman, *Vice Pres*
Lindsay Placona, *Vice Pres*
Dawn Dizeo, *Human Res Dir*
Mandy Bubel, *Buyer*
Thomas Novello, *Buyer*
EMP: 300
SALES (corp-wide): 9B **Publicly Held**
WEB: www.matterkind.com
SIC: 7311 Advertising consultant
HQ: Mediabrands Worldwide, Inc.
   100 W 33rd St Fl 3
   New York NY 10001
   646 808-1282

(P-17034)
MEDIAPLEX INC (DH)
30699 Russell Ranch Rd # 2, Westlake Village (91362-7315)
PHONE...................................818 575-4500
EMP: 100
SALES (est): 6.3MM
SALES (corp-wide): 29.8MM **Privately Held**
WEB: www.conversantmedia.com
SIC: 7311 Advertising Agencies, Nsk
HQ: Conversant, Llc
   30699 Russell Ranch Rd # 250
   Westlake Village CA 60606
   818 575-4500

(P-17035)
MH SUB I LLC (PA)
Also Called: Internet Brands
909 N Pacific Coast Hwy # 11, El Segundo (90245-2724)
PHONE...................................310 280-4000
Michelle Barrington, *Executive Asst*
Chris Braun, *Vice Pres*
Phil Oester, *Vice Pres*
John Harrison, *General Mgr*
Willard Hu, *General Mgr*
EMP: 818 **EST:** 2013
SALES (est): 705MM **Privately Held**
WEB: www.internetbrands.com
SIC: 7311 Advertising agencies

(P-17036)
MOB SCENE LLC (PA)
Also Called: Mob Scene Creative Productions
8447 Wilshire Blvd # 100, Beverly Hills (90211-3228)
PHONE...................................323 648-7200
Brian Daly,
Brett Abbey, *CFO*
Toddrick Spalding, *Vice Pres*
Gregg Temkin, *Vice Pres*
Nick Wakefield, *Vice Pres*
EMP: 134 **EST:** 2005 **Privately Held**
WEB: www.mobscene.com
SIC: 7311 7929 3993 7812 Advertising consultant; entertainment service; advertising artwork; television film production

(P-17037)
MUTESIX GROUP INC
Also Called: Mutesix, An Iprospect Company
5800 Bristol Pkwy Ste 500, Culver City (90230-6899)
PHONE...................................310 215-3467
Steve Weiss, *CEO*
Daniel Rutberg, *President*
EMP: 120 **EST:** 2018

SALES (est): 10.6MM **Privately Held**
WEB: www.mutesix.com
SIC: 7311 Advertising agencies
HQ: Dentsu Uk Limited
   10 Triton Street
   London NW1 3
   207 430-6000

(P-17038)
NATIONAL PROMOTIONS & ADVG INC
Also Called: N P A
3434 Overland Ave, Los Angeles (90034-5406)
PHONE...................................310 558-8555
Peter Zackery, *President*
Gary Shafner, *Vice Pres*
Nena Hunt, *Contractor*
EMP: 45 **EST:** 1981
SQ FT: 15,000
SALES (est): 2MM **Privately Held**
WEB: www.alchemymedia.net
SIC: 7311 2752 Advertising agencies; commercial printing, offset

(P-17039)
NEXSTAR DIGITAL LLC
12777 W Jefferson Blvd, Los Angeles (90066-7048)
PHONE...................................310 971-9300
Morgan Harris, *Branch Mgr*
EMP: 100
SALES (corp-wide): 4.5B **Publicly Held**
WEB: www.nexstardigital.com
SIC: 7311 Advertising agencies
HQ: Nexstar Digital, Llc
   545 E John Carpenter Fwy
   Irving TX 75062
   972 373-8800

(P-17040)
OMELET LLC (PA)
3540 Hayden Ave, Culver City (90232-2413)
PHONE...................................213 427-6400
Thas Naseemuddeen, *CEO*
Chelsea Obrien, *Partner*
Don Kurz, *CEO*
Naj Allana, *CFO*
Sarah Ceglarski, *Chief Mktg Ofcr*
EMP: 64 **EST:** 2004
SQ FT: 7,500
SALES (est): 10MM **Privately Held**
WEB: www.omelet.com
SIC: 7311 Advertising consultant

(P-17041)
OPENX TECHNOLOGIES INC (DH)
888 E Walnut St Fl 2, Pasadena (91101-1897)
PHONE...................................855 673-6948
Tim Cadogan, *CEO*
Wendy Myotsang, *Partner*
Hsiao-CHI Weng, *Partner*
John Gentry, *President*
Tom Fuelling, *CFO*
▲ **EMP:** 356 **EST:** 2008
SALES (est): 162.6MM **Privately Held**
WEB: www.openx.com
SIC: 7311 Advertising agencies

(P-17042)
OVERSEENET (PA)
550 S Hope St Ste 200, Los Angeles (90071-2672)
PHONE...................................213 408-0080
Debra Domeyer, *CEO*
Lawrence Ng, *President*
Dwayne Walker, *President*
Elizabeth Murray, *CFO*
Gene Chuang, *CTO*
EMP: 170 **EST:** 2000
SQ FT: 54,000
SALES (est): 18.5MM **Privately Held**
WEB: www.oversee.net
SIC: 7311 Advertising agencies

(P-17043)
PALISADES MEDIA GROUP INC (PA)
Also Called: Palisades Interactive
1601 Clver Feld Bvld Ste, Santa Monica (90404)
PHONE...................................310 564-5400

Roger Schaffner, *Ch of Bd*
Laura Jean Bracken, *President*
Bruce Dennler, *President*
Rhona Dass, *Senior VP*
Lauren Foley, *Senior VP*
EMP: 58 **EST:** 1996
SQ FT: 13,000
SALES (est): 27.1MM **Privately Held**
WEB: www.palisadesmedia.com
SIC: 7311 Advertising consultant

(P-17044)
PETROL ADVERTISING INC
443 N Varney St, Burbank (91502-1733)
PHONE...................................323 644-3720
Alan Hunter, *CEO*
Neel Kar, *Creative Dir*
Andrea Voskanian, *Creative Dir*
Breanna Lam, *Hum Res Coord*
Patrick Cervantes, *Corp Comm Staff*
EMP: 50 **EST:** 2003
SALES (est): 16MM
SALES (corp-wide): 65.8MM **Privately Held**
WEB: www.petrolad.com
SIC: 7311 Advertising consultant
PA: Enad Global 7 Ab (Publ)
   Ringvagen 100
   Stockholm 118 6
   708 887-252

(P-17045)
PHELPS GROUP
12121 W Bluff Dr Ste 200, Playa Vista (90094)
PHONE...................................310 752-4400
Jose Lozano, *CEO*
Robert Berry, *CFO*
Myles Watling, *CFO*
Craig Denton, *Vice Pres*
Judy Lynes, *Vice Pres*
EMP: 50
SQ FT: 17,000
SALES (est): 21MM **Privately Held**
WEB: www.thephelpsgroup.com
SIC: 7311 Advertising consultant

(P-17046)
POSTAER RUBIN AND ASSOCIATES (PA)
Also Called: R P Direct
2525 Colorado Ave Ste 100, Santa Monica (90404-5576)
PHONE...................................310 394-4000
Willam C Hagelstein, *CEO*
Gerrold R Rubin, *Ch of Bd*
Vincent Mancuso, *CFO*
Larry Postaer, *Exec VP*
Gayle Gray, *Vice Pres*
EMP: 402 **EST:** 1986
SQ FT: 130,000
SALES (est): 91.7MM **Privately Held**
SIC: 7311 Advertising consultant

(P-17047)
QUIGLY-SIMPSON HEPPELWHITE INC
Also Called: Quigley-Simpson La
11601 Wilshire Blvd Fl 7, Los Angeles (90025-0509)
PHONE...................................310 996-5800
Kathryn Browne, *CFO*
Gerald Bagg, *Ch of Bd*
Renee Hill Young, *Ch of Bd*
Duryea Ruffins, *President*
Alissa Stakgold, *President*
EMP: 150 **EST:** 2002
SQ FT: 10,500
SALES (est): 41.1MM **Privately Held**
WEB: www.quigleysimpson.com
SIC: 7311 7319 Advertising agencies; media buying service

(P-17048)
RAPP WORLDWIDE CALIFORNIA INC (PA)
12777 W Jefferson Blvd, Los Angeles (90066-7048)
PHONE...................................310 563-7200
Marco Scognamiglio, *CEO*
Michael Tinaza, *Senior VP*
Milton Weaver, *Vice Pres*
Natalie Degrvel, *Office Mgr*
Sebastian Werner, *Info Tech Dir*
EMP: 109 **EST:** 2004

SALES (est): 11.4MM **Privately Held**
WEB: www.rapp.com
SIC: 7311 Advertising consultant

(P-17049)
RAPP WORLDWIDE INC
12777 W Jefferson Blvd, Los Angeles
(90066-7048)
PHONE.....................................310 563-7200
Collins Rapp, *Branch Mgr*
EMP: 55
SALES (corp-wide): 13.1B **Publicly Held**
WEB: www.rappusa.com
SIC: 7311 Advertising consultant
HQ: Rapp Worldwide Inc.
    437 Madison Ave
    New York NY 10022

(P-17050)
RATESPECIAL INTERACTIVE LLC (PA)
46 Smith Aly Ste 230, Pasadena
(91103-3663)
PHONE.....................................626 376-4702
David Tam, *CEO*
Tom McErlane, *President*
Joshua Armstrong, *CFO*
Bert Seow, *CTO*
Joe Reymann, *Web Dvlpr*
EMP: 52 EST: 2011
SALES (est): 686.4K **Privately Held**
WEB: www.ratespecial.com
SIC: 7311 Advertising consultant

(P-17051)
REACHLOCAL INC (DH)
21700 Oxnard St Ste 1600, Woodland Hills
(91367-7586)
PHONE.....................................818 274-0260
Sharon T Rowlands, *CEO*
Steven Dollar, *Partner*
Anthony Gallace, *Partner*
Jonathan Greer, *Partner*
Katie McCullin, *Partner*
EMP: 876 EST: 2004
SQ FT: 38,592
SALES (est): 276.7MM
SALES (corp-wide): 3.4B **Publicly Held**
WEB: www.reachlocal.com
SIC: 7311 7375 Advertising consultant;
    on-line data base information retrieval
HQ: Gannett Media Corp.
    7950 Jones Branch Dr
    Mc Lean VA 22102
    703 854-6000

(P-17052)
RED INTERACTIVE AGENCY LLC (PA)
3420 Ocean Park Blvd # 3080, Santa Monica (90405-3325)
PHONE.....................................310 399-4242
Brian Lovell, *CEO*
Donny Makower, *President*
Derek Van Den Bosch, *COO*
Derek Bosch, *COO*
Andrew Feldman, *Vice Pres*
EMP: 95 EST: 2010
SALES (est): 13.3MM **Privately Held**
WEB: www.wearered.com
SIC: 7311 Advertising consultant

(P-17053)
S CALLAN COMPANY INC
Also Called: Callan Advertising Company
1126 N Hollywood Way, Burbank
(91505-2527)
PHONE.....................................818 841-3284
Sheri E Calinoff, *President*
Mike Whamond, *Vice Pres*
Erika Forkel, *Executive Asst*
Al Chang, *Marketing Staff*
Josh Allen, *Director*
EMP: 62 EST: 1993
SALES (est): 20.3MM **Privately Held**
WEB: www.scallan.com
SIC: 7311 Advertising consultant

(P-17054)
SAATCHI & SAATCHI N AMER LLC
Team One
13031 W Jefferson Blvd, Los Angeles
(90094-7000)
PHONE.....................................310 437-2500
Amanda Taft, *President*
John McGonigle, *Vice Pres*
Katie Costopoulos, *Executive*
Ashley McAlpin, *Associate Dir*
Craig Crawford, *Creative Dir*
EMP: 250
SALES (corp-wide): 29.1MM **Privately Held**
WEB: www.saatchi.com
SIC: 7311 Advertising agencies
HQ: Saatchi & Saatchi North America, Llc.
    375 Hudson St
    New York NY 10014
    212 463-2000

(P-17055)
SCDRG INC
473 S Carnegie Dr, San Bernardino
(92408-4207)
PHONE.....................................818 874-0830
Richard Seiglery, *President*
Richard Seigler, *President*
Mark Seigler, *Creative Dir*
EMP: 66 EST: 1997
SQ FT: 10,000
SALES (est): 7MM **Privately Held**
SIC: 7311 Advertising consultant

(P-17056)
SPECIFIC MEDIA LLC (DH)
2722 Michelson Dr Ste 100, Irvine
(92612-8905)
PHONE.....................................949 861-8888
Timothy C Vanderhook, *President*
Christopher Vanderhook, *COO*
Jason Knapp, *Exec VP*
Russell Vanderhook, *Senior VP*
Josh Hare, *Vice Pres*
EMP: 81 EST: 2010
SALES (est): 28.7MM
SALES (corp-wide): 165.2MM **Publicly Held**
WEB: www.specificmedia.com
SIC: 7311 7313 5999 Advertising agencies; newspaper advertising representative; banners
HQ: Interactive Media Holdings, Inc.
    2722 Michelson Dr Ste 100
    Irvine CA 92612
    949 861-8888

(P-17057)
STARCOM WORLDWIDE INC
5200 Lankershim Blvd # 60, North Hollywood (91601-3155)
PHONE.....................................818 753-7200
Kim Colweck, *Exec VP*
Matthew Jimenez, *Vice Pres*
David Breh, *Associate Dir*
Sarah Sinitean, *Associate Dir*
Melva Kupiainen, *Executive Asst*
EMP: 129
SALES (corp-wide): 29.1MM **Privately Held**
WEB: www.starcomww.com
SIC: 7311 Advertising agencies
HQ: Starcom Worldwide, Inc.
    35 W Wacker Dr Fl 11
    Chicago IL 60601
    312 220-3535

(P-17058)
STEELHOUSE INC
3644 Eastham Dr, Culver City
(90232-2411)
P.O. Box 5286 (90231-5286)
PHONE.....................................310 773-3331
Mark Douglas, *CEO*
Rory Mitchell, *Ch Credit Ofcr*
Vin Bhardwaj, *Vice Pres*
Lindsey Breeden, *Vice Pres*
Keith Dale, *Vice Pres*
EMP: 160 EST: 2009
SALES (est): 16MM **Privately Held**
WEB: www.mountain.com
SIC: 7311 Advertising agencies

(P-17059)
SUISSA MILLER ADVERTISING LLC
8687 Melrose Ave, West Hollywood
(90069-5701)
PHONE.....................................310 392-9666
David Suissa,
Bruce Miller,
EMP: 100 EST: 1985
SQ FT: 40,000
SALES (est): 2.4MM **Privately Held**
SIC: 7311 Advertising agencies

(P-17060)
TBWA WORLDWIDE INC
Also Called: Media Arts Lab
1017 16th St Apt C, Santa Monica
(90403-4330)
PHONE.....................................310 305-4400
Larry Kelly, *Owner*
Kristen McCoy, *Executive Asst*
Greg Lizanich, *Opers Staff*
Lisa Le, *Producer*
Richard Oldfield, *Corp Comm Staff*
EMP: 133
SALES (corp-wide): 13.1B **Publicly Held**
SIC: 7311 Advertising consultant
HQ: Tbwa Worldwide Inc.
    488 Madison Ave
    New York NY 10022

(P-17061)
TEAM GARAGE LLC
Also Called: Garage Team Mazda
3200 Bristol St Ste 300, Costa Mesa
(92626-1838)
PHONE.....................................714 913-9900
Michael Buttlar, *CEO*
Brad Audet, *Exec VP*
Brian Rogers, *Exec VP*
Benjamin Chung, *Senior VP*
Scott Magie, *Senior VP*
EMP: 70 EST: 2012
SALES (est): 10.2MM **Privately Held**
WEB: www.garageteammazda.com
SIC: 7311 Advertising agencies

(P-17062)
TRAILER PARK INC
6922 Hollywood Blvd Fl 12, Los Angeles
(90028-6132)
PHONE.....................................310 845-8400
Joel Johnston, *President*
EMP: 60 **Privately Held**
WEB: www.trailerpark.com
SIC: 7311 7812 Advertising agencies; motion picture & video production
PA: Trailer Park Inc.
    6922 Hollywood Blvd # 1200
    Los Angeles CA 90028

(P-17063)
TRAILER PARK INC
9000 W Sunset Blvd # 915, Los Angeles
(90069-5801)
PHONE.....................................310 845-3000
Tim Nett, *President*
Jake Katz, *Senior VP*
Tyler Herkenhoff, *Production*
Emily Paul, *Producer*
Matt Brubaker, *Senior Mgr*
EMP: 60 **Privately Held**
WEB: www.trailerpark.com
SIC: 7311 7822 Advertising agencies; motion picture distribution
PA: Trailer Park Inc.
    6922 Hollywood Blvd # 1200
    Los Angeles CA 90028

(P-17064)
TRAILER PARK INC (PA)
6922 Hollywood Blvd # 1200, Los Angeles
(90028-6132)
P.O. Box 2950 (90078-2950)
PHONE.....................................310 845-3000
Tim Nett, *President*
James Hale, *Shareholder*
Ali Aleisawi, *COO*
Kevin Van Belois, *Exec VP*
Jake Katz, *Senior VP*
EMP: 100
SQ FT: 8,000

SALES (est): 32.7MM **Privately Held**
WEB: www.trailerpark.com
SIC: 7311 Advertising agencies

(P-17065)
UNFOLD AGENCY INC (PA)
11801 Teale St, Culver City (90230-7701)
PHONE.....................................323 963-3108
Brick Rucker, *Principal*
Daniel Weisinger, *Co-Owner*
Colin Stephens, *Executive Asst*
Paul Caparotta, *CIO*
Derek Javier, *CIO*
EMP: 64 EST: 2014
SALES (est): 2.6MM **Privately Held**
WEB: www.unfoldagency.com
SIC: 7311 Advertising agencies

(P-17066)
UNITED ONLINE ADVG NETWRK INC
21301 Burbank Blvd, Woodland Hills
(91367-6679)
PHONE.....................................818 287-3000
Mark Goldston, *President*
Kenneth Coleman, *Director*
EMP: 56 EST: 2005
SALES (est): 4.9MM **Publicly Held**
WEB: www.brileyfin.com
SIC: 7311 Advertising agencies
PA: B. Riley Financial, Inc.
    11100 Santa Monica Blvd
    Los Angeles CA 90025

(P-17067)
US INTERNATIONAL MEDIA LLC (PA)
Also Called: US Outdoor
3415 S Sepulveda Blvd # 8, Los Angeles
(90034-6060)
PHONE.....................................310 482-6700
Dennis Holt, *CEO*
Sixto Castillo, *Exec VP*
Sherry Catchpole, *Exec VP*
DOT Dilorenzo, *Exec VP*
Mike Haggerty, *Exec VP*
EMP: 117 EST: 2003
SQ FT: 5,000
SALES (est): 20.7MM **Privately Held**
WEB: www.theusim.com
SIC: 7311 Advertising consultant

(P-17068)
VIANT TECHNOLOGY LLC (HQ)
Also Called: Viant US
2722 Michelson Dr Ste 100, Irvine
(92612-8905)
PHONE.....................................949 861-8888
Tim Vanderhook, *Ch of Ed*
Chris Vanderhook, *COO*
Larry Madden, *CFO*
Brian Bell, *Vice Pres*
Adam Paz, *Vice Pres*
EMP: 50 EST: 1999
SQ FT: 47,000
SALES (est): 52.7MM
SALES (corp-wide): 165.2MM **Publicly Held**
WEB: www.viantinc.com
SIC: 7311 Advertising consultant
PA: Viant Technology Inc.
    2722 Michelson Dr Ste 100
    Irvine CA 92612
    949 861-8888

(P-17069)
WALKER ADVERTISING LLC
20101 Hamilton Ave # 300, Torrance
(90502-1351)
PHONE.....................................310 519-4050
Mary Ann Walker, *CEO*
John Pan, *Vice Pres*
Andy Rogers, *Vice Pres*
Miriam Serrano, *Vice Pres*
Josephine Nguyen, *Software Dev*
EMP: 50 EST: 1979
SALES (est): 14.1MM **Privately Held**
WEB: www.walkeradvertising.com
SIC: 7311 Advertising consultant

(P-17070)
WONDERFUL AGENCY
11444 W Olympic Blvd # 210, Los Angeles
(90064-1559)
PHONE.....................................310 966-8600

748   2022 Southern California Business
Directory and Buyers Guide   ▲ = Import ▼=Export
◆ =Import/Export

Stewart A Resnick, *CEO*
Margaret Keene, *Officer*
EMP: 3601 **EST:** 2016
SALES (est): 9.9MM
SALES (corp-wide): 2B **Privately Held**
WEB: www.wonderful.com
SIC: 7311 Advertising consultant
PA: The Wonderful Company Llc
11444 W Olympic Blvd # 210
Los Angeles CA 90064
310 966-5700

(P-17071)
WONGDOODY INC
Also Called: Digital Sherpas
8500 Steller Dr Ste 5, Culver City
(90232-2455)
PHONE...................310 280-7800
Brian Thompson, *Office Mgr*
Josh Mooney, *Senior VP*
Christy Ferguson, *Vice Pres*
Matt Burgess, *Creative Dir*
Z Gevorkian, *Creative Dir*
EMP: 50 **Privately Held**
WEB: www.wongdoody.com
SIC: 7311 4813 Advertising consultant;
HQ: Wongdoody, Inc.
1011 Western Ave Ste 900
Seattle WA 98104

(P-17072)
YOUNG & RUBICAM LLC
Also Called: Y&R-Wcj Spectrum
7535 Irvine Center Dr, Irvine (92618-2962)
PHONE...................949 754-2000
David Murphy, *President*
EMP: 300
SALES (corp-wide): 15.9B **Privately Held**
WEB: www.vmlyr.com
SIC: 7311 Advertising agencies
HQ: Young & Rubicam Llc
3 Columbus Cir Frnt 3 # 3
New York NY 10019
212 210-3000

(P-17073)
YOUNG & RUBICAM LLC
Also Called: Landor Associates
7535 Irvine Center Dr, Irvine (92618-2962)
PHONE...................949 754-2100
Rick Eisermas, *Manager*
EMP: 250
SALES (corp-wide): 15.9B **Privately Held**
WEB: www.vmlyr.com
SIC: 7311 Advertising agencies
HQ: Young & Rubicam Llc
3 Columbus Cir Frnt 3 # 3
New York NY 10019
212 210-3000

(P-17074)
YOUNG & RUBICAM LLC
Wunderman Cato Jhnsn-Los Angle
4751 Wilshire Blvd # 201, Los Angeles
(90010-3827)
PHONE...................213 930-5000
Andy Bielanski, *Managing Dir*
Sydney Quirk, *President*
Paul Katzka, *Vice Pres*
Jim Smith, *Vice Pres*
Yoki Nakajima, *VP Sales*
EMP: 135
SALES (corp-wide): 15.9B **Privately Held**
WEB: www.vmlyr.com
SIC: 7311 Advertising consultant
HQ: Young & Rubicam Llc
3 Columbus Cir Frnt 3 # 3
New York NY 10019
212 210-3000

7312 Outdoor Advertising Svcs

(P-17075)
BRIMAD ENTERPRISES INC
Also Called: Creative Outdoor Advertising
2900 Adams St Ste B16, Riverside
(92504-4396)
PHONE...................951 354-8187
Eric Glaub, *President*
David Burr, *District Mgr*
Chris Grigg, *District Mgr*
Robert Polan, *District Mgr*

Caryn Gediman, *Office Mgr*
EMP: 27 **EST:** 1984
SQ FT: 10,000
SALES (est): 4.5MM **Privately Held**
WEB: www.coasigns.com
SIC: 7312 3993 Billboard advertising;
signs & advertising specialties

(P-17076)
OUTFRONT MEDIA LLC
1731 Workman St, Los Angeles
(90031-3334)
PHONE...................323 222-7171
Dennis Kuhl, *Manager*
Lyly Stefanowicz, *Executive*
Sally Chen, *Production*
Lorena Martinez, *Sales Staff*
Shery Baumann, *Manager*
EMP: 27
SALES (corp-wide): 1.2B **Publicly Held**
WEB: www.outfrontmedia.com
SIC: 7312 3993 Outdoor advertising serv-
ices; signs & advertising specialties
HQ: Outfront Media Llc
405 Lexington Ave Fl 14
New York NY 10174
212 297-6400

(P-17077)
SILTANEN INC
Also Called: Siltanen & Partners Advg
353 Coral Cir, El Segundo (90245-4620)
PHONE...................310 321-5200
Rob Siltanen, *CEO*
Joe Hemp, *Partner*
Timothy Murphy, *President*
Alec Hodgman, *Executive*
Ashley Munoz, *Executive*
EMP: 62 **EST:** 1999
SQ FT: 12,000
SALES (est): 4.4MM **Privately Held**
WEB: www.siltanen.com
SIC: 7312 Billboard advertising

7313 Radio, TV & Publishers Adv Reps

(P-17078)
ATTN INC
729 Seward St, Los Angeles (90038-3503)
PHONE...................323 413-2878
Jarrett Moreno, *CEO*
Matthew Segel, *President*
Mike Hadgis, *Officer*
Jesse Hicks, *Creative Dir*
Devon Romo, *CIO*
EMP: 200 **EST:** 2014
SQ FT: 100,000
SALES (est): 11.8MM **Privately Held**
WEB: www.attn.com
SIC: 7313 Electronic media advertising
representatives

(P-17079)
BEACHBODY LLC (HQ)
3301 Exposition Blvd Fl 3, Santa Monica
(90404-5082)
P.O. Box 1227, Pico Rivera (90660-1227)
PHONE...................310 883-9000
Carl Daikeler, *CEO*
Sue Collyns, *CFO*
Jon Congdon, *Chief Mktg Ofcr*
Brad Ramberg, *Exec VP*
Joe Sagona, *Vice Pres*
▲ **EMP:** 500 **EST:** 1998
SALES (est): 663.5MM **Publicly Held**
WEB: www.beachbody.com
SIC: 7313 7999 Electronic media advertis-
ing representatives; physical fitness in-
struction
PA: The Beachbody Company Inc
3301 Exposition Blvd
Santa Monica CA 90404
310 883-9000

(P-17080)
BREITBART NEWS NETWORK LLC
Also Called: Bnn
149 S Barrington Ste 735, Los Angeles
(90049)
PHONE...................424 371-0585
Laurence Solov, *Mng Member*
Ana Barrera, *CFO*

EMP: 60 **EST:** 2011
SALES (est): 3.6MM **Privately Held**
WEB: www.breitbart.com
SIC: 7313 Electronic media advertising
representatives

(P-17081)
CANVAS WORLDWIDE LLC
12015 Bluff Creek Dr, Los Angeles
(90094-2930)
PHONE...................424 303-4300
Paul Woolmington, *CEO*
Gregory Johns, *Officer*
Madhavi Tadikonda, *Exec VP*
Jen Bochner, *Vice Pres*
Christi Cicerelli, *Vice Pres*
EMP: 250 **EST:** 2015
SALES (est): 62.4MM **Privately Held**
WEB: www.canvasworldwide.com
SIC: 7313 Electronic media advertising
representatives
PA: Innocean Worldwide Inc.
308 Gangnam-Daero, Gangnam-Gu
Seoul 06253

(P-17082)
CITYSEARCH (HQ)
8833 W Sunset Blvd # 101, West Holly-
wood (90069-2110)
PHONE...................310 360-4555
Jay Herratti, *CEO*
Gerald Douglas, *Senior Mgr*
Kate Wu, *Manager*
EMP: 73 **EST:** 2002
SALES (est): 13.3MM
SALES (corp-wide): 2.3B **Publicly Held**
WEB: www.citysearch.com
SIC: 7313 Electronic media advertising
representatives
PA: Match Group, Inc.
8750 N Cntl Expy Ste 1400
Dallas TX 75231
214 576-9352

(P-17083)
DANIEL J EDELMAN INC
Also Called: Edelman Public Relations
5900 Wilshire Blvd # 2400, Los Angeles
(90036-5022)
PHONE...................323 857-9100
EMP: 53
SALES (corp-wide): 790.4MM **Privately
Held**
SIC: 7313 8743 Advertising Representa-
tive Public Relations Services
HQ: Daniel J. Edelman, Inc.
200 E Randolph St Fl 63
Chicago IL 60601
312 240-3000

(P-17084)
EDMUNDSCOM INC (HQ)
2401 Colorado Ave Ste P1, Santa Monica
(90404-3175)
PHONE...................310 309-6300
Peter Steinlauf, *Ch of Bd*
Seth Berkowitz, *President*
AVI Steinlauf, *CEO*
Allen Ollis, *CFO*
Elizabeth Steinlauf, *Admin Sec*
▲ **EMP:** 550 **EST:** 1966
SALES (est): 212MM **Privately Held**
WEB: www.edmunds.com
SIC: 7313 Electronic media advertising
representatives

(P-17085)
GHOST MANAGEMENT GROUP LLC
41 Discovery, Irvine (92618-3150)
PHONE...................949 870-1400
Justin Hartfield, *CEO*
Doug Francis, *President*
Albert Lopez, *CFO*
Hendrik Davel, *Controller*
Chris Beals, *General Counsel*
EMP: 175 **EST:** 2012
SQ FT: 44,820
SALES (est): 40MM **Privately Held**
SIC: 7313 7371 Electronic media advertis-
ing representatives; computer software
development & applications; custom com-
puter programming services

(P-17086)
GRABIT INTERACTIVE INC
Also Called: Kerv Interactive
14724 Ventura Blvd, Sherman Oaks
(91403-3501)
PHONE...................844 472-2488
Gary Mittman, *CEO*
Grant Gorton, *Vice Pres*
Jason Gibson, *VP Sls/Mktg*
EMP: 34 **EST:** 2016
SALES (est): 1.1MM **Privately Held**
WEB: www.grabit.media
SIC: 7313 7372 Printed media advertising
representatives; application computer
software

(P-17087)
KARGO GLOBAL INC
1437 4th St Ste 200, Santa Monica
(90401-2377)
PHONE...................212 979-9000
Natalie Nelson, *Branch Mgr*
Emily Demichele, *Manager*
EMP: 139 **Privately Held**
WEB: www.kargo.com
SIC: 7313 7372 7374 Electronic media
advertising representatives; application
computer software; computer graphics
service
PA: Kargo Global, Inc.
826 Broadway Fl 5
New York NY 10003

(P-17088)
LIVEUNIVERSE INC
9255 W Sunset Blvd # 1010, West Holly-
wood (90069-3309)
PHONE...................310 492-2200
Bradley D Greenspan, *CEO*
Toan Nguyen, *CTO*
EMP: 60 **EST:** 2005
SQ FT: 10,137
SALES (est): 2.6MM **Privately Held**
WEB: www.liveuniverse.com
SIC: 7313 Electronic media advertising
representatives

(P-17089)
SABIO MOBILE INC
16350 Ventura Blvd D82, Encino
(91436-5300)
PHONE...................818 805-3678
Aziz Rahim, *CEO*
Joe Camacho, *Chief Mktg Ofcr*
Helen Lum, *Vice Pres*
Ashley Perkins, *Vice Pres*
Missaka Wijekoon, *CTO*
EMP: 50 **EST:** 2014
SQ FT: 1,500
SALES (est): 5.9MM **Privately Held**
WEB: www.sabio.inc
SIC: 7313 Electronic media advertising
representatives

(P-17090)
STUDIO 71 LP
Also Called: Collective Digital Studio, LLC
8383 Wilshire Blvd # 1050, Beverly Hills
(90211-2415)
PHONE...................323 370-1500
Reza Isad, *CEO*
Matthew Brannen, *Partner*
Matt Crowley, *Officer*
Joseph Hodorowicz, *Vice Pres*
Dave Devries, *Executive*
EMP: 150 **EST:** 2011
SQ FT: 15,000
SALES (est): 33.9MM
SALES (corp-wide): 4.7B **Privately Held**
WEB: www.studio71.com
SIC: 7313 Electronic media advertising
representatives
PA: Prosiebensat.1 Media Se
Medienallee 7
Unterfohring BY 85774
899 507-10

(P-17091)
TRADE NEWS INTERNATIONAL INC
4444 W Riverside Dr # 202, Burbank
(91505-4073)
PHONE...................818 848-6397
Mark Deitch, *President*
Bruce Loria, *Advt Staff*

P R O D U C T S & S V C S

Natalie Tolila, *Director*
EMP: 33 **EST:** 1981
SALES (est): 2.3MM **Privately Held**
WEB: www.911media.com
SIC: 7313 2721 8742 Electronic media advertising representatives; printed media advertising representatives; periodicals: publishing & printing; marketing consulting services

(P-17092)
WALDBERG INC
Also Called: Refinery, The
15301 Ventura Blvd # 300, Sherman Oaks (91403-5813)
PHONE..................818 843-0004
Adam Waldman, *CEO*
Brad Hochberg, *President*
Ed Bonderant, *Info Tech Dir*
Seth Ward, *Graphic Designe*
Noelle Beltran, *Accountant*
EMP: 100 **EST:** 2006
SALES (est): 9.1MM **Privately Held**
WEB: www.therefinerycreative.com
SIC: 7313 Electronic media advertising representatives; printed media advertising representatives

---

7319 Advertising, NEC

(P-17093)
ADVERTISING CONSULTANTS INC (PA)
Also Called: American Crclation Innovations
330 Golden Shore Ste 410, Long Beach (90802-4271)
PHONE..................310 233-2750
Keith Somers, *President*
John G Walsh, *COO*
Kent Brown, *CFO*
Robert Somers, *Chairman*
Sheri Cassidy, *Finance*
EMP: 50 **EST:** 1966
SQ FT: 60,000
SALES (est): 13.6MM **Privately Held**
SIC: 7319 Distribution of advertising material or sample services

(P-17094)
CIE DIGITAL LABS LLC
Also Called: Choice Internet
19600 Fairchild Ste 350, Irvine (92612-2519)
PHONE..................949 381-6200
Anderee Berengian, *CEO*
Alvin Fong, *Officer*
Trent Johnson, *Senior VP*
Pranav Khandelwal, *Software Dev*
Glen Kim, *Finance*
EMP: 55 **EST:** 1999
SALES (est): 11.8MM **Privately Held**
WEB: www.ciedigital.com
SIC: 7319 Display advertising service

(P-17095)
DIVERSFIED MRCURY CMMNCTONS LL
Also Called: Mercury Media
11620 Wilshire Blvd, Los Angeles (90025-1706)
P.O. Box 57499, Sherman Oaks (91413-2499)
PHONE..................508 598-3569
Janet Campbell, *Branch Mgr*
Ruth Nightengale, *Senior VP*
Joe Kochberg, *Vice Pres*
David Reinbach, *VP Bus Dvlpt*
Angela Pupo, *Associate Dir*
EMP: 64
SALES (corp-wide): 24.3MM **Privately Held**
SIC: 7319 7313 Media buying service; television & radio time sales
HQ: Diversified Mercury Communications, Llc
3 Speen St Ste 140
Framingham MA 01701

(P-17096)
DRISSI ADVERTISING INC (PA)
6721 Romaine St, Los Angeles (90038-2425)
PHONE..................323 466-4700

Tomy Drissi, *President*
David Crvelin, *Exec VP*
Zuleika Carvajal, *Executive Asst*
Ashley Zerah, *Executive Asst*
Julian Gurrola, *Engineer*
EMP: 62 **EST:** 2011
SALES (est): 5.5MM **Privately Held**
WEB: www.drissi.com
SIC: 7319 7311 Display advertising service; advertising agencies

(P-17097)
FASTCLICK INC
Also Called: Fastclick.com
530 E Montecito St, Santa Barbara (93103-3245)
PHONE..................805 689-9839
Kurt A Johnson, *President*
Fred Krupica, *CFO*
James Aviani, *CTO*
EMP: 342 **EST:** 2000
SQ FT: 14,900
SALES (est): 4.5MM
SALES (corp-wide): 29.1MM **Privately Held**
WEB: www.epsilon.com
SIC: 7319 Circular & handbill distribution
HQ: Conversant, Llc
101 N Wacker Dr
Chicago IL 60606

(P-17098)
GILS DISTRIBUTING SERVICE
Also Called: Great Western Distributing Svc
718 E 8th St, Los Angeles (90021-1802)
PHONE..................213 627-0539
Feleciano Gil, *President*
Gloria Gil, *Treasurer*
Fidel Gil, *Vice Pres*
EMP: 112 **EST:** 1967
SQ FT: 5,000
SALES (est): 2.6MM **Privately Held**
SIC: 7319 4215 Circular & handbill distribution; courier services, except by air

(P-17099)
IMAGE OPTIONS
80 Icon, Foothill Ranch (92610-3000)
PHONE..................949 586-7665
Tim Bennett, *CEO*
Brian Hite, *President*
Dave Bales, *COO*
Dave Brewer, *Vice Pres*
David Brewer, *Vice Pres*
EMP: 101 **EST:** 1999
SQ FT: 22,000
SALES (est): 23.1MM **Privately Held**
WEB: www.imageoptions.net
SIC: 7319 7336 Display advertising service; commercial art & graphic design; art design services

(P-17100)
KSL MEDIA INC
15910 Ventura Blvd # 900, Encino (91436-2802)
PHONE..................212 468-3395
Kalman Liebowitz, *Ch of Bd*
Hank Cohen, *President*
Russell Meisels, *CFO*
EMP: 130 **EST:** 1981
SQ FT: 13,000
SALES (est): 13.9MM **Privately Held**
SIC: 7319 Media buying service

(P-17101)
SMALL BUSINESS ADVERTISING INC
5304 Derry Ave Ste L, Agoura Hills (91301-6047)
PHONE..................818 262-8923
Stephen Tackett, *President*
EMP: 50 **EST:** 2017
SALES (est): 3.7MM **Privately Held**
SIC: 7319 8742 Advertising; marketing consulting services

(P-17102)
WEST COAST COUPON INC
9400 Oso Ave, Chatsworth (91311-6020)
PHONE..................818 341-2400
Mark Fischer, *President*
Doug Rewers, *Vice Pres*
EMP: 26 **EST:** 2004
SQ FT: 30,000

SALES (est): 1MM **Privately Held**
WEB: www.westcoastcoupon.com
SIC: 7319 2731 5961 Coupon distribution; books: publishing & printing; computer software, mail order

(P-17103)
ZAMBEZI LLC
10441 Jefferson Blvd, Culver City (90232-3512)
PHONE..................310 450-6800
Jean Freeman, *Mng Member*
Jill Burgeson, *Officer*
Channing Rossi, *IT/INT Sup*
Ling Ly, *Production*
James Freeman,
EMP: 65 **EST:** 2015
SALES (est): 7.7MM **Privately Held**
WEB: www.zmbz.com
SIC: 7319 7389 Advertising; advertising, promotional & trade show services

---

7322 Adjustment & Collection Svcs

(P-17104)
ATTORNEY RECOVERY SYSTEMS INC (PA)
18757 Burbank Blvd # 225, Tarzana (91356-3346)
PHONE..................818 774-1420
Gene Bloom, *President*
Jack Weitz, *Sales Executive*
EMP: 70 **EST:** 1989
SALES (est): 5.7MM **Privately Held**
WEB: www.legalcollection.com
SIC: 7322 8111 Collection agency, except real estate; legal services

(P-17105)
CAINE & WEINER COMPANY INC (PA)
5805 Sepulvda Blvd # 400, Van Nuys (91411-2546)
P.O. Box 55848, Sherman Oaks (91413-0848)
PHONE..................818 226-6000
Greg A Cohen, *President*
Lisa Newberg, *President*
Roy Jones, *COO*
Joe Batie, *Officer*
Brad Schaffer, *Senior VP*
EMP: 90 **EST:** 1930
SQ FT: 14,400
SALES (est): 20.2MM **Privately Held**
WEB: www.caine-weiner.com
SIC: 7322 Collection agency, except real estate

(P-17106)
CMRE FINANCIAL SERVICES INC
3075 E Imperial Hwy # 200, Brea (92821-6753)
PHONE..................714 528-3200
Jeffrey Nieman, *President*
EMP: 450 **EST:** 2000
SQ FT: 35,000
SALES (est): 24.3MM **Privately Held**
WEB: www.cmrefsi.com
SIC: 7322 Collection agency, except real estate

(P-17107)
COLLECTION TECHNOLOGY INC
Also Called: C T I
10801 6th St Ste 200, Rancho Cucamonga (91730-5904)
P.O. Box 2200 (91729-2200)
PHONE..................800 743-4284
Chris Van Dellen, *CEO*
Paul Van Dellen, *President*
EMP: 100 **EST:** 1953
SALES (est): 10.8MM **Privately Held**
WEB: www.collectiontechnology.com
SIC: 7322 Collection agency, except real estate

(P-17108)
CPS RECEIVABLES FIVE LLC
19500 Jamboree Rd, Irvine (92612-2411)
PHONE..................949 753-6800
EMP: 68 **EST:** 2016

SALES (est): 4.5MM **Publicly Held**
WEB: www.consumerportfolio.com
SIC: 7322 Collection agency, except real estate
PA: Consumer Portfolio Services, Inc.
3800 Howard Hughes Pkw
Las Vegas NV 89169

(P-17109)
CREDITORS ADJUSTMENT BUR INC
14226 Ventura Blvd, Sherman Oaks (91423-2715)
P.O. Box 5932, Van Nuys (914 3-5932)
PHONE..................818 990-4800
Robert Mitteldorf, *CEO*
Brian L Mitteldorf, *President*
Henry Hou, *Vice Pres*
Laura Levy, *Managing Dir*
Lori D 'itri, *Sales Executive*
EMP: 53 **EST:** 1954
SQ FT: 4,500
SALES (est): 5.3MM **Privately Held**
WEB: www.cabcollects.com
SIC: 7322 Collection agency, except real estate

(P-17110)
EGS FINANCIAL CARE INC (DH)
5 Park Plz Ste 1100, Irvine (92614-8502)
PHONE..................877 217-4423
Jay King, *President*
Steven Winokur, *CFO*
Joshua Gindin, *Admin Sec*
Marieta San Pedro, *Technology*
Peter Brillhart, *Engineer*
▲ **EMP:** 300 **EST:** 1966
SALES (est): 194.1MM
SALES (corp-wide): 845.1MM **Privately Held**
WEB: www.alorica.com
SIC: 7322 Collection agency, except real estate

(P-17111)
FCI LENDER SERVICES INC
Also Called: F C I
8180 E Kaiser Blvd, Anaheim (92808-2277)
PHONE..................800 931-2424
Michael W Griffith, *CEO*
Teri Snyder, *Exec VP*
Sylvia Derdall, *CIO*
Leigh Eddy, *Loan*
EMP: 105
SQ FT: 19,000
SALES (est): 27.8MM **Privately Held**
WEB: www.trustfci.com
SIC: 7322 Adjustment & collection services

(P-17112)
FINANCIAL CREDIT NETWORK INC (PA)
1300 W Main St, Visalia (93291-5825)
P.O. Box 3084 (93278-3084)
PHONE..................559 733-7550
Alicia Sundstrom, *President*
Kris Davisson, *COO*
Jeanie Weber, *IT/INT Sup*
Wendy Anderson, *Representative*
Venita Jourdan, *Representative*
EMP: 62 **EST:** 1958
SQ FT: 11,000
SALES (est): 12.6K **Privately Held**
WEB: www.fcnetwork.com
SIC: 7322 Collection agency, except real estate

(P-17113)
GRANT & WEBER (PA)
Also Called: Grant & Weber Travel
26610 Agoura Rd Ste 20S, Calabasas (91302-2975)
P.O. Box 8669 (91372-8669)
PHONE..................818 878-7700
Jimi Bingham, *CEO*
Denise Williams, *Vice Pres*
Mary Kempski, *CIO*
Robert Nye, *Info Tech Dir*
Reid Steinfeld, *General Counsel*
▲ **EMP:** 168 **EST:** 1976
SQ FT: 30,000

SALES (est): 27.3MM Privately Held
WEB: www.grantweber.com
SIC: 7322 Collection agency, except real estate

(P-17114)
JJ MAC INTYRE CO INC (PA)
4160 Temescal Canyon Rd, Corona (92883-4625)
P.O. Box 78150 (92877-0138)
PHONE..................................951 898-4300
Scott M Hall, CEO
Kenneth A Lee, President
EMP: 115 EST: 1959
SQ FT: 28,254
SALES (est): 2.9MM Privately Held
SIC: 7322 Collection agency, except real estate

(P-17115)
NATIONAL COMMERCIAL SERVICES
6644 Valjean Ave Ste 100, Van Nuys (91406-5816)
PHONE..................................818 701-4400
Zoran Jovanoski, President
Zoran Jovanovski, President
Natalie Mansour, Vice Pres
Darlene Martinez, Legal Staff
Ryan Keyaerts, Manager
EMP: 52 EST: 1996
SQ FT: 4,500
SALES (est): 5.9MM Privately Held
WEB: www.ncssubro.com
SIC: 7322 Collection agency, except real estate

(P-17116)
RM GALICIA INC
Also Called: Progressive Management Systems
1521 W Cameron Ave # 100, West Covina (91790-2738)
P.O. Box 2220 (91793-2220)
PHONE..................................626 813-6200
Timothy Chase Banta, CEO
Carol Ryan, Exec VP
Carole Ryan, Vice Pres
Juan Vargas, Vice Pres
Gabriela Sanabria, Manager
EMP: 125 EST: 1978
SQ FT: 20,000
SALES (est): 15.2MM Privately Held
SIC: 7322 Collection agency, except real estate

(P-17117)
SEQUOIA CONCEPTS INC
Also Called: Sequoia Financial Services
28632 Roadside Dr Ste 110, Agoura Hills (91301-6074)
PHONE..................................818 409-6000
Roy Duplessis, President
King Bechtel, Chief Mktg Ofcr
Denise Duplessis, Vice Pres
Roy Deplessis II, Admin Sec
Mischaulette Johnson, Legal Staff
EMP: 75 EST: 1992
SQ FT: 9,100
SALES (est): 8.4MM Privately Held
WEB: www.sequoiafinancial.com
SIC: 7322 Collection agency, except real estate

(P-17118)
USCB INC (PA)
Also Called: Uscb America
355 S Grand Ave Ste 3200, Los Angeles (90071-1591)
PHONE..................................213 985-2111
Albert Cadena, CEO
David Georgescu, President
Melvin F Shaw, President
John McCrosky, CFO
Astrid Blackmon, Officer
EMP: 213 EST: 1915
SQ FT: 34,000
SALES (est): 41.5MM Privately Held
WEB: www.uscbamerica.com
SIC: 7322 8741 Collection agency, except real estate; management services

7323 Credit Reporting Svcs

(P-17119)
A-CHECK AMERICA INC (PA)
Also Called: A-Check America, Member Act 1
1501 Research Park Dr, Riverside (92507-2114)
P.O. Box 29048, Glendale (91209-9048)
PHONE..................................951 750-1501
Janice B Howryd, CEO
Carlos Lacambra, President
Michael Hoyal, CFO
Don Shimizu, Exec VP
Gregg Hassler, Vice Pres
▲ EMP: 170
SQ FT: 30,000
SALES (est): 25.3MM Privately Held
WEB: www.acheckglobal.com
SIC: 7323 7375 Credit reporting services; information retrieval services

(P-17120)
CORELOGIC CREDCO LLC (DH)
40 Pacifica Ste 900, Irvine (92618-7487)
PHONE..................................800 255-0792
Frank Martel, President
Jim Balas, CFO
Mercedes Vela, Vice Pres
Barry Sando, Managing Dir
Keith Curran, Area Mgr
EMP: 220 EST: 2005
SALES (est): 54MM
SALES (corp-wide): 1.6B Privately Held
WEB: www.corelogic.com
SIC: 7323 8748 Credit bureau & agency; business consulting
HQ: Corelogic, Inc.
40 Pacifica Ste 900
Irvine CA 92618
866 873-3651

(P-17121)
CREDIT MONKEY LLC
Also Called: Credit Repair
8484 Wilshire Blvd # 515, Beverly Hills (90211-3227)
PHONE..................................877 701-7307
EMP: 76
SALES (est): 1MM Privately Held
WEB: www.creditmonkey.com
SIC: 7323 Credit Reporting Services

(P-17122)
EXPERIAN CORPORATION
475 Anton Blvd, Santa Ana (92704)
PHONE..................................714 830-7000
Rick Cortese, CEO
Craig Smith, Ch of Bd
Chris Callero, President
Margaret B Smith, President
Deborah Zuccarini, President
EMP: 223 EST: 1996
SQ FT: 323,000
SALES (est): 13.3MM
SALES (corp-wide): 5.3B Privately Held
WEB: www.experian.com
SIC: 7323 Credit bureau & agency
HQ: Experian Na Unlimited
Landmark House
Nottingham NOTTS

(P-17123)
EXPERIAN HOLDINGS INC (DH)
475 Anton Blvd, Costa Mesa (92626-7037)
PHONE..................................714 830-7000
Victor Nichols, CEO
Scott Bagwell, President
Caroline Donahue, Bd of Directors
Ek Koh, Senior VP
Tammy Marge, Senior VP
EMP: 152 EST: 1997
SALES (est): 1B
SALES (corp-wide): 5.3B Privately Held
WEB: www.experian.com
SIC: 7323 Credit bureau & agency
HQ: Experian Finance Plc
Landmark House
Nottingham NOTTS NG80
115 992-2777

(P-17124)
EXPERIAN INFO SOLUTIONS INC (DH)
475 Anton Blvd, Costa Mesa (92626-7037)
P.O. Box 5001 (92628-5001)
PHONE..................................714 830-7000
Chris Callero, CEO
Steve Platt, Exec VP
Stephen Burnside, Senior VP
Maryam Damavandi, Vice Pres
Mindy Ferguson, Vice Pres
EMP: 3700 EST: 1996
SQ FT: 323,000
SALES (est): 973.8MM
SALES (corp-wide): 5.3B Privately Held
WEB: www.experian.com
SIC: 7323 Credit bureau & agency
HQ: Experian Holdings, Inc.
475 Anton Blvd
Costa Mesa CA 92626
714 830-7000

(P-17125)
EXPERIAN MKTG SOLUTIONS LLC
475 Anton Blvd, Costa Mesa (92626-7037)
PHONE..................................714 830-7000
Kevin Dean, President
Klaudette Christensen, COO
EMP: 501 EST: 2016
SQ FT: 4,000
SALES (est): 46.7MM
SALES (corp-wide): 621MM Privately Held
WEB: www.experian.com
SIC: 7323 Credit bureau & agency
PA: Vector Capital Management, L.P.
1 Market St Ste 2300
San Francisco CA 94105
415 293-5000

(P-17126)
PRESIDENTAL SERVICES INC (PA)
23404 Lyons Ave Ste 223, Santa Clarita (91321-2511)
PHONE..................................661 259-8987
Kevin Wessell, Principal
EMP: 133 EST: 1998
SALES (est): 419.8K Privately Held
SIC: 7323 Credit investigation service

7331 Direct Mail Advertising Svcs

(P-17127)
AARON THOMAS & ASSOCIATES INC
Also Called: Aaron Group, The
21344 Superior St, Chatsworth (91311-4312)
PHONE..................................818 727-9040
Fred Thomas, President
Gary Thomas, Admin Sec
Cristina Agopian, Accountant
EMP: 35 EST: 1980
SQ FT: 18,500
SALES (est): 2.1MM Privately Held
WEB: www.atacampaigns.com
SIC: 7331 2759 Mailing service; commercial printing

(P-17128)
ACE DIRECT
Also Called: Ace Printing
948 Vella Rd, Palm Springs (92264-3469)
PHONE..................................760 969-5500
Mark Lawrence, President
Greg Lawrence, Vice Pres
Sandy Miller, Cust Mgr
EMP: 22 EST: 1979
SQ FT: 8,000
SALES (est): 1.2MM Privately Held
WEB: www.acedirect.com
SIC: 7331 2752 Direct mail advertising services; commercial printing, lithographic

(P-17129)
ADVANCED IMAGE DIRECT LLC
Also Called: Fht Printing
1415 S Acacia Ave, Fullerton (92831-5317)
PHONE..................................714 502-3900

Ty McMillin,
Michael Shevitz, CFO
Hugo Solorio, Plant Mgr
Scott Dempster, Natl Sales Mgr
Vidal Gallardo, Warehouse Mgr
▲ EMP: 50 EST: 2008
SALES (est): 9.7MM
SALES (corp-wide): 29MM Privately Held
WEB: www.advancedimagedirect.com
SIC: 7331 2752 Mailing service; commercial printing, lithographic
PA: Real Estate Image, Inc.
1415 S Acacia Ave
Fullerton CA 92831
714 502-3900

(P-17130)
ADVANTAGE MAILING LLC (PA)
Also Called: Advantage Mailing Service
1600 N Kraemer Blvd, Anaheim (92806-1410)
P.O. Box 66013 (92816-6013)
PHONE..................................714 538-3881
Thomas Ling, Mng Member
Thomas C Ling, President
Tom Ling, President
Brett Noss, CFO
Cara Cohan, Vice Pres
EMP: 125 EST: 1994
SQ FT: 60,000
SALES (est): 105.7MM Privately Held
WEB: www.advantageinc.com
SIC: 7331 Mailing service

(P-17131)
DATABASE MARKETING GROUP INC
300 Commerce Ste 200, Irvine (92602-1305)
PHONE..................................714 727-0800
John A Engstrom, President
Sharon M Engstrom, Vice Pres
Sharon Engstrom, Vice Pres
Yan Thomas, Vice Pres
Yan Xia, Vice Pres
EMP: 64 EST: 1991
SALES (est): 8.5MM Privately Held
WEB: www.dbmgroup.com
SIC: 7331 8742 Mailing service; marketing consulting services

(P-17132)
FINANCIAL STATEMENT SVCS INC (PA)
Also Called: Fssi
3300 S Fairview St, Santa Ana (92704-7004)
PHONE..................................714 436-3326
Jennifer Dietz, CEO
Henry Perez, COO
Karen Elsbury, CFO
Dick O 'neil, Vice Pres
Jon Dietz, Admin Sec
EMP: 144 EST: 1984
SQ FT: 167,000
SALES (est): 25.1MM Privately Held
WEB: www.fssi-ca.com
SIC: 7331 7374 2759 Mailing service; data processing & preparation; laser printing

(P-17133)
M M DIRECT MARKETING INC
14271 Corporate Dr, Garden Grove (92843-5000)
PHONE..................................714 265-4100
Godfred P Otueye, President
EMP: 133 EST: 1995
SALES (est): 3.3MM
SALES (corp-wide): 45.4MM Privately Held
WEB: www.moneymailer.com
SIC: 7331 6794 Mailing service; franchises, selling or licensing
PA: Money Mailer, Llc
128 Se 8th Pl
Cape Coral FL 33990
714 889-3800

(P-17134)
MRT INC
19781 Pauling, Foothill Ranch (92610-2606)
PHONE..................................949 348-2292
Rick Theder, President

Tracy Vanevery, *Admin Sec*
EMP: 63 **EST:** 1976
SQ FT: 18,000
SALES (est): 2.7MM **Privately Held**
SIC: 7331 Direct mail advertising services

(P-17135)
ORANGE COUNTY DIRECT MAIL INC
Also Called: Ocdm
2672 Dow Ave, Tustin (92780-7208)
PHONE..................714 444-4412
Mark Cretz, *CEO*
Donna Crane, *Business Mgr*
Carlos Solorio, *Prdtn Mgr*
Pablo Hernandez, *Production*
Jason Cliff, *Sales Executive*
EMP: 45
SQ FT: 35,000
SALES (est): 5MM **Privately Held**
WEB: www.ocdm.com
SIC: 7331 7313 7389 2752 Mailing service; printed media advertising representatives; printers' services: folding, collating; commercial printing, lithographic

(P-17136)
POMONA COLLEGE
333 N College Way, Claremont (91711-4429)
PHONE..................909 621-8000
David W Oxtoby, *President*
Richard Worthington, *Partner*
Elizabeth Crighton, *Vice Pres*
Kitty Maryatt, *Vice Pres*
Ann Quinley, *Vice Pres*
EMP: 85
SALES (corp-wide): 223.1MM **Privately Held**
WEB: www.pomona.edu
SIC: 7331 8221 Addressing service; college, except junior
PA: Pomona College
550 N College Ave
Claremont CA 91711
909 621-8135

(P-17137)
PREMIER MAILING INC
Also Called: Premier Mailing Services
14522 Garfield Ave, Paramount (90723-3426)
PHONE..................562 408-2134
Ramon Arribeno, *President*
▲ **EMP:** 50
SQ FT: 5,200
SALES (est): 8.4MM **Privately Held**
SIC: 7331 Mailing service

(P-17138)
PRESORT CENTER OF FRESNO LLC
496 S Uruapan Way, Dinuba (93618-2719)
PHONE..................559 498-6151
Rebecca Kozlowski,
Lynn Payne, *Human Res Dir*
EMP: 40 **EST:** 2015
SQ FT: 92,000
SALES (est): 5MM **Privately Held**
SIC: 7331 2759 Mailing service; commercial printing

(P-17139)
R R DONNELLEY & SONS COMPANY
Also Called: RR Donnelley
18915 S Laurel Park Rd, Rancho Dominguez (90220-6005)
PHONE..................310 784-8485
Kelly Martinez, *Vice Pres*
EMP: 50
SALES (corp-wide): 4.7B **Publicly Held**
WEB: www.rrd.com
SIC: 7331 Mailing service
PA: R. R. Donnelley & Sons Company
35 W Wacker Dr
Chicago IL 60601
312 326-8000

(P-17140)
REAL ESTATE IMAGE INC (PA)
Also Called: Advanced Image Direct
1415 S Acacia Ave, Fullerton (92831-5317)
PHONE..................714 502-3900
Ty McMillin, *President*

Scott Dempster, *Exec VP*
Hugo Solorio, *Vice Pres*
Steven Chan, *Opers Mgr*
Frank Gil, *Production*
EMP: 150 **EST:** 1981
SQ FT: 136,000
SALES (est): 29MM **Privately Held**
SIC: 7331 2752 Mailing service; commercial printing, lithographic

(P-17141)
SPECTRUM INFORMATION SVCS LLC (PA)
16 Technology Dr Ste 107, Irvine (92618-2323)
PHONE..................949 752-7070
Curtis Pilon, *President*
Jim Bradford, *CFO*
Amy Thatcher, *CFO*
Glenn O Dell, *Vice Pres*
Steve Selinsky, *Vice Pres*
EMP: 70 **EST:** 1991
SQ FT: 142,000
SALES (est): 8.5MM **Privately Held**
WEB: www.spectruminformation.com
SIC: 7331 7375 4731 Mailing service; information retrieval services; shipping documents preparation

(P-17142)
STAMPSCOM INC (PA)
1990 E Grand Ave, El Segundo (90245-5013)
PHONE..................310 482-5800
Nathan Jones, *CEO*
Tran CHI, *Partner*
Kyle Huebner, *President*
Jeff Carberry, *CFO*
Mohan Ananda, *Bd of Directors*
EMP: 400 **EST:** 1996
SQ FT: 99,600
SALES (est): 757.9MM **Privately Held**
WEB: www.stamps.com
SIC: 7331 5961 4813 Mailing service; catalog & mail-order houses;

7334 Photocopying & Duplicating Svcs

(P-17143)
ABI ATTORNEYS SERVICE INC (PA)
Also Called: ABI VIP Attorney Service
2015 W Park Ave, Redlands (92373-6271)
P.O. Box 9240 (92375-2440)
PHONE..................909 793-0613
Alice J Benge, *President*
Chuck Benge, *Corp Secy*
EMP: 80 **EST:** 1985
SQ FT: 7,500
SALES (est): 6.1MM **Privately Held**
SIC: 7334 Photocopying & duplicating services

(P-17144)
AMERICAN REPROGRAPHICS CO LLC
Also Called: ARC Imaging Resources
616 Monterey Pass Rd, Monterey Park (91754-2419)
PHONE..................626 289-5021
Doug Elffers, *Sales Mgr*
Mike Bottitta, *Info Tech Mgr*
EMP: 52
SALES (corp-wide): 289.4MM **Publicly Held**
WEB: www.ryansallans.com
SIC: 7334 Photocopying & duplicating services
HQ: American Reprographics Company, L.L.C.
1981 N Broadway Ste 385
Walnut Creek CA 94596
925 949-5100

(P-17145)
ARC (PA)
345 Clinton St, Costa Mesa (92626-6011)
PHONE..................714 424-8500
Arthur G Lundeen, *President*
Jim Chamberlain, *Treasurer*
Dick French, *Vice Pres*
Mark Sipes, *Vice Pres*

EMP: 20 **EST:** 1965
SALES (est): 25.1MM **Privately Held**
WEB: www.crestaurant.com
SIC: 7334 7389 2752 Blueprinting service; mimeographing; drafting service, except temporary help; commercial printing, offset

(P-17146)
CONCORD DOCUMENT SERVICES INC (PA)
1321 W 12th St, Los Angeles (90015-2008)
PHONE..................213 745-3175
Fernando B Flores, *CEO*
Hector Flores, *President*
EMP: 51 **EST:** 1996
SQ FT: 9,000
SALES (est): 4.8MM **Privately Held**
WEB: www.concorddt.com
SIC: 7334 3577 Photocopying & duplicating services; optical scanning devices

(P-17147)
CRISP ENTERPRISES INC (PA)
Also Called: C2 Imaging
3180 Pullman St, Costa Mesa (92626-3323)
PHONE..................714 668-5955
Gary Crisp, *CEO*
William Govaars II, *Shareholder*
Arthur Gregory Lundeen III, *Shareholder*
Barry Malkin, *COO*
Julie Crisp, *Exec VP*
EMP: 60 **EST:** 2000
SQ FT: 28,000
SALES (est): 21.5MM **Privately Held**
WEB: www.crispimg.com
SIC: 7334 Blueprinting service

(P-17148)
CYBERCOPY INC (PA)
2766 S La Cienega Blvd, Los Angeles (90034-2642)
P.O. Box 507, Culver City (90232-0507)
PHONE..................310 736-1001
Paul Fridrich, *CEO*
Alex Gaytan, *Opers Mgr*
Braxton Leonard, *Accounts Exec*
EMP: 30 **EST:** 1997
SALES (est): 6.5MM **Privately Held**
WEB: www.cybercopyusa.com
SIC: 7334 2754 2741 2732 Blueprinting service; commercial printing, gravure; art copy & poster publishing; book printing

(P-17149)
DVS MEDIA SERVICES (PA)
Also Called: D V S Mdia Srvces/Intelestream
2625 W Olive Ave, Burbank (91505-4526)
PHONE..................818 841-6750
Rick Appell, *Mng Member*
EMP: 18 **EST:** 2020
SALES (est): 5.1MM **Privately Held**
WEB: www.dvs.tv
SIC: 7334 2759 Photocopying & duplicating services; commercial printing

(P-17150)
FEDEX OFFICE & PRINT SVCS INC
15951 Goldenwest St, Huntington Beach (92647-3127)
PHONE..................714 892-1452
EMP: 22
SALES (corp-wide): 47.4B **Publicly Held**
SIC: 7334 2791 2789 2752 Photocopying Service Typesetting Services Bookbinding/Related Work Lithographic Coml Print
HQ: Fedex Office And Print Services, Inc.
7900 Legacy Dr
Dallas TX 75024
214 550-7000

(P-17151)
LASR INC
Also Called: First Reprographic
1517 Beverly Blvd, Los Angeles (90026-5704)
P.O. Box 749469 (90074-9469)
PHONE..................877 591-9979
Martin Kayondo, *President*
Rick Matsumoto, *Opers Mgr*
EMP: 120 **EST:** 2002
SALES (est): 5.2MM **Privately Held**
SIC: 7334 Photocopying & duplicating services

(P-17152)
MAINSTREET COMMUNICATIONS INC (PA)
Also Called: PIP Printing
4093 Market St, Riverside (92501-3542)
PHONE..................951 682-2005
Justin Tracy, *President*
Christa Shewbridge, *Technician*
EMP: 15 **EST:** 1968
SQ FT: 5,500
SALES (est): 4.1MM **Privately Held**
WEB: www.printmystuff.com
SIC: 7334 2752 Photocopying & duplicating services; commercial printing, offset

(P-17153)
PRECISION COPY (PA)
1413 E Edinger Ave, Santa Ana (92705-4814)
PHONE..................949 833-1213
Judy Branch, *President*
Lee Gorrin, *Vice Pres*
EMP: 13 **EST:** 1989
SALES (est): 832K **Privately Held**
SIC: 7334 7389 2759 Photocopying & duplicating services; microfilm recording & developing service; commercial printing

(P-17154)
SECOND IMAGE NATIONAL LLC (PA)
170 E Arrow Hwy, San Dimas (91773-3336)
P.O. Box 52969, Houston TX (77052-2969)
PHONE..................800 229-7477
Norman Fogwell, *CEO*
Mason Ross, *Branch Mgr*
EMP: 145 **EST:** 1982
SQ FT: 25,500
SALES (est): 23.7MM **Privately Held**
WEB: www.ontellus.com
SIC: 7334 Photocopying & duplicating services

(P-17155)
TAYLOR MORSE LTD
23422 Mill Creek Dr # 135, Laguna Hills (92653-7921)
PHONE..................949 707-5031
Mace Morse, *Owner*
Mark Taylor, *Partner*
EMP: 21 **EST:** 2000
SQ FT: 2,000
SALES (est): 1.6MM **Privately Held**
WEB: www.taylormorse.com
SIC: 7334 7389 2759 Photocopying & duplicating services; legal & tax services; commercial printing

(P-17156)
UCLA COPY SERVICES
555 Westwood Plz Ste B, Los Angeles (90095-8351)
PHONE..................310 794-6371
James Muh, *Director*
Alex Caro, *Admin Asst*
Sue Chang, *Network Analyst*
David Aberbush, *Director*
Bill Lundy, *Manager*
EMP: 32 **EST:** 1998
SALES (est): 667.5K **Privately Held**
WEB: www.ucla.edu
SIC: 7334 2759 Photocopying & duplicating services; commercial printing

---

7335 Commercial Photography

(P-17157)
AHTINEB NVELS PHOTOS BY DESIGN
473 Ecarnegie Dr Ste 200, San Bernardino (92408)
P.O. Box 2162, Helendae (92342-2162)
PHONE..................442 327-9234
Benitha Brown, *Owner*
EMP: 13
SQ FT: 1,700
SALES (est): 60K **Privately Held**
SIC: 7335 7336 2731 Commercial photography; graphic arts & related design; book publishing

(P-17158)
BRANDED ENTRMT NETWRK INC (PA)
15250 Ventura Blvd # 300, Sherman Oaks (91403-3201)
PHONE..................310 342-1500
Gary Shenk, *CEO*
Joe Schick, *CFO*
Jim Mitchell, *Senior VP*
Lauren Knowles, *Executive Asst*
Brian Cohee, *CTO*
EMP: 233 EST: 1989
SALES (est): 96.3MM Privately Held
WEB: www.ben.productplacement.com
SIC: 7335 Photographic studio, commercial

(P-17159)
ULTRAGRAPHICS INC
2800 N Naomi St, Burbank (91504-2023)
PHONE..................818 295-3994
E Alexander Kilgo, *CEO*
Jon E Crossley, *President*
John T Crossley, *CEO*
Nancy E Pasch Erlandsen, *Vice Pres*
Javier Beltran, *Sales Associate*
EMP: 44 EST: 1980
SQ FT: 19,000
SALES (est): 5.4MM Privately Held
WEB: www.ultragraphicsla.com
SIC: 7335 2752 Photographic studio, commercial; commercial printing, offset

---

7336 Commercial Art & Graphic Design

(P-17160)
ASSOCIATED STUDENTS UCLA
Also Called: Ucla Dept of Design Media
11000 Kinross Ave Ave # 245, Los Angeles (90095-2000)
P.O. Box 951615 (90095-1615)
PHONE..................310 206-8282
Diane Mills, *Principal*
EMP: 201
SALES (corp-wide): 54.7MM Privately Held
WEB: www.asucla.ucla.edu
SIC: 8221 7336 University; graphic arts & related design
PA: Associated Students U.C.L.A.
    308 Westwood Plz
    Los Angeles CA 90095
    310 794-8836

(P-17161)
ATELIER ACE LLC
3191 Casitas Ave Ste 116, Los Angeles (90039-2470)
PHONE..................503 546-6836
Bradford Wilson, *President*
Kelly Sawdon, *Vice Pres*
Lindsay Skillman, *General Mgr*
Amanda Dissinger, *Pub Rel Staff*
Meriem Soliman, *General Counsel*
EMP: 50 EST: 2008 Privately Held
WEB: www.atelierace.com
SIC: 7336 Creative services to advertisers, except writers

(P-17162)
BLT & ASSOCIATES INC
6430 W Sunset Blvd # 800, Los Angeles (90028-7901)
PHONE..................323 860-4000
Clive Baillie, *President*
Dawn Baillie, *CFO*
Kaz Dugandzic, *Vice Pres*
Rick Lynch, *Vice Pres*
Alon Amir, *Creative Dir*
EMP: 170 EST: 1992
SQ FT: 15,000
SALES (est): 39MM Privately Held
WEB: www.bltomato.com
SIC: 7336 Graphic arts & related design

(P-17163)
CINNABAR
4571 Electronics Pl, Los Angeles (90039-1007)
PHONE..................818 842-8190
Jonathan Katz, *President*
Juan Corral, *Technical Staff*

Randy Morgan, *Manager*
EMP: 200 EST: 1982
SQ FT: 60,000
SALES (est): 21.6MM Privately Held
WEB: www.cinnabar.com
SIC: 7336 3999 7819 Graphic arts & related design; theatrical scenery; sound (effects & music production), motion picture; visual effects production

(P-17164)
CINNABAR CALIFORNIA INC
4571 Electronics Pl, Los Angeles (90039-1007)
PHONE..................818 842-8190
Leslie Crawford, *CFO*
Basil Katz, *CEO*
Jonathan Katz, *Chairman*
Joseph Dunham, *Technical Mgr*
Jeff Crocker, *Project Mgr*
EMP: 60 EST: 1982
SQ FT: 55,271
SALES (est): 10.6MM Privately Held
WEB: www.cinnabar.com
SIC: 7336 8712 1796 Art design services; architectural services; installing building equipment

(P-17165)
CLASSICAL SILK INC (PA)
2016 E 15th St, Los Angeles (90021-2823)
PHONE..................213 488-0909
Morris Peykar, *President*
◆ EMP: 62 EST: 2007
SALES (est): 1MM Privately Held
WEB: www.classicalsilk.com
SIC: 5632 5699 7336 Blouses; dressmakers, custom; knit dresses, made to order; commercial art & graphic design; art design services; silk screen design

(P-17166)
CONSOLIDATED DESIGN WEST INC
Also Called: Cdw
1345 S Lewis St, Anaheim (92805-6431)
PHONE..................714 999-1476
Victor John Perrillo, *CEO*
Rick Gaulden, *Sales Executive*
Sandra Gonzalez,
Yvonne Kiely,
Kim Garriot, *Accounts Mgr*
▲ EMP: 50 EST: 1990
SQ FT: 7,500
SALES (est): 23.2MM Privately Held
WEB: www.consolidateddesignwest.com
SIC: 7336 2754 Package design; commercial printing, gravure

(P-17167)
CONTINENTAL GRAPHICS CORP (HQ)
Also Called: Continental Data Graphics
4060 N Lakewood Blvd, Long Beach (90808-1700)
PHONE..................714 503-4200
David Malmo, *CEO*
James Mills, *CFO*
Michael Parven, *Exec VP*
Charlie Kirkpatrick, *Executive*
Jane Grafton, *Surgery Dir*
EMP: 200 EST: 1986
SQ FT: 45,000
SALES (est): 98.7MM
SALES (corp-wide): 58.1B Publicly Held
WEB: www.cdgnow.com
SIC: 7336 8741 8711 8999 Commercial art & graphic design; management services; engineering services; technical writing
PA: The Boeing Company
    100 N Riverside Plz
    Chicago IL 60606
    312 544-2000

(P-17168)
CREATIVE INTELLIGENCE INC
4988 Venice Blvd, Los Angeles (90019-5547)
PHONE..................323 936-9009
Marc P Friedland, *President*
Arturo Valadez, *Engineer*
Rebecca Drooks, *Accounts Mgr*
EMP: 14 EST: 1991

SALES (est): 541.8K Privately Held
WEB: www.marcfriedland.com
SIC: 7336 2759 Graphic arts & related design; invitation & stationery printing & engraving

(P-17169)
CUSTOMLINE PROFESSIONAL
567 S Melrose St, Placentia (92870-6305)
PHONE..................714 996-1333
EMP: 300
SQ FT: 60,000
SALES (est): 26.1MM Privately Held
WEB: www.quikturnusa.com
SIC: 7336 Commercial Art And Graphic Design

(P-17170)
DANDREA GRAPHIC CORPORTION
Also Called: D'Andrea Graphics
6100 Gateway Dr, Cypress (90630-4840)
PHONE..................310 642-0260
David D'Andrea, *CEO*
Jim Musgrove, *Executive*
Scott Pekar, *Executive*
Ray Minter, *CIO*
Taylor Fenster, *Project Mgr*
▲ EMP: 80
SQ FT: 25,000
SALES (est): 17.8MM Privately Held
WEB: www.dandreavisual.com
SIC: 7336 Graphic arts & related design

(P-17171)
DESIGNORY INC (HQ)
211 E Ocean Blvd Ste 100, Long Beach (90802-4850)
PHONE..................562 624-0200
Paul Hosea, *CEO*
Matt Radigan, *CFO*
Joel Fuller, *Exec VP*
Jeff Wright, *Associate Dir*
Janet M Thompson, *Principal*
EMP: 115 EST: 1970
SALES (est): 26.4MM
SALES (corp-wide): 13.1B Publicly Held
WEB: www.designory.com
SIC: 7336 Graphic arts & related design
PA: Omnicom Group Inc.
    280 Park Ave Fl 31w
    New York NY 10017
    212 415-3600

(P-17172)
DYNAMIC DEZIGN
32 S Broadway, Los Angeles (90012)
PHONE..................562 735-3060
Dave Thompson, *Owner*
EMP: 50 EST: 2010
SALES (est): 784.2K Privately Held
SIC: 7336 Commercial art & graphic design

(P-17173)
ELLENS SILK SCREENING INC
1500 Mission St, South Pasadena (91030-3216)
PHONE..................626 441-4415
Ellen Daigle, *President*
Joe Daigle, *Admin Sec*
Precy Vidal, *Accountant*
Ann M Kent, *Representative*
EMP: 24 EST: 1975
SQ FT: 2,200
SALES (est): 3.4MM Privately Held
WEB: www.ellenssilkscreening.com
SIC: 7336 3552 Silk screen design; silk screens for textile industry

(P-17174)
EXPLOREMYPC
Also Called: Web Design
1968 S Coast Hwy 402, Laguna Beach (92651-3681)
PHONE..................877 497-1650
Julius Ryan, *Principal*
EMP: 50 EST: 2018
SALES (est): 4MM Privately Held
WEB: www.exploremypc.com
SIC: 7336 Commercial art & graphic design

(P-17175)
FINAL FILM
Also Called: Flash Point Graphix
3620 W Valhalla Dr, Burbank (91505-1127)
PHONE..................323 467-0700
Thomas L Saliba, *Ch of Bd*
Guy S Claudy, *President*
Gregory D Davidiian, *CEO*
Raymond Hebrank, *CFO*
Brian Rahming, *Info Tech Dir*
EMP: 62 EST: 1986
SQ FT: 20,000
SALES (est): 10MM Privately Held
SIC: 7336 Graphic arts & related design

(P-17176)
GRAPHIC DESIGN SERVICES INC
1059 West Rd, La Habra Heights (90631-8681)
PHONE..................562 282-8000
Jan Noller, *President*
John Lorenzini, *Vice Pres*
Dorothy Sheraga, *Vice Pres*
▲ EMP: 40 EST: 1975
SALES (est): 4MM Privately Held
WEB: www.gdsflexo.com
SIC: 7336 7384 2791 Graphic arts & related design; photofinish laboratories; linotype composition, for the printing trade

(P-17177)
GRAPHIC INK CORP
Also Called: Graphic Ink and Graphic Ink
5382 Industrial Dr, Huntington Beach (92649-1517)
PHONE..................714 901-2805
Vincent De La Torre, *President*
Jenny Lynn Quilico, *Vice Pres*
EMP: 45 EST: 2005
SQ FT: 6,000
SALES (est): 6.1MM Privately Held
WEB: www.graphicink.org
SIC: 7336 2262 Commercial art & graphic design; finishing plants, manmade fiber & silk fabrics

(P-17178)
HOG INC
Also Called: House of Graphics
9519 Rush St Ste A, South El Monte (91733-1556)
PHONE..................626 279-5275
Michael Harada, *President*
EMP: 15 EST: 1975
SALES (est): 1MM Privately Held
WEB: www.hogprinter.com
SIC: 7336 2752 Graphic arts & related design; commercial printing, lithographic

(P-17179)
IDENTIGRAPHIX INC
19866 Quiroz Ct, Walnut (91789-2828)
PHONE..................909 468-4741
A Fred Mendoza, *President*
Guillermo Quiroz, *Plant Mgr*
Olivia Nguyen, *Sales Staff*
Rosa Obregon, *Cust Mgr*
EMP: 25 EST: 1982
SQ FT: 17,000
SALES (est): 2.7MM Privately Held
WEB: www.identigraphix.com
SIC: 7336 2396 Silk screen design; automotive & apparel trimmings

(P-17180)
MOTION THEORY INC
Also Called: Mirada
444 W Ocean Blvd Ste 1400, Long Beach (90802-4522)
PHONE..................310 396-9433
Andrew Merkin, *Director*
Janell Perez, *CFO*
Chris Riehl, *Creative Dir*
Matthew Cullen,
EMP: 110 EST: 2000
SQ FT: 25,000
SALES (est): 8.5MM Privately Held
WEB: www.motiontheory.com
SIC: 7336 7371 7812 Graphic arts & related design; computer software development & applications; motion picture production

PRODUCTS & SVCS

(P-17181)
NEW-INDY TRIPAQ LLC (PA)
16069 Shoemaker Ave, Cerritos
(90703-2234)
PHONE.....................562 404-6965
Lynn Liddle, *Sales Dir*
Julia Artaserse, *Cust Mgr*
EMP: 80 EST: 2016
SALES (est): 9.1MM **Privately Held**
WEB: www.tripaq.com
SIC: 7336 Package design

(P-17182)
P5 GRAPHICS AND DISPLAYS INC
625 Fee Ana St, Placentia (92870-6704)
PHONE.....................714 808-1645
Amit Patel, *President*
Kirit Ramani, *Vice Pres*
Jimmy Patel, *Systems Dir*
Randy Myers, *Accounts Exec*
EMP: 21 EST: 2015
SALES (est): 2.7MM **Privately Held**
WEB: www.p5graphics.net
SIC: 7336 2782 Graphic arts & related design; account books

(P-17183)
PRIMARY COLOR INC
11130 Holder St, Cypress (90630-5162)
PHONE.....................714 824-8930
Lindsay Parton, *Principal*
Ivan Debucquois, *Asst Controller*
Tony Leo, *Production*
Eva Alexander-Gutie, *Sales Staff*
Nancy Firestone, *Sales Staff*
EMP: 51 EST: 2018
SALES (est): 10.3MM **Privately Held**
WEB: www.primarycolor.com
SIC: 7336 Commercial art & graphic design

(P-17184)
PULP STUDIO INCORPORATED
Also Called: CGB
2100 W 139th St, Gardena (90249-2412)
P.O. Box 16231, Beverly Hills (90209-2231)
PHONE.....................310 815-4999
Bernard Lax, *CEO*
Lynda N Lax, *President*
Oscar Ramirez, *Vice Pres*
Kirk Johnson, *Exec Dir*
Henry Marquis, *Technician*
▲ EMP: 60 EST: 1940
SQ FT: 36,000
SALES (est): 12MM **Privately Held**
WEB: www.pulpstudio.com
SIC: 7336 3229 Commercial art & graphic design; glass furnishings & accessories

(P-17185)
REFINERY AV LLC
15301 Ventura Blvd # 300, Sherman Oaks
(91403-5813)
PHONE.....................818 843-0004
Adam Waldman, *Mng Member*
EMP: 50 EST: 2013
SALES (est): 1.6MM **Privately Held**
WEB: www.therefinerycreative.com
SIC: 7336 Graphic arts & related design

(P-17186)
RYOT CORP
11995 Bluff Creek Dr, Playa Vista
(90094-2929)
PHONE.....................323 356-1787
Bryn Mooser, *CEO*
Hayley Pappas, *Officer*
Ricky Baba, *Creative Dir*
Katie Katz, *Project Mgr*
Tarik Benbrahim, *Producer*
EMP: 100 EST: 2013
SALES (est): 1MM **Privately Held**
WEB: www.ryot.org
SIC: 7336 7371 Still film producer; computer software development & applications

(P-17187)
SESA INC (PA)
Also Called: Signco
20391 Via Guadalupe, Yorba Linda
(92887-3133)
PHONE.....................714 779-9700
Elaine M Roach, *CEO*

EMP: 23 EST: 1986
SQ FT: 18,000
SALES (est): 4.7MM **Privately Held**
SIC: 7336 2759 3993 2396 Silk screen design; screen printing; signs & advertising specialties; automotive & apparel trimmings; color printing, gravure

(P-17188)
SPLASH EVENTS INC (PA)
80 Icon, Foothill Ranch (92610-3000)
PHONE.....................408 287-8600
David Payne, *President*
Cy Nakbayaski, *Vice Pres*
Jason Lemus, *Prgrmr*
Brian Hergenroether, *Project Mgr*
Alvin Molina, *Graphic Designe*
EMP: 53 EST: 1987
SALES (est): 10.1MM **Privately Held**
WEB: www.imageoptions.net
SIC: 7336 Commercial art & graphic design

(P-17189)
STAR LINK COMPANY INC
3300 Fujita St, Torrance (90505-4017)
PHONE.....................310 787-8299
Steven Chan, *President*
Heidi Chan, *Vice Pres*
EMP: 15 EST: 1988
SALES (est): 2.3MM **Privately Held**
WEB: www.starlinkco.com
SIC: 7336 7374 2759 Graphic arts & related design; service bureau, computer; commercial printing

(P-17190)
STYLE CRAFT MARKETING INC
Also Called: Style Cft Grphic Cmmunications
22922 Avenida Empresa, Rcho STA Marg
(92688-2665)
PHONE.....................949 709-2000
Sonja E Tripodi, *President*
John Barnhart, *Vice Pres*
Diana Chambers, *Manager*
▲ EMP: 20 EST: 1976
SQ FT: 26,000
SALES (est): 1.6MM **Privately Held**
WEB: www.stylecraft.net
SIC: 7336 2752 Graphic arts & related design; commercial printing, offset; photo-offset printing

(P-17191)
TREND DESIGN INC
Also Called: Trend Graphics Screenprinting
1200 Lawrence Dr Ste 465, Newbury Park
(91320-1342)
PHONE.....................805 498-0457
Steve Dilallo, *President*
Kim Di Lallo, *Corp Secy*
Chris Kaul, *Vice Pres*
Gloria Castillo, *Executive*
EMP: 17 EST: 1987
SQ FT: 3,000
SALES (est): 1.4MM **Privately Held**
SIC: 7336 2759 Silk screen design; screen printing

(P-17192)
TWENTIETH CNTURY FOX JAPAN INC
Also Called: News Corp - Fox
10201 W Pico Blvd, Los Angeles
(90064-2606)
PHONE.....................310 369-4636
Robert B Cohen, *CEO*
EMP: 4000 EST: 1981
SALES (est): 45MM
SALES (corp-wide): 65.3B **Publicly Held**
WEB: www.thewaltdisneycompany.com
SIC: 7336 Film strip & slide producer
HQ: Tfcf Corporation
1211 Ave Of The Americas
New York NY 10036
212 852-7000

7338 Secretarial & Court Reporting Svcs

(P-17193)
ASAB INC (DH)
500 N Brand Blvd Fl 3, Glendale
(91203-4725)
P.O. Box 29054 (91209-9054)
PHONE.....................818 551-7300
Alan Atkinson Baker, *CEO*
Sheila Atkinson-Baker, *President*
Ryan Atkinson-Baker, *Vice Pres*
Ryan Atkinson Baker, *Vice Pres*
Adrienne Macdonald, *Vice Pres*
EMP: 150 EST: 1987
SQ FT: 23,000
SALES (est): 36MM
SALES (corp-wide): 192.1MM **Privately Held**
WEB: www.depo.com
SIC: 7338 Court reporting service
HQ: Veritext, Llc
290 W Mount Pleasant Ave # 3
Livingston NJ 07039
973 410-4040

(P-17194)
SOFTSCRIPT INC
2215 Campus Dr, El Segundo
(90245-0001)
PHONE.....................310 451-2110
Howard Wisnicki, *CEO*
Braden Andreassi, *Vice Pres*
Claudia Mendoza, *Vice Pres*
Irene Oseguera, *Vice Pres*
Carla Rigdon, *Vice Pres*
EMP: 1200 EST: 1996
SALES (est): 25.2MM **Privately Held**
WEB: www.softscript.com
SIC: 7338 Court reporting service

(P-17195)
VERITXT/CLFORNIA REPORTING LLC
20 Corporate Park, Irvine (92606-5139)
PHONE.....................714 432-1711
John Olsen, ---
Una Elias, *President*
Paul Hilts, *Executive*
Rebecca Minadeo, *Opers Mgr*
Debbie Saline, *Director*
EMP: 50 EST: 1984
SALES (est): 15.3MM
SALES (corp-wide): 192.1MM **Privately Held**
WEB: www.veritext.com
SIC: 7338 Court reporting service
HQ: Veritext, Llc
290 W Mount Pleasant Ave # 3
Livingston NJ 07039
973 410-4040

7342 Disinfecting & Pest Control Svcs

(P-17196)
A-ABLE INC (PA)
Also Called: Fume-A-Pest & Termite Control
17801 Ventura Blvd, Encino (91316-3616)
PHONE.....................323 658-5779
Michael Herson, *President*
Jack Herson, *Vice Pres*
EMP: 65 EST: 1971
SQ FT: 9,026
SALES (est): 4.3MM **Privately Held**
WEB: www.fumeapest.com
SIC: 7342 1799 Pest control in structures; termite control; steam cleaning of building exteriors

(P-17197)
ASSOCIATES INSECTARY
1400 E Santa Paula St, Santa Paula
(93060-2335)
P.O. Box 969 (93061-0969)
PHONE.....................805 933-1301
Jonathan Pinkerton, *Ch of Bd*
Brett Chandler, *General Mgr*
Manuel Merino, *Office Mgr*
Michelle Haase, *Advisor*
EMP: 53 EST: 1928
SQ FT: 200,000

SALES (est): 2.6MM **Privately Held**
WEB: www.associatesinsectary.com
SIC: 7342 Pest control services

(P-17198)
BANKS PEST CONTROL
7440 District Blvd Ste A, Bakersfield
(93313-4821)
P.O. Box 113 (93302-0113)
PHONE.....................661 323-7858
Don Banks, *President*
Orland Banks, *Admin Sec*
Janet Banks, *Director*
EMP: 139 EST: 1969
SALES (est): 3.2MM
SALES (corp-wide): 2.1B **Publicly Held**
WEB: www.bankspest.com
SIC: 7342 Pest control in structures
PA: Rollins, Inc.
2170 Piedmont Rd Ne
Atlanta GA 30324
404 888-2000

(P-17199)
BUSY BEE LLC
36798 Pictor Ave, Murrieta (92563-4202)
PHONE.....................951 404-9900
EMP: 131
SALES (corp-wide): 87.2K **Privately Held**
SIC: 7342 Disinfecting & pest control services
PA: Busy Bee Llc
27100 Sunnyridge Rd
Pls Vrds Pnsl CA

(P-17200)
CARTWRIGHT TERMITE & PEST CTRL
51360 Calle Guatemala, La Quinta
(92253-2916)
P.O. Box 658 (92247-0658)
PHONE.....................760 771-6091
Fax: 760 771-4881
EMP: 50
SALES (est): 2.6MM **Privately Held**
SIC: 7342 Disinfecting/Pest Services

(P-17201)
CATS USA INC
Also Called: Cats U S A Pest Control
5683 Whitnall Hwy, North Hollywood
(91601-2213)
P.O. Box 151 (91603-0151)
PHONE.....................818 506-1000
Hirotaka Otomo, *Ch of Bd*
Yoshi Tada, *Vice Pres*
Ad Beal, *Supervisor*
EMP: 100 EST: 1971
SQ FT: 3,900
SALES (est): 8.9MM **Privately Held**
WEB: www.cats.co.jp
SIC: 7342 Pest control in structures
HQ: Cats, Inc.
15-13, Nampeidaicho
Shibuya-Ku TKY 150-0

(P-17202)
ECOLA SERVICES INC
15314 Devonshire St Ste F, Mission Hills
(91345-2773)
PHONE.....................818 920-7301
Susan Fries, *President*
Dennis McClure, *Regional Mgr*
Daniel Soto, *General Mgr*
Angie Gutierrez, *Cust Mgr*
EMP: 52 EST: 1983
SQ FT: 10,000
SALES (est): 5.1MM **Privately Held**
WEB: www.ecolatermite.com
SIC: 7342 Pest control in structures; pest control services

(P-17203)
MOXIE PEST CTRL ORANGE CNTY LP
18 Technology Dr Ste 154, Irvine
(92618-2312)
PHONE.....................951 272-4000
David Royce, *Partner*
Omar Matute, *Manager*
EMP: 50 EST: 2006
SQ FT: 6,600

SALES (est): 1.3MM **Privately Held**
WEB: www.moxieservices.com
SIC: 7342 Pest control in structures

(P-17204)
PEST OPTIONS INC
Also Called: Landscape Pest Management
135 N Manchester Ave, Anaheim
(92802-1007)
P.O. Box 5827, Orange (92863-5827)
PHONE.................................714 224-7378
Tracy Thompson, *President*
Bryan Thompson, *Vice Pres*
EMP: 83 EST: 1976
SALES (est): 2.8MM **Privately Held**
WEB: www.pestoptions.com
SIC: 7342 Pest control in structures

(P-17205)
ROLLINS INC
2585 Commerce Way, Commerce
(90040-1446)
P.O. Box 911520, Los Angeles (90091-1239)
PHONE.................................323 722-2279
EMP: 115
SALES (corp-wide): 2.1B **Publicly Held**
WEB: www.rollins.com
SIC: 7342 Disinfecting/Pest Services
PA: Rollins, Inc.
2170 Piedmont Rd Ne
Atlanta GA 30324
404 888-2000

(P-17206)
WESTERN EXTERMINATOR COMPANY
Also Called: Target Specialty Products
15415 Marquardt Ave, Santa Fe Springs
(90670-5711)
P.O. Box 3408 (90670-1408)
PHONE.................................562 802-2238
Rich Records, *Manager*
Jeffrey Bastian, *Branch Mgr*
Gary Singh, *Administration*
EMP: 100
SALES (corp-wide): 3.7B **Privately Held**
WEB: www.westernexterminator.com
SIC: 7342 Pest control in structures
HQ: Western Exterminator Company
305 N Crescent Way
Anaheim CA 92801
714 517-9000

(P-17207)
YOUR WAY FUMIGATION INC
1660 Chicago Ave Ste N9, Riverside
(92507-2053)
PHONE.................................951 699-9116
Jose Manuel Aguilar, *President*
EMP: 90 EST: 2006
SALES (est): 7.3MM **Privately Held**
WEB: www.ywfumigation.com
SIC: 7342 Pest control in structures

7349 Building Cleaning & Maintenance Svcs, NEC

(P-17208)
A B C UNIFIED SCHOOL DISTRICT
Also Called: Maintainance Department
11865 178th St, Artesia (90701-4101)
PHONE.................................562 865-1676
Chit Bao, *Principal*
Tamara Bachant, *Teacher*
Rosa Lamoureux, *Teacher*
Sue Highland, *Supervisor*
EMP: 65
SALES (corp-wide): 36K **Privately Held**
WEB: www.abcusd.us
SIC: 8211 7349 Public elementary school;
building maintenance services
PA: A B C Unified School District
16700 Norwalk Blvd
Cerritos CA 90703
562 926-5567

(P-17209)
ABM ELCTRCAL LTG SOLUTIONS INC (DH)
14201 Franklin Ave, Tustin (92780-7008)
PHONE.................................866 226-2838

Henrick C Slipsager, *CEO*
James S Lusk, *Exec VP*
Tracy K Price, *Exec VP*
Scott Tapia, *Sales Staff*
Sue Bremner, *Director*
EMP: 50 EST: 2003
SQ FT: 4,803
SALES (est): 18.7MM
SALES (corp-wide): 5.9B **Publicly Held**
SIC: 7349 Lighting maintenance service
HQ: Abm Facility Solutions Group, Llc
1201 Louisiana St
Houston TX 77002
832 214-5500

(P-17210)
ABM JANITORIAL SERVICES INC
1335 N Plaza Dr Ste C, Visalia
(93291-8838)
PHONE.................................559 651-1612
Tony Bautista, *Branch Mgr*
EMP: 90
SALES (corp-wide): 5.9B **Publicly Held**
WEB: www.abm.com
SIC: 7349 Janitorial service, contract basis
HQ: Abm Janitorial Services, Inc.
1111 Fannin St Ste 1500
Houston TX 77002
866 624-1520

(P-17211)
ACCELERATED ENVMTL SVCS INC
23601 Taft Hwy, Bakersfield (93311)
P.O. Box 398, Taft (93268-0398)
PHONE.................................661 765-4003
John E Neumann, *President*
Joe Hernandez, *Safety Mgr*
EMP: 53 EST: 2004
SQ FT: 25,440
SALES (est): 1.9MM **Privately Held**
WEB: www.ae-as.com
SIC: 7349 Cleaning service, industrial or
commercial

(P-17212)
ADVANCED CLNROOM MCRCLEAN CORP
Also Called: A C M
3250 S Susan St Ste A, Santa Ana
(92704-6807)
PHONE.................................714 751-1152
Janet Ford, *CEO*
David Agostine, *COO*
Daniel M Brandt, *Vice Pres*
Brian Enright, *General Mgr*
Stephen Shukur, *Sales Executive*
▲ EMP: 200 EST: 1982
SQ FT: 3,500
SALES (est): 19.6MM **Privately Held**
WEB: www.advancedcleanroom.com
SIC: 7349 8734 Cleaning service, indus-
trial or commercial; testing laboratories

(P-17213)
ALL-RITE LEASING COMPANY INC
950 S Coast Dr Ste 110, Costa Mesa
(92626-1778)
PHONE.................................714 957-1822
Chris Schran, *President*
Pauline Rosenberg, *Corp Secy*
EMP: 269 EST: 1991
SALES (est): 3.2MM **Privately Held**
SIC: 7349 Building maintenance services

(P-17214)
AMERI-KLEEN
Also Called: Ameri-Kleen Building Services
1023 E Grand Ave, Arroyo Grande
(93420-2504)
PHONE.................................805 546-0706
Dan Erpenbach, *Branch Mgr*
EMP: 190 **Privately Held**
WEB: www.ameri-kleen.com
SIC: 7349 Janitorial service, contract basis
PA: Ameri-Kleen
119 W Beach St
Watsonville CA 95076

(P-17215)
ARAMARK FACILITY SERVICES LLC
941 W 35th St, Los Angeles (90007-4002)
PHONE.................................213 740-8968
Ron Cote, *Manager*
EMP: 110 **Publicly Held**
WEB: www.aramark.es
SIC: 7349 Janitorial service, contract basis
HQ: Aramark Facility Services, Llc
2400 Market St 209
Philadelphia PA 19103
215 238-3000

(P-17216)
AVALON BUILDING MAINT INC (PA)
3148 E La Palma Ave Ste A, Anaheim
(92806-2805)
PHONE.................................714 693-2407
Steve J Healis, *CEO*
Tom Poston, *CFO*
Tom Devlin, *Admin Sec*
EMP: 220 EST: 1988
SQ FT: 5,000
SALES (est): 11.1MM **Privately Held**
WEB: www.avalonbuildingmaintenance-
ie.com
SIC: 7349 Janitorial service, contract basis

(P-17217)
AVERY GROUP INC
8941 Dalton Ave, Los Angeles
(90047-3631)
PHONE.................................310 217-1070
Leatora Jefferson, *President*
Julisa Garcia, *Executive*
EMP: 300 EST: 2006 **Privately Held**
WEB: www.averygroup-inc.com
SIC: 5963 7349 Food services, direct
sales; janitorial service, contract basis

(P-17218)
BENS ASPHALT INC
2200 S Yale St, Santa Ana (92704-4404)
PHONE.................................714 540-1700
Bill Skeffington, *President*
EMP: 24 EST: 1992
SALES (est): 553.1K **Privately Held**
WEB: www.bensasphalt.com
SIC: 7349 1795 1389 Building mainte-
nance services; demolition, buildings &
other structures; construction, repair &
dismantling services

(P-17219)
BIELSKI SERVICES INC
Also Called: Bielski Window & Masonry Clng.
1200 N Lance Ln, Anaheim (92806-1812)
PHONE.................................714 630-2316
Tim Bielski, *President*
EMP: 53 EST: 1979
SQ FT: 4,500
SALES (est): 2.5MM **Privately Held**
WEB: www.bielskiservices.com
SIC: 7349 1741 Window cleaning; ma-
sonry & other stonework

(P-17220)
BRITEWORKS INC
620 N Commercial Ave, Covina
(91723-1309)
PHONE.................................626 337-0099
Anita Ron, *President*
Gracie Corona, *Office Mgr*
EMP: 75 EST: 2001
SQ FT: 4,800
SALES (est): 4.1MM **Privately Held**
WEB: www.briteworks.com
SIC: 7349 Janitorial service, contract basis

(P-17221)
C&W FACILITY SERVICES INC
Also Called: Dtz
3011 Townsgate Rd Ste 410, Westlake Vil-
lage (91361-5882)
PHONE.................................805 267-7123
EMP: 215
SALES (corp-wide): 7.8B **Privately Held**
WEB: www.cwservices.com
SIC: 7349 Janitorial service, contract basis
HQ: C&W Facility Services Inc.
140 Kendrick St Ste C120
Needham Heights MA 02494
888 751-9100

(P-17222)
CALICO BUILDING SERVICES INC
15550 Rockfield Blvd C, Irvine
(92618-2791)
PHONE.................................949 380-8707
Ron Strand, *President*
Orlando Fernandez, *Vice Pres*
Christopher Guidry, *Vice Pres*
Thomas Miquelon, *Vice Pres*
Marisa Personius, *Executive Asst*
EMP: 185 EST: 1986
SQ FT: 1,700
SALES (est): 18.1MM **Privately Held**
WEB: www.calicoweb.com
SIC: 7349 Janitorial service, contract basis

(P-17223)
CCS LOS ANGELES JANITORIAL LLC (HQ)
Also Called: Commercial Cleaning Services
16514 Arminta St, Van Nuys (91406-1744)
PHONE.................................818 455-4551
Troy Coker, *CEO*
Stephen Testa, *CFO*
EMP: 50 EST: 2013
SALES (est): 397.1K
SALES (corp-wide): 85.2MM **Privately
Held**
WEB: www.ccsbts.com
SIC: 7349 Building maintenance services
PA: Commercial Cleaning Systems, Inc.
1485 S Lipan St
Denver CO 80223
303 733-8997

(P-17224)
CCS LOS ANGELES JANITORIAL LLC
10540 Talbert Ave 300w, Fountain Valley
(92708-6027)
PHONE.................................714 966-5600
Stephen Testa, *Branch Mgr*
EMP: 3161
SALES (corp-wide): 85.2MM **Privately
Held**
SIC: 7349 Building maintenance services
HQ: Ccs Los Angeles Janitorial Llc
16514 Arminta St
Van Nuys CA 91406
818 455-4551

(P-17225)
CERTIFIED WTR DMAGE RSTRTION E
Also Called: Cwdre
5319 University Dr, Irvine (92612-2965)
PHONE.................................800 417-1776
Cyrus Fatoure, *President*
EMP: 48 EST: 2016
SALES (est): 2.7MM **Privately Held**
SIC: 7349 1389 6331 1521 Building
maintenance services; construction, repair & dismantling services; property
damage insurance; repairing fire damage,
single-family houses; construction management

(P-17226)
CHIMNEY PRODUCTS INC
11011 Glenoaks Blvd, Pacoima
(91331-1634)
PHONE.................................818 272-2011
Julian Margo, *CEO*
EMP: 15 EST: 2015
SALES (est): 597K **Privately Held**
WEB: www.chimneyproductsinc.com
SIC: 7349 3444 Chimney cleaning;
awnings & canopies

(P-17227)
CLEANING FOR KING INC
Also Called: Office Pride
720 E Center Ave Ste A, Visalia
(93292-6433)
PHONE.................................559 733-3856
Steve Smith Jr, *President*
EMP: 120 EST: 2001
SALES (est): 2.1MM **Privately Held**
WEB: www.officepride.com
SIC: 7349 Janitorial service, contract basis

P R O D U C T S & S V C S

(P-17228)
COASTAL BUILDING SERVICES INC
1433 W Central Park Ave N, Anaheim (92802-1417)
PHONE..................................714 775-2855
Hipolito G Arias, *CEO*
Brett Dunstan, *CFO*
Marina Pohl, *Office Mgr*
Dalila Baltazar, *Administration*
Alberto Melendez, *Opers Staff*
EMP: 300 **EST:** 1998
SALES (est): 8.7MM **Privately Held**
WEB: www.coastalbuildingservice.com
SIC: 7349 Janitorial service, contract basis

(P-17229)
COME LAND INC (PA)
Also Called: Come Land Maintenance Company
1419 N San Fernando Blvd, Burbank (91504-4141)
PHONE..................................818 567-2455
Grace H Lee, *President*
Robert Makowski, *Vice Pres*
William Lee, *Admin Sec*
Yessenia Echeverria, *Manager*
EMP: 334 **EST:** 2012 **Privately Held**
WEB: www.comeland.com
SIC: 7349 Janitorial service, contract basis

(P-17230)
COME LAND MAINT SVC CO INC
1419 N San Fernando Blvd # 250, Burbank (91504-4141)
PHONE..................................818 567-2455
Grace H Lee, *President*
William Lee, *Admin Sec*
EMP: 513 **EST:** 1992
SQ FT: 12,750
SALES (est): 3.9MM **Privately Held**
WEB: www.comeland.com
SIC: 7349 Janitorial service, contract basis
PA: Come Land, Inc.
1419 N San Fernando Blvd
Burbank CA 91504

(P-17231)
COMMON AREA MAINT SVCS INC (PA)
Also Called: CAM Services
21811 S Western Ave, Torrance (90501-3724)
PHONE..................................310 390-3552
Jim Swindle, *CEO*
David A Herrera, *President*
Sidney Young, *Principal*
Jeff Hellerud, *Division Mgr*
Crystal Rangel, *Admin Asst*
EMP: 91 **EST:** 1987
SALES (est): 11.6MM **Privately Held**
WEB: www.camservices.com
SIC: 7349 Janitorial service, contract basis

(P-17232)
CONTRACT SERVICES GROUP INC
Also Called: Celex Solutions
480 Capricorn St, Brea (92821-3203)
P.O. Box 8815 (92822-5815)
PHONE..................................714 582-1800
John Pearce, *CEO*
Casey Pearce, *President*
Eric Pelayo, *Manager*
EMP: 250 **EST:** 2003
SALES (est): 24.5MM **Privately Held**
WEB: www.csgcares.com
SIC: 7349 Janitorial service, contract basis

(P-17233)
CREATIVE MAINTENANCE SYSTEMS
1340 Reynolds Ave Ste 111, Irvine (92614-5503)
PHONE..................................949 852-2871
Bill Koop, *President*
Christina Alexander, *Vice Pres*
EMP: 100 **EST:** 2000
SQ FT: 2,000
SALES (est): 2.5MM **Privately Held**
WEB: www.cmsjanitorial.com
SIC: 7349 Janitorial service, contract basis

(P-17234)
CROWN BUILDING MAINTENANCE CO
Also Called: Able Building Maintenance
3300 W Macarthur Blvd, Santa Ana (92704-6804)
PHONE..................................714 434-9494
Robert Hughes, *CEO*
Robert Martinez, *Chief Engr*
EMP: 285
SALES (corp-wide): 270.5MM **Privately Held**
WEB: www.ableserve.com
SIC: 7349 Janitorial service, contract basis
PA: Crown Building Maintenance Co.
868 Folsom St
San Francisco CA 94107
415 981-8070

(P-17235)
CROWN ENERGY SERVICES INC
Also Called: Able Engineering Services
2601 S Fgroa St Bldg Fl 1, Los Angeles (90007)
PHONE..................................213 765-7800
Ed Figueroa, *Manager*
Bill Paxton, *Engineer*
EMP: 698 **Privately Held**
WEB: www.ableserve.com
SIC: 7349 Janitorial service, contract basis
PA: Crown Energy Services, Inc.
868 Folsom St
San Francisco CA 94107

(P-17236)
CROWN FACILITY SOLUTIONS
3617 W Macarthur Blvd, Santa Ana (92704-6847)
PHONE..................................657 266-0821
Brent Shears, *President*
EMP: 50 **EST:** 2018
SQ FT: 1,950
SALES (est): 1.2MM **Privately Held**
WEB: www.crownfacilitysolutions.com
SIC: 7349 Building maintenance, except repairs; janitorial service, contract basis

(P-17237)
DESERT AREA RESOURCES TRAINING (PA)
Also Called: DART
201 E Ridgecrest Blvd, Ridgecrest (93555-3919)
PHONE..................................760 375-9787
Jinny Deangelis, *CEO*
Robert Beecroft, *COO*
Jeannie Luke, *Administration*
EMP: 100 **EST:** 1961
SQ FT: 10,800
SALES (est): 2.8MM **Privately Held**
WEB: www.dartontarget.org
SIC: 5932 7349 8322 Clothing & shoes, secondhand; janitorial service, contract basis; association for the handicapped; child related social services

(P-17238)
DIMAR ENTERPRISES INC
Also Called: Drymaster
26021 Pala Ste 150, Mission Viejo (92691-2718)
PHONE..................................949 492-1100
Diane Combs, *CEO*
Crystal Heckman, *Office Mgr*
Gary Bittner, *Director*
Kandice Larsen, *Manager*
EMP: 182 **EST:** 2014
SALES (est): 10.5MM **Privately Held**
WEB: www.drymaster.com
SIC: 7349 Building maintenance services

(P-17239)
DMS FACILITY SERVICES INC
2861 E Coronado St, Anaheim (92806-2504)
PHONE..................................949 975-1366
Douglas Gregory, *Principal*
Justin Marchello, *Project Mgr*
Ken Cogliano, *Chief Engr*
Malhaz Dediashvili, *Teacher*
Loren Dotts, *Manager*
EMP: 1245

SALES (corp-wide): 29MM **Privately Held**
WEB: www.dmsfacilityservices.com
SIC: 7349 Janitorial service, contract basis
PA: Dms Facility Services, Inc.
1040 Arroyo Dr
South Pasadena CA 91030
626 305-8500

(P-17240)
ELITE CRAFTSMAN (PA)
Also Called: Stockmar Industrial
2763 Saint Louis Ave, Long Beach (90755-2025)
P.O. Box 90458 (90809-0458)
PHONE..................................562 989-3511
William C Stockmar, *President*
George N Negrete, *Vice Pres*
Linda Pierson, *Admin Sec*
EMP: 130 **EST:** 1972
SQ FT: 10,000
SALES (est): 7.8MM **Privately Held**
SIC: 7349 Building maintenance services

(P-17241)
EMPIRE BUILDING SERVICES INC
1570 E Edinger Ave Ste D, Santa Ana (92705-4909)
P.O. Box 26, Tustin (92781-0026)
PHONE..................................714 836-7700
Suzanne De Rossett, *President*
Rebecca Ewald, *Executive*
Rebecca Johnson, *Representative*
EMP: 62 **EST:** 1980
SALES (est): 11.6MM **Privately Held**
WEB: www.ebuildingservices.com
SIC: 7349 Janitorial service, contract basis

(P-17242)
FAME SYSTEMS INC
301 Hearst Dr, Oxnard (93030-5158)
PHONE..................................805 485-0808
Sal Mejia, *President*
Jesus Mejia, *Vice Pres*
EMP: 50 **EST:** 2006 **Privately Held**
WEB: www.famesystemsinc.com
SIC: 7349 Janitorial service, contract basis

(P-17243)
FLUOR INDUSTRIAL SERVICES INC
1 Enterprise, Aliso Viejo (92656-2606)
PHONE..................................949 439-2000
▲ **EMP:** 101 **EST:** 1986
SALES (est): 4.8MM
SALES (corp-wide): 15.6B **Publicly Held**
WEB: www.fluor.com
SIC: 7349 Building maintenance services
HQ: Fluor Enterprises, Inc.
6700 Las Colinas Blvd
Irving TX 75039
469 398-7000

(P-17244)
GAMBOA SERVICE INC
Also Called: Corporate Image Maintenance
2116 S Wright St, Santa Ana (92705-5314)
PHONE..................................714 966-5325
Gilbert Gamboa, *President*
EMP: 55 **EST:** 1998
SQ FT: 2,800
SALES (est): 1.9MM **Privately Held**
SIC: 7349 Janitorial service, contract basis

(P-17245)
GARDEN GROVE UNIFIED SCHL DST
Also Called: Maintenance Department
8211 Lampson Ave, Garden Grove (92841-3115)
PHONE..................................714 663-6185
Casey Pijl, *Manager*
Dante Urzua, *Teacher*
EMP: 62
SALES (corp-wide): 658.3MM **Privately Held**
WEB: www.ggusd.us
SIC: 8211 7349 Public elementary & secondary schools; building maintenance services
PA: Garden Grove Unified School District
10331 Stanford Ave
Garden Grove CA 92840
714 663-6000

(P-17246)
GHOSSAIN & TRUELOCK ENTPS INC
Also Called: Custom Service Systems
783 Palmyrita Ave Ste A, Riverside (92507-1817)
P.O. Box 5596 (92517-5596)
PHONE..................................951 781-9345
Donna Little, *CEO*
Kenneth Truelock, *President*
David L Truelock, *CEO*
Robert K Ghossain, *Bd of Directors*
EMP: 50 **EST:** 1974
SALES (est): 3MM **Privately Held**
SIC: 7349 Janitorial service, contract basis

(P-17247)
GLOBAL BUILDING SERVICES INC (PA)
27433 Tourney Rd Ste 280, Valencia (91355-5619)
PHONE..................................800 675-6643
Julio Belloso, *President*
Eddie Gaitan, *Director*
Mike Lewis, *Supervisor*
EMP: 907 **EST:** 1986
SALES (est): 19.7MM **Privately Held**
WEB: www.globalbuildingservices.com
SIC: 7349 Janitorial service, contract basis

(P-17248)
HARBOR BUILDING SERVICES
2761 Plaza Del Amo # 901, Torrance (90503-7320)
PHONE..................................310 320-2966
Peter Lescord, *Owner*
EMP: 86 **EST:** 1994
SALES (est): 2.3MM **Privately Held**
WEB: www.harborbldgservices.com
SIC: 7349 Janitorial service, contract basis

(P-17249)
HAYNES BUILDING SERVICE LLC
16027 Arrow Hwy Ste I, Baldwin Park (91706-2064)
PHONE..................................626 359-6100
John P Scharler, *President*
Michael Franco, *Vice Pres*
EMP: 175 **EST:** 1982
SQ FT: 20,000
SALES (est): 4.6MM **Privately Held**
WEB: www.haynesservices.com
SIC: 7349 Janitorial service, contract basis

(P-17250)
HUNTER EASTERDAY CORPORATION
1475 N Hundley St, Anaheim (92806-1323)
PHONE..................................714 238-3400
Sam Easterday, *CEO*
Manny Jones, *President*
Joanne Easterday, *CFO*
Gilbert Anzaldua, *Vice Pres*
EMP: 135 **EST:** 1976
SQ FT: 4,400
SALES (est): 6.1MM **Privately Held**
WEB: www.ebmcorp.com
SIC: 7349 5087 Janitorial service, contract basis; building maintenance, except repairs; janitors' supplies

(P-17251)
INNOVATIONS BUILDING SVCS LLC
402 S Orange Ave Apt D, Monterey Park (91755-7554)
PHONE..................................323 787-6068
Helbert Daniel Torres, *Principal*
EMP: 100 **EST:** 2016
SALES (est): 1MM **Privately Held**
WEB:
www.innovationsbuildingservices.com
SIC: 7349 Janitorial service, contract basis

(P-17252)
J & S BUILDING MAINTENANCE INC
Also Called: J&S Janitorial Services
7400 E Slauson Ave Ste 3w, Commerce (90040-3308)
PHONE..................................562 714-4033
Carolina Alvarez, *President*
EMP: 50 **EST:** 2016

SALES (est): 2.5MM **Privately Held**
SIC: 7349 7389 Janitorial service, contract basis; building cleaning service; cleaning service, industrial or commercial; building maintenance, except repairs;

(P-17253)
JAN PRO CLG SYSTEMS STHERN CAL
Also Called: Jan-Pro Cleaning Systems
2401 E Katella Ave # 525, Anaheim (92806-5939)
PHONE...................................714 220-0500
Dave Rhodes, *Manager*
EMP: 50
SALES (corp-wide): 2.8MM **Privately Held**
WEB: www.jan-pro.com
SIC: 7349 5087 Janitorial service, contract basis; service establishment equipment
PA: Jan Pro Cleaning Systems Of Southern California
3875 Hopyard Rd Ste 194
Pleasanton CA 94588
714 220-0500

(P-17254)
JANITORIAL EQUIPMENT SVCS INC
Also Called: King Janitorial Equipment Svcs
11752 Garden Grove Blvd, Garden Grove (92843-1423)
PHONE...................................951 205-8937
Javier Brito, *CFO*
EMP: 55 EST: 2010 **Privately Held**
SIC: 7349 Janitorial service, contract basis

(P-17255)
K & P JANITORIAL SERVICES
412 S Pcf Cast Hwy Ste 20, Redondo Beach (90277)
PHONE...................................310 540-8878
Kelly Lynch, *President*
Beth Lynch, *Controller*
EMP: 100 EST: 1991
SALES (est): 3.2MM **Privately Held**
WEB: www.kandpjanitorial.com
SIC: 7349 Janitorial service, contract basis

(P-17256)
LANDMARK SERVICES INC
410 N Fairview St, Santa Ana (92703-3412)
PHONE...................................714 547-6308
Dan Rogers, *President*
EMP: 60 EST: 2000
SQ FT: 130,000
SALES (est): 4.1MM **Privately Held**
WEB: www.landmarkservices.com
SIC: 7349 Janitorial service, contract basis

(P-17257)
LEES MAINTENANCE SERVICE INC
14740 Keswick St, Van Nuys (91405-1205)
PHONE...................................818 988-6644
Tyrone P Ingram, *President*
Jutta Doerrstein, *Bookkeeper*
EMP: 275 EST: 1961
SQ FT: 3,000
SALES (est): 9.1MM **Privately Held**
WEB: www.leesmaint.com
SIC: 7349 5087 Janitorial service, contract basis; laundry & dry cleaning equipment & supplies

(P-17258)
M-N-Z JANITORIAL SERVICES INC
2109 W Burbank Blvd, Burbank (91506-1231)
PHONE...................................323 851-4115
Marc De Mauregne, *Exec VP*
Dennis Krebs, *Shareholder*
Zorina Russell Kroop, *President*
Gene Figueroa, *Project Mgr*
George Buendia, *Supervisor*
EMP: 110 EST: 1979
SQ FT: 1,000
SALES (est): 5MM **Privately Held**
WEB: www.mnz.com
SIC: 7349 1799 Building maintenance, except repairs; construction site cleanup

(P-17259)
MASTER & SONS INC
Also Called: ServiceMaster
24922 Anza Dr Ste B, Valencia (91355-1231)
PHONE...................................661 299-9090
Wayne Neyhart, *President*
EMP: 56 EST: 1989
SALES (est): 869.3K **Privately Held**
WEB: www.servicemaster.com
SIC: 7349 Building maintenance services

(P-17260)
MERCHANTS BUILDING MAINT CO
1639 E Edinger Ave Ste C, Santa Ana (92705-5013)
PHONE...................................714 973-9272
George Rodriguez, *Branch Mgr*
EMP: 81
SALES (corp-wide): 79.3MM **Privately Held**
WEB: www.mbmonline.com
SIC: 7349 Janitorial service, contract basis
PA: Merchants Building Maintenance Company
1190 Monterey Pass Rd
Monterey Park CA 91754
323 881-6701

(P-17261)
MERCHANTS BUILDING MAINT CO (PA)
1190 Monterey Pass Rd, Monterey Park (91754-3615)
PHONE...................................323 881-6701
Theodore Haas, *CEO*
David Haas, *President*
Karen T Haas, *Treasurer*
Krista M Haas, *Vice Pres*
Adam Navarrette, *Vice Pres*
EMP: 1576 EST: 1961
SQ FT: 8,000
SALES (est): 79.3MM **Privately Held**
WEB: www.mbmonline.com
SIC: 7349 Janitorial service, contract basis

(P-17262)
MERCHANTS BUILDING MAINT CO
1995 W Holt Ave, Pomona (91768-3352)
PHONE...................................909 622-8260
Angel Meza, *Branch Mgr*
EMP: 81
SALES (corp-wide): 79.3MM **Privately Held**
WEB: www.mbmonline.com
SIC: 7349 7381 Janitorial service, contract basis; security guard service
PA: Merchants Building Maintenance Company
1190 Monterey Pass Rd
Monterey Park CA 91754
323 881-6701

(P-17263)
MERCHANTS BUILDING MAINT CO
606 Monterey Paca Rd 20, Monterey Park (91754)
PHONE...................................323 881-8902
Michael Anthony Palma,
Marco Ferrel, *Vice Pres*
Amanda Haas, *Business Dir*
Shenny Reyes, *CTO*
Karla Martinez, *Project Mgr*
EMP: 130
SALES (corp-wide): 79.3MM **Privately Held**
WEB: www.mbmonline.com
SIC: 7349 7381 Janitorial service, contract basis; detective & armored car services
PA: Merchants Building Maintenance Company
1190 Monterey Pass Rd
Monterey Park CA 91754
323 881-6701

(P-17264)
MIDA INDUSTRIES INC
6101 Obispo Ave, Long Beach (90805-3799)
PHONE...................................562 616-1020
Michael T Drake, *President*
John Durfee, *President*

Dawit Kidane, *CFO*
John Valencia, *Vice Pres*
EMP: 250
SQ FT: 10,000
SALES (est): 14.9MM **Privately Held**
WEB: www.midaindustries.com
SIC: 7349 1799 Janitorial service, contract basis; asbestos removal & encapsulation

(P-17265)
MINTIE CORPORATION (PA)
Also Called: Mintie Technologies
777 N Georgia Ave, Azusa (91702-2207)
PHONE...................................323 225-4111
Kevin J Mintie, *CEO*
James M Mintie, *Exec VP*
Ambar Torres, *Admin Asst*
Jim Bieritz, *Sales Staff*
EMP: 138 EST: 1940
SALES (est): 12.6MM **Privately Held**
WEB: www.mintie.com
SIC: 7349 Building cleaning service

(P-17266)
ONE SILVER SERVE INC
Also Called: SERVPRO Encino/Sherman Oaks
17835 Ventura Blvd # 108, Encino (91316-3667)
PHONE...................................818 995-6444
Alan Reed, *CEO*
Artemio Diaz, *Technician*
EMP: 50 EST: 2005
SALES (est): 5.8MM **Privately Held**
WEB:
www.servproencinoshermanoaks.com
SIC: 7349 Building maintenance services

(P-17267)
OPEN AMERICA INC
Also Called: Openworks
4300 Long Beach Blvd # 45, Long Beach (90807-2011)
PHONE...................................562 428-9210
John Palmer, *Branch Mgr*
EMP: 125
SALES (corp-wide): 25.6MM **Privately Held**
WEB: www.openworksweb.com
SIC: 7349 Janitorial service, contract basis
PA: O.P.E.N. America, Inc.
4742 N 24th St Ste 450
Phoenix AZ 85016
602 224-0440

(P-17268)
PACIFIC BUILDING CARE INC (PA)
3001 Red Hill Ave 6-210, Costa Mesa (92626-4529)
PHONE...................................949 261-1234
Ian Bress, *CEO*
Ted Geissler, *President*
Holly Papa, *Treasurer*
Jennifer Corbett, *Vice Pres*
Jesus Guerrero, *Vice Pres*
EMP: 310 EST: 1970
SQ FT: 5,200
SALES (est): 21MM **Privately Held**
WEB: www.occhildcarecouncil.org
SIC: 7349 Building cleaning service; building maintenance, except repairs

(P-17269)
PACIFIC BUILDING MAINT INC
Also Called: Servicmster Clean By Integrity
130 Garden St Ste B, Santa Barbara (93101-1832)
PHONE...................................805 969-5221
EMP: 64
SALES (corp-wide): 5.6MM **Privately Held**
WEB:
www.pacificbuildingmaintenance.com
SIC: 7349 Building Maintenance Services
PA: Pacific Building Maintenance, Inc.
1601 Ives Ave Ste E
Oxnard CA 93033
805 642-0214

(P-17270)
PACIFIC BUILDING MAINT INC (PA)
Also Called: Servicmster Clean By Integrity
1601 Ives Ave Ste E, Oxnard (93033-1908)
PHONE...................................805 642-0214

Aaron Shia, *President*
Aaron Shiah, *President*
EMP: 88 EST: 2002
SQ FT: 1,600
SALES (est): 4.4MM **Privately Held**
WEB:
www.pacificbuildingmaintenance.com
SIC: 7349 Janitorial service, contract basis

(P-17271)
PASADENA UNIFIED SCHOOL DST
Also Called: District Service
740 W Woodbury Rd, Pasadena (91104)
PHONE...................................626 798-9171
Mark Gutheinz, *Director*
Nadia Zendejas, *Exec Sec*
EMP: 60
SALES (corp-wide): 275.4MM **Privately Held**
WEB: www.pusd.us
SIC: 8211 7349 Public elementary & secondary schools; building maintenance, except repairs
PA: Pasadena Unified School District
351 S Hudson Ave
Pasadena CA 91101
626 396-3600

(P-17272)
PEERLESS MAINTENANCE SVC INC
1100 S Euclid St, La Habra (90631-6807)
P.O. Box 3900 (90632-3900)
PHONE...................................714 871-3380
Linda Gabriel, *President*
David Gabriel, *Corp Secy*
Ralph Dergazarian, *Vice Pres*
Deanne Louise, *Cust Mgr*
Deanne Derg, *Manager*
EMP: 300 EST: 1979
SQ FT: 2,000
SALES (est): 8.8MM **Privately Held**
WEB: www.peerlesssvc.com
SIC: 7349 Janitorial service, contract basis

(P-17273)
PERFORMANCE BUILDING SERVICES
Also Called: Performance Cleanroom Services
22642 Lambert St Ste 409, Lake Forest (92630-1645)
PHONE...................................949 364-4364
James Chriss, *President*
Robert Lynch, *Vice Pres*
Ron Matthews, *Vice Pres*
Jacque Argil, *Office Mgr*
Jesse Cayetano, *Opers-Prdtn-Mfg*
EMP: 104 EST: 2001
SALES (est): 5.7MM **Privately Held**
WEB: www.performance-now.com
SIC: 7349 7699 Janitorial service, contract basis; cleaning services

(P-17274)
PERSONAL TOUCH CLG & MAINT INC (PA)
340 Goddard, Irvine (92618-4601)
PHONE...................................949 727-4135
Patrick Obrien, *President*
Mary O'Brien, *Vice Pres*
Bianka Sandoval, *Mktg Coord*
EMP: 77 EST: 1984
SALES (est): 6.6MM **Privately Held**
WEB: www.ptchoa.com
SIC: 7349 Janitorial service, contract basis

(P-17275)
PLATINUM CLG INDIANAPOLIS LLC
1522 2nd St, Santa Monica (90401-2303)
PHONE...................................310 584-8000
William Hertz,
Sally Lockett, *Property Mgr*
Mike Hodges, *Maint Spvr*
Bernardine Baca, *Manager*
Stephanie Farnan, *Manager*
EMP: 460 EST: 2008
SALES (est): 10.8MM **Privately Held**
SIC: 7349 Building & office cleaning services

(P-17276)
PRIORITY BUILDING SERVICES LLC (PA)
Also Called: Priority Landscape Services
521 Mercury Ln, Brea (92821-4831)
PHONE...................................714 255-2940
Simon Rocha, *President*
Eddie Rocha, *Regional Mgr*
David Kraushaar, *Sales Mgr*
Scott Nankervis,
EMP: 321 EST: 2004
SQ FT: 6,000
SALES (est): 21.1MM **Privately Held**
WEB: www.priorityservices.net
SIC: 7349 Janitorial service, contract basis

(P-17277)
PRO BUILDING MAINTENANCE INC
149 N Maple St Ste H, Corona (92878-3273)
PHONE...................................951 279-3386
Carl Hoff, *CEO*
Christina L Hoff, *Principal*
Sara Johns, *Office Mgr*
Jackie Troglia, *Representative*
EMP: 120 EST: 2006
SQ FT: 1,600 **Privately Held**
WEB: www.probuildingmaintenance.com
SIC: 7349 Janitorial service, contract basis

(P-17278)
PRONTO JANITORIAL SERVICES INC
12561 Persing Dr, Whittier (90606-2713)
PHONE...................................562 273-5997
Edgar Rodas, *President*
EMP: 80 EST: 2019
SALES (est): 959.8K **Privately Held**
SIC: 7349 Janitorial service, contract basis

(P-17279)
PROPERTY CARE BUILDING SVC LLC
126 La Porte St Ste F, Arcadia (91006-7190)
P.O. Box 661690 (91066-1690)
PHONE...................................626 623-6420
Everardo Amezcua,
Victoria Amezcua, *Vice Pres*
EMP: 26 EST: 2013
SALES (est): 820.1K **Privately Held**
WEB: www.propertycarebuildingservice.com
SIC: 7349 2842 7342 Janitorial service, contract basis; sanitation preparations, disinfectants & deodorants; disinfecting services

(P-17280)
RANSCAPES INC
30 Hughes Ste 209, Irvine (92618-1916)
P.O. Box 50580 (92619-0580)
PHONE...................................866 883-9297
Ran Tomaino, *President*
Susan Tomaino, *Corp Secy*
Daniel Martin, *IT/INT Sup*
Joel Conchas, *Project Mgr*
EMP: 50 EST: 2010
SQ FT: 2,000
SALES (est): 7.6MM **Privately Held**
WEB: www.ranscapes.com
SIC: 7349 Janitorial service, contract basis

(P-17281)
RESOURCE COLLECTION INC
Also Called: Command Guard Services
3771 W 242nd St Ste 205, Torrance (90505-6566)
PHONE...................................310 219-3272
Martin Benom, *Ch of Bd*
Steven Jacobson, *Corp Secy*
Paula Benom, *Vice Pres*
Marilyn Jacobson, *Vice Pres*
EMP: 58 EST: 1962
SQ FT: 15,000
SALES (est): 2MM **Privately Held**
WEB: www.resourcecollection.com
SIC: 7349 7381 0782 3564 Air duct cleaning; guard services; lawn & garden services; air cleaning systems

(P-17282)
SCV FACILITIES SERVICES INC
1907 W 75th St, Los Angeles (90047-2325)
PHONE...................................310 803-4588
Samuel Valdez, *Owner*
EMP: 72 EST: 2013
SALES (est): 1.6MM **Privately Held**
WEB: www.scvfs.com
SIC: 7349 7389 Janitorial service, contract basis; cleaning service, industrial or commercial;

(P-17283)
SERVICEMASTER BY BEST PROS INC
6474 Western Ave, Riverside (92505-2130)
PHONE...................................951 515-9051
Filip Busuioc, *CEO*
EMP: 99 EST: 2018
SALES (est): 1.2MM **Privately Held**
WEB: www.servicemaster.com
SIC: 7349 1799 Building maintenance services; construction site cleanup

(P-17284)
SITE CREW INC
3185 Airway Ave Ste G, Costa Mesa (92626-4601)
PHONE...................................714 668-0100
Tina Manavi, *CEO*
Maria Candle, *Manager*
EMP: 300 EST: 2005
SQ FT: 2,160
SALES (est): 10.9MM **Privately Held**
WEB: www.sitecrewinc.com
SIC: 7349 Janitorial service, contract basis

(P-17285)
SKYLSTAD-SCHOELEN CO INC
Also Called: ServiceMaster
3130 Skyway Dr Ste 701, Santa Maria (93455-1800)
PHONE...................................805 349-0503
Jeffrey Hopson, *CEO*
Nicole Southaphanh, *Bookkeeper*
EMP: 64 EST: 1980
SALES (est): 760K **Privately Held**
WEB: www.servicemaster.com
SIC: 7349 Building maintenance services

(P-17286)
SO CAL LAND MAINTENANCE INC
3121 E La Palma Ave Ste K, Anaheim (92806-2804)
PHONE...................................714 231-1454
Stephen Guise, *Principal*
EMP: 72 EST: 2011
SALES (est): 3.7MM **Privately Held**
SIC: 7349 Building maintenance services

(P-17287)
SOUTHERN COUNTIES BLDG MAINT (PA)
1035 N Armando St Ste F, Anaheim (92806-2607)
PHONE...................................805 928-9900
Ruben Garcia, *President*
EMP: 125 EST: 1978
SALES (est): 4MM **Privately Held**
SIC: 7349 Janitorial service, contract basis

(P-17288)
SOUTHERN MANAGEMENT CORP
808 S Olive St, Los Angeles (90014-3006)
PHONE...................................213 312-2268
EMP: 127
SALES (corp-wide): 5.9B **Publicly Held**
SIC: 7349 Building maintenance services
HQ: Southern Management Corp.
6478e Highway 90
Milton FL 32570

(P-17289)
TCI SUPPLY INC
121 E 18th St, Los Angeles (90015-3648)
PHONE...................................213 745-7756
Isidro Rojas Benitez, *CEO*
EMP: 26 EST: 2003
SALES (est): 265.7K **Privately Held**
WEB:
SIC: 7349 2674 Janitorial service, contract basis; bags: uncoated paper & multiwall

(P-17290)
TIM HOFER INC
Also Called: Environment Control
148 N Akers St, Visalia (93291-5121)
P.O. Box 6445 (93290-6445)
PHONE...................................559 732-6676
Timothy Hofer, *President*
Suzanne Hofer, *Admin Sec*
EMP: 103 EST: 1984
SQ FT: 5,700
SALES (est): 2.6MM **Privately Held**
WEB: www.environmentcontrol.com
SIC: 7349 Janitorial service, contract basis

(P-17291)
TRIANGLE SERVICES INC
7032 Comstock Ave Ste 207, Whittier (90602-1390)
PHONE...................................562 696-0712
EMP: 63 **Privately Held**
WEB: www.triangleservices.com
SIC: 7349 Janitorial service, contract basis
PA: Triangle Services, Inc.
10 5th St Ste 200
Valley Stream NY 11581

(P-17292)
TRICOM SERVICE CORP (PA)
2384 -1801 W Olympic Blvd, Pasadena (91199-0001)
PHONE...................................888 415-6911
Ian Hodge, *President*
EMP: 50 EST: 2020
SALES (est): 500K **Privately Held**
WEB: www.tricomservice.com
SIC: 7349 Janitorial service, contract basis

(P-17293)
TSCM CORPORATION
17791 Jamestown Ln, Huntington Beach (92647-7134)
PHONE...................................714 841-1988
Margaret Pappano, *President*
Frank Pappano, *Vice Pres*
Jacki Wun, *Office Mgr*
Paul Abler, *Opers Staff*
Mendez Carlos, *Opers Staff*
EMP: 55 EST: 1986
SALES (est): 4MM **Privately Held**
WEB: www.tscmcorp.com
SIC: 7349 1799 Cleaning service, industrial or commercial; steam cleaning of building exteriors

(P-17294)
TUTTLE FAMILY ENTERPRISES INC
Also Called: Peerless Building Maint Co
9510 Topanga Canyon Blvd, Chatsworth (91311-4011)
PHONE...................................818 534-2566
Tim Tuttle, *CEO*
EMP: 350 EST: 1948
SALES (est): 10.9MM **Privately Held**
SIC: 7349 Building maintenance, except repairs

(P-17295)
ULTIMATE MAINTENANCE SVCS INC
4237 Redondo Beach Blvd, Lawndale (90260-3341)
PHONE...................................310 542-1474
Paul Marmol, *President*
Claudia Salomon, *CFO*
Sherly Garcia,
EMP: 50
SALES (est): 2.2MM **Privately Held**
WEB: www.umscorporation.com
SIC: 7349 Janitorial service, contract basis

(P-17296)
UNISERVE FACILITIES SVCS CORP (PA)
Also Called: Union Building Maintenance
2363 S Atlantic Blvd, Commerce (90040-1256)
PHONE...................................213 533-1000
Sam M Hwang, *Ch of Bd*
Anthony Santana, *COO*
Marlene Gatica, *Admin Asst*
Frank Maldonado, *CIO*
Casimiro Pascual, *Opers Staff*
EMP: 500 EST: 1966

SQ FT: 5,000
SALES (est): 16.3MM **Privately Held**
WEB: www.uniservecorp.com
SIC: 7349 Janitorial service, contract basis

(P-17297)
UNISERVE FACILITIES SVCS CORP
1200 Getty Center Dr, Los Angeles (90049-1657)
PHONE...................................310 440-6747
F Jackson, *Opers Staff*
EMP: 325
SALES (corp-wide): 16.3MM **Privately Held**
WEB: www.uniservecorp.com
SIC: 7349 Janitorial service, contract basis
PA: Uniserve Facilities Services Corporation
2363 S Atlantic Blvd
Commerce CA 90040
213 533-1000

(P-17298)
UNIVERSAL SERVICES AMERICA LP
1815 E Wilshire Ave # 91, Santa Ana (92705-4646)
PHONE...................................714 923-3700
Mark Olivas, *Branch Mgr*
EMP: 999
SALES (corp-wide): 8.6B **Privately Held**
WEB: www.legacy.aus.com
SIC: 7349 Janitorial service, contract basis
HQ: Universal Services Of America, Lp
1551 N Tustin Ave Fl 6
Santa Ana CA 92705
866 877-1965

(P-17299)
US METRO GROUP INC
Also Called: Metro Building Maintenance
135 S State College Blvd, Brea (92821-5823)
PHONE...................................213 382-6435
Brian Lee, *President*
Evelyn Kim, *CEO*
Jennifer Park, *CFO*
Philip Gregg, *General Mgr*
Jose Alcala, *Opers Staff*
EMP: 800 EST: 1998
SQ FT: 40,000
SALES (est): 37.1MM **Privately Held**
WEB: www.usmetrogroup.com
SIC: 7349 Janitorial service, contract basis

(P-17300)
VARSITY CONTRACTORS INC
24155 Laguna Hills Mall, Laguna Hills (92653-3667)
PHONE...................................949 586-8283
EMP: 118
SALES (corp-wide): 620.5MM **Privately Held**
WEB: www.varsityfs.com
SIC: 7349 Janitorial service, contract basis
HQ: Varsity Contractors, Inc.
1055 S 3600 W Ste 101
Salt Lake City UT 84104
208 232-8598

(P-17301)
WURMS JANITORIAL SERVICE INC
544 Bateman Cir, Corona (92878-4011)
PHONE...................................951 582-0003
Larry Stewart, *President*
Pam Costa, *Vice Pres*
EMP: 80 EST: 1986
SALES (est): 2.3MM **Privately Held**
WEB: www.wurmsjanitorialservices.com
SIC: 7349 Janitorial service, contract basis

7352 Medical Eqpt Rental & Leasing

(P-17302)
APRIA HEALTHCARE LLC (DH)
26220 Enterprise Ct, Lake Forest (92630-8405)
P.O. Box 610 (92609-0610)
PHONE...................................949 639-2000
Daniel J Stark, *CEO*

Donna Blake, *President*
Matt Gallagher, *President*
Stephanie Christensen, *COO*
Debra Morris, *CFO*
◆ **EMP:** 350 **EST:** 1984
SALES (est): 1B
SALES (corp-wide): 1.1B **Publicly Held**
WEB: www.apria.com
SIC: 7352 5999 5047 Medical equipment rental; medical apparatus & supplies; hospital equipment & furniture

(P-17303)
OPTION ONE HOME MED EQP INC
1220 Research Dr Ste A, Redlands (92374-4563)
P.O. Box 40700, Mesa AZ (85274-0700)
PHONE..............................909 478-5413
David Scheven, *CEO*
▲ **EMP:** 54 **EST:** 1981
SQ FT: 36,000
SALES (est): 3.3MM **Privately Held**
WEB: www.optiononehomemedical.com
SIC: 7352 5999 Medical equipment rental; medical apparatus & supplies

---

7353 Heavy Construction Eqpt Rental & Leasing

(P-17304)
AL ASHER & SONS INC
5301 Valley Blvd, Los Angeles (90032-3930)
PHONE..............................800 896-2480
James A Asher, *CEO*
Robert L Asher, *Treasurer*
◆ **EMP:** 25 **EST:** 1914
SQ FT: 80,000
SALES (est): 9.5MM **Privately Held**
WEB: www.alasher.com
SIC: 5511 7353 3531 Trucks, tractors & trailers: new & used; heavy construction equipment rental; construction machinery

(P-17305)
BIGRENTZ INC (PA)
Also Called: Bigrentz.com
1063 Mcgaw Ave Ste 200, Irvine (92614-5553)
PHONE..............................855 999-5438
Scott Cannon, *CEO*
Dallas Imbimbo, *Ch of Bd*
Neda Imbimbo, *CFO*
Stephen Jesson, *Exec VP*
Nicholas Kovacevich, *Vice Pres*
EMP: 54 **EST:** 2012
SQ FT: 15,852
SALES (est): 31.8MM **Privately Held**
WEB: www.bigrentz.com
SIC: 7353 Earth moving equipment, rental or leasing

(P-17306)
BRAGG INVESTMENT COMPANY INC (PA)
Also Called: Bragg Crane & Rigging
6251 N Paramount Blvd, Long Beach (90805-3713)
P.O. Box 727 (90801-0727)
PHONE..............................562 984-2400
M Scott Bragg, *President*
Ian Johnson, *COO*
Dennis Ferguson, *CFO*
Mike Roy, *Exec VP*
Herman Buck Baird, *Vice Pres*
◆ **EMP:** 300 **EST:** 1946
SQ FT: 50,000
SALES (est): 489.5MM **Privately Held**
WEB: www.braggequipment.com
SIC: 7353 4213 7389 1791 Cranes & aerial lift equipment, rental or leasing; heavy hauling; crane & aerial lift service; structural steel erection

(P-17307)
DOWNS EQUIPMENT RENTALS INC (PA)
4800 Saco Rd, Bakersfield (93308-9626)
P.O. Box 80536 (93380-0536)
PHONE..............................661 615-6119
Gordon L Downs, *President*
Joyce M Downs, *Vice Pres*

Robert Battiston, *Executive*
Tim Burns, *Opers Mgr*
Kristine Hudson, *Opers Staff*
EMP: 78 **EST:** 1976
SALES (est): 11.1MM **Privately Held**
WEB: www.downsequip.com
SIC: 7353 1794 Earth moving equipment, rental or leasing; excavation work

(P-17308)
EXTERRAN INC
3449 Santa Anita Ave, El Monte (91731-2424)
PHONE..............................626 455-0739
EMP: 51
SALES (corp-wide): 3.1B **Publicly Held**
SIC: 7353 Heavy Construction Equipment Rental
HQ: Exterran, Inc.
16666 Northchase Dr
Houston TX 77060
281 836-7000

(P-17309)
GLOBAL RENTAL CO INC
1253 Price Ave, Pomona (91767-5839)
PHONE..............................909 469-5160
James Dixon, *Branch Mgr*
EMP: 107
SALES (corp-wide): 1.2B **Privately Held**
WEB: www.globalrental.com
SIC: 7353 5082 Heavy construction equipment rental; contractors' materials
HQ: Global Rental Co., Inc.
33 Inverness Center Pkwy # 250
Hoover AL 35242

(P-17310)
HARBOR INDUSTRIAL SERVICES
211 N Marine Ave, Wilmington (90744-5724)
PHONE..............................310 522-1193
W Michael Hawk, *President*
Maria Gray, *Officer*
Steve Hessenauer, *VP Bus Dvlpt*
Phil Torrano, *Maintence Staff*
▲ **EMP:** 80 **EST:** 1993
SALES (est): 10.7MM **Privately Held**
WEB: www.harborindustrial.com
SIC: 7353 Cranes & aerial lift equipment, rental or leasing

(P-17311)
KING EQUIPMENT LLC
1690 Ashley Way, Colton (92324-4000)
PHONE..............................909 986-5300
Ernie Quijada,
Sydney Reitz, *General Mgr*
Casey Wheeler, *Admin Asst*
Ronnie Kozna, *Info Tech Mgr*
Jennifer Waltman, *Credit Mgr*
EMP: 73 **EST:** 2007
SALES (est): 9.4MM **Privately Held**
WEB: www.sunbeltrentals.com
SIC: 7353 Heavy construction equipment rental

(P-17312)
NATIONAL BUSINESS GROUP INC (PA)
Also Called: National Tube & Steel
15319 Chatsworth St, Mission Hills (91345-2040)
PHONE..............................818 221-6000
James Mooneyham, *President*
EMP: 85 **EST:** 1985
SQ FT: 24,000
SALES (est): 123.1MM **Privately Held**
SIC: 7353 5039 7359 3496 Earth moving equipment, rental or leasing; wire fence, gates & accessories; garage facility & tool rental; fencing, made from purchased wire; utility trailer rental

(P-17313)
NATIONAL TRENCH SAFETY LLC
Also Called: Trench Plate Rental
13217 Laureldale Ave, Downey (90242-5140)
PHONE..............................562 602-1642
Dexter Poston, *Branch Mgr*
EMP: 185

SALES (corp-wide): 104MM **Privately Held**
WEB: www.ntsafety.com
SIC: 7353 Heavy construction equipment rental
PA: National Trench Safety, Llc
260 N Sam Houston Pkwy E
Houston TX 77060
832 200-0988

(P-17314)
NOBLE RENTS INC
8314 Slauson Ave, Pico Rivera (90660-4323)
PHONE..............................855 767-4424
Nabil Kassam, *CEO*
Suzy Taherian, *Corp Secy*
EMP: 65 **EST:** 2011
SQ FT: 62,766
SALES (est): 6.2MM **Privately Held**
WEB: www.nobleiron.com
SIC: 7353 Heavy construction equipment rental

(P-17315)
NORTHWEST EXCAVATING INC
18201 Napa St, Northridge (91325-3374)
PHONE..............................818 349-5861
Susan Groff, *CEO*
Robbie Groff, *Vice Pres*
Cecille Bandalaria, *Executive Asst*
Richard Marshall, *Controller*
Jane Sotto, *Controller*
EMP: 72 **EST:** 1959
SQ FT: 2,500
SALES (est): 9MM **Privately Held**
WEB: www.nwexc.com
SIC: 7353 1794 Heavy construction equipment rental; excavation & grading, building construction

(P-17316)
OFFSHORE CRANE & SERVICE CO (PA)
Also Called: T & T Truck & Crane Service
1375 N Olive St Ste A, Ventura (93001-1375)
P.O. Box 1748 (93002-1748)
PHONE..............................805 648-3348
Earl G Holder, *CEO*
Tim Holder, *President*
Kimberly A Loft, *Treasurer*
Shawn Paul, *Vice Pres*
Tracy Everett, *Sales Staff*
EMP: 52
SQ FT: 11,000
SALES (est): 12.8MM **Privately Held**
WEB: www.truckandcrane.com
SIC: 7353 4212 Cranes & aerial lift equipment, rental or leasing; truck rental with drivers

(P-17317)
PEED EQUIPMENT COMPANY
43466 Business Park Dr, Temecula (92590-5526)
PHONE..............................951 657-0900
Carolyn Peed, *President*
Michael Peed, *Treasurer*
David Peed, *General Mgr*
Frank Loera, *Opers Staff*
EMP: 50 **EST:** 1982
SQ FT: 17,000
SALES (est): 14.6MM **Privately Held**
WEB: www.peedequipment.com
SIC: 7353 7699 Heavy construction equipment rental; construction equipment repair

(P-17318)
RJ ALLEN INC
10392 Stanford Ave, Garden Grove (92840-6301)
PHONE..............................714 539-1022
Ron Markham, *Vice Pres*
Liz Wood, *Human Res Mgr*
Shawn Ellis, *Plant Mgr*
Abel Diaz, *Superintendent*
EMP: 65 **EST:** 1969
SQ FT: 20,000
SALES (est): 19.6MM **Privately Held**
WEB: www.rjalleninc.com
SIC: 7353 Heavy construction equipment rental

(P-17319)
SAVALA EQUIPMENT COMPANY INC (PA)
Also Called: Savala Equipment Rentals
16402 Construction Cir E, Irvine (92606-4408)
PHONE..............................949 552-1859
Sean Savala, *President*
Aaron Dyer, *Vice Pres*
Julie Stafford, *Office Mgr*
Scott Damon, *VP Sales*
Brigham Florentin, *Sales Staff*
EMP: 54 **EST:** 1978
SQ FT: 3,200
SALES (est): 9.9MM **Privately Held**
WEB: www.savala.com
SIC: 7353 Cranes & aerial lift equipment, rental or leasing

(P-17320)
WASTE MGT COLLECTN RECYCL INC
1800 S Grand Ave, Santa Ana (92705-4800)
PHONE..............................714 637-3010
Lee Hicks, *Principal*
Angelica Dulce, *Manager*
Osvaldo Jauregui, *Manager*
EMP: 68 **EST:** 1969
SALES (est): 19.2MM
SALES (corp-wide): 15.2B **Publicly Held**
WEB: www.santaanadumpsterrental-prices.com
SIC: 7353 4953 Heavy construction equipment rental; refuse collection & disposal services
PA: Waste Management, Inc.
800 Capitol St Ste 3000
Houston TX 77002
713 512-6200

(P-17321)
WESTERN ENERGY SERVICES CORP
3430 Getty St, Bakersfield (93308-5248)
PHONE..............................403 984-5916
Alex Rn Macausland, *CEO*
Jeffrey K Bowers, *Vice Pres*
EMP: 200 **EST:** 2005
SALES (est): 6MM **Privately Held**
WEB: www.wesc.ca
SIC: 7353 Oil well drilling equipment, rental or leasing

(P-17322)
WESTERN PCF CRANE & EQP LLC (DH)
8600 Calabash Ave, Fontana (92335-3018)
PHONE..............................562 286-6618
Robert G Johnson, *President*
Robert G Jonhson, *President*
Steve Felkins, *Regional Mgr*
Dennis Piatek, *Branch Mgr*
Thomas Aguirre, *Manager*
EMP: 50 **EST:** 2011
SQ FT: 45,000
SALES (est): 25.8MM
SALES (corp-wide): 178.7MM **Privately Held**
WEB: www.wpcrane.com
SIC: 7353 Cranes & aerial lift equipment, rental or leasing
HQ: Mi-Jack Products Inc.
3111 167th St
Hazel Crest IL 60429
708 596-5200

(P-17323)
WHITES CRANE SERVICE INC
Also Called: White Crane
45524 Towne St, Indio (92201-4446)
PHONE..............................760 347-3401
Edwin Neumeyer, *President*
Jim Bozlino, *Controller*
EMP: 70 **EST:** 1999
SALES (est): 2.3MM
SALES (corp-wide): 14.6MM **Privately Held**
WEB: www.whitescraneservice.net
SIC: 7353 Cranes & aerial lift equipment, rental or leasing
PA: White's Steel, Inc.
45524 Towne St
Indio CA 92201
760 347-3401

(PA)=Parent Co (HQ)=Headquarters (DH)=Div Headquarters
✪ = New Business established in last 2 years

7359 Equipment Rental & Leasing, NEC

(P-17324)
A-THRONE CO INC
1850 E 33rd St, Long Beach (90807-5208)
PHONE..................................562 981-1197
Michael L Rice, *President*
Minerva Songco, *CFO*
Corey Vane, *Opers Mgr*
Ricardo Miranda, *Sales Staff*
EMP: 55 **EST:** 1980
SALES (est): 7.2MM **Privately Held**
WEB: www.unitedsiteservices.com
SIC: 7359 1799 Portable toilet rental; fence construction

(P-17325)
AERCAP GLOBAL AVIATION TRUST (HQ)
10250 Constellation Blvd, Los Angeles (90067-6200)
PHONE..................................310 788-1999
Sean Sullivan, *President*
Keith Helming, *CFO*
EMP: 143 **EST:** 2014
SALES (est): 27.8MM
SALES (corp-wide): 1B **Privately Held**
WEB: www.aercap.com
SIC: 7359 6159 Aircraft rental; equipment & vehicle finance leasing companies
PA: Aercap Holdings N.V.
Onbekend Nederlands Adres
Onbekend
353 163-6065

(P-17326)
AEROTURBINE LLC (DH)
Also Called: Aeroturbine, Inc.
10250 Constellation Blvd, Los Angeles (90067-6200)
PHONE..................................305 406-3090
Michael King, *CEO*
Garry Failler, *COO*
David Crull, *CFO*
Al Wood, *Exec VP*
Scott Loescher, *Vice Pres*
◆ **EMP:** 137 **EST:** 1997
SQ FT: 14,834
SALES (est): 51.3MM
SALES (corp-wide): 1B **Privately Held**
SIC: 7359 5088 Aircraft rental; aircraft engines & engine parts
HQ: International Lease Finance Corporation
10250 Constellation Blvd
Los Angeles CA 90067
310 788-1999

(P-17327)
AES HEAVY EQUIPMENT RENTAL INC
10880 Wilshire Blvd, Los Angeles (90024-4101)
PHONE..................................213 892-9720
Mark Wright, *Principal*
Marcy Gram, *Principal*
EMP: 52
SALES: 7.3MM **Privately Held**
SIC: 7359 Equipment rental & leasing

(P-17328)
AFTER-PARTY2 INC
1120 Mark Ave, Carpinteria (93013-2918)
PHONE..................................805 563-3800
Sindy Ceja, *Human Resources*
Richard Good, *Manager*
Maria Mejia, *Manager*
EMP: 74 **Publicly Held**
WEB: www.bright.com
SIC: 7359 Party supplies rental services
HQ: After-Party2, Inc.
901 W Hillcrest Blvd
Inglewood CA 90301
310 202-0011

(P-17329)
AFTER-PARTY2 INC (HQ)
Also Called: Classic Party Rentals
901 W Hillcrest Blvd, Inglewood (90301-2100)
PHONE..................................310 202-0011
Jeff Black, *President*
Jenna Coonce, *Department Mgr*

Jenna Florentino, *Department Mgr*
Jim Incavo, *General Mgr*
Janet Vasquez, *Office Mgr*
▲ **EMP:** 200 **EST:** 1996
SALES (est): 68MM **Publicly Held**
WEB: www.apollo.com
SIC: 7359 Party supplies rental services

(P-17330)
AIR LEASE CORP (PA)
7520 Hayvenhurst Ave, Van Nuys (91406-2844)
PHONE..................................818 387-8924
Sabrina Lemmens, *President*
Aj Abedin, *Treasurer*
Daniel Verwholt, *Treasurer*
Kishore Korde, *Exec VP*
Michael Bai, *Vice Pres*
EMP: 56 **EST:** 2013
SALES (est): 402.7K **Privately Held**
WEB: www.airleasecorp.com
SIC: 7359 Home appliance, furniture & entertainment rental services

(P-17331)
AIR LEASE CORPORATION (PA)
2000 Avenue Of The Stars 1000n, Los Angeles (90067-4734)
PHONE..................................310 553-0555
John L Plueger, *President*
Steven F Udvar-Hazy, *Ch of Bd*
Gregory B Willis, *CFO*
Carol H Forsyte, *Ch Credit Ofcr*
Jie Chen, *Exec VP*
EMP: 112 **EST:** 2010
SALES (est): 2B **Publicly Held**
WEB: www.airleasecorp.com
SIC: 7359 7389 Aircraft rental; aircraft & industrial truck rental services; financial services

(P-17332)
ALL-IN PRDCTONS CSINO RNTALS L
Also Called: Casino Table Rentals
7222 Garden Grove Blvd, Westminster (92683-2225)
PHONE..................................866 875-8628
Andrew Litwin, *CEO*
EMP: 63 **EST:** 2009
SALES (est): 3.9MM **Privately Held**
WEB: www.all-inproductions.net
SIC: 7359 Equipment rental & leasing

(P-17333)
AUDIO VISUAL HEADQUARTERS (DH)
Also Called: Psav
16320 Arthur St, Cerritos (90703-2129)
PHONE..................................310 603-0652
Michael O'Brien, *President*
Pat Gephardt, *CFO*
Todd Hester, *Vice Pres*
Jacob Vanvolkenburgh, *Technician*
Jonathan Kwon, *Technology*
EMP: 50 **EST:** 1967
SQ FT: 70,000
SALES (est): 23.5MM
SALES (corp-wide): 434.2MM **Privately Held**
SIC: 7359 7389 Audio-visual equipment & supply rental; convention & show services
HQ: Encore Group (Usa) Llc
24105 Frampton Ave
Harbor City CA 90710
562 366-0620

(P-17334)
BRANVID LTD INC
Also Called: Pumpkin Patch
4920 E La Palma Ave, Anaheim (92807-1912)
PHONE..................................714 630-0661
Fax: 714 630-0662
EMP: 23
SQ FT: 11,600
SALES (est): 2.4MM **Privately Held**
SIC: 7359 2394 Equipment Rental/Leasing Mfg Canvas/Related Prdts Whol Toys/Hobby Goods

(P-17335)
BRIGHT EVENT RENTALS LLC (PA)
Also Called: Wine Country Party & Events
1640 W 190th St Ste A, Torrance (90501-1113)
PHONE..................................310 202-0011
Michael Bjornstad, *Mng Member*
Michael Persson, *Partner*
Holly Thach, *General Mgr*
Christine Pease, *Accounting Mgr*
Joe Leahy, *Business Mgr*
▲ **EMP:** 240 **EST:** 2013
SALES (est): 34.4MM **Privately Held**
WEB: www.bright.com
SIC: 7359 Party supplies rental services

(P-17336)
CHOURA EVENTS
540 Hawaii Ave, Torrance (90503-5148)
PHONE..................................310 320-6200
James Ryan Choura, *CEO*
Damon Guilfoyle, *Vice Pres*
Jim Choura, *General Mgr*
Matthew Maldonado, *Project Mgr*
Jessica Pekar, *Sales Mgr*
EMP: 80 **EST:** 2014
SALES (est): 12MM **Privately Held**
WEB: www.choura.co
SIC: 7359 Party supplies rental services

(P-17337)
CLAIRMONT CAMERA INC (PA)
15411 Mulholland Dr, Los Angeles (90077-1624)
PHONE..................................818 761-4440
Denny Clairmont, *President*
Alan Albert, *Exec VP*
Irving Correa, *Vice Pres*
Mardrie Mullen, *Vice Pres*
EMP: 78 **EST:** 1980
SQ FT: 33,000
SALES (est): 7.4MM **Privately Held**
SIC: 7359 Audio-visual equipment & supply rental

(P-17338)
COMPASS GROUP USA INC
Also Called: Canteen Vending
12640 Knott St, Garden Grove (92841-3902)
PHONE..................................714 899-2520
Ron Wanamaker, *Vice Pres*
Mike Pulsipher, *Manager*
Kaila Thompson, *Manager*
EMP: 125
SALES (corp-wide): 26B **Privately Held**
WEB: www.compass-usa.com
SIC: 7359 7699 5962 Vending machine rental; vending machine repair; merchandising machine operators
HQ: Compass Group Usa, Inc.
2400 Yorkmont Rd
Charlotte NC 28217

(P-17339)
CP OPCO LLC
Also Called: Classic Party Rentals
333 S Grand Ave Ste 4070, Los Angeles (90071-1544)
PHONE..................................209 524-1966
EMP: 59
SALES (corp-wide): 1.9MM **Privately Held**
SIC: 7359 Equipment Rental/Leasing
HQ: Cp Opco, Llc
901 W Hillcrest Blvd A
Inglewood CA 90301
310 966-4900

(P-17340)
CP OPCO LLC
Also Called: Classic Party Rentals
11766 Wilshire Blvd # 380, Los Angeles (90025-6538)
PHONE..................................310 966-4900
EMP: 59
SALES (corp-wide): 1.9MM **Privately Held**
SIC: 7359 Equipment Rental/Leasing
HQ: Cp Opco, Llc
901 W Hillcrest Blvd A
Inglewood CA 90301
310 966-4900

(P-17341)
CP OPCO LLC
Also Called: Classic Party Rentals
1120 Mark Ave, Carpinteria (93013-2918)
PHONE..................................805 566-3566
Fax: 805 566-3599
EMP: 59
SALES (corp-wide): 1.9MM **Privately Held**
SIC: 7359 Equipment Rental/Leasing
HQ: Cp Opco, Llc
901 W Hillcrest Blvd A
Inglewood CA 90301
310 966-4900

(P-17342)
CP OPCO LLC
Also Called: Classic Party Rentals
3101 S Harbor Blvd, Santa Ana (92704-6826)
PHONE..................................714 540-6111
EMP: 100
SALES (corp-wide): 1.9MM **Privately Held**
SIC: 7359 Equipment Rental/Leasing
HQ: Cp Opco, Llc
901 W Hillcrest Blvd A
Inglewood CA 90301
310 966-4900

(P-17343)
CREATIVE TECHNOLOGY GROUP INC (DH)
14000 Arminta St, Panorama City (91402-6080)
PHONE..................................818 779-2400
Graham Andrews, *President*
Stephen Gray, *COO*
Augie Dellapi, *General Mgr*
Phyllis Huber, *Office Mgr*
Nicholas S Conn, *Admin Sec*
▲ **EMP:** 80 **EST:** 1985
SALES (est): 51.2MM
SALES (corp-wide): 102.1MM **Privately Held**
WEB: www.ct-group.com
SIC: 7359 Audio-visual equipment & supply rental
HQ: Creative Technology Group Limited
Unit 2 - 4
Crawley W SUSSEX FH10
129 358-3400

(P-17344)
CWF INC
Also Called: A-1 Party Rentals
251 E Front St, Covina (91723-1613)
PHONE..................................626 967-0500
Chet Fortney, *President*
Angela Barrera, *Project Mgr*
▲ **EMP:** 51 **EST:** 2001 **Privately Held**
WEB: www.a1partyrental.com
SIC: 7359 Party supplies rental services

(P-17345)
DIRECT CHASSISLINK INC
Also Called: Dcli
7777 Center Ave Ste 325, Huntington Beach (92647-9132)
PHONE..................................657 216-5846
Don Peltier, *Manager*
EMP: 134
SALES (corp-wide): 93.5MM **Privately Held**
WEB: www.dcli.com
SIC: 7359 Equipment rental & leasing
PA: Direct Chassislink, Inc.
3525 Whitehall Park Dr
Charlotte NC 28273
704 594-3800

(P-17346)
DISPATCH TRANSPORTATION LLC
Also Called: Dispatch Commodity Trucking
14032 Santa Ana Ave, Fontana (92337-7035)
PHONE..................................909 355-5531
Bruce Degler,
Bob Titular, *Info Tech Dir*
Julio Figueredo, *Opers Mgr*
John Miller, *Sales Staff*
Kim Pugmire,
EMP: 50 **EST:** 1986
SQ FT: 3,500

SALES (est): 2.2MM **Privately Held**
WEB: www.dispatchtrans.com
SIC: 7359 Equipment rental & leasing

(P-17347)
ELECTRO RENT CORPORATION (HQ)
Also Called: Rush Computer Rentals
8511 Fllbrook Ave Ste 200, West Hills (91304)
P.O. Box 605, Newbury Park (91319-0605)
PHONE...........................818 787-2100
Michael Clark, *CEO*
Jay Geldmacher, *President*
Nathan Hurst, *CFO*
Allen Sciarillo, *CFO*
Meryl Evans, *Vice Pres*
EMP: 142 EST: 1965
SALES (est): 128.7MM
SALES (corp-wide): 254.4MM **Privately Held**
WEB: www.electrorent.com
SIC: 7359 7377 5065 5045 Electronic equipment rental, except computers; computer rental & leasing; electronic parts & equipment; computers & accessories, personal & home entertainment
PA: Elecor Intermediate Holding Ii Corporation
360 N Crescent Dr
Beverly Hills CA 90210
310 712-1850

(P-17348)
FENIX MARINE SERVICES LTD (HQ)
614 Terminal Way, San Pedro (90731-7453)
PHONE...........................310 548-8877
Sean Pierce, *President*
◆ EMP: 50 EST: 1978
SQ FT: 2,500
SALES (est): 34.7MM
SALES (corp-wide): 68MM **Privately Held**
WEB: www.fenixmarineservices.com
SIC: 7359 Shipping container leasing
PA: P5 Infrastructure Llc
6263 N Scottsdale Rd # 3
Scottsdale AZ 85250
206 696-3648

(P-17349)
FINNCO SERVICES INCORPORATED
8241 Beech Ave, Fontana (92335-3210)
PHONE...........................909 355-0707
Matthew Finnerty, *Vice Pres*
Cynthia Finnerty, *CFO*
Art Torres, *Director*
Trenton Finnerty, *Parts Mgr*
EMP: 52 EST: 2006
SALES (est): 6MM **Privately Held**
WEB: www.finncoservices.com
SIC: 7359 7699 Equipment rental & leasing; elevators: inspection, service & repair

(P-17350)
GFN NORTH AMERICA CORP (HQ)
260 S Los Robles Ave # 217, Pasadena (91101-2824)
PHONE...........................626 584-9722
Lawrence Glascott, *Ch of Bd*
Ronald F Valenta, *CEO*
Charles Barrantes, *CFO*
EMP: 50 EST: 2008
SALES (est): 235.1MM **Privately Held**
WEB: www.unitedrentals.com
SIC: 7359 5085 Shipping container leasing; bins & containers, storage

(P-17351)
HANA FINANCIAL INC (PA)
1000 Wilshire Blvd # 2000, Los Angeles (90017-5645)
PHONE...........................213 240-1234
Sunnie S Kim, *CEO*
Young Shim, *CFO*
Dave Lee, *Officer*
Toni Rios, *Officer*
Kevin Thomas, *Senior VP*
▲ EMP: 85
SQ FT: 24,000

SALES (est): 13.6MM **Privately Held**
WEB: www.hanafinancial.com
SIC: 7359 6153 6159 Equipment rental & leasing; factoring services; small business investment companies

(P-17352)
HD SUPPLY FACILITIES MAINT LTD
21651 Baker Pkwy, City of Industry (91789-5235)
PHONE...........................909 594-3843
Mary Sullivan, *Branch Mgr*
Francisco Cervantes, *Accounts Mgr*
EMP: 69
SALES (corp-wide): 132.1B **Publicly Held**
WEB: www.hdsupply.com
SIC: 7359 Equipment rental & leasing
HQ: Hd Supply Facilities Maintenance, Ltd.
3400 Cumberland Blvd Se
Atlanta GA 30339
770 852-9000

(P-17353)
HOME DEPOT USA INC
Also Called: Home Depot, The
6345 Variel Ave, Woodland Hills (91367-2515)
PHONE...........................818 716-9141
EMP: 200
SALES (corp-wide): 132.1B **Publicly Held**
WEB: www.homedepot.com
SIC: 5211 7359 Ret Lumber/Building Materials Equipment Rental/Leasing
HQ: Home Depot U.S.A., Inc.
2455 Paces Ferry Rd Se
Atlanta GA 30339

(P-17354)
HOME DEPOT USA INC
Also Called: Home Depot, The
22855 Victory Blvd, Canoga Park (91307-3956)
PHONE...........................818 887-7083
EMP: 150
SALES (corp-wide): 132.1B **Publicly Held**
WEB: www.homedepot.com
SIC: 5211 7359 Ret Lumber/Building Materials Equipment Rental/Leasing
HQ: Home Depot U.S.A., Inc.
2455 Paces Ferry Rd Se
Atlanta GA 30339

(P-17355)
HUB CONSTRUCTION SPC INC (DH)
Also Called: Hub Construction Sups & Eqp
379 S I St, San Bernardino (92410-2409)
PHONE...........................909 889-0161
Edward Dainko, *President*
Vince French, *CFO*
Larry Clause, *Branch Mgr*
Phil Lujan, *Branch Mgr*
Dean Overton, *Branch Mgr*
EMP: 50 EST: 1958
SQ FT: 25,000
SALES (est): 31.8MM
SALES (corp-wide): 6.7B **Privately Held**
WEB: www.whitecap.com
SIC: 7359 5082 Equipment rental & leasing; construction & mining machinery
HQ: Construction Supply Holdings, Llc
9 Greenway Plz Ste 2400
Houston TX 77046
713 877-8257

(P-17356)
INTERNATIONAL LEASE FIN CORP (DH)
10250 Constellation Blvd, Los Angeles (90067-6200)
PHONE...........................310 788-1999
Henri Courpron, *CEO*
Alan Lund, *Vice Chairman*
Ed Fanning, *President*
Pinella Shapiro, *President*
Elias Habayeb, *CFO*
EMP: 504 EST: 1990
SQ FT: 149,000

SALES (est): 244.5MM
SALES (corp-wide): 1B **Privately Held**
WEB: www.aercap.com
SIC: 5599 7359 8741 Aircraft dealers; aircraft rental; business management
HQ: Aercap U.S. Global Aviation Llc
10250 Constellation Blvd
Los Angeles CA 90067
310 788-1999

(P-17357)
J L FISHER INC
1000 W Isabel St, Burbank (91506-1404)
PHONE...........................818 846-8366
James L Fisher, *President*
Cary Clayton, *Vice Pres*
Mark Gregory, *Technician*
Nancy Bowers, *Personnel*
Lucy Soghomonian, *Marketing Staff*
▲ EMP: 60 EST: 1951
SALES (est): 5.2MM **Privately Held**
WEB: www.jlfisher.com
SIC: 7359 3861 3663 Equipment rental & leasing; motion picture apparatus & equipment; radio & TV communications equipment

(P-17358)
JC PARTY RENTALS INC
11562 Vanowen St, North Hollywood (91605-6229)
PHONE...........................818 765-4819
Delmy Chavarria, *CEO*
Jose Urquilla, *President*
EMP: 52 EST: 2003
SQ FT: 6,600
SALES (est): 653K **Privately Held**
WEB: www.jcpartyrentals.com
SIC: 7359 Party supplies rental services

(P-17359)
JULES AND ASSOCIATES INC
515 S Figueroa St # 1900, Los Angeles (90071-3336)
PHONE...........................213 362-5600
Jules Buenabenta, *President*
Michael Behar, *Senior VP*
Scott Monroe, *Senior VP*
Ryan Murphy, *Executive*
Patrick Tully, *Executive*
EMP: 51 EST: 1992
SQ FT: 15,000
SALES (est): 22.8MM **Privately Held**
WEB: www.julesandassociates.com
SIC: 7359 Equipment rental & leasing

(P-17360)
L A PARTY RENTS INC
13520 Saticoy St, Van Nuys (91402-6428)
PHONE...........................818 989-4300
Gerome Nehus, *President*
Kevin Dwyer, *Vice Pres*
Jerry Nehus, *CIO*
Ella Rosenberg, *Human Res Dir*
David Searcy, *Human Res Mgr*
EMP: 100 EST: 1987
SALES (est): 9.5MM **Privately Held**
WEB: www.lapartyrents.com
SIC: 7359 Party supplies rental services

(P-17361)
MAGIC JUMP INC
9165 Glenoaks Blvd, Sun Valley (91352-2612)
PHONE...........................818 847-1313
Andranik Bagumyan, *President*
Arthur Bagumyan, *Vice Pres*
Sam Bagumyan, *Vice Pres*
Arsen Ambartsumyan, *Sales Mgr*
◆ EMP: 20 EST: 1996
SQ FT: 20,000
SALES (est): 3.4MM **Privately Held**
WEB: www.magicjump.com
SIC: 7359 3069 Party supplies rental services; balloons, advertising & toy: rubber

(P-17362)
MICROFINANCIAL INCORPORATED
2801 Townsgate Rd, Westlake Village (91361-3003)
PHONE...........................805 367-8900
Richard Latour, *CEO*
EMP: 113

SALES (corp-wide): 95.2MM **Privately Held**
WEB: www.timepayment.com
SIC: 7359 Business machine & electronic equipment rental services
HQ: Microfinancial Incorporated
200 Summit Dr Ste 100
Burlington MA 01803
781 994-4800

(P-17363)
MICROLEASE INC (DH)
6060 Sepulveda Blvd, Van Nuys (91411-2512)
PHONE...........................866 520-0200
Gordon Curwen, *Vice Pres*
Michael E Clark, *CEO*
EMP: 85 EST: 2001
SQ FT: 20,000
SALES (est): 45.4MM
SALES (corp-wide): 254.4MM **Privately Held**
WEB: www.electrorent.com
SIC: 7359 Rental store, general
HQ: Electro Rent Uk Limited
Unit 1 Waverley Industrial Estate Hailsham Drive
Harrow MIDDX HA1 4
208 420-0200

(P-17364)
MUFG AMERICAS LEASING CORP (DH)
445 S Figueroa St # 2700, Los Angeles (90071-1602)
PHONE...........................213 488-3700
Hideya Takaishi, *CEO*
Rory Laughna, *President*
David A Meehan, *President*
Paul Nolan, *CFO*
Paul F Nolan, *Treasurer*
EMP: 100 EST: 1973
SALES (est): 24.5MM **Privately Held**
WEB: www.mufgamericas.com
SIC: 7359 Equipment rental & leasing
HQ: Mufg Americas Holdings Corporation
1251 Ave Of The Americas
New York NY 10020
212 782-6800

(P-17365)
NATIONAL CNSTR RENTALS INC (HQ)
15319 Chatsworth St, Mission Hills (91345-2040)
PHONE...........................818 221-6000
James R Mooneyham, *President*
W Robert Mooneyham, *President*
Fabrizio Carrillo, *Admin Asst*
William Prigge, *Info Tech Dir*
Walter Rigler, *Finance*
◆ EMP: 85 EST: 1961
SQ FT: 23,000
SALES (est): 99.3MM
SALES (corp-wide): 123.1MM **Privately Held**
WEB: www.rentnational.com
SIC: 7359 Equipment rental & leasing
PA: The National Business Group Inc
15319 Chatsworth St
Mission Hills CA 91345
818 221-6000

(P-17366)
PANAVISION INC (PA)
Also Called: Panavision Group
6101 Variel Ave, Woodland Hills (91367-3722)
PHONE...........................818 316-1000
Ronald O Perelman, *Ch of Bd*
William C Bevins, *President*
Kimberly Snyder, *CEO*
Ross Landsbaum, *COO*
John Suh, *CFO*
▲ EMP: 550 EST: 1990
SQ FT: 150,000
SALES (est): 156.7MM **Privately Held**
WEB: www.panavision.com
SIC: 7359 3861 3648 5063 Equipment rental & leasing; cameras & related equipment; stage lighting equipment; lighting fixtures

(P-17367)
PICO RENTS INC
Also Called: Pico Party Rents
4646 E Los Angeles Ave, Simi Valley
(93063-3407)
PHONE..................310 275-9431
William Edwards, *President*
Darren G Edwards, *Admin Sec*
Lisa Chocooj, *Human Res Mgr*
EMP: 60 **EST:** 1926
SALES (est): 6.8MM **Privately Held**
WEB: www.picopartyrents.com
SIC: 7359 Party supplies rental services

(P-17368)
PRODUCERS INC
Also Called: Muse Presentation Technologies
1751 Langley Ave, Irvine (92614-5621)
P.O. Box 16214 (92623-6214)
PHONE..................714 850-1008
Jim Muse, *CEO*
Joyce Muse, *CFO*
Kevin Hara, *Vice Pres*
Adam Bendig, *CTO*
Adam CTS, *CTO*
EMP: 64 **EST:** 1973
SQ FT: 11,000
SALES (est): 2.6MM **Privately Held**
SIC: 7359 Audio-visual equipment & supply rental

(P-17369)
PSAV HOLDINGS LLC (PA)
111 W Ocean Blvd Ste 1110, Long Beach
(90802-4688)
PHONE..................562 366-0138
J Michael McIlwain, *CEO*
Ben Erwin, *President*
Michael Leone, *Ch Credit Ofcr*
Whit Markowitz,
Arthur Clyne, *Senior VP*
EMP: 323 **EST:** 2013
SALES (est): 434.2MM **Privately Held**
WEB: www.encoreglobal.com
SIC: 7359 Audio-visual equipment & supply rental

(P-17370)
RSI LEASING LLC
1314 E Puente Ave, West Covina
(91790-1361)
PHONE..................626 966-6129
Ronadl Chaplen, *Principal*
EMP: 85 **EST:** 2010
SALES (est): 99K
SALES (corp-wide): 818.1MM **Publicly Held**
WEB: www.soterahealth.com
SIC: 7359 Equipment rental & leasing
PA: Sotera Health Company
9100 S Hills Blvd Ste 300
Broadview Heights OH 44147
440 262-1410

(P-17371)
SHOWBIZ ENTERPRISES INC (PA)
Also Called: Showbiz Drapery
15541 Lanark St, Van Nuys (91406-1471)
PHONE..................818 989-5005
Scott Webley, *President*
▲ **EMP:** 50 **EST:** 1977
SQ FT: 35,000
SALES (est): 3.3MM **Privately Held**
WEB: www.showbizenterprises.com
SIC: 5714 7359 Draperies; rental store, general

(P-17372)
SHOWROOM INTERIORS LLC
Also Called: Vesta Luxury Home Staging
8905 Rex Rd, Pico Rivera (90660-3799)
PHONE..................323 348-1551
Julianne Buckner, *Mng Member*
Everett Bumbalough, *Vice Pres*
Alexander Gomez, *Manager*
EMP: 105 **EST:** 2016
SALES (est): 5MM **Privately Held**
SIC: 7359 Furniture rental
PA: Showroom, Inc
8905 Rex Rd
Pico Rivera CA 90660
323 348-1551

(P-17373)
SOLA RENTALS INC
8629 S Vermont Ave, Los Angeles
(90044-4868)
PHONE..................323 306-4648
John Lusk, *President*
Malcolm Rivera, *Associate Dir*
Alexis Lujan, *Principal*
Martin Muoto, *Principal*
Hector Ala, *Regional Mgr*
EMP: 50 **EST:** 2013
SALES (est): 5.8MM **Privately Held**
WEB: www.solarentals.com
SIC: 7359 Equipment rental & leasing

(P-17374)
SOUNDBOKS INC
800 Wilshire Blvd, Los Angeles
(90017-2604)
PHONE..................310 774-0480
Jesper Theil Thomsen, *CEO*
EMP: 15 **EST:** 2015
SALES (est): 4.1MM
SALES (corp-wide): 1.2MM **Privately Held**
WEB: www.soundboks.com
SIC: 7359 7819 1731 3651 Sound & lighting equipment rental; sound (effects & music production), motion picture; sound equipment specialization; sound reproducing equipment
HQ: Soundboks Aps
Esromgade 15, Sal 11
KObenhavn
607 200-15

(P-17375)
SOUTHWEST SITE SERVICES INC
963 Main St, Riverside (92501-1017)
PHONE..................866 892-8451
Steve Morales, *CEO*
Blanca Morales, *Vice Pres*
Jessica Morales, *Human Res Mgr*
EMP: 53 **EST:** 2012
SALES (est): 5.6MM **Privately Held**
WEB: www.southwestsiteservices.com
SIC: 7359 Portable toilet rental

(P-17376)
STATEWIDE SAFETY & SIGNS INC (HQ)
522 Lindon Ln, Nipomo (93444-9222)
P.O. Box 5299, Irvine (92616-5299)
PHONE..................805 929-5070
Don Louis Nicholas, *CEO*
Gregory E Grosch, *President*
Steve Vogel, *Officer*
Kory Fivecoat, *Branch Mgr*
Carrie Jensen, *Admin Asst*
EMP: 21 **EST:** 1987
SQ FT: 15,000
SALES (est): 12MM **Privately Held**
WEB: www.statewidess.com
SIC: 7359 5088 3993 5087 Work zone traffic equipment (flags, cones, barrels, etc.); transportation equipment & supplies; signs, not made in custom sign painting shops; service establishment equipment; industrial supplies

(P-17377)
SUMMIT EQUIPMENT RENTALS LLC
Also Called: Summit Rentals
26105 Sherman Rd A, Menifee
(92585-9249)
PHONE..................951 246-3313
Gedrse Courtney, *Mng Member*
Robert J Kushner, *Principal*
Tanner Harris, *Opers Staff*
Sam Melendez, *Foreman/Supr*
Nic Sandoval, *Sales Staff*
EMP: 51 **EST:** 2007
SALES (est): 9.8MM **Privately Held**
WEB: www.summitrentals.net
SIC: 7359 Equipment rental & leasing

(P-17378)
SUNN AMERICA INC
Also Called: Classe Party Rentals
10280 Indiana Ct, Rancho Cucamonga
(91730-5332)
PHONE..................909 944-5756
Vishnu Reddy, *CEO*

Saritha Reddy, *President*
Ronald Francis, *Principal*
EMP: 30 **EST:** 1999
SALES (est): 4.5MM **Privately Held**
WEB: www.reddyworld.com
SIC: 7359 7299 3999 Party supplies rental services; tent & tarpaulin rental; party planning service; stage hardware & equipment, except lighting

(P-17379)
TOWN & CNTRY EVENT RENTALS INC (PA)
Also Called: Tacer
7725 Airport Bus Pkwy, Van Nuys (91406)
PHONE..................818 908-4211
Richard Loguercio, *CEO*
Sandy Hasson, *CFO*
Christopher Keesler, *Vice Pres*
Chris Mackey, *Vice Pres*
Jaclyn Ludford, *Branch Mgr*
▲ **EMP:** 400 **EST:** 1998
SQ FT: 1,100
SALES (est): 64.1MM **Privately Held**
WEB: www.tacer.biz
SIC: 7359 Party supplies rental services

(P-17380)
TOWN & CNTRY EVENT RENTALS INC
1 N Calle Cesar Chavez, Santa Barbara
(93103-3662)
PHONE..................805 770-5729
Jaclynn Ludford, *Branch Mgr*
Nasreen Jadmani, *Assistant*
EMP: 398
SALES (corp-wide): 64.1MM **Privately Held**
WEB: www.tacer.biz
SIC: 7359 Party supplies rental services
PA: Town & Country Event Rentals, Inc.
7725 Airport Bus Pkwy
Van Nuys CA 91406
818 908-4211

(P-17381)
UNITED SITE SERVICES CAL INC (PA)
242 Live Oak Ave, Irwindale (91706-1311)
PHONE..................626 462-9110
Debbi Thornton, *Manager*
EMP: 50 **EST:** 1998
SQ FT: 2,400
SALES (est): 5.4MM **Privately Held**
WEB: www.unitedsiteservices.com
SIC: 7359 Portable toilet rental

(P-17382)
VARCO DE MEXICO HOLDINGS INC
Also Called: Varco Systems
743 N Eckhoff St, Orange (92868-1080)
PHONE..................714 978-1900
Richard Kertson, *VP Finance*
▲ **EMP:** 86 **EST:** 1983
SALES (est): 18.9MM
SALES (corp-wide): 6B **Publicly Held**
WEB: www.nov.com
SIC: 7359 3533 Equipment rental & leasing; oil & gas field machinery
PA: Nov Inc.
7909 Parkwood Circle Dr
Houston TX 77036
713 346-7500

(P-17383)
VCI EVENT TECHNOLOGY INC
Also Called: Videocam
1261 S Simpson Cir, Anaheim
(92806-5530)
PHONE..................714 772-2002
Toll Free:..................888 -
Evan H Goldschlag, *President*
Kirk Rhinehart, *COO*
Becky Moore, *Engineer*
Jessica Baxter, *Opers Staff*
Todd Dale, *Accounts Mgr*
▲ **EMP:** 166 **EST:** 1993
SALES (est): 18.3MM **Privately Held**
WEB: www.vcievents.com
SIC: 7359 Audio-visual equipment & supply rental

(P-17384)
WESTERN OILFIELDS SUPPLY CO (PA)
Also Called: Rain For Rent
3404 State Rd, Bakersfield (93308-4538)
P.O. Box 2248 (93303-2248)
PHONE..................661 399-9124
Robert Lake, *CEO*
Maston Cunningham, *CFO*
Steve Bayda, *Vice Pres*
Chris Lake, *Vice Pres*
Myles Dockter, *Executive*
▲ **EMP:** 150 **EST:** 1934
SQ FT: 57,000
SALES (est): 250.8MM **Privately Held**
WEB: www.rainforrent.com
SIC: 7359 3523 5083 Equipment rental & leasing; farm machinery & equipment; irrigation equipment

7361 Employment Agencies

(P-17385)
24-HOUR MED STAFFING SVCS LLC
21700 Copley Dr Ste 270, Diamond Bar
(91765-5489)
PHONE..................909 895-8960
Erlinda R Stone,
Ron Elamparo, *Vice Pres*
Carlo Tan, *Accountant*
Karen Sagad, *Assistant*
Janus Yambao, *Assistant*
EMP: 110 **EST:** 2000
SALES (est): 6.9MM **Privately Held**
WEB: www.24-hrmed.com
SIC: 7361 Employment agencies

(P-17386)
5 STAR JOB SOURCE
12025 Garfield Ave, South Gate
(90280-7822)
PHONE..................562 788-7391
Fernando Carrillo Morales, *CEO*
EMP: 70 **EST:** 2018
SALES (est): 3MM **Privately Held**
SIC: 7361 Employment agencies

(P-17387)
ACCELON INC
19075 Wells Dr, Tarzana (91356-3936)
PHONE..................925 216-5735
Aizad Kamal, *CEO*
Unsa Kazmi Kamal, *CFO*
Andy Paul, *Tech Recruiter*
EMP: 50 **EST:** 2014
SALES (est): 2.4MM **Privately Held**
WEB: www.acceloninc.com
SIC: 7361 8742 Executive placement; labor contractors (employment agency); construction project management consultant; business consultant

(P-17388)
ACT 1 GROUP INC (PA)
Also Called: Agileone
1999 W 190th St, Torrance (90504-6202)
P.O. Box 2886 (90509-2886)
PHONE..................310 750-3400
Janice B Howroyd, *CEO*
Bernard Howroyd, *President*
Carlton Bryant, *Exec VP*
Jean Barrick, *Vice Pres*
Cynthia M Futvoye, *Vice Pres*
EMP: 90 **EST:** 1978
SQ FT: 18,026
SALES (est): 628.6MM **Privately Held**
WEB: www.actonegroup.com
SIC: 7361 8741 Employment agencies; administrative management

(P-17389)
ALL HEALTH SERVICES CORP (PA)
11104 Bonneyview Ln, Hanford
(93230-6308)
PHONE..................559 583-9101
Dave Matthews, *President*
Brenda Matthews, *CFO*
Michael Ross, *Vice Pres*
Jeremy Matthews, *Admin Sec*
Robert Garcia, *Director*
EMP: 65 **EST:** 2004

SALES (est): 9MM **Privately Held**
WEB: www.allhs.net
SIC: **7361** Employment agencies

(P-17390)
ALLS WELL INC (PA)
Also Called: All's Well Healthcare Staffing
327 W Broadway, Glendale (91204-1301)
P.O. Box 29048 (91209-9048)
PHONE..................................818 240-8688
Janice Bryant Howroyd, *President*
EMP: 59 EST: 1992
SALES (est): 16.4MM **Privately Held**
WEB: www.allswell.com
SIC: **7361 7363** Placement agencies;
medical help service

(P-17391)
ASSISTED HOME RECOVERY INC (PA)
Also Called: Assisted Home Care
8550 Balboa Blvd Lbby, Northridge
(91325-5808)
PHONE..................................818 894-8117
Elaine S Donley, *President*
Bill Donley, *Ch of Bd*
Michele Myers, *Hum Res Coord*
Sheena Bob, *Nurse*
Tatyana Krifuks, *Nurse*
EMP: 110 EST: 1979
SQ FT: 4,000
SALES (est): 11.4MM **Privately Held**
WEB: www.assistedcares.com
SIC: **7361** Nurses' registry

(P-17392)
AT-TECH STAFFING SERVICES INC (PA)
327 W Broadway, Glendale (91204-1301)
PHONE..................................818 240-8688
Bernard Howroyd, *President*
Michael Hoyal, *CFO*
EMP: 98 EST: 2001
SALES (est): 7.1MM **Privately Held**
WEB: www.appleonetechnical.com
SIC: **7361** Executive placement

(P-17393)
B2 SERVICES LLC
Also Called: At Work
17291 Irvine Blvd Ste 258, Tustin
(92780-2949)
PHONE..................................714 363-3481
Lori Brower, *President*
EMP: 100 EST: 2017
SALES (est): 2.2MM **Privately Held**
WEB: www.atwork.com
SIC: **7361** Employment agencies

(P-17394)
BARONHR LLC
13085 Central Ave Ste 4, Chino
(91710-4184)
PHONE..................................909 517-3800
EMP: 86
SALES (corp-wide): 51.3MM **Privately Held**
WEB: www.baronhr.com
SIC: **7361** Employment agencies
PA: Baronhr, Llc
8101 E Kaiser Blvd
Anaheim CA 92808
714 860-7800

(P-17395)
BARRETT BUSINESS SERVICES INC
862 E Hospitality Ln, San Bernardino
(92408-3530)
PHONE..................................909 890-3633
Walter Kilifi, *Business Mgr*
EMP: 3049
SALES (corp-wide): 880.8MM **Publicly Held**
WEB: www.bbsi.com
SIC: **7361** Employment agencies
PA: Barrett Business Services Inc
8100 Ne Parkway Dr # 200
Vancouver WA 98662
360 828-0700

(P-17396)
BARRETT BUSINESS SERVICES INC
Also Called: Bbsi Camarillo
815 Camarillo Springs Rd C, Camarillo
(93012-9457)
PHONE..................................805 987-0331
Dee Levy, *Area Mgr*
Tucker Smith, *Area Mgr*
Kirk Manchester, *Manager*
Chris McCarthy, *Manager*
EMP: 3049
SALES (corp-wide): 880.8MM **Publicly Held**
WEB: www.bbsi.com
SIC: **7361 8742** Employment agencies;
human resource consulting services
PA: Barrett Business Services Inc
8100 Ne Parkway Dr # 200
Vancouver WA 98662
360 828-0700

(P-17397)
BOILING POINT REST S CA INC
13668 Valley Blvd Unit C2, City of Industry
(91746-2572)
PHONE..................................626 551-5181
CHI How Chou, *Chairman*
Michael Lin, *Vice Pres*
EMP: 300 EST: 2012
SALES (est): 23.8MM **Privately Held**
SIC: **7361 5812** Employment agencies;
Chinese restaurant

(P-17398)
BOT TRAVEL & STAFFING
5900 Wilshire Blvd # 243, Los Angeles
(90036-5013)
PHONE..................................323 272-4911
Sam Murphy, *Ch of Bd*
EMP: 55 EST: 2014
SALES (est): 1.3MM **Privately Held**
SIC: **7361** Employment agencies

(P-17399)
BUTLER AMERICA HOLDINGS INC
12625 Frederick St Ste E2, Moreno Valley
(92553-5253)
PHONE..................................951 563-0020
Yvonne Rodriguez, *Branch Mgr*
EMP: 177
SALES (corp-wide): 81.8MM **Privately Held**
WEB: www.butler.com
SIC: **7361** Employment agencies
PA: Butler America Holdings, Inc.
3820 State St Ste B
Santa Barbara CA 93105
805 880-1978

(P-17400)
BUTLER AMERICA HOLDINGS INC (PA)
3820 State St Ste B, Santa Barbara
(93105-3182)
PHONE..................................805 880-1978
Robert Olson, *CEO*
Stephen Morrison, *CFO*
Shannon P Sorensen, *Director*
EMP: 246 EST: 2014
SALES (est): 81.8MM **Privately Held**
WEB: www.butler.com
SIC: **7361** Employment agencies

(P-17401)
BUTLER AMERICA HOLDINGS INC
8647 Haven Ave Ste 100, Rancho Cuca-
monga (91730-4887)
PHONE..................................909 417-3660
Cecilia La Tour, *Branch Mgr*
Gloria Dominguez, *Branch Mgr*
Ian Stephens, *Sales Staff*
Erin Aumrin, *Manager*
Brandon Hedges, *Manager*
EMP: 177
SALES (corp-wide): 81.8MM **Privately Held**
WEB: www.butler.com
SIC: **7361** Employment agencies
PA: Butler America Holdings, Inc.
3820 State St Ste B
Santa Barbara CA 93105
805 880-1978

(P-17402)
BUTLER INTERNATIONAL INC (PA)
3820 State St Ste A, Santa Barbara
(93105-3182)
PHONE..................................805 882-2200
Edward M Kopko, *Ch of Bd*
Mark Koscinski, *CFO*
James J Beckley, *Senior VP*
Al Moreno, *Vice Pres*
Chris Hamel, *VP Bus Dvlpt*
EMP: 200 EST: 1985
SALES (est): 168.4MM **Privately Held**
WEB: www.butler.com
SIC: **7361 8742** Employment agencies;
management consulting services

(P-17403)
CAREER GROUP INC (PA)
Also Called: Fourthfloor Fashion Talent
10100 Santa Monica Blvd # 900, Los Ange-
les (90067-4138)
PHONE..................................310 277-8188
Michael B Levine, *CEO*
Susan Levine, *President*
Scott H Pick, *CFO*
Melissa Bucchino, *Vice Pres*
Emily Levine, *Vice Pres*
▲ EMP: 2100 EST: 1980
SQ FT: 11,986
SALES (est): 50.8MM **Privately Held**
WEB: www.careergroupcompanies.com
SIC: **7361** Executive placement

(P-17404)
CAREER STRATEGIES TMPRY INC
719 N Victory Blvd, Burbank (91502-1629)
PHONE..................................213 385-0440
Darin Rado, *President*
Jim King, *CFO*
Julie Maddox, *Vice Pres*
Minh Pho, *Administration*
Ethel Smith, *Info Tech Mgr*
EMP: 67 EST: 1990
SQ FT: 6,000
SALES (est): 8.1MM **Privately Held**
WEB: www.csi4jobs.com
SIC: **7361** Executive placement

(P-17405)
CENTURY HLTH STAFFING SVCS INC
1701 Westwind Dr Ste 101, Bakersfield
(93301-3045)
PHONE..................................661 322-0606
Richard Ochieng, *President*
Lissa Harris-Soto, *Vice Pres*
Michelle Phillips, *Manager*
EMP: 213 EST: 2006
SQ FT: 2,000
SALES (est): 10.1MM **Privately Held**
WEB: www.centurynurse.com
SIC: **7361** Nurses' registry

(P-17406)
CITISTAFF SOLUTIONS INC (PA)
1865 E 4th St, Ontario (91764-2652)
PHONE..................................310 763-1636
Erika M Sanchez, *President*
Javier Chavolla, *CFO*
April Venegas, *Vice Pres*
Charles Slater, *General Counsel*
David Duenas, *Director*
EMP: 126 EST: 2004
SALES (est): 15.9MM **Privately Held**
WEB: www.citistaffsolutions.com
SIC: **7361** Executive placement

(P-17407)
CLOUDSTAFF LLC (PA)
Also Called: 1st Class Event Services
1165 E San Antonio Dr, Long Beach
(90807-2374)
PHONE..................................888 551-5339
Patrick Allen,
EMP: 393 EST: 2018
SALES (est): 19.9MM **Privately Held**
WEB: www.cloudstaffllc.com
SIC: **7361** Employment agencies

(P-17408)
CREATIVE CIRCLE LLC (DH)
5900 Wilshire Blvd # 1100, Los Angeles
(90036-5036)
PHONE..................................323 930-2333
Lawrence Serf, *Mng Member*
Jenna Briggs, *Executive*
Alexa Kornemann, *Executive*
Jena Lepkowski, *Executive*
Kyle Pressley, *Executive*
EMP: 60 EST: 2008
SALES (est): 23.2MM
SALES (corp-wide): 3.9B **Publicly Held**
WEB: www.creativecircle.com
SIC: **7361** Executive placement
HQ: Mscp V Cc Parent, Llc
5900 Wilshire Blvd # 110
Los Angeles CA 90036
323 634-0156

(P-17409)
CYBERCODERS INC
Also Called: Cyberscientific
6591 Irvine Center Dr # 200, Irvine
(92618-2131)
PHONE..................................949 885-5151
Heidi Golledge, *CEO*
Matt Miller, *COO*
Eric Coe, *Vice Pres*
Aaron Frankel, *Vice Pres*
Yassen Matt, *Executive*
EMP: 140 EST: 1999
SALES (est): 41MM
SALES (corp-wide): 3.9B **Publicly Held**
WEB: www.cybercoders.com
SIC: **7361** Executive placement
PA: Asgn Incorporated
4400 Cox Rd Ste 110
Glen Allen VA 23060
888 482-8068

(P-17410)
DAWSON & DAWSON STAFFING INC (PA)
26522 La Alameda Ste 110, Mission Viejo
(92691-8579)
PHONE..................................949 421-3966
Kathy Dawson, *President*
Larry Dawson, *CFO*
Erika Young, *Recruiter*
Gina Brehmer, *Director*
EMP: 74 EST: 2008
SALES (est): 2.9MM **Privately Held**
WEB: www.dawsondawsoninc.com
SIC: **7361** Executive placement

(P-17411)
DECTON INC (PA)
Also Called: Decton Trade Solutions
15635 Alton Pkwy Ste 475, Irvine
(92618-7361)
PHONE..................................949 851-0111
Stephen Beal, *President*
Steve Stenerodden, *COO*
Erlene Stevenson-Freem, *Payroll Mgr*
EMP: 206 EST: 2002
SQ FT: 2,000
SALES (est): 30.1MM **Privately Held**
WEB: www.dectoninc.com
SIC: **7361** Labor contractors (employment agency)

(P-17412)
DIAMOND PEO LLC
27442 Calle Arroyo Ste A, San Juan Capis-
trano (92675-6753)
PHONE..................................714 728-5186
Veronica Lake,
Sandra Moreno, *General Mgr*
Veronica Cruz, *Director*
EMP: 180 EST: 2016
SALES (est): 500K **Privately Held**
WEB: www.diamondpeo.com
SIC: **7361** Employment agencies

(P-17413)
DIVERSITY BUS SOLUTIONS INC
2515 S Euclid Ave, Ontario (91762-6620)
PHONE..................................909 395-0243
Sandy Tribby, *CEO*
Marisol Nieves, *Human Resources*
EMP: 200 EST: 2011
SALES (est): 6.2MM **Privately Held**
WEB: www.dbsinc.org
SIC: **7361** Employment agencies

(P-17414)
DYNASTY STAFFING SOLUTIONSINC
17255 Sycamore St, Hesperia
(92345-2141)
PHONE....................909 727-3801
Rocio Lopez, *Branch Mgr*
EMP: 52
SALES (corp-wide): 617.4K **Privately Held**
SIC: 7361 Employment agencies
PA: Dynasty Staffing Solutions.Inc.
9668 Milliken Ave 104-3
Rancho Cucamonga CA 91730
909 802-4803

(P-17415)
E Z STAFFING INC (PA)
200 N Maryland Ave # 303, Glendale
(91206-4276)
PHONE....................818 845-2500
Abraham F Abirafeh, *President*
EMP: 298 **EST:** 1994
SALES (est): 11.9MM **Privately Held**
WEB: www.ezstaffing.com
SIC: 7361 Nurses' registry

(P-17416)
ELITE NURSING SERVICES INC
1915 W Orangewood Ave # 110, Orange
(92868-2084)
PHONE....................714 919-7898
Lee Hadfield, *President*
EMP: 56 **EST:** 1998
SQ FT: 2,000
SALES (est): 1MM **Privately Held**
WEB: www.elitenursingusa.com
SIC: 7361 Nurses' registry

(P-17417)
EMCARE INC
3916 State St 200, Santa Barbara
(93105-5602)
PHONE....................805 564-5097
Jill Meredith, *Branch Mgr*
Donna Davis, *Office Mgr*
EMP: 51 **Publicly Held**
SIC: 7361 8011 Labor contractors (employment agency); medical centers
HQ: Emcare, Inc.
13737 Noel Rd Ste 1600
Dallas TX 75240
214 712-2000

(P-17418)
EMPLOYBRIDGE LLC (HQ)
Also Called: Select Staffing
301 Mentor Dr 210, Santa Barbara
(93111-3339)
PHONE....................805 882-2200
Thomas A Bickes, *President*
Fred R Herbert, *President*
Julie Mellin, *President*
Steve Mills, *President*
Paul J Sorensen, *President*
EMP: 190 **EST:** 1989
SALES (est): 560.9MM
SALES (corp-wide): 32B **Privately Held**
WEB: www.employbridge.com
SIC: 7361 Employment agencies
PA: Employbridge Holding Company
1040 Crown Pointe Pkwy
Atlanta GA 30338
770 671-1900

(P-17419)
EMPLOYNET INC
123 E 9th St Ste 103, Upland
(91786-6033)
PHONE....................909 458-0961
EMP: 174
SALES (corp-wide): 90.1MM **Privately Held**
WEB: www.employnet.com
SIC: 7361 Employment agencies
PA: Employnet, Inc.
2555 Garden Rd Ste H
Monterey CA 93940
866 527-4473

(P-17420)
EPLICA INC
17785 Center Court Dr N, Cerritos
(90703-8573)
PHONE....................562 977-4300
Jade Jenkins, *Branch Mgr*

EMP: 156
SALES (corp-wide): 136.9MM **Privately Held**
WEB: www.eastridge.com
SIC: 7361 Employment agencies
PA: Eplica, Inc.
2385 Northside Dr Ste 250
San Diego CA 92108
619 260-2000

(P-17421)
ESPARZA ENTERPRISES INC
3851 Fruitvale Ave A, Bakersfield
(93308-5111)
PHONE....................661 831-0002
Irene Borland, *Manager*
EMP: 284
SALES (corp-wide): 135MM **Privately Held**
WEB: www.esparzainc.com
SIC: 7361 Labor contractors (employment agency)
PA: Esparza Enterprises, Inc.
3851 Fruitvale Ave
Bakersfield CA 93308
661 831-0002

(P-17422)
ESPARZA ENTERPRISES INC
51335 Harrison St Ste 112, Coachella
(92236-1528)
PHONE....................760 398-0349
Manuel Padilla, *Manager*
EMP: 284
SALES (corp-wide): 135MM **Privately Held**
WEB: www.esparzainc.com
SIC: 7361 Labor contractors (employment agency)
PA: Esparza Enterprises, Inc.
3851 Fruitvale Ave
Bakersfield CA 93308
661 831-0002

(P-17423)
ESPARZA ENTERPRISES INC
222 S Union Ave, Bakersfield (93307-3325)
PHONE....................661 631-0347
EMP: 284
SALES (corp-wide): 135MM **Privately Held**
WEB: www.esparzainc.com
SIC: 7361 Labor contractors (employment agency)
PA: Esparza Enterprises, Inc.
3851 Fruitvale Ave
Bakersfield CA 93308
661 831-0002

(P-17424)
EXECUTIVE PERSONNEL SERVICES
1526 Brookhollow Dr # 83, Santa Ana
(92705-5421)
PHONE....................714 310-9506
Mario Mendoza, *President*
Alinne Espinoza, *Vice Pres*
Alejandra Quinonez, *Admin Asst*
EMP: 300 **EST:** 2013
SALES (est): 10.1MM **Privately Held**
SIC: 7361 Executive placement

(P-17425)
GO-STAFF INC
240 W Lincoln Ave, Anaheim (92805-2903)
PHONE....................657 242-9350
EMP: 210
SALES (corp-wide): 27.1MM **Privately Held**
WEB: www.go-staff.com
SIC: 7361 Executive placement
PA: Go-Staff, Inc.
8798 Complex Dr
San Diego CA 92123
858 292-8562

(P-17426)
HARDESTY LLC (PA)
19800 Macarthur Blvd # 820, Irvine
(92612-2427)
PHONE....................949 407-6625
Karl Hardesty, *CEO*
Dave Aguero, *Partner*
Natl Arthur Cohen, *Partner*
Dan Corredor, *Partner*
Skip D'Orazio, *Partner*

EMP: 50 **EST:** 2011
SQ FT: 5,000
SALES (est): 12.9MM **Privately Held**
WEB: www.hardestyllc.com
SIC: 7361 Executive placement

(P-17427)
HORIZON PERSONNEL SERVICES (PA)
770 The Cy Dr S Ste 2000, Orange
(92868)
PHONE....................714 912-7500
Wally Ramirez, *VP Opers*
Maralice Stokes, *Regional*
EMP: 141 **EST:** 2013
SALES (est): 5.1MM **Privately Held**
WEB: www.horizonpersonnelservices.com
SIC: 7361 Placement agencies

(P-17428)
HOWROYD-WRIGHT EMPLYMNT AGCY (HQ)
Also Called: Apple One Employment
327 W Broadway, Glendale (91204-1301)
PHONE....................818 240-8688
Janice Bryant Howroyd, *CEO*
Bernard Howroyd, *President*
Michael Hoyal, *CFO*
Brett Howroyd, *Vice Pres*
Jan Speight, *Vice Pres*
EMP: 175 **EST:** 1964
SQ FT: 27,000
SALES (est): 145.3MM **Privately Held**
WEB: www.appleone.com
SIC: 7361 Labor contractors (employment agency); executive placement

(P-17429)
HOWROYD-WRIGHT EMPLYMNT AGCY
Also Called: Appleone Employment Services
325 W Broadway, Glendale (91204-1301)
PHONE....................818 240-8688
Marie Rounsavell, *Manager*
Rachel Borowski, *President*
Michael Hoyal, *CFO*
Jasmine Fishpaw, *Executive*
Roberta Lyon, *Executive*
EMP: 120 **Privately Held**
WEB: www.appleone.com
SIC: 7361 Labor contractors (employment agency)
HQ: Howroyd-Wright Employment Agency, Inc.
327 W Broadway
Glendale CA 91204
818 240-8688

(P-17430)
IBFTECH INC
Also Called: Image Business Forms
343 Main St, El Segundo (90245-3814)
PHONE....................424 217-8010
John Koch, *President*
Patricia Padilla, *Human Res Mgr*
Stephen Takahashi, *Recruiter*
EMP: 100 **EST:** 1979
SQ FT: 4,000
SALES (est): 5.6MM **Privately Held**
SIC: 7361 Executive placement

(P-17431)
JT RESOURCES
26372 Ruether Ave, Santa Clarita
(91350-2990)
PHONE....................661 367-6827
Darren Jackson, *Principal*
Jessica Jackson, *Contractor*
EMP: 110 **EST:** 2015
SALES (est): 9MM **Privately Held**
WEB: www.jtresources.com
SIC: 7361 Labor contractors (employment agency)

(P-17432)
KIMCO STAFFING SERVICES INC
3415 S Sepulveda Blvd # 1100, Los Angeles (90034-7090)
PHONE....................310 622-1616
EMP: 696
SALES (corp-wide): 89.9MM **Privately Held**
WEB: www.kimco.com
SIC: 7361 Placement agencies

PA: Kimco Staffing Services, Inc.
17872 Cowan
Irvine CA 92614
949 331-1199

(P-17433)
KIMCO STAFFING SERVICES INC
Also Called: Kimco Services
4295 Jurupa St Ste 107, Ontario
(91761-1429)
PHONE....................909 390-9881
Pammy Burton, *Manager*
Azeddine Ouhida, *Info Tech Dir*
Karla Austin, *Opers Staff*
Karla Chensam, *Opers Staff*
Kathie Niekowal, *Sales Staff*
EMP: 696
SALES (corp-wide): 89.9MM **Privately Held**
WEB: www.kimco.com
SIC: 7361 Labor contractors (employment agency)
PA: Kimco Staffing Services, Inc.
17872 Cowan
Irvine CA 92614
949 331-1199

(P-17434)
KIMCO STAFFING SERVICES INC
Also Called: Kimco Staffing Solutions
1770 Iowa Ave Ste 160, Riverside
(92507-7400)
P.O. Box 25190, Santa Ana 92799-5190)
PHONE....................951 686-3800
Silvia Roberts, *Manager*
EMP: 696
SALES (corp-wide): 89.9MM **Privately Held**
WEB: www.kimco.com
SIC: 7361 Employment agencies
PA: Kimco Staffing Services, Inc.
17872 Cowan
Irvine CA 92614
949 331-1199

(P-17435)
KORN FERRY (PA)
1900 Avenue Of The Stars # 2600, Los Angeles (90067-4507)
PHONE....................310 552-1834
Gary D Burnison, *Presiden*
David Armstrong, *Senior Partner*
Cara Capretta, *Senior Partner*
Dan Quinn, *Senior Partner*
Jamey Cummings, *Partner*
EMP: 136 **EST:** 1969
SALES: 1.8B **Publicly Held**
WEB: www.kornferry.com
SIC: 7361 8742 Employment agencies; executive placement; management consulting services

(P-17436)
L&T STAFFING INC (PA)
Also Called: Staffing Solutions
950 W 17th St Ste E, Santa Ana
(92706-3573)
PHONE....................714 558-1821
Fortino Rivera, *CEO*
Lucia Montellano, *CFO*
Rayel Christiansen, *Business Anlyst*
Tobi Barmen, *Human Resources*
Sherry Hicks, *Nurse*
EMP: 349 **EST:** 2004
SQ FT: 1,500 **Privately Held**
WEB: www.staffingsolutions.us
SIC: 7361 Executive placement

(P-17437)
LOAN ADMINISTRATION NETWRK INC
Also Called: Lani
2082 Bus Ctr Dr Ste 250, Irvine (92612)
PHONE....................949 752-5246
Charlene Nichols, *President*
Ernie Hernandez, *Vice Pres*
Candace Elaine, *Human Resources*
Bobbi Everett, *Recruiter*
Elizabeth Pino, *Manager*
EMP: 100 **EST:** 1992

SALES (est): 5.7MM **Privately Held**
WEB: www.lani.com
SIC: 7361 8742 Employment agencies; financial consultant; training & development consultant; banking & finance consultant

(P-17438)
MEDISCAN DIAGNOSTIC SVCS LLC
Also Called: Mediscan Staffing Services
21050 Califa St Ste 100, Woodland Hills (91367-5103)
PHONE....................................818 758-4224
Val Serebryany, *President*
EMP: 100 EST: 1995
SALES (est): 19.6MM
SALES (corp-wide): 836.4MM **Publicly Held**
WEB: www.crosscountryeducation.com
SIC: 7361 Employment agencies
HQ: Mediscan Nursing Staffing, Llc
21050 Califa St Ste 100
Woodland Hills CA 91367
818 758-8680

(P-17439)
MSCP V CC PARENT LLC (HQ)
5900 Wilshire Blvd # 110, Los Angeles (90036-5013)
PHONE....................................323 634-0156
Lawrence Serf,
EMP: 60 EST: 2012
SALES (est): 23.2MM
SALES (corp-wide): 3.9B **Publicly Held**
WEB: www.asgn.com
SIC: 7361 6719 Employment agencies; investment holding companies, except banks
PA: Asgn Incorporated
4400 Cox Rd Ste 110
Glen Allen VA 23060
888 482-8068

(P-17440)
NOVATIME TECHNOLOGY INC (HQ)
9680 Haven Ave Ste 200, Rancho Cucamonga (91730-5342)
PHONE....................................909 895-8100
Frank Su, *President*
Ian Sexton, *Senior VP*
Gil Sidhom, *Vice Pres*
Eric Su, *Info Tech Dir*
Christopher Stoliker, *IT/INT Sup*
▲ EMP: 60 EST: 1999
SQ FT: 6,000
SALES (est): 18.8MM
SALES (corp-wide): 27MM **Privately Held**
WEB: www.novatime.com
SIC: 7361 Executive placement
PA: Ascentis Corporation
11995 Singletree Ln # 400
Eden Prairie MN 55344
866 382-6229

(P-17441)
OFFICEWORKS INC
11801 Pierce St Fl 2, Riverside (92505-4400)
PHONE....................................951 784-2534
EMP: 85
SALES (corp-wide): 28.6MM **Privately Held**
WEB: www.officeworksrx.com
SIC: 7361 Employment agencies
PA: Officeworks, Inc.
3200 E Guasti Rd Ste 100
Ontario CA 91761
909 606-4100

(P-17442)
OSI STAFFING INC
10913 La Reina Ave Ste B, Downey (90241-3654)
PHONE....................................562 261-5753
Jose Vazquez, *CEO*
Sid Dakoria, *CFO*
EMP: 100 EST: 2018
SALES (est): 6.9MM **Privately Held**
SIC: 7361 Placement agencies

(P-17443)
PDS TECH INC
3100 S Harbor Blvd # 135, Santa Ana (92704-6823)
PHONE....................................214 647-9600
Dj Englert, *Manager*
Hemant Sachdev, *Tech Recruiter*
EMP: 188
SALES (corp-wide): 262.4MM **Privately Held**
WEB: www.pdstech.com
SIC: 7361 Employment agencies
PA: Pds Tech, Inc.
300 E John Carpenter Fwy # 700
Irving TX 75062
214 647-9600

(P-17444)
PEOPLES CHOICE STAFFING INC
4218 Green River Rd # 101, Corona (92878-3834)
PHONE....................................951 735-0550
EMP: 100
SALES (est): 14.5MM **Privately Held**
WEB: www.peopleschoicestaffing.com
SIC: 7361 Employment Agencies, Nsk

(P-17445)
PRECISE FIT LIMITED ONE LLC
Also Called: Pfitech
17011 Beach Blvd Ste 900, Huntington Beach (92647-5998)
PHONE....................................310 824-1800
Richard Hernandez, *Marketing Staff*
Carl Cook, *Executive*
Renae Miller, *CIO*
Tony Galindo, *CTO*
Brandon Asire, *Comp Tech*
EMP: 380 EST: 2001
SQ FT: 10,000 **Privately Held**
SIC: 7361 Employment agencies

(P-17446)
PREMIER HEALTHCARE SVCS LLC (DH)
Also Called: Phs Staffing
3030 Old Ranch Pkwy # 100, Seal Beach (90740-2752)
PHONE....................................626 204-7930
Anthony H Strange, *CEO*
Jerin Johnson, *Vice Pres*
Yesenia Macedo, *Finance Mgr*
Sherial Walker, *Finance Mgr*
Melissa Awe, *Recruiter*
EMP: 200 EST: 2005
SALES (est): 25.4MM
SALES (corp-wide): 1.5B **Publicly Held**
WEB: www.advantageoncall.com
SIC: 7361 Nurses' registry
HQ: Aveanna Healthcare Llc
400 Interstate North Pkwy
Atlanta GA 30339
770 441-1580

(P-17447)
PRIME ONE INC
22410 Hawthorne Blvd # 4, Torrance (90505-2539)
PHONE....................................310 378-1944
Elvira Musell, *President*
Laura Hernandez, *VP Sales*
EMP: 156 EST: 2001
SQ FT: 1,000
SALES (est): 5.8MM **Privately Held**
SIC: 7361 Employment agencies

(P-17448)
PRO CORPORATION
17682 Mitchell N Ste 100, Irvine (92614-6037)
PHONE....................................949 660-9544
Stephen Carew, *Principal*
EMP: 116 **Privately Held**
SIC: 7361 Employment agencies
HQ: Pro Corporation
999 Stewart Ave Ste 100
Bethpage NY 11714
516 437-3300

(P-17449)
PTS ADVANCE
1775 Flight Way Ste 100, Tustin (92782-1845)
PHONE....................................949 268-4000

June Stein, *President*
Randy Nodalo, *Vice Pres*
David Stein, *Vice Pres*
Ronald Stein, *Vice Pres*
Russell Stein, *Vice Pres*
EMP: 220 EST: 1995
SALES (est): 30.6MM **Privately Held**
WEB: www.ptsadvance.com
SIC: 7361 Employment agencies

(P-17450)
QUANTUM WORLD TECHNOLOGIES INC
199 W Hillcrest Dr Ste 11, Thousand Oaks (91360-7892)
PHONE....................................805 834-0532
Ekta Srivastava, *President*
Abhinav Garg, *Vice Pres*
Sajal Singhal, *CIO*
Vinay Singh, *Technical Staff*
Anshul Kumar, *Business Mgr*
EMP: 360 EST: 2016
SALES (est): 12.9MM **Privately Held**
WEB: www.quantumworld.us
SIC: 7361 Placement agencies

(P-17451)
RAMCO ENTERPRISES LP
325 Plaza Dr Ste 1, Santa Maria (93454-6929)
PHONE....................................805 922-9888
EMP: 558
SALES (corp-wide): 92.8MM **Privately Held**
WEB: www.ramcoenterpriseslp.com
SIC: 7361 Executive placement
PA: Ramco Enterprises, L.P.
710 La Guardia St
Salinas CA 93905
831 758-5272

(P-17452)
RANDSTAD PROFESSIONALS US LLC
Also Called: Mergis Group, The
3333 Michelson Dr Ste 210, Irvine (92612-1682)
PHONE....................................781 213-1500
EMP: 86
SALES (corp-wide): 24.5B **Privately Held**
WEB: www.randstadusa.com
SIC: 7361 Employment agencies
HQ: Randstad Professionals Us, Llc
150 Presidential Way Fl 4
Woburn MA 01801

(P-17453)
RANDSTAD PROFESSIONALS US LLC
Also Called: Randstad Finance & Accounting
17777 Center Court Dr N # 225, Cerritos (90703-9320)
PHONE....................................562 468-0111
EMP: 86
SALES (corp-wide): 24.5B **Privately Held**
WEB: www.randstadusa.com
SIC: 7361 Executive placement
HQ: Randstad Professionals Us, Llc
150 Presidential Way Fl 4
Woburn MA 01801

(P-17454)
READYLINK INC
72030 Metroplex Dr, Thousand Palms (92276)
PHONE....................................760 343-7000
Daniel Caliendo, *Principal*
EMP: 99 EST: 2017
SALES (est): 11.4MM **Privately Held**
WEB: www.readylinkstaffing.com
SIC: 7361 Employment agencies

(P-17455)
READYLINK HEALTHCARE
72030 Metroplex Dr, Thousand Palms (92276)
P.O. Box 1047 (92276-1047)
PHONE....................................760 343-7000
Barry L Treash, *President*
Sheri Price, *Manager*
EMP: 85 EST: 2002

SALES (est): 17.6MM **Privately Held**
WEB: www.readylinkstaffing.com
SIC: 7361 Nurses' registry

(P-17456)
RECRUIT 360
457 Ogle St, Costa Mesa (92627-3243)
PHONE....................................949 250-4420
Greg Kennedy, *President*
EMP: 115 EST: 2007
SALES (est): 3.5MM **Privately Held**
WEB: www.recruit360.net
SIC: 7361 Executive placement

(P-17457)
REDLANDS EMPLOYMENT SERVICES
Also Called: Redlands Staffing Services
4295 Jurupa St Ste 110, Ontario (91761-1429)
PHONE....................................951 688-0083
Matt Tahlmeyer, *President*
Kimber Minix, *Branch Mgr*
EMP: 115 **Privately Held**
WEB: www.arrowstaffing.com
SIC: 7361 Placement agencies
PA: Redlands Employment Services Inc
499 W State St
Redlands CA 92373

(P-17458)
REDLANDS EMPLOYMENT SERVICES (PA)
Also Called: Arrow Staffing
499 W State St, Redlands (92373-4647)
PHONE....................................909 792-3413
Matthew Thalmayer, *President*
Jeffrey Thalmayer, *Vice Pres*
Meggie Diaz, *Branch Mgr*
Reinhard Thalmayer, *Admin Sec*
Connie Carpenter, *Mktg Dir*
EMP: 284 EST: 1992
SQ FT: 3,000
SALES (est): 11.2MM **Privately Held**
WEB: www.arrowstaffing.com
SIC: 7361 Placement agencies

(P-17459)
REHABABILITIES INC
Also Called: Social Service Professionals
11835 W Olympic Blvd, Los Angeles (90064-5001)
PHONE....................................310 473-4448
Marina Rodriguez, *Social Worker*
EMP: 235
SALES (corp-wide): 12.4MM **Privately Held**
WEB: www.rehababilities.com
SIC: 7361 Registries
PA: Rehababilities, Inc.
8655 Haven Ste 200
Rancho Cucamonga CA 91730
909 989-5699

(P-17460)
RESOURCES CONNECTION LLC (HQ)
Also Called: Resources Global Professionals
17101 Armstrong Ave # 100, Irvine (92614-5742)
PHONE....................................714 430-6400
Donald B Murray, *Ch of Bd*
Kate W Duchene, *President*
Herbert M Mueller, *CFO*
Tanja Cebula, *Exec VP*
Shared Dallas, *Exec VP*
EMP: 60 EST: 1999
SQ FT: 16,366
SALES (est): 583.4MM **Publicly Held**
WEB: www.rgp.com
SIC: 7361 8742 Executive placement; management consulting services

(P-17461)
ROBERT HALF INTERNATIONAL INC
2280 Market St Ste 220, Riverside (92501-2120)
PHONE....................................951 779-9081
EMP: 92
SALES (corp-wide): 5.1B **Publicly Held**
WEB: www.roberthalf.com
SIC: 7361 Employment Agency

PA: Robert Half International Inc.
2884 Sand Hill Rd Ste 200
Menlo Park CA 94025
650 234-6000

(P-17462)
ROBERT QUINTERO LABOR CONTG
1827 S Bardo St, Visalia (93277-4848)
PHONE................................559 732-6954
EMP: 50
SALES: 1MM Privately Held
SIC: 7361 Employment Agency

(P-17463)
SEARCH ASSOCIATES INC
Also Called: S A I
5900 Sepulveda Blvd # 104, Van Nuys (91411-2511)
PHONE................................818 988-5600
Lee Woodward, Co-President
Bernard Sharf, Co-President
EMP: 74 EST: 1982
SALES: 1.1MM Privately Held
WEB: www.csajobs.com
SIC: 7361 Executive placement

(P-17464)
SELECT TEMPORARIES LLC (DH)
Also Called: Select Personnel Services
3820 State St, Santa Barbara (93105-3182)
PHONE................................805 882-2200
Thomas A Bickes, President
Shawn W Poole, CFO
Michael Parrish, Vice Pres
Rachelle Vargas, Vice Pres
Tina Haas, Regional Mgr
▲ EMP: 90 EST: 1985
SQ FT: 30,000
SALES (est): 44.1MM
SALES (corp-wide): 32B Privately Held
WEB: www.select.com
SIC: 7361 Employment agencies
HQ: Employment Solutions Management, Inc.
1040 Crown Pointe Pkwy
Atlanta GA 30338
770 671-1900

(P-17465)
SIRACUSA ENTERPRISES INC
Also Called: Quality Temp Staffing
17737 Chtswrth St Ste 200, Granada Hills (91344-5628)
PHONE................................818 831-1130
Joe Alas, President
Marie Alas, Vice Pres
Angie Londono, Recruiter
EMP: 70 EST: 1988 Privately Held
WEB: www.qualitytempstaffing.com
SIC: 7361 Employment agencies

(P-17466)
SMART CHOICE INVESTMENTS INC (PA)
Also Called: Brightstar Health
7121 Magnolia Ave, Riverside (92504-3805)
PHONE................................310 944-6985
Maurice Geyen, President
EMP: 67 EST: 2008
SALES (est): 6.4MM Privately Held
SIC: 7361 8082 Nurses' registry; home health care services

(P-17467)
SOLEMNITY PERSONNEL
5670 E Washington Blvd, Commerce (90040-1406)
PHONE................................323 718-3979
Peter Diaz, Principal
EMP: 50 EST: 2017
SALES (est): 2.5MM Privately Held
SIC: 7361 Employment agencies

(P-17468)
STAFF ASSISTANCE INC
Also Called: Assisted Home Care
72 Moody Ct Ste 100, Thousand Oaks (91360-7426)
PHONE................................805 371-9980
Elaine Thinney, Branch Mgr
Nicolle Sapo, Analyst

Seth Baxter, Recruiter
Teresa Casas, Recruiter
Jolene Velasquez, Recruiter
EMP: 300 Privately Held
WEB: www.assistedcares.com
SIC: 7361 8082 Nurses' registry; home health care services
PA: Staff Assistance, Inc.
72 Moody Ct Ste 100
Thousand Oaks CA 91360

(P-17469)
STAFFCHEX INC
20537 Devonshire St, Chatsworth (91311-3208)
PHONE................................818 709-6100
Steven Zingerman, Principal
EMP: 652
SALES (corp-wide): 49.1MM Privately Held
WEB: www.staffchex.com
SIC: 7361 Employment agencies
PA: Staffchex, Inc.
770 The Cy Dr S Ste 2000
Orange CA 92868
714 912-7500

(P-17470)
T L C TRANSPORTATION STAFFING (HQ)
1600 E 4th St Ste 340, Santa Ana (92701-5194)
PHONE................................714 541-5415
Toll Free:................................888 -
Paul C Driskell, Ch of Bd
EMP: 60 EST: 1981
SQ FT: 13,543
SALES (est): 894.2K Privately Held
SIC: 7361 7363 Labor contractors (employment agency); temporary help service

(P-17471)
TEAM-ONE EMPLYMENT SPCLSTS LLC
Also Called: Team One
15720 Ventura Blvd # 607, Encino (91436-2914)
PHONE................................310 481-4480
Frank Moran,
Joanne Geishecker, Marketing Staff
EMP: 52 EST: 2001 Privately Held
SIC: 7361 Placement agencies

(P-17472)
TEAM-ONE STAFFING SERVICES INC
Also Called: Teamone Employment
15720 Ventura Blvd # 607, Encino (91436-2914)
PHONE................................951 616-3515
EMP: 2629 Privately Held
WEB: www.teamone.com
SIC: 7361 Placement agencies
PA: Team-One Staffing Services, Inc.
10801 National Blvd # 104
Los Angeles CA 90064

(P-17473)
TEMPS PLUS INC
Also Called: Sales Advantage Group
268 N Lincoln Ave Ste 12, Corona (92882-7103)
PHONE................................951 549-8309
Louie S Norwood, CEO
Kenneth Post, Vice Pres
Nadine Rini, Vice Pres
Karen Beanblossom, Recruiter
Kirk Chittick, Sales Staff
EMP: 84 EST: 1996
SALES (est): 10.7MM Privately Held
WEB: www.tempsplus.com
SIC: 7361 Executive placement

(P-17474)
TEMPUS LLC
Also Called: Emerald Health Services
2041 Rosecrans Ave # 245, El Segundo (90245-4707)
PHONE................................800 917-5055
Mark Siegel, CEO
Mark Stagen, CEO
Adam Guttmann, Vice Pres
Beverly Scott, Vice Pres

Jeffrey Murray, Human Res Dir
EMP: 70 EST: 2002
SALES (est): 20.9MM Privately Held
WEB: www.emeraldhs.com
SIC: 7361 Nurses' registry

(P-17475)
TETRA TECH EXECUTIVE SVCS INC
3475 E Foothill Blvd, Pasadena (91107-6024)
PHONE................................626 470-2400
Sam Box, Principal
EMP: 162 EST: 2013
SALES (est): 26MM
SALES (corp-wide): 2.9B Publicly Held
WEB: www.tetratech.com
SIC: 7361 Employment agencies
PA: Tetra Tech, Inc.
3475 E Foothill Blvd
Pasadena CA 91107
626 351-4664

(P-17476)
TOTAL MANAGEMENT SVCS AMER INC
Also Called: Tms America
21151 S Wstn Ave Ste 139, Torrance (90501)
PHONE................................310 328-0867
Pakaco Shimakage, President
EMP: 50 EST: 2014
SALES (est): 1MM Privately Held
WEB: www.tmsjob.com
SIC: 7361 Executive placement

(P-17477)
VOLT CONSULTING GROUP LTD
2401 N Glassell St, Orange (92865-2705)
PHONE................................800 654-2624
Linda Perneau, President
Ludwig Guarino, Treasurer
Elizabeth Bush Y, Senior VP
Jerome Shaw, Vice Pres
Howard Weinreich, Admin Sec
EMP: 172 EST: 2000
SALES (est): 26.1MM
SALES (corp-wide): 822MM Publicly Held
WEB: www.voltconsultinggroup.com
SIC: 7361 Executive placement
PA: Volt Information Sciences Inc
2401 N Glassell St
Orange CA 92865
714 921-8800

(P-17478)
WESTERN STAFFING SOLUTIONS LLC
1235 Carbide Dr, Corona (92881-7269)
PHONE................................951 545-4449
Jerry Edwards, CEO
EMP: 123 EST: 2014
SALES (est): 450K Privately Held
WEB: www.westernstaffingsolutions.net
SIC: 7361 Employment agencies

(P-17479)
WORKFORCE ENTERPRISES WFE INC
800 N Haven Ave Ste 330, Ontario (91764-4976)
PHONE................................909 718-8915
Andrew Hernandez, President
Luis Garicia, Director
EMP: 50 EST: 2013
SALES (est): 6.2MM Privately Held
SIC: 7361 Employment agencies

(P-17480)
WORKWAY INC
19742 Macarthur Blvd # 235, Irvine (92612-2446)
PHONE................................949 553-8700
Jill Burdock, Branch Mgr
EMP: 227 Privately Held
WEB: www.workway.com
SIC: 7361 Labor contractors (employment agency)
PA: Workway, Inc.
5151 Belt Line Rd
Dallas TX 75254

(P-17481)
WYNDEN STARK LLC (HQ)
Also Called: Gqr
1038 Princeton Dr Ste B, Marina Del Rey (90292-6680)
PHONE................................424 271-4156
Steven Talbot, Mng Member
Anjuli Patel, Marketing Staff
James Richter, Sr Associate
Hugo Sugden, Mng Member
EMP: 107 EST: 2016
SALES (est): 25.8MM
SALES (corp-wide): 32MM Privately Held
WEB: www.wyndenstark.gqrgrn.com
SIC: 7361 6799 Employment agencies; investors

(P-17482)
YORK EMPLOYMENT SERVICES INC
980 Ontario Mills Dr C, Ontario (91764-5241)
PHONE................................909 581-0181
Roberta Pierce, President
Steven Healis, Treasurer
Robin Engstron, Vice Pres
Jon Grasso, Business Anlyst
EMP: 56 EST: 2000
SALES (est): 3.8MM Privately Held
WEB: www.yorkemployment.com
SIC: 7361 Employment agencies

7363 Help Supply Svcs

(P-17483)
A P R INC
Also Called: Alpha Professional Resources
100 E Thsnd Oaks Blvd, Thousand Oaks (91360)
PHONE................................805 379-3400
Salvador Ramirez, President
Cliff Goodwin, CFO
Clifton Goodwin Jr, CFO
Sean Pennel, Senior Mgr
EMP: 125 EST: 1993
SQ FT: 1,100
SALES (est): 10.3MM Privately Held
WEB: www.alphaprotemps.com
SIC: 7363 7361 Temporary help service; employment agencies

(P-17484)
ADVANCED MEDICAL REVIEWS LLC
600 Crprate Pinte Ste 300, Culver City (90230)
PHONE................................310 575-0900
Barak Mevorak, CEO
Nelson F Dunham, Vice Pres
Hollymarie Britt, Human Res Mgr
Stephanie Nguyen, Opers Mgr
Quinn Jorgenson, Opers Staff
EMP: 61 EST: 2005
SQ FT: 10,000
SALES (est): 17MM Privately Held
WEB: www.admere.com
SIC: 7363 Medical help service
PA: Examworks Group, Inc.
3280 Peachtree Rd Ne # 26
Atlanta GA 30305

(P-17485)
ANDERSON ASSOC STAFFING CORP (PA)
8200 Wilshire Blvd # 20C, Beverly Hills (90211-2328)
PHONE................................323 930-3170
Tom Anderson, President
EMP: 200 EST: 1997
SALES (est): 13.5MM Privately Held
SIC: 7363 Temporary help service

(P-17486)
B2B STAFFING SERVICES INC
Also Called: B2b Payroll Services
4501 Cerritos Ave Ste 201, Cypress (90630-4215)
PHONE................................714 243-4104
Brian Wigdor, President
Bruce Underwood, CFO
EMP: 350 EST: 2006

SALES (est): 12MM **Privately Held**
WEB: www.b2bstaffingservices.com
SIC: 7363 Temporary help service

(P-17487)
BUTLER SERVICE GROUP INC (HQ)
3820 State St Ste A, Santa Barbara
(93105-3182)
PHONE.................................201 891-5312
Edward M Kopko, *President*
Michael C Hellriegel, *CFO*
R Scott Silver Hill, *Senior VP*
EMP: 100 **EST:** 1965
SQ FT: 82,000
SALES (est): 74.6MM
SALES (corp-wide): 168.4MM **Privately Held**
WEB: www.butler.com
SIC: 7363 8711 8748 3661 Engineering help service; engineering services; communications consulting; telephone & telegraph apparatus; general automotive repair shops
PA: Butler International, Inc.
3820 State St Ste A
Santa Barbara CA 93105
805 882-2200

(P-17488)
CANON RECRUITING GROUP LLC
27651 Lincoln Pl Ste 250, Santa Clarita
(91387-8818)
PHONE.................................661 252-7400
Laurie Grayem, *CEO*
Tim Grayem, *President*
EMP: 500 **EST:** 1980
SQ FT: 7,500
SALES (est): 22.3MM **Privately Held**
WEB: www.canonrecruiting.com
SIC: 7363 7361 Office supply service; executive placement

(P-17489)
CULINARY SERVICES AMERICA INC
Also Called: Culinary Staffing Service
6404 Wilshire Blvd # 500, Los Angeles
(90048-5507)
PHONE.................................323 965-7582
Randy Hopp, *President*
David Crego, *Recruiter*
Jessica Sapia, *Manager*
EMP: 50 **EST:** 1999
SQ FT: 1,200
SALES (est): 8MM **Privately Held**
WEB: www.culinarystaffing.com
SIC: 7363 7361 Temporary help service; employment agencies

(P-17490)
CULINARY STAFFING OF AMERICA (PA)
2950 S Mooney Blvd Ste G, Visalia
(93277-7357)
PHONE.................................559 741-1314
John M Anderson, *President*
Nancy Anderson, *Vice Pres*
EMP: 64 **EST:** 2003
SALES (est): 11.2MM **Privately Held**
WEB: www.staffing-america.com
SIC: 7363 Temporary help service

(P-17491)
EMERGNCY MDCINE SPCLIST ORNGE
Also Called: Emsoc
1310 W Stewart Dr Ste 212, Orange
(92868-3837)
PHONE.................................714 543-8911
Matthey Mallarky, *Mng Member*
Jonathen Blair, *Partner*
Mark Falcone, *Partner*
Daniel Starr, *Associate Dir*
Claudia Gold, *Emerg Med Spec*
EMP: 129 **EST:** 1976
SALES (est): 7.2MM **Privately Held**
WEB: www.emsoc.net
SIC: 7363 Medical help service

(P-17492)
ESPARZA ENTERPRISES INC (PA)
3851 Fruitvale Ave, Bakersfield
(93308-5111)
PHONE.................................661 831-0002
Luis Esparza, *President*
Maria Esparza, *Corp Secy*
Luis Esparza Jr, *Vice Pres*
Tandy Greiner, *Admin Asst*
Justice Gradowitz, *Controller*
EMP: 1840 **EST:** 1999
SQ FT: 5,800
SALES (est): 135MM **Privately Held**
WEB: www.esparzainc.com
SIC: 7363 7361 Help supply services; labor contractors (employment agency)

(P-17493)
GET HEAL INC
528 Palisades Dr Ste 176, Pacific Palisades
(90272-2844)
PHONE.................................310 528-4957
Greg Drobnick, *Exec VP*
Steve Friedman, *Controller*
Dany Danny, *Med Doctor*
EMP: 52
SALES (corp-wide): 14.6MM **Privately Held**
WEB: www.heal.com
SIC: 7363 Medical help service
PA: Get Heal, Inc.
11845 W Olympic Blvd 900w
Los Angeles CA 90064
310 528-4957

(P-17494)
H M H EMERGENCY MEDICAL GROUP
100 W California Blvd, Pasadena
(91105-3010)
PHONE.................................626 397-5106
Stanley Kalter MD, *Director*
James Luna MD, *Vice Pres*
Robert Goldwebber, *Admin Sec*
EMP: 66 **EST:** 1973
SALES (est): 677.2K **Privately Held**
WEB: www.huntingtonhospital.org
SIC: 7363 Medical help service

(P-17495)
I N C BUILDERS INC
Also Called: Acme Staffing
1560 Ocotillo Dr Ste L, El Centro
(92243-4237)
PHONE.................................760 352-4200
Rebecca Deal, *Manager*
EMP: 350
SALES (corp-wide): 11MM **Privately Held**
WEB: www.algodonesrx.com
SIC: 7363 Help supply services
PA: I N C Builders, Inc.
550 E 32nd St Ste 5a
Yuma AZ 85365
928 344-8367

(P-17496)
LAB SUPPORT LLC (HQ)
26745 Malibu Hills Rd, Calabasas
(91301-5355)
PHONE.................................818 878-7900
Christina Gibson, *President*
Nancy Pawar, *Admin Sec*
Reginald Wright, *IT/INT Sup*
Carol Rubens, *Tech Recruiter*
Cassidy Lavigne, *Recruiter*
EMP: 146 **EST:** 1996
SALES (est): 35.7MM
SALES (corp-wide): 3.9B **Publicly Held**
WEB: www.asgn.com
SIC: 7363 Temporary help service
PA: Asgn Incorporated
4400 Cox Rd Ste 110
Glen Allen VA 23060
888 482-8068

(P-17497)
LLOYD STAFFING INC
18000 Studebaker Rd # 700, Cerritos
(90703-2679)
PHONE.................................631 777-7600
Luly Santana, *President*
EMP: 456

SALES (corp-wide): 52.2MM **Privately Held**
WEB: www.lloydstaffing.com
SIC: 7363 Temporary help service
PA: Lloyd Staffing, Inc.
445 Broadhollow Rd # 119
Melville NY 11747
631 777-7600

(P-17498)
MAXIM HEALTHCARE SERVICES INC
28470 Ave Stnford Ste 250, Valencia
(91355)
PHONE.................................661 964-6350
Kowalczyk David, *Manager*
EMP: 92 **Privately Held**
WEB: www.maximhealthcare.com
SIC: 7363 8099 8748 Medical help service; blood related health services; testing services
PA: Maxim Healthcare Services, Inc.
7227 Lee Deforest Dr
Columbia MD 21046

(P-17499)
MAXIM HEALTHCARE SERVICES INC
104 Traffic Way Ste A, Arroyo Grande
(93420-3451)
PHONE.................................805 489-2685
Jeremiah Lee, *Branch Mgr*
EMP: 92 **Privately Held**
WEB: www.maximhealthcare.com
SIC: 7363 8099 8748 Medical help service; blood related health services; testing services
PA: Maxim Healthcare Services, Inc.
7227 Lee Deforest Dr
Columbia MD 21046

(P-17500)
MAXIM HEALTHCARE SERVICES INC
500 E Esplanade Dr, Oxnard (93036-2110)
PHONE.................................805 278-4593
Rowena Garcia, *Manager*
EMP: 92 **Privately Held**
WEB: www.maximhealthcare.com
SIC: 7363 Medical help service
PA: Maxim Healthcare Services, Inc.
7227 Lee Deforest Dr
Columbia MD 21046

(P-17501)
MAXIM HEALTHCARE SERVICES INC
Also Called: Temecula Homecare
1 Ridgegate Dr Ste 130, Temecula
(92590-5505)
PHONE.................................951 694-0100
Jeff Abbott, *Manager*
EMP: 92 **Privately Held**
WEB: www.maximhealthcare.com
SIC: 7363 Medical help service
PA: Maxim Healthcare Services, Inc.
7227 Lee Deforest Dr
Columbia MD 21046

(P-17502)
MAXIM HEALTHCARE SERVICES INC
Also Called: Riverside Companion Services
1845 Bus Ctr Dr Ste 112, San Bernardino
(92408)
PHONE.................................951 684-4148
Elijah Hall, *Manager*
EMP: 92 **Privately Held**
WEB: www.maximhealthcare.com
SIC: 7363 Medical help service
PA: Maxim Healthcare Services, Inc.
7227 Lee Deforest Dr
Columbia MD 21046

(P-17503)
MAXIM HEALTHCARE SERVICES INC
Also Called: Bakersfield Respite Homecare
5201 California Ave # 200, Bakersfield
(93309-1674)
PHONE.................................661 322-3039
Reyes Robles, *Branch Mgr*
EMP: 92 **Privately Held**
WEB: www.maximhealthcare.com
SIC: 7363 Medical help service
PA: Maxim Healthcare Services, Inc.
7227 Lee Deforest Dr
Columbia MD 21046

(P-17504)
MAXIM HEALTHCARE SERVICES INC
801 Corporate Center Dr # 21, Pomona
(91768-2628)
PHONE.................................626 962-6453
Kirk Grant, *Manager*
EMP: 92 **Privately Held**
WEB: www.maximhealthcare.com
SIC: 7363 7361 Medical help service; nurses' registry
PA: Maxim Healthcare Services, Inc.
7227 Lee Deforest Dr
Columbia MD 21046

(P-17505)
MEDICAL MANAGEMENT CONS INC (PA)
Also Called: MMC
8150 Beverly Blvd, Los Angeles
(90048-4513)
PHONE.................................310 659-3835
Mashi Rahmani, *President*
Marc Peralejo, *Administration*
Raymond Chen, *Accountant*
Chris Platt, *Human Res Mgr*
Nancy Melamed, *Human Resources*
▲ **EMP:** 50 **EST:** 1982
SQ FT: 21,000
SALES (est): 39.8MM **Privately Held**
WEB: www.mmchr.com
SIC: 7363 8742 8748 8721 Help supply services; hospital & health services consultant; employee programs administration; payroll accounting service

(P-17506)
PERRIS VALLEY AVI SVCS INC
Also Called: Perris Valley Government Svcs
2091 Goetz Rd, Perris (92570-9315)
P.O. Box 1823 (92572-1823)
PHONE.................................951 657-3904
Patrick Conatser, *President*
Melanie Conatser, *Vice Pres*
EMP: 57 **EST:** 1990
SALES (est): 2.8MM **Privately Held**
WEB: www.skydiveperris.com
SIC: 7363 Pilot service, aviation

(P-17507)
PHOENIX ENGINEERING CO INC
Also Called: Phoenix Personnel
2480 Armacost Ave, Los Angeles
(90064-2714)
P.O. Box 66395 (90066-0395)
PHONE.................................310 532-1134
Silvia Maron, *President*
Silvia Lugo, *President*
EMP: 100 **EST:** 1974
SQ FT: 1,700
SALES (est): 4.9MM **Privately Held**
WEB: www.phoenix-engineering.com
SIC: 7363 7361 Office help supply service; employment agencies

(P-17508)
PLATINUM EMPIRE GROUP INC
Also Called: Platinum Healthcare Staffing
2430 Amsler St Ste B, Torrance
(90505-5302)
P.O. Box 10338 (90505-1238)
PHONE.................................310 821-5888
Arun Mahtani, *President*
Rajat Bhattacharya, *Exec VP*
Erika Malicdem, *Technical Staff*
Naveen Yadav, *Technical Staff*
Goutam Mitra, *Engineer*
EMP: 120 **EST:** 2005

(PA)=Parent Co (HQ)=Headquarters (DH)=Div Headquarters
✪ = New Business established in last 2 years

SALES (est): 9.7MM **Privately Held**
WEB: www.platinumhealthcarestaffing.com
SIC: **7363** Temporary help service

(P-17509)
PROCEL TEMPORARY SERVICES INC
108 W Walnut St Fl 1, Gardena
(90248-3107)
PHONE..............................310 372-0560
Marilyn Stephens, *President*
Bert Soriano, *Department Mgr*
Robert Stephens, *Purch Mgr*
EMP: 70 EST: 1988
SALES (est): 7.7MM **Privately Held**
WEB: www.procelnurses.com
SIC: **7363** Temporary help service

(P-17510)
RANDSTAD PROFESSIONALS US LLC
Also Called: Randstad Engineering
2321 Rosecrans Ave # 2215, El Segundo
(90245-4903)
PHONE..............................424 246-4400
Joe Davis, *Branch Mgr*
Alyssa Woodruff, *Tech Recruiter*
EMP: 86
SALES (corp-wide): 24.5B **Privately Held**
WEB: www.randstadusa.com
SIC: **7363** Temporary help service
HQ: Randstad Professionals Us, Llc
　　150 Presidential Way Fl 4
　　Woburn MA 01801

(P-17511)
REMEDY INTLLIGENT STAFFING LLC (DH)
3820 State St Ste A, Santa Barbara
(93105-3182)
PHONE..............................805 882-2200
Thomas A Bickes, *President*
Shawn W Poole, *CFO*
Bonnie Cox, *Vice Pres*
Kammie Gargan, *Vice Pres*
Kristen Nelson, *Vice Pres*
EMP: 60 EST: 2014
SALES (est): 26.9MM
SALES (corp-wide): 32B **Privately Held**
WEB: www.remedystaffing.com
SIC: **7363** Temporary help service

(P-17512)
REMEDYTEMP INC (DH)
Also Called: Remedy Intelligent Staffing
101 Enterprise Ste 100, Aliso Viejo
(92656-2604)
PHONE..............................949 425-7600
David Stephen Sorensen, *CEO*
Jeff R Mitchell, *CFO*
Richard Hulme, *Exec VP*
EMP: 143 EST: 1974
SQ FT: 51,000
SALES (est): 43.4MM
SALES (corp-wide): 32B **Privately Held**
WEB: www.remedystaffing.com
SIC: **7363 7361** Temporary help service;
　　employment agencies

(P-17513)
RIGHTSOURCING INC (HQ)
9 Executive Cir Ste 290, Irvine
(92614-4704)
PHONE..............................800 660-9544
Andrew Schultz, *Ch of Bd*
Terry McGoldrick, *Officer*
Richey Brownfield, *Vice Pres*
Hillary Degraffenreid, *Vice Pres*
Akbar Vanterpool, *Program Mgr*
EMP: 87 EST: 2003
SALES (est): 65.2MM **Privately Held**
WEB: www.rightsourcingusa.com
SIC: **7363** Help supply services

(P-17514)
ROTH STAFFING COMPANIES LP (PA)
Also Called: Ultimate Staffing Services
450 N State College Blvd, Orange
(92868-1708)
PHONE..............................714 939-8600
Adam Roth, *CEO*
Ben Roth, *Ch of Bd*
Homze Stephen, *Treasurer*

Pam Sexauer, *Exec VP*
Gail Ferrari, *Vice Pres*
◆ EMP: 80 **Privately Held**
WEB: www.rothstaffing.com
SIC: **7363** Help supply services

(P-17515)
SAGE STAFFING CONSULTANTS INC (PA)
27441 Tourney Rd Ste 150, Valencia
(91355-5312)
PHONE..............................661 254-4026
Laura Kincaid, *CEO*
Greg Kincaid, *President*
EMP: 190 EST: 1987
SQ FT: 5,000
SALES (est): 9.8MM **Privately Held**
WEB: www.sagestaffing.com
SIC: **7363** Temporary help service

(P-17516)
SFN GROUP INC
114 Pacifica Ste 210, Irvine (92618-3320)
PHONE..............................949 727-8500
Tammy Hawkins, *Manager*
EMP: 715
SALES (corp-wide): 24.5B **Privately Held**
WEB: www.spherion.com
SIC: **7363** Temporary help service
HQ: Sfn Group, Inc.
　　2050 Spectrum Blvd
　　Fort Lauderdale FL 33309
　　954 308-7600

(P-17517)
TAD PGS INC
12062 Valley View St # 108, Garden Grove
(92845-1737)
PHONE..............................800 261-3779
Latonya Walker, *Director*
EMP: 797
SALES (corp-wide): 775.3MM **Privately Held**
WEB: www.tadpgs.com
SIC: **7363** Temporary help service
HQ: Tad Pgs, Inc.
　　1001 3rd Ave W Ste 460
　　Bradenton FL 34205
　　941 746-4434

(P-17518)
TAD PGS INC
10805 Holder St Ste 250, Cypress
(90630-5142)
PHONE..............................571 451-2428
Wendy Harkins, *CFO*
Marisela Vega, *Manager*
EMP: 797
SALES (corp-wide): 775.3MM **Privately Held**
WEB: www.tadpgs.com
SIC: **7363** Temporary help service
HQ: Tad Pgs, Inc.
　　1001 3rd Ave W Ste 460
　　Bradenton FL 34205
　　941 746-4434

(P-17519)
TWO ROADS PROF RESOURCES INC
5122 Bolsa Ave Ste 112, Huntington Beach
(92649-1050)
PHONE..............................714 901-3804
Tammy Gottschalk, *President*
Chris Hoff, *Vice Pres*
Michele Hoff, *Vice Pres*
Barry Vince, *Vice Pres*
Molly Kidder, *HR Admin*
EMP: 56 EST: 1996
SQ FT: 4,000
SALES (est): 7.2MM **Privately Held**
WEB: www.2roads.com
SIC: **7363** Temporary help service

(P-17520)
USA STAFFING INC
505 Higuera St, San Luis Obispo
(93401-6107)
PHONE..............................805 269-2677
Susan Elson, *Principal*
EMP: 75 EST: 2010
SALES (est): 2.9MM **Privately Held**
WEB: www.unitedwestaff.com
SIC: **7363** Temporary help service

(P-17521)
VASINDA INVESTMENTS INC
Also Called: Around The Clock Care
5353 Truckston Ave, Bakersfield (93309)
PHONE..............................661 324-4277
Mary Vasinda, *President*
John Vasinda, *Vice Pres*
Stacie Dollar, *Regional Mgr*
Juliana Kabwe, *Lic Prac Nurse*
EMP: 75 EST: 1994
SALES (est): 3.5MM **Privately Held**
WEB: www.bakersfieldcare.com
SIC: **7363** Domestic help service

(P-17522)
VOLT INFORMATION SCIENCES INC (PA)
2401 N Glassell St, Orange (92865-2705)
PHONE..............................714 921-8800
Linda Perneau, *President*
William J Grubbs, *Ch of Bd*
Herbert M Mueller, *CFO*
Nancy T Avedissian,
Lori Schultz, *Senior VP*
EMP: 50 EST: 1950
SQ FT: 200,000
SALES: 822MM **Publicly Held**
WEB: www.volt.com
SIC: **7363** Help supply services; temporary
　　help service

(P-17523)
VOLT MANAGEMENT CORP
715 6th St, Paso Robles (93446-2871)
PHONE..............................805 237-0882
EMP: 75
SALES (corp-wide): 822MM **Publicly Held**
WEB: www.arctern.com
SIC: **7363** Help supply services
HQ: Volt Management Corp.
　　2401 N Glassell St
　　Orange CA 92865

(P-17524)
VOLT MANAGEMENT CORP
Also Called: Volt Workforce Solutions
19191 S Vt Ave Ste 950, Torrance
(90502-1098)
PHONE..............................310 316-8523
Rhona Driggs, *Branch Mgr*
Bob Barber, *Analyst*
Lindsay Brock, *Analyst*
Nicollette Tomseth, *Recruiter*
Danielle Cattaneo, *Director*
EMP: 75
SALES (corp-wide): 822MM **Publicly Held**
WEB: www.arctern.com
SIC: **7363** Temporary help service
HQ: Volt Management Corp.
　　2401 N Glassell St
　　Orange CA 92865

(P-17525)
VOLT MANAGEMENT CORP
Also Called: Volt Temporary Services
2411 N Glassell St, Orange (92865-2717)
PHONE..............................800 654-2624
Rhona Driggs, *Branch Mgr*
EMP: 300
SALES (corp-wide): 822MM **Publicly Held**
WEB: www.arctern.com
SIC: **7363 7373** Temporary help service;
　　computer integrated systems design
HQ: Volt Management Corp.
　　2401 N Glassell St
　　Orange CA 92865

(P-17526)
VOLT MANAGEMENT CORP
Also Called: Volt Workforce Solutions
100 N Citrus St Ste 150, West Covina
(91791-1656)
PHONE..............................626 931-1437
Rhona Driggs, *Branch Mgr*
EMP: 75
SALES (corp-wide): 822MM **Publicly Held**
WEB: www.arctern.com
SIC: **7363** Temporary help service

HQ: Volt Management Corp.
　　2401 N Glassell St
　　Orange CA 92865

(P-17527)
VOLT MANAGEMENT CORP
Also Called: Volt Workforce Solutions
1400 N Harbor Blvd # 103, Fullerton
(92835-4126)
PHONE..............................714 879-9330
Scott Giroux, *Branch Mgr*
EMP: 75
SQ FT: 11,000
SALES (corp-wide): 822MM **Publicly Held**
WEB: www.arctern.com
SIC: **7363** Temporary help service
HQ: Volt Management Corp.
　　2401 N Glassell St
　　Orange CA 92865

(P-17528)
VOLT MANAGEMENT CORP
Also Called: Volt Workforce Solutions
1300 Santa Barbara St A, Santa Barbara
(93101-6041)
PHONE..............................805 560-8658
Scott Giroux, *Branch Mgr*
EMP: 75
SALES (corp-wide): 822MM **Publicly Held**
WEB: www.arctern.com
SIC: **7363** Temporary help service
HQ: Volt Management Corp.
　　2401 N Glassell St
　　Orange CA 92865

(P-17529)
VOLT MANAGEMENT CORP (HQ)
Also Called: Volt Workforce Solutions
2401 N Glassell St, Orange (92865-2705)
PHONE..............................800 654-2624
Linda Perneau, *President*
Lou Grossi, *Director*
Diana Rojas, *Manager*
EMP: 50
SQ FT: 41,000
SALES (est): 196.3MM
SALES (corp-wide): 822MM **Publicly Held**
WEB: www.arctern.com
SIC: **7363** Temporary help service; domes-
　　tic help service
PA: Volt Information Sciences Inc
　　2401 N Glassell St
　　Orange CA 92865
　　714 921-8800

(P-17530)
VOLT MANAGEMENT CORP
Also Called: Volt Workforce Solutions
1650 Iowa Ave Ste 140, Riverside
(92507-2432)
PHONE..............................951 789-8133
Scott Giroux, *Branch Mgr*
EMP: 75
SALES (corp-wide): 822MM **Publicly Held**
WEB: www.arctern.com
SIC: **7363** Help supply services
HQ: Volt Management Corp.
　　2401 N Glassell St
　　Orange CA 92865

(P-17531)
VOLT MANAGEMENT CORP
Also Called: Volt Workforce Solutions
1701 Solar Dr Ste 145, Oxnard
(93030-0137)
PHONE..............................805 485-0506
Scott Giroux, *Branch Mgr*
EMP: 75
SALES (corp-wide): 822MM **Publicly Held**
WEB: www.arctern.com
SIC: **7363** Help supply services
HQ: Volt Management Corp.
　　2401 N Glassell St
　　Orange CA 92865

(P-17532)
WORK FORCE SERVICES INC
Also Called: Work Force Staffing
1811 Oak St, Bakersfield (93301-3062)
PHONE..................661 327-5019
Brooks Whitehead, *President*
Brenda Bynum, *Accounting Dir*
Morgan Corvett, *Manager*
EMP: 250 **EST:** 1981
SALES (est): 10.2MM **Privately Held**
WEB: www.wfskern.com
SIC: 7363 Temporary help service

7371 Custom Computer Programming Svcs

(P-17533)
1NTEGER LLC
Also Called: Kharon
1999 Avenue Of The Stars, Los Angeles
(90067-6022)
PHONE..................424 320-2977
Frazer Burkart, *Administration*
Victoria Lumb, *Vice Pres*
Darci Kovacs, *Project Mgr*
William Harrington, *Manager*
Diogo Palhano, *Account Dir*
EMP: 50 **EST:** 2016
SALES (est): 5.3MM **Privately Held**
SIC: 7371 Computer software systems
analysis & design, custom

(P-17534)
3DNA CORP (PA)
Also Called: Nationbuilder
520 S Grand Ave Fl 2, Los Angeles
(90071-2600)
PHONE..................213 394-4623
Jim H Gilliam, *President*
Gabi Loeb, *CFO*
Gina Davis, *Vice Pres*
Laura Harris, *Vice Pres*
Ryann McQuilton, *Software Engr*
EMP: 99 **EST:** 2009
SALES (est): 21.7MM **Privately Held**
WEB: www.nationbuilder.com
SIC: 7371 Computer software development

(P-17535)
3I INFOTECH INC
555 Chorro St Ste B, San Luis Obispo
(93405-2398)
PHONE..................805 544-8327
Mathew Philip, *CFO*
Scott Huerta, *Vice Pres*
Prashant Ambre, *Executive*
Ruchira Vaidya, *Senior Mgr*
Ginamarie Gaughan, *Director*
EMP: 14 **Privately Held**
WEB: www.3i-infotech.com
SIC: 7371 7372 7373 7379 Computer
software development; prepackaged soft-
ware; computer integrated systems de-
sign; computer related consulting services
HQ: 3i Infotech Inc
450 Rritan Ctr Pkwy Ste B
Edison NJ 08837

(P-17536)
9EDGE INC
200 Sandpointe Ave # 575, Santa Ana
(92707-5751)
P.O. Box 1004, Manhattan Beach (90267-
1004)
PHONE..................657 229-3343
Dale Kaplan, *Managing Prtnr*
Ashish Kalawadia, *Managing Prtnr*
Tushar Mehta, *Managing Prtnr*
Palash Jain, *Technology*
Sujata Savekar, *Recruiter*
EMP: 20 **EST:** 2012
SQ FT: 2,500
SALES (est): 1MM **Privately Held**
WEB: www.9edge.co
SIC: 7371 8243 8748 7373 Computer
software development; software training;
computer; systems engineering consult-
ant, ex. computer or professional; value-
added resellers, computer systems;
prepackaged software

(P-17537)
ACOM SOLUTIONS INC (PA)
2850 E 29th St, Long Beach (90806-2313)
PHONE..................562 424-7899
Patrick S McMahon, *President*
Jason Pisetsky, *COO*
Edward J Kennedy, *Chairman*
Mark Firmin, *Vice Pres*
James Scott, *Vice Pres*
▲ **EMP:** 50 **EST:** 1984
SQ FT: 23,000
SALES (est): 21.7MM **Privately Held**
WEB: www.acom.com
SIC: 7371 Computer software develop-
ment

(P-17538)
ADCOLONY INC
11400 W Olympic Blvd # 1200, Los Angeles
(90064-1583)
PHONE..................650 625-1262
William Kassoy, *CEO*
David Pokress, *Vice Pres*
Clifford Hillyer, *Technical Mgr*
Joshua Conner, *Software Engr*
Britt Mullen, *Software Engr*
EMP: 100 **EST:** 2008
SALES (est): 20.5MM
SALES (corp-wide): 38.1MM **Privately
Held**
WEB: www.jirbo.com
SIC: 7371 Computer software develop-
ment
PA: Adcolony Holdings Us, Inc.
1875 S Grant St Ste 800
San Mateo CA 94402
650 625-1262

(P-17539)
ADVANCED REALTIME SYSTEMS INC
110 Conejo Cir, Palm Desert (92260-0383)
PHONE..................760 636-0444
Richard Roter, *President*
EMP: 15
SALES (est): 906.5K **Privately Held**
WEB: www.arsi.com
SIC: 7371 7372 7373 7376 Computer
software development; prepackaged software; computer integrated systems design; computer facilities management;
computer related consulting services; educational services

(P-17540)
ADVANCEDWARE CORPORATION
13844 Alton Pkwy Ste 136, Irvine
(92618-1689)
PHONE..................949 609-1240
Michael Serrato, *President*
Paul Batten, *Vice Pres*
Frankie Rosario, *Vice Pres*
Serene Lee, *Executive Asst*
Jeff Zonick, *Info Tech Dir*
EMP: 17 **EST:** 1999
SALES (est): 649.1K **Privately Held**
WEB: www.advancedware.com
SIC: 7371 7372 Computer software devel-
opment; prepackaged software

(P-17541)
ADVANTAGE SYSTEMS INC
34 Executive Park Ste 100, Irvine
(92614-6721)
PHONE..................949 250-0260
Brian Lynch, *President*
Joe Ludlow, *Vice Pres*
Thomas Pugh, *Sr Software Eng*
Frank Paladino, *Software Dev*
EMP: 14 **EST:** 1991
SALES (est): 1.4MM **Privately Held**
WEB: www.mortgageaccounting.com
SIC: 7371 7372 Computer software devel-
opment; application computer software

(P-17542)
ADVENT RESOURCES INC
235 W 7th St, San Pedro (90731-3321)
PHONE..................310 241-1500
Ysidro Salinas, *Ch of Bd*
Robert Ford, *Managing Prtnr*
Timothy Gill, *CEO*
Vishal Ghelani, *Vice Pres*
Benjamin Gill, *Executive*
EMP: 80 **EST:** 1984
SQ FT: 22,000
SALES (est): 13.6MM **Privately Held**
WEB: www.adventresources.com
SIC: 7371 Computer software develop-
ment

(P-17543)
AF TECHNOLOGY LLC
Also Called: Aims360
12130 Millennium 3-154, Playa Vista
(90094-2945)
PHONE..................310 361-5710
Shahin Kohan, *President*
Kim Kerr, *Vice Pres*
Scott Chaban, *Principal*
Martha Rodriguez, *Controller*
EMP: 50 **EST:** 2010
SALES (est): 3MM **Privately Held**
SIC: 7371 Custom computer programming
services

(P-17544)
AFTERSHOCK LA STUDIOS INC
3633 Lenawee Ave Ste 100, Los Angeles
(90016-4319)
PHONE..................650 450-9660
Kent Wakeford, *CEO*
EMP: 60 **EST:** 2016
SALES (est): 1.3MM **Privately Held**
SIC: 7371 Computer software develop-
ment & applications

(P-17545)
ALPHA SOFT SUPPORT LLC
8605 Santa Monica Blvd, West Hollywood
(90069-4109)
PHONE..................857 219-5505
Kim Johnny, *CEO*
EMP: 51
SALES (est): 8MM **Privately Held**
SIC: 7371 Computer software develop-
ment & applications

(P-17546)
ANAMEX CORPORATION (PA)
250 S Peralta Way, Anaheim (92807-3618)
PHONE..................714 779-7055
Cung Phan, *President*
EMP: 47 **EST:** 1986
SQ FT: 10,000
SALES (est): 2.6MM **Privately Held**
SIC: 7371 7372 8711 Computer software
development; prepackaged software;
business oriented computer software;
electrical or electronic engineering

(P-17547)
ANCHORE INC
800 Presidio Ave Ste B, Santa Barbara
(93101-2210)
PHONE..................805 456-8981
Said Ziouani, *CEO*
Emily Long, *Officer*
Daniel Nurmi, *Officer*
Paul Holt, *Senior VP*
Zach Hill, *Chief*
EMP: 50 **EST:** 2017
SALES (est): 5.1MM **Privately Held**
WEB: www.anchore.com
SIC: 7371 Computer software develop-
ment

(P-17548)
ANJANA SOFTWARE SOLUTIONS INC
1445 E Los Angeles Ave 301t, Simi Valley
(93065-2862)
PHONE..................805 583-0121
Saravana Kumarasamy, *President*
Kritik A Govindan, *Treasurer*
Venkatesh Ramachandran, *Vice Pres*
▲ **EMP:** 75
SQ FT: 3,000
SALES: 15.9MM **Privately Held**
WEB: www.anjanasoft.com
SIC: 7371 Computer software develop-
ment
PA: Anjana Software Solutions Private Lim-
ited
Module No. 306, Nsic Software Tech-
nology Park
Chennai TN 60003

(P-17549)
ANRE TECHNOLOGIES INC
741 W Woodbury Rd, Altadena
(91001-5310)
PHONE..................818 627-5433
Roubina Keshish-Moses, *Ch of Bd*
Eugean Hacopians, *CTO*
EMP: 150 **EST:** 2010
SQ FT: 600
SALES (est): 9.9MM **Privately Held**
WEB: www.anretech.com
SIC: 7371 7376 7379 Computer software
development & applications; computer fa-
cilities management; computer related
maintenance services

(P-17550)
APPLIED COMPUTER SOLUTIONS (DH)
15461 Springdale St, Huntington Beach
(92649-1335)
PHONE..................714 861-2200
Elaine Bellock, *President*
Michael Davis, *COO*
Warren Barnes, *CFO*
Bob Goetz, *Vice Pres*
David Altman, *Executive*
EMP: 70 **EST:** 1989
SQ FT: 60,000
SALES (est): 70.7MM
SALES (corp-wide): 7.2B **Privately Held**
WEB: www.acsacs.com
SIC: 7371 Custom computer programming
services
HQ: Pivot Technology Solutions Inc
55 Renfrew Dr Suite 200
Markham ON L3R 8
416 360-4777

(P-17551)
APPLIED ENGINEERING MGT CORP
Also Called: Aem Corporation
760 Paseo Camarillo # 101, Camarillo
(93010-6000)
P.O. Box 1263 (93011-1263)
PHONE..................805 484-1909
Anne Morgan, *Exec VP*
Sharon Demonsabert, *President*
Kelley Pecheux, *Bd of Directors*
Dave Brady, *Assoc VP*
Ana Echemendia, *Assoc VP*
EMP: 250
SALES (corp-wide): 40MM **Privately
Held**
WEB: www.aemcorp.com
SIC: 7371 Computer software develop-
ment
PA: Virginia Aem Corporation
13880 Dulles Corner Ln # 300
Herndon VA 20171
703 464-7030

(P-17552)
APRISO CORPORATION
301 E Ocean Blvd Ste 1200, Long Beach
(90802-4839)
PHONE..................562 951-8000
James Henderson, *CEO*
Bill Cohn, *CFO*
Carey Tokirio, *CFO*
Chris Brecher, *Exec VP*
Tom Comstock, *Exec VP*
EMP: 200 **EST:** 1993
SALES (est): 25.2MM
SALES (corp-wide): 2B **Privately Held**
WEB: www.apriso.com
SIC: 7371 Computer software develop-
ment
PA: Dassault Systemes
10 Rue Marcel Dassault
Velizy Villacoublay 78140
161 623-000

(P-17553)
ARCULES INC
17875 Von Karman Ave # 450, Irvine
(92614-6212)
PHONE..................949 439-0053
Andreas Pettersson, *CEO*
Nigel Waterton, *Risk Mgmt Dir*
Jesse Hazen, *IT Specialist*
Sakura Mizuno, *Engineer*
Jon Kenyon, *Finance*
EMP: 70 **EST:** 2017

SALES (est): 6.5MM **Privately Held**
WEB: www.arcules.com
SIC: **7371** Software programming applications

(P-17554)
ASHUNYA INC
642 N Eckhoff St, Orange (92868-1004)
PHONE..........................714 385-1900
Melanie Merchant, *Principal*
EMP: 88 EST: 2001
SALES (est): 7.8MM **Privately Held**
WEB: www.ashunya.com
SIC: **7371** 7372 7373 Computer software development & applications; application computer software; office computer automation systems integration; turnkey vendors, computer systems; value-added resellers, computer systems

(P-17555)
ATLAS DATABASE SOFTWARE CORP (PA)
Also Called: Atlas Development
26679 Agoura Rd Ste 200, Calabasas (91302-3812)
PHONE..........................818 340-7080
Robert D Atlas, *CEO*
Steven Atlas, *Vice Pres*
Michelle Del Guercio, *Vice Pres*
Dan Nelson, *Vice Pres*
Russell Vonblanck, *Vice Pres*
EMP: 154 EST: 1993
SQ FT: 15,000
SALES (est): 32.8MM **Privately Held**
SIC: **7371** Computer software development

(P-17556)
AUDITBOARD INC (PA)
12900 Park Plaza Dr # 200, Cerritos (90703-9329)
PHONE..........................877 769-5444
Daniel Kim, *CEO*
Karen Gift, *CFO*
Hayes Kim, *Senior VP*
Kevin Mayeda, *Business Dir*
Robert Craven, *Administration*
EMP: 50 EST: 2014
SQ FT: 10,000
SALES (est): 26.5MM **Privately Held**
WEB: www.auditboard.com
SIC: **7371** Computer software development

(P-17557)
AUGUSTINE GAMING MGT CORP
Also Called: Augustine Casino
84001 Avenue 54, Coachella (92236-9780)
PHONE..........................760 391-9500
Jeff Bauer, *General Mgr*
John Corrigan, *Finance Dir*
EMP: 99
SALES (est): 7.4MM **Privately Held**
WEB: www.augustinecasino.com
SIC: **7371** Computer software development & applications

(P-17558)
AVANQUEST NORTH AMERICA LLC (HQ)
Also Called: Nova Development
23801 Calabasas Rd # 2005, Calabasas (91302-1547)
PHONE..........................818 591-9600
Roger Bloxberg, *CEO*
Todd Helfstein, *President*
Sharon Chiu, *CFO*
Cynthia Esters, *Officer*
Mike Addante, *Exec VP*
▲ EMP: 80 EST: 1984
SQ FT: 12,000
SALES (est): 55.9MM
SALES (corp-wide): 1.8MM **Privately Held**
WEB: www.claranova.com
SIC: **7371** Computer software development
PA: Claranova S.E.
Avanquest Blue Squad Bvrp Software Immeuble Vision Defense
La Garenne Colombes 92250
962 557-603

(P-17559)
AXON NETWORKS INC
15420 Laguna Canyon Rd # 15, Irvine (92618-2119)
PHONE..........................949 310-4429
Martin Manniche, *CEO*
EMP: 100 EST: 2020
SALES (est): 1.3MM **Privately Held**
SIC: **7371** 8742 Custom computer programming services; general management consultant

(P-17560)
B JACQUELINE AND ASSOC INC
Also Called: J B A
1192 N Lake Ave, Pasadena (91104-3739)
PHONE..........................626 844-1400
Jacqueline Buickians, *President*
Gary Buickians, *Admin Sec*
Ronal Velez, *Human Res Mgr*
EMP: 51 EST: 1979
SQ FT: 4,000
SALES (est): 1.6MM **Privately Held**
WEB: www.jba.com
SIC: **7371** 7379 Computer software development & applications; computer related consulting services

(P-17561)
BABYFIRST AMERICAS LLC
10390 Santa Monica Blvd, Los Angeles (90025-5058)
PHONE..........................310 442-9853
Guy Oranim, *CEO*
Sharon Rechter, *President*
Karl Knipliy, *CFO*
EMP: 75 EST: 2010
SALES (est): 13MM **Privately Held**
WEB: www.shop.babyfirsttv.com
SIC: **7371** Computer software development & applications
PA: Bftv, Llc
10390 Santa Monica Blvd # 310
Los Angeles CA 90025
310 442-9853

(P-17562)
BELLROCK MEDIA INC (PA)
11500 W Olympic Blvd # 400, Los Angeles (90064-1525)
PHONE..........................310 315-2727
Peter Levin, *President*
EMP: 30 EST: 2005
SALES (est): 4.7MM **Privately Held**
SIC: **7371** 3661 Software programming applications; headsets, telephone

(P-17563)
BIRD RIDES INC
2501 Colorado Ave, Santa Monica (90404-3500)
PHONE..........................866 205-2442
Evan Conroy, *Manager*
Robert Whittlesey, *Program Mgr*
Amy Lan, *General Mgr*
Tristan Gardner, *Software Engr*
Salmaan Rizvi, *Software Engr*
EMP: 100
SALES (corp-wide): 3.4MM **Privately Held**
WEB: www.bird.co
SIC: **7371** Computer software development & applications
PA: Bird Rides, Inc.
406 Broadway Ste 369
Santa Monica CA 90401
866 205-2442

(P-17564)
BIRD RIDES INC (PA)
406 Broadway Ste 369, Santa Monica (90401-2314)
PHONE..........................866 205-2442
Travis Vanderzanden, *CEO*
Dennis Cinelli, *Vice Pres*
Yibo Ling, *Vice Pres*
Natalie Sawyer, *Comms Mgr*
Ravi Goyal, *CIO*
EMP: 373 EST: 2017
SALES (est): 3.4MM **Privately Held**
WEB: www.bird.co
SIC: **7371** 3751 Computer software development & applications; bicycles & related parts

(P-17565)
BIS COMPUTER SOLUTIONS INC (PA)
Also Called: Business Information Systems
5500 Alta Canyada Rd, La Canada Flintridge (91011-1610)
PHONE..........................818 248-4282
Miro J Macho, *President*
Michael Macho, *CFO*
Jan Macho, *Vice Pres*
Mike Norton, *Vice Pres*
Karen Johnson, *Controller*
EMP: 25 EST: 1971
SALES (est): 3.8MM **Privately Held**
WEB: www.biscomputer.com
SIC: **7371** 7379 5045 7372 Computer software development; computer related consulting services; computers, peripherals & software; prepackaged software

(P-17566)
BITFONE CORPORATION (PA)
32451 Golden Lantern # 301, Laguna Niguel (92677-5344)
PHONE..........................949 234-7000
Gene Wang, *President*
Hang Michael Xu, *CFO*
Harri Okkonen, *Senior VP*
Chris Cassapakis, *Vice Pres*
Carla Fitzgerald, *Vice Pres*
EMP: 50 EST: 2000
SALES (est): 5.1MM **Privately Held**
SIC: **7371** Computer software development

(P-17567)
BLAZE SOLUTIONS INC
4590 Macarthur Blvd # 500, Newport Beach (92660-2030)
PHONE..........................415 964-5689
Chris Violas, *CEO*
Justin Kirk,
EMP: 55 EST: 2018
SALES (est): 700K **Privately Held**
SIC: **7371** Computer software development & applications

(P-17568)
BLU DIGITAL GROUP INC
Also Called: Blufocus
2233 N Ontario St 130, Burbank (91504-4503)
PHONE..........................818 294-7695
Paulette E Pantoja, *CEO*
David Roesner, *Project Mgr*
Amy Carlos, *Opers Mgr*
John Choi, *Production*
EMP: 84 EST: 2007
SQ FT: 7,000
SALES (est): 5.8MM **Privately Held**
WEB: www.blufocus.com
SIC: **7371** 8748 7379 Software programming applications; systems analysis & engineering consulting services; computer related consulting services

(P-17569)
BLUEBEAM INC (PA)
443 S Raymond Ave, Pasadena (91105-2630)
PHONE..........................626 788-4100
Jon Elliott, *CEO*
Richard Lee, *President*
Jim Atkinson, *Officer*
Jason Bonifay, *Officer*
Phillip Yang, *Administration*
EMP: 200 EST: 2002
SALES (est): 81.5MM **Privately Held**
WEB: www.bluebeam.com
SIC: **7371** Computer software development

(P-17570)
BLUR STUDIO INC
3960 Ince Blvd, Culver City (90232-2635)
PHONE..........................424 258-3145
Tim Miller, *President*
David Stinnett, *Vice Pres*
Jennifer Miller, *Creative Dir*
Zachary Hardy, *Executive Asst*
Duane Powell, *Admin Asst*
EMP: 70 EST: 1995
SQ FT: 20,000

SALES (est): 9MM **Privately Held**
WEB: www.blur.com
SIC: **7371** Custom computer programming services

(P-17571)
BOULEVARD LABS INC
1041 N Formosa Ave Bldg W, West Hollywood (90046-6703)
PHONE..........................323 310-2093
Matthew Danna, *CEO*
EMP: 60 EST: 2016
SALES (est): 2.8MM **Privately Held**
WEB: www.joinblvd.com
SIC: **7371** 7389 7372 Computer software development & applications; prepackaged software

(P-17572)
BPO MANAGEMENT SERVICES INC (PA)
8175 E Kaiser Blvd 100, Anaheim (92808-2214)
PHONE..........................714 972-2670
Patrick A Dolan, *Ch of Bd*
James Cortens, *President*
Donald W Rutherford, *CFO*
Koushik Dutta, *CTO*
Angel Lopez, *Software Dev*
EMP: 73 EST: 1982
SQ FT: 5,871
SALES (est): 36.5MM **Privately Held**
SIC: **7371** Computer software development

(P-17573)
CALLFIRE INC
Also Called: EZ Texting
1410 2nd St Ste 200, Santa Monica (90401-3349)
PHONE..........................213 221-2289
Michel Veys, *Principal*
Komnieve Singh, *President*
Tj Thinakaran, *COO*
Tridivesh Kidambi, *CFO*
Vijesh Mehta, *Corp Secy*
EMP: 61 EST: 2004
SALES (est): 13.3MM **Privately Held**
WEB: www.callfire.com
SIC: **7371** Computer software development

(P-17574)
CAREER ENGAGEMENT GROUP LLC
Also Called: Fuel50
30025 Alicia Pkwy, Laguna Niguel (92677-2090)
PHONE..........................212 235-1470
EMP: 70
SALES: 4.5MM **Privately Held**
WEB: www.fuel50.com
SIC: **7371** Custom Computer Programing

(P-17575)
CARRIERX LLC (PA)
4300 E Pacific Coast Hwy, Long Beach (90804-2114)
PHONE..........................562 437-1411
Eugene Tcipnjatov, *CTO*
EMP: 61 EST: 2016
SALES (est): 5MM **Privately Held**
WEB: www.carrierx.com
SIC: **7371** Computer software development

(P-17576)
CHEQUE GUARD INC
512 S Verdugo Dr, Burbank (91502-2344)
PHONE..........................818 563-9335
Emil Ramzy, *President*
Alfred Ramzi, *CEO*
Louris Khalaf, *COO*
EMP: 54 EST: 2002
SQ FT: 6,000
SALES (est): 1.6MM **Privately Held**
WEB: www.cheque-guard.com
SIC: **7371** 2893 Computer software development; printing ink

(P-17577)
CIMATRON GIBBS LLC
Also Called: Gibbs & Associates
323 Science Dr, Moorpark (93021-2092)
PHONE..........................805 523-0004
Bill Gibbs, *Owner*

Bruce King, *Engineer*
Don Meifert, *Finance*
William F Gibbs,
Danny Moore, *Asst Mgr*
EMP: 61 **EST:** 1982
SQ FT: 22,500
SALES (est): 12MM **Publicly Held**
WEB: www.3dsystems.com
SIC: 7371 Computer software development
PA: 3d Systems Corporation
333 Three D Systems Cir
Rock Hill SC 29730

(P-17578)
CITRUSBYTE LLC
Also Called: Theorem LLC
21550 Oxnard St Ste 300, Woodland Hills (91367-7109)
PHONE..................888 969-2983
William Jessup, *Mng Member*
Michel Charlery, *Vice Pres*
Ezequiel Becerra, *Software Engr*
Eugene Howe, *Software Engr*
Gregory Kenenitz, *Software Engr*
EMP: 30 **EST:** 2007
SALES (est): 5.5MM **Privately Held**
WEB: www.theorem.co
SIC: 7371 7372 7373 Computer software development & applications; computer software systems analysis & design, custom; computer software writing services; computer software development; business oriented computer software; computer integrated systems design

(P-17579)
COALITION TECHNOLOGIES LLC
445 S Figueroa St # 3100, Los Angeles (90071-1635)
PHONE..................310 905-8268
Joel Gross, *CEO*
Bridget Beehler, *Analyst*
Alfonso Flores, *Recruiter*
Igor Kholkin, *Opers Staff*
Jordan Gross, *Mktg Dir*
EMP: 24 **EST:** 2011
SALES (est): 1.7MM **Privately Held**
WEB: www.coalitiontechnologies.com
SIC: 7371 8743 8243 7372 Computer software writers, freelance; computer software development; public relations services; public relations & publicity; software training, computer; business oriented computer software

(P-17580)
CODAZEN INC
60 Bunsen, Irvine (92618-4210)
PHONE..................949 916-6266
Michael Merchant, *President*
Michael H Merchant, *President*
Angela Merchant, *Vice Pres*
Danny Petrovich, *Exec Dir*
Austin Okamuro, *CIO*
EMP: 85 **EST:** 2007
SALES (est): 4.5MM **Privately Held**
WEB: www.codazen.com
SIC: 7371 Computer software development

(P-17581)
COMMISSION JUNCTION LLC (DH)
530 E Montecito St, Santa Barbara (93103-3245)
PHONE..................805 730-8000
Bryan Kennedy, *CEO*
Mayuresh Kshetramade, *Senior VP*
Dave Duckwitz, *Vice Pres*
Kenya Feinberg, *Vice Pres*
Sean Longman, *Vice Pres*
EMP: 85 **EST:** 2015
SQ FT: 16,000
SALES (est): 16.7MM
SALES (corp-wide): 29.1MM **Privately Held**
WEB: www.cj.com
SIC: 7371 Computer software development & applications

(P-17582)
COMPULINK MANAGEMENT CTR INC (PA)
Also Called: Laserfiche Document Imaging
3545 Long Beach Blvd, Long Beach (90807-3941)
PHONE..................562 988-1688
Nien-Ling Wacker, *President*
Alex Wilson, *Partner*
Karl Chan, *Vice Pres*
Jereb Cheatham, *Vice Pres*
Channing Fleetwood, *Vice Pres*
▲ **EMP:** 199 **EST:** 1976
SQ FT: 30,000
SALES (est): 56MM **Privately Held**
WEB: www.laserfiche.com
SIC: 7371 Computer software development

(P-17583)
COMPUTRITION INC (HQ)
8521 Fllbrook Ave Ste 100, Canoga Park (91304)
PHONE..................818 961-3999
Scott Saklad, *President*
Stephen Conner, *Vice Pres*
Kim C Goldberg, *Vice Pres*
Kim Helmey, *Project Mgr*
Heather Martin, *Sales Staff*
EMP: 60 **EST:** 1981
SQ FT: 16,763
SALES (est): 13.3MM
SALES (corp-wide): 3.9B **Privately Held**
WEB: www.computrition.com
SIC: 7371 7372 Computer software development; prepackaged software

(P-17584)
CORPTAX LLC
21550 Oxnard St Ste 700, Woodland Hills (91367-7170)
PHONE..................818 316-2400
Dale S Deobler, *Technology*
Patrick Hickey, *Analyst*
Olga Guler, *QC Mgr*
Lindsey Petramala, *Marketing Staff*
Nancy Tominaga, *Director*
EMP: 68 **Privately Held**
WEB: www.corptax.com
SIC: 7371 Computer software development
PA: Corptax, Llc
2100 E Lake Cook Rd # 800
Buffalo Grove IL 60089

(P-17585)
COUNTY OF LOS ANGELES
Also Called: Internal Services
1100 N Eastern Ave, Los Angeles (90063-3200)
PHONE..................562 940-4324
David Wesolik, *General Mgr*
EMP: 2000
SALES (corp-wide): 25.2B **Privately Held**
WEB: www.lacounty.gov
SIC: 7371 Computer software development & applications
PA: County Of Los Angeles
500 W Temple St Ste 437
Los Angeles CA 90012
213 974-1101

(P-17586)
CREATIVE DGTAL SYSTEMS INTGRTI
670 E Easy St, Simi Valley (93065-1808)
PHONE..................805 364-0555
Norman Lamarra, *CEO*
Nancy Konysky, *Treasurer*
Anand Kelkar, *Vice Pres*
Luc Gravelle, *Admin Sec*
Cory Lamarra, *Manager*
◆ **EMP:** 16 **EST:** 2006
SQ FT: 15,000
SALES (est): 3.5MM **Privately Held**
WEB: www.cdsi-simi.com
SIC: 7371 3812 Computer software development; defense systems & equipment; search & detection systems & instruments

(P-17587)
CU DIRECT CORPORATION (PA)
Also Called: Cudc
2855 E Guasti Rd Ste 500, Ontario (91761-1253)
P.O. Box 51482 (91761-0082)
PHONE..................909 481-2300
Antony Boutelle, *President*
Craig S Montesanti, *CFO*
Keith Sultemeier, *Chairman*
Erin Mendez, *Treasurer*
Paul Kirkbride, *Ch Credit Ofcr*
EMP: 175 **EST:** 1994
SQ FT: 30,000 **Privately Held**
WEB: www.cudirect.com
SIC: 7371 Computer software development

(P-17588)
CYBERDEFENDER CORPORATION
617 W 7th St Fl 10, Los Angeles (90017-3879)
PHONE..................323 449-0774
Kevin Harris, *CEO*
Igor Barash, *COO*
Sarah B Hicks, *Senior VP*
Steven R Okun, *Senior VP*
Richard Barnes, *CIO*
EMP: 30 **EST:** 2003
SALES (est): 4.2MM **Privately Held**
WEB: www.cyberdefender.com
SIC: 7371 7372 Custom computer programming services; prepackaged software

(P-17589)
DAQRI LLC (HQ)
1201 W 5th St Ste T800, Los Angeles (90017-1452)
P.O. Box 15548, Long Beach (90815-0548)
PHONE..................213 375-8830
Roy Ashok, *CEO*
Robert Brass, *CFO*
Brass Rob, *CFO*
Brian Selzer, *Vice Pres*
Troy West, *VP Bus Dvlpt*
EMP: 92 **EST:** 2007
SALES (est): 23.3MM
SALES (corp-wide): 2.5B **Publicly Held**
WEB: www.daqri.com
SIC: 7371 Computer software development
PA: Snap Inc.
2772 Dnald Douglas Loop N
Santa Monica CA 90405
310 399-3339

(P-17590)
DATA PROCESSING DESIGN INC
1409 Glenneyre St Ste B, Laguna Beach (92651-3171)
PHONE..................714 695-1000
Brendan Nolan, *CEO*
Tom Politowski, *President*
Shane Rothenberger, *Finance*
Stuart Egli, *Director*
EMP: 13 **EST:** 1976
SALES: 3.6MM **Privately Held**
SIC: 7371 7372 Computer software development; prepackaged software

(P-17591)
DAZ SYSTEMS LLC
1003 E 4th Pl Ste 800, Los Angeles (90013-2775)
PHONE..................310 640-1300
Walt Zipperman, *CEO*
Deborah Arnold, *President*
David Binkley, *COO*
Lisa Savage, *Human Resources*
David Hurst, *Sales Staff*
EMP: 375 **EST:** 1995
SALES (est): 44.5MM **Privately Held**
WEB: www.accenture.com
SIC: 7371 7372 Computer software development; prepackaged software
HQ: Accenture Llp
161 N Clark St.Ste 1100
Chicago IL 60601
312 693-0161

(P-17592)
DEALERSOCKET INC (PA)
100 Avenida La Pata, San Clemente (92673-6304)
P.O. Box 96020, Southlake TX (76092-0111)
PHONE..................949 900-0300
Sejal Pietrzak, *President*
Jose Arcilla, *COO*
Cameron Darby, *COO*
Byron McDuffee, *COO*
Gary Ito, *CFO*
EMP: 60 **EST:** 2005
SALES (est): 44.3MM **Privately Held**
WEB: www.dealersocket.com
SIC: 7371 Computer software systems analysis & design, custom

(P-17593)
DENKEN SOLUTIONS INC
9170 Irvine Center Dr # 200, Irvine (92618-4614)
PHONE..................949 630-5263
Rajendra Maddula, *Exec Dir*
Eddie Gallardo, *CEO*
Anna Zufi, *Executive*
Mastan Basha Sk, *Administration*
Manikanta Kumar, *IT Executive*
EMP: 250 **EST:** 2010
SQ FT: 4,000
SALES (est): 29.2MM **Privately Held**
WEB: www.denkensolutions.com
SIC: 7371 8742 8748 Computer software systems analysis & design, custom; computer software development & applications; management consulting services; business consulting; systems analysis & engineering consulting services

(P-17594)
DESIGN SCIENCE INC
444 W Ocean Blvd Ste 800, Long Beach (90802-4529)
PHONE..................562 432-2920
Paul Topping, *President*
Paul R Topping, *President*
John Schnell, *Software Dev*
Michael Won, *Controller*
EMP: 30 **EST:** 1986
SALES (est): 5.6MM **Privately Held**
WEB: www.wiris.com
SIC: 7371 7379 7372 5045 Computer software development; computer related consulting services; prepackaged software; computers, peripherals & software

(P-17595)
DESTINATIONRX INC (DH)
Also Called: D R X
600 Wilshire Blvd # 1100, Los Angeles (90017-3212)
PHONE..................800 379-9060
Randell P Herman, *President*
▲ **EMP:** 72 **EST:** 2000
SALES (est): 17.3MM
SALES (corp-wide): 96.5MM **Privately Held**
WEB: www.destinationrx.com
SIC: 7371 Computer software development
HQ: Connecture, Inc.
18500 W Corp Dr Ste 250
Brookfield WI 53045
262 432-8282

(P-17596)
DFUSION SOFTWARE INC
Also Called: Total Immersion
5900 Wilshire Blvd # 2550, Los Angeles (90036-5013)
PHONE..................323 617-5577
Didier Lesteven, *CEO*
Bruno Uzzan, *Principal*
EMP: 50 **EST:** 2006
SQ FT: 3,000
SALES (est): 3.9MM **Privately Held**
SIC: 7371 Computer software development

(P-17597)
DISNEY INTERACTIVE STUDIOS INC
601 Circle Seven Dr, Glendale (91201-2332)
PHONE..................818 560-1000
Peter Casciani, *Manager*

Alex Eiserloh, *Creative Dir*
EMP: 270
SALES (corp-wide): 65.3B **Publicly Held**
SIC: 7371 Computer software development
HQ: Disney Interactive Studios, Inc.
500 S Buena Vista St
Burbank CA 91521
818 560-1000

(P-17598)
DISNEY INTERACTIVE STUDIOS INC
681 W Buena Vista St, Burbank (91521-0001)
PHONE....................818 553-5000
Gram Hoper, *Branch Mgr*
EMP: 270
SALES (corp-wide): 65.3B **Publicly Held**
SIC: 7371 Computer software development
HQ: Disney Interactive Studios, Inc.
500 S Buena Vista St
Burbank CA 91521
818 560-1000

(P-17599)
DISTILLERY TECH INC
1914 Huntington Ln A, Redondo Beach (90278-4220)
PHONE....................310 776-6234
Andrey Kudievskiy, *CEO*
Sam Wheeler, *Sales Staff*
EMP: 220 **EST:** 2012
SALES (est): 13.7MM **Privately Held**
WEB: www.distillery.com
SIC: 7371 7372 7373 Computer software development; computer software systems analysis & design, custom; application computer software; business oriented computer software; computer systems analysis & design

(P-17600)
DOCUPACE TECHNOLOGIES LLC
11766 Wilshire Blvd # 1120, Los Angeles (90025-6578)
P.O. Box 92117, Las Vegas NV (89193-2117)
PHONE....................310 445-7722
Michael Pinsker, *Mng Member*
Kim Pederson, *Exec VP*
Patrick McMahon, *Vice Pres*
Sharon Ross, *VP Bus Dvlpt*
James Caulkins, *Risk Mgmt Dir*
EMP: 200 **EST:** 2002
SQ FT: 1,500
SALES (est): 18.7MM **Privately Held**
WEB: www.docupace.com
SIC: 7371 Computer software development

(P-17601)
DOLPHIN IMAGING SYSTEMS LLC
9200 Oakdale Ave, Chatsworth (91311-6500)
PHONE....................818 435-1368
Chester H Wang,
Joseph Bautista, *Technology*
Ryan Escobar, *Technical Staff*
Kathy Moss, *Purch Agent*
Matthew Yamamoto, *Sales Staff*
EMP: 211 **EST:** 1995
SALES: 5.7MM
SALES (corp-wide): 5.9B **Publicly Held**
WEB: www.dolphinimaging.com
SIC: 7371 Computer software development
HQ: Patterson Dental Supply, Inc.
1031 Mendota Heights Rd
Saint Paul MN 55120
651 686-1600

(P-17602)
DP TECHNOLOGY LLC (HQ)
Also Called: Esprit
1150 Avenida Acaso, Camarillo (93012-8719)
PHONE....................805 388-6000
Daniel Frayssinet, *CEO*
Paul Ricard, *President*
Graham Starfelt, *Administration*
Manoj Rade, *Software Engr*
Simone Petruzzi, *Prgrmr*

EMP: 60 **EST:** 1982
SQ FT: 12,000
SALES (est): 21.6MM
SALES (corp-wide): 4.5B **Privately Held**
WEB: www.espritcam.com
SIC: 7371 7373 7372 Computer software development; computer integrated systems design; prepackaged software
PA: Hexagon Ab
Lilla Bantorget 15
Stockholm 111 2
860 126-20

(P-17603)
DRIVENBI LLC
1606 Camino Lindo, South Pasadena (91030-4130)
PHONE....................626 795-2088
Benjamin Tai, *CEO*
Sheree Chang, *Manager*
EMP: 60 **EST:** 2006
SALES (est): 1.5MM **Privately Held**
WEB: www.drivenbi.com
SIC: 7371 Computer software development

(P-17604)
E Z DATA INC (HQ)
251 S Lake Ave Ste 200, Pasadena (91101-3075)
PHONE....................626 585-3505
Dale Okuno, *President*
EMP: 51 **EST:** 1986
SALES (est): 10.1MM
SALES (corp-wide): 625.6MM **Publicly Held**
WEB: www.ebixcrm.com
SIC: 7371 Computer software development
PA: Ebix, Inc.
1 Ebix Way
Duluth GA 30097
678 281-2020

(P-17605)
E4SITE INC (PA)
Also Called: Visionaire
6700 E Pacific Coast Hwy # 201, Long Beach (90803-4213)
PHONE....................714 242-5700
Sukant S Jain, *CEO*
Ameeta Jain, *CFO*
EMP: 19 **EST:** 2001
SALES (est): 3.6MM **Privately Held**
WEB: www.visionaire-us.com
SIC: 7371 7372 Computer software systems analysis & design, custom; application computer software; business oriented computer software

(P-17606)
EIM CORPORATION
315 Meigs Rd, Santa Barbara (93109-1900)
PHONE....................805 963-2935
Mircea Oprea, *Branch Mgr*
EMP: 50
SALES (corp-wide): 134.1K **Privately Held**
WEB: www.eim.com
SIC: 7371 Software programming applications
PA: Eim Corporation
3926 Kendall St
San Diego CA
619 846-9085

(P-17607)
ELLIE MAE INC
24025 Park Sorrento # 210, Calabasas (91302-4018)
PHONE....................818 223-2000
Marc Sackeli, *Software Engr*
Jeannette Chadwick, *Research*
Kedar Ghatpande, *Engineer*
John Love, *Engineer*
Vitalii Sukhomlynov, *Engineer*
EMP: 231
SALES (corp-wide): 6B **Publicly Held**
WEB: www.icemortgagetechnology.com
SIC: 7371 Computer software systems analysis & design, custom
HQ: Ice Mortgage Technology, Inc.
4420 Rosewood Dr Ste 500
Pleasanton CA 94588
855 224-8572

(P-17608)
EPITOME ENTERPRISES LLC
821 Mary Pl, Claremont (91711-2273)
PHONE....................909 625-4728
EMP: 60
SALES: 1.8MM **Privately Held**
WEB: www.epitomeenterprises.com
SIC: 7371 Software Development

(P-17609)
EQUATOR LLC (DH)
Also Called: Equator Business Solutions
6060 Center Dr Ste 500, Los Angeles (90045-8857)
PHONE....................310 469-9500
Chris Saitta, *CEO*
Robert McKinley, *President*
Moira Polius, *Program Mgr*
Amit Aggarwal, *Info Tech Dir*
Binod Gurung, *Software Dev*
EMP: 200
SALES (est): 45.4MM
SALES (corp-wide): 1.1B **Publicly Held**
WEB: www.equator.com
SIC: 7371 Computer software development & applications

(P-17610)
ERP INTEGRATED SOLUTIONS LLC
1501 Hughes Way Ste 320, Long Beach (90810-1880)
PHONE....................562 425-7800
Joseph Cabrera, *President*
Doug Cole, *Vice Pres*
Nick Felix, *Executive*
Anthony Raimo, *CTO*
Shekhar Katariya, *Software Dev*
EMP: 100 **EST:** 2008
SQ FT: 5,000
SALES (est): 9.8MM **Privately Held**
WEB: www.shiperp.com
SIC: 7371 Computer software development

(P-17611)
EVEG INC
16540 Aston, Irvine (92606-4805)
PHONE....................844 221-3359
Peter Krish, *Mng Member*
EMP: 50 **EST:** 2013
SALES (est): 1.5MM **Privately Held**
WEB: www.evegtech.com
SIC: 7371 Computer software development & applications

(P-17612)
EVOX PRODUCTIONS LLC (PA)
2363 E Pacifica Pl 305, Compton (90220-6212)
PHONE....................310 605-1400
David Falstrup,
Carol Falstrup, *CFO*
Peter Avildsen, *Chief Mktg Ofcr*
Chris Williams, *Vice Pres*
Christopher Williams, *VP Bus Dvlpt*
EMP: 58 **EST:** 1994
SQ FT: 37,500
SALES (est): 10.6MM **Privately Held**
WEB: www.evoximages.com
SIC: 7371 7335 Custom computer programming services; commercial photography

(P-17613)
FAHETAS LLC
Also Called: Green Tomato Grill
1419 N Tustin St Ste A, Orange (92867-3922)
PHONE....................949 280-1983
Kyle Markt, *Mng Member*
Michael Moore,
Nicole Piscetelli,
Chris Stern,
Bruce Whistnant,
EMP: 100 **EST:** 2012
SALES (est): 4MM **Privately Held**
SIC: 5812 7371 Fast-food restaurant, chain; computer software development & applications

(P-17614)
FENDER DIGITAL LLC (DH)
1575 N Gower St Ste 170, Los Angeles (90028-7179)
PHONE....................323 462-2198

Ethan Katlan,
EMP: 74 **EST:** 2015
SQ FT: 25,000
SALES (est): 50MM
SALES (corp-wide): 1.8B **Privately Held**
WEB: www.fenderdigital.com
SIC: 7371 Computer software development & applications
HQ: Fender Musical Instruments Corporation
17600 N Perimeter Dr # 100
Scottsdale AZ 85255
480 596-9690

(P-17615)
FINANCIAL INFO NETWRK INC
Also Called: F I N
11164 Bertrand Ave, Granada Hills (91344-4005)
P.O. Box 7954, Van Nuys (91409-7954)
PHONE....................818 782-0331
Jerry Sears, *President*
Stephen Seig, *Vice Pres*
Mario Uribe, *Administration*
Steve Seig, *MIS Mgr*
Ron Watson, *Business Mgr*
EMP: 33 **EST:** 1969
SQ FT: 6,000
SALES (est): 2.8MM **Privately Held**
WEB: www.fingps.com
SIC: 7371 7372 Custom computer programming services; prepackaged software

(P-17616)
FOCUS 360 INC
27721 La Paz Rd Ste B, Laguna Niguel (92677-3949)
PHONE....................949 234-0008
Steven G Ormonde, *President*
Brent C Chase, *Vice Pres*
Katelyn Rigler, *Project Mgr*
Carol Byrnes, *Controller*
Geoff Preston, *Production*
EMP: 52 **EST:** 1989
SQ FT: 18,300
SALES (est): 9.5MM **Privately Held**
WEB: www.focus360.com
SIC: 7371 Computer software development

(P-17617)
FOREMAY INC (PA)
225 S Lake Ave Ste 300, Pasadena (91101-3009)
PHONE....................408 228-3468
Haining Fan, *CEO*
Tiffany Fan, *President*
Yanlei Yao, *Principal*
Jason Hoover, *VP Mktg*
EMP: 46 **EST:** 2002
SALES (est): 7.3MM **Privately Held**
WEB: www.foremay.net
SIC: 7371 7373 3572 Computer software systems analysis & design, custom; computer software development & applications; computer systems analysis & design; computer storage devices; computer auxiliary storage units

(P-17618)
FORMULA CONSULTANTS INC
222 S Harbor Blvd Ste 650, Anaheim (92805-3756)
P.O. Box 544 (92815-0544)
PHONE....................714 778-0123
R Joseph Dale, *President*
Tony Sapienza, *Vice Pres*
Frank Schultz, *Executive*
Tony J Sapienza, *Admin Sec*
Bonita Chavis, *Administration*
EMP: 13 **EST:** 1978
SQ FT: 7,000
SALES (est): 2.2MM **Privately Held**
WEB: www.formula.com
SIC: 7371 7379 7372 Computer software development; computer related consulting services; prepackaged software

(P-17619)
FOXNEXT GAMES LLC (PA)
12121 Bluff Creek Dr # 400, Playa Vista (90094-3158)
PHONE....................424 222-5889
Sebastian Kriese, *Mng Member*
EMP: 166 **EST:** 2017

SALES (est): 10.5MM Privately Held
SIC: 7371 Custom computer programming services

(P-17620)
FUEL CYCLE INC (PA)
11859 Wilshire Blvd # 400, Los Angeles (90025-6600)
PHONE..................................323 556-5400
Bahram Nour-Omid, *CEO*
Ramesh Pidikiti, *President*
Steve Howe, *COO*
Gordon Morris, *Vice Pres*
Thomas Hoffer, *Research*
EMP: 58 EST: 2006
SQ FT: 15,000
SALES (est): 10.6MM Privately Held
WEB: www.fuelcycle.com
SIC: 7371 Computer software development

(P-17621)
FUEL50 INC
30025 Alicia Pkwy 20-23, Laguna Niguel (92677-2090)
PHONE..................................833 844-1103
Ron Shah, *Administration*
Steven Todd, *Vice Pres*
Roel Deuss, *Sales Mgr*
Rhonda Taylor, *Director*
Jessica Towicz, *Consultant*
EMP: 72 EST: 2020
SALES: 4.5MM Privately Held
WEB: www.fuel50.com
SIC: 7371 Computer software development

(P-17622)
FUJITSU GLOVIA INC (HQ)
200 Continental Blvd Fl 3, El Segundo (90245-4510)
PHONE..................................310 563-7000
Chikara Ono, *CEO*
Masahiro Cho, *CFO*
Jim Errington, *Exec VP*
Kentaro Ueda, *Sales Mgr*
Doreen Weinheimer, *Marketing Staff*
EMP: 150 EST: 1970
SQ FT: 53,000
SALES (est): 46.7MM Privately Held
WEB: www.glovia.com
SIC: 7371 7372 Computer software development; prepackaged software

(P-17623)
GAN LIMITED
400 Spectrum Center Dr # 19, Irvine (92618-4934)
PHONE..................................702 964-5777
Dermot S Smurfit, *President*
Seamus McGill, *Ch of Bd*
Donald Ryan, *COO*
Karen Flores, *CFO*
Jeffrey Berman, *Ch Credit Ofcr*
EMP: 288 EST: 2002
SALES (est): 35.1MM Privately Held
WEB: www.gan.com
SIC: 7371 7374 Custom computer programming services; custom computer programming services; data processing & preparation; data processing service

(P-17624)
GEHRY TECHNOLOGIES INC (HQ)
12181 Bluff Creek Dr # 200, Playa Vista (90094-2992)
PHONE..................................310 862-1200
Meaghan Lloyd, *CEO*
Michael Lin, *CFO*
James Porter, *Managing Dir*
Dhruba Kalita, *CIO*
Dennis Sheldon, *CTO*
EMP: 94 EST: 2002
SQ FT: 2,000
SALES (est): 14.3MM
SALES (corp-wide): 3.2B Publicly Held
WEB: www.trimbleconsulting.com
SIC: 7371 Computer software development & applications
PA: Trimble Inc.
    935 Stewart Dr
    Sunnyvale CA 94085
    408 481-8000

(P-17625)
GENEX (HQ)
800 Corporate Pointe # 100, Culver City (90230-7667)
PHONE..................................424 672-9500
Walter Schild, *CEO*
Gretchen Humbert, *CFO*
EMP: 130 EST: 1995
SQ FT: 12,000
SALES (est): 11.1MM
SALES (corp-wide): 2.9B Publicly Held
WEB: www.mxm.com
SIC: 7371 7379 4813 Computer software development & applications; computer related consulting services;
PA: Meredith Corporation
    1716 Locust St
    Des Moines IA 50309
    515 284-3000

(P-17626)
GLOBAL SERVICE RESOURCES INC
Also Called: Computerworks Technologies
711 S Victory Blvd, Burbank (91502-2426)
P.O. Box 4057 (91503-4057)
PHONE..................................800 679-7658
Nick Sefayan, *President*
Val Casagrande, *Recruiter*
▲ EMP: 80 EST: 1991
SQ FT: 7,000
SALES (est): 3.7MM Privately Held
WEB: www.globalserviceresources.com
SIC: 7371 7363 Computer software development; labor resource services; employee leasing service; engineering help service; medical help service

(P-17627)
GLORY GLOBAL SOLUTIONS INC
11135 Knott Ave Ste C, Cypress (90630-5139)
PHONE..................................714 897-7545
Gari Sithamaraju, *Branch Mgr*
EMP: 68 Privately Held
WEB: www.glory-global.com
SIC: 7371 Computer software development
HQ: Glory Global Solutions Inc.
    3333 Warrenville Rd # 310
    Lisle IL 60532
    920 262-3300

(P-17628)
GOLDEN FIVE LLC
Also Called: Golden Five Consulting
3045 Auburn Ct, Simi Valley (93063-1627)
PHONE..................................323 489-8001
Prabhat Nigam, *Ch of Bd*
EMP: 50 EST: 2016
SQ FT: 1,100
SALES (est): 3.6MM Privately Held
SIC: 7371 8748 8999 8742 Computer software development & applications; systems analysis & engineering consulting services; scientific consulting; management consulting services; computer related consulting services

(P-17629)
GOOD SPORTS PLUS LTD
Also Called: ARC
370 Amapola Ave Ste 208, Torrance (90501-7241)
PHONE..................................310 671-4400
Brad Lupien, *President*
Gary Lipsky, *President*
Elmer Axume, *COO*
Kitty Cohen, *Vice Pres*
Nicholas Silva, *Regional Mgr*
EMP: 300 EST: 2002
SQ FT: 3,500
SALES (est): 30.4MM Privately Held
WEB: www.arc-experience.com
SIC: 7371 7997 Computer software development & applications; outdoor field clubs

(P-17630)
HEALTHCARE SYNERGY INC
5555 Corporate Ave, Cypress (90630-4708)
PHONE..................................714 229-8700
Jude Mercado, *President*
Kailash Naik, *Administration*

Mark Bella, *Info Tech Mgr*
Omo Oloye, *Associate*
EMP: 53 EST: 1982
SQ FT: 2,000
SALES (est): 3.5MM Privately Held
WEB: www.healthcaresynergy.com
SIC: 7371 Computer software development

(P-17631)
HOME JUNCTION INC
1 Venture Ste 300, Irvine (92618-7416)
PHONE..................................858 777-9533
John Perkins, *CEO*
Pete Yunker, *Vice Pres*
Andrew Wilcox, *CTO*
Myles Tryder, *MIS Mgr*
Mike Domzalski, *Engineer*
EMP: 88 EST: 2013
SALES (est): 16.6MM
SALES (corp-wide): 17.2MM Privately Held
WEB: www.homejunction.com
SIC: 7371 Computer software development
PA: Attom Data Solutions, Llc
    505 Technology Dr Ste 100
    Irvine CA 92618
    949 502-8300

(P-17632)
HONEY SCIENCE LLC
963 E 4th St Ste 100, Los Angeles (90013-2645)
PHONE..................................949 795-1695
George Ruan, *Mng Member*
Chris Arreguin, *Senior VP*
Dave Hsu, *Senior VP*
Brian Kim, *Vice Pres*
Maryam Mahdaviani, *Vice Pres*
EMP: 112 EST: 2012
SALES (est): 26.6MM
SALES (corp-wide): 21.4B Publicly Held
WEB: www.joinhoney.com
SIC: 7371 Software programming applications
PA: Paypal Holdings, Inc.
    2211 N 1st St
    San Jose CA 95131
    408 967-1000

(P-17633)
HTEC GROUP INC (PA)
10250 Constellation Blvd, Los Angeles (90067-6200)
P.O. Box 5545, Redwood City (94063-0545)
PHONE..................................213 785-7824
Aleksandar Cabrilo, *President*
Jeffrey Landres, *Vice Pres*
Gail Rackliffe, *Vice Pres*
Timothy Gens, *Admin Sec*
Eric Helphrey, *Manager*
EMP: 822 EST: 2015 Privately Held
WEB: www.htecgroup.com
SIC: 7371 Computer software development

(P-17634)
HVANTAGE TECHNOLOGIES INC
6700 Fllbrook Ave Ste 222, West Hills (91307)
PHONE..................................818 661-6301
Krishna Baderia, *CEO*
Riya Dubal, *Senior Mgr*
EMP: 80 EST: 2017
SALES (est): 3.3MM Privately Held
WEB: www.hvantagetechnologies.com
SIC: 7371 8748 7372 7373 Computer software development; systems engineering consultant, ex. computer or professional; application computer software; business oriented computer software; systems engineering, computer related

(P-17635)
IBASET FEDERAL SERVICES LLC (PA)
27442 Portola Pkwy # 300, Foothill Ranch (92610-2823)
PHONE..................................949 598-5200
Ladeira Poonian, *Chairman*
Vic Sial, *President*
Naveen Poonian, *COO*
Louis Columbus, *Vice Pres*
Len Lisewsky, *Vice Pres*

EMP: 75 EST: 1986
SQ FT: 30,000
SALES (est): 22.2MM Privately Held
WEB: www.ibaset.com
SIC: 7371 Computer software development

(P-17636)
IEPC CORP
Also Called: Interntnal Engrg PDT Cnsulting
15179 Springdale St, Huntington Beach (92649-1154)
P.O. Box 2180 (92647-0180)
PHONE..................................714 892-4443
Ron Flores, *President*
Kaoru Nakagawa, *CFO*
EMP: 13 EST: 1997
SQ FT: 3,219
SALES (est): 677.5K Privately Held
WEB: www.anaya2k.com
SIC: 7371 8711 3612 Computer software development; electrical or electronic engineering; transformers, except electric

(P-17637)
IMAGE-X ENTERPRISES INC
Also Called: Image X
6464 Hollister Ave Ste 7g, Goleta (93117-3110)
PHONE..................................805 964-3535
Mohammed Shaikh, *Ch of Bd*
Joseph Stupar, *Info Tech Mgr*
EMP: 23 EST: 1989
SQ FT: 4,000
SALES (est): 1.5MM Privately Held
WEB: www.imagexx.com
SIC: 7371 3577 Computer software development; computer peripheral equipment

(P-17638)
INDIZEN OPTICAL TECH AMER LLC
Also Called: Iot Photochromics
2925 California St # 201, Torrance (90503-3914)
PHONE..................................310 783-1533
Daniel Crespo, *Mng Member*
EMP: 26 EST: 2012
SALES (est): 2.5MM Privately Held
WEB: www.iotlenses.com
SIC: 7371 3827 Computer software systems analysis & design, custom; optical instruments & lenses
HQ: Indizen Optical Technologies Sl
    Calle Suero De Quilones, 34 - 36 3 Plt
    Madrid 28002
    918 333-786

(P-17639)
INFINITE TECHNOLOGIES LLC
1667 N Batavia St, Orange (92867-3508)
PHONE..................................786 408-7995
Nicholas Robertson,
EMP: 147 EST: 2017
SALES (est): 2.5MM Privately Held
SIC: 7371 Custom computer programming services

(P-17640)
INTEGRATED DATA SERVICES INC (PA)
2141 Rosecrans Ave # 2050, El Segundo (90245-4747)
PHONE..................................310 647-3439
Jerry Murray, *CEO*
Michelle Elliott, *Executive*
John Cole, *CTO*
Bruce Armstrong, *Info Tech Dir*
Kim Nguyen, *Software Dev*
EMP: 92 EST: 1997
SALES (est): 15.1MM Privately Held
WEB: www.get-integrated.com
SIC: 7371 Computer software development

(P-17641)
INTELLITIME SYSTEMS CORP
1118 E 17th St, Santa Ana (92701-2620)
PHONE..................................714 444-3020
Dennis Peters, *President*
Alexander Chalakov, *Vice Pres*
Leslie Van Exel, *Software Dev*
Anirban Ghosh, *Project Mgr*
EMP: 54 EST: 1997
SQ FT: 11,000

SALES (est): 7.3MM **Privately Held**
WEB: www.intellitime.com
SIC: **7371** Computer software development

(P-17642)
INVISION NETWORKING LLC
333 City Blvd W Ste 1700, Orange
(92868-5905)
PHONE..........................949 309-3441
Justin Johnson, *CEO*
Erica Thorsen, *Vice Pres*
EMP: 135 EST: 2006
SALES (est): 3.7MM **Privately Held**
WEB: www.invisionnetworking.com
SIC: **7371** Custom computer programming services

(P-17643)
INVOCA INC
419 State St, Santa Barbara (93101-2304)
PHONE..........................855 977-3154
Juan Leal, *Sr Software Eng*
Eric Wert, *Technical Staff*
Ariel Middleton, *Marketing Mgr*
Sarah Bachetti, *Sales Staff*
Sandro Lobo, *Sales Staff*
EMP: 71 EST: 2020
SALES (est): 6.6MM **Privately Held**
WEB: www.invoca.com
SIC: **7371** Computer software development

(P-17644)
IRISE (PA)
2381 Rosecrans Ave # 100, El Segundo
(90245-4917)
PHONE..........................800 556-0399
Emmet B Keeffe III, *CEO*
Maurice Martin, *President*
Lionel Etrillard, *CFO*
Mitch Bishop, *Chief Mktg Ofcr*
Stephen Brickley, *Exec VP*
▲ EMP: 94 EST: 1997
SALES (est): 21.5MM **Privately Held**
WEB: www.irise.com
SIC: **7371** Computer software development

(P-17645)
IT DIVISION INC
Also Called: Apeiro Technologies
9170 Irvine Center Dr # 200, Irvine
(92618-4614)
PHONE..........................678 648-2709
Lavanya Nilagiri, *CEO*
Shruti Nilagiri, *COO*
Neeta Prasad, *CFO*
Vivek Jaiswal, *Finance*
EMP: 103 EST: 2006
SALES (est): 5.1MM **Privately Held**
WEB: www.apeiro.us
SIC: **8243** 7371 7373 Software training, computer; computer software systems analysis & design, custom; computer software development & applications; software programming applications; systems software development services; systems engineering, computer related

(P-17646)
IV INC
Also Called: Iv. Ai
1211 Westerly Ter Ste 300, Los Angeles
(90026-7251)
PHONE..........................310 658-7374
Vince Lynch, *CEO*
John Martin, *CTO*
Uri Guzman, *Manager*
EMP: 53 EST: 2016
SQ FT: 4,000
SALES (est): 3.5MM **Privately Held**
WEB: www.iv.ai
SIC: **7371** Computer software development

(P-17647)
JUMPSTART GAMES INC
830 S Pcf Cast Hwy Ste 20, El Segundo
(90245)
PHONE..........................424 645-4311
David Lord, *CEO*
James Czulewicz, *Admin Sec*
EMP: 59 EST: 1993

SALES (est): 12.5MM **Privately Held**
WEB: www.jumpstart.com
SIC: **7371** 5734 Computer software systems analysis & design, custom; computer software development; software, computer games
HQ: Netdragon Websoft Holdings Limited
Rm 2001-05&11 20/F Harbour Ctr
Wan Chai HK

(P-17648)
KODER INC
9541 Irvine Center Dr, Irvine (92618-4654)
P.O. Box 62633 (92602-6087)
PHONE..........................415 906-4157
Elmer Morales, *CEO*
Mildred Morales, *Principal*
Richard Barnes, *CIO*
EMP: 50 EST: 2016
SALES (est): 3.3MM **Privately Held**
WEB: www.koder.com
SIC: **7371** Computer software development & applications

(P-17649)
KOFAX INC (PA)
15211 Laguna Canyon Rd, Irvine
(92618-3146)
PHONE..........................949 783-1000
Reynolds Bish, *CEO*
Cort Townsend, *CFO*
Kathleen Delaney, *Chief Mktg Ofcr*
John Cowley, *Officer*
Chris Huff, *Officer*
▼ EMP: 500 EST: 1985
SQ FT: 100,000
SALES (est): 760.9MM **Privately Held**
WEB: www.kofax.com
SIC: **7371** 3577 Computer software development; input/output equipment, computer

(P-17650)
KRG TECHNOLOGIES INC
25000 Ave Stnford Ste 243, Valencia
(91355)
PHONE..........................661 257-9967
Balamurugan Subbiah, *President*
Hemalatha Rajagopala, *CEO*
Nivethan Niv, *Executive*
Brian Adam, *IT/INT Sup*
Suresh Kumar, *IT/INT Sup*
EMP: 500 EST: 2003
SQ FT: 780
SALES (est): 32.4MM **Privately Held**
WEB: www.krgtech.com
SIC: **7371** Computer software development & applications

(P-17651)
LANDSLIDE TECHNOLOGIES INC (DH)
6922 Hollywood Blvd # 500, Los Angeles
(90028-6125)
PHONE..........................412 489-1705
Rick Faulk, *President*
Tom Costa, *COO*
Rick Brostowin, *CFO*
Karen Leavitt, *Chief Mktg Ofcr*
Edward J McGowan, *CTO*
EMP: 102 EST: 2004
SQ FT: 5,000
SALES (est): 3.3MM
SALES (corp-wide): 1.4B **Publicly Held**
WEB: www.j2global.com
SIC: **7371** Computer software development

(P-17652)
LANGUAGE WEAVER INC
Also Called: Sdl
6060 Center Dr Ste 150, Los Angeles
(90045-8808)
PHONE..........................310 437-7300
Mark Tapling, *CEO*
Daniel Marcu, *COO*
Kevin Knight, *Vice Pres*
Kirti Vashee, *Vice Pres*
Amos Kariuki, *Software Dev*
EMP: 55 EST: 2002
SQ FT: 6,000
SALES (est): 10.2MM **Privately Held**
WEB: www.languageweaver.com
SIC: **7371** Computer software development

PA: Sdl Limited
New Globe House
Maidenhead BERKS SL6 4

(P-17653)
LIMINEX INC
Also Called: Goguardian
2030 E Maple Ave, El Segundo
(90245-5170)
PHONE..........................888 310-0410
Advait Shinde, *CEO*
Michael Jonas, *CFO*
Zahir Zubair, *Program Mgr*
Manny Sevillano, *Manager*
EMP: 220 EST: 2014
SQ FT: 30,000
SALES (est): 46.7MM **Privately Held**
WEB: www.goguardian.com
SIC: **7371** Computer software development; computer software development & applications;

(P-17654)
LOGIC MATE INC
412 W Broadway Fl 3, Glendale
(91204-1297)
PHONE..........................213 623-4422
Roger Khadarian, *President*
Chris Hawatian, *Principal*
EMP: 18 EST: 1989
SALES (est): 1.1MM **Privately Held**
WEB: www.logicmate.com
SIC: **7371** 7372 5734 Computer software development; prepackaged software; software, business & non-game

(P-17655)
LOS ANGELES INTL CH CHRST
Also Called: Los Angeles Church of Christ
2716 Ocean Park Blvd # 20, Santa Monica
(90405-5207)
PHONE..........................213 351-2300
Brian Gold, *COO*
Chris Yen, *CFO*
Michael Wooten, *Admin Sec*
EMP: 160 EST: 1989
SALES (est): 13MM **Privately Held**
WEB: www.laicc.net
SIC: **8661** 7371 Miscellaneous denomination church; computer software development & applications

(P-17656)
MAINTECH INCORPORATED
2401 N Glassell St, Orange (92865-2705)
P.O. Box 13500 (92857-8500)
PHONE..........................714 921-8000
Tony Donato, *Vice Pres*
Richard Olohan, *Info Tech Dir*
Craig Saffell, *Network Enginr*
Dwayne Paoner, *Network Tech*
Tony Diaz, *Senior Engr*
EMP: 200
SQ FT: 1,200
SALES (corp-wide): 301.3MM **Privately Held**
SIC: **7371** 3577 Computer software systems analysis & design, custom; computer peripheral equipment
HQ: Maintech, Incorporated
14 Commerce Dr Ste 200
Cranford NJ 07016
973 330-3200

(P-17657)
MARKET SCAN INFO SYSTEMS INC
815 Camarillo Springs Rd, Camarillo
(93012-9457)
PHONE..........................800 658-7226
Russell West, *President*
Brent Taylor, *COO*
Mathew Hermann, *CFO*
Carsten Preisz, *Chief Mktg Ofcr*
Jose Galvan, *Officer*
EMP: 80 EST: 1987
SQ FT: 10,500
SALES (est): 10.8MM **Privately Held**
WEB: www.marketscan.com
SIC: **7371** Computer software development

(P-17658)
MAVENLINK INC (PA)
6501 Irvine Center Dr # 25, Irvine
(92618-2133)
PHONE..........................949 336-7610
Raymond Grainger, *CEO*
Piero Broccardo, *CFO*
Michael Lin, *CFO*
Chris Scalia, *Senior VP*
Doug Tilford, *Senior VP*
EMP: 171 EST: 2010
SALES (est): 10.4MM **Privately Held**
WEB: www.mavenlink.com
SIC: **7371** Computer software development

(P-17659)
MEDIACHASE LTD
8447 Wilshire Blvd # 102, Beverly Hills
(90211-3226)
PHONE..........................323 988-1071
Julie Magbojos, *President*
Chad Wolf, *Exec VP*
Sue Bergamo, *Vice Pres*
Peter Yeung, *Manager*
EMP: 57 EST: 1997
SQ FT: 4,700
SALES (est): 2.9MM **Privately Held**
SIC: **7371** Computer software development & applications
HQ: Episerver Inc.
542 Amherst St
Nashua NH 03063
603 594-0249

(P-17660)
MERGE MOBILE INC
1311 Calle Batido Ste 240, San Clemente
(92673-6316)
PHONE..........................949 234-6248
Jeff Stay, *President*
Pat Hustad, *Executive*
Patrick McCarthy, *Sales Mgr*
Jon Lathrop, *Marketing Staff*
Andrew Lathrop, *Manager*
EMP: 50 EST: 2012
SALES (est): 2.8MM **Privately Held**
WEB: www.fastfieldforms.com
SIC: **7371** Computer software development; computer software development & applications

(P-17661)
MINDSPARK INC
21021 Ventura Blvd # 220, Woodland Hills
(91364-2214)
PHONE..........................310 396-9292
David Aspinall, *CEO*
Gray Benoist, *President*
Isha Dash, *Manager*
EMP: 50 EST: 2013
SQ FT: 1,700
SALES (est): 2.6MM **Privately Held**
WEB: www.mindsparktech.com
SIC: **7371** Computer software development & applications

(P-17662)
MOBILITYWARE LLC (PA)
440 Exchange Ste 100, Irvine
(92602-1390)
PHONE..........................949 788-9900
John Libby, *President*
Lee McElroy, *CFO*
Kathy De Lay, *Vice Pres*
Robert Jackson, *Vice Pres*
Steve Wetherill, *Vice Pres*
EMP: 58 EST: 2014
SALES (est): 8MM **Privately Held**
WEB: www.mobilityware.com
SIC: **7371** Computer software development

(P-17663)
MODERN CAMPUS USA INC
1320 Flynn Rd Ste 100, Camarillo
(93012-8745)
PHONE..........................805 484-9400
Lance Merker, *President*
Tom Nalevanko, *Vice Pres*
Owen Savage, *Vice Pres*
Shelly Lee, *Administration*
Beau Pellowski, *Administration*
EMP: 60 EST: 1982
SQ FT: 6,600

SALES (est): 10MM **Privately Held**
WEB: www.moderncampus.com
SIC: 7371 7372 Computer software development; prepackaged software

(P-17664)
MODRINE LIMITED
750 N Diamond Bar Blvd, Diamond Bar (91765-1023)
PHONE...................213 269-5466
Fang He, *Sales Mgr*
Lisa Cagnolatti, *Vice Pres*
EMP: 69
SALES (est): 275K **Privately Held**
SIC: 7371 Computer software development & applications

(P-17665)
MOTHERSHIP TECHNOLOGIES INC
3213 S La Cienega Blvd, Los Angeles (90016-3112)
P.O. Box 515381 (90051-6681)
PHONE...................310 905-8677
Aaron Peck, *CEO*
Jennifer Edwards, *Officer*
Gregory Luskin, *CTO*
EMP: 56 **EST:** 2017
SALES (est): 6.8MM **Privately Held**
WEB: www.mothership.com
SIC: 7371 Computer software development & applications

(P-17666)
MTI FILM LLC
1016 N Sycamore Ave, Los Angeles (90038-2308)
PHONE...................323 465-6487
EMP: 13
SALES (corp-wide): 3.6MM **Privately Held**
SIC: 7371 7819 7372 Provides Computer Programming Services
HQ: Mti Film, L.L.C.
209 Angell St
Providence RI 02906
401 831-1315

(P-17667)
MYEVALUATIONSCOM INC
11111 W Olympic Blvd, Los Angeles (90064-1842)
PHONE...................646 422-0554
David Melamed, *Exec Dir*
EMP: 25 **EST:** 2005
SALES (est): 1.6MM **Privately Held**
WEB: www.myevaluations.com
SIC: 7371 7372 Computer software systems analysis & design, custom; educational computer software

(P-17668)
NEASI-WEBER INTERNATIONAL LLC (PA)
Also Called: Nwi
25115 Ave Stnford Ste 220, Valencia (91355)
P.O. Box 800514, Santa Clarita (91380-0514)
PHONE...................818 895-6900
Dennis J Neasi, *Partner*
James S Weber, *Partner*
Francis Chen, *Chief*
EMP: 50 **EST:** 1977
SQ FT: 13,900
SALES (est): 6.1MM **Privately Held**
WEB: www.nwintl.com
SIC: 5734 7371 Software, business & non-game; custom computer programming services

(P-17669)
NEONROOTS LLC
8560 W Sunset Blvd # 500, West Hollywood (90069-2311)
PHONE...................310 907-9210
Benjamin C Lee, *CEO*
EMP: 125 **EST:** 2012
SALES (est): 6.1MM **Privately Held**
WEB: www.neonroots.com
SIC: 7371 Computer software development & applications

(P-17670)
NEUDESIC LLC (PA)
Also Called: Neuron Esb
200 Spectrum Center Dr # 2000, Irvine (92618-5013)
PHONE...................949 754-4500
Parsa Rohani, *CEO*
Don Lukasek, *Partner*
Manny Singh, *Partner*
Zeeshan Subzwari, *Partner*
Dan Alecia, *Executive*
EMP: 125
SQ FT: 15,150
SALES (est): 65.8MM **Privately Held**
WEB: www.neudesic.com
SIC: 7371 Computer software development

(P-17671)
NEUINTEL LLC (PA)
Also Called: Pricespider
20 Pacifica Ste 1000, Irvine (92618-7462)
PHONE...................949 625-6117
Anthony Ferry, *CEO*
Jon Pfortmiller, *President*
Lucas Baerg, *CFO*
Sean Reiter, *Vice Pres*
Bryce Thornton, *Vice Pres*
EMP: 80 **EST:** 2004
SQ FT: 17,000
SALES (est): 33.9MM **Privately Held**
WEB: www.pricespider.com
SIC: 7371 Computer software development

(P-17672)
NEVERSOFT ENTERTAINMENT INC
21255 Burbank Blvd # 600, Woodland Hills (91367-6610)
PHONE...................818 610-4100
Joel Jewett, *President*
Sandy Jewett, *Data Proc Staff*
EMP: 30 **EST:** 1994
SALES (est): 2.2MM
SALES (corp-wide): 8B **Publicly Held**
WEB: www.activisionblizzard.com
SIC: 7371 7372 Computer code authors; prepackaged software
PA: Activision Blizzard, Inc.
3100 Ocean Park Blvd
Santa Monica CA 90405
310 255-2000

(P-17673)
NEW CAM COMMERCE SOLUTIONS LLC
5555 Garden Grove Blvd # 100, Westminster (92683-8227)
PHONE...................714 338-0200
Doug Roberson, *Mng Member*
EMP: 77 **EST:** 2010
SQ FT: 26,000
SALES (est): 7.1MM
SALES (corp-wide): 19.7MM **Privately Held**
WEB: www.celerant.com
SIC: 7371 Computer software development
PA: Celerant Technology Corp.
4830 Arthur Kill Rd Ste 3
Staten Island NY 10309
718 351-2000

(P-17674)
NEXGENIX INC (PA)
2 Peters Canyon Rd # 200, Irvine (92606-1798)
PHONE...................714 665-6240
Rick Dutta, *CEO*
Don Ganguly, *Ch of Bd*
Mark Iwanowski, *COO*
Ravi Renduchintala, *Vice Pres*
EMP: 258 **EST:** 1990
SQ FT: 14,264
SALES (est): 19.9MM **Privately Held**
SIC: 7371 8748 4813 Computer software development; systems analysis or design;

(P-17675)
NEXTGEN HEALTHCARE INFO SYSTEM (HQ)
18111 Von Karman Ave # 800, Irvine (92612-7111)
PHONE...................949 255-2600

John Frantz, *President*
Scott E Bostick, *COO*
Daniel J Morefield, *COO*
Paul Holt, *CFO*
John Stumpf, *CFO*
EMP: 65
SALES (est): 400MM
SALES (corp-wide): 540.2MM **Publicly Held**
WEB: www.nextgen.com
SIC: 7371 5072 Computer software systems analysis & design, custom; hardware
PA: Nextgen Healthcare, Inc.
18111 Von Karman Ave # 800
Irvine CA 30305
949 255-2600

(P-17676)
NGA 911 LLC
Also Called: Telecommunication
8383 Wilshire Blvd # 800, Beverly Hills (90211-2425)
PHONE...................877 899-8337
Don Ferguson, *CEO*
Jackie Barnes, *President*
Michelle Bland, *COO*
Darold Whitmer, *Vice Pres*
Dustin Becker, *Accounts Exec*
EMP: 80 **EST:** 2016
SALES (est): 20MM **Privately Held**
WEB: www.nga911.com
SIC: 7371 Computer software development & applications

(P-17677)
NKSFB LLC
10960 Wilshire Blvd Fl 5, Los Angeles (90024-3708)
PHONE...................310 277-4657
Mickey Segal, *Mng Member*
EMP: 32 **EST:** 2018
SALES (est): 8.5MM **Privately Held**
WEB: www.nksfb.com
SIC: 7371 7372 Computer software systems analysis & design, custom; business oriented computer software

(P-17678)
NORTHROP GRUMMAN SYSTEMS CORP
1762 Glenn Curtiss St, Carson (90746-4034)
PHONE...................310 764-3000
Neil Siegel, *Branch Mgr*
Alice Reed, *Analyst*
EMP: 150 **Publicly Held**
WEB: www.northropgrumman.com
SIC: 7371 Computer software development
HQ: Northrop Grumman Systems Corporation
2980 Fairview Park Dr
Falls Church VA 22042
703 280-2900

(P-17679)
NOVALOGIC INC (PA)
27489 Agoura Rd Ste 300, Agoura Hills (91301-2419)
PHONE...................818 880-1997
John Garcia, *Ch of Bd*
John Butrovich, *Vice Pres*
Kyle Freeman, *Vice Pres*
David Seeholzer, *Vice Pres*
EMP: 89 **EST:** 1985
SALES (est): 7.1MM **Privately Held**
WEB: www.novalogic.com
SIC: 7371 5734 7372 Computer software development; software, business & non-game; prepackaged software

(P-17680)
NUBITY INC (PA)
2767 Tumbleweed Ave, Simi Valley (93065-1337)
PHONE...................213 408-4675
EMP: 50 **EST:** 2013
SALES (est): 129.8K **Privately Held**
WEB: www.nubity.com
SIC: 7371 Computer software development & applications

(P-17681)
NUMERICAL CTRL CMPT SCIENCES (PA)
Also Called: Nccs
2600 Michelson Dr # 1700, Irvine (92612-1550)
PHONE...................949 852-3664
Donald Schultz, *President*
EMP: 13 **EST:** 1976
SALES (est): 1.6MM **Privately Held**
WEB: www.nccs.com
SIC: 7371 7372 Computer software development; prepackaged software

(P-17682)
OBLONG INDUSTRIES INC (HQ)
923 E 3rd St Ste 111, Los Angeles (90013-1867)
PHONE...................213 683-8863
Peter Holst, *CEO*
Gabriel Abejon, *Vice Pres*
Mark Backman, *Vice Pres*
David Kung, *Vice Pres*
Darrin Montague, *Vice Pres*
EMP: 129 **EST:** 2007
SALES (est): 20.9MM **Publicly Held**
WEB: www.oblong.com
SIC: 7371 Computer software development & applications

(P-17683)
ONE IDENTITY LLC (DH)
4 Polaris Way, Aliso Viejo (92656-5356)
PHONE...................949 754-8000
Jeff Hawn, *CEO*
David Earhart, *President*
Meryl Seely, *Principal*
Bradley Haque, *Admin Sec*
Rachit Goel, *Software Dev*
EMP: 50 **EST:** 2016
SALES (est): 83.4MM
SALES (corp-wide): 2.6B **Privately Held**
WEB: www.oneidentity.com
SIC: 7371 7379 Computer software development; computer related consulting services
HQ: Quest Software, Inc.
4 Polaris Way
Aliso Viejo CA 92656
949 754-8000

(P-17684)
OPERATION TECHNOLOGY INC (PA)
Also Called: Etap
17 Goodyear Ste 100, Irvine (92618-1822)
PHONE...................949 462-0100
Farrokh Shokooh, *President*
Ben Boronow, *Vice Pres*
Nikta Nikzad Shokooh, *Admin Sec*
EMP: 89 **EST:** 1986
SQ FT: 32,000
SALES (est): 31.7MM **Privately Held**
WEB: www.etap.com
SIC: 7371 8732 8249 Computer software development; research services, except laboratory; business training services

(P-17685)
ORANGE COUNTY PIKE ALUMNI ASSN
6653 Iron Horse Ln, Eastvale (92880-9127)
PHONE...................702 832-6211
Howie Palmer, *President*
EMP: 300
SALES (est): 3.1MM **Privately Held**
SIC: 7371 Computer software development & applications

(P-17686)
ORANGE HEALTH SOLUTIONS INC
28480 Ave Stnford Ste 300, Valencia (91355)
PHONE...................661 310-9333
Nicole Bradberry, *Branch Mgr*
EMP: 62
SALES (corp-wide): 25.2MM **Privately Held**
WEB: www.cedargate.com
SIC: 7371 Custom computer programming services

HQ: Orange Health Solutions, Inc.
500 Southborough Dr
South Portland ME 04106
207 253-2131

(P-17687)
OSHYN INC
100 W Broadway Ste 330, Long Beach
(90802-4431)
PHONE..........................213 483-1770
Diego Rebosio, *CEO*
Byron Calisto, *Software Dev*
Kimberly McCabe, *Sales Staff*
Jim Meyer, *Manager*
Aleksandar Radonjic, *Manager*
EMP: 75 EST: 2001
SALES (est): 10.8MM Privately Held
WEB: www.oshyn.com
SIC: 7371 Computer software development

(P-17688)
P MURPHY & ASSOCIATES INC
359 E Magnolia Blvd Ste G, Burbank
(91502-3211)
PHONE..........................818 841-2002
Phyliss Murphy, *President*
EMP: 121 EST: 1981
SQ FT: 1,200
SALES (est): 12.2MM
SALES (corp-wide): 42.5MM Privately Held
WEB: www.pmurphy.com
SIC: 7371 7361 Computer software development; employment agencies; executive placement
PA: Intelliswift Software, Inc.
39600 Balentine Dr # 200
Newark CA 94560
510 490-9240

(P-17689)
PERFORMIO USA INC (PA)
18191 Von Karman Ave # 1, Irvine
(92612-7102)
PHONE..........................833 817-7084
Grayson Morris, *CEO*
Luke Teeple, *COO*
EMP: 58 EST: 2019
SALES (est): 3.6MM Privately Held
WEB: www.performio.co
SIC: 7371 Computer software development

(P-17690)
PHONE CHECK SOLUTIONS LLC
Also Called: Software
16027 Ventura Bllvd 605, Encino (91436)
PHONE..........................310 365-1855
Chris Sabeti, *CEO*
EMP: 358 EST: 2016
SALES (est): 7.5MM Privately Held
WEB: www.phonecheck.com
SIC: 7371 Software programming applications

(P-17691)
PROCORE TECHNOLOGIES INC (PA)
6309 Carpinteria Ave, Carpinteria
(93013-2924)
PHONE..........................866 477-6267
Craig F Courtemanche Jr, *President*
Paul Lyandres, *CFO*
Benjamin C Singer,
Patricia Wadors, *Officer*
Dennis Lyandres, *Risk Mgmt Dir*
EMP: 2024 EST: 2002
SQ FT: 235,000
SALES: 113.9MM Publicly Held
WEB: www.procore.com
SIC: 7371 Computer software development

(P-17692)
PRODEGE LLC (PA)
Also Called: Swagbucks
2030 E Maple Ave Ste 200, El Segundo
(90245-5171)
PHONE..........................310 294-9599
Chuck Davis, *CEO*
Jay Hoag, *General Ptnr*
Mendy Pinson, *President*
David Weinrot, *COO*
Brad Kates, *CFO*

EMP: 430 EST: 2005
SALES (est): 35.5MM Privately Held
WEB: www.prodege.com
SIC: 7371 8742 Computer software development & applications; marketing consulting services

(P-17693)
PROLIFICS TESTING INC
24025 Park Sorrento # 405, Calabasas
(91302-4018)
PHONE..........................925 485-9535
Danis Yadegar, *President*
Claude Fenner, *Vice Pres*
Dale Lampson, *Vice Pres*
Rutesh Shah, *Vice Pres*
Armen Tekerian, *Vice Pres*
EMP: 45 EST: 1988
SQ FT: 6,500
SALES (est): 3.2MM Privately Held
WEB: www.prolifics.com
SIC: 7371 7372 Computer software development; prepackaged software
HQ: Prolifics Application Services, Inc.
24025 Park Sorrento # 405
Calabasas CA 91302
646 201-4967

(P-17694)
QUESTSOFT CORPORATION
24411 Ridge Route Dr # 220, Laguna Hills
(92653-1698)
PHONE..........................949 837-9506
Michael Berman, *CEO*
Leonard William Ryan, *President*
Daryl Nickerson, *Prgrmr*
Carmen Mullery, *Accountant*
Ken Kovaleski, *Natl Sales Mgr*
EMP: 43 EST: 1995
SALES (est): 9.5MM Privately Held
WEB: www.ncontracts.com
SIC: 7371 7372 Computer software development; business oriented computer software
PA: Ncontracts, Llc
214 Overlook Cir Ste 152
Brentwood TN 37027

(P-17695)
RAINTREE SYSTEMS INC
30650 Rancho California R, Temecula
(92591-3279)
PHONE..........................951 252-9400
Richard V Welty, *CEO*
Terrence Sims, *COO*
Jatin Burman, *Software Engr*
Jessica Ogne-Klinkhamme, *Project Mgr*
Traci Stewart, *Project Mgr*
EMP: 190 EST: 1982
SALES (est): 21MM Privately Held
WEB: www.raintreeinc.com
SIC: 7371 5045 5734 Computer software development; computer software; computer & software stores

(P-17696)
REAL ESTATE DIGITAL LLC
20411 Sw Birch St Ste 250, Newport Beach
(92660-1771)
PHONE..........................800 234-2139
Jay Gaskill, *CEO*
Monisha Bawa, *Vice Pres*
Stephanie Estrada, *Office Mgr*
Brent Marchbanks, *Info Tech Mgr*
John Hensley, *Technology*
EMP: 108 EST: 2011
SALES (est): 23.3MM
SALES (corp-wide): 3.9B Privately Held
WEB: www.constellation1.com
SIC: 7371 Software programming applications
HQ: Constellation Homebuilder Systems Corp
8133 Warden Ave 7 Fl
Markham ON L6G 1
888 723-2222

(P-17697)
RENTSPREE INC
15303 Ventura Blvd # 1150, Sherman Oaks
(91403-6623)
PHONE..........................323 515-7757
Michael Lucarelli, *CEO*
Potsawee Vechpanich, *CTO*
Jirat Boondum, *Software Engr*

Vudhidej Dejmul, *Software Engr*
Thanawat Pinya, *Software Engr*
EMP: 50 EST: 2016
SALES (est): 2.9MM Privately Held
WEB: www.rentspree.com
SIC: 7371 Computer software development & applications

(P-17698)
RIGHTSCALE INC
402 E Gutierrez St, Santa Barbara
(93101-1709)
PHONE..........................805 500-4164
EMP: 112
SALES (est): 9.2MM Privately Held
WEB: www.flexera.com
SIC: 7371 Custom Computer Programing

(P-17699)
RIOT GAMES INC (DH)
12333 W Olympic Blvd, Los Angeles
(90064-1021)
PHONE..........................310 207-1444
Brandon Beck, *CEO*
Mark Marrill, *President*
Shauna Spenley, *President*
A Dyoan Jadeja, *CFO*
Dylan A Jadeja, *CFO*
▲ EMP: 880 EST: 2006
SALES (est): 798.3MM Privately Held
WEB: www.riotgames.com
SIC: 7371 7993 Custom computer programming services; video game arcade

(P-17700)
RISA TECH INC
26632 Towne Cntre Dr 210, Foothill Ranch
(92610)
PHONE..........................949 951-5815
Amber Freund, *CEO*
Gail Reynolds, *Office Mgr*
Gail A Reynolds, *Office Mgr*
Michelle Stamm, *Office Mgr*
Adam Cristiano, *Software Engr*
EMP: 22
SQ FT: 1,000
SALES (est): 3.4MM
SALES (corp-wide): 705.9MM Privately Held
WEB: www.risa.com
SIC: 7371 7372 Computer software development; prepackaged software
PA: Nemetschek Se
Konrad-Zuse-Platz 1
Munchen 81829
895 404-590

(P-17701)
ROGUE GAMES INC
4056 Ventura Canyon Ave, Sherman Oaks
(91423-4715)
PHONE..........................650 483-8008
Michael C Delaet, *Manager*
EMP: 20 EST: 2017
SALES (est): 1.2MM Privately Held
WEB: www.rogueco.com
SIC: 7371 2741 Computer software development & applications; miscellaneous publishing

(P-17702)
ROOTSTRAP INC
8306 Wilshire Blvd # 249, Beverly Hills
(90211-2304)
PHONE..........................310 907-9210
David Jarrett, *CEO*
Fernando Colman, *President*
Anthony Figueroa, *CTO*
EMP: 134 EST: 2015
SALES (est): 7.6MM Privately Held
WEB: www.rootstrap.com
SIC: 7371 Computer software development & applications

(P-17703)
ROSE INTERNATIONAL INC
450 N Brand Blvd Fl 6, Glendale
(91203-2349)
PHONE..........................636 812-4000
EMP: 107 Privately Held
WEB: www.roseint.com
SIC: 7371 8748 Computer software development; systems engineering consultant, ex. computer or professional

PA: Rose International, Inc.
16305 Swingley Ridge Rd # 350
Chesterfield MO 63017

(P-17704)
RUNA HR HOLDINGS INC
3067 E 1st St, Long Beach (90803-2536)
PHONE..........................562 883-3546
Courtney McColgan, *CEO*
EMP: 55
SALES (est): 120K Privately Held
SIC: 7371 Computer software development & applications

(P-17705)
SAFRAN PASS INNOVATIONS LLC (HQ)
Also Called: Zodiac Inflight Innovations US
3151 E Imperial Hwy, Brea (92821-6720)
PHONE..........................714 854-8600
Matt Smith, *CEO*
Ed Barrera, *CFO*
Shannon Biggs, *Senior VP*
Steve Hawkins, *CTO*
Francis Memole, *Director*
EMP: 73 EST: 1996
SALES (est): 55.1MM
SALES (corp-wide): 639.8MM Privately Held
WEB: www.imsco-us.com
SIC: 7371 Computer software systems analysis & design, custom
PA: Safran
2 Bd Du General Martial Valin
Paris 75015
140 608-080

(P-17706)
SECOND SPECTRUM INC
312 E 1st St, Los Angeles (90012-3900)
PHONE..........................213 995-6860
Yu-Han Chang, *Owner*
Lai Ki Wong, *Officer*
Tracey Ho, *Vice Pres*
Lai-Ki Wong, *Vice Pres*
Michael D'auria, *VP Bus Drlpt*
EMP: 51 EST: 2013
SALES (est): 6.5MM Privately Held
WEB: www.secondspectrum.com
SIC: 7371 Software programming applications

(P-17707)
SECURE CHANNELS INC (PA)
Also Called: Proximity Technologies
2102 Bus Ctr Dr Ste 130, Irvine (92612)
PHONE..........................949 208-7525
Richard Blech, *CEO*
Mike Rash, *CFO*
Deirdre Murphy, *Officer*
Michael Feinberg, *CIO*
Adam Firestone, *Engineer*
EMP: 17 EST: 2015
SQ FT: 2,500
SALES (est): 3.4MM Privately Held
WEB: www.securechannels.com
SIC: 7371 7372 7373 Computer software development; business oriented computer software; utility computer software; systems software development services

(P-17708)
SECUREAUTH CORPORATION (PA)
38 Discovery Ste 100, Irvine (92618-3128)
PHONE..........................949 777-6959
Ahmed Rubaie, *CEO*
Craig J Lund, *CEO*
Justin Dolly, *COO*
Jeffrey Kukowski, *COO*
Tom Moyes, *CFO*
EMP: 97 EST: 2005
SALES (est): 12MM Privately Held
WEB: www.secureauth.com
SIC: 7371 Computer software development

(P-17709)
SELECT DATA INC
4175 E La Palma Ave # 205, Anaheim
(92807-1842)
PHONE..........................714 577-1000
Edward A Buckley, *CEO*
Pete Poulis, *CFO*
Susan Carmichael, *Officer*

Ginger Voss, *Officer*
Martha Case, *Vice Pres*
EMP: 121 **EST:** 1991
SALES (est): 20MM **Privately Held**
WEB: www.selectdata.com
SIC: 7371 7372 Computer code authors;
prepackaged software

(P-17710)
SERCO SERVICES INC
Also Called: Lompoc-Vandenberg Afb
701 N St Ste A, Lompoc (93437-6210)
PHONE.....................805 736-3584
Nedra Engleson, *Branch Mgr*
EMP: 90
SALES (corp-wide): 5.1B **Privately Held**
WEB: www.serco.com
SIC: 7371 8711 7375 Computer software
development; petroleum engineering;
data base information retrieval
HQ: Serco Services, Inc.
12930 Worldgate Dr # 600
Herndon VA 20170
703 939-6000

(P-17711)
SERVICETITAN INC (PA)
801 N Brand Blvd Ste 700, Glendale
(91203-3255)
PHONE.....................855 899-0970
ARA Mahdessian, *CEO*
Justin Lu, *Partner*
Vahe Kuzoyan, *President*
Guy Longworth, *Chief Mktg Ofcr*
Chris Trombetta,
EMP: 97 **EST:** 2015
SALES (est): 43.6MM **Privately Held**
WEB: www.servicetitan.com
SIC: 7371 Computer software develop-
ment

(P-17712)
SHELL NEW ENERGIES US LLC (HQ)
Also Called: Greenlots
767 S Alameda St Ste 200, Los Angeles
(90021-1664)
PHONE.....................888 751-8560
EMP: 50 **EST:** 2002
SALES (est): 53.3MM
SALES (corp-wide): 180.5B **Privately Held**
WEB: www.shell.com
SIC: 7371 Computer software systems
analysis & design, custom
PA: Royal Dutch Shell Plc
Shell Centre
London
207 934-1234

(P-17713)
SKILLZ INC (PA)
2121 Avenue Of The Stars, Los Angeles
(90067-5010)
P.O. Box 445, San Francisco (94104-0445)
PHONE.....................415 762-0511
Andrew Paradise, *Ch of Bd*
Ian Lee, *CFO*
Vatsal Bhardwaj, *Officer*
Casey Chafkin, *Risk Mgmt Dir*
Miriam Aguirre, *CTO*
EMP: 320 **EST:** 2020
SALES (est): 230.1MM **Publicly Held**
WEB: www.games.skillz.com
SIC: 7371 Computer software develop-
ment & applications

(P-17714)
SLEEPY GIANT ENTERTAINMENT INC
4 San Joaquin Plz Ste 200, Newport Beach
(92660-5934)
PHONE.....................949 464-7986
EMP: 150 **EST:** 2007
SALES (est): 11.2MM **Privately Held**
SIC: 7371 Custom Computer Programing

(P-17715)
SMART ENERGY SYSTEMS INC (PA)
15495 Sand Canyon Ave # 100, Irvine
(92618-3152)
PHONE.....................909 703-9609
Ray Howlett, *Principal*
Deepak Garg, *CEO*

EMP: 134 **EST:** 2012
SALES (est): 10.1MM **Privately Held**
WEB: www.sew.ai
SIC: 7371 Computer software develop-
ment

(P-17716)
SNAP INC (PA)
Also Called: SNAPCHAT
2772 Dnald Douglas Loop N, Santa Monica
(90405-2951)
PHONE.....................310 399-3339
Evan Spiegel, *CEO*
Michael Lynton, *Ch of Bd*
Derek Andersen, *CFO*
Alan Lafley, *Bd of Directors*
Jeremi Gorman, *Officer*
EMP: 1967 **EST:** 2010
SQ FT: 553,000
SALES (est): 2.5B **Publicly Held**
WEB: www.snap.com
SIC: 7371 7372 Computer software devel-
opment & applications; software program-
ming applications; application computer
software

(P-17717)
SNAPCOMMS INC
155 N Lake Ave Fl 9, Pasadena
(91101-1849)
PHONE.....................805 715-0300
Chris Leonard, *CEO*
EMP: 80 **EST:** 2012
SALES (est): 6.2MM
SALES (corp-wide): 271.1MM **Publicly Held**
WEB: www.snapcomms.com
SIC: 7371 Computer software develop-
ment
PA: Everbridge, Inc.
155 N Lake Ave Ste 100
Pasadena CA 91101
818 230-9700

(P-17718)
SNAPPAYS MOBILE INC
14140 Ventura Blvd, Sherman Oaks
(91423-2774)
PHONE.....................310 869-6942
Patrick Kahn, *CEO*
Jason Meltzer, *Principal*
EMP: 50 **EST:** 2016
SALES (est): 1.8MM **Privately Held**
SIC: 7371 Computer software develop-
ment & applications

(P-17719)
SOFTWARE MANAGEMENT CONS INC
Also Called: Smci
959 S Coast Dr Ste 415, Costa Mesa
(92626-7839)
PHONE.....................714 662-1841
Cesar Sanchez, *Principal*
Lori Boone, *Business Anlyst*
EMP: 140
SALES (corp-wide): 275MM **Privately Held**
WEB: www.smci.com
SIC: 7371 Computer software systems
analysis & design, custom
HQ: Software Management Consultants,
Llc
500 N Brand Blvd Ste 1100
Glendale CA 91203
818 240-3177

(P-17720)
SOLARTIS LLC
1601 N Sepulveda Blvd # 6, Manhattan
Beach (90266-5111)
PHONE.....................310 251-4861
Nicholas Richardson, *President*
Jonathan Kaplan, *Vice Pres*
Carol M McKenzie, *Vice Pres*
Siby Nidhiry, *CTO*
Sharon Mercier, *Business Anlyst*
EMP: 21 **EST:** 2000
SALES (est): 797.5K **Privately Held**
WEB: www.solartis.com
SIC: 7371 7374 7372 Computer software
development; data processing & prepara-
tion; business oriented computer software

(P-17721)
SPIREON INC (PA)
Also Called: Goldstar
16802 Aston Ste 150, Irvine (92606-4840)
PHONE.....................800 557-1449
Kevin Weiss, *CEO*
Brian Skutta, *President*
Tim Welch, *COO*
Rita Parvaneh, *CFO*
Carla Fitzgerald, *Chief Mktg Ofcr*
EMP: 175 **EST:** 2002
SALES (est): 172.3MM **Privately Held**
WEB: www.spireon.com
SIC: 7371 8741 Computer software devel-
opment; business management

(P-17722)
ST JHNS LTHRAN CH BAKERSFIELD
Also Called: St Johns Lthran Schl Chldren C
4500 Buena Vista Rd, Bakersfield
(93311-9702)
PHONE.....................661 665-7815
Dennis Hilken, *Pastor*
Sara Ablin, *Administration*
Mike Kinsey, *CIO*
Michelle Fox, *Finance Asst*
Fox Michelle, *Finance Asst*
EMP: 105 **EST:** 1904
SQ FT: 40,000
SALES (est): 7MM **Privately Held**
WEB: www.sjlchurch.org
SIC: 8661 8211 7371 Lutheran Church;
private elementary school; computer soft-
ware development & applications

(P-17723)
STARTEL CORPORATION (PA)
16 Goodyear B-125, Irvine (92618-3758)
PHONE.....................949 863-8700
William Lane, *President*
Renita Dorty, *Officer*
Isaac Thompson, *Business Mgr*
David Abrams, *Purch Mgr*
Jim Graham, *Opers Staff*
EMP: 60 **EST:** 1980
SQ FT: 27,000
SALES (est): 11.2MM **Privately Held**
WEB: www.startel.com
SIC: 7371 3661 Computer software devel-
opment; communication headgear, tele-
phone

(P-17724)
STONEFIRE GRILL INC (PA)
30401 Agoura Rd Ste 130, Agoura Hills
(91301-2084)
PHONE.....................805 413-0300
Mary Harrigan, *President*
Matthew Calabrese, *CFO*
Cindy Escobedo, *Area Mgr*
Matt Francisco, *General Mgr*
Shannon Francisco, *General Mgr*
EMP: 353 **EST:** 2000
SALES (est): 93.1MM **Privately Held**
WEB: www.stonefiregrill.com
SIC: 5812 7371 Grills (eating places);
computer software development & appli-
cations

(P-17725)
STONERIVER INC
770 The Cy Dr S Ste 5000, Orange
(92868)
PHONE.....................714 705-8227
John Grundman, *Principal*
EMP: 91 **Privately Held**
WEB: www.sapiens.com
SIC: 7371 Computer software develop-
ment
HQ: Stoneriver, Inc.
20 Horseneck Ln Ste 1
Greenwich CT 06830
303 729-7500

(P-17726)
STRATACARE LLC
17838 Gillette Ave Ste D, Irvine
(92614-6502)
P.O. Box 19600 (92623-9600)
PHONE.....................949 743-1200
Scott R Green, *CEO*
Steve Ditman, *CFO*
Robert McCaffrey, *Officer*
John Zavoli, *Officer*
Michael Josephs, *Vice Pres*

▲ **EMP:** 250 **EST:** 1998
SALES (est): 30.5MM
SALES (corp-wide): 4.1B **Publicly Held**
WEB: www.conduent.com
SIC: 7371 Computer software develop-
ment & applications
HQ: Conduent Workers Compensation
Holdings, Inc.
17838 Gillette Ave
Irvine CA 92614

(P-17727)
SYSTECH SOLUTIONS INC (PA)
500 N Brand Blvd Ste 1900, Glendale
(91203-3308)
PHONE.....................818 550-9690
Arun Gollapudi, *President*
Ashish Parikh, *CFO*
Srinivasan Ramaswamy, *Vice Pres*
Sudha Gopal, *Managing Dir*
Mercy David, *Software Dev*
EMP: 81
SQ FT: 1,500
SALES (est): 23.8MM **Privately Held**
WEB: www.systechusa.com
SIC: 7371 Computer software systems
analysis & design, custom

(P-17728)
SYXSENSE INC
Also Called: Cloud Management Suite
65 Enterprise Ste 375, Aliso Viejo
(92656-2705)
PHONE.....................949 270-1903
Ashley Leonard, *CEO*
Mike Jager, *Technical Staff*
EMP: 53 **EST:** 2011
SQ FT: 1,700
SALES (est): 5MM **Privately Held**
WEB: www.syxsense.com
SIC: 7371 Computer software develop-
ment

(P-17729)
TALENT & ACQUISITION LLC
Also Called: Stand 8
100 W Broadway Ste 650, Long Beach
(90802-4466)
PHONE.....................213 742-1972
Quinn Fillmon, *Exec Dir*
Andrew Moreno, *Vice Pres*
Scott Banks, *Technical Staff*
Ryan Pollard, *Sales Staff*
Jennifer Gordon, *Director*
EMP: 150 **EST:** 2009
SALES (est): 10.4MM **Privately Held**
WEB: www.stand8.io
SIC: 7371 7379 7363 7361 Computer
software development & applications;
computer related consulting services;
help supply services; employment agen-
cies

(P-17730)
TALESPIN REALITY LABS INC (PA)
600 Corporate Pointe # 1130, Culver City
(90230-7600)
PHONE.....................323 452-6998
Kyle Jackson, *CEO*
Doug Lorenzen, *CFO*
Jeroen De Cloe, *Officer*
Jasmine Bulin, *Vice Pres*
Travis Falstad, *Vice Pres*
EMP: 65 **EST:** 2015
SQ FT: 7,000
SALES (est): 5.8MM **Privately Held**
WEB: www.talespin.com
SIC: 7371 Computer software develop-
ment & applications

(P-17731)
TCG SOFTWARE SERVICES INC
320 Commerce Ste 200, Irvine
(92602-1363)
PHONE.....................714 665-6200
Greg Blevins, *Branch Mgr*
EMP: 278 **Privately Held**
SIC: 7371 Custom computer programming
services; computer software development
PA: Tcg Software Services, Inc.
265 Davidson Ave Ste 220
Somerset NJ 08873

(P-17732)
TECH TOWN INC
1157 N Brand Blvd, Glendale (91202-2503)
PHONE..............................818 621-2744
Shant Chorbadjian, *CEO*
EMP: 50 **EST:** 2016
SALES (est): 3.3MM **Privately Held**
WEB: www.techtown.co
SIC: 7371 Custom computer programming
services

(P-17733)
THE FIFTY FIVE FOUNDRY INC
Also Called: Fifty Five Foundry, The
1100 Highland Ave, Manhattan Beach
(90266-5311)
PHONE..............................612 760-5900
Jonn Schumacher, *Principal*
EMP: 50 **EST:** 2018
SQ FT: 14,000
SALES (est): 2.9MM **Privately Held**
SIC: 7371 Software programming applica-
tions

(P-17734)
**THOMAS GALLAWAY
CORPORATION (PA)**
Also Called: Technologent
100 Spectrum Center Dr # 700, Irvine
(92618-4970)
PHONE..............................949 716-9500
Lezlie Gallaway, *CEO*
Marco Mohajer, *President*
Thomas Gallaway, *Chairman*
Jim Bevis, *Vice Pres*
David Gill, *Vice Pres*
EMP: 70 **EST:** 2002
SQ FT: 4,500
SALES: 515.9MM **Privately Held**
WEB: www.technologent.com
SIC: 7371 Computer software develop-
ment

(P-17735)
TICKETSOCKET INC
2901 W Coast Hwy Ste 200, Newport
Beach (92663-4045)
PHONE..............................917 283-0436
Mark Miller, *CEO*
EMP: 50 **EST:** 2016
SALES (est): 3.7MM **Privately Held**
WEB: www.ticketsocket.com
SIC: 7371 Software programming applica-
tions

(P-17736)
TIKTOK INC (DH)
5800 Bristol Pkwy, Culver City
(90230-6696)
PHONE..............................844 523-3993
Shou Zi Chew, *CEO*
Luyu Yang, *Treasurer*
Ole Obermann, *Vice Pres*
Lee Hunter, *General Mgr*
Richard Waterworth, *General Mgr*
EMP: 147 **EST:** 2015
SALES (est): 16MM **Privately Held**
WEB: www.tiktok.com
SIC: 7371 7389 Software programming
applications; music & broadcasting serv-
ices

(P-17737)
TK CARSITES INC
2975 Red Hill Ave, Costa Mesa
(92626-1201)
PHONE..............................714 937-1239
Richard J Valenta, *CEO*
James Bradford, *President*
James Rucker, *Chief Mktg Ofcr*
Philip Sahyoun, *CTO*
EMP: 90 **EST:** 1997
SQ FT: 8,000
SALES (est): 3.3MM
SALES (corp-wide): 17.4MM **Privately
Held**
WEB: www.searchoptics.com
SIC: 7371 Computer software develop-
ment
PA: Search Optics, Llc
531 Vester St
Ferndale MI 48220
858 678-0707

(P-17738)
TOMITRIBE CORPORATION
1519 6th St Apt 503, Santa Monica
(90401-2532)
PHONE..............................310 526-7676
David Blevins, *CEO*
Amelia Eiras, *COO*
Jean-Louis Monteiro, *Engineer*
Jonathan Gallimore, *Director*
EMP: 20 **EST:** 2012
SALES (est): 1.3MM **Privately Held**
WEB: www.tomitribe.com
SIC: 7371 7372 8742 Computer software
development; prepackaged software; pro-
grammed instruction service

(P-17739)
TOUCHTONE CORPORATION
3151 Airway Ave Ste I3, Costa Mesa
(92626-4624)
P.O. Box 5719, Irvine (92616-5719)
PHONE..............................714 755-2810
Reza H Saraf, *President*
EMP: 20 **EST:** 1991
SQ FT: 5,000
SALES (est): 1.5MM **Privately Held**
WEB: www.touchtonecorp.com
SIC: 7371 7372 Computer software writing
services; prepackaged software

(P-17740)
TRACKR INC
7410 Hollister Ave, Santa Barbara
(93117-2583)
PHONE..............................855 981-1690
Christopher G Herbert, *CEO*
Christian J Smith, *President*
Nathan Kelly, *COO*
Matthew Pigeon, *CFO*
Mark Jenkins, *Sales Staff*
EMP: 100 **EST:** 2009
SQ FT: 40,000
SALES (est): 44MM **Privately Held**
WEB: www.thetrackr.com
SIC: 7371 Computer software develop-
ment

(P-17741)
TRADE DESK INC (PA)
Also Called: Thetradedesk
42 N Chestnut St, Ventura (93001-2662)
PHONE..............................805 585-3434
Jeff T Green, *Ch of Bd*
Michelle E Hulst, *COO*
Blake J Grayson, *CFO*
Susan Vobejda, *Chief Mktg Ofcr*
Jay R Grant,
EMP: 1046 **EST:** 2009
SALES (est): 836MM **Publicly Held**
WEB: www.thetradedesk.com
SIC: 7371 7372 Software programming
applications; prepackaged software; busi-
ness oriented computer software; publish-
ers' computer software

(P-17742)
TRENDSHIFT LLC
13274 Fiji Way Ste 250, Marina Del Rey
(90292-7298)
P.O. Box 691233, West Hollywood (90069-
9233)
PHONE..............................866 644-8877
EMP: 55
SALES (est): 2MM **Privately Held**
SIC: 7371 Custom Computer Programing

(P-17743)
TRI-TECH SYSTEMS INC (PA)
Also Called: Triad Systems International
23801 Calabasas Rd # 2022, Calabasas
(91302-1547)
PHONE..............................818 222-6811
Cyril Cianflone, *President*
John Gerber, *Vice Pres*
Thomas Pickett, *Admin Sec*
Michael Nguyen, *Technical Staff*
EMP: 373 **EST:** 1992
SQ FT: 3,500
SALES (est): 51MM **Privately Held**
WEB: www.triadsystems.com
SIC: 7371 7373 Custom computer pro-
gramming services; computer integrated
systems design

(P-17744)
TRIBRIDGE HOLDINGS LLC
523 W 6th St Ste 830, Los Angeles
(90014-1243)
PHONE..............................813 287-8887
Criatritinia Valentin, *Branch Mgr*
Ted Potter, *Technical Mgr*
Gladys Tseng, *Senior Mgr*
EMP: 337 **Privately Held**
SIC: 7371 Computer software develop-
ment
PA: Tribridge Holdings, Llc
4830 W Kennedy Blvd # 89
Tampa FL 33609

(P-17745)
TRINUS CORPORATION
1030 Fallen Leaf Rd, Arcadia (91006-1903)
PHONE..............................818 246-1143
Sanjay Kucheria, *CEO*
Harshada Kucheria, *President*
Sudhir Vannadil, *CIO*
EMP: 50 **EST:** 1995
SALES (est): 6.5MM **Privately Held**
WEB: www.trinus.com
SIC: 7371 Custom computer programming
services

(P-17746)
TRUECAR INC (PA)
120 Broadway Ste 200, Santa Monica
(90401-2385)
PHONE..............................800 200-2000
Michael D Darrow, *President*
Nathan Roark, *Partner*
Christopher W Claus, *Ch of Bd*
Kristin Slanina, *COO*
Jantoon E Reigersman, *CFO*
EMP: 50 **EST:** 2005
SALES (est): 278.6MM **Publicly Held**
WEB: www.truecar.com
SIC: 7371 7299 Custom computer pro-
gramming services; information services,
consumer

(P-17747)
**UNIVERSAL ASSET LNDING
INFO SY (DH)**
Also Called: Unalisys
505 N Brand Blvd Ste 830, Glendale
(91203-3964)
PHONE..............................678 854-9451
David Keaton,
Steven Bush,
EMP: 56 **EST:** 2006
SALES (est): 955.2K
SALES (corp-wide): 15.2MM **Privately
Held**
WEB: www.theglenwoodgroup.net
SIC: 7371 Computer software develop-
ment & applications
HQ: Glenwood Financial Group, Inc.
3795 La Crescenta Ave # 2
Glendale CA 91208
818 956-9100

(P-17748)
UST GLOBAL INC (HQ)
5 Polaris Way, Aliso Viejo (92656-5374)
PHONE..............................949 716-8757
Krishna Sudheendra, *CEO*
Matthew Nocks, *Partner*
Arun Narayanan, *COO*
Paras Chandaria, *Chairman*
Murali Gopalan, *Ch Credit Ofcr*
EMP: 100 **EST:** 2007
SQ FT: 20.000
SALES (est): 511.4MM **Privately Held**
WEB: www.ust.com
SIC: 7371 Computer software develop-
ment

(P-17749)
**UTILITY SYSTEMS SCNCE
SFTWR IN (PA)**
Also Called: US 3
601 Parkcenter Dr Ste 209, Santa Ana
(92705-3542)
PHONE..............................714 542-1004
Gabriel A Chavez, *CEO*
Anthony Chavez, *CFO*
Tony Chavez, *CFO*
Mark Serres, *Vice Pres*
Ryan Trisnojoyo, *Software Engr*

EMP: 70 **EST:** 2002
SALES (est): 8.5MM **Privately Held**
WEB: www.uscubed.com
SIC: 7371 Computer software development
ment

(P-17750)
VEGATEK CORPORATION
Also Called: Intellective
470 Wald, Irvine (92618-4638)
P.O. Box 436057, Louisville KY (40253-
6057)
PHONE..............................949 502-0090
Matthew Barnickle, *CEO*
Boris Zhilin, *President*
Dan Rotelli, *Bd of Directors*
John McConville, *Vice Pres*
Chris Schassler, *Vice Pres*
EMP: 70 **EST:** 2005
SQ FT: 6,000
SALES (est): 9.1MM **Privately Held**
WEB: www.intellective.com
SIC: 7371 7379 6411 Computer software
development; computer software systems
analysis & design, custom; computer soft-
ware development & applications; com-
puter related consulting services;
computer related maintenance services;
insurance information & consulting serv-
ices

(P-17751)
**VENDOR DIRECT SOLUTIONS
LLC (PA)**
515 S Figueroa St # 1900, Los Angeles
(90071-3336)
PHONE..............................213 362-5622
Jules Buenabenta, *Principal*
Jim Young, *Exec VP*
Leslie Barton, *Human Res Mgr*
Stephanie Simmons, *Human Resources*
Angel E Nevarez, *General Counsel*
EMP: 249 **EST:** 2006
SQ FT: 1,200
SALES (est): 23.4MM **Privately Held**
WEB: www.teamvds.com
SIC: 7371 Computer software develop-
ment

(P-17752)
VENTURE AVIATOR
4136 Del Rey Ave Ste 662, Marina Del Rey
(90292-5604)
PHONE..............................212 913-9746
Don Oparah, *CEO*
Lam Nguyen, *Vice Pres*
Roy Malkin, *Manager*
EMP: 50 **EST:** 2012
SALES (est): 1.9MM **Privately Held**
WEB: www.ventureaviator.com
SIC: 7371 5047 Computer software devel-
opment; medical equipment & supplies

(P-17753)
VERITAS TECHNOLOGIES LLC
16501 Ventura Blvd # 400, Encino
(91436-2007)
PHONE..............................310 202-0757
EMP: 200
SALES (corp-wide): 2.9B **Publicly Held**
WEB: www.veritas.com
SIC: 7371 7375 Computer software devel-
opment & applications; data base infor-
mation retrieval
HQ: Veritas Technologies Llc
2625 Augustine Dr
Santa Clara CA 95054
866 837-4827

(P-17754)
VISION SOLUTIONS INC (PA)
15300 Barranca Pkwy, Irvine (92618-2200)
PHONE..............................949 253-6500
Nicolaas Vlok, *President*
Maureen Eubeler, *Partner*
Don Scott, *CFO*
Wm Edward Vesely, *Chief Mktg Ofcr*
Alan Arnold, *Exec VP*
▲ **EMP:** 90 **EST:** 1989
SQ FT: 25,000
SALES (est): 49.6MM **Privately Held**
WEB: www.visionsolutions-
optometrist.business.site
SIC: 7371 7373 Computer software devel-
opment; systems integration services

(P-17755)
VIVID DIGITAL
Also Called: Vivid Interactive
1933 N Bronson Ave # 209, Los Angeles
(90068-5603)
PHONE.................................818 908-0481
David James,
Bill Dellara, *Purch Agent*
EMP: 60
SALES (est): 1.9MM **Privately Held**
WEB: www.vividtv.com
SIC: 7371 7812 Computer software development & applications; motion picture & video production

(P-17756)
VWISE INC
85 Enterprise Ste 320, Aliso Viejo
(92656-2504)
PHONE.................................949 716-1276
Tony F Mingo, *CEO*
Dave Ferrigno, *CFO*
Lucio Marino, *Vice Pres*
EMP: 60 **EST:** 2007
SALES (est): 4.1MM **Privately Held**
WEB: www.vwise.com
SIC: 7371 Computer software development

(P-17757)
WAVEFUNCTION INC
18401 Von Karman Ave # 370, Irvine
(92612-1542)
PHONE.................................949 955-2120
Warren J Hehre, *CEO*
Pam Chua, *Administration*
Michelle Fitzpatrick, *Administration*
Jacob Tredwell, *Technician*
Susan Kurz, *Sales Staff*
EMP: 19 **EST:** 1991
SALES (est): 2.7MM **Privately Held**
WEB: www.wavefun.com
SIC: 7371 7372 5734 Computer software development; prepackaged software; software, business & non-game

(P-17758)
WAYFORWARD TECHNOLOGIES INC
28738 The Old Rd, Valencia (91355-1084)
PHONE.................................661 286-2769
Voldi Way, *President*
Matt Bozon, *Creative Dir*
James Guintu, *Software Engr*
Andrew Aitchison, *Prgrmr*
Byron Choy, *Prgrmr*
EMP: 50 **EST:** 1996
SQ FT: 10,000
SALES (est): 10.2MM **Privately Held**
WEB: www.wayforward.com
SIC: 7371 Computer software development

(P-17759)
WEB4 INC
8175 E Kaiser Blvd 100, Anaheim
(92808-2214)
PHONE.................................714 974-2670
Dutta Koushik, *Principal*
Raj Kavari, *Director*
EMP: 64 **EST:** 2010
SALES (est): 224.6K
SALES (corp-wide): 65.8MM **Privately Held**
WEB: www.neudesic.com
SIC: 7371 Computer software development
PA: Neudesic, Llc
200 Spectrum Center Dr # 2000
Irvine CA 92618
949 754-4500

(P-17760)
WESTMONT COLLEGE
Also Called: Martin Inst For Chrstnity Cltu
955 La Paz Rd, Santa Barbara
(93108-1099)
PHONE.................................805 565-6000
EMP: 322
SALES (corp-wide): 81.9MM **Privately Held**
WEB: www.westmont.edu
SIC: 7371 Computer software development & applications

PA: Westmont College
955 La Paz Rd
Santa Barbara CA 93108
805 565-6000

(P-17761)
WETRANSFER CORPORATION
2116 Zeno Pl, Venice (90291-4855)
PHONE.................................626 626-5565
EMP: 51
SALES (est): 2.5MM **Privately Held**
WEB: www.wetransfer.com
SIC: 7371 Custom Computer Programing

(P-17762)
WYNNE SYSTEMS INC (DH)
2601 Main St Ste 270, Irvine (92614-4203)
PHONE.................................949 224-6300
John Bureau, *President*
Patrick Stephens, *Vice Pres*
Mike Stilwagner, *Vice Pres*
Jerome Kern, *Administration*
Tran Ly, *Info Tech Dir*
EMP: 82 **EST:** 1989
SALES (est): 16.1MM
SALES (corp-wide): 3.9B **Privately Held**
WEB: www.wynnesystems.com
SIC: 7371 7372 Computer software development; prepackaged software
HQ: Volaris Group Inc
5060 Spectrum Way Suite 100
Mississauga ON L4W 5
647 951-9345

(P-17763)
X1 DISCOVERY INC
617 W 7th St Ste 604, Los Angeles
(90017-3817)
PHONE.................................877 999-1347
John Patzakis, *CEO*
Georges Sabongui, *Officer*
Carine Sergeant, *Manager*
EMP: 36 **EST:** 2011
SQ FT: 2,000
SALES (est): 3MM **Privately Held**
WEB: www.x1.com
SIC: 7371 7372 Computer software development; prepackaged software

(P-17764)
XCAST LABS INC (PA)
1880 Century Park E # 1415, Los Angeles
(90067-1600)
PHONE.................................310 861-4700
Cliff Rees, *President*
Susan Kelley, *Exec VP*
Larry Anthony, *Senior VP*
Roman Marchevsky, *Senior VP*
Michael Henderson, *Vice Pres*
EMP: 147 **EST:** 2008
SALES (est): 5.9MM **Privately Held**
WEB: www.xcastlabs.com
SIC: 7371 8748 4813 Computer software development & applications; telecommunications consultant; voice telephone communications

(P-17765)
YARDI SYSTEMS INC (PA)
430 S Fairview Ave, Santa Barbara
(93117-3637)
PHONE.................................951 203-6951
Keith Jones, *CEO*
Jonathan Delong, *President*
Gordon Morrell, *Exec VP*
John Pendergast, *Senior VP*
Fritz Schindelbeck, *Senior VP*
EMP: 380 **EST:** 1982
SQ FT: 160,000
SALES (est): 856.6MM **Privately Held**
WEB: www.yardi.com
SIC: 7371 Computer software development

(P-17766)
ZEFR INC
Also Called: Movieclips.com
4101 Redwood Ave, Los Angeles
(90066-5603)
PHONE.................................310 392-3555
Rich Raddon, *CEO*
Toby Byrne, *President*
Kelsey Garigan, *Exec VP*
Ryan Barker, *Vice Pres*
Robert Cukierman, *Vice Pres*
EMP: 200 **EST:** 2010

SALES (est): 18.1MM **Privately Held**
WEB: www.zefr.com
SIC: 7371 Software programming applications

(P-17767)
ZESTFINANCE INC
Also Called: Zest.ai
3900 W Alameda Ave Fl 30, Burbank
(91505-4316)
PHONE.................................323 450-3000
Mike De Vere, *CEO*
Michelle Sangster, *President*
Douglas Merrill, *CEO*
Paul SRI, *Vice Pres*
Jose Valentin, *Vice Pres*
EMP: 85 **EST:** 2012
SALES (est): 7.5MM **Privately Held**
WEB: www.zest.ai
SIC: 7371 Computer software development

(P-17768)
ZYNX HEALTH INCORPORATED (DH)
6420 Wilshire Blvd # 1250, Los Angeles
(90048-5502)
PHONE.................................310 954-1950
Scott Weingarten, *President*
Kevin Daly, *President*
Richard P Malloch, *Treasurer*
Robert D Wilbanks, *Treasurer*
Bertina Yen, *Exec VP*
EMP: 50 **EST:** 1996
SQ FT: 9,422
SALES (est): 26.7MM
SALES (corp-wide): 4.2B **Privately Held**
WEB: www.zynxhealth.com
SIC: 7371 Computer software development; custom computer programming services
HQ: Hearst Business Media Corp
2620 Barrett Rd
Gainesville GA 30507
770 532-4111

7372 Prepackaged Software

(P-17769)
3BD HOLDINGS INC (PA)
Also Called: 3blackdot
717 Mateo St, Los Angeles (90021-1709)
PHONE.................................323 524-0541
Reginald Cash, *CEO*
Luke Stepleton, *President*
Shelby Brown, *COO*
Vince Cortese, *CFO*
Boris Chang, *Creative Dir*
EMP: 22 **EST:** 2014
SQ FT: 10,000
SALES (est): 4.2MM **Privately Held**
SIC: 7372 5699 Application computer software; home entertainment computer software; T-shirts, custom printed

(P-17770)
3BECOM INC (PA)
2400 Lincoln Ave Ste 216, Altadena
(91001-5425)
PHONE.................................818 726-0007
Bob Ntoya, *President*
Brian Jones, *COO*
Brennon Neff, *CFO*
Adam Gerber, *Principal*
Simon Wise, *Principal*
EMP: 15 **EST:** 2010
SALES (est): 2.1MM **Privately Held**
WEB: www.3becom.com
SIC: 7372 Prepackaged software

(P-17771)
48FORTY SOLUTIONS
2641 Hall Ave, Riverside (92509-2240)
PHONE.................................951 682-3095
Ian High, *General Mgr*
Gregg Elam, *Regional*
EMP: 14 **EST:** 2019
SALES (est): 673.3K **Privately Held**
WEB: www.48forty.com
SIC: 7372 Prepackaged software

(P-17772)
ABLE SOFTWARE INC
20251 Sw Acacia St # 220, Newport Beach
(92660-0768)
PHONE.................................949 274-8321
Ming LI, *President*
Garth Stern, *Sales Mgr*
Yolande Pawley, *Cust Mgr*
Sing Lee, *Manager*
EMP: 13 **EST:** 2001
SALES (est): 534.6K **Privately Held**
WEB: www.able-soft.com
SIC: 7372 Prepackaged software

(P-17773)
ACTIVISION BLIZZARD INC (PA)
3100 Ocean Park Blvd, Santa Monica
(90405-3032)
PHONE.................................310 255-2000
Robert A Kotick, *CEO*
Brian G Kelly, *Ch of Bd*
Daniel Alegre, *President*
Armin Zerza, *CFO*
Julie Hodges,
EMP: 333 **EST:** 1979
SALES (est): 8B **Publicly Held**
WEB: www.activisionblizzard.com
SIC: 7372 Prepackaged software; home entertainment computer software

(P-17774)
ACTIVISION BLIZZARD INC
Blizzard Entertainment
3 Blizzard, Irvine (92618-3628)
P.O. Box 18979 (92623-8979)
PHONE.................................949 955-1380
Frank Pearce, *Principal*
Jesse Meschuk, *Vice Pres*
Jonathan Zweig, *Vice Pres*
Callie Carrington, *Program Mgr*
Jason Scott, *Sr Software Eng*
EMP: 85
SALES (corp-wide): 8B **Publicly Held**
WEB: www.activisionblizzard.com
SIC: 7372 Prepackaged software
PA: Activision Blizzard, Inc.
3100 Ocean Park Blvd
Santa Monica CA 90405
310 255-2000

(P-17775)
ACUANT INC (HQ)
Also Called: Card Scanning Solutions
6080 Center Dr Ste 850, Los Angeles
(90045-9229)
PHONE.................................213 867-2621
Yossi Zekri, *CEO*
Rob Scheschareg, *Partner*
Kevin O'Connor, *CFO*
Iuval Hatzav, *Exec VP*
Varun Garg, *Vice Pres*
▲ **EMP:** 121 **EST:** 2013
SALES (est): 26.9MM
SALES (corp-wide): 151.1MM **Privately Held**
WEB: www.acuant.com
SIC: 7372 Business oriented computer software
PA: Audax Management Company, Llc
101 Huntington Ave Fl 23
Boston MA 02199
617 859-1500

(P-17776)
ADAPTIVE INC (PA)
Also Called: Adaptiv I/S
340 S Lemon Ave, Walnut (91789-2706)
P.O. Box 305, Chesterfield VA (23832-0005)
PHONE.................................631 760-6577
Jeff Goins, *CEO*
Sandra Foster, *Partner*
Rich Hatlen, *Vice Pres*
James F Bedford, *Executive*
Paul Koerber, *Sr Software Eng*
EMP: 22 **EST:** 2011
SQ FT: 5,000
SALES (est): 6.6MM **Privately Held**
WEB: www.adaptive.com
SIC: 7372 Prepackaged software

(P-17777)
ADDING TECHNOLOGY INC (PA)
27 W Anapamu St, Santa Barbara
(93101-3107)
PHONE.................................805 252-6971

Natalie Browne, *Principal*
EMP: 15 EST: 2011
SALES (est): 257.2K **Privately Held**
WEB: www.addingtechnology.com
SIC: 7372 Prepackaged software

(P-17778)
ADEXA INC (PA)
5777 W Century Blvd # 1100, Los Angeles
(90045-5643)
PHONE................................310 642-2100
Khosrow Cyrus Hadavi, *CEO*
Mario A Disandro, *CFO*
Kameron Hadavi, *Vice Pres*
John Hosford, *Vice Pres*
William Green, *VP Business*
EMP: 50 EST: 1994
SQ FT: 31,000
SALES (est): 17.5MM **Privately Held**
WEB: www.adexa.com
SIC: 7372 Business oriented computer
software

(P-17779)
AGENCYCOM LLC
5353 Grosvenor Blvd, Los Angeles
(90066-6913)
PHONE................................415 817-3800
Chan Suh, *CEO*
Jordan Warren, *President*
Rob Elliott, *CFO*
EMP: 400 EST: 1995
SQ FT: 130,000
SALES (est): 31.5MM
SALES (corp-wide): 13.1B **Publicly Held**
WEB: www.omnicomgroup.com
SIC: 7372 Application computer software
PA: Omnicom Group Inc.
280 Park Ave Fl 31w
New York NY 10017
212 415-3600

(P-17780)
ALLDIGITAL HOLDINGS INC
1405 Warner Ave Ste A, Tustin
(92780-6405)
PHONE................................949 250-7340
Michael Linos, *President*
Brad Eisenstein, *COO*
Steve Smith, *Vice Pres*
Leonard Wanger, *Director*
EMP: 15 EST: 2011
SQ FT: 3,769
SALES (est): 1.2MM **Privately Held**
WEB: www.alldigital.com
SIC: 7372 Prepackaged software

(P-17781)
ALPHA STAR CORPORATION
2601 Main St Ste 660, Irvine (92614-4257)
PHONE................................562 961-7827
Frank Abdi, *Ch of Bd*
Kay Matin, *President*
Anil Mehta, *VP Bus Dvlpt*
Cody Godines, *Engineer*
Sarah Abdi, *Marketing Staff*
EMP: 45 EST: 1989
SQ FT: 3,800
SALES (est): 4.3MM **Privately Held**
WEB: www.alphastarcorp.com
SIC: 7372 7371 3724 Prepackaged soft-
ware; computer software development;
research & development on aircraft en-
gines & parts

(P-17782)
ANNEX PRO INC
4100 W Alameda Ave Fl 3, Burbank
(91505-4191)
PHONE................................800 682-6639
Kerry Corlett, *CEO*
Kalinka Corlett, *Director*
EMP: 20 EST: 2017
SALES (est): 12MM **Privately Held**
WEB: www.annexpro.com
SIC: 7372 5734 8731 5946 Application
computer software; computer peripheral
equipment; computer (hardware) develop-
ment; camera & photographic supply
stores; video cameras, recorders & ac-
cessories

(P-17783)
APEX COMMUNICATIONS INC
(DH)
21700 Oxnard St Ste 1060, Woodland Hills
(91367-7571)
PHONE................................818 379-8400
Ben Levy, *President*
EMP: 15 EST: 1989
SQ FT: 7,500
SALES (est): 5.1MM
SALES (corp-wide): 376.4MM **Privately
Held**
WEB: www.apexvoice.com
SIC: 7372 Application computer software

(P-17784)
APOTHEKA SYSTEMS INC
14040 Panay Way, Marina Del Rey
(90292-6697)
P.O. Box 1251, Beverly Hills (90213-1251)
PHONE................................844 777-4455
Dennis Maliani, *CEO*
EMP: 30 EST: 2018
SALES (est): 1.8MM **Privately Held**
WEB: www.apotheka.co
SIC: 7372 Application computer software

(P-17785)
APPETIZE TECHNOLOGIES INC
6601 Center Dr W Ste 700, Los Angeles
(90045-1545)
PHONE................................877 559-4225
Max Roper, *CEO*
Jason Pratts, *COO*
Dan Machock, *CFO*
Daniel Machock, *CFO*
Mark Eastwood, *Officer*
EMP: 110 EST: 2011
SALES (est): 16.2MM **Privately Held**
WEB: www.appetize.com
SIC: 7372 Application computer software

(P-17786)
APPFOLIO INC (PA)
50 Castilian Dr Ste 101, Goleta
(93117-5578)
PHONE................................805 364-6093
Jason Randall, *President*
Andreas Von Blottnitz, *Ch of Bd*
Michael Gordon, *COO*
Ida Kane, *CFO*
Janet Kerr, *Bd of Directors*
EMP: 584 EST: 2006
SQ FT: 79,200
SALES (est): 310MM **Publicly Held**
WEB: www.appfolio.com
SIC: 7372 Business oriented computer
software

(P-17787)
**APPLIED BUSINESS SOFTWARE
INC**
Also Called: A B S
2847 Gundry Ave, Signal Hill (90755-1812)
PHONE................................562 426-2188
Jerry Delgado, *President*
Jasen Portero, *COO*
Elizabeth Morales, *Chief Mktg Ofcr*
Eddy Delgado, *Vice Pres*
Gerardo Delgado, *Vice Pres*
EMP: 31 EST: 1979
SQ FT: 7,200
SALES (est): 9MM **Privately Held**
WEB: www.themortgageoffice.com
SIC: 7372 5045 5734 Prepackaged soft-
ware; computers, peripherals & software;
computer & software stores

(P-17788)
APPLIED STATISTICS & MGT INC
Also Called: Md-Staff
32848 Wolf Store Rd Ste A, Temecula
(92592-8277)
P.O. Box 891329 (92589-1329)
PHONE................................951 699-4600
Trung Phan, *President*
Nickolaus Phan, *COO*
Daniel Cairney, *Vice Pres*
Michael Garcia, *Admin Sec*
Jeff Holder, *Administration*
EMP: 45 EST: 1981
SQ FT: 4,000

SALES (est): 8.6MM **Privately Held**
WEB: www.mdstaff.com
SIC: 7372 7371 Prepackaged software;
computer software systems analysis &
design, custom

(P-17789)
ARCORO HOLDINGS CORP
27001 Agoura Rd Ste 280, Calabasas
(91301-5139)
PHONE................................877 252-2168
John Ohara, *CEO*
John Austin, *Partner*
Aaron Olney, *Vice Pres*
Karen Williams, *Vice Pres*
Anna Taylor, *Administration*
EMP: 17 EST: 2018
SALES (est): 1.4MM **Privately Held**
WEB: www.arcoro.com
SIC: 7372 Business oriented computer
software

(P-17790)
ARXIS TECHNOLOGY INC
2468 Tapo Canyon Rd, Simi Valley
(93063-2361)
PHONE................................805 306-7890
Christopher L Hamilton, *CEO*
Jedi Johnson, *CPA*
Jan Goodman, *Marketing Staff*
Mark Severance, *Marketing Staff*
Janna Crowther, *Sr Consultant*
EMP: 24 EST: 1994
SALES (est): 6.8MM **Privately Held**
WEB: www.rklesolutions.com
SIC: 7372 Prepackaged software

(P-17791)
ATLANTIS COMPUTING INC
900 Glenneyre St, Laguna Beach
(92651-2707)
PHONE................................650 917-9471
Jason Donahue, *CEO*
Timm Hoyt, *Partner*
Richard Van Hoesen, *CFO*
David Cumberworth, *Vice Pres*
Toby Coleridge, *CTO*
EMP: 35 EST: 2006
SQ FT: 5,000
SALES (est): 8.8MM **Privately Held**
WEB: www.hiveio.com
SIC: 7372 Business oriented computer
software

(P-17792)
AXIA TECHNOLOGIES INC
Also Called: Axiamed
4183 State St, Santa Barbara
(93110-1817)
PHONE................................855 376-2942
Randal Clark, *President*
Dan Berger, *Sales Staff*
Patrick Schreifels, *Director*
Ben Ingalls, *Accounts Exec*
EMP: 21 EST: 2016
SALES (est): 5.5MM
SALES (corp-wide): 93.7B **Publicly Held**
WEB: www.axiamed.com
SIC: 7372 Prepackaged software
HQ: Bank Of America, National Association
100 S Tryon St
Charlotte NC 28202
704 386-5681

(P-17793)
AXIA TECHNOLOGIES INC
4183 State St, Santa Barbara
(93110-1817)
PHONE................................855 376-2942
EMP: 21
SALES (est): 397.7K **Privately Held**
WEB: www.axiamed.com
SIC: 7372 Prepackaged Software

(P-17794)
BEN GROUP INC
14724 Ventura Blvd # 1200, Sherman Oaks
(91403-3512)
PHONE................................310 342-1500
Gary R Shenk, *CEO*
EMP: 15 EST: 2017
SALES (est): 1MM **Privately Held**
WEB: www.ben.productplacement.com
SIC: 7372 Home entertainment computer
software

(P-17795)
**BENEFIT SOFTWARE
INCORPORATED**
212 Cottage Grove Ave A, Santa Barbara
(93101-3450)
PHONE................................805 679-6200
Larry S Dubois, *President*
EMP: 16 EST: 1986
SQ FT: 5,105
SALES (est): 2.4MM **Privately Held**
WEB: www.bsiweb.com
SIC: 7372 Prepackaged software

(P-17796)
BETHEBEAST INC
3738 W 181st St, Torrance (90504-3921)
PHONE................................424 206-1081
Michael Mahoney, *President*
Steve Brodzinski, *Business Dir*
EMP: 27 EST: 2011
SALES (est): 2.9MM **Privately Held**
WEB: www.bethebeast.com
SIC: 7372 Educational computer software

(P-17797)
BITVORE CORP
15300 Barranca Pkwy # 150, Irvine
(92618-2257)
PHONE................................866 869-5151
David Mandel, *Ch of Bd*
Jeff Curie, *CEO*
Bill Ruehle, *CFO*
Greg Bolcer, *Officer*
Michael Heberle, *Vice Pres*
EMP: 33 EST: 2009
SALES (est): 1.2MM **Privately Held**
WEB: www.bitvore.com
SIC: 7372 7371 Business oriented com-
puter software; computer software devel-
opment & applications

(P-17798)
BLACKLINE INC (PA)
21300 Victory Blvd Fl 12, Woodland Hills
(91367-7734)
PHONE................................818 223-9008
Marc Huffman, *President*
Therese Tucker, *Ch of Bd*
Mark Partin, *CFO*
Karole Morgan-Prager, *Vice Pres*
Mark Woodhams, *Risk Mgmt Dir*
EMP: 468 EST: 2001
SQ FT: 89,000
SALES (est): 351.7MM **Publicly Held**
WEB: www.blackline.com
SIC: 7372 Business oriented computer
software

(P-17799)
BLACKLINE SYSTEMS INC (HQ)
21300 Victory Blvd Fl 12, Woodland Hills
(91367-7734)
PHONE................................877 777-7750
Therese Tucker, *CEO*
Jennifer T Pottle, *Partner*
Mark Partin, *CFO*
Graham Smith, *Bd of Directors*
David Downing, *Chief Mktg Ofcr*
EMP: 98 EST: 2001
SQ FT: 66,447
SALES (est): 61.4MM
SALES (corp-wide): 351.7MM **Publicly
Held**
WEB: www.blackline.com
SIC: 7372 Business oriented computer
software
PA: Blackline, Inc.
21300 Victory Blvd Fl 12
Woodland Hills CA 91367
818 223-9008

(P-17800)
BLIND SQUIRREL GAMES INC
7545 Irvine Center Dr # 150, Irvine
(92618-2935)
PHONE................................714 460-0860
Bradford Hendricks, *CEO*
Patrick Ghiocel, *Sr Software Eng*
Ron Bitzer, *Info Tech Dir*
Handerson Lee, *Prgmr*
Masana Pawlan, *Prgmr*
EMP: 23 EST: 2010
SALES (est): 4.6MM **Privately Held**
WEB: www.blindsquirrelentertainment.com
SIC: 7372 Home entertainment computer
software

(P-17801)
BLIZZARD ENTERTAINMENT INC (HQ)
1 Blizzard, Irvine (92618-3628)
P.O. Box 18979 (92623-8979)
PHONE..................................949 955-1380
Mike Morhaime, *President*
Stephanie Johnson, *Partner*
J Allen Brack, *President*
Paul Sams, *President*
Chris Metzen, *Senior VP*
▲ EMP: 85 EST: 2004
SALES (est): 155.3MM
SALES (corp-wide): 8B **Publicly Held**
WEB: www.blizzard.com
SIC: 7372 5734 7819 Prepackaged software; software, computer games; reproduction services, motion picture production
PA: Activision Blizzard, Inc.
3100 Ocean Park Blvd
Santa Monica CA 90405
310 255-2000

(P-17802)
BLUE MARBLE REHAB INC
Also Called: Blue Marble Game Co
2400 Lincoln Ave, Altadena (91001-5425)
PHONE..................................626 296-6400
Sheryl Flynn, *CEO*
Sheryl Maureen Flynn, *CEO*
William Smith, *Research*
Kevin McLaughlin, *Controller*
EMP: 15 EST: 2009
SQ FT: 60,000
SALES (est): 1.8MM **Privately Held**
WEB: www.bluemarblehealthco.com
SIC: 7372 5734 8731 Prepackaged software; software, business & non-game; biotechnical research, commercial

(P-17803)
BMC
300 Continental Blvd # 570, El Segundo (90245-5072)
PHONE..................................310 321-5555
Sean Allen, *CEO*
Wade Watson, *Director*
Gary Kellermeier, *Manager*
EMP: 27 EST: 2009
SALES (est): 260.5K **Privately Held**
WEB: www.bmcgroup.com
SIC: 7372 Prepackaged software

(P-17804)
BPO MANAGEMENT SERVICES INC (HQ)
8175 E Kaiser Blvd 100, Anaheim (92808-2214)
PHONE..................................714 974-2670
Patrick Dolan, *Ch of Bd*
James Cortens, *President*
Don Rutherford, *CFO*
Koushik Dutta, *CTO*
EMP: 202 EST: 1996
SQ FT: 3,500
SALES (est): 6.6MM
SALES (corp-wide): 36.5MM **Privately Held**
SIC: 7372 7371 Prepackaged software; custom computer programming services
PA: Bpo Management Services, Inc
8175 E Kaiser Blvd 100
Anaheim CA 92808
714 972-2670

(P-17805)
BQE SOFTWARE INC
3825 Del Amo Blvd Trrance Torrance, Torrance (90503)
PHONE..................................310 602-4020
Shafat Qazi, *CEO*
Austin Miller, *Chief Mktg Ofcr*
Sharone Strauss, *Vice Pres*
Nazia Fazili, *Prgrmr*
Jake Alvarez, *Technical Staff*
EMP: 95 EST: 1995
SQ FT: 20,000
SALES (est): 12.5MM **Privately Held**
WEB: www.bqe.com
SIC: 7372 5734 Application computer software; software, business & non-game

(P-17806)
BRAINCHIP INC (HQ)
65 Enterprise Ste 325, Aliso Viejo (92656-2705)
PHONE..................................949 330-6750
Louis Dinardo, *CEO*
Roman Kochan, *Sr Software Eng*
Peter Van Der Made, *CTO*
Kristofor Carlson, *Research*
Gilles Bezard, *Engineer*
EMP: 15 EST: 2014
SQ FT: 2,500
SALES (est): 5.1MM **Privately Held**
WEB: www.brainchipinc.com
SIC: 7372 Prepackaged software

(P-17807)
BRAINS OUT MEDIA INC
2629 Foothill Blvd # 111, La Crescenta (91214-3511)
PHONE..................................818 296-1036
Fermin Iglesias, *President*
EMP: 15
SALES (est): 850K **Privately Held**
WEB: www.brainsout.media
SIC: 7372 7374 Application computer software; computer graphics service

(P-17808)
BTRADE LLC
701 N Brand Blvd Ste 205, Glendale (91203-3212)
PHONE..................................818 334-4433
Steve Zapata, *Mng Member*
Don Miller, *COO*
Clifton Gonsalves, *Vice Pres*
Teresa Perez, *Vice Pres*
Scott Beland, *Director*
EMP: 25 EST: 2008 **Privately Held**
WEB: www.btrade.com
SIC: 7372 Business oriented computer software

(P-17809)
CADENCE DESIGN SYSTEMS INC
7505 Irvine Center Dr # 250, Irvine (92618-3078)
PHONE..................................949 788-6080
EMP: 34
SALES (corp-wide): 1.9B **Publicly Held**
SIC: 7372 Prepackaged Software Services
PA: Cadence Design Systems, Inc.
2655 Seely Ave Bldg 5
San Jose CA 95134
408 943-1234

(P-17810)
CATALYST DEVELOPMENT CORP
56925 Yucca Trl, Yucca Valley (92284-7913)
PHONE..................................760 228-9653
Cary Harwin, *President*
Todd Clapp, *Partner*
Brian Rich, *Managing Prtnr*
Mike Stefanik, *Senior VP*
Samantha Lexton, *Vice Pres*
EMP: 24 EST: 1995
SALES (est): 1.6MM **Privately Held**
WEB: www.catalyst.com
SIC: 7372 Business oriented computer software

(P-17811)
CATAPULT COMMUNICATIONS CORP (DH)
26601 Agoura Rd, Calabasas (91302-1959)
PHONE..................................818 871-1800
Richard A Karp, *Ch of Bd*
David Mayfield, *President*
Chris Stephenson, *CFO*
Terry Eastham, *Vice Pres*
Barbara J Fairhurst, *Vice Pres*
▲ EMP: 98 EST: 1985
SQ FT: 39,000
SALES (est): 3.1MM
SALES (corp-wide): 4.2B **Publicly Held**
WEB: www.support.ixiacom.com
SIC: 7372 3661 Application computer software; telephone & telegraph apparatus

HQ: Ixia
26601 Agoura Rd
Calabasas CA 91302
818 871-1800

(P-17812)
CERTEMY INC
14876 Raymer St Ste 200, Van Nuys (91405-1219)
PHONE..................................866 907-4088
Zorik Gordon, *CEO*
Oleg Shvarts, *President*
Herman Berger, *CEO*
Shawn Cantor, *COO*
Erich Kaiser, *Vice Pres*
EMP: 18 EST: 2017
SALES (est): 1MM **Privately Held**
SIC: 7372 7371 7379 Business oriented computer software; custom computer programming services; computer related services

(P-17813)
CFORIA SOFTWARE INC
4333 Park Terrace Dr # 201, Westlake Village (91361-5656)
PHONE..................................818 871-9687
Dave McIntyre, *President*
Chris Caparon, *President*
Denise Mills, *IT/INT Sup*
Mary Strege, *Engineer*
Mollie McIntyre, *Mktg Dir*
EMP: 22 EST: 2001
SQ FT: 4,000
SALES (est): 5.7MM **Privately Held**
WEB: www.cforia.com
SIC: 7372 Business oriented computer software

(P-17814)
CFS TAX SOFTWARE
Also Called: CFS Income Tax
1445 E Los Angeles Ave # 214, Simi Valley (93065-2828)
P.O. Box 941659 (93094-1659)
PHONE..................................805 522-1157
Ted Sullivan, *President*
Duy Tran, *Vice Pres*
Tyler Monroe, *Software Dev*
Greg Hatfield, *Prgrmr*
Roger Stock, *Technical Staff*
EMP: 23 EST: 1982
SALES (est): 4.3MM **Privately Held**
WEB: www.taxtools.com
SIC: 7372 8721 Business oriented computer software; accounting, auditing & bookkeeping

(P-17815)
CHOWNOW INC
12181 Bluff Creek Dr, Playa Vista (90094-2992)
PHONE..................................888 707-2469
Eric Jaffe, *President*
Stuart Hathaway, *CFO*
Andre Mancl, *COO*
Kent Ngo, *Executive*
Amy Larion, *Business Dir*
EMP: 100 EST: 2010
SQ FT: 25,000
SALES (est): 16.1MM **Privately Held**
WEB: www.get.chownow.com
SIC: 7372 Business oriented computer software

(P-17816)
CHROME RIVER TECHNOLOGY
Also Called: Sag-Aftra Plaza
5757 Wilshire Blvd # 270, Los Angeles (90036-5814)
PHONE..................................888 781-0088
EMP: 41 EST: 2007
SALES (est): 1.8MM **Privately Held**
SIC: 7372 Prepackaged software

(P-17817)
CITRIX SYSTEMS INC
7414 Hollister Ave Goleta, Los Angeles (90074-0001)
PHONE..................................800 424-8749
EMP: 17 **Publicly Held**
WEB: www.citrix.com
SIC: 7372 Prepackaged software

PA: Citrix Systems, Inc.
851 W Cypress Creek Rd
Fort Lauderdale FL 33309

(P-17818)
CLEARLAKE CAPITAL PARTNERS
233 Wilshire Blvd Ste 800, Santa Monica (90401-1207)
PHONE..................................310 400-8800
John A McKenna Jr, *President*
EMP: 1832 EST: 2012
SALES (est): 51.2MM **Privately Held**
SIC: 7372 Prepackaged software

(P-17819)
CLOUDCOVER IOT INC
14 Goodyear Ste 125b, Irvine (92618-3759)
PHONE..................................888 511-2022
Jeffrey Huggins, *CEO*
Aaron Zeper, *Exec VP*
Jeff Huggins, *Principal*
EMP: 37 EST: 2015
SALES (est): 14.7MM **Privately Held**
WEB: www.cloudcover.it
SIC: 7372 7379 7373 Prepackaged software; business oriented computer software; computer related maintenance services; computer related consulting services; systems engineering, computer related

(P-17820)
CLOUDVIRGA INC
5291 California Ave # 300, Irvine (92617-3221)
PHONE..................................949 799-2643
Daniel Akiva, *CEO*
Steve Desantis, *CFO*
Maria Moskver, *Officer*
James Vinci, *Exec VP*
Kelly Kucera, *Senior VP*
EMP: 59 EST: 2015
SALES (est): 24.1MM
SALES (corp-wide): 2.2B **Publicly Held**
WEB: www.cloudvirga.com
SIC: 7372 Prepackaged software
PA: Stewart Information Services Corporation
1360 Post Oak Blvd Ste 10
Houston TX 77056
713 625-8100

(P-17821)
CLUB SPEED LLC
400 Spectrum Center Dr # 1900, Irvine (92618-5025)
PHONE..................................951 817-7073
Romir Bosu, *CEO*
Caleb Everett, *President*
Gerardo Cortez, *Analyst*
EMP: 42 EST: 2007
SALES (est): 3.4MM **Privately Held**
WEB: www.clubspeed.com
SIC: 7372 Prepackaged software

(P-17822)
COMMERCE VELOCITY LLC
1 Technology Dr Ste J725, Irvine (92618-2353)
PHONE..................................949 756-8950
Umesh Verma,
Ajay Chopra,
EMP: 49 EST: 2000
SQ FT: 5,000
SALES (est): 19.5MM **Publicly Held**
WEB: www.fnf.com
SIC: 7372 Business oriented computer software
PA: Fidelity National Financial, Inc.
601 Riverside Ave Fl 4
Jacksonville FL 32204

(P-17823)
COMPUGROUP MEDICAL INC
25 B Tech Dr Ste 200, Irvine (92618)
PHONE..................................949 789-0500
John Tangredi, *COO*
EMP: 25
SALES (corp-wide): 990.1MM **Privately Held**
WEB: www.cgm.com
SIC: 7372 Prepackaged software

PRODUCTS & SVCS

HQ: Compugroup Medical, Inc.
3838 N Central Ave # 1600
Phoenix AZ 85012
855 270-6700

(P-17824)
COMPULINK BUSINESS SYSTEMS INC (PA)
Also Called: Compulink Healthcare Solutions
1100 Business Center Cir, Newbury Park
(91320-1124)
PHONE.................................805 446-2050
Link Wilson, *President*
Cole Galbarith, *Officer*
Link L Wilson, *Executive*
Richard Barnes, *CIO*
Cole Galbraith, *CTO*
EMP: 117 **EST:** 1985
SQ FT: 15,000
SALES (est): 23.1MM **Privately Held**
WEB: www.compulinkadvantage.com
SIC: 7372 Business oriented computer software

(P-17825)
CONNECTPOINT INC
175 Cremona Dr Ste 160, Goleta
(93117-3197)
PHONE.................................805 682-8900
Frederick A Wood, *CEO*
Jennifer Evans, *Opers Staff*
EMP: 20 **EST:** 2018
SALES (est): 1.6MM **Privately Held**
WEB: www.connectpointdigital.com
SIC: 7372 Prepackaged software

(P-17826)
CONSENSUS CLOUD SOLUTIONS INC ✪
700 S Flower St Fl 15, Los Angeles
(90017-4101)
PHONE.................................323 860-9200
Scott Turicchi, *CEO*
John Nebergall, *COO*
Jeffrey Sullivan, *CTO*
Steve Emberland, *Controller*
EMP: 440 **EST:** 2021
SALES (est): 678.4MM **Privately Held**
SIC: 7372 Prepackaged software

(P-17827)
CONVERSIONPOINT HOLDINGS INC
840 Nwport Cntr Dr Ste 45, Newport Beach
(92660)
PHONE.................................888 706-6764
Robert Tallack, *President*
Jonathan Gregg, *President*
Don Walker Barrett III, *COO*
Raghu Kilambi, *CFO*
Tom Furukawa, *CTO*
EMP: 85
SALES (est): 1.3MM **Privately Held**
WEB: www.conversionpoint.com
SIC: 7372 Prepackaged software

(P-17828)
CORNERSTONE ONDEMAND INC (PA)
1601 Cloverf Blvd 620s, Santa Monica
(90404-4178)
PHONE.................................310 752-0200
Philip S Saunders, *CEO*
Jeffrey Lautenbach, *President*
Chirag Shah, *CFO*
Richard Haddrill, *Co-COB*
Adam L Miller, *Co-COB*
EMP: 2323 **EST:** 1999
SQ FT: 94,000
SALES (est): 740.9MM **Privately Held**
WEB: www.cornerstoneondemand.com
SIC: 7372 Business oriented computer software

(P-17829)
CROSSROADS SOFTWARE INC
210 W Birch St Ste 207, Brea
(92821-4504)
PHONE.................................714 990-6433
Jeff Cullen, *President*
Memduh Gorkem, *Software Dev*
EMP: 15 **EST:** 1992
SQ FT: 1,000

SALES (est): 873.3K **Privately Held**
WEB: www.web.crossroadssoftware.com
SIC: 7372 Prepackaged software

(P-17830)
CULTURE AMP INC (HQ)
16501 Ventura Blvd # 400, Encino
(91436-2007)
PHONE.................................415 326-8453
Didier Raoul Elzinga, *CEO*
Douglas Mark English, *CFO*
Alannah Reaborn, *General Mgr*
Rodney James Hamilton, *Admin Sec*
Riley Jones, *CIO*
EMP: 37 **EST:** 2013
SALES (est): 15.5MM **Privately Held**
WEB: www.cultureamp.com
SIC: 7372 Prepackaged software

(P-17831)
CYBREX CONSULTING INC
4470 W Sunset Blvd # 961, Los Angeles
(90027-6302)
PHONE.................................513 999-2109
James Whitmore, *Managing Dir*
EMP: 100 **EST:** 2010
SQ FT: 1,000
SALES (est): 2MM **Privately Held**
SIC: 7372 8742 Prepackaged software; real estate consultant

(P-17832)
D3PUBLISHER OF AMERICA INC
Also Called: D3 Go
15910 Ventura Blvd # 800, Encino
(91436-2810)
PHONE.................................310 268-0820
Yoji Takenaka, *President*
Yuji ITOH, *Ch of Bd*
Hidetaka Tachibana, *CFO*
Brian Etheridge, *Vice Pres*
Josh Austin, *Director*
EMP: 63 **EST:** 2004
SQ FT: 6,129
SALES (est): 18.5MM **Privately Held**
WEB: www.d3go.com
SIC: 7372 Home entertainment computer software
HQ: D3 Publisher Inc.
3-2-3, Kandajimbocho
Chiyoda-Ku TKY 101-0

(P-17833)
DATA LINKAGE SOFTWARE INC
2421 W 205th St Ste D207, Torrance
(90501-1469)
PHONE.................................310 781-3056
Marwan Dajani, *President*
▲ **EMP:** 13 **EST:** 1985
SQ FT: 1,900
SALES (est): 630.6K **Privately Held**
WEB: www.datalinkage.com
SIC: 7372 Business oriented computer software

(P-17834)
DATABASE WORKS INC
500 S Kraemer Blvd # 110, Brea
(92821-6766)
PHONE.................................714 203-8800
Terry Young, *President*
Joshua Milus, *Manager*
EMP: 13 **EST:** 1983
SQ FT: 2,500
SALES (est): 1.5MM **Privately Held**
WEB: www.dbworks.com
SIC: 7372 3577 Business oriented computer software; application computer software; optical scanning devices

(P-17835)
DATAZEO INC
8655 Morro Rd Ste C, Atascadero
(93422-3913)
PHONE.................................805 461-3458
Tim L Alexander, *CEO*
EMP: 16 **EST:** 2010
SALES (est): 240.3K **Privately Held**
SIC: 7372 5065 Prepackaged software; mobile telephone equipment

(P-17836)
DE NOVO SOFTWARE LLC
207 N Sierra Madre Blvd # 1, Pasadena
(91107-3302)
PHONE.................................213 814-1240
David Novo, *CEO*
Hemant Agrawal, *Technical Staff*
Andrea Valle, *Technical Staff*
Christopher Concannon, *Opers Staff*
EMP: 21 **EST:** 2003
SALES (est): 2MM **Privately Held**
WEB: www.denovosoftware.com
SIC: 7372 Prepackaged software

(P-17837)
DEFINITIVE MEDIA CORP (PA)
155 El Camino Real Ste B, Tustin
(92780-3601)
PHONE.................................714 305-5900
Jeff Fazier, *CEO*
EMP: 23 **EST:** 2008
SALES (est): 2.1MM **Privately Held**
WEB: www.threadresearch.com
SIC: 7372 Business oriented computer software

(P-17838)
DINCLOUD INC
27520 Hawthorne Blvd # 185, Rllng HLS Est (90274-3576)
PHONE.................................310 929-1101
Mark Briggs, *CEO*
Steven M Kawalick, *Officer*
Mike L Chase, *Exec VP*
Ali M Dincmo, *Vice Pres*
Farhan Mirza, *Vice Pres*
EMP: 53
SQ FT: 1,500
SALES (est): 4MM
SALES (corp-wide): 43.7MM **Privately Held**
WEB: www.dincloud.com
SIC: 7372 Business oriented computer software
PA: Premier Bpo, Inc.
128 N 2nd St Ste 210
Clarksville TN 37040
931 551-8888

(P-17839)
DM SOFTWARE INC
1842 Park Skyline Rd, Santa Ana
(92705-3120)
PHONE.................................714 953-2653
Bill Parson, *Owner*
EMP: 20
SALES (corp-wide): 4.1MM **Privately Held**
SIC: 7372 Prepackaged software
PA: Dm Software Inc
654 Jack Cir
Stateline NV 89449
775 589-6049

(P-17840)
DOMO COMPANY LLC (PA)
15925 Canary Ave, La Mirada
(90638-5506)
PHONE.................................626 407-0015
Tina Hebner, *Principal*
EMP: 20 **EST:** 2018
SALES (est): 401.5K **Privately Held**
SIC: 7372 Prepackaged software

(P-17841)
DOZUKI
1330 Monterey St, San Luis Obispo
(93401-3106)
PHONE.................................805 464-0573
Richard Barnes, *CIO*
David Rans, *Software Dev*
Richard Mishler, *Mfg Staff*
Leslie Bloom, *Mktg Dir*
Brian Sallee, *Sales Staff*
EMP: 20 **EST:** 2015
SALES (est): 1.3MM **Privately Held**
WEB: www.dozuki.com
SIC: 7372 Prepackaged software

(P-17842)
EEYE INC (HQ)
Also Called: Eeye Digital Security
65 Enterprise Ste 100, Aliso Viejo
(92656-2503)
PHONE.................................949 333-1900
Kevin Hickey, *CEO*

Tyler Hanson, *CFO*
Raj Cherukuri, *Exec VP*
Marc Maiffret, *CTO*
Kyle Young, *Analyst*
EMP: 54 **EST:** 1998
SALES (est): 10.1MM
SALES (corp-wide): 18.8MM **Privately Held**
WEB: www.beyondtrust.com
SIC: 7372 Business oriented computer software
PA: Beyondtrust Software, Inc.
578 Highland Colony Pkw
Ridgeland MS 39157
623 455-6499

(P-17843)
EKRAN SYSTEM INC
260 Nwport Ctr Dr Ste 425, Newport Beach
(92660)
PHONE.................................424 242-8838
Dennis Turpitka, *CEO*
Neil Butchart, *President*
Oleg Shomonko, *CFO*
EMP: 30 **EST:** 2014
SALES (est): 1.1MM **Privately Held**
WEB: www.ekransystem.com
SIC: 7372 Prepackaged software

(P-17844)
ELECTRONIC CLEARING HOUSE INC (HQ)
730 Paseo Camarillo, Camarillo
(93010-6064)
PHONE.................................805 419-8700
Charles J Harris, *President*
Alice L Cheung, *CFO*
Karl Asplund, *Senior VP*
Rick Slater, *Vice Pres*
William Wied, *CIO*
EMP: 100 **EST:** 1981
SQ FT: 32,669
SALES (est): 58MM
SALES (corp-wide): 9.6B **Publicly Held**
WEB: www.echo-inc.com
SIC: 7372 Business oriented computer software
PA: Intuit Inc.
2700 Coast Ave
Mountain View CA 94043
650 944-6000

(P-17845)
ELEVATE INC
180 Avnida La Pata Ste 20, San Clemente
(92673)
PHONE.................................949 276-5428
Wright W Thurston, *CEO*
Rod Place, *COO*
Bryan Ferre, *Chief Mktg Ofcr*
Alexander Chester, *Officer*
EMP: 13 **EST:** 2011
SALES (est): 613K **Privately Held**
WEB: www.goelevate.com
SIC: 7372 Prepackaged software

(P-17846)
EMPOWER SOFTWARE TECH LLC
28999 Old Town Front St # 203, Temecula
(92590-5806)
PHONE.................................951 672-6257
Thomas V Smith, *Partner*
Charlie Smith, *Asst Controller*
Kevin Kerr, *Marketing Mgr*
Denee Burns, *Sales Staff*
Ed Power, *CEO*
EMP: 13 **EST:** 1998
SALES (est): 3MM **Privately Held**
WEB: www.storagecommander.com
SIC: 7372 Business oriented computer software

(P-17847)
EPIRUS INC
12831 Weber Way, Hawthorne
(90250-5536)
P.O. Box 3927, Redondo Beach (90277-1725)
PHONE.................................310 620-8678
Leigh Madden, *CEO*
Joseph Lonsdale, *Ch of Bd*
Nathan Mintz, *CEO*
Max Mednik, *COO*
Ken Bedingfield, *CFO*
EMP: 26 **EST:** 2018

SALES (est): 1MM **Privately Held**
WEB: www.epirusinc.com
SIC: 7372 7373 0781 1771 Prepackaged software; computer integrated systems design; landscape counseling & planning; stucco, gunite & grouting contractors; commercial physical research

(P-17848)
EQUIMINE INC
26457 Rancho Pkwy S, Lake Forest (92630-8326)
PHONE.....................877 437-8464
Rabih Zahr, *President*
Nedal Mackarem, *Vice Pres*
EMP: 16 EST: 2006
SALES (est): 1.4MM **Privately Held**
WEB: www.propstream.com
SIC: 7372 3429 Business oriented computer software; keys, locks & related hardware

(P-17849)
ETURNS INC
19700 Fairchild Ste 290, Irvine (92612-2521)
PHONE.....................949 265-2626
Richard Rockwell, *CEO*
Donald Anderson, *Vice Pres*
Julie Watson, *Vice Pres*
John Jackson, *VP Bus Dvlpt*
EMP: 32 EST: 2010
SALES (est): 2.5MM **Privately Held**
WEB: www.eturns.com
SIC: 7372 7371 Application computer software; computer software development & applications

(P-17850)
EVENTURE INTERACTIVE INC
3420 Bristol St Fl 6, Costa Mesa (92626-7170)
PHONE.....................855 986-5669
Gannon Giguiere, *Ch of Bd*
Jason Harvey, *CEO*
Michael D Rountree, *CFO*
EMP: 13 EST: 2012
SQ FT: 2,000
SALES (est): 1MM **Privately Held**
WEB: www.eventure.com
SIC: 7372 Application computer software

(P-17851)
EVERBRIDGE INC (PA)
155 N Lake Ave Ste 100, Pasadena (91101-1857)
PHONE.....................818 230-9700
David Meredith, *CEO*
Jaime Ellertson, *Ch of Bd*
Robert Hughes, *President*
Patrick Brickley, *CFO*
Joel Rosen, *Chief Mktg Ofcr*
EMP: 120 EST: 2002
SQ FT: 45,000
SALES (est): 271.1MM **Publicly Held**
WEB: www.everbridge.com
SIC: 7372 4899 Prepackaged software; data communication services

(P-17852)
EVOCATIVE INC
600 W 7th St Ste 510, Los Angeles (90017-3864)
PHONE.....................888 365-2656
Patrick Rigney, *CEO*
Erin Mac Arthur, *COO*
Savi Singh, *Vice Pres*
Melik Manukyan, *Engineer*
Alexandra Stone, *Mktg Coord*
EMP: 75 EST: 1996
SQ FT: 15,000
SALES (est): 11MM
SALES (corp-wide): 45.6MM **Privately Held**
SIC: 7372 Application computer software
PA: Evodc, Llc
600 W 7th St Ste 510
Los Angeles CA 90017
888 365-2656

(P-17853)
EVOLUTION ROBOTICS INC
1055 E Colo Blvd Ste 320, Pasadena (91106)
PHONE.....................626 993-3300
Paolo Pirjanian, *CEO*

Bill Gross, *President*
Doug McPherson, *Asst Sec*
EMP: 75 EST: 2001
SALES (est): 11.6MM **Publicly Held**
WEB: www.evolution.com
SIC: 7372 Application computer software
PA: Irobot Corporation
8 Crosby Dr
Bedford MA 01730

(P-17854)
EXACTUALS LLC
1100 Glendon Ave Fl 17, Los Angeles (90024-3588)
PHONE.....................310 689-7491
Michael Hurst, *CEO*
Bryan Walley, *COO*
Ilie Ardelean,
Sean Spradlin, *Sr Software Eng*
Jason Hiller, *CTO*
EMP: 15 EST: 2012
SALES (est): 6.4MM
SALES (corp-wide): 31.1B **Privately Held**
WEB: www.exactuals.com
SIC: 7372 Prepackaged software
HQ: City National Bank
555 S Flower St Ste 2500
Los Angeles CA 90071
310 888-6000

(P-17855)
FGR 1 LLC
Also Called: Fresh Griller
3191 Red Hill Ave Ste 100, Costa Mesa (92626-3451)
PHONE.....................800 653-3517
Anand Gala, *Mng Member*
EMP: 40 EST: 2011
SALES (est): 1.5MM **Privately Held**
SIC: 5812 7372 American restaurant; application computer software

(P-17856)
FIELDCENTRIX INC
24001 Mrlnds Blvd Spc 125, Lake Forest (92630)
PHONE.....................949 784-5000
Renee Labran, *President*
Helen Fuerst, *Office Admin*
Mark Borgeson, *Sr Software Eng*
Stephen Omnus, *Project Mgr*
Bob Ansari, *VP Sales*
EMP: 13 EST: 1994
SALES (est): 701.8K **Privately Held**
WEB: www.ifs.com
SIC: 7372 Business oriented computer software

(P-17857)
FLASH CODE SOLUTIONS LLC
4727 Wilshire Blvd # 302, Los Angeles (90010-3806)
PHONE.....................800 633-7467
James B Davis, *Principal*
EMP: 17 EST: 2015
SQ FT: 2,600
SALES (est): 1MM **Privately Held**
WEB: www.flashcodesolutions.com
SIC: 7372 Application computer software

(P-17858)
FLOOR COVERING SOFT
221 E Walnut St Ste 110, Pasadena (91101-1554)
PHONE.....................626 683-9188
Steven Wang, *CEO*
Ariel Fu, *Manager*
▼ EMP: 23 EST: 2001
SQ FT: 2,500
SALES (est): 1.6MM **Privately Held**
WEB: www.measuresquare.com
SIC: 7372 Prepackaged software

(P-17859)
FOUNDATION 9 ENTERTAINMENT INC (PA)
30211 A De Las Bandera200, Rancho Santa Margari (92688)
PHONE.....................949 698-1500
James N Hearn, *CEO*
John Goldman, *Ch of Bd*
David Mann, *President*
Kim Le, *Accounts Mgr*
EMP: 200 EST: 2005

SALES (est): 59.5MM **Privately Held**
SIC: 7372 Home entertainment computer software

(P-17860)
FOUNDATION INC
Also Called: Foundation Ai
17632 Irvine Blvd Ste 225, Tustin (92780-3181)
PHONE.....................310 294-8955
Vivek RAO, *Principal*
Victor Gebhardt, *Principal*
Vamsi Kasivajjala, *Principal*
EMP: 38 EST: 2017
SALES (est): 1.1MM **Privately Held**
SIC: 7372 7371 Prepackaged software; custom computer programming services

(P-17861)
FOUNDSTONE INC
27201 Puerta Real Ste 400, Mission Viejo (92691-8517)
PHONE.....................949 297-5600
George Kurtz, *CEO*
Stuart McClure, *President*
Larry McIntosh, *Chief Mktg Ofcr*
William Chan, *Vice Pres*
Chris Prosise, *Vice Pres*
EMP: 36 EST: 1999
SQ FT: 15,000
SALES (est): 5.6MM
SALES (corp-wide): 1.5B **Publicly Held**
WEB: www.foundstone.com
SIC: 7372 Application computer software
HQ: Mcafee, Llc
6220 America Center Dr
San Jose CA 95002

(P-17862)
FREIGHTGATE INC
Also Called: Edi Ideas
10055 Slater Ave Ste 231, Fountain Valley (92708-4722)
PHONE.....................714 799-2833
Martin Hubert, *President*
Raymond Chen, *Software Engr*
Nathan Huang, *Software Engr*
Andrea Hubert, *VP Mktg*
Greg Hudgens, *Sales Staff*
EMP: 32 EST: 2000
SALES (est): 6MM **Privately Held**
WEB: www.ediidea.com
SIC: 7372 7371 Application computer software; utility computer software; computer software development & applications
PA: Edi Ideas Inc
16051 Springdale St # 111
Huntington Beach CA 92649
714 841-2833

(P-17863)
GAMECLOUD STUDIOS INC
30111 Tech Dr Ste 110, Murrieta (92563)
PHONE.....................951 677-2345
EMP: 20 EST: 2010
SALES (est): 1.2MM **Privately Held**
SIC: 7372 Prepackaged Software Services

(P-17864)
GAMEMINE LLC
2341 Wilson Ave, Venice (90291-4738)
PHONE.....................310 310-3105
Flaviu Rus, *Mng Member*
Daneil Starr,
EMP: 35 EST: 2017
SALES (est): 50MM **Privately Held**
SIC: 7372 Publishers' computer software

(P-17865)
GENESIS GROUP SFTWR DEVELOPERS
Also Called: Ggsdi
16027 Brookhurst St Ste G, Fountain Valley (92708-1562)
PHONE.....................714 630-4297
EMP: 25
SALES (est): 2.2MM **Privately Held**
WEB: www.ggsdi.com
SIC: 7372 7371 Prepackaged Software Services Custom Computer Programing

(P-17866)
GLOBAL EDGE LLC
5230 Las Virgenes Rd # 265, Calabasas (91302-3459)
PHONE.....................888 315-2692
EMP: 30 **Privately Held**
SIC: 7372 8721 Prepackaged Software Services Accounting/Auditing/Bookkeeping
PA: Global Edge, Llc
5230 Las Virgenes Rd # 265
Calabasas CA

(P-17867)
GLOBAL WAVE GROUP
26970 Aliso Viejo Pkwy # 250, Aliso Viejo (92656-2621)
PHONE.....................949 916-9800
Zubin Mehta, *CEO*
Randy M Ruckle, *COO*
Rhett Rowe, *Senior VP*
EMP: 18 EST: 2007
SALES (est): 615.8K **Privately Held**
WEB: www.globalwavegroup.com
SIC: 7372 Prepackaged software

(P-17868)
GOODRX INC (PA)
2701 Olympic Blvd A, Santa Monica (90404-4183)
PHONE.....................855 268-2822
Douglass Hirsch, *CEO*
Gracye Cheng, *Vice Pres*
Michael Dlugos, *Vice Pres*
Greg Hanna, *Vice Pres*
Rohit Malhotra, *VP Bus Dvlpt*
EMP: 16 EST: 2011
SALES (est): 10.9MM **Privately Held**
WEB: www.goodrx.com
SIC: 7372 Application computer software

(P-17869)
GOVERNMENTJOBSCOM INC
Also Called: Neogov
300 Continental Blvd # 565, El Segundo (90245-5042)
PHONE.....................310 426-6304
Damir Davidovic, *CEO*
Scott Letourneau, *President*
Stephen Koo, *CFO*
Matthew Geber, *Administration*
Hal Blakeslee, *Sr Software Eng*
EMP: 130 EST: 2000
SQ FT: 5,000
SALES (est): 29.7MM **Privately Held**
WEB: www.neogov.com
SIC: 7372 Prepackaged software

(P-17870)
GRANITE SOFTWARE INC
7590 N Glenoaks Blvd # 102, Burbank (91504-1011)
PHONE.....................818 252-1950
Elmer Vasquez, *President*
Christopher Negron, *Prgrmr*
Gloria McClain, *Supervisor*
EMP: 14 EST: 1999
SALES (est): 1MM **Privately Held**
WEB: www.granitesoftwareinc.com
SIC: 7372 Prepackaged software

(P-17871)
GRAYPAY LLC
6345 Balboa Blvd Ste 115, Encino (91316-1517)
PHONE.....................818 387-6735
Marc Geolina, *Mng Member*
Christa Pizzolanti, *Executive*
Beau Geolina, *Marketing Mgr*
Bryan Rainey,
Jaimie Smith, *Manager*
EMP: 14 EST: 2015
SALES (est): 999.1K **Privately Held**
WEB: www.graypay.com
SIC: 7372 Business oriented computer software

(P-17872)
GREEN HILLS SOFTWARE LLC (HQ)
30 W Sola St, Santa Barbara (93101-2599)
PHONE.....................805 965-6044
Daniel O Dowd, *CEO*
Dave Kleidermacher, *President*
Michael W Liacko, *President*

Daniel O'Dowd, *CEO*
Brad Jackson, *COO*
EMP: 105 **EST:** 1986
SALES (est): 124.9MM
SALES (corp-wide): 128.9MM **Privately Held**
WEB: www.ghs.com
SIC: 7372 Prepackaged software
PA: Ghs Holding Company
30 W Sola St
Santa Barbara CA 93101
805 965-6044

(P-17873)
GREENGRO TECHNOLOGIES INC (PA)
1676 W Lincoln Ave, Anaheim
(92801-5501)
PHONE..................714 367-6538
Matthew Burden, *CEO*
Aaron R Thomas, *President*
Robert Martinez, *CEO*
Owen Naccarato, *CFO*
David L Rudat, *CFO*
EMP: 24 **EST:** 2009
SALES (est): 3.5MM **Privately Held**
WEB: www.greengrotech.com
SIC: 7372 Prepackaged software

(P-17874)
GUIDANCE SOFTWARE INC (HQ)
1055 E Colo Blvd Ste 400, Pasadena
(91106)
PHONE..................626 229-9191
Patrick Dennis, *President*
Barry Plaga, *COO*
Michael Harris, *Chief Mktg Ofcr*
Alfredo Gomez, *Senior VP*
Christopher Blake, *Executive*
EMP: 215 **EST:** 2006
SQ FT: 90,000
SALES: 110.5MM
SALES (corp-wide): 3.1B **Privately Held**
WEB: www.security.opentext.com
SIC: 7372 3572 Business oriented computer software; computer storage devices
PA: Open Text Corporation
275 Frank Tompa Dr
Waterloo ON N2L 0
519 888-7111

(P-17875)
GUIDANCE SOFTWARE INC
215 N Marengo Ave Ste 250, Pasadena
(91101-1532)
PHONE..................626 229-9199
EMP: 32
SALES (est): 1.6MM **Privately Held**
WEB: www.guidancesoftware.com
SIC: 7372 Prepackaged Software Services

(P-17876)
GUMGUM SPORTS INC ◆
1314 7th St Fl 4, Santa Monica
(90401-1608)
PHONE..................310 400-0396
Brian Kim, *CEO*
EMP: 45 **EST:** 2021
SALES (est): 2.5MM **Privately Held**
SIC: 7372 Business oriented computer software

(P-17877)
GURUCUL SOLUTIONS LLC
222 N Pcf Cast Hwy Ste 13, El Segundo
(90245)
PHONE..................213 291-6888
Kanchan Nayyar,
Jasen Meece, *President*
Saryu Nayyar, *CEO*
Amol Bhagwat, *Vice Pres*
Beau Hutto, *Vice Pres*
EMP: 30 **EST:** 2010
SQ FT: 4,360
SALES (est): 13.9MM **Privately Held**
WEB: www.gurucul.com
SIC: 5734 7372 Software, business & non-game; publishers' computer software

(P-17878)
H2 WELLNESS INCORPORATED
15414 Milldale Dr, Los Angeles
(90077-1601)
PHONE..................310 362-1888
Hooman Fakki, *CEO*

Houman Arasteh, *COO*
Esfandiar Behrouz, *Director*
EMP: 22 **EST:** 2005
SALES (est): 1.5MM **Privately Held**
WEB: www.h2wellness.com
SIC: 7372 Application computer software

(P-17879)
HOLLYWOOD SOFTWARE INC
5000 Van Nuys Blvd # 460, Van Nuys
(91403-1854)
PHONE..................818 205-2121
Carol Dibattiste, *CEO*
Karl Anderson, *COO*
Kim Lockhart, *Senior VP*
Larry McCourt, *Senior VP*
Susan Wells, *Senior VP*
EMP: 20 **EST:** 1997
SALES (est): 622.6K **Privately Held**
WEB: www.hollywoodsoftware.com
SIC: 7372 Operating systems computer software

(P-17880)
HR CLOUD INC (PA)
222 N Pcf Cast Hwy Ste 20, El Segundo
(90245)
PHONE..................510 909-1993
Damir Davidovic, *Principal*
Dijana Davidovic, *Controller*
EMP: 97 **EST:** 2016
SQ FT: 10,000
SALES (est): 3.2MM **Privately Held**
WEB: www.hrcloud.com
SIC: 7372 Business oriented computer software

(P-17881)
IAMPLUS ELECTRONICS INC (PA)
809 N Cahuenga Blvd, Los Angeles
(90038-3703)
PHONE..................323 210-3852
Will Adams, *CEO*
Phil Molyneux, *President*
Rosemary Peschken, *CFO*
Travis Lopez, *Finance*
Chandrasekar Rathakrishnan, *Director*
EMP: 38 **EST:** 2013
SQ FT: 6,000
SALES (est): 10.9MM **Privately Held**
WEB: www.iamplus.services
SIC: 7372 Prepackaged software

(P-17882)
ILLUMNATE EDUCATN HOLDINGS INC (PA)
6531 Irvine Center Dr # 10, Irvine
(92618-2146)
PHONE..................949 656-3133
Christine Willig, *CEO*
Dick Davidson, *CFO*
Jane Snyder, *Chief Mktg Ofcr*
Pam Demond, *Officer*
Shawn Mahoney, *Officer*
EMP: 77 **EST:** 2009
SALES (est): 14.7MM **Privately Held**
WEB: www.illuminateed.com
SIC: 7372 Educational computer software

(P-17883)
INDABA GROUP INC (HQ)
6144 Calle Real Ste 200, Santa Barbara
(93117-2012)
PHONE..................805 964-3313
Gregory Boden, *President*
EMP: 50 **EST:** 1999
SALES (est): 1MM **Publicly Held**
WEB: www.aiadvertising.com
SIC: 7372 7371 Prepackaged software; computer software systems analysis & design, custom

(P-17884)
INDUSTRIOUS SOFTWARE SOLUTION
Also Called: Industrious Software Solutions
8901 S La Cnga Blvd # 202, Inglewood
(90301-4495)
PHONE..................310 672-8700
Stephen Ryza, *President*
Gina Lynn Tan, *Controller*
EMP: 13 **EST:** 1982
SQ FT: 10,000

SALES (est): 507.1K **Privately Held**
WEB: www.issweb.com
SIC: 7372 Business oriented computer software; business forms

(P-17885)
INFORM DECISIONS INC
30162 Tomas 101, Rcho STA Marg
(92688-2124)
PHONE..................949 709-5838
Dan Forester, *President*
EMP: 16 **EST:** 2002
SALES (est): 1.4MM **Privately Held**
WEB: www.informdecisions.com
SIC: 7372 Business oriented computer software

(P-17886)
INFORM SOLUTION INCORPORATED
201 Mentor Dr, Santa Barbara
(93111-3337)
PHONE..................805 879-6000
Rey Hugh, *President*
EMP: 18 **EST:** 1994
SALES (est): 3.1MM
SALES (corp-wide): 82.5B **Publicly Held**
WEB: www.mentordirect.com
SIC: 7372 Prepackaged software
HQ: Mentor Worldwide Llc
31 Technology Dr Ste 200
Irvine CA 92618
800 636-8678

(P-17887)
INFORMTION INTGRTION GROUP INC
457 Palm Dr Ste 200, Glendale
(91202-4339)
PHONE..................818 956-3744
Alec Baghdasaryan, *President*
Jay Hersey, *Vice Pres*
EMP: 46 **EST:** 1995
SALES (est): 3.8MM **Privately Held**
WEB: www.iigservices.com
SIC: 7372 7371 Prepackaged software; computer software development

(P-17888)
INNOVATE LABS LLC
556 S Fair Oaks Ave Ste 5, Pasadena
(91105-2656)
PHONE..................917 753-2673
Adam Fisk,
EMP: 14 **EST:** 2015
SALES (est): 633.6K **Privately Held**
SIC: 7372 7389 Application computer software;

(P-17889)
INTELLECTYX INC
680 E Colo Blvd Ste 180, Pasadena
(91101)
PHONE..................720 256-7540
Raj Joseph, *CEO*
EMP: 70 **EST:** 2010
SALES (est): 1.9MM **Privately Held**
WEB: www.intellectyx.com
SIC: 7372 Business oriented computer software

(P-17890)
INTOUCH TECHNOLOGIES INC (HQ)
Also Called: Intouch Health
7402 Hollister Ave, Goleta (93117-2583)
PHONE..................805 562-8686
Yulun Wang, *CEO*
David Jahns, *Managing Prtnr*
Susan Wang, *Shareholder*
David Adornetto, *COO*
Stephen L Wilson, *CFO*
EMP: 299 **EST:** 2002
SQ FT: 1,600
SALES (est): 99.5MM **Publicly Held**
WEB: www.intouchhealth.com
SIC: 7372 Business oriented computer software

(P-17891)
INVISBLE PRTECTION SYSTEMS INC
8847 S Halldale Ave, Los Angeles
(90047-3428)
P.O. Box 452963 (90045-8541)
PHONE..................213 254-0463
Gregory Bryant, *Principal*
EMP: 20 **EST:** 2018
SALES (est): 724.1K **Privately Held**
WEB: www.ipsitech.com
SIC: 7372 Prepackaged software

(P-17892)
INVOTECH SYSTEMS INC
20951 Burbank Blvd Ste B, Woodland Hills
(91367-6696)
PHONE..................318 461-9800
Harvey Welles, *President*
Jennifer Despain, *CFO*
Robert Andrews, *Technical Staff*
Oscar Estacio, *Technical Staff*
Oswald Lares, *Sales Staff*
EMP: 15 **EST:** 1991
SQ FT: 10,000
SALES (est): 2.6MM **Privately Held**
WEB: www.invotech.com
SIC: 7372 Business oriented computer software

(P-17893)
IPRESSROOM INC
Also Called: Ipr Software
16501 Ventura Blvd # 424, Encino
(91436-2007)
PHONE..................310 499-0544
Chris Bechtel, *President*
Tom Madden, *Chairman*
Vadim Derkach, *Director*
EMP: 20 **EST:** 2000
SQ FT: 10,000
SALES (est): 511.3K **Privately Held**
WEB: www.iprsoftware.com
SIC: 7372 Application computer software

(P-17894)
IQMS LLC (HQ)
2231 Wisteria Ln, Paso Robles
(93446-9820)
PHONE..................805 227-1122
Gary Nemmers, *President*
Matt Ouska, *CFO*
Steve Bieszczat, *Chief Mktg Ofcr*
Shannon Holloway, *Officer*
Cheri Williams, *Senior VP*
EMP: 130 **EST:** 1989
SQ FT: 60,000
SALES: 61.9MM
SALES (corp-wide): 2B **Privately Held**
WEB: www.iqms.com
SIC: 7372 Prepackaged software
PA: Dassault Systemes
10 Rue Marcel Dassault
Velizy Villacoublay 73140
161 623-000

(P-17895)
ISOLUTECOM INC (PA)
9 Northam Ave, Newbury Park
(91320-3323)
PHONE..................805 498-6259
Byron Nutley, *Ch of Bd*
Don Hyun, *President*
Thomas Mangle, *CFO*
Michael Brown, *CTO*
EMP: 50 **EST:** 1999
SALES (est): 3.9MM **Privately Held**
SIC: 7372 Business oriented computer software

(P-17896)
ITC SFTWARE SLUTIONS GROUP LLC (PA)
Also Called: Itcssg
201 Sandpointe Ave # 305, Santa Ana
(92707-5778)
PHONE..................877 248-2774
Del Husain, *CEO*
Ray Jandga, *President*
Guru Gurumoorthy, *Vice Pres*
Thanigaimani Subramanian, *Software Dev*
Arulselvam Venkatasubbu, *Recruiter*
EMP: 398 **EST:** 2008
SQ FT: 3,000

SALES (est): 24MM **Privately Held**
WEB: www.rencata.com
SIC: 7372 7371 7373 Prepackaged software; computer software systems analysis & design, custom; systems software development services

(P-17897)
JAM CITY INC (PA)
Also Called: Social Gaming Network
3562 Eastham Dr, Culver City
(90232-2409)
PHONE....................310 205-4800
Chris Dewolfe, *CEO*
Rachel Levine, *Vice Chairman*
Josh Yguado, *COO*
Zakari Rob, *Exec VP*
Josh Brooks, *Senior VP*
EMP: 249 EST: 2009
SALES (est): 59.5MM **Privately Held**
WEB: www.jamcity.com
SIC: 7372 Prepackaged software

(P-17898)
JESTA DIGITAL ENTRMT INC (HQ)
15303 Ventura Blvd # 900, Sherman Oaks
(91403-3199)
PHONE....................323 648-4200
Jason Aintabi, *CEO*
Mark Anderson, *COO*
EMP: 50 EST: 2005
SALES (est): 1.9MM **Privately Held**
SIC: 7372 Prepackaged software

(P-17899)
JUSTENOUGH SOFTWARE CORP INC (HQ)
15440 Laguna Canyon Rd # 100, Irvine
(92618-2139)
PHONE....................949 706-5400
Malcolm Buxton, *President*
Robert Rackleff, *CFO*
Fabien Lamon, *Vice Pres*
Wikus Van Dyk, *Development*
Tonya Nicholls, *Human Res Dir*
EMP: 30 EST: 2001
SALES (est): 11.3MM
SALES (corp-wide): 20.5MM **Privately Held**
WEB: www.justenoughsoftware.com
SIC: 7372 Prepackaged software
PA: Mi9 Retail Inc.
12000 Biscayne Blvd # 600
North Miami FL 33181
647 849-1101

(P-17900)
KINGCOM(US) LLC (HQ)
3100 Ocean Park Blvd, Santa Monica
(90405-3032)
PHONE....................424 744-5697
EMP: 50 EST: 2016
SALES (est): 53.4MM
SALES (corp-wide): 8B **Publicly Held**
WEB: www.activisionblizzard.com
SIC: 7372 Home entertainment computer software
PA: Activision Blizzard, Inc.
3100 Ocean Park Blvd
Santa Monica CA 90405
310 255-2000

(P-17901)
KLEVERNESS INCORPORATED
340 S Lemon Ave 2291, Walnut
(91789-2706)
PHONE....................213 559-2480
Dan Nurko Elliot, *CEO*
Alex Fraind-Dorfsman, *CFO*
EMP: 15 EST: 2017
SALES (est): 1MM **Privately Held**
WEB: www.kleverness.com
SIC: 5734 7372 Computer peripheral equipment; application computer software

(P-17902)
KLOOMA HOLDINGS INC
113 N San Vicente Blvd, Beverly Hills
(90211-2329)
PHONE....................305 747-3315
Gary Merisier, *CEO*
EMP: 20 EST: 2017
SALES (est): 1.1MM **Privately Held**
SIC: 7372 Application computer software

(P-17903)
KOFAX LIMITED (DH)
15211 Laguna Canyon Rd, Irvine
(92618-3146)
PHONE....................949 783-1000
Reynolds C Bish, *CEO*
James Arnold Jr, *CFO*
Grant Johnson, *Chief Mktg Ofcr*
Bradford Weller, *Exec VP*
Anthony Macciola, *CTO*
EMP: 1399 EST: 1985
SQ FT: 91,000
SALES (est): 74.7MM **Privately Held**
WEB: www.kofax.com
SIC: 7372 Business oriented computer software

(P-17904)
LCPTRACKER INC
117 E Chapman Ave, Orange
(92866-1401)
P.O. Box 187 (92856-6187)
PHONE....................714 669-0052
Mark Douglas, *President*
Loren Doll, *Vice Pres*
Parker Douglas,
Kathryn Reger, *Admin Asst*
Kayla Taormina, *Admin Asst*
EMP: 20 EST: 1992
SQ FT: 1,500
SALES (est): 6MM **Privately Held**
WEB: www.lcptracker.com
SIC: 7372 Business oriented computer software

(P-17905)
LIGHTSPEED SOFTWARE INC
1800 19th St, Bakersfield (93301-4315)
PHONE....................661 716-7600
Eileen Shihadeh, *Chief Mktg Ofcr*
Michael Durando, *Vice Pres*
Greg Funk, *Vice Pres*
Johnathan Genter, *Vice Pres*
Max Hardy, *Administration*
EMP: 21 EST: 2017
SALES (est): 943.2K **Privately Held**
WEB: www.lightspeedsystems.com
SIC: 7372 Prepackaged software

(P-17906)
LIVEOFFICE LLC
Also Called: Advisorsquare
900 Corporate Pointe, Culver City
(90230-7609)
PHONE....................877 253-2793
Alexander Rusich,
Matt Hardy,
Jeffrey W Hausman,
Nikhil Menta,
Matt Smith,
EMP: 64 EST: 2007
SQ FT: 15,000
SALES (est): 9.2MM
SALES (corp-wide): 2.5B **Publicly Held**
WEB: www.liveoffice.com
SIC: 7372 Prepackaged software
PA: Nortonlifelock Inc.
60 E Rio Salado Pkwy # 1
Tempe AZ 85281
650 527-8000

(P-17907)
LUNA IMAGING INC
2702 Media Center Dr, Los Angeles
(90065-1733)
PHONE....................323 908-1400
Marlo Lee, *President*
Lori Richmeier, *Admin Mgr*
Drake Zabriskie, *Systems Dir*
Robert Amesbury, *Finance*
Amesbury Robert, *Finance*
EMP: 22 EST: 1993
SQ FT: 6,000
SALES (est): 2.9MM **Privately Held**
WEB: www.lunaimaging.com
SIC: 7372 7373 Publishers' computer software; computer integrated systems design

(P-17908)
M NEXON INC
Also Called: Nexon America
222 N Pacific Coast Hwy # 300, El Segundo (90245-5614)
PHONE....................213 858-5930
John Robinson, *CEO*
Christina Song, *Marketing Staff*
Roy Shin, *Director*
Richard Mejiaalonzo, *Supervisor*
Mary Whiting, *Associate*
EMP: 52 EST: 2011
SALES (est): 4.2MM **Privately Held**
WEB: www.company.nexon.co.jp
SIC: 7372 5092 Application computer software; video games
PA: Nexon Co.,Ltd.
1-4-5, Roppongi
Minato-Ku TKY 106-0

(P-17909)
M29 TECHNOLOGY AND DESIGN
133 Bridge St Ste B, Arroyo Grande
(93420-3366)
PHONE....................805 489-9402
John Herlihy, *Owner*
Corey Knowlton, *Sales Dir*
EMP: 17 EST: 1999
SQ FT: 1,200
SALES (est): 3.1MM **Privately Held**
WEB: www.m29.com
SIC: 7372 7371 Prepackaged software; custom computer programming services

(P-17910)
MAGIC SOFTWARE ENTERPRISES INC
24422 Avnida De La Crlota Carlota, Laguna Hills (92653)
P.O. Box 52020, Irvine (92619-2020)
PHONE....................949 250-1718
Eyal Karny, *CEO*
Fred Esquillo, *Vice Pres*
Glenn Johnson, *Vice Pres*
Jarred Parris, *Vice Pres*
Brian Pitoniak, *Vice Pres*
EMP: 20 EST: 1991
SQ FT: 7,000
SALES (est): 6.5MM **Privately Held**
WEB: www.magicsoftware.com
SIC: 7372 7379 7371 Prepackaged software; computer related consulting services; custom computer programming services
PA: Magic Software Enterprises Ltd.
1 Yahadut Canada
Or Yehuda 60375
-

(P-17911)
MARKZWARE
Also Called: Markzware Software
1805 E Dyer Rd Ste 101, Santa Ana
(92705-5742)
P.O. Box 1059, Dayton NV (89403-1059)
PHONE....................949 756-5100
Patrick Marchese, *President*
Ron Crandall, *Vice Pres*
Long Nguyen, *CIO*
Valerie Consalvi, *Info Tech Dir*
Breck Auten, *Prgrmr*
EMP: 38 EST: 1995
SQ FT: 5,000
SALES (est): 1.2MM **Privately Held**
WEB: www.markzware.com
SIC: 7372 Business oriented computer software

(P-17912)
MAXXESS SYSTEMS INC (PA)
22661 Old Canal Rd, Yorba Linda
(92887-4601)
PHONE....................714 772-1000
Kevin Charles Daly, *CEO*
Nancy Islas, *President*
Joel Slutzky, *Chairman*
Erik Wade, *Business Dir*
Lee Copland, *Managing Dir*
EMP: 18 EST: 2003
SQ FT: 12,000
SALES (est): 5MM **Privately Held**
WEB: www.maxxess-systems.com
SIC: 7372 Business oriented computer software

(P-17913)
MEDATA INC (PA)
5 Peters Canyon Rd # 250, Irvine
(92606-1791)
PHONE....................714 918-1310
Cy King, *CEO*
Tom Herndon, *President*
Thomas Herndon, *COO*
Dana Joanou, *CFO*
Bryan Lowe, *CFO*
EMP: 51 EST: 1975
SQ FT: 17,192
SALES (est): 97.2MM **Privately Held**
WEB: www.medata.com
SIC: 7372 6411 Business oriented computer software; medical insurance claim processing, contract or fee basis

(P-17914)
MEDIA GOBBLER INC
6427 W Sunset Blvd, Los Angeles
(90028-7314)
PHONE....................323 203-3222
Chris Kantrowitz, *CEO*
Phil Kinkade, *President*
Olivier Albin, *Office Mgr*
Richard Misenheimer, *Info Tech Dir*
Aaron McCullough, *Manager*
EMP: 21 EST: 2010
SALES (est): 1.6MM **Privately Held**
WEB: www.gobbler.com
SIC: 7372 Application computer software

(P-17915)
METRONOME SOFTWARE LLC
2 S Pointe Dr Ste 140, Lake Forest
(92630-2296)
PHONE....................949 273-5190
Chieu Nguyen, *Mng Member*
Huy Nguyen, *President*
David Lim, *CTO*
Wou Kuo, *Software Engr*
Samantha Keith, *Controller*
EMP: 20 EST: 2008
SQ FT: 6,500
SALES (est): 1.4MM **Privately Held**
WEB: www.metronome-software.com
SIC: 7372 Prepackaged software

(P-17916)
MIDRANGE SOFTWARE INC
12223 Otsego St, Valley Village
(91607-3007)
PHONE....................818 762-8539
Jacques Ohana, *President*
Simon Ohana, *Vice Pres*
EMP: 15 EST: 1987
SALES (est): 1MM **Privately Held**
SIC: 7372 Prepackaged software

(P-17917)
MINDSHOW
333 S Grand Ave Ste 4325, Los Angeles
(90071-1522)
PHONE....................213 531-0277
Angelo Warner, *Opers Mgr*
Daniel Bellezza, *Manager*
EMP: 23 EST: 2017
SALES (est): 3.6MM **Privately Held**
WEB: www.mindshow.com
SIC: 7372 Prepackaged software

(P-17918)
MIRTH CORPORATION
611 Anton Blvd Ste 500, Costa Mesa
(92626-1934)
PHONE....................714 389-1200
Jon Teichrow, *President*
Samuel Sippl, *CFO*
Gary Teichrow, *Vice Pres*
Andrew Thorson, *Vice Pres*
Jeff Cardenas, *Software Engr*
EMP: 81 EST: 1993
SQ FT: 10,000
SALES (est): 4.2MM
SALES (corp-wide): 556.8MM **Publicly Held**
WEB: www.nextgen.com
SIC: 7372 Business oriented computer software
PA: Nextgen Healthcare, Inc.
3525 Piedmont Rd Ne # 700
Atlanta GA 30305
404 467-1500

(P-17919)
MITRATECH HOLDINGS INC
5900 Wilshire Blvd # 1500, Los Angeles
(90036-5031)
PHONE....................323 964-0000
Jason Parkman, *CEO*
Tamara Wasserman, *Executive*
Georg Zunner, *Technical Staff*

PRODUCTS & SVCS

Dakota Wright, *Analyst*
Laura Paynter, *Hum Res Coord*
EMP: 125
SALES (corp-wide): 47MM **Privately Held**
WEB: www.mitratech.com
SIC: 7372 Business oriented computer software
PA: Mitratech Holdings, Inc.
5001 Plz On The Lk Ste 11
Austin TX 78746
512 382-7322

(P-17920)
MOBILE NET POSA INC
835 Wilshire Blvd Ste 200, Los Angeles (90017-2655)
P.O. Box 811160 (90081-0003)
PHONE..................213 863-0351
Sharoz Yroshalmiane, *CEO*
▲ **EMP:** 17 **EST:** 2010
SALES (est): 577K **Privately Held**
WEB: www.us1316639364cypn.trustpass.alibaba.com
SIC: 7372 Application computer software

(P-17921)
MOD2 INC
Also Called: Mod 2
3317 S Broadway, Los Angeles (90007-4114)
PHONE..................213 747-8424
Javid Nia, *President*
Albert Jumaquio, *Software Dev*
Omeed Nia, *Software Dev*
Ronald Bantayan, *Manager*
EMP: 24 **EST:** 1992
SQ FT: 12,000
SALES (est): 1.2MM **Privately Held**
WEB: www.mod2.com
SIC: 7372 7371 Business oriented computer software; application computer software; computer software systems analysis & design, custom

(P-17922)
MODEL MATCH INC
209 Avnida Fbrcnte Ste 15, San Clemente (92672)
PHONE..................949 525-9405
Kirk Waldfogel, *Principal*
Eric Levin, *Principal*
Eric Petersen, *Principal*
Steve Rennie, *Principal*
Drew Waterhouse, *Principal*
EMP: 18 **EST:** 2014
SQ FT: 3,400
SALES (est): 1.1MM **Privately Held**
WEB: www.modelmatch.com
SIC: 7372 Application computer software

(P-17923)
MSCSOFTWARE CORPORATION (HQ)
5161 California Ave # 200, Irvine (92617-8002)
PHONE..................714 540-8900
Roger Assaker, *CEO*
Alex Montgomery, *CFO*
Kais Bouchiba, *Vice Pres*
John Janevic, *Vice Pres*
Doug Neill, *Vice Pres*
EMP: 245 **EST:** 1963
SALES (est): 120.3MM
SALES (corp-wide): 4.5B **Privately Held**
WEB: www.mscsoftware.com
SIC: 7372 Business oriented computer software
PA: Hexagon Ab
Lilla Bantorget 15
Stockholm 111 2
860 126-20

(P-17924)
MSCSOFTWARE CORPORATION (PA)
815 Colorado Blvd, Los Angeles (90041-1720)
PHONE..................323 258-9111
Ennie Gonzaga, *Principal*
Peter Mendoza, *Principal*
Main Andrew, *Technology*
James Fillon, *Engineer*
Ted Rose, *Engineer*
EMP: 103 **EST:** 1994

SALES (est): 1.1MM **Privately Held**
SIC: 7372 Prepackaged software

(P-17925)
MY EYE MEDIA LLC
2211 N Hollywood Way, Burbank (91505-1113)
PHONE..................818 559-7200
Michael Kadenacy, *President*
Rodd Feingold, *CFO*
Jane C Hawley, *Senior VP*
Raphael Morozov, *Vice Pres*
Jannie WEI, *Office Mgr*
EMP: 80 **EST:** 2004
SQ FT: 20,000
SALES (est): 10.2MM
SALES (corp-wide): 17.8MM **Privately Held**
WEB: www.eurofins-dms.com
SIC: 7372 Business oriented computer software
HQ: Eurofins Product Testing Us Holdings, Inc.
11720 N Creek Pkwy N # 400
Bothell WA 98011
800 383-0085

(P-17926)
NAVER BAND INC
5750 Wilshire Blvd # 640, Los Angeles (90036-4494)
PHONE..................323 847-1750
Hakseon Lee, *CEO*
Doyon Kim, *Principal*
EMP: 14 **EST:** 2014
SALES (est): 3.7MM **Privately Held**
WEB: www.band.us
SIC: 7372 Application computer software
PA: Naver Corporation
6 Buljeong-Ro, Bundang-Gu
Seongnam 13561

(P-17927)
NAZCA SOLUTIONS INC
4 First American Way, Santa Ana (92707-5913)
PHONE..................612 279-6100
Robert Karraa, *President*
Ted Mondale, *Vice Pres*
EMP: 42 **EST:** 2003
SQ FT: 45,000
SALES (est): 6.5MM **Publicly Held**
WEB: www.firstam.com
SIC: 7372 Application computer software
PA: First American Financial Corporation
1 First American Way
Santa Ana CA 92707

(P-17928)
NC4 SOLTRA LLC
21515 Hawthorne Blvd # 52, Torrance (90503-6501)
PHONE..................408 489-5579
Tommy McDowell, *Mng Member*
EMP: 67 **EST:** 2016
SALES (est): 8.4MM
SALES (corp-wide): 10.3MM **Privately Held**
WEB: www.everbridge.com
SIC: 7372 Prepackaged software
PA: Celerium Inc.
21515 Hawthorne Blvd # 520
Torrance CA 90503
408 489-5579

(P-17929)
NEIGHBORHOOD MENNONITE
Also Called: Neighborhood Church
5505 W Riggin Ave, Visalia (93291-9084)
PHONE..................559 732-9107
Forrest Jenan, *Pastor*
Dale Best, *Comms Dir*
Heather Stafford, *Finance Dir*
Kelly Thomas, *Assoc Pastor*
Steve Harms, *Pastor*
EMP: 24 **EST:** 1950
SALES (est): 1.5MM **Privately Held**
WEB: www.ncvisalia.com
SIC: 8661 7372 Miscellaneous denomination church; churches, temples & shrines; application computer software

(P-17930)
NETSOL TECHNOLOGIES INC (PA)
23975 Park Sorrento # 250, Calabasas (91302-4016)
PHONE..................818 222-9197
Najeeb Ghauri, *Ch of Bd*
Naeem Ghauri, *President*
Usman Idrees, *President*
Boo Ali, *CFO*
Roger Almond, *Officer*
EMP: 1046 **EST:** 1997
SQ FT: 5,000
SALES: 54.9MM **Publicly Held**
WEB: www.netsoltech.com
SIC: 7372 7373 7299 Business oriented computer software; computer integrated systems design; personal document & information services

(P-17931)
NETWORK AUTOMATION INC
3530 Wilshire Blvd # 1800, Los Angeles (90010-2335)
PHONE..................213 738-1700
Dustin Snell, *CEO*
Graham Taylor, *CTO*
Esther Suh, *Agent*
EMP: 50 **EST:** 2004
SQ FT: 9,000
SALES (est): 13.1MM
SALES (corp-wide): 562.3MM **Privately Held**
SIC: 7372 Business oriented computer software
HQ: Help/Systems, Llc
6455 City West Pkwy
Eden Prairie MN 55344
952 933-0609

(P-17932)
NETWRIX CORPORATION (HQ)
300 Spectrum Center Dr # 200, Irvine (92618-4925)
PHONE..................888 638-9749
Steve Dickson, *CEO*
Anthony Chin, *Vice Pres*
Jim Smith, *Vice Pres*
Ilia Sotnikov, *Vice Pres*
Marina PO, *CIO*
EMP: 55 **EST:** 2006
SQ FT: 12,000
SALES (est): 64MM **Privately Held**
WEB: www.netwrix.com
SIC: 7372 Business oriented computer software

(P-17933)
NILE AI INC
15260 Ventura Blvd # 141, Sherman Oaks (91403-5307)
PHONE..................818 689-9107
Artin Davidian, *Administration*
EMP: 25 **EST:** 2020
SALES (est): 884.3K **Privately Held**
SIC: 7372 Application computer software

(P-17934)
NIS AMERICA INC
4 Hutton Cntre Dr Ste 650, Santa Ana (92707)
PHONE..................714 540-1199
Souhei Niikawa, *CEO*
Harusato Akenaga, *President*
Johanna Hirota, *CFO*
Mitsuharu Hiraoka, *Vice Pres*
Mizuki Nishida, *Production*
▲ **EMP:** 40 **EST:** 2003
SQ FT: 1,000
SALES (est): 13.9MM **Privately Held**
WEB: www.nisamerica.com
SIC: 7372 Publishers' computer software
PA: Nipponichi K.K.
1-8-4, Nihombashihoridomecho
Chuo-Ku TKY 103-0

(P-17935)
NOVASTOR CORPORATION (PA)
29209 Canwood St Ste 200, Agoura Hills (91301-1908)
PHONE..................805 579-6700
Peter Means, *President*
Martin Albert, *Chairman*
Mike D Andrews, *Managing Dir*
Bridget Giacinto, *Marketing Staff*

Nathan Fouarge, *Products*
EMP: 30 **EST:** 1987
SQ FT: 7,800
SALES (est): 4.9MM **Privately Held**
WEB: www.novastor.com
SIC: 7372 7371 5734 Business oriented computer software; custom computer programming services; software, business & non-game

(P-17936)
NTRUST INFOTECH INC
230 Commerce Ste 180, Irvine (92602-1336)
PHONE..................562 207-1600
Srikanth Ramachandran, *CEO*
Kevin Harrigan, *President*
Ramesh Narayanan, *Vice Pres*
Sameer Sarvate, *Vice Pres*
Sundararajan Varadarajan, *Vice Pres*
EMP: 65
SALES (est): 5.5MM **Privately Held**
WEB: www.ntrustinfotech.com
SIC: 7372 7371 Business oriented computer software; computer software development & applications
PA: Ntrust Infotech Private Limited
3rd Floor Ganesh Towers
Chennai TN 60000

(P-17937)
NUMECENT INC
530 Technology Dr Ste 375, Irvine (92618-3505)
PHONE..................949 833-2800
Tom Lagatta, *CEO*
Osman Kent, *Ch of Bd*
Ed Corrente, *CFO*
Hildy Shandell, *CFO*
Huy Huynh, *Vice Pres*
EMP: 30 **EST:** 2012
SALES (est): 2.9MM **Privately Held**
WEB: www.numecent.com
SIC: 7372 Application computer software

(P-17938)
NUORDER INC (PA)
1901 Avenue Of The Stars # 175, Los Angeles (90067-6000)
PHONE..................310 954-1313
Heath Wells, *CEO*
Nicole McElroy, *Partner*
Adam Schneider, *COO*
Kevin Sagarchi, *Executive*
Andrew Santistevan, *Administration*
EMP: 19 **EST:** 2011
SALES (est): 2.9MM **Privately Held**
WEB: www.nuorder.com
SIC: 7372 Application computer software

(P-17939)
NWP SERVICES CORPORATION (DH)
535 Anton Blvd Ste 1100, Costa Mesa (92626-7699)
P.O. Box 19661, Irvine (92623-9661)
PHONE..................949 253-2500
Ron Reed, *President*
Lana Reeve,
Mike Haviken, *Exec VP*
Weston Thomas, *Software Engr*
John Deretich, *Analyst*
EMP: 141 **EST:** 1995
SQ FT: 21,171
SALES (est): 48.8MM **Privately Held**
WEB: www.nwp.com
SIC: 7372 8721 Utility computer software; billing & bookkeeping service
HQ: Realpage, Inc.
2201 Lakeside Blvd
Richardson TX 75082
972 820-3000

(P-17940)
ODDWORLD INHABITANTS INC
869 Monterey St, San Luis Obispo (93401-3224)
PHONE..................805 503-3000
Sherry McKenna, *CEO*
Lorne Lanning, *President*
Maurice Konkle, *COO*
Raymond Swanland, *Production*
EMP: 17 **EST:** 1997
SQ FT: 15,000

SALES (est): 749.4K **Privately Held**
SIC: 7372 Application computer software

(P-17941)
ONCEHUB INC
Also Called: Reschedge
340 S Lemon Ave Ste 5585, Walnut
(91789-2706)
PHONE..................................650 206-5585
Rami Goraly, *CEO*
Gilad Goraly, *CTO*
Jonathan Gee, *Finance*
EMP: 13 EST: 2013
SALES (est): 810.7K **Privately Held**
WEB: www.oncehub.com
SIC: 7372 Operating systems computer
software

(P-17942)
ONLINE MEDIA TECHNOLOGIES LTD
1633 Amador Ln, Newbury Park
(91320-1804)
PHONE..................................209 279-5320
William Stewart, *CEO*
EMP: 14
SALES (est): 289.1K **Privately Held**
SIC: 7372 Prepackaged software

(P-17943)
OPTIMIS SERVICES INC
225 Mantua Rd, Pacific Palisades
(90272-3349)
PHONE..................................310 230-2780
Alan Morelli, *President*
Dan Dourney, *COO*
Scott Schroeder, *Bd of Directors*
Tiffany Manning, *Director*
EMP: 13 EST: 2013
SALES (est): 491.1K **Privately Held**
WEB: www.optimiscorp.com
SIC: 7372 Business oriented computer
software

(P-17944)
OPTIMISCORP
200 Mantua Rd, Pacific Palisades
(90272-3349)
PHONE..................................310 230-2780
Alan Morelli, *CEO*
William Horne, *CFO*
Peter Rogers, *Officer*
Kelly Beam, *Vice Pres*
Mark Hopkins, *Software Engr*
EMP: 36 EST: 2006
SALES (est): 2.5MM **Privately Held**
WEB: www.optimiscorp.com
SIC: 7372 Business oriented computer
software

(P-17945)
ORACLE CORPORATION
1 Bolero, Mission Viejo (92692-5164)
PHONE..................................626 315-7513
Hemesh Surana, *Branch Mgr*
Jim Wharrie, *Vice Pres*
Ann Hohisel, *Engineer*
Ben Staveley-Taylor, *Engineer*
EMP: 302
SALES (corp-wide): 40.4B **Publicly Held**
WEB: www.oracle.com
SIC: 7372 Prepackaged software
PA: Oracle Corporation
2300 Oracle Way
Austin TX 78741
737 867-1000

(P-17946)
ORANGEGRID LLC
145 S State College Blvd, Brea
(92821-5818)
PHONE..................................657 220-1519
Todd Mobraten, *Mng Member*
Michele McCoy, *VP Bus Dvlpt*
Denise Alvarez, *Administration*
Bryan Nguyen, *QC Mgr*
Dustin Sauter,
EMP: 28 EST: 2014
SALES (est): 4.7MM **Privately Held**
SIC: 7372 Prepackaged software

(P-17947)
OSR ENTERPRISES INC
1910 E Stowell Rd, Santa Maria
(93454-8002)
PHONE..................................805 925-1831

James O Rice, *CEO*
Owen S Rice, *Ch of Bd*
Betty E Rice, *Vice Pres*
EMP: 45
SQ FT: 1,500
SALES (est): 8.3MM **Privately Held**
WEB: www.osrenterprises.com
SIC: 7372 Publishers' computer software

(P-17948)
OUTPUT INC
1418 N Spring St Ste 102, Los Angeles
(90012-1924)
PHONE..................................310 795-6099
Gregg Lehrmann, *President*
EMP: 18 EST: 2013
SALES (est): 3.1MM **Privately Held**
WEB: www.output.com
SIC: 7372 Application computer software

(P-17949)
PACIOLAN LLC (DH)
Also Called: Ticketswest
5291 California Ave # 100, Irvine
(92617-3223)
PHONE..................................866 722-4652
Dave Butler, *CEO*
Jane Kleinberger, *Ch of Bd*
Kimberly Boren, *CFO*
Steve Shaw, *CFO*
Craig Ricks, *Chief Mktg Ofcr*
EMP: 112 EST: 1980
SALES (est): 29.9MM **Privately Held**
WEB: www.paciolan.com
SIC: 7372 5045 Business oriented com-
puter software; computers
HQ: Learfield Communications, Llc
2400 Dallas Pkwy Ste 510
Plano TX 75093
336 464-0224

(P-17950)
PAKEDGE DEVICE & SOFTWARE INC
17011 Beach Blvd Ste 600, Huntington
Beach (92647-5962)
PHONE..................................714 880-4511
Dusan Jankov, *Branch Mgr*
EMP: 23
SALES (corp-wide): 855.6MM **Publicly Held**
WEB: www.pakedge.com
SIC: 7372 Application computer software
HQ: Pakedge Device & Software Inc.
11734 S Election Rd
Draper UT 84020
650 385-8700

(P-17951)
PANORAMIC SOFTWARE CORPORATION
Also Called: Panosoft
9650 Research Dr, Irvine (92618-4666)
PHONE..................................877 558-8526
Jeff Von Waldburg, *President*
EMP: 17 EST: 1990
SQ FT: 1,500
SALES (est): 325MM **Privately Held**
WEB: www.panosoft.com
SIC: 7372 7371 Prepackaged software;
custom programming services

(P-17952)
PARENTSQUARE INC
6144 Calle Real Ste 200a, Goleta
(93117-2012)
PHONE..................................888 496-3168
Sohit Wadhwa, *CEO*
Jay Klanfer, *Vice Pres*
Anupama Vaid, *Principal*
Valerie Wilson, *Sales Staff*
EMP: 65 EST: 2011
SALES (est): 4.8MM **Privately Held**
WEB: www.parentsquare.com
SIC: 7372 Educational computer software

(P-17953)
PATIENTPOP INC
214 Wilshire Blvd, Santa Monica
(90401-1202)
PHONE..................................844 487-8399
Travis Schneider, *CEO*
David McNeil, *President*
Jason Gardner, *CFO*
Luke Kervin, *Co-CEO*
Carla Nichols, *Senior VP*

EMP: 51 EST: 2015
SALES (est): 5.5MM **Privately Held**
WEB: www.patientpop.com
SIC: 7372 Business oriented computer
software

(P-17954)
PATRON SOLUTIONS LLC
5171 California Ave # 200, Irvine
(92617-3068)
PHONE..................................949 823-1700
Steve Shaw, *Owner*
EMP: 245 EST: 2015
SALES (est): 13.4MM **Privately Held**
SIC: 7372 Application computer software

(P-17955)
PAYROLLCENTRIC INC
2100 W Century Blvd, Los Angeles
(90047-4006)
PHONE..................................310 258-9703
Christian Zaky, *District Mgr*
Meegan Johnson, *VP Sales*
Josephine Mikhail, *Accounts Exec*
EMP: 20 EST: 2012
SALES (est): 2.7MM **Privately Held**
WEB: www.payrollcentric.com
SIC: 7372 Prepackaged software

(P-17956)
PHOENIX TECHNOLOGIES LTD (HQ)
150 S Los Robles Ave # 5, Pasadena
(91101-2441)
PHONE..................................408 570-1000
Rich Geruson, *President*
Debasish N Biswas, *President*
Steven S Chan, *President*
Brian Stein, *CFO*
Richard Arnold, *Exec VP*
◆ EMP: 20 EST: 1979
SQ FT: 47,000
SALES (est): 36.2MM **Privately Held**
WEB: www.phoenix.com
SIC: 7372 6794 Prepackaged software;
patent owners & lessors

(P-17957)
PIPELINER CRM
15243 La Cruz Dr Unit 492, Pacific Pal-
isades (90272-5328)
PHONE..................................424 280-6445
Nikoluas Kimla, *CEO*
Nina Peery, *Partner*
Gerald Toumayan, *COO*
John Golden, *Officer*
Don Araldi, *Exec VP*
EMP: 14 EST: 2014
SALES (est): 230.2K **Privately Held**
WEB: www.pipelinersales.com
SIC: 7372 Business oriented computer
software

(P-17958)
PIPELINERSALES CORPORATION (PA)
15243 La Cruz Dr Unit 492, Pacific Pal-
isades (90272-5328)
P.O. Box 492 (90272-0492)
PHONE..................................888 843-6699
Nikolaus Kimla, *CEO*
Gerald Toumayan, *COO*
Thomas Kattnigg, *Vice Pres*
Todd Martin, *Vice Pres*
Lucia Schmidt, *Software Dev*
EMP: 36 EST: 2011
SALES (est): 2MM **Privately Held**
WEB: www.pipelinersales.com
SIC: 7372 Business oriented computer
software

(P-17959)
PLUGG ME LNC
18100 Von Karman Ave # 850, Irvine
(92612-0169)
PHONE..................................949 705-4472
Clarissa Watkins, *CEO*
EMP: 25 EST: 2019
SALES (est): 920.8K **Privately Held**
SIC: 7372 Application computer software

(P-17960)
PRATA INC
202 Bicknell Ave, Santa Monica
(90405-2317)
PHONE..................................512 823-1002

Rajat Jain, *CEO*
EMP: 20 EST: 2020
SALES (est): 714.2K **Privately Held**
SIC: 7372 Application computer software

(P-17961)
PRISM SOFTWARE CORPORATION
184 Technology Dr Ste 201, Irvine
(92618-2434)
PHONE..................................949 855-3100
Carl S Von Bibra, *Chairman*
David Ayres, *President*
Michael Cheever, *CFO*
Conrad Von Bibra, *Admin Sec*
John Campbell, *CIO*
EMP: 25 EST: 1970
SALES (est): 5.6MM **Privately Held**
WEB: www.prismsoftware.com
SIC: 7372 Publishers' computer software;
utility computer software; word processing
computer software; operating systems
computer software

(P-17962)
PRODUCTPLAN LLC
10 E Yanonali St Ste 2a, Santa Barbara
(93101-1878)
PHONE..................................805 618-2975
James Semick,
Diana Ciontea, *Finance*
Breanna Davis, *Producer*
Sierra Newell, *Marketing Staff*
Andrea Thies, *Marketing Staff*
EMP: 20 EST: 2013
SALES (est): 1.3MM **Privately Held**
WEB: www.productplan.com
SIC: 7372 Business oriented computer
software

(P-17963)
QAD INC (PA)
100 Innovation Pl, Santa Barbara
(93108-2268)
PHONE..................................805 566-6000
Anton Chilton, *CEO*
Peter R Van Cuylenburg, *Ch of Bd*
Pamela M Lopker, *President*
Daniel Lender, *CFO*
John Neale, *Treasurer*
EMP: 1401 EST: 1979
SQ FT: 120,000
SALES (est): 307.8MM **Publicly Held**
WEB: www.qad.com
SIC: 7372 Prepackaged software; busi-
ness oriented computer software

(P-17964)
QAD INC
6450 Via Real, Carpinteria (93013-2903)
PHONE..................................805 684-6614
Mark Rasmussen, *Branch Mgr*
Vince Niedzielski, *Exec VP*
Vincent P Niedzielski, *Exec VP*
Murray Ray, *Exec VP*
Evan M Bishop, *Vice Pres*
EMP: 17
SALES (corp-wide): 307.8MM **Publicly Held**
WEB: www.qad.com
SIC: 7372 Business oriented computer
software
PA: Qad Inc.
100 Innovation Pl
Santa Barbara CA 93108
805 566-6000

(P-17965)
QED SOFTWARE LLC
Also Called: Trinium Technologies
304 Tejon Pl, Palos Verdes Estates
(90274-1204)
PHONE..................................310 214-3118
Michael Thomas, *CEO*
Guillermo Chinchilla, *Administration*
Barry Assadi, *CTO*
Michael Gould, *Business Anlyst*
Keith Bowers, *Director*
▲ EMP: 27 EST: 2001
SQ FT: 2,500
SALES (est): 9.2MM **Privately Held**
WEB: www.triniumtech.com
SIC: 7372 Business oriented computer
software

PA: Wisetech Global Limited
U 3 72 O'riordan St
Alexandria NSW 2015
-

(P-17966)
QSI 2011 INC (PA)
Also Called: Questys Solutions
2302 Martin Ste 475, Irvine (92612-7402)
PHONE...................................949 855-6885
Rodney Anderson, *President*
Michael Richard, *CFO*
Laura Lechien, *Sales Mgr*
Vickie McGee, *Corp Comm Staff*
Brett Barnes, *Manager*
EMP: 16 **EST:** 1980
SQ FT: 5,050
SALES (est): 2.4MM **Privately Held**
SIC: 7372 Business oriented computer
software

(P-17967)
**QUADROTECH SOLUTIONS INC
(PA)**
4 Polaris Way, Aliso Viejo (92656-5356)
PHONE...................................302 660-0166
Thomas Madsen, *CEO*
Dan Clark, *Officer*
Paul Robichaux, *CTO*
EMP: 17 **EST:** 2013
SALES (est): 9.9MM **Privately Held**
SIC: 7372 Application computer software

(P-17968)
QUEST SOFTWARE INC
Also Called: Cloud Automation Division
4 Polaris Way, Aliso Viejo (92656-5356)
PHONE...................................949 754-8000
Sydney Curtis, *Partner*
Alexa Ives, *Partner*
Katherine Tate, *Officer*
Steve Harvey, *Vice Pres*
Dwight Hood, *Exec Dir*
EMP: 80
SALES (corp-wide): 2.6B **Privately Held**
WEB: www.quest.com
SIC: 7372 Prepackaged software
HQ: Quest Software, Inc.
4 Polaris Way
Aliso Viejo CA 92656
949 754-8000

(P-17969)
RAILSTECH INC
730 Arizona Ave, Santa Monica
(90401-1702)
PHONE...................................267 315-2998
EMP: 23 **EST:** 2020
SALES (est): 3.6MM
SALES (corp-wide): 3.5MM **Privately
Held**
WEB: www.railsbank.com
SIC: 7372 Business oriented computer
software
PA: Railsbank Technology Limited
1 Snowden Street
London EC2A

(P-17970)
RAZZOR TECHNOLOGIES INC
1 Park Plz Fl 6, Irvine (92614-5910)
PHONE...................................949 202-5846
EMP: 13 **EST:** 2013
SALES (est): 505K **Privately Held**
WEB: www.razzortech.com
SIC: 7372 Prepackaged software

(P-17971)
**REAL SOFTWARE SYSTEMS
LLC (PA)**
21255 Burbank Blvd # 220, Woodland Hills
(91367-6681)
PHONE...................................818 313-8000
Kent Sahin, *Mng Member*
Rita Feldman, *Sr Software Eng*
David Engh, *Software Dev*
Swanny Juwono, *Programmer Anys*
Jeremy Fingerman, *Sales Staff*
EMP: 50 **EST:** 1993
SALES (est): 10.3MM **Privately Held**
WEB: www.realsoftwaresystems.com
SIC: 7372 Business oriented computer
software

(P-17972)
RED GATE SOFTWARE INC
144 W Colo Blvd Ste 200, Pasadena
(91105)
PHONE...................................626 993-3949
Tom Curtis, *President*
Michelle Medd, *Partner*
Drew Lawrence, *Sales Staff*
Pete Ruiz, *Sales Staff*
Nina Tompkin, *Sales Staff*
EMP: 23 **EST:** 2011
SQ FT: 5,500
SALES (est): 4.4MM
SALES (corp-wide): 72.2MM **Privately
Held**
WEB: www.red-gate.com
SIC: 7372 Business oriented computer
software
HQ: Red Gate Software Limited
Newnham House
Cambridge CAMBS
122 342-0397

(P-17973)
RELATIONAL CENTER
2717 S Robertson Blvd # 1, Los Angeles
(90034-2442)
PHONE...................................323 935-1807
Traci Bivens Davis, *Principal*
Jami Winkel, *Opers Staff*
Dan Fink, *Deputy Dir*
Jayme Davis, *Instructor*
Penny Timmons, *Internal Med*
EMP: 17 **EST:** 2008
SALES (est): 721.1K **Privately Held**
WEB: www.relationalcenter.org
SIC: 7372 Prepackaged software

(P-17974)
RFL GLOBAL INC
732 E Jefferson Blvd, Los Angeles
(90011-2435)
PHONE...................................323 235-2580
EMP: 15 **EST:** 2014
SALES (est): 690K **Privately Held**
SIC: 7372 Prepackaged Software Services

(P-17975)
**SAGE SOFTWARE HOLDINGS
INC (HQ)**
6561 Irvine Center Dr, Irvine (92618-2118)
PHONE...................................866 530-7243
Stev Swenson, *CEO*
Mack Lout, *CFO*
Doug Meyer, *Vice Pres*
Sabby Gill, *Managing Dir*
Douglas Thorpe, *Training Spec*
EMP: 400 **EST:** 2000
SALES (est): 870.2MM
SALES (corp-wide): 2.4B **Privately Held**
WEB: www.sage.com
SIC: 7372 Business oriented com-
puter software; 7371 custom computer pro-
gramming services
PA: The Sage Group Plc.
North Park Avenue
Newcastle-Upon-Tyne NE13
800 923-0344

(P-17976)
SALESFORCECOM INC
1442 2nd St, Santa Monica (90401-2302)
PHONE...................................310 752-7000
Andy Demari, *Manager*
Paolo Bergamo, *Vice Pres*
Aqeel Syed, *Sr Software Eng*
Devon Prince, *IT/INT Sup*
Kevin Ota, *Senior Mgr*
EMP: 40
SALES (corp-wide): 17.1B **Publicly Held**
WEB: www.salesforce.com
SIC: 7372 Business oriented computer
software
PA: Salesforce.Com, Inc.
415 Mission St Fl 3
San Francisco CA 94105
415 901-7000

(P-17977)
SCOPELY INC (PA)
3530 Hayden Ave Ste A, Culver City
(90232-2413)
PHONE...................................323 400-6618
Walter Driver, *President*
Javier Ferreira, *Co-CEO*
Roxane Lukas,

Tim Obrien, *Officer*
Jake Bales, *Vice Pres*
EMP: 200 **EST:** 2011
SALES (est): 109.7MM **Privately Held**
WEB: www.scopely.com
SIC: 7372 Home entertainment computer
software

(P-17978)
SCRIPLA LLC
11134 Sepulveda Blvd, Mission Hills
(91345-1114)
PHONE...................................818 925-1460
David Deleplane,
EMP: 13 **EST:** 2019
SALES (est): 300K **Privately Held**
SIC: 7372 Publishers' computer software

(P-17979)
SE SOFTWARE INC
3340 Ocean Park Blvd # 1005, Santa Mon-
ica (90405-3255)
P.O. Box 341469, Los Angeles (90034-
9469)
PHONE...................................888 504-9876
Greg Hermanovic, *President*
Sean Lee, *Accountant*
EMP: 15 **EST:** 1995
SALES (est): 967.8K **Privately Held**
SIC: 7372 Prepackaged software

(P-17980)
SELAROM
3234 Concord Ave, Alhambra (91803-1153)
PHONE...................................626 614-6744
Michael A Morales, *President*
EMP: 13 **EST:** 2011
SALES (est): 699.7K **Privately Held**
SIC: 7372 Business oriented computer
software

(P-17981)
SHORTCUTS SOFTWARE INC
7711 Center Ave Ste 550, Huntington
Beach (92647-3075)
PHONE...................................714 622-6600
Rebecca Randall, *CEO*
Malcom Raward, *Treasurer*
Paul Tate, *Vice Pres*
EMP: 30 **EST:** 2005
SALES (est): 4.7MM **Privately Held**
WEB: www.shortcuts.net
SIC: 7372 Business oriented computer
software
HQ: Shortcuts Software Pty Ltd
L 2 South Tower 10 Browning St
South Brisbane QLD 4101

(P-17982)
SIGNAL SCIENCES CORP
600 Corporate Pointe # 1200, Culver City
(90230-7626)
PHONE...................................424 289-0342
Andrew Peterson, *CEO*
Jonathan Divincenzo, *Vice Pres*
Randy Paulk, *Vice Pres*
David Knight, *Technical Staff*
Jonathan Speigner, *Engineer*
EMP: 13 **EST:** 2014
SALES (est): 4.2MM
SALES (corp-wide): 290.8MM **Publicly
Held**
WEB: www.signalsciences.com
SIC: 7372 Application computer software
PA: Fastly, Inc.
475 Brannan St Ste 300
San Francisco CA 94107
844 432-7859

(P-17983)
**SINGULARITY 6 CORPORATION
(PA)**
12203 W Pico Blvd, Los Angeles
(90064-1134)
PHONE...................................310 963-1655
Anthony Leung, *President*
Jeremy Fenske, *Art Dir*
EMP: 19 **EST:** 2018
SALES (est): 1.6MM **Privately Held**
WEB: www.singularity6.com
SIC: 7372 Prepackaged software

(P-17984)
SMART ACTION COMPANY LLC
300 Continental Blvd # 350, El Segundo
(90245-5042)
PHONE...................................3 0 776-9200
Tom Lewis, *CEO*
Brian Morin, *Chief Mktg Ofcr*
Michael Vanca, *Senior VP*
Stuart Bailey, *Vice Pres*
Louise Gold, *Vice Pres*
EMP: 26 **EST:** 2008
SALES (est): 3.7MM **Privately Held**
WEB: www.smartaction.ai
SIC: 7372 Prepackaged software

(P-17985)
SMARTEST EDU INC
Also Called: Formative
10880 Wilshire Blvd # 11, Los Angeles
(90024-4101)
PHONE...................................333 463-6761
Craig Jones, *CEO*
Kevin McFarland, *COO*
Matt Kane, *Risk Mgmt Dir*
Lauren Sprowl, *Business Mgr*
EMP: 14 **EST:** 2013
SALES (est): 2.5MM **Privately Held**
WEB: www.formative.com
SIC: 7372 Prepackaged software

(P-17986)
SMD HOLDINGS 2019 INC
121 W Lexington Dr # 412, Glendale
(91203-2203)
PHONE...................................310 953-4800
Dave Skibinski, *CEO*
George Tierney, *COO*
Deric Frost, *Risk Mgmt Dir*
Douglas Campbell, *Principal*
Christie Threlkeld, *Director*
EMP: 13 **EST:** 2013
SQ FT: 2,200
SALES (est): 1.4MM **Privately Held**
SIC: 7372 Business oriented computer
software

(P-17987)
SMITH MICRO SOFTWARE INC
Mobility Solutions
120 Vantis Dr Ste 350, Aliso Viejo
(92656-2686)
PHONE...................................949 362-5800
Biju Nair, *Branch Mgr*
Ken Shebek, *CIO*
Jonathan Horvath, *Engineer*
Syl Corbin, *Analyst*
Steven Martinez, *Sales Staff*
EMP: 14
SALES (corp-wide): 51.3MM **Publicly
Held**
WEB: www.smithmicro.com
SIC: 7372 Prepackaged software
PA: Smith Micro Software, Inc.
5800 Corporate Dr Ste 500
Pittsburgh PA 15237
412 837-5300

(P-17988)
SPRINGCOIN INC
4551 Glencoe Ave Ste 100, Marina Del Rey
(90292-7902)
PHONE...................................847 322-6349
Katie Fegen, *Principal*
Michael Young, *Sr Software Eng*
David Kravitz, *Research*
Halle McQuilton, *Opers Staff*
EMP: 56
SALES (corp-wide): 4.2MM **Privately
Held**
WEB: www.springlabs.com
SIC: 7372 Prepackaged software
PA: Springcoin, Inc.
20 W Kinzie St Ste 1700
Chicago IL 60654
323 577-9322

(P-17989)
STRATEGY COMPANION CORP
3240 El Camino Real # 120, Irvine
(92602-1384)
PHONE...................................714 460-8398
Robert Sterling, *President*
Eric Halverson, *Partner*
Mandy Lin, *Human Res Mgr*
Bill Tang, *Marketing Staff*
EMP: 70 **EST:** 2006

SALES (est): 5.5MM **Privately Held**
WEB: www.strategycompanion.com
SIC: **7372** Prepackaged software
PA: Strategy Companion Corp.
Scotia Centre 4th Floor
George Town GR CAYMAN

(P-17990)
SUGARSYNC INC
Also Called: Sharpcast
6922 Hollywood Blvd # 500, Los Angeles (90028-6117)
PHONE.....................650 571-5105
Laura Yecies, *President*
Peter Chantel, *CFO*
Mike Ureste, *Administration*
Soumya Sarita, *Accounts Exec*
EMP: 30 EST: 2004
SQ FT: 11,000
SALES (est): 8.4MM **Privately Held**
WEB: www.sugarsync.com
SIC: **7372** Business oriented computer software

(P-17991)
SUPPORT TECHNOLOGIES INC
1939 Deere Ave, Irvine (92606-4818)
PHONE.....................949 442-2957
Tayo Daramole, *President*
Ian Yhap, *Engineer*
George Yu, *Manager*
EMP: 15 EST: 1992
SQ FT: 2,000
SALES (est): 1.1MM **Privately Held**
WEB: www.alexusinfo.com
SIC: **7372** Prepackaged software

(P-17992)
TEACHERZONE INC
31899 Del Obispo St, San Juan Capistrano (92675-3234)
PHONE.....................855 970-9663
Christopher Bates, *CEO*
Tyler Marolf, *Owner*
EMP: 16 EST: 2015
SALES (est): 194.3K **Privately Held**
WEB: www.teacherzone.com
SIC: **7372** Business oriented computer software; educational computer software

(P-17993)
TELESIGN HOLDINGS INC (DH)
13274 Fiji Way Ste 600, Marina Del Rey (90292-7293)
PHONE.....................310 740-9700
Ryan Disraeli, *CEO*
Philipp Gast, *CFO*
Justin Hart, *Chief Mktg Ofcr*
Tom Powledge, *Officer*
Joe Amadea, *Sales Staff*
EMP: 30 EST: 2016
SALES (est): 7.8MM **Privately Held**
WEB: www.telesign.com
SIC: **7372** Prepackaged software

(P-17994)
THEBRAIN TECHNOLOGIES LP
11522 W Washington Blvd, Los Angeles (90066-5914)
PHONE.....................310 751-5000
Harlan Hugh, *General Ptnr*
Shelley Hayduk, *Partner*
EMP: 15 EST: 1996
SQ FT: 2,850
SALES (est): 1.1MM **Privately Held**
WEB: www.thebrain.com
SIC: **7372** Business oriented computer software; home entertainment computer software

(P-17995)
THERMEON CORPORATION (PA)
1175 Warner Ave, Tustin (92780-6458)
PHONE.....................714 731-9191
Rollo S Pickford, *Ch of Bd*
Scott Sampson, *President*
Sharon Miller, *CFO*
Roland Keogh, *Officer*
Chris Anders, *Managing Dir*
EMP: 14 EST: 1967
SQ FT: 5,000

SALES (est): 2.2MM **Privately Held**
WEB: www.thermeon.com
SIC: **7372 5045** Prepackaged software; computer systems analysis & design; computers, peripherals & software

(P-17996)
TI LIMITED LLC (PA)
20335 Ventura Blvd, Woodland Hills (91364-2444)
PHONE.....................323 877-5991
ARI Daniels,
Alberto Gamez,
EMP: 52
SQ FT: 9,000
SALES (est): 9MM **Privately Held**
SIC: **7372 8748** Business oriented computer software; business consulting

(P-17997)
TIMEVALUE SOFTWARE
22 Mauchly, Irvine (92618-2306)
P.O. Box 50250 (92619-0250)
PHONE.....................949 727-1800
Michael Applegate, *President*
Linda Applegate, *Vice Pres*
Charles Miller, *Vice Pres*
Chuck Miller, *Vice Pres*
Terry Reagan, *Vice Pres*
EMP: 25 EST: 1983
SQ FT: 18,000
SALES (est): 4.7MM **Privately Held**
WEB: www.timevalue.com
SIC: **7372 7371** Prepackaged software; computer software development

(P-17998)
TMD WORLDWIDE INCORPORATED
12 Alisal Ct, Aliso Viejo (92656-1850)
PHONE.....................949 306-8877
Timothy Derose, *Principal*
Claudia Sanges, *Administration*
John Lowery, *Software Dev*
Mike Nguyen, *Software Dev*
Nanci Chau, *Technology*
EMP: 13 EST: 2014
SALES (est): 290.3K **Privately Held**
SIC: **7372** Prepackaged software

(P-17999)
TOTAL CMMNICATOR SOLUTIONS INC
Also Called: Spark Compass
11150 Santa Monica Blvd # 600, Los Angeles (90025-3380)
PHONE.....................619 277-1488
Brent Erik Bjoegard, *CEO*
EMP: 95 EST: 2012
SALES (est): 5MM **Privately Held**
WEB: www.sparkcompass.com
SIC: **7372** Application computer software

(P-18000)
TRANSPLANT CONNECT INC
Also Called: I Transplant Enterprise Tech
12121 Wilshire Blvd # 205, Los Angeles (90025-1164)
PHONE.....................310 392-1400
John Piano, *CEO*
Brian Buroker, *Partner*
Lucia Lopez, *Admin Asst*
Nicole Williams, *Admin Asst*
Anukool Gandhi, *Software Dev*
EMP: 28 EST: 2003
SALES (est): 4.6MM **Privately Held**
WEB: www.transplantconnect.com
SIC: **7372 7371** Prepackaged software; custom computer programming services

(P-18001)
TRIBEWORX LLC
4 San Joaquin Plz Ste 150, Newport Beach (92660-5934)
PHONE.....................800 949-3432
EMP: 75
SQ FT: 10,000
SALES (est): 4.9MM **Privately Held**
SIC: **7372** Prepackaged Software Services

(P-18002)
TUTORING EXPERT SERVICES LLC
Also Called: Tradestyle
3751 Motor Ave Unit 34394, Los Angeles (90034-8018)
PHONE.....................424 297-8318
Emmanouil Kantzios, *Owner*
EMP: 15 EST: 2016
SALES (est): 45.1K **Privately Held**
SIC: **8299 8221 7372 7812** Tutoring school; professional schools; educational computer software; educational motion picture production, television; school, college, university consultant; education & teacher association

(P-18003)
UNBROKEN STUDIOS LLC
2121 Park Pl Ste 100, El Segundo (90245-4180)
PHONE.....................310 741-2670
Paul Ohanian, *CEO*
Anthony Scott, *COO*
EMP: 80 EST: 2018
SALES (est): 8.6MM **Privately Held**
WEB: www.poundsand.com
SIC: **7372** Prepackaged software
PA: Pound Sand, Llc
2121 Park Pl
El Segundo CA 90245
310 741-2670

(P-18004)
UPSTANDING LLC
Also Called: Mobilityware
440 Exchange Ste 100, Irvine (92602-1390)
PHONE.....................949 788-9900
Dave Yonamine,
Steve Wetherill, *Vice Pres*
Jill Wilder, *Vice Pres*
Claudia Avitabile, *Admin Mgr*
Lee H McElroy, *Administration*
EMP: 180 EST: 1990
SQ FT: 48,000
SALES (est): 10.5MM **Privately Held**
WEB: www.mobilityware.com
SIC: **7372** Business oriented computer software

(P-18005)
VIDEOAMP INC (PA)
2229 S Carmelina Ave, Los Angeles (90064-1001)
PHONE.....................949 294-0351
Ross McCray, *CEO*
Michael Parkes, *Officer*
Nick Chakalos, *Senior VP*
Anthony Psacharopoulos, *Senior VP*
Rachel Acker, *Vice Pres*
EMP: 93 EST: 2014
SALES (est): 9.2MM **Privately Held**
WEB: www.videoamp.com
SIC: **7372** Prepackaged software

(P-18006)
VISIONARY VR INC
409 N Plymouth Blvd, Los Angeles (90004-3001)
PHONE.....................323 868-7443
Gil Baron, *Principal*
EMP: 18 EST: 2014
SALES (est): 382.3K **Privately Held**
WEB: www.mindshow.com
SIC: **7372** Prepackaged software

(P-18007)
WEB EDUCATIONAL SERVICES INC
Also Called: Lightningfasttrafficschool.com
524 N Mtn View Ave Ste 3, San Bernardino (92401-1208)
PHONE.....................866 719-2159
Efren Morera, *President*
Kathrina Morera, *Associate*
EMP: 13 EST: 2019
SQ FT: 5,000
SALES (est): 953.6K **Privately Held**
SIC: **5999 7372 7374** Educational aids & electronic training materials; educational computer software; service bureau, computer

(P-18008)
WEBEDOCTOR INC
335 N Puente St Ste B, Brea (92821-5274)
PHONE.....................714 990-3999
Anwer Siddiqi, *CEO*
Elizabeth Heath, *Business Mgr*
Tanwer Siddiqi, *Marketing Mgr*
EMP: 17 EST: 1999
SALES (est): 1.6MM **Privately Held**
WEB: www.new.webedoctor.com
SIC: **7372** Application computer software

(P-18009)
WEST COAST CONSULTING LLC
9233 Research Dr Ste 200, Irvine (92618-4294)
PHONE.....................949 250-4102
Rajat Khurana, *CEO*
Vivek Singh, *Tech Recruiter*
Sachin Kaushal, *Technology*
Karam Singh, *Technical Staff*
Reena Rawat, *Business Mgr*
EMP: 125 EST: 1997
SALES (est): 10.9MM **Privately Held**
WEB: www.westcoastllc.com
SIC: **7372** Prepackaged software

(P-18010)
WM TECHNOLOGY INC
41 Discovery, Irvine (92618-3150)
PHONE.....................844 933-3627
Christopher Beals, *CEO*
Scott Gordon, *Ch of Bd*
Juanjo Feijoo, *COO*
Arden Lee, *CFO*
Brian Camire, *Admin Sec*
EMP: 434 EST: 2008 **Privately Held**
SIC: **7372** Prepackaged software; business oriented computer software

(P-18011)
WONDERWARE CORPORATION (DH)
26561 Rancho Pkwy S, Lake Forest (92630-8301)
PHONE.....................949 727-3200
Rick Bullotta, *Vice Pres*
Paula Larson, *Officer*
Brian Dibenedetto, *Senior VP*
Karen Hamilton, *Senior VP*
Peter Kent, *Senior VP*
EMP: 300 EST: 1987
SQ FT: 32,000
SALES (est): 77.6MM **Privately Held**
WEB: www.aveva.com
SIC: **7372** Prepackaged software

(P-18012)
XLSOFT CORPORATION
12 Mauchly Ste K, Irvine (92618-6304)
PHONE.....................949 453-2781
Mitsutoshi Watanabe, *President*
Nanako Watanabe, *CFO*
EMP: 15 EST: 1987
SQ FT: 7,000
SALES (est): 1.9MM **Privately Held**
WEB: www.xlsoft.com
SIC: **7372 7371** Publishers' computer software; custom computer programming services

(P-18013)
YARDI KUBE INC
Also Called: Wun
430 S Fairview Ave, Goleta (93117-3637)
PHONE.....................805 699-2040
John Bennett, *Vice Pres*
Laurie Diaz, *Vice Pres*
Fritz Schindelbeck, *Vice Pres*
Sheila Anderson, *Executive*
Eric Bourassa, *Executive*
EMP: 41 EST: 2018
SALES (est): 7.1MM **Privately Held**
WEB: www.yardikube.com
SIC: **7372** Prepackaged software

(P-18014)
YELLOW MAGIC INCORPORATED
41571 Date St, Murrieta (92562-7086)
P.O. Box 3033, Fallbrook (92088-3033)
PHONE.....................951 506-4005
Ronald G Mintle, *CEO*
Beverly Mintle, *Treasurer*

P
R
O
D
U
C
T
S

&

S
V
C
S

Sam Pretorius, *Vice Pres*
James Snyder, *Vice Pres*
EMP: 17 **EST:** 1984
SALES (est): 2.5MM **Privately Held**
WEB: www.yellowmagic.com
SIC: 7372 7389 Home entertainment computer software; educational computer software;

(P-18015)
ZWIFT INC (PA)
111 W Ocean Blvd Ste 1800, Long Beach
(90802-7936)
PHONE..................................855 469-9438
Eric Min, *CEO*
Jason Kaplan, *Business Dir*
Vinh Tran, *Web Dvlpr*
Alper Akture, *Software Engr*
Ian Gonzalez, *Technician*
EMP: 385 **EST:** 2014
SALES (est): 26.5MM **Privately Held**
WEB: www.zwift.com
SIC: 7372 5961 Publishers' computer software; fitness & sporting goods, mail order

7373 Computer Integrated Systems Design

(P-18016)
ABLE MICROSYSTEMS CORPORATION
Also Called: K I S Computer Center
2021 Las Lomitas Dr, Hacienda Heights
(91745-4131)
PHONE..................................626 723-7777
Richard Chan, *President*
Vivien Mak, *CFO*
Alina Chu, *Admin Sec*
Brent Schmidt, *Sr Ntwrk Engine*
EMP: 22 **EST:** 1985
SALES: 10.6MM **Privately Held**
SIC: 7373 5045 3571 7378 Computer integrated systems design; computers, peripherals & software; electronic computers; computer maintenance & repair

(P-18017)
ALTERYX INC (PA)
3345 Michelson Dr Ste 400, Irvine
(92612-7683)
PHONE..................................888 836-4274
Mark Anderson, *CEO*
Dean A Stoecker, *Ch of Bd*
Robert S Jones, *President*
Scott Davidson, *COO*
Kevin Rubin, *CFO*
EMP: 25 **EST:** 1997
SQ FT: 70,000
SALES (est): 495.3MM **Publicly Held**
WEB: www.alteryx.com
SIC: 7373 7372 Systems software development services; prepackaged software

(P-18018)
ART & LOGIC INC
Also Called: Artlogic
87 N Raymond Ave, Pasadena
(91103-3932)
PHONE..................................818 500-1933
Bob Bajoras, *President*
Paul Hershenson, *Co-Owner*
Tom Bajoras, *Owner*
Andrew Sherbrooke, *Vice Pres*
John Boynton, *Sr Software Eng*
EMP: 55 **EST:** 1991
SQ FT: 1,500
SALES (est): 6.5MM **Privately Held**
WEB: www.artandlogic.com
SIC: 7373 7371 7379 Systems software development services; custom computer programming services; computer related consulting services

(P-18019)
AVEVA SOFTWARE LLC (DH)
Also Called: Wonderware
26561 Rancho Pkwy S, Lake Forest
(92630-8301)
PHONE..................................949 727-3200
Ravi Gopinath, *President*
James Danley, *Treasurer*
Paul Forney, *Vice Pres*
Jeff Greene, *Vice Pres*

Stephen Halsey, *Vice Pres*
EMP: 350 **EST:** 2014
SALES: 264.3MM **Privately Held**
WEB: www.wonderware.com
SIC: 7373 Computer integrated systems design
HQ: Aveva Inc.
920 Mmrial Cy Way Ste 120
Houston TX 77024
713 977-1225

(P-18020)
AZTEK INCORPORATED
13765 Alton Pkwy Ste F, Irvine
(92618-1627)
PHONE..................................949 770-8406
Pamela Lippincott, *President*
EMP: 24 **EST:** 1978
SQ FT: 12,000
SALES (est): 1.2MM **Privately Held**
WEB: www.aztek.com
SIC: 7373 7372 5734 Turnkey vendors, computer systems; prepackaged software; printers & plotters: computers

(P-18021)
CA INC
6100 Center Dr Ste 700, Los Angeles
(90045-9228)
PHONE..................................310 670-6500
Bob Wright, *Manager*
EMP: 89
SALES (corp-wide): 23.8B **Publicly Held**
WEB: www.broadcom.com
SIC: 7373 Computer integrated systems design
HQ: Ca, Inc.
520 Madison Ave
New York NY 10022
800 225-5224

(P-18022)
CGTECH (HQ)
Also Called: Cgtech Vericut
9000 Research Dr, Irvine (92618-4214)
PHONE..................................949 753-1050
Jon L Prun, *President*
Heidi Edmonston, *Admin Asst*
Jia Yan, *Sr Software Eng*
Kelly Anderson, *Info Tech Mgr*
Andy Sosnowski, *Technical Mgr*
EMP: 50 **EST:** 1988
SQ FT: 27,000
SALES: 26.5MM
SALES (corp-wide): 9.9B **Privately Held**
WEB: www.cgtech.com
SIC: 7373 8243 Computer-aided design (CAD) systems service; computer-aided manufacturing (CAM) systems service; software training, computer
PA: Sandvik Ab
Hogbovagen 45
Sandviken 811 3
262 600-00

(P-18023)
COAST TO COAST CMPT PDTS INC
4277 Valley Fair St, Simi Valley
(93063-2940)
PHONE..................................805 244-9500
Rick Roussin, *President*
Wendy Roussin, *Treasurer*
Stacy Schulman, *Senior VP*
Cathy Olwell, *Vice Pres*
Melissa Servatdjoo, *Vice Pres*
▼ **EMP:** 110 **EST:** 1985
SQ FT: 8,800
SALES (est): 49.8MM **Privately Held**
WEB: www.coastcoast.com
SIC: 5734 7373 7371 5112 Magnetic disks; computer tapes; computer systems analysis & design; computer software systems analysis & design, custom; stationery & office supplies

(P-18024)
COMPUTRZED VHCL RGSTRATION INC (HQ)
Also Called: Cvr
1100 W Twn Cntry Rd, Orange
(92868-4600)
PHONE..................................800 386-1746
Scott Heberes, *Principal*
EMP: 50 **EST:** 1985
SQ FT: 7,000

SALES (est): 1.4MM
SALES (corp-wide): 1.6B **Publicly Held**
WEB: www.cvrconnect.com
SIC: 7373 Computer integrated systems design
PA: Cdk Global, Inc.
1950 Hassell Rd
Hoffman Estates IL 60169
847 397-1700

(P-18025)
CONNECTALL LLC
177 E Colo Blvd Ste 200, Pasadena
(91105)
PHONE..................................800 913-7457
Brett Taylor, *CEO*
EMP: 21 **EST:** 2020
SALES (est): 1.9MM **Privately Held**
WEB: www.connectall.com
SIC: 7373 5045 7374 7372 Systems software development services; computers, peripherals & software; computer processing services; application computer software

(P-18026)
CORDOBA CORPORATION
1401 N Broadway, Los Angeles
(90012-1410)
PHONE..................................213 895-0224
George Pla, *President*
Maria Mehranian, *COO*
Christian Rodriguez, *Technical Staff*
Brenda Valencia, *Project Engr*
Christian Diaz, *Engineer*
EMP: 60 **EST:** 1993
SALES (est): 1.2MM **Privately Held**
WEB: www.cordobacorp.com
SIC: 7373 Computer integrated systems design

(P-18027)
CORE BTS INC
5250 Lankershim Blvd # 62, North Hollywood (91601-3186)
PHONE..................................818 766-2400
Josselyn Flores, *Business Anlyst*
Sunal Gupta, *Sr Consultant*
Sunil Mangam, *Sr Consultant*
Patrick Okula, *Manager*
Simon Rilkoff, *Manager*
EMP: 106
SALES (corp-wide): 93.8MM **Privately Held**
WEB: www.corebts.com
SIC: 7373 Systems integration services
HQ: Core Bts, Inc.
5875 Castle Creek Parkway
Indianapolis IN 46250
317 566-6200

(P-18028)
DECISIONPOINT SYSTEMS INTL INC (HQ)
8697 Research Dr, Irvine (92618-4204)
PHONE..................................949 465-0065
Donald W Rowley, *CFO*
Ralph S Hubregsen, *COO*
Melinda Wohl, *Treasurer*
John E Chis, *Senior VP*
EMP: 39 **EST:** 2011
SQ FT: 7,500
SALES (est): 8.7MM
SALES (corp-wide): 31.1MM **Privately Held**
WEB: www.decisionpt.com
SIC: 7373 7372 Systems integration services; prepackaged software
PA: Decisionpoint Systems, Inc.
8697 Research Dr
Irvine CA 92618
949 465-0065

(P-18029)
DISCO PRINT WHL 46 SUP CMPNIES
1891 Alton Pkwy Ste A, Irvine
(92606-4985)
P.O. Box 19337 (92623-9337)
PHONE..................................949 261-8457
Elias G Khamis, *Partner*
Ibrahim G Khamis, *Partner*
ISA G Khamis, *Partner*
Juliette Khamis, *Partner*
Violette Khamis, *Partner*
EMP: 16 **EST:** 1972

SQ FT: 70,500
SALES (est): 2MM **Privately Held**
WEB: www.discoprint.com
SIC: 7373 5734 5712 5943 Systems software development services; computer & software stores; office furniture; office forms & supplies; telephone & telegraph apparatus; furniture

(P-18030)
FASTXCHANGE INC
4640 Admiralty Way # 710, Marina Del Rey
(90292-6621)
PHONE..................................310 827-2445
George Fan, *President*
Paul Postel, *President*
Shepal Patel, *Finance*
EMP: 50 **EST:** 1997
SQ FT: 5,000
SALES (est): 6.4MM **Privately Held**
WEB: www.fastx.com
SIC: 7373 Systems software development services

(P-18031)
FINANCE EXPRESS LLC (HQ)
30071 Tomas Ste 250, Rcho STA Marg
(92688-2186)
P.O. Box 74866, San Clemente (92673-0163)
PHONE..................................949 635-5892
David Huber, *President*
EMP: 53 **EST:** 2003
SQ FT: 6,000
SALES (est): 6.6MM
SALES (corp-wide): 44.3MM **Privately Held**
WEB: www.financeexpress.com
SIC: 7373 6159 Systems integration services; automobile finance leasing
PA: Dealersocket, Inc.
100 Avenida La Pata
San Clemente CA 92673
949 900-0300

(P-18032)
GBL SYSTEMS CORPORATION
760 Paseo Camarillo # 401, Camarillo
(93010-6002)
PHONE..................................805 987-4345
James Buscemi, *President*
Lee Manko, *Sr Software Eng*
Jim Bak, *Info Tech Mgr*
Jessica Smith, *Prgrmr*
Aaron Gavino, *Chief Engr*
EMP: 35 **EST:** 1990
SQ FT: 8,228
SALES (est): 10.3MM **Privately Held**
WEB: www.gblsys.com
SIC: 7373 3559 Computer integrated systems design; electronic component making machinery

(P-18033)
GEMALTO COGENT NC (DH)
2964 Bradley St, Pasadena (91107-1560)
PHONE..................................626 325-9600
Alan Pelligrini, *President*
Alan Pellegrini, *President*
Alan Ball, *Treasurer*
Antonio Lo Brutto, *Exec VF*
Daniel Asraf, *Vice Pres*
▲ **EMP:** 360 **EST:** 1990
SQ FT: 151,000
SALES (est): 49.9MM
SALES (corp-wide): 279.3MM **Privately Held**
WEB: www.sconnect.com
SIC: 7373 Computer-aided system services

(P-18034)
GENEA ENERGY PARTNERS INC
19100 Von Karman Ave # 550, Irvine
(92612-1539)
PHONE..................................714 694-0536
Jon Haahr, *Chairman*
David Balkin, *President*
Joseph Nugent, *President*
Keith Voysey, *CEO*
Rolland Zeleznik, *Vice Pres*
EMP: 85 **EST:** 2006
SQ FT: 10,000

SALES (est): 7.6MM **Privately Held**
WEB: www.getgenea.com
SIC: **7373** Systems software development services

(P-18035)
GREENWAVE REALITY INC
Also Called: Greenwave Systems
15420 Laguna Canyon Rd # 15, Irvine
(92618-2119)
PHONE........................714 805-9283
Martin Manniche, *CEO*
Peter Wilmar Christensen, *CFO*
Peter Christensen, *CFO*
Peter Wilmar Christensen, *CFO*
Troy Pliska, *Exec VP*
▲ EMP: 20 EST: 2008
SALES (est): 4.6MM **Privately Held**
WEB: www.greenwavesystems.com
SIC: **7373** 7372 Systems software development services; prepackaged software

(P-18036)
ICL SYSTEMS INC (PA)
19782 Macarthur Blvd # 260, Irvine
(92612-2486)
PHONE........................877 425-8725
Pat Donahoe, *President*
Michelle Gundy, *Officer*
Brian Hook, *Vice Pres*
Steve Tripp, *Vice Pres*
Scott Rosenau, *Lab Dir*
EMP: 81 EST: 2000
SALES (est): 8.6MM **Privately Held**
WEB: www.iclsystems.com
SIC: **7373** Systems integration services

(P-18037)
IGNIFY INC (DH)
Also Called: Ignify Consulting
200 Pine Ave Ste 400, Long Beach
(90802-3039)
PHONE........................562 219-2000
Sandeep Walia, *CEO*
Christopher Small, *Vice Pres*
Phil Ignify, *Executive*
Pankaj Kumar, *CTO*
Sunil Tehalani, *Technical Staff*
EMP: 35 EST: 1998
SQ FT: 5,000
SALES (est): 46.2MM **Privately Held**
SIC: **5734** 7373 7372 Software, business & non-game; computer integrated systems design; business oriented computer software

(P-18038)
INFORMATION MGT RESOURCES INC (PA)
Also Called: Imri
85 Argonaut Ste 215, Aliso Viejo
(92656-4105)
PHONE........................949 215-8889
Martha Daniel, *CEO*
Brian Berger, *Exec VP*
Adrian Scharf, *Executive Asst*
Doris Joyner, *Admin Asst*
Conor Czyzniejewski, *Network Enginr*
EMP: 130 EST: 1986
SQ FT: 5,000
SALES (est): 16.6MM **Privately Held**
WEB: www.imri.com
SIC: **7373** 8742 7371 Computer integrated systems design; management consulting services; computer software systems analysis & design, custom

(P-18039)
INTERNET CORP FOR ASSGNED NMES (PA)
Also Called: I CANN
12025 Waterfront Dr # 300, Los Angeles
(90094-3220)
PHONE........................310 823-9358
Cherine Chalaby, *Chairman*
Xavier Calvez, *CFO*
Adiel Akplogan, *Vice Pres*
Kathryn A Carver, *Vice Pres*
Larisa Gurnick, *Vice Pres*
EMP: 155 EST: 1998
SALES (est): 149.5MM **Privately Held**
WEB: www.icann.org
SIC: **7373** Systems software development services

(P-18040)
INTERNTNAL COMMUNICATIONS CORP
Also Called: ICC Networking
11801 Pierce St Fl 2, Riverside
(92505-4400)
PHONE........................951 934-0531
Keith Alexis, *CEO*
Mark Spangler, *Partner*
Keith M Alexis, *President*
Amanda Frazier, *COO*
Amada Frazier, *Vice Pres*
▲ EMP: 25 EST: 2011
SALES (est): 3.4MM **Privately Held**
WEB: www.intcomcorp.com
SIC: **7373** 4812 7389 3663 Local area network (LAN) systems integrator; radio telephone communication; ; mobile communication equipment

(P-18041)
JUNIPER NETWORKS INC
Aurrion
6868 Cortona Dr Ste C, Goleta
(93117-1363)
PHONE........................805 880-2000
Volkan Kaman, *Director*
EMP: 60 **Publicly Held**
WEB: www.juniper.net
SIC: **7373** Computer integrated systems design
PA: Juniper Networks, Inc.
1133 Innovation Way
Sunnyvale CA 94089

(P-18042)
LEADINGWAY CORPORATION (PA)
Also Called: Leadingway Knowledge Systems
4199 Campus Dr Ste 550, Irvine
(92612-4694)
PHONE........................949 509-6589
James LI, *President*
WEI-WEI Fang, *CFO*
EMP: 18
SQ FT: 6,600
SALES (est): 1.4MM **Privately Held**
SIC: **7373** 7379 8742 7375 Systems software development services; computer related consulting services; management consulting services; information retrieval services; prepackaged software; custom computer programming services

(P-18043)
LIFERAY INC (PA)
1400 Montefino Ave # 100, Diamond Bar
(91765-5501)
PHONE........................877 543-3729
Bryan Cheung, *CEO*
Karen Newnam, *Partner*
Scott Tachiki, *CFO*
Paul Hinz, *Chief Mktg Ofcr*
Caris Chan, *Officer*
EMP: 187 EST: 2006
SALES (est): 45MM **Privately Held**
WEB: www.liferay.com
SIC: **7373** Systems software development services

(P-18044)
LIGHTCREST LLC
1112 Montana Ave 705, Santa Monica
(90403-1652)
PHONE........................888 320-8495
Zachary Fierstadt,
Denice Legree, *Admin Asst*
Thomas Swigert, *Administration*
Stephen Richter, *Database Admin*
Zeke Dauer, *Engineer*
EMP: 50 EST: 2007
SALES (est): 9.4MM **Privately Held**
WEB: www.lightcrest.com
SIC: **7373** Systems integration services

(P-18045)
LIQUIDATE DIRECT LLC
Also Called: Solid Commerce
2929 Washington Blvd Fl 2, Marina Del Rey
(90292-5546)
PHONE........................800 750-7617
Eran Pick, *CEO*
Alon Berkovich, *COO*
Shawna Snukst, *Bus Dvlpt Dir*

EMP: 50 EST: 2003
SALES (est): 3.8MM **Privately Held**
WEB: www.solidcommerce.com
SIC: **7373** 7371 7379 Computer integrated systems design; custom computer programming services; computer related maintenance services

(P-18046)
LOCKHEED MARTIN UNMANNED
125 Venture Dr Ste 110, San Luis Obispo
(93401-9103)
PHONE........................805 503-4340
Jesse May, *CEO*
EMP: 80 **Publicly Held**
WEB: www.lockheedmartin.com
SIC: **7373** Computer systems analysis & design
HQ: Lockheed Martin Unmanned Integrated Systems, Inc.
133 W Park Loop Nw
Huntsville AL 35806

(P-18047)
MORPHOTRAK LLC (DH)
Also Called: Safran
5515 E La Palma Ave # 100, Anaheim
(92807-2127)
PHONE........................714 238-2000
Celeste Thomasson, *CEO*
Florian Hebras, *CFO*
Clark Nelson, *Vice Pres*
Katie Murphy, *Admin Sec*
Jenny Pelayo, *Administration*
EMP: 175 EST: 1985
SQ FT: 32,000
SALES (est): 42.7MM
SALES (corp-wide): 1.3B **Privately Held**
WEB: www.morphotrak.com
SIC: **7373** Computer integrated systems design

(P-18048)
NANTHEALTH INC (HQ)
2040 E Mariposa Ave, El Segundo
(90245-5027)
PHONE........................310 883-1300
Patrick Soon-Shiong, *Ch of Bd*
Ronald A Louks, *COO*
Bob Petrcu, *CFO*
Tiffany Avery, *Chief Mktg Ofcr*
Sarah Chavarria, *Officer*
EMP: 376 EST: 2010
SQ FT: 8,000
SALES (est): 73.1MM
SALES (corp-wide): 158.2K **Publicly Held**
WEB: www.nanthealth.com
SIC: **7373** Computer integrated systems design
PA: Nantworks, Llc
9920 Jefferson Blvd
Culver City CA 90232
310 883-1300

(P-18049)
NANTWORKS LLC (PA)
9920 Jefferson Blvd, Culver City
(90232-3506)
PHONE........................310 883-1300
Charles N Kenworthy, *Mng Member*
Patrick Soon-Shiong, *Founder*
Steven Zakaio, *Exec VP*
Carl Averion, *Vice Pres*
Maureen Horst Becker, *Vice Pres*
EMP: 112 EST: 2011
SALES: 158.2K **Publicly Held**
WEB: www.nantworks.com
SIC: **7373** Computer-aided system services

(P-18050)
NETAPP INC
6320 Canoga Ave Ste 1500, Woodland Hills
(91367-2563)
PHONE........................818 227-5025
James McCormick III, *Manager*
Teresa Tolentino, *Comms Mgr*
Cecelia Taylor, *Marketing Staff*
EMP: 209
SALES (corp-wide): 6.3B **Publicly Held**
WEB: www.netapp.com
SIC: **7373** Computer integrated systems design

PA: Netapp, Inc.
495 E Java Dr
Sunnyvale CA 95128
408 822-6000

(P-18051)
NETWORK INTGRTION PARTNERS INC
Also Called: Nic Partners
11981 Jack Benny Dr # 10, Rancho Cucamonga (91739-9232)
PHONE........................909 919-2800
Franklin P Spaeth, *President*
EMP: 80 EST: 2007
SQ FT: 6,000
SALES (est): 21.8MM **Privately Held**
WEB: www.nicpartersinc.com
SIC: **7373** Local area network (LAN) systems integrator

(P-18052)
NEW DIRECTIONS TECH INC (PA)
Also Called: Ndti
137 W Drummond Ave Ste A, Ridgecrest
(93555-3583)
PHONE........................760 384-2444
Cedric Knight, *President*
Bert Belisch, *Officer*
Michele E Hoopes, *Exec VP*
Michele Hoopes, *Exec VP*
John Dermatas, *Business Dir*
EMP: 65 EST: 1992
SQ FT: 6,000
SALES (est): 24.2MM **Privately Held**
WEB: www.ndti.net
SIC: **7373** 7374 8711 7371 Systems software development services; data processing & preparation; engineering services; computer software development & applications; computer facilities management

(P-18053)
NORTHROP GRUMMAN SYSTEMS CORP
Also Called: Northrop Grumman CMS
21240 Burbank Blvd, Woodland Hills
(91367-6680)
PHONE........................818 715-4854
Roy Medland, *Branch Mgr*
EMP: 133 **Publicly Held**
WEB: www.northropgrumman.com
SIC: **7373** 3812 Systems integration services; search & navigation equipment
HQ: Northrop Grumman Systems Corporation
2980 Fairview Park Dr
Falls Church VA 22042
703 280-2900

(P-18054)
NORTHROP GRUMMAN SYSTEMS CORP
5161 Verdugo Way, Camarillo
(93012-8603)
PHONE........................805 987-9739
Jim Lueck, *Branch Mgr*
EMP: 133 **Publicly Held**
WEB: www.northropgrumman.com
SIC: **7373** 8731 8711 7371 Computer systems analysis & design; commercial physical research; engineering services; custom computer programming services
HQ: Northrop Grumman Systems Corporation
2980 Fairview Park Dr
Falls Church VA 22042
703 280-2900

(P-18055)
NTT DATA INC
1000 Corporate Center Dr # 140, Monterey Park (91754-7610)
PHONE........................213 228-2500
Fax: 323 261-3030
EMP: 93
SALES (corp-wide): 93.3B **Privately Held**
SIC: **7373** Computer Systems Design
HQ: Ntt Data, Inc.
5601 Gran Pkwy Ste 1000
Plano TX 75024
800 745-3263

PRODUCTS & SVCS

(P-18056)
OBERMAN TIVOLI & PICKERT INC
Also Called: Media Services
500 S Sepulveda Blvd # 500, Los Angeles
(90049-3551)
PHONE.................................310 440-9600
Robert Oberman, *President*
Barry Oberman, *CEO*
Sanaa Wadsworth, *CFO*
Steve Bizenov, *Vice Pres*
Anthony Lopez, *Vice Pres*
EMP: 230 **EST:** 1989
SALES (est): 26MM **Privately Held**
WEB: www.mediaservices.com
SIC: 7373 8721 8741 Systems software development services; payroll accounting service; business management

(P-18057)
P-COVE ENTERPRISES INC
8745 Remmet Ave, Canoga Park
(91304-1519)
PHONE.................................818 341-1101
Jonathan Manhan, *CEO*
EMP: 59 **EST:** 2011
SALES (est): 17MM **Privately Held**
SIC: 7373 Value-added resellers, computer systems

(P-18058)
PRESENTATION PRODUCTS INC (PA)
Also Called: Spinitar
16751 Knott Ave, La Mirada (90638-6013)
PHONE.................................714 367-2900
Joseph J Rogina Jr, *CEO*
James Jeffrey Irvin, *President*
Scott Kroeze, *Exec VP*
David Taccone, *Exec VP*
Dan Tompkins, *Exec VP*
▲ **EMP:** 80
SQ FT: 18,000
SALES (est): 36.2MM **Privately Held**
WEB: www.spinitar.com
SIC: 5999 7373 7622 Audio-visual equipment & supplies; computer systems analysis & design; tape recorder repair; video repair

(P-18059)
PRODUCT DATA INTGRTION TECH IN (PA)
Also Called: Modulant
111 W Ocean Blvd Fl 4, Long Beach
(90802-4633)
PHONE.................................562 495-6500
Alfred Johnson, *President*
Dawn Porter, *Vice Pres*
EMP: 56 **EST:** 1989
SALES (est): 7.9MM **Privately Held**
WEB: www.modulant.com
SIC: 7373 Systems integration services

(P-18060)
QUEST SOFTWARE INC (HQ)
4 Polaris Way, Aliso Viejo (92656-5356)
PHONE.................................949 754-8000
Patrick Nichols, *CEO*
Carol Oberle, *Partner*
Gary Broadwater, *President*
Kevin E Brooks, *Vice Pres*
Carolyn McCarthy, *Vice Pres*
EMP: 600 **EST:** 1987
SQ FT: 170,000
SALES (est): 647.6MM
SALES (corp-wide): 2.6B **Privately Held**
WEB: www.quest.com
SIC: 7373 7379 7372 Computer integrated systems design; computer related consulting services; business oriented computer software
PA: Francisco Partners Management, L.P.
1 Letterman Dr Ste 410
San Francisco CA 94129
415 418-2900

(P-18061)
QUOTIT CORPORATION
721 S Parker St Ste 330, Orange
(92868-4739)
PHONE.................................714 564-5000
Chad Hogan, *Senior VP*
Majchrowski Thomas, *Vice Pres*
Kimberly Longenecker, *Analyst*
Ken Banfill, *Sales Staff*
Rick Newman, *Maintence Staff*
EMP: 162 **EST:** 1999
SQ FT: 2,400
SALES (est): 5MM **Publicly Held**
WEB: www.quotit.com
SIC: 7373 Systems software development services
HQ: National General Holdings Corp.
59 Maiden Ln Fl 38
New York NY 10038

(P-18062)
RESULT GROUP INC
2603 Main St Ste 710, Irvine (92614-4263)
PHONE.................................480 777-7130
William Derick Robson, *President*
David Griffiths, *Admin Sec*
EMP: 13 **EST:** 2003
SALES (est): 921.1K
SALES (corp-wide): 3.9B **Privately Held**
WEB: www.wynnesystems.com
SIC: 7373 7372 Systems software development services; business oriented computer software
HQ: Wynne Systems, Inc.
2601 Main St Ste 270
Irvine CA 92614

(P-18063)
SAVEDAILYCOM INC (HQ)
1503 S Coast Dr Ste 330, Costa Mesa
(92626-1509)
PHONE.................................562 795-7500
Jeff Mahony, *CEO*
Gregory D Vacca, *President*
Jeffrey Mahony, *COO*
Mike Cronin, *CFO*
EMP: 59 **EST:** 1999
SQ FT: 3,000
SALES (est): 6.8MM **Privately Held**
WEB: www.savedaily.com
SIC: 7373 6282 Computer system selling services; investment advice
PA: Savedaily Holdings Corp.
1503 S Coast Dr Ste 330
Costa Mesa CA 92626
562 795-7500

(P-18064)
SECOM INTERNATIONAL (PA)
15905 S Broadway, Gardena (90248-2405)
PHONE.................................310 641-1290
Ted Burton, *President*
Amir Behic, *CFO*
Terry Bixler, *Vice Pres*
Linda Vose, *Admin Sec*
George Horner, *Software Engr*
EMP: 52 **EST:** 1978
SALES (est): 8.2MM **Privately Held**
WEB: www.secomintl.com
SIC: 7373 3446 3559 7371 Turnkey vendors, computer systems; architectural metalwork; parking facility equipment & supplies; computer software systems analysis & design, custom

(P-18065)
SIMULATIONS PLUS INC (PA)
42505 10th St W Ste 103, Lancaster
(93534-7059)
PHONE.................................661 723-7723
Shawn O'Connor, *CEO*
Walter S Woltosz, *Ch of Bd*
John A Dibella, *President*
Will Frederick, *CFO*
Renee Bouche, *Officer*
EMP: 62 **EST:** 1996
SQ FT: 13,500
SALES: 46.4MM **Publicly Held**
WEB: www.simulations-plus.com
SIC: 7373 Systems software development services

(P-18066)
SOFTWARE DYNAMICS INCORPORATED
8501 Fllbrook Ave Ste 200, Canoga Park
(91304)
PHONE.................................818 992-3299
Matthew Hale, *President*
Christopher J Stein, *Treasurer*
Richard Dobb, *Admin Sec*
EMP: 133 **EST:** 1982
SQ FT: 40,000
SALES (est): 1.3MM **Publicly Held**
WEB: www.aciworldwide.com
SIC: 7373 7371 Computer systems analysis & design; computer software development
HQ: S1 Corporation
705 Westech Dr
Norcross GA 30092
678 966-9499

(P-18067)
SOLESTAGE INC
Also Called: Store & Online
17651 Railroad St, City of Industry
(91748-1194)
PHONE.................................909 576-1309
Lane Wang, *CEO*
EMP: 50 **EST:** 2013
SALES (est): 15MM **Privately Held**
SIC: 7373 7371 Value-added resellers, computer systems; computer software development & applications

(P-18068)
SOLUGENIX CORPORATION (PA)
601 Valencia Ave Ste 260, Brea
(92823-6357)
PHONE.................................866 749-7658
Shashi Jasthi, *CEO*
Abhay Jajoo, *Senior VP*
Damola Akinola, *Vice Pres*
Crystal A Kolosick, *Executive Asst*
Christie Crisman, *Admin Asst*
EMP: 138
SQ FT: 1,600
SALES (est): 35.5MM **Privately Held**
WEB: www.solugenix.com
SIC: 7373 Computer integrated systems design

(P-18069)
SOURCE IT USA INC
1150 S Olive St, Los Angeles (90015-2211)
PHONE.................................714 318-4428
Peter Deralas, *CEO*
Robert Easton, *Senior Partner*
Fatana Deralas, *Vice Pres*
Stephen Beardsley, *Managing Dir*
Gerald Chidowe, *Managing Dir*
EMP: 22 **EST:** 2005
SALES (est): 1.8MM **Privately Held**
WEB: www.sourceitusa.com
SIC: 7373 3577 Value-added resellers, computer systems; computer peripheral equipment

(P-18070)
SURVIOS INC
4501 Glencoe Ave, Marina Del Rey
(90292-6372)
PHONE.................................310 736-1503
Nathan Burba, *CEO*
Ben Kim, *President*
Emily Procek, *Office Mgr*
Richard Barnes, *Sr Software Eng*
Lewis Hu, *Research*
EMP: 24 **EST:** 2013
SALES (est): 2.5MM **Privately Held**
WEB: www.survios.com
SIC: 7373 7372 Computer integrated systems design; prepackaged software; home entertainment computer software; publishers' computer software

(P-18071)
TRAMS INC (DH)
7 Lower Blackwater Cyn Rd, Rolling Hills
(90274-4053)
PHONE.................................310 641-8726
Lee B Rosen, *President*
Jay Jones, *Vice Pres*
Ronald Larson, *Vice Pres*
EMP: 65 **EST:** 1984
SALES (est): 8.2MM **Publicly Held**
WEB: www.trestechnologies.com
SIC: 7373 Systems software development services
HQ: Sabre Glbl Inc.
3150 Sabre Dr
Southlake TX 76092
682 605-1000

(P-18072)
TRANSCENTRA INC
20500 Belshaw Ave, Carson (90746-3506)
PHONE.................................310 603-0105
Dwayne Moore, *Branch Mgr*
EMP: 530
SALES (corp-wide): 1.2B **Publicly Held**
WEB: www.exelatech.com
SIC: 7373 Systems software development services
HQ: Transcentra, Inc.
4145 Shackleford Rd # 330
Norcross GA 30093
678 728-2500

(P-18073)
URBAN INSIGHT INC
3530 Wilshire Blvd # 128, Los Angeles
(90010-2328)
PHONE.................................213 792-2000
Chris Steins, *CEO*
Abhijeet Chavan, *COO*
EMP: 18 **EST:** 1997
SQ FT: 4,000 **Privately Held**
WEB: www.urbaninsight.com
SIC: 7373 7372 7371 8748 Computer integrated systems design; business oriented computer software; application computer software; custom computer programming services; custom computer programming services; systems engineering consultant, ex. computer or professional

(P-18074)
WEST PUBLISHING CORPORATION
Also Called: Elite
800 Crprate Pinte Ste 150, Culver City
(90230)
P.O. Box 51606, Los Angeles (90051-5906)
PHONE.................................424 243-2100
Salim Sunderji, *Vice Pres*
EMP: 178
SALES (corp-wide): 10.6B **Publicly Held**
WEB: www.thomsonreuters.com
SIC: 7373 7371 Computer integrated systems design; custom computer programming services
HQ: West Publishing Corporation
610 Opperman Dr
Eagan MN 55123
651 687-7000

(P-18075)
WYTCOTE INC
3 Park Plz Ste 480, Irvine (92614-2568)
PHONE.................................877 472-5587
Frank Gomez, *CEO*
John Wilkerson, *President*
Bo Larsson, *COO*
Jason Derry, *Info Tech Dir*
EMP: 15 **EST:** 2016
SALES (est): 1.1MM **Privately Held**
WEB: www.wytcote.com
SIC: 7373 3821 3826 3823 Systems integration services; laboratory apparatus & furniture; analytical instruments; industrial instrmnts msrmnt display/control process variable; telephone communication, except radio; radio telephone communication

(P-18076)
XP SYSTEMS CORPORATION (HQ)
405 Science Dr, Moorpark (93021-2247)
PHONE.................................805 532-9100
John Edwards, *President*
Diane Atkins, *Vice Pres*
Drew Foley, *Principal*
Tina Laramie, *Executive Asst*
Teresa Farrow, *Human Res Mgr*
EMP: 200 **EST:** 1992
SQ FT: 109,256
SALES (est): 22.6MM
SALES (corp-wide): 14.8B **Publicly Held**
WEB: www.fiserv.com
SIC: 7373 Computer integrated systems design
PA: Fiserv, Inc.
255 Fiserv D
Brookfield W 53045
262 879-5000

▲ = Import ▼=Export
◆ =Import/Export

(P-18077)
YANG-MING INTERNATIONAL CORP
Also Called: Rackmountpro.com
595 Yorbita Rd, La Puente (91744-5956)
PHONE..................626 956-0100
Betty B Shou, *President*
Stephen Shou, *Vice Pres*
Aron Liu, *General Mgr*
Guang Kong, *Engineer*
Sunny Kwong, *Opers Staff*
◆ **EMP:** 25 **EST:** 1994
SQ FT: 10,000
SALES (est): 13.9MM **Privately Held**
WEB: www.rackmountpro.com
SIC: 7373 3571 Systems integration services; electronic computers

---

7374 Data & Computer Processing & Preparation

(P-18078)
4MEDICA INC (PA)
13160 Mindanao Way # 350, Marina Del Rey (90292-7915)
PHONE..................310 695-3300
Oleg Bess, *CEO*
Amy Muradyan, *CFO*
Brian Keefe, *Vice Pres*
Ramesh Natarajan, *Director*
EMP: 95 **EST:** 1999
SQ FT: 6,000
SALES (est): 8.6MM **Privately Held**
WEB: www.4medica.com
SIC: 7374 Computer processing services

(P-18079)
AUTOMATIC DATA PROCESSING INC
Also Called: ADP
3972 Barranca Pkwy J610, Irvine (92606-1204)
PHONE..................949 751-0360
Cory Simons, *Agent*
EMP: 165
SALES (corp-wide): 14.5B **Publicly Held**
WEB: www.adp.com
SIC: 7374 Data processing service
PA: Automatic Data Processing, Inc.
1 Adp Blvd Ste 1 # 1
Roseland NJ 07068
973 974-5000

(P-18080)
AUTOMATIC DATA PROCESSING INC
Also Called: ADP
400 W Covina Blvd, San Dimas (91773-2954)
PHONE..................800 225-5237
Rodney Hroblak, *Principal*
Sheryll Cannon, *Vice Pres*
Eileen McCormick, *Vice Pres*
Susan Gabriel, *Business Anlyst*
Shari Kelly, *Project Mgr*
EMP: 117
SALES (corp-wide): 14.5B **Publicly Held**
WEB: www.adp.com
SIC: 7374 8721 Data processing service; accounting, auditing & bookkeeping
PA: Automatic Data Processing, Inc.
1 Adp Blvd Ste 1 # 1
Roseland NJ 07068
973 974-5000

(P-18081)
BIRCH STREET SYSTEMS LLC
Also Called: Birchstreet
1301 Dove St Ste 300, Newport Beach (92660-2462)
PHONE..................949 567-7100
Sushil Garg, *CEO*
Doug Sanborn, *President*
Bill Hirsch, *Vice Pres*
Jim Oquinn, *Vice Pres*
Sue Pfister, *Vice Pres*
EMP: 59 **EST:** 2002
SALES (est): 8.5MM **Privately Held**
WEB: www.birchstreetsystems.com
SIC: 7374 Data processing & preparation

(P-18082)
BLACK KNIGHT INFOSERV LLC
2500 Redhill Ave Ste 100, Santa Ana (92705-5518)
PHONE..................904 854-5100
Miriam Moore, *Branch Mgr*
EMP: 120
SALES (corp-wide): 1.2B **Publicly Held**
WEB: www.blackknightinc.com
SIC: 7374 Data processing & preparation
HQ: Black Knight Infoserv, Llc
601 Riverside Ave
Jacksonville FL 32204

(P-18083)
DESIGN PEOPLE
1700 E Walnut Ave Ste 400, El Segundo (90245-2609)
PHONE..................800 969-5799
Jon Krabbe, *Officer*
Tiger Bitanga, *CEO*
Eve Sastre, *Officer*
Luigi Amante, *Vice Pres*
Joey Perez, *Project Mgr*
EMP: 160 **EST:** 1998
SQ FT: 9,200
SALES (est): 11.8MM **Privately Held**
WEB: www.thedesignpeople.com
SIC: 7374 Computer graphics service

(P-18084)
ELEVATED RESOURCES INC
3990 Westerly Pl Ste 270, Newport Beach (92660-2348)
PHONE..................949 419-6632
Robert Morris, *CEO*
Bruce Ferguson, *Vice Pres*
Mike Willner, *Principal*
Nambi Balasubramamani, *Info Tech Dir*
Nambi Balasubramaniya, *Info Tech Dir*
EMP: 225 **EST:** 2007
SQ FT: 1,900
SALES (est): 23.1MM **Privately Held**
WEB: www.elevatedresources.com
SIC: 7374 Data processing & preparation

(P-18085)
ENCLARITY INC
16815 Von Karman Ave # 1, Irvine (92606-2404)
PHONE..................949 797-7160
Sean Downs, *CEO*
Paul Perleberg, *President*
Warren Gouk Andrea, *CFO*
Scott Marber, *Vice Pres*
Brian Smith, *Vice Pres*
EMP: 997 **EST:** 2005
SQ FT: 3,500
SALES (est): 2.2MM
SALES (corp-wide): 9.4B **Privately Held**
WEB: www.risk.lexisnexis.com
SIC: 7374 Data processing service
HQ: Lexisnexis Risk Solutions Inc.
1000 Alderman Dr
Alpharetta GA 30005
678 694-6000

(P-18086)
ENERVEE CORPORATION
1746 Abbot Kinney Blvd, Venice (90291-4839)
PHONE..................650 996-7048
Matthias Kurwig, *CEO*
Donald Epperson, *Ch of Bd*
Alex Katzman, *Vice Pres*
Brian Leung, *Software Engr*
Regina Sasin, *Software Engr*
EMP: 73 **EST:** 2009
SALES: 11.2MM **Privately Held**
WEB: www.enervee.com
SIC: 7374 Computer processing services

(P-18087)
EPOCHCOM LLC
3110 Main St Ste 220, Santa Monica (90405-5353)
PHONE..................310 664-5700
Joel Hall, *Mng Member*
Esther Martinez, *COO*
David Bonsukan, *Officer*
Harmik Gharapetian, *Vice Pres*
Gharapetian Harmik, *Vice Pres*
EMP: 150 **EST:** 2004
SQ FT: 22,000
SALES (est): 14.6MM **Privately Held**
WEB: www.epoch.com
SIC: 7374 Data processing service

(P-18088)
ESP COMPUTER SERVICES INC (PA)
12444 Victory Blvd Fl 4, North Hollywood (91606-3156)
PHONE..................818 487-4500
Jack Miller, *President*
Joe Hamby, *CTO*
Bill Coffman, *Director*
Illescas Mitchell, *Manager*
Chris Barnes, *Accounts Mgr*
EMP: 85 **EST:** 1969
SALES (est): 9.9MM **Privately Held**
WEB: www.espcomp.com
SIC: 7374 7371 Data processing service; custom computer programming services

(P-18089)
FISERV INC
8413 Fallbrook Ave, West Hills (91304-3226)
PHONE..................818 226-4400
EMP: 100
SALES (corp-wide): 14.8B **Publicly Held**
WEB: www.fiserv.com
SIC: 7374 Data Processing/Preparation
PA: Fiserv, Inc.
255 Fiserv Dr
Brookfield WI 53045
262 879-5000

(P-18090)
FLYR INC
3205 Pico Blvd, Santa Monica (90405-2113)
PHONE..................415 841-3597
Alexander Mans, *CEO*
Andrew Jing, *Director*
EMP: 70 **EST:** 2013
SALES (est): 2.8MM **Privately Held**
WEB: www.flyrlabs.com
SIC: 7374 Data processing & preparation

(P-18091)
GOODRX HOLDINGS INC (PA)
2701 Olympic Blvd, Santa Monica (90404-4183)
PHONE..................855 268-2822
Douglas Hirsch, *Co-CEO*
Bansi Nagji, *President*
Andrew Slutsky, *President*
Karsten Voermann, *CFO*
Trevor Bezdek, *Co-CEO*
EMP: 217 **EST:** 2011
SQ FT: 29,000
SALES (est): 550.7MM **Publicly Held**
WEB: www.goodrx.com
SIC: 7374 Computer processing services

(P-18092)
GREENSOFT TECHNOLOGY INC
155 S El Molino Ave # 100, Pasadena (91101-2563)
PHONE..................323 254-5961
Larry Yen, *President*
Jon Wu, *Vice Pres*
Linda Yin, *Project Engr*
EMP: 121 **EST:** 2002
SALES (est): 5.9MM **Privately Held**
WEB: www.greensofttech.com
SIC: 7374 Data processing service

(P-18093)
HEALTH DATA VISION INC (PA)
425 W Broadway Ste 100, Glendale (91204-1269)
PHONE..................866 969-3222
Jay Ackerman, *President*
Rita Young, *COO*
Ryan Peterson, *Senior VP*
EMP: 65 **EST:** 2009
SQ FT: 2,200
SALES (est): 9.9MM **Privately Held**
WEB: www.reveleer.com
SIC: 7374 Data processing & preparation

(P-18094)
HONK TECHNOLOGIES INC
2251 Barry Ave, Los Angeles (90064-1401)
P.O. Box 910 (90078-0910)
PHONE..................800 979-3162
Corey Brundage, *CEO*
Dan Rosenthal, *CFO*
Rochelle Thielen, *Exec VP*
Carlo Macalagay, *Finance Mgr*
Brian Colsell, *Director*
EMP: 151 **EST:** 2014
SQ FT: 8,000
SALES (est): 75MM **Privately Held**
WEB: www.honkforhelp.com
SIC: 7374 7372 7371 Data processing & preparation; business oriented computer software; custom computer programming services

(P-18095)
I HOT LEADS
19671 Beach Blvd Ste 204, Huntington Beach (92648-5905)
PHONE..................714 960-8028
EMP: 56
SALES (est): 1.9MM **Privately Held**
WEB: www.ihotleads.com
SIC: 7374 Data Processing/Preparation

(P-18096)
IKANO COMMUNICATIONS INC (PA)
Also Called: A & S Technologies
9221 Corbin Ave Ste 260, Northridge (91324-1625)
PHONE..................801 924-0900
Jim Murphy, *CEO*
Sam Ghahremanpour, *President*
George Mitsopoulos, *COO*
Dean Russ, *Vice Pres*
Michelle Chance, *Technical Staff*
EMP: 91 **EST:** 1991
SQ FT: 50,000
SALES (est): 17.4MM **Privately Held**
WEB: www.ikano.com
SIC: 7374 Data processing & preparation

(P-18097)
LEAF GROUP LTD (PA)
1655 26th St, Santa Monica (90404-4016)
PHONE..................310 656-6253
Sean Moriarty, *CEO*
Deborah A Benton, *Ch of Bd*
Brian Pike, *COO*
Brian Gephart, *CFO*
Brian Regan, *Bd of Directors*
EMP: 290 **EST:** 2006
SQ FT: 52,000
SALES (est): 212MM **Privately Held**
WEB: www.leafgroup.com
SIC: 7374 Data processing & preparation

(P-18098)
LEGALZOOMCOM INC (PA)
101 N Brand Blvd Fl 11, Glendale (91203-2638)
PHONE..................323 962-8600
Dan Wernikoff, *CEO*
Kamal Akwara, *Partner*
Jeffrey Stibel, *Ch of Bd*
Noel Watson, *CFO*
John Buchanan, *Chief Mktg Ofcr*
EMP: 300 **EST:** 2000
SQ FT: 56,000
SALES (est): 470.6MM **Publicly Held**
WEB: www.legalzoom.com
SIC: 7374 8111 Data processing & preparation; legal services

(P-18099)
MANAGEMENT APPLIED PRGRM INC (PA)
Also Called: BENEFIT PROGRAMS ADMINISTRATIO
13191 Crossroads Pkwy N # 205, City of Industry (91746-3434)
PHONE..................562 463-5000
Phiroze Dalal, *CEO*
Hormazd Dalal, *CFO*
Edward Simon, *Vice Pres*
Judi Knore, *Asst Admin*
Tout Sanh, *Programmer Anys*
EMP: 176 **EST:** 1964
SALES (est): 7.4MM **Privately Held**
WEB: www.mapinc.com
SIC: 7374 Data processing service

(P-18100)
MERCURY SYSTEMS INC
10855 Bus Ctr Dr Ste A, Cypress (90630)
PHONE..................714 898-8200
Mark Aslett, *President*

EMP: 85
SALES (corp-wide): 924MM **Publicly Held**
WEB: www.mrcy.com
SIC: 7374 Data processing service
PA: Mercury Systems, Inc.
50 Minuteman Rd
Andover MA 01810
978 256-1300

(P-18101)
MINDBODY INC (PA)
4051 Broad St Ste 220, San Luis Obispo (93401-8723)
PHONE....................877 755-4279
Richard Stollmeyer, *Ch of Bd*
Michelle Van Horn, *Partner*
Michael Mansbach, *President*
Josh McCarter, *President*
Brett White, *COO*
EMP: 109 EST: 2001
SQ FT: 160,000
SALES (est): 182.6MM **Privately Held**
WEB: www.mindbodyonline.com
SIC: 7374 7372 8741 Data processing & preparation; business oriented computer software; business management

(P-18102)
MOCEAN LLC
2440 S Sepulveda Blvd # 150, Los Angeles (90064-1786)
PHONE....................310 481-0808
Craig R Murray, *Mng Member*
Stuart Boone, *President*
Michael McIntyre, *President*
Roshone Harmon, *Vice Pres*
Kelsey Anderson, *Creative Dir*
EMP: 200 EST: 2000
SALES (est): 19.9MM **Privately Held**
WEB: www.moceanla.com
SIC: 7374 7822 Computer graphics service; motion picture distribution

(P-18103)
ORDERMARK INC
12045 Waterfront Dr # 400, Playa Vista (90094-3226)
P.O. Box 260206, Encino (91426-0206)
PHONE....................833 673-3762
Alex Canter, *CEO*
Mike Jacobs, *COO*
Paul Allen, *Officer*
Arpan Desai, *CTO*
Liz Coster, *Director*
EMP: 71 EST: 2017
SALES (est): 5.6MM **Privately Held**
WEB: www.ordermark.com
SIC: 7374 Data processing & preparation

(P-18104)
PROSUM INC (PA)
Also Called: Prosum Technology Services
2201 Park Pl Ste 102, El Segundo (90245-5167)
PHONE....................310 426-0600
Ravi Chatwani, *COO*
Emily Fortenberry, *Partner*
John Petri, *CFO*
Ken Aster, *Co-CEO*
Amy Chidthai, *Vice Pres*
EMP: 57 EST: 1996
SALES (est): 23.1MM **Privately Held**
WEB: www.prosum.com
SIC: 7374 8748 Computer graphics service; systems engineering consultant, ex. computer or professional

(P-18105)
PROSUM INC
3990 Westerly Pl Ste 100, Newport Beach (92660-2300)
PHONE....................949 732-1122
Ken Aster, *Branch Mgr*
Amit Bhatia, *Vice Pres*
Nisha Ranganath, *Executive Asst*
Lukasz Buchwald, *Info Tech Mgr*
Aaron Heydinger, *Tech Recruiter*
EMP: 54
SALES (corp-wide): 23.1MM **Privately Held**
WEB: www.prosum.com
SIC: 7374 8748 Computer graphics service; systems engineering consultant, ex. computer or professional

PA: Prosum Inc.
2201 Park Pl Ste 102
El Segundo CA 90245
310 426-0600

(P-18106)
QUESTUS INC (PA)
3350 E Birch St Ste 110, Brea (92821-6290)
PHONE....................415 677-5719
Jordan Berg, *CEO*
Debbie Dumont, *Exec VP*
Jeff Wagener, *Exec VP*
Will Chamberlin, *Vice Pres*
Debrianna Obara, *Vice Pres*
EMP: 50 EST: 1998
SQ FT: 4,000
SALES (est): 9MM **Privately Held**
WEB: www.questus.com
SIC: 7374 Computer graphics service

(P-18107)
RUITENG INTERNET TECHNOLOGY CO
1344 W Foothill Blvd D, Azusa (91702-2846)
PHONE....................302 597-7438
Canzhi Zhen, *Principal*
Wendy Huang, *Principal*
Chris Zhang, *Principal*
◆ EMP: 220 EST: 2018
SQ FT: 500
SALES (est): 3.5MM **Privately Held**
SIC: 7374 Computer graphics service

(P-18108)
SARITASA LLC (PA)
Also Called: Clickbrand
20411 Sw Birch St Ste 330, Newport Beach (92660-1771)
PHONE....................949 200-6839
Nik Froehlich, *CEO*
Quan Dao, *Vice Pres*
Aaron Franko, *Vice Pres*
Melinda McCartney, *Vice Pres*
Max Maximov, *Technical Mgr*
EMP: 92 EST: 2005
SQ FT: 12,000
SALES (est): 8.7MM **Privately Held**
WEB: www.saritasa.com
SIC: 7374 8742 7336 7371 Computer graphics service; marketing consulting services; graphic arts & related design; custom computer programming services; computer software development & applications; software programming applications

(P-18109)
SECURE ONE DATA SOLUTIONS LLC
11090 Artesia Blvd Ste D, Cerritos (90703-2545)
PHONE....................562 924-7056
David Sandobal, *President*
EMP: 90 **Privately Held**
WEB: www.secure1outsource.com
SIC: 7374 Data punch service; data processing service
PA: Secure One Data Solutions, Llc
2801 N 33rd Ave Ste 1
Phoenix AZ 85009

(P-18110)
SOCIETY6 LLC
1655 26th St, Santa Monica (90404-4016)
PHONE....................310 394-6400
Sean Moriarty,
Andrea Stanford, *Vice Pres*
Rory Wood, *Marketing Staff*
EMP: 66 EST: 2011
SQ FT: 25,000
SALES (est): 9.8MM **Privately Held**
WEB: www.society6.com
SIC: 7374 Computer graphics service
PA: Leaf Group Ltd.
1655 26th St
Santa Monica CA 90404

(P-18111)
SONY PICTURES IMAGEWORKS INC
9050 Washington Blvd, Culver City (90232-2518)
PHONE....................310 840-8000
Bob Osher, *President*
Robin Garcia, *Treasurer*
Linda Riewe, *Treasurer*
Ken Ralston, *Vice Pres*
Stephanie Greco, *Department Mgr*
EMP: 1000 EST: 1992
SALES (est): 98.4MM **Privately Held**
WEB: www.imageworks.com
SIC: 7374 Computer graphics service
HQ: Sony Pictures Entertainment, Inc.
10202 Washington Blvd
Culver City CA 90232
310 244-4000

(P-18112)
STARK SERVICES
12444 Victory Blvd # 300, North Hollywood (91606-3173)
PHONE....................818 985-2003
Maricel Zabel, *President*
Steve Pugh, *Vice Pres*
Simon Kojayan, *Manager*
EMP: 75 EST: 1975
SALES (est): 4.5MM **Privately Held**
WEB: www.starkservices.com
SIC: 7374 Data processing service

(P-18113)
TECHNOSOCIALWORKCOM LLC
Also Called: Stria
4300 Resnik Ct Unit 103, Bakersfield (93313-4836)
P.O. Box 21660 (93390-1660)
PHONE....................661 617-6601
Jim Damian, *Mng Member*
Rory Banks, *Vice Pres*
Scott Garrison, *Vice Pres*
Taryn Powers, *Project Mgr*
Sandra Ayala, *Opers Staff*
EMP: 75 EST: 2002
SQ FT: 10,000
SALES (est): 9.5MM **Privately Held**
WEB: www.stria.com
SIC: 7374 Computer graphics service

(P-18114)
VELOCITY TECH SOLUTIONS INC
111 Pacifica Ste 320, Irvine (92618-7428)
PHONE....................949 417-0260
EMP: 70 **Privately Held**
WEB: www.navisite.com
SIC: 7374 Data processing & preparation
HQ: Velocity Technology Solutions, Inc.
1901 Roxborough Rd # 406
Charlotte NC 28211

(P-18115)
VERITONE INC (PA)
575 Anton Blvd Ste 100, Costa Mesa (92626-7672)
PHONE....................888 507-1737
Chad Steelberg, *Ch of Bd*
Ryan Steelberg, *President*
Peter F Collins, *CFO*
Michael L Zemetra, *CFO*
Jeffrey B Coyne, *Exec VP*
EMP: 67 EST: 2014
SALES (est): 57.7MM **Publicly Held**
WEB: www.veritone.com
SIC: 7374 Data processing & preparation

(P-18116)
VERIZON CONNECT TELO INC (DH)
15505 Sand Canyon Ave, Irvine (92618-3114)
PHONE....................949 389-5500
Ralph Mason, *CTO*
Brendan Kieffer, *Partner*
Brian Calhoun, *Managing Prtnr*
Tyson Haas, *Managing Prtnr*
Jason Koch, *President*
▼ EMP: 150 EST: 2001

SALES (est): 64.8MM
SALES (corp-wide): 128.2B **Publicly Held**
WEB: www.verizonconnect.com
SIC: 7374 Data processing & preparation
HQ: Verizon Connect Inc.
5055 N Point Pkwy
Alpharetta GA 30022
404 573-5800

7375 Information Retrieval Svcs

(P-18117)
ACCURATE BACKGROUND LLC (PA)
Also Called: Selectforce
7515 Irvine Center Dr, Irvine (92618-2930)
PHONE....................800 784-3911
David C Dickerson, *CEO*
Brenda Marin, *Partner*
Tim Dowd, *President*
Russell Doll, *CFO*
Peter Harker, *CFO*
EMP: 315
SQ FT: 98,024
SALES (est): 117.6MM **Privately Held**
WEB: www.accurate.com
SIC: 7375 Information retrieval services

(P-18118)
AMBULNZ HEALTH LLC (PA)
1907 Border Ave, Torrance (90501-3606)
PHONE....................877 311-5555
Stan Vashovsky,
Andre Oberholzer, *CFO*
Michael Witkowski, *Officer*
Kelly Adair, *Vice Pres*
Anthony Capone, *CTO*
EMP: 292 EST: 2015
SALES (est): 18.7MM **Privately Held**
WEB: www.ambulnz.com
SIC: 7375 4119 Information retrieval services; ambulance service

(P-18119)
COUNTY OF LOS ANGELES
Also Called: Department of Mental Health
320 W Temple St Fl 9, Los Angeles (90012-3217)
PHONE....................213 974-0515
Jacqueline Criddell, *Manager*
Mona Teebay, *Officer*
Kenneth Bjork, *Network Mgr*
Erica Greene, *Analyst*
Don Yuan, *Manager*
EMP: 150
SALES (corp-wide): 25.2B **Privately Held**
WEB: www.lacounty.gov
SIC: 7375 9131 Information retrieval services;
PA: County Of Los Angeles
500 W Temple St Ste 437
Los Angeles CA 90012
213 974-1101

(P-18120)
DIGITAL INSIGHT CORPORATION
5601 Lindero Canyon Rd # 100, Westlake Village (91362-6494)
PHONE....................818 879-1010
Paul Nieman, *Principal*
Woody Woodruff, *Info Tech Mgr*
EMP: 52
SALES (corp-wide): 6.2B **Publicly Held**
WEB: www.ncr.com
SIC: 7375 Information retrieval services
HQ: Digital Insight Corporation
1300 Seaport Blvd Ste 300
Redwood City CA 94063

(P-18121)
E-TIMES CORPORATION LTD
601 S Figueroa St # 5000, Los Angeles (90017-3883)
PHONE....................213 452-6720
Chiharu Nakahara, *President*
Ken Yasuda, *CFO*
EMP: 300 EST: 2003

SALES (est): 9.3MM **Privately Held**
WEB: www.etimesltd.com
SIC: 7375 7374 8742 Information retrieval services; computer graphics service; administrative services consultant

(P-18122)
EDMUNDS HOLDING COMPANY (PA)
Also Called: Edmunds.com
2401 Colorado Ave, Santa Monica (90404-3585)
PHONE....................310 309-6300
AVI Steinlauf, *CEO*
Seth Berkowitz, *President*
Charles Farrell, *CFO*
Stephen Felisan, *CTO*
EMP: 650 **EST:** 1962
SALES (est): 212MM **Privately Held**
SIC: 7375 Information retrieval services

(P-18123)
GROUNDWORK OPEN SOURCE INC
23332 Mill Creek Dr # 155, Laguna Hills (92653-7911)
PHONE....................415 992-4500
Dave Lilly, *CEO*
Hans Kriel, *Vice Pres*
Roger Ruttimann, *Engineer*
Wayne Dahler, *Sales Staff*
EMP: 100 **EST:** 2004
SALES (est): 10.8MM
SALES (corp-wide): 562.3MM **Privately Held**
WEB: www.gwos.com
SIC: 7375 7371 On-line data base information retrieval; custom computer programming services
HQ: Fox Technologies, Inc.
6455 City West Pkwy
Eden Prairie MN 55344
800 328-1000

(P-18124)
GUIDANCE SOLUTIONS INC
4134 Del Rey Ave, Marina Del Rey (90292-5604)
PHONE....................310 754-4000
Jason Meugniot, *CEO*
Jeff Herrera, *Partner*
John Provisor, *President*
Mike Hill, *Exec VP*
EMP: 50
SQ FT: 10,000
SALES (est): 8.8MM **Privately Held**
WEB: www.guidance.com
SIC: 7375 4813 On-line data base information retrieval;

(P-18125)
IRDETO USA INC (DH)
5250 Lankershim Blvd, North Hollywood (91601-3186)
PHONE....................818 508-2333
Barry Coleman, *Senior VP*
Niels Haverkorn, *Senior VP*
Lawrence Low, *VP Bus Dvlpt*
Marissa Cruz, *Office Admin*
Sameera Ramagiri, *Database Admin*
EMP: 414 **EST:** 2000
SALES (est): 48.2MM
SALES (corp-wide): 355.8K **Privately Held**
WEB: www.irdeto.com
SIC: 7375 On-line data base information retrieval
HQ: Irdeto B.V.
Taurusavenue 105
Hoofddorp 2132
235 562-222

(P-18126)
ISN GLOBAL ENTERPRISES INC
678 S Indian Hill Blvd # 300, Claremont (91711-6003)
P.O. Box 1391 (91711-1391)
PHONE....................909 670-0601
Edgar Reece, *President*
Scott Miller, *CFO*
James Lewis, *Vice Pres*
J T Reece, *Vice Pres*
Gabriel Caustrita, *Administration*
EMP: 15 **EST:** 1995
SQ FT: 1,500

SALES (est): 2.5MM **Privately Held**
WEB: www.isnglobal.com
SIC: 7375 5999 1731 3575 Information retrieval services; hospital equipment & supplies; telephone & telephone equipment installation; computer terminals, monitors & components; telephone & communication line construction; data telephone communications

(P-18127)
KAJABI LLC
17100 Laguna Canyon Rd # 100, Irvine (92618-5401)
PHONE....................855 452-5224
James A Jenkins,
Kenny Rueter, *CEO*
Jared Loman, *Vice Pres*
EMP: 50 **EST:** 2011
SALES (est): 4.6MM **Privately Held**
WEB: www.kajabi.com
SIC: 7375 On-line data base information retrieval

(P-18128)
LOGICMONITOR INC (PA)
820 State St Fl 5, Santa Barbara (93101-3271)
PHONE....................805 394-8632
Kevin McGibben, *CEO*
Steven Francis,
Mark Kelly, *Senior VP*
Collin Chan, *Vice Pres*
Richard Gerdis, *Vice Pres*
EMP: 574 **EST:** 2007
SALES (est): 50.4MM **Privately Held**
WEB: www.logicmonitor.com
SIC: 7375 Information retrieval services

(P-18129)
MOLINA INFORMATION SYSTEMS LLC (HQ)
Also Called: Molina Medicaid Solutions
200 Oceangate Ste 100, Long Beach (90802-4317)
PHONE....................916 561-8540
Joseph M Molina,
John C Molina,
EMP: 880 **EST:** 2009
SQ FT: 320,000
SALES (est): 56.5MM
SALES (corp-wide): 17.7B **Publicly Held**
WEB: www.dxc.com
SIC: 7375 On-line data base information retrieval
PA: Dxc Technology Company
1775 Tysons Blvd Fl 8
Tysons VA 22102
703 245-9675

(P-18130)
REPRINTS DESK INC
15821 Ventura Blvd # 165, Encino (91436-2915)
PHONE....................310 477-0354
Alan Urban, *CFO*
Rogier Vanerkel, *Officer*
Rafael Murguia, *Data Proc Staff*
Marie Nyblom, *Technology*
Tracy Forrester, *Opers Staff*
EMP: 92 **EST:** 2006
SQ FT: 2,500
SALES (est): 9.2MM **Publicly Held**
WEB: www.researchsolutions.com
SIC: 7375 Information retrieval services
PA: Research Solutions, Inc.
16350 Ventura Blvd Ste D
Encino CA 91436

(P-18131)
SPRINT COMMUNICATIONS CO LP
31754 Temecula Pkwy Ste A, Temecula (92592-6805)
PHONE....................951 303-8501
EMP: 177
SALES (corp-wide): 68.4B **Publicly Held**
SIC: 7375 5065 4813 4812 On-line data base information retrieval; telephone & telegraphic equipment; local & long distance telephone communications; cellular telephone services

HQ: Sprint Communications Company L.P.
6391 Sprint Pkwy
Overland Park KS 66251
800 829-0965

(P-18132)
SPRINT COMMUNICATIONS CO LP
12913 Harbor Blvd Ste Q4, Garden Grove (92840-5856)
PHONE....................714 534-2107
EMP: 177
SALES (corp-wide): 68.4B **Publicly Held**
SIC: 7375 4813 4812 On-line data base information retrieval; local & long distance telephone communications; cellular telephone services
HQ: Sprint Communications Company L.P.
6391 Sprint Pkwy
Overland Park KS 66251
800 829-0965

(P-18133)
SPRINT COMMUNICATIONS CO LP
1316 N Azusa Ave, Covina (91722-1259)
PHONE....................626 339-0430
EMP: 177
SALES (corp-wide): 68.4B **Publicly Held**
SIC: 7375 4813 4812 On-line data base information retrieval; local & long distance telephone communications; cellular telephone services
HQ: Sprint Communications Company L.P.
6391 Sprint Pkwy
Overland Park KS 66251
800 829-0965

(P-18134)
TROJAN PROFESSIONAL SVCS INC
4410 Cerritos Ave, Los Alamitos (90720-2549)
P.O. Box 1270 (90720-1270)
PHONE....................714 816-7169
Mark Dunn, *CEO*
Ingrid M Kidd, *President*
Chris Iseri, *Admin Sec*
Daniel Jara, *IT/INT Sup*
Gina Lopez, *Human Res Dir*
EMP: 99 **EST:** 1976
SQ FT: 12,000
SALES (est): 9.8MM **Privately Held**
WEB: www.trojanonline.com
SIC: 7375 Data base information retrieval

(P-18135)
WESTERN FELD INVSTIGATIONS INC (PA)
Also Called: Releasepoint
405 W Foothill Blvd # 204, Claremont (91711-2786)
P.O. Box 246, Glendora (91740-0246)
PHONE....................800 999-9589
Gerard F Halvey, *President*
Clair Halvey, *Vice Pres*
Derrick Halvey, *Vice Pres*
Christina Tsang-Reveche, *Info Tech Dir*
Marlo Hamby, *Opers Staff*
EMP: 96 **EST:** 1972
SALES (est): 8.1MM **Privately Held**
WEB: www.releasepointonline.com
SIC: 7375 Information retrieval services

(P-18136)
WORLD ACCEPTANCE GROUP CORP (PA)
Also Called: Secure Data Recovery Services
3255 Chnga Blvd W Ste 301, Los Angeles (90068-1778)
PHONE....................800 388-1266
Dmitri T Kardashev, *President*
Yelena Tselenchuk, *Marketing Staff*
Moore Mitchell, *Representative*
EMP: 59 **EST:** 2007
SQ FT: 1,800
SALES (est): 5.4MM **Privately Held**
SIC: 7375 7371 Data base information retrieval; computer software development

(P-18137)
ZOOMINFO TECHNOLOGIES LLC
Dept La 24789, Pasadena (91185-0001)
PHONE....................360 783-6924

Henry Schuck, *Mng Member*
EMP: 201
SALES (corp-wide): 58.9MM **Privately Held**
WEB: www.discoverorg.com
SIC: 7375 Information retrieval services
PA: Zoominfo Technologies Llc
805 Broadway St Ste 900
Vancouver WA 98660
360 783-6800

7376 Computer Facilities Management Svcs

(P-18138)
ALLIED DIGITAL SERVICES LLC (HQ)
680 Knox St Ste 200, Torrance (90502-1358)
PHONE....................310 431-2375
Paresh Shah, *CEO*
Gaurav Bahirvani, *Chief Mktg Ofcr*
Kapil Mehta, *Officer*
Sair Muhammad, *Exec VP*
Ajit Bhosale, *Executive*
EMP: 144 **EST:** 2008
SQ FT: 14,516
SALES (est): 26.5MM **Privately Held**
WEB: www.allieddigital.net
SIC: 7376 Computer facilities management

(P-18139)
TPUSA - FHCS INC (DH)
Also Called: Teleperformance
215 N Marengo Ave Ste 160, Pasadena (91101-1524)
PHONE....................213 873-5100
Jeff Balagna, *President*
Shayne Murray, *President*
Dean Duncan, *Treasurer*
Michael Evans, *Exec VP*
Michael Hutchison, *Exec VP*
EMP: 273 **EST:** 1998
SQ FT: 1,029,146
SALES (est): 19.5MM
SALES (corp-wide): 164.9MM **Privately Held**
WEB: www.teleperformance.com
SIC: 7376 7373 Computer facilities management; systems integration services
HQ: Tpusa, Inc.
5295 S Commerce Dr # 600
Murray UT 84107
801 257-5800

7377 Computer Rental & Leasing

(P-18140)
INSIGHT INVESTMENTS LLC (DH)
611 Anton Blvd Ste 700, Costa Mesa (92626-7050)
PHONE....................714 939-2300
John W Ford, *CEO*
Christopher Czaja, *CFO*
Jim Lindley, *Exec VP*
Mark Castellanos, *Vice Pres*
Michael Dundon, *Vice Pres*
EMP: 56 **EST:** 2009
SQ FT: 30,000
SALES (est): 102.4MM **Privately Held**
WEB: www.insightinvestments.com
SIC: 7377 5045 Computer peripheral equipment rental & leasing; computer peripheral equipment
HQ: Insight Investments Holdings, Llc
611 Anton Blvd Ste 700
Costa Mesa CA 92626
714 939-2300

P R O D U C T S & S V C S

7378 Computer Maintenance & Repair

(P-18141)
ALPHA OMEGA CMPT NTWRK SVCS IN
20042 Beach Blvd Ste 202, Huntington Beach (92648-3702)
PHONE..................714 962-3129
Darryl Santa, *President*
Jeremiah Vergara, *Consultant*
EMP: 13 EST: 1999
SALES (est): 1MM **Privately Held**
WEB: www.aobiz.com
SIC: 7378 7373 3571 1731 Computer & data processing equipment repair/maintenance; computer integrated systems design; local area network (LAN) systems integrator; personal computers (microcomputers); computer installation

(P-18142)
ALQUEST TECHNOLOGIES INC
1760 Yeager Ave, La Verne (91750-5850)
PHONE..................909 592-8708
Henry J Wojcik, *CEO*
Henry Wojcik, *President*
Melody Mahmoud, *Human Resources*
EMP: 70 EST: 2000
SALES (est): 7.7MM **Privately Held**
WEB: www.alquestonline.com
SIC: 7378 Computer maintenance & repair

(P-18143)
APEX COMPUTER SYSTEMS INC
13875 Cerritos Corprt Dr A, Cerritos (90703-2470)
P.O. Box 4859 (90703-4859)
PHONE..................562 926-6820
Philip C Chen, *CEO*
Dennis Rice, *President*
Jessica C Chow, *CFO*
Michael Da Silva, *Vice Pres*
Roy Chan, *Administration*
EMP: 60 EST: 1983
SQ FT: 18,146 **Privately Held**
WEB: www.acsi2000.com
SIC: 7378 5734 Computer maintenance & repair; computer & software stores

(P-18144)
BCP SYSTEMS INC
1560 S Sinclair St, Anaheim (92806-5933)
PHONE..................714 202-3900
Carlos P Torres, *CEO*
William W Price, *President*
Wes Price, *Vice Pres*
Dianna Rodriguez, *Vice Pres*
David Garcia, *Engineer*
EMP: 60
SALES (est): 9.1MM **Privately Held**
WEB: www.bcpsystems.com
SIC: 7378 3571 5063 Computer & data processing equipment repair/maintenance; computer peripheral equipment repair & maintenance; electronic computers; electrical apparatus & equipment

(P-18145)
FAKOURI ELECTRICAL ENGRG INC
Also Called: F E E
30001 Comercio, Rcho STA Marg (92688-2106)
PHONE..................949 888-2400
Maryam Ewalt, *President*
Charles Ewalt, *COO*
John Oveisi, *CFO*
Bijan Ewalt, *Vice Pres*
Kavita Agarwal, *Human Res Mgr*
▲ EMP: 79 EST: 1979
SQ FT: 15,000
SALES (est): 11.5MM **Privately Held**
WEB: www.fee-ups.com
SIC: 7378 8742 Computer maintenance & repair; maintenance management consultant

(P-18146)
GOLDEN STAR TECHNOLOGY INC
1215 Columbia Ave Ste C3, Riverside (92507-2115)
PHONE..................951 778-8930
Jia P Wang, *Branch Mgr*
Aracely Ramirez, *Project Mgr*
Jeff Ting, *Project Mgr*
Alice Ramos, *Human Res Mgr*
Victoria Sanchez, *Buyer*
EMP: 50
SALES (corp-wide): 200.9MM **Privately Held**
WEB: www.gstinc.com
SIC: 5734 7378 5045 Computer peripheral equipment; computer maintenance & repair; computers, peripherals & software
PA: Golden Star Technology Inc.
12881 166th St
Cerritos CA 90703
562 345-8700

(P-18147)
GOLDEN STAR TECHNOLOGY INC (PA)
Also Called: G S T
12881 166th St, Cerritos (90703-2103)
PHONE..................562 345-8700
Jia Peir Wang, *CEO*
Alice Wang, *President*
Dennise Wang, *COO*
Henry Ngo, *Senior VP*
Nathan Castillo, *Executive*
▲ EMP: 70 EST: 1985
SQ FT: 55,000
SALES: 200.9MM **Privately Held**
WEB: www.gstinc.com
SIC: 5734 7378 5045 Computer peripheral equipment; computer software & accessories; computer maintenance & repair; computers, peripherals & software

(P-18148)
INHOUSEIT INC
400 Exchange Ste 100, Irvine (92602-1340)
PHONE..................949 660-5655
Glen Ackerman, *CEO*
Steve Bender, *President*
Scott V Essen, *Director*
John Mitchell, *Accounts Mgr*
EMP: 70 EST: 1998
SALES (est): 9.3MM **Privately Held**
WEB: www.inhouse-it.de
SIC: 7378 Computer & data processing equipment repair/maintenance

(P-18149)
NEOCOMP SYSTEMS INC
21541 Nordhoff St Ste F, Chatsworth (91311-6986)
PHONE..................818 700-8722
Dennis Flugard, *President*
James Bailey, *Vice Pres*
EMP: 52 EST: 1979
SQ FT: 8,500
SALES (est): 3.6MM **Privately Held**
WEB: www.neocomp.com
SIC: 7378 Computer maintenance & repair

(P-18150)
QUEST INTL MONITOR SVC INC (PA)
60-65 Parker, Irvine (92618)
PHONE..................949 581-9900
Shahnam Arshadi, *President*
Robert Cort, *Vice Pres*
Kamyar Katouzian, *Vice Pres*
Ben Arshadi, *General Mgr*
Inam Siddiqui, *Project Mgr*
▲ EMP: 60 EST: 1985
SALES (est): 31.5MM **Privately Held**
WEB: www.questinc.com
SIC: 7378 7379 7371 7373 Computer maintenance & repair; computer related maintenance services; custom computer programming services; systems integration services; cathode ray tubes, including rebuilt; computer & software stores

(P-18151)
RAKWORX INC
23122 Alcalde Dr Ste C, Laguna Hills (92653-1459)
PHONE..................949 215-1362
Yue Cong, *Vice Pres*
Zhiyong Ding, *President*
Isamu Tanaka, *Opers Staff*
EMP: 150 EST: 2016
SALES (est): 5.2MM **Privately Held**
WEB: www.rakworx.com
SIC: 7378 3577 Computer & data processing equipment repair/maintenance; data conversion equipment, media-to-media: computer

(P-18152)
TURNER TECHTRONICS INC
17845 Sky Park Cir, Irvine (92614-6112)
PHONE..................949 724-1339
Nefi Calderon, *IT/INT Sup*
Andrew Ehlen, *Technician*
Javier Hernandez, *Technician*
Christopher Vavro, *Technology*
Pierre Bernard, *Analyst*
EMP: 118
SALES (corp-wide): 18.2MM **Privately Held**
WEB: www.turnertech.com
SIC: 7378 7372 Computer maintenance & repair; prepackaged software
PA: Turner Techtronics, Inc.
7675 N San Fernando Rd
Burbank CA 91505
818 973-1060

(P-18153)
VALTRON TECHNOLOGIES INC
28309 Avenue Crocker, Santa Clarita (91355-1251)
PHONE..................805 257-0333
Andrew Hart, *President*
Steve Nober, *Vice Pres*
Cindy Breneman, *Accounting Mgr*
EMP: 95 EST: 1988
SQ FT: 48,000
SALES (est): 1.7MM **Privately Held**
SIC: 7378 5734 Computer & data processing equipment repair/maintenance; modems, monitors, terminals & disk drives: computers

7379 Computer Related Svcs, NEC

(P-18154)
A P R CONSULTING INC
17852 17th St Ste 206, Tustin (92780-2143)
PHONE..................714 544-3696
Darryl Stone, *Branch Mgr*
EMP: 417 **Privately Held**
WEB: www.aprconsulting.com
SIC: 7379 7371 Computer related maintenance services; custom computer programming services
PA: A P R Consulting, Inc.
1370 Valley Vista Dr # 280
Diamond Bar CA 91765

(P-18155)
ACCESS NETWORKS INC (PA)
28482 Constellation Rd, Valencia (91355-5081)
PHONE..................310 453-1800
Hagai Feiner, *CEO*
Mark Andrew, *COO*
Bryce Nordstrand, *Vice Pres*
Brett Canter, *CTO*
Chris Leffler, *Network Enginr*
EMP: 75 EST: 2004
SALES (est): 5.2MM **Privately Held**
WEB: www.accessnetworks.com
SIC: 7379 Computer related consulting services

(P-18156)
ADAMS COMM & ENGRG TECH INC
1875 Century Park E # 1130, Los Angeles (90067-2253)
PHONE..................301 861-5000
Charles Adams, *President*
EMP: 250
SALES (corp-wide): 262.3MM **Privately Held**
WEB: www.adamscomm.com
SIC: 7379
PA: Adams Communication & Engineering Technology, Inc.
10740 Parkridge Blvd # 70
Reston VA 20191
703 391-1682

(P-18157)
ADCOM INTERACTIVE MEDIA INC
Also Called: Admedia
21200 Oxnard St 429, Woodland Hills (91367-5014)
PHONE..................800 296-7104
Danny E Bibi, *CEO*
Liora Berg, *Sales Staff*
Chaunci Toney, *Manager*
EMP: 100 EST: 2009
SALES (est): 6.9MM **Privately Held**
WEB: www.admedia.com
SIC: 7379

(P-18158)
AIMINSIGHT SOLUTIONS INC
Also Called: A.I.M. Services
4127 Berryman Ave, Los Angeles (90066-5425)
PHONE..................310 313-0047
Amjad Khanmohamed, *President*
Amjad Khan, *Vice Pres*
Imtiaz Khanmohamed, *Vice Pres*
EMP: 14 EST: 2011
SALES (est): 1.4MM **Privately Held**
WEB: www.aiminsight.com
SIC: 7379 7371 8742 7372 Computer related consulting services; computer software systems analysis & design, custom; management consulting services; business oriented computer software

(P-18159)
ASI NETWORKS INC
19331 E Walnut Dr N, City of Industry (91748-1436)
P.O. Box 867, San Dimas (91773-0867)
PHONE..................800 251-1336
Jeff Plumley, *President*
EMP: 15 EST: 1997
SQ FT: 3,300
SALES (est): 4.4MM **Privately Held**
WEB: www.asi-networks.com
SIC: 7379 3825 Disk & diskette conversion service; network analyzers

(P-18160)
ASSIGN CORPORATION
200 N Maryland Ave # 204, Glendale (91206-4262)
PHONE..................818 247-7100
Umesh Lalwani, *CEO*
Rachel Wagoner, *Admin Asst*
Liandra Sapien, *Controller*
Ashish Madan, *Consultant*
EMP: 120 EST: 1997
SQ FT: 1,300
SALES (est): 5.1MM **Privately Held**
SIC: 7379

(P-18161)
AVENTE INC
200 Spectrum Dr Ste 300, Irvine (92618)
PHONE..................844 385-1556
Jason Pammer, *CEO*
EMP: 50
SALES (est): 1.4MM **Privately Held**
WEB: www.avente.com
SIC: 7379

(P-18162)
AVIDEX INDUSTRIES LLC
20382 Hermana Cir, Lake Forest (92630-8701)
PHONE..................949 428-6333
Mike Stammire, *Branch Mgr*
EMP: 100 **Privately Held**
WEB: www.avidex.com

SIC: 7379 1731 Computer related consulting services; computer hardware requirements analysis; electrical work; communications specialization; cable television installation; sound equipment specialization
HQ: Avidex Industries, L.L.C.
13555 Ne Bel Red Rd # 226
Bellevue WA 98005
425 643-0330

(P-18163)
BESTITCOM INC (PA)
1464 Madera Rd, Simi Valley (93065-3077)
PHONE...................................602 667-5613
Harry Curtin, *CEO*
Susan Silberstein, *COO*
Rich Hybner, *CFO*
Fred Chen, *CTO*
John Yu, *Opers Staff*
EMP: 65 EST: 2004
SQ FT: 20,000
SALES (est): 5.2MM **Privately Held**
WEB: www.bestit.com
SIC: 7379 Computer related consulting services; computer related maintenance services

(P-18164)
BEYOND LIMITS INC (PA)
400 N Brand Blvd Ste 700, Glendale (91203-2364)
PHONE...................................818 643-2344
Aj Abdallat, *CEO*
Mark James, *Officer*
Maggi Baldieri, *Human Resources*
EMP: 191 EST: 2004
SALES (est): 2.6MM **Privately Held**
WEB: www.beyond.ai
SIC: 7379

(P-18165)
BIKEEXCHANGE INC
21 Spectrum Pointe Dr # 101, Lake Forest (92630-2224)
PHONE...................................949 344-2616
Matthew Gordin, *CEO*
Sara Hopp, *Project Mgr*
JP Lamunyon, *Sales Staff*
EMP: 13 EST: 2014
SALES (est): 678.5K **Privately Held**
WEB: www.bikeexchange.com
SIC: 7379 3312 5139 ; wheels; shoes

(P-18166)
BLYTHECO INC (PA)
23161 Mill Creek Dr # 200, Laguna Hills (92653-1649)
PHONE...................................949 583-9500
Stephen P Blythe, *CEO*
Ruth Menter, *COO*
Lori Seal, *COO*
Phil Sim, *Officer*
Barry Tietz, *Vice Pres*
EMP: 45 EST: 1980
SQ FT: 15,000
SALES (est): 24.2MM **Privately Held**
WEB: www.blytheco.com
SIC: 7379 7372 7371 Computer related consulting services; prepackaged software; computer software systems analysis & design, custom

(P-18167)
CHARTEC LLC
1600 Mill Rock Way, Bakersfield (93311-1320)
PHONE...................................661 281-4000
David Bellini,
Nick Points, *Executive*
Roger Lawrence, *Software Dev*
Jason Rock, *Technician*
Jacob Thompson, *Technician*
EMP: 74 EST: 2010
SALES (est): 6.1MM **Privately Held**
WEB: www.chartec.net
SIC: 7379

(P-18168)
CJ SETO SUPPORT SERVICES LLC (PA)
2300 Knoll Dr Ste G, Ventura (93003-8058)
PHONE...................................805 644-1214
Chet Seto, *Director*
Rick Lindsay, *Program Mgr*
Chad Tapie, *Technician*

Alisha Rhodes, *Director*
EMP: 68 EST: 1999
SQ FT: 2,800
SALES (est): 11.8MM **Privately Held**
WEB: www.cjseto.com
SIC: 7379 8748 Computer related consulting services; environmental consultant

(P-18169)
CLOUD CREATIONS INC
790 E Colorado Blvd Fl 9, Pasadena (91101-2193)
PHONE...................................800 951-7651
Justin Davis, *CEO*
Justin Paul Davis, *CEO*
Felicia Duarte, *COO*
Nayeli Castro, *Project Mgr*
Evelyn Portillo, *Project Mgr*
EMP: 68 EST: 2015
SQ FT: 5,000
SALES (est): 3.1MM **Privately Held**
WEB: www.cloudcreations.com
SIC: 7379 Computer related consulting services

(P-18170)
COMMERCIAL PRGRM SYSTEMS INC (PA)
Also Called: CPS
4400 Cldwtr Cyn Ave, Studio City (91604-1480)
P.O. Box 3436, Pls Vrds Pnsl (90274-9436)
PHONE...................................818 308-8560
Alan Strong, *CEO*
Phil Sawyer, *President*
Michele Stewart, *Treasurer*
Marjorie Kram, *Vice Pres*
Donna Preston, *Vice Pres*
EMP: 146 EST: 1978
SQ FT: 8,000
SALES (est): 10.6MM **Privately Held**
WEB: www.cpsinc.com
SIC: 7379 Data processing consultant

(P-18171)
CONSTELLATION HOMEBUILDER (HQ)
888 S Dsnyland Dr Ste 430, Tustin (92780)
PHONE...................................714 768-6100
Dexter Salna, *President*
Chris Graham, *Vice Pres*
Bob Swainhart, *General Mgr*
Linda Lane, *Administration*
Diptee Mehta, *Software Engr*
EMP: 50 EST: 2006
SALES (est): 102.3MM
SALES (corp-wide): 3.9B **Privately Held**
WEB: www.constellationhb.com
SIC: 7379

(P-18172)
DELTA COMPUTER CONSULTING
25550 Hawthorne Blvd # 106, Torrance (90505-6831)
PHONE...................................310 541-9440
Marzieh Daneshvar, *President*
Laurent Verrando, *Managing Prtnr*
Masih Hakimpour, *Vice Pres*
Dane Encarnacion, *IT/INT Sup*
Michael Maranhas, *Manager*
EMP: 180 EST: 1987
SQ FT: 2,000
SALES (est): 10.8MM **Privately Held**
WEB: www.deltacci.com
SIC: 7379 Computer related consulting services

(P-18173)
DISNEY WORLDWIDE SERVICES INC
589 Paula Ave, Glendale (91201)
PHONE...................................818 560-1250
Steve Finney, *Branch Mgr*
EMP: 78
SQ FT: 33,350
SALES (corp-wide): 65.3B **Publicly Held**
SIC: 7379 Computer related maintenance services
HQ: Disney Worldwide Services Inc
1375 E Buena Vista Dr 4n
Lake Buena Vista FL 32830

(P-18174)
DTI SERVICES INC (PA)
601 S Figueroa St # 4300, Los Angeles (90017-5757)
PHONE...................................213 670-1100
Satoru Amano, *President*
Chad D Harmon, *CEO*
Ken Yasuda, *CFO*
Michael Frick, *Info Tech Dir*
EMP: 60 EST: 1996
SALES (est): 7.9MM **Privately Held**
WEB: www.dtiservices.com
SIC: 7379 4813 7374 7389 ; ; telephone communications broker; computer graphics service;

(P-18175)
DYNTEK INC (PA)
5241 California Ave # 150, Irvine (92617-3215)
PHONE...................................949 271-6700
Ron Ben-Yishay, *CEO*
Wade Stevenson, *President*
Karen Rosenberger, *COO*
Karen S Rosenberger, *CFO*
Michael Gullard, *Chairman*
EMP: 105 EST: 1989
SQ FT: 10,250
SALES (est): 101.1MM **Publicly Held**
WEB: www.dyntek.com
SIC: 7379 ; computer related consulting services

(P-18176)
ETAIROS CONSULTING
6711 Studio Pl, Riverside (92509-5900)
PHONE...................................844 219-7027
EMP: 50
SQ FT: 4,000
SALES (est): 1.9MM **Privately Held**
SIC: 7379 Computer Related Services

(P-18177)
ETHERWAN SYSTEMS INC
2301 E Winston Rd, Anaheim (92806-5542)
PHONE...................................714 779-3800
Mitch Yang, *President*
John Marchiando, *President*
Cara Rising, *Administration*
Mars Pao, *Engineer*
David Anderson, *Regl Sales Mgr*
▲ EMP: 100 EST: 1996
SQ FT: 5,000
SALES (est): 18.4MM
SALES (corp-wide): 2.7B **Privately Held**
WEB: www.etherwan.com
SIC: 7379 3577 Computer related maintenance services; computer peripheral equipment
HQ: Etherwan Systems, Inc.
8f, No. 2, Alley 6, Lane 235, Baoqiao Rd.
New Taipei City TAP 23145

(P-18178)
EXPERTS EXCHANGE LLC
Also Called: Experts Exch Exprts-Xchange-com
7301 Morro Rd Ste 105a, Atascadero (93422-4458)
P.O. Box 1229, San Luis Obispo (93406-1229)
PHONE...................................805 787-0603
Randy Redberg, *Mng Member*
David Kelly, *Web Dvlpr*
Anthony Pangilinan, *Software Dev*
Mikkel Sandberg, *Software Dev*
Jan Louwerens, *Software Engr*
EMP: 55 EST: 2003
SQ FT: 13,400
SALES (est): 6.5MM **Privately Held**
WEB: www.experts-exchange.com
SIC: 7379

(P-18179)
FUNNY OR DIE INC
1013 N Orange Dr, Los Angeles (90038-2317)
PHONE...................................650 461-3929
Richard Glover, *CEO*
Mitch Galbraith, *COO*
Michele Rosette, *Officer*
Jim Ziegler, *Senior VP*
Chris Bruss, *Vice Pres*

EMP: 50 EST: 2007
SALES (est): 17.1MM **Privately Held**
WEB: www.funnyordie.io
SIC: 7379

(P-18180)
GA SERVICES LLC
1681 Kettering, Irvine (92614-5613)
PHONE...................................949 752-6515
Fax: 949 606-1990
EMP: 50
SQ FT: 10,500
SALES (est): 3.6MM **Privately Held**
WEB: www.gasllc.com
SIC: 7379 7378 Computer Related Services Computer Maintenance/Repair

(P-18181)
GDR GROUP INC
3 Park Plz Ste 1700, Irvine (92614-8540)
PHONE...................................949 453-8818
Ellen Dorse, *Principal*
Lacie Oots, *COO*
Bruce Greenburg, *Principal*
Robert Redwitz, *Principal*
Zack Stigall, *Administration*
EMP: 76
SALES (est): 18.1MM **Privately Held**
WEB: www.gdrgroup.com
SIC: 7379

(P-18182)
GEBBS SOFTWARE INTL INC
4640 Admiralty Way Fl 9, Marina Del Rey (90292-6630)
PHONE...................................201 227-0088
Nitin Thakor, *CEO*
EMP: 52 EST: 1997
SQ FT: 2,500
SALES (est): 3.4MM **Privately Held**
WEB: www.gebbs.com
SIC: 7379 Computer related consulting services
PA: Gebbs Software International Private Limited
Gebbs House
Mumbai MH 40009

(P-18183)
GEEK SQUAD INC
12989 Park Plaza Dr, Cerritos (90703-8565)
PHONE...................................562 402-1555
EMP: 88
SALES (corp-wide): 47.2B **Publicly Held**
WEB: www.bestbuy.com
SIC: 7379 Computer related consulting services
HQ: Geek Squad, Inc.
1213 Washington Ave N
Minneapolis MN 55401

(P-18184)
GENERAL NETWORKS CORPORATION
3524 Ocean View Blvd, Glendale (91208-1212)
PHONE...................................818 249-1962
Robert Todd Withers, *President*
Randall C Wise, *Ch of Bd*
Todd Withers, *President*
Cort Baker, *Vice Pres*
David Horwatt, *Vice Pres*
EMP: 60 EST: 1986
SQ FT: 3,600
SALES (est): 12MM **Privately Held**
WEB: www.gennet.com
SIC: 7379 5045 7372 Computer related consulting services; terminals, computer; prepackaged software

(P-18185)
IDRIVE INC
Also Called: Ibackup.com
26115 Mureau Rd Ste A, Calabasas (91302-3179)
PHONE...................................818 594-5972
Raghu Kulkarni, *Principal*
Ajit Sirohi, *Software Engr*
Doug Little, *Sales Staff*
Palak Bhakta, *General Counsel*
Zachary Manzer, *Accounts Exec*
EMP: 70 EST: 1995

SALES (est): 10.5MM **Privately Held**
WEB: www.idrive.com
SIC: **7379** Computer related maintenance services; computer related consulting services

(P-18186)
INFOGEN LABS INC
18223 Charlton Ln, Porter Ranch (91326-3617)
PHONE................................818 825-5024
Sanjeev Kuwadeker, *President*
Priya Pillai, *Executive*
Shrinath Kopare, *Sr Software Eng*
Sid Patti, *VP Sales*
EMP: 70 EST: 2017
SALES (est): 5MM **Privately Held**
SIC: **7379** Computer related consulting services

(P-18187)
INFORMATION TECH PARTNERS INC
Also Called: I T P
3003 N San Fernando Blvd, Burbank (91504-2525)
PHONE................................800 789-7487
Michael Thompson, *President*
Chuck Newberry, *Software Dev*
Christian Thompson, *Director*
EMP: 60 EST: 1991
SQ FT: 10,000
SALES (est): 20.5MM **Privately Held**
WEB: www.itpnet.com
SIC: **7379** Computer related consulting services

(P-18188)
INQBRANDS INC
Also Called: Ft USA
1150 S Milliken Ave, Ontario (91761-7840)
PHONE................................909 390-7788
Zhen Qin, *CEO*
Jinhua Shen, *CFO*
Alexander Calvo, *Sales Staff*
Lora Kojak, *Sales Staff*
John Xin, *Senior Mgr*
▲ EMP: 55 EST: 2013
SALES (est): 8.3MM **Privately Held**
WEB: www.inqbrands.com
SIC: **7379**
PA: Focus Technology Co., Ltd.
No.7, Lijing Rd., Jiangbei New Dist.
Nanjing 21003

(P-18189)
INTEGRATED INTERMODAL SVCS INC
8600 Banana Ave, Fontana (92335-3033)
PHONE................................909 355-4100
Greg Philip Steffire, *President*
EMP: 100 EST: 1991
SALES (est): 2.2MM **Privately Held**
SIC: **7379** Computer related maintenance services

(P-18190)
INTERBASE CORPORATION (PA)
22485 La Palma Ave # 200, Yorba Linda (92887-3812)
PHONE................................714 701-3600
Tejas Modi, *President*
Parul Modi, *Admin Sec*
Andrew Paulino, *Software Dev*
Harry Sagar, *Software Dev*
Hiren Sagar, *Technology*
EMP: 88 EST: 1997
SQ FT: 1,100
SALES (est): 20.5MM **Privately Held**
WEB: www.interbasecorp.com
SIC: **7379** Computer related consulting services

(P-18191)
INTRATEK COMPUTER INC
9950 Irvine Center Dr, Irvine (92618-4357)
PHONE................................949 334-4200
Parviz Ramezani, *CEO*
Anthony Battey, *Shareholder*
Mohsen Fahami, *Shareholder*
Rodney Holdren, *Shareholder*
Bahi Ghobbeh, *CFO*
EMP: 150
SQ FT: 9,800

SALES: 16.5MM **Privately Held**
WEB: www.intrapc.com
SIC: **7379** Computer related consulting services

(P-18192)
IP ACCESS INTERNATIONAL
31831 Camn Capistrano, San Juan Capistrano (92675-3211)
PHONE................................949 655-1000
Bryan Hill, *President*
Ben Glover, *Engineer*
Kim Graville, *Sales Staff*
Mike Gregg, *Sales Staff*
Brian Roland, *Director*
EMP: 50 EST: 1999
SQ FT: 10,000
SALES (est): 7.3MM **Privately Held**
WEB: www.ipinternational.net
SIC: **7379**

(P-18193)
ISPACE INC
2381 Rosecrans Ave # 110, El Segundo (90245-4920)
PHONE................................310 563-3800
Suresh Kothapalli, *CEO*
Ram Davaloor, *Vice Pres*
Ravi Kottapalli, *Vice Pres*
Shilpa Khanolkar, *Business Anlyst*
Kiran Chalasani, *Technology*
EMP: 120 EST: 2000
SALES (est): 15.9MM **Privately Held**
WEB: www.ispace.com
SIC: **7379**

(P-18194)
ITEK SERVICES INC
25501 Arctic Ocean Dr, Lake Forest (92630-8827)
PHONE................................949 770-4835
Donald W Rowley, *CEO*
John Curl, *President*
Robert Tintner, *Executive*
Jon Thornton, *Project Mgr*
Kenn Frank, *Business Mgr*
EMP: 100
SQ FT: 12,000
SALES (est): 24MM **Privately Held**
WEB: www.itekservices.com
SIC: **7379** Computer related maintenance services

(P-18195)
KODELLA LLC
17922 Fitch Ste 200, Irvine (92614-1611)
PHONE................................786 408-7995
Eric Bibi, *Principal*
EMP: 104 EST: 2016
SALES (est): 5.2MM **Privately Held**
WEB: www.kodella.com
SIC: **7379** **8243** Computer related consulting services; software training, computer

(P-18196)
KORE1 INC
530 Technology Dr Ste 150, Irvine (92618-1368)
PHONE................................949 706-6990
Brian Hunt, *CEO*
Steven Quarles, *Managing Dir*
Kevin Shearer, *Managing Dir*
Sara Ferry, *Tech Recruiter*
Alex Kumar, *Tech Recruiter*
EMP: 100 EST: 2005
SALES (est): 11.2MM **Privately Held**
WEB: www.kore1.com
SIC: **7379**

(P-18197)
LASER IMAGE PLUS
14751 Franklin Ave Ste B, Tustin (92780-7272)
PHONE................................714 556-5277
Robert Pool, *Owner*
Caryn Frawley, *Manager*
EMP: 28 EST: 1986
SALES (est): 1.2MM **Privately Held**
WEB: www.laserimageplus.com
SIC: **7379** **3955** Computer related maintenance services; print cartridges for laser & other computer printers

(P-18198)
LEIDOS GOVERNMENT SERVICES INC
500 N Via Val Verde, Montebello (90640-2358)
PHONE................................323 721-6979
Nate Sadorian, *Branch Mgr*
EMP: 188 **Publicly Held**
SIC: **7379** **7372** Computer related consulting services; prepackaged software
HQ: Leidos Government Services, Inc.
9737 Washingtonian Blvd
Gaithersburg MD 20878
856 486-5156

(P-18199)
LOGIN CONSULTING SERVICES INC
300 Continental Blvd # 405, El Segundo (90245-5042)
PHONE................................310 607-9091
Elece J Otten, *President*
Dan McKee, *Officer*
Shawn Reagan, *Vice Pres*
Rose Villa, *Vice Pres*
Thomas Seavey, *Exec Dir*
EMP: 75 EST: 1996
SQ FT: 3,200
SALES (est): 5.3MM **Privately Held**
WEB: www.loginconsult.com
SIC: **7379**

(P-18200)
MAGMA CONSULTING GROUP LLC
Also Called: Magmalabs
830 Traction Ave 3a, Los Angeles (90013-1816)
PHONE................................415 315-9364
Carlos Rocha, *CEO*
Joe Moreno, *Executive*
Alejandro Espinoza, *Sr Software Eng*
Edwin Cruz, *CTO*
Alejandra Torres, *Finance*
EMP: 60 EST: 2015
SALES (est): 2MM **Privately Held**
SIC: **7379** Computer related consulting services

(P-18201)
MEDIACENTRIC INTEGRATION INC
20610 Manhattan Pl # 128, Torrance (90501-1836)
PHONE................................310 325-7900
David Lopez, *President*
Annette Simpson, *Admin Asst*
Mauro Fernandez, *Technician*
Tito Lezama, *Technician*
Samuel Pinto, *Technician*
EMP: 55 EST: 2001
SQ FT: 950
SALES (est): 4.6MM **Privately Held**
WEB: www.mediacentric.net
SIC: **7379** **1731** ; electronic controls installation

(P-18202)
NC INTERACTIVE LLC
Also Called: Ncsoft
1 Polaris Way Ste 110, Aliso Viejo (92656-5358)
PHONE................................512 623-8700
Songyee Yoon, *Principal*
Josh Taylor, *Project Mgr*
EMP: 100 **Privately Held**
SIC: **7379** Computer related consulting services
HQ: Nc Interactive Llc
3180 139th Ave Se Ste 500
Bellevue WA 98005
206 588-7200

(P-18203)
NIMBUS DATA INC
5151 California Ave # 100, Irvine (92617-3205)
PHONE................................650 276-4500
Thomas Isakovich, *CEO*
◆ EMP: 50 EST: 2003
SALES (est): 9.8MM **Privately Held**
WEB: www.nimbusdata.com
SIC: **7379** Computer related consulting services

(P-18204)
NOWCOM LLC
Also Called: Hankey Group
4751 Wilshire Blvd # 205, Los Angeles (90010-3860)
PHONE................................323 746-6888
Jay Kamdar, *President*
Rahul Sonthalia, *President*
Robert Kozak, *Vice Pres*
Jesse Martin, *Vice Pres*
Letty Aguiar, *Administration*
EMP: 165 EST: 1996
SQ FT: 4,800
SALES (est): 27.7MM **Privately Held**
WEB: www.nowcom.com
SIC: **7379**

(P-18205)
OMNIKRON SYSTEMS INC
20920 Warner Center Ln A, Woodland Hills (91367-6526)
PHONE................................818 591-7890
EMP: 100
SALES (est): 4.9MM **Privately Held**
WEB: www.omnikron.com
SIC: **7379** **7375** **5045** **8243** Computer Related Svcs Information Retrieval Sv Whol Computer/Peripheral Data Processing School Computer Programming Svc

(P-18206)
ORGANIC INC
390 Amapola Ave Ste 8, Torrance (90501-1400)
PHONE................................310 543-4600
EMP: 71
SALES (corp-wide): 15.3B **Publicly Held**
SIC: **7379** Computer Related Services
HQ: Organic, Inc.
600 California St Fl 8
San Francisco CA 10017
415 581-5300

(P-18207)
OSI DIGITAL INC (PA)
5950 Canoga Ave Ste 300, Woodland Hills (91367-5041)
PHONE................................818 992-2700
Kumar Yamani, *CEO*
Suzette White, *President*
Martin Mathias, *COO*
Pavlos Alexandrou, *Vice Pres*
Karen Dosanjh, *Vice Pres*
EMP: 40 EST: 1995
SALES (est): 24.4MM **Privately Held**
WEB: www.osidigital.com
SIC: **7379** **7372** **7371** 8741 ; application computer software; computer software development; management services

(P-18208)
OUTLOOK AMUSEMENTS INC
3746 Foothill Blvd, La Crescenta (91214-1740)
PHONE................................818 433-3800
Jason Freeland, *CEO*
Cyrus Pejoumand, *President*
Tim Youd, *Co-President*
Tom Wszalek, *Senior VP*
Isaac Abecassis, *Vice Pres*
EMP: 150 EST: 2003
SALES (est): 26MM **Privately Held**
WEB: www.outlookamusements.com
SIC: **7379**

(P-18209)
PARTNERS INFORMATION TECH (HQ)
Also Called: Calance
888 S Disneyland Dr # 500, Anaheim (92802-1847)
PHONE................................714 736-4487
Amit Govil, *Chairman*
Bill Darden, *CFO*
Asit Govil, *Treasurer*
Michell Casey, *Business Dir*
Robert Dlugos, *Info Tech Mgr*
EMP: 100 EST: 2011
SALES (est): 48.9MM **Privately Held**
WEB: www.calanceus.com
SIC: **7379**

(P-18210)
PEGASUS SQUIRE INC
12021 Wilshire Blvd # 77, Los Angeles (90025-1206)
PHONE..................................866 208-6837
Scott Cooper, *CEO*
EMP: 100 **EST:** 2002
SALES (est): 2.9MM **Privately Held**
WEB: www.pegasussquire.com
SIC: 7379 Computer related consulting services

(P-18211)
PEXS INTERNATIONAL INC
1400 Midvale Ave Apt 408, Los Angeles (90024-7812)
PHONE..................................626 365-6706
Shi Chang Lin, *CEO*
Pien LI, *CFO*
EMP: 124 **EST:** 2017
SALES (est): 50K **Privately Held**
SIC: 7379 7371 Computer related consulting services; computer software development & applications

(P-18212)
PIVOT TECHNOLOGY SOLUTIONS
15461 Springdale St, Huntington Beach (92649-1335)
PHONE..................................714 845-4547
Michael May, *President*
Carmen Collado, *Manager*
Stephen Guynn, *Manager*
EMP: 200 **EST:** 2017
SALES (est): 5.8MM **Privately Held**
WEB: www.acsacs.com
SIC: 7379

(P-18213)
PLANNET CONSULTING LLC
180 N Rverview Dr Ste 240, Anaheim (92808)
PHONE..................................714 982-5800
Steve Miano, *CEO*
Andrew Harrod, *President*
Gary Cox, *Principal*
Kamyar Ghazimorad, *Consultant*
EMP: 52 **EST:** 2001
SALES (est): 8.8MM **Privately Held**
WEB: www.plannet.com
SIC: 7379 8742 8748 ; management consulting services; telecommunications consultant

(P-18214)
PRAMIRA INC
2552 Walnut Ave Ste 200, Tustin (92780-6983)
PHONE..................................800 678-1169
Omar Houari, *CEO*
Edward Krol, *Vice Pres*
Elisabeth Miller, *Project Mgr*
MAI Thao, *Project Mgr*
Darin Huynh, *Engineer*
EMP: 125 **EST:** 2014
SQ FT: 6,000
SALES (est): 13.7MM **Privately Held**
SIC: 7379 8711 Computer related consulting services; engineering services

(P-18215)
PRECISEQ INC
11601 Wilshire Blvd Fl 5, Los Angeles (90025-0509)
PHONE..................................310 709-6094
Mark Dorner, *Partner*
Guy Livneh, *Managing Prtnr*
EMP: 80 **EST:** 2015
SQ FT: 1,200
SALES (est): 4.8MM **Privately Held**
SIC: 7379 Computer related consulting services

(P-18216)
PRO-TEK CONSULTING (PA)
21300 Victory Blvd # 240, Woodland Hills (91367-2525)
PHONE..................................805 807-5571
Raj Kessireddy, *CEO*
Divya Reddy Pyreddy, *Chairman*
EMP: 110 **EST:** 2010
SQ FT: 2,400
SALES (est): 7.8MM **Privately Held**
WEB: www.pro-tekconsulting.com
SIC: 7379

(P-18217)
QUANTUM SOLUTIONS INC
5146 Douglas Fir Rd # 205, Calabasas (91302-1405)
PHONE..................................818 577-4555
Hamid Akhavan, *CEO*
Eva Farooqi, *Administration*
EMP: 50 **EST:** 2013
SQ FT: 14,641
SALES (est): 5.9MM **Privately Held**
WEB: www.quantumsolutions.com
SIC: 7379 8742 ; business consultant

(P-18218)
SACA TECHNOLOGIES INC
5101 E La Palma Ave # 200, Anaheim (92807-2056)
PHONE..................................888 603-9030
Alexander Saca, *CEO*
Wasif Ehsan, *Software Dev*
Jaime Aguayo, *IT/INT Sup*
Andy Nackoud, *IT/INT Sup*
Andrew Saca, *Technical Staff*
EMP: 67 **EST:** 2008
SALES (est): 16.8MM **Privately Held**
WEB: www.sacatech.com
SIC: 7379 ; computer related consulting services

(P-18219)
SADA SYSTEMS INC
5250 Lankershim Blvd # 620, North Hollywood (91601-3188)
PHONE..................................818 766-2400
Tony Safoian, *CEO*
Dana Berg, *COO*
Matt Lawrence, *CFO*
Annie Safoian, *CFO*
Patrick Monaghan,
EMP: 106 **EST:** 2000
SQ FT: 10,503
SALES (est): 42.5MM **Privately Held**
WEB: www.sada.com
SIC: 7379 Computer related consulting services

(P-18220)
SAPPHIRE SOFTECH SOLUTIONS LLC
123 E 9th St Ste 323, Upland (91786-6050)
P.O. Box 6220, Corona (92878-6220)
PHONE..................................888 357-5222
Nitin Makkar,
Jasmeer Oberoi,
Rajdeep Singh Oberoi,
EMP: 60 **EST:** 2015
SALES (est): 2.8MM **Privately Held**
WEB: www.sapphiresoftech.com
SIC: 7379 Computer related maintenance services

(P-18221)
SEATECH CONSULTING GROUP INC
609 Deep Valley Dr # 200, Rllng HLS Est (90274-3614)
PHONE..................................310 356-6828
EMP: 50
SALES: 3.5MM **Privately Held**
SIC: 7379 Computer Related Services

(P-18222)
SOFTWARE MANAGEMENT CONS LLC (HQ)
Also Called: Smci
500 N Brand Blvd Ste 1100, Glendale (91203-3943)
PHONE..................................818 240-3177
Spencer L Karpf, *CEO*
Bob Maltzman, *COO*
Clara Nersissian, *CFO*
Deborah House, *Vice Pres*
Elena Zacky, *Executive*
EMP: 320 **EST:** 1976
SQ FT: 4,500
SALES (est): 39.9MM
SALES (corp-wide): 275MM **Privately Held**
WEB: www.smci.com
SIC: 7379 7361 Computer related consulting services; placement agencies

PA: Milestone Technologies Inc.
3101 Skyway Ct
Fremont CA 94539
510 651-2454

(P-18223)
SYNECTIC SOLUTIONS INC (PA)
Also Called: S S I
1701 Pacific Ave Ste 260, Oxnard (93033-1887)
PHONE..................................805 483-4800
Lynn Dines, *President*
Joel Dines, *CFO*
Toby Doane, *Vice Pres*
Pam Pullman, *Director*
EMP: 78
SQ FT: 5,000
SALES (est): 13.4MM **Privately Held**
WEB: www.synecticsolutions.com
SIC: 7379 8331 ; job training services

(P-18224)
SYNOPTEK INC (PA)
19520 Jamboree Rd Ste 110, Irvine (92612-2429)
PHONE..................................949 241-8600
Tim Britt, *CEO*
John Frazier, *COO*
Ricardo Ordonez, *CFO*
Phil Crippen, *Officer*
Glenn Mulhare, *Officer*
EMP: 67 **EST:** 1988
SALES (est): 148.5MM **Privately Held**
WEB: www.synoptek.com
SIC: 7379 Computer related consulting services

(P-18225)
T & T SOLUTIONS INC
7018 Owensmouth Ave # 201, Canoga Park (91303-2073)
PHONE..................................818 676-1786
Fax: 818 676-1272
EMP: 70
SQ FT: 2,100
SALES (est): 6.2MM **Privately Held**
WEB: www.ttsus.com
SIC: 7379 Computer Related Services

(P-18226)
TECHNOLOGY RESOURCE CENTER INC (PA)
2101 E 4th St Ste 130a, Santa Ana (92705-3843)
PHONE..................................714 542-1004
Gabriel Chavez, *President*
Anthony Chavez, *CFO*
Mark Serres, *Vice Pres*
EMP: 59 **EST:** 1996
SQ FT: 2,000
SALES (est): 5.4MM **Privately Held**
WEB: www.trcinc.net
SIC: 7379 7361 Computer related consulting services; employment agencies

(P-18227)
TENTEK INC (PA)
101 N Brand Blvd Ste 1660, Glendale (91203-2664)
PHONE..................................818 551-7100
Allen Teng, *President*
Henry Lee, *Vice Pres*
Carlos Regalado, *Tech Recruiter*
Christine Sagherian, *Opers Staff*
Calli Clemons, *Account Dir*
EMP: 124 **EST:** 1989
SALES (est): 16.2MM **Privately Held**
WEB: www.tentek.com
SIC: 7379 Computer related consulting services

(P-18228)
TRIAGE PARTNERS LLC
15717 Texaco Ave, Paramount (90723-3923)
PHONE..................................562 634-0058
EMP: 78
SALES (corp-wide): 25.6MM **Privately Held**
SIC: 7379 Computer Related Services
PA: Triage Partners, L.L.C.
1715 N West Shore Blvd # 250
Tampa FL 33607
813 801-9869

(P-18229)
TRUTHMD LLC
32932 Pcf Cast Hwy Ste 14, Dana Point (92629)
PHONE..................................949 637-4296
Gemma Turi,
John Utz, *COO*
Todd Sabath, *Officer*
Samarith Srey, *Vice Pres*
Vicki Gagliardi, *Administration*
EMP: 54 **EST:** 2013
SALES (est): 5.9MM **Privately Held**
SIC: 7379

(P-18230)
U-NAV MICROELECTRONICS CORP
8 Hughes, Irvine (92618-2072)
PHONE..................................949 453-2727
Russ Garcia, *CEO*
Alan Ross, *Ch of Bd*
Greg Winner, *COO*
Frank Hettmann, *CFO*
Brad Anderson, *Director*
EMP: 55 **EST:** 2001
SQ FT: 10,000
SALES (est): 4.9MM **Privately Held**
SIC: 7379 8711 Computer related consulting services; engineering services

(P-18231)
UNITED STATES TECHNICAL SVCS
Also Called: Usts
16541 Gothard St Ste 214, Huntington Beach (92647-4436)
PHONE..................................714 374-6300
Bob Polk, *President*
John Courtney, *CEO*
Cynthia Dugger, *Treasurer*
EMP: 122 **EST:** 1998
SQ FT: 2,500
SALES (est): 10.8MM **Privately Held**
WEB: www.usts.com
SIC: 7379

(P-18232)
UNITEK LEARNING INC (PA)
Also Called: Unitek It Education
1401 Dove St Ste 340, Newport Beach (92660-2420)
PHONE..................................510 249-1060
Janis Paulson, *CEO*
Shiva Jahan, *CFO*
Navraj Bawa, *Vice Pres*
Don Corvin, *Vice Pres*
Jamie Holcomb, *Vice Pres*
EMP: 55 **EST:** 1992
SALES (est): 27.1MM **Privately Held**
WEB: www.uniteklearning.com
SIC: 7379 7371 Computer related consulting services; custom computer programming services

(P-18233)
US DATA MANAGEMENT LLC (PA)
Also Called: Usdm Life Science
535 Chapala St, Santa Barbara (93101-3411)
PHONE..................................888 231-0816
Kevin Brown, *Managing Prtnr*
Vega Finucan, *Managing Prtnr*
Kim Hutchings, *Vice Pres*
Robert Lucchesi, *Vice Pres*
Erin Northington, *Vice Pres*
EMP: 100
SQ FT: 4,000
SALES (est): 19.7MM **Privately Held**
WEB: www.usdm.com
SIC: 7379 Computer related consulting services

(P-18234)
VERIZON DIGITAL MEDIA SVCS INC (HQ)
13031 W Jefferson Blvd, Los Angeles (90094-7000)
PHONE..................................310 396-7400
Ralf Jacob, *President*
Dhruva Patel, *Partner*
Jonathan Divincenzo, *Vice Pres*
Daniel Franklin, *Vice Pres*
Jeff Geiser, *Vice Pres*
EMP: 424 **EST:** 2006

SQ FT: 50,000
SALES (est): 89.7MM
SALES (corp-wide): 128.2B **Publicly Held**
WEB: www.verizon.com
SIC: 7379
PA: Verizon Communications Inc.
1095 Ave Of The Americas
New York NY 10036
212 395-1000

(P-18235)
VISION 33 INC (PA)
6 Hughes Ste 220, Irvine (92618-2063)
PHONE...........................949 420-3300
Tony Whalen, *President*
Blake Barkhouse, *Vice Pres*
Neil Feingold, *Vice Pres*
Scott McMahon, *Vice Pres*
Alexander Rooney, *Vice Pres*
▲ **EMP:** 150 **EST:** 2003
SQ FT: 1,500
SALES (est): 36.4MM **Privately Held**
WEB: www.vision33.com
SIC: 5734 7379 Computer & software stores; computer related consulting services

(P-18236)
WHERE 2 GET IT INC (HQ)
Also Called: Brandify
222 S Harbor Blvd Ste 600, Anaheim (92805-3794)
PHONE...........................714 660-4870
Manish Patel, *President*
Jeff Hix, *Partner*
Mike Pycha, *Officer*
Geoffrey Infeld, *Vice Pres*
Andy Roy, *Vice Pres*
EMP: 69 **EST:** 1994
SALES (est): 10MM **Privately Held**
WEB: www.brandify.com
SIC: 7379 Computer related maintenance services
PA: Soci, Inc.
225 Broadway Ste 600
San Diego CA 92101
858 225-4110

7381 Detective & Armored Car Svcs

(P-18237)
ABM ONSITE SERVICES INC
3337 Michelson Dr Ste Cn7, Irvine (92612-1699)
PHONE...........................949 863-9100
EMP: 572
SALES (corp-wide): 5.9B **Publicly Held**
WEB: www.abm.com
SIC: 7381 7521 8711 7349 Security guard service; automobile parking; engineering services; janitorial service, contract basis
HQ: Abm Onsite Services, Inc.
1 Liberty Plz Fl 7
New York NY 10006

(P-18238)
ACCESS CONTROL SECURITY INC (PA)
21049 Devonshire St # 211, Chatsworth (91311-2375)
P.O. Box 3791 (91313-3791)
PHONE...........................714 835-3800
Reza Jalala, *President*
Salman Sarfraz, *Opers Mgr*
Jerry Bashin, *Sales Mgr*
Fahim Abid, *Manager*
EMP: 99 **EST:** 2004
SALES (est): 5.2MM **Privately Held**
WEB: www.accesscontrolsecurity.com
SIC: 7381 Security guard service; guard services

(P-18239)
AEGIS SEC & INVESTIGATIONS INC
10866 Wash Blvd Ste 308, Culver City (90232-3610)
PHONE...........................310 838-2787
Jeffrey Nathaniel Zisner, *CEO*
EMP: 102 **EST:** 2010

SALES (est): 9.3MM **Privately Held**
WEB: www.aegis.com
SIC: 7381 Security guard service

(P-18240)
ALLIED GUARD SERVICES INC (PA)
110 S La Brea Ave Ste 425, Inglewood (90301-8725)
PHONE...........................424 227-9912
Ibrahim Tchiany, *Principal*
EMP: 88 **EST:** 2016
SALES (est): 411.7K **Privately Held**
WEB: www.alliedguardservices.com
SIC: 7381 Security guard service

(P-18241)
ALLIED PROTECTION SERVICES INC
Also Called: Armed/Xctive Prtction Armed Un
19164 Van Ness Ave, Torrance (90501-1101)
PHONE...........................310 330-8314
Leon Brooks, *President*
Corbin Howard, *Executive Asst*
EMP: 178 **EST:** 1999
SALES (est): 7.1MM **Privately Held**
WEB: www.alliedprotection.com
SIC: 7381 Security guard service

(P-18242)
AMERICAN CORPORATE SEC INC (PA)
1 World Trade Ctr # 1240, Long Beach (90831-1240)
PHONE...........................562 216-7440
Larry J Saye, *CEO*
Dina Christopher, *Officer*
Yvonne Mercado, *Officer*
Sean Ramsden, *Officer*
Tim Lovette, *Human Res Mgr*
EMP: 407 **EST:** 2003
SALES (est): 35.5MM **Privately Held**
WEB: www.amcorpsec.com
SIC: 7381 8721 Security guard service; payroll accounting service

(P-18243)
AMERICAN EGLE PRTCTIVE SVCS IN
Also Called: American Eagle Protective Svcs
425 W Kelso St, Inglewood (90301-2539)
PHONE...........................310 412-0019
Joelle Fopoussi Epoh, *CEO*
Alma Serrano, *Admin Sec*
EMP: 90 **EST:** 2011
SALES (est): 6.3MM **Privately Held**
WEB: www.aeprotectiveservices.com
SIC: 7381 Security guard service

(P-18244)
AMERICAN GUARD SERVICES INC (PA)
1125 W 190th St, Gardena (90248-4303)
PHONE...........................310 645-6200
Sherine Assal, *President*
Douglas Lopez, *Officer*
Jason Johnson, *Branch Mgr*
Cash Foster, *General Mgr*
Arnold Garcia, *Technician*
EMP: 400 **EST:** 1997
SQ FT: 28,000
SALES (est): 97.9MM **Privately Held**
WEB: www.americanguardservices.com
SIC: 7381 Security guard service

(P-18245)
AMERICAN POWER SEC SVC INC
1451 Rimpau Ave Ste 207, Corona (92879-7522)
PHONE...........................866 974-9994
Mohamed Faty, *President*
EMP: 85 **EST:** 2015
SALES (est): 550K **Privately Held**
WEB: www.americanpowersecurity.com
SIC: 7381 Security guard service

(P-18246)
AMERICAN PROTECTION GROUP INC (PA)
Also Called: Apg
8551 Vesper Ave, Panorama City (91402-2914)
PHONE...........................818 279-2433
Anthony Brown, *President*
EMP: 107 **EST:** 2012
SQ FT: 3,000
SALES (est): 5.4MM **Privately Held**
WEB: www.apg-svcs.com
SIC: 7381 5063 7382 Security guard service; burglary protection service; detective agency; alarm systems; burglar alarm maintenance & monitoring

(P-18247)
AMERICAN PRTCTIVE SVCS INVSTGT
12471 Balsam Rd, Victorville (92395-9474)
P.O. Box 4640, Diamond Bar (91765-0640)
PHONE...........................626 705-8600
Allan Bailey, *President*
EMP: 225 **EST:** 1998
SALES (est): 1.7MM **Privately Held**
SIC: 7381 Security guard service

(P-18248)
AMERICAN SECURITY FORCE INC
5400 E Olympic Blvd # 225, Commerce (90022-5154)
PHONE...........................323 722-8585
Albert Williams, *President*
Yesenia Zambrano, *Admin Asst*
Jose Robledo, *Accounts Mgr*
EMP: 70 **EST:** 1993
SQ FT: 3,700
SALES (est): 9.4MM **Privately Held**
WEB: www.americansecurityforce.com
SIC: 7381 7382 Protective services, guard; private investigator; guard dog rental; detective agency; burglar alarm maintenance & monitoring

(P-18249)
ANDREWS INTERNATIONAL INC
455 N Moss St, Burbank (91502-1727)
PHONE...........................818 260-9586
EMP: 177
SALES (corp-wide): 139.5MM **Privately Held**
SIC: 7381 Detective/Armored Car Services
PA: Andrews International, Inc.
455 N Moss St
Burbank CA 91502
818 487-4060

(P-18250)
ANDREWS INTERNATIONAL INC
Also Called: Vance Executive Protection
11601 Wilshire Blvd # 50, Los Angeles (90025-0509)
PHONE...........................310 575-4844
Rocco Barnes, *Director*
EMP: 172
SALES (corp-wide): 120.3MM **Privately Held**
SIC: 7381 Security guard service
HQ: Andrews International, Inc.
5870 Trinity Pkwy Ste 300
Centreville VA 20120
703 592-1400

(P-18251)
ANDREWS INTERNATIONAL INC (PA)
455 N Moss St, Burbank (91502-1727)
PHONE...........................818 487-4060
Randy Andrews, *President*
Ty Richmond, *COO*
James Wood, *COO*
Michael Topf, *CFO*
Jackson Demars, *Officer*
EMP: 1700 **EST:** 1986
SQ FT: 5,000
SALES (est): 120.3MM **Privately Held**
WEB: www.andrewsinternational.com
SIC: 7381 Security guard service

(P-18252)
ARMORED TRANSPORT INC (DH)
20325 E Walnut Dr N, Walnut (91789-2916)
PHONE...........................909 468-2229
Vic Schunstein, *General Mgr*
EMP: 50 **EST:** 2000
SALES (est): 1MM
SALES (corp-wide): 145.8MM **Privately Held**
WEB: www.garda.com
SIC: 7381 Armored car services

(P-18253)
BABYLON SECURITY SERVICES INC
6032 One Half Vneland Ave, North Hollywood (91606)
PHONE...........................818 766-8122
Arvin Younan, *Principal*
EMP: 85 **EST:** 1997
SALES (est): 2MM **Privately Held**
SIC: 7381 Security guard service

(P-18254)
BARRYS SECURITY SERVICES INC (PA)
16739 Van Buren Blvd, Riverside (92504-5744)
PHONE...........................951 789-7575
Michelle Barry, *CEO*
Martin Morales, *Vice Pres*
Heidi Falls-Hand, *Controller*
EMP: 188 **EST:** 1999
SQ FT: 5,000
SALES (est): 8.3MM **Privately Held**
WEB: www.weguard.biz
SIC: 7381 Security guard service

(P-18255)
BARRYS SECURITY SERVICES INC
5480 Katella Ave Ste 203, Los Alamitos (90720-6823)
PHONE...........................562 493-7007
EMP: 125
SALES (corp-wide): 8.3MM **Privately Held**
WEB: www.weguard.biz
SIC: 7381 Detective And Armored Car Services, Nsk
PA: Barry's Security Services, Inc.
16739 Van Buren Blvd
Riverside CA 92504
951 789-7575

(P-18256)
BOYD & ASSOCIATES
3151 Airway Ave Ste K105, Costa Mesa (92626-4613)
PHONE...........................714 835-5423
Fax: 714 835-5641
EMP: 150
SQ FT: 3,012
SALES (corp-wide): 19.4MM **Privately Held**
SIC: 7381 Security Protection Services
PA: Boyd & Associates
2191 E Thompson Blvd
Ventura CA 93001
818 752-1888

(P-18257)
BOYD AND ASSOCIATES
445 E Esplanade Dr # 210, Oxnard (93036-2126)
PHONE...........................805 988-8298
Kathy Correll, *Manager*
EMP: 75
SALES (corp-wide): 14.2MM **Privately Held**
WEB: www.boydsecurity.com
SIC: 7381 Security guard service
PA: Boyd And Associates
2191 E Thompson Blvd
Ventura CA 93001
818 752-1888

(P-18258)
BOYD AND ASSOCIATES (PA)
2191 E Thompson Blvd Ventura (93001-3538)
PHONE...........................818 752-1888
Raymond G Boyd Sr, *Ch of Bd*

Daniel Boyd, *President*
Barbara K Boyd, *Vice Pres*
Jeff Krieger, *Consultant*
EMP: 160
SQ FT: 8,000
SALES (est): 14.2MM **Privately Held**
WEB: www.boydsecurity.com
SIC: 7381 7382 Security guard service; detective services; security systems services

(P-18259)
BRINKS INCORPORATED
7191 Patterson Dr, Garden Grove (92841-1415)
PHONE....................714 903-9272
Al Kent, *Manager*
John Bui, *Opers Staff*
EMP: 120
SALES (corp-wide): 3.6B **Publicly Held**
WEB: www.us.brinks.com
SIC: 7381 Armored car services
HQ: Brink's, Incorporated
1801 Bayberry Ct Ste 400
Richmond VA 23226
804 289-9600

(P-18260)
CALIFORNIA SAFETY AGENCY
8932 Katella Ave Ste 108, Anaheim (92804-6299)
PHONE....................866 996-6990
EMP: 50
SALES (est): 1MM **Privately Held**
SIC: 7381 Detective/Armored Car Services

(P-18261)
CENTURION SECURITY SVCS INC (PA)
20102 Sw Cypress St, Newport Beach (92660-0713)
PHONE....................949 474-0444
Robyn Hamilton, *President*
Jeff Hamilton, *Vice Pres*
EMP: 54 **EST:** 2009
SALES (est): 1.8MM **Privately Held**
WEB: www.centurionssi.com
SIC: 7381 Security guard service

(P-18262)
CHG SECURITY INC
16431 Grayville Dr, La Mirada (90638-2719)
PHONE....................562 284-6260
Owusu Boateng, *CEO*
EMP: 50 **EST:** 2018
SALES (est): 910.1K **Privately Held**
SIC: 7381 Protective services, guard

(P-18263)
COMMERCIAL PROTECTIVE SVCS INC
Also Called: CPS Security
3400 E Airport Way, Long Beach (90806-2412)
PHONE....................310 515-5290
Christopher Coffey, *President*
William R Babcock, *CFO*
EMP: 1800 **EST:** 1997
SQ FT: 10,000
SALES (est): 57MM **Privately Held**
SIC: 7381 Security guard service

(P-18264)
COMMUNITY PATROL
1420 E Edinger Ave # 213, Santa Ana (92705-4816)
PHONE....................657 247-4744
Alicia Ledesma, *Owner*
EMP: 90 **EST:** 2019
SALES (est): 1.3MM **Privately Held**
SIC: 7381 Security guard service

(P-18265)
CONTEMPORARY SERVICES CORP (PA)
Also Called: C S C
17101 Superior St, Northridge (91325-1961)
PHONE....................818 885-5150
Damon Zumwalt, *CEO*
Jim Granger, *President*
Mark Camillo, *Vice Pres*
Chris Martinez, *Vice Pres*
Nick Ryter, *Office Mgr*

▲ **EMP:** 3144 **EST:** 1967
SQ FT: 20,000
SALES (est): 297.4MM **Privately Held**
WEB: www.rnstaffing.com
SIC: 7381 Security guard service

(P-18266)
COTTRELL PAUL ENTERPRISES LLC (PA)
Also Called: Unique Protective Services
16654 Soledad Canyon Rd # 23, Santa Clarita (91387-3217)
PHONE....................661 212-2357
Paul Cottrell, *Mng Member*
EMP: 120
SQ FT: 400
SALES (est): 4.3MM **Privately Held**
SIC: 7381 Security guard service

(P-18267)
CPS SECURITY SOLUTIONS INC (PA)
3400 E Airport Way, Long Beach (90806-2412)
PHONE....................310 818-1030
Chris Coffey, *President*
William Babcock, *CFO*
Scott R Barnes, *Exec VP*
EMP: 963 **EST:** 2007
SQ FT: 14,000
SALES (est): 37.9MM **Privately Held**
SIC: 7381 Security guard service

(P-18268)
CROSSING GUARD COMPANY
10440 Pioneer Blvd Ste 5, Santa Fe Springs (90670-8238)
PHONE....................310 202-8284
Chris O 'connor, *Opers Staff*
EMP: 112 **EST:** 2011
SALES (est): 282.6K
SALES (corp-wide): 63.7MM **Privately Held**
WEB: www.thecrossingguardcompany.com
SIC: 7381 Guard services
PA: All-City Management Services, Inc.
10440 Pioneer Blvd Ste 5
Santa Fe Springs CA 90670
310 202-8284

(P-18269)
DAVID SHIELD SECURITY INC
Also Called: Dss
23945 Calabasas Rd # 108, Calabasas (91302-1503)
PHONE....................310 849-4950
Athan Bazaz, *President*
Snir Warshaziak, *CEO*
EMP: 100 **EST:** 2015
SALES (est): 5MM **Privately Held**
WEB: www.davidshieldsecurity.com
SIC: 7381 Security guard service

(P-18270)
DINASTY SECURITY SERVICES
640 S Ford Blvd, Los Angeles (90022-2412)
PHONE....................310 507-7848
Oliva Chavez, *President*
EMP: 50 **EST:** 2009
SALES (est): 1.1MM **Privately Held**
WEB: www.dinastysecurity.com
SIC: 7381 Security guard service

(P-18271)
DREW CHAIN SECURITY CORP
55 S Raymond Ave Ste 303, Alhambra (91801-7100)
PHONE....................626 457-8626
Kenneth Y Lee, *President*
EMP: 71 **EST:** 2004
SQ FT: 800
SALES (est): 1MM **Privately Held**
WEB: www.drewchain.com
SIC: 7381 Security guard service

(P-18272)
EAGLE SECURITY SERVICES INC
12903 S Normandie Ave, Gardena (90249-2123)
PHONE....................310 642-0656
Mohsen Kamel, *President*
EMP: 150 **EST:** 2003
SQ FT: 5,000

SALES (est): 6.2MM **Privately Held**
WEB: www.eagless.com
SIC: 7381 Security guard service

(P-18273)
ELITE ENFRCMENT SEC SLTONS INC (PA)
1290 N Hancock St Ste 101, Anaheim (92807-1942)
PHONE....................866 354-8308
Alex Solorio, *President*
Kevin Roncevich, *Vice Pres*
Matt Trujillo, *Director*
EMP: 144 **EST:** 2012
SQ FT: 2,400
SALES (est): 5MM **Privately Held**
WEB: www.eliteenforcement.com
SIC: 7381 7389 Security guard service;

(P-18274)
FIDELITY SECURITY SERVICES INC
25133 Avenue Tibbitts H, Valencia (91355-3494)
PHONE....................661 295-5007
Ahmadshah Ahmadi, *President*
Nazifa Ahmadi, *CFO*
EMP: 51 **EST:** 2005
SQ FT: 1,000
SALES (est): 675K **Privately Held**
WEB: www.fidelitysecurityservices.com
SIC: 7381 Security guard service; guard services

(P-18275)
FPK SECURITY INC
Also Called: Fpk Investigaions
28348 Constellation Rd # 880, Valencia (91355-5097)
P.O. Box 55597 (91385-0597)
PHONE....................661 702-9091
Mark David, *CEO*
Robert Esquivel, *President*
Kamy Bassiri, *Vice Pres*
EMP: 365 **EST:** 2005
SQ FT: 1,200
SALES (est): 10.8MM **Privately Held**
WEB: www.fpksecurity.com
SIC: 7381 Security guard service

(P-18276)
FRASCO INC (PA)
Also Called: Frasco Investigative Services
215 W Alameda Ave Ste 105, Burbank (91502-3061)
PHONE....................818 848-3888
John C Simmers, *President*
Laura Pfaffman, *CFO*
Laura S Pfaffman, *CFO*
Scott Cornelison, *Vice Pres*
Noelle Harling, *Vice Pres*
EMP: 65
SQ FT: 10,000
SALES (est): 19.6MM **Privately Held**
WEB: www.frasco.com
SIC: 7381 Private investigator

(P-18277)
FRAUD FIGHTERS INC
Also Called: Prodigy Investigations
2600 Michelson Dr Ste 160, Irvine (92612-6505)
PHONE....................800 576-6116
Todd M Gullett, *CEO*
Stephanie Mic Lapointe, *Director*
Gina Evangelisti, *Accounts Mgr*
EMP: 50 **EST:** 1977
SQ FT: 4,000
SALES (est): 1.8MM **Privately Held**
WEB: www.factsnotfiction.com
SIC: 7381 Private investigator

(P-18278)
GARDA CL WEST INC (DH)
Also Called: Gcl W
1612 W Pico Blvd, Los Angeles (90015-2410)
PHONE....................213 383-3611
Stephan Cretier, *President*
Chris W Jamroz, *President*
Chantal Baril, *Vice Pres*
Jean-Michel Filiatrault, *Vice Pres*
Christian Paradis, *Vice Pres*
▲ **EMP:** 375 **EST:** 1947
SQ FT: 25,000

SALES (est): 290.5MM
SALES (corp-wide): 145.8MM **Privately Held**
WEB: www.garda.com
SIC: 7381 Security guard service

(P-18279)
GOLDEN WEST SECURITY
Also Called: Golden West K-9
12502 Van Nuys Blvd Ste 2, Pacoima (91331-1321)
PHONE....................818 897-5965
Chris Monica, *CEO*
Ralf Santarelli, *President*
Gary Jeffrey, *VP Sales*
Mic Montalvo, *Director*
EMP: 120 **EST:** 1971
SALES (est): 7.5MM **Privately Held**
WEB: www.goldenwestsecurityinc.com
SIC: 7381 Security guard service; guard services

(P-18280)
GUARD-SYSTEMS INC
1910 S Archibald Ave M2, Ontario (91761-8502)
PHONE....................909 947-5400
Patrick Crawford, *Manager*
EMP: 568
SALES (corp-wide): 15.5MM **Privately Held**
WEB: www.guardsystemsinc.com
SIC: 7381 Protective services, guard; guard services; security guard service
PA: Guard-Systems, Inc.
1190 Monterey Pass Rd
Monterey Park CA 91754
626 443-0031

(P-18281)
GUARD-SYSTEMS INC
Also Called: Guard Systems District 1
1190 Monterey Pass Rd, Monterey Park (91754-3615)
PHONE....................323 881-6715
Theodore Haas, *Owner*
Lindsey Livacich, *Mktg Dir*
EMP: 568
SALES (corp-wide): 15.5MM **Privately Held**
WEB: www.guardsystemsinc.com
SIC: 7381 Security guard service
PA: Guard-Systems, Inc.
1190 Monterey Pass Rd
Monterey Park CA 91754
626 443-0031

(P-18282)
GUARDNOW INC
18663 Ventura Blvd # 217, Tarzana (91356-4162)
P.O. Box 67, Manhattan Beach (90267-0067)
PHONE....................877 482-7366
Mike Kator, *President*
EMP: 50 **EST:** 2011
SQ FT: 115
SALES (est): 5MM **Privately Held**
WEB: www.guardnow.com
SIC: 7381 Security guard service

(P-18283)
GUARDSMARK LLC
1225 W 190th St Ste 280, Gardena (90248-4305)
PHONE....................310 522-9603
EMP: 60
SALES (corp-wide): 741.7MM **Privately Held**
SIC: 7381 Detective/Armored Car Services
HQ: Guardsmark, Llc
1551 N Tustin Ave Ste 650
Santa Ana CA 92705
714 619-9700

(P-18284)
GUARDSMARK LLC (DH)
1551 N Tustin Ave Ste 650, Santa Ana (92705-8664)
PHONE....................714 619-9700
Steven S Jones, *CEO*
James Hartman, *Portfolio Mgr*
Penny Estes, *Business Mgr*
EMP: 88 **EST:** 2002
SQ FT: 32,107

SALES (est): 195.1MM
SALES (corp-wide): 592.4MM **Privately Held**
SIC: **7381** 8742 2721 Security guard service; private investigator; industry specialist consultants; periodicals: publishing only
HQ: Universal Protection Service, Lp
1551 N Tustin Ave Ste 650
Santa Ana CA 92705
714 619-9700

(P-18285)
GUARDSMARK LLC
5300 Lennox Ave Ste 102, Bakersfield (93309-1662)
PHONE..................661 325-5906
EMP: 111
SALES (corp-wide): 928.7MM **Privately Held**
SIC: **7381** Detective/Armored Car Services
HQ: Guardsmark, Llc
6363 Poplar Ave Ste 300
Memphis TN 92705
901 761-2288

(P-18286)
HAYES PROTECTIVE SERVICES INC
2930 W Imperial Hwy 200b, Inglewood (90303-3143)
P.O. Box 4684, Carson (90749-4684)
PHONE..................323 755-2282
Berlin Hayes, *President*
Jim Marin, *CFO*
EMP: 210 EST: 1986
SALES (est): 4MM **Privately Held**
SIC: **7381** Security guard service

(P-18287)
HMI ASSOCIATES INC
6800 Owensmouth Ave # 330, Canoga Park (91303-3159)
PHONE..................818 887-6800
EMP: 200
SALES (est): 1.8MM **Privately Held**
SIC: **7381** Detective/Armored Car Services

(P-18288)
HORSEMEN INC
16911 Algonquin St, Huntington Beach (92649-3812)
PHONE..................714 847-4243
Patrick Carroll, *President*
Melissa Turrieta, *Office Mgr*
Andy Crimmins, *Accounts Mgr*
Cheryl Gall, *Consultant*
EMP: 100 EST: 1995
SALES (est): 7.1MM **Privately Held**
WEB: www.horsemeninc.com
SIC: **7381** Private investigator

(P-18289)
INTER-CON INVESTIGATORS INC
Also Called: Inter Con Systems
210 S De Lacey Ave, Pasadena (91105-2048)
PHONE..................626 535-2200
Enrique Hernandez Jr, *President*
Roland Hernandez, *Vice Pres*
EMP: 51 EST: 1980
SQ FT: 17,000
SALES (est): 541.4K **Privately Held**
WEB: www.icsecurity.com
SIC: **7381** Security guard service

(P-18290)
J&E PRIVATE SECURITY CORP
3227 Producer Way Ste 110, Pomona (91768-3919)
PHONE..................909 594-1111
Megan Hsu, *Admin Sec*
Edwin Inocencio, *CFO*
EMP: 60 EST: 2016
SALES (est): 1.7MM **Privately Held**
WEB: www.jeprivatesecurity.com
SIC: **7381** Security guard service

(P-18291)
JONES BOLD SECURITY INC
Also Called: Jbsprotection
1611 S Catalina Ave L50, Redondo Beach (90277-5255)
PHONE..................323 800-2542
Brandon Jones, *CEO*

EMP: 100 EST: 2018
SALES (est): 3.4MM **Privately Held**
SIC: **7381** Guard services

(P-18292)
LANDMARK EVENT STAFFING
4790 Irvine Blvd Ste 105, Irvine (92620-1998)
PHONE..................714 293-4248
Peter Kranske, *President*
EMP: 876 **Privately Held**
WEB: www.landmarkeventstaff.com
SIC: **7381** Security guard service
PA: Landmark Event Staffing Services, Inc.
4131 Harbor Walk Dr
Fort Collins CO 80525

(P-18293)
LANTZ SECURITY SYSTEMS INC
101 N Westlake Blvd # 20, Westlake Village (91362-3753)
PHONE..................805 496-5775
Terry Oestreich, *Manager*
EMP: 146 **Privately Held**
WEB:
SIC: **7381** 7382 Security guard service; security systems services
PA: Lantz Security Systems, Inc.
43440 Sahuayo St
Lancaster CA 93535

(P-18294)
LANTZ SECURITY SYSTEMS INC (PA)
43440 Sahuayo St, Lancaster (93535-4659)
PHONE..................661 949-3565
Jack E Lantz, *President*
Jehry Miller, *Officer*
Jose Reyes, *Vice Pres*
Damon Lantz, *Marketing Staff*
EMP: 60 EST: 1994
SQ FT: 2,100
SALES (est): 14.6MM **Privately Held**
WEB: www.lantzsecurity.com
SIC: **7381** Security guard service

(P-18295)
LYONS SECURITY SERVICE INC (PA)
505 S Villa Real Ste 203a, Anaheim (92807-3448)
P.O. Box 18955 (92817-8955)
PHONE..................714 401-4850
Kathleen Guidice, *President*
EMP: 130 EST: 1982
SQ FT: 750
SALES (est): 2.5MM **Privately Held**
WEB: www.lyonssecurityinc.com
SIC: **7381** Security guard service

(P-18296)
M & S SECURITY SERVICES INC
Also Called: Westside Security Patrol
2900 L St, Bakersfield (93301-2351)
PHONE..................661 397-9616
Marvin Fuller Jr, *President*
Steve Fuller, *President*
Darlene Fuller, *Corp Secy*
EMP: 100 EST: 1972
SQ FT: 3,000
SALES (est): 7.4MM **Privately Held**
WEB: www.mssecurityservices.com
SIC: **7381** 7382 1731 Protective services, guard; security systems services; burglar alarm maintenance & monitoring; fire detection & burglar alarm systems specialization

(P-18297)
MORGAN TURNER FREEMAN (PA)
Also Called: Morgan Trner Frman Invstgators
433 N Camden Dr, Beverly Hills (90210-4409)
PHONE..................310 800-3502
Monte Frank, *Principal*
David Giovannitti, *Manager*
EMP: 60 EST: 2010
SALES (est): 208.2K **Privately Held**
WEB: www.morganturnerinvestigators.com
SIC: **7381** Private investigator

(P-18298)
MULHOLLAND SEC & PATROL INC
Also Called: Centurion Group, The
11454 San Vicente Blvd, Los Angeles (90049-6208)
PHONE..................818 755-0202
David Rosenberg, *President*
Steven Lemmer, *Partner*
Daniel Campbell, *Vice Pres*
EMP: 350 EST: 1992
SQ FT: 2,500
SALES (est): 15.7MM **Privately Held**
WEB: www.centuriongroup.com
SIC: **7381** Protective services, guard; security guard service

(P-18299)
MURANO GROUP
30211 Avnida De Las Bndra Ste, Rancho Santa Margari (92688)
PHONE..................949 409-1079
Tristan Murano, *CEO*
EMP: 52 EST: 2019
SQ FT: 2,000
SALES (est): 1.2MM **Privately Held**
WEB: www.themuranogroup.com
SIC: **7381** 7389 Security guard service; explosives recovery or extraction services

(P-18300)
NAFEES MEMON
Also Called: Nafees Mmon Cmmand Intl SEC Sv
6819 Sepulveda Blvd # 312, Van Nuys (91405-4463)
PHONE..................818 997-1666
Nafees Memon, *Owner*
Kim Newbill, *Manager*
EMP: 90 EST: 2008
SQ FT: 700
SALES (est): 3MM **Privately Held**
WEB: www.commandinternational.com
SIC: **7381** Security guard service

(P-18301)
NATIONWIDE GUARD SERVICES INC
9327 Frway View Pl Ste 20, Rancho Cucamonga (91730)
PHONE..................909 608-1112
James Woolen, *President*
John Woolen, *President*
Adrienne Johnson, *Admin Sec*
Dean Kendrick, *Supervisor*
Johnathan Sullivan, *Supervisor*
EMP: 325 EST: 1984
SALES (est): 12.3MM **Privately Held**
WEB: www.nwguards.com
SIC: **7381** Security guard service

(P-18302)
NORTH AMRCN SEC INVESTIGATIONS
550 E Carson Plaza Dr # 22, Carson (90746-3229)
PHONE..................323 634-1911
Kenny Hillman, *President*
Arthur Lopez, *CEO*
EMP: 100 EST: 2004
SQ FT: 6,000
SALES (est): 4.8MM **Privately Held**
WEB: www.nasi-pi.com
SIC: **7381** Security guard service

(P-18303)
NU-WAY SEC INVSTGTIVE SVCS INC
14368 St Andrews Dr Ste D, Victorville (92395-4315)
PHONE..................760 243-7577
Willie Patton, *President*
Audra D Patton, *Info Tech Mgr*
EMP: 59 EST: 1999
SALES (est): 688.5K **Privately Held**
WEB: www.nuwaysecurity.com
SIC: **7381** Security guard service

(P-18304)
OPSEC SPECIALIZED PROTECTION
44262 Division St Ste A, Lancaster (93535-3548)
PHONE..................661 942-3999

Fred Porras, *Owner*
Jeannie Groff, *Owner*
Sue Imperial, *General Mgr*
EMP: 99 EST: 2001
SALES (est): 4.9MM **Privately Held**
WEB: www.opsecpro.com
SIC: **7381** Security guard service

(P-18305)
PACIFIC EAGLE INTERNATIONAL (PA)
12674 Hoover St, Garden Grove (92841-4173)
P.O. Box 2647, Los Alamitos (90720-7647)
PHONE..................562 972-3813
Mach Nguyen, *President*
So Fan Ip, *Vice Pres*
Rpa Robin Andrews, *Property Mgr*
EMP: 293 EST: 1990
SALES (est): 7.7MM **Privately Held**
SIC: **7381** Security guard service

(P-18306)
PACIFIC PROTECTION SVCS INC (PA)
22144 Clarendon St # 110, Woodland Hills (91367-8201)
PHONE..................818 313-9369
Melvin Staples, *CEO*
Steven W Frye, *CFO*
EMP: 187 EST: 1984
SQ FT: 3,000
SALES (est): 13.2MM **Privately Held**
WEB: www.garda.com
SIC: **7381** Security guard service

(P-18307)
PACWEST SECURITY SERVICES
2990 Inland Empire Blvd, Ontario (91764-4899)
PHONE..................909 948-0279
Jery Winkfield, *Branch Mgr*
EMP: 130 **Privately Held**
WEB: www.pacwestsecurity.com
SIC: **7381** Security guard service
PA: Pacwest Security Services
3303 Harbor Blvd Ste A103
Costa Mesa CA 92626

(P-18308)
PACWEST SECURITY SERVICES
1545 Wilshire Blvd # 302, Los Angeles (90017-4501)
PHONE..................213 413-3500
Salvador Crespo, *Branch Mgr*
Ashleigh Parker, *Officer*
David Harris, *Regional Mgr*
Hilda Soberanes, *Opers Staff*
Ricardo Molina, *Accounts Mgr*
EMP: 130 **Privately Held**
WEB: www.pacwestsecurity.com
SIC: **7381** Security guard service
PA: Pacwest Security Services
3303 Harbor Blvd Ste A103
Costa Mesa CA 92626

(P-18309)
PATROL BLACK KNIGHT INC
505 S Pcf Ave Unit 201, San Pedro (90731)
PHONE..................213 985-6499
Manuel Jimenez, *CEO*
EMP: 70 EST: 2015
SALES (est): 6MM **Privately Held**
WEB: www.blackknightpatrol.com
SIC: **7381** Security guard service

(P-18310)
PLATINUM BOSS INTL INTLLGNCE L
18735 Gilmore St, Reseda (91335-6017)
PHONE..................818 416-5216
Gurpinder Singh Sagoo, *President*
EMP: 100 EST: 2019
SQ FT: 6,014
SALES (est): 1.3MM **Privately Held**
SIC: **7381** 7382 7389 3699 Security guard service; protective devices, security; personal service agents, brokers & bureaus; security devices; security cable locking system

(P-18311)
PLATINUM BOSS INTL PRTCTION SV
18735 Gilmore St, Reseda (91335-6017)
PHONE......................................818 416-5216
Gurpinder Singh Sagoo, *President*
EMP: 50 **EST:** 2020
SALES (est): 1MM **Privately Held**
SIC: 7381 Protective services, guard; security guard service

(P-18312)
PROFESSIONAL SECURITY CONS (PA)
11454 San Vicente Blvd # 2, Los Angeles (90049-6208)
PHONE......................................310 207-7729
Moshe Alon, *President*
Hector Acevedo, *Vice Pres*
Ilene Alon, *Vice Pres*
Mike Lambos, *Vice Pres*
Vicente Guerrero, *Security Dir*
EMP: 2019 **EST:** 1985
SALES (est): 59.1MM **Privately Held**
WEB: www.pscsite.com
SIC: 7381 7382 Security guard service; security systems services

(P-18313)
PROTECT-US
12391 Lewis St Ste 201, Garden Grove (92840-4668)
PHONE......................................714 721-8127
Nadiya Aziz, *Principal*
Steven Norman, *Opers Staff*
EMP: 180 **EST:** 2018
SALES (est): 5.1MM **Privately Held**
WEB: www.protect.us
SIC: 7381 Security guard service

(P-18314)
PROTECTED OUTCOMES CORPORATION
9663 Santa Monica Blvd, Beverly Hills (90210-4303)
PHONE......................................203 545-9565
EMP: 87
SALES: 950K **Privately Held**
SIC: 7381 Detective/Armored Car Services

(P-18315)
REEL SECURITY CALIFORNIA INC
15303 Ventura Blvd # 1080, Sherman Oaks (91403-5800)
PHONE......................................818 928-4737
Mario Inez Ramirez, *CEO*
Bradley Bush, *COO*
EMP: 99 **EST:** 2017
SALES (est): 1.5MM **Privately Held**
WEB: www.reelsecurity.com
SIC: 7381 Security guard service

(P-18316)
RICHMAN MANAGEMENT CORPORATION
35400 Bob Hope Dr Ste 107, Rancho Mirage (92270-1772)
PHONE......................................760 832-8520
Jake Simpson, *Branch Mgr*
EMP: 323
SALES (corp-wide): 592.4MM **Privately Held**
WEB: www.heritagesecurity.com
SIC: 7381 Security guard service
HQ: Richman Management Corporation
　　7840 Mssion Ctr Ct Ste 10
　　San Diego CA 92108
　　619 275-7007

(P-18317)
RICHMAN MANAGEMENT CORPORATION
Also Called: Heritage Security Services
41743 Entp Cir N Ste 209, Temecula (92590)
PHONE......................................909 296-6189
Liam Burke, *Branch Mgr*
EMP: 323
SALES (corp-wide): 592.4MM **Privately Held**
WEB: www.heritagesecurity.com
SIC: 7381 Security guard service
HQ: Richman Management Corporation
　　7840 Mssion Ctr Ct Ste 10
　　San Diego CA 92108
　　619 275-7007

(P-18318)
RJN INVESTIGATIONS INC
360 E 1st St Ste 696, Tustin (92780-3211)
P.O. Box 55451, Riverside (92517-0451)
PHONE......................................951 686-7638
Robert Nagle, *President*
Michael Gomez, *President*
Fred Martino, *Administration*
EMP: 80 **EST:** 1992
SALES (est): 5.2MM **Privately Held**
WEB: www.rjninv.com
SIC: 7381 Detective agency; private investigator

(P-18319)
SAFEGUARD ON DEMAND INC
Also Called: Security and Patrol Services
11037 Warner Ave 297, Fountain Valley (92708-4007)
PHONE......................................800 640-2327
Ahmad B Nawabi, *CEO*
Ahmad Nawabi, *CEO*
Umar Mohammad, *Administration*
EMP: 125 **EST:** 2015
SALES (est): 4.1MM **Privately Held**
WEB: www.safeguardondemand.com
SIC: 7381 Security guard service

(P-18320)
SAFETY SECURITY PATROL LLC
560 N Arrowhead Ave 3b, San Bernardino (92401-1219)
PHONE......................................909 888-7778
EMP: 63
SALES (est): 86.1K **Privately Held**
SIC: 7381 Detective/Armored Car Services

(P-18321)
SECTRAN SECURITY INCORPORATED (PA)
Also Called: Sectran Armored Truck Service
7633 Industry Ave, Pico Rivera (90660-4301)
P.O. Box 7267, Los Angeles (90022-0967)
PHONE......................................562 948-1446
Fred Kunik, *President*
Harlen Rueda, *Vice Pres*
Oscar Colocho, *Branch Mgr*
Martin Hematsiraki, *Branch Mgr*
Erryna Pinon, *General Mgr*
EMP: 141
SQ FT: 19,736
SALES (est): 17.3MM **Privately Held**
WEB: www.sectransecurity.com
SIC: 7381 Armored car services

(P-18322)
SECURITAS SEC SVCS USA INC
Also Called: Western Operations Center
4330 Park Terrace Dr, Westlake Village (91361-4630)
PHONE......................................818 706-6800
Edie Stafford, *Manager*
Paul R Amour, *President*
Norman Chavosky, *Branch Mgr*
Nathan Coyle, *Branch Mgr*
Danny Gould, *Branch Mgr*
EMP: 350
SALES (corp-wide): 12.4B **Privately Held**
WEB: www.securitasinc.com
SIC: 7381 Security guard service
HQ: Securitas Security Services Usa, Inc.
　　9 Campus Dr Ste 25
　　Parsippany NJ 07054
　　973 267-5300

(P-18323)
SECURITAS SEC SVCS USA INC
Also Called: Shared.Services
400 Crenshaw Blvd Ste 200, Torrance (90503-1736)
PHONE......................................310 787-0747
EMP: 181
SALES (corp-wide): 9.4B **Privately Held**
SIC: 7381 Detective/Armored Car Services
HQ: Securitas Security Services Usa, Inc.
　　2 Campus Dr
　　Parsippany NJ 07054
　　973 267-5300

(P-18324)
SECURITAS SEC SVCS USA INC
4330 Park Terrace Dr, Westlake Village (91361-4630)
PHONE......................................818 706-6800
EMP: 116
SALES (corp-wide): 10.9B **Privately Held**
SIC: 7381 Detective/Armored Car Services
HQ: Securitas Security Services Usa, Inc.
　　9 Campus Dr
　　Parsippany NJ 07054
　　973 267-5300

(P-18325)
SECURITECH SECURITY SVCS INC
2733 N San Fernando Rd, Los Angeles (90065-1318)
P.O. Box 65097 (90065-0097)
PHONE......................................213 387-5050
Serge Tachdjian, *President*
Marianna Amirkhanyan, *CFO*
Adriana Alvarez, *Admin Sec*
EMP: 110 **EST:** 1999
SALES (est): 5.7MM **Privately Held**
WEB: www.securitechguards.com
SIC: 7381 Security guard service

(P-18326)
SECURITY BASE GROUP INC
2447 Pacific Coast Hwy # 2, Hermosa Beach (90254-2714)
PHONE......................................213 444-1555
Musa Hussain, *CEO*
EMP: 50 **EST:** 2020
SALES (est): 1MM **Privately Held**
WEB: www.securitybasegroup.com
SIC: 7381 Security guard service

(P-18327)
SECURITY INDUST SPCIALISTS INC
477 N Oak St, Inglewood (90302-3314)
PHONE......................................323 924-9147
Chris Cochrane, *Manager*
EMP: 210
SALES (corp-wide): 143.8MM **Privately Held**
WEB: www.sis.us
SIC: 7381 Detective services
PA: Security Industry Specialists, Inc.
　　6071 Bristol Pkwy
　　Culver City CA 90230
　　310 215-5100

(P-18328)
SECURITY INDUST SPCIALISTS INC (PA)
Also Called: SIS
6071 Bristol Pkwy, Culver City (90230-6601)
PHONE......................................310 215-5100
John Spesak, *President*
Tom Seltz, *President*
Kit Knudsen, *COO*
Chuck Calderhead, *Officer*
Tom Stevens, *Vice Pres*
EMP: 4739 **EST:** 1999
SQ FT: 9,000
SALES (est): 143.8MM **Privately Held**
WEB: www.sis.us
SIC: 7381 5065 Security guard service; security control equipment & systems

(P-18329)
SECURTAS CRTCAL INFRSTRCTURE S
1835 W Orangewood Ave # 2, Orange (92868-2011)
PHONE......................................310 817-2177
Elijah Kimble, *Manager*
Mark Howell, *Vice Pres*
EMP: 271
SALES (corp-wide): 12.4B **Privately Held**
WEB: www.parasys.com
SIC: 7381 Security guard service
HQ: Securitas Critical Infrastructure Services, Inc.
　　13900 Lincoln Park Dr # 37
　　Herndon VA 20171

(P-18330)
SECURTAS CRTCAL INFRSTRCTURE S
Rm 117 Bldg 7525, Vandenberg Afb (93437)
PHONE......................................805 685-1100
Paul Jensen, *Branch Mgr*
EMP: 271
SALES (corp-wide): 12.4B **Privately Held**
WEB: www.parasys.com
SIC: 7381 Security guard service
HQ: Securitas Critical Infrastructure Services, Inc.
　　13900 Lincoln Park Dr # 37
　　Herndon VA 20171

(P-18331)
SECURTAS CRTCAL INFRSTRCTURE S
360 N Pacific Coast Hwy # 30, El Segundo (90245-4460)
PHONE......................................310 426-3300
Michael Kemppainen, *Branch Mgr*
EMP: 271
SALES (corp-wide): 12.4B **Privately Held**
WEB: www.parasys.com
SIC: 7381 Security guard service
HQ: Securitas Critical Infrastructure Services, Inc.
　　13900 Lincoln Park Dr # 37
　　Herndon VA 20171

(P-18332)
SERVEXO
Also Called: Servexo Protective Service
1515 W 190th St Ste 170, Gardena (90248-4927)
P.O. Box 9017, San Pedro (90734-9017)
PHONE......................................323 527-9994
John Palmer, *President*
Suzanne Bohrer, *Human Resources*
Mike Dalton, *Manager*
EMP: 500 **EST:** 2012
SALES: 5.3MM **Privately Held**
WEB: www.servexousa.com
SIC: 7381 Protective services, guard; security guard service

(P-18333)
SHIELD SECURITY INC (DH)
1551 N Tustin Ave Ste 650, Santa Ana (92705-8664)
PHONE......................................714 210-1501
Ed Klosterman Jr, *President*
Kenneth Klosterman, *Vice Pres*
EMP: 300 **EST:** 1964
SQ FT: 5,500
SALES (est): 84.1MM
SALES (corp-wide): 592.4MM **Privately Held**
SIC: 7381 Security guard service
HQ: Universal Protection Service, Lp
　　1551 N Tustin Ave Ste 650
　　Santa Ana CA 92705
　　714 619-9700

(P-18334)
SHIELD SECURITY INC
21110 Vanowen St, Canoga Park (91303-2821)
PHONE......................................818 239-5800
Kenneth Klosterman, *Branch Mgr*
EMP: 333
SALES (corp-wide): 592.4MM **Privately Held**
SIC: 7381 Security guard service
HQ: Shield Security, Inc.
　　1551 N Tustin Ave Ste 650
　　Santa Ana CA 92705
　　714 210-1501

(P-18335)
SHIELD SECURITY INC
150 E Wardlow Rd, Long Beach (90807-4417)
PHONE......................................562 283-1100
Leo Green, *Manager*
EMP: 333
SALES (corp-wide): 592.4MM **Privately Held**
SIC: 7381 Security guard service

PRODUCTS & SVCS

HQ: Shield Security, Inc.
1551 N Tustin Ave Ste 650
Santa Ana CA 92705
714 210-1501

(P-18336)
SHIELD SECURITY INC
265 N Euclid Ave, Upland (91786-6038)
PHONE..................................909 920-1173
Paul Srankowski, *Manager*
EMP: 333
SALES (corp-wide): 592.4MM **Privately
Held**
SIC: 7381 Security guard service
HQ: Shield Security, Inc.
1551 N Tustin Ave Ste 650
Santa Ana CA 92705
714 210-1501

(P-18337)
SOS SECURITY INCORPORATED
3000 S Robertson Blvd # 100, Los Angeles
(90034-3145)
PHONE..................................310 392-9600
Doug Hamilton, *Manager*
Fred Silverman, *Vice Pres*
EMP: 61
SALES (corp-wide): 97.7MM **Privately
Held**
WEB: www.sossecurity.com
SIC: 7381 Security guard service; detec-
tive agency
PA: Sos Security Incorporated
1915 Us Highway 46 Ste 1
Parsippany NJ 07054
973 402-6600

(P-18338)
SOS SECURITY LLC
331 N Beverly Dr Ste 3, Beverly Hills
(90210-4729)
PHONE..................................310 859-8248
EMP: 70
SALES (corp-wide): 4.7B **Privately Held**
WEB: www.sossecurity.com
SIC: 7381 Security Officers/Investigations
HQ: Sos Security Llc
1915 Us Highway 46 Ste 2
Parsippany NJ 07054
973 402-6600

(P-18339)
SOUTHWEST PATROL INC
556 N Dmnd Bar Blvd # 207, Diamond Bar
(91765-1054)
PHONE..................................909 861-1884
John Stirn, *President*
Richard Stirn, *CFO*
Pete Macias, *Opers Mgr*
EMP: 70 EST: 1992
SQ FT: 1,400
SALES (est): 5.6MM **Privately Held**
WEB: www.southwestpatrol.com
SIC: 7381 Security guard service

(P-18340)
SOUTHWEST PROTECTIVE SVCS INC
Also Called: Southwest Security
404 W Heil Ave, El Centro (92243-3328)
P.O. Box 2915 (92244-2915)
PHONE..................................760 996-1285
Jason Jackson, *Manager*
Cinnamon Hack, *Officer*
EMP: 250 EST: 2015
SALES (est): 9.7MM **Privately Held**
SIC: 7381 Guard services

(P-18341)
SRS PROTECTION INC
2064 Eastman Ave Ste 110, Ventura
(93003-7787)
PHONE..................................805 744-7122
James Allen Rita, *CEO*
Robin Neubert, *Vice Pres*
Matt Harbin, *Opers Mgr*
Jeff Sarge Gish, *Director*
EMP: 150 EST: 2013
SQ FT: 1,200
SALES (est): 2MM **Privately Held**
WEB: www.srsprotection.com
SIC: 7381 Security guard service

(P-18342)
STAR PRO SECURITY PATROL INC
3303 Harbor Blvd Ste B3, Costa Mesa
(92626-1517)
PHONE..................................714 617-5056
Sally Covington, *President*
EMP: 124 EST: 2016
SALES (est): 8.7MM **Privately Held**
WEB: www.starprosecurity.com
SIC: 7381 Security guard service

(P-18343)
SURVEILLANCE SYSTEMS GROUP INC
Also Called: Corinthian Group
3175 Sedona Ct, Ontario (91764-6560)
PHONE..................................877 687-3939
Claude Ammons, *CEO*
Kim Ammons, *Admin Sec*
EMP: 15 EST: 2007
SALES (est): 661.9K **Privately Held**
WEB: www.corinthian-group.com
SIC: 7381 8111 7389 1382 Private inves-
tigator; criminal law; personal investiga-
tion service; aerial geophysical
exploration oil & gas; inspection & investi-
gation services, insurance; business man-
agement

(P-18344)
SYNOLO SECURITY
Also Called: Security Guard Services
7231 Boulder Ave Pmb 650, Highland
(92346-3313)
PHONE..................................909 907-4605
Jeffrey Trent, *CEO*
EMP: 50 EST: 2020
SALES (est): 100K **Privately Held**
WEB: www.synolosecurity.com
SIC: 7381 Security guard service

(P-18345)
TRANS-WEST SERVICES INC
8503 Crippen St, Bakersfield (93311-8993)
PHONE..................................661 381-2900
Brooke L Antonioni, *President*
Duane Williams, *Exec VP*
Katy Williams, *Vice Pres*
Gilbert Cota, *Opers Mgr*
Monique Williams, *Manager*
EMP: 300 EST: 1973
SQ FT: 8,500
SALES (est): 17.4MM **Privately Held**
WEB: www.trans-west.net
SIC: 7381 Security guard service

(P-18346)
TRANSCENDENT SECURITY SERVICES
3553 Atl Ave Ste 1197, Long Beach
(90807)
PHONE..................................562 850-3313
John Harris, *President*
EMP: 50 EST: 2018
SALES (est): 1MM **Privately Held**
SIC: 7381 Security guard service

(P-18347)
TYAN INC
Also Called: Security Specialists
1500 Glenoaks Blvd, San Fernando
(91340-1740)
P.O. Box 3472, Van Nuys (91407-3472)
PHONE..................................818 785-5831
Nick Tsotsikyan, *President*
EMP: 55 EST: 2001
SQ FT: 2,000
SALES (est): 5.2MM **Privately Held**
WEB: www.securityspecialists.pro
SIC: 7381 Security guard service

(P-18348)
UNITED FACILITY SOLUTIONS INC
Also Called: Command Gard Srvces Wsa
Srvces
19208 S Vermont Ave # 200, Gardena
(90248-4414)
PHONE..................................310 743-3000
Martin Benom, *CEO*
Mark Myers, *President*
Annette Phillips, *Accounts Exec*
EMP: 400 EST: 2015

SALES (est): 9.3MM **Privately Held**
SIC: 7381 7349 Security guard service;
janitorial service, contract basis

(P-18349)
UNITED GUARD SECURITY INC (PA)
879 W 190th St Ste 280, Gardena
(90248-4223)
PHONE..................................800 228-2505
Ismael Zita, *CEO*
Chawki Nouizi, *Treasurer*
EMP: 294 EST: 2012
SALES (est): 17.6MM **Privately Held**
WEB: www.unitedguardsecurity.net
SIC: 7381 Security guard service

(P-18350)
UNIVERSAL PROTECTION GP LLC (PA)
1551 N Tustin Ave Ste 650, Santa Ana
(92705-8664)
PHONE..................................714 619-9700
Brian Cescolini, *Chairman*
Sarah Ellwood, *CEO*
Scott Savoie, *CFO*
Michael Coutre, *Vice Pres*
Steve Pounds, *Vice Pres*
EMP: 198 EST: 2013
SQ FT: 6,000
SALES (est): 592.4MM **Privately Held**
SIC: 7381 Security guard service

(P-18351)
UNIVERSAL PROTECTION SVC LP (HQ)
Also Called: Allied Universal Security Svcs
1551 N Tustin Ave Ste 650, Santa Ana
(92705-8664)
PHONE..................................714 619-9700
Brian Cescolini, *Partner*
Steve Jones, *Partner*
Paul Sova, *President*
Lawrence O'Brien, *COO*
Billy Thompson, *Officer*
EMP: 1903 EST: 2009
SALES (est): 592.4MM **Privately Held**
SIC: 7381 Security guard service
PA: Universal Protection Gp, Llc
1551 N Tustin Ave Ste 650
Santa Ana CA 92705
714 619-9700

(P-18352)
UNIVERSAL PRTCTION SEC SYSTEMS (DH)
1815 E Wilshire Ave # 91, Santa Ana
(92705-4646)
PHONE..................................714 288-2227
Steve Jones, *Partner*
Robert Wood, *Partner*
Kelly Snyder, *Administration*
Ryan Weisbrod, *Opers Mgr*
Brandon Newell, *Manager*
EMP: 50 EST: 2009
SALES (est): 13.7MM **Privately Held**
WEB: www.legacy.aus.com
SIC: 7381 Security guard service
HQ: Universal Services Of America, Lp
1551 N Tustin Ave Fl 6
Santa Ana CA 92705
866 877-1965

(P-18353)
UNIVERSAL SERVICES AMERICA LP
77725 Enfield Ln, Palm Desert
(92211-0468)
PHONE..................................760 200-2865
Peter Moyer, *Manager*
EMP: 999
SALES (corp-wide): 8.6B **Privately Held**
WEB: www.legacy.aus.com
SIC: 7381 Security guard service
HQ: Universal Services Of America, Lp
1551 N Tustin Ave Fl 6
Santa Ana CA 92705
866 877-1965

(P-18354)
UNIVERSAL SERVICES AMERICA LP (DH)
Also Called: Allied Universal
1551 N Tustin Ave Fl 6, Santa Ana
(92705-8634)
PHONE..................................866 877-1965
Steve Jones, *CEO*
Toni Ippolito, *CEO*
Jennifer Jimenez, *Officer*
Chris Johnson, *Officer*
Ron Rabena, *Officer*
EMP: 100 EST: 2001
SALES (est): 1.2B
SALES (corp-wide): 8.6B **Privately Held**
WEB: www.legacy.aus.com
SIC: 7381 7349 Security guard service;
janitorial service, contract basis
HQ: Allied Universal Holdco LLC
1551 N Tustin Ave Ste 650
Santa Ana CA 92705
866 877-1965

(P-18355)
US SECURITY ASSOCIATES INC
Also Called: US Security Associates
455 N Moss St, Burbank (91502-1727)
PHONE..................................818 697-1809
EMP: 451
SALES (corp-wide): 17.7MM **Privately
Held**
WEB: www.ussecurityassociates.com
SIC: 7381 Security guard service
HQ: U.S. Security Associates, Inc.
200 Mansell Ct E Fl 5
Roswell GA 30076

(P-18356)
US SECURITY ASSOCIATES INC
2275 W 190th St Ste 100, Torrance
(90504-6007)
PHONE..................................714 352-0773
Richard L Wyckoff, *Branch Mgr*
EMP: 451
SALES (corp-wide): 17.7MM **Privately
Held**
WEB: www.ussecurityassociates.com
SIC: 7381 Security guard service
HQ: U.S. Security Associates, Inc.
200 Mansell Ct E Fl 5
Roswell GA 30076

(P-18357)
VENUE MANAGEMENT SYSTEMS INC
Also Called: V M S
2041 E Gladstone St Ste A, Glendora
(91740-5385)
P.O. Box 25, San Dimas (91773-0025)
PHONE..................................626 445-6000
Charles E McIntyre, *President*
EMP: 6000 EST: 2001
SQ FT: 35,000
SALES (est): 8.6B **Privately Held**
WEB: www.crowdservices.com
SIC: 7381 7363 8742 Detective & ar-
mored car services; employee leasing
service; human resource consulting serv-
ices

(P-18358)
VESCOM CORPORATION (PA)
1125 W 190th St, Gardena (90248-4303)
PHONE..................................207 945-5051
Sherif Assal, *President*
Pamela J Treadwell, *Vice Pres*
EMP: 622 EST: 1986
SALES (est): 14.2MM **Privately Held**
SIC: 7381 Security guard service

(P-18359)
WHELAN SECURITY CO
400 Continental Blvd, E Segundo
(90245-5076)
PHONE..................................310 343-8628
Gregory Twardowski, *Branch Mgr*
EMP: 301
SALES (corp-wide): 115.8MM **Privately
Held**
WEB: www.garda.com
SIC: 7381 Security guard service

HQ: Whelan Security Co.
1699 S Hanley Rd Ste 350
Saint Louis MO 63144
314 644-3227

(P-18360)
WORLD PRIVATE SECURITY INC
16921 Parthenia St # 201, Northridge
(91343-4568)
PHONE..........................818 894-1800
Fred Youssif, *President*
Jeannette Youssif, *Co-Owner*
EMP: 200 EST: 1997 **Privately Held**
WEB: www.worldsecurityinc.com
SIC: 7381 Security guard service

(P-18361)
WORLDWIDE SECURITY ASSOC INC (HQ)
10311 S La Cienega Blvd, Los Angeles
(90045-6109)
PHONE..........................310 743-3000
Andres Martinez, *President*
EMP: 300 EST: 1991
SQ FT: 5,000
SALES (est): 25.4MM **Privately Held**
SIC: 7381 Security guard service

(P-18362)
WSA GROUP INC (PA)
19208 S Vermont Ave 200, Gardena
(90248-4414)
PHONE..........................310 743-3000
Andres Martinez, *President*
James E Bush, *Vice Pres*
EMP: 50 EST: 1991
SQ FT: 10,000
SALES (est): 68.8MM **Privately Held**
SIC: 7381 7349 Security guard service;
janitorial service, contract basis

7382 Security Systems Svcs

(P-18363)
313 ACQUISITION LLC
1111 Citrus St Ste 1, Riverside
(92507-1735)
PHONE..........................801 234-6374
Jakob Imig, *Branch Mgr*
Brianna Pritchett, *Partner*
Pat Kelliher, *Officer*
Stephen Haynes, *Vice Pres*
Neal Rogers, *Vice Pres*
EMP: 4236
SALES (corp-wide): 631.5MM **Privately
Held**
SIC: 7382 Security systems services
PA: 313 Acquisition Llc
4931 N 300 W
Provo UT 84604
877 404-4129

(P-18364)
ADVANCED PROTECTION INDS LLC
Also Called: National Monitoring Center
25341 Commercentre Dr, Lake Forest
(92630-8856)
PHONE..........................800 662-1711
Woodie Andrawos, *President*
Frank Farag, *CFO*
Mark Matlock, *Vice Pres*
Nicola Oakie, *Vice Pres*
Todd Shuff, *Vice Pres*
EMP: 99 EST: 2018
SALES (est): 18.4MM **Privately Held**
SIC: 7382 Burglar alarm maintenance &
monitoring

(P-18365)
AERO PORT SERVICES INC (PA)
216 W Florence Ave, Inglewood
(90301-1213)
PHONE..........................310 623-8230
Chris Paik, *President*
Stephan Park, *CFO*
Jake Yoon, *CFO*
Julie Hong, *Treasurer*
Walter Vergara, *Chief Mktg Ofcr*
▲ EMP: 806 EST: 2002
SALES (est): 36.6MM **Privately Held**
WEB: www.aeroportservices.com
SIC: 7382 Security systems services

(P-18366)
AM-TEC TOTAL SECURITY INC (PA)
Also Called: Am-TEC Security
4075 Schaefer Ave, Chino (91710-5446)
PHONE..........................909 573-4678
Jeff Torok, *President*
EMP: 54 EST: 1984
SQ FT: 7,000
SALES (est): 280K **Privately Held**
WEB: www.am-tecsecurity.com
SIC: 7382 Security systems services

(P-18367)
BOLIDE TECHNOLOGY GROUP INC
Also Called: Bolide International
468 S San Dimas Ave, San Dimas
(91773-4045)
PHONE..........................909 305-8889
David Liu, *President*
Richard Barnes, *CIO*
Camilo Avila, *Engineer*
Fiona Du, *Accountant*
Ron Budiarto, *Sales Mgr*
◆ EMP: 70 EST: 1994
SQ FT: 16,000
SALES (est): 6.3MM **Privately Held**
WEB: www.bolideco.com
SIC: 7382 Security systems services

(P-18368)
COAST2COAST PUBLIC SAFETY LLC
1733 S Douglass Rd Ste H, Anaheim
(92806-6034)
PHONE..........................833 262-7877
John Cox,
Sean Riley,
Jason Villa,
EMP: 50 EST: 2018
SALES (est): 1.7MM **Privately Held**
WEB: www.c2cpublicsafety.com
SIC: 7382 7363 Security systems serv-
ices; medical help service

(P-18369)
CORPORATE ALNCE STRATEGIES INC
3410 La Sierra Ave F244, Riverside
(92503-5270)
PHONE..........................877 777-7487
Leah Pinto, *CEO*
Zeriah McKnight, *Advisor*
EMP: 115 EST: 2015
SALES (est): 5.8MM **Privately Held**
WEB: www.corporatealliancestrategies.com
SIC: 7382 Security systems services

(P-18370)
DELTA SCIENTIFIC CORPORATION (PA)
40355 Delta Ln, Palmdale (93551-3616)
PHONE..........................661 575-1100
Harry D Dickinson, *CEO*
Richard I Winger, *CFO*
Keith Bobrosky, *Senior VP*
David Dickinson, *Vice Pres*
Greg Hamm, *Vice Pres*
◆ EMP: 188 EST: 1974
SQ FT: 200,000
SALES (est): 25.7MM **Privately Held**
WEB: www.deltascientific.com
SIC: 7382 Security systems services

(P-18371)
DIAL SECURITY INC (PA)
Also Called: Dial Communications
760 W Ventura Blvd, Camarillo
(93010-8382)
P.O. Box 34781, Bethesda MD (20827-
0781)
PHONE..........................805 389-6700
William H Dundas, *President*
Erica Ayala, *Admin Asst*
Mike McDermott, *Sales Mgr*
EMP: 250
SQ FT: 12,000
SALES (est): 17.3MM **Privately Held**
WEB: www.dialcomm.com
SIC: 7382 7381 Protective devices, secu-
rity; detective & armored car services

(P-18372)
ECAMSECURE
3400 E Airport Way, Long Beach
(90806-2412)
PHONE..........................888 246-0556
Christopher Coffey, *President*
William R Babcock, *CFO*
Danny Mize, *Technical Staff*
Henry Flores, *Sales Staff*
EMP: 67 EST: 1985
SQ FT: 3,500
SALES (est): 8.1MM **Privately Held**
WEB: www.ecamsecure.garda.com
SIC: 7382 5065 Security systems serv-
ices; electronic parts & equipment

(P-18373)
EDGEWORTH INTEGRATION LLC
2360 Shasta Way Ste F, Simi Valley
(93065-1800)
PHONE..........................805 915-0211
EMP: 78
SALES (corp-wide): 4.2MM **Privately
Held**
WEB: www.edgeworthsecurity.com
SIC: 7382 Security systems services
PA: Edgeworth Integration, Llc
1000 Commerce Dr Fl 2
Pittsburgh PA 15275
800 421-9130

(P-18374)
ELITE INTRACTIVE SOLUTIONS INC
1200 W 7th St Ste L1-180, Los Angeles
(90017-6411)
PHONE..........................310 740-5426
Aria Kozak, *President*
John Valdez, *Exec VP*
Jonathan Kozak, *Info Tech Dir*
Lauren Sorrels, *Opers Mgr*
Lauren Sorrells, *Opers Staff*
EMP: 32 EST: 2001
SQ FT: 8,000
SALES (est): 4.9MM **Privately Held**
WEB: www.eiteisi.com
SIC: 7382 1731 3629 3669 Burglar alarm
maintenance & monitoring; electrical
work; electronic generation equipment; vi-
sual communication systems

(P-18375)
EMERGENCY TECHNOLOGIES INC
Also Called: American Two-Way
7345 Varna Ave, North Hollywood
(91605-4009)
PHONE..........................818 765-4421
Christopher Baskin, *CEO*
Verny Grajeda, *Info Tech Mgr*
EMP: 72 EST: 1995
SQ FT: 13,000
SALES (est): 7.7MM **Privately Held**
SIC: 7382 Security systems services

(P-18376)
ENTERPRISE SECURITY INC (PA)
Also Called: Enterprise Security Solutions
22860 Savi Ranch Pkwy, Yorba Linda
(92887-4610)
PHONE..........................714 630-9100
Samuel Troy Laughlin, *CEO*
Troy Laughlin, *President*
Joseph Emens, *COO*
Daniel Steiner, *Vice Pres*
Dave Toon, *Executive*
EMP: 74 EST: 2000
SALES (est): 10.7MM **Privately Held**
WEB: www.entersecurity.com
SIC: 7382 3699 3429 6211 Protective de-
vices, security; security devices; security
control equipment & systems; security
cable locking system; dealers, security;
security control equipment & systems

(P-18377)
EON INNOVATIVE TECHNOLOGY INC
Also Called: KT&c USA
10645 W Vanowen St, Burbank
(91505-1136)
PHONE..........................213 381-0061
Jason JC Ra, *President*

H S Kwon, *CEO*
Joe Troiano, *Vice Pres*
Danny Han, *Technical Staff*
Daniel Choi, *Sales Executive*
▲ EMP: 53 EST: 2000
SALES (est): 5.5MM **Privately Held**
WEB: www.ktncusa.com
SIC: 7382 Security systems services
PA: Kt&C Co.,Ltd
7 Yangcheon-Ro 11-Gil, Gangseo-Gu
Seoul 07516

(P-18378)
EZVIZ INC
908 Canada Ct, City of Industry
(91748-1136)
PHONE..........................855 693-9849
Jeffrey He, *CEO*
Hsin Lin, *Admin Sec*
Miki Barr, *Marketing Staff*
Liz Van Dyke, *Sales Staff*
Rod St Michel, *Director*
EMP: 200 EST: 2015
SQ FT: 32,000
SALES (est): 12.2MM **Privately Held**
WEB: www.ezvizlife.com
SIC: 7382 Confinement surveillance sys-
tems maintenance & monitoring
HQ: Hikvision Usa Inc.
18639 Railroad St
City Of Industry CA 91748
909 895-0400

(P-18379)
FIRST INTERSTATE SERVICES INC
635 W Colo St Ste 108a, Glendale (91204)
PHONE..........................818 638-3435
Mohab Ahmed, *President*
EMP: 300 EST: 2008
SALES (est): 3.7MM **Privately Held**
SIC: 7382 7381 Security systems serv-
ices; security guard service

(P-18380)
G4S JUSTICE SERVICES LLC
Also Called: G4s Government Services
1290 N Hancock St Ste 103, Anaheim
(92807-1925)
PHONE..........................800 589-6003
Robert Contestabile, *CEO*
Misty Fry, *Nurse*
EMP: 56 EST: 1995
SALES (est): 8.6MM
SALES (corp-wide): 94.1MM **Privately
Held**
WEB: www.sentineladvantage.com
SIC: 7382 3669 Fire alarm maintenance &
monitoring; emergency alarms
PA: Sentinel Offender Services Llc
1290 N Hancock St Ste 103
Anaheim CA 92807
949 453-1550

(P-18381)
GO GET EM INC
45248 Trevor Ave, Lancaster (93534-1614)
PHONE..........................702 985-5637
Michael Sprague, *President*
EMP: 60 EST: 2017
SALES (est): 1.3MM **Privately Held**
SIC: 7382 Security systems services

(P-18382)
GREATER ALARM COMPANY INC (DH)
3750 Schaufele Ave # 200, Long Beach
(90808-1779)
PHONE..........................949 474-0555
George De Marco, *President*
James De Marco, *Vice Pres*
Ken McDowell, *Regl Sales Mgr*
EMP: 71 EST: 1981
SQ FT: 11,500
SALES (est): 5.2MM
SALES (corp-wide): 170.7MM **Privately
Held**
WEB: www.interfacesystems.com
SIC: 7382 Security systems services
HQ: Interface Security Systems, Llc
3773 Corporate Centre Dr
Earth City MO 63045
314 595-0100

(P-18383)
HIKVISION USA INC (HQ)
18639 Railroad St, City of Industry
(91748-1317)
PHONE..............................909 895-0400
Jeffrey He, *CEO*
Tony Yang, *President*
Nick Tang, *Executive*
Eric Chen, *General Mgr*
Ning Tang, *Admin Sec*
▲ EMP: 120 EST: 2007
SALES (est): 79MM Privately Held
WEB: www.us.hikvision.com
SIC: 7382 Confinement surveillance systems maintenance & monitoring

(P-18384)
HILLQUEST SEC PATROL SVCS INC
Also Called: Hillquest Security Services
8383 Wilshire Blvd # 800, Beverly Hills
(90211-2425)
PHONE..............................213 213-9763
John Bouzy, *CEO*
EMP: 50 EST: 2016
SALES (est): 1.6MM Privately Held
WEB: www.hillquestsecurity.com
SIC: 7382 Security systems services

(P-18385)
I C U SECURITY INC
2530 Calcite Cir, Newbury Park
(91320-1203)
PHONE..............................805 498-9620
Ali Omidfar, *President*
Fred Dorrani, *Vice Pres*
Reed Harrison, *Agent*
EMP: 52 EST: 1998
SQ FT: 200,000
SALES (est): 1.6MM Privately Held
WEB: www.icusecurity.com
SIC: 7382 Security systems services

(P-18386)
IDENTITY INTLLIGENCE GROUP LLC
Also Called: Idiq
43454 Business Park Dr, Temecula
(92590-5530)
PHONE..............................626 522-7993
Scott Hermann, *Mng Member*
EMP: 232 EST: 2010
SALES (est): 12.5MM Privately Held
SIC: 7382 Security systems services

(P-18387)
INTER-CON SECURITY SYSTEMS INC (PA)
210 S De Lacey Ave, Pasadena
(91105-2048)
PHONE..............................626 535-2200
Enrique Hernandez Jr, *Ch of Bd*
Roland A Hernandez, *Treasurer*
Donte Harris, *Officer*
Destiny O'Connor, *Officer*
Steve Vasquez, *Officer*
EMP: 24016 EST: 1973
SQ FT: 17,000
SALES (est): 362.1MM Privately Held
WEB: www.icsecurity.com
SIC: 7382 Security systems services

(P-18388)
JAM FIRE PROTECTION INC (PA)
Also Called: J A M
1930 S Myrtle Ave, Monrovia (91016-4835)
PHONE..............................626 256-4400
John A Mongillo, *CEO*
Michael Deushane, *CFO*
Sal Cervantes, *Project Mgr*
Lisa Brennan, *VP Opers*
Mike Mongillo, *Opers Staff*
EMP: 99 EST: 1993
SQ FT: 15,000
SALES (est): 13.6MM Privately Held
WEB: www.jamcorporation.com
SIC: 7382 Security systems services

(P-18389)
JOHNSON CONTROLS
12728 Shoemaker Ave, Santa Fe Springs
(90670-6345)
PHONE..............................562 405-3817
Andy Bernot, *Manager*

EMP: 150 Publicly Held
WEB: www.tycosimplexgrinnell.com
SIC: 7382 Security systems services; fire detection & burglar alarm systems specialization; plumbing, heating, air-conditioning contractors
HQ: Johnson Controls Fire Protection Lp
6600 Congress Ave
Boca Raton FL 33487
561 988-7200

(P-18390)
KERN SECURITY CORPORATION
Also Called: Kern Security Systems
2701 Fruitvale Ave, Bakersfield
(93308-5905)
PHONE..............................661 363-6874
John Affeld, *President*
Ronald C McVicar, *CFO*
EMP: 84 EST: 1982
SQ FT: 4,000
SALES (est): 4.3MM
SALES (corp-wide): 26.8MM Privately Held
WEB: www.ssdalarm.com
SIC: 7382 5999 1731 Burglar alarm maintenance & monitoring; fire alarm maintenance & monitoring; alarm signal systems; closed circuit television installation
PA: Security Signal Devices, Inc.
1740 N Lemon St
Anaheim CA 92801
800 888-0444

(P-18391)
KESA INCORPORATED
Also Called: Constrction Instlltion Mint Gr
960 E Discovery Ln, Anaheim
(92801-1149)
PHONE..............................714 956-2827
Connie Moreno, *Payroll Mgr*
Bill Morrill, *Manager*
EMP: 40 EST: 2003
SALES (est): 9.3MM Privately Held
WEB: www.kesacorp.com
SIC: 7382 3577 Burglar alarm maintenance & monitoring; computer peripheral equipment

(P-18392)
LANTZ SECURITY SYSTEMS INC
4111 Las Virgenes Rd # 202, Calabasas
(91302-1886)
PHONE..............................818 871-0193
EMP: 114
SALES (corp-wide): 9.7MM Privately Held
SIC: 7382 Security Systems Services
PA: Lantz Security Systems Inc
43440 Sahuayo St
Lancaster CA 93535
661 949-3565

(P-18393)
LIFE ALERT EMRGNCY RSPONSE INC (PA)
16027 Ventura Blvd # 400, Encino
(91436-2728)
PHONE..............................800 247-0000
Isaac Shepher, *President*
Heidi Nestor, *President*
Felix Leung, *CFO*
Miriam Shepher, *Senior VP*
Olga Vlasova, *Vice Pres*
▲ EMP: 175 EST: 1987
SQ FT: 29,489
SALES (est): 51.3MM Privately Held
WEB: www.lifealert.net
SIC: 7382 5731 Confinement surveillance systems maintenance & monitoring; consumer electronic equipment

(P-18394)
LOUROE ELECTRONICS INC
6955 Valjean Ave, Van Nuys (91406-4716)
PHONE..............................818 994-6498
Louis Weiss, *President*
Richard S Brent, *CEO*
Sara Rollens, *General Mgr*
Donald Schiffer, *Admin Sec*
Wayne Paes, *Software Engr*
▼ EMP: 28 EST: 1979
SQ FT: 17,000

SALES (est): 8.2MM Privately Held
WEB: www.louroe.com
SIC: 7382 3651 Burglar alarm maintenance & monitoring; audio electronic systems

(P-18395)
PLEXICOR INC (PA)
3598 Cadillac Ave, Costa Mesa
(92626-1416)
PHONE..............................714 918-8700
Robert Klemme, *CEO*
EMP: 50 EST: 2002
SALES (est): 5.5MM Privately Held
SIC: 7382 5063 1731 Security systems services; electric alarms & signaling equipment; safety & security specialization

(P-18396)
POST ALARM SYSTEMS (PA)
Also Called: Post Alarm Systems Patrol Svcs
47 E Saint Joseph St, Arcadia
(91006-2861)
PHONE..............................626 446-7159
William Post, *President*
Bill Post, *Owner*
Rob Post, *CFO*
Lois Post, *Treasurer*
Fred Dunner, *Vice Pres*
EMP: 98 EST: 1956
SQ FT: 10,500
SALES (est): 12.4MM Privately Held
WEB: www.postalarm.com
SIC: 7382 1731 5063 Burglar alarm maintenance & monitoring; fire alarm maintenance & monitoring; protective devices, security; fire detection & burglar alarm systems specialization; electrical apparatus & equipment

(P-18397)
SECURITY SIGNAL DEVICES INC (PA)
Also Called: Ssd Systems
1740 N Lemon St, Anaheim (92801-1047)
PHONE..............................800 888-0444
John F Affeld, *CEO*
Scott Hollis, *Vice Pres*
Sheila Rossi, *Admin Sec*
Kristen Clark, *Admin Asst*
George Saad, *Sr Software Eng*
EMP: 50 EST: 1969
SQ FT: 20,000
SALES (est): 26.8MM Privately Held
WEB: www.ssdalarm.com
SIC: 7382 1731 Security systems services; safety & security specialization

(P-18398)
SENTINEL MONITORING CORP (HQ)
220 Technology Dr Ste 200, Irvine
(92618-2424)
PHONE..............................949 453-1550
Robert Contestabile, *President*
EMP: 100 EST: 1993
SALES (est): 9.5MM
SALES (corp-wide): 94.1MM Privately Held
WEB: www.sentineladvantage.com
SIC: 7382 Confinement surveillance systems maintenance & monitoring
PA: Sentinel Offender Services Llc
1290 N Hancock St Ste 103
Anaheim CA 92807
949 453-1550

(P-18399)
SENTINEL OFFENDER SERVICES LLC (PA)
1290 N Hancock St Ste 103, Anaheim
(92807-1925)
PHONE..............................949 453-1550
Robert Contestabile,
Melissa Starr, *Vice Pres*
Alan Velasquez, *Vice Pres*
Dj Williamson, *Executive*
Margaret Duenas, *Regional Mgr*
EMP: 85 EST: 1993
SALES (est): 94.1MM Privately Held
WEB: www.sentineladvantage.com
SIC: 7382 Confinement surveillance systems maintenance & monitoring

(P-18400)
SKYLINE SECURITY MGT INC (PA)
10642 Downey Ave Ste 205, Downey
(90241-3442)
PHONE..............................562 622-7114
Edwin Arroyave, *CEO*
Aftab Hussein, *CFO*
David Sheldon, *Asst Controller*
Darrell Olsen, *Opers Mgr*
Ivan Mejia, *Sales Mgr*
EMP: 59 EST: 2004
SALES (est): 11.7MM Privately Held
WEB: www.skylinesecurity.com
SIC: 7382 Protective devices, security

(P-18401)
SMART SYSTEMS TECHNOLOGIES (PA)
9 Goodyear, Irvine (92618-2001)
PHONE..............................949 367-9375
Craig Steven Curran, *CEO*
Peter Scolara, *CFO*
Melissa Ramos, *Office Mgr*
Raquel Navarro, *Purchasing*
Naeem Siddiqui, *Opers Staff*
EMP: 62 EST: 1999
SQ FT: 7,000
SALES (est): 13.1MM Privately Held
WEB: www.sstsun.com
SIC: 7382 Security systems services

(P-18402)
STAFF PRO INC (PA)
Also Called: Allied Universal Event Svcs
1400 N Harbor Blvd # 700, Fullerton
(92835-4109)
PHONE..............................714 230-7200
Cory Meredith, *CEO*
David Avila, *Branch Mgr*
Jose Martinez, *Branch Mgr*
Tracy Neff, *Branch Mgr*
Mary J Becker, *Admin Asst*
EMP: 700 EST: 1987
SALES (est): 102.8MM Privately Held
WEB: www.staffpro.com
SIC: 7382 8741 Security systems services; management services

(P-18403)
TAD GROUP LLC
5000 Birch St Ste 3000, Newport Beach
(92660-2140)
PHONE..............................949 476-3601
Izan Todorov,
EMP: 150 EST: 2007
SALES (est): 2.8MM Privately Held
WEB: www.tadgroup.com
SIC: 7382 7373 Security systems services; computer integrated systems design

(P-18404)
VIRTIS-US LLC (PA)
11601 Wilshire Blvd 5thf, Los Angeles
(90025-0509)
PHONE..............................855 796-1457
Michelle Wilner, *Mng Member*
Dan Wilner, *Vice Pres*
Kerri Gosnell, *VP Business*
Joel Schluter,
EMP: 15 EST: 2016
SQ FT: 3,000
SALES (est): 6MM Privately Held
WEB: www.virtis-us.com
SIC: 7382 7371 7373 7372 Security systems services; software programming applications; computer integrated systems design; prepackaged software

(P-18405)
WEST CAST FIRE NTEGRATION INC
891 Iowa Ave, Riverside (92507-1614)
PHONE..............................909 824-7980
EMP: 71
SALES (corp-wide): 13.2MM Privately Held
WEB: www.westcoastfreinc.com
SIC: 7382 Security systems services
PA: West Coast Fire & Integration, Inc.
22405 La Palma Ave
Yorba Linda CA 92887
714 957-5750

7383 News Syndicates

(P-18406)
BUENA VISTA TELEVISION (DH)
Also Called: Buena Vista TV Advg Sls
500 S Buena Vista St, Burbank
(91521-0001)
PHONE..................................818 560-1878
Janice Marinelli, *CEO*
Mort Marcus, *President*
Sal Sardo, *President*
Anne L Buettner, *CFO*
Mercedes Cregar, *Treasurer*
EMP: 129 **EST:** 1985
SALES (est): 22MM
SALES (corp-wide): 65.3B **Publicly Held**
WEB: www.gargoyles-fans.org
SIC: 7383 News feature syndicate
HQ: Disney Enterprises, Inc.
    500 S Buena Vista St
    Burbank CA 91521
    818 560-1000

(P-18407)
MARKETWIRE INC (HQ)
100 N Pacific Coast Hwy # 32, El Segundo
(90245-4359)
PHONE..................................310 765-3200
Michael Nowlan, *President*
James H Delaney, *COO*
Stephen Devito, *CFO*
Michael Shuler, *Senior VP*
Suresh Kumar, *Vice Pres*
EMP: 55 **EST:** 1998
SALES (est): 12.1MM
SALES (corp-wide): 5.6B **Publicly Held**
WEB: www.globenewswire.com
SIC: 7383 News reporting services for
    newspapers & periodicals
PA: Nasdaq, Inc.
    151 W 42nd St Fl 26
    New York NY 10036
    212 401-8700

(P-18408)
WRAP NEWS INC
Also Called: Wrap, The
2260 S Centinela Ave # 15, Los Angeles
(90064-1007)
PHONE..................................424 248-0612
Sharon Waxman, *President*
Sarah Lindsay, *Executive*
Steve Root, *Editor*
EMP: 50 **EST:** 2008
SALES (est): 7.5MM **Privately Held**
WEB: www.thewrap.com
SIC: 7383 News correspondents, inde-
    pendent; news pictures, gathering & dis-
    tributing

7384 Photofinishing Labs

(P-18409)
JAKE HEY INCORPORATED
Also Called: A & I Color Laboratory
257 S Lake St, Burbank (91502-2111)
PHONE..................................323 856-5280
David Alexander, *President*
John Gaeta, *CFO*
James Ishihara, *Vice Pres*
EMP: 144 **EST:** 1978
SQ FT: 16,000
SALES (est): 6.5MM **Privately Held**
WEB: www.aandi.com
SIC: 7384 Photofinishing laboratory

(P-18410)
LONGS DRUG STORES CAL INC
155 W Los Angeles Ave, Moorpark
(93021-1822)
PHONE..................................805 530-0283
Fax: 805 517-1148
EMP: 60
SALES (corp-wide): 177.5B **Publicly Held**
SIC: 5912 7384 5999 Ret Drugs/Sundries
    Photofinishing Laboratory Ret Misc Mer-
    chandise
HQ: Longs Drug Stores California Inc.
    1 Cvs Dr
    Woonsocket RI 02895
    925 937-1170

(P-18411)
LONGS DRUG STORES CAL INC
451 S Reino Rd, Newbury Park
(91320-4267)
PHONE..................................805 499-4006
Fax: 805 499-8525
EMP: 50
SALES (corp-wide): 177.5B **Publicly Held**
SIC: 5912 7384 5999 Ret Drugs/Sundries
    Photofinishing Laboratory Ret Misc Mer-
    chandise
HQ: Longs Drug Stores California Inc.
    1 Cvs Dr
    Woonsocket RI 02895
    925 937-1170

(P-18412)
LONGS DRUG STORES CAL INC
1540 E Highland Ave, San Bernardino
(92404-4614)
PHONE..................................909 886-4984
Fax: 909 881-9562
EMP: 60
SQ FT: 26,058
SALES (corp-wide): 177.5B **Publicly Held**
SIC: 5912 7384 Ret Drugs/Sundries Pho-
    tofinishing Laboratory
HQ: Longs Drug Stores California Inc.
    1 Cvs Dr
    Woonsocket RI 02895
    925 937-1170

(P-18413)
LONGS DRUG STORES CAL INC
4400 Coffee Rd, Bakersfield (93308-5032)
PHONE..................................805 588-0290
Fax: 661 588-1931
EMP: 60
SALES (corp-wide): 177.5B **Publicly Held**
SIC: 5912 7384 5999 Ret Drugs/Sundries
    Photofinishing Laboratory Ret Misc Mer-
    chandise
HQ: Longs Drug Stores California Inc.
    1 Cvs Dr
    Woonsocket RI 02895
    925 937-1170

(P-18414)
LONGS DRUG STORES CAL INC
25880 Mcbean Pkwy, Santa Clarita
(91355-2004)
PHONE..................................661 254-3766
EMP: 60
SALES (corp-wide): 177.5B **Publicly Held**
SIC: 5912 7384 5999 Ret Drugs/Sundries
    Photofinishing Laboratory Ret Misc Mer-
    chandise
HQ: Longs Drug Stores California Inc.
    1 Cvs Dr
    Woonsocket RI 02895
    925 937-1170

(P-18415)
LONGS DRUG STORES CAL INC
3935 Cochran St, Simi Valley (93063-2364)
PHONE..................................805 581-1504
Fax: 805 581-5315
EMP: 50
SALES (corp-wide): 177.5B **Publicly Held**
SIC: 5912 5331 7384 5999 Ret
    Drugs/Sundries Variety Store Photofinish
    Laboratory Ret Misc Merchandise
HQ: Longs Drug Stores California Inc.
    1 Cvs Dr
    Woonsocket RI 02895
    925 937-1170

(P-18416)
LONGS DRUG STORES CAL LLC
1822 E Avnida De Los Arbl, Thousand Oaks
(91362)
PHONE..................................805 493-1502
Sid Rehka, *Branch Mgr*
EMP: 208
SALES (corp-wide): 268.7B **Publicly Held**
WEB: www.cvs.com
SIC: 5912 7384 5999 Drug stores; photo-
    finishing laboratory; toiletries, cosmetics &
    perfumes

(P-18417)
LONGS DRUG STORES CAL LLC
901 Silver Spur Rd, Rllng HLS Est
(90274-3895)
PHONE..................................310 377-6728
Gary Lofstrom, *Manager*
EMP: 208
SQ FT: 23,009
SALES (corp-wide): 268.7B **Publicly Held**
WEB: www.cvs.com
SIC: 5912 5331 7384 Drug stores; variety
    stores; photofinishing laboratory
HQ: Longs Drug Stores California L.L.C.
    1 Cvs Dr
    Woonsocket RI 02895

(P-18418)
LONGS DRUG STORES CAL LLC
1785 E Palm Canyon Dr, Palm Springs
(92264-1630)
PHONE..................................760 327-1374
Dennis Pompa, *Manager*
EMP: 208
SALES (corp-wide): 268.7B **Publicly Held**
WEB: www.cvs.com
SIC: 5912 5331 7384 5999 Drug stores;
    variety stores; photofinishing laboratory;
    cosmetics
HQ: Longs Drug Stores California L.L.C.
    1 Cvs Dr
    Woonsocket RI 02895

(P-18419)
LONGS DRUG STORES CAL LLC
404 E Base Line St, San Bernardino
(92410-3919)
PHONE..................................909 884-5364
Denise Pompa, *Branch Mgr*
EMP: 208
SALES (corp-wide): 268.7B **Publicly Held**
WEB: www.cvs.com
SIC: 5912 5331 7384 5999 Drug stores;
    variety stores; photofinishing laboratory;
    toiletries, cosmetics & perfumes
HQ: Longs Drug Stores California L.L.C.
    1 Cvs Dr
    Woonsocket RI 02895

(P-18420)
NEW ALBERTSONS INC
Also Called: Albertsons - Savon 6153
21804 Hawthorne Blvd, Torrance
(90503-4613)
PHONE..................................310 540-6824
Arnold Walder, *Manager*
EMP: 115
SALES (corp-wide): 69.6B **Publicly Held**
WEB: www.albertsonscompanies.com
SIC: 5411 7384 5992 5461 Supermar-
    kets, chain; photofinish laboratories;
    florists; bakeries
HQ: New Albertson's, Inc.
    250 E Parkcenter Blvd
    Boise ID 83706

(P-18421)
TECHNICOLOR INC
Also Called: Technicolor Lab
2255 N Ontario St Ste 180, Burbank
(91504-4509)
PHONE..................................818 260-4577
Joe Berchtold, *President*
Rene Abeyta, *Purch Mgr*
EMP: 400 **EST:** 1966
SALES (est): 39.4MM **Privately Held**
SIC: 7384 Photofinish laboratories

(P-18422)
WITHIN UNLIMITED INC
3760 Motor Ave, Los Angeles
(90034-6404)
PHONE..................................310 664-1400
EMP: 50 **EST:** 2016

SALES (est): 3.1MM **Privately Held**
WEB: www.with.in
SIC: 7384 Home movies, developing &
    processing

7389 Business Svcs, NEC

(P-18423)
117 GLOBAL LLC (PA)
Also Called: One Seventeen Global
32861 Camn Capistrano, San Juan Capis-
trano (92675-4529)
PHONE..................................949 570-1552
Greg Maselli, *President*
EMP: 14 **EST:** 2016
SALES (est): 1.2MM **Privately Held**
WEB: www.117global.com
SIC: 7389 2657 2326 Design, commercial
    & industrial; food containers, folding;
    made from purchased material; medical &
    hospital uniforms, men's

(P-18424)
2310 CATALINA LLC
1507 Western Ave, Glendale (91201-1215)
PHONE..................................818 696-2040
Ararat Yesayan, *Branch Mgr*
EMP: 73
SALES (corp-wide): 721.7K **Privately Held**
SIC: 7389 Personal service agents, bro-
    kers & bureaus
PA: 2310 Catalina Llc
    635 W Colorado St Ste 109
    Glendale CA 91204
    818 824-6304

(P-18425)
603 N LA CIENEGA BOULEVARD LLC
603 N La Cienega Blvd, West Hollywood
(90069-5201)
PHONE..................................310 855-9955
EMP: 56
SALES (corp-wide): 410.9K **Privately Held**
WEB: www.melroserooftoptheatre.com
SIC: 7389 Personal service agents, bro-
    kers & bureaus
PA: 603 N. La Cienega Boulevard, Llc
    6666 Whitley Ter
    Los Angeles CA 90068
    310 721-2731

(P-18426)
A J PARENT COMPANY INC (PA)
Also Called: Americas Printer.com
6910 Aragon Cir Ste 6, Buena Park
(90620-8103)
PHONE..................................714 521-1100
Arthur Parent, *CEO*
Mike Roccio, *Vice Pres*
Nathan Williams, *Information Mgr*
Benny Gallego, *Technician*
Julio Sandoval, *Technician*
EMP: 75 **EST:** 1997
SALES (est): 18.1MM **Privately Held**
WEB: www.americasprinter.com
SIC: 7389 2752 Printers' services: folding,
    collating; commercial printing, lithographic

(P-18427)
A THREAD AHEAD INC
1925 1st St, San Fernando (91340-2609)
P.O. Box 889 (91341-0889)
PHONE..................................818 837-1984
Lori Banks, *President*
Julio Moreno, *Prdtn Mgr*
EMP: 20 **EST:** 2010
SALES (est): 3MM **Privately Held**
WEB: www.athreadahead.com
SIC: 7389 2759 Advertising, promotional &
    trade show services; screen printing

(P-18428)
AARON THOMAS COMPANY INC (PA)
7421 Chapman Ave, Garden Grove
(92841-2115)
PHONE..................................714 894-4468
James T Chang, *CEO*
Thomas Bacon, *President*
Linda Bacon, *Treasurer*
Brian Robinson, *Principal*

Jean Chang, *Admin Sec*
▲ **EMP:** 125
SQ FT: 207,000
SALES (est): 44.3MM **Privately Held**
WEB: www.packaging.com
SIC: 7389 Packaging & labeling services

(P-18429)
ABI DOCUMENT SUPPORT SVCS LLC
10459 Mountain View Ave E, Loma Linda
(92354-2033)
PHONE..................909 793-0613
David Benge, *Branch Mgr*
Judy Bible, *CIO*
Steven Thue, *CIO*
Derrick Chan-Sew, *Info Tech Dir*
Derrick Sew, *Info Tech Dir*
EMP: 79 **Privately Held**
WEB: www.abidss.com
SIC: 7389 5044 Microfilm recording & developing service; office equipment
HQ: Abi Document Support Services, Llc
3534 E Sunshine St Ste L
Springfield MO 65809

(P-18430)
ABLE RISE LIMITED CORP
11100 Valley Blvd Ste 306, El Monte
(91731-2533)
PHONE..................626 416-5680
Yuanyuan Liu, *President*
EMP: 50 **EST:** 2016
SQ FT: 966
SALES (est): 1.3MM **Privately Held**
SIC: 7389 Styling of fashions, apparel, furniture, textiles, etc.

(P-18431)
ACCESS FINANCE INC
3415 S Sepulveda Blvd # 400, Los Angeles
(90034-6094)
PHONE..................310 826-4000
Raquel Aguirre, *Manager*
EMP: 50 **EST:** 2014
SALES (est): 1.3MM **Privately Held**
WEB: www.accessfinanceinc.com
SIC: 7389 Financial services

(P-18432)
ACCO ENGINEERED SYSTEMS INC
6446 E Washington Blvd, Commerce
(90040-1820)
PHONE..................323 201-0931
Matt Deluca, *Principal*
Greg Guizado, *Regional Mgr*
Jeff Ban, *Project Mgr*
David Cellini, *Project Mgr*
Brandon Ellis, *Project Engr*
EMP: 50
SALES (corp-wide): 1.4B **Privately Held**
WEB: www.accoes.com
SIC: 7389 Automobile recovery service
PA: Acco Engineered Systems, Inc.
888 E Walnut St
Pasadena CA 91101
818 244-6571

(P-18433)
ACE ATTRNEY SVC INC A CAL CORP (PA)
811 Wilshire Blvd Ste 900, Los Angeles
(90017-2637)
P.O. Box 71036 (90071-0036)
PHONE..................213 623-3979
Mahmoud Moussaoui, *President*
Menelik Mendaye, *President*
Michael Moussoaui, *CFO*
Abdi Mohammad, *Vice Pres*
EMP: 91 **EST:** 1989
SALES (est): 9.3MM **Privately Held**
WEB: www.acelegal.com
SIC: 7389 8111 4215 Courier or messenger service; legal services; courier services, except by air

(P-18434)
ADVANSTAR COMMUNICATIONS INC
2901 28th St Ste 100, Santa Monica
(90405-2975)
PHONE..................310 857-7500
Danny Phillips, *Manager*

Jessica Davies, *Sales Executive*
Melissa Stillwell, *Manager*
EMP: 18
SALES (corp-wide): 1.3B **Privately Held**
WEB: www.epay.advanstar.com
SIC: 7389 2721 7331 Trade show arrangement; magazines: publishing only, not printed on site; direct mail advertising services
HQ: Advanstar Communications Inc.
2501 Colorado Ave Ste 280
Santa Monica CA 90404
310 857-7500

(P-18435)
AEGEAN STONEWORKS INC
880 N Eckhoff St, Orange (92868-1008)
PHONE..................800 762-9089
Adriana Callas, *President*
Adriana Eallas, *President*
EMP: 58 **EST:** 1973
SALES (est): 3MM **Privately Held**
WEB: www.aswca.com
SIC: 7389 1799 Design services; counter top installation; kitchen & bathroom remodeling

(P-18436)
AFFILIATED COMMUNICATIONS INC
Also Called: Alert Communications
3601 Calle Tecate, Camarillo (93012-5056)
P.O. Box 5720, Ventura (93005-0720)
PHONE..................805 447-2101
Richard Starr, *President*
Nick Giacopuzzi, *Vice Pres*
Monte L Widders, *Vice Pres*
Crystal Razo, *Business Mgr*
Matthew Ashman, *Marketing Mgr*
EMP: 105 **EST:** 1965
SQ FT: 5,000
SALES (est): 7.4MM **Privately Held**
WEB: www.alertcommunications.com
SIC: 7389 5999 Telephone answering service; telephone & communication equipment

(P-18437)
AFM & SG-FTRA INTLLCTUAL PRPRT
4705 Laurel Canyon Blvd # 40, Valley Village (91607-3960)
PHONE..................818 255-7980
Dennis Dreith, *Director*
Shari Hoffman, *COO*
Jennifer Leblanc, *CFO*
Eric Cowden, *Associate Dir*
Cindy Jara, *Admin Asst*
EMP: 70
SQ FT: 21,600
SALES: 68.5MM **Privately Held**
WEB: www.afmsagaftrafund.org
SIC: 7389 Fund raising organizations

(P-18438)
AIA HOLDINGS INC (PA)
Also Called: Associated Bond
26560 Agoura Rd Ste 100, Calabasas
(91302-2015)
PHONE..................818 222-4999
Brian N Nairin, *President*
Robert Kersnick, *COO*
Mark Francis, *CFO*
Norman Konvitz, *Exec VP*
Fred Mitterhoff, *Exec VP*
EMP: 51 **EST:** 2003
SQ FT: 8,000
SALES (est): 9.5MM **Privately Held**
WEB: www.aiasurety.com
SIC: 7389 Bail bonding

(P-18439)
ALIN PARTY SUPPLY CO
6493 Magnolia Ave, Riverside
(92506-2409)
PHONE..................951 682-7441
Sherry Bauer, *Manager*
EMP: 28 **Privately Held**
WEB: www.alinpartysupply.com
SIC: 5947 7389 2759 Party favors; balloons, novelty & toy; invitation & stationery printing & engraving
PA: Alin Party Supply Co.
4139 Woodruff Ave
Lakewood CA 90713

(P-18440)
ALORICA INC (PA)
5161 California Ave # 100, Irvine
(92617-8002)
PHONE..................949 527-4600
Andy Lee, *CEO*
Colleen Beers, *President*
Brian Delaney, *President*
Jay King, *President*
Greg Haller, *COO*
▲ **EMP:** 100 **EST:** 1999
SALES (est): 845.1MM **Privately Held**
WEB: www.alorica.com
SIC: 7389 Telephone answering service; telemarketing services

(P-18441)
ALTEC PRODUCTS INC (PA)
23422 Mill Creek Dr # 225, Laguna Hills
(92653-7910)
PHONE..................949 727-1248
Mark Ford, *CEO*
Brandt Morell, *President*
Frank Sansone, *CFO*
Mark Tague, *CFO*
Howren Don, *Officer*
EMP: 74 **EST:** 1985
SQ FT: 12,500
SALES (est): 12.9MM **Privately Held**
WEB: www.altecproductsinc.com
SIC: 7389 Telemarketing services

(P-18442)
AMERICAN COPAK CORPORATION
9175 Eton Ave, Chatsworth (91311-5806)
PHONE..................818 576-1000
Steven A Brooker, *President*
Kenneth Oconnor, *CTO*
EMP: 150 **EST:** 1987
SQ FT: 150,000
SALES (est): 7.3MM **Privately Held**
WEB: www.americancopak.com
SIC: 7389 Packaging & labeling services

(P-18443)
AMERICAN HEALTH CONNECTION
8484 Wilshire Blvd # 501, Beverly Hills
(90211-3243)
PHONE..................424 226-0420
Yuriy Koltyar, *CEO*
Azabeh Williamson, *President*
Raymond Miller, *Business Dir*
Mel Saturnino, *Accounting Mgr*
Michael McWilliams, *Opers Staff*
EMP: 850 **EST:** 2011
SQ FT: 3,500
SALES (est): 13.6MM **Privately Held**
WEB: www.americanhealthconnection.com
SIC: 7389 Telemarketing services

(P-18444)
ANAHEIM/ORANGE CNTY VISITOR BU (PA)
Also Called: Visit Anaheim
2099 S State College Blvd, Anaheim
(92806-6142)
P.O. Box 4270 (92803-4270)
PHONE..................714 765-8888
Jay Burress, *CEO*
Charles Ahlers, *President*
Christina Dawson, *Vice Pres*
Harriet Porter, *Vice Pres*
Gina McQuade, *Planning*
EMP: 56 **EST:** 1961
SQ FT: 3,000
SALES: 16.5MM **Privately Held**
WEB: www.visitanaheim.org
SIC: 7389 Convention & show services; tourist information bureau

(P-18445)
ANDREW LAUREN COMPANY INC
15225 Alton Pkwy Unit 300, Irvine
(92618-2345)
PHONE..................949 861-4222
Mark Noonan, *Principal*
Heather Collins, *Director*
Carrie Outlaw, *Manager*
EMP: 134 **Privately Held**
WEB: www.int.andrewlauren.com
SIC: 7389 5713 Interior design services; carpets

PA: The Andrew Lauren Company Inc
8909 Kenamar Dr Ste 101
San Diego CA 92121

(P-18446)
ANSIRA PARTNERS INC
Also Called: Co-Optimum
5000 Van Nuys Blvd, Sherman Oaks
(91403-1793)
PHONE..................818 461-6100
EMP: 60
SALES (corp-wide): 73.9MM **Privately Held**
SIC: 7389 7331 Business Services Direct Mail Advertising Services Management Consulting Services
PA: Ansira Partners, Inc.
2300 Locust St
Saint Louis MO 63103
314 783-2300

(P-18447)
ANSWER FINANCIAL INC (HQ)
15910 Ventura Blvd Fl 6, Encino
(91436-2803)
PHONE..................818 644-4000
Robert J Slingerland, *CEO*
Darren Howard, *Chief Mktg Ofcr*
Jimmy Lee, *Chief Mktg Ofcr*
Daniel John Bryce, *Senior VP*
Peter Foley, *Senior VP*
EMP: 200 **EST:** 2006
SQ FT: 45,000
SALES (est): 80MM **Publicly Held**
WEB: www.allstate.com
SIC: 7389 6411 Brokers, business: buying & selling business enterprises; property & casualty insurance agent

(P-18448)
AP PARPRO INC (PA)
2700 S Fairview St, Santa Ana
(92704-5947)
PHONE..................714 545-8886
Hsiu-PI Wu, *CEO*
Tucky Wong, *Vice Pres*
Eduardo Serrano Luna, *Admin Sec*
Quin Dang, *Engineer*
Wen-Chia Liao, *Director*
EMP: 133 **EST:** 2005
SALES (est): 7.6MM **Privately Held**
WEB: www.parpro.com
SIC: 7389 3559 3679 Design services; electronic component making machinery; electronic circuits

(P-18449)
ARRIVAL COMMUNICATIONS INC (DH)
1800 19th St, Bakersfield (93301-4315)
PHONE..................661 716-2100
Richard Jalkut, *CEO*
Warren Heffelfinger, *President*
David Riordan, *COO*
Geoffrey Whynot, *CFO*
Tony Distefano, *Principal*
EMP: 75 **EST:** 1991
SQ FT: 4,000
SALES (est): 10.2MM **Privately Held**
WEB: www.arrivalcommunications.com
SIC: 7389 Design services
HQ: U.S. Telepacific Corp.
515 S Flower St Ste 4500
Los Angeles CA 90071
877 487-8722

(P-18450)
ASSOCTED LDSCP DSPLAY GROUP IN
Also Called: Associated Group
1005 Mateo St, Los Angeles (90021-1715)
PHONE..................714 558-6100
Laurie Resnick, *President*
Greg Salmeri, *Vice Pres*
Richard Ordaz, *Purchasing*
EMP: 90 **EST:** 1986
SALES (est): 9.7MM **Privately Held**
WEB: www.ag-ca.com
SIC: 7389 0781 Plant care service; decoration service for special events; landscape services

(P-18451)
ATLANTC-PCFIC PROC SYSTEMS INC (PA)
18350 Mount Langley St # 20, Fountain Val-ley (92708-6900)
PHONE....................714 241-1402
Abe Maghaguian, *CEO*
Robyn Hickman, *President*
Frank A Dicrisi III, *COO*
Lee Morgan, *CFO*
Hadia Fadial, *Treasurer*
EMP: 126 **EST:** 2004
SQ FT: 10,000
SALES (est): 33.1MM **Privately Held**
WEB: www.approcessing.com
SIC: 7389 Credit card service

(P-18452)
AUTHORITY TAX SERVICES LLC
Also Called: Tax Problem Center
777 S Figueroa St # 1900, Los Angeles (90017-5817)
PHONE....................213 486-5135
EMP: 60
SALES (est): 3.9MM **Privately Held**
SIC: 7389 Business Services

(P-18453)
AUTOCRIB INC
2882 Dow Ave, Tustin (92780-7258)
PHONE....................714 274-0400
Stephen Pixley, *CEO*
Jim McMahon, *Vice Pres*
Mark Van Bloem, *Vice Pres*
Mark Bloem, *Regional Mgr*
Jonathan Kim, *CTO*
▲ **EMP:** 150 **EST:** 1999
SQ FT: 58,000
SALES (est): 43.8MM
SALES (corp-wide): 3.5B **Publicly Held**
WEB: www.autocrib.com
SIC: 7389 3581 Inventory computing serv-ice; automatic vending machines
PA: Snap-On Incorporated
2801 80th St
Kenosha WI 53143
262 656-5200

(P-18454)
AZTECS TELECOM INC
1353 Walker Ln, Corona (92879-1775)
PHONE....................714 373-1560
Robert Lopez, *CEO*
Charley Cole, *Vice Pres*
EMP: 80 **EST:** 2000
SALES (est): 11.6MM **Privately Held**
WEB: www.aztecs.net
SIC: 7389 1731 Telephone services; com-munications specialization

(P-18455)
B RILEY RETAIL SOLUTIONS LLC
30870 Russell Ranch Rd, Westlake Village (91362-7347)
PHONE....................818 884-3737
Andrew Gumaer, *CEO*
Harvey Yellen, *President*
Michael A Petruski, *Exec VP*
Peter Wyke, *Senior VP*
Paul Brown, *Vice Pres*
EMP: 91 **EST:** 2000
SQ FT: 10,000
SALES (est): 12.2MM **Publicly Held**
WEB: www.brileyfin.com
SIC: 7389 Merchandise liquidators
PA: B. Riley Financial, Inc.
11100 Santa Monica Blvd
Los Angeles CA 90025

(P-18456)
BANKCARD SERVICES (PA)
21281 S Western Ave, Torrance (90501-2958)
PHONE....................213 365-1122
Jacky Tam, *Admin Sec*
Boahe Hyun, *Manager*
EMP: 110 **EST:** 2012
SALES (est): 19.4MM **Privately Held**
WEB: www.navyz.com
SIC: 7389 Credit card service

(P-18457)
BANKCARD USA MERCHANT SRVC
5701 Lindero Canyon Rd, Westlake Village (91362-4060)
PHONE....................818 597-7000
Shawn Skelton, *President*
Alan Griefer, *Exec VP*
Charlie Cicack, *Executive*
Mike Dom, *Info Tech Dir*
Sean Smith, *Sales Staff*
EMP: 85 **EST:** 1993
SQ FT: 20,000
SALES (est): 146.1K **Privately Held**
WEB: www.bankcardusa.com
SIC: 7389 Credit card service

(P-18458)
BAXALTA US INC
17511 Armstrong Ave, Irvine (92614-5725)
PHONE....................949 474-6301
EMP: 288 **Privately Held**
SIC: 7389 Personal service agents, bro-kers & bureaus
HQ: Baxalta Us Inc.
1200 Lakeside Dr
Bannockburn IL 60015
224 948-2000

(P-18459)
BERSHTEL ENTERPRISES LLC (PA)
Also Called: We Pack It All
2745 Huntington Dr, Duarte (91010-2302)
PHONE....................626 301-9214
Jack Bershtel, *President*
Sharon Bershtel, *CFO*
Gaby Gaiz, *Treasurer*
George Gellert, *Vice Pres*
Robert Gellert, *Vice Pres*
EMP: 145 **EST:** 1972
SQ FT: 50,000
SALES (est): 25.1MM **Privately Held**
WEB: www.wepackitall.com
SIC: 7389 Packaging & labeling services

(P-18460)
BEST SIGNS INC (PA)
1550 S Gene Autry Trl, Palm Springs (92264-3505)
PHONE....................760 320-3042
Jesse Cross, *Vice Pres*
Jim Cross, *Vice Pres*
John Cross, *Project Mgr*
EMP: 26 **EST:** 1960
SQ FT: 6,000
SALES (est): 5.2MM **Privately Held**
WEB: www.bestsignsinc.com
SIC: 7389 3993 1799 Sign painting & let-tering shop; signs & advertising special-ties; sign installation & maintenance

(P-18461)
BLUE LAGOON TEXTILE INC
317 N Palm Dr Apt 4d, Beverly Hills (90210-5800)
PHONE....................213 590-4545
Kamran Amirianfar, *CEO*
John Malonie, *Vice Pres*
EMP: 50 **EST:** 2010
SALES (est): 1.6MM **Privately Held**
WEB: www.bluelagoontextile.com
SIC: 7389 Textile & apparel services

(P-18462)
BROKER SOLUTIONS INC
11820 Pierce St, Riverside (92505-4403)
PHONE....................951 637-2300
Neil Wachsberger, *Manager*
EMP: 69 **Privately Held**
WEB: www.newamericanfunding.com
SIC: 7389 Personal service agents, bro-kers & bureaus
PA: Broker Solutions, Inc.
14511 Myford Rd Ste 100
Tustin CA 92780

(P-18463)
BUDGET BLINDS LLC (HQ)
19000 Macarthur Blvd # 100, Irvine (92612-1416)
PHONE....................949 404-1100
Shirin Behzadi, *Mng Member*
Marjorie Kahre, *President*

Brent Hallock, *Exec VP*
Tami Stepp, *Vice Pres*
Carlin Anderson, *Office Mgr*
EMP: 65 **EST:** 1992
SALES (est): 26.5MM
SALES (corp-wide): 43.6MM **Privately Held**
WEB: www.budgetblinds.com
SIC: 5719 7389 Window furnishings;
PA: Home Franchise Concepts, Llc
19000 Macarthur Blvd # 100
Irvine CA 92612
949 404-1100

(P-18464)
CALIFORNIA CREDITS GROUP LLC
87 N Raymond Ave Ste 526, Pasadena (91103-3904)
PHONE....................626 584-9800
John Simpson,
Jay Parker, *Vice Pres*
Lan Hai, *Opers Staff*
Heather Smith, *Opers Staff*
Marianne Serpa, *Manager*
EMP: 50 **EST:** 2002
SALES (est): 10MM **Privately Held**
WEB: www.ccg.com
SIC: 7389 Personal service agents, kers & bureaus

(P-18465)
CALIFORNIA TRAFFIC CONTROL
Also Called: California Traffic Ctrl Svcs
3333 Cherry Ave, Long Beach (90807-4901)
PHONE....................562 595-7575
Delores Kepl, *CFO*
Dolores Reza Nix, *General Mgr*
EMP: 70 **EST:** 2010
SALES (est): 5.1MM **Privately Held**
WEB: www.californiatrafficcontrol.com
SIC: 7389 Flagging service (traffic control)

(P-18466)
CALIFRNIA GRNHSE FRM II LTD PR
17712 Adobe Rd, Bakersfield (93307-9756)
PHONE....................949 715-3987
LI Hui Lo, *President*
EMP: 78 **EST:** 2012
SALES (est): 1MM **Privately Held**
SIC: 7389

(P-18467)
CARBON 38 INC
10000 Wash Blvd Ste 800, Culver City (90232-2784)
PHONE....................888 723-5838
Katherine Johnson, *CEO*
Jem Berke, *CFO*
Lisa Kraynak, *Chief Mktg Ofcr*
Peter Bohnert, *Vice Pres*
Jenny Neymark, *Creative Dir*
EMP: 90 **EST:** 2012
SALES (est): 11.7MM **Privately Held**
WEB: www.carbon38.com
SIC: 7389 Styling of fashions, apparel, fur-niture, textiles, etc.

(P-18468)
CARDFLEX INC
2900 Bristol St Ste F, Costa Mesa (92626-7911)
PHONE....................714 361-1900
Andrew M Phillips, *President*
Todd Gordon, *Manager*
Martin Phillips, *Manager*
EMP: 75 **EST:** 2008
SALES (est): 15.9MM **Privately Held**
WEB: www.cardflexprepaid.com
SIC: 7389 Credit card service

(P-18469)
CARDSERVICE INTERNATIONAL INC
Also Called: Csi
1538 W Commonwealth Ave, Fullerton (92833-2754)
PHONE....................714 773-1778
EMP: 56
SALES (corp-wide): 2B **Privately Held**
SIC: 7389 Business Services

HQ: Cardservice International, Inc.
5898 Condor Dr 220
Moorpark CA 93021
805 648-1425

(P-18470)
CARDSERVICE INTERNATIONAL INC (DH)
5898 Condor Dr 220, Moorpark (93021-2603)
PHONE....................805 648-1425
Don Headlund, *President*
Charles Burtzloff, *CEO*
EMP: 450 **EST:** 2002
SQ FT: 34,000
SALES (est): 58.2MM
SALES (corp-wide): 14.8B **Publicly Held**
WEB: www.ceocardservice.com
SIC: 7389 6153 Credit card service; short-term business credit

(P-18471)
CASECENTRAL INC (DH)
Also Called: Casecentral
1055 E Colo Blvd Ste 400, Pasadena (91106)
PHONE....................415 989-2300
Christopher S Kruse, *President*
Peter H Kruse, *Vice Pres*
Jay O'Connor, *Vice Pres*
Philip Sakakihara, *Vice Pres*
Ted Sergott, *Vice Pres*
EMP: 60 **EST:** 1993
SALES (est): 15.6MM
SALES (corp-wide): 3.1B **Privately Held**
WEB: www.casecentral.com
SIC: 7389 4813 4226 Legal & tax serv-ices; ; document & office records storage
HQ: Guidance Software, Inc.
1055 E Colo Blvd Ste 400
Pasadena CA 91106
626 229-9191

(P-18472)
CAUSEFORCE INC (PA)
12301 Wilshire Blvd # 430, Los Angeles (90025-1024)
PHONE....................323 654-9255
Brian Pendelton, *CEO*
Bev Deeth, *COO*
Mike Brown, *Production*
Robert Facer, *Marketing Staff*
Vanessa Wan, *Sales Staff*
EMP: 68 **EST:** 2003
SALES (est): 9.6MM **Privately Held**
WEB: www.causeforce.com
SIC: 7389 Fund raising organizations

(P-18473)
CAW COWIE INC (PA)
Also Called: Colin Cowie Lifestyle
7 Ginger Root Ln, Rancho Palos Verdes (90275-5907)
PHONE....................212 396-9007
Colin Cowie, *CEO*
Stuart Brownstein, *President*
David Berke, *COO*
Alia Wilcox, *Creative Dir*
Nadia Ahmed, *Executive Asst*
EMP: 25 **EST:** 1994
SALES (est): 4.9MM **Privately Held**
WEB: www.rsclarkenergy.com
SIC: 7389 7299 5023 2731 Interior de-sign services; party planning service; dec-orative home furnishings & supplies; book publishing

(P-18474)
CENTECH GROUP INC
2 Draco Dr Bldg 8352, Edwards (93524-7801)
PHONE....................661 275-5688
Carson Chism, *General Mgr*
EMP: 50
SALES (corp-wide): 53MM **Privately Held**
WEB: www.centechgroup.com
SIC: 7389 Personal service agents, bro-kers & bureaus
PA: The Centech Group Inc
4437 Brkfeld Corp Dr Ste
Chantilly VA 20151
703 525-4444

P R O D U C T S & S V C S

(P-18475)
CENTURY BANKCARD SERVICES
25129 The Old Rd Ste 222, Stevenson Ranch (91381-2281)
PHONE...................................818 700-3100
Scott Scherr, *President*
EMP: 51 EST: 1999
SQ FT: 4,200
SALES (est): 2.1MM
SALES (corp-wide): 150.1MM **Publicly Held**
WEB: www.pacepayment.com
SIC: 7389 Credit card service
HQ: Pace Payment Systems, Inc.
30 Burton Hills Blvd
Nashville TN 37215

(P-18476)
CERAMIC DECORATING COMPANY INC
4651 Sheila St, Commerce (90040-1003)
PHONE...................................323 268-5135
Chad A Johnson, *CEO*
Allan Johnson, *President*
W Allan Johnson, *CEO*
Sheryl Sellers, *Executive Asst*
Burnell D Johnson, *Admin Sec*
EMP: 50 EST: 1934
SQ FT: 30,290
SALES (est): 9.2MM **Privately Held**
WEB: www.ceramicdecoratingco.com
SIC: 7389 2396 Labeling bottles, cans, cartons, etc.; lettering service; automotive & apparel trimmings

(P-18477)
CETERA FINANCIAL GROUP INC (PA)
200 N Pacific Coast Hwy # 11, El Segundo (90245-5628)
PHONE...................................866 489-3100
Adam Antoniades, *President*
Thomas B Taylor, *President*
Jeffrey Buchheister, *CFO*
Michael Zuna, *Chief Mktg Ofcr*
Jason Mullens, *Officer*
EMP: 78 EST: 2009
SQ FT: 70,000
SALES (est): 315.7K **Privately Held**
WEB: www.cetera.com
SIC: 7389 6282 Financial services; investment advisory service

(P-18478)
CHINESEINVESTORSCOM INC (PA)
Also Called: Chinesefn
227 W Valley Blvd 208a, San Gabriel (91776-3764)
PHONE...................................626 589-2468
Warren Wang, *Principal*
Patrick Leung, *CFO*
Keevin Gillespie, *Vice Pres*
EMP: 52 EST: 1999
SALES: 6.4MM **Publicly Held**
WEB: www.chineseinvestors.com
SIC: 8299 7389 8742 Educational services; language school; financial services; management consulting services

(P-18479)
CINTAS CORPORATION
Also Called: Cintas Fire
4320 E Miraloma Ave, Anaheim (92807-1886)
P.O. Box 636525, Cincinnati OH (45263-6525)
PHONE...................................714 646-2550
Winter Barry, *General Mgr*
Dan Berkemeyer, *Vice Pres*
Leticia Holcomb, *Admin Asst*
Boyd Mannie, *Sales Staff*
Sharon Crall, *Corp Comm Staff*
EMP: 80
SALES (corp-wide): 7.1B **Publicly Held**
WEB: www.cintas.com
SIC: 5699 7389 8711 Uniforms; fire protection service other than forestry or public; fire protection engineering
PA: Cintas Corporation
6800 Cintas Blvd
Cincinnati OH 45262
513 459-1200

(P-18480)
CIRTECH INC
Also Called: Apct Anaheim
250 E Emerson Ave, Orange (92865-3317)
PHONE...................................714 921-0860
Brad Reese, *President*
Frank E Reese, *CEO*
Karen Bever, *Manager*
EMP: 50 EST: 1965
SQ FT: 30,000
SALES (est): 729.1K
SALES (corp-wide): 7MM **Privately Held**
WEB: www.apct.com
SIC: 7389 3672 Printed circuitry graphic layout; printed circuit boards; wiring boards
PA: Apct Holdings, Llc
3495 De La Cruz Blvd
Santa Clara CA 95054
408 727-6442

(P-18481)
CLARO POOL SERVICES INC
42161 Beacon Hl, Palm Desert (92211-5108)
PHONE...................................760 341-3377
Stephen Little, *CEO*
EMP: 53 EST: 2012
SQ FT: 8,000
SALES (est): 6.9MM **Privately Held**
WEB: www.claropool.com
SIC: 7389 Swimming pool & hot tub service & maintenance

(P-18482)
COASTAL CLOSEOUTS INC
Also Called: West Coast Rags
100 Oceangate Ste 1200, Long Beach (90802-4324)
PHONE...................................323 589-7900
EMP: 52
SQ FT: 68,000
SALES (est): 4.1MM **Privately Held**
SIC: 7389 Business Services

(P-18483)
COASTAL INTL HOLDINGS LLC
2832 Walnut Ave Ste B, Tustin (92780-7002)
PHONE...................................714 635-1200
Robert Hill, *Branch Mgr*
Rich Sotir, *Vice Pres*
Richard Rebecky, *General Mgr*
Kathy Spangler, *CIO*
Boone Michael, *Director*
EMP: 219
SALES (corp-wide): 28MM **Privately Held**
WEB: www.coastalintl.com
SIC: 7389 Trade show arrangement
PA: Coastal International Holdings, Llc
3 Harbor Dr Ste 211
Sausalito CA 94965
415 339-1700

(P-18484)
COLOR DESIGN LABORATORY INC
21329 Nordhoff St, Chatsworth (91311-5819)
PHONE...................................818 341-8200
Gilberto Amparo, *CEO*
EMP: 50 **Privately Held**
WEB: www.colordesignlaboratory.com
SIC: 7389 Design services
PA: Color Design Laboratory Inc
19151 Parthenia St Ste H
Northridge CA 91324

(P-18485)
COMMERCIAL GRINDING CO INC
6829 Walthall Way, Paramount (90723-2028)
P.O. Box 1267, La Mirada (90637-1267)
PHONE...................................562 531-9970
Gale Sturdevant, *President*
Teresa Schwappach, *CFO*
Carolyn Sturdevant, *Vice Pres*
EMP: 53 EST: 1945
SQ FT: 35,000
SALES (est): 1.5MM **Privately Held**
WEB: www.wegrind.com
SIC: 7389 Business Services

(P-18486)
COMPTON UNIFIED SCHOOL DST
2600 N Central Ave, Compton (90222-1640)
PHONE...................................310 639-4321
Jesse Jones, *Principal*
EMP: 72
SALES (corp-wide): 342.2MM **Privately Held**
WEB: www.compton.k12.ca.us
SIC: 8211 7389 Public elementary & secondary schools; personal service agents, brokers & bureaus
PA: Compton Unified School District
501 S Santa Fe Ave
Compton CA 90221
310 604-6508

(P-18487)
COMPUTER EMB SPECIALISTS
17312 Gillette Ave, Irvine (92614-5606)
PHONE...................................949 852-8888
Fax: 949 852-8383
EMP: 20
SALES (est): 1.4MM **Privately Held**
SIC: 7389 2395 Business Services Pleating/Stitching Services

(P-18488)
CONSEJOSANO INC
5200 Lankershim Blvd # 31, North Hollywood (91601-3155)
PHONE...................................855 735-6726
Abner Mason, *CEO*
Vikram Bakhru, *Officer*
Nicole Cook, *Vice Pres*
Kate Jenkins, *Comms Dir*
John Solis, *Software Engr*
EMP: 60 EST: 2009
SALES (est): 3.7MM **Privately Held**
WEB: www.consejosanous.com
SIC: 7389 Business services

(P-18489)
CONSOLDTED FIRE PROTECTION LLC (HQ)
153 Technology Dr Ste 200, Irvine (92618-2461)
PHONE...................................949 727-3277
Rob Salek, *CEO*
Keith Fielding, *President*
Peter Chung, *COO*
Jeff Murtari, *Info Tech Dir*
Jacob Broderick, *Sales Staff*
EMP: 800 EST: 1999
SALES (est): 54.2MM **Privately Held**
WEB: www.cfpfire.com
SIC: 7389 Fire protection service other than forestry or public

(P-18490)
CONTINENTAL EXCH SOLUTIONS INC
Also Called: Ria Financial Services
7001 Village Dr Ste 200, Buena Park (90621-2232)
PHONE...................................562 345-2100
EMP: 70 **Publicly Held**
WEB: www.us.riafinancial.com
SIC: 7389 Financial services
HQ: Continental Exchange Solutions Inc.
6565 Knott Ave
Buena Park CA 90620

(P-18491)
CONTRACT LABELING SERVICE INC
13885 Ramona Ave, Chino (91710-5426)
PHONE...................................909 937-0344
Trevor Metcalf, *CEO*
Carolyn Johnson, *Corp Secy*
Alexander Riff, *Vice Pres*
▲ EMP: 48 EST: 1992
SALES (est): 8.4MM **Privately Held**
WEB: www.contractlabel.com
SIC: 7389 3552 Packaging & labeling services; silk screens for textile industry

(P-18492)
COOK HAMMOND AND KELL INC
Also Called: Chk America
115 S La Cumbre Ln # 201, Santa Barbara (93105-6127)
PHONE...................................805 682-8900
EMP: 15
SALES (est): 1.2MM **Privately Held**
WEB: www.chkamerica.com
SIC: 7389 3993 Business Services, Nec, Nsk

(P-18493)
COWAN PRECISION GRINDING INC
12864 Foothill Blvd, Sylmar (91342-5330)
PHONE...................................318 361-3512
Phillip E Cowan, *President*
Gail Cowan, *Vice Pres*
Philip S Kevin, *Vice Pres*
Jerry DOE, *Supervisor*
EMP: 58 EST: 1967
SQ FT: 5,000
SALES (est): 1.2MM **Privately Held**
WEB: www.cowanprecisiongrinding.com
SIC: 7389 Grinding, precision: commercial or industrial

(P-18494)
CPPG INC
3905 E Miraloma Ave, Anaheim (92806-6201)
PHONE...................................714 572-3662
Louis Torres, *President*
Justino Cantu, *Vice Pres*
EMP: 30 EST: 1987
SQ FT: 15,000
SALES (est): 643.6K **Privately Held**
WEB: www.cppginc.com
SIC: 7389 3471 Grinding, precision: commercial or industrial; chromium plating of metals or formed products

(P-18495)
CREATE MUSIC GROUP INC
1320 N Wilton Pl, Los Angeles (90028-8527)
PHONE...................................310 623-0696
Jonathan Strauss, *CEO*
Alexandre Williams, *COO*
Ethan Baer, *Senior VP*
Robert Cheek, *General Mgr*
Darlene Hall, *Administration*
EMP: 85 EST: 2015
SALES (est): 30MM **Privately Held**
WEB: www.createmusicgroup.com
SIC: 7389 7371 Music distribution systems; computer software development & applications

(P-18496)
CREATIVE DESIGN CONSULTANTS (PA)
Also Called: C D C
2915 Red Hill Ave G201, Costa Mesa (92626-7948)
PHONE...................................714 641-4868
Dana Eggerts, *Principal*
Brian Richardson, *Info Tech Mgr*
Rick Betts, *Project Mgr*
Jeff Cooley, *Project Mgr*
Debra Harrison, *Project Mgr*
EMP: 95 EST: 1994
SQ FT: 9,988
SALES (est): 11.2MM **Privately Held**
WEB: www.cdcdesigns.com
SIC: 7389 Interior designer

(P-18497)
CREDIT CARD SERVICES INC (PA)
Also Called: Bankcard Services
21281 S Western Ave, Torrance (90501-2958)
PHONE...................................213 365-1122
Patrick S Hong, *CEO*
Denise Hunt, *Admin Sec*
Jina Han, *Supervisor*
EMP: 95 EST: 1996
SQ FT: 17,000
SALES (est): 41.7MM **Privately Held**
WEB: www.navyz.com
SIC: 7389 Credit card service

(P-18498)

CURRENCY CAPITAL LLC
12100 Wilshire Blvd # 1800, Los Angeles
(90025-7136)
PHONE...................310 571-9600
Blake Johnson, *Mng Member*
Kote Flosse, *COO*
Tim Hill, *Business Dir*
Chris Pirch, *Project Mgr*
Nami Ghahremani, *Credit Staff*
EMP: 65 **EST:** 2016
SALES (est): 5.1MM **Privately Held**
WEB: www.gocurrency.com
SIC: 7389 Financial services

(P-18499)

DAILYLOOK INC
2445 E 12th St Ste B, Los Angeles
(90021-2937)
PHONE...................888 888-6645
Brian Ree, *CEO*
Eric Marston, *Officer*
Henry Barahona, *Director*
Vinece Barlow, *Director*
Valerie Marsalli, *Director*
EMP: 86 **EST:** 2011
SALES (est): 11.8MM **Privately Held**
WEB: www.dailylook.com
SIC: 7389 Styling of fashions, apparel, furniture, textiles, etc.

(P-18500)

DAKO NORTH AMERICA INC
6392 Via Real, Carpinteria (93013-2921)
PHONE...................805 566-3037
EMP: 94 **EST:** 1979
SALES (est): 2.7MM **Privately Held**
SIC: 7389 Business services

(P-18501)

DAVINCI SCHOOLS
201 N Douglas St, El Segundo
(90245-4637)
PHONE...................310 725-5800
Matthew Wunder, *Administration*
Tom Cox, *Executive*
David Brown, *Exec Dir*
Jackie Martinez, *Office Mgr*
Sabrina Harris, *Business Anlyst*
EMP: 50 **EST:** 2017
SALES (est): 720.6K **Privately Held**
WEB: www.davincischools.org
SIC: 7389 Design services

(P-18502)

DEKRA-LITE INDUSTRIES INC
Also Called: DI Imaging
3102 W Alton Ave, Santa Ana
(92704-6817)
PHONE...................714 436-0705
Jeffrey Lopez, *CEO*
Mike Sterling, *General Mgr*
Amber Ledesma, *Admin Asst*
Elaine Hernandez, *Opers Mgr*
Eddie De La Rosa, *Manager*
▲ **EMP:** 80 **EST:** 1987
SQ FT: 30,000
SALES (est): 12.8MM **Privately Held**
WEB: www.dekra-lite.com
SIC: 7389 5999 3999 Decoration service for special events; art, picture frames & decorations; Christmas lights & decorations; advertising curtains

(P-18503)

DNICK24 ACADEMY
3054 E Via Corvina, Ontario (91764-7401)
PHONE...................310 904-4545
Dekel Nichols, *CEO*
Myoshia Nichols, *COO*
EMP: 50 **EST:** 2016
SALES (est): 1.4MM **Privately Held**
SIC: 7389 8322 ; meal delivery program

(P-18504)

DOCMAGIC INC
Also Called: Document Systems
1800 W 213th St, Torrance (90501-2832)
PHONE...................800 649-1362
Dominic Iannitti, *President*
Gavin Ales, *Officer*
Melanie Feliciano, *Officer*
Shandi Smith, *Executive*
Jimmy Chen, *Administration*
EMP: 79 **EST:** 1987
SQ FT: 20,000

SALES (est): 23.1MM **Privately Held**
WEB: www.docmagic.com
SIC: 7389 Legal & tax services

(P-18505)

DOUBLELINE CAPITAL LP
333 S Grand Ave Fl 18, Los Angeles
(90071-1504)
PHONE...................213 633-8200
Jeffery E Gundlach, *Partner*
Philip A Barach, *Partner*
Henry V Chase, *Partner*
Henry Chase, *CFO*
Susan Nichols, *Treasurer*
EMP: 111
SQ FT: 35,000
SALES (est): 20MM **Privately Held**
WEB: www.doubleline.com
SIC: 7389 6719 Financial services; investment holding companies, except banks

(P-18506)

DRIVER SPG LLC
468 N Rosemead Blvd, Pasadena
(91107-3010)
PHONE...................855 300-4774
Dana J Roberts, *CEO*
Karl Kreutziger, *President*
Matt Loorya, *Senior VP*
Aimee Siemianowsk, *Senior VP*
Daniel Maeng, *Project Engr*
EMP: 50 **EST:** 2011
SALES (est): 74MM **Privately Held**
WEB: www.driverspg.com
SIC: 7389 Drive-a-way automobile service

(P-18507)

DUN & BRDSTREET EMRGING BSNSSE (DH)
22761 Pacific Coast Hwy, Malibu
(90265-5098)
PHONE...................310 456-8271
Anthony Jabbour, *Director*
Bryan Hipsher, *Treasurer*
Joe Reinhardt, *Officer*
Susan D Beriont, *Vice Pres*
Chad Buechler, *Vice Pres*
EMP: 145 **EST:** 2010
SALES (est): 361.6MM
SALES (corp-wide): 1.7B **Publicly Held**
WEB: www.dandb.com
SIC: 7389 Financial services
HQ: Dun & Bradstreet, Inc
    101 John F Kennedy Pkwy # 5
    Short Hills NJ 07078
    973 921-5500

(P-18508)

E & C FASHION INC
Also Called: Pacific Concept Laundry
1420 Esperanza St, Los Angeles
(90023-3914)
PHONE...................323 262-0099
William Moo Han Bae, *CEO*
Maria Bae, *President*
Elizabeth Bae, *Vice Pres*
Claudia Kye, *Vice Pres*
▲ **EMP:** 300 **EST:** 1989
SALES (est): 10.2MM **Privately Held**
WEB: www.atomicdenim.com
SIC: 7389 Sewing contractor

(P-18509)

EAGLE MED PCKG STRLIZATION INC
Also Called: Eagle Med Packg Sterilization
2921 Union Rd Ste A, Paso Robles
(93446-7316)
P.O. Box 1228 (93447-1228)
PHONE...................805 238-7401
Doyle Timmons, *President*
Roy Morgan, *Vice Pres*
Jody Birks, *QC Dir*
EMP: 35 **EST:** 1992
SQ FT: 10,000
SALES (est): 4.2MM **Privately Held**
WEB: www.eaglemed.com
SIC: 7389 3841 Packaging & labeling services; surgical & medical instruments

(P-18510)

EAGLERIDER FINANCE LLC
11860 S La Cienega Blvd, Hawthorne
(90250-3461)
P.O. Box 2346 (90251-2346)
PHONE...................310 321-3191

Chris Macintyre,
Jeff Brown,
EMP: 87 **EST:** 2008
SALES (est): 946.1K **Privately Held**
WEB: www.eaglerider.com
SIC: 7389 Financial services
PA: J.C. Bromac Corporation
    11860 S La Cienega Blvd
    Hawthorne CA 90250

(P-18511)

EDCO HEALTH INFO SOLUTION
Also Called: ABI Document Support Services
17316 Edwards Rd Ste 280, Cerritos
(90703-2477)
PHONE...................909 793-0613
Matt Pokorski, *Branch Mgr*
EMP: 83
SALES (corp-wide): 38.6MM **Privately Held**
SIC: 7389 5044 Microfilm recording & developing services; office equipment
PA: Edco Health Information Solution Inc
    10411 Clayton Rd Ste 211
    Saint Louis MO 63131
    417 862-4351

(P-18512)

EMERALD HOLDING INC (PA)
31910 Del Obispo St # 200, San Juan
Capistrano (92675-3195)
PHONE...................949 226-5700
Herve Sedky, *President*
Konstantin Gilis, *Ch of Bd*
Brian Field, *COO*
David Doft, *CFO*
Eric Lisman, *Exec VP*
EMP: 117 **EST:** 2013
SALES (est): 234.4MM **Publicly Held**
WEB: www.emeraldx.com
SIC: 7389 Advertising, promotional & trade show services

(P-18513)

EMERALD X LLC (HQ)
Also Called: Emerald Expositions, LLC
31910 Del Obispo St # 20, San Juan Capistrano (92675-3182)
PHONE...................949 226-5700
Kosty Gilis, *CEO*
Erin Odonnell, *Vice Pres*
Jennifer Sutherland, *Finance*
Kara Kobrzycki, *Opers Dir*
Megan Hill, *Opers Staff*
▲ **EMP:** 116 **EST:** 1994
SQ FT: 6,500
SALES (est): 109.4MM
SALES (corp-wide): 234.4MM **Publicly Held**
WEB: www.emeraldx.com
SIC: 7389 Trade show arrangement
PA: Emerald Holding, Inc.
    31910 Del Obispo St # 200
    San Juan Capistrano CA 92675
    949 226-5700

(P-18514)

EONSTAR LEDLIGHT CORP
18835 San Jose Ave, City of Industry
(91748-1326)
PHONE...................626 693-8084
EMP: 131
SALES (corp-wide): 162.7K **Privately Held**
SIC: 7389 Personal service agents, brokers & bureaus
PA: Eonstar Ledlight Corp.
    204 N Vineyard Ave
    Ontario CA 91764
    805 601-5095

(P-18515)

EZCARETECH USA INC
21081 S Wstn Ave Ste 130, Torrance
(90501)
PHONE...................424 558-3191
Justin Chung, *CEO*
Justin Park, *Administration*
Kyungho Min, *Manager*
EMP: 350 **EST:** 2019
SALES (est): 5.8MM **Privately Held**
WEB: www.ezcaretech.com
SIC: 7389 Business services

(P-18516)

FACT FOUNDATION
303 N Glenoaks Blvd, Burbank
(91502-1116)
PHONE...................818 729-8105
Donna Shaw, *Principal*
Tim Detmen, *President*
EMP: 402 **EST:** 1990
SALES (est): 1.6MM
SALES (corp-wide): 158.2MM **Privately Held**
WEB: www.frontporch.net
SIC: 7389 Fund raising organizations
PA: Front Porch Communities And Services - Casa De Manana, Llc
    800 N Brand Blvd Fl 19
    Glendale CA 91203
    818 729-8100

(P-18517)

FACTER DIRECT LTD
4751 Wilshire Blvd # 140, Los Angeles
(90010-3827)
PHONE...................323 634-1999
Larry Keefer, *Controller*
EMP: 252
SALES (corp-wide): 9.4MM **Privately Held**
SIC: 7389 8742 Telemarketing services; marketing consulting services
PA: Facter Direct Ltd
    11500 W Olympic Blvd
    Los Angeles CA
    310 788-9000

(P-18518)

FEDERAL EXPRESS CORPORATION
Also Called: Fedex
7000 Barranca Pkwy, Irvine (92618-3112)
PHONE...................800 463-3339
EMP: 350
SALES (corp-wide): 47.4B **Publicly Held**
SIC: 7389 4731 4581 4513 Business Services Freight Trans Arrangmt Airport/Airport Services Air Courier Service Courier Service
HQ: Federal Express Corporation
    3610 Hacks Cross Rd
    Memphis TN 38125
    901 369-3600

(P-18519)

FOSSIL ENERGY RESEARCH CORP
Also Called: Ferco
23342 S Pointe Dr Ste C, Laguna Hills
(92653-1470)
PHONE...................949 859-4466
Richard Thompson, *President*
Larry Muzio, *Vice Pres*
Jun Canaveral, *Engineer*
EMP: 14 **EST:** 1984
SQ FT: 7,875
SALES (est): 2.5MM **Privately Held**
WEB: www.ferco.com
SIC: 7389 3829 Air pollution measuring service; measuring & controlling devices

(P-18520)

FRED BROWNS RECOVERY SVCS INC
Also Called: ABSTINATE LIVING CENTERS
270 W 14th St, San Pedro (90731-4396)
P.O. Box 2743 (90731-0182)
PHONE...................310 519-8723
Roxanna Natale-Brown, *Exec Dir*
Roxanna Lynn Natale-Brown, *Exec Dir*
Fred Brown, *Director*
Mark Malone, *Director*
EMP: 55 **EST:** 1991
SALES (est): 4.5MM **Privately Held**
WEB: www.fredbrown.org
SIC: 7389 8069 8322 8361 Explosives recovery or extraction services; substance abuse hospitals; individual & family services; residential care

(P-18521)

FREEMAN EXPOSITIONS LLC
2170 S Towne Centre Pl, Anaheim
(92806-6127)
PHONE...................714 254-3400
Pattie Balding, *Manager*
Tom Intagliata, *General Mgr*

P
R
O
D
U
C
T
S

&

S
V
C
S

John Kennedy, *General Mgr*
James Ligoretti, *IT/INT Sup*
David Spain, *Business Mgr*
EMP: 200
SALES (corp-wide): 1.5B **Privately Held**
WEB: www.freeman.com
SIC: 7389 Trade show arrangement
HQ: Freeman Expositions, Llc
   1600 Viceroy Dr Ste 100
   Dallas TX 75235
   214 445-1000

(P-18522)
FRESH GRILL LLC
111 E Garry Ave, Santa Ana (92707-4201)
PHONE..............................714 444-2126
Jeff Heavirland, *Mng Member*
Iris Rodriguez, *Purch Mgr*
Phil Abreo, *Sales Staff*
▲ **EMP:** 200 **EST:** 1996
SQ FT: 27,000
SALES (est): 47.4MM **Privately Held**
WEB: www.freshgrillfoods.com
SIC: 7389 Packaging & labeling services
PA: Fb Holding Company, Llc
   111 E Garry Ave
   Santa Ana CA 92707
   714 444-2126

(P-18523)
FUSE LLC (DH)
Also Called: Fuse Media
700 N Central Ave Ste 600, Glendale
(91203-3438)
PHONE..............................323 256-8900
Miguel Roggero,
George Greenberg, *Senior VP*
Adrienne Cooksey, *Director*
Kyle Whited, *Director*
EMP: 215 **EST:** 2003
SALES (est): 36.2MM
SALES (corp-wide): 41.7MM **Privately
Held**
WEB: www.fuse.tv
SIC: 7389 4833 Music & broadcasting
   services; television broadcasting stations

(P-18524)
GBS FINANCIAL CORP
Also Called: Wagner Financials
904 Manhattan Ave Ste 3, Manhattan
Beach (90266-5538)
PHONE..............................310 937-0073
EMP: 60
SALES (est): 1.9MM **Privately Held**
SIC: 7389 Business Services

(P-18525)
**GELFAND RENNERT &
FELDMAN LLP (PA)**
1880 Century Park E # 1600, Los Angeles
(90067-1661)
PHONE..............................310 553-1707
Marshall M Gelfand, *Managing Prtnr*
Tyson Beem, *Partner*
Todd Gelfand, *Partner*
Andrew Harwood, *CFO*
Christopher Fazzolari, *Managing Dir*
EMP: 200 **EST:** 1967
SALES (est): 67.8K **Privately Held**
WEB: www.grfllp.com
SIC: 7389 8721 8741 Legal & tax serv-
   ices; accounting, auditing & bookkeeping;
   business management

(P-18526)
GENTLE GIANT STUDIOS INC
7511 N San Fernando Rd, Burbank
(91505-1044)
PHONE..............................818 504-3555
Karl Z Meyer, *President*
Jewell Morson, *Administration*
Kevin Monge, *Production*
Aaron White, *Manager*
Stephen Casa, *Editor*
▲ **EMP:** 56 **EST:** 1996
SQ FT: 20,000
SALES (est): 11.6MM **Publicly Held**
WEB: www.gentlegiantstudios.com
SIC: 7389 Design services
HQ: 3d Systems, Inc.
   333 Three D Systems Cir
   Rock Hill SC 29730
   803 326-3900

(P-18527)
GLARE TECHNOLOGY USA INC
30898 Wealth St, Murrieta (92563-2534)
PHONE..............................909 437-6999
Laith Salih, *CEO*
EMP: 120 **EST:** 2015
SALES (est): 5.9MM **Privately Held**
SIC: 7389

(P-18528)
**GLOBAL DEBT MANAGEMENT
LLC (PA)**
18881 Von Karman Ave # 1500, Irvine
(92612-1582)
PHONE..............................949 825-7800
Banir Ganatra, *Mng Member*
Robert Guy,
Bill Davis, *Accounts Exec*
EMP: 59 **EST:** 2008
SQ FT: 3,400
SALES (est): 1.6MM **Privately Held**
SIC: 7389 Financial services

(P-18529)
**GLOBAL EXPRNCE
SPECIALISTS INC**
Also Called: Ges
18504 Beach Blvd Unit 511, Huntington
Beach (92648-0915)
PHONE..............................619 498-6300
Tom Robins, *Manager*
EMP: 166 **Publicly Held**
WEB: www.ges.com
SIC: 7389 Convention & show services
HQ: Global Experience Specialists, Inc.
   7000 Lindell Rd
   Las Vegas NV 89118
   702 515-5500

(P-18530)
**GLOBAL LANGUAGE
SOLUTIONS LLC**
19800 Macarthur Blvd # 750, Irvine
(92612-2402)
PHONE..............................949 798-1400
Olga Smirnova, *CEO*
Inna Kassatkina, *President*
Consol Casablanca, *Surgery Dir*
Thanh V Dong, *Project Mgr*
Mana Mishina, *Project Mgr*
EMP: 100 **EST:** 1994
SQ FT: 7,500
SALES (est): 12.2MM **Privately Held**
WEB: www.welocalize.com
SIC: 7389 Translation services
PA: Welocalize, Inc.
   15 W 37th St Fl 4
   New York NY 10018

(P-18531)
GOOD TRADING CO
4085 Flat Rock Dr, Riverside (92505-5859)
PHONE..............................951 688-2495
Ellen Lee, *Branch Mgr*
▲ **EMP:** 50
SALES (corp-wide): 134.8K **Privately
Held**
WEB: www.goodtradingco.com
SIC: 7389 Personal service agents, bro-
   kers & bureaus
PA: Good Trading Co
   6881 Stanton Ave Ste K
   Buena Park CA
   714 879-5801

(P-18532)
**GOODWILL SRVING THE PPLE
STHER (PA)**
Also Called: Links Sign Lngage Intrprting S
800 W Pacific Coast Hwy, Long Beach
(90806-5243)
PHONE..............................562 435-3411
Janet McCarthy, *CEO*
Julie Beck, *Admin Asst*
Rob Boyajian, *Director*
EMP: 100 **EST:** 1939
SQ FT: 80,000
SALES (est): 24.4MM **Privately Held**
WEB: www.linksinterpreting.com
SIC: 7389 8331 5932 Translation serv-
   ices; job training & vocational rehabilita-
   tion services; vocational training agency;
   used merchandise stores

(P-18533)
**GRANDALL DISTRIBUTING CO
INC**
321 El Bonito Ave, Glendale (91204-2707)
PHONE..............................818 242-6640
Jose M Granda, *President*
Jessica J Granda, *Treasurer*
Jessica Granda, *Treasurer*
Melisa J Granda, *Vice Pres*
Joseph J Granda, *Admin Sec*
EMP: 30 **EST:** 1966
SQ FT: 18,000
SALES (est): 3.6MM **Privately Held**
WEB: www.grandall.com
SIC: 7389 2844 Cosmetic kits, assembling
   & packaging; cosmetic preparations

(P-18534)
**GREAT WESTERN GRINDING
INC**
15292 Bolsa Chica St, Huntington Beach
(92649-1243)
PHONE..............................714 890-6592
Michael Del Medico, *President*
Revona Del Medico, *Vice Pres*
EMP: 15 **EST:** 1984
SQ FT: 8,000
SALES (est): 1.5MM **Privately Held**
WEB: www.greatwesterngrinding.com
SIC: 7389 3812 3769 Grinding, precision:
   commercial or industrial; search & naviga-
   tion equipment; guided missile & space
   vehicle parts & auxiliary equipment

(P-18535)
GSA DESIGN INC
4551 San Fernando Rd # 102, Glendale
(91204-3227)
PHONE..............................818 241-2558
Grigor Grigoryan, *President*
Narine Khachatryan, *CFO*
EMP: 28 **EST:** 1998
SQ FT: 20,000
SALES (est): 1.1MM **Privately Held**
WEB: www.gsa2000.com
SIC: 7389 2386 Sewing contractor; gar-
   ments, leather

(P-18536)
H&S ENERGY LLC (HQ)
2860 N Santiago Blvd, Orange
(92867-1722)
PHONE..............................714 761-5426
Salaheddin Hassan, *Mng Member*
EMP: 307 **EST:** 2015
SALES (est): 150.7MM
SALES (corp-wide): 321.1MM **Privately
Held**
WEB: www.hnsenergyproducts.com
SIC: 5541 5411 7389 Filling stations,
   gasoline; convenience stores; business
   services
PA: Hassan & Sons, Inc.
   17108 Dogwood Way
   Cobb CA 95426
   714 761-5426

(P-18537)
HARINGA INC (PA)
Also Called: Premier Packaging/Assembly
14422 Best Ave, Santa Fe Springs
(90670-5133)
P.O. Box 4707, Cerritos (90703-4707)
PHONE..............................800 499-9991
Victoria Haringa, *CEO*
Vicki Haringa, *President*
Randy Haringa, *General Mgr*
Candice Olson, *Opers Mgr*
Vincent Olson, *QC Mgr*
▲ **EMP:** 77 **EST:** 1991
SQ FT: 200,000
SALES (est): 14.5MM **Privately Held**
SIC: 7389 Packaging & labeling services

(P-18538)
**HARRIS WATER CONDITIONING
INC**
Also Called: Culligan
1025 S Rose Ave, Oxnard (93030-5180)
P.O. Box 3217, Ventura (93006-3217)
PHONE..............................805 656-4411
Robert Stevens, *President*
Dennis Harris, *Ch of Bd*
Phyllis Harris, *CFO*
Robin Harris, *Corp Secy*

EMP: 52 **EST:** 1962
SQ FT: 20,000
SALES (est): 7.6MM **Privately Held**
WEB: www.culliganventura.com
SIC: 5999 7389 5499 Water purification
   equipment; water softener service; water:
   distilled mineral or spring

(P-18539)
HCT PACKAGING INC (FA)
2800 28th St Ste 240, Santa Monica
(90405-6214)
PHONE..............................310 260-7680
Tim Thorpe, *President*
Tara Corcoran, *Controller*
Christina Blanchard, *Director*
◆ **EMP:** 125 **EST:** 1996
SQ FT: 1,500
SALES (est): 23.3MM **Privately Held**
WEB: www.hctgroup.com
SIC: 7389 Packaging & labeling services

(P-18540)
**HEARTLAND PAYMENT
SYSTEMS INC**
510 Cerritos Way, Cathedral City
(92234-1617)
PHONE..............................760 324-0133
EMP: 97
SALES (corp-wide): 2B **Publicly Held**
SIC: 7389 Business Services
PA: Heartland Payment Systems, Inc.
   90 Nassau St
   Princeton NJ 30328
   609 683-3831

(P-18541)
HERITAGE AUCTIONS INC
9478 W Olympic Blvd, Beverly Hills
(90212-4246)
PHONE..............................310 300-8390
Greg Rohan, *President*
Noah Fleisher, *Vice Pres*
Bruce Scott, *Vice Pres*
Jennifer Marsh, *Hum Res Coord*
John Hickey, *Sales Mgr*
EMP: 100 **EST:** 2010
SALES (est): 2.5MM **Privately Held**
WEB: www.ha.com
SIC: 7389 Auctioneers, fee basis

(P-18542)
HG INSIGHTS INC
1 N Calle Cesar Chavez # 1, Santa Barbara
(93103-3662)
PHONE..............................805 880-1100
Elizabeth Cholawsky, *CEO*
Craig Harris, *Ch of Bd*
Tim Baskerville, *President*
Dave Ruehlman, *COO*
John Connell, *Exec VP*
EMP: 83 **EST:** 2010
SALES (est): 12.7MM **Privately Held**
WEB: www.hginsights.com
SIC: 7389 Subscription fulfillment services:
   magazine, newspaper, etc.

(P-18543)
**HIRSCH BEDNER ASSOCIATES
(PA)**
Also Called: H B A
3216 Nebraska Ave, Santa Monica
(90404-4214)
PHONE..............................310 829-9087
Howard Pharr, *Principal*
Jacques Coetzee, *Partner*
Eugene Bedner, *Officer*
Michael Bedner, *Executive*
Paul Fialkowski, *Business Dir*
EMP: 138 **EST:** 2012
SALES (est): 12.8MM **Privately Held**
WEB: www.hba.com
SIC: 7389 Interior designer

(P-18544)
HIRSCH/BEDNER INTL INC (PA)
Also Called: Hba International
3216 Nebraska Ave, Santa Monica
(90404-4214)
PHONE..............................310 829-9087
Rene G Kaerskov, *CEO*
Caren Disney,
Sayeli Ayaydin, *Managing Prtnr*
Michael J Bedner, *Ch of Bd*
Howard Pharr, *President*
EMP: 70 **EST:** 1964

SQ FT: 14,000
SALES (est): 21MM **Privately Held**
WEB: www.hba.com
SIC: 7389 Interior designer; interior design services

(P-18545)
HOLLYWOOD SPORTS PARK LLC
Also Called: Giant Sportz Paintball Park
9030 Somerset Blvd, Bellflower (90706-3402)
PHONE.................................562 867-9600
Dennis Bukowski, *Mng Member*
Judy Bukowski,
Giovanni D'Egido,
▲ EMP: 100 EST: 1999
SQ FT: 20,000
SALES (est): 7.2MM **Privately Held**
WEB: www.hollywoodsports.com
SIC: 7389 Personal service agents, brokers & bureaus

(P-18546)
IMG (PA)
Also Called: Demo Deluxe
4560 Dorinda Rd, Yorba Linda (92887-1800)
PHONE.................................714 974-1700
Jim Smith, *Partner*
Michael Allwein, *Partner*
Jerry Smith, *Partner*
Mark Ervin, *Vice Pres*
Rachel Sugita, *Project Mgr*
▲ EMP: 50 EST: 1983
SQ FT: 3,600
SALES (est): 35.2MM **Privately Held**
WEB: www.imgprestige.com
SIC: 7389 Demonstration service

(P-18547)
IMPERIAL HOTEL GROUP LLC
2532 Dupont Dr, Irvine (92612-1524)
PHONE.................................949 474-7368
Eric Bonnett,
EMP: 50 EST: 2014
SALES (est): 1.4MM **Privately Held**
SIC: 7389 Business services

(P-18548)
INDUSTRIAL STITCHTECH INC
520 Library St, San Fernando (91340-2524)
PHONE.................................818 361-6319
Ed Perez, *President*
Amber Quinn, *Vice Pres*
Adriana Pena, *Manager*
EMP: 150 EST: 1996
SQ FT: 35,000
SALES (est): 9MM **Privately Held**
WEB: www.industrialstitchtech.com
SIC: 7389 Sewing contractor

(P-18549)
INSPECTORATE AMERICA CORP
3401 Jack Northrop Ave, Hawthorne (90250-4428)
PHONE.................................800 424-0099
Jamie Murnahan, *Clerk*
EMP: 148
SALES (corp-wide): 156.7MM **Privately Held**
WEB: www.commodities.bureauveritas.com
SIC: 7389 Petroleum refinery inspection service
PA: Bureau Veritas Commodities And Trade, Inc.
1300 Hercules Ave
Houston TX 77058
713 944-2000

(P-18550)
INTEGRATED VOTING SYSTEMS INC
496 S Uruapan Way, Dinuba (93618-2719)
PHONE.................................559 498-0281
Rebecca Kozlowski, *President*
Joey Rocha, *Info Tech Mgr*
EMP: 45 EST: 2015

SALES (est): 4.7MM **Privately Held**
WEB: www.integravote.com
SIC: 7389 7331 8742 2741 Presorted mail service; direct mail advertising services; marketing consulting services; business service newsletters; publishing & printing; offset & photolithographic printing

(P-18551)
INTERIOR LOGIC GROUP INC (HQ)
10 Bunsen, Irvine (92618-4210)
PHONE.................................800 959-8333
Mark Fikse, *CEO*
Lee Robinson, *CFO*
Richard Strulson, *Exec VP*
Jeff Trapp, *Exec VP*
Randy Brown, *Vice Pres*
EMP: 623 EST: 2013
SALES (est): 269.1MM
SALES (corp-wide): 448.8MM **Privately Held**
WEB: www.interiorlogicgroup.com
SIC: 7389 Interior designer
PA: Interior Logic Group Holdings, Llc
10 Bunsen
Irvine CA 92618
800 959-8333

(P-18552)
INTERPRETING SERVICES INTL LLC
700 N Brand Blvd Ste 950, Glendale (91203-1207)
PHONE.................................818 753-9181
ISI Solutions, *Administration*
EMP: 60 EST: 1982
SALES (est): 2.2MM **Privately Held**
SIC: 7389 Translation services

(P-18553)
INVESTLINC GROUP LLC (PA)
Also Called: Investlinc Group, The
1230 Rosecrans Ave # 600, Manhattan Beach (90266-2477)
PHONE.................................310 997-0580
Troy D Wiseman,
Leroy H Paris II,
Tim Morgan, *Director*
EMP: 85
SALES (est): 2.9MM **Privately Held**
WEB: www.trilincglobal.com
SIC: 7389 Financial services

(P-18554)
IPAYMENT INC
3325 Wilshire Blvd # 535, Los Angeles (90010-1703)
PHONE.................................213 387-1353
Guillermo Ramirez, *Branch Mgr*
EMP: 76
SALES (corp-wide): 1.4MM **Privately Held**
WEB: www.paysafe.com
SIC: 7389 Credit card service
HQ: Ipayment, Inc.
30721 Russell Ranch Rd # 200
Westlake Village CA 91362
212 802-7200

(P-18555)
IPAYMENT INC (DH)
30721 Russell Ranch Rd # 200, Westlake Village (91362-7383)
PHONE.................................212 802-7200
Mark C Monaco, *CFO*
Philip J Ragona, *Exec VP*
Philip Ragona, *Exec VP*
Robert N Purcell,
Mike Breidert, *Software Dev*
EMP: 215 EST: 2001
SQ FT: 3,800
SALES (est): 53.2MM
SALES (corp-wide): 1.4MM **Privately Held**
WEB: www.paysafe.com
SIC: 7389 Credit card service

(P-18556)
IPAYMENT HOLDINGS INC (HQ)
30721 Russell Ranch Rd # 200, Westlake Village (91362-7383)
PHONE.................................310 436-5294
Ob Rawls IV, *President*
Greg Cohen, *COO*

Robert Purcell, *CFO*
Philip Ragona, *Exec VP*
Guy Dimaggio, *Senior VP*
EMP: 50 EST: 2001
SALES (est): 62.1MM
SALES (corp-wide): 1.4MM **Privately Held**
WEB: www.paysafe.com
SIC: 7389 Personal service agents, brokers & bureaus

(P-18557)
ISOVAC ENGINEERING INC
614 Justin Ave, Glendale (91201-2327)
PHONE.................................818 552-6200
George R Neff, *President*
EMP: 25 EST: 1957
SALES (est): 2.8MM **Privately Held**
WEB: www.isovac.com
SIC: 7389 3825 3829 3826 Inspection & testing services; semiconductor test equipment; measuring & controlling devices; analytical instruments

(P-18558)
JENCO PRODUCTIONS INC (PA)
401 S J St, San Bernardino (92410-2605)
PHONE.................................909 381-9453
Jennifer Imbriani, *President*
John Imbriani, *Vice Pres*
Nelson Escobar, *Executive*
Hector Ramos, *Purchasing*
Teresa Fiero, *Production*
◆ EMP: 160 EST: 1995
SQ FT: 50,000
SALES (est): 40.4MM **Privately Held**
WEB: www.jencoproductions.com
SIC: 7389 2789 2653 7331 Packaging & labeling services; bookbinding & related work; boxes, corrugated: made from purchased materials; mailing service; letter folding, stuffing & sealing machines

(P-18559)
JF FIXTURES & DESIGN LLC
Also Called: Manufacturing/Distributrion
546 W Esther St, Long Beach (90813-1529)
PHONE.................................562 437-7466
Jaideep Ahluwalia, *Mng Member*
EMP: 15 EST: 2019
SALES (est): 1MM **Privately Held**
SIC: 7389 2542 2541 Design services; office & store showcases & display fixtures; store & office display cases & fixtures; display fixtures, wood; showcases, except refrigerated: wood

(P-18560)
JOHN CHAPMAN INC
21648 Nutmeg Ln, Santa Clarita (91350-1622)
PHONE.................................661 212-5053
John Chapman, *Branch Mgr*
EMP: 50 **Privately Held**
SIC: 7389
PA: John Chapman, Inc.
9210 San Fernando Rd
Sun Valley CA

(P-18561)
JOMAR INDUSTRIES INC
1500 W 139th St, Gardena (90249-2604)
PHONE.................................323 770-0505
John H Stern, *President*
Margaret H Stern, *Corp Secy*
Jeff Stern, *Vice Pres*
▲ EMP: 22 EST: 1959
SQ FT: 25,000
SALES (est): 1.2MM **Privately Held**
WEB: www.jomarpackaging.com
SIC: 7389 3089 Packaging & labeling services; coloring & finishing of plastic products

(P-18562)
KENNETH BRDWICK INTR DSGNS INC
Also Called: Beverly Hills Luxury Interiors
1615 Westwood Blvd # 202, Los Angeles (90024-5653)
PHONE.................................310 274-9999
Kenneth Bordewick, *CEO*
Robert Morrison, *Manager*
EMP: 73 EST: 2004

SALES (est): 2.7MM **Privately Held**
WEB: www.beverlyhillsluxuryinteriors.com
SIC: 7389 Interior designer

(P-18563)
KIM CHONG
Also Called: Union 76
2105 E 25th St, Los Angeles (90058-1125)
PHONE.................................323 581-4700
Chong Kim, *Owner*
EMP: 25 EST: 1987
SQ FT: 10,300
SALES (est): 1.6MM **Privately Held**
SIC: 7389 2395 Embroidering of advertising on shirts, etc.; embroidery products, except schiffli machine

(P-18564)
KIMOA BROADCAST TV NETWRK
12222 Grfield Ave Apt 222, South Gate (90280)
PHONE.................................213 364-9558
Melvin Rixey, *CEO*
EMP: 16
SALES (corp-wide): 62.7K **Privately Held**
WEB: www.kimoabroadcasttvnetwork.net
SIC: 7389 2741 Music & broadcasting services;
PA: Kimoa Broadcast Television Network, Corp
594 Howard Ave
Brooklyn NY 11212
800 754-3309

(P-18565)
KIRSCHENMAN ENTERPRISES SLS LP
12826 Edison Hwy, Edison (93220)
P.O. Box 27 (93220-0027)
PHONE.................................661 366-5736
Wayde Kirschenman, *General Ptnr*
EMP: 120 EST: 2009
SQ FT: 5,000
SALES (est): 100MM **Privately Held**
WEB: www.kirschenman.com
SIC: 7389 Brokers, business: buying & selling business enterprises

(P-18566)
KNG BRNDS INC DBA PSTOLA DBA D
2211 E 27th St, Vernon (90058-1132)
PHONE.................................323 588-6903
Kevin NA, *CEO*
EMP: 50 EST: 2017
SALES (est): 1.6MM **Privately Held**
SIC: 7389 Design services

(P-18567)
KOOS MANUFACTURING INC
Also Called: Big Star
2741 Seminole Ave, South Gate (90280-5550)
PHONE.................................323 249-1000
U Yul Ku, *President*
Kee H Fong, *Vice Pres*
John Hur, *Vice Pres*
Nan J Ku, *Admin Sec*
David Gumpel, *Business Anlyst*
▲ EMP: 800 EST: 1985
SQ FT: 180,000
SALES (est): 39.6MM **Privately Held**
WEB: www.koos.com
SIC: 7389 Sewing contractor

(P-18568)
KUKDONG APPAREL AMERICA INC
17100 Pioneer Blvd # 230, Artesia (90701-2776)
PHONE.................................562 403-0044
Sang Ki Pyon, *CEO*
Caz Eyun, *CFO*
Claudia Bogran, *Purchasing*
Rebecca Kim, *Manager*
▲ EMP: 20 EST: 1999
SQ FT: 5,000
SALES (est): 75MM **Privately Held**
WEB: www.kd.co.kr
SIC: 7389 2386 Apparel designers, commercial; garments, leather

PRODUCTS & SVCS

PA: Kukdong Corporation
405 Cheonho-Daero, Dongdaemun-Gu
Seoul 02633

(P-18569)
LA JOLLA GROUP INC (PA)
Also Called: Ljg
14350 Myford Rd, Irvine (92606-1002)
PHONE..................................949 428-2800
Daniel Neukomm, *CEO*
Cindy Picado, *Store Mgr*
Michelle Riell, *Admin Sec*
Debbie Dufour, *Technical Staff*
Regina Diaz, *Accounting Mgr*
▲ **EMP:** 235 **EST:** 2007
SALES (est): 27.2MM **Privately Held**
WEB: www.lajollagroup.com
SIC: 7389 6794 2326 Apparel designers,
commercial; copyright buying & licensing;
men's & boys' work clothing

(P-18570)
LAG AND ASSOCIATES LLC
1514 E Adams Park Dr, Covina
(91724-3101)
PHONE..................................909 242-4394
Roland Irvin, *Mng Member*
EMP: 62 **EST:** 2019
SALES (est): 854.2K **Privately Held**
SIC: 7389 Financial services

(P-18571)
LAKEWOOD PARK HEALTH CTR INC (PA)
12023 Lakewood Blvd, Downey
(90242-2699)
PHONE..................................562 869-0978
Daniel Zilafro, *President*
Emilio Florita, *Human Resources*
EMP: 285 **EST:** 1985
SALES (est): 5.9MM **Privately Held**
WEB: www.lwhealthcare.com
SIC: 7389 Personal service agents, brokers & bureaus

(P-18572)
LARK INDUSTRIES INC (DH)
Also Called: Residential Design Service
10 Bunsen, Irvine (92618-4210)
PHONE..................................714 701-4200
Kendall Hoyd, *President*
Kip Cruze, *Exec VP*
V Eitler, *Exec VP*
Tim Comstock, *Vice Pres*
Helen Rettberg, *Vice Pres*
EMP: 218 **EST:** 1988
SALES (est): 126.2MM
SALES (corp-wide): 448.8MM **Privately Held**
WEB: www.interiorlogicgroup.com
SIC: 7389 3281 Interior design services;
cut stone & stone products
HQ: Interior Logic Group, Inc.
10 Bunsen
Irvine CA 92618
800 959-8333

(P-18573)
LAUREE LLC
25901 Commercentre Dr, Lake Forest
(92630-8805)
PHONE..................................949 446-9900
EMP: 62
SALES (est): 57.9K **Privately Held**
WEB: www.laureelabs.com
SIC: 7389 Business Services, Nec, Nsk

(P-18574)
LE VAL OF CALIFORNIA INC
3305 Pasadena Ave, Los Angeles
(90031-1995)
PHONE..................................323 221-9116
EMP: 45
SQ FT: 18,000
SALES (est): 900K **Privately Held**
SIC: 7389 2339 Business Services Mfg
Women's/Misses' Outerwear

(P-18575)
LEGAL SUPPORT NETWORK LLC
Also Called: Express Network
1533 Wilshire Blvd, Los Angeles
(90017-2205)
PHONE..................................213 975-9850
Gary Camara, *Owner*
Michael Barretto, *Opers Staff*
Lyn Bartlett, *Sales Staff*
Roxana Zavala, *Sales Staff*
Gibby Carrillo, *Manager*
EMP: 53 **EST:** 2012
SALES (est): 3.6MM **Privately Held**
WEB: www.expressnetworkas.com
SIC: 7389 Courier or messenger service

(P-18576)
LENNAR PARTNERS OF LOS ANGELES (PA)
4350 Von Karman Ave # 200, Newport
Beach (92660-2041)
PHONE..................................949 885-8500
David Team, *Division Pres*
EMP: 79 **EST:** 1996
SALES (est): 10.1MM **Privately Held**
SIC: 7389 Personal service agents, brokers & bureaus

(P-18577)
LFP ECOMMERCE LLC
210 N Sunset Ave, West Covina
(91790-2257)
PHONE..................................314 428-5069
EMP: 52
SALES (corp-wide): 2.5MM **Privately Held**
SIC: 7389 Personal service agents, brokers & bureaus
PA: Lfp Ecommerce, Llc
8484 Wilshire Blvd # 900
Beverly Hills CA 90211
323 651-5400

(P-18578)
LINDSEY & SONS ✪
Also Called: Flo-CHI
1226 E 76th St, Los Angeles (90001-2416)
PHONE..................................657 306-5369
Andre Lindsey Sr, *President*
EMP: 100 **EST:** 2021
SALES (est): 1.1MM **Privately Held**
SIC: 7389

(P-18579)
LITIGTION RSRCES OF AMERICA-CA (PA)
Also Called: Legal Enterprise
4232-1 Las Virgenes Rd, Calabasas
(91302-3589)
PHONE..................................818 878-9227
Tony Maddocks, *President*
Rick Matsumoto, *Manager*
EMP: 75 **EST:** 1993
SALES (est): 4MM **Privately Held**
SIC: 7389 8111 Document storage service; general practice attorney, lawyer

(P-18580)
LIVE NATION ENTERTAINMENT INC (PA)
9348 Civic Center Dr Lbby, Beverly Hills
(90210-3642)
PHONE..................................310 867-7000
Michael Rapino, *President*
Greg Maffei, *Ch of Bd*
Joe Berchtold, *President*
Arthur Fogel, *President*
John Reid, *President*
▲ **EMP:** 200 **EST:** 2005
SALES (est): 1.8B **Publicly Held**
WEB: www.livenationentertainment.com
SIC: 7389 7922 7941 Promoters of shows
& exhibitions; entertainment promotion;
theatrical production services; theatrical
companies; legitimate live theater producers; sports clubs, managers & promoters

(P-18581)
LMS CORPORATION
300 Crprate Pinte Ste 301, Culver City
(90230)
PHONE..................................310 641-4222
EMP: 50
SQ FT: 2,712

SALES (est): 1.6MM **Privately Held**
WEB: www.thelmscorp.com
SIC: 7389 8742 Business Services Management Consulting Services

(P-18582)
LOS ANGLES TRISM CONVENTION BD (PA)
633 W 5th St Ste 1800, Los Angeles
(90071-2087)
PHONE..................................213 624-7300
Adam Burke, *President*
Alan I Rothenberg, *Ch of Bd*
Stefan J Dietrich, *CFO*
Jamie Foley, *Vice Pres*
Darren K Green, *Vice Pres*
EMP: 50 **EST:** 1971
SALES (est): 27.9MM **Privately Held**
WEB: www.discoverlosangeles.com
SIC: 7389 Convention & show services;
tourist information bureau

(P-18583)
LPS AGENCY SALES & POSTING INC (PA)
3210 El Cmino Real Ste 20, Irvine (92602)
PHONE..................................714 247-7503
Michelle Barney, *Senior VP*
EMP: 70 **EST:** 1983
SALES (est): 562.9K **Privately Held**
SIC: 7389 Personal service agents, brokers & bureaus

(P-18584)
MACRO-PRO INC (PA)
Also Called: Micro-Pro Microfilming Svcs
2400 Grand Ave, Long Beach
(90815-1762)
P.O. Box 90459 (90809-0459)
PHONE..................................562 595-0900
Patty Waldeck, *President*
Diann Cohen, *Vice Pres*
Monique Villano, *Info Tech Mgr*
Zuly Arguello, *Clerk*
Jennifer Blair, *Clerk*
EMP: 140
SQ FT: 24,000
SALES (est): 12.1MM **Privately Held**
WEB: www.macropro.com
SIC: 7389 7334 Legal & tax services; microfilm recording & developing service;
photocopying & duplicating services

(P-18585)
MAHAVAIPULYA BUDDHIST ASSN
8781 Knott Ave, Buena Park (90620-3854)
PHONE..................................714 220-0028
Howard Yaag, *President*
▲ **EMP:** 50 **EST:** 1993
SALES (est): 49.3K **Privately Held**
SIC: 8661 7389 Buddhist Temple; lecture
bureau

(P-18586)
MARINE TECHNICAL SERVICES INC
Also Called: Dockside Machine & Ship Repair
211 N Marine Ave, Wilmington
(90744-5724)
P.O. Box 1301, San Pedro (90733-1301)
PHONE..................................310 549-8030
Dianne Marie Hawke, *President*
▼ **EMP:** 75 **EST:** 1989
SQ FT: 20,000
SALES (est): 7.2MM **Privately Held**
WEB: www.marinetechserv.com
SIC: 7389 7699 Crane & aerial lift service;
nautical repair services

(P-18587)
MARSH CONSULTING GROUP
2626 Summer Ranch Rd, Paso Robles
(93446-8473)
PHONE..................................239 433-5500
Brad Heinrichs, *President*
Anne Dansereau, *Analyst*
Jill Marsh, *Opers Staff*
Robin Schwartz, *Corp Comm Staff*
Geoffrey Marsh, *Consultant*
EMP: 70 **EST:** 2005
SALES (est): 4.2MM
SALES (corp-wide): 6MM **Privately Held**
WEB: www.foster-foster.com
SIC: 7389 Financial services

PA: Foster & Foster Consulting Actuaries, Inc.
13420 Parker Commons Blvd
Fort Myers FL 33912
239 433-5500

(P-18588)
MARTYS CUTTING INC
Also Called: Marty's Cutting Service
2615 Fruitland Ave, Vernon (90058-2219)
PHONE..................................323 582-5758
Fax: 323 582-5272
EMP: 80
SQ FT: 57,000
SALES (est): 3.8MM **Privately Held**
WEB: www.marty-howard.com
SIC: 7389 Cutting And Fusing Service

(P-18589)
MB COATINGS INC
571 N Poplar St Ste G, Orange
(92868-1023)
PHONE..................................714 625-2118
Michael Bartle, *President*
Amanda Bartle, *Vice Pres*
Monica Sanchez, *Office Mgr*
Brandon Boehm, *Project Mgr*
Guy Bruno, *Project Mgr*
EMP: 80 **EST:** 1996
SQ FT: 2,000
SALES (est): 5.9MM **Privately Held**
WEB: www.mbcoatings.com
SIC: 7389 Hand painting, textile

(P-18590)
MEDUSIND SOLUTIONS INC (PA)
31103 Rancho Viejo Rd, San Juan Capistrano (92675-1759)
PHONE..................................949 240-8895
Rajiv Sahney, *Chairman*
Robert Beck, *President*
Vipul Bansal, *CEO*
Dhiren Kapadia, *CFO*
Kranti Munje, *Senior VP*
EMP: 749 **EST:** 2002
SALES (est): 18.6MM **Privately Held**
WEB: www.medusind.com
SIC: 7389 Personal service agents, brokers & bureaus

(P-18591)
MEGA APPRAISERS INC
14724 Ventura Blvd # 800, Sherman Oaks
(91403-3501)
PHONE..................................818 246-7370
Levon Hairapetian, *President*
EMP: 600 **EST:** 2003
SALES (est): 1.2MM **Privately Held**
WEB: www.megaappraisers.com
SIC: 7389 Appraisers, except real estate

(P-18592)
MERCHANT OF TENNIS INC
1118 S La Cienega Blvd, Los Angeles
(90035-2519)
PHONE..................................310 855-1946
Jay Banks, *Branch Mgr*
EMP: 663
SALES (corp-wide): 158.4MM **Privately Held**
WEB: www.usmerchants.com
SIC: 7389 Packaging & labeling services
HQ: The Merchant Of Tennis Inc
8737 Wilshire Blvd
Beverly Hills CA 90211
310 228-4000

(P-18593)
MERCHANT OF TENNIS INC
1625 Proforma Ave, Ontario (91761-7607)
PHONE..................................909 923-3388
Larry Khemlani, *Principal*
EMP: 663
SALES (corp-wide): 158.4MM **Privately Held**
WEB: www.usmerchants.com
SIC: 7389 Packaging & labeling services
HQ: The Merchant Of Tennis Inc
8737 Wilshire Blvd
Beverly Hills CA 90211
310 228-4000

(P-18594)
MERIBEAR PRODUCTIONS INC
Also Called: Meredith Baer & Associates
4100 Ardmore Ave, South Gate
(90280-3246)
PHONE.................................310 204-5353
Meridith Baer, *President*
Richard Yoon, *CFO*
Renee Becnel, *Vice Pres*
Anna Viola, *Office Mgr*
Kelsey Carleton, *Project Mgr*
▲ EMP: 90 EST: 1980
SQ FT: 55,000
SALES (est): 14.9MM **Privately Held**
WEB: www.meridithbaer.com
SIC: 7389 Interior design services; interior decorating

(P-18595)
MERICAL LLC (PA)
2995 E Miraloma Ave, Anaheim
(92806-1805)
PHONE.................................714 238-7225
Mark Walsh, *CEO*
Jeffrey Stallings, *President*
Richard Gates, *COO*
Marc Goedemans, *CFO*
Tom Bovich, *Exec VP*
EMP: 237 EST: 1960
SQ FT: 92,000
SALES (est): 177MM **Privately Held**
WEB: www.merical.com
SIC: 7389 Packaging & labeling services

(P-18596)
MERRILL LYNCH PRCE FNNER SMITH
1096 Coast Village Rd, Santa Barbara
(93108-0723)
PHONE.................................805 695-7028
EMP: 113
SALES (corp-wide): 93.7B **Publicly Held**
WEB: www.ml.com
SIC: 7389 6211 6021 Finishing services; bond dealers & brokers; national commercial banks
HQ: Merrill Lynch, Pierce, Fenner & Smith Incorporated
111 8th Ave
New York NY 10011
800 637-7455

(P-18597)
MESSAGE BROADCAST LLC
4685 Macarthur Ct Ste 250, Newport Beach
(92660-1893)
PHONE.................................949 428-3111
William H Potter, *Mng Member*
Gary Temme, *Vice Pres*
Scott Wendrick, *Vice Pres*
Kyle Manchester, *Technology*
Tiffany Trinh, *Controller*
EMP: 50
SQ FT: 8,000
SALES (est): 5.7MM **Privately Held**
WEB: www.messagebroadcast.com
SIC: 7389 Telemarketing services

(P-18598)
MKTG INC
5800 Bristol Pkwy Ste 500, Culver City
(90230-6899)
PHONE.................................310 972-7900
Patty Hubbard, *Branch Mgr*
Alyse Courtines, *Vice Pres*
EMP: 1212 **Privately Held**
WEB: www.mktg.com
SIC: 7389 Advertising, promotional & trade show services
HQ: Mktg, Inc.
32 Avenue Of The Americas # 1
New York NY 10013

(P-18599)
MME FLORIDA LLC (PA)
Also Called: Medmen
10115 Jefferson Blvd, Culver City
(90232-3519)
PHONE.................................678 826-8622
Adam Bierman, *President*
Jim Miller, *Vice Pres*
Morgan Thomas, *Vice Pres*
Justin Bunton, *Human Resources*
John McQueeney, *Director*
EMP: 67 EST: 2018

SALES (est): 5.2MM **Privately Held**
SIC: 7389

(P-18600)
MOBILE MESSENGER AMERICAS INC (PA)
6601 Center Dr W Ste 700, Los Angeles
(90045-1545)
PHONE.................................310 957-3300
Darcy Wedd, *CEO*
Daniel Machock, *CFO*
EMP: 130 EST: 2005
SALES (est): 18.2MM **Privately Held**
SIC: 7389 Courier or messenger service

(P-18601)
MODERN DEV CO A LTD PARTNR
Also Called: Paramount Swap Meet
7900 All America City Way, Paramount
(90723-3400)
PHONE.................................949 646-6400
Darren Kurkowski, *Branch Mgr*
EMP: 57
SALES (corp-wide): 17.7MM **Privately Held**
SIC: 7389 Flea market
PA: Modern Development Co, A Limited Partnership
496 N Coast Hwy Ste A
Laguna Beach CA 92651
949 646-6400

(P-18602)
MODERN OUTDOOR DESIGNS LLC
16787 Schoenborn St, North Hills
(91343-6107)
PHONE.................................818 785-0171
Janel Sobeck, *Principal*
Rose Petrosyan, *Executive*
EMP: 13 EST: 2009
SALES (est): 790.3K **Privately Held**
WEB: www.modernoutdoor.com
SIC: 7389 2531 Design services; public building & related furniture

(P-18603)
MONKEE INC
16104 E Cypress St, Covina (91722-2208)
PHONE.................................626 848-1555
Qing Ye, *Branch Mgr*
EMP: 50 **Privately Held**
SIC: 7389
PA: Monkee Inc.
9834 Longden Ave
Temple City CA

(P-18604)
MOTION PICTURE LICENSING CORP (PA)
5455 S Centinela Ave, Los Angeles
(90066-6942)
P.O. Box 66970 (90066-0970)
PHONE.................................800 462-8855
Peter Kuyper, *Ch of Bd*
Peter J Kane, *CFO*
Lyn Lim, *Treasurer*
Julie Maresca, *Exec VP*
Mike Weatherley, *Exec VP*
▲ EMP: 57 EST: 1985
SALES (est): 7.1MM **Privately Held**
WEB: www.mplc.org
SIC: 7389 Legal & tax services

(P-18605)
MOTIVATIONAL MARKETING INC (PA)
Also Called: Motivtnal Flfllment Lgstics Sv
15820 Euclid Ave, Chino (91708-9162)
PHONE.................................909 517-2200
Hal Altman, *CEO*
Andrea Stuhley, *Exec VP*
Anthony Altman, *Senior VP*
Tony Altman, *Vice Pres*
Cheryl Nataren, *Vice Pres*
▲ EMP: 229 EST: 1977
SQ FT: 300,000
SALES (est): 54.3MM **Privately Held**
WEB: www.mfals.com
SIC: 7389 8748 4225 Telemarketing services; mailing & messenger services; business consulting; general warehousing & storage

(P-18606)
MULTI-PAK CORPORATION
Also Called: Multipak
20131 Bahama St, Chatsworth
(91311-6202)
PHONE.................................818 709-0508
Randall B Unthank, *President*
EMP: 60 EST: 1955
SQ FT: 20,000
SALES (est): 6.6MM **Privately Held**
WEB: www.multi-pak.com
SIC: 7389 Packaging & labeling services

(P-18607)
MVENTIX INC (PA)
21600 Oxnard St Ste 1700, Woodland Hills
(91367-4972)
PHONE.................................818 337-3747
Kristian Beloff, *CEO*
Vesselin Kavrakov, *Officer*
Alok Devkota, *Administration*
Pavel Monev, *CTO*
Koh Mina, *Accountant*
EMP: 385 EST: 2004
SQ FT: 6,606
SALES (est): 17.4MM **Privately Held**
WEB: www.mventix.com
SIC: 7389 8732 7372 Advertising, promotional & trade show services; survey service: marketing, location, etc.; business oriented computer software; educational computer software

(P-18608)
NATIONAL BUS INVSTIGATIONS INC
Also Called: MPS Security
25020 Las Brisas Rd Ste A, Murrieta
(92562-4064)
PHONE.................................951 677-3500
Michael D Julian, *President*
Lisa Pons, *Administration*
Ryan Hanhardt, *Manager*
Sam Grothe, *Accounts Mgr*
EMP: 60 EST: 1967
SQ FT: 2,000
SALES (est): 7MM **Privately Held**
WEB: www.investigations-nbi.com
SIC: 7389 7381 Personal investigation service; private investigator

(P-18609)
NATIONAL ORANGE SHOW (PA)
Also Called: Orange Show Fairgrounds The
689 S E St, San Bernardino (92408-1987)
PHONE.................................909 888-6788
Larry Curti, *Chairman*
Leslie Bischoff, *Marketing Staff*
Albert Villegas, *Manager*
EMP: 105 EST: 1911
SQ FT: 6,500
SALES (est): 4MM **Privately Held**
WEB: www.nosevents.com
SIC: 5812 7389 7299 Caterers; convention & show services; banquet hall facilities

(P-18610)
NEFTALY IMPORTS LLC
1700 S Milliken Ave, Ontario (91761-2338)
PHONE.................................909 329-1276
Armand Puyolt,
EMP: 260 EST: 2018
SALES (est): 2.7MM **Privately Held**
SIC: 7389

(P-18611)
NETTWERK MUSIC GROUP LLC (DH)
1545 Wilcox Ave Ste 103, Los Angeles
(90028-7324)
PHONE.................................323 301-4200
Terry Mc Bride, *CEO*
Danielle Romeo, *Vice Pres*
Brayman Mallory, *Office Mgr*
Ellen Gildersleeve, *CIO*
Liz Erman, *Mktg Dir*
EMP: 50 EST: 1999
SQ FT: 7,000
SALES (est): 6.8MM
SALES (corp-wide): 1.6MM **Privately Held**
WEB: www.nettwerk.com
SIC: 7389 Music recording producer

HQ: Nettwerk Records Inc
345 7th Ave Fl 11
New York NY 10001
212 760-1540

(P-18612)
NETWORK TELEPHONE SERVICES INC (PA)
Also Called: N T S
21135 Erwin St, Woodland Hills
(91367-3713)
PHONE.................................800 742-5687
Joseph Preston, *CEO*
Dan Coleman, *Vice Pres*
Daniel Coleman, *Vice Pres*
Marlene Tanner, *Vice Pres*
Paruyr Safaryan, *Administration*
EMP: 87 EST: 1988
SQ FT: 70,000
SALES (est): 29.4MM **Privately Held**
WEB: www.nts.net
SIC: 7389 4813 7374 Telephone services; ; data processing & preparation

(P-18613)
NEW CREW PRODUCTION CORP
1100 W 135th St, Gardena (90247-1919)
PHONE.................................323 234-8880
Kris Park, *President*
Joseph Park, *Admin Sec*
▲ EMP: 110 EST: 2002
SALES (est): 4.7MM **Privately Held**
WEB: www.newcrewproductioncorp.com
SIC: 7389 Sewing contractor

(P-18614)
NOR-CAL BEVERAGE CO INC
Also Called: Norcal Beverage Co
1226 N Olive St, Anaheim (92801-2543)
PHONE.................................714 526-8600
William McFarland, *Manager*
EMP: 39
SALES (corp-wide): 231.7MM **Privately Held**
WEB: www.ncbev.com
SIC: 7389 2033 Packaging & labeling services; canned fruits & specialties
PA: Nor-Cal Beverage Co., Inc.
2150 Stone Blvd
West Sacramento CA 95691
916 372-0600

(P-18615)
NSI GROUP LLC (PA)
Also Called: Nsi - Natural Sourcing Intl
17031 Ventura Blvd, Encino (91316-4128)
PHONE.................................818 639-8335
Vincent Grignon,
Kimberly Khournso, *Project Mgr*
Chris Mon, *Accountant*
Mariolle Jean-Victor, *VP Sales*
Elisabetta Brinis,
EMP: 23 EST: 2013
SQ FT: 7,000
SALES (est): 7.5MM **Privately Held**
WEB: www.nsifood.com
SIC: 7389 2034 Packaging & labeling services; dried & dehydrated fruits

(P-18616)
NUVIA WATER TECHNOLOGIES INC
108 Business Center Dr, Corona
(92878-3218)
PHONE.................................951 734-7400
Kellie Johnson, *President*
Kelley Johnson, *Vice Pres*
EMP: 60 EST: 2011
SALES (est): 6.9MM **Privately Held**
WEB: www.nuviawater.com
SIC: 7389 Personal service agents, brokers & bureaus

(P-18617)
OCEANX LLC (HQ)
100 N Pcf Cast Hwy Ste 15, El Segundo
(90245)
PHONE.................................310 774-4088
Steve Adams, *Mng Member*
Marc Kallick, *CFO*
Chris Accardo, *Vice Pres*
Kevin Gorman, *Vice Pres*
Jessica Perez, *Vice Pres*
EMP: 98 EST: 2015

SALES (est): 137MM **Privately Held**
WEB: www.oceanx.com
SIC: 7389 4731 Subscription fulfillment services: magazine, newspaper, etc.; freight transportation arrangement

(P-18618)
OCS AMERICA INC (DH)
Also Called: Ocs Bookstore
11100 Hindry Ave, Los Angeles
(90045-6224)
PHONE.........................310 417-0650
Yutaka Otake, *Ch of Bd*
Takuya Hiraiwa, *CEO*
Susan Onuman, *Admin Sec*
▲ EMP: 39
SQ FT: 15,200
SALES (est): 12.5MM **Privately Held**
WEB: www.ocs-india.com
SIC: 7389 5192 2711 5942 Courier or messenger service; newspapers; newspapers: publishing only, not printed on site; books, foreign

(P-18619)
ONEIL DIGITAL SOLUTIONS LLC
12655 Beatrice St, Los Angeles
(90066-7300)
PHONE.........................310 448-6407
David Woodley, *Controller*
Alfredo Aleman, *Software Engr*
Gina Kwong, *Engineer*
Leo Grin, *Manager*
EMP: 201
SALES (corp-wide): 335.6MM **Privately Held**
WEB: www.oneildigitalsolutions.com
SIC: 7389 2752 5045 Mailbox rental & related service; commercial printing, lithographic; computer software
HQ: O'neil Digital Solutions, Llc
3100 E Plano Pkwy
Plano TX 75074
972 881-1282

(P-18620)
ONTARIO CONVENTION CENTER CORP
Also Called: Smg Management Facility
2000 E Convention Ctr Way, Ontario
(91764-5633)
PHONE.........................909 937-3000
Dick Walsh, *Mayor*
Michael K Krouse, *CEO*
Debra Dorst-Porada, *Mayor*
EMP: 240 EST: 1995
SQ FT: 225,000
SALES (est): 11MM
SALES (corp-wide): 374.3MM **Privately Held**
WEB: www.gocvb.org
SIC: 7389 Convention & show services
PA: City Of Ontario
303 E B St
Ontario CA 91764
909 395-2012

(P-18621)
ORANGE COAST TITLE COMPANY (PA)
1551 N Tustin Ave Ste 300, Santa Ana
(92705-8638)
P.O. Box 11825 (92711-1825)
PHONE.........................714 558-2836
Mike Kaluger, *President*
Shannon Staley, *Bd of Directors*
Larry Bowser, *Officer*
Christi Cobain-Freeman, *Officer*
Marilyn Eschenbaum, *Officer*
EMP: 100 EST: 1973
SQ FT: 24,000
SALES (est): 427.5MM **Privately Held**
WEB: www.octitle.com
SIC: 7389 6361 6541 Personal service agents, brokers & bureaus; title insurance; title & trust companies

(P-18622)
ORANGE COURIER INC
15300 Desman Rd, La Mirada
(90638-5762)
P.O. Box 5308, Santa Ana (92704-0308)
PHONE.........................714 384-3600
Evell T Stanley, *President*
Michelle Cannon,
Roy Requena, *Manager*

Brandon Ruben, *Manager*
Tim Thompson, *Manager*
▲ EMP: 300 EST: 1992
SALES (est): 21.4MM **Privately Held**
WEB: www.orangecourier.com
SIC: 7389 4213 4225 Courier or messenger service; trucking, except local; general warehousing & storage

(P-18623)
OST TRUCKS AND CRANES INC
Also Called: Ost Crane Service
2951 N Ventura Ave, Ventura (93001-1210)
P.O. Box 237 (93002-0237)
PHONE.........................805 643-9963
L Dennis Zermeno, *President*
Don D Zermeno, *Vice Pres*
Ron J Zermeno, *Vice Pres*
Rose Kurta, *Controller*
EMP: 73 EST: 1962
SQ FT: 3,000
SALES (est): 12.9MM **Privately Held**
WEB: www.ostcranes.com
SIC: 7389 4212 4225 Crane & aerial lift service; local trucking, without storage; general warehousing & storage

(P-18624)
OVERLAND PACIFIC & CUTLER LLC (PA)
Also Called: Pacific Relocation Consultants
5000 Arprt Plz Dr Ste 250, Long Beach
(90815)
PHONE.........................800 400-7356
Ray Armstrong Sr, *CEO*
Mike Leber, *CFO*
Marty Zvirbulis, *Officer*
Michele Folk Sr, *Vice Pres*
Mark Labonte Sr, *Vice Pres*
▲ EMP: 55 EST: 1980
SALES (est): 20.8MM **Privately Held**
WEB: www.opcservices.com
SIC: 7389 Relocation service

(P-18625)
PACIFIC ASIAN ENTERPRISES INC (PA)
Also Called: Nordhavn Yachts
25001 Dana Dr, Dana Point (92629-3005)
P.O. Box 874 (92629-0874)
PHONE.........................949 496-4848
Dan Streech, *President*
James Leishman, *CFO*
Jeffrey Leishman, *Admin Sec*
Trever Smith, *Project Mgr*
Josh Lloyd, *Controller*
◆ EMP: 30
SQ FT: 3,500
SALES (est): 8MM **Privately Held**
WEB: www.nordhavn.com
SIC: 7389 3732 Yacht brokers; yachts, building & repairing

(P-18626)
PACIFIC EMBROIDERY LLC
1189 N Kraemer Blvd, Anaheim
(92806-1917)
PHONE.........................714 630-4757
Sam Choe,
Joel Choi,
EMP: 19 EST: 1988
SQ FT: 3,600
SALES (est): 1.3MM **Privately Held**
WEB: www.pacificemb.com
SIC: 7389 2395 Sewing contractor; pleating & stitching

(P-18627)
PARADIGM INDUSTRIES INC
2522 E 37th St, Vernon (90058-1725)
PHONE.........................310 965-1900
William Jun, *CEO*
Chu Kim, *President*
Miri Nino, *Manager*
▲ EMP: 80 EST: 2000
SALES (est): 5.1MM **Privately Held**
WEB: www.paradigmindustries.net
SIC: 7389 Textile & apparel services

(P-18628)
PARAGON LANGUAGE SERVICES INC (PA)
5055 Wilshire Blvd # 835, Los Angeles
(90036-5092)
PHONE.........................323 966-4655

Hanne R Mintz, *President*
Marina G Mintz, *Vice Pres*
Maybelline Racca, *Vice Pres*
Marissa Goodman, *Project Mgr*
Irina Gunthart, *Project Mgr*
EMP: 13 EST: 1991
SQ FT: 1,300
SALES (est): 2.1MM **Privately Held**
WEB: www.paragonls.com
SIC: 7389 2791 8732 Translation services; typesetting, computer controlled; market analysis, business & economic research

(P-18629)
PARTNERS CAPITAL GROUP INC (PA)
201 Sandpointe Ave # 220, Santa Ana
(92707-5778)
PHONE.........................949 916-3900
Mark Davin, *CEO*
Jason Altunian, *Vice Pres*
Jared Berggren, *Vice Pres*
Laramie Smith, *Vice Pres*
David So, *Vice Pres*
EMP: 80 EST: 2005
SQ FT: 25,000
SALES (est): 37.5MM **Privately Held**
WEB: www.partnerscapitalgrp.com
SIC: 7389 Financial services

(P-18630)
PASADENA CENTER OPERATING CO
Also Called: PASADENA CONVENTION CENTER
300 E Green St, Pasadena (91101-2399)
PHONE.........................626 795-9311
Michael Ross, *CEO*
Anthony Burgess, *Officer*
Tara Gadsby, *Executive*
Jessica Gonzales, *Administration*
Vicki Carrillo, *Technician*
EMP: 116 EST: 1973
SQ FT: 32,000
SALES (est): 25.5MM **Privately Held**
WEB: www.visitpasadena.com
SIC: 7389 Convention & show services

(P-18631)
PERFECT IMPRESSION INC
Also Called: Perfect Banner, The
27111 Aliso Creek Rd # 145, Aliso Viejo
(92656-3365)
PHONE.........................949 305-0797
Suzie Abrahams, *President*
Stephanie Auriemma, *Sales Staff*
Susan Abrahams,
EMP: 28 EST: 2008
SALES (est): 3MM **Privately Held**
WEB: www.theperfectimpression.com
SIC: 7389 2395 Embroidering of advertising on shirts, etc.; embroidery & art needlework; art goods for embroidering, stamped; purchased materials

(P-18632)
PHOENIX TEXTILE INC
910 S Los Angeles St, Los Angeles
(90015-1726)
PHONE.........................213 239-9640
Fax: 213 228-1109
EMP: 70
SALES (corp-wide): 42.4MM **Privately Held**
SIC: 7389 Business Services
PA: Phoenix Textile, Inc.
14600 S Broadway
Gardena CA 90248
310 715-7090

(P-18633)
PHX INVESTMENT PROPERTIES LLC
2532 Dupont Dr, Irvine (92612-1524)
PHONE.........................949 474-7368
Tim Busch, *Vice Pres*
Paul McCormick, *COO*
EMP: 50 EST: 2019
SALES (est): 1.6MM **Privately Held**
SIC: 7389

(P-18634)
PIONEER THEATRES INC
Also Called: Roadium Open Air Market
2500 Redondo Beach Blvd, Torrance
(90504-1529)
PHONE.........................310 532-8183
William Fleischman, *President*
William Warnick, *Vice Pres*
Paul Hengehold, *General Mgr*
Mike Romo, *Opers Staff*
EMP: 110 EST: 1949
SQ FT: 3,000
SALES (est): 6.6MM **Privately Held**
WEB: www.roadium.com
SIC: 7389 5431 Flea market; fruit & vegetable markets

(P-18635)
PIXIOR LLC (PA)
5901 S Eastern Ave, Commerce
(90040-4003)
PHONE.........................323 721-2221
Yassine Amallal, *CEO*
Elena Pickett, *Senior VP*
Janet Ingle, *Vice Pres*
Kiet Huynh, *Accounting Mgr*
Galina Turetskaya, *Personne*
◆ EMP: 160 EST: 2000
SQ FT: 192,000
SALES (est): 18MM **Privately Held**
SIC: 7389 Advertising, promotional & trade show services

(P-18636)
PLUM HEALTHCARE GROUP LLC
Also Called: Redlands Health Care Group
1620 W Fern Ave, Redlands (92373-4918)
PHONE.........................909 793-2609
Mark Baliff,
Vicenta Hollingshead, *Records Dir*
Nanci Wilson, *Officer*
Rick Burke, *Creative Dir*
Anita Hubbard, *Administration*
EMP: 67 EST: 1998
SALES (est): 1MM **Privately Held**
WEB: www.redlandshealthcarecenter.com
SIC: 7389 Personal service agents, brokers & bureaus

(P-18637)
PML INC
Also Called: Precision Measurement Labs
201 W Beach Ave, Inglewood
(90302-2902)
PHONE.........................310 671-4345
David Tolin, *President*
EMP: 62 EST: 1986
SQ FT: 3,900
SALES (est): 2.2MM **Privately Held**
WEB: www.yourcovers.com
SIC: 7389 3543 Inspection & testing services; industrial & commercial equipment inspection service; industrial patterns

(P-18638)
PRECISION NETWRK SOLUTIONS LLC
4259 Deeboyar Ave, Lakewood
(90712-3901)
PHONE.........................562 318-4242
Amanda Hunt, *President*
Steven Hunt, *Principal*
Fernando Ornelas, *Principal*
Korey Ornelas, *Principal*
EMP: 60 EST: 2018
SALES (est): 1.7MM **Privately Held**
WEB: www.precisionnetsolutions.com
SIC: 7389

(P-18639)
PREMIER OFFICE CENTERS LLC (PA)
Also Called: Premier Business Centers
2102 Business Center Dr, Irvine
(92612-1001)
PHONE.........................949 253-4616
Jeffrey Reinstein, *CEO*
William Gutierrez, *COO*
Jeff Reinstein, *COO*
Laura Allen, *General Mgr*
Nancy Colella, *General Mgr*
▲ EMP: 50 EST: 2002

SALES (est): 109.7MM **Privately Held**
WEB: www.premierworkspaces.com
SIC: **7389** Office facilities & secretarial service rental

(P-18640)
PRIDE CLEANING CO INC
Also Called: Pride Companies
1900 W Burbank Blvd, Burbank
(91506-1317)
PHONE..................................818 295-2510
Lilit Marzbetuny, *President*
Vahe Marzbetuny, *Vice Pres*
Zareh Marzbetuny, *Admin Sec*
EMP: 50 EST: 1974
SQ FT: 4,000
SALES (est): 2.3MM **Privately Held**
WEB: www.pridecompanies.com
SIC: **7389** Fire protection service other than forestry or public

(P-18641)
PRO-TECH DESIGN & MFG INC
14561 Marquardt Ave, Santa Fe Springs
(90670-5137)
PHONE..................................562 207-1680
Pamela Mc Master, *CEO*
Aaron Swanson, *President*
David Mc Master, *CFO*
Jeff Swanson, *Vice Pres*
Jonathan Contreras, *Production*
▲ EMP: 60 EST: 1979
SALES (est): 14MM **Privately Held**
WEB: www.protechdesign.com
SIC: **7389 8711** Packaging & labeling services; industrial engineers

(P-18642)
PRODUCTIVE PLAYHOUSE INC
25231 Paseo De Alicia # 2, Laguna Hills
(92653-4645)
PHONE..................................323 250-3445
Harry Ralston, *CEO*
EMP: 268 EST: 2009
SALES (est): 20MM **Privately Held**
WEB: www.productiveplayhouse.com
SIC: **7389** Translation services

(P-18643)
PROFESSNAL CMMNCTONS NETWRK LP (PA)
6774 Magnolia Ave, Riverside
(92506-2908)
PHONE..................................951 275-9149
Diann K Johnston, *Partner*
Brian White, *Partner*
Jeff White, *Partner*
Diann Johnston, *General Mgr*
Donna Wuersch, *Finance Mgr*
EMP: 50 EST: 1990
SQ FT: 4,000
SALES (est): 4.3MM **Privately Held**
WEB: www.pcnanswers.com
SIC: **7389** Telephone answering service

(P-18644)
PROLOGIC RDMPTION SLUTIONS INC (PA)
2121 Rosecrans Ave, El Segundo
(90245-4743)
PHONE..................................310 322-7774
William Atkinson, *CEO*
Paul Cooley, *President*
Robb Warwick, *CFO*
Kelly Fuller, *Ch Credit Ofcr*
Ross Ely, *Chief Mktg Ofcr*
EMP: 700 EST: 2008
SALES (est): 61.2MM **Privately Held**
SIC: **7389** Coupon redemption service

(P-18645)
PROMPT DELIVERY INC
Also Called: Southern California Messenger
5757 Wilshire Blvd Ph 3, Los Angeles
(90036-3681)
PHONE..................................858 549-8000
Mike Dysland, *Manager*
EMP: 100 **Privately Held**
SIC: **7389 4212** Courier or messenger service; delivery service, vehicular
PA: Prompt Delivery, Inc.
5757 Wilshire Blvd # 120
Los Angeles CA 90036

(P-18646)
QOLOGY DIRECT LLC
Also Called: Centerfield Media
12130 Millennium Ste 600, Los Angeles
(90094-2945)
PHONE..................................310 341-4420
Brett Cravatt, *President*
Jason Cohen, *President*
EMP: 170 EST: 2012
SQ FT: 90,000
SALES (est): 20.3MM
SALES (corp-wide): 60.5MM **Privately Held**
WEB: www.centerfield.com
SIC: **7389** Telephone services; telemarketing services
HQ: Qology Direct Holdings, Inc.
12130 Millennium Ste 600
Los Angeles CA 90094

(P-18647)
R G CANNING ENTERPRISES INC
4515 E 59th Pl, Maywood (90270-3201)
PHONE..................................323 560-7469
Richard G Canning, *President*
Charles R Canning, *Vice Pres*
EMP: 215 EST: 1955
SQ FT: 50,000
SALES (est): 8.6MM **Privately Held**
WEB: www.rgcshows.com
SIC: **7389** Promoters of shows & exhibitions

(P-18648)
RAYTHEON COMPANY
75 Coromar Dr, Goleta (93117-3088)
PHONE..................................805 562-2941
EMP: 66
SALES (corp-wide): 23.2B **Publicly Held**
SIC: **7389** Business Services
PA: Raytheon Company
870 Winter St
Waltham MA 02451
781 522-3000

(P-18649)
REASON FOUNDATION
5737 Mesmer Ave, Los Angeles
(90230-6316)
PHONE..................................310 391-2245
David Nott, *President*
Mike Alissi, *Vice Pres*
Leonard Gilroy, *Vice Pres*
Adrian Moore, *Vice Pres*
Chris Mitchell, *Comms Dir*
EMP: 35 EST: 1968
SQ FT: 6,300
SALES (est): 16.1MM **Privately Held**
WEB: www.reason.org
SIC: **7389 2741 2721** Speakers' bureau; newsletter publishing; magazines: publishing & printing

(P-18650)
REGISTRATION CTRL SYSTEMS INC (PA)
Also Called: Rcs World Travel
1833 Portola Rd Unit B, Ventura
(93003-7797)
PHONE..................................805 654-0171
Edgar A Bolton, *President*
Gary Bolton, *Vice Pres*
Rick Bradd, *Vice Pres*
Sam Hamilton, *Vice Pres*
Jim Lecroy, *Vice Pres*
EMP: 55 EST: 1971
SQ FT: 15,000
SALES (est): 5.2MM **Privately Held**
WEB: www.home.rcsreg.com
SIC: **7389** Convention & show services

(P-18651)
RGIS LLC
500 E Olive Ave Ste 240, Burbank
(91501-2171)
PHONE..................................248 651-2511
EMP: 140
SALES (corp-wide): 6.1B **Publicly Held**
WEB: www.rgis.com
SIC: **7389** Business Services

HQ: Rgis, Llc
2000 Taylor Rd
Auburn Hills MI 48326
248 651-2511

(P-18652)
RGIS LLC
1937 W Chapman Ave, Orange
(92868-2632)
PHONE..................................714 938-0663
EMP: 133
SALES (corp-wide): 6.1B **Publicly Held**
WEB: www.rgis.com
SIC: **7389** Inventory computing service
HQ: Rgis, Llc
2000 Taylor Rd
Auburn Hills MI 48326
248 651-2511

(P-18653)
RGIS LLC
6529 Riverside Ave Ste 215, Riverside
(92506)
PHONE..................................951 369-7131
Katherine Barton, *Manager*
Ruth Vallejo, *District Mgr*
EMP: 65
SALES (corp-wide): 6.1B **Publicly Held**
WEB: www.rgis.com
SIC: **7389** Inventory computing service
HQ: Rgis, Llc
2000 Taylor Rd
Auburn Hills MI 48326
248 651-2511

(P-18654)
RIA ENVIA INC (HQ)
6565 Knott Ave, Buena Park (90620-1139)
PHONE..................................714 543-8448
Juan Beanchi, *President*
Humberto Espinosa, *Opers Staff*
Roberto Guzman, *Director*
EMP: 824 EST: 2000
SALES (est): 3.8MM **Publicly Held**
WEB: www.euronetworldwide.com
SIC: **7389** Financial services

(P-18655)
ROMAN CTHLIC DIOCESE OF ORANGE
Also Called: St Josephs School
801 N Bradford Ave, Placentia
(92870-4515)
PHONE..................................714 528-1794
Joann Telles, *Principal*
Rica Mendoza, *Teacher*
Matt Raya, *Teacher*
Andreina Rodriguez, *Teacher*
Michael Spillman, *Director*
EMP: 175
SALES (corp-wide): 100.3MM **Privately Held**
WEB: www.rcbo.org
SIC: **8211 8661 7389** Catholic junior high school; Catholic Church; fund raising organizations
PA: The Roman Catholic Diocese Of Orange
13280 Chapman Ave
Garden Grove CA 92840
714 282-3000

(P-18656)
RONSIN PHOTOCOPY INC (PA)
215 Lemon Creek Dr, Walnut (91789-2643)
PHONE..................................909 594-5995
Dennis Grant, *President*
Robert Alkema, *Ch of Bd*
Cheryl Alkema, *Corp Secy*
Valarie Gudino, *Vice Pres*
Gina Bruno, *Sales Executive*
EMP: 60 EST: 1976
SQ FT: 12,000
SALES (est): 7.6MM **Privately Held**
WEB: www.ronsinphotocopy.com
SIC: **7389** Microfilm recording & developing service

(P-18657)
ROSE & SHORE INC
5151 Alcoa Ave, Vernon (90058-3715)
P.O. Box 58225 (90058-0225)
PHONE..................................323 826-2144
Irwin Miller, *President*
James Craig, *Vice Pres*
Carol Miller, *Admin Sec*

Warren Barber, *Controller*
Guadalupe Contreras, *Human Res Mgr*
EMP: 320 EST: 1968
SQ FT: 60,000
SALES (est): 21.5MM **Privately Held**
WEB: www.roseandshore.com
SIC: **7389 5147** Packaging & labeling services; meats, cured or smoked

(P-18658)
RTI SERVICES INC
2836 Vail Ave, Commerce (90040-2697)
PHONE..................................323 725-6370
Kelly McLeland, *Manager*
EMP: 77
SALES (corp-wide): 12.2MM **Privately Held**
SIC: **7389** Salvaging of damaged merchandise, service only
PA: Rti Services, Inc.
800 Berkshire Ln N
Plymouth MN 55441
952 475-0242

(P-18659)
RUZANNAS DECOR
608 S Hill St Ste Gl118, Los Angeles
(90014-4750)
PHONE..................................323 472-0505
Ruzanna Sargsyan, *CEO*
EMP: 50 EST: 2020
SALES (est): 690K **Privately Held**
SIC: **7389** Interior design services

(P-18660)
RYAN SHROADS
5110 E Washington Blvd, Commerce
(90040-1290)
P.O. Box 78850, Los Angeles (90016-0850)
PHONE..................................310 936-5966
Marquesha Green, *Principal*
Monique Palmer, *Principal*
EMP: 50
SALES (est): 641.1K **Privately Held**
SIC: **7389**

(P-18661)
SCA ENTERPRISES INC (PA)
Also Called: Southern Cal Appraisal Co
3817 W Magnolia Blvd, Burbank
(91505-2820)
P.O. Box 1455 (91507-1455)
PHONE..................................818 845-7621
Timothy S Davis, *CEO*
Paula Davis, *CFO*
Phil Langley, *Vice Pres*
Grey Logan, *Admin Asst*
Dan Karlson, *Info Tech Mgr*
▲ EMP: 65 EST: 1979
SQ FT: 1,200
SALES (est): 14.3MM **Privately Held**
WEB: www.sca-appraisal.com
SIC: **7389** Appraisers, except real estate

(P-18662)
SCHERZER INTERNATIONAL CORP (PA)
21650 Oxnard St Ste 300, Woodland Hills
(91367-4989)
PHONE..................................818 227-2770
Larry S Scherzer, *President*
Joseph Stone, *Officer*
Jessica Staheli, *Exec VP*
Jennifer Jackson, *Managing Dir*
David Lazar, *Managing Dir*
EMP: 60 EST: 1991
SQ FT: 11,400
SALES (est): 10.1MM **Privately Held**
WEB: www.scherzer.com
SIC: **7389** Financial services

(P-18663)
SCRATCH FINANCIAL INC
Also Called: Scratchpay
225 S Lake Ave Ste 250, Pasadena
(91101-4895)
PHONE..................................855 727-2395
John Keatley, *CEO*
Cherie Goerisch, *Partner*
Caleb Morse, *COO*
Paul Farina, *Vice Pres*
Jin Han, *Vice Pres*
EMP: 61 EST: 2016
SQ FT: 3,000

PRODUCTS & SVCS

(PA)=Parent Co (HQ)=Headquarters (DH)=Div Headquarters
✪ = New Business established in last 2 years

SALES (est): 5.3MM **Privately Held**
WEB: www.scratchpay.com
SIC: 7389 Financial services

(P-18664)
SEVEN ONE INC (PA)
Also Called: Professional Tele Answering Svc
21540 Prairie St Ste E, Chatsworth
(91311-5814)
PHONE..................................818 904-3435
James Thompson, *President*
EMP: 83 EST: 1983
SQ FT: 4,000
SALES (est): 2.5MM **Privately Held**
WEB: www.answer24live.com
SIC: 7389 Telephone answering service

(P-18665)
SHERYL LOWE DESIGNS LLC
1187 Coast Village Rd # 156, Santa Barbara (93108-2737)
PHONE..................................805 969-1742
Sheryl Lowe, *CEO*
Jaden Levit, *CFO*
Samantha Bryant, *Prdtn Mgr*
Jane Davis, *Opers Staff*
EMP: 20 EST: 2010
SQ FT: 1,500
SALES (est): 6MM **Privately Held**
WEB: www.sheryllowejewelry.com
SIC: 7389 3911 Design services; jewelry apparel

(P-18666)
SIGUE CORPORATION (PA)
13190 Telfair Ave., Sylmar (91342-3573)
PHONE..................................818 837-5939
Guillermo Dela Vina, *CEO*
Christina M Pappas, *President*
Victor Cohen, *CFO*
Alfredo Dela Vina, *CFO*
Christina Pappas, *Bd of Directors*
EMP: 100 EST: 1996
SQ FT: 3,000
SALES (est): 116.2MM **Privately Held**
WEB: www.sigue.com
SIC: 7389 4822 Financial services; telegraph & other communications

(P-18667)
SIMPLE SCIENCE INC
1626 Ohms Way, Costa Mesa
(92627-4329)
PHONE..................................949 335-1099
Christian Henderson, *President*
John Spilman, *President*
Andy Nidzieko, *Marketing Mgr*
Brooke Henderson, *Marketing Staff*
EMP: 35 EST: 2009
SALES (est): 3.8MM **Privately Held**
WEB: www.simple.science
SIC: 7389 7812 7371 7311 Design services; video production; audio-visual program production; software programming applications; advertising agencies;

(P-18668)
SINECERA INC
Also Called: Crown Vly Precision Machining
5397 3rd St, Irwindale (91706-2085)
PHONE..................................626 962-1087
Donald Brown, *CEO*
Dale B Mikus, *CFO*
EMP: 80 EST: 1984
SQ FT: 10,500
SALES (est): 24.7MM
SALES (corp-wide): 101.9MM **Privately Held**
WEB: www.h-dam.com
SIC: 7389 3492 Grinding, precision: commercial or industrial; control valves, aircraft: hydraulic & pneumatic
PA: H-D Advanced Manufacturing Company
2200 Georgetown Dr # 300
Sewickley PA 15143
724 759-2850

(P-18669)
SMG FOOD AND BEVERAGE LLC (PA)
Also Called: Ontario Convention Center
2000 E Convention Ctr Way, Ontario
(91764-5633)
PHONE..................................909 937-3000
Victoria Van Damme, *Mng Member*

John Burns,
Maureen Ginty,
EMP: 76 EST: 1999
SALES (est): 11.9MM **Privately Held**
WEB: www.gocvb.org
SIC: 7389 Convention & show services

(P-18670)
SNOWKAP ENTERPRISES INC (PA)
1405 E Washington St, Colton
(92324-4611)
PHONE..................................909 370-4444
EMP: 50 EST: 2018
SALES (est): 364.2K **Privately Held**
SIC: 7389 Business services

(P-18671)
SOBOBA BAND LUISENO INDIANS
Also Called: Soboba Casino
22777 Soboba Rd, San Jacinto
(92583-2935)
PHONE..................................951 665-1000
Toll Free:..................................888 -
Richard Kline, *Branch Mgr*
Chad Delgado, *Exec Dir*
Charlotte Golden, *Admin Asst*
Catherine Gonzalez, *Admin Asst*
Steven Nino, *CIO*
EMP: 900 **Privately Held**
WEB: www.soboba-nsn.gov
SIC: 7389 7011 Personal service agents, brokers & bureaus; casino hotel
PA: Soboba Band Of Luiseno Indians
23906 Soboba Rd
San Jacinto CA 92583
951 654-2765

(P-18672)
SOUTH BAY FABRICATION INC
15421 Electronic Ln, Huntington Beach
(92649-1333)
PHONE..................................714 894-1314
Cliff Klein, *CEO*
EMP: 34 EST: 2004
SALES (est): 2.3MM **Privately Held**
WEB: www.southbayfab.com
SIC: 7389 3441 Metal cutting services; metal slitting & shearing; fabricated structural metal

(P-18673)
SOUTHWEST DEALER SERVICES INC (PA)
8659 Research Dr Ste 100, Irvine
(92618-4204)
PHONE..................................949 707-4200
Eric Hamann, *President*
Steve Alderson, *Vice Pres*
Annie Melzer, *Case Mgr*
Chris Evans, *Manager*
▲ EMP: 226 EST: 1987
SQ FT: 3,387
SALES (est): 21.4MM **Privately Held**
WEB: www.swds.net
SIC: 7389 8742 Brokers, contract services; marketing consulting services

(P-18674)
SOUTHWEST INSPECTION AND TSTG
Also Called: Southwest Inspection Testing
441 Commercial Way, La Habra
(90631-6168)
PHONE..................................562 941-2990
Steven L Godbey, *President*
Kathy Godbey, *Treasurer*
Charles L Godbey, *Vice Pres*
Steven Ballesteros, *Manager*
EMP: 61 EST: 1956
SQ FT: 2,400
SALES (est): 9.8MM **Privately Held**
WEB: www.southwesttesting.com
SIC: 7389 Building inspection service

(P-18675)
SOUTHWEST MATERIAL HDLG INC (PA)
Also Called: Southwest Toyota Lift
3725 Nobel Ct, Jurupa Valley (91752-3267)
P.O. Box 1070, Mira Loma (91752-8070)
PHONE..................................951 727-0477
Kirt Little, *CEO*
Joseph G Little, *President*

Brad Christman, *Vice Pres*
Barry Westenhaver, *Opers Mgr*
Raelene Vega, *Sales Staff*
▲ EMP: 115 EST: 1962
SQ FT: 10,000
SALES (est): 71.1MM **Privately Held**
WEB: www.toyota.com
SIC: 5511 7389 7699 7359 Automobiles, new & used; design, commercial & industrial; industrial machinery & equipment repair; equipment rental & leasing; building site preparation

(P-18676)
STANDARD TEXTILE CO INC
Also Called: Western Distribution Center
6980 Sycamore Canyon Blvd, Riverside
(92507-0781)
PHONE..................................800 999-0400
Pete Staylor, *Manager*
Daniel Esquibel, *Supervisor*
EMP: 65
SALES (corp-wide): 393.5MM **Privately Held**
WEB: www.standardtextile.com
SIC: 7389 Textile & apparel services
PA: Standard Textile Co., Inc.
1 Knollcrest Dr
Cincinnati OH 45237
513 761-9255

(P-18677)
STANTEC ARCHITECTURE INC
Also Called: Rnl Design
801 S Figueroa St Ste 300, Los Angeles
(90017-3007)
PHONE..................................213 955-9775
Patrick McKelvey, *Branch Mgr*
Daigo Murakami, *Engineer*
Katie O 'neill, *Engineer*
Min Bikhram, *Manager*
EMP: 214
SALES (corp-wide): 3.6B **Privately Held**
WEB: www.stantec.com
SIC: 7389 8712 Interior designer; architectural engineering
HQ: Stantec Architecture Inc.
224 S Michigan Ave # 1400
Chicago IL 60604
336 714-7413

(P-18678)
STARCO GROUP INC (PA)
9160 Hyssop Dr, Rancho Cucamonga
(91730-6100)
PHONE..................................909 989-9898
Ross Sklar, *CEO*
▲ EMP: 60 EST: 2013
SALES (est): 36.7MM **Privately Held**
WEB: www.starcogp.com
SIC: 7389 Design services

(P-18679)
STERILE PROC SVCS AMER LLC (PA)
2240 E Artesia Blvd, Long Beach
(90805-1739)
PHONE..................................562 428-5858
Jacob Anderson,
Greg Anderson,
EMP: 64 EST: 2018
SQ FT: 36,000
SALES (est): 10MM **Privately Held**
WEB: www.spsausa.com
SIC: 7389 7349 Product sterilization service; hospital housekeeping

(P-18680)
STERILTEK INC
Also Called: SPD Department
637 S Lucas St, Los Angeles (90046)
PHONE..................................213 977-2298
Michele Gibson, *Manager*
EMP: 59 **Privately Held**
SIC: 7389 8621 Product sterilization service; health association
PA: Steriltek, Inc.
11910 Briarwyck Woods Dr
Concord Township OH 44077

(P-18681)
SUGAR FOODS CORPORATION
Also Called: Sygma Network, The
9500 El Dorado Ave, Sun Valley
(91352-1339)
PHONE..................................818 768-7900
Stephen Odell, *Partner*
EMP: 200
SALES (corp-wide): 286.3MM **Privately Held**
WEB: www.sugarfoods.com
SIC: 7389 2099 2062 Packaging & labeling services; food preparations; cane sugar refining
PA: Sugar Foods Corporation
950 3rd Ave Fl 21
New York NY 10022
212 753-6900

(P-18682)
SWIFT MEDIA ENTERTAINMENT INC
5340 Alla Rd Ste 101, Los Angeles
(90066-7036)
PHONE..................................310 308-3694
Andy Dinh, *CEO*
EMP: 75 EST: 2017
SALES (est): 5.8MM **Privately Held**
WEB: www.swiftmedia.net
SIC: 7389 Advertising, promotional & trade show services

(P-18683)
SWISSTEX CALIFORNIA INC (PA)
13660 S Figueroa St, Los Angeles
(90061-1023)
PHONE..................................310 516-6800
Henry Bassett, *President*
Michel Morger, *Vice Pres*
Thomas Schrieder, *Vice Pres*
Thomas Niessner, *Maintence Staff*
▲ EMP: 84 EST: 1995
SALES (est): 31.6MM **Privately Held**
WEB: www.swisstex-ca.com
SIC: 7389 Textile & apparel services

(P-18684)
T P R TRAFFIC SOLUTIONS (PA)
13217 Laureldale Ave, Downey
(90242-5140)
PHONE..................................800 821-2913
EMP: 15 EST: 2011
SALES (est): 657.9K **Privately Held**
WEB: www.tprts.tprco.com
SIC: 7389 3812 Flagging service (traffic control); air traffic control systems & equipment, electronic

(P-18685)
TBWA CHIAT/DAY INC
5353 Grosvenor Blvd, Los Angeles
(90066-6913)
PHONE..................................310 305-5000
Lee Clow, *Branch Mgr*
Chris Beresford-Hill, *Officer*
Gary Scheiner, *Exec VP*
Nora Chivelly, *Executive*
George Ashbrook, *Managing Dir*
EMP: 299
SALES (corp-wide): 13.1B **Publicly Held**
SIC: 7389 Interior design services
HQ: Tbwa Chiat/Day Inc.
488 Madison Ave Fl 7
New York NY 10022
212 804-1000

(P-18686)
TECHNICON DESIGN CORPORATION
26522 La Alameda Ste 150, Mission Viejo
(92691-6545)
PHONE..................................949 218-1300
David Shall, *President*
Helen Thomas, *Exec VP*
Rudolf Ludwig, *Manager*
Lauren Delgado, *Consultant*
Brenda Ramirez, *Consultant*
EMP: 61 EST: 1989
SQ FT: 1,000
SALES (est): 6.1MM
SALES (corp-wide): 10MM **Privately Held**
WEB: www.technicondesign.com
SIC: 7389 Design services

PA: Technicon Design Limited
Technicon House
Luton BEDS LU1 3
158 250-6600

(P-18687)
TECHNOLOGY TRAINING CORP (PA)
Also Called: Avalon Communications
369 Van Ness Way Ste 735, Torrance
(90501-6247)
P.O. Box 119 (90507-0119)
PHONE.....................310 320-8110
Hyman Silver, *CEO*
Steven Silver, *President*
Rick Hahn, *Treasurer*
Brad Barrett, *Director*
EMP: 15 EST: 1974
SQ FT: 4,300
SALES (est): 9.7MM **Privately Held**
WEB: www.ttcus.com
SIC: 7389 8742 2741 Lecture bureau;
business consultant; technical manuals:
publishing & printing

(P-18688)
THE/STUDIO
800 Wilshire Blvd Ste 200, Los Angeles
(90017-2608)
P.O. Box 1045, South Pasadena (91031-1045)
PHONE.....................877 647-6447
Joseph Heller, *President*
Jehan Loren, *Manager*
EMP: 13 EST: 2006
SALES (est): 932.4K **Privately Held**
WEB: www.thestudio.com
SIC: 5699 7389 2395 Shirts, custom
made; embroidering of advertising on
shirts, etc.; embroidery & art needlework

(P-18689)
THOUSAND OAKS PRTG & SPC INC
Also Called: T/O Printing
5334 Sterling Center Dr, Westlake Village
(91361-4612)
PHONE.....................818 706-8330
Steve Mahr, *President*
Michael Berry, *Technology*
Alan Forbes, *Credit Mgr*
Beth Digirolamo, *Human Res Dir*
Timothy Hayes, *Purch Mgr*
▲ EMP: 140 EST: 1981
SQ FT: 60,000
SALES (est): 21.8MM
SALES (corp-wide): 4.7B **Publicly Held**
WEB: www.rrd.com
SIC: 7389 2752 Printing broker; commercial printing, offset
HQ: Consolidated Graphics, Inc.
5858 Westheimer Rd # 200
Houston TX 77057
713 787-0977

(P-18690)
THRIO INC
5230 Las Virgenes Rd # 21, Calabasas
(91302-3448)
PHONE.....................858 299-7191
Edwin Margulies, *CEO*
Rose Sinicrope, *COO*
Ran Ezerzer, *Principal*
EMP: 20 EST: 2017
SALES (est): 1.2MM **Privately Held**
WEB: www.thrio.com
SIC: 7389 7372 Telephone services; telephone answering service; telemarketing
services; prepackaged software

(P-18691)
THYDE INC (PA)
300 El Sobrante Rd, Corona (92879-5757)
PHONE.....................951 817-2300
Tim Hyde, *President*
EMP: 200 EST: 1984
SQ FT: 70,000
SALES (est): 29.8MM **Privately Held**
SIC: 7389 Packaging & labeling services

(P-18692)
TIDAVATER INC
Also Called: Le Courier
2107 W Alameda Ave, Burbank
(91506-2934)
PHONE.....................818 848-4151

Fax: 818 848-5294
EMP: 150
SQ FT: 3,000
SALES (est): 5.2MM **Privately Held**
SIC: 7389 4513 4215 Business Services
Air Courier Services Courier Service

(P-18693)
TRAFFIC MANAGEMENT INC (PA)
4900 Arprt Plz Dr Ste 300, Long Beach
(90815)
PHONE.....................562 595-4278
Christopher H Spano, *CEO*
Jonathan Spano, *COO*
William Kearney, *Vice Pres*
Fernando Soriano, *Vice Pres*
Michael Sprouse, *Vice Pres*
▲ EMP: 144 EST: 1992
SALES (est): 120.3MM **Privately Held**
WEB: www.trafficmanagement.com
SIC: 7389 8741 Flagging service (traffic
control); business management

(P-18694)
TRANS-PAK INCORPORATED
Also Called: Transpak Los Angeles
2601 S Garnsey St, Santa Ana
(92707-3338)
PHONE.....................310 618-6937
Charles Frasier, *Principal*
EMP: 108
SALES (corp-wide): 187.9MM **Privately Held**
WEB: www.transpak.com
SIC: 7389 Packaging & labeling services
PA: Transpak, Inc.
520 Marburg Way
San Jose CA 95133
408 254-0500

(P-18695)
TRAP
Also Called: Task Force For Reg Autostaff
1833 S Mountain Ave, Monrovia
(91016-4270)
PHONE.....................626 572-5610
EMP: 80
SALES (est): 2.4MM **Privately Held**
SIC: 7389 Business Services

(P-18696)
TROPHIES ETC
2255 Pleasant Valley Rd K, Camarillo
(93012-8569)
PHONE.....................805 484-4121
EMP: 14
SQ FT: 10,000
SALES: 900K **Privately Held**
WEB: www.trophiesetc.com
SIC: 5999 7389 5199 3993 Ret Trophies
& Plaques Engraving & Whol Advertising
Specialties & Mfg Banners & Signs

(P-18697)
UBIQUITY BROADCASTING CORP (HQ)
9801 Research Dr, Irvine (92618-4304)
PHONE.....................949 489-7600
EMP: 50 EST: 2004
SQ FT: 29,000
SALES (est): 438.6K **Publicly Held**
WEB: www.ubiquitysci.com
SIC: 7389 Music & broadcasting services
PA: Ubiquity, Inc.
9801 Research Dr
Irvine CA 92618
949 489-7600

(P-18698)
UNITED EXCHANGE CORP (PA)
Also Called: Uec
5836 Corp Ave Ste 200, Cypress (90630)
PHONE.....................562 977-4500
Eugene W Choi, *CEO*
Carol J Choi, *President*
Lynn Chang, *Controller*
Jocelyn Jocson, *Marketing Mgr*
Amy Erdmann, *Sales Staff*
◆ EMP: 69 EST: 1993
SQ FT: 100,000
SALES (est): 37.5MM **Privately Held**
WEB: www.ueccorp.com
SIC: 7389 5122 Packaging & labeling
services; drugs, proprietaries & sundries

(P-18699)
UNITED PARCEL SERVICE INC
Also Called: UPS
2747 Vail Ave, Commerce (90040-2611)
PHONE.....................323 837-1220
Steven Hill, *Principal*
EMP: 61
SALES (corp-wide): 84.6B **Publicly Held**
WEB: www.ups.com
SIC: 7389 Mailing & messenger services
HQ: United Parcel Service, Inc.
55 Glenlake Pkwy
Atlanta GA 30328
404 828-6000

(P-18700)
UNITED PARCEL SERVICE INC
Also Called: UPS
1820 Railroad St, Oceano (93445-9552)
PHONE.....................805 474-9134
EMP: 61
SALES (corp-wide): 84.6B **Publicly Held**
WEB: www.ups.com
SIC: 7389 Mailing & messenger services
HQ: United Parcel Service, Inc.
55 Glenlake Pkwy
Atlanta GA 30328
404 828-6000

(P-18701)
UNITED PARCEL SERVICE INC
Also Called: UPS
22 Brookline, Aliso Viejo (92656-1461)
PHONE.....................949 643-6634
EMP: 61
SALES (corp-wide): 84.6B **Publicly Held**
WEB: www.ups.com
SIC: 7389 Telephone services
HQ: United Parcel Service, Inc.
55 Glenlake Pkwy
Atlanta GA 30328
404 828-6000

(P-18702)
UNITED PARCEL SERVICE INC
Also Called: UPS
3221 E Jurupa, Ontario (91764)
PHONE.....................909 974-7250
Richard Ricardo, *General Mgr*
EMP: 61
SALES (corp-wide): 84.6B **Publicly Held**
WEB: www.ups.com
SIC: 7389 Mailing & messenger services
HQ: United Parcel Service, Inc.
55 Glenlake Pkwy
Atlanta GA 30328
404 828-6000

(P-18703)
UNITED PARCEL SERVICE INC
Also Called: UPS
201 W Garvey Ave Ste 102, Monterey Park
(91754-7425)
PHONE.....................626 280-8012
Francis Fong, *Owner*
EMP: 61
SALES (corp-wide): 84.6B **Publicly Held**
WEB: www.ups.com
SIC: 7389 Mailing & messenger services
HQ: United Parcel Service, Inc.
55 Glenlake Pkwy
Atlanta GA 30328
404 828-6000

(P-18704)
UNITED PARCEL SERVICE INC
Also Called: UPS
4607 Lakeview Canyon Rd, Westlake Village (91361-4028)
PHONE.....................818 735-0945
Jim Penna, *Manager*
EMP: 61
SALES (corp-wide): 84.6B **Publicly Held**
WEB: www.ups.com
SIC: 7389 Mailing & messenger services
HQ: United Parcel Service, Inc.
55 Glenlake Pkwy
Atlanta GA 30328
404 828-6000

(P-18705)
UNITED PARCEL SERVICE INC
Also Called: UPS
11811 Landon Dr, Eastvale (91752-4002)
PHONE.....................951 749-3400
Paul Slater, *Principal*

Mario Dimen, *Consultant*
EMP: 61
SALES (corp-wide): 84.6B **Publicly Held**
WEB: www.ups.com
SIC: 7389 Mailing & messenger services
HQ: United Parcel Service, Inc.
55 Glenlake Pkwy
Atlanta GA 30328
404 828-6000

(P-18706)
UNITED PARCEL SERVICE INC
Also Called: UPS
91 W Easy St, Simi Valley (93065-1601)
PHONE.....................866 553-1069
Louis Moody, *Principal*
EMP: 61
SALES (corp-wide): 84.6B **Publicly Held**
WEB: www.ups.com
SIC: 7389 Mailing & messenger services
HQ: United Parcel Service, Inc.
55 Glenlake Pkwy
Atlanta GA 30328
404 828-6000

(P-18707)
UNITED TRANSPORT SERVICE INC
6750 Black Forest Dr, Eastvale
(92880-3922)
PHONE.....................844 258-2262
Felipe Mercado, *CEO*
EMP: 50 EST: 1990
SALES (est): 1.2MM **Privately Held**
SIC: 7389

(P-18708)
UNIVERSAL CARD INC
Also Called: Merchant Services
9012 Research Dr Ste 200, Irvine
(92618-4254)
PHONE.....................949 861-4000
Jason Moore, *President*
Jason W Moore, *CEO*
Robert Parisi, *Vice Pres*
Michael Carro, *Executive*
Marc Lewis, *Executive*
EMP: 400 EST: 2000
SQ FT: 40,000
SALES (est): 26.6MM **Privately Held**
SIC: 7389 Credit card service

(P-18709)
UNIVERSAL MUS GROUP DIST CORP
111 Unvrsal Hllywood Dr S, Universal City
(91608-1054)
PHONE.....................818 508-9550
Clarence McDonald, *Branch Mgr*
EMP: 59
SALES (corp-wide): 108MM **Privately Held**
WEB: www.universalmusic.com
SIC: 7389 Music recording producer
HQ: Umg Commercial Services, Inc.
2220 Colorado Ave
Santa Monica CA 90404
310 235-4700

(P-18710)
UNIVERSAL MUS INVESTMENTS INC (HQ)
2220 Colorado Ave, Santa Monica
(90404-3506)
PHONE.....................888 583-7176
Lucian C Grainge, *CEO*
Vikram Tuli, *Senior VP*
Alessandra Breton, *Vice Pres*
Christine Buckley, *Vice Pres*
Wendy Goldstein, *Vice Pres*
▲ EMP: 80 EST: 1996
SALES (est): 100.6MM
SALES (corp-wide): 108MM **Privately Held**
WEB: www.universalmusic.com
SIC: 7389 7929 Music recording producer;
musical entertainers; musicians
PA: Vivendi Se
42 Avenue De Friedland
Paris 75008
145 639-909

(P-18711)
UNIVERSAL MUSIC GROUP INC (PA)
2220 Colorado Ave, Santa Monica (90404-3506)
PHONE....................310 865-4000
Lucian Grainge, *Co-CEO*
Mauro Deceglie, *Partner*
Jules Ferree, *Partner*
Darcus Beese, *President*
Joie Manda, *President*
▲ EMP: 100 EST: 1996
SALES (est): 509.2MM **Privately Held**
WEB: www.universalmusic.com
SIC: 7389 2741 Music recording producer; miscellaneous publishing

(P-18712)
UNIVERSAL TECHNICAL INST INC
Also Called: Uti
9494 Haven Ave, Rancho Cucamonga (91730-5843)
PHONE....................909 484-1929
Suzanne Cabral, *Vice Pres*
Dani Castro, *Executive*
Aurora Schmiedel, *Admin Asst*
Todd Gaither, *CIO*
George Potter, *Technical Staff*
EMP: 53
SALES (corp-wide): 300.7MM **Publicly Held**
SIC: 8249 7389 Trade school; personal service agents, brokers & bureaus
PA: Universal Technical Institute, Inc.
4225 E Windrose Dr # 200
Phoenix AZ 85032
623 445-9500

(P-18713)
US ALLIANCE GROUP INC
Also Called: Usag
29883 Snta Mrgrita Pkwy S, Rcho STA Marg (92688-3611)
PHONE....................949 888-8580
Fadi Cheikha, *CEO*
Lisa Poyner, *Vice Pres*
Nathan Johnston, *Executive*
Cody Fields, *MIS Mgr*
Kimberly Cheikha, *Director*
EMP: 50 EST: 2007
SALES (est): 10.6MM **Privately Held**
WEB: www.usag-inc.com
SIC: 7389 Credit card service

(P-18714)
US BANKCARD SERVICES INC
17171 Gale Ave Ste 110, City of Industry (91745-1822)
PHONE....................888 888-8872
Christopher J Chang, *President*
Martin Lanyan, *Vice Pres*
Iris Chang, *Products*
Rick Chen, *Sales Staff*
Gary Lau, *Asst Mgr*
▲ EMP: 75 EST: 1996
SQ FT: 3,000
SALES (est): 15.8MM **Privately Held**
WEB: www.usbsi.com
SIC: 7389 Credit card service

(P-18715)
V A ANDERSON ENTERPRISES INC (PA)
Also Called: Kopy Kat Attorney Service
400 Atlas St, Brea (92821-3117)
P.O. Box 1029 (92822-1029)
PHONE....................714 990-6100
Pat Flynn, *President*
Bob Flynn, *Vice Pres*
Chuck Cunningham, *Manager*
Perry Miller, *Manager*
▲ EMP: 62 EST: 1973
SQ FT: 10,000
SALES (est): 7.9MM **Privately Held**
SIC: 7389 Microfilm recording & developing service

(P-18716)
VALLEY INDUS X-RAY INSPTN SVCS
3700 Pegasus Dr Ste 100, Bakersfield (93308-6805)
PHONE....................661 399-8497
Larry Williams, *President*

Terry Campbell, *Vice Pres*
EMP: 51 EST: 1978
SQ FT: 18,000
SALES (est): 1.7MM
SALES (corp-wide): 65.5MM **Privately Held**
WEB: www.applus.com
SIC: 7389 Inspection & testing services
HQ: Rontgen Technische Dienst B.V.
Delftweg 144
Rotterdam 3046
107 166-000

(P-18717)
VIVOPOOLS INC
825 S Primrose Ave Ste H, Monrovia (91016-3413)
PHONE....................818 952-2121
William Johnson, *CEO*
EMP: 55 EST: 2010
SQ FT: 1,300
SALES (est): 5MM **Privately Held**
WEB: www.vivopools.com
SIC: 7389 Swimming pool & hot tub service & maintenance

(P-18718)
VIVOPOOLS LLC
Also Called: North Bay Pool and Spa
245 W Foothill Blvd, Monrovia (91016-2152)
PHONE....................888 702-8486
EMP: 63
SQ FT: 4,000
SALES (est): 7.6MM **Privately Held**
WEB: www.vivopools.com
SIC: 7389 3589 5734 5091 Business Services Mfg Svc Industry Mach Ret Computers/Software Whol Sporting Goods/Supp Ret Misc Merchandise

(P-18719)
VOLCOM LLC (HQ)
Also Called: Stone Entertainment
1740 Monrovia Ave, Costa Mesa (92627-4407)
PHONE....................949 646-2175
Todd Hymel, *Mng Member*
Nicole Abbott, *Partner*
Elizabeth Krause, *Vice Pres*
Ed Shaver, *Vice Pres*
Tyler Middleton, *Regional Mgr*
EMP: 200 EST: 1991
SQ FT: 104,000
SALES (est): 103.8MM **Privately Held**
WEB: www.volcom.com
SIC: 7389 2253 7822 5136 Design services; bathing suits & swimwear, knit; motion picture & tape distribution; men's & boys' clothing; women's & children's clothing; unisex clothing stores

(P-18720)
VPET USA LLC
12925 Marlay Ave, Fontana (92337-6939)
PHONE....................909 605-1668
Jeff Kellar, *CEO*
Steven Saull, *CFO*
EMP: 96 EST: 2001
SALES (est): 9.9MM **Privately Held**
WEB: www.vpetusa.com
SIC: 7389 Packaging & labeling services

(P-18721)
VXI GLOBAL SOLUTIONS LLC (PA)
220 W 1st St Fl 3, Los Angeles (90012-4105)
PHONE....................213 739-4720
Eva Yi Hui Wang, *President*
Mark Hauge, *President*
Jared Morrison, *COO*
David Zhou, *COO*
Michael Festa, *CFO*
EMP: 1200 EST: 1998
SALES (est): 321.7MM **Privately Held**
WEB: www.vxi.com
SIC: 7389 Telemarketing services

(P-18722)
WARNER BROS RECORDS INC (DH)
777 S Santa Fe Ave, Los Angeles (90021-1750)
PHONE....................818 846-9090
Todd Moscowitz, *President*

Rob Cavallo, *Ch of Bd*
Livia Tortella, *President*
Marty Greenfield, *CFO*
Michele Nadelman, *CFO*
EMP: 460 EST: 1958
SALES (est): 198.9MM **Publicly Held**
WEB: www.warnerrecords.com
SIC: 7389 Music recording producer; recording studio, noncommercial records

(P-18723)
WATT COMMUNITIES
2716 Ocean Park Blvd # 2025, Santa Monica (90405-5209)\
PHONE....................310 314-2430
Brett Trebil, *Vice Pres*
Dave Johnson, *VP Engrg*
Efrem Joelson, *Project Mgr*
Jim Severns, *Superintendent*
EMP: 52 EST: 1947
SALES (est): 5.8MM **Privately Held**
WEB: www.wattcommunities.com
SIC: 7389 Business services

(P-18724)
WESTPOINT MARKETING INTL INC
5901 Avalon Blvd, Los Angeles (90003-1309)
P.O. Box 30144 (90030-0144)
PHONE....................323 233-0233
EMP: 85
SALES (est): 2.9MM **Privately Held**
SIC: 7389 Business Services

(P-18725)
WET (PA)
Also Called: Wet Design
10847 Sherman Way, Sun Valley (91352-4829)
PHONE....................818 769-6200
Mark W Fuller, *CEO*
Shemi Hart, *CFO*
Tania Avedissian, *Senior VP*
Helen Park, *Senior VP*
Maria Villamil, *Senior VP*
▲ EMP: 178 EST: 1983
SQ FT: 112,000
SALES (est): 69.2MM **Privately Held**
WEB: www.wetdesign.com
SIC: 7389 8711 3443 Design services; engineering services; metal parts

(P-18726)
WILLITS PERPETUAL LLC
21600 Oxnard St, Woodland Hills (91367-4976)
PHONE....................818 668-6800
EMP: 75
SALES (est): 3.2MM **Privately Held**
SIC: 7389 Business Services

(P-18727)
WILMAY INC
893 Oak Ave, Fillmore (93015-9621)
PHONE....................805 524-2603
EMP: 80
SALES (est): 2.2MM **Privately Held**
SIC: 7389 Business Services

(P-18728)
WINNING PERFORMANCE PDTS INC
Also Called: Diplomat Packaging
13010 Bradley Ave, Sylmar (91342-3831)
PHONE....................818 367-1041
Todd J Harding, *President*
Kim Harding, *Officer*
Barbara Rogers, *Officer*
▲ EMP: 50 EST: 1974
SQ FT: 60,000
SALES (est): 6MM **Privately Held**
SIC: 7389 5013 Packaging & labeling services; motorcycle parts

(P-18729)
WOLFGANG ENTERPRISE INC
Also Called: Fh Packaging
13977 The Merge St Unit B, Eastvale (92880-3860)
PHONE....................951 848-7680
Gang Wu, *CEO*
William Kittinger, *Officer*
EMP: 15 EST: 2014

SALES (est): 1.7MM **Privately Held**
WEB: www.fhpkg.com
SIC: 7389 3221 5199 Packaging & labeling services; glass containers bottles for packing, bottling & canning; glass; packaging materials

(P-18730)
WORLDLINK LLC (PA)
Also Called: Worldlink East
6100 Wilshire Blvd # 1400, Los Angeles (90048-5111)
PHONE....................323 866-5900
Toni E Knight, *Mng Member*
Ryan Brommer, *Sales Staff*
Rex Janechuti, *Sales Staff*
Gary Jenkins, *Sales Staff*
Ryan Schumaker, *Sales Staff*
EMP: 60 EST: 1997
SQ FT: 20,000
SALES (est): 9.7MM **Privately Held**
WEB: www.worldlinkmedia.com
SIC: 7389 Personal service agents, brokers & bureaus

(P-18731)
YELLOWPAGESCOM LLC (DH)
Also Called: Dexyp
611 N Brand Blvd Ste 500, Glendale (91203-3293)
PHONE....................818 937-5500
David Krantz,
Williams Clenney, *CFO*
Derek Wood, *Executive*
Brad Mohs, *CTO*
Alberto Mata, *Software Engr*
EMP: 260 EST: 2004
SALES (est): 48.1MM
SALES (corp-wide): 1.4B **Publicly Held**
WEB: www.anywho.com
SIC: 7389 Telephone directory distribution, contract or fee basis
HQ: Thryv, Inc.
2200 W Airfield Dr
Dfw Airport TX 75261
972 453-7000

(P-18732)
YOURTEX FASHIONS INC
2060 E Via Arado, Compton (90220-6112)
PHONE....................323 581-6600
Sam Oster, *President*
Joo Park, *Vice Pres*
EMP: 120 EST: 1984
SALES (est): 1.5MM **Privately Held**
SIC: 7389 Sewing contractor

(P-18733)
ZENITH AMERICAN SOLUTIONS INC
1325 N Grand Ave Ste 100, Covina (91724-4044)
PHONE....................626 732-2100
Alan P Fazer, *Branch Mgr*
EMP: 180
SALES (corp-wide): 1.23 **Privately Held**
WEB: www.zenith-american.com
SIC: 7389 8741 Financial services; administrative management
HQ: Zenith American Solutions, Inc.
302 Knights Run Ave # 1100
Tampa FL 33602
813 666-6900

7513 Truck Rental & Leasing, Without Drivers

(P-18734)
DART TRANSPORTATION SVC A CORP (PA)
Also Called: Dart Entities
1430 S Eastman Ave Ste 1, Commerce (90023-4096)
P.O. Box 23931, Los Angeles (90023-0931)
PHONE....................323 981-8205
Terrence Dedeaux, *President*
Ashok Aggarwal, *Treasurer*
Joseph M Medlin, *Vice Pres*
Larry Nelson, *Vice Pres*
James Hunter, *IT/INT Sup*
EMP: 236 EST: 1938
SQ FT: 800

SALES (est): 107.1MM **Privately Held**
WEB: www.dartentities.com
SIC: **7513** 6798 Truck leasing, without drivers; realty investment trusts

(P-18735)
PENSKE MOTOR GROUP LLC
2010 E Garvey Ave S, West Covina (91791-1911)
PHONE..................................626 859-1200
Glen Hightman, *Branch Mgr*
Harout Boyadjian, *General Mgr*
Ralph Cerulli, *General Mgr*
Evelyn Rivas, *Office Mgr*
Josh McIntyre, *Technician*
EMP: 377
SALES (corp-wide): 5.1B **Privately Held**
WEB: www.penskemotorgroup.com
SIC: **7513** 7538 Truck rental & leasing, no drivers; general automotive repair shops
HQ: Penske Motor Group, Llc
3534 Peck Rd
El Monte CA 91731

(P-18736)
ROLLINS LEASING LLC
Also Called: Rollins Truck Rental-Leasing
18305 Arenth Ave, City of Industry (91748-1226)
PHONE..................................626 913-7186
Dave Bettson, *Manager*
EMP: 90
SQ FT: 10,370
SALES (corp-wide): 5.1B **Privately Held**
WEB: www.baltimorehammondstruck-rental.com
SIC: **7513** Truck rental & leasing, no drivers
HQ: Rollins Leasing Llc
2200 Concord Pike
Wilmington DE 19803
302 426-2700

(P-18737)
RYDER INTGRTED LGSTICS CAL LLC
10641 Almond Ave, Fontana (92337-7154)
PHONE..................................909 356-8555
R E Sanchez, *President*
Robert E Sanchez, *President*
Trisha Summers, *Senior Mgr*
Amy Cook, *Manager*
EMP: 76 EST: 2010
SALES (est): 10.2MM
SALES (corp-wide): 2.1B **Publicly Held**
WEB: www.ryder.com
SIC: **7513** Truck rental, without drivers; truck leasing, without drivers
PA: Ryder System, Inc.
11690 Nw 105th St
Medley FL 33178
305 500-3726

(P-18738)
WESTRUX INTERNATIONAL INC (PA)
15555 Valley View Ave, Santa Fe Springs (90670-5718)
PHONE..................................562 404-1020
David M Kenney, *President*
John M Reynolds, *CFO*
Juan Vasquez, *Finance Mgr*
Tamara Ashbaker, *Asst Controller*
Tamara D Ashbaker, *Asst Controller*
▲ EMP: 70 EST: 1982
SALES (est): 135.2MM **Privately Held**
WEB: www.westrux.com
SIC: **5511** 5531 7513 7538 Trucks, tractors & trailers: new & used; truck equipment & parts; truck rental, without drivers; truck leasing, without drivers; truck engine repair, except industrial

7514 Passenger Car Rental

(P-18739)
ENTERPRISE RNT—CAR LOS ANGLES (DH)
333 City Blvd W Ste 1000, Orange (92868-5917)
PHONE..................................657 221-4400
Jack C Taylor, *Ch of Bd*
Pamela Nicholson, *COO*

William W Snyder, *CFO*
Andrew C Taylor, *Chairman*
Rose Langhorst, *Treasurer*
▲ EMP: 90 EST: 1957
SQ FT: 30,000
SALES (est): 755.1MM
SALES (corp-wide): 6.8B **Privately Held**
WEB: www.enterprise.com
SIC: **7514** 7513 5511 Rent-a-car service; truck rental & leasing, no drivers; trucks, tractors & trailers: new & used
HQ: Enterprise Holdings, Inc.
600 Corporate Park Dr
Saint Louis MO 63105
314 512-5000

(P-18740)
FOX RENT A CAR INC
325 Baker St, Costa Mesa (92626-4518)
PHONE..................................310 342-5155
Trent Dennis, *Branch Mgr*
EMP: 68
SALES (corp-wide): 7.7MM **Privately Held**
WEB: www.foxrentacar.com
SIC: **7514** Passenger car rental
HQ: Fox Rent A Car, Inc.
5500 W Century Blvd
Los Angeles CA 90045

(P-18741)
FOX RENT A CAR INC (HQ)
5500 W Century Blvd, Los Angeles (90045-5914)
PHONE..................................310 342-5155
Allen Rezapour, *President*
Mike Jaberi, *Treasurer*
Jose Giraldo, *Officer*
Joe Knight, *Exec VP*
Jerame Jackson, *Vice Pres*
EMP: 50 EST: 1989
SQ FT: 73,500
SALES (est): 101.7MM
SALES (corp-wide): 7.7MM **Privately Held**
WEB: www.foxrentacar.com
SIC: **7514** Passenger car rental
PA: Europcar Mobility Group
13 T Boulevard Berthier
Paris 75017
130 449-144

(P-18742)
HERTZ CLAIM MANAGEMENT CORP
2923 Bradley St Ste 190, Pasadena (91107-1502)
P.O. Box 7857, Burbank (91510)
PHONE..................................626 296-4760
Fax: 626 296-4799
EMP: 84
SALES (corp-wide): 8.8B **Publicly Held**
SIC: **7514** Rent-A-Car Service
HQ: Hertz Claim Management Corporation
8501 Williams Rd
Estero FL 06120
239 301-7000

(P-18743)
KEYSTONE FORD INC (PA)
12000 Firestone Blvd, Norwalk (90650-2907)
PHONE..................................562 868-0825
Norman P Stutzke, *President*
Paul Stutzke, *Treasurer*
Lamberto Colon, *Vice Pres*
EMP: 130 EST: 1968
SQ FT: 14,000
SALES (est): 30.5MM **Privately Held**
WEB: www.ford.com
SIC: **5511** 5531 7514 Automobiles, new & used; pickups, new & used; vans, new & used; automotive parts; rent-a-car service

(P-18744)
MIDWAY RENT A CAR INC
6225 W Century Blvd, Los Angeles (90045-5311)
PHONE..................................310 330-4600
George Garavullo, *Manager*
EMP: 51 **Privately Held**
WEB: www.midwaycarrental.com
SIC: **7514** Rent-a-car service

PA: Midway Rent A Car, Inc.
4751 Wilshire Blvd # 120
Los Angeles CA 90010

(P-18745)
MIDWAY RENT A CAR INC
11231 S La Cienega Blvd, Los Angeles (90045-6112)
PHONE..................................424 293-4855
EMP: 51 **Privately Held**
WEB: www.midwaycarrental.com
SIC: **7514** Rent-a-car service
PA: Midway Rent A Car, Inc.
4751 Wilshire Blvd # 120
Los Angeles CA 90010

(P-18746)
MIDWAY RENT A CAR INC
Also Called: Midway Clinic Cars
1800 S Sepulveda Blvd, Los Angeles (90025-4314)
PHONE..................................310 445-4355
Steve Rosen, *Manager*
Ben Hemmet, *Admin Asst*
Jeffrey Riesenberg, *Manager*
EMP: 51 **Privately Held**
WEB: www.midwaycarrental.com
SIC: **7514** Rent-a-car service
PA: Midway Rent A Car, Inc.
4751 Wilshire Blvd # 120
Los Angeles CA 90010

7515 Passenger Car Leasing

(P-18747)
ALLEN GWYNN CHEVROLET INC
1400 S Brand Blvd, Glendale (91204-2895)
PHONE..................................818 240-0000
Gwynn G Bacon, *President*
Steve Bacon, *Sales Mgr*
Chris Gouzoubachian, *Manager*
Tom Pina, *Manager*
Erick Cea, *Consultant*
EMP: 76 EST: 1930
SALES (est): 31.6MM **Privately Held**
WEB: www.lovemychevy.com
SIC: **5511** 7515 Automobiles, new & used; passenger car leasing

(P-18748)
CU VEHICLES LLC
20131 Prairie St B, Chatsworth (91311-6106)
PHONE..................................818 885-1226
Jean Faenza, *Exec VP*
Marisol Winetrs, *CFO*
Telesis Community Credit Union,
EMP: 65 EST: 2007
SALES (est): 4.1MM **Privately Held**
WEB: www.telesiscu.com
SIC: **5511** 7515 Automobiles, new & used; passenger car leasing
PA: Telesis Community Credit Union
9301 Winnetka Ave
Chatsworth CA 91311

(P-18749)
GEORGE CHEVROLET
17000 Lakewood Blvd, Bellflower (90706-5594)
PHONE..................................562 925-2500
Jeffery Estabrooks, *President*
Patricia Estabrooks, *Vice Pres*
Juana Araujo, *Finance Mgr*
Jilma Blanco, *Finance Mgr*
Blanco Jilma, *Finance Mgr*
EMP: 100 EST: 1961
SQ FT: 56,000
SALES (est): 37.6MM **Privately Held**
WEB: www.georgechevy.com
SIC: **5511** 7515 7538 Automobiles, new & used; passenger car leasing; general automotive repair shops

(P-18750)
LEO HOFFMAN CHEVROLET INC (PA)
Also Called: Puente Hills Chevrolet
17300 Gale Ave, City of Industry (91748-1512)
P.O. Box 90428 (91715-0428)
PHONE..................................626 968-8411
Thomas L Hoffman, *President*
Kurt Hoffman, *Treasurer*
Gary A Campbell, *Vice Pres*
EMP: 149 EST: 1944
SQ FT: 75,000
SALES (est): 38.5MM **Privately Held**
WEB: www.chevroletofpuentehills.com
SIC: **5511** 7515 Automobiles, new & used; passenger car leasing

(P-18751)
LOS FELIZ FORD INC (PA)
Also Called: Star Ford Lincoln Mercury
1101 S Brand Blvd, Glendale (91204-2313)
PHONE..................................818 502-1901
Steve Bussjaeger, *President*
Tad Okumoto, *Corp Secy*
Alex Tamez, *General Mgr*
Freddy Camacho, *Finance Mgr*
Agnes Gurida, *Accountant*
EMP: 80 EST: 1970
SQ FT: 75,000
SALES (est): 19MM **Privately Held**
WEB: www.starford.com
SIC: **5511** 7515 Automobiles, new & used; vans, new & used; pickups, new & used; passenger car leasing

(P-18752)
MIDWAY RENT A CAR INC
Also Called: Midway Car Rental
4201 Lankershim Blvd, North Hollywood (91602-2856)
PHONE..................................818 985-9770
Jeff Riesenberg, *Branch Mgr*
Mark Despres, *Vice Pres*
Caroline Kim, *Director*
Arbi Ghazarian, *Asst Mgr*
EMP: 51 **Privately Held**
WEB: www.midwaycarrental.com
SIC: **7515** 7514 Passenger car leasing; passenger car rental
PA: Midway Rent A Car, Inc.
4751 Wilshire Blvd # 120
Los Angeles CA 90010

(P-18753)
SELMAN CHEVROLET COMPANY
1800 E Chapman Ave, Orange (92867-7797)
P.O. Box 31 (92856-9031)
PHONE..................................714 633-3521
William H Selman Jr, *CEO*
William H Selman III, *Vice Pres*
Theresa Schaffer, *Office Mgr*
Daisy Kan, *Admin Sec*
Sonia Lamas, *Finance Dir*
EMP: 107 EST: 1951
SQ FT: 4,000
SALES (est): 44.9MM **Privately Held**
WEB: www.selmanchevy.com
SIC: **5511** 7515 Automobiles, new & used; passenger car leasing

(P-18754)
STERLING MOTORS LTD
Also Called: Sterling BMW
3000 W Coast Hwy, Newport Beach (92663-4004)
PHONE..................................949 645-5900
Wayne Minor, *CEO*
John Belanger, *President*
David Mattice, *CFO*
Steve Army, *Principal*
Vince Del RE, *Principal*
EMP: 80 EST: 1955
SQ FT: 27,000
SALES (est): 32.2MM **Privately Held**
WEB: www.sterlingbmw.com
SIC: **5511** 7515 Automobiles, new & used; passenger car leasing

7519 Utility Trailers & Recreational Vehicle Rental

(P-18755)
EL MONTE RENTS INC (HQ)
Also Called: El Monte Rv
12818 Firestone Blvd, Santa Fe Springs
(90670-5404)
PHONE...................................562 404-9300
Kenneth Schork, *CEO*
Todd Schork, *Vice Pres*
Mike Haugen, *General Mgr*
Annemarie De Cort, *Marketing Mgr*
Lynn Van Geene, *Marketing Mgr*
EMP: 110 **EST:** 1970
SALES (est): 53MM **Privately Held**
WEB: www.elmonterv.com
SIC: 7519 5561 Motor home rental; motor homes

7521 Automobile Parking Lots & Garages

(P-18756)
ACE PARKING MANAGEMENT INC
11500 W Olympic Blvd, Los Angeles
(90064-1524)
PHONE...................................310 575-3192
Vince Garrido, *Branch Mgr*
EMP: 53
SALES (corp-wide): 257.4MM **Privately Held**
WEB: www.aceparking.com
SIC: 7521 Parking lots
PA: Ace Parking Management, Inc.
   645 Ash St
   San Diego CA 92101
   619 233-6624

(P-18757)
ACE PARKING MANAGEMENT INC
18150 Von Karman Ave A, Irvine
(92612-7173)
PHONE...................................949 769-3696
Michael Schuster, *Owner*
EMP: 53
SALES (corp-wide): 257.4MM **Privately Held**
WEB: www.aceparking.com
SIC: 7521 Parking lots
PA: Ace Parking Management, Inc.
   645 Ash St
   San Diego CA 92101
   619 233-6624

(P-18758)
ACE PARKING MANAGEMENT INC
1221 Ocean Ave, Santa Monica
(90401-1034)
PHONE...................................310 393-9863
EMP: 53
SALES (corp-wide): 257.4MM **Privately Held**
WEB: www.aceparking.com
SIC: 7521 Parking lots; parking structure
PA: Ace Parking Management, Inc.
   645 Ash St
   San Diego CA 92101
   619 233-6624

(P-18759)
ACE PARKING MANAGEMENT INC
6200 W 98th St, Los Angeles (90045-5327)
PHONE...................................310 645-6025
EMP: 53
SALES (corp-wide): 257.4MM **Privately Held**
WEB: www.aceparking.com
SIC: 7521 Parking lots
PA: Ace Parking Management, Inc.
   645 Ash St
   San Diego CA 92101
   619 233-6624

(P-18760)
ACE PARKING MANAGEMENT INC
21500 Pacific Coast Hwy, Huntington
Beach (92648-5300)
PHONE...................................714 845-8000
Trevor Waiton, *Branch Mgr*
EMP: 53
SALES (corp-wide): 257.4MM **Privately Held**
WEB: www.aceparking.com
SIC: 7521 Parking lots
PA: Ace Parking Management, Inc.
   645 Ash St
   San Diego CA 92101
   619 233-6624

(P-18761)
ACE PARKING MANAGEMENT INC
610 Newport Center Dr # 50, Newport
Beach (92660-6419)
PHONE...................................949 724-0963
Scott Ashcraft, *Manager*
EMP: 53
SALES (corp-wide): 257.4MM **Privately Held**
WEB: www.aceparking.com
SIC: 7521 Parking lots
PA: Ace Parking Management, Inc.
   645 Ash St
   San Diego CA 92101
   619 233-6624

(P-18762)
ACE PARKING MANAGEMENT INC
332 W Broadway, Long Beach
(90802-4435)
PHONE...................................562 437-6700
Mark Ruiz, *Manager*
EMP: 53
SALES (corp-wide): 257.4MM **Privately Held**
WEB: www.aceparking.com
SIC: 7521 Parking lots
PA: Ace Parking Management, Inc.
   645 Ash St
   San Diego CA 92101
   619 233-6624

(P-18763)
AMERIPARK LLC
17165 Von Karman Ave # 110, Irvine
(92614-0905)
PHONE...................................949 279-7525
Josh Hess, *Branch Mgr*
EMP: 300
SALES (corp-wide): 1.7B **Privately Held**
WEB: www.ameripark.com
SIC: 7521 Parking lots
HQ: Ameripark, Llc
   233 Peachtree St Ne # 2600
   Atlanta GA 30303

(P-18764)
AUTOMATE PARKING INC
8405 Pershing Dr Ste 301, Playa Del Rey
(90293-7861)
PHONE...................................310 674-3396
EMP: 60
SQ FT: 1,000
SALES (est): 1MM **Privately Held**
SIC: 7521 Operates Parking Lots

(P-18765)
EVERPARK INC
3470 Wilshire Blvd # 940, Los Angeles
(90010-2207)
PHONE...................................310 987-6922
Alazar Asmamaw, *CEO*
Abbi Abebe, *COO*
Abiy Wouldgerema, *CFO*
EMP: 200 **EST:** 2007
SALES (est): 4.3MM **Privately Held**
WEB: www.everpark.com
SIC: 7521 Automobile parking

(P-18766)
IMPERIAL PARKING INDS INC (PA)
Also Called: I P I
6404 Wilshire Blvd B, Los Angeles
(90048-5501)
PHONE...................................323 651-5588
Ali Yeganeh, *President*
Paul Gnasso, *Vice Pres*
Jose Mazariego, *Manager*
Francisco Lira, *Accounts Mgr*
EMP: 91 **EST:** 1997
SALES (est): 6MM **Privately Held**
WEB: www.ipicorp.net
SIC: 7521 Parking lots

(P-18767)
L AND R AUTO PARKS INC
Also Called: Joe's Auto Parks
707 Wilshire Blvd # 4700, Los Angeles
(90017-3601)
PHONE...................................213 784-3018
Charles Bassett, *President*
Mark Funk, *CFO*
Gabriel Rubin, *Corp Secy*
Jeff Matsuno, *Vice Pres*
Jeff Lumer, *Opers Staff*
EMP: 250 **EST:** 1951
SQ FT: 5,000
SALES (est): 19.7MM **Privately Held**
WEB: www.joesautoparks.com
SIC: 7521 7542 7371 Parking lots; car-washes; computer software development & applications

(P-18768)
LRW INVESTMENTS LLC
Also Called: Wally Park
9700 Bellanca Ave, Los Angeles
(90045-5510)
PHONE...................................310 337-1944
Gilad Lumer, *Branch Mgr*
EMP: 58 **Privately Held**
SIC: 7521 Parking lots
PA: Lrw Investments Llc
   990 W 8th St Ste 600
   Los Angeles CA 90017

(P-18769)
MODERN PARKING INC
14110 Palawan Way, Marina Del Rey
(90292-6231)
PHONE...................................310 821-1081
Arisur Rahnan, *Principal*
EMP: 334 **Privately Held**
WEB: www.modernparking.com
SIC: 7521 Parking garage
PA: Modern Parking, Inc.
   303 S Union Ave Fl 1
   Los Angeles CA 90017

(P-18770)
PARKING COMPANY OF AMERICA
Also Called: Pcamp
3165 Garfield Ave, Commerce
(90040-3217)
PHONE...................................562 862-2118
Alex Martin Chaves Jr, *President*
Eric Chaves, *President*
Aaron Chaves, *Vice Pres*
John Watkins, *Vice Pres*
Lupe Alvarado, *Human Resources*
EMP: 100 **EST:** 1990
SALES (est): 8.9MM **Privately Held**
WEB: www.parkpca.com
SIC: 7521 Parking lots

(P-18771)
PARKING CONCEPTS INC
1020 W Civic Center Dr, Santa Ana
(92703-2303)
PHONE...................................714 543-5725
Gilbert Bernick, *Branch Mgr*
Adrian Gonzalez, *Manager*
EMP: 169
SALES (corp-wide): 42.5MM **Privately Held**
WEB: www.parkingconcepts.com
SIC: 7521 Parking lots

(P-18772)
PARKING CONCEPTS INC
1036 Broxton Ave, Los Angeles
(90024-2824)
PHONE...................................310 208-1611
Jorge Lopez, *Manager*
Angelica Urquizu, *Facilities Mgr*
David Martil, *Manager*
EMP: 169
SALES (corp-wide): 42.5MM **Privately Held**
WEB: www.parkingconcepts.com
SIC: 7521 Parking lots
PA: Parking Concepts, Inc.
   12 Mauchly Ste I
   Irvine CA 92618
   949 753-7525

(P-18773)
PARKING CONCEPTS INC
1801 Georgia St, Los Angeles
(90015-3477)
PHONE...................................213 746-5764
Bob Hindle, *Manager*
Richard Inthavong, *Accountant*
Steve Picard, *Director*
Ulla Bjorkqvist, *Manager*
EMP: 169
SALES (corp-wide): 42.5MM **Privately Held**
WEB: www.parkingconcepts.com
SIC: 7521 8748 Parking lots; traffic con-sultant
PA: Parking Concepts, Inc.
   12 Mauchly Ste I
   Irvine CA 92618
   949 753-7525

(P-18774)
PARKING CONCEPTS INC
14110 Palawan Way Lab, Venice
(90292-6231)
PHONE...................................310 821-1081
Frank Vargas, *General Mgr*
EMP: 169
SALES (corp-wide): 42.5MM **Privately Held**
WEB: www.parkingconcepts.com
SIC: 7521 8741 Parking lots; management services
PA: Parking Concepts, Inc.
   12 Mauchly Ste I
   Irvine CA 92618
   949 753-7525

(P-18775)
PARKING CONCEPTS INC
800 Wilshire Blvd, Los Angeles
(90017-2604)
PHONE...................................213 623-2661
Juan Cortes, *Branch Mgr*
David Martil, *Manager*
EMP: 169
SALES (corp-wide): 42.5MM **Privately Held**
WEB: www.parkingconcepts.com
SIC: 7521 Parking lots
PA: Parking Concepts, Inc.
   12 Mauchly Ste I
   Irvine CA 92618
   949 753-7525

(P-18776)
PARKING CONCEPTS INC
12001 Vista Del Mar, Playa Del Rey
(90293-8518)
PHONE...................................310 322-5008
Zahid Hossian, *Branch Mgr*
EMP: 169
SALES (corp-wide): 42.5MM **Privately Held**
WEB: www.parkingconcepts.com
SIC: 7521 Parking lots
PA: Parking Concepts, Inc.
   12 Mauchly Ste I
   Irvine CA 92618
   949 753-7525

▲ = Import ▼=Export
◆ =Import/Export

(P-18777)
PROFESSIONAL PARKING (DH)
2799 E 21st St, Signal Hill (90755-1007)
PHONE..............................714 722-0242
Ralph Caldin, *President*
EMP: 118 EST: 2009
SALES (est): 7.6MM **Privately Held**
WEB: www.professional-parking.com
SIC: 7521 Parking garage
HQ: Laz Parking Ltd, Llc
1 Financial Plz Fl 14
Hartford CT 06103
860 713-2030

(P-18778)
RESORT PARKING SERVICES INC
39755 Berkey Dr B, Palm Desert (92211-1106)
PHONE..............................760 328-4041
Mario Gardner, *President*
Richard Barnes, *CIO*
EMP: 120 EST: 1973
SQ FT: 1,100
SALES (est): 3.7MM **Privately Held**
WEB: www.resortparkingservices.com
SIC: 7521 7299 Parking lots; indoor parking services; personal item care & storage services

(P-18779)
SAFETYPARK CORPORATION (PA)
13420 Beach Ave, Marina Del Rey (90292-5624)
PHONE..............................310 899-0490
Lisane Menezes, *Vice Pres*
EMP: 132 EST: 2012
SALES (est): 6.2MM **Privately Held**
WEB: www.safetypark.net
SIC: 7521 Parking lots

(P-18780)
UNIFIED VALET PARKING INC
99 S Chester Ave Fl 2, Pasadena (91106-5805)
PHONE..............................818 822-5807
Mike Madjid Sabet, *President*
EMP: 57 EST: 2009
SALES (est): 1.5MM **Privately Held**
WEB: www.unifiedparking.com
SIC: 7521 Parking lots

(P-18781)
VALET PARKING SVC A CAL PARTNR (PA)
6933 Hollywood Blvd, Los Angeles (90028-6146)
PHONE..............................323 465-5873
Anthony Policella, *CEO*
EMP: 1268 EST: 1946
SQ FT: 10,000
SALES (est): 24.4MM **Privately Held**
WEB: www.valetparkingservice.com
SIC: 7521 7299 Parking lots; valet parking

7532 Top, Body & Upholstery Repair & Paint Shops

(P-18782)
ADVANTAGE FORD LINCOLN MERCURY
1031 Central Ave, Duarte (91010-2424)
PHONE..............................626 305-9188
Gary W Hoecker, *President*
Isela Orellana, *Business Mgr*
Jeff Piatt, *Finance*
Zareh Chiranian, *Sales Mgr*
Rick Covani, *Sales Mgr*
EMP: 97 EST: 1997
SQ FT: 20,280
SALES (est): 21.5MM **Privately Held**
WEB: www.advantageford.com
SIC: 5511 7532 Automobiles, new & used; top & body repair & paint shops

(P-18783)
ANAHEIM HILLS AUTO BODY INC
3500 E La Palma Ave, Anaheim (92806-2116)
PHONE..............................714 632-8266

Robert Smith, *President*
Patrick Smith, *Vice Pres*
Janelle Rogers, *Auditor*
Brian Sievers, *Facilities Mgr*
EMP: 60 EST: 1978
SQ FT: 33,000
SALES (est): 5.2MM **Privately Held**
WEB: www.anaheimhillsautobody.com
SIC: 7532 Body shop, automotive

(P-18784)
CALIBER BODYWORKS TEXAS INC
Also Called: Caliber Collision Centers
5 Auto Center Dr, Tustin (92782-8402)
PHONE..............................714 665-3905
David Adams, *Branch Mgr*
Justin Frost, *Manager*
EMP: 100
SALES (corp-wide): 824.4MM **Privately Held**
WEB: www.calibercollision.com
SIC: 7532 Body shop, automotive
PA: Caliber Bodyworks Of Texas, Inc.
2941 Lake Vista Dr
Lewisville TX 75067
469 948-9500

(P-18785)
CALIBER HOLDINGS CORPORATION
Also Called: Classic Collision Center 2
3020 Riverside Dr, Los Angeles (90039-2014)
P.O. Box 39437 (90039-0437)
PHONE..............................323 913-4000
Madjid Berenji, *Branch Mgr*
EMP: 60 **Privately Held**
WEB: www.calibercollision.com
SIC: 7532 Body shop, automotive
PA: Caliber Holdings Corporation
2941 Lake Vista Dr
Lewisville TX 75067

(P-18786)
CV & DA HOLDINGS INC (PA)
Also Called: Cerwin Vega & Diamond Audio
3761 S Hill St, Los Angeles (90007-4339)
PHONE..............................213 261-4161
Henry Razipour, *President*
▲ EMP: 62 EST: 2012
SQ FT: 5,000
SALES (est): 797.5K **Privately Held**
WEB: www.cerwinvegamobile.com
SIC: 7532 3651 Antique & classic automobile restoration; household audio equipment

(P-18787)
DEPENDABLE DODGE INC
21415 Roscoe Blvd, Canoga Park (91304-4162)
PHONE..............................818 883-9060
Ed Sternfeld Jr, *President*
Jonathan Booth, *Sales Staff*
Joe Garcia, *Sr Associate*
EMP: 50 EST: 1971
SQ FT: 5,000
SALES (est): 6.5MM **Privately Held**
WEB: www.depcdjr.com
SIC: 5511 7532 5531 7538 Automobiles, new & used; pickups, new & used; paint shop, automotive; automobile & truck equipment & parts; general automotive repair shops

(P-18788)
EL MONTE AUTOMOTIVE GROUP INC
Also Called: Longo Lexus
3530 Peck Rd, El Monte (91731-3526)
PHONE..............................626 580-6200
Greg Penske, *President*
Toni Kennedy, *Executive Asst*
Edgar Arriola, *Technician*
Fabian Cortes, *Technician*
David Lieu, *Technician*
EMP: 104 EST: 1989
SALES (est): 33.7MM **Privately Held**
WEB: www.longolexus.com
SIC: 5511 7532 7515 5521 Automobiles, new & used; top & body repair & paint shops; passenger car leasing; used car dealers; truck rental & leasing, no drivers; automobiles & other motor vehicles

(P-18789)
FAITH QUALITY AUTO BODY INC
41130 Nick Ln, Murrieta (92562-7012)
PHONE..............................951 698-8215
Lee Amaradio, *President*
EMP: 60 EST: 1979
SALES (est): 5.4MM **Privately Held**
WEB: www.faithqualityautobody.com
SIC: 7532 Body shop, automotive

(P-18790)
GENERAL MOTORS LLC
5350 Biloxi Ave, North Hollywood (91601-3531)
PHONE..............................818 752-6619
Phil Tanioka, *Branch Mgr*
Frank Saucedo, *Exec Dir*
Jeff Harbach, *Area Mgr*
Simone Thompson, *Engineer*
Tom Gordon, *Director*
EMP: 62 **Publicly Held**
WEB: www.gm.com
SIC: 7532 Top & body repair & paint shops
HQ: General Motors Llc
300 Renaissance Ctr L1
Detroit MI 48243

(P-18791)
HARRYS AUTO BODY INC
Also Called: Harry's Auto Collision
1013 S La Brea Ave, Los Angeles (90019-6902)
PHONE..............................323 933-4600
Harry Barseghian, *President*
Sally Courtois, *Marketing Staff*
Debbie Hall, *Director*
▲ EMP: 65 EST: 1979
SQ FT: 5,000
SALES (est): 7.1MM **Privately Held**
WEB: www.harryscollision.com
SIC: 7532 Body shop, automotive

(P-18792)
HOLMES BODY SHOP-ALHAMBRA
1130 E Main St, Alhambra (91801-4111)
PHONE..............................626 282-6173
Thomas V Holmes, *President*
EMP: 81 EST: 1992
SALES (est): 197.7K
SALES (corp-wide): 7.3MM **Privately Held**
WEB: www.holmesbodyshop.com
SIC: 7532 Body shop, automotive
PA: Holmes Body Shop-Alhambra, Inc.
466 Foothill Blvd
La Canada Flintridge CA 91011
626 795-6447

(P-18793)
HOLMES BODY SHOP-ALHAMBRA INC (PA)
466 Foothill Blvd, La Canada Flintridge (91011-3518)
PHONE..............................626 795-6447
Thomas V Holmes, *President*
EMP: 64 EST: 1970
SQ FT: 300,000
SALES (est): 7.3MM **Privately Held**
WEB: www.holmesbodyshop.com
SIC: 7532 Body shop, automotive; collision shops, automotive

(P-18794)
LABAYA BEACHCOMBER LP
3101 Sturgis Rd, Oxnard (93030-7791)
PHONE..............................805 278-6688
Daniel Mohr, *Managing Prtnr*
Edward Mohr, *Partner*
EMP: 50 EST: 2003
SQ FT: 25,000
SALES (est): 1.7MM **Privately Held**
SIC: 7532 Collision shops, automotive

(P-18795)
MAIMONE LIQUIDATING CORP (PA)
Also Called: Marco's Auto Body
1390 E Palm St, Altadena (91001-2042)
PHONE..............................626 286-5691
Marco G Maimone, *President*
Mike Gregorian, *President*
Lillian Maimone, *Treasurer*
Carl Canzano, *Vice Pres*

EMP: 100 EST: 1974
SQ FT: 14,000
SALES (est): 4.3MM **Privately Held**
WEB: www.serviceking.com
SIC: 7532 7539 Body shop, automotive; frame & front end repair services

(P-18796)
MOUNTAIN VIEW CHEVROLET INC
1079 W Foothill Blvd, Upland (91786-3731)
P.O. Box 758 (91785-0758)
PHONE..............................909 985-2866
Christopher Leggio, *President*
Christopher M Leggio, *President*
Nick Cacucciolo, *Vice Pres*
Amir Henin, *Finance Dir*
Yuri Hernandez, *Finance Mgr*
EMP: 54 EST: 1966
SQ FT: 14,000
SALES (est): 26.6MM **Privately Held**
WEB: www.mountainviewchevrolet.com
SIC: 5511 7532 Automobiles, new & used; top & body repair & paint shops

(P-18797)
PARK PLACE FORD LLC
555 W Foothill Blvd, Upland (91786-3853)
PHONE..............................909 946-5555
Timothy Park,
Ann Reid, *Office Mgr*
Basem Yousef, *Sales Staff*
Barbara Schilder, *Manager*
Vince Vanhook, *Manager*
EMP: 83 EST: 2012
SQ FT: 15,000
SALES (est): 23.8MM **Privately Held**
WEB: www.uplandford.com
SIC: 5511 7532 7549 5561 Automobiles, new & used; collision shops, automotive; emissions testing without repairs, automotive; inspection & diagnostic service, automotive; travel trailers: automobile, new & used

(P-18798)
PLATINUM PERFORMANCE INC
760 Mcmurray Rd, Buellton (93427-2510)
PHONE..............................800 553-2400
Kristin Peck, *CEO*
Kate Russo, *Director*
EMP: 80 EST: 1997
SALES (est): 590.6K **Privately Held**
WEB: www.platinumperformance.com
SIC: 7532 Body shop, automotive

(P-18799)
PRESTIGE AUTO COLLISION INC
23726 Via Fabricante, Mission Viejo (92691-3145)
PHONE..............................949 470-6031
Bernie Gates, *President*
Laurie Gates, *Treasurer*
Amy Beckner, *General Mgr*
EMP: 65 EST: 1984
SQ FT: 10,000
SALES (est): 7.4MM **Privately Held**
WEB: www.prestigeac.co
SIC: 7532 Body shop, automotive

(P-18800)
PRIDE COLLISION CENTERS INC (HQ)
Also Called: Pride Auto Body
7950 Haskell Ave, Van Nuys (91406-1923)
PHONE..............................818 909-0660
Randy Stabler, *President*
Robert Turchan, *Vice Pres*
Addie Silva, *Office Mgr*
EMP: 65 EST: 1982
SQ FT: 44,000
SALES (est): 9.7MM **Privately Held**
WEB: www.classiccollision.net
SIC: 7532 Body shop, automotive

(P-18801)
RANCHO FORD INC
26895 Ynez Rd, Temecula (92591-4695)
PHONE..............................951 699-1302
Eric Gosch, *President*
Marc L Gosch, *Vice Pres*
Issac Lizarrago, *General Mgr*
Keith Thamma, *Finance Mgr*
Jim Smith, *Foreman/Supr*

EMP: 124 EST: 1984
SQ FT: 40,000
SALES (est): 26.1MM **Privately Held**
WEB: www.goschfordtemecula.com
SIC: 5511 7532 7515 5521 Automobiles, new & used; top & body repair & paint shops; passenger car leasing; used car dealers

(P-18802)
REDLANDS FORD INC
1121 W Colton Ave, Redlands (92374-2935)
PHONE.................................909 793-3211
Steve Rojas, *CEO*
Tracey Hooper, *Treasurer*
Tina Abbott, *Finance Mgr*
Monica Alvarado, *Sales Staff*
Jay Yerman, *Sales Staff*
EMP: 85 EST: 2002
SALES (est): 14.9MM **Privately Held**
WEB: www.redlandsford.com
SIC: 7532 5511 Body shop, automotive; automobiles, new & used

(P-18803)
SEIDNER-MILLER INC
Also Called: Toyota of Glendora
1949 Auto Centre Dr, Glendora (91740-6714)
PHONE.................................909 305-2000
Murrey Seidner, *President*
Peter Miller, *Vice Pres*
Maria Fanning, *Manager*
EMP: 180 EST: 1993
SQ FT: 65,000
SALES (est): 41.5MM **Privately Held**
WEB: www.toyotaofglendora.com
SIC: 5511 7532 7515 5521 Automobiles, new & used; top & body repair & paint shops; passenger car leasing; used car dealers

(P-18804)
SHOWTIME CUSTOM COACH INC
2461 Deep Creek Dr, Running Springs (92382)
P.O. Box 2409 (92382-2409)
PHONE.................................909 867-7025
Armando Nava, *President*
Martha Nava, *Treasurer*
Lisa Makeig, *Admin Sec*
EMP: 34 EST: 1986
SQ FT: 7,000
SALES (est): 1.7MM **Privately Held**
WEB: www.showtimeautobody.com
SIC: 7532 3711 Collision shops, automotive; customizing services, non-factory basis; body shop, automotive; automobile assembly, including specialty automobiles

(P-18805)
STERLING COLLISION LLC (PA)
Also Called: Sea Breeze Collision
1111 Bell Ave Ste A, Tustin (92780-6463)
PHONE.................................714 259-1111
Ray Shaai, *General Ptnr*
Nancy Routtenberg, *Controller*
EMP: 65 EST: 1999
SALES (est): 5.7MM **Privately Held**
WEB: www.sterlingcollisioncenter.com
SIC: 7532 Body shop, automotive

(P-18806)
UNIVERSAL METAL PLATING (PA)
1526 W 1st St, Irwindale (91702-3201)
PHONE.................................626 969-7931
Jesus Martinez, *Partner*
EMP: 18 EST: 1978
SQ FT: 20,000
SALES (est): 1.8MM **Privately Held**
WEB: www.universalmetalplating.com
SIC: 7532 3471 Bump shops, automotive repair; plating of metals or formed products

(P-18807)
VILLA FORD INC
Also Called: David Wilson's Villa Ford
2550 N Tustin St, Orange (92865-3099)
PHONE.................................714 637-8222
Toll Free:.................................888
Peggy Baldwin-Butler, *President*
Karen Baldwin, *Treasurer*

Peggy Butler, *Treasurer*
Brian Butler, *Vice Pres*
Scott V Wade, *General Mgr*
EMP: 132 EST: 1970
SQ FT: 38,745
SALES (est): 42.5MM **Privately Held**
WEB: www.villaford.com
SIC: 5511 7532 7549 Automobiles, new & used; body shop, automotive; automotive maintenance services

(P-18808)
VOLKSWAGEN SANTA MONICA INC (PA)
Also Called: Lexus Santa Monica
2440 Santa Monica Blvd, Santa Monica (90404-2039)
PHONE.................................310 829-1888
Toll Free:.................................888
Michael Sullivan, *President*
Hazel R Sullivan, *CEO*
Kerry Sullivan, *Treasurer*
Jeff La Plant, *Vice Pres*
Liz Kennedy, *Executive Asst*
EMP: 170 EST: 1964
SQ FT: 10,000
SALES (est): 95.7MM **Privately Held**
WEB: www.volkswagensantamonica.com
SIC: 5511 7532 7538 Automobiles, new & used; body shop, automotive; general automotive repair shops

---

7534 Tire Retreading & Repair Shops

(P-18809)
BRIDGESTONE AMERICAS
Also Called: GCR Tires & Service 185
14521 Hawthorne Ave, Fontana (92335-2508)
PHONE.................................909 770-8523
EMP: 89 **Privately Held**
WEB: www.bridgestoneamericas.com
SIC: 7534 5531 Tire repair shop; automotive tires
HQ: Bridgestone Americas Tire Operations, Llc
200 4th Ave S Ste 100
Nashville TN 37201
615 937-1000

(P-18810)
SANTA MARIA TIRE INC (PA)
Also Called: SM Tire
2170 Hutton Rd Bldg A, Nipomo (93444-9717)
P.O. Box 6007, Santa Maria (93456-6007)
PHONE.................................805 347-4793
Craig Stephens, *President*
Cameron Stephens, *CEO*
Brenee Stephens, *Corp Secy*
C Kent Stephens, *Vice Pres*
Scott Carranza, *Branch Mgr*
EMP: 75 EST: 1946
SALES (est): 20.6MM **Privately Held**
WEB: www.goodyear.com
SIC: 5531 7534 Automotive tires; rebuilding & retreading tires; tire repair shop

---

7537 Automotive Transmission Repair Shops

(P-18811)
H & A TRANSMISSIONS INC
8727 Rochester Ave, Rancho Cucamonga (91730-4908)
PHONE.................................909 941-9020
Gilbert H Dickason, *CEO*
Corina Dickason, *CFO*
Carol Sprague, *Human Res Mgr*
▲ EMP: 26 EST: 1992
SQ FT: 3,500
SALES (est): 6MM **Privately Held**
WEB: www.handatrans.com
SIC: 7537 3714 Automotive transmission repair shops; axle housings & shafts, motor vehicle

---

7538 General Automotive Repair Shop

(P-18812)
10-8 RETROFIT INC
415 W Main St, Ontario (91762-3845)
PHONE.................................909 986-5551
Daniel Keenan, *President*
Jerry Keenan, *Principal*
Mario Montes, *Sales Mgr*
EMP: 15 EST: 2000
SQ FT: 6,800
SALES (est): 2.1MM **Privately Held**
WEB: www.10-8retrofit.com
SIC: 7538 3711 5087 General automotive repair shops; ambulances (motor vehicles), assembly of; service establishment equipment

(P-18813)
ALLIED LUBE INC
Also Called: Jiffy Lube
3087 Edinger Ave, Tustin (92780-7240)
PHONE.................................949 651-8814
Lillian Kline, *Accountant*
EMP: 99 **Privately Held**
WEB: www.jiffylube.com
SIC: 7538 7549 General automotive repair shops; lubrication service, automotive
PA: Allied Lube, Inc.
27240 La Paz Rd
Mission Viejo CA 92692

(P-18814)
ATV INC (PA)
Also Called: American Tire Depot
4490 Ayers Ave, Vernon (90058-4317)
PHONE.................................562 977-8565
ARA Tchaghlassian, *President*
Craig Anderson, *CFO*
Shant Halajian, *Opers Staff*
◆ EMP: 70 EST: 1994
SQ FT: 15,000
SALES (est): 265.9MM **Privately Held**
WEB: www.americantiredepot.com
SIC: 5531 7538 Automotive tires; general automotive repair shops

(P-18815)
CABE BROTHERS
Also Called: Cabe Toyota
2895 Long Beach Blvd, Long Beach (90806-1533)
PHONE.................................562 595-7411
John Cabe, *President*
Glenda Favilla, *Treasurer*
Marilyn Gidden, *Vice Pres*
Myra Cabe, *Admin Sec*
Phil Henry, *Administration*
EMP: 81 EST: 1956
SQ FT: 11,080
SALES (est): 40.6MM **Privately Held**
WEB: www.cabetoyota.com
SIC: 5511 7538 Automobiles, new & used; general automotive repair shops

(P-18816)
CENTRAL CALIFORNIA POWER
19487 Broken Ct, Shafter (93263-3146)
P.O. Box 1934, Bakersfield (93303-1934)
PHONE.................................661 589-2870
Rhoderick E Headley, *CEO*
Blake Headley, *Vice Pres*
Jaime Moreno, *Manager*
Larry Rouell, *Manager*
Raul Portugal, *Consultant*
EMP: 25 EST: 1982
SQ FT: 15,000
SALES (est): 10.4MM **Privately Held**
WEB: www.gensets.com
SIC: 7538 7359 3569 Truck engine repair, except industrial; equipment rental & leasing; gas generators

(P-18817)
CENTURY WEST BMW
4245 Lankershim Blvd, North Hollywood (91602-2802)
PHONE.................................818 432-5800
Dennis Lin, *President*
Monique Vasquez, *Business Mgr*
Quyen Le, *Finance Mgr*
Jarod Loux, *Finance Mgr*

Dixie Stanton, *Controller*
EMP: 92 EST: 1995
SALES (est): 30.8MM **Privately Held**
WEB: www.centurywestbmw.com
SIC: 5511 7538 Automobiles, new & used; general automotive repair shops

(P-18818)
CITRUS MOTORS ONTARIO INC (PA)
Also Called: Citrus Ford
1375 S Woodruff Way, Ontario (91761-2233)
P.O. Box 4270 (91761-8970)
PHONE.................................909 390-0930
Dennis Shannon, *President*
Alice Van Dentoorn, *Vice Pres*
Traci Ramos, *Office Admin*
Francisco Luna, *Finance Asst*
Lisa Ford, *Human Resources*
EMP: 218 EST: 1950
SALES (est): 54.3MM **Privately Held**
WEB: www.citrusmotors.com
SIC: 5511 7538 Automobiles, new & used; general automotive repair shops

(P-18819)
CJM AUTOMOTIVE GROUP INC
Also Called: Bakersfield Mazda
3101 Cattle Dr, Bakersfield (93313-2604)
P.O. Box 41117 (93384-1117)
PHONE.................................661 832-3000
Masoud Bashirtash, *President*
Farhad Bashirtash, *Treasurer*
Ali Reza Bashirtash, *Executive*
Alex Kargaran, *General Mgr*
James Haddad, *Admin Sec*
EMP: 70 EST: 1960
SALES (est): 24.3MM **Privately Held**
WEB: www.nissanusa.com
SIC: 5511 7538 Automobiles, new & used; pickups, new & used; general automotive repair shops

(P-18820)
D C H CALIFORNIA MOTORS INC
Also Called: Toyota of Oxnard
1631 Auto Center Dr, Oxnard (93036-8972)
PHONE.................................805 988-7900
Shau-Wai Lam, *President*
John Hautman, *General Mgr*
Lee Jaitt, *Finance Mgr*
Andres Santander, *Finance Mgr*
Oscar Gutierrez, *Sales Mgr*
EMP: 95 EST: 1991
SALES (est): 21.7MM
SALES (corp-wide): 13.1B **Publicly Held**
WEB: www.toyota.com
SIC: 5511 7538 7532 Automobiles, new & used; general automotive repair shops; top & body repair & paint shops
HQ: Dch North America Inc.
955 Rt 9 N
South Amboy NJ
732 727-9168

(P-18821)
D LONGO INC
Also Called: Longo Scion
3534 Peck Rd, El Monte (91731-3526)
PHONE.................................626 580-6000
Greg Penske, *President*
Daniel Pineda, *General Mgr*
Denise Pineda, *Executive Asst*
Adrian Hernandez, *Information Mgr*
Jeffrey Chang, *Web Dvlpr*
EMP: 380 EST: 1967
SALES (est): 168.5MM
SALES (corp-wide): 5.1B **Privately Held**
WEB: www.longotoyota.com
SIC: 5511 7538 Automobiles, new & used; general automotive repair shops
PA: Penske Corporation
2555 S Telegraph Rd
Bloomfield Hills MI 48302
248 648-2000

(P-18822)
DAVID A CAMPBELL CORPORATION
Also Called: B M W of Riverside
3060 Adams St, Riverside (92504-4014)
P.O. Box 4007 (92514-4007)
PHONE.................................951 785-4444
Allen David Franklin, *CEO*
Patrick Smith, *Officer*

Patrick Campbell, *Vice Pres*
Steven Campbell, *Vice Pres*
Gidget Santoliquido, *Executive Asst*
EMP: 150 **EST:** 1975
SQ FT: 45,000
SALES (est): 28.1MM **Privately Held**
WEB: www.bmwgroup.com
SIC: 5511 7538 Automobiles, new & used;
general automotive repair shops

(P-18823)
DCH GARDENA HONDA
15541 S Western Ave, Gardena
(90249-4320)
P.O. Box 3220 (90247-1420)
PHONE..................................310 515-5700
Shauwai Lam, *Principal*
Raul Alarcon, *Sales Staff*
Charles Fisher, *Sales Staff*
Fernando Padilla, *Sales Staff*
Yim Hom,
EMP: 140 **EST:** 1979
SQ FT: 290,000
SALES (est): 45.2MM
SALES (corp-wide): 13.1B **Publicly Held**
WEB: www.gardenahonda.com
SIC: 5511 7538 Automobiles, new & used;
general automotive repair shops
HQ: Dch North America Inc.
955 Rt 9 N
South Amboy NJ
732 727-9168

(P-18824)
DICK DEWESE CHEVROLET INC
Also Called: Tom Bell Chevrolet
800 Alabama St, Redlands (92374-2806)
PHONE..................................909 793-2681
Tom O Bell, *President*
Lynn Drysdale, *Corp Secy*
Derek Hanson, *Vice Pres*
Jessica Hosino, *Office Mgr*
Jonathan Pease, *Finance Dir*
EMP: 102 **EST:** 1951
SQ FT: 10,000
SALES (est): 32.8MM **Privately Held**
WEB: www.tombellchevrolet.com
SIC: 5511 7538 5531 5521 Automobiles,
new & used; general automotive repair
shops; automotive & home supply stores;
used car dealers

(P-18825)
EZ LUBE LLC
24043 Hawthorne Blvd, Torrance
(90505-5901)
PHONE..................................310 791-8480
Alex Gomez, *Branch Mgr*
EMP: 84
SALES (corp-wide): 22.5MM **Privately
Held**
WEB: www.vioc.com
SIC: 7538 7549 General automotive repair
shops; lubrication service, automotive
PA: Ez Lube, Llc
3540 Howard Way Ste 200
Costa Mesa CA

(P-18826)
FAA BEVERLY HILLS INC
Also Called: Beverly Hills BMW
5070 Wilshire Blvd, Los Angeles
(90036-4381)
PHONE..................................323 801-1430
Step Jones, *General Mgr*
Sandra Cooper, *Executive*
Sandy Cooper, *Executive*
Sean Ramezani, *General Mgr*
Michelle Pinkston, *Controller*
EMP: 85 **EST:** 1991
SQ FT: 4,000
SALES (est): 28.5MM
SALES (corp-wide): 9.7B **Publicly Held**
WEB: www.bmwofbeverlyhills.com
SIC: 5511 7538 Automobiles, new & used;
general automotive repair shops
PA: Sonic Automotive, Inc.
4401 Colwick Rd
Charlotte NC 28211
704 566-2400

(P-18827)
FELIX CHEVROLET LP (PA)
714 W Olympic Blvd Ste 11, Los Angeles
(90015-1425)
PHONE..................................213 748-6141
Nicholas N Shammas, *Partner*
George Damaa, *Partner*
EMP: 113 **EST:** 1921
SALES (est): 62.3MM **Privately Held**
WEB: www.felixchevrolet.com
SIC: 5511 7538 7532 5531 Automobiles,
new & used; general automotive repair
shops; top & body repair & paint shops;
automotive & home supply stores; pas-
senger car leasing

(P-18828)
FIESTA FORD INC
Also Called: Fiesta Ford Lincoln-Mercury
79015 Avenue 40, Indio (92203-9499)
PHONE..................................760 775-7777
Paul J Thiel, *CEO*
EMP: 126 **EST:** 1966
SQ FT: 304,920
SALES (est): 42.2MM **Privately Held**
WEB: www.fiestafordinc.com
SIC: 5511 7538 Automobiles, new & used;
general automotive repair shops

(P-18829)
FORD OF SIMI VALLEY INC
2440 1st St, Simi Valley (93065-0916)
PHONE..................................805 583-0333
Larry Hibbler, *President*
Kathleen Lindsey, *Admin Sec*
Chris Gomar, *Technology*
EMP: 70 **EST:** 2001
SQ FT: 28,000
SALES (est): 30.3MM **Privately Held**
WEB: www.simivalleyford.net
SIC: 5511 7538 Automobiles, new & used;
general automotive repair shops

(P-18830)
FORTRESS RESOURCES LLC (HQ)
Also Called: Royal Truck Body
24200 Main St, Carson (90745-6325)
PHONE..................................562 633-9951
Daryl Adams, *President*
John Campbell, *Purch Mgr*
EMP: 142 **EST:** 2009
SQ FT: 53,000
SALES (est): 10.6MM
SALES (corp-wide): 146.2MM **Publicly
Held**
WEB: www.royaltruckbody.com
SIC: 7538 General truck repair
PA: The Shyft Group Inc
41280 Bridge St
Novi MI 48375
517 543-6400

(P-18831)
FOX HILLS AUTO INC (PA)
Also Called: Airport Marina Ford
5880 W Centinela Ave, Los Angeles
(90045-1504)
PHONE..................................310 649-3673
Norris J Bishton Jr, *CEO*
Doug Goodrow, *General Mgr*
Dan Theroux, *General Mgr*
Jose Villapando, *CIO*
Jay Felix, *Finance Mgr*
▲ **EMP:** 140 **EST:** 1989
SQ FT: 35,000
SALES (est): 70MM **Privately Held**
WEB: www.quicklane.com
SIC: 5511 7538 5531 5521 Automobiles,
new & used; general automotive repair
shops; automotive & home supply stores;
used car dealers

(P-18832)
GALPIN MOTORS INC (PA)
Also Called: Galpin Ford
15505 Roscoe Blvd, North Hills
(91343-6598)
PHONE..................................818 787-3800
Herbert F Boeckman II, *President*
Jane Boeckmann, *Treasurer*
Brad Boeckmann, *Vice Pres*
Bradley M Boeckmann, *Vice Pres*
Karl L Boeckmann, *Vice Pres*
▼ **EMP:** 500 **EST:** 1946
SQ FT: 175,000

SALES (est): 372.2MM **Privately Held**
WEB: www.galpin.com
SIC: 5511 7538 7515 Automobiles,
new & used; used car dealers; general
automotive repair shops; passenger car
leasing; passenger car rental; automotive
& home supply stores

(P-18833)
GIANT INLAND EMPIRE RV CTR INC (PA)
Also Called: Giant Rv
9150 Benson Ave, Montclair (91763-1688)
PHONE..................................909 981-0444
Behzad Barouti, *CEO*
Nasser Etebar, *Treasurer*
Mellanie Ingle, *Vice Pres*
Robert Barouti, *Branch Mgr*
Dick Torres, *General Mgr*
EMP: 125 **EST:** 1986
SQ FT: 50,000
SALES (est): 64MM **Privately Held**
WEB: www.giantrv.com
SIC: 5561 7538 Recreational vehicle parts
& accessories; recreational vehicle re-
pairs

(P-18834)
GIBBS INTERNATIONAL INC (PA)
Also Called: Gibbs International Truck Ctrs
2201 Ventura Blvd, Oxnard (93036-7902)
P.O. Box 5206 (93031-5206)
PHONE..................................805 485-0551
Edward A Gibbs, *President*
Scott Wittwer, *General Mgr*
Mark S Rapin, *Sales Mgr*
John Limoli, *Sales Staff*
George Wishart, *Sales Staff*
EMP: 83 **EST:** 1970
SQ FT: 25,000
SALES (est): 24.8MM **Privately Held**
WEB: www.gibbstrucks.com
SIC: 7538 5511 4212 Truck engine repair,
except industrial; trucks, tractors & trail-
ers: new & used; local trucking, without
storage

(P-18835)
GPI CA-NIII INC
Also Called: Performance Nissan
1434 Buena Vista St, Duarte (91010-2402)
PHONE..................................626 305-3000
John C Rickel, *CEO*
Frank Grese Jr, *Principal*
EMP: 68 **EST:** 1991
SALES (est): 3MM **Publicly Held**
WEB: www.nissanofduarte.com
SIC: 5511 7538 7515 5531 Automobiles,
new & used; general automotive repair
shops; passenger car leasing; automotive
& home supply stores
PA: Group 1 Automotive, Inc.
800 Gessner Rd Ste 500
Houston TX 77024

(P-18836)
GREGORY CONSULTING INC (PA)
6350 Leland St, Ventura (93003-8585)
PHONE..................................805 642-0111
Toll Free:..................................888
Robert Gregory, *President*
Nancy Gregory, *Vice Pres*
EMP: 135 **EST:** 1986
SQ FT: 54,000
SALES (est): 12MM **Privately Held**
WEB: www.paradisechevrolet.com
SIC: 5511 7538 5521 Automobiles, new &
used; general automotive repair shops;
used car dealers

(P-18837)
GRIMMWAY ENTERPRISES INC
2171 W Bannister Rd, Brawley
(92227-9653)
PHONE..................................760 344-0204
Cheryl Chaney, *Principal*
EMP: 242
SALES (corp-wide): 1.8B **Privately Held**
WEB: www.grimmway.com
SIC: 7538 General automotive repair
shops

PA: Grimmway Enterprises, Inc.
14141 Di Giorgio Rd
Arvin CA 93203
800 301-3101

(P-18838)
H W HUNTER INC (PA)
Also Called: Hunter Dodge Chrysler Jeep
Ram
1130 Auto Mall Dr, Lancaster (93534-6302)
PHONE..................................661 948-8411
Timothy H Fuller, *CEO*
Gus Briones, *General Mgr*
Bethany Curtin, *Office Mgr*
Sean Rodgers, *Finance Mgr*
Mark Greenwald, *Finance*
EMP: 80 **EST:** 1956
SQ FT: 5,000
SALES (est): 84MM **Privately Held**
WEB: www.hunterdodgechryslerjeep.net
SIC: 5511 7538 Automobiles, new & used;
pickups, new & used; general automotive
repair shops

(P-18839)
HABERFELDE FORD (PA)
Also Called: Jim Burke Ford
2001 Oak St, Bakersfield (93301-3010)
P.O. Box 2088 (93303-2088)
PHONE..................................661 328-3600
Daniel George Hay, *President*
Beverly Burke, *Corp Secy*
Joe Hay, *Corp Secy*
Troy Fringer, *Vice Pres*
Michelle Hay, *Vice Pres*
EMP: 246 **EST:** 1913
SQ FT: 102,000
SALES (est): 50.5MM **Privately Held**
WEB: www.quicklane.com
SIC: 5511 7538 Automobiles, new & used;
pickups, new & used; general automotive
repair shops

(P-18840)
HABERFELDE FORD
Also Called: Jim Burke Ford
5300 Gasoline Alley Dr, Bakersfield
(93313-3213)
PHONE..................................661 837-6400
Joe Hay, *Branch Mgr*
Maria Paine, *Vice Pres*
Sathi Sanghera, *Sales Executive*
Temo Martinez, *Sales Mgr*
Chad Yost, *Sales Associate*
EMP: 54
SALES (corp-wide): 50.5MM **Privately
Held**
WEB: www.quicklane.com
SIC: 5511 7538 Automobiles, new & used;
general automotive repair shops
PA: Ford Haberfelde
2001 Oak St
Bakersfield CA 93301
661 328-3600

(P-18841)
HAMBLINS BDY PNT FRAME SP INC
Also Called: Hamblin's Auto & Body Shop
7590 Cypress Ave, Riverside (92503-1904)
PHONE..................................951 689-8440
Rod Perry, *President*
EMP: 70 **EST:** 1965
SALES (est): 5.8MM **Privately Held**
WEB: www.hamblinsbodyandpaint.com
SIC: 7538 7532 General automotive repair
shops; body shop, automotive

(P-18842)
JACK GOSCH FORD INC
Also Called: Gosch Ford Lincoln Mercury
150 Carriage Cir, Hemet (92545-9610)
PHONE..................................951 658-3181
Jack E Gosch, *President*
Mark E Gosch, *President*
Richard Rodgers, *CFO*
Eric Gosch, *Vice Pres*
Marc Gosch, *Admin Sec*
EMP: 100 **EST:** 1964
SQ FT: 35,000
SALES (est): 38.3MM **Privately Held**
WEB: www.goschauto.com
SIC: 5511 7538 Automobiles, new & used;
general automotive repair shops

(P-18843)
JEEP CHRYSLER OF ONTARIO
Also Called: Jeep Chrysler Ddge Ram Ontario
1202 Auto Center Dr, Ontario (91761-2208)
PHONE............................909 390-9898
Richard D Romero, *Ch of Bd*
R J Romero, *President*
Kathy Brown, *CFO*
Valerie Romero, *Vice Pres*
J B Butterwick, *Admin Sec*
EMP: 95 EST: 1993
SQ FT: 30,000
SALES (est): 18.5MM **Privately Held**
WEB: www.jcofontario.com
SIC: 5511 7538 5531 Automobiles, new & used; general automotive repair shops; automotive & home supply stores

(P-18844)
JOHNSON FORD (PA)
Also Called: Antelope Valley Lincoln
1155 Auto Mall Dr, Lancaster (93534-5867)
PHONE............................888 483-0454
Michael H Johnson, *President*
Doug Killebrew, *General Mgr*
Ramsey Esteva, *Sales Mgr*
Bob Heninger, *Sales Mgr*
Christian Mejia, *Sales Staff*
EMP: 120 EST: 1957
SQ FT: 70,000
SALES (est): 58.4MM **Privately Held**
WEB: www.diamondfordav.com
SIC: 5511 7538 5561 Automobiles, new & used; general automotive repair shops; camper & travel trailer dealers

(P-18845)
JURUPA UNIFIED SCHOOL DISTRICT
Riverside Ca 92509, Riverside (92509)
PHONE............................951 222-7756
Benita Roberts, *Superintendent*
EMP: 61
SALES (corp-wide): 287.2MM **Privately Held**
SIC: 8211 7538 Public elementary school; general automotive repair shops
PA: Jurupa Unified School District
4850 Pedley Rd
Jurupa Valley CA 92509
951 360-4100

(P-18846)
JVAC INC
Also Called: Keller Lincoln Ford
1073 Cadillac Ln, Hanford (93230-4966)
PHONE............................559 584-5531
Jon Keller, *President*
Valerie Keller, *Vice Pres*
EMP: 70 EST: 2008
SALES (est): 14.3MM **Privately Held**
WEB: www.quicklane.com
SIC: 5511 7538 Automobiles, new & used; general automotive repair shops

(P-18847)
KEN GRODY REDLANDS LLC
Also Called: Ken Grody Ford - Redlands
1121 W Colton Ave, Redlands (92374-2935)
PHONE............................909 793-3211
Ken Grody,
Brandi Desherlia,
William Raymond,
EMP: 85 EST: 2019
SALES (est): 16.8MM **Privately Held**
WEB: www.kengrodyfordinlandempire.com
SIC: 5511 7538 New & used car dealers; general automotive repair shops

(P-18848)
KEYES MOTORS INC (PA)
Also Called: Keyes Toyota
5855 Van Nuys Blvd, Van Nuys (91401-4219)
PHONE............................818 782-0122
Howard Keyes, *President*
Lawrence Abramson, *Vice Pres*
Jim Sarvey, *General Mgr*
Andrew Carl, *Technology*
Anna Ramirez, *Business Mgr*
EMP: 80 EST: 1968
SQ FT: 20,000

SALES (est): 75.8MM **Privately Held**
WEB: www.keyestoyota.com
SIC: 5511 7538 5531 5012 Automobiles, new & used; general automotive repair shops; passenger car leasing; automobiles & other motor vehicles

(P-18849)
KEYLEX INC (PA)
Also Called: Keyes Lexus
5905 Van Nuys Blvd, Van Nuys (91401-3624)
PHONE............................818 379-4000
Howard Keyes, *President*
Vivian Fowler, *Finance Dir*
Russell Roshandel, *Finance Dir*
Marina Sanusi, *Finance Mgr*
Alex Ayyoub, *Sales Mgr*
EMP: 89 EST: 1989
SQ FT: 32,376
SALES (est): 56.7MM **Privately Held**
WEB: www.lexus.com
SIC: 5511 7538 5531 Automobiles, new & used; general automotive repair shops; passenger car leasing; automotive & home supply stores

(P-18850)
KIRBY OLDSMOBILE
Also Called: Kirby Jeep-Eagle Suzuki
6424 Auto Center Dr, Ventura (93003-7289)
PHONE............................805 644-2241
John W Kirby, *President*
Chet Bredemeier, *CFO*
Jeffrey Sukay, *Vice Pres*
Miguel Hurtado, *Consultant*
EMP: 55 EST: 1966
SQ FT: 10,000
SALES (est): 21.5MM **Privately Held**
WEB: www.kirbycollision.com
SIC: 5511 7538 Automobiles, new & used; general automotive repair shops

(P-18851)
LANCASTER CMNTY SVCS FNDTION I
Also Called: Development Services
46008 7th St W, Lancaster (93534-7602)
PHONE............................661 723-6230
Randy Williams, *Manager*
EMP: 200 **Privately Held**
WEB: www.cityoflancasterca.org
SIC: 7538 9111 General automotive repair shops; mayors' offices
PA: The Lancaster Community Services Foundation Inc
44933 Fern Ave
Lancaster CA 93534
661 723-6000

(P-18852)
MAGIC ACQUISITION CORP
Also Called: Autonation Ford Valencia
23920 Creekside Rd, Valencia (91355-1701)
PHONE............................661 382-4700
Chance Corbitt, *Manager*
Mark Leccompte, *Controller*
EMP: 350 EST: 1996
SALES (est): 71.8MM
SALES (corp-wide): 20.3B **Publicly Held**
WEB: www.autonation.com
SIC: 5511 7538 5531 New & used car dealers; general automotive repair shops; automotive & home supply stores
HQ: Magic Acquisition Holding, Llc
200 Sw 1st Ave
Fort Lauderdale FL 33301
954 769-7000

(P-18853)
MARTIN AUTOMOTIVE INC
Also Called: Glendora Chevrolet
1959 Auto Centre Dr, Glendora (91740-6714)
PHONE............................909 394-9899
Michael W Martin, *CEO*
Melissa Alvarez, *Controller*
EMP: 65 EST: 2014
SALES (est): 2.7MM **Privately Held**
WEB: www.martinautomotivegroup.com
SIC: 7538 General automotive repair shops

(P-18854)
MARTIN CHEVROLET
23505 Hawthorne Blvd, Torrance (90505-4739)
P.O. Box 2895 (90509-2895)
PHONE............................323 772-6494
Toll Free:............................888 -
Joe Giacomin, *President*
Fran Williams, *Corp Secy*
Lewis Cook, *General Mgr*
Raul Ruiz, *Finance Mgr*
Milian Andy, *Sales Mgr*
EMP: 100 EST: 1947
SQ FT: 10,000
SALES (est): 28.9MM **Privately Held**
WEB: www.martinchevrolet.com
SIC: 5511 7538 Automobiles, new & used; general automotive repair shops

(P-18855)
MILLER AUTOMOTIVE GROUP INC (HQ)
Also Called: Miller Nissan
5425 Van Nuys Blvd, Sherman Oaks (91401-5628)
PHONE............................818 787-8400
Fred Miller, *Ch of Bd*
Michael Miller, *President*
Doug Stewart, *CFO*
Mark Miller, *Vice Pres*
Dante Ayala, *Finance Mgr*
▲ EMP: 350 EST: 1989
SQ FT: 40,000
SALES (est): 138.9MM **Publicly Held**
WEB: www.nissanofvannuys.com
SIC: 5511 7538 5521 Automobiles, new & used; general automotive repair shops; automobiles, used cars only

(P-18856)
MISSION SERVICE INC
1800 Avenue Of The Stars # 1400, Los Angeles (90067-4216)
PHONE............................323 266-2593
John E Anderson Jr, *President*
Ken Sims, *VP Sales*
EMP: 590 EST: 1976
SALES (est): 1MM
SALES (corp-wide): 446.1MM **Privately Held**
WEB: www.topaequities.com
SIC: 7538 Truck engine repair, except industrial
PA: Topa Equities, Ltd.
1800 Avenue Of The Stars # 1400
Los Angeles CA 90067
310 203-9199

(P-18857)
MISSION VOLKSWAGEN INC
Also Called: Capistrano Volkswagen
32922 Valle Rd, San Juan Capistrano (92675-4802)
PHONE............................949 493-4511
Miles Braden, *President*
Miles Brandon, *President*
Jorge Babiczuk, *Technician*
Joey Robustelli, *Finance Mgr*
Brenda Mongillo, *Controller*
EMP: 80 EST: 1993
SQ FT: 3,997
SALES (est): 26.6MM **Privately Held**
WEB: www.capovw.com
SIC: 5511 7538 Automobiles, new & used; general automotive repair shops

(P-18858)
NOARUS INVESTMENTS INC
Also Called: Airport Honda
5850 W Centinela Ave, Los Angeles (90045-1504)
PHONE............................310 649-2440
Norris J Bishton, *President*
Dan Theroux, *General Mgr*
Brian Twoomey, *General Mgr*
Richard Lee, *Finance Mgr*
Stanley Salinas, *Sales Executive*
EMP: 100 EST: 1998
SALES (est): 27.6MM **Privately Held**
WEB: www.airportmarinahonda.com
SIC: 5511 5521 5531 7538 Automobiles, new & used; automobiles, used cars only; automotive parts; general automotive repair shops

(P-18859)
NOARUS TGG
Also Called: Toyota Scion Place
9444 Trask Ave, Garden Grove (92844-2824)
PHONE............................714 895-5595
Norris J Bishton, *President*
Gary Alwood, *CFO*
William Hurst, *Vice Pres*
Nick Posada, *Controller*
Delicia Rivera, *Human Res Dir*
EMP: 97 EST: 1979
SQ FT: 30,000
SALES (est): 37.1MM **Privately Held**
WEB: www.occardealers.com
SIC: 5511 7538 Automobiles, new & used; automotive parts; general automotive repair shops

(P-18860)
PALM SPRINGS MOTORS INC
Also Called: Palm Sprng Ford Lincoln Mercury
69-200a Highway 111, Cathedral City (92234)
PHONE............................760 699-6695
Paul J Thiel, *CEO*
William S Torrance, *Vice Pres*
Michael Beaty, *Finance Dir*
Darla Lizarraga, *Finance Ass*
Raymond Magdaleno, *Finance*
EMP: 200 EST: 1950
SALES (est): 37.5MM **Privately Held**
WEB: www.palmspringsmazda.com
SIC: 5511 7538 Automobiles, new & used; pickups, new & used; general automotive repair shops

(P-18861)
PMB MOTORCARS LLC (HQ)
Also Called: Penske Motorcars Mercedes Benz
2010 E Garvey Ave S, West Covina (91791-1911)
PHONE............................626 859-1200
Greg Penske, *President*
Walter Krukowski, *Sales Staff*
Philip Fong, *Manager*
EMP: 60 EST: 1995
SQ FT: 81,013
SALES: 65MM
SALES (corp-wide): 5.1B **Privately Held**
WEB: www.mbwestcovina.com
SIC: 5511 7538 Automobiles, new & used; general automotive repair shops
PA: Penske Corporation
2555 S Telegraph Rd
Bloomfield Hills MI 48302
248 648-2000

(P-18862)
QUALIS AUTOMOTIVE LLC
21046 Figueroa St, Carson (90745-1906)
PHONE............................859 689-7772
EMP: 93
SALES (corp-wide): 3.3B **Privately Held**
WEB: www.centricparts.com
SIC: 7538 General automotive repair shops
HQ: Qualis Automotive, L.L.C.
14528 Bonelli St
City Of Industry CA 91746
310 218-1082

(P-18863)
RACEWAY FORD INC
Also Called: Quick Lane
5800 Sycamore Canyon Blvd, Riverside (92507-0706)
PHONE............................951 571-9300
John Barry McCallan Jr, *President*
Brij Desai, *Principal*
Betty Fernandez, *General Mgr*
Tammy Northup, *IT/INT Sup*
Ulaina Clark, *Finance Mgr*
EMP: 145 EST: 1956
SALES (est): 27.2MM **Privately Held**
WEB: www.racewayford.com
SIC: 5511 7538 Automobiles, new & used; general automotive repair shops

(P-18864)
RAMONA AUTO SERVICES INC
Also Called: Firestone
2451 S Euclid Ave, Ontario (91762-6617)
P.O. Box 960, Hemet (92546-0960)
PHONE............................909 986-1785

▲ = Import ▼=Export
◆ =Import/Export

Chris Wyborny, *Branch Mgr*
EMP: 74 **Privately Held**
WEB: www.ramonatire.com
SIC: 5531 7538 Automotive tires; general
    automotive repair shops
PA: Ramona Auto Services, Inc.
    2350 W Menlo Ave
    Hemet CA 92545

(P-18865)
RAYMAK AUTOMOTIVE INC
Also Called: Falcon Auto Repair
15600 S Main St, Gardena (90248-2219)
PHONE..............................310 329-8910
Kamyar Najmi, *President*
Eddy Basterio, *Consultant*
EMP: 50
SQ FT: 38,000
SALES: 7.4MM **Privately Held**
WEB: www.falcontowing.com
SIC: 7538 General automotive repair
    shops

(P-18866)
RESEDA DODGE SALES INC
Also Called: Simi Valley Chrysler
4470 Winnetka Ave, Woodland Hills
(91364-4608)
PHONE..............................805 581-9090
Salem Aranout, *Manager*
Jackie Baker, *Officer*
Jeff Sukay, *Sales Dir*
Bruce Holley, *Marketing Staff*
Austin Dietz, *Sales Staff*
EMP: 69
SALES (corp-wide): 24.6MM **Privately
Held**
WEB: www.dodge.com
SIC: 5511 7538 5531 Automobiles, new &
    used; general automotive repair shops;
    automotive parts
PA: Reseda Dodge Sales, Inc.
    4470 Winnetka Ave
    Woodland Hills CA 91364
    818 345-4001

(P-18867)
RHI INC (PA)
Also Called: Robertson Honda
5841 Lankershim Blvd, North Hollywood
(91601-1035)
PHONE..............................818 508-3800
Robert Robertson, *President*
Vic Simonian, *General Mgr*
Roberto Verdasco, *Sales Mgr*
Andrew Cruz, *Sales Staff*
Dennesses Martinez, *Sales Staff*
▼ **EMP:** 126 **EST:** 1970
SQ FT: 130,000
SALES (est): 39.6MM **Privately Held**
WEB: www.oceanhondanoho.com
SIC: 5511 5531 7532 5531 Automobiles,
    new & used; general automotive repair
    shops; body shop, automotive; automo-
    tive parts

(P-18868)
ROTOLO CHEVROLET INC
16666 S Highland Ave, Fontana
(92336-1213)
P.O. Box 457 (92334-0457)
PHONE..............................866 756-9776
Marie Waddingham, *President*
Nina Rotolo, *Treasurer*
Darinda Madeiros, *Corp Secy*
Lynn West, *Exec VP*
Michael Caposio, *General Mgr*
EMP: 137
SQ FT: 51,000
SALES: 197.8MM **Privately Held**
WEB: www.rotolochevy.com
SIC: 5511 5521 7538 Automobiles, new &
    used; used car dealers; general automo-
    tive repair shops

(P-18869)
S T MOLL INC (PA)
Also Called: Integrity Tires
3223 W Florida Ave, Hemet (92545-3638)
PHONE..............................951 658-3145
Steve Moll, *President*
EMP: 56 **EST:** 2000

SALES (est): 3.7MM **Privately Held**
WEB: www.integritytire.com
SIC: 5531 7538 5014 Automotive tires;
    general automotive repair shops; automo-
    bile tires & tubes

(P-18870)
SAN FERNANDO VALLEY AUTO LLC
Also Called: Rydell Chevrolet-Northridge
18600 Devonshire St, Northridge
(91324-1309)
PHONE..............................818 832-1600
Kelly Cashman, *Director*
John Turner, *Finance Mgr*
Mark Vanloo, *Sales Associate*
S Chris Olwell, *Sales Staff*
EMP: 148
SALES (corp-wide): 100.1MM **Privately
Held**
WEB: www.chevrolet.com
SIC: 5511 7538 7532 Automobiles, new &
    used; general automotive repair shops;
    body shop, automotive
PA: San Fernando Valley Automotive, Llc
    6001 Van Nuys Blvd
    Van Nuys CA 91401
    818 817-4600

(P-18871)
SANGERA BUICK INC
Also Called: Mercedes Benz of Bakersfield
5600 Gasoline Alley Dr, Bakersfield
(93313-3737)
PHONE..............................661 833-5200
Damon Culbertson, *President*
Mehnga Sangera, *Ch of Bd*
Hardev Sangera, *Vice Pres*
Tiffany Maldonado, *Office Mgr*
Nick Lightle, *Sales Mgr*
EMP: 85 **EST:** 1969
SQ FT: 20,000
SALES (est): 10.6MM **Privately Held**
WEB: www.sangera.com
SIC: 7538 5531 5511 General automotive
    repair shops; automotive parts; automo-
    biles, new & used

(P-18872)
SOUTH BAY FORD INC (PA)
Also Called: Quick Lane
5100 W Rosecrans Ave, Hawthorne
(90250-6620)
P.O. Box 1550 (90251-1550)
PHONE..............................310 644-0211
Gary Premeaux, *CEO*
Lars Brandt, *Vice Chairman*
Cynthia Palm, *CFO*
Dan Mueller, *General Mgr*
Steve Wood, *Admin Sec*
▼ **EMP:** 150 **EST:** 1993
SALES (est): 84.9MM **Privately Held**
WEB: www.southbayford.com
SIC: 5511 5531 7538 5521 Automobiles,
    new & used; automotive parts; automotive
    accessories; general automotive repair
    shops; used car dealers

(P-18873)
SOUTH BAY TOYOTA
18416 S Western Ave, Gardena
(90248-3823)
PHONE..............................310 323-7800
David Wilson, *President*
David Ortiz, *Vice Pres*
Pam Kompleski, *General Mgr*
Martin Contreras, *Technician*
Roger Lopez, *Technician*
EMP: 141 **EST:** 1989
SQ FT: 33,000
SALES (est): 39.9MM **Privately Held**
WEB: www.southbaytoyota.com
SIC: 5511 7538 7515 Automobiles, new &
    used; general automotive repair shops;
    passenger car leasing

(P-18874)
SOUTHERN CAL DISC TIRE CO INC
4640 Telephone Rd, Ventura (93003-5630)
PHONE..............................805 639-0166
Thomas Gensen, *Manager*
EMP: 106
SQ FT: 4,500

SALES (corp-wide): 3.6B **Privately Held**
WEB: www.discounttire.com
SIC: 5531 7538 Automotive tires; general
    automotive repair shops
HQ: Southern California Discount Tire Co.,
    Inc.
    16100 N Grnway Hyden Loop
    Scottsdale AZ 85260
    602 996-0201

(P-18875)
SOUTHERN CALIFORNIA MAR ASSN
3333 Fairview Rd, Costa Mesa
(92626-1610)
PHONE..............................714 850-4004
Betty Chew, *Director*
Greg Backley, *Vice Pres*
Jim Doran, *Empl Rel Mgr*
Jensen Rei-NA, *Marketing Mgr*
Ewa Goetz, *Manager*
EMP: 64 **EST:** 2011
SALES (est): 5.3MM **Privately Held**
SIC: 7538 General automotive repair
    shops

(P-18876)
SUNLAND FORD INC
Also Called: Sunland Ford-Lincoln-Mercury
15330 Palmdale Rd, Victorville
(92392-2498)
PHONE..............................760 241-7751
Ken Chambers, *President*
Wes Canfield, *Sales Mgr*
Andrew Anthony, *Sales Associate*
Sharon Burkhart, *Sales Associate*
Shane Simpson, *Sales Associate*
EMP: 90 **EST:** 1969
SQ FT: 10,000
SALES (est): 32.3MM **Privately Held**
WEB: www.sunlandfordinc.com
SIC: 5511 7538 5531 5521 Automobiles,
    new & used; general automotive repair
    shops; automotive & home supply stores;
    used car dealers

(P-18877)
SYMES CADILLAC INC
Also Called: Symes Cadillac of Pasadena
3475 E Colorado Blvd, Pasadena
(91107-3879)
PHONE..............................626 689-4386
John C Symes II, *CEO*
Bill Symes, *CEO*
Peter C Symes, *Vice Pres*
John Canales, *Parts Mgr*
EMP: 64 **EST:** 1948
SQ FT: 40,000
SALES (est): 12.7MM **Privately Held**
WEB: www.symescadillac.com
SIC: 5511 7538 5521 Automobiles, new &
    used; general automotive repair shops;
    automobiles, used cars only

(P-18878)
TED FORD JONES INC (PA)
Also Called: Ken Grody Ford
6211 Beach Blvd, Buena Park
(90621-2307)
P.O. Box 2154 (90621-0654)
PHONE..............................714 521-3110
Kenneth B Grody, *President*
Ken Grody, *President*
Billy Raymond, *CFO*
Curt Maletych, *Vice Pres*
Kurt Maletych, *Vice Pres*
▼ **EMP:** 110 **EST:** 1995
SQ FT: 4,500
SALES (est): 36.4MM **Privately Held**
WEB: www.quicklane.com
SIC: 7538 5511 General automotive repair
    shops; automobiles, new & used

(P-18879)
THOMAS BAVARIAN MTR WORKS INC
Also Called: Steve Thomas BMW
411 E Daily Dr, Camarillo (93010-5818)
PHONE..............................805 482-8878
Steve Thomas Jr, *President*
Stephanie Thomas, *Treasurer*
Mary Schroeder, *Vice Pres*
Christine Thomas, *Vice Pres*
Fredy Herrera, *Office Mgr*
EMP: 69 **EST:** 1983
SQ FT: 21,000

SALES (est): 14MM **Privately Held**
WEB: www.bmwgroup.com
SIC: 5511 7538 Automobiles, new & used;
    general automotive repair shops

(P-18880)
TOYOTA OF RIVERSIDE INC
7870 Indiana Ave, Riverside (92504-4109)
PHONE..............................951 687-1622
David Wilson, *President*
Tye Gutierrez, *Comp Spec*
Robert Arreola, *Finance Mgr*
Perry Ellis, *Finance Mgr*
Cedar Lanmon, *Finance Mgr*
EMP: 109 **EST:** 1969
SQ FT: 100,000
SALES (est): 44.7MM **Privately Held**
WEB: www.toyotaofriverside.com
SIC: 5511 5531 7538 5521 Automobiles,
    new & used; automotive parts; general
    automotive repair shops; used car deal-
    ers; automobiles & other motor vehicles

(P-18881)
TUTTLE-CLICK FORD INC
Also Called: Tuttle Click Ford
43 Auto Center Dr, Irvine (92618-2898)
PHONE..............................949 855-1704
Bob Tuttle, *President*
Elvia Morales, *CFO*
Chris Cotter, *Corp Secy*
James H Click, *Vice Pres*
EMP: 225 **EST:** 1980
SQ FT: 50,000
SALES (est): 35.7MM **Privately Held**
WEB: www.tuttleclickford.com
SIC: 5511 5521 7538 Automobiles, new &
    used; used car dealers; general automo-
    tive repair shops

(P-18882)
UNITED PANAM FINANCIAL CORP (PA)
1071 Camelback St Ste 100, Newport
Beach (92660-3046)
PHONE..............................949 224-1226
James Vagim, *President*
Guillermo Bron, *Ch of Bd*
Steve Singh, *COO*
Ravi Gandhi, *CFO*
Ravi R Gandhi, *Exec VP*
EMP: 454 **EST:** 1998
SQ FT: 31,214
SALES (est): 84.6MM **Privately Held**
SIC: 7538 General automotive repair
    shops

(P-18883)
USA EXPRESS TIRE AND SERVICE
350 Broadway St Ste A, Laguna Beach
(92651-4336)
PHONE..............................949 494-7111
Richard Minser, *Branch Mgr*
EMP: 52
SALES (corp-wide): 7.2MM **Privately
Held**
WEB: www.usaexpresstire.com
SIC: 7538 5531 General automotive repair
    shops; automotive tires
PA: Usa Express Tire And Service Inc
    3400 Cerritos Ave
    Los Alamitos CA 90720
    714 826-1001

(P-18884)
VAHI TOYOTA INC (PA)
Also Called: Valley-HI Toyota Honda
14612 Valley Center Dr, Victorville
(92395-4205)
P.O. Box 1508 (92393-1508)
PHONE..............................760 241-6484
Kent Browning, *President*
Alex Atalla, *Finance Mgr*
Efrain Ramirez, *Sales Mgr*
Byron Powell, *Sales Staff*
Frank Yegge, *Sales Staff*
EMP: 120 **EST:** 1971
SQ FT: 17,000
SALES (est): 26.3MM **Privately Held**
WEB: www.valleyhitoyota.com
SIC: 5511 7538 5561 5531 Automobiles,
    new & used; general automotive repair
    shops; recreational vehicle dealers; auto-
    motive & home supply stores

(P-18885)

VISTA FORD INC
Also Called: Vista Ford of Oxnard
1501 Auto Center Dr, Oxnard (93036-7916)
PHONE..............................805 983-6511
Randy Haddock, *Manager*
Aj Johnson, *General Mgr*
Laura Romero, *Office Mgr*
Christian Martinez, *Info Tech Dir*
Patti Chiaro, *Business Mgr*
EMP: 77
SALES (corp-wide): 122.6MM **Privately Held**
WEB: www.quicklane.com
SIC: 5511 5521 7538 Automobiles, new & used; used car dealers; general automotive repair shops
PA: Vista Ford Inc.
    21501 Ventura Blvd
    Woodland Hills CA 91364
    818 884-7600

(P-18886)

VOLKSWAGEN OF VAN NUYS INC
300 Hitchcock Way, Santa Barbara (93105-4002)
PHONE..............................323 873-3311
Ludwig Pflock, *President*
Ashraf Graies, *Sales Staff*
EMP: 100 EST: 1991
SALES (est): 25.3MM **Privately Held**
WEB: www.vw.com
SIC: 5511 7538 Automobiles, new & used; general automotive repair shops

(P-18887)

WALTER TIMMONS ENTERPRISES INC
Also Called: Timmons Volkswagen
3940 Cherry Ave, Long Beach (90807-3727)
PHONE..............................562 595-4601
Erika Timmons, *President*
Greg Timmons, *Vice Pres*
Mike Meltebeke, *Administration*
Bill Looney, *Technician*
Mario J Philippe, *Finance Mgr*
EMP: 60 EST: 1971
SQ FT: 32,000
SALES (est): 22.3MM **Privately Held**
WEB: www.timmonsvw.com
SIC: 5511 7538 5531 Automobiles, new & used; general automotive repair shops; automobile & truck equipment & parts

(P-18888)

YORK ENTERPRISES SOUTH INC
Also Called: Huntington Beach Ford
18255 Beach Blvd, Huntington Beach (92648-1351)
PHONE..............................714 842-6611
Oscar Bakhtiari, *CEO*
Catherine Barrett, *Business Mgr*
Donna Graham, *Business Mgr*
Lennon Gomez, *Sales Staff*
EMP: 100 EST: 1989
SALES (est): 30.7MM **Privately Held**
WEB: www.quicklane.com
SIC: 5511 7538 Automobiles, new & used; general automotive repair shops

7539 Automotive Repair Shops, NEC

(P-18889)

AIRDRAULICS INC
13261 Saticoy St, North Hollywood (91605-3401)
PHONE..............................818 982-1400
Dan Tracey, *CEO*
Joseph Melendez, *Technician*
Denise Tracey, *Purch Mgr*
Laura Triggs, *Sales Staff*
Devin Tracey, *Manager*
EMP: 25 EST: 1986
SQ FT: 5,000

SALES (est): 8.5MM **Privately Held**
WEB: www.airdraulicsinc.com
SIC: 7539 3599 5013 5084 Automotive repair shops; machine & other job shop work; automotive servicing equipment; industrial machinery & equipment; compressor repair; service station equipment installation, maintenance & repair

(P-18890)

AKH COMPANY INC
Also Called: Discount Tire Center 025
7120 Laurel Canyon Blvd, North Hollywood (91605-5740)
PHONE..............................818 691-1978
Leo Gonzalez, *Manager*
EMP: 110
SALES (corp-wide): 31MM **Privately Held**
WEB: www.discounttires.com
SIC: 7539 5014 5531 Wheel alignment, automotive; automobile tires & tubes; automotive tires
PA: Akh Company, Inc.
    1160 N Anaheim Blvd
    Anaheim CA 92801
    800 999-2878

(P-18891)

AKH COMPANY INC
Also Called: Discount Tire Center 038
1647 W Rdlands Blvd Ste C, Redlands (92373)
PHONE..............................909 748-5016
Marc Fortin, *Manager*
EMP: 88
SALES (corp-wide): 31MM **Privately Held**
WEB: www.discounttires.com
SIC: 5531 7539 5014 Automotive tires; wheel alignment, automotive; automobile tires & tubes
PA: Akh Company, Inc.
    1160 N Anaheim Blvd
    Anaheim CA 92801
    800 999-2878

(P-18892)

ALASKA DIESEL ELECTRIC
425 S Hacienda Blvd, City of Industry (91745-1123)
PHONE..............................626 934-6211
Peter B Hill Jr, *President*
EMP: 109 EST: 1999
SALES (est): 2MM
SALES (corp-wide): 178.7MM **Privately Held**
WEB: www.valleypowersystems.com
SIC: 7539 Automotive repair shops
PA: Valley Power Systems, Inc.
    425 S Hacienda Blvd
    City Of Industry CA 91745
    626 333-1243

(P-18893)

AUTO GALLERY (PA)
5711 Van Nuys Blvd, Van Nuys (91401-4217)
PHONE..............................818 884-4411
Darrin Chrisman, *General Mgr*
Harrison Gray, *Principal*
Tony Schwartz, *Principal*
Kathy Wilson, *Office Mgr*
Kayla Nelson, *Admin Asst*
EMP: 55 EST: 2001
SALES (est): 28.8MM **Privately Held**
WEB: www.theautogallery.com
SIC: 5511 5531 7539 7538 Automobiles, new & used; automobile & truck equipment & parts; tune-up service, automotive; general automotive repair shops

(P-18894)

CARLI SUSPENSION INC
596 Crane St, Lake Elsinore (92530-2737)
PHONE..............................951 403-6570
Sage Carli, *President*
EMP: 68 EST: 2004
SQ FT: 30,000
SALES (est): 3.3MM **Privately Held**
WEB: www.carlisuspension.com
SIC: 7539 Machine shop, automotive

(P-18895)

CHINO MFG & REPAIR INC
13563 12th St, Chino (91710-5297)
P.O. Box 516 (91708-0516)
PHONE..............................909 628-0519
Bernie Vander Molen, *President*
Jeanette Vander Molen, *Treasurer*
Jeanette Molen, *Treasurer*
Marlin J Vander Molen, *Vice Pres*
EMP: 18 EST: 1973
SQ FT: 12,500
SALES (est): 1.5MM **Privately Held**
WEB: www.chinomfg.com
SIC: 7539 3535 3523 Trailer repair; conveyors & conveying equipment; trailers & wagons, farm; elevators, farm

(P-18896)

DCH ACURA OF TEMECULA
Also Called: Lithia
26705 Ynez Rd, Temecula (92591-4693)
P.O. Box 9043 (92589-9043)
PHONE..............................877 847-9532
Kenneth Colson, *Vice Pres*
EMP: 100 EST: 2014
SALES (est): 10.9MM **Privately Held**
WEB: www.dchacuraoftemecula.com
SIC: 5511 7539 5531 Automobiles, new & used; automotive repair shops; automotive parts

(P-18897)

EIGHT POINT TRAILER CORP
14770 Slover Ave, Fontana (92337-7234)
PHONE..............................909 357-9227
Gregory Anderson, *President*
Dan Paul, *Purchasing*
EMP: 27 EST: 1948
SQ FT: 28,000
SALES (est): 1.8MM **Privately Held**
WEB: www.eightpointtrailer.com
SIC: 7539 3715 5013 Trailer repair; truck trailers; truck parts & accessories

(P-18898)

HONDA WORLD WESTMINSTER
13600 Beach Blvd, Westminster (92683-3202)
PHONE..............................714 890-8900
Jim Kitzmiller, *President*
Tom Chadwell, *CFO*
Hieu Tran, *Finance Mgr*
Kelli Gorman, *Controller*
Randy Hickerson, *Opers Staff*
EMP: 175 EST: 1989
SQ FT: 6,000
SALES (est): 62.1MM
SALES (corp-wide): 114.1MM **Privately Held**
WEB: www.ochondaworld.com
SIC: 5511 7539 5012 Automobiles, new & used; automotive repair shops; motor vehicle parts, used; automobiles & other motor vehicles
PA: Piercey Management Services, Inc.
    16901 Millikan Ave
    Irvine CA 92606
    949 379-3701

(P-18899)

JAMES MAGNA LTD
Also Called: Northstar Engineering
8782 Lanyard Ct, Rancho Cucamonga (91730-0804)
PHONE..............................909 391-2025
Mike Maedel, *CEO*
Gene Gregory, *Vice Pres*
Michael Maedel, *Program Mgr*
◆ EMP: 17 EST: 1991
SQ FT: 19,696
SALES (est): 4MM **Privately Held**
WEB: www.northstar-e.com
SIC: 7539 3599 Fuel system repair, motor vehicle; machine shop, jobbing & repair

(P-18900)

NGP MOTORS INC
Also Called: Sunrise Ford
5500 Lankershim Blvd, North Hollywood (91601-2724)
P.O. Box 908, Fontana (92334-0908)
PHONE..............................818 980-9800
Robert Burncati, *President*
James Bruncati, *COO*
Maureen Burncati, *Vice Pres*
Juan Arellano, *Finance Dir*

Albert Miramontes, *Finance Dir*
EMP: 131
SQ FT: 75,000
SALES (est): 48.5MM **Privately Held**
WEB: www.sunrisefordnoho.com
SIC: 5511 7539 7538 Automobiles, new & used; automotive repair shops; general automotive repair shops

(P-18901)

PEARSON FORD CO (PA)
5900 Sycamore Canyon Blvd, Riverside (92507-0719)
PHONE..............................877 743-0421
John McCallan, *President*
Randy Olds, *CIO*
Ricky Meyer, *Sales Mgr*
Gary Thiem, *Manager*
EMP: 180 EST: 1940
SQ FT: 275,000
SALES (est): 38MM **Privately Held**
WEB: www.racewayford.com
SIC: 5511 7539 7538 5521 Automobiles, new & used; automotive repair shops; general automotive repair shops; used car dealers

(P-18902)

PENDRAGON NORTH AMER AUTO INC
26400 La Alameda Ste 112, Mission Viejo (92691-8305)
PHONE..............................949 365-8750
Trevor Garry Finn, *CEO*
EMP: 60 EST: 1999
SALES (est): 22.6MM
SALES (corp-wide): 3.8B **Privately Held**
WEB: www.pendragonplc.com
SIC: 5511 7539 New & used car dealers; automotive repair shops
PA: Pendragon Plc
    Loxley House
    Nottingham NOTTS NG15
    162 372-5200

(P-18903)

RICHLAND CHEVROLET CO CORP
511 Central Ave, Shafter (93263-2121)
P.O. Box 1120 (93263-1120)
PHONE..............................661 746-4981
Jeffrey Millwee, *President*
Lana Harvey, *Office Mgr*
Keith Stewart, *Manager*
EMP: 59 EST: 1947
SQ FT: 30,000
SALES (est): 14.8MM **Privately Held**
WEB: www.rldchev.com
SIC: 5511 7539 5531 Automobiles, new & used; automotive repair shops; automotive parts

(P-18904)

SIMPSON AUTOMOTIVE INC
Also Called: Simpson Buick Pontiac GMC
6600 Auto Center Dr, Buena Park (90621-2927)
PHONE..............................714 690-6200
David A Simpson, *President*
Diana Ramsey, *Treasurer*
Dianna Ramsey, *Corp Secy*
George Heugel, *General Mgr*
Steve Cnywar, *Finance Mgr*
EMP: 91 EST: 1951
SQ FT: 46,000
SALES (est): 32.9MM **Privately Held**
WEB:
www.simpsonbuickgmcbuenapark.com
SIC: 5511 5531 7539 Automobiles, new & used; automobile & truck equipment & parts; automotive repair shops

(P-18905)

SOUTHBAY EUROPEAN INC
Also Called: Southbay BMW
18800 Hawthorne Blvd, Torrance (90504-5507)
PHONE..............................310 939-7300
Fritz Hitchcock, *President*
Peter Boesen, *Vice Pres*
Brian Wong, *Finance Mgr*
Kenny Jumps, *Manager*
Fe Celestial, *Advisor*
EMP: 100 EST: 1968
SQ FT: 150,000

SALES (est): 36.3MM Privately Held
WEB: www.southbaybmw.com
SIC: 5511 5531 7539 Automobiles, new & used; automotive parts; automotive accessories; automotive repair shops

(P-18906)
ST GEORGE AUTO CENTER INC (PA)
Also Called: Stg Auto Group
10325 Central Ave, Montclair (91763-4402)
PHONE..................................909 341-1189
Tony Bacily, *President*
Mina Ghandor, *Sales Mgr*
Mariea Dalluge, *Marketing Staff*
Javier Cuevas, *Manager*
Jesse Gonzalez, *Parts Mgr*
EMP: 85 EST: 2005
SALES (est): 15.1MM Privately Held
WEB: www.stgautogroup.com
SIC: 7539 7538 Automotive repair shops; general automotive repair shops

7542 Car Washes

(P-18907)
BOWIE ENTERPRISES
Also Called: Red Carpet Car Wash
1920 S Mooney Blvd, Visalia (93277-4450)
PHONE..................................559 732-2988
EMP: 53
SALES (corp-wide): 14.8MM Privately Held
WEB: www.chevronwithtechron.com
SIC: 7542 Carwash
PA: Bowie Enterprises
    4411 N Blackstone Ave
    Fresno CA 93726
    559 227-6221

(P-18908)
CAR WASH PARTNERS INC
2619 Mount Vernon Ave, Bakersfield (93306-2900)
PHONE..................................661 377-1020
EMP: 426
SALES (corp-wide): 574.9MM Publicly Held
WEB: www.mistercarwash.com
SIC: 7542 Washing & polishing, automotive
HQ: Car Wash Partners, Inc.
    222 E 5th St
    Tucson AZ 85705
    520 615-4000

(P-18909)
CAR WASH PARTNERS INC
5375 Olive Dr, Bakersfield (93308-2921)
PHONE..................................661 231-3689
EMP: 88
SALES (corp-wide): 1.1B Privately Held
SIC: 7542 Washing & polishing, automotive
HQ: Car Wash Partners, Inc.
    1503 S Collins St
    Plant City FL 33563

(P-18910)
CONICO CORO INC (HQ)
4520 E Thsand Oaks Blvd S, Westlake Village (91362)
PHONE..................................805 373-1880
Peter Hong, *President*
Toni Kim, *Controller*
EMP: 55 EST: 2000
SALES (est): 13.2MM
SALES (corp-wide): 131.8MM Privately Held
WEB: www.conicooil.com
SIC: 5411 5541 7542 Convenience stores; filling stations, gasoline; carwashes
PA: Hong Holdings, Llc
    4520 E Thsand Oaks Blvd S
    Westlake Village CA 91361
    805 777-7938

(P-18911)
CONICO RORO INC (HQ)
Also Called: Victory Shell
4520 E Thsand Oaks Blvd S, Westlake Village (91362)
PHONE..................................818 716-1238
Peter Hong, *President*
Danny Baillargeon, *General Counsel*
Miriam Vera, *Manager*
EMP: 50 EST: 2000
SALES (est): 39.6MM
SALES (corp-wide): 131.8MM Privately Held
WEB: www.conicooil.com
SIC: 5541 7542 ; carwashes
PA: Hong Holdings, Llc
    4520 E Thsand Oaks Blvd S
    Westlake Village CA 91361
    805 777-7938

(P-18912)
DYNAMIC AUTO IMAGES INC
Also Called: Dynamic Detail
2860 Michelle Ste 140, Irvine (92606-1007)
PHONE..................................714 771-3400
EMP: 300 EST: 2004
SALES (est): 14.4MM Privately Held
WEB: www.dynamicautoimages.com
SIC: 7542 7532 Washing & polishing, automotive; collision shops, automotive

(P-18913)
ENCINO CENTER CAR WASH INC
16300 Ventura Blvd, Encino (91436-2116)
PHONE..................................818 788-6300
EMP: 50
SALES (est): 1MM Privately Held
SIC: 7542 5541 5947 Car Wash

(P-18914)
EXECUTIVE AUTO RECONDITIONING
Also Called: Dealership Auto Dtail Rstrtons
522 E Duarte Rd, Monrovia (91016-4604)
PHONE..................................626 416-3322
Miguel Alvarado, *CEO*
EMP: 45 EST: 2017
SALES (est): 1.2MM Privately Held
SIC: 7542 7532 3842 Carwashes; body shop, automotive; cosmetic restorations

(P-18915)
MADRONA CARWASH INC (PA)
Also Called: Chevron
3405 Sepulveda Blvd, Torrance (90505-2606)
PHONE..................................310 373-9736
Rekha Bajaria, *President*
Jay Bajaria, *CFO*
Neha Bajaria, *Corp Secy*
EMP: 50 EST: 1979
SQ FT: 4,000
SALES (est): 17.8MM Privately Held
WEB: www.gasandwash.com
SIC: 5541 7542 5947 Filling stations, gasoline; carwash, automatic; gift shop

(P-18916)
RUSSELL FISHER PARTNERSHIP
Also Called: Bella Terra Carwash
16061 Beach Blvd, Huntington Beach (92647-3802)
PHONE..................................714 842-4453
Ruben Hernandez, *Site Mgr*
Alphonso Perez, *Manager*
Juan Rojas, *Manager*
EMP: 50
SALES (corp-wide): 6.8MM Privately Held
SIC: 7542 Washing & polishing, automotive
PA: The Russell Fischer Partnership Lp
    18971 Beach Blvd
    Huntington Beach CA 92648
    714 847-4924

(P-18917)
TEAM DYKSPRA (PA)
2315 California Ave, Corona (92881-6655)
PHONE..................................951 898-6482
Lenny Dykstra, *President*
EMP: 60 EST: 1992

SALES (est): 3.4MM Privately Held
SIC: 7542 7549 Washing & polishing, automotive; automotive maintenance services

(P-18918)
WASH DEPOT AUTO CENTERS LP
Also Called: Simoniz Janss Mall Car Wash
467 N Moorpark Rd, Thousand Oaks (91360-3706)
PHONE..................................805 379-4900
Craig Barknikel, *Manager*
EMP: 54
SALES (corp-wide): 45.2MM Privately Held
WEB: www.washdepot.com
SIC: 7542 Washing & polishing, automotive
HQ: Wash Depot Auto Centers, L.P.
    435 Eastern Ave
    Malden MA 02148

7549 Automotive Svcs, Except Repair & Car Washes

(P-18919)
ABSOLUTE TWING - HLLNBECK DIV
4760 Valley Blvd, Los Angeles (90032-3834)
PHONE..................................323 225-9294
Todd Q Smart, *President*
EMP: 50 EST: 1998
SQ FT: 111,000
SALES (est): 2.8MM Privately Held
WEB: www.viertels.com
SIC: 7549 Towing service, automotive

(P-18920)
ALLEN/CLARK CADILLAC
Also Called: Crestview Cadillac
2700 E Garvey Ave S, West Covina (91791-2114)
PHONE..................................626 966-7441
Scott Allen, *President*
Beverly Harmon, *Finance*
Peter Yang, *Sales Mgr*
Mark Michie, *Sales Staff*
Kara Sacks, *Sales Staff*
▲ EMP: 68 EST: 1957
SQ FT: 10,000
SALES (est): 28.1MM Privately Held
WEB: www.cadillac.com
SIC: 5511 5531 7549 Automobiles, new & used; automotive parts; do-it-yourself garages

(P-18921)
AMERIT FLEET SOLUTIONS INC
15325 Manila St, Fontana (92337-7261)
PHONE..................................909 357-0100
David Kristy, *Manager*
EMP: 884 Privately Held
WEB: www.ameritfleetsolutions.com
SIC: 7549 Inspection & diagnostic service, automotive
HQ: Amerit Fleet Solutions Inc.
    1331 N Calif Blvd Ste 150
    Walnut Creek CA 94596
    877 512-6374

(P-18922)
AUTOMOTIVE TSTG & DEV SVCS INC (PA)
400 Etiwanda Ave, Ontario (91761-8637)
PHONE..................................909 390-1100
Devon Larry Smith, *CEO*
Kay Smith, *Corp Secy*
Steve Arnold, *Vice Pres*
Dave Kovach, *Manager*
Jason Link, *Manager*
▲ EMP: 185 EST: 1989
SQ FT: 24,000
SALES (est): 16.4MM Privately Held
WEB: www.automotivetesting.com
SIC: 7549 8734 8711 Emissions testing without repairs, automotive; testing laboratories; engineering services

(P-18923)
COMPLETE COACH WORKS (HQ)
Also Called: John Deere Authorized Dealer
1863 Service Ct, Riverside (92507-2341)
PHONE..................................951 682-2557
Dale E Carson, *President*
Elliott Carson, *Exec Dir*
Natalie Esparza, *Admin Asst*
Oliver Davis, *CIO*
Keith Bulter, *Info Tech Dir*
▲ EMP: 253 EST: 2007
SALES (est): 100.4MM
SALES (corp-wide): 105.7MM Privately Held
WEB: www.completecoach.com
SIC: 7549 5082 Trailer maintenance; construction & mining machinery
PA: D/T Carson Enterprises, Inc.
    42882 Ivy St
    Murrieta CA 92562
    951 684-9585

(P-18924)
EVGO SERVICES LLC
11835 W Olympic Blvd 900e, Los Angeles (90064-5001)
P.O. Box 642830 (90064-8287)
PHONE..................................310 954-2900
Cathy Zoi, *CEO*
Olga Shevorenkova, *CFO*
Jay Goldman, *Vice Pres*
Jonathan Levy, *Vice Pres*
Jeffrey Ricketts, *Vice Pres*
EMP: 130 EST: 2011
SQ FT: 10,000
SALES (est): 120.3MM Publicly Held
WEB: www.evgo.com
SIC: 7549 Automotive maintenance services
PA: Ls Power Equity Partners, L.P.
    1700 Broadway Fl 35
    New York NY 10019

(P-18925)
EZ LUBE LLC
Also Called: E Z Lube No 54
201 S La Brea Ave, Los Angeles (90036-3022)
PHONE..................................323 930-9389
Marco Cabrera, *Manager*
EMP: 67
SALES (corp-wide): 22.5MM Privately Held
WEB: www.vioc.com
SIC: 7549 Lubrication service, automotive; inspection & diagnostic service, automotive
PA: Ez Lube, Llc
    3540 Howard Way Ste 200
    Costa Mesa CA

(P-18926)
EZ LUBE LLC
Also Called: EZ Lube- Costco
13421 Washington Blvd, Marina Del Rey (90292-5658)
PHONE..................................310 821-2517
Doug Paysse, *Manager*
EMP: 67
SALES (corp-wide): 22.5MM Privately Held
WEB: www.vioc.com
SIC: 7549 Lubrication service, automotive; inspection & diagnostic service, automotive
PA: Ez Lube, Llc
    3540 Howard Way Ste 200
    Costa Mesa CA

(P-18927)
EZ LUBE LLC
1460 E Foothill Blvd, Upland (91786-4024)
PHONE..................................909 920-0476
Ben Daughenbaugh, *Manager*
EMP: 67
SALES (corp-wide): 22.5MM Privately Held
WEB: www.vioc.com
SIC: 7549 Lubrication service, automotive

PA: Ez Lube, Llc
3540 Howard Way Ste 200
Costa Mesa CA

(P-18928)
EZ LUBE LLC
11827 Santa Monica Blvd, Los Angeles (90025-2201)
PHONE....................310 479-4704
Alfred Lopez, *Branch Mgr*
EMP: 67
SALES (corp-wide): 22.5MM **Privately Held**
SIC: 7549 Lubrication service, automotive
PA: Ez Lube, Llc
3540 Howard Way Ste 200
Costa Mesa CA

(P-18929)
EZ LUBE LLC
Also Called: E-Z Lube 13
10800 Riverside Dr, North Hollywood (91602-2360)
PHONE....................818 761-5696
Guillermo Campos, *Branch Mgr*
EMP: 67
SALES (corp-wide): 22.5MM **Privately Held**
WEB: www.vioc.com
SIC: 7549 7538 Lubrication service, automotive; general automotive repair shops
PA: Ez Lube, Llc
3540 Howard Way Ste 200
Costa Mesa CA

(P-18930)
EZ LUBE LLC
21000 Ventura Blvd, Woodland Hills (91364-2201)
PHONE....................818 610-8866
Hugo Luveano, *Branch Mgr*
EMP: 67
SALES (corp-wide): 22.5MM **Privately Held**
WEB: www.vioc.com
SIC: 7549 Lubrication service, automotive
PA: Ez Lube, Llc
3540 Howard Way Ste 200
Costa Mesa CA

(P-18931)
EZ LUBE LLC
4002 N Harbor Blvd, Fullerton (92835-1037)
PHONE....................714 871-9980
Nick Salcedo, *Branch Mgr*
EMP: 67
SALES (corp-wide): 22.5MM **Privately Held**
WEB: www.vioc.com
SIC: 7549 Lubrication service, automotive
PA: Ez Lube, Llc
3540 Howard Way Ste 200
Costa Mesa CA

(P-18932)
EZ LUBE LLC
Also Called: Valvoline Instant Oil Change
3599 Harbor Blvd, Costa Mesa (92626-1405)
PHONE....................714 966-1647
Abdul Keium, *Branch Mgr*
EMP: 67
SALES (corp-wide): 22.5MM **Privately Held**
WEB: www.vioc.com
SIC: 7549 Automotive maintenance services
PA: Ez Lube, Llc
3540 Howard Way Ste 200
Costa Mesa CA

(P-18933)
FUGRO ROADWARE INC
17752 Sky Park Cir, Irvine (92614-6419)
PHONE....................949 536-5175
Edwin Houthuijzen, *President*
EMP: 52
SALES (corp-wide): 1B **Privately Held**
SIC: 7549 Road service, automotive

HQ: Fugro Roadware, Inc.
3104 Northside Ave
Richmond VA 23228
804 264-2982

(P-18934)
GLOBAL AUTO PROC SVCS INC (PA)
Also Called: Gaps
567 W Channel Islands Blv, Port Hueneme (93041-2133)
PHONE....................805 382-9601
Jay Song, *Ch of Bd*
Robert Miller, *President*
Michael W Song, *Vice Pres*
EMP: 69 EST: 2001
SALES (est): 9.9MM **Privately Held**
SIC: 7549 7521 Automotive customizing services, non-factory basis; automobile parking

(P-18935)
JABI ENTERPRISES INC
Also Called: Hisham's Towing
14201 Halldale Ave, Gardena (90249-2631)
PHONE....................310 323-8436
Hisham A Jabi, *President*
Khaled H Jabi, *Vice Pres*
EMP: 52 EST: 1983
SQ FT: 99,000
SALES (est): 1.3MM **Privately Held**
SIC: 7549 Towing service, automotive; towing services

(P-18936)
JANS TOWING INC (PA)
1045 W Kirkwall Rd, Azusa (91702-5127)
PHONE....................626 334-1383
Jan Qualkenbush, *President*
EMP: 158 EST: 1994
SQ FT: 5,896
SALES (est): 2.4MM **Privately Held**
WEB: www.janstowing.com
SIC: 7549 Towing service, automotive; towing services

(P-18937)
M K SMITH CHEVROLET
12845 Central Ave, Chino (91710-4120)
P.O. Box 455 (91708-0455)
PHONE....................909 628-8961
Marc Smith, *CEO*
Carolyn Coble, *Treasurer*
Cheryl Smith, *Admin Sec*
Todd Smith, *Opers Staff*
Don Harshfield, *Manager*
EMP: 120 EST: 1941 **Privately Held**
WEB: www.mksmithchevrolet.com
SIC: 5511 7549 5531 Automobiles, new & used; automotive maintenance services; automotive parts

(P-18938)
METROPRO ROAD SERVICES INC (PA)
Also Called: A & P Towing-Metropro Rd Svcs
957 W 17th St, Costa Mesa (92627-4402)
PHONE....................714 556-7600
Bradley T Humphreys, *CEO*
Jody Campbell, *President*
Michael Kirkland, *Manager*
EMP: 85 EST: 1998
SALES (est): 7.7MM **Privately Held**
WEB: www.metro-pro.com
SIC: 7549 Towing service, automotive

(P-18939)
NICK ALEXANDER IMPORTS
6333 S Alameda St, Los Angeles (90001-1812)
PHONE....................800 800-6425
Elizabeth Alexander, *CEO*
Brad Kim, *CFO*
Nick Alexander, *Treasurer*
Mary Alexander, *Vice Pres*
Daniel Campos, *Department Mgr*
EMP: 110 EST: 1978
SQ FT: 32,500
SALES (est): 61.4MM **Privately Held**
WEB: www.alexanderbmw.com
SIC: 5511 7549 Automobiles, new & used; automotive maintenance services

(P-18940)
PRECISION AERIAL SERVICES INC
2020 Lowell St, Rialto (92377-3722)
PHONE....................909 484-8259
Bill Payne Jr, *CEO*
Tina Zanardi, *General Mgr*
Rachel Huston, *Info Tech Mgr*
EMP: 16 EST: 2012
SALES (est): 2.4MM **Privately Held**
WEB: www.precisionaerialservices.com
SIC: 7549 7694 High performance auto repair & service; electric motor repair

(P-18941)
PRESTIGE STATIONS INC (DH)
Also Called: Am/PM Mini Market
4 Centerpointe Dr, La Palma (90623-1015)
PHONE....................714 670-5145
John Lannan, *Vice Pres*
Vicki Flies, *Vice Pres*
Faisal Afsari, *Site Mgr*
Lupe Alvarez, *Site Mgr*
Aman Azizi, *Site Mgr*
EMP: 200
SQ FT: 7,000
SALES (est): 270.6MM
SALES (corp-wide): 278.4B **Privately Held**
WEB: www.ampm.com
SIC: 5411 7549 5541 Convenience stores, chain; automotive maintenance services; filling stations, gasoline
HQ: Atlantic Richfield Company Inc
4 Centerpointe Dr
La Palma CA 90623
800 333-3991

(P-18942)
ROSS BAKER TOWING INC
Also Called: Ross Baker Towing Service
8750 Vanalden Ave, Northridge (91324-3656)
PHONE....................818 886-7411
Greg Baker, *President*
EMP: 101 EST: 1960
SQ FT: 2,000
SALES (est): 3.3MM
SALES (corp-wide): 92.4MM **Privately Held**
WEB: www.rossbakertowing.com
SIC: 7549 Towing service, automotive
HQ: United Road Towing, Inc.
9550 Bormet Dr Ste 304
Mokena IL 60448

(P-18943)
SOUTH CNTY LXUS AT MSSION VEJO
28242 Marguerite Pkwy, Mission Viejo (92692-3704)
PHONE....................949 347-3400
Patrick Lustin, *General Mgr*
Peggy Brunworth, *Administration*
Chuck Chadwick, *Controller*
Andrea Bracken, *Sales Mgr*
Fardad Mahjoob, *Sales Mgr*
EMP: 200 EST: 2013
SALES (est): 37.3MM **Privately Held**
WEB: www.southcountylexus.com
SIC: 5511 7549 Automobiles, new & used; automotive maintenance services

7622 Radio & TV Repair Shops

(P-18944)
MINILEC SERVICE INC
Also Called: Minilec Service-Los Angeles BR
9207 Deering Ave Ste A, Chatsworth (91311-6959)
PHONE....................818 341-1125
EMP: 50
SQ FT: 7,000
SALES (corp-wide): 6.6MM **Privately Held**
SIC: 7622 4812 Radio/Television Repair Radiotelephone Communication
PA: Minilec Service Inc.
9207 Deering Ave Ste A
Chatsworth CA 91311
818 773-6300

7623 Refrigeration & Air Conditioning Svc & Repair Shop

(P-18945)
CLIMA-TECH INC
1820 Town And Country Dr, Norco (92860-3616)
PHONE....................909 613-5513
William C Valenzuela, *CEO*
Ada Roberts, *CFO*
Husein Aziz, *Exec VP*
Dolores Garcia, *Administration*
Frank Eppelheimer, *Techniciar*
EMP: 89 EST: 2004
SALES (est): 12.3MM **Privately Held**
WEB: www.climatechref.com
SIC: 7623 1711 Refrigeration service & repair; refrigeration contractor; heating & air conditioning contractors

(P-18946)
COOLSYS INC (HQ)
145 S State College Blvd, Brea (92821-5818)
PHONE....................714 510-9577
Anesa Chaibi, *CEO*
Adam Coffey, *President*
Amy Freeman, *COO*
Andy Mandell, *CFO*
Burton Hong, *Exec VP*
EMP: 355 EST: 2017
SALES (est): 1.1B
SALES (corp-wide): 1.7B **Publicly Held**
WEB: www.coolsys.com
SIC: 7623 Air conditioning repair
PA: Ares Management Corporation
2000 Avenue Of The Stars # 12
Los Angeles CA 90067
310 201-4100

(P-18947)
GMH INC
Also Called: West Coast Air Conditioning
561 Kinetic Dr Ste A, Oxnard (93030-7947)
PHONE....................805 485-1410
Michael C Haase, *President*
Gina Haase, *Vice Pres*
Todd Smith, *General Mgr*
Greg Hellmann, *Project Mgr*
Alex Banales, *Manager*
EMP: 50 EST: 1976
SQ FT: 5,600
SALES (est): 10.8MM **Privately Held**
WEB: www.honeywell.com
SIC: 7623 1711 Refrigeration repair service; refrigeration contractor

(P-18948)
MRV SERVICE AIR INC
Also Called: Mrv Crane
937 High St, Delano (93215-1704)
P.O. Box 535 (93216-0535)
PHONE....................661 725-3400
Manuel Valdovinos, *President*
EMP: 18 EST: 2007
SQ FT: 7,200
SALES (est): 2.7MM **Privately Held**
WEB: www.mrvserviceair.com
SIC: 7623 3444 Air conditioning repair; sheet metalwork

(P-18949)
VARIABLE SPEED SOLUTIONS INC
16182 Gothard St Ste I, Huntington Beach (92647-3642)
PHONE....................714 847-5957
Brian Pavloff, *President*
Tracy Pavloff, *Corp Secy*
William Pavloff, *Vice Pres*
EMP: 13 EST: 2003
SQ FT: 2,000
SALES (est): 2.9MM **Privately Held**
WEB: www.variablespeedsolutions.com
SIC: 7623 1731 3699 3561 Air conditioning repair; electrical work; electrical equipment & supplies; pumps & pumping equipment; pumps & pumping equipment repair; motor controls & accessories

7629 Electrical & Elex Repair Shop, NEC

(P-18950)
ABLE CABLE INC (PA)
Also Called: A C I Communications
5115 Douglas Fir Rd Ste A, Calabasas (91302-2588)
PHONE..................818 223-3600
Russell Ramas, *President*
David Gardner, *CFO*
Michael Collette, *Vice Pres*
Curtis Quillin, *Vice Pres*
Melisa McNiece, *Controller*
EMP: 175
SQ FT: 3,500
SALES (est): 12MM **Privately Held**
WEB: www.acicommunications.com
SIC: 7629 1731 4813 Telephone set repair; telephone & telephone equipment installation; fiber optic cable installation; telephone communication, except radio

(P-18951)
AMERICAN ELC COMPONENTS INC
4901 Fruitland Ave, Vernon (90058-2728)
PHONE..................323 771-4888
Raul Bauelos Sr, *President*
Victor M Banuelos, *Corp Secy*
Antonio Camacho, *Vice Pres*
Luis Lopez, *Purchasing*
EMP: 15 EST: 1995
SALES (est): 3MM **Privately Held**
WEB: www.aecinc1.com
SIC: 7629 3612 Electrical equipment repair services; power transformers, electric

(P-18952)
AUTHORIZED CELLULAR SERVICE
Also Called: ACS
8808 S Sepulveda Blvd, Los Angeles (90045-4810)
PHONE..................310 466-4144
Ray Diab, *Co-Owner*
Rami Radi, *Co-Owner*
Eric Goettman, *Manager*
Carlos Espinoza, *Superintendent*
EMP: 100 EST: 1993
SQ FT: 10,000
SALES (est): 2MM **Privately Held**
SIC: 7629 5999 Telephone set repair; telephone equipment & systems

(P-18953)
BSH HOME APPLIANCES CORP (DH)
1901 Main St Ste 600, Irvine (92614-0521)
PHONE..................949 440-7100
Michael Traub, *President*
Christofer Von Nagel, *President*
Stefan Koss, *CFO*
John Iacoviello, *Vice Pres*
Christopher Kaeser, *Vice Pres*
◆ EMP: 220 EST: 1996
SQ FT: 52,000
SALES (est): 529.9MM
SALES (corp-wide): 297.8MM **Privately Held**
WEB: www.bosch-home.com
SIC: 7629 Electrical household appliance repair
HQ: Bsh Hausgerate Gmbh
Carl-Wery-Str. 34
Munchen BY 81739
894 590-01

(P-18954)
DUTHIE ELECTRIC SERVICE CORP
Also Called: Duthie Power Services
2335 E Cherry Indus Cir, Long Beach (90805-4416)
PHONE..................562 790-1772
Christina Duthie, *President*
Richard Duthie, *Corp Secy*
Carlos Cestero, *Controller*
Kevin Gates, *Sales Mgr*
Karen Cooper, *Manager*
EMP: 50 EST: 1965
SQ FT: 17,000
SALES (est): 13.5MM **Privately Held**
WEB: www.duthiepower.com
SIC: 7629 7359 Generator repair; equipment rental & leasing

(P-18955)
RUBEN & LEON INC
Also Called: Takyo Tyco
5002 Venice Blvd, Los Angeles (90019-5308)
PHONE..................323 937-4445
Ruben Cielak, *President*
Leon Cielak, *Vice Pres*
Craig Posey, *Project Mgr*
EMP: 20 EST: 1983
SQ FT: 8,000
SALES (est): 2.7MM **Privately Held**
WEB: www.tykosigns.com
SIC: 7629 5063 5719 3993 Electrical equipment repair services; light bulbs & related supplies; lighting, lamps & accessories; advertising artwork

(P-18956)
SCOTTEL VOICE & DATA INC
Also Called: Black Box Network Services
6100 Center Dr Ste 720, Los Angeles (90045-9228)
PHONE..................310 737-7300
George Robertson, *General Mgr*
Alex Kobe, *Administration*
Linda Hunt, *Engineer*
EMP: 130 EST: 1984
SQ FT: 5,200
SALES (est): 33.5MM
SALES (corp-wide): 573.9MM **Privately Held**
WEB: www.blackbox.com
SIC: 7629 1731 Telecommunication equipment (except telephones); telephone & telephone equipment installation
HQ: Black Box Corporation
1000 Park Dr
Lawrence PA 15055
724 746-5500

(P-18957)
SERVICE QUICK INC (PA)
18724 S Broadwick St, Compton (90220-6426)
PHONE..................213 700-4332
Kil Won Jin, *CEO*
Joseph Hong, *Manager*
EMP: 228 EST: 2013
SALES (est): 2.3MM **Privately Held**
WEB: www.servicequick.com
SIC: 7629 Telecommunication equipment repair (except telephones)

(P-18958)
TELENET VOIP INC
850 N Park View Dr, El Segundo (90245-4914)
PHONE..................310 253-9000
Asghar Ghassemy, *President*
Nicol Payab, *Vice Pres*
Doug Amos, *Executive*
Michael Merkel, *General Mgr*
Moises Sarabia, *Project Mgr*
EMP: 65
SQ FT: 11,000
SALES (est): 11.9MM **Privately Held**
WEB: www.telenetvoip.com
SIC: 7629 7379 7382 3612 Telephone set repair; computer related consulting services; security systems services; transmission & distribution voltage regulators

(P-18959)
TESTEQUITY LLC (PA)
6100 Condor Dr, Moorpark (93021-2608)
PHONE..................805 498-9933
Steve Newland, *President*
Nick Hawtrey, *CFO*
Neil McKinnon, *CFO*
John Glass, *Chief Mktg Ofcr*
Michael Hade, *Senior VP*
▲ EMP: 168 EST: 1973
SQ FT: 75,000
SALES (est): 163.8MM **Privately Held**
WEB: www.jensentools.com
SIC: 7629 3825 Electrical equipment repair services; test equipment for electronic & electrical circuits

(P-18960)
TOTAL TELCO SPECIALISTS INC
Also Called: Tts
602 W Southern Ave, Orange (92865-3219)
PHONE..................805 541-2232
Earl J Darway, *President*
Phil Calkins, *Senior VP*
Eric Larson, *Vice Pres*
Doug Miller, *General Mgr*
Jesse Peralta, *General Mgr*
EMP: 60 EST: 1995
SQ FT: 14,000
SALES (est): 9.4MM **Privately Held**
WEB: www.totaltelco.net
SIC: 7629 Telecommunication equipment repair (except telephones)

(P-18961)
WILLIS ELECTRIC INC
Also Called: Willis Electric Company
4465 Buck Owens Blvd, Bakersfield (93308-4939)
P.O. Box 81085 (93380-1085)
PHONE..................661 324-2781
William A Willis, *President*
Dave Bosse, *Manager*
EMP: 28 EST: 1987
SQ FT: 8,500
SALES (est): 1.4MM **Privately Held**
WEB: www.williselectricmotorcompany.com
SIC: 7629 5999 7694 Electrical repair shops; motors, electric; electric motor repair

7631 Watch, Clock & Jewelry Repair

(P-18962)
ROLEX WATCH USA INC
Also Called: Rolex Watch Service Center Cal
9420 Wilshire Blvd # 400, Beverly Hills (90212-3151)
PHONE..................310 271-6200
Hines Imhof, *Vice Pres*
EMP: 60
SQ FT: 56,124
SALES (corp-wide): 240.2MM **Privately Held**
WEB: www.rolex.com
SIC: 7631 Watch, clock & jewelry repair
HQ: Rolex Watch U.S.A., Inc.
665 5th Ave Fl 6
New York NY 10022
212 758-7700

7641 Reupholstery & Furniture Repair

(P-18963)
GUYS PATIO INC
Also Called: Patio Guys
2907 Oak St, Santa Ana (92707-3722)
PHONE..................844 968-7485
Jan Vanderlinden, *President*
EMP: 25 EST: 1978
SALES (est): 1.4MM **Privately Held**
WEB: www.patioguys.com
SIC: 7641 5712 5021 2514 Furniture repair & maintenance; furniture stores; outdoor & lawn furniture; metal household furniture

(P-18964)
MOYES CUSTOM FURNITURE INC
3431 E La Palma Ave Ste 3, Anaheim (92806-2022)
PHONE..................714 729-0234
Brian Moyes, *President*
Jane Moyes, *Corp Secy*
Ildi Girba, *Office Mgr*
David Moyes, *Administration*
EMP: 50 EST: 1961
SQ FT: 59,000
SALES (est): 2.5MM **Privately Held**
WEB: www.moyesfurniture.com
SIC: 7641 2512 Reupholstery; upholstered household furniture

7692 Welding Repair

(P-18965)
A AND M WELDING INC
16935 S Broadway, Gardena (90248-3111)
PHONE..................310 329-2700
Tom A Jorgenson, *President*
Linda Jorgenson, *Vice Pres*
EMP: 22 EST: 1952
SQ FT: 25,000
SALES (est): 972.1K **Privately Held**
WEB: www.ammetalforming.com
SIC: 7692 Welding repair

(P-18966)
AEROSPACE WELDING INC
2035 Granville Ave, Los Angeles (90025-6103)
PHONE..................310 914-0324
EMP: 19
SQ FT: 20,000
SALES (est): 1.4MM
SALES (corp-wide): 44.2MM **Privately Held**
SIC: 7692 Welding Repair
HQ: Williams Aerospace & Manufacturing Inc.
1283 Flynn Rd
Camarillo CA 93012
805 446-2700

(P-18967)
AG-WELD INC
1236 G St, Wasco (93280-2359)
P.O. Box 637 (93280-0637)
PHONE..................661 758-3061
Jeff Mehlberg, *CEO*
Bedi Mehlberg, *Vice Pres*
Ben Coyle, *General Mgr*
Patty Mehlberg, *Controller*
▲ EMP: 23 EST: 1980
SQ FT: 20,000
SALES (est): 3.3MM **Privately Held**
WEB: www.ag-weld.com
SIC: 7692 Welding repair

(P-18968)
AGNALDOS WELDING INC
828 S Burnett Rd, Tipton (93272)
P.O. Box 154 (93272-0154)
PHONE..................559 752-4254
Agnaldo Tamariz, *President*
Delores Tamariz, *Treasurer*
James Tamariz, *Director*
EMP: 18 EST: 1980
SALES (est): 1MM **Privately Held**
WEB: www.agnaldoswelding.com
SIC: 7692 7699 5083 Welding repair; farm machinery repair; farm equipment parts & supplies

(P-18969)
ALL SPEC WELDING SOLUTIONS
10406 Enterprise St, Rancho Cucamonga (91730-5822)
PHONE..................909 794-4828
Nathaniel Kluz, *Principal*
EMP: 16 EST: 2012
SALES (est): 1MM **Privately Held**
SIC: 7692 Welding repair

(P-18970)
BILL WILLIAMS WELDING CO
1735 Santa Fe Ave, Long Beach (90813-1292)
PHONE..................562 432-5421
Martha Williams-Hermon, *President*
EMP: 70 EST: 1945
SQ FT: 30,000
SALES (est): 607K **Privately Held**
WEB: www.cwindustries.us
SIC: 7692 3441 Automotive welding; fabricated structural metal

(P-18971)
CAMERON WELDING SUPPLY (PA)
11061 Dale Ave, Stanton (90680-3247)
P.O. Box 266 (90680-0266)
PHONE..................714 530-9353
Elizabeth Perry, *CEO*
Joseph Churilla, *President*
Robert Rodriguez, *Branch Mgr*

Rick Tull, *Branch Mgr*
Geno Sanchez, *Store Mgr*
▲ **EMP:** 36 **EST:** 1963
SQ FT: 4,500 **Privately Held**
WEB: www.cameronwelding.com
SIC: 7692 5999 Welding repair; welding
supplies

(P-18972)
CAMLAND INC
3152 Canopy Dr, Camarillo (93012-7763)
PHONE....................805 485-9242
Darlene Camarillo, *CEO*
Dave Green, *Vice Pres*
EMP: 16 **EST:** 1999
SQ FT: 15,000
SALES (est): 466.3K **Privately Held**
SIC: 7692 3713 Welding repair; truck &
bus bodies

(P-18973)
CW INDUSTRIES INC (PA)
1735 Santa Fe Ave, Long Beach
(90813-1242)
PHONE....................562 432-5421
Craig Wildvank, *President*
EMP: 49 **EST:** 1979
SQ FT: 22,000
SALES (est): 7.8MM **Privately Held**
WEB: www.cwindustries.us
SIC: 7692 Welding repair

(P-18974)
**DEANS CERTIFIED WELDING
INC**
27645 Commerce Center Dr, Temecula
(92590-2521)
PHONE....................951 676-0242
Michael W Deam, *CEO*
Elizabeth Scott, *Office Mgr*
EMP: 18 **EST:** 2015
SALES (est): 1.3MM **Privately Held**
WEB: www.deanswelding.com
SIC: 7692 Welding repair

(P-18975)
DIP BRAZE INC
9131 De Garmo Ave, Sun Valley
(91352-2696)
PHONE....................818 768-1555
Gail Brown, *President*
Robert Gebo, *President*
EMP: 29 **EST:** 1956
SQ FT: 10,500
SALES (est): 2.8MM **Privately Held**
WEB: www.dipbraze.com
SIC: 7692 3398 Brazing; metal heat treat-
ing

(P-18976)
DOUG DELEO WELDING INC
249 N Ashland Ave, Lindsay (93247-2430)
P.O. Box 878 (93247-0878)
PHONE....................559 562-3700
Doug Deleo, *CEO*
Pam Deleo, *Vice Pres*
Robert Howard, *Prdtn Mgr*
EMP: 13 **EST:** 1990
SQ FT: 9,600
SALES (est): 3.4MM **Privately Held**
SIC: 7692 1799 Welding repair; welding
on site

(P-18977)
**ELECTRON BEAM
ENGINEERING INC**
1425 S Allec St, Anaheim (92805-6306)
PHONE....................714 491-5990
Richard Trillwood, *CEO*
Hilary Hurt, *Admin Sec*
Camille Chauvin, *Admin Asst*
Thomas Hurt, *Prdtn Mgr*
Tom Hurt, *Prdtn Mgr*
EMP: 14 **EST:** 1991
SQ FT: 17,000 **Privately Held**
WEB: www.electronbeamwelding.com
SIC: 7692 3548 Welding repair; welding
apparatus

(P-18978)
GALAXY BRAZING CO INC
10015 Freeman Ave, Santa Fe Springs
(90670-3405)
PHONE....................562 946-9039
John Mc Gee, *President*
Donna Mc Gee, *Treasurer*

EMP: 27 **EST:** 1961
SQ FT: 13,144
SALES (est): 2.2MM **Privately Held**
WEB: www.galaxybrazing.com
SIC: 7692 3398 1799 Brazing; metal heat
treating; welding on site

(P-18979)
GOULD WELDING INC
3725 Alisos Rd, Arroyo Grande
(93420-6151)
P.O. Box 112 (93421-0112)
PHONE....................805 489-9353
Aaron Gould, *Principal*
EMP: 16 **EST:** 2011
SALES (est): 669.1K **Privately Held**
SIC: 7692 Welding repair

(P-18980)
HANSENS WELDING INC
358 W 168th St, Gardena (90248-2733)
PHONE....................310 329-6888
Gary D Hansen, *CEO*
Robert Hansen, *Vice Pres*
Shauna Hansen, *Admin Sec*
EMP: 25 **EST:** 1949
SQ FT: 26,000
SALES (est): 4.6MM **Privately Held**
WEB: www.hansenswelding.com
SIC: 7692 Welding repair

(P-18981)
HAYES WELDING INC (PA)
Also Called: Valew Welding & Fabrication
12522 Violet Rd, Adelanto (92301-2704)
P.O. Box 310 (92301-0310)
PHONE....................760 246-4878
Roger L Hayes, *CEO*
Velma D Hayes, *President*
Vernon L Hayes, *Vice Pres*
Justin Dittemore, *Manager*
Keseloff Manya, *Clerk*
▲ **EMP:** 92 **EST:** 1954
SQ FT: 45,000
SALES (est): 14.2MM **Privately Held**
WEB: www.valew.com
SIC: 7692 3465 3714 3713 Welding re-
pair; automotive stampings; body parts,
automobile: stamped metal; fenders, au-
tomobile: stamped or pressed metal; fuel
systems & parts, motor vehicle; truck &
bus bodies; fabricated plate work (boiler
shop)

(P-18982)
IRONMAN INC
20555 Superior St, Chatsworth
(91311-4418)
PHONE....................818 341-0980
Joe Salem, *CEO*
Ben Salem, *Vice Pres*
Ziva Salem, *Vice Pres*
Tish Byrne, *Admin Sec*
EMP: 25 **EST:** 1987
SALES (est): 5.4MM **Privately Held**
WEB: www.ironmaninc.net
SIC: 7692 Welding repair

(P-18983)
**J AND D STL FBRICATION REPR
LP**
2360 Westgate Rd, Santa Maria
(93455-1046)
P.O. Box 5487 (93456-5487)
PHONE....................805 928-9674
Joe Trevino, *Partner*
David Cox, *Partner*
Yvonne Miller, *Manager*
EMP: 17 **EST:** 2018
SALES: 185.3K **Privately Held**
WEB: www.jdfabandweld.com
SIC: 7692 Welding repair

(P-18984)
JETI INC (PA)
Also Called: Jet I
14578 Hawthorne Ave, Fontana
(92335-2507)
PHONE....................909 357-2966
John Lowery, *President*
Jose Gradilla, *Vice Pres*
EMP: 13 **EST:** 1983
SQ FT: 10,000
SALES (est): 827K **Privately Held**
SIC: 7692 Welding repair

(P-18985)
JOBSITE STUD WELDING
9445 Washburn Rd, Downey (90242-2912)
PHONE....................855 885-7883
Julie Blanchard, *Human Res Mgr*
EMP: 14 **EST:** 2018
SALES (est): 5.9MM **Privately Held**
WEB: www.jobsitestud.com
SIC: 7692 Welding repair

(P-18986)
JON STEEL ERECTORS INC
1431 S Gage St, San Bernardino
(92408-2835)
PHONE....................909 799-0005
Octavio Arellano, *President*
EMP: 22 **EST:** 2005
SALES (est): 2.6MM **Privately Held**
WEB: www.jonsteelinc.com
SIC: 7692 5082 1791 Welding repair;
general construction machinery & equip-
ment; structural steel erection

(P-18987)
K C WELDING INC
1549 Dogwood Rd, El Centro
(92243-9605)
PHONE....................760 352-3832
C Mostrong, *Principal*
Rita Novak, *Info Tech Mgr*
Blake Stiff, *Sales Staff*
EMP: 13 **EST:** 1997
SALES (est): 1.2MM **Privately Held**
WEB: www.kcweldingandrentals.com
SIC: 7692 Welding repair

(P-18988)
KATHLEEN BRUGGER
Also Called: J&K Welding
6815 Foxtail Ct, Rancho Cucamonga
(91739-1577)
PHONE....................909 226-1372
Kathleen Brugger, *Owner*
EMP: 20 **EST:** 1982
SALES (est): 720.5K **Privately Held**
SIC: 7692 Welding repair

(P-18989)
MARLEON INC
Also Called: Hanley Welding
3202 W Rosecrans Ave, Hawthorne
(90250-8225)
PHONE....................310 679-1242
Leon Hanley, *President*
EMP: 28 **EST:** 1960
SQ FT: 3,000
SALES (est): 1.2MM **Privately Held**
SIC: 7692 2431 Welding repair; stair-
cases, stairs & railings

(P-18990)
**MIKES PRECISION WELDING
INC**
28073 Diaz Rd Ste D, Temecula
(92590-3464)
P.O. Box 891929 (92589-1929)
PHONE....................951 676-4744
Michael Prunty, *President*
Jeanette Prunty, *Admin Sec*
EMP: 17 **EST:** 2000
SQ FT: 3,000
SALES (est): 1MM **Privately Held**
SIC: 7692 Welding repair

(P-18991)
**MORGAN & SLATES MFG & SUP
INC (PA)**
12918 Hanford Armona Rd, Hanford
(93230-9023)
PHONE....................559 582-4417
Leroy Morgan, *CEO*
Gloria Morgan, *Corp Secy*
Brad Morgan, *Vice Pres*
Leonard Ramirez, *Buyer*
EMP: 17 **EST:** 1973
SQ FT: 15,000
SALES (est): 8.5MM **Privately Held**
WEB: www.morganandslates.com
SIC: 5251 7692 3523 Hardware; welding
repair; farm machinery & equipment

(P-18992)
**PHILLIPS MACHINE & WLDG CO
INC**
16125 Gale Ave, City of Industry
(91745-1709)
PHONE....................626 855-4600
Don McKenna, *Branch Mgr*
EMP: 42
SALES (corp-wide): 8.5MM **Privately
Held**
WEB: www.phillipsaerospace.com
SIC: 7692 Welding repair
PA: Phillip's Machine And Welding Com-
pany, Inc.
16125 Gale Ave
City Of Industry CA 91745
626 855-4600

(P-18993)
R B WELDING INC
155 E Redondo Beach Blvd, Gardena
(90248-2347)
PHONE....................310 324-8680
Nabil Abeskharoun, *President*
EMP: 20 **EST:** 1973
SQ FT: 2,500
SALES (est): 2MM **Privately Held**
WEB: www.rb-welding.net
SIC: 7692 3441 Welding repair; fabricated
structural metal

(P-18994)
**RANDY NIX CSTM WLDG & MFG
INC**
22700 Road 196, Lindsay (93247-9832)
P.O. Box 730, Strathmore (93267-0730)
PHONE....................559 562-1958
Guy Randy Nix, *President*
Traci L Nix, *Corp Secy*
EMP: 26 **EST:** 2006
SQ FT: 74,880
SALES (est): 2.7MM **Privately Held**
WEB: www.customweldingca.com
SIC: 7692 3556 Welding repair; packing
house machinery

(P-18995)
RETTIG MACHINE INC
301 Kansas St, Redlands (92373-8153)
P.O. Box 7460 (92375-0460)
PHONE....................909 793-7811
Franz A Rettig Sr, *President*
Susan L Rettig, *Corp Secy*
Bob Rettig, *Vice Pres*
Franz A Rettig Jr, *Vice Pres*
Robert A Rettig, *Vice Pres*
EMP: 25
SQ FT: 37,000
SALES (est): 1.6MM **Privately Held**
WEB: www.rettigmachine.com
SIC: 7692 3599 Welding repair; machine
shop, jobbing & repair

(P-18996)
**SO CAL TRACTOR SALES CO
INC**
30517 The Old Rd, Castaic (91384-3709)
PHONE....................818 252-1900
Utz James, *President*
EMP: 19 **EST:** 1993
SQ FT: 26,000
SALES (est): 682.5K **Privately Held**
WEB: www.socalturfandtractor.com
SIC: 7692 7549 1799 Welding repair; high
performance auto repair & service; steam
cleaning of building exteriors

(P-18997)
**STAINLESS TECHNOLOGIES
LLC**
19425 W Grove Ave, Visalia (93291)
PHONE....................559 651-0460
Robert Krikorian, *President*
Manny Hoy, *CFO*
Freddy Perales, *General Mgr*
Curt Nelson, *Project Mgr*
Richard Perales, *Project Mgr*
EMP: 13 **EST:** 2007
SQ FT: 5,000
SALES (est): 181.5K **Privately Held**
WEB: www.stainlesstech.com
SIC: 7692 Welding repair

(P-18998)
STAINLESS WORKS INC
201 E Owens Ave, Tulare (93274-5434)
PHONE..........................559 688-4310
Richard Perales, *President*
Margaret Perales, *Treasurer*
David Munoz, *Vice Pres*
Judy Munoz, *Admin Sec*
EMP: 17 **EST:** 1998
SQ FT: 2,200
SALES (est): 2.7MM **Privately Held**
WEB: www.stainless-works-specialties-inc.hub.biz
SIC: 7692 Welding repair

(P-18999)
T L FABRICATIONS LP
2921 E Coronado St, Anaheim
(92806-2502)
PHONE..........................562 802-3980
Ryan Kerrigan, *President*
Michael Hsu, *Vice Pres*
Jorge Hernandez, *Manager*
▲ **EMP:** 60 **EST:** 1980
SQ FT: 30,000
SALES (est): 6.5MM **Privately Held**
WEB: www.tlfab.com
SIC: 7692 Welding repair

(P-19000)
THEODORE B MARTIN
Also Called: Mmiw Welding & Fabrication
17530 Doran Dr, Springville (93265-9386)
PHONE..........................559 360-2559
Theodore Martin, *Owner*
EMP: 20 **EST:** 2002
SALES (est): 1.5MM **Privately Held**
SIC: 7692 Welding repair

(P-19001)
TIKOS TANKS INC
Also Called: Rte Welding
14561 Hawthorne Ave, Fontana
(92335-2508)
PHONE..........................951 757-8014
Ruben Gutierrez III, *Founder*
Richard Barnes, *CIO*
EMP: 41 **EST:** 2007
SALES (est): 1.4MM **Privately Held**
WEB: www.rtewelding.com
SIC: 7692 Welding repair

(P-19002)
WELDLOGIC INC
2651 Lavery Ct, Newbury Park
(91320-1502)
PHONE..........................805 375-1670
Robert Elizarraz, *President*
Jack Froschauer, *Vice Pres*
Rick Heminuk, *VP Engrg*
▲ **EMP:** 65 **EST:** 1980
SQ FT: 25,000
SALES (est): 10.2MM **Privately Held**
WEB: www.weldlogic.com
SIC: 7692 Welding repair

(P-19003)
WEST COAST WELDING & CNSTR
390 S Del Norte Blvd, Oxnard
(93030-7914)
PHONE..........................805 604-1222
Micheal Edward Barbey, *CEO*
Tamara Barbey, *CFO*
Stella Delgado, *Admin Sec*
John Bricker, *Superintendent*
EMP: 14 **EST:** 2005
SALES (est): 501.6K **Privately Held**
SIC: 7692 Welding repair

(P-19004)
WEST COAST WLDG & PIPING INC
Also Called: PIPLINE
640 W Hueneme Rd, Oxnard (93033-9012)
PHONE..........................805 246-5841
Gabriel Nunez, *Mng Member*
Mike Barbey,
Jose Vargas,
EMP: 80 **EST:** 2018
SALES (est): 1.2MM **Privately Held**
WEB: www.wcwpiping.com
SIC: 7692 Welding repair

(P-19005)
WYMORE INC
697 S Dogwood Rd, El Centro
(92243-9747)
P.O. Box 2618 (92244-2618)
PHONE..........................760 352-2045
Marla Wymore Stilwell, *President*
Michael Mouser, *Treasurer*
Mike Mouser, *Purchasing*
Richard C Wymore, *Director*
Thomas A Wymore, *Director*
EMP: 30 **EST:** 1947
SQ FT: 25,200
SALES (est): 4.3MM **Privately Held**
WEB: www.wymoreinc.com
SIC: 7692 3599 5251 5085 Welding repair; machine shop, jobbing & repair; tools; tools

7694 Armature Rewinding Shops

(P-19006)
BAKERSFIELD ELC MTR REPR INC
Also Called: B E M R
121 W Sumner St, Bakersfield
(93301-4137)
PHONE..........................661 327-3583
Michael Wayne Langston, *President*
Jerry Endicott, *President*
Nina Endicott, *Vice Pres*
EMP: 67 **EST:** 1949
SQ FT: 12,350
SALES (est): 1.3MM **Privately Held**
SIC: 7694 5063 Rewinding services; electric motor repair; motors, electric

(P-19007)
BRECKS ELECTRIC MOTORS INC
30510 Road 68, Visalia (93291-9585)
PHONE..........................559 651-1475
Breck Bruce Altaffer, *CEO*
EMP: 13 **EST:** 2000
SALES (est): 896.1K **Privately Held**
WEB: www.breckselectricmotors.com
SIC: 7694 5063 Armature rewinding shops; electrical supplies

(P-19008)
DEMARIA ELECTRIC INC
Also Called: Demaria Electric Motor Svcs
7048 Marcelle St, Paramount
(90723-4839)
PHONE..........................310 549-4980
Daniel Demaria, *President*
Gary Demaria, *Information Mgr*
EMP: 21 **EST:** 1977
SQ FT: 6,500
SALES (est): 1.3MM **Privately Held**
WEB: www.demariaelectric.com
SIC: 7694 7699 Electric motor repair; engine repair & replacement, non-automotive

(P-19009)
E & L ELECTRIC
12322 Los Nietos Rd, Santa Fe Springs
(90670-2912)
PHONE..........................562 903-9272
Mike Fitch, *President*
Adam Fitch, *Sales Staff*
Orlanda Sosa, *Accounts Mgr*
EMP: 17 **EST:** 1959
SQ FT: 10,000
SALES (est): 4.1MM **Privately Held**
WEB: www.eandlelectric.com
SIC: 7694 5063 Electric motor repair; motors, electric

(P-19010)
ELECTRIC MOTOR WORKS INC
803 Inyo St, Bakersfield (93305-5127)
P.O. Box 3349 (93385-3349)
PHONE..........................661 327-4271
L B Thomasl B Thomas, *CEO*
Chuck Thomas, *Vice Pres*
Austin Schwebel, *General Mgr*
Melody Alther, *Office Mgr*
Mike Anderson, *Sales Mgr*
EMP: 20 **EST:** 1939
SQ FT: 7,600
SALES (est): 2.4MM **Privately Held**
WEB: www.electricmotorworks.com
SIC: 7694 5063 Electric motor repair; motors, electric

(P-19011)
EURTON ELECTRIC COMPANY INC
9920 Painter Ave, Santa Fe Springs
(90670)
P.O. Box 2113 (90670-0113)
PHONE..........................562 946-4477
John Buchanan, *President*
Heather Buchanan, *Vice Pres*
Rick Arellano, *General Mgr*
Julie Galaviz-Macias, *Office Mgr*
Ashley Tallis, *Admin Asst*
▲ **EMP:** 34 **EST:** 1973
SQ FT: 10,000
SALES (est): 1.7MM **Privately Held**
WEB: www.eurtonelectric.com
SIC: 7694 5063 Rewinding services; electrical supplies

(P-19012)
G POWELL ELECTRIC
Also Called: GP Electric
1020 Price Ave, Pomona (91767-5739)
PHONE..........................909 865-2291
Geepi Powell, *President*
EMP: 34 **EST:** 1978
SQ FT: 19,000
SALES (est): 674.4K **Privately Held**
SIC: 7694 5063 Electric motor repair; motors, electric

(P-19013)
GRECH MOTORS LLC (PA)
6915 Arlington Ave, Riverside
(92504-1905)
PHONE..........................951 688-8347
Edward P Grech, *Mng Member*
Aj Thurber, *Vice Pres*
Steve Little, *Executive*
Brian Neill, *Executive*
Sue Reagan, *Executive Asst*
EMP: 42 **EST:** 2012
SALES (est): 24.5MM **Privately Held**
WEB: www.grechmotors.com
SIC: 7694 Electric motor repair

(P-19014)
MAGNETECH INDUSTRIAL SVCS INC
7515 W Sunnyview Ave, Visalia
(93291-9602)
PHONE..........................559 651-0606
EMP: 27 **EST:** 2014
SALES (est): 207.3K **Privately Held**
WEB: www.magnetech.com
SIC: 7694 Electric motor repair

(P-19015)
R A REED ELECTRIC COMPANY (PA)
Also Called: Reed Electric & Field Service
5503 S Boyle Ave, Vernon (90058-3932)
PHONE..........................323 587-2284
John A Richard Jr, *President*
Alex Wong, *CFO*
Dorothy J Richard, *Treasurer*
John Corral, *Vice Pres*
Tim Durnil, *Sales Staff*
EMP: 29 **EST:** 1929
SQ FT: 55,000
SALES (est): 6.2MM **Privately Held**
WEB: www.reed-electric.com
SIC: 7694 5063 Electric motor repair; motors, electric

(P-19016)
SULZER ELECTRO-MECHANICAL SERV
620 S Rancho Ave, Colton (92324-3243)
PHONE..........................909 825-7971
Gary Patton, *Branch Mgr*
EMP: 50
SALES (corp-wide): 3.6B **Privately Held**
WEB: www.sulzer.com
SIC: 7694 5063 Electric motor repair; motors, electric
HQ: Sulzer Electro-Mechanical Services
(Us) Inc.
1910 Jasmine Dr
Pasadena TX 77503
713 473-3231

(P-19017)
SUPERIOR ELECTRIC MTR SVC INC
4622 Alcoa Ave, Vernon (90058-2416)
PHONE..........................323 583-1040
Vicky Marachelian, *President*
Art Marachelian, *Vice Pres*
Christopher Marachelian, *Vice Pres*
Mark Frank, *Consultant*
EMP: 18 **EST:** 1963
SQ FT: 12,000
SALES (est): 4.5MM **Privately Held**
WEB: www.superiorelectricmotors.com
SIC: 7694 5063 Electric motor repair; motors, electric

(P-19018)
VISALIA ELECTRIC MOTOR SP INC
Also Called: Visalia Electric Motor Service
7515 W Sunnyview Ave, Visalia
(93291-9602)
PHONE..........................559 651-0606
Gene Quesnoy, *President*
EMP: 45 **EST:** 1945
SQ FT: 30,000
SALES (est): 2.9MM **Publicly Held**
WEB: www.magnetech.com
SIC: 7694 Electric motor repair
HQ: Magnetech Industrial Services, Inc.
800 Nave Rd Se
Massillon OH 44646
330 830-3500

7699 Repair Shop & Related Svcs, NEC

(P-19019)
ADVANCED CMBSTN PRCESS CNTRLS
1648 Art St, Bakersfield (93312-2165)
P.O. Box 22225 (93390-2225)
PHONE..........................661 615-1193
Stephen David Bopp, *President*
▲ **EMP:** 14 **EST:** 2008
SALES (est): 3MM **Privately Held**
WEB: www.advancedcombustionpro.com
SIC: 7699 1382 4931 Engine repair & replacement, non-automotive; oil & gas exploration services;

(P-19020)
AER TECHNOLOGIES INC
650 Columbia St, Brea (92821-2912)
PHONE..........................714 871-7357
Kim Quick, *CEO*
Michael McGroarty, *President*
Ingrid Osborne, *Admin Sec*
Vivek Menon, *Engineer*
Elaine Hernandez, *Human Res Mgr*
EMP: 320 **EST:** 1953
SQ FT: 50,000
SALES (est): 25.8MM **Privately Held**
WEB: www.aertech.com
SIC: 7699 Precision instrument repair

(P-19021)
AEROWORX INC
Also Called: Aero Worx
2565 W 237th St, Torrance (90505-5216)
PHONE..........................310 891-0300
Gary E Furlong, *President*
Carol Furlong, *Admin Sec*
Bob Smith, *Engineer*
▼ **EMP:** 30 **EST:** 1999
SQ FT: 38,800
SALES: 8.6MM **Privately Held**
WEB: www.aero-worx.com
SIC: 7699 3569 3492 3724 Industrial equipment services; industrial shock absorbers; control valves; aircraft: hydraulic & pneumatic; electrohydraulic servo valves; metal; pumps, aircraft engine; aircraft parts & equipment; aircraft assemblies, subassemblies & parts

PRODUCTS & SVCS

(P-19022)
AMERICAN COOLING TOWER INC (PA)
3130 W Harvard St, Santa Ana
(92704-3937)
PHONE..................714 898-2436
Erik Johnson, *President*
Brandi Reyes, *Project Mgr*
Kayte Meyer, *Opers Staff*
Chris Dahlen, *Sales Mgr*
Robert Spragg, *Sales Staff*
EMP: 19 **EST:** 1990
SQ FT: 3,500
SALES (est): 5.3MM **Privately Held**
WEB: www.americancoolingtower.com
SIC: 7699 3444 Tank repair & cleaning services; cooling towers, sheet metal

(P-19023)
AMERICAN VISION WINDOWS INC
2125 N Madera Rd Ste A, Simi Valley
(93065-7709)
PHONE..................805 582-1833
William Herren, *CEO*
Gabriela Herrera, *COO*
Frank Kolesar, *CFO*
Al Alfieri, *Vice Pres*
Monica Estrada, *Vice Pres*
EMP: 215 **EST:** 1999
SALES (est): 39.9MM **Privately Held**
WEB: www.americanvisionwindows.com
SIC: 7699 1799 5031 Door & window repair; home/office interiors finishing, furnishing & remodeling; metal doors, sash & trim

(P-19024)
AMKO SERVICE COMPANY
17909 Adelanto Rd, Adelanto
(92301-1745)
PHONE..................760 246-3600
Michael Medsker, *Manager*
EMP: 70 **Privately Held**
WEB: www.amkotech.com
SIC: 7699 Tank repair & cleaning services
HQ: Amko Service Company
3211 Brightwood Rd
Midvale OH 44653
330 364-8857

(P-19025)
BRIDPORT ERIE AVIATION INC
Also Called: Amsafe Bridport
2220 E Cerritos Ave, Anaheim
(92806-5709)
PHONE..................714 634-8801
Sal Valle, *Manager*
Keith McConnell, *President*
Habib Enayetullah, *Treasurer*
Dennis Gilbert, *Vice Pres*
Harold Handelsman, *Admin Sec*
EMP: 61 **EST:** 2000
SQ FT: 7,500
SALES (est): 953.3K **Privately Held**
WEB: www.amsafebridport.com
SIC: 7699 7363 3728 Aircraft & heavy equipment repair services; pilot service, aviation; aircraft body & wing assemblies & parts

(P-19026)
CALI FRAMING SUPPLIES LLC
20450 Plummer St, Chatsworth
(91311-5372)
PHONE..................818 899-7777
Barry Kaufman, *Mng Member*
Chaim Neuberg,
▲ **EMP:** 20 **EST:** 2009
SALES (est): 5.3MM **Privately Held**
WEB: www.califraming.com
SIC: 7699 3999 Picture framing, custom; framed artwork

(P-19027)
CALIFRNIA ELCTRMECHANICAL REPR
Also Called: Delta Plastics
606 W Doran St, Glendale (91203-1626)
PHONE..................818 840-9211
Fax: 818 840-8231
EMP: 14
SQ FT: 4,000

SALES (est): 664K **Privately Held**
SIC: 7699 3089 3599 3559 Repair Services Mfg Plastic Products Mfg Industrial Machinery Mfg Misc Industry Mach

(P-19028)
CARBIDE SAW AND TOOL INC
336 S Waterman Ave Ste P, San Bernardino
(92408-1534)
PHONE..................909 884-9956
Mark Mackamul, *Director*
Philip Mackamul, *Admin Sec*
EMP: 15 **EST:** 1991
SQ FT: 2,500
SALES (est): 650K **Privately Held**
WEB: www.carbidesawandtool.com
SIC: 7699 3545 3546 Knife, saw & tool sharpening & repair; machine tool accessories; saws & sawing equipment

(P-19029)
CASH CONVENIENCE INDS LLC
Also Called: Atmpartmart.com
733 Lakefield Rd Ste Aa, Westlake Village
(91361-2625)
PHONE..................805 381-0806
Kathleen Fischer,
Patrick Conner,
Ted Fischer,
Art Leigh,
Nazanin Shams,
▲ **EMP:** 14 **EST:** 2007
SQ FT: 5,000
SALES (est): 1.7MM **Privately Held**
WEB: www.atmpartmart.com
SIC: 7699 3578 Automated teller machine (ATM) repair; automatic teller machines (ATM)

(P-19030)
CDSRVS LLC
840 W Grove Ave, Orange (92865-3216)
PHONE..................714 912-8353
Steven Fenzel, *President*
Jim Philipps, *Exec VP*
Danielle Thompson, *Admin Asst*
Gordon McTavish,
Jerramie Argo, *Manager*
EMP: 56 **EST:** 2010
SQ FT: 10,000
SALES (est): 6MM **Privately Held**
WEB: www.cleanacanoc.com
SIC: 7699 Metal reshaping & replating services; plastics products repair

(P-19031)
COLLECTORS UNIVERSE INC (PA)
1610 E Saint Andrew Pl, Santa Ana
(92705-4941)
P.O. Box 6280, Newport Beach (92658-6280)
PHONE..................949 567-1234
Joseph J Orlando, *CEO*
Nichole Schembre, *Receiver*
Bruce A Stevens, *Ch of Bd*
Joseph J Wallace, *CFO*
Joseph R Martin, *Bd of Directors*
EMP: 375 **EST:** 1986
SQ FT: 62,755
SALES: 78.8MM **Privately Held**
WEB: www.collectors.com
SIC: 7699 Hobby & collectors services

(P-19032)
CROTHALL SERVICES GROUP
14710 Northam St, La Mirada
(90638-5620)
PHONE..................714 562-9275
Frank Arcos, *Branch Mgr*
EMP: 620
SALES (corp-wide): 26B **Privately Held**
WEB: www.crothall.com
SIC: 7699 Hospital equipment repair services
HQ: Crothall Services Group
1500 Liberty Ridge Dr # 210
Chesterbrook PA 19087

(P-19033)
DK VALVE & SUPPLY INC
Also Called: DK Amans Valve & Supply
2385 E Artesia Blvd, Long Beach
(90805-1707)
PHONE..................562 529-8400

David Kinzler, *CEO*
Eddie Kinzler, *Director*
EMP: 33 **EST:** 1987
SALES (est): 1.1MM **Privately Held**
WEB: www.dkamans.com
SIC: 7699 3491 Valve repair, industrial; industrial valves

(P-19034)
DUCLOS LENSES INC
20222 Bahama St, Chatsworth
(91311-6203)
PHONE..................818 773-0600
Paul Duclos, *President*
Michelle Duclos, *Officer*
Kelsey Fisher, *Admin Asst*
Evelyn Frederick, *Admin Asst*
David Pannkuk, *Technician*
EMP: 17 **EST:** 2013
SALES (est): 2.5MM **Privately Held**
WEB: www.ducloslenses.com
SIC: 7699 5731 3861 Camera repair shop; video cameras & accessories; lens shades, camera

(P-19035)
EDN AVIATION INC
6720 Valjean Ave, Van Nuys (91406-5818)
PHONE..................818 988-8826
Motti Kurzweil, *President*
Edan Kurzweil, *General Mgr*
Nishan Bostanian, *Manager*
EMP: 45 **EST:** 1987
SQ FT: 15,000
SALES (est): 7.6MM
SALES (corp-wide): 49.8MM **Privately Held**
WEB: www.ednaviation.com
SIC: 7699 3728 Aircraft & heavy equipment repair services; research & dev by manuf., aircraft parts & auxiliary equip
PA: Velocity Aerospace Group, Inc.
7460 Warren Pkwy Ste 180
Frisco TX 75034
214 988-9898

(P-19036)
EVANS HYDRO INC
18128 S Santa Fe Ave, Compton
(90221-5517)
PHONE..................310 608-5801
James R Byrom, *President*
James Byrom, *Accounts Mgr*
Jimmy Byrom, *Accounts Mgr*
EMP: 28 **EST:** 1929
SQ FT: 16,000
SALES (est): 8MM
SALES (corp-wide): 91.1MM **Privately Held**
WEB: www.hydroinc.com
SIC: 7699 7694 5084 Pumps & pumping equipment repair; armature rewinding shops; pumps & pumping equipment
PA: Hydro, Inc.
834 W Madison St
Chicago IL 60607
312 738-3000

(P-19037)
EXCEL PICTURE FRAMES INC
647 E 59th St, Los Angeles (90001-1001)
PHONE..................323 231-0244
Rafael Delgado, *CEO*
Antonio Delgado Sr, *President*
EMP: 50 **EST:** 1992
SALES (est): 1.8MM **Privately Held**
WEB: www.excelpictureframes.com
SIC: 7699 2791 Picture framing, custom; photocomposition, for the printing trade

(P-19038)
FLEETWOOD MOTOR HOMES-CALIF INC
Also Called: Fleetwood Homes
2350 Fleetwood Dr, Riverside
(92509-2409)
PHONE..................951 274-2000
David Lewis, *Branch Mgr*
EMP: 185 **Privately Held**
WEB: www.fleetwoodhomes.com
SIC: 7699 5271 Mobile home repair; mobile homes
HQ: Fleetwood Motor Homes-Calif.Inc
3125 Myers St
Riverside CA 92503
951 354-3000

(P-19039)
GENESIS TECH PARTNERS LLC
21540 Plummer St Ste A, Chatsworth
(91311-4143)
PHONE..................800 950-2647
Sandy D Morford,
Haresh Satiani,
EMP: 240 **EST:** 1998
SQ FT: 3,000
SALES (est): 1MM
SALES (corp-wide): 35.2B **Privately Held**
SIC: 7699 Medical equipment repair, non-electric
HQ: Cohr, Inc.
10510 Twin Lakes Pkwy
Charlotte NC 28269
704 948-5700

(P-19040)
HAWKER PACIFIC AEROSPACE
11240 Sherman Way, Sun Valley
(91352-4942)
PHONE..................818 765-6201
Bernd Riggers, *CEO*
Troy Trower, *CFO*
Brian Carr, *Vice Pres*
Dennis Jelinek, *Technician*
David Benitez, *Engineer*
◆ **EMP:** 355 **EST:** 1980
SQ FT: 193,000
SALES (est): 51.6MM
SALES (corp-wide): 16B **Privately Held**
WEB: www.hawker.com
SIC: 7699 5088 3728 Hydraulic equipment repair; aircraft & parts; aircraft parts & equipment
HQ: Lufthansa Technik Ag
Weg Beim Jager 193
Hamburg HH 22335
405 070-3667

(P-19041)
HOGUE INC
550 Linne Rd, Paso Robles (93446-8454)
P.O. Box 91360, Henderson NV (89009-1360)
PHONE..................805 239-1440
Aaron Hogue, *President*
EMP: 53 **EST:** 1990
SALES (est): 20.8MM **Privately Held**
WEB: www.hogueinc.com
SIC: 7699 5099 Gun services; machine guns

(P-19042)
HRD AERO SYSTEMS INC (PA)
25555 Avenue Stanford, Valencia
(91355-1101)
PHONE..................661 295-0670
Tom Salamone, *President*
Tim McBride, *CFO*
Rich OHM, *Executive*
Paul Zapata, *Regional Mgr*
Albert Leon, *CIO*
◆ **EMP:** 108 **EST:** 1986
SQ FT: 70,000
SALES (est): 12.2MM **Privately Held**
WEB: www.hrd-aerosystems.com
SIC: 7699 8711 Aircraft & heavy equipment repair services; aircraft flight instrument repair; aviation propeller & blade repair; aviation &/or aeronautical engineering

(P-19043)
IMAGE 2000 INC (PA)
26037 Huntington Ln, Valencia
(91355-1145)
PHONE..................818 781-2200
Joe Blatchford, *CEO*
Richard Campbell, *President*
Michael McGuigan, *Vice Pres*
Kevin Amezquita, *Executive*
Mitch Claman, *Executive*
▲ **EMP:** 50 **EST:** 1992
SQ FT: 22,557
SALES (est): 28MM **Privately Held**
WEB: www.image-2000.com
SIC: 7699 5999 Photographic equipment repair; photocopy machines

(P-19044)
INNOVATIVE EMERGENCY EQUIPMENT
1616 Marlborough Ave, Riverside (92507-2041)
PHONE..................................951 222-2270
EMP: 22 EST: 2016
SALES (est): 2.2MM Privately Held
WEB: www.idsmp.com
SIC: 7699 3669 Repair services; sirens, electric: vehicle, marine, industrial & air raid

(P-19045)
INTERFACE WELDING
20722 Belshaw Ave, Carson (90746-3510)
PHONE..................................310 323-4944
A S Wadleigh, President
EMP: 20 EST: 1967
SQ FT: 12,000
SALES (est): 3MM Privately Held
WEB: www.interfacewelding.com
SIC: 7699 7692 3769 3728 Welding equipment repair; welding repair; guided missile & space vehicle parts & auxiliary equipment; aircraft parts & equipment

(P-19046)
KONE INC
11165 Knott Ave Ste B, Cypress (90630-5148)
PHONE..................................714 890-7080
Jeff Schultz, Branch Mgr
Jon Rodgers, Branch Mgr
Ali Shamsa, Superintendent
EMP: 25
SALES (corp-wide): 11.7B Privately Held
WEB: www.kone.us
SIC: 7699 3534 1796 Elevators: inspection, service & repair; elevators & moving stairways; installing building equipment
HQ: Kone Inc.
4225 Naperville Rd # 400
Lisle IL 60532
630 577-1650

(P-19047)
LA HYDRO-JET ROOTER SVC INC
Also Called: La Hydrojet
10639 Wixom St, Sun Valley (91352-4603)
PHONE..................................818 768-4225
Daniel Baldwin, President
Lori Baldwin, CFO
Philip Abraham, Controller
Dean Buckley, Controller
Janet Parker, Assistant
EMP: 68 EST: 1991
SALES (est): 10.5MM Privately Held
WEB: www.lahydrojet.com
SIC: 7699 Sewer cleaning & rodding

(P-19048)
LINDER EQUIPMENT CO
311 E Kern Ave, Tulare (93274-4107)
P.O. Box 1139 (93275-1139)
PHONE..................................559 685-5000
Frances Linder, President
Troy D Allen, Corp Secy
Francine Linder, Vice Pres
Mike Stevenson, Sales Executive
Jonathan Hodson, Sales Staff
▲ EMP: 50 EST: 1947
SQ FT: 40,000
SALES (est): 28.3MM Privately Held
WEB: www.linderequipment.com
SIC: 5999 7699 Farm equipment & supplies; farm machinery repair

(P-19049)
LTP MODERN MACHINE INC
10900 Walker St, Cypress (90630-5013)
PHONE..................................562 795-1701
Thanh Phan, President
Loan Phan, Vice Pres
Gabriel Quintero, General Mgr
John Hunter, Production
Alex Gomez, Manager
EMP: 15
SQ FT: 30,000
SALES (est): 1.5MM Privately Held
WEB: www.ltpmodernmachine.com
SIC: 7699 3441 Industrial machinery & equipment repair; fabricated structural metal

(P-19050)
MCKENNA BOILER WORKS INC
1510 N Spring St, Los Angeles (90012-1925)
PHONE..................................323 221-1171
Howard Smith, President
Richard R Smith, President
James F Smith, Treasurer
EMP: 35 EST: 1921
SQ FT: 14,000
SALES (est): 4.5MM Privately Held
WEB: www.mckennaboiler.com
SIC: 7699 3823 Boiler repair shop; boiler controls: industrial, power & marine type

(P-19051)
MONARCH ART & FRAME INC
7700 Gloria Ave, Van Nuys (91406-1819)
PHONE..................................818 373-6180
Jaime V Mizrahi, CEO
EMP: 50 EST: 1997
SQ FT: 16,000
SALES (est): 3.4MM Privately Held
WEB: www.monarchframe.com
SIC: 7699 Picture framing, custom; cesspool cleaning

(P-19052)
OMNI OPTICAL PRODUCTS INC
22605 La Palma Ave # 502, Yorba Linda (92887-6713)
PHONE..................................714 692-1400
Jeffrey Frank, Branch Mgr
Chet Henry, Sales Dir
EMP: 31
SALES (corp-wide): 5.9MM Privately Held
WEB: www.omnisurvey.com
SIC: 7699 5048 3827 Photographic & optical goods equipment repair services; optometric equipment & supplies; optical instruments & lenses
PA: Omni Optical Products, Inc.
17282 Eastman
Irvine CA 92614
714 634-5700

(P-19053)
PACIFIC COAST ELEVATOR CORP
Also Called: Amtech Elevator Services
3041 Roswell St, Los Angeles (90065-2213)
PHONE..................................323 345-2550
Tom Bertsch, Branch Mgr
EMP: 101
SALES (corp-wide): 12.7B Publicly Held
WEB: www.amtechelevator.com
SIC: 7699 1796 Elevators: inspection, service & repair; elevator installation & conversion
HQ: Pacific Coast Elevator Corporation
1 Farm Springs Rd
Farmington CT 06032
860 676-6000

(P-19054)
PACWEST INSTRUMENT LABS INC
Also Called: Pacific Southwest Instruments
1721 Railroad St, Corona (92878-5011)
PHONE..................................951 737-0790
Jim Joubert, President
Boon Lee, CFO
Ray McDonald, Vice Pres
Tim Hernandez, Info Tech Mgr
David Bishop, Opers Mgr
EMP: 51 EST: 1982
SQ FT: 37,000
SALES (est): 9.5MM Privately Held
WEB: www.psilabs.com
SIC: 7699 7629 Aircraft flight instrument repair; aircraft electrical equipment repair

(P-19055)
PASSPORT TECHNOLOGY USA INC
Also Called: Asai
101 N Brand Blvd Ste 1230, Glendale (91203-2677)
PHONE..................................818 957-5471
Cleve Tzung, CEO
John Steely, COO
Paul Nielsen, CFO
Scott Dowty, Chairman
Jacqueline Sarcinelli, Senior VP
EMP: 33 EST: 1997
SQ FT: 1,200
SALES (est): 8.4MM Privately Held
WEB: www.passporttechnology.com
SIC: 7699 3578 6099 Automated teller machine (ATM) repair; automatic teller machines (ATM); automated teller machine (ATM) network

(P-19056)
PEGGS COMPANY INC (PA)
4851 Felspar St, Riverside (92509-3024)
PHONE..................................253 584-9548
Chresten Revelle Nelson, President
John L Peggs, President
Kristin Bywater, Asst Controller
Frank Loera, Purchasing
Stephen Forde, Opers Staff
◆ EMP: 100 EST: 1964
SQ FT: 80,000
SALES (est): 32.1MM Privately Held
WEB: www.thepeggscompany.com
SIC: 7699 3496 5046 7359 Shopping cart repair; miscellaneous fabricated wire products; commercial equipment; equipment rental & leasing

(P-19057)
PORTER BOILER SERVICE INC
1166 E 23rd St, Signal Hill (90755-3447)
PHONE..................................562 426-2528
George Hrebien, President
Nooshin Singhal, Admin Sec
Mohan Singhal, Project Mgr
EMP: 25 EST: 1958
SQ FT: 5,000
SALES (est): 4.5MM Privately Held
WEB: www.porterboiler.com
SIC: 7699 1711 3443 Boiler repair shop; boiler maintenance contractor; fabricated plate work (boiler shop)

(P-19058)
PSC INDUSTRIAL OUTSOURCING LP
Also Called: Hydrochempsc
19340 Van Ness Ave, Torrance (90501-1103)
PHONE..................................310 325-1600
EMP: 137
SALES (corp-wide): 750MM Privately Held
SIC: 7699 Repair Services
PA: Psc Industrial Outsourcing, Lp
900 Georgia Ave
Deer Park TX 77536
713 393-5600

(P-19059)
RAY GASKIN SERVICE
14312 Arrow Hwy, Baldwin Park (91706-1352)
PHONE..................................909 574-7000
Bill McIntosh, President
Gladys McIntosh, Office Mgr
EMP: 27 EST: 1941
SQ FT: 17,000
SALES (est): 524.1K Privately Held
WEB: www.raygaskinservice.com
SIC: 7699 5511 3713 Hydraulic equipment repair; trucks, tractors & trailers: new & used; garbage, refuse truck bodies

(P-19060)
REDMAN EQUIPMENT & MFG CO
19800 Normandie Ave, Torrance (90502-1182)
PHONE..................................310 329-1134
Donald Redman, Co-President
Gerald E Redman, CEO
Janelle Redman, Corp Secy
▲ EMP: 48 EST: 1962
SQ FT: 8,000
SALES (est): 9.4MM
SALES (corp-wide): 8.8B Publicly Held
WEB: www.redmaneq.com
SIC: 7699 3443 Boiler & heating repair services; heat exchangers, condensers & components
HQ: Ohmstede Ltd.
895 N Main St
Beaumont TX 77701
409 833-6375

(P-19061)
SA CAMP PUMP COMPANY
Also Called: SA Camp Pump and Drilling Co
17876 Zerker Rd, Bakersfield (93308-9221)
P.O. Box 82575 (93380-2575)
PHONE..................................661 399-2976
James S Camp, President
Greg Clerico, Sales Engr
Josh Alvidrez, Sales Staff
Gerrit Otten, Sales Staff
Don Pedersen, Sales Staff
EMP: 60 EST: 1952
SQ FT: 10,000
SALES (est): 18.4MM
SALES (corp-wide): 21.8MM Privately Held
WEB: www.sacampcompanies.com
SIC: 7699 3561 Agricultural equipment repair services; pumps & pumping equipment
PA: S A Camp Companies
17876 Zerker Rd
Bakersfield CA 93308
661 399-4451

(P-19062)
SAM SCHAFFER INC
Also Called: Weld-It Co
4477 Sheila St, Commerce (90023-4331)
PHONE..................................323 263-7524
Stephen Schaffer, Vice Pres
EMP: 43 EST: 1946
SQ FT: 54,000
SALES (est): 4.4MM Privately Held
WEB: www.welditco.com
SIC: 7699 3559 Industrial machinery & equipment repair; petroleum refinery equipment

(P-19063)
SCHINDLER ELEVATOR CORPORATION
16450 Fthill Blvd Ste 200, Sylmar (91342)
PHONE..................................818 336-3000
Lance Howard, Manager
Ronan Lebaut, General Mgr
Seth Stodghill, Project Mgr
John Meadows, Sales Staff
Lance Kiefer, Manager
EMP: 240
SALES (corp-wide): 753.4MM Privately Held
WEB: www.schindler.com
SIC: 7699 Elevators: inspection, service & repair
HQ: Schindler Elevator Corporation
20 Whippany Rd
Morristown NJ 07960
973 397-6500

(P-19064)
SCHRADER-BRIDGEPORT INTL INC
Amflo Products
2018 E Cedar St, Ontario (91761-8012)
PHONE..................................909 930-2475
George Alvarez, Manager
EMP: 198
SALES (corp-wide): 3B Privately Held
WEB: www.schrader-pacific.com
SIC: 7699 Industrial machinery & equipment repair
HQ: Schrader-Bridgeport International Inc.
205 Frazier Rd
Altavista VA 24517
434 369-4741

(P-19065)
SEARS ROEBUCK AND CO
100 Brea Mall, Brea (92821-5796)
PHONE..................................714 256-7328
EMP: 200
SALES (corp-wide): 16.7B Publicly Held
SIC: 7699 Repair Services
HQ: Sears, Roebuck And Co.
3333 Beverly Rd
Hoffman Estates IL 60179
847 286-2500

(PA)=Parent Co (HQ)=Headquarters (DH)=Div Headquarters
✪ = New Business established in last 2 years

(P-19066)
SEARS ROEBUCK AND CO
Also Called: Direct Delivery Center
5691 E Philadelphia St, Ontario
(91761-2805)
PHONE..................909 390-4210
EMP: 125
SALES (corp-wide): 16.7B **Publicly Held**
SIC: 7699 7629 Repair Services Electrical
   Repair
HQ: Sears, Roebuck And Co.
   3333 Beverly Rd
   Hoffman Estates IL 60179
   847 286-2500

(P-19067)
SEARS ROEBUCK AND CO
3845 State St, Santa Barbara
(93105-3161)
PHONE..................805 569-6700
EMP: 113
SALES (corp-wide): 16.7B **Publicly Held**
SIC: 5311 7699 Department Store
HQ: Sears, Roebuck And Co.
   3333 Beverly Rd
   Hoffman Estates IL 60179
   847 286-2500

(P-19068)
SHOP SERVICES INC
27622 Highway 33, Fellows (93224-9626)
PHONE..................661 768-1775
Joy Steve Swenson, *President*
EMP: 15 EST: 1979
SALES (est): 1.4MM **Privately Held**
SIC: 7699 3491 Valve repair, industrial;
   pressure valves & regulators, industrial

(P-19069)
SOUTHWEST PPLINE
TRNCHLESS COR (PA)
22118 S Vermont Ave, Torrance
(90502-2131)
PHONE..................310 329-8717
Justin Duchaineau, *President*
John Colich, *Director*
▲ EMP: 54 EST: 1999
SQ FT: 3,000 **Privately Held**
WEB: www.swpipeline.com
SIC: 7699 Sewer cleaning & rodding

(P-19070)
STAVROS ENTERPRISES INC
Also Called: Facilitec West
681 Arrow Grand Cir, Covina (91722-2146)
PHONE..................888 463-2293
Anthony Emanuel Stavros, *CEO*
Frank Martinez, *Branch Mgr*
Karina De Leon, *Office Mgr*
Teri Hamann, *Sales Staff*
Brian Houser, *Sales Staff*
EMP: 30 EST: 2006
SALES (est): 2.6MM **Privately Held**
WEB: www.facilitecwest.com
SIC: 7699 3272 Cleaning services; grease
   traps, concrete

(P-19071)
SUN COUNTRY MARINE INC
17092 Pullman St, Irvine (92614-5542)
PHONE..................909 390-6600
Joseph Michael Basso, *President*
Greg Glogow, *Exec VP*
Jeff Mellin, *Vice Pres*
Jim Cabral, *General Mgr*
Jeremiah Parkinson, *Store Mgr*
EMP: 52 EST: 1990
SALES (est): 11.3MM **Privately Held**
WEB: www.suncountrymarinegroup.com
SIC: 5551 7699 Motor boat dealers; boat
   repair

(P-19072)
SUNVAIR AEROSPACE GROUP
INC (PA)
29145 The Old Rd, Valencia (91355-1015)
PHONE..................661 294-3777
Udo Reider, *CEO*
Glenn Miller, *CFO*
Puya Parniani, *Officer*
Eduardo Escobedo, *Program Mgr*
Jennifer Niedrich, *Program Mgr*
EMP: 80
SQ FT: 77,000

SALES (est): 30MM **Privately Held**
WEB: www.sunvair.com
SIC: 7699 Aircraft & heavy equipment re-
   pair services

(P-19073)
TARSCO HOLDINGS LLC
11905 Regentview Ave, Downey
(90241-5515)
PHONE..................562 869-0200
Terry S Warren, *Mng Member*
Kim Wales, *Project Mgr*
Tyler Casteel, *Engineer*
James Combs, *Business Mgr*
Patrick Fitzgerald, *Controller*
EMP: 121 EST: 2007
SALES (est): 13.6MM
SALES (corp-wide): 164.4MM **Privately
Held**
WEB: www.tfwarren.com
SIC: 7699 Tank repair
PA: T.F. Warren Group Inc
   57 Old Onondaga Rd W
   Brantford ON N3T 5
   519 756-8222

(P-19074)
TAYLORS APPLIANCE
6140 Magnolia Ave, Riverside
(92506-2522)
PHONE..................951 683-6365
Scott Taylor, *President*
Harold Taylor Jr, *CFO*
Lola Taylor, *Admin Sec*
Sherry Esterberg, *Bookkeeper*
Nate Thomas, *Sales Mgr*
EMP: 50 EST: 1946
SQ FT: 12,000
SALES (est): 6.6MM **Privately Held**
WEB: www.taylorsappliance.com
SIC: 5722 7699 Electric household appli-
   ances, major; appliance parts; household
   appliance repair services

(P-19075)
TEAGUE CUSTOM MARINE INC
28115 Avenue Stanford, Valencia
(91355-1106)
PHONE..................661 295-7000
Robert Teague, *President*
EMP: 33 EST: 1992
SQ FT: 30,000
SALES (est): 1.1MM **Privately Held**
WEB: www.teaguecustommarine.com
SIC: 7699 5088 3732 7948 Boat repair;
   marine crafts & supplies; motorboats, in-
   board or outboard: building & repairing;
   boat racing; boat accessories & parts

(P-19076)
TECH KNOWLEDGE
ASSOCIATES LLC
Also Called: Tka
1 Centerpointe Dr Ste 200, La Palma
(90623-2529)
PHONE..................714 735-3810
Joe Randolph, *CEO*
Ed Wong, *CFO*
Steve Gilbert, *Exec VP*
EMP: 80 EST: 2011
SALES (est): 24.6MM
SALES (corp-wide): 32.7MM **Privately
Held**
WEB: www.ii-techknow.com
SIC: 7699 Medical equipment repair, non-
   electric
HQ: St. Joseph Health System
   3345 Michelson Dr Ste 100
   Irvine CA 92612
   949 381-4000

(P-19077)
TED LEVINE DRUM CO (PA)
1817 Chico Ave, South El Monte
(91733-2943)
P.O. Box 3246 (91733-0246)
PHONE..................626 579-1084
Ozzie Levine, *President*
Mario Hernandez, *Department Mgr*
Luis Serrano, *Maintence Staff*
Eli Bloch, *Manager*
EMP: 80 EST: 1983
SQ FT: 200,000

SALES (est): 10.7MM **Privately Held**
WEB: www.tldrumco.com
SIC: 7699 4959 3412 Industrial equipment services; sanitary services; metal
   barrels, drums & pails

(P-19078)
THARP TRUCK RENTAL INC
(PA)
Also Called: Depot
15243 Road 192, Porterville (93257-8967)
PHONE..................559 782-5800
Morris A Tharp, *CEO*
Carol R Tharp, *Corp Secy*
Casey O Tharp, *Vice Pres*
Loyd Crabtree, *Purchasing*
◆ EMP: 125 EST: 1936
SQ FT: 5,000
SALES (est): 10.8MM **Privately Held**
WEB: www.emtharp.com
SIC: 7699 5013 5511 5012 Agricultural
   equipment repair services; motor vehicle
   supplies & new parts; trucks, tractors &
   trailers: new & used; automobiles & other
   motor vehicles

(P-19079)
UNITED SERVICE TECH INC
181 W Orangethorpe Ave D, Placentia
(92870-6931)
PHONE..................714 224-1406
Robert Heidkamp, *CEO*
Patrick Mahoney, *CFO*
Sandra Smelcer, *Treasurer*
Rodger Smelcer, *Vice Pres*
Terrie Heidkamp, *Admin Sec*
EMP: 56 EST: 1995
SQ FT: 2,400
SALES (est): 16.5MM **Privately Held**
WEB: www.ustservice.com
SIC: 7699 5963 Industrial equipment serv-
   ices; food services, direct sales

(P-19080)
UNIVERSAL SAW COMPANY
INC
13316 Arctic Cir, Santa Fe Springs
(90670-5543)
PHONE..................562 921-8832
John Nostrand, *President*
Thelma Nostrand, *Treasurer*
Dale Nostrand, *Vice Pres*
Thelma Denton, *Admin Sec*
EMP: 15 EST: 1965
SQ FT: 8,000
SALES (est): 1.1MM **Privately Held**
WEB: www.universalsaw.com
SIC: 7699 3541 Knife, saw & tool sharp-
   ening & repair; machine tool replacement
   & repair parts, metal cutting types

(P-19081)
USOC MEDICAL
Also Called: Usoc Bio-Medical Services
20 Morgan, Irvine (92618-2022)
PHONE..................949 243-9109
Ali Nazem Youssef, *CEO*
Alexander Truong, *Software Dev*
Gadier Rodriguez, *Technician*
Pranil Singh, *Purchasing*
Hailey Larson, *Sales Staff*
EMP: 60 EST: 2010
SALES (est): 11.8MM **Privately Held**
WEB: www.usocmedical.com
SIC: 5999 7699 Medical apparatus & sup-
   plies; medical equipment repair, non-elec-
   tric

(P-19082)
VELOCITY AROSPC - BURBANK
INC (HQ)
2840 N Ontario St, Burbank (91504-2015)
PHONE..................818 246-8431
Dale Gable, *CEO*
Dennis Suedkamp, *President*
Jeff Black, *Exec VP*
Josephine Demetriou, *Vice Pres*
Coya Davis, *Executive*
EMP: 77 EST: 2013
SALES (est): 6.5MM
SALES (corp-wide): 49.8MM **Privately
Held**
WEB: www.velocityaero.com
SIC: 7699 Aircraft & heavy equipment re-
   pair services

PA: Velocity Aerospace Group, Inc.
   7460 Warren Pkwy Ste 180
   Frisco TX 75034
   214 988-9898

(P-19083)
WARDLOW 2 LP (PA)
333 S Grand Ave Ste 4070, Los Angeles
(90071-1544)
PHONE..................562 432-8066
Steven B McLeod, *Partner*
Joe Gregorio, *Partner*
Del Conte, *Vice Pres*
Porter Travis, *Vice Pres*
Scott Baker, *General Mgr*
EMP: 99 EST: 2007
SALES (est): 37.2MM **Privately Held**
SIC: 7699 Construction equipment repair

(P-19084)
WHITE HOUSE SANITATION INC
18916 Seaton Ave, Perris (92570-8720)
P.O. Box 3038, Whittier (90605-0038)
PHONE..................951 943-1550
Karen A Blackburn, *CEO*
Tim Blackburn, *Principal*
EMP: 65 EST: 1985
SQ FT: 6,000
SALES (est): 1.1MM
SALES (corp-wide): 39.2MM **Privately
Held**
WEB: www.uwscompany.com
SIC: 7699 7359 Septic tank cleaning serv-
   ice; portable toilet rental
PA: Universal Waste Systems, Inc.
   9016 Norwalk Blvd
   Santa Fe Springs CA 90670
   562 695-8236

(P-19085)
WHITING DOOR MFG CORP
301 S Milliken Ave, Ontario 91761-7800)
PHONE..................909 877-0120
Abdullah Eren, *Branch Mgr*
Chris Ericksen, *Area Mgr*
Paul Zola, *Area Mgr*
EMP: 93
SQ FT: 5,400
SALES (corp-wide): 103.2MM **Privately
Held**
WEB: www.whitingdoor.com
SIC: 7699 3713 5531 5211 Door & win-
   dow repair; truck & bus bodies; truck
   equipment & parts; garage doors, sale &
   installation
PA: Whiting Door Mfg Corp
   113 Cedar St
   Akron NY 14001
   716 542-5427

(P-19086)
WILLITTS EQUIPMENT
COMPANY INC
Also Called: Water Well Solutions
30548 Road 196, Exeter (93221-9773)
P.O. Box 1110 (93221-7110)
PHONE..................559 594-5020
Ken Williams, *President*
Kenneth W Williams, *President*
Jean Jones, *Corp Secy*
Korina Zimmerman, *Human Resources*
EMP: 36 EST: 1954
SALES (est): 9.8MM **Privately Held**
WEB: www.willittspump.com
SIC: 5251 5999 7699 7694 Pumps &
   pumping equipment; motors, electric;
   pumps & pumping equipment repair; elec-
   tric motor repair

7812 Motion Picture & Video Tape Production

(P-19087)
3ALITY DIGITAL LLC (PA)
Also Called: 3ality Technica
895 N Todd Ave, Azusa (91702-2224)
PHONE..................818 970-7756
Steve Schklair, *CEO*
Gari Ann Douglass, *COC*
Hector Ortega, *Senior VP*
Stephen Pizzo, *Senior VP*
Jonathan Shapiro,
▲ EMP: 58 EST: 2006
SQ FT: 25,000

SALES (est): 6.6MM **Privately Held**
WEB: www.3alitytechnica.com
SIC: 7812 Video production

(P-19088)
88RISING INC
5735 Melrose Ave, Los Angeles
(90038-3807)
PHONE..............................626 372-7387
Sean Miyashiro, *CEO*
EMP: 50 EST: 2015
SALES (est): 2.8MM **Privately Held**
SIC: 7812 Music video production

(P-19089)
A ITS LAUGH PRODUCTIONS INC
914 N Victory Blvd, Burbank (91502-1632)
PHONE..............................818 848-8787
EMP: 100
SALES (est): 17.2MM
SALES (corp-wide): 65.3B **Publicly Held**
SIC: 7812 Motion Picture And Video Production, Nsk
PA: The Walt Disney Company
500 S Buena Vista St
Burbank CA 91521
818 560-1000

(P-19090)
ABC FAMILY WORLDWIDE INC (HQ)
500 S Buena Vista St, Burbank
(91521-0001)
PHONE..............................818 560-1000
Elery Borton, *Manager*
EMP: 500 EST: 1996
SALES (est): 237.5MM
SALES (corp-wide): 65.3B **Publicly Held**
WEB: www.thewaltdisneycompany.com
SIC: 7812 4841 Cartoon production, television; cable & other pay television services
PA: The Walt Disney Company
500 S Buena Vista St
Burbank CA 91521
818 560-1000

(P-19091)
ADVANCED DIGITAL SERVICES INC (PA)
Also Called: A D S
948 N Cahuenga Blvd, Los Angeles
(90038-2615)
PHONE..............................323 962-8585
Thomas Engdahl, *President*
Andrew McIntyre, *Ch of Bd*
Brad Weyl, *COO*
Valerie Kroll, *Vice Pres*
Marvin Morales, *Opers Staff*
▲ EMP: 87 EST: 1989
SQ FT: 33,000
SALES (est): 15.7MM **Privately Held**
WEB: www.adshollywood.com
SIC: 7812 7819 Video tape production; film processing, editing & titling: motion picture

(P-19092)
ALL3MEDIA AMERICA LLC (DH)
6060 Center Dr Ste 400, Los Angeles
(90045-8855)
PHONE..............................424 732-6600
Sara Geater, *Mng Member*
Ivan Garel-Jones, *COO*
Kelsey Boxser,
Rich Leist, *Vice Pres*
Rebekah Fry, *CIO*
EMP: 67 EST: 2008
SALES (est): 21.2MM
SALES (corp-wide): 872.8MM **Privately Held**
WEB: www.all3a.com
SIC: 7812 Motion picture production

(P-19093)
ALLIED ENTERTAINMENT GROUP INC (PA)
Also Called: Allied Artists International
273 W Allen Ave, City of Industry (91746)
PHONE..............................626 330-0600
Greg Hammond, *President*
Robert Fitzpatrick, *Treasurer*
John Mason, *Vice Pres*
Ashley D Posner, *Vice Pres*

Kim Richards, *Admin Sec*
◆ EMP: 325
SQ FT: 60,000 **Privately Held**
WEB: www.alliedartists.com
SIC: 7812 Video production

(P-19094)
AND SYNDICATED PRODUCTIONS INC
3500 W Olive Ave Ste 1000, Burbank
(91505-5515)
PHONE..............................818 308-5200
▲ EMP: 100
SALES (est): 6.2MM **Privately Held**
SIC: 7812 Television Production

(P-19095)
ANONYMOUS CONTENT LLC (PA)
3532 Hayden Ave, Culver City
(90232-2413)
PHONE..............................310 558-6000
Steven Golin,
Michael Conway, *Officer*
Kathryn Thal, *Executive*
Tor Fitzwilliams, *Managing Dir*
Kelcey Maguire, *Executive Asst*
▲ EMP: 60
SALES (est): 250MM **Privately Held**
WEB: www.anonymouscontent.com
SIC: 7812 Video production

(P-19096)
ARTISAN ENTERTAINMENT INC
2700 Colorado Ave Ste 200, Santa Monica
(90404-5502)
PHONE..............................310 449-9200
Wayne Levin, *President*
James W Barge, *CFO*
Brian James Gladstone, *Exec VP*
Agapy Kapouranis, *Exec VP*
Kristine Klimczak, *Exec VP*
EMP: 1000 EST: 1988
SALES (est): 51.7MM
SALES (corp-wide): 3.8B **Privately Held**
WEB: www.lionsgate.com
SIC: 7812 Motion picture production; motion picture production & distribution; music video production; video tape production
HQ: Lions Gate Entertainment Inc.
2700 Colorado Ave Ste 200
Santa Monica CA 90404
310 449-9200

(P-19097)
ASSOCIATED ENTRMT RELEASING (PA)
Also Called: Associated Television Intl
4401 Wilshire Blvd, Los Angeles
(90010-3703)
P.O. Box 4180 (90078-4180)
PHONE..............................323 556-5600
David McKenzie, *President*
Murray Drechsler, *CFO*
Murray Dreschler, *CFO*
Richard Casares, *Vice Pres*
Barry Thurston, *Administration*
EMP: 50 EST: 1982
SQ FT: 35,000
SALES (est): 10.7MM **Privately Held**
SIC: 7812 Motion picture production & distribution

(P-19098)
ATLAS DIGITAL LLC (PA)
170 S Flower St, Burbank (91502-2122)
P.O. Box 4110 (91503-4110)
PHONE..............................323 762-2626
Shawn Sanbar, *Owner*
Dan Warner, *COO*
Carrie Iino, *Admin Mgr*
Peter Heinrich, *Branch Mgr*
Greg Evanski, *Technician*
EMP: 74 EST: 2003
SQ FT: 13,000
SALES (est): 11MM **Privately Held**
WEB: www.atlasdigital.tv
SIC: 7812 Video production

(P-19099)
ATLAS ENTERTAINMENT INC
9200 W Sunset Blvd Ste 10, West Hollywood (90069-3608)
PHONE..............................310 786-4900

Charles V Roven, *President*
Yesenia Cruz, *VP Finance*
EMP: 50 EST: 1987
SALES (est): 3.2MM **Privately Held**
SIC: 7812 Motion picture production & distribution

(P-19100)
BENTO BOX ENTERTAINMENT LLC
5161 Lankershim Blvd, North Hollywood
(91601-4962)
PHONE..............................818 333-7700
Scott Greenberg, *CEO*
Brett Coker, *Partner*
Joel Kuwahara, *President*
Holly Bright, *Business Dir*
Paige Vehlewald, *Executive Asst*
EMP: 300 EST: 2009
SALES (est): 40.5MM
SALES (corp-wide): 12.9B **Publicly Held**
WEB: www.bentoboxent.com
SIC: 7812 Motion picture production & distribution
HQ: Fox Television Stations, Inc.
1999 S Bundy Dr
Los Angeles CA 90025
310 584-2000

(P-19101)
BLIND DECKER PRODUCTIONS INC (PA)
8621 Hayden Pl, Culver City (90232-2901)
PHONE..............................310 264-4247
Kevin Hyman, *Admin Sec*
EMP: 59 EST: 1995
SALES (est): 252.7K **Privately Held**
SIC: 7812 Motion picture production

(P-19102)
BRC IMAGINATION ARTS INC (PA)
2711 Winona Ave, Burbank (91504-2535)
PHONE..............................818 841-8084
Robert Rogers, *President*
Tom McDonald, *CFO*
Tom Seib, *CFO*
Christian Lachel, *Ch Credit Ofcr*
Carmel Lewis, *Vice Pres*
EMP: 64 EST: 1971
SQ FT: 42,000
SALES (est): 10.6MM **Privately Held**
WEB: www.brcweb.com
SIC: 7812 Television film production

(P-19103)
BRILLSTEIN ENTRMT PARTNERS LLC (PA)
Also Called: Brillstein Grey Entertainment
9150 Wilshire Blvd # 350, Beverly Hills
(90212-3427)
PHONE..............................310 205-5100
Brad Grey, *President*
Aleen Keshishian, *Managing Prtnr*
Amy Weiss, *Executive*
Laura Brown, *Admin Asst*
Naren Ramanuj, *Controller*
EMP: 90 EST: 1980
SALES (est): 16.2MM **Privately Held**
WEB: www.bepmedia.com
SIC: 7812 Television film production

(P-19104)
BUENA VISTA INTERNATIONAL INC
350 S Buena Vista St, Burbank
(91521-0004)
PHONE..............................818 295-5200
EMP: 115
SALES (corp-wide): 65.3B **Publicly Held**
SIC: 7812 7822 3695 Video tape production; video tapes, recorded: wholesale; video recording tape, blank
HQ: Buena Vista International Inc
500 S Buena Vista St
Burbank CA 91521
818 560-1000

(P-19105)
BUNIM-MURRAY PRODUCTIONS
Also Called: Bmp
1015 Grandview Ave, Glendale
(91201-2205)
PHONE..............................818 756-5100
Jonathan Murray, *CEO*

Julie Pizzi, *President*
Gil Goldschein, *CEO*
John Greco, *COO*
Mark Lebowitz, *CFO*
▲ EMP: 150 EST: 1989
SQ FT: 20,000
SALES (est): 44.1MM
SALES (corp-wide): 12.6MM **Privately Held**
WEB: www.bunim-murray.com
SIC: 7812 Television film production
HQ: Banijay Entertainment
5 Rue Francois 1er
Paris
143 189-191

(P-19106)
BVS ENTERTAINMENT INC (DH)
500 S Buena Vista St, Burbank
(91521-0001)
PHONE..............................818 460-6917
Griffith Foxley, *President*
David K Thompson, *Admin Sec*
EMP: 50 EST: 1981
SQ FT: 111,000
SALES (est): 17.5MM
SALES (corp-wide): 65.3B **Publicly Held**
SIC: 7812 7822 Cartoon production, television; motion picture distribution
HQ: Abc Family Worldwide, Inc.
500 S Buena Vista St
Burbank CA 91521
818 560-1000

(P-19107)
CARA COMMUNICATIONS CORP
Also Called: Vin Dibona Productions
12233 W Olympic Blvd # 170, Los Angeles
(90064-1034)
PHONE..............................310 442-5600
Vincent Dibona, *President*
Lisa Black, *Exec VP*
Sharon Arnett, *Vice Pres*
Alexandra Kyle, *Vice Pres*
Sara Mullins, *Producer*
EMP: 50 EST: 1989
SALES (est): 7.6MM **Privately Held**
WEB: www.vindibonaproductions.com
SIC: 7812 7819 Television film production; directors, independent; motion picture; television program, including commercial producers

(P-19108)
CBS STUDIOS INC (DH)
Also Called: CBS Paramount Television
6100 Wilshire Blvd # 1000, Los Angeles
(90048-5109)
PHONE..............................323 634-3519
Leslie Moonves, *President*
EMP: 480 EST: 2005
SALES (est): 25.6MM
SALES (corp-wide): 25.3B **Publicly Held**
WEB: www.cbssc.com
SIC: 7812 Television film production
HQ: Viacomcbs Inc.
1515 Broadway
New York NY 10036
212 258-6000

(P-19109)
COLUMBIA PICTURES INDS INC (DH)
10202 Washington Blvd, Culver City
(90232-3119)
PHONE..............................310 244-4000
Michael Lynton, *CEO*
Doug Belgrad, *President*
Andrew Gumpert, *President*
Hannah Minghella, *President*
Matt Tolmach, *President*
EMP: 200 EST: 1987
SALES (est): 125.9MM **Privately Held**
WEB: www.sonypictures.com
SIC: 7812 Motion picture production & distribution
HQ: Sony Pictures Entertainment, Inc.
10202 Washington Blvd
Culver City CA 90232
310 244-4000

PRODUCTS & SVCS

(P-19110)
CONCORDE-NEW HORIZONS CORP
Also Called: New Horizons Picture
11600 San Vicente Blvd, Los Angeles
(90049-5102)
PHONE....................310 820-6733
Roger Corman, *President*
Julie Corman, *Exec VP*
Max Yodhikawa, *Vice Pres*
EMP: 53 **EST:** 1971
SQ FT: 7,000
SALES (est): 2.2MM **Privately Held**
SIC: 7812 Motion picture production & distribution; motion picture production & distribution, television; television film production

(P-19111)
CORDAY PRODUCTIONS INC (PA)
3400 W Olive Ave Ste 170, Burbank
(91505-5539)
PHONE....................818 295-2821
Ken Corday, *President*
Mike Russell, *CFO*
Greg Meng, *Principal*
Maya Frangie, *Director*
Stephen Reinhardt, *Supervisor*
EMP: 50 **EST:** 1954
SALES (est): 1.6MM **Privately Held**
SIC: 7812 Motion picture & video production

(P-19112)
CREATIVE PARK PRODUCTIONS LLC
Also Called: Universal Studios
100 Universal City Plz, Universal City
(91608-1002)
PHONE....................818 622-3702
Richard Cotton,
Theresa McCann, *Partner*
Donna Langley, *Bd of Directors*
Austin Barker, *Exec VP*
Sean Gamble, *Exec VP*
EMP: 257 **EST:** 2002
SALES (est): 38.6MM **Privately Held**
SIC: 7812 Motion picture & video production

(P-19113)
CRENSHAW CHRSTN CTR CH LOS ANG (PA)
Also Called: Ever Increasing Faith Ministry
7901 S Vermont Ave, Los Angeles
(90044-3531)
P.O. Box 90000 (90009-9201)
PHONE....................323 758-3777
Frederick K C Price, *CEO*
Angela Evans, *CEO*
Cheryl Price, *CFO*
Craig Hays, *Vice Pres*
Jeanette Fant, *Admin Sec*
▲ **EMP:** 294
SALES (est): 14.1MM **Privately Held**
WEB: www.crenshawchristiancenter.net
SIC: 8661 7812 Community church; motion picture & video production

(P-19114)
CRYSTAL CATHEDRAL MINISTRIES (PA)
12901 Lewis St, Garden Grove
(92840-6207)
P.O. Box 100 (92842-0100)
PHONE....................714 622-2900
Robert V Schuller, *CEO*
Fred Southard, *CFO*
▲ **EMP:** 250 **EST:** 1955
SQ FT: 135,000
SALES (est): 9.9MM **Privately Held**
SIC: 8661 7812 Apostolic Church; television film production

(P-19115)
DEBMAR/MERCURY LLC
2700 Colorado Ave, Santa Monica
(90404-3553)
PHONE....................310 393-6000
Mort Marcus,
Lonnie Burstein, *Exec VP*
Ira Bernstein,
Lynn Dilworth, *Director*
EMP: 50 **EST:** 2005

SALES (est): 10MM
SALES (corp-wide): 3.8B **Privately Held**
WEB: www.debmarmercury.com
SIC: 7812 Video production
HQ: Lions Gate Entertainment Inc.
2700 Colorado Ave Ste 200
Santa Monica CA 90404
310 449-9200

(P-19116)
DIGITAL DOMAIN 30 INC (PA)
12641 Beatrice St, Los Angeles
(90066-7003)
PHONE....................310 314-2800
Daniel Seah, *CEO*
Frank Ming WEI, *Vice Chairman*
Od Welch, *President*
Amit Chopra, *COO*
Joseph Gabriel, *Vice Pres*
EMP: 300 **EST:** 2012
SALES (est): 75MM **Privately Held**
WEB: www.digitaldomain.com
SIC: 7812 Video production

(P-19117)
DISNEY ENTERPRISES INC
1313 S Harbor Blvd, Anaheim
(92802-2309)
PHONE....................407 397-6000
Marlene Madrid, *Manager*
Eric Freihoff, *Engineer*
David Edmondson, *Training Spec*
EMP: 100
SALES (corp-wide): 65.3B **Publicly Held**
WEB: www.en.disneyme.com
SIC: 7812 Motion picture production & distribution, television
HQ: Disney Enterprises, Inc.
500 S Buena Vista St
Burbank CA 91521
818 560-1000

(P-19118)
DISNEY INCORPORATED (DH)
500 S Buena Vista St, Burbank
(91521-0001)
PHONE....................818 560-1000
Matthew L McGinnis, *CEO*
Sanford M Litvack, *President*
Floriane Mathieu, *President*
Bill Frew, *Senior VP*
Cyndi Cruz, *Vice Pres*
▲ **EMP:** 150 **EST:** 1952
SALES (est): 411.7MM
SALES (corp-wide): 65.3B **Publicly Held**
WEB: www.disney.com
SIC: 7812 Motion picture production & distribution
HQ: Disney Enterprises, Inc.
500 S Buena Vista St
Burbank CA 91521
818 560-1000

(P-19119)
DREAMWORKS ANIMATION PUBG LLC
1000 Flower St, Glendale (91201-3007)
PHONE....................818 695-5000
EMP: 775 **EST:** 2014
SALES (est): 1.7MM
SALES (corp-wide): 103.5B **Publicly Held**
WEB: www.dreamworks.com
SIC: 7812 Motion picture & video production
HQ: Dwa Holdings, Llc
1000 Flower St
Glendale CA 91201
818 695-5000

(P-19120)
DWA HOLDINGS LLC (DH)
1000 Flower St, Glendale (91201-3007)
PHONE....................818 695-5000
Mellody Hobson, *Principal*
Ann Daly, *President*
Jeffrey Katzenberg, *CEO*
Fazal Merchant, *CFO*
Steven A Adams,
EMP: 75 **EST:** 1994
SQ FT: 500,000

SALES (est): 540.8MM
SALES (corp-wide): 103.5B **Publicly Held**
WEB: www.research.dreamworks.com
SIC: 7812 Cartoon motion picture production

(P-19121)
EFILM LLC
Also Called: E Film Digital Labratories
1144 N Las Palmas Ave, Los Angeles
(90038-1209)
PHONE....................323 463-7041
Aria Mehrabi,
Al Cleland, *Vice Pres*
Marvin Boonmee, *Software Engr*
Terry Morrison, *Senior Engr*
Kit Young, *Senior Engr*
EMP: 150 **EST:** 2002
SALES (est): 22.9MM **Privately Held**
WEB: www.company3.com
SIC: 7812 Video production

(P-19122)
EVOLUTION FILM & TAPE INC
Also Called: Evolution Media
3310 W Vanowen St, Burbank
(91505-1239)
PHONE....................818 260-0300
Douglas A Ross, *CEO*
Alex Baskin, *President*
Greg B Stewart, *CFO*
Robert Carroll, *Vice Pres*
Sara Hansemann, *Vice Pres*
EMP: 95 **EST:** 1987
SQ FT: 25,000
SALES (est): 7.4MM **Privately Held**
WEB: www.evolutionusa.com
SIC: 7812 Video production

(P-19123)
FILM ROMAN LLC
6320 Canoga Ave, Woodland Hills
(91367-2526)
PHONE....................818 748-4000
Dana Booton, *Manager*
EMP: 214
SQ FT: 87,000
SALES (corp-wide): 3.8B **Privately Held**
WEB: www.filmroman.com
SIC: 7812 Cartoon motion picture production; cartoon production, television
HQ: Film Roman, Llc.
8900 Liberty Cir
Englewood CO 80112
720 852-6327

(P-19124)
FONCO CREATIVE SERVICES
Also Called: Fonco Studios
1310 N San Fernando Rd, Los Angeles
(90065-1237)
PHONE....................415 254-5460
Phuong Davis, *Owner*
EMP: 20 **EST:** 1997
SALES (est): 1.6MM **Privately Held**
WEB: www.foncostudios.com
SIC: 7812 7819 7336 3999 Video production; equipment & prop rental, motion picture production; studio property rental, motion picture; editing services, motion picture production; commercial art & graphic design; miniatures; costume & scenery design services; photographer, still or video

(P-19125)
FOX ANIMATION STUDIOS INC
5700 Wilshire Blvd # 325, Los Angeles
(90036-3659)
PHONE....................323 857-8800
John McKenna, *President*
▲ **EMP:** 106 **EST:** 1994
SALES (est): 5.4MM
SALES (corp-wide): 65.3B **Publicly Held**
SIC: 7812 Motion picture production & distribution; video tape production; motion picture production & distribution, television; cartoon motion picture production
HQ: Twentieth Century Fox Film Corporation
10201 W Pico Blvd
Los Angeles CA 90064
310 369-1000

(P-19126)
FOX NET INC
Also Called: 20th Century Fox Studio
10201 W Pico Blvd, Los Angeles
(90064-2606)
PHONE....................310 369-1000
Chase Carey, *President*
EMP: 2599 **EST:** 1992
SALES (est): 25.1MM
SALES (corp-wide): 65.3B **Publicly Held**
WEB: www.foxcredit.org
SIC: 7812 Motion picture & video production
HQ: Twentieth Television, Inc.
10201 W Pico Blvd
Los Angeles CA 90064

(P-19127)
FTP PRODUCTIONS LLC (PA)
Also Called: Kimoyo Productions
500 S Buena Vista St, Burbank
(91521-0001)
PHONE....................818 560-2977
John F Cooke, *Mng Member*
EMP: 187 **EST:** 2006
SALES (est): 14.5MM **Privately Held**
SIC: 7812 Television film production

(P-19128)
FUNIMATION GLOBAL GROUP LLC (DH)
Also Called: Funimation Entertainment
10202 Washington Blvd, Culver City
(90232-3119)
PHONE....................972 355-7300
Gen Fukunaga, *President*
Greg Stevenson, *CFO*
▲ **EMP:** 147 **EST:** 1994
SALES (est): 33.4MM **Privately Held**
WEB: www.funimation.com
SIC: 7812 4813 7822 Cartoon production, television; ; video tapes, recorded: wholesale
HQ: Sony Pictures Entertainment, Inc.
10202 Washington Blvd
Culver City CA 90232
310 244-4000

(P-19129)
GLOBAL ASYLUM INCORPORATED
Also Called: Asylum, The
440 W Los Feliz Rd, Glendale
(91204-2776)
PHONE....................323 850-1214
Paul Bales, *CFO*
Brian Brinkman, *Editor*
EMP: 50 **EST:** 1997
SALES (est): 3.9MM **Privately Held**
SIC: 7812 Motion picture production & distribution

(P-19130)
HARPO PRODUCTIONS INC
Also Called: Harpo Entertainment Group
1041 N Formosa Ave, West Hollywood
(90046-6703)
PHONE....................312 633-1000
Oprah Winfrey, *Ch of Ed*
Tim Bennett, *President*
Doug Pattison, *CFO*
Bill Becker, *Vice Pres*
John Boekeloo, *Info Tech Dir*
EMP: 200 **EST:** 1988
SQ FT: 100,000
SALES (est): 2.7MM **Privately Held**
SIC: 7812 Television film production; video tape production

(P-19131)
HIGH TECHNOLOGY VIDEO INC
Also Called: H T V
10900 Ventura Blvd, Studio City
(91604-3340)
PHONE....................323 969-8822
Jim Hardy, *CEO*
Steve Weiner, *Chairman*
Sandy Crawford, *Exec VP*
Steve Galloway, *Senior VP*
Richard Gelles, *Vice Pres*
EMP: 73 **EST:** 1995
SQ FT: 30,000

SALES (est): 11MM **Privately Held**
WEB: www.illuminatehollywood.com
SIC: 7812 Video production

(P-19132)
HULA POST PRODUCTIONS INC
Also Called: Llc, Hula Media Services
1111 S Victory Blvd, Burbank (91502-2550)
PHONE..................................818 954-0200
Denine James Nio, *President*
EMP: 61 EST: 1998
SQ FT: 2,500
SALES (est): 24.7MM **Privately Held**
WEB: www.hulapost.com
SIC: 7812 Audio-visual program production
HQ: H.I.G. Capital, L.L.C.
1450 Brickell Ave Fl 31
Miami FL 33131
305 379-2322

(P-19133)
HUNGRY HEART MEDIA INC
Also Called: Wondros
5450 W Washington Blvd, Los Angeles
(90016-1135)
PHONE..................................323 951-0010
Jesse Dylan, *CEO*
Tyler Peters, *Creative Dir*
Claire Andreae, *Executive Asst*
Kelly Alsip, *Prgrmr*
Kate Correll, *Project Mgr*
EMP: 140 EST: 2011
SALES (est): 21.1MM **Privately Held**
WEB: www.wondros.com
SIC: 7812 8742 Motion picture & video
production; marketing consulting services

(P-19134)
IF LIVE LLC (PA)
2254 S Sepulveda Blvd, Los Angeles
(90064-1812)
PHONE..................................323 957-6868
Alan Walter Fields,
Peter Frankfurt,
Francis Houghton,
EMP: 69 EST: 2001
SALES (est): 1.5MM **Privately Held**
WEB: www.lalive.com
SIC: 7812 Motion picture & video production

(P-19135)
IGNITION CREATIVE LLC
1201 W 5th St Ste T1100, Los Angeles
(90017-5158)
PHONE..................................310 315-6300
Ron Moler,
Dale Lanier, *Exec VP*
Jenna Doneen, *Vice Pres*
Eric Breshears, *Creative Dir*
Paul Spencer, *Creative Dir*
EMP: 91 EST: 2003
SALES (est): 10.1MM **Privately Held**
WEB: www.ignitioncreative.com
SIC: 7812 Video production

(P-19136)
JEOPARDY PRODUCTIONS INC
10202 Washington Blvd, Culver City
(90232-3119)
PHONE..................................310 244-8855
Rocky Schmitt, *CEO*
EMP: 105 EST: 1984
SALES (est): 6.7MM **Privately Held**
WEB: www.jeopardy.com
SIC: 7812 Television film production
HQ: Sony Pictures Entertainment, Inc.
10202 Washington Blvd
Culver City CA 90232
310 244-4000

(P-19137)
JERRY BRUCKHEIMER INC
Also Called: Bruckheimer, Jerry Films
1631 10th St, Santa Monica (90404-3705)
PHONE..................................310 664-6260
Jerry Bruckheimer, *President*
Michael Singer, *Vice Pres*
Matthew Wolfe, *Info Tech Dir*
Charles Fitzer, *Director*
Linda Bruckheimer, *Assistant*
EMP: 56 EST: 1987
SALES (est): 8.2MM **Privately Held**
WEB: www.jbfilms.com
SIC: 7812 Television film production

(P-19138)
**JIM HENSON COMPANY INC
(PA)**
Also Called: Henson Recording Studio
1416 N La Brea Ave, Los Angeles
(90028-7506)
PHONE..................................323 856-6680
Lisa Henson, *CEO*
Cheryl Henson, *President*
Peter Schube, *President*
Halle Stanford, *President*
Brian Henson, *CEO*
EMP: 55 EST: 1965
SQ FT: 7,000
SALES (est): 22.5MM **Privately Held**
WEB: www.henson.com
SIC: 7812 Motion picture production & distribution

(P-19139)
**KINGDOM ENTERPRISE FILMS
LLC**
10812 Bothwell Rd, Chatsworth
(91311-1915)
PHONE..................................818 963-2513
Gregory Nalbandian,
Armando Talian,
EMP: 50 EST: 2019
SALES (est): 264.1K **Privately Held**
SIC: 7812 Motion picture & video production

(P-19140)
LEGEND3D INC
1500 Cotner Ave Ste 1, Los Angeles
(90025-3303)
PHONE..................................858 793-4420
Ian Jessel, *President*
Shamitha Kattukandy, *COO*
Tom Sinnott, *COO*
Steven Wolkenstein, *CFO*
Barry Sandrew, *Ch Credit Ofcr*
EMP: 79 EST: 2002
SQ FT: 50,000
SALES (est): 14.3MM **Privately Held**
WEB: www.legend3d.com
SIC: 7812 Video production

(P-19141)
**LEGENDARY ENTERTAINMENT
LLC**
2900 W Alameda Ave, Burbank
(91505-4220)
PHONE..................................818 688-7006
Thomas Tull, *CEO*
Sirena Liu, *CEO*
Dawn Castro, *Officer*
Alex Garcia, *Exec VP*
Pearl Wible, *Senior VP*
EMP: 53 EST: 2012
SALES (est): 12.8MM **Privately Held**
WEB: www.legendary.com
SIC: 7812 Motion picture production; television film production

(P-19142)
LEMONLIGHT MEDIA INC
226 S Glasgow Ave, Inglewood
(90301-2106)
PHONE..................................310 402-0275
Hope Horner, *CEO*
EMP: 67 EST: 2018
SALES (est): 3.3MM **Privately Held**
WEB: www.lemonlight.com
SIC: 7812 Video tape production

(P-19143)
**LIONS GATE ENTERTAINMENT
INC (HQ)**
2700 Colorado Ave Ste 200, Santa Monica
(90404-5502)
PHONE..................................310 449-9200
Jon Feltheimer, *Ch of Bd*
Michael Burns, *Vice Chairman*
Steven Beeks, *President*
Joseph Drake, *President*
Erik Feig, *President*
EMP: 55 EST: 1998
SALES: 3.2B
SALES (corp-wide): 3.8B **Privately Held**
WEB: www.lionsgate.com
SIC: 7812 Motion picture production & distribution

PA: Lions Gate Entertainment Corp
250 Howe St Fl 20
Vancouver BC V6C 3
877 848-3866

(P-19144)
LIONS GATE FILMS INC
2700 Colorado Ave, Santa Monica
(90404-3553)
PHONE..................................310 449-9200
Jon Feltheimer, *President*
Steve Beeks, *COO*
James Keegan, *CFO*
David Diamond, *Vice Pres*
Christian Perala, *Vice Pres*
EMP: 147 EST: 1998
SQ FT: 30,000
SALES (est): 43.7MM
SALES (corp-wide): 3.8B **Privately Held**
WEB: www.lionsgate.com
SIC: 7812 Motion picture production
HQ: Lions Gate Entertainment Inc.
2700 Colorado Ave Ste 200
Santa Monica CA 90404
310 449-9200

(P-19145)
LMNO PRODUCTIONS INC
Also Called: Lmno Cable Group
15821 Ventura Blvd # 320, Encino
(91436-2928)
PHONE..................................818 995-5555
Eric Schotz, *President*
Ned Davis, *Vice Pres*
Ed Horowitz, *Vice Pres*
Jeff Rice, *Vice Pres*
EMP: 56 EST: 1986
SALES (est): 4.7MM **Privately Held**
WEB: www.lmnotv.com
SIC: 7812 Television film production

(P-19146)
LUMA PICTURES INC
1453 3rd Street Promenade # 400, Santa
Monica (90401-3428)
PHONE..................................310 888-8738
Payam Shohadai, *President*
Grady Gamble, *COO*
John Betdul, *Principal*
Chadd Dombrova, *Director*
Vanessa Krejcir, *Manager*
EMP: 171 EST: 2002
SALES (est): 14.7MM **Privately Held**
WEB: www.luma.inc
SIC: 7812 Motion picture & video production

(P-19147)
MEDIUM LARGE LLC
Also Called: Digital Publisher
13247 Jamboree Rd, Tustin (92782-9158)
PHONE..................................424 271-9411
Ian Chin, *President*
EMP: 14 EST: 2012
SALES (est): 751.4K **Privately Held**
WEB: www.mediumlarge.la
SIC: 7812 2741 Video production;

(P-19148)
**MERLOT FILM PRODUCTIONS
INC**
Also Called: CBS Network News
7800 Beverly Blvd, Los Angeles
(90036-2112)
PHONE..................................323 575-2906
Bruce C Taub, *CEO*
Lesile Moondes, *President*
David Strauss, *CFO*
Claudia E Morf, *Treasurer*
Leo Gorius, *Vice Pres*
EMP: 130 EST: 1996
SALES (est): 11.7MM
SALES (corp-wide): 25.3B **Publicly Held**
WEB: www.cbswatchmagazine.com
SIC: 7812 4833 Motion picture & video
production; television broadcasting stations
HQ: Cbs Broadcasting Inc.
524 W 57th St
New York NY 10019
212 975-4321

(P-19149)
METHOD STUDIOS LLC
3401 Exposition Blvd, Santa Monica
(90404-5050)
PHONE..................................310 434-6500
Ed Ulbrich, *President*
Erika Burton, *Exec VP*
Bryan Farhy, *Senior VP*
Deborah Giarratana, *Vice Pres*
Wensen Ho, *Creative Dir*
EMP: 68 EST: 2007
SALES (est): 13.9MM **Privately Held**
WEB: www.methodstudios.com
SIC: 7812 Video production

(P-19150)
**METRO-GOLDWYN-MAYER INC
(DH)**
Also Called: MGM
245 N Beverly Dr, Beverly Hills
(90210-5319)
PHONE..................................310 449-3000
Gary Barber, *CEO*
Ken Schapiro, *COO*
Kenneth Kay, *CFO*
Katie Martin Kelley, *Officer*
Matt Davidson, *Exec VP*
EMP: 300 EST: 1996
SQ FT: 131,400
SALES (est): 1B
SALES (corp-wide): 1.1B **Privately Held**
WEB: www.mgm.com
SIC: 7812 Motion picture production & distribution
HQ: Mgm Holdings Ii, Inc.
245 N Beverly Dr
Beverly Hills CA 90210
310 449-3000

(P-19151)
MGM HOLDINGS II INC (HQ)
Also Called: MGM Studios
245 N Beverly Dr, Beverly Hills
(90210-5319)
PHONE..................................310 449-3000
Daniel J Taylor, *CEO*
Steve Hendry, *CFO*
Charles Cohen, *Exec VP*
Scott Packman, *Exec VP*
Cindy Wilford Perez, *Vice Pres*
EMP: 96 EST: 2005
SQ FT: 131,400
SALES (est): 1B
SALES (corp-wide): 1.1B **Privately Held**
WEB: www.mgm.com
SIC: 7812 Motion picture & video production
PA: Mgm Holdings, Inc.
245 N Beverly Dr
Beverly Hills CA 90210
310 449-3000

(P-19152)
MIRAMAX LLC
1901 Avenue Of The Stars # 2000, Los Angeles (90067-6021)
PHONE..................................310 409-4321
Bill Block, *CEO*
Denise Evans, *President*
Michael Lachance, *Exec VP*
Jill Silfen, *Exec VP*
Katelyn Crabb, *Executive Asst*
EMP: 109 EST: 2011
SALES (est): 16.7MM **Privately Held**
WEB: www.miramax.com
SIC: 7812 Motion picture production & distribution
PA: Bein Media Group Wll
Behind Ahli Hospital, Al Asmakh
Tower No. 864, Zone 63
Doha

(P-19153)
MIRAMAX FILM NY LLC (HQ)
1901 Avenue Of The Stars # 2000, Los Angeles (90067-6021)
PHONE..................................310 409-4321
Bill Block, *CEO*
Steven Schoch, *Exec VP*
EMP: 76 EST: 2010
SALES (est): 15.9MM **Privately Held**
WEB: www.miramax.com
SIC: 7812 Video production

(P-19154)
MODERN VIDEOFILM INC
Also Called: Mod Vid Film
1733 Flower St, Glendale (91201-2022)
PHONE..................................818 637-6800
EMP: 125
SALES (corp-wide): 24.8MM **Privately Held**
WEB: www.point360.com
SIC: **7812** Motion Picture/Video Production
PA: Modern Videofilm, Inc.
2300 W Empire Ave
Burbank CA 91504
818 840-1700

(P-19155)
NBC UNIVERSAL STUDIOS INC (HQ)
3900 Lnkrshim Blvd Ste 42, Universal City (91608)
PHONE..................................818 777-5000
Ted Hughes, *Info Tech Mgr*
Steven O 'neill, *Vice Pres*
◆ EMP: 96 EST: 2004
SALES (est): 16.8MM
SALES (corp-wide): 103.5B **Publicly Held**
WEB: www.nbcuniversal.com
SIC: **7812** Motion picture & video production
PA: Comcast Corporation
1701 John F Kennedy Blvd
Philadelphia PA 19103
215 286-1700

(P-19156)
NEW REGENCY PRODUCTIONS INC (PA)
Also Called: Regency Enterprises
10201 W Pico Blvd Bldg 12, Los Angeles (90064-2606)
PHONE..................................310 369-8300
Arnon Milchan, *Principal*
Yariv Milchan, *President*
Brad Weston, *CEO*
Jonathan Fischer, *COO*
Mimi Mtseng, *CFO*
▼ EMP: 60 EST: 1991
SQ FT: 13,000
SALES (est): 17.1MM **Privately Held**
SIC: **7812** Video production

(P-19157)
NW ENTERTAINMENT INC (PA)
Also Called: New Wave Entertainment
2660 W Olive Ave, Burbank (91505-4525)
PHONE..................................818 295-5000
Paul Apel, *CEO*
Brian Volk-Weiss, *President*
Kieran Dotti, *COO*
Greg Woertz, *CFO*
Gary Lister, *Senior VP*
▲ EMP: 172 EST: 1986
SQ FT: 40,000
SALES (est): 37.2MM **Privately Held**
SIC: **7812** Motion picture production

(P-19158)
ORION PICTURES CORPORATION
245 N Beverly Dr, Beverly Hills (90210-5319)
PHONE..................................310 449-3000
Alex Yemenidjian, *Ch of Bd*
Daniel J Taylor, *Treasurer*
EMP: 1000 EST: 1995
SALES (est): 16MM
SALES (corp-wide): 1.1B **Privately Held**
WEB: www.mgm.com
SIC: **7812** Motion picture production & distribution
HQ: Metro-Goldwyn-Mayer, Inc.
245 N Beverly Dr
Beverly Hills CA 90210

(P-19159)
PARAMOUNT PICTURES CORPORATION (DH)
Also Called: Paramount Studios
5555 Melrose Ave, Los Angeles (90038-3197)
PHONE..................................323 956-5000
Brian Robbins, *President*
Jim Gianopulos, *Ch of Bd*

Chris Aronson, *President*
Fred T Gallo, *President*
Adam Goodman, *President*
◆ EMP: 1700 EST: 1912
SALES (est): 705MM
SALES (corp-wide): 25.3B **Publicly Held**
WEB: www.paramountstudiotour.com
SIC: **7812** 4833 7829 5099 Motion picture production & distribution, television; motion picture production & distribution; television broadcasting stations; motion picture distribution services; video cassettes, accessories & supplies
HQ: Viacomcbs Inc.
1515 Broadway
New York NY 10036
212 258-6000

(P-19160)
PARTICIPANT MEDIA LLC (PA)
331 Foothill Rd Fl 3, Beverly Hills (90210-3669)
PHONE..................................310 550-5100
Jeff Skoll, *CEO*
Joshua Couch, *President*
Jeffrey Ivers, *COO*
Andy Kim, *CFO*
Diane Weyermann, *Ch Credit Ofcr*
EMP: 55 EST: 2004
SALES: 3.6K **Privately Held**
WEB: www.participant.com
SIC: **7812** Video production

(P-19161)
PEGASUS COMMUNICATIONS INC (PA)
16633 Ventura Blvd # 1010, Encino (91436-1801)
PHONE..................................818 907-1900
James E Porep Sr, *President*
Julie Scanlon, *Admin Sec*
EMP: 50 EST: 1986
SQ FT: 4,000
SALES (est): 3.5MM **Privately Held**
WEB: www.pegasuscommunications.tv
SIC: **7812** Video tape production

(P-19162)
PICKLEBACK NOLA LLC
1102 7th Pl, Hermosa Beach (90254-4911)
PHONE..................................504 605-0911
EMP: 50 EST: 2018
SALES (est): 866.3K **Privately Held**
SIC: **7812** Television film production

(P-19163)
PIE TOWN PRODUCTIONS INC
5433 Laurel Canyon Blvd, North Hollywood (91607-2114)
PHONE..................................818 255-9300
Tara Sandler, *President*
Dana Besnoy, *Vice Pres*
Eric Black, *Vice Pres*
Nicole Henrich, *Vice Pres*
Stacey Davis-Jackson, *Producer*
EMP: 51 EST: 1994
SALES (est): 6.8MM **Privately Held**
WEB: www.pietown.tv
SIC: **7812** Video production

(P-19164)
PLAYBOY ENTRMT GROUP INC (DH)
2300 W Empire Ave, Burbank (91504-3341)
PHONE..................................323 276-4000
Brinda Viloa, *Director*
James Griffiths, *President*
Brian Middleton, *Senior Mgr*
Anna Peries, *Director*
EMP: 139 EST: 1984
SALES (est): 22.1MM **Publicly Held**
WEB: www.criticalcontent.com
SIC: **7812** Video tape production
HQ: Playboy Enterprises, Inc.
10960 Wilshire Blvd Fl 22
Los Angeles CA 90024
310 424-1800

(P-19165)
PLUTO INC (DH)
Also Called: Pluto TV
6100 Wilshire Blvd # 1550, Los Angeles (90048-5109)
PHONE..................................323 746-0500
Thomas Ryan, *CEO*

Scott Reich, *Senior VP*
EMP: 54 EST: 2008
SALES (est): 21.3MM
SALES (corp-wide): 25.3B **Publicly Held**
WEB: www.pluto.tv
SIC: **7812** Motion picture production & distribution, television
HQ: Viacomcbs Inc.
1515 Broadway
New York NY 10036
212 258-6000

(P-19166)
POST MODERN EDIT LLC (PA)
1821 E Dyer Rd Ste 125, Santa Ana (92705-5894)
PHONE..................................949 608-8700
Rick Warren,
Hamid Samnani,
◆ EMP: 51 EST: 1994
SALES (est): 5.8MM **Privately Held**
WEB: www.postmoderngroup.com
SIC: **7812** Video production

(P-19167)
PRODUCTION ASSOCIATES INC (PA)
77899 Wolf Rd Ste 107, Palm Desert (92211-1137)
PHONE..................................310 598-7200
Michael Thuney, *President*
Christopher Cheek, *CFO*
EMP: 64 EST: 2008
SALES (est): 298.5K **Privately Held**
SIC: **7812** Motion picture production

(P-19168)
QUADRA PRODUCTIONS INC
Also Called: Wheel of Forturne
10202 Washington Blvd, Culver City (90232-3119)
PHONE..................................310 244-1234
Harry Friedman, *President*
EMP: 60 EST: 1988
SALES (est): 4.3MM **Privately Held**
WEB: www.sonypictures.com
SIC: **7812** Television film production
HQ: Sony Pictures Entertainment, Inc.
10202 Washington Blvd
Culver City CA 90232
310 244-4000

(P-19169)
RADLEYS
3780 Wilshire Blvd # 110, Los Angeles (90010-2805)
PHONE..................................310 765-2223
Christian Thompson, *Mng Member*
Keith Orden, *COO*
Drake Chandler, *Graphic Designe*
Kevin Velasquez, *Graphic Designe*
Elizabeth Lisk, *Controller*
EMP: 50 EST: 2010
SALES (est): 4.7MM **Privately Held**
WEB: www.radleystudios.tv
SIC: **7812** Television film production

(P-19170)
RHYTHM AND HUES INC (PA)
Also Called: Rhythm & Hues Studios
2100 E Grand Ave Ste A, El Segundo (90245-5055)
PHONE..................................310 448-7500
John Hughes, *President*
Keith Goldfarb, *Shareholder*
Pauline TSO, *Corp Secy*
Steve Fong, *Software Engr*
Rodney Montague, *VP Prdtn*
EMP: 229 EST: 1987
SALES (est): 13.5MM **Privately Held**
WEB: www.rhythm.com
SIC: **7812** Cartoon production, television

(P-19171)
ROCK PAPER SCISSORS LLC
2308 Broadway, Santa Monica (90404-2916)
PHONE..................................310 586-0600
Angus Wall,
Arleen Rosenberg, *CFO*
Eve Kornblum, *Managing Dir*
Kimberly Frole, *Office Mgr*
Rob Larose, *Engineer*
EMP: 50 EST: 1992
SQ FT: 9,000

SALES (est): 15.5MM **Privately Held**
WEB: www.makemakeentertainment.com
SIC: **7812** 8999 Commercials, television: tape or film; editorial service

(P-19172)
RODAX DISTRIBUTORS
7230 Coldwater Canyon Ave, North Hollywood (91605-4203)
P.O. Box 16539 (91615-6539)
PHONE..................................818 765-6400
Daniel Mamane, *President*
Tom Yofee, *CFO*
EMP: 78 EST: 1995
SALES (est): 1.2MM **Privately Held**
SIC: **7812** Video tape production

(P-19173)
ROUNDABOUT ENTERTAINMENT INC
Also Called: Secuto Music
217 S Lake St, Burbank (91502-2111)
PHONE..................................818 842-9300
Craig S Clark, *CEO*
Mike Esfahanian, *Vice Pres*
Vincent Pirozzi, *Vice Pres*
Paul Rodriguez, *Vice Pres*
Tiffany Price, *Office Mgr*
EMP: 84 EST: 1992
SQ FT: 6,000
SALES (est): 10.8MM **Privately Held**
WEB: www.roundabout.com
SIC: **7812** Video production

(P-19174)
SAINT JSEPH COMMUNICATIONS INC (PA)
Also Called: Catholic Resource Center
1243 E Shamwood St, West Covina (91790-2348)
P.O. Box 720 (91793-0720)
PHONE..................................626 331-3549
Terry Barber, *President*
EMP: 25 EST: 1988
SALES (est): 306.1K **Privately Held**
WEB: www.cedarhouse.co
SIC: **7812** 2741 7822 Motion picture & video production; miscellaneous publishing; motion picture & tape distribution

(P-19175)
SCREEN GEMS INC
10202 Washington Blvd, Culver City (90232-3119)
P.O. Box 3277, Manhattan Beach (90266-1277)
PHONE..................................310 244-4000
Clint Culpepper, *Presiden*
EMP: 67 EST: 1960
SALES (est): 3.3MM **Privately Held**
WEB: www.sonypictures.com
SIC: **7812** Motion picture & video production
HQ: Sony Pictures Entertainment, Inc.
10202 Washington Blvd
Culver City CA 90232
310 244-4000

(P-19176)
SDI MEDIA USA INC (HQ)
Also Called: Iyuno-Sdi Group
6060 Center Dr Ste 100, Los Angeles (90045-8835)
PHONE..................................310 388-8800
Mark Howorth, *President*
Gina Chang, *Vice Pres*
Olivier Christmann, *Vice Pres*
Sharyn Hopkins, *Vice Pres*
Alexis Martinez, *Vice Pres*
EMP: 586 EST: 1974
SQ FT: 13,000
SALES (est): 63.4MM **Privately Held**
WEB: www.iyuno-sdi.com
SIC: **7812** Video production
PA: Iyuno Media Group
3601 W Olive Ave Ste 650
Burbank CA 91505
818 812-1213

(P-19177)
SHADOW ANIMATION LLC
940 N Mansfield Ave, Los Angeles (90038-2312)
PHONE..................................323 466-7771
Alex Bulkley, *Owner*
Hana Masters, *IT/INT Sup*

Corey Campodonico,
Chris Lee, *Sr Project Mgr*
EMP: 50 **EST:** 2004
SALES (est): 2.7MM **Privately Held**
SIC: 7812 Audio-visual program production

(P-19178)
SHADOWMACHINE LLC (PA)
940 N Mansfield Ave, Los Angeles
(90038-2312)
PHONE....................323 466-7388
Alex Bulkley, *Mng Member*
Kyle Bowman, *Vice Pres*
Kristina Soderquist, *Accountant*
Marci Levine, *Controller*
Melanie Coombs, *Producer*
EMP: 58 **EST:** 2007
SALES (est): 5.7MM **Privately Held**
WEB: www.shadowmachine.com
SIC: 7812 Motion picture & video production

(P-19179)
SONY MEDIA CLOUD SERVICES LLC
10202 Washington Blvd, Culver City
(90232-3119)
PHONE....................877 683-9124
Naomi Climer,
Jared Jussim, *Exec VP*
Amy Kondo, *Site Mgr*
Kira Thompson, *Director*
EMP: 50 **EST:** 2013
SALES (est): 1MM **Privately Held**
WEB: www.sonymcs.com
SIC: 7812 7372 Video production; business oriented computer software
PA: Sony Group Corporation
1-7-1, Konan
Minato-Ku TKY 108-0
-

(P-19180)
SONY PCTRES HM ENTRMT ONLINE I (DH)
10202 Washington Blvd, Culver City
(90232-3119)
PHONE....................310 244-4000
David Bishop, *CEO*
EMP: 211 **EST:** 1991
SALES (est): 42.5MM **Privately Held**
WEB: www.sonypictures.com
SIC: 7812 Motion picture & video production
HQ: Sony Pictures Entertainment, Inc.
10202 Washington Blvd
Culver City CA 90232
310 244-4000

(P-19181)
SONY PCTRES WRLDWIDE ACQSTONS
10202 Washington Blvd, Culver City
(90232-3119)
PHONE....................310 244-4000
Rory Bruer, *President*
EMP: 87 **EST:** 1988
SALES (est): 3MM **Privately Held**
WEB: www.sonypictures.com
SIC: 7812 Video production
PA: Sony Group Corporation
1-7-1, Konan
Minato-Ku TKY 108-0
-

(P-19182)
SONY PICTURES ENTRMT INC (DH)
Also Called: Sony Pictures Studios
10202 Washington Blvd, Culver City
(90232-3119)
PHONE....................310 244-4000
Tony Vinciquerra, *CEO*
Annie Dimascio, *Partner*
Kristine Belson, *President*
David Bishop, *President*
Rory Bruer, *President*
▲ **EMP:** 3000 **EST:** 1982

SALES (est): 1.5B **Privately Held**
WEB: www.sonypictures.com
SIC: 7812 7822 7832 Motion picture production & distribution; motion picture production & distribution, television; distribution, exclusive of production: motion picture; distribution for television: motion picture; motion picture theaters, except drive-in

(P-19183)
SONY PICTURES TELEVISION INC (DH)
10202 Washington Blvd, Culver City
(90232-3119)
PHONE....................310 244-7625
Ravi Ahuja, *Chairman*
Jason Clodfelter, *President*
Jeff Frost, *President*
Wayne Garvie, *President*
Keith Le Goy, *Chairman*
▲ **EMP:** 300 **EST:** 1982
SALES (est): 16.1MM **Privately Held**
WEB: www.sonypicturestelevision.com
SIC: 7812 Motion picture production & distribution, television
HQ: Sony Pictures Entertainment, Inc.
10202 Washington Blvd
Culver City CA 90232
310 244-4000

(P-19184)
SSI/ADVANCED POST SERVICES LLC
Also Called: Sound Services
7165 W Sunset Blvd, West Hollywood
(90046-4417)
PHONE....................323 969-9333
Robert T Walker, *President*
Steven J Alteri, *COO*
Doug Dear, *CFO*
John Warren, *Admin Sec*
Tyler Fradkin, *Technician*
EMP: 67 **EST:** 1968
SQ FT: 30,000
SALES (est): 4.2MM **Privately Held**
WEB: www.ssipost.com
SIC: 7812 7819 Audio-visual program production; services allied to motion pictures

(P-19185)
STARGATE FILMS INC (PA)
Also Called: Stargate Digital
1001 El Centro St, South Pasadena
(91030-5206)
PHONE....................626 403-8403
Samuel Nicholson, *CEO*
Jason Lucas, *CFO*
Jim Riley, *Exec VP*
Darren Frankel, *Vice Pres*
Pete Ware, *Principal*
EMP: 64 **EST:** 1989
SQ FT: 50,000
SALES (est): 8.9MM **Privately Held**
WEB: www.stargatestudios.net
SIC: 7812 Motion picture production

(P-19186)
STUDIO DISTRIBUTION SVCS LLC
4000 Warner Blvd, Burbank (91522-0001)
PHONE....................818 954-6000
Eddie Cunningham, *Mng Member*
Daniel Weinberger, *Asst Sec*
EMP: 140 **EST:** 2020
SALES (est): 1.8MM **Privately Held**
SIC: 7812 Motion picture production & distribution

(P-19187)
TRIAGE ENTERTAINMENT LLC
6701 Center Dr W Ste 300, Los Angeles
(90045-2482)
PHONE....................310 417-4800
Stuart M Schreiber, *President*
John Bravakis, *COO*
Stephen Kroopnick, *Exec VP*
Rochelle Matsubara,
EMP: 60 **EST:** 1995
SQ FT: 15,000
SALES (est): 10.3MM **Privately Held**
WEB: www.levitylive.com
SIC: 7812 Motion picture & video production

(P-19188)
TTT WEST COAST INC
3000 W Alameda Ave # 125, Burbank
(91505-4437)
PHONE....................818 972-0500
Mike Darnell, *President*
EMP: 75 **EST:** 1993
SALES (est): 5.4MM
SALES (corp-wide): 2.9B **Publicly Held**
WEB: www.meredith.com
SIC: 7812 Motion picture production; television film production
HQ: Ti Gotham Inc.
225 Liberty St
New York NY 10281
212 522-8282

(P-19189)
TWENTETH CNTURY FOX HM ENTRMT (DH)
10201 W Pico Blvd, Los Angeles
(90064-2606)
PHONE....................310 369-1000
K Rupert Murdoch,
Eileen Ige, *Vice Pres*
EMP: 1000 **EST:** 1953
SQ FT: 25,000
SALES (est): 66.7MM
SALES (corp-wide): 65.3B **Publicly Held**
SIC: 7812 Television film production
HQ: Twentieth Century Fox Film Corporation
10201 W Pico Blvd
Los Angeles CA 90064
310 369-1000

(P-19190)
TWENTIETH CNTURY FOX FILM CORP (DH)
Also Called: Fox Films Entertainment
10201 W Pico Blvd, Los Angeles
(90064-2606)
P.O. Box 900, Beverly Hills (90213-0900)
PHONE....................310 369-1000
Rupert Murdoch, *Ch of Bd*
Florence Grace, *Vice Pres*
◆ **EMP:** 75 **EST:** 1915
SQ FT: 25,000
SALES (est): 926.6MM
SALES (corp-wide): 65.3B **Publicly Held**
WEB: www.fox.com
SIC: 7812 Motion picture production & distribution
HQ: Fox Entertainment Group, Llc
1211 Ave Of The Americas
New York NY 10036
212 852-7000

(P-19191)
TWENTIETH CNTURY FOX FILM CORP
Fox Video International
2121 Avenue Of The Stars, Los Angeles
(90067-5010)
PHONE....................310 369-2582
Marc Dilorenzo, *President*
Peter Byrne, *Exec VP*
Mary Daily, *Exec VP*
James Finn, *Senior VP*
David Shall, *Senior VP*
EMP: 80
SALES (corp-wide): 65.3B **Publicly Held**
SIC: 7812 Television film production
HQ: Twentieth Century Fox Film Corporation
10201 W Pico Blvd
Los Angeles CA 90064
310 369-1000

(P-19192)
UNITED ARTISTS PICTURES INC (DH)
10250 Constellation Blvd, Los Angeles
(90067-6200)
PHONE....................310 449-3000
Alex Yemenitjian, *CEO*
EMP: 187 **EST:** 1919
SALES (est): 58MM
SALES (corp-wide): 1.1B **Privately Held**
WEB: www.007.com
SIC: 7812 Video production
HQ: Metro-Goldwyn-Mayer Studios Inc.
245 N Beverly Dr
Beverly Hills CA 90210
310 449-3000

(P-19193)
UNIVERSAL CY STDIOS PRDCTONS L (DH)
Also Called: Nbcuniversal Television Dist
100 Universal City Plz, Universal City
(91608-1002)
PHONE....................818 777-1000
Ron Meyer, *President*
Lynn A Calpeter, *CFO*
Maren Christensen, *Exec VP*
Richard Cotton, *Exec VP*
Rick Finkelstein, *Exec VP*
▲ **EMP:** 926 **EST:** 2002
SALES (est): 190.2MM
SALES (corp-wide): 103.5B **Publicly Held**
SIC: 7812 3652 2741 5947 Motion picture production & distribution; phonograph records, prerecorded; music, sheet: publishing & printing; gift shop; jewelry stores; gift items, mail order
HQ: Vivendi Universal Entertainment Lllp
30 Rockefeller Plz
New York NY 10112
212 664-4444

(P-19194)
UNIVERSAL PCTRES HM ENTRMT LLC (DH)
100 Unvrsal Cy Plz Bldg 1, Universal City
(91608)
PHONE....................818 777-1000
Ed Cunningham, *President*
Erik Baiers, *Exec VP*
Kathleen Gallagher, *Exec VP*
Matt Reilly, *Exec VP*
Jay Polidoro, *Vice Pres*
EMP: 681 **EST:** 1965
SALES (est): 65.3MM
SALES (corp-wide): 103.5B **Publicly Held**
WEB: www.nbcuniversal.com
SIC: 7812 Motion picture & video production
HQ: Nbcuniversal, Llc
1221 Ave Of The Amrcas St
New York NY 10020
212 664-4444

(P-19195)
UNIVERSAL STUDIOS COMPANY LLC (DH)
100 Universal City Plz, North Hollywood
(91608-1002)
PHONE....................818 777-1000
Adam Fogelson, *Chairman*
Ron Meyer, *President*
Sean Gamble, *CFO*
Donna Langley, *Chairman*
Michael Daruty, *Vice Pres*
▲ **EMP:** 397 **EST:** 1958
SQ FT: 100,000
SALES (est): 986.3MM
SALES (corp-wide): 103.5B **Publicly Held**
WEB: www.universalstudioshollywood.com
SIC: 7812 3652 2741 5947 Motion picture production & distribution; television film production; phonograph records, prerecorded; magnetic tape (audio): prerecorded; compact laser discs, prerecorded; music, sheet: publishing & printing; gift shop; novelties; jewelry stores; gift items, mail order; novelty merchandise, mail order; jewelry, mail order

(P-19196)
VIACOM NETWORKS
Also Called: Mtv Networks
1575 N Gower St Ste 100, Los Angeles
(90028-6488)
PHONE....................310 752-8000
Anthony Disanto, *President*
Jeremy Gonzalez, *President*
Joshua Vodnoy, *Vice Pres*
Lauren Hentschel, *Manager*
EMP: 51 **EST:** 2010
SALES (est): 8.8MM **Privately Held**
SIC: 7812 7822 Television film production; motion picture & tape distribution

---

(PA)=Parent Co (HQ)=Headquarters (DH)=Div Headquarters
✪ = New Business established in last 2 years

(P-19197)
**VILLAGE RDSHOW ENTRMT
GROUP US (PA)**
10100 Santa Monica Blvd, Los Angeles
(90067-4003)
PHONE....................310 385-4300
Greg Basser, *CEO*
Susan Bracey, *CFO*
Pollyanna Kwok, *Vice Pres*
Kevin Berg, *General Counsel*
EMP: 50 **EST:** 2006
SALES (est): 3.5MM **Privately Held**
WEB: www.vreg.com
SIC: 7812 Motion picture & video production

(P-19198)
**VILLAGE RDSHOW ENTRMT
GROUP US**
9268 W 3rd St, Beverly Hills (90210-3713)
PHONE....................310 867-8000
James P Moore, *CEO*
EMP: 50
SALES (corp-wide): 3.5MM **Privately
Held**
WEB: www.vreg.com
SIC: 7812 Motion picture & video production
PA: Village Roadshow Entertainment Group
Usa Inc.
10100 Santa Monica Blvd
Los Angeles CA 90067
310 385-4300

(P-19199)
**VILLAGE ROAD SHOW
PICTURES USA**
10100 Santa Monica Blvd, Los Angeles
(90067-4003)
PHONE....................310 385-4300
Greg Basser, *Chairman*
Simon Phillipson, *President*
Bruce Berman, *CEO*
Matthew Velkes, *COO*
▲ **EMP:** 66 **EST:** 1988
SQ FT: 9,000
SALES (est): 12.8MM **Privately Held**
WEB: www.vreg.com
SIC: 7812 Motion picture production & distribution
HQ: Village Roadshow Pty Ltd
L 1 500 Chapel St
South Yarra VIC 3141

(P-19200)
VIVID ENTERTAINMENT LLC
3599 Cahuenga Blvd W, Los Angeles
(90068-1397)
PHONE....................323 845-4557
Steven Hirsch,
Ken Boenish, *President*
Michael H Klein, *President*
David Guerra, *Vice Pres*
Kristin Harrah, *Production*
EMP: 50 **EST:** 1984
SQ FT: 15,000
SALES (est): 7.5MM **Privately Held**
WEB: www.vivid.com
SIC: 7812 5099 Video tape production;
video & audio equipment

(P-19201)
WAD PRODUCTIONS INC
Also Called: Ellen Degeneres Show, The
3500 W Olive Ave Ste 1000, Burbank
(91505-5515)
PHONE....................818 260-5673
Greg Gorden, *President*
Lauren Blincoe, *Vice Pres*
Alissa Cote, *Producer*
Ryan Kawamoto, *Producer*
Corey Palent, *Producer*
EMP: 64 **EST:** 2002
SALES (est): 7.4MM **Privately Held**
SIC: 7812 Motion picture & video production

(P-19202)
**WALT DISNEY MUSIC COMPANY
(DH)**
500 S Buena Vista St, Burbank
(91521-0007)
P.O. Box 3232, Anaheim (92803-3232)
PHONE....................818 560-1000

Tom Macdougall, *President*
Robert Cavallo, *Ch of Bd*
Cathleen M Taff, *CFO*
Cathleen Tass, *Treasurer*
Kary McHoul, *Senior VP*
▲ **EMP:** 611 **EST:** 1947
SALES (est): 103.4MM
SALES (corp-wide): 65.3B **Publicly Held**
WEB: www.disneyanimation.com
SIC: 7812 Motion picture & video production
HQ: Disney Enterprises, Inc.
500 S Buena Vista St
Burbank CA 91521
818 560-1000

(P-19203)
**WALT DISNEY RECORDS
DIRECT (DH)**
500 S Buena Vista St, Burbank
(91521-0007)
PHONE....................818 560-1000
Alan H Bergman, *Senior VP*
Rob Moore, *CFO*
Nick Franklin, *Senior VP*
Tonya Agurto, *Vice Pres*
Marsha Reed, *Admin Sec*
◆ **EMP:** 2990 **EST:** 1983
SQ FT: 600,000
SALES (est): 112.3MM
SALES (corp-wide): 65.3B **Publicly Held**
WEB: www.disneyanimation.com
SIC: 7812 Motion picture production & distribution
HQ: Disney Enterprises, Inc.
500 S Buena Vista St
Burbank CA 91521
818 560-1000

(P-19204)
**WARNER BROS ENTERPRISES
LLC (DH)**
4000 Warner Blvd, Burbank (91522-0002)
PHONE....................818 954-6000
Stephen Carroll, *Principal*
▲ **EMP:** 60 **EST:** 2005
SALES (est): 95.7MM
SALES (corp-wide): 171.7B **Publicly
Held**
WEB: www.warnerbros.com
SIC: 7812 Television film production
HQ: Warner Bros. Entertainment Inc.
4000 Warner Blvd
Burbank CA 91522
818 954-6000

(P-19205)
**WARNER BROS
ENTERTAINMENT INC (DH)**
Also Called: Victory Studio
4000 Warner Blvd, Burbank (91522-0002)
P.O. Box 29113, Hot Springs AR (71903-
9113)
PHONE....................818 954-6000
Ann Sarnoff, *CEO*
Tom Ascheim, *President*
Alan Horn, *President*
Lynne Frank, *Exec VP*
Johanna Fuentes, *Exec VP*
◆ **EMP:** 3877 **EST:** 2001
SALES (est): 542.4MM
SALES (corp-wide): 171.7B **Publicly
Held**
WEB: www.warnerbros.com
SIC: 7812 Television film production

(P-19206)
**WARNER BROS
ENTERTAINMENT INC**
Also Called: Warner Bros Studio Facilities
3500 W Olive Ave Ste 200, Burbank
(91505-4644)
PHONE....................818 954-2209
Steven Singer, *Branch Mgr*
EMP: 168
SALES (corp-wide): 171.7B **Publicly
Held**
WEB: www.warnerbros.com
SIC: 7812 Television film production
HQ: Warner Bros. Entertainment Inc.
4000 Warner Blvd
Burbank CA 91522
818 954-6000

(P-19207)
WARNER BROS FE INC (DH)
4000 Warner Blvd Bldg 178, Burbank
(91522-0002)
PHONE....................212 484-8000
Mark Brown, *Vice Pres*
Melinda Hage, *Vice Pres*
Christopher Mack, *Vice Pres*
Jennifer Pettit, *Exec Dir*
Hank Lachmund, *Technology*
EMP: 184 **EST:** 1932
SALES (est): 8.1MM
SALES (corp-wide): 171.7B **Publicly
Held**
WEB: www.warnermedia.com
SIC: 7812 Motion picture production

(P-19208)
**WARNER BROS HOME ENTRMT
INC**
4000 Warner Blvd Bldg 160, Burbank
(91522-0002)
P.O. Box 9153, Canton MA (02021-9153)
PHONE....................818 954-6000
James Cardwell, *President*
Jeff Nagler, *Exec VP*
David Haddad, *Senior VP*
Peter Axelrad, *Vice Pres*
Jeff Baker, *Vice Pres*
▲ **EMP:** 600 **EST:** 1978
SQ FT: 12,000
SALES (est): 126.3MM
SALES (corp-wide): 171.7B **Publicly
Held**
WEB: www.warnerbros.com
SIC: 7812 Television film production
HQ: Warner Bros. Entertainment Inc.
4000 Warner Blvd
Burbank CA 91522
818 954-6000

(P-19209)
**WARNER BROS INTL TV DIST
INC**
4000 Warner Blvd, Burbank (91522-0002)
PHONE....................818 954-6000
Robert Blair, *President*
Monique Esclavissat, *Exec VP*
Eric Wilker, *Exec Dir*
Kelly Findley, *Administration*
Margee Schubert, *Director*
EMP: 99 **EST:** 2003
SALES (est): 12.7MM
SALES (corp-wide): 171.7B **Publicly
Held**
WEB: www.warnerbros.com
SIC: 7812 -Television film production
HQ: Warner Bros. Entertainment Inc.
4000 Warner Blvd
Burbank CA 91522
818 954-6000

(P-19210)
WARNER BROS PICTURES INC
4000 Warner Blvd, Burbank (91522-0002)
PHONE....................818 954-6000
Steven S Spira, *President*
Andrew Cripps, *President*
Lynne Frank, *President*
Blair Rich, *President*
JP Richards, *President*
EMP: 50 **EST:** 2003
SALES (est): 8.6MM **Privately Held**
WEB: www.wbphotolab.com
SIC: 7812 Video production

(P-19211)
WESTBROOK OPS LLC
24151 Ventura Blvd # 200, Calabasas
(91302-1276)
PHONE....................818 832-2300
Kosako Yada,
EMP: 78 **EST:** 2019
SALES (est): 1MM **Privately Held**
SIC: 7812 Motion picture & video production

(P-19212)
**WPA WORLDWIDE
PRODUCTION AGCY (PA)**
144 N Robertson Blvd, West Hollywood
(90048-3131)
PHONE....................310 659-9965
Steven Jacob, *President*
Frank Balkin, *Partner*

Brian J Goldberg, *Partner*
Trevor Kossack, *Partner*
Barnaby Laws, *Director*
EMP: 64 **EST:** 2017
SALES (est): 325.2K **Privately Held**
SIC: 7812 Motion picture & video production

(P-19213)
YOBS TECHNOLOGIES INC
615 Childs Way 370, Los Angeles
(90089-0024)
PHONE....................213 713-3825
Raphael Danilo, *President*
Federico Dubini, *CFO*
EMP: 50 **EST:** 2016
SALES (est): 2.8MM **Privately Held**
WEB: www.yobstech.com
SIC: 7812 8742 7389 3652 Educational
motion picture production; industrial motion picture production; audio-visual program production; programmed instruction
service; ; pre-recorded records & tapes

(P-19214)
ZOIC INC
Also Called: Zoic Studios
3582 Eastham Dr, Culver City
(90232-2409)
PHONE....................310 838-0770
Loni Peristere, *CEO*
Chris Jones, *President*
Tim McBride, *Treasurer*
Gina Fiore, *Vice Pres*
Johnny Uribe, *Engineer*
EMP: 125 **EST:** 2002
SQ FT: 15,000
SALES (est): 12.9MM **Privately Held**
WEB: www.zoicstudios.com
SIC: 7812 Video production

(P-19215)
ZOO DIGITAL PRODUCTION LLC
2201 Park Pl Ste 100, El Segundo
(90245-5167)
PHONE....................310 220-3939
Laura Herbers, *Administration*
Tony Ferkranus, *Vice Pres*
Chris Oakley, *Vice Pres*
Chris Reilly, *Vice Pres*
Todd Schwartz, *Vice Pres*
EMP: 98 **EST:** 2010
SALES (est): 25MM **Privately Held**
WEB: www.zoodigital.com
SIC: 7812 Video production; video tape
production

7819 Services Allied To
Motion Picture Prdtn

(P-19216)
A FILML INC
Also Called: FILML.A
6255 W Sunset Blvd Fl 12, Los Angeles
(90028-7428)
PHONE....................213 977-8600
Paul Audley, *President*
Denise Gutches, *Officer*
Philip Sokoloski, *Comms Dir*
Daniel Poissant, *Office Admin*
Corina Sandru, *Admin Sec*
EMP: 70 **EST:** 1995
SALES (est): 10.7MM **Privately Held**
WEB: www.filmla.com
SIC: 7819 Services allied to motion pictures

(P-19217)
ACADEMY FOUNDATION (HQ)
8949 Wilshire Blvd, Beverly Hills
(90211-1907)
PHONE....................310 247-3000
Bruce Davis, *Exec Dir*
Dawn Mori, *Director*
EMP: 50 **EST:** 1944
SQ FT: 35,000
SALES (est): 71MM
SALES (corp-wide): 158.3MM **Privately
Held**
WEB: www.oscars.org
SIC: 7819 Services allied to motion pictures

PA: Academy Of Motion Picture Arts & Sciences
8949 Wilshire Blvd
Beverly Hills CA 90211
310 247-3000

(P-19218)
ALAN GORDON ENTERPRISES INC
5625 Melrose Ave, Los Angeles
(90038-3909)
PHONE..................................323 466-3561
Grant Loucks, *President*
Martha Garcia, *CFO*
Don Sahlein, *Senior VP*
Isabel Cardenap, *General Mgr*
Mark Mondok, *Administration*
◆ **EMP:** 24 **EST:** 1945
SQ FT: 15,000
SALES (est): 2.7MM **Privately Held**
WEB: www.alangordon.com
SIC: 7819 3861 Equipment rental, motion picture; photographic equipment & supplies

(P-19219)
ASPECT RATIO INC (HQ)
5161 Lankershim Blvd # 30, North Hollywood (91601-4962)
PHONE..................................323 467-2121
Robert Israel, *CEO*
Mark Trugman, *President*
Dennis Hamilton, *CFO*
Phillip Gershwin, *Opers Mgr*
EMP: 85 **EST:** 1978
SQ FT: 11,000
SALES (est): 6.1MM
SALES (corp-wide): 11.4MM **Privately Held**
WEB: www.teamaspect.com
SIC: 7819 Film processing, editing & titling: motion picture
PA: Aspect Group Llc
1347 N Cahuenga Blvd
Los Angeles CA 90028
323 467-2121

(P-19220)
AVONGARD PRODUCTS USA LTD
Also Called: Hydraulx
12855 Runway Rd Apt 1208, Playa Vista (90094-2666)
PHONE..................................310 319-2300
David Strause, *President*
Gregor D Strause, *CEO*
Colin Strause, *Vice Pres*
Linda Strause, *Admin Sec*
EMP: 50 **EST:** 1979
SALES (est): 11.4MM **Privately Held**
SIC: 7819 Visual effects production

(P-19221)
BEAR NASH PRODUCTIONS
521 E Sycamore Ave, El Segundo (90245-2406)
PHONE..................................310 428-5167
Albert CHI, *Principal*
EMP: 65 **EST:** 2019
SALES (est): 233.3K **Privately Held**
SIC: 7819 Developing & laboratory services, motion picture

(P-19222)
CHAPMN/LNARD STDIO EQP CNADA I (PA)
12950 Raymer St, North Hollywood (91605-4211)
PHONE..................................323 877-5309
Leonard Chapman, *President*
Michael Chapman, *Corp Secy*
David Bullard, *Prdtn Mgr*
David Gasparian, *Prdtn Mgr*
Frank Requena, *Relations*
▲ **EMP:** 145 **EST:** 1945
SQ FT: 300,000
SALES (est): 20.9MM **Privately Held**
WEB: www.chapman-leonard.com
SIC: 7819 Studio property rental, motion picture; equipment rental, motion picture

(P-19223)
CONDOR PRODUCTIONS LLC
245 N Beverly Dr, Beverly Hills (90210-5319)
PHONE..................................310 449-3000
Kathryn Rose-Remlinger, *Accountant*
EMP: 99
SQ FT: 5,000
SALES (est): 376.1K **Privately Held**
SIC: 7819 TV tape services: editing, transfers, etc.

(P-19224)
DE LA MARE ENGINEERING INC
1908 1st St, San Fernando (91340-2691)
PHONE..................................818 365-9208
George Jackman, *President*
EMP: 39 **EST:** 1952
SALES (est): 1.4MM **Privately Held**
SIC: 7819 3679 Services allied to motion pictures; electronic circuits

(P-19225)
DELUXE ENTERTAINMENT SVCS INC
2400 W Empire Ave, Burbank (91504-3331)
PHONE..................................323 960-7303
Stefanie Liquori, *Principal*
Anatol Sapleu, *Software Engr*
Victor Dominguez, *IT/INT Sup*
Akhil Conner, *Technical Staff*
Karineh Carapetian, *Director*
EMP: 53 **EST:** 2019
SALES (est): 8.1MM **Privately Held**
WEB: www.customframestore.com
SIC: 7819 Services allied to motion pictures

(P-19226)
DELUXE LABORATORIES INC (HQ)
Also Called: Color By Deluxe
2400 W Empire Ave Ste 400, Burbank (91504-3355)
PHONE..................................323 462-6171
Cyril Drabinsky, *CEO*
Mike Gunter, *CFO*
Scott Ehrlich, *Exec VP*
Dashiell Morrison, *Exec VP*
Warren Stein, *Exec VP*
▲ **EMP:** 626 **EST:** 1990
SQ FT: 150,000
SALES (est): 46.9MM **Privately Held**
SIC: 7819 Film processing, editing & titling: motion picture

(P-19227)
DELUXE MEDIA INC (PA)
Also Called: Deluxe Digital Studios
2400 W Empire Ave Ste 400, Burbank (91504-3355)
PHONE..................................818 565-3697
Cyril Drabinsky, *CEO*
Warren Stein, *COO*
Michael Gunter, *CFO*
Les Roy, *Manager*
Mallory Larsen, *Accounts Mgr*
EMP: 2986 **EST:** 2013
SALES (est): 151.8MM **Privately Held**
WEB: www.bydeluxe.com
SIC: 7819 Sound (effects & music production), motion picture

(P-19228)
DIRECTORS GUILD AMERICA INC (PA)
Also Called: D G A
7920 W Sunset Blvd, Los Angeles (90046-3300)
PHONE..................................310 289-2000
Jay D Roth, *Exec Dir*
Lesli Linka Glatter, *President*
Brian O'Rourke, *CFO*
Michael Apted, *Treasurer*
Scott Berger, *Treasurer*
EMP: 110 **EST:** 1936
SQ FT: 100,000
SALES (est): 26.2MM **Privately Held**
WEB: www.dga.org
SIC: 7819 8631 Directors, independent: motion picture; labor unions & similar labor organizations

(P-19229)
DNEG NORTH AMERICA INC (PA)
Also Called: Prime Focus World
5750 Hannum Ave Ste 100, Culver City (90230-6666)
PHONE..................................323 461-7887
Namit Malhotra, *CEO*
Robert Hummel, *CEO*
Oliver Welch, *COO*
Sue Murphree, *CFO*
Anjay Nagpal, *Senior VP*
EMP: 85 **EST:** 1985
SQ FT: 50,000
SALES (est): 12.8MM **Privately Held**
SIC: 7819 Sound (effects & music production), motion picture

(P-19230)
DTS INC (DH)
5220 Las Virgenes Rd, Calabasas (91302-1064)
PHONE..................................818 436-1000
Jon E Kirchner, *CEO*
Brian D Towne, *President*
Melvin L Flanigan, *CFO*
Victor Smith, *CFO*
Kevin Doohan, *Chief Mktg Ofcr*
▲ **EMP:** 150 **EST:** 1990
SQ FT: 89,000
SALES (est): 92.9MM
SALES (corp-wide): 892MM **Publicly Held**
WEB: www.dts.com
SIC: 7819 3651 Services allied to motion pictures; household audio & video equipment
HQ: Xperi Corporation
3025 Orchard Pkwy
San Jose CA 95134
408 321-6000

(P-19231)
EDGEBROOK PRODUCTIONS INC
10806 Ventura Blvd, Studio City (91604-3300)
PHONE..................................818 766-6789
Alan O Grady, *President*
EMP: 52
SALES (est): 415.9K **Privately Held**
WEB: www.edgebrookproductions.com
SIC: 7819 Developing & laboratory services, motion picture

(P-19232)
F J & J CORPORATION
Also Called: Leonetti Company
6938 Shadygrove St, Tujunga (91042-3144)
PHONE..................................505 452-1700
Frank Leonetti, *President*
Matthew Leonetti, *Vice Pres*
EMP: 17 **EST:** 1955
SQ FT: 28,250
SALES (est): 1.2MM **Privately Held**
SIC: 7819 3861 Equipment rental, motion picture; motion picture apparatus & equipment

(P-19233)
FOR CALI PRODUCTIONS LLC (DH)
5808 W Sunset Blvd, Los Angeles (90028-6607)
PHONE..................................323 956-9508
EMP: 219 **EST:** 2017
SALES (est): 21.6MM **Publicly Held**
SIC: 7819 Services allied to motion pictures
HQ: Netflix Studios, Llc
100 Winchester Cir
Los Gatos CA 95032
408 540-3700

(P-19234)
FOR CALI PRODUCTIONS LLC
5555 Melrose Ave Bldg 213, Los Angeles (90038-3996)
PHONE..................................323 956-9500
EMP: 81 **Publicly Held**
SIC: 7819 Services allied to motion pictures

HQ: For Cali Productions, Llc
5808 W Sunset Blvd
Los Angeles CA 90028
323 956-9508

(P-19235)
FOTO-KEM INDUSTRIES INC (PA)
Also Called: Foto Kem Film & Video
2801 W Alameda Ave, Burbank (91505-4405)
P.O. Box 7755 (91510-7755)
PHONE..................................818 846-3102
William F Brodersen, *CEO*
Kam Schumacher, *Bd of Directors*
Rosanna Marino, *Senior VP*
Gerald D Brodersen Jr, *Vice Pres*
Jeff Charles, *Vice Pres*
▲ **EMP:** 401 **EST:** 1963
SQ FT: 43,000
SALES (est): 43.4MM **Privately Held**
WEB: www.fotokem.com
SIC: 7819 Laboratory service, motion picture

(P-19236)
FUSEFX LLC
14823 Califa St, Van Nuys (91411-3108)
PHONE..................................818 237-5052
David Altenau, *CEO*
Tim Jacobsen, *Officer*
Johnny Fisk, *Vice Pres*
Jim Rygiel, *Executive*
Brad Kalinoski, *Admin Sec*
EMP: 300 **EST:** 2006
SQ FT: 12,500
SALES (est): 21.8MM **Privately Held**
SIC: 7819 Visual effects production

(P-19237)
HOLLYWOOD RNTALS PROD SVCS LLC (PA)
5300 Melrose Ave, Los Angeles (90038-5111)
PHONE..................................818 407-7800
Mark A Rosenthal, *Mng Member*
▲ **EMP:** 100 **EST:** 2000
SQ FT: 100,000
SALES (est): 10.2MM **Privately Held**
WEB: www.mbsequipmentco.com
SIC: 7819 Equipment rental, motion picture

(P-19238)
INDUSTRIAL MEDIA INC
6007 Sepulveda Blvd, Van Nuys (91411-2502)
PHONE..................................310 777-1940
Peter Hurwitz, *CEO*
Scott Frosch, *CFO*
Lara Geer, *Vice Pres*
Meron Bratzel, *Finance*
EMP: 250 **EST:** 2016
SALES (est): 150MM **Privately Held**
SIC: 7819 Reproduction services, motion picture production

(P-19239)
JACKSON SHRUB SUPPLY INC
11505 Vanowen St, North Hollywood (91605-6232)
PHONE..................................818 982-0100
Gary Jackson, *President*
EMP: 60 **EST:** 1936
SQ FT: 16,000
SALES (est): 5MM **Privately Held**
WEB: www.jacksonshrub.com
SIC: 7819 Services allied to motion pictures

(P-19240)
LATINO FILM INST YUTH CNEMA PR
143 S Glendale Ave # 204, Glendale (91205-4933)
PHONE..................................626 222-9252
Rafael Agustin Guerrero, *CEO*
EMP: 56 **EST:** 2016
SALES (est): 579.1K **Privately Held**
WEB: www.youthcinemaproject.org
SIC: 7819 Services allied to motion pictures

P
R
O
D
U
C
T
S

&

S
V
C
S

(P-19241)
NATIONAL FILM LABORATORIES
Also Called: Crest Digital
900 Glenneyre St, Laguna Beach
(92651-2707)
PHONE....................323 466-0281
Stephen R Stein, *CEO*
Ronald Stein, *President*
Lorraine Ross, *Corp Secy*
EMP: 86 **EST:** 1961
SQ FT: 50,000
SALES (est): 1.3MM **Privately Held**
SIC: 7819 7812 Film processing, editing & titling: motion picture; reproduction services, motion picture production; motion picture & video production

(P-19242)
NETFLIX WRLDWIDE PRDCTIONS LLC (DH)
5808 W Sunset Blvd Fl 11, Los Angeles
(90028-6607)
PHONE....................310 734-2900
EMP: 836 **EST:** 2018
SALES (est): 9MM **Publicly Held**
SIC: 7819 7841 Sound (effects & music production), motion picture; video tape rental; video disk/tape rental to the general public
HQ: Netflix Studios, Llc
100 Winchester Cir
Los Gatos CA 95032
408 540-3700

(P-19243)
OMEGA/CINEMA PROPS INC
1515 E 15th St, Los Angeles (90021-2711)
PHONE....................323 466-8201
E Jay Krause, *President*
Cheryl Jordan, *Corp Secy*
Josh Ziegert, *Info Tech Mgr*
Allan Songer, *Opers Mgr*
▲ **EMP:** 90 **EST:** 1967
SQ FT: 300,000
SALES (est): 9.3MM **Privately Held**
WEB: www.omegacinemaprops.com
SIC: 7819 Equipment rental, motion picture

(P-19244)
PIXELOGIC MEDIA PARTNERS LLC (DH)
4000 W Alameda Ave # 110, Burbank
(91505-4305)
PHONE....................818 861-2001
John Suh,
Barry Doyle, *Vice Pres*
Rick Soto, *Vice Pres*
Joselito David, *Technician*
Nicholas Colla, *Project Mgr*
EMP: 240 **EST:** 2016
SQ FT: 20,000
SALES (est): 20.6MM **Privately Held**
WEB: www.pixelogicmedia.com
SIC: 7819 Reproduction services, motion picture production

(P-19245)
POINT360 (PA)
Also Called: Digital Film Labs
2701 Media Center Dr, Los Angeles
(90065-1700)
PHONE....................818 565-1400
Haig S Bagerdjian, *Ch of Bd*
Alan R Steel, *CFO*
Alan Steel, *CFO*
John Schweizer, *Vice Pres*
Sally Fenton, *Managing Dir*
EMP: 146 **EST:** 1997
SQ FT: 64,600
SALES (est): 19.2MM **Privately Held**
WEB: www.point360.com
SIC: 7819 7822 7829 Video tape or disk reproduction; motion picture & tape distribution; television & video tape distribution; motion picture distribution services

(P-19246)
POST GROUP INC (PA)
1415 N Cahuenga Blvd, Los Angeles
(90028-8198)
PHONE....................323 462-2300
Frederic Rheinstein, *Chairman*
Lloyd Guillen, *President*
Vincent Lyons, *President*

Winston Whitmarsh, *Office Mgr*
Duke Gallagher, *Admin Sec*
EMP: 110 **EST:** 1974
SQ FT: 40,000
SALES (est): 8.6MM **Privately Held**
WEB: www.postgroup.com
SIC: 7819 7812 Editing services, motion picture production; film processing, editing & titling: motion picture; TV tape services: editing, transfers, etc.; motion picture & video production

(P-19247)
RUNWAY INC
1330 Vine St, Los Angeles (90028-8140)
P.O. Box 1536 (90078-1536)
PHONE....................310 636-2000
Roberta Margolis, *President*
Kit Lubold, *Opers Staff*
Richard Venezian, *Sales Executive*
Melissa Sonderegger, *Director*
Erica Villafane, *Director*
EMP: 91 **EST:** 1974
SQ FT: 17,500
SALES (est): 4.7MM **Privately Held**
WEB: www.runway.com
SIC: 7819 Video tape or disk reproduction

(P-19248)
TECHNCLOR CRATIVE SVCS USA INC (DH)
6040 W Sunset Blvd, Los Angeles
(90028-6402)
PHONE....................818 260-3800
Timothy Sarnoff, *CEO*
Richard Andrews, *President*
Claude Gagnon, *CEO*
Mark Bradford, *Vice Pres*
Keith Woody, *Vice Pres*
EMP: 300 **EST:** 1980
SQ FT: 25,000
SALES (est): 26.9MM
SALES (corp-wide): 57.9MM **Privately Held**
WEB: www.technicolor.com
SIC: 7819 Video tape or disk reproduction
HQ: Technicolor Thomson Group, Inc
2233 N Ontario St Ste 300
Burbank CA 91504
818 260-3600

(P-19249)
TECHNCLOR CRATIVE SVCS USA INC
Technicolor Complete Post
8921 Lindblade St, Culver City
(90232-2438)
PHONE....................323 467-1244
Mike Doggett, *Manager*
Michael Peters, *Manager*
EMP: 50
SALES (corp-wide): 57.9MM **Privately Held**
WEB: www.technicolor.com
SIC: 7819 Video tape or disk reproduction; sound (effects & music production), motion picture
HQ: Technicolor Creative Services Usa, Inc.
6040 W Sunset Blvd
Los Angeles CA 90028
818 260-3800

(P-19250)
TECHNCLOR VDOCASSETTE MICH INC (DH)
Also Called: Technicolor Video Service
3233 Mission Oaks Blvd, Camarillo
(93012-5138)
PHONE....................805 445-1122
Lanni Ormonvo, *President*
John H Oliphant, *Admin Sec*
▲ **EMP:** 500 **EST:** 1987
SQ FT: 300,000
SALES (est): 49.8MM
SALES (corp-wide): 57.9MM **Privately Held**
SIC: 7819 Video tape or disk reproduction
HQ: Technicolor Thomson Group, Inc
2233 N Ontario St Ste 300
Burbank CA 91504
818 260-3600

(P-19251)
TECHNICOLOR HM ENTRMT SVCS INC (HQ)
Also Called: Technicolor Video Services
3233 Mission Oaks Blvd, Camarillo
(93012-5097)
PHONE....................805 445-1122
Lanny Raimondo, *CEO*
Orlando F Raimondo, *President*
Patricia Dave, *CFO*
◆ **EMP:** 500 **EST:** 1983
SQ FT: 5,000
SALES (est): 484.9MM
SALES (corp-wide): 57.9MM **Privately Held**
WEB: www.technicolor.com
SIC: 7819 Video tape or disk reproduction

(P-19252)
TEN PUBLISHING MEDIA LLC (PA)
831 S Douglas St Ste 100, El Segundo
(90245-4956)
PHONE....................310 531-9900
Scott P Dickey, *CEO*
Peter H Englehart, *Ch of Bd*
Chris Argentieri, *President*
Bill Sutman, *CFO*
Jonathan Anastas, *Chief Mktg Ofcr*
EMP: 230 **EST:** 1991
SALES (est): 54.2MM **Privately Held**
SIC: 7819 Visual effects production

(P-19253)
TESTRONIC INC
Also Called: Testronic Labs
111 N First St Ste 204, Burbank
(91502-1851)
PHONE....................818 845-3223
Dominic Wheatley, *CEO*
Mike Betti, *Officer*
Ron Taylor, *General Mgr*
Kevin Lebre, *Project Mgr*
Andy Riddle, *Project Mgr*
▲ **EMP:** 112 **EST:** 1996
SALES (est): 6MM **Privately Held**
WEB: www.testroniclabs.com
SIC: 7819 Video tape or disk reproduction

(P-19254)
WALT DISNEY IMAGINEERING (DH)
1401 Flower St, Glendale (91201-2421)
P.O. Box 25020 (91221-5020)
PHONE....................818 544-6500
Thomas O Staggs, *CEO*
Martin A Sklar, *Vice Ch Bd*
Craig Russell, *Exec VP*
Markus Gross, *Vice Pres*
Jessica Hodgins, *Vice Pres*
▲ **EMP:** 1011 **EST:** 1986
SQ FT: 100,000
SALES (est): 74.9MM
SALES (corp-wide): 65.3B **Publicly Held**
WEB: www.disneyimaginations.com
SIC: 7819 8712 1542 8741 Visual effects production; architectural services; custom builders, non-residential; management services; engineering services
HQ: Disney Enterprises, Inc.
500 S Buena Vista St
Burbank CA 91521
818 560-1000

(P-19255)
WALT DISNEY PICTURES
811 Sonora Ave, Glendale (91201-2433)
PHONE....................818 409-2200
Meredith Roberts, *Senior VP*
Heather Lanza, *Department Mgr*
Ben Dejean, *Opers Staff*
Rosemary White, *Production*
Clay Price, *Manager*
EMP: 300 **EST:** 1983
SQ FT: 461,000
SALES (est): 51.7MM
SALES (corp-wide): 65.3B **Publicly Held**
WEB: www.movies.disney.com
SIC: 7819 TV tape services: editing, transfers, etc.
PA: The Walt Disney Company
500 S Buena Vista St
Burbank CA 91521
818 560-1000

7822 Motion Picture & Video Tape Distribution

(P-19256)
BAD ROBOT PRODUCTIONS INC
1221 Olympic Blvd, Santa Monica
(90404-3721)
PHONE....................310 664-3456
Mike Silver, *Manager*
Brian Weinstein, *COO*
James Kerr, *Executive*
Tim Keenan, *Creative Dir*
Scott Struna, *Office Mgr*
EMP: 64
SALES (corp-wide): 1.9MM **Privately Held**
SIC: 7822 Motion picture & tape distribution
PA: Bad Robot Productions, Inc.
1925 Century Park E Fl 22
Los Angeles CA 90067
310 664-3456

(P-19257)
BUENA VISTA INTERNATIONAL INC (DH)
500 S Buena Vista St, Burbank
(91521-0001)
PHONE....................818 560-1000
David M Hollis, *CEO*
Mark D Zoradi, *President*
David Hughes, *Treasurer*
▲ **EMP:** 50 **EST:** 1961
SALES (est): 39.2MM
SALES (corp-wide): 65.3B **Publicly Held**
WEB: www.thewaltdisneycompany.com
SIC: 7822 Distribution, exclusive of production: motion picture

(P-19258)
DELUXE NMS INC
4499 Glencoe Ave, Marina Del Rey
(90292-6357)
PHONE....................310 760-8500
Cyril Drabinsky, *CEO*
Arlyn Vizcarra, *Accounts Mgr*
EMP: 200 **EST:** 2010
SQ FT: 20,000
SALES (est): 17.2MM
SALES (corp-wide): 1.7B **Publicly Held**
WEB: www.dadcdigital.com
SIC: 7822 7374 Motion picture & tape distribution; data processing & preparation
PA: Deluxe Corporation
3680 Victoria St N
Shoreview MN 55126
651 483-7111

(P-19259)
IMAGE ENTERTAINMENT INC (DH)
6320 Canoga Ave Ste 790, Woodland Hills
(91367-2561)
PHONE....................818 407-9100
Miguel Penella, *COO*
Drew Wilson, *CFO*
▲ **EMP:** 77 **EST:** 1975
SQ FT: 30,000
SALES (est): 11.7MM
SALES (corp-wide): 2.8B **Publicly Held**
WEB: www.image-entertainment.com
SIC: 7822 Motion picture & tape distribution
HQ: Rlj Entertainment, Inc.
8515 Georgia Ave Ste 650
Silver Spring MD 20910
301 608-2115

(P-19260)
LIONSGATE PRODUCTIONS INC
2700 Colorado Ave Ste 200, Santa Monica
(90404-5502)
PHONE....................310 255-3937
Jon Feltheimer, *CEO*
Steve Beeks, *COO*
Sandra Stern, *COO*
Patricia Laucella, *Exec VP*
Wayne Levin, *Exec VP*
EMP: 587 **EST:** 2010

SALES (est): 54.6MM
SALES (corp-wide): 3.8B Privately Held
WEB: www.lionsgate.com
SIC: 7822 Motion picture & tape distribution
HQ: Lions Gate Entertainment Inc.
2700 Colorado Ave Ste 200
Santa Monica CA 90404
310 449-9200

(P-19261)
SONAR ENTERTAINMENT INC (PA)
2834 Colorado Ave Ste 300, Santa Monica (90404-3644)
PHONE................................424 230-7140
Thomas F Lesinski, *CEO*
Joel E Denton, *President*
William J Aliber, *CFO*
Henry S Hoberman, *Exec VP*
Matt Loze, *Exec VP*
EMP: 394 EST: 2007
SALES (est): 35.1MM Privately Held
WEB: www.sonarent.com
SIC: 7822 Motion picture & tape distribution

(P-19262)
STX PRODUCTIONS LLC (PA)
3900 W Alameda Ave Fl 32, Burbank (91505-4316)
PHONE................................310 742-2300
Jada Miranda, *Exec VP*
Llewellyn Radley, *Exec VP*
Lisa Dimartino, *Vice Pres*
Shari Hardison, *Vice Pres*
Stephen Murphy, *Vice Pres*
EMP: 53 EST: 2014
SALES (est): 2.7MM Privately Held
WEB: www.erosstx.com
SIC: 7822 Motion picture & tape distribution

(P-19263)
TWENTIETH CNTURY FOX INTL CORP (DH)
Also Called: FOX INTERACTIVE
10201 W Pico Blvd Bldg 1, Los Angeles (90064-2606)
P.O. Box 900, Beverly Hills (90213-0900)
PHONE................................310 969-5300
Pat Wyatt, *Ch of Bd*
Bob Delellis, *President*
Craig Sloan, *President*
Dean Hallett, *CFO*
David Miller, *Treasurer*
◆ EMP: 629 EST: 1972
SQ FT: 115,000
SALES: 1.4MM
SALES (corp-wide): 65.3B Publicly Held
WEB: www.fox.com
SIC: 7822 7922 Motion picture distribution; television program, including commercial producers
HQ: Twentieth Century Fox Film Corporation
10201 W Pico Blvd
Los Angeles CA 90064
310 369-1000

(P-19264)
UNITED ARTISTS PRODUCTIONS INC
10250 Constellation Blvd, Los Angeles (90067-6200)
PHONE................................310 449-3000
Christopher McGurk, *President*
EMP: 199 EST: 1995
SALES (est): 1.4MM
SALES (corp-wide): 1.1B Privately Held
SIC: 7822 Distribution, exclusive of production: motion picture
HQ: United Artists Pictures Inc.
10250 Constellation Blvd
Los Angeles CA 90067

(P-19265)
UNITED ARTISTS TELEVISION CORP
10250 Constellation Blvd, Los Angeles (90067-6200)
PHONE................................310 449-3000
EMP: 114 EST: 1931

SALES (est): 782.7K
SALES (corp-wide): 1.1B Privately Held
SIC: 7822 Distribution, exclusive of production: motion picture
HQ: United Artists Pictures Inc.
10250 Constellation Blvd
Los Angeles CA 90067
-

(P-19266)
WARNER BROS TRANSATLANTIC INC (DH)
4000 Warner Blvd, Burbank (91522-0002)
PHONE................................818 977-0018
Barry M Meyer, *CEO*
Ralph Peterson, *Treasurer*
Richard Fox, *Exec VP*
Stuart Krasnow, *Exec VP*
Andy Lewis, *Exec VP*
▲ EMP: 1321 EST: 1929
SALES (est): 287.2MM
SALES (corp-wide): 171.7B Publicly Held
WEB: www.warnerbroscanada.com
SIC: 7822 Distribution, exclusive of production: motion picture

---

7829 Services Allied To Motion Picture Distribution

(P-19267)
WALT DISNEY PICTURES AND TV
500 S Buena Vista St, Burbank (91521-0007)
PHONE................................818 560-1000
Richard W Cook, *Chairman*
Robert Matschullat, *Vice Chairman*
Ravi Ahuja, *President*
Alan Bergman, *President*
Peter Rice, *Chairman*
▲ EMP: 56 EST: 1986
SALES (est): 17.7MM
SALES (corp-wide): 65.3B Publicly Held
WEB: www.disney.com
SIC: 7829 Motion picture distribution services
HQ: Disney Enterprises, Inc.
500 S Buena Vista St
Burbank CA 91521
818 560-1000

7832 Motion Picture Theaters, Except Drive-In

(P-19268)
AMERICAN CINEMAS GROUP INC (PA)
Also Called: Ultrastar Cinemas
1180 Nevada St Ste 100, Redlands (92374-2894)
PHONE................................760 597-5777
Russell Seheult, *President*
John Ellison, *COO*
Adam Saks, *VP Opers*
EMP: 178 EST: 2004
SALES (est): 6.2MM Privately Held
SIC: 7832 Motion picture theaters, except drive-in

(P-19269)
AMERICAN MULTI-CINEMA INC
Also Called: AMC
42 Miller Aly, Pasadena (91103-3643)
PHONE................................626 585-8900
EMP: 50 Publicly Held
SIC: 7832 Motion Picture Theater
HQ: American Multi-Cinema, Inc.
1 Amc Way
Leawood KS 66211
913 213-2000

(P-19270)
ARCLIGHT CINEMA COMPANY
15301 Ventura Blvd Bldg A, Sherman Oaks (91403-3102)
PHONE................................818 501-0753
EMP: 92

SALES (corp-wide): 13.5MM Privately Held
WEB: www.arclightcinemas.com
SIC: 7832 Motion Picture Theater
PA: Arclight Cinema Company
6360 W Sunset Blvd
Los Angeles CA 90028
323 464-4226

(P-19271)
ARCLIGHT CINEMA COMPANY
120 N Robertson Blvd Fl 3, Los Angeles (90048-3115)
PHONE................................323 464-1465
EMP: 170
SALES (corp-wide): 13.5MM Privately Held
WEB: www.arclightcinemas.com
SIC: 7832 Motion Picture Theater
PA: Arclight Cinema Company
6360 W Sunset Blvd
Los Angeles CA 90028
323 464-4226

(P-19272)
DECURION CORPORATION (PA)
120 N Robertson Blvd Fl 3, Los Angeles (90048-3115)
PHONE................................310 659-9432
Michael R Forman, *President*
Greg Hambly, *Treasurer*
Bryan Ungard, *Vice Pres*
James Cotter, *Vice Pres*
Jerome Forman, *Vice Pres*
EMP: 100
SQ FT: 31,000
SALES (est): 175.8MM Privately Held
WEB: www.decurion.com
SIC: 7832 7833 Motion picture theaters, except drive-in; drive-in motion picture theaters

(P-19273)
EDWARDS THEATRES CIRCUIT INC
Also Called: Mesa Pointe Stadium 12
901 S Coast Dr, Costa Mesa (92626-1747)
PHONE................................714 428-0962
Minh Duong, *Branch Mgr*
EMP: 171 Privately Held
SIC: 7832 Motion picture theaters, except drive-in
HQ: Edwards Theatres Circuit, Inc.
300 Newport Center Dr
Newport Beach CA 92660
949 640-4600

(P-19274)
EDWARDS THEATRES CIRCUIT INC
Also Called: Kaleidioscope Stadium Cinema
27741 Crown Valley Pkwy, Mission Viejo (92691-6532)
PHONE................................949 582-4078
EMP: 171 Privately Held
SIC: 7832 Motion picture theaters, except drive-in
HQ: Edwards Theatres Circuit, Inc.
300 Newport Center Dr
Newport Beach CA 92660
949 640-4600

(P-19275)
EDWARDS THEATRES CIRCUIT INC
Also Called: Aliso Viejo Stadium Cinemas 10
26701 Aliso Creek Rd, Aliso Viejo (92656-2887)
PHONE................................949 425-3838
EMP: 62 Privately Held
SIC: 7832 Motion picture theaters, except drive-in
HQ: Edwards Theatres Circuit, Inc.
300 Newport Center Dr
Newport Beach CA 92660
949 640-4600

(P-19276)
EDWARDS THEATRES CIRCUIT INC (DH)
300 Newport Center Dr, Newport Beach (92660-7529)
PHONE................................949 640-4600
W James Edwards III, *Ch of Bd*
Steve Coffey, *President*

Joan Randolph, *Vice Pres*
Marcella Sheldon, *Admin Sec*
EMP: 118 EST: 1930
SQ FT: 30,000
SALES (est): 249.7MM Privately Held
WEB: www.regmovies.com
SIC: 7832 Motion picture theaters, except drive-in

(P-19277)
EDWARDS THEATRES CIRCUIT INC
Also Called: Temecula Stadium Cinemas 15
40750 Winchester Rd, Temecula (92591-5524)
PHONE................................951 296-0144
EMP: 171 Privately Held
SIC: 7832 Motion picture theaters, except drive-in
HQ: Edwards Theatres Circuit, Inc.
300 Newport Center Dr
Newport Beach CA 92660
949 640-4600

(P-19278)
EDWARDS THEATRES CIRCUIT INC
Also Called: Edwards Cinemas University
4245 Campus Dr, Irvine (92612-2752)
PHONE................................949 854-8811
Mike Peterson, *Branch Mgr*
EMP: 171 Privately Held
SIC: 7832 Motion picture theaters, except drive-in
HQ: Edwards Theatres Circuit, Inc.
300 Newport Center Dr
Newport Beach CA 92660
949 640-4600

(P-19279)
EDWARDS THEATRES CIRCUIT INC
Also Called: Santa Maria Cinema 10
1521 S Bradley Rd, Santa Maria (93454-8014)
PHONE................................805 347-1164
Santa Edwards, *Manager*
EMP: 171 Privately Held
SIC: 7832 Motion picture theaters, except drive-in
HQ: Edwards Theatres Circuit, Inc.
300 Newport Center Dr
Newport Beach CA 92660
949 640-4600

(P-19280)
IMAX CORPORATION (HQ)
Also Called: Imax Theatre Marketing
12582 Millennium, Los Angeles (90094-2823)
PHONE................................310 255-5559
Richard Gelfond, *CEO*
Greg Foster, *President*
Carrie Lindzon-Jacobs, *Officer*
MO Rhim, *Senior VP*
Joseph Findley, *Executive*
◆ EMP: 265 EST: 1967
SALES (est): 33.8MM
SALES (corp-wide): 137MM Privately Held
WEB: www.imax.com
SIC: 7832 Motion picture theaters, except drive-in
PA: Imax Corporation
2525 Speakman Dr
Mississauga ON L5K 1
905 403-6500

(P-19281)
KRIKORIAN PREMIERE THEATRE LLC
8290 La Palma Ave, Buena Park (90620)
PHONE................................714 826-7469
Ted Goldbeck, *Vice Pres*
Steve Bowen, *VP Finance*
Elizabeth Holliday, *Sales Associate*
EMP: 93
SALES (corp-wide): 25.6MM Privately Held
SIC: 7832 Motion picture theaters, except drive-in
PA: Krikorian Premiere Theatre Llc
2275 W 190th St
Torrance CA 90504
310 856-1270

(PA)=Parent Co (HQ)=Headquarters (DH)=Div Headquarters
✪ = New Business established in last 2 years

(P-19282)
KRIKORIAN PREMIERE THEATRE LLC
8540 Whittier Blvd, Pico Rivera (90660-2520)
PHONE...............................562 205-3456
Todd Cummings, *Branch Mgr*
EMP: 93
SALES (corp-wide): 25.6MM **Privately Held**
SIC: 7832 Motion picture theaters, except drive-in
PA: Krikorian Premiere Theatre Llc
　　2275 W 190th St
　　Torrance CA 90504
　　310 856-1270

(P-19283)
MAYA BKRSFELD CINEMAS OPER LLC
Also Called: Maya Cinemas Bakersfield
1000 California Ave, Bakersfield (93304-1520)
PHONE...............................213 805-5333
Heidi Garcia, *Opers Staff*
EMP: 50 EST: 2001
SALES (est): 476K **Privately Held**
WEB: www.mayacinemas.com
SIC: 7832 Motion picture theaters, except drive-in

(P-19284)
MAYA DELANO CINEMAS OPER LLC
Also Called: Maya Cinemas Delano
401 Woollomes Ave, Delano (93215-9557)
PHONE...............................213 805-5333
Heidi Garcia, *Opers Staff*
EMP: 50 EST: 2016
SALES (est): 428.6K **Privately Held**
WEB: www.mayacinemas.com
SIC: 7832 Motion picture theaters, except drive-in

(P-19285)
PACIFIC THEATERS INC (PA)
120 N Robertson Blvd Fl 3, Los Angeles (90048-3113)
PHONE...............................310 657-8420
EMP: 120
SQ FT: 25,000
SALES (est): 8.3MM **Privately Held**
WEB: www.pacifictheatres.com
SIC: 7832 7812 Motion Picture Theater, Except Drive-In

(P-19286)
PACIFIC THEATRES ENTRMT CORP (HQ)
120 N Robertson Blvd Fl 3, Los Angeles (90048-3113)
PHONE...............................310 659-9432
EMP: 100
SQ FT: 3,000
SALES (est): 7.8MM
SALES (corp-wide): 175.8MM **Privately Held**
WEB: www.pacifictheatres.com
SIC: 7832 Motion Picture Theater
PA: The Decurion Corporation
　　120 N Robertson Blvd Fl 3
　　Los Angeles CA 90048
　　310 659-9432

(P-19287)
READING ENTERTAINMENT INC (HQ)
500 Citadel Dr Ste 300, Commerce (90040-1575)
PHONE...............................213 235-2226
Robert F Smerling, *President*
Andrzej Matyczynski, *CFO*
Ellen Cotter, *Vice Pres*
Charles Grohon, *Vice Pres*
John Willey, *Vice Pres*
▲ EMP: 78 EST: 1996
SQ FT: 3,300
SALES (est): 11.6MM
SALES (corp-wide): 77.8MM **Publicly Held**
WEB: www.readingrdi.com
SIC: 7832 Motion picture theaters, except drive-in

PA: Reading International, Inc.
　　5995 Sepulveda Blvd # 300
　　Culver City CA 90230
　　213 235-2240

(P-19288)
READING INTERNATIONAL INC (PA)
5995 Sepulveda Blvd # 300, Culver City (90230-6415)
PHONE...............................213 235-2240
Ellen M Cotter, *President*
Margaret Cotter, *Ch of Bd*
Robert F Smerling, *President*
Gilbert Avanes, *CFO*
Andrzej Matyczynski, *Exec VP*
EMP: 562 EST: 1833
SQ FT: 11,700
SALES (est): 77.8MM **Publicly Held**
WEB: www.readingrdi.com
SIC: 7832 7922 6512 6531 Motion picture theaters, except drive-in; theatrical producers & services; nonresidential building operators; real estate agents & managers

(P-19289)
SILVER CINEMAS ACQUISITION CO (HQ)
Also Called: Landmark Theatres
700 N San Vicnte Blvd G460, West Hollywood (90069-5078)
PHONE...............................310 473-6701
George T Mundorff, *CEO*
Paul Serwitz, *President*
Jason Sachs, *Officer*
Bob Shaw, *Exec VP*
Dale Friddell, *Vice Pres*
EMP: 52 EST: 1974
SALES (est): 90.9MM
SALES (corp-wide): 129.1MM **Privately Held**
WEB: www.landmarktheatres.com
SIC: 7832 Motion picture theaters, except drive-in
PA: Cohen Media Group Llc
　　750 Lexington Ave Ste 500
　　New York NY 10022
　　646 380-7929

(P-19290)
WESTSTAR CINEMAS INC
Also Called: Plant 16
7876 Van Nuys Blvd, Van Nuys (91402-6069)
PHONE...............................818 779-0323
Randy Dingwall, *Branch Mgr*
EMP: 155
SALES (corp-wide): 25.7MM **Privately Held**
SIC: 7832 Motion picture theaters, except drive-in
PA: Weststar Cinemas, Inc.
　　16530 Ventura Blvd # 500
　　Encino CA 91436
　　818 784-6266

(P-19291)
WESTSTAR CINEMAS INC
Also Called: Village 8
180 Promenade Way Ste R, Westlake Village (91362-3826)
PHONE...............................805 379-8966
Joseph Leptore, *Manager*
EMP: 155
SALES (corp-wide): 25.7MM **Privately Held**
SIC: 7832 Motion picture theaters, except drive-in
PA: Weststar Cinemas, Inc.
　　16530 Ventura Blvd # 500
　　Encino CA 91436
　　818 784-6266

(P-19292)
WESTSTAR CINEMAS INC
Also Called: Buenaventura 6
1440 Eastman Ave, Ventura (93003-7784)
PHONE...............................805 658-6544
Lyndon Golin, *Branch Mgr*
Andrew Gualtieri, *District Mgr*
Crystal Whittaker, *Marketing Staff*
EMP: 155

SALES (corp-wide): 25.7MM **Privately Held**
SIC: 7832 Motion picture theaters, except drive-in
PA: Weststar Cinemas, Inc.
　　16530 Ventura Blvd # 500
　　Encino CA 91436
　　818 784-6266

(P-19293)
WESTSTAR CINEMAS INC
Also Called: Agoura Hills 8 Cinema Center
29045 Agoura Rd, Agoura Hills (91301-2572)
PHONE...............................818 707-9987
Raymond Cornelio, *General Mgr*
EMP: 155
SALES (corp-wide): 25.7MM **Privately Held**
SIC: 7832 Motion picture theaters, except drive-in
PA: Weststar Cinemas, Inc.
　　16530 Ventura Blvd # 500
　　Encino CA 91436
　　818 784-6266

7833 Drive-In Motion Picture Theaters

(P-19294)
CENTURY THEATRES INC
Also Called: Century Downtown 10
555 E Main St, Ventura (93001-2628)
PHONE...............................805 641-6555
EMP: 237 **Publicly Held**
SIC: 7833 Drive-in motion picture theaters; motion picture theaters, except drive-in
HQ: Century Theatres, Inc
　　3900 Dallas Pkwy Ste 500
　　Plano TX 75093
　　972 665-1000

(P-19295)
CENTURY THEATRES INC
Also Called: Century 8
12827 Victory Blvd, North Hollywood (91606-3012)
PHONE...............................818 508-1943
Terrell Hammack, *Branch Mgr*
EMP: 237 **Publicly Held**
WEB: www.cinemark.com
SIC: 7833 7832 Drive-in motion picture theaters; motion picture theaters, except drive-in
HQ: Century Theatres, Inc
　　3900 Dallas Pkwy Ste 500
　　Plano TX 75093
　　972 665-1000

(P-19296)
NATIONWIDE THEATRES CORP (HQ)
120 N Robertson Blvd Fl 3, Los Angeles (90048-3115)
PHONE...............................310 657-8420
Christopher Forman, *President*
Nora Dashwood, *COO*
EMP: 75 EST: 1956
SQ FT: 25,000
SALES (est): 77.9MM
SALES (corp-wide): 175.8MM **Privately Held**
WEB: www.decurion.com
SIC: 7833 7832 Drive-in motion picture theaters; motion picture theaters, except drive-in
PA: The Decurion Corporation
　　120 N Robertson Blvd Fl 3
　　Los Angeles CA 90048
　　310 659-9432

7841 Video Tape Rental

(P-19297)
EROS STX GLOBAL CORPORATION
3900 W Alameda Ave Fl 32, Burbank (91505-4316)
PHONE...............................818 524-7000
Robert B Simonds Jr, *Ch of Bd*
Kishore Lulla, *Ch of Bd*

Noah Fogelson, *President*
Rishika Lulla Singh, *President*
Pradeep Dwivedi, *CEO*
EMP: 502 EST: 1977
SALES: 434.2MM **Privately Held**
WEB: www.erosstx.com
SIC: 7841 Video disk/tape rental to the general public

7911 Dance Studios, Schools & Halls

(P-19298)
FOUNDATION FOR DANCE EDUCATION
Also Called: Inland Pacific Balle
9061 Central Ave, Montclair (91763-1622)
PHONE...............................909 482-1590
Victoria Koenig, *Exec Dir*
▲ EMP: 64 EST: 2008
SALES (est): 588.8K **Privately Held**
WEB: www.ipballet.org
SIC: 7911 Dance studio & school

(P-19299)
I2K LLC
748 N Mckeever Ave, Azusa (91702-2349)
PHONE...............................626 969-7780
Stephen Gray,
Meril Gray,
Stacy Gray,
EMP: 20 EST: 2015
SALES (est): 596.5K **Privately Held**
SIC: 7911 3061 Dance studio & school; medical & surgical rubber tubing (extruded & lathe-cut)

7922 Theatrical Producers & Misc Theatrical Svcs

(P-19300)
ADVENTIST MEDIA CENTER INC (PA)
Also Called: It Is Written
11291 Pierce St, Riverside (92505-2705)
P.O. Box 101, Simi Valley (93062-0101)
PHONE...............................805 955-7777
Daniel R Jackson, *CEO*
Daniel Jackson, *Ch of Bd*
Marshall Chase, *Presiden*
Coleen Dolinsky, *Treasurer*
Charles Reel, *Treasurer*
▲ EMP: 220 EST: 1972
SQ FT: 76,000
SALES (est): 14.7MM **Privately Held**
WEB: www.adventistmediaministries.com
SIC: 7922 Television program, including commercial producers

(P-19301)
AEG PRESENTS LLC (DH)
425 W 11th St, Los Angeles (90015-3459)
PHONE...............................323 930-5700
Jay Marciano, *CEO*
Leslie Millis, *COO*
Jorge Melendez, *CFO*
Ron Chiu, *Officer*
Brooke Kain, *Officer*
▲ EMP: 140 EST: 2002
SQ FT: 16,400
SALES (est): 28.7MM **Privately Held**
WEB: www.aegpresents.com
SIC: 7922 Entertainment promotion
HQ: Anschutz Entertainment Group, Inc.
　　800 W Olympic Blvd # 305
　　Los Angeles CA 90015
　　213 763-7700

(P-19302)
AGENCY FOR PERFORMING ARTS INC
405 S Beverly Dr Ste 500, Beverly Hills (90212-4425)
PHONE...............................310 888-4200
Andy Somers, *Vice Pres*
Wilson Becca, *Marketing Staff*
Gabe Berenson, *Assistant*
Ross Shenker, *Assistant*
Evan Tomlinson, *Assistant*
EMP: 71

SALES (corp-wide): 39.9MM **Privately Held**
WEB: www.apa-agency.com
SIC: 7922 Theatrical producers & services
PA: Agency For The Performing Arts, Inc.
405 S Beverly Dr Ste 500
Beverly Hills CA 90212
310 557-9049

(P-19303)
AGENCY FOR PERFORMING ARTS INC (PA)
405 S Beverly Dr Ste 500, Beverly Hills (90212-4425)
PHONE....................................310 557-9049
James Gosnell, *President*
Stuart Nichols, *CFO*
Jeff Witjas, *Senior VP*
Betsy Berg, *Vice Pres*
Alex Chaykin, *Vice Pres*
EMP: 100 **EST:** 1962
SALES (est): 39.9MM **Privately Held**
WEB: www.apa-agency.com
SIC: 7922 Theatrical producers & services; talent agent, theatrical

(P-19304)
BEN BOLLINGER PRODUCTIONS INC
Also Called: Bollingers Candelight Pavilion
455 W Foothill Blvd, Claremont (91711-2701)
PHONE....................................909 626-3296
Ben Bollinger, *President*
Mindy Teuber, *Executive*
Michael Ryan, *Administration*
Ezequiel Gonzalez, *Technical Staff*
John Lalonde, *Director*
EMP: 71 **EST:** 1985
SALES (est): 5.1MM **Privately Held**
SIC: 7922 8999 Legitimate live theater producers; music arranging & composing

(P-19305)
CALIFORNIA TICKETSCOM INC (DH)
555 Anton Blvd Fl 11, Costa Mesa (92626-7811)
PHONE....................................714 327-5400
Joe Choti, *President*
Christopher Farrar, *Partner*
Derek Goodnature, *President*
Chris Hurley, *CFO*
Cristine Hurley, *CFO*
▲ **EMP:** 196 **EST:** 1997
SALES (est): 39.9MM
SALES (corp-wide): 434.8MM **Privately Held**
WEB: www.tickets.com
SIC: 7922 7999 5961 5045 Ticket agency, theatrical; ticket sales office for sporting events, contract; catalog & mail-order houses; computers, peripherals & software
HQ: Mlb Advanced Media, L.P.
1271 Ave Of The Americas
New York NY 10020
212 485-3444

(P-19306)
CENTER THTRE GROUP LOS ANGELES (PA)
601 W Temple St, Los Angeles (90012-2621)
PHONE....................................213 972-7344
Meghan Pressman, *CEO*
William Ahmanson, *Ch of Bd*
Kiki Gindler, *President*
Cheryl Shepherd, *CFO*
Sarah Gonta, *Treasurer*
▲ **EMP:** 130 **EST:** 1966
SQ FT: 20,000
SALES (est): 46MM **Privately Held**
WEB: www.centertheatregroup.org
SIC: 7922 Theatrical companies

(P-19307)
CITY OF CERRITOS
Also Called: Cerritos Ctr For Prfrmg Arts
18125 Bloomfield Ave, Cerritos (90703-8577)
PHONE....................................562 916-8500
Dianne Cheney, *Exec Dir*
Gary W Hopkins PH, *Admin Sec*
Laurie Kajiwara, *Marketing Staff*

Wyman Wong, *Associate*
EMP: 150
SALES (corp-wide): 79.2MM **Privately Held**
WEB: www.safercerritos.com
SIC: 9111 7922 ; legitimate live theater producers
PA: City Of Cerritos
18125 Bloomfield Ave
Cerritos CA 90703
562 860-0311

(P-19308)
CREATIVE ARTSTS AGCY HLDNGS LL (PA)
Also Called: C A A
2000 Avenue Of The Stars, Los Angeles (90067-4700)
PHONE....................................424 288-2000
Steve Hasker, *CEO*
Kevin Gelbard, *Partner*
Rob Light, *Managing Prtnr*
Rick Nicita, *Chairman*
Ian Doody, *Vice Pres*
EMP: 800 **EST:** 1975
SALES (est): 668.1MM **Privately Held**
WEB: www.caa.com
SIC: 7922 Agent or manager for entertainers

(P-19309)
DELICATE PRODUCTIONS INC (PA)
874 Verdulera St, Camarillo (93010-8371)
PHONE....................................415 484-1174
James Steve Dabbs, *CEO*
Brian Boy, *COO*
Christopher Smyth, *CFO*
Harvey Ross, *Exec VP*
Angus Thomson, *Vice Pres*
EMP: 75 **EST:** 1978
SQ FT: 19,937
SALES (est): 10.2MM **Privately Held**
WEB: www.delicate.com
SIC: 7922 7359 Equipment rental, theatrical; sound & lighting equipment rental

(P-19310)
FRIENDS OF CULTURAL CENTER INC
Also Called: MCCALLUM THEATRE
73000 Fred Waring Dr, Palm Desert (92260-2800)
PHONE....................................760 346-6505
Jamie Grant, *President*
Robert McConnaughey, *CFO*
William Towers, *Chairman*
Ron Gregroire, *Treasurer*
Thomas Head, *Vice Pres*
EMP: 100 **EST:** 1973
SQ FT: 66,000
SALES (est): 15.4MM **Privately Held**
WEB: www.mccallumtheatre.com
SIC: 7922 Legitimate live theater producers

(P-19311)
GERSH AGENCY INC (PA)
9465 Wilshire Blvd Fl 6, Beverly Hills (90212-2605)
PHONE....................................310 274-6611
Robert Gersh, *President*
David Decamillo, *Senior Partner*
Stephen M Kravit, *Exec VP*
Beatrice Gersh, *Vice Pres*
David Gersh, *Vice Pres*
EMP: 100 **EST:** 1949
SQ FT: 15,000
SALES (est): 29.5MM **Privately Held**
WEB: www.gersh.com
SIC: 7922 Talent agent, theatrical

(P-19312)
HARPO INC
Also Called: Harpo Studios
1041 N Formosa Ave, West Hollywood (90046-6703)
PHONE....................................312 633-1000
Oprah Winfrey, *President*
Erik Logan, *President*
Sheri Salata, *President*
Douglas J Pattison, *CFO*
Jon Sinclair, *Vice Pres*
EMP: 57 **EST:** 1986
SQ FT: 88,000

SALES (est): 3.7MM **Privately Held**
WEB: www.oprah.com
SIC: 7922 Television program, including commercial producers

(P-19313)
INDEPENDENT STUDIO SVCS LLC
9545 Wentworth St, Sunland (91040-1626)
PHONE....................................818 951-5600
Rick Caprarelli,
Gregg H Bilson Jr,
EMP: 78 **EST:** 2012
SALES (est): 5.2MM
SALES (corp-wide): 12.2MM **Privately Held**
WEB: www.issprops.com
SIC: 5999 Theatrical equipment & supplies; equipment rental, theatrical
PA: Independent Studio Services Inc.
9545 Wentworth St
Sunland CA 91040
818 951-5600

(P-19314)
INNOVTIVE ARTSTS TLENT LTRARY (PA)
1505 10th St, Santa Monica (90401-2805)
PHONE....................................310 656-0400
Scott Harris, *President*
Nevin Dolcefino, *Exec VP*
Maury Dimauro, *Vice Pres*
Jonathan Howard, *Vice Pres*
Wahed Khaliqi, *Technology*
EMP: 75 **EST:** 1982
SALES (est): 6.6MM **Privately Held**
WEB: www.innovativeartists.com
SIC: 7922 7819 Talent agent, theatrical; casting bureau, motion picture

(P-19315)
INTERACT THEATRE CO
5215 Bakman Ave, North Hollywood (91601-3102)
PHONE....................................818 765-8732
John Rubinstein, *President*
Michale Manuel, *Treasurer*
Matt Ashford, *Vice Pres*
James Harper, *Admin Sec*
EMP: 50 **EST:** 1991
SALES (est): 36.6K **Privately Held**
WEB: www.interactla.org
SIC: 7922 6512 Legitimate live theater producers; theater building, ownership & operation

(P-19316)
INTERNATIONAL CREATIVE MGT INC (HQ)
Also Called: I C M
10250 Constellation Blvd, Los Angeles (90067-6200)
PHONE....................................310 550-4000
Jeff Berg, *Ch of Bd*
Celestine Au, *Partner*
Rick Farrell, *Partner*
Amy Grgich, *Partner*
Robert Murphy, *CFO*
▲ **EMP:** 220 **EST:** 1975
SQ FT: 72,000
SALES (est): 73.7MM **Privately Held**
WEB: www.icmpartners.com
SIC: 7922 8699 Talent agent, theatrical; literary, film or cultural club
PA: Icm Holdings
40 W 57th St Fl 16
New York NY 10019
212 556-5600

(P-19317)
INTERNATIONAL CREATIVE MGT INC
Also Called: I C M
10250 Constellation Blvd, Los Angeles (90067-6200)
PHONE....................................310 550-4000
Jeff Derg, *Manager*
EMP: 50
SALES (corp-wide): 73.7MM **Privately Held**
WEB: www.icmpartners.com
SIC: 7922 Booking agency, theatrical

HQ: International Creative Management, Inc.
10250 Constellation Blvd
Los Angeles CA 90067
310 550-4000

(P-19318)
J C ENTERTAINMENT LTG SVCS INC
Also Called: E L S
5435 W San Fernando Rd, Los Angeles (90039-1014)
PHONE....................................818 252-7481
John Allen Chuck, *CEO*
Todd Richards, *CFO*
Kevin Dowling, *Vice Pres*
Derek Smith, *Vice Pres*
EMP: 75 **EST:** 1991
SQ FT: 69,000
SALES (est): 6.7MM **Privately Held**
WEB: www.4wall.com
SIC: 7922 5719 Equipment rental, theatrical; lighting, lamps & accessories

(P-19319)
JUKIN MEDIA INC (DH)
5764 W Jefferson Blvd, Los Angeles (90016-3107)
PHONE....................................323 932-0960
Jonathan Skogmo, *CEO*
Anton Reut, *COO*
Matt Wells, *CFO*
Lee Essner, *Co-CEO*
Zach Alter, *Vice Pres*
EMP: 166 **EST:** 2010
SALES (est): 34.5MM **Privately Held**
WEB: www.jukinmedia.com
SIC: 7922 Entertainment promotion
HQ: Trusted Media Brands, Inc.
485 Lexington Ave Lbby 1
New York NY 10017
914 238-1000

(P-19320)
LA LIVE PROPERTIES LLC
800 W Olympic Blvd Ste 30, Los Angeles (90015-1360)
PHONE....................................213 763-7700
Donna Johnson, *VP Finance*
EMP: 50 **EST:** 2007
SALES (est): 108.3K **Privately Held**
WEB: www.lalive.com
SIC: 7922 6512 Theatrical producers & services; property operation, auditoriums & theaters
HQ: Anschutz Entertainment Group, Inc.
800 W Olympic Blvd # 305
Los Angeles CA 90015
213 763-7700

(P-19321)
LAGUNA PLAYHOUSE (PA)
606 Laguna Canyon Rd, Laguna Beach (92651-1837)
P.O. Box 1747 (92652-1747)
PHONE....................................949 497-2787
Karen Wood, *CEO*
Bob Crowson, *CFO*
Ellen Richard, *Exec Dir*
Richard Stein, *Exec Dir*
Louisa Balch, *General Mgr*
EMP: 225 **EST:** 1920
SQ FT: 19,000
SALES (est): 5.4MM **Privately Held**
WEB: www.lagunaplayhouse.com
SIC: 7922 Legitimate live theater producers

(P-19322)
LIVE NATION MTOURS (USA) INC (HQ)
9348 Civic Center Dr, Beverly Hills (90210-3624)
PHONE....................................310 867-7000
Michael Rapino, *CEO*
EMP: 85 **EST:** 2006
SALES (est): 8.1MM **Publicly Held**
WEB: www.livenationentertainment.com
SIC: 7922 7389 7941 Entertainment promotion; promoters of shows & exhibitions; sports clubs, managers & promoters

(P-19323)
MANAGEMENT 360
9111 Wilshire Blvd, Beverly Hills
(90210-5508)
P.O. Box A (90213-3087)
PHONE..................310 272-7000
Evelyn O Neill, *Principal*
Dylan Conklin, *Partner*
Brianna Pitan, *Partner*
Guymon Casady, *Vice Pres*
Reed Cousins, *Executive Asst*
EMP: 71 **EST:** 1992
SALES (est): 5.4MM **Privately Held**
SIC: 7922 Agent or manager for entertainers

(P-19324)
MCGUIRE TALENT INC
8608 Utica Ave Ste 220, Rancho Cucamonga (91730-4879)
PHONE..................909 527-7006
EMP: 80
SQ FT: 2,200
SALES: 2MM **Privately Held**
SIC: 7922 Talent Agency

(P-19325)
PARADIGM MUSIC LLC (PA)
360 N Crescent Dr, Beverly Hills
(90210-4874)
PHONE..................310 288-8000
Sam Gores, *Ch of Bd*
Lucy Stille, *Partner*
Courtney Dondelinger, *Trust Officer*
Sam Alpert, *Vice Pres*
April Perroni, *Vice Pres*
EMP: 70 **EST:** 1993
SALES (est): 24.9MM **Privately Held**
WEB: www.paradigmagency.com
SIC: 7922 Talent agent, theatrical

(P-19326)
PARADIGM TALENT AGENCY LLC
6725 W Sunset Blvd, Los Angeles
(90028-7119)
PHONE..................310 288-8000
Sofia Pasternack, *General Mgr*
Jessica McCrary, *Executive Asst*
Chantal Walker, *Executive Asst*
Wilson Rubinoff, *Administration*
Scott Peyatt, *Accountant*
EMP: 72
SALES (corp-wide): 11MM **Privately Held**
WEB: www.paradigmagency.com
SIC: 7922 Talent agent, theatrical
PA: Paradigm Talent Agency, Llc
8942 Wilshire Blvd
Beverly Hills CA 90211
310 288-8000

(P-19327)
PERFORMING ARTS CTR LOS ANGLES
Also Called: Music Center
135 N Grand Ave Ste 314, Los Angeles
(90012-3018)
PHONE..................213 972-7512
John Emerson, *Ch of Bd*
Lucy Zepeda, *Partner*
Lisa Specht, *Ch of Bd*
Stephen Rountree, *President*
Howard Sherman, *COO*
▲ **EMP:** 250 **EST:** 1961
SQ FT: 24,000
SALES (est): 37.3MM **Privately Held**
WEB: www.musiccenter.org
SIC: 7922 Theatrical production services
PA: The Music Center Of Los Angeles
County Inc
135 N Grand Ave Ste 201
Los Angeles CA 90012
213 972-8007

(P-19328)
PRDCTIONS N FREMANTLE AMER INC (DH)
Also Called: Fremantle Media
2900 W Alameda Ave # 800, Burbank
(91505-4220)
PHONE..................818 748-1100
Thom Beers, *CEO*
Nicholas Dale, *Partner*
Donna Redier Linsk, *COO*
Stefanie Berk, *Exec VP*

Daniel Funk, *Exec VP*
EMP: 100 **EST:** 1995
SALES (est): 39MM
SALES (corp-wide): 147.7MM **Privately Held**
WEB: www.fremantle.com
SIC: 7922 Television program, including commercial producers
HQ: Fremantlemedia Group Limited
1 Stephen Street
London
207 691-6000

(P-19329)
PREMIERE RADIO NETWORK INC (DH)
Also Called: Prn Radio Networks
15260 Ventura Blvd # 400, Sherman Oaks
(91403-5307)
PHONE..................818 377-5300
Stephen C Lehman, *CEO*
Kraig T Kitchin, *President*
Timothy M Kelly, *Exec VP*
Alan Korowitz, *Exec VP*
Bill Barker, *Vice Pres*
EMP: 200 **EST:** 1987
SQ FT: 15,000
SALES (est): 33.7MM **Publicly Held**
WEB: www.premierenetworks.com
SIC: 7922 7389 4832 Radio producers; advertising, promotional & trade show services; radio broadcasting stations
HQ: Jacor Communications Company
200 E Basse Rd
San Antonio TX 78209
210 822-2828

(P-19330)
RADFORD STUDIO CENTER INC
Also Called: CBS Studio Center
4024 Radford Ave, Studio City
(91604-2101)
PHONE..................818 655-5000
Michael Klausman, *President*
Nina Tassler, *Ch of Bd*
Brian Lovell, *Vice Pres*
Joseph Soukup, *Vice Pres*
Adam Hersh, *Planning*
EMP: 300 **EST:** 1987
SALES (est): 61.4MM
SALES (corp-wide): 25.3B **Publicly Held**
WEB: www.cbswatchmagazine.com
SIC: 7922 6512 7999 Television program, including commercial producers; nonresidential building operators; martial arts school
HQ: Cbs Broadcasting Inc.
524 W 57th St
New York NY 10019
212 975-4321

(P-19331)
ROSE BRAND WIPERS INC
11440 Sheldon St, Sun Valley
(91352-1121)
PHONE..................818 505-6290
Tina Carlin, *Principal*
EMP: 72
SALES (corp-wide): 81.5MM **Privately Held**
WEB: www.rosebrand.com
SIC: 7922 Costume & scenery design services
PA: Rose Brand Wipers, Inc.
4 Emerson Ln
Secaucus NJ 07094
201 809-1730

(P-19332)
SOUTH COAST REPERTORY INC
Also Called: S C R
655 Town Center Dr, Costa Mesa
(92626-1918)
P.O. Box 2197 (92628-2197)
PHONE..................714 708-5500
Martin Benson, *Art Dir*
David Krajanowski, *Vice Pres*
Martha Guzman, *Associate Dir*
David Emmes, *Principal*
Paula Tomei, *Managing Dir*
EMP: 60 **EST:** 1964
SQ FT: 40,000
SALES (est): 16.2MM **Privately Held**
WEB: www.scr.org
SIC: 7922 Legitimate live theater producers

(P-19333)
TENNIS CHANNEL INC (HQ)
3003 Exposition Blvd, Santa Monica
(90404-5026)
PHONE..................310 392-1920
Ken Solomon, *CEO*
William Simon, *COO*
Bob Whyley, *Senior VP*
John Macdonald, *Vice Pres*
ARI Brock, *Products*
EMP: 70 **EST:** 2001
SALES (est): 30.2MM
SALES (corp-wide): 5.9B **Publicly Held**
WEB: www.azteca48.com
SIC: 7922 Television program, including commercial producers
PA: Sinclair Broadcast Group, Inc.
10706 Beaver Dam Rd
Hunt Valley MD 21030
410 568-1500

(P-19334)
THEATREDREAMS LA/CHI L P
Also Called: Dolby Theatre
6801 Hollywood Blvd # 18, Los Angeles
(90028-6136)
PHONE..................323 308-6363
Annette Bethers, *Partner*
Jay Thomas, *Vice Pres*
Jared Peter, *Prdtn Mgr*
Mark Jenkins, *Director*
EMP: 50 **EST:** 2005
SALES (est): 8.4MM **Privately Held**
SIC: 7922 Theatrical producers & services

(P-19335)
THINKWELL GROUP INC (PA)
2710 Media Center Dr, Los Angeles
(90065-1746)
PHONE..................818 333-3444
Joseph Zenas, *CEO*
Francois Bergeron, *COO*
Craig Hanna, *Officer*
Regina Eise, *Vice Pres*
Randy Ewing, *Vice Pres*
▲ **EMP:** 73 **EST:** 2002
SQ FT: 23,000
SALES (est): 16.1MM **Privately Held**
WEB: www.thinkwellgroup.com
SIC: 7922 Theatrical producers & services; interior design services

(P-19336)
TICKETSCOM LLC (DH)
Also Called: Tickets.com, Inc.
535 Anton Blvd Ste 250, Costa Mesa
(92626-7694)
PHONE..................714 327-5400
Joe Choti, *President*
Larry D Witherspoon, *President*
Cristine Hurley, *CFO*
Gene Whitright, *Treasurer*
John Walker, *Principal*
EMP: 211 **EST:** 1995
SALES (est): 75MM
SALES (corp-wide): 434.8MM **Privately Held**
WEB: www.tickets.com
SIC: 7922 7372 Ticket agency, theatrical; application computer software
HQ: Mlb Advanced Media, L.P.
1271 Ave Of The Americas
New York NY 10020
212 485-3444

(P-19337)
TRAPDOOR ENSEMBLE
11236 Valley Spring Ln, North Hollywood
(91602-2611)
PHONE..................310 951-4836
William M Swadley, *Chairman*
EMP: 50 **EST:** 2004
SALES (est): 597.1K **Privately Held**
WEB: www.trapdoorensemble.com
SIC: 7922 Theatrical producers & services

(P-19338)
TRISTAR TELEVISION MUSIC INC
10202 Washington Blvd, Culver City
(90232-3119)
PHONE..................310 244-4000
EMP: 50
SALES (est): 696.3K **Privately Held**
SIC: 7922 Theatrical Producers/Services

HQ: Sony Pictures Releasing International Corporation
10202 Washington Blvd
Culver City CA 90232
310 244-4000

(P-19339)
WILLIAM MRRIS ENDVCR ENTRMT FN (DH)
Also Called: William Morris Endeavor Entrmt
9601 Wilshire Blvd Fl 3, Beverly Hills
(90210-5219)
PHONE..................310 285-9000
Tom Strickler, *President*
Jeff Gorin, *Partner*
Peter Klein, *CFO*
Michelle Walter, *CFO*
Lisa Burelli, *Vice Pres*
EMP: 180 **EST:** 2000
SALES (est): 43.5MM
SALES (corp-wide): 880.5MM **Publicly Held**
WEB: www.wmeagency.com
SIC: 7922 Talent agent, theatrical
HQ: William Morris Endeavor Entertainment, Llc
11 Madison Ave Fl 18
New York NY 10010
212 586-5100

(P-19340)
WILLIAM MRRIS ENDVOR ENTRMT LL
Also Called: William Morris Consulting
9601 Wilshire Blvd Fl 3, Beverly Hills
(90210-5219)
PHONE..................310 285-9000
Chris Newman, *Branch Mgr*
Tim Curtis, *Partner*
Seth Krauss, *Officer*
Bria Dotson, *Vice Pres*
Sam Kirby, *Vice Pres*
EMP: 393
SALES (corp-wide): 880.5MM **Publicly Held**
WEB: www.wmespeakers.com
SIC: 7922 Talent agent, theatrical
HQ: William Morris Endeavor Entertainment, Llc
11 Madison Ave Fl 18
New York NY 10010
212 586-5100

7929 Bands, Orchestras, Actors & Entertainers

(P-19341)
51 MINDS ENTERTA NMENT LLC
Also Called: Mindless Entertainment
5200 Lankershim Blvd # 200, North Hollywood (91601-3155)
PHONE..................818 643-8200
Mark Cronin,
Jessica Bofshever, *Vice Pres*
Courtland Cox, *Vice Pres*
Isabella Jorbajian, *Executive Asst*
Ruba Zarour, *Executive Asst*
▼ **EMP:** 60 **EST:** 2004
SALES (est): 10MM
SALES (corp-wide): 12.3MM **Privately Held**
WEB: www.51minds.com
SIC: 7929 7812 Entertainers; television film production
HQ: Endemol Usa Holding, Inc.
5161 Lankershim Blvd # 400
North Hollywood CA 91601
310 860-9914

(P-19342)
ALLEN MEDIA LLC (HQ)
1925 Century Park E Fl 10, Los Angeles
(90067-2701)
PHONE..................310 277-3500
Byron Allen Folks, *President*
Tom O'Brien, *Exec VP*
EMP: 133 **EST:** 2018
SALES (est): 23MM **Privately Held**
WEB: www.entertainmentstudios.com
SIC: 7929 Entertainment service

(P-19343)
ANSCHUTZ ENTRMT GROUP INC (HQ)
Also Called: AEG Worldwide
800 W Olympic Blvd # 305, Los Angeles
(90015-1366)
PHONE..................................213 763-7700
Tim Leiweke, *President*
Jonathan Moeis, *Partner*
Casie Nguyen, *COO*
Dan Beckerman, *CFO*
Dennis Dennehy, *Ch Credit Ofcr*
EMP: 79 **EST:** 1994
SALES: 431.3K **Privately Held**
WEB: www.aegworldwide.com
SIC: 7929 Entertainment service

(P-19344)
ARTISTIC ENTRMT SVCS LLC
120 N Aspan Ave, Azusa (91702-4224)
PHONE..................................626 334-9388
Craig Bugajski, *Mng Member*
Rob Pearson, *Creative Dir*
Jason Degrande, *Project Mgr*
Tim Johnson, *Project Mgr*
Steve Shewman, *Electrical Engi*
EMP: 60 **EST:** 2003
SALES (est): 12.2MM **Privately Held**
WEB: www.aescreative.com
SIC: 7929 Entertainment service

(P-19345)
BONANZA PRODUCTIONS INC
4000 Warner Blvd, Burbank (91522-0001)
P.O. Box 1667 (91507-1667)
PHONE..................................818 954-4212
John A Rogovin, *CEO*
Jonathan Rosenfeld, *Director*
EMP: 1000 **EST:** 1991
SALES (est): 31.3MM **Privately Held**
SIC: 7929 Entertainment group

(P-19346)
CZND INC
8444 Wilshire Blvd Fl 5, Beverly Hills
(90211-3200)
PHONE..................................323 378-6505
Luigi Picarazzi, *President*
EMP: 68 **EST:** 2015
SALES (est): 287.4K **Privately Held**
SIC: 7929 Entertainment service

(P-19347)
DELUXE ENTRMT SVCS GROUP INC (PA)
2400 W Empire Ave Ste 200, Burbank
(91504-3355)
PHONE..................................818 565-3600
EMP: 98 **EST:** 1932
SALES (est): 38.3MM **Privately Held**
SIC: 7929 Entertainer/Entertainment Group

(P-19348)
ENTERTIMENT STUDIOS MEDIA INC (PA)
1925 Century Park E # 1025, Los Angeles
(90067-2701)
PHONE..................................310 277-3500
Byron Allen Folks, *CEO*
Nora Zimmett, *Ch Credit Ofcr*
Melissa Squaires, *Senior VP*
Jessica Goss, *Vice Pres*
Susan Vadner, *Vice Pres*
EMP: 65 **EST:** 1993
SQ FT: 5,000
SALES (est): 199.8MM **Privately Held**
WEB: www.entertainmentstudios.com
SIC: 7929 Entertainers & entertainment groups

(P-19349)
ENTERTNMENT STDIOS MTION PCTRE
1925 Century Park E Fl 10, Los Angeles
(90067-2701)
PHONE..................................310 277-3500
Byron Allen, *Principal*
EMP: 50 **EST:** 2015
SALES (est): 1.3MM **Privately Held**
SIC: 7929 Entertainers & entertainment groups

(P-19350)
ENTITLEMENT LLC
1236 Euclid St, Santa Monica
(90404-1041)
PHONE..................................224 336-2669
Ted Lauck, *President*
EMP: 50 **EST:** 2018
SALES (est): 188.5K **Privately Held**
SIC: 7929 Entertainment service

(P-19351)
ESL GAMING AMERICA INC
Also Called: Turtle Entertainment America,
1212 Chestnut St, Burbank (91506-1627)
PHONE..................................818 861-7315
Han Park, *President*
Yvette Marinez-Ray, *COO*
Craig Levine, *Exec VP*
Paul Brewer, *Vice Pres*
Kevin Rosenblatt, *Vice Pres*
EMP: 50 **EST:** 2014
SALES (est): 8.3MM
SALES (corp-wide): 462.1MM **Privately Held**
WEB: www.eslgaming.com
SIC: 7929 Entertainment service
HQ: Esl Gaming Gmbh
Schanzenstr. 23
Koln NW 51063
221 880-4490

(P-19352)
HOB ENTERTAINMENT LLC
1350 Disneyland Dr, Anaheim (92802)
PHONE..................................714 778-2583
Kristen Kowlminsky, *Branch Mgr*
EMP: 58 **Publicly Held**
WEB: www.houseofblues.com
SIC: 7929 Entertainment service
HQ: Hob Entertainment, Llc
7060 Hollywood Blvd
Los Angeles CA 90028

(P-19353)
HOB ENTERTAINMENT LLC
8430 W Sunset Blvd, West Hollywood
(90069-1910)
PHONE..................................323 848-5100
Arich Berghammer, *Principal*
EMP: 58 **Publicly Held**
WEB: www.houseofblues.com
SIC: 7929 Entertainment service
HQ: Hob Entertainment, Llc
7060 Hollywood Blvd
Los Angeles CA 90028

(P-19354)
HOB ENTERTAINMENT LLC (DH)
Also Called: House of Blues
7060 Hollywood Blvd, Los Angeles
(90028-6014)
PHONE..................................323 769-4600
Michael Rapino, *CEO*
Joseph C Kaczorowski, *President*
Peter Cyffka, *Senior VP*
Dwight Payne, *Director*
Laura Cancro, *Manager*
EMP: 172 **EST:** 1993
SQ FT: 53,000
SALES (est): 305.7MM **Publicly Held**
WEB: www.houseofblues.com
SIC: 7929 Entertainment service
HQ: Live Nation Worldwide, Inc.
430 W 15th St
New York NY 10011
917 421-5100

(P-19355)
HOUSE BLUES HOUSTON REST CORP
9348 Civic Center Dr, Beverly Hills
(90210-3624)
PHONE..................................310 867-7000
Scott Kapp, *Manager*
EMP: 102 **EST:** 2014
SALES (est): 4.4MM **Publicly Held**
WEB: www.houseofblues.com
SIC: 7929 Entertainers & entertainment groups

(P-19356)
HOUSE BLUES ORLANDO REST CORP
9348 Civic Center Dr, Beverly Hills
(90210-3624)
PHONE..................................310 867-7000
Michael Rowles, *Principal*
EMP: 102 **EST:** 2014
SALES (est): 5.3MM **Publicly Held**
WEB: www.houseofblues.com
SIC: 7929 Entertainment service
HQ: Hob Entertainment, Llc
7060 Hollywood Blvd
Los Angeles CA 90028

(P-19357)
HOUSE OF BLUES CONCERTS INC (DH)
6255 W Sunset Blvd Fl 16, Los Angeles
(90028-7403)
PHONE..................................323 769-4977
Joe Kazoworski, *President*
EMP: 150 **EST:** 1978
SALES (est): 24.2MM **Publicly Held**
WEB: www.houseofblues.com
SIC: 7929 Entertainers & entertainment groups

(P-19358)
INSOMNIAC INC
9441 W Olympic Blvd, Beverly Hills
(90212-4541)
PHONE..................................323 874-7020
Pasquale Rotella, *CEO*
Simon Rust Lamb, *CFO*
John Boyle, *Officer*
Sara Napolitano, *Officer*
Katherine Gonzalez, *Technical Mgr*
▲ **EMP:** 229 **EST:** 1998
SALES (est): 21.6MM **Privately Held**
WEB: www.insomniac.com
SIC: 7929 Entertainment service

(P-19359)
INSOMNIAC HOLDINGS LLC (HQ)
9441 W Olympic Blvd, Beverly Hills
(90212-4541)
PHONE..................................323 874-7020
Michael Rapino, *President*
George Chan, *Accounting Mgr*
Pasquale Rotella,
EMP: 124 **EST:** 2013
SQ FT: 5,000
SALES (est): 29.6MM **Publicly Held**
WEB: www.insomniac.com
SIC: 7929 Entertainment service

(P-19360)
KACE ENTERTAINMENT INC (PA)
Also Called: Vox DJS
2988 Columbia St, Torrance (90503-3806)
PHONE..................................310 372-2222
Kc Campbell, *CEO*
Robert Corrall, *Office Mgr*
Richard Hayes, *Opers Mgr*
Maxwell Averill, *Production*
Tommy O 'sullivan, *Production*
EMP: 63 **EST:** 2008
SALES (est): 3.1MM **Privately Held**
SIC: 7929 Disc jockey service

(P-19361)
KADEN CASH LLC
15845 Jackson Dr, Fontana (92336-1763)
PHONE..................................818 714-4665
Kevin Buckley,
EMP: 50 **EST:** 2017
SALES (est): 406.9K **Privately Held**
SIC: 7929 Entertainment service

(P-19362)
LIVE NATION CONCERTS INC
9348 Civic Center Dr Lbby, Beverly Hills
(90210-3642)
PHONE..................................310 867-7132
Michael Rowles, *President*
Kathy Willard, *Treasurer*

EMP: 50 **EST:** 1996
SALES (est): 2.3MM **Publicly Held**
WEB: www.livenationentertainment.com
SIC: 7929 Entertainers & entertainment groups
PA: Live Nation Entertainment, Inc.
9348 Civic Center Dr Lbby
Beverly Hills CA 90210

(P-19363)
LIVE NATION WORLDWIDE INC
9348 Civic Center Dr Lbby, Beverly Hills
(90210-3642)
PHONE..................................310 867-7000
Kathy Willard, *CEO*
Jonathan Dolgen, *Bd of Directors*
John Hopmans, *Exec VP*
EMP: 8800 **EST:** 1997
SALES (est): 116.8MM **Publicly Held**
WEB: www.livenationentertainment.com
SIC: 7929 Entertainers & entertainment groups
PA: Live Nation Entertainment, Inc.
9348 Civic Center Dr Lbby
Beverly Hills CA 90210

(P-19364)
LOS ANGELES PHILHARMONIC ASSN (PA)
Also Called: L A Philharmonic
151 S Grand Ave, Los Angeles
(90012-3034)
P.O. Box 1951 (90078-1951)
PHONE..................................213 972-7300
Chad Smith, *CEO*
Thomas L Beckmen, *Ch of Bd*
Virginia Farrell, *President*
Gail Samuel, *President*
Karen Sturges, *CFO*
EMP: 200 **EST:** 1934
SQ FT: 13,467
SALES: 187.1MM **Privately Held**
WEB: www.laphil.com
SIC: 7929 Symphony orchestras

(P-19365)
LOS ANGELES PHILHARMONIC ASSN
Also Called: Hollywood Bowl
2301 N Highland Ave, Los Angeles
(90068-2742)
PHONE..................................323 850-2060
Ed Tom, *Opers Staff*
Nora Brady, *Vice Pres*
Kathleen Kane, *Vice Pres*
Daniel Song, *Vice Pres*
Mark Ladd, *Associate Dir*
EMP: 1270
SALES (corp-wide): 187.1MM **Privately Held**
WEB: www.laphil.com
SIC: 7929 Entertainment group
PA: Los Angeles Philharmonic Association
151 S Grand Ave
Los Angeles CA 90012
213 972-7300

(P-19366)
LOS ANGELES CHMBER ORCHSTRA SOC
510 W 6th St Ste 1001, Los Angeles
(90014-1321)
PHONE..................................213 622-7001
Andrea Laguni, *Exec Dir*
Ruth L Eliel, *Vice Chairman*
Thomas Mallen, *CFO*
Laurie Zimmerman, *Officer*
Ben Cadwallader, *Exec Dir*
EMP: 51 **EST:** 1968
SALES (est): 6.3MM **Privately Held**
WEB: www.laco.org
SIC: 7929 Orchestras or bands

(P-19367)
LUX SOLUTIONS LLC (PA)
12123 Barringer St, South El Monte
(91733-4137)
PHONE..................................770 591-0463
Stephen Tolopilo,
Kyle Sherrick, *Technical Staff*
EMP: 63 **EST:** 2016

SALES (est): 904.4K **Privately Held**
WEB: www.luxsolutions.com
SIC: 7929 Entertainers & entertainment groups

(P-19368)
LVL 10 ENTERTAINMENT LLC
6444 San Fernando Rd # 55, Glendale (91201-2124)
PHONE.................424 298-5119
EMP: 50
SALES (est): 500K **Privately Held**
SIC: 7929 Entertainers And Entertainment Groups

(P-19369)
MAKER STUDIOS INC (DH)
3515 Eastham Dr, Culver City (90232-2440)
PHONE.................310 606-2182
Courtney Holt, *CEO*
Lisa Donovan, *CFO*
EMP: 250 EST: 2009
SQ FT: 20,000
SALES (est): 50.4MM
SALES (corp-wide): 65.3B **Publicly Held**
WEB: www.thewaltdisneycompany.com
SIC: 7929 Entertainment service

(P-19370)
MPC PRODUCTIONS LLC
12035 Killion St, Sherman Oaks (91401)
PHONE.................310 418-8115
Rick Nicolet,
EMP: 75 EST: 2016
SALES (est): 152K **Privately Held**
SIC: 7929 Entertainment service

(P-19371)
MUSIC ACADEMY OF WEST
1070 Fairway Rd, Santa Barbara (93108-2899)
PHONE.................805 969-4726
Nancybell Coe, *President*
James Davidson, *Chairman*
Benjamin J Cohen, *Treasurer*
Jon Steiner, *Officer*
Ana Papakhian, *Vice Pres*
EMP: 78 EST: 1947
SQ FT: 8,000
SALES (est): 10.6MM **Privately Held**
WEB: www.musicacademy.org
SIC: 8299 7929 Music school; entertainers & entertainment groups

(P-19372)
ORCHARD HORROR FILM LLC
15715 Woodvale Rd, Encino (91436-3416)
PHONE.................212 203-6147
Brandon Menchen, *Mng Member*
EMP: 50 EST: 2017
SALES (est): 568.1K **Privately Held**
SIC: 7929 Entertainment service

(P-19373)
PACIFIC SYMPHONY
17620 Fitch Ste 100, Irvine (92614-6081)
PHONE.................714 755-5788
Jjohn Forsyte, *President*
John E Forsyte, *CEO*
Rhonda Halverson, *Vice Pres*
Judy Huck, *Administration*
Jesse Hiser, *Finance*
EMP: 60 EST: 1980
SQ FT: 5,750
SALES (est): 17.6MM **Privately Held**
WEB: www.pacificsymphony.org
SIC: 7929 Symphony orchestras

(P-19374)
POP MEDIA NETWORKS LLC (DH)
Also Called: Tvguide.com
5510 Lincoln Blvd Ste 400, Playa Vista (90094-1900)
PHONE.................323 856-4000
Allen Shapiro, *Chairman*
Ryan O'Hara, *President*
Brad Schwartz, *President*
Debra Wichser, *CFO*
David Mandell, *Exec VP*
EMP: 124 EST: 1998

SALES (est): 27.8MM
SALES (corp-wide): 25.3B **Publicly Held**
WEB: www.poptv.com
SIC: 7929 7313 7379 Entertainment service; electronic media advertising representatives;
HQ: Viacomcbs Inc.
1515 Broadway
New York NY 10036
212 258-6000

(P-19375)
ROVI GUIDES INC (DH)
2233 N Ontario St Ste 100, Burbank (91504-4500)
PHONE.................323 817-4600
Richard Battista, *CEO*
Anthea Disney, *Ch of Bd*
Thomas Carson, *President*
Doug Macrae, *President*
Akitaka Nishimura, *President*
EMP: 77 EST: 2000
SQ FT: 22,000
SALES (est): 78.4MM
SALES (corp-wide): 892MM **Publicly Held**
WEB: www.ir.tivo.com
SIC: 7929 7313 7379 Entertainment service; electronic media advertising representatives;
HQ: Tivo Corporation
2160 Gold St
San Jose CA 95002
408 519-9100

(P-19376)
RUN THE PLAY ENTERTAINMENT LLC
9350 Wilshire Blvd, Beverly Hills (90212-3214)
PHONE.................800 978-9638
EMP: 13
SALES (est): 54.1K **Privately Held**
SIC: 7929 3651 7812 Entertainer/Entertainment Group Mfg Home Audio/Video Equipment Motion Picture/Video Production

(P-19377)
SAS ENTERTAINMENT PARTNERS INC
6224 Greenleaf Ave, Whittier (90601-3528)
PHONE.................213 400-1901
Miles Williams, *President*
EMP: 50 EST: 2018
SALES (est): 252.4K **Privately Held**
SIC: 7929 Entertainment service

(P-19378)
SKY ZONE LLC (HQ)
1201 W 5th St Ste T340, Los Angeles (90017-1489)
PHONE.................310 734-0300
Jeffrey Platt, *CEO*
Chas Hallis, *Partner*
Matt Lambeth, *Vice Pres*
Deann Rexroad, *Regional Mgr*
Lindsay Murray, *General Mgr*
▲ EMP: 119 EST: 2014
SALES (est): 7.8MM
SALES (corp-wide): 27.1MM **Privately Held**
WEB: www.skyzone.com
SIC: 7929 Entertainment service

(P-19379)
SLEEPY GIANT ENTERTAINMENT INC
3501 Jamboree Rd Ste 5000, Newport Beach (92660-2959)
PHONE.................714 460-4113
◆ EMP: 58
SALES (est): 1.5MM **Privately Held**
SIC: 7929 Entertainers And Entertainment Groups

(P-19380)
SPSV ENTERTAINMENT LLC
Also Called: Skypark At Santa's Village
28950 State Highway 18, Skyforest (92385-0460)
P.O. Box 369 (92385-0369)
PHONE.................909 744-9373
William Johnson, *Mng Member*
EMP: 99 EST: 2016

SALES (est): 2.2MM **Privately Held**
SIC: 7929 Entertainers & entertainment groups

(P-19381)
TWENTY MILE PRODUCTIONS LLC
11833 Miss Ave Ste 101, Los Angeles (90025-6135)
PHONE.................412 251-0767
Karen Wacker,
Margaret Ellison,
EMP: 150 EST: 2013
SALES (est): 930.2K **Privately Held**
SIC: 7929 Entertainment group

(P-19382)
UNITED ARTISTS ENTRMT LLC (PA)
245 N Beverly Dr, Beverly Hills (90210-5319)
PHONE.................310 449-3000
Paula Wagner, *Principal*
Tom Cruise, *Principal*
EMP: 54 EST: 2007
SALES (est): 339.7K **Privately Held**
SIC: 7929 Entertainment service

(P-19383)
UNIVERSAL CBLE PRODUCTIONS LLC
100 Universal City Plz, Universal City (91608-1002)
PHONE.................818 777-0351
Steve Burke, *CEO*
Matt Bond, *Chairman*
Patricia Fili-Krushel, *Exec VP*
EMP: 58 EST: 2015
SALES (est): 5.6MM **Privately Held**
WEB: www.nbcuniversal.com
SIC: 7929 Entertainment group

(P-19384)
WARNER BROS HOME ENTRMT GROUP (DH)
4000 Warner Blvd, Burbank (91522-0002)
PHONE.................818 954-6000
Thomas Gewecke, *President*
Adam Schlagman, *Creative Dir*
EMP: 100 EST: 2005
SALES (est): 38.8MM
SALES (corp-wide): 171.7B **Publicly Held**
WEB: www.warnerbroscanada.com
SIC: 7929 Entertainment service

(P-19385)
WEBTOON ENTERTAINMENT INC (PA)
5700 Wilshire Blvd # 220, Los Angeles (90036-3659)
PHONE.................323 297-3410
Jun Koo Kim, *CEO*
Eugene Kim, *General Counsel*
Elywill M Zamora, *Counsel*
EMP: 88 EST: 2017
SALES (est): 5.1MM **Privately Held**
WEB: www.apply.workable.com
SIC: 7929 Entertainers & entertainment groups

(P-19386)
WORKS ENTERTAINMENT LLC
11333 Iowa Ave, Los Angeles (90025-4214)
PHONE.................310 623-7436
Simon Painter, *Partner*
Tim Lawson, *Partner*
EMP: 50 EST: 2018
SALES (est): 495.2K **Privately Held**
WEB: www.theworksent.com
SIC: 7929 Entertainers & entertainment groups

7933 Bowling Centers

(P-19387)
BOWLERO CORP
Also Called: Brunswick Covino Lanes
1060 W San Bernardino Rd, Covina (91722-4160)
PHONE.................626 339-1286
Javier Guzman, *Manager*

EMP: 65
SALES (corp-wide): 530.3MM **Publicly Held**
WEB: www.bowlmor.com
SIC: 7933 Ten pin center
PA: Bowlero Corp.
222 W 44th St
New York NY 10036
212 777-2214

(P-19388)
BOWLERO CORP
Also Called: West Covina Lanes
675 S Glendora Ave, West Covina (91790-3705)
PHONE.................626 960-3636
Joe Carridoza, *Manager*
Randy Avila, *Engineer*
EMP: 65
SQ FT: 57,259
SALES (corp-wide): 530.3MM **Publicly Held**
WEB: www.bowlmor.com
SIC: 7933 Ten pin center
PA: Bowlero Corp.
222 W 44th St
New York NY 10036
212 777-2214

(P-19389)
BOWLERO CORP
Also Called: Brunswick Moreno Valley Lanes
24666 Sunnymead Blvd, Moreno Valley (92553-3713)
PHONE.................951 924-6008
Bob Osborn, *General Mgr*
EMP: 65
SALES (corp-wide): 530.3MM **Publicly Held**
WEB: www.bowlmor.com
SIC: 7933 Ten pin center
PA: Bowlero Corp.
222 W 44th St
New York NY 10036
212 777-2214

(P-19390)
BOWLERO CORP
Also Called: Bz Upland Bowl
451 W Foothill Blvd, Upland (91786-3857)
PHONE.................909 946-7006
Bill Breadeu, *Manager*
EMP: 65
SALES (corp-wide): 530.3MM **Publicly Held**
WEB: www.bowlmor.com
SIC: 7933 Ten pin center
PA: Bowlero Corp.
222 W 44th St
New York NY 10036
212 777-2214

(P-19391)
BOWLERO CORP
Also Called: Brunswick Classic Lanes
1800 Hamner Ave, Norco (92860-2945)
PHONE.................951 734-8410
Jon Diso, *Manager*
EMP: 65
SALES (corp-wide): 530.3MM **Publicly Held**
WEB: www.bowlmor.com
SIC: 7933 Ten pin center
PA: Bowlero Corp.
222 W 44th St
New York NY 10036
212 777-2214

(P-19392)
BOWLERO CORP
Also Called: B B & B
38241 30th St E, Palmdale (93550-4936)
PHONE.................661 274-2878
Brad Roseling, *Manager*
EMP: 65
SALES (corp-wide): 530.3MM **Publicly Held**
WEB: www.bowlmor.com
SIC: 7933 Ten pin center
PA: Bowlero Corp.
222 W 44th St
New York NY 10036
212 777-2214

(P-19393)
BOWLERO CORP
Also Called: Brunswick Deer Creks Lnes 213
7930 Haven Ave Ste 101, Rancho Cuca-
monga (91730-3056)
PHONE...................................909 945-9392
Venesa Boudreau, *Assistant VP*
EMP: 65
SALES (corp-wide): 530.3MM **Publicly
Held**
WEB: www.bowlmor.com
SIC: 7933 Ten pin center
PA: Bowlero Corp.
222 W 44th St
New York NY 10036
212 777-2214

(P-19394)
BOWLERO CORP
Also Called: Brunswick Cal Oaks Bowl
40440 California Oaks Rd, Murrieta
(92562-5828)
PHONE...................................951 698-2202
John Tang, *Branch Mgr*
EMP: 65
SALES (corp-wide): 530.3MM **Publicly
Held**
WEB: www.bowlmor.com
SIC: 7933 Ten pin center
PA: Bowlero Corp.
222 W 44th St
New York NY 10036
212 777-2214

(P-19395)
BOWLERO CORP
Also Called: Brunswick Foothill Lanes
17238 Foothill Blvd, Fontana (92335-9043)
PHONE...................................909 822-9900
Jeremy Dewhirst, *Manager*
EMP: 65
SALES (corp-wide): 530.3MM **Publicly
Held**
WEB: www.bowlmor.com
SIC: 7933 Ten pin center
PA: Bowlero Corp.
222 W 44th St
New York NY 10036
212 777-2214

(P-19396)
**CHAMPIONS BOWLING &
EMBROIDERY**
3058 Capri Ln, Costa Mesa (92626-3502)
PHONE...................................714 968-5033
Barry Asher, *Executive Asst*
EMP: 13 EST: 2007
SALES (est): 259.3K **Privately Held**
SIC: 7933 5941 5699 2395 Ten pin cen-
ter; bowling equipment & supplies; sports
apparel; embroidery & art needlework

(P-19397)
**CONCOURSE RECREATION
CENTER (PA)**
Also Called: Concourse Bowling Center
3364 E La Palma Ave, Anaheim
(92806-2814)
PHONE...................................714 666-2695
Bert C Rainone, *General Ptnr*
Ron Hughes, *General Mgr*
EMP: 52 EST: 1984
SQ FT: 42,000
SALES (est): 2.3MM **Privately Held**
WEB: www.concoursebowling.com
SIC: 7933 5813 5812 7993 Ten pin cen-
ter; bar (drinking places); eating places;
video game arcade

(P-19398)
GABLE HOUSE INC
Also Called: Gable House Bowl
22501 Hawthorne Blvd, Torrance
(90505-2509)
PHONE...................................310 378-2265
Michael Cogan, *President*
EMP: 100 EST: 1959
SQ FT: 80,000
SALES (est): 5.1MM **Privately Held**
WEB: www.gablehousebowl.com
SIC: 7933 5813 5812 Ten pin center; bar
(drinking places); snack bar

(P-19399)
**LUCKY STRIKE
ENTERTAINMENT INC**
800 W Olympic Blvd # 250, Los Angeles
(90015-1366)
PHONE...................................213 542-4880
Bobby Braydoy, *Branch Mgr*
Kirsten Carpenter, *Vice Pres*
Darla Walcoff, *CPA*
Alyssa Kite, *Sales Mgr*
Nabil Pierre, *Sales Staff*
EMP: 247 **Privately Held**
WEB: www.luckystrikeent.com
SIC: 7933 5813 5812 Ten pin center; tav-
ern (drinking places); American restaurant
PA: Lucky Strike Entertainment, Inc.
15260 Ventura Blvd # 1110
Sherman Oaks CA 91403

(P-19400)
**LUCKY STRIKE
ENTERTAINMENT LLC**
6801 Hollywood Blvd # 143, Los Angeles
(90028-6138)
PHONE...................................818 933-3752
David Bradley, *General Mgr*
Shannon Martin, *Vice Pres*
Bill Hovey, *General Mgr*
Rick Kotikian, *Planning*
Tim Killeen, *Opers Staff*
EMP: 104
SALES (corp-wide): 61.2MM **Privately
Held**
WEB: www.luckystrikeent.com
SIC: 7933 Ten pin center
PA: Lucky Strike Entertainment, Llc
15260 Ventura Blvd # 1110
Sherman Oaks CA 91403
323 467-7776

(P-19401)
**LUCKY STRIKE
ENTERTAINMENT LLC**
Also Called: Lucky Strike Novi
15260 Ventura Blvd # 1110, Sherman Oaks
(91403-5346)
PHONE...................................248 374-3420
Eddie Bourque, *Branch Mgr*
Darius Collins, *Technician*
Nancy Cowden, *Technician*
Amber Sanders, *Opers Mgr*
Jim Bennington, *Director*
EMP: 104
SALES (corp-wide): 61.2MM **Privately
Held**
WEB: www.luckystrikeent.com
SIC: 7933 Ten pin center
PA: Lucky Strike Entertainment, Llc
15260 Ventura Blvd # 1110
Sherman Oaks CA 91403
323 467-7776

(P-19402)
**LUCKY STRIKE
ENTERTAINMENT LLC**
15260 Ventura Blvd # 1110, Sherman Oaks
(91403-5346)
PHONE...................................818 933-0872
Mark P'Pool, *Branch Mgr*
EMP: 104
SALES (corp-wide): 61.2MM **Privately
Held**
WEB: www.luckystrikeent.com
SIC: 7933 Ten pin center
PA: Lucky Strike Entertainment, Llc
15260 Ventura Blvd # 1110
Sherman Oaks CA 91403
323 467-7776

(P-19403)
**LUCKY STRIKE
ENTERTAINMENT LLC**
20 City Blvd W Ste G2, Orange
(92868-3131)
PHONE...................................248 374-3420
Ismail Saleem, *Branch Mgr*
Tom Calpito, *Vice Pres*
Bryan Reis, *General Mgr*
EMP: 104
SALES (corp-wide): 61.2MM **Privately
Held**
WEB: www.luckystrikeent.com
SIC: 7933 Ten pin center

PA: Lucky Strike Entertainment, Llc
15260 Ventura Blvd # 1110
Sherman Oaks CA 91403
323 467-7776

(P-19404)
NATIONWIDE THEATRES CORP
Also Called: Cal Coffee Shop
2500 Carson St, Lakewood (90712-4107)
PHONE...................................562 421-8448
Tom Moeller, *Manager*
EMP: 2720
SALES (corp-wide): 175.8MM **Privately
Held**
SIC: 7933 5813 5812 Ten pin center;
cocktail lounge; coffee shop
HQ: Nationwide Theatres Corp.
120 N Robertson Blvd Fl 3
Los Angeles CA 90048
310 657-8420

7941 Professional Sports
Clubs & Promoters

(P-19405)
**ANAHEIM ARENA
MANAGEMENT LLC**
Also Called: AAM
2695 E Katella Ave, Anaheim (92806-5904)
PHONE...................................714 704-2400
Tim Ryan, *President*
Ryan Cordes, *Partner*
Michael Schulman, *Ch of Bd*
Nestor Blanco, *Vice Pres*
Chris Johnston, *Vice Pres*
EMP: 600 EST: 2001
SQ FT: 106,000
SALES (est): 81.4MM **Privately Held**
WEB: www.hondacenter.com
SIC: 7941 Sports field or stadium operator,
promoting sports events

(P-19406)
**ANAHEIM DUCKS HOCKEY
CLUB LLC (PA)**
2695 E Katella Ave, Anaheim (92806-5904)
PHONE...................................714 940-2900
Michel Schulman, *Mng Member*
Bill Pedigo, *Officer*
Gina Galasso, *Exec VP*
Bob Murray, *Exec VP*
Tim Ryan, *Exec VP*
EMP: 149 EST: 2005
SALES (est): 25.3MM **Privately Held**
WEB: www.nhl.com
SIC: 7941 Sports clubs, managers & pro-
moters

(P-19407)
ANGELS BASEBALL LP (PA)
Also Called: Los Angeles Angels of Anaheim
2000 E Gene Autry Way, Anaheim
(92806-6143)
PHONE...................................714 940-2000
Dennis Kuhl, *General Ptnr*
Bill Beverage, *Partner*
Molly Jolly, *Partner*
Richard McClemmy, *Partner*
Tim Mead, *Partner*
EMP: 790 EST: 1996
SALES (est): 87.2MM **Privately Held**
WEB: www.mlb.com
SIC: 7941 Baseball club, professional &
semi-professional

(P-19408)
**ANSCHUTZ STHERN CAL SPT
CMPLEX**
Also Called: Stop Hop Center
18400 Avalon Blvd Ste 100, Carson
(90746-2180)
PHONE...................................310 630-2000
Kedie Pendolfo,
Anschutz Grp,
EMP: 160 EST: 2000
SALES (est): 346.8K **Privately Held**
WEB: www.dignityhealthsportspark.com
SIC: 7941 Soccer club
HQ: Anschutz Entertainment Group, Inc.
800 W Olympic Blvd # 305
Los Angeles CA 90015
213 763-7700

(P-19409)
**BIG LGUE DREAMS
CONSULTING LLC**
2155 Trumble Rd, Perris (92571-9211)
PHONE...................................619 846-8855
EMP: 98
SALES (corp-wide): 52.4MM **Privately
Held**
WEB: www.bigleaguedreams.com
SIC: 7941 Sports field or stadium operator,
promoting sports events
PA: Big League Dreams Consulting, Llc
16333 Fairfield Ranch Rd
Chino Hills CA 91709
909 287-1700

(P-19410)
**BIG LGUE DREAMS
CONSULTING LLC**
2100 S Azusa Ave, West Covina
(91792-1507)
PHONE...................................626 839-1100
Jeffrey Odekirk, *Principal*
EMP: 98
SALES (corp-wide): 52.4MM **Privately
Held**
WEB: www.bigleaguedreams.com
SIC: 7941 Sports field or stadium operator,
promoting sports events
PA: Big League Dreams Consulting, Llc
16333 Fairfield Ranch Rd
Chino Hills CA 91709
909 287-1700

(P-19411)
BIG3 BASKETBALL LLC
644 S Figueroa St, Los Angeles
(90017-3411)
PHONE...................................213 417-2013
Jeff Kwatinetz, *CEO*
O'Shea Jackson Sr, *Principal*
Rahul Mishra, *Project Engr*
Liam Kincaid, *Opers-Prdtn-Mfg*
Jerry Fortuna, *Marketing Staff*
EMP: 67 EST: 2016
SALES (est): 3MM **Privately Held**
WEB: www.big3.com
SIC: 7941 Basketball club

(P-19412)
CAA SPORTS LLC (HQ)
2000 Avenue Of The Stars # 100, Los An-
geles (90067-4705)
PHONE...................................424 288-2000
Michael A Rubel,
Bruce King, *Principal*
Alex Newell, *Manager*
EMP: 88 EST: 2006
SALES: 38.9MM
SALES (corp-wide): 668.1MM **Privately
Held**
WEB: www.caa.com
SIC: 7941 Sports promotion
PA: Creative Artists Agency Holdings, Llc
2000 Avenue Of The Stars
Los Angeles CA 90067
424 288-2000

(P-19413)
**CHARGERS FOOTBALL
COMPANY LLC (PA)**
Also Called: Los Angeles Chargers
3333 Susan St, Costa Mesa (92626-1632)
PHONE...................................619 280-2121
Dean A Spanos, *President*
Jeanne Bonk, *CFO*
Alex Spanos, *Chairman*
Jeanne M Bonk, *Exec VP*
Jim Steeg, *Exec VP*
EMP: 70 EST: 1959
SALES (est): 691.7K **Privately Held**
WEB: www.chargers.com
SIC: 7941 Football club

(P-19414)
**COTO DE CAZA GOLF CLUB
INC**
25291 Vista Del Verde, Trabuco Canyon
(92679-4900)
PHONE...................................949 766-7886
Jack Deal, *Director*
Marc Chasman, *Director*
EMP: 135 EST: 1989

SALES (est): 1.3MM
SALES (corp-wide): 8.1MM **Privately Held**
WEB: www.cotobobbi.com
SIC: 7941 5813 7992 7991 Professional & semi-professional sports clubs; drinking places; public golf courses; physical fitness facilities; eating places
PA: Coto De Caza Limited
   24800 Chrisanta Dr
   Mission Viejo CA

(P-19415)
ENDEAVOR GROUP HOLDINGS INC (PA)
9601 Wilshire Blvd, Beverly Hills (90210-5213)
PHONE...................................310 285-9000
ARI Emanuel, *CEO*
Mark Shapiro, *President*
Jason Lublin, *CFO*
Seth Krauss,
Howard Heller, *Controller*
EMP: 53 EST: 2019
SQ FT: 300,000
SALES (est): 880.5MM **Publicly Held**
SIC: 7941 Sports field or stadium operator, promoting sports events

(P-19416)
FOX BASEBALL HOLDINGS INC
1000 Vin Scully Ave, Los Angeles (90090-1112)
PHONE...................................323 224-1500
Frank McCourt, *President*
EMP: 736 EST: 2000
SALES (est): 3MM
SALES (corp-wide): 65.3B **Publicly Held**
WEB: www.fox.com
SIC: 7941 Baseball club, professional & semi-professional
HQ: Fox Entertainment Group, Llc
   1211 Ave Of The Americas
   New York NY 10036
   212 852-7000

(P-19417)
IMMORTALS LLC
11460 W Washington Blvd A, Los Angeles (90066-6030)
P.O. Box 641729 (90064-6729)
PHONE...................................310 554-8267
ARI Segal, *COO*
Noah Whinston, *CEO*
Jmr Luna, *Vice Pres*
Jonathan Stein, *Vice Pres*
Tomi Kovanen, *General Mgr*
EMP: 85 EST: 2015
SQ FT: 30,000
SALES (est): 10.2MM **Privately Held**
SIC: 7941 Professional & semi-professional sports clubs

(P-19418)
INLAND EMPIRE 66ERS BSBAL CLB
280 S E St, San Bernardino (92401-2009)
PHONE...................................909 888-9922
David Elmore, *CEO*
Donna Tuttle, *President*
Jhon Fonsaker, *CFO*
Dave Oldham, *VP Bus Dvlpt*
Jarrett Stark, *Executive*
EMP: 110 EST: 1993
SQ FT: 600
SALES: 37.7K
SALES (corp-wide): 34.1MM **Privately Held**
WEB: www.inlandempire.66ers.milb.com
SIC: 7941 Baseball club, professional & semi-professional
PA: The Elmore Group Ltd
   19 N Grant St Ste 2
   Hinsdale IL
   630 325-6228

(P-19419)
LA CLIPPERS LLC
1212 S Flower Fl 5, Los Angeles (90015-2123)
PHONE...................................213 742-7500
Steven A Ballmer, *Mng Member*
Jason Green, *Vice Pres*
Liseth Castillo, *Executive*
Amber Costà, *Executive*

Richard Craig, *Executive*
EMP: 77 EST: 2014
SALES (est): 12.1MM **Privately Held**
WEB: www.clippers.com
SIC: 7941 Basketball club

(P-19420)
LA SPORTS PROPERTIES INC
Also Called: Los Angeles Clippers
1212 S Flower St Fl 5, Los Angeles (90015-2123)
PHONE...................................213 742-7500
Dick Parsons, *CEO*
Sam Borst-Smith, *Partner*
Steve Ballmer, *Vice Chairman*
Larry Abney, *COO*
Andrew Roeser, *Exec VP*
EMP: 195 EST: 1946
SQ FT: 5,000
SALES (est): 27.3MM **Privately Held**
WEB: www.clippers.com
SIC: 7941 Basketball club

(P-19421)
LOS ANGELES DODGERS LLC
1000 Vin Scully Ave, Los Angeles (90090-1112)
PHONE...................................323 224-1507
Stan Kasten, *President*
Ralph Esquibel, *Vice Pres*
Michael Wandell, *Vice Pres*
Mark Langill, *Publications*
Corey Schimmel, *Director*
EMP: 1360 EST: 2003
SALES (est): 20.4MM **Privately Held**
WEB: www.mlb.com
SIC: 7941 Stadium event operator services

(P-19422)
LOS ANGELES RAMS LLC (PA)
Also Called: St Louis Rams
29899 Agoura Rd, Agoura Hills (91301-2493)
PHONE...................................314 982-7267
E Stanley Kroenke, *Mng Member*
Kate Kost, *Opers Staff*
Nick Scott, *Advt Staff*
Daleyna Adkinson, *Marketing Staff*
Chase Isaacs, *Corp Comm Staff*
EMP: 100 EST: 1939
SALES (est): 63.3MM **Privately Held**
WEB: www.therams.com
SIC: 7941 Football club

(P-19423)
MANDALAY SPT ACTION ENTRMT LLC (PA)
Also Called: Mandalay Baseball Properties
4751 Wilshire Blvd Fl 3, Los Angeles (90010-3844)
PHONE...................................323 549-4300
Hank Stickney, *CEO*
Anthony Lott, *Ch of Bd*
Peter Guber, *CEO*
Jimmy Bailey, *CFO*
Shelly Riney, *Senior VP*
EMP: 59 EST: 1997
SALES (est): 10.7MM **Privately Held**
WEB: www.peterguber.com
SIC: 7941 Sports clubs, managers & promoters

(P-19424)
MISSION VIEJO PATEADORES INC
7 El Corzo, Rcho STA Marg (92688-3507)
PHONE...................................949 350-5590
EMP: 50 EST: 2010
SALES (est): 368.7K **Privately Held**
SIC: 7941 Soccer club

(P-19425)
NFL PROPERTIES LLC
Also Called: Nfl Network
10950 Wash Blvd Ste 100, Culver City (90232-4032)
PHONE...................................310 840-4635
Steve Bernstein, *Principal*
Lorey Zlotnick, *Vice Pres*
Trent Cooper, *Creative Dir*
Chia-Ho Chen, *Software Engr*
Andrew Le, *Software Engr*
EMP: 100

SALES (corp-wide): 603.2MM **Privately Held**
WEB: www.nfl.com
SIC: 7941 Football club
PA: Nfl Properties Llc
   345 Park Ave
   New York NY 10154
   212 450-2000

(P-19426)
NIKE USA INC
222 E Redondo Beach Blvd C, Gardena (90248-2302)
PHONE...................................310 670-6770
EMP: 461
SALES (corp-wide): 44.5B **Publicly Held**
WEB: www.nike.com
SIC: 7941 Sports clubs, managers & promoters
HQ: Nike Usa, Inc.
   1 Sw Bowerman Dr
   Beaverton OR 97005

(P-19427)
PALM SPRNG PWR BASBAL CLB INC
1901 E Baristo Rd, Palm Springs (92262-7119)
PHONE...................................760 778-4487
Andrew Starke, *Principal*
EMP: 55 EST: 2003
SALES (est): 1.1MM **Privately Held**
WEB: www.palmspringspowerbaseball.com
SIC: 7941 Sports clubs, managers & promoters

(P-19428)
PSE HOLDING LLC (DH)
Also Called: Palace Sports & Entrmt LLC
360 N Crescent Dr, Beverly Hills (90210-4874)
PHONE...................................248 377-0165
Tom Gores,
Paul Rapier, *Manager*
EMP: 300 EST: 1985
SALES (est): 115.2MM **Privately Held**
SIC: 7941 7922 Stadium event operator services; summer theater
HQ: Pistons Palace Holdings, Llc
   360 N Crescent Dr
   Beverly Hills CA 90210
   310 228-9521

7948 Racing & Track Operations

(P-19429)
CALIFORNIA SPEEDWAY CORP
Also Called: Auto Club Speedway
9300 Cherry Ave, Fontana (92335-2562)
PHONE...................................909 429-5000
William Miller, *President*
Ray Wilkings, *Vice Pres*
Erin Macdonald, *Executive*
David Talley, *Comms Mgr*
Sandy Carnes, *Exec Dir*
EMP: 50 EST: 1994
SALES (est): 14.9MM **Privately Held**
WEB: www.autoclubspeedway.com
SIC: 7948 Automotive race track operation
HQ: 88 Corporation
   1801 W Intl Speedway Blvd
   Daytona Beach FL 32114
   386 254-2700

(P-19430)
LOS ALAMITOS RACE COURSE
Also Called: Vessels Club Restaurant
4961 Katella Ave, Cypress (90720-2721)
PHONE...................................714 820-2800
Edward Allred, *Partner*
Jorge Avina, *Officer*
Tom Seibly, *Vice Pres*
Cathy Moji, *Office Mgr*
George Yniguez, *Admin Sec*
EMP: 200 EST: 1943
SQ FT: 2,000
SALES (est): 15.9MM **Privately Held**
WEB: www.losalamitos.com
SIC: 5812 7948 5813 5963 Eating places; horses, racing; bar (drinking places); direct selling establishments

(P-19431)
LOS ANGELES TURF CLUB INC (DH)
Also Called: Santa Anita Park
285 W Huntington Dr, Arcadia (91007-3439)
P.O. Box 60014 (91066-6014)
PHONE.................................€26 574-6330
Gregory C Avioli, *CEO*
Frank Stronach, *Ch of Bd*
George Haines II, *President*
Sherrie Thayer, *President*
Sherwood Chillingworth, *Exec VP*
▲ EMP: 440 EST: 1964
SALES (est): 71.2MM
SALES (corp-wide): 32.6B **Privately Held**
WEB: www.santaanita.com
SIC: 7948 Horse race track operation
HQ: Magna Car Top Systems Of America, Inc.
   456 Wimpole Dr
   Rochester Hills MI 48309
   248 836-4500

(P-19432)
MB2 RACEWAY INC (PA)
13943 Balboa Blvd, Sylmar (91342-1084)
PHONE...................................818 364-8000
Chris Brooks, *President*
Jared Sheff, *Manager*
EMP: 63 EST: 2006
SALES (est): 3.5MM **Privately Held**
WEB: www.mb2raceway.com
SIC: 7948 Motor vehicle racing & drivers

(P-19433)
NATIONAL HOT ROD ASSOCIATION (PA)
Also Called: Nhra
2035 E Financial Way, Glendora (91741-4602)
PHONE...................................626 914-4761
Wally Parks, *Director*
Tom Compton, *President*
Kasey Coler, *Vice Pres*
Bob Lang, *Vice Pres*
Josh Peterson, *Vice Pres*
EMP: 200 EST: 1951
SQ FT: 30,000
SALES (est): 43MM **Privately Held**
WEB: www.nhra.com
SIC: 7948 2711 2741 Automotive race track operation; newspapers: publishing only, not printed on site; miscellaneous publishing

(P-19434)
POLE POSITION RACEWAY INC (PA)
1594 E Bentley Dr, Corona (92879-1741)
P.O. Box 1344, Murrieta 92564-1344)
PHONE...................................951 817-5032
Jason Williams, *President*
Debbie Cocanour, *Executive Asst*
Bryant Mark, *Manager*
EMP: 69 EST: 2005
SALES (est): 7MM **Privately Held**
WEB: www.polepositionraceway.com
SIC: 7948 Race track operation

(P-19435)
SPEEDWAY USA INC
14800 Seventh St, Victorville (92395-4024)
PHONE...................................760 245-6211
Gene Woods, *President*
EMP: 50
SALES (est): 478.1K **Privately Held**
SIC: 7948 Race track operation

(P-19436)
YOUBETCOM INC (HQ)
2600 W Olive Ave Fl 5, Burbank (91505-4572)
PHONE...................................818 668-2100
David Goldberg, *President*
Susan Bracey, *CFO*
Michael D Nelson,
EMP: 56 EST: 1995
SQ FT: 3,000
SALES (est): 5.9MM
SALES (corp-wide): 1B **Publicly Held**
WEB:
www.churchilldownsincorporated.com
SIC: 7948 Race track operation

PA: Churchill Downs Incorporated
600 N Hurstbourne Pkwy # 400
Louisville KY 40222
502 636-4400

7991 Physical Fitness Facilities

(P-19437)
ADVENTUREPLEX
1701 Marine Ave, Manhattan Beach
(90266-4100)
PHONE...............................310 546-7708
EMP: 50
SALES (est): 583.8K **Privately Held**
WEB: www.adventureplex.org
SIC: 7991 Physical Fitness Facilities

(P-19438)
BARRYS BOOTCAMP LLC (PA)
Also Called: Barry's Boot Camp
7373 Beverly Blvd, Los Angeles
(90036-2502)
PHONE...............................323 452-0037
Joey Consolis, *CEO*
Rachel Mumford, *Co-Owner*
John Mumford, *Founder*
Tracy McIntosh, *Officer*
Leah Eisenhauer, *Graphic Designe*
EMP: 452 **EST:** 2015
SALES (est): 28.9MM **Privately Held**
SIC: 7991 Physical fitness facilities

(P-19439)
BLISS WORLD LLC
6250 Hollywood Blvd Fl 4, Los Angeles
(90028-5325)
PHONE...............................323 500-0921
EMP: 70 **Privately Held**
WEB: www.blissworld.com
SIC: 7991 Spas
HQ: Bliss World Llc
145 S Fairfax Ave Ste 400
Los Angeles CA 90036
212 931-6383

(P-19440)
BOXUNION SANTA MONICA LLC (PA)
1755 Ocean Ave, Santa Monica
(90401-3615)
PHONE...............................310 882-5508
Todd Wadler,
EMP: 75 **EST:** 2016
SALES (est): 19.5MM **Privately Held**
WEB: www.boxunion.com
SIC: 7991 Physical fitness facilities

(P-19441)
CRUNCH LLC
19867 Prairie St Ste 200, Chatsworth
(91311-6533)
PHONE...............................951 327-0202
Todd Neely, *Branch Mgr*
Angela Fernandez, *Opers Mgr*
EMP: 59 **Privately Held**
WEB: www.crunch.com
SIC: 7991 Physical fitness facilities
PA: Crunch, Llc
220 W 19th St
New York NY 10011

(P-19442)
CRUNCH LLC
Also Called: Crunch Fitness
19867 Prairie St Ste 200, Chatsworth
(91311-6533)
PHONE...............................719 301-1760
Robert Brito, *General Mgr*
EMP: 59 **Privately Held**
WEB: www.crunch.com
SIC: 7991 Physical fitness facilities
PA: Crunch, Llc
220 W 19th St
New York NY 10011

(P-19443)
CRUNCH FITNESS
19867 Prairie St Ste 200, Chatsworth
(91311-6533)
PHONE...............................805 522-5454
Teresa Frost, *General Mgr*

Daniel Gallagher, *CFO*
EMP: 65 **EST:** 1980
SALES (est): 4.2MM **Privately Held**
WEB: www.crunch.com
SIC: 7991 Athletic club & gymnasiums,
membership

(P-19444)
EQUINOX-76TH STREET INC
5400 W Rosecrans Ave Up, Hawthorne
(90250-6682)
PHONE...............................310 727-9543
Larry Schneider, *Branch Mgr*
EMP: 72
SALES (corp-wide): 2B **Privately Held**
SIC: 7991 Health club
HQ: Equinox-76th Street, Inc.
895 Broadway Fl 3
New York NY 10003

(P-19445)
EQUINOX-76TH STREET INC
1550 Vine St, Hollywood (90028-7305)
PHONE...............................323 471-0130
EMP: 72
SALES (corp-wide): 2B **Privately Held**
SIC: 7991 Health club
HQ: Equinox-76th Street, Inc.
895 Broadway Fl 3
New York NY 10003

(P-19446)
EQUINOX-76TH STREET INC
112 S Lakeview Canyon Rd, Westlake Village (91362-3925)
PHONE...............................805 367-3925
Katie Kim, *Manager*
EMP: 72
SALES (corp-wide): 2B **Privately Held**
SIC: 7991 Health club
HQ: Equinox-76th Street, Inc.
895 Broadway Fl 3
New York NY 10003

(P-19447)
EQUINOX-76TH STREET INC
1835 S Sepulveda Blvd, Los Angeles
(90025-6941)
PHONE...............................310 479-5200
Tonya Jacobs, *Manager*
EMP: 72
SALES (corp-wide): 2B **Privately Held**
SIC: 7991 Health club
HQ: Equinox-76th Street, Inc.
895 Broadway Fl 3
New York NY 10003

(P-19448)
EQUINOX-76TH STREET INC
Also Called: Equinox Fitness Club
19540 Jamboree Rd, Irvine (92612-8448)
PHONE...............................949 296-1700
Herb Umphreyville, *General Mgr*
Anna Burns, *Advisor*
EMP: 90
SALES (corp-wide): 2B **Privately Held**
SIC: 7991 Health club
HQ: Equinox-76th Street, Inc.
895 Broadway Fl 3
New York NY 10003

(P-19449)
EQUINOX-76TH STREET INC
Also Called: Equinox Fitness Club
550 Deep Valley Dr, Rlling HLS Est
(90274-3664)
PHONE...............................310 697-1016
EMP: 72
SALES (corp-wide): 2B **Privately Held**
SIC: 7991 Health club
HQ: Equinox-76th Street, Inc.
895 Broadway Fl 3
New York NY 10003

(P-19450)
EQUINOX-76TH STREET INC
Also Called: Equinox Fitness Club
10250 Santa Monica Blvd, Los Angeles
(90067-6404)
PHONE...............................310 552-0420

Mathew Herbert, *Branch Mgr*
EMP: 72
SALES (corp-wide): 2B **Privately Held**
SIC: 7991 Health club
HQ: Equinox-76th Street, Inc.
895 Broadway Fl 3
New York NY 10003

-

(P-19451)
GRIT MANAGEMENT LLC
Also Called: Gritcycle
864 W 16th St, Newport Beach
(92663-2802)
PHONE...............................949 220-7765
Gail Gray,
EMP: 60 **EST:** 2020
SALES (est): 469.6K **Privately Held**
SIC: 7991 Physical fitness facilities

(P-19452)
JURLIQUE HLISTIC SKIN CARE INC (PA)
234 E Colo Blvd Ste 450, Pasadena
(91101)
PHONE...............................914 998-8800
Sam McKay, *CEO*
EMP: 50 **EST:** 2005
SALES (est): 11MM **Privately Held**
WEB: www.jurlique.com
SIC: 7991 Spas

(P-19453)
LA BONNE VIE INC
2723 Shell Beach Rd, Shell Beach
(93449-1629)
PHONE...............................805 773-5003
Maureen Raynaud-Loughead, *Principal*
EMP: 100 **EST:** 2005
SALES (est): 236.1K **Privately Held**
SIC: 7991 Spas

(P-19454)
LA BOXING FRANCHISE CORP
1241 E Dyer Rd Ste 100, Santa Ana
(92705-5611)
PHONE...............................714 668-0911
Anthony Geisler, *President*
▲ **EMP:** 247 **EST:** 1992
SALES (est): 4.6MM
SALES (corp-wide): 99.9MM **Privately Held**
WEB: www.ufcgym.com
SIC: 7991 Physical fitness facilities
PA: U Gym, Llc
1501 Quail St Ste 100
Newport Beach CA 92660
714 668-0911

(P-19455)
LA WORKOUT INC
Also Called: La Workout Camarillo West
500 Paseo Camarillo, Camarillo
(93010-5900)
PHONE...............................805 482-8884
Steve Rivera, *Branch Mgr*
EMP: 115 **Privately Held**
WEB: www.laworkout.com
SIC: 7991 Health club
PA: La Workout, Inc.
2510g Las Posas Rd Ste 44
Camarillo CA 93010

(P-19456)
LIFE TIME INC
Also Called: Life Time Fitness
111 Avenida Vista Montana, San Clemente
(92672-6094)
PHONE...............................949 492-1515
Steve Johnson, *President*
Cameron Wallace, *Accounts Mgr*
EMP: 103
SALES (corp-wide): 948.3MM **Privately Held**
WEB: www.lifetime.life
SIC: 7991 Health club
HQ: Life Time, Inc.
2902 Corporate Pl
Chanhassen MN 55317

(P-19457)
LOS ANGELES ATHLETIC CLUB INC
431 W 7th St, Los Angeles (90014-1691)
PHONE...............................213 625-2211
Karen Hathaway, *President*
Bryan Cusworth, *CFO*
Gretchen Crookes, *Opers Staff*
Stela Tasu, *Director*
Cory Hathaway, *Manager*
EMP: 106 **EST:** 1986
SALES (est): 1.6MM
SALES (corp-wide): 96.2MM **Privately Held**
WEB: www.laac.com
SIC: 7991 Athletic club & gymnasiums,
membership
PA: Laaco, Ltd.
431 W 7th St
Los Angeles CA 90014
213 622-1254

(P-19458)
LOUNGE SPA INC
4016 East Blvd, Los Angeles (90066-4608)
PHONE...............................310 745-1646
Alice Koskas, *Branch Mgr*
EMP: 66
SALES (corp-wide): 55.2K **Privately Held**
WEB: www.redcat.org
SIC: 7991 Spas
PA: Lounge Spa Inc
3830 Vly Cntre Dr Ste 70
San Diego CA

(P-19459)
MADONNA INN INC
100 Madonna Rd, San Luis Obispo
(93405-5489)
PHONE...............................805 543-3000
Phyllis Madonna, *CEO*
Alexandra Sutton, *General Mgr*
Brian Ogden, *CIO*
Cory Scamara, *Info Tech Mgr*
Ron Griffin, *Auditor*
EMP: 200 **EST:** 1951
SQ FT: 9,200
SALES (est): 23.2MM **Privately Held**
WEB: www.madonnainn.com
SIC: 5461 5812 5813 7991 Bakeries;
cafe; steak restaurant; steak & barbecue
restaurants; bar (drinking places); tavern
(drinking places); spas; inns

(P-19460)
MERIDAN SPORT CLUB LLC (PA)
12100 W Olympic Blvd, Los Angeles
(90064-1048)
PHONE...............................818 698-2900
Charles H Grieve, *Principal*
EMP: 61 **EST:** 2006
SALES (est): 367.1K **Privately Held**
SIC: 7991 Health club

(P-19461)
MONIQUE SURACI
Also Called: Murrieta Day Spa
41885 Ivy St, Murrieta (92562-8607)
PHONE...............................951 677-8111
Monique Suraci, *Owner*
EMP: 60 **EST:** 1989
SALES (est): 4.8MM **Privately Held**
WEB: www.mdayspa.com
SIC: 7991 Spas

(P-19462)
NUZUNA CORPORATION
Also Called: Nuzuna Fitness
1451 Quail St Ste 104, Newport Beach
(92660-2747)
PHONE...............................949 432-4824
Charlie Laverty, *CEO*
Aileen Pham, *COO*
Gwen Nguyen, *Vice Pres*
EMP: 90 **EST:** 2019
SALES (est): 4.5MM **Privately Held**
WEB: www.nuzunafit.com
SIC: 7991 Physical fitness facilities

(PA)=Parent Co (HQ)=Headquarters (DH)=Div Headquarters
✪ = New Business established in last 2 years

(P-19463)
OCFIT LB LLC (PA)
151 Kalmus Dr Ste F3a, Costa Mesa
(92626-7974)
PHONE....................949 701-7702
Marc Thomas, *President*
EMP: 63 **EST:** 2016
SALES (est): 594.7K **Privately Held**
SIC: 7991 Physical fitness facilities

(P-19464)
OLYMPIX FITNESS LLC
4101 E Olympic Plz, Long Beach
(90803-2807)
PHONE....................562 366-4600
Eden Paul,
EMP: 91 **EST:** 2016
SALES (est): 792K **Privately Held**
WEB: www.iconixfit.com
SIC: 7991 Physical fitness facilities

(P-19465)
RACHAS INC
Also Called: Chuze Fitness
9080 Foothill Blvd, Rancho Cucamonga
(91730-3450)
PHONE....................626 671-2440
EMP: 50
SALES (corp-wide): 62.6MM **Privately Held**
SIC: 7991 Physical fitness facilities
PA: Rachas, Inc.
1011 Cmino Del Rio S Ste
San Diego CA 92108
619 780-0141

(P-19466)
RACHAS INC
Also Called: Chuze Fitness
135 N Beach Blvd, Anaheim (92801-6135)
PHONE....................714 290-0636
Cory Brightwell, *Branch Mgr*
EMP: 50
SALES (corp-wide): 62.6MM **Privately Held**
SIC: 7991 Physical fitness facilities
PA: Rachas, Inc.
1011 Cmino Del Rio S Ste
San Diego CA 92108
619 780-0141

(P-19467)
SANTEE SYSTEMS SERVICES II LL
229 E Gage Ave, Los Angeles
(90003-1533)
PHONE....................323 445-0044
EMP: 50 **EST:** 2012
SQ FT: 10,000
SALES (est): 1.4MM **Privately Held**
SIC: 7991 Physical Fitness Facility

(P-19468)
SKIN HEALTH EXPERTS LLC
8428 Melrose Pl, Los Angeles
(90069-5300)
PHONE....................323 655-7546
Michelle Taylor, *Mng Member*
Laura Shass,
EMP: 61 **EST:** 2004
SALES (est): 1.8MM **Privately Held**
WEB: www.katesomerville.com
SIC: 7991 Spas
PA: Skin Health Experts Medical Corporation
8428 Melrose Pl
Los Angeles CA 90069

(P-19469)
SWEATHEORY LLC
1503 N Cahuenga Blvd, Los Angeles
(90028-7312)
PHONE....................310 956-2307
Julian Ledesma,
EMP: 64 **EST:** 2016
SALES (est): 800.7K **Privately Held**
WEB: www.sweatheory.com
SIC: 7991 Health club

(P-19470)
THINK TOGETHER
12016 Telegraph Rd, Santa Fe Springs
(90670-3784)
PHONE....................562 236-3835
Johanna Lizarraga, *General Mgr*
EMP: 365
SALES (est): 66.3MM **Privately Held**
WEB: www.thinktogether.org
SIC: 7991 Physical fitness facilities
PA: Think Together
2101 E 4th St Ste 200b
Santa Ana CA 92705
714 543-3807

(P-19471)
U GYM LLC (PA)
Also Called: Ufc Gym
1501 Quail St Ste 100, Newport Beach
(92660-2797)
PHONE....................714 668-0911
Adam Sedlack, *CEO*
Kim Hayoung, *Partner*
Michael Pilatos, *CFO*
Mark Mastrov, *Chairman*
Taylor Whisenand, *Exec VP*
EMP: 70 **EST:** 2008
SALES (est): 99.9MM **Privately Held**
WEB: www.ufcgym.com
SIC: 7991 5699 6794 Health club; shirts, custom made; franchises, selling or licensing

(P-19472)
WEST SIDE RECREATION & PK DST ✪
500 Cascade Pl, Taft (93268-2641)
PHONE....................661 763-4246
Leslie Clark III, *Director*
EMP: 50 **EST:** 2021
SALES (est): 946.8K **Privately Held**
SIC: 7991 Physical fitness facilities

(P-19473)
XI ENTERPRISE INC
2140 E Palmdale Blvd, Palmdale
(93550-1202)
PHONE....................661 266-3200
Shah Roshan, *CEO*
EMP: 74 **EST:** 2011
SALES (est): 1.3MM **Privately Held**
SIC: 7991 Physical fitness facilities

(P-19474)
XPONENTIAL FITNESS INC (HQ)
17877 Von Karman Ave # 100, Irvine
(92614-4227)
PHONE....................949 346-3000
Anthony Geisler, *CEO*
Mark Grabowski, *Ch of Bd*
Sarah Luna, *President*
Ryan Junk, *COO*
John Meloun, *CFO*
EMP: 270 **EST:** 2017
SALES (est): 106.4MM **Publicly Held**
SIC: 7991 Athletic club & gymnasiums, membership
PA: H&W Investco Lp
17 Palmer Ln
Riverside CT 06878
949 346-3000

(P-19475)
YOGA WORKS INC (DH)
Also Called: Yogaworks
2215 Main St, Santa Monica (90405-2217)
PHONE....................310 664-6470
Phillip Swain, *CEO*
Jay Decoons, *President*
Kiernan Aileen, *General Mgr*
Taylor Barragan, *Sales Mgr*
Lee Janet, *Marketing Staff*
EMP: 50 **EST:** 1987
SALES (est): 37.4MM
SALES (corp-wide): 461.8MM **Privately Held**
WEB: www.yogaworks.com
SIC: 7991 5961 5651 Exercise salon; mail order house; unisex clothing stores
HQ: Yogaworks, Inc.
5780 Uplander Way
Culver City CA 90230
310 664-6470

7992 Public Golf Courses

(P-19476)
BLACK GOLD GOLF CLUB
1 Black Gold Dr, Yorba Linda (92886-2383)
PHONE....................714 961-0060
Eric Lohman, *General Mgr*
Mark Blakely, *Technology*
Dave Bosak, *Technology*
Josh Hunhoff, *Sales Staff*
Cara Young, *Sales Staff*
EMP: 75 **EST:** 2001
SALES (est): 3.1MM **Privately Held**
WEB: www.blackgoldgolf.com
SIC: 7992 Public golf courses

(P-19477)
CITY OF PASADENA
Also Called: Brookside Golf Course
1133 Rosemont Ave, Pasadena
(91103-2401)
PHONE....................626 543-4708
EMP: 60 **Privately Held**
SIC: 7992 9111 Public Golf Course Executive Office
PA: City Of Pasadena
100 N Garfield Ave
Pasadena CA 91101
626 744-4386

(P-19478)
CONCERT GOLF PARTNERS LLC
1 Coastal Oak, Newport Coast
(92657-1655)
PHONE....................949 715-0602
Peter J Nanula, *Mng Member*
Susan Dunnavant, *COO*
Aaron Straub, *Vice Pres*
Gabby McCalister, *Director*
Yvonne Turnbull, *Director*
EMP: 2000 **EST:** 2011
SALES (est): 33.3MM **Privately Held**
WEB: www.concertgolfpartners.com
SIC: 7992 Public golf courses

(P-19479)
COUNTY OF LOS ANGELES
8640 Rush St, Rosemead (91770-3739)
PHONE....................626 280-8225
Peter Nenula, *Branch Mgr*
EMP: 51
SALES (corp-wide): 25.2B **Privately Held**
WEB: www.lacounty.gov
SIC: 7992 9111 Public golf courses; county supervisors' & executives' offices
PA: County Of Los Angeles
500 W Temple St Ste 437
Los Angeles CA 90012
213 974-1101

(P-19480)
COUNTY OF LOS ANGELES
Also Called: Parks and Recreation Dept
3101 Carson St, Lakewood (90712-4005)
PHONE....................562 429-9711
Gary Kossick, *Manager*
EMP: 51
SALES (corp-wide): 25.2B **Privately Held**
WEB: www.lacounty.gov
SIC: 7992 9512 Public golf courses; recreational program administration, government;
PA: County Of Los Angeles
500 W Temple St Ste 437
Los Angeles CA 90012
213 974-1101

(P-19481)
COUNTY OF LOS ANGELES
Also Called: Parks and Recreation Dept
1875 Fairplex Dr, Pomona (91768-1240)
PHONE....................909 231-0549
Chad Hackman, *General Mgr*
EMP: 51
SALES (corp-wide): 25.2B **Privately Held**
WEB: www.lacounty.gov
SIC: 7992 9512 7299 Public golf courses; recreational program administration, government; ; wedding chapel, privately operated
PA: County Of Los Angeles
500 W Temple St Ste 437
Los Angeles CA 90012
213 974-1101

(P-19482)
COUNTY OF LOS ANGELES
Also Called: Parks and Recreation, Dept of
1235 Figueroa Pl, Wilmington
(90744-2312)
PHONE....................310 549-4953
Beverly Cox, *Manager*
EMP: 51
SALES (corp-wide): 25.2B **Privately Held**
WEB: www.lacounty.gov
SIC: 7992 9512 Public golf courses; recreational program administration, government;
PA: County Of Los Angeles
500 W Temple St Ste 437
Los Angeles CA 90012
213 974-1101

(P-19483)
COUNTY OF LOS ANGELES
Also Called: Sepulveda Golf Course
16821 Burbank Blvd Ste 4, Encino
(91436-1025)
PHONE....................818 995-1170
Jim Dodds, *Branch Mgr*
EMP: 51
SALES (corp-wide): 25.2B **Privately Held**
WEB: www.lacounty.gov
SIC: 7992 9512 Public golf courses; land management agency, government
PA: County Of Los Angeles
500 W Temple St Ste 437
Los Angeles CA 90012
213 974-1101

(P-19484)
DESERT WILLOW GOLF RESORT INC
Also Called: Desert Willow Golf Course
38995 Desert Willow Dr, Palm Desert
(92260-1674)
PHONE....................760 346-0015
Richard Mogensen, *General Mgr*
Derek White, *General Mgr*
EMP: 150 **EST:** 1997
SQ FT: 33,000
SALES (est): 2.7MM **Privately Held**
WEB: www.desertwillow.com
SIC: 7992 Public golf courses

(P-19485)
EAGLE GLEN COUNTRY CLUB LLC
Also Called: Eagle Glen Golf Club
1800 Eagle Glen Pkwy, Corona
(92883-0620)
PHONE....................951 272-4653
Jim Previty, *Chairman*
EMP: 60 **EST:** 1999
SQ FT: 26,000
SALES (est): 5.7MM **Privately Held**
WEB: www.eagleglencc.com
SIC: 7992 Public golf courses

(P-19486)
EL PRADO GOLF COURSE LP
6555 Pine Ave, Chino (91708-9192)
PHONE....................909 597-1751
Bruce Jenke, *General Ptnr*
Anthony Foo, *Partner*
G Barton Heuler, *Partner*
Walter Heuler, *Partner*
Jacob Perry, *Director*
EMP: 80 **EST:** 1975
SQ FT: 5,000
SALES (est): 5.6MM **Privately Held**
WEB: www.elpradogolfcourses.com
SIC: 7992 Public golf courses

(P-19487)
EVERGREEN ALLIANCE GOLF LTD LP
299 S Moorpark Rd, Thousand Oaks
(91361-1006)
PHONE....................805 495-6421
John Dillin, *General Mgr*
EMP: 56
SALES (corp-wide): 70.4MM **Privately Held**
WEB: www.eaglgolf.com
SIC: 7992 Public golf courses
PA: Evergreen Alliance Golf Limited, L.P.
13727 Noel Rd Ste 1000
Dallas TX 75240
214 722-6000

(P-19488)
EVERGREEN ALLIANCE GOLF LTD LP
3750 Olivas Park Dr, Ventura (93001-4324)
PHONE..................................805 650-1794
EMP: 56
SALES (corp-wide): 70.4MM **Privately Held**
WEB: www.eaglgolf.com
SIC: 7992 Public golf courses
PA: Evergreen Alliance Golf Limited, L.P.
13727 Noel Rd Ste 1000
Dallas TX 75240
214 722-6000

(P-19489)
GLEN ANNIE GOLF CLUB
405 Glen Annie Rd, Goleta (93117-1427)
PHONE..................................805 968-6400
Richard Nahas, *General Mgr*
Rich Nahas, *General Mgr*
Brad Van Horn, *General Mgr*
EMP: 80 EST: 1997
SALES (est): 2.7MM **Privately Held**
WEB: www.glenanniegolf.com
SIC: 7992 Public golf courses

(P-19490)
GREEN RIVER GOLF CORPORATION
Also Called: Green River Golf Course
5215 Green River Rd, Corona (92878-9404)
PHONE..................................714 970-8411
Judy Saguchi, *President*
Katie Hinks, *Sales Staff*
Stephnie McNulty, *Sales Staff*
Sandra Scubla, *Sales Staff*
Michael Dooley, *Superintendent*
EMP: 100 EST: 1977
SQ FT: 30,000
SALES (est): 11.8MM **Privately Held**
WEB: www.courseco.com
SIC: 7992 5941 5813 5812 Public golf courses; sporting goods & bicycle shops; drinking places; eating places
PA: Courseco, Inc.
5341 Old Redwood Hwy # 202
Petaluma CA 94954

(P-19491)
HENRY C COX II AND JOHN L WEST
Also Called: Indian Hills Country Club
5700 Club House Dr, Riverside (92509-7002)
P.O. Box 3617 (92519-3617)
PHONE..................................951 360-2090
Henry C Cox II, *Partner*
John L West, *Partner*
EMP: 52 EST: 1965
SQ FT: 20,680
SALES (est): 1.5MM **Privately Held**
WEB: www.indianhillsgolf.com
SIC: 7992 Public golf courses

(P-19492)
HERITAGE GOLF GROUP LLC
Also Called: Talega Golf Club
990 Avenida Talega, San Clemente (92673-6849)
PHONE..................................949 369-6226
David Foster, *Branch Mgr*
EMP: 104
SALES (corp-wide): 97.9MM **Privately Held**
WEB: www.heritagegolfgroup.com
SIC: 7992 Public golf courses
PA: Heritage Golf Group, Llc
12750 High Bluff Dr Fl 4
San Diego CA 92130
858 720-0694

(P-19493)
HERITAGE GOLF GROUP LLC
Also Called: Valencia Country Club
27330 Tourney Rd, Valencia (91355-1806)
PHONE..................................661 254-4401
Jim Fitzsimmons, *Manager*
Andrew Kingsley, *General Mgr*
Kaylah Hurst, *Marketing Staff*
Darin Jarosz, *Director*
Mark Kowalski, *Director*
EMP: 104

SALES (corp-wide): 97.9MM **Privately Held**
WEB: www.heritagegolfgroup.com
SIC: 7992 Public golf courses
PA: Heritage Golf Group, Llc
12750 High Bluff Dr Fl 4
San Diego CA 92130
858 720-0694

(P-19494)
HERITAGE PALMS HOA
Also Called: Heritage Palms Golf Club
44291 Heritage Palms Dr S, Indio (92201-2713)
PHONE..................................760 772-7334
Dennis Elem, *General Mgr*
Kirk Muldarry, *Security Dir*
Ann Lachance, *Receptionist*
EMP: 53 EST: 1996
SQ FT: 2,200
SALES (est): 4.1MM **Privately Held**
WEB: www.heritagepalmsgolfclub.com
SIC: 7992 Public golf courses

(P-19495)
HIGH TIDE AND GREEN GRASS INC
Also Called: River Ridge Golf Club
2401 W Vineyard Ave, Oxnard (93036-2218)
PHONE..................................805 981-8722
Carl Kanny, *President*
John Kanny, *Vice Pres*
Otto Kanny, *Vice Pres*
EMP: 50 EST: 1993
SQ FT: 27,000
SALES (est): 1.9MM **Privately Held**
WEB: www.riverridge-golfclub.com
SIC: 7992 5812 Public golf courses; snack bar

(P-19496)
LAKESIDE GOLF CLUB
4500 W Lakeside Dr, Burbank (91505-4088)
P.O. Box 2386, Toluca Lake (91610-0386)
PHONE..................................818 984-0601
Jerry Fard, *Manager*
Michael E Henry, *CEO*
James Baker, *General Mgr*
Hans Telleson, *Engineer*
Isabel Cruz, *Controller*
EMP: 98 EST: 1924
SQ FT: 25,000
SALES (est): 11.4MM **Privately Held**
WEB: www.lakesidegolfclub.com
SIC: 7992 Public golf courses

(P-19497)
LOS SERRANOS GOLF CLUB
Also Called: Los Serranos Golf & Cntry CLB
15656 Yorba Ave, Chino Hills (91709-3129)
PHONE..................................909 597-1769
John A Kramer Jr, *CEO*
Gloria Kramer, *Shareholder*
John A Kramer Sr, *President*
David Kramer, *Treasurer*
Ronald Kramer, *Vice Pres*
EMP: 135 EST: 1953
SQ FT: 41,896
SALES (est): 6.6MM **Privately Held**
WEB: www.losserranoscountryclub.com
SIC: 7992 5812 5813 Public golf courses; American restaurant; snack shop; cocktail lounge

(P-19498)
MADISON CLUB OWNERS ASSN
Also Called: Madison Club, The
53035 Meriwether Way, La Quinta (92253-5535)
P.O. Box 1558 (92247-1558)
PHONE..................................760 777-9320
Douglas Siebold, *CEO*
Brian Ellis, *Principal*
EMP: 125 EST: 2006
SQ FT: 70,000
SALES (est): 10.6MM
SALES (corp-wide): 567.4MM **Privately Held**
WEB: www.madisonclubca.com
SIC: 7992 Public golf courses
PA: Discovery Land Company, Llc
14605 N 73rd St
Scottsdale AZ 85260
480 624-5200

(P-19499)
MCMILLIN COMMUNITIES INC
Also Called: Temeku Hills
41687 Temeku Dr, Temecula (92591-3909)
PHONE..................................951 506-3303
Sonia Howard, *Branch Mgr*
EMP: 174
SALES (corp-wide): 45.3MM **Privately Held**
WEB: www.mcmillin.com
SIC: 7992 Public golf courses
PA: Mcmillin Communities, Inc.
2750 Womble Rd Ste 102
San Diego CA 92106
619 477-4117

(P-19500)
MESA VERDE PARTNERS
Also Called: Costa Mesa Country Club
1701 Golf Course Dr, Costa Mesa (92626-5049)
PHONE..................................714 540-7500
Scott Henderson, *Partner*
EMP: 120 EST: 1992
SQ FT: 12,000
SALES (est): 2MM
SALES (corp-wide): 10.8MM **Privately Held**
WEB: www.costamesacountryclub.com
SIC: 7992 7997 5813 5812 Public golf courses; membership sports & recreation clubs; drinking places; eating places
PA: Santa Anita Associates
405 S Santa Anita Ave
Arcadia CA 91006
626 447-2764

(P-19501)
MILE SQUARE GOLF COURSE
10401 Warner Ave, Fountain Valley (92708-1604)
PHONE..................................714 962-5541
David A Rainville, *Partner*
EMP: 109 EST: 1969
SQ FT: 12,000
SALES (est): 5.4MM **Privately Held**
WEB: www.milesquaregolfcourse.com
SIC: 7992 7999 5812 Public golf courses; golf driving range; American restaurant

(P-19502)
MONARCH BEACH GOLF LINKS (HQ)
50 Monarch Beach Resort N, Dana Point (92629-4084)
PHONE..................................949 240-8247
Hale Kelly, *Director*
Katy Gorelick, *Manager*
Ryan Sheffer, *Manager*
EMP: 80 EST: 1983
SALES (est): 15MM **Privately Held**
WEB: www.monarchbeachgolf.com
SIC: 7992 Public golf courses

(P-19503)
PALMS GOLF CLUB INC
57000 Palms Dr, La Quinta (92253-8767)
P.O. Box 29 (92247-0029)
PHONE..................................760 771-2606
JD Eberbsberger, *President*
J D Ebersberger, *Director*
▲ EMP: 55 EST: 1997
SALES (est): 2.7MM **Privately Held**
WEB: www.thepalmsgc.org
SIC: 7992 Public golf courses

(P-19504)
QUARRY AT LA QUINTA INC (PA)
41865 Boardwalk Ste 214, Palm Desert (92211-9033)
PHONE..................................760 777-1100
William Morrow, *President*
EMP: 60 EST: 1993
SALES (est): 5.5MM **Privately Held**
WEB: www.thequarrygc.com
SIC: 7992 Public golf courses

(P-19505)
RANCHO VISTA DEVELOPMENT CO
Also Called: Rancho Vista Golf Course
3905 Club Rancho Dr, Palmdale (93551-5334)
PHONE..................................661 272-9082
Mark Frugal, *Branch Mgr*

Mark Fragale, *General Mgr*
Jonathan Hand, *Director*
Brianne Harding, *Manager*
Ellena Paterson, *Manager*
EMP: 60
SALES (corp-wide): 4.6MM **Privately Held**
WEB: www.ranchovistagolfclub.com
SIC: 7992 5941 Public golf courses; golf goods & equipment
PA: Rancho Vista Development Co
3011 Rancho Vista Blvd
Palmdale CA 93551
661 266-9785

(P-19506)
SAN JUAN GOLF INC
Also Called: San Juan Hill Country Club
32120 San Juan Creek Rd, San Juan Capistrano (92675-3840)
PHONE..................................949 493-1167
Tony Kato, *President*
Mike Abee, *General Mgr*
Christian Pierre, *Opers Staff*
Stacey Strausbaugh, *Director*
Michelle Roberts, *Supervisor*
EMP: 77 EST: 1994
SALES (est): 2.9MM **Privately Held**
WEB: www.sanjuanhillsgolf.com
SIC: 7992 5812 5941 Public golf courses; eating places; golf goods & equipment

(P-19507)
SANDPIPER GOLF TRUST LLC
Also Called: Sandpiper Golf Course
7925 Hollister Ave, Goleta (93117-2421)
PHONE..................................805 968-1541
Ty Warner, *Owner*
Carson Franzman, *Sales Staff*
Albert Corral, *Assistant*
EMP: 73 EST: 1998
SQ FT: 3,000
SALES (est): 3.8MM **Privately Held**
SIC: 7992 5812 Public golf courses; grills (eating places)

(P-19508)
SANTA ANITA ASSOCIATES (PA)
Also Called: Santa Anita Golf Course
405 S Santa Anita Ave, Arcadia (91006-3509)
PHONE..................................626 447-2764
Scott L Henderson, *Managing Prtnr*
Mike Donavan, *Partner*
EMP: 60 EST: 1986
SQ FT: 16,000
SALES (est): 10.8MM **Privately Held**
WEB: www.santaanitagc.com
SIC: 7992 5812 7999 7299 Public golf courses; American restaurant; golf cart, power, rental; golf driving range; banquet hall facilities

(P-19509)
SILVER ROCK RESORT GOLF CLUB
79179 Ahmanson Ln, La Quinta (92253-5715)
PHONE..................................760 777-8884
EMP: 100 EST: 2005
SALES (est): 10.2MM
SALES (corp-wide): 76MM **Privately Held**
WEB: www.silverrock.org
SIC: 7992 Public golf courses
PA: City Of La Quinta
78495 Calle Tampico
La Quinta CA 92253
760 777-7000

(P-19510)
STRAWBERRY FARMS GOLF CLUB LLC
11 Strawberry Farm Rd, Irvine (92612-2300)
PHONE..................................949 551-2560
Doug Decinese,
Patti Ross, *General Mgr*
EMP: 115 EST: 1997
SALES (est): 2.3MM **Privately Held**
WEB: www.sf-golf.com
SIC: 7992 Public golf courses

PRODUCTS & SVCS

(P-19511)
TRILOGY GOLF AT LA QUINTA
60151 Trilogy Pkwy, La Quinta
(92253-7640)
PHONE....................760 771-0707
Tom Williams, *Manager*
Ralph Bernhisel, *General Mgr*
Marge Deschaak, *Office Admin*
EMP: 185 **EST:** 2004
SALES (est): 4.1MM
SALES (corp-wide): 2.1B **Privately Held**
WEB: www.coralmountaingolfclub.com
SIC: 7992 Public golf courses
HQ: J.F. Shea Construction, Inc.
  655 Brea Canyon Rd
  Walnut CA 91789
  909 594-9500

(P-19512)
WON & JAY INC
Also Called: Talega Golf Club
990 Avenida Talega, San Clemente
(92673-6849)
PHONE....................949 369-6226
Won Sik Cho, *President*
Alex An, *Controller*
Jesse Pacheco, *Superintendent*
EMP: 50 **EST:** 2008
SALES (est): 3.1MM **Privately Held**
WEB: www.talegagolfclub.com
SIC: 7992 Public golf courses

7993 Coin-Operated Amusement Devices & Arcades

(P-19513)
PLAYERS WEST AMUSEMENTS INC (PA)
Also Called: Toy Barn
2360 Sturgis Rd Ste A, Oxnard
(93030-8956)
PHONE....................805 983-1400
Jack G Mann, *President*
Sylvester Mack, *CIO*
▲ **EMP:** 109 **EST:** 1991
SALES (est): 3.8MM **Privately Held**
WEB: www.toybarn.com
SIC: 7993 5092 3942 Amusement machine rental, coin-operated; toys & hobby goods & supplies; amusement goods; dolls & stuffed toys; stuffed toys, including animals

(P-19514)
THATGAMECOMPANY INC
Also Called: VIDEO GAME
1520 Cloverfield Blvd D, Santa Monica
(90404-5563)
PHONE....................310 453-4906
Jenova Chen, *CEO*
Nancy Bautista, *Manager*
Yui Tanabe, *Manager*
EMP: 50 **EST:** 2006
SALES (est): 5.1MM **Privately Held**
WEB: www.thatgamecompany.com
SIC: 7993 Video game arcade

(P-19515)
US ARCADES LLC (PA)
11684 Ventura Blvd, Studio City
(91604-2699)
PHONE....................818 888-8738
EMP: 54 **EST:** 2016
SALES (est): 542.2K **Privately Held**
SIC: 7993 Arcades

7996 Amusement Parks

(P-19516)
CASINO MORONGO
49500 Seminole Dr, Cabazon
(92230-2202)
P.O. Box 366 (92230-0366)
PHONE....................951 849-3080
Gene Stachowksi, *Principal*
Koehler Daniel, *Training Super*
EMP: 57
SALES (est): 5MM **Privately Held**
WEB: www.morongocasinoresort.com
SIC: 7996 Amusement parks

(P-19517)
DISNEYLAND INTERNATIONAL (DH)
1313 S Harbor Blvd, Anaheim
(92802-2309)
PHONE....................714 781-4565
James Thomas, *President*
James Cora, *Ch of Bd*
Robert S Risteen, *Treasurer*
Laura Nathanson, *Exec VP*
Lori Cohen-Elias, *Vice Pres*
EMP: 200 **EST:** 1961
SALES (est): 260.4MM
SALES (corp-wide): 65.3B **Publicly Held**
WEB: www.disneyland.disney.go.com
SIC: 7996 Theme park, amusement
HQ: Disney Enterprises, Inc.
  500 S Buena Vista St
  Burbank CA 91521
  818 560-1000

(P-19518)
KNOTTS BERRY FARM LLC (HQ)
Also Called: Knott's Berry Farm
8039 Beach Blvd, Buena Park
(90620-3225)
P.O. Box 5002 (90622-5002)
PHONE....................714 827-1776
Jack Falfas, *Partner*
Larry Daniel, *Vice Pres*
Jeff Gahagan, *Vice Pres*
Raffi Kaprelyan, *Vice Pres*
Kent Maulsby, *Vice Pres*
▲ **EMP:** 500 **EST:** 1920
SQ FT: 5,000
SALES (est): 49.5MM
SALES (corp-wide): 181.5MM **Publicly Held**
WEB: www.knotts.com
SIC: 7996 Theme park, amusement
PA: Cedar Fair, L.P.
  1 Cedar Point Dr
  Sandusky OH 44870
  419 626-0830

(P-19519)
MALIBU CASTLE
27061 Aliso Creek Rd # 100, Aliso Viejo
(92656-5322)
PHONE....................210 341-6663
EMP: 50
SQ FT: 6,980
SALES (est): 3.1MM **Privately Held**
SIC: 7996 Amusement Park
HQ: Festival Fun Parks, Llc
  4590 Macarthur Blvd # 400
  Newport Beach CA 92660
  949 261-0404

(P-19520)
MOUNTASIA FAMILY FUN CENTER
21516 Golden Triangle Rd, Santa Clarita
(91350-2612)
PHONE....................661 253-4386
EMP: 60
SQ FT: 22,000
SALES (est): 2.4MM **Privately Held**
WEB: www.mountasiafuncenter.com
SIC: 7996 Amusement Park
PA: Mb2 Raceway, Inc.
  13943 Balboa Blvd
  Sylmar CA 91342

(P-19521)
MULLIGAN LIMITED (PA)
Also Called: Mulligan Family Fun Center
1801 S Catalina Ave # 306, Redondo Beach (90277-5513)
PHONE....................714 484-6799
Rob Thomas, *Principal*
Georgia Claessens, *Partner*
EMP: 58 **EST:** 1993
SALES (est): 10.2MM **Privately Held**
SIC: 7996 Amusement parks

(P-19522)
RAGING WATERS GROUP INC
111 Raging Waters Dr, San Dimas
(91773-3998)
PHONE....................909 802-2200
Randy Drew, *President*
Armando Pickett, *President*
Riley Villa, *President*
Mary Papadopoulos, *Chief Mktg Ofcr*
Christine Miller, *Officer*
EMP: 808 **EST:** 2000
SALES (est): 9.9MM
SALES (corp-wide): 53.9MM **Privately Held**
WEB: www.ragingwaters.com
SIC: 7996 Theme park, amusement
PA: Alfa Smartparks, Inc
  1 W Adams St Ste 200
  Jacksonville FL 32202
  904 358-1027

(P-19523)
RAVINE WATERPARK LLC
Also Called: Ravine Waterpark, The
2301 Airport Rd, Paso Robles
(93446-8549)
PHONE....................805 237-8500
James Walsh, *Principal*
Brett Butterfield, *Principal*
EMP: 205 **EST:** 2004
SALES (est): 5.9MM **Privately Held**
WEB: www.ravinewaterpark.com
SIC: 7996 Theme park, amusement

(P-19524)
SANTA MONICA AMUSEMENTS LLC
Also Called: Pacific Park
380 Santa Monica Pier, Santa Monica
(90401-3128)
PHONE....................310 451-9641
Mary Ann Powell, *CEO*
David Gillam, *CFO*
Jeff Klocke, *Vice Pres*
Dana Wyatt, *Opers Staff*
Nathan Smithson, *Marketing Staff*
EMP: 325 **EST:** 1992
SQ FT: 70,000
SALES (est): 21.7MM **Privately Held**
WEB: www.pacpark.com
SIC: 7996 Theme park, amusement

(P-19525)
WALT DISNEY COMPANY (PA)
500 S Buena Vista St, Burbank
(91521-0007)
PHONE....................818 560-1000
Robert A Chapek, *CEO*
Robert A Iger, *Ch of Bd*
Ayo Davis, *President*
K Madhavan, *President*
Christine M McCarthy, *CFO*
EMP: 22519 **EST:** 1923
SALES (est): 65.3B **Publicly Held**
WEB: www.thewaltdisneycompany.com
SIC: 7996 4841 Amusement parks; cable television services

7997 Membership Sports & Recreation Clubs

(P-19526)
1334 PARTNERS LP
Also Called: Manhattan Country Club
1330 Park View Ave, Manhattan Beach
(90266-3704)
PHONE....................310 546-5656
Keith Brackpool, *Partner*
Anne Wharton, *General Mgr*
Mark McGuire, *Director*
EMP: 100 **EST:** 1982
SQ FT: 80,000
SALES (est): 54.7K **Privately Held**
WEB: www.manhattanccc.com
SIC: 7997 6512 7991 5813 Country club, membership; commercial & industrial building operation; physical fitness facilities; drinking places; eating places

(P-19527)
ACADEMY SWIM CLUB
Also Called: Santa Clarita Swim Club
28079 Smyth Dr, Valencia (91355-4023)
PHONE....................661 702-8585
Nikki Miller, *President*
Jim Miller, *Vice Pres*
Dakota Miller, *Program Dir*
EMP: 55 **EST:** 2004
SALES (est): 642.8K **Privately Held**
WEB: www.swim4life.com
SIC: 7997 7999 Swimming club, membership; swimming instruction

(P-19528)
AGI HOLDING CORP (HQ)
Also Called: Affinity Group
2575 Vista Del Mar Dr, Ventura
(93001-3900)
P.O. Box 6888, Englewood CO (80155-6888)
PHONE....................805 667-4100
Mr Stephen Adams, *CEO*
Joe McAdams, *President*
Michael Schneider, *COO*
Mark Boggess, *CFO*
Ankur Gupta, *Principal*
◆ **EMP:** 960 **EST:** 1988
SQ FT: 74,000
SALES (est): 377.9MM **Privately Held**
WEB: www.coastresorts.com
SIC: 7997 2741 Membership sports & recreation clubs; directories: publishing & printing

(P-19529)
ALTA VISTA COUNTRY CLUB LLC
777 Alta Vista St, Placentia (92870-5101)
PHONE....................714 524-1591
Karl Reul, *Mng Member*
Ashley Knorr, *Marketing Staff*
Danielle Scarsone, *Sales Staff*
Ruby Juarez, *Manager*
Henry Templeton, *Manager*
EMP: 60 **EST:** 1998
SQ FT: 6,751,800
SALES (est): 2.9MM **Privately Held**
WEB: www.altavistacc.com
SIC: 7997 Country club, membership

(P-19530)
ALTADENA TOWN AND COUNTRY CLUB
2290 Country Club Dr, Altadena
(91001-3202)
PHONE....................626 345-9088
David Edens, *President*
Kelly Bash, *Office Mgr*
Stephanie Duran, *Manager*
Ashley Owens, *Manager*
EMP: 80
SQ FT: 50,000
SALES (est): 4MM **Privately Held**
WEB: www.altaclub.com
SIC: 7997 Country club, membership

(P-19531)
AMERICAN GOLF CORPORATION
Also Called: Desert Rose Golf Course
68311 Paseo Real, Cathedral City
(92234-6767)
PHONE....................702 431-2191
EMP: 78
SALES (corp-wide): 560.6MM **Privately Held**
SIC: 7997 7999 7992 Membership Sport/Recreation Club Amusement/Recreation Services Public Golf Course
PA: American Golf Corporation
  6080 Center Dr Ste 500
  Los Angeles CA 75231
  310 664-4000

(P-19532)
ANNANDALE GOLF CLUB
1 N San Rafael Ave, Pasadena
(91105-1299)
PHONE....................626 796-6125
Christoff Granger, *General Mgr*
Rebecca Bedrick, *Vice Pres*
Toni Crockett, *Admin Sec*
Susy Gorlach, *Human Res Dir*
Rene Morales, *Purch Agent*
EMP: 125
SQ FT: 10,000
SALES: 11.8MM **Privately Held**
WEB: www.annandalegolf.com
SIC: 7997 Golf club, membership

(P-19533)
ANTELOPE VLY CNTRY CLB IMPRV
39800 Country Club Dr, Palmdale
(93551-2970)
PHONE....................661 947-3142
Mark Range, *General Mgr*

EMP: 150 EST: 1952
SQ FT: 22,000
SALES (est): 6.5MM Privately Held
WEB: www.antelopevalleycountryclub.com
SIC: 7997 Country club, membership

(P-19534)
ARROWHEAD COUNTRY CLUB GOLF SP
Also Called: ARROWHEAD COUNTRY CLUB PRO SHO
3433 Parkside Dr, San Bernardino (92404-2499)
PHONE..................................909 882-1735
Scott Daniels, President
EMP: 51 EST: 1981
SQ FT: 3,000
SALES (est): 1.2MM Privately Held
WEB: www.arrowheadcc.org
SIC: 7997 Country club, membership

(P-19535)
BAKERSFIELD COUNTRY CLUB
4200 Country Club Dr, Bakersfield (93306-3700)
P.O. Box 6007 (93386-6007)
PHONE..................................661 871-4000
Jon Van Boening, President
Christy Solari, Controller
Eric Kuhn, Manager
EMP: 75 EST: 1948
SQ FT: 30,000
SALES: 5.5MM Privately Held
WEB: www.bakersfieldcountryclub.com
SIC: 7997 5812 5813 Country club, membership; eating places; bar (drinking places)

(P-19536)
BALBOA BAY CLUB INC (HQ)
1221 W Coast Hwy Ste 145, Newport Beach (92663-5092)
PHONE..................................949 645-5000
David Wooten, President
W D Ray, CEO
Sergio Pineda, Finance
Rachel Reitkopp,
Melanie Hertrick, Manager
EMP: 260 EST: 1948
SALES (est): 26.6MM
SALES (corp-wide): 47.3MM Privately Held
WEB: www.balboabayclub.com
SIC: 7997 7011 Country club, membership; resort hotel
PA: International Bay Clubs, Llc
1221 W Coast Hwy Ste 145
Newport Beach CA 92663
949 645-5000

(P-19537)
BALBOA YACHT CLUB
1801 Bayside Dr, Corona Del Mar (92625-1898)
PHONE..................................949 673-3515
Howard Ness, President
Martha Guzman, Controller
Katie Tinder, Director
Israel Castell, Manager
Gracie Kinder, Receptionist
EMP: 50 EST: 1924
SQ FT: 23,000
SALES (est): 7MM Privately Held
WEB: www.balboayachtclub.com
SIC: 7997 Yacht club, membership

(P-19538)
BEACH CLUB
201 Palisades Beach Rd, Santa Monica (90402-1401)
PHONE..................................310 395-3254
Gregg Patterson, Exec Dir
EMP: 60 EST: 1923
SQ FT: 35,000
SALES: 8.5MM Privately Held
WEB: www.thebc.org
SIC: 7997 5812 5813 Beach club, membership; eating places; bar (drinking places)

(P-19539)
BEAR CREEK GOLF CLUB INC
Also Called: Bear Creek Golf & Country Club
22640 Bear Creek Dr N, Murrieta (92562-3015)
PHONE..................................951 677-8621

Peter Hanson, General Mgr
Rich Gillete, President
Tim Gardner, Director
EMP: 94 EST: 1983
SQ FT: 28,000
SALES (est): 2.9MM Privately Held
WEB: www.bearcreekgc.com
SIC: 7997 7992 Golf club, membership; public golf courses

(P-19540)
BEL-AIR BAY CLUB LTD
16801 Pacific Coast Hwy, Pacific Palisades (90272-3399)
PHONE..................................310 230-4700
William Howard, CEO
Christine Kamps-Silver, Director
Mauricio Lopez, Director
Dale Porteous, Manager
EMP: 200
SQ FT: 7,500
SALES (est): 12MM Privately Held
WEB: www.belairbayclub.com
SIC: 7997 Membership sports & recreation clubs

(P-19541)
BEL-AIR COUNTRY CLUB
10768 Bellagio Rd, Los Angeles (90077-3799)
PHONE..................................310 472-9563
Joseph Wagner, General Mgr
Peter Best, CEO
Adam Fannon, CIO
Karen Decker, Human Res Mgr
Martha Gamez, Purch Dir
EMP: 140 EST: 1924
SQ FT: 10,000
SALES: 13.9MM Privately Held
WEB: www.bel-aircc.golf
SIC: 7997 5941 Country club, membership; golf goods & equipment

(P-19542)
BELLA COLLINA SAN CLEMENTE
200 Avenida La Pata, San Clemente (92673-6301)
PHONE..................................949 498-6604
Mark Freilich, Mng Member
Tom Frost, Principal
Dawn Chapman,
EMP: 80 EST: 2009
SALES (est): 2.5MM Privately Held
WEB: www.bellacollinasanclemente.com
SIC: 7997 Golf club, membership

(P-19543)
BELMONT ATHLETIC CLUB
4918 E 2nd St, Long Beach (90803-5318)
PHONE..................................562 438-3816
John Doyle, Partner
Bill Fraser, Ltd Ptnr
Patrick Gormley, Ltd Ptnr
Barry Miller, Ltd Ptnr
Joyce Pokstaff, Ltd Ptnr
EMP: 57 EST: 1980
SQ FT: 25,000
SALES (est): 5MM Privately Held
WEB: www.belmontathleticclub.com
SIC: 7997 7991 Racquetball club, membership; athletic club & gymnasiums, membership

(P-19544)
BERMUDA DUNES COUNTRY CLUB
42765 Adams St, Bermuda Dunes (92203-7937)
PHONE..................................760 360-2481
Ed Cooney, CEO
Steve Hubbard, President
Perry Dickey, COO
George Neidhardt, Treasurer
Leon Webrand, Vice Pres
EMP: 50 EST: 1965
SQ FT: 40,000
SALES (est): 4.5MM Privately Held
WEB: www.bermudadunescc.com
SIC: 7997 Country club, membership

(P-19545)
BIG CANYON COUNTRY CLUB
1 Big Canyon Dr, Newport Beach (92660-5299)
PHONE..................................949 644-5404

Donald Tippett, CEO
William Stamply, President
Barbara Griffith, CFO
Lisa Curlee, Comms Mgr
David Voorhees, General Mgr
EMP: 180 EST: 1971
SQ FT: 50,000
SALES (est): 22.5MM Privately Held
WEB: www.bigcanyoncc.org
SIC: 7997 Country club, membership

(P-19546)
BIGHORN GOLF CLUB CHARITIES
255 Palowet Dr, Palm Desert (92260-7311)
PHONE..................................760 773-2468
Carl T Cardinalli, President
Joe Curtis, Treasurer
Marilyn Gillespie, Administration
Martin Islas, Engineer
Carl Williams, Asst Director
EMP: 190 EST: 1990
SALES (est): 1.3MM Privately Held
WEB: www.bighorngolf.com
SIC: 7997 7992 Country club, membership; public golf courses

(P-19547)
BIRNAM WOOD GOLF CLUB (PA)
1941 E Valley Rd, Santa Barbara (93108-1427)
PHONE..................................805 969-2223
Robert Thornburgh, President
Michael-Mc Gardner, COO
Robert Trent Jones, Principal
ARI Kreisler, General Mgr
Tito Arriaza, Administration
EMP: 144 EST: 1967
SQ FT: 45,000
SALES (est): 13.1MM Privately Held
WEB: www.bwgc.net
SIC: 7997 7992 5812 Golf club, membership; public golf courses; eating places

(P-19548)
BOYS AND GIRLS CLUB
22450 Mulholland Hwy, Calabasas (91302-5180)
PHONE..................................818 225-8406
Natalie Gonzales, Director
EMP: 50 EST: 2016
SALES (est): 229.3K Privately Held
SIC: 7997 Membership sports & recreation clubs

(P-19549)
BRAEMAR COUNTRY CLUB INC
4001 Reseda Blvd, Tarzana (91356-5330)
P.O. Box 570217 (91357-0217)
PHONE..................................323 873-6880
Steven Held, Manager
EMP: 199 EST: 1959
SQ FT: 20,000
SALES (est): 14.8MM
SALES (corp-wide): 1B Privately Held
WEB: www.braemarclub.com
SIC: 7997 Country club, membership
HQ: Clubcorp Usa, Inc.
3030 Lyndon B Johnson Fwy
Dallas TX 75234
972 243-6191

(P-19550)
BRENTWOOD COUNTRY CLUB
590 S Burlingame Ave, Los Angeles (90049-4896)
PHONE..................................310 451-8011
Linda Briskman, President
Cindy Doherty, Buyer
Rosemary Bryan, Director
Patrick Casey, Director
Steve Cluett, Director
EMP: 120 EST: 2015
SALES (est): 14.1MM Privately Held
WEB: www.brentwoodcc.net
SIC: 7997 7999 Country club, membership; golf services & professionals

(P-19551)
CALIFORNIA COUNTRY CLUB
Also Called: S R Mutual Funds
1509 Workman Mill Rd, City of Industry (90601-1499)
PHONE..................................626 333-4571
Will Bayer, General Mgr

Helen Bates, Executive
ARA Cho, Executive
Timothy Gore, General Mgr
Ted Parker, Director
EMP: 69 EST: 1956
SALES (est): 5MM Privately Held
WEB: www.golfccc.com
SIC: 7997 Country club, membership

(P-19552)
CANYON CREST COUNTRY CLUB INC
Also Called: Golf Pro Shop
975 Country Club Dr, Riverside (92506-3699)
PHONE..................................951 274-7900
Robert H Dedman, Ch of Bd
James Maser, Officer
Frank Gore, Exec VP
Richard S Poole, Exec VP
Sidney Simmons, Exec VP
EMP: 75 EST: 1967
SQ FT: 4,000
SALES (est): 7.9MM
SALES (corp-wide): 1B Privately Held
WEB: www.canyoncrestcc.com
SIC: 7997 5812 5813 Golf club, membership; American restaurant; bar (drinking places)
HQ: Clubcorp Usa, Inc.
3030 Lyndon B Johnson Fwy
Dallas TX 75234
972 243-6191

(P-19553)
CF VALENCIA ARCIS LLC
Also Called: Valencia Country Club
27330 Tourney Rd, Valencia (91355-1806)
PHONE..................................661 254-4401
Matt Zuckerman, General Mgr
Deborah Turcios, Admin Asst
Lyon Lazare, Sales Staff
Molly Smith,
Alison Cady, Director
EMP: 57 EST: 2014
SALES (est): 7.5MM Privately Held
WEB: www.valenciagolfclub.com
SIC: 7997 Golf club, membership

(P-19554)
CHAPMAN GOLF DEVELOPMENT LLC
Also Called: Tradition Golf Club
78505 Avenue 52, La Quinta (92253-2802)
PHONE..................................760 564-8723
David Chapman, Mng Member
Al Castro, General Mgr
Julie Harris,
Donna Long,
Melissa Glazier, Director
EMP: 100 EST: 1999
SALES (est): 10.6MM Privately Held
SIC: 7997 Golf club, membership

(P-19555)
CLAREMONT TENNIS CLUB
Also Called: Claremont Club, The
1777 Monte Vista Ave, Claremont (91711-2916)
PHONE..................................909 625-9515
Michael G Alpert, President
Geoffrey Clark, Vice Pres
Natalie Levangie, Instructor
Sara White, Instructor
Cathleen Garner, Director
EMP: 200 EST: 1973
SQ FT: 40,000
SALES (est): 13.1MM Privately Held
WEB: www.claremontclub.com
SIC: 7997 7991 5812 Membership sports & recreation clubs; health club; eating places

(P-19556)
COMEDY CLUB OXNARD LLC
Also Called: Levity Live
591 Collection Blvd, Oxnard (93036-5454)
PHONE..................................805 535-5400
Alireza Ghaemian, Principal
EMP: 88 EST: 2015
SALES (est): 1MM Privately Held
SIC: 7997 Membership sports & recreation clubs

(P-19557)
DEL REY YACHT CLUB
13900 Palawan Way, Marina Del Rey
(90292-6294)
PHONE...................................310 823-4664
Ilona Fellows, *CEO*
EMP: 66 EST: 1954
SQ FT: 10,000
SALES (est): 8.9MM **Privately Held**
WEB: www.dryc.org
SIC: 7997 Yacht club, membership

(P-19558)
DESERT FALLS COUNTRY CLUB INC
1111 Desert Falls Pkwy, Palm Desert
(92211-1709)
PHONE...................................760 340-5646
Tim Scogan, *President*
EMP: 66 EST: 1994
SALES (est): 3.1MM
SALES (corp-wide): 1B **Privately Held**
WEB: www.desert-falls.com
SIC: 7997 5812 7992 7299 Golf club,
  membership; eating places; public golf
  courses; banquet hall facilities
HQ: Clubcorp Usa, Inc.
  3030 Lyndon B Johnson Fwy
  Dallas TX 75234
  972 243-6191

(P-19559)
DESERT PRNCESS HM OWNERS CLB I
28555 Landau Blvd, Cathedral City
(92234-3508)
PHONE...................................760 322-1655
Lynn Gilliam, *President*
EMP: 50 EST: 1992
SALES (est): 1.5MM **Privately Held**
WEB: www.desertprincesscc.com
SIC: 7997 Country club, membership

(P-19560)
DHCCNP
Also Called: Desert Horizons Country Club
44900 Desert Horizons Dr, Indian Wells
(92210-7401)
PHONE...................................760 340-4646
Jurgen Gross, *Manager*
Al Castro, *General Mgr*
Janet Rodgers, *Controller*
Armida Trujillo, *Buyer*
Krista Simmons, *Director*
EMP: 86 EST: 1979
SQ FT: 30,000
SALES (est): 4.4MM **Privately Held**
WEB: www.deserthorizons.org
SIC: 7997 7992 5812 Country club, mem-
  bership; public golf courses; eating places

(P-19561)
EL CABALLERO COUNTRY CLUB
18300 Tarzana Dr, Tarzana (91356-4216)
PHONE...................................818 654-3000
Bary West, *President*
Phil Lopez, *COO*
Kristin Charness, *CFO*
Peter Jimenez, *CFO*
Gary Diamond, *Treasurer*
EMP: 125 EST: 1956
SQ FT: 20,000
SALES (est): 9.3MM **Privately Held**
WEB: www.elcaballerocc.com
SIC: 7997 7992 5812 Country club, mem-
  bership; public golf courses; eating places

(P-19562)
ELDORADO COUNTRY CLUB
46000 Fairway Dr, Indian Wells
(92210-8631)
PHONE...................................760 346-8081
Geoff Hasley, *President*
Pamela Jaymes, *Controller*
Maria Cintron, *Human Res Mgr*
Jesse Badillo, *Director*
Terry Beardsley, *Director*
EMP: 200 EST: 1959
SQ FT: 50,000
SALES (est): 15.4MM **Privately Held**
WEB: www.eldoradocc.com
SIC: 7997 5812 Golf club, membership;
  eating places

(P-19563)
FRIENDLY HLLS CNTRY CLB FNDTIO
8500 Villaverde Dr, Whittier (90605-1342)
PHONE...................................562 698-0331
Dave Goodrich, *COO*
Russ Onizuka, *General Mgr*
Brittany Kuramoto, *Sales Staff*
Nicole Yasui, *Sales Staff*
Chris Banner, *Director*
EMP: 110 EST: 1969
SQ FT: 42,000
SALES (est): 4.5MM **Privately Held**
WEB: www.friendlyhillscc.com
SIC: 7997 Country club, membership

(P-19564)
GLENDORA COUNTRY CLUB
2400 Country Club Dr, Glendora (91741)
PHONE...................................626 335-4051
Jack Stoughton, *CEO*
Mike Kerstetter, *President*
Jim Leahy, *CEO*
Bill McKinley, *Treasurer*
Arthur Barajas, *General Mgr*
EMP: 90
SQ FT: 10,000
SALES (est): 5.2MM **Privately Held**
WEB: www.glendoracountryclub.com
SIC: 7997 5812 5813 Country club, mem-
  bership; eating places; drinking places

(P-19565)
GOLF INVESTMENT LLC (PA)
200 Avenida La Pata, San Clemente
(92673-6301)
PHONE...................................949 498-6604
Shahin Vosough,
EMP: 60 EST: 2002
SQ FT: 42,250
SALES (est): 2.7MM **Privately Held**
SIC: 7997 7992 Golf club, membership;
  public golf courses

(P-19566)
HACIENDA GOLF CLUB
718 East Rd, La Habra Heights
(90631-8155)
PHONE...................................562 694-1081
Frank Cordeiro, *General Mgr*
Lane Greenlee, *CFO*
Veronica Barajas, *Admin Asst*
Carina Najera, *Controller*
EMP: 95 EST: 1919
SQ FT: 30,000
SALES: 6.5MM **Privately Held**
WEB: www.haciendagolfclub.com
SIC: 7997 5812 5813 Golf club, member-
  ship; American restaurant; bar (drinking
  places)

(P-19567)
HIDEAWAY CLUB
80440 Hideaway Club Ct, La Quinta
(92253-7867)
P.O. Box 1540 (92247-1540)
PHONE...................................760 777-7400
Brian J Ellis, *CEO*
EMP: 527 EST: 2015
SALES (est): 18MM
SALES (corp-wide): 567.4MM **Privately
Held**
WEB: www.hideawaygolfclub.com
SIC: 7997 6531 Membership sports &
  recreation clubs; real estate agents &
  managers
PA: Discovery Land Company, Llc
  14605 N 73rd St
  Scottsdale AZ 85260
  480 624-5200

(P-19568)
HILLCREST COUNTRY CLUB
10000 W Pico Blvd, Los Angeles
(90064-3400)
PHONE...................................310 553-8911
John Jameson, *President*
John Goldsmith, *CEO*
Tom Dreifus, *CFO*
Tom Driefus, *CFO*
Chester Firestien, *Principal*
EMP: 180 EST: 1920
SQ FT: 69,081
SALES: 22.1MM **Privately Held**
WEB: www.hcc-la.com
SIC: 7997 Country club, membership

(P-19569)
INDIAN WELLS COUNTRY CLUB INC
46000 Club Dr, Indian Wells (92210-8870)
PHONE...................................760 345-2561
Gabe Codding, *General Mgr*
James Hinckley, *President*
Jack Lupton, *Treasurer*
Douglas Howe, *Exec VP*
Erin Dougherty, *General Mgr*
EMP: 60 EST: 1956
SQ FT: 65,000
SALES (est): 6.6MM
SALES (corp-wide): 1B **Privately Held**
WEB: www.indianwellsclub.com
SIC: 7997 Country club, membership
HQ: Clubcorp Usa, Inc.
  3030 Lyndon B Johnson Fwy
  Dallas TX 75234
  972 243-6191

(P-19570)
INTERNATIONAL BAY CLUBS LLC (PA)
Also Called: Balboa Bay Club and Resort
1221 W Coast Hwy Ste 145, Newport
Beach (92663-5037)
PHONE...................................949 645-5000
Todd M Pickup, *CEO*
David Wooten, *President*
Nicole Coleman, *Natl Sales Mgr*
Danielle Kangas, *Sales Mgr*
Paul Voita, *Sales Mgr*
EMP: 195 EST: 1948
SQ FT: 330,000
SALES (est): 47.3MM **Privately Held**
WEB: www.balboabayclub.com
SIC: 7997 4493 6552 7011 Country club,
  membership; marinas; land subdividers &
  developers; residential; hotels & motels

(P-19571)
JACK KRAMER CLUB
11 Montecillo Dr, Rllng HLS Est
(90274-4297)
PHONE...................................310 326-4404
Craig Purcell, *General Mgr*
Connie Spencer, *President*
Bruce Ostermann, *General Mgr*
Amanda Romero, *Manager*
EMP: 50 EST: 1957
SQ FT: 4,000
SALES (est): 3.6MM **Privately Held**
WEB: www.jackkramerclub.com
SIC: 7997 5941 5812 7999 Tennis club,
  membership; swimming club, member-
  ship; tennis goods & equipment; snack
  bar; swimming instruction; aerobic dance
  & exercise classes

(P-19572)
JONATHAN CLUB
Also Called: Jonathan Beach Club
850 Palisades Beach Rd, Santa Monica
(90403-1008)
PHONE...................................310 393-9245
Ernie Dunn, *Manager*
Matthew Allnatt, *General Mgr*
Julio Portillo, *Buyer*
Heidi Llovet, *Nutritionist*
Ivet Vargas,
EMP: 100
SQ FT: 12,784
SALES (corp-wide): 39.4MM **Privately
Held**
WEB: www.jc.org
SIC: 7997 5812 8641 Beach club, mem-
  bership; grills (eating places); civic social
  & fraternal associations
PA: Jonathan Club
  545 S Figueroa St
  Los Angeles CA 90071
  213 624-0881

(P-19573)
KNIGHT-CALABASAS LLC (PA)
Also Called: Calabasas Country Club
4515 Park Entrada, Calabasas
(91302-1453)
PHONE...................................818 222-3200
Mike Calabassas,
Greg Elowe, *CFO*
Robert W Linn, *General Mgr*
Pam Lydon, *Accounting Mgr*
Karen Seidman, *Controller*
EMP: 51 EST: 1973

SQ FT: 2,000
SALES (est): 10.7MM **Privately Held**
WEB: www.calabasasgolf.com
SIC: 7997 Country club, membership

(P-19574)
LA CANADA FLINTRIDGE CNTRY CLB
5500 Godbey Dr, La Canada (91011-1836)
PHONE...................................818 790-0611
Gilbert Dreyfus, *President*
Shi Wang, *CFO*
Evelyn Dreyfus, *Admin Sec*
Victor Ortega, *Controller*
Nicole Martinez, *Sales Staff*
EMP: 80 EST: 1977
SQ FT: 24,000
SALES (est): 6MM **Privately Held**
WEB: www.lcfcountryclub.com
SIC: 7997 Country club, membership

(P-19575)
LA CUMBRE COUNTRY CLUB
4015 Via Laguna, Santa Barbara
(93110-2298)
PHONE...................................805 687-2421
Brian Bahman, *General Mgr*
Pam Grossman,
Karen Webb, *Director*
EMP: 100 EST: 1956
SQ FT: 8,000
SALES (est): 7.9MM **Privately Held**
WEB: www.lacumbrecc.org
SIC: 7997 Country club, membership

(P-19576)
LA QUINTA COUNTRY CLUB
77750 Avenue 50, La Quinta (92253-2204)
PHONE...................................760 564-4151
Ernest Moore, *CFO*
Bruce Zahn, *COO*
Teresa Windsor, *Controller*
Lynn Reehl, *Buyer*
Kelly O 'day, *Director*
EMP: 55 EST: 1959
SQ FT: 36,000
SALES: 6.9MM **Privately Held**
WEB: www.lqcc.org
SIC: 7997 Country club, membership

(P-19577)
LAKES COUNTRY CLUB ASSN INC (PA)
Also Called: Lakes Country Club, The
161 Old Ranch Rd, Palm Desert
(92211-3211)
PHONE...................................760 568-4321
Gerald Lee Hagood, *President*
Sandy Seddon, *COO*
Ron Phipps, *CFO*
Frank Melon, *Principal*
Ken Limes, *General Mgr*
EMP: 299 EST: 1982
SQ FT: 3,600
SALES (est): 14.3MM **Privately Held**
WEB: www.thelakescc.com
SIC: 7997 5941 5812 Country club, mem-
  bership; sporting goods & bicycle shops;
  eating places

(P-19578)
LAS POSAS COUNTRY CLUB
Also Called: Lpcc
955 Fairway Dr, Camarillo (93010-8499)
PHONE...................................805 482-4518
Sandy McNolty, *Controller*
Charles Burns, *CEO*
Thomas Walling, *CEO*
Dena Levy, *Principal*
Todd Keefer, *General Mgr*
EMP: 100 EST: 1957
SALES: 4.8MM **Privately Held**
WEB: www.lasposascc.com
SIC: 7997 7992 5812 0781 Country club,
  membership; tennis club, membership;
  public golf courses; eating places; land-
  scape counseling & planning

(P-19579)
LEVITY OF BREA LLC
180 S Brea Blvd, Brea (92821-4989)
PHONE...................................714 482-0700
Alireza Ghaemian, *Principal*
EMP: 92 EST: 2015

SALES (est): 1.9MM **Privately Held**
WEB: www.improv.com
SIC: **5813** 7997 5812 Bars & lounges; membership sports & recreation clubs; buffet (eating places)

(P-19580)
LONG BEACH YACHT CLUB
6201 E Appian Way, Long Beach (90803-4199)
PHONE...................................562 598-9401
Louis Izurieta, *General Mgr*
Robert Frazer, *Ch of Bd*
Matthew Williston, *Executive*
Louis Izurieta, *General Mgr*
Kim Eastwood, *Asst Controller*
EMP: 63
SQ FT: 25,000
SALES: 4.4MM **Privately Held**
WEB: www.lbyc.org
SIC: **7997** Yacht club, membership

(P-19581)
LOS ANGELES COUNTRY CLUB
10101 Wilshire Blvd, Los Angeles (90024-4703)
PHONE...................................310 276-6104
Kirk O Reese, *Principal*
Janet Welsh, *CFO*
James H Brewer, *General Mgr*
Shannon Dunne, *Executive Asst*
Jaime Flores, *Chief Engr*
EMP: 250 EST: 1898
SQ FT: 75,000
SALES: 17.6MM **Privately Held**
WEB: www.thelacc.org
SIC: **7997** Country club, membership; golf club, membership; tennis club, membership

(P-19582)
LOS ANGELES ORGANIZING
10900 Wilshire Blvd # 710, Los Angeles (90024-6515)
PHONE...................................310 407-0539
Casey Wasserman, *Chairman*
John Harper, *COO*
Brence Culp, *Officer*
Brian Nelson, *Officer*
Richard Barnes, *CIO*
EMP: 50
SALES: 17.7MM **Privately Held**
WEB: www.la28.org
SIC: **7997** Membership sports & recreation clubs

(P-19583)
LOS ANGELES RYAL VSTA GOLF CRSE
Also Called: Los Angles Ryal Vsta Golf Crse
20055 Colima Rd, Walnut (91789-3502)
PHONE...................................909 595-7441
Don Crooker, *Manager*
EMP: 74
SALES (corp-wide): 2.3MM **Privately Held**
SIC: **7997** 5941 Golf club, membership; country club, membership; golf goods & equipment
HQ: Los Angeles Royal Vista Golf Courses, Inc.
770 Kapiolani Blvd # 506
Honolulu HI 96813
808 592-4800

(P-19584)
MAGIC CASTLES INC
7001 Franklin Ave, Los Angeles (90028-8600)
PHONE...................................323 851-3313
Milton P Larsen, *CEO*
Ron Wilson, *President*
Emily Ruebl, *Executive Asst*
Bruce Cervon, *Admin Sec*
Michael Fogiel, *IT/INT Sup*
EMP: 100 EST: 1962
SQ FT: 20,000
SALES (est): 7.9MM **Privately Held**
WEB: www.magiccastle.com
SIC: **5812** 7997 7991 Eating places; membership sports & recreation clubs; physical fitness facilities

(P-19585)
MARBELLA COUNTRY CLUB
30800 Golf Club Dr, San Juan Capistrano (92675-5415)
PHONE...................................949 248-3700
Dan Riker, *Manager*
Ted Clark, *Treasurer*
Jeffrey Krifle, *General Mgr*
Phil Kempler, *Admin Sec*
EMP: 140 EST: 1993
SQ FT: 43,000
SALES (est): 2.7MM **Privately Held**
WEB: www.marbellacc.net
SIC: **7997** Country club, membership
PA: National Golf Properties Llc
2951 28th St Ste 3000
Santa Monica CA 90405

(P-19586)
MESA VERDE COUNTRY CLUB
3000 Club House Rd, Costa Mesa (92626-3599)
PHONE...................................714 549-0377
John Hayhoe, *CEO*
Robert Heflin, *President*
Jeremy Samson, *General Mgr*
Randy Myers, *CIO*
Michele Green, *Human Res Dir*
EMP: 125 EST: 1959
SQ FT: 34,000
SALES: 8.9MM **Privately Held**
WEB: www.mesaverdecc.com
SIC: **7997** Country club, membership

(P-19587)
MISSION HILLS COUNTRY CLUB INC
34600 Mission Hills Dr, Rancho Mirage (92270-1300)
PHONE...................................760 324-9400
Josh Tanner, *General Mgr*
Doug Howe, *Exec VP*
EMP: 130 EST: 1983
SQ FT: 75,000
SALES (est): 8.2MM
SALES (corp-wide): 1B **Privately Held**
WEB: www.missionhills.com
SIC: **7997** 7992 5812 Country club, membership; public golf courses; eating places
HQ: Clubcorp Usa, Inc.
3030 Lyndon B Johnson Fwy
Dallas TX 75234
972 243-6191

(P-19588)
MISSION VIEJO COUNTRY CLUB
26200 Country Club Dr, Mission Viejo (92691-5905)
PHONE...................................949 582-1550
Michael Lance Kennedy, *Mng Member*
Enrique Martinez, *Principal*
Chad Pettit, *Principal*
Veronica Alva Roman, *Accountant*
Andrew Slone, *Manager*
EMP: 103
SALES (est): 7.4MM **Privately Held**
WEB: www.missionviejocc.com
SIC: **7997** 7991 5812 7299 Country club, membership; physical fitness facilities; eating places; banquet hall facilities

(P-19589)
MONTECITO COUNTRY CLUB INC
920 Summit Rd, Santa Barbara (93108-2326)
P.O. Box 1170 (93102-1170)
PHONE...................................805 969-0800
Tai Warner, *President*
Hiro Suzuki, *General Mgr*
Johanna Dearinger,
EMP: 100 EST: 1921
SQ FT: 10,000
SALES (est): 9.7MM **Privately Held**
WEB: www.montecitoclub1918.com
SIC: **7997** 5812 5813 Country club, membership; eating places; bar (drinking places)
PA: Tsukamoto Corporation Co., Ltd.
1-6-5, Nihombashihoncho
Chuo-Ku TKY 103-0

(P-19590)
MOUNTAIN VIEW COUNTRY CLUB INC
80375 Pomelo, La Quinta (92253-8502)
PHONE...................................760 771-4311
Todd Connelly, *Manager*
Johnathan Curci, *Director*
EMP: 51 EST: 2004
SALES (est): 3.9MM **Privately Held**
WEB: www.mountainviewatlaquinta.com
SIC: **7997** Country club, membership

(P-19591)
NETBALL AMERICA INC
5101 Audrey Dr, Huntington Beach (92649-2404)
P.O. Box 11531, Westminster (92685-1531)
PHONE...................................888 221-3650
Sonya Ottaway, *President*
EMP: 50 EST: 2009
SALES (est): 596.6K **Privately Held**
WEB: www.netballamerica.com
SIC: **7997** Membership sports & recreation clubs

(P-19592)
NEWPORT BEACH COUNTRY CLUB INC
1 Clubhouse Dr, Newport Beach (92660-7107)
PHONE...................................949 644-9550
David Wooten, *President*
Gerald Johnson, *CFO*
Jerry Anderson, *Vice Pres*
EMP: 90 EST: 1985
SALES (est): 13.3MM
SALES (corp-wide): 47.3MM **Privately Held**
WEB: www.newportbeachcc.com
SIC: **7997** 7991 5941 5813 Country club, membership; physical fitness facilities; sporting goods & bicycle shops; drinking places; eating places
PA: International Bay Clubs, Llc
1221 W Coast Hwy Ste 145
Newport Beach CA 92663
949 645-5000

(P-19593)
NITRO CIRCUS LIVE USA INC
946 W 17th St, Costa Mesa (92627-4403)
PHONE...................................760 231-1840
Kurt Nicoll, *General Mgr*
Dave Mateus, *Senior VP*
Taylor Trip, *Vice Pres*
Ryan Casselman, *Executive Asst*
Joshua Geduld, *Graphic Designe*
▲ EMP: 75 EST: 2013
SALES (est): 14.8MM **Privately Held**
WEB: www.nitrocircus.com
SIC: **7997** Membership sports & recreation clubs
PA: Nitro Circus Live Pty Ltd
U 10a 2 Daydream St
Warriewood NSW 2102

(P-19594)
NORTH RANCH COUNTRY CLUB
4761 Valley Spring Dr, Westlake Village (91362-4399)
PHONE...................................818 889-3531
Mark Bagaaso, *CEO*
Scott London, *Treasurer*
Jenny Duce, *General Mgr*
Scott Miller, *CIO*
Westbrook Jonathan, *Controller*
EMP: 160 EST: 1976
SQ FT: 53,000
SALES (est): 14.8MM **Privately Held**
WEB: www.northranchcc.org
SIC: **7997** 5812 5941 Country club, membership; eating places; sporting goods & bicycle shops

(P-19595)
OAKMONT COUNTRY CLUB
3100 Country Club Dr, Glendale (91208-1799)
PHONE...................................818 542-4260
Pat Dahlson, *CEO*
John Schiller, *President*
Michael Hyler, *COO*
Logan Scott, *Instructor*

Matt McLean, *Director*
EMP: 125 EST: 1955
SQ FT: 37,000
SALES: 10.3MM **Privately Held**
WEB: www.oakmontcc.com
SIC: **7997** Country club, membership; golf club, membership; swimming club, membership

(P-19596)
OJAI VALLEY ATHLETIC CLUB
409 Fox St, Ojai (93023-3399)
PHONE...................................805 646-7213
Nancy Prather, *Exec Dir*
Shaena Strubing, *Managing Dir*
Ryan Gaston, *General Mgr*
Rosalinda Mendoza, *Opers Staff*
Malinda Chambers, *Instructor*
EMP: 53 EST: 1976
SQ FT: 3,000
SALES (est): 5MM **Privately Held**
WEB: www.ovac.caclubs.com
SIC: **7997** Tennis club, membership; swimming club, membership

(P-19597)
PACIFIC CLUB (PA)
4110 Macarthur Blvd, Newport Beach (92660-2012)
PHONE...................................949 955-1123
Joe Gatto, *President*
Ray Madro, *Controller*
Michelle Malegni, *Controller*
Karen Ringer,
Rick Cervantes, *Director*
EMP: 77
SQ FT: 28,000
SALES (est): 6.8MM **Privately Held**
WEB: www.pacficclub.org
SIC: **7997** 5812 5813 Country club, membership; bar (drinking places); eating places

(P-19598)
PALOS VERDES GOLF CLUB
Also Called: Palos Verdes Golf & Cntry CLB
3301 Via Campesina, Palos Verdes Estates (90274-1468)
PHONE...................................310 375-2759
Gerald Kouzmanoff, *CEO*
David Conforti, *General Mgr*
Steve Hockett, *General Mgr*
Jackie Ferguson, *Controller*
Janice Riscinto, *Controller*
EMP: 100 EST: 1967
SQ FT: 55,000
SALES: 11.3MM **Privately Held**
WEB: www.pvgc.com
SIC: **5813** 5941 7997 5812 Bar (drinking places); golf goods & equipment; golf club, membership; eating places; public golf courses

(P-19599)
PLANTATION GOLF CLUB INC
50994 Monroe St, Indio (92201-9709)
P.O. Box 1657, La Quinta (92247-1657)
PHONE...................................760 775-3688
Art Schillings, *General Mgr*
EMP: 62 EST: 1994
SQ FT: 16,000
SALES (est): 2.6MM **Privately Held**
WEB: www.theplantationgc.com
SIC: **7997** Golf club, membership

(P-19600)
PORTER VALLEY COUNTRY CLUB
Also Called: Porter Valley Catering
19216 Singing Hills Dr, Northridge (91326-1799)
PHONE...................................818 360-1071
Robert H Dedman, *Ch of Bd*
John Beckett, *President*
Doug Howe, *Exec VP*
EMP: 110 EST: 1966
SQ FT: 18,000
SALES (est): 7.3MM
SALES (corp-wide): 1B **Privately Held**
WEB: www.portervalley.com
SIC: **7997** 5812 5941 Golf club, membership; steak restaurant; sporting goods & bicycle shops

HQ: Clubcorp Usa, Inc.
3030 Lyndon B Johnson Fwy
Dallas TX 75234
972 243-6191

(P-19601)
PREMIER AQUATIC SERVICES LLC
6 Journey Ste 160, Aliso Viejo
(92656-5319)
PHONE..................949 716-3333
Daniel Berzansky, President
EMP: 57 EST: 2011
SALES (est): 3.5MM Privately Held
WEB: www.swimoc.com
SIC: 7997 Swimming club, membership

(P-19602)
RED HILL COUNTRY CLUB
8358 Red HI Cntry Clb Dr, Rancho Cucamonga (91730-1899)
PHONE..................909 982-1358
Rob Mocskley, President
Kimberly Bennett-Ross, Admin Asst
Rick Swartout, Technical Staff
Von San Luis, Superintendent
EMP: 92 EST: 1921
SQ FT: 20,000
SALES (est): 4.8MM Privately Held
WEB: www.redhillcc.com
SIC: 7997 5812 Country club, membership; eating places

(P-19603)
REDLANDS COUNTRY CLUB
1749 Garden St, Redlands (92373-7248)
PHONE (909) 793-2661
Scott Reding, President
Pamela Dvorak, Comms Dir
Jason Murphy, General Mgr
Erica Banda, Office Mgr
EMP: 80 EST: 1946
SQ FT: 22,000
SALES (est): 5.6MM Privately Held
WEB: www.redlandscountryclub.com
SIC: 7997 5812 5813 Country club, membership; snack shop; bar (drinking places)

(P-19604)
RESERVE CLUB
49400 Desert Butte Trl, Indian Wells
(92210-7075)
PHONE..................760 674-2222
Kenneth Novack, President
C Ted McCarter, Treasurer
EMP: 80 EST: 1998
SQ FT: 10,000
SALES (est): 8.8MM Privately Held
WEB: www.thereserveclub.com
SIC: 7997 Country club, membership

(P-19605)
ROSE BOWL AQUATICS CENTER
360 N Arroyo Blvd, Pasadena
(91103-3201)
PHONE..................626 564-0330
Judy Biggs, Exec Dir
Robert Kamins, Ch of Bd
Raymond Butner, Treasurer
Alison Laster, Vice Ch Bd
Daniel Leyson, Bd of Directors
EMP: 80 EST: 1992
SALES (est): 8MM Privately Held
WEB: www.rosebowlaquatics.org
SIC: 7997 Swimming club, membership

(P-19606)
SAN DIMAS GOLF INC
Also Called: Via Verde Country Club
1400 Avenida Entrada, San Dimas
(91773-4004)
PHONE..................909 599-8486
Kwan O Lee, President
Dal Eun Lee, Shareholder
Dal H Lee, Vice Pres
Dal K Lee, Admin Sec
EMP: 114 EST: 1975
SQ FT: 21,887
SALES (est): 1.2MM Privately Held
WEB: www.viaverdecc.com
SIC: 7997 Country club, membership

(P-19607)
SAN GABRIEL COUNTRY CLUB
350 E Hermosa Dr, San Gabriel
(91775-2346)
PHONE..................626 287-9671
Tom Dukes, President
Terry Deasy, Admin Sec
Debora Escobar, Director
Debora Sinclair, Director
Dylan Torcoletti, Director
EMP: 80 EST: 1904
SQ FT: 48,000
SALES (est): 9.2MM Privately Held
WEB: www.sangabrielcc.com
SIC: 7997 Country club, membership

(P-19608)
SAN LUIS OBISPO GOLF CNTRY CLB
Also Called: Slogcc
255 Country Club Dr, San Luis Obispo
(93401-8939)
PHONE..................805 543-3400
David Cole, President
Carol Kerwin, Admin Sec
Christopher Simpson, Manager
EMP: 110 EST: 1958
SQ FT: 10,000
SALES (est): 6.5MM Privately Held
WEB: www.slocountryclub.com
SIC: 7997 Country club, membership

(P-19609)
SANTA ANA COUNTRY CLUB
20382 Newport Blvd, Santa Ana
(92707-5396)
PHONE..................714 556-3000
Joseph J Wagner, CEO
Rob Tanaka, General Mgr
Justin Rocha, Chief Engr
Pamela Paulson, Director
Joseph Alberici, Manager
EMP: 100 EST: 1914
SALES (est): 10.1MM Privately Held
WEB: www.santaanacc.org
SIC: 7997 Country club, membership

(P-19610)
SATICOY COUNTRY CLUB
4450 Clubhouse Dr, Somis (93066-9798)
PHONE..................805 647-1153
Douglas Taxton, President
James R Van Wyck, CEO
Robert Nagelberg, General Mgr
Kathy Sube, Financial Exec
Gloria Slocum, Controller
EMP: 80 EST: 1921
SALES (est): 34.1K Privately Held
WEB: www.thesaticoyclub.com
SIC: 7997 Country club, membership; golf club, membership

(P-19611)
SEVEN OAKS COUNTRY CLUB
2000 Grand Lakes Ave, Bakersfield
(93311-2931)
P.O. Box 11165 (93389-1165)
PHONE..................661 664-6404
David H Murdock, CEO
Bruce Freeman, President
Don Ciota, General Mgr
Tasha Moon, Controller
Martha Lozada, Human Resources
EMP: 125 EST: 1991
SQ FT: 39,000
SALES (est): 14.7MM Privately Held
WEB: www.sevenoakscountryclub.com
SIC: 7997 Country club, membership

(P-19612)
SHADY CANYON GOLF CLUB INC
100 Shady Canyon Dr, Irvine (92603-0301)
PHONE..................949 856-7000
James T Wood, CEO
Thomas Heggi, President
Mike Brewer, Officer
Robert Leenhouts, Principal
Lloyd Gillespie, General Mgr
EMP: 117 EST: 2003
SALES: 269.4K Privately Held
WEB: www.shadycanyongolfclub.com
SIC: 7997 Country club, membership

(P-19613)
SHERWOOD COUNTRY CLUB
320 W Stafford Rd, Thousand Oaks
(91361-5087)
PHONE..................805 496-3036
Lance Fisher, General Mgr
Lenny Fisher, General Mgr
Melanie Kohagen, Executive Asst
Andrea Sidman, Admin Asst
Daryn Wood, Controller
EMP: 124 EST: 1989
SALES (est): 14.5MM Privately Held
WEB: www.sherwoodcc.com
SIC: 7997 Country club, membership

(P-19614)
SNOWBOUNDERS SKI CLUB
5402 Tattershall Ave, Westminster
(92683-3447)
PHONE..................714 892-4897
EMP: 80
SALES: 47.9K Privately Held
SIC: 7997 Membership Sport/Recreation Club

(P-19615)
SOUTH HILLS COUNTRY CLUB
2655 S Citrus St, West Covina
(91791-3405)
PHONE..................626 339-1231
James Wendoll, CEO
Chris Banner, General Mgr
Lynn Aparicio, Controller
Benita Bodnar, Manager
Joey Davis, Manager
EMP: 78 EST: 1852
SQ FT: 34,000
SALES (est): 4.6MM Privately Held
WEB: www.southhillscountryclub.org
SIC: 7997 5813 5812 Country club, membership; golf club, membership; bar (drinking places); American restaurant

(P-19616)
SPANISH HILLS CLUB LLC
999 Crestview Ave, Camarillo
(93010-7429)
PHONE..................805 388-5000
Alain O'Connor, Mng Member
EMP: 99
SALES (est): 263.2K Privately Held
SIC: 7997 Country club, membership

(P-19617)
SPANISH HILLS COUNTRY CLUB (PA)
999 Crestview Ave, Camarillo
(93010-8493)
PHONE..................805 389-1644
Joe Topper, President
Steve Thomas, CEO
Jacqui Kaplan, Controller
Grant Webster, Controller
Estella Arguelles, Human Resources
EMP: 150 EST: 1989
SQ FT: 42,000
SALES (est): 10MM Privately Held
WEB: www.thespanishhillsclub.com
SIC: 7997 Country club, membership

(P-19618)
SPRINGS CLUB INC
Also Called: SPRINGS COUNTRY CLUB, THE
1 Duke Dr, Rancho Mirage (92270-3647)
PHONE..................760 328-0254
Robert Middlemas, CEO
Rick Cabasal, COO
Daniel Cooper, COO
Richard Yehling, Officer
Ronda Allen, Principal
EMP: 65 EST: 1973
SQ FT: 36,000
SALES (est): 5MM Privately Held
WEB: www.club.thespringsrm.com
SIC: 7997 5812 5813 Golf club, membership; tennis club, membership; American restaurant; cocktail lounge

(P-19619)
STOCKDALE COUNTRY CLUB
7001 Stockdale Hwy, Bakersfield
(93309-1313)
P.O. Box 9727 (93389-9727)
PHONE..................661 832-0310
Sam Monroe, President

Michael Davis, CEO
Linda Voiland, Vice Pres
Susan Greer, General Mgr
Hank Pfister, Director
EMP: 100
SQ FT: 12,000
SALES: 6.7MM Privately Held
WEB: www.stockdalecc.com
SIC: 7997 Country club, membership

(P-19620)
SUNRISE CNTRY CLB RANCHO MRAGE
71601 Country Club Dr, Rancho Mirage
(92270-3598)
PHONE..................760 328-6549
Bill Athan, General Mgr
EMP: 63 EST: 1975
SQ FT: 15,000
SALES (est): 877.3K Privately Held
WEB: www.sunrisecountryclub.com
SIC: 7997 5812 5941 Country club, membership; American restaurant; golf, tennis & ski shops

(P-19621)
THE VALLEY CLUB OF MONTECITO
1901 E Valley Rd, Santa Barbara
(93108-1427)
PHONE..................805 969-2215
John S Degroot, CEO
Palmer Jackson, President
EMP: 50
SQ FT: 3,000
SALES: 7.5MM Privately Held
WEB: www.valleyclub.org
SIC: 7997 Golf club, membership

(P-19622)
THUNDERBIRD COUNTRY CLUB
70737 Country Club Dr, Rancho Mirage
(92270-3500)
P.O. Box 5005 (92270-1005)
PHONE..................760 328-2161
Brian Rice, CEO
Chris Olson, Executive
Michaell Crandall, General Mgr
David Shepler, General Mgr
Martha Martinez, Human Res Mgr
EMP: 60 EST: 1954
SQ FT: 30,000
SALES: 9.3MM Privately Held
WEB: www.thunderbirdcountryclub.com
SIC: 7997 5812 7011 Country club, membership; eating places; hotels & motels

(P-19623)
TOSCANA COUNTRY CLUB INC
76009 Via Club Villa, Indian Wells
(92210-7851)
PHONE..................760 404-1444
Paul K Levy, CEO
Rick Sall, Vice Pres
Lori Benavides, Office Mgr
Joseph Byrne, Engineer
Beth Hunter, Controller
EMP: 150 EST: 2004
SALES (est): 15.7MM Privately Held
WEB: www.toscanacc.com
SIC: 7997 Country club, membership

(P-19624)
TRADITION GOLF CLUB ASSOCIATES
78505 Avenue 52, La Quinta (92253-2802)
PHONE..................760 564-3355
David Champman, General Mgr
EMP: 82 EST: 1997
SALES (est): 699.8K Privately Held
WEB: www.traditiongc.com
SIC: 7997 Golf club, membership

(P-19625)
VINTAGE CLUB
75001 Vintage Dr W, Indian Wells
(92210-7304)
PHONE..................760 340-0500
John Buttemiller, Broker, Sales Staff
Marc D Ray, COO
Neal Hoffman, Officer
Diana Luna, Officer
Carol Daniels, Comms Dir
EMP: 90 EST: 1979
SQ FT: 86,000

▲ = Import ▼=Export
◆ =Import/Export

SALES: 25.6MM **Privately Held**
WEB: www.thevintageclub.com
SIC: 7997 5813 5812 5941 Country club, membership; bar (drinking places); American restaurant; golf goods & equipment; tennis services & professionals; real estate agents & managers

(P-19626)
VIRGINIA CNTRY CLB OF LONG BCH
4602 N Virginia Rd, Long Beach (90807-1999)
PHONE....................562 427-0924
Jamie Mulligan, *CEO*
Liz Sarkisyan, *Manager*
Barnuy Viloabas, *Asst Mgr*
EMP: 110 EST: 1909
SQ FT: 15,000
SALES: 6.7MM **Privately Held**
WEB: www.vcc1909.org
SIC: 7997 Country club, membership

(P-19627)
VISALIA COUNTRY CLUB
625 N Ranch St, Visalia (93291-4317)
P.O. Box 3410 (93278-3410)
PHONE....................559 734-3733
Steve Beargeon, *Principal*
Sharon Robison, *Vice Pres*
Dawn Kakutani, *Controller*
Jessica Alderete, *Director*
EMP: 80
SQ FT: 60,000
SALES: 4.5MM **Privately Held**
WEB: www.visaliacc.net
SIC: 7997 Country club, membership

(P-19628)
WILSHIRE COUNTRY CLUB
301 N Rossmore Ave, Los Angeles (90004-2499)
PHONE....................323 934-6050
Jeffrey Ornstein, *CEO*
Norman Branchflower, *President*
Todd Keefer, *COO*
Mirion Bowers MD, *Vice Pres*
Peter Jimenez, *Controller*
EMP: 94 EST: 1919
SQ FT: 50,000
SALES: 10.6MM **Privately Held**
WEB: www.wilshirecountryclub.com
SIC: 7997 5941 5812 Country club, membership; sporting goods & bicycle shops; eating places

---

7999 Amusement & Recreation Svcs, NEC

(P-19629)
29 PALMS ENTERPRISES CORP
Also Called: Spotlight 29 Casino
46200 Harrison Pl, Coachella (92236-2031)
PHONE....................760 775-5566
Darrel Mike, *President*
Michael Frawley, *COO*
Marcia R Martin, *CFO*
Gordon Howe, *MIS Staff*
Judy Maldonado, *Purchasing*
EMP: 600 EST: 1995
SQ FT: 70,000
SALES (est): 71.3MM **Privately Held**
WEB: www.spotlight29.com
SIC: 7999 5812 Gambling establishment; eating places

(P-19630)
3RD STREET BILLIARD CLUB INC
Also Called: Yankee Doodles
3111 Via Dolce Apt 403, Marina Del Rey (90292-5076)
PHONE....................310 434-1000
Fax: 310 576-7754
EMP: 85
SQ FT: 15,000
SALES (est): 2.6MM **Privately Held**
SIC: 5812 5813 7999 Eating Places

(P-19631)
ADVENTURE CITY INC
1238 S Beach Blvd, Anaheim (92804-4828)
PHONE....................714 821-3311
Allan Ansdell Jr, *President*
Yvonne Ansdell, *Treasurer*
Trina Ansdell, *Human Res Mgr*
EMP: 100 EST: 1992
SALES (est): 5.9MM **Privately Held**
WEB: www.adventurecity.com
SIC: 7999 7996 Tourist attractions, amusement park concessions & rides; amusement parks

(P-19632)
ALPINE CAMP CONFERENCE CTR INC
415 Clubhouse Dr, Blue Jay (92317)
P.O. Box 155 (92317-0155)
PHONE....................909 337-6287
Kim Polson, *Administration*
Anthony Xepolis, *President*
Joel Rude, *Principal*
John Gehrig, *Director*
EMP: 57 EST: 2015
SALES (est): 1.7MM **Privately Held**
WEB: www.alpine-cc.org
SIC: 7999 7032 Instruction schools, camps & services; youth camps

(P-19633)
APEX PARKS GROUP LLC
Also Called: Malibu Castle
27061 Aliso Creek Rd # 100, Aliso Viejo (92656-5322)
PHONE....................210 341-6663
EMP: 100
SALES (corp-wide): 39.9MM **Privately Held**
SIC: 7999 5599 Amusement/Recreation Services Ret Misc Vehicles
PA: Apex Parks Group, Llc
27061 Aliso Creek Rd # 100
Aliso Viejo CA 92612
949 349-8461

(P-19634)
ARIZONA CHANNEL ISLA
300 W 9th St, Oxnard (93030-7060)
PHONE....................480 788-0755
EMP: 75
SQ FT: 60,000
SALES (est): 282.9K **Privately Held**
SIC: 7999 Amusement And Recreation, Nec, Nsk

(P-19635)
AROMA SPA & SPORTS LLC
Also Called: Aroma Wilshire Center
3680 Wilshire Blvd # 301, Los Angeles (90010-2708)
PHONE....................213 387-2111
Byoung G Choi,
Chris Mader, *Officer*
Jae Whang, *Controller*
Keejune Huh,
EMP: 60 EST: 2000
SALES (est): 2.1MM **Privately Held**
WEB: www.aromaresort.com
SIC: 7999 7991 Recreation center; health club

(P-19636)
ARTISTS STUDIO GALLERY (PA)
550 Deep Valley Dr # 327, Rllng HLS Est (90274-3664)
PHONE....................310 265-2592
George Chirinian, *Principal*
EMP: 59 EST: 2001
SALES (est): 450K **Privately Held**
WEB: www.artists-studio-pvac.com
SIC: 7999 5947 Art gallery, commercial; artcraft & carvings

(P-19637)
BELL GARDENS BICYCLE CLUB INC
Also Called: Bicycle Club Casino
888 Bicycle Casino Dr, Bell Gardens (90201-7617)
PHONE....................562 806-4646
George Hardie, *President*
George G Hardie, *President*
Claire Markham, *Personnel Assit*

Onassis Yumul, *Marketing Staff*
EMP: 1300 EST: 1984
SQ FT: 110,000
SALES (est): 42.3MM **Privately Held**
WEB: www.thebike.com
SIC: 7999 5812 Card rooms; coffee shop

(P-19638)
CAHUILLA CREEK REST & CASINO
Also Called: Cahuilla Creek Casino
52702 Us Highway 371, Anza (92539-8707)
PHONE....................951 763-1200
Leonardo Pasquarelli, *General Mgr*
Jon Gregory, *General Mgr*
Susan Bellamy, *Mktg Dir*
Hoshi Henry, *Marketing Mgr*
Melissa Asmus, *Marketing Staff*
EMP: 103 EST: 1996
SQ FT: 14,000
SALES (est): 11.1MM **Privately Held**
WEB: www.cahuillacasinohotel.com
SIC: 7999 5812 5813 Gambling establishment; American restaurant; bar (drinking places); tavern (drinking places)

(P-19639)
CHUMASH CASINO RESORT (HQ)
3400 E Highway 246, Santa Ynez (93460-9405)
PHONE....................805 686-0855
Carol Clearwater, *CFO*
John Featherstone, *Executive*
John Martino, *Exec Dir*
William Peters, *General Mgr*
Juanita Castro, *Office Mgr*
EMP: 114 EST: 1994
SQ FT: 29,000
SALES (est): 140.7MM **Privately Held**
WEB: www.chumashcasino.com
SIC: 7999 7011 Gambling establishment; resort hotel

(P-19640)
CITY WIDE AQUATICS (PA)
Also Called: Dept of Recreation Parks Cy La
3900 Chevy Chase Dr, Los Angeles (90039-1221)
PHONE....................323 906-7953
John Mukri, *President*
EMP: 75 EST: 2002
SALES (est): 456K **Privately Held**
WEB: www.laparks.org
SIC: 7999 Swimming pool, non-membership

(P-19641)
CTOUR HOLIDAY LLC
222 E Huntington Dr # 221, Monrovia (91016-8014)
PHONE....................323 261-8811
Charlie Lu, *Mng Member*
Heidi Ju, *Controller*
EMP: 300 EST: 2016
SALES (est): 9.9MM **Privately Held**
WEB: www.ctourholiday.ca
SIC: 7999 Tour & guide services

(P-19642)
DESERT RECREATION DISTRICT (PA)
45305 Oasis St, Indio (92201-4337)
PHONE....................760 347-3484
Rudy Acosta, *President*
Joanne Gilbert, *COO*
Laura McGalliard, *Vice Pres*
Kevin Kalman, *General Mgr*
Delia Granados, *Admin Sec*
EMP: 54 EST: 1950
SQ FT: 40,000
SALES (est): 6MM **Privately Held**
WEB: www.myrecreationdistrict.com
SIC: 7999 Recreation center

(P-19643)
DISNEY REGIONAL ENTRMT INC (DH)
500 S Buena Vista St, Burbank (91521-0001)
PHONE....................818 560-1000
Arthur Levitt, *President*
Gary Marcotte, *CFO*
Laurie Mazar, *Opers Staff*

Joan Lane, *Ch Life Und*
EMP: 200 EST: 1996
SALES: 117.8MM
SALES (corp-wide): 65.3B **Publicly Held**
WEB: www.thewaltdisneycompany.com
SIC: 7999 5812 5813 Recreation center; eating places; drinking places

(P-19644)
DROPZONE WATERPARK
2165 Trumble Rd, Perris (92571-9211)
PHONE....................951 210-1600
Erica Bice, *Director*
EMP: 150 EST: 2014
SALES (est): 509.9K **Privately Held**
WEB: www.dropzonewaterpark.com
SIC: 7999 Recreation services

(P-19645)
EAST VALLEY TOURIST DEV AUTH
Also Called: Fantasy Springs Resort Casino
84245 Indio Springs Dr, Indio (92203-3405)
PHONE....................760 342-5000
John James, *Ch of Bd*
Angela Roosevelt, *Corp Secy*
Mark Benitez, *Vice Ch Bd*
Brenda Soulliere, *Vice Ch Bd*
Eric Amidei, *Officer*
EMP: 1200 EST: 1983
SQ FT: 94,000
SALES (est): 79.1MM **Privately Held**
SIC: 7999 Gambling establishment

(P-19646)
FAIRPLEX ENTERPRISES INC
1101 W Mckinley Ave, Pomona (91768-1650)
PHONE....................909 623-3111
James Henwood, *President*
Michelle Demott, *Vice Pres*
John Gilbert, *Vice Pres*
Judi Brooks, *Admin Asst*
Smaranda Fetila, *Comp Spec*
▲ EMP: 72 EST: 2011
SALES (est): 20.8MM
SALES (corp-wide): 66.3MM **Privately Held**
WEB: www.fairplex.com
SIC: 7999 Fair
PA: Los Angeles County Fair Association
1101 W Mckinley Ave
Pomona CA 91768
909 623-3111

(P-19647)
FAZE CLAN INC
7288 Mulholland Dr, Los Angeles (90068-2032)
PHONE....................818 538-5204
Lee Trink, *CEO*
Ben Sack, *CTO*
Tyler Rayne, *Info Tech Mgr*
EMP: 56 EST: 2016
SALES (est): 6.2MM **Privately Held**
WEB: www.fazeclan.com
SIC: 7999 5961 Games, instruction;

(P-19648)
FESTIVAL FUN PARKS LLC
Also Called: Boomers
4590 Macarthur Blvd # 400, Newport Beach (92660-2027)
PHONE....................954 921-1411
EMP: 150 **Privately Held**
SIC: 7999 Amusement Rides Go-Carts
HQ: Festival Fun Parks, Llc
4590 Macarthur Blvd # 400
Newport Beach CA 92660
949 261-0404

(P-19649)
FESTIVAL OF ARTS LAGUNA BEACH
650 Laguna Canyon Rd, Laguna Beach (92651-1899)
PHONE....................949 494-1145
Fredric Sattler, *CEO*
Gary Fowler, *COO*
Wayne Baglin, *Bd of Directors*
Tom Lamb, *Vice Pres*
David Perry, *Vice Pres*
EMP: 51 EST: 1934
SQ FT: 6,500

PRODUCTS & SVCS

SALES (est): 1MM **Privately Held**
WEB: www.foapom.com
SIC: 7999 Festival operation

(P-19650)
FORTISS LLC
1100 S Flower St Ste 3100, Los Angeles
(90015-2127)
PHONE.................................323 415-4900
John Park, *VP Pub Rel*
Kirk Newman, *Vice Pres*
Nicholas Grimshaw, *IT/INT Sup*
Anthony Arballo, *Payroll Mgr*
Lisa Grewohl, *Human Resources*
EMP: 68 EST: 2004
SALES (est): 9.5MM **Privately Held**
WEB: www.fortiss.com
SIC: 7999 Card & game services

(P-19651)
GLACIAL GARDEN INC (PA)
Also Called: Glacial Garden Skating Arena
3975 Pixie Ave, Lakewood (90712-4147)
PHONE.................................714 502-9029
Ronald R White, *President*
Pam King, *CFO*
Teri Taluto, *Treasurer*
Rose White, *Exec VP*
Laura Ellis, *Vice Pres*
EMP: 52 EST: 1992
SQ FT: 125,000
SALES (est): 2.7MM **Privately Held**
WEB: www.glacialgardens.com
SIC: 7999 7941 Ice skating rink operation;
sports field or stadium operator, promoting sports events

(P-19652)
HAPPY JUMP INC
9749 Independence Ave, Chatsworth
(91311-4318)
P.O. Box 1025, Sun Valley (91353-1025)
PHONE.................................818 886-3991
Roubik Amirian, *President*
Yolanda Beatriz Ibarra, *Administration*
▲ EMP: 13 EST: 2000
SALES (est): 7.6MM **Privately Held**
WEB: www.happyjump.com
SIC: 7999 3944 Festival operation;
games, toys & children's vehicles

(P-19653)
LAKE ELSINORE HOTEL & CASINO
Also Called: Lake Elsinore Resort & Casino
20930 Malaga Rd, Lake Elsinore
(92530-4508)
PHONE.................................951 674-3101
Ted Kingston, *Managing Prtnr*
Elden Kingston, *Partner*
Justin Jones, *Marketing Staff*
Ian Geering, *Director*
Pat Wilmes, *Manager*
▲ EMP: 102 EST: 1968
SALES (est): 16.2MM **Privately Held**
WEB: www.lercasino.com
SIC: 5812 5813 7999 7011 Eating
places; cocktail lounge; card rooms; hotels & motels

(P-19654)
LOS ANGELES COUNTY FAIR ASSN (PA)
Also Called: Fairplex Rv Park
1101 W Mckinley Ave, Pomona
(91768-1639)
PHONE.................................909 623-3111
Ronald Bolding, *Director*
Micheal Seder, *Vice Pres*
Tammy Roush, *Manager*
EMP: 100 EST: 1922
SALES (est): 66.3MM **Privately Held**
WEB: www.fairplex.com
SIC: 7999 8412 Fair; museums & art galleries

(P-19655)
MOUNT SAN JCNTO WINTER PK AUTH
1 Tramway Rd, Palm Springs
(92262-1827)
PHONE.................................760 325-1449
Nancy Nichols, *President*
Rob Parkins, *President*
Jim Whitmore, *COO*

Tara Meinkey, *CFO*
Marjorie Dela Cruz, *Vice Pres*
▲ EMP: 73
SQ FT: 50,000
SALES: 16.9MM **Privately Held**
WEB: www.pstramway.com
SIC: 7999 Aerial tramway or ski lift, amusement or scenic

(P-19656)
MOUNTAIN VISTA GOLF COURSE AT
38180 Del Webb Blvd, Palm Desert
(92211-1256)
PHONE.................................760 200-2200
Andrea Goodwin, *President*
Bill Wirian, *Treasurer*
Reginia Cain, *Bd of Directors*
Chuck Carpenter, *Bd of Directors*
John Celli, *Vice Pres*
EMP: 85 EST: 1992
SQ FT: 300
SALES (est): 30MM **Privately Held**
WEB: www.mountainvistagolfclub.com
SIC: 7999 Golf services & professionals

(P-19657)
NORMANDIE CLUB LP
Also Called: Normandie Casino & Showroom
57 Via Malona, Rancho Palos Verdes
(90275-4882)
PHONE.................................310 352-3486
Lawrence F Miller, *Managing Prtnr*
Russel Miller Jr, *General Ptnr*
Greg Miller, *Partner*
Steve Miller, *Partner*
▲ EMP: 57 EST: 1936
SQ FT: 44,000
SALES (est): 3MM **Privately Held**
WEB: www.mobile-casino.com
SIC: 7999 5812 Bingo hall; eating places

(P-19658)
OAK VIEW GROUP LLC (PA)
11755 Wilshire Blvd Fl 9, Los Angeles
(90025-1540)
PHONE.................................310 209-3164
Tim Leiweke, *CEO*
Erin Diaz, *Partner*
Jaclyn Sigmen, *President*
Stephen Collins, *COO*
Steven Selcer, *CFO*
EMP: 170 EST: 2015
SALES (est): 11MM **Privately Held**
WEB: www.oakviewgroup.com
SIC: 7999 6799 Ticket sales office for
sporting events, contract; investors

(P-19659)
PACIFIC COAST CHEER INC (PA)
25815 Jefferson Ave, Murrieta
(92562-6961)
PHONE.................................951 894-7438
Kellie Elliott, *CEO*
EMP: 54 EST: 2005
SALES (est): 501.3K **Privately Held**
WEB: www.pacificcoastmagic.com
SIC: 7999 Gymnastic instruction, non-
membership; tennis club, non-membership

(P-19660)
PALACE ENTERTAINMENT INC (DH)
5160 Campus Dr, Newport Beach
(92660-2101)
PHONE.................................949 261-0404
Alexander Weber Jr, *CEO*
John Cora, *President*
Albert Cabuco, *Vice Pres*
James Judy, *Vice Pres*
Bill Lentz, *Vice Pres*
EMP: 50 EST: 1998
SALES (est): 139.1MM
SALES (corp-wide): 177.9K **Privately Held**
WEB: www.palaceentertainment.com
SIC: 7999 7993 Miniature golf course operation; arcades
HQ: Parque De Atracciones Madrid Sa
Lugar Parque Atracciones (Casa De
Campo), S/N
Madrid 28011
902 345-001

(P-19661)
PSYCHIC EYE BOOK SHOPS INC (PA)
13435 Ventura Blvd, Sherman Oaks
(91423-3812)
PHONE.................................818 906-8263
Robert Leysen, *CEO*
Mary Karahalios, *CFO*
Mary Kara, *Admin Sec*
EMP: 80 EST: 1984
SQ FT: 5,000
SALES (est): 10.2MM **Privately Held**
WEB: www.pebooks.com
SIC: 5942 5947 7999 Book stores; gift
shop; fortune tellers

(P-19662)
PYRAMID ENTERPRISES INC (PA)
Also Called: Lake Piru Marina
28368 Constellation Rd # 380, Valencia
(91355-5005)
PHONE.................................661 702-1420
Chester Roberts, *President*
Traci Roberts, *General Mgr*
Richard Barnes, *CIO*
Shirley Stambaugh, *Manager*
EMP: 60 EST: 1975
SQ FT: 1,300
SALES (est): 9.7MM **Privately Held**
WEB: www.rockymountainrec.com
SIC: 7999 4493 Beach & water sports
equipment rental & services; marinas

(P-19663)
QUECHAN INDIAN TRIBE
Also Called: Quechan Gaming Commission
450 Quechan Rd, Winterhaven
(92283-9676)
P.O. Box 2737, Yuma AZ (85366-2573)
PHONE.................................760 572-2413
Mike Jackson, *President*
Juan Gabriel Leyva, *Comp Spec*
Kristian Welch, *Cashier*
EMP: 74 **Privately Held**
WEB: www.quechantribe.com
SIC: 7999 5812 Gambling establishment;
eating places
PA: Quechan Indian Tribe
350 Picacho Rd
Winterhaven CA 92283
760 572-0213

(P-19664)
RAINBOW CAMP INC
26619 Marigold Ct, Calabasas
(91302-2945)
PHONE.................................310 456-3066
EMP: 50
SALES: 165K **Privately Held**
WEB: www.rainbowcamp.com
SIC: 7999 Amusement/Recreation Services

(P-19665)
RASPADOXPRESS
13796 Foothill Blvd, Sylmar (91342-3128)
PHONE.................................818 367-9838
Maria Aguirre, *Branch Mgr*
EMP: 61
SALES (corp-wide): 1.5MM **Privately Held**
WEB: www.raspadoxpress.com
SIC: 7999 Ice skating rink operation
PA: Raspadoxpress
9765 Laurel Canyon Blvd
Pacoima CA 91331
818 890-4111

(P-19666)
S J S ENTERPRISE INC
Also Called: S C Village
9030 Somerset Blvd, Bellflower
(90706-3402)
PHONE.................................949 489-9000
Dennis Bukowski, *President*
Judy Bukowski, *Vice Pres*
Gio Degidio, *Vice Pres*
Noel Castillo, *Accountant*
Leilanie Marshal, *Manager*
EMP: 150 EST: 1987
SALES (est): 5.1MM **Privately Held**
SIC: 7999 Indoor court clubs

(P-19667)
SAN CLEMENTE SPORTFISHING INC
Also Called: Dana Wharf Sportfishing
34675 Golden Lantern St, Dana Point
(92629-2908)
PHONE.................................949 496-5794
Donald K Hansen, *President*
Sheri Hockmeyer, *Sales Staff*
EMP: 73 EST: 1946
SQ FT: 5,000
SALES (est): 4.1MM **Privately Held**
WEB: www.danawharf.com
SIC: 7999 5941 Fishing boats, party: operation; fishing equipment

(P-19668)
SAN MANUEL INDIAN BINGO CASINO (PA)
777 San Manuel Blvd, Highland
(92346-6713)
PHONE.................................909 864-5050
James Ramos, *Chairman*
Rikki Tanenbaum, *COO*
Rebecca Spalding, *CFO*
Audrey Martinez, *Treasurer*
Peter Watts, *Chief Mktg Ofcr*
▲ EMP: 2950 EST: 1987
SALES (est): 154.8MM **Privately Held**
WEB: www.yaamava.com
SIC: 7999 Bingo hall

(P-19669)
SIERRA CANYON INC
Also Called: Sierra Canyon Day Camp
11052 Independence Ave, Chatsworth
(91311-1562)
PHONE.................................818 882-8121
Jim Skruneis, *President*
Javy Martinez, *Ch of Bd*
Tom Perry, *Ch of Bd*
Howard Wang, *President*
Matthew Brown, *Officer*
EMP: 60 EST: 1971
SQ FT: 35,000
SALES (est): 6.9MM **Privately Held**
WEB: www.sierracanyondaycamp.com
SIC: 8211 7999 Private elementary & secondary schools; day camp

(P-19670)
SNOW SUMMIT SKI CORPORATION
Also Called: Snow Summit Mountain Resort
43101 Goldmine Dr, Big Bear City (92314)
P.O. Box 77, Big Bear Lake (92315-0077)
PHONE.................................909 585-2517
Richard C Kun, *Branch Mgr*
EMP: 52
SALES (corp-wide): 59.8MM **Privately Held**
WEB: www.bigbearmountainresort.com
SIC: 7999 7011 5941 7992 Aerial
tramway or ski lift, amusement or scenic;
ski lodge; skiing equipment; public golf
courses
PA: Snow Summit Ski Corporation
880 Summit Blvd
Big Bear Lake CA 92315
909 866-5766

(P-19671)
SPEARMAN CLUBS INC (PA)
Also Called: Laguna Niguel Racquet Club
23500 Clubhouse Dr, Laguna Niguel
(92677-2902)
PHONE.................................949 496-2070
Cecil E Spearman Jr, *Ch of Bd*
Mark Spearman, *President*
Steven Spearman, *CFO*
Jean Spearman, *Vice Ch Bd*
Scott Spearman, *Vice Pres*
EMP: 50 EST: 1979
SQ FT: 20,000
SALES (est): 7MM **Privately Held**
WEB: www.spearmansportsclubs.com
SIC: 7999 7991 Tennis club, non-membership; physical fitness clubs with training
equipment

(P-19672)
SPORT CHALET LLC
16242 Beach Blvd, Huntington Beach
(92647-3702)
PHONE.................................714 848-0988

EMP: 75
SALES (corp-wide): 443.9MM **Privately Held**
SIC: 5941 7999 5091 Ret Sporting Goods/Bicycles Amusement/Recreation Services Whol Sporting/Recreational Goods
HQ: Sport Chalet Llc
160 Corporate Ct
Meriden CT 06450
818 790-2717

(P-19673)
SPORT CHALET LLC
2983 Michelson Dr, Irvine (92612-0623)
PHONE..................................949 476-9555
EMP: 80
SALES (corp-wide): 443.9MM **Privately Held**
SIC: 5941 5699 7999 5091 Ret Sport Goods/Bicycles Ret Misc Apparel/Access Amusement/Recreation Svc Whol Sporting Goods/Supp
HQ: Sport Chalet Llc
160 Corporate Ct
Meriden CT 06450
818 790-2717

(P-19674)
T ALLANCE ONE - PALM SPRNG LLC
Also Called: Doubltree Palm Sprng Golf Rsor
67967 Vista Chino, Cathedral City (92234-7408)
PHONE..................................760 322-7000
Bhavesh Patel,
Laurie Miller, *Marketing Staff*
EMP: 99 **EST:** 2013
SALES (est): 3.7MM **Privately Held**
SIC: 7999 Golf professionals

(P-19675)
TICKETMASTER ENTERTAINMENT LLC
8800 W Sunset Blvd, West Hollywood (90069-2105)
PHONE..................................800 653-8000
Ron Bension, *Mng Member*
Adam Goldberg, *Partner*
Dave Scarborough, *Officer*
Michael Baugh, *Vice Pres*
Gary Brosius, *Vice Pres*
EMP: 4390 **EST:** 2010
SALES (est): 103.9MM **Publicly Held**
WEB: www.livenationentertainment.com
SIC: 7999 Ticket sales office for sporting events, contract; tennis club, non-membership
PA: Live Nation Entertainment, Inc.
9348 Civic Center Dr Lbby
Beverly Hills CA 90210

(P-19676)
TICKETMSTER NEW VNTRES HLDNGS (HQ)
7060 Hollywood Blvd Fl 2, Los Angeles (90028-6015)
PHONE..................................800 653-8000
Irving Azoff, *CEO*
Casey Klein, *Partner*
Tom Bray, *Senior VP*
Brendan Lynch, *Senior VP*
Kurt Schwartzkopf, *Senior VP*
EMP: 2970 **EST:** 1996
SALES (est): 66.6MM **Publicly Held**
WEB: www.livenationentertainment.com
SIC: 7999 Ticket sales office for sporting events, contract

(P-19677)
TIERRA DEL SOL FOUNDATION
Also Called: Tierra Del Soul
250 W 1st St Ste 120, Claremont (91711-4741)
PHONE..................................909 626-8301
Rebecca Hamm, *Branch Mgr*
EMP: 85
SALES (corp-wide): 18.8MM **Privately Held**
WEB: www.tierradelsol.org
SIC: 7999 5999 Art gallery, commercial; art dealers

PA: Tierra Del Sol Foundation
9919 Sunland Blvd
Sunland CA 91040
818 352-1419

(P-19678)
TUMBLEWEED EDUCTL ENTPS INC
Also Called: Tumbleweed Day Camp
1024 Hanley Ave, Los Angeles (90049-1306)
P.O. Box 49291 (90049-0291)
PHONE..................................310 444-3232
Erin Benfield, *President*
Michael Sagner, *Maintenance Dir*
Laura Lynch, *Manager*
EMP: 160 **EST:** 1954
SQ FT: 6,500
SALES (est): 11.8MM **Privately Held**
WEB: www.tumbleweedtransportation.com
SIC: 7999 4151 Day camp; school buses

(P-19679)
VALLEY WIDE RECREATION PK DST (PA)
901 W Esplanade Ave, San Jacinto (92582-4501)
P.O. Box 907 (92581-0907)
PHONE..................................951 654-1505
Nick Schouton, *President*
Kenneth Hyatt, *President*
Sam Goepp, *General Mgr*
EMP: 86 **EST:** 1972
SQ FT: 30,000
SALES (est): 161.4K **Privately Held**
WEB: www.gorecreation.org
SIC: 7999 7996 Recreation services; amusement parks

(P-19680)
VOLUME SERVICES INC
5333 Zoo Dr, Los Angeles (90027-1451)
PHONE..................................323 644-6038
Greg Edgar, *Manager*
EMP: 135
SALES (corp-wide): 158.5MM **Privately Held**
WEB: www.us.sodexo.com
SIC: 7999 Concession operator
HQ: Volume Services, Inc.
2187 Atlantic St Ste 6
Stamford CT 06902

(P-19681)
WHITTIER NARROW GOLF COURSE
8640 Rush St, Rosemead (91770-3739)
PHONE..................................626 288-1044
Peter Nenula, *President*
David Beyer, *General Mgr*
EMP: 112 **EST:** 1991
SQ FT: 3,000
SALES (est): 3.9MM **Publicly Held**
WEB: www.whittiernarrowsgc.com
SIC: 7999 Golf services & professionals
HQ: American Golf Corporation
10670 N Cntl Expy Ste 700
Dallas TX 75231
310 664-4000

(P-19682)
YOGAWORKS INC (HQ)
Also Called: Myyogaworks
5780 Uplander Way, Culver City (90230-6606)
PHONE..................................310 664-6470
Rosanna C McCollough, *President*
Peter L Garran, *Ch of Bd*
Vance Y Chang, *CFO*
Cate Rubenstein, *Senior VP*
Jamie Haddad, *Regional Mgr*
EMP: 60 **EST:** 1987
SQ FT: 6,800
SALES: 59.5MM
SALES (corp-wide): 461.8MM **Privately Held**
WEB: www.yogaworks.com
SIC: 7999 5961 7991 Yoga instruction; mail order house; exercise salon
PA: Great Hill Equity Partners V, L.P.
200 Clarendon St Ste 2901
Boston MA 02116
617 790-9400

(P-19683)
YOUNG MNS CHRSTN ASSN STHAST V
Also Called: Simi Valley Family YMCA
3200 Cochran St, Simi Valley (93065-2769)
PHONE..................................805 583-5338
Dan Jaeger, *Director*
Lynda Wiggins, *Director*
EMP: 62
SALES (corp-wide): 10.2MM **Privately Held**
WEB: www.sevymca.org
SIC: 7999 8351 8641 7997 Recreation center; child day care services; civic social & fraternal associations; membership sports & recreation clubs
PA: Young Men's Christian Association Of Southeast Ventura County
31105 E Thusand Oaks Blvd
Thousand Oaks CA 91362
805 497-3081

8011 Offices & Clinics Of Doctors Of Medicine

(P-19684)
ADVANCED AMBLTORY SRGERY CTR L
1901 W Lugonia Ave # 100, Redlands (92374-9703)
PHONE..................................909 557-1700
John Steinmann,
Ronny Ghazal, *Mng Member*
EMP: 50 **EST:** 2003
SALES (est): 5.8MM **Privately Held**
SIC: 8011 Surgeon

(P-19685)
ADVANCED PROF IMGING MED GROUP (PA)
6905 Oslo Cir Ste F, Buena Park (90621-4673)
PHONE..................................714 995-5400
Sim C Hoffman, *President*
EMP: 108 **EST:** 1986
SALES (est): 1MM **Privately Held**
SIC: 8011 Radiologist

(P-19686)
ADVENTIST HEALTH SYSTEM
Also Called: Adventist Health Cmnty. Care
250 W El Monte Way, Dinuba (93618-1554)
PHONE..................................559 595-9890
Wayne Ferch, *Branch Mgr*
EMP: 2683 **Privately Held**
WEB: www.adventhealth.com
SIC: 8011 Offices & clinics of medical doctors
PA: Adventist Health System Sunbelt Healthcare Corporation
900 Hope Way
Altamonte Springs FL 32714

(P-19687)
AHMC INC
100 S Raymond Ave, Alhambra (91801-3166)
PHONE..................................626 570-1606
Jonathan Wu, *President*
EMP: 71 **EST:** 1998
SALES (est): 2.7MM **Privately Held**
SIC: 8011 General & family practice, physician/surgeon

(P-19688)
ALEX A KHADAVI MD INC
Also Called: Encino Drmtology Laser Med Ctr
16260 Ventura Blvd # 140, Encino (91436-2203)
PHONE..................................818 528-2500
Alex Khadavi, *Principal*
EMP: 20 **EST:** 2010
SALES (est): 2.6MM **Privately Held**
WEB: www.dermatologycenteria.com
SIC: 8011 2834 Dermatologist; allergist; dermatologicals

(P-19689)
ALL CARE MEDICAL GROUP INC
Also Called: Professional Svcs Med Group
31 Crescent St, Huntington Park (90255)
PHONE..................................408 278-3550
Samuel Rotenberg MD, *Director*
Joan Wright, *Surgeon*
Reza Yazdi, *Med Doctor*
EMP: 85 **EST:** 1946
SQ FT: 33,000
SALES (est): 7.5MM **Privately Held**
SIC: 8011 Physicians' office, including specialists

(P-19690)
ALL FOR HLTH HLTH FOR ALL INC (PA)
519 E Broadway, Glendale (91205-1110)
PHONE..................................818 409-3020
Adrineh Ebrahimian, *CEO*
Juliet Gurjian, *Bd of Directors*
Ninet Abgarian, *Executive*
Kristina Karapetyan, *Admin Sec*
Berge Simonian, *Finance Mgr*
EMP: 136 **EST:** 1999
SALES (est): 20.8MM **Privately Held**
WEB: www.all4health.org
SIC: 8011 Clinic, operated by physicians

(P-19691)
ALLERGY & ASTHMA ASSOC CAL
Also Called: Southern Asthma Assoc Southern
27800 Med Ctr Rd Ste 244, Mission Viejo (92691)
PHONE..................................949 364-2900
William Berger, *Principal*
William E Berger MD, *President*
Shivam Patel, *Research*
EMP: 66 **EST:** 1981
SALES (est): 5.2MM **Privately Held**
WEB: www.socalallergy.com
SIC: 8011 Allergist

(P-19692)
ALLIANCE ONCOLOGY LLC (DH)
100 Bayview Cir Ste 400, Newport Beach (92660-2984)
PHONE..................................949 242-5345
Richard J Hall, *President*
Josh Eaves, *Vice Pres*
Michael F Frisch, *Vice Pres*
Douglas McCracken, *Vice Pres*
Craig Weeks, *Vice Pres*
EMP: 50 **EST:** 2007
SALES (est): 88.6MM
SALES (corp-wide): 512.6MM **Privately Held**
WEB: www.alliancehealthcareservices-us.com
SIC: 8011 Radiologist
HQ: Alliance Healthcare Services, Inc.
18201 Von Karman Ave # 6
Irvine CA 92612
949 242-5300

(P-19693)
ALTA CALIFORNIA MED GROUP INC
2925 Sycamore Dr Ste 204, Simi Valley (93065-1208)
PHONE..................................805 578-9622
Alberto Jose Odio, *Principal*
EMP: 57 **EST:** 2008
SALES (est): 6.7MM **Privately Held**
WEB: www.altacaliforniamedicalgroup.com
SIC: 8011 General & family practice, physician/surgeon

(P-19694)
ALTA VISTA HEALTHCARE AND WELL
9020 Garfield St, Riverside (92503-3903)
PHONE..................................951 688-8200
EMP: 105
SALES (est): 5.5MM **Privately Held**
SIC: 8011 Skilled Nursing Services

(P-19695)
ALTAMED HEALTH SERVICES CORP
Also Called: Ultimate
12130 Paramount Blvd, Downey
(90242-2339)
PHONE......................562 923-9414
Chikita Emel, *Director*
EMP: 112
SALES (corp-wide): 702MM **Privately Held**
WEB: www.altamed.org
SIC: 8011 Gynecologist; pediatrician; radiologist
PA: Altamed Health Services Corporation
2040 Camfield Ave
Commerce CA 90040
323 725-8751

(P-19696)
ALTAMED HEALTH SERVICES CORP
Also Called: Altamed Adhc Golden Age
3820 Mrtin Lther King Jr, Lynwood
(90262-3625)
PHONE......................310 632-0415
Peter M Feldman, *Principal*
EMP: 112
SALES (corp-wide): 702MM **Privately Held**
WEB: www.altamed.org
SIC: 8011 8099 Gynecologist; pediatrician; radiologist; medical services organization
PA: Altamed Health Services Corporation
2040 Camfield Ave
Commerce CA 90040
323 725-8751

(P-19697)
ALTAMED HEALTH SERVICES CORP
5427 Whittier Blvd, Los Angeles
(90022-4101)
PHONE......................323 980-4466
Irene Avilar, *Principal*
EMP: 112
SALES (corp-wide): 702MM **Privately Held**
WEB: www.altamed.org
SIC: 8011 Clinic, operated by physicians
PA: Altamed Health Services Corporation
2040 Camfield Ave
Commerce CA 90040
323 725-8751

(P-19698)
ALTAMED HEALTH SERVICES CORP
1325 N Anaheim Blvd 101, Anaheim
(92801-1202)
PHONE......................714 635-0593
EMP: 112
SALES (corp-wide): 702MM **Privately Held**
WEB: www.altamed.org
SIC: 8011 Gynecologist
PA: Altamed Health Services Corporation
2040 Camfield Ave
Commerce CA 90040
323 725-8751

(P-19699)
ALTAMED HEALTH SERVICES CORP
6330 Rugby Ave Ste 200, Huntington Park
(90255-6938)
PHONE......................323 277-7678
Yorka Rodriguez, *Manager*
Anna Sigal, *Design Engr*
Josephine Chumley, *Technical Staff*
Ashley Dapson, *Production*
Susan Fisher, *Manager*
EMP: 112
SALES (corp-wide): 702MM **Privately Held**
WEB: www.altamed.org
SIC: 8011 8322 Gynecologist; individual & family services
PA: Altamed Health Services Corporation
2040 Camfield Ave
Commerce CA 90040
323 725-8751

(P-19700)
ALTAMED HEALTH SERVICES CORP
268 Bloom St, Los Angeles (90012-1973)
PHONE......................323 276-0267
EMP: 112
SALES (corp-wide): 702MM **Privately Held**
WEB: www.altamed.org
SIC: 8011 Clinic, operated by physicians
PA: Altamed Health Services Corporation
2040 Camfield Ave
Commerce CA 90040
323 725-8751

(P-19701)
ALTAMED HEALTH SERVICES CORP (PA)
2040 Camfield Ave, Commerce
(90040-1574)
PHONE......................323 725-8751
Castulo De La Rocha, *CEO*
Jose U Esparza, *CFO*
Marie S Torres, *Senior VP*
Zoila D Escobar, *Vice Pres*
Carmen Flores, *Recruiter*
EMP: 135 EST: 1970
SQ FT: 27,345
SALES: 702MM **Privately Held**
WEB: www.altamed.org
SIC: 8011 8099 Gynecologist; pediatrician; radiologist; medical services organization

(P-19702)
ALTAMED HEALTH SERVICES CORP
1776 E Century Blvd, Los Angeles
(90002-3050)
PHONE......................323 374-6848
EMP: 112
SALES (corp-wide): 702MM **Privately Held**
WEB: www.altamed.org
SIC: 8011 Offices & clinics of medical doctors
PA: Altamed Health Services Corporation
2040 Camfield Ave
Commerce CA 90040
323 725-8751

(P-19703)
ALTAMED HEALTH SERVICES CORP
Also Called: Senior Health and Activity Ctr
5425 Pomona Blvd, Los Angeles
(90022-1716)
PHONE......................323 728-0411
Mariela Bauer, *Branch Mgr*
EMP: 112
SQ FT: 24,369
SALES (corp-wide): 702MM **Privately Held**
WEB: www.altamed.org
SIC: 8011 8099 Gynecologist; medical services organization
PA: Altamed Health Services Corporation
2040 Camfield Ave
Commerce CA 90040
323 725-8751

(P-19704)
ALTAMED HEALTH SERVICES CORP
2219 E 1st St, Los Angeles (90033-3901)
PHONE......................323 269-0421
Shi Y Wong, *Branch Mgr*
EMP: 112
SALES (corp-wide): 702MM **Privately Held**
WEB: www.altamed.org
SIC: 8011 8099 Gynecologist; pediatrician; radiologist; medical services organization
PA: Altamed Health Services Corporation
2040 Camfield Ave
Commerce CA 90040
323 725-8751

(P-19705)
ALTURA CENTERS FOR HEALTH
1201 N Cherry St, Tulare (93274-2233)
PHONE......................559 686-9097
Graciela Soto-Perez, *President*
Niel Fishback, *Officer*

Evelyn Benson, *Exec Dir*
Amy Azevedo, *Admin Asst*
Manuel Pedroza, *CIO*
EMP: 83 EST: 1996
SQ FT: 18,000
SALES: 26.5MM **Privately Held**
WEB: www.altura.org
SIC: 8011 8021 Clinic, operated by physicians; primary care medical clinic; offices & clinics of dentists

(P-19706)
AMEN CLINICS INC A MED CORP (PA)
3150 Bristol St Ste 400, Costa Mesa
(92626-3054)
PHONE......................888 564-2700
Daniel Amen, *President*
Kim Schneider, *Executive Asst*
Catherine J Hanlon, *Administration*
▲ EMP: 75 EST: 2000
SALES (est): 27.4MM **Privately Held**
WEB: www.amenclinics.com
SIC: 8011 Psychiatric clinic; neurologist

(P-19707)
AMERICAN EYE INSTITUTE
8635 W 3rd St Ste 390, Los Angeles
(90048-6150)
PHONE......................310 652-1396
Anthony Nesburn, *President*
Lawrence Shortz MD, *Partner*
James Salz MD, *Principal*
EMP: 67 EST: 1971
SALES (est): 8.3MM **Privately Held**
WEB: www.americaneyeinstitutelosangeles.com
SIC: 8011 Ophthalmologist

(P-19708)
AMERICAN HEALTH SERVICES LLC
Also Called: Palmdale Med Mental Hlth Svcs
26460 Summit Cir, Santa Clarita
(91350-2991)
P.O. Box 801809 (91380-1809)
PHONE......................661 254-6630
Stan Sharma, *CEO*
Leni Legaspi, *CFO*
Hamir Sinha, *Treasurer*
Sean Sharma, *Vice Pres*
Arlyn Barner, *Admin Sec*
EMP: 66 EST: 1996
SALES (est): 6.3MM **Privately Held**
WEB: www.americanhealthservices.org
SIC: 8011 8361 Offices & clinics of medical doctors; rehabilitation center, residential; health care incidental

(P-19709)
ANAHEIM HARBOR MEDICAL GROUP (PA)
Also Called: Family Urgent Care Center
710 N Euclid St, Anaheim (92801-4122)
PHONE......................714 533-4511
David L Tsoong MD, *President*
Joseph M Mule MD, *Admin Sec*
Miguel Estrada, *VP Finance*
Andrea Moroso, *Business Mgr*
EMP: 50 EST: 1984
SQ FT: 10,000
SALES (est): 10.1MM **Privately Held**
WEB: www.pmcamd.com
SIC: 8011 Pediatrician

(P-19710)
ANESTHSIA MED GROUP SNTA BRBAR
Also Called: Anesthsia Med Group Snta Brbar
514 W Pueblo St Fl 2, Santa Barbara
(93105-6219)
PHONE......................805 682-7751
Eric Amador, *Director*
John King, *President*
Douglas Etsel, *Chairman*
Clinton Lagrange, *Vice Pres*
Derrick Willsey, *Admin Sec*
EMP: 66 EST: 1970
SALES (est): 6.2MM **Privately Held**
WEB: www.amgsb.com
SIC: 8011 Anesthesiologist

(P-19711)
ANGELES CLINIC & RES INST INC
11818 Wilshire Blvd, Los Angeles
(90025-6646)
PHONE......................310 582-7900
Barbara Quinn, *Principal*
Dr Lawrence D Piro, *CEO*
Gina Olvera, *Human Res Dir*
Decio M Rangel, *Oncology*
Melani Shaum, *Med Doctor*
EMP: 67 EST: 1999
SALES (est): 7.8MM **Privately Held**
WEB: www.theangelesclinic.org
SIC: 8011 Clinic, operated by physicians

(P-19712)
ANTELOPE VALLEY HOSPITAL INC
Ob Clinic
1600 W Avenue J, Lancaster (93534-2894)
PHONE......................661 726-6180
Vikki Haley, *Principal*
EMP: 84
SALES (corp-wide): 450.4MM **Privately Held**
WEB: www.avhospital.org
SIC: 8011 Offices & clinics of medical doctors
PA: Antelope Valley Hospital Inc.
1600 W Avenue J
Lancaster CA 93534
661 949-5000

(P-19713)
ANTELOPE VALLEY SURGERY CTR LP
44301 Lorimer Ave, Lancaster
(93534-3700)
PHONE......................661 947-4600
Daniel Taheri, *CEO*
EMP: 50 EST: 2011
SALES (est): 13MM
SALES (corp-wide): 257.13 **Publicly Held**
WEB: www.antelopevalleysurgerycenter.com
SIC: 8011 Surgeon
PA: Unitedhealth Group Incorporated
9900 Bren Rd E Ste 300w
Minnetonka MN 55343
952 936-1300

(P-19714)
APLA HEALTH & WELLNESS
611 S Kingsley Dr, Los Angeles
(90005-2319)
PHONE......................213 201-1600
Craig Thompson, *CEO*
Robyn Goldman, *CFO*
EMP: 56 EST: 2010
SALES (est): 55.5MM
SALES (corp-wide): 10.3MM **Privately Held**
WEB: www.aplahealth.org
SIC: 8011 Primary care medical clinic
PA: Aids Project Los Angeles
611 S Kingsley Dr
Los Angeles CA 90005
213 201-1600

(P-19715)
ARROYO SECO MEDICAL GROUP (PA)
301 S Fair Oaks Ave # 300, Pasadena
(91105-2561)
PHONE......................626 795-7556
Henry Sideropoulos MD, *President*
Andrew Muller MD, *Vice Pres*
Andrew N Muller, *Director*
EMP: 65 EST: 1978
SQ FT: 9,145
SALES (est): 5.8MM **Privately Held**
WEB: www.arroyoseco.net
SIC: 8011 Internal medicine, physician/surgeon; general & family practice, physician/surgeon

(P-19716)
ARROYO VSTA FMLY HLTH FNDATION
Also Called: Arroyo Vista Family Health Ctr
2411 N Broadway, Los Angeles
(90031-2218)
PHONE......................323 224-2188

Line Fernandez, *Manager*
Najma Qamar, *Pediatrics*
Francisco Gonzalez, *Fmly & Gen Dent*
EMP: 100
SQ FT: 13,435 **Privately Held**
WEB: www.arroyovista.org
SIC: 8011 Clinic, operated by physicians
PA: Arroyo Vista Family Health Foundation
  6000 N Figueroa St
  Los Angeles CA 90042
  -

(P-19717)
ASSOCIATED STUDENTS UCLA
Also Called: Ucla Mdcn SC Phrmclgy
650 Chrles Yung Dr S Rm 2, Los Angeles (90095-0001)
PHONE...............................310 825-9451
Michael Phelps, *Principal*
EMP: 227
SALES (corp-wide): 54.7MM **Privately Held**
WEB: www.asucla.edu
SIC: 8011 General & family practice, physician/surgeon
PA: Associated Students U.C.L.A.
  308 Westwood Plz
  Los Angeles CA 90095
  310 794-8836

(P-19718)
AXMINSTER MEDICAL GROUP INC (PA)
8540 S Sepulveda Blvd # 818, Los Angeles (90045-3808)
PHONE...............................310 670-3255
Raymond Jing MD, *CEO*
Huey-Jer Su MD, *Treasurer*
Spencer H Wenger MD, *Vice Pres*
Stanley E Golden MD, *Admin Sec*
Rudo Benjamin, *Med Doctor*
EMP: 56 **EST:** 1961
SQ FT: 20,000
SALES (est): 13.3MM **Privately Held**
WEB: www.axminstermedicalgroup.com
SIC: 8011 Internal medicine, physician/surgeon; pediatrician; gynecologist

(P-19719)
BAY CITIS SURGERY CENTRE L P
Also Called: Surgery Center of South Bay
23500 Madison St, Torrance (90505-4702)
PHONE...............................310 784-2710
Barry Rodgveller, *Partner*
EMP: 71 **EST:** 2004
SALES (est): 10.4MM **Privately Held**
WEB: www.surgerycentersouthbay.com
SIC: 8011 Surgeon

(P-19720)
BEAUTOLOGIE MGT GROUP INC
4850 Commerce Dr, Bakersfield (93309-0415)
P.O. Box 4199, Malibu (90264-4199)
PHONE...............................661 327-3800
Darshan Shah, *CEO*
Darshan R Shah, *CEO*
James Knoetgen, *Surgeon*
Nancy Solorio, *Manager*
EMP: 50 **EST:** 2002
SALES (est): 4.5MM **Privately Held**
WEB: www.beautologie.com
SIC: 8011 Plastic surgeon

(P-19721)
BEAVER MEDICAL CLINIC INC (PA)
1615 Orange Tree Ln, Redlands (92374-2804)
P.O. Box 10069, San Bernardino (92423-0069)
PHONE...............................909 793-3311
Robert Klein, *President*
Regan Douty, *Internal Med*
Lori Duerr,
EMP: 190 **EST:** 1945
SQ FT: 79,212
SALES (est): 342.5K **Privately Held**
WEB: www.beavermedicalgroup.com
SIC: 8011 Clinic, operated by physicians

(P-19722)
BEAVER MEDICAL GROUP LP (HQ)
Also Called: Beaver Medical Clinic
7000 Boulder Ave, Highland (92346-3348)
PHONE...............................909 425-3321
John Goodman, *CEO*
James Watson M D, *Partner*
Robert Bourne M D, *Partner*
Robert Rentschler, *Partner*
Richard J Hall, *Anesthesiology*
EMP: 166 **EST:** 1995
SALES (est): 34.4MM **Privately Held**
WEB: www.beavermedicalgroup.com
SIC: 8011 General & family practice, physician/surgeon

(P-19723)
BECKMAN RES INST OF THE CY HOP
1500 Duarte Rd, Duarte (91010-3012)
PHONE...............................626 359-8111
Michael A Friedman, *CEO*
Robert Stone, *President*
Harlan Levine, *CEO*
William Sargeant, *COO*
Terry Blackwood, *CFO*
EMP: 250 **EST:** 1979
SALES (est): 59.1MM
SALES (corp-wide): 592.4MM **Privately Held**
WEB: www.cityofhope.org
SIC: 8011 Offices & clinics of medical doctors
PA: City Of Hope
  1500 Duarte Rd
  Duarte CA 91010
  626 256-4673

(P-19724)
BREAST CARE CENTER OF ORANGE (PA)
230 S Main St Ste 100, Orange (92868-3851)
PHONE...............................714 541-0101
John West, *President*
David Margileth, *Treasurer*
Peter Hinckle, *Vice Pres*
Rena Munoz, *Administration*
Shlomit Ein-Gal, *Internal Med*
EMP: 59 **EST:** 1988
SALES (est): 5MM **Privately Held**
WEB: www.breastlink.com
SIC: 8011 Physicians' office, including specialists

(P-19725)
BRIGHT HEALTH PHYSICIANS (PA)
15725 Whittier Blvd # 500, Whittier (90603-2350)
PHONE...............................562 947-8478
William H Stimmler MD, *Ch of Bd*
Keith Miyamoto MD, *President*
Don T Eli, *Principal*
Berent Gray MD, *Admin Sec*
Dan Ogletree, *Social Worker*
EMP: 140 **EST:** 1991
SQ FT: 50,000
SALES (est): 38.7MM **Privately Held**
WEB: www.pihhealth.org
SIC: 8011 Physicians' office, including specialists

(P-19726)
BUENA PARK MEDICAL GROUP INC (PA)
6301 Beach Blvd Ste 101, Buena Park (90621-4030)
P.O. Box 277 (90621-0277)
PHONE...............................714 994-5290
Martin Ahn, *CEO*
EMP: 50 **EST:** 1989
SQ FT: 20,000
SALES (est): 6.6MM **Privately Held**
WEB: www.buenaparkmedical.com
SIC: 8011 General & family practice, physician/surgeon

(P-19727)
BUENAVENTURA MEDICAL GROUP (PA)
888 S Hill Rd, Ventura (93003-8400)
PHONE...............................805 477-6000

James Malone, *CEO*
David Grahm, *COO*
Kevin Moore, *CFO*
EMP: 170 **EST:** 1950
SQ FT: 27,000
SALES (est): 13.5MM **Privately Held**
SIC: 8011 Clinic, operated by physicians

(P-19728)
BUENAVENTURA MEDICAL GROUP
2601 E Main St Ste 104, Ventura (93003-2801)
PHONE...............................805 477-6220
James Malone, *CEO*
G Dennis Horvath, *Surgeon*
EMP: 62
SALES (corp-wide): 13.5MM **Privately Held**
WEB: www.primarymedical.net
SIC: 8011 Clinic, operated by physicians
PA: Buenaventura Medical Group Inc
  888 S Hill Rd
  Ventura CA 93003
  805 477-6000

(P-19729)
BURBANK EMRGNCY MED GROUP INC
501 S Buena Vista St, Burbank (91505-4809)
PHONE...............................818 506-5778
Philip Schwarzman, *CEO*
Robert Proulx MD, *Partner*
EMP: 54 **EST:** 1985
SALES (est): 2.7MM **Privately Held**
WEB: www.bemg.net
SIC: 8011 Offices & clinics of medical doctors

(P-19730)
CABRILLO CRDOLGY MED GROUP INC
2241 Wankel Way Ste C, Oxnard (93030-0191)
PHONE...............................805 983-0922
David Schmidt MD, *President*
David E Schmidt, *President*
Richard Rothchild MD, *Treasurer*
Khamaj Dave, *Director*
Esam Obed, *Director*
EMP: 65 **EST:** 1971
SALES (est): 9.2MM **Privately Held**
WEB: www.cabrillocardiology.com
SIC: 8011 Cardiologist & cardio-vascular specialist

(P-19731)
CADUCEUS PHYSCANS MED GROUP A
18200 Yorba Linda Blvd # 401, Yorba Linda (92886-4061)
PHONE...............................714 646-8000
Gregg Denicola, *Chairman*
Dennis Ponzio, *President*
EMP: 57 **EST:** 1998
SALES (est): 5.2MM **Privately Held**
WEB: www.caduceusmedicalgroup.com
SIC: 8011 General & family practice, physician/surgeon

(P-19732)
CALIFORNIA HEART ASSOCIATES
18111 Brookhurst St # 5100, Fountain Valley (92708-6728)
PHONE...............................714 546-2238
Steven M Schiff, *Med Doctor*
Robert Greenfield, *Partner*
Thuy Le, *Partner*
Steven Schiff MD, *Partner*
Marvin E Turbow MD, *Partner*
EMP: 53 **EST:** 1979
SALES (est): 8.8MM **Privately Held**
WEB: www.californiaheart.com
SIC: 8011 Cardiologist & cardio-vascular specialist

(P-19733)
CALIFRNIA CLNIC PLSTIC SURGERY (PA)
100 E California Blvd, Pasadena (91105-3205)
PHONE...............................626 817-0818
Tom Phang, *Owner*

EMP: 61 **EST:** 2013
SALES (est): 1.1MM **Privately Held**
SIC: 8011 Surgeon

(P-19734)
CAREMARK RX INC
Also Called: US Family Care
2150 N Waterman Ave # 200, San Bernardino (92404-4811)
PHONE...............................909 887-7951
Al Scott, *Branch Mgr*
EMP: 54
SALES (corp-wide): 268.7B **Publicly Held**
SIC: 8011 Surgeon
HQ: Caremark Rx, Inc.
  445 Great Circle Rd
  Nashville TN 37228

(P-19735)
CAREMARK RX INC
Also Called: US Family Care
1851 N Riverside Ave, Rialto (92376-8069)
PHONE...............................909 822-1164
Steve Heide, *Administration*
EMP: 54
SALES (corp-wide): 268.7B **Publicly Held**
SIC: 8011 General & family practice, physician/surgeon; internal medicine, physician/surgeon; obstetrician; gynecologist
HQ: Caremark Rx, Inc.
  445 Great Circle Rd
  Nashville TN 37228

(P-19736)
CAREMARK RX INC
Also Called: US Family Care
15576 Main St, Hesperia (92345-3482)
PHONE...............................760 948-6606
Rochelle Steen, *Principal*
EMP: 54
SALES (corp-wide): 268.7B **Publicly Held**
SIC: 8011 General & family practice, physician/surgeon
HQ: Caremark Rx, Inc.
  445 Great Circle Rd
  Nashville TN 37228

(P-19737)
CAREMORE HEALTH PLAN (HQ)
Also Called: Caremore Insurance Services
12900 Park Plaza Dr # 150, Cerritos (90703-9329)
PHONE...............................562 622-2950
Toll Free:...............................888 -
Leeba R Lessin, *President*
Jason Barker, *President*
John KAO, *President*
Allan Hoops, *CEO*
Vish Sankaran, *COO*
EMP: 135 **EST:** 1996
SALES (est): 85.9MM
SALES (corp-wide): 121.8B **Publicly Held**
WEB: www.caremore.com
SIC: 8011 6411 Offices & clinics of medical doctors; insurance agents, brokers & service
PA: Anthem, Inc.
  220 Virginia Ave
  Indianapolis IN 46204
  800 331-1476

(P-19738)
CAREONSITE INC (PA)
1250 Pacific Ave, Long Beach (90813-3026)
P.O. Box 11389, Carson (90749-1389)
PHONE...............................562 437-0831
Helen Tang, *President*
Brian Tang, *Vice Pres*
Mary Boktor-Grisard, *General Mgr*
Ciana Bataineh, *Analyst*
Emily McIntyre, *Opers-Prdtn-Mfg*
EMP: 50 **EST:** 2011
SALES (est): 23MM **Privately Held**
WEB: www.tangandcompany.com
SIC: 8011 Occupational & industrial specialist, physician/surgeon

PRODUCTS & SVCS

(P-19739)
CEDARS-SINAI MEDICAL CENTER
8700 Beverly Blvd, West Hollywood (90048-1804)
P.O. Box 200, Whittier (90608-0200)
PHONE......................................800 233-2771
Terri W Cammarano, *President*
Larry Platt, *Bd of Directors*
Marilyn Ader, *Associate Dir*
Maureen Chin, *Exec Dir*
Karen Geiser, *Executive Asst*
EMP: 100 **EST:** 2016
SALES (est): 37.6MM **Privately Held**
WEB: www.cedars-sinai.org
SIC: 8011 Offices & clinics of medical doctors

(P-19740)
CEDARS-SINAI MEDICAL CENTER
Also Called: Cardiac Noninvasive Laboratory
127 S San Vicente Blvd # 3417, Los Angeles (90048-3311)
PHONE......................................310 423-3849
Timothy Henry, *Director*
Edward Prunchunas, *Exec VP*
Won Choi, *Administration*
Erick Galvez, *Technician*
Susan Lei, *Technician*
EMP: 132
SALES (corp-wide): 4.1B **Privately Held**
WEB: www.cedars-sinai.org
SIC: 8011 Cardiologist & cardio-vascular specialist
PA: Cedars-Sinai Medical Center
8700 Beverly Blvd
West Hollywood CA 90048
310 423-3277

(P-19741)
CEDARS-SINAI MEDICAL CENTER
8631 W 3rd St Ste 730, Los Angeles (90048-5911)
P.O. Box 48955 (90048-0955)
PHONE......................................323 866-8483
Graham Woolf, *Principal*
Catherine Bambridge,
Jonathan Gray,
EMP: 132
SALES (corp-wide): 4.1B **Privately Held**
WEB: www.cedars-sinai.org
SIC: 8011 Medical centers
PA: Cedars-Sinai Medical Center
8700 Beverly Blvd
West Hollywood CA 90048
310 423-3277

(P-19742)
CENTRAL CARDIOLOGY MED CLINIC
2901 Sillect Ave Ste 100, Bakersfield (93308-6372)
P.O. Box 1139 (93302-1139)
PHONE......................................661 395-0000
Brijesh Bahmbi, *Partner*
Peter Nalos MD, *Partner*
William Nyitray MD, *Partner*
Kay Bravo, *Asst Admin*
Jaclyn Osthimer, *Research*
EMP: 120 **EST:** 1974
SALES (est): 21.4MM **Privately Held**
WEB: www.heart24.com
SIC: 8011 Cardiologist & cardio-vascular specialist; medical centers

(P-19743)
CHA HEALTH SYSTEMS INC (PA)
Also Called: Cha Renetative Medicine
3731 Wilshire Blvd # 850, Los Angeles (90010-2851)
PHONE......................................213 487-3211
Dr K Cha, *CEO*
Jean Yi, *COO*
Thomas J May,
EMP: 1650 **EST:** 2004
SALES (est): 281.2MM **Privately Held**
WEB: www.kulaio.com
SIC: 8011 Clinic, operated by physicians

(P-19744)
CHARLES C MANGER III MD INC
Also Called: Saddleback Eye Center
23161 Moulton Pkwy, Laguna Hills (92653-1206)
PHONE......................................949 951-4641
Charles C Manger III, *President*
Jessica Harbin, *Marketing Staff*
Laurie Manger, *Director*
EMP: 51 **EST:** 1980
SQ FT: 7,500
SALES (est): 8.8MM **Privately Held**
WEB: www.saddlebackeye.com
SIC: 8011 Ophthalmologist; surgeon

(P-19745)
CHEN DVID MD DGNSTC MED GROUP
208 N Garfield Ave, Monterey Park (91754-1705)
PHONE......................................626 288-8029
Anthony Tsun, *CEO*
EMP: 81 **Privately Held**
WEB: www.airqualityremediation.com
SIC: 8011 Radiologist
PA: Chen, David Md Diagnostic Medical Group Inc
1129 S San Gabriel Blvd
San Gabriel CA 91776

(P-19746)
CHILDRENS CLNIC SRVING CHLDREN
701 E 28th St Ste 200, Long Beach (90806-2784)
PHONE......................................562 264-4638
Elisa A Nicholas, *CEO*
Jina Lee Lawler, *COO*
Maria Y Chandler, *CFO*
Albert P Ocampo, *CFO*
Knut P Thune, *CFO*
EMP: 320 **EST:** 1939
SQ FT: 24,000
SALES (est): 36.8MM **Privately Held**
WEB: www.thechildrensclinic.org
SIC: 8011 Clinic, operated by physicians

(P-19747)
CHILDRENS HEALTH CENTER
Also Called: Yvonne J Bryson MD
200 Ucla Med Ctr Plz 265, Los Angeles (90095-0001)
PHONE......................................310 825-0867
Wendy Songer, *Manager*
Maureen Jonas, *Med Doctor*
EMP: 55 **EST:** 2001
SALES (est): 5.2MM **Privately Held**
WEB: www.uclahealth.org
SIC: 8011 Gastronomist

(P-19748)
CHILDRENS HEALTHCARE CAL
Also Called: Pediatric Cancer Research
455 S Main St, Orange (92868-3835)
P.O. Box 5700 (92863-5700)
PHONE......................................714 997-3000
Kimberly Crite, *CEO*
EMP: 300 **Privately Held**
WEB: www.choc.org
SIC: 8011 Pediatrician
PA: Children's Healthcare Of California
1201 W La Veta Ave
Orange CA 92868

(P-19749)
CHINO MEDICAL GROUP INC
5475 Walnut Ave, Chino (91710-2699)
PHONE......................................909 591-6446
J A Lira MD, *President*
Fidel F Pinzon MD, *Vice Pres*
Steven Pulverman, *Vice Pres*
Jeffrey R Unger MD, *Vice Pres*
Uju Rivera, *Nurse Practr*
EMP: 100 **EST:** 1977
SQ FT: 36,000
SALES (est): 10.1MM **Privately Held**
WEB: www.myfamilymg.com
SIC: 8011 8031 Clinic, operated by physicians; offices & clinics of osteopathic physicians

(P-19750)
CIRRUS HEALTH II LP
Also Called: Laguna Hills Surgery Center
24331 El Toro Rd Ste 150, Laguna Hills (92637-8818)
PHONE......................................949 855-0562
Kim Wood, *Principal*
EMP: 113
SALES (corp-wide): 12.1MM **Privately Held**
SIC: 8011 Clinic, operated by physicians
PA: Cirrus Health Ii, L.P.
2800 E Highway 114 # 300
Trophy Club TX 76262
214 217-0100

(P-19751)
CLINIC INC
Also Called: TO HELP EVERYONE HEALTH AND WE
3834 S Western Ave, Los Angeles (90062-1104)
PHONE......................................323 730-1920
Jamesina E Henderson, *CEO*
Marlin Abramian, *Financial Analy*
Lilian Alvarez, *Human Res Dir*
Naureen Tareen, *Internal Med*
Nnennaya Omerigbo, *Pediatrics*
EMP: 85 **EST:** 1974
SQ FT: 26,000
SALES: 15.1MM **Privately Held**
WEB: www.tohelpeveryone.org
SIC: 8011 Clinic, operated by physicians

(P-19752)
CLINICA MSR OSCAR A ROMERO (PA)
123 S Alvarado St, Los Angeles (90057-2201)
PHONE......................................213 989-7700
Carlos Antonio H Vaquerano, *President*
Pablo F Lopez, *Treasurer*
Marcello Villagomez, *Vice Pres*
Jonathan Miranda Canas C, *Admin Sec*
Eduardo Gonzalez, *Director*
EMP: 52 **EST:** 1983
SALES (est): 13.6MM **Privately Held**
WEB: www.clinicaromero.com
SIC: 8011 Clinic, operated by physicians

(P-19753)
CLINICA SIERRA VISTA (PA)
Also Called: Lamont Community Health Center
1430 Truxtun Ave Ste 400, Bakersfield (93301-5220)
P.O. Box 1559 (93302-1559)
PHONE......................................661 635-3050
Stacy Ferreira, *CEO*
Matthew Clark, *Ch of Bd*
Ana Medina, *COO*
Emily Garcia, *CFO*
Roberto Rivera, *Treasurer*
EMP: 90 **EST:** 1971
SQ FT: 14,599
SALES: 134.9MM **Privately Held**
WEB: www.clinicasierravista.org
SIC: 8011 Clinic, operated by physicians

(P-19754)
CLINICAS DE SLUD DEL PEBLO INC (PA)
852 Danenberg Dr, El Centro (92243-8517)
P.O. Box 1279, Brawley (92227-1279)
PHONE......................................760 344-9951
Yvonne Bell, *CEO*
Gloria Santillan, *CFO*
Greg Gilbert, *Radiology Dir*
Josie Godinez, *Administration*
Priscilla Galvan, *Personnel Assit*
EMP: 62 **EST:** 1970
SQ FT: 15,251
SALES: 65.7MM **Privately Held**
WEB: www.cdsdp.org
SIC: 8011 8049 Clinic, operated by physicians; gynecologist; nutrition specialist; dental hygienist

(P-19755)
CO D L PHAM MD
Also Called: Bolsa Medical Group
10362 Bolsa Ave Ste 110, Westminster (92683-6763)
PHONE......................................714 531-2091
Co L Pham MD, *President*
Tuan V Pham, *Family Practiti*
EMP: 50 **EST:** 1979
SALES (est): 5.3MM **Privately Held**
SIC: 8011 Gynecologist

(P-19756)
COASTAL RDTION ONCLOGY MED GRO
1240 S Westlake Blvd # 1, Westlake Village (91361-1929)
PHONE......................................805 494-4483
Kimberly Commins, *Director*
Lauren Lovett, *Director*
EMP: 99 **EST:** 2018
SALES (est): 2.6MM **Privately Held**
WEB: www.coastalradiationoncology.com
SIC: 8011 Oncologist

(P-19757)
COMMUNITY HEALTH SYSTEMS INC
Also Called: Moreno Valley Family Hlth Ctr
21801 Alessandro Blvd, Moreno Valley (92553-8202)
PHONE......................................951 571-2300
Lori Holeman, *CEO*
Yolanda Gomez, *Director*
EMP: 130 **EST:** 1984
SALES: 26.1MM **Privately Held**
WEB: www.chsica.org
SIC: 8011 Primary care medical clinic

(P-19758)
COMMUNITY HLTH CTRS OF CNTL CA (PA)
150 Tejas Pl, Nipomo (93444-9123)
P.O. Box 430 (93444-0430)
PHONE......................................805 929-3211
Ronald E Castle, *CEO*
Denise Stewart, *COO*
Bob Lotwala, *CFO*
Robert Beaudry, *Exec VP*
Ginger Smith, *Vice Pres*
EMP: 112 **EST:** 1978
SQ FT: 10,000
SALES: 141.5MM **Privately Held**
WEB: www.communityhealthcenters.org
SIC: 8011 Clinic, operated by physicians

(P-19759)
COMMUNITY HLTHCARE PARTNER INC
Also Called: Colorado River Medical Center
1401 Bailey Ave, Needles (92363-3103)
PHONE......................................760 326-4531
Bing Lum, *Exec VP*
Joy Papa, *Lab Dir*
Celia Ulibarri, *Radiology Dir*
Pamela Barrett, *Human Res Dir*
Linda Proa, *Purchasing*
EMP: 100 **EST:** 1999
SQ FT: 46,000
SALES: 9.7MM **Privately Held**
WEB: www.crmccares.com
SIC: 8011 8062 Clinic, operated by physicians; general medical & surgical hospitals

(P-19760)
COMMUNITY ORTHPD MED GROUP PRT
26401 Crown Valley Pkwy, Mission Viejo (92691-6302)
PHONE......................................949 348-4000
Kent Adamson, *President*
Ellen Castillo,
Scott Stephan, *Physician Asst*
Drew Parton, *Assistant*
EMP: 89 **EST:** 1973
SALES (est): 10.7MM **Privately Held**
WEB: www.comg.com
SIC: 8011 Orthopedic physician

(P-19761)
COMPREHENSIVE CMNTY HLTH CTR
5059 York Blvd, Los Angeles (90042-1713)
PHONE......................................323 344-4144
EMP: 50
SALES (est): 78K **Privately Held**
SIC: 8011 Medical Doctor's Office

(P-19762)
COR MEDICA TECHNOLOGY (PA)
188 Technology Dr Ste F, Irvine (92618-2459)
PHONE.....................949 353-4554
Fouad Ghaly, *CEO*
David Sestini, *President*
Kevin Cousins, *Exec VP*
Rachel Everett, *Senior VP*
Robert Prestwood, *Vice Pres*
EMP: 22 EST: 2015
SQ FT: 2,200
SALES (est): 5MM Privately Held
SIC: 8011 3841 Cardiologist & cardio-vascular specialist; diagnostic apparatus, medical

(P-19763)
COUNTY OF LOS ANGELES
Also Called: Health Department
711 Del Amo Blvd, Torrance (90502-1362)
PHONE.....................310 354-2300
Helen Rivera, *Manager*
EMP: 57
SALES (corp-wide): 25.2B Privately Held
WEB: www.lacounty.gov
SIC: 8011 Clinic, operated by physicians
PA: County Of Los Angeles
500 W Temple St Ste 437
Los Angeles CA 90012
213 974-1101

(P-19764)
COUNTY OF LOS ANGELES
1212 Pico St, San Fernando (91340-3503)
PHONE.....................818 837-6969
Gretchen McGinley, *Principal*
Hadi Rahnamoon, *Med Doctor*
EMP: 57
SALES (corp-wide): 25.2B Privately Held
WEB: www.lacounty.gov
SIC: 8011 9111 Clinic, operated by physicians; executive offices
PA: County Of Los Angeles
500 W Temple St Ste 437
Los Angeles CA 90012
213 974-1101

(P-19765)
COUNTY OF LOS ANGELES
Also Called: Hudson H Clude Cmplete Hlth Ct
2829 S Grand Ave, Los Angeles (90007-3304)
PHONE.....................213 744-3919
Michael Mills, *Administration*
Huy Han, *Nephrology*
EMP: 57
SALES (corp-wide): 25.2B Privately Held
WEB: www.lacounty.gov
SIC: 8011 9431 8093 Medical centers; administration of public health programs; ; specialty outpatient clinics
PA: County Of Los Angeles
500 W Temple St Ste 437
Los Angeles CA 90012
213 974-1101

(P-19766)
COUNTY OF LOS ANGELES
Also Called: Health Services, Dept of
15930 Central Ave Ste 100, La Puente (91744-5410)
PHONE.....................626 968-3711
Mary Anne Moreno, *Manager*
EMP: 57
SALES (corp-wide): 25.2B Privately Held
WEB: www.lacounty.gov
SIC: 8011 9431 Medical centers; administration of public health programs;
PA: County Of Los Angeles
500 W Temple St Ste 437
Los Angeles CA 90012
213 974-1101

(P-19767)
COUNTY OF LOS ANGELES
Also Called: Health Services, Dept of
1200 N State St Rm 3250, Los Angeles (90089-1001)
PHONE.....................323 226-3373
David Peng, *Chairman*
EMP: 57

SALES (corp-wide): 25.2B Privately Held
WEB: www.lacounty.gov
SIC: 8011 9431 Dermatologist; child health program administration, government
PA: County Of Los Angeles
500 W Temple St Ste 437
Los Angeles CA 90012
213 974-1101

(P-19768)
COUNTY OF LOS ANGELES
Also Called: Harbor Ucla Medical Center
1403 Lomita Blvd, Harbor City (90710-2076)
PHONE.....................310 257-4989
EMP: 57
SALES (corp-wide): 25.2B Privately Held
WEB: www.lacounty.gov
SIC: 8011 Offices & clinics of medical doctors
PA: County Of Los Angeles
500 W Temple St Ste 437
Los Angeles CA 90012
213 974-1101

(P-19769)
COUNTY OF LOS ANGELES
Also Called: Health Services, Dept of
10005 E Flower Ave, Bellflower (90706)
PHONE.....................562 804-8111
Earnst Espinoza, *Director*
EMP: 57
SALES (corp-wide): 25.2B Privately Held
WEB: www.lacounty.gov
SIC: 8011 9431 Medical centers; administration of public health programs;
PA: County Of Los Angeles
500 W Temple St Ste 437
Los Angeles CA 90012
213 974-1101

(P-19770)
COUNTY OF LOS ANGELES
Also Called: Health Services, Dept of
3834 S Western Ave, Los Angeles (90062-1104)
PHONE.....................323 730-3507
Bernard Wilite, *Administration*
Jan King, *Hlthcr Dir*
EMP: 57
SALES (corp-wide): 25.2B Privately Held
WEB: www.lacounty.gov
SIC: 8011 9431 8031 Medical centers; administration of public health programs; ; offices & clinics of osteopathic physicians
PA: County Of Los Angeles
500 W Temple St Ste 437
Los Angeles CA 90012
213 974-1101

(P-19771)
COUNTY OF LOS ANGELES
Also Called: Health Services, Dept of
1325 Broad Ave, Wilmington (90744-2604)
PHONE.....................310 518-8800
Dr Jesus Gutierrez, *Director*
EMP: 57
SALES (corp-wide): 25.2B Privately Held
WEB: www.lacounty.gov
SIC: 8011 9431 Offices & clinics of medical doctors; administration of public health programs;
PA: County Of Los Angeles
500 W Temple St Ste 437
Los Angeles CA 90012
213 974-1101

(P-19772)
COUNTY OF LOS ANGELES
Also Called: Los Angeles County
13300 Van Nuys Blvd, Pacoima (91331-3004)
PHONE.....................818 896-1903
Miriam Sanchez, *Administration*
EMP: 57
SQ FT: 47,532
SALES (corp-wide): 25.2B Privately Held
WEB: www.lacounty.gov
SIC: 8011 Clinic, operated by physicians
PA: County Of Los Angeles
500 W Temple St Ste 437
Los Angeles CA 90012
213 974-1101

(P-19773)
COUNTY OF LOS ANGELES
Also Called: Health Services, Dept of
150 N Azusa Ave, Azusa (91702-3521)
PHONE.....................626 969-7885
Carmelida Ruffles, *Manager*
EMP: 57
SALES (corp-wide): 25.2B Privately Held
WEB: www.lacounty.gov
SIC: 8011 9431 Clinic, operated by physicians; administration of public health programs;
PA: County Of Los Angeles
500 W Temple St Ste 437
Los Angeles CA 90012
213 974-1101

(P-19774)
COUNTY OF LOS ANGELES
Also Called: Health Services, Dept of
1900 Zonal Ave, Los Angeles (90033-1033)
P.O. Box 866001 (90086-6001)
PHONE.....................323 226-7131
Linda Guerra, *Manager*
EMP: 57
SALES (corp-wide): 25.2B Privately Held
WEB: www.lacounty.gov
SIC: 8011 9431 Offices & clinics of medical doctors; administration of public health programs;
PA: County Of Los Angeles
500 W Temple St Ste 437
Los Angeles CA 90012
213 974-1101

(P-19775)
COUNTY OF LOS ANGELES
Also Called: Mental Health Dept of
2600 Redondo Ave 3, Long Beach (90806-2325)
PHONE.....................562 599-9200
Margie Pappas, *Chief*
Sherletta Carter, *Social Worker*
EMP: 57
SALES (corp-wide): 25.2B Privately Held
WEB: www.lacounty.gov
SIC: 8011 9431 Offices & clinics of medical doctors; administration of public health programs;
PA: County Of Los Angeles
500 W Temple St Ste 437
Los Angeles CA 90012
213 974-1101

(P-19776)
COVID CLINIC INC
18800 Delaware St Ste 800, Huntington Beach (92648-6019)
PHONE.....................877 219-8378
Matthew Collins, *CEO*
Matthew Abinante, *CFO*
EMP: 68 EST: 2020
SALES (est): 10.5MM Privately Held
WEB: www.covidclinic.org
SIC: 8011 Offices & clinics of medical doctors

(P-19777)
CRESTWOOD BEHAVIORAL HLTH INC
Also Called: 116 Angwin Mhrc
6700 Eucalyptus Dr Ste A, Bakersfield (93306-6076)
PHONE.....................661 363-0124
Delphina Deleon, *Exec Dir*
EMP: 547
SALES (corp-wide): 238MM Privately Held
WEB: www.crestwoodbehavioralhealth.com
SIC: 8011 Offices & clinics of medical doctors
PA: Crestwood Behavioral Health, Inc.
520 Capitol Mall Ste 800
Sacramento CA 95814
510 651-1244

(P-19778)
CROWN SURGERY MED GROUP INC (PA)
25470 Med Ctr Dr Ste 203, Murrieta (92562)
PHONE.....................951 973-7290
Festus Dada, *President*
EMP: 84 EST: 2002

SALES (est): 2.7MM Privately Held
WEB: www.crownsurgery.com
SIC: 8011 Surgeon

(P-19779)
DARIUS E LIN MD INC
15 Blessing, Irvine (92612-3274)
PHONE.....................215 601-6899
Darius E Lin, *Branch Mgr*
EMP: 87
SALES (corp-wide): 800.3K Privately Held
SIC: 8011 Offices & clinics of medical doctors
PA: Darius E. Lin, M.D., Inc.
11160 Warner Ave Ste 311
Fountain Valley CA 92708
215 601-6899

(P-19780)
DAVID S BOYER MD INC
12840 Rverside Dr Ste 402, North Hollywood (91607)
PHONE.....................818 754-2090
David Boyer, *Branch Mgr*
EMP: 52
SALES (corp-wide): 1MM Privately Held
WEB: www.laretina.com
SIC: 8011 Ophthalmologist
PA: David S. Boyer, M.D., Inc.
1127 Wilshire Blvd # 1620
Los Angeles CA 90017
310 854-6201

(P-19781)
DAVITA MAGAN MANAGEMENT INC (DH)
Also Called: M M C
420 W Rowland St, Covina (91723-2943)
PHONE.....................626 331-6411
Bradley J Rosenberg, *Principal*
Connie Solorza, *Division VP*
Howard Ort MD, *Exec VP*
Miguel Garcia, *Vice Pres*
Blair Johnson, *Executive*
EMP: 250 EST: 1975
SQ FT: 66,000
SALES (est): 93.8MM Publicly Held
WEB: www.optumcare.com
SIC: 8011 Clinic, operated by physicians; urologist; internal medicine, physician/surgeon; ophthalmologist

(P-19782)
DAVITA MEDICAL MANAGEMENT LLC
Also Called: Medical Group
9810 Las Tunas Dr, Temple City (91780-2208)
PHONE.....................626 309-7600
Mariln Williams, *Branch Mgr*
Sandra Nicolas, *Admin Asst*
Yvette David, *Med Doctor*
Gil Eng, *Med Doctor*
Marlon Farley, *Med Doctor*
EMP: 60 Publicly Held
SIC: 8011 Internal medicine practitioners
HQ: Davita Medical Management, Llc
2175 Park Pl
El Segundo CA 90245

(P-19783)
DAVITA MEDICAL MANAGEMENT LLC
4281 Katella Ave Ste 220, Los Alamitos (90720-6506)
PHONE.....................714 252-1135
Dennis Kogod, *Branch Mgr*
Craig L Olsen, *Med Doctor*
EMP: 60 Publicly Held
SIC: 8011 Group health association
HQ: Davita Medical Management, Llc
2175 Park Pl
El Segundo CA 90245

(P-19784)
DAVITA MEDICAL MANAGEMENT LLC
Also Called: Healthcare Partners Med Group
3932 Long Beach Blvd, Long Beach (90807-2615)
PHONE.....................562 304-2100
Kenny Heine, *Branch Mgr*

PRODUCTS & SVCS

EMP: 60 **Publicly Held**
SIC: **8011** Group health association
HQ: Davita Medical Management, Llc
2175 Park Pl
El Segundo CA 90245

(P-19785)
DAVITA MEDICAL MANAGEMENT LLC
Also Called: Health Care Partners
6226 E Spring St Ste 100, Long Beach
(90815-1442)
PHONE..................562 420-1338
Lorraine Keating, *Administration*
Kimberly A Arsi, *Principal*
James Linden, *Psychologist*
Robert Cohen, *Med Doctor*
Anh Pham, *Med Doctor*
EMP: 60 **Publicly Held**
SIC: **8011** Clinic, operated by physicians
HQ: Davita Medical Management, Llc
2175 Park Pl
El Segundo CA 90245

(P-19786)
DAVITA MEDICAL MANAGEMENT LLC
Harriman Jones Medical
2600 Redondo Ave Ste 405, Long Beach
(90806-2330)
PHONE..................562 988-7000
Jill R Cortese, *Principal*
Suzanne Hansen, *Vice Pres*
Jim Kostick, *Vice Pres*
Michael McArthur, *Vice Pres*
Dan Reynolds, *Vice Pres*
EMP: 60 **Publicly Held**
SIC: **8011** Clinic, operated by physicians
HQ: Davita Medical Management, Llc
2175 Park Pl
El Segundo CA 90245

(P-19787)
DAVITA MEDICAL MANAGEMENT LLC
502 Torrance Blvd, Redondo Beach
(90277-3413)
PHONE..................310 316-0811
Mark Moser, *Branch Mgr*
Mary Rowe, *Office Mgr*
Richard Tibor, *Psychologist*
Nevine Salama, *Med Doctor*
John Tsao, *Med Doctor*
EMP: 60
SQ FT: 23,000 **Publicly Held**
SIC: **8011** General & family practice, physician/surgeon
HQ: Davita Medical Management, Llc
2175 Park Pl
El Segundo CA 90245

(P-19788)
DAVITA MEDICAL MANAGEMENT LLC
Also Called: Healthcare Partners Med Group
2601 Via Campo, Montebello (90640-1807)
PHONE..................323 720-1144
Sonia Flores, *Branch Mgr*
Kathleen Savage, *Psychologist*
Kwei J Quartey, *Internal Med*
Brittina Rollins, *Manager*
EMP: 60 **Publicly Held**
SIC: **8011** Clinic, operated by physicians
HQ: Davita Medical Management, Llc
2175 Park Pl
El Segundo CA 90245

(P-19789)
DAVITA MEDICAL MANAGEMENT LLC
Also Called: Healthcare Partners Med Group
3144 Santa Anita Ave # 2, El Monte
(91733-1316)
PHONE..................626 444-0333
Joseph Soto, *Branch Mgr*
EMP: 60 **Publicly Held**
SIC: **8011** Clinic, operated by physicians

HQ: Davita Medical Management, Llc
2175 Park Pl
El Segundo CA 90245

(P-19790)
DAVITA MEDICAL MANAGEMENT LLC
Memorial Medical Group
2699 Atlantic Ave, Long Beach
(90806-2710)
PHONE..................562 426-3333
Marc W Sonne MD, *Branch Mgr*
EMP: 60 **Publicly Held**
SIC: **8011** Physicians' office, including specialists
HQ: Davita Medical Management, Llc
2175 Park Pl
El Segundo CA 90245

(P-19791)
DAVITA MEDICAL MANAGEMENT LLC (HQ)
Also Called: Healthcare Partners Med Group
2175 Park Pl, El Segundo (90245-4705)
PHONE..................310 354-4200
Robert J Margolis, *CEO*
Marianne Garrity, *President*
Karen Hayes, *CFO*
Kevin Littlefield, *Officer*
Matthew Mazdyasni, *Exec VP*
EMP: 600 **EST:** 1994
SQ FT: 38,000
SALES (est): 258.2MM **Publicly Held**
WEB: www.davita.com
SIC: **8011** Group health association

(P-19792)
DAVITA MEDICAL MANAGEMENT LLC
931 Buena Vista St # 405, Duarte
(91010-1712)
PHONE..................626 358-0269
Robert Margolis, *Branch Mgr*
EMP: 60 **Publicly Held**
SIC: **8011** Physicians' office, including specialists
HQ: Davita Medical Management, Llc
2175 Park Pl
El Segundo CA 90245

(P-19793)
DESERT CRDLGY CONS MED GROUP I
Also Called: Desert Cardiology Cons Med G
39000 Bob Hope Dr, Rancho Mirage
(92270-3221)
PHONE..................760 346-0642
Keenan F Barber, *Vice Pres*
Barry Hackshaw, *President*
Merle R Bolton, *Treasurer*
Charles W Shaeffer Jr, *Admin Sec*
Philip Patel, *Cardiology*
EMP: 78 **EST:** 1974
SALES (est): 9.9MM **Privately Held**
WEB: www.desertcard.com
SIC: **8011** Cardiologist & cardio-vascular specialist

(P-19794)
DESERT HEART PHYSICIANS INC
1180 N Indian Canyon Dr, Palm Springs
(92262-4800)
PHONE..................760 325-1203
Narasimha RAO MD, *President*
EMP: 79 **EST:** 1982
SALES (est): 5.5MM **Privately Held**
WEB: www.desertheartphysicians.com
SIC: **8011** Cardiologist & cardio-vascular specialist

(P-19795)
DESERT MEDICAL GROUP INC (PA)
Also Called: Desert Oasis Healthcare
275 N El Cielo Rd D-402, Palm Springs
(92262-6972)
PHONE..................760 320-8814
Richard E Merkin MD, *President*
EMP: 240 **EST:** 1981
SQ FT: 13,000

SALES (est): 50.5MM **Privately Held**
WEB: www.mydohc.com
SIC: **8011** General & family practice, physician/surgeon

(P-19796)
DESERT ORTHPD CTR A MED GROUP (PA)
39000 Bob Hope Dr Ste W30, Rancho Mirage (92270-3221)
PHONE..................760 568-2684
Ronald Lamb MD, *President*
Robert Murphy MD, *Ch of Bd*
Stephen O Connell MD, *CFO*
Carol Alvarez, *Vice Pres*
James Bell MD, *Vice Pres*
EMP: 78 **EST:** 1990
SQ FT: 23,000
SALES (est): 17.3MM **Privately Held**
WEB: www.desertortho.com
SIC: **8011** Orthopedic physician

(P-19797)
DESERT RADIOLOGY MEDICAL GROUP
1150 N Indian Canyon Dr, Palm Springs
(92262-4872)
P.O. Box 2829 (92263-2829)
PHONE..................760 778-5900
David Conston MD, *Partner*
Dennis Blafberg MD, *Partner*
Linda Gordon MD, *Partner*
John Leary MD, *Partner*
Barry Mantell MD, *Partner*
EMP: 62 **EST:** 1964
SALES (est): 1.1MM **Privately Held**
WEB: www.eisenhowerradiology.com
SIC: **8011** Radiologist

(P-19798)
DESERT VALLEY MED GROUP INC (PA)
16850 Bear Valley Rd, Victorville
(92395-5794)
PHONE..................760 241-8000
Prem Reddy MD, *CEO*
Lex Reddy, *President*
M Mansukhani, *CFO*
Diane Van Velkinburg, *Project Mgr*
EMP: 300 **EST:** 1981
SQ FT: 15,000
SALES (est): 51.1MM **Privately Held**
WEB: www.desertvalleymedicalgroup.com
SIC: **8011** Physicians' office, including specialists

(P-19799)
DIAGNSTIC INTRVNTNAL SRGCAL CT
13160 Mindanao Way # 150, Marina Del Rey (90292-6358)
PHONE..................310 574-0400
Robert S Bray Jr, *President*
Keren Reiter, *COO*
Amer Khalil, *Surgeon*
Richard Kim, *Surgeon*
Hamid Mir, *Surgeon*
EMP: 100 **EST:** 2006 **Privately Held**
WEB: www.discmdgroup.com
SIC: **8011** Orthopedic physician

(P-19800)
DIGESTIVE CARE CONSULTANTS
23451 Madison St Ste 290, Torrance
(90505-4737)
PHONE..................310 375-1246
Kenneth Holt MD, *Partner*
Karl Fukunaga MD, *Partner*
James Sattler, *Partner*
Therese Botkin, *Office Mgr*
Pam Phillips, *Admin Sec*
EMP: 61 **EST:** 2001
SALES (est): 19.6MM **Privately Held**
WEB: www.digestivecareconsultants.net
SIC: **8011** Gastronomist

(P-19801)
DIGITAL RDLGIC IMGING ASSOC IN
29122 Rncho Vejo Rd Ste 1, San Juan Capistrano (92675)
PHONE..................949 499-1311
Elliot Wagner, *President*
EMP: 61

SALES (corp-wide): 3.6MM **Privately Held**
SIC: **8011** Radiologist
PA: Digital And Radiologic Imaging Associates, Inc., A Medical Group
27800 Med Ctr Rd Ste 108
Mission Viejo CA 92691
949 364-6900

(P-19802)
EDINGER MEDICAL GROUP INC
Also Called: Willis, Burton F MD
18682 Beach Blvd Ste 150, Huntington Beach (92648-2050)
PHONE..................714 965-2500
Burton Willis, *Manager*
MAI Tran, *Pediatrics*
Alan Viglione, *Med Doctor*
Lana Nguyen, *Nurse*
Robyne Thibodeau, *Director*
EMP: 61
SALES (corp-wide): 14.5MM **Privately Held**
WEB: www.edingermedicalgroup.com
SIC: **8011** General & family practice, physician/surgeon
PA: Edinger Medical Group, Inc.
9900 Talbert Ave 302
Fountain Valley CA 92708
714 965-2500

(P-19803)
EDWARDS LIFESCIENCES LLC (HQ)
1 Edwards Way, Irvine (92614-5688)
PHONE..................949 250-2500
Michael A Mussallem, *CEO*
Huimin Wang MD, *President*
Aik Doumanian, *Officer*
Jeremy Curtis, *Vice Pres*
Patricia Garvey, *Vice Pres*
▲ EMP: 1700 **EST:** 1958
SALES (est): 420.3MM
SALES (corp-wide): 4.3B **Publicly Held**
WEB: www.edwards.com
SIC: **8011** Cardiologist & cardio-vascular specialist
PA: Edwards Lifesciences Corp
1 Edwards Way
Irvine CA 92614
949 250-2500

(P-19804)
ELITE DIAGNOSTIC IMAGING LLC
Also Called: Elite Imaging
17260 Bear Valley Rd # 109, Victorville
(92395-7778)
PHONE..................760 962-9866
Michael Atwood,
Hector Torres,
EMP: 60 **EST:** 2006
SQ FT: 9,000
SALES (est): 1MM **Privately Held**
SIC: **8011** Radiologist

(P-19805)
EMANATE HEALTH
1722 Desire Ave Ste 206, Rowland Heights
(91748-2970)
PHONE..................626 912-5282
EMP: 229
SALES (corp-wide): 464.3MM **Privately Held**
WEB: www.emanatehealth.org
SIC: **8011** Physicians' office, including specialists
PA: Emanate Health Medical Center
1115 S Sunset Ave
West Covina CA 91790
626 962-4011

(P-19806)
EMERGENT MEDICAL ASSOCIATES (PA)
111 N Sepulveda Blvd # 210, Manhattan Beach (90266-6849)
PHONE..................310 379-2134
Mark Bell, *Principal*
David Limoges, *CTO*
Wilma Kanwar, *Accountant*
▲ EMP: 122 **EST:** 2005
SALES (est): 22.6MM **Privately Held**
WEB: www.ema.us
SIC: **8011** Medical centers

(P-19807)
ENKI HEALTH AND RES SYSTEMS
Also Called: Enki Health Care
160 S 7th Ave, La Puente (91746-3211)
PHONE...........................626 961-8971
Maria M Carmichael, *Director*
Joseph Avila, *Admin Asst*
Sharlene Silva, *Psychologist*
Cecilia Hsia, *Psychiatry*
EMP: 55
SALES (corp-wide): 31.1MM **Privately Held**
WEB: www.ehrs.com
SIC: 8011 8733 Psychiatric clinic; medical research
PA: Enki Health And Research Systems
150 E Olive Ave Ste 203
Burbank CA 91502
818 973-4899

(P-19808)
EXER HOLDING COMPANY LLC
15503 Ventura Blvd, Encino (91436-3114)
PHONE...........................818 287-0894
Cherlin Johnson,
Gary Turner, *Vice Pres*
Scott Whitney, *Vice Pres*
Jerry Winklhofer, *Controller*
Eva Kurtin,
EMP: 50 EST: 2014
SALES (est): 17.9MM **Privately Held**
WEB: www.exerurgentcare.com
SIC: 8011 Clinic, operated by physicians

(P-19809)
EYE PHYSCANS LONG BCH A MED GR
2925 Palo Verde Ave, Long Beach (90815-1552)
PHONE...........................562 421-2757
Carlos E Martinez, *President*
EMP: 72 EST: 1978
SALES (est): 16.4MM **Privately Held**
WEB: www.eyephysiciansoflongbeach.com
SIC: 8011 Ophthalmologist

(P-19810)
FACEY MEDICAL FOUNDATION (PA)
15451 San Frnndo Mssion B, Mission Hills (91345-1368)
PHONE...........................818 365-9531
Bill Gill, *CEO*
Jim Corwin, *CFO*
Steven Watson, *Administration*
James Moreno, *Technical Staff*
Anna Ventura, *OB/GYN*
EMP: 170 EST: 1991
SQ FT: 306,000
SALES (est): 96.9MM **Privately Held**
WEB: www.facey.com
SIC: 8011 Physicians' office, including specialists

(P-19811)
FACEY MEDICAL FOUNDATION
27924 Seco Canyon Rd, Santa Clarita (91350-3870)
PHONE...........................661 513-2100
Joan Rhee, *Manager*
Maria Catheri Asuncion, *Internal Med*
Jong Lee, *Internal Med*
Cindy Abernethy,
EMP: 147
SALES (corp-wide): 96.9MM **Privately Held**
WEB: www.facey.com
SIC: 8011 Physicians' office, including specialists
PA: Facey Medical Foundation
15451 San Frnndo Mssion B
Mission Hills CA 91345
818 365-9531

(P-19812)
FACEY MEDICAL FOUNDATION
11165 Sepulveda Blvd, Mission Hills (91345-1125)
PHONE...........................818 365-9531
Judy Breen, *Branch Mgr*
Roscoe Marter, *Vice Pres*
Ashley Johann, *Opers Staff*
Donald Huey, *Internal Med*
Poonam Gorakshakar, *Med Doctor*

EMP: 147
SALES (corp-wide): 96.9MM **Privately Held**
WEB: www.facey.com
SIC: 8011 Physicians' office, including specialists
PA: Facey Medical Foundation
15451 San Frnndo Mssion B
Mission Hills CA 91345
818 365-9531

(P-19813)
FACEY MEDICAL GROUP PC (HQ)
11333 Sepulveda Blvd, Mission Hills (91345-1116)
PHONE...........................818 365-9531
Frederick Russo MD, *President*
Magaly Beilke, *Vice Pres*
Roscoe Marter, *Vice Pres*
Susan Slack, *Admin Dir*
Peter Richman, *CTO*
EMP: 116 EST: 1991
SALES (est): 12.7MM
SALES (corp-wide): 96.9MM **Privately Held**
WEB: www.facey.com
SIC: 8011 8741 Pediatrician; management services
PA: Facey Medical Foundation
15451 San Frnndo Mssion B
Mission Hills CA 91345
818 365-9531

(P-19814)
FAMILY HEALTHCARE NETWORK
501 N Bridge St, Visalia (93291-5014)
PHONE...........................559 734-1939
Travis Chapin, *Principal*
Sarah De Leon, *Executive Asst*
Daryl Sanchez, *Financial Analy*
Elizabeth Enderton, *Director*
Jeanine Bailey, *Manager*
EMP: 114
SALES (corp-wide): 209.5MM **Privately Held**
WEB: www.fhcn.org
SIC: 8011 General & family practice, physician/surgeon
PA: Family Healthcare Network
305 E Center Ave
Visalia CA 93291
559 737-4700

(P-19815)
FAMILY HEALTHCARE NETWORK
Also Called: Porterville Annex
1137 W Poplar Ave, Porterville (93257-5839)
PHONE...........................559 781-7242
EMP: 114
SALES (corp-wide): 209.5MM **Privately Held**
WEB: www.fhcn.org
SIC: 8011 Primary care medical clinic
PA: Family Healthcare Network
305 E Center Ave
Visalia CA 93291
559 737-4700

(P-19816)
FAMILY HEALTHCARE NETWORK
400 E Oak Ave, Visalia (93291-5034)
PHONE...........................559 741-4500
Harry Foste, *Exec Dir*
Max E Yankes, *Internal Med*
EMP: 114
SQ FT: 20,182
SALES (corp-wide): 209.5MM **Privately Held**
WEB: www.fhcn.org
SIC: 8011 General & family practice, physician/surgeon; clinic, operated by physicians
PA: Family Healthcare Network
305 E Center Ave
Visalia CA 93291
559 737-4700

(P-19817)
FAMILY HEALTHCARE NETWORK
801 W Center Ave, Visalia (93291-6013)
PHONE...........................559 737-4700
Harry Foster, *Branch Mgr*
Alfred Alvarado, *Technology*
EMP: 114
SALES (corp-wide): 209.5MM **Privately Held**
WEB: www.fhcn.org
SIC: 8011 Clinic, operated by physicians
PA: Family Healthcare Network
305 E Center Ave
Visalia CA 93291
559 737-4700

(P-19818)
FAMILY HEALTHCARE NETWORK
250 W 5th St, Hanford (93230-5029)
PHONE...........................559 582-2013
EMP: 114
SALES (corp-wide): 209.5MM **Privately Held**
WEB: www.fhcn.org
SIC: 8011 Primary care medical clinic
PA: Family Healthcare Network
305 E Center Ave
Visalia CA 93291
559 737-4700

(P-19819)
FAMILY HEALTHCARE NETWORK
33025 159th Rd, Ivanhoe (93235)
PHONE...........................559 798-1877
Yterry Abbott, *Manager*
EMP: 114
SALES (corp-wide): 209.5MM **Privately Held**
WEB: www.fhcn.org
SIC: 8011 8021 Physicians' office, including specialists; offices & clinics of dentists
PA: Family Healthcare Network
305 E Center Ave
Visalia CA 93291
559 737-4700

(P-19820)
FAMILY PLG ASSOC MED GROUP (PA)
3050 E Airport Way, Long Beach (90806-2404)
PHONE...........................213 738-7283
Edward C Allred MD, *Principal*
EMP: 52 EST: 1968
SQ FT: 14,000
SALES (est): 39.7MM **Privately Held**
WEB: www.fpamg.net
SIC: 8011 Clinic, operated by physicians

(P-19821)
FANG INC
12235 Beach Blvd Ste 20h, Stanton (90680-3965)
PHONE...........................714 898-7785
Kaung-King Fang, *President*
Kaung Fang, *General Mgr*
EMP: 55 EST: 1990
SALES (est): 5MM **Privately Held**
WEB: www.fanginc.com
SIC: 8011 Offices & clinics of medical doctors

(P-19822)
FCS MEDICAL CORPORATION
Also Called: Family Care Specialists
815 Washington Blvd, Montebello (90640-6123)
PHONE...........................323 728-3955
Alma Espana, *Manager*
EMP: 87 **Privately Held**
WEB: www.fcsmg.com
SIC: 8011 Internal medicine, physician/surgeon
PA: Fcs Medical Corporation
5823 York Blvd Ste 1
Los Angeles CA 90042

(P-19823)
FIRST CHOICE PHYSCN PARTNERS (HQ)
Also Called: Fcpp
1400 S Douglass Rd # 250, Anaheim (92806-6904)
PHONE...........................714 428-2311
Ronald L Kaufman, *CEO*
EMP: 50 EST: 2010
SALES (est): 8.1MM
SALES (corp-wide): 17.6B **Publicly Held**
WEB: www.fcpp.com
SIC: 8011 Clinic, operated by physicians
PA: Tenet Healthcare Corporation
14201 Dallas Pkwy
Dallas TX 75254
469 893-2200

(P-19824)
FOUR SEASONS SURGERY CENTERS
1211 W 6th St, Ontario (91762-1103)
PHONE...........................909 933-6576
Andrea Amanda, *Principal*
EMP: 15 EST: 2004
SALES (est): 2.4MM **Privately Held**
WEB: www.fssc22000.com
SIC: 8011 3842 Ambulatory surgical center; grafts, artificial: for surgery

(P-19825)
FRIEDMAN PROFESSIONAL MGT CO
Also Called: Post Surgical Recovery Center
17752 Beach Blvd Side, Huntington Beach (92647-6838)
PHONE...........................714 842-1426
EMP: 70 EST: 1975
SQ FT: 35,500
SALES (est): 4.1MM **Privately Held**
SIC: 8011 Minor Surgical Clinic

(P-19826)
FULLERTON ORTHPD SRGERY MED GR
Also Called: Wagner, Kendall S MD
680 Langsdorf Dr, Fullerton (92831-3702)
PHONE...........................714 879-0050
Philip H Mc Farland MD, *President*
Kendall S Wagner MD, *Treasurer*
Harry L Gibson MD, *Vice Pres*
John F Parker MD, *Admin Sec*
Eugene D Williams, *Asst Treas*
EMP: 68 EST: 1974
SALES (est): 6MM **Privately Held**
WEB: www.fcppfullertonortho.com
SIC: 8011 Orthopedic physician

(P-19827)
GARDEN GROVE ADVANCED IMAGING
1510 Cotner Ave, Los Angeles (90025-3303)
PHONE...........................310 445-2800
EMP: 107 EST: 2015
SALES (est): 5.3MM **Publicly Held**
WEB: www.radnet.com
SIC: 8011 Radiologist
HQ: Radnet Management Iii, Inc.
1510 Cotner Ave
Los Angeles CA 90025
310 445-2800

(P-19828)
GARFIELD IMAGING CENTER INC
555 N Garfield Ave, Monterey Park (91754-1202)
PHONE...........................626 572-0912
Clark Gardner MD, *President*
EMP: 107 EST: 1980
SQ FT: 3,000
SALES (est): 5.9MM
SALES (corp-wide): 359.9MM **Privately Held**
WEB: www.garfieldimaging.com
SIC: 8011 Radiologist
HQ: Insight Health Services Corp.
5775 Wayzata Blvd Ste 400
Minneapolis MN 55416

(P-19829)
GARRISON FAMILY MED GROUP INC
41210 11th St W Ste K, Palmdale (93551-1447)
PHONE..................661 947-7100
Ric Garrison, *President*
Mary Tockstein, *Assistant*
EMP: 60 **EST:** 1980
SALES (est): 6.6MM **Privately Held**
WEB:
www.garrisonfamilymedicalgroup.com
SIC: 8011 General & family practice, physician/surgeon

(P-19830)
GEORGE M RAJACICH MD PC
Also Called: Valley Eye Center Group
14914 Sherman Way, Van Nuys (91405-2113)
PHONE..................818 787-2020
George M Rajacich MD, *President*
Dorcas Fikejs, *Office Mgr*
EMP: 50 **EST:** 1985
SQ FT: 12,000
SALES (est): 6.4MM **Privately Held**
WEB: www.amerisight.com
SIC: 8011 Ophthalmologist

(P-19831)
GLENDALE EYE MEDICAL GROUP (PA)
Also Called: Amsurg
607 N Central Ave Ste 203, Glendale (91203-1845)
PHONE..................818 956-1010
Richard Weise, *Partner*
Stephen Chang, *Partner*
Candy Sorgani, *Administration*
Heather McKinney,
Carolyn Wang,
EMP: 63 **EST:** 1981
SALES (est): 5.7MM **Privately Held**
WEB: www.glendaleeye.com
SIC: 8011 Physicians' office, including specialists; ophthalmologist

(P-19832)
GOLDEN RAIN FOUNDATION
1661 Golden Rain Rd, Seal Beach (90740-4999)
P.O. Box 2685 (90740-1685)
PHONE..................562 493-9581
EMP: 104
SALES (corp-wide): 15MM **Privately Held**
WEB: www.lwsb.com
SIC: 8011 Geriatric specialist, physician/surgeon
PA: Rain Golden Foundation
13531 Saint Andrews Dr
Seal Beach CA 90740
562 431-6586

(P-19833)
GOOD SAMARITAN HOSPITAL AUX
1225 Wilshire Blvd, Los Angeles (90017-1901)
PHONE..................213 977-2121
Andrew Leeka, *CEO*
Claus Von Zychlin, *COO*
EMP: 131 **EST:** 2001
SALES (est): 4.2MM **Privately Held**
WEB: www.pihhealth.org
SIC: 8011 Medical centers

(P-19834)
GREGORY A STAINER MD FACS
Also Called: 2nd Location, SW Eye Care
215 China Grade Loop, Bakersfield (93308-1707)
PHONE..................661 393-2331
Gregory A Stainer MD, *President*
EMP: 51 **EST:** 1980
SQ FT: 3,000
SALES (est): 5.2MM **Privately Held**
WEB: www.bakersfieldlasik.com
SIC: 8011 Ophthalmologist

(P-19835)
GROVE DIAGNSTC IMAGING CTR INC
8805 Haven Ave Ste 120, Rancho Cucamonga (91730-5149)
PHONE..................909 982-8638
Broc Larouche, *General Mgr*
EMP: 568 **Publicly Held**
WEB: www.radnet.com
SIC: 8011 Radiologist
HQ: Grove Diagnostic Imaging Center, Inc.
8283 Grove Ave Ste 101
Rancho Cucamonga CA 91730

(P-19836)
GROVE DIAGNSTC IMAGING CTR INC (DH)
8283 Grove Ave Ste 101, Rancho Cucamonga (91730-3138)
PHONE..................909 982-8638
Elena Kogan, *President*
EMP: 50 **EST:** 1995
SALES (est): 7.7MM **Publicly Held**
WEB: www.radnet.com
SIC: 8011 Radiologist
HQ: Radnet Management Iii, Inc.
1510 Cotner Ave
Los Angeles CA 90025
310 445-2800

(P-19837)
HEALTHPOINTE MEDICAL GROUP INC (PA)
Also Called: Southern Cal Orthopedics
16702 Valley View Ave, La Mirada (90638-5824)
PHONE..................714 956-2663
Ismael Silva, *President*
Ernest Medina, *Exec Dir*
Carmen Aceves, *Administration*
Patricia Garnette, *Administration*
Daniel Santos, *Sales Mgr*
EMP: 52 **EST:** 1986
SQ FT: 10,000
SALES (est): 25.7MM **Privately Held**
WEB: www.healthpointe.net
SIC: 8011 Orthopedic physician; sports medicine specialist, physician; surgeon

(P-19838)
HEALTHSMART PACIFIC INC
Also Called: Health Smart Clinic
2683 Pacific Ave, Long Beach (90806-2610)
PHONE..................562 595-1911
Mike Drobot, *CEO*
EMP: 311
SALES (corp-wide): 29.6MM **Privately Held**
SIC: 8011 Clinic, operated by physicians
PA: Healthsmart Pacific, Inc.
5150 E Pacific Cst Hwy # 200
Long Beach CA 90804
562 595-1911

(P-19839)
HEART CENTER A MEDICAL CORP
Also Called: Kumar, Vinod MD Facc
5020 Commerce Dr, Bakersfield (93309-0631)
PHONE..................661 324-4100
Vinod Kumar MD, *President*
Marcella Sunseri, *Executive*
EMP: 51 **EST:** 1992
SQ FT: 4,600
SALES (est): 10.8MM **Privately Held**
WEB: www.vascularhealth.com
SIC: 8011 Cardiologist & cardio-vascular specialist

(P-19840)
HENRY MAYO NEWHALL MEM HOSP
23845 Mcbean Pkwy, Valencia (91355-2001)
PHONE..................661 253-8112
EMP: 94 **EST:** 2013
SALES (est): 245.5MM **Privately Held**
SIC: 8011 Medical Doctor's Office

(P-19841)
HERALD CHRISTIAN HEALTH CENTER
1661 Hanover Rd Ste 103, City of Industry (91748-5705)
PHONE..................626 286-8700
Spencer Tsui, *Branch Mgr*
EMP: 60 **Privately Held**
WEB: www.hchcla.org
SIC: 8011 Clinic, operated by physicians
PA: Christian Herald Health Center
3401 Aero Jet Ave
El Monte CA 91731

(P-19842)
HERALD CHRISTIAN HEALTH CENTER (PA)
3401 Aero Jet Ave, El Monte (91731-2801)
PHONE..................626 286-8700
David Lee, *CEO*
Carolin Eng, *COO*
Emily Szeto, *CFO*
Amanda Yang, *Business Dir*
Thomas Harang, *Human Res Dir*
EMP: 80 **EST:** 2005
SALES (est): 15.1MM **Privately Held**
WEB: www.hchcla.org
SIC: 8011 8021 Primary care medical clinic; dental clinics & offices

(P-19843)
HERITAGE MEDICAL GROUP INC (PA)
Also Called: Bakersfield Family Medical Ctr
4580 California Ave, Bakersfield (93309-1104)
P.O. Box 10749 (93389-0749)
PHONE..................661 327-4411
Stanley Wohl, *CEO*
Richard Merkin, *Owner*
Ardelle Covington, *Admin Sec*
Flo Meador, *Info Tech Mgr*
Mark Lin, *Med Doctor*
EMP: 119 **EST:** 1984
SALES (est): 25.2MM **Privately Held**
WEB: www.bfmc.com
SIC: 8011 Offices & clinics of medical doctors

(P-19844)
HIGH DSERT MED CORP A MED GROU (PA)
Also Called: Heritage Health Care
43839 15th St W, Lancaster (93534-4756)
P.O. Box 7007 (93539-7007)
PHONE..................661 945-5984
Richard N Merkin, *CEO*
Ian Drew, *Records Dir*
David Pfafman, *Records Dir*
Rafael Gonzalez, *Administration*
Nathaniel Bautista, *CTO*
EMP: 120 **EST:** 1984
SQ FT: 25,000
SALES (est): 51MM **Privately Held**
WEB: www.hdmg.net
SIC: 8011 Clinic, operated by physicians

(P-19845)
HONDA STEPHAN T MD INC
Also Called: Bayside Medical Center
2301 W El Segundo Blvd, Hawthorne (90250-3315)
PHONE..................323 757-2118
Stephan T Honda, *President*
Claudia Valtierra, *Admin Sec*
Steve Browning, *Director*
EMP: 52 **EST:** 1960
SQ FT: 5,000
SALES (est): 7.2MM **Privately Held**
WEB: www.baysidemedicalcenter.com
SIC: 8011 General & family practice, physician/surgeon

(P-19846)
HOUSE EAR CLINIC INC (PA)
2100 W 3rd St Ste 111, Los Angeles (90057-1999)
P.O. Box 52001, Phoenix AZ (85072-2001)
PHONE..................213 483-9930
Derald E Brackmann MD, *President*
John W House MD, *Treasurer*
Antonio D La Cruz MD, *Admin Sec*
Gonzalez Alyssa, *Admin Asst*
Alyssa Gonzalez, *Admin Asst*
EMP: 88 **EST:** 1969
SQ FT: 25,500
SALES (est): 9.6MM **Privately Held**
WEB: www.houseinstitute.com
SIC: 8011 5999 Ears, nose & throat specialist: physician/surgeon; hearing aids

(P-19847)
HUNTINGTON AMBLTRY SURG CTR
625 S Fair Oaks Ave, Pasadena (91105-2613)
P.O. Box 840189, Los Angeles (90084-0189)
PHONE..................626 229-8999
Harry Bowles, *Mng Member*
Bernadette Molino,
James Noble,
Stephen Ralph,
Robin Waldvogel, *Director*
EMP: 50 **EST:** 2010
SALES (est): 10.5MM **Privately Held**
WEB: www.huntingtonhospital.org
SIC: 8011 Surgeon

(P-19848)
HUNTINGTON MEDICAL FOUNDATION
10 Congress St Ste 208, Pasadena (91105-3027)
PHONE..................626 795-4210
Donna Ellis, *Office Mgr*
George Jung, *Med Doctor*
EMP: 66 **Privately Held**
WEB: www.huntingtonhospital.org
SIC: 8011 Internal medicine, physician/surgeon
PA: The Huntington Medical Foundation
100 W California Blvd
Pasadena CA 91105

(P-19849)
HUNTINGTON RADIOLOGY
11525 Brookshire Ave # 11, Downey (90241-4985)
PHONE..................562 904-1111
Eugene Tsimerinov, *Branch Mgr*
EMP: 56 **Privately Held**
SIC: 8011 Radiologist
PA: Huntington Radiology
2679 Zoe Ave
Huntington Park CA 90255

(P-19850)
HUNTINGTON REPRODCTVE CTR INC (PA)
Also Called: Hrc Fertility
135 S Rosemead Blvd, Pasadena (91107-3955)
PHONE..................626 204-9699
Timothy J McGinley, *CEO*
John Wilcox, *Treasurer*
Jeffery Nelson, *President*
Jeffrey R Nelson, *Vice Pres*
Lu Jiao, *CTO*
EMP: 50 **EST:** 1988
SQ FT: 22,394
SALES (est): 33.8MM **Privately Held**
WEB: www.havingbabies.com
SIC: 8011 Fertility specialist, physician

(P-19851)
INDUSTRIAL MEDICAL GROUP
2501 G St, Bakersfield (93301-2811)
PHONE..................661 327-2225
Larry M Cho, *Owner*
Jimmy Shiu, *Marketing Staff*
Larry Cho, *Med Doctor*
EMP: 70 **EST:** 1984
SQ FT: 4,000
SALES (est): 9.4MM **Privately Held**
SIC: 8011 Occupational & industrial specialist, physician/surgeon

(P-19852)
INLAND EYE INST MED GROUP INC (PA)
1900 E Washington St, Colton (92324-4698)
P.O. Box 1427 (92324-0836)
PHONE..................909 825-3425
Loren Denler MD, *President*
Harold P Wallar, *Treasurer*

Wayne B Isaeff, *Vice Pres*
Melissa Goins, *Nursing Dir*
EMP: 70 **EST:** 1976
SQ FT: 12,500
SALES (est): 15.8MM **Privately Held**
WEB: www.inlandeye.com
SIC: 8011 Ophthalmologist

(P-19853)
INPATIENT CONSULTANTS FLA INC (DH)
Also Called: IPC of Florida
4605 Lankershim Blvd # 216, North Hollywood (91602-1818)
PHONE...................888 447-2362
Adam D Singer, *CEO*
R Jeffrey Taylor, *President*
Rick Kline, *CFO*
Fernando J Sarria, *Officer*
Patrick McHorney, *Manager*
EMP: 156 **EST:** 2004
SALES (est): 26.3MM
SALES (corp-wide): 3.6B **Privately Held**
SIC: 8011 Physical medicine, physician/surgeon
HQ: Ipc Healthcare, Inc.
    4605 Lankershim Blvd
    North Hollywood CA 91602
    888 447-2362

(P-19854)
INSITE DIGESTIVE HEALTH CARE
7320 Woodlake Ave Ste 310, West Hills (91307-1471)
PHONE...................818 346-9911
Margarita Joaquin, *Branch Mgr*
Calin Arimie, *Gastroenterlgy*
Cyrus Badii, *Gastroenterlgy*
Ron Chitayat, *Gastroenterlgy*
EMP: 84
SALES (corp-wide): 25.1MM **Privately Held**
WEB: www.insitedigestive.com
SIC: 8011 Gastronomist
PA: Insite Digestive Health Care
    5525 Etiwanda Ave Ste 110
    Tarzana CA 91356
    818 437-8105

(P-19855)
INSITE DIGESTIVE HEALTH CARE
225 W Broadway Ste 350, Glendale (91204-1303)
PHONE...................626 817-2900
Alaa Abousaif, *Branch Mgr*
EMP: 84
SALES (corp-wide): 25.1MM **Privately Held**
WEB: www.insitedigestive.com
SIC: 8011 2834 General & family practice, physician/surgeon; chlorination tablets & kits (water purification)
PA: Insite Digestive Health Care
    5525 Etiwanda Ave Ste 110
    Tarzana CA 91356
    818 437-8105

(P-19856)
IPC HEALTHCARE INC (DH)
Also Called: Intrepid Healthcare Svcs Inc
4605 Lankershim Blvd, North Hollywood (91602-1818)
PHONE...................888 447-2362
Adam D Singer, *CEO*
R Jeffrey Taylor, *President*
Richard H Kline III, *CFO*
Kerry E Weiner, *Chief Mktg Ofcr*
Richard G Russell, *Exec VP*
EMP: 886 **EST:** 1995
SALES (est): 409.7MM
SALES (corp-wide): 3.6B **Privately Held**
WEB: www.teamhealth.com
SIC: 8011 Physicians' office, including specialists
HQ: Team Health Holdings, Inc.
    265 Brookview Centre Way
    Knoxville TN 37919
    865 693-1000

(P-19857)
JOHN J OHARA MD A MEDICAL CORP
Also Called: Torrance Orthpdic Spt Medicine
23456 Hawthorne Blvd # 300, Torrance (90505-4716)
PHONE...................310 316-7095
John J O Hara MD, *President*
Pamela Watanabe, *Administration*
John Fleming III, *Surgeon*
Kenneth Park, *Med Doctor*
▲ **EMP:** 58 **EST:** 1962
SQ FT: 8,000
SALES (est): 5.4MM **Privately Held**
WEB: www.coastalorthoca.com
SIC: 8011 Orthopedic physician

(P-19858)
KAISER FOUNDATION HOSPITALS
Also Called: Lakeview Medical Offices
411 N Lakeview Ave, Anaheim (92807-3028)
PHONE...................714 279-4675
Suzie Characky, *Manager*
Martha Dispoto, *Executive*
Dave McLaughlin, *Info Tech Dir*
Kerry Teplinsky, *Cardiology*
Jose Baeza, *Internal Med*
EMP: 235
SALES (corp-wide): 30.5B **Privately Held**
WEB: www.kaisercenter.com
SIC: 8011 Medical centers
HQ: Kaiser Foundation Hospitals Inc
    1 Kaiser Plz
    Oakland CA 94612
    510 271-6611

(P-19859)
KAISER FOUNDATION HOSPITALS
1011 Baldwin Park Blvd, Baldwin Park (91706-5806)
PHONE...................310 922-8916
Abdalla Mallouk, *Branch Mgr*
Susannah Patton, *Vice Pres*
James Landers, *Technology*
Ramin Davidoff, *Urology*
Amanda Higgins, *Manager*
EMP: 235
SALES (corp-wide): 30.5B **Privately Held**
WEB: www.kaisercenter.com
SIC: 8011 Physicians' office, including specialists
HQ: Kaiser Foundation Hospitals Inc
    1 Kaiser Plz
    Oakland CA 94612
    510 271-6611

(P-19860)
KAISER FOUNDATION HOSPITALS
Also Called: Aliso Viejo Medical Offices
24502 Pacific Park Dr, Aliso Viejo (92656-3033)
PHONE...................949 425-3150
Bruce Sogioka, *Branch Mgr*
Majdah Saleh, *Project Mgr*
Richard Moldawsky, *Psychiatry*
EMP: 235
SALES (corp-wide): 30.5B **Privately Held**
WEB: www.kaisercenter.com
SIC: 8011 Medical centers
HQ: Kaiser Foundation Hospitals Inc
    1 Kaiser Plz
    Oakland CA 94612
    510 271-6611

(P-19861)
KAISER FOUNDATION HOSPITALS
15446 S Western Ave, Gardena (90249-4319)
PHONE...................310 325-5111
Angel Schaffer, *Branch Mgr*
EMP: 235
SALES (corp-wide): 30.5B **Privately Held**
WEB: www.kaisercenter.com
SIC: 8011 Medical centers
HQ: Kaiser Foundation Hospitals Inc
    1 Kaiser Plz
    Oakland CA 94612
    510 271-6611

(P-19862)
KAISER FOUNDATION HOSPITALS
3900 Alamo St, Simi Valley (93063-2111)
PHONE...................805 582-0100
David Carrington, *Branch Mgr*
EMP: 235
SALES (corp-wide): 30.5B **Privately Held**
WEB: www.kaisercenter.com
SIC: 8011 Physicians' office, including specialists
HQ: Kaiser Foundation Hospitals Inc
    1 Kaiser Plz
    Oakland CA 94612
    510 271-6611

(P-19863)
KAISER FOUNDATION HOSPITALS
Also Called: Kaiser Permanente
12100 Euclid St, Garden Grove (92840-3304)
PHONE...................714 741-3448
Betty Bohner, *Administration*
Eun Lee, *Family Practti*
Ashley Brown, *Dermatology*
Leo Maffey, *Internal Med*
Dan Hoang, *Pediatrics*
EMP: 235
SALES (corp-wide): 30.5B **Privately Held**
WEB: www.kaisercenter.com
SIC: 8011 Medical centers
HQ: Kaiser Foundation Hospitals Inc
    1 Kaiser Plz
    Oakland CA 94612
    510 271-6611

(P-19864)
KAISER FOUNDATION HOSPITALS
6 Willard, Irvine (92604-4694)
PHONE...................949 262-5760
Scott Allan Murray, *Branch Mgr*
EMP: 235
SALES (corp-wide): 30.5B **Privately Held**
WEB: www.kaisercenter.com
SIC: 8011 General & family practice, physician/surgeon
HQ: Kaiser Foundation Hospitals Inc
    1 Kaiser Plz
    Oakland CA 94612
    510 271-6611

(P-19865)
KAISER FOUNDATION HOSPITALS
5601 De Soto Ave, Woodland Hills (91367-6701)
PHONE...................818 719-2000
Pei Chen, *Branch Mgr*
Nabil Odeh, *Technology*
EMP: 235
SALES (corp-wide): 30.5B **Privately Held**
WEB: www.kaisercenter.com
SIC: 8011 General & family practice, physician/surgeon
HQ: Kaiser Foundation Hospitals Inc
    1 Kaiser Plz
    Oakland CA 94612
    510 271-6611

(P-19866)
KAISER FOUNDATION HOSPITALS
13652 Cantara St, Panorama City (91402-5423)
PHONE...................818 375-4023
Andrea D Mason Otr, *Branch Mgr*
Kathy Kigerl, *Officer*
Michael Flores, *Radiology Dir*
Vicki Gradjyan, *Project Mgr*
Brent Slutski, *Engineer*
EMP: 235
SALES (corp-wide): 30.5B **Privately Held**
WEB: www.kaisercenter.com
SIC: 8011 Internal medicine practitioners
HQ: Kaiser Foundation Hospitals Inc
    1 Kaiser Plz
    Oakland CA 94612
    510 271-6611

(P-19867)
KAISER FOUNDATION HOSPITALS
4950 W Sunset Blvd # 200, Los Angeles (90027-5822)
PHONE...................323 783-7695
EMP: 235
SALES (corp-wide): 30.5B **Privately Held**
WEB: www.kaisercenter.com
SIC: 8011 Offices & clinics of medical doctors
HQ: Kaiser Foundation Hospitals Inc
    1 Kaiser Plz
    Oakland CA 94612
    510 271-6611

(P-19868)
KAISER FOUNDATION HOSPITALS
6650 Alton Pkwy, Irvine (92618-3734)
PHONE...................949 932-2604
Johnny Kim, *Branch Mgr*
EMP: 235
SALES (corp-wide): 30.5B **Privately Held**
WEB: www.kaisercenter.com
SIC: 8011 Offices & clinics of medical doctors
HQ: Kaiser Foundation Hospitals Inc
    1 Kaiser Plz
    Oakland CA 94612
    510 271-6611

(P-19869)
KAISER FOUNDATION HOSPITALS
2081 Palos Verdes Dr N, Lomita (90717-3701)
PHONE...................310 325-6542
EMP: 235
SALES (corp-wide): 30.5B **Privately Held**
WEB: www.kaisercenter.com
SIC: 8011 Medical centers
HQ: Kaiser Foundation Hospitals Inc
    1 Kaiser Plz
    Oakland CA 94612
    510 271-6611

(P-19870)
KAISER FOUNDATION HOSPITALS
1515 N Vermont Ave Fl 1, Los Angeles (90027-5337)
PHONE...................323 783-8191
Kenneth WEI, *Branch Mgr*
EMP: 235
SALES (corp-wide): 30.5B **Privately Held**
WEB: www.kaisercenter.com
SIC: 8011 Medical centers
HQ: Kaiser Foundation Hospitals Inc
    1 Kaiser Plz
    Oakland CA 94612
    510 271-6611

(P-19871)
KAISER FOUNDATION HOSPITALS
8220 Woodman Ave, Panorama City (91402-5427)
PHONE...................818 375-3475
Teresa Park, *Branch Mgr*
EMP: 235
SALES (corp-wide): 30.5B **Privately Held**
WEB: www.kaisercenter.com
SIC: 8011 Offices & clinics of medical doctors
HQ: Kaiser Foundation Hospitals Inc
    1 Kaiser Plz
    Oakland CA 94612
    510 271-6611

(P-19872)
KAISER FOUNDATION HOSPITALS
2055 Kellogg Ave, Corona (92879-3111)
PHONE...................951 898-7370
Christopher Cheng, *Branch Mgr*
EMP: 235
SALES (corp-wide): 30.5B **Privately Held**
WEB: www.kaisercenter.com
SIC: 8011 Physicians' office, including specialists

PRODUCTS & SVCS

HQ: Kaiser Foundation Hospitals Inc
1 Kaiser Plz
Oakland CA 94612
510 271-6611

(P-19873)
KAISER FOUNDATION HOSPITALS
400 S Sepulveda Blvd, Manhattan Beach
(90266-6814)
PHONE....................626 405-2589
EMP: 235
SALES (corp-wide): 30.5B **Privately Held**
WEB: www.kaisercenter.com
SIC: **8011** Offices & clinics of medical doctors
HQ: Kaiser Foundation Hospitals Inc
1 Kaiser Plz
Oakland CA 94612
510 271-6611

(P-19874)
KAISER FOUNDATION HOSPITALS
6041 Cadillac Ave, Los Angeles
(90034-1700)
PHONE....................323 857-2000
Kenneth Nudelman, *Branch Mgr*
Tien Winarko, *Pharmacy Dir*
Holly Bowser, *Admin Sec*
Cyndra Poe, *Admin Sec*
Shukla Sen, *Admin Asst*
EMP: 235
SALES (corp-wide): 30.5B **Privately Held**
WEB: www.kaisercenter.com
SIC: **8011** Physicians' office, including specialists
HQ: Kaiser Foundation Hospitals Inc
1 Kaiser Plz
Oakland CA 94612
510 271-6611

(P-19875)
KAISER FOUNDATION HOSPITALS
14305 Meridian Pkwy, March ARB
(92518-3034)
PHONE....................951 251-7300
EMP: 235
SALES (corp-wide): 30.5B **Privately Held**
WEB: www.kaisercenter.com
SIC: **8011** Offices & clinics of medical doctors
HQ: Kaiser Foundation Hospitals Inc
1 Kaiser Plz
Oakland CA 94612
510 271-6611

(P-19876)
KAISER FOUNDATION HOSPITALS
Also Called: Kaiser Permanente
1301 California St, Redlands (92374-2910)
PHONE....................888 750-0036
Cindy Wong, *Director*
Yohan Shin, *Pediatrics*
EMP: 235
SALES (corp-wide): 30.5B **Privately Held**
WEB: www.kaisercenter.com
SIC: **8011** Medical centers
HQ: Kaiser Foundation Hospitals Inc
1 Kaiser Plz
Oakland CA 94612
510 271-6611

(P-19877)
KAISER FOUNDATION HOSPITALS
Also Called: Kaiser Permanente
1900 E Lambert Rd, Brea (92821-4371)
PHONE....................714 672-5100
David Jeng, *Principal*
Alia Khalil, *Family Practiti*
Kevin Liao, *Family Practiti*
Shawn Nguyen, *Family Practiti*
Tri Tran, *Family Practiti*
EMP: 235
SQ FT: 9,240
SALES (corp-wide): 30.5B **Privately Held**
WEB: www.kaisercenter.com
SIC: **8011** Medical centers
HQ: Kaiser Foundation Hospitals Inc
1 Kaiser Plz
Oakland CA 94612
510 271-6611

(P-19878)
KAISER FOUNDATION HOSPITALS
10800 Magnolia Ave, Riverside
(92505-3000)
PHONE....................951 353-3790
Laura Estrada, *Branch Mgr*
Diane Hallihan, *Food Svc Dir*
Jennifer Chou, *Obstetrician*
EMP: 235
SALES (corp-wide): 30.5B **Privately Held**
WEB: www.kaisercenter.com
SIC: **8011** Offices & clinics of medical doctors
HQ: Kaiser Foundation Hospitals Inc
1 Kaiser Plz
Oakland CA 94612
510 271-6611

(P-19879)
KAISER FOUNDATION HOSPITALS
7825 Atlantic Ave, Cudahy (90201-5022)
PHONE....................323 562-6400
Robert Escalera, *Branch Mgr*
EMP: 235
SALES (corp-wide): 30.5B **Privately Held**
WEB: www.kaisercenter.com
SIC: **8011** Offices & clinics of medical doctors
HQ: Kaiser Foundation Hospitals Inc
1 Kaiser Plz
Oakland CA 94612
510 271-6611

(P-19880)
KAISER FOUNDATION HOSPITALS
13640 Roscoe Blvd, Panorama City
(91402-3904)
PHONE....................818 375-2369
Michelle Sanchez, *Branch Mgr*
EMP: 235
SALES (corp-wide): 30.5B **Privately Held**
WEB: www.kaisercenter.com
SIC: **8011** Offices & clinics of medical doctors
HQ: Kaiser Foundation Hospitals Inc
1 Kaiser Plz
Oakland CA 94612
510 271-6611

(P-19881)
KAISER FOUNDATION HOSPITALS
Also Called: Kaiser Prmnnte W Los Angles Me
6041 Cadillac Ave, Los Angeles
(90034-1700)
PHONE....................323 857-2000
Howard Fullman, *Admin Director*
Merrick Schneider, *Ch Radiology*
Tracy Fietz, *Officer*
David Venegas, *Admin Sec*
Faith Kone, *Administration*
EMP: 235
SALES (corp-wide): 30.5B **Privately Held**
WEB: www.kaisercenter.com
SIC: **8011** Medical centers
HQ: Kaiser Foundation Hospitals Inc
1 Kaiser Plz
Oakland CA 94612
510 271-6611

(P-19882)
KAISER FOUNDATION HOSPITALS
Also Called: Kaiser Permanente
13651 Willard St, Panorama City (91402)
PHONE....................818 375-2000
Dev Mahadevan, *Principal*
Jane Ryang, *Business Dir*
Eugene Kenigsberg, *Research*
Gerald R Higgins, *Pathologist*
Abdi T Sherif, *Surgeon*
EMP: 235
SALES (corp-wide): 30.5B **Privately Held**
WEB: www.kaisercenter.com
SIC: **8011** Medical centers
HQ: Kaiser Foundation Hospitals Inc
1 Kaiser Plz
Oakland CA 94612
510 271-6611

(P-19883)
KAISER FOUNDATION HOSPITALS
10740 4th St, Rancho Cucamonga
(91730-0973)
PHONE....................562 658-3441
EMP: 235
SALES (corp-wide): 30.5B **Privately Held**
WEB: www.kaisercenter.com
SIC: **8011** Offices & clinics of medical doctors
HQ: Kaiser Foundation Hospitals Inc
1 Kaiser Plz
Oakland CA 94612
510 271-6611

(P-19884)
KAISER FOUNDATION HOSPITALS
17284 Slover Ave, Fontana (92337-7584)
PHONE....................909 609-3800
Gregory Christian, *President*
EMP: 235
SALES (corp-wide): 30.5B **Privately Held**
WEB: www.kaisercenter.com
SIC: **8011** General & family practice, physician/surgeon
HQ: Kaiser Foundation Hospitals Inc
1 Kaiser Plz
Oakland CA 94612
510 271-6611

(P-19885)
KAISER FOUNDATION HOSPITALS
Also Called: Rancho Cucamonga Medical Offs
10850 Arrow Rte, Rancho Cucamonga
(91730-4833)
PHONE....................888 750-0036
EMP: 235
SALES (corp-wide): 30.5B **Privately Held**
WEB: www.kaisercenter.com
SIC: **8011** Medical centers
HQ: Kaiser Foundation Hospitals Inc
1 Kaiser Plz
Oakland CA 94612
510 271-6611

(P-19886)
KAISER FOUNDATION HOSPITALS
Also Called: Anaheim Hills Medical Offices
5475 E La Palma Ave # 20, Anaheim
(92807-2075)
PHONE....................888 988-2800
EMP: 235
SALES (corp-wide): 30.5B **Privately Held**
WEB: www.kaisercenter.com
SIC: **8011** Offices & clinics of medical doctors
HQ: Kaiser Foundation Hospitals Inc
1 Kaiser Plz
Oakland CA 94612
510 271-6611

(P-19887)
KAISER FOUNDATION HOSPITALS
Also Called: Central Medical Offices
3733 San Dimas St, Bakersfield
(93301-1407)
PHONE....................877 524-7373
EMP: 235
SALES (corp-wide): 30.5B **Privately Held**
WEB: www.kaisercenter.com
SIC: **8011** Medical centers
HQ: Kaiser Foundation Hospitals Inc
1 Kaiser Plz
Oakland CA 94612
510 271-6611

(P-19888)
KAISER FOUNDATION HOSPITALS
Also Called: Anaheim Kraemer Medical Offs
3460 E La Palma Ave, Anaheim
(92806-2020)
PHONE....................888 988-2800
EMP: 235
SALES (corp-wide): 30.5B **Privately Held**
WEB: www.kaisercenter.com
SIC: **8011** Medical centers

HQ: Kaiser Foundation Hospitals Inc
1 Kaiser Plz
Oakland CA 94612
510 271-6611

(P-19889)
KAISER FOUNDATION HOSPITALS
Also Called: Chester Avenue Medical Offices
2531 Chester Ave, Bakersfield
(93301-2012)
PHONE....................877 524-7373
EMP: 235
SALES (corp-wide): 30.5B **Privately Held**
WEB: www.kaisercenter.com
SIC: **8011** Medical centers
HQ: Kaiser Foundation Hospitals Inc
1 Kaiser Plz
Oakland CA 94612
510 271-6611

(P-19890)
KAISER FOUNDATION HOSPITALS
Also Called: Chester Avenue Medical Offs II
2620 Chester Ave, Bakersfield
(93301-2015)
PHONE....................661 337-7160
EMP: 235
SALES (corp-wide): 30.5B **Privately Held**
WEB: www.kaisercenter.com
SIC: **8011** Medical centers
HQ: Kaiser Foundation Hospitals Inc
1 Kaiser Plz
Oakland CA 94612
510 271-6611

(P-19891)
KAISER FOUNDATION HOSPITALS
Also Called: Discovery Plz Med & Admin Offs
1200 Discovery Dr, Bakersfield
(93309-7032)
PHONE....................877 524-7373
Peggy Kasinger, *Nurse Practr*
EMP: 235
SALES (corp-wide): 30.5B **Privately Held**
WEB: www.kaisercenter.com
SIC: **8011** Medical centers
HQ: Kaiser Foundation Hospitals Inc
1 Kaiser Plz
Oakland CA 94612
510 271-6611

(P-19892)
KAISER FOUNDATION HOSPITALS
Also Called: Cerritos Medical Office Bldg
10820 183rd St, Cerritos (90703-8010)
PHONE....................800 823-4040
EMP: 235
SALES (corp-wide): 30.5B **Privately Held**
WEB: www.kaisercenter.com
SIC: **8011** Medical centers
HQ: Kaiser Foundation Hospitals Inc
1 Kaiser Plz
Oakland CA 94612
510 271-6611

(P-19893)
KAISER FOUNDATION HOSPITALS
Also Called: Las Posas Road Medical Offices
2620 Las Posas Rd, Camarillo
(93010-3400)
PHONE....................888 515-3500
EMP: 235
SALES (corp-wide): 30.5B **Privately Held**
WEB: www.kaisercenter.com
SIC: **8011** Medical centers
HQ: Kaiser Foundation Hospitals Inc
1 Kaiser Plz
Oakland CA 94612
510 271-6611

(P-19894)
KAISER FOUNDATION HOSPITALS
Also Called: Ming Medical Offices
8800 Ming Ave, Bakersfield (93311-1308)
PHONE....................877 524-7373
EMP: 235
SALES (corp-wide): 30.5B **Privately Held**
WEB: www.kaisercenter.com
SIC: **8011** Medical centers

HQ: Kaiser Foundation Hospitals Inc
1 Kaiser Plz
Oakland CA 94612
510 271-6611

(P-19895)
KAISER FOUNDATION HOSPITALS
Also Called: Crossroads Medical Offices
12801 Crssrads Pkwy S Ste, City of Industry (91746)
PHONE....................562 463-4377
EMP: 235
SALES (corp-wide): 30.5B **Privately Held**
WEB: www.kaisercenter.com
SIC: **8011** Medical centers
HQ: Kaiser Foundation Hospitals Inc
1 Kaiser Plz
Oakland CA 94612
510 271-6611

(P-19896)
KAISER FOUNDATION HOSPITALS
Also Called: Orchard Medical Offices
9449 Imperial Hwy, Downey (90242-2814)
PHONE....................800 823-4040
Leon Randolph, *President*
EMP: 235
SALES (corp-wide): 30.5B **Privately Held**
WEB: www.kaisercenter.com
SIC: **8011** Medical centers
HQ: Kaiser Foundation Hospitals Inc
1 Kaiser Plz
Oakland CA 94612
510 271-6611

(P-19897)
KAISER FOUNDATION HOSPITALS
Also Called: Diamond Bar Medical Offices
1336 Bridgegate Dr, Diamond Bar (91765-3955)
PHONE....................800 780-1277
EMP: 235
SALES (corp-wide): 30.5B **Privately Held**
WEB: www.kaisercenter.com
SIC: **8011** Medical centers
HQ: Kaiser Foundation Hospitals Inc
1 Kaiser Plz
Oakland CA 94612
510 271-6611

(P-19898)
KAISER FOUNDATION HOSPITALS
Also Called: Garden Medical Offices
9353 Imperial Hwy, Downey (90242-2812)
PHONE....................800 823-4040
Wendy De Vreugd, *Opers Staff*
Danielle Manalo, *Family Practiti*
Madhav Boddula, *Surgeon*
Elizabeth Norheim, *Surgeon*
Nicholas Jung, *Anesthesiology*
EMP: 235
SALES (corp-wide): 30.5B **Privately Held**
WEB: www.kaisercenter.com
SIC: **8011** Medical centers
HQ: Kaiser Foundation Hospitals Inc
1 Kaiser Plz
Oakland CA 94612
510 271-6611

(P-19899)
KAISER FOUNDATION HOSPITALS
Also Called: Foothill Ranch Medical Offices
26882 Towne Centre Dr # 1, Foothill Ranch (92610-2862)
PHONE....................800 922-2000
EMP: 235
SALES (corp-wide): 30.5B **Privately Held**
WEB: www.kaisercenter.com
SIC: **8011** Medical centers
HQ: Kaiser Foundation Hospitals Inc
1 Kaiser Plz
Oakland CA 94612
510 271-6611

(P-19900)
KAISER FOUNDATION HOSPITALS
Also Called: Fontana Mental Health Offices
9310 Sierra Ave, Fontana (92335-5711)
PHONE....................866 205-3595

EMP: 235
SALES (corp-wide): 30.5B **Privately Held**
WEB: www.kaisercenter.com
SIC: **8011** Psychiatrists & psychoanalysts
HQ: Kaiser Foundation Hospitals Inc
1 Kaiser Plz
Oakland CA 94612
510 271-6611

(P-19901)
KAISER FOUNDATION HOSPITALS
Also Called: Carson Medical Offices
18600 S Figueroa St, Gardena (90248-4505)
PHONE....................800 780-1230
EMP: 235
SALES (corp-wide): 30.5B **Privately Held**
WEB: www.kaisercenter.com
SIC: **8011** Medical centers
HQ: Kaiser Foundation Hospitals Inc
1 Kaiser Plz
Oakland CA 94612
510 271-6611

(P-19902)
KAISER FOUNDATION HOSPITALS
Also Called: Balboa Plaza Admin Offices
10605 Balboa Blvd Ste 330, Granada Hills (91344-6358)
PHONE....................818 832-7200
Dennis C Benton, *Exec Dir*
EMP: 235
SALES (corp-wide): 30.5B **Privately Held**
WEB: www.kaisercenter.com
SIC: **8011** Health maintenance organization
HQ: Kaiser Foundation Hospitals Inc
1 Kaiser Plz
Oakland CA 94612
510 271-6611

(P-19903)
KAISER FOUNDATION HOSPITALS
Also Called: Glendale Orange St Med Offs
501 N Orange St, Glendale (91203-1970)
PHONE....................800 954-8000
EMP: 235
SALES (corp-wide): 30.5B **Privately Held**
WEB: www.kaisercenter.com
SIC: **8011** Medical centers
HQ: Kaiser Foundation Hospitals Inc
1 Kaiser Plz
Oakland CA 94612
510 271-6611

(P-19904)
KAISER FOUNDATION HOSPITALS
Also Called: Indio Medical Offices
46900 Monroe St, Indio (92201-4827)
PHONE....................866 984-7483
EMP: 235
SALES (corp-wide): 30.5B **Privately Held**
WEB: www.kaisercenter.com
SIC: **8011** Medical centers
HQ: Kaiser Foundation Hospitals Inc
1 Kaiser Plz
Oakland CA 94612
510 271-6611

(P-19905)
KAISER FOUNDATION HOSPITALS
Also Called: Behavioral Health
44444 20th St W, Lancaster (93534-2714)
PHONE....................661 951-0070
EMP: 235
SALES (corp-wide): 30.5B **Privately Held**
WEB: www.kaisercenter.com
SIC: **8011** Psychiatrists & psychoanalysts
HQ: Kaiser Foundation Hospitals Inc
1 Kaiser Plz
Oakland CA 94612
510 271-6611

(P-19906)
KAISER FOUNDATION HOSPITALS
Also Called: Lomita Medical Offices
2081 Palos Verdes Dr N, Lomita (90717-3701)
PHONE....................310 325-6542

EMP: 235
SALES (corp-wide): 30.5B **Privately Held**
WEB: www.kaisercenter.com
SIC: **8011** Medical centers
HQ: Kaiser Foundation Hospitals Inc
1 Kaiser Plz
Oakland CA 94612
510 271-6611

(P-19907)
KAISER FOUNDATION HOSPITALS
Also Called: Lynwood Medical Offices
3830 Mrtin Lther King Jr, Lynwood (90262-3625)
PHONE....................310 604-5700
Sepehr Katiraie MD, *CEO*
EMP: 235
SALES (corp-wide): 30.5B **Privately Held**
WEB: www.kaisercenter.com
SIC: **8011** Medical centers
HQ: Kaiser Foundation Hospitals Inc
1 Kaiser Plz
Oakland CA 94612
510 271-6611

(P-19908)
KAISER FOUNDATION HOSPITALS
Also Called: North Hollywood Medical Offs
5250 Lankershim Blvd, North Hollywood (91601-3186)
PHONE....................888 778-5000
EMP: 235
SALES (corp-wide): 30.5B **Privately Held**
WEB: www.kaisercenter.com
SIC: **8011** Medical centers
HQ: Kaiser Foundation Hospitals Inc
1 Kaiser Plz
Oakland CA 94612
510 271-6611

(P-19909)
KAISER FOUNDATION HOSPITALS
Also Called: Norwalk Medical Offices
12501 Imperial Hwy Ste 40, Norwalk (90650-3179)
PHONE....................562 807-6100
EMP: 235
SALES (corp-wide): 30.5B **Privately Held**
WEB: www.kaisercenter.com
SIC: **8011** Offices & clinics of medical doctors
HQ: Kaiser Foundation Hospitals Inc
1 Kaiser Plz
Oakland CA 94612
510 271-6611

(P-19910)
KAISER FOUNDATION HOSPITALS
Also Called: Ontario Vineyard Medical Offs
2295 S Vineyard Ave, Ontario (91761-7925)
PHONE....................909 724-5000
EMP: 235
SALES (corp-wide): 30.5B **Privately Held**
WEB: www.kaisercenter.com
SIC: **8011** Medical centers
HQ: Kaiser Foundation Hospitals Inc
1 Kaiser Plz
Oakland CA 94612
510 271-6611

(P-19911)
KAISER FOUNDATION HOSPITALS
Also Called: Oxnard 2200 E Gnzles Rd Med Of
2200 E Gonzales Rd, Oxnard (93036-0619)
PHONE....................888 515-3500
EMP: 235
SALES (corp-wide): 30.5B **Privately Held**
WEB: www.kaisercenter.com
SIC: **8011** Medical centers
HQ: Kaiser Foundation Hospitals Inc
1 Kaiser Plz
Oakland CA 94612
510 271-6611

(P-19912)
KAISER FOUNDATION HOSPITALS
Also Called: Kaiser Permanente Member Svcs
73733 Fred Waring Dr # 1, Palm Desert (92260-2589)
PHONE....................800 777-1256
Virginia McLain, *Branch Mgr*
EMP: 235
SALES (corp-wide): 30.5B **Privately Held**
WEB: www.kaisercenter.com
SIC: **8011** Health maintenance organization
HQ: Kaiser Foundation Hospitals Inc
1 Kaiser Plz
Oakland CA 94612
510 271-6611

(P-19913)
KAISER FOUNDATION HOSPITALS
Also Called: Oxnard 2103 E Gnzles Rd Med Of
2103 E Gonzales Rd, Oxnard (93036-3757)
PHONE....................805 988-6300
EMP: 235
SALES (corp-wide): 30.5B **Privately Held**
WEB: www.kaisercenter.com
SIC: **8011** Medical centers
HQ: Kaiser Foundation Hospitals Inc
1 Kaiser Plz
Oakland CA 94612
510 271-6611

(P-19914)
KAISER FOUNDATION HOSPITALS
Also Called: Palm Desert Medical Offices
University Park Ctr, Palm Desert (92211)
PHONE....................866 984-7483
EMP: 593
SALES (corp-wide): 19.1B **Privately Held**
SIC: **8011** Medical Doctor's Office
PA: Kaiser Foundation Hospitals Inc
1 Kaiser Plz Ste 2600
Oakland CA 94612
510 271-5800

(P-19915)
KAISER FOUNDATION HOSPITALS
Also Called: Canyon Crest Mental Hlth Offs
5225 Canyon Crest Dr # 10, Riverside (92507-6301)
PHONE....................951 248-4000
EMP: 235
SALES (corp-wide): 30.5B **Privately Held**
WEB: www.kaisercenter.com
SIC: **8011** Psychiatrists & psychoanalysts
HQ: Kaiser Foundation Hospitals Inc
1 Kaiser Plz
Oakland CA 94612
510 271-6611

(P-19916)
KAISER FOUNDATION HOSPITALS
Also Called: Meridian Medical Offices
14305 Meridian Pkwy, Riverside (92518-3034)
PHONE....................866 984-7483
EMP: 235
SALES (corp-wide): 30.5B **Privately Held**
WEB: www.kaisercenter.com
SIC: **8011** Medical centers
HQ: Kaiser Foundation Hospitals Inc
1 Kaiser Plz
Oakland CA 94612
510 271-6611

(P-19917)
KAISER FOUNDATION HOSPITALS
Also Called: Harbor Corporate Park
3601 S Harbor Blvd, Santa Ana (92704-7909)
PHONE....................714 223-2606
EMP: 235
SALES (corp-wide): 30.5B **Privately Held**
WEB: www.kaisercenter.com
SIC: **8011** Psychiatric clinic

HQ: Kaiser Foundation Hospitals Inc
1 Kaiser Plz
Oakland CA 94612
510 271-6611

(P-19918)
KAISER FOUNDATION HOSPITALS
Also Called: Canyon Country Medical Offices
26415 Carl Boyer Dr, Santa Clarita
(91350-5824)
PHONE...................................888 778-5000
EMP: 235
SALES (corp-wide): 30.5B **Privately Held**
WEB: www.kaisercenter.com
SIC: **8011** Medical centers
HQ: Kaiser Foundation Hospitals Inc
1 Kaiser Plz
Oakland CA 94612
510 271-6611

(P-19919)
KAISER FOUNDATION HOSPITALS
Also Called: Thosand Oaks 145 Hdncamp Rd Me
145 Hodencamp Rd, Thousand Oaks
(91360-5810)
PHONE...................................888 515-3500
EMP: 235
SALES (corp-wide): 30.5B **Privately Held**
WEB: www.kaisercenter.com
SIC: **8011** Medical centers
HQ: Kaiser Foundation Hospitals Inc
1 Kaiser Plz
Oakland CA 94612
510 271-6611

(P-19920)
KAISER FOUNDATION HOSPITALS
Also Called: Thousand Oaks 322 E Thsand Oak
322 E Thousand Oaks Blvd, Thousand Oaks (91360-5804)
PHONE...................................888 515-3500
EMP: 235
SALES (corp-wide): 30.5B **Privately Held**
WEB: www.kaisercenter.com
SIC: **8011** Medical centers
HQ: Kaiser Foundation Hospitals Inc
1 Kaiser Plz
Oakland CA 94612
510 271-6611

(P-19921)
KAISER FOUNDATION HOSPITALS
Also Called: Tustin Ranch Medical Offices
2521 Michelle Dr, Tustin (92780-7014)
PHONE...................................888 988-2800
EMP: 235
SALES (corp-wide): 30.5B **Privately Held**
WEB: www.kaisercenter.com
SIC: **8011** Offices & clinics of medical doctors
HQ: Kaiser Foundation Hospitals Inc
1 Kaiser Plz
Oakland CA 94612
510 271-6611

(P-19922)
KAISER FOUNDATION HOSPITALS
9521 Dalen St, Downey (90242-4847)
PHONE...................................817 372-8201
EMP: 235
SALES (corp-wide): 30.5B **Privately Held**
WEB: www.kaisercenter.com
SIC: **8011** Offices & clinics of medical doctors
HQ: Kaiser Foundation Hospitals Inc
1 Kaiser Plz
Oakland CA 94612
510 271-6611

(P-19923)
KAISER FOUNDATION HOSPITALS
5 Centerpointe Dr, La Palma (90623-1050)
PHONE...................................714 562-3420
Gary Edwards, *Branch Mgr*
EMP: 235

SALES (corp-wide): 30.5B **Privately Held**
WEB: www.kaisercenter.com
SIC: **8011** Offices & clinics of medical doctors
HQ: Kaiser Foundation Hospitals Inc
1 Kaiser Plz
Oakland CA 94612
510 271-6611

(P-19924)
KAISER FOUNDATION HOSPITALS
Also Called: Kaiser Permanente
3401 S Harbor Blvd, Santa Ana
(92704-7933)
PHONE...................................714 830-6500
Kip Taylor, *Branch Mgr*
Sheila Marsh, *Family Practiti*
Tatianne Velo, *Family Practiti*
Megan Johnson, *Obstetrician*
Eline Wilson, *Obstetrician*
EMP: 235
SALES (corp-wide): 30.5B **Privately Held**
WEB: www.kaisercenter.com
SIC: **8011** Medical centers
HQ: Kaiser Foundation Hospitals Inc
1 Kaiser Plz
Oakland CA 94612
510 271-6611

(P-19925)
KAISER FOUNDATION HOSPITALS
10850 Arrow Rte, Rancho Cucamonga
(91730-4833)
PHONE...................................909 988-0379
Glen Moore, *Branch Mgr*
EMP: 235
SALES (corp-wide): 30.5B **Privately Held**
WEB: www.kaisercenter.com
SIC: **8011** Offices & clinics of medical doctors
HQ: Kaiser Foundation Hospitals Inc
1 Kaiser Plz
Oakland CA 94612
510 271-6611

(P-19926)
KAISER FOUNDATION HOSPITALS
Also Called: Kaiser Permanente
12001 W Washington Blvd, Los Angeles
(90066-5801)
PHONE...................................310 915-5000
James Corb, *Exec Dir*
Beauvoir Joseph, *Network Enginr*
Millie Olarve, *Prgrmr*
Calvin Okey, *Radiology*
Valentina Zamora,
EMP: 235
SQ FT: 46,281
SALES (corp-wide): 30.5B **Privately Held**
WEB: www.kaisercenter.com
SIC: **8011** Medical centers
HQ: Kaiser Foundation Hospitals Inc
1 Kaiser Plz
Oakland CA 94612
510 271-6611

(P-19927)
KAISER FOUNDATION HOSPITALS
18600 S Figueroa St, Gardena
(90248-4505)
PHONE...................................310 325-5111
Ernest Lee, *Executive*
EMP: 235
SALES (corp-wide): 30.5B **Privately Held**
WEB: www.kaisercenter.com
SIC: **8011** Offices & clinics of medical doctors
HQ: Kaiser Foundation Hospitals Inc
1 Kaiser Plz
Oakland CA 94612
510 271-6611

(P-19928)
KAISER FOUNDATION HOSPITALS
Also Called: Kaiser Permanente 24 Hour
5330 San Bernardino St, Montclair
(91763-2952)
PHONE...................................909 427-5521
Harlan Omlid, *Branch Mgr*
Michael Dinh, *Analyst*

Ana Osorio, *Psychiatry*
EMP: 235
SALES (corp-wide): 30.5B **Privately Held**
WEB: www.kaisercenter.com
SIC: **8011** Medical centers
HQ: Kaiser Foundation Hospitals Inc
1 Kaiser Plz
Oakland CA 94612
510 271-6611

(P-19929)
KAISER FOUNDATION HOSPITALS
Also Called: Kaiser Permanente
25825 Vermont Ave, Harbor City
(90710-3518)
PHONE...................................310 325-5111
Mary Ann Barnes, *Branch Mgr*
Michael Kusunoki, *Officer*
Cristeta L Lozon, *Top Exec*
Sue Lee, *Quality Imp Dir*
Christine Sandaval, *Project Mgr*
EMP: 235
SALES (corp-wide): 30.5B **Privately Held**
WEB: www.kaisercenter.com
SIC: **8011** Medical centers
HQ: Kaiser Foundation Hospitals Inc
1 Kaiser Plz
Oakland CA 94612
510 271-6611

(P-19930)
KAISER FOUNDATION HOSPITALS
Also Called: Vision Essntals By Kser Prmnnt
9000 Ming Ave, Bakersfield (93311-1318)
PHONE...................................877 524-7373
Michelle Quiogue, *Family Practiti*
EMP: 235
SALES (corp-wide): 30.5B **Privately Held**
WEB: www.kaisercenter.com
SIC: **8011** Medical centers
HQ: Kaiser Foundation Hospitals Inc
1 Kaiser Plz
Oakland CA 94612
510 271-6611

(P-19931)
KAISER FOUNDATION HOSPITALS
1550 N Edgemont St, Los Angeles
(90027-5210)
PHONE...................................323 783-7955
EMP: 235
SALES (corp-wide): 30.5B **Privately Held**
WEB: www.kaisercenter.com
SIC: **8011** Offices & clinics of medical doctors
HQ: Kaiser Foundation Hospitals Inc
1 Kaiser Plz
Oakland CA 94612
510 271-6611

(P-19932)
KAISER FOUNDATION HOSPITALS
Also Called: Kaiser Permanente
9961 Sierra Ave, Fontana (92335-6720)
PHONE...................................909 427-5000
William Meyer, *Principal*
Martha Sikkens, *Officer*
David Young, *Officer*
Lindsay Gem, *Nursing Mgr*
Esther Cohen, *CIO*
EMP: 235
SALES (corp-wide): 30.5B **Privately Held**
WEB: www.kaisercenter.com
SIC: **8011** Medical centers
HQ: Kaiser Foundation Hospitals Inc
1 Kaiser Plz
Oakland CA 94612
510 271-6611

(P-19933)
KAISER FOUNDATION HOSPITALS
Also Called: Stockdale Medical Offices
3501 Stockdale Hwy, Bakersfield
(93309-2150)
PHONE...................................661 398-5011
KY P Ho, *Principal*
Jinsun Kim, *Family Practiti*
Kyi Aung, *Internal Med*
Sandra Lara, *Accounts Mgr*
EMP: 235

SALES (corp-wide): 30.5B **Privately Held**
WEB: www.kaisercenter.com
SIC: **8011** Medical centers
HQ: Kaiser Foundation Hospitals Inc
1 Kaiser Plz
Oakland CA 94612
510 271-6611

(P-19934)
KAISER FOUNDATION HOSPITALS
Also Called: Kaiser Permanente
3951 Van Buren Blvd, Riverside
(92503-3620)
PHONE...................................951 352-0292
Nancy Kingson, *Branch Mgr*
Terri Lynch, *Manager*
EMP: 235
SALES (corp-wide): 30.5B **Privately Held**
WEB: www.kaisercenter.com
SIC: **8011** Medical centers
HQ: Kaiser Foundation Hospitals Inc
1 Kaiser Plz
Oakland CA 94612
510 271-6611

(P-19935)
KAISER FOUNDATION HOSPITALS
Also Called: La Palma Medical Offices
5 Centerpointe Dr, La Palma (90623-1050)
PHONE...................................714 562-3420
Josefina Guzman-Inouye, *Manager*
Merve Karabulut, *Family Practiti*
Binh Nguyen, *Family Practiti*
Diane V Pham, *Family Practiti*
Margarita Enriquez, *Manager*
EMP: 235
SALES (corp-wide): 30.5B **Privately Held**
WEB: www.kaisercenter.com
SIC: **8011** Offices & clinics of medical doctors
HQ: Kaiser Foundation Hospitals Inc
1 Kaiser Plz
Oakland CA 94612
510 271-6611

(P-19936)
KAISER FOUNDATION HOSPITALS
Also Called: Glendale Medical Offices
444 W Glenoaks Blvd, Glendale
(91202-2917)
PHONE...................................818 552-3000
Avetis Tashyan, *Branch Mgr*
Atieh Hajianpour, *Technical Staff*
Letitia Ho, *Family Practiti*
Melineh Shajanian, *Family Practiti*
EMP: 235
SALES (corp-wide): 30.5B **Privately Held**
WEB: www.kaisercenter.com
SIC: **8011** Medical centers
HQ: Kaiser Foundation Hospitals Inc
1 Kaiser Plz
Oakland CA 94612
510 271-6611

(P-19937)
KAISER FOUNDATION HOSPITALS
Also Called: Kaiser Prmnnt Psadena Med Off
3280 E Foothill Blvd, Pasadena
(91107-3103)
P.O. Box 7005 (91109-7005)
PHONE...................................626 440-5639
Indu Ramachandran, *IT/NT Sup*
Hai Linh, *Research*
Roger Vasquez, *Finance*
Minerva Donnell, *Analyst*
Rosemary Lee, *Opers Staff*
EMP: 235
SALES (corp-wide): 30.5B **Privately Held**
WEB: www.kaisercenter.com
SIC: **8011** Medical centers
HQ: Kaiser Foundation Hospitals Inc
1 Kaiser Plz
Oakland CA 94612
510 271-6611

(P-19938)
KAISER FOUNDATION HOSPITALS
2521 Michelle Dr, Tustin (92780-7014)
PHONE...................................310 325-5111

Genie Kim, *Branch Mgr*
EMP: 235
SALES (corp-wide): 30.5B **Privately Held**
WEB: www.kaisercenter.com
SIC: 8011 Offices & clinics of medical doctors
HQ: Kaiser Foundation Hospitals Inc
1 Kaiser Plz
Oakland CA 94612
510 271-6611

(P-19939)
KAISER FOUNDATION HOSPITALS
Also Called: Kaiser Psychiatry Srvs Div
325 W Hospitality Ln, San Bernardino
(92408-3243)
PHONE..................866 205-3595
Katie Easterwood, *Branch Mgr*
Joy Oltman,
EMP: 235
SALES (corp-wide): 30.5B **Privately Held**
WEB: www.kaisercenter.com
SIC: 8011 Psychiatric clinic
HQ: Kaiser Foundation Hospitals Inc
1 Kaiser Plz
Oakland CA 94612
510 271-6611

(P-19940)
KAISER FOUNDATION HOSPITALS
Also Called: Kaiser Permanente
1515 N Vermont Ave Fl 3, Los Angeles
(90027-5337)
PHONE..................323 783-8306
Cecilia Militante, *Principal*
Jennifer Christian-Herma, *Exec Dir*
C K E Lin, *Project Mgr*
Ryan Church, *Dermatology*
Melissa Reyes Merin, *Dermatology*
EMP: 235
SALES (corp-wide): 30.5B **Privately Held**
WEB: www.kaisercenter.com
SIC: 8011 Dermatologist
HQ: Kaiser Foundation Hospitals Inc
1 Kaiser Plz
Oakland CA 94612
510 271-6611

(P-19941)
KAISER FOUNDATION HOSPITALS
Also Called: Kaiser Permanente
27107 Tourney Rd, Santa Clarita
(91355-1860)
PHONE..................661 222-2323
Pat Kenney, *Principal*
Steve Miller, *Pharmacy Dir*
Magdalena Stevens, *Family Practiti*
Kathleen Metcalf, *Obstetrician*
Mano Thanam, *Med Doctor*
EMP: 235
SQ FT: 70,835
SALES (corp-wide): 30.5B **Privately Held**
WEB: www.kaisercenter.com
SIC: 8011 Medical centers
HQ: Kaiser Foundation Hospitals Inc
1 Kaiser Plz
Oakland CA 94612
510 271-6611

(P-19942)
KAISER FOUNDATION HOSPITALS
Also Called: Kaiser Foundation Health Plan
42575 Washington St, Palm Desert
(92211-8850)
PHONE..................760 360-1475
EMP: 235
SALES (corp-wide): 30.5B **Privately Held**
WEB: www.kaisercenter.com
SIC: 8011 Medical centers
HQ: Kaiser Foundation Hospitals Inc
1 Kaiser Plz
Oakland CA 94612
510 271-6611

(P-19943)
KAISER FOUNDATION HOSPITALS
Also Called: Kaiser Foundation Health Plan
1717 Date Pike, San Bernardino (92404)
PHONE..................888 750-0036
Jim Morrison, *Manager*

EMP: 235
SQ FT: 18,253
SALES (corp-wide): 30.5B **Privately Held**
WEB: www.healthy.kaiserpermanente.org
SIC: 8011 6324 Medical centers; hospital & medical service plans
HQ: Kaiser Foundation Hospitals Inc
1 Kaiser Plz
Oakland CA 94612
510 271-6611

(P-19944)
KAISER FOUNDATION HOSPITALS
Also Called: Riverside Medical Center
10800 Magnolia Ave, Riverside
(92505-3000)
PHONE..................951 353-2000
Vita Willett, *Director*
Donise Farnum, *Executive*
Jessica Grimes, *Social Dir*
Caitlin Chau, *Family Practiti*
Paul Hsiang, *Family Practiti*
EMP: 235
SALES (corp-wide): 30.5B **Privately Held**
WEB: www.kaisercenter.com
SIC: 8011 8062 Medical centers; general medical & surgical hospitals
HQ: Kaiser Foundation Hospitals Inc
1 Kaiser Plz
Oakland CA 94612
510 271-6611

(P-19945)
KAISER FOUNDATION HOSPITALS
Also Called: Kaiser Prmnnte Mreno Vly Med C
27300 Iris Ave, Moreno Valley
(92555-4802)
PHONE..................951 243-0811
Tom Mc Ciltock, *Manager*
Nataly Romero, *Auditing Mgr*
Elizabeth Guardia, *Accountant*
Ytb Grayson, *Auditor*
David Condon, *Gastroenterlgy*
EMP: 235
SALES (corp-wide): 30.5B **Privately Held**
WEB: www.kaisercenter.com
SIC: 8011 Medical centers
HQ: Kaiser Foundation Hospitals Inc
1 Kaiser Plz
Oakland CA 94612
510 271-6611

(P-19946)
KAISER FOUNDATION HOSPITALS
Also Called: Kaiser Permanente
110 N La Brea Ave, Inglewood
(90301-1708)
PHONE..................310 419-3303
Victor Ahaiwe, *President*
Lamar Nelson, *Executive*
Jennifer Rysso, *Internal Med*
EMP: 235
SALES (corp-wide): 30.5B **Privately Held**
WEB: www.kaisercenter.com
SIC: 8011 Medical centers
HQ: Kaiser Foundation Hospitals Inc
1 Kaiser Plz
Oakland CA 94612
510 271-6611

(P-19947)
KAISER FOUNDATION HOSPITALS
25825 Vermont Ave, Harbor City
(90710-3518)
PHONE..................310 517-3400
Richard Guest, *Branch Mgr*
EMP: 235
SALES (corp-wide): 30.5B **Privately Held**
WEB: www.kaisercenter.com
SIC: 8011 Physicians' office, including specialists
HQ: Kaiser Foundation Hospitals Inc
1 Kaiser Plz
Oakland CA 94612
510 271-6611

(P-19948)
KAISER PRMNNTE SCHL ANESTHESIA
100 S Los Robles Ave # 501, Pasadena
(91101-2453)
PHONE..................626 564-3016
Kaiser Permanente, *Owner*
Adam Miller, *Administration*
Francine Demers, *Prgrmr*
Alberto Garcia, *Network Analyst*
Vijyendra Karpatne, *Project Mgr*
EMP: 74 **EST:** 2009
SALES (est): 24.6MM **Privately Held**
WEB: www.kpsan.org
SIC: 8011 Anesthesiologist

(P-19949)
KERLAN-JOBE ORTHOPEDIC CLINIC (PA)
6801 Park Ter Ste 500, Los Angeles
(90045-9212)
PHONE..................310 665-7200
Ralph A Gambardella, *CEO*
Vernon Williams, *Managing Dir*
Stephen Lombardo, *Admin Sec*
Jae Chon, *Med Doctor*
Neal S Elattrache, *Med Doctor*
EMP: 78 **EST:** 1973
SQ FT: 37,000
SALES (est): 13.8MM **Privately Held**
WEB: www.kerlanjobe.org
SIC: 8011 Orthopedic physician

(P-19950)
KERN HEALTH SYSTEMS INC
Also Called: Kern Family Healthcare
2900 Buck Owens Blvd, Bakersfield
(93308-6316)
P.O. Box 85000 (93380-5000)
PHONE..................661 664-5000
Carol L Sorrell, *CEO*
Martha Tasinga, *Chief Mktg Ofcr*
Irwin Harris, *Associate Dir*
Leslie Scerbo, *Program Mgr*
Justin Burt, *Administration*
EMP: 98 **EST:** 1995
SQ FT: 16,000
SALES (est): 28.8MM **Privately Held**
WEB: www.kernfamilyhealthcare.com
SIC: 8011 Clinic, operated by physicians

(P-19951)
KERN RDLGY IMAGING SYSTEMS INC (PA)
2301 Bahamas Dr, Bakersfield
(93309-0663)
PHONE..................661 326-9600
David P Schale, *CEO*
Jeff Child MD, *Treasurer*
John Gundzik MD, *Vice Pres*
EMP: 65 **EST:** 1968
SQ FT: 20,000
SALES (est): 29.6MM **Privately Held**
WEB: www.radnet.com
SIC: 8011 Radiologist

(P-19952)
KERN RDLGY IMAGING SYSTEMS INC
4100 Truxtun Ave Ste 306, Bakersfield
(93309-0657)
PHONE..................661 322-9958
John M Gundzik, *Principal*
EMP: 70
SALES (corp-wide): 29.6MM **Privately Held**
WEB: www.radnet.com
SIC: 8011 Radiologist
PA: Kern Radiology Imaging Systems, Inc.
2301 Bahamas Dr
Bakersfield CA 93309
661 326-9600

(P-19953)
KRISTIE L LIN MD INC (PA)
100 E California Blvd, Pasadena
(91105-3205)
PHONE..................626 272-4408
Kristie L Lin, *CEO*
EMP: 77 **EST:** 2013
SALES (est): 842.8K **Privately Held**
SIC: 8011 Physicians' office, including specialists

(P-19954)
LA PEER SURGERY CENTER LLC
Also Called: La Peer Health Systems
8920 Wilshire Blvd # 101, Beverly Hills
(90211-2007)
PHONE..................310 360-9119
Dr Siamak Tabib, *Mng Member*
Juselle Cortes, *Administration*
Nick Camacho, *Controller*
Babak Azizzadeh, *Med Doctor*
EMP: 78 **EST:** 2000
SQ FT: 2,300
SALES (est): 28.3MM
SALES (corp-wide): 1.9B **Publicly Held**
WEB: www.lapeerhealth.com
SIC: 8011 Surgeon
HQ: Surgery Partners, Inc.
310 Sven Sprng Way Ste 50
Brentwood TN 37027
615 234-5900

(P-19955)
LAC & USC MEDICAL CENTER
2051 Marengo St, Los Angeles
(90033-1352)
P.O. Box 861749 (90086-1749)
PHONE..................323 409-2345
Marisa Danbee, *Principal*
Gualberto Escobedo, *Engineer*
Deepa Nanayakkara, *Infectious Dis*
Eric Basler, *Surgeon*
Artur Fahradyan, *Surgeon*
EMP: 143 **EST:** 2009
SALES (est): 25.4MM **Privately Held**
WEB: www.dhs.lacounty.gov
SIC: 8011 Primary care medical clinic

(P-19956)
LANCASTER CRDLGY MED GROUP INC (PA)
Also Called: Physicians Referral Service
43847 Heaton Ave Ste B, Lancaster
(93534-4922)
PHONE..................661 726-3058
Shun K Sunder MD, *President*
E Ekong MD, *Vice Pres*
Kanagarath Sivalingam MD, *Admin Sec*
EMP: 80
SQ FT: 30,000
SALES (est): 5.2MM **Privately Held**
SIC: 8011 Cardiologist & cardio-vascular specialist

(P-19957)
LANDMARK IMAGING LLC
11620 Wilshire Blvd Fl 10, Los Angeles
(90025-6821)
PHONE..................310 914-7336
Brian King, *Med Doctor*
Jeffrey Silverman, *Med Doctor*
Douglas Brown,
Jeff Silverman, *Director*
EMP: 88 **EST:** 2002
SALES (est): 1.7MM **Privately Held**
WEB: www.landmarkimaging.com
SIC: 8011 Radiologist

(P-19958)
LANE & KUSCHNER MEDICAL GROUP
9001 Wilshire Blvd # 200, Beverly Hills
(90211-1838)
P.O. Box 16197 (90209-2197)
PHONE..................310 858-0104
Charles S Lane, *Partner*
Stuart Kuschner, *Partner*
EMP: 54 **EST:** 1960
SQ FT: 5,200
SALES (est): 1.5MM **Privately Held**
WEB: www.cedars-sinai.org
SIC: 8011 Orthopedic physician

(P-19959)
LAS ISLAS FAMILY MED GROUP PC
325 W Chnnel Islands Blvd, Oxnard
(93033-4501)
PHONE..................805 385-8662
Miguel Cervantes, *Director*
EMP: 52 **EST:** 1991
SALES (est): 6.9MM **Privately Held**
WEB: www.lasislas.org
SIC: 8011 General & family practice, physician/surgeon

(PA)=Parent Co (HQ)=Headquarters (DH)=Div Headquarters
✪ = New Business established in last 2 years

(P-19960)
LASERAWAY MEDICAL GROUP INC (PA)
9615 Brighton Way Ste 202, Beverly Hills (90210-5158)
PHONE................................888 252-7497
Andrea Heckmann, President
Marla Esposito, Exec Dir
Jade Heglie, Administration
Danelle Forcier, VP Sales
Michael Jenkot, Sales Mgr
EMP: 116 EST: 2005
SALES (est): 25.8MM Privately Held
WEB: www.laseraway.com
SIC: 8011 Dermatologist

(P-19961)
LINDA LOMA UNIV HLTH CARE (PA)
11175 Campus St, Loma Linda (92350-1700)
PHONE................................909 558-4729
Roger Hadley MD, President
David B Hinshaw Jr, Vice Chairman
Barbara Sharp, Vice Pres
Brian Bull MD, Admin Sec
Nikki McCutchan, Admin Asst
EMP: 850 EST: 1989
SQ FT: 70,000
SALES (est): 166.4MM Privately Held
WEB: www.fmg.lluh.org
SIC: 8011 Clinic, operated by physicians

(P-19962)
LOBUE LASER & EYE MEDICAL CTRS (PA)
40700 California Oaks Rd, Murrieta (92562-5795)
PHONE................................951 696-1135
Thomas David Lobue, President
Ryan Miller,
EMP: 57 EST: 2008
SALES (est): 7.1MM Privately Held
WEB: www.lobue2020eyes.com
SIC: 8011 Ophthalmologist

(P-19963)
LOMA LNDA UNIV FMLY MED GROUP
25455 Barton Rd Ste 204b, Loma Linda (92354-3130)
PHONE................................909 558-6600
John Testerman, President
Richard Kim, Med Doctor
Lauren Simon, Med Doctor
Lauren M Simon, Director
EMP: 92 EST: 1980
SALES (est): 3MM Privately Held
WEB: www.lluh.org
SIC: 8011 Clinic, operated by physicians

(P-19964)
LONG BCH - LKWOOD ORTHPD MED G
Also Called: Wassef, E W MD Facs
5750 Downey Ave Ste 308, Lakewood (90712-1482)
PHONE................................562 633-3787
Ezzat W Wasses MD, Partner
Perry R Secor MD, Partner
EMP: 78 EST: 1975
SQ FT: 5,000
SALES (est): 6.6MM Privately Held
WEB: www.lborthoinstitute.com
SIC: 8011 Orthopedic physician

(P-19965)
LOS ANGELES CARDIOLOGY ASSOC (HQ)
1245 Wilshire Blvd # 703, Los Angeles (90017-4810)
PHONE................................213 977-0419
Guy Mayeda, CEO
Dale Hill, Office Mgr
Guy S Mayeda, Internal Med
Edward Abdullah, Med Doctor
Ivan Ho, Med Doctor
EMP: 65 EST: 1989
SQ FT: 12,000
SALES (est): 10MM
SALES (corp-wide): 923K Privately Held
WEB: www.pihhealth.org
SIC: 8011 Cardiologist & cardio-vascular specialist

PA: Pih Health, Inc.
12401 Washington Blvd
Whittier CA 90602
562 698-0811

(P-19966)
LOS ANGELES FREE CLINIC
5205 Melrose Ave, Los Angeles (90038-3144)
PHONE................................323 653-1990
EMP: 111
SALES (corp-wide): 43.3MM Privately Held
WEB: www.sabancommunityclinic.org
PA: The Los Angeles Free Clinic
8405 Beverly Blvd
Los Angeles CA 90048
323 653-8622

(P-19967)
LOS ANGELES FREE CLINIC (PA)
Also Called: SABAN COMMUNITY CLINIC
8405 Beverly Blvd, Los Angeles (90048-3401)
PHONE................................323 653-8622
Jeffrey Bujer, CEO
Maria Unzueta, CIO
Dave Shortt, Technician
Mario Rivas, Technology
Robynn Cameros, Accountant
EMP: 79 EST: 1967
SQ FT: 26,615
SALES (est): 43.3MM Privately Held
WEB: www.sabancommunityclinic.org
SIC: 8011 Clinic, operated by physicians

(P-19968)
LOS ANGLES FREE CLNIC HLLYWOOD
8405 Beverly Blvd, Los Angeles (90048-3401)
PHONE................................323 653-8622
Abbe Land, CEO
EMP: 99
SALES (est): 89.4K Privately Held
WEB: www.sabancommunityclinic.org
SIC: 8011 Clinic, operated by physicians

(P-19969)
LOS ROBLES REGIONAL MED CTR
150 Via Merida, Westlake Village (91362-3816)
PHONE................................805 370-4531
Simin Shandiz, Principal
Cynthia Johnson, Ch Nursing Ofcr
Don Adler, Administration
Sonny Bui, Administration
John Ortega, Purch Dir
EMP: 138 Publicly Held
WEB: www.losrobleshospital.com
SIC: 8011 Medical centers
HQ: Los Robles Regional Medical Center
215 W Janss Rd
Thousand Oaks CA 91360

(P-19970)
MADISON RADIOLOGY MED GROUP
65 N Madison Ave Ste M250, Pasadena (91101-2000)
PHONE................................626 793-8189
Terry S Becker, President
Jeanette Velasco, Radiology
Eric Becker, Director
Terry Becker, Director
EMP: 55 EST: 1979
SALES (est): 6MM Privately Held
WEB: www.madisonradiology.net
SIC: 8011 Radiologist

(P-19971)
MARK KISLINGER MD INC
Also Called: Foothill Eye Surgical Center
210 S Grand Ave Ste 106, Glendora (91741-4276)
PHONE................................626 335-2020
Mark B Kislinger MD, President
EMP: 58 EST: 1985

SALES (est): 7.5MM Privately Held
WEB: www.foothilleyeinstitute.com
SIC: 8011 Ears, nose & throat specialist: physician/surgeon

(P-19972)
MEDICAL GROUP BVERLY HILLS INC
Also Called: Cedar Sinai Medical Group
250 N Robertson Blvd # 60, Beverly Hills (90211-1788)
PHONE................................310 247-4646
Tom Gordon, Branch Mgr
John Andrews, Med Doctor
James L Caplan, Med Doctor
EMP: 50
SALES (corp-wide): 447.7MM Privately Held
WEB: www.cedars-sinai.org
SIC: 8011 General & family practice, physician/surgeon
PA: Medical Group Of Beverly Hills, Inc.
6500 Wilshire Blvd # 150
Los Angeles CA 90048
310 385-3200

(P-19973)
MEDICAL IMAGING PARTNERS LLC
Also Called: Arcadia Mri Centre
638 W Duarte Rd Ste 2, Arcadia (91007-7622)
PHONE................................626 446-0080
Bryan Sotomayor, Mng Member
Patty Higa, Executive
Mary Morrissey, Administration
EMP: 61 EST: 1991
SQ FT: 7,000
SALES (est): 6.2MM Privately Held
SIC: 8011 Radiologist

(P-19974)
MEDICL IMGNG CTR OF SOUTHRN CA
2811 Wilshire Blvd # 100, Santa Monica (90403-4803)
PHONE................................310 829-9788
Bradley Jabour MD, President
Nicole Pelissier, COO
Ulli Butzke, Executive
EMP: 65
SQ FT: 22,000
SALES (est): 7.4MM Privately Held
WEB: www.micsc.com
SIC: 8011 Radiologist

(P-19975)
MEDPOINT MANAGEMENT
6400 Canoga Ave Ste 163, Woodland Hills (91367-2435)
PHONE................................818 702-0100
Sheldon Lewenfuff Preident, Principal
Sheldon Lewenfuf, President
Derek Schneider, CFO
Linda Deaktor, Vice Pres
Tom Diaz, Vice Pres
EMP: 50 EST: 1993
SALES (est): 23.9MM Privately Held
WEB: www.medpointmanagement.com
SIC: 8011 Health maintenance organization

(P-19976)
MEMOR ORTHO SURGIC GROUP A M
Also Called: Southern California Cen
2760 Atlantic Ave, Long Beach (90806-2755)
PHONE................................562 424-6666
Peter R Kurzweil, CEO
Douglas W Jackson MD, President
Curtis W Spencer III, Vice Pres
Leang Prum, Office Mgr
David S Morrison MD, Admin Sec
▲ EMP: 70 EST: 1977
SQ FT: 12,000
SALES (est): 14MM Privately Held
WEB: www.memorialorthopaedic.com
SIC: 8011 Orthopedic physician; sports medicine specialist, physician; surgeon; physical medicine, physician/surgeon

(P-19977)
MICHA-RETTENMAIER PARTNERSHIP
Also Called: Gynecologic Oncology Assoc
351 Hospital Rd Ste 507, Newport Beach (92663-3500)
PHONE................................714 280-1645
John P Micha MD, Partner
Mark A Rettenmaier MD, Partner
Cheri Graham, Exec Dir
Michelle Aylward, Administration
Vilma Thompson, Administration
EMP: 88 EST: 1989
SQ FT: 3,500
SALES (est): 13.7MM Privately Held
WEB: www.axik.net
SIC: 8011 Gynecologist; oncologist

(P-19978)
MICHAEL D MOLINARI MD FACG INC
Also Called: Molinari, Michael D MD
341 Magnolia Ave Ste 207, Corona (92879-3332)
PHONE................................951 734-9930
Michael D Molinari MD, President
EMP: 13 EST: 1978
SALES (est): 778.1K Privately Held
SIC: 8011 2834 Gastronomist; internal medicine, physician/surgeon; drugs acting on the gastrointestinal or genitourinary system

(P-19979)
MINAL INC (PA)
1080 N Western Ave, Los Angeles (90029-2310)
PHONE................................323 957-8787
Minal Borsada, Manager
EMP: 81 EST: 2010
SALES (est): 318.2K Privately Held
SIC: 8011 Offices & clinics of medical doctors

(P-19980)
MINERAL KING RDLGCAL MED GROUP
1700 S Court St Ste F, Visalia (93277-4931)
PHONE................................559 734-9244
Gaine Aguet, President
Michael Bowers, President
Thu Le, Diag Radio
Erika Balderas, Director
EMP: 80 EST: 1964
SQ FT: 1,200
SALES (est): 9.1MM Privately Held
WEB: www.visaliaopenmri.net
SIC: 8011 Radiologist

(P-19981)
MISSION INTERNAL MED GROUP INC
Also Called: Arthur Loussararian MD
26800 Crown Valley Pkwy # 103, Mission Viejo (92691-6389)
PHONE................................949 364-3570
Arthur Loussararian, Principal
David Kovacs, Internal Med
Khadija Mayet, Internal Med
EMP: 91
SALES (corp-wide): 19.1MM Privately Held
SIC: 8011 Primary care medical clinic
PA: Mission Internal Medical Group, Inc.
26732 Crown Valley Pkwy # 351
Mission Viejo CA 92691
949 282-1600

(P-19982)
MISSION INTERNAL MED GROUP INC
Also Called: West Coast Physical Therapy
27882 Forbes Rd Ste 110, Laguna Niguel (92677-1267)
PHONE................................949 364-3605
Joan Shrum-Brown, Principal
EMP: 91
SALES (corp-wide): 19.1MM Privately Held
SIC: 8011 8049 Cardiologist & cardio-vascular specialist; physical therapist

PA: Mission Internal Medical Group, Inc.
26732 Crown Valley Pkwy # 351
Mission Viejo CA 92691
949 282-1600

(P-19983)
MOHAWK MEDICAL GROUP INC
9500 Stockdale Hwy # 200, Bakersfield
(93311-3621)
PHONE....................661 324-4747
Jorge Deltoro, *President*
Luis Cousin, *Vice Pres*
Julie Rice, *Office Mgr*
Gene A Anderson, *Family Practiti*
Albert Peinado, *Internal Med*
EMP: 80 **EST:** 1985
SQ FT: 18,500
SALES (est): 5.6MM **Privately Held**
SIC: 8011 General & family practice, physician/surgeon

(P-19984)
MOLINA HEALTHCARE INC (PA)
200 Oceangate Ste 100, Long Beach
(90802-4317)
P.O. Box 22813 (90801-5813)
PHONE....................562 435-3666
Joseph M Zubretsky, *President*
Dale B Wolf, *Ch of Bd*
Mark L Keim, *CFO*
Ronna E Romney, *Vice Ch Bd*
Jeff D Barlow,
EMP: 2800 **EST:** 1980
SALES (est): 19.4B **Publicly Held**
WEB: www.molinahealthcare.com
SIC: 8011 6324 Health maintenance organization; hospital & medical service plans; health maintenance organization (HMO), insurance only

(P-19985)
MOLINA HEALTHCARE CALIFORNIA
200 Oceangate Ste 100, Long Beach
(90802-4317)
PHONE....................800 526-8196
EMP: 245 **EST:** 2016
SALES (est): 2.6MM
SALES (corp-wide): 19.4B **Publicly Held**
WEB: www.molinahealthcare.com
SIC: 8011 Offices & clinics of medical doctors
PA: Molina Healthcare, Inc.
200 Oceangate Ste 100
Long Beach CA 90802
562 435-3666

(P-19986)
MOLINA HEALTHCARE NEW YORK INC
200 Oceangate Ste 100, Long Beach
(90802-4317)
PHONE....................888 562-5442
EMP: 110 **EST:** 2019
SALES (est): 2.9MM
SALES (corp-wide): 19.4B **Publicly Held**
WEB: www.molinahealthcare.com
SIC: 8011 Health maintenance organization
PA: Molina Healthcare, Inc.
200 Oceangate Ste 100
Long Beach CA 90802
562 435-3666

(P-19987)
MOLINA PATHWAYS LLC
200 Oceangate Ste 100, Long Beach
(90802-4317)
PHONE....................562 491-5773
Craig Bass, *CEO*
EMP: 321 **EST:** 2011
SALES (est): 3.8MM
SALES (corp-wide): 19.4B **Publicly Held**
WEB: www.molinahealthcare.com
SIC: 8011 Health maintenance organization
PA: Molina Healthcare, Inc.
200 Oceangate Ste 100
Long Beach CA 90802
562 435-3666

(P-19988)
MONARCH HEALTHCARE A MEDICAL (HQ)
11 Technology Dr, Irvine (92618-2302)
PHONE....................949 923-3200
Bartley Asner, *CEO*
Marcie Greene, *CEO*
Marvin Gordon MD, *CFO*
Jay J Cohen MD, *Vice Pres*
Olga Kosenko, *Vice Pres*
EMP: 396 **EST:** 1986
SQ FT: 75,000
SALES (est): 95MM
SALES (corp-wide): 257.1B **Publicly Held**
WEB: www.monarchhealthcare.com
SIC: 8011 Group health association
PA: Unitedhealth Group Incorporated
9900 Bren Rd E Ste 300w
Minnetonka MN 55343
952 936-1300

(P-19989)
MONTEBELLO ORTHPD MED GROUP
Also Called: M O M G Orthopedics
6758 Passons Blvd, Pico Rivera
(90660-3666)
PHONE....................562 654-6899
Charles Alexander, *President*
Yung Cho, *Principal*
EMP: 64 **EST:** 1980
SQ FT: 4,000
SALES (est): 3.6MM **Privately Held**
SIC: 8011 Orthopedic physician

(P-19990)
N S C CHANNEL ISLANDS INC
Also Called: HealthSouth
2300 Wankel Way, Oxnard (93030-2665)
PHONE....................805 485-1908
Susan Clark, *Administration*
EMP: 426 **EST:** 1995
SQ FT: 14,000
SALES (est): 16.7MM
SALES (corp-wide): 4.6B **Publicly Held**
WEB: www.channelislandssurgicenter.com
SIC: 8011 Surgeon
HQ: Healthsouth Rehabilitation Hospital Of Cypress, Llc
9001 Liberty Pkwy
Birmingham AL 35242

(P-19991)
NEUROSURGICAL ASSOCIATES (PA)
25751 Mcbean Pkwy Ste 305, Valencia
(91355-3701)
PHONE....................661 799-2542
Mark A Liker, *Principal*
EMP: 92 **EST:** 2008
SALES (est): 6.6MM **Privately Held**
WEB: www.californianeurosurgicalinstitute.com
SIC: 8011 Orthopedic physician

(P-19992)
NEW SPIRIT NATURALS INC (PA)
615 W Allen Ave, San Dimas (91773-1447)
PHONE....................909 592-4445
Larry Milam, *President*
Victoria Dauer, *Director*
Gina Famiglietti, *Director*
◆ **EMP:** 26 **EST:** 1982
SQ FT: 25,000
SALES (est): 6.7MM **Privately Held**
WEB: www.newspirit.com
SIC: 8011 5122 2032 2844 Offices & clinics of medical doctors; drugs, proprietaries & sundries; canned specialties; shampoos, rinses, conditioners: hair

(P-19993)
NEWPORT BEACH SURGERY CTR LLC
361 Hospital Rd Ste 124, Newport Beach
(92663-3521)
PHONE....................949 631-0988
John McNutt, *Managing Dir*
Madonna Molinari, *Exec VP*
Bruce Albert,
Robert Anderson,
Perter Broekelschen, *Mng Member*

EMP: 120 **EST:** 1992
SQ FT: 10,000
SALES (est): 15.6MM **Privately Held**
WEB:
www.newportbeachsurgerycenter.com
SIC: 8011 Surgeon

(P-19994)
NEWPORT CENTER MEDICAL GROUP
400 Nwport Ctr Dr Ste 502, Newport Beach
(92660)
PHONE....................949 644-3555
Bradley Kayes, *Partner*
Susan Cederstrom, *Partner*
Paul Fakuda, *Partner*
Dr Gilbert Goodman, *Partner*
Amy Teresi, *Partner*
EMP: 56 **EST:** 1992
SQ FT: 10,000
SALES (est): 8.6MM **Privately Held**
WEB: www.newportchildren.com
SIC: 8011 Physicians' office, including specialists

(P-19995)
NEWPORT DIAGNOSTIC CENTER INC (PA)
1605 Avocado Ave, Newport Beach
(92660-7725)
PHONE....................949 760-3025
Hazem H Chehabi, *President*
Kathy Wortham, *Exec Dir*
Brigit Lieb, *Technology*
Janet Crider, *Finance*
Hang Le, *Accountant*
EMP: 55 **EST:** 1991
SQ FT: 26,000
SALES (est): 10MM **Privately Held**
WEB: www.newportdiagnosticcenter.com
SIC: 8011 Radiologist

(P-19996)
NEXTHEALTH WEST HOLLYWOOD INC
24955 Pacific Coast Hwy, Malibu
(90265-4700)
PHONE....................310 295-2075
Darshan Shah, *CEO*
Kevin Peake, *President*
EMP: 15
SALES (est): 2MM **Privately Held**
SIC: 8011 7372 Physicians' office, including specialists; application computer software

(P-19997)
NORTHEAST VALLEY HEALTH CORP
531 5th St Unit A, San Fernando
(91340-2269)
PHONE....................818 361-8464
Rebecca Macmillan, *Branch Mgr*
Teda Arunrut, *Med Doctor*
Tim Farrell, *Med Doctor*
Shabnam Jacobson, *Med Doctor*
Hyejung Kang, *Med Doctor*
EMP: 65
SALES (corp-wide): 104.7MM **Privately Held**
SIC: 8011 Clinic, operated by physicians
PA: Northeast Valley Health Corp
1172 N Maclay Ave
San Fernando CA 91340
818 898-1388

(P-19998)
NORTHEAST VALLEY HEALTH CORP
23763 Valencia Blvd, Valencia
(91355-2105)
PHONE....................661 287-1551
Raquel Heximer, *Manager*
Mona Shah, *Med Doctor*
EMP: 65
SALES (corp-wide): 104.7MM **Privately Held**
SIC: 8011 Clinic, operated by physicians
PA: Northeast Valley Health Corp
1172 N Maclay Ave
San Fernando CA 91340
818 898-1388

(P-19999)
NORTHEAST VALLEY HEALTH CORP
Also Called: San Fernando Health Center
1600 San Fernando Rd, San Fernando
(91340-3115)
PHONE....................818 365-8086
Beverly Jenkins, *Manager*
Margaret Natarajan, *Admin Sec*
Mary Wakim, *Pediatrics*
Karla Nungaray, *Pediatrics*
Joy Ahrens, *Director*
EMP: 65
SALES (corp-wide): 104.7MM **Privately Held**
SIC: 8011 Clinic, operated by physicians
PA: Northeast Valley Health Corp
1172 N Maclay Ave
San Fernando CA 91340
818 898-1388

(P-20000)
NORTHEAST VALLEY HEALTH CORP
7138 Van Nuys Blvd, Van Nuys
(91405-3005)
PHONE....................818 778-6240
Gary Morris, *Manager*
Lisa Valdez, *Med Doctor*
EMP: 65
SALES (corp-wide): 104.7MM **Privately Held**
SIC: 8011 Clinic, operated by physicians
PA: Northeast Valley Health Corp
1172 N Maclay Ave
San Fernando CA 91340
818 898-1388

(P-20001)
NORTHEAST VALLEY HEALTH CORP
Also Called: Homeless Care
7843 Lankershim Blvd, North Hollywood
(91605-2523)
PHONE....................818 765-8656
Kathy Proctor, *Director*
EMP: 65
SALES (corp-wide): 104.7MM **Privately Held**
SIC: 8011 Clinic, operated by physicians
PA: Northeast Valley Health Corp
1172 N Maclay Ave
San Fernando CA 91340
818 898-1388

(P-20002)
NORTHEAST VALLEY HEALTH CORP
12756 Van Nuys Blvd, Pacoima
(91331-1696)
PHONE....................818 896-0531
Kathreen Dayanim, *Manager*
Jesse Sanders, *Associate Dir*
Denise Torres, *Program Mgr*
Yanira Valencia, *Program Mgr*
Frederick Choi, *General Mgr*
EMP: 65
SQ FT: 11,645
SALES (corp-wide): 104.7MM **Privately Held**
SIC: 8011 8071 Clinic, operated by physicians; medical laboratories
PA: Northeast Valley Health Corp
1172 N Maclay Ave
San Fernando CA 91340
818 898-1388

(P-20003)
NORTHEAST VALLEY HEALTH CORP
8215 Van Nuys Blvd Ste 21, Panorama City
(91402-4810)
PHONE....................818 988-6335
Nick Rocca, *Director*
Jose Paredes, *Administration*
EMP: 65
SALES (corp-wide): 104.7MM **Privately Held**
SIC: 8011 8099 Clinic, operated by physicians; health screening service
PA: Northeast Valley Health Corp
1172 N Maclay Ave
San Fernando CA 91340
818 898-1388

PRODUCTS & SVCS

(P-20004)
NORTHERN ORNGE CNTY ENT MDCL (PA)
1955 Sunny Crest Dr # 108, Fullerton (92835-3654)
PHONE...................714 441-0133
James J Lee, *President*
EMP: 59 **EST:** 2001
SALES (est): 1.7MM **Privately Held**
WEB: www.ocentmed.com
SIC: 8011 Eyes, ears, nose & throat specialist: physician/surgeon

(P-20005)
NORTHRIDGE DIAGNOSTIC CENTER
Also Called: Beverly Radiology
8227 Reseda Blvd, Reseda (91335-1247)
PHONE...................818 773-6500
Dr Leo Rain, *General Ptnr*
Dr Chin Lon Lin, *Ltd Ptnr*
Dr Raj Wick, *Ltd Ptnr*
EMP: 103 **EST:** 1985
SQ FT: 3,300
SALES (est): 2.7MM **Privately Held**
WEB: www.radnet.com
SIC: 8011 Cardiologist & cardio-vascular specialist

(P-20006)
NVISION LASER EYE CENTERS INC
24022 Calle De La Plata, Laguna Hills (92653-3626)
PHONE...................949 951-1457
Norman Peterson, *Branch Mgr*
EMP: 52
SALES (corp-wide): 40.5MM **Privately Held**
WEB: www.nvisioncenters.com
SIC: 8011 Ophthalmologist
PA: Nvision Laser Eye Centers Inc.
75 Enterprise Ste 200
Aliso Viejo CA 92656
877 455-9942

(P-20007)
OAK GROVE INST FOUNDATION INC (PA)
Also Called: Oak Grove Center
24275 Jefferson Ave, Murrieta (92562-7285)
PHONE...................951 677-5599
Tamara L Wilson, *CEO*
Barry Soper, *Ch of Bd*
Fe Santiago, *CFO*
April Honore, *Teacher*
Athene Banche, *Education*
EMP: 368 **EST:** 1986
SQ FT: 39,000
SALES: 20.9MM **Privately Held**
WEB: www.oakgrovecenter.org
SIC: 8011 8211 8361 Psychiatric clinic; specialty education; residential care

(P-20008)
OAKS DIAGNOSTICS INC (PA)
Also Called: California Imaging Nework
6310 San Vicente Blvd, Los Angeles (90048-5426)
P.O. Box 5355, Beverly Hills (90209-5355)
PHONE...................310 855-0035
Ronald Grusd MD, *CEO*
EMP: 60 **EST:** 1989
SQ FT: 9,000
SALES (est): 11.7MM **Privately Held**
SIC: 8011 Radiologist

(P-20009)
OJAI VLY FMLY MEDICINE GROUP
117 Pirie Rd Ste D, Ojai (93023-3166)
PHONE...................805 646-7246
Halverson J R MD, *Partner*
Mary Dial MD, *Partner*
Carl Gross MD, *Partner*
James Halverson MD, *Partner*
Michelle Gorrell, *Admin Sec*
EMP: 75 **EST:** 1979
SALES (est): 10MM **Privately Held**
WEB: www.ojaiusd.org
SIC: 8011 General & family practice, physician/surgeon

(P-20010)
OLIVE VIEW-UCLA MEDICAL CENTER (PA)
Also Called: Valley Care Olive View Med Ctr
14445 Olive View Dr, Sylmar (91342-1438)
PHONE...................818 364-1555
Carolyn Rhee, *CEO*
EMP: 1810 **EST:** 2001
SALES (est): 128.3MM **Privately Held**
WEB: www.uclaoliveview.org
SIC: 8011 Medical centers

(P-20011)
OMNI FAMILY HEALTH (PA)
Also Called: Community Health Center
4900 California Ave 400b, Bakersfield (93309-7024)
P.O. Box 1060, Shafter (93263-1060)
PHONE...................661 459-1900
Francisco L Castillon, *CEO*
Novira Irawan, *CFO*
David Brust, *Treasurer*
Diego Martinez, *Officer*
Mark Millan, *Officer*
EMP: 80
SQ FT: 14,000
SALES: 66.4MM **Privately Held**
WEB: www.omnifamilyhealth.org
SIC: 8011 Clinic, operated by physicians

(P-20012)
ONRAD INC
Also Called: Onrad Medical Group
1770 Iowa Ave Ste 280, Riverside (92507-7401)
PHONE...................800 848-5876
David Engert, *President*
Samuel Salen, *Ch of Bd*
Joseph Artino, *CFO*
Scott Castle, *CFO*
Anthony Freire, *Vice Pres*
EMP: 79
SQ FT: 1,500
SALES (est): 9MM **Privately Held**
WEB: www.onradinc.com
SIC: 8011 Radiologist

(P-20013)
OPHTHALMIC FACIAL PLASTIC (PA)
9735 Wilshire Blvd # 300, Beverly Hills (90212-2105)
PHONE...................310 276-0044
Sam Goldberger, *Principal*
Denae Loughrie, *Office Mgr*
EMP: 62 **EST:** 2006
SALES (est): 1MM **Privately Held**
WEB: www.neweyelids.com
SIC: 8011 Plastic surgeon

(P-20014)
OPTHAMOLOGY ASSOCIATES OF VLY
Also Called: Ophthalmology Assoc of Vly
16311 Ventura Blvd # 750, Encino (91436-2124)
PHONE...................818 990-3623
Peter Zeegen, *President*
Kelly Starr, *Research*
Jeanie Clark, *Surgeon*
Ana Robles, *Surgeon*
Stacy Mincheva, *Supervisor*
EMP: 64 **EST:** 1974
SALES (est): 7.7MM **Privately Held**
WEB: www.oaveyes.com
SIC: 8011 Ophthalmologist

(P-20015)
ORTHOPEDIC CONSULTANTS (PA)
16311 Ventura Blvd # 800, Encino (91436-2140)
PHONE...................818 788-7343
Lester Cohn, *President*
EMP: 50 **EST:** 1961
SQ FT: 8,300
SALES (est): 5.6MM **Privately Held**
SIC: 8011 Orthopedic physician

(P-20016)
OVATION FERTILITY (PA)
15821 Ventura Blvd # 625, Encino (91436-4780)
PHONE...................818 858-1074
Paul Kappelman, *CEO*

Conor Beardsley, *President*
Goldie Gupta, *CFO*
Ian Koons, *Vice Pres*
Cassie Miller, *Risk Mgmt Dir*
EMP: 94 **EST:** 2018
SALES (est): 17.5MM **Privately Held**
WEB: www.ovationfertility.com
SIC: 8011 Fertility specialist, physician

(P-20017)
PACIFIC SHORES MED GROUP INC (HQ)
1043 Elm Ave Ste 104, Long Beach (90813-3244)
PHONE...................562 590-0345
Simon Tchekmedyian, *CEO*
Jonathan Rigutto, *District Mgr*
Christina Hamilton, *Research*
Arturo Medina, *Technology*
Helene Au, *Hematology*
EMP: 60 **EST:** 1995
SQ FT: 3,300
SALES (est): 17.7MM
SALES (corp-wide): 592.4MM **Privately Held**
WEB: www.cityofhope.org
SIC: 8011 Medical centers; oncologist
PA: City Of Hope
1500 Duarte Rd
Duarte CA 91010
626 256-4673

(P-20018)
PAMONA VALLEY MEDICAL GROUP (PA)
Also Called: Pro Med Hlth Netwrk Pomona Vly
600 City Pkwy W Ste 800, Orange (92868-2948)
PHONE...................909 932-1045
Kishon Thapar, *CEO*
Victor Pappoe MD, *Treasurer*
Randy Karu MD, *Admin Sec*
Diane Cacho, *Author*
EMP: 80 **EST:** 1988 **Privately Held**
SIC: 8011 8741 General & family practice, physician/surgeon; administrative management

(P-20019)
PAVILION SURGERY CENTER LLC
1140 W La Veta Ave, Orange (92868-4225)
PHONE...................714 744-8850
David Yomtoob, *Ch of Bd*
EMP: 70 **EST:** 2016
SQ FT: 49,000
SALES (est): 19.6MM **Privately Held**
WEB: www.pavilionsurgery.com
SIC: 8011 Surgeon

(P-20020)
PEDIATRIC & FAMILY MEDICAL CTR
Also Called: EISNER PEDIATRIC & FAMILY MEDI
1530 S Olive St, Los Angeles (90015-3023)
PHONE...................213 342-3325
Carl Coan, *CEO*
Edward Matthews III, *Ch of Bd*
Kevin Rossi, *Ch of Bd*
Herb Schultz, *President*
Carl Edward Coan, *CEO*
EMP: 160 **EST:** 1920
SQ FT: 21,000
SALES: 54.1MM **Privately Held**
WEB: www.eisnerhealth.org
SIC: 8011 Clinic, operated by physicians

(P-20021)
PEOPLE CREATING SUCCESS INC
380 Arneill Rd, Camarillo (93010-6406)
PHONE...................805 644-9480
Marie McManus, *Branch Mgr*
EMP: 132
SALES (corp-wide): 14MM **Privately Held**
WEB: www.pcs-services.org
SIC: 8011 Offices & clinics of medical doctors

PA: People Creating Success, Inc.
2585 Teller Rd
Newbury Park CA 91320
805 375-9222

(P-20022)
PERMANENTE MEDICAL GROUP INC
Also Called: S C P M G
25825 Vermont Ave, Harbor City (90710-3518)
PHONE...................310 325-5111
Leroy Foster, *Manager*
Abraham Schlossberg, *Med Doctor*
Peter Tsai, *Med Doctor*
EMP: 628
SALES (corp-wide): 30.5B **Privately Held**
WEB: www.permanente.org
SIC: 8011 Medical centers
HQ: The Permanente Medical Group Inc
1950 Franklin St Fl 18th
Oakland CA 94612
866 858-2226

(P-20023)
PHYSICIANS AUTOMATED LAB INC
Also Called: Physicians Automated Labs
9830 Brimhall Rd Unit 100, Bakersfield (93312-2790)
P.O. Box 1536 (93302-1536)
PHONE...................661 431-1176
EMP: 67 **Privately Held**
WEB: www.westpaclab.com
SIC: 8011 Pathologist
HQ: Physician's Automated Laboratory, Inc.
820 34th St Ste 102
Bakersfield CA 93301
661 325-0744

(P-20024)
PREMIER OTPTENT SRGERY CTR INC
Also Called: Amsurg
900 E Washington St # 155, Colton (92324-7111)
PHONE...................909 370-2190
David Wood, *President*
Nancy Bito, *Nurse*
Carrie BSN, *Nurse*
Darril Duthie,
Cristina Marquez, *Receptionist*
EMP: 119 **EST:** 2000
SQ FT: 70,000
SALES (est): 22.3MM **Privately Held**
WEB: www.premierosc.com
SIC: 8011 Surgeon

(P-20025)
PREMIERE MEDICAL GROUP
Also Called: Family Health Center
1770 N Orng Grv Ave, Pomona (91767-3027)
PHONE...................909 469-9498
Duane Styles, *Partner*
EMP: 54 **EST:** 1976
SQ FT: 5,300
SALES (est): 650.6K **Privately Held**
SIC: 8011 General & family practice, physician/surgeon

(P-20026)
PRIMARY CRITICAL CARE MEDICAL
620 N Brand Blvd Ste 500, Glendale (91203-4218)
P.O. Box 998, North Hollywood (91603-0998)
PHONE...................818 847-9950
EMP: 164 **EST:** 1995
SALES (est): 1.8MM
SALES (corp-wide): 287.4MM **Privately Held**
SIC: 8011 Medical Doctor's Office
HQ: Team Health Holdings, Inc.
265 Brookview Centre Way
Knoxville TN 37919
865 693-1000

(P-20027)
PRIMECARE MORENO VALLEY INC
2275 Sampson Ave Ste 111, Corona (92879-3401)
PHONE...................951 371-8440

EMP: 58 EST: 1995
SALES (est): 3.8MM
SALES (corp-wide): 257.1B **Publicly Held**
WEB: www.unitedhealthgroup.com
SIC: 8011 Offices & clinics of medical doctors
PA: Unitedhealth Group Incorporated
9900 Bren Rd E Ste 300w
Minnetonka MN 55343
952 936-1300

(P-20028)
PROSPECT MEDICAL HOLDINGS INC (PA)
3415 S Sepulveda Blvd # 9, Los Angeles (90034-6060)
PHONE....................310 943-4500
Samuel Lee, *Ch of Bd*
Mike Heather, *CFO*
Debbie Berry, *Officer*
Laura Lacorte, *Officer*
Cindra Syverson, *Officer*
EMP: 260 **EST:** 1993
SQ FT: 7,154
SALES (est): 3.4B **Privately Held**
WEB: www.pmh.com
SIC: 8011 Health maintenance organization

(P-20029)
PROVIDENCE ST JOSEPH HEALTH
4 Park Plz Ste 150, Irvine (92614-2525)
PHONE....................949 430-3963
John Michael Dannelley, *Branch Mgr*
EMP: 3076
SALES (corp-wide): 32.7MM **Privately Held**
WEB: www.psjhealth.org
SIC: 8011 Offices & clinics of medical doctors
PA: Providence St. Joseph Health
1801 Lind Ave Sw
Renton WA 98057
425 525-3355

(P-20030)
PROVIDENCE ST JOSEPH HEALTH
501 S Buena Vista St, Burbank (91505-4809)
PHONE....................818 843-5111
Heidi Lennartz, *COO*
Cynthia Lloyd, *Radiology Dir*
Gisho Tatsutani, *Radiology Dir*
Alexander Koretz, *Principal*
Casey Silva, *IT/INT Sup*
EMP: 3076
SALES (corp-wide): 32.7MM **Privately Held**
WEB: www.psjhealth.org
SIC: 8011 Offices & clinics of medical doctors
PA: Providence St. Joseph Health
1801 Lind Ave Sw
Renton WA 98057
425 525-3355

(P-20031)
QUEENSCARE HEALTH CENTERS
Also Called: Queenscare Fmly Clinics-Eastsd
4816 E 3rd St, Los Angeles (90022-1602)
PHONE....................323 780-4510
Evelyn Moody, *Manager*
EMP: 83
SALES (corp-wide): 28.1MM **Privately Held**
WEB: www.queenscare.org
SIC: 8011 Clinic, operated by physicians
PA: Queenscare Health Centers
950 Suth Grnd Ave Fl 2 Flr 2
Los Angeles CA 90015
323 669-4301

(P-20032)
QUEENSCARE HEALTH CENTERS
4618 Fountain Ave, Los Angeles (90029-1830)
PHONE....................323 644-6180
Guillermo Diaz, *Branch Mgr*
Marina Snitman, *Pharmacy Dir*
Cynthia Borders, *Director*

Emma Nkwam, *Director*
Erica Macias, *Manager*
EMP: 83
SALES (corp-wide): 28.1MM **Privately Held**
WEB: www.queenscare.org
SIC: 8011 Clinic, operated by physicians
PA: Queenscare Health Centers
950 Suth Grnd Ave Fl 2 Flr 2
Los Angeles CA 90015
323 669-4301

(P-20033)
RAD ONC INC
Also Called: Radiation Oncology
2650 Elm Ave Ste 201, Long Beach (90806-1600)
PHONE....................562 492-6695
Ajmel A Puthawala, *President*
Zia Ziaulla, *CFO*
EMP: 58 **EST:** 1988
SQ FT: 10,000
SALES (est): 6.4MM **Privately Held**
SIC: 8011 Oncologist

(P-20034)
RAD-IMAGE MED GROUP INC A CAL
Also Called: Nexxrad Teleradiology Partners
2651 Walnut Ave, Signal Hill (90755-1830)
PHONE....................562 912-2500
Michael Gordon, *Vice Pres*
Shawn Jackson, *Info Tech Dir*
Darissa Kon, *Radiology*
Gabriel Ramirez, *Radiology*
Yvonne Beltran, *Med Doctor*
EMP: 52 **EST:** 2002
SALES (est): 9MM **Privately Held**
WEB: www.nexxrad.com
SIC: 8011 Radiologist

(P-20035)
RADIOLOGY PARTNERS INC (HQ)
2101 E El Segundo Blvd # 40, El Segundo (90245-4518)
PHONE....................424 290-8004
Richard Whitney, *CEO*
Steve Tumbarello, *CFO*
Basak Ertan, *Officer*
Tom Usilton, *Senior VP*
Nina Kottler, *Vice Pres*
EMP: 500 **EST:** 2012
SALES (est): 126.7MM
SALES (corp-wide): 148.7MM **Privately Held**
WEB: www.radpartners.com
SIC: 8011 Radiologist
PA: Radiology Partners Holdings, Llc
2330 Utah Ave Ste 200
El Segundo CA 90245
424 290-8004

(P-20036)
RADNET MANAGEMENT I INC
44725 10th St W Ste 150, Lancaster (93534-3000)
PHONE....................661 945-5855
Mike Buxton, *Manager*
EMP: 201 **EST:** 1982
SQ FT: 1,600
SALES (est): 6MM **Publicly Held**
WEB: www.radnet.com
SIC: 8011 Radiologist
PA: Radnet, Inc.
1510 Cotner Ave
Los Angeles CA 90025

(P-20037)
RADNET MNAGED IMAGING SVCS INC (HQ)
1510 Cotner Ave, Los Angeles (90025-3303)
PHONE....................310 445-2800
Howard G Berger, *CEO*
EMP: 118 **EST:** 1995
SALES (est): 14MM **Publicly Held**
WEB: www.radnet.com
SIC: 8011 Radiologist

(P-20038)
REDLANDS FMLY PRCTICE MED GROU
1520 Barton Rd, Redlands (92373-5467)
PHONE....................909 793-3208
EMP: 52 **EST:** 2006
SALES (est): 434.1K **Privately Held**
WEB: www.redlandshospital.org
SIC: 8011 General & family practice, physician/surgeon

(P-20039)
REGENTS OF UC
4560 Admiralty Way # 100, Marina Del Rey (90292-5423)
PHONE....................310 827-3700
Bernard J Katz, *Director*
Kelly McCarthy, *Manager*
EMP: 61 **EST:** 2007
SALES (est): 3.7MM
SALES (corp-wide): 59MM **Privately Held**
WEB:
www.regents.universityofcalifornia.edu
SIC: 8011 Freestanding emergency medical center
PA: Uc San Francisco
1111 Franklin St Fl 12
Oakland CA 94607
858 534-7323

(P-20040)
REHABILITATION ASSOC MED GROUP
2840 Long Beach Blvd # 13, Long Beach (90806-1516)
PHONE....................562 424-8111
Eric Feldman, *Partner*
Richard Adams, *Partner*
Fred Batkin, *Partner*
Ann Vasile, *Partner*
EMP: 71 **EST:** 1964
SQ FT: 1,500
SALES (est): 2.7MM **Privately Held**
SIC: 8011 Physical medicine, physician/surgeon; physicians' office, including specialists

(P-20041)
RESPONSIBLE MED SOLUTIONS CORP
Also Called: Temecula 24 Hour Care
41715 Winchester Rd # 101, Temecula (92590-4808)
PHONE....................951 308-0024
Steven J Schutz, *President*
Paul Schutz, *Admin Sec*
Adrianna Tolles, *Marketing Staff*
Nadine Schneider,
Kayla Drake, *Assistant*
EMP: 50 **EST:** 2007
SQ FT: 5,000 **Privately Held**
WEB:
www.responsiblemedicalsolutions.com
SIC: 8011 Freestanding emergency medical center

(P-20042)
RETINA ASSOCIATES ORANGE CNTY (PA)
23521 Paseo De Valencia, Laguna Hills (92653-3107)
PHONE....................949 707-5125
Desmond E McGuire, *President*
Laura Harris, *Manager*
EMP: 56 **EST:** 2008
SALES (est): 3.2MM **Privately Held**
WEB: www.retinaorangecounty.com
SIC: 8011 Ophthalmologist

(P-20043)
RIVERSD-SAN BRNRDINO CNTY INDI (PA)
11980 Mount Vernon Ave, Grand Terrace (92313-5172)
PHONE....................909 864-1097
Jackie Wisespirit, *President*
Bill Thomsen, *COO*
Mark Jensen, *CFO*
Brandie Miranda, *Treasurer*
Charles Castello, *Vice Pres*
EMP: 291 **EST:** 1974
SQ FT: 38,000

SALES (est): 54.9MM **Privately Held**
WEB: www.rsbcihi.org
SIC: 8011 8093 Clinic, operated by physicians; specialty outpatient clinics

(P-20044)
RIVERSIDE MEDICAL CLINIC INC (PA)
Also Called: Riverside Med Clnic Ptient Ctr
3660 Arlington Ave, Riverside (92506-3987)
PHONE....................951 683-6370
Steven E Larson, *President*
Judy Carpenter, *President*
Tony Lazcano, *Vice Pres*
Sondra Smith, *Vice Pres*
Ruben Muradyan, *Executive*
EMP: 434 **EST:** 1993
SQ FT: 65,000
SALES (est): 102.2MM **Privately Held**
WEB: www.riversidemedicalclinic.com
SIC: 8011 Clinic, operated by physicians

(P-20045)
ROLLING OAKS RADIOLOGY INC
Also Called: Westlake Diagnostic Center
415 Rolling Oaks Dr # 16, Thousand Oaks (91361-1029)
PHONE....................805 778-1513
Robert A Princethal MD, *President*
Roy Gottlieb, *Vice Pres*
Josephine Lee, *Admin Sec*
Steven Barret, *Med Doctor*
Jeff Williams, *Director*
EMP: 195 **EST:** 1993
SQ FT: 2,500
SALES (est): 27.7MM **Publicly Held**
WEB: www.radnet.com
SIC: 8011 Radiologist
PA: Radnet, Inc.
1510 Cotner Ave
Los Angeles CA 90025

(P-20046)
SADDLBACK VLY SRGCAL MED GROUP
Also Called: Mission Viejo Surgicenter
26732 Crown Valley Pkwy, Mission Viejo (92691-6306)
PHONE....................949 364-1007
Thomas E Shaver MD, *Partner*
Marcello Borzatta MD, *Partner*
Stephen A Desantis MD, *Partner*
Kenneth Kushner MD, *Partner*
Ralph H Maeda Jr, *Partner*
EMP: 102 **EST:** 1972
SQ FT: 4,000
SALES (est): 4.7MM **Privately Held**
WEB: www.saddlebackvalleysurgery.com
SIC: 8011 Surgeon

(P-20047)
SAINT JHNS HLTH CTR FOUNDATION
Wayne, John Cancer Institute
2200 Santa Monica Blvd, Santa Monica (90404-2312)
PHONE....................310 315-6111
Donald Mortan, *Director*
Lynne Cabus, *Technician*
Lien Hua-Feng, *Nurse*
Chris Silvalski, *Manager*
EMP: 125
SQ FT: 7,100
SALES (corp-wide): 2.8B **Privately Held**
WEB: www.pacificneuroscienceinstitute.org
SIC: 8011 8731 Primary care medical clinic; commercial physical research
HQ: Saint John's Health Center Foundation
2121 Santa Monica Blvd
Santa Monica CA 90404
310 829-5511

(P-20048)
SAN ANTNIO AMBLTORY SRGCAL CTR
901 San Bernardino Rd 2n, Upland (91786-4912)
PHONE....................909 579-1500
C Perry Chu, *President*
Tomi Bortolizo, *Shareholder*
Henry Gonzales, *Shareholder*

(PA)=Parent Co (HQ)=Headquarters (DH)=Div Headquarters

✿ = New Business established in last 2 years

EMP: 53 EST: 1999
SALES (est): 6.4MM **Privately Held**
WEB: www.sanantonioasc.com
SIC: **8011** Surgeon

(P-20049)
SAN DIMAS MEDICAL GROUP INC
100 Old River Rd, Bakersfield
(93311-8823)
PHONE..................661 663-4800
Frank Ynostroza MD, *Ch of Bd*
Ken Knutson, *CFO*
Kandi N Knudsen, *Executive*
Wendy Crenshaw MD, *Principal*
Philip H Davis MD, *Principal*
EMP: 60 EST: 1971
SQ FT: 20,000
SALES (est): 13.6MM **Privately Held**
WEB: www.sandimasmedical.com
SIC: **8011** Gynecologist

(P-20050)
SAN FRNNDO VLY URLGCAL MED GRO
Also Called: Urological Associates
18370 Burbank Blvd # 407, Tarzana
(91356-2804)
PHONE..................818 996-4242
Leonard Skaist MD, *President*
Richard Leff, *Treasurer*
Richard Shapiro, *Admin Sec*
EMP: 68 EST: 1969
SQ FT: 4,000
SALES (est): 9MM **Privately Held**
WEB: www.sfvua.com
SIC: **8011** Urologist

(P-20051)
SAN GBRIEL AMBLTORY SRGERY CTR
207 S Santa Anita St, San Gabriel
(91776-1146)
PHONE..................626 300-5300
Brenda Durgin, *Manager*
EMP: 320 EST: 2003
SALES (est): 27.9MM
SALES (corp-wide): 17.6B **Publicly Held**
WEB: www.acuityeyegroup.com
SIC: **8011** Ophthalmologist
HQ: United Surgical Partners International, Inc.
14201 Dallas Pkwy
Dallas TX 75254
972 713-3500

(P-20052)
SAN LUIS DGNSTC CTR A CAL LTD
Also Called: San Luis Diagnostic Med Assoc
1100 Monterey St, San Luis Obispo
(93401-3102)
PHONE..................805 542-9700
Fred Vernacchia, *Partner*
EMP: 72 EST: 1994
SALES (est): 9.7MM **Privately Held**
WEB: www.dignityhealth.org
SIC: **8011** Clinic, operated by physicians; radiologist

(P-20053)
SANSUM CLINIC (PA)
470 S Patterson Ave, Santa Barbara
(93111-2404)
P.O. Box 1200 (93102-1200)
PHONE..................805 681-7700
Kurt Ransohoff MD, *President*
Alexander Bauer, *CFO*
Chad Hine, *CFO*
Jonathan Andrews, *Assoc VP*
Thomas Colbert, *Vice Pres*
EMP: 60 EST: 1921
SQ FT: 10,944
SALES (est): 303.9MM **Privately Held**
WEB: www.sansumclinic.org
SIC: **8011** Clinic, operated by physicians

(P-20054)
SANTA ANA CLNICA MDICA GEN MED
2208 W 7th St, Los Angeles (90057-4002)
PHONE..................323 221-1111
Juan Carlos Garcia, *Principal*
EMP: 50 EST: 2001

SALES (est): 1MM **Privately Held**
WEB: www.cmghc.com
SIC: **8011** Offices & clinics of medical doctors

(P-20055)
SANTA ANA RADIOLOGY CENTER
Also Called: West Coast Radiology Center
1100 N Tustin Ave Ste A, Santa Ana
(92705-3509)
PHONE..................714 835-6055
Tim Chavez, *CEO*
EMP: 100 EST: 1987
SQ FT: 15,000
SALES (est): 4.8MM **Privately Held**
SIC: **8011** 8071 Radiologist; X-ray laboratory, including dental

(P-20056)
SANTA BARBARA SURGICAL CTR INC
3045 De La Vina St, Santa Barbara
(93105-3351)
PHONE..................805 569-3226
Gary Anderson, *CEO*
Donald Rhodes, *Vice Pres*
Diane Hadighi, *Admin Sec*
Daniel Curhan, *Director*
EMP: 67 EST: 1999
SALES (est): 9.8MM **Privately Held**
WEB: www.santabarbarasurgerycenter.com
SIC: **8011** Surgeon

(P-20057)
SANTA MNICA WLSHIRE IMGING LLC
Also Called: Tower St John Imaging
5455 Wilshire Blvd # 112, Los Angeles
(90036-4201)
PHONE..................323 549-3055
Gerald Roth MD,
EMP: 50 EST: 2002
SALES (est): 3.3MM **Privately Held**
SIC: **8011** Radiologist

(P-20058)
SANTA MONICA BAY PHYSCIANS
881 Alma Real Dr Ste 214, Pacific Palisades (90272-3750)
PHONE..................310 459-2363
Mark R Needham, *President*
Ronen Kalay, *Family Practiti*
EMP: 55 EST: 1982
SALES (est): 1.5MM **Privately Held**
SIC: **8011** General & family practice, physician/surgeon

(P-20059)
SANTA MONICA BAY PHYSICIANS HE (PA)
Also Called: Bay Area Community Med Group
5767 W Century Blvd, Los Angeles
(90045-5631)
PHONE..................310 417-5900
Eileen McGrath, *President*
Dr Richard Zachrich, *Treasurer*
Dr Steven Seizer, *Vice Pres*
Dr David Cutler, *Admin Sec*
EMP: 85 EST: 1985
SALES (est): 15.4MM **Privately Held**
WEB: www.uclahealth.org
SIC: **8011** Clinic, operated by physicians

(P-20060)
SANTA MONICA ORTHOPEDIC (PA)
2020 Santa Monica Blvd # 230, Santa Monica (90404-2124)
PHONE..................310 315-2018
Ramin M Modabber MD, *President*
Kevin M Erhardt MD, *Vice Pres*
Kenton S Horacek MD, *Admin Sec*
Kenton Horacek, *Med Doctor*
EMP: 52 EST: 1988
SQ FT: 28,242
SALES (est): 15.8MM **Privately Held**
WEB: www.santamonicaoms.com
SIC: **8011** Orthopedic physician

(P-20061)
SB WATERMAN HOLDINGS INC (PA)
1700 N Waterman Ave, San Bernardino
(92404-5115)
PHONE..................909 883-8611
James Malin, *CEO*
Thomas Hellwig, *President*
James W Malin, *CEO*
Louis Francisco MD, *Treasurer*
Paul G Godfrey MD, *Vice Pres*
EMP: 150 EST: 1954
SQ FT: 55,000
SALES (est): 21.3MM **Privately Held**
WEB: www.sbmed.com
SIC: **8011** Clinic, operated by physicians

(P-20062)
SCRIBEMD LLC
1310 W Stewart Dr Ste 212, Orange
(92868-3837)
PHONE..................714 543-8911
Coutney Aldama, *CEO*
Matthew Mullarky, *Managing Prtnr*
EMP: 90 EST: 2009
SALES (est): 1.6MM **Privately Held**
WEB: www.scribemd.com
SIC: **8011** Offices & clinics of medical doctors

(P-20063)
SERRA COMMUNITY MED CLINIC INC
9375 San Fernando Rd, Sun Valley
(91352-1418)
PHONE..................818 768-3000
Sadayappa K Durairaj, *CEO*
Kumar Soundar, *CFO*
Dr Arnold Jacobs, *Treasurer*
Dr Carlos Jimenez, *Admin Sec*
Dan Bumgarner, *Administration*
EMP: 163
SQ FT: 60,000
SALES (est): 18MM **Privately Held**
WEB: www.serramedicalgroup.com
SIC: **8011** Clinic, operated by physicians

(P-20064)
SHYAM BHASKAR MD INC (PA)
231 W Noble Ave, Visalia (93277-2631)
PHONE..................559 635-7100
Bhaskar M Shyam, *President*
Shyam Bhaskar, *Med Doctor*
EMP: 76 EST: 2009
SALES (est): 2.8MM **Privately Held**
SIC: **8011** Internal medicine, physician/surgeon

(P-20065)
SIERRA PRIMARY CARE MEDICAL (PA)
Also Called: Sierra Medical Group
44469 10th St W, Lancaster (93534-3396)
PHONE..................661 945-9411
Karunyan Arul MD, *President*
Kay Arul, *President*
Jessica Lara, *Vice Pres*
Belinda Hartson, *Admin Asst*
Lori Gabbard, *Administration*
EMP: 63 EST: 1984
SQ FT: 14,000
SALES (est): 13.7MM **Privately Held**
WEB: www.heritagesmg.com
SIC: **8011** Primary care medical clinic

(P-20066)
SIERRA VIEW DST HOSP LEAG INC (PA)
Also Called: Sierra View Medical Center
465 W Putnam Ave, Porterville
(93257-3320)
PHONE..................559 784-1110
Donna Hefner, *President*
Debbie Zebofkey, *Records Dir*
John Chivers, *CFO*
Douglas Dickson, *CFO*
Ruth Gonzalez, *CFO*
◆ EMP: 569 EST: 1948
SQ FT: 135,000
SALES (est): 147.9MM **Privately Held**
WEB: www.sierra-view.com
SIC: **8011** 8062 Offices & clinics of medical doctors; general medical & surgical hospitals

(P-20067)
SOUTH CENTRAL FAMILY HLTH CTR
4425 S Central Ave, Los Angeles
(90011-3629)
PHONE..................323 908-4200
Richard Veloz, *President*
Paul Ramos, *CFO*
Ruby Raya Morones, *Chief Mktg Ofcr*
Sandra Tatum Green, *Human Res Dir*
EMP: 92 EST: 1983
SQ FT: 13,000
SALES (est): 25.3MM **Privately Held**
WEB: www.scfhc.org
SIC: **8011** Clinic, operated by physicians

(P-20068)
SOUTH CNTY ORTHPD SPCLSTS A ME
Also Called: Orthowest
24331 El Toro Rd Ste 200, Laguna Hills
(92637-3116)
PHONE..................949 586-3200
James Mullen, *President*
Kyle W Coker, *Principal*
Larry M Gursten, *Principal*
Lance R Montgomery, *Principal*
Lance Montgomery, *Principa*
EMP: 87 EST: 1994
SALES (est): 21.4MM **Privately Held**
WEB: www.scosortho.com
SIC: **8011** Orthopedic physician

(P-20069)
SOUTH COAST EYE CARE CENTERS
24022 Calle De La Plata, Laguna Hills
(92653-3626)
PHONE..................949 588-2020
Andrew Henry, *President*
Andrew Henrick, *President*
Tobi Foisy, *Executive*
Basil Mijares, *Manager*
EMP: 71 EST: 1967
SALES (est): 7.7MM **Privately Held**
WEB: www.southcoasteye.com
SIC: **8011** Ophthalmologist

(P-20070)
SOUTH COAST GLOBAL MED CTR INC
1301 N Tustin Ave, Santa Ana
(92705-8619)
PHONE..................714 953-3582
Matt Whaley, *CEO*
EMP: 53 EST: 2015
SALES (est): 8.1MM **Privately Held**
WEB: www.kpchealth.com
SIC: **8011** Medical centers

(P-20071)
SOUTH ORNGE CNTY SRGCAL MED GR
24411 Health Center Dr # 350, Laguna Hills
(92653-3651)
PHONE..................949 457-7900
William Wallace, *CEO*
David Dearing, *Gnrl Med Prac*
Robert Duensing, *Med Doctor*
Chirag Patel, *Med Docto*
EMP: 61 EST: 1971
SALES (est): 6.2MM **Privately Held**
WEB: www.theocsurgeons.com
SIC: **8011** Surgeon

(P-20072)
SOUTHERN CA HLTH & RHBLTN PRG
2610 Industry Way Ste A, Lynwood
(90262-4028)
PHONE..................310 631-8004
Dr Jack M Barbour, *CEO*
Rita Floyd, *President*
EMP: 165 EST: 1993
SQ FT: 6,000
SALES (est): 10.4MM **Privately Held**
WEB: www.scharpca.com
SIC: **8011** Psychiatric clinic

(P-20073)
SOUTHERN CAL DGNSTC IMGING INC (PA)
Also Called: Imaging Center
408 S Beach Blvd Ste 106, Anaheim
(92804-1873)
PHONE...................714 995-5471
Steven Chao, *Principal*
EMP: 84 **EST:** 2010
SALES (est): 9.8MM **Privately Held**
WEB: www.socaldiagnostics.com
SIC: 8011 Radiologist

(P-20074)
SOUTHERN CAL ORTHPD INST LP (PA)
6815 Noble Ave Ste 400, Van Nuys
(91405-6516)
PHONE...................818 901-6600
Marc J Friedman, *Partner*
Robert Horowitz, *Office Mgr*
Victoria Hannah, *Administration*
Susan Nadeau, *Administration*
Carol Weiske, *Administration*
EMP: 135 **EST:** 1992
SALES (est): 171.1K **Privately Held**
WEB: www.scoi.com
SIC: 8011 8249 Orthopedic physician; medical training services

(P-20075)
SOUTHERN CAL PRMNNTE MED GROUP
6 Willard, Irvine (92604-4694)
PHONE...................949 262-5780
Debra Dannemeyer, *Administration*
EMP: 234
SALES (corp-wide): 30.5B **Privately Held**
SIC: 8011 Clinic, operated by physicians
HQ: Southern California Permanente Medical Group
393 Walnut Dr
Pasadena CA 91107
626 405-5704

(P-20076)
SOUTHERN CAL PRMNNTE MED GROUP
3501 Stockdale Hwy, Bakersfield
(93309-2150)
PHONE...................661 398-5085
EMP: 234
SALES (corp-wide): 30.5B **Privately Held**
SIC: 8011 Medical centers
HQ: Southern California Permanente Medical Group
393 Walnut Dr
Pasadena CA 91107
626 405-5704

(P-20077)
SOUTHERN CAL PRMNNTE MED GROUP
3830 Mrtin Lther King Jr, Lynwood
(90262-3625)
PHONE...................310 604-5700
EMP: 234
SALES (corp-wide): 30.5B **Privately Held**
SIC: 8011 Medical centers
HQ: Southern California Permanente Medical Group
393 Walnut Dr
Pasadena CA 91107
626 405-5704

(P-20078)
SOUTHERN CAL PRMNNTE MED GROUP
6041 Cadillac Ave, Los Angeles
(90034-1702)
PHONE...................323 857-2000
Larry Poston, *Director*
Yosef Zibari, *Med Doctor*
EMP: 234
SALES (corp-wide): 30.5B **Privately Held**
SIC: 8011 Radiologist
HQ: Southern California Permanente Medical Group
393 Walnut Dr
Pasadena CA 91107
626 405-5704

(P-20079)
SOUTHERN CAL PRMNNTE MED GROUP
25825 Vermont Ave, Harbor City
(90710-3518)
PHONE...................800 780-1230
EMP: 234
SALES (corp-wide): 30.5B **Privately Held**
SIC: 8011 Medical centers
HQ: Southern California Permanente Medical Group
393 Walnut Dr
Pasadena CA 91107
626 405-5704

(P-20080)
SOUTHERN CAL PRMNNTE MED GROUP
4841 Hollywood Blvd, Los Angeles
(90027-5301)
PHONE...................323 783-5455
Maria Montes, *Project Mgr*
EMP: 234
SALES (corp-wide): 30.5B **Privately Held**
SIC: 8011 Medical centers
HQ: Southern California Permanente Medical Group
393 Walnut Dr
Pasadena CA 91107
626 405-5704

(P-20081)
SOUTHERN CAL PRMNNTE MED GROUP
Also Called: Orthopedics Department
4760 W Sunset Blvd, Los Angeles
(90027-6063)
PHONE...................323 783-4893
Dolores Cobbarrubias, *Office Mgr*
EMP: 234
SALES (corp-wide): 30.5B **Privately Held**
SIC: 8011 Orthopedic physician
HQ: Southern California Permanente Medical Group
393 Walnut Dr
Pasadena CA 91107
626 405-5704

(P-20082)
SOUTHERN CAL PRMNNTE MED GROUP
Also Called: S C P M G
789 E Cooley Dr, Colton (92324-4007)
PHONE...................909 370-2501
EMP: 234
SALES (corp-wide): 30.5B **Privately Held**
SIC: 8011 Medical centers
HQ: Southern California Permanente Medical Group
393 Walnut Dr
Pasadena CA 91107
626 405-5704

(P-20083)
SOUTHERN CAL PRMNNTE MED GROUP
Also Called: S C P M G
5620 Mesmer Ave, Culver City
(90230-6315)
PHONE...................310 737-4900
Olive Goldsmith, *Manager*
EMP: 234
SALES (corp-wide): 30.5B **Privately Held**
SIC: 8011 Medical centers
HQ: Southern California Permanente Medical Group
393 Walnut Dr
Pasadena CA 91107
626 405-5704

(P-20084)
SOUTHERN CAL PRMNNTE MED GROUP
Also Called: S C P M G
110 N La Brea Ave, Inglewood
(90301-1708)
PHONE...................310 419-3306
Helen Jones, *Manager*
EMP: 234
SALES (corp-wide): 30.5B **Privately Held**
SIC: 8011 Medical centers

HQ: Southern California Permanente Medical Group
393 Walnut Dr
Pasadena CA 91107
626 405-5704

(P-20085)
SOUTHERN CAL PRMNNTE MED GROUP
18081 Beach Blvd, Huntington Beach
(92648-1304)
PHONE...................714 841-7293
EMP: 234
SALES (corp-wide): 30.5B **Privately Held**
SIC: 8011 Medical centers
HQ: Southern California Permanente Medical Group
393 Walnut Dr
Pasadena CA 91107
626 405-5704

(P-20086)
SOUTHERN CAL PRMNNTE MED GROUP
Also Called: S C P M G
411 N Lakeview Ave, Anaheim
(92807-3028)
PHONE...................714 279-4675
Ryan Williams, *Manager*
Janet Hartmann Jones, *Hematology*
EMP: 234
SALES (corp-wide): 30.5B **Privately Held**
SIC: 8011 Offices & clinics of medical doctors
HQ: Southern California Permanente Medical Group
393 Walnut Dr
Pasadena CA 91107
626 405-5704

(P-20087)
SOUTHERN CAL PRMNNTE MED GROUP
Also Called: S C P M G
30400 Camino Capistrano, San Juan Capistrano (92675-1300)
PHONE...................949 234-2139
EMP: 234
SALES (corp-wide): 30.5B **Privately Held**
SIC: 8011 Medical centers
HQ: Southern California Permanente Medical Group
393 Walnut Dr
Pasadena CA 91107
626 405-5704

(P-20088)
SOUTHERN CAL PRMNNTE MED GROUP
Also Called: S C P M G
1900 E 4th St, Santa Ana (92705-3910)
PHONE...................714 967-4760
Julie White-Dahlgren, *Branch Mgr*
EMP: 234
SALES (corp-wide): 30.5B **Privately Held**
SIC: 8011 8049 Obstetrician; psychiatric social worker
HQ: Southern California Permanente Medical Group
393 Walnut Dr
Pasadena CA 91107
626 405-5704

(P-20089)
SOUTHERN CAL PRMNNTE MED GROUP
Also Called: S C P M G
7825 Atlantic Ave, Cudahy (90201-5022)
PHONE...................323 562-6459
Maria Gonzalez, *Principal*
EMP: 234
SALES (corp-wide): 30.5B **Privately Held**
SIC: 8011 Medical centers
HQ: Southern California Permanente Medical Group
393 Walnut Dr
Pasadena CA 91107
626 405-5704

(P-20090)
SOUTHERN CAL PRMNNTE MED GROUP
Also Called: S C P M G
21263 Erwin St, Woodland Hills
(91367-3715)
PHONE...................818 592-3038
Cary Glass, *Branch Mgr*
EMP: 234
SALES (corp-wide): 30.5B **Privately Held**
SIC: 8011 Medical centers
HQ: Southern California Permanente Medical Group
393 Walnut Dr
Pasadena CA 91107
626 405-5704

(P-20091)
SOUTHERN CAL PRMNNTE MED GROUP
Also Called: S C P M G
27107 Tourney Rd, Santa Clarita
(91355-1860)
PHONE...................661 222-2150
EMP: 234
SALES (corp-wide): 30.5B **Privately Held**
SIC: 8011 Medical centers
HQ: Southern California Permanente Medical Group
393 Walnut Dr
Pasadena CA 91107
626 405-5704

(P-20092)
SOUTHERN CAL PRMNNTE MED GROUP
5055 California Ave, Bakersfield
(93309-0701)
PHONE...................661 334-2020
Geckeley, *Principal*
EMP: 234
SALES (corp-wide): 30.5B **Privately Held**
SIC: 8011 Medical centers
HQ: Southern California Permanente Medical Group
393 Walnut Dr
Pasadena CA 91107
626 405-5704

(P-20093)
SOUTHLAND ARTHRITIS OSTEO
949 Calhoun Pl Ste F, Hemet (92543-4403)
PHONE...................951 672-1866
Chantra V Mehta, *Owner*
Ratan Tiwari, *Cardiology*
Naishadh Raghuwanshi, *Gastroenterlgy*
Amal Mehta, *Internal Med*
Dharmarajan Ramaswamy, *Internal Med*
EMP: 50 **EST:** 2011
SALES (est): 4.8MM **Privately Held**
WEB: www.southlandarthritis.com
SIC: 8011 Rheumatology specialist, physician/surgeon

(P-20094)
SOUTHWESTERN ORTHPD MED CORP
Also Called: Downey Orthopedic Med Group
3416 The Strand, Manhattan Beach
(90266-3350)
P.O. Box 4489, Montebello (90640-9309)
PHONE...................562 803-0600
Lucy Guttierez, *Branch Mgr*
EMP: 50
SALES (corp-wide): 6.6MM **Privately Held**
SIC: 8011 Orthopedic physician
PA: Southwestern Orthopedic Medical Corporation
905 S A St
Oxnard CA 93030
805 486-4501

(P-20095)
SPECIALTY SURGICAL CENTERS
15825 Laguna Canyon Rd # 200, Irvine
(92618-2127)
PHONE...................949 341-3499
Andrew Brooks MD, *President*
Terry Weisman, *Director*
EMP: 50 **EST:** 1997
SALES (est): 7MM **Privately Held**
WEB: www.sscirvine.com
SIC: 8011 Surgeon

P R O D U C T S & S V C S

(P-20096)
ST JSEPH HERITG MED GROUP LLC (PA)
Also Called: Yorba Park Medical Group
2212 E 4th St Ste 201, Santa Ana
(92705-3872)
PHONE..........................714 633-1011
Charles Foster, *President*
C R Burke, *CFO*
Dennis Long MD, *Treasurer*
Marc Bennette MD, *Vice Pres*
Joseph Brown MD, *Vice Pres*
▲ EMP: 134 EST: 1964
SQ FT: 58,000
SALES (est): 15.2MM **Privately Held**
WEB: www.psjhmedgroups.org
SIC: 8011 General & family practice, physician/surgeon

(P-20097)
ST JUDE HERITAGE MEDICAL GROUP
4300 Rose Dr, Yorba Linda (92886-2026)
PHONE..........................714 528-4211
Lytton Smith MD, *President*
Richard Kenfield MD, *Treasurer*
R S Hall MD, *Vice Pres*
Kenneth Tan MD, *Admin Sec*
Richard Barnes, *CIO*
EMP: 52 EST: 1959
SALES (est): 1.1MM **Privately Held**
SIC: 8011 Clinic, operated by physicians; general & family practice, physician/surgeon

(P-20098)
STEPHEN B MEISEL MD A MED CORP (HQ)
Also Called: Med Focus/California Radiology
2811 Wilshire Blvd # 900, Santa Monica
(90403-4803)
PHONE..........................310 828-8843
Joseph P Delaney, *President*
EMP: 52 EST: 1977
SQ FT: 14,000
SALES (est): 10.5MM **Privately Held**
WEB: www.onecallcm.com
SIC: 8011 Radiologist

(P-20099)
SUMMIT VNTRES SANTA BARBARA LP
Also Called: Summit Surgery Center
231 W Pueblo St, Santa Barbara
(93105-3804)
PHONE..........................805 898-2797
Richard Ryu, *Partner*
David Odell, *Partner*
Denise Phelps, *Partner*
Steve Shot, *Partner*
Jennifer Bowman, *CIO*
EMP: 65 EST: 2000
SALES (est): 13.3MM **Privately Held**
WEB: www.summitsurgerycenter.com
SIC: 8011 Surgeon

(P-20100)
SURGICAL CENTER OF WEST COVINA
Also Called: San Gabriel Vly Surgical Ctr
1250 S Sunset Ave Ste 100, West Covina
(91790-3912)
PHONE..........................626 960-6623
Donna Ferguson, *Manager*
EMP: 63 EST: 1981
SQ FT: 9,350
SALES (est): 3.5MM **Privately Held**
WEB: www.sangabrielvalley-sc.com
SIC: 8011 Surgeon; ambulatory surgical center

(P-20101)
SURGICARE LA VETA LTD A CAL LT
681 S Parker St Ste 150, Orange
(92868-4761)
PHONE..........................714 744-0900
Richard L Sharff, *Vice Pres*
EMP: 51 EST: 1993
SALES (est): 10.6MM
SALES (corp-wide): 257.1B **Publicly Held**
WEB: www.lavetasurgical.com
SIC: 8011 Ambulatory surgical center

PA: Unitedhealth Group Incorporated
9900 Bren Rd E Ste 300w
Minnetonka MN 55343
952 936-1300

(P-20102)
T JOSEPH RAOOF MD INC
16133 Ventura Blvd # 340, Encino
(91436-2403)
PHONE..........................818 788-5060
Tooraj Joseph Raoof, *President*
Sarah Emert, *Research*
EMP: 15 EST: 1989
SQ FT: 2,200
SALES (est): 1.3MM **Privately Held**
WEB: www.drraoof.com
SIC: 8011 3444 5561 7631 Dermatologist; sheet metalwork; recreational vehicle parts & accessories; jewelry repair services

(P-20103)
TEMPLETON SURGERY CENTER LLC
1310 Las Tablas Rd # 104, Templeton
(93465-9746)
PHONE..........................805 434-3550
Brenda Gray, *Mng Member*
Sue Vineyard, *Manager*
EMP: 471 EST: 2005
SALES (est): 15.7MM
SALES (corp-wide): 17.6B **Publicly Held**
WEB: www.uspi.com
SIC: 8011 Surgeon
HQ: United Surgical Partners International, Inc.
14201 Dallas Pkwy
Dallas TX 75254
972 713-3500

(P-20104)
TENET HEALTHSYSTEM MEDICAL INC
Also Called: Lakewood Regional Medical Ctr
3700 South St, Lakewood (90712-1419)
PHONE..........................562 531-2550
Carol Mammolite, *Branch Mgr*
Mary L Okuhara, *Human Resources*
Irwin Cohen, *Pharmacist*
Joshua Daniels, *Manager*
EMP: 57
SALES (corp-wide): 17.6B **Publicly Held**
WEB: www.tenethealth.com
SIC: 8011 8062 Medical centers; general medical & surgical hospitals
HQ: Tenet Healthsystem Medical, Inc.
14201 Dallas Pkwy
Dallas TX 75254
469 893-2000

(P-20105)
TENET HEALTHSYSTEM MEDICAL INC
Also Called: Western Regional Cancer Center
1301 N Tustin Ave, Santa Ana
(92705-8619)
PHONE..........................714 524-4820
Dr Robert Egan, *Branch Mgr*
EMP: 57
SALES (corp-wide): 17.6B **Publicly Held**
WEB: www.tenethealth.com
SIC: 8011 Oncologist
HQ: Tenet Healthsystem Medical, Inc.
14201 Dallas Pkwy
Dallas TX 75254
469 893-2000

(P-20106)
TENET HEALTHSYSTEM MEDICAL INC
Los Alamitos Med Ctr
3751 Katella Ave, Los Alamitos
(90720-3113)
PHONE..........................805 546-7698
Michelle Finney, *Principal*
Don Gierman, *Purch Agent*
Azar Daneshbod, *Pathologist*
Diane Mielke, *Director*
EMP: 57
SALES (corp-wide): 17.6B **Publicly Held**
WEB: www.tenethealth.com
SIC: 8011 8062 Offices & clinics of medical doctors; general medical & surgical hospitals

HQ: Tenet Healthsystem Medical, Inc.
14201 Dallas Pkwy
Dallas TX 75254
469 893-2000

(P-20107)
TENET HEALTHSYSTEM MEDICAL INC
Also Called: Leisure World Pharmacy
1661 Golden Rain Rd, Seal Beach
(90740-4907)
P.O. Box 2685 (90740-1685)
PHONE..........................562 493-9581
Diana Doyle, *Manager*
EMP: 57
SALES (corp-wide): 17.6B **Publicly Held**
WEB: www.mygnp.com
SIC: 8011 5912 Offices & clinics of medical doctors; drug stores
HQ: Tenet Healthsystem Medical, Inc.
14201 Dallas Pkwy
Dallas TX 75254
469 893-2000

(P-20108)
THE COMMUNITY MEDICAL GROUP OF (PA)
8510 Balboa Blvd Ste 150, Northridge
(91325-5810)
PHONE..........................818 707-9603
Marvin Kanter, *Principal*
EMP: 58 EST: 1980
SALES (est): 10.1MM **Privately Held**
SIC: 8011 Medical insurance associations

(P-20109)
THE ORTHOPEDIC INSTITUTE OF
616 Witmer St, Los Angeles (90017-2308)
PHONE..........................213 977-2010
Andrew B Leeka, *CEO*
EMP: 4173 EST: 1990
SALES (est): 3.1MM
SALES (corp-wide): 923K **Privately Held**
WEB: www.pihhealth.org
SIC: 8011 Orthopedic physician
HQ: Pih Health Good Samaritan Hospital
1225 Wilshire Blvd
Los Angeles CA 90017
213 977-2121

(P-20110)
TOWER HMTLOGY ONCLOGY MED GROU
9090 Wilshire Blvd # 200, Beverly Hills
(90211-1848)
P.O. Box 5624 (90209-5605)
PHONE..........................310 888-8680
Robert W Decker MD, *Partner*
Leland M Green MD, *Partner*
Heydi Ellis, *Admin Asst*
Kevin Scher, *Hematology*
Maryliza El-Masry, *Internal Med*
EMP: 100 EST: 1992
SQ FT: 13,000
SALES (est): 10MM **Privately Held**
WEB: www.cedars-sinai.org
SIC: 8011 Hematologist; oncologist

(P-20111)
TRANSLTNAL PLMNARY IMMNLGY RE
Also Called: Southern Cal Fd Allergy Inst
701 E 28th St Ste 419, Long Beach
(90806-2775)
PHONE..........................562 490-9900
Dr Inderpal Randhawa, *Principal*
Natasha Levy, *Manager*
EMP: 90 EST: 2016
SALES (est): 5.2MM **Privately Held**
WEB: www.socalfoodallergy.org
SIC: 8011 Allergist

(P-20112)
TRUXTUN PSYCHTRIC MED GROUP LP
Also Called: Sipa Medical Group
6313 Schirra Ct, Bakersfield (93313-2191)
PHONE..........................661 323-6410
S A Manohare MD, *President*
EMP: 62 EST: 1993
SALES (est): 10.8MM **Privately Held**
WEB: www.truxtunpsych.com
SIC: 8011 Psychiatrist

(P-20113)
TRUXTUN RADIOLOGY MED GROUP LP (HQ)
1817 Truxtun Ave, Bakersfield
(93301-5008)
PHONE..........................661 325-6800
Girish Patel MD, *Partner*
Pragati Patel, *Principal*
John Roefs, *Med Doctor*
Martha Wiedman, *Med Doctor*
Sireesha Iruvuri, *Diag Radio*
EMP: 371 EST: 1997
SQ FT: 30,000
SALES (est): 26.4MM **Publicly Held**
WEB: www.radnet.com
SIC: 8011 8071 Radiologist; X-ray laboratory, including dental

(P-20114)
TURNER JOHN MCDONALD MD
Also Called: Seal Beach Family Med Group
1198 Pacific Coast Hwy I, Seal Beach
(90740-6248)
PHONE..........................562 799-7071
John M Turner MD, *Owner*
EMP: 56 EST: 1979
SALES (est): 1.1MM **Privately Held**
WEB:
www.sealbeachfamilymedicalgroup.com
SIC: 8011 General & family practice, physician/surgeon

(P-20115)
TWIN CITIES COMMUNITY HOSP INC
1100 Las Tablas Rd, Templeton
(93465-9704)
PHONE..........................805 434-3500
Mark P Lisa, *CEO*
Paul Posmosga, *CFO*
Aiga Charles, *Obstetrician*
Chad Bateman, *Director*
Shelby Peri, *Manager*
EMP: 450 EST: 1977
SQ FT: 120,000
SALES (est): 17.7K
SALES (corp-wide): 17.6B **Publicly Held**
WEB: www.tenethealthcentralcoast.com
SIC: 8011 8062 Medical centers; general medical & surgical hospitals
PA: Tenet Healthcare Corporation
14201 Dallas Pkwy
Dallas TX 75254
469 893-2200

(P-20116)
UNITED FMLY CARE INC A MED COR
8110 Mango Ave Ste 104, Fontana
(92335-3603)
PHONE..........................909 874-1679
Keith Schauermann, *President*
EMP: 120 EST: 1999
SALES (est): 10.6MM **Privately Held**
WEB: www.pinnaclemedical.com
SIC: 8011 General & family practice, physician/surgeon

(P-20117)
UNITED MEDICAL DOCTORS
Also Called: United Gastroenterologists
28078 Baxter Rd Ste 530, Murrieta
(92563-1405)
PHONE..........................951 566-5229
Samantha Cottrell, *Principal*
Stephen OH, *Pathologist*
Gary Annunziata, *Gastroenterlgy*
Shruti Ariza, *Gastroenterlgy*
Philip Chen, *Gastroenterlgy*
EMP: 69 EST: 2003
SALES (est): 14.4MM **Privately Held**
WEB: www.unitedmd.com
SIC: 8011 Gastronomist

(P-20118)
UNITED MEDICAL IMAGING INC (PA)
1762 Westwood Blvd # 230, Los Angeles
(90024-5648)
PHONE..........................310 943-8400
Nasser Hiekali, *CEO*
Mitra Afrooz, *Administration*
EMP: 85 EST: 2006

SALES (est): 12.3MM **Privately Held**
WEB: www.umih.com
SIC: **8011** Radiologist

(P-20119)
UNITED SRGCAL PRTNERS INTL INC
3445 Pcf Cast Hwy Ste 110, Torrance (90505)
PHONE...........................310 325-4555
Rosemary Hawkins, *Branch Mgr*
EMP: 52
SALES (corp-wide): 17.6B **Publicly Held**
WEB: www.uspi.com
SIC: **8011** Surgeon
HQ: United Surgical Partners International, Inc.
    14201 Dallas Pkwy
    Dallas TX 75254
    972 713-3500

(P-20120)
UNIVERSAL PAIN MGT MED CORP (PA)
819 Auto Center Dr Ste A, Palmdale (93551-4599)
PHONE...........................661 267-6876
Francis X Riegler, *President*
Francis Riegler, *Manager*
Debbie Castillo, *Assistant*
EMP: 69 EST: 2000
SALES (est): 10.4MM **Privately Held**
WEB: www.universalpain.com
SIC: **8011** Orthopedic physician

(P-20121)
UNIVERSITY CALIFORNIA IRVINE
Also Called: UIC
101 The City Dr S Ste 313, Orange (92868-3201)
PHONE...........................714 456-6966
Sharon McCarthy, *Manager*
Helena Easterday, *Senior Mgr*
EMP: 136 **Privately Held**
WEB: www.uci.edu
SIC: **8011** 8221 9411 Surgeon; university; administration of educational programs
HQ: University Of California, Irvine
    510 Aldrich Hall
    Irvine CA 92697
    949 824-5011

(P-20122)
UNIVERSITY CALIFORNIA IRVINE
Also Called: Uc Irvine Hlth Rgonal Burn Ctr
101 The City Dr S Bldg 1a, Orange (92868-3201)
PHONE...........................714 456-6170
Howard Federoff, *Vice Chancellor*
Ralph Cygan, *Exec Dir*
Linda Ketchersid, *Administration*
Jason Hu, *Programmer Anys*
Anh Nguyen, *Programmer Anys*
EMP: 1757 **Privately Held**
WEB: www.uci.edu
SIC: **8011** 8221 9411 Medical centers; university; administration of educational programs;
HQ: University Of California, Irvine
    510 Aldrich Hall
    Irvine CA 92697
    949 824-5011

(P-20123)
UNIVERSITY CALIFORNIA IRVINE
Also Called: UCI Family Health Center
800 N Main St, Santa Ana (92701-3576)
PHONE...........................714 480-2443
Nancy D Hurtado, *Manager*
Ivan Coziahr, *Exec Dir*
Kelly Schoby, *Analyst*
Aaron Barth, *Professor*
Marco Angulo, *Family Practiti*
EMP: 136
SQ FT: 49,361 **Privately Held**
WEB: www.uci.edu
SIC: **8011** 8221 9411 Medical centers; university; administration of educational programs;

HQ: University Of California, Irvine
    510 Aldrich Hall
    Irvine CA 92697
    949 824-5011

(P-20124)
UNIVERSITY CALIFORNIA IRVINE
43 Cambria Dr, Corona Del Mar (92625-1004)
PHONE...........................949 644-5245
EMP: 136 **Privately Held**
WEB: www.uci.edu
SIC: **8011** Offices & clinics of medical doctors
HQ: University Of California, Irvine
    510 Aldrich Hall
    Irvine CA 92697
    949 824-5011

(P-20125)
UNIVERSITY CALIFORNIA IRVINE
1640 Newport Blvd Ste 340, Costa Mesa (92627-7730)
PHONE...........................949 646-2267
Olivia Reil, *Branch Mgr*
Thelma Castro, *Purchasing*
Jessica Greenwood, *Assistant*
EMP: 136 **Privately Held**
WEB: www.uci.edu
SIC: **8011** 8221 9411 Gynecologist; university; administration of educational programs
HQ: University Of California, Irvine
    510 Aldrich Hall
    Irvine CA 92697
    949 824-5011

(P-20126)
UNIVERSITY CALIFORNIA IRVINE
Also Called: Barr, Ronald J MD /UCI Med Gro
101 The City Dr S, Orange (92868-3201)
PHONE...........................714 456-7890
Ronald J Barr MD, *Dermatology*
Scott Capps, *Vice Pres*
Jamie L Garcia, *Med Doctor*
Hooshang Meshkinpour, *Med Doctor*
EMP: 136 **Privately Held**
WEB: www.uci.edu
SIC: **8011** 8221 9411 Dermatologist; university; administration of educational programs
HQ: University Of California, Irvine
    510 Aldrich Hall
    Irvine CA 92697
    949 824-5011

(P-20127)
US HEALTHWORKS INC (DH)
Also Called: U.S. Healthworks Medical Group
28035 Avenue Stanford, Valencia (91355-1104)
PHONE...........................661 678-2300
Keith Newton, *President*
Su Zan Nelson, *CFO*
John Anderson, *Chief Mktg Ofcr*
John Delorimier, *Exec VP*
Jim Talalai, *Senior VP*
EMP: 60 EST: 1995
SALES (est): 156.9MM
SALES (corp-wide): 5B **Publicly Held**
WEB: www.concentra.com
SIC: **8011** Clinic, operated by physicians
HQ: Concentra Inc.
    5080 Spectrum Dr Ste 400w
    Addison TX 75001
    972 364-8000

(P-20128)
USC CRDIOTHORACIC SURGEONS INC
1520 San Pablo St # 4300, Los Angeles (90033-5310)
PHONE...........................323 442-5849
Vaughn A Starnes MD, *President*
Vaughn Starnes MD, *Chairman*
Bertha Acosta, *Treasurer*
Thanh Diep, *Principal*
Seon H Ha, *Principal*
EMP: 63 EST: 1998
SALES (est): 20MM **Privately Held**
WEB: www.usc.edu
SIC: **8011** Thoracic physician

(P-20129)
USC EMERGENCY MEDICINE ASSOC
1200 N State St Ste 1011, Los Angeles (90033-1029)
PHONE...........................323 226-6667
Fax: 323 226-6806
EMP: 80
SALES (est): 3.9MM **Privately Held**
SIC: **8011** Medical Doctor's Office

(P-20130)
USC SURGEONS INCORPORATED
Also Called: Usc Srgcal Edcatn RES Fndation
1510 San Pablo St Ste 514, Los Angeles (90033-5324)
PHONE...........................323 442-5910
Tom Demeester MD, *President*
Eric Alcorn, *Exec VP*
Albert Yellin MD, *Admin Sec*
Anita Chan, *Administration*
EMP: 51 EST: 1991
SQ FT: 15,000
SALES (est): 2.4MM **Privately Held**
WEB: www.keckmedicine.org
SIC: **8011** Specialized medical practitioners, except internal

(P-20131)
VALLEY COMMUNITY HEALTHCARE
6801 Coldwater Canyon Ave 1b, North Hollywood (91605-5164)
PHONE...........................818 763-8836
Paula Wilson, *CEO*
Lee Huey, *CFO*
Irina Pogosyan, *Vice Pres*
Sunny Lucas, *Info Tech Dir*
Fidel Gruber, *Network Enginr*
EMP: 300 EST: 1970
SQ FT: 15,000
SALES (est): 23.8MM **Privately Held**
WEB: www.valleycommunityhealthcare.org
SIC: **8011** Clinic, operated by physicians

(P-20132)
VANGUARD HEALTH SYSTEMS INC
Also Called: North Anaheim Surgery Center
1154 N Euclid St, Anaheim (92801-1955)
PHONE...........................714 635-6272
Jeanette Rasmussen, *Administration*
EMP: 309 EST: 1991
SQ FT: 12,000
SALES (est): 27.6MM
SALES (corp-wide): 17.6B **Publicly Held**
WEB: www.tenethealth.com
SIC: **8011** 5999 Ambulatory surgical center; medical apparatus & supplies
HQ: Vanguard Health Systems, Inc.
    20 Burton Hills Blvd # 100
    Nashville TN 37215
    615 665-6000

(P-20133)
VANOWEN MEDICAL ASSOCIATES
Also Called: Silverstein, Sylvain S MD
15211 Vanowen St Ste 100, Van Nuys (91405-3628)
PHONE...........................818 778-1920
Sylvain Silberstein MD, *Owner*
Dr Steven L Rouff, *Partner*
Linda Sevilla, *Endocrinology*
EMP: 72 EST: 1978
SQ FT: 7,250
SALES (est): 2.8MM **Privately Held**
SIC: **8011** Internal medicine, physician/surgeon; endocrinologist

(P-20134)
VENICE FMLY CLINIC FOUNDATION (PA)
604 Rose Ave, Venice (90291-2767)
PHONE...........................310 664-7703
Elizabeth Forer, *CEO*
Gordon Lee, *Treasurer*
Stewart Seradsky, *Treasurer*
Jeffrey E Sinaiko, *Treasurer*
Lee Rosenberg, *Vice Pres*
EMP: 211 EST: 1970

SALES (est): 58.6MM **Privately Held**
WEB: www.venicefamilyclinic.org
SIC: **8011** Clinic, operated by physicians

(P-20135)
VENTURA COUNTY MEDICAL CENTER
Also Called: Santa Paula Hospital
845 N 10th St Ste 3, Santa Paula (93060-1348)
PHONE...........................805 933-8600
Wes Clark, *Food Svc Dir*
Teresa Hulett, *Director*
Dee Pupa, *Director*
EMP: 103
SALES (corp-wide): 68.6MM **Privately Held**
WEB: www.vchca.org
SIC: **8011** Medical centers
PA: Ventura County Medical Center
    3291 Loma Vista Rd
    Ventura CA 93003
    805 652-6000

(P-20136)
VENTURA COUNTY MEDICAL CENTER (PA)
3291 Loma Vista Rd, Ventura (93003-3099)
PHONE...........................805 652-6000
Ronald O'Halloran, *Principal*
Jon Nothwang,
Barry Sanchez,
William Starr,
Robert Levin, *Officer*
EMP: 190 EST: 2000
SALES (est): 68.6MM **Privately Held**
WEB: www.vchca.org
SIC: **8011** Medical centers

(P-20137)
VENTURA COUNTY MEDICAL CENTER
Also Called: Ana Nacapa Surgical Associates
3291 Loma Vista Rd # 343, Ventura (93003-3099)
PHONE...........................805 652-6201
Scott Arnold, *Principal*
Chau Nguyen, *Otolaryngology*
EMP: 103
SALES (corp-wide): 68.6MM **Privately Held**
WEB: www.vchca.org
SIC: **8011** Medical centers
PA: Ventura County Medical Center
    3291 Loma Vista Rd
    Ventura CA 93003
    805 652-6000

(P-20138)
VERDUGO HILLS PSYCHTHERAPY CTR (PA)
Also Called: Pacific Child and Family Assoc
410 Arden Ave Ste 201, Glendale (91203-4006)
PHONE...........................818 241-6780
Ira Heilveil, *President*
Celina Lopez, *Exec Dir*
Rachael Schneider, *Exec Dir*
Daniel Matas, *Comp Spec*
Paul Pieri, *Controller*
EMP: 59 EST: 1988
SALES (est): 13.3MM **Privately Held**
SIC: **8011** Psychoanalyst

(P-20139)
VERITY MEDICAL FOUNDATION (PA)
Also Called: San Jose Medical Group / MGT
6300 Canoga Ave Ste 1500, Woodland Hills (91367-8015)
PHONE...........................408 278-3000
Ernest Wallerstein, *CEO*
Christine Hoskinson, *CFO*
Arthur Feldman, *Med Doctor*
Arthur B Feldman, *Director*
EMP: 80 EST: 2011
SALES (est): 9.6MM **Privately Held**
WEB: www.verity.org
SIC: **8011** 8741 Medical centers; management services

PRODUCTS & SVCS

(P-20140)
VETERANS AFFAIRS US DEPT
888 W Santa Ana Blvd, Santa Ana
(92701-4561)
PHONE..................714 568-9802
Erin Potter, *Branch Mgr*
EMP: 62 **Publicly Held**
WEB: www.va.gov
SIC: **8011** 9451 Cardiologist & cardio-vascular specialist;
HQ: United States Department Of Veterans
Affairs
810 Vermont Ave Nw
Washington DC 20420
800 827-1000

(P-20141)
VETERANS HEALTH ADMINISTRATION
16111 Plummer St, North Hills
(91343-2036)
PHONE..................818 895-9344
EMP: 111 **Publicly Held**
WEB: www.va.gov
SIC: **8011** 9451 Clinic, operated by physicians;
HQ: Veterans Health Administration
810 Vermont Ave Nw
Washington DC 20420

(P-20142)
VETERANS HEALTH ADMINISTRATION
Also Called: West Los Angeles V A Med Ctr
11301 Wilshire Blvd, Los Angeles
(90073-1003)
PHONE..................310 478-3711
Donna Beiter, *Director*
Jessica Oconnell, *Opers Staff*
Joan Scheibel, *Professor*
Deniz Ahmadinia, *Psychologist*
Mark Sawicki, *Surgeon*
EMP: 111 **Publicly Held**
WEB: www.benefits.va.gov
SIC: **8011** 9451 Clinic, operated by physicians; psychiatric clinic;
HQ: Veterans Health Administration
810 Vermont Ave Nw
Washington DC 20420

(P-20143)
VETERANS HEALTH ADMINISTRATION
Also Called: San Luis Obispo VA Cboc
1288 Morro St Ste 200, San Luis Obispo
(93401-6302)
PHONE..................805 543-1233
Mark Donaldson, *Branch Mgr*
EMP: 111 **Publicly Held**
WEB: www.va.gov
SIC: **8011** 9451 Clinic, operated by physicians;
HQ: Veterans Health Administration
810 Vermont Ave Nw
Washington DC 20420

(P-20144)
VETERANS HEALTH ADMINISTRATION
Also Called: VA Santa Maria Cboc
1550 E Main St, Santa Maria (93454-4819)
PHONE..................805 354-6000
EMP: 111 **Publicly Held**
WEB: www.benefits.va.gov
SIC: **8011** 9451 Ambulatory surgical center;
HQ: Veterans Health Administration
810 Vermont Ave Nw
Washington DC 20420

(P-20145)
VETERANS HEALTH ADMINISTRATION
Also Called: Oxnard Veterans Center
250 Citrus Grove Ln # 250, Oxnard
(93036-9030)
PHONE..................805 983-6384
EMP: 263 **Publicly Held**
SIC: **8011** 9451 Medical Doctor's Office
Administrative Veterans' Affairs

HQ: Veterans Health Administration
810 Vermont Ave Nw
Washington DC 20420

(P-20146)
VETERANS HEALTH ADMINISTRATION
Also Called: Palm Desert Veterans Center
41865 Boardwalk Ste 103, Palm Desert
(92211-9031)
PHONE..................760 341-5570
Roberta Murphy, *Manager*
EMP: 111 **Publicly Held**
WEB: www.va.gov
SIC: **8011** 9451 Medical centers;
HQ: Veterans Health Administration
810 Vermont Ave Nw
Washington DC 20420

(P-20147)
VETERANS HEALTH ADMINISTRATION
Also Called: Sepulveda Ambltory Care Ctr Cl
16111 Plummer St, North Hills
(91343-2036)
PHONE..................818 891-7711
Dolly G Whitehead, *Manager*
Christopher Godfrey, *Vice Chairman*
EMP: 111 **Publicly Held**
WEB: www.va.gov
SIC: **8011** 9451 Medical centers;
HQ: Veterans Health Administration
810 Vermont Ave Nw
Washington DC 20420

(P-20148)
VETERANS HEALTH ADMINISTRATION
Also Called: Santa Brbara V A Otptent Clnic
4440 Calle Real, Santa Barbara
(93110-1002)
PHONE..................805 683-1491
Dr Robert Gaines, *Branch Mgr*
EMP: 111 **Publicly Held**
WEB: www.va.gov
SIC: **8011** 9451 Clinic, operated by physicians;
HQ: Veterans Health Administration
810 Vermont Ave Nw
Washington DC 20420

(P-20149)
VETERANS HEALTH ADMINISTRATION
Also Called: Loma Linda Healthcare Sys 605
11201 Benton St, Loma Linda
(92357-1000)
PHONE..................909 825-7084
Debbie Romero, *Branch Mgr*
Shane Elliott, *Associate Dir*
EMP: 111 **Publicly Held**
WEB: www.benefits.va.gov
SIC: **8011** 9451 Medical centers;
HQ: Veterans Health Administration
810 Vermont Ave Nw
Washington DC 20420

(P-20150)
VETERANS HEALTH ADMINISTRATION
Also Called: VA HSR&d Center of Excellence
16111 Plummer St, North Hills
(91343-2036)
PHONE..................818 895-9449
Lisa Rubenstein, *Branch Mgr*
EMP: 111 **Publicly Held**
WEB: www.va.gov
SIC: **8011** 9451 Medical centers; administration of veterans' affairs
HQ: Veterans Health Administration
810 Vermont Ave Nw
Washington DC 20420

(P-20151)
VETERANS HEALTH ADMINISTRATION
Also Called: Anaheim V A Clinic
1801 W Romneya Dr Ste 303, Anaheim
(92801-1825)
PHONE..................714 780-5400
Teresa Carpenter, *Branch Mgr*
EMP: 111 **Publicly Held**
WEB: www.va.gov
SIC: **8011** 9451 Clinic, operated by physicians; administration of veterans' affairs
HQ: Veterans Health Administration
810 Vermont Ave Nw
Washington DC 20420

(P-20152)
VETERANS HEALTH ADMINISTRATION
Also Called: Bakersfield Cmnty Bsed Otptent
1801 Westwind Dr, Bakersfield
(93301-3028)
PHONE..................661 632-1871
Joan Van Horn, *Manager*
EMP: 111 **Publicly Held**
WEB: www.va.gov
SIC: **8011** 9451 Clinic, operated by physicians;
HQ: Veterans Health Administration
810 Vermont Ave Nw
Washington DC 20420

(P-20153)
VETERANS HEALTH ADMINISTRATION
Also Called: Los Angles Ambulatory Care Ctr
351 E Temple St, Los Angeles
(90012-3328)
PHONE..................213 253-2677
Lane Turzan, *General Mgr*
EMP: 111 **Publicly Held**
WEB: www.va.gov
SIC: **8011** 9451 Medical centers; psychiatric clinic;
HQ: Veterans Health Administration
810 Vermont Ave Nw
Washington DC 20420

(P-20154)
VETERANS HEALTH ADMINISTRATION
Also Called: Bakersfield Vet Center
1110 Golden Valley Fwy, Bakersfield
(93301)
PHONE..................661 323-8387
Jenney Frank, *Office Mgr*
EMP: 111 **Publicly Held**
WEB: www.va.gov
SIC: **8011** 9451 Medical centers;
HQ: Veterans Health Administration
810 Vermont Ave Nw
Washington DC 20420

(P-20155)
VIA CARE CMNTY HLTH CTR INC
Also Called: BIENVENIDOS COMMUNITY HEALTH C
507 S Atlantic Blvd, Los Angeles
(90022-2621)
PHONE..................323 268-9191
Deborah Villar, *CEO*
Joe Gotsill, *CFO*
Eduardo Vasquez, *Director*
Vanessa Fuentes, *Supervisor*
EMP: 60 **EST:** 2010
SALES: 12.6MM **Privately Held**
WEB: www.viacarela.org
SIC: **8011** Primary care medical clinic

(P-20156)
VISALIA MEDICAL CLINIC INC (PA)
Also Called: Multi Specialty Medical Svc
5400 W Hillsdale Ave, Visalia (93291-5140)
PHONE..................559 733-5222
Richard E Strid, *CEO*
Russ Desch, *CFO*
Lynn Carillo, *Executive Asst*
Benjamin Brennan, *Family Practiti*
Angelina Mallari, *Family Practiti*
EMP: 289 **EST:** 1973

SQ FT: 70,000
SALES (est): 49.4MM **Privately Held**
WEB: www.kaweahhealthmedicalgroup.org
SIC: **8011** 8071 Clinic, operated by physicians; medical laboratories

(P-20157)
VISTA COMMUNITY CLINIC
30195 Fraser Dr, Lake Elsinore
(92530-7006)
PHONE..................951 245-2735
EMP: 88
SALES (corp-wide): 69MM **Privately Held**
WEB: www.vistacommunityclinic.org
SIC: **8011** Clinic, operated by physicians
PA: Vista Community Clinic
1000 Vale Terrace Dr
Vista CA 92084
760 631-5000

(P-20158)
WATTS HEALTHCARE CORPORATION
700 W Imperial Hwy, Los Angeles
(90044-4127)
PHONE..................323 241-1780
EMP: 162
SALES (corp-wide): 34.1MM **Privately Held**
SIC: **8011** Nonclassified Establishment
PA: Watts Healthcare Corporation
10300 Compton Ave
Los Angeles CA 90002
323 568-3059

(P-20159)
WATTS HEALTHCARE CORPORATION (PA)
10300 Compton Ave, Los Angeles
(90002-3628)
PHONE..................323 564-4331
Roderick Seamster, *President*
Carroll J McNeely, *CFO*
Yoko Sugihara, *Treasurer*
Mary Cortez, *Bd of Directors*
Linda Daniels, *Bd of Directors*
EMP: 180 **EST:** 2002
SALES: 39.3MM **Privately Held**
WEB: www.wattshealth.org
SIC: **8011** Clinic, operated by physicians

(P-20160)
WEST COVINA MEDICAL CLINIC INC (PA)
1500 W West Covina Pkwy, West Covina
(91790-2708)
PHONE..................626 960-8614
Dr Ziad Dabuni, *President*
Dr Suntheetha Ali, *Treasurer*
Dr Shivani Shah, *Exec VF*
Dr Jose Bautista, *Asst Treas*
Carolina Mc Dowell, *Manager*
EMP: 222 **EST:** 1950
SQ FT: 50,000
SALES (est): 12.5MM **Privately Held**
WEB: www.westcovinadentalandorthodontics.com
SIC: **8011** Clinic, operated by physicians

(P-20161)
WEST DERMATOLOGY MED MGT INC
680 Nwport Ctr Dr Ste 150, Newport Beach
(92660)
PHONE..................909 793-3000
J Robert West, *Presiden*
Espy Byrd, *Recruiter*
Tanya J Foreman, *Med Doctor*
EMP: 140 **EST:** 2004
SALES (est): 17.3MM **Privately Held**
WEB: www.westdermatology.com
SIC: **8011** Dermatologist

(P-20162)
WESTERN UNIV HLTH SCIENCES
Also Called: Mission Medical Clinic
360 E Mission Blvd, Pomona (91766-1847)
PHONE..................909 865-2565
Alan D Cundari, *Principal*
EMP: 75

SALES (corp-wide): 223.1MM **Privately Held**
WEB: www.westernu.edu
SIC: **8011** 8221 Clinic, operated by physicians; university
PA: Western University Of Health Sciences
309 E 2nd St
Pomona CA 91766
909 623-6116

(P-20163)
WESTSIDE CRDVSCLAR MED GROUP I (PA)
Also Called: Westside Medical ASC Los Ang
99 N La Cienega Blvd # 10, Beverly Hills (90211-2222)
PHONE...................310 623-1150
Norman E Lepor, *Principal*
Norman Lepor, *President*
EMP: 75 EST: 2002
SALES (est): 8.5MM **Privately Held**
SIC: **8011** Radiologist

(P-20164)
WHITE MEM CMNTY HLTH CTR A CAL
1828 E Cesar E Chavez Ave # 5000, Los Angeles (90033-2400)
PHONE...................323 987-1222
Carl Coan, *CEO*
EMP: 61 EST: 2016
SALES (est): 5MM **Privately Held**
SIC: **8011** Physical medicine, physician/surgeon

(P-20165)
WHITE MEMORIAL MED GROUP INC (PA)
1701 E Cesar E Chavez Ave, Los Angeles (90033-2464)
P.O. Box 51741 (90051-6041)
PHONE...................323 987-1300
Alan Lau, *President*
EMP: 71 EST: 1983
SQ FT: 20,000
SALES (est): 14.5MM **Privately Held**
WEB: www.adventisthealth.org
SIC: **8011** 8742 Medical centers; hospital & health services consultant

(P-20166)
WHITE MEMORIAL MEDICAL CENTER
1720 E Cesar E Chavez Ave, Los Angeles (90033-2414)
PHONE...................323 260-5739
Beth D Zachary, *Branch Mgr*
EMP: 800
SALES (corp-wide): 4.5B **Privately Held**
WEB: www.adventisthealth.org
SIC: **8011** Medical centers
HQ: White Memorial Medical Center Inc
1720 E Cesar E Chavez Ave
Los Angeles CA 90033
323 268-5000

(P-20167)
WILLOW SPRINGS LLC
17241 Van Buren Blvd, Riverside (92504-5942)
PHONE...................951 789-4405
Joseph McCoy, *Branch Mgr*
EMP: 55
SALES (corp-wide): 11.5B **Publicly Held**
WEB: www.uhs.com
SIC: **8011** Psychiatric clinic
HQ: Willow Springs, Llc
6640 Carothers Pkwy # 400
Franklin TN 37067
615 312-5700

8021 Offices & Clinics Of Dentists

(P-20168)
ACCESS DENTAL PLAN (PA)
Also Called: Access Dental Centers
530 S Main St Ste 100, Orange (92868-4555)
PHONE...................916 922-5000
Reza M Abbaszadeh, *President*
Teri Abbaszadeh, *President*
Charlotte Quider, *Exec Officer*

Myles Hokama, *Officer*
▲ EMP: 70 EST: 1989
SALES (est): 22.3MM **Privately Held**
WEB: www.westerndental.com
SIC: **8021** Dental clinic

(P-20169)
ALENE LE DDS MS INC (PA)
511 E 1st St Ste C, Tustin (92780-3333)
PHONE...................626 332-6291
Alene Le, *Principal*
EMP: 77 EST: 2010
SALES (est): 133.7K **Privately Held**
SIC: **8021** Offices & clinics of dentists

(P-20170)
BOYD DENTAL CORPORATION (PA)
599 Inland Center Dr # 110, San Bernardino (92408-1819)
PHONE...................909 384-1111
Anthony Q Boyd, *President*
EMP: 80 EST: 2000
SALES (est): 331.4K **Privately Held**
SIC: **8021** Dentists' office

(P-20171)
C BRENT PEEKE DDS INC (PA)
264 N Highland Sprng Ave S, Banning (92220-3082)
PHONE...................951 845-4685
EMP: 56 EST: 2015
SALES (est): 532.2K **Privately Held**
SIC: **8021** Dentists' office

(P-20172)
DAVID C HAN DDS A PROF CORP (PA)
41253 12th St W Ste B, Palmdale (93551-1413)
PHONE...................661 254-1924
David C Han, *President*
▲ EMP: 52 EST: 2005
SALES (est): 1.4MM **Privately Held**
SIC: **8021** Offices & clinics of dentists

(P-20173)
DEDICATED DENTAL SYSTEMS INC
9800 S La Cnga Blvd, Inglewood (90301-4440)
PHONE...................661 397-5513
Arthur Kaiser, *President*
Heather Martinez, *Manager*
EMP: 65 EST: 1987
SQ FT: 5,000
SALES (est): 4.8MM
SALES (corp-wide): 119.8MM **Privately Held**
WEB: www.dedicated-dental.com
SIC: **8021** 6324 Dental clinic; hospital & medical service plans
HQ: Interdent Service Corporation
9800 S La Cnga Blvd # 800
Inglewood CA 90301

(P-20174)
DENTAL IMAGING TECH CORP
1717 W Collins Ave, Orange (92867-5422)
PHONE...................714 516-7868
Tammy Manning, *President*
EMP: 2074 EST: 2015
SALES (est): 5.8MM
SALES (corp-wide): 2.2B **Publicly Held**
WEB: www.kavo.com
SIC: **8021** Offices & clinics of dentists
PA: Envista Holdings Corporation
200 S Kraemer Blvd Bldg E
Brea CA 92821
714 817-7000

(P-20175)
DONGSUK PARK DDS INC
14 Crestwood, Irvine (92620-1273)
PHONE...................714 734-0900
Dongsuk Park, *Branch Mgr*
EMP: 70 **Privately Held**
SIC: **8021** Dentists' office
PA: Park Dongsuk Dds Inc
1352 Irvine Blvd
Tustin CA

(P-20176)
ELIAS ELLIOTT LAMPASI FEHN (PA)
7251 Magnolia Ave, Riverside (92504-3811)
PHONE...................951 689-5031
Douglass R Gerald, *CEO*
Jay Elliot, *Vice Pres*
Dee Elias, *Admin Sec*
EMP: 59 EST: 1986
SALES (est): 10.3MM **Privately Held**
WEB: www.riversidedentalgroup.com
SIC: **8021** Dentists' office

(P-20177)
FARBOD PARVINJAH DMD INC (PA)
4128 Whitsett Ave Apt 111, Studio City (91604-2461)
PHONE...................805 583-5589
Farbod Parvinjah, *CEO*
EMP: 63 EST: 2015
SALES (est): 544.4K **Privately Held**
SIC: **8021** Dentists' office

(P-20178)
FUTUREDONTICS INC (HQ)
Also Called: 1-800 Dentist
11209 National Blvd # 409, Los Angeles (90064-3902)
PHONE...................310 215-6400
Michael Turner, *CEO*
Ronald Joyal, *COO*
Gary St Denis, *Chairman*
Todd Daum, *Chief Mktg Ofcr*
Jonathan Kass, *Vice Pres*
EMP: 247 EST: 1986
SQ FT: 35,000
SALES (est): 55.9MM
SALES (corp-wide): 3.3B **Publicly Held**
WEB: www.1800dentist.com
SIC: **8021** Dental clinic
PA: Dentsply Sirona Inc.
13320b Balntyn Corp Pl
Charlotte NC 28277
844 848-0137

(P-20179)
GENTLE DENTAL SERVICE CORP (DH)
9800 S La Cnga Blvd Fl 2, Inglewood (90301-4408)
PHONE...................800 277-1112
Fred Vanerden, *CFO*
Rebecca Kriegshauser, *Practice Mgr*
Bernadette Armstrong, *Business Anlyst*
Aide Morales, *Opers Staff*
Erica Sevilla, *Opers Staff*
EMP: 66 EST: 2007
SALES (est): 115.8MM **Privately Held**
WEB: www.interdent.com
SIC: **8021** Dental clinic
HQ: H.I.G. Capital, L.L.C.
1450 Brickell Ave Fl 31
Miami FL 33131
305 379-2322

(P-20180)
GREGORY W PETERSON DDS (PA)
25260 La Paz Rd Ste I, Laguna Hills (92653-5132)
PHONE...................626 354-4223
Gregory Peterson, *Principal*
EMP: 52 EST: 2017
SALES (est): 855.5K **Privately Held**
SIC: **8021** Offices & clinics of dentists

(P-20181)
INTERDENT INC (HQ)
Also Called: Smile Keepers
9800 S La Cnga Blvd # 800, Inglewood (90301-4442)
PHONE...................310 765-2400
Ivar S Chhina, *President*
Robert W Hill, *CFO*
Matthew Wickesberg, *CFO*
Mark Backstrom, *Vice Pres*
John Bukowski, *Vice Pres*
EMP: 55 EST: 1992
SQ FT: 10,000
SALES (est): 119.8MM **Privately Held**
WEB: www.interdent.com
SIC: **8021** Dentists' office

PA: H.I.G. Middle Market Llc
1 Sansome St Fl 37
San Francisco CA 94104
415 439-5500

(P-20182)
INTERDENT SERVICE CORPORATION
3630 Central Ave, Riverside (92506-5908)
PHONE...................951 682-1720
Carlos Espadas, *Branch Mgr*
EMP: 105
SALES (corp-wide): 119.8MM **Privately Held**
SIC: **8021** Offices & clinics of dentists
HQ: Interdent Service Corporation
9800 S La Cnga Blvd # 800
Inglewood CA 90301

(P-20183)
INTERDENT SERVICE CORPORATION (DH)
9800 S La Cnga Blvd # 800, Inglewood (90301-4442)
PHONE...................310 765-2400
Marshal Salomon, *CEO*
Matthew Wickesberg, *CFO*
Irma Duron, *Manager*
EMP: 50 EST: 1991
SQ FT: 10,000
SALES (est): 55.6MM
SALES (corp-wide): 119.8MM **Privately Held**
WEB: www.interdent.com
SIC: **8021** Dental clinic
HQ: Interdent, Inc.
9800 S La Cnga Blvd # 800
Inglewood CA 90301
310 765-2400

(P-20184)
JONG S YOON DMD INC (PA)
520 S Virgil Ave Ste 101, Los Angeles (90020-1425)
PHONE...................213 383-0010
EMP: 53 EST: 2008
SALES (est): 84.6K **Privately Held**
SIC: **8021** Offices & clinics of dentists

(P-20185)
LANCE RYGG DENTAL CORP (PA)
2860 Michelle Fl 2, Irvine (92606-1008)
PHONE...................714 508-3600
Carolyn Ghazal, *Principal*
EMP: 153 EST: 2005
SALES (est): 168.5K **Privately Held**
SIC: **8021** Dental clinic

(P-20186)
LEONID M GLSMAN DDS A DNTL COR
Also Called: Dentalville
5021 Florence Ave, Bell (90201-3802)
PHONE...................323 560-4514
EMP: 130
SALES (corp-wide): 5.6MM **Privately Held**
WEB: www.belldentistca.com
SIC: **8021** Dentists' office
PA: Leonid M. Glosman, D.D.S., A Dental Corporation
7864 Van Nuys Blvd
Panorama City CA 91402
323 266-1000

(P-20187)
MANSKE DENTAL CORPORATION (PA)
1355 N Sierra Bonita Ave, West Hollywood (90046-8515)
PHONE...................424 354-9336
Jessica Lynn Manske, *Principal*
EMP: 63 EST: 2015
SALES (est): 317.9K **Privately Held**
SIC: **8021** Offices & clinics of dentists

(P-20188)
MICHAEL P BYKO DDS A PROF CORP (PA)
164 W Hospitality Ln # 14, San Bernardino (92408-3316)
PHONE...................909 888-7817

Michael Boyko, *President*
Heather Dunham, *Manager*
◆ **EMP:** 60 **EST:** 1980
SQ FT: 3,000
SALES (est): 11.1MM **Privately Held**
SIC: 8021 Dental clinic; orthodontist

(P-20189)
MY KIDS DENTIST
24635 Madison Ave Ste E, Murrieta
(92562-7556)
PHONE....................................951 600-1062
Theresa Gomez, *Branch Mgr*
EMP: 400
SALES (corp-wide): 5.4MM **Privately
Held**
WEB: www.blainedentists.com
SIC: 8021 Dentists' office
PA: My Kid's Dentist
      17000 Red Hill Ave
      Irvine CA 92614
      909 854-1437

(P-20190)
MY KIDS DENTIST (PA)
17000 Red Hill Ave, Irvine (92614-5626)
PHONE....................................909 854-1437
Scott Ngai, *President*
EMP: 66 **EST:** 2009
SALES (est): 5.4MM **Privately Held**
WEB: www.blainedentists.com
SIC: 8021 Dentists' office

(P-20191)
NGORK DENTAL CORPORATION (PA)
275 S Arroyo Pkwy # 511, Pasadena
(91105-5209)
PHONE....................................714 200-4095
Tim Ngork, *Principal*
EMP: 59 **EST:** 2016
SALES (est): 116.9K **Privately Held**
SIC: 8021 Offices & clinics of dentists

(P-20192)
PACIFIC DENTAL SERVICES LLC (PA)
Also Called: Pds
17000 Red Hill Ave, Irvine (92614-5626)
P.O. Box 19723 (92623-9723)
PHONE....................................714 845-8500
Stephen E Thorne IV, *President*
Simon W Abrahms, *Partner*
Scott Beck, *Vice Chairman*
Brady Aase, *CFO*
Dan Burke, *Senior VP*
▲ **EMP:** 300 **EST:** 1991
SQ FT: 40,000
SALES (est): 595.6MM **Privately Held**
WEB: www.pacificdentalservices.com
SIC: 8021 6794 Dental clinic; franchises,
selling or licensing

(P-20193)
PEACE KIM DENTISTRY INC (PA)
4 Longbourn Aisle, Irvine (92603-5722)
PHONE....................................949 679-8762
Peace P Kim, *Principal*
EMP: 61 **EST:** 2018
SALES (est): 194.4K **Privately Held**
SIC: 8021 Offices & clinics of dentists

(P-20194)
PETER WYLAN DDS
Also Called: Bellflower Dental Group
10318 Rosecrans Ave, Bellflower
(90706-2702)
PHONE....................................562 925-3765
Peter Wylan DDS, *Owner*
EMP: 100 **EST:** 1955
SQ FT: 2,000
SALES (est): 8.2MM **Privately Held**
SIC: 8021 8072 Dentists' office; orthodontist; dental laboratories

(P-20195)
PLAYHOUSE DENTAL (PA)
3000 Whittier Blvd, Los Angeles
(90023-1637)
PHONE....................................323 269-5437
Amir Korouri, *Principal*
EMP: 60 **EST:** 2010

SALES (est): 662.1K **Privately Held**
WEB: www.phddental.com
SIC: 8021 Dental clinic

(P-20196)
SAC HEALTH SYSTEM (PA)
1455 3rd Ave, San Bernardino
(92408-0218)
PHONE....................................909 382-7100
Richard H Hart MD, *President*
George Cencel, *CFO*
Barry Randolph, *Opers Staff*
EMP: 66 **EST:** 1995
SALES (est): 61.6MM **Privately Held**
WEB: www.sachealth.org
SIC: 8021 8011 8093 Offices & clinics of
dentists; offices & clinics of medical doctors; mental health clinic, outpatient

(P-20197)
SALAMEH & MAHMOOD DDS INC (PA)
24102 El Toro Rd Ste A, Laguna Woods
(92637-3123)
PHONE....................................949 830-6510
Mohsin Mahmood, *Principal*
EMP: 55 **EST:** 2010
SALES (est): 525.8K **Privately Held**
SIC: 8021 Offices & clinics of dentists

(P-20198)
SCHNIEROW DENTAL CARE
Also Called: Piehl, Joel J DDS
13450 Hawthorne Blvd, Hawthorne
(90250-5806)
PHONE....................................310 377-6453
Burton Schnierow, *President*
EMP: 77 **EST:** 1948
SQ FT: 3,200
SALES (est): 8.5MM **Privately Held**
WEB: www.310drsmile.com
SIC: 8021 Dentists' office

(P-20199)
SETAREHSHENAS DENTAL CORP
1197 E Los Angeles Ave, Simi Valley
(93065-2868)
PHONE....................................805 583-5700
Katayoun Setarehshenas, *Branch Mgr*
EMP: 105 **EST:** 1991
WEB: www.firststreetdental.com
SIC: 8021 Dentists' office
PA: Setarehshenas Dental Corp
      2860 Michelle Fl 2
      Irvine CA 92606

(P-20200)
ST JHNS WELL CHILD FMLY CTR I (PA)
Also Called: Saint John's Well Child Center
808 W 58th St, Los Angeles (90037-3632)
PHONE....................................323 541-1600
James J Mangia, *CEO*
Liz Meisler, *CFO*
EMP: 74 **EST:** 1963
SALES (est): 82.3MM **Privately Held**
WEB: www.wellchild.org
SIC: 8021 8011 Dental clinic; offices &
clinics of medical doctors

(P-20201)
TOAN D NGUYEN DDS INC (PA)
511 E 1st St Ste C, Tustin (92780-3333)
PHONE....................................562 926-3354
Toan D Nguyen, *President*
▲ **EMP:** 73 **EST:** 2005
SALES (est): 313.6K **Privately Held**
SIC: 8021 Dentists' office

(P-20202)
TOIYABE INDIAN HEALTH PRJ INC (PA)
250 N See Vee Ln, Bishop (93514-8130)
PHONE....................................760 873-8461
David Lent, *CEO*
Libby Watanabe, *COO*
Mary Daniel, *CFO*
Monty Bengochia, *Chairman*
Rick Maddux, *Treasurer*
EMP: 86 **EST:** 1971
SQ FT: 66,300

SALES (est): 16.4MM **Privately Held**
WEB: www.toiyabe.us
SIC: 8021 8011 Dental clinic; clinic, operated by physicians; psychiatric clinic

(P-20203)
WADE MELVIN BANNER DMD (PA)
2060 E Route 66 Ste 105, Glendora
(91740-4691)
PHONE....................................626 594-0374
EMP: 52 **EST:** 2016
SALES (est): 1.2MM **Privately Held**
SIC: 8021 Dentists' office

(P-20204)
WESTERN DENTAL SERVICES INC (HQ)
Also Called: Western Dental & Orthodontics
530 S Main St Ste 600, Orange
(92868-4544)
P.O. Box 14227 (92863-1227)
PHONE....................................714 480-3000
Daniel D Crowley, *CEO*
Preet M Takkar, *COO*
William Dembereckyj, *CFO*
Paul Holt, *CFO*
Leslie Gibbs, *Chief Mktg Ofcr*
EMP: 350 **EST:** 1984
SALES (est): 225.7MM
SALES (corp-wide): 328.1MM **Privately
Held**
WEB: www.westerndental.com
SIC: 8021 Dentists' office
PA: Premier Dental Holdings, Inc.
      530 S Main St Ste 600
      Orange CA 92868
      714 480-3000

8042 Offices & Clinics Of Optometrists

(P-20205)
FIRSTSIGHT VISION SERVICES INC (DH)
1202 Monte Vista Ave # 17, Upland
(91786-8208)
PHONE....................................909 920-5008
Robert K Patton, *President*
Joseph T Heidelman, *CFO*
EMP: 50 **EST:** 1995
SALES (est): 17.9MM
SALES (corp-wide): 1.7B **Publicly Held**
WEB: www.firstsightvision.net
SIC: 8042 Specialized optometrists

(P-20206)
FOCUS VSION CLNIC OPTMETRY INC (PA)
Also Called: Focu Vision Clinic
1668 E Second St Ste B, Beaumont
(92223-3168)
PHONE....................................951 845-4749
Tanya L Vanguilder, *CEO*
EMP: 65 **EST:** 2007
SALES (est): 2.6MM **Privately Held**
WEB: www.focusvisionopt.com
SIC: 8042 Offices & clinics of optometrists

(P-20207)
TOTAL VISION LLC
27271 Las Ramblas 200a, Mission Viejo
(92691-8041)
PHONE....................................949 652-7242
Scott Strachan, *President*
Doug Lattime, *Senior VP*
Broke Jakovich, *VP Opers*
EMP: 194 **EST:** 2014
SQ FT: 3,000
SALES (est): 19MM **Privately Held**
SIC: 8042 Group & corporate practice optometrists
PA: Total Vision Holdings, Llc
      277 Park Ave Fl 27
      New York NY 10172
      212 704-5364

8049 Offices & Clinics Of Health Practitioners, NEC

(P-20208)
BEHAVIOR FRONTIERS LLC
18726 S Wstn Ave Ste 408, Gardena
(90248)
PHONE....................................310 856-0800
Helen Mader, *CEO*
Darian Salazar, *COO*
Bryan Mader, *CFO*
Alysia Wyatt, *Admin Asst*
Christina Chang, *Technician*
EMP: 58 **EST:** 2004
SALES (est): 15.1MM **Privately Held**
WEB: www.behaviorfrontiers.com
SIC: 8049 Offices of health practitioner

(P-20209)
CALIFORNIA PSYCHCARE INC (PA)
9201 Oakdale Ave Ste 101, Chatsworth
(91311-6546)
PHONE....................................818 401-0661
Ali Sadeghi, *President*
Adriana Garcia, *Department Mgr*
Alicia Ramsey, *Office Mgr*
Paulette Torres, *Office Mgr*
Mayra Sencion, *Admin Asst*
EMP: 72 **EST:** 2003
SALES (est): 11.7MM **Privately Held**
WEB: www.jamesgeorge.me
SIC: 8049 Psychologist, psychotherapist &
hypnotist

(P-20210)
CASA COLINA HOSPTAL AND CENTE
910 E Alosta Ave, Azusa (91702-2709)
PHONE....................................626 334-8735
Felice L Loverso, *Presiden*
EMP: 149
SALES (corp-wide): 123MM **Privately
Held**
WEB: www.casacolina.org
SIC: 8049 Physical therapist
HQ: Casa Colina Hospital And Centers For
      Healthcare
      255 E Bonita Ave
      Pomona CA 91767
      909 596-7733

(P-20211)
CENTER FOR ATISM RLTED DSRDERS (PA)
21600 Oxnard St Ste 1800, Woodland Hills
(91367-7807)
PHONE....................................818 345-2345
Doreen Granpeesheh, *Director*
Mark Keller, *CFO*
Dennis Dixon, *Officer*
Vardui Chilingaryan, *Regional Mgr*
Aubrey Nigoza, *Admin Mgr*
EMP: 143 **EST:** 1990
SALES (est): 120.8MM **Privately Held**
WEB: www.centerforautism.com
SIC: 8049 Clinical psychologist

(P-20212)
COMMUNITY THERAPIES LLC
Also Called: Community Therapies Baby
Steps
19040 Soledad Canyon Rd # 25, Santa
Clarita (91351-3363)
P.O. Box 432, Lancaster (93584-0432)
PHONE....................................661 945-7878
Roy Jensen, *Owner*
Shelli Hughes, *Supervisor*
EMP: 50 **EST:** 1996
SALES (est): 2.6MM **Privately Held**
WEB: www.communitytherapies.com
SIC: 8049 Speech therapist

(P-20213)
COMPREHENSIVE AUTISM CTR INC (PA)
40485 Mrreta Hot Sprng Rd, Murrieta
(92563-6436)
PHONE....................................951 813-4034
Chris Macken, *Vice Pres*
EMP: 62 **EST:** 2007

SALES (est): 7.9MM **Privately Held**
WEB: www.cac.co
SIC: **8049** Physical therapist

(P-20214)
EQUINOX-76TH STREET INC
Also Called: Health Fitness America
1980 Main St Fl 4, Irvine (92614-7200)
PHONE.................................949 975-8400
Ian McFodden, *Manager*
Mike Gallegos, *Maintence Staff*
EMP: 86
SALES (corp-wide): 2B **Privately Held**
SIC: **8049** 7991 Physical therapist; health club
HQ: Equinox-76th Street, Inc.
895 Broadway Fl 3
New York NY 10003

(P-20215)
HOLMAN FAMILY COUNSELING INC (PA)
Also Called: Holman Group, The
8511 Fllbrook Ave Ste 400, West Hills (91304)
PHONE.................................818 704-1444
Ron Holman PHD, *President*
Elizabeth Holman, *President*
Jane Galvin, *Vice Pres*
Marcus Sola, *Vice Pres*
Nikkole Galvin, *Personnel Assit*
EMP: 66 EST: 1979
SALES (est): 9.6MM **Privately Held**
SIC: **8049** Clinical psychologist

(P-20216)
INLAND EMPIRE THERAPY PROVIDER (PA)
Also Called: Life Enchancing Therapies
1150 N Mountain Ave # 214, Upland (91786-3668)
PHONE.................................909 985-7905
James W Milton, *President*
EMP: 65 EST: 1997
SALES (est): 2MM **Privately Held**
SIC: **8049** Physical therapist; speech therapist; occupational therapist

(P-20217)
INLAND VALLEY PARTNERS LLC
Also Called: Inland Valley Care & Rehab Ctr
250 W Artesia St, Pomona (91768-1807)
PHONE.................................909 623-7100
Robert Nelson,
Elizabeth Casey,
Phil Chase,
Susan Chase,
EMP: 250 EST: 1998
SALES (est): 25.9MM **Privately Held**
WEB: www.inlandvalleyhopepartners.org
SIC: **8049** Nurses & other medical assistants

(P-20218)
INSTITUTE FOR APPLIED BEHAVIOR
9221 Corbin Ave, Northridge (91324-2483)
PHONE.................................818 341-1933
EMP: 84
SALES (corp-wide): 25.8MM **Privately Held**
WEB: www.iaba.com
SIC: **8049** Nutrition specialist
PA: Institute For Applied Behavior Analysis, A Psychological Corporation
5777 W Century Blvd # 675
Los Angeles CA 90045
310 649-0499

(P-20219)
INSTITUTE FOR APPLIED BEHAVIOR (PA)
Also Called: Iaba
5777 W Century Blvd # 675, Los Angeles (90045-5600)
PHONE.................................310 649-0499
Gary W Lavigna PHD, *President*
Amber Kerns, *Analyst*
Kendra Oliver, *Asst Director*
Marvin Drummond, *Supervisor*
Diana Figueroa, *Supervisor*
▲ EMP: 140 EST: 1982
SQ FT: 3,000

SALES (est): 25.8MM **Privately Held**
WEB: www.iaba.com
SIC: **8049** 8741 8093 Clinical psychologist; management services; specialty outpatient clinics

(P-20220)
INSTITUTE FOR APPLIED BEHAVIOR
Also Called: Institute Applied Bhvior Anlis
19510 Ventura Blvd # 204, Tarzana (91356-2969)
PHONE.................................818 881-1933
Fax: 818 881-1835
EMP: 61
SALES (corp-wide): 17.3MM **Privately Held**
SIC: **8049** 8322 8093 Health Practitioner's Office Individual/Family Services Specialty Outpatient Clinic
PA: Institute For Applied Behavior Analysis, A Psychological Corporation
5777 W Century Blvd # 675
Los Angeles CA 90045
310 649-0499

(P-20221)
INSTITUTE FOR APPLIED BHVIOR A
Also Called: Iaba
2310 E Ponderosa Dr Ste 1, Camarillo (93010-4747)
PHONE.................................805 987-5886
Gary Lavigna, *Director*
EMP: 84
SALES (corp-wide): 25.8MM **Privately Held**
WEB: www.iaba.com
SIC: **8049** 8399 Clinical psychologist; community development groups
PA: Institute For Applied Behavior Analysis, A Psychological Corporation
5777 W Century Blvd # 675
Los Angeles CA 90045
310 649-0499

(P-20222)
INTERCARE THERAPY INC
4221 Wilshire Blvd 300a, Los Angeles (90010-3537)
PHONE.................................323 866-1880
Naomi Heller, *President*
Eri Heller, *Vice Pres*
Simone Presley, *Program Mgr*
Fernando Martinez, *Supervisor*
EMP: 130 EST: 1979
SALES (est): 16.2MM **Privately Held**
WEB: www.intercaretherapy.com
SIC: **8049** Psychologist, psychotherapist & hypnotist; occupational therapist; speech specialist

(P-20223)
INTERFACE REHAB INC
774 S Placentia Ave # 200, Placentia (92870-6826)
PHONE.................................714 646-8300
Anant B Desai, *CEO*
Falguni Desai, *Admin Sec*
EMP: 657 EST: 1995
SQ FT: 10,000
SALES (est): 79.1MM **Privately Held**
WEB: www.interfacerehab.com
SIC: **8049** Physical therapist; speech specialist

(P-20224)
INTERGRO REHAB SERVICE
1922 N Broadway, Santa Ana (92706-2610)
PHONE.................................714 901-4200
Sherrilyn Tong, *President*
Alma Rolle, *Administration*
Masaru Okajima, *Director*
EMP: 80 EST: 1990
SQ FT: 2,000
SALES (est): 16.7MM **Privately Held**
WEB:
SIC: **8049** Physical therapist; speech specialist; occupational therapist

(P-20225)
KAISER FOUNDATION HOSPITALS
Also Called: Polk Street Offices
10689 Magnolia Ave, Riverside (92505-1879)
PHONE.................................951 353-4670
EMP: 157
SALES (corp-wide): 30.5B **Privately Held**
WEB: www.kaisercenter.com
SIC: **8049** Physical therapist
HQ: Kaiser Foundation Hospitals Inc
1 Kaiser Plz
Oakland CA 94612
510 271-6611

(P-20226)
MCHAEL G FORTANSCE PHYSCL THRA
Also Called: Fortanasce & Associates
24630 Washington Ave # 200, Murrieta (92562-6131)
P.O. Box 661150, Arcadia (91066-1150)
PHONE.................................626 446-7027
Michael Fortanasce, *President*
EMP: 120 EST: 1981
SALES (est): 6.9MM **Privately Held**
SIC: **8049** Physiotherapist; physical therapist

(P-20227)
MONTE NIDO HOLDINGS LLC
520 S Sepulveda Blvd # 208, Los Angeles (90049-3521)
PHONE.................................310 472-3728
Carolyn Costin, *Branch Mgr*
EMP: 52
SALES (corp-wide): 60MM **Privately Held**
WEB: www.montenido.com
SIC: **8049** Clinical psychologist
PA: Monte Nido Holdings, Llc
6100 Sw 76th St
South Miami FL 33143
310 457-9958

(P-20228)
MYNELA LLC
Also Called: Mynela Staffing
1025 W 190th St Ste 220, Gardena (90248-4332)
PHONE.................................323 522-9080
Michelle Nguyen, *CEO*
Mireya Arguelles, *President*
EMP: 50 EST: 2015
SQ FT: 1,500
SALES (est): 5.2MM **Privately Held**
WEB: www.mynela.com
SIC: **8049** 7363 7361 Physical therapist; nurses & other medical assistants; nurses, registered & practical; help supply services; employment agencies

(P-20229)
QUANTUM BHVIORAL SOLUTIONS INC (PA)
445 S Figueroa St # 3100, Los Angeles (90071-1602)
PHONE.................................626 531-6999
Gevork Gevojanyan, *Principal*
EMP: 71 EST: 2012
SALES (est): 18MM **Privately Held**
WEB:
www.quantumbehavioralsolutions.com
SIC: **8049** Clinical psychologist

(P-20230)
QUANTUM BHVIORAL SOLUTIONS INC
2400 E Katella Ave # 800, Anaheim (92806-5945)
PHONE.................................626 531-6999
Miranda Marshall, *Analyst*
EMP: 70
SALES (corp-wide): 18MM **Privately Held**
WEB:
www.quantumbehavioralsolutions.com
SIC: **8049** Clinical psychologist
PA: Quantum Behavioral Solutions, Inc.
445 S Figueroa St # 3100
Los Angeles CA 90071
626 531-6999

(P-20231)
RANCHO PHYSICAL THERAPY INC (PA)
24630 Washington Ave # 200, Murrieta (92562-6177)
PHONE.................................951 696-9353
John Waite, *CEO*
Greg Smith, *Principal*
Amy Taylor, *Office Mgr*
Bill Atkins,
Meagan Andrew, *Director*
EMP: 220 EST: 1984
SALES (est): 19.1MM **Privately Held**
WEB: www.ranchopt.com
SIC: **8049** 8093 Physical therapist; respiratory therapy clinic

(P-20232)
ROBERT BALLARD REHAB HOSPITAL (HQ)
Also Called: Ballard Rehabilitation Hosp
1760 W 16th St, San Bernardino (92411-1160)
PHONE.................................909 473-1200
Edward Palacios, *CEO*
Mary Hunt, *COO*
Ravon McDaniel, *Admin Sec*
Michelle Diaz, *Human Res Dir*
Eric Eblen, *Food Svc Dir*
▲ EMP: 136 EST: 1993
SALES (est): 22.8MM
SALES (corp-wide): 759.7MM **Privately Held**
WEB: www.vibrahealthcare.com
SIC: **8049** 8051 8069 Physical therapist; skilled nursing care facilities; specialty hospitals, except psychiatric
PA: Vibra Healthcare, Llc
4600 Lena Dr Ste 100
Mechanicsburg PA 17055
717 591-5700

(P-20233)
SERENDIPITY HEARING INC (PA)
Also Called: Sonus Hring Care Professionals
5555 Garden Grove Blvd # 200, Westminster (92683-1886)
PHONE.................................562 922-1718
Willard Gililland, *CEO*
Willard Clayton Gililland, *CEO*
EMP: 61 EST: 2010
SALES (est): 5.4MM **Privately Held**
WEB: www.serendipityhearing.com
SIC: **8049** 3842 Audiologist; hearing aids

(P-20234)
SOUTHERN CAL UNIV HLTH SCENCES
Also Called: Los Angles Cllege Chiropractic
16200 Amber Valley Dr, Whittier (90604-4051)
P.O. Box 1166 (90609-1166)
PHONE.................................562 947-8755
J Scaringe, *Exec Dir*
EMP: 50
SALES (corp-wide): 28.9MM **Privately Held**
WEB: www.scuhs.edu
SIC: **8221** 8049 University;
PA: Southern California University Of Health Sciences
16200 Amber Valley Dr
Whittier CA 90604
562 947-8755

(P-20235)
VENTURA COUNTY MEDICAL CENTER
300 Hillmont Ave, Ventura (93003-1651)
PHONE.................................805 652-6729
Myung Ryang, *Principal*
Diana Zenner, *COO*
Kimberly Milstien, *Officer*
Jason Arimura, *Pharmacy Dir*
Rebecca Macias, *Education*
EMP: 69
SALES (corp-wide): 68.6MM **Privately Held**
WEB: www.vchca.org
SIC: **8049** Clinical psychologist
PA: Ventura County Medical Center
3291 Loma Vista Rd
Ventura CA 93003
805 652-6000

8051 Skilled Nursing Facilities

(P-20236)
1135 N LEISURE CT INC
Also Called: Leisure Court Nursing Center
1135 N Leisure Ct, Anaheim (92801-2939)
PHONE..................................714 772-1353
Patricia Smith, *Director*
Aura Galindo, *Administration*
EMP: 66 EST: 1965
SQ FT: 15,000
SALES (est): 10.4MM **Privately Held**
SIC: 8051 Skilled nursing care facilities

(P-20237)
3067 ORANGE AVENUE LLC
Also Called: Anaheim Crest Nursing Center
3067 W Orange Ave, Anaheim
(92804-3156)
PHONE..................................714 827-2440
Alireza Talebi,
Roxanne Barquero, *Office Mgr*
Betsy Pascual, *Nursing Dir*
Jacob Wintner,
EMP: 60 EST: 2000
SALES (est): 12.3MM **Privately Held**
WEB: www.anaheimcrest.com
SIC: 8051 Convalescent home with contin-
uous nursing care

(P-20238)
ACCREDITED NURSING SERVICES
Also Called: Accredited Nursing Care
80 S Lake Ave Ste 630, Pasadena
(91101-4971)
PHONE..................................626 573-1234
Teresa Salvino, *Manager*
EMP: 222
SALES (corp-wide): 16.8MM **Privately
Held**
WEB: www.accreditednursing.com
SIC: 8051 Skilled nursing care facilities
PA: Accredited Nursing Services
17141 Ventura Blvd # 201
Encino CA
818 986-6017

(P-20239)
AHMC GARFIELD MEDICAL CTR LP
525 N Garfield Ave, Monterey Park
(91754-1202)
PHONE..................................626 573-2222
Patrick Petre, *CEO*
Jose Reyes,
Steve Maekewa, *Partner*
Erik Jiang, *Officer*
Stanley Toy Jr, *Officer*
EMP: 150 EST: 1997
SALES (est): 110.3MM
SALES (corp-wide): 574.5MM **Privately
Held**
WEB: www.garfieldmedicalcenter.com
SIC: 8051 8062 Skilled nursing care facili-
ties; general medical & surgical hospitals
PA: Ahmc Healthcare Inc.
506 W Valley Blvd Ste 300
San Gabriel CA 91776
626 943-7526

(P-20240)
AIR FORCE VILLAGE WEST INC
Also Called: Village West Health Center
17050 Arnold Dr, Riverside (92518-2806)
PHONE..................................951 697-2000
Mary Carruthers, *CEO*
Ervin Reed, *CFO*
Charles Dalton, *Vice Pres*
Ruby Duque, *Social Dir*
Veronica Silva, *Human Res Dir*
EMP: 350 EST: 1985
SQ FT: 494,000
SALES (est): 5.7MM **Privately Held**
WEB: www.westmontliving.com
SIC: 8051 8052 Convalescent home with
continuous nursing care; intermediate
care facilities

(P-20241)
ALAMITOS-BELMONT REHAB INC
Also Called: Alamitos Blmont Rhblttion Hosp
3901 E 4th St, Long Beach (90814-1632)
PHONE..................................562 434-8421
Shaun Dahl, *Administration*
Elsa Santillano, *Records Dir*
Darian Dahl, *Administration*
Chona Rodriguez, *Human Res Dir*
Rose Posadas, *Nursing Dir*
EMP: 150 EST: 1969
SQ FT: 30,000
SALES (est): 10.5MM **Privately Held**
WEB: www.alamitosbelmont.com
SIC: 8051 Skilled nursing care facilities;
convalescent home with continuous nurs-
ing care

(P-20242)
AMADA ENTERPRISES INC
Also Called: View Heights Convalescent Hosp
12619 Avalon Blvd, Los Angeles
(90061-2727)
PHONE..................................323 757-1881
Shedrick D Jones, *CEO*
John Jones, *Administration*
Brizeida Martinez, *Clerk*
EMP: 135 EST: 1968
SQ FT: 36,600
SALES (est): 13.6MM **Privately Held**
WEB: www.viewheights.com
SIC: 8051 Convalescent home with contin-
uous nursing care

(P-20243)
AMERICAN RETIREMENT CORP
2107 Ocean Ave, Santa Monica
(90405-2299)
PHONE..................................310 399-3227
EMP: 121
SALES (corp-wide): 3.5B **Publicly Held**
WEB: www.brookdale.com
SIC: 8051 Skilled nursing care facilities
HQ: American Retirement Corporation
111 Westwood Pl Ste 200
Brentwood TN 37027
615 221-2250

(P-20244)
ANAHEIM HEALTHCARE CENTER LLC
501 S Beach Blvd, Anaheim (92804-1810)
PHONE..................................714 816-0540
Irv Bauman,
Michael Parker, *Office Mgr*
German Martinez, *Administration*
Michael Wexler, *Psychiatry*
Frank Johnson,
EMP: 78 EST: 1995
SALES (est): 23.9MM **Privately Held**
WEB: www.anaheimhealthcare.com
SIC: 8051 Convalescent home with contin-
uous nursing care

(P-20245)
ANTELOPE VLY RETIREMENT HM INC
Also Called: Antelope Vly Retirement Manor
44523 15th St W, Lancaster (93534-2847)
PHONE..................................661 949-5584
Mark Aronoss, *Branch Mgr*
EMP: 214
SALES (corp-wide): 11.4MM **Privately
Held**
WEB: www.avcsnf.com
SIC: 8051 8361 Skilled nursing care facili-
ties; residential care
PA: Antelope Valley Retirement Home, Inc.
44523 15th St W
Lancaster CA 93534
661 949-5584

(P-20246)
ARCADIA CONVALESCENT HOSP INC
Also Called: Shadow Hills Convalescent
Home
10158 Sunland Blvd, Sunland
(91040-1651)
PHONE..................................818 352-4438
Orlando Clarizio, *Administration*
EMP: 74

SALES (corp-wide): 11.7MM **Privately
Held**
SIC: 8051 Convalescent home with contin-
uous nursing care
PA: Arcadia Convalescent Hospital, Inc.
1601 S Baldwin Ave
Arcadia CA 91007
626 445-2170

(P-20247)
ASH HOLDINGS LLC
Also Called: Redlands Healthcare Center
1620 W Fern Ave, Redlands (92373-4918)
PHONE..................................909 793-2600
Novie Sitanggang, *Mng Member*
EMP: 85 EST: 1999
SALES (est): 8.9MM **Privately Held**
WEB: www.redlandshealthcarecenter.com
SIC: 8051 Skilled nursing care facilities

(P-20248)
ASTORIA CONVALESCENT HOSPITAL
Also Called: Astoria Nursing & Rehab Center
14040 Astoria St, Sylmar (91342-2998)
PHONE..................................818 367-5881
Grace Mercado, *Exec Dir*
EMP: 90 EST: 1969
SQ FT: 50,000
SALES (est): 2.2MM **Privately Held**
WEB: www.astorianrc.com
SIC: 8051 8059 8322 Convalescent home
with continuous nursing care; convales-
cent home; rehabilitation services

(P-20249)
ATHERTON BAPTIST HOMES
214 S Atlantic Blvd, Alhambra
(91801-3298)
PHONE..................................626 863-1710
Craig Statton, *President*
Jessica Litchfield, *Volunteer Dir*
Dennis E McFadden, *President*
Jackie Pascual, *CFO*
Dale Torry, *Vice Pres*
EMP: 200 EST: 1914
SQ FT: 42,000
SALES: 23.3MM **Privately Held**
WEB: www.abh.org
SIC: 8051 Convalescent home with contin-
uous nursing care; extended care facility

(P-20250)
ATLANTIC MEM HEALTHCARE ASSOC (PA)
Also Called: Atlantic Mem Healthcare Ctr
2750 Atlantic Ave, Long Beach
(90806-2713)
PHONE..................................562 424-8101
Jake Rothey, *Administration*
Gladys Valenzuela, *Records Dir*
Brenda Parker, *Office Mgr*
April Infante, *Marketing Staff*
Josephine Flores, *Food Svc Dir*
EMP: 75 EST: 2002
SALES (est): 11MM **Privately Held**
WEB: www.atlanticmemorial.com
SIC: 8051 Convalescent home with contin-
uous nursing care

(P-20251)
BAKERSFIELD HEALTHCARE
Also Called: Rehablttion Cntre of Bkrsfield
2211 Mount Vernon Ave, Bakersfield
(93306-3309)
PHONE..................................661 872-2121
EMP: 99
SALES (est): 2.6MM **Privately Held**
SIC: 8051 Skilled Nursing Care Facilities,
Nsk

(P-20252)
BAYSHORE HEALTHCARE INC
Also Called: Bella Vsta Trnstional Care Ctr
3033 Augusta St, San Luis Obispo
(93401-5820)
PHONE..................................805 544-5100
Benjamin Flinders, *CEO*
Paul McLean, *CFO*
Johannah Tamba, *Administration*
EMP: 160 EST: 1975
SQ FT: 43,000
SALES (est): 9.4MM **Privately Held**
SIC: 8051 Convalescent home with contin-
uous nursing care

(P-20253)
BELL VILLA CARE ASSOCIATES LLC
Also Called: Rose Villa Healthcare Center
9028 Rose St, Bellflower (90706-6418)
PHONE..................................562 925-4252
David Howell, *Exec Dir*
EMP: 95 EST: 2003
SALES (est): 2.7MM **Privately Held**
SIC: 8051 Convalescent home with contin-
uous nursing care

(P-20254)
BEVERLY WEST HEALTH CARE INC
1020 S Fairfax Ave, Los Angeles
(90019-4401)
PHONE..................................323 938-2451
Louise Koss, *President*
Lydia Cruz, *President*
EMP: 85 EST: 1981
SQ FT: 23,848
SALES (est): 8.7MM **Privately Held**
SIC: 8051 Convalescent home with contin-
uous nursing care

(P-20255)
BIJOU HEALTHCARE INC
29222 Rncho Vejo Rd Ste 1, San Juan
Capistrano (92675)
PHONE..................................949 487-9500
EMP: 63
SALES (est): 82.9K
SALES (corp-wide): 2.4B **Publicly Held**
SIC: 8051 Skilled Nursing Care Facilities,
Nsk
PA: The Ensign Group Inc
29222 Rncho Vejo Rd Ste 1
San Juan Capistrano CA 92675
949 487-9500

(P-20256)
BISHOP CARE CENTER
151 Pioneer Ln, Bishop (93514-2557)
PHONE..................................760 872-1000
Steve Hendrickson, *CEO*
Bill Adams, *Administration*
Ethan Flake, *Administration*
Mary Chesler, *Director*
Sergio Hernandez, *Director*
EMP: 76 EST: 2003
SALES (est): 7MM **Privately Held**
WEB: www.bishopcarecenter.com
SIC: 8051 Skilled nursing care facilities

(P-20257)
BRASWLLS MDTERRANEAN GRDNS INC
Also Called: Braswell Ivy Retreat
2278 Nice Ave, Mentone (92359-9655)
PHONE..................................909 794-1189
Jan Alexander, *Director*
James Braswell, *CTO*
Maryann Shadwick, *Director*
EMP: 59
SALES (corp-wide): 11.3MM **Privately
Held**
SIC: 8051 Convalescent home with contin-
uous nursing care
PA: Braswell's Mediterranean Gardens, Inc.
12295 4th St
Yucaipa CA 92399
909 797-1131

(P-20258)
BRASWLLS MDTERRANEAN GRDNS INC
620 E Highland Ave, Redlands
(92374-6231)
PHONE..................................909 793-0433
Janie Hesner, *Manager*
EMP: 59
SALES (corp-wide): 11.8MM **Privately
Held**
SIC: 8051 Skilled nursing care facilities
PA: Braswell's Mediterranean Gardens, Inc.
12295 4th St
Yucaipa CA 92399
909 797-1131

(P-20259)
BRASWLLS MDTERRANEAN GRDNS INC
Also Called: Braswells Chateau Villa
620 E Highland Ave, San Bernardino (92404-4004)
PHONE.....................909 793-0433
Collete Schacht, *Manager*
EMP: 59
SALES (corp-wide): 11.8MM **Privately Held**
SIC: 8051 Skilled nursing care facilities
PA: Braswell's Mediterranean Gardens, Inc.
12295 4th St
Yucaipa CA 92399
909 797-1131

(P-20260)
BRASWLLS MDTERRANEAN GRDNS INC
Also Called: Braswells Yucaipa Leisre Manor
32195 Avenue E, Yucaipa (92399-1731)
PHONE.....................909 797-1314
Janet Piccinati, *Branch Mgr*
Linda Woofter, *Director*
EMP: 59
SALES (corp-wide): 11.8MM **Privately Held**
SIC: 8051 Skilled nursing care facilities
PA: Braswell's Mediterranean Gardens, Inc.
12295 4th St
Yucaipa CA 92399
909 797-1131

(P-20261)
BRASWLLS MDTERRANEAN GRDNS INC
Also Called: Hospital
13542 2nd St, Yucaipa (92399-5396)
PHONE.....................909 795-2421
Betty Dennett, *Director*
Dorinda Stottlemyer, *Info Tech Mgr*
EMP: 59
SALES (corp-wide): 11.8MM **Privately Held**
SIC: 8051 Skilled nursing care facilities
PA: Braswell's Mediterranean Gardens, Inc.
12295 4th St
Yucaipa CA 92399
909 797-1131

(P-20262)
BRASWLLS MDTERRANEAN GRDNS INC
Also Called: Braswlls Ycipa Vly Cnvlscent H
35253 Avenue H, Yucaipa (92399-5415)
PHONE.....................909 795-2476
Jennifer Suniega, *Manager*
EMP: 59
SALES (corp-wide): 11.8MM **Privately Held**
SIC: 8051 Skilled nursing care facilities
PA: Braswell's Mediterranean Gardens, Inc.
12295 4th St
Yucaipa CA 92399
909 797-1131

(P-20263)
BRIARCREST NURSING CENTER INC
5648 Gotham St, Bell (90201-5413)
PHONE.....................562 927-2641
Jack Silverman, *President*
Wilson Park, *CFO*
Lisa Turner, *Hlthcr Dir*
EMP: 56 EST: 1994
SALES (est): 6.9MM **Privately Held**
WEB: www.briarcrestnursing.com
SIC: 8051 Convalescent home with continuous nursing care

(P-20264)
BRIDGESTONE LIVING LLC
27101 Puerta Real Ste 450, Mission Viejo (92691-8566)
PHONE.....................949 487-9500
John Gurrieri, *President*
EMP: 68 EST: 2014
SALES (est): 6.2MM
SALES (corp-wide): 2.4B **Publicly Held**
WEB: www.ensigngroup.net
SIC: 8051 Skilled nursing care facilities

PA: The Ensign Group Inc
29222 Rncho Vejo Rd Ste 1
San Juan Capistrano CA 92675
949 487-9500

(P-20265)
BROOKDALE BREA
285 W Central Ave, Brea (92821-3374)
PHONE.....................714 706-9968
Chuck Uceusa, *Exec Dir*
EMP: 50 EST: 2015
SALES (est): 1MM **Privately Held**
SIC: 8051 Skilled nursing care facilities

(P-20266)
BUENA VENTURA CARE CENTER INC (PA)
1016 S Record Ave, Los Angeles (90023-2533)
PHONE.....................323 268-0106
Vernon Aguirre, *Administration*
Steve Keh, *Vice Pres*
EMP: 75 EST: 1971
SQ FT: 15,000
SALES (est): 6.6MM **Privately Held**
WEB: www.buenaventurarehab.com
SIC: 8051 Convalescent home with continuous nursing care

(P-20267)
BURLINGTON CONVALESCENT HOSP (PA)
Also Called: View Park Convalescent Center
845 S Burlington Ave, Los Angeles (90057-4296)
PHONE.....................213 381-5585
Jacob Friedman, *President*
Ervin Friedman, *Vice Pres*
Kathleen Becker, *Administration*
EMP: 100 EST: 1967
SQ FT: 5,000
SALES (est): 10.9MM **Privately Held**
SIC: 8051 8059 8052 Convalescent home with continuous nursing care; convalescent home; intermediate care facilities

(P-20268)
BURLINGTON CONVALESCENT HOSP
Also Called: View Park Convalescent Center
3737 Don Felipe Dr, Los Angeles (90008-4210)
PHONE.....................323 295-7737
Joe Voltes, *Manager*
Dalia Sor, *Records Dir*
Sheila Beckom, *Social Dir*
Roldan Rapisora, *Education*
Patricia Chavez, *Food Svc Dir*
EMP: 179
SQ FT: 40,000
SALES (corp-wide): 10.9MM **Privately Held**
SIC: 8051 Convalescent home with continuous nursing care
PA: Burlington Convalescent Hospital
845 S Burlington Ave
Los Angeles CA 90057
213 381-5585

(P-20269)
CALIFORNIA CONVALESCENT HOSP
Also Called: Santa Barbara Convalescent Ctr
2225 De La Vina St, Santa Barbara (93105-3815)
PHONE.....................805 682-1355
Dorothy Shea, *President*
Laurie Shea, *President*
Roger Shea, *Treasurer*
S Laurie Anderson, *Admin Sec*
Kathleen Shea, *Admin Sec*
EMP: 56 EST: 1960
SQ FT: 25,000
SALES (est): 9.3MM **Privately Held**
WEB: www.californiancare.com
SIC: 8051 Convalescent home with continuous nursing care

(P-20270)
CALIFORNIA DEPT OF PUB HLTH
681 S Parker St Ste 200, Orange (92868-4719)
PHONE.....................714 567-2906
Jacqueline Lincer, *Branch Mgr*

Marivn Agustin, *Admin Sec*
Tom Ahrens, *Planning*
EMP: 95 **Privately Held**
WEB: www.cdph.ca.gov
SIC: 9199 8051 ; extended care facility
HQ: The California Department Of Public Health
1615 Capitol Ave
Sacramento CA 95814
916 558-1784

(P-20271)
CALIFRNIA NRSING RHBLTTION CTR
Also Called: Califrnia Nrsing Rhblttion Ctr
2299 N Indian Ave, Palm Springs (92262)
PHONE.....................760 325-2937
Kennon Shea, *Administration*
Victoria Shea, *Treasurer*
Linda Jackson, *Administration*
Shlomo Rechnitz,
EMP: 66 EST: 1965
SQ FT: 22,000
SALES (est): 21.2MM **Privately Held**
WEB: www.californianursingrc.com
SIC: 8051 Convalescent home with continuous nursing care

(P-20272)
CALIMESA OPERATIONS LLC
Also Called: Calimesa Post Acute
13542 2nd St, Yucaipa (92399-5396)
PHONE.....................909 795-2421
Jordan Thompson,
Covey Christensen,
EMP: 105 EST: 2015
SALES (est): 9.9MM **Privately Held**
SIC: 8051 Skilled nursing care facilities

(P-20273)
CAMBRIDGE SIERRA HOLDINGS LLC
Also Called: Reche Cyn Regional Rehab Ctr
1350 Reche Canyon Rd, Colton (92324-9528)
PHONE.....................909 370-4411
RB Bridges, *CEO*
EMP: 350 EST: 1991
SALES (est): 25.9MM **Privately Held**
SIC: 8051 Convalescent home with continuous nursing care

(P-20274)
CAMELLIA GARDENS CARE CTR
Also Called: Camellia Gardens Care Center
1920 N Fair Oaks Ave, Pasadena (91103-1623)
PHONE.....................626 798-6777
EMP: 80
SALES: 8.3MM **Privately Held**
SIC: 8051 Skilled Nursing Care Facility

(P-20275)
CARE TECH INC
Also Called: Hill Cress Home
4280 Cypress Dr, San Bernardino (92407-2960)
PHONE.....................909 882-2965
Carol Dichman, *Administration*
James Fitzgerald, *Vice Pres*
Annette Elchert, *Executive*
Thelma Benison, *Admin Asst*
Gowri Kunda, *Administration*
EMP: 50
SALES (corp-wide): 10.4MM **Privately Held**
WEB: www.caretech.com
SIC: 8051 Skilled nursing care facilities
PA: Care Tech, Inc.
401 N Central Ave Ste B
Upland CA 91786
909 373-3766

(P-20276)
CASTLE PEAK RESOURCES LLC
1000 Town Center Dr Fl 6, Oxnard (93036-1132)
PHONE.....................805 535-2000
Andrew Prestridge, *Manager*
EMP: 50 **Privately Held**
SIC: 8051 Skilled nursing care facilities

PA: Castle Peak Resources Llc
8401 N Central Expy # 525
Dallas TX 75225

(P-20277)
CEDAR HOLDINGS LLC
Also Called: Highland Palms Healthcare Ctr
7534 Palm Ave, Highland (92346-3736)
PHONE.....................909 862-0611
Ryan McCook, *Mng Member*
Myrna De Guzman,
Paul Hubbard,
EMP: 99 EST: 2001
SALES (est): 10.2MM **Privately Held**
WEB: www.highlandpalmshc.com
SIC: 8051 Convalescent home with continuous nursing care

(P-20278)
CEDAR OPERATIONS LLC
Also Called: Cedar Mountain Post Acute
11970 4th St, Yucaipa (92399-2720)
PHONE.....................909 790-2273
Covey Christensen,
EMP: 140 EST: 2001
SALES (est): 19.2MM
SALES (corp-wide): 26.6MM **Privately Held**
WEB: www.madison-creek-partners-llc.business.site
SIC: 8051 Skilled nursing care facilities
PA: Madison Creek Partners, Llc
26522 La Alameda Ste 300
Mission Viejo CA 92691
949.449-2500

(P-20279)
CENTURY SKILL CARE
Also Called: Century Skilled Nursing Care
301 Centinela Ave, Inglewood (90302-3231)
PHONE.....................310 672-1012
Oscar Parel, *Exec Dir*
Christopher Arias, *Administration*
Evangeline Estavillo, *Nursing Dir*
EMP: 52 EST: 2004
SALES (est): 3.5MM **Privately Held**
SIC: 8051 Skilled nursing care facilities

(P-20280)
CHAPMAN HBR SKLLED NRSING CARE
Also Called: Chapmn-Hrbor Sklled Nrsing Ctr
12232 Chapman Ave, Garden Grove (92840-3717)
PHONE.....................714 971-5517
Lydia Goodell, *President*
Aaron Victor, *President*
EMP: 55 EST: 1969
SQ FT: 15,000
SALES (est): 8.2MM **Privately Held**
WEB: www.chapmancare.com
SIC: 8051 Convalescent home with continuous nursing care

(P-20281)
CHRISTIAN ATASCADERO HOME
Also Called: COUNTY CARE COVELECEST HOSPITA
611 Hollyhock Ln, Templeton (93465-9614)
PHONE.....................805 466-0281
Paul Simpson, *President*
Bill Zeiders, *Treasurer*
Jessica Guerrero, *Manager*
EMP: 51 EST: 1960
SQ FT: 10,000
SALES (est): 8.4MM **Privately Held**
WEB: www.atascaderocc.org
SIC: 8051 8059 Skilled nursing care facilities; nursing home, except skilled & intermediate care facility

(P-20282)
CLARA BLDWIN STCKER HM FOR WME
527 S Valinda Ave, West Covina (91790-3008)
PHONE.....................626 962-7151
Laura Qualls, *Administration*
Barabara Giesa, *Trustee*
Alfred Giese, *Trustee*
Ann Koecritz, *Trustee*
Ann E Koeckritz, *Administration*

PRODUCTS & SVCS

EMP: 50 **EST:** 1963
SQ FT: 12,218
SALES: 3.8MM **Privately Held**
WEB: www.clarabaldwinstocker.com
SIC: 8051 Skilled nursing care facilities

(P-20283)
COASTAL HEALTH CARE INC
Also Called: Brentwood Health Care Center
1321 Franklin St, Santa Monica
(90404-2603)
PHONE..............................310 828-5596
John Sorensen, *President*
Marlo Ilagan, *Records Dir*
Tim Paulsen, *Exec VP*
Pauline Martin, *Human Res Dir*
Jessica Kari, *Rector*
EMP: 75 **EST:** 1987
SALES: 10.9MM **Privately Held**
WEB: www.brentwoodnursing.com
SIC: 8051 Convalescent home with contin-
uous nursing care

(P-20284)
COMPASS HEALTH INC
Also Called: Compas Health
290 Heather Ct, Templeton (93465-9738)
PHONE..............................805 434-3035
Mark Woolpert, *President*
Kim Elliott, *Executive*
Martrise Austin, *Education*
Amy Fanning, *Education*
Christine Chavez, *Asst Director*
EMP: 174 **Privately Held**
WEB: www.compass-health.com
SIC: 8051 Convalescent home with contin-
uous nursing care
PA: Compass Health, Inc.
200 S 13th St Ste 208
Grover Beach CA 93433

(P-20285)
COMPASS HEALTH INC
Also Called: Alto Lucero Transitional Care
3880 Via Lucero, Santa Barbara
(93110-1605)
PHONE..............................805 687-6651
Kirk Klotthor, *Administration*
Darren Smith, *CEO*
Roslyn Payne, *Office Mgr*
Annette Gonzales, *Food Svc Dir*
EMP: 174 **Privately Held**
WEB: www.compass-health.com
SIC: 8051 Convalescent home with contin-
uous nursing care
PA: Compass Health, Inc.
200 S 13th St Ste 208
Grover Beach CA 93433

(P-20286)
COMPASS HEALTH INC
Also Called: Mission View Health Center
1425 Woodside Dr, San Luis Obispo
(93401-5936)
PHONE..............................805 543-0210
Linda Lindsey, *Manager*
Kim Hyde, *Education*
EMP: 174 **Privately Held**
WEB: www.compass-health.com
SIC: 8051 Skilled nursing care facilities
PA: Compass Health, Inc.
200 S 13th St Ste 208
Grover Beach CA 93433

(P-20287)
COMPASS HEALTH INC
Also Called: Bayside Care Center
1405 Teresa Dr, Morro Bay (93442-2457)
PHONE..............................805 772-7372
Harold Carder, *Manager*
Cindi Murray, *Social Dir*
Rebecca Nolan, *Office Mgr*
Erica Gomez, *Human Res Dir*
ERA-Lynn Ridge, *Chf Purch Ofc*
EMP: 174 **Privately Held**
WEB: www.compass-health.com
SIC: 8051 Skilled nursing care facilities
PA: Compass Health, Inc.
200 S 13th St Ste 208
Grover Beach CA 93433

(P-20288)
COMPASS HEALTH INC
Also Called: Arroyo Grande Care Center
1212 Farroll Ave, Arroyo Grande
(93420-3718)
PHONE..............................805 489-8137
Harold Carder, *Administration*
Darren Smith, *COO*
Cecilia Hernandez, *Human Res Dir*
Tammy Risner, *Food Svc Dir*
Rosie Moreno, *Hlthcr Dir*
EMP: 174 **Privately Held**
WEB: www.compass-health.com
SIC: 8051 Skilled nursing care facilities
PA: Compass Health, Inc.
200 S 13th St Ste 208
Grover Beach CA 93433

(P-20289)
COMPASS HEALTH INC
Also Called: Danish Care Center
10805 El Camino Real, Atascadero
(93422-8868)
PHONE..............................805 466-9254
Mark Woolpert, *President*
Sheila Brown, *Records Dir*
Sharon Ray, *Office Mgr*
Linda Lindsay, *Administration*
Marissa Pickens, *Administration*
EMP: 174 **Privately Held**
WEB: www.compass-health.com
SIC: 8051 Skilled nursing care facilities
PA: Compass Health, Inc.
200 S 13th St Ste 208
Grover Beach CA 93433

(P-20290)
CONGAREE HEALTH HOLDINGS LLC
29222 Rncho Vejo Rd Ste 1, San Juan
Capistrano (92675)
PHONE..............................949 487-9500
EMP: 60 **EST:** 2015
SALES (est): 5.4MM
SALES (corp-wide): 2.4B **Publicly Held**
WEB: www.ensigngroup.net
SIC: 8051 Skilled nursing care facilities
PA: The Ensign Group Inc
29222 Rncho Vejo Rd Ste 1
San Juan Capistrano CA 92675
949 487-9500

(P-20291)
CORECARE V A CAL LTD PARTNR
Also Called: Park Vista At Morningside
2525 Brea Blvd, Fullerton (92835-2787)
PHONE..............................714 256-1000
Gary R Stork, *Principal*
Melody Olmstead, *Controller*
Jennifer Martinez, *Education*
Karrie Castles, *Food Svc Dir*
EMP: 101 **EST:** 1992
SALES (est): 11.2MM **Privately Held**
WEB: www.parkvista.net
SIC: 8051 Convalescent home with contin-
uous nursing care

(P-20292)
COUNTRY OAKS CARE CENTER INC
830 E Chapel St, Santa Maria
(93454-4699)
PHONE..............................805 922-6657
John Henning, *President*
Sharon Henning, *Principal*
Geraldine Bombard, *Marketing Staff*
Patricia Penrod, *Asst Mgr*
EMP: 70 **EST:** 1968
SQ FT: 14,000
SALES (est): 4.4MM **Privately Held**
WEB: www.countryoakscarecenter.com
SIC: 8051 Convalescent home with contin-
uous nursing care

(P-20293)
COUNTRY VILLA NURSING CTR INC
Also Called: Country Vlla Nrsing Rhbltttion
340 S Alvarado St, Los Angeles
(90057-2915)
PHONE..............................213 484-9730
Stephen Reissman, *CEO*

Steven Reissman, *CEO*
Diane Reissman, *Senior VP*
Eddie Rowles, *Vice Pres*
EMP: 125 **EST:** 1990
SQ FT: 18,000
SALES (est): 9.5MM **Privately Held**
WEB: www.losangelesrehabhc.com
SIC: 8051 Convalescent home with contin-
uous nursing care

(P-20294)
COUNTRY VILLA SERVICE CORP
1208 S Central Ave, Glendale
(91204-2504)
PHONE..............................818 246-5516
Adam Mitchel, *Administration*
Laila Hanna, *Director*
EMP: 206
SALES (corp-wide): 78.2MM **Privately
Held**
SIC: 8051 Skilled nursing care facilities
PA: Country Villa Service Corp.
2400 E Katella Ave # 800
Anaheim CA 92806
310 574-3733

(P-20295)
COUNTRY VILLA SERVICE CORP
400 W Huntington Dr, Arcadia
(91007-3470)
PHONE..............................626 445-2421
Shelly Andresen, *Principal*
Anita Perez, *Director*
EMP: 206
SALES (corp-wide): 78.2MM **Privately
Held**
WEB: www.huntingtondrivehcc.com
SIC: 8051 Skilled nursing care facilities
PA: Country Villa Service Corp.
2400 E Katella Ave # 800
Anaheim CA 92806
310 574-3733

(P-20296)
COUNTRY VILLA SERVICE CORP
3611 E Imperial Hwy, Lynwood
(90262-2608)
PHONE..............................310 537-2500
Jacob Wintner, *Branch Mgr*
EMP: 206
SALES (corp-wide): 78.2MM **Privately
Held**
SIC: 8051 Skilled nursing care facilities
PA: Country Villa Service Corp.
2400 E Katella Ave # 800
Anaheim CA 92806
310 574-3733

(P-20297)
COVENANT CARE CALIFORNIA LLC
Also Called: Royal Care Skilled Nursing Ctr
2725 Pacific Ave, Long Beach
(90806-2612)
PHONE..............................562 427-7493
Nasreen Pervaiz, *Branch Mgr*
Djuan Jester, *Director*
EMP: 55 **Privately Held**
WEB: www.covenantcare.com
SIC: 8051 Convalescent home with contin-
uous nursing care
HQ: Covenant Care California, Llc
120 Vantis Dr Ste 200
Aliso Viejo CA 92656

(P-20298)
COVENANT CARE CALIFORNIA LLC
Also Called: Shoreline Care Center
5225 S J St, Oxnard (93033-8320)
PHONE..............................805 488-3696
Cindy Poulsen, *Exec Dir*
Florence Gapasin, *Records Dir*
Krystine Morales, *Human Res Dir*
Juanito Joseph, *Maint Spvr*
Nina Ebete, *Director*
EMP: 55 **Privately Held**
WEB: www.covenantcare.com
SIC: 8051 Convalescent home with contin-
uous nursing care
HQ: Covenant Care California, Llc
120 Vantis Dr Ste 200
Aliso Viejo CA 92656

(P-20299)
COVENANT CARE CALIFORNIA LLC
Also Called: Huntington Park Nursing Center
6425 Miles Ave, Huntington Park
(90255-4315)
PHONE..............................323 589-5941
Toni Mazzeo, *Branch Mgr*
Michelle Solorio, *Business Dir*
EMP: 55 **Privately Held**
WEB: www.covenantcare.com
SIC: 8051 Convalescent home with contin-
uous nursing care
HQ: Covenant Care California, Llc
120 Vantis Dr Ste 200
Aliso Viejo CA 92656

(P-20300)
COVENANT CARE CALIFORNIA LLC
Also Called: Buena Vista Care Center
160 S Patterson Ave, Santa Barbara
(93111-2006)
PHONE..............................805 964-4871
David Hibarger, *Branch Mgr*
Jeannette Lopez, *Records Dir*
Ethel Thomas, *Exec Dir*
Jaime Mejia, *Office Mgr*
Michael Malloy, *Business Anlyst*
EMP: 55 **Privately Held**
WEB: www.covenantcare.com
SIC: 8051 Convalescent home with contin-
uous nursing care
HQ: Covenant Care California, Llc
120 Vantis Dr Ste 200
Aliso Viejo CA 92656

(P-20301)
COVENANT CARE CALIFORNIA LLC (HQ)
120 Vantis Dr Ste 200, Aliso Viejo
(92656-2677)
PHONE..............................949 349-1200
Robert Levin, *President*
Miriam Orozco, *Records Dir*
Dalia Velasquez, *Records Dir*
Mary A Evans, *COO*
Christine Sims, *CFO*
EMP: 50 **EST:** 1994
SQ FT: 10,000
SALES (est): 551.4MM **Privately Held**
WEB: www.covenantcare.com
SIC: 8051 Convalescent home with contin-
uous nursing care

(P-20302)
COVENANT CARE CALIFORNIA LLC
Also Called: St. Edna Sb-Cute Rhbltttion Ctr
1929 N Fairview St, Santa Ana
(92706-2205)
PHONE..............................714 554-9700
Joshua Torres, *Manager*
Donna Durkin, *Office Mgr*
Edna Zarco, *Director*
EMP: 55 **Privately Held**
WEB: www.covenantcare.com
SIC: 8051 Convalescent home with contin-
uous nursing care
HQ: Covenant Care California, Llc
120 Vantis Dr Ste 200
Aliso Viejo CA 92656

(P-20303)
COVENANT CARE DUBUQUE LLC
120 Vantis Dr Ste 200, Aliso Viejo
(92656-2677)
PHONE..............................949 349-1200
Christine M Sims,
Robert A Levin,
Christine Sims,
Andrew F Torok,
EMP: 66 **EST:** 2010
SALES (est): 6.6MM **Privately Held**
WEB: www.covenantcare.com
SIC: 8051 Convalescent home with contin-
uous nursing care
HQ: Covenant Care California, Llc
120 Vantis Dr Ste 200
Aliso Viejo CA 92656

(P-20304)
COVENANT RTIREMENT COMMUNITIES
2550 Treasure Dr, Santa Barbara (93105-4148)
PHONE..............................805 687-0701
Rick K Fisk, *President*
EMP: 100 **Privately Held**
WEB: www.covliving.org
SIC: 8051 Skilled nursing care facilities
HQ: Covenant Living West
5700 Old Orchard Rd # 10
Skokie IL 60077

(P-20305)
COVENTRY COURT HEALTH CENTER
2040 S Euclid St, Anaheim (92802-3111)
PHONE..............................714 636-2800
Saun Dohl, *CEO*
Shaun Dahl, *Administration*
Jeffery Deguzman, *Software Dev*
Charisse Gamboa, *Marketing Mgr*
Erin Hawley, *Marketing Staff*
EMP: 200
SALES: 13MM **Privately Held**
WEB: www.coventrycourt.org
SIC: 8051 Skilled nursing care facilities

(P-20306)
COVINA REHABILITATION CENTER
Also Called: Regency Health Services
261 W Badillo St, Covina (91723-1907)
PHONE..............................626 967-3874
Teresa Dearmond, *Director*
Agnes Maron, *Director*
EMP: 110 **EST:** 1971
SQ FT: 27,800
SALES (est): 11.6MM **Privately Held**
SIC: 8051 Skilled nursing care facilities

(P-20307)
CRESTWOOD BEHAVIORAL HLTH INC
Also Called: 1170 Lompoc Mhrc
303 S C St, Lompoc (93436-7305)
PHONE..............................805 308-8720
Marc Sabi, *Branch Mgr*
EMP: 85
SALES (corp-wide): 238MM **Privately Held**
WEB: www.crestwoodbehavioralhealth.com
SIC: 8051 Skilled nursing care facilities
PA: Crestwood Behavioral Health, Inc.
520 Capitol Mall Ste 800
Sacramento CA 95814
510 651-1244

(P-20308)
DEL AMO GRDNS CNVLSCENT HOSP S
Also Called: Del AMO Grdns Cnvalescent Hosp
22419 Kent Ave, Torrance (90505-2303)
PHONE..............................310 378-4233
Morris Weiss, *President*
Barry Weiss, *Vice Pres*
Daniella Gonzalez, *Office Mgr*
Harry Jacobs, *Admin Sec*
Michael Gruenbaum, *Director*
EMP: 85 **EST:** 1960
SQ FT: 21,298
SALES (est): 13.6MM **Privately Held**
WEB: www.delamogardens.com
SIC: 8051 Convalescent home with continuous nursing care

(P-20309)
DEL RIO SANITARIUM INC
Also Called: Del Rio Convalescent
7002 Gage Ave, Bell Gardens (90201-2014)
PHONE..............................562 927-6586
Joy Thune, *President*
EMP: 150 **EST:** 1963
SALES (est): 11.3MM **Privately Held**
SIC: 8051 Skilled nursing care facilities

(P-20310)
DEL ROSA VILLA INC
2018 Del Rosa Ave, San Bernardino (92404-5642)
PHONE..............................909 885-3261
Carol Wagner, *Administration*
Thomas S Plott, *President*
Elizabeth Plott, *Corp Secy*
EMP: 85 **EST:** 1965
SQ FT: 20,000
SALES (est): 7.3MM **Privately Held**
SIC: 8051 Convalescent home with continuous nursing care

(P-20311)
DELANO DST SKLLED NRSING FCLTY
1509 Tokay St, Delano (93215-3603)
PHONE..............................661 720-2100
Dennis Karnowski, *Administration*
Janice Calzo, *Business Dir*
Michelle Alacar, *Nursing Dir*
EMP: 94 **EST:** 1991
SQ FT: 30,000
SALES (est): 10.1MM **Privately Held**
WEB: www.nksthd.org
SIC: 8051 Convalescent home with continuous nursing care

(P-20312)
DELTA NRSING RHBLTTION HOSP IN
Also Called: Delta Nrsing Rhabilitation Ctr
514 N Bridge St, Visalia (93291-5015)
PHONE..............................559 625-4003
Mark Fisher, *President*
Amanda Cooke, *Regional*
EMP: 50 **EST:** 2006
SALES (est): 6.7MM **Privately Held**
WEB: www.missioncg.com
SIC: 8051 Convalescent home with continuous nursing care

(P-20313)
DEVELOPMENTAL SVCS CAL DEPT
Also Called: Porterville Developmental Ctr
26501 Avenue 140, Porterville (93257-9109)
P.O. Box 2000 (93258-2000)
PHONE..............................559 782-2222
Theresa Villeci, *Principal*
EMP: 1800 **Privately Held**
WEB: www.ca.gov
SIC: 8051 9431 Mental retardation hospital; administration of public health programs
HQ: California Department Of Developmental Services
1215 O St
Sacramento CA 95814

(P-20314)
DIAMOND VLY HLTH HOLDINGS LLC
29222 Rncho Vejo Rd Ste 1, San Juan Capistrano (92675)
PHONE..............................949 487-9500
EMP: 60 **EST:** 2015
SALES (est): 5.4MM
SALES (corp-wide): 2.4B **Publicly Held**
WEB: www.ensigngroup.net
SIC: 8051 Skilled nursing care facilities
PA: The Ensign Group Inc
29222 Rncho Vejo Rd Ste 1
San Juan Capistrano CA 92675
949 487-9500

(P-20315)
DOUGLAS FIR HOLDINGS LLC
Also Called: Huntington Vly Healthcare Ctr
8382 Newman Ave, Huntington Beach (92647-7038)
PHONE..............................714 842-5551
Brad Truhar, *Administration*
Angie Gonzalez, *Social Dir*
EMP: 145 **EST:** 2000
SALES (est): 16.8MM **Privately Held**
WEB: www.hvhcc.com
SIC: 8051 Convalescent home with continuous nursing care

(P-20316)
DOWNEY COMMUNITY HEALTH CENTER
8425 Iowa St, Downey (90241-4929)
P.O. Box 340 (90241-0340)
PHONE..............................562 862-6506
Rich Coberly, *Administration*
Stanley Diller, *Partner*
Elsa Conv, *Office Mgr*
EMP: 175 **EST:** 1980
SQ FT: 60,000
SALES (est): 17.3MM **Privately Held**
WEB: www.downeycommunityhealthcenter.com
SIC: 8051 Convalescent home with continuous nursing care

(P-20317)
EDGEWATER CONVALESCENT HOSP
Also Called: Edgewater Skilled Nursing Ctr
2625 E 4th St, Long Beach (90814-1299)
PHONE..............................562 434-0974
Debbie Grani, *President*
Beth Rabin, *Records Dir*
Norma Cowles, *Vice Pres*
Sylvia Gandara, *Social Dir*
Joe Yu, *Office Mgr*
EMP: 66 **EST:** 1954
SQ FT: 18,000
SALES (est): 10.8MM **Privately Held**
WEB: www.edgewaterrehab.com
SIC: 8051 Convalescent home with continuous nursing care

(P-20318)
EL ENCANTO HEALTHCARE & REHAB
Also Called: EL ENCANTO HOME HEALTH CARE
555 El Encanto Rd, City of Industry (91745-1017)
PHONE..............................626 336-1274
Steve Blackwell, *Administration*
EMP: 62 **EST:** 1944
SQ FT: 70,000
SALES (est): 11.6MM **Privately Held**
WEB: www.eehc.org
SIC: 8051 Convalescent home with continuous nursing care; mental retardation hospital

(P-20319)
EL MONTE CONVALESCENT HOSPITAL
4096 Easy St, El Monte (91731-1054)
PHONE..............................626 442-1500
Jesse Telles, *CEO*
EMP: 98 **EST:** 1964
SQ FT: 21,208
SALES (est): 7.3MM **Privately Held**
WEB: www.elmonteconvalescent.com
SIC: 8051 Convalescent home with continuous nursing care

(P-20320)
EMERITUS CORPORATION
Also Called: Emeritus At San Dimas
1740 S San Dimas Ave, San Dimas (91773-5108)
PHONE..............................909 394-0304
George Dualan, *Branch Mgr*
EMP: 155
SALES (corp-wide): 3.5B **Publicly Held**
WEB: www.brookdale.com
SIC: 8051 Skilled nursing care facilities
HQ: Emeritus Corporation
6737 W Wa St Ste 2300
Milwaukee WI 53214

(P-20321)
EMERITUS CORPORATION
1001 N Lyon Ave, Hemet (92545-1753)
PHONE..............................951 744-9861
EMP: 155
SALES (corp-wide): 3.5B **Publicly Held**
WEB: www.brookdale.com
SIC: 8051 Skilled nursing care facilities
HQ: Emeritus Corporation
6737 W Wa St Ste 2300
Milwaukee WI 53214

(P-20322)
EMERITUS CORPORATION
142 S Prospect St, Orange (92869-3842)
PHONE..............................714 639-3590
Bernice Holmes, *Exec Dir*
Alysa Agan, *Director*
EMP: 155
SALES (corp-wide): 3.5B **Publicly Held**
WEB: www.brookdale.com
SIC: 8051 Skilled nursing care facilities
HQ: Emeritus Corporation
6737 W Wa St Ste 2300
Milwaukee WI 53214

(P-20323)
EMERITUS CORPORATION
Also Called: Emeritus At Casa Glendale
426 Piedmont Ave, Glendale (91206-3448)
PHONE..............................818 246-7457
David Wilkens, *Branch Mgr*
EMP: 155
SALES (corp-wide): 3.5B **Publicly Held**
WEB: www.brookdale.com
SIC: 8051 Skilled nursing care facilities
HQ: Emeritus Corporation
6737 W Wa St Ste 2300
Milwaukee WI 53214

(P-20324)
EMERITUS CORPORATION
Also Called: Emeritus At Villa Colima
19850 Colima Rd, Walnut (91789-3411)
PHONE..............................909 595-5030
Wanda Reynolds, *Branch Mgr*
EMP: 155
SALES (corp-wide): 3.5B **Publicly Held**
WEB: www.brookdale.com
SIC: 8051 Skilled nursing care facilities
HQ: Emeritus Corporation
6737 W Wa St Ste 2300
Milwaukee WI 53214

(P-20325)
EMERITUS CORPORATION
Also Called: Terrace, The
22325 Barton Rd, Grand Terrace (92313-5006)
PHONE..............................909 420-0153
Larry Smith, *Director*
EMP: 155
SALES (corp-wide): 3.5B **Publicly Held**
WEB: www.brookdale.com
SIC: 8051 Skilled nursing care facilities
HQ: Emeritus Corporation
6737 W Wa St Ste 2300
Milwaukee WI 53214

(P-20326)
ENDURA HEALTHCARE INC
29222 Rncho Vejo Rd Ste 1, San Juan Capistrano (92675)
PHONE..............................949 487-9500
EMP: 60 **EST:** 2014
SALES (est): 5.4MM
SALES (corp-wide): 2.4B **Publicly Held**
WEB: www.ensigngroup.net
SIC: 8051 Skilled nursing care facilities
PA: The Ensign Group Inc
29222 Rncho Vejo Rd Ste 1
San Juan Capistrano CA 92675
949 487-9500

(P-20327)
ENSIGN GROUP INC
340 Victoria St, Costa Mesa (92627-1914)
PHONE..............................949 642-0387
Cindy Ramirez, *Director*
EMP: 80
SALES (corp-wide): 2.4B **Publicly Held**
WEB: www.ensigngroup.net
SIC: 8051 Convalescent home with continuous nursing care
PA: The Ensign Group Inc
29222 Rncho Vejo Rd Ste 1
San Juan Capistrano CA 92675
949 487-9500

(P-20328)
ENSIGN GROUP INC
Also Called: Downey Care Center
13007 Paramount Blvd, Downey
(90242-4329)
PHONE.....................562 923-9301
Marc Brian, *Principal*
EMP: 80
SALES (corp-wide): 2.4B **Publicly Held**
WEB: www.ensigngroup.net
SIC: 8051 Convalescent home with continuous nursing care
PA: The Ensign Group Inc
29222 Rncho Vejo Rd Ste 1
San Juan Capistrano CA 92675
949 487-9500

(P-20329)
ENSIGN GROUP INC
Also Called: Panaroma Gardens
9541 Van Nuys Blvd, Panorama City
(91402-1315)
PHONE.....................818 893-6385
Alicia Gamero, *Executive*
Paloma Sanchez, *Records Dir*
Susana Sanchez, *Social Dir*
Rafael Lopez, *Office Mgr*
Manuel Sanchez, *Chf Purch Ofc*
EMP: 80
SALES (corp-wide): 2.4B **Publicly Held**
WEB: www.ensigngroup.net
SIC: 8051 Convalescent home with continuous nursing care
PA: The Ensign Group Inc
29222 Rncho Vejo Rd Ste 1
San Juan Capistrano CA 92675
949 487-9500

(P-20330)
ENSIGN GROUP INC
Also Called: Whittier Hills Health Care Ctr
10426 Bogardus Ave, Whittier
(90603-2642)
PHONE.....................562 947-7817
Lisa Matarazzo, *Administration*
Huong Butel, *Social Dir*
EMP: 80
SQ FT: 36,316
SALES (corp-wide): 2.4B **Publicly Held**
WEB: www.ensigngroup.net
SIC: 8051 8059 Convalescent home with continuous nursing care; rest home, with health care
PA: The Ensign Group Inc
29222 Rncho Vejo Rd Ste 1
San Juan Capistrano CA 92675
949 487-9500

(P-20331)
ENSIGN GROUP INC
Also Called: Mission Care Center
4800 Delta Ave, Rosemead (91770-1127)
PHONE.....................626 607-2400
Tin Nelson, *Director*
Sheila Manapat, *Human Res Dir*
Roger Nieto, *Director*
EMP: 80
SALES (corp-wide): 2.4B **Publicly Held**
WEB: www.ensigngroup.net
SIC: 8051 Convalescent home with continuous nursing care
PA: The Ensign Group Inc
29222 Rncho Vejo Rd Ste 1
San Juan Capistrano CA 92675
949 487-9500

(P-20332)
ENSIGN PALM I LLC
Also Called: Premier Care Ctr For Palm Sprn
2990 E Ramon Rd, Palm Springs
(92264-7931)
PHONE.....................760 323-2638
Soon Burnam, *Treasurer*
Donna Andres, *Office Mgr*
Leeron Hever, *Administration*
Misty Edgemon, *Train & Dev Mgr*
Carmelo Avalos, *Director*
EMP: 172 EST: 2001
SALES (est): 15.6MM
SALES (corp-wide): 2.4B **Publicly Held**
WEB: www.premiercarecenter.net
SIC: 8051 Convalescent home with continuous nursing care

PA: The Ensign Group Inc
29222 Rncho Vejo Rd Ste 1
San Juan Capistrano CA 92675
949 487-9500

(P-20333)
ENSIGN SERVICES INC
29222 Rncho Vejo Rd Ste 1, San Juan
Capistrano (92675)
PHONE.....................949 487-9500
Christopher Christensen, *CEO*
Snapper Suzanne, *CFO*
Beverly B Wittekind, *Treasurer*
Debbie Miller, *Officer*
Craig Fitch, *Vice Pres*
EMP: 90 EST: 2002
SALES (est): 8.2MM
SALES (corp-wide): 2.4B **Publicly Held**
WEB: www.ensigngroup.net
SIC: 8051 Convalescent home with continuous nursing care
PA: The Ensign Group Inc
29222 Rncho Vejo Rd Ste 1
San Juan Capistrano CA 92675
949 487-9500

(P-20334)
ENSIGN SOUTHLAND LLC
Also Called: Southland Care
29222 Rncho Vejo Rd Ste 1, San Juan
Capistrano (92675)
PHONE.....................949 487-9500
Allan Norman,
EMP: 300 EST: 2000
SALES (est): 27.3MM
SALES (corp-wide): 2.4B **Publicly Held**
WEB: www.ensigngroup.net
SIC: 8051 Extended care facility
PA: The Ensign Group Inc
29222 Rncho Vejo Rd Ste 1
San Juan Capistrano CA 92675
949 487-9500

(P-20335)
ENSIGN WHITTIER EAST LLC
Also Called: Whittier Hills Health Care Ctr
10426 Bogardus Ave, Whittier
(90603-2642)
PHONE.....................562 947-7817
Jesse Kim,
EMP: 120 EST: 2001
SALES (est): 10.9MM
SALES (corp-wide): 2.4B **Publicly Held**
WEB: www.whittierhillshealthcare.com
SIC: 8051 Convalescent home with continuous nursing care
PA: The Ensign Group Inc
29222 Rncho Vejo Rd Ste 1
San Juan Capistrano CA 92675
949 487-9500

(P-20336)
EPISCOPAL COMMUNITIES & SERVIC
Also Called: Canterbury, The
5801 Crestridge Rd, Pls Vrds Pnsl
(90275-4961)
PHONE.....................310 544-2204
Consuelo Haire, *Branch Mgr*
Sharon Pewtress, *Vice Pres*
Dave Hone, *Exec Dir*
Joann Afusia, *Director*
Diana Ernandes, *Director*
EMP: 100
SALES (corp-wide): 86.4MM **Privately Held**
WEB: www.ecsforseniors.org
SIC: 8051 8361 8059 Extended care facility; home for the aged; personal care home, with health care
PA: Episcopal Communities & Services For
Seniors
605 E Huntington Dr # 207
Monrovia CA 91016
626 403-5880

(P-20337)
ESTRELLA INC
Also Called: Woodruff Convalescent Center
1340 Highland Ave 12, Duarte
(91010-2520)
PHONE.....................562 925-6418
Liberation De Leon MD, *President*
EMP: 110 EST: 1969

SALES (est): 6.2MM **Privately Held**
SIC: 8051 Convalescent home with continuous nursing care

(P-20338)
EVERGREEN AT LAKEPORT LLC
Also Called: Evergreen Healthcare Center
6212 Tudor Way, Bakersfield (93306-7067)
PHONE.....................661 871-3133
Gloria Melliti, *Manager*
EMP: 100
SALES (corp-wide): 8.1B **Privately Held**
SIC: 8051 Convalescent home with continuous nursing care
PA: Evergreen At Lakeport Llc
1291 Craig Ave
Lakeport CA 95453
707 263-6382

(P-20339)
EVERGREEN HEALTH CARE LLC
323 Campus Dr, Arvin (93203-1047)
PHONE.....................661 854-4475
Cody Rasmussen, *Exec Dir*
Rush Melliti, *Manager*
EMP: 592 EST: 1985
SALES (est): 34.9MM
SALES (corp-wide): 5MM **Privately Held**
WEB: www.arvinpostacute.com
SIC: 8051 Convalescent home with continuous nursing care
HQ: Evergreen At Chico, L.L.C.
4601 Ne 77th Ave Ste 300
Vancouver WA 98662
530 342-4885

(P-20340)
EXTENDED CARE HOSP WESTMINSTER
206 Hospital Cir, Westminster
(92683-3910)
PHONE.....................714 891-2769
George Rhodes, *Administration*
Connie Black, *Partner*
Fred Landry, *Partner*
Mark Landry, *Partner*
Chad Wolfgang, *Technician*
EMP: 104 EST: 1977
SALES (est): 21.4MM **Privately Held**
WEB: www.westminsterec.com
SIC: 8051 8069 Convalescent home with continous nursing care; specialty hospitals, except psychiatric

(P-20341)
FAR WEST INC
Also Called: Linwood Grdns Convalescent Ctr
4444 W Meadow Ave, Visalia (93277-1652)
PHONE.....................559 627-1241
Robert Barker, *Manager*
Aaron Burrup, *Administration*
Jackie Dees, *Education*
Adam Salow, *Director*
EMP: 69 **Privately Held**
WEB: www.farwest.org
SIC: 8051 8059 Convalescent home with continuous nursing care; convalescent home
HQ: Far West, Inc.
4020 Sierra College Blvd
Rocklin CA 95677

(P-20342)
FAR WEST INC
Also Called: South Gate Care Centers
8455 State St, South Gate (90280-2339)
PHONE.....................323 564-7761
James Hagar, *Administration*
EMP: 69 **Privately Held**
WEB: www.farwest.org
SIC: 8051 8059 Convalescent home with continuous nursing care; convalescent home
HQ: Far West, Inc.
4020 Sierra College Blvd
Rocklin CA 95677

(P-20343)
FAR WEST INC
Also Called: Medical Center
467 E Gilbert St, San Bernardino
(92404-5318)
PHONE.....................909 884-4781

Frank De Leosa, *Manager*
EMP: 69 **Privately Held**
WEB: www.farwest.org
SIC: 8051 8059 Convalescent home with continuous nursing care; rest home, with health care
HQ: Far West, Inc.
4020 Sierra College Blvd
Rocklin CA 95677

(P-20344)
FH & HF-TORRANCE I LLC
Also Called: Sunnyside Nursing Center
22617 S Vermont Ave, Torrance
(90502-2550)
PHONE.....................310 320-4130
Larry Bell, *Principal*
EMP: 164 EST: 1975
SQ FT: 35,000
SALES (est): 23.6MM **Privately Held**
WEB: www.sunnysidenursing.com
SIC: 8051 8361 8069 8052 Convalescent home with continuous nursing care; residential care; specialty hospitals, except psychiatric; intermediate care facilities

(P-20345)
FLAGSTONE HEALTHCARE SOUTH LLC
29222 Rncho Vejo Rd Ste 1, San Juan
Capistrano (92675)
PHONE.....................949 487-9500
EMP: 56 EST: 2019
SALES (est): 5.1MM
SALES (corp-wide): 2.4B **Publicly Held**
WEB: www.ensigngroup.net
SIC: 8051 Skilled nursing care facilities
PA: The Ensign Group Inc
29222 Rncho Vejo Rd Ste 1
San Juan Capistrano CA 92675
949 487-9500

(P-20346)
FREEDOM VILLAGE HEALTHCARE CTR
Also Called: Rehabworks At Freedom Village
23442 El Toro Rd Bldg 2, Lake Forest
(92630-6992)
PHONE.....................949 472-4733
Joel Niblett, *Administration*
Mary Beth Melby, *Records Dir*
Chery Roscamp, *CFO*
Stephanie Martinez, *Social Dir*
Marianne Casino, *Exec Dir*
EMP: 106 EST: 1977
SALES (est): 11.3MM **Privately Held**
WEB:
www.freedomvillageorangecounty.org
SIC: 8051 8052 Convalescent home with continuous nursing care; intermediate care facilities

(P-20347)
FRONT PRCH CMMNTIES SVCS - CAS
Also Called: Apple Valley Care Center
11959 Apple Valley Rd, Apple Valley
(92308-7507)
PHONE.....................760 240-5051
Terry Blumer, *Manager*
EMP: 152
SQ FT: 36,151
SALES (corp-wide): 152.2MM **Privately Held**
WEB: www.frontporch.net
SIC: 8051 Convalescent home with continuous nursing care
PA: Front Porch Communities And Services
- Casa De Manana Llc
800 N Brand Blvd Fl 19
Glendale CA 91203
818 729-8100

(P-20348)
FULLERTON HLTHCARE WLLNESS CNT
Also Called: Evergreen Fullerton Healthcare
2222 N Harbor Blvd, Fullerton
(92835-2605)
PHONE.....................714 992-5701
Shlomo Rechnitz, *Partner*
Sharrod Brooks, *Partner*
Tyler Smith, *Hlthcr Dir*
EMP: 125 EST: 2013

SALES (est): 22.7MM **Privately Held**
SIC: 8051 Convalescent home with continuous nursing care

(P-20349)
GARDEN CREST CNVLSCENT HOSP IN
Also Called: Garden Crest Rtrment Residence
909 Lucile Ave, Los Angeles (90026-1598)
PHONE..................323 663-8281
Paul Barron, *CEO*
Vera Barron, *Vice Pres*
EMP: 90
SQ FT: 30,000
SALES (est): 6.5MM **Privately Held**
WEB: www.gardencrestweb.com
SIC: 8051 8059 8322 Convalescent home with continuous nursing care; convalescent home; old age assistance

(P-20350)
GARDEN GROVE MEDICAL INVESTORS (HQ)
Also Called: Garden Grove Rehabilitation
12332 Garden Grove Blvd, Garden Grove (92843-1804)
PHONE..................714 534-1041
Nelia Yonzen, *Exec Dir*
Donna Devera, *Hlthcr Dir*
EMP: 58 **EST:** 1976
SQ FT: 10,000
SALES (est): 13.5MM
SALES (corp-wide): 1.5B **Privately Held**
WEB: www.lcca.com
SIC: 8051 8069 Convalescent home with continuous nursing care; specialty hospitals, except psychiatric
PA: Life Care Centers Of America, Inc.
3570 Keith St Nw
Cleveland TN 37312
423 472-9585

(P-20351)
GARDEN VIEW CARE CENTER INC
14475 Garden View Ln, Baldwin Park (91706-6000)
PHONE..................626 962-7095
John Sorensen, *President*
Vicente Iracheta, *Maint Spvr*
Madelly Mendoza, *Asst Director*
Josefa Custodia, *Director*
Velia Hernandez, *Supervisor*
EMP: 50 **EST:** 1990
SALES (est): 12MM **Privately Held**
WEB: www.gardenviewrehab.com
SIC: 8051 Convalescent home with continuous nursing care

(P-20352)
GARDENA FLORES
Also Called: Las Flores Convalescent Hosp
14165 Purche Ave, Gardena (90249-2824)
PHONE..................310 323-4570
Keith Fortune, *Director*
Diana Fortune, *Treasurer*
EMP: 58 **EST:** 1964
SQ FT: 10,000
SALES (est): 9MM **Privately Held**
SIC: 8051 Skilled nursing care facilities

(P-20353)
GARDENA RETIREMENT CENTER INC
14741 S Vermont Ave, Gardena (90247-3098)
PHONE..................310 327-4091
EMP: 96
SALES (corp-wide): 7.3MM **Privately Held**
WEB: www.gardenaretirement.com
SIC: 8051 Skilled nursing care facilities
PA: Gardena Retirement Center, Inc.
11627 Telg Rd Ste 200
Santa Fe Springs CA 90670
310 327-4091

(P-20354)
GATE THREE HEALTHCARE LLC
Also Called: Palm Ter Hlth Care Rhblitation
24962 Calle Aragon, Laguna Hills (92637-3883)
PHONE..................949 770-3348
Soon Burnam,

EMP: 208 **EST:** 2004
SALES (est): 18.9MM
SALES (corp-wide): 2.4B **Publicly Held**
WEB: www.palmterracecares.com
SIC: 8051 Convalescent home with continuous nursing care
PA: The Ensign Group Inc
29222 Rncho Vejo Rd Ste 1
San Juan Capistrano CA 92675
949 487-9500

(P-20355)
GEM TRANSITIONAL CARE CENTER
Also Called: Gem Trans Care
716 S Fair Oaks Ave, Pasadena (91105-2618)
PHONE..................626 737-0560
Rupert Ouano, *Director*
Hrag H Bekerian, *Exec Dir*
Manuel Dellana, *Administration*
Dione Gil, *Education*
Jeanette Abram, *Director*
EMP: 50 **EST:** 2000
SALES (est): 11.6MM **Privately Held**
WEB: www.gemtransitional.com
SIC: 8051 Convalescent home with continuous nursing care

(P-20356)
GENESIS HEALTHCARE LLC
Also Called: Spring Senior Assisted Living
20900 Earl St Ste 100, Torrance (90503-4309)
PHONE..................310 370-3594
EMP: 211 **Privately Held**
WEB: www.genesishcc.com
SIC: 8051 Skilled nursing care facilities
HQ: Genesis Healthcare Llc
101 E State St
Kennett Square PA 19348

(P-20357)
GENESIS HEALTHCARE LLC
425 Barcellus Ave, Santa Maria (93454-6901)
PHONE..................805 922-3558
Arlene Gonzales, *Director*
EMP: 211 **Privately Held**
WEB: www.genesishcc.com
SIC: 8051 Convalescent home with continuous nursing care
HQ: Genesis Healthcare Llc
101 E State St
Kennett Square PA 19348

(P-20358)
GEORGIA ATKISON SNF LLC
Also Called: Alliance Nrsing Rhbltation Ctr
3825 Durfee Ave, El Monte (91732-2505)
PHONE..................626 444-2535
Eli Quinones, *Mng Member*
EMP: 52 **EST:** 1996
SQ FT: 30,000
SALES (est): 8.7MM **Privately Held**
SIC: 8051 Convalescent home with continuous nursing care

(P-20359)
GERI-CARE INC
Also Called: Harbor Post Accute Care Center
21521 S Vermont Ave, Torrance (90502-1939)
PHONE..................310 320-0961
Emmanuel David, *President*
EMP: 100 **EST:** 1975
SQ FT: 30,000
SALES (est): 10MM **Privately Held**
WEB: www.harborpostacute.com
SIC: 8051 Convalescent home with continuous nursing care

(P-20360)
GLENWOOD CORPORATION
Also Called: Glenwood Care Center
1300 N C St, Oxnard (93030-4006)
PHONE..................805 983-0305
Jerry E Wells, *President*
Frank Chung MD, *Treasurer*
Wallace Tamoyose MD, *Vice Pres*
Gladys Hernandez, *Office Mgr*
Harvey Wilson, *Admin Sec*
EMP: 65 **EST:** 1968
SQ FT: 30,000

SALES (est): 12.1MM **Privately Held**
WEB: www.glenwoodcarecenter.com
SIC: 8051 Convalescent home with continuous nursing care

(P-20361)
GOLDEN CROSS CARE INC
Also Called: Golden Cross Health Care
1450 N Fair Oaks Ave, Pasadena (91103-1801)
PHONE..................626 791-1948
Marlene Robertson, *President*
Richard Barnes, *CIO*
Vida Arevalo, *Nursing Dir*
EMP: 56 **EST:** 1991
SQ FT: 30,000
SALES (est): 10.6MM **Privately Held**
WEB: www.goldencrosshealthcare.com
SIC: 8051 Skilled nursing care facilities

(P-20362)
GOLDEN STATE HABILITATION CONV (PA)
Also Called: Golden State Care Center
1758 Big Dalton Ave, Baldwin Park (91706-5910)
PHONE..................626 962-3274
Eden Salceda, *President*
Claudio Hernandez, *Vice Pres*
Emmanuel David, *Admin Sec*
EMP: 175 **EST:** 1971
SALES (est): 10.7MM **Privately Held**
WEB: www.gsccdd.com
SIC: 8051 8361 8052 Convalescent home with continuous nursing care; residential care; intermediate care facilities

(P-20363)
GOLDEN STATE HEALTH CTRS INC (PA)
13347 Ventura Blvd, Sherman Oaks (91423-3979)
PHONE..................818 385-3200
Martin J Weiss, *CEO*
Ronald Mayer, *CFO*
David B Weiss, *Chairman*
Bernard Friedman, *Exec Dir*
Howard Weiss, *Admin Sec*
EMP: 220 **EST:** 1984
SQ FT: 2,000
SALES: 62.1MM **Privately Held**
WEB: www.goldenstatehealth.com
SIC: 8051 Skilled nursing care facilities

(P-20364)
GPH MEDICAL & LEGAL SERVICES (PA)
Also Called: G P H Medical Services
468 N Camden Dr, Beverly Hills (90210-4507)
PHONE..................213 207-2700
Summer Reed, *President*
Olen Maxwell PHD, *Shareholder*
William Maxwell PHD, *Shareholder*
Alvin Thomas Jr, *Shareholder*
Michael McBay MD, *Vice Pres*
▲ **EMP:** 217 **EST:** 1986
SQ FT: 4,000
SALES (est): 12.1MM **Privately Held**
WEB: www.nulegal.com
SIC: 8051 8059 7361 7812 Skilled nursing care facilities; convalescent home; nurses' registry; television film production

(P-20365)
GR8 CARE INC
14518 Los Angeles St, Baldwin Park (91706-2636)
PHONE..................626 337-7229
Edwin Raquel, *CEO*
Napoleon Garcia, *Principal*
EMP: 73 **EST:** 2007
SQ FT: 9,710
SALES (est): 4.4MM **Privately Held**
SIC: 8051 Skilled nursing care facilities

(P-20366)
GRAND AVENUE HLTH HOLDINGS LLC
29222 Rncho Vejo Rd Ste 1, San Juan Capistrano (92675)
PHONE..................949 487-9500
EMP: 80 **EST:** 2018

SALES (est): 7.2MM
SALES (corp-wide): 2.4B **Publicly Held**
WEB: www.ensigngroup.net
SIC: 8051 Skilled nursing care facilities
PA: The Ensign Group Inc
29222 Rncho Vejo Rd Ste 1
San Juan Capistrano CA 92675
949 487-9500

(P-20367)
GRAND TERRACE CARE CENTER (PA)
12000 Mount Vernon Ave, Grand Terrace (92313-5174)
PHONE..................909 825-5221
John Sorenson, *CEO*
Ashley Luna, *Records Dir*
Chrystal Ortiz, *Office Mgr*
EMP: 67 **EST:** 2001
SALES (est): 9.2MM **Privately Held**
WEB: www.grandterracecare.com
SIC: 8051 Convalescent home with continuous nursing care

(P-20368)
GRIFFITH PK RHBLTATION CTR LLC
Also Called: Griffith Park Healthcare Ctr
201 Allen Ave, Glendale (91201-2803)
PHONE..................818 845-8507
Crystal Solorzano,
EMP: 75 **EST:** 2015
SALES (est): 11.3MM **Privately Held**
SIC: 8051 Convalescent home with continuous nursing care

(P-20369)
GVA ENTERPRISES INC (PA)
Also Called: Angels Nursing Center
316 S Westlake Ave, Los Angeles (90057-2906)
PHONE..................213 484-0510
George Rabinowitz, *President*
Maria Silva, *Social Dir*
Elizabeth Austra, *Office Mgr*
Risse Derayu, *Education*
Cristine Veldes, *Food Svc Dir*
EMP: 66 **EST:** 1970
SQ FT: 22,578
SALES (est): 8.4MM **Privately Held**
SIC: 8051 Skilled nursing care facilities

(P-20370)
HACIENDA RHBLTTION HLTH CARE C
Also Called: Hacienda Health Care
361 E Grangeville Blvd, Hanford (93230-3054)
PHONE..................559 582-9221
Rex Moore, *Branch Mgr*
EMP: 120
SALES (corp-wide): 5.5MM **Privately Held**
WEB: www.haciendacares.com
SIC: 8051 8069 Convalescent home with continuous nursing care; specialty hospitals, except psychiatric
PA: Hacienda Rehabilitation & Health Care Center, Inc
1440 S State College Blvd 2a
Anaheim CA 92806
714 778-0221

(P-20371)
HARBOR GLEN CARE CENTER
1033 E Arrow Hwy, Glendora (91740-6110)
PHONE..................626 963-7531
Kevin Thomas, *Owner*
Diane Robinson, *Records Dir*
Joy Devera, *Social Dir*
EMP: 268 **EST:** 2000
SALES (est): 24.4MM
SALES (corp-wide): 2.4B **Publicly Held**
WEB: www.arborglencare.com
SIC: 8051 Convalescent home with continuous nursing care
PA: The Ensign Group Inc
29222 Rncho Vejo Rd Ste 1
San Juan Capistrano CA 92675
949 487-9500

PRODUCTS & SVCS

(P-20372)
HEALTH CARE INVESTMENTS INC
Also Called: Rosecrans Care Center
1140 W Rosecrans Ave, Gardena
(90247-2664)
PHONE..................310 323-3194
Pompeyo Rosales, *President*
Lakaya Strickland, *Social Dir*
Gonzalo Delrosario, *Admin Sec*
Lady Leano, *Food Svc Dir*
EMP: 106 **EST:** 1991
SALES (est): 11.1MM **Privately Held**
WEB: www.rosecranscc.com
SIC: 8051 Convalescent home with continuous nursing care

(P-20373)
HEALTHCARE CTR OF DOWNEY LLC
Also Called: Lakewood Healthcare Center
12023 Lakewood Blvd, Downey
(90242-2635)
PHONE..................562 869-0978
Vince Hambright, *CEO*
Ken Lehmann,
EMP: 250 **EST:** 2011
SQ FT: 1,076,391
SALES (est): 19.4MM **Privately Held**
WEB: www.lwhealthcare.com
SIC: 8051 Mental retardation hospital

(P-20374)
HERITAGE HEALTH CARE INC
Also Called: Heritage Gardens Hlth Care Ctr
25271 Barton Rd, Loma Linda
(92354-3013)
PHONE..................909 796-0216
Stephen Flood, *CEO*
Gregory S Goings, *CEO*
Jim Kilian, *CFO*
James Kilian, *Officer*
Elizabeth Ambriz, *VP Finance*
EMP: 150 **EST:** 1963
SALES (est): 11.6MM **Privately Held**
WEB: www.progressivecarecenters.com
SIC: 8051 8059 Skilled nursing care facilities; rest home, with health care

(P-20375)
HIGHLAND PK SKLLED NRSING WLLN
5125 Monte Vista St, Los Angeles
(90042-3931)
PHONE..................323 254-6125
Shlomo Rechnitz,
EMP: 72 **EST:** 2008
SALES (est): 7MM **Privately Held**
WEB: www.highlandparkskillednursing.com
SIC: 8051 Convalescent home with continuous nursing care

(P-20376)
HUNTINGTON BCH CNVLSCENT HOSP
29222 Rncho Vejo Rd Ste 1, San Juan
Capistrano (92675)
PHONE..................949 487-9500
EMP: 56
SALES (est): 5.1MM
SALES (corp-wide): 2.4B **Publicly Held**
WEB: www.ensigngroup.net
SIC: 8051 Skilled nursing care facilities
PA: The Ensign Group Inc
29222 Rncho Vejo Rd Ste 1
San Juan Capistrano CA 92675
949 487-9500

(P-20377)
HYDE PK CONVALESCENT HOSP INC
6520 West Blvd, Los Angeles (90043-4311)
PHONE..................323 753-1354
Jeff Mendell, *President*
Elaine Wiesel, *Admin Sec*
EMP: 50 **EST:** 1965
SQ FT: 15,258
SALES (est): 7.2MM **Privately Held**
SIC: 8051 Convalescent home with continuous nursing care

(P-20378)
IN GRANADA HLLS CNVLSCENT HOSP
Also Called: Granada Hills Care Center
16123 Chatsworth St, Granada Hills
(91344-7045)
PHONE..................818 891-1745
Seid Sadat, *President*
Abraham Birnbaum, *President*
Kim Marconet, *Vice Pres*
EMP: 64 **EST:** 1963
SQ FT: 96,680
SALES (est): 5.5MM **Privately Held**
WEB: www.ghcarecenter.com
SIC: 8051 Convalescent home with continuous nursing care

(P-20379)
INLAND CHRSTN HM FUNDATION INC
1950 S Mountain Ave Ofc, Ontario
(91762-6709)
PHONE..................909 395-9322
David Stienstra, *President*
Christian Uduefe, *Administration*
Mary Wolff, *Administration*
Joe Whitford, *Opers Staff*
Jennifer Dreiling, *Marketing Staff*
EMP: 114 **EST:** 1973
SQ FT: 100,000
SALES (est): 112.9K **Privately Held**
WEB: www.ichome.org
SIC: 8051 8052 6513 8361 Skilled nursing care facilities; intermediate care facilities; retirement hotel operation; residential care

(P-20380)
INTERCOMMUNITY CARE CENTERS
2626 Grand Ave, Long Beach
(90815-1707)
PHONE..................562 427-8915
Russel Boydston, *Branch Mgr*
Paula Curry, *Records Dir*
Rosemary Valentin, *Office Mgr*
Armida Faussler, *Administration*
Monique Robinette, *Human Res Dir*
EMP: 141
SQ FT: 32,159
SALES (corp-wide): 9.5MM **Privately Held**
WEB: www.iccare.org
SIC: 8051 Convalescent home with continuous nursing care
PA: Intercommunity Care Centers Inc
2660 Grand Ave
Long Beach CA
562 426-1368

(P-20381)
J P H CONSULTING INC (PA)
1101 Crenshaw Blvd, Los Angeles
(90019-3112)
PHONE..................323 934-5660
Jeoung H Lee, *President*
Greda Bernabe, *CFO*
Kyle Watanabe, *Director*
EMP: 50 **EST:** 1998
SALES (est): 56.7MM **Privately Held**
SIC: 8051 Skilled nursing care facilities

(P-20382)
J P H CONSULTING INC
4515 Huntington Dr S, Los Angeles
(90032-1940)
PHONE..................323 934-5660
EMP: 65
SALES (corp-wide): 56.7MM **Privately Held**
SIC: 8051 Skilled nursing care facilities
PA: J P H Consulting, Inc.
1101 Crenshaw Blvd
Los Angeles CA 90019
323 934-5660

(P-20383)
JOHNRE CARE LLC
461 E Johnston Ave, Hemet (92543-7113)
PHONE..................951 658-6374
EMP: 60
SALES (est): 1.8MM **Privately Held**
SIC: 8051 Skilled Nursing Care Facility

(P-20384)
KATELLA PROPERTIES
Also Called: Alamitos W Convalescent Hosp
3902 Katella Ave, Los Alamitos
(90720-3304)
PHONE..................562 596-5561
Marilyn Gelgincolin, *Director*
Catherine Beltran, *Social Dir*
Dora Hernandez, *Technology*
Esperanza Farrell, *Food Svc Dir*
Marilyn Elgincolin, *Nursing Dir*
EMP: 142
SALES (corp-wide): 12.3MM **Privately Held**
WEB: www.katellaseniorliving.com
SIC: 8051 Convalescent home with continuous nursing care
PA: Katella Properties
3952 Katella Ave
Los Alamitos CA 90720
562 596-2773

(P-20385)
KERN VALLEY HOSP FOUNDATION (PA)
6412 Laurel Ave, Lake Isabella
(93240-9529)
P.O. Box 1628 (93240-1628)
PHONE..................760 379-2681
Clarence Semonious, *President*
Mary Completo, *Treasurer*
Anne Litz, *Vice Pres*
Charlie Busch, *Admin Sec*
Kay Knight, *Admin Sec*
EMP: 300 **EST:** 1964
SQ FT: 65,000
SALES: 36.4K **Privately Held**
WEB: www.kvhd.org
SIC: 5912 8051 Drug stores; extended care facility

(P-20386)
KINDRED HEALTHCARE LLC
3220 S Higuera St, San Luis Obispo
(93401-6987)
PHONE..................805 544-4472
EMP: 142
SALES (corp-wide): 6B **Privately Held**
WEB: www.kindredhealthcare.com
SIC: 8051 Skilled nursing care facilities
HQ: Kindred Healthcare, Llc
680 S 4th St
Louisville KY 40202
502 596-7300

(P-20387)
KINGS NRSING RHBLTTION HOSP IN
Also Called: Kings Nrsing Rhabilitation Ctr
851 Leslie Ln, Hanford (93230-5643)
PHONE..................559 582-4414
Mark Allan Fisher, *President*
Sharon A Fisher, *President*
Mike Owen, *Maint Spvr*
Steve Grossman, *Director*
EMP: 50 **EST:** 2005
SALES (est): 7.4MM **Privately Held**
WEB: www.missioncg.com
SIC: 8051 Convalescent home with continuous nursing care

(P-20388)
KNOLLS CONVALESCENT HOSP INC (PA)
Also Called: Desert Knlls Convalescent Hosp
16890 Green Tree Blvd, Victorville
(92395-5618)
PHONE..................760 245-5361
Gary L Bechtold, *President*
Fred Bechtold, *Vice Pres*
Larry Bechtold, *Vice Pres*
Alyssa Ornelas, *Assistant*
EMP: 130 **EST:** 1971
SQ FT: 5,421
SALES (est): 12.6MM **Privately Held**
WEB: www.knollswestpostacute.com
SIC: 8051 8052 Convalescent home with continuous nursing care; intermediate care facilities

(P-20389)
KNOLLS WEST ENTERPRISE
Also Called: Knolls West Residential Care
16890 Green Tree Blvd, Victorville
(92395-5618)
PHONE..................760 245-0107
Larry Bechtold, *Partner*
Fred Bechtold, *Partner*
Gary Bechtold, *Partner*
Michelle Schmidt, *Human Res Dir*
EMP: 132 **EST:** 1979
SQ FT: 44,000
SALES (est): 8.1MM
SALES (corp-wide): 12.6MM **Privately Held**
WEB: www.knollswestpostacute.com
SIC: 8051 Convalescent home with continuous nursing care
PA: Knolls Convalescent Hospital, Inc.
16890 Green Tree Blvd
Victorville CA 92395
760 245-5361

(P-20390)
KSM HEALTHCARE INC
Also Called: Dreier's Nursing Care Center
1400 W Glenoaks Blvd, Glendale
(91201-1911)
PHONE..................818 242-1183
John Haedrich, *President*
EMP: 76 **EST:** 1947
SQ FT: 40,000
SALES (est): 7.6MM **Privately Held**
SIC: 8051 Skilled nursing care facilities

(P-20391)
LIFE CARE CENTERS AMERICA INC
Also Called: Life Care Center of La Habra
1233 W La Habra Blvd, La Habra
(90631-5226)
PHONE..................562 690-0852
Daniel Husband, *Administration*
Marilyn Mallari, *Records Dir*
Lupe Rosas, *Hlthcr Dir*
Juan Jimenez, *Director*
EMP: 105
SALES (corp-wide): 1.5B **Privately Held**
WEB: www.lcca.com
SIC: 8051 Convalescent home with continuous nursing care
PA: Life Care Centers Of America, Inc.
3570 Keith St Nw
Cleveland TN 37312
423 472-9585

(P-20392)
LIFE CARE CENTERS AMERICA INC
Also Called: Mirada Hlls Rehb Cnvlscent Hos
12200 La Mirada Blvd, La Mirada
(90638-1306)
PHONE..................562 947-8691
Selina Stewart, *Branch Mgr*
EMP: 105
SALES (corp-wide): 1.5B **Privately Held**
WEB: www.lcca.com
SIC: 8051 Convalescent home with continuous nursing care
PA: Life Care Centers Of America, Inc.
3570 Keith St Nw
Cleveland TN 37312
423 472-9585

(P-20393)
LIFE CARE CENTERS AMERICA INC
Also Called: Life Care Center San Gabriel
909 W Santa Anita Ave, San Gabriel
(91776-1018)
PHONE..................626 289-5365
Eunice Fletcher, *Manager*
EMP: 105
SALES (corp-wide): 1.5B **Privately Held**
WEB: www.lcca.com
SIC: 8051 Convalescent home with continuous nursing care
PA: Life Care Centers Of America, Inc.
3570 Keith St Nw
Cleveland TN 37312
423 472-9585

(P-20394)

LIFE CARE CENTERS AMERICA INC

901 W Santa Anita Ave, San Gabriel (91776-1018)
PHONE.................................626 289-8889
Eunice Fletcher, *Director*
EMP: 105
SALES (corp-wide): 1.5B **Privately Held**
WEB: www.lcca.com
SIC: 8051 8052 Convalescent home with continuous nursing care; intermediate care facilities
PA: Life Care Centers Of America, Inc.
3570 Keith St Nw
Cleveland TN 37312
423 472-9585

(P-20395)

LIFE CARE CENTERS AMERICA INC

Also Called: Lake Forest Nursing Center
25652 Old Trabuco Rd, Lake Forest (92630-2776)
PHONE.................................949 380-9380
Kim Le, *Branch Mgr*
Richard Daiz, *Business Mgr*
Kaye Browe, *Human Res Dir*
Sharon Allman, *Director*
EMP: 105
SALES (corp-wide): 1.5B **Privately Held**
WEB: www.lcca.com
SIC: 8051 Convalescent home with continuous nursing care
PA: Life Care Centers Of America, Inc.
3570 Keith St Nw
Cleveland TN 37312
423 472-9585

(P-20396)

LIFE CARE CENTERS AMERICA INC

Also Called: Imperial Convalescent
11926 La Mirada Blvd, La Mirada (90638-1303)
PHONE.................................562 943-7156
Ted Stultz, *Manager*
EMP: 105
SALES (corp-wide): 1.5B **Privately Held**
WEB: www.lcca.com
SIC: 8051 8741 Convalescent home with continuous nursing care; management services
PA: Life Care Centers Of America, Inc.
3570 Keith St Nw
Cleveland TN 37312
423 472-9585

(P-20397)

LIFE CARE CENTERS AMERICA INC

Also Called: Life Care Center of Bellflower
16910 Woodruff Ave, Bellflower (90706-6036)
PHONE.................................562 867-1761
Tooren Bel, *Manager*
Mary Helen Gomez, *Director*
EMP: 105
SALES (corp-wide): 1.5B **Privately Held**
WEB: www.lcca.com
SIC: 8051 Convalescent home with continuous nursing care
PA: Life Care Centers Of America, Inc.
3570 Keith St Nw
Cleveland TN 37312
423 472-9585

(P-20398)

LIFE CARE CENTERS AMERICA INC

Also Called: Life Care Center of Norwalk
12350 Rosecrans Ave, Norwalk (90650-5064)
PHONE.................................562 921-6624
Steve Ramsdel, *Vice Pres*
EMP: 105
SALES (corp-wide): 1.5B **Privately Held**
WEB: www.lcca.com
SIC: 8051 Convalescent home with continuous nursing care
PA: Life Care Centers Of America, Inc.
3570 Keith St Nw
Cleveland TN 37312
423 472-9585

(P-20399)

LIFE CARE CENTERS AMERICA INC

27555 Rimrock Rd, Barstow (92311-4230)
PHONE.................................760 252-2515
Leshawn Mitchell, *Social Dir*
Veronica McArthur, *Human Res Dir*
Robert Scott, *Maintence Staff*
EMP: 105
SALES (corp-wide): 1.5B **Privately Held**
WEB: www.lcca.com
SIC: 8051 Convalescent home with continuous nursing care
PA: Life Care Centers Of America, Inc.
3570 Keith St Nw
Cleveland TN 37312
423 472-9585

(P-20400)

LIGHTHOUSE HEALTHCARE CTR LLC

2222 Santa Ana S, Los Angeles (90059-1350)
PHONE.................................323 564-4461
Sharrod Brooks,
EMP: 99 EST: 2007
SALES (est): 9.9MM **Privately Held**
SIC: 8051 Skilled nursing care facilities

(P-20401)

LITTLE SSTERS OF THE POOR LOS

Also Called: Jeanne Jugan, A Residence
2100 S Western Ave, San Pedro (90732-4331)
PHONE.................................310 548-0625
Margaret McArthy, *President*
Clotilde Jardim, *Treasurer*
Michael Mugan, *Vice Pres*
Victor Salcido, *Human Res Dir*
EMP: 100 EST: 1905
SQ FT: 145,530
SALES (est): 5.9MM **Privately Held**
WEB: www.littlesistersofthepoorsanpedro.org
SIC: 8051 8361 8052 Extended care facility; residential care; intermediate care facilities

(P-20402)

LOMA LINDA UNIVERSITY MED CTR

Also Called: Loma Linda Hospice
268 W Hospitality Ln # 300, San Bernardino (92408-3241)
PHONE.................................909 824-6904
Jan Hutkins, *Manager*
Lauren Ball, *Admin Dir*
EMP: 81
SALES (corp-wide): 284.6MM **Privately Held**
WEB: www.home.llu.edu
SIC: 8051 Extended care facility
HQ: Loma Linda University Medical Center
11234 Anderson St
Loma Linda CA 92354
909 558-4000

(P-20403)

LONG BEACH CARE CENTER INC

2615 Grand Ave, Long Beach (90815-1708)
PHONE.................................562 426-6141
William A Nelson, *President*
EMP: 108
SQ FT: 43,962
SALES (est): 14.6MM **Privately Held**
WEB: www.iccare.org
SIC: 8051 Convalescent home with continuous nursing care

(P-20404)

LONGWOOD MANAGEMENT CORP

Also Called: Imperial Crest Healthcare Ctr
11834 Inglewood Ave, Hawthorne (90250-2731)
PHONE.................................310 679-1461
Robert Villalub, *Administration*
Zaid Pervaiz, *CFO*
Cary Baker, *Planning*
Wilma Ross, *Benefits Mgr*
Christina Rosas, *Nurse*
EMP: 124
SALES (corp-wide): 179.6MM **Privately Held**
WEB: www.longwoodmgmt.com
SIC: 8051 Convalescent home with continuous nursing care
PA: Longwood Management Corp.
4032 Wilshire Blvd Fl 6
Los Angeles CA 90010
213 389-6900

(P-20405)

LONGWOOD MANAGEMENT CORP

Also Called: Magnolia Grdns Convalescent HM
17922 San Frnando Msn, Granada Hills (91344-4043)
PHONE.................................818 360-1864
Oijjoji Gervacio, *Principal*
Annalynn Barrion, *Executive*
EMP: 124
SALES (corp-wide): 179.6MM **Privately Held**
WEB: www.longwoodmgmt.com
SIC: 8051 Convalescent home with continuous nursing care
PA: Longwood Management Corp.
4032 Wilshire Blvd Fl 6
Los Angeles CA 90010
213 389-6900

(P-20406)

LONGWOOD MANAGEMENT CORP

Also Called: Green Acres Lodge
8101 Hill Dr, Rosemead (91770-4169)
PHONE.................................626 280-2293
Karen Fugate, *Administration*
Jun Virola, *Office Mgr*
EMP: 124
SALES (corp-wide): 179.6MM **Privately Held**
WEB: www.longwoodmgmt.com
SIC: 8051 Convalescent home with continuous nursing care
PA: Longwood Management Corp.
4032 Wilshire Blvd Fl 6
Los Angeles CA 90010
213 389-6900

(P-20407)

LONGWOOD MANAGEMENT CORP

Also Called: San Gabriel Convalescent Ctr
8035 Hill Dr, Rosemead (91770-4116)
PHONE.................................626 280-4820
Gigi Garcia, *Branch Mgr*
Tom Yeh, *Director*
EMP: 124
SALES (corp-wide): 179.6MM **Privately Held**
WEB: www.longwoodmgmt.com
SIC: 8051 Convalescent home with continuous nursing care
PA: Longwood Management Corp.
4032 Wilshire Blvd Fl 6
Los Angeles CA 90010
213 389-6900

(P-20408)

LONGWOOD MANAGEMENT CORP

Also Called: Crenshaw Nursing
1900 S Longwood Ave, Los Angeles (90016-1408)
PHONE.................................323 933-1560
Gilbert Fimbres, *Manager*
EMP: 124
SALES (corp-wide): 179.6MM **Privately Held**
WEB: www.longwoodmgmt.com
SIC: 8051 8052 Convalescent home with continuous nursing care; intermediate care facilities
PA: Longwood Management Corp.
4032 Wilshire Blvd Fl 6
Los Angeles CA 90010
213 389-6900

(P-20409)

LOS ANGLES JEWISH HM FOR AGING (PA)

Also Called: Grancell Village
7150 Tampa Ave, Reseda (91335-3700)
PHONE.................................818 774-3000
Andrew Berman, *Ch of Bd*
Joyce Brandman, *Vice Chairman*
James Gerson, *Vice Chairman*
Jeffrey Glassman, *Vice Chairman*
Les Granow, *Vice Chairman*
EMP: 400 EST: 1912
SQ FT: 35,000
SALES: 172.6MM **Privately Held**
WEB: www.jha.org
SIC: 8051 8361 Skilled nursing care facilities; residential care

(P-20410)

LOS ANGLES JEWISH HM FOR AGING

Also Called: Eisenberg Village
18855 Victory Blvd, Reseda (91335-6445)
PHONE.................................818 774-3000
Kathleen Glass, *Manager*
Edith Morales, *Records Dir*
Hadi Pourbeheshtian, *Engineer*
Anna Haro, *Human Res Dir*
Sherry Cunningham, *Opers Spvr*
EMP: 500
SALES (corp-wide): 172.6MM **Privately Held**
WEB: www.jha.org
SIC: 8051 Convalescent home with continuous nursing care
PA: Los Angeles Jewish Home For The Aging
7150 Tampa Ave
Reseda CA 91335
818 774-3000

(P-20411)

MADISON CREEK PARTNERS LLC (PA)

26522 La Alameda Ste 300, Mission Viejo (92691-8302)
PHONE.................................949 449-2500
Covey Christensen,
James Gamett,
Anthony Geronimo, *Senior Mgr*
EMP: 76 EST: 2015
SALES (est): 26.6MM **Privately Held**
WEB: www.madison-creek-partners-llc.business.site
SIC: 8051 Skilled nursing care facilities

(P-20412)

MANCHSTER MNOR CNVLESCENT HOSP

837 W Manchester Ave, Los Angeles (90044-4913)
PHONE.................................323 753-1789
Phadra Johnson-Fenton, *Administration*
Wilisha Jackson, *Office Mgr*
Phadra Fenton, *Administration*
Mary Morales, *Human Res Dir*
Nita Lee, *Hlthcr Dir*
EMP: 65 EST: 1963
SQ FT: 10,000
SALES (est): 5.1MM **Privately Held**
WEB: www.manchestermanorch.com
SIC: 8051 Convalescent home with continuous nursing care

(P-20413)

MARK & FRED ENTERPRISES

Also Called: West Anaheim Care Center
645 S Beach Blvd, Anaheim (92804-3102)
PHONE.................................714 821-1993
Mark Landry, *Managing Prtnr*
Connie Black, *Partner*
Donna Meyer, *Officer*
Mary Loether, *Office Mgr*
Charlene Hawelu, *Marketing Staff*
EMP: 125 EST: 1989
SQ FT: 39,000
SALES (est): 14.2MM **Privately Held**
WEB: www.westanaheimec.com
SIC: 8051 Convalescent home with continuous nursing care

(P-20414)
MARLORA INVESTMENTS LLC
Also Called: Marlora Post Accute Rhblttion
3801 E Anaheim St, Long Beach
(90804-4004)
PHONE....................................562 494-3311
Marilyn A Hauser,
Gabriela Patheco, *Officer*
Cathy Hernandez, *Marketing Staff*
Imelda Tolentino, *Hlthcr Dir*
EMP: 100 **EST:** 1998
SQ FT: 22,118
SALES (est): 8.6MM **Privately Held**
SIC: 8051 Convalescent home with contin-
uous nursing care

(P-20415)
**MARY HLTH SCK CNVLSCNT
&NRSNG**
2929 Theresa Dr, Newbury Park
(91320-3136)
PHONE....................................805 498-3644
Jody Rupp, *Administration*
Sister Purificaion Fererro, *CEO*
Diane Zimanski, *Office Mgr*
EMP: 92
SQ FT: 5,000
SALES: 7.2MM **Privately Held**
WEB: www.maryhealth.com
SIC: 8051 Convalescent home with contin-
uous nursing care

(P-20416)
MEDICREST OF CALIFORNIA 1
Also Called: Montclair Mnor Cnvlescent Hosp
5119 Bandera St, Montclair (91763-4410)
PHONE....................................909 626-1294
Melinda Mabini, *Administration*
EMP: 59 **Privately Held**
SIC: 8051 Convalescent home with contin-
uous nursing care
HQ: Medicrest Of California 1, Inc
4020 Sierra College Blvd
Rocklin CA 95677
916 624-6238

(P-20417)
**MESA VRDE CNVALESCENT
HOSP INC**
Also Called: Mesa Verde Prosecute Care
661 Center St, Costa Mesa (92627-2708)
PHONE....................................949 548-5584
Rita Simms, *Administration*
Joseph Munoz, *Administration*
Joye Tsuchiyama, *Administration*
Lucy Garcilazo, *Food Svc Dir*
Elsa Almazon, *Director*
EMP: 200 **EST:** 1972
SALES (est): 22.7MM **Privately Held**
WEB: www.mesaverdehealthcare.com
SIC: 8051 Convalescent home with contin-
uous nursing care

(P-20418)
**MIRAMONTE ENTERPRISES
LLC**
Also Called: San Jacinto Healthcare
275 N San Jacinto St, Hemet (92543-4453)
PHONE....................................951 658-9441
Emmanuel B David, *President*
EMP: 134 **EST:** 2005
SQ FT: 22,968
SALES (est): 8.2MM **Privately Held**
WEB: www.sjsnf.com
SIC: 8051 Skilled nursing care facilities

(P-20419)
MONTECITO RETIREMENT ASSN
Also Called: Casa Dorinda
300 Hot Springs Rd, Santa Barbara
(93108-2037)
PHONE....................................805 969-8011
Robin Drew, *CFO*
Sam Aguilar, *Asst Director*
Melissa Gill, *Director*
Melissa Gill-Hausz, *Director*
Marilu Greene, *Manager*
EMP: 265
SQ FT: 350,000
SALES: 27.7MM **Privately Held**
WEB: www.casadorinda.org
SIC: 8051 8052 8361 Skilled nursing care
facilities; personal care facility; rest home,
with health care incidental

(P-20420)
**MOYLES CENTL VLY HLTH
CARE INC (PA)**
999 N M St, Tulare (93274-2019)
PHONE....................................559 688-0288
Ken Moyel III, *President*
EMP: 241 **EST:** 1990
SALES (est): 14.4MM **Privately Held**
SIC: 8051 Skilled nursing care facilities

(P-20421)
**MOYLES CENTL VLY HLTH
CARE INC**
Also Called: Porterville Convalescent Hosp
1100 W Morton Ave, Porterville
(93257-1947)
PHONE....................................559 782-1509
James Higbee, *CFO*
EMP: 99
SALES (corp-wide): 14.4MM **Privately
Held**
SIC: 8051 Convalescent home with contin-
uous nursing care
PA: Moyle's Central Valley Health Care Inc.
999 N M St
Tulare CA 93274
559 688-0288

(P-20422)
**MT RUBIDOUXIDENCE OPCO
LLC**
Also Called: Jurupa Hills Post Acute
6401 33rd St, Riverside (92509-1404)
PHONE....................................951 681-2200
Jason Murray, *Principal*
Debra Gogerty, *Principal*
Mark Hancock, *Principal*
EMP: 199 **EST:** 2015
SALES (est): 6.5MM **Privately Held**
SIC: 8051 Skilled nursing care facilities

(P-20423)
NAVIGAGE FOUNDATION (PA)
849 Foothill Blvd Ste 8, La Canada
(91011-3368)
PHONE....................................818 790-2522
Judy Vallas, *CEO*
EMP: 100 **EST:** 1932
SQ FT: 90,000
SALES (est): 579.6K **Privately Held**
SIC: 8051 8059 8052 Skilled nursing care
facilities; rest home, with health care; in-
termediate care facilities

(P-20424)
**NEWPORT SBACUTE
HEALTHCARE CTR**
Also Called: Milestone Health Care Center
2570 Newport Blvd, Costa Mesa
(92627-1331)
PHONE....................................949 631-4282
Tony Ricci, *President*
EMP: 81 **EST:** 1998
SQ FT: 22,000
SALES (est): 13.6MM **Privately Held**
SIC: 8051 Skilled nursing care facilities

(P-20425)
**NORWALK MEADOWS NURSING
CTR LP**
10625 Leffingwell Rd, Norwalk
(90650-3434)
PHONE....................................562 864-2541
Pnina Graff, *Partner*
Jacob Graff, *Partner*
Lisa Thomashow, *Administration*
EMP: 106 **EST:** 1997
SQ FT: 23,632
SALES (est): 32.7MM **Privately Held**
WEB: www.norwalkmeadows.com
SIC: 8051 Convalescent home with contin-
uous nursing care

(P-20426)
OASIS HCP 2 LLC (PA)
4601 Wilshire Blvd # 220, Los Angeles
(90010-3880)
PHONE....................................323 987-5954
EMP: 139 **EST:** 2017
SALES (est): 9.4MM **Privately Held**
SIC: 8051 Convalescent home with contin-
uous nursing care

(P-20427)
ODYSSEY HEALTHCARE INC
525 Cabrillo Park Dr # 150, Santa Ana
(92701-5017)
PHONE....................................714 245-7420
EMP: 52
SALES (corp-wide): 6B **Privately Held**
SIC: 8051 Skilled Nursing Care Facility
HQ: Odyssey Healthcare, Inc.
7801 Mesquite Bend Dr # 105
Irving TX 75063

(P-20428)
**ORANGE HLTHCARE WLLNESS
CNTRE**
920 W La Veta Ave, Orange (92868-4302)
PHONE....................................714 633-3568
Jonathan Weiss,
Sharrod Brooks,
Maricris Guray, *Director*
EMP: 110 **EST:** 2009
SALES (est): 10MM **Privately Held**
WEB: www.orangerehabilitation.com
SIC: 8051 Convalescent home with contin-
uous nursing care

(P-20429)
**ORCHARD - POST ACUTE CARE
CTR**
12385 Washington Blvd, Whittier
(90606-2502)
PHONE....................................562 693-7701
Rich Jorgensen, *Principal*
EMP: 148 **EST:** 2011
SALES (est): 15.6MM
SALES (corp-wide): 2.4B **Publicly Held**
WEB: www.theorchardpostacute.com
SIC: 8051 Convalescent home with contin-
uous nursing care
PA: The Ensign Group Inc
29222 Rncho Vejo Rd Ste 1
San Juan Capistrano CA 92675
949 487-9500

(P-20430)
**P R N CONVALESCENT
HOSPITAL**
Also Called: High Valley Lodge
7912 Topley Ln, Sunland (91040-3336)
PHONE....................................818 352-3158
Pauline Albert, *President*
Luis Albert Jr, *Vice Pres*
EMP: 54 **EST:** 1989
SQ FT: 11,712
SALES (est): 3.7MM **Privately Held**
SIC: 8051 Convalescent home with contin-
uous nursing care

(P-20431)
**PACIFIC PALMS HEALTHCARE
LLC (PA)**
1020 Termino Ave, Long Beach
(90804-4123)
PHONE....................................562 433-6791
Emmanuel B David,
Brandie D Kaneshiro,
Marybeth D Martinez,
EMP: 114 **EST:** 2003
SALES: 8.3MM **Privately Held**
WEB: www.ppsnf.com
SIC: 8051 Convalescent home with contin-
uous nursing care

(P-20432)
**PALMCREST GRAND CARE CTR
INC**
3501 Cedar Ave, Long Beach
(90807-3809)
PHONE....................................562 595-4551
William Nelson, *President*
EMP: 99
SALES (est): 5.7MM **Privately Held**
WEB: www.palmcrestgrandretirement.com
SIC: 8051 Skilled nursing care facilities

(P-20433)
**PARKVIEW JLIAN CNVLESCENT
HOSP**
1801 Julian Ave, Bakersfield (93304-6419)
PHONE....................................661 831-9150
Ligia Denham, *Vice Pres*
Sylvia Velasco, *Office Mgr*
Douglas Rice, *Administration*

Raju Patel, *Director*
EMP: 130
SQ FT: 8,000
SALES: 12.3MM **Privately Held**
WEB: www.parkviewjulian-snf.com
SIC: 8051 Convalescent home with contin-
uous nursing care

(P-20434)
PARKVIEW JULIAN LLC
Also Called: Parkview Julian Healthcare Ctr
1801 Julian Ave, Bakersfield (93304-6419)
PHONE....................................661 831-9150
David Levy, *Mng Member*
Moshe Frankel, *Mng Member*
EMP: 150 **EST:** 2017
SALES (est): 11.2MM **Privately Held**
SIC: 8051 Convalescent home with contin-
uous nursing care

(P-20435)
**PASADENA HOSPITAL ASSN
LTD (PA)**
Also Called: Huntington Memorial Hospital
100 W California Blvd, Pasadena
(91105-3010)
P.O. Box 440746, Houston TX (77244-
0746)
PHONE....................................626 397-5000
Lori J Morgan, *CEO*
Jonathan Maskin,
Paul Ouyang, *Ch of Bd*
Stephen A Ralph, *President*
Steven L Mohr, *CFO*
EMP: 2100 **EST:** 1892
SQ FT: 928,000
SALES: 654.4MM **Privately Held**
WEB: www.huntingtonhospital.org
SIC: 5912 8051 8063 Drug stores; skilled
nursing care facilities; psychiatric hospi-
tals

(P-20436)
**PASADENA HOSPITAL ASSN
LTD**
Also Called: Huntington Extended Care Ctr
716 S Fair Oaks Ave, Pasadena
(91105-2618)
PHONE....................................626 397-3322
Ken Hoff, *Manager*
EMP: 445
SALES (corp-wide): 654.4MM **Privately
Held**
WEB: www.huntingtonhospital.org
SIC: 8051 Skilled nursing care facilities
PA: Pasadena Hospital Association, Ltd.
100 W California Blvd
Pasadena CA 91105
626 397-5000

(P-20437)
**PASADENA MADOWS NURSING
CTR LP**
150 Bellefontaine St, Pasadena
(91105-3102)
PHONE....................................626 796-1103
Pnina Graff, *Partner*
Khristine Bondoc, *Marketing Mgr*
EMP: 99 **EST:** 2012
SALES (est): 5MM **Privately Held**
WEB: www.pasadenameadows.com
SIC: 8051 Skilled nursing care facilities

(P-20438)
PCI CARE VENTURE I
Also Called: Prestige Asssted Lving At Lncs
43454 30th St W Ofc, Lancaster
(93536-5307)
PHONE....................................661 949-2177
Pat Elliott, *Manager*
Nancy Seagar, *Chf Purch Ofc*
Gustavo Velasco-Rivera, *Food Svc Dir*
EMP: 70
SALES (corp-wide): 381.6MM **Privately
Held**
SIC: 8051 Skilled nursing care facilities
HQ: Pci Care Venture I
7700 Ne Parkway Dr # 300
Vancouver WA 98662

(P-20439)
PCI CARE VENTURE I
Also Called: Prestige Asssted Lving At Vsli
3120 W Caldwell Ave, Visalia (93277-7003)
PHONE..................................559 735-0828
Helen Hurley, *Manager*
EMP: 70
SQ FT: 42,457
SALES (corp-wide): 381.6MM **Privately Held**
SIC: **8051** Skilled nursing care facilities
HQ: Pci Care Venture I
7700 Ne Parkway Dr # 300
Vancouver WA 98662

(P-20440)
PENNANT HEALTHCARE INC (HQ)
Also Called: ENSIGN
27101 Puerta Real Ste 450, Mission Viejo
(92691-8566)
PHONE..................................949 487-9500
Owen Hammond, *President*
Soon Burnam, *Treasurer*
Beverly Wittekind, *Admin Sec*
EMP: 112 EST: 2011
SALES (est): 1.9MM
SALES (corp-wide): 2.4B **Publicly Held**
WEB: www.pennanthealthcare.com
SIC: **8051** Skilled nursing care facilities
PA: The Ensign Group Inc
29222 Rncho Vejo Rd Ste 1
San Juan Capistrano CA 92675
949 487-9500

(P-20441)
PLOTT MANAGEMENT CO
Also Called: Plott Family Home Care
264 E 18th St, San Bernardino
(92404-4708)
PHONE..................................909 883-0288
EMP: 88
SALES (est): 3.6MM **Privately Held**
SIC: **8051** Skilled Nursing Care Facility

(P-20442)
RAMONA CARE INC
Also Called: Ramona Nrsing Rhbilitation Ctr
11900 Ramona Blvd, El Monte
(91732-2314)
PHONE..................................626 442-5721
Michael Hyer, *President*
Jeffrey Daly, *Treasurer*
Victor Lundquist, *Admin Sec*
Alvaro Lemus, *Maint Spvr*
Marie Dor-Oscar, *Nursing Dir*
EMP: 140 EST: 1990
SQ FT: 35,000
SALES (est): 10MM **Privately Held**
WEB: www.ramonarehab.com
SIC: **8051** Convalescent home with contin-
uous nursing care

(P-20443)
REHABLTION CNTRE OF BVRLY HLLS
580 S San Vicente Blvd, Los Angeles
(90048-4621)
PHONE..................................323 782-1500
Eldon Teper, *President*
EMP: 200 EST: 1998
SALES (est): 26.5MM **Privately Held**
WEB: www.rehabcentre.com
SIC: **8051** Convalescent home with contin-
uous nursing care

(P-20444)
REHABLTTION CTR OF ORNGE CNTY
9021 Knott Ave, Buena Park (90620-4138)
PHONE..................................714 826-2330
Peter Madigan, *President*
Robert Nelson, *President*
EMP: 125 EST: 1967
SALES (est): 15.3MM **Privately Held**
SIC: **8051 8059** Convalescent home with
continuous nursing care; rest home, with
health care

(P-20445)
RHF PLYMOUTH TOWER
3401 Lemon St Ofc, Riverside
(92501-2817)
PHONE..................................951 248-0456

Wes Jones, *Administration*
EMP: 65 EST: 2004
SALES (est): 2.7MM **Privately Held**
SIC: **8051** Convalescent home with contin-
uous nursing care

(P-20446)
RIDGECREST HEALTHCARE INC (PA)
1131 N China Lake Blvd, Ridgecrest
(93555-3131)
PHONE..................................323 344-0601
Oscar Abaya Parel, *President*
Ginggaew Kaspar, *Food Svc Dir*
EMP: 136 EST: 2003
SALES (est): 12.9MM **Privately Held**
WEB: www.windsorridgecrest.com
SIC: **8051** Convalescent home with contin-
uous nursing care

(P-20447)
RIVERA SANITARIUM INC
Also Called: Colonial Gardens Nursing Home
7246 Rosemead Blvd, Pico Rivera
(90660-4010)
P.O. Box 2098 (90662-2098)
PHONE..................................562 949-2591
Elizabeth Stephens, *President*
Kent Stephens, *Administration*
EMP: 86 EST: 1959
SQ FT: 30,000
SALES (est): 8.7MM **Privately Held**
SIC: **8051** Convalescent home with contin-
uous nursing care

(P-20448)
RIVERSIDE CARE INC
Also Called: VALENCIA GARDENS HEALTH
CARE CENTER
4301 Caroline Ct, Riverside (92506-2902)
PHONE..................................951 683-7111
Ted Holt, *President*
Spencer E Olsen, *Treasurer*
Jenny Ortiz, *Office Mgr*
EMP: 130 EST: 1971
SALES (est): 6.9MM **Privately Held**
WEB: www.valenciagardenshealth.com
SIC: **8051** Convalescent home with contin-
uous nursing care
PA: North American Client Services, Inc.
25910 Acero Ste 350
Mission Viejo CA 92691

(P-20449)
RIVERSIDE EQUITIES LLC
Also Called: Mission Care Center
8487 Magnolia Ave, Riverside
(92504-3222)
PHONE..................................951 688-2222
Frank Johnson, *CEO*
Irving Bauman, *COO*
Roger Groves, *Administration*
EMP: 141 EST: 2008
SALES (est): 6.5MM **Privately Held**
WEB: www.missioncarecenter.com
SIC: **8051** Convalescent home with contin-
uous nursing care
PA: Sun Mar Management Services
3050 Saturn St Ste 201
Brea CA 92821

(P-20450)
RIVIERA NURSING & CONVA
Also Called: Riviera Health Care Center
8203 Telegraph Rd, Pico Rivera
(90660-4905)
PHONE..................................562 806-2576
Morris Weiss, *President*
Bessie Weiss, *Vice Pres*
Rolan Calungsod, *Office Mgr*
EMP: 118 EST: 1966
SQ FT: 60,000
SALES (est): 10.8MM **Privately Held**
WEB: www.rivierahealthcare.com
SIC: **8051 8059** Convalescent home with
continuous nursing care; convalescent
home

(P-20451)
ROCKPORT ADM SVCS LLC
Also Called: Montecito Heights
4585 N Figueroa St, Los Angeles
(90065-3026)
PHONE..................................323 223-3441

EMP: 63 **Privately Held**
SIC: **8051** Skilled nursing care facilities
PA: Rockport Administrative Services, Llc
5900 Wilshire Blvd # 1600
Los Angeles CA 90036

(P-20452)
ROWLAND CONVALESCENT HOSP INC
Also Called: Rowland, The
330 W Rowland St, Covina (91723-2941)
PHONE..................................626 967-2741
Anthony Kalomas, *President*
EMP: 100 EST: 1979
SQ FT: 30,000
SALES (est): 8.3MM **Privately Held**
WEB: www.rowlandconvalescent.com
SIC: **8051** Convalescent home with contin-
uous nursing care

(P-20453)
ROYAL TERRACE HEALTHCARE
1340 Highland Ave, Duarte (91010-2520)
PHONE..................................626 256-4654
Eloisa Heiser, *Director*
Alma Hechanova, *Director*
Anabell Reyes, *Director*
EMP: 60 EST: 2003
SALES (est): 5.7MM **Privately Held**
SIC: **8051** Convalescent home with contin-
uous nursing care

(P-20454)
RRT ENTERPRISES LP (PA)
Also Called: Country Vlla Mar Vsta Nrsing C
3966 Marcasel Ave, Los Angeles
(90066-4616)
PHONE..................................310 397-2372
Stephen Reissman, *General Ptnr*
Myla Cari, *Records Dir*
Rita Luhar, *Records Dir*
Virginia Muniz, *Records Dir*
Karen Quintanar, *Records Dir*
EMP: 390 EST: 1972
SQ FT: 18,000
SALES (est): 16.4MM **Privately Held**
SIC: **8051** Skilled nursing care facilities

(P-20455)
RRT ENTERPRISES LP
855 N Fairfax Ave, Los Angeles
(90046-7207)
PHONE..................................323 653-1521
Stephen Reissman, *Branch Mgr*
EMP: 344
SALES (corp-wide): 16.4MM **Privately Held**
SIC: **8051** Skilled nursing care facilities
PA: Rrt Enterprises L.P.
3966 Marcasel Ave
Los Angeles CA 90066
310 397-2372

(P-20456)
S&F MANAGEMENT COMPANY LLC (PA)
9200 W Sunset Blvd # 700, West Holly-
wood (90069-3502)
PHONE..................................310 385-1090
Lee C Samson, *President*
EMP: 1343 EST: 2006
SALES (est): 191.7MM **Privately Held**
SIC: **8051** Convalescent home with contin-
uous nursing care

(P-20457)
SAN PEDRO CONVALESCENT HM INC
Also Called: Los Palos Convalescent Hosp
1430 W 6th St, San Pedro (90732-3503)
PHONE..................................310 832-6431
Celia Valdomar, *President*
Ruth Angeles, *Office Mgr*
Nestor Alegre, *Administration*
Christine Yim, *Hlthcr Dir*
EMP: 90 EST: 1963
SQ FT: 10,000
SALES (est): 10MM **Privately Held**
WEB: www.lpconv.com
SIC: **8051** Convalescent home with contin-
uous nursing care

(P-20458)
SANDHRST CNVLSCENT GROUP LTD A
Also Called: Windsor Grdns Cnvlscent Ctr Hw
13922 Cerise Ave, Hawthorne
(90250-8118)
PHONE..................................310 675-3304
Anne Josafat, *Principal*
Becca Catlett, *Sales Staff*
EMP: 63 EST: 1993
SALES (est): 5MM **Privately Held**
SIC: **8051** Convalescent home with contin-
uous nursing care

(P-20459)
SANTA ANITA CNVLSCENT HOSP RTR
5522 Gracewood Ave, Temple City (91780)
PHONE..................................626 579-0310
Miriam Weiss, *President*
Jacob Kasirer, *Vice Pres*
EMP: 150 EST: 1968
SQ FT: 88,615
SALES (est): 11.6MM
SALES (corp-wide): 62.1MM **Privately Held**
WEB: www.goldenstatehealth.com
SIC: **8051** Convalescent home with contin-
uous nursing care
PA: Golden State Health Centers, Inc.
13347 Ventura Blvd
Sherman Oaks CA 91423
818 385-3200

(P-20460)
SEA BREEZE HEALTH CARE INC
Also Called: Beachside Nursing Center
7781 Garfield Ave, Huntington Beach
(92648-2026)
PHONE..................................714 847-9671
Tim Paulson, *President*
Nate Beck, *Administration*
ARI Corona, *Payroll Mgr*
Ethel Bartolome, *Sales Executive*
Brandi Guzman, *Nurse*
EMP: 132 EST: 2003
SQ FT: 14,895
SALES (est): 9.9MM **Privately Held**
WEB: www.beachsidenursing.com
SIC: **8051** Convalescent home with contin-
uous nursing care
PA: North American Client Services, Inc.
25910 Acero Ste 350
Mission Viejo CA 92691

(P-20461)
SEACREST CONVALESCENT HOSP INC
1416 W 6th St, San Pedro (90732-3550)
PHONE..................................310 833-3526
Cecelia Valdomar, *President*
Cecelia D Valdomar, *President*
Joy Nacionales, *Admin Sec*
Chris Tui, *Director*
Jose Valdomar, *Director*
EMP: 70 EST: 1962
SALES (est): 8.9MM **Privately Held**
WEB: www.scconv.com
SIC: **8051** Convalescent home with contin-
uous nursing care

(P-20462)
SELA HEALTHCARE INC (PA)
Also Called: Holiday Manor Care Center
867 E 11th St, Upland (91786-4867)
PHONE..................................909 985-1981
Philip Weinberger, *CEO*
Marylnynn Mahan, *CFO*
EMP: 140 EST: 2002
SQ FT: 60,000
SALES (est): 13.3MM **Privately Held**
SIC: **8051** Skilled nursing care facilities

(P-20463)
SELA HEALTHCARE INC
Also Called: Holiday Manor Care Center
20554 Roscoe Blvd, Canoga Park
(91306-1746)
PHONE..................................818 341-9800
Victorio Ocbena Sosing, *Principal*
EMP: 310

SALES (corp-wide): 13.3MM **Privately Held**
SIC: **8051** Convalescent home with continuous nursing care
PA: Sela Healthcare, Inc.
867 E 11th St
Upland CA 91786
909 985-1981

(P-20464)
SHADOW HLLS CNVLSCENT HOSP INC
10158 Sunland Blvd, Sunland
(91040-1651)
PHONE..................818 352-4438
Orlando Clarizio Jr, *President*
Dino Clarizio, *Treasurer*
Michale Clarizio, *Admin Sec*
EMP: 67 EST: 1968
SQ FT: 13,000
SALES (est): 4.2MM **Privately Held**
SIC: **8051** Convalescent home with continuous nursing care

(P-20465)
SILVERADO SENIOR LIVING INC
Also Called: Beach Cities Memory Care
Cmnty
514 N Prospect Ave # 120, Redondo Beach
(90277-3036)
PHONE..................424 257-6418
Christine Garcia, *Food Svc Dir*
Michael Barron, *Director*
EMP: 59
SALES (corp-wide): 173.8MM **Privately Held**
WEB: www.silverado.com
SIC: **8051** Skilled nursing care facilities
PA: Senior Silverado Living Inc
6400 Oak Cyn Ste 200
Irvine CA 92618
949 240-7200

(P-20466)
SILVERADO SENIOR LIVING INC (PA)
6400 Oak Cyn Ste 200, Irvine
(92618-5233)
PHONE..................949 240-7200
George L Chapman, *CEO*
Daizel Gasperian, *President*
Kathy Greene, *President*
Shannon Gutierrez, *President*
Loren B Shook, *President*
EMP: 65
SQ FT: 65,000
SALES (est): 173.8MM **Privately Held**
WEB: www.silverado.com
SIC: **8051** Skilled nursing care facilities

(P-20467)
SILVERADO SENIOR LIVING INC
Also Called: Los Angeles At Home
601 S Glenoaks Blvd, Burbank
(91502-1474)
PHONE..................747 477-2618
EMP: 59
SALES (corp-wide): 173.8MM **Privately Held**
WEB: www.silverado.com
SIC: **8051** Skilled nursing care facilities
PA: Senior Silverado Living Inc
6400 Oak Cyn Ste 200
Irvine CA 92618
949 240-7200

(P-20468)
SILVERADO SENIOR LIVING INC
Also Called: Orange County At Home
6400 Oak Cyn Ste 150, Irvine
(92618-5205)
PHONE..................858 869-0538
Angela Mouton, *Vice Pres*
EMP: 59
SALES (corp-wide): 173.8MM **Privately Held**
WEB: www.silverado.com
SIC: **8051** Skilled nursing care facilities
PA: Senior Silverado Living Inc
6400 Oak Cyn Ste 200
Irvine CA 92618
949 240-7200

(P-20469)
SILVERADO SENIOR LIVING INC
Also Called: Orange County Hospice
6400 Oak Cyn Ste 150, Irvine
(92618-5205)
PHONE..................949 240-7744
EMP: 59
SALES (corp-wide): 173.8MM **Privately Held**
WEB: www.silverado.com
SIC: **8051** Skilled nursing care facilities
PA: Senior Silverado Living Inc
6400 Oak Cyn Ste 200
Irvine CA 92618
949 240-7200

(P-20470)
SILVERADO SENIOR LIVING INC
Also Called: Ventura Hospice
4520 E Thousand Oaks Blvd, Westlake Village (91362-7220)
PHONE..................805 230-2626
EMP: 59
SALES (corp-wide): 173.8MM **Privately Held**
WEB: www.silverado.com
SIC: **8051** Skilled nursing care facilities
PA: Senior Silverado Living Inc
6400 Oak Cyn Ste 200
Irvine CA 92618
949 240-7200

(P-20471)
SILVERADO SENIOR LIVING INC
Also Called: Newport Mesa Memory Care
Cmnty
350 W Bay St, Costa Mesa (92627-2020)
PHONE..................949 945-0189
Michelle Egrer, *Principal*
Lee Riggs, *COO*
Modesto Trujillo, *Food Svc Dir*
Jamie Langston, *Hlthcr Dir*
Dorothy Washington, *Director*
EMP: 59
SQ FT: 20,331
SALES (corp-wide): 173.8MM **Privately Held**
WEB: www.silverado.com
SIC: **8051** Skilled nursing care facilities
PA: Senior Silverado Living Inc
6400 Oak Cyn Ste 200
Irvine CA 92618
949 240-7200

(P-20472)
SILVERADO SENIOR LIVING INC
Also Called: San Juan Cpstrano Mmory Care
C
30311 Camino Capistrano, San Juan Capistrano (92675-1303)
PHONE..................949 988-0921
Carol Shaw, *Manager*
Doreen Cregg, *Hlthcr Dir*
EMP: 59
SALES (corp-wide): 173.8MM **Privately Held**
WEB: www.silverado.com
SIC: **8051** Skilled nursing care facilities
PA: Senior Silverado Living Inc
6400 Oak Cyn Ste 200
Irvine CA 92618
949 240-7200

(P-20473)
SILVERADO SENIOR LIVING INC
Also Called: Huntington Memory Care Cmnty
1118 N Stoneman Ave, Alhambra
(91801-1007)
PHONE..................626 872-3941
Vida Gwin, *Administration*
Tamra Mitchell, *Human Res Dir*
Maria Quizon, *Director*
EMP: 59
SALES (corp-wide): 173.8MM **Privately Held**
WEB: www.silverado.com
SIC: **8051** Skilled nursing care facilities
PA: Senior Silverado Living Inc
6400 Oak Cyn Ste 200
Irvine CA 92618
949 240-7200

(P-20474)
SILVERADO SENIOR LIVING INC
Also Called: Calabasas Memory Care Cmnty
25100 Calabasas Rd, Calabasas
(91302-1435)
PHONE..................818 746-2583
Rachel Dardeau, *Administration*
EMP: 59
SALES (corp-wide): 173.8MM **Privately Held**
WEB: www.silverado.com
SIC: **8051** Skilled nursing care facilities
PA: Senior Silverado Living Inc
6400 Oak Cyn Ste 200
Irvine CA 92618
949 240-7200

(P-20475)
SILVERADO SENIOR LIVING INC
Also Called: Beverly Pl Memory Care Cmnty
330 N Hayworth Ave, Los Angeles
(90048-2702)
PHONE..................323 984-7313
Beth Medina, *Principal*
EMP: 59
SALES (corp-wide): 173.8MM **Privately Held**
WEB: www.silverado.com
SIC: **8051** Skilled nursing care facilities
PA: Senior Silverado Living Inc
6400 Oak Cyn Ste 200
Irvine CA 92618
949 240-7200

(P-20476)
SKYLINE HLTHCARE WLLNESS CTR L
Also Called: Skyline Healthcare Center
3032 Rowena Ave, Los Angeles
(90039-2005)
PHONE..................323 665-1185
Bernon Aguilar, *Administration*
Sharrod Brooks,
EMP: 99 EST: 2010
SALES (est): 9.9MM **Privately Held**
WEB: www.skylinehc.com
SIC: **8051** Convalescent home with continuous nursing care

(P-20477)
SLCH INC (PA)
Also Called: Sophia Lyn Convalescent Hosp
1920 N Fair Oaks Ave, Pasadena
(91103-1623)
PHONE..................626 798-0558
Phillip Rosales, *President*
Lolita Asero, *Administration*
EMP: 50
SQ FT: 16,757
SALES (est): 3.2MM **Privately Held**
SIC: **8051** Extended care facility

(P-20478)
SOUTH COAST HEALTH WELLNESS
Also Called: Community Care On Palm
4768 Palm Ave, Riverside (92501-4012)
PHONE..................951 686-9001
Cheryl B Jumonville, *President*
Tony Hunter, *Administration*
Peter Anes, *Maint Spvr*
EMP: 50 EST: 1989
SALES (est): 5MM **Privately Held**
WEB: www.cconpalm.com
SIC: **8051** Convalescent home with continuous nursing care

(P-20479)
SPRING VALLEY POST ACUTE LLC
14973 Hesperia Rd, Victorville
(92395-3923)
PHONE..................760 245-6477
David Johnson, *Mng Member*
Matheson Chambers, *Mng Member*
Thomas Chambers, *Mng Member*
Nicola Harris, *Assistant*
EMP: 200
SALES: 11.5MM **Privately Held**
WEB: www.springvalleypostacute.com
SIC: **8051** Convalescent home with continuous nursing care

(P-20480)
STJOHN GOD RTIREMENT CARE CTR
2468 S St Andrews Pl, Los Angeles
(90018-2042)
PHONE..................323 731-0641
Michael Bessimer, *Administration*
Angelita Trinidad, *Office Mgr*
Marinor Ifurung, *Human Res Dir*
Jonathon Harris, *Human Resources*
Ada Guevara, *Hlthcr Dir*
EMP: 200 EST: 1942
SQ FT: 99,392
SALES: 16MM **Privately Held**
SIC: **8051 8052** Skilled nursing care facilities; intermediate care facilities

(P-20481)
SUMMIT TRAIL HLTH HOLDINGS LLC
29222 Rncho Vejo Rd Ste 1, San Juan Capistrano (92675)
PHONE..................949 487-9500
EMP: 56 EST: 2019
SALES (est): 5.1MM
SALES (corp-wide): 2.4B **Publicly Held**
WEB: www.ensigngroup.net
SIC: **8051** Skilled nursing care facilities
PA: The Ensign Group Inc
29222 Rncho Vejo Rd Ste 1
San Juan Capistrano CA 92675
949 487-9500

(P-20482)
SUN HAVEN CARE INC
Also Called: Terrace View Care Center
201 E Bastanchury Rd, Fullerton
(92835-2604)
PHONE..................714 870-0060
John Sworenson, *CEO*
Rina Abaya, *Records Dir*
Brendon Bahl, *Vice Pres*
Claudia Valdez, *Office Mgr*
EMP: 58 EST: 1997
SALES (est): 12.4MM **Privately Held**
SIC: **8051** Convalescent home with continuous nursing care

(P-20483)
SUN MAR MANAGEMENT SERVICES
8171 Magnolia Ave, Riverside
(92504-3409)
PHONE..................951 687-3842
Robert Ginn, *Administration*
Amy Wood, *Director*
Lorie Rodriguez, *Consultant*
EMP: 117 **Privately Held**
SIC: **8051** Skilled nursing care facilities
PA: Sun Mar Management Services
3050 Saturn St Ste 201
Brea CA 92821

(P-20484)
SUNBRDGE SHNDIN HLLS RHBLTTION
Also Called: Shandin Hlls Ehvior Thrapy Ctr
4164 N 4th Ave, San Bernardino
(92407-2908)
PHONE..................909 881-3896
Mike Gasis, *Manager*
Crystal Gecse, *Hlthcr Dir*
EMP: 53 **Privately Held**
WEB: www.shandinhillsbhc.com
SIC: **8051** Convalescent home with continuous nursing care
HQ: Sunbridge Shandin Hills Rehabilitation Center
4164 N 4th Ave
San Bernardino CA 92407
909 881-3896

(P-20485)
SUNFLOWER GARDENS INC
3730 S Greenville St, Santa Ana
(92704-7092)
PHONE..................714 641-0959
Isaac Neches, *President*
Stella Neches, *Vice Pres*
EMP: 59 EST: 1992
SQ FT: 5,783
SALES (est): 4.4MM **Privately Held**
SIC: **8051** Skilled nursing care facilities

(P-20486)

SUNRISE SENIOR LIVING LLC

31741 Rancho Viejo Rd, San Juan Capistrano (92675-6722)
PHONE................................949 248-8855
Tiffany Calahan, *Manager*
EMP: 58
SALES (corp-wide): 418.2MM **Privately Held**
WEB: www.sunriseseniorliving.com
SIC: 8051 8361 Convalescent home with continuous nursing care; residential care
HQ: Sunrise Senior Living, Llc
7902 Westpark Dr
Mc Lean VA 22102

(P-20487)

TORRANCE CARE CENTER WEST INC

4333 Torrance Blvd, Torrance (90503-4401)
PHONE................................310 370-4561
Vicki P Rollins, *President*
EMP: 180
SALES: 17.8MM **Privately Held**
WEB: www.torranceca.gov
SIC: 8051 Skilled nursing care facilities

(P-20488)

TOWN CNTRY MNOR OF CHRSTN MSSN

555 E Memory Ln Ofc Ofc, Santa Ana (92706-1753)
PHONE................................714 547-7581
Dirk De Wolfe, *Administration*
Gina Kolb, *CFO*
Shauna Stratton, *Admin Sec*
Dirk D Wolfe, *Administration*
Nancy Melendez, *Nursing Dir*
EMP: 210 EST: 1975
SQ FT: 208,000
SALES: 21.7MM **Privately Held**
WEB: www.tcmanor.com
SIC: 8051 8059 8052 Skilled nursing care facilities; nursing home, except skilled & intermediate care facility; intermediate care facilities

(P-20489)

TREASURE HLLS HLTH HLDINGS LLC

29222 Rncho Vejo Rd Ste 1, San Juan Capistrano (92675)
PHONE................................949 487-9500
EMP: 80 EST: 2019
SALES (est): 7.2MM
SALES (corp-wide): 2.4B **Publicly Held**
WEB: www.ensigngroup.net
SIC: 8051 Skilled nursing care facilities
PA: The Ensign Group Inc
29222 Rncho Vejo Rd Ste 1
San Juan Capistrano CA 92675
949 487-9500

(P-20490)

TRINITY HEALTH SYSTEMS (PA)

Also Called: Villa Maria Care Center
14318 Ohio St, Baldwin Park (91706-2553)
PHONE................................626 960-1971
Randal Kleis, *President*
Bob Wardwell, *CFO*
Frances Ruiz, *Social Dir*
Shelley Jackson, *Principal*
Teresa Steele, *Principal*
EMP: 80 EST: 1989
SQ FT: 35,000
SALES (est): 10.3MM **Privately Held**
WEB: www.sierraviewcarecenter.com
SIC: 8051 Convalescent home with continuous nursing care

(P-20491)

TULARE NRSING RHBLTTION HOSP I

Also Called: Tulare Nrsing Rhbilitation Ctr
680 E Merritt Ave, Tulare (93274-2135)
PHONE................................559 686-8581
Mark Fisher, *President*
Norm Christianson, *CFO*
Sharon A Fisher, *Admin Sec*
EMP: 51 EST: 2006

SALES (est): 10.4MM **Privately Held**
WEB: www.missioncg.com
SIC: 8051 Convalescent home with continuous nursing care

(P-20492)

UPLAND COMMUNITY CARE INC

Also Called: Upland Rehabilitation Care Ctr
1221 E Arrow Hwy, Upland (91786-4911)
PHONE................................909 985-1903
Owen Hammond, *CEO*
Beverly Hughes, *Chf Purch Ofc*
Connie Chacon, *Education*
Elsa Beltran, *Food Svc Dir*
Corey N Procuniar, *Director*
EMP: 192 EST: 2008
SALES (est): 17.5MM
SALES (corp-wide): 2.4B **Publicly Held**
WEB: www.uplandcare.com
SIC: 8051 Convalescent home with continuous nursing care
PA: The Ensign Group Inc
29222 Rncho Vejo Rd Ste 1
San Juan Capistrano CA 92675
949 487-9500

(P-20493)

US SKILLSERVE INC

Also Called: Community Cnvlscent Hosp Mntcl
9620 Fremont Ave, Montclair (91763-2320)
PHONE................................909 621-4751
Johannes Simanjuntak, *Manager*
Irena Jerak, *Social Dir*
Veronica Esperar, *Office Mgr*
Sharon Collins, *Marketing Staff*
Carlos Rios, *Food Svc Dir*
EMP: 987
SALES (corp-wide): 18.1MM **Privately Held**
WEB: www.communityech.com
SIC: 8051 Convalescent home with continuous nursing care
PA: U.S. Skillserve Inc
4115 E Broadway Ste A
Long Beach CA 90803
562 930-0777

(P-20494)

VALLEY CAREIDENCE OPCO LLC

Also Called: Gateway Post Acute
661 W Poplar Ave, Porterville (93257-5926)
PHONE................................559 784-8371
Jason Murray, *CEO*
Mark Hancock, *CFO*
EMP: 75 EST: 2014
SALES (est): 8.9MM **Privately Held**
WEB: www.gatewaypostacute.com
SIC: 8051 Convalescent home with continuous nursing care
PA: Providence Group Of California, Llc
140 N Union Ave Ste 320
Farmington UT 84025
619 756-6800

(P-20495)

VALLEY VSTA NRSING TRNSTNAL CA

Also Called: Valley Vsta Nrsing Trnstnal Ca
6120 Vineland Ave, North Hollywood (91606-4914)
PHONE................................818 763-6275
Crystal Solorzano,
EMP: 170 EST: 2017
SALES (est): 5.3MM **Privately Held**
SIC: 8051 Convalescent home with continuous nursing care

(P-20496)

VICTORIA CARE CENTER

5445 Everglades St, Ventura (93003-6523)
PHONE................................805 642-1736
Scott Porter, *Exec Dir*
Jay Brady, *President*
EMP: 100 EST: 1987
SQ FT: 85,000
SALES (est): 25MM **Privately Held**
WEB: www.victoriacarecenter.com
SIC: 8051 Convalescent home with continuous nursing care

PA: Beverly Health Care Corporation
5445 Everglades St
Ventura CA 93003

(P-20497)

VILLA CONVALESCENT HOSP INC

8965 Magnolia Ave, Riverside (92503-4432)
PHONE................................951 689-5788
Jacob Paulson, *Administration*
Spencer E Olsen, *CFO*
Stephanie Rivera, *Social Dir*
Ryan Leet, *Administration*
Holly Christensen, *Marketing Staff*
EMP: 90 EST: 1971
SQ FT: 25,000
SALES: 9.2MM **Privately Held**
WEB: www.villahealthcare.com
SIC: 8051 Convalescent home with continuous nursing care

(P-20498)

VILLA SERENA HEALTHCARE CENTER

723 E 9th St, Long Beach (90813-4611)
PHONE................................562 437-2797
Matt Carp, *President*
EMP: 70 EST: 2014
SALES (est): 3.7MM **Privately Held**
SIC: 8051 Skilled nursing care facilities

(P-20499)

VILLAGE PACIFIC MGT GROUP INC

Also Called: Village At Sydney Creek
1234 Laurel Ln, San Luis Obispo (93401-5860)
PHONE................................805 543-2350
Leona Baker, *Manager*
Jane Lefebre, *Director*
EMP: 53 **Privately Held**
WEB: www.villagesofslo.com
SIC: 8051 Skilled nursing care facilities
PA: Village Pacific Management Group, Inc.
55 Broad St
San Luis Obispo CA 93405

(P-20500)

VILLAGE PACIFIC MGT GROUP INC (PA)

Also Called: Village At Sydney Creek
55 Broad St, San Luis Obispo (93405-1745)
PHONE................................805 543-2300
Patrick Smith, *Principal*
Kenny Espinal, *Exec Dir*
EMP: 55 EST: 1999
SALES (est): 9.4MM **Privately Held**
WEB: www.villagesofslo.com
SIC: 8051 Skilled nursing care facilities

(P-20501)

VISTA PACIFICA ENTERPRISES INC (PA)

Also Called: Vista Pacifica Center
3674 Pacific Ave, Jurupa Valley (92509-1948)
PHONE................................951 682-4833
Cheryl Jumonville, *CEO*
James Braswell, *Shareholder*
Ruth Braswell, *Shareholder*
A L Braswell Jr, *President*
Cheryl Tumonbille, *Vice Pres*
EMP: 180 EST: 1988
SALES (est): 3.7MM **Privately Held**
WEB: www.vistapacificaent.com
SIC: 8051 8059 Convalescent home with continuous nursing care; domiciliary care

(P-20502)

WATERMAN CONVALESCENT HOSP INC (PA)

Also Called: Mt Rubidoux Convalescent Hosp
1850 N Waterman Ave, San Bernardino (92404-4895)
PHONE................................909 882-1215
Thomas Plott, *President*
Elizabeth Plott, *Corp Secy*
Mr Terry Steege, *Account Dir*
EMP: 109 EST: 1964
SQ FT: 13,000

SALES (est): 10.1MM **Privately Held**
SIC: 8051 Convalescent home with continuous nursing care

(P-20503)

WATERMARK RTRMENT CMMNTIES INC

Also Called: Fountains At The Carlotta, The
41505 Carlotta Dr, Palm Desert (92211-3279)
PHONE................................760 346-5420
Richard M Howell, *Managing Dir*
Craig Meyer, *Office Mgr*
Bill Zachau, *Sales Staff*
Cjill Hofer, *Corp Comm Staff*
Chris Casteel, *Hlthcr Dir*
EMP: 223 **Privately Held**
WEB: www.watermarkcommunities.com
SIC: 8051 8052 Skilled nursing care facilities; intermediate care facilities
HQ: Watermark Retirement Communities, Inc.
2020 W Rudasill Rd
Tucson AZ 85704

(P-20504)

WESCORDON INCORPORATED (PA)

Also Called: Valley Care Center
661 W Poplar Ave, Porterville (93257-5926)
P.O. Box 3566 (93258-3566)
PHONE................................559 784-8371
Donald C Smith, *President*
EMP: 70 EST: 1948
SQ FT: 14,000
SALES (est): 5.8MM **Privately Held**
SIC: 8051 Convalescent home with continuous nursing care

(P-20505)

WEST CNTINELA VLY CARE CTR INC

Also Called: Centinela Skld Nrng Wlns Cntr
950 S Flower St, Inglewood (90301-4186)
PHONE................................310 674-3216
EMP: 99
SALES (est): 5.7MM **Privately Held**
SIC: 8051 Skilled Nursing Care Facilities, Nsk

(P-20506)

WESTGATE GARDENS CARE CTR INC

4525 W Tulare Ave, Visalia (93277-1560)
PHONE................................559 733-0901
Eric Tolman, *Administration*
Christina Lopez, *Social Dir*
Benjamin Carter, *Administration*
Eddie Cook, *Administration*
Erica Harmatz, *Analyst*
EMP: 97 **Privately Held**
WEB: www.westgategardenscarecenter.com
SIC: 8051 Convalescent home with continuous nursing care
HQ: Westgate Gardens Care Center, Inc.
4020 Sierra College Blvd # 19
Rocklin CA 95677
916 624-6230

(P-20507)

WESTLAKE HEALTH CARE CENTER

1101 Crenshaw Blvd, Los Angeles (90019-3112)
PHONE................................805 494-1233
Jeoung Lee, *President*
EMP: 391 EST: 2001
SALES (est): 21.4MM
SALES (corp-wide): 56.7MM **Privately Held**
SIC: 8051 Skilled nursing care facilities
PA: J P H Consulting, Inc.
1101 Crenshaw Blvd
Los Angeles CA 90019
323 934-5660

(P-20508)

WESTVIEW SERVICES INC

Also Called: Westview Cmnty Arts Program
1701 S Euclid St Ste E, Anaheim (92802-2408)
PHONE................................714 956-4199

Britain Semain, *Manager*
EMP: 193
SALES (corp-wide): 15.8MM **Privately Held**
WEB: www.westviewservices.org
SIC: 8051 8322 Mental retardation hospital; adult day care center
PA: Westview Services, Inc
10522 Katella Ave
Anaheim CA 92804
714 517-6606

(P-20509)
WESTWOOD HEALTHCARE CENTER LP
Also Called: Country Vlla Wstwood Nrsing Ct
12121 Santa Monica Blvd, Los Angeles (90025-2515)
PHONE..................310 826-0821
Stephen Reissman, *General Ptnr*
Hillard Torgan, *Partner*
Rachel Bennett, *COO*
Jerry Allgood, *Administration*
Kathie Rock, *Manager*
EMP: 83 **EST:** 1970
SQ FT: 18,000
SALES (est): 7.2MM **Privately Held**
SIC: 8051 Skilled nursing care facilities

(P-20510)
WINDSOR ANAHEIM HEALTHCARE
Also Called: Windsor Gardens of Long Beach
3232 E Artesia Blvd, Long Beach (90805-2811)
PHONE..................562 422-9219
Calcin Warren, *Administration*
Rosario Jackson, *Records Dir*
Lauren Weiss, *Social Dir*
Joshua Reuben, *Office Mgr*
Jon Peralez, *Administration*
EMP: 50 **Privately Held**
WEB: www.anaheimhealthcare.com
SIC: 8051 Convalescent home with continuous nursing care
PA: Windsor Anaheim Healthcare, Ltd
3415 W Ball Rd
Anaheim CA 92804

(P-20511)
WINDSOR ANAHEIM HEALTHCARE
Also Called: Southwest Convalesant
13922 Cerise Ave, Hawthorne (90250-8118)
PHONE..................310 675-3304
Michael Gamet, *Administration*
EMP: 50 **Privately Held**
WEB: www.anaheimhealthcare.com
SIC: 8051 Skilled nursing care facilities
PA: Windsor Anaheim Healthcare, Ltd
3415 W Ball Rd
Anaheim CA 92804

(P-20512)
WINDSOR ANAHEIM HEALTHCARE (PA)
Also Called: Windsor Grdns Cnvlescent Ctr A
3415 W Ball Rd, Anaheim (92804-3708)
PHONE..................714 826-8950
Lee Samson, *President*
Matt Diaz, *Facilities Dir*
Joan Drexler, *Director*
EMP: 164 **EST:** 1996
SQ FT: 37,245
SALES (est): 23.1MM **Privately Held**
WEB: www.anaheimhealthcare.com
SIC: 8051 Convalescent home with continuous nursing care

(P-20513)
WINDSOR CRT ASSSTED LIVING LLC
201 S Sunrise Way, Palm Springs (92262-6783)
PHONE..................760 327-8351
Jeanne Reller Brownstein, *Principal*
Lee Samson,
EMP: 50 **EST:** 1999
SALES (est): 11.2MM **Privately Held**
WEB: www.wincourt.com
SIC: 8051 Skilled nursing care facilities

(P-20514)
WINDSOR GRDNS CNVLSCENT HOSP I
9200 W Sunset Blvd, West Hollywood (90069-3502)
PHONE..................888 234-4442
Lee C Samson, *CEO*
EMP: 58 **EST:** 1990
SALES (est): 1MM **Privately Held**
WEB: www.windsorcares.com
SIC: 8051 Convalescent home with continuous nursing care

(P-20515)
WINDSOR GRDNS CNVLSCENT HOSP I
915 Crenshaw Blvd, Los Angeles (90019-1938)
PHONE..................323 937-5466
Nathan Alyeshmerni, *Administration*
Lee Samson, *President*
EMP: 99 **EST:** 1988
SALES (est): 6.8MM **Privately Held**
WEB: www.windsorgardenslosangeles.com
SIC: 8051 8742 Convalescent home with continuous nursing care; hospital & health services consultant

(P-20516)
WINDSOR GRDNS HLTHCARE CTR FLL
Also Called: Windsor Gardens of Fullerton
245 E Wilshire Ave, Fullerton (92832-1935)
PHONE..................714 871-6020
Lee Samson,
EMP: 94 **EST:** 2005
SALES (est): 21.4MM **Privately Held**
SIC: 8051 Convalescent home with continuous nursing care
PA: Lexington Group International, Inc
9200 W Sunset Blvd # 600
West Hollywood CA 90069

(P-20517)
WINDSOR TWIN PLMS HLTHCARE CTR
Also Called: Windsor Palms Care Ctr Artesia
11900 Artesia Blvd, Artesia (90701-4039)
PHONE..................562 865-0271
John Ryan, *Administration*
Lee Samson, *Partner*
James Hagar, *Administration*
Matthew Galang, *Hlthcr Dir*
Carrie Marigny, *Social Worker*
EMP: 133 **EST:** 2005
SALES (est): 25.9MM **Privately Held**
WEB: www.windsorartesia.com
SIC: 8051 Convalescent home with continuous nursing care
PA: Lexington Group International, Inc
9200 W Sunset Blvd # 600
West Hollywood CA 90069

8052 Intermediate Care Facilities

(P-20518)
A-1 HOSPICE CARE INC
217 E Alameda Ave Ste 306, Burbank (91502-2621)
PHONE..................818 237-2700
Femi Samuel, *CFO*
EMP: 65 **EST:** 2012
SQ FT: 2,800
SALES (est): 1.6MM **Privately Held**
WEB: www.a-1hospice.com
SIC: 8052 Personal care facility

(P-20519)
ADMIRAL HOSPICE CARE INC
4010 Watson Plaza Dr # 120, Lakewood (90712-4035)
PHONE..................562 429-1500
Josie Austria Jones, *President*
EMP: 59 **EST:** 2003
SALES (est): 3.8MM **Privately Held**
WEB: www.admiralhospicecare.com
SIC: 8052 Personal care facility

(P-20520)
ALLIANCE FOR HOUSING & HEALING (PA)
Also Called: AID FOR AIDS
825 Colorado Blvd Ste 100, Los Angeles (90041-1741)
PHONE..................323 344-4885
Terry Goddard II, *Exec Dir*
Warren R Wimmer, *President*
Ella Noflin, *Program Mgr*
Tacarra Logan, *Executive Asst*
Rina Oktarinah, *Financial Analy*
EMP: 62 **EST:** 1987
SQ FT: 1,620
SALES: 9.9MM **Privately Held**
WEB: www.alliancehh.org
SIC: 8052 Personal care facility

(P-20521)
ALTA VERDUGO CONSULTING INC
Also Called: Verdugo Hospice Care Center
4170 Verdugo Rd, Los Angeles (90065-3821)
PHONE..................323 257-5715
Robina Kirkorian, *President*
Robina Krikorian, *President*
Rima Khajetourian, *Office Mgr*
EMP: 52 **EST:** 2002
SALES (est): 11.4MM **Privately Held**
SIC: 8052 Personal care facility

(P-20522)
ANGELS HAND HOSPICE CARE INC (PA)
2501 W Burbank Blvd # 310, Burbank (91505-2347)
PHONE..................818 782-2516
Ani Badalyan, *President*
EMP: 76 **EST:** 2017
SALES (est): 3MM **Privately Held**
WEB: www.angelshandhospicecare.business.site
SIC: 8052 Personal care facility

(P-20523)
ARCADIA GARDENS MGT CORP
Also Called: Independnt Asstd Lvng & Memory
720 W Camino Real Ave, Arcadia (91007-7839)
PHONE..................626 574-8571
Julie Chirikian, *President*
David Chirikian, *Vice Pres*
EMP: 100 **EST:** 2004
SQ FT: 120,320
SALES (est): 10MM **Privately Held**
WEB: www.arcadiagardensretirement.com
SIC: 8052 Intermediate care facilities

(P-20524)
BLYTH/WNDSOR CNTRY PK HLTHCARE
3232 E Artesia Blvd, Long Beach (90805-2811)
PHONE..................310 385-1090
Jon Peralez, *Principal*
EMP: 99 **EST:** 2013
SALES (est): 2.7MM **Privately Held**
SIC: 8052 Intermediate care facilities

(P-20525)
BRISTOL HOSPICE FOUNDATION CAL
3200 E 19th St, Signal Hill (90755-1244)
PHONE..................562 494-7687
EMP: 68
SALES (corp-wide): 170.2K **Privately Held**
WEB: www.bristolhospicefoundationca.org
SIC: 8052 Personal care facility
PA: Bristol Hospice Foundation Of California
1227 Chester Ave Ste A
Bakersfield CA 93301
661 410-3000

(P-20526)
BRISTOL HOSPICE FOUNDATION CAL
Also Called: Optimal Hospice Care
1675 Chester Ave Ste 401, Bakersfield (93301-5225)
PHONE..................661 716-4000
Doug Clary, *CEO*

EMP: 68
SALES (corp-wide): 170.2K **Privately Held**
WEB: www.bristolhospicefoundationca.org
SIC: 8052 Personal care facility
PA: Bristol Hospice Foundation Of California
1227 Chester Ave Ste A
Bakersfield CA 93301
661 410-3000

(P-20527)
CHARTER HOSPICE COLTON LLC
1007 E Cooley Dr Ste 100, Colton (92324-3901)
PHONE..................909 825-2969
Fred Frank, *President*
Sabina Del Rosario, *Sales Staff*
Sabina Rosario, *Sales Staff*
EMP: 120 **EST:** 2008
SALES (est): 14.3MM **Privately Held**
SIC: 8052 Personal care facility

(P-20528)
COUNTY OF ORANGE
405 W 5th St Ofc, Santa Ana (92701-4519)
PHONE..................714 834-6021
David L Riley, *Director*
Lydia Garcia, *Purch Mgr*
Candace Alas, *Manager*
Rhonda Childs, *Supervisor*
EMP: 95
SALES (corp-wide): 4.3B **Privately Held**
WEB: www.ocgov.com
SIC: 8052 Intermediate care facilities
PA: County Of Orange
333 W Santa Ana Blvd
Santa Ana CA 92701
714 834-6200

(P-20529)
FAMILY HOSPICE LTD
Also Called: Hospice Family
9253 Reseda Blvd, Northridge (91324-3137)
PHONE..................818 571-2870
Sunil Thukral, *Branch Mgr*
EMP: 102
SALES (corp-wide): 1.1B **Privately Held**
SIC: 8052 Personal care facility
HQ: Family Hospice, Ltd
4800 N Scottsdale Rd # 5
Scottsdale AZ 85251

(P-20530)
GLEN PARK RETIREMENT HOTEL
5527 Laurel Canyon Blvd, North Hollywood (91607-2116)
PHONE..................818 769-6626
Esther Agpaoa, *Administration*
EMP: 53 **Privately Held**
SIC: 8052 8361 Intermediate care facilities; rest home, with health care incidental
PA: Glen Park Retirement Hotel
1220 Mariposa S
Glendale CA 91205

(P-20531)
HILLSIDE HOUSE
1235 Veronica Springs Rd, Santa Barbara (93105-4522)
PHONE..................805 687-0788
Michael Rassler, *Exec Dir*
Chuck Klein, *Principal*
Peter Troesch, *Principal*
Gail Metzger, *Exec Dir*
Angela De Bruyn, *Executive Asst*
EMP: 98 **EST:** 1945
SQ FT: 24,000
SALES (est): 5.5MM **Privately Held**
WEB: www.hillsidesb.org
SIC: 8052 Home for the mentally retarded, with health care

(P-20532)
HOFFMAN HOSPICE OF THE VALLEY
4325 Buena Vista Rd, Bakersfield (93311-8701)
PHONE..................661 410-1010
Beth Hosman, *President*

Marissa Slayton, *Executive Asst*
Ross Hoffmann, *Opers Staff*
Erin Gish-Stiles, *Social Worker*
EMP: 67 **EST:** 1994
SALES (est): 21.2MM **Privately Held**
WEB: www.hoffmannhospice.org
SIC: 8052 Personal care facility

(P-20533)
JONBEC CARE INCORPORATED (PA)
1711 Plum Ln, Redlands (92374-2874)
P.O. Box 10788, San Bernardino (92423-0788)
PHONE..............................909 798-4003
Jonathan Joseph, *President*
Cindy Collins, *Treasurer*
Becky Joseph, *Vice Pres*
Oynnie Joseph, *Admin Sec*
Francisco Gonzalez, *Program Dir*
EMP: 52 **EST:** 1990
SQ FT: 13,000
SALES (est): 12.2MM **Privately Held**
WEB: www.jonbeccare.com
SIC: 8052 Home for the mentally retarded, with health care

(P-20534)
L & A CARE CORPORATION
Also Called: Roze Room Hospice
5000 Overland Ave Ste 101, Culver City (90230-4969)
PHONE..............................310 202-7693
Lena M Beker, *Branch Mgr*
Raisa Adler, *Executive*
Ana Cartmel, *Principal*
Euler Ferrer, *CIO*
Josefa Azcueta, *Director*
EMP: 85
SALES (corp-wide): 5.5MM **Privately Held**
WEB: www.rozeroom.org
SIC: 8052 Personal care facility
PA: L & A Care Corporation
18107 Sherman Way Ste 100
Reseda CA 91335
323 938-1155

(P-20535)
LEISURE CARE LLC
Also Called: Fairwinds-West Hills
8138 Woodlake Ave, West Hills (91304-3500)
PHONE..............................818 713-0900
Pat Luc, *General Mgr*
EMP: 470
SALES (corp-wide): 175.2MM **Privately Held**
WEB: www.leisurecare.com
SIC: 8052 Intermediate care facilities
HQ: Leisure Care, Llc
999 3rd Ave Ste 4550
Seattle WA 98104
206 436-7827

(P-20536)
LOS ANGELES CTY RNCH LOS AMGOS
7601 Imperial Hwy, Downey (90242-3456)
PHONE..............................562 385-7111
Jorge Orozco, *CEO*
Pattie Soltero Sanchez, *Director*
EMP: 1400 **EST:** 2009
SALES (est): 32.8MM **Privately Held**
WEB: www.losamigosgc.com
SIC: 8052 Personal care facility

(P-20537)
MLIFE HOSPICE INC (PA)
7786 Lemon Pepper Ave, Fontana (92336-3407)
PHONE..............................909 996-2508
Gladys L Smedley, *CEO*
EMP: 62 **EST:** 2018
SALES (est): 2.7MM **Privately Held**
SIC: 8052 Personal care facility

(P-20538)
NEW VISTA BEHAVIORAL HLTH LLC
3 Park Plz Ste 550, Irvine (92614-2537)
PHONE..............................949 284-0095
Jennifer Hale, *Branch Mgr*
EMP: 99

SALES (corp-wide): 3MM **Privately Held**
WEB: www.avalonmalibu.com
SIC: 8052 Home for the mentally retarded, with health care
PA: New Vista Behavioral Health, Llc
1901 Newport Blvd Ste 204
Costa Mesa CA
888 316-3665

(P-20539)
QUAIL PARK RETIREMENT VLG LLC
4520 W Cypress Ave, Visalia (93277-1577)
PHONE..............................559 624-3500
Denis Bryant, *Manager*
EMP: 65 **EST:** 2001
SALES (est): 5MM **Privately Held**
WEB: www.livingcarelifestyles.com
SIC: 8052 6513 Intermediate care facilities; apartment building operators

(P-20540)
RES-CARE INC
45691 Monroe St Ste 6, Indio (92201-3943)
PHONE..............................760 775-2887
EMP: 82
SALES (corp-wide): 2B **Privately Held**
WEB: www.rescare.com
SIC: 8052 Home for the mentally retarded, with health care
HQ: Res-Care, Llc
805 N Whittington Pkwy
Louisville KY 40222
502 394-2100

(P-20541)
RES-CARE INC
22635 Alessandro Blvd, Moreno Valley (92553-8550)
PHONE..............................951 653-1311
EMP: 82
SALES (corp-wide): 2B **Privately Held**
WEB: www.rescare.com
SIC: 8052 Home for the mentally retarded, with health care
HQ: Res-Care, Inc.
805 N Whittington Pkwy
Louisville KY 40222
502 394-2100

(P-20542)
RES-CARE INC
2120 Foothill Blvd # 205, La Verne (91750-2941)
PHONE..............................909 596-5360
Jill Crowell, *Manager*
EMP: 82
SALES (corp-wide): 2B **Privately Held**
WEB: www.rescare.com
SIC: 8052 Home for the mentally retarded, with health care
HQ: Res-Care, Inc.
805 N Whittington Pkwy
Louisville KY 40222
502 394-2100

(P-20543)
SHERMAN OAKS HSPICE CARE GROUP
Also Called: Graceland Hospice Care
1855 W Katella Ave # 255, Orange (92867-3451)
PHONE..............................714 733-1333
Michele Lovato, *CEO*
Marlyn Munguia, *General Mgr*
EMP: 50 **EST:** 2015
SALES (est): 7.4MM **Privately Held**
WEB: www.gracelandhospicecare.com
SIC: 8052 Personal care facility

(P-20544)
UNITED CRBRAL PLSY/SPSTIC CHLD
Also Called: White Oak Housing Foundation
9205 White Oak Ave, Northridge (91325-2335)
PHONE..............................818 727-1067
Ronald Cohen, *Branch Mgr*
EMP: 97
SALES (corp-wide): 26.7MM **Privately Held**
WEB: www.momentum4all.org
SIC: 8052 Home for the mentally retarded, with health care

PA: United Cerebral Palsy/Spastic Children's Foundation Of Los Angeles And Ventura Counties
6430 Independence Ave
Woodland Hills CA 91367
818 782-2211

(P-20545)
VALLEY VILLAGE
8727 Fenwick St, Sunland (91040-1952)
PHONE..............................818 446-0366
EMP: 157
SALES (corp-wide): 20.3MM **Privately Held**
WEB: www.valleyvillage.org
SIC: 8052 Intermediate care facilities
PA: Valley Village
20830 Sherman Way
Winnetka CA 91306
818 587-9450

(P-20546)
VITAS HEALTHCARE CORPORATION
9106 Pulsar Ct Ste D, Corona (92883-4632)
PHONE..............................858 805-6254
EMP: 78
SALES (corp-wide): 2B **Publicly Held**
WEB: www.vitas.com
SIC: 8052 Personal care facility
HQ: Vitas Healthcare Corporation
201 S Biscayne Blvd # 400
Miami FL 33131
305 374-4143

(P-20547)
VITAS HEALTHCARE CORPORATION
333 N Lantana St Ste 124, Camarillo (93010-9007)
PHONE..............................805 437-2100
Rita Peddycoart, *Manager*
EMP: 78
SALES (corp-wide): 2B **Publicly Held**
WEB: www.vitas.com
SIC: 8052 Personal care facility
HQ: Vitas Healthcare Corporation
201 S Biscayne Blvd # 400
Miami FL 33131
305 374-4143

(P-20548)
WATTS HEALTH FOUNDATION INC (HQ)
Also Called: Uhp Healthcare
3405 W Imperial Hwy # 304, Inglewood (90303-2219)
PHONE..............................310 424-2220
Dr Clyde W Oden, *President*
Jennifer Stapalding, *CEO*
Dr Darryl Leong, *MIS Dir*
EMP: 400 **EST:** 1967
SALES (est): 69.5MM
SALES (corp-wide): 69.9MM **Privately Held**
WEB: www.wattshealthsystems.com
SIC: 8052 8011 8741 Intermediate care facilities; health maintenance organization; management services
PA: Watts Health Systems, Inc.
3405 W Imperial Hwy
Inglewood CA
310 424-2220

8059 Nursing & Personal Care Facilities, NEC

(P-20549)
A CORI PARTNERSHIP
Also Called: Casitas Care Center
10626 Balboa Blvd, Granada Hills (91344-6329)
PHONE..............................818 368-2802
Claire Badama, *Partner*
Sonia Joshi, *Administration*
EMP: 50 **EST:** 1982
SALES (est): 4.8MM **Privately Held**
WEB: www.casitascarecenter.com
SIC: 8059 8051 Convalescent home; nursing home, except skilled & intermediate care facility; skilled nursing care facilities

(P-20550)
AMBERWOOD CONVALESCENT HOSP
6071 York Blvd, Los Angeles (90042-3503)
PHONE..............................323 254-3407
Jeanie Barrett, *Administration*
Ben Garrett, *President*
Gloria Galeano, *Executive*
Eileen M Robles, *Office Mgr*
Marilyn Spaun, *Administration*
EMP: 100 **EST:** 1967
SALES (est): 5MM **Privately Held**
WEB: www.yorkhealthcareandwellness.com
SIC: 8059 Convalescent home
PA: Casner Consolidated, Llc.
1020 Huntington Dr
San Marino CA 91108
626 282-8443

(P-20551)
ANTELOPE VLY RETIREMENT HM INC
Also Called: Antelope Vly Convalecent Hosp
44445 15th St W, Lancaster (93534-2801)
PHONE..............................661 948-7501
Marsha Weldon, *Director*
EMP: 161
SALES (corp-wide): 11.4MM **Privately Held**
WEB: www.avcsnf.com
SIC: 8059 8051 Convalescent home; skilled nursing care facilities
PA: Antelope Valley Retirement Home, Inc.
44523 15th St W
Lancaster CA 93534
661 949-5584

(P-20552)
ANTELOPE VLY RETIREMENT HM INC
Also Called: A V Nursing Care Center
44567 15th St W, Lancaster (93534-2803)
PHONE..............................661 949-5524
Alfred Jones, *Manager*
EMP: 161
SALES (corp-wide): 11.4MM **Privately Held**
WEB: www.avcsnf.com
SIC: 8059 8051 Convalescent home; skilled nursing care facilities
PA: Antelope Valley Retirement Home, Inc.
44523 15th St W
Lancaster CA 93534
661 949-5584

(P-20553)
ARARAT HOME LOS ANGELES INC
Also Called: Ararat Nursing Facility
15099 Mission Hills Rd, Mission Hills (91345-1102)
PHONE..............................818 837-1800
M Kebhichien, *Administration*
Derik Ghookasian, *COO*
EMP: 120
SALES (corp-wide): 37.5MM **Privately Held**
WEB: www.ararathome.org
SIC: 8059 8051 Nursing home, except skilled & intermediate care facility; skilled nursing care facilities
PA: Ararat Home Of Los Angeles, Inc.
15105 Mission Hills Rd
Mission Hills CA 91345
818 365-3000

(P-20554)
ARARAT HOME LOS ANGELES INC
Also Called: Ararat Convalescent Hospital
2373 Colorado Blvd, Los Angeles (90041-1157)
PHONE..............................323 256-8012
Violette Alahaidoyan, *Finance Other*
Sose Shirinian, *Social Dir*
Margarita Kechichian, *Exec Dir*
Christine Karapetian, *Administration*
EMP: 120
SQ FT: 9,104
SALES (corp-wide): 37.5MM **Privately Held**
WEB: www.ararathome.org
SIC: 8059 8051 Convalescent home; skilled nursing care facilities

PA: Ararat Home Of Los Angeles, Inc.
15105 Mission Hills Rd
Mission Hills CA 91345
818 365-3000

(P-20555)
ARCADIA CONVALESCENT HOSP INC (PA)
Also Called: Arcadia Health Care Center
1601 S Baldwin Ave, Arcadia (91007-7910)
PHONE....................626 445-2170
Orlando Clarizio Jr, *CEO*
EMP: 117 **EST:** 1962
SQ FT: 21,342
SALES (est): 11.7MM **Privately Held**
SIC: 8059 8051 Convalescent home; skilled nursing care facilities

(P-20556)
ARTESIA CHRISTIAN HOME INC
11614 183rd St, Artesia (90701-5506)
PHONE....................562 865-5218
Elroy Van Derley, *Exec Dir*
Elroy Vander Ley, *Exec Dir*
Sharon Kim, *Office Mgr*
Deborah Rouwenhorst, *Accountant*
Eggy Ruiz, *QC Dir*
EMP: 140 **EST:** 1947
SQ FT: 43,223
SALES: 12.1MM **Privately Held**
WEB: www.achome.org
SIC: 8059 8052 8051 Convalescent home; intermediate care facilities; skilled nursing care facilities

(P-20557)
B & E CONVALESCENT CENTER INC (PA)
Also Called: Gardena Convalescent Center
11627 Telg Rd Ste 200, Santa Fe Springs (90670)
PHONE....................562 923-9449
Barry J Weiss, *President*
Esther Weiss, *Treasurer*
EMP: 60 **EST:** 1968
SALES (est): 5.9MM **Privately Held**
SIC: 8059 Convalescent home

(P-20558)
BAKERSFELD HLTHCARE WLLNESS CN
Also Called: Rehabilitation Ctr Bakersfield
2211 Mount Vernon Ave, Bakersfield (93306-3309)
PHONE....................661 872-2121
Cheryl Petterson,
EMP: 99 **EST:** 2009
SALES (est): 10.6MM **Privately Held**
WEB:
www.rehabilitationcenterbakersfield.com
SIC: 8059 Nursing home, except skilled & intermediate care facility

(P-20559)
BEGROUP (PA)
516 Burchett St, Glendale (91203-1014)
PHONE....................818 638-4563
John H Cochrane III, *President*
David L Pierce, *CFO*
Daniel S Ogus, *Exec VP*
EMP: 75 **EST:** 1989
SALES (est): 41.7MM **Privately Held**
WEB: www.humangood.org
SIC: 8059 Nursing home, except skilled & intermediate care facility

(P-20560)
BEN BENNETT INC (PA)
Also Called: Community Care Rhbltation Ctr
3419 Via Lido 646, Newport Beach (92663-3908)
PHONE....................949 209-9712
Bruce Bennett, *President*
▲ **EMP:** 200 **EST:** 1965
SQ FT: 50,000
SALES (est): 15.6MM **Privately Held**
SIC: 8059 8069 8051 Convalescent home; specialty hospitals, except psychiatric; skilled nursing care facilities

(P-20561)
BERKELEY E CONVALESCENT HOSP
Also Called: Berkeley E Convalescent Hosp
2021 Arizona Ave, Santa Monica (90404-1335)
PHONE....................310 829-5377
Paul Bartolucce, *President*
Saul Galper, *Corp Secy*
EMP: 150 **EST:** 1965
SQ FT: 10,000
SALES (est): 11.3MM **Privately Held**
SIC: 8059 Convalescent home

(P-20562)
BMB 1 LLC
Also Called: Ride At Home Care
495 E Rincon St Ste 211, Corona (92879-1379)
PHONE....................951 741-0663
Michael Barboza, *Mng Member*
EMP: 65 **EST:** 2017
SALES (est): 1.4MM **Privately Held**
SIC: 8059 8051 Nursing & personal care; convalescent home with continuous nursing care

(P-20563)
BONNIE BRAE CNVLSCENT HOSP INC (PA)
Also Called: California Convalescent Center
420 S Bonnie Brae St, Los Angeles (90057-3010)
PHONE....................213 483-8144
Elma Cayton, *CEO*
Albert Ballo, *Treasurer*
Divina Matabalan-Billing, *Clerk*
EMP: 60 **EST:** 1960
SALES (est): 6MM **Privately Held**
SIC: 8059 8051 Convalescent home; skilled nursing care facilities

(P-20564)
BRIERWOOD TERRACE VENTURA INC (HQ)
4904 Telegraph Rd, Ventura (93003-4109)
PHONE....................805 642-4101
Sanford Weiss, *President*
Frances Foy, *President*
EMP: 77 **EST:** 1962
SALES (est): 2.5MM
SALES (corp-wide): 4.8MM **Privately Held**
WEB: www.theventuran.com
SIC: 8059 Convalescent home
PA: D S I Corporation
1611 S Pacific Coast Hwy # 301
Redondo Beach CA 90277
310 273-1770

(P-20565)
BRIGHTON CONVALESCENT CENTER
1836 N Fair Oaks Ave, Pasadena (91103-1619)
PHONE....................626 798-9124
Alex Makabuhay, *Administration*
Pat Capello, *Administration*
Rose Wilson, *Systems Mgr*
EMP: 100
SALES: 9.4MM **Privately Held**
WEB: www.brighton1836.com
SIC: 8059 8051 Convalescent home; skilled nursing care facilities

(P-20566)
BUENA VENTURA CARE CENTER INC
Also Called: Leisure Glen Convalescent Ctr
1505 Colby Dr, Glendale (91205-3307)
PHONE....................818 247-4476
Yolanda Wise, *Administration*
EMP: 80
SALES (corp-wide): 6.6MM **Privately Held**
WEB: www.buenaventurarehab.com
SIC: 8059 8051 Convalescent home; skilled nursing care facilities
PA: Buena Ventura Care Center Inc
1016 S Record Ave
Los Angeles CA 90023
323 268-0106

(P-20567)
BV GENERAL INC
Also Called: Kennedy Care Center
619 N Fairfax Ave, Los Angeles (90036-1714)
PHONE....................323 651-0043
James Kargol, *Branch Mgr*
EMP: 111 **Privately Held**
WEB: www.leisurevale.com
SIC: 8059 Rest home, with health care
PA: B.V. General, Inc.
1332 S Glendale Ave
Glendale CA 91205

(P-20568)
CANTALOUPE HOLDINGS LLC
Also Called: Beachwood Post-Acute & Rehab
1340 15th St, Santa Monica (90404-1802)
PHONE....................310 451-9706
Anton Novitsky, *Administration*
EMP: 58 **EST:** 2011
SALES (est): 19MM **Privately Held**
WEB: www.beachwoodpostacute.com
SIC: 8059 8322 Nursing home, except skilled & intermediate care facility; rehabilitation services

(P-20569)
CANYON OAKS NURSING AND REHAB
22029 Saticoy St, Canoga Park (91303-1133)
PHONE....................818 887-7050
Jason Nagy, *Administration*
Tess Santiago, *Nursing Dir*
EMP: 57 **EST:** 2008
SALES (est): 12MM **Privately Held**
WEB: www.lifegen.net
SIC: 8059 8051 Nursing home, except skilled & intermediate care facility; skilled nursing care facilities

(P-20570)
CHANCELLOR HLTH CARE CAL I INC (PA)
Also Called: Linda Valley Care Center
25383 Cole St, Loma Linda (92354-3103)
PHONE....................909 796-0235
Corbin Swafford, *Exec Dir*
Carol Romo, *Records Dir*
Edmond Peters, *Vice Ch Bd*
Hoselito Acuna, *Office Mgr*
Dave Green, *Administration*
EMP: 69 **EST:** 1960
SQ FT: 32,000
SALES (est): 9.4MM **Privately Held**
WEB: www.lindavalleycare.com
SIC: 8059 6513 8051 Convalescent home; nursing home, except skilled & intermediate care facility; apartment building operators; skilled nursing care facilities

(P-20571)
CHASE CARE CENTER INC
1101 Crenshaw Blvd, Los Angeles (90019-3112)
PHONE....................323 935-8490
Jeoung H Lee, *President*
John Yoo, *Administration*
EMP: 81 **EST:** 1996
SQ FT: 83,000
SALES (est): 16.4MM **Privately Held**
SIC: 8059 8051 Convalescent home; skilled nursing care facilities

(P-20572)
COASTAL VIEW HALTHCARE CTR LLC
4904 Telegraph Rd, Ventura (93003-4109)
PHONE....................805 642-4101
Sim Mandelbaum,
Debbie Smith, *Marketing Staff*
Frances Foy, *Director*
Renee Jones, *Director*
EMP: 96 **EST:** 2012
SALES (est): 9.6MM **Privately Held**
WEB: www.coastalviewhcc.com
SIC: 8059 Convalescent home

(P-20573)
COUNTRY VILLA SERVICE CORP
112 E Broadway, San Gabriel (91776-1805)
PHONE....................626 285-2165
J Caballero, *Administration*
EMP: 154
SALES (corp-wide): 78.2MM **Privately Held**
SIC: 8059 Nursing home, except skilled & intermediate care facility
PA: Country Villa Service Corp
2400 E Katella Ave # 800
Anaheim CA 92806
310 574-3733

(P-20574)
COUNTRY VILLA TERRACE (PA)
Also Called: Country Vlla Convalescent Hosp
6050 W Pico Blvd, Los Angeles (90035-2647)
PHONE....................323 653-3980
Steven Reissman, *President*
Diana Reissman, *Vice Pres*
EMP: 75 **EST:** 1963
SQ FT: 6,000
SALES (est): 6.6MM **Privately Held**
SIC: 8059 8361 Convalescent home; residential care

(P-20575)
CPCC INC
Also Called: Chatsworth Park Hlth Care Ctr
10610 Owensmouth Ave, Chatsworth (91311-2151)
PHONE....................818 882-3200
John Sorensen, *President*
Greg Ethington, *Administration*
Sonia Ly, *Administration*
Jennifer Espinola, *Director*
Carmen Lemus, *Director*
EMP: 99 **EST:** 1982
SALES (est): 5.2MM **Privately Held**
WEB: www.chatsworthparkcare.com
SIC: 8059 8051 Convalescent home; skilled nursing care facilities

(P-20576)
CULVER WEST HEALTH CENTER LLC
4035 Grand View Blvd, Los Angeles (90066-5211)
PHONE....................310 390-9506
Harry Jacobs,
Rose Jimenea, *Hlthcr Dir*
Joy Camtan, *Director*
EMP: 90 **EST:** 1996
SQ FT: 25,000
SALES (est): 9.2MM **Privately Held**
WEB: www.culverwest.com
SIC: 8059 Convalescent home

(P-20577)
D K FORTUNE & ASSOCIATES INC
Also Called: Marina Care Center
5240 Sepulveda Blvd, Culver City (90230-5214)
PHONE....................310 391-7266
Fax: 310 397-4998
EMP: 130
SALES: 9.2MM **Privately Held**
SIC: 8059 8051 Nursing/Personal Care Skilled Nursing Care Facility

(P-20578)
ELENA VILLA HEALTHCARE CENTER
13226 Studebaker Rd, Norwalk (90650-2532)
PHONE....................562 868-0591
Floyd Loupot, *President*
Everett E Goings, *Vice Pres*
EMP: 62 **EST:** 1968
SQ FT: 24,000
SALES (est): 11.2MM **Privately Held**
WEB: www.progressivecarecenters.com
SIC: 8059 8051 Convalescent home; skilled nursing care facilities

(P-20579)
ENSIGN SAN DIMAS LLC
Also Called: Arbor Glen Care Center
1033 E Arrow Hwy, Glendora (91740-6110)
PHONE....................626 963-7531

Steve Powell, *Opers Staff*
Don R Bybee, *Principal*
EMP: 152 **EST:** 2010
SALES (est): 9.9MM
SALES (corp-wide): 2.4B **Publicly Held**
WEB: www.arborglencare.com
SIC: 8059 Convalescent home
PA: The Ensign Group Inc
29222 Rncho Vejo Rd Ste 1
San Juan Capistrano CA 92675
949 487-9500

(P-20580)
FAR WEST INC
Also Called: Westgage Grdn Convalescent
Ctr
4525 W Tulare Ave, Visalia (93277-1560)
PHONE...................................559 733-0901
Ellen Rioux, *Principal*
EMP: 51 **Privately Held**
WEB: www.farwest.org
SIC: 8059 8051 Convalescent home;
skilled nursing care facilities
HQ: Far West, Inc.
4020 Sierra College Blvd
Rocklin CA 95677

(P-20581)
FILLMORE CONVALESCENT CTR LLC
118 B St, Fillmore (93015-1763)
PHONE...................................805 524-0083
Fax: 805 524-7260
EMP: 80
SQ FT: 13,800
SALES (est): 4.5MM **Privately Held**
WEB: www.fillmoreconvalescentcenter.com
SIC: 8059 8051 Skilled / Rehabilitation
Nursing Facility

(P-20582)
FOCUS ON ALL CHILD THRPIES INC
Also Called: FAMILY, ADULT AND CHILD
THERAP
1880 Century Park E # 512, Los Angeles
(90067-1600)
PHONE...................................310 475-9620
Lania Glaude, *President*
Zoe Giesberg, *Executive Asst*
John Causey, *Admin Sec*
Lenord Felder,
Laureen Sills,
EMP: 68 **EST:** 1999
SALES (est): 4.5MM **Privately Held**
WEB: www.factfamily.org
SIC: 8059 8351 Home for the mentally re-
tarded, exc. skilled or intermediate; child
day care services

(P-20583)
FRONT PRCH CMMNTIES OPRTING GR
Also Called: FREDERICKA MANOR CARE
CENTER
800 N Brand Blvd Fl 19, Glendale
(91203-1231)
PHONE...................................800 233-3709
John Woodward, *CEO*
EMP: 190 **EST:** 2013
SALES: 84.6MM **Privately Held**
WEB: www.frontporch.net
SIC: 8059 Nursing & personal care

(P-20584)
FRONT PRCH CMMNTIES SVCS - CAS
Also Called: Walnut Manor Care Center
1401 W Ball Rd, Anaheim (92802-1711)
PHONE...................................714 776-7150
Sondra Coughlin, *Manager*
EMP: 114
SALES (corp-wide): 158.2MM **Privately
Held**
WEB: www.frontporch.net
SIC: 8059 8051 Rest home, with health
care; skilled nursing care facilities
PA: Front Porch Communities And Services
- Casa De Manana, Llc
800 N Brand Blvd Fl 19
Glendale CA 91203
818 729-8100

(P-20585)
FRONT PRCH CMMNTIES SVCS - CAS (PA)
Also Called: FREDERICKA MANOR CARE
CENTER
800 N Brand Blvd Fl 19, Glendale
(91203-1231)
PHONE...................................818 729-8100
Gary Wheeler, *CEO*
Sharon Jansen, *Managing Prtnr*
Roberta Jacobsen, *President*
Bill Jennings, *CFO*
Mary Miller, *CFO*
EMP: 100 **EST:** 1995
SQ FT: 20,000
SALES: 158.2MM **Privately Held**
WEB: www.frontporch.net
SIC: 8059 8051 Rest home, with health
care; skilled nursing care facilities

(P-20586)
FRONT PRCH CMMNTIES SVCS - CAS
Also Called: Claremont Manor
650 Harrison Ave, Claremont (91711-4536)
PHONE...................................909 626-1227
Joseph Peduzzi, *Branch Mgr*
Kari Miner, *President*
Tanya Madrid, *Social Dir*
Greg Hirst, *Exec Dir*
Gregory Pippen, *Food Svc Dir*
EMP: 114
SQ FT: 167,053
SALES (corp-wide): 158.2MM **Privately
Held**
WEB: www.frontporch.net
SIC: 8059 8052 6513 Convalescent
home; intermediate care facilities; apart-
ment building operators
PA: Front Porch Communities And Services
- Casa De Manana, Llc
800 N Brand Blvd Fl 19
Glendale CA 91203
818 729-8100

(P-20587)
FRONT PRCH CMMNTIES SVCS - CAS
3775 Modoc Rd, Santa Barbara
(93105-4474)
PHONE...................................805 687-0793
Roberta Jacobsen, *Branch Mgr*
Laurie Yttri, *Exec Dir*
Mark McGilvray, *Council Mbr*
Michael Pointer, *Director*
EMP: 114
SQ FT: 68,000
SALES (corp-wide): 158.2MM **Privately
Held**
WEB: www.frontporch.net
SIC: 8059 8051 Rest home, with health
care; skilled nursing care facilities
PA: Front Porch Communities And Services
- Casa De Manana, Llc
800 N Brand Blvd Fl 19
Glendale CA 91203
818 729-8100

(P-20588)
FRONT PRCH CMMNTIES SVCS - CAS
Also Called: Lutheran Health Facility
303 N Glenoaks Blvd # 100, Burbank
(91502-1116)
PHONE...................................626 570-5293
EMP: 60
SALES (corp-wide): 165.1MM **Privately
Held**
WEB: www.frontporch.net
SIC: 8059 8011 Nursing/Personal Care
Medical Doctor's Office
PA: Front Porch Communities And Services
- Casa De Manana, Llc
800 N Brand Blvd Fl 19
Glendale CA 91203
818 729-8100

(P-20589)
FRONT PRCH CMMNTIES SVCS - CAS
Also Called: Southland Lutheran Home
11701 Studebaker Rd, Norwalk
(90650-7544)
PHONE...................................562 868-9761
Covy Christiansen, *Manager*

Joy Corcuera, *Records Dir*
Margie Cruz, *Social Dir*
Mary Delarosa, *Social Dir*
Annalisa Canlas, *Office Mgr*
EMP: 114
SALES (corp-wide): 158.2MM **Privately
Held**
WEB: www.frontporch.net
SIC: 8059 8011 8052 8051 Rest home,
with health care; geriatric specialist,
physician/surgeon; intermediate care fa-
cilities; skilled nursing care facilities
PA: Front Porch Communities And Services
- Casa De Manana, Llc
800 N Brand Blvd Fl 19
Glendale CA 91203
818 729-8100

(P-20590)
GENESIS HEALTHCARE LLC
Also Called: Fountain View Cnvalescent Hosp
5310 Fountain Ave, Los Angeles
(90029-1005)
PHONE...................................323 461-9961
Jennifer Gans, *Records Dir*
Claire Padama, *Vice Pres*
Jamila Gaines, *Social Dir*
Rogaciaonno Morales, *Envir Svcs Dir*
Pia Banaag, *Office Mgr*
EMP: 158 **Privately Held**
WEB: www.genesishcc.com
SIC: 8059 8051 8069 Convalescent
home; skilled nursing care facilities; spe-
cialty hospitals, except psychiatric
HQ: Genesis Healthcare Llc
101 E State St
Kennett Square PA 19348

(P-20591)
GERI-CARE II INC
Also Called: Vermont Care Center
22035 S Vermont Ave, Torrance
(90502-2120)
P.O. Box 6069 (90504-0069)
PHONE...................................310 328-0812
Emmanuel David, *President*
Engelica Vivillanueva, *Vice Pres*
Richard Barnes, *CIO*
EMP: 250 **EST:** 1989
SQ FT: 40,000
SALES (est): 10.7MM **Privately Held**
SIC: 8059 8051 Convalescent home;
skilled nursing care facilities

(P-20592)
GIBRALTER CONVALESCENT HOSP (PA)
Also Called: Del Mar Convalescent Hospital
600 E Washington Ave, Santa Ana
(92701-3843)
PHONE...................................714 550-5380
Blaine Hendrickson, *President*
Carol Leggett, *Vice Pres*
EMP: 60 **EST:** 1972
SALES (est): 9.3MM **Privately Held**
SIC: 8059 Convalescent home

(P-20593)
GIBRALTER CONVALESCENT HOSP
Also Called: Sunset Manor Convalescent
Hosp
2720 Nevada Ave, El Monte (91733-2318)
PHONE...................................626 443-9425
Marcel Morales, *Manager*
CHI Lam, *Director*
EMP: 100
SALES (corp-wide): 9.3MM **Privately
Held**
WEB: www.sunsetmanorcare.com
SIC: 8059 8051 Convalescent home;
skilled nursing care facilities
PA: Gibralter Convalescent Hospital
600 E Washington Ave
Santa Ana CA 92701
714 550-5380

(P-20594)
GOLDEN STATE HEALTH CTRS INC
Also Called: King David Convalescent Hosp
1340 15th St, Santa Monica (90404-1802)
PHONE...................................310 451-9706
Dina Closas Rn, *Director*
EMP: 200

SALES (corp-wide): 62.1MM **Privately
Held**
WEB: www.goldenstatehealth.com
SIC: 8059 8051 Convalescent home;
skilled nursing care facilities
PA: Golden State Health Centers, Inc.
13347 Ventura Blvd
Sherman Oaks CA 91423
818 385-3200

(P-20595)
HILLSDALE GROUP LP
Also Called: Sherman Village Hlth Care Ctr
12750 Riverside Dr, North Hollywood
(91607-3319)
PHONE...................................818 623-2170
Rich Terrell, *Principal*
EMP: 147
SALES (corp-wide): 20.1MM **Privately
Held**
SIC: 8059 8051 8093 8011 Convalescent
home; skilled nursing care facilities; reha-
bilitation center, outpatient treatment;
clinic, operated by physicians
PA: The Hillsdale Group L P
1199 Howard Ave Ste 200
Burlingame CA

(P-20596)
HUMANGOOD NORCAL
Also Called: Rosewood Retirement Commu-
nity
1401 New Stine Rd, Bakersfield
(93309-3530)
PHONE...................................661 834-0620
Ellen Renner, *Branch Mgr*
Rebecca Humes, *Records Dir*
Brenda Ocheao, *Office Mgr*
Wayne Watroús, *CIO*
Sally Parker, *Food Svc Dir*
EMP: 77
SALES (corp-wide): 25.9MM **Privately
Held**
WEB: www.humangood.org
SIC: 8059 8052 8051 Rest home, with
health care; intermediate care facilities;
skilled nursing care facilities
HQ: Humangood Norcal
6120 Stnrdge Mall Rd Ste
Pleasanton CA 94588
925 924-7100

(P-20597)
HUMANGOOD NORCAL
Also Called: Plymouth Village
900 Salem Dr, Redlands (92373-6147)
PHONE...................................909 793-1233
Keith Kasin, *Exec Dir*
Valerie Sponheim, *Director*
EMP: 77
SQ FT: 8,000
SALES (corp-wide): 25.9MM **Privately
Held**
WEB: www.humangood.org
SIC: 8059 8051 Rest home, with health
care; skilled nursing care facilities
HQ: Humangood Norcal
6120 Stnrdge Mall Rd Ste
Pleasanton CA 94588
925 924-7100

(P-20598)
IN GARDEN GROVE CNVLSCENT HOSP
Also Called: Garden Grove Post Acute
12882 Shackelford Ln, Garden Grove
(92841-5109)
PHONE...................................714 638-9470
Aurea Sarigan, *Administration*
Uri Mandelbaum, *President*
EMP: 52 **EST:** 1969
SQ FT: 6,000
SALES (est): 11.6MM **Privately Held**
SIC: 8059 8051 Convalescent home;
skilled nursing care facilities

(P-20599)
KF ONTARIO HEALTHCARE LLC
Also Called: Ontario Healthcare Center
1661 S Euclid Ave, Ontario (91762-5826)
PHONE...................................909 984-6713
Jacob Wintner, *CEO*
Edward S Shea, *President*
Gordon Buechs, *CFO*
Robin Harrison, *General Mgr*

PRODUCTS & SVCS

Julie Lerma, *Office Mgr*
EMP: 50 **EST:** 1969
SALES (est): 4.6MM **Privately Held**
WEB: www.ontariohealthcarecenter.com
SIC: 8059 8051 Convalescent home;
nursing home, except skilled & intermediate care facility; skilled nursing care facilities

(P-20600)
LOMITA VERDE INC
Also Called: Lomita Care Center
1955 Lomita Blvd, Lomita (90717-1807)
PHONE....................310 325-1970
Donald G Laws, *President*
David E Sorenson, *Treasurer*
Mary Pettway, *Social Dir*
Wayne Fortin, *Administration*
Tracy Baca, *Director*
EMP: 60 **EST:** 1986
SALES (est): 9.9MM **Privately Held**
WEB: www.lomitacare.com
SIC: 8059 8322 Convalescent home; individual & family services

(P-20601)
LONGWOOD MANAGEMENT CORP
Also Called: Sunny View Care Center
2000 W Washington Blvd, Los Angeles (90018-1637)
PHONE....................323 735-5146
Amber Gooden, *Administration*
EMP: 93
SALES (corp-wide): 179.6MM **Privately Held**
WEB: www.longwoodmgmt.com
SIC: 8059 Convalescent home
PA: Longwood Management Corp.
4032 Wilshire Blvd Fl 6
Los Angeles CA 90010
213 389-6900

(P-20602)
LONGWOOD MANAGEMENT CORP
Also Called: Broadway Manor Care Center
605 W Broadway, Glendale (91204-1007)
PHONE....................818 246-7174
Dolly Piper, *Manager*
EMP: 93
SQ FT: 7,000
SALES (corp-wide): 179.6MM **Privately Held**
WEB: www.longwoodmgmt.com
SIC: 8059 8051 Convalescent home; skilled nursing care facilities
PA: Longwood Management Corp.
4032 Wilshire Blvd Fl 6
Los Angeles CA 90010
213 389-6900

(P-20603)
LONGWOOD MANAGEMENT CORP
Also Called: Western Convelescence
2190 W Adams Blvd, Los Angeles (90018-2039)
PHONE....................323 737-7778
Emma Camanag, *Administration*
EMP: 93
SALES (corp-wide): 179.6MM **Privately Held**
WEB: www.longwoodmgmt.com
SIC: 8059 6512 Convalescent home; commercial & industrial building operation
PA: Longwood Management Corp.
4032 Wilshire Blvd Fl 6
Los Angeles CA 90010
213 389-6900

(P-20604)
LONGWOOD MANAGEMENT CORP
Also Called: Aldon Ter Convalsent Hosptial
1240 S Hoover St, Los Angeles (90006-3606)
PHONE....................213 382-8461
John Sicat, *Principal*
EMP: 93
SALES (corp-wide): 179.6MM **Privately Held**
WEB: www.longwoodmgmt.com
SIC: 8059 8051 Convalescent home; skilled nursing care facilities

PA: Longwood Management Corp.
4032 Wilshire Blvd Fl 6
Los Angeles CA 90010
213 389-6900

(P-20605)
LONGWOOD MANAGEMENT CORP
Also Called: Imperial Care Center
11429 Ventura Blvd, Studio City (91604-3143)
PHONE....................818 980-8200
Emma Dellanuoni, *Manager*
EMP: 93
SQ FT: 29,525
SALES (corp-wide): 179.6MM **Privately Held**
WEB: www.longwoodmgmt.com
SIC: 8059 8051 Convalescent home; skilled nursing care facilities
PA: Longwood Management Corp.
4032 Wilshire Blvd Fl 6
Los Angeles CA 90010
213 389-6900

(P-20606)
LONGWOOD MANAGEMENT CORP
Also Called: Live Oak Rehab
537 W Live Oak St, San Gabriel (91776-1149)
PHONE....................626 289-3763
Ranita Phan, *Manager*
EMP: 93
SALES (corp-wide): 179.6MM **Privately Held**
WEB: www.longwoodmgmt.com
SIC: 8059 8051 Convalescent home; skilled nursing care facilities
PA: Longwood Management Corp.
4032 Wilshire Blvd Fl 6
Los Angeles CA 90010
213 389-6900

(P-20607)
LONGWOOD MANAGEMENT CORP
Also Called: Colonial Care Center
1913 E 5th St, Long Beach (90802-2024)
PHONE....................562 432-5751
Laura McCuphen, *Manager*
Cindy Seilhamer, *Human Res Dir*
EMP: 93
SALES (corp-wide): 179.6MM **Privately Held**
WEB: www.longwoodmgmt.com
SIC: 8059 8051 Convalescent home; skilled nursing care facilities
PA: Longwood Management Corp.
4032 Wilshire Blvd Fl 6
Los Angeles CA 90010
213 389-6900

(P-20608)
LUNWOOD DEVELOPMENTAL CARE
Also Called: Lynwood Adult Day Care
14925 S Atlantic Ave, Compton (90221-3005)
PHONE....................310 223-5920
James E Logan, *President*
Lavern L Neal, *Treasurer*
Bev Logan, *Sales Executive*
Lavern Logan, *Director*
EMP: 57 **EST:** 1994
SALES (est): 7.5MM **Privately Held**
WEB: www.compton-cadhc.com
SIC: 8059 Personal care home, with health care

(P-20609)
MAGNOLIA RHBLTTION NURSING CTR
Also Called: Magnolia Convalescent Hospital
8133 Magnolia Ave, Riverside (92504-3409)
PHONE....................951 688-4321
Larry Mays, *President*
Grant Edgeson, *Treasurer*
Bennie J Mays, *Vice Pres*
Bobbie N Mays, *Admin Sec*
Kimberly Richards, *Administration*
EMP: 140 **EST:** 1971
SQ FT: 25,000

SALES (est): 9.4MM **Privately Held**
WEB: www.magnolia-rehab.com
SIC: 8059 8051 Convalescent home; skilled nursing care facilities

(P-20610)
MARLINDA MANAGEMENT INC (PA)
Also Called: Sherwood Guest Home
3351 E Imperial Hwy, Lynwood (90262-3305)
PHONE....................310 631-6122
Martha Lang, *President*
Linda Gassoumis, *CFO*
EMP: 120 **EST:** 1961
SALES (est): 5.2MM **Privately Held**
SIC: 8059 Convalescent home

(P-20611)
MARNA HEALTH SERVICES INC
Also Called: Sillcrest Nursing Home
4280 Cypress Dr, San Bernardino (92407-2960)
PHONE....................909 882-2965
Maria Barrios, *President*
Napoleon Garcia, *Vice Pres*
EMP: 70 **EST:** 2013
SQ FT: 120
SALES (est): 4.6MM **Privately Held**
SIC: 8059 7389 8049 Personal care home, with health care; ; physical therapist

(P-20612)
MARYCREST MANOR
10664 Saint James Dr, Culver City (90230-5498)
PHONE....................310 838-2778
SIS V Del Carmen, *Administration*
SIS Veronica Del Carmen, *Administration*
EMP: 152 **EST:** 1961
SQ FT: 43,449
SALES (est): 27.5MM **Privately Held**
WEB: www.marycrestculvercity.com
SIC: 8059 8051 Convalescent home; skilled nursing care facilities

(P-20613)
MIRADA HILLS REHABILITATION
12200 La Mirada Blvd, La Mirada (90638-1306)
PHONE....................562 947-8691
Ryan Maguét, *Exec Dir*
Erika Garcia, *Office Mgr*
Renee Valera, *Director*
EMP: 53 **EST:** 2008
SALES (est): 3.9MM **Privately Held**
WEB: www.lcca.com
SIC: 8059 Nursing home, except skilled & intermediate care facility; convalescent home

(P-20614)
MONTEREY PK CONVALESCENT HOSP
Also Called: Sun Mar Management Service
416 N Garfield Ave, Monterey Park (91754-1203)
PHONE....................626 280-0280
Irving Bauman, *President*
William Presnell, *Treasurer*
Bi WEI, *Social Dir*
Frank Johnson, *Principal*
Eli Marmur, *Principal*
EMP: 57 **EST:** 1965
SQ FT: 22,000
SALES (est): 18.1MM **Privately Held**
WEB: www.montereyparkcare.com
SIC: 8059 8051 Convalescent home; skilled nursing care facilities

(P-20615)
MOYLES HEALTH CARE INC
604 E Merritt Ave, Tulare (93274-2135)
PHONE....................559 686-1601
Kensett J Moyle III, *President*
Kensett J Moyle IV, *Vice Pres*
Mark Harris, *Admin Sec*
EMP: 550 **EST:** 1971 **Privately Held**
SIC: 8059 Convalescent home

(P-20616)
NEW VISTA HEALTH SERVICES
Also Called: New Vsta Post Acute Care Ctr W
1516 Sawtelle Blvd, Los Angeles (90025-3207)
PHONE....................310 477-5501
Eugene Tipo, *Administration*
Vernon Gayares, *Hlthcr Dir*
Gina Hernandez, *Director*
EMP: 224
SALES (corp-wide): 17MM **Privately Held**
WEB: www.newvista.us
SIC: 8059 8051 Nursing home, except skilled & intermediate care facility; skilled nursing care facilities
PA: New Vista Health Services, Inc
1987 Vartikian Ave
Clovis CA 93611
559 298-3236

(P-20617)
NEW VISTA HEALTH SERVICES
Also Called: New Vsta Nrsing Fhbltation Ctr
8647 Fenwick St, Sunland (91040-1957)
PHONE....................818 352-1421
Robert Craig, *President*
Alexis Remington-Perez, *Vice Pres*
EMP: 224
SALES (corp-wide): 17MM **Privately Held**
WEB: www.newvista.us
SIC: 8059 8361 Nursing home, except skilled & intermediate care facility; rehabilitation center, residential health care incidental
PA: New Vista Health Services, Inc
1987 Vartikian Ave
Clovis CA 93611
559 298-3236

(P-20618)
NOTELLAGE CORPORATION
Also Called: College Vsta Convalescent Hosp
4681 Eagle Rock Blvd, Los Angeles (90041-3036)
PHONE....................323 257-8151
Michael Stifere, *Administration*
EMP: 51 **EST:** 1976
SQ FT: 10,000
SALES (est): 13.2MM **Privately Held**
SIC: 8059 Convalescent home

(P-20619)
OLYMPIA CONVALESCENT HOSPITAL
1100 S Alvarado St, Los Angeles (90006-4110)
PHONE....................213 487-3000
Otto Schwartz, *Administration*
Sam Lidell, *Ltd Ptnr*
Andre Pollak, *Ltd Ptnr*
EMP: 115 **EST:** 1971
SQ FT: 25,000
SALES (est): 6.8MM **Privately Held**
WEB: www.olympia.com
SIC: 8059 8051 Convalescent home; skilled nursing care facilities

(P-20620)
ORANGE COUNTY ROYALE CONVLSCNT (PA)
1030 W Warner Ave, Santa Ana (92707-3147)
PHONE....................714 546-6450
Mitchell Kantor, *President*
Laura Guzman, *Office Mgr*
Donald Connelly, *Administration*
Michael Pierson, *Administration*
Vicky Limalima, *Director*
EMP: 330 **EST:** 1965
SQ FT: 87,000
SALES (est): 17MM **Privately Held**
WEB: www.royalehealth.com
SIC: 8059 8051 Convalescent home; skilled nursing care facilities

(P-20621)
PACIFIC HAVEN CONVALESCENT HM
Also Called: Pacific Haven Convalescent HM
12072 Trask Ave, Garden Grove (92843-3881)
PHONE....................714 534-1942
Mike Uranga, *Administration*

Nick Duran, *Opers Staff*
Long Vu,
Melody Cruz, *Director*
Emily Alvea, *Manager*
EMP: 100 **EST:** 1978
SALES (est): 11.3MM **Privately Held**
WEB: www.pachaven.com
SIC: 8059 8051 Convalescent home; skilled nursing care facilities

(P-20622)
PARK MARINO CONVALESCENT CTR
2585 E Washington Blvd, Pasadena (91107-1446)
PHONE..................626 463-4105
William Kite, *Administration*
EMP: 121 **EST:** 1966
SALES (est): 7.1MM
SALES (corp-wide): 10.1MM **Privately Held**
WEB: www.parkmarino.com
SIC: 8059 8051 Convalescent home; skilled nursing care facilities
PA: Diversified Health Services (Del)
136 Washington Ave
Richmond CA 94801
510 231-6200

(P-20623)
PILGRIM PLACE IN CLAREMONT (PA)
625 Mayflower Rd, Claremont (91711-4240)
PHONE..................909 399-5500
William R Cunitz, *President*
Sue Fairley, *Vice Pres*
Bernard Valek, *Vice Pres*
Joyce Yarborough, *Vice Pres*
Mary Ann Macias, *Director*
EMP: 175
SQ FT: 2,000
SALES: 19.7MM **Privately Held**
WEB: www.pilgrimplace.org
SIC: 8059 8051 8052 Rest home, with health care; skilled nursing care facilities; intermediate care facilities

(P-20624)
REDLANDS CMNTY HOSP FOUNDATION
Also Called: Asistencia Villa
1875 Barton Rd, Redlands (92373-5308)
PHONE..................909 793-1382
EMP: 101
SALES (corp-wide): 1.1MM **Privately Held**
WEB: www.redlandshospital.org
SIC: 8059 8051 8093 Nursing/Personal Care Skilled Nursing Care Facility Specialty Outpatient Clinic
PA: Redlands Community Hospital Foundation
350 Terracina Blvd
Redlands CA 92373
909 335-5540

(P-20625)
SAN BERNARDINO CARE COMPANY
467 E Gilbert St, San Bernardino (92404-5318)
PHONE..................909 884-4781
Jenq Chen, *President*
EMP: 110 **EST:** 2004
SALES (est): 9.6MM **Privately Held**
SIC: 8059 Convalescent home

(P-20626)
SECROM INC
Also Called: Carson Senior Assisted Living
345 E Carson St, Carson (90745-2709)
PHONE..................310 830-4010
Shlomo Rechnitz, *CEO*
Ginger Enriquez, *Administration*
EMP: 55 **EST:** 2005
SALES (est): 2.6MM **Privately Held**
WEB: www.carsonassistedliving.net
SIC: 8059 Rest home, with health care

(P-20627)
SILVERSCREEN HEALTHCARE INC
Also Called: Asistencia Villa Rehab & Care
1875 Barton Rd, Redlands (92373-5308)
PHONE..................909 793-1382
EMP: 135
SALES (est): 4.4MM **Privately Held**
WEB: www.yolocare2.com
SIC: 8059 8322 Nursing/Personal Care Individual/Family Services

(P-20628)
STANLEY HEALTHCARE CENTER
14102 Springdale St, Westminster (92683-3538)
PHONE..................714 893-0026
William Larson, *Partner*
Everett Goings, *Partner*
Malcolm Williams, *Director*
EMP: 66 **EST:** 1977
SQ FT: 6,000
SALES (est): 32.4MM **Privately Held**
WEB: www.progressivecarecenters.com
SIC: 8059 8051 Convalescent home; skilled nursing care facilities

(P-20629)
SUN MAR MANAGEMENT SERVICES
Also Called: Sun Mar Healthcare
500 N State College Blvd, Orange (92868-1604)
PHONE..................714 385-1006
Toni Gutierrez, *Info Tech Dir*
John Tao, *Business Anlyst*
EMP: 88 **Privately Held**
SIC: 8059 Nursing home, except skilled & intermediate care facility
PA: Sun Mar Management Services
3050 Saturn St Ste 201
Brea CA 92821

(P-20630)
SUN MAR NURSING CENTER INC
Also Called: Sun Mar Management Services
1720 W Orange Ave, Anaheim (92804-2699)
PHONE..................714 776-1720
Chris William, *Administration*
Blaine Hendrickson, *President*
Bill Presnell, *Corp Secy*
Anne Sitchon, *Office Mgr*
Camille Velasco, *Office Mgr*
EMP: 51 **EST:** 1979
SQ FT: 10,000
SALES (est): 12.9MM **Privately Held**
WEB: www.sunmarnursing.com
SIC: 8059 Nursing home, except skilled & intermediate care facility

(P-20631)
TEMPLE PK CNVALESCENT HOSP INC
2411 W Temple St, Los Angeles (90026-4817)
PHONE..................213 380-2035
Barry Kohn, *President*
Toby Kohn, *Vice Pres*
EMP: 77 **EST:** 1976
SALES (est): 5.5MM **Privately Held**
SIC: 8059 Convalescent home

(P-20632)
TWO PALMS NURSING CENTER INC (PA)
2637 E Washington Blvd, Pasadena (91107-1412)
PHONE..................626 798-8991
Marthann Demchuk, *CEO*
EMP: 50 **EST:** 1970
SALES (est): 9.6MM **Privately Held**
SIC: 8059 Convalescent home

(P-20633)
TWO PALMS NURSING CENTER INC
Also Called: Marlinda Imperial Hospital
150 Bellefontaine St, Pasadena (91105-3102)
PHONE..................626 796-1103

EMP: 185
SQ FT: 28,955
SALES (corp-wide): 9.6MM **Privately Held**
WEB: www.pasadenameadows.com
SIC: 8059 8051 Convalescent home; skilled nursing care facilities
PA: Two Palms Nursing Center, Inc.
2637 E Washington Blvd
Pasadena CA 91107
626 798-8991

(P-20634)
UNITED CONVALESCENT FACILITIES
Also Called: University Park Healthcare Ctr
230 E Adams Blvd, Los Angeles (90011-1426)
PHONE..................626 629-6950
Doug Easton, *Owner*
Bill Ingram, *Hlthcr Dir*
EMP: 80 **EST:** 1998
SQ FT: 1,300
SALES (est): 4MM **Privately Held**
WEB: www.universityparkhcc.com
SIC: 8059 Nursing home, except skilled & intermediate care facility

(P-20635)
UNITED CRBRAL PLSY/SPSTIC CHLD
Also Called: Ucp Dronfield North
13272 Dronfield Ave, Sylmar (91342-2961)
PHONE..................818 364-5911
Liz McLaughlin, *Administration*
EMP: 76
SALES (corp-wide): 26.7MM **Privately Held**
WEB: www.momentum4all.org
SIC: 8059 Home for the mentally retarded, exc. skilled or intermediate
PA: United Cerebral Palsy/Spastic Children's Foundation Of Los Angeles And Ventura Counties
6430 Independence Ave
Woodland Hills CA 91367
818 782-2211

(P-20636)
UNITED MEDICAL MANAGEMENT INC
Also Called: Valley Healthcare
1680 N Waterman Ave, San Bernardino (92404-5113)
PHONE..................909 886-5291
Alan Hull, *Administration*
James Kilian, *Med Doctor*
EMP: 125 **EST:** 1982
SQ FT: 30,000
SALES (est): 7.2MM **Privately Held**
SIC: 8059 8051 8322 Convalescent home; skilled nursing care facilities; rehabilitation services

(P-20637)
VAN NUYS CARE CENTER INC
Also Called: Lake Balboa Care Center
16955 Vanowen St, Van Nuys (91406-4542)
PHONE..................818 343-0700
Chad Thornton, *President*
John Thornton, *President*
Wayne A Evans, *Vice Pres*
Craig Barron, *Administration*
Jose Aldunate, *Chf Purch Ofc*
EMP: 67 **EST:** 1972
SQ FT: 12,500
SALES (est): 9.1MM **Privately Held**
WEB: www.lakebalboacare.com
SIC: 8059 8051 Convalescent home; skilled nursing care facilities

(P-20638)
VIACARE INC (PA)
Also Called: Chez Bon Guest Home
1206 Walnut Ave, Long Beach (90813-3823)
PHONE..................562 591-1411
Marcia Rubin, *President*
EMP: 66 **EST:** 1968
SALES (est): 3MM **Privately Held**
WEB: www.viacarela.org
SIC: 8059 Home for the mentally retarded, exc. skilled or intermediate

(P-20639)
WALDEN ENVIRONMENT
Also Called: Walden Family Services
6345 Balboa Blvd Ste 130, Encino (91316-1510)
PHONE..................818 365-3665
Olga Sizon, *Manager*
Nayely Perez, *Recruiter*
Leslie Lucas, *Program Dir*
Kathryn Stephens, *Director*
Jill Harris, *Supervisor*
EMP: 70
SALES (corp-wide): 17.1MM **Privately Held**
WEB: www.waldenfamily.org
SIC: 8059 Convalescent home
PA: Walden Environment
8525 Gibbs Dr Ste 100
San Diego CA 92123
619 727-5884

(P-20640)
WESTMINSTER GARDENS
1420 Santo Domingo Ave, Duarte (91010-2698)
PHONE..................626 359-2571
Judy Thorndyke, *Exec Dir*
EMP: 82 **EST:** 1950
SQ FT: 1,306,800
SALES (est): 6.3MM **Privately Held**
WEB: www.humangood.org
SIC: 8059 Rest home, with health care; nursing home, except skilled & intermediate care facility

(P-20641)
WICORO INC (HQ)
Also Called: Colonial Mnor Cnvalescent Hosp
919 N Sunset Ave, West Covina (91790-1244)
PHONE..................626 962-4489
C David Benfield, *President*
Amber Felix, *Manager*
EMP: 50 **EST:** 1970
SQ FT: 15,000
SALES (est): 7.1MM
SALES (corp-wide): 10.4MM **Privately Held**
WEB: www.caretech.com
SIC: 8059 Convalescent home
PA: Care Tech, Inc.
401 N Central Ave Ste B
Upland CA 91786
909 373-3766

(P-20642)
WINDSOR CYPRESS GRDNS HLTHCARE
9025 Colorado Ave, Riverside (92503-2157)
PHONE..................951 688-3643
Lee Samson, *CEO*
Stanley Angermeir, *President*
Edward Erzen, *Vice Pres*
EMP: 2773 **EST:** 1972
SALES (est): 27.8MM **Privately Held**
WEB: www.cypressgardenscare.com
SIC: 8059 8051 Convalescent home; skilled nursing care facilities
PA: S&F Management Company, Llc
9200 W Sunset Blvd # 700
West Hollywood CA 90069

8062 General Medical & Surgical Hospitals

(P-20643)
ADVENTIST HEALTH MED TEHACHAPI (PA)
305 S Robinson St, Tehachapi (93561-1726)
P.O. Box 669 (93581-0669)
PHONE..................661 750-4848
Eugene Suksi, *CEO*
Allen Burgess, *Principal*
Lisa Hughes, *Business Mgr*
Bridget Thomason, *Controller*
Elizabeth McGehee,
EMP: 101 **EST:** 1949
SQ FT: 18,000

SALES: 2.9MM **Privately Held**
WEB: www.tvhd.org
SIC: **8062** General medical & surgical hospitals

(P-20644)
ADVENTIST HEALTH SYSTEM/WEST
31872 Coast Hwy, Laguna Beach (92651-6773)
PHONE......................949 499-7175
Mindra Fielding, *Info Tech Dir*
Kathryn M Cvar, *Oncology*
Andrew Henrick, *Ophthalmology*
EMP: 61
SALES (corp-wide): 4.5B **Privately Held**
WEB: www.adventisthealth.org
SIC: **8062** General medical & surgical hospitals
PA: Adventist Health System/West, Corporation
    1 Adventist Health Way
    Roseville CA 95661
    844 574-5686

(P-20645)
ADVENTIST HEALTH SYSTEM/WEST
1040 7th St, Wasco (93280-1934)
PHONE......................661 869-6700
EMP: 61
SALES (corp-wide): 4.5B **Privately Held**
WEB: www.adventisthealth.org
SIC: **8062** General medical & surgical hospitals
PA: Adventist Health System/West, Corporation
    1 Adventist Health Way
    Roseville CA 95661
    844 574-5686

(P-20646)
ADVENTIST HEALTH SYSTEM/WEST
1524 W Lacey Blvd Ste 102, Hanford (93230-5966)
PHONE......................559 537-0305
Aaron S Currie, *Physician Asst*
EMP: 61
SALES (corp-wide): 4.5B **Privately Held**
WEB: www.adventisthealth.org
SIC: **8062** General medical & surgical hospitals
PA: Adventist Health System/West, Corporation
    1 Adventist Health Way
    Roseville CA 95661
    844 574-5686

(P-20647)
ADVENTIST HEALTH SYSTEM/WEST
Also Called: Adventist Hlth Cmnty Care-Taft
501 6th St, Taft (93268-2704)
PHONE......................661 763-5131
Alan Ferch, *Branch Mgr*
EMP: 61
SALES (corp-wide): 4.5B **Privately Held**
WEB: www.adventisthealth.org
SIC: **8062** General medical & surgical hospitals
PA: Adventist Health System/West, Corporation
    1 Adventist Health Way
    Roseville CA 95661
    844 574-5686

(P-20648)
ADVENTIST HEALTH SYSTEM/WEST
301 Science Dr Ste 150, Moorpark (93021-2097)
PHONE......................805 955-7000
EMP: 61
SALES (corp-wide): 4.5B **Privately Held**
WEB: www.adventisthealth.org
SIC: **8062** General medical & surgical hospitals
PA: Adventist Health System/West, Corporation
    1 Adventist Health Way
    Roseville CA 95661
    844 574-5686

(P-20649)
ADVENTIST HEALTH SYSTEM/WEST
Also Called: Hanford Community Center
470 Greenfield Ave, Hanford (93230-3576)
PHONE......................559 537-2510
Kenny MAI, *Surgeon*
Frank Buchanan, *Med Doctor*
Prem Sahasranam, *Med Doctor*
EMP: 61
SALES (corp-wide): 4.5B **Privately Held**
WEB: www.adventisthealth.org
SIC: **8062** General medical & surgical hospitals
PA: Adventist Health System/West, Corporation
    1 Adventist Health Way
    Roseville CA 95661
    844 574-5686

(P-20650)
ADVENTIST HEALTH TULARE
869 N Cherry St, Tulare (93274-2207)
PHONE......................559 688-0821
Andrea Kofl, *President*
Sharon Fong, *Lab Dir*
Annette Machado, *Technician*
Daniel Sedano, *Technical Staff*
Charlene Dawson, *Nursing Dir*
EMP: 500 EST: 2018
SALES (est): 72.8MM **Privately Held**
WEB: www.adventisthealth.org
SIC: **8062** General medical & surgical hospitals

(P-20651)
ADVENTIST HLTH SYSTM/WEST CORP
337 E Kings St, Avenal (93204-1630)
PHONE......................559 386-5200
EMP: 61
SALES (corp-wide): 4.5B **Privately Held**
WEB: www.adventisthealth.org
SIC: **8062** General medical & surgical hospitals
PA: Adventist Health System/West, Corporation
    1 Adventist Health Way
    Roseville CA 95661
    844 574-5686

(P-20652)
ADVENTIST HLTH SYSTM/WEST CORP
3191 Casitas Ave Ste 216, Los Angeles (90039-2470)
PHONE......................323 646-2858
Juan A Silva, *Family Practiti*
Robbin Cohen, *Med Doctor*
EMP: 61
SALES (corp-wide): 4.5B **Privately Held**
WEB: www.adventisthealth.org
SIC: **8062** General medical & surgical hospitals
PA: Adventist Health System/West, Corporation
    1 Adventist Health Way
    Roseville CA 95661
    844 574-5686

(P-20653)
ADVENTIST HLTH SYSTM/WEST CORP
Also Called: Adventist Health Job Care
444 W El Monte Way, Dinuba (93618-1500)
PHONE......................559 591-1906
EMP: 61
SALES (corp-wide): 4.5B **Privately Held**
WEB: www.adventisthealth.org
SIC: **8062** General medical & surgical hospitals
PA: Adventist Health System/West, Corporation
    1 Adventist Health Way
    Roseville CA 95661
    844 574-5686

(P-20654)
ADVENTIST HLTH SYSTM/WEST CORP
1025 N Douty St, Hanford (93230-3722)
PHONE......................888 443-2273
EMP: 61

SALES (corp-wide): 4.5B **Privately Held**
WEB: www.adventisthealth.org
SIC: **8062** General medical & surgical hospitals
PA: Adventist Health System/West, Corporation
    1 Adventist Health Way
    Roseville CA 95661
    844 574-5686

(P-20655)
ADVENTIST HLTH SYSTM/WEST CORP
41696 Road 128, Orosi (93647-2059)
PHONE......................559 528-6966
EMP: 61
SALES (corp-wide): 4.5B **Privately Held**
WEB: www.adventisthealth.org
SIC: **8062** General medical & surgical hospitals
PA: Adventist Health System/West, Corporation
    1 Adventist Health Way
    Roseville CA 95661
    844 574-5686

(P-20656)
ADVENTIST HLTH SYSTM/WEST CORP
Also Called: Adventist Hlth Med Foundation
381 Merrill Ave, Glendale (91206-4178)
PHONE......................818 409-8540
Iris Weil, *CEO*
EMP: 61
SALES (corp-wide): 4.5B **Privately Held**
WEB: www.adventisthealth.org
SIC: **8062** General medical & surgical hospitals
PA: Adventist Health System/West, Corporation
    1 Adventist Health Way
    Roseville CA 95661
    844 574-5686

(P-20657)
ADVENTIST HLTH SYSTM/WEST CORP
Also Called: Central Vly Fmly Health-Dinuba
1451 E El Monte Way, Dinuba (93618-1812)
PHONE......................559 591-3342
Ronald Ray Ruminson, *Principal*
EMP: 61
SALES (corp-wide): 4.5B **Privately Held**
WEB: www.adventisthealth.org
SIC: **8062** General medical & surgical hospitals
PA: Adventist Health System/West, Corporation
    1 Adventist Health Way
    Roseville CA 95661
    844 574-5686

(P-20658)
ADVENTIST HLTH SYSTM/WEST CORP
Also Called: Central Valley Family Health
216 E Fresno St, Avenal (93204-1525)
PHONE......................559 386-5364
Madaline Andrade, *Manager*
EMP: 61
SALES (corp-wide): 4.5B **Privately Held**
WEB: www.adventisthealth.org
SIC: **8062** General medical & surgical hospitals
PA: Adventist Health System/West, Corporation
    1 Adventist Health Way
    Roseville CA 95661
    844 574-5686

(P-20659)
ADVENTIST HLTH SYSTM/WEST CORP
Also Called: Central Vly Fmly Halthcorcoran
1212 Hanna Ave, Corcoran (93212-2313)
PHONE......................559 992-2800
Randy Dodd, *Manager*
EMP: 61
SALES (corp-wide): 4.5B **Privately Held**
WEB: www.adventisthealth.org
SIC: **8062** General medical & surgical hospitals

PA: Adventist Health System/West, Corporation
    1 Adventist Health Way
    Roseville CA 95661
    844 574-5686

(P-20660)
ADVENTIST HLTH SYSTM/WEST CORP
Also Called: Central Vly Fmly Hlth-Lmoore E
810 E D St, Lemoore (93245-9545)
PHONE......................559 924-7711
N Bartell, *Branch Mgr*
EMP: 61
SALES (corp-wide): 4.5B **Privately Held**
WEB: www.adventisthealth.org
SIC: **8062** General medical & surgical hospitals
PA: Adventist Health System/West, Corporation
    1 Adventist Health Way
    Roseville CA 95661
    844 574-5686

(P-20661)
ADVENTIST HLTH SYSTM/WEST CORP
Also Called: Schn
1509 Wilson Ter, Glendale (91206-4007)
PHONE......................818 409-8050
Mari Abrams, *Manager*
Susan Leyba, *Vice Pres*
Seth Wade, *Regional Mgr*
Lorenzo Zendejas, *Technology*
Aileen Legaspi, *Recruiter*
EMP: 61
SALES (corp-wide): 4.5B **Privately Held**
WEB: www.adventisthealth.org
SIC: **8062** General medical & surgical hospitals
PA: Adventist Health System/West, Corporation
    1 Adventist Health Way
    Roseville CA 95661
    844 574-5686

(P-20662)
ADVENTIST MED CENTER-HANFORD (HQ)
115 Mall Dr, Hanford (93230-5786)
PHONE......................559 582-9000
Eric Martinson, *CFO*
Frank Gavini, *Officer*
Andrea Kofl, *Officer*
Stephen Avalos, *Pathologist*
Laurie Taggart, *Nursing Dir*
EMP: 50 EST: 2010
SALES (est): 260.4MM
SALES (corp-wide): 4.5B **Privately Held**
WEB: www.adventisthealth.org
SIC: **8062** General medical & surgical hospitals
PA: Adventist Health System/West, Corporation
    1 Adventist Health Way
    Roseville CA 95661
    844 574-5686

(P-20663)
ADVENTIST MED CENTER-HANFORD
125 Mall Dr, Hanford (93230-5787)
PHONE......................559 537-1377
Ashley Clabeaux, *Administration*
EMP: 466
SALES (corp-wide): 4.5B **Privately Held**
WEB: www.adventisthealth.org
SIC: **8062** General medical & surgical hospitals
HQ: Adventist Medical Center-Hanford
    115 Mall Dr
    Hanford CA 93230
    559 582-9000

(P-20664)
AHM GEMCH INC
Also Called: Greater El Monte Cmnty Hosp
1701 Santa Anita Ave, El Monte (91733-3411)
PHONE......................626 579-7777
Jeffrey Flocken, *CEO*
James Lin Jr, *Ch Radiology*
Patrick Steinhauser, *COO*
Gary Louis, *CFO*
Stanley Toy Jr, *Officer*

▲ = Import ▼=Export
◆ =Import/Export

EMP: 180 EST: 1973
SQ FT: 71,500
SALES (est): 50.5MM
SALES (corp-wide): 574.5MM Privately Held
WEB: www.greaterelmonte.com
SIC: 8062 General medical & surgical hospitals
PA: Ahmc Healthcare Inc.
506 W Valley Blvd Ste 300
San Gabriel CA 91776
626 943-7526

(P-20665)
AHMC HEALTHCARE INC (PA)
506 W Valley Blvd Ste 300, San Gabriel (91776-5716)
PHONE.....................626 943-7526
Jonathan Wu MD, *CEO*
Suzanne Hsu,
Amitabh Prakash, *Chief Mktg Ofcr*
Eunice Andaya, *Vice Pres*
Charles Dong, *Vice Pres*
EMP: 150 EST: 2004
SALES (est): 574.5MM Privately Held
WEB: www.ahmchealth.com
SIC: 8062 8641 General medical & surgical hospitals; civic social & fraternal associations

(P-20666)
AHMC HEALTHCARE INC
1701 Santa Anita Ave, South El Monte (91733-3411)
PHONE.....................626 579-7777
Teresita Pascual, *Accountant*
Linda Du, *Controller*
Mark Underwood, *Director*
EMP: 2906
SALES (corp-wide): 574.5MM Privately Held
WEB: www.ahmchealth.com
SIC: 8062 General medical & surgical hospitals
PA: Ahmc Healthcare Inc.
506 W Valley Blvd Ste 300
San Gabriel CA 91776
626 943-7526

(P-20667)
AHMC WHITTIER HOSP MED CTR LP
9080 Colima Rd, Whittier (90605-1600)
PHONE.....................562 945-3561
Richard Castro, *CEO*
Lee Panton, *Lab Dir*
Michael Nakamura, *Business Dir*
Sarkis Vartanian, *Ch Nursing Ofcr*
Marie Trembath, *Exec Dir*
EMP: 850 EST: 2001
SQ FT: 16,782
SALES (est): 183MM
SALES (corp-wide): 574.5MM Privately Held
WEB: www.whittierhospital.com
SIC: 8062 General medical & surgical hospitals
PA: Ahmc Healthcare Inc.
506 W Valley Blvd Ste 300
San Gabriel CA 91776
626 943-7526

(P-20668)
ALAKOR HEALTHCARE LLC
Also Called: Monrovia Memorial Hospital
323 S Heliotrope Ave, Monrovia (91016-2914)
PHONE.....................626 408-9800
Kevin Smith,
Amanda Morales, *Executive Asst*
Katty Johnson, *Human Res Dir*
Ron Kupferstein,
Jon Woods,
EMP: 126 EST: 2004
SQ FT: 10,000
SALES (est): 23.5MM Privately Held
WEB: www.monroviamemorial.com
SIC: 8062 General medical & surgical hospitals

(P-20669)
ALHAMBRA HOSPITAL MED CTR LP
Also Called: Alhambra Hospital Medical Ctr
100 S Raymond Ave, Alhambra (91801-3166)
PHONE.....................626 570-1606
Iris Lai, *Marketing Staff*
Elizabeth Sabandit, *Exec Dir*
Juan Rodriquez, *Purchasing*
Tai Phung, *Nurse*
Grace Wu, *Hlthcr Dir*
EMP: 160 EST: 1920
SQ FT: 200,000
SALES (est): 91MM
SALES (corp-wide): 574.5MM Privately Held
WEB: www.alhambrahospital.com
SIC: 8062 General medical & surgical hospitals
PA: Ahmc Healthcare Inc.
506 W Valley Blvd Ste 300
San Gabriel CA 91776
626 943-7526

(P-20670)
ALTA HEALTHCARE SYSTEM LLC (HQ)
4081 E Olympic Blvd, Los Angeles (90023-3330)
PHONE.....................323 267-0477
David Topper, *Mng Member*
Bruce Grimshaw, *Vice Pres*
Sam Lee,
Leslia Gomez, *Director*
Venice Bacani, *Case Mgr*
EMP: 250 EST: 1998
SALES (est): 92.4MM
SALES (corp-wide): 3.4B Privately Held
WEB: www.sch-culvercity.com
SIC: 8062 General medical & surgical hospitals
PA: Prospect Medical Holdings, Inc.
3415 S Sepulveda Blvd # 9
Los Angeles CA 90034
310 943-4500

(P-20671)
ALTA HOSPITALS SYSTEM LLC
Also Called: Foothill Regional Medical Ctr
14662 Newport Ave, Tustin (92780-6064)
PHONE.....................714 619-7700
EMP: 575
SALES (corp-wide): 3.4B Privately Held
WEB: www.pmh.com
SIC: 8062 General medical & surgical hospitals
HQ: Alta Hospitals System, Llc
3415 S Sepulveda Blvd # 900
Los Angeles CA 90034

(P-20672)
ALTA HOSPITALS SYSTEM LLC (HQ)
3415 S Sepulveda Blvd # 900, Los Angeles (90034-6060)
PHONE.....................310 943-4500
Samuel S Lee, *Mng Member*
Kenneth Auguster, *Records Dir*
Leslie Miller, *Records Dir*
Nestor Lopez, *Officer*
Nina Rosenfeld, *Officer*
EMP: 50 EST: 2007
SALES (est): 334.2MM
SALES (corp-wide): 3.4B Privately Held
WEB: www.foothillregionalmedicalcenter.com
SIC: 8062 General medical & surgical hospitals
PA: Prospect Medical Holdings, Inc.
3415 S Sepulveda Blvd # 9
Los Angeles CA 90034
310 943-4500

(P-20673)
AMI-HTI TRZANA ENCINO JINT VNT
Also Called: A M I Encn-Trzana Rgnal Med Ce
18321 Clark St, Tarzana (91356-3501)
PHONE.....................818 881-0800
Dale Surowitz, *Managing Prtnr*
Jo Ann Lewis, *Director*
EMP: 123 EST: 1993

SQ FT: 180,000
SALES (est): 11MM Privately Held
SIC: 8062 General medical & surgical hospitals

(P-20674)
AMISUB OF CALIFORNIA INC (DH)
18321 Clark St, Tarzana (91356-3501)
PHONE.....................818 881-0800
Dale Surowitz, *CEO*
Don Kreitz, *COO*
Nick Lymberopolous, *CFO*
EMP: 900 EST: 1979
SQ FT: 180,000
SALES (est): 100.8MM
SALES (corp-wide): 17.6B Publicly Held
WEB: www.tenethealth.com
SIC: 8062 General medical & surgical hospitals
HQ: Tenet Healthsystem Medical, Inc.
14201 Dallas Pkwy
Dallas TX 75254
469 893-2000

(P-20675)
ANAHEIM GLOBAL MEDICAL CENTER
1025 S Anaheim Blvd, Anaheim (92805-5806)
PHONE.....................714 533-6220
Jamie You, *CEO*
Marven E Howard, *CEO*
Jason Liu, *Principal*
George Bandy, *Security Dir*
Robert Lank, *Engineer*
EMP: 975 EST: 1981
SALES (est): 162.5MM
SALES (corp-wide): 1.9B Privately Held
WEB: www.anaheimglobalmedicalcenter.com
SIC: 8062 General medical & surgical hospitals
PA: Kpc Healthcare, Inc.
1301 N Tustin Ave
Santa Ana CA 92705
714 953-3652

(P-20676)
ANAHEIM REGIONAL MEDICAL CTR
Also Called: Cardiac Unit
1111 W La Palma Ave, Anaheim (92801-2804)
PHONE.....................714 774-1450
EMP: 116
SALES (corp-wide): 113.9MM Privately Held
WEB: www.anaheimregionalmc.com
SIC: 8062 General medical & surgical hospitals
PA: Anaheim Regional Medical Center
1111 W La Palma Ave
Anaheim CA 92801
714 774-1450

(P-20677)
ANAHEIM REGIONAL MEDICAL CTR
Also Called: Ahmc
1211 W La Palma Ave, Anaheim (92801-2815)
PHONE.....................714 999-3847
Patrick Petre, *Branch Mgr*
Trina Viveros, *Executive Asst*
Karen Ashley,
Guillermina Lopez, *Manager*
EMP: 116
SALES (corp-wide): 113.9MM Privately Held
WEB: www.anaheimregionalmc.com
SIC: 8062 General medical & surgical hospitals
PA: Anaheim Regional Medical Center
1111 W La Palma Ave
Anaheim CA 92801
714 774-1450

(P-20678)
ANTELOPE VALLEY HOSPITAL INC (PA)
Also Called: Antelope Valley Healthcare Dst
1600 W Avenue J, Lancaster (93534-2894)
P.O. Box 7001 (93539-7001)
PHONE.....................661 949-5000

Edward Mirzabegian, *CEO*
Jennifer Hill, *Ch Radiology*
Marcelo Spector, *Ch Radiology*
Jack Burke, *COO*
Dennis Empey, *CFO*
EMP: 1660 EST: 1955
SQ FT: 300,000
SALES: 450.4MM Privately Held
WEB: www.avhospital.org
SIC: 8062 General medical & surgical hospitals

(P-20679)
ANTELOPE VALLEY HOSPITAL INC
Also Called: Antelope Valley Home Care
44335 Lowtree Ave, Lancaster (93534-4167)
PHONE.....................661 949-5936
Patti Sheldon, *Manager*
Linda Robinson, *Manager*
EMP: 186
SALES (corp-wide): 450.4MM Privately Held
WEB: www.avhospital.org
SIC: 8062 8082 General medical & surgical hospitals; home health care services
PA: Antelope Valley Hospital, Inc.
1600 W Avenue J
Lancaster CA 93534
661 949-5000

(P-20680)
ANTELOPE VALLEY HOSPITAL INC
Also Called: Antelope Valley Hlth Care Dst
44335 Lowtree Ave, Lancaster (93534-4167)
PHONE.....................661 949-5000
Cheryl Akerly, *Branch Mgr*
Dennis Empey, *Officer*
Nana Deeb, *Vice Pres*
Ross Bauman, *Business Dir*
Sheryl Chavez, *Admin Sec*
EMP: 186
SALES (corp-wide): 450.4MM Privately Held
WEB: www.avhospital.org
SIC: 8062 General medical & surgical hospitals
PA: Antelope Valley Hospital, Inc.
1600 W Avenue J
Lancaster CA 93534
661 949-5000

(P-20681)
ANTELOPE VALLEY HOSPITAL INC
Antelope Otpatient Imaging Ctr
44105 15th St W Ste 100, Lancaster (93534-4090)
PHONE.....................661 726-6050
Veronica Munoz-Rivera, *Branch Mgr*
Kayla Tyndall, *Office Mgr*
Barbara Kirwan, *Recruiter*
EMP: 186
SALES (corp-wide): 450.4MM Privately Held
WEB: www.avhospital.org
SIC: 8062 8099 General medical & surgical hospitals; medical services organization
PA: Antelope Valley Hospital, Inc.
1600 W Avenue J
Lancaster CA 93534
661 949-5000

(P-20682)
ANTELOPE VALLEY HOSPITAL INC
44335 Lowtree Ave, Lancaster (93534-4167)
PHONE.....................661 949-5938
Patti Sheldon, *Manager*
Jessica Biehl,
Taylor Wade,
EMP: 186
SALES (corp-wide): 450.4MM Privately Held
WEB: www.avhospital.org
SIC: 8062 8082 General medical & surgical hospitals; home health care services

PA: Antelope Valley Hospital, Inc.
1600 W Avenue J
Lancaster CA 93534
661 949-5000

(P-20683)
ARROWHEAD REGIONAL MEDICAL CTR
Also Called: Armc
400 N Pepper Ave, Colton (92324-1819)
PHONE..................909 580-1000
Patrick Petre, *Director*
June Malone, *COO*
Sam Hessami, *Chief Mktg Ofcr*
Barbara Hanson, *Officer*
Theodore Friedman, *Lab Dir*
EMP: 2500 **EST:** 1952
SQ FT: 950,000
SALES (est): 574.1MM
SALES (corp-wide): 4B **Privately Held**
WEB: www.arrowheadregional.org
SIC: 8062 General medical & surgical hospitals
PA: County Of San Bernardino
385 N Arrowhead Ave
San Bernardino CA 92415
909 387-3841

(P-20684)
AUXILARY OF MSSION HOSP MSSION
27700 Medical Center Rd, Mission Viejo (92691-6426)
PHONE..................949 364-1400
Eduardo Jordan, *Ch of Bd*
Kenn McFarland, *President*
Vicki J Veal, *CEO*
EMP: 1242 **EST:** 2011
SALES: 443.3K
SALES (corp-wide): 322.5MM **Privately Held**
WEB: www.mission4health.com
SIC: 8062 General medical & surgical hospitals
PA: Mission Hospital Regional Medical Center Inc
27700 Medical Center Rd
Mission Viejo CA 92691
949 364-1400

(P-20685)
BAKERSFIELD MEMORIAL HOSPITAL
Also Called: MEMORIAL CENTER
420 34th St, Bakersfield (93301-2237)
P.O. Box 1888 (93303-1888)
PHONE..................661 327-1792
Jon Van Boening, *CEO*
David Schale, *Ch Radiology*
Gordon K Foster, *Ch of Bd*
R Mark R Root, *Vice Pres*
Gary De Risio, *Opers Mgr*
EMP: 1100 **EST:** 1953
SQ FT: 364,000
SALES: 540.8MM **Privately Held**
WEB: www.dignityhealth.org
SIC: 8062 Hospital, affiliated with AMA residency
HQ: Dignity Health
185 Berry St Ste 200
San Francisco CA 94107
415 438-5500

(P-20686)
BEAR VLY CMNTY HEALTHCARE DST (PA)
41870 Garstin Dr, Big Bear Lake (92315-2088)
PHONE..................909 866-6501
Raymond Hino, *CEO*
Donna Nicely, *Treasurer*
Mary Norman, *Officer*
Barbara Espinoza, *Vice Pres*
Kerri Jex, *Ch Nursing Ofcr*
EMP: 150 **EST:** 1985
SQ FT: 25,000
SALES: 341.3K **Privately Held**
WEB:
www.bearvalleycommunityhospital.com
SIC: 8062 General medical & surgical hospitals

(P-20687)
BEVERLY COMMUNITY HOSP ASSN (PA)
Also Called: BEVERLY HOSPITAL
309 W Beverly Blvd, Montebello (90640-4308)
PHONE..................323 726-1222
Gary Kiff, *CEO*
Wendy Beesley, *COO*
Larry Pugh, *CFO*
Renee D Martinez, *Treasurer*
Lester Fujimoto, *Vice Pres*
EMP: 954 **EST:** 1949
SQ FT: 274,000
SALES: 189.9MM **Privately Held**
WEB: www.beverly.org
SIC: 8062 General medical & surgical hospitals

(P-20688)
BHC ALHAMBRA HOSPITAL INC
4619 Rosemead Blvd, Rosemead (91770-1478)
PHONE..................626 286-1191
Margaret Minnick, *Manager*
EMP: 65 **EST:** 1996
SALES (est): 16MM **Privately Held**
WEB: www.bhcalhambra.com
SIC: 8062 General medical & surgical hospitals

(P-20689)
BIO-MED SERVICES INC
Also Called: Prime Healthcare Services
3300 E Guasti Rd, Ontario (91761-8655)
PHONE..................909 235-4400
Prem Reddy, *CEO*
Christopher Doan, *Officer*
Paula Ellis, *Ch Nursing Ofcr*
Karen McComb, *Analyst*
Norell Vacharapornsoph, *Analyst*
EMP: 85 **EST:** 2006
SALES (est): 26MM
SALES (corp-wide): 1B **Privately Held**
WEB: www.primehealthcare.com
SIC: 8062 General medical & surgical hospitals
HQ: Prime Healthcare Services Inc
3480 E Guasti Rd
Ontario CA 91761

(P-20690)
BROTMAN MEDICAL CENTER INC
Also Called: Southern Cal Hosp At Culver Cy
3828 Delmas Ter, Culver City (90232-6806)
PHONE..................310 836-7000
Michael Klepin, *CEO*
Stanley Otake, *Administration*
Melinda Hakim, *Ophthalmology*
Fred Hafezi, *Surg-Orthopdc*
Larry L Smith, *Hlthcr Dir*
EMP: 300 **EST:** 1961
SQ FT: 183,000
SALES (est): 61MM
SALES (corp-wide): 3.4B **Privately Held**
WEB: www.pmh.com
SIC: 8062 General medical & surgical hospitals
PA: Prospect Medical Holdings, Inc.
3415 S Sepulveda Blvd # 9
Los Angeles CA 90034
310 943-4500

(P-20691)
CALIFRNIA HOSP MED CTR FNDTION
1401 S Grand Ave, Los Angeles (90015-3010)
PHONE..................213 748-2411
Phillip C Hill, *Ch of Bd*
Nathan R Nusbaum, *President*
Margaret R Peterson, *President*
Harold Newton, *COO*
Clark Underwood, *CFO*
▲ **EMP:** 1500 **EST:** 1926
SQ FT: 800,000
SALES (est): 396.8MM **Privately Held**
WEB: www.supportcaliforniahospital.org
SIC: 8062 Hospital, medical school affiliated with nursing & residency

HQ: Dignity Health
185 Berry St Ste 200
San Francisco CA 94107
415 438-5500

(P-20692)
CALIFRNIA RHBLITATION INST LLC
2070 Century Park E, Los Angeles (90067-1907)
PHONE..................424 363-1003
Michael Tarvin, *Vice Pres*
EMP: 90 **EST:** 2014
SALES (est): 98.9MM
SALES (corp-wide): 5B **Publicly Held**
WEB: www.californiarehabinstitute.com
SIC: 8062 General medical & surgical hospitals
PA: Select Medical Holdings Corporation
4714 Gettysburg Rd
Mechanicsburg PA 17055
717 972-1100

(P-20693)
CASA COLINA HOSPITAL AND CENTE (HQ)
Also Called: Casa Clina Ctrs For Rhbltation
255 E Bonita Ave, Pomona (91767-1933)
P.O. Box 6001 (91769-6001)
PHONE..................909 596-7733
Felice Loverso, *CEO*
Bill Loverso, *COO*
Steve Norin, *Chairman*
Randy Blackman, *Treasurer*
Stephen Graeber, *Treasurer*
▲ **EMP:** 500 **EST:** 1936
SQ FT: 90,000
SALES (est): 53.4MM
SALES (corp-wide): 123MM **Privately Held**
WEB: www.casacolina.org
SIC: 8062 General medical & surgical hospitals
PA: Casa Colina, Inc.
255 E Bonita Ave
Pomona CA 91767
909 596-7733

(P-20694)
CEDARS-SINAI MEDICAL CENTER
Also Called: Nephrology
8635 W 3rd St Ste 1195, Los Angeles (90048-6146)
P.O. Box 48956 (90048-0956)
PHONE..................310 824-3664
Larry Froch, *Principal*
Neel Joshi, *Principal*
Silvia Guzman, *Executive Asst*
James Hawes, *Administration*
Stuart Noah, *Prgrmr*
EMP: 293
SALES (corp-wide): 4.1B **Privately Held**
WEB: www.cedars-sinai.org
SIC: 8062 General medical & surgical hospitals
PA: Cedars-Sinai Medical Center
8700 Beverly Blvd
West Hollywood CA 90048
310 423-3277

(P-20695)
CEDARS-SINAI MEDICAL CENTER
Also Called: Cedars Surgical Research Ctr
8700 Beverly Blvd 4018, West Hollywood (90048-1804)
PHONE..................310 855-7701
Linda Protcor, *Division Mgr*
Boulton Linda, *Vice Pres*
Glenn Bautista, *Pathologist*
EMP: 293
SALES (corp-wide): 4.1B **Privately Held**
WEB: www.cedars-sinai.org
SIC: 8062 8733 General medical & surgical hospitals; medical research
PA: Cedars-Sinai Medical Center
8700 Beverly Blvd
West Hollywood CA 90048
310 423-3277

(P-20696)
CEDARS-SINAI MEDICAL CENTER
8797 Beverly Blvd Ste 220, West Hollywood (90048-1892)
PHONE..................310 423-5468
Alan Weinberger, *Med Doctor*
EMP: 293
SALES (corp-wide): 4.1B **Privately Held**
WEB: www.cedars-sinai.org
SIC: 8062 General medical & surgical hospitals
PA: Cedars-Sinai Medical Center
8700 Beverly Blvd
West Hollywood CA 90048
310 423-3277

(P-20697)
CEDARS-SINAI MEDICAL CENTER
8727 W 3rd St, Los Angeles 90048-3843)
PHONE..................310 423-6451
Eric Fee, *General Mgr*
Olga Garcia, *Executive Asst*
Eric See, *Administration*
Karyn Solky, *Obstetrician*
EMP: 293
SALES (corp-wide): 4.1B **Privately Held**
WEB: www.cedars-sinai.org
SIC: 8062 General medical & surgical hospitals
PA: Cedars-Sinai Medical Center
8700 Beverly Blvd
West Hollywood CA 90048
310 423-3277

(P-20698)
CEDARS-SINAI MEDICAL CENTER
Also Called: Clinical Translational RES Ctr
8723 Alden Dr, Los Angeles (90048)
PHONE..................310 423-8965
Quyen Hurlburt, *Associate Dir*
Stephen Bettini, *Recruiter*
Roy Silver, *Obstetrician*
Randy Harris, *Med Doctor*
Maryam Ahmadian, *Nurse Practr*
EMP: 293
SALES (corp-wide): 4.1B **Privately Held**
WEB: www.cedars-sinai.org
SIC: 8062 General medical & surgical hospitals
PA: Cedars-Sinai Medical Center
8700 Beverly Blvd
West Hollywood CA 90048
310 423-3277

(P-20699)
CEDARS-SINAI MEDICAL CENTER
Anesthesiology Department
8700 Beverly Blvd # 8211, West Hollywood (90048-1804)
PHONE..................310 423-5841
Tom Pirscelac, *Administration*
EMP: 293
SALES (corp-wide): 4.1B **Privately Held**
WEB: www.cedars-sinai.org
SIC: 8062 3841 General medical & surgical hospitals; anesthesia apparatus
PA: Cedars-Sinai Medical Center
8700 Beverly Blvd
West Hollywood CA 90048
310 423-3277

(P-20700)
CEDARS-SINAI MEDICAL CENTER
8700 Beverly Blvd # 2213, West Hollywood (90048-1804)
PHONE..................310 423-5147
Thomas Priselac, *President*
Quyen Hurlburt, *Associate Dir*
Mark Pimentel, *Director*
EMP: 293
SALES (corp-wide): 4.1B **Privately Held**
WEB: www.cedars-sina.org
SIC: 8062 General medical & surgical hospitals
PA: Cedars-Sinai Medical Center
8700 Beverly Blvd
West Hollywood CA 90048
310 423-3277

(P-20701)
CEDARS-SINAI MEDICAL CENTER
310 N San Vicente Blvd, West Hollywood (90048-1810)
PHONE..................310 423-9310
Sylvia Salgado Estrada, *Principal*
Soussan Semerciyan, *Associate Dir*
Sharon Fawcett,
EMP: 293
SALES (corp-wide): 4.1B **Privately Held**
WEB: www.cedars-sinai.org
SIC: **8062** General medical & surgical hospitals
PA: Cedars-Sinai Medical Center
8700 Beverly Blvd
West Hollywood CA 90048
310 423-3277

(P-20702)
CEDARS-SINAI MEDICAL CENTER
99 N La Cienega Blvd Me, Beverly Hills (90211-2222)
PHONE..................310 967-1884
Lloyd Greig, *Branch Mgr*
Anthony Galante, *Vice Chairman*
Jon Rasak, *Internal Med*
Arash Moradzadeh, *Plastic Surgeon*
EMP: 293
SALES (corp-wide): 4.1B **Privately Held**
WEB: www.cedars-sinai.org
SIC: **8062** General medical & surgical hospitals
PA: Cedars-Sinai Medical Center
8700 Beverly Blvd
West Hollywood CA 90048
310 423-3277

(P-20703)
CEDARS-SINAI MEDICAL CENTER
200 N Robertson Blvd, Beverly Hills (90211-1769)
PHONE..................310 385-3326
Arnel Mendoza, *President*
James Caplan, *Vice Pres*
Cynthia Litt Deculus, *Vice Pres*
Rachel Joven, *Exec Dir*
Gregg Sannes, *Research*
EMP: 293
SALES (corp-wide): 4.1B **Privately Held**
WEB: www.cedars-sinai.org
SIC: **8062** General medical & surgical hospitals
PA: Cedars-Sinai Medical Center
8700 Beverly Blvd
West Hollywood CA 90048
310 423-3277

(P-20704)
CEDARS-SINAI MEDICAL CENTER
Also Called: Cedars-Sinai Home Care
8635 W 3rd Ste 1165w, Los Angeles (90048-6134)
PHONE..................310 423-3277
Sheldon King, *President*
Linda Burnes-Bolton, *Vice Pres*
Jeffrey Deeter, *Vice Pres*
Nicole Leonard, *Vice Pres*
Lorraine Kimura, *Associate Dir*
EMP: 293
SALES (corp-wide): 4.1B **Privately Held**
WEB: www.cedars-sinai.org
SIC: **8062** General medical & surgical hospitals
PA: Cedars-Sinai Medical Center
8700 Beverly Blvd
West Hollywood CA 90048
310 423-3277

(P-20705)
CEDARS-SINAI MEDICAL CENTER
Also Called: Medical Genetics
444 S San Vicente Blvd # 1001, Los Angeles (90048-4170)
PHONE..................310 423-9520
David Rimoin, *Manager*
Fabrizio Palanca, *Associate Dir*
Debbie Valdes, *Exec Dir*
Mary Kostikyan, *Research*
Mallory Burgess, *Technology*
EMP: 293

SALES (corp-wide): 4.1B **Privately Held**
WEB: www.cedars-sinai.org
SIC: **8062** 8099 General medical & surgical hospitals; health screening service
PA: Cedars-Sinai Medical Center
8700 Beverly Blvd
West Hollywood CA 90048
310 423-3277

(P-20706)
CEDARS-SINAI MEDICAL CENTER
4100 W 190th St, Torrance (90504-5513)
PHONE..................310 967-1900
Clyde Goldman, *Principal*
Linda B Bolton, *Vice Pres*
Andrew Ortiz, *Vice Pres*
Soledad Gonzalez-Olivar, *Supervisor*
EMP: 293
SALES (corp-wide): 4.1B **Privately Held**
WEB: www.cedars-sinai.org
SIC: **8062** 8011 General medical & surgical hospitals; medical centers
PA: Cedars-Sinai Medical Center
8700 Beverly Blvd
West Hollywood CA 90048
310 423-3277

(P-20707)
CEDARS-SINAI MEDICAL CENTER
Also Called: Health System Medical Network
250 N Robertson Blvd # 101, Beverly Hills (90211-1788)
PHONE..................310 385-3400
Tom Gordon, *CEO*
Jeffery Wilkins, *Vice Chairman*
Kc Miller, *Officer*
Mark Gavens, *Senior VP*
Mahmoud Samie, *Exec Dir*
EMP: 293
SALES (corp-wide): 4.1B **Privately Held**
WEB: www.cedars-sinai.org
SIC: **8062** 8011 General medical & surgical hospitals; offices & clinics of medical doctors
PA: Cedars-Sinai Medical Center
8700 Beverly Blvd
West Hollywood CA 90048
310 423-3277

(P-20708)
CEDARS-SINAI MEDICAL CENTER
Emergency Services
8700 Beverly Blvd # 1103, West Hollywood (90048-1804)
PHONE..................310 423-8780
Joel Giderman, *Director*
Robert Ravinsky, *Surgeon*
Wendy Lin, *Emerg Med Spec*
Paula Whiteman, *Emerg Med Spec*
EMP: 293
SALES (corp-wide): 4.1B **Privately Held**
WEB: www.cedars-sinai.org
SIC: **8062** General medical & surgical hospitals
PA: Cedars-Sinai Medical Center
8700 Beverly Blvd
West Hollywood CA 90048
310 423-3277

(P-20709)
CEDARS-SNAI IMGING MED GROUP A
8700 Beverly Blvd, West Hollywood (90048-1804)
P.O. Box 48750, Los Angeles (90048-0750)
PHONE..................310 423-8000
Barry D Pressman, *Ch of Bd*
EMP: 77 EST: 1992
SALES (est): 20.6MM **Privately Held**
WEB: www.cedars-sinai.org
SIC: **8062** General medical & surgical hospitals

(P-20710)
CFHS HOLDINGS INC
Also Called: Centinela Frman Rgonal Med Ctr
4650 Lincoln Blvd, Marina Del Rey (90292-6306)
PHONE..................310 823-8911
EMP: 264
SQ FT: 150,000

SALES (corp-wide): 4.1B **Privately Held**
WEB: www.marinahospital.com
SIC: **8062** General medical & surgical hospitals
HQ: Cfhs Holdings, Inc.
4650 Lincoln Blvd
Marina Del Rey CA 90292

(P-20711)
CFHS HOLDINGS INC
Also Called: Centinela Frman Rgonal Med Ctr
4640 Admiralty Way # 650, Marina Del Rey (90292-6667)
PHONE..................310 448-7800
Bob Bokern, *Principal*
EMP: 264
SALES (corp-wide): 4.1B **Privately Held**
WEB: www.marinahospital.com
SIC: **8062** General medical & surgical hospitals
HQ: Cfhs Holdings, Inc.
4650 Lincoln Blvd
Marina Del Rey CA 90292

(P-20712)
CFHS HOLDINGS INC (HQ)
Also Called: MARINA DEL REY HOSPITAL
4650 Lincoln Blvd, Marina Del Rey (90292-6306)
PHONE..................310 823-8911
Stacy Sean Fowler, *CEO*
Walter Watson,
Michael A Rembis, *President*
Kathy Hammack, *CFO*
Vanessa Colaco, *Business Dir*
EMP: 1982 EST: 2004
SALES: 139.9MM
SALES (corp-wide): 4.1B **Privately Held**
WEB: www.marinahospital.com
SIC: **8062** 8093 8011 General medical & surgical hospitals; weight loss clinic, with medical staff; orthopedic physician; sports medicine specialist, physician; surgeon
PA: Cedars-Sinai Medical Center
8700 Beverly Blvd
West Hollywood CA 90048
310 423-3277

(P-20713)
CFHS HOLDINGS INC
Also Called: Centinela Frman Rgonal Med Ctr
555 E Hardy St, Inglewood (90301-4011)
PHONE..................310 673-4660
Michael Rembis, *Branch Mgr*
EMP: 264
SALES (corp-wide): 4.1B **Privately Held**
WEB: www.marinahospital.com
SIC: **8062** General medical & surgical hospitals
HQ: Cfhs Holdings, Inc.
4650 Lincoln Blvd
Marina Del Rey CA 90292

(P-20714)
CHA HOLLYWOOD MEDICAL CTR LP (HQ)
Also Called: Hollywood Presbyterian Med Ctr
1300 N Vermont Ave, Los Angeles (90027-6098)
PHONE..................213 413-3000
Jeff A Nelson, *CEO*
Romeo Velasco,
Galen Gorman, *CFO*
Irene Ruiz, *Vice Pres*
Ronora Sayaman, *Controller*
▲ EMP: 1474 EST: 1924
SQ FT: 900,000
SALES (est): 288.9MM **Privately Held**
WEB: www.hollywoodpresbyterian.com
SIC: **8062** 8351 Hospital, affiliated with AMA residency; child day care services

(P-20715)
CHAPMAN GLOBAL MEDICAL CENTER
Also Called: CHAPMAN FAMILY HEALTH
2601 E Chapman Ave, Orange (92869-3206)
PHONE..................714 633-0011
Matt Whaley, *CEO*
Robert Heinemeier, *CFO*
Charlotte Woods, *CIO*
EMP: 425 EST: 1968

SQ FT: 96,000
SALES (est): 98.3K
SALES (corp-wide): 1.9B **Privately Held**
WEB: www.chapmanmedicalcenter.com
SIC: **8062** General medical & surgical hospitals
PA: Kpc Healthcare, Inc.
1301 N Tustin Ave
Santa Ana CA 92705
714 953-3652

(P-20716)
CHHP HOLDINGS II LLC (HQ)
Also Called: Community Hosp Huntington Pk
2623 E Slauson Ave, Huntington Park (90255-2926)
PHONE..................323 583-1931
Hector Hernandez, *CEO*
Patrick Githens, *Radiology Dir*
Olga Ortiz, *Security Dir*
Julio Morales, *Safety Dir*
James De La Torre, *Med Doctor*
EMP: 275 EST: 2011
SQ FT: 6,000
SALES (est): 68.8MM
SALES (corp-wide): 375.9MM **Privately Held**
WEB: www.pipelinehealth.us
SIC: **8062** General medical & surgical hospitals
PA: Avanti Hospitals, Llc
898 N Pcf Cast Hwy Ste 70
El Segundo CA 90245
310 356-0550

(P-20717)
CHHP MANAGEMENT LLC
Also Called: Community Hosp Huntington Pk
2623 E Slauson Ave, Huntington Park (90255-2926)
PHONE..................323 583-1931
Joel Freedman, *Principal*
Mark Bell, *Principal*
Jamie Macpherson, *Principal*
EMP: 99 EST: 2010
SALES: 49.7MM
SALES (corp-wide): 375.9MM **Privately Held**
SIC: **8062** General medical & surgical hospitals
HQ: Chhp Holdings Ii, Llc
2623 E Slauson Ave
Huntington Park CA 90255
323 583-1931

(P-20718)
CHILDRENS HOSP LOS ANGLES MED (PA)
Also Called: CHILDRENS HOSPITAL LOS ANGELES
6430 W Sunset Blvd # 600, Los Angeles (90028-7901)
PHONE..................323 361-2336
Robert Adler, *President*
EMP: 60 EST: 1977
SQ FT: 10,000
SALES (est): 214.2MM **Privately Held**
WEB: www.chla.org
SIC: **8062** General medical & surgical hospitals

(P-20719)
CHILDRENS HOSPITAL LOS ANGELES
Also Called: Saban Research Institute, The
4661 W Sunset Blvd, Los Angeles (90027-6042)
PHONE..................323 361-2751
Cheryl Saban, *Branch Mgr*
EMP: 450
SALES (corp-wide): 1.3B **Privately Held**
WEB: www.chla.org
SIC: **8062** General medical & surgical hospitals
PA: The Childrens Hospital Los Angeles
4650 W Sunset Blvd
Los Angeles CA 90027
323 660-2450

(P-20720)
CHILDRENS HOSPITAL ORANGE CNTY (PA)
Also Called: CHOC
1201 W La Veta Ave, Orange (92868-4203)
PHONE..................714 997-3000
Kimberly Cripe, *President*

PRODUCTS & SVCS

Eric Ontiveros,
L Kenneth Heuler DDS, *Ch of Bd*
Sally Gallagher, *President*
Bill Feaster, *Officer*
EMP: 2573 **EST:** 1950
SQ FT: 328,200
SALES: 992MM **Privately Held**
WEB: www.choc.org
SIC: 8062 General medical & surgical hospitals

(P-20721)
CHILDRENS HOSPITAL ORANGE CNTY
Also Called: Choc Mission
455 S Main St, Orange (92868-3835)
PHONE..................949 365-2416
Kerri Ruppert Schiller, *Principal*
Susan Burrows, *Vice Pres*
Barbara Sanchez, *Vice Pres*
Jordan Schunk, *Associate Dir*
Angela Bermudez, *Nursing Mgr*
EMP: 163
SALES (corp-wide): 992MM **Privately Held**
WEB: www.choc.org
SIC: 8062 General medical & surgical hospitals
PA: Children's Hospital Of Orange County
1201 W La Veta Ave
Orange CA 92868
714 997-3000

(P-20722)
CHILDRENS HOSPITAL ORANGE CNTY
980 Roosevelt, Irvine (92620-3672)
PHONE..................949 387-2586
EMP: 163
SALES (corp-wide): 992MM **Privately Held**
WEB: www.choc.org
SIC: 8062 8099 8082 6321 General medical & surgical hospitals; childbirth preparation clinic; home health care services; accident & health insurance
PA: Children's Hospital Of Orange County
1201 W La Veta Ave
Orange CA 92868
714 997-3000

(P-20723)
CITRUS VLY HLTH PARTNERS INC
Also Called: Queen of The Valley Campus
1115 S Sunset Ave, West Covina
(91790-3940)
PHONE..................626 962-4011
Debbie Segaram, *Branch Mgr*
Abel Mesa, *Executive Asst*
Michael Walker, *Network Mgr*
Cassandra Valizan, *Technician*
John Graffius, *Engineer*
EMP: 954 **Privately Held**
WEB: www.emanatehealth.org
SIC: 8062 General medical & surgical hospitals
PA: Emanate Health Medical Group
210 W San Bernardino Rd
Covina CA 91723

(P-20724)
CITY HOPE NATIONAL MEDICAL CTR
1500 Duarte Rd, Duarte (91010-3012)
PHONE..................626 256-4673
Michael A Friedman, *CEO*
Michael Sullivan,
Robert Stone, *CEO*
Kristin Bertell, *Officer*
Mark Hulse, *Officer*
EMP: 1900 **EST:** 1948
SALES: 1.3B
SALES (corp-wide): 592.4MM **Privately Held**
WEB: www.cityofhope.org
SIC: 8062 General medical & surgical hospitals
PA: City Of Hope
1500 Duarte Rd
Duarte CA 91010
626 256-4673

(P-20725)
COAST PLZ DCTORS HOSP A CAL LT (HQ)
13100 Studebaker Rd, Norwalk
(90650-2531)
PHONE..................562 868-3751
John Ferrelli, *CEO*
Craig B Garner, *CEO*
Mihi Lee, *CFO*
Joel Freedman, *Principal*
EMP: 308 **EST:** 1968
SQ FT: 58,000
SALES (est): 35.4MM
SALES (corp-wide): 375.9MM **Privately Held**
WEB: www.pipelinehealth.us
SIC: 8062 Hospital, medical school affiliation
PA: Avanti Hospitals, Llc
898 N Pcf Cast Hwy Ste 70
El Segundo CA 90245
310 356-0550

(P-20726)
COMMUNITY HLTH ALANCE PASADENA (PA)
Also Called: CHAP
1855 N Fair Oaks Ave, Pasadena
(91103-1620)
P.O. Box 94873 (91109-4873)
PHONE..................626 398-6300
Margaret Martinez, *CEO*
Sergio Bautista, *COO*
Michael P Hernandez, *Treasurer*
Marcy Chavez, *Office Mgr*
Mauricette Montredon, *Admin Sec*
EMP: 65 **EST:** 1995
SALES: 21.8MM **Privately Held**
WEB: www.chapcare.org
SIC: 8062 General medical & surgical hospitals

(P-20727)
COMMUNITY HOSP SAN BERNARDINO (DH)
1805 Medical Center Dr, San Bernardino
(92411-1217)
PHONE..................909 887-6333
June Collisone, *President*
Gonzalo Cazas,
Ed Sorenson, *CFO*
Dave Evans, *General Mgr*
Faviola Garcia, *Admin Sec*
EMP: 350 **EST:** 1938
SALES (est): 246.7MM **Privately Held**
WEB: www.dignityhealth.org
SIC: 8062 Hospital, affiliated with AMA residency
HQ: Dignity Health
185 Berry St Ste 200
San Francisco CA 94107
415 438-5500

(P-20728)
COMMUNITY HOSPITAL LONG BEACH
1760 Termino Ave Ste 105, Long Beach
(90804-2157)
PHONE..................562 494-0600
John Bishop, *CEO*
Krikor Jansian, *President*
Kevin Peterson, *CEO*
Matthew Faulkner, *Exec Dir*
Linda Tatum, *Planning*
EMP: 570 **EST:** 2000
SALES: 5.4K **Privately Held**
WEB: www.chlbfoundation.org
SIC: 8062 Hospital, affiliated with AMA residency
PA: Memorial Health Services
17360 Brookhurst St # 160
Fountain Valley CA 92708

(P-20729)
COMMUNITY MEM HOSP SAN BNVNTUR
Also Called: Purchasing Department
147 N Brent St, Ventura (93003-2809)
PHONE..................805 652-5072
Chuck Gray, *Manager*
▲ **EMP:** 55 **EST:** 1927

SALES (est): 29.8MM **Privately Held**
WEB: www.cmhshealth.org
SIC: 8062 General medical & surgical hospitals

(P-20730)
COMMUNITY MEMORIAL HEALTH SYS (PA)
Also Called: Community Memorial Hospital
147 N Brent St, Ventura (93003-2809)
PHONE..................805 652-5011
Gary Wilde, *President*
Diane Cornell,
Theodore Tuschka,
Mary Jane Greene, *Records Dir*
Steve Caryer, *President*
▲ **EMP:** 1881 **EST:** 1933
SQ FT: 174,000
SALES: 432.7MM **Privately Held**
WEB: www.cmhshealth.org
SIC: 8062 General medical & surgical hospitals

(P-20731)
COMMUNITY MEMORIAL HEALTH SYS
Also Called: Ojai Valley Community Hospital
1306 Maricopa Hwy, Ojai (93023-3131)
PHONE..................805 646-1401
Gary Wilde, *President*
Christopher McKinney, *Internal Med*
Timothy Williamson, *Pediatrics*
Camille Yannantuono, *Nurse*
Sheila Dedrick,
EMP: 120
SALES (corp-wide): 432.7MM **Privately Held**
WEB: www.cmhshealth.org
SIC: 8062 General medical & surgical hospitals
PA: Community Memorial Health System
147 N Brent St
Ventura CA 93003
805 652-5011

(P-20732)
COTTAGE HEALTH
1035 Peach St Ste 203, San Luis Obispo
(93401-2700)
PHONE..................805 541-9113
EMP: 63
SALES (corp-wide): 152.8MM **Privately Held**
WEB: www.cottagehealth.org
SIC: 8062 General medical & surgical hospitals
PA: Cottage Health
400 W Pueblo St
Santa Barbara CA 93105
805 682-7111

(P-20733)
COTTAGE HEALTH
2050 Viborg Rd, Solvang (93463-2220)
PHONE..................805 688-6432
Wende Cappetta, *Vice Pres*
Judy Blokdyk, *Purchasing*
John McCaffery, *Med Doctor*
Kristin Tufvesson, *Director*
Jo Dambrosio, *Manager*
EMP: 63
SALES (corp-wide): 152.8MM **Privately Held**
WEB: www.cottagehealth.org
SIC: 8062 General medical & surgical hospitals
PA: Cottage Health
400 W Pueblo St
Santa Barbara CA 93105
805 682-7111

(P-20734)
COTTAGE HEALTH SYSTEM
351 S Patterson Ave, Goleta (93111-2403)
PHONE..................805 967-3411
Pamela Washburn, *Director*
EMP: 63
SALES (corp-wide): 152.8MM **Privately Held**
WEB: www.cottagehealth.org
SIC: 8062 General medical & surgical hospitals
PA: Cottage Health
400 W Pueblo St
Santa Barbara CA 93105
805 682-7111

(P-20735)
COTTAGE REHABILITATION HOSP
2415 De La Vina St, Santa Barbara
(93105-3819)
PHONE..................805 569-8999
Ron Werft, *CEO*
Arie Dejong, *Vice Pres*
EMP: 50 **EST:** 2010
SALES (est): 1.3MM
SALES (corp-wide): 152.8MM **Privately Held**
WEB: www.sbch.org
SIC: 8062 General medical & surgical hospitals
PA: Cottage Health
400 W Pueblo St
Santa Barbara CA 93105
805 682-7111

(P-20736)
COUNTY OF KERN
Public Health Dept
1700 Mount Vernon Ave, Bakersfield
(93306-4018)
P.O. Box 3519 (93385-3519)
PHONE..................661 326-2054
Peter Bryan, *CEO*
Misty Dominguez, *Planning*
John Aguilar, *Info Tech Dir*
Melanie Brassfield, *Recruiter*
Miguel Sandoval, *Purch Dir*
EMP: 800 **Privately Held**
WEB: www.kerncounty.com
SIC: 8062 9431 General medical & surgical hospitals; administration of public health programs;
PA: County Of Kern
1115 Truxtun Ave Rm 505
Bakersfield CA 93301
661 868-3690

(P-20737)
COUNTY OF LOS ANGELES
Also Called: Health Services Dept
1000 W Carson St Fl 8 Flr E, Palos Verdes Peninsu (90274)
PHONE..................310 222-2401
Miguel Ortiz Marroquin, *CEO*
Susan Black, *Director*
EMP: 127
SALES (corp-wide): 25.2E **Privately Held**
WEB: www.lacounty.gov
SIC: 8062 9431 General medical & surgical hospitals; administration of public health programs;
PA: County Of Los Angeles
500 W Temple St Ste 437
Los Angeles CA 90012
213 974-1101

(P-20738)
COUNTY OF LOS ANGELES
Also Called: Health Services, Dept of
12025 Wilmington Ave, Los Angeles
(90059-3019)
PHONE..................310 668-4545
Willie T May, *Exec Dir*
EMP: 127
SALES (corp-wide): 25.2B **Privately Held**
WEB: www.lacounty.gov
SIC: 8062 9431 General medical & surgical hospitals; administration of public health programs;
PA: County Of Los Angeles
500 W Temple St Ste 437
Los Angeles CA 90012
213 974-1101

(P-20739)
COUNTY OF LOS ANGELES
Also Called: Health Services Dept
1100 N Mission Rd Rm 236, Los Angeles
(90033-1017)
PHONE..................323 226-6021
Scott Drewgan, *Director*
EMP: 127
SALES (corp-wide): 25.2B **Privately Held**
WEB: www.lacounty.gov
SIC: 8062 9431 General medical & surgical hospitals; administration of public health programs
PA: County Of Los Angeles
500 W Temple St Ste 437
Los Angeles CA 90012
213 974-1101

(P-20740)
COUNTY OF LOS ANGELES
Also Called: Los Angeles Cnty Cntl Jail Hosp
450 Bauchet St, Los Angeles (90012-2907)
PHONE....................213 473-6100
Don Knable, *Ch of Bd*
Tom Crabson, *Officer*
Cabrera Tony, *Officer*
Kathleen Allen, *Executive Asst*
Gabriela Martinez, *Admin Asst*
EMP: 127
SALES (corp-wide): 25.2B **Privately Held**
WEB: www.lacounty.gov
SIC: 8062 9431 General medical & surgical hospitals;
PA: County Of Los Angeles
500 W Temple St Ste 437
Los Angeles CA 90012
213 974-1101

(P-20741)
COUNTY OF SAN LUIS OBISPO
Also Called: County General Hospital
2180 Johnson Ave, San Luis Obispo (93401-4558)
PHONE....................805 781-4753
Nancy Rosen, *Manager*
Jeff Hamm, *Director*
EMP: 107
SQ FT: 4,500 **Privately Held**
WEB: www.slocounty.ca.gov
SIC: 8062 8721 General medical & surgical hospitals; accounting, auditing & bookkeeping
PA: County Of San Luis Obispo
Government Center Rm 300
San Luis Obispo CA 93408
805 781-5040

(P-20742)
CPH HOSPITAL MANAGEMENT LLC
Also Called: Coast Plaza Hospital
13100 Studebaker Rd, Norwalk (90650-2531)
PHONE....................562 838-3751
James Paul Macpherson,
Thomas Trice, *Records Dir*
Patrick Rafferty, *Officer*
Enrique Trujillo, *Officer*
Mila Uyan, *Lab Dir*
EMP: 1166 **EST:** 2011
SALES (est): 44.3MM
SALES (corp-wide): 375.9MM **Privately Held**
WEB: www.cph.avantihospitals.com
SIC: 8062 General medical & surgical hospitals
PA: Avanti Hospitals, Llc
898 N Pcf Cast Hwy Ste 70
El Segundo CA 90245
310 356-0550

(P-20743)
DEANCO HEALTHCARE LLC
Also Called: Mission Community Hospital
14850 Roscoe Blvd, Panorama City (91402-4618)
PHONE....................818 787-2222
James Theiring,
Denise Sandoval, *Records Dir*
Craig Garner, *Officer*
Dianne Wagner, *Officer*
Joe Magpantay, *Lab Dir*
EMP: 700 **EST:** 2010
SALES (est): 176MM **Privately Held**
WEB: www.mchonline.org
SIC: 8062 General medical & surgical hospitals

(P-20744)
DEPARTMENT OF ARMY
Also Called: Weed Army Community Hospital
390 N Loop Rd, Fort Irwin (92310)
P.O. Box 105067 (92310-5067)
PHONE....................760 380-3114
EMP: 54 **EST:** 2012
SALES (est): 24.6MM **Privately Held**
WEB: www.irwin.amedd.army.mil
SIC: 8062 General medical & surgical hospitals

(P-20745)
DESERT REGIONAL MED CTR INC
Also Called: Tenet
47647 Caleo Bay Dr # 260, La Quinta (92253-8854)
PHONE....................760 771-6158
EMP: 52
SALES (corp-wide): 17.6B **Publicly Held**
WEB: www.desertcarenetwork.com
SIC: 8062 General medical & surgical hospitals
HQ: Desert Regional Medical Center, Inc.
1150 N Indian Canyon Dr
Palm Springs CA 92262
760 323-6511

(P-20746)
DESERT REGIONAL MED CTR INC (HQ)
Also Called: Tenet
1150 N Indian Canyon Dr, Palm Springs (92262-4872)
P.O. Box 2739 (92263-2739)
PHONE....................760 323-6511
Toll Free:....................888 -
Michele Finney, *President*
Robert Rosser, *Ch Pathology*
Frank Ercoli, *Chairman*
Raymond Foster, *Radiology Dir*
Ralph M Steiger, *Principal*
EMP: 1200 **EST:** 1948
SQ FT: 400,000
SALES (est): 200.1MM
SALES (corp-wide): 17.6B **Publicly Held**
WEB: www.desertcarenetwork.com
SIC: 8062 General medical & surgical hospitals
PA: Tenet Healthcare Corporation
14201 Dallas Pkwy
Dallas TX 75254
469 893-2200

(P-20747)
DESERT REGIONAL MED CTR INC
Also Called: Tenet
1180 N Indian Canyon Dr, Palm Springs (92262-4800)
PHONE....................760 416-4613
Leonard Spitsner, *Pharmacist*
Louis A Stabile, *Surgeon*
EMP: 52
SALES (corp-wide): 17.6B **Publicly Held**
WEB: www.desertcarenetwork.com
SIC: 8062 General medical & surgical hospitals
HQ: Desert Regional Medical Center, Inc.
1150 N Indian Canyon Dr
Palm Springs CA 92262
760 323-6511

(P-20748)
DESERT VALLEY HOSPITAL INC (DH)
16850 Bear Valley Rd, Victorville (92395-5794)
PHONE....................760 241-8000
Margaret R Peterson, *CEO*
Roger Krissman, *CFO*
Michael Sarrao, *Vice Pres*
▲ **EMP:** 225 **EST:** 1985
SQ FT: 63,000
SALES: 140.5MM
SALES (corp-wide): 1B **Privately Held**
WEB: www.dvmc.com
SIC: 8062 General medical & surgical hospitals

(P-20749)
DIGNITY HEALTH
Also Called: Marian Regional Medical Center
1400 E Church St, Santa Maria (93454-5906)
PHONE....................805 739-3000
Charles Cova, *President*
John Mulder, *Business Dir*
Patricia Haase, *Info Tech Dir*
Tayari Anderson, *Technology*
Brian Crisp, *Obstetrician*
EMP: 400 **Privately Held**
WEB: www.dignityhealth.org
SIC: 8062 8011 General medical & surgical hospitals; offices & clinics of medical doctors

HQ: Dignity Health
185 Berry St Ste 200
San Francisco CA 94107
415 438-5500

(P-20750)
DIGNITY HEALTH
Also Called: Saint John's Hospital X Ray
200 Oceangate, Long Beach (90802-4302)
PHONE....................805 988-2868
Steve Higgs, *Manager*
EMP: 474 **Privately Held**
WEB: www.dignityhealth.org
SIC: 8062 General medical & surgical hospitals
HQ: Dignity Health
185 Berry St Ste 200
San Francisco CA 94107
415 438-5500

(P-20751)
DIGNITY HEALTH
Northridge Family Practice Med
18460 Roscoe Blvd, Northridge (91325-4107)
PHONE....................818 993-4054
Pamela Davis, *Systems Mgr*
Darlene Underwood, *Executive*
Wendy Hagen, *Family Practiti*
Jeffrey Wang, *Family Practiti*
Roxanne Rahimi, *Oncology*
EMP: 50 **Privately Held**
WEB: www.dignityhealth.org
SIC: 8062 8011 General medical & surgical hospitals; physicians' office, including specialists
HQ: Dignity Health
185 Berry St Ste 200
San Francisco CA 94107
415 438-5500

(P-20752)
DIGNITY HEALTH
Also Called: Northridge Hospital Med Ctr
18300 Roscoe Blvd, Northridge (91325-4105)
PHONE....................818 885-8500
Paul Watkins, *President*
Cheryl Lovett, *Records Dir*
EMP: 1750 **Privately Held**
WEB: www.dignityhealth.org
SIC: 8062 General medical & surgical hospitals
HQ: Dignity Health
185 Berry St Ste 200
San Francisco CA 94107
415 438-5500

(P-20753)
DIGNITY HEALTH
Also Called: St. Johns Pleasant Valley Hosp
2309 Antonio Ave, Camarillo (93010-1414)
PHONE....................805 389-5800
Daniel Herlinger, *Branch Mgr*
Mark Sharma,
M Eugene Fussell, *Vice Pres*
Israel Medina, *Purch Dir*
Erin Stevens, *Education*
EMP: 250 **Privately Held**
WEB: www.dignityhealth.org
SIC: 8062 General medical & surgical hospitals
HQ: Dignity Health
185 Berry St Ste 200
San Francisco CA 94107
415 438-5500

(P-20754)
DIGNITY HEALTH
Also Called: St Johns Regional Medical Ctr
1600 N Rose Ave, Oxnard (93030-3722)
PHONE....................805 988-2500
George West, *Vice Pres*
Chris Champlin, *Vice Pres*
Catherine Barbiera, *Managing Dir*
Richard Park, *Internal Med*
Juula Roman, *Internal Med*
EMP: 1900 **Privately Held**
WEB: www.dignityhealth.org
SIC: 8062 General medical & surgical hospitals
HQ: Dignity Health
185 Berry St Ste 200
San Francisco CA 94107
415 438-5500

(P-20755)
DIGNITY HEALTH MED FOUNDATION
2901 N Ventura Rd Ste 100, Oxnard (93036-1126)
PHONE....................805 981-6101
EMP: 74 **Privately Held**
WEB: www.dignityhealth.org
SIC: 8062 General medical & surgical hospitals
HQ: Dignity Health Medical Foundation
3400 Data Dr
Rancho Cordova CA 95670

(P-20756)
DJ JOHN PARK MD INC (PA)
180 Nwport Ctr Dr Ste 170, Newport Beach (92660)
PHONE....................714 326-7715
EMP: 52 **EST:** 2013
SALES (est): 954.2K **Privately Held**
WEB: www.johnparkmd.com
SIC: 8062 General medical & surgical hospitals

(P-20757)
DOCTORS HOSPITAL RIVERSIDE LLC (PA)
3865 Jackson St, Riverside (92503-3919)
PHONE....................951 354-7404
Jonathan Wu, *CEO*
EMP: 50 **EST:** 2018
SALES (est): 162.7MM **Privately Held**
WEB: www.pchmc.org
SIC: 8062 General medical & surgical hospitals

(P-20758)
DOCTORS HOSPITAL W COVINA INC
Also Called: WEST COVINA PHYSICAL THERAPY
725 S Orange Ave, West Covina (91790-2614)
PHONE....................626 338-8481
Pareed Mohamed, *CEO*
Cami Horvat, *CFO*
Jong Kim MD, *Treasurer*
Akbar Omar MD, *Vice Pres*
Gerald Wallman, *Executive*
EMP: 155 **EST:** 1958
SQ FT: 50,000
SALES (est): 16MM **Privately Held**
SIC: 8062 8049 General medical & surgical hospitals; physical therapist

(P-20759)
EAST VALLEY GLENDORA HOSP LLC
Also Called: Glendora Oaks Bhvral Hlth Hosp
150 W Route 66, Glendora (91740-6207)
PHONE....................626 852-5000
Joseph Chang,
Kim Bui, *Executive*
Ben Ortega, *Recruiter*
Nagasamudra Ashok, *Med Doctor*
Robert Gordon,
EMP: 448 **EST:** 1957
SQ FT: 60,592
SALES (est): 29.3MM **Privately Held**
WEB: www.glendorahospital.com
SIC: 8062 General medical & surgical hospitals
PA: College Health Enterprises, Llc
11627 Telg Rd Ste 200
Santa Fe Springs CA 90670

(P-20760)
EISENHOWER MEDICAL CENTER (PA)
Also Called: EISENHOWER HEALTH
39000 Bob Hope Dr, Rancho Mirage (92270-3221)
PHONE....................760 340-3911
G Aubrey Serfling, *CEO*
Barbara Comess, *Ch Pathology*
Kimberly Osborne, *CFO*
David Friscia, *Treasurer*
Barry Hackshaw, *Trustee*
▲ **EMP:** 2000 **EST:** 1971
SQ FT: 240,000

PRODUCTS & SVCS

SALES: 3.8MM **Privately Held**
WEB: www.eisenhowerhealth.org
SIC: **8062** 8082 General medical & surgical hospitals; home health care services

(P-20761)
EL CENTRO RGNAL MED CTR FNDTIO (PA)
Also Called: E C R M C
1415 Ross Ave, El Centro (92243-4306)
PHONE.................................760 339-7100
Robert R Frantz, *President*
Erica Whannel, *Records Dir*
Barbara Blevins, *President*
Kathy Farmer, *CFO*
Louis Castro, *Officer*
EMP: 603 EST: 2005
SQ FT: 187,044
SALES: 212.3K **Privately Held**
WEB: www.ecrmc.org
SIC: **8062** General medical & surgical hospitals

(P-20762)
ELADH LP
Also Called: East Los Angeles Doctors Hosp
4060 Whittier Blvd, Los Angeles (90023-2526)
PHONE.................................323 268-5514
Gerald Clute, *CEO*
Hector Hernandez, *Managing Prtnr*
Janine King, *Bd of Directors*
Lillian Ramos, *Social Dir*
Konivi Attipoe, *Engineer*
EMP: 99 EST: 1999
SALES (est): 72.1MM
SALES (corp-wide): 375.9MM **Privately Held**
WEB: www.eladoctorshospital.com
SIC: **8062** General medical & surgical hospitals
PA: Avanti Hospitals, Llc
898 N Pcf Cast Hwy Ste 70
El Segundo CA 90245
310 356-0550

(P-20763)
EMANATE HEALTH
Also Called: Citrus Vly Hlth Care Partners
427 W Carroll Ave, Glendora (91741-4214)
PHONE.................................626 857-3477
Sue Benson, *Director*
EMP: 508
SALES (corp-wide): 464.3MM **Privately Held**
WEB: www.emanatehealth.org
SIC: **8062** General medical & surgical hospitals
PA: Emanate Health Medical Center
1115 S Sunset Ave
West Covina CA 91790
626 962-4011

(P-20764)
EMANATE HEALTH MEDICAL CENTER (PA)
1115 S Sunset Ave, West Covina (91790-3940)
P.O. Box 6108, Covina (91722-5108)
PHONE.................................626 962-4011
Robert Curry, *President*
Elvia Foulke, *COO*
Roger Sharma, *CFO*
Debbie Cooper, *VP Finance*
Annette Macias, *Mktg Dir*
EMP: 1229 EST: 1959
SQ FT: 285,000
SALES: 464.3MM **Privately Held**
WEB: www.emanatehealth.org
SIC: **8062** General medical & surgical hospitals

(P-20765)
EMANATE HEALTH MEDICAL CENTER
Also Called: Human Resources Department
140 W College St, Covina (91723-2007)
PHONE.................................626 858-8515
Robert H Curry, *Administration*
EMP: 508
SALES (corp-wide): 464.3MM **Privately Held**
WEB: www.emanatehealth.org
SIC: **8062** General medical & surgical hospitals

PA: Emanate Health Medical Center
1115 S Sunset Ave
West Covina CA 91790
626 962-4011

(P-20766)
EMANATE HEALTH MEDICAL CENTER
Also Called: Queen of The Valley Hospital
1115 S Sunset Ave, West Covina (91790-3940)
PHONE.................................626 963-8411
Robert Curry, *President*
Stephanie Oliver, *Purchasing*
EMP: 508
SALES (corp-wide): 464.3MM **Privately Held**
WEB: www.emanatehealth.org
SIC: **8062** General medical & surgical hospitals
PA: Emanate Health Medical Center
1115 S Sunset Ave
West Covina CA 91790
626 962-4011

(P-20767)
EMANATE HEALTH MEDICAL CENTER
Also Called: Inter Community Hospital
210 W San Bernardino Rd, Covina (91723-1515)
PHONE.................................626 331-7331
Toll Free:.................................877 -
Jim Yoshioka, *President*
Armando Munoz, *Engineer*
Maria Palacios, *Analyst*
Kathy Trujillo, *Opers Staff*
Sherry Schwan, *Marketing Staff*
EMP: 508
SALES (corp-wide): 464.3MM **Privately Held**
WEB: www.emanatehealth.org
SIC: **8062** General medical & surgical hospitals
PA: Emanate Health Medical Center
1115 S Sunset Ave
West Covina CA 91790
626 962-4011

(P-20768)
EMANATE HEALTH MEDICAL GROUP (PA)
Also Called: Emanate Hlth Intr-Cmmnity Hosp
210 W San Bernardino Rd, Covina (91723-1515)
P.O. Box 6108 (91722-5108)
PHONE.................................626 331-7331
Robert Curry, *CEO*
Uri Zisblatt, *Ch Radiology*
James Yoshioka, *President*
Alvia Polk, *COO*
Lois Conyers, *CFO*
EMP: 1200 EST: 1983
SQ FT: 237,000
SALES (est): 75.4MM **Privately Held**
WEB: www.emanatehealth.org
SIC: **8062** General medical & surgical hospitals

(P-20769)
ENCINO TRZANA REGIONAL MED CTR
16237 Ventura Blvd, Encino (91436-2201)
PHONE.................................818 995-5000
EMP: 450
SALES: 41.7MM **Privately Held**
SIC: **8062** General Hospital

(P-20770)
FLEXOGENIX GROUP INC (PA)
1000 S Hope St Ste 101, Los Angeles (90015-4057)
PHONE.................................213 622-6010
Sean Whalen, *CEO*
Paul Mogannam, *President*
Lj Dalmata, *Office Mgr*
Prutha Patel, *Med Doctor*
Dinoshka Acevedo, *Manager*
EMP: 86 EST: 2015
SQ FT: 5,322
SALES (est): 20.5MM **Privately Held**
SIC: **8062** General medical & surgical hospitals

(P-20771)
FOOTHILL HSPTL-MRRIS L JHNSTON (PA)
Also Called: FOOTHILL PRESBYTERIAN HOSPITAL
250 S Grand Ave, Glendora (91741-4218)
PHONE.................................626 857-3145
Robert Curry, *President*
Melissa Howard, *Administration*
Diana Zenner, *Administration*
Ed Tronez,
EMP: 97 EST: 1973
SQ FT: 104,371
SALES: 109.4MM **Privately Held**
SIC: **8062** Hospital, affiliated with AMA residency

(P-20772)
FOUNTAIN VLY RGNAL HOSP MED CT
17100 Euclid St, Fountain Valley (92708-4004)
P.O. Box 8010 (92728-8010)
PHONE.................................714 966-7200
Clay Farell, *CEO*
Edward F Littlejohn, *COO*
Ken Jordan, *CFO*
CJ Lee, *Officer*
Cari Welsh, *Controller*
EMP: 1200 EST: 1969
SALES (est): 239.5MM
SALES (corp-wide): 17.6B **Publicly Held**
WEB: www.fountainvalleyhospital.com
SIC: **8062** Hospital, affiliated with AMA residency
HQ: Tenet Healthsystem Medical, Inc.
14201 Dallas Pkwy
Dallas TX 75254
469 893-2000

(P-20773)
FRENCH HOSPITAL MEDICAL CENTER (DH)
1911 Johnson Ave, San Luis Obispo (93401-4197)
PHONE.................................805 543-5353
Jim Copeland, *Chairman*
Allan Iftiniuk, *President*
Sue Anderson, *CFO*
Julia Fogelson, *Ch Nursing Ofcr*
Patricia Herrera, *Benefits Mgr*
EMP: 480 EST: 1946
SQ FT: 80,000
SALES (est): 86.2MM **Privately Held**
WEB: www.dignityhealth.org
SIC: **8062** Hospital, affiliated with AMA residency
HQ: Dignity Health
185 Berry St Ste 200
San Francisco CA 94107
415 438-5500

(P-20774)
GARDENA HOSPITAL LP
Also Called: Memorial Hospital of Gardena
1145 W Redondo Beach Blvd, Gardena (90247-3511)
PHONE.................................310 532-4200
Kathy Wojno, *CEO*
John N Loizeaux-Witte, *Partner*
David Lee, *CFO*
Mahua Biswas, *Treasurer*
Christy Tercero, *Social Dir*
EMP: 760 EST: 1999
SALES: 143.5MM
SALES (corp-wide): 464.5MM **Privately Held**
WEB: www.memorialhospitalgardena.com
SIC: **8062** General medical & surgical hospitals
PA: Pipeline Health, Llc
111 N Sepulveda Blvd # 21
Manhattan Beach CA 90266
310 379-2134

(P-20775)
GATEWAYS HOSP MENTAL HLTH CTR
340 N Madison Ave, Los Angeles (90004-3504)
PHONE.................................323 644-2026
Mara Pelsman, *Branch Mgr*
Priscilla Ortega, *Systems Dir*
EMP: 63

SALES (corp-wide): 31.7MM **Privately Held**
WEB: www.gatewayshospital.org
SIC: **8062** General medical & surgical hospitals
PA: Gateway's Hospital And Mental Health Center Inc
1891 Effie St
Los Angeles CA 90026
323 644-2000

(P-20776)
GLENDALE ADVENTIST MEDICAL CTR (HQ)
1509 Wilson Ter, Glendale (91206-4007)
PHONE.................................818 409-8000
Kevin A Roberts, *President*
Randy L Bivens, *Ch Radiology*
Irene Bourdon, *President*
Warren Tetz, *COO*
Carlton Jacobson, *CFO*
EMP: 2550 EST: 1905
SQ FT: 700,000
SALES: 502MM
SALES (corp-wide): 4.5B **Privately Held**
WEB: www.healthyglendale.org
SIC: **8062** 8093 8011 General medical & surgical hospitals; mental health clinic, outpatient; freestanding emergency medical center
PA: Adventist Health System West, Corporation
1 Adventist Health Way
Roseville CA 95661
844 574-5686

(P-20777)
GLENDALE MEM HOSP & HLTH CTR
1420 S Central Ave, Glendale (91204-2508)
PHONE.................................818 502-1900
Carmen Rezak, *Principal*
Kelly Brady, *Facilities Mgr*
Bob Rose,
Steven Wong, *Diag Radio*
Lorie Vasquez, *Representative*
EMP: 96 EST: 2011
SALES (est): 1.9MM **Privately Held**
WEB: www.dignityhealth.org
SIC: **8062** General medical & surgical hospitals
HQ: Dignity Health
185 Berry St Ste 200
San Francisco CA 94107
415 438-5500

(P-20778)
GLENOAKS CONVALESCENT HOSPITAL
409 W Glenoaks Blvd, Glendale (91202-2916)
PHONE.................................818 240-4300
Elaine Levine, *Partner*
Tova Shallman, *Marketing Staff*
EMP: 85 EST: 1984
SQ FT: 22,306
SALES (est): 5.3MM **Privately Held**
WEB: www.gshci.com
SIC: **8062** General medical & surgical hospitals

(P-20779)
GOLETA VALLEY COTTAGE HOSP AUX
Also Called: Cottage Health System
351 S Patterson Ave, Santa Barbara (93111-2403)
P.O. Box 689 (93102-0639)
PHONE.................................805 681-6468
Ronald C Werft, *President*
Robert Knight, *Ch of Bd*
Joan Bricher, *CFO*
Ron Biscaro, *Vice Pres*
Ronald Biscaro, *Vice Pres*
EMP: 300 EST: 1966
SQ FT: 92,273
SALES: 79MM
SALES (corp-wide): 152.8MM **Privately Held**
WEB: www.cottagehealth.org
SIC: **8062** General medical & surgical hospitals

PA: Cottage Health
400 W Pueblo St
Santa Barbara CA 93105
805 682-7111

(P-20780)
GOOD SMRTAN HOSP A CAL LTD PRT
901 Olive Dr, Bakersfield (93308-4137)
P.O. Box 85002 (93380-5002)
PHONE..................661 903-9555
Amandeep Basra, *President*
David Huff, *Partner*
Sakrepatna Manohara, *President*
Andrew B Leeka, *CEO*
Anand Manohara, *CEO*
EMP: 400 **EST:** 1965
SQ FT: 49,001
SALES (est): 111.5MM **Privately Held**
WEB: www.goodsamhospital.com
SIC: 8062 8063 8069 General medical & surgical hospitals; psychiatric hospitals; specialty hospitals, except psychiatric

(P-20781)
HANFORD COMMUNITY HOSPITAL (HQ)
Also Called: Hanford Community Medical Ctr
115 Mall Dr, Hanford (93230-5786)
P.O. Box 240 (93232-0240)
PHONE..................559 582-9000
Lori Ruffner, *Opers Staff*
Stephen M Avalos, *Pathologist*
Michael Crawford, *Pathologist*
Gerardo Princesa, *Anesthesiology*
William Wilson, *Emerg Med Spec*
EMP: 640 **EST:** 1956
SQ FT: 52,060
SALES (est): 321MM
SALES (corp-wide): 4.5B **Privately Held**
WEB: www.adventisthealth.org
SIC: 8062 General medical & surgical hospitals
PA: Adventist Health System/West, Corporation
1 Adventist Health Way
Roseville CA 95661
844 574-5686

(P-20782)
HEALTH RESOURCES CORP
Also Called: Coastal Community Hospital
2701 S Bristol St, Santa Ana (92704-6201)
PHONE..................714 754-5454
Trevor Fetter, *President*
EMP: 400 **EST:** 1984
SALES (est): 25.2MM
SALES (corp-wide): 1.9B **Privately Held**
WEB: www.kpchealth.com
SIC: 8062 General medical & surgical hospitals
PA: Kpc Healthcare, Inc.
1301 N Tustin Ave
Santa Ana CA 92705
714 953-3652

(P-20783)
HEALTHSMART PACIFIC INC (PA)
Also Called: Long Beach Pain Center
5150 E Pacific Cst Hwy # 200, Long Beach (90804-3312)
PHONE..................562 595-1911
Michael Ddrobot, *CEO*
Michael D Drobot, *CEO*
EMP: 610 **EST:** 1932
SALES (est): 29.6MM **Privately Held**
SIC: 8062 General medical & surgical hospitals

(P-20784)
HEART HOSPITAL OF BK LLC
Also Called: Bakersfield Heart Hospital
3001 Sillect Ave, Bakersfield (93308-6337)
PHONE..................661 316-6000
Michelle Oxford, *President*
Houshang Abd, *CFO*
Judy Littrell, *Vice Pres*
Charles Clayton, *Lab Dir*
Cherie Cadena, *Analyst*
EMP: 336 **EST:** 1996
SALES (est): 443MM
SALES (corp-wide): 1.9B **Publicly Held**
WEB: www.bakersfieldhearthospital.com
SIC: 8062 General medical & surgical hospitals

HQ: Surgery Partners, Inc.
310 Sven Sprng Way Ste 50
Brentwood TN 37027
615 234-5900

(P-20785)
HENRY MAYO NEWHALL MEM HOSP (PA)
23845 Mcbean Pkwy, Valencia (91355-2001)
PHONE..................661 253-8000
Roger E Seaver, *President*
Elizabeth Hopp, *Ch of Bd*
Mimi Baum, *President*
Jim Sapienza, *President*
Debra Weyand, *President*
EMP: 1528 **EST:** 1972
SQ FT: 210,000
SALES (est): 411.3MM **Privately Held**
WEB: www.henrymayo.com
SIC: 8062 General medical & surgical hospitals

(P-20786)
HENRY MAYO NWHALL MEM HLTH FND
23845 Mcbean Pkwy, Santa Clarita (91355-2001)
PHONE..................661 253-8000
Dianna Vose, *Director*
C R Bob Hutson, *CFO*
EMP: 66 **EST:** 1980
SALES (est): 650.8K **Privately Held**
WEB: www.henrymayo.com
SIC: 8062 General medical & surgical hospitals

(P-20787)
HENRY MAYO NWHALL MEM HLTH FND
Also Called: Henrymayo Newhall Mem Hosp
23845 Mcbean Pkwy, Valencia (91355-2001)
P.O. Box 55279 (91385-0279)
PHONE..................661 253-8000
Roger Seaver, *President*
Mark Puleo, *Vice Pres*
Cecelia Hann, *Admin Sec*
EMP: 1500 **EST:** 1972
SALES (est): 411.3MM **Privately Held**
WEB: www.henrymayo.com
SIC: 8062 General medical & surgical hospitals

(P-20788)
HOAG FAMILY CANCER INSTITUTE (PA)
1 Hoag Dr Bldg 41, Newport Beach (92663-4162)
PHONE..................949 722-6237
Burt Eisenberg, *Director*
Blair Azamian, *Officer*
Camille Schwan, *Officer*
Kris Iyer, *Senior VP*
Nicole Balsamo, *Vice Pres*
EMP: 83 **EST:** 2006
SALES (est): 12.7MM **Privately Held**
WEB: www.hoag.org
SIC: 8062 General medical & surgical hospitals

(P-20789)
HOAG HOSPITAL FOUNDATION (HQ)
330 Placentia Ave Ste 100, Newport Beach (92663-3309)
P.O. Box 6100 (92658-6100)
PHONE..................949 764-7217
Toll Free:..................877 -
Karen Linden, *CEO*
Leslie Scarborough, *Records Dir*
Flynn A Andrizzi, *CEO*
Colette Crandall, *Chairman*
Roger T Kirwan, *Chairman*
▲ **EMP:** 50 **EST:** 1944
SQ FT: 500,000
SALES (est): 99.1MM **Privately Held**
WEB: www.hoaghospitalfoundation.org
SIC: 8062 General medical & surgical hospitals

(P-20790)
HOAG MEMORIAL HOSPITAL PRESBT (PA)
1 Hoag Dr, Newport Beach (92663-4162)
P.O. Box 6100 (92658-6100)
PHONE..................949 764-4624
Robert Braithwaite, *President*
William Vandalsem, *Ch Radiology*
Leslie Scarborough, *Records Dir*
Pauline Jackson, *Partner*
Rachel Leyva, *Partner*
EMP: 3600 **EST:** 1944
SALES (est): 894MM **Privately Held**
WEB: www.hoag.org
SIC: 8062 General medical & surgical hospitals

(P-20791)
HOAG ORTHOPEDIC INSTITUTE LLC
16250 Sand Canyon Ave, Irvine (92618-3714)
PHONE..................949 764-8690
Kim Mikes, *CEO*
James Caillouette, *Ch of Bd*
Flynn A Andrizzi, *President*
Steven Barnett, *Chief Mktg Ofcr*
Jay Patel, *Officer*
EMP: 73 **EST:** 2008
SALES (est): 57.6MM **Privately Held**
WEB: www.hoagorthopedicinstitute.com
SIC: 8062 General medical & surgical hospitals

(P-20792)
HOLLYWOOD CMNTY HOSP MED CTR I
Also Called: Hollywood Cmnty Hosp Hollywood
6245 De Longpre Ave, Los Angeles (90028-8253)
PHONE..................323 462-2271
Robert Starling, *CEO*
Kenneth Auguster, *Records Dir*
Ron Messenger, *President*
Manfred Krukemeyer, *Vice Ch Bd*
Eldino Defensor, *Lab Dir*
EMP: 220 **EST:** 1982
SQ FT: 100,000
SALES (est): 26.9MM
SALES (corp-wide): 3.4B **Privately Held**
WEB: www.sch-hollywood.com
SIC: 8062 Hospital, affiliated with AMA residency
HQ: Southern California Healthcare System, Inc.
3415 S Sepulveda Blvd # 9
Los Angeles CA 90034

(P-20793)
HOLLYWOOD MEDICAL CENTER LP
Also Called: Hollywood Presbyterian Med Ctr
1300 N Vermont Ave, Los Angeles (90027-6098)
PHONE..................213 413-3000
Jeff Nelson, *Partner*
Esther Villegas, *Teacher*
Pam Tuszynski, *Director*
EMP: 1250 **EST:** 1928
SALES (est): 281.2MM **Privately Held**
WEB: www.hollywoodpresbyterian.com
SIC: 8062 General medical & surgical hospitals
PA: Cha Health Systems, Inc
3731 Wilshire Blvd # 850
Los Angeles CA 90010

(P-20794)
HOSPITAL OF BARSTOW INC (DH)
Also Called: BARSTOW COMMUNITY HOSPITAL
820 E Mountain View St, Barstow (92311-3004)
PHONE..................760 256-1761
Justin Sheridan, *CEO*
Shawn Curtis, *CFO*
Rene Capule, *Lab Dir*
Michelle Brooks, *Purch Mgr*
EMP: 214 **EST:** 1958
SQ FT: 54,000

SALES (est): 40.6K
SALES (corp-wide): 1.6B **Privately Held**
WEB: www.barstowhospital.com
SIC: 8062 Hospital, affiliated with AMA residency

(P-20795)
HOSPITALIST CORP INLAND EMPIRE
840 Towne Center Dr, Pomona (91767-5900)
PHONE..................909 398-1550
Irf Brown, *Principal*
EMP: 59 **EST:** 2011
SALES (est): 1MM **Privately Held**
WEB: www.iehospitalists.com
SIC: 8062 General medical & surgical hospitals

(P-20796)
HUNTINGTON MEDICAL FOUNDATION
65 N Madison Ave Ste 800, Pasadena (91101-2038)
PHONE..................626 792-3141
Laura Hernandez, *Manager*
EMP: 146 **Privately Held**
WEB: www.huntingtonhospital.org
SIC: 8062 General medical & surgical hospitals
PA: The Huntington Medical Foundation
100 W California Blvd
Pasadena CA 91105

(P-20797)
INLAND HLTH ORGNZTION OF STHER (DH)
1980 Orange Tree Ln # 200, Redlands (92374-4534)
P.O. Box 10457, San Bernardino (92423-0457)
PHONE..................909 335-7171
Jeff Winter, *President*
Paula Lamar, *Vice Pres*
EMP: 50 **EST:** 1994
SQ FT: 12,000
SALES (est): 20.9MM **Privately Held**
WEB: www.dignityhealth.org
SIC: 8062 General medical & surgical hospitals
HQ: Dignity Health
185 Berry St Ste 200
San Francisco CA 94107
415 438-5500

(P-20798)
INLAND VLY RGIONAL MED CTR INC
36485 Inland Valley Dr, Wildomar (92595-9681)
PHONE..................951 677-1111
Alan B Miller, *CEO*
Barry Thorfinnson, *CFO*
Alan Coates, *Purch Dir*
EMP: 500 **EST:** 1983
SQ FT: 77,000
SALES (est): 67.7MM
SALES (corp-wide): 11.5B **Publicly Held**
WEB: www.inlandvalleymedcenter.com
SIC: 8062 8011 General medical & surgical hospitals; clinic, operated by physicians
PA: Universal Health Services, Inc.
367 S Gulph Rd
King Of Prussia PA 19406
610 768-3300

(P-20799)
JOHN F KENNEDY MEM HOSP AUX
Also Called: John F Knnedy Mem Hosp Emrgncy
47111 Monroe St, Indio (92201-6799)
PHONE..................760 347-6191
Gary Honts, *Officer*
Ralph Ho, *Ch Radiology*
Robert Galvan, *Radiology Dir*
Robert Macdonald, *Engineer*
Jorge Cebreros, *Buyer*
EMP: 650 **EST:** 1986

SALES (est): 78MM
SALES (corp-wide): 72.9MM **Privately Held**
WEB: www.desertcarenetwork.com
SIC: 8062 Hospital, affiliated with AMA residency
HQ: St. Luke's Des Peres Episcopal-Presbyterian Hospital
2345 Dougherty Ferry Rd
Saint Louis MO 63122
314 966-9100

(P-20800)
KAISER FOUNDATION HOSPITALS
Also Called: Barranca Medical Offices
6 Willard, Irvine (92604-4694)
PHONE...........................949 262-5780
George Disalvo, *Owner*
Sohrab Barkhordar, *Pediatrics*
Vivian Fan,
EMP: 522
SQ FT: 51,080
SALES (corp-wide): 30.5B **Privately Held**
WEB: www.kaisercenter.com
SIC: 8062 General medical & surgical hospitals
HQ: Kaiser Foundation Hospitals Inc
1 Kaiser Plz
Oakland CA 94612
510 271-6611

(P-20801)
KAISER FOUNDATION HOSPITALS
Also Called: Kaiser Permanente
5601 De Soto Ave, Woodland Hills
(91367-6701)
PHONE...........................818 719-2000
Cathy Casas, *Senior VP*
Donna Moore, *Executive*
Darrick Cheyno, *Radiology Dir*
Daniel Torres, *Administration*
Karun Kapur, *Info Tech Dir*
EMP: 1200
SALES (corp-wide): 30.5B **Privately Held**
WEB: www.kaisercenter.com
SIC: 8062 General medical & surgical hospitals
HQ: Kaiser Foundation Hospitals Inc
1 Kaiser Plz
Oakland CA 94612
510 271-6611

(P-20802)
KAISER FOUNDATION HOSPITALS
Also Called: Kaiser Permanente
12620 Prescott Ave, Tustin (92782-1066)
PHONE...........................951 353-4000
Danh V Le, *Director*
EMP: 522
SALES (corp-wide): 30.5B **Privately Held**
WEB: www.kaisercenter.com
SIC: 8062 General medical & surgical hospitals
HQ: Kaiser Foundation Hospitals Inc
1 Kaiser Plz
Oakland CA 94612
510 271-6611

(P-20803)
KAISER FOUNDATION HOSPITALS
Also Called: Kaiser Permanente
8800 Ming Ave, Bakersfield (93311-1308)
PHONE...........................661 412-6777
Jennifer Fletcher, *Office Mgr*
EMP: 522
SALES (corp-wide): 30.5B **Privately Held**
WEB: www.kaisercenter.com
SIC: 8062 General medical & surgical hospitals
HQ: Kaiser Foundation Hospitals Inc
1 Kaiser Plz
Oakland CA 94612
510 271-6611

(P-20804)
KAISER FOUNDATION HOSPITALS
Also Called: Kaiser Permanente
43112 15th St W, Lancaster (93534-6219)
PHONE...........................661 726-2500
Barbara Fordice, *General Mgr*

Willie Delarosa, *Analyst*
Zhongheng Tu, *Family Practiti*
Ivy Semenez, *Internal Med*
Zin Win, *Internal Med*
EMP: 522
SALES (corp-wide): 30.5B **Privately Held**
WEB: www.kaisercenter.com
SIC: 8062 Hospital, affiliated with AMA residency
HQ: Kaiser Foundation Hospitals Inc
1 Kaiser Plz
Oakland CA 94612
510 271-6611

(P-20805)
KAISER FOUNDATION HOSPITALS
Also Called: Kaiser Permanente
4867 W Sunset Blvd, Los Angeles
(90027-5969)
PHONE...........................323 783-4011
Vicken Aharonian, *Director*
Sima Hartounian, *Officer*
Carlotta Jemison, *Administration*
Raj Mallichetty, *Info Tech Dir*
Leonard Champion, *Project Mgr*
EMP: 60
SALES (corp-wide): 30.5B **Privately Held**
WEB: www.kaisercenter.com
SIC: 8062 8099 6321 6324 General medical & surgical hospitals; physical examination service, insurance; health insurance carriers; hospital & medical service plans
HQ: Kaiser Foundation Hospitals Inc
1 Kaiser Plz
Oakland CA 94612
510 271-6611

(P-20806)
KAISER FOUNDATION HOSPITALS
Also Called: Kaiser Prmnnte Ornge Cnty-Nhei
3440 E La Palma Ave, Anaheim
(92806-2020)
PHONE...........................714 644-2000
Patrick Steinhauser, *Director*
Steinhauser Pat, *Engineer*
Mohamed Moussa, *Surgeon*
Nina Agarwal, *Obstetrician*
Stella Sien, *Obstetrician*
EMP: 522
SQ FT: 125,000
SALES (corp-wide): 30.5B **Privately Held**
WEB: www.kaisercenter.com
SIC: 8062 8011 General medical & surgical hospitals; general & family practice, physician/surgeon
HQ: Kaiser Foundation Hospitals Inc
1 Kaiser Plz
Oakland CA 94612
510 271-6611

(P-20807)
KAISER FOUNDATION HOSPITALS
4733 W Sunset Blvd Fl 2, Los Angeles
(90027-6021)
PHONE...........................323 783-4011
Ryan P Clare, *Internal Med*
Jennifer L Tran, *Otolaryngology*
Alexander Miric, *Med Doctor*
Andy Tien, *Med Doctor*
EMP: 522
SALES (corp-wide): 30.5B **Privately Held**
WEB: www.kaisercenter.com
SIC: 8062 General medical & surgical hospitals
HQ: Kaiser Foundation Hospitals Inc
1 Kaiser Plz
Oakland CA 94612
510 271-6611

(P-20808)
KAISER FOUNDATION HOSPITALS
Also Called: Kaiser Permanente
1255 W Arrow Hwy, San Dimas
(91773-2340)
PHONE...........................909 394-2530
Will Tatum, *Manager*
Veena Bhatarakamol, *Family Practiti*
Jennie Chang, *Obstetrician*
EMP: 522
SQ FT: 23,801

SALES (corp-wide): 30.5B **Privately Held**
WEB: www.kaisercenter.com
SIC: 8062 8011 General medical & surgical hospitals; general & family practice, physician/surgeon
HQ: Kaiser Foundation Hospitals Inc
1 Kaiser Plz
Oakland CA 94612
510 271-6611

(P-20809)
KAISER FOUNDATION HOSPITALS
Also Called: San Joaquin Community Hospital
2615 Chester Ave, Bakersfield
(93301-2014)
PHONE...........................661 395-3000
EMP: 522
SALES (corp-wide): 30.5B **Privately Held**
WEB: www.kaisercenter.com
SIC: 8062 General medical & surgical hospitals
HQ: Kaiser Foundation Hospitals Inc
1 Kaiser Plz
Oakland CA 94612
510 271-6611

(P-20810)
KAISER FOUNDATION HOSPITALS
Also Called: Antelope Valley Hospital
1600 W Avenue J, Lancaster (93534-2814)
PHONE...........................661 949-5000
Harriet R Lee, *Administration*
EMP: 522
SALES (corp-wide): 30.5B **Privately Held**
WEB: www.kaisercenter.com
SIC: 8062 General medical & surgical hospitals
HQ: Kaiser Foundation Hospitals Inc
1 Kaiser Plz
Oakland CA 94612
510 271-6611

(P-20811)
KAISER FOUNDATION HOSPITALS
Also Called: Wildomar Medical Offices
36450 Inland Valley Dr # 2, Wildomar
(92595-9583)
PHONE...........................951 353-2000
Geoffrey Gomez, *Principal*
EMP: 522
SALES (corp-wide): 30.5B **Privately Held**
WEB: www.kaisercenter.com
SIC: 8062 General medical & surgical hospitals
HQ: Kaiser Foundation Hospitals Inc
1 Kaiser Plz
Oakland CA 94612
510 271-6611

(P-20812)
KAISER FOUNDATION HOSPITALS
Also Called: Cudahy Medical Offices
7825 Atlantic Ave, Cudahy (90201-5022)
PHONE...........................323 562-6400
Karen Warren, *Manager*
Robert L Escalera, *Family Practiti*
Mariela Garcia, *Family Practiti*
Edwin Solorzano, *Family Practiti*
Maria Gonzalez, *Psychologist*
EMP: 522
SALES (corp-wide): 30.5B **Privately Held**
WEB: www.kaisercenter.com
SIC: 8062 General medical & surgical hospitals
HQ: Kaiser Foundation Hospitals Inc
1 Kaiser Plz
Oakland CA 94612
510 271-6611

(P-20813)
KAISER FOUNDATION HOSPITALS
Also Called: Gardena Medical Offices
15446 S Western Ave, Gardena
(90249-4319)
PHONE...........................310 517-2956
Mary Mauch, *Manager*
Jennifer Wang, *Family Practiti*
Marilou Puga,
EMP: 522

SQ FT: 114,575
SALES (corp-wide): 30.5B **Privately Held**
WEB: www.kaisercenter.com
SIC: 8062 General medical & surgical hospitals
HQ: Kaiser Foundation Hospitals Inc
1 Kaiser Plz
Oakland CA 94612
510 271-6611

(P-20814)
KAISER FOUNDATION HOSPITALS
Also Called: Erwin Street Medical Offices
21263 Erwin St, Woodland Hills
(91367-3715)
PHONE...........................818 592-3100
Karen Kim, *Executive*
Sylva Murdaian, *Family Practiti*
Donald Eknoyan, *Psychiatry*
EMP: 522
SQ FT: 28,398
SALES (corp-wide): 30.5B **Privately Held**
WEB: www.kaisercenter.com
SIC: 8062 General medical & surgical hospitals
HQ: Kaiser Foundation Hospitals Inc
1 Kaiser Plz
Oakland CA 94612
510 271-6611

(P-20815)
KAISER FOUNDATION HOSPITALS
Also Called: Kaiser Permanente
1055 E Colo Blvd Ste 100, Pasadena
(91106)
PHONE...........................626 440-5659
Jeanine Boudakian, *Branch Mgr*
George Di Salvo, *CFO*
Patti Harvey, *Vice Pres*
Barbara Farrell, *Admin Ass*
Frank Kuo, *Administration*
EMP: 500
SALES (corp-wide): 30.5B **Privately Held**
WEB: www.kaisercenter.com
SIC: 8062 General medical & surgical hospitals
HQ: Kaiser Foundation Hospitals Inc
1 Kaiser Plz
Oakland CA 94612
510 271-6611

(P-20816)
KAISER FOUNDATION HOSPITALS
Also Called: Kaiser Permanente
250 W San Jose Ave, Claremont
(91711-5295)
PHONE...........................888 750-0036
Bell Pacific, *Manager*
Wednesday Biscocho, *Family Practiti*
Karen Langdon,
EMP: 522
SQ FT: 17,908
SALES (corp-wide): 30.5B **Privately Held**
WEB: www.kaisercenter.com
SIC: 8062 General medical & surgical hospitals
HQ: Kaiser Foundation Hospitals Inc
1 Kaiser Plz
Oakland CA 94612
510 271-6611

(P-20817)
KAWEAH DELTA HEALTH CARE DST
355 Monte Vista Dr, Dinuba (93618-9228)
PHONE...........................559 591-5513
Gary K Herbst, *CFO*
EMP: 118
SALES (corp-wide): 734.3MM **Privately Held**
WEB: www.kdhcd.org
SIC: 8062 Hospital, AMA approved residency
PA: Kaweah Delta Health Care District Guild
400 W Mineral King Ave
Visalia CA 93291
559 624-2000

▲ = Import ▼=Export
◆ =Import/Export

(P-20818)
KAWEAH DELTA HEALTH CARE DST
1014 San Juan Ave, Exeter (93221-1312)
PHONE..................................559 592-7128
EMP: 118
SALES (corp-wide): 734.3MM **Privately Held**
WEB: www.kdhcd.org
SIC: **8062** General medical & surgical hospitals
PA: Kaweah Delta Health Care District Guild
400 W Mineral King Ave
Visalia CA 93291
559 624-2000

(P-20819)
KAWEAH DELTA HEALTH CARE DST
1110 S Ben Maddox Way, Visalia (93292-3643)
PHONE..................................559 624-4800
EMP: 118
SALES (corp-wide): 734.3MM **Privately Held**
WEB: www.kdhcd.org
SIC: **8062** General medical & surgical hospitals
PA: Kaweah Delta Health Care District Guild
400 W Mineral King Ave
Visalia CA 93291
559 624-2000

(P-20820)
KAWEAH DELTA HEALTH CARE DST (PA)
Also Called: Kaweah Delta Medical Center
400 W Mineral King Ave, Visalia (93291-6237)
PHONE..................................559 624-2000
Donna Archer, *CEO*
Lindsay K Mann, *CEO*
Thomas Rayner, *COO*
Gary Herbst, *CFO*
Toni Boniske, *Treasurer*
EMP: 1800
SQ FT: 250,255
SALES: 734.3MM **Privately Held**
WEB: www.kdhcd.org
SIC: **8062** Hospital, AMA approved residency

(P-20821)
KAWEAH DLTA HLTH CARE DST GILD
400 W Mineral King Ave, Visalia (93291-6237)
PHONE..................................559 624-2000
Susan Kordell, *Manager*
EMP: 118
SALES (corp-wide): 734.3MM **Privately Held**
WEB: www.kdhcd.org
SIC: **8062** General medical & surgical hospitals
PA: Kaweah Delta Health Care District Guild
400 W Mineral King Ave
Visalia CA 93291
559 624-2000

(P-20822)
KECK HOSPITAL OF USC
1500 San Pablo St, Los Angeles (90033-5313)
PHONE..................................800 872-2273
Thomas E Jackiewicz, *CEO*
Rodney B Hanners, *COO*
James J Uli Jr, *CFO*
Paul Craig, *Officer*
Tammy Capretta,
▲ EMP: 282 EST: 2009
SALES (est): 247.5MM **Privately Held**
WEB: www.keckmedicine.org
SIC: **8062** General medical & surgical hospitals

(P-20823)
KEIRO NURSING HOME
2221 Lincoln Park Ave, Los Angeles (90031-2998)
PHONE..................................323 276-5700
EMP: 150

SALES (corp-wide): 16.5MM **Privately Held**
WEB: www.keiro.org
SIC: **8062** 8052 8051 General Hospital Intermediate Care Facility Skilled Nursing Care Facility
PA: Keiro Nursing Home
325 S Boyle Ave
Los Angeles CA 90033
323 263-9655

(P-20824)
KENNETH CORP
Also Called: GARDEN GROVE HOSPITAL
12601 Garden Grove Blvd, Garden Grove (92843-1908)
PHONE..................................714 537-5160
Edward Mirzabegian, *CEO*
Hassan Alkhouli, *Ch of Bd*
EMP: 615 EST: 1951
SQ FT: 133,083
SALES (est): 108.4MM **Privately Held**
WEB: www.gardengrovehospital.com
SIC: **8062** General medical & surgical hospitals

(P-20825)
KERN COUNTY HOSPITAL AUTHORITY (PA)
1700 Mount Vernon Ave, Bakersfield (93306-4018)
PHONE..................................661 326-2102
Russell Judd, *CEO*
Tyler Whitezell, *COO*
Andrew Cantu, *CFO*
EMP: 978 EST: 1865
SQ FT: 29,800
SALES (est): 43.8MM **Privately Held**
WEB: www.kernmedical.com
SIC: **8062** General medical & surgical hospitals

(P-20826)
KINDRED HEALTHCARE LLC
550 N Monterey Ave, Ontario (91764-3318)
PHONE..................................909 391-0333
Robin Rapp, *Branch Mgr*
Cherie Snyder, *Nursing Mgr*
EMP: 142
SALES (corp-wide): 6B **Privately Held**
WEB: www.kindredhealthcare.com
SIC: **8062** General medical & surgical hospitals
HQ: Kindred Healthcare, Llc
680 S 4th St
Louisville KY 40202
502 596-7300

(P-20827)
KINDRED HEALTHCARE LLC
2224 Medical Center Dr, Perris (92571-2638)
PHONE..................................951 436-3535
James Linhares, *CEO*
Tawanda Whitaker, *Records Dir*
Lorelei Garrison, *Radiology Dir*
Emma Duran, *Technician*
Pam Lani, *Purch Dir*
EMP: 142
SALES (corp-wide): 6B **Privately Held**
WEB: www.kindredhealthcare.com
SIC: **8062** General medical & surgical hospitals
HQ: Kindred Healthcare, Llc
680 S 4th St
Louisville KY 40202
502 596-7300

(P-20828)
KINDRED HEALTHCARE LLC
Also Called: Kindred Hospital Santa Ana
1901 College Ave, Santa Ana (92706-2334)
PHONE..................................714 564-7800
Trish Kemble, *Pharmacy Dir*
Robert Bendzsel, *Facilities Mgr*
Hector Cisneros, *Food Svc Dir*
Sheila Frias, *Director*
EMP: 142
SALES (corp-wide): 6B **Privately Held**
WEB: www.kindredhealthcare.com
SIC: **8062** 8011 General medical & surgical hospitals; offices & clinics of medical doctors

HQ: Kindred Healthcare, Llc
680 S 4th St
Louisville KY 40202
502 596-7300

(P-20829)
KINDRED HEALTHCARE LLC
Also Called: Kindred Hospital Paramount
16453 Colorado Ave, Paramount (90723-5011)
PHONE..................................562 531-3110
Mary Reed, *Controller*
Rosio Hobbs, *Mktg Dir*
EMP: 142
SALES (corp-wide): 6B **Privately Held**
WEB: www.kindredhealthcare.com
SIC: **8062** General medical & surgical hospitals
HQ: Kindred Healthcare, Llc
680 S 4th St
Louisville KY 40202
502 596-7300

(P-20830)
KND DEVELOPMENT 52 LLC
Also Called: Kindred Hospital - Baldwin Pk
14148 Francisquito Ave, Baldwin Park (91706-6120)
PHONE..................................626 388-2700
Swenda Moreh, *CEO*
Dina Garrow, *COO*
Nancy Batac, *Lab Dir*
Evalee Fajardo, *Opers Staff*
EMP: 54 EST: 2011
SALES (est): 50.2MM **Privately Held**
SIC: **8062** General medical & surgical hospitals

(P-20831)
KND DEVELOPMENT 55 LLC
Also Called: Kindred Hospital - Rancho
10841 White Oak Ave, Rancho Cucamonga (91730-3817)
PHONE..................................909 581-6400
Miller Debroah, *Director*
James Rudolph, *Lab Dir*
Lisa Hernandez, *Social Dir*
Jenny Hicks, *Radiology Dir*
Cody Anderson, *Director*
EMP: 77 EST: 2007
SALES (est): 51.8MM **Privately Held**
SIC: **8062** General medical & surgical hospitals

(P-20832)
LAKEWOOD REGIONAL MED CTR INC
Also Called: Lakewood Regional Medical Ctr
3700 South St, Lakewood (90712-1419)
P.O. Box 6070 (90714-6070)
PHONE..................................562 531-2550
John Grah, *CEO*
Mark Korth, *President*
Ronald Galonsky, *CEO*
Michael Paul Amos, *COO*
Lani Dickinson, *COO*
EMP: 900 EST: 2001
SALES (est): 128.6MM
SALES (corp-wide): 17.6B **Publicly Held**
WEB: www.lakewoodregional.com
SIC: **8062** Hospital, affiliated with AMA residency
PA: Tenet Healthcare Corporation
14201 Dallas Pkwy
Dallas TX 75254
469 893-2200

(P-20833)
LINDA LOMA UNIV HLTH CARE (HQ)
11370 Anderson St # 3900, Loma Linda (92354-3450)
P.O. Box 2000 (92354-0200)
PHONE..................................909 558-2806
Richard Hart, *President*
Rosita Fike, *CEO*
Andrea Champlin, *Program Mgr*
Ester Boloix-Chapman, *Executive Asst*
Becky Brewster, *Admin Sec*
EMP: 1233 EST: 1967

SALES: 171.2MM
SALES (corp-wide): 284.6MM **Privately Held**
WEB: www.home.llu.edu
SIC: **8062** 8011 8051 5999 Hospital, medical school affiliated with residency; medical centers; extended care facility; convalescent equipment & supplies
PA: Loma Linda University
11060 Anderson St
Loma Linda CA 92350
909 558-4540

(P-20834)
LITTLE COMPANY MARY HOSPITAL
Also Called: Leader Drug Store
4101 Torrance Blvd, Torrance (90503-4664)
PHONE..................................310 540-7676
Joseph Zanetta, *CEO*
Elizabeth Zuanich, *CFO*
Kasey Lai, *Internal Med*
Christian McClung, *Emerg Med Spec*
Robert Marcus, *Diag Radio*
▲ EMP: 1200 EST: 1957
SQ FT: 300,000
SALES (est): 203.4MM
SALES (corp-wide): 32.7MM **Privately Held**
WEB: www.providence.org
SIC: **8062** 8051 General medical & surgical hospitals; skilled nursing care facilities
HQ: Providence Health System-Southern California
1801 Lind Ave Sw
Renton WA 98057
425 525-3355

(P-20835)
LOMA LINDA UNIVERSITY MED CTR
26780 Barton Rd, Redlands (92373-4308)
PHONE..................................909 558-4000
Susan L Beaman, *Ch of Bd*
Edward L Field, *Exec Dir*
Richard Rice, *Professor*
Bryant H Nguyen, *Director*
Mary E Moline, *Representative*
EMP: 81
SALES (corp-wide): 284.6MM **Privately Held**
WEB: www.home.llu.edu
SIC: **8062** General medical & surgical hospitals
HQ: Loma Linda University Medical Center
11234 Anderson St
Loma Linda CA 92354
909 558-4000

(P-20836)
LOMA LINDA UNIVERSITY MED CTR
Also Called: Craniofacial Department
11370 Anderson St 2100, Loma Linda (92354-3450)
P.O. Box 982 (92354-0982)
PHONE..................................909 558-2100
Leonard Bailey MD, *Principal*
Joe Ruga, *Analyst*
EMP: 81
SALES (corp-wide): 284.6MM **Privately Held**
WEB: www.home.llu.edu
SIC: **8062** 8221 Hospital, medical school affiliation; university
HQ: Loma Linda University Medical Center
11234 Anderson St
Loma Linda CA 92354
909 558-4000

(P-20837)
LOMA LINDA UNIVERSITY MED CTR (DH)
Also Called: LLUMC
11234 Anderson St, Loma Linda (92354-2871)
P.O. Box 2000 (92354-0200)
PHONE..................................909 558-4000
Richard H Hart, *Vice Chairman*
Robert Martin,
David Hinshaw Jr, *Ch Radiology*
Richard H Hart, *Vice Chairman*
James Jesse, *President*
EMP: 4600 EST: 1967

PRODUCTS & SVCS

SQ FT: 630,000
SALES: 1.5B
SALES (corp-wide): 284.6MM **Privately Held**
WEB: www.lluh.org
SIC: 8062 8011 8051 5999 Hospital, medical school affiliated with residency; medical centers; extended care facility; medical apparatus & supplies
HQ: Loma Linda University Health Care
　11370 Anderson St # 3900
　Loma Linda CA 92354
　909 558-2806

(P-20838)
LOMA LINDA UNIVERSITY MED CTR
Also Called: Loma Linda Catering Center
11175 Campus St, Loma Linda (92350-1700)
PHONE................................909 558-8244
Najwa Medina, *Manager*
Debbie Johnson, *Admin Sec*
Brent Boyko, *IT/INT Sup*
Jon Paulien, *Dean*
David J Michelson, *Neurology*
EMP: 81
SALES (corp-wide): 284.6MM **Privately Held**
WEB: www.home.llu.edu
SIC: 8062 Hospital, medical school affiliation
HQ: Loma Linda University Medical Center
　11234 Anderson St
　Loma Linda CA 92354
　909 558-4000

(P-20839)
LOMA LINDA UNIVERSITY MED CTR
Also Called: Behavioral Medicine Center
1710 Barton Rd, Redlands (92373-5304)
PHONE................................909 558-9275
Ruthita Fike, *Manager*
Diana Deandrea, *Business Dir*
Edward L Field, *Exec Dir*
Carol Barnes-Reid, *Food Svc Dir*
Jennifer Weniger, *Psychologist*
EMP: 81
SQ FT: 62,476
SALES (corp-wide): 284.6MM **Privately Held**
WEB: www.home.llu.edu
SIC: 8062 8221 Hospital, medical school affiliation; university
HQ: Loma Linda University Medical Center
　11234 Anderson St
　Loma Linda CA 92354
　909 558-4000

(P-20840)
LOMA LINDA UNIVERSITY MED CTR
11370 Anderson St, Loma Linda (92354-3450)
P.O. Box 728 (92354-0728)
PHONE................................909 558-4385
EMP: 81
SALES (corp-wide): 284.6MM **Privately Held**
WEB: www.home.llu.edu
SIC: 8062 General medical & surgical hospitals
HQ: Loma Linda University Medical Center
　11234 Anderson St
　Loma Linda CA 92354
　909 558-4000

(P-20841)
LOMA LINDA UNIVERSITY MED CTR
Also Called: Loma Linda Pharmacy
11223 Campus St, Loma Linda (92354-3203)
PHONE................................909 558-4216
Bill Robinson, *Manager*
EMP: 81
SALES (corp-wide): 284.6MM **Privately Held**
WEB: www.home.llu.edu
SIC: 8062 General medical & surgical hospitals

HQ: Loma Linda University Medical Center
　11234 Anderson St
　Loma Linda CA 92354
　909 558-4000

(P-20842)
LOMA LINDA UNIVERSITY MED CTR
Also Called: Loma Linda Community Hospital
25333 Barton Rd, Loma Linda (92350-0210)
PHONE................................909 796-0167
Todd Nelson, *Manager*
Mark Hubbard, *Vice Pres*
Romy Reyes, *Lab Dir*
David Gentry, *Radiology Dir*
Debra Thomas, *QA Dir*
EMP: 81
SQ FT: 79,580
SALES (corp-wide): 284.6MM **Privately Held**
WEB: www.home.llu.edu
SIC: 8062 General medical & surgical hospitals
HQ: Loma Linda University Medical Center
　11234 Anderson St
　Loma Linda CA 92354
　909 558-4000

(P-20843)
LOMPOC VALLEY MEDICAL CENTER
Also Called: Mammography Center
1111 E Ocean Ave Ste 2, Lompoc (93436-2500)
PHONE................................805 735-9229
Jim Raggio, *Branch Mgr*
EMP: 174
SALES (corp-wide): 104.2MM **Privately Held**
WEB: www.lompocvmc.com
SIC: 8062 General medical & surgical hospitals
PA: Lompoc Valley Medical Center
　1515 E Ocean Ave
　Lompoc CA 93436
　805 737-3300

(P-20844)
LOMPOC VALLEY MEDICAL CENTER (PA)
Also Called: LOMPOC SKILLED CARE CENTER
1515 E Ocean Ave, Lompoc (93436-7092)
P.O. Box 1058 (93438-1058)
PHONE................................805 737-3300
Jim Raggio, *CEO*
Naishadh Buch, *COO*
Dustin Cheney, *CFO*
Ray Down, *Bd of Directors*
John Lonsbury, *Bd of Directors*
EMP: 325
SQ FT: 150,000
SALES: 104.2MM **Privately Held**
WEB: www.lompocvmc.com
SIC: 8062 8051 Hospital, affiliated with AMA residency; skilled nursing care facilities

(P-20845)
LOMPOC VALLEY MEDICAL CENTER
Also Called: Lompoc Convlsnt Care Ctr
216 N 3rd St, Lompoc (93436-6104)
PHONE................................805 736-3466
EMP: 150
SALES (corp-wide): 104.2MM **Privately Held**
WEB: www.lompocvmc.com
SIC: 8062 General medical & surgical hospitals
PA: Lompoc Valley Medical Center
　1515 E Ocean Ave
　Lompoc CA 93436
　805 737-3300

(P-20846)
LONG BEACH MEDICAL CENTER
Also Called: Infusion Care
450 E Spring St Ste 11, Long Beach (90806-1625)
PHONE................................562 933-7701
Gerald Nichrossan, *Branch Mgr*
Jeffrey N Luther, *Principal*
Lauren A Barnes, *Family Practiti*

Nicholas Doan, *Med Doctor*
EMP: 318 **Privately Held**
WEB: www.memorialcare.org
SIC: 8062 General medical & surgical hospitals
HQ: Long Beach Medical Center
　2801 Atlantic Ave Fl 2
　Long Beach CA 90806
　562 933-2000

(P-20847)
LONG BEACH MEDICAL CENTER (HQ)
Also Called: Miller Children's Hospital
2801 Atlantic Ave Fl 2, Long Beach (90806-1701)
PHONE................................562 933-2000
John Bishop, *CEO*
Barry Arbuckle PHD, *President*
Tamra Kaplan, *COO*
Suize Reinsvold, *COO*
Joseph C Hirt, *CFO*
EMP: 2000 **EST:** 1907
SQ FT: 1,100,000
SALES: 633.6MM **Privately Held**
WEB: www.memorialcare.org
SIC: 8062 General medical & surgical hospitals

(P-20848)
LONG BEACH MEDICAL CENTER
1720 Termino Ave, Long Beach (90804-2104)
PHONE................................562 933-0085
Tom Collins, *President*
Martin Collen, *Principal*
Donna Carnegie, *Opers Staff*
Edwin M Ashley, *Surgeon*
Stanley Katz, *Surgeon*
EMP: 318 **Privately Held**
WEB: www.memorialcare.org
SIC: 8062 General medical & surgical hospitals
HQ: Long Beach Medical Center
　2801 Atlantic Ave Fl 2
　Long Beach CA 90806
　562 933-2000

(P-20849)
LONG BEACH MEMORIAL MED CTR
1057 Pine Ave, Long Beach (90813-3118)
PHONE................................562 933-0432
Renee May, *Branch Mgr*
Caroline Gordon,
EMP: 318 **Privately Held**
WEB: www.memorialcare.org
SIC: 8062 General medical & surgical hospitals
HQ: Long Beach Medical Center
　2801 Atlantic Ave Fl 2
　Long Beach CA 90806
　562 933-2000

(P-20850)
LONGWOOD MANAGEMENT CORP
Also Called: Shea Convalescent Hospital
7716 Pickering Ave, Whittier (90602-2001)
PHONE................................562 693-5240
Richard Esconrias, *Manager*
Eva Santiago, *Human Res Dir*
Dory Alcazar, *Marketing Staff*
Kesheng Wu, *Director*
EMP: 124
SALES (corp-wide): 179.6MM **Privately Held**
WEB: www.longwoodmgmt.com
SIC: 8062 8011 General medical & surgical hospitals; skilled nursing facilities; offices & clinics of medical doctors
PA: Longwood Management Corp.
　4032 Wilshire Blvd Fl 6
　Los Angeles CA 90010
　213 389-6900

(P-20851)
LONGWOOD MANAGEMENT CORP
Also Called: Northridge Nursing Center
7836 Reseda Blvd, Reseda (91335-1902)
PHONE................................818 881-7414
Deffie Biczi, *General Mgr*
EMP: 124

SALES (corp-wide): 179.6MM **Privately Held**
WEB: www.longwoodmgmt.com
SIC: 8062 General medical & surgical hospitals
PA: Longwood Management Corp.
　4032 Wilshire Blvd Fl 6
　Los Angeles CA 90010
　213 389-6900

(P-20852)
LOS ALAMITOS MEDICAL CTR INC (HQ)
3751 Katella Ave, Los Alamitos (90720-3113)
P.O. Box 533 (90720-0533)
PHONE................................714 826-6400
Kent Clayton, *CEO*
Alice Livingood, *President*
Margaret Watkins, *President*
Richard Gonsalves, *Lab Dir*
Min Sung, *Business Dir*
EMP: 1100 **EST:** 1970
SQ FT: 900
SALES (est): 157.9MM
SALES (corp-wide): 17.6B **Publicly Held**
WEB: www.losalamitosmedctr.com
SIC: 8062 General medical & surgical hospitals
PA: Tenet Healthcare Corporation
　14201 Dallas Pkwy
　Dallas TX 75254
　469 893-2200

(P-20853)
LOS ROBLES REGIONAL MED CTR
Also Called: Neuroscience Gamma Knife Ctr
2200 Lynn Rd, Thousand Oaks (91360-2071)
PHONE................................805 494-0880
Cherrie De La La Cruz, *Principal*
James Modlinger, *Med Doctor*
Michael Papanicolaou, *Med Doctor*
Alan Rashkin, *Med Doctor*
EMP: 306 **Publicly Held**
WEB: www.losrobleshospital.com
SIC: 8062 General medical & surgical hospitals
HQ: Los Robles Regional Medical Center
　215 W Janss Rd
　Thousand Oaks CA 91360

(P-20854)
LOS ROBLES REGIONAL MED CTR (DH)
Also Called: HCA HEALTHCARE
215 W Janss Rd, Thousand Oaks (91360-1847)
P.O. Box 550, Nashville TN (37202-0550)
PHONE................................805 497-2727
Natalie Mussi, *Officer*
Laurie Holoff, *Records Dir*
Maureen Nicols, *COO*
Nancy Weeks, *COO*
Craig Corley, *Officer*
◆ **EMP:** 1119 **EST:** 1978
SQ FT: 475
SALES: 334K **Publicly Held**
WEB: www.losrobleshospital.com
SIC: 8062 General medical & surgical hospitals
HQ: Hca Inc.
　1 Park Plz
　Nashville TN 37203
　615 344-9551

(P-20855)
MAIN STREET SPECIALTY SURGERY
280 S Mn St Ste 100, Orange (92868)
PHONE................................714 704-1900
Betty Hoogenban, *Director*
Tammy Tanner, *Manager*
EMP: 60 **EST:** 2002
SALES (est): 36.7MM **Privately Held**
WEB: www.hoagorthopedicinstitute.com
SIC: 8062 General medical & surgical hospitals

(P-20856)
MARIAN COMMUNITY CLINIC
117 W Bunny Ave, Santa Maria
(93458-2805)
PHONE.....................805 739-3867
Eugen Alarco, *CEO*
Lupe Terrones, *Director*
EMP: 240 EST: 1997
SALES (est): 6.6MM **Privately Held**
WEB: www.dignityhealth.org
SIC: **8062** General medical & surgical hospitals
HQ: Dignity Health
185 Berry St Ste 200
San Francisco CA 94107
415 438-5500

(P-20857)
MEDICAL CENTER GIFT SHOP
Also Called: Medical Center of Garden Grove
12601 Garden Grove Blvd, Garden Grove
(92843-1908)
PHONE.....................714 537-7100
Prem Reddy, *Ch of Bd*
Virg Nabutas, *CEO*
Hassan Alkhouli, *Officer*
Asaad Hakim, *Med Doctor*
EMP: 68 EST: 1989
SALES (est): 1MM **Privately Held**
WEB: www.gardengrovehospital.com
SIC: **8062** General medical & surgical hospitals

(P-20858)
MEMORIAL HEALTH SERVICES (PA)
Also Called: MEMORIAL CARE MEDICAL CENTERS
17360 Brookhurst St # 160, Fountain Valley
(92708-3720)
P.O. Box 20894 (92728-0894)
PHONE.....................714 377-2900
Barry Arbuckle, *President*
Aaron Coley, *CFO*
Karen Testman, *CFO*
Rick Graniere, *Treasurer*
Peter Knudson, *Bd of Directors*
EMP: 1435 EST: 1937
SALES: 2.5B **Privately Held**
WEB: www.memorialcare.org
SIC: **8062** General medical & surgical hospitals

(P-20859)
MEMORIAL HEALTHTEC LABRATORIES (DH)
2865 Atlantic Ave Ste 203, Long Beach
(90806-7426)
PHONE.....................562 933-0777
Sandra Reese, *President*
Jeanine Haller, *Opers Staff*
Robert Nagourney, *Oncology*
Brooke Caldwell, *Med Doctor*
Renee Lee, *Med Doctor*
EMP: 50 EST: 1995
SALES (est): 5.2MM **Privately Held**
WEB: www.memorialcare.org
SIC: **8062** General medical & surgical hospitals
HQ: Long Beach Medical Center
2801 Atlantic Ave Fl 2
Long Beach CA 90806
562 933-2000

(P-20860)
MEMORIAL HLTH SVCS - UNIV CAL (PA)
2801 Atlantic Ave, Long Beach
(90806-1701)
PHONE.....................562 933-2000
Edward Quilligan, *CEO*
Diana Hendel, *President*
Darrel Brownell, *Treasurer*
Michael Perry, *Vice Pres*
Kelly Hales, *Business Dir*
EMP: 3816 EST: 1907
SQ FT: 1,000,000
SALES (est): 363.5MM **Privately Held**
WEB: www.memorialcare.org
SIC: **8062** 8741 General medical & surgical hospitals; management services

(P-20861)
MEMORLCARE SRGCAL CTR AT ORNGE
Also Called: Orange Coast Ctr For Surgl Cr
18111 Brookhurst St # 3200, Fountain Valley (92708-6728)
PHONE.....................714 369-1100
Dana Pratt, *CEO*
David Chim, *Technician*
Amanda Justus, *Purch Dir*
Amanda Bonanno, *Materials Mgr*
Marcia Lanum, *Opers Staff*
EMP: 65 EST: 2011
SALES (est): 66.7MM
SALES (corp-wide): 257.1B **Publicly Held**
WEB: www.orangecoastcenter.com
SIC: **8062** General medical & surgical hospitals
PA: Unitedhealth Group Incorporated
9900 Bren Rd E Ste 300w
Minnetonka MN 55343
952 936-1300

(P-20862)
METHODIST HOSP SOUTHERN CAL (PA)
300 W Huntington Dr, Arcadia
(91007-3402)
PHONE.....................626 898-8000
Dan F Ausman, *CEO*
Rose Dealba, *Officer*
Clifford R Daniels, *Senior VP*
William E Grigg, *Senior VP*
Steven A Sisto, *Senior VP*
EMP: 933 EST: 1903
SQ FT: 100,000
SALES (est): 299MM **Privately Held**
WEB: www.methodisthospital.org
SIC: **8062** General medical & surgical hospitals

(P-20863)
MISSION AMBLTORY SRGCENTER LTD
26730 Crown Valley Pkwy, Mission Viejo
(92691-6364)
PHONE.....................949 364-2201
Peter F Bastone, *President*
Kenneth McFarland, *CFO*
Eileen Ihauble, *Exec Dir*
EMP: 77 EST: 1990
SQ FT: 15,000
SALES (est): 36.3MM **Privately Held**
WEB: www.mission4health.com
SIC: **8062** General medical & surgical hospitals

(P-20864)
MISSION HOSP REGIONAL MED CTR (PA)
27700 Medical Center Rd, Mission Viejo
(92691-6426)
PHONE.....................949 364-1400
Seth Peigen, *CEO*
Robert Deshaies, *Treasurer*
Katherine Davis, *Officer*
Terri Covert, *Vice Pres*
Martha Ann Fitzpatrick, *Vice Pres*
EMP: 1349 EST: 1941
SQ FT: 750,000
SALES (est): 322.5MM **Privately Held**
WEB: www.mission4health.com
SIC: **8062** General medical & surgical hospitals

(P-20865)
MONTEREY PARK HOSPITAL
Also Called: Monterey Park Hospital
900 S Atlantic Blvd, Monterey Park
(91754-4780)
PHONE.....................626 570-9000
Philip A Cohen, *CEO*
Jose Reyes,
Bobbi Diamond, *Records Dir*
Robert M Dubbs, *President*
Andrew Grim, *CFO*
EMP: 150 EST: 1972
SQ FT: 90,575
SALES (est): 74.7MM
SALES (corp-wide): 574.5MM **Privately Held**
WEB: www.montereyparkhosp.com
SIC: **8062** General medical & surgical hospitals

PA: Ahmc Healthcare Inc.
506 W Valley Blvd Ste 300
San Gabriel CA 91776
626 943-7526

(P-20866)
MOTION PICTURE AND TV FUND (PA)
Also Called: Bob Hope Health Center
23388 Mulholland Dr # 200, Woodland Hills
(91364-2733)
P.O. Box 51151, Los Angeles (90051-5451)
PHONE.....................818 876-1777
Robert Beitcher, *CEO*
Bob Pisano, *Ch of Bd*
Jay Roth, *Treasurer*
Sharon Siefert, *Vice Pres*
Robert Jensen, *Executive*
EMP: 688 EST: 1924
SQ FT: 50,000
SALES: 23MM **Privately Held**
WEB: www.mptf.com
SIC: **8062** 8051 8011 8351 General medical & surgical hospitals; convalescent home with continuous nursing care; medical centers; child day care services; individual & family services; retirement hotel operation

(P-20867)
MOUNTAIN VIEW CHILD CARE INC (PA)
Also Called: Totally Kids Rhbilitation Hosp
1720 Mountain View Ave, Loma Linda
(92354-1799)
PHONE.....................909 796-6915
Doug Pagett, *CEO*
Toni Callicott, *Vice Chairman*
Cynthia Capetillo, *CFO*
Donald Nydam, *Vice Pres*
Cindy Capetillo, *Executive*
EMP: 275 EST: 1972
SALES (est): 51.8MM **Privately Held**
WEB: www.totallykids.com
SIC: **8062** 8052 8051 General medical & surgical hospitals; intermediate care facilities; skilled nursing care facilities

(P-20868)
MOUNTAINS COMMUNITY HOSP FNDTN
29101 Hospital Rd, Lake Arrowhead
(92352-9706)
P.O. Box 70 (92352-0070)
PHONE.....................909 336-3651
Don Willerth, *CEO*
Debra Saddlemire, *Opers Staff*
Renee Limpus, *Education*
Steve Early, *Nursing Dir*
Cyndy Davidson-Bennet, *Hlthcr Dir*
EMP: 180 EST: 1957
SQ FT: 18,500 **Privately Held**
WEB: www.mchcares.com
SIC: **8062** 8051 General medical & surgical hospitals; skilled nursing care facilities

(P-20869)
NIX HOSPITALS SYSTEM LLC (HQ)
Also Called: Nix Healthcare System
3415 S Sepulveda Blvd # 900, Los Angeles
(90034-6981)
PHONE.....................210 271-1800
John F Strieby, *President*
Rob Elders, *Admin Sec*
EMP: 101 EST: 2011
SALES (est): 72.3MM
SALES (corp-wide): 3.4B **Privately Held**
WEB: www.nixhealth.com
SIC: **8062** General medical & surgical hospitals
PA: Prospect Medical Holdings, Inc.
3415 S Sepulveda Blvd # 9
Los Angeles CA 90034
310 943-4500

(P-20870)
NORTH KERN S TULARE HOSP DST
Also Called: Delano Dst Sklled Nrsing Fclty
1509 Tokay St, Delano (93215-3603)
PHONE.....................661 720-2126
Silva Soto, *President*
Femme Adebayo, *Principal*
Heather McDougal, *Principal*

Jaime Mendoza, *Principal*
Dio Telmo, *Administration*
EMP: 230 EST: 1966
SALES (est): 13.8MM **Privately Held**
WEB: www.nksthd.org
SIC: **8062** General medical & surgical hospitals

(P-20871)
NORTHERN INYO HEALTHCARE DST
Also Called: NORTHERN INYO HOSPITAL
150 Pioneer Ln, Bishop (93514-2556)
PHONE.....................760 873-5811
Victoria Alexander-Lane, *CEO*
Nickoline Hathaway, *Partner*
Marie Boyd, *Vice Chairman*
M C Hubbard, *President*
Peter Watercott, *Treasurer*
EMP: 402 EST: 1946
SQ FT: 55,000
SALES (est): 25MM **Privately Held**
WEB: www.nih.org
SIC: **8062** General medical & surgical hospitals

(P-20872)
NORTHRIDGE EMERGENCY MED GROUP
18300 Roscoe Blvd, Northridge
(91325-4105)
PHONE.....................818 700-5603
Stephen Jones, *Partner*
EMP: 60 EST: 1988
SQ FT: 120
SALES (est): 711.5K **Privately Held**
SIC: **8062** General medical & surgical hospitals

(P-20873)
NORTHRIDGE HOSP FOUNDATION AUX
18300 Roscoe Blvd, Northridge
(91325-4105)
PHONE.....................818 885-5341
Brian Hammel, *President*
Dr Frederick Gruneck, *Principal*
EMP: 60 EST: 1959
SQ FT: 1,500
SALES (est): 6MM **Privately Held**
WEB: www.supportnorthridge.org
SIC: **8062** General medical & surgical hospitals

(P-20874)
OLYMPIA HEALTH CARE LLC
Also Called: Olympia Medical Center
5900 W Olympic Blvd, Los Angeles
(90036-4671)
P.O. Box 351209 (90035-9609)
PHONE.....................323 938-3161
John A Calderone, *CEO*
Babur Ozkan, *CFO*
Eli Mingail, *Business Dir*
Bruce Com, *Office Mgr*
Maria Shah, *CTO*
EMP: 875 EST: 2004
SQ FT: 500,000
SALES (est): 185.8MM **Privately Held**
WEB: www.olympiamc.com
SIC: **8062** Hospital, affiliated with AMA residency
PA: Alecto Healthcare Services Llc
16310 Bake Pkwy Ste 200
Irvine CA 92618

(P-20875)
ORANGE COAST MEMORIAL MED CTR (HQ)
9920 Talbert Ave, Fountain Valley
(92708-5153)
PHONE.....................714 378-7000
Toll Free:.....................888
Marcia Manker, *President*
Aaron Coley, *CFO*
Steve McNamara, *CFO*
Xiaodong LI, *Executive*
Stan Hill, *Business Dir*
EMP: 984 EST: 1995
SQ FT: 40,361
SALES (est): 259MM **Privately Held**
WEB: www.memorialcare.org
SIC: **8062** General medical & surgical hospitals

(P-20876)
ORANGETREE CONVALESCENT HOSP
Also Called: Plott Family Care Centers
4000 Harrison St, Riverside (92503-3599)
PHONE..................951 785-6060
Elizabeth Plott, *President*
EMP: 120 EST: 1983
SALES (est): 11.4MM **Privately Held**
SIC: 8062 8051 General medical & surgical hospitals; skilled nursing care facilities

(P-20877)
ORTHOPAEDIC HOSPITAL (PA)
Also Called: ORTHOPAEDIC INSTITUTE FOR CHIL
403 W Adams Blvd, Los Angeles (90007-2664)
P.O. Box 60132 (90060-0132)
PHONE..................213 742-1000
Anthony A Scaduto, *President*
Diane Moon, *CFO*
Nicholas V McClure, *Bd of Directors*
Harry McKellop, *Professor*
Doris Quon, *Director*
EMP: 168 EST: 1923
SQ FT: 105,000
SALES: 62.3MM **Privately Held**
WEB: www.ortho-institute.org
SIC: 8062 8011 General medical & surgical hospitals; primary care medical clinic

(P-20878)
PACIFIC HEALTH CORPORATION
Also Called: Anaheim General Hospital
3699 Wilshire Blvd # 540, Los Angeles (90010-2723)
PHONE..................714 619-7797
Fax: 714 761-1295
EMP: 500
SALES (corp-wide): 93MM **Privately Held**
SIC: 8062 General Acute Care Hospital
HQ: Pacific Health Corporation
14642 Newport Ave
Tustin CA 92780
714 838-9600

(P-20879)
PACIFIC OCCPTNAL MEDICINE SVCS
2776 Pacific Ave, Long Beach (90806-2613)
PHONE..................562 997-2290
EMP: 50
SALES (est): 753.3K **Privately Held**
SIC: 8062 General Medical And Surgical Hosps,Nsk

(P-20880)
PACIFICA OF VALLEY CORPORATION
Also Called: Pacifica Hospital of Valley
9449 San Fernando Rd, Sun Valley (91352-1421)
PHONE..................818 767-3310
Paul Tuft, *Ch of Bd*
Ayman Mousa, *CEO*
Maria Gomez, *Social Dir*
Michelle Koupai, *Security Dir*
Dean Morford, *Engineer*
EMP: 607 EST: 1996
SQ FT: 148,020
SALES (est): 121.1MM **Privately Held**
WEB: www.pacificahospital.com
SIC: 8062 Hospital, affiliated with AMA residency

(P-20881)
PALO VERDE HEALTH CARE DST
Also Called: Palo Verde Hospital
250 N 1st St, Blythe (92225-1702)
PHONE..................760 922-4115
Sandra J Anaya, *CEO*
Dennis Rutherford, *CFO*
EMP: 180 EST: 1938
SALES: 23.8MM **Privately Held**
WEB: www.paloverdehospital.org
SIC: 8062 8069 General medical & surgical hospitals; specialty hospitals, except psychiatric

(P-20882)
PALO VERDE HOSPITAL ASSN
250 N 1st St, Blythe (92225-1702)
PHONE..................760 922-4115
Sandra J Anaya, *CEO*
Jim Carney, *President*
Larry Blitz, *CEO*
Christa Rohde, *CFO*
Samuel Burton, *Treasurer*
EMP: 135 EST: 1948
SQ FT: 44,000
SALES (est): 30.1MM **Privately Held**
WEB: www.paloverdehospital.org
SIC: 8062 General medical & surgical hospitals

(P-20883)
PALOS VRDES FMLY IMMDATE MED C
Also Called: Immediate Medical Care Center
26516 Crenshaw Blvd, Pls Vrds Pnsl (90274-3970)
PHONE..................310 541-7911
Dr Christopher Traughber, *Partner*
Nasim Golzar, *Partner*
Dirk Ruffin, *Partner*
EMP: 50 EST: 1982
SALES (est): 9.7MM **Privately Held**
SIC: 8062 General medical & surgical hospitals

(P-20884)
PAMC LTD (PA)
Also Called: Pamc Health Foundation
531 W College St, Los Angeles (90012-2315)
PHONE..................213 624-8411
John Edwards, *CEO*
Jessica Baird, *Manager*
Lisa Young, *Relations*
EMP: 530 EST: 1989
SQ FT: 75,600
SALES (est): 35.3MM **Privately Held**
SIC: 8062 General medical & surgical hospitals

(P-20885)
PARACELSUS LOS ANGELES COMM
4081 E Olympic Blvd, Los Angeles (90023-3330)
PHONE..................323 267-0477
Lou Rubino, *Acting CEO*
Robert Vasquez, *Records Dir*
Omar Ramirez, *COO*
Ketih Levy, *Officer*
Andrew Perez, *Security Dir*
EMP: 250
SALES: 141.6MM **Privately Held**
WEB: www.lach-la.com
SIC: 8062 General medical & surgical hospitals

(P-20886)
PARKVIEW CMNTY HOSP MED CTR
3865 Jackson St, Riverside (92503-3919)
PHONE..................951 354-7404
Norm Martin, *President*
Doug Drumwright, *CEO*
Carlos Carreron, *CFO*
Ken Culver, *Business Dir*
Karen Descent, *Ch Nursing Ofcr*
EMP: 1149
SQ FT: 132,651
SALES: 162.7MM **Privately Held**
WEB: www.pchmc.org
SIC: 8062 8011 General medical & surgical hospitals; offices & clinics of medical doctors
PA: Doctors Hospital Of Riverside Llc
3865 Jackson St
Riverside CA 92503
951 354-7404

(P-20887)
PERRIS VALLEY CMNTY HOSP LLC (PA)
Also Called: Vista Specialty Hosp Riverside
2224 Medical Center Dr, Perris (92571-2638)
PHONE..................951 436-5000
James Linhares, *Mng Member*
Robert Vanbuskirk, *Purch Dir*
Marc C Ferrell, *Mng Member*

Marc A Furstman, *Mng Member*
ARA Tavitian, *Mng Member*
EMP: 226 EST: 2006
SALES (est): 24.7MM **Privately Held**
WEB: www.kindredhealthcare.com
SIC: 8062 General medical & surgical hospitals

(P-20888)
PHYSICIANS FOR HEALTHY HOSPITA
Also Called: Menifee Valley Hospital Center
28400 Mccall Blvd, Sun City (92585-9658)
PHONE..................951 679-8888
Jeffrey Lang, *CEO*
David S Johnson, *Med Doctor*
EMP: 300
SALES (corp-wide): 1.9B **Privately Held**
WEB:
www.physiciansforhealthyhospitals.com
SIC: 8062 General medical & surgical hospitals
HQ: Kpc Global Medical Canters, Inc.
1117 E Devonshire Ave
Hemet CA 92543
951 652-2811

(P-20889)
PIH HEALTH INC (PA)
Also Called: Integrted Healthcare Dlvry Sys
12401 Washington Blvd, Whittier (90602-1006)
PHONE..................562 698-0811
Jane Dicus, *Ch of Bd*
Richard Atwood, *Vice Chairman*
Anita Chou, *CFO*
Kenton Woods, *Treasurer*
Daniel Adams, *Vice Pres*
EMP: 1100 EST: 1981
SQ FT: 500,000
SALES (est): 923K **Privately Held**
WEB: www.pihhealth.org
SIC: 8062 8011 General medical & surgical hospitals; offices & clinics of medical doctors

(P-20890)
PIH HEALTH GOOD SAMARITAN HOSP (HQ)
Also Called: General Acute Care Hospital
1225 Wilshire Blvd, Los Angeles (90017-1901)
PHONE..................213 977-2121
James West, *CEO*
Charles Munger, *Ch of Bd*
Alan Ino, *CFO*
Robert Richards, *Treasurer*
Nancy Clark, *Vice Pres*
▲ EMP: 29709 EST: 1885
SQ FT: 10,000
SALES: 6MM
SALES (corp-wide): 923K **Privately Held**
WEB: www.pihhealth.org
SIC: 8062 Hospital, affiliated with AMA residency
PA: Pih Health, Inc.
12401 Washington Blvd
Whittier CA 90602
562 698-0811

(P-20891)
PIH HEALTH HOSPITAL - DOWNEY (HQ)
Also Called: General Acute Care Hospital
11500 Brookshire Ave, Downey (90241-4917)
PHONE..................562 698-0811
James R West, *President*
Bryan Smolskis, *COO*
Greg Williams, *CFO*
Kenton Woods, *Treasurer*
Rosalio Lopez MD, *Senior VP*
EMP: 1149 EST: 1956
SQ FT: 225,000
SALES (est): 154.8MM
SALES (corp-wide): 651.1MM **Privately Held**
WEB: www.pihhealth.org
SIC: 8062 General medical & surgical hospitals
PA: Pih Health Whittier Hospital
12401 Washington Blvd
Whittier CA 90602
562 698-0811

(P-20892)
PIH HEALTH HOSPITAL - WHITTI
Also Called: Downey Regional Medical Center
11500 Brookshire Ave, Downey (90241-4917)
PHONE..................562 904-5482
James R West, *CEO*
Elnaz Shahabi-Abney, *Family Practiti*
Kelly Murray, *Anesthesiology*
George Torres, *Anesthesiolog*
Jeremiah Pamer, *Internal Med*
EMP: 1150
SALES (corp-wide): 651.1MM **Privately Held**
WEB: www.pihhealth.org
SIC: 8062 8071 General medical & surgical hospitals; medical laboratories
PA: Pih Health Whittier Hospial
12401 Washington Blvd
Whittier CA 90602
562 698-0811

(P-20893)
PIH HEALTH WHITTIER HOSPITAL (PA)
Also Called: General Acute Ca e Hospital
12401 Washington Blvd, Whittier (90602-1006)
PHONE..................562 698-0811
James R West, *CEO*
Nancy Stoner, *Records Dir*
Anita Chou, *CFO*
Peggy Chulack, *Officer*
Ramona Pratt, *Officer*
EMP: 1900 EST: 1954
SQ FT: 500,000
SALES (est): 651.1MM **Privately Held**
WEB: www.pihhealth.org
SIC: 8062 General medica & surgical hospitals

(P-20894)
PIONEER MEDICAL GROUP INC
10230 Artesia Blvd # 300, Bellflower (90706-6763)
PHONE..................562 867-8681
Tanya Lee, *Manager*
Illya Quinones, *Hum Res Coord*
Jane Kong, *Family Practiti*
Kathleen Morgan, *Family Practiti*
Angelyn Moultrie-Lizana, *Family Practiti*
EMP: 72
SALES (corp-wide): 41.9MM **Privately Held**
WEB: www.pihhealth.org
SIC: 8062 General medical & surgical hospitals
PA: Pioneer Medical Group, Inc.
6557 Greenleaf Ave
Whittier CA 90601
562 597-4181

(P-20895)
PIONEER MEDICAL GROUP INC
2220 Clark Ave, Long Beach (90815-2521)
PHONE..................562 597-4181
Sadalia Sousa, *Manager*
EMP: 72
SALES (corp-wide): 41.9MM **Privately Held**
WEB: www.pihhealth.org
SIC: 8062 General medical & surgical hospitals
PA: Pioneer Medical Group, Inc.
6557 Greenleaf Ave
Whittier CA 90601
562 597-4181

(P-20896)
PIONEERS MEM HEALTHCARE DST (PA)
Also Called: PIONEERS MEMORIAL HOSPITAL
207 W Legion Rd, Brawley (92227-7780)
PHONE..................760 351-3333
Richard L Mendoza, *CEO*
Christopher C Lai,
Roger Armstrong, *CFO*
Daniel Heckathorne, *CFO*
Justina Aguirre, *Vice Pres*
EMP: 571 EST: 1947
SQ FT: 171,445
SALES: 115.4MM **Privately Held**
SIC: 8062 Hospital, affiliated with AMA residency

(P-20897)
PIPELINE HEALTH LLC (PA)
111 N Sepulveda Blvd # 21, Manhattan Beach (90266-6861)
PHONE..................310 379-2134
Andrei Soran, *CEO*
Mark R Bell,
EMP: 285 **EST:** 2014
SALES (est) 464.5MM **Privately Held**
WEB: www.pipelinehealth.us
SIC: 8062 General medical & surgical hospitals

(P-20898)
POMONA VALLEY HOSPITAL MED CTR (PA)
Also Called: Pvhmc
1798 N Garey Ave, Pomona (91767-2918)
PHONE..................909 865-9500
Richard E Yochum, *CEO*
Jasvir Sandhu,
Kurt Weinmeister, *COO*
Michael Nelson, *CFO*
Alan Smith, *Chairman*
EMP: 2121
SQ FT: 362,000
SALES: 658MM **Privately Held**
WEB: www.pvhmc.org
SIC: 8062 Hospital, medical school affiliated with residency

(P-20899)
PRESBYTERIAN HEALTH PHYSICIANS
6557 Greenleaf Ave, Whittier (90601-4108)
PHONE..................562 464-4717
Marvin Rice, *President*
Walter Price, *Director*
EMP: 311 **EST:** 1970
SQ FT: 72,000
SALES (est): 19.2MM
SALES (est): 923K **Privately Held**
WEB: www.pihhealth.org
SIC: 8062 General medical & surgical hospitals
PA: Pih Health, Inc.
12401 Washington Blvd
Whittier CA 90602
562 698-0811

(P-20900)
PRIME HALTHCARE FOUNDATION INC (PA)
3480 E Guasti Rd, Ontario (91761-7684)
PHONE..................909 235-4400
Prem Reddy, *CEO*
Jon Aquino, *COO*
Kavitha Bhatia, *Chief Mktg Ofcr*
Cheryl Johnson, *IT/INT Sup*
Marwa Ghouse, *Project Mgr*
EMP: 52 **EST:** 2006
SALES (est): 1B **Privately Held**
WEB: www.primehealthcare.com
SIC: 8062 General medical & surgical hospitals

(P-20901)
PRIME HEALTHCARE ANAHEIM LLC
Also Called: WEST ANAHEIM MEDICAL CENTER
3033 W Orange Ave, Anaheim (92804-3156)
PHONE..................714 827-3000
Virg Narbutas, *CEO*
Raghav Sharma, *Records Dir*
Kora Guoyavatin, *CFO*
Reena Mahadevan, *Engineer*
EMP: 800 **EST:** 1963
SQ FT: 180,000
SALES: 123.9MM
SALES (corp-wide): 1B **Privately Held**
WEB: www.westanaheimmedctr.com
SIC: 8062 Hospital, affiliated with AMA residency
HQ: Prime Healthcare Services Inc
3480 E Guasti Rd
Ontario CA 91761

(P-20902)
PRIME HEALTHCARE CENTINELA LLC
Also Called: Centinela Hospital Medical Ctr
555 E Hardy St, Inglewood (90301-4011)
PHONE..................310 673-4660
Linda Bradley, *CEO*
Mohammed Albark, *Lab Dir*
Jeffrey Benson, *Administration*
Matt Ewert, *Technician*
Kavya Kandula, *Technology*
EMP: 1500 **EST:** 1952
SALES (est): 269.9MM
SALES (corp-wide): 1B **Privately Held**
WEB: www.centinelamed.com
SIC: 8062 General medical & surgical hospitals
HQ: Prime Healthcare Services Inc
3480 E Guasti Rd
Ontario CA 91761

(P-20903)
PRIME HEALTHCARE SERVICES-MONT
5000 San Bernardino St, Montclair (91763-2326)
PHONE..................909 625-5411
EMP: 1142
SALES (est): 89MM
SALES (corp-wide): 1B **Privately Held**
WEB: www.montclair-hospital.org
SIC: 8062 General medical & surgical hospitals
PA: Prime Healthcare Foundation, Inc.
3480 E Guasti Rd
Ontario CA 91761
909 235-4400

(P-20904)
PRIME HLTHCARE HNTNGTON BCH LL
Also Called: Huntington Beach Hospital
17772 Beach Blvd, Huntington Beach (92647-6819)
PHONE..................714 843-5000
Prem Reddy, *CEO*
Ravi Alla, *Vice Pres*
Mark Bell, *Med Doctor*
Patricia Cody,
Eileen Fisler,
EMP: 480 **EST:** 1957
SQ FT: 100,000
SALES (est): 140.3MM
SALES (corp-wide): 1B **Privately Held**
WEB: www.hbhospital.org
SIC: 8062 General medical & surgical hospitals
HQ: Prime Healthcare Services Inc
3480 E Guasti Rd
Ontario CA 91761

(P-20905)
PRIME HLTHCARE SRVCS-MNTCLAIR
Also Called: Urgent Care Center
5000 San Bernardino St, Montclair (91763-2326)
PHONE..................909 625-5411
David Chu, *Manager*
Anthony Ramirez, *Director*
EMP: 88
SALES (corp-wide): 1B **Privately Held**
WEB: www.montclair-hospital.org
SIC: 8062 General medical & surgical hospitals
HQ: Prime Healthcare Services-Montclair, Llc
5000 San Bernardino St
Montclair CA 91763
909 625-5411

(P-20906)
PRIME HLTHCARE SRVCS-MNTCLAIR (DH)
Also Called: Prime Healthcare Svcs III LLC
5000 San Bernardino St, Montclair (91763-2326)
PHONE..................909 625-5411
Jennifer Ramirez, *Exec Sec*
Prem Reddy, *Chairman*
David Chu, *Manager*
EMP: 362 **EST:** 1999

SALES: 55.5MM
SALES (corp-wide): 1B **Privately Held**
WEB: www.montclair-hospital.org
SIC: 8062 General medical & surgical hospitals

(P-20907)
PRIME HLTHCARE SVCS - ENCINO H
16237 Ventura Blvd, Encino (91436-2201)
PHONE..................818 995-5000
Bockhi Park, *CEO*
Prem Reddy, *President*
EMP: 400 **EST:** 2008
SALES: 52.4MM
SALES (corp-wide): 1B **Privately Held**
WEB: www.encinomed.org
SIC: 8062 General medical & surgical hospitals
HQ: Prime Healthcare Services Inc
3480 E Guasti Rd
Ontario CA 91761

(P-20908)
PRIME HLTHCARE SVCS - PMPA LLC (DH)
Also Called: Pampa Regional Medical Center
3300 E Guasti Rd Ste 300, Ontario (91761-8657)
PHONE..................909 235-4400
Brad Morse, *CEO*
Steven Smith, *CFO*
Mandie McMahon, *QA Dir*
Joy Patton, *Info Tech Dir*
Michelle Arnold, *Surgeon*
EMP: 268 **EST:** 1960
SQ FT: 150,000
SALES (est): 37.1MM
SALES (corp-wide): 1B **Privately Held**
WEB: www.primehealthcare.com
SIC: 8062 General medical & surgical hospitals

(P-20909)
PRIME HLTHCARE SVCS - SAN DMAS
Also Called: San Dimas Community Hospital
1350 W Covina Blvd, San Dimas (91773-3245)
PHONE..................909 599-6811
Gregory Brentano, *CEO*
Sumana Chenna, *Records Dir*
Dan Galles, *CFO*
Maria Cordon,
EMP: 350 **EST:** 1982
SQ FT: 90,000
SALES (est): 50.2MM
SALES (corp-wide): 1B **Privately Held**
WEB: www.sandimashospital.com
SIC: 8062 General medical & surgical hospitals
HQ: Prime Healthcare Services Inc
3480 E Guasti Rd
Ontario CA 91761

(P-20910)
PRIME HLTHCARE SVCS - SHRMAN O
Also Called: Sherman Oaks Hospital
4929 Van Nuys Blvd, Sherman Oaks (91403-1702)
PHONE..................818 981-7111
Prem Reddy, *CEO*
John Deady, *CFO*
Micaela Tetangco, *Hum Res Coord*
Gail Goldstein, *Director*
EMP: 500 **EST:** 2006
SQ FT: 36,000
SALES (est): 103.4MM
SALES (corp-wide): 1B **Privately Held**
WEB: www.shermanoakshospital.org
SIC: 8062 General medical & surgical hospitals
HQ: Prime Healthcare Services Inc
3480 E Guasti Rd
Ontario CA 91761

(P-20911)
PRIME HLTHCARE SVCS - ST JOHN (DH)
3500 S 4th St, Ontario (91761)
PHONE..................913 680-6000

Randall G Nyp, *CEO*
EMP: 50 **EST:** 1864
SQ FT: 96,000
SALES (est): 89.1MM
SALES (corp-wide): 1B **Privately Held**
WEB: www.montclair-hospital.org
SIC: 8062 General medical & surgical hospitals
WEB: www.stjohnleavenworth.com
SIC: 8062 General medical & surgical hospitals

(P-20912)
PROVIDENCE HEALTH & SERVICES F
Also Called: Providnce Holy Cross Foundation
501 S Buena Vista St, Burbank (91505-4809)
PHONE..................818 843-5111
Patricia Modrzejewski, *CEO*
James Reiner, *CFO*
Lee Kanon Alpert, *Chairman*
EMP: 2000 **EST:** 1980
SALES (est): 19.1MM **Privately Held**
SIC: 8062 General medical & surgical hospitals

(P-20913)
PROVIDENCE HEALTH & SERVICES S
Also Called: Providence Little Company of M
1300 W 7th St, San Pedro (90732-3505)
PHONE..................310 832-3311
EMP: 99
SALES (est): 4.7MM **Privately Held**
SIC: 8062 General Medical And Surgical Hospitals, Nsk

(P-20914)
PROVIDENCE HEALTH & SVCS - ORE
Also Called: Providence Holy Cross Med Ctr
15031 Rinaldi St, Mission Hills (91345-1207)
PHONE..................818 365-8051
David Mast, *Branch Mgr*
Daniel Rohrer, *Managing Dir*
Cynthia Simmons, *Executive Asst*
Sonia Ramos, *Administration*
Georgia Colkitt, *Research*
EMP: 117
SALES (corp-wide): 32.7MM **Privately Held**
WEB: www.providence.org
SIC: 8062 General medical & surgical hospitals
HQ: Providence Health & Services - Oregon
1801 Lind Ave Sw
Renton WA 98057
425 525-3355

(P-20915)
PROVIDENCE HEALTH SYSTEM
Providence St Joseph Med Ctr
501 S Buena Vista St, Burbank (91505-4809)
PHONE..................818 843-5111
Georgianne Johnson, *COO*
Arnie Schaffer, *CEO*
Cathy Boucher, *Office Mgr*
Kumar Doshi, *Finance*
Andrew Werts, *Marketing Staff*
EMP: 2000
SALES (corp-wide): 32.7MM **Privately Held**
WEB: www.providence.org
SIC: 8062 General medical & surgical hospitals
HQ: Providence Health System-Southern California
1801 Lind Ave Sw
Renton WA 98057
425 525-3355

(P-20916)
PROVIDENCE HOLY CROSS MEDICAL (PA)
15031 Rinaldi St, Mission Hills (91345-1207)
PHONE..................818 365-8051
Lee Kanon Alpert, *Chairman*
Peter Richman, *Vice Chairman*
June E Drake, *CEO*
Chloe Medrano, *Officer*
Jennifer Mau, *Comms Dir*
▲ **EMP:** 1558 **EST:** 1960

PRODUCTS & SVCS

SALES (est): 207MM **Privately Held**
SIC: **8062** General medical & surgical hospitals

(P-20917)
PROVIDENCE ST JOHNS HLTH CTR
2121 Santa Monica Blvd, Santa Monica (90404-2303)
PHONE..................................310 829-6562
Marcel Loh, *CEO*
Donald Larsen Jr, *Officer*
Virginia Borncamp, *Vice Pres*
Justin Freed, *Vice Pres*
Leanne Park, *Risk Mgmt Dir*
EMP: 350 EST: 1940
SQ FT: 60,000
SALES (est): 88MM **Privately Held**
SIC: **8062** General medical & surgical hospitals

(P-20918)
PROVIDENCE TARZANA MEDICAL CTR
18321 Clark St, Tarzana (91356-3501)
PHONE..................................818 881-0800
Dale Surowitz, *CEO*
Amgad Elsibai,
Nojan Toomari,
Diana Lau, *Records Dir*
Kathy Evans, *CEO*
EMP: 1300
SALES (est): 199.1MM **Privately Held**
WEB: www.tarzanacme.com
SIC: **8062** General medical & surgical hospitals

(P-20919)
QUEEN OF VALLEY HOSPITAL
1115 S Sunset Ave, West Covina (91790-3940)
PHONE..................................626 962-4011
Louis Conyers, *CFO*
Robert Curry, *CEO*
Elvia Foulke, *COO*
Gilbert Martin, *Med Doctor*
EMP: 80 EST: 2001
SALES (est): 67MM **Privately Held**
WEB: www.emanatehealth.org
SIC: **8062** General medical & surgical hospitals

(P-20920)
RAMONA RHBLTTION POST ACUTE CA
Also Called: Ramona Rhblttion Post Acute Ca
485 W Johnston Ave, Hemet (92543-7012)
PHONE..................................951 652-0011
Stan Leland, *President*
Heidi Vickers, *Officer*
Meredith Shipley, *Social Dir*
Jenny Kovar, *Administration*
Joy Bolechowski,
EMP: 120 EST: 1995
SQ FT: 30,000
SALES (est): 11.5MM **Privately Held**
WEB: www.ramona-rehab.com
SIC: **8062** 8051 General medical & surgical hospitals; convalescent home with continuous nursing care

(P-20921)
RANCHO CCAMONGA CMNTY HOSP LLC
Also Called: Rancho Speciality Hospital
10841 White Oak Ave, Rancho Cucamonga (91730-3817)
PHONE..................................909 581-6400
Marc C Ferrell,
Debroah Miller, *Business Dir*
Mark Ferrell,
Vartan Hovsetian,
ARA Tavitian,
EMP: 51 EST: 2005
SQ FT: 100,000
SALES (est): 10.1MM **Privately Held**
WEB: www.kindredhealthcare.com
SIC: **8062** Hospital, affiliated with AMA residency

(P-20922)
REDLANDS COMMUNITY HOSPITAL (PA)
350 Terracina Blvd, Redlands (92373-4897)
PHONE..................................909 335-5500
James R Holmes, *CEO*
Cherie Towers, *Bd of Directors*
Harvey Hansen, *Vice Pres*
Debbie Evans, *Social Dir*
Justin Miles, *Pharmacy Dir*
EMP: 97 EST: 1927
SALES: 372.7MM **Privately Held**
WEB: www.redlandshospital.org
SIC: **8062** General medical & surgical hospitals

(P-20923)
RIDGECREST REGIONAL HOSPITAL (PA)
Also Called: Southern Sierra Medical Clinic
1081 N China Lake Blvd, Ridgecrest (93555-3130)
PHONE..................................760 446-3551
James A Suver, *CEO*
Earl Ferguson, *Records Dir*
Charity Sevaaetasi, *Records Dir*
Barbara Badertscher, *COO*
Donna Kiser, *CFO*
EMP: 476 EST: 1962
SQ FT: 80,000
SALES (est): 129.9MM **Privately Held**
WEB: www.rrh.org
SIC: **8062** General medical & surgical hospitals

(P-20924)
RIVERSIDE CMNTY HLTH SYSTEMS (DH)
Also Called: Riverside Community Hospital
4445 Magnolia Ave Fl 6, Riverside (92501-4135)
PHONE..................................951 788-3000
Partrick Brilliant, *President*
Mukesh Gupta,
Donald Massee, *Ch Radiology*
Doug Long, *COO*
Tracey Fernandez, *CFO*
EMP: 1186 EST: 1901
SQ FT: 386,100
SALES (est): 245.2MM **Publicly Held**
WEB: www.riversidecommunityhospital.com
SIC: **8062** 8011 General medical & surgical hospitals; offices & clinics of medical doctors
HQ: Hca Inc.
1 Park Plz
Nashville TN 37203
615 344-9551

(P-20925)
RIVERSIDE UNIV HLTH SYS FNDTIO (PA)
Also Called: RIVERSIDE COUNTY REGIONAL MEDI
4065 County Circle Dr, Riverside (92503-3410)
PHONE..................................951 358-5000
Douglas D Bagley, *CEO*
Monica Kief-Garcia, *Ch Radiology*
Dana Kearney, *Records Dir*
Ellie Bennett, *COO*
David Runke, *CFO*
EMP: 773 EST: 1989
SALES: 2MM **Privately Held**
WEB: www.ruhealth.org
SIC: **8062** General medical & surgical hospitals

(P-20926)
SADDLEBACK MEMORIAL MED CTR (HQ)
24451 Health Center Dr # 1, Laguna Hills (92653-3689)
PHONE..................................949 837-4500
Steve Geidt, *CEO*
Julio Duarte,
Barry Arbuckle, *President*
Catherine Shitara, *COO*
Adolfo Chanez, *CFO*
EMP: 1020 EST: 1969
SQ FT: 195,000

SALES (est): 349.1MM **Privately Held**
WEB: www.memorialcare.org
SIC: **8062** 8011 8093 8099 General medical & surgical hospitals; medical centers; diabetes specialist, physician/surgeon; cardiologist & cardio-vascular specialist; pediatrician; rehabilitation center, outpatient treatment; blood related health services; medical laboratories; cancer hospital; maternity hospital; orthopedic hospital

(P-20927)
SAINT JHNS HLTH CTR FOUNDATION
Also Called: St John's Health Centre
2020 Santa Monica Blvd, Santa Monica (90404-2023)
PHONE..................................310 829-8970
Lou Laztin, *CEO*
EMP: 53
SALES (corp-wide): 2.8B **Privately Held**
WEB: www.pacificneuroscienceinstitute.org
SIC: **8062** General medical & surgical hospitals
HQ: Saint John's Health Center Foundation.
2121 Santa Monica Blvd
Santa Monica CA 90404
310 829-5511

(P-20928)
SAN ANTONIO REGIONAL HOSPITAL (PA)
999 San Bernardino Rd, Upland (91786-4920)
PHONE..................................909 985-2811
Jim Milhiser, *Chairman*
Donna Vig, *Records Dir*
Jim R Milhiser, *Vice Chairman*
John Chapman, *President*
Roger Parsons, *CFO*
▲ EMP: 1900 EST: 1920
SQ FT: 349,000
SALES (est): 364.9MM **Privately Held**
WEB: www.sarh.org
SIC: **8062** 5912 General medical & surgical hospitals; drug stores & proprietary stores

(P-20929)
SAN GABRIEL VALLEY MEDICAL CTR
438 W Las Tunas Dr, San Gabriel (91776-1216)
PHONE..................................626 289-5454
Thomas Mone, *CEO*
Harold Way, *CFO*
Richard Polver, *Treasurer*
Edward Shuey, *Admin Sec*
EMP: 850 EST: 1964
SQ FT: 42,000
SALES (est): 2.5K **Privately Held**
WEB: www.sgvmc.com
SIC: **8062** General medical & surgical hospitals
HQ: Dignity Health
185 Berry St Ste 200
San Francisco CA 94107
415 438-5500

(P-20930)
SAN GORGONIO MEMORIAL HOSPITAL
600 N Highland Sprng Ave, Banning (92220-3046)
PHONE..................................951 845-1121
Steve Barron, *CEO*
EMP: 819 EST: 1990
SALES (est): 6.3MM **Privately Held**
SIC: **8062** General medical & surgical hospitals

(P-20931)
SAN GRGNIO MEM HOSP FOUNDATION (PA)
600 N Highland Sprng Ave, Banning (92220-3046)
PHONE..................................951 845-1121
Steven Barron, *CEO*
Mark Beck, *Ch Pathology*
Dave Recupero, *CFO*
Dorothy Ellis, *Chairman*
Jerilynn Kaibel, *Chairman*
EMP: 245 EST: 1990

SQ FT: 76,000
SALES: 67.3MM **Privately Held**
WEB: www.sgmh.org
SIC: **8062** Hospital, affiliated with AMA residency

(P-20932)
SAN JOAQUIN COMMUNITY HOSPITAL (PA)
Also Called: Adventist Health Bakersfield
2615 Chester Ave, Bakersfield (93301-2014)
PHONE..................................661 395-3000
Sharlet Briggs, *President*
Brent Soper, *CFO*
Nancy Garcia, *CTO*
Viral Mehta, *Cardiology*
Charles T Tam, *Cardiovascular*
EMP: 850
SQ FT: 137,000
SALES (est): 200.8MM **Privately Held**
WEB: www.bakersfield.com
SIC: **8062** 8011 General medical & surgical hospitals; offices & clinics of medical doctors

(P-20933)
SANTA BARBARA COTTAGE
5333 Hollister Ave # 250, Santa Barbara (93111-2341)
P.O. Box 8180, Goleta (93118-8180)
PHONE..................................805 879-8900
Robert E M Nourse, *Chairman*
EMP: 52 EST: 2009
SALES (est): 34.4MM **Privately Held**
SIC: **8062** General medical & surgical hospitals

(P-20934)
SANTA BRBARA CTTAGE HOSP FNDTI (HQ)
Also Called: Cottage Childrens Medical Ctr
400 W Pueblo St, Santa Barbara (93105-4353)
P.O. Box 689 (93102-0689)
PHONE..................................805 682-7111
Ronald C Werft, *CEO*
Patricia Dooley, *Volunteer Dir*
Brett Tande, *CFO*
Alejandro Soffici, *Treasurer*
Sandra Wilson, *Treasurer*
EMP: 1612 EST: 1982
SQ FT: 485,874
SALES (est): 25.1MM
SALES (corp-wide): 152.8MM **Privately Held**
WEB: www.cottagehealth.org
SIC: **8062** Hospital, AMA approved residency
PA: Cottage Health
400 W Pueblo St
Santa Barbara CA 93105
805 682-7111

(P-20935)
SANTA PAULA MEMORIAL HOSPITAL
845 N 10th St Ste 3, Santa Paula (93060-1348)
P.O. Box 270 (93061-0270)
PHONE..................................805 933-9131
Mark Gregson, *CEO*
Phil Romney, *Chairman*
Marsha Rae, *Treasurer*
Angie Morales, *Admir Sec*
Scott Wilson, *Purchasing*
EMP: 54 EST: 1959
SQ FT: 40,000
SALES (est): 2.7MM **Privately Held**
WEB: www.santapaulahospital.u9v.net
SIC: **8062** General medical & surgical hospitals

(P-20936)
SANTA TERESITA INC (PA)
Also Called: Manor At Santa Teresita Hosp
819 Buena Vista St, Duarte (91010-1703)
PHONE..................................626 359-3243
Sister Mary Clare Mancini, *CEO*
EMP: 264 EST: 1955
SQ FT: 232,165
SALES (est): 13.1MM **Privately Held**
WEB: www.santa-teresita.org
SIC: **8062** 8051 General medical & surgical hospitals; skilled nursing care facilities

(P-20937)
SANTA YNEZ VLY CTTAGE HOSP INC
2050 Viborg Rd, Solvang (93463-2220)
P.O. Box 689, Santa Barbara (93102-0689)
PHONE..................805 688-6431
Ron Werft, *President*
EMP: 75 **EST:** 1962
SQ FT: 30,000
SALES (est): 17.5MM
SALES (corp-wide): 152.8MM **Privately Held**
WEB: www.cottagehealth.org
SIC: 8062 General medical & surgical hospitals
PA: Cottage Health
400 W Pueblo St
Santa Barbara CA 93105
805 682-7111

(P-20938)
SHERMAN OAKS HEALTH SYSTEM
4929 Van Nuys Blvd, Sherman Oaks (91403-1702)
PHONE..................818 981-7111
David Levinsohn, *CEO*
EMP: 71 **EST:** 1997
SALES (est): 341.2K **Privately Held**
WEB: www.shermanoakshospital.org
SIC: 8062 General medical & surgical hospitals

(P-20939)
SIERRA VISTA HOSPITAL INC (HQ)
Also Called: Sierra Vista Regional Med Ctr
1010 Murray Ave, San Luis Obispo (93405-8801)
P.O. Box 1367 (93406-1367)
PHONE..................805 546-7600
Joseph Deschryver, *CEO*
Candace Markwith, *President*
Ikenna Mmeje, *COO*
Richard Phillips, *CFO*
Rollie Pirkl, *CFO*
EMP: 575 **EST:** 1968
SQ FT: 138,690
SALES (est): 150MM
SALES (corp-wide): 17.6B **Publicly Held**
WEB: www.tenethealthcentralcoast.com
SIC: 8062 General medical & surgical hospitals
PA: Tenet Healthcare Corporation
14201 Dallas Pkwy
Dallas TX 75254
469 893-2200

(P-20940)
SIMI VLY HOSP & HLTH CARE SVCS
Also Called: Aspen Surgery Center
2750 Sycamore Dr, Simi Valley (93065-1502)
PHONE..................805 955-6000
EMP: 237
SALES (corp-wide): 4.5B **Privately Held**
WEB: www.adventisthealth.org
SIC: 8062 General medical & surgical hospitals
HQ: Simi Valley Hospital And Health Care Services
2975 Sycamore Dr
Simi Valley CA 93065

(P-20941)
SIMI VLY HOSP & HLTH CARE SVCS (HQ)
Also Called: Simi Vly Hosp & Hlth Care Svcs
2975 Sycamore Dr, Simi Valley (93065-1201)
PHONE..................805 955-6000
Margaret Peterson, *President*
Craig Inouye, *Ch Radiology*
Marine Baghumyan, *Records Dir*
Caroline Esparza, *President*
Clif Patten, *CFO*
EMP: 553 **EST:** 1960
SALES (est): 163MM
SALES (corp-wide): 4.5B **Privately Held**
WEB: www.adventisthealth.org
SIC: 8062 General medical & surgical hospitals

PA: Adventist Health System/West, Corporation
1 Adventist Health Way
Roseville CA 95661
844 574-5686

(P-20942)
SISTERS OF ST JOSEPH ORANGE
240 Ocean Ave, Seal Beach (90740-6029)
PHONE..................562 430-4638
Catherine Gray, *Principal*
EMP: 705
SALES (corp-wide): 32.7MM **Privately Held**
WEB: www.thecsd.org
SIC: 8661 8062 Convent; general medical & surgical hospitals
HQ: Sisters Of St. Joseph Of Orange
480 S Batavia St
Orange CA 92868
714 633-8121

(P-20943)
SOUTHERN CAL HALTHCARE SYS INC
Also Called: Southern Cal Hosp At Culver Cy
3828 Delmas Ter, Culver City (90232-2713)
PHONE..................310 836-7000
EMP: 74
SALES (corp-wide): 3.4B **Privately Held**
SIC: 8062 General medical & surgical hospitals
HQ: Southern California Healthcare System, Inc.
3415 S Sepulveda Blvd # 9
Los Angeles CA 90034

(P-20944)
SOUTHERN CAL HALTHCARE SYS INC (HQ)
3415 S Sepulveda Blvd # 9, Los Angeles (90034-6060)
PHONE..................310 943-4500
David R Topper, *CEO*
EMP: 169 **EST:** 1998
SALES (est): 108.5MM
SALES (corp-wide): 3.4B **Privately Held**
WEB: www.pmh.com
SIC: 8062 General medical & surgical hospitals
PA: Prospect Medical Holdings, Inc.
3415 S Sepulveda Blvd # 9
Los Angeles CA 90034
310 943-4500

(P-20945)
SOUTHERN CAL PRMNNTE MED GROUP
26415 Carl Boyer Dr, Santa Clarita (91350-5824)
PHONE..................661 290-3100
EMP: 519
SALES (corp-wide): 30.5B **Privately Held**
SIC: 8062 General medical & surgical hospitals
HQ: Southern California Permanente Medical Group
393 Walnut Dr
Pasadena CA 91107
626 405-5704

(P-20946)
SOUTHERN CAL PRMNNTE MED GROUP
Also Called: S C P M G
9961 Sierra Ave, Fontana (92335-6720)
PHONE..................909 427-5000
Gerald McCall, *Branch Mgr*
Aaron L Rubin, *Med Doctor*
Arlene Sarocca, *Med Doctor*
Kelly Johnson, *Consultant*
EMP: 519
SALES (corp-wide): 30.5B **Privately Held**
SIC: 8062 General medical & surgical hospitals
HQ: Southern California Permanente Medical Group
393 Walnut Dr
Pasadena CA 91107
626 405-5704

(P-20947)
SOUTHERN CAL SPCIALTY CARE INC
Also Called: Kindred Hospital Santa Ana
1901 College Ave, Santa Ana (92706-2334)
PHONE..................714 564-7800
Rich McCarthy, *Principal*
EMP: 250
SALES (corp-wide): 6B **Privately Held**
WEB: www.kindredhealthcare.com
SIC: 8062 General medical & surgical hospitals
HQ: Southern California Specialty Care, Inc.
14900 Imperial Hwy
La Mirada CA 90638

(P-20948)
SOUTHERN CAL SPCIALTY CARE INC
Also Called: Kindred Hospital La Mirata
845 N Lark Ellen Ave, West Covina (91791-1069)
PHONE..................626 339-5451
Nenda Estudillo, *Director*
Elvira Gonzalez, *Food Svc Dir*
Victor Reyes, *Director*
EMP: 250
SQ FT: 34,082
SALES (corp-wide): 6B **Privately Held**
WEB: www.kindredhealthcare.com
SIC: 8062 General medical & surgical hospitals
HQ: Southern California Specialty Care, Inc.
14900 Imperial Hwy
La Mirada CA 90638

(P-20949)
SOUTHERN CAL SPCIALTY CARE INC (DH)
Also Called: Kindred Hospital La Mirada
14900 Imperial Hwy, La Mirada (90638-2172)
PHONE..................562 944-1900
Ty Richardson, *President*
George Burkley, *COO*
Robin Rapp, *COO*
Judie Sheldon, *Ch Credit Ofcr*
Roy Vera, *Vice Pres*
EMP: 100 **EST:** 1994
SQ FT: 74,074
SALES (est): 109.3MM
SALES (corp-wide): 6B **Privately Held**
WEB: www.kindredhealthcare.com
SIC: 8062 General medical & surgical hospitals
HQ: Specialty Healthcare Services, Inc
680 S 4th St
Louisville KY 40202
502 596-7300

(P-20950)
SOUTHERN INYO HEALTHCARE DST
501 E Locust St, Lone Pine (93545-8044)
PHONE..................760 876-5501
Peter Spiers, *CEO*
Charles Carson, *Vice Pres*
George Lahey, *Lab Dir*
Stacey Young, *Social Dir*
Jeff Sheffield, *Director*
EMP: 112
SQ FT: 29,000
SALES (est): 20.4MM **Privately Held**
WEB: www.sihd.org
SIC: 8062 General medical & surgical hospitals

(P-20951)
SOUTHERN SIERRA MEDICAL CENTER
105 E Sydnor Ave 100, Ridgecrest (93555-5546)
PHONE..................760 446-6404
Katherine Ferguson, *President*
EMP: 52 **EST:** 1996
SALES (est): 4.5MM **Privately Held**
WEB: www.rrh.org
SIC: 8062 General medical & surgical hospitals

(P-20952)
SOUTHWEST HEALTHCARE SYS AUX
Also Called: Business Department
38977 Sky Canyon Dr # 200, Murrieta (92563-2681)
PHONE..................800 404-6627
Paula Dalbeck, *Controller*
EMP: 712
SALES (corp-wide): 11.5B **Publicly Held**
WEB: www.swhealthcaresystem.com
SIC: 8062 General medical & surgical hospitals
HQ: Southwest Healthcare System Auxiliary
25500 Medical Center Dr
Murrieta CA 92562

(P-20953)
SOUTHWEST HEALTHCARE SYS AUX (HQ)
Also Called: Rancho Springs Medical Center
25500 Medical Center Dr, Murrieta (92562-5965)
PHONE..................951 696-6000
Brad Neet, *CEO*
Jared Chase,
Vimi Kapur,
David Lawson, *Ch Radiology*
Diane Moon, *CFO*
▲ **EMP:** 450 **EST:** 1989
SALES (est): 72.5K
SALES (corp-wide): 11.5B **Publicly Held**
WEB: www.swhealthcaresystem.com
SIC: 8062 8051 8059 4119 General medical & surgical hospitals; skilled nursing care facilities; convalescent home; ambulance service
PA: Universal Health Services, Inc.
367 S Gulph Rd
King Of Prussia PA 19406
610 768-3300

(P-20954)
SOVEREIGN HEALTHCARE OC LLC (PA)
27401 Los Altos Ste 200, Mission Viejo (92691-8008)
PHONE..................949 706-9900
Jeremy Hogue, *President*
Jay McKim, *CFO*
Lisa Allen, *Vice Pres*
Lynn Dugan, *Vice Pres*
Jim Rice, *Vice Pres*
EMP: 51 **EST:** 2007
SALES (est): 95.1MM **Privately Held**
WEB: www.sovereignhealthcare.net
SJC: 8062 General medical & surgical hospitals

(P-20955)
SPECILTY HOSP SAN GBRIEL VLY M
Also Called: Sgvmi
845 N Lark Ellen Ave, West Covina (91791-1069)
PHONE..................626 339-5451
Ninda Espadillo, *Director*
Joseph Roserollo, *Treasurer*
RAO Atluri MD, *Admin Sec*
Tony Macaraeg, *Manager*
EMP: 82 **EST:** 1979
SQ FT: 39,000
SALES (est): 1.1MM **Privately Held**
WEB: www.kindredhealthcare.com
SIC: 8062 General medical & surgical hospitals

(P-20956)
ST BERNARDINE MED CTR AUX INC
Also Called: Inland Empire Heart Institute
2101 N Waterman Ave, San Bernardino (92404-4836)
PHONE..................909 881-4320
Toll Free:..................877 -
Ed Langden, *Director*
EMP: 107 **Privately Held**
WEB:
SIC: 8062 General medical & surgical hospitals

PRODUCTS & SVCS

HQ: St. Bernardine Medical Center Auxiliary, Inc.
2101 N Waterman Ave
San Bernardino CA 92404
909 883-8711

(P-20957)
ST BERNARDINE MEDICAL CENTER
2101 N Waterman Ave, San Bernardino (92404-4836)
PHONE.............................909 883-8711
Darryl Vandenbosch, *President*
Paul Steinke, *CFO*
EMP: 292 EST: 1931
SQ FT: 433,484
SALES (est): 60.3MM **Privately Held**
WEB: www.dignityhealth.org
SIC: 8062 General medical & surgical hospitals
HQ: Dignity Health
185 Berry St Ste 200
San Francisco CA 94107
415 438-5500

(P-20958)
ST FRANCIS MEDICAL CENTER (DH)
Also Called: Sfmc
3630 E Imperial Hwy, Lynwood (90262-2609)
P.O. Box 1387, San Carlos (94070-7387)
PHONE.............................310 900-8900
Richard Adcock, *CEO*
Gerald Kozai, *CEO*
Derek Drake, *Ch Nursing Ofcr*
Karen Chapman, *Exec Dir*
Eileen Williams, *CTO*
EMP: 77 EST: 2001
SALES: 282.6MM
SALES (corp-wide): 1B **Privately Held**
WEB: www.stfrancismedicalcenter.com
SIC: 8062 General medical & surgical hospitals

(P-20959)
ST JOSEPH HOSPITAL
1000 W La Veta Ave, Orange (92868-4304)
PHONE.............................714 744-8601
Jay K Harness, *Principal*
Ray Casciari, *Chief Mktg Ofcr*
Valerie Vega, *Officer*
Yvonne Grayson, *Radiology Dir*
Katie Skelton, *Ch Nursing Ofcr*
EMP: 50 EST: 2008
SALES (est): 25.8MM **Privately Held**
WEB: www.sjo.org
SIC: 8062 General medical & surgical hospitals

(P-20960)
ST JOSEPH HOSPITAL OF ORANGE
Also Called: St Josephs Physical Rehab Svcs
1310 W Stewart Dr Ste 203, Orange (92868-3837)
PHONE.............................714 771-8222
Paul Pursell, *Director*
Brian Phipps, *Manager*
EMP: 170
SALES (corp-wide): 32.7MM **Privately Held**
WEB: www.sjo.org
SIC: 8062 8322 General medical & surgical hospitals; rehabilitation services
HQ: St. Joseph Hospital Of Orange
1100 W Stewart Dr
Orange CA 92868
714 633-9111

(P-20961)
ST JOSEPH HOSPITAL OF ORANGE
Also Called: Information Systems
363 S Main St Ste 211, Orange (92868-3825)
PHONE.............................714 771-8006
Dennise Masiello, *Director*
Michael Malouf, *Principal*
EMP: 170
SQ FT: 15,605

SALES (corp-wide): 32.7MM **Privately Held**
WEB: www.sjo.org
SIC: 8062 General medical & surgical hospitals
HQ: St. Joseph Hospital Of Orange
1100 W Stewart Dr
Orange CA 92868
714 633-9111

(P-20962)
ST JOSEPH HOSPITAL OF ORANGE (DH)
1100 W Stewart Dr, Orange (92868-3891)
P.O. Box 5600 (92863-5600)
PHONE.............................714 633-9111
Larry K Ainsworth, *President*
Tina Nycroft, *CFO*
Jim Cora, *Chairman*
Warren D Johnson, *Vice Ch Bd*
Patti Aube, *Officer*
EMP: 2100 EST: 1929
SQ FT: 448,000
SALES: 627.2MM
SALES (corp-wide): 32.7MM **Privately Held**
WEB: www.sjo.org
SIC: 8062 General medical & surgical hospitals
HQ: St. Joseph Health System
3345 Michelson Dr Ste 100
Irvine CA 92612
949 381-4000

(P-20963)
ST JOSEPH HOSPITAL OF ORANGE
Also Called: Business Office
3345 Michelson Dr Ste 100, Irvine (92612-0693)
PHONE.............................714 568-5500
Marina Lopez, *Manager*
Afshin Arianjam, *Surgeon*
Sharon Hayes,
Joan Vandermeulen,
Kelly Logan, *Manager*
EMP: 170
SALES (corp-wide): 32.7MM **Privately Held**
WEB: www.sjo.org
SIC: 8062 General medical & surgical hospitals
HQ: St. Joseph Hospital Of Orange
1100 W Stewart Dr
Orange CA 92868
714 633-9111

(P-20964)
ST JOSEPH HOSPITAL OF ORANGE
Also Called: Renal Center
1100 W Stewart Dr, Orange (92868-3891)
P.O. Box 5600 (92863-5600)
PHONE.............................714 771-8037
Mary McKenzie, *Director*
Phillip Beaudry, *IT/INT Sup*
Malissa Lewis, *Recruiter*
Helen Cha, *Marketing Staff*
Jeffrey Feiner, *Cardiology*
EMP: 170
SALES (corp-wide): 32.7MM **Privately Held**
WEB: www.sjo.org
SIC: 8062 General medical & surgical hospitals
HQ: St. Joseph Hospital Of Orange
1100 W Stewart Dr
Orange CA 92868
714 633-9111

(P-20965)
ST JUDE HERITAGE MED GROUP
Also Called: Sisters of Saint Joseph
1835 Sunny Crest Dr, Fullerton (92835-3616)
PHONE.............................714 449-6200
Michael Fabricant, *Med Doctor*
EMP: 55 EST: 1997
SALES (est): 14.3MM **Privately Held**
WEB: www.stjudemedicalcenter.org
SIC: 8062 General medical & surgical hospitals

(P-20966)
ST JUDE HOSPITAL (DH)
Also Called: St Jude Medical Center
101 E Valencia Mesa Dr, Fullerton (92835-3875)
PHONE.............................714 871-3280
Robert Fraschetti, *President*
Patrick L Fitzgibbons, *Ch Pathology*
Doreen Dann, *CEO*
Lee Penrose, *CEO*
Don Miller, *Business Dir*
▲ EMP: 2582 EST: 1942
SQ FT: 190,000
SALES: 557.5MM
SALES (corp-wide): 32.7MM **Privately Held**
WEB: www.stjudemedicalcenter.org
SIC: 8062 General medical & surgical hospitals
HQ: St. Joseph Health System
3345 Michelson Dr Ste 100
Irvine CA 92612
949 381-4000

(P-20967)
ST MARY MEDICAL CENTER (DH)
Also Called: St Mary's School of Nursing
1050 Linden Ave, Long Beach (90813-3321)
P.O. Box 887 (90801-0887)
PHONE.............................562 491-9000
Trammie McMann, *CEO*
Alan Garrett, *CEO*
Tammie McMann, *CEO*
Tiffany Caster, *COO*
Carolyn Caldwell, *Officer*
EMP: 1929 EST: 1924
SQ FT: 700,000
SALES (est): 270.6MM **Privately Held**
WEB: www.dignityhealth.org
SIC: 8062 Hospital, medical school affiliated with nursing & residency
HQ: Dignity Health
185 Berry St Ste 200
San Francisco CA 94107
415 438-5500

(P-20968)
ST MARY MEDICAL CENTER LLC
Also Called: Materals MGT At St Mary Med Ct
16000 Kasota Rd, Apple Valley (92307)
P.O. Box 7025 (92307-0731)
PHONE.............................760 946-8767
Leland Glisson, *Manager*
EMP: 85
SALES (corp-wide): 174.2MM **Privately Held**
WEB: www.stmaryapplevalley.com
SIC: 8062 General medical & surgical hospitals
PA: St. Mary Medical Center, Llc
18300 Us Highway 18
Apple Valley CA 92307
760 242-2311

(P-20969)
ST MARY MEDICAL CENTER LLC (PA)
18300 Us Highway 18, Apple Valley (92307-2206)
PHONE.............................760 242-2311
David Klein, *President*
Kelly Linden, *COO*
Tracey Fernandez, *CFO*
Mark Lauron, *Treasurer*
Diana Carloni - O'Malley, *Trustee*
EMP: 1265 EST: 1956
SQ FT: 92,000
SALES (est): 174.2MM **Privately Held**
WEB: www.stmaryapplevalley.com
SIC: 8062 General medical & surgical hospitals

(P-20970)
SUTTER HEALTH
25 W Micheltorena St, Santa Barbara (93101-2509)
PHONE.............................805 966-1600
EMP: 169
SALES (corp-wide): 13.2B **Privately Held**
SIC: 8062 General medical & surgical hospitals

PA: Sutter Health
2200 River Plaza Dr
Sacramento CA 95833
916 733-8800

(P-20971)
TENET HEALTH SYSTEMS NORRIS
Also Called: Kenneth Norris Cancer Hospital
1441 Eastlake Ave, Los Angeles (90089-1019)
PHONE.............................323 865-3000
Scott Evans, *CEO*
Strawn Steele, *CFO*
Arjun Ratnam, *Vice Pres*
Shirley Sian, *Project Mgr*
Syma Iqbal, *Professor*
EMP: 352 EST: 1982
SQ FT: 175,000
SALES (est): 179.2MM **Privately Held**
WEB: www.keckmedicine.org
SIC: 8062 General medical & surgical hospitals

(P-20972)
TENET HEALTHSYSTEM MEDICAL INC
13032 Earlham St, Santa Ana (92705-2113)
PHONE.............................714 966-8191
Tim Smith, *CEO*
EMP: 127
SALES (corp-wide): 17.6B **Publicly Held**
WEB: www.tenethealth.com
SIC: 8062 General medical & surgical hospitals
HQ: Tenet Healthsystem Medical, Inc.
14201 Dallas Pkwy
Dallas TX 75254
469 893-2000

(P-20973)
TENET HEALTHSYSTEM MEDICAL INC
16331 Arthur St, Cerritos (90703-2128)
PHONE.............................562 531-2550
John R Nickens, *Principal*
EMP: 127
SALES (corp-wide): 17.6B **Publicly Held**
WEB: www.tenethealth.com
SIC: 8062 8011 General medical & surgical hospitals; offices & clinics of medical doctors
HQ: Tenet Healthsystem Medical, Inc.
14201 Dallas Pkwy
Dallas TX 75254
469 893-2000

(P-20974)
TENET HEALTHSYSTEM MEDICAL INC
Also Called: Irvine Regional Hospital
1400 S Duglaca Rd Ste 250, Anaheim (92806)
PHONE.............................714 428-6800
Donald Lorack, *CEO*
EMP: 127
SALES (corp-wide): 17.6B **Publicly Held**
WEB: www.tenethealth.com
SIC: 8062 General medical & surgical hospitals
HQ: Tenet Healthsystem Medical, Inc.
14201 Dallas Pkwy
Dallas TX 75254
469 893-2000

(P-20975)
TENNESSEE HOSPITALISTS INC
4605 Lankershim Blvd, North Hollywood (91602-1818)
PHONE.............................888 447-2362
EMP: 51 EST: 2011
SALES (est): 6MM
SALES (corp-wide): 3.5B **Privately Held**
SIC: 8062 General medical & surgical hospitals
HQ: Ipc Healthcare, Inc.
4605 Lankershim Blvd
North Hollywood CA 91602
888 447-2362

(P-20976)
THC - ORANGE COUNTY INC
5525 W Slauson Ave, Los Angeles
(90056-1047)
PHONE........................310 642-0325
Arthur L Rothgerber, *Principal*
EMP: 242 **EST:** 2008
SALES (est): 27.8MM
SALES (corp-wide): 6B **Privately Held**
WEB: www.kindredhealthcare.com
SIC: 8062 General medical & surgical hospitals
HQ: Kindred Healthcare, Llc
680 S 4th St
Louisville KY 40202
502 596-7300

(P-20977)
THOUSAND OAKS SURGICAL HOSP LP
401 Rolling Oaks Dr, Thousand Oaks
(91361-1050)
PHONE........................805 777-7750
Micheal Bass, *Partner*
Marissa Mc Arthur, *Exec Sec*
Inga Jones, *Director*
EMP: 100 **EST:** 1999
SQ FT: 50,000
SALES (est): 13.9MM **Privately Held**
WEB: www.losrobleshospital.com
SIC: 8062 General medical & surgical hospitals

(P-20978)
TORRANCE HEALTH ASSN INC (PA)
Also Called: PHYSICIAN OFFICE SUPPORT SERVI
3330 Lomita Blvd, Torrance (90505-5002)
P.O. Box 13717 (90503-0717)
PHONE........................310 325-9110
Craig Leach, *CEO*
Bill Larson, *CFO*
Sally Eberhard, *Senior VP*
John McNamara, *Senior VP*
Bernadette Reid, *Vice Pres*
EMP: 3000 **EST:** 1985
SQ FT: 180,000
SALES: 913.8MM **Privately Held**
WEB: www.torrancememorialipa.org
SIC: 8062 General medical & surgical hospitals

(P-20979)
TORRANCE MEM PHYSICIANS NETWRK (HQ)
Also Called: Torrance Family Medicine Ctr
855 Manhattan Beach Blvd, Manhattan Beach (90266-4965)
PHONE........................310 939-7847
Mark Lurie, *Principal*
Michelle Lopez, *Principal*
EMP: 50 **EST:** 1998
SALES (est): 90MM **Privately Held**
WEB: www.torrancememorial.org
SIC: 8062 General medical & surgical hospitals

(P-20980)
TORRANCE MEMORIAL MEDICAL CTR
3333 Skypark Dr Ste 200, Torrance
(90505-5035)
PHONE........................310 784-6316
Donnie Watson, *Program Dir*
Minh Dang, *Manager*
Khalid Shariff, *Manager*
EMP: 505 **Privately Held**
WEB: www.torrancememorial.org
SIC: 8062 General medical & surgical hospitals
HQ: Torrance Memorial Medical Center
3330 Lomita Blvd
Torrance CA 90505
310 325-9110

(P-20981)
TORRANCE MEMORIAL MEDICAL CTR
22411 Hawthorne Blvd, Torrance
(90505-2507)
PHONE........................310 784-3740
EMP: 505 **Privately Held**
WEB: www.torrancememorial.org

SIC: **8062** Hospital, affiliated with AMA residency
HQ: Torrance Memorial Medical Center
3330 Lomita Blvd
Torrance CA 90505
310 325-9110

(P-20982)
TORRANCE MEMORIAL MEDICAL CTR (HQ)
3330 Lomita Blvd, Torrance (90505-5002)
PHONE........................310 325-9110
Craig Leach, *President*
Shanna Hall, *Vice Pres*
Debby Kelley, *Vice Pres*
Alex Cluge, *Executive*
Pattie Drew, *Lab Dir*
EMP: 1500 **EST:** 1925
SALES: 724.6MM **Privately Held**
WEB: www.torrancememorial.org
SIC: 8062 Hospital, affiliated with AMA residency

(P-20983)
TORRANCE MEMORIAL MEDICAL CTR
Also Called: Torrance Memorial Breast Diagn
855 Manhattan Beach Blvd # 208, Manhattan Beach (90266-4965)
PHONE........................310 939-7847
Shireen Alwani, *Branch Mgr*
Elaine Stevens, *Office Mgr*
William Mealer, *Orthopedist*
Anthony Zoppi, *Surgeon*
Michelle Lopez, *Manager*
EMP: 505 **Privately Held**
WEB: www.torrancememorial.org
SIC: 8062 General medical & surgical hospitals
HQ: Torrance Memorial Medical Center
3330 Lomita Blvd
Torrance CA 90505
310 325-9110

(P-20984)
TULARE LOCAL HEALTH CARE DST
Also Called: TULARE DISTRICT HOSPITAL
869 N Cherry St, Tulare (93274-2207)
PHONE........................559 685-3462
Shawn Bolouki, *CEO*
Sherrie Bell, *President*
Fred Capozello, *CFO*
Lee Gardner, *Pharmacy Dir*
Prem Camboj, *Admin Sec*
EMP: 700
SQ FT: 140,000
SALES: 14.2MM **Privately Held**
WEB: www.tularelocalhealthcaredistrict.org
SIC: 8062 General medical & surgical hospitals

(P-20985)
UCLA HEALTH
Also Called: Ronald Reagan Building
757 Westwood Plz, Los Angeles
(90095-8358)
PHONE........................310 825-9111
Dr David T Feinberg, *CEO*
Suzie Morrel, *Officer*
Susi Takeuchi, *Officer*
Marlene Lozano, *Admin Asst*
Aniket Tiwari, *Network Enginr*
EMP: 58 **EST:** 2012
SALES (est): 115.7MM **Privately Held**
WEB: www.uclahealth.org
SIC: 8062 General medical & surgical hospitals

(P-20986)
UCLA HEALTHCARE
1821 Wilshire Blvd Fl 6, Santa Monica
(90403-5618)
PHONE........................310 319-4560
Tami Dennis, *Exec Dir*
Dennis Slamon, *Hematology*
EMP: 77 **EST:** 2007
SALES (est): 20.7MM **Privately Held**
WEB: www.ucla.edu
SIC: 8062 9411 General medical & surgical hospitals; administration of educational programs;
HQ: University Of California, Los Angeles
405 Hilgard Ave
Los Angeles CA 90095

(P-20987)
UHS-CORONA INC (HQ)
Also Called: Corona Regional Med Ctr Hosp
800 S Main St, Corona (92882-3420)
PHONE........................951 737-4343
Marvin Pember, *CEO*
Kristin Mercado, *Records Dir*
Alan B Miller, *President*
Ken Rivers, *CEO*
Lisa Giarraputo, *Lab Dir*
▲ **EMP:** 900 **EST:** 1978
SALES: 169.5MM
SALES (corp-wide): 11.5B **Publicly Held**
WEB: www.coronaregional.com
SIC: 8062 General medical & surgical hospitals
PA: Universal Health Services, Inc.
367 S Gulph Rd
King Of Prussia PA 19406
610 768-3300

(P-20988)
UNIVERSITY CAL LOS ANGELES
Also Called: Ronald Reagan Ucla Medical Ctr
757 Westwood Plz, Los Angeles
(90095-8358)
PHONE........................310 825-9111
Tatiana Orloff, *Branch Mgr*
Art Rocha, *Admin Asst*
Emily Manczuk, *Administration*
Dean Childers, *Project Mgr*
Richard Lee, *Project Mgr*
EMP: 2056 **Privately Held**
WEB: www.ucla.edu
SIC: 8062 8221 9411 General medical & surgical hospitals; university; administration of educational programs;
HQ: University Of California, Los Angeles
405 Hilgard Ave
Los Angeles CA 90095

(P-20989)
UNIVERSITY CALIFORNIA IRVINE
Also Called: Uc Irvine Medical Center
101 The City Dr S, Orange (92868-3201)
PHONE........................714 456-6011
Mary Piccione, *Exec Dir*
Janet Shigei, *Admin Dir*
Angela Monroe, *Admin Asst*
Thomas Wen, *Administration*
Kim Ritorto, *Network Enginr*
EMP: 3000 **Privately Held**
WEB: www.uci.edu
SIC: 8062 8221 9411 General medical & surgical hospitals; university;
HQ: University Of California, Irvine
510 Aldrich Hall
Irvine CA 92697
949 824-5011

(P-20990)
UNIVERSITY CALIFORNIA IRVINE
Also Called: Irvine Medical Center
200 S Manchester Ave # 400, Orange
(92868-3220)
PHONE........................714 456-5558
Joy Grosse, *Director*
Maurice Espinoza, *Nursing Mgr*
Chelsea Anorma, *Research*
Matt Deines, *Associate*
EMP: 302 **Privately Held**
WEB: www.uci.edu
SIC: 8062 8221 9411 General medical & surgical hospitals; university; administration of educational programs;
HQ: University Of California, Irvine
510 Aldrich Hall
Irvine CA 92697
949 824-5011

(P-20991)
UNIVERSITY CALIFORNIA IRVINE
Also Called: UCI Westminster Medical Center
15355 Brookhurst St # 102, Westminster
(92683-7077)
PHONE........................714 775-3066
Toll Free:........................888 -
Nhu Ngo, *Manager*
Huan V Nguyen, *Internal Med*
EMP: 302 **Privately Held**
WEB: www.uci.edu

SIC: **8062 8221 9411** General medical & surgical hospitals; university; administration of educational programs;
HQ: University Of California, Irvine
510 Aldrich Hall
Irvine CA 92697
949 824-5011

(P-20992)
UNIVERSITY CALIFORNIA IRVINE
Also Called: Social Sciences
3151 Social Science Plz, Irvine
(92697-5100)
PHONE........................949 824-7725
Barbara Venook, *Principal*
Patty Furukawa, *IT/INT Sup*
Sheila Mercer, *Analyst*
Zuzanna Siwy, *Professor*
Daniel Bogart, *Assoc Prof*
EMP: 121 **Privately Held**
WEB: www.uci.edu
SIC: 8221 9411 8062 University; administration of educational programs; general medical & surgical hospitals
HQ: University Of California, Irvine
510 Aldrich Hall
Irvine CA 92697
949 824-5011

(P-20993)
UNIVERSITY SOUTHERN CALIFORNIA
Also Called: Usc University Hospital
1500 San Pablo St, Los Angeles
(90033-5313)
PHONE........................323 442-8500
Paul Vivano, *Director*
Alan Levine, *Managing Prtnr*
Kevin Farr, *CFO*
Reginald Harpur, *Exec VP*
Stender Sweeney, *Exec VP*
EMP: 875
SALES (corp-wide): 641.8MM **Privately Held**
WEB: www.usc.edu
SIC: 8062 8011 General medical & surgical hospitals; offices & clinics of medical doctors
PA: University Of Southern California
3720 S Flower St Fl 3
Los Angeles CA 90089
213 740-7762

(P-20994)
USC CARE MEDICAL GROUP INC (PA)
Also Called: Cardiology Department
1510 San Pablo St Ste 649, Los Angeles
(90033-5404)
PHONE........................323 442-5100
Smitha Ravipudi, *CEO*
David Peng, *President*
Eileen Kohan, *Exec Dir*
Stephanie Mullin, *Research*
Sandra Galvez, *Professor*
EMP: 108 **EST:** 1995
SALES (est): 116.2MM **Privately Held**
WEB: www.usc.edu
SIC: 8062 Hospital, medical school affiliated with nursing & residency

(P-20995)
USC KECK SCHOOL OF MEDICINE (HQ)
1975 Zonal Ave Ste Kam500, Los Angeles
(90089-5601)
PHONE........................323 442-2830
Carmen A Puliafito, *Dean*
Coreen A Rodgers, *COO*
Jon Samet, *Chairman*
Jean Chan, *Associate Dir*
Christina Ortiz, *Executive Asst*
EMP: 113 **EST:** 2011
SALES (est): 66.8MM
SALES (corp-wide): 641.8MM **Privately Held**
WEB: www.keckmedicine.org
SIC: 8062 Hospital, medical school affiliated with residency
PA: University Of Southern California
3720 S Flower St Fl 3
Los Angeles CA 90089
213 740-7762

(P-20996)
USC VERDUGO HILLS HOSPITAL LLC
1812 Verdugo Blvd, Glendale (91208-1407)
PHONE..................818 790-7100
Armand Dorian, *CEO*
Hack Lash, *CFO*
Tracy Valenzuela, *Program Mgr*
James Plaza, *Info Tech Mgr*
Paul Celuch, *VP Human Res*
EMP: 750 **EST:** 2013
SQ FT: 45,000
SALES (est): 223.3MM
SALES (corp-wide): 641.8MM **Privately Held**
WEB: www.uscvhh.org
SIC: 8062 Hospital, affiliated with AMA residency
PA: University Of Southern California
3720 S Flower St Fl 3
Los Angeles CA 90089
213 740-7762

(P-20997)
USC VRDUGO HLLS HOSP FUNDATION (HQ)
Also Called: U S C
1812 Verdugo Blvd, Glendale (91208-1407)
PHONE..................800 872-2273
Paul Craig, *CEO*
Debbie L Walsh, *President*
Armand H Dorian, *Principal*
John Blaha, *Technology*
Asfike Koulloukian, *Accountant*
EMP: 446 **EST:** 1947
SQ FT: 225,000
SALES: 891.2K
SALES (corp-wide): 641.8MM **Privately Held**
WEB: www.uscvhh.org
SIC: 8062 General medical & surgical hospitals
PA: University Of Southern California
3720 S Flower St Fl 3
Los Angeles CA 90089
213 740-7762

(P-20998)
VALLEY HEALTH SYSTEM SVC CORP
301 N San Jacinto St, Hemet (92543-3119)
PHONE..................951 765-4702
Patrick Searl, *President*
EMP: 55 **EST:** 1985
SALES (est): 1.1MM **Privately Held**
SIC: 8062 General medical & surgical hospitals

(P-20999)
VALLEY MED GROUP LOMPOC INC
Also Called: Bailey, Rollin C MD
136 N 3rd St, Lompoc (93436-7002)
PHONE..................805 736-1253
William H Gausman Jr, *President*
B J Coughlin MD, *Corp Secy*
Eldon Elam MD, *Vice Pres*
Rollin C Bailey, *Managing Dir*
Thomas E Fritch, *Managing Dir*
EMP: 81 **EST:** 1965
SQ FT: 10,700
SALES (est): 4.6MM **Privately Held**
WEB: www.lompocvmc.com
SIC: 8062 General medical & surgical hospitals; hospital, affiliated with AMA residency

(P-21000)
VALLEY PRESBYTERIAN HOSPITAL
Also Called: V P H
15107 Vanowen St, Van Nuys (91405-4597)
PHONE..................818 782-6600
Gustavo Valdespino, *CEO*
Janice Klostermeier, *CFO*
Kelly Anderson, *Officer*
Clyde Wesp, *Officer*
Gayathri S Jith, *Senior VP*
EMP: 1600 **EST:** 1948
SQ FT: 400,000

SALES: 486.6MM
SALES (corp-wide): 68.3MM **Privately Held**
WEB: www.valleypres.org
SIC: 8062 General medical & surgical hospitals
PA: Barlow Respiratory Hospital
2000 Stadium Way
Los Angeles CA 90026
213 250-4200

(P-21001)
VERDUGO HILLS HOSPITAL INC
1812 Verdugo Blvd, Glendale (91208-1409)
PHONE..................818 790-7100
Leonard Labella, *President*
Elen Borja, *Executive Asst*
Armand Dorian, *Emerg Med Spec*
Vivienne Uytana,
Ofelia Geragosian, *Manager*
EMP: 133 **EST:** 1947
SALES (est): 49.5MM **Privately Held**
WEB: www.uscvhh.org
SIC: 8062 Hospital, affiliated with AMA residency

(P-21002)
VERITAS HEALTH SERVICES INC
Also Called: Chino Valley Medical Center
5451 Walnut Ave, Chino (91710-2609)
PHONE..................909 464-8600
Parrish Scarboro, *CEO*
Irv E Edwards, *President*
Jacob Jensen, *Podiatrist*
Anna Zvansky, *Med Doctor*
EMP: 600 **EST:** 2000
SALES: 92MM
SALES (corp-wide): 1B **Privately Held**
WEB: www.cvmc.com
SIC: 8062 General medical & surgical hospitals
HQ: Prime Healthcare Services Inc
3480 E Guasti Rd
Ontario CA 91761

(P-21003)
VERITY HEALTH SYSTEM CAL INC
3680 E Imperial Hwy # 306, Lynwood (90262-2659)
PHONE..................310 900-2000
EMP: 100
SALES (corp-wide): 225.4MM **Privately Held**
SIC: 8062 General Hospital
PA: Verity Health System Of California, Inc.
2040 E Mariposa Ave
El Segundo CA 91367
650 551-6650

(P-21004)
VINCENT HAYLEY ENTERPRISES
Also Called: St Vincent Health Care
1810 N Fair Oaks Ave, Pasadena (91103-1619)
PHONE..................626 398-8182
Rob Barrett, *President*
Cipriano Baustista, *Administration*
EMP: 75 **EST:** 1990
SALES: 8.1MM **Privately Held**
SIC: 8062 General medical & surgical hospitals

(P-21005)
VISTA SPCLTY HOSP STHERN CAL L
Also Called: Vista Hospital San Gabriel Vly
14148 Francisquito Ave, Baldwin Park (91706-6120)
PHONE..................626 388-2700
Marc C Ferrell, *Partner*
Tawanda Whitaker, *Records Dir*
Christine Saltonstall, *CFO*
Rick Revkalla, *Nurse*
Rick Rezkalla, *Director*
EMP: 103 **EST:** 2003
SQ FT: 44,400
SALES (est): 28.2MM **Privately Held**
WEB: www.kindredhealthcare.com
SIC: 8062 General medical & surgical hospitals

(P-21006)
WAVE PLASTIC SURGERY CTR INC (PA)
Also Called: Wave Plstic Srgery Asthtic Lse
3680 Wilshire Blvd Fl 2, Los Angeles (90010-2707)
PHONE..................213 383-4800
Peter G Lee, *CEO*
Sunny Gao, *Opers Staff*
Tina Lin, *Sr Consultant*
Morgan Detienne, *Manager*
EMP: 70 **EST:** 2009
SALES (est): 38.7MM **Privately Held**
WEB: www.waveplasticsurgery.com
SIC: 8062 8011 General medical & surgical hospitals; plastic surgeon

(P-21007)
WEST SIDE DST HOSP FOUNDATION
Also Called: Skilled Nursing Facility
110 E North St, Taft (93268-3606)
PHONE..................805 763-4211
Morgan Clayton, *Ch of Bd*
John Ruffner, *Administration*
EMP: 84 **EST:** 1950
SQ FT: 30,000
SALES (est): 5.2MM **Privately Held**
WEB: www.wshcd.org
SIC: 8062 8051 8011 General medical & surgical hospitals; skilled nursing care facilities; offices & clinics of medical doctors

(P-21008)
WESTERN MEDICAL CENTER AUX (HQ)
Also Called: Western Med Center-Santa Ana
1301 N Tustin Ave, Santa Ana (92705-8619)
PHONE..................714 835-3555
Dan Brothman, *CEO*
Patricia Stites, *CEO*
EMP: 200 **EST:** 1998
SALES (est): 105.8MM
SALES (corp-wide): 1.9B **Privately Held**
WEB: www.orangecountyglobalmedicalcenter.com
SIC: 8062 General medical & surgical hospitals
PA: Kpc Healthcare, Inc.
1301 N Tustin Ave
Santa Ana CA 92705
714 953-3652

(P-21009)
WHITE MEM PEDIATRICS MED GROUP
1701 E Cesar E Chavez Ave # 456, Los Angeles (90033-2496)
PHONE..................323 987-1200
Samuel Bruttomesso, *Partner*
Danielle Borut, *Partner*
EMP: 51 **EST:** 1984
SQ FT: 12,000
SALES (est): 6.1MM **Privately Held**
WEB: www.adventisthealth.org
SIC: 8062 General medical & surgical hospitals

(P-21010)
WHITE MEMORIAL MEDICAL CENTER (HQ)
Also Called: CECILLA GONZALEZ DE AL HOYA CA
1720 E Cesar E Chavez Ave, Los Angeles (90033-2414)
PHONE..................323 268-5000
Beth D Zachary, *CEO*
Mark J Newmyer, *President*
John G Raffoul, *CEO*
Terri Day, *CFO*
Mara C Bryant, *Vice Pres*
EMP: 1200 **EST:** 1913
SQ FT: 454,000
SALES: 504MM
SALES (corp-wide): 4.5B **Privately Held**
WEB: www.adventisthealth.org
SIC: 8062 General medical & surgical hospitals
PA: Adventist Health System/West, Corporation
1 Adventist Health Way
Roseville CA 95661
844 574-5686

(P-21011)
WHITTIER HOSPITAL MED CTR INC
9080 Colima Rd, Whittier (90605-1600)
PHONE..................562 945-3561
Richard Castro, *CEO*
Vicki Aguilar, *Records Dir*
Sheilah Creus, *QA Dir*
Jesse Garrido, *Purch Dir*
Freida Wenzara, *Mktg Dir*
EMP: 180 **EST:** 1962
SQ FT: 144,000
SALES (est): 27.1MM
SALES (corp-wide): 574.5MM **Privately Held**
WEB: www.whittierhospital.com
SIC: 8062 General medical & surgical hospitals
PA: Ahmc Healthcare Inc.
506 W Valley Blvd Ste 300
San Gabriel CA 91776
626 943-7526

8063 Psychiatric Hospitals

(P-21012)
ALTA HLLYWOOD CMNTY HOSP VAN N
14433 Emelita St, Van Nuys (91401-4213)
PHONE..................818 787-1511
Irving Loube, *President*
Claude Lowen, *Corp Secy*
EMP: 537 **EST:** 1969
SQ FT: 34,192
SALES (est): 5.4MM
SALES (corp-wide): 3.4B **Privately Held**
WEB: www.sch-vannuys.com
SIC: 8063 Psychiatric hospitals
HQ: Southern California Healthcare System, Inc.
3415 S Sepulveda Blvd # 9
Los Angeles CA 90034

(P-21013)
AURORA BHVIORAL HEALTHCARE LLC (HQ)
4238 Green River Rd, Corona (92878-3869)
PHONE..................951 549-8032
EMP: 50 **EST:** 2000
SALES (est): 48.5MM
SALES (corp-wide): 4.5B **Publicly Held**
WEB: www.magellanhealth.com
SIC: 8063 Hospital for the mentally ill
PA: Magellan Health, Inc.
4801 E Washington St # 100
Phoenix AZ 85034
800 642-1716

(P-21014)
AURORA LAS ENCINAS LLC
Also Called: Aurora Las Encinas Hospital
2900 E Del Mar Blvd, Pasadena (91107-4375)
PHONE..................626 795-9901
James Wilcox,
Brenda Nocon Rn,
Will Williams, *Director*
EMP: 236 **EST:** 1903
SQ FT: 132,000
SALES (est): 33.1MM **Publicly Held**
WEB: www.lasencinashospital.com
SIC: 8063 8069 Hospital for the mentally ill; alcoholism rehabilitation hospital
HQ: Hca Inc.
1 Park Plz
Nashville TN 37203
615 344-9551

(P-21015)
BAKERSFIELD BHVRAL HLTHCARE HOS
5201 White Ln, Bakersfield (93309-6200)
PHONE..................661 398-1800
Jeff Chinn, *CEO*
May C Villegas, *Nursing Mgr*
Gavino Salas, *Opers Staff*
Sergio Herrera, *Food Svc Dir*
Prayag Bhakta,
EMP: 235 **EST:** 2015

SALES (est): 28.7MM **Privately Held**
WEB: www.bakersfieldbehavioral.com
SIC: 8063 8011 Psychiatric hospitals;
medical centers

(P-21016)
CANYON RIDGE HOSPITAL INC
Also Called: UHS
5353 G St, Chino (91710-5250)
PHONE..................909 590-3700
Peggy Minnick, *CEO*
Stephanie Bernier, *Officer*
Maria Patterson, *Safety Mgr*
EMP: 677 **EST:** 1990
SALES (est): 35.3MM
SALES (corp-wide): 11.5B **Publicly Held**
WEB: www.canyonridgehospital.com
SIC: 8063 8093 Hospital for the mentally
ill; mental health clinic, outpatient
HQ: Willow Springs, Llc
6640 Carothers Pkwy # 400
Franklin TN 37067
615 312-5700

(P-21017)
CHARTER BHVRAL HLTH SYS S C/CH
Also Called: Charter Oak Hospital
1161 E Covina Blvd, Covina (91724-1523)
PHONE..................626 966-1632
Todd Smith, *CEO*
Janet Ray Perkins, *Officer*
Christine De La Paz, *Executive*
Martha Rojas, *Food Svc Dir*
Crescent Real Estate Funding L,
EMP: 146 **EST:** 1997
SALES (est): 18.6MM **Privately Held**
WEB: www.charteroakhospital.com
SIC: 8063 Psychiatric hospitals

(P-21018)
COLLEGE HOSPITAL INC (PA)
Also Called: College Hospital Cerritos
10802 College Pl, Cerritos (90703-1579)
PHONE..................562 924-9581
Stephen A Witt, *President*
Bessie Weiss, *Corp Secy*
Holly McKittrick, *Ch Nursing Ofcr*
EMP: 300 **EST:** 1973
SQ FT: 60,000
SALES (est): 70.3MM **Privately Held**
WEB: www.chc.la
SIC: 8063 Hospital for the mentally ill

(P-21019)
GATEWAYS HOSP MENTAL HLTH CTR (PA)
1891 Effie St, Los Angeles (90026-1711)
PHONE..................323 644-2000
Mara Pelsman, *CEO*
Jeff Emery, *CFO*
George King, *CFO*
Phil Wong, *Officer*
Joshua Ly, *Pharmacy Dir*
EMP: 150
SQ FT: 40,000
SALES (est): 29.8MM **Privately Held**
WEB: www.gatewayshospital.org
SIC: 8063 8093 Hospital for the mentally
ill; mental health clinic, outpatient

(P-21020)
KAISER FOUNDATION HOSPITALS
Also Called: Kaiser Mental Health Center
765 W College St, Los Angeles
(90012-1181)
PHONE..................213 580-7200
Kurt Hastings, *Manager*
Siv Hour, *Psychiatry*
EMP: 392
SQ FT: 66,697
SALES (corp-wide): 30.5B **Privately Held**
WEB: www.kaisercenter.com
SIC: 8063 Psychiatric hospitals
HQ: Kaiser Foundation Hospitals Inc
1 Kaiser Plz
Oakland CA 94612
510 271-6611

(P-21021)
KAWEAH DLTA HLTH CARE DST GILD
1100 S Akers St, Visalia (93277-8311)
PHONE..................559 624-3300

Don Myers, *Director*
Liz Pannell, *Executive Asst*
Geoff Sanders, *IT/INT Sup*
Rebecca Kroeze, *Nurse*
Dee Vernon,
EMP: 88
SALES (corp-wide): 734.3MM **Privately Held**
WEB: www.kdhcd.org
SIC: 8063 Psychiatric hospitals
PA: Kaweah Delta Health Care District
Guild
400 W Mineral King Ave
Visalia CA 93291
559 624-2000

(P-21022)
KEDREN COMMUNITY HLTH CTR INC (PA)
Also Called: Kedren Acute Psychtric Hosp Cm
4211 Avalon Blvd, Los Angeles
(90011-5622)
PHONE..................323 233-0425
John Griffith, *President*
Maria Dia, *CFO*
Robert Lawson, *Treasurer*
Lupe Ross, *Admin Sec*
Araceli Lomeli, *Personnel Assit*
EMP: 400 **EST:** 1965
SQ FT: 144,000
SALES (est): 54.8MM **Privately Held**
WEB: www.kedren.org
SIC: 8063 8093 Hospital for the mentally
ill; specialty outpatient clinics

(P-21023)
KNOLLWOOD PSYCHTRIC HOSP CHEM
Also Called: Knollwood Center
5900 Brockton Ave, Riverside
(92506-1862)
PHONE..................951 275-8400
Robert B Summerour, *President*
Byron Defour, *Shareholder*
EMP: 63 **EST:** 1995
SQ FT: 50,000
SALES (est): 2.9MM **Privately Held**
WEB: www.pacificgrovehospital.com
SIC: 8063 Psychiatric hospitals

(P-21024)
LANDMARK MEDICAL SERVICES INC
Also Called: Landmark Medical Center
2030 N Garey Ave, Pomona (91767-2722)
PHONE..................909 593-2585
Rose Horsman, *President*
EMP: 100 **EST:** 1971
SQ FT: 27,500
SALES (est): 11.2MM **Privately Held**
WEB: www.landmarkmedicalcenter.net
SIC: 8063 Hospital for the mentally ill

(P-21025)
ONTRAK INC (PA)
2120 Colorado Ave Ste 230, Santa Monica
(90404-3768)
PHONE..................310 444-4300
Jonathan Mayhew, *CEO*
Terren S Peizer, *Ch of Bd*
Brandon H Laverne, *CFO*
Sara E Armstrong, *Senior VP*
Pat Traynor, *Senior VP*
EMP: 714 **EST:** 2003
SALES (est): 82.8MM **Publicly Held**
WEB: www.ontrakhealth.com
SIC: 8063 Psychiatric hospitals

(P-21026)
PINE GROVE HOSPITAL CORP
9449 San Fernando Rd, Sun Valley
(91352-1421)
PHONE..................818 348-0500
Paul R Tuft, *President*
EMP: 180 **EST:** 1998
SALES (est): 2.5MM **Privately Held**
SIC: 8063 Psychiatric hospitals

(P-21027)
STATE HOSPITALS CAL DEPT
Also Called: Fairview Developmental Center
2501 Harbor Blvd, Costa Mesa
(92626-6143)
PHONE..................714 957-5000

Michael Hatton, *Principal*
EMP: 456 **Privately Held**
WEB: www.ca.gov
SIC: 8063 9431 Hospital for the mentally
ill; mental health agency administration,
government;
HQ: California Department Of State Hospi-
tals
1600 9th St Ste 350
Sacramento CA 95814

(P-21028)
STATE HOSPITALS CAL DEPT
Also Called: Patton State Hospital
3102 E Highland Ave, Patton (92369-7813)
PHONE..................909 425-7000
Bruce Parks, *Director*
EMP: 456 **Privately Held**
WEB: www.ca.gov
SIC: 8063 9431 Hospital for the mentally
ill; mental health agency administration,
government;
HQ: California Department Of State Hospi-
tals
1600 9th St Ste 350
Sacramento CA 95814

(P-21029)
STATE HOSPITALS CAL DEPT
Also Called: Atascadero State Hospital
10333 El Camino Real, Atascadero
(93422-5808)
P.O. Box 7001 (93423-7001)
PHONE..................805 468-2000
John De Morales, *Branch Mgr*
EMP: 456 **Privately Held**
WEB: www.ca.gov
SIC: 8063 9431 8062 Hospital for the
mentally ill; mental health agency admin-
istration, government; ; general medical &
surgical hospitals
HQ: California Department Of State Hospi-
tals
1600 9th St Ste 350
Sacramento CA 95814

8069 Specialty Hospitals, Except Psychiatric

(P-21030)
AKUA BEHAVIORAL HEALTH INC (PA)
Also Called: Akua Mind & Body
20271 Sw Birch St Ste 200, Newport Beach
(92660-1752)
PHONE..................949 777-2283
Kenny Dewan, *CEO*
Nikki Vaughn, *Marketing Staff*
EMP: 161 **EST:** 2014
SALES (est): 15.6MM **Privately Held**
WEB: www.akuamindbody.com
SIC: 8069 8322 Drug addiction rehabilita-
tion hospital; rehabilitation services

(P-21031)
ANAHEIM REGIONAL MEDICAL CTR (PA)
1111 W La Palma Ave, Anaheim
(92801-2804)
PHONE..................714 774-1450
Patrick Petre, *CEO*
Roy L Dorman, *Ch Radiology*
Deborah Webber, *COO*
Rick Castro, *Officer*
Phyllis Snyder, *Ch Nursing Ofcr*
EMP: 968 **EST:** 1958
SALES (est): 113.9MM **Privately Held**
WEB: www.anaheimregionalmc.com
SIC: 8069 8062 Children's hospital; gen-
eral medical & surgical hospitals

(P-21032)
BARLOW GROUP (PA)
Also Called: Barlow Respitory Hospital
2000 Stadium Way, Los Angeles
(90026-2606)
PHONE..................213 250-4200
Margaret W Crane, *CEO*
Aclita Velasco, *Admin Asst*
Kaitlyn Dombrowski, *Personnel Assit*
Julia Shimizu, *Pub Rel Dir*

Melissa Wong, *Pharmacist*
EMP: 250 **EST:** 1994
SALES (est): 3.2MM **Privately Held**
WEB: www.barlowhospital.org
SIC: 8069 7389 8733 Specialty hospitals,
except psychiatric; fund raising organiza-
tions; medical research

(P-21033)
BARLOW RESPIRATORY HOSPITAL (PA)
2000 Stadium Way, Los Angeles (90026-2606)
PHONE..................213 250-4200
Margaret W Crane, *CEO*
Edward Engesser, *CFO*
Martin Hesky, *Pharmacy Dir*
Kaitlyn Dombrowski, *Personnel Assit*
Donna Kraus, *Purchasing*
EMP: 250 **EST:** 1902
SQ FT: 80,000
SALES (est): 68.3MM **Privately Held**
WEB: www.barlowhospital.org
SIC: 8069 Specialty hospitals, except psy-
chiatric

(P-21034)
BARLOW RESPIRATORY HOSPITAL
12401 Washington Blvd, Whittier
(90602-1006)
PHONE..................562 698-0811
Priscilla Jahangiri, *Branch Mgr*
Christy Doan, *Pharmacy Dir*
Rick Culp, *CIO*
Sandra Harlan, *Finance*
Armando Serrato, *Facilities Mgr*
EMP: 50
SALES (corp-wide): 68.3MM **Privately Held**
WEB: www.barlowhospital.org
SIC: 8069 Respiratory hospital
PA: Barlow Respiratory Hospital
2000 Stadium Way
Los Angeles CA 90026
213 250-4200

(P-21035)
BEVERLY HLLS ONCOLGY MED GROUP
8900 Wilshire Blvd, Beverly Hills
(90211-1958)
PHONE..................310 432-8900
Afshin Gabayan, *CEO*
EMP: 74 **EST:** 2007
SALES (est): 10.3MM **Privately Held**
WEB: www.bhcancercenter.com
SIC: 8069 Cancer hospital

(P-21036)
CHAPMAN HOUSE INC
1412 E Chapman Ave, Orange
(92866-2229)
PHONE..................714 288-6100
Timothy P Chapman, *President*
EMP: 115 **EST:** 1985
SALES (est): 9.6MM **Privately Held**
WEB: www.chapmanrehab.com
SIC: 8069 Drug addiction rehabilitation
hospital; alcoholism rehabilitation hospital

(P-21037)
CHILDRENS HEALTHCARE CAL (PA)
Also Called: CHOC CHILDREN'S
1201 W La Veta Ave, Orange (92868-4203)
PHONE..................714 997-3000
Kimberly C Cripe, *President*
Chris Furman, *Vice Chairman*
Thomas Brotherton, *COO*
Kerri Ruppert, *CFO*
Maria Minon MD, *Vice Pres*
EMP: 1500 **EST:** 1986
SALES (est): 38.2MM **Privately Held**
WEB: www.choc.org
SIC: 8069 Children's hospital

(P-21038)
CHILDRENS HOSPITAL LOS ANGELES (PA)
4650 W Sunset Blvd, Los Angeles
(90027-6062)
PHONE..................323 660-2450
Richard Cordova, *President*
Randall Wetzel,

PRODUCTS & SVCS

Dawn Wilcox, *President*
Lannie Tonnu, *CFO*
Alexandra Carter, *Senior VP*
▲ **EMP:** 2491 **EST:** 1901
SQ FT: 750,000
SALES: 1.3B **Privately Held**
WEB: www.chla.org
SIC: 8069 8062 Children's hospital; general medical & surgical hospitals

(P-21039)
CLARE MATRIX (PA)
2644 30th St Ste 100, Santa Monica (90405-3051)
PHONE..............................310 314-6200
Dan George, *CEO*
Kevin Fahy, *President*
Jennifer Hemphill, *Officer*
Julia Lundeberg, *Officer*
Scott Van Camp, *Officer*
EMP: 65 **EST:** 1970
SALES (est): 7.4MM **Privately Held**
WEB: www.clarematrix.org
SIC: 8069 Drug addiction rehabilitation hospital

(P-21040)
COMFORT CARE HOSPICE INC
5170 Sepulveda Blvd # 290, Sherman Oaks (91403-1186)
PHONE..............................818 501-3129
David Friedman, *CEO*
EMP: 55 **EST:** 2009
SALES (est): 4.9MM **Privately Held**
WEB: www.comfortcarehospice.com
SIC: 8069 Specialty hospitals, except psychiatric

(P-21041)
COUNTY OF LOS ANGELES
Also Called: Health Services, Dept of
30500 Arrastre Canyon Rd, Acton (93510-2160)
P.O. Box 25 (93510-0025)
PHONE..............................661 223-8700
Suzanna Kassinger, *Administration*
Peggy Sun, *Technology*
EMP: 57
SALES (corp-wide): 25.2B **Privately Held**
WEB: www.lacounty.gov
SIC: 8069 9431 8361 Alcoholism rehabilitation hospital; administration of public health programs; ; residential care
PA: County Of Los Angeles
500 W Temple St Ste 437
Los Angeles CA 90012
213 974-1101

(P-21042)
COUNTY OF LOS ANGELES
515 E 6th St, Los Angeles (90021-1009)
PHONE..............................213 974-7284
Maria Lopez, *Manager*
EMP: 57
SALES (corp-wide): 25.2B **Privately Held**
WEB: www.lacounty.gov
SIC: 8069 9111 Tuberculosis hospital; executive offices
PA: County Of Los Angeles
500 W Temple St Ste 437
Los Angeles CA 90012
213 974-1101

(P-21043)
COUNTY OF LOS ANGELES
Also Called: Department of Health Services
1240 N Mission Rd, Los Angeles (90033-1019)
PHONE..............................323 226-3468
Barbara Oliver, *Exec Dir*
William Walton, *Manager*
EMP: 57
SALES (corp-wide): 25.2B **Privately Held**
WEB: www.lacounty.gov
SIC: 8069 9431 8062 Specialty hospitals, except psychiatric; administration of public health programs; ; general medical & surgical hospitals
PA: County Of Los Angeles
500 W Temple St Ste 437
Los Angeles CA 90012
213 974-1101

(P-21044)
COUNTY OF LOS ANGELES
Also Called: Health Services, Dept of
38200 Lake Hughes Rd, Castaic (91384-4100)
PHONE..............................661 223-8700
Lynne Dahl, *Administration*
EMP: 57
SALES (corp-wide): 25.2B **Privately Held**
WEB: www.lacounty.gov
SIC: 8069 9431 Drug addiction rehabilitation hospital; administration of public health programs;
PA: County Of Los Angeles
500 W Temple St Ste 437
Los Angeles CA 90012
213 974-1101

(P-21045)
EXODUS RECOVERY CTR AT BROTMAN (PA)
3828 Delmas Ter, Culver City (90232-2713)
PHONE..............................310 253-9494
Luana Murphy, *Principal*
Lezlie Murch, *Vice Pres*
Geniesha Robertson, *Accountant*
EMP: 59 **EST:** 1999
SALES (est): 10.5MM **Privately Held**
WEB: www.exodusrecovery.com
SIC: 8069 Drug addiction rehabilitation hospital

(P-21046)
GOODEN CENTER
191 N El Molino Ave, Pasadena (91101-1804)
PHONE..............................626 356-0078
Budd Williams, *Exec Dir*
Molly Dhuet, *Program Mgr*
Thomas Gallo, *Opers Staff*
Andrew G Ewing III,
Joshua A Moore, *Director*
EMP: 85 **EST:** 1962
SALES: 7MM **Privately Held**
WEB: www.goodencenter.org
SIC: 8069 8361 8093 Alcoholism rehabilitation hospital; drug addiction rehabilitation hospital; rehabilitation center, residential: health care incidental; mental health clinic, outpatient

(P-21047)
KOREAN COMMUNITY SERVICES INC
Also Called: KC SERVICES
451 W Lincoln Ave Ste 100, Anaheim (92805-2912)
PHONE..............................714 527-6561
Ellen Ahn, *CEO*
Kay Ahn, *Director*
EMP: 120 **EST:** 1977
SALES (est): 8.1MM **Privately Held**
WEB: www.kcservices.org
SIC: 8069 8322 8011 Drug addiction rehabilitation hospital; social service center; offices & clinics of medical doctors

(P-21048)
NATIONWIDE MEDICAL GROUP INC
Also Called: Aegis Medical Systems
501 W Columbus St Ste A, Bakersfield (93301-1263)
PHONE..............................661 328-0245
Udi Barkai, *President*
EMP: 63 **EST:** 1998
SALES (est): 516.9K **Privately Held**
SIC: 8069 Drug addiction rehabilitation hospital

(P-21049)
SHIELDS FOR FAMILIES (PA)
11601 S Western Ave, Los Angeles (90047-5006)
P.O. Box 59129 (90059-0129)
PHONE..............................323 242-5000
Kathryn S Icenhower, *CEO*
Xylina Bean, *President*
Norma Mtume, *CFO*
Gerald Phillips, *Chairman*
Susan Haynes, *Treasurer*
EMP: 82 **EST:** 1991

SALES (est): 20.3MM **Privately Held**
WEB: www.shieldsforfamilies.org
SIC: 8069 Drug addiction rehabilitation hospital

(P-21050)
SHIELDS FOR FAMILIES
Also Called: Ark Program
11705 Deputy Yamamoto Pl A, Lynwood (90262-4031)
P.O. Box 59129, Los Angeles (90059-0129)
PHONE..............................310 603-1050
Shalanda Body, *Branch Mgr*
EMP: 63
SALES (corp-wide): 20.3MM **Privately Held**
WEB: www.shieldsforfamilies.org
SIC: 8069 8322 Drug addiction rehabilitation hospital; individual & family services
PA: Shields For Families
11601 S Western Ave
Los Angeles CA 90047
323 242-5000

(P-21051)
SHIELDS FOR FAMILIES
3209 N Alameda St, Compton (90222-1406)
PHONE..............................310 604-4446
Kathryn Icenhower, *Branch Mgr*
EMP: 63
SALES (corp-wide): 20.3MM **Privately Held**
WEB: www.shieldsforfamilies.org
SIC: 8069 Specialty hospitals, except psychiatric
PA: Shields For Families
11601 S Western Ave
Los Angeles CA 90047
323 242-5000

(P-21052)
SHRINERS HSPITALS FOR CHILDREN
Also Called: Shriner's Hospital
909 S Fair Oaks Ave, Pasadena (91105-2625)
PHONE..............................213 388-3151
Terence Cunningham, *Principal*
G Frank Labonte, *Administration*
Janet Amirkhanian, *Director*
Robert Cho, *Director*
Dawn Musser, *Director*
EMP: 132 **Privately Held**
WEB: www.shrinerschildrens.org
SIC: 8069 8062 Children's hospital; general medical & surgical hospitals
HQ: Shriners Hospitals For Children
12502 Usf Pine Dr
Tampa FL 33612
813 972-2250

(P-21053)
SOCIAL SCIENCE SERVICE CENTER
Also Called: Cedar House Rehabilitation Ctr
18612 Santa Ana Ave, Bloomington (92316-2636)
PHONE..............................909 421-7120
Daniel Gakgolla, *CEO*
Daniel Chagolla, *Officer*
Allen Eisenman, *Admin Sec*
Amelia Toledo, *Controller*
Jamie Vergilio, *Persnl Mgr*
EMP: 82 **EST:** 1973
SQ FT: 29,000
SALES (est): 19.6MM **Privately Held**
WEB: www.cedarhouse.org
SIC: 8069 8322 Alcoholism rehabilitation hospital; individual & family services

(P-21054)
SPECIAL NEEDS NETWORK
4401 Crenshaw Blvd # 215, Los Angeles (90043-1200)
PHONE..............................323 291-7100
Julia Djeke, *President*
Edguin Castellanos, *Officer*
Juan Garcia, *Prgrmr*
Hannah Chung, *Technician*
Amarilis Paredes, *Technician*
EMP: 50 **EST:** 2013
SALES (est): 4.7MM **Privately Held**
WEB: www.snnla.org
SIC: 8069 Children's hospital

(P-21055)
TENET HEALTHSYSTEM MEDICAL INC
Also Called: Placentia Linda Hospital
1301 N Rose Dr, Placentia (92870-3802)
PHONE..............................714 993-2000
Kent Clayton, *CEO*
Ann Marie Watkins, *Ch Nursing Ofcr*
Mary Ann Railey, *Planning*
Freddie Sanchez, *MIS Dir*
Fred Valtairo, *QA Dir*
EMP: 57
SALES (corp-wide): 17.6B **Publicly Held**
WEB: www.tenethealth.com
SIC: 8069 8011 8062 Specialty hospitals, except psychiatric; offices & clinics of medical doctors; general medical & surgical hospitals
HQ: Tenet Healthsystem Medical, Inc.
14201 Dallas Pkwy
Dallas TX 75254
469 893-2000

(P-21056)
WATERMAN CONVALESCENT HOSP INC
Mt Rubidoux Convalescent Hosp
6401 33rd St, Riverside (92509-1404)
PHONE..............................951 681-2200
Magda Williams, *Director*
EMP: 51
SALES (corp-wide): 10.1MM **Privately Held**
SIC: 8069 8051 Specialty hospitals, except psychiatric; skilled nursing care facilities
PA: Waterman Convalescent Hospital, Inc.
1850 N Waterman Ave
San Bernardino CA 92404
909 882-1215

(P-21057)
WATTS HEALTH FOUNDATION INC
Also Called: House of Uhuru
8005 S Figueroa St, Los Angeles (90003-2720)
PHONE..............................323 750-5284
Sharon Allen, *Director*
EMP: 78
SALES (corp-wide): 69.9MM **Privately Held**
WEB: www.wattshealth.org
SIC: 8069 Alcoholism rehabilitation hospital
HQ: Watts Health Foundation, Inc.
3405 W Imperial Hwy # 304
Inglewood CA 90303
310 424-2220

8071 Medical Laboratories

(P-21058)
ALLIANCE HEALTHCARE SVCS INC (DH)
18201 Von Karman Ave # 6, Irvine (92612-1000)
P.O. Box 19532 (92623-9532)
PHONE..............................949 242-5300
Rhonda Longmore-Grund, *CEO*
Carol Glejzer, *President*
Percy C Tomlinson, *CEO*
Howard Aihara, *CFO*
Richard W Johns,
EMP: 250 **EST:** 1983
SALES: 505.5MM
SALES (corp-wide): 512.6MM **Privately Held**
WEB: www.alliancehealthcareservices-us.com
SIC: 8071 Ultrasound laboratory
HQ: Akumin Corp.
8300 W Sunrise Blvd
Plantation FL 33322
954 475-2368

(P-21059)
AMBRY GENETICS CORPORATION (DH)
Also Called: Konica Mnlta Hlthcare Amrcas I
1 Enterprise, Aliso Viejo (92656-2606)
PHONE..............................949 900-5500
Tom Schoenherr, *CEO*

Ardy Arianpour, *President*
Charles Lm Dunlop, *President*
Jessica Rios, *COO*
Charles Caporale, *CFO*
EMP: 84 **EST:** 1999
SQ FT: 20,000
SALES (est): 65.3MM **Privately Held**
WEB: www.ambrygen.com
SIC: 8071 Medical laboratories
HQ: Konica Minolta Healthcare Americas,
Inc.
411 Newark Pompton Tpke
Wayne NJ 07470
973 633-1500

(P-21060)
BEDFORD SURGICAL CENTER INC
436 N Bedford Dr Ste 305, Beverly Hills
(90210-4320)
PHONE....................................310 271-6996
EMP: 55 **EST:** 2009
SALES (est): 224.9K **Privately Held**
WEB: www.bedfordsurgicalcenter.com
SIC: 8071 Medical laboratories

(P-21061)
CAP DIAGNOSTICS LLC
Also Called: Pathnostics
17661 Cowan, Irvine (92614-6031)
PHONE....................................714 966-1221
David A Baunoch,
Lukas Pieter, *CFO*
Matt Tate, *Vice Pres*
Maher Badir, *Lab Dir*
Pamela Nakamoto, *Executive Asst*
EMP: 75 **EST:** 2014
SALES (est): 18.4MM **Privately Held**
WEB: www.pathnostics.com
SIC: 8071 Medical laboratories

(P-21062)
CENTRAL CAST PTHLOGY CONS INC (DH)
Also Called: Western Dermato Pathology
Svcs
3701 S Higuera St, San Luis Obispo
(93401-7462)
P.O. Box 3160 (93403-3160)
PHONE....................................805 541-6033
Ronald E Rocha, *Med Doctor*
Ron Rocha, *President*
Greg Hohman, *Info Tech Mgr*
Sonya Bryars, *Software Dev*
Michael Frost, *Pathologist*
EMP: 87 **EST:** 1984
SQ FT: 18,000
SALES (est): 26.4MM **Privately Held**
WEB: www.westpaclab.com
SIC: 8071 Medical laboratories
HQ: Physician's Automated Laboratory, Inc.
820 34th St Ste 102
Bakersfield CA 93301
661 325-0744

(P-21063)
CERRITOS REFERENCE LABS INC
3848 Del Amo Blvd Ste 303, Torrance
(90503-7714)
PHONE....................................562 865-3609
Arturo Pamintuan, *President*
Nija Wade, *IT/INT Sup*
Mary Moreno, *Technician*
Terri Negrete, *Instructor*
Amanda Mathews, *Clerk*
EMP: 69 **EST:** 1998
SALES (est): 1.9MM **Privately Held**
WEB: www.cerritos.us
SIC: 8071 Testing laboratories

(P-21064)
CONSOLDTED MED BO-ANALYSIS INC (PA)
Also Called: Cmb Laboratory
10700 Walker St, Cypress (90630-4703)
P.O. Box 2369 (90630-1869)
PHONE....................................714 657-7369
Chin Kuo Fan, *President*
Gloria Fan, *Shareholder*
CAM Chinh Fan, *Senior VP*
Michelle Fan, *Vice Pres*
Anh Nguyen, *Executive*
EMP: 100 **EST:** 1979
SQ FT: 11,000

SALES (est): 10.1MM **Privately Held**
WEB: www.cmblabs.com
SIC: 8071 Testing laboratories

(P-21065)
CSA SILICON VALLEY LLC
Also Called: Cannasafe
7027 Hayvenhurst Ave, Van Nuys
(91406-3802)
PHONE....................................818 922-2416
EMP: 61 **EST:** 2019
SALES (est): 653.3K **Privately Held**
SIC: 8071 Medical laboratories

(P-21066)
CURATIVE-KORVA LLC
430 S Cataract Ave, San Dimas
(91773-2902)
PHONE....................................424 645-7575
Jonathan Martin, *Mng Member*
EMP: 85 **EST:** 2020
SALES (est): 8.8MM **Privately Held**
SIC: 8071 Medical laboratories

(P-21067)
FOCUS DIAGNOSTICS INC
11331 Valley View St # 150, Cypress
(90630-5300)
PHONE....................................714 220-1900
John Hurrell PHD, *President*
Michelle Tabb, *Vice Pres*
Anh Ha, *Research*
Yvette Parocua, *Research*
Susan Vogeli, *Technical Staff*
EMP: 400 **EST:** 1978
SQ FT: 36,000
SALES (est): 58.9MM
SALES (corp-wide): 9.4B **Publicly Held**
WEB: www.focusdx.com
SIC: 8071 Testing laboratories
PA: Quest Diagnostics Incorporated
500 Plaza Dr Ste G
Secaucus NJ 07094
973 520-2700

(P-21068)
FOCUS TECHNOLOGIES HOLDING CO
10703 Progress Way, Cypress
(90630-4714)
PHONE....................................800 838-4548
Charles C Harwood, *President*
Edward Caffrey, *Vice Pres*
Don Mooney, *Vice Pres*
Laurence R McCarthy, *CTO*
EMP: 22 **EST:** 1985
SQ FT: 28,000
SALES (est): 755.8K **Privately Held**
WEB: www.focusdx.com
SIC: 8071 3826 Testing laboratories; analytical instruments

(P-21069)
GRIFOLS DIAGNSTC SOLUTIONS INC (HQ)
2410 Lillyvale Ave, Los Angeles
(90032-3514)
PHONE....................................323 225-2221
David Bell, *Exec VP*
Laura Gardner, *Associate Dir*
Feng Jiang, *Prgrmr*
Josh Farrand, *IT/INT Sup*
Elizabeth Booth, *Research*
EMP: 621 **EST:** 2013
SALES (est): 500.5MM
SALES (corp-wide): 657.6MM **Privately Held**
WEB: www.diagnostic.grifols.com
SIC: 8071 Testing laboratories; biological laboratory; blood analysis laboratory; pathological laboratory
PA: Grifols Sa
Calle Jesus I Maria 6
Barcelona 08022
935 710-000

(P-21070)
HEALTH CARE PROVIDER LABS INC
14411 Palmrose Ave, Baldwin Park
(91706-3318)
P.O. Box 1287, West Covina (91793-1287)
PHONE....................................626 813-3800
Emilio Villarba, *CEO*
EMP: 55 **EST:** 1995

SALES (est): 2.5MM **Privately Held**
WEB:
www.healthcareproviderslaboratory.us
SIC: 8071 Medical laboratories

(P-21071)
HEALTHQUEST LABORATORIES INC (PA)
18023 Sky Park Cir # 66, Irvine
(92614-6521)
PHONE....................................714 418-5867
Thomas Giancursio, *CEO*
Edward Hickey, *CFO*
Joy REA, *Director*
EMP: 55 **EST:** 2015
SALES (est): 3.1MM **Privately Held**
WEB: www.hqesoterics.com
SIC: 8071 Testing laboratories

(P-21072)
INSIGHT HLTH SVCS HLDINGS CORP (PA)
26250 Entp Ct Ste 100, Lake Forest
(92630)
PHONE....................................949 282-6000
Louis E Hallman III, *President*
Robert V Baumgartner, *CEO*
Bernard J O'Rourke, *COO*
Keith S Kelson, *CFO*
Patricia R Blank, *Exec VP*
EMP: 195 **EST:** 1991
SQ FT: 30,000
SALES (est): 359.9MM **Privately Held**
SIC: 8071 Testing laboratories

(P-21073)
KAN-DI-KI LLC (HQ)
Also Called: Diagnostic Labs & Rdlgy
2820 N Ontario St, Burbank (91504-2015)
PHONE....................................818 549-1880
David F Smith III, *Mng Member*
Jennifer Saeturn, *Info Tech Mgr*
Lorette Kelsey, *Purchasing*
Barbara Palau, *Purchasing*
Eric Somes, *Opers Staff*
EMP: 879 **EST:** 2008
SQ FT: 7,000
SALES (est): 136.5MM **Privately Held**
WEB: www.tridentcare.com
SIC: 8071 Testing laboratories

(P-21074)
LATARA ENTERPRISE INC (PA)
Also Called: Foundation Laboratory
1716 W Holt Ave, Pomona (91768-3333)
PHONE....................................909 623-9301
Stepan Vartanian, *CEO*
Michelle Lewis, *CFO*
ARA Vartanian, *Treasurer*
Sam Azatyan, *Executive*
Kim Carter, *Executive*
EMP: 120 **EST:** 1966
SQ FT: 19,000
SALES (est): 25.3MM **Privately Held**
WEB: www.foundationlaboratory.com
SIC: 8071 Pathological laboratory

(P-21075)
LOTUS CLINICAL RESEARCH LLC
100 W California Blvd, Pasadena
(91105-3010)
PHONE....................................626 381-9830
Neil Singla, *Security Dir*
Anne Arriaga, *COO*
Mark Ubert, *CFO*
Jeff Kopplin, *Exec VP*
Peggy Schrammel, *Senior VP*
EMP: 100 **EST:** 2008
SALES (est): 11.4MM **Privately Held**
WEB: www.lotuscr.com
SIC: 8071 Medical laboratories

(P-21076)
MAX/MR IMAGING INC
17530 Ventura Blvd # 105, Encino
(91316-3818)
PHONE....................................818 382-2220
Javad Ahmadian, *President*
Rafi Hedvat, *CFO*
Majid Ahmadian, *Vice Pres*
Laura Melendez, *Administration*
EMP: 59 **EST:** 1991

SALES (est): 2.2MM **Privately Held**
WEB: www.maxmrimaging.com
SIC: 8071 X-ray laboratory, including dental

(P-21077)
MEDICAL LAB SVCS MED GROUP INC
25470 Med Ctr Dr Ste 105, Murrieta
(92562)
PHONE....................................951 834-9020
Ernest Holburt MD, *Director*
Susan Holburt, *Corp Secy*
EMP: 57 **EST:** 1972
SQ FT: 6,600
SALES (est): 8MM **Privately Held**
WEB: www.medicallaboratoryservices.com
SIC: 8071 Medical laboratories

(P-21078)
MID RCKLAND IMGING PRTNERS INC (HQ)
1510 Cotner Ave, Los Angeles
(90025-3303)
PHONE....................................310 445-2800
Howard G Berger, *CEO*
▲ **EMP:** 50 **EST:** 1986
SQ FT: 1,000
SALES (est): 31.4MM **Publicly Held**
WEB:
SIC: 8071 Ultrasound laboratory; X-ray laboratory, including dental; neurological laboratory

(P-21079)
NICHOLS INST REFERENCE LABS (DH)
33608 Ortega Hwy, San Juan Capistrano
(92675-2042)
PHONE....................................949 728-4000
Douglas Harrington, *President*
Charles Olson, *CFO*
Jolene Kahn, *Treasurer*
Michael O'Gorman, *Vice Pres*
Murugan R Pandian, *Vice Pres*
EMP: 525 **EST:** 1971
SQ FT: 240,000
SALES (est): 41.2MM
SALES (corp-wide): 9.4B **Publicly Held**
WEB: www.questdiagnostics.com
SIC: 8071 Testing laboratories
HQ: Quest Diagnostics Nichols Institute
33608 Ortega Hwy
San Juan Capistrano CA 92675
949 728-4000

(P-21080)
NKMAX AMERICA INC
3001 Daimler St, Santa Ana (92705-5812)
PHONE....................................949 396-6830
Daeyoung Kwon, *Principal*
Amber Kaplan, *Officer*
Paul Song, *Officer*
Stephen Chen, *CTO*
Kim Beaudette, *Human Resources*
EMP: 68 **EST:** 2017
SALES (est): 11.9MM **Privately Held**
WEB: www.nkgenbiotech.com
SIC: 8071 Medical laboratories

(P-21081)
PACIFIC DIAGNOSTIC LABS LLC (PA)
454 S Patterson Ave, Santa Barbara
(93111-2404)
P.O. Box 689 (93102-0689)
PHONE....................................805 879-8100
Mark Epply, *Mng Member*
Brent McClendon, *CFO*
Susanne Peterson, *Technical Staff*
Bill Reitz, *Buyer*
Lisa Heinrichsen, *Manager*
EMP: 142 **EST:** 2006
SALES (est): 16.9MM **Privately Held**
WEB: www.pdllabs.com
SIC: 8071 Testing laboratories

(P-21082)
PACIFIC TOXICOLOGY LABS
Also Called: Forensic Toxicology Associates
9348 De Soto Ave, Chatsworth
(91311-4926)
PHONE....................................818 598-3110
Jeff Lanzolatta, *CEO*
Sue Barbosa, *COO*

PRODUCTS & SVCS

Greg Carroll, *CFO*
Neil Patel Carroll, *CFO*
Neil Patel, *CFO*
EMP: 75 **EST:** 1984
SQ FT: 19,000
SALES (est): 13.7MM **Privately Held**
WEB: www.pactox.com
SIC: 8071 Testing laboratories

(P-21083)
PENTRON CLINICAL TECH LLC
1717 W Collins Ave, Orange (92867-5422)
PHONE...........................203 265-7397
EMP: 85
SALES (est): 2.3MM
SALES (corp-wide): 16.8MM **Privately Held**
SIC: 8071 Medical Laboratory
PA: Pentron Corporation
53 N Plains Industrial Rd
Wallingford CT 06492
203 265-7397

(P-21084)
PHYSICIANS AUTOMATED LAB INC (DH)
Also Called: Central Coast Pathology Lab
820 34th St Ste 102, Bakersfield (93301-1933)
P.O. Box 1536 (93302-1536)
PHONE...........................661 325-0744
Ken Botta, *CEO*
William R Schmalhorst MD, *President*
Bruce Smith, *CEO*
Kara Stephen, *Officer*
Joyce Hulen, *Admin Sec*
EMP: 69 **EST:** 1967
SQ FT: 63,000
SALES (est): 26.6MM **Privately Held**
WEB: www.westpaclab.com
SIC: 8071 Medical laboratories

(P-21085)
PHYSICIANS AUTOMATED LAB INC
2920 F St Ste A2, Bakersfield (93301-1829)
PHONE...........................661 325-0744
Lori Larkins, *Principal*
Angela Roberts, *Officer*
EMP: 67 **Privately Held**
WEB: www.westpaclab.com
SIC: 8071 Medical laboratories
HQ: Physician's Automated Laboratory, Inc.
820 34th St Ste 102
Bakersfield CA 93301
661 325-0744

(P-21086)
POLYPEPTIDE LABORATORIES INC (DH)
365 Maple Ave, Torrance (90503-2602)
PHONE...........................310 782-3569
Timothy Culbreth, *President*
Jane Salik, *CEO*
Tim Culbreth, *Vice Pres*
Nagana Goud, *Vice Pres*
Michael Verlander, *Vice Pres*
▲ **EMP:** 85 **EST:** 1996
SQ FT: 19,200
SALES (est): 50.9MM **Privately Held**
WEB: www.polypeptide.com
SIC: 8071 2836 8731 2834 Medical laboratories; biological products, except diagnostic; biotechnical research, commercial; pharmaceutical preparations
HQ: Polypeptide Laboratories Holding (Ppl) Ab
Soldattorpsv 5
Limhamn 216 1
403 662-00

(P-21087)
PRIMEX CLINICAL LABS INC (PA)
16742 Stagg St Ste 120, Van Nuys (91406-1641)
PHONE...........................818 779-0496
Oshin Hartoonian, *President*
ARA Hartoonian, *COO*
Erik Avaniss-Aghajano, *Vice Pres*
Andre Aslanian, *Info Tech Dir*
Maria Acosta, *Technology*
EMP: 80 **EST:** 1996
SQ FT: 3,000

SALES (est): 30.1MM **Privately Held**
WEB: www.primexlab.com
SIC: 8071 Blood analysis laboratory

(P-21088)
PRODUCTION ENGINEERING & MCH
14955 Hilton Dr, Fontana (92336-2082)
PHONE...........................909 721-2455
Thomas Kearns, *Principal*
Carl Reynolds, *Principal*
Steven Espinosa, *QC Mgr*
Char Wolosuk, *Production*
EMP: 21 **EST:** 2012
SALES (est): 1.2MM **Privately Held**
WEB: www.pemmachining.com
SIC: 8071 3599 Medical laboratories; machine shop, jobbing & repair

(P-21089)
PROFORM INC
Also Called: Proform Labs
1140 S Rockefeller Ave, Ontario (91761-2201)
PHONE...........................707 752-9010
Sean Phillip Thomas, *CEO*
Jim Starr, *Sales Staff*
EMP: 100 **EST:** 2016
SALES (est): 3.1MM **Privately Held**
SIC: 8071 Biological laboratory

(P-21090)
QUEST DGNSTICS CLNCAL LABS INC
26081 Avenue Hall 150, Valencia (91355-1241)
PHONE...........................661 964-6582
Dennis Hogle, *Branch Mgr*
EMP: 62
SQ FT: 40,000
SALES (corp-wide): 9.4B **Publicly Held**
WEB: www.questdiagnostics.com
SIC: 8071 Medical laboratories
HQ: Quest Diagnostics Clinical Laboratories, Inc.
1201 S Collegeville Rd
Collegeville PA 19426
610 454-6000

(P-21091)
QUEST DGNSTICS CLNCAL LABS INC
701 E 28th St Ste 113, Long Beach (90806-2759)
PHONE...........................562 424-3039
Ann Foresz, *Branch Mgr*
EMP: 62
SALES (corp-wide): 9.4B **Publicly Held**
WEB: www.questdiagnostics.com
SIC: 8071 Medical laboratories
HQ: Quest Diagnostics Clinical Laboratories, Inc.
1201 S Collegeville Rd
Collegeville PA 19426
610 454-6000

(P-21092)
QUEST DGNSTICS CLNCAL LABS INC
15141 Whittier Blvd # 12, Whittier (90603-2145)
PHONE...........................562 945-7771
Veronica Ochoa, *Branch Mgr*
EMP: 62
SALES (corp-wide): 9.4B **Publicly Held**
WEB: www.questdiagnostics.com
SIC: 8071 Testing laboratories
HQ: Quest Diagnostics Clinical Laboratories, Inc.
1201 S Collegeville Rd
Collegeville PA 19426
610 454-6000

(P-21093)
RADNET INC (PA)
1510 Cotner Ave, Los Angeles (90025-3303)
PHONE...........................310 445-2800
Howard G Berger, *Ch of Bd*
Mark D Stolper, *CFO*
Ranjan Jayanathan, *Exec VP*
David J Katz, *Exec VP*
Michael M Murdock, *Exec VP*
EMP: 365 **EST:** 1985

SALES (est): 1.1B **Publicly Held**
WEB: www.radnet.com
SIC: 8071 Ultrasound laboratory; X-ray laboratory, including dental

(P-21094)
RHEUMATOLOGY DIAGNOSTICS LAB
Also Called: Rdl Reference Laboratory
324 S Beverly Dr, Beverly Hills (90212-4801)
P.O. Box 34020, Los Angeles (90034-0020)
PHONE...........................310 253-5455
Morris Robert I, *President*
Laura Lehrhoff, *COO*
Rick Kazdan, *CFO*
Kristine Azarraga, *Ch Credit Ofcr*
Allan Metzger MD, *Vice Pres*
EMP: 60 **EST:** 1976
SALES (est): 11MM **Privately Held**
SIC: 8071 Pathological laboratory

(P-21095)
SAMARITAN IMAGING CENTER
1245 Wilshire Blvd # 205, Los Angeles (90017-4812)
PHONE...........................213 977-2140
Andrew B Leeka, *CEO*
EMP: 1102 **EST:** 2010
SALES (est): 1MM
SALES (corp-wide): 923K **Privately Held**
WEB: www.pihhealth.org
SIC: 8071 Medical laboratories
HQ: Pih Health Good Samaritan Hospital
1225 Wilshire Blvd
Los Angeles CA 90017
213 977-2121

(P-21096)
SPECIALTY LABORATORIES INC (DH)
Also Called: Quest Dgnstics Nchols Inst Vln
27027 Tourney Rd, Valencia (91355-5386)
PHONE...........................661 799-6543
R Keith Laughman, *President*
Vicki Difrancesco, *Vice Pres*
Michael Bond, *Administration*
Nicole Larkins, *Administration*
Sam Hart, *Info Tech Mgr*
▲ **EMP:** 633 **EST:** 1975
SALES (est): 71.3MM
SALES (corp-wide): 9.4B **Publicly Held**
WEB: www.ameripath.com
SIC: 8071 Testing laboratories
HQ: Ameripath, Inc.
7108 Fairway Dr Ste 335
Palm Beach Gardens FL 33418
561 712-6200

(P-21097)
SPECTRA CLINICAL LABS INC
14601 S Broadway, Gardena (90248-1811)
P.O. Box 2989 (90247-1189)
PHONE...........................562 776-8440
Nagi N Abdelsayed, *President*
EMP: 52 **EST:** 1991
SALES (est): 4.6MM **Privately Held**
SIC: 8071 Testing laboratories

(P-21098)
TESTING COMPANY LLC (PA)
12802 Valley View St, Garden Grove (92845-2511)
PHONE...........................714 379-0280
Christopher Crock, *Mng Member*
Brittaney Crock,
EMP: 146 **EST:** 2020
SALES (est): 4.6MM **Privately Held**
SIC: 8071 Testing laboratories

(P-21099)
THAIHOT INVESTMENT CO US LTD
18201 Von Karman Ave # 60, Irvine (92612-1000)
PHONE...........................949 242-5300
Tom Gaston, *Opers Staff*
Paula Whaley, *Opers Staff*
EMP: 2450 **EST:** 2017
SALES (est): 58.9MM **Privately Held**
WEB: www.tahoeinvest.com
SIC: 8071 Medical laboratories

PA: Tahoe Investment Group Co., Ltd.
Floor 2, Aolinpike Building No.43,
Hudong Ro Ad, Gulou Dis rict
Fuzhou 35000

(P-21100)
UNILAB CORPORATION (HQ)
Also Called: Quest Diagnostics
8401 Fallbrook Ave, West Hills (91304-3226)
PHONE...........................318 737-6000
Surya Mohapatra, *CEO*
Robert Moverley, *Managing Dir*
Tony Gouveia, *VP Finance*
Alexis Pacheco, *Training Spec*
Callie Poindexter, *Marketing Staff*
EMP: 400 **EST:** 1992
SALES (est): 251MM
SALES (corp-wide): 9.4B **Publicly Held**
WEB: www.questdiagnostics.com
SIC: 8071 Testing laboratories
PA: Quest Diagnostics Incorporated
500 Plaza Dr Ste G
Secaucus NJ 07094
973 520-2700

(P-21101)
WESTPAC LABS INC (PA)
10200 Pioneer Blvd # 500, Santa Fe Springs (90670-6000)
PHONE...........................562 906-5227
Phillp Chen, *CEO*
Brian Patchett, *Officer*
Michael Mosunic, *Vice Pres*
Mimi Breslin, *Controller*
Manny Jaime, *Senior Mgr*
EMP: 296 **EST:** 2009
SALES (est): 91.3MM **Privately Held**
WEB: www.westpaclab.com
SIC: 8071 Testing laboratories

(P-21102)
WHITEFIELD MEDICAL LAB INC (PA)
Also Called: Whitefield Medical Lab & Rdlgy
764 Indigo Ct Ste A, Pomona (91767-2269)
PHONE...........................909 625-2114
Jatin Laxpati, *President*
Shaila Laxpati, *Treasurer*
EMP: 50 **EST:** 1986
SQ FT: 7,000
SALES (est): 6.2MM **Privately Held**
WEB: www.whitefieldlabs.com
SIC: 8071 Testing laboratories

8072 Dental Laboratories

(P-21103)
BURBANK DENTAL LABORATORY INC
2101 Floyd St, Burbank (91504-3411)
PHONE...........................818 841-2256
Anatony Sedler, *CEO*
Tony Sedler, *President*
David French, *Vice Pres*
Robert Vartanian, *Vice Pres*
Denise Hernandez, *Surgeon*
▲ **EMP:** 175 **EST:** 1980
SALES (est): 19.6MM **Privately Held**
WEB: www.burbankdental.com
SIC: 8072 Dental laboratories

(P-21104)
CONTINENTAL DNTL CERAMICS INC
1873 Western Way, Torrance (90501-1124)
PHONE...........................310 618-8821
Jerry Doviack, *President*
Krystina Doviack, *Corp Secy*
Karen Chamberlain, *Mktg Dir*
Robert Gonzalez, *Manager*
EMP: 50 **EST:** 1971
SQ FT: 12,000
SALES (est): 3.7MM **Privately Held**
WEB: www.continentaldental.com
SIC: 8072 Crown & bridge production

(P-21105)
DLH DAVINCI LLC
22135 Roscoe Blvd Ste 101, West Hills (91304-3857)
PHONE...........................818 703-5100
Thomas Rochefort, *Vice Pres*

EMP: 65 EST: 2012
SALES (est): 604.6K Privately Held
SIC: 8072 Dental laboratories

(P-21106)
GKY DENTAL ARTS INC (PA)
4212 Artesia Blvd, Torrance (90504-3106)
PHONE..................310 214-8007
Glen Yamamoto, President
Brian Smith, Vice Pres
Kiichi Yamamoto, Vice Pres
Emiko Onda, Accountant
▲ EMP: 79 EST: 1982
SQ FT: 4,500 Privately Held
WEB: www.gkydentalarts.com
SIC: 8072 Crown & bridge production

(P-21107)
JAMES R GLDWELL DNTL CRMICS IN (PA)
Also Called: Glidewell Laboratories
4141 Macarthur Blvd, Newport Beach (92660-2015)
PHONE..................949 440-2600
James R Glidewell, CEO
Dudley Michael, Partner
Ryan Shiroishi, Partner
Sherry Vitalone, Partner
Greg Minzenmayer, COO
▲ EMP: 1100 EST: 1969
SQ FT: 72,000
SALES (est): 519.4MM Privately Held
WEB: www.glidewelldental.com
SIC: 8072 Crown & bridge production

(P-21108)
JOONG-ANG DAILY NEWS CAL INC
2880 W Olympic Blvd Ste 2, Los Angeles (90006-2644)
PHONE..................213 487-2355
Jonathan Lee, Branch Mgr
EMP: 85 Privately Held
SIC: 8072 Dental laboratories
HQ: The Joong-Ang Daily News California Inc
690 Wilshire Pl
Los Angeles CA 90005
213 368-2500

(P-21109)
JP CROWN HOUSE DENTAL LAB INC (PA)
6481 Orangethorpe Ave # 8, Buena Park (90620-1365)
PHONE..................714 323-8555
Gwisoon Park, CEO
EMP: 57 EST: 2018
SALES (est): 772.4K Privately Held
SIC: 8072 Dental laboratories

(P-21110)
KEATING DENTAL ARTS
16881 Hale Ave Ste A, Irvine (92606-5068)
PHONE..................949 955-2100
Shaun Keating, President
Gloria Macias, Admin Asst
Jeanette Crabb, Manager
Matthew Keating, Manager
Jeff Sugimura, Manager
EMP: 105 EST: 2002
SQ FT: 26,000
SALES (est): 13MM Privately Held
WEB: www.keatingdentallab.com
SIC: 8072 Crown & bridge production

(P-21111)
NOBEL BIOCARE USA LLC
22715 Savi Ranch Pkwy, Yorba Linda (92887-4609)
PHONE..................714 282-4800
Thomas Olsen, President
Jim Lazaroff, COO
Frederick Walther, Treasurer
Hans Geiselhoringer, Exec VP
Natalia Hess, Vice Pres
▲ EMP: 500 EST: 2004
SQ FT: 150,000
SALES (est): 68.6MM
SALES (corp-wide): 22.2B Publicly Held
WEB: www.nobelbiocare.com
SIC: 8072 Dental laboratories

HQ: Nobel Biocare Ab
Vastra Hamngatan 12
Goteborg 411 1
318 188-00

(P-21112)
POSCA BROTHERS DENTAL LAB INC
641 W Willow St, Long Beach (90806-2832)
PHONE..................562 427-1811
Alex Posca, President
Yanette Posca, Corp Secy
Aj Posca, Vice Pres
Angel Jorge Posca, Vice Pres
▲ EMP: 55 EST: 1965
SQ FT: 5,000
SALES (est): 4.6MM Privately Held
WEB: www.poscabrothers.com
SIC: 8072 3843 Dental laboratories; teeth, artificial (not made in dental laboratories)

(P-21113)
TRIDENT LABS LLC
Also Called: Trident Dental Labratories
12000 Aviation Blvd, Hawthorne (90250-3438)
PHONE..................310 915-9121
Laurence K Fishman, President
Richard B Mc Donald, CFO
Richard McDonald, CFO
Rachelle Selmon, Vice Pres
Tim Goldstein, Supervisor
▲ EMP: 125 EST: 1988
SQ FT: 16,000
SALES (est): 20.8MM
SALES (corp-wide): 165.1MM Privately Held
WEB: www.tridentlab.com
SIC: 8072 Crown & bridge production
PA: Gdc Holdings, Inc.
11601 Kew Gardens Ave # 200
Palm Beach Gardens FL 33410
763 398-0654

8082 Home Health Care Svcs

(P-21114)
24-7 CAREGIVERS REGISTRY INC
6800 Owensmouth Ave # 420, Canoga Park (91303-4238)
PHONE..................800 687-8066
Piroska Zalkadi, CEO
Richard Weatherman, CFO
EMP: 110 EST: 2013
SALES (est): 4.2MM Privately Held
WEB: www.24-7caregiversregistry.com
SIC: 8082 Home health care services

(P-21115)
24HR HOMECARE LLC (PA)
300 N Pacific Coast Hwy # 1065, El Segundo (90245-4490)
PHONE..................310 906-3683
Sonia Aouriri, Principal
Ryan Iwamoto, Chief Mktg Ofcr
Arlyn Carbonell, Administration
Jacque Davis, Controller
Amaris Coutee, Opers Staff
EMP: 2370
SALES (est): 70.7MM Privately Held
WEB: www.24hrcares.com
SIC: 8082 Home health care services

(P-21116)
24HR HOMECARE LLC
Also Called: 24 Hour Home Care
200 N Pcf Cast Hwy Ste 30, El Segundo (90245)
PHONE..................310 375-5353
David Allerby, Mng Member
Blake Naudin, Managing Dir
Jesse Thomas, Managing Dir
Stephanie Aguilera, Program Mgr
Charles Munoz, Business Mgr
EMP: 217 EST: 2008
SALES (est): 25.4MM Privately Held
WEB: www.24hrcares.com
SIC: 8082 Oxygen tent service

(P-21117)
24HR HOMECARE LLC
5901 Green Valley Cir, Culver City (90230-6938)
PHONE..................310 258-9525
EMP: 53
SALES (corp-wide): 70.7MM Privately Held
WEB: www.24hrcares.com
SIC: 8082 Home health care services
PA: 24hr Homecare L.L.C.
300 N Pacific Coast Hwy # 1065
El Segundo CA 90245
310 906-3683

(P-21118)
24HR HOMECARE LLC
17141 Ventura Blvd # 205, Encino (91316-4027)
PHONE..................818 385-0227
David Allerby, President
Sarina Saldana, Managing Dir
EMP: 53
SALES (corp-wide): 70.7MM Privately Held
WEB: www.24hrcares.com
SIC: 8082 Home health care services
PA: 24hr Homecare L.L.C.
300 N Pacific Coast Hwy # 1065
El Segundo CA 90245
310 906-3683

(P-21119)
24HR HOMECARE LLC
1440 N Harbor Blvd # 715, Fullerton (92835-4127)
PHONE..................714 881-4245
EMP: 53
SALES (corp-wide): 70.7MM Privately Held
WEB: www.24hrcares.com
SIC: 8082 Home health care services
PA: 24hr Homecare L.L.C.
300 N Pacific Coast Hwy # 1065
El Segundo CA 90245
310 906-3683

(P-21120)
24HR HOMECARE LLC
16485 Laguna Canyon Rd # 110, Irvine (92618-3837)
PHONE..................949 607-8115
EMP: 53
SALES (corp-wide): 70.7MM Privately Held
WEB: www.24hrcares.com
SIC: 8082 Home health care services
PA: 24hr Homecare L.L.C.
300 N Pacific Coast Hwy # 1065
El Segundo CA 90245
310 906-3683

(P-21121)
24HR HOMECARE LLC
2401 E Gonzales Rd # 170, Oxnard (93036-0679)
PHONE..................805 988-2205
EMP: 53
SALES (corp-wide): 70.7MM Privately Held
WEB: www.24hrcares.com
SIC: 8082 Home health care services
PA: 24hr Homecare L.L.C.
300 N Pacific Coast Hwy # 1065
El Segundo CA 90245
310 906-3683

(P-21122)
24HR HOMECARE LLC
21311 Hawthorne Blvd # 101, Torrance (90503-5681)
PHONE..................310 375-5353
EMP: 53
SALES (corp-wide): 70.7MM Privately Held
WEB: www.24hrcares.com
SIC: 8082 Home health care services
PA: 24hr Homecare L.L.C.
300 N Pacific Coast Hwy # 1065
El Segundo CA 90245
310 906-3683

(P-21123)
A CAREGIVER LLC
31520 Rr Cyn Rd Ste A, Canyon Lake (92587-9499)
PHONE..................951 676-4190
EMP: 50
SALES (est): 841.8K Privately Held
SIC: 8082 Home Health Care Services

(P-21124)
ACCENTCARE HM HLTH EL CNTRO IN
2344 S 2nd St Ste A, El Centro (92243-5606)
PHONE..................760 352-4022
Melanie Ihler, CEO
EMP: 248 EST: 1994
SALES (est): 963.8K
SALES (corp-wide): 1.3B Privately Held
SIC: 8082 Home health care services
HQ: Accentcare Home Health, Inc.
135 Technology Dr Ste 150
Irvine CA 92618

(P-21125)
ACCENTCARE HOME HLTH YUMA INC
1455 Auto Center Dr # 200, Ontario (91761-2239)
PHONE..................909 605-7000
Connie Morris, President
Anna Trappett, Vice Pres
Melanie Ihler, Admin Sec
EMP: 495 EST: 1992
SALES (est): 17.1MM
SALES (corp-wide): 1.3B Privately Held
SIC: 8082 Home health care services
HQ: Accentcare Home Health, Inc.
135 Technology Dr Ste 150
Irvine CA 92618

(P-21126)
ACCREDITED NURSING SERVICES
Also Called: Accredited Nursing Care
950 S Coast Dr Ste 215, Costa Mesa (92626-7850)
PHONE..................714 973-1234
Meryll Jones, Manager
EMP: 111
SALES (corp-wide): 16.8MM Privately Held
WEB: www.accreditednursing.com
SIC: 8082 Home health care services
PA: Accredited Nursing Services
17141 Ventura Blvd # 201
Encino CA
818 986-6017

(P-21127)
ACTION HOME HEALTH CARE INC
6300 Wilshire Blvd # 710, Los Angeles (90048-5206)
PHONE..................310 659-9930
Renee C Steele, President
EMP: 50 EST: 1996
SALES (est): 8MM Privately Held
WEB: www.action-health.com
SIC: 8082 Home health care services

(P-21128)
AEGIS SENIOR COMMUNITIES LLC
Also Called: Aegis of Ventura
4964 Telegraph Rd, Ventura (93003-8181)
PHONE..................805 650-1114
Hugh Carter, Manager
Mary Sawyer, Mktg Dir
Brenda Plascencia, Food Svc Dir
EMP: 106
SALES (corp-wide): 137.2MM Privately Held
WEB: www.aegisliving.com
SIC: 8082 8051 Home health care services; skilled nursing care facilities
PA: Senior Aegis Communities Llc
415 118th Ave Se
Bellevue WA 98005
866 688-5829

PRODUCTS & SVCS

(P-21129)
AEGIS SENIOR COMMUNITIES LLC
Also Called: Aegis of Granada Hills
10801 Lindley Ave, Granada Hills
(91344-4441)
PHONE..............................818 363-3373
Bill Phelps, *Branch Mgr*
Samantha Shippee, *Nursing Dir*
Scott Eckstein, *Manager*
EMP: 106
SALES (corp-wide): 137.2MM **Privately Held**
WEB: www.aegisliving.com
SIC: **8082** 8052 8051 8361 Home health care services; intermediate care facilities; skilled nursing care facilities; residential care
PA: Senior Aegis Communities Llc
415 118th Ave Se
Bellevue WA 98005
866 688-5829

(P-21130)
ALL CARE HOME HEALTH PROVIDER
1218 E Broadway, Glendale (91205-1408)
PHONE..............................818 241-2473
Apolonio Pagsisihaw, *President*
Apolonio Pagsisihan, *President*
Gennie Espinosa,
EMP: 60 EST: 1995
SALES (est): 5.7MM **Privately Held**
WEB: www.allcareprovider.com
SIC: **8082** Home health care services

(P-21131)
ALLIED PROF NURSING CARE INC
2345 W Fthlls Blvd Ste 14, Upland (91786)
PHONE..............................909 949-1066
Michael Gutierrez, *President*
Karen Gutierrez, *Administration*
EMP: 88 EST: 1996
SALES (est): 7.3MM **Privately Held**
WEB:
www.alliedprofessionalnursingcare.com
SIC: **8082** Visiting nurse service

(P-21132)
AMDAL IN-HOME CARE INC (PA)
147 N K St, Tulare (93274-4003)
P.O. Box 1318 (93275-1318)
PHONE..............................559 686-6611
Deanne Martin Soares, *CEO*
Julian Mack, *Shareholder*
Charles Mack, *Admin Sec*
EMP: 50 EST: 1999
SALES (est): 10.7MM **Privately Held**
WEB: www.amdalinhome.com
SIC: **8082** Home health care services

(P-21133)
AMERICAN PRIVATE DUTY INC
Also Called: American Untd HM Care Crp-Priv
13111 Ventura Blvd # 100, Studio City
(91604-2218)
PHONE..............................818 386-6358
Ann Koshy, *President*
Levi Ferencz, *Controller*
Ray Tran,
EMP: 80 EST: 1999
SALES (est): 7.4MM **Privately Held**
WEB: www.americanunitedhomecare.com
SIC: **8082** Visiting nurse service

(P-21134)
ANGELS IN MOTION LLC
Also Called: Visiting Angels
4091 Riverside Dr Ste 111, Chino
(91710-3195)
PHONE..............................909 590-9102
Dominique Alvarez, *Mng Member*
EMP: 70 EST: 2010
SALES (est): 7.3MM **Privately Held**
WEB: www.visitingangels.com
SIC: **8082** Home health care services

(P-21135)
APRIA HEALTHCARE GROUP LLC (HQ)
26220 Enterprise Ct, Lake Forest
(92630-8405)
PHONE..............................949 639-2000

Daniel J Stark, *CEO*
Debra L Morris, *CFO*
Connie Lai, *Officer*
Kimberlie Rogers-Bowers, *Senior VP*
James Bowers, *Vice Pres*
◆ EMP: 350 EST: 1995
SQ FT: 100,000
SALES (est): 1.1B
SALES (corp-wide): 1.1B **Publicly Held**
WEB: www.apria.com
SIC: **8082** Home health care services
PA: Apria, Inc.
7353 Company Dr
Indianapolis IN 46237
800 990-9799

(P-21136)
ASSISTED HOME RECOVERY INC
1900 W Garvey Ave S # 210, West Covina
(91790-2656)
PHONE..............................626 915-5595
EMP: 62
SALES (corp-wide): 11.4MM **Privately Held**
WEB: www.assistedcares.com
SIC: **8082** Home health care services
PA: Assisted Home Recovery, Inc.
8550 Balboa Blvd Lbby
Northridge CA 91325
818 894-8117

(P-21137)
AXELACARE HOLDINGS INC
12604 Hiddencreek Way C, Cerritos
(90703-2137)
PHONE..............................714 522-8802
EMP: 648 **Privately Held**
WEB: www.specialty.optumrx.com
SIC: **8082** Home health care services
PA: Axelacare Holdings, Inc.
15529 College Blvd
Lenexa KS 66219

(P-21138)
BJZ LLC
Also Called: Always Best Care Desert Cities
45150 Club Dr, Indian Wells (92210-8806)
PHONE..............................760 851-0740
Neil Zwack, *Administration*
Bonnie Zwack, *Mng Member*
EMP: 140 EST: 2013
SALES (est): 3.1MM **Privately Held**
WEB: www.alwaysbestcare.com
SIC: **8082** Home health care services

(P-21139)
BLUEBRIDGE PROF SVCS INC
Also Called: Comfort Keepers
420 W Baseline Rd Ste D, Claremont
(91711-1621)
PHONE..............................909 625-6151
Michael Craig II, *CEO*
EMP: 68 EST: 2005
SALES (est): 2.8MM **Privately Held**
WEB: www.comfortkeepers.com
SIC: **8082** Home health care services

(P-21140)
BRANLYN PROMINENCE INC
Also Called: Home Instead Senior Care
13334 Amargosa Rd, Victorville
(92392-8504)
PHONE..............................760 843-5655
Chris Parmelee, *General Mgr*
EMP: 130
SQ FT: 1,800 **Privately Held**
WEB: www.homeinstead.com
SIC: **8082** Home health care services
PA: Branlyn Prominence, Inc.
9213 Archibald Ave
Rancho Cucamonga CA 91730

(P-21141)
BRANLYN PROMINENCE INC (PA)
Also Called: Home Instead Senior Care
9213 Archibald Ave, Rancho Cucamonga
(91730-5207)
PHONE..............................909 476-9030
Brandi Johnson, *CEO*
Lynda Patriquin, *Vice Pres*
EMP: 100 EST: 2000

SALES (est): 10.4MM **Privately Held**
WEB: www.homeinstead.com
SIC: **8082** Home health care services

(P-21142)
BRIGHT CARE HOME HEALTH INC (PA)
3925 Rosemead Blvd 205a, Rosemead
(91770-1933)
PHONE..............................626 285-9698
Chris Lam, *President*
EMP: 55 EST: 2005
SALES (est): 1.2MM **Privately Held**
WEB: www.brightcarehomehealth.com
SIC: **8082** Home health care services

(P-21143)
BRIGHT EXPECTATIONS INC
8175 Limonite Ave Ste C, Riverside
(92509-6121)
PHONE..............................951 360-2070
Charley Cox, *President*
EMP: 50 EST: 1993
SQ FT: 1,000
SALES (est): 6.1MM **Privately Held**
SIC: **8082** Home health care services

(P-21144)
BRITTNEY HOUSE
5401 E Centralia St, Long Beach
(90808-1494)
PHONE..............................562 421-4717
Major Chief, *Owner*
EMP: 72
SALES (est): 295K **Privately Held**
WEB: www.activcareliving.com
SIC: **8082** 8051 Home health care services; skilled nursing care facilities

(P-21145)
C MBA RN INC
Also Called: Interim Services
4801 Truxtun Ave, Bakersfield
(93309-0605)
PHONE..............................661 395-1700
Darlyn Baker, *President*
Chuck Baker, *Vice Pres*
EMP: 76 EST: 1993
SQ FT: 5,000
SALES (est): 10.6MM **Privately Held**
WEB: www.interimhealthcare.com
SIC: **8082** Home health care services

(P-21146)
CARE STFFING PROFESSIONALS INC
2151 E Cnvntion Ctr Way S, Ontario
(91764-5429)
PHONE..............................909 906-2060
D'Andre Lampkin, *CEO*
EMP: 80 EST: 2016
SALES (est): 6.7MM **Privately Held**
WEB: www.carestaffingprofessionals.com
SIC: **8082** 7363 Home health care services; medical help service

(P-21147)
CENTRAL HEALTH PLAN CAL INC
1540 Bridgegate Dr, Diamond Bar
(91765-3912)
PHONE..............................626 938-7120
Sam Kam, *President*
EMP: 175 EST: 2001
SQ FT: 16,144
SALES (est): 37.2MM
SALES (corp-wide): 1.2B **Publicly Held**
WEB: www.centralhealthplan.com
SIC: **8082** Home health care services
PA: Bright Health Group, Inc.
8000 Norman Center Dr # 1200
Minneapolis MN 55437
612 238-1321

(P-21148)
CK FRANCHISING INC (DH)
Also Called: Comfort Keepers
1 Park Plz Ste 300, Irvine (92614-2510)
PHONE..............................800 498-8144
Sarosh Mistry, *CEO*
Phillip Celani, *Vice Pres*
Tim Purcey, *Vice Pres*
Carol Carbutti, *General Mgr*
Shannon Haws, *General Mgr*
EMP: 314 EST: 1999

SQ FT: 11,160
SALES (est): 34.6MM
SALES (corp-wide): 158.5MM **Privately Held**
WEB: www.comfortkeepersfranchise.com
SIC: **8082** 6794 Home health care services; franchises, selling or licensing
HQ: Sodexo, Inc.
9801 Washingtonian Blvd # 1
Gaithersburg MD 20878
301 987-4000

(P-21149)
CLINICS ON DEMAND   NC
11000 Wilshire Blvd, Los Angeles
(90024-3601)
PHONE..............................310 709-7355
Shahrouz Ghodsian, *CEO*
EMP: 81 EST: 2015
SALES (est): 8.5MM **Privately Held**
SIC: **8082** Home health care services

(P-21150)
COASTAL CMNTY SENIOR CARE LLC
Also Called: Home Instead Senior Care
5500 E Atherton St # 216, Long Beach
(90815-4016)
PHONE..............................562 596-4884
Donald Pierce, *Mng Member*
EMP: 140 EST: 2015
SQ FT: 2,300
SALES (est): 10.2MM **Privately Held**
WEB: www.homeinstead.com
SIC: **8082** Home health care services

(P-21151)
COMFORT KEEPERS (PA)
29970 Tech Dr Ste 213, Murrieta (92563)
PHONE..............................951 696-2710
Jennifer Ramos, *Owner*
Erin Beck, *Opers Staff*
Wyatt Howell, *Manager*
EMP: 111 EST: 2012
SALES (est): 103.1K **Privately Held**
WEB: www.comfortkeepers.com
SIC: **8082** Home health care services

(P-21152)
COMMUNITY SENIOR SERV INC
VIP Adult Day Health Care
1101 S Grand Ave Ste K, Santa Ana
(92705-4100)
PHONE..............................714 558-1216
Louise Obester, *Director*
EMP: 51
SALES (corp-wide): 17.1MM **Privately Held**
WEB: www.mealsonwheelssoc.org
SIC: **8082** 8322 Home health care services; geriatric social service
PA: Community Seniorserv, Inc.
1200 N Knollwood C
Anaheim CA 92801
714 220-0224

(P-21153)
COMPETENT CARE INC
Also Called: Competent Care HM Hlth Nursing
2900 Bristol St Ste D107, Costa Mesa
(92626-5940)
PHONE..............................714 545-4818
Lynett Laroche, *President*
EMP: 70 EST: 1988
SALES (est): 5.1MM **Privately Held**
WEB: www.competentcare.com
SIC: **8082** 7299 Visiting nurse service; information services, consumer

(P-21154)
COMPPARTNERS INC
333 City Blvd W Ste 1500, Orange
(92868-5913)
PHONE..............................949 253-3111
Bruce Carlin, *CEO*
Bernard J Mansheim, *Chief Mktg Ofcr*
Eleanor Marciniak, *CTO*
Andrea Laughlin, *Technical Staff*
Maria Fugrad, *Supervisor*
EMP: 50 EST: 1998
SQ FT: 15,000
SALES (est): 1.7MM **Privately Held**
WEB: www.comppartners.com
SIC: **8082** Home health care services

(P-21155)
CONFIDO LLC
Also Called: 123 Home Care
3407 W 6th St Ste 709, Los Angeles (90020-2554)
PHONE..................................310 361-8558
Graeme Freeman, *CEO*
Brendan Bodi, *Sales Executive*
Ryan Baxter, *Director*
Cristal Munoz, *Director*
Mark Schellinger, *Director*
EMP: 1900 EST: 2018
SALES (est): 54.9MM **Privately Held**
SIC: 8082 Home health care services

(P-21156)
CRESCENT HEALTHCARE INC
1640 Newport Blvd Ste 435, Costa Mesa (92627-7730)
PHONE..................................949 646-2267
EMP: 53
SALES (corp-wide): 132.5B **Publicly Held**
WEB: www.crescenthealthcare.com
SIC: 8082 Home health care services
HQ: Crescent Healthcare, Inc.
11980 Telg Rd Ste 100
Santa Fe Springs CA 90670

(P-21157)
CRESCENT HEALTHCARE INC
11980 Telg Rd Ste 102, Santa Fe Springs (90670)
PHONE..................................562 347-2800
Lori Zsitek, *Branch Mgr*
EMP: 53
SALES (corp-wide): 132.5B **Publicly Held**
WEB: www.crescenthealthcare.com
SIC: 8082 Home health care services
HQ: Crescent Healthcare, Inc.
11980 Telg Rd Ste 100
Santa Fe Springs CA 90670

(P-21158)
CRESCENT HEALTHCARE INC (DH)
11980 Telg Rd Ste 100, Santa Fe Springs (90670)
PHONE..................................714 520-6300
Paul Mastrapa, *CEO*
Virginia Havai, *President*
David Zelaskowski, *President*
William P Forster, *CFO*
Pamela Bowen, *CIO*
EMP: 150 EST: 1992
SQ FT: 26,000
SALES (est): 58.8MM
SALES (corp-wide): 132.5B **Publicly Held**
WEB: www.crescenthealthcare.com
SIC: 8082 Home health care services
HQ: Walgreen Co.
200 Wilmot Rd Ste 2002
Deerfield IL 60015
847 940-2500

(P-21159)
CRESCENT HEALTHCARE INC
11980 Telg Rd Ste 100, Santa Fe Springs (90670)
PHONE..................................562 347-2900
Robert Funari, *Manager*
EMP: 53
SALES (corp-wide): 132.5B **Publicly Held**
WEB: www.crescenthealthcare.com
SIC: 8082 Home health care services
HQ: Crescent Healthcare, Inc.
11980 Telg Rd Ste 100
Santa Fe Springs CA 90670

(P-21160)
DUNN & BERGER INC
Also Called: Accredited Nursing Care
5955 De Soto Ave Ste 160, Woodland Hills (91367-5101)
PHONE..................................818 986-1234
Barry Berger, *President*
EMP: 500 EST: 1980
SALES (est): 31.6MM **Privately Held**
SIC: 8082 Home health care services

(P-21161)
DYNAMIC HOME CARE SERVICE INC (PA)
14260 Ventura Blvd # 301, Sherman Oaks (91423-2734)
PHONE..................................818 981-4446
Nissan Pardo, *CEO*
Carol Silver, *President*
Marilyn Flick, *Human Res Mgr*
Jeff Friedman, *Sales Staff*
EMP: 100 EST: 1987
SALES (est): 12.5MM **Privately Held**
WEB: www.dynamicnursing.com
SIC: 8082 Visiting nurse service

(P-21162)
E R G HOME HEALTH PROVIDER
11700 South St Ste 200, Artesia (90701-6619)
PHONE..................................562 403-1070
Fax: 562 403-1068
EMP: 60
SALES (est): 2.2MM **Privately Held**
SIC: 8082 Home Health Care Services

(P-21163)
EVERGREEN HOSPICE CARE INC (PA)
17215 Studebaker Rd # 100, Cerritos (90703-2548)
PHONE..................................562 865-9006
Lydia Ahn, *President*
EMP: 111 EST: 2004
SALES (est): 13.3MM **Privately Held**
WEB: www.evergreenhospicecare.com
SIC: 8082 Home health care services

(P-21164)
EXCELLENT IN-HOME CARE INC
22041 Clarendon St 100, Woodland Hills (91367-6305)
PHONE..................................818 755-4900
Khosrow Assadi, *President*
Jay Isaacs, *CEO*
Gilda Anvari, *Director*
EMP: 69 EST: 1998
SALES (est): 3.8MM **Privately Held**
WEB: www.excellenthomecare.com
SIC: 8082 Visiting nurse service

(P-21165)
GENTIVA HEALTH SERVICES INC
Also Called: Gentiva Home Health Care
3220 S Higuera St Ste 101, San Luis Obispo (93401-6983)
PHONE..................................805 549-0801
Elaine Clark, *Manager*
EMP: 77
SALES (corp-wide): 1.1B **Privately Held**
WEB: www.kindredathome.com
SIC: 8082 Home health care services
PA: Gentiva Health Services, Inc.
3350 Rvrwood Pkwy Se # 140
Atlanta GA 30339
770 951-6450

(P-21166)
GENTIVA HOSPICE
5001 E Cmmrccnter Dr Ste, Bakersfield (93309)
PHONE..................................661 324-1232
EMP: 228 EST: 2013
SALES (est): 2.7MM
SALES (corp-wide): 6B **Privately Held**
WEB: www.kindredhealthcare.com
SIC: 8082 Home health care services
HQ: Kindred Healthcare, Llc
680 S 4th St
Louisville KY 40202
502 596-7300

(P-21167)
GLENDALE ADVENTIST MEDICAL CTR
Also Called: Adventist Health Homecare Svcs
281 Harvey Dr Unit B, Glendale (91206-4112)
PHONE..................................818 409-8379
Bruce Nelson, *Med Doctor*
Kathleen Mershon, *Nutritionist*
EMP: 50
SALES (corp-wide): 4.5B **Privately Held**
WEB: www.healthyglendale.org
SIC: 8082 Home health care services

HQ: Glendale Adventist Medical Center Inc
1509 Wilson Ter
Glendale CA 91206
818 409-8000

(P-21168)
GRANDCARE HEALTH SERVICES LLC (PA)
3452 E Fthill Blvd Ste 70, Pasadena (91107)
PHONE..................................866 554-2447
David Bell, *Mng Member*
Dylan Garland, *Bd of Directors*
Jeaneen Cockrell, *VP Business*
Sumith Fernando, *Accountant*
Carolyn Cowie,
EMP: 150 EST: 2014
SALES (est): 19MM **Privately Held**
WEB: www.grandcarehealth.com
SIC: 8082 Home health care services

(P-21169)
HELP UNLMTED PERSONNEL SVC INC
3202 E Ojai Ave, Ojai (93023-9320)
PHONE..................................805 962-4646
Leanna McNealy, *Manager*
EMP: 675 **Privately Held**
WEB: www.helpunlimited.com
SIC: 8082 7363 Visiting nurse service; medical help service
PA: Help Unlimited Personnel Service, Inc.
1957 Eastman Ave
Ventura CA 93003

(P-21170)
HOSPICE REDLAND COMMUNITY HOSP
Also Called: Hospice Prgram Rdlnds Cmnty Ho
350 Terracina Blvd, Redlands (92373-4850)
PHONE..................................909 335-5643
Julie Crocetti, *Director*
EMP: 51 EST: 1988
SALES (est): 815.3K **Privately Held**
WEB: www.redlandshospital.org
SIC: 8082 Home health care services

(P-21171)
HOSPICE TOUCH INC (PA)
3070 Bristol St Ste 100, Costa Mesa (92626-7334)
PHONE..................................714 327-1936
Larry Nab, *CEO*
Mandy Ayers,
Divya RAO, *Social Worker*
Tiffany Kinchen-Andrews, *Manager*
Tami Holden, *Consultant*
EMP: 76 EST: 2002
SALES (est): 10.1MM **Privately Held**
WEB: www.bristolhospice.com
SIC: 8082 Home health care services

(P-21172)
HUNTINGTON CARE LLC
Also Called: Huntington Home Care
3452 E Fthill Blvd Ste 76, Pasadena (91107)
PHONE..................................877 405-6990
Carlo Stepanians, *CEO*
Sergio Varela, *President*
EMP: 200 EST: 2007
SALES (est): 3.9MM
SALES (corp-wide): 19MM **Privately Held**
WEB: www.24hrcares.com
SIC: 8082 Home health care services
PA: Grandcare Health Services Llc
3452 E Fthill Blvd Ste 70
Pasadena CA 91107
866 554-2447

(P-21173)
IMMEDATE CLINIC HEALTHCARE INC (HQ)
27101 Puerta Real Ste 450, Mission Viejo (92691-8566)
PHONE..................................949 487-9500
Mike Dalton, *President*
Soon Burnam, *Treasurer*
EMP: 52 EST: 2012

SALES (est): 22.2MM
SALES (corp-wide): 2.4B **Publicly Held**
WEB: www.ensigngroup.net
SIC: 8082 Home health care services
PA: The Ensign Group Inc
29222 Rncho Vejo Rd Ste 1
San Juan Capistrano CA 92675
949 487-9500

(P-21174)
IN HOME COMFORT AND CARE INC
Also Called: Right At Home
17155 Newhope St Ste O, Fountain Valley (92708-4233)
PHONE..................................714 485-4120
Greg James, *CEO*
Cat Koehler, *Relations*
EMP: 55 EST: 2012
SALES (est): 6.2MM **Privately Held**
WEB: www.rightathome.net
SIC: 8082 Home health care services

(P-21175)
INFINITE HOME HEALTH INC
22151 Ventura Blvd # 102, Woodland Hills (91364-1666)
PHONE..................................818 888-7772
Taimoor Bidari, *President*
EMP: 60 EST: 2003
SQ FT: 4,000
SALES (est): 2.5MM **Privately Held**
WEB: www.infinitehha.com
SIC: 8082 Home health care services

(P-21176)
INTERHEALTH SERVICES INC (HQ)
Also Called: Presbyterian Inter Cmnty Hosp
12401 Washington Blvd, Whittier (90602-1006)
PHONE..................................562 698-0811
Daniel F Adams, *President*
Jim West, *President*
Gary Koger, *CFO*
Raul Castillo, *Vice Pres*
Paulette Heitmeyer, *Ch Nursing Ofcr*
EMP: 143 EST: 1983
SQ FT: 1,000
SALES (est): 103.4MM
SALES (corp-wide): 923K **Privately Held**
WEB: www.pihhealth.org
SIC: 8082 8062 Home health care services; general medical & surgical hospitals
PA: Pih Health, Inc.
12401 Washington Blvd
Whittier CA 90602
562 698-0811

(P-21177)
KAISER FOUNDATION HOSPITALS
Also Called: Tustin Executive Center
17542 17th St, Tustin (92780-1959)
PHONE..................................714 734-4500
EMP: 261
SALES (corp-wide): 30.5B **Privately Held**
WEB: www.kaisercenter.com
SIC: 8082 Home health care services
HQ: Kaiser Foundation Hospitals Inc
1 Kaiser Plz
Oakland CA 94612
510 271-6611

(P-21178)
KEARN ALTERNATIVE CARE INC (PA)
2029 21st St, Bakersfield (93301-4219)
PHONE..................................661 631-2036
Jean Schamblin, *President*
J R Doty, *Admin Sec*
EMP: 300 EST: 1998
SALES (est): 10.4MM **Privately Held**
WEB: www.eldercarebakersfieldca.com
SIC: 8082 Visiting nurse service

(P-21179)
KINDRED HEALTHCARE LLC
17290 Jasmine St Ste 104, Victorville (92395-8300)
PHONE..................................760 241-7044
EMP: 71
SALES (corp-wide): 6B **Privately Held**
WEB: www.kindredhealthcare.com
SIC: 8082 Home health care services

HQ: Kindred Healthcare, Llc
680 S 4th St
Louisville KY 40202
502 596-7300

(P-21180)
KINDRED HEALTHCARE LLC
Also Called: Odyssey Healthcare Bakersfield
5001 E Cmmrccnter Dr Ste, Bakersfield
(93309)
PHONE....................661 324-1232
EMP: 71
SALES (corp-wide): 6B Privately Held
WEB: www.kindredhealthcare.com
SIC: 8082 Home health care services
HQ: Kindred Healthcare, Llc
680 S 4th St
Louisville KY 40202
502 596-7300

(P-21181)
KINDRED HEALTHCARE LLC
735 Carnegie Dr Ste 240, San Bernardino
(92408-3574)
PHONE....................909 890-1226
EMP: 71
SALES (corp-wide): 6B Privately Held
WEB: www.kindredhealthcare.com
SIC: 8082 Home health care services
HQ: Kindred Healthcare, Llc
680 S 4th St
Louisville KY 40202
502 596-7300

(P-21182)
L & A CARE CORPORATION (PA)
18107 Sherman Way Ste 100, Reseda
(91335-4564)
PHONE....................323 938-1155
Lena Beker, President
EMP: 59 EST: 2001
SALES (est): 5.5MM Privately Held
SIC: 8082 Visiting nurse service

(P-21183)
LANDMARK HEALTH LLC (PA)
7755 Center Ave Ste 630, Huntington
Beach (92647-9152)
PHONE....................657 237-2450
Nick Loporcaro, CEO
Lily Fu, Partner
Carol Devol, COO
Brandon Kerns, CFO
Michael Le, Chief Mktg Ofcr
EMP: 292 EST: 2013
SALES (est): 44.7MM Privately Held
WEB: www.landmarkhealth.org
SIC: 8082 Home health care services

(P-21184)
LINCARE INC
Also Called: United Medical-IV Pharmacy
17777 Center Court Dr N # 55, Cerritos
(90703-9320)
PHONE....................870 972-8839
Brian Nannie, Administration
EMP: 52 Privately Held
WEB: www.lincare.com
SIC: 8082 Home health care services
HQ: Lincare Inc.
19387 Us Highway 19 N
Clearwater FL 33764
727 530-7700

(P-21185)
LINCARE INC
4300 Stine Rd Ste 603, Bakersfield
(93313-2364)
PHONE....................661 833-3333
Frank Gurriola, Sales/Mktg Mgr
EMP: 52 Privately Held
WEB: www.lincare.com
SIC: 8082 Home health care services
HQ: Lincare Inc.
19387 Us Highway 19 N
Clearwater FL 33764
727 530-7700

(P-21186)
LIVHOME INC (PA)
5670 Wilshire Blvd # 500, Los Angeles
(90036-5682)
PHONE....................800 807-5854
Toll Free:....................877 -
Mike Nicholson, Ch of Bd
Cody D Legler, Officer

Leslie Saller, Office Mgr
Aleksandra Rozenfeld, Accounting Mgr
Bill Thomas, Med Doctor
EMP: 1299 EST: 1999
SQ FT: 7,454
SALES (est): 75.7MM Privately Held
WEB: www.arosacare.com
SIC: 8082 Home health care services

(P-21187)
LU & WEBER CORPORATION
Also Called: Preferred Excellent Care Phrm
10521 Garden Grove Blvd, Garden Grove
(92843-1128)
PHONE....................714 590-3620
Rosalie Lu Weber, President
Phong Lu, Vice Pres
Rudolf Weber, VP Finance
EMP: 76 EST: 1992
SQ FT: 14,000
SALES (est): 8MM Privately Held
WEB: www.preferredexcellentcare.com
SIC: 8082 Home health care services

(P-21188)
LUMINA HEALTHCARE LLC (PA)
Also Called: Lumina At Home
5220 Pcf Cncrse Dr Ste 12, Los Angeles
(90045)
PHONE....................888 958-6462
Mary Ellen Hardin, President
Robert C Mathuny, Vice Pres
Jennifer Brown, Administration
Gina Medeiros, Administration
EMP: 55 EST: 2006
SALES (est): 8MM Privately Held
WEB: www.luminahealthcare.com
SIC: 8082 Home health care services

(P-21189)
LUXE HOMECARE INC (PA)
Also Called: Home Health Care Dept
881 Alma Real Dr, Pacific Palisades
(90272-3731)
PHONE....................310 454-5500
Seyedeh Vahdani, CEO
EMP: 53 EST: 2013
SALES (est): 3.7MM Privately Held
WEB: www.luxehomecare.com
SIC: 8082 Visiting nurse service

(P-21190)
**MAXIM HEALTHCARE SERVICES
INC**
3580 Wilshire Blvd # 100, Los Angeles
(90010-2501)
PHONE....................866 465-5678
Maxim Indianapolis, Recruiter
EMP: 184 Privately Held
WEB: www.maximhealthcare.com
SIC: 8082 Home health care services
PA: Maxim Healthcare Services, Inc.
7227 Lee Deforest Dr
Columbia MD 21046

(P-21191)
**MAXIM HEALTHCARE SERVICES
INC**
Also Called: Victorville Homecare
560 E Hospitality Ln # 400, San Bernardino
(92408-3545)
PHONE....................760 243-3377
Angie R Wiechert, Manager
EMP: 184 Privately Held
WEB: www.maximhealthcare.com
SIC: 8082 Home health care services
PA: Maxim Healthcare Services, Inc.
7227 Lee Deforest Dr
Columbia MD 21046

(P-21192)
MOMS ORANGE COUNTY
1128 W Santa Ana Blvd, Santa Ana
(92703-3833)
PHONE....................714 972-2610
Pamela Pimentel Rn, Exec Dir
Patricia Bartlett, Exec VP
Barbara Overholser, Executive Asst
Yvonne Sanders, Marketing Mgr
Molly Jensen, Nurse
EMP: 50 EST: 1992
SALES (est): 1.5MM Privately Held
WEB: www.momsorangecounty.org
SIC: 8082 Home health care services

(P-21193)
**NURSES TUCH HM HLTH
PRVDER INC**
135 S Jackson St Ste 100, Glendale
(91205-4917)
PHONE....................818 500-4877
Evangeline Ursua, President
EMP: 50 EST: 2003
SALES (est): 1.4MM Privately Held
WEB: www.nursestouchhh.com
SIC: 8082 Home health care services

(P-21194)
**OPTIMAL HOME HEALTH CARE
INC**
1227 Chester Ave, Bakersfield
(93301-5445)
PHONE....................661 410-4000
Doug Clary, President
Sarah Shelbourne, CFO
Dennis Black,
Kevin Fabrizio, Director
Shelly Marquez, Director
EMP: 75 EST: 1992
SALES (est): 11.9MM Privately Held
WEB: www.bristolhospice.com
SIC: 8082 Visiting nurse service

(P-21195)
**ORANGE COUNTY HOMECARE
LLC (PA)**
Also Called: Salus Homecare
630 Roosevelt, Irvine (92620-3621)
PHONE....................949 390-7308
Boad Swanson,
Tyson Manning, CFO
Debbie Robson, Vice Pres
Sue Tulley, Nurse
Kimberly Hayden, Case Mgr
EMP: 63 EST: 2006
SALES (est): 7MM Privately Held
WEB: www.salushomecare.com
SIC: 8082 Visiting nurse service

(P-21196)
OUR WATCH
Also Called: Assistance In Home Care
12832 Valley View St # 211, Garden Grove
(92845-2524)
PHONE....................714 622-5852
Ramona Streit, Principal
EMP: 52 EST: 2007
SALES (est): 5.2MM Privately Held
SIC: 8082 Home health care services

(P-21197)
**PACIFICARE HEALTH SYSTEMS
LLC (HQ)**
5995 Plaza Dr, Cypress (90630-5028)
PHONE....................714 952-1121
Howard Phanstiel, CEO
Paul Bihm, Vice Pres
Daniel Bohmfalk, Vice Pres
Paul Drago, Executive
WEI Wu, Administration
EMP: 550 EST: 1996
SQ FT: 104,000
SALES (est): 2B
SALES (corp-wide): 257.1B Publicly
Held
WEB: www.unitedhealthgroup.com
SIC: 8082 6321 Home health care serv-
ices; accident & health insurance carriers
PA: Unitedhealth Group Incorporated
9900 Bren Rd E Ste 300w
Minnetonka MN 55343
952 936-1300

(P-21198)
PARAMOUNT HOME CARE INC
12235 Beach Blvd Ste 102, Stanton
(90680-3943)
PHONE....................714 994-1250
Nickolas Lacson, CEO
Lordus Velez, President
Deborah Miller, Director
EMP: 60 EST: 1994
SALES (est): 3.1MM Privately Held
WEB: www.paramounthomecareinc.com
SIC: 8082 Home health care services

(P-21199)
PATHFINDER HEALTH INC
10051 Lampson Ave, Garden Grove
(92840-4716)
PHONE....................714 636-5649
Avelina Cumbis, President
Scott Morcott, Chief Mktg Ofcr
EMP: 50 EST: 1993
SALES (est): 1.3MM Privately Held
WEB: www.pathfinderhealth.org
SIC: 8082 Visiting nurse service

(P-21200)
**PEGASUS HM HLTH CARE A
CAL COR**
Also Called: Pegasus Home Health Services
132 N Artsakh Ave, Glendale (91206-4094)
PHONE....................818 551-1932
Pamela Spiszman, President
Isabelle Davidian, Director
Pilar Huliganga, Supervisor
▼ EMP: 80 EST: 1994
SQ FT: 2,800
SALES (est): 7.4MM Privately Held
WEB: www.pegasushomecare.com
SIC: 8082 Visiting nurse service

(P-21201)
PEOPLES CARE INC
13901 Amargosa Rd Ste 101, Victorville
(92392-2409)
PHONE....................760 962-1900
Stacey Minwalla, Owner
EMP: 189
SALES (corp-wide): 62.2MM Privately
Held
WEB: www.peoplescare.com
SIC: 8082 Home health care services
PA: Peoples Care Inc.
13920 City Center Dr # 290
Chino Hills CA 91709
855 773-6753

(P-21202)
PHARMACO INC
Also Called: Premier Infusion Care
19500 Normandie Ave, Torrance
(90502-1108)
PHONE....................310 328-3897
Saman Refua, CEO
Christina Armendariz, Officer
Rhamil Rana, Info Tech Dir
Sean Basilio, Technology
April Cable, Opers Mgr
EMP: 99 EST: 2004
SALES (est): 26.1MM Privately Held
SIC: 8082 Home health care services

(P-21203)
**PHYSICIANS CHOICE HM HLTH
INC**
3220 Sepulveda Blvd # 100, Torrance
(90505-8160)
PHONE....................310 793-1616
Shari Sunada, President
EMP: 50 EST: 1993
SQ FT: 2,500
SALES (est): 3.5MM Privately Held
WEB: www.physchoicehh.com
SIC: 8082 Home health care services

(P-21204)
PROVIDENCE HEALTH SYSTEM
Also Called: Trinity Home Care
4101 Torrance Blvd, Torrance
(90503-4607)
PHONE....................310 370-5895
EMP: 200
SALES (corp-wide): 17.6B Privately Held
SIC: 8082 8051 Home Health Care Serv-
ices Skilled Nursing Care Facility
HQ: Providence Health System-Southern
California
1801 Lind Ave Sw
Renton WA 98057
425 525-3355

(P-21205)
**PROVIDENCE ST JOSEPH
HEALTH**
57 Prism, Irvine (92618-3148)
PHONE....................949 430-3960
EMP: 3418

SALES (corp-wide): 32.7MM **Privately Held**
WEB: www.psjhealth.org
SIC: **8082** Home health care services
PA: Providence St. Joseph Health
1801 Lind Ave Sw
Renton WA 98057
425 525-3355

(P-21206)
RAMONA COMMUNITY SERVICES CORP (HQ)
Also Called: Ramona Vna & Hospice
890 W Stetson Ave Ste A, Hemet
(92543-7311)
PHONE..................................951 658-9288
Patricia McBe, *Branch Mgr*
Patrick Searl, *Ch of Bd*
Carol Wood, *CEO*
Lauien Mahieu, *COO*
John Brudin, *Treasurer*
EMP: 150 EST: 1987
SQ FT: 14,000
SALES (est): 22.8MM **Privately Held**
WEB: www.arborhospicecare.org
SIC: **8082** Visiting nurse service

(P-21207)
REHABFOCUS HOME HEALTH INC (DH)
Also Called: Focus Health
27071 Aliso Creek Rd, Aliso Viejo
(92656-3399)
PHONE..................................209 524-8700
Robert Levin, *CEO*
EMP: 50 EST: 2003
SALES (est): 24.5MM
SALES (corp-wide): 1MM **Privately Held**
WEB: www.rehabfocus.net
SIC: **8082** Home health care services
HQ: Focus Healthcare Holdings, Inc.
27071 Aliso Creek Rd # 100
Aliso Viejo CA 92656
949 349-1200

(P-21208)
ROBERTS & ASSOCIATES INC
Also Called: Visiting Angels Riverside Cnty
8175 Limonite Ave Ste A, Riverside
(92509-6120)
PHONE..................................951 727-4357
Joan Roberts, *President*
Robert Roberts, *Treasurer*
Benita Roberts, *Vice Pres*
EMP: 55 EST: 2004
SQ FT: 400
SALES (est): 7MM **Privately Held**
WEB: www.visitingangels.com
SIC: **8082** Home health care services

(P-21209)
ROCK CANYON HEALTHCARE INC
Also Called: Riverwalk PST-Cute Rhblitation
27101 Puerta Real Ste 450, Mission Viejo
(92691-8566)
PHONE..................................719 404-1000
Dave Jorgensen, *President*
Soon Burnam, *Treasurer*
Ron Cook, *Exec Dir*
Beverly Wittekind, *Admin Sec*
Theresa Miller, *Hlthcr Dir*
EMP: 250 EST: 2014
SALES (est): 22.7MM
SALES (corp-wide): 2.4B **Publicly Held**
WEB: www.rockcanyonrehab.com
SIC: **8082** Home health care services
PA: The Ensign Group Inc
29222 Rncho Vejo Rd Ste 1
San Juan Capistrano CA 92675
949 487-9500

(P-21210)
SELECT HOME CARE
2393 Townsgate Rd Ste 100, Westlake Village (91361-2513)
PHONE..................................805 777-3855
Dylan Hull, *CEO*
EMP: 100 EST: 2007
SALES (est): 6.9MM **Privately Held**
WEB: www.selecthomecare.com
SIC: **8082** Home health care services

(P-21211)
SFV LLC
Also Called: Brightstar Care NW San Frnndo
8949 Reseda Blvd 227-2, Northridge
(91324-3916)
PHONE..................................818 839-8881
Ivan Yeung, *Mng Member*
EMP: 50 EST: 2018
SALES (est): 2.5MM **Privately Held**
SIC: **8082** Home health care services

(P-21212)
SMITH RESIDENTIAL CARE FCILTY (PA)
318 E 4th St, Hanford (93230-5125)
P.O. Box 1093 (93232-1093)
PHONE..................................559 584-8451
Catherine Smith, *Owner*
EMP: 60 EST: 1983
SALES (est): 2MM **Privately Held**
SIC: **8082** Home health care services

(P-21213)
SOUTH BAY SENIOR SERVICES INC
Also Called: Homewatch Caregivers
8929 S Sepulveda Blvd # 314, Los Angeles
(90045-3616)
PHONE..................................310 338-8558
Richard Williams, *President*
Patricia Greaney, *Admin Sec*
EMP: 77 EST: 2006
SQ FT: 700
SALES (est): 3.2MM **Privately Held**
WEB: www.homewatchcaregivers.com
SIC: **8082** Home health care services

(P-21214)
ST JOSEPH HEALTH PER CARE SVCS (PA)
Also Called: Nurse Next Door
200 W Center St Promenade, Anaheim
(92805-3960)
PHONE..................................714 712-7100
Ryan Berger, *Vice Pres*
Eric Lisker, *Opers Staff*
EMP: 76 EST: 2016
SQ FT: 1,450
SALES (est): 7.7MM **Privately Held**
WEB: www.nursenextdoor.com
SIC: **8082** Home health care services

(P-21215)
ST JOSEPH HEALTH PER CARE SVCS
1315 Corona Pointe Ct, Corona
(92879-1785)
PHONE..................................800 365-1110
Greg Henderson, *Principal*
EMP: 99
SALES (corp-wide): 7.7MM **Privately Held**
WEB: www.nursenextdoor.com
SIC: **8082** Home health care services
PA: St Joseph Health Personal Care Services
200 W Center St Promenade
Anaheim CA 92805
714 712-7100

(P-21216)
ST JSEPH HLTH SYS HM CARE SVC
200 W Center St Promenade, Anaheim
(92805-3960)
PHONE..................................714 712-9500
Jeffrey Hammond, *Mng Member*
Susan Harvey, *CFO*
Lydia Thangaiyan, *Finance*
EMP: 800 EST: 2015
SALES (est): 71.9MM
SALES (corp-wide): 32.7MM **Privately Held**
WEB: www.stjhs.org
SIC: **8082** Home health care services
HQ: St. Joseph Health System
3345 Michelson Dr Ste 100
Irvine CA 92612
949 381-4000

(P-21217)
STAFF ASSISTANCE INC (PA)
72 Moody Ct Ste 100, Thousand Oaks
(91360-7426)
PHONE..................................818 894-7879
Bill Donley, *Ch of Bd*
Elaine S Donley, *President*
Wendy Blum, *Administration*
Teri Whittaker, *Nurse*
Debra Morgan, *Assistant*
EMP: 300 EST: 1992
SQ FT: 800
SALES (est): 23.9MM **Privately Held**
WEB: www.assistedcares.com
SIC: **8082** Home health care services

(P-21218)
STEP UP ON SECOND STREET INC (PA)
1328 2nd St Ofc, Santa Monica
(90401-1123)
PHONE..................................310 394-6889
Todd Lipka, *CEO*
Barbara Bloom, *COO*
Kim Carson, *CFO*
EMP: 60 EST: 1984
SQ FT: 7,500
SALES (est): 27.9MM **Privately Held**
WEB: www.stepup.org
SIC: **8082** **8052** **8059** Home health care
services; home for the mentally retarded,
with health care; personal care home,
with health care

(P-21219)
SUCCESS HEALTHCARE 1 LLC (PA)
Also Called: Silver Lake Medical Center
1711 W Temple St, Los Angeles
(90026-5421)
PHONE..................................213 989-6100
Peter R Baronoff,
Brian Dunn, *CEO*
James Hopwood, *CFO*
Lawrence Leder, *Principal*
Lina Hernandez, *Technology*
EMP: 690 EST: 2008
SALES (est): 47.8MM **Privately Held**
SIC: **8082** Home health care services

(P-21220)
TANDEM CARE PLG A PUB BNEFT CO
1925 Century Park E # 1700, Los Angeles
(90067-2701)
PHONE..................................310 281-0028
Joshua Greer, *Ch of Bd*
EMP: 92 EST: 2012
SALES (est): 10.1MM **Privately Held**
WEB: www.tandemcareplanning.com
SIC: **8082** Home health care services

(P-21221)
TENDER HOME HEALTHCARE INC
Also Called: Home Instead Senior Care
3550 Wilshire Blvd # 700, Los Angeles
(90010-2401)
PHONE..................................323 466-2345
EMP: 80
SALES (est): 2.3MM **Privately Held**
WEB: www.homeinstead.com
SIC: **8082** Home Health Care Services

(P-21222)
TEXAS HOME HEALTH AMERICA LP (PA)
1455 Auto Center Dr # 200, Ontario
(91761-2239)
PHONE..................................972 201-3800
Steve Abshire, *Partner*
Judy Bishop, *Partner*
Mark Lamp, *Partner*
Duff Whitaker, *Partner*
Julie Porras, *Nurse*
EMP: 100 EST: 1969
SQ FT: 18,000
SALES (est): 129.9MM **Privately Held**
WEB: www.accentcare.com
SIC: **8082** Home health care services

(P-21223)
TIFFANY HOMECARE INC (PA)
Also Called: Always Right Home Care
9700 Reseda Blvd Ste 105, Northridge
(91324-5516)
PHONE..................................818 886-1602
Larry S Spaeter, *CEO*
EMP: 322 EST: 2003
SQ FT: 1,200
SALES (est): 11.3MM **Privately Held**
SIC: **8082** Home health care services

(P-21224)
TRINITYCARE LLC (PA)
Also Called: Trinity Care & Nutria
13030 Alondra Blvd, Cerritos (90703-2246)
PHONE..................................818 709-4221
Peggy Chris,
EMP: 50 EST: 1998
SALES (est): 3.8MM **Privately Held**
WEB: www.chgseniorliving.com
SIC: **8082** Home health care services

(P-21225)
UCLA HEALTH SYSTEM AUXILIARY
10920 Wilshire Blvd, Los Angeles
(90024-6502)
PHONE..................................310 267-4327
David T Feinberg, *President*
Ryan Hatoum, *Officer*
Patricia Kapur, *Exec VP*
Patty Cuen, *Exec Dir*
Chiuling Ta, *Project Mgr*
EMP: 287 EST: 1981
SALES (est): 86.3MM **Privately Held**
WEB: www.uclahealth.org
SIC: **8082** Home health care services

(P-21226)
UNIVERSAL HOME CARE INC
151 N San Vicente Blvd, Beverly Hills
(90211-2323)
PHONE..................................323 653-9222
Marina Greenberg, *CEO*
Stephen Shapiro MD, *Vice Pres*
Roy Eisenberg, *Sales Executive*
Michelle Gougis-Hayes, *Director*
Bonnie Siegal, *Director*
EMP: 200 EST: 1995
SALES (est): 3.5MM **Privately Held**
WEB: www.universalhomecare.org
SIC: **8082** Home health care services

(P-21227)
US CARENET SERVICES LLC
42225 10th St W Ste 2b, Lancaster
(93534-7080)
PHONE..................................661 945-7350
Michelle Shah, *Director*
EMP: 106
SALES (corp-wide): 98.3MM **Privately Held**
WEB: www.navcare.com
SIC: **8082** Visiting nurse service
HQ: Us Carenet Services, Llc
699 Broad St Ste 1001
Augusta GA 30901

(P-21228)
VISITING NRSE ASSN OF INLAND C (PA)
Also Called: Vnaic
600 W Santa Ana Blvd # 1, Santa Ana
(92701-4558)
P.O. Box 1649, Riverside (92502-1649)
PHONE..................................951 413-1200
Mike A Rusnak, *President*
Joseph Allen, *Officer*
Gerrard Gier, *Info Tech Dir*
Mary Reed, *Info Tech Mgr*
Erika Ronska, *Nurse*
EMP: 720 EST: 1960
SALES (est): 14.9MM **Privately Held**
WEB: www.vnacalifornia.org
SIC: **8082** Visiting nurse service

(P-21229)
VISITING NRSE ASSN ORANGE CNTY (PA)
Also Called: Vna Home Health Systems
2520 Redhill Ave, Santa Ana (92705-5542)
PHONE..................................949 263-4700
Jeneane A Brian, *President*

Joan Randall, *COO*
Walid Yosafi, *Info Tech Dir*
Andrea Arambula, *Marketing Mgr*
▼ **EMP:** 55 **EST:** 1947
SQ FT: 30,000
SALES (est): 2MM **Privately Held**
WEB: www.vnahomehealthandhospice.com
SIC: 8082 Home health care services

(P-21230)
VISITING NURSE & HOSPICE CARE (PA)
Also Called: Visiting Nurse & Hospice Care
509 E Montecito St # 200, Santa Barbara
(93103-3293)
PHONE..............................805 965-5555
Lynda Tanner, *CEO*
Karen Wallace, *CFO*
Michelle Martinich, *Chairman*
Mary Pritchard, *Treasurer*
Michael Bordofsky, *Bd of Directors*
EMP: 120 **EST:** 1910
SQ FT: 13,765
SALES: 24.6MM **Privately Held**
WEB: www.vna.health
SIC: 8082 Home health care services

(P-21231)
VITAS HEALTHCARE CORP CAL (DH)
7888 Mission Grove Pkwy S, Riverside
(92508-5089)
PHONE..............................305 374-4143
David A Wester, *President*
Peggy Pettit, *COO*
Barry M Kinzbrunner, *Chief Mktg Ofcr*
Kal Mistry, *Senior VP*
EMP: 50 **EST:** 1993
SALES: 22.7MM
SALES (corp-wide): 2B **Publicly Held**
WEB: www.vitas.com
SIC: 8082 8011 Home health care services; physical medicine, physician/surgeon
HQ: Vitas Healthcare Corporation
201 S Biscayne Blvd # 400
Miami FL 33131
305 374-4143

(P-21232)
VNA HSPICE PLLTIVE CARE STHERN (PA)
Also Called: Vna Private Duty Care
412 E Vanderbilt Way # 10, San Bernardino
(92408-3552)
P.O. Box 908, Claremont (91711-0908)
PHONE..............................909 624-3574
Marsha Fox, *President*
Cindy Cameron, *CFO*
Valerie Hogman, *Human Res Dir*
Fiona Salazar, *Recruiter*
Linda Adams, *Marketing Staff*
EMP: 220 **EST:** 1952
SALES (est): 26.1MM **Privately Held**
WEB: www.vnasocal.org
SIC: 8082 Visiting nurse service

8092 Kidney Dialysis Centers

(P-21233)
AUSTIN DIALYSIS CENTERS LP (HQ)
601 Hawaii St, El Segundo (90245-4814)
PHONE..............................310 536-2400
Marina Acosta, *Principal*
EMP: 50 **EST:** 2009
SALES (est): 19.2MM **Publicly Held**
WEB: www.davita.com
SIC: 8092 Kidney dialysis centers

(P-21234)
CENTRAL KY DIALYSIS CTRS LLC (HQ)
601 Hawaii St, El Segundo (90245-4814)
PHONE..............................310 536-2400
EMP: 50 **EST:** 2009
SALES (est): 6.8MM **Publicly Held**
WEB: www.davita.com
SIC: 8092 Kidney dialysis centers

(P-21235)
CONTINENTAL DIALYSIS CTR INC (HQ)
601 Hawaii St, El Segundo (90245-4814)
PHONE..............................310 536-2400
Joseph Mello, *Principal*
Joseph C Mello, *Principal*
EMP: 50 **EST:** 2009
SALES (est): 10.8MM **Publicly Held**
WEB: www.davita.com
SIC: 8092 Kidney dialysis centers

(P-21236)
DALLAS-FORT WRTH NEPHROLOGY LP (HQ)
601 Hawaii St, El Segundo (90245-4814)
PHONE..............................310 536-2400
Thomas Georgouses, *Principal*
EMP: 50 **EST:** 2009
SALES (est): 7MM **Publicly Held**
WEB: www.davita.com
SIC: 8092 Kidney dialysis centers

(P-21237)
DAVITA - RIVERSIDE LLC (HQ)
601 Hawaii St, El Segundo (90245-4814)
PHONE..............................310 536-2400
Tim Burke, *Principal*
Mark Pierce, *President*
EMP: 50 **EST:** 2009
SALES (est): 22.5MM **Publicly Held**
WEB: www.davita.com
SIC: 8092 Kidney dialysis centers

(P-21238)
DAVITA INC
Also Called: Davita Hesperia Dialysis Ctr
14135 Main St Ste 501, Hesperia
(92345-8097)
PHONE..............................310 536-2406
Javier J Rodriguez, *CEO*
Cynthia Baxter Diggles, *Vice Pres*
Caren Weakley, *Vice Pres*
Angela Brunelle, *Admin Asst*
Holly Beppler, *Administration*
EMP: 175 **EST:** 1994
SALES (est): 25.4MM **Privately Held**
WEB: www.davita.com
SIC: 8092 Kidney dialysis centers

(P-21239)
DAVITA INC
15271 Laguna Canyon Rd, Irvine
(92618-3146)
PHONE..............................949 930-4400
Viki Anderson, *Branch Mgr*
Andrew Kin, *Vice Pres*
Patricia Ruiz, *Admin Asst*
Cameron McKim, *Database Admin*
Chad Luminarias, *Technician*
EMP: 270 **Publicly Held**
WEB: www.davita.com
SIC: 8092 Kidney dialysis centers
PA: Davita Inc.
2000 16th St
Denver CO 80202

(P-21240)
DIALYSIS NORTH ATLANTA LLC (HQ)
601 Hawaii St, El Segundo (90245-4814)
PHONE..............................310 536-2400
EMP: 50 **EST:** 2009
SALES (est): 8.9MM **Publicly Held**
WEB: www.davita.com
SIC: 8092 Kidney dialysis centers

(P-21241)
DVA HEALTHCARE TUSCALOOSA LLC (HQ)
601 Hawaii St, El Segundo (90245-4814)
PHONE..............................310 536-2400
EMP: 50 **EST:** 2009
SALES (est): 8.3MM **Publicly Held**
WEB: www.davita.com
SIC: 8092 Kidney dialysis centers

(P-21242)
FRESENIUS MED CARE SAN JUAN CP
31001 Rncho Vejo Rd Ste 1, San Juan
Capistrano (92675)
PHONE..............................949 240-0221

Mary Garber, *Mng Member*
EMP: 56
SALES (corp-wide): 333.6K **Privately Held**
WEB: www.freseniuskidneycare.com
SIC: 8092 Kidney dialysis centers
PA: Fresenius Medical Care San Juan
Capistrano, Llc
920 Winter St
Waltham MA 02451
781 699-4000

(P-21243)
GREATER LAS VEGAS DIALYSIS LLC (HQ)
601 Hawaii St, El Segundo (90245-4814)
PHONE..............................310 536-2400
Scott Macleod, *Director*
EMP: 50 **EST:** 2009
SALES (est): 14.6MM **Publicly Held**
WEB: www.davita.com
SIC: 8092 Kidney dialysis centers

(P-21244)
HAEMO-STAT INC (DH)
Also Called: Haemo Stat Acute Services
7247 Hayvenhurst Ave A1, Van Nuys
(91406-2871)
PHONE..............................818 908-0371
Karol Stein, *President*
Christy Martinez, *Director*
Tina Holt, *Manager*
EMP: 89 **EST:** 1975
SQ FT: 1,700
SALES (est): 1.5MM
SALES (corp-wide): 21.1B **Privately Held**
WEB: www.fmcna.com
SIC: 8092 Kidney dialysis centers

(P-21245)
HARBOR-UCLA MED FOUNDATION INC
Also Called: Ucla Hbr Dlysis Ctr Med Fndtio
21602 S Vermont Ave, Torrance
(90502-1940)
PHONE..............................310 533-0413
Patricia Hall, *Manager*
EMP: 300 **Privately Held**
WEB: www.harborucladocs.org
SIC: 8092 Kidney dialysis centers
PA: Harbor-Ucla Medical Foundation, Inc.
21840 Normandie Ave Ste 1
Torrance CA 90502

(P-21246)
HEMODIALYSIS INC (PA)
Also Called: Glentrans
710 W Wilson Ave, Glendale (91203-2409)
PHONE..............................818 500-8736
John R Depalma, *President*
EMP: 50 **EST:** 1978
SQ FT: 1,500
SALES (est): 11.9MM **Privately Held**
WEB: www.hemodialysis-inc.com
SIC: 8092 Kidney dialysis centers

(P-21247)
HEMODIALYSIS INC
Also Called: Holy Cross Renal Center
14901 Rinaldi St Ste 100, Mission Hills
(91345-1253)
PHONE..............................818 365-6961
John R Depalma, *Branch Mgr*
EMP: 109
SALES (corp-wide): 11.9MM **Privately Held**
WEB: www.hemodialysis-inc.com
SIC: 8092 Kidney dialysis centers
PA: Hemodialysis, Inc.
710 W Wilson Ave
Glendale CA 91203
818 500-8736

(P-21248)
HOUSTON KIDNEY CENTER/TOTAL R (HQ)
601 Hawaii St, El Segundo (90245-4814)
PHONE..............................310 536-2400
EMP: 50 **EST:** 2009
SALES (est): 38.9MM **Publicly Held**
WEB: www.davita.com
SIC: 8092 Kidney dialysis centers

(P-21249)
HUNTINGTON PARK DIALYSIS LLC
5942 Rugby Ave, Huntington Park
(90255-2803)
PHONE..............................323 585-7605
Rauhie Sadeghpour, *Principal*
EMP: 53 **EST:** 2000
SALES (est): 2MM **Publicly Held**
WEB: www.davita.com
SIC: 8092 Kidney dialysis centers
PA: Davita Inc.
2000 16th St
Denver CO 80202

(P-21250)
JAMBOOR MEDICAL CORPORATION
Also Called: Desert Cities Dialysis
12675 Hesperia Rd, Victorville
(92395-5878)
PHONE..............................760 241-8063
Jay Shankar, *President*
Saguna Jayashankar, *Admin Sec*
EMP: 65 **EST:** 1988
SQ FT: 7,000
SALES (est): 11.6MM **Privately Held**
WEB: www.desertcitiesdialysis.com
SIC: 8092 Kidney dialysis centers

(P-21251)
KAISER FOUNDATION HOSPITALS
Also Called: La Punte Prtneal Dialysis Unit
1813 N Hacienda Blvd, La Puente
(91744-1142)
PHONE..............................626 931-3580
EMP: 209
SALES (corp-wide): 30.5E **Privately Held**
WEB: www.kaisercenter.com
SIC: 8092 Kidney dialysis centers
HQ: Kaiser Foundation Hospitals Inc
1 Kaiser Plz
Oakland CA 94612
510 271-6611

(P-21252)
KIDNEY CENTER VENTURA INC
Also Called: Kidney Dialysis Center Verdugo
50 Moreland Rd, Simi Valley (93065-1659)
P.O. Box 940838 (93094-0838)
PHONE..............................805 433-7777
Kant Tucker MD, *CEO*
Ushakant Thakkar, *President*
Rajesh Thakkar, *Vice Pres*
Kumar Ullal, *Info Tech Dir*
EMP: 59 **EST:** 1997
SQ FT: 10,000
SALES (est): 10.8MM **Privately Held**
WEB: www.kidneycenter.com
SIC: 8092 Kidney dialysis centers

(P-21253)
KIDNEY CENTERS MICHIGAN LLC (HQ)
601 Hawaii St, El Segundo (90245-4814)
PHONE..............................310 536-2400
EMP: 50 **EST:** 2009
SALES (est): 7.7MM **Publicly Held**
WEB: www.davita.com
SIC: 8092 Kidney dialysis centers

(P-21254)
MOUNTAIN W DIALYSIS SVCS LLC (HQ)
601 Hawaii St, El Segundo (90245-4814)
PHONE..............................310 536-2400
EMP: 50 **EST:** 2009
SALES (est): 10MM **Publicly Held**
WEB: www.davita.com
SIC: 8092 Kidney dialysis centers

(P-21255)
NEW BAY DIALYSIS LLC (HQ)
601 Hawaii St, El Segundo (90245-4814)
PHONE..............................310 536-2400
EMP: 50 **EST:** 2009
SALES (est): 15.6MM **Publicly Held**
WEB: www.davita.com
SIC: 8092 Kidney dialysis centers

(P-21256)
OHIO RIVER DIALYSIS LLC (HQ)
601 Hawaii St, El Segundo (90245-4814)
PHONE..................................310 536-2400
Marina Acosta, *Principal*
James V Hilger, *Officer*
EMP: 50 **EST:** 2009
SALES (est): 6.4MM **Publicly Held**
WEB: www.davita.com
SIC: 8092 Kidney dialysis centers

(P-21257)
PACIFIC SOUTH BAY DIALYSIS LLC (HQ)
Also Called: U.S. Rnal Care Earl St Dalysis
20911 Earl St Ste 160, Torrance
(90503-4353)
PHONE..................................310 371-4244
Edallie Padilla Ferniz, *CEO*
Allen Fulmer, *President*
EMP: 50 **EST:** 1991
SALES (est): 4.9MM **Privately Held**
WEB: www.usrenalcare.com
SIC: 8092 Kidney dialysis centers

(P-21258)
PHYSICANS DALYSIS ACQUISITIONS (HQ)
601 Hawaii St, El Segundo (90245-4814)
PHONE..................................310 536-2400
Marina Acosta, *Principal*
EMP: 50 **EST:** 2009
SALES (est): 19.4MM **Publicly Held**
WEB: www.davita.com
SIC: 8092 Kidney dialysis centers

(P-21259)
PORTERVILLE DIALYSIS CENTER
Also Called: Porterville Hemodialysis
385 Pearson Dr, Porterville (93257-3305)
PHONE..................................559 781-5551
Sonia Duran-Aguilar, *CEO*
EMP: 353 **EST:** 1987
SALES (est): 426.2K
SALES (corp-wide): 734.3MM **Privately Held**
WEB: www.sierra-view.com
SIC: 8092 8051 Kidney dialysis centers; skilled nursing care facilities
PA: Kaweah Delta Health Care District Guild
400 W Mineral King Ave
Visalia CA 93291
559 624-2000

(P-21260)
RAI CARE CTRS STHERN CAL II LL
Rai Monroe Indio
46767 Monroe St Ste 101, Indio
(92201-5593)
PHONE..................................760 347-3986
April Thompson, *Branch Mgr*
EMP: 96
SALES (corp-wide): 21.1B **Privately Held**
SIC: 8092 Kidney dialysis centers
HQ: Rai Care Centers Of Southern California Ii, Llc
920 Winter St
Waltham MA 02451
781 699-9000

(P-21261)
RAI CARE CTRS STHERN CAL II LL
Also Called: Rai Centinela Inglewood
1416 Centinela Ave, Inglewood
(90302-1142)
PHONE..................................310 673-6865
Monique Hartell, *Branch Mgr*
EMP: 96
SALES (corp-wide): 21.1B **Privately Held**
SIC: 8092 Kidney dialysis centers
HQ: Rai Care Centers Of Southern California Ii, Llc
920 Winter St
Waltham MA 02451
781 699-9000

(P-21262)
RAI CARE CTRS STHERN CAL II LL
Also Called: Rai Corporate Way Palm Desert
41501 Corporate Way, Palm Desert
(92260-1974)
PHONE..................................760 346-7588
Monique Hartell, *Branch Mgr*
EMP: 96
SALES (corp-wide): 21.1B **Privately Held**
SIC: 8092 Kidney dialysis centers
HQ: Rai Care Centers Of Southern California Ii, Llc
920 Winter St
Waltham MA 02451
781 699-9000

(P-21263)
RIVER VALLEY DIALYSIS LLC (HQ)
601 Hawaii St, El Segundo (90245-4814)
PHONE..................................310 536-2400
EMP: 50 **EST:** 2009
SALES (est): 6.3MM **Publicly Held**
WEB: www.davita.com
SIC: 8092 Kidney dialysis centers

(P-21264)
ROCKY MTN DIALYSIS SVCS LLC (HQ)
601 Hawaii St, El Segundo (90245-4814)
PHONE..................................310 536-2400
EMP: 50 **EST:** 2009
SALES (est): 14.3MM **Publicly Held**
WEB: www.davita.com
SIC: 8092 Kidney dialysis centers

(P-21265)
SHINING STAR DIALYSIS INC (HQ)
601 Hawaii St, El Segundo (90245-4814)
PHONE..................................310 536-2400
Javier Rodriguez, *President*
EMP: 50 **EST:** 2001
SALES (est): 18.6MM **Publicly Held**
WEB: www.davita.com
SIC: 8092 Kidney dialysis centers

(P-21266)
SOUTHWEST ATLANTA DIA (HQ)
601 Hawaii St, El Segundo (90245-4814)
PHONE..................................310 536-2400
EMP: 50 **EST:** 2009
SALES (est): 19.6MM **Publicly Held**
WEB: www.davita.com
SIC: 8092 Kidney dialysis centers

(P-21267)
TOTAL RENAL CARE INC
Also Called: Davita Hesperia Dialysis Ctr
14135 Main St Ste 501, Hesperia
(92345-8097)
PHONE..................................760 947-7405
EMP: 60
SALES (corp-wide): 12.8B **Publicly Held**
SIC: 8092 Kidney Dialysis Centers
HQ: Total Renal Care, Inc.
601 Hawaii St
El Segundo CA 80202
310 536-2400

(P-21268)
TRC-INDIANA LLC (HQ)
601 Hawaii St, El Segundo (90245-4814)
PHONE..................................310 536-2400
Toni McClenny, *CEO*
Courtney Barefoot, *Recruiter*
Susan Nadolski, *Opers Staff*
Brian Olsen, *Director*
Romeo Matining, *Supervisor*
EMP: 50 **EST:** 2009
SALES (est): 6.5MM **Publicly Held**
WEB: www.davita.com
SIC: 8092 Kidney dialysis centers

8093 Specialty Outpatient Facilities, NEC

(P-21269)
ABILITIES RECOVERY CENTER INC
909 N Beverly Glen Blvd, Los Angeles
(90077-3117)
PHONE..................................310 488-1122
EMP: 51
SALES (corp-wide): 73.3K **Privately Held**
WEB: www.arc-la.com
SIC: 8093 Substance abuse clinics (outpatient)
PA: Abilities Recovery Center, Inc.
1662 Hillhurst Ave Ste A
Los Angeles CA

(P-21270)
AGENDIA INC
22 Morgan, Irvine (92618-2022)
PHONE..................................949 540-6300
Mark R Straley, *CEO*
Brian Dow, *CFO*
Glen Fredenberg, *CFO*
Kurt Schmidt, *CFO*
M William Audeh, *Chief Mktg Ofcr*
EMP: 107 **EST:** 2008
SALES (est): 58.4MM
SALES (corp-wide): 49.8MM **Privately Held**
WEB: www.agendia.com
SIC: 8093 Drug clinic, outpatient
PA: Agendia N.V.
Radarweg 60
Amsterdam
204 621-500

(P-21271)
ALCOTT CTR FOR MNTAL HLTH SVCS
1433 S Robertson Blvd, Los Angeles
(90035-3414)
PHONE..................................310 785-2121
Nicholas Maiorino, *CEO*
Alannah Robb, *Admin Asst*
Sarah Cummings, *Manager*
EMP: 120 **EST:** 1979
SALES (est): 5.7MM **Privately Held**
WEB: www.alcottcenter.org
SIC: 8093 Mental health clinic, outpatient; speech defect clinic

(P-21272)
ALGOS INC A MEDICAL CORP (PA)
Also Called: Pasadena Rehabilitation Inst
224 N Fair Oaks Ave, Pasadena
(91103-3618)
PHONE..................................626 696-1400
Clayton Varga, *President*
Matt Talbot, *COO*
Robert Castaneda, *CFO*
Daniel Pencak, *CFO*
Gerri Summe, *CFO*
EMP: 57 **EST:** 1989
SQ FT: 8,000
SALES (est): 12.7MM **Privately Held**
WEB: www.olioshealth.com
SIC: 8093 8049 8011 Rehabilitation center, outpatient treatment; physical therapist; specialized medical practitioners, except internal

(P-21273)
AMANECER CMNTY COUNSELING SVC
1200 Wilshire Blvd # 200, Los Angeles
(90017-1908)
PHONE..................................213 481-7464
Tim Ryder, *Exec Dir*
Frank Chargualaf, *CFO*
Linda Sanner, *CFO*
Laura Gonzalez, *Executive Asst*
Kanisha McReynolds, *QA Dir*
EMP: 100 **EST:** 1975
SALES: 11MM **Privately Held**
WEB: www.amanecerla.org
SIC: 8093 Mental health clinic, outpatient

(P-21274)
ARC - IMPERIAL VALLEY
340 E 1st St, Calexico (92231-2732)
PHONE..................................760 768-1944
Alex King, *Principal*
Ramon Aguirre, *Transportation*
EMP: 48
SALES (corp-wide): 15.2MM **Privately Held**
WEB: www.arciv.org
SIC: 8093 4783 2051 5812 Rehabilitation center, outpatient treatment; packing goods for shipping; bakery: wholesale or wholesale/retail combined; delicatessen (eating places); caterers
PA: Arc - Imperial Valley
298 E Ross Ave
El Centro CA 92243
760 352-0180

(P-21275)
ASANA RECOVERY
Also Called: Asana Rcvery Alchol DRG Trtmnt
1730 Pomona Ave Ste 3, Costa Mesa
(92627-3628)
PHONE..................................702 786-2396
Adam Shandrow, *Exec Dir*
EMP: 50 **EST:** 2017
SQ FT: 2,000
SALES (est): 6.1MM **Privately Held**
WEB: www.asanarecovery.com
SIC: 8093 8069 Substance abuse clinics (outpatient); substance abuse hospitals

(P-21276)
BEACON HEALTHCARE SERVICES
Also Called: Newport Bay Hospital
1501 E 16th St, Newport Beach
(92663-5924)
PHONE..................................949 650-9750
James E Parkhurst, *President*
Clint Salo, *Psychiatry*
Lynn Crosby, *Nurse*
Sherine Legge, *Director*
Juan Osorio, *Director*
EMP: 73 **EST:** 1994
SALES (est): 10.3MM **Privately Held**
WEB: www.newportbayhospital.com
SIC: 8093 Mental health clinic, outpatient

(P-21277)
BEHAVIOR ONE ATISM SLTIONS LLC
3002 Dow Ave Ste 206, Tustin
(92780-7234)
PHONE..................................657 294-5113
Kenneth Burg, *Mng Member*
EMP: 57 **EST:** 2018
SALES (est): 1.3MM **Privately Held**
WEB: www.beonebehavior.com
SIC: 8093 Mental health clinic, outpatient

(P-21278)
BEHAVIORAL HEALTH WORKS INC
1301 E Orangewood Ave, Anaheim
(92805-6807)
PHONE..................................800 249-1266
Robert Douk, *CEO*
Michael Comer, *CFO*
Michelle Douk, *Opers Dir*
Ruth Estrada,
Adam Price, *Manager*
EMP: 99 **EST:** 2011
SALES (est): 17.1MM **Privately Held**
WEB: www.bhwcares.com
SIC: 8093 Mental health clinic, outpatient

(P-21279)
BETTY FORD CENTER (HQ)
39000 Bob Hope Dr, Rancho Mirage
(92270-3297)
P.O. Box 1560 (92270-1056)
PHONE..................................760 773-4100
Mark Mishek, *President*
James Blaha, *CFO*
Briar Geraci, *Vice Pres*
Jim Steinhagen, *Vice Pres*
James Ahlman, *Exec Dir*
EMP: 250 **EST:** 1983

SALES (est): 38.3MM
SALES (corp-wide): 186.2MM **Privately Held**
WEB: www.hazeldenbettyford.org
SIC: **8093** Substance abuse clinics (outpatient)
PA: Hazelden Betty Ford Foundation
15251 Pleasant Valley Rd
Center City MN 55012
651 213-4000

(P-21280)
BRIDGES AT SN PDRO PNNSLA HSPT
1300 W 7th St Fl 4, San Pedro (90732-3505)
PHONE..................310 514-5359
EMP: 55
SALES (est): 804.6K **Privately Held**
SIC: **8093** Specialty Outpatient Clinics, Nec

(P-21281)
CAMDEN CENTER INC
10780 Santa Monica Blvd, Los Angeles (90025-4749)
PHONE..................844 422-6336
Jason Schiffman MD, *CEO*
EMP: 130 EST: 2011
SALES (est): 12MM **Privately Held**
WEB: www.camdencenter.com
SIC: **8093** Mental health clinic, outpatient

(P-21282)
CASA CLINA CMPRHNSIVE OTPTENT
255 E Bonita Ave, Pomona (91767-1923)
PHONE..................909 596-7733
Felice Loverso, *CEO*
Susan Stanley, *Vice Pres*
Ross Lessons, *MIS Dir*
EMP: 52 EST: 1984
SQ FT: 35,000
SALES (est): 704.7K **Privately Held**
WEB: www.casacolina.org
SIC: **8093** Rehabilitation center, outpatient treatment

(P-21283)
CASTLEWOOD TREATMENT CTR LLC (PA)
Also Called: Alsana
2545 W Hillcrest Dr # 20, Thousand Oaks (91320-2296)
PHONE..................805 273-5217
Jennifer Steiner, *CEO*
Clodagh Rafferty, *COO*
Bart Thielen, *CFO*
Nicole Siegfried, *Officer*
Tammy Beasley, *Vice Pres*
EMP: 54 EST: 1999
SQ FT: 5,000
SALES (est): 1.7MM **Privately Held**
WEB: www.alsana.com
SIC: **8093** Mental health clinic, outpatient

(P-21284)
CENTER FOR AUTISM &
106 Discovery, Irvine (92618-3131)
PHONE..................949 203-8872
Adrienne Tran, *Supervisor*
EMP: 50 **Privately Held**
WEB: www.centerforautism.com
SIC: **8093** Mental health clinic, outpatient
PA: Center For Autism And Related Disorders, Llc.
21600 Oxnard St Ste 1800
Woodland Hills CA 91367

(P-21285)
CENTRAL VLY REGIONAL CTR INC
5441 W Cypress Ave, Visalia (93277-8341)
PHONE..................559 738-2200
Lorraine Bortes, *General Mgr*
Chris Soares, *Bd of Directors*
Lynn Fjeld, *Case Mgmt Dir*
Ed Araim, *Exec Dir*
Sandra Juniel, *Case Mgr*
EMP: 120

SALES (corp-wide): 277.3MM **Privately Held**
WEB: www.cvrc.org
SIC: **8093** **8399** Mental health clinic, outpatient; social service information exchange
PA: Central Valley Regional Center, Inc.
4615 N Marty Ave
Fresno CA
559 276-4300

(P-21286)
CENTRE FOR NEURO SKILLS (PA)
5215 Ashe Rd, Bakersfield (93313-2069)
PHONE..................661 872-3408
Mark J Ashley, *CEO*
Susan Ashley, *Vice Pres*
Elaine Roberts, *Business Dir*
Brent Masel, *Adv Board Mem*
Bobbie Miller, *Executive Asst*
EMP: 386 EST: 1980
SQ FT: 14,000
SALES (est): 320.2K **Privately Held**
WEB: www.neuroskills.com
SIC: **8093** Rehabilitation center, outpatient treatment

(P-21287)
CHILD AND FAMILY GUIDANCE CTR (PA)
Also Called: NORTHPOINT DAY TREATMENT SCH
9650 Zelzah Ave, Northridge (91325-2003)
PHONE..................818 739-5140
Roy Marshall, *Exec Dir*
Russell Jones, *Ch of Bd*
Robert Garcia, *President*
Mary Becker, *COO*
Ronald Call, *Treasurer*
EMP: 200 EST: 1961
SQ FT: 35,000
SALES: 33.9MM **Privately Held**
WEB: www.childguidance.org
SIC: **8093** Mental health clinic, outpatient

(P-21288)
COMMUNITY ACTION PRTNR SAN LUI
Also Called: E O C Health Services
705 Grand Ave, San Luis Obispo (93401-2639)
PHONE..................805 544-2478
Janice Wolf, *Manager*
EMP: 134
SALES (corp-wide): 93.2MM **Privately Held**
WEB: www.capslo.org
SIC: **8093** Family planning clinic
PA: Community Action Partnership Of San Luis Obispo County, Inc.
1030 Southwood Dr
San Luis Obispo CA 93401
805 544-4355

(P-21289)
COMMUNITY FAMILY GUIDANCE CTR (PA)
10929 South St Ste 208b, Cerritos (90703-5391)
PHONE..................562 865-6444
Richard Murase, *President*
Lesley Watkins, *CFO*
Patricia Taylor PH, *Training Dir*
EMP: 58 EST: 1976
SALES (est): 6.6MM **Privately Held**
WEB: www.cfgcenter.com
SIC: **8093** Mental health clinic, outpatient

(P-21290)
COUNTY OF LOS ANGELES
Also Called: Health Services, Dept of
7601 Imperial Hwy, Downey (90242-3456)
PHONE..................562 401-7088
Valeria Orange, *Director*
Aries Limbaga, *Ch Nursing Ofcr*
EMP: 51
SALES (corp-wide): 25.2B **Privately Held**
WEB: www.lacounty.gov
SIC: **8093** **9431** Rehabilitation center, outpatient treatment;
PA: County Of Los Angeles
500 W Temple St Ste 437
Los Angeles CA 90012
213 974-1101

(P-21291)
COUNTY OF LOS ANGELES
Also Called: Health Dept
5850 S Main St, Los Angeles (90003-1215)
PHONE..................323 897-6187
Floretta Taylor, *Admin Director*
Anthony Fedon, *Analyst*
Hubert Humphrey, *Mayor*
EMP: 51
SALES (corp-wide): 25.2B **Privately Held**
WEB: www.lacounty.gov
SIC: **8093** **8011** Specialty outpatient clinics; administration of public health programs; ; offices & clinics of medical doctors
PA: County Of Los Angeles
500 W Temple St Ste 437
Los Angeles CA 90012
213 974-1101

(P-21292)
COUNTY OF LOS ANGELES
Also Called: Health Services, Dept of
5205 Melrose Ave, Los Angeles (90038-3144)
PHONE..................323 769-7800
Rosa Pinon, *Branch Mgr*
EMP: 51
SALES (corp-wide): 25.2B **Privately Held**
WEB: www.lacounty.gov
SIC: **8093** **9431** Family planning & birth control clinics; administration of public health programs;
PA: County Of Los Angeles
500 W Temple St Ste 437
Los Angeles CA 90012
213 974-1101

(P-21293)
COUNTY OF LOS ANGELES
Also Called: Mental Health Dept of
17707 Studebaker Rd, Artesia (90703-2640)
PHONE..................562 402-0688
Latisha Guvman, *Manager*
EMP: 51
SALES (corp-wide): 25.2B **Privately Held**
WEB: www.lacounty.gov
SIC: **8093** **9431** Specialty outpatient clinics; administration of public health programs;
PA: County Of Los Angeles
500 W Temple St Ste 437
Los Angeles CA 90012
213 974-1101

(P-21294)
COUNTY OF LOS ANGELES
Also Called: Antelope Valley Health Center
335 E Avenue K6 Ste B, Lancaster (93535-4645)
PHONE..................661 524-2005
Mary Nolan, *Manager*
EMP: 51
SALES (corp-wide): 25.2B **Privately Held**
WEB: www.lacounty.gov
SIC: **8093** Family planning clinic
PA: County Of Los Angeles
500 W Temple St Ste 437
Los Angeles CA 90012
213 974-1101

(P-21295)
CRC HEALTH CORPORATE
Also Called: Recovery Solutions Santa Ana
2101 E 1st St, Santa Ana (92705-4007)
PHONE..................714 542-3581
Tfu Bach Tran, *Manager*
EMP: 1318 **Publicly Held**
SIC: **8093** Drug clinic, outpatient
HQ: Crc Health Corporate
20400 Stevns Crk Blvd
Cupertino CA 95014
408 367-0044

(P-21296)
CRC HEALTH GROUP INC
1021 W La Cadena Dr, Riverside (92501-1413)
PHONE..................951 784-8010
Tammy Elkins, *Branch Mgr*
EMP: 75 **Publicly Held**
SIC: **8093** Mental health clinic, outpatient

HQ: Crc Health Group, Inc.
6100 Tower Cir Ste 1000
Franklin TN 37067

(P-21297)
DEL AMO HOSPITAL INC
23700 Camino Del Sol, Torrance (90505-5000)
PHONE..................310 530-1151
Lisa Moncen, *CEO*
Alan B Miller, *Ch of Bd*
Kirk E Gorman, *Treasurer*
Steven Hytry, *Officer*
Sidney Miller, *Exec VP*
EMP: 300 EST: 1991
SQ FT: 88,000
SALES: 42.9MM
SALES (corp-wide): 11.5B **Publicly Held**
WEB: www.delamohospital.com
SIC: **8093** Mental health clinic, outpatient
PA: Universal Health Services, Inc.
367 S Gulph Rd
King Of Prussia PA 19406
610 768-3300

(P-21298)
DEVEREUX FOUNDATION
Also Called: Devereux California Center
7055 Seaway Dr, Goleta (93117-4358)
P.O. Box 6784, Santa Barbara (93160-6784)
PHONE..................805 968-2525
Amy Evans, *Principal*
Veronica Arenas, *Human Res Mgr*
Mory Alvarez, *Manager*
EMP: 63
SALES (corp-wide): 460.5MM **Privately Held**
WEB: www.devereux.org
SIC: **8093** Mental health clinic, outpatient
PA: Devereux Foundation
2012 Renaissance Blvd # 200
King Of Prussia PA 19085
610 542-3057

(P-21299)
DEVEREUX FOUNDATION
6980 Falberg Way, Goleta (93117)
PHONE..................805 968-2525
EMP: 63
SALES (corp-wide): 460.5MM **Privately Held**
WEB: www.devereux.org
SIC: **8093** Mental health clinic, outpatient
PA: Devereux Foundation
2012 Renaissance Blvd # 200
King Of Prussia PA 19085
610 542-3057

(P-21300)
DUAL DIAGNOSIS TRTMNT CTR INC (PA)
Also Called: Sovereign Health of California
1211 Puerta Del Sol # 200, San Clemente (92673-6342)
PHONE..................949 276-5553
Tonmoy Sharma, *CEO*
Rishi Barkataki, *President*
Veena Kumari, *Officer*
Nidhi Grover, *Executive*
Nader Faraji, *Administration*
EMP: 470 EST: 1983
SALES (est): 52.9MM **Privately Held**
WEB: www.sovcal.com
SIC: **8093** Mental health clinic, outpatient

(P-21301)
DUBNOFF CTR FOR CHILD DEVL & (PA)
10526 Dubnoff Way, North Hollywood (91606-3921)
PHONE..................818 755-4950
Sandra Babcock, *President*
Sandra Sternig-Babcock, *President*
EMP: 94 EST: 1948
SQ FT: 13,968
SALES (est): 5.5MM **Privately Held**
SIC: **8211** **8093** **8361** Specialty education; specialty outpatient clinics; residential care

(P-21302)
EAST VALLEY CMNTY HLTH CTR INC (PA)
420 S Glendora Ave, West Covina
(91790-3001)
PHONE...............................626 919-3402
Alicia Mardini, *CEO*
Sophia Shavira, *Ch Of Bd*
Alicia Thomas, *CEO*
Eva Elser, *Opers Staff*
Kimberly Rios, *Corp Comm Staff*
EMP: 65
SQ FT: 24,000
SALES: 25.9MM **Privately Held**
WEB: www.evchc.org
SIC: 8093 Family planning clinic

(P-21303)
ELEMENTS BEHAVIORAL HEALTH INC (PA)
5000 Arprt Plz Dr Ste 100, Long Beach
(90815)
PHONE...............................562 741-6470
David Sack, *Chief Mktg Ofcr*
James Adams, *CFO*
Rob Mahan, *CFO*
Keith Arnold, *Exec VP*
Kayleen Hittesdorf, *Vice Pres*
EMP: 205 **EST:** 2010
SALES (est): 113.5MM **Privately Held**
WEB: www.promisesbehavioralhealth.com
SIC: 8093 8049 Substance abuse clinics (outpatient); nutrition specialist

(P-21304)
ELWYN PENNSYLVANIA AND DEL
Also Called: Elwyn Cal Rehabilitation Ctr
18325 Mount Baldy Cir, Fountain Valley
(92708-6115)
PHONE...............................714 557-6313
Joan McKinney, *Director*
Ken Ager, *General Mgr*
Kathryn Pfister, *Admin Asst*
Henry Michaels, *Program Dir*
Cheryl Westley, *Director*
EMP: 57
SQ FT: 16,000
SALES (corp-wide): 314.5MM **Privately Held**
WEB: www.elwyn.org
SIC: 8211 8093 Private special education school; rehabilitation center, outpatient treatment
PA: Elwyn Of Pennsylvania And Delaware
111 Elwyn Rd
Media PA 19063
610 891-2000

(P-21305)
EXODUS RECOVERY INC (PA)
9808 Venice Blvd Ste 700, Culver City
(90232-6824)
PHONE...............................310 945-3350
Luana Murphy, *CEO*
Leeann Skorohod, *President*
Aaron Ikuru, *Officer*
Cesar Martinez, *Officer*
Lezlie Murch, *Senior VP*
EMP: 105 **EST:** 1988
SALES (est): 103.3MM **Privately Held**
WEB: www.exodusrecovery.com
SIC: 8093 Mental health clinic, outpatient

(P-21306)
GHC OF LOMPOC LLC
Also Called: Lompoc Sklled Nrsing Rhblttion
1428 W North Ave, Lompoc (93436-3961)
PHONE...............................805 735-4010
Thomas Olds,
Mark Hall, *Administration*
Lois Mastrocola,
EMP: 87 **EST:** 2006
SALES (est): 7.9MM
SALES (corp-wide): 112.7MM **Privately Held**
SIC: 8093 Rehabilitation center, outpatient treatment
PA: Life Generations Healthcare Llc
6 Hutton Cntre Dr Ste 400
Santa Ana CA 92707
714 241-5600

(P-21307)
GRASSHOPPER HOUSE PARTNERS LLC
Also Called: Passages
6428 Meadows Ct, Malibu (90265-4492)
PHONE...............................310 589-2880
Chris Prentiss,
Pax Prentiss,
Alexander Maroto, *Director*
EMP: 105
SQ FT: 16,000
SALES (est): 11.5MM **Privately Held**
WEB: www.passagesmalibu.com
SIC: 8093 Rehabilitation services

(P-21308)
GREATER VALLEY MEDICAL GROUP (PA)
11600 Indian Hills Rd # 300, Mission Hills
(91345-1225)
PHONE...............................818 838-4500
Don Rebhun MD, *President*
Howard Sawyer MD, *Corp Secy*
Mohyi Soleiman MD, *Vice Pres*
EMP: 75 **EST:** 1977
SALES (est): 12.2MM **Privately Held**
SIC: 8093 Specialty outpatient clinics

(P-21309)
GREATER VALLEY MEDICAL GROUP
Also Called: Healthcare Partners
14600 Sherman Way Ste 300, Van Nuys
(91405-2272)
PHONE...............................818 781-7097
Cris Kalal, *Manager*
EMP: 147
SALES (corp-wide): 12.2MM **Privately Held**
SIC: 8093 8011 Specialty outpatient clinics; offices & clinics of medical doctors
PA: Greater Valley Medical Group Inc
11600 Indian Hills Rd # 300
Mission Hills CA 91345
818 838-4500

(P-21310)
HARBOR COMMUNITY CLINIC
593 W 6th St, San Pedro (90731-2521)
PHONE...............................310 547-0202
Rick Paars, *Director*
Michele Ruple, *President*
EMP: 67 **EST:** 1970
SQ FT: 2,000
SALES (est): 7MM **Privately Held**
WEB: www.harborcommunityclinic.com
SIC: 8093 8011 Specialty outpatient clinics; clinic, operated by physicians

(P-21311)
HELP GROUP WEST (PA)
13130 Burbank Blvd, Sherman Oaks
(91401-6000)
PHONE...............................818 781-0360
Barbara Firestone, *President*
Michael Love, *CFO*
Susan Berman PH, *Exec VP*
Elena Brewer, *Vice Pres*
Heather Humphrey, *Accounts Mgr*
EMP: 200 **EST:** 1999
SQ FT: 100,000
SALES: 17.8MM **Privately Held**
WEB: www.thehelpgroup.org
SIC: 8093 Speech defect clinic

(P-21312)
HILLVIEW MENTAL HEALTH CTR INC
12450 Van Nuys Blvd Ste 2, Pacoima
(91331-1391)
PHONE...............................818 896-1161
Eva S McCraven, *President*
Carl C Mc Craven, *Treasurer*
Julie E Jones, *Vice Pres*
Beth K Meltzer, *Vice Pres*
Hazel Westbrook, *Office Mgr*
EMP: 80 **EST:** 1984
SQ FT: 17,600
SALES: 10.7MM **Privately Held**
WEB: www.hillviewmhc.org
SIC: 8093 Mental health clinic, outpatient

(P-21313)
INTERSTATE RHBLTATION SVCS LLC
333 E Glenoaks Blvd # 204, Glendale
(91207-2074)
PHONE...............................818 244-5656
James Pietsch, *Owner*
Glenn Dabatos, *COO*
Beth Cera-Celo,
Sandy Pietsch,
Lot Tanpinco, *Assistant*
EMP: 120 **EST:** 1986
SALES (est): 21.7MM **Privately Held**
WEB: www.interstaterehab.com
SIC: 8093 Rehabilitation center, outpatient treatment

(P-21314)
KAISER FOUNDATION HOSPITALS
Also Called: Montclair Mental Health Offs
5330 San Bernardino St, Montclair
(91763-2952)
PHONE...............................909 399-3700
David Rodriguez, *Director*
EMP: 209
SALES (corp-wide): 30.5B **Privately Held**
WEB: www.kaisercenter.com
SIC: 8093 Mental health clinic, outpatient
HQ: Kaiser Foundation Hospitals Inc
1 Kaiser Plz
Oakland CA 94612
510 271-6611

(P-21315)
KAISER FOUNDATION HOSPITALS
Also Called: Kaiser Permanente
333 S Hope St, Los Angeles (90071-1406)
PHONE...............................213 217-4514
Estivali Villa, *Sr Project Mgr*
Lizbeth Illingworth, *Manager*
EMP: 209
SALES (corp-wide): 30.5B **Privately Held**
WEB: www.kaisercenter.com
SIC: 8093 8062 8049 8031 Mental health clinic, outpatient; general medical & surgical hospitals; nutrition specialist; offices & clinics of osteopathic physicians
HQ: Kaiser Foundation Hospitals Inc
1 Kaiser Plz
Oakland CA 94612
510 271-6611

(P-21316)
KAISER FOUNDATION HOSPITALS
Also Called: Oak Street Physical Therapy
2040 Pacific Coast Hwy, Lomita
(90717-2660)
PHONE...............................424 251-7000
EMP: 209
SALES (corp-wide): 30.5B **Privately Held**
WEB: www.kaisercenter.com
SIC: 8093 Rehabilitation center, outpatient treatment
HQ: Kaiser Foundation Hospitals Inc
1 Kaiser Plz
Oakland CA 94612
510 271-6611

(P-21317)
KAISER FOUNDATION HOSPITALS
Also Called: Health Educatn Psychiatry Offs
5105 W Goldleaf Cir, Los Angeles
(90056-1269)
PHONE...............................323 298-3300
Natasha Elliott, *Branch Mgr*
Margarita Somova, *Psychiatry*
EMP: 209
SALES (corp-wide): 30.5B **Privately Held**
WEB: www.kaisercenter.com
SIC: 8093 Specialty outpatient clinics
HQ: Kaiser Foundation Hospitals Inc
1 Kaiser Plz
Oakland CA 94612
510 271-6611

(P-21318)
KAISER FOUNDATION HOSPITALS
Also Called: Kaiser Permanente
23621 Main St, Carson (90745-5743)
PHONE...............................310 513-6707
Lora Griffin, *Branch Mgr*
Ann La Fever, *Executive*
EMP: 209
SALES (corp-wide): 30.5B **Privately Held**
WEB: www.kaisercenter.com
SIC: 8093 8062 Specialty outpatient clinics; general medical & surgical hospitals
HQ: Kaiser Foundation Hospitals Inc
1 Kaiser Plz
Oakland CA 94612
510 271-6611

(P-21319)
MFI RECOVERY CENTER (PA)
5870 Arlington Ave # 103, Riverside
(92504-2037)
PHONE...............................951 683-6596
Craig Lamdon, *Exec Dir*
Jennifer Gordon, *Program Mgr*
EMP: 98 **EST:** 1972
SQ FT: 864
SALES: 15.8MM **Privately Held**
WEB: www.mfirecovery.com
SIC: 8093 8322 Alcohol clinic, outpatient; family counseling services

(P-21320)
MHM SERVICES INC
230 Station Way, Arroyo Grande
(93420-3358)
PHONE...............................805 904-6678
EMP: 148 **Publicly Held**
WEB: www.mhm-services.com
SIC: 8093 Mental health clinic, outpatient
HQ: Mhm Services, Inc.
1593 Spring Hill Rd # 600
Vienna VA 22182
703 749-4600

(P-21321)
MODIVCARE INC
1021 4th St, Taft (93268-2433)
PHONE...............................661 765-7025
Courtney Morris, *Branch Mgr*
EMP: 50
SALES (corp-wide): 1.3B **Publicly Held**
WEB: www.prsholdings.com
SIC: 8093 Mental health clinic, outpatient
PA: Modivcare Inc.
4700 S Syracuse St # 410
Denver CO 80237
404 888-5800

(P-21322)
NATIONAL THERAPEUTIC SVCS INC (PA)
Also Called: Northbound Treatment Services
3822 Campus Dr Ste 100, Newport Beach
(92660-2674)
PHONE...............................866 311-0003
Michael Neatherton, *President*
Paul Alexander, *COO*
Devon Wayt, *COO*
Ray Pacini, *CFO*
Paul Tangonan, *Technician*
EMP: 98 **EST:** 1995
SALES (est): 22.8MM **Privately Held**
WEB: www.northboundtreatment.com
SIC: 8093 Alcohol clinic, outpatient

(P-21323)
OPTIONS FAMILY OF SERVICES
5755 Valentina Ave, Atascadero
(93422-3532)
PHONE...............................805 462-8544
EMP: 50
SQ FT: 576
SALES (corp-wide): 5.6MM **Privately Held**
SIC: 8093 Services-Misc
PA: Options Family Of Services, Inc
800 Quintana Rd Ste 2c
Morro Bay CA 93442
805 772-6066

(P-21324)
PEDIATRIC THERAPY NETWORK
1815 W 213th St Ste 100, Torrance
(90501-2852)
PHONE.................................310 328-0276
Zoe Mailloux, *Exec Dir*
Terri Nishimura, *Exec Dir*
Gloria Gonzalez-Karch, *General Mgr*
Kelly Peterson, *CTO*
Adrian Harewood, *Controller*
EMP: 101 EST: 1996
SQ FT: 20,000
SALES (est): 21.2MM **Privately Held**
WEB: www.pediatrictherapynetwork.org
SIC: 8093 Rehabilitation center, outpatient
treatment

(P-21325)
PLANNED PARENTHOOD LOS ANGELES (PA)
400 W 30th St, Los Angeles (90007-3320)
PHONE.................................213 284-3200
Sue Dunlap, *President*
Mark Kimura, *CFO*
Linda Pahl, *CFO*
Kate Ceredona, *Officer*
Adrianne Black, *Vice Pres*
EMP: 80 EST: 1965
SQ FT: 30,000
SALES (est): 81.3MM **Privately Held**
WEB: www.plannedparenthood.org
SIC: 8093 Family planning clinic; birth con-
trol clinic

(P-21326)
PLANNED PRNTHOOD CAL CNTL CAST (PA)
518 Garden St, Santa Barbara
(93101-1606)
PHONE.................................805 963-2445
Cheryl Rollings, *Exec Dir*
Tiana Riskowski, *CFO*
Jenna Tosh, *Exec Dir*
Lindsay Soleimani, *Director*
EMP: 54 EST: 1964
SQ FT: 9,000
SALES: 23.3MM **Privately Held**
WEB: www.plannedparenthood.org
SIC: 8093 Family planning clinic

(P-21327)
POSITIVE BEHAVIOR STEPS CORP
1050 Lakes Dr Ste 225, West Covina
(91790-2910)
PHONE.................................626 940-5180
David Sandoval, *CEO*
David Alberto Sandoval, *CEO*
EMP: 73 EST: 2017
SALES (est): 1.1MM **Privately Held**
WEB: www.pbxsteps.org
SIC: 8093 Mental health clinic, outpatient

(P-21328)
PRIME MSO LLC
550 N Brand Blvd Ste 900, Glendale
(91203-4721)
PHONE.................................818 937-9969
Caroline Tchamanian, *COO*
Raffi Tchamanian, *CFO*
Brian Owens, *Radiology Dir*
Patricia Khamis, *CIO*
Shadi Yassine, *Accountant*
EMP: 85 EST: 1998
SALES (est): 45MM **Privately Held**
WEB: www.primemso.com
SIC: 8093 Specialty outpatient clinics

(P-21329)
PRINCIPLES INC (PA)
Also Called: Impact DRG Alcohol Trtmnt Ctr
1680 N Fair Oaks Ave, Pasadena
(91103-1642)
P.O. Box 93607 (91109-3607)
PHONE.................................323 681-2575
James M Stillwell, *CEO*
Lois Gonzales, *Controller*
Mark Paquet, *Hlthcr Dir*
Patty Despain-Fiendel, *Manager*
EMP: 51 EST: 1971
SQ FT: 40,000
SALES (est): 13.5MM **Privately Held**
WEB: www.impacthouse.com
SIC: 8093 Rehabilitation center, outpatient
treatment

(P-21330)
PROVIDENCE SPEECH HEARING CTR
Also Called: Word and Brown Hearing Ctr
1301 W Providence Ave, Orange
(92868-3892)
PHONE.................................714 639-4990
Linda Smith, *CEO*
Bill Ross, *President*
Jack Shradder, *Treasurer*
Margaret A Inman PH, *Founder*
Jerry O'Connor, *Exec VP*
EMP: 50 EST: 1966
SQ FT: 15,000
SALES (est): 9.7MM **Privately Held**
WEB: www.pshc.org
SIC: 8093 Speech defect clinic

(P-21331)
PURE AUTISM COUNSELING CTR INC
Also Called: Pacc
17728 Sierra Hwy, Canyon Country
(91351-1635)
PHONE.................................661 360-7730
Arevik Karamyan, *President*
EMP: 65 EST: 2018
SALES (est): 5.8MM **Privately Held**
WEB: www.paccenter.net
SIC: 8093 Mental health clinic, outpatient

(P-21332)
QUALITY BEHAVIOR SOLUTIONS INC
1212 W Avenue J Ste 200, Lancaster
(93534-2940)
PHONE.................................818 991-7722
Rosa Hernandez, *Branch Mgr*
EMP: 53
SALES (corp-wide): 4.3MM **Privately Held**
WEB: www.qbssocal.com
SIC: 8093 Mental health clinic, outpatient
PA: Quality Behavior Solutions, Inc.
16600 Sherman Way Ste 105
Van Nuys CA 91406
818 991-7722

(P-21333)
REIMAGINE NETWORK (PA)
Also Called: Rehabilitation Inst Orange Cnty
1601 E Saint Andrew Pl, Santa Ana
(92705-4940)
PHONE.................................714 633-7400
Praim S Singh, *Director*
Dana Patton, *Executive Asst*
Bernardo Lahoz III, *Bookkeeper*
Roberta Ybarra, *Human Resources*
Lisa Jenks, *Director*
EMP: 130 EST: 1950
SALES (est): 8.3MM **Privately Held**
WEB: www.riorehab.org
SIC: 8093 Rehabilitation center, outpatient
treatment

(P-21334)
RIO
Also Called: Rehabilitation Inst of Sthrn C
1800 E La Veta Ave, Orange (92866-2902)
PHONE.................................714 633-7400
Glenn Motola, *Exec Dir*
John Berry, *Principal*
EMP: 233 EST: 1964
SQ FT: 3,000
SALES (est): 8.6MM **Privately Held**
SIC: 8093 8351 Rehabilitation center, out-
patient treatment; child day care services

(P-21335)
SAFE REFUGE
Also Called: Sobriety House
1041 Redondo Ave, Long Beach
(90804-3928)
PHONE.................................562 987-5722
Kathryn Romo, *Exec Dir*
Annette Mulinix, *Manager*
EMP: 80
SQ FT: 2,300
SALES: 7.1MM **Privately Held**
WEB: www.asaferefuge.org
SIC: 8093 Substance abuse clinics (outpa-
tient)

(P-21336)
SAN FERNANDO CITY OF INC
10605 Balboa Blvd Ste 100, Granada Hills
(91344-6367)
PHONE.................................818 832-2400
Wendi Tovey, *Branch Mgr*
EMP: 96
SALES (corp-wide): 28.8MM **Privately Held**
WEB: www.ci.san-fernando.ca.us
SIC: 8093 9111 Mental health clinic, out-
patient; county supervisors' & executives'
offices
PA: San Fernando, City Of Inc
117 N Macneil St
San Fernando CA 91340
818 898-1201

(P-21337)
SAN FRNNDO VLY CMNTY MNTAL HLT (PA)
16360 Roscoe Blvd Fl 2, Van Nuys
(91406-1219)
PHONE.................................818 901-4830
Ian Hunter PHD, *President*
Emily Chen, *CFO*
Jennifer Calderon, *Program Mgr*
Christina Giles, *Program Mgr*
John Putman, *Program Mgr*
EMP: 55 EST: 1970
SQ FT: 13,000
SALES: 44MM **Privately Held**
WEB: www.movinglivesforward.org
SIC: 8093 Substance abuse clinics (outpa-
tient)

(P-21338)
SARAH ELIZABETH TREUSDELL
921 W Avenue J Ste C, Lancaster
(93534-3443)
PHONE.................................661 949-0131
S E Treusdell, *Principal*
Sarah Elizabeth Treusdell, *Principal*
EMP: 50
SALES (est): 124.3K **Privately Held**
SIC: 8093 Mental health clinic, outpatient

(P-21339)
SMILE HOUSING CORPORATION
800 Quintana Rd Ste 2c, Morro Bay
(93442-2300)
P.O. Box 877 (93443-0877)
PHONE.................................805 772-6066
Debbie Bertrando, *CEO*
Jennifer Gaalswyk, *CFO*
EMP: 99
SALES: 106.9K **Privately Held**
WEB: www.smile-housing-corporation-
morro-bay-ca.assistance-from-
nonprofits.aidpage.com
SIC: 8093 Specialty outpatient clinics

(P-21340)
SOBER LIVING BY SEA INC (HQ)
2800 Lafayette Rd Ste D, Newport Beach
(92663-3753)
PHONE.................................949 673-6696
Carl Mosen, *President*
Barbara Mosen, *Corp Secy*
Andrej Kukric, *Marketing Staff*
Jessica Piersall, *Hlthcr Dir*
Ashley Mansfield, *Program Dir*
EMP: 76 EST: 1986
SQ FT: 4,000
SALES (est): 5MM **Publicly Held**
WEB: www.sierrabythesea.com
SIC: 8093 Substance abuse clinics (outpa-
tient)

(P-21341)
SOUTH BAYLO UNIVERSITY
Also Called: South Baylo Acupuncture Clinic
2727 W 6th St, Los Angeles (90057-3111)
PHONE.................................213 999-0297
David J Park, *President*
Mimi Park, *Officer*
Jennifer E Park, *Vice Pres*
Pia Melen, *Dean*
Seon Kim, *Hlthcr Dir*
EMP: 136
SALES (corp-wide): 3.3MM **Privately Held**
WEB: www.southbaylo.edu
SIC: 8093 8221 8049 Specialty outpatient
clinics; university; acupuncturist

PA: South Baylo University
1126 N Brookhurst St
Anaheim CA 92801
714 533-1495

(P-21342)
SOUTH CNTL HLTH RHBLTTION PRGR
Also Called: Barbour & Floyd Medical Assoc
2620 Industry Way, Lynwood 90262-4024)
PHONE.................................310 667-4070
Jack M Barbour, *Principal*
EMP: 98 **Privately Held**
WEB: www.barbourandfloydla.org
SIC: 8093 Rehabilitation center, outpatient
treatment
PA: South Central Health & Rehabilitation
Program
2610 Industry Way Ste A
Lynwood CA 90262

(P-21343)
SOUTHERN CAL ALCHOL DRG PRGRAM (PA)
11500 Paramount Blvd, Downey
(90241-4530)
PHONE.................................562 923-4545
Lynne Appel, *CEO*
Gary Munger, *Ch of Bd*
Marsie Alford, *CFO*
Judith Edwards, *Treasurer*
Leon Emerson, *Treasurer*
EMP: 60 EST: 1972
SALES (est): 8.8MM **Privately Held**
WEB: www.scadpinc.org
SIC: 8093 Substance abuse clinics (outpa-
tient)

(P-21344)
SPENCER RECOVERY CENTERS INC (PA)
1316 S Coast Hwy, Laguna Beach
(92651-3118)
P.O. Box 9296 (92652-7261)
PHONE.................................949 376-3705
Chris Spencer, *President*
Cindy Spencer, *Admin Sec*
EMP: 60 EST: 1987
SQ FT: 2,000
SALES (est): 9.2MM **Privately Held**
WEB: www.spencerrecovery.com
SIC: 8093 Alcohol clinic, outpatient; sub-
stance abuse clinics (outpatient)

(P-21345)
STAFFREHAB
5000 Birch St, Newport Beach
(92660-2127)
PHONE.................................888 835-0894
Sara Palmer, *CEO*
Lindsay Joseph, *CTO*
EMP: 677 EST: 2009
SALES (est): 3.1MM
SALES (corp-wide): 165MM **Privately Held**
WEB: www.thesteppingstonesgroup.com
SIC: 8093 Rehabilitation center, outpatient
treatment
PA: Pediatric Therapy Services, Llc
2586 Trailridge Dr E # 100
Lafayette CO 80026
800 337-5965

(P-21346)
SUNSHINE BEHAVIORAL HEALTH LLC (PA)
30950 Rncho Vejo Rd Ste 2, San Juan
Capistrano (92675)
PHONE.................................949 835-4375
Tahnil Oconnor, *Mng Member*
EMP: 64 EST: 2013
SALES (est): 11.3MM **Privately Held**
WEB: www.sunshinebehavioralhealth.com
SIC: 8093 Substance abuse clinics (outpa-
tient)

(P-21347)
TARZANA TREATMENT CENTERS INC
320 E Palmdale Blvd Palmdale
(93550-4598)
PHONE.................................818 654-3815
Albert Senella, *President*
Phyllis Cohen, *Family Practiti*

EMP: 93
SALES (corp-wide): 96MM Privately Held
WEB: www.tarzanatc.org
SIC: 8093 Substance abuse clinics (outpatient)
PA: Tarzana Treatment Centers, Inc.
18646 Oxnard St
Tarzana CA 91356
818 996-1051

(P-21348)
TARZANA TREATMENT CENTERS INC (PA)
18646 Oxnard St, Tarzana (91356-1411)
PHONE...................................818 996-1051
Albert Senella, *President*
Sylvia Cadena, *CFO*
Bobbi Sloan, *Corp Secy*
Robert Obogeanu, *Vice Pres*
Rochelle Price, *Admin Asst*
EMP: 160 EST: 1972
SQ FT: 14,000
SALES: 96MM Privately Held
WEB: www.tarzanatc.org
SIC: 8093 8322 8063 Mental health clinic, outpatient; individual & family services; psychiatric hospitals

(P-21349)
TARZANA TREATMENT CENTERS INC
Also Called: Tarzana Trtmnt Ctrs LNG Bch O
5190 Atlantic Ave, Lakewood (90805-6510)
PHONE...................................562 428-4111
EMP: 93
SALES (corp-wide): 96MM Privately Held
WEB: www.tarzanatc.org
SIC: 8093 8299 Substance abuse clinics (outpatient); airline training
PA: Tarzana Treatment Centers, Inc.
18646 Oxnard St
Tarzana CA 91356
818 996-1051

(P-21350)
TARZANA TREATMENT CENTERS INC
2101 Magnolia Ave, Long Beach (90806-4521)
PHONE...................................562 218-1868
Angela Knox, *Branch Mgr*
Ronald Voeltner, *Technician*
Shaun Flax, *Research*
Glenn Metken, *Technology*
Dianne Sanchez, *Analyst*
EMP: 93
SQ FT: 11,482
SALES (corp-wide): 96MM Privately Held
WEB: www.tarzanatc.org
SIC: 8093 Substance abuse clinics (outpatient)
PA: Tarzana Treatment Centers, Inc.
18646 Oxnard St
Tarzana CA 91356
818 996-1051

(P-21351)
TARZANA TREATMENT CENTERS INC
Also Called: Tarzana Treatment Ctr
44447 10th St W, Lancaster (93534-3324)
PHONE...................................661 726-2630
Theresa Scott, *Director*
Norma Chavez-Barrales, *Case Mgr*
EMP: 93
SALES (corp-wide): 96MM Privately Held
WEB: www.tarzanatc.org
SIC: 8093 8069 8011 Drug clinic, outpatient; drug addiction rehabilitation hospital; clinic, operated by physicians
PA: Tarzana Treatment Centers, Inc.
18646 Oxnard St
Tarzana CA 91356
818 996-1051

(P-21352)
TELECARE ACT 7
12440 Firestone Blvd # 30, Norwalk (90650-4328)
PHONE...................................562 929-6688
Bryan Sawlsville, *Director*

Verlonda Vaughn, *Supervisor*
EMP: 85 EST: 1996
SALES (est): 2.2MM
SALES (corp-wide): 140.9MM Privately Held
WEB: www.telecarecorp.com
SIC: 8093 Mental health clinic, outpatient
PA: Telecare Corporation
1080 Marina Village Pkwy # 100
Alameda CA 94501
510 337-7950

(P-21353)
TELECARE CORPORATION
Also Called: La Casa Mhrc
6060 N Paramount Blvd, Long Beach (90805-3711)
PHONE...................................562 630-8672
Anne Bakar, *CEO*
Joshua Hartman, *Administration*
Kier Taylor, *Director*
Anthony Thai, *Director*
EMP: 120 EST: 1965
SALES (est): 12.5MM
SALES (corp-wide): 140.9MM Privately Held
WEB: www.telecarecorp.com
SIC: 8093 Mental health clinic, outpatient
PA: Telecare Corporation
1080 Marina Village Pkwy # 100
Alameda CA 94501
510 337-7950

(P-21354)
THERAPY FOR KIDS INC
Also Called: Gallagher Pediatric Therapy
233 Orangefair Mall, Fullerton (92832-3038)
PHONE...................................714 870-6116
Mary K Gallagher, *President*
Gene Riddle, *CFO*
Ariane Miyakawa, *Analyst*
Jessica Alter,
Stacy Cobbs,
EMP: 57 EST: 1994
SALES (est): 10.3MM Privately Held
SIC: 8093 Rehabilitation center, outpatient treatment

(P-21355)
TRANSITIONS - MENTAL HLTH ASSN (PA)
Also Called: SLO TRANSITIONS
784 High St, San Luis Obispo (93401-5243)
P.O. Box 15408 (93406-5408)
PHONE...................................805 540-6500
Jill B White, *Exec Dir*
Maria Perez, *Partner*
Casey Appell, *Exec VP*
Doris Bell, *Program Mgr*
Savannah Williams, *Technician*
EMP: 60 EST: 1980
SQ FT: 8,000
SALES: 15.1MM Privately Held
WEB: www.t-mha.org
SIC: 8093 Mental health clinic, outpatient

(P-21356)
TRI-CITY MENTAL HEALTH AUTH (PA)
Also Called: Tri City Mental Health Center
2008 N Garey Ave, Pomona (91767-2722)
PHONE...................................909 623-6131
Toll Free:...................................866 -
Diana Acosta, *CFO*
Jed Leano, *Vice Chairman*
Nancy Gill, *Officer*
Antonette Navarro, *Exec Dir*
Mica Olmos, *Executive Asst*
EMP: 85
SQ FT: 12,000
SALES: 10.2MM Privately Held
WEB: www.tricitymhs.org
SIC: 8093 8322 Mental health clinic, outpatient; individual & family services

(P-21357)
TRUVIDA RECOVERY
45 Timberland, Aliso Viejo (92656-2108)
PHONE...................................949 283-4679
Vince Bindi, *Partner*
EMP: 64 EST: 2016

SALES (est): 3MM Privately Held
WEB: www.truvida.com
SIC: 8093 Substance abuse clinics (outpatient)

(P-21358)
TULE RIVER INDIAN HLTH CTR INC
380 N Reservation Rd, Porterville (93257-9673)
P.O. Box 768 (93258-0768)
PHONE...................................559 784-2316
Zahid Sheikh, *CEO*
Casey Carrillo, *CFO*
Jan L Trigleth, *Physician Asst*
Nancy Batres, *Dental Hygenist*
EMP: 65 EST: 1973
SQ FT: 15,000
SALES: 10.9MM Privately Held
WEB: www.trihci.org
SIC: 8093 Specialty outpatient clinics

(P-21359)
UHS-CORONA INC
Also Called: Corona Rgnal Med Ctr Rhbltion
730 Magnolia Ave, Corona (92879-3117)
PHONE...................................951 736-7200
Pat Sanders, *Director*
Beverly Montiel, *Hlthcr Dir*
EMP: 200
SALES (corp-wide): 11.5B Publicly Held
WEB: www.coronaregional.com
SIC: 8093 8062 8069 8051 Rehabilitation center, outpatient treatment; general medical & surgical hospitals; specialty hospitals, except psychiatric; skilled nursing care facilities
HQ: Uhs-Corona, Inc.
800 S Main St
Corona CA 92882
951 737-4343

(P-21360)
UNITED AMRCN INDIAN INVLVMENT (PA)
1125 W 6th St Ste 103, Los Angeles (90017-1896)
PHONE...................................213 202-3970
Joseph Quintana, *Director*
Luis Cervantes, *CFO*
David L Rambeau, *Exec Dir*
Tamara Bolding,
Carrie Johnson PHD, *Director*
EMP: 123 EST: 1974
SQ FT: 26,000
SALES (est): 10.3MM Privately Held
WEB: www.uaii.org
SIC: 8093 Rehabilitation center, outpatient treatment

(P-21361)
UNIVERSAL CARE INC (PA)
Also Called: Smile Wide Dental
19762 Macarthur Blvd # 100, Irvine (92612-2424)
PHONE...................................562 424-6200
Howard E Davis, *CEO*
Mark Gunter, *CFO*
Jay Davis, *Vice Pres*
Jeffrey Davis, *Admin Sec*
Allen Wong, *Analyst*
EMP: 350 EST: 1983
SQ FT: 73,000
SALES (est): 31.4MM Privately Held
WEB: www.bndhmo.com
SIC: 8093 Specialty outpatient clinics

(P-21362)
VERDUGO MENTAL HEALTH
1540 E Colorado St, Glendale (91205-1514)
PHONE...................................818 244-7257
Jeff Smith, *Exec Dir*
Karo Povolitis, *Ch of Bd*
David Igler, *Vice Ch Bd*
Lois Neil, *Vice Pres*
Richard Slavett, *Admin Sec*
EMP: 85 EST: 1957
SALES (est): 6.9MM Privately Held
SIC: 8093 Mental health clinic, outpatient

(P-21363)
VICTOR CMNTY SUPPORT SVCS INC
15095 Amargosa Rd Ste 201, Victorville (92394-1875)
PHONE...................................760 987-8225
Angie R Wiechert, *Manager*
EMP: 137
SALES (corp-wide): 62.2MM Privately Held
WEB: www.victor.org
SIC: 8093 Mental health clinic, outpatient
PA: Victor Community Support Services, Inc.
1360 E Lassen Ave
Chico CA 95973
530 893-0758

(P-21364)
VICTOR CMNTY SUPPORT SVCS INC
Also Called: Desert Mountain Fics
14360 St Andrews Dr Ste 1, Victorville (92395-4341)
PHONE...................................760 245-4695
Alan Mann, *Branch Mgr*
EMP: 137
SALES (corp-wide): 62.2MM Privately Held
WEB: www.victor.org
SIC: 8093 Mental health clinic, outpatient
PA: Victor Community Support Services, Inc.
1360 E Lassen Ave
Chico CA 95973
530 893-0758

(P-21365)
VICTOR CMNTY SUPPORT SVCS INC
Also Called: San Bernardino Fics
1908 Bsneca Ctr Dr Ste 10, San Bernardino (92408)
PHONE...................................909 890-5930
Paula Quijano, *Branch Mgr*
Jill Morgan, *Psychologist*
Jasmine Bradley, *Manager*
EMP: 137
SALES (corp-wide): 62.2MM Privately Held
WEB: www.victor.org
SIC: 8093 Mental health clinic, outpatient
PA: Victor Community Support Services, Inc.
1360 E Lassen Ave
Chico CA 95973
530 893-0758

(P-21366)
VILLAGE FAMILY SERVICES (PA)
6736 Laurel Canyon Blvd # 200, North Hollywood (91606-1576)
PHONE...................................818 755-8786
Hugo C Villa, *CEO*
Irma Seilicovich, *COO*
Krista Brown, *Vice Pres*
Charles Robbins, *Vice Pres*
Ivonne Wolovich, *Vice Pres*
EMP: 63 EST: 1997
SQ FT: 1,000
SALES: 19.2MM Privately Held
WEB: www.thevillagefs.org
SIC: 8093 8322 Mental health clinic, outpatient; family counseling services

(P-21367)
WORKING WITH AUTISM INC
14724 Ventura Blvd # 1110, Sherman Oaks (91403-3511)
PHONE...................................818 501-4240
Jennifer Sabin, *Founder*
Christine Allen, *Supervisor*
Christine Craighead, *Supervisor*
Adam Di Panni, *Supervisor*
Traci Oberg, *Supervisor*
EMP: 100 EST: 1997
SALES (est): 5.2MM Privately Held
WEB: www.workingwithautism.com
SIC: 8093 Mental health clinic, outpatient

(P-21368)
YOUTH ENTERPRISE INC
231 E Alessndro Blvd, Riverside (92508-5084)
PHONE...................................310 902-9266

Alina C Whitmore, *Exec Dir*
EMP: 50 **EST:** 2020
SALES (est): 766.7K **Privately Held**
SIC: 8093 Mental health clinic, outpatient

8099 Health & Allied Svcs, NEC

(P-21369)
ABRAXIS HEALTH INC (PA)
11755 Wilshire Blvd, Los Angeles
(90025-1506)
PHONE..........................310 883-1300
Patrick Soon-Shiong MD, *Exec CHB*
EMP: 55 **EST:** 2009
SALES (est): 236.8K **Privately Held**
SIC: 8099 Health screening service

(P-21370)
ACCOUNTBLE HLTH CRE IPA A PROF
2525 Cherry Ave Ste 225, Signal Hill
(90755-2057)
PHONE..........................562 435-3333
Thomas Lam, *CEO*
EMP: 122 **EST:** 1993
SALES (est): 1.2MM **Publicly Held**
SIC: 8099 Physical examination & testing services
HQ: Apc-Lsma Designated Shareholder
Medical Corporation
1668 S Garfield Ave Fl 2
Alhambra CA 91801
626 282-0288

(P-21371)
AGILON HEALTH MANAGEMENT INC
1 World Trade Ctr Ste 200, Long Beach
(90831-0200)
PHONE..........................562 256-3800
Steven J Sell, *President*
Ron Williams, *Ch of Bd*
Timothy S Bensley, *CFO*
Ravi Sachdev, *Vice Ch Bd*
Joan Danieley, *Officer*
EMP: 552 **EST:** 2016
SQ FT: 18,350
SALES (est): 1.2B **Privately Held**
WEB: www.agilonhealth.com
SIC: 8099 Medical services organization

(P-21372)
AHMC HEALTHCARE INC
506 W Valley Blvd Ste 300, San Gabriel
(91776-5716)
PHONE..........................626 248-3452
EMP: 1163
SALES (corp-wide): 574.5MM **Privately Held**
WEB: www.ahmchealth.com
SIC: 8099 8062 Blood bank; general medical & surgical hospitals
PA: Ahmc Healthcare Inc.
506 W Valley Blvd Ste 300
San Gabriel CA 91776
626 943-7526

(P-21373)
ALIGNMENT HEALTHCARE USA LLC (PA)
1100 W Twn Cntry Rd, Orange
(92868-4600)
PHONE..........................844 310-2247
John KAO, *CEO*
David Jarboe, *President*
Matt Malin, *President*
Matthew Malin, *President*
Scott Powers, *President*
EMP: 67 **EST:** 2012
SALES (est): 49.6MM **Privately Held**
WEB: www.alignmenthealthcare.com
SIC: 8099 Medical services organization

(P-21374)
ALLURE MEDICAL STAFFING INC
23152 Verdugo Dr Ste 120, Laguna Hills
(92653-1373)
PHONE..........................888 310-1020
Jeff Trusiak, *CEO*
EMP: 62 **EST:** 1999

SALES (est): 693.8K **Privately Held**
WEB: www.ams4nurses.com
SIC: 8099 Health & allied services

(P-21375)
ALTAMED HEALTH SERVICES CORP
1515 S Broadway Ste A, Santa Ana
(92707-2253)
PHONE..........................714 919-0280
Alberto Gedissman, *Branch Mgr*
EMP: 99
SALES (corp-wide): 702MM **Privately Held**
WEB: www.altamed.org
SIC: 8099 Blood related health services
PA: Altamed Health Services Corporation
2040 Camfield Ave
Commerce CA 90040
323 725-8751

(P-21376)
ALTAMED HEALTH SERVICES CORP
10454 Valley Blvd, El Monte (91731-2444)
PHONE..........................323 889-7847
EMP: 99
SALES (corp-wide): 702MM **Privately Held**
WEB: www.altamed.org
SIC: 8099 Childbirth preparation clinic
PA: Altamed Health Services Corporation
2040 Camfield Ave
Commerce CA 90040
323 725-8751

(P-21377)
ALTAMED HEALTH SERVICES CORP
Also Called: Altamed Med & Dntl Group Bell
8627 Atlantic Ave, South Gate
(90280-3501)
PHONE..........................323 562-6700
Erika Sockaci, *Branch Mgr*
EMP: 99
SALES (corp-wide): 702MM **Privately Held**
WEB: www.altamed.org
SIC: 8099 8011 Medical services organization; gynecologist; pediatrician; radiologist
PA: Altamed Health Services Corporation
2040 Camfield Ave
Commerce CA 90040
323 725-8751

(P-21378)
ALTAMED HEALTH SERVICES CORP
Also Called: Altamed Med Dntl Grp Whttier W
3945 Whittier Blvd, Los Angeles
(90023-2440)
PHONE..........................323 307-0400
Angela Arredondo, *Branch Mgr*
EMP: 99
SALES (corp-wide): 702MM **Privately Held**
WEB: www.altamed.org
SIC: 8099 8011 Medical services organization; gynecologist; pediatrician; radiologist
PA: Altamed Health Services Corporation
2040 Camfield Ave
Commerce CA 90040
323 725-8751

(P-21379)
ALTAMED HEALTH SERVICES CORP
Also Called: Altamed Ltc Trnsp Dept
5255 Pomona Blvd Ste 11, Los Angeles
(90022-1770)
PHONE..........................323 890-8767
Gloria Marquez, *Branch Mgr*
EMP: 99
SALES (corp-wide): 702MM **Privately Held**
WEB: www.altamed.org
SIC: 8099 8011 Medical services organization; gynecologist; pediatrician; radiologist
PA: Altamed Health Services Corporation
2040 Camfield Ave
Commerce CA 90040
323 725-8751

(P-21380)
ALTAMED HEALTH SERVICES CORP
Also Called: Slauson Plaza Med Group
9436 Slauson Ave, Pico Rivera
(90660-4748)
PHONE..........................562 949-8717
Alfredo Nunez, *Branch Mgr*
EMP: 99
SALES (corp-wide): 702MM **Privately Held**
WEB: www.altamed.org
SIC: 8099 8011 Medical services organization; clinic, operated by physicians
PA: Altamed Health Services Corporation
2040 Camfield Ave
Commerce CA 90040
323 725-8751

(P-21381)
ALTAMED HEALTH SERVICES CORP
Also Called: Youth Services
711 E Wardlow Rd Ste 203, Long Beach
(90807-4650)
PHONE..........................562 595-8040
Galiah Richmond, *Branch Mgr*
EMP: 99
SALES (corp-wide): 702MM **Privately Held**
WEB: www.altamed.org
SIC: 8099 8011 Medical services organization; pediatrician
PA: Altamed Health Services Corporation
2040 Camfield Ave
Commerce CA 90040
323 725-8751

(P-21382)
ALTAMED HEALTH SERVICES CORP
Also Called: Alta Med Health Services
10418 Valley Blvd Ste B, El Monte
(91731-3600)
PHONE..........................626 453-8466
Juan Esquivez, *Branch Mgr*
EMP: 99
SALES (corp-wide): 702MM **Privately Held**
WEB: www.altamed.org
SIC: 8099 8011 Medical services organization; gynecologist; pediatrician; radiologist
PA: Altamed Health Services Corporation
2040 Camfield Ave
Commerce CA 90040
323 725-8751

(P-21383)
AMERICAN INDIAN HEALTH & SVCS
4141 State St Ste B11, Santa Barbara
(93110-1898)
PHONE..........................805 681-7356
Scott Black, *Exec Dir*
Brad Stoltey, *CFO*
Merin McCabe, *Administration*
Paul Hennig, *Family Practiti*
Bradley Hope, *Family Practiti*
EMP: 50
SQ FT: 4,000
SALES (est): 9.1MM **Privately Held**
WEB: www.aihscorp.org
SIC: 8099 Health screening service

(P-21384)
APC-LSMA DSMC (HQ)
1668 S Garfield Ave Fl 2, Alhambra
(91801-5400)
PHONE..........................626 282-0288
Thomas Lam, *CEO*
EMP: 146 **EST:** 2012
SALES (est): 16.9MM **Publicly Held**
WEB: www.apollomed.net
SIC: 8099 Medical services organization

(P-21385)
ARAMARK HEALTHCARE SUPPORT
Also Called: Aramark Healthcare Sprt Serv
1400 E Church St, Santa Maria
(93454-5906)
PHONE..........................805 739-3000
EMP: 166 **Publicly Held**
WEB: www.aramark.com

SIC: 8099 Childbirth preparation clinic
HQ: Aramark Healthcare Support Services,
Llc
2400 Market St 209
Philadelphia PA 19103

(P-21386)
ARBORMED INC (PA)
725 W Town And Country Rd, Orange
(92868-4703)
PHONE..........................714 689-1500
Charles Morf, *President*
William Shaw, *CFO*
Scott Everson, *Vice Pres*
EMP: 123 **EST:** 1995
SQ FT: 11,000
SALES (est): 6.5MM **Privately Held**
SIC: 8099 8742 Medical services organization; management consulting services

(P-21387)
BENEVOLENCE HEALTH CENTER (PA)
1010 Crenshaw Blvd # 100, Torrance
(90501-2056)
PHONE..........................323 732-0100
Kwabena Oben, *President*
Matthew Mariano,
Taronda Mikell, *Assistant*
EMP: 56 **EST:** 2014
SALES (est): 3.2MM **Privately Held**
WEB: www.bhchealth.org
SIC: 8099 Medical services organization

(P-21388)
BHC ALHAMBRA HOSPITAL INC
4619 Rosemead Blvd, Rosemead
(91770-1478)
PHONE..........................626 286-1191
Debbie Irvin, *Records Dir*
Anthony Babcock, *Engineer*
EMP: 350 **EST:** 2009
SALES (est): 35.6MM **Privately Held**
SIC: 8099 Blood related health services

(P-21389)
BIO-MEDICS INC
371 W Highland Ave, San Bernardino
(92405-4011)
PHONE..........................909 883-9501
Gary Crandall, *Manager*
EMP: 126 **Privately Held**
SIC: 8099 Blood bank
PA: Bio-Medics, Inc.
2187 Monitor Dr
Park City UT

(P-21390)
BIOMAT USA INC (DH)
2410 Lillyvale Ave, Los Angeles
(90032-3514)
PHONE..........................323 225-2221
Gregory Rich, *CEO*
Max Debrouwer, *CFO*
Cheryl Lawrence, *Treasurer*
Steve Wong, *Treasurer*
Shinji Wada, *Exec VP*
◆ **EMP:** 50 **EST:** 1988
SQ FT: 20,000
SALES (est): 1.9B
SALES (corp-wide): 657.6MM **Privately Held**
WEB: www.grifolsplasma.com
SIC: 8099 Blood bank
HQ: Grifols Shared Services North America, Inc.
2410 Lillyvale Ave
Los Angeles CA 90032
323 225-2221

(P-21391)
BLOOD BNK SAN BRNRDINO RVRSIDE (HQ)
Also Called: Lifestream
384 W Orange Show Rd, San Bernardino
(92408-2028)
P.O. Box 1429 (92402-1429)
PHONE..........................909 885-6503
Frederick B Axelrod, *CEO*
Jim Schraith, *Treasurer*
Joseph Dunn, *Vice Pres*
Michelle Johnson, *Vice Pres*
Susan Marquez, *Vice Pres*
EMP: 240 **EST:** 1951

SQ FT: 50,000
SALES (est): 64.5MM
SALES (corp-wide): 526.6MM **Privately Held**
WEB: www.lstream.org
SIC: 8099 2836 Blood bank; blood donor station; blood derivatives
PA: Vitalant
     6210 E Oak St
     Scottsdale AZ 85257
     800 288-2199

(P-21392)
BMS HEALTHCARE INC
8925 Mines Ave, Pico Rivera (90660-3006)
PHONE.................................562 942-7019
Mordechai Stock, *Principal*
EMP: 130 EST: 2010
SALES (est): 3.6MM **Privately Held**
SIC: 8099 Health & allied services

(P-21393)
BREATHE LA LHC LLC
Also Called: Breathe Life Healing Centers
8060 Melrose Ave Fl 3, Los Angeles (90046-7039)
PHONE.................................212 989-9332
EMP: 50
SALES (est): 46.2K **Privately Held**
WEB: www.breathelifehealingcenters.com
SIC: 8099 Health/Allied Services

(P-21394)
BREATHE LA LHC LLC
Also Called: Healthcare
8060 Melrose Ave Fl 3, Los Angeles (90046-7039)
PHONE.................................800 929-5904
Brad Lamm, *Partner*
EMP: 51 EST: 2013
SALES (est): 5.3MM **Privately Held**
SIC: 8099 Health & allied services

(P-21395)
CALIFORNIA CRYOBANK LLC (PA)
11915 La Grange Ave, Los Angeles (90025-5213)
PHONE.................................310 496-5691
Richards Jennings, *CEO*
Lorraine Kirby, *Owner*
Pamela Richardson, *President*
Charles A Sims MD, *CEO*
Scott Brown, *Vice Pres*
EMP: 75 EST: 1977
SQ FT: 21,300
SALES (est): 59.9MM **Privately Held**
WEB: www.cryobank.com
SIC: 8099 Blood bank

(P-21396)
CALIFRNIA FRNSIC MED GROUP INC
800 S Victoria Ave, Ventura (93009-0001)
PHONE.................................805 654-3343
Elaine Hustedt, *Vice Pres*
EMP: 98
SALES (corp-wide): 33.7MM **Privately Held**
SIC: 8099 Medical services organization
PA: California Forensic Medical Group, Incorporated
     1283 Murfreesboro Pike # 500
     Nashville TN 37217
     831 649-8994

(P-21397)
CARE 1ST HEALTH PLAN (PA)
601 Potrero Grande Dr # 2, Monterey Park (91755-7430)
PHONE.................................323 889-6638
Maureen Tyson, *President*
Olivia Mendoza, *CEO*
Anna Tran, *CEO*
Janet Jan, *CFO*
Joseph Hakimian, *Vice Pres*
EMP: 165 EST: 1994
SALES (est): 34.9MM **Privately Held**
WEB: www.care1st.com
SIC: 8099 Blood related health services

(P-21398)
CITRUS VLY HLTH PARTNERS INC
1325 N Grand Ave Ste 300, Covina (91724-4046)
PHONE.................................626 732-3100
Carol Eaton, *Principal*
Diane L Martin, *Marketing Staff*
EMP: 382 **Privately Held**
WEB: www.emanatehealth.org
SIC: 8099 Blood related health services
PA: Emanate Health Medical Group
     210 W San Bernardino Rd
     Covina CA 91723

(P-21399)
COMPRHNSIVE INDUS DSBLITY MGT
Also Called: Cid Management
2555 Towngate Rd Ste 125, Westlake Village (91361-2605)
P.O. Box 4379 (91359-1379)
PHONE.................................866 301-6568
Steven Cardinale, *CEO*
Andy Smith, *CFO*
EMP: 67 EST: 2002
SQ FT: 5,500
SALES (est): 22.5MM **Publicly Held**
WEB: www.genexservices.com
SIC: 8099 8741 Medical services organization; nursing & personal care facility management
HQ: Genex Services, Llc
     440 E Swedesford Rd Ste 1
     Wayne PA 19087
     610 964-5100

(P-21400)
CONDUENT WKRS CMPNSTION HLDNGS (HQ)
17838 Gillette Ave, Irvine (92614-6502)
PHONE.................................860 678-7877
Paul Glover, *President*
Diane Hicks, *Consultant*
EMP: 50 EST: 2008
SALES (est): 30.5MM
SALES (corp-wide): 4.1B **Publicly Held**
WEB: www.conduent.com
SIC: 8099 7371 Medical services organization; computer software development & applications
PA: Conduent Incorporated
     100 Campus Dr Ste 200
     Florham Park NJ 07932
     844 663-2638

(P-21401)
CORE MEDICAL GROUP INC
Also Called: Cedars- Sinai Medical Group
8635 W 3rd St Ste 1, Los Angeles (90048-6102)
PHONE.................................310 967-1884
Rosalina Kohagura, *Principal*
Susan Essenfeld, *Office Mgr*
Marion McRae, *Nurse Practr*
EMP: 64 EST: 2011
SALES (est): 1.8MM **Privately Held**
WEB: www.coremedicalgroup.com
SIC: 8099 Health & allied services

(P-21402)
COUNTY OF LOS ANGELES
Also Called: Countywide Childrens Case MGT
600 S Commwl Ave Fl 2 Flr 2, Los Angeles (90005)
PHONE.................................213 739-2360
Bryan Mershon, *Branch Mgr*
Suthep Chantorn, *Program Mgr*
Yeongeon OH, *Supervisor*
EMP: 51
SALES (corp-wide): 25.2B **Privately Held**
WEB: www.lacounty.gov
SIC: 8099 Blood related health services
PA: County Of Los Angeles
     500 W Temple St Ste 437
     Los Angeles CA 90012
     213 974-1101

(P-21403)
COUNTY OF LOS ANGELES
Also Called: Compton Family Mhc Fsp
546 W Compton Blvd, Compton (90220-3011)
PHONE.................................310 885-2100
Phillip Mobley, *Manager*
EMP: 51
SALES (corp-wide): 25.2B **Privately Held**
WEB: www.lacounty.gov
SIC: 8099 Blood related health services
PA: County Of Los Angeles
     500 W Temple St Ste 437
     Los Angeles CA 90012
     213 974-1101

(P-21404)
COUNTY OF LOS ANGELES
Also Called: Specilzed Fster Care Chtsworth
20151 Nordhoff St, Chatsworth (91311-6215)
PHONE.................................818 717-4644
Philip L Browning, *Director*
Jackie Solomon, *Vice Chairman*
Jeff Dorsey, *Branch Mgr*
Laura Morgan, *Admin Sec*
Rosella Yousef, *Administration*
EMP: 51
SALES (corp-wide): 25.2B **Privately Held**
WEB: www.lacounty.gov
SIC: 8099 Childbirth preparation clinic
PA: County Of Los Angeles
     500 W Temple St Ste 437
     Los Angeles CA 90012
     213 974-1101

(P-21405)
COUNTY OF LOS ANGELES
921 E Compton Blvd, Compton (90221-3303)
PHONE.................................310 668-6845
Marvin Southard, *Branch Mgr*
Euronda Davis, *Admin Sec*
Carrie Wilson, *Director*
EMP: 51
SALES (corp-wide): 25.2B **Privately Held**
WEB: www.lacounty.gov
SIC: 8099 Blood related health services
PA: County Of Los Angeles
     500 W Temple St Ste 437
     Los Angeles CA 90012
     213 974-1101

(P-21406)
COUNTY OF LOS ANGELES
Also Called: Specilzed Foster Care Pasadena
532 E Colorado Blvd Fl 8, Pasadena (91101-2044)
PHONE.................................626 229-3825
Jonathan E Sherin, *Director*
Gloria Rodriguez-Vasqu, *Supervisor*
EMP: 51
SALES (corp-wide): 25.2B **Privately Held**
WEB: www.lacounty.gov
SIC: 8099 Blood related health services
PA: County Of Los Angeles
     500 W Temple St Ste 437
     Los Angeles CA 90012
     213 974-1101

(P-21407)
COUNTY OF LOS ANGELES
Also Called: Department of Health
3530 Wilshire Blvd Fl 9, Los Angeles (90010-2344)
PHONE.................................213 351-7800
Michelle Parra PHD, *Manager*
Melanie Barr, *Director*
Wendi Cate, *Director*
Eloisa Gonzalez, *Director*
EMP: 51
SALES (corp-wide): 25.2B **Privately Held**
WEB: www.lacounty.gov
SIC: 8099 9431 Medical services organization; administration of public health programs
PA: County Of Los Angeles
     500 W Temple St Ste 437
     Los Angeles CA 90012
     213 974-1101

(P-21408)
COUNTY OF LOS ANGELES
Also Called: Los Angeles County Pub Works
5525 Imperial Hwy, South Gate (90280-7417)
PHONE.................................562 861-0316
Phil Doudar, *Manager*
Cheri Stabell, *Deputy Dir*
Alfred Ben Carrillo, *Superintendent*
EMP: 51
SALES (corp-wide): 25.2B **Privately Held**
WEB: www.lacounty.gov
SIC: 8099 9111 Blood related health services; executive offices
PA: County Of Los Angeles
     500 W Temple St Ste 437
     Los Angeles CA 90012
     213 974-1101

(P-21409)
COUNTY OF RIVERSIDE
Also Called: Fire Department Station 29
56560 State Hwy 371, Anza (92539)
P.O. Box 391489 (92539-1489)
PHONE.................................951 763-5611
Han Bolowich, *Chief*
EMP: 110
SALES (corp-wide): 4B **Privately Held**
WEB: www.rivco.org
SIC: 9224 8099 Fire department, not including volunteer; ; medical rescue squad
PA: County Of Riverside
     4080 Lemon St Fl 11
     Riverside CA 92501
     951 955-1110

(P-21410)
DAVID-KLEIS II LLC
Also Called: Palm Grove Healthcare
1665 E Eighth St, Beaumont (92223-2512)
PHONE.................................951 845-3125
Madelyn V Smith,
EMP: 86 EST: 2013
SALES (est): 5.3MM **Privately Held**
WEB: www.pghsnf.com
SIC: 8099 Health & allied services

(P-21411)
DAVITA MEDICAL MANAGEMENT LLC
Also Called: Talbert Medical Center
8311 Florence Ave, Downey (90240-3928)
PHONE.................................562 923-4911
Dag Jacobson, *General Mgr*
Reyna Deluna-Sandoval, *Supervisor*
EMP: 53 **Publicly Held**
SIC: 8099 8011 Medical services organization; hearing testing service; general & family practice, physician/surgeon
HQ: Davita Medical Management, Llc
     2175 Park Pl
     El Segundo CA 90245

(P-21412)
DAVITA MEDICAL MANAGEMENT LLC
Also Called: Talbert Medical Group
1081 Long Beach Blvd # 10, Long Beach (90813-3217)
PHONE.................................562 432-5661
Barbara Blaser, *Administration*
Meyoung Ryu, *Podiatrist*
EMP: 53 **Publicly Held**
SIC: 8099 Medical services organization
HQ: Davita Medical Management, Llc
     2175 Park Pl
     El Segundo CA 90245

(P-21413)
DAVITA MEDICAL MANAGEMENT LLC
1236 N Magnolia Ave, Anaheim (92801-2607)
PHONE.................................714 995-1000
Kathy Porter, *Admin Asst*
Babak Firoozi, *Med Doctor*
Bertha Varallo, *Manager*
EMP: 53 **Publicly Held**
SIC: 8099 8011 Medical services organization; offices & clinics of medical doctors

PRODUCTS & SVCS

HQ: Davita Medical Management, Llc
2175 Park Pl
El Segundo CA 90245

(P-21414)
DAVITA MEDICAL MANAGEMENT LLC
19066 Magnolia St, Huntington Beach (92646-2232)
PHONE................714 968-0068
Robert Hunn, *Principal*
Cristina Lacy, *Business Anlyst*
Vincent Zorrilla, *Manager*
Shaun Torbati, *Supervisor*
EMP: 53 **Publicly Held**
SIC: 8099 Medical services organization
HQ: Davita Medical Management, Llc
2175 Park Pl
El Segundo CA 90245

(P-21415)
DAVITA MEDICAL MANAGEMENT LLC
Also Called: Talbert Medical Center
901 W Civic Center Dr # 120, Santa Ana (92703-2352)
PHONE................714 835-8501
Linda Journet, *Manager*
EMP: 53 **Publicly Held**
SIC: 8099 8011 Medical services organization; general & family practice, physician/surgeon
HQ: Davita Medical Management, Llc
2175 Park Pl
El Segundo CA 90245

(P-21416)
DAVITA MEDICAL MANAGEMENT LLC
7301 Med Ctr Dr Ste 500, West Hills (91307-4101)
PHONE................818 226-3666
Nina Dandrea, *Manager*
EMP: 53 **Publicly Held**
SIC: 8099 Childbirth preparation clinic
HQ: Davita Medical Management, Llc
2175 Park Pl
El Segundo CA 90245

(P-21417)
DAVITA MEDICAL MANAGEMENT LLC
Also Called: Healthcare Partners Med Group
2160 W 190th St, Torrance (90504-6103)
PHONE................310 783-5567
EMP: 53 **Publicly Held**
SIC: 8099 Medical services organization
HQ: Davita Medical Management, Llc
2175 Park Pl
El Segundo CA 90245

(P-21418)
DAVITA MEDICAL MANAGEMENT LLC
Also Called: Family Health Program
4910 Airport Plaza Dr, Long Beach (90815-1376)
PHONE................562 429-2473
Rhonda Luster, *Director*
Masoomeh Djodeir, *Family Practiti*
Lyle Nalli, *Med Doctor*
EMP: 53 **Publicly Held**
SIC: 8099 8011 Medical services organization; clinic, operated by physicians
HQ: Davita Medical Management, Llc
2175 Park Pl
El Segundo CA 90245

(P-21419)
DAVITA MEDICAL MANAGEMENT LLC
3501 S Harbor Blvd, Santa Ana (92704-6919)
PHONE................714 964-6229
Francis Gale, *Manager*
Lee Win, *Family Practiti*
Patrick Nguyen, *Director*
EMP: 53 **Publicly Held**
SIC: 8099 Blood related health services

HQ: Davita Medical Management, Llc
2175 Park Pl
El Segundo CA 90245

(P-21420)
DEVELOPMENTAL SVCS CAL DEPT
Also Called: CA Department Development Svc
696 Ramon, Cathedral City (92234)
PHONE................760 770-6248
Kathleen Waegner, *Director*
EMP: 593 **Privately Held**
WEB: www.ca.gov
SIC: 8099 Physical examination & testing services
HQ: California Department Of Developmental Services
1215 O St
Sacramento CA 95814

(P-21421)
EASY CARE MSO LLC
3900 Kilroy Airport Way, Long Beach (90806-6809)
PHONE................562 676-9600
Michelle Bui, *President*
EMP: 161 **EST:** 2014
SALES (est): 10.4MM
SALES (corp-wide): 19.4B **Publicly Held**
WEB: www.easycaremso.com
SIC: 8099 Medical services organization
PA: Molina Healthcare, Inc.
200 Oceangate Ste 100
Long Beach CA 90802
562 435-3666

(P-21422)
ELECTRONIC HEALTH PLANS INC
Also Called: Ehp Administrators
9131 Oakdale Ave Ste 150, Chatsworth (91311-6502)
P.O. Box 4449 (91313-4449)
PHONE................818 734-4700
Alina Green, *Vice Pres*
Laura Copeland, *CIO*
Manuel Garcia, *Opers Staff*
Gina Girard, *Nurse*
Lea Torno, *Nurse*
EMP: 78
SALES (corp-wide): 11.1MM **Privately Held**
WEB: www.electronichealthplans.com
SIC: 8099 Medical services organization
PA: Electronic Health Plans, Inc.
1111 Route 1110 Ste 378
Farmingdale NY 11735
631 845-5680

(P-21423)
ELIZABETH GLASER PEDIA
16130 Ventura Blvd # 250, Encino (91436-2503)
PHONE................310 231-0400
Charles Lyons, *Branch Mgr*
Parker Bryant, *Officer*
Doug Horner, *Vice Pres*
Aida Awaj, *Accounting Mgr*
Stephanie Bruno, *Manager*
EMP: 52
SALES (corp-wide): 202.2MM **Privately Held**
WEB: www.pedaids.org
SIC: 8099 Medical services organization
PA: Elizabeth Glaser Pediatric Aids Foundation
1140 Conn Ave Nw Ste 200
Washington DC 20036
920 770-0103

(P-21424)
FACEY MEDICAL FOUNDATION
11211 Sepulveda Blvd, Mission Hills (91345-1115)
PHONE................818 837-5677
Cathy Hawes, *Branch Mgr*
Susan Slack, *Administration*
Jeffrey Caputo, *Family Practiti*
Calvin Hung, *Family Practiti*
Nicholas Tuso, *Obstetrician*
EMP: 131

SALES (corp-wide): 96.9MM **Privately Held**
WEB: www.facey.com
SIC: 8099 8042 8011 Medical services organization; offices & clinics of optometrists; offices & clinics of medical doctors
PA: Facey Medical Foundation
15451 San Frnndo Mssion B
Mission Hills CA 91345
818 365-9531

(P-21425)
FACEY MEDICAL FOUNDATION
Also Called: Facey Medical Group
17909 Soledad Canyon Rd, Santa Clarita (91387-3210)
PHONE................661 250-5225
Leslie Holland, *Branch Mgr*
Khai Kim T Tram, *Director*
EMP: 131
SALES (corp-wide): 96.9MM **Privately Held**
WEB: www.facey.com
SIC: 8099 8011 Medical services organization; offices & clinics of medical doctors
PA: Facey Medical Foundation
15451 San Frnndo Mssion B
Mission Hills CA 91345
818 365-9531

(P-21426)
FACEY MEDICAL FOUNDATION
Also Called: Marshall, Spector MD
1237 E Main St, San Gabriel (91776)
PHONE................626 576-0800
Ana Ventura, *Manager*
EMP: 131
SALES (corp-wide): 96.9MM **Privately Held**
WEB: www.facey.com
SIC: 8099 8011 Medical services organization; pediatrician
PA: Facey Medical Foundation
15451 San Frnndo Mssion B
Mission Hills CA 91345
818 365-9531

(P-21427)
FOCUS HEALTHCARE HOLDINGS INC (HQ)
27071 Aliso Creek Rd # 100, Aliso Viejo (92656-3399)
PHONE................949 349-1200
Robert Levin, *CEO*
Sam Sepulveda, *Social Dir*
EMP: 50 **EST:** 2013
SALES (est): 24.5MM
SALES (corp-wide): 1MM **Privately Held**
WEB: www.elevatehomehealth.com
SIC: 8099 Health screening service
PA: Elevate Home Health, Llc
120 Vantis Dr Ste 200
Aliso Viejo CA 92656
562 438-3181

(P-21428)
FRONT PORCH COMMUNITIES
621 W Bonita Ave, Claremont (91711-4513)
PHONE................909 626-3490
Robin Aspinall, *Vice Pres*
Tanya Madrid, *Social Dir*
Donna Guardado, *Office Mgr*
Gregory Pippen, *Food Svc Dir*
Amy McFarland, *Hlthcr Dir*
EMP: 61
SALES (corp-wide): 158.2MM **Privately Held**
WEB: www.frontporch.net
SIC: 8099 Childbirth preparation clinic
PA: Front Porch Communities And Services - Casa De Manana, Llc
800 N Brand Blvd Fl 19
Glendale CA 91203
818 729-8100

(P-21429)
FYEO APPAREL INC
757 E 14th Pl, Los Angeles (90021-2117)
PHONE................213 278-0435
Alexandra Vince, *CEO*
EMP: 50 **EST:** 2019
SALES (est): 455K **Privately Held**
SIC: 8099 7221 Medical photography & art; photographer, still or video

(P-21430)
GOLDEN STATE PRVDERS A MED COR (PA)
865 Patriot Dr, Moorpark (93021-3407)
PHONE................805 523-8250
Paul Beaupre, *President*
EMP: 57 **EST:** 2014
SALES (est): 145.1K **Privately Held**
SIC: 8099 Health & allied services

(P-21431)
GRIFOLS WRLDWIDE OPRTONS USA I
13111 Temple Ave, City of Industry (91746-1500)
PHONE................626 435-2600
Red Fredericksen, *General Mgr*
EMP: 70
SALES (corp-wide): 657.6MM **Privately Held**
SIC: 8099 Blood bank
HQ: Grifols Worldwide Operations Usa, Inc.
5555 Valley Blvd
Los Angeles CA 90032
323 225-2221

(P-21432)
HALO UNLIMTED INC
Also Called: Infant Hring Scrning Spcalists
1867 California Ave # 101, Corona (92881-7281)
P.O. Box 77010 (92877-0100)
PHONE................714 692-2270
Leonard Machado, *CEO*
Martha Hawkins, *President*
Bradley Northcutt, *COO*
Nina Murcia, *Area Mgr*
Maricela Guzman, *Manager*
EMP: 59 **EST:** 2002
SQ FT: 7,500
SALES (est): 7.3MM **Privately Held**
WEB: www.ihssca.com
SIC: 8099 Hearing testing service

(P-21433)
HARBOR HEALTH SYSTEMS LLC
3501 Jamboree Rd Ste 540, Newport Beach (92660-2950)
P.O. Box 1145, Elk Grove Village IL (60009-1145)
PHONE................949 273-7020
Gregory Moore, *CEO*
James W Dolan, *CEO*
EMP: 95 **EST:** 2001
SALES (est): 2.4MM **Privately Held**
WEB: www.harborhealthsystems.com
SIC: 8099 7372 Blood related health services; business oriented computer software
PA: One Call Medical, Inc.
841 Prudential Dr Ste 204
Jacksonville FL 32207

(P-21434)
HEALTH SERVICE ALLIANCE
Also Called: Montclair Community Health Ctr
13193 Central Ave Ste 100, Chino (91710-4179)
PHONE................909 464-9675
Dr Terry Chase, *CEO*
Sue Montoya-Bell, *Director*
EMP: 54 **EST:** 2008
SALES (est): 887.8K **Privately Held**
WEB: www.montclair-hospital.org
SIC: 8099 Health & allied services

(P-21435)
HEALTHY MEDICA_ SOLUTIONS INC
5943 Rhodes Ave, Valley Village (91607-1131)
PHONE................818 974-1980
Mori Bennissan, *CEO*
EMP: 77 **EST:** 2005
SALES (est): 6MM **Privately Held**
SIC: 8099 Childbirth preparation clinic

(P-21436)

HEMACARE CORPORATION (HQ)

8500 Balboa Blvd Ste 130, Northridge (91325-5802)
PHONE.....................877 310-0717
James C Foster, *President*
Anna Stock, *CFO*
Rochelle Martel, *CFO*
Lou Juliano, *Senior VP*
Maria Muniz, *Vice Pres*
EMP: 97 **EST:** 1978
SQ FT: 19,600
SALES (est): 45.4MM
SALES (corp-wide): 2.9B **Publicly Held**
WEB: www.hemacare.com
SIC: 8099 5122 Blood related health services; blood bank; blood donor station; blood plasma
PA: Charles River Laboratories International, Inc.
251 Ballardvale St
Wilmington MA 01887
781 222-6000

(P-21437)

HERITAGE MEDICAL GROUP

12370 Hesperia Rd Ste 6, Victorville (92395-4787)
PHONE.....................760 956-1286
Stanley Wohl, *Branch Mgr*
Lynn Richardson, *Marketing Staff*
Cindy Carroll, *Director*
EMP: 169 **Privately Held**
WEB: www.bfmc.com
SIC: 8099 Blood related health services
PA: Heritage Medical Group, Inc.
4580 California Ave
Bakersfield CA 93309

(P-21438)

HONEYBEE HEALTH INC (PA)

3515 Helms Ave, Culver City (90232-2414)
PHONE.....................310 559-5903
Jessica Nouhavandi, *Owner*
Ben Nelson, *Manager*
EMP: 125 **EST:** 2017
SALES (est): 11.6MM **Privately Held**
WEB: www.honeybeehealth.com
SIC: 8099 Health & allied services

(P-21439)

HOUCHIN BLOOD SERVICES (PA)

11515 Bolthouse Dr, Bakersfield (93311-8822)
PHONE.....................661 323-4222
Greg Gallion, *CEO*
Walter Heisey, *President*
Joe Engel, *Vice Pres*
EMP: 69 **EST:** 1951
SQ FT: 6,000
SALES (est): 4.8MM **Privately Held**
WEB: www.westcoastblood.org
SIC: 8099 Blood bank

(P-21440)

HOUCHIN BLOOD SERVICES

11515 Bolthouse Dr, Bakersfield (93311-8822)
PHONE.....................661 327-8541
EMP: 60
SALES (corp-wide): 8.6MM **Privately Held**
WEB: www.hcbb.com
SIC: 8099 Health/Allied Services
PA: Houchin Blood Services
11515 Bolthouse Dr
Bakersfield CA 93311
661 323-4222

(P-21441)

HOUCHIN COMMUNITY BLOOD BANK

11515 Bolthouse Dr, Bakersfield (93311-8822)
PHONE.....................661 323-4222
Sean McNally, *President*
Brad Bryan, *COO*
Randy Greenlee, *Officer*
Josie Pippert, *Vice Pres*
Susan Bowser, *VP Bus Dvlpt*
EMP: 59 **EST:** 2012

SALES (est): 11.2MM **Privately Held**
WEB: www.westcoastblood.org
SIC: 8099 Blood bank

(P-21442)

INDUSTRIAL MEDICAL SUPPORT INC

3320 E Airport Way, Long Beach (90806-2410)
PHONE.....................877 878-9185
Michael Donoghue, *CEO*
Ryan La Bounty,
EMP: 800 **EST:** 2014
SALES (est): 24MM **Privately Held**
SIC: 8099 Medical services organization

(P-21443)

INLAND BHAVIORAL HLTH SVCS INC (PA)

1963 N E St, San Bernardino (92405-3919)
PHONE.....................909 881-6146
Temetry Ann Lindsey, *President*
Vernon Bragg Jr, *Ch of Bd*
Rachel Jones, *CEO*
John Wilson, *COO*
Peter Demel, *CFO*
EMP: 68 **EST:** 1978
SQ FT: 13,500
SALES: 12.1MM **Privately Held**
WEB: www.ibhealth.com
SIC: 8099 8093 Medical services organization; drug clinic, outpatient; alcohol clinic, outpatient

(P-21444)

INSTITUTE FOR BHVORAL HLTH INC

1905 Bus Ctr Dr S Ste 100, San Bernardino (92408)
PHONE.....................909 289-1041
Azadeh K Jebelli, *President*
EMP: 265 **EST:** 2013
SALES (est): 13MM **Privately Held**
WEB: www.ibhcare.com
SIC: 8099 Childbirth preparation clinic

(P-21445)

JWCH INSTITUTE INC

14371 Clark Ave, Bellflower (90706-2901)
PHONE.....................562 867-7999
Alvaro Ballesteros, *Branch Mgr*
Steve Lopez, *Assistant*
EMP: 323
SALES (corp-wide): 86.3MM **Privately Held**
WEB: www.jwchinstitute.org
SIC: 8099 Blood related health services
PA: Jwch Institute, Inc.
5650 Jillson St
Commerce CA 90040
323 477-1171

(P-21446)

KAISER FOUNDATION HOSPITALS

Also Called: Kaiser Foundation Health Plan
1050 Commerce Center Dr, Lancaster (93534-5860)
PHONE.....................661 729-7250
Barbara Wheeler, *Principal*
EMP: 209
SALES (corp-wide): 30.5B **Privately Held**
WEB: www.kaisercenter.com
SIC: 8099 Blood related health services
HQ: Kaiser Foundation Hospitals Inc
1 Kaiser Plz
Oakland CA 94612
510 271-6611

(P-21447)

KAISER FOUNDATION HOSPITALS

Also Called: Kaiser Foundation Health Plan
2055 Kellogg Ave, Corona (92879-3111)
PHONE.....................866 984-7483
Ruth Jasse, *Administration*
Richard Liu, *Family Practiti*
EMP: 209
SALES (corp-wide): 30.5B **Privately Held**
WEB: www.kaisercenter.com
SIC: 8099 Childbirth preparation clinic
HQ: Kaiser Foundation Hospitals Inc
1 Kaiser Plz
Oakland CA 94612
510 271-6611

(P-21448)

KAWEAH DELTA HEALTH CARE

101 S Floral St, Visalia (93291-6258)
PHONE.....................559 624-2854
Barbara Mayeda, *Exec Dir*
Soozee Edminster, *Instructor*
EMP: 57 **EST:** 2004
SALES (est): 5.9MM **Privately Held**
WEB: www.kaweahhealth.org
SIC: 8099 Medical services organization

(P-21449)

LEGACY HEALTHCARE CENTER LLC

1570 N Fair Oaks Ave, Pasadena (91103-1822)
PHONE.....................626 798-0558
Raphael Oscherowitz, *Principal*
Dov Jacobs, *Principal*
EMP: 90 **EST:** 2016
SALES (est): 3MM **Privately Held**
SIC: 8099 Health & allied services

(P-21450)

LIFE TIME FITNESS INC

28221 Crown Valley Pkwy, Laguna Niguel (92677-1427)
PHONE.....................949 238-2700
Tracy Graf, *Mktg Dir*
EMP: 165
SALES (corp-wide): 948.3MM **Privately Held**
WEB: www.lifetime.life
SIC: 8099 7991 7299 Nutrition services; physical fitness clubs with training equipment; personal appearance services
HQ: Life Time, Inc.
2902 Corporate Pl
Chanhassen MN 55317

(P-21451)

LOS ANGLES CNTY DVLPMNTAL SVCS

Also Called: FRANK D LANTERMAN REGIONAL CEN
3303 Wilshire Blvd # 700, Los Angeles (90010-1704)
PHONE.....................213 383-1300
Dianne Anand, *Exec Dir*
Frank Lara, *Bd of Directors*
Patrick Aulicino, *Associate Dir*
Sonia Garibay, *Regional Mgr*
Karen Chacana, *Human Res Dir*
EMP: 180 **EST:** 1979
SQ FT: 80,000
SALES (est): 238.1MM **Privately Held**
WEB: www.lanterman.org
SIC: 8099 8322 8093 Medical services organization; individual & family services; mental health clinic, outpatient

(P-21452)

MARTIN LTHER KING JR-LOS ANGLE

Also Called: MARTIN LUTHER KING, JR. COMMUN
1680 E 120th St, Los Angeles (90059-3026)
PHONE.....................424 338-8000
Elaine E Batchlor, *CEO*
Casey Hebert, *COO*
Pablo Jacobo, *Officer*
Bruce Pollack, *Senior VP*
Susan Burrows, *Vice Pres*
EMP: 193 **EST:** 2010
SALES: 344.1MM **Privately Held**
WEB: www.mlkch.org
SIC: 8099 Childbirth preparation clinic

(P-21453)

MEDASEND BIOMEDICAL INC (PA)

1402 Daisy Ave, Long Beach (90813-1521)
PHONE.....................800 200-3581
Steve Grand, *CEO*
Stephanie Harrison, *Vice Pres*
EMP: 150 **EST:** 1999
SQ FT: 10,000
SALES (est): 5MM **Privately Held**
WEB: www.medasend.com
SIC: 8099 4953 Health screening service; hazardous waste collection & disposal

(P-21454)

MEDITECH HEALTH SERVICES INC (PA)

1650 Palma Dr Ste 101, Ventura (93003-5749)
PHONE.....................800 538-0900
Sharon J Bick, *President*
EMP: 312 **EST:** 1986
SALES (est): 8.8MM **Privately Held**
WEB: www.seniorplanningservices.com
SIC: 8099 7361 8082 Medical services organization; nurses' registry; home health care services

(P-21455)

MOLINA HEALTHCARE INC

790 E Foothill Blvd, Rialto (92376-5269)
PHONE.....................909 546-7116
EMP: 68
SALES (corp-wide): 19.4B **Publicly Held**
WEB: www.molinahealthcare.com
SIC: 8099 Blood related health services
PA: Molina Healthcare, Inc.
200 Oceangate Ste 100
Long Beach CA 90802
562 435-3666

(P-21456)

MOLINA HEALTHCARE INC

604 Pine Ave, Long Beach (90802-1329)
PHONE.....................888 562-5442
Deidre Palmer, *Manager*
EMP: 68
SALES (corp-wide): 19.4B **Publicly Held**
WEB: www.molinahealthcare.com
SIC: 8099 Blood related health services
PA: Molina Healthcare, Inc.
200 Oceangate Ste 100
Long Beach CA 90802
562 435-3666

(P-21457)

MOLINA HEALTHCARE INC

1 Golden Shore, Long Beach (90802-4202)
PHONE.....................562 435-3666
Sriram Bharadwaj, *Branch Mgr*
Robert Gordon, *President*
Rajan Jain, *President*
Victor Hurtado, *Vice Pres*
Domenico Pagone, *Vice Pres*
EMP: 68
SALES (corp-wide): 19.4B **Publicly Held**
WEB: www.molinahealthcare.com
SIC: 8099 Blood related health services
PA: Molina Healthcare, Inc.
200 Oceangate Ste 100
Long Beach CA 90802
562 435-3666

(P-21458)

NAVY UNITED STATES DEPARTMENT

Also Called: Naval Hosp Twntynine Plms Gfeb
1145 Sturgis Rd, Twentynine Palms (92278)
PHONE.....................760 830-2124
Eugene Dearstine, *CFO*
EMP: 99 **Publicly Held**
WEB: www.navy.mil
SIC: 8099 Blood related health services
HQ: United States Department Of Navy
1200 Navy Pentagon
Washington DC 20350

(P-21459)

NEIGHBORHOOD HEALTHCARE

41840 Enterprise Cir N, Temecula (92590-5654)
PHONE.....................951 225-6400
EMP: 78
SALES (corp-wide): 101.7MM **Privately Held**
WEB: www.nhcare.org
SIC: 8099 Childbirth preparation clinic
PA: Neighborhood Healthcare
425 N Date St Ste 203
Escondido CA 92025
760 520-8372

(P-21460)
NEWPORT MESA UNIFIED SCHL DST
Also Called: Nutrition Services Department
2985 Barrish St Bldg E, Costa Mesa (92626)
PHONE....................714 424-5090
Dale Ellis, *Director*
EMP: 69
SALES (corp-wide): 378.9MM **Privately Held**
WEB: www.web.nmusd.us
SIC: **8211** 8099 Public combined elementary & secondary school; nutrition services
PA: Newport Mesa Unified School District
2985 Bear St Ste A
Costa Mesa CA 92626
714 424-5000

(P-21461)
NEXUS HEALTHCARE SOLUTIONS INC
648 N St Andrews Pl, Los Angeles (90004-1704)
PHONE....................310 448-2693
Akiva Greenfield, *CEO*
Julia Li, *Director*
EMP: 50 EST: 2016
SALES (est): 4.9MM **Privately Held**
WEB: www.nexushs.com
SIC: **8099** Medical services organization

(P-21462)
NORTHEAST VALLEY HEALTH CORP
7107 Remmet Ave, Canoga Park (91303-2016)
PHONE....................818 340-3570
Gary Morris, *Branch Mgr*
EMP: 58
SALES (corp-wide): 104.7MM **Privately Held**
SIC: **8099** Blood related health services
PA: Northeast Valley Health Corp
1172 N Maclay Ave
San Fernando CA 91340
818 898-1388

(P-21463)
NORTHEAST VALLEY HEALTH CORP
26974 Rainbow Glen Dr, Canyon Country (91351-4875)
PHONE....................661 673-8888
Kimberly Wyard, *CEO*
EMP: 58
SALES (corp-wide): 104.7MM **Privately Held**
SIC: **8099** Childbirth preparation clinic
PA: Northeast Valley Health Corp
1172 N Maclay Ave
San Fernando CA 91340
818 898-1388

(P-21464)
NORTHEAST VALLEY HEALTH CORP
7223 Fair Ave, Sun Valley (91352-4964)
PHONE....................818 432-4400
Jeannette Correa, *Executive Asst*
Prudence Oey, *Administration*
EMP: 58
SALES (corp-wide): 104.7MM **Privately Held**
SIC: **8099** Childbirth preparation clinic
PA: Northeast Valley Health Corp
1172 N Maclay Ave
San Fernando CA 91340
818 898-1388

(P-21465)
NORTHERN PIONR HEALTHCARE INC (HQ)
27101 Puerta Real, Mission Viejo (92691-8518)
PHONE....................949 487-9500
Cory Monette, *President*
Sunny Chahal, *Director*
EMP: 50 EST: 2006
SALES (est): 67.9MM
SALES (corp-wide): 2.4B **Publicly Held**
WEB: www.ensigngroup.net
SIC: **8099** Medical services organization

PA: The Ensign Group Inc
29222 Rncho Vejo Rd Ste 1
San Juan Capistrano CA 92675
949 487-9500

(P-21466)
NOVA SKILLED HOME HEALTH INC
3300 N San Fernando Blvd, Burbank (91504-2530)
PHONE....................323 658-6232
Nelson Aguilar, *CEO*
Julita Fraley, *CFO*
Carol Vega, *Administration*
EMP: 136 EST: 2018
SALES (est): 4.8MM **Privately Held**
WEB: www.novaskilledhomehealth.net
SIC: **8099** Health & allied services

(P-21467)
OASIS REHABILITATION CENTER (HQ)
Also Called: Oasis Mental Health Treatment
2283 N Viminal Rd, Palm Springs (92262-3852)
PHONE....................760 863-8638
Mary Jane Gross, *President*
EMP: 50 EST: 2000
SALES (est): 2.4MM
SALES (corp-wide): 34.6MM **Privately Held**
WEB: www.starsinc.com
SIC: **8099** Medical services organization
PA: Stars Behavioral Health Group, Inc.
1501 Hughes Way Ste 150
Long Beach CA 90810
310 221-6336

(P-21468)
ONELEGACY (PA)
221 S Figueroa St Ste 500, Los Angeles (90012-2526)
PHONE....................213 625-0665
Thomas D Mone, *CEO*
Robert Mendez, *President*
Jose Del Real, *COO*
Prasad Garimella, *Officer*
Rachel Grayczyk, *Executive Asst*
EMP: 60 EST: 1977
SALES (est): 115MM **Privately Held**
WEB: www.onelegacy.org
SIC: **8099** Organ bank

(P-21469)
PANCRTIC CNCER ACTION NTWRK IN (PA)
Also Called: PANCAN
1500 Rosecrans Ave # 200, Manhattan Beach (90266-3763)
PHONE....................310 725-0025
Julie Fleshman, *President*
Hilarie Koplow-Mcadams, *Ch of Bd*
Jeanne Weaver Ruesch, *Ch of Bd*
Abigail Winston, *CFO*
Anne-Marie Duliege, *Officer*
EMP: 127 EST: 1999
SALES (est): 36.6MM **Privately Held**
WEB: www.pancan.org
SIC: **8099** 8399 Medical services organization; social service information exchange

(P-21470)
PERFORMANCE HEALTH MED GROUP (PA)
21707 Hawthorne Blvd # 20, Torrance (90503-7009)
PHONE....................310 540-9699
Brian D Carrico, *Principal*
Bob Poirier, *Vice Pres*
EMP: 50 EST: 2008
SALES (est): 2.6MM **Privately Held**
WEB: www.performancehealth.com
SIC: **8099** 8049 Blood related health services; physical therapist

(P-21471)
PLASMA BIOLIFE SERVICES L P
2065 E Highland Ave, San Bernardino (92404-4625)
PHONE....................909 863-3025
Pamela Hughes, *Branch Mgr*
EMP: 50 **Privately Held**
SIC: **8099** Plasmapherous center

HQ: Biolife Plasma Services L.P.
1200 Lakeside Dr
Bannockburn IL 60015
224 940-2000

(P-21472)
PPONEXT WEST INC
1501 Hughes Way Ste 400, Long Beach (90810-1881)
PHONE....................888 446-6098
Barbara E Rodin PHD, *President*
EMP: 385 EST: 1999
SALES (est): 1.8MM
SALES (corp-wide): 5B **Publicly Held**
WEB: www.beechstreet.com
SIC: **8099** Medical services organization
HQ: Beech Street Corporation
25550 Commercentre Dr # 200
Lake Forest CA 92630
949 672-1000

(P-21473)
QTC MANAGEMENT INC (DH)
924 Overland Ct, San Dimas (91773-1742)
PHONE....................800 260-1515
Stephanie Hill, *CEO*
Tony Buratti, *Vice Pres*
Virginia Mao, *Vice Pres*
Carrie Blackburn, *Office Mgr*
Benjamin Yu, *Sr Ntwrk Engine*
▼ EMP: 99 EST: 1981
SQ FT: 20,000
SALES (est): 61.6MM **Publicly Held**
WEB: www.qtcm.com
SIC: **8099** Medical services organization
HQ: Qtc Holdings Inc.
9737 Washingtonian Blvd
Gaithersburg MD 20878
909 859-2100

(P-21474)
QTC MDCAL GROUP INC A MED CORP
924 Overland Ct, San Dimas (91773-1742)
PHONE....................800 260-1515
Brant Kim, *CEO*
Francisco Guzman, *Software Engr*
EMP: 1000 EST: 1984
SALES (est): 27.8MM **Privately Held**
WEB: www.qtcm.com
SIC: **8099** Medical services organization

(P-21475)
REGENTS OF THE UNIVERSITY CAL
Also Called: Santa Monica Ucla Medical Ctr
1250 16th St, Santa Monica (90404-1249)
PHONE....................310 267-9308
Johnese Spisso, *Principal*
Felicia Rue, *Principal*
Paul Staton, *Principal*
EMP: 99 EST: 1996
SALES (est): 8.3MM **Privately Held**
SIC: **8099** Health & allied services

(P-21476)
SAJE NATURAL WELLNESS USA INC (HQ)
1421 Abbot Kinney Blvd, Venice (90291-3740)
PHONE....................310 317-0421
Katie Drechsel, *Vice Pres*
EMP: 52
SALES (est): 5.8MM
SALES (corp-wide): 73MM **Privately Held**
WEB: www.saje.com
SIC: **8099** Health & allied services
PA: Saje Natural Business Inc
22 5th Ave E Suite 500
Vancouver BC V5T 1
877 275-7253

(P-21477)
SAN ANTNIO BEHAVIORAL HLTH LLC (PA)
1333 2nd St Ste 650, Santa Monica (90401-4103)
PHONE....................310 566-0640
EMP: 51 EST: 2016
SALES (est): 616.4K **Privately Held**
WEB: www.sanantoniobehavioral.com
SIC: **8099** Health & allied services

(P-21478)
SCRIBEAMERICA LLC
840 Apollo St Ste 231, El Segundo (90245-4762)
PHONE....................877 819-5900
Michael Murphy, *Branch Mgr*
EMP: 112 **Privately Held**
WEB: www.scribeamerica.com
SIC: **8099** Blood related health services
HQ: Scribeamerica, Llc
1200 E Las Olas Blvd # 201
Fort Lauderdale FL 33301

(P-21479)
SHARE OUR SELVES CORPORATION
1 Purpose Dr, Lake Forest (92630-8717)
PHONE....................949 609-8199
EMP: 85 **Privately Held**
WEB: www.shareourselves.org
SIC: **8099** Childbirth preparation clinic
PA: Share Our Selves Corporation
1550 Superior Ave
Costa Mesa CA 92627

(P-21480)
SIERRA VISTA FAMILY MEDICAL
1227 E Los Angeles Ave, Simi Valley (93065-2871)
PHONE....................805 582-4000
EMP: 80 EST: 2009
SALES (est): 2.6MM **Privately Held**
SIC: **8099** Health/Allied Services

(P-21481)
SOBALIVING LLC
22669 Pacific Coast Hwy, Malibu (90265-5036)
PHONE....................800 595-3803
EMP: 50
SALES (est): 4.1MM **Privately Held**
WEB: www.sobarecovery.com
SIC: **8099** Health/Allied Services

(P-21482)
SOUTHERN CAL PRMNNTE MED GROUP
23781 Maquina, Mission Viejo (92691-2716)
PHONE....................949 376-8619
EMP: 208
SALES (corp-wide): 30.5B **Privately Held**
SIC: **8099** Blood related health services
HQ: Southern California Permanente Medical Group
393 Walnut Dr
Pasadena CA 91107
626 405-5704

(P-21483)
STAR OF CA LLC
299 W Hillcrest Dr, Thousand Oaks (91360-4264)
PHONE....................805 379-1401
Doug Moes, *Branch Mgr*
Keegan Tangeman, *Director*
Michelle Wenzel, *Director*
Jessica Haro, *Supervisor*
EMP: 95
SALES (corp-wide): 165MM **Privately Held**
WEB: www.starofca.com
SIC: **8099** Medical services organization
HQ: Star Of Ca, Llc
4880 Market St
Ventura CA 93003

(P-21484)
STAR OF CA LLC
15260 Ventura Blvd, Sherman Oaks (91403-5307)
PHONE....................818 986-7827
Alison Stanley, *Branch Mgr*
EMP: 95
SALES (corp-wide): 165MM **Privately Held**
WEB: www.starofca.com
SIC: **8099** Medical services organization
HQ: Star Of Ca, Llc
4880 Market St
Ventura CA 93003

(P-21485)
STAR OF CA LLC (HQ)
4880 Market St, Ventura (93003-7783)
PHONE..................................805 644-7827
Doug Moes, *President*
Quy Neel, *Ch Credit Ofcr*
Tom Forde, *Controller*
Faye Carter, *Director*
Jennifer Johnson, *Director*
EMP: 110 **EST:** 2006
SQ FT: 6,640
SALES (est): 46.3MM
SALES (corp-wide): 165MM **Privately Held**
WEB: www.starofca.com
SIC: 8099 8049 8322 Medical services organization; clinical psychologist; individual & family services
PA: Pediatric Therapy Services, Llc
2586 Trailridge Dr E # 100
Lafayette CO 80026
800 337-5965

(P-21486)
STAR OF CALIFORNIA
8834 Morro Rd, Atascadero (93422-3953)
PHONE..................................805 466-1638
EMP: 95
SALES (corp-wide): 165MM **Privately Held**
WEB: www.starofca.com
SIC: 8099 Medical services organization
HQ: Star Of Ca, Llc
4880 Market St
Ventura CA 93003

(P-21487)
SWEATHEORY WELLNESS LLC
6427 W Sunset Blvd 106, Los Angeles (90028-7314)
PHONE..................................310 844-3662
Julian Ledesma, *Mng Member*
EMP: 64 **EST:** 2018
SALES (est): 1.2MM **Privately Held**
WEB: www.sweatheory.com
SIC: 8099 5812 Health & allied services; snack bar

(P-21488)
SWEETGRACE HOME HLTH SVCS LLC
6101 Cherry Ave, Fontana (92336-5362)
PHONE..................................909 463-7400
Lourdes Garcia,
EMP: 65 **EST:** 2012
SALES (est): 982.4K **Privately Held**
SIC: 8099 Health & allied services

(P-21489)
TELEMEDICINE CORP
8920 Wilshire Blvd # 310, Beverly Hills (90211-2003)
PHONE..................................888 472-2853
David Woroboff, *CEO*
George Willard, *COO*
EMP: 50 **EST:** 2015
SQ FT: 2,000
SALES (est): 3.9MM **Privately Held**
WEB: www.247calladoc.com
SIC: 8099 Childbirth preparation clinic

(P-21490)
TENET HEALTHSYSTEM MEDICAL INC
47111 Monroe St, Indio (92201-6739)
PHONE..................................760 347-6191
Matt Keating, *CFO*
Ruben Garcia, *Administration*
Anne Engleman, *QC Mgr*
Gary Harris, *Director*
EMP: 51
SALES (corp-wide): 17.6B **Publicly Held**
WEB: www.tenethealth.com
SIC: 8099 Blood related health services
HQ: Tenet Healthsystem Medical, Inc.
14201 Dallas Pkwy
Dallas TX 75254
469 893-2000

(P-21491)
UNI HEALTHCARE INC
25129 The Old Rd Ste 204, Stevenson Ranch (91381-2274)
PHONE..................................661 222-9984

Benzie Roy Davidson, *President*
EMP: 50 **EST:** 1990
SALES (est): 1.4MM **Privately Held**
SIC: 8099 Health & allied services

(P-21492)
UNIFIED INV PROGRAMS INC (PA)
Also Called: Palm Grove Health Care
2368 Torrance Blvd # 200, Torrance (90501-2500)
PHONE..................................310 782-1878
Cynthia Schein, *Owner*
Emmanuel B David, *President*
EMP: 50 **EST:** 1997
SALES (est): 3.8MM **Privately Held**
SIC: 8099 8051 Medical services organization; skilled nursing care facilities

(P-21493)
UNIVERSITY CALIFORNIA IRVINE
31865 Circle Dr, Laguna Beach (92651-6860)
PHONE..................................949 939-7106
EMP: 121 **Privately Held**
WEB: www.uci.edu
SIC: 8099 Blood related health services
HQ: University Of California, Irvine
510 Aldrich Hall
Irvine CA 92697
949 824-5011

(P-21494)
UNIVERSITY CALIFORNIA IRVINE
Also Called: UCI Health Blood Donor Center
106 B Student Ctr, Irvine (92697-0001)
PHONE..................................949 824-2662
EMP: 121 **Privately Held**
WEB: www.uci.edu
SIC: 8099 Blood donor station
HQ: University Of California, Irvine
510 Aldrich Hall
Irvine CA 92697
949 824-5011

(P-21495)
VENTURA COUNTY MEDI-CAL MANAGE
Also Called: Gold Coast Health Plan
711 E Daily Dr Ste 106, Camarillo (93010-6082)
PHONE..................................888 301-1228
Michael P Engelhard, *CEO*
EMP: 79 **EST:** 2010
SALES (est): 24.6MM **Privately Held**
WEB: www.goldcoasthealthplan.org
SIC: 8099 Medical services organization

(P-21496)
VITALANT
Also Called: United Blood Svcs Centl Coast
2223 Eastman Ave Ste A, Ventura (93003-8050)
PHONE..................................805 654-1603
Susan Noone, *Director*
EMP: 60
SALES (corp-wide): 526.6MM **Privately Held**
WEB: www.laboratories.vitalant.org
SIC: 8099 Blood bank; blood donor station
PA: Vitalant
6210 E Oak St
Scottsdale AZ 85257
800 288-2199

(P-21497)
VU HOLDINGS LLC
55 Fair Dr, Costa Mesa (92626-6520)
PHONE..................................661 808-4004
Vanguard University, *Principal*
Joshua Freeman, *Assistant*
EMP: 57 **EST:** 2014
SALES (est): 18.7MM **Privately Held**
WEB: www.vanguard.edu
SIC: 8099 Health & allied services

(P-21498)
WILD CREEK HEALTHCARE INC (DH)
27101 Puerta Real Ste 450, Mission Viejo (92691-8566)
PHONE..................................775 359-3161
Cory Monette, *President*

Soon Burnam, *Treasurer*
Christopher Christensen, *Director*
EMP: 50 **EST:** 2011
SALES (est): 10.4MM
SALES (corp-wide): 2.4B **Publicly Held**
SIC: 8099 Medical services organization
HQ: Northern Pioneer Healthcare, Inc.
27101 Puerta Real
Mission Viejo CA 92691
949 487-9500

8111 Legal Svcs

(P-21499)
A BUCHALTER PROFESSIONAL CORP (PA)
1000 Wilshire Blvd # 150, Los Angeles (90017-2457)
PHONE..................................213 891-0700
Adam Bass, *CEO*
Mia Blackler, *Shareholder*
Mark Bonenfant, *Shareholder*
Howard Ellman, *Shareholder*
Martin Florman, *Shareholder*
EMP: 209 **EST:** 1970
SQ FT: 84,000
SALES (est): 96.7MM **Privately Held**
WEB: www.buchalter.com
SIC: 8111 General practice law office

(P-21500)
AKERMAN LLP
601 W 5th St Ste 300, Los Angeles (90071-3506)
PHONE..................................213 688-9500
Justin Balser, *Partner*
EMP: 56
SALES (corp-wide): 178.8MM **Privately Held**
WEB: www.akerman.com
SIC: 8111 General practice attorney, lawyer
PA: Akerman Llp
98 Se 7th St Ste 1100
Miami FL 33131
305 374-5600

(P-21501)
ALBERT & MACKENZIE LLP (PA)
28216 Dorothy Dr Ste 200, Agoura Hills (91301-4973)
PHONE..................................818 575-9876
Bruce Albert, *Managing Prtnr*
Peter Mackenzie, *Partner*
Peter N Mackenzie, *Partner*
Mackenzie Peter, *Partner*
Russ Neault, *Exec Dir*
EMP: 161 **EST:** 2000
SALES (est): 23.4MM **Privately Held**
WEB: www.albmac.com
SIC: 8111 Real estate law

(P-21502)
ALLEN MTKINS LECK GMBLE MLLORY (PA)
865 S Figueroa St # 2800, Los Angeles (90017-2543)
PHONE..................................213 622-5555
David L Osias, *Managing Prtnr*
Frederick L Allen, *Partner*
Dwight Armstrong, *Partner*
Michael J Betz, *Partner*
Keith Paul Bishop, *Partner*
EMP: 130 **EST:** 1986
SQ FT: 40,000
SALES (est): 55.8MM **Privately Held**
WEB: www.allenmatkins.com
SIC: 8111 General practice law office; labor & employment law; corporate, partnership & business law; real estate law

(P-21503)
ALSTON & BIRD LLP
333 S Hope St Ste 1600, Los Angeles (90071-1410)
PHONE..................................213 576-1000
Wayne Mitchell, *Branch Mgr*
Mark Hahs, *Managing Prtnr*
Karen Schmid, *Vice Pres*
Michael Siska, *Regional Mgr*
Julie Hite, *Branch Mgr*
EMP: 65

SALES (corp-wide): 216.9MM **Privately Held**
WEB: www.alston.com
SIC: 8111 General practice attorney, lawyer
PA: Alston & Bird Llp
1201 W Peachtree St Nw # 4000
Atlanta GA 30309
404 881-7000

(P-21504)
ALSTON & BIRD LLP
2815 Townsgate Rd Ste 200, Westlake Village (91361-3091)
PHONE..................................202 239-3673
Michael D Bradbury, *Principal*
EMP: 65
SALES (corp-wide): 216.9MM **Privately Held**
WEB: www.alston.com
SIC: 8111 General practice attorney, lawyer
PA: Alston & Bird Llp
1201 W Peachtree St Nw # 4000
Atlanta GA 30309
404 881-7000

(P-21505)
ANDERSON MCPHARLIN CONNERS LLP (PA)
Also Called: AMC&
707 Wilshire Blvd # 4000, Los Angeles (90017-3501)
PHONE..................................213 688-0080
David T Dibiase, *Partner*
Mark E Aronson, *Partner*
Carleton R Burch, *Partner*
Colleen A Dziel, *Partner*
Jesse S Hernandez, *Partner*
EMP: 57 **EST:** 1947
SQ FT: 23,000
SALES (est): 13.8MM **Privately Held**
WEB: www.amclaw.com
SIC: 8111 General practice attorney, lawyer

(P-21506)
ATKINSON ANDLSON LOYA RUUD ROM (PA)
Also Called: Atkinson Andelson Loya
12800 Center Court Dr S # 300, Cerritos (90703-9363)
PHONE..................................562 653-3200
James C Romo, *CEO*
Mark T Palin, *Managing Prtnr*
Steven Atkinson, *President*
Steven Andelson, *Vice Pres*
Paul Loya, *Principal*
EMP: 150 **EST:** 1979
SALES (est): 38.2MM **Privately Held**
WEB: www.aalrr.com
SIC: 8111 General practice attorney, lawyer

(P-21507)
BAKER & HOSTETLER LLP
11601 Wilshire Blvd Fl 14, Los Angeles (90025-0509)
PHONE..................................310 820-8800
John F Cermak Jr, *Partner*
Cathryn Rowley, *Partner*
Hernandez Bernard, *IT/INT Sup*
Bob Lofton,
Teresa R Tracy,
EMP: 86
SALES (corp-wide): 320.8K **Privately Held**
WEB: www.bakerlaw.com
SIC: 8111 General practice attorney, lawyer; bankruptcy law; labor & employment law; real estate law
PA: Baker & Hostetler Llp
127 Public Sq Ste 2000
Cleveland OH 44114
216 621-0200

(P-21508)
BAKER & HOSTETLER LLP
600 Anton Blvd Ste 900, Costa Mesa (92626-7193)
PHONE..................................714 754-6600
George T Mooradian, *Partner*
Marcus McCutcheon, *Assistant*
Joe Souza, *Supervisor*
EMP: 86
SQ FT: 6,000

SALES (corp-wide): 320.8K **Privately Held**
WEB: www.bakerlaw.com
SIC: **8111** General practice attorney, lawyer; bankruptcy law; labor & employment law; real estate law
PA: Baker & Hostetler Llp
127 Public Sq Ste 2000
Cleveland OH 44114
216 621-0200

(P-21509)
BAKER & MCKENZIE LLP
10250 Constellation Blvd, Los Angeles (90067-6200)
PHONE..................310 201-4728
EMP: 125
SALES (corp-wide): 782.2MM **Privately Held**
WEB: www.bakermckenzie.com
SIC: **8111** General practice law office
PA: Baker & Mckenzie Llp
300 E Randolph St # 5000
Chicago IL 60601
312 861-8000

(P-21510)
BALLARD SPAHR LLP
2029 Century Park E # 800, Los Angeles (90067-2901)
PHONE..................424 204-4400
Alan Petlak, *Branch Mgr*
Irma Williams, *Marketing Mgr*
Ashley Kissinger, *Counsel*
EMP: 76
SALES (corp-wide): 224.2MM **Privately Held**
WEB: www.consumerfinancemonitor.com
SIC: **8111** General practice attorney, lawyer
PA: Ballard Spahr Llp
1735 Market St Fl 51
Philadelphia PA 19103
215 665-8500

(P-21511)
BARNES & THORNBURG LLP
2029 Century Park E # 300, Los Angeles (90067-2904)
PHONE..................310 284-3880
Paul J Laurin, *Partner*
Charles La Bella, *Counsel*
Garrett Llewellyn, *Counsel*
Bryan Thompson, *Counsel*
Mary Garnett, *Manager*
EMP: 113
SALES (corp-wide): 102MM **Privately Held**
WEB: www.btlaw.com
SIC: **8111** General practice attorney, lawyer
PA: Barnes & Thornburg Llp
11 S Meridian St Ste 1313
Indianapolis IN 46204
317 236-1313

(P-21512)
BARTHOLOMEW BARRY & ASSOCIATES
701 N Brand Blvd Ste 800, Glendale (91203-3279)
PHONE..................818 543-4000
EMP: 73
SALES (est): 3.7MM **Privately Held**
SIC: **8111** Attorney

(P-21513)
BERGER KAHN A LAW CORPORATION (PA)
Also Called: Simon and Gladstone A Prof
1 Park Plz Ste 340, Irvine (92614-2511)
PHONE..................949 474-1880
Craig Simon, *CEO*
Ron Alberts, *Partner*
Jason Wallach, *Partner*
Heather Whitmore, *Partner*
Mike Aiken, *Principal*
▲ EMP: 70 EST: 1928
SQ FT: 22,250
SALES (est): 15.6MM **Privately Held**
WEB: www.bergerkahn.com
SIC: **8111** General practice attorney, lawyer

(P-21514)
BEST BEST & KRIEGER LLP (PA)
Also Called: BB&k
3390 University Ave # 500, Riverside (92501-3369)
P.O. Box 1028 (92502-1028)
PHONE..................951 686-1450
Eric L Garner, *Managing Prtnr*
Jason M Ackerman, *Partner*
Franklin C Adams, *Partner*
Franklin Adams, *Partner*
Clark Alsop, *Partner*
EMP: 188 EST: 1891
SQ FT: 57,000
SALES (est): 49.1MM **Privately Held**
WEB: www.bbklaw.com
SIC: **8111** General practice attorney, lawyer

(P-21515)
BEST BEST & KRIEGER LLP
18101 Von Karman Ave # 1000, Irvine (92612-0164)
PHONE..................949 263-2600
Monica Elmar, *Branch Mgr*
EMP: 50
SALES (corp-wide): 49.1MM **Privately Held**
WEB: www.bbklaw.com
SIC: **8111** General practice attorney, lawyer
PA: Best Best & Krieger Llp
3390 University Ave # 500
Riverside CA 92501
951 686-1450

(P-21516)
BET TZEDEK
3250 Wilshire Blvd Fl 13, Los Angeles (90010-1601)
PHONE..................323 939-0506
Diego Cartagena, *President*
Stanley Kandel, *Partner*
Michael D Seplow, *Partner*
David Lash, *President*
Zoe Engel, *Officer*
EMP: 51
SALES: 11.2MM **Privately Held**
WEB: www.bettzedek.org
SIC: **8111** Legal aid service

(P-21517)
BIRD MRLLA BXER WLPERT NSSIM
Also Called: Bird Marella
1875 Century Park E Fl 23, Los Angeles (90067-2253)
PHONE..................310 201-2100
Vincent Marella, *Partner*
Terry Bird, *Partner*
Joel Boxer, *Partner*
Dorothy Wolpert, *Partner*
Sandy Palmieri, *President*
EMP: 60 EST: 1981
SALES (est): 9.2MM **Privately Held**
WEB: www.birdmarella.com
SIC: **8111** General practice law office

(P-21518)
BLOOM HERGOTT DIEMER COOK LLC
Also Called: Bloom, Jacob A
9665 Wilshire Blvd # 500, Beverly Hills (90212-2312)
PHONE..................310 859-6800
Jacob A Bloom, *Partner*
Lawrence H Graves, *Partner*
Candice S Hansen, *Partner*
Allen Hergott, *Partner*
Tina J Kahn, *Partner*
EMP: 52 EST: 1971
SALES (est): 2.5MM **Privately Held**
WEB: www.stacykeibler.com
SIC: **8111** General practice law office

(P-21519)
BMC GROUP INC
Also Called: Bankruptcy Management Cons
300 N Cntntl Blvd Ste 570, El Segundo (90245)
PHONE..................310 321-5555
Shawn Allen, *President*
Walter Bracken, *Vice Pres*
Jeff Kalina, *Vice Pres*
Patrick Schnepf, *Vice Pres*

John R Burge, *Managing Dir*
EMP: 100 **Privately Held**
WEB: www.bmcgroup.com
SIC: **8111** Bankruptcy referee
PA: The Bmc Group Inc
3732 W 120th St
Hawthorne CA 90250

(P-21520)
BONNE BRDGES MLLER OKEFE NCHOL (PA)
355 S Grand Ave Ste 1750, Los Angeles (90071-1562)
PHONE..................213 480-1900
David J O'Keefe, *President*
Thomas M O 'neil, *Shareholder*
Peter R Osinoff, *Shareholder*
George Peterson, *Corp Secy*
James D Nichols, *Vice Pres*
EMP: 100 EST: 1961
SALES (est): 17.4MM **Privately Held**
WEB: www.bonnebridges.com
SIC: **8111** General practice attorney, lawyer

(P-21521)
BOOTH MITCHEL & STRANGE LLP
979 Osos St Ste C1, San Luis Obispo (93401-3253)
PHONE..................805 400-0703
Christpher Levwi, *Branch Mgr*
EMP: 76
SALES (corp-wide): 7.2MM **Privately Held**
WEB: www.boothmitchel.com
SIC: **8111** General practice law office
PA: Booth Mitchel & Strange, L.L.P.
707 Wilshire Blvd # 3000
Los Angeles CA 90017
213 738-0100

(P-21522)
BRADY VORWERCK RYDR & CSPNO (PA)
19200 Von Karman Ave, Irvine (92612-8553)
PHONE..................480 456-9888
James Brady, *CEO*
Robert Ryder, *Principal*
Gregg Vorwerck, *Principal*
EMP: 75 EST: 1996
SALES (est): 10.1MM **Privately Held**
SIC: **8111** Legal services

(P-21523)
BREMER WHYTE BROWN OMEARA LLP (PA)
Also Called: Bremer Whyte Brown Omeara
20320 Sw Birch St Ste 200, Newport Beach (92660-1791)
PHONE..................949 221-1000
Keith Bremer, *Partner*
Nicole Whyte, *Partner*
Arash Arabi, *Managing Prtnr*
Shawn Reutter, *President*
Brenda Newkirk, *General Mgr*
EMP: 50 EST: 1997
SQ FT: 6,000
SALES (est): 16.7MM **Privately Held**
WEB: www.bremerwhyte.com
SIC: **8111** General practice law office

(P-21524)
BURKE WILLIAMS & SORENSEN LLP (PA)
444 S Flower St Ste 2400, Los Angeles (90071-2953)
PHONE..................213 236-0600
John J Welsh, *Managing Prtnr*
James T Bradshaw Jr, *Partner*
Harold Bridges, *Partner*
Steven J Dawson, *Partner*
Leland C Dolley, *Partner*
EMP: 90 EST: 1927
SQ FT: 51,000
SALES (est): 31.4MM **Privately Held**
WEB: www.bwslaw.com
SIC: **8111** General practice attorney, lawyer

(P-21525)
BURT L HOWE & ASSOCIATES
Also Called: Howe Construction Co
5415 E La Palma Ave, Anaheim (92807-2022)
PHONE..................714 701-9180
Bert L Howe, *Partner*
Susan A Howe, *Partner*
Don Macgregor, *Vice Pres*
Mark Chapman, *Project Mgr*
Brad Hughes, *Project Mgr*
EMP: 52 EST: 1984
SALES (est): 3.1MM **Privately Held**
WEB: www.berthowe.com
SIC: **8111** 8711 Product liability law; building construction consultant

(P-21526)
CALL & JENSEN APC
610 Nwport Ctr Dr Ste 700, Newport Beach (92660)
PHONE..................949 717-3000
Wayne W Call, *President*
Kent Christensen, *Shareholder*
Alyvia Moss, *Admin Asst*
Jon Jensen, *Administration*
Janelle Lford, *Legal Staff*
EMP: 50 EST: 1985
SALES (est): 6.4MM **Privately Held**
WEB: www.calljensen.com
SIC: **8111** General practice attorney, lawyer

(P-21527)
CARROLL KLLY TRTTER FRNZEN A L (PA)
111 W Ocean Blvd Fl 14, Long Beach (90802-4646)
P.O. Box 22636 (90801-5636)
PHONE..................562 432-5855
Richard Caroll, *CEO*
John Kelly, *Treasurer*
Katherine Maguire, *Admin Sec*
Troy Totter, *Admin Sec*
Michael Trotter, *Admin Sec*
EMP: 57 EST: 1994
SALES (est): 10.9MM **Privately Held**
WEB: www.cktfmlaw.com
SIC: **8111** General practice law office

(P-21528)
CARSON KURTZMAN CONSULTANTS (DH)
Also Called: K C C
2335 Alaska Ave, El Segundo (90245-4808)
PHONE..................310 823-9000
Jon A Orr, *President*
Albert Kass, *Exec VP*
James Le Transitions, *Exec VP*
Jonathan Carameros, *Vice Pres*
Robert Dewitte, *Vice Pres*
EMP: 180 EST: 2001
SQ FT: 46,000
SALES (est): 63.1MM **Privately Held**
WEB: www.kccllc.com
SIC: **8111** Specialized legal services

(P-21529)
CHILDRENS LAW CENTER CAL (PA)
101 Centre Plaza Dr, Monterey Park (91754-2155)
PHONE..................323 980-8700
Leslie Starr Heimov, *CEO*
Jessica Wilde, *Executive Asst*
Lela Getzler, *Admin Sec*
Sarah Tam, *Admin Sec*
Patricia Salcido, *Administration*
EMP: 108 EST: 1989
SALES: 55.6MM **Privately Held**
WEB: www.clccal.org
SIC: **8111** Legal aid service

(P-21530)
CITIZNSHIP IMMIGRATION SVCS US
9251 Garvey Ave Ste N, El Monte (91733-4611)
PHONE..................626 448-0135
EMP: 110 **Publicly Held**
SIC: **9721** 8111 International Affairs Legal Services Office

HQ: Citizenship & Immigration Services,
U.S.
20 Ma Ave Nw Rm 3000
Washington DC 20529
-

(P-21531)
CITIZNSHIP IMMIGRATION SVCS US
Also Called: Phoenix Immigration & Educatn
113 N I St, Lompoc (93436-6758)
PHONE..................................805 588-7002
EMP: 70 **Publicly Held**
WEB: www.uscis.gov
SIC: 9721 8111 Immigration services, gov-
ernment; immigration & naturalization law
HQ: Citizenship & Immigration Services,
U.S.
20 Ma Ave Nw Rm 3000
Washington DC 20529

(P-21532)
CLARK & TREVITHICK A PROF CORP
800 Wilshire Blvd # 1200, Los Angeles
(90017-2617)
PHONE..................................213 629-5700
Donald P Clark, *President*
James S Arico, *Vice Pres*
Philip W Bartenetti, *Vice Pres*
Leonard Brazil, *Vice Pres*
Dean I Friedman, *Vice Pres*
EMP: 51 EST: 1977
SQ FT: 13,500
SALES (est): 5MM **Privately Held**
WEB: www.clarktrev.com
SIC: 8111 General practice law office

(P-21533)
COLLINS CLLINS MUIR STWART LLP
790 E Colo Blvd Ste 600, Pasadena
(91101)
PHONE..................................626 243-1100
John Collins, *Partner*
Samuel J Muir, *Partner*
Brian Stewart, *Partner*
Laurey Carpenter, *President*
Chelsea Reyes, *Admin Sec*
EMP: 50 EST: 1964
SALES (est): 9.5MM **Privately Held**
WEB: www.ccllp.law
SIC: 8111 General practice attorney,
lawyer

(P-21534)
COMMUNITY ACTION PARTNERSHIP
1152 E Grand Ave, Arroyo Grande
(93420-2583)
PHONE..................................805 489-4026
Raye Flemming, *Branch Mgr*
EMP: 84
SALES (corp-wide): 93.2MM **Privately
Held**
WEB: www.capslo.org
SIC: 8111 General practice law office
PA: Community Action Partnership Of San
Luis Obispo County, Inc.
1030 Southwood Dr
San Luis Obispo CA 93401
805 544-4355

(P-21535)
COMPEX LEGAL SERVICES INC (PA)
325 Maple Ave, Torrance (90503-2602)
PHONE..................................310 782-1801
Paul Boroditsch, *CEO*
Venkat Raman, *COO*
Humildad Pasimio, *CFO*
Nitin Mehta, *Chairman*
Anthony Bazurto, *Officer*
▲ EMP: 120 EST: 1974
SQ FT: 47,740
SALES (est): 60.2MM **Privately Held**
WEB: www.cpxlegal.com
SIC: 8111 7338 7334 Specialized legal
services; secretarial & court reporting;
photocopying & duplicating services

(P-21536)
CONSILIO LLC
605 E Huntington Dr # 211, Monrovia
(91016-6352)
PHONE..................................626 921-1600
Dale Bowen, *CFO*
Amy Hinzmann, *Officer*
Adam Pollitt, *Exec VP*
Tamara Buie, *Vice Pres*
Karen Hornbeck, *Vice Pres*
EMP: 228 **Privately Held**
WEB: www.consilio.com
SIC: 8111 8748 7374 Legal services;
business consulting; data processing &
preparation
HQ: Consilio, Llc
1828 L St Nw Ste 1070
Washington DC 20036
202 822-6222

(P-21537)
COOKSEY TLEN GAGE DFFY WOOG A (PA)
535 Anton Blvd Fl 10, Costa Mesa
(92626-1947)
PHONE..................................714 431-1100
David Cooksey, *President*
Robert L Toolen, *Vice Pres*
Dalin Suon, *Admin Sec*
Richard C Buck,
Kim Patterson Gage,
EMP: 91 EST: 1970
SALES (est): 9.3MM **Privately Held**
WEB: www.cookseylaw.com
SIC: 8111 General practice attorney,
lawyer

(P-21538)
COUNTY OF LOS ANGELES
Also Called: District Attorney
42011 4th St W Ste 3530, Lancaster
(93534-7196)
PHONE..................................661 974-7700
Steve Cooley, *Administration*
Tracy Holcombe, *Asst Director*
EMP: 127
SALES (corp-wide): 25.2B **Privately Held**
WEB: www.lacounty.gov
SIC: 9222 8111 District Attorneys' offices; ;
general practice attorney, lawyer
PA: County Of Los Angeles
500 W Temple St Ste 437
Los Angeles CA 90012
213 974-1101

(P-21539)
COUNTY OF ORANGE
Also Called: District Attorney
901 W Civic Center Dr # 200, Santa Ana
(92703-2383)
PHONE..................................714 796-8200
Jo Escobar, *Branch Mgr*
EMP: 100
SALES (corp-wide): 4.3B **Privately Held**
WEB: www.ocgov.com
SIC: 9222 8111 District Attorneys' offices; ;
general practice attorney, lawyer
PA: County Of Orange
333 W Santa Ana Blvd
Santa Ana CA 92701
714 834-6200

(P-21540)
COUNTY OF RIVERSIDE
Also Called: Public Defender- Main Office
4075 Main St, Riverside (92501-3701)
PHONE..................................951 955-6000
Gary Windom, *Administration*
EMP: 200
SALES (corp-wide): 4B **Privately Held**
WEB: www.rivco.org
SIC: 8111 9222 Legal services; public de-
fenders' offices;
PA: County Of Riverside
4080 Lemon St Fl 11
Riverside CA 92501
951 955-1110

(P-21541)
COURTCALL LLC (PA)
2158 W 190th St, Torrance (90504-6103)
PHONE..................................310 342-0888
Robert Alvarado,
Edie Liu, *COO*
Marcia Wood, *Administration*
Charles Reeves, *Prgrmr*

Gustavo Gonzalez, *IT/INT Sup*
EMP: 61 EST: 1995
SALES (est): 8MM **Privately Held**
WEB: www.courtcall.com
SIC: 8111 Legal services

(P-21542)
COX CASTLE & NICHOLSON LLP (PA)
Also Called: Cox Castle
2029 Century Park E # 2100, Los Angeles
(90067-3007)
PHONE..................................310 284-2200
Gary A Glick, *Partner*
Lindsey H Barr, *Partner*
Robin L Bennett, *Partner*
Kenneth B Bley, *Partner*
Erica A Bose, *Partner*
EMP: 165 EST: 1968
SQ FT: 60,000
SALES (est): 41.4MM **Privately Held**
WEB: www.coxcastle.com
SIC: 8111 General practice attorney,
lawyer

(P-21543)
DANNING GILL DAMND KOLLITZ LLP
1901 Avenue Of The Stars # 450, Los An-
geles (90067-6006)
PHONE..................................310 277-0077
David A Gill, *Partner*
Richard K Diamond, *Partner*
Howard Kollitz, *Partner*
David M Poitras, *Partner*
Eric P Israel PC, *Partner*
EMP: 70 EST: 1952
SALES (est): 9.7MM **Privately Held**
WEB: www.danninggill.com
SIC: 8111 General practice law office

(P-21544)
DAVIS WRIGHT TREMAINE LLP
865 S Figueroa St # 2400, Los Angeles
(90017-2566)
PHONE..................................213 633-6800
Mary Haas, *Partner*
EMP: 91
SALES (corp-wide): 238.7MM **Privately
Held**
WEB: www.dwtholiday.com
SIC: 8111 General practice attorney,
lawyer
PA: Davis Wright Tremaine Llp
920 5th Ave Ste 3300
Seattle WA 98104
206 622-3150

(P-21545)
DE CASTRO W CHDROW MNDLER GLCK
10960 Wilshire Blvd # 14, Los Angeles
(90024-3702)
PHONE..................................310 478-2541
Hugo Decastro, *President*
Marcia Denton, *Office Mgr*
Richard Furman, *Planning*
Leonard S Perlman, *Planning*
Merna Figoten, *Info Tech Mgr*
EMP: 65 EST: 1963
SQ FT: 19,400
SALES (est): 9.2MM **Privately Held**
WEB: www.dwclaw.com
SIC: 8111 General practice law office

(P-21546)
DEMLER ARMSTRONG & ROWLAND LLP
4500 E Pcf Cast Hwy Ste 4, Long Beach
(90804)
PHONE..................................562 597-0029
Robert Armstrong, *Partner*
Bjorn C Green, *Senior Partner*
Sean Beatty, *Partner*
Edison Demler, *Partner*
Terry Rowland, *Partner*
EMP: 50
SQ FT: 13,500
SALES (est): 6.9MM **Privately Held**
WEB: www.darlaw.com
SIC: 8111 General practice attorney,
lawyer

(P-21547)
DENTONS US LLP
Also Called: A Dentons Innovation Wirthlin
601 S Figueroa St # 2500, Los Angeles
(90017-5704)
PHONE..................................213 623-9300
Edwin Reeser, *General Mgr*
Michael Lubic, *Partner*
John Walker, *Partner*
Laurie Soledad, *Admin Sec*
Paterson Lee,
EMP: 150
SALES (corp-wide): 509MM **Privately
Held**
WEB: www.dentons.com
SIC: 8111 Specialized law offices, attor-
neys
HQ: Dentons Us Llp
233 S Wacker Dr Ste 5900
Chicago IL 60606
312 876-8000

(P-21548)
DIRECTCNNECT LGAL SLUTIONS INC
9431 Hven Ave Ste 100-280, Rancho Cuca-
monga (91730)
PHONE..................................888 685-7771
EMP: 50 EST: 2014
SALES (est): 1.6MM **Privately Held**
SIC: 8111 Legal services

(P-21549)
DISABILITY RIGHTS CALIFORNIA
350 S Bixel St, Los Angeles (90017-1418)
PHONE..................................213 213-8000
Kathy Blakemore, *President*
EMP: 76
SALES (corp-wide): 36MM **Privately
Held**
WEB: www.disabilityrightsca.org
SIC: 8111 Legal aid service
PA: Disability Rights California
1831 K St
Sacramento CA 95811
916 488-9950

(P-21550)
DOMINGUEZ FIRM INC
Also Called: Law Offices Juan J. Dominguez
3250 Wilshire Blvd # 2200, Los Angeles
(90010-1612)
PHONE..................................213 388-7788
Juan J Dominguez, *President*
Estela Barraza, *Administration*
Francisco Frias, *Human Res Mgr*
Larry Litzky, *Personnel*
Steven P Blye, *Legal Staff*
EMP: 100 EST: 1988
SQ FT: 5,000
SALES (est): 12.3MM **Privately Held**
WEB: www.dominguezfirm.com
SIC: 8111 General practice attorney,
lawyer; general practice law office

(P-21551)
ENGSTROM LIPSCOMB AND LACK A (PA)
10100 Santa Monica Blvd # 1200, Los An-
geles (90067-4113)
PHONE..................................310 552-3800
Paul Engstrom, *President*
Lee G Lipscomb, *Vice Pres*
Walter J Lack, *Admin Sec*
Brittan Cortney,
Rick Kinnan,
EMP: 70 EST: 1974
SQ FT: 22,000
SALES (est): 12.2MM **Privately Held**
WEB: www.elllaw.com
SIC: 8111 General practice law office

(P-21552)
EPSTEIN BECKER & GREEN PC
1875 Century Park E # 500, Los Angeles
(90067-2253)
PHONE..................................310 556-8861
Sandy Siciliano, *Manager*
Adam C Abrahms, *Bd of Directors*
Jennifer Nutter, *Executive*
Joy Ingoglia, *Admin Sec*
James Flynn, *General Counsel*
EMP: 81

SALES (corp-wide): 117MM **Privately Held**
WEB: www.ebglaw.com
SIC: 8111 General practice attorney, lawyer
PA: Epstein Becker & Green, P.C.
875 3rd Ave Fl 19
New York NY 10022
212 351-4500

(P-21553)
FERRUZZO & FERRUZZO LLP
3737 Birch St Ste 400, Newport Beach (92660-2671)
PHONE..................................949 608-6900
James Ferruzzo, *Partner*
Gregory J Ferruzzo, *Partner*
Thomas G Ferruzzo, *Partner*
John R Pelle, *Partner*
Maria A Newkirk,
EMP: 54 **EST:** 1972
SALES (est): 5.6MM **Privately Held**
WEB: www.ferruzzo.com
SIC: 8111 General practice attorney, lawyer

(P-21554)
FIRST LEGAL SUPPORT SVCS LLC (PA)
1517 Beverly Blvd, Los Angeles (90026-5704)
PHONE..................................213 250-1111
Elisha Gilboa, *Mng Member*
Brian Malouf, *Regional Mgr*
Christopher Daum, *Division Mgr*
Gian Ghio, *Office Mgr*
Matt Carter, *Technology*
EMP: 54
SQ FT: 3,000
SALES (est): 16.4MM **Privately Held**
WEB: www.firstlegal.com
SIC: 8111 Legal aid service

(P-21555)
FLOYD SKEREN & KELLY LLP (PA)
Also Called: FS&k
101 Moody Ct Ste 200, Thousand Oaks (91360-6068)
PHONE..................................818 206-9222
Thomas M Skeren Jr, *President*
Todd Kelly, *Principal*
Thomas Skeren, *Principal*
Aimee Haverlah, *Administration*
Tim Jurich, *Administration*
EMP: 55 **EST:** 1990
SALES (est): 13.3MM **Privately Held**
WEB: www.floydskerenlaw.com
SIC: 8111 General practice law office

(P-21556)
FOLEY BEZEK BEHLE & CURTIS LLP
Also Called: Foley Bezek & Komoroske
15 W Carrillo St, Santa Barbara (93101-8215)
PHONE..................................805 962-9495
Thomas G Foley Jr, *Partner*
Peter J Bezek, *Partner*
Frances E Komoroske, *Partner*
Jacqueline Phlgar, *CFO*
Jeannine Kassity, *Legal Staff*
EMP: 53 **EST:** 1993
SQ FT: 5,000
SALES (est): 5MM **Privately Held**
WEB: www.foleybezek.com
SIC: 8111 General practice law office

(P-21557)
FORD WLKER HAGGERTY BEHAR LLP (PA)
1 World Trade Ctr Ste 270, Long Beach (90831-0002)
PHONE..................................562 983-2500
William C Haggerty, *Principal*
Jeffrey S Behar, *Principal*
G Richard Ford, *Principal*
Timothy Walker, *Principal*
Ingrid Pena, *Admin Sec*
EMP: 63 **EST:** 1991
SQ FT: 23,000
SALES (est): 14MM **Privately Held**
WEB: www.fwhb.com
SIC: 8111 General practice attorney, lawyer

(P-21558)
FRAGOMEN DEL REY BERNSE
18401 Von Karman Ave # 255, Irvine (92612-1596)
PHONE..................................949 660-3504
EMP: 81
SALES (corp-wide): 248.2MM **Privately Held**
SIC: 8111 Legal Services Office
PA: Fragomen, Del Rey, Bernsen & Loewy, Llp
90 Matawan Rd
Matawan NJ 07747
732 862-5000

(P-21559)
FRANDZEL SHARE ROBINS BLOOM LC
1000 Wilshire Blvd # 190, Los Angeles (90017-2457)
PHONE..................................323 852-1000
Steve N Bloom, *President*
Lawrence Grosberg, *Shareholder*
Thomas Robins, *Vice Pres*
Monica Celis, *Executive*
Debra Gray, *Administration*
EMP: 55 **EST:** 1979
SQ FT: 40,000
SALES (est): 7.7MM **Privately Held**
WEB: www.frandzel.com
SIC: 8111 General practice attorney, lawyer; general practice law office

(P-21560)
FREEMAN FREEMAN & SMILEY (PA)
Also Called: Freeman Freeman & Smiley LLP
1888 Century Park E Fl 19, Los Angeles (90067-1702)
PHONE..................................310 398-6100
Bruce M Smiley, *Principal*
Jill Draffin, *Partner*
Teresa Tracy, *Partner*
Steven Ziven, *Managing Prtnr*
Elyse Henry, *President*
EMP: 78 **EST:** 1976
SQ FT: 25,000
SALES (est): 21.5MM **Privately Held**
WEB: www.ffslaw.com
SIC: 8111 General practice law office; general practice attorney, lawyer

(P-21561)
FULWIDER AND PATTON LLP
111 W Ocean Blvd, Long Beach (90802-4633)
PHONE..................................310 824-5555
Richard A Bardin, *Managing Prtnr*
Drucker Sommers, *Senior Partner*
Scott Hansen, *Partner*
Katherine McDaniel, *Partner*
David Pitman, *Partner*
EMP: 100 **EST:** 1938
SALES (est): 13.6MM **Privately Held**
WEB: www.fulpat.com
SIC: 8111 General practice law office

(P-21562)
GANG TYRE RAMER & BROWN INC
Also Called: Shandon Properties
132 S Rodeo Dr Ste 306, Beverly Hills (90212-2414)
PHONE..................................310 777-7158
Norman R Tyre, *President*
Donald S Passman, *Treasurer*
Bruce M Ramer, *Vice Pres*
Hermione K Brown, *Admin Sec*
Nancy Boxwell,
EMP: 50 **EST:** 1943
SALES (est): 12.8K **Privately Held**
WEB: www.jordanzucker.com
SIC: 8111 General practice attorney, lawyer

(P-21563)
GIBBS GIDEN LOCHER
1880 Century Park E # 1200, Los Angeles (90067-1621)
PHONE..................................310 552-3400
Richard J Wittbrodt, *Principal*
Kenneth C Gibbs, *Principal*
Joseph M Giden, *Principal*
William D Locher, *Principal*
Amelia Walker, *Admin Sec*

EMP: 70 **EST:** 1978
SQ FT: 27,000
SALES (est): 11.4MM **Privately Held**
WEB: www.gibbsgiden.com
SIC: 8111 General practice attorney, lawyer

(P-21564)
GIBSON DUNN & CRUTCHER LLP (PA)
333 S Grand Ave Ste 4600, Los Angeles (90071-1512)
PHONE..................................213 229-7000
Kenneth M Doran, *Managing Prtnr*
Nicholas Aleksander, *Partner*
Peter Alexiadis, *Partner*
Lisa A Alfaro, *Partner*
Terrence R Allen, *Partner*
EMP: 500 **EST:** 1880
SQ FT: 250,000
SALES (est): 497.3MM **Privately Held**
WEB: www.gibsondunn.com
SIC: 8111 General practice law office

(P-21565)
GILBERT KLLY CRWLEY JNNETT LLP (PA)
550 S Hope St Ste 2200, Los Angeles (90071-3200)
PHONE..................................213 615-7000
Jon H Tisdale, *Managing Prtnr*
Paul Bigley, *Partner*
Timothy Kenna, *Partner*
Arthur J Mc Keon III, *Partner*
Lisa Braham, *President*
EMP: 75 **EST:** 1936
SQ FT: 30,000
SALES (est): 12.6MM **Privately Held**
SIC: 8111 General practice law office

(P-21566)
GILCHRIST & RUTTER PROF CORP
1299 Ocean Ave Ste 900, Santa Monica (90401-1058)
PHONE..................................310 393-4000
Jonathan Gross, *President*
Frank Gooch, *Treasurer*
Brad Cox, *Principal*
Jeanette Rodriguez, *Office Admin*
Paul Rutter, *Admin Sec*
EMP: 50 **EST:** 1985
SQ FT: 3,000
SALES (est): 5.6MM **Privately Held**
WEB: www.gilchristrutter.com
SIC: 8111 General practice attorney, lawyer

(P-21567)
GIPSON HFFMAN PNCONE A PROF CO
1901 Avenue Of The Stars, Los Angeles (90067-6001)
PHONE..................................310 556-4660
Lawrence R Barnett, *President*
Richard P Solomon, *Partner*
Kenneth I Sidle, *President*
Robert E Gipson, *Vice Pres*
Robert H Steinberg, *Vice Pres*
EMP: 70 **EST:** 1982
SQ FT: 27,000
SALES (est): 8.8MM **Privately Held**
WEB: www.ghplaw.com
SIC: 8111 General practice attorney, lawyer; corporate, partnership & business law; bankruptcy law

(P-21568)
GIRARDI KEESE (PA)
1126 Wilshire Blvd, Los Angeles (90017-1904)
PHONE..................................213 977-0211
Thomas V Girardi, *Partner*
Robert M Keese, *Partner*
Elizabeth Escobedo, *President*
Shelby Fujioka, *President*
Luis Jimenez, *Office Mgr*
EMP: 95 **EST:** 1976
SQ FT: 5,000
SALES (est): 10.9MM **Privately Held**
WEB: www.girardikeese.com
SIC: 8111 General practice law office

(P-21569)
GLASER WEIL FINK JACOBS (PA)
10250 Constellation Blvd # 1900, Los Angeles (90067-6229)
PHONE..................................310 553-3000
Terry Christensen, *Managing Prtnr*
Barry E Fink, *Partner*
Patricia L Glaser, *Partner*
John Mason, *Partner*
Richard Volpert, *Partner*
EMP: 160 **EST:** 1988
SQ FT: 76,000
SALES (est): 34.4MM **Privately Held**
WEB: www.glaserweil.com
SIC: 8111 General practice law office

(P-21570)
GORDON EDLSTEIN KRPACK GRANT F
Also Called: Gordon Edelstein & Krepack
3580 Wilshire Blvd # 180, Los Angeles (90010-2501)
PHONE..................................213 739-7000
Roger L Gordon, *Partner*
Mark Edelstein, *Partner*
Richard Felton, *Partner*
Irwin Goldstein, *Partner*
Larry Goldstein, *Partner*
EMP: 50 **EST:** 1985
SALES (est): 12.8MM **Privately Held**
WEB: www.geklaw.com
SIC: 8111 General practice attorney, lawyer

(P-21571)
GREENBERG GLSKER FLDS CLMAN MC
2049 Century Park E # 2600, Los Angeles (90067-3101)
PHONE..................................310 553-3610
Jonathan R Fitzgarrald, *Principal*
ARI B Brumer, *Partner*
Ricardo P Cestero, *Partner*
Stephen Claman, *Partner*
Bert Fields, *Partner*
EMP: 200 **EST:** 1959
SQ FT: 80,000
SALES (est): 38.4MM **Privately Held**
WEB: www.greenbergglusker.com
SIC: 8111 General practice attorney, lawyer

(P-21572)
GREENBERG TRAJRIG LLP
1840 Century Park E # 1900, Los Angeles (90067-2121)
PHONE..................................310 586-7708
Richard Rowan, *Branch Mgr*
Matthew Gershman, *Shareholder*
John McBride, *Shareholder*
Edward Schultz, *Shareholder*
Howard Steinberg, *Shareholder*
EMP: 76
SALES (corp-wide): 1.1B **Privately Held**
WEB: www.eb5insights.com
SIC: 8111 General practice attorney, lawyer
HQ: Greenberg Traurig, Llp
1 Intl Pl Ste 2000
Boston MA 02110

(P-21573)
GRESHAM SAVAGE NOLAN & TILDEN (PA)
550 E Hospitality Ln # 300, San Bernardino (92408-4205)
PHONE..................................619 794-0050
Mark A Ostoich, *President*
Bob Ritter, *Partner*
Paige Gosney, *Shareholder*
Matthew Wilcox, *Shareholder*
Christie Bowman, *President*
EMP: 50 **EST:** 1920
SQ FT: 16,500
SALES (est): 8.5MM **Privately Held**
WEB: www.greshamsavage.com
SIC: 8111 General practice law office

▲ = Import ▼=Export
◆ =Import/Export

(P-21574)

HADSELL STRMER KENY RCHRDSON R

Also Called: Hadsell & Stormer Attorneys
128 N Fair Oaks Ave Fl 2, Pasadena
(91103-3664)
PHONE.................626 585-9600
Dan Stormer, *President*
Barbara Hadsell, *Vice Pres*
Maria Stroud, *Legal Staff*
Nancy Hanna, *Associate*
David Washington, *Associate*
EMP: 51 **EST:** 1991
SALES (est): 6.4MM **Privately Held**
WEB: www.hadsellstormer.com
SIC: 8111 General practice law office; general practice attorney, lawyer

(P-21575)

HAIGHT BROWN & BONESTEEL LLP (PA)

555 S Flwr St Frty Ffth F Forty, Los Angeles
(90071)
PHONE.................213 542-8000
S Christian Stouder, *Managing Prtnr*
Carolyn Harper, *CFO*
Lisa Muzycka, *Vice Pres*
Wendy Franco, *Admin Sec*
Michael Parme, *CIO*
EMP: 80 **EST:** 1980
SQ FT: 36,265
SALES (est): 22.7MM **Privately Held**
WEB: www.hbblaw.com
SIC: 8111 General practice law office

(P-21576)

HARRIS STOCKWELL (PA)

3580 Wilshire Blvd Fl 19, Los Angeles
(90010-2532)
PHONE.................310 277-6669
Steven I Harris, *CEO*
John Billingslea, *Vice Pres*
Anne Bobchick, *Vice Pres*
Anthony Cannizzo, *Vice Pres*
Edward Muehl, *Vice Pres*
EMP: 50 **EST:** 1970
SALES (est): 20MM **Privately Held**
WEB: www.shww.com
SIC: 8111 General practice attorney, lawyer

(P-21577)

HART KING A PROFESSIONAL CORP

4 Hutton Cntre Dr Ste 900, Santa Ana
(92707)
PHONE.................714 432-8700
Robert S Coldren, *President*
Gary R King, *Treasurer*
William R Hart, *Admin Sec*
William Hart, *CTO*
Ann Moriya, *Sales Executive*
EMP: 60 **EST:** 1982
SQ FT: 20,000
SALES (est): 7.9MM **Privately Held**
WEB: www.hartkinglaw.com
SIC: 8111 General practice attorney, lawyer

(P-21578)

HEALTH ADVOCATES (PA)

Also Called: Leibovic & Tysch
13412 Ventura Blvd # 300, Sherman Oaks
(91423-3965)
PHONE.................818 995-9500
Al Leibovic, *Partner*
Aaron J Leibovic, *Partner*
Steve Levine, *COO*
Nuria Morales, *Administration*
Cindy Castellenos, *Business Anlyst*
EMP: 89 **EST:** 1990
SQ FT: 7,500
SALES (est): 8.8MM **Privately Held**
WEB: www.healthadvocates.com
SIC: 8111 General practice law office

(P-21579)

HEMAR ROUSSO & HEALD L L P

Also Called: Hemar & Rousso Attys At Law
15910 Ventura Blvd # 1201, Encino
(91436-2829)
PHONE.................818 501-3800
Richard P Hemar, *Managing Prtnr*
Daniel E Heald, *Partner*
Martin J Rousso, *Partner*

Tammy Dunn, *President*
Mary Granzow, *CIO*
EMP: 50 **EST:** 1974
SQ FT: 10,000
SALES (est): 6.4MM **Privately Held**
SIC: 8111 General practice law office

(P-21580)

HILL FARRER & BURRILL

Also Called: One California Plaza
300 S Grand Ave Ste 3700, Los Angeles
(90071-3147)
PHONE.................213 620-0460
Scott Gilmore, *Partner*
Steven W Bacon, *Partner*
Julia L Birkel, *Partner*
William M Bitting, *Partner*
Michael S Blanton, *Partner*
EMP: 100 **EST:** 1923
SQ FT: 32,000
SALES (est): 13.7MM **Privately Held**
WEB: www.hillfarrer.com
SIC: 8111 General practice law office

(P-21581)

HOGAN LOVELLS US LLP

1999 Avenue Of The Stars, Los Angeles
(90067-6022)
PHONE.................310 785-4600
Neil O'Hanlon, *Manager*
Jennifer Hjerleid, *Admin Sec*
Anthony Webb, *Data Admn*
Tracy Troke, *Project Mgr*
Matthew Hocking, *Technical Staff*
EMP: 63
SALES (corp-wide): 473.1MM **Privately Held**
WEB: www.hlregulation.com
SIC: 8111 Corporate, partnership & business law
PA: Hogan Lovells Us Llp
555 13th St Nw
Washington DC 20004
202 637-5600

(P-21582)

HUESTON HENNIGAN LLP

523 W 6th St Ste 400, Los Angeles
(90014-1208)
PHONE.................213 788-4340
Marshall A Camp, *Partner*
Douglas J Dixon, *Partner*
Alexander C D Giza, *Partner*
Brian J Hennigan, *Partner*
John C Hueston, *Partner*
EMP: 80 **EST:** 2015
SQ FT: 25,000
SALES (est): 10.7MM **Privately Held**
WEB: www.hueston.com
SIC: 8111 General practice attorney, lawyer

(P-21583)

HUNT ORTMANN PALFFY NIEVES

301 N Lake Ave Fl 7, Pasadena
(91101-5118)
PHONE.................626 440-5200
Dale A Ortmann, *Co-Founder*
Thomas Palffy, *Treasurer*
Gordon Hunt, *Principal*
Laurence Lubka, *Principal*
Omel Nieves, *Principal*
EMP: 50 **EST:** 1990
SQ FT: 18,000
SALES (est): 12.3MM **Privately Held**
WEB: www.huntortmann.com
SIC: 8111 General practice law office

(P-21584)

IMHOFF & ASSOCIATES PC

Also Called: Miller and Associates
12424 Wilshire Blvd # 770, Los Angeles
(90025-1065)
PHONE.................310 691-2200
Jim Stefanucci, *Manager*
Vincent Imhoff, *Managing Dir*
Brett Schoneman, *Marketing Staff*
Jason Betts, *Manager*
EMP: 100 **EST:** 2001
SALES (est): 11.4MM **Privately Held**
WEB: www.criminalattorney.com
SIC: 8111 Legal services

(P-21585)

IMPROV TVS INC (PA)

Also Called: Improvstnal Cmedy Traffic Schl
5455 Wilshire Blvd # 1812, Los Angeles
(90036-4201)
PHONE.................323 937-5030
Gary Aleksintser, *President*
Gerson Freidman, *Vice Pres*
Mark Aleksintser, *Admin Sec*
EMP: 50 **EST:** 1988
SQ FT: 3,000
SALES (est): 2.5MM **Privately Held**
SIC: 8299 8111 Vehicle driving school; legal services

(P-21586)

IRELL & MANELLA LLP (PA)

1800 Avenue Of The Stars # 900, Los Angeles (90067-4276)
PHONE.................310 277-1010
Elliot Brown, *Managing Prtnr*
Dick Borow, *Partner*
Chuck Collier, *Partner*
Milt Hyman, *Partner*
Edebeatu Ibekwe, *Partner*
EMP: 400
SQ FT: 154,000
SALES (est): 34.6K **Privately Held**
WEB: www.irell.com
SIC: 8111 General practice law office

(P-21587)

IRELL & MANELLA LLP

840 Nwport Ctr Dr Ste 400, Newport Beach
(92660)
PHONE.................949 760-0991
Nancy Adams, *Manager*
Daniel Lefler, *Partner*
Leah Theilacker, *Admin Sec*
Sherman Richard,
Robert W Stedman,
EMP: 150
SALES (corp-wide): 34.6K **Privately Held**
WEB: www.irell.com
SIC: 8111 General practice attorney, lawyer
PA: Irell & Manella Llp
1800 Avenue Of The Stars # 900
Los Angeles CA 90067
310 277-1010

(P-21588)

IVIE MCNEILL WYATT A PROF LAW

444 S Flower St Ste 1800, Los Angeles
(90071-2919)
PHONE.................213 489-0028
Robert H Mc Neill Jr, *President*
Marie Maurice, *Partner*
Rickey Ivie, *Vice Pres*
Keith Wyatt, *Managing Dir*
Antonio Kizzie,
EMP: 50 **EST:** 1971
SALES (est): 9.4MM **Privately Held**
WEB: www.imwlaw.com
SIC: 8111 General practice attorney, lawyer

(P-21589)

JACKOWAY TYREMAN WERTHEIMER AU

1925 Century Park E Fl 2, Los Angeles
(90067-2701)
PHONE.................310 553-0305
Barry Hirsch, *President*
Eric Weissler, *Shareholder*
Laurie Anderson, *Legal Staff*
EMP: 100 **EST:** 1976
SQ FT: 3,000
SALES (est): 9.3MM **Privately Held**
WEB: www.jtwamm.com
SIC: 8111 General practice law office

(P-21590)

JACKSON TIDUS A LAW CORP (PA)

2030 Main St Ste 1200, Irvine
(92614-7256)
P.O. Box 19703 (92623-9703)
PHONE.................949 752-8585
M Alim Malik, *CEO*
James Demarco, *President*
Thomas D Peckenpaugh, *President*
Ruth Mijuskovic, *CEO*
Michael Tidus, *CFO*

EMP: 70 **EST:** 1983
SQ FT: 23,000
SALES (est): 11.3MM **Privately Held**
WEB: www.jdtplaw.com
SIC: 8111 General practice attorney, lawyer

(P-21591)

JEFFER MNGELS BTLR MTCHELL LLP (PA)

Also Called: Jmbm
1900 Avenue Of The Stars 7th, Los Angeles
(90067-4301)
PHONE.................310 203-8080
Bruce P Jeffer, *Partner*
James R Butler Jr, *Partner*
Dan E Chambers, *Partner*
Greg Cordrey, *Partner*
Stan M Gibson, *Partner*
▲ **EMP:** 190 **EST:** 1981
SALES (est): 46.2MM **Privately Held**
WEB: www.jmbm.com
SIC: 8111 General practice attorney, lawyer

(P-21592)

JONES DAY LIMITED PARTNERSHIP

3161 Michelson Dr Ste 800, Irvine
(92612-4408)
PHONE.................949 851-3939
EMP: 85
SQ FT: 22,500
SALES (corp-wide): 663.1MM **Privately Held**
WEB: www.jonesday.com
SIC: 8111 Legal Services Office
PA: Jones Day Limited Partnership
901 Lakeside Ave E Ste 2
Cleveland OH 44114
216 586-3939

(P-21593)

JOSEPH C SANSONE COMPANY (PA)

Also Called: Tobin Lucks
21300 Victory Blvd # 300, Woodland Hills
(91367-2525)
P.O. Box 4502 (91365-4502)
PHONE.................818 226-3400
Irvin Lucks, *Managing Prtnr*
Edwin Lucks, *Partner*
Donald Tobin, *Partner*
Irv Lucks, *Managing Prtnr*
Kimberly G Davidson, *CIO*
EMP: 97 **EST:** 1982
SALES (est): 25.5MM **Privately Held**
WEB: www.tobinlucks.com
SIC: 8111 General practice law office

(P-21594)

KASDAN SMNDS RILEY VAUGHAN LLP (PA)

19900 Macarthur Blvd # 850, Irvine
(92612-8422)
PHONE.................949 851-9000
Kenneth Kasdan, *Partner*
EMP: 56 **EST:** 2000
SQ FT: 20,000
SALES (est): 5.3MM **Privately Held**
SIC: 8111 General practice law office

(P-21595)

KATTEN MUCHIN ROSENMAN LLP

515 S Flower St, Los Angeles
(90071-2201)
PHONE.................310 788-4498
Susan Taylor, *Branch Mgr*
EMP: 75
SALES (corp-wide): 195.6MM **Privately Held**
WEB: www.katten.com
SIC: 8111 General practice law office
PA: Katten Muchin Rosenman Llp
525 W Monroe St Ste 1900
Chicago IL 60661
312 902-5200

(P-21596)

KATTEN MUCHIN ROSENMAN LLP

2029 Century Park E # 2600, Los Angeles
(90067-3012)
PHONE.................310 788-4400

Tanya Russell, *Branch Mgr*
Michael Jacobson, *Partner*
Zia Modabber, *Partner*
Bernadette Aronson, *Executive Asst*
Travis Mogren, *IT/INT Sup*
EMP: 75
SALES (corp-wide): 195.6MM **Privately
Held**
WEB: www.katten.com
SIC: 8111 General practice law office
PA: Katten Muchin Rosenman Llp
525 W Monroe St Ste 1900
Chicago IL 60661
312 902-5200

(P-21597)
**KEESAL YOUNG LOGAN A PROF
CORP (PA)**
400 Oceangate Ste 1400, Long Beach
(90802-4325)
PHONE..............................562 436-2000
Samuel A Keesal Jr, *CEO*
Lisa Beazley, *Shareholder*
Chris Stecher, *Shareholder*
J Stephen Young, *Corp Secy*
Maricel Schilt, *Admin Sec*
EMP: 90 **EST:** 1970
SQ FT: 65,000
SALES (est): 20.5MM **Privately Held**
WEB: www.kyl.com
SIC: 8111 General practice law office

(P-21598)
**KING HLMES PTERNO
SORIANO LLP**
1900 Avenue Of The Stars, Los Angeles
(90067-4301)
PHONE..............................310 282-8989
Howard King, *Partner*
Keith Holmes, *Partner*
Peter Paterno, *Partner*
Lori Soriano, *Partner*
Aurora Gomez, *President*
EMP: 50 **EST:** 1991
SALES (est): 8.5MM **Privately Held**
WEB: www.khpslaw.com
SIC: 8111 General practice attorney,
lawyer

(P-21599)
**KLEIN DENATALE GOLDNER ET
AL (PA)**
Also Called: Klein Dntale Gldner Cper Rsnli
4550 California Ave Fl 2, Bakersfield
(93309-7012)
P.O. Box 11172 (93389-1172)
PHONE..............................661 401-7755
Anthony J Klein, *Partner*
Anthony Klein, *Senior Partner*
Jennifer A Adams, *Partner*
Hagop T Bedoyan, *Partner*
David J Cooper, *Partner*
EMP: 103 **EST:** 2007
SQ FT: 25,000
SALES (est): 13.5MM **Privately Held**
WEB: www.kleinlaw.com
SIC: 8111 General practice attorney,
lawyer

(P-21600)
**KNOBBE MARTENS OLSON
BEAR LLP (PA)**
2040 Main St Fl 14, Irvine (92614-8214)
PHONE..............................949 760-0404
Steven J Nataupsky, *Managing Prtnr*
William B Bunker, *Partner*
Drew S Hamilton, *Partner*
Ned Israelsen, *Partner*
Baraa Kahf, *Partner*
EMP: 350 **EST:** 1962
SQ FT: 120,000
SALES (est): 66.7MM **Privately Held**
WEB: www.knobbe.com
SIC: 8111 General practice law office

(P-21601)
**KOELLER NBKER CRLSON
HLUCK LLP (PA)**
3 Park Plz Ste 1500, Irvine (92614-8558)
P.O. Box 19799 (92623-9799)
PHONE..............................949 864-3400
Keith Koeller, *Managing Prtnr*
Bob Carlson, *Managing Prtnr*
William Haluck, *Managing Prtnr*
Bill Nebeker, *Managing Prtnr*

Erin Moore, *Office Mgr*
EMP: 56 **EST:** 2005
SALES (est): 21.2MM **Privately Held**
WEB: www.knchlaw.com
SIC: 8111 General practice law office

(P-21602)
**LA FOLLETTE JOHNSON DE
HAAS (PA)**
701 N Brand Blvd Ste 600, Glendale
(91203-9877)
PHONE..............................213 426-3600
Daren T Johnson, *President*
Michael L Bazzo, *Shareholder*
Donald Fesler, *Shareholder*
Mark Stewart, *Shareholder*
James Wallace, *Shareholder*
EMP: 105 **EST:** 1953
SALES (est): 17.9MM **Privately Held**
WEB: www.ljdfa.com
SIC: 8111 General practice law office

(P-21603)
**LAQUER URBAN CLFFORD
HODGE LLP**
225 S Lake Ave Ste 200, Pasadena
(91101-3009)
PHONE..............................626 449-1882
Chris Laquer, *Owner*
Robert Scott Clifford, *Partner*
Mark Hallen, *Partner*
Brian Ray Hodge, *Partner*
Michael A Urban, *Partner*
EMP: 56 **EST:** 1972
SQ FT: 5,000
SALES (est): 3.3MM **Privately Held**
WEB: www.luch.com
SIC: 8111 General practice attorney,
lawyer

(P-21604)
LATHAM & WATKINS LLP (PA)
555 W 5th St Ste 300, Los Angeles
(90013-1020)
PHONE..............................213 485-1234
David Gordon, *Partner*
Christopher Allen, *Partner*
Christopher J Allen, *Partner*
James Beaubien, *Partner*
Joseph Bevash, *Partner*
EMP: 570 **EST:** 1934
SALES (est): 1.1B **Privately Held**
WEB: www.lw.com
SIC: 8111 General practice attorney,
lawyer

(P-21605)
**LAW OFFCES LES ZEVE A PROF
COR**
30 Corporate Park Ste 450, Irvine
(92606-3401)
PHONE..............................714 848-7920
Les Zieve, *Principal*
Erin McCartney, *Partner*
Joanna Develasco, *Officer*
Mark Kayton, *Principal*
Jennifer Spagnoli, *Department Mgr*
EMP: 105 **EST:** 1991
SQ FT: 1,000
SALES (est): 10.1MM **Privately Held**
SIC: 8111 General practice attorney,
lawyer

(P-21606)
**LAW OFFICES BERGLUND &
JOHNSON (PA)**
Also Called: Berglund & Johnson Law Office
21550 Oxnard St Ste 900, Woodland Hills
(91367-7144)
PHONE..............................951 276-4783
David W Berglund, *Partner*
Daniel W Johnson, *Partner*
Christopher Townsley, *Litigation*
EMP: 56 **EST:** 1975
SALES (est): 2.5MM **Privately Held**
WEB: www.berglundandjohnson.com
SIC: 8111 General practice law office

(P-21607)
LE BEAU THELEN LLP
5001 E Commercecenter Dr, Bakersfield
(93309-1659)
P.O. Box 12092 (93389-2092)
PHONE..............................661 325-8962
Bernard Le Beau, *Partner*

Thomas Crear, *Partner*
David Lampe, *Partner*
Thomas Mc Intosh, *Partner*
Dennis Thelen, *Partner*
EMP: 52 **EST:** 1985
SALES (est): 5MM **Privately Held**
WEB: www.lebeauthelen.com
SIC: 8111 General practice attorney,
lawyer

(P-21608)
**LEGAL SOLUTIONS HOLDINGS
INC**
Also Called: Getmedlegal
955 Overland Ct Ste 200, San Dimas
(91773-1747)
PHONE..............................800 244-3495
Greg Webber, *CEO*
Kenneth Gleockler, *CFO*
Keahi Kakugawa, *Principal*
Chris Bermudez, *Marketing Staff*
EMP: 237 **EST:** 1986
SALES (est): 29.3MM **Privately Held**
WEB: www.getmedlegal.com
SIC: 8111 Legal services

(P-21609)
**LEWIS BRSBOIS BSGARD
SMITH LLP**
28765 Single Oak Dr # 14, Temecula
(92590-3661)
PHONE..............................951 252-6150
Robert F Lewis, *Managing Prtnr*
EMP: 81
SALES (corp-wide): 284.9MM **Privately
Held**
WEB: www.lewisbrisbois.com
SIC: 8111 General practice law office
PA: Lewis Brisbois Bisgaard & Smith Llp
633 W 5th St Ste 4000
Los Angeles CA 90071
213 250-1800

(P-21610)
**LEWIS BRSBOIS BSGARD
SMITH LLP (PA)**
633 W 5th St Ste 4000, Los Angeles
(90071-2074)
PHONE..............................213 250-1800
Robert F Lewis, *Managing Prtnr*
William S Helfand, *Senior Partner*
Judd Uhl, *Senior Partner*
Christopher P Bisgaard, *Partner*
Roy M Brisbois, *Partner*
EMP: 650
SQ FT: 80,000
SALES (est): 284.9MM **Privately Held**
WEB: www.lewisbrisbois.com
SIC: 8111 General practice law office

(P-21611)
**LEWIS BRSBOIS BSGARD
SMITH LLP**
650 E Hospitality Ln # 600, San Bernardino
(92408-3535)
PHONE..............................909 387-1130
John Lowenthal, *Manager*
Carrie Mattison, *Assistant*
EMP: 81
SQ FT: 6,203
SALES (corp-wide): 284.9MM **Privately
Held**
WEB: www.lewisbrisbois.com
SIC: 8111 General practice law office
PA: Lewis Brisbois Bisgaard & Smith Llp
633 W 5th St Ste 4000
Los Angeles CA 90071
213 250-1800

(P-21612)
**LEWIS MARENSTEIN WICKE
SHERWIN**
20750 Ventura Blvd # 400, Woodland Hills
(91364-2390)
PHONE..............................818 703-6000
Michael B Lewis, *Partner*
Alan B Marenstein, *Partner*
Robert Sherwin, *Partner*
Thomas Wicke, *Partner*
Stephanie Rowlett, *Admin Sec*
EMP: 50 **EST:** 1971
SQ FT: 15,000
SALES (est): 5.9MM **Privately Held**
WEB: www.lmwslaw.com
SIC: 8111 General practice law office

(P-21613)
LFK LAW
9595 Wilshire Blvd # 900, Beverly Hills
(90212-2512)
PHONE..............................310 300-8464
Louis Fkmontcho, *CFO*
EMP: 55 **EST:** 2018
SALES (est): 1.2MM **Privately Held**
SIC: 8111 Legal services

(P-21614)
LIMNEXUS LLP (PA)
707 Wilshire Blvd # 4600, Los Angeles
(90017-3612)
PHONE..............................213 955-9500
John S C Lim, *Administration*
Pio Kim, *Partner*
Lisa Yang, *General Mgr*
Luong Eva, *Accounting Mgr*
Bryan Sheldon,
EMP: 65 **EST:** 2017
SALES (est): 9.9MM **Privately Held**
WEB: www.limnexus.com
SIC: 8111 General practice law office

(P-21615)
LINER LLP
Also Called: Liner Law
1100 Glendon Ave 14th, Los Angeles
(90024-3503)
PHONE..............................310 500-3500
Stuart A Liner, *Managing Prtnr*
Mitchell C Regenstreif, *Manager*
EMP: 104 **EST:** 1996
SQ FT: 21,000
SALES (est): 24.4MM **Privately Held**
WEB: www.bottlefish.com
SIC: 8111 General practice law office
HQ: Dla Piper Llp (Us)
6225 Smith Ave Ste 200
Baltimore MD 21209
410 580-3000

(P-21616)
LOEB & LOEB LLP (PA)
10100 Santa Monica Blvd # 2200, Los An-
geles (90067-4120)
PHONE..............................310 282-2000
Barry I Slotnick, *Chairman*
Kenneth B Anderson, *Partner*
Daniel D Frohling, *Partner*
Douglas N Masters, *Partner*
Mickey Mayerson, *Partner*
EMP: 134 **EST:** 1909
SALES (est): 66.8MM **Privately Held**
WEB: www.loeb.com
SIC: 8111 General practice attorney,
lawyer

(P-21617)
**LOS ANGELES DEPENDENCY
LAWYERS**
901 Corporate Center Dr # 52, Monterey
Park (91754-7630)
PHONE..............................323 859-5546
Kenneth Krekorian, *Owner*
Melissa Tellez, *Admin Sec*
Katie McShane, *Social Worker*
Alexa Bicos, *Clerk*
EMP: 83 **EST:** 2017
SALES (est): 34.6MM **Privately Held**
WEB: www.ladlinc.org
SIC: 8111 General practice attorney,
lawyer

(P-21618)
**LOUIE ALMEIDA & SETTLER
(PA)**
303 N Glenoaks Blvd # 400, Burbank
(91502-1116)
PHONE..............................818 461-9559
Peter Louie, *Partner*
David Stettler, *Senior Partner*
Donald Leiber, *Partner*
Sandra De Tovar, *Executive*
Nishitha Reddy, *Nurse*
EMP: 54 **EST:** 1986
SALES (est): 3.9MM **Privately Held**
WEB: www.louielaw.com
SIC: 8111 General practice law office

(P-21619)
LYNBERG & WATKINS A PROF CORP (PA)
Also Called: Lynberg & Watkins Attys At Law
1150 S Olive St Fl 18, Los Angeles
(90015-3989)
PHONE................................213 624-8700
Norman J Watkins, *President*
Charles A Lynberg, *President*
Randall J Peters, *CEO*
Sierra Fruhn, *Assistant*
Susan Susebach, *Assistant*
EMP: 50
SQ FT: 32,108
SALES (est): 13.8MM **Privately Held**
WEB: www.lynberg.com
SIC: 8111 General practice law office

(P-21620)
MALCOLM & CISNEROS A LAW CORP
Also Called: Malcolm Cisneros
2112 Business Center Dr # 100, Irvine
(92612-7136)
PHONE................................949 252-1039
William Malcolm, *CEO*
Arturo Cisneros, *CFO*
Ashley Malcolm, *QC Mgr*
Courtney Domer, *Manager*
EMP: 110 EST: 1992
SALES (est): 12.3MM **Privately Held**
WEB: www.malcolmcisneros.com
SIC: 8111 General practice law office

(P-21621)
MANATT PHELPS & PHILLIPS LLP
695 Town Center Dr # 1400, Costa Mesa
(92626-7223)
PHONE................................714 371-2500
Shierley Hands, *Manager*
John Grosvenor, *Partner*
Tracey Dunn, *President*
EMP: 50
SALES (corp-wide): 208.5MM **Privately Held**
WEB: www.manatt.com
SIC: 8111 General practice attorney, lawyer
PA: Manatt, Phelps & Phillips, Llp
2049 Century Park E # 1700
Los Angeles CA 90067
310 312-4000

(P-21622)
MANNING KASS ELLROD RMREZ TRST (PA)
801 S Figueroa St Fl 15, Los Angeles
(90017-5504)
PHONE................................213 624-6900
Steven D Manning, *Managing Prtnr*
Steve Manning, *Partner*
Steven Manning, *Partner*
Martha Alfaro, *Admin Sec*
Linda Lopez, *Admin Sec*
EMP: 150 EST: 1994
SALES (est): 33.9MM **Privately Held**
WEB: www.manningllp.com
SIC: 8111 General practice attorney, lawyer

(P-21623)
MCGUIREWOODS LLP
1800 Century Park E Fl 8, Los Angeles
(90067-1501)
PHONE................................310 315-8200
Richard Grant, *Managing Prtnr*
Thomas Becket, *Vice Pres*
Betty Smith, *Sales Staff*
Simon Davidson, *Counsel*
Leslie M Werlin Jr, *Manager*
EMP: 50
SALES (corp-wide): 157.2MM **Privately Held**
WEB: www.mcguirewoods.com
SIC: 8111 General practice attorney, lawyer
PA: Mcguirewoods Llp
800 E Canal St
Richmond VA 23219
804 775-1000

(P-21624)
MCGUIREWOODS LLP
355 S Grand Ave Ste 4200, Los Angeles
(90071-3103)
PHONE................................213 627-2268
David P Pusateri, *Branch Mgr*
Gregory Evans, *Managing Prtnr*
EMP: 50
SALES (corp-wide): 157.2MM **Privately Held**
WEB: www.mcguirewoods.com
SIC: 8111 General practice attorney, lawyer
PA: Mcguirewoods Llp
800 E Canal St
Richmond VA 23219
804 775-1000

(P-21625)
MCKOOL SMITH HENNIGAN
300 S Grand Ave Ste 2900, Los Angeles
(90071-3139)
PHONE................................213 694-1200
J Michael Hennigan, *Partner*
Bruce Bennett, *Partner*
James W Mercer, *Partner*
Bruce Mac Leod,
EMP: 90 EST: 1995
SQ FT: 35,000
SALES (est): 9.5MM **Privately Held**
WEB: www.mckoolsmith.com
SIC: 8111 General practice attorney, lawyer

(P-21626)
MED-LEGAL LLC (PA)
955 Overland Ct Ste 200, San Dimas
(91773-1747)
PHONE................................626 653-5160
Moonesh Arora, *CEO*
Michael Salzano, *President*
Gregory Webber, *Bd of Directors*
Kenneth E Gleockler, *Vice Pres*
James Tuthill, *Executive*
EMP: 136 EST: 2010
SALES (est): 14MM **Privately Held**
WEB: www.getmedlegal.com
SIC: 8111 Legal aid service

(P-21627)
MELMET STEVEN J LAW OFC
2912 Daimler St, Santa Ana (92705-5811)
PHONE................................949 263-1000
EMP: 70
SALES (est): 10MM **Privately Held**
SIC: 8111 6531 Law Officereal Estate Agent

(P-21628)
MICHAEL SULLIVAN & ASSOC LLP
400 Continental Blvd # 250, El Segundo
(90245-5076)
P.O. Box 85059, San Diego (92186-5059)
PHONE................................310 337-4480
Michael W Sullivan, *Partner*
Bart R Sullivan, *Senior Partner*
Eric H De Wames, *Managing Prtnr*
Megan Sullivan, *Managing Prtnr*
Ivette Lopez, *Office Spvr*
EMP: 147 EST: 2012
SALES (est): 22.6MM **Privately Held**
WEB: www.sullivanattorneys.com
SIC: 8111 General practice attorney, lawyer

(P-21629)
MILBANK TWEED HDLEY MCCLOY LLP
Also Called: Milbank Global Securities
2029 Century Park E # 3300, Los Angeles
(90067-2901)
PHONE................................424 386-4000
David C Frauman, *Director*
Lona Kelly, *Vice Pres*
Dino T Barajas,
Patrick Park, *Director*
Joi Ruther, *Manager*
EMP: 120
SQ FT: 40,000
SALES (corp-wide): 133.6MM **Privately Held**
WEB: www.milbank.com
SIC: 8111 Corporate, partnership & business law

PA: Milbank Llp
55 Hudson Yards
New York NY 10001
212 530-5000

(P-21630)
MITCHELL SILBERBERG KNUPP LLP (PA)
Also Called: Mitchell Slbrberg Knupp Fndtio
2049 Century Park E Fl 18, Los Angeles
(90067-3120)
PHONE................................310 312-2000
Jeffrey K Eisen, *Principal*
Jeffrey L Richardson, *Partner*
Steven M Schneider, *Partner*
Thomas P Lambert, *Managing Prtnr*
Kevin E Gaut, *COO*
EMP: 260 EST: 1908
SALES (est): 27.7K **Privately Held**
WEB: www.msk.com
SIC: 8111 General practice law office; real estate law; taxation law; labor & employment law

(P-21631)
MOADDEL LAW FIRM APC
3435 Wilshire Blvd # 243, Los Angeles
(90010-1901)
PHONE................................323 999-5099
Daniel Moaddel, *President*
Claudia Martinez, *Associate*
EMP: 50 EST: 2014
SALES (est): 4.6MM **Privately Held**
WEB: www.mdlfirm.com
SIC: 8111 General practice law office

(P-21632)
MOORE LAW GROUP A PROF CORP
3710 S Susan St Ste 210, Santa Ana
(92704-6956)
P.O. Box 25145 (92799-5145)
PHONE................................714 431-2000
Harvey Moore, *President*
Donnie Pangburn, *Treasurer*
Donna Aguirre,
Chad M Biggerstaff,
Vincent Creta,
EMP: 65 EST: 2008
SALES (est): 7.1MM **Privately Held**
WEB: www.collectmoore.com
SIC: 8111 General practice law office

(P-21633)
MORRIS POLICH & PURDY LLP (PA)
1055 W 7th St Ste 2400, Los Angeles
(90017-2550)
PHONE................................213 891-9100
Theodore D Levin, *Partner*
Jeff Barron, *Partner*
William M Betley, *Partner*
Anthony Brazil, *Partner*
James Chantland, *Partner*
EMP: 100 EST: 1969
SQ FT: 40,000
SALES (est): 18.9MM **Privately Held**
WEB: www.mpplaw.leveelabs.com
SIC: 8111 General practice attorney, lawyer

(P-21634)
MORRISON & FOERSTER LLP
707 Wilshire Blvd # 6000, Los Angeles
(90017-3501)
PHONE................................213 892-5200
Gregory Koltun, *Managing Prtnr*
John W Alden Jr, *Partner*
Mark T Gillett, *Partner*
Dan Marmalefsky, *Partner*
A Max Olson, *Partner*
EMP: 250
SALES (corp-wide): 392.2MM **Privately Held**
WEB: www.mofo.com
SIC: 8111 General practice attorney, lawyer
PA: Morrison & Foerster Llp
425 Market St Fl 32
San Francisco CA 94105
415 268-7000

(P-21635)
MULLEN & HENZELL LLP
112 E Victoria St, Santa Barbara
(93101-2068)
P.O. Box 789 (93102-0789)
PHONE................................805 966-1501
Dennis W Reilly, *Mng Member*
Erin Costigan, *President*
Brooke McDermott, *Bd of Directors*
Greg Faulkner, *Officer*
Nicole Herrera, *Admin Sec*
EMP: 50 EST: 1931
SQ FT: 15,000
SALES (est): 9.5MM **Privately Held**
WEB: www.mullenlaw.com
SIC: 8111 Real estate law; will, estate & trust law; general practice attorney, lawyer

(P-21636)
MUNGER TOLLES & OLSON LLP
350 S Grand Ave Fl 50, Los Angeles
(90071-3426)
PHONE................................213 683-9100
Sandra Seville-Jones, *Partner*
Thomas B Edwards, *Exec Dir*
Caroline Litten, *Litigation*
EMP: 168 EST: 2001
SALES (est): 27.4MM **Privately Held**
WEB: www.mto.com
SIC: 8111 Corporate, partnership & business law

(P-21637)
MUNGER TOLLES OLSON FOUNDATION (PA)
350 S Grand Ave Fl 50, Los Angeles
(90071-3426)
PHONE................................213 683-9100
O'Malley M Miller, *CEO*
Robert Johnson, *President*
Larry Kleinberg, *CFO*
Mark Helm, *Vice Pres*
Steven B Weisburd, *Vice Pres*
EMP: 420 EST: 1962
SQ FT: 100,000
SALES: 1.2MM **Privately Held**
SIC: 8111 General practice attorney, lawyer

(P-21638)
MURCHISON & CUMMING LLP (PA)
Also Called: M & C
801 S Grand Ave Ste 900, Los Angeles
(90017-4624)
PHONE................................213 623-7400
Friedrich W Seitz, *Partner*
Gina Bazaz, *Senior Partner*
Edmund G Farrell, *Senior Partner*
Edmund Farrell, *Senior Partner*
Guy R Gruppie, *Senior Partner*
EMP: 100 EST: 1952
SQ FT: 30,000
SALES (est): 26.7MM **Privately Held**
WEB: www.murchisonlaw.com
SIC: 8111 General practice law office

(P-21639)
MURPHY & BEANE INC
5901 Green Valley Cir # 145, Culver City
(90230-6991)
PHONE................................310 649-4470
Edward J Murphy Sr, *Manager*
Rose De Leon, *Supervisor*
EMP: 63
SALES (corp-wide): 8MM **Privately Held**
WEB: www.murphy-beane.com
SIC: 8111 6411 General practice attorney, lawyer; insurance adjusters
PA: Murphy & Beane Inc
15 Broad St Ste 305
Boston MA 02109
617 723-0871

(P-21640)
MURTAUGH MYER NLSON TRGLIA LLP
2603 Main St Ste 900, Irvine (92614-4270)
P.O. Box 19627 (92623-9627)
PHONE................................949 794-4000
Michael J Nelson, *Managing Prtnr*
Rod Stern, *Senior Partner*
Lawrencea Treglia, *Senior Partner*

Harry A Halkowich, *Partner*
Mark S Himmelstein, *Partner*
EMP: 60 **EST:** 1979
SALES (est): 10MM **Privately Held**
WEB: www.murtaughlaw.com
SIC: 8111 General practice law office

(P-21641)
MUSICK PEELER & GARRETT LLP (PA)
624 S Grand Ave Ste 2000, Los Angeles
(90017-3321)
PHONE................................213 629-7600
R Joseph De Briyn, *Managing Prtnr*
Peter J Diedrich, *Partner*
Susan Field, *Partner*
Edward Landrey, *Partner*
Catherine Lee, *Partner*
EMP: 168 **EST:** 1937
SQ FT: 100,000
SALES (est): 39.5MM **Privately Held**
WEB: www.musickpeeler.com
SIC: 8111 General practice law office; taxation law; corporate, partnership & business law; labor & employment law

(P-21642)
NATIONAL ATTNY COLLECTION SVCS
700 N Brand Blvd Fl 2, Glendale
(91203-1247)
PHONE................................818 547-9760
A Donovan, *CEO*
John Weinstein, *CFO*
EMP: 251 **EST:** 2005
SALES (est): 5.5MM **Privately Held**
SIC: 8111 Debt collection law

(P-21643)
NATIONWIDE LEGAL LLC (PA)
Also Called: Headquarters
1609 James M Wood Blvd, Los Angeles
(90015-1005)
P.O. Box 15012 (90015-0012)
PHONE................................213 249-9999
Tony Davoodi, *CEO*
Joe Caamal, *COO*
Louis Nelson, *Exec VP*
Michael Lazcano, *Senior VP*
Sigrid Propper, *Executive*
EMP: 129 **EST:** 2007
SALES (est): 29.8MM **Privately Held**
WEB: www.nationwidelegal.com
SIC: 8111 General practice attorney, lawyer

(P-21644)
NEWMEYER & DILLION LLP (PA)
895 Dove St Fl 5, Newport Beach
(92660-2999)
PHONE................................949 854-7000
Gregory L Dillion, *Partner*
Michael S Cucchissi, *Partner*
Joseph A Ferrentino, *Partner*
John A O Hara, *Partner*
Jon J Janecek, *Partner*
EMP: 115 **EST:** 1984
SQ FT: 52,000 **Privately Held**
WEB: www.newmeyerdillion.com
SIC: 8111 General practice attorney, lawyer

(P-21645)
NOSSAMAN LLP (PA)
777 S Figueroa St # 3400, Los Angeles
(90017-5834)
PHONE................................213 612-7800
E George Joseph, *Managing Prtnr*
Ashley K Dunning, *Partner*
Barbara Virga, *Bd of Directors*
Christopher Flaherty, *Officer*
Amy Freeman, *Officer*
EMP: 74 **EST:** 1944
SQ FT: 20,000
SALES (est): 43.4MM **Privately Held**
WEB: www.nossaman.com
SIC: 8111 General practice attorney, lawyer

(P-21646)
NOSSAMAN LLP
777 S Figueroa St # 3400, Los Angeles
(90017-5834)
PHONE................................760 918-0500
EMP: 51

SALES (corp-wide): 43.4MM **Privately Held**
WEB: www.nossaman.com
SIC: 8111 General practice attorney, lawyer
PA: Nossaman Llp
777 S Figueroa St # 3400
Los Angeles CA 90017
213 612-7800

(P-21647)
NOSSAMAN LLP
18101 Von Karman Ave # 1800, Irvine
(92612-0177)
PHONE................................949 833-7800
George Joseph, *Partner*
Elena Apodaca, *Admin Sec*
Robin Golder, *Admin Sec*
Patricia Cooper, *Administration*
Chris Hubbard, *Information Mgr*
EMP: 51
SALES (corp-wide): 43.4MM **Privately Held**
WEB: www.nossaman.com
SIC: 8111 General practice attorney, lawyer
PA: Nossaman Llp
777 S Figueroa St # 3400
Los Angeles CA 90017
213 612-7800

(P-21648)
OMELVENY & MYERS LLP (PA)
400 S Hope St Fl 19, Los Angeles
(90071-2801)
PHONE................................213 430-6000
Arthur Culvahouse Jr, *Managing Prtnr*
Geoff Kuziemko, *Partner*
Christopher Brearton, *Managing Prtnr*
Stephen Brody, *Managing Prtnr*
Riccardo Celli, *Managing Prtnr*
EMP: 850 **EST:** 1885
SQ FT: 250,000
SALES (est): 208.1MM **Privately Held**
WEB: www.omm.com
SIC: 8111 General practice law office

(P-21649)
ONE LLP (PA)
4000 Macarthur Blvd # 500, Newport Beach
(92660-2517)
PHONE................................949 502-2870
Peter R Afrasiabi, *Partner*
Chris Arledge, *Partner*
Robin Golder, *Legal Staff*
Nate Lichtenberger, *Legal Staff*
Stacey Messina, *Legal Staff*
EMP: 73 **EST:** 2012
SALES (est): 4.9MM **Privately Held**
WEB: www.onellp.com
SIC: 8111 General practice law office

(P-21650)
PACHULSKI STANG ZEHL JONES LLP (PA)
Also Called: Pszyjw
10100 Santa Monica Blvd # 1300, Los Angeles (90067-4114)
PHONE................................310 277-6910
Richard M Pachulski, *President*
Tanya Thompson, *President*
Airika Kimble, *Officer*
Dean A Ziehl, *Vice Pres*
Melisa Desjardien, *Admin Sec*
EMP: 90 **EST:** 1983
SQ FT: 21,000
SALES (est): 33.5MM **Privately Held**
WEB: www.pszjlaw.com
SIC: 8111 General practice law office

(P-21651)
PALMIERI TYLER WNER WLHELM WLD
1900 Main St Ste 700, Irvine (92614-7328)
P.O. Box 19712 (92623-9712)
PHONE................................949 851-9400
James E Wilhelm, *Partner*
Mike Greene, *Partner*
Robert Ihrke, *Partner*
David Parr, *Partner*
L Richard Rawls, *Partner*
EMP: 100 **EST:** 1986
SQ FT: 34,000

SALES (est): 15.3MM **Privately Held**
WEB: www.ptwww.com
SIC: 8111 General practice attorney, lawyer

(P-21652)
PALUMBO LAWYERS LLP (PA)
20 Journey, Aliso Viejo (92656-3317)
PHONE................................949 442-0300
Diane O Palumbo, *Partner*
Jay Bergstrom, *Partner*
Julia Bergstrom, *Partner*
Patty Holt, *Finance Dir*
Donna Mann, *Legal Staff*
EMP: 52 **EST:** 2003
SALES (est): 7.9MM **Privately Held**
WEB: www.palumbolawyers.com
SIC: 8111 General practice attorney, lawyer

(P-21653)
PARKER MILLIKEN CLARK OHAR
555 S Flower St Ste 3000, Los Angeles
(90071-2440)
PHONE................................818 784-8087
Larry Ivanjack, *Shareholder*
Gary Ganchrow, *Shareholder*
David McLeod, *Shareholder*
Gary Meyer, *Shareholder*
Gary A Meyer, *Shareholder*
EMP: 70 **EST:** 1914
SQ FT: 25,000
SALES (est): 10.2MM **Privately Held**
WEB: www.parkermilliken.com
SIC: 8111 General practice law office

(P-21654)
PARKER STANBURY LLP (PA)
444 S Flower St Ste 1900, Los Angeles
(90071-2909)
PHONE................................619 528-1259
Robert Lo Presti, *Partner*
Graham J Baldwin, *Partner*
John D Barrett Jr, *Partner*
John W Dannhausen, *Partner*
Douglas M Degrade, *Partner*
EMP: 60 **EST:** 1922
SQ FT: 17,152
SALES (est): 10.1MM **Privately Held**
WEB: www.parkstan.com
SIC: 8111 General practice law office

(P-21655)
PATTERSON RITNER LOCKWOOD (PA)
620 N Brand Blvd Fl 3, Glendale
(91203-4221)
P.O. Box 361, Pacific Palisades (90272-0361)
PHONE................................818 241-8001
William F Ritner, *Partner*
Harold H Gartner III, *Partner*
John A Jurich, *Partner*
Clyde E Lockwood, *Partner*
James McGahan, *Partner*
EMP: 50 **EST:** 1968
SQ FT: 16,000
SALES (est): 2.6MM **Privately Held**
WEB: www.pattersonlockwood.com
SIC: 8111 General practice law office

(P-21656)
PAUL HASTINGS LLP (PA)
515 S Flower St Fl 25, Los Angeles
(90071-2228)
PHONE................................213 683-6000
Greg Nitzkowski, *Partner*
George W Abele, *Partner*
Jesse H Austin, *Partner*
Elena R Baca, *Partner*
Dino T Barajas, *Partner*
EMP: 1639 **EST:** 2011
SQ FT: 209,000
SALES (est): 851.8MM **Privately Held**
WEB: www.paulhastings.com
SIC: 8111 General practice law office

(P-21657)
PAYNE & FEARS LLP (PA)
4 Park Plz Ste 1100, Irvine (92614-8550)
PHONE................................949 851-1101
James L Payne, *Partner*
Jeffrey Brown, *Partner*
Jeffrey K Brown, *Partner*
Daniel Fears, *Partner*

Eric Fohlgren, *Partner*
EMP: 57 **EST:** 1992
SQ FT: 22,000
SALES (est): 16.5MM **Privately Held**
WEB: www.paynefears.com
SIC: 8111 Corporate, partnership & business law; labor & employment law

(P-21658)
PEARLMAN BROWN & WAX LLP (PA)
15910 Ventura Blvd Fl 18, Encino
(91436-2819)
PHONE................................818 501-4343
Barry S Pearlman, *Partner*
Elliot F Borska, *Partner*
Dean Brown, *Partner*
Steven H Wax, *Partner*
Tiffany Fong, *Human Res Dir*
EMP: 60
SQ FT: 4,000
SALES (est): 13.3MM **Privately Held**
WEB: www.pbw-law.com
SIC: 8111 General practice law office

(P-21659)
PERONA LANGER BECK A PROF CORP
300 E San Antonio Dr, Long Beach
(90807-2002)
PHONE................................562 426-6155
James T Perona, *President*
Todd Harrison, *Managing Prtnr*
Major A Langer, *CFO*
Ronald Beck, *Admin Sec*
EMP: 53 **EST:** 1966
SQ FT: 18,000
SALES (est): 7.2MM **Privately Held**
WEB: www.plbsh.com
SIC: 8111 General practice attorney, lawyer

(P-21660)
PIRCHER NICHOLS & MEEKS (PA)
1925 Century Park E # 1700, Los Angeles
(90067-2740)
PHONE................................310 201-0132
Gary Laughlin, *Senior Partner*
Stevens Carey, *Partner*
Eugene Leone, *Partner*
Leo Pircher, *Partner*
Belinda Lambert, *President*
EMP: 95 **EST:** 1983
SQ FT: 35,000
SALES (est): 17.1MM **Privately Held**
WEB: www.pircher.com
SIC: 8111 General practice attorney, lawyer

(P-21661)
POLSINELLI PC
Also Called: Polsinelli LLP
2049 Century Park E, Los Angeles
(90067-3101)
PHONE................................310 556-1801
Norma Ayala, *Administration*
Lisa Quateman, *Partner*
Vivian Grigorians, *Shareholder*
Todd Malynn, *Shareholder*
Randye Soref, *Admin Sec*
EMP: 70
SALES (corp-wide): 227.6MM **Privately Held**
SIC: 8111 General practice attorney, lawyer
PA: Polsinelli Pc
900 W 48th Pl Ste 900 # 900
Kansas City MO 64112
816 753-1000

(P-21662)
PRICE LAW GROUP A PROF CORP (PA)
15760 Ventura Blvd # 1100, Encino
(91436-3044)
PHONE................................818 995-4540
Stuart M Price, *President*
Mako Shuttleworth, *Asst Mgr*
EMP: 115 **EST:** 1991
SQ FT: 15,000
SALES (est): 11.5MM **Privately Held**
WEB: www.pricelawgroup.com
SIC: 8111 General practice law office; debt collection law

(P-21663)
PRICE POSTEL AND PARMA LLP
200 E Carrillo St Ste 400, Santa Barbara
(93101-2190)
P.O. Box 99 (93102-0099)
PHONE..................................805 962-0011
Terry J Schwartz, *Partner*
Lonni Meanley Collins, *Partner*
James H Hurley Jr, *Partner*
Gerald S Thede, *Partner*
David W Van Horne, *Partner*
EMP: 60 EST: 1952
SQ FT: 5,000
SALES (est): 9.2MM **Privately Held**
WEB: www.ppplaw.com
SIC: 8111 General practice attorney,
lawyer

(P-21664)
PRINDLE DECKER & AMARO LLP (PA)
310 Golden Shore Fl 4, Long Beach
(90802-4232)
PHONE..................................562 436-3946
R Joseph Decker, *Partner*
Michael Amaro, *Partner*
Kenneth Prindle, *Partner*
Greg Fox, *COO*
Kim Fine, *Admin Sec*
EMP: 85 EST: 1990
SALES (est): 8.4MM **Privately Held**
WEB: www.prindlelaw.com
SIC: 8111 Specialized law offices, attorneys

(P-21665)
PROBER & RAPHAEL A LAW CORP
Also Called: Prober & Raphael, ALC
20750 Ventura Blvd # 100, Woodland Hills
(91364-2338)
P.O. Box 4365 (91365-4365)
PHONE..................................818 227-0100
Dean R Prober, *President*
Lee Raphael, *Managing Prtnr*
Lee S Raphael, *Principal*
Caren Fajardo, *CIO*
Verzhine Khachatryan, *Accountant*
EMP: 70 EST: 1984
SALES (est): 9.3MM **Privately Held**
WEB: www.pralc.com
SIC: 8111 General practice attorney,
lawyer

(P-21666)
PUBLIC COUNSEL
610 S Ardmore Ave, Los Angeles
(90005-2322)
PHONE..................................213 385-2977
Margaret Morrow, *President*
Madaline Kleiner, *Ch of Bd*
Benjamin Harville, *Counsel*
David Bubis, *Director*
Jill Thompson, *Director*
EMP: 94 EST: 1970
SQ FT: 12,000
SALES: 14MM **Privately Held**
WEB: www.publiccounsel.org
SIC: 8111 Specialized law offices, attorneys

(P-21667)
QUINN EMNUEL URQHART SLLVAN LL (PA)
865 S Figueroa St Fl 10, Los Angeles
(90017-5003)
PHONE..................................213 443-3000
John B Quinn, *Partner*
Dale H Oliver, *Senior Partner*
Adam Abensohn, *Partner*
Anthony Alden, *Partner*
Wayne Alexander, *Partner*
EMP: 366 EST: 1986
SALES (est): 131MM **Privately Held**
WEB: www.quinnemanuel.com
SIC: 8111 Specialized law offices, attorneys

(P-21668)
REED SMITH LLP
355 S Grand Ave Ste 2900, Los Angeles
(90071-1514)
PHONE..................................213 457-8000
Peter Kennedy, *Partner*
Patty Carr, *President*

Socorro Dominguez, *President*
Sonia Martinez, *President*
Griselda Munoz, *President*
EMP: 158
SALES (corp-wide): 632.8MM **Privately Held**
WEB: www.adlawbyrequest.com
SIC: 8111 General practice attorney,
lawyer
PA: Reed Smith Llp
225 5th Ave Ste 1200
Pittsburgh PA 15222
412 288-3131

(P-21669)
RICHARDS WATSON & GERSHON PC (PA)
Also Called: RW&g
355 S Grand Ave Fl 40, Los Angeles
(90071-1560)
PHONE..................................213 626-8484
Laurence S Wiener, *CEO*
Saskia Asamura, *Shareholder*
Robert Ceccon, *Shareholder*
Jim G Grayson, *Shareholder*
Steven Kaufmann, *Shareholder*
EMP: 120
SQ FT: 45,000
SALES (est): 17.4MM **Privately Held**
WEB: www.rwglaw.com
SIC: 8111 General practice law office

(P-21670)
ROPERS MAJESKI A PROF CORP
445 S Figueroa St # 3000, Los Angeles
(90071-1619)
PHONE..................................213 312-2000
Allan Anderson, *Manager*
EMP: 217
SALES (corp-wide): 5.2MM **Privately Held**
WEB: www.ropers.com
SIC: 8111 General practice law office
PA: Ropers Majeski, A Professional Corporation
1001 Marshall St Fl 5
Redwood City CA 94063
650 364-8200

(P-21671)
RUTAN & TUCKER LLP (PA)
18575 Jamboree Rd Ste 900, Irvine
(92612-2559)
P.O. Box 1950, Costa Mesa (92628-1950)
PHONE..................................714 641-5100
Richard Boden, *Mng Member*
William F Meehan, *Partner*
Tony Malkani, *Officer*
Josette Cann, *Managing Dir*
Shelley Aronson, *Admin Sec*
EMP: 243 EST: 1935
SALES (est): 51.9MM **Privately Held**
WEB: www.rutan.com
SIC: 8111 General practice attorney,
lawyer

(P-21672)
SAN BERNARDINO CALIFORNIA CITY (PA)
290 N D St, San Bernardino (92401-1734)
PHONE..................................909 384-7272
R Carey Davis, *Mayor*
David Kennedy, *Treasurer*
Deborah Lewis, *Treasurer*
Emil Kokesh, *Bd of Directors*
Samuel Abbott, *Officer*
EMP: 352 EST: 1854
SALES: 170.3MM **Privately Held**
WEB: www.sbcity.org
SIC: 8111 Administrative & government law

(P-21673)
SAVIN & BURSK LAW OFFICES OF
Also Called: George J Savin Jr
10663 Yarmouth Ave, Granada Hills
(91344-5936)
PHONE..................................818 368-8646
George Savin Jr, *Partner*
Bonnie Marie Bursk, *Partner*
Martha Andrews, *Admin Sec*
Lindsay Savin, *Sr Associate*
Paul Lacayo, *Receptionist*
EMP: 58 EST: 1996

SQ FT: 1,958
SALES (est): 8.6MM **Privately Held**
WEB: www.savinbursklaw.com
SIC: 8111 Bankruptcy law; criminal law

(P-21674)
SEYFARTH SHAW LLP
601 S Figueroa St # 3300, Los Angeles
(90017-5793)
P.O. Box 17961 (90017-0961)
PHONE..................................213 270-9600
Arthur Wood IV, *Branch Mgr*
Hilary White, *Office Mgr*
Steven Malm, *Counsel*
Michael Stevens, *Sr Associate*
Elizabeth Tingey, *Director*
EMP: 141
SALES (corp-wide): 330MM **Privately Held**
WEB: www.seyfarth.com
SIC: 8111 General practice law office
PA: Seyfarth Shaw Llp
233 S Wacker Dr Ste 8000
Chicago IL 60606
312 460-5000

(P-21675)
SEYFARTH SHAW LLP
2029 Century Park E # 3400, Los Angeles
(90067-3020)
PHONE..................................310 277-7200
Sandy Abrahamian, *Branch Mgr*
Michael Marino, *Partner*
Susie Diaz, *Office Admin*
Kathy Truesdale, *Admin Sec*
Rachel Victor, *Admin Sec*
EMP: 200
SALES (corp-wide): 330MM **Privately Held**
WEB: www.seyfarth.com
SIC: 8111 General practice law office
PA: Seyfarth Shaw Llp
233 S Wacker Dr Ste 8000
Chicago IL 60606
312 460-5000

(P-21676)
SHEPPARD MLLIN RCHTER HMPTON L (PA)
Also Called: SHEPPARD MULLIN
333 S Hope St Fl 43, Los Angeles
(90071-1422)
PHONE..................................213 620-1780
Guy N Halgren, *Partner*
Charles Barker, *Partner*
Robert Beall, *Partner*
Lawrence Braun, *Partner*
Justine M Casey, *Partner*
EMP: 370 EST: 1927
SQ FT: 52,820
SALES (est): 956.5K **Privately Held**
WEB: www.sheppardmullin.com
SIC: 8111 General practice law office

(P-21677)
SHOOK HARDY & BACON LLP
5 Park Plz Ste 1600, Irvine (92614-2546)
PHONE..................................949 475-1500
Michelle Fujimoto, *Manager*
Vaveca Moss, *Director*
EMP: 239
SALES (corp-wide): 147.9MM **Privately Held**
WEB: www.shb.com
SIC: 8111 General practice law office
PA: Shook, Hardy & Bacon L.L.P.
2555 Grand Blvd
Kansas City MO 64108
816 474-6550

(P-21678)
SKADDEN ARPS SLATE MEAGHER & F
300 S Grand Ave Ste 3400, Los Angeles
(90071-3137)
PHONE..................................213 687-5000
Rand S April, *Partner*
Michael Beinus, *Partner*
Kenneth J Betts, *Partner*
Brian J McCarthy, *Partner*
Jeffrey Mishkin, *Exec VP*
EMP: 250 **Privately Held**
SIC: 8111 General practice attorney,
lawyer

HQ: Skadden, Arps, Slate, Meagher & Flom Llp
1 Manhattan Pl
New York NY 10007
212 735-3000

(P-21679)
SMS TRANSPORTATION INC
18516 S Broadway, Gardena (90248-4615)
PHONE..................................310 527-9200
John W Harris, *Principal*
Jennifer Wiltz, *COO*
EMP: 100 EST: 2005
SALES (est): 3.2MM **Privately Held**
WEB: www.smstransportation.net
SIC: 8111 Legal services

(P-21680)
SNELL & WILMER LLP
600 Anton Blvd Ste 1400, Costa Mesa
(92626-7689)
PHONE..................................714 427-7000
Andrea Bryant, *Principal*
Alexander L Conti, *Partner*
Frank Cronin, *Partner*
Christy D Joseph, *Partner*
William S O'Hare, *Officer*
EMP: 64
SQ FT: 3,000
SALES (corp-wide): 77.1MM **Privately Held**
WEB: www.swlaw.com
SIC: 8111 General practice attorney,
lawyer; specialized law offices, attorneys
PA: Snell & Wilmer L.L.P.
400 E Van Buren St Fl 10
Phoenix AZ 85004
602 382-6000

(P-21681)
STRADLING YCCA CRLSON RUTH A P (PA)
660 Nwport Ctr Dr Ste 160, Newport Beach
(92660)
PHONE..................................949 725-4000
John F Cannon, *Principal*
Sean Absher, *Shareholder*
Marc G Alcser, *Shareholder*
Salil Bali, *Shareholder*
Sarah Brooks, *Shareholder*
EMP: 200 EST: 1975
SQ FT: 64,000
SALES (est): 40.6MM **Privately Held**
WEB: www.stradlinglaw.com
SIC: 8111 General practice law office

(P-21682)
STRETTO INC (PA)
410 Exchange Ste 100, Irvine
(92602-1331)
PHONE..................................949 222-1212
Steve Moore, *CEO*
James M Le, *COO*
Scott Barna, *Officer*
Patrick Shaughnessy, *Vice Pres*
Dear Terry, *Vice Pres*
EMP: 56 EST: 2003
SALES (est): 44.5MM **Privately Held**
WEB: www.stretto.com
SIC: 8111 Bankruptcy referee

(P-21683)
STROOCK & STROOCK & LAVAN LLP
2029 Century Park E # 1800, Los Angeles
(90067-3086)
PHONE..................................310 556-5800
Diane Cohen, *Branch Mgr*
Howard Lavin, *Partner*
Arjun Ghosh-Dastidar, *Exec Dir*
Tracy Garcia, *Admin Sec*
Ronald Tolan, *Business Anlyst*
EMP: 150
SALES (corp-wide): 26.4K **Privately Held**
WEB: www.stroock.com
SIC: 8111 General practice attorney,
lawyer
PA: Stroock & Stroock & Lavan Llp
180 Maiden Ln Fl 17
New York NY 10038
212 806-5400

(P-21684)
STUTMAN TRSTER GLATT PROF CORP
Also Called: Stutman Treister Glatt Prof Co
1901 Avenue Of The, Los Angeles (90067)
PHONE................310 228-5600
Scott H Yun, *CEO*
Frank Merola, *Shareholder*
Charles D Axelrod, *Vice Pres*
Michael H Goldstein, *Vice Pres*
Robert A Greenfield, *Vice Pres*
EMP: 75 **EST:** 1969
SQ FT: 40,000
SALES (est): 12.1MM **Privately Held**
SIC: 8111 General practice law office

(P-21685)
SULMEYERKUPETZ A PROF CORP (PA)
333 S Hope St Ste 3500, Los Angeles (90071-3044)
PHONE..................213 617-5221
Alan Tippie, *President*
Arnold L Kupetz, *Partner*
Alan G Tippie, *President*
Richard G Baumann, *Vice Pres*
Carol K Leemon, *Exec Dir*
EMP: 56 **EST:** 1952
SQ FT: 22,000
SALES (est): 4.7MM **Privately Held**
WEB: www.sulmeyerlaw.com
SIC: 8111 General practice law office

(P-21686)
TESTAN LAW A PROFESSIONAL CORP (PA)
31330 Oak Crest Dr, Westlake Village (91361-4632)
PHONE..................805 604-1816
Steven Testan, *President*
Kathleen Brundo, *Partner*
Melissa Bryant, *Partner*
Debra Tobias, *Partner*
Michelle Wu, *Partner*
EMP: 50 **EST:** 1996
SQ FT: 17,900
SALES (est): 44.2MM **Privately Held**
WEB: www.testanlaw.com
SIC: 8111 Labor & employment law

(P-21687)
THARPE & HOWELL (PA)
15250 Ventura Blvd Fl 9, Sherman Oaks (91403-3221)
PHONE..................818 205-9955
John Maile, *Managing Prtnr*
Todd R Howell, *Partner*
Timothy D Lake, *Partner*
Christopher S Maile, *Partner*
Stacey A Miller, *Partner*
EMP: 78 **EST:** 1977
SQ FT: 13,500
SALES (est): 8.4MM **Privately Held**
WEB: www.tharpe-howell.com
SIC: 8111 General practice law office

(P-21688)
THOMPSON & COLEGATE LLP
3610 14th St Lowr, Riverside (92501-3852)
P.O. Box 1299 (92502-1299)
PHONE..................951 682-5550
John W Marshall, *Partner*
John A Boyd, *Partner*
Donald G Grant, *Partner*
J E Holmes III, *Partner*
Michael J Marlatt, *Partner*
EMP: 50 **EST:** 1920
SQ FT: 28,500
SALES (est): 6.6MM **Privately Held**
WEB: www.tclaw.net
SIC: 8111 General practice attorney, lawyer

(P-21689)
TROUTMAN PPPER HMLTON SNDERS L
Also Called: Troutman Sanders
5 Park Plz Ste 1400, Irvine (92614-2545)
PHONE..................949 622-2700
David B Allen, *Partner*
Koenig V Crime, *Administration*
Samrah Mahmoud, *Counsel*
EMP: 86

SALES (corp-wide): 161.1MM **Privately Held**
WEB: www.troutman.com
SIC: 8111 General practice attorney, lawyer
PA: Troutman Pepper Hamilton Sanders Llp
600 Peachtree St Ne # 300
Atlanta GA 30308
404 885-3000

(P-21690)
TROYGOULD PC
1801 Century Park E # 1600, Los Angeles (90067-2367)
PHONE..................310 553-4441
Sanford J Hillsberg, *Principal*
Diane Gordon, *Exec Dir*
Sandy Anderson, *Admin Sec*
Steve Hernandez, *Office Spvr*
Lea McCormick, *Info Tech Mgr*
EMP: 80 **EST:** 1970
SQ FT: 24,000
SALES (est): 12.4MM **Privately Held**
WEB: www.troygould.com
SIC: 8111 General practice attorney, lawyer

(P-21691)
VEATCH CARLSON GROGAN & NELSON
1055 Wilshire Blvd Fl 11, Los Angeles (90017-2431)
PHONE..................213 381-2861
Jim Galloway, *Partner*
David Failer, *Partner*
Juana Guevara, *President*
Anna Sepulveda, *Officer*
Cyril Czajkowskyj, *Executive*
EMP: 50 **EST:** 1974
SALES (est): 6.2MM **Privately Held**
WEB: www.veatchfirm.com
SIC: 8111 General practice law office

(P-21692)
WADE & LOWE A PROF CORP
7700 Irvine Center Dr # 700, Irvine (92618-3042)
PHONE..................949 753-1000
James Crandall, *Manager*
Arhlene Buning-Perez, *Admin Sec*
EMP: 52
SALES (corp-wide): 7.4MM **Privately Held**
WEB: www.wllegal.com
SIC: 8111 General practice attorney, lawyer
PA: Wade & Lowe, A Professional Corporation
3200 Inland Empire Blvd # 160
Ontario CA 91764
909 483-6700

(P-21693)
WALSWRTH FRNKLIN BEVINS MCCALL (PA)
Also Called: Walsworth Franklin & Bevins
1 City Blvd W Ste 500, Orange (92868-3677)
PHONE..................714 634-2522
Jeffrey P Walsworth, *Partner*
Ronald H Bevins Jr, *Partner*
Ian P Dillon, *Partner*
Ferdie F Franklin, *Partner*
Daniel R Jacobs, *Partner*
EMP: 55
SQ FT: 2,800
SALES (est): 14.9MM **Privately Held**
WEB: www.wfbm.com
SIC: 8111 General practice law office

(P-21694)
WARREN DRYE KELLEY
10100 Santa Monica Blvd # 2300, Los Angeles (90067-4135)
PHONE..................310 712-6100
Andrew White, *Managing Prtnr*
Michael O'Connor, *Managing Prtnr*
EMP: 50 **EST:** 1997
SALES (est): 1.1MM **Privately Held**
WEB: www.kelleydrye.com
SIC: 8111 General practice attorney, lawyer

(P-21695)
WASSERMAN COMDEN & CASSELMAN (PA)
5567 Reseda Blvd Ste 330, Tarzana (91356-2699)
P.O. Box 7033 (91357-7033)
PHONE..................323 872-0995
Steve Wasserman, *Partner*
David B Casselman, *Partner*
Leonard J Comden, *Partner*
Clifford H Pearson, *Partner*
EMP: 88 **EST:** 1976
SQ FT: 15,000
SALES (est): 8.4MM **Privately Held**
WEB: www.wassermanlawgroup.com
SIC: 8111 General practice law office

(P-21696)
WEITZ & LUXENBERG PC
1880 Century Park E # 700, Los Angeles (90067-1618)
PHONE..................310 247-0921
Christina Shackelford, *Receptionist*
Erin M Boyle, *Associate*
Tyler Stock, *Associate*
EMP: 57 **Privately Held**
WEB: www.weitzlux.com
SIC: 8111 General practice attorney, lawyer
PA: Weitz & Luxenberg, P.C.
700 Broadway Lbby A
New York NY 10003

(P-21697)
WOLF RFKIN SHPIRO SCHLMAN RBK (PA)
Also Called: Grant, Richard S
11400 W Olympic Blvd, Los Angeles (90064-1550)
PHONE..................310 445-8817
Michael Wolf, *Senior Partner*
Jeff W Lane, *Partner*
Stephen Levine, *Partner*
Leslie Marks, *Partner*
Barry Mitidiere, *Partner*
EMP: 66 **EST:** 1978
SALES (est): 9.7MM **Privately Held**
WEB: www.wrslawyers.com
SIC: 8111 General practice attorney, lawyer

(P-21698)
WOLF FIRM A LAW CORPORATION
1851 E 1st St Ste 100, Santa Ana (92705-4036)
PHONE..................949 720-9200
Alan S Wolf, *President*
Jenny Giacopelli, *Partner*
Krys Fuller, *COO*
Brenda Britten, *Trustee*
Scott Jackson, *Exec VP*
EMP: 60 **EST:** 1993
SALES (est): 18.1MM **Privately Held**
WEB: www.wolffirm.com
SIC: 8111 General practice law office; specialized law offices, attorneys

(P-21699)
WOMBLE BOND DICKINSON (US) LLP
12400 Wilshire Blvd # 600, Los Angeles (90025-1040)
PHONE..................310 207-3800
EMP: 240
SALES (corp-wide): 218.4MM **Privately Held**
WEB: www.womblebonddickinson.com
SIC: 8111 Specialized law offices, attorneys
PA: Womble Bond Dickinson (Us) Llp
1 W 4th St
Winston Salem NC 27101
336 721-3600

(P-21700)
WOOD SMITH HENNING BERMAN LLP (PA)
Also Called: WSH&b
10960 Wilshire Blvd Fl 18, Los Angeles (90024-3804)
PHONE..................310 481-7600
David Wood, *Partner*
Daniel Berman, *Partner*

Steven Henning, *Partner*
Kevin Smith, *Partner*
Stewart Reid, *Managing Prtnr*
EMP: 50 **EST:** 1997
SQ FT: 24,500
SALES (est): 52.8MM **Privately Held**
WEB: www.wshblaw.com
SIC: 8111 General practice law office

(P-21701)
WOODRUFF SPRADLIN & SMART
555 Anton Blvd Ste 1200, Costa Mesa (92626-7670)
PHONE..................714 558-7000
Ken Smart, *President*
Bradley Hogin, *Shareholder*
Kennard Smart, *Shareholder*
Thomas L Woodruff, *Treasurer*
Lois E Jeffrey, *Vice Pres*
EMP: 62 **EST:** 1975
SALES (est): 8.4MM **Privately Held**
WEB: www.wss-law.com
SIC: 8111 General practice attorney, lawyer

(P-21702)
WRIGHT FINLAY & ZAK LLP
4665 Macarthur Ct Ste 200, Newport Beach (92660-1811)
PHONE..................949 477-5050
Robin P Wright, *Managing Prtnr*
Robert Finley, *Partner*
Dana Nitz, *Partner*
Jonathan Zak, *Partner*
Robin Wright, *Managing Prtnr*
EMP: 60 **EST:** 2002
SALES (est): 18.1MM **Privately Held**
WEB: www.wrightlegal.net
SIC: 8111 General practice attorney, lawyer

(P-21703)
YUKEVICH / CVANAUGH A LAW CORP (PA)
355 S Grand Ave Fl 15, Los Angeles (90071-3180)
PHONE..................213 362-7777
James J Yukevich, *Managing Prtnr*
Alexander Calfo, *Principal*
Todd Cavanaugh, *Principal*
Jennifer Rodriguez, *Executive Asst*
Vivian Powers, *Administration*
EMP: 62 **EST:** 1994
SALES (est): 5.5MM **Privately Held**
WEB: www.yukelaw.com
SIC: 8111 General practice law office

(P-21704)
ZBS LAW LLP
30 Corporate Park Ste 450, Irvine (92606-3401)
PHONE..................714 848-7920
Les Zieve, *Partner*
Paul Kim, *Principal*
EMP: 85 **EST:** 2020
SALES (est): 3.2MM **Privately Held**
WEB: www.zbslaw.com
SIC: 8111 Real estate law

(P-21705)
ZIFFREN B B F G-L S&C FND
1801 Century Park W, Los Angeles (90067-6409)
PHONE..................310 552-3388
Kenneth Ziffren, *Owner*
John G Branca, *Principal*
Harry M Brittenham, *Principal*
Steven Burkow, *Principal*
David Byrnes, *Principal*
EMP: 103 **EST:** 1979
SQ FT: 33,000
SALES (est): 17.1MM **Privately Held**
WEB: www.ziffrenlaw.com
SIC: 8111 General practice law office

8322 Individual & Family Social Svcs

(P-21706)
A PLUS SENIOR CARE INC
4701 Arrow Hwy, Montclair (91763-1229)
PHONE..................909 989-2563

Gahta Lutfi, *Owner*
EMP: 50 **EST:** 2011
SALES (est): 1MM **Privately Held**
SIC: 8322 Senior citizens' center or association

(P-21707)
ABRAZAR INC
Also Called: Abrazar Elderly Assistance
7101 Wyoming St, Westminster
(92683-3811)
PHONE..................714 893-3581
Gloria Reyes, *CEO*
Mario Ortega, *COO*
EMP: 80
SALES: 8.2MM **Privately Held**
WEB: www.abrazarinc.com
SIC: 8322 Social service center

(P-21708)
AIDS PROJECT LOS ANGELES (PA)
Also Called: Aids Project La
611 S Kingsley Dr, Los Angeles
(90005-2319)
PHONE..................213 201-1600
Craig E Thompson, *CEO*
Robyn Goldman, *CFO*
EMP: 90 **EST:** 1983
SALES: 10.3MM **Privately Held**
WEB: www.aplahealth.org
SIC: 8322 Social service center

(P-21709)
AIDS SVCS FNDATION ORANGE CNTY
Also Called: AIDS WALK ORANGE COUNTY
17982 Sky Park Cir Ste J, Irvine
(92614-6482)
PHONE..................949 809-5700
Alan Witchey, *Exec Dir*
Duane Vajgrt, *Vice Pres*
Stefanie Kochen, *Nurse*
Sharon Petrillo, *Nurse*
Sandra Boodman, *Director*
EMP: 66 **EST:** 1985
SQ FT: 16,051
SALES (est): 11.1MM **Privately Held**
WEB: www.radianthealthcenters.org
SIC: 8322 8011 Social service center; clinic, operated by physicians

(P-21710)
ALCOHOLISM CENTER FOR WOMEN
Also Called: A C W
1147 S Alvarado St, Los Angeles
(90006-4100)
P.O. Box 17640 (90017-0640)
PHONE..................213 381-8500
Lorette Herman, *Manager*
EMP: 50 **EST:** 1974
SALES (est): 2.3MM **Privately Held**
WEB: www.alcoholismcenterforwomen.org
SIC: 8322 Alcoholism counseling, nontreatment

(P-21711)
ALZHEIMERS GREATER LOS ANGELES
4221 Wilshire Blvd # 400, Los Angeles
(90010-3512)
PHONE..................323 938-3379
Heather Cooper Ortner, *President*
Debra Cherry, *Exec VP*
Kara Bonela, *Vice Pres*
John Seiber, *Vice Pres*
Sara Mikael, *Admin Asst*
EMP: 58 **EST:** 2012
SALES (est): 5.8MM **Privately Held**
WEB: www.alzheimersla.org
SIC: 8322 Senior citizens' center or association

(P-21712)
AMERICAN RED CROSS LOS ANGLES (PA)
1320 Newton St, Los Angeles
(90021-2724)
PHONE..................310 445-9900
Roger Dixon, *CEO*
Kirk Richard Hyde, *Ch of Bd*
Scott J Olmsted, *Ch of Bd*
Michelle McCarthy, *CFO*
Thomas E Stephenson, *CFO*
EMP: 150 **EST:** 1916
SALES (est): 27.5MM **Privately Held**
WEB: www.redcross.org
SIC: 8322 Social service center

(P-21713)
ANTELOPE VLY DOM VLNCE COUNCIL (PA)
Also Called: VALLEY OASIS
1150 W Avenue I, Lancaster (93534-2246)
P.O. Box 2980 (93539-2980)
PHONE..................661 949-1916
Carol Crabson, *Exec Dir*
Darryl Kniss, *CFO*
Toni Severino, *Accountant*
EMP: 117 **EST:** 1981
SQ FT: 16,500
SALES: 15.3MM **Privately Held**
WEB: www.valleyoasis.org
SIC: 8322 8361 Social service center; halfway group home, persons with social or personal problems

(P-21714)
ARC - IMPERIAL VALLEY (PA)
298 E Ross Ave, El Centro (92243-9303)
P.O. Box 1828 (92244-1828)
PHONE..................760 352-0180
Arturo Santos, *CEO*
Poli Flores, *President*
Martha Carrillo, *General Mgr*
Sherri Gutierrez, *Admin Sec*
Lorie Weaver, *Human Res Dir*
EMP: 60 **EST:** 1973
SQ FT: 22,000
SALES (est): 15.2MM **Privately Held**
WEB: www.arciv.org
SIC: 8322 4729 8361 Adult day care center; carpool/vanpool arrangement; home for the mentally handicapped

(P-21715)
ARC RIVERSIDE
Also Called: Pass Resources Center
702 E Eleventh St, Beaumont
(92223-1909)
PHONE..................951 845-3385
Patricia Duncan, *Manager*
EMP: 62
SALES (corp-wide): 5.5MM **Privately Held**
WEB: www.arcriverside.org
SIC: 8322 Social service center
PA: Arc Riverside
8138 Mar Vista Ct
Riverside CA

(P-21716)
ASANA INTEGRATED MEDICAL GROUP
6200 Canoga Ave Ste 350, Woodland Hills
(91367-7782)
PHONE..................888 212-7545
Nitin Nanda, *Principal*
EMP: 53 **EST:** 2010
SALES (est): 9.4MM
SALES (corp-wide): 3.6B **Privately Held**
SIC: 8322 General counseling services
HQ: Ipc Healthcare, Inc.
4605 Lankershim Blvd
North Hollywood CA 91602
888 447-2362

(P-21717)
ASIAN YOUTH CENTER
Also Called: Ayc
100 Clary Ave, San Gabriel (91776-1374)
PHONE..................626 309-0622
Ken Tcheng, *CEO*
Sally Baldwin, *President*
Gay Yuren, *President*
Michelle Ferige, *Exec Dir*
Verena Kwan, *Manager*
EMP: 65 **EST:** 1989
SALES: 2.9MM **Privately Held**
WEB: www.aycla.org
SIC: 8322 Youth center

(P-21718)
ASSOCIATED STUDENTS INC (PA)
Also Called: ASSICIATED STUDENTS
University Un Bldg 65, San Luis Obispo
(93407)
PHONE..................805 756-1281
Richard Johnson, *Director*
Dwayne Brummett, *Business Mgr*
EMP: 70 **EST:** 1964
SQ FT: 110,000
SALES (est): 24MM **Privately Held**
WEB: www.calpoly.edu
SIC: 8322 8221 Multi-service center; colleges universities & professional schools

(P-21719)
AVIVA FAMILY & CHILDRENS SVCS (PA)
1701 Camino Palmero St, Los Angeles
(90046-2902)
PHONE..................323 876-0550
Ira J Kruskol, *Director*
Jennifer Wong, *Program Mgr*
Genevieve Morgan, *Psychologist*
EMP: 84 **EST:** 1976
SALES (est): 8.4MM **Privately Held**
WEB: www.aviva.org
SIC: 8322 Child related social services

(P-21720)
BEHAVIORAL HEALTH SERVICES INC (PA)
15519 Crenshaw Blvd, Gardena
(90249-4525)
PHONE..................310 679-9031
Henry Van Oudheudsen, *CEO*
Lawrence T Gentile, *President*
Donna Stanovich, *CEO*
Andy Worrell, *CFO*
Theresa Cannon, *Officer*
EMP: 50 **EST:** 1973
SQ FT: 35,000
SALES (est): 45.8MM **Privately Held**
WEB: www.bhs-inc.org
SIC: 8322 Substance abuse counseling

(P-21721)
BEHAVIORAL LEARNING CENTER INC
13400 Riverside Dr Ste 209, Sherman Oaks
(91423)
PHONE..................661 254-7086
Jody Stiegemeyer, *President*
Shanna Munoz, *Admin Sec*
Danielle Sheehy, *Admin Sec*
Jasmine Sancedo, *Technician*
Victor Chata, *Human Resources*
EMP: 99 **EST:** 2007
SQ FT: 4,000
SALES (est): 5.5MM **Privately Held**
WEB: www.blcca.com
SIC: 8322 Child related social services

(P-21722)
BEHAVORAL AUTISM THERAPIES LLC (PA)
2930 Inland Empire Blvd, Ontario
(91764-4802)
PHONE..................909 483-5000
Mia Humphreys, *Admin Dir*
Larry Humphreys, *Exec Dir*
Jackie Robinson, *Office Mgr*
Beatriz Barragan, *Executive Asst*
ABI Delgado, *Human Res Mgr*
EMP: 247 **EST:** 2013
SQ FT: 2,000
SALES (est): 10.4MM **Privately Held**
WEB: www.behavioralautismtherapies.com
SIC: 8322 General counseling services

(P-21723)
BENEVOLENCE INDUSTRIES INC
3533 W Pico Blvd, Los Angeles
(90019-4534)
PHONE..................310 800-7963
Kwabena Obeng, *President*
EMP: 50 **EST:** 2005
SALES: 9.9MM **Privately Held**
WEB: www.bhchealth.org
SIC: 8322 Individual & family services

(P-21724)
BERKSHIRE HATHAWAY HOME SERVIC
881 Alma Real Dr, Pacific Palisades
(90272-3731)
PHONE..................310 230-3700
Cecile Gifford, *Principal*
EMP: 147
SALES (corp-wide): 53.4MM **Privately Held**
SIC: 8322 Homemakers' service
PA: Berkshire Hathaway Home Services California Properties
12770 El Cmino Real Ste 1
San Diego CA 92130
858 792-6085

(P-21725)
BLC RESIDENTIAL CARE INC
1455 W 112th St, Los Angeles
(90047-4926)
PHONE..................310 722-7541
Brenda Chandler, *President*
EMP: 80 **EST:** 2004
SALES (est): 2.1MM **Privately Held**
SIC: 8322 Adult day care center

(P-21726)
BRAILLE INSTITUTE AMERICA INC (PA)
741 N Vermont Ave, Los Angeles
(90029-3594)
PHONE..................323 663-1111
Lester M Sussman, *Ch of Bd*
George E Thomas, *Partner*
Peter Mindnich, *President*
Les Stocker, *President*
Janice Herzberg, *Assoc VP*
EMP: 208 **EST:** 1919
SQ FT: 167,079
SALES: 34MM **Privately Held**
WEB: www.brailleinstitute.org
SIC: 8322 8231 2731 2759 Individual & family services; specialized libraries; textbooks: publishing & printing; commercial printing

(P-21727)
CALIFORNIA PEDIATRIC FMLY SVCS
Also Called: Able
326 E Foothill Blvd, Azusa (91702-2515)
PHONE..................626 812-0055
Louise Vanzee PHD, *President*
Faviola Acevedo, *Manager*
EMP: 52 **EST:** 1988
SQ FT: 2,417
SALES: 113.2K **Privately Held**
WEB: www.cal-peds.com
SIC: 8322 Family counseling services

(P-21728)
CAREWORKS HEALTH SERVICES
5151 Oceanus Dr Ste 102, Huntington Beach (92649-1057)
PHONE..................949 859-4700
Anh Tu Dang, *President*
Meagan Truglio, *Pain Mangement*
EMP: 65 **EST:** 2015
SALES (est): 2.7MM **Privately Held**
WEB: www.careworkshealthservices.com
SIC: 8322 Senior citizens' center or association

(P-21729)
CAROLYN E WYLIE CTR FOR CHLDRE
4164 Brockton Ave, Riverside
(92501-3400)
PHONE..................951 683-5193
Mickey Rubinson, *CEO*
Melody Amaral, *CEO*
EMP: 100 **EST:** 1976
SQ FT: 3,000
SALES (est): 3.4MM **Privately Held**
WEB: www.wyliecenter.org
SIC: 8322 8093 8049 Individual & family services; child related social services; social service center; mental health clinic, outpatient; psychotherapist, except M.D.

(P-21730)
CASA CLINA HOSP CTRS FOR HLTHC
Also Called: Rancho Pino Verdi
11981 Midway Ave, Lucerne Valley
(92356-7517)
P.O. Box 1760 (92356-1760)
PHONE..........................760 248-6245
Michael Stayer, *Manager*
EMP: 149
SQ FT: 2,934
SALES (corp-wide): 123MM **Privately Held**
WEB: www.casacolina.org
SIC: 8322 Rehabilitation services
HQ: Casa Colina Hospital And Centers For Healthcare
255 E Bonita Ave
Pomona CA 91767
909 596-7733

(P-21731)
CASA COLINA INC (PA)
Also Called: CASA COLINA HOSPITAL AND CENTE
255 E Bonita Ave, Pomona (91767-1933)
PHONE..........................909 596-7733
Felice L Loverso, *CEO*
Gary Jensen, *Ch Radiology*
Stephanie Bradhurst, *Chief Mktg Ofcr*
Karen Dupont, *Officer*
Robert Jones, *Officer*
EMP: 800 EST: 1981
SALES: 123MM **Privately Held**
WEB: www.casacolina.org
SIC: 8322 8011 Rehabilitation services; ambulatory surgical center

(P-21732)
CASA PCFICA CTRS FOR CHLDREN F (PA)
1722 S Lewis Rd, Camarillo (93012-8520)
PHONE..........................805 482-3260
Shawna Morris, *CEO*
Polly Huffer, *Partner*
Felice Ginsberg, *CFO*
Michael Redard, *CFO*
Allyson Bell, *Program Mgr*
EMP: 175 EST: 1988
SQ FT: 63,000
SALES (est): 28.5MM **Privately Held**
WEB: www.casapacifica.org
SIC: 8322 8361 8211 Child related social services; residential care for children; specialty education

(P-21733)
CATHOLIC CHARITIES OF LA INC
21600 Hart St, Canoga Park (91303)
PHONE..........................818 883-6015
EMP: 50
SALES (corp-wide): 29MM **Privately Held**
SIC: 8322 Individual/Family Services
PA: Catholic Charities Of Los Angeles, Inc.
1531 James M Wood Blvd
Los Angeles CA 90015
213 251-3400

(P-21734)
CATHOLIC CHRTIES SNTA CLARA CN
303 N Ventura Ave Ste A, Ventura (93001-1961)
PHONE..........................805 643-4694
Robert Batdazian, *Director*
EMP: 88
SALES (corp-wide): 36.6MM **Privately Held**
WEB: www.catholiccharitiesscc.org
SIC: 8322 Social service center
PA: Catholic Charities Of Santa Clara County
2625 Zanker Rd Ste 200
San Jose CA 95134
408 468-0100

(P-21735)
CHILD & FAMILY CENTER
21545 Centre Pointe Pkwy, Santa Clarita (91350-2947)
PHONE..........................661 259-9439
Joan Aschoff, *CEO*
Victor Chavira, *Exec VP*

Bert Paras, *Vice Pres*
Melissa Mercer, *Admin Sec*
Anissa Lee, *Asst Controller*
EMP: 120 EST: 1976
SQ FT: 26,581
SALES (est): 13.2MM **Privately Held**
WEB: www.childfamilycenter.org
SIC: 8322 8099 8093 8049 Family counseling services; childbirth preparation clinic; mental health clinic, outpatient; clinical psychologist

(P-21736)
CHILD ABUSE LSTENING MEDIATION
Also Called: C A L M
1236 Chapala St, Santa Barbara (93101-3116)
PHONE..........................805 965-2376
Anna M Kokotovic, *Exec Dir*
Andrew McGowan, *Program Mgr*
Caroline Powers, *Admin Sec*
Mireya Hernandez, *Info Tech Mgr*
Benjamin Kortuem, *Technician*
EMP: 50
SALES: 7MM **Privately Held**
WEB: www.calm4kids.org
SIC: 8322 Crisis intervention center; general counseling services

(P-21737)
CHILD CARE RESOURCE CENTER INC (PA)
20001 Prairie St, Chatsworth (91311-6508)
PHONE..........................818 717-1000
Michael Olenick, *CEO*
Casey Quinn, *CFO*
Denise Trinh, *CFO*
Ellen Cervantes, *Vice Pres*
Rick Robertss, *Vice Pres*
EMP: 130 EST: 1981
SALES: 335.1MM **Privately Held**
WEB: www.ccrcca.org
SIC: 8322 Child related social services

(P-21738)
CHILD CARE RESOURCE CENTER INC
250 Grand Cypress Ave # 601, Palmdale (93551-3675)
PHONE..........................661 723-3246
Ann Bubont, *Principal*
Beth Chiaro, *Director*
Cynthia Renteria, *Director*
EMP: 184
SALES (corp-wide): 335.1MM **Privately Held**
WEB: www.ccrcca.org
SIC: 8322 Child related social services
PA: Child Care Resource Center, Inc.
20001 Prairie St
Chatsworth CA 91311
818 717-1000

(P-21739)
CHILD DEV RSRCES OF VNTURA CNT (PA)
Also Called: C D R
221 Ventura Blvd, Oxnard (93036-0277)
PHONE..........................805 485-7878
Jack Hinojosa, *CEO*
Alec Hairabedian, *CFO*
Stuart Orlinsky, *Officer*
Dana Johnson, *Exec Dir*
Alex Solis, *Technician*
EMP: 200 EST: 1974
SQ FT: 67,007
SALES (est): 53.5MM **Privately Held**
WEB: www.cdrv.org
SIC: 8322 8699 Child guidance agency; charitable organization

(P-21740)
CHILD DEVELOPMENT INSTITUTE
Also Called: CDI
18050 Vanowen St, Reseda (91335-5638)
PHONE..........................818 888-4559
Joan Samaltese, *Exec Dir*
Tessa Graham, *Principal*
Dana Kalek, *Principal*
Steve Lenhert, *Principal*
Joan Maltese, *Exec Dir*
EMP: 93 EST: 1995

SALES (est): 5.6MM **Privately Held**
WEB: www.cdikids.org
SIC: 8322 Child related social services

(P-21741)
CHILDHELP INC
Also Called: Childhelp Foster Family
1955 Hunts Ln Ste 200, San Bernardino (92408-3344)
PHONE..........................909 335-1164
Edward Siahaan, *Manager*
EMP: 59
SALES (corp-wide): 36MM **Privately Held**
WEB: www.childhelp.org
SIC: 8322 Child related social services
PA: Childhelp, Inc.
6730 N Scottsdale Rd # 150
Scottsdale AZ 85253
480 922-8212

(P-21742)
CHILDNET YOUTH & FMLY SVCS INC (PA)
4155 Outer Traffic Cir, Long Beach (90804-2111)
P.O. Box 4550 (90804-0550)
PHONE..........................562 498-5500
Kathy L Hughes, *CEO*
Donna Skees, *President*
Kathy Hughes, *COO*
Yolanda Hullum, *Vice Pres*
Ana Barraza, *Exec Dir*
EMP: 177 EST: 1970
SQ FT: 16,073
SALES: 32.5MM **Privately Held**
WEB: www.childnet.net
SIC: 8322 Child related social services

(P-21743)
CHILDRENS BUREAU SOUTHERN CAL (PA)
1910 Magnolia Ave, Los Angeles (90007-1220)
PHONE..........................213 342-0100
Alex Morales, *President*
Sona Chandwani, *CFO*
Ron Brown, *Officer*
Susan J Wood, *CIO*
Kathryn Reimer, *Research*
EMP: 107 EST: 1904
SQ FT: 43,000
SALES: 46.2MM **Privately Held**
WEB: www.all4kids.org
SIC: 8322 Child related social services

(P-21744)
CHILDRENS HUNGER FUND (PA)
13931 Balboa Blvd, Sylmar (91342-1084)
PHONE..........................818 979-7100
Dav Phillips, *President*
Steve McCormick, *Vice Chairman*
Christopher Sue, *CFO*
Morgan Owen, *Exec Dir*
Maureen McTeer, *Office Admin*
EMP: 60 EST: 1991
SQ FT: 60,000
SALES (est): 38.6MM **Privately Held**
WEB: www.childrenshungerfund.org
SIC: 8322 Social service center

(P-21745)
CHILDRENS INST LOS ANGELES
679 S New Hampshire Ave, Los Angeles (90005-1355)
PHONE..........................213 383-2765
Mary Emmons, *Branch Mgr*
Ron Smith, *Analyst*
EMP: 850
SALES (corp-wide): 392K **Privately Held**
WEB: www.childrensinstitute.org
SIC: 8322 Social service center
PA: Children's Institute Of Los Angeles
2121 W Temple St
Los Angeles CA 90026
213 385-5100

(P-21746)
CHILDRENS INSTITUTE INC (PA)
2121 W Temple St, Los Angeles (90026-4915)
PHONE..........................213 385-5100
Martine Singer, *CEO*
Shahram Aminian, *President*
Tarek Kutrieh, *Treasurer*
Todd Sosna,

Dr Steve Ambrose, *Senior VP*
EMP: 190 EST: 1906
SQ FT: 18,000
SALES: 86.9MM **Privately Held**
WEB: www.childrensinstitute.org
SIC: 8322 8699 Child related social services; charitable organization

(P-21747)
COACHELLA VLY RESCUE MISSION
Also Called: Cvrm
82873 Via Venecia, Indio (92201-6971)
P.O. Box 10660 (92202-2564)
PHONE..........................760 347-3512
Floyd Rhoades, *Ch of Bd*
Pete Del Rio, *Vice Chairman*
Joseph Hayes, *Treasurer*
Jim Parrish, *Vice Ch Bd*
Darla Burkett, *Exec Dir*
EMP: 64 EST: 1971
SQ FT: 43,000
SALES: 8.7MM **Privately Held**
WEB: www.cvrm.org
SIC: 8322 8661 Social service center; non-church religious organizations

(P-21748)
COALITION FOR FAMLY HARMONY
1030 N Ventura Rd, Oxnard (93030-3855)
PHONE..........................805 983-6014
Cherie Douval, *President*
Alma Plazola, *Office Admin*
Sherrie Houston, *Accountant*
Gerry STA, *Controller*
Sandy Gomez, *Education*
EMP: 63 EST: 1978
SQ FT: 20,000
SALES (est): 2.9MM **Privately Held**
WEB: www.thecoalition.org
SIC: 8322 Social service center

(P-21749)
COMMUNITY ACCESS NTWRK NON PRF (PA)
2275 S Main St Ste 201, Corona (92882-5303)
PHONE..........................951 279-1333
Rafik Philobos, *President*
Karen Shah, *Vice Pres*
Magaly Sevillano, *Admin Sec*
EMP: 55 EST: 1999
SQ FT: 10,000
SALES (est): 6.6MM **Privately Held**
WEB: www.fosterkidscan.org
SIC: 8322 8361 Social service center; family counseling services; residential care

(P-21750)
COMMUNITY ACTION PARTNERSHIP
3970 Short St, San Luis Obispo (93401-7567)
PHONE..........................805 541-4122
EMP: 100
SALES (corp-wide): 93.2MM **Privately Held**
WEB: www.capslo.org
SIC: 8322 Individual & family services
PA: Community Action Partnership Of San Luis Obispo County, Inc.
1030 Southwood Dr
San Luis Obispo CA 93401
805 544-4355

(P-21751)
COMMUNITY ACTION PARTNR KERN
3000 Sterling Rd, Bakersfield (93306-4569)
PHONE..........................661 871-6055
Kim Lisby, *Manager*
EMP: 74
SALES (corp-wide): 63.1MM **Privately Held**
WEB: www.capk.org
SIC: 8322 8661 Child related social services; religious organizations
PA: Community Action Partnership Of Kern
5005 Business Park N
Bakersfield CA 93309
661 336-5236

(P-21752)
COMMUNITY ACTION PARTNR KERN (PA)
5005 Business Park N, Bakersfield
(93309-1651)
PHONE...................661 336-5236
Jeremy Tobias, *Exec Dir*
Pam Pritchard, *Officer*
Letisha Brooks, *Program Mgr*
Jackie Guerra, *Program Mgr*
Lois Hannible, *Program Mgr*
EMP: 50 **EST:** 1965
SQ FT: 14,500
SALES (est): 63.1MM **Privately Held**
WEB: www.capk.org
SIC: 8322 Social service center; senior citizens' center or association; child guidance agency; public welfare center

(P-21753)
COMMUNITY ACTION PRTNR ORNGE C
Also Called: OC FOOD BANK
11870 Monarch St, Garden Grove
(92841-2113)
PHONE...................714 897-6670
Gregory C Scott, *CEO*
Janice Holley, *Admin Asst*
Sherrie Paull, *Human Res Dir*
John Nguyen, *Corp Comm Staff*
Kristin Kvesic, *Senior Mgr*
EMP: 105 **EST:** 1965
SQ FT: 86,300
SALES: 24.4MM **Privately Held**
WEB: www.capoc.org
SIC: 8322 Social service center

(P-21754)
COMMUNITY COLLEGE FOUNDATION
3530 Wilshire Blvd # 610, Los Angeles
(90010-2372)
PHONE...................213 427-6910
Nanette Fowler, *President*
EMP: 50
SALES (corp-wide): 4.5MM **Privately Held**
WEB: www.communitycollege.org
SIC: 8322 Child related social services
PA: Community College Foundation
1901 Royal Oaks Dr # 100
Sacramento CA 95815
916 418-5100

(P-21755)
COMMUNITY SUPPORT OPTIONS INC
1401 Poso Dr, Wasco (93280-2584)
P.O. Box 8018 (93280-8108)
PHONE...................661 758-5331
John Stockton, *CEO*
Anna Poggi, *President*
Ben Goosen, *Treasurer*
Melissa Stockton, *Officer*
Jose Hernandez, *Vice Pres*
EMP: 102 **EST:** 1974
SQ FT: 9,000
SALES (est): 5.8MM **Privately Held**
WEB: www.cso-svd.org
SIC: 8322 Association for the handicapped

(P-21756)
COMPTON UNIFIED SCHOOL DST
Also Called: Edward G Chester Adult Center
1104 E 148th St, Compton (90220-1339)
PHONE...................310 898-6470
Saundra T Bishop, *Director*
Saundra Bishop, *Exec Dir*
Zuniga Maria, *Admin Sec*
EMP: 72
SALES (corp-wide): 342.2MM **Privately Held**
WEB: www.compton.k12.ca.us
SIC: 8211 8322 Public elementary & secondary schools; adult day care center
PA: Compton Unified School District
501 S Santa Fe Ave
Compton CA 90221
310 604-6508

(P-21757)
COUNCIL ON AGING - STHERN CAL
2 Executive Cir Ste 175, Irvine
(92614-6773)
PHONE...................714 479-0107
Lisa Wright Jenkins, *CEO*
Rim Hussin, *Manager*
Lee Woolery, *Manager*
Sara Yu, *Manager*
Richard Barnes, *Supervisor*
EMP: 83 **EST:** 1973
SALES (est): 4.6MM **Privately Held**
WEB: www.coasc.org
SIC: 8322 Senior citizens' center or association

(P-21758)
COUNTRY VILLA RANCHO
39950 Vista Del Sol, Rancho Mirage
(92270-3206)
PHONE...................760 340-0053
Scott Gillis, *Administration*
EMP: 200 **EST:** 2007
SALES (est): 9.5MM **Privately Held**
WEB: www.ranchomiragehcc.com
SIC: 8322 Rehabilitation services

(P-21759)
COUNTRY VILLA SERVICE CORP
3000 N Gate Rd, Seal Beach (90740-2535)
PHONE...................562 598-2477
Jennifer Rose, *Branch Mgr*
EMP: 62
SALES (corp-wide): 78.2MM **Privately Held**
SIC: 8322 8011 Rehabilitation services; medical centers
PA: Country Villa Service Corp.
2400 E Katella Ave # 800
Anaheim CA 92806
310 574-3733

(P-21760)
COUNTY OF RIVERSIDE
Also Called: District Attorney's Office
2001 Iowa Ave Ste 218, Riverside
(92507-2480)
P.O. Box 1260 (92502-1260)
PHONE...................951 955-5659
John Replogle, *Branch Mgr*
John Browning, *Officer*
Claudia Juarez, *Officer*
Roger Medina, *Officer*
Cathryn Piech, *Admin Sec*
EMP: 73
SALES (corp-wide): 4B **Privately Held**
WEB: www.rivco.org
SIC: 9222 8322 District Attorneys' offices; ; child related social services
PA: County Of Riverside
4080 Lemon St Fl 11
Riverside CA 92501
951 955-1110

(P-21761)
COUNTY OF SAN BERNARDINO
Also Called: Aging & Adult Services
17270 Bear Valley Rd # 108, Victorville
(92395-7751)
PHONE...................760 843-5100
EMP: 51 **Privately Held**
SIC: 8322 9441 Individual/Family Services Executive Office
PA: County Of San Bernardino
385 N Arrowhead Ave
San Bernardino CA 92415
909 387-5455

(P-21762)
COUNTY OF VENTURA
Also Called: County Ventura Human Resources
800 S Victoria Ave, Ventura (93009-0003)
PHONE...................805 654-2561
Jodi Lee Prior, *Branch Mgr*
Robert McMahan, *Ch Radiology*
Jed Chernabaeff, *Officer*
Joseph Vasquez, *Officer*
Leah Velador, *Officer*
EMP: 104
SALES (corp-wide): 1.5B **Privately Held**
WEB: www.ventura.org
SIC: 8322 9441 Individual & family services; administration of social & human resources

PA: County Of Ventura
800 S Victoria Ave
Ventura CA 93009
805 654-2644

(P-21763)
COUNTY OF VENTURA
Also Called: Ventura Yuth Conservation Camp
2800 Wright Rd, Camarillo (93010-8350)
PHONE...................805 983-1332
Steve Heil, *Chief*
EMP: 115
SALES (corp-wide): 1.5B **Privately Held**
WEB: www.ventura.org
SIC: 9224 8322 ; youth center
PA: County Of Ventura
800 S Victoria Ave
Ventura CA 93009
805 654-2644

(P-21764)
CRESTWOOD BEHAVIORAL HLTH INC
Also Called: 1115 Bakersfield Mhrc
6700 Eucalyptus Dr Ste A, Bakersfield
(93306-6076)
PHONE...................661 363-8127
Sukhdeep Kaur, *Principal*
Ronda Banclive, *Director*
EMP: 82
SALES (corp-wide): 238MM **Privately Held**
WEB: www.crestwoodbehavioralhealth.com
SIC: 8322 8011 Rehabilitation services; psychiatric clinic
PA: Crestwood Behavioral Health, Inc.
520 Capitol Mall Ste 800
Sacramento CA 95814
510 651-1244

(P-21765)
CRYSTAL STAIRS INC (PA)
5110 W Goldleaf Cir # 150, Los Angeles
(90056-1287)
PHONE...................323 299-8998
Jackie B Majors, *CEO*
Dianna Torres, *Ch of Bd*
Dr Karen Hill-Scott, *President*
Javier La Fianza, *COO*
Robert Trujillo, *Treasurer*
EMP: 330 **EST:** 1980
SQ FT: 83,000
SALES: 218.2MM **Privately Held**
WEB: www.crystalstairs.org
SIC: 8322 Social service center

(P-21766)
DEAN L DAVIS MD
Also Called: Mercy Hospital
2215 Truxtun Ave, Bakersfield
(93301-3602)
P.O. Box 119 (93302-0119)
PHONE...................661 632-5000
Dean L Davis MD, *Owner*
Keith Jennings, *CIO*
Rose Dela Cruz, *Surgeon*
Jon Ehrhardt, *Radiology*
Spencer Todd, *Med Doctor*
EMP: 20 **EST:** 1996
SALES (est): 10.1MM **Privately Held**
SIC: 8322 3842 Community center; gynecological supplies & appliances

(P-21767)
DESERT AIDS PROJECT (PA)
Also Called: REVIVALS THRIFT STORES
1695 N Sunrise Way # 101, Palm Springs
(92262-5572)
P.O. Box 2890 (92263-2890)
PHONE...................760 323-2118
David Brinkman, *CEO*
Mary Park, *CFO*
Nick Valenziano, *Executive Asst*
John Hueste, *Controller*
Bryan Sypherd, *Inv Control Mgr*
EMP: 65 **EST:** 1984
SQ FT: 46,050
SALES (est): 49MM **Privately Held**
WEB: www.daphealth.org
SIC: 8322 5932 8011 General counseling services; used merchandise stores; clinic, operated by physicians

(P-21768)
DESERTARC
Also Called: DESERT VALLEY INDUSTRIES
73255 Country Club Dr, Palm Desert
(92260-2309)
PHONE...................760 346-1611
Lori Serfling, *Treasurer*
Robert Anzalone, *President*
Robin Keagen, *CFO*
Jay Chesterton, *Treasurer*
Rosemary Fausel, *Vice Pres*
EMP: 256 **EST:** 1959
SQ FT: 12,000
SALES: 18.5MM **Privately Held**
WEB: www.desertarc.org
SIC: 8322 Association for the handicapped; social services for the handicapped

(P-21769)
DIDI HIRSCH PSYCHIATRIC SVC (PA)
Also Called: DIDI HIRSCH COMMUNITY MENTAL H
4760 Sepulveda Blvd, Culver City
(90230-4820)
PHONE...................310 390-6612
Michael Wierwille, *Chairman*
Kita S Curry, *President*
Martin Frank, *Treasurer*
Nick Bacon, *Vice Pres*
Robbi Shulman, *Admin Mgr*
EMP: 150 **EST:** 1944
SQ FT: 35,000
SALES: 54.6MM **Privately Held**
WEB: www.didihirsch.org
SIC: 8322 8093 Family counseling services; mental health clinic, outpatient

(P-21770)
DIOCESE FRESNO EDUCATION CORP
Also Called: Catholic Social Services
1638 N Dinuba Blvd, Visalia (93291-3019)
PHONE...................559 734-1572
Marcy Ramirez, *Director*
EMP: 53
SALES (corp-wide): 100.8MM **Privately Held**
WEB: www.dioceseoffresno.org
SIC: 8211 8322 Catholic elementary & secondary schools; individual & family services
PA: Diocese Of Fresno Education Corporation
1550 N Fresno St
Fresno CA 93703
559 488-7400

(P-21771)
DIVERSE JOURNEYS INC (PA)
525 S Douglas St Ste 210, El Segundo
(90245-4827)
PHONE...................310 643-7403
Amanda Gerhart, *President*
Laura Broderrick, *Director*
EMP: 78 **EST:** 2005
SQ FT: 2,000
SALES (est): 4.9MM **Privately Held**
WEB: www.diversejourneys.org
SIC: 8322 Social services for the handicapped

(P-21772)
DIVINITY RECOVERY
20301 Ventura Blvd # 121, Woodland Hills
(91364-2447)
PHONE...................866 757-0474
Lea Hummel, *Principal*
EMP: 50 **EST:** 2020
SALES (est): 829.4K **Privately Held**
SIC: 8322 Rehabilitation services

(P-21773)
DREW CHILD DEV CORP INC (PA)
1770 E 118th St, Los Angeles
(90059-2518)
PHONE...................323 249-2950
Michael Jackson, *President*
James Hays, *CEO*
Jacqueline Clarke, *Officer*
Diann Fauntleroy, *Education*
Gricelda Perez, *Education*
EMP: 122 **EST:** 1987

(PA)=Parent Co (HQ)=Headquarters (DH)=Div Headquarters

✪ = New Business established in last 2 years

2022 Southern California Business
Directory and Buyers Guide

957

PRODUCTS & SVCS

SALES (est): 34.9MM **Privately Held**
WEB: www.drewcdc.org
SIC: 8322 Child guidance agency

(P-21774)
EAST LOS ANGLES RMRKBLE CTZENS
Also Called: EL ARCA
3839 Selig Pl, Los Angeles (90031-3143)
PHONE..................................323 223-3079
Carlos Madrid, *Exec Dir*
Laurence Ramirez, *Treasurer*
Karina Andrade, *Vice Pres*
John Menchaca, *Vice Pres*
Melissa Trancoso,
EMP: 100 EST: 1969
SQ FT: 23,360
SALES (est): 5.8MM **Privately Held**
WEB: www.elarcainc.org
SIC: 8322 Social services for the handicapped

(P-21775)
EASTER SEALS SOUTHERN CAL INC
531 W 8th St, Upland (91786-6512)
PHONE..................................909 981-4668
Angela Okey, *Administration*
Jeff Fine, *Program Dir*
EMP: 62
SQ FT: 17,000
SALES (corp-wide): 295.6MM **Privately Held**
WEB: www.easterseals.com
SIC: 8322 Social service center
PA: Easter Seals Southern California, Inc.
   1063 Mcgaw Ave Ste 100
   Irvine CA 92614
   714 834-1111

(P-21776)
EASTERN LOS ANGELES RE (PA)
1000 S Fremont Ave # 40, Alhambra
(91803-8873)
P.O. Box 7916 (91802-7916)
PHONE..................................626 299-4700
Gloria Wong, *Exec Dir*
Sophia Tang Hao, *Controller*
Lily Ortega, *Training Spec*
Heike Ballmaier, *Psychologist*
Frances Jacobs, *Manager*
EMP: 242
SQ FT: 31,704
SALES: 196.3MM **Privately Held**
WEB: www.elarc.org
SIC: 8322 Association for the handicapped

(P-21777)
EASTERN STAR HOMES CALIFORNIA (PA)
Also Called: EASTERN STAR PROFESSIONAL BUIL
16850 Bastanchury Rd, Yorba Linda
(92886-1608)
PHONE..................................714 986-2380
Norma Stillwell, *President*
Danna Willoughby, *President*
EMP: 56 EST: 1930
SQ FT: 15,604
SALES (est): 3.4MM **Privately Held**
SIC: 8322 Geriatric social service

(P-21778)
EGGLESTON YOUTH CENTERS INC (PA)
13001 Ramona Blvd Ste E, Irwindale
(91706-3752)
P.O. Box 638, Baldwin Park (91706-0638)
PHONE..................................626 480-8107
Clarence Brown, *Exec Dir*
April Mitchell, *President*
Don Gutierrez, *Administration*
Adrianna Vermilion, *Director*
EMP: 90 EST: 1975
SQ FT: 7,616
SALES (est): 6.4MM **Privately Held**
WEB: www.egglestonyouthcenter.org
SIC: 8322 Social service center; youth center

(P-21779)
EL NIDO FAMILY CENTERS (PA)
10200 Sepulveda Blvd # 350, Mission Hills
(91345-3318)
PHONE..................................818 830-3646
Liz Herrera, *Director*
Mike Still, *Administration*
Sandy Rodriguez, *Program Dir*
Desiree Vega, *Director*
EMP: 130 EST: 1957
SQ FT: 3,650
SALES (est): 12.2MM **Privately Held**
WEB: www.elnidofamilycenters.org
SIC: 8322 Social service center

(P-21780)
FAMILIES CHICE HM CARE SVCS IN
545 N Mountain Ave # 209, Upland
(91786-5073)
PHONE..................................909 303-9377
Kendal Ingram, *CEO*
Tim Ingram, *Vice Pres*
Nancy Ingram, *Office Mgr*
EMP: 65 EST: 2014
SALES (est): 1.5MM **Privately Held**
WEB: www.familieschoicehomecare.com
SIC: 8322 Individual & family services

(P-21781)
FAMILY ASSISTANCE PROGRAM
Also Called: OUR HOUSE
15075 Seventh St, Victorville (92395-3810)
PHONE..................................760 843-0701
Darryl Evey, *CEO*
Elsa Scott, *CFO*
Lori Kilgore, *Bd of Directors*
Caroline Reyna, *Program Mgr*
EMP: 92 EST: 1985
SQ FT: 4,960
SALES (est): 5.9MM **Privately Held**
WEB: www.familyassist.org
SIC: 8322 Social service center

(P-21782)
FAMILY ASSSSMENT CNSLING EDCAT
1651 E 4th St Ste 128, Santa Ana
(92701-5141)
PHONE..................................714 447-9024
Mary O Harris, *Branch Mgr*
Karen L Mfti, *Director*
EMP: 69 **Privately Held**
WEB: www.facescounseling.org
SIC: 8322 Family counseling services; general counseling services
PA: Family Assessment Counseling Education Services
   2601 E Chapman Ave # 114
   Fullerton CA 92831

(P-21783)
FAMILY CIRCLE INC
Also Called: Oxnard Family Circle Adhc
2100 Outlet Center Dr # 380, Oxnard
(93036-0612)
PHONE..................................805 385-4180
Katy Krul, *CEO*
Inna Berger, *CEO*
Dina Treglia, *Accounts Mgr*
EMP: 56 EST: 2001
SQ FT: 12,000
SALES (est): 6.8MM **Privately Held**
WEB: www.oxnardfamilycircle.com
SIC: 8322 Adult day care center

(P-21784)
FAMILY SERVICE ASSOCIATION
21801 Alessandro Blvd, Moreno Valley
(92553-8202)
PHONE..................................951 653-8109
Marc Salveson, *Branch Mgr*
EMP: 53 **Privately Held**
WEB: www.fsaca.org
SIC: 8322 Social service center
PA: Family Service Association
   21250 Box Springs Rd # 21
   Moreno Valley CA 92557

(P-21785)
FAMILY SERVICE ASSOCIATION
Also Called: K Ceniceros Community Center
29995 Evans Rd, Sun City (92586-3607)
PHONE..................................951 672-9673
Leslie Covey, *Manager*
EMP: 53 **Privately Held**
WEB: www.fsaca.org
SIC: 8322 Social service center
PA: Family Service Association
   21250 Box Springs Rd # 21
   Moreno Valley CA 92557

(P-21786)
FAMILY SERVICES TULARE COUNTY
815 W Oak Ave, Visalia (93291-6033)
P.O. Box 429 (93279-0429)
PHONE..................................559 732-1970
Caity Meader, *Exec Dir*
Heather Reed, *Hum Res Coord*
Mary Boylan, *Manager*
EMP: 59 EST: 1983
SQ FT: 2,000
SALES (est): 6.2MM **Privately Held**
WEB: www.fstc.net
SIC: 8322 Family counseling services

(P-21787)
FAMILY SVC AGCY SNTA BRBARA CN
123 W Gutierrez St, Santa Barbara
(93101-3424)
PHONE..................................805 965-1001
Denise Cicourel, *Administration*
Steven Delira, *Exec Dir*
Christie Ontjes, *Opers Spvr*
Tracy Thompson,
Deann Rosenberry, *Manager*
EMP: 100 EST: 1901
SALES: 13MM **Privately Held**
WEB: www.fsacares.org
SIC: 8322 Social service center

(P-21788)
FIREFIGHTER CANCER SUPPORT NTW
3460 Fletcher Ave, El Monte (91731-3002)
PHONE..................................866 994-3276
Dan Crow, *President*
Jeffrey Howe, *Treasurer*
Steve Fisher, *Vice Pres*
Donna Macdonald, *Vice Pres*
Lisa Raggio, *Exec Dir*
EMP: 50 EST: 2009
SALES (est): 228.2K **Privately Held**
WEB: www.firefightercancersupport.org
SIC: 8322 Social service center

(P-21789)
FIRST 5 LA
750 N Alameda St Ste 300, Los Angeles
(90012-3870)
PHONE..................................213 482-9487
Kim Belsh, *Principal*
Maria Aquino, *Officer*
Leticia Ches, *Officer*
Tina Chinakarn, *Officer*
Amelia Cobb, *Officer*
EMP: 61 EST: 2008
SALES (est): 33.9MM **Privately Held**
WEB: www.first5la.org
SIC: 8322 Child guidance agency

(P-21790)
FOUNDTION FOR ERLY CHLDHOOD ED (PA)
3450 E Sierra Madre Blvd, Pasadena
(91107-1934)
PHONE..................................626 572-5107
Sharyn Muhammad-Beeker, *CEO*
Pablo Ocasio, *Bd of Directors*
Angelica Orozco, *Bd of Directors*
Qi Xu, *Officer*
Abdi Ahmed, *Vice Pres*
EMP: 101 EST: 1965
SALES (est): 10.5MM **Privately Held**
WEB: www.foundationheadstart.org
SIC: 8322 Child guidance agency

(P-21791)
FRESHLUNCHES INC
19431 Business Center Dr, Northridge
(91324-3507)
PHONE..................................318 885-1718
Alan Razzaghi, *CEO*
EMP: 50 EST: 2006
SALES (est): 5.3MM **Privately Held**
WEB: www.freshlunches.com
SIC: 8322 5812 Meal delivery program; contract food services

(P-21792)
GOOD SAMARITAN SHELTER
245 Inger Dr Ste 103b, Santa Maria
(93454-8669)
PHONE..................................805 346-8185
Sylvia Barnard, *Director*
EMP: 51 EST: 1989
SQ FT: 2,400
SALES (est): 8.7MM **Privately Held**
WEB: www.goodsamaritanshelter.org
SIC: 8322 Social service center

(P-21793)
GOODWILL CENTRAL COAST
Also Called: Goodwill Inds San Luis Obispo
880 Industrial Way, San Luis Obispo
(93401-7666)
PHONE..................................805 544-0542
James Burke, *Branch Mgr*
EMP: 168
SALES (corp-wide): 32MM **Privately Held**
WEB: www.ccgoodwill.com
SIC: 5932 8322 Used merchandise stores; rehabilitation services
PA: Goodwill Central Coast
   1566 Moffett St
   Salinas CA 93905
   831 423-8611

(P-21794)
GRACEFUL SNSCNCE ADULT DAY HLT
120 W El Segundo Blvd, Los Angeles
(90061-1628)
PHONE..................................310 538-5808
Ladale Jackson, *President*
EMP: 14 EST: 1998
SALES (est): 518.4K **Privately Held**
SIC: 8322 3679 7371 Adult day care center; electronic circuits; custom computer programming services

(P-21795)
GUARDIAN HEALTH CARE SVCS INC
16561 Graham St, Huntington Beach
(92649-3732)
PHONE..................................714 377-7767
John Emma, *CFO*
EMP: 50 EST: 2016
SALES (est): 1.4MM **Privately Held**
SIC: 8322 Individual & family services

(P-21796)
HATHAWY-SYCMRES CHILD FMLY SVC
Also Called: Hathaway Children and Family
12502 Van Nuys Blvd Ste 1, Pacoima
(91331-1321)
PHONE..................................626 395-7100
Muriel Gaudin, *Manager*
Jonathan Wu, *Exec VP*
Cherrie Rodriguez, *Admin Asst*
Veronica Munoz, *Analyst*
Janette Baucham, *Director*
EMP: 195
SALES (corp-wide): 64.2MM **Privately Held**
WEB: www.hathaway-sycamores.org
SIC: 8322 Child related social services
PA: Hathaway-Sycamores Child And Family Services
   100 W Walnut St Ste 375
   Pasadena CA 91124
   626 395-7100

(P-21797)
HATHAWY-SYCMRES CHILD FMLY SVC
3741 Stocker St Ste 01, View Park
(90008-5150)
PHONE..................................323 733-0322

Debbie Manners, *Branch Mgr*
Mary Wilson, *Asst Director*
Elika Ramirez, *Director*
Judy Cardona, *Manager*
Norma Ramirez, *Manager*
EMP: 195
SALES (corp-wide): 64.2MM **Privately Held**
WEB: www.hathaway-sycamores.org
SIC: 8322 Child related social services
PA: Hathaway-Sycamores Child And Family Services
  100 W Walnut St Ste 375
  Pasadena CA 91124
  626 395-7100

(P-21798)
HAVEN HILLS INC
7112 Owensmouth Ave, Canoga Park (91303-2007)
P.O. Box 260 (91305-0260)
PHONE.................................818 887-7481
Lila Aurich, *Vice Pres*
Joanne David, *Principal*
Sara Berdine, *Exec Dir*
Jacqueline Harris, *Teacher*
Ivy Panlilio, *Program Dir*
EMP: 67 **EST:** 1977
SALES (est): 3.6MM **Privately Held**
WEB: www.havenhills.org
SIC: 8322 Social service center

(P-21799)
HEALTH SOUTH TUSTIN REHAB HOSP
14851 Yorba St, Tustin (92780-2925)
PHONE.................................714 832-9200
Paula Redman, *Controller*
EMP: 120 **EST:** 1988
SQ FT: 90,000
SALES (est): 3.6MM
SALES (corp-wide): 4.6B **Publicly Held**
WEB: www.encompasshealth.com
SIC: 8322 8069 Rehabilitation services; specialty hospitals, except psychiatric
PA: Encompass Health Corporation
  9001 Liberty Pkwy
  Birmingham AL 35242
  205 967-7116

(P-21800)
HELP CHILDREN WORLD FOUNDATION
Also Called: INTERNATIONAL CHILDREN'S CHARI
26500 Agoura Rd Ste 657, Calabasas (91302-1952)
PHONE.................................818 706-9848
Lev M Leznik, *President*
Andrew Grey, *Vice Pres*
Veronica Duval, *Director*
Michael Teilmann, *Director*
EMP: 300 **EST:** 1991
SQ FT: 2,200
SALES (est): 387K **Privately Held**
WEB: www.tohelpthechildren.org
SIC: 8322 Children's aid society

(P-21801)
HELP HOSPITALIZED VETERANS (PA)
36585 Penfield Ln, Winchester (92596-9672)
PHONE.................................951 926-4500
Mike Lynch, *Exec Dir*
Joe McClain, *CEO*
Tracey Bridges, *Admin Asst*
Wende Caha, *Administration*
Chip Purkey, *Prdtn Mgr*
EMP: 86 **EST:** 1971
SQ FT: 25,000
SALES (est): 12.2MM **Privately Held**
WEB: www.healvets.org
SIC: 8322 Individual & family services

(P-21802)
HELPLINE YOUTH COUNSELING INC (PA)
14181 Telegraph Rd, Whittier (90604-2554)
PHONE.................................562 273-0722
Deepak Nanda, *Ch of Bd*
Jacques Welche C P A, *Treasurer*
Jeff Farber, *Exec Dir*
Jeffrey Farber, *Exec Sec*
Pam Van Alstyne, *Admin Sec*

EMP: 50 **EST:** 1971
SQ FT: 9,000
SALES (est): 7.4MM **Privately Held**
WEB: www.hycinc.org
SIC: 8322 Family (marriage) counseling; social service center

(P-21803)
HOMEBOY INDUSTRIES (PA)
Also Called: Homeboy Bakery
130 Bruno St, Los Angeles (90012-1815)
PHONE.................................323 526-1254
Greg Boyle, *Exec Dir*
John Brady, *Ch of Bd*
Jack Faherty, *CFO*
Francis Ota, *CFO*
James Burk, *Treasurer*
EMP: 270 **EST:** 2000
SQ FT: 3,690
SALES (est): 14.4MM **Privately Held**
WEB: www.homeboyindustries.org
SIC: 8322 Rehabilitation services

(P-21804)
HOPE OF VALLEY RESCUE MISSION
11076 Norris Ave Fl 2, Pacoima (91331-2468)
P.O. Box 7609, Mission Hills (91346-7609)
PHONE.................................818 392-0020
Ken Craft, *President*
Michael Klausman, *Ch of Bd*
David Faustina, *COO*
Chris Delaplane, *Treasurer*
Rowan Vansleve, *Officer*
EMP: 54 **EST:** 2010
SQ FT: 22,000
SALES (est): 7.7MM **Privately Held**
WEB: www.hopeofthevalley.org
SIC: 8322 Emergency shelters

(P-21805)
HORRIGAN ENTERPRISES INC
Also Called: Crossrads Adult Hlth Care
7945 Cartilla Ave, Rancho Cucamonga (91730-3076)
PHONE.................................909 481-9663
Judy Lowe, *Manager*
EMP: 153
SALES (corp-wide): 4.7MM **Privately Held**
WEB: www.industry386.com
SIC: 8322 Adult day care center
PA: Horrigan Enterprises, Inc.
  11130 White Birch Dr
  Rancho Cucamonga CA 91730
  909 484-5561

(P-21806)
HUMAN OPTIONS INC
1901 Newport Blvd Ste 240, Costa Mesa (92627-2294)
PHONE.................................949 757-3635
Maricela Rios, *Branch Mgr*
Jessica Reynaga, *Education*
EMP: 50 **Privately Held**
WEB: www.humanoptions.org
SIC: 8322 Social service center
PA: Human Options, Inc.
  5540 Trabuco Rd Ste 100
  Irvine CA 92620

(P-21807)
HUMAN SERVICES ASSOCIATION (PA)
Also Called: Hsa Bell Gardens Laup
6800 Florence Ave, Bell (90201-4957)
PHONE.................................562 806-5400
Susanne Sundberg, *Principal*
Ricardo Mota, *Officer*
Josie Alston Williams, *Exec Dir*
Laura Avila, *Executive Asst*
Bre Onna Mathis, *Project Dir*
EMP: 75
SQ FT: 10,000
SALES (est): 20.6MM **Privately Held**
WEB: www.hsala.org
SIC: 8322 Social service center

(P-21808)
IDEAL PROGRAM SERVICES INC
3970 W Mrtn Lther King Jr, Los Angeles (90008-1732)
PHONE.................................323 296-2255
Omolara Okunubi, *CEO*
Ivan Martinez, *COO*
Lara Okunubi, *Administration*
Tara Mitchell, *Manager*
Nakia Powell, *Manager*
EMP: 71 **EST:** 1989
SQ FT: 8,880
SALES (est): 7.1MM **Privately Held**
WEB: www.idealprogramsservices.org
SIC: 8322 5999 Social services for the handicapped; technical aids for the handicapped

(P-21809)
IN-ROADS CREATIVE PROGRAMS
9057 Arrow Rte Ste 120, Rancho Cucamonga (91730-4452)
PHONE.................................909 989-9944
Sharon Barton, *Branch Mgr*
EMP: 69 **Privately Held**
WEB: www.in-roads.net
SIC: 8322 Adult day care center
PA: In-Roads Creative Programs, Inc
  7955 Webster St Ste 7
  Highland CA 92346

(P-21810)
IN-ROADS CREATIVE PROGRAMS
1951 E Saint Andrews Dr, Ontario (91761-6447)
PHONE.................................909 947-9142
Sharon Barton, *Branch Mgr*
EMP: 69 **Privately Held**
WEB: www.in-roads.net
SIC: 8322 Children's aid society
PA: In-Roads Creative Programs, Inc
  7955 Webster St Ste 7
  Highland CA 92346

(P-21811)
IN-ROADS CREATIVE PROGRAMS (PA)
7955 Webster St Ste 7, Highland (92346-3880)
PHONE.................................909 864-1551
Sharon Barton, *CEO*
EMP: 622 **EST:** 2000
SQ FT: 1,200
SALES (est): 13.4MM **Privately Held**
WEB: www.in-roads.net
SIC: 8322 Children's aid society

(P-21812)
INCLUSION SERVICES LLC
7255 Greenleaf Ave Ste 20, Whittier (90602-1340)
PHONE.................................562 945-2000
Cesar Torres, *Mng Member*
Israel Ibenez, *Mng Member*
Christina Gotay, *Director*
Nicole Geames, *Manager*
EMP: 103 **EST:** 2009
SALES (est): 10.3MM **Privately Held**
WEB: www.inclusionsvs.com
SIC: 8322 8331 Social services for the handicapped; skill training center

(P-21813)
INDEPNDENT LVING CTR KERN CNTY
5251 Office Park Dr # 200, Bakersfield (93309-0404)
PHONE.................................661 325-1063
Jimmie Soto, *Exec Dir*
David Hendrickson, *Technology*
EMP: 58 **EST:** 1981
SALES (est): 1.2MM **Privately Held**
WEB: www.ilcofkerncounty.org
SIC: 8322 Social service center

(P-21814)
INDUSTRIAL RELATIONS CAL DEPT
28 Civic Center Plz # 239, Santa Ana (92701-4024)
PHONE.................................714 558-4121
George Gomez, *Manager*
EMP: 60 **Privately Held**
SIC: 9199 8322 ; rehabilitation services
HQ: California Department Of Industrial Relations
  455 Golden Gate Ave Fl 10
  San Francisco CA 94102

(P-21815)
INLAND CNTIES REGIONAL CTR INC (PA)
Also Called: INLAND REGIONAL CENTER
1365 S Waterman Ave, San Bernardino (92408-2804)
P.O. Box 19037 (92423-9037)
PHONE.................................909 890-3000
Carol A Fitzgibbons, *CEO*
Carol Fitzgibbons, *Exec Dir*
Mia Gurri, *Program Mgr*
Sandra Fortino, *Admin Sec*
Denise Fanelli, *Director*
EMP: 535 **EST:** 1971
SQ FT: 82,000
SALES (est): 641.7MM **Privately Held**
WEB: www.inlandrc.org
SIC: 8322 Social service center

(P-21816)
INTERFACE COMMUNITY (PA)
Also Called: INTERFACE CHILDREN FAMILY SERV
4001 Mission Oaks Blvd, Camarillo (93012-5121)
PHONE.................................805 485-6114
Charles T Watson, *President*
Dale Stoeber, *CFO*
Terryl Miller,
Kim Mora, *Officer*
Erik Sternad, *Exec Dir*
EMP: 93 **EST:** 1975
SQ FT: 3,000
SALES: 14.6MM **Privately Held**
WEB: www.icfs.org
SIC: 8322 Social service center

(P-21817)
INTERNATIONAL INST LOS ANGELES (PA)
3845 Selig Pl, Los Angeles (90031-3143)
PHONE.................................323 224-3800
E Stephen Voss, *CEO*
Hasmik Ktoian, *Administration*
Lilian Alba, *Director*
Robert Foss, *Director*
Lupe Granados, *Director*
EMP: 52 **EST:** 1935
SQ FT: 18,000
SALES (est): 432K **Privately Held**
WEB: www.iilosangeles.org
SIC: 8322 Family service agency

(P-21818)
INTERNATIONAL MEDICAL CORPS (PA)
12400 Wilshire Blvd # 1500, Los Angeles (90025-1030)
PHONE.................................310 826-7800
Nancy Aossey, *President*
Barry A Porter, *General Ptnr*
Jonathan M Glaser, *Managing Prtnr*
Jan Brandt, *Vice Chairman*
Michael Burns, *Vice Chairman*
EMP: 93 **EST:** 1984
SALES: 176MM **Privately Held**
WEB: www.internationalmedicalcorps.org
SIC: 8322 Disaster service

(P-21819)
INTERVAL HOUSE
6615 E Pcf Cast Hwy Ste 1, Long Beach (90803)
P.O. Box 3356, Seal Beach (90740-2356)
PHONE.................................562 594-4555
Robert Armstrong, *President*
Carol Williams, *Exec Dir*
Elizabeth Lambert, *Admin Sec*
Christine Delabre, *Director*
Thyda Duong, *Director*

EMP: 110 EST: 1979
SALES (est): 9.6MM **Privately Held**
WEB: www.intervalhouse.org
SIC: 8322 Emergency shelters; crisis center

(P-21820)
JEWISH COMMUNITY CTR LONG BCH
Also Called: ALPERT JEWISH COMMUNITY CENTRE
3801 E Willow St, Long Beach
(90815-1734)
PHONE..................562 426-7601
Gordon Lentzner, *President*
Winston Abigail, *CFO*
Eugene Ross, *Treasurer*
Deborah Goldfarb, *Exec Dir*
Jeannette Bastin, *Executive Asst*
EMP: 150
SQ FT: 90,000
SALES: 6.4MM **Privately Held**
WEB: www.alpertjcc.org
SIC: 8322 Community center

(P-21821)
JEWISH FAMILY SERVICE OF
16439 Vanowen St, Van Nuys
(91406-4730)
PHONE..................818 988-7682
Terry Friedman, *President*
Todd Sosna, *Vice Pres*
Laura Diepenbrock, *Program Mgr*
Brooke Moore, *Social Worker*
Kristina Sobko, *Social Worker*
EMP: 57 EST: 2012
SALES (est): 10.5MM **Privately Held**
WEB: www.jfsla.org
SIC: 8322 Social service center

(P-21822)
JEWISH FAMILY SVC LOS ANGELES
Also Called: Senior Nutrition Program
330 N Fairfax Ave, Los Angeles
(90036-2109)
PHONE..................323 937-5900
Eileen McCouliffe, *Director*
Edwin Avedian, *Administration*
EMP: 66
SALES (corp-wide): 45.4MM **Privately Held**
WEB: www.jfla.org
SIC: 8322 Social service center
PA: Jewish Family Service Of Los Angeles
330 N Fairfax Ave
Los Angeles CA 90036
323 761-8800

(P-21823)
JEWISH FAMILY SVC LOS ANGELES
Also Called: Valley Store Front Jwish Fmly
12821 Victory Blvd, North Hollywood
(91606-3012)
PHONE..................818 984-0276
Karen Leaf, *Director*
EMP: 66
SALES (corp-wide): 45.4MM **Privately Held**
WEB: www.jfsla.org
SIC: 8322 5331 Social service center; variety stores
PA: Jewish Family Service Of Los Angeles
330 N Fairfax Ave
Los Angeles CA 90036
323 761-8800

(P-21824)
JEWISH FAMILY SVC LOS ANGELES
Senior Citizens Center
330 N Fairfax Ave, Los Angeles
(90036-2109)
PHONE..................323 937-5900
Doreen Klee, *Owner*
EMP: 66
SALES (corp-wide): 45.4MM **Privately Held**
WEB: www.jfla.org
SIC: 8322 Social service center
PA: Jewish Family Service Of Los Angeles
330 N Fairfax Ave
Los Angeles CA 90036
323 761-8800

(P-21825)
JEWISH FAMILY SVC LOS ANGELES
4311 Wilshire Blvd, Los Angeles
(90010-3708)
PHONE..................323 935-5303
Susan Mendlowitz, *Branch Mgr*
Dora Escalante, *Manager*
EMP: 66
SALES (corp-wide): 45.4MM **Privately Held**
WEB: www.jfla.org
SIC: 8322 Social service center
PA: Jewish Family Service Of Los Angeles
330 N Fairfax Ave
Los Angeles CA 90036
323 761-8800

(P-21826)
JEWISH FMLY CHLD SVC LONG BCH-
Also Called: Jewish Family and Chld Svc
3801 E Willow St Ste 217, Long Beach
(90815-1734)
PHONE..................562 426-7601
Debbie Freeman, *Principal*
Richard Ruby, *President*
Rachel Gordon, *Opers Staff*
Pattie Davidson, *Director*
Karen Eddington, *Director*
EMP: 50 EST: 1958
SALES: 3.5MM **Privately Held**
WEB: www.jfcslongbeach.org
SIC: 8322 Social service center

(P-21827)
JOHN HENRY FOUNDATION
403 N Susan St, Santa Ana (92703-3433)
PHONE..................714 554-8906
M Andrews, *Exec Dir*
Mindy Andrews, *Exec Dir*
Allison Martin, *Exec Dir*
John Baxter, *General Mgr*
EMP: 61 EST: 1989
SQ FT: 6,400
SALES: 1.7MM **Privately Held**
WEB: www.johnhenry.org
SIC: 8322 Social services for the handicapped

(P-21828)
JONI AND FRIENDS FOUNDATION (PA)
30009 Ladyface Ct, Agoura (91301-2583)
PHONE..................818 707-5664
Joni E Tada, *CEO*
Billy Burnett, *Exec VP*
Douglas Mazza, *Exec VP*
Catherine Cobb, *Corp Comm Staff*
Glen Garcia, *Editor*
◆ EMP: 84 EST: 1979
SQ FT: 30,000
SALES: 35.9MM **Privately Held**
WEB: www.joniandfriends.org
SIC: 8322 Association for the handicapped

(P-21829)
JWCH INSTITUTE INC
Also Called: Jwch Medical Center
3591 E Imperial Hwy, Lynwood
(90262-2654)
PHONE..................310 223-1035
Al Basceros, *Manager*
EMP: 242
SALES (corp-wide): 86.3MM **Privately Held**
WEB: www.jwchinstitute.org
SIC: 8322 8093 Individual & family services; family planning clinic
PA: Jwch Institute, Inc.
5650 Jillson St
Commerce CA 90040
323 477-1171

(P-21830)
KEDREN COMMUNITY HLTH CTR INC
3800 S Figueroa St, Los Angeles
(90037-1206)
PHONE..................323 524-0634
John Griffith, *President*
Frank L Williams, *Bd of Directors*
Kristina Ledesma-Davies, *Officer*
Merced Pereda, *Controller*
Amelia Huckabee, *Human Res Dir*

EMP: 116
SALES (corp-wide): 54.8MM **Privately Held**
WEB: www.kedren.org
SIC: 8322 Community center
PA: Kedren Community Health Center, Inc.
4211 Avalon Blvd
Los Angeles CA 90011
323 233-0425

(P-21831)
KINGS CMNTY ACTION ORGNZTION I (PA)
Also Called: KCAO
1130 N 11th Ave, Hanford (93230-3608)
PHONE..................559 582-4386
David Droker, *Exec Dir*
Jennifer Hoffmaster, *Director*
EMP: 93 EST: 1965
SQ FT: 15,000
SALES: 25.3MM **Privately Held**
WEB: www.kcao.org
SIC: 8322 8399 Individual & family services; antipoverty board

(P-21832)
KINGS REHABILITATION CTR INC (PA)
490 E Hanford Armona Rd, Hanford
(93230-6129)
P.O. Box 719 (93232-0719)
PHONE..................559 582-9234
Carol Rogers, *Marketing Staff*
Sherrie Martin, *Manager*
EMP: 57 EST: 1965
SQ FT: 13,000
SALES (est): 8.6MM **Privately Held**
WEB: www.kingsrehab.com
SIC: 8322 8361 Rehabilitation services; rehabilitation center, residential: health care incidental

(P-21833)
KOREAN HLTH EDCATN INFO RES CT (PA)
Also Called: Kheir
3727 W 6th St Ste 210, Los Angeles
(90020-5108)
PHONE..................213 427-4000
Erin K Pak, *CEO*
Chakma Nadesh, *Technology*
Crystal Cruz, *Hum Res Coord*
Papehn Navid, *Director*
Damian Kelly, *Manager*
EMP: 59 EST: 1986
SQ FT: 800
SALES (est): 16.2MM **Privately Held**
WEB: www.lakheir.org
SIC: 8322 8011 Individual & family services; offices & clinics of medical doctors

(P-21834)
LA ASCCION NCNAL PRO PRSNAS MY
Also Called: National Assn For Hispanic
1452 W Temple St Ste 100, Los Angeles
(90026-5649)
PHONE..................213 202-5900
Zecia Soto, *Principal*
EMP: 85
SALES (corp-wide): 15.3MM **Privately Held**
SIC: 8322 7361 8611 Social service center; employment agencies; business associations
PA: La Asociacion Nacional Pro Personas Mayores
234 E Colo Blvd Ste 300
Pasadena CA 91101
626 564-1988

(P-21835)
LA ASCCION NCNAL PRO PRSNAS MY (PA)
Also Called: NAT'L ASSN FOR HISPANIC ELDERL
234 E Colo Blvd Ste 300, Pasadena
(91101)
PHONE..................626 564-1988
Carmela G Lacayo, *President*
Maria Ramirez, *Ch of Bd*
Carole Kracer, *Treasurer*
Therese Grenier, *Admin Sec*
EMP: 552 EST: 1975
SQ FT: 11,000

SALES: 15.3MM **Privately Held**
SIC: 8322 Social service center

(P-21836)
LACBA COUNSEL FOR JUSTICE
200 S Spring St, Los Angeles
(90012-3710)
PHONE..................951 489-2919
Stanley Bissey, *CEO*
EMP: 66 EST: 2015
SALES (est): 1.4MM **Privately Held**
WEB: www.lacba.org
SIC: 8322 General counseling services

(P-21837)
LAURAS HOUSE
33 Journey Ste 150, Aliso Viejo
(92656-5364)
PHONE..................949 361-3775
Margaret Bayston, *Exec Dir*
Barry Villines, *CFO*
Dan Weeks, *Treasurer*
Sandra Condello, *Principal*
Mike James, *Exec Dir*
EMP: 92
SALES: 4MM **Privately Held**
WEB: www.laurashouse.org
SIC: 8322 Social service center

(P-21838)
LIFE STEPS FOUNDATION INC
Also Called: Santa Maria Wisdom Center
2255 S Depot St, Santa Maria
(93455-1216)
PHONE..................805 349-9810
Susan Chang, *Branch Mgr*
Alice Reyes, *Branch Mgr*
EMP: 85
WEB: www.lifestepsfoundation.org
SIC: 8322 Social service center
PA: Life Steps Foundation, Inc.
5757 W Century Blvc # 575
Los Angeles CA 90045

(P-21839)
LIFE STEPS FOUNDATION INC
Also Called: Lsf Central Ca Adult Svcs
218 Carmen Ln Ste 108, Santa Maria
(93458-7773)
PHONE..................805 474-8431
EMP: 85 **Privately Held**
WEB: www.lifestepsfoundation.org
SIC: 8322 Social service center
PA: Life Steps Foundation, Inc.
5757 W Century Blvd # 575
Los Angeles CA 90045

(P-21840)
LIFE STEPS FOUNDATION INC
500 E 4th St, Long Beach (90802-2501)
PHONE..................562 436-0751
Kristine Engels, *Director*
Robert Turner, *Manager*
EMP: 85 **Privately Held**
WEB: www.lifestepsfoundation.org
SIC: 8322 8399 Social service center; community development groups
PA: Life Steps Foundation, Inc.
5757 W Century Blvd # 575
Los Angeles CA 90045

(P-21841)
LIFE STEPS FOUNDATION INC
1107 Johnson Ave, San Luis Obispo
(93401-3303)
PHONE..................805 549-0150
Virginia Franco, *Manager*
EMP: 85 **Privately Held**
WEB: www.lifestepsfoundation.org
SIC: 8322 Social service center
PA: Life Steps Foundation, Inc.
5757 W Century Blvd # 575
Los Angeles CA 90045

(P-21842)
LONG BCH RSCUE MSSION FNDATION
Also Called: SAMARITIN HOUSE
1430 Pacific Ave, Long Beach
(90813-1717)
P.O. Box 1969 (90801-1969)
PHONE..................562 423-2500

James Lewis, *Deputy Dir*
EMP: 67 **EST:** 1971
SQ FT: 30,000
SALES: 129.2K **Privately Held**
WEB: www.lbrm.org
SIC: 8322 Social service center

(P-21843)
LOS ANGELES HOMELESS SVCS AUTH
Also Called: L A H S A
707 Wilshire Blvd # 1000, Los Angeles (90017-3729)
PHONE.................................213 683-3333
Heidi Marston, *Exec Dir*
Ahmad Chapman, *Comms Dir*
Peter Lynn, *Exec Dir*
Allura M Graham, *Admin Asst*
Debra Neal, *Admin Asst*
EMP: 558 **EST:** 1993
SALES (est): 55.4MM **Privately Held**
WEB: www.lahsa.org
SIC: 8322 Social service center

(P-21844)
LOS ANGELES REGIONAL FOOD BANK
1734 E 41st St, Vernon (90058-1502)
PHONE.................................323 234-3030
Michael Flood, *President*
Whitney Jones Roy, *Ch of Bd*
Edward McCarthy, *COO*
Czarina Luna, *CFO*
Paxeli Moreira, *CFO*
EMP: 120 **EST:** 1977
SQ FT: 100,000
SALES: 380.5MM **Privately Held**
WEB: www.lafoodbank.org
SIC: 8322 Meal delivery program

(P-21845)
LOS ANGLES SCTION NAT CNCIL JW (PA)
Also Called: NCJW LA
543 N Fairfax Ave, Los Angeles (90036-1715)
PHONE.................................323 651-2930
Hillary Sullivan, *Exec Dir*
Shelli Dodell, *President*
Sofiya Dubinsky, *CFO*
Sophia Orshansky, *Vice Pres*
Carrie Jacoves, *Comms Dir*
EMP: 50 **EST:** 1909
SALES: 722K **Privately Held**
WEB: www.ncjwla.org
SIC: 8322 Multi-service center

(P-21846)
LUMINA ALLIANCE
Also Called: Stand Strong
51 Zaca Ln Ste 150, San Luis Obispo (93401-7319)
P.O. Box 125 (93406-0125)
PHONE.................................805 781-6400
Jennifer Adams, *CEO*
Marianne Kennedy, *Principal*
EMP: 75 **EST:** 2001
SALES (est): 5.3MM **Privately Held**
WEB: www.standstrongnow.org
SIC: 8322 Social service center

(P-21847)
MARK 1 RESTORATION SERVICE LLC
3360 E La Palma Ave, Anaheim (92806-2814)
PHONE.................................714 283-9990
Gary Moore,
EMP: 78 **EST:** 2020
SALES (est): 1MM **Privately Held**
WEB: www.mark1restoration.net
SIC: 8322 Disaster service

(P-21848)
MARTHAS VILLAGE & KITCHEN
83791 Date Ave, Indio (92201-4737)
PHONE.................................760 347-4741
Joe Carol, *President*
Matthew Packard, *Vice Pres*
Claudia Castorena, *Director*
Rachelle Flores, *Director*
Gloria Gomez, *Director*
EMP: 65

SALES: 4.6MM **Privately Held**
WEB: www.marthasvillage.org
SIC: 8322 Social service center

(P-21849)
MEN TKING OVER RFRMING SOC INC
6630 Crenshaw Blvd, Los Angeles (90043-4102)
PHONE.................................323 338-6633
Toni Wells, *CEO*
David Thomas, *President*
Ronald Burnette, *Bd of Directors*
Tylo James, *Development*
EMP: 61 **EST:** 2016
SALES (est): 2.8MM **Privately Held**
WEB: www.operationbrightlights.org
SIC: 8322 Emergency shelters; community center

(P-21850)
MEXICAN AMRCN OPRTNTY FNDATION (PA)
Also Called: MAOF
401 N Garfield Ave, Montebello (90640-2901)
P.O. Box 4602 (90640-9311)
PHONE.................................323 890-9600
Martin Vasquez Castro, *President*
Orlando M Sayson, *CFO*
Carolina Rodriguez, *Officer*
Carlos J Viramontes, *Principal*
Estela Morales, *Admin Asst*
EMP: 100 **EST:** 1963
SQ FT: 25,000
SALES: 109.4MM **Privately Held**
WEB: www.maof.org
SIC: 8322 Social service center

(P-21851)
MIXTEC/NDGENA CMNTY ORGNZING P
Also Called: Micop
135 Magnolia Ave, Oxnard (93030-5336)
P.O. Box 20543 (93034-0543)
PHONE.................................805 483-1166
Arcenio Lopez, *Exec Dir*
Margaret Sawyer, *Exec Dir*
Vanessa Teran, *Program Mgr*
Donna Foster, *Opers Mgr*
EMP: 75
SALES: 4.8MM **Privately Held**
WEB: www.mixteco.org
SIC: 8322 Social service center

(P-21852)
MIZELL SENIOR CENTER INC
Also Called: PALM SPRINGS SENIOR CENTER
480 S Sunrise Way, Palm Springs (92262-7697)
PHONE.................................760 323-5689
Marty Hoffmen, *Director*
Ginny Foat, *Exec Dir*
Suzanne Spencer,
Laura Castillo, *Director*
Ian Murray, *Director*
EMP: 63 **EST:** 1980
SQ FT: 12,000
SALES (est): 2.7MM **Privately Held**
WEB: www.mizell.org
SIC: 8322 Senior citizens' center or association

(P-21853)
MOTHERS CLUB FAMILY LRNG CTR
980 N Fair Oaks Ave, Pasadena (91103-3009)
PHONE.................................626 792-2687
Susan Kujawa, *Exec Dir*
Hector Lafarga, *Exec Dir*
Elva Sandoval, *Exec Dir*
Martha Murillo, *Office Mgr*
Julie Espinoza, *Education*
EMP: 54 **EST:** 1961
SQ FT: 10,000
SALES (est): 1.6MM **Privately Held**
WEB: www.familiesforwardlc.org
SIC: 8322 Social service center

(P-21854)
NEW DIRECTIONS INC (PA)
Also Called: New Directions For Veterans
11303 Wilshire Blvd, Los Angeles (90025-5069)
P.O. Box 25536 (90025-0536)
PHONE.................................310 914-4045
Edgar H Howell, *CEO*
Usha Murthy, *CFO*
Tony Reinis, *Exec Dir*
Duane Byrdsong, *Program Mgr*
Ren Ross, *Project Mgr*
EMP: 80 **EST:** 1989
SQ FT: 60,000
SALES (est): 15.3MM **Privately Held**
WEB: www.ndvets.org
SIC: 8322 Substance abuse counseling

(P-21855)
NEW ECONOMICS FOR WOMEN (PA)
303 Loma Dr, Los Angeles (90017-1103)
PHONE.................................213 483-2060
Maggie Cervantes, *Exec Dir*
Liz Garcia, *Admin Asst*
Cheryl Bates, *Project Mgr*
Edith Martinez, *Project Mgr*
Romeo Reyes, *Finance Mgr*
EMP: 66 **EST:** 1985
SQ FT: 25,000
SALES: 4.5MM **Privately Held**
WEB: www.neweconomicsforwomen.org
SIC: 8322 Settlement house

(P-21856)
NEXCARE COLLABORATIVE (PA)
15477 Ventura Blvd, Sherman Oaks (91403-3006)
PHONE.................................818 907-0322
Pejman Salimpour, *President*
Ralph Salimpour MD, *Corp Secy*
Pedram Salimpour MD, *Exec VP*
EMP: 50 **EST:** 2001
SQ FT: 15,000
SALES (est): 16MM **Privately Held**
SIC: 8322 Child related social services

(P-21857)
NORTHEAST VALLEY HEALTH CORP (PA)
1172 N Maclay Ave, San Fernando (91340-1328)
PHONE.................................818 898-1388
Kimberly Wyard, *CEO*
Missy Nitescu, *COO*
Vince Avila, *CFO*
Patricia Moraga, *CFO*
Nelson Wong, *Chairman*
EMP: 75 **EST:** 1971
SALES: 104.7MM **Privately Held**
SIC: 8322 Community center

(P-21858)
NUEVO AMNECER LATINO CHLD SVCS (PA)
5400 Pomona Blvd, Los Angeles (90022-1717)
PHONE.................................323 720-9951
Norma Duque-Acosta, *President*
Enrique Danwing, *Administration*
Veronica Hernandez, *Administration*
Ofelia Medina, *Administration*
Jose Ruvalcaba, *Administration*
EMP: 54 **EST:** 1995
SQ FT: 2,600
SALES (est): 11.8MM **Privately Held**
WEB: www.nalcs.org
SIC: 8322 Adoption services

(P-21859)
OPERATION SAFE HOUSE INC (PA)
Also Called: SAFE HOUSE SHELTER
9685 Hayes St, Riverside (92503-3660)
PHONE.................................951 358-4418
Kathy McAdara, *Exec Dir*
Pam Johnsen, *Human Resources*
Shawn Johnson, *Director*
Jackie Moot, *Director*
EMP: 95 **EST:** 1990
SALES (est): 4.9MM **Privately Held**
WEB: www.operationsafehouse.org
SIC: 8322 Crisis intervention center

(P-21860)
ORANGE CNTY ADULT ACHVMENT CTR
Also Called: My Day Counts
225 W Carl Karcher Way, Anaheim (92801-2499)
PHONE.................................714 744-5301
Michael Galliano, *CEO*
Patrick Faraday, *Vice Pres*
Richard Farmer, *Vice Pres*
Laurie Vinkavich, *Vice Pres*
Judy Penaloza, *Human Resources*
▲ **EMP:** 135 **EST:** 1955
SQ FT: 57,000
SALES: 10.1MM **Privately Held**
WEB: www.mydaycounts.org
SIC: 8322 Social service center

(P-21861)
ORANGE CNTY RESCUE MISSION INC (PA)
1 Hope Dr, Tustin (92782-0221)
PHONE.................................714 247-4300
Jim Palmer, *President*
Bryan Crain, *COO*
John Luker, *CFO*
Georgan Browning, *Officer*
Ryan K Burris, *Officer*
EMP: 52 **EST:** 1963
SALES: 18.3MM **Privately Held**
WEB: www.rescuemission.org
SIC: 8661 8322 Religious organizations; emergency shelters

(P-21862)
ORANGEWOOD FOUNDATION
1575 E 17th St, Santa Ana (92705-8506)
PHONE.................................714 619-0200
Chris Simonsen, *CEO*
John Luker, *CFO*
L A Songstad,
Alicia Daddio, *Director*
Jeff Gilstrap, *Manager*
EMP: 85 **EST:** 1980
SQ FT: 22,340
SALES: 22MM **Privately Held**
WEB: www.orangewoodfoundation.org
SIC: 8322 Child related social services

(P-21863)
PASADENA SENIOR CENTER
Also Called: Scott's Pavillon
85 E Holly St, Pasadena (91103-3907)
PHONE.................................626 795-4331
Archana Carey, *Exec Dir*
Karine Kadyan, *Comms Dir*
Peggy Buchanan, *Exec Dir*
Nancy Meeker, *Finance*
Charmaine Nelson, *Director*
EMP: 53 **EST:** 1958
SALES: 1.2MM **Privately Held**
WEB: www.pasadenaseniorcenter.org
SIC: 8322 Senior citizens' center or association

(P-21864)
PATHWAYS I SOBER LIVING INC (PA)
13312 Ranchero Rd, Oak Hills (92344-4812)
PHONE.................................626 373-6006
Timothy Evans, *CEO*
EMP: 85 **EST:** 2017
SALES (est): 615.6K **Privately Held**
SIC: 8322 Substance abuse counseling

(P-21865)
PATHWAYS LA (PA)
3325 Wilshire Blvd # 110, Los Angeles (90010-1703)
PHONE.................................213 427-2700
Karen Park, *President*
Carla Buck, *Vice Pres*
Les Guttman, *Principal*
Lisa Cahill, *Exec Dir*
Duane Dennis, *Exec Dir*
EMP: 50 **EST:** 1978
SQ FT: 24,000
SALES: 28MM **Privately Held**
WEB: www.pathwaysla.org
SIC: 8322 Child related social services

PRODUCTS & SVCS

(P-21866)
PEOPLE ASSISTING HOMELESS
Also Called: P A T H
340 N Madison Ave, Los Angeles
(90004-3504)
PHONE.................323 644-2216
Joel John Roberts, *President*
Shane Goldsmith, *President*
Marsha J Moutrie, *President*
Jennifer Hark-Dietz, *COO*
Jesus Torres, *Associate Dir*
EMP: 167 **EST:** 1984
SALES (est): 88.5MM **Privately Held**
WEB: www.epath.org
SIC: 8322 Social service center

(P-21867)
PEOPLE CONCERN
Safe Haven
1751 Cloverfield Blvd, Santa Monica
(90404-4007)
PHONE.................310 883-1222
Andrew Schwich, *Director*
EMP: 143
SALES (corp-wide): 68MM **Privately Held**
WEB: www.thepeopleconcern.org
SIC: 8322 Emergency shelters; emergency social services
PA: The People Concern
2116 Arlington Ave # 100
Los Angeles CA 90018
323 334-9000

(P-21868)
PEOPLE CONCERN
Daybreak
1751 Cloverfield Blvd, Santa Monica
(90404-4007)
PHONE.................310 450-0650
Anya Booker, *Director*
EMP: 143
SALES (corp-wide): 68MM **Privately Held**
WEB: www.thepeopleconcern.org
SIC: 8322 Community center
PA: The People Concern
2116 Arlington Ave # 100
Los Angeles CA 90018
323 334-9000

(P-21869)
PEOPLE CREATING SUCCESS INC
1607 E Palmdale Blvd H, Palmdale
(93550-7801)
PHONE.................661 225-9700
Robert Donery, *Branch Mgr*
Knechele Reed, *Human Resources*
Angela Buse, *Director*
EMP: 88
SALES (corp-wide): 14MM **Privately Held**
WEB: www.pcs-services.org
SIC: 8322 Individual & family services
PA: People Creating Success, Inc.
2585 Teller Rd
Newbury Park CA 91320
805 375-9222

(P-21870)
PEOPLE CREATING SUCCESS INC
5350 Hollister Ave Ste I, Santa Barbara
(93111-2326)
PHONE.................805 692-5290
Brian Fay, *Manager*
EMP: 88
SALES (corp-wide): 14MM **Privately Held**
WEB: www.pcs-services.org
SIC: 8322 Social service center
PA: People Creating Success, Inc.
2585 Teller Rd
Newbury Park CA 91320
805 375-9222

(P-21871)
PORTO INC
Also Called: A Quality In Home Care
12 S San Gorgonio Ave # 2, Banning
(92220-6005)
PHONE.................760 709-3737
Darrell R Marble, *Exec Dir*
EMP: 60 **EST:** 2015

SQ FT: 1,800
SALES (est): 2MM **Privately Held**
SIC: 8322 Adult day care center

(P-21872)
PRIORITY CTR ENDING THE GNRTNA
Also Called: Welcome Baby
1940 E Deere Ave Ste 100, Santa Ana
(92705-5718)
PHONE.................714 543-4333
Scott Trotter, *Exec Dir*
Bill Tornquist, *Officer*
Stephanie Enano, *Principal*
Linda Sarabia, *Controller*
EMP: 99
SALES: 6.3MM **Privately Held**
WEB: www.theprioritycenter.org
SIC: 8322 Child related social services

(P-21873)
PROJECT ACCESS INC (PA)
2100 W Orangewood Ave # 2, Orange
(92868-1952)
PHONE.................949 253-6200
Kathy McCarrell, *Principal*
Teresa Ichsan, *Officer*
Claudia Beaty, *Vice Pres*
Karyn Mendoza, *Vice Pres*
Khassaundra Whitehead, *Principal*
EMP: 70 **EST:** 1999
SALES: 11.9MM **Privately Held**
WEB: www.project-access.org
SIC: 8322 Social service center

(P-21874)
PROTOTYPES CENTERS FOR INNOV
1000 N Alameda St Ste 390, Los Angeles
(90012-1804)
PHONE.................213 542-3838
Cassandra Loch, *President*
Maryann Fraser, *Exec VP*
Dylan Grattidge, *Info Tech Dir*
John Baldrias, *Nurse*
Erica McKee, *Program Dir*
EMP: 250 **EST:** 1986
SQ FT: 8,400
SALES (est): 20.1MM **Privately Held**
WEB: www.prototypes.org
SIC: 8322 General counseling services

(P-21875)
PULSE ONE CARE LLC
1260 S La Cienega Blvd, Los Angeles
(90035-2548)
PHONE.................310 657-9300
E AVI Arshadnia,
Leeor Arshadnia,
MA Kristina Pasco,
EMP: 50 **EST:** 2016
SALES (est): 2.3MM **Privately Held**
WEB: www.pulseonecare.com
SIC: 8322 Family service agency

(P-21876)
RANCHO LOS AMIGOS NATIONA (PA)
7601 Imperial Hwy, Downey (90242-3456)
PHONE.................562 401-7111
Jorge R Orozco, *CEO*
Benjamin Ovando Sr, *COO*
Robin Bayus, *CFO*
Elizabeth Jacobi, *Officer*
Bryan Kakehashi, *Business Dir*
EMP: 1327 **EST:** 1988
SALES (est): 137.7MM **Privately Held**
WEB: www.dhs.lacounty.gov
SIC: 8322 Rehabilitation services

(P-21877)
REGIONAL CTR ORANGE CNTY INC (PA)
Also Called: DEVELOPMENT DISABILITIES CENTE
1525 N Tustin Ave, Santa Ana
(92705-8621)
P.O. Box 22010 (92702-2010)
PHONE.................714 796-5100
William J Bowman, *Exec Dir*
Theresa Ta, *Area Spvr*
Derek Bush, *CIO*
Erminia Gomez, *CIO*
Derrick Shepard, *Technical Staff*
EMP: 309 **EST:** 1977

SQ FT: 41,128
SALES: 522.7MM **Privately Held**
WEB: www.rcocdd.com
SIC: 9431 8322 Mental health agency administration, government; ; individual & family services

(P-21878)
RIO HONDO EDUCATION CONSORTIUM
Also Called: LEARN
7200 Greenleaf Ave # 300, Whittier
(90602-1383)
PHONE.................562 945-0150
Robert Arellanes, *CEO*
Brenda Carrillo, *COO*
Adrianna Ortega, *COO*
Carolina Arce, *Principal*
Robert Bell, *Principal*
EMP: 58 **EST:** 1986
SALES: 7.2MM **Privately Held**
SIC: 8322 Individual & family services

(P-21879)
SAFE PLACE FOR YOUTH INC
1821 E 68th St Apt 108, Long Beach
(90805-1683)
PHONE.................310 902-2283
Alison Hurst, *Exec Dir*
Ben Perkins, *Program Mgr*
Savanna Lamb, *Admin Asst*
Tony Rodriguez, *Maintence Staff*
Cody Metzger, *Sr Associate*
EMP: 53 **EST:** 2018
SALES (est): 5.1MM **Privately Held**
WEB: www.safeplaceforyouth.org
SIC: 8322 Social service center

(P-21880)
SALVATION ARMY (HQ)
Also Called: Salvation Army Western Ttry
16941 Keegan Ave, Carson (90746-1307)
PHONE.................562 264-3600
James M Knaggs, *CEO*
Commissioner Carolyn R Knaggs, *President*
Ellen OH, *Officer*
Jose Galan, *Social Dir*
Rachael Fowler, *Comms Mgr*
▼ **EMP:** 140 **EST:** 1865
SALES: 516.5K
SALES (corp-wide): 2.4B **Privately Held**
WEB: www.salvationarmy.org
SIC: 8322 Social service center
PA: The Salvation Army National Corporation
615 Slaters Ln
Alexandria VA 22314
703 684-5500

(P-21881)
SALVATION ARMY
10200 Pioneer Rd, Tustin (92782-1418)
PHONE.................714 832-7100
Nigel Cross, *Director*
Al Hoeft, *Admin Sec*
Jack Ames, *Finance*
Stacie Hurst, *Finance*
Carolynn Barkhouse, *Director*
EMP: 72
SALES (corp-wide): 2.4B **Privately Held**
WEB: www.centralusa.salvationarmy.org
SIC: 8322 8661 8699 Social service center; religious organizations; charitable organization
HQ: The Salvation Army
5550 Prairie Stone Pkwy # 130
Hoffman Estates IL 60192
847 294-2000

(P-21882)
SAN BRNRDINO CNTY PRBTION OFFC
4370 Hallmark Pkwy # 105, San Bernardino
(92407-7710)
PHONE.................909 887-2544
Laura Pleasant, *Vice Pres*
EMP: 407 **EST:** 2007
SALES: 493.8K **Privately Held**
SIC: 8322 Probation office

(P-21883)
SAN FERNANDO CITY OF INC
Also Called: Las Palmas Park
505 S Huntington St, San Fernando
(91340-3917)
PHONE.................818 898-7340
Virginia Usano, *Principal*
EMP: 60
SALES (corp-wide): 28.8MM **Privately Held**
WEB: www.ci.san-fernando.ca.us
SIC: 9199 8322 ; senior citizens' center or association
PA: San Fernando, City Of Inc
117 N Macneil St
San Fernando CA 91340
818 898-1201

(P-21884)
SAN FRNNDO VLY INTRFITH CNCIL
8956 Vanalden Ave, Northridge
(91324-3753)
PHONE.................818 885-5220
EMP: 70
SALES (corp-wide): 4.1MM **Privately Held**
WEB: www.vic-la.org
SIC: 8322 Senior citizens' center or association
PA: San Fernando Valley Interfaith Council, Inc.
4505 Las Virgenes Rd # 21
Calabasas CA 91302
818 880-4842

(P-21885)
SAN GBRL/PMONA VLLEYS DVLPMNTA
Also Called: SAN GABRIEL/POMONA REGIONAL CE
75 Rancho Camino Dr, Pomona
(91766-4728)
PHONE.................909 620-7722
R Keith Penman, *Exec Dir*
John Hunt, *CFO*
Rosa Chavez, *Associate Dir*
Dara Mikesell, *Associate Dir*
Arlene Godinez, *Sr Associate*
EMP: 323 **EST:** 1986
SQ FT: 100,000
SALES: 287.8MM **Privately Held**
WEB: www.sgprc.org
SIC: 8322 Social service center

(P-21886)
SANTA CLRITA VLY CMMTTEE ON AG
Also Called: SANTA CLARITA VALLEY SENIOR CE
22900 Market St, Santa Clarita
(91321-3608)
PHONE.................661 259-9444
Brad Berens, *Director*
Jeff Pollard, *President*
Greg Kory, *CFO*
Don Kimball, *Vice Pres*
EMP: 65 **EST:** 1976
SQ FT: 10,000
SALES (est): 7.3MM **Privately Held**
WEB: www.myscvcoa.org
SIC: 8322 Senior citizens' center or association

(P-21887)
SECOND HRVEST FD BNK ORNGE CNT
8014 Marine Way, Irvine (92618-2235)
PHONE.................949 653-2900
Joyce Foley, *Administration*
Joe Schoeningh, *Principal*
Jane Van Dyke, *Human Resources*
EMP: 80 **EST:** 2008
SALES (est): 92MM **Privately Held**
WEB: www.feedoc.org
SIC: 8322 Social service center

(P-21888)
SEXUAL RECOVERY INSTITUTE INC
1964 Westwood Blvd # 400, Los Angeles
(90025-4695)
PHONE.................310 360-0130
David A Sack, *CEO*
Robert Weiss, *President*

Miriam Commisso, *Marketing Staff*
Terry Gatewood, *Commissioner*
Nancy Koplow, *Director*
EMP: 305 **EST:** 1955
SALES (est): 11.6MM
SALES (corp-wide): 113.5MM **Privately Held**
WEB: www.sexualrecovery.com
SIC: 8322 General counseling services
PA: Elements Behavioral Health, Inc.
5000 Arprt Plz Dr Ste 100
Long Beach CA 90815
562 741-6470

(P-21889)
SOCIAL SERVICES CAL DEPT
Also Called: Community Care Licensing
3737 Main St Ste 700, Riverside
(92501-3349)
PHONE..................951 782-4200
Robert Gonzales, *Branch Mgr*
EMP: 55 **Privately Held**
WEB: www.ca.gov
SIC: 9441 8322 Administration of social & manpower programs; ; offender self-help agency
HQ: California Dept Of Social Services
744 P St
Sacramento CA 95814

(P-21890)
SOUTH BAY CTR FOR COUNSELING
Also Called: South Bay Center For Cmnty Dev
540 N Marine Ave, Wilmington
(90744-5528)
PHONE..................310 414-2090
Colleen Mooney, *Exec Dir*
Gina Lomibao-Budnick, *Info Tech Mgr*
Gina Lomibao, *Controller*
Liliana Villa, *Coordinator*
Jones Robert, *Superintendent*
EMP: 90 **EST:** 1974
SALES (est): 5.4MM **Privately Held**
WEB: www.sbccthrivela.org
SIC: 8322 General counseling services

(P-21891)
SOUTH COAST CHILDRENS SOC INC
24950 Redlands Blvd, Loma Linda
(92354-4032)
PHONE..................909 478-3377
EMP: 186
SALES (corp-wide): 36MM **Privately Held**
WEB: www.sccs4kids.org
SIC: 8322 Social service center; rehabilitation services; community center
PA: South Coast Children's Society, Inc.
27261 Las Ramblas Ste 220
Mission Viejo CA 92691
714 966-8650

(P-21892)
SOUTH COAST CHILDRENS SOC INC
11780 Central Ave, Chino (91710-6498)
PHONE..................909 364-9788
EMP: 135
SALES (corp-wide): 30MM **Privately Held**
SIC: 8322 Individual/Family Services
PA: South Coast Children's Society, Inc.
27261 Las Ramblas Ste 220
Mission Viejo CA 92691
714 966-8650

(P-21893)
SOUTHERN CAL HSING RIGHTS CTR
3255 Wilshire Blvd, Los Angeles
(90010-1404)
PHONE..................213 387-8400
Aaron B Bloom, *President*
Danny A Batalla, *Officer*
Frances Espinoza, *Exec Dir*
EMP: 60 **EST:** 1968
SQ FT: 6,000
SALES (est): 12.6MM **Privately Held**
WEB: www.housingrightscenter.org
SIC: 8322 Social service center

(P-21894)
ST BRNBAS SNIOR CTR LOS ANGLE
Also Called: Saint Barnabas Senior Services
675 S Carondelet St, Los Angeles
(90057-3309)
PHONE..................213 388-4444
Rigo Sabareo, *President*
Nick Dumicreseu, *Treasurer*
Johnathon Ferguson, *Administration*
Corazon Velazco, *Controller*
Liz Torres, *Manager*
EMP: 61 **EST:** 1908
SQ FT: 27,000
SALES (est): 4.9MM **Privately Held**
WEB: www.sbssla.org
SIC: 8322 Senior citizens' center or association

(P-21895)
ST JOSEPH CENTER
Also Called: SAINT JOSEPH CENTER VOLUNTEER
204 Hampton Dr, Venice (90291-8633)
PHONE..................310 396-6468
Felecia Adams, *Vice Pres*
John McGann, *CFO*
VA Lecia Adams Kellum, *Exec Dir*
Richard Barnes, *CIO*
Tifara Monroe, *Director*
EMP: 85 **EST:** 1976
SQ FT: 32,000
SALES (est): 39.6MM **Privately Held**
WEB: www.stjosephctr.org
SIC: 8322 8331 8351 Social service center; child related social services; temporary relief service; job training services; vocational rehabilitation agency; child day care services

(P-21896)
ST JOSEPH HOSPICE
Also Called: Saint Joseph Hlth Sys Hospice
200 W Center St Promenade, Anaheim
(92805-3960)
PHONE..................714 712-7100
Linda Glomp, *Director*
Ron Nagano, *CFO*
Maire Blaistell, *Director*
EMP: 206 **EST:** 1994
SQ FT: 3,000
SALES (est): 2.8MM
SALES (corp-wide): 32.7MM **Privately Held**
WEB: www.stjosephhomehealth.org
SIC: 8322 8063 Geriatric social service; psychiatric hospitals
HQ: St Joseph Home Health Network
441 College Ave
Santa Rosa CA 95401
714 712-9500

(P-21897)
ST VINCENTS INSTITUTION
Also Called: SAINT VINCENT'S INSTITUTION
4200 Calle Real, Santa Barbara
(93110-1454)
PHONE..................805 683-6381
Sister Margaret Keaveney, *President*
Rosa Paredes, *CFO*
Sonia Diaz Ebadi, *Manager*
EMP: 60 **EST:** 1858
SQ FT: 25,000
SALES (est): 6.1MM **Privately Held**
SIC: 8322 Social service center

(P-21898)
STAR VIEW CHLDREN FMLY SVCS IN
1085 W Victoria St, Compton (90220-5817)
PHONE..................310 868-5379
Paul Stansbury, *CEO*
Kent Dunlap, *Vice Pres*
Maryjane Gross, *Admin Sec*
Ontson Placide, *Director*
EMP: 51 **EST:** 1995
SALES (est): 597.3K **Privately Held**
WEB: www.starsinc.com
SIC: 8322 Family counseling services

(P-21899)
STRAIGHT TALK INC
Also Called: Straight Talk Counseling Ctr
13710 La Mirada Blvd, La Mirada
(90638-3028)
PHONE..................562 943-0195
Meg Kalugan, *Manager*
Robin Miller, *Office Mgr*
EMP: 90
SALES (corp-wide): 1.3MM **Privately Held**
WEB: www.straighttalkcounseling.org
SIC: 8322 General counseling services
PA: Straight Talk Inc
5712 Camp St
Cypress CA 90630
714 828-2000

(P-21900)
SU CASA ENDING DOM VIOLENCE
Also Called: USA
3750 E Anaheim St Ste 100, Long Beach
(90804-4016)
PHONE..................562 421-6537
Anna Cont, *Exec Dir*
Anna Conti, *Exec Dir*
Miriam Gomez, *Admin Mgr*
Rosalie Rowe, *Finance*
Philip Bui, *Accountant*
EMP: 64 **EST:** 1980
SALES (est): 2.4MM **Privately Held**
WEB: www.sucasadv.org
SIC: 8322 8699 Crisis intervention center; charitable organization

(P-21901)
TESSIE CLVLAND CMNTY SVCS CORP
Also Called: Tccsc
8019 Compton Ave Ste 219, Los Angeles
(90001-3409)
PHONE..................323 586-7333
Forescee Hogan-Rowles, *CEO*
Tyrone Ingram, *President*
Carolyn Chadwick, *CFO*
Deborah Mayes, *Officer*
Moses Chadwick, *Exec Dir*
EMP: 100 **EST:** 2003 **Privately Held**
WEB: www.tccsc.org
SIC: 8322 Child related social services

(P-21902)
TIFFANYS LIU
9465 Wilshire Blvd, Beverly Hills
(90212-2612)
PHONE..................415 644-0846
Liu Tiffanys, *Owner*
EMP: 57
SALES (est): 6MM **Privately Held**
SIC: 8322 8742 Individual & family services; management consulting services

(P-21903)
TOT SQUAD SERVICES LLC
13412 Ventura Blvd # 300, Sherman Oaks
(91423-6201)
PHONE..................310 895-9983
Jen Saxton, *CEO*
EMP: 17 **EST:** 2011
SALES (est): 529.2K **Privately Held**
WEB: www.totsquad.com
SIC: 8322 7372 Individual & family services; prepackaged software

(P-21904)
TRI-CNTIES ASSN FOR DVLPMNTLLY (PA)
Also Called: TRI-COUNTIES REGIONAL CENTER
520 E Montecito St, Santa Barbara
(93103-3245)
PHONE..................805 962-7881
Bob Cobbs, *President*
Omar Noorzad, *Exec Dir*
Dominic Namnath, *CIO*
Tom Harm, *Auditor*
Phil Stucky, *Controller*
EMP: 60 **EST:** 1968
SQ FT: 16,000
SALES: 352.8MM **Privately Held**
WEB: www.tri-counties.org
SIC: 8322 Association for the handicapped

(P-21905)
TRI-CNTIES ASSN FOR DVLPMNTLLY
Also Called: Tri-Counties Regional Center
1146 Farmhouse Ln, San Luis Obispo
(93401-8362)
PHONE..................805 543-2833
Frank Bush, *Director*
Anna Welling, *Admin Sec*
Silvia Bordin, *Analyst*
Darris Lange, *Analyst*
Liz Aced, *Sales Staff*
EMP: 111
SALES (corp-wide): 352.8MM **Privately Held**
WEB: www.tri-counties.org
SIC: 8322 Association for the handicapped
PA: Tri-Counties Association For The Developmentally Disabled, Inc.
520 E Montecito St
Santa Barbara CA 93103
805 962-7881

(P-21906)
TRYVISION
15056 Dakota St, Victorville (92394-2019)
PHONE..................760 780-0408
Kevin O Shannon, *President*
EMP: 50 **EST:** 2019
SALES (est): 332.4K **Privately Held**
WEB: www.tryvision1.weebly.com
SIC: 8322 Individual & family services

(P-21907)
UNITED CRBRAL PLSY ASSN ORNGE
1251 E Dyer Rd Ste 150, Santa Ana
(92705-5662)
PHONE..................949 333-6400
Ramin Baschshi, *CEO*
EMP: 400 **EST:** 1953
SQ FT: 5,000
SALES (est): 6.2MM **Privately Held**
WEB: www.ucpoc.org
SIC: 8322 Social service center

(P-21908)
VALLEY VILLAGE (PA)
20830 Sherman Way, Winnetka
(91306-2707)
PHONE..................818 587-9450
Debra Donovan, *CEO*
Steve Beilinson, *Treasurer*
Vania Garcia, *Human Res Mgr*
Susan Schepps, *Human Resources*
Jenny D Freese, *Marketing Staff*
EMP: 75 **EST:** 1973
SQ FT: 14,000
SALES: 20.3MM **Privately Held**
WEB: www.valleyvillage.org
SIC: 8322 Individual & family services

(P-21909)
VINTAGE SENIOR MANAGEMENT INC
2721 W Willow St, Burbank (91505-4544)
PHONE..................818 954-9500
Brian Flornes, *Branch Mgr*
EMP: 241 **Privately Held**
WEB: www.vintagehousing.com
SIC: 8322 Geriatric social service
PA: Senior Vintage Management Inc
23 Corporate Plaza Dr # 190
Newport Beach CA 92660

(P-21910)
VOLUNTEERS OF AMER LOS ANGELES
1032 W 18th St, Los Angeles (90015-3324)
PHONE..................213 749-0362
Ernest Green, *Director*
EMP: 94
SALES (corp-wide): 100.1MM **Privately Held**
WEB: www.voala.org
SIC: 8322 Social service center
PA: Volunteers Of America Of Los Angeles
3600 Wilshire Blvd # 1500
Los Angeles CA 90010
213 389-1500

PRODUCTS & SVCS

(P-21911)
VOLUNTEERS OF AMER LOS ANGELES
10896 Lehigh Ave, Pacoima (91331-2584)
PHONE 818 834-9097
Paloma Cisneros, *Manager*
EMP: 94
SALES (corp-wide): 100.1MM **Privately Held**
WEB: www.voala.org
SIC: 8322 Social service center
PA: Volunteers Of America Of Los Angeles
3600 Wilshire Blvd # 1500
Los Angeles CA 90010
213 389-1500

(P-21912)
VOLUNTEERS OF AMER LOS ANGELES
13550 Herron St, Sylmar (91342-3119)
PHONE 818 367-8841
EMP: 94
SALES (corp-wide): 100.1MM **Privately Held**
WEB: www.voala.org
SIC: 8322 Social service center
PA: Volunteers Of America Of Los Angeles
3600 Wilshire Blvd # 1500
Los Angeles CA 90010
213 389-1500

(P-21913)
VOLUNTEERS OF AMER LOS ANGELES
522 N Dangler Ave, Los Angeles (90022-1218)
PHONE 323 780-3770
EMP: 94
SALES (corp-wide): 100.1MM **Privately Held**
WEB: www.voala.org
SIC: 8322 Social service center
PA: Volunteers Of America Of Los Angeles
3600 Wilshire Blvd # 1500
Los Angeles CA 90010
213 389-1500

(P-21914)
VOLUNTEERS OF AMER LOS ANGELES
1760 W Cameron Ave # 104, West Covina (91790-2739)
PHONE 626 337-9878
EMP: 94
SALES (corp-wide): 100.1MM **Privately Held**
WEB: www.voala.org
SIC: 8322 Social service center
PA: Volunteers Of America Of Los Angeles
3600 Wilshire Blvd # 1500
Los Angeles CA 90010
213 389-1500

(P-21915)
VOLUNTEERS OF AMER LOS ANGELES
25141 Avenida Rondel, Valencia (91355-3205)
PHONE 661 290-2829
EMP: 94
SALES (corp-wide): 100.1MM **Privately Held**
WEB: www.voala.org
SIC: 8322 Social service center
PA: Volunteers Of America Of Los Angeles
3600 Wilshire Blvd # 1500
Los Angeles CA 90010
213 389-1500

(P-21916)
VOLUNTEERS OF AMER LOS ANGELES
Also Called: Voa Plainview Head Start
10819 Plainview Ave, Tujunga (91042-1633)
PHONE 818 352-5974
EMP: 94
SALES (corp-wide): 100.1MM **Privately Held**
WEB: www.voala.org
SIC: 8322 Social service center

PA: Volunteers Of America Of Los Angeles
3600 Wilshire Blvd # 1500
Los Angeles CA 90010
213 389-1500

(P-21917)
VOLUNTEERS OF AMER LOS ANGELES
2100 N Broadway Ste 300, Santa Ana (92706-2624)
PHONE 714 426-9834
EMP: 94
SALES (corp-wide): 100.1MM **Privately Held**
WEB: www.voala.org
SIC: 8322 Social service center
PA: Volunteers Of America Of Los Angeles
3600 Wilshire Blvd # 1500
Los Angeles CA 90010
213 389-1500

(P-21918)
VOLUNTEERS OF AMER LOS ANGELES
6724 Tujunga Ave, North Hollywood (91606-1910)
PHONE 818 769-3617
EMP: 94
SALES (corp-wide): 100.1MM **Privately Held**
WEB: www.voala.org
SIC: 8322 Social service center
PA: Volunteers Of America Of Los Angeles
3600 Wilshire Blvd # 1500
Los Angeles CA 90010
213 389-1500

(P-21919)
VOLUNTEERS OF AMER LOS ANGELES
Also Called: Maud Booth Family Center
11243 Kittridge St, North Hollywood (91606-2605)
PHONE 818 506-0597
Felix Cruz, *Manager*
EMP: 94
SALES (corp-wide): 100.1MM **Privately Held**
WEB: www.voala.org
SIC: 8322 Social service center
PA: Volunteers Of America Of Los Angeles
3600 Wilshire Blvd # 1500
Los Angeles CA 90010
213 389-1500

(P-21920)
VOLUNTEERS OF AMER LOS ANGELES
Also Called: Voa
515 E 6th St Fl 9, Los Angeles (90021-1009)
PHONE 213 627-8002
Jim Howat, *Dir Ops-Prd-Mfg*
EMP: 94
SQ FT: 15,346
SALES (corp-wide): 100.1MM **Privately Held**
WEB: www.voala.org
SIC: 8322 Social service center
PA: Volunteers Of America Of Los Angeles
3600 Wilshire Blvd # 1500
Los Angeles CA 90010
213 389-1500

(P-21921)
VOLUNTEERS OF AMER LOS ANGELES
12550 Van Nuys Blvd, Pacoima (91331-1354)
PHONE 818 834-8957
Letecia Aguirre, *Principal*
EMP: 94
SALES (corp-wide): 100.1MM **Privately Held**
WEB: www.voala.org
SIC: 8322 Social service center
PA: Volunteers Of America Of Los Angeles
3600 Wilshire Blvd # 1500
Los Angeles CA 90010
213 389-1500

(P-21922)
VOLUNTEERS OF AMER LOS ANGELES
334 Figueroa St, Wilmington (90744-4804)
PHONE 310 830-3404
EMP: 94
SALES (corp-wide): 100.1MM **Privately Held**
WEB: www.voala.org
SIC: 8322 Social service center
PA: Volunteers Of America Of Los Angeles
3600 Wilshire Blvd # 1500
Los Angeles CA 90010
213 389-1500

(P-21923)
WATTS LABOR COMMUNITY ACTION
Also Called: Wlcac
4142 Palmwood Dr Apt 11, Los Angeles (90008-2355)
PHONE 323 563-5639
Timothy Watkins, *CEO*
Cindy Dominguez, *General Mgr*
Charles Standokes, *Administration*
Julie Rodriguez, *Production*
Karen Holtzclaw,
EMP: 136
SALES (corp-wide): 21.9MM **Privately Held**
WEB: www.wlcac.org
SIC: 8322 7299 Social service center; handyman service
PA: Watts Labor Community Action Committee
10950 S Central Ave
Los Angeles CA 90059
323 563-5639

(P-21924)
WAYMAKERS (PA)
1221 E Dyer Rd Ste 120, Santa Ana (92705-5634)
PHONE 714 492-1010
Margot R Carlson, *Exec Dir*
Jeff Cadieux, *Treasurer*
Kristine Brooks, *Bd of Directors*
Thomas Coad, *Bd of Directors*
Robert Hutson, *Bd of Directors*
EMP: 60 **EST:** 1974
SQ FT: 16,000
SALES (est): 24.6MM **Privately Held**
WEB: www.waymakersoc.org
SIC: 8322 Social service center

(P-21925)
WEINGART CENTER ASSOCIATION
Also Called: WEINGART CENTER FOR THE HOMELE
566 S San Pedro St, Los Angeles (90013-2102)
PHONE 213 622-6359
Kevin Murray, *President*
Warren Loui, *Partner*
Tonja Boykin, *COO*
Sonny Santa Ines, *CFO*
Peter Getoff, *Director*
EMP: 150
SQ FT: 175,000
SALES: 13.8MM **Privately Held**
WEB: www.weingart.org
SIC: 8322 Emergency social services

(P-21926)
WELLNEST EMTONAL HLTH WELLNESS (PA)
3031 S Vermont Ave, Los Angeles (90007-3033)
PHONE 323 373-2400
Charlene Dimas-Peinado, *CEO*
Margaret Lopez, *CFO*
Laura Alvarez, *Vice Pres*
Tiffany Rodriguez, *Vice Pres*
Andrea Salazar, *Vice Pres*
EMP: 110 **EST:** 1924
SALES: 25.9MM **Privately Held**
WEB: www.wellnestla.org
SIC: 8322 Child guidance agency

(P-21927)
WESTVIEW SERVICES INC
301 E Glenoaks Blvd Ste 2, Glendale (91207-2076)
PHONE 818 242-0068

Marina Margaryan, *Director*
EMP: 58
SALES (corp-wide): 15.8MM **Privately Held**
WEB: www.westviewservices.org
SIC: 8322 Association for the handicapped
PA: Westview Services, Inc
10522 Katella Ave
Anaheim CA 92804
714 517-6606

(P-21928)
WESTVIEW SERVICES INC
Also Called: Day Star Educational Center
626 W Commonwealth Ave, Fullerton (92832-1725)
PHONE 714 879-3980
EMP: 88
SQ FT: 4,419
SALES (corp-wide): 15.4MM **Privately Held**
WEB: www.westviewservices.org
SIC: 8322 Individual/Family Services
PA: Westview Services, Inc
10522 Katella Ave
Anaheim CA 92804
714 517-6606

(P-21929)
WHITTIER UNION HIGH SCHL DIST
Also Called: Capc Adult Services
7200 Greenleaf Ave # 17C, Whittier (90602-1367)
PHONE 562 693-8826
Dan Hulbert, *Director*
James Mendez, *Officer*
Jennifer Suter, *Technology*
Guiterrez Alma, *Teacher*
Jeffrey Maginnis, *Teacher*
EMP: 106
SALES (corp-wide): 205.5MM **Privately Held**
WEB: www.wuhsd.org
SIC: 8211 8322 Public elementary & secondary schools; social services for the handicapped
PA: Whittier Union High School Dist
9401 Painter Ave
Whittier CA 90605
562 698-8121

(P-21930)
WISE & HEALTHY AGING
23388 Mulholland Dr # 60, Woodland Hills (91364-2733)
PHONE 818 876-1402
Grace Cheng Braun, *Principal*
Phyllis Amaral, *Principal*
Grace Braun, *Principal*
Molly Davies, *Principal*
Charles Hardie, *Principal*
EMP: 70 **EST:** 1972
SALES (est): 708.9K **Privately Held**
WEB: www.wiseandhealthyaging.org
SIC: 8322 Senior citizens' center or association

(P-21931)
WORK INC
3070 Skyway Dr Ste 104, Santa Maria (93455-1830)
PHONE 805 739-0451
Ed Hartman, *President*
Kathy Webb, *Exec Dir*
EMP: 164 **EST:** 1968
SALES (est): 825.4K **Privately Held**
WEB: www.momentum4work.org
SIC: 8322 Adult day care center
HQ: The Chimes Inc
4815 Seton Dr
Baltimore MD 21215
410 358-6400

(P-21932)
YOUNG MEN CHRSTN ASSOC W SAN G (PA)
Also Called: YMCA
401 Corto St, Alhambra (91801-4553)
PHONE 626 576-0226
Valarie Gomez, *CEO*
EMP: 70 **EST:** 1912
SQ FT: 17,000
SALES: 1.7MM **Privately Held**
SIC: 8661 8322 Religious organizations; youth center

(P-21933)
YUE FENG INC
145 S Fairfax Ave, Los Angeles
(90036-2166)
PHONE...................................310 253-9795
Cheng Chen, *President*
EMP: 72 **EST:** 2013
SQ FT: 8,500
SALES (est): 7MM **Privately Held**
SIC: 8322 Individual & family services

8331 Job Training & Vocational Rehabilitation Svcs

(P-21934)
ABILITY COUNTS INC (PA)
775 Trademark Cir Ste 101, Corona
(92879-2084)
PHONE...................................951 734-6595
Joyce Hearn, *CEO*
Amanda Rivera, *Manager*
Veronica Salanga, *Manager*
EMP: 97 **EST:** 1980
SQ FT: 28,000
SALES: 7.5MM **Privately Held**
WEB: www.abilitycounts.org
SIC: 8331 Sheltered workshop

(P-21935)
ABLE INDUSTRIES INC
8929 W Goshen Ave, Visalia (93291-7969)
PHONE...................................559 651-8150
Wende Ayers, *Exec Dir*
Brandi Miller, *Technician*
Bill Little, *Controller*
Sheree Hooper, *Production*
Gerald Ormonde, *Mktg Coord*
▲ **EMP:** 52 **EST:** 1960
SQ FT: 75,000
SALES: 4.2MM **Privately Held**
WEB: www.ableindustries.org
SIC: 8331 Community service employment training program; job counseling

(P-21936)
ADVOCACY FOR RSPECT CHICE - LO (PA)
Also Called: HILLSIDE ENTERPRISES - AR & C
4519 E Stearns St, Long Beach
(90815-2540)
PHONE...................................562 597-7716
Marion Lieberman, *CEO*
EMP: 81 **EST:** 1952
SQ FT: 35,000
SALES (est): 5.9MM **Privately Held**
WEB: www.hillsideenterprises.org
SIC: 8331 Sheltered workshop

(P-21937)
AMERICAN ASSN CRTCAL CARE NRSE
Also Called: A A C N
27071 Aliso Creek Rd, Aliso Viejo
(92656-3399)
PHONE...................................949 362-2000
Dana Woods, *CEO*
Vicki Good, *President*
Teri Lynn Kiss, *President*
Michael Willett, *CFO*
Linda Bay, *Treasurer*
EMP: 128 **EST:** 1969
SALES: 34.6MM **Privately Held**
WEB: www.aacn.org
SIC: 8299 8331 8621 Educational services; job training & vocational rehabilitation services; professional membership organizations

(P-21938)
APPRENTICE JRNYMEN TRNING TR F
Also Called: COMPTON TRAINING CENTER
7850 Haskell Ave, Van Nuys (91406-1907)
PHONE...................................310 604-0892
Raymond Levangie III, *Exec Dir*
EMP: 222 **EST:** 1956
SALES (est): 28.4MM **Privately Held**
WEB: www.ajtraining.org
SIC: 8331 Job training services

(P-21939)
ARC LOS ANGLES ORANGE COUNTIES (PA)
Also Called: Southeast Industries
12049 Woodruff Ave, Downey
(90241-5669)
PHONE...................................562 803-1556
Kevin Mac Donald, *Exec Dir*
EMP: 75 **EST:** 1962
SQ FT: 9,800
SALES (est): 3.8MM **Privately Held**
WEB: www.thearclaoc.org
SIC: 8331 5932 Skill training center; vocational training agency; used merchandise stores

(P-21940)
ASIAN REHABILITATION SVC INC (PA)
7009 Washington Ave, Whittier
(90602-1416)
PHONE...................................562 632-1141
Si Ho, *Exec Dir*
Cherry Habacon, *Executive*
EMP: 62
SQ FT: 28,000
SALES: 2.1MM **Privately Held**
WEB: www.asianrehab.org
SIC: 8331 Vocational rehabilitation agency

(P-21941)
ASIAN REHABILITATION SVC INC
Also Called: ARS
312 N Spring St Ste B30, Los Angeles
(90012-3152)
PHONE...................................213 680-3790
George Allen, *Manager*
EMP: 120
SALES (corp-wide): 2.1MM **Privately Held**
WEB: www.asianrehab.org
SIC: 8331 Vocational rehabilitation agency
PA: Asian Rehabilitation Service, Inc.
7009 Washington Ave
Whittier CA 90602
562 632-1141

(P-21942)
BAKERSFIELD ASSN FOR RTRDED CTZ
2240 S Union Ave, Bakersfield
(93307-4158)
PHONE...................................661 834-2272
Jim Baldwin, *President*
Kenneth Schmitz, *Vice Pres*
EMP: 126 **EST:** 1951
SQ FT: 30,000
SALES (est): 9.7MM **Privately Held**
WEB: www.barc-inc.org
SIC: 8331 Sheltered workshop; skill training center; work experience center

(P-21943)
BENEFITVISION INC
5550 Topanga Canyon Blvd # 180, Woodland Hills (91367-6478)
PHONE...................................818 348-3100
Terry Fuzue, *Branch Mgr*
EMP: 81 **Privately Held**
WEB: www.benefitvision.com
SIC: 8331 Job training & vocational rehabilitation services
PA: Benefitvision, Inc.
4522 Rfd
Long Grove IL 60047
877 737-5526

(P-21944)
BEST OPPORTUNITIES INC
Also Called: Best Opportunities
22450 Headquarters Ave, Apple Valley
(92307-4304)
PHONE...................................760 628-0111
Karin Etheridge, *CEO*
Richard O'Brien, *President*
Karin Etheride, *General Mgr*
EMP: 140
SQ FT: 5,000
SALES: 3.3MM **Privately Held**
WEB: www.bestopportunities.org
SIC: 8331 Vocational rehabilitation agency

(P-21945)
CHINATOWN SERVICE CENTER (PA)
767 N Hill St Ste 400, Los Angeles
(90012-2381)
PHONE...................................213 808-1701
Peter Ng, *President*
Yeryca Ramos, *CFO*
Gloria Tang, *Treasurer*
Henry Kwong, *Admin Sec*
Jack Cheng, *Opers Staff*
EMP: 132 **EST:** 1975
SQ FT: 20,000
SALES: 14.7MM **Privately Held**
WEB: www.cscla.org
SIC: 8331 8322 8011 Job counseling; family (marriage) counseling; clinic, operated by physicians

(P-21946)
CONSERVATION CORPS LONG BEACH
340 Nieto Ave, Long Beach (90814-1845)
PHONE...................................562 986-1249
Samara Ashley, *Principal*
Mike Bassett, *CEO*
John Dunay, *CFO*
Mario R Beas, *Admin Sec*
Rhonda Head, *Accountant*
EMP: 165
SQ FT: 10,000
SALES: 3.5MM **Privately Held**
WEB: www.cclb-corps.org
SIC: 8331 8322 Community service employment training program; individual & family services

(P-21947)
CORNERSTONE ONDMAND GLOBL OPRT (HQ)
1601 Cloverf Blvd Ste 60, Santa Monica
(90404-4082)
PHONE...................................310 752-0200
Adam Miller, *President*
EMP: 330 **EST:** 2010
SALES (est): 3.7MM
SALES (corp-wide): 740.9MM **Privately Held**
WEB: www.cornerstoneondemand.org
SIC: 8331 Skill training center
PA: Cornerstone Ondemand, Inc.
1601 Cloverf Blvd 620s
Santa Monica CA 90404
310 752-0200

(P-21948)
COUNCIL OF ORANGE COUNTY OF ST (PA)
Also Called: Council Program Serv & Admin
1505 E 17th St Ste 109, Santa Ana
(92705-8520)
PHONE...................................949 653-2900
Andrew Saavedra, *President*
Rich Gorham, *Vice Pres*
Woody Smith, *Marketing Staff*
Debbie Gordon, *Manager*
Susan Martin, *Manager*
EMP: 56 **EST:** 1976
SQ FT: 121,000
SALES (est): 53.1MM **Privately Held**
SIC: 5932 8331 8093 8322 Used merchandise stores; job training services; specialty outpatient clinics; individual & family services

(P-21949)
DEVELOPMENTAL SVCS CAL DEPT
Also Called: Fairview Developmental Center
2501 Harbor Blvd, Costa Mesa
(92626-6143)
PHONE...................................714 957-5151
Bill Wilson, *Exec Dir*
EMP: 445 **Privately Held**
WEB: www.ca.gov
SIC: 8331 9431 8361 Job training & vocational rehabilitation services; administration of public health programs; ; residential care
HQ: California Department Of Developmental Services
1215 O St
Sacramento CA 95814

(P-21950)
EXCEPTIONAL CHLD FOUNDATION (PA)
Also Called: PAR SERVICES
5350 Machado Ln, Culver City
(90230-8800)
PHONE...................................310 204-3300
Scott Bowling, *President*
Monica Jaramillo, *Chief Mktg Ofcr*
Maryam Hamedaninia, *Officer*
Maryam Hamedininia, *Officer*
Karen Kato, *Officer*
EMP: 120 **EST:** 1946
SQ FT: 45,000
SALES: 26.7MM **Privately Held**
WEB: www.ecf.net
SIC: 8331 Vocational training agency; vocational rehabilitation agency

(P-21951)
EXCEPTIONAL CHLD FOUNDATION
Also Called: Par Services
1430 Venice Blvd, Los Angeles
(90006-4818)
PHONE...................................213 748-3556
Nanette Cruz, *Principal*
EMP: 197
SALES (corp-wide): 26.7MM **Privately Held**
WEB: www.ecf.net
SIC: 8331 Job training & vocational rehabilitation services
PA: Exceptional Children's Foundation
5350 Machado Ln
Culver City CA 90230
310 204-3300

(P-21952)
FONTANA RESOURCES AT WORK
Also Called: INDUSTRIAL SUPPORT SYSTEMS
8608 Live Oak Ave, Fontana (92335-3172)
P.O. Box 848 (92334-0848)
PHONE...................................909 428-3833
Ulric Jones, *CFO*
Sylvia Anderson, *Exec Dir*
Joseph Varela, *Opers Staff*
Danny Cervera, *Production*
EMP: 140 **EST:** 1965
SQ FT: 22,600
SALES: 2MM **Privately Held**
WEB: www.fontanaresources.com
SIC: 8331 3444 Vocational rehabilitation agency; sheet metalwork

(P-21953)
GIANT STEPS TRNING PRGRAMS INC
2228 Crenshaw Blvd, Los Angeles
(90016-1808)
PHONE...................................323 733-6401
Billy Richard, *CEO*
EMP: 60 **EST:** 2001
SQ FT: 2,500
SALES (est): 3.9MM **Privately Held**
WEB: www.giantsteps.net
SIC: 8331 Vocational rehabilitation agency

(P-21954)
GOODWILL INDS ORANGE CNTY CAL
2910 W Garry Ave, Santa Ana
(92704-6510)
PHONE...................................714 754-7808
EMP: 110
SALES (corp-wide): 126.7MM **Privately Held**
SIC: 8331 Job Training/Related Services
PA: Goodwill Industries Of Orange County, California
410 N Fairview St
Santa Ana CA 92703
714 547-6308

(P-21955)
GOODWILL INDS ORANGE CNTY CAL
5880 Edinger Ave, Huntington Beach
(92649-1705)
PHONE...................................714 881-3986
EMP: 78

PRODUCTS & SVCS

SALES (corp-wide): 126.7MM **Privately Held**
WEB: www.ocgoodwill.org
SIC: 8331 Job training & vocational rehabilitation services
PA: Goodwill Industries Of Orange County, California
410 N Fairview St
Santa Ana CA 92703
714 547-6308

(P-21956)
GOODWILL INDS SOUTHERN CAL (PA)
342 N San Fernando Rd, Los Angeles (90031-1730)
PHONE...................................323 223-1211
Patrick McClenahan, *President*
Gari Douglass, *CFO*
Peter Starrett, *Treasurer*
Gesenia Guzman, *Officer*
Lowell King, *Officer*
▲ EMP: 880 EST: 1919
SQ FT: 200,000
SALES (est): 253.6MM **Privately Held**
WEB: www.goodwillsocal.org
SIC: 5331 8331 Variety stores; vocational rehabilitation agency; vocational training agency; community service employment training program

(P-21957)
JEWISH VOCATIONAL SERVICES (PA)
Also Called: JVSLA
6505 Wilshire Blvd # 200, Los Angeles (90048-4957)
PHONE...................................323 761-8888
Vivian B Seigel, *CEO*
Claudia Finkel, *COO*
Olwen Brown, *CFO*
Stacy Goodman, *Bd of Directors*
Mark Edwards, *Vice Pres*
EMP: 50 EST: 1931
SQ FT: 11,000
SALES (est): 14.7MM **Privately Held**
WEB: www.jvsla.jvs-socal.org
SIC: 8331 Vocational rehabilitation agency

(P-21958)
KERN CMNTY CLLEGE DST FNDATION
Also Called: Central Envmtl Training Ctr
2100 Chester Ave, Bakersfield (93301-4014)
PHONE...................................661 336-5117
Richard Casagrande, *Manager*
EMP: 54
SALES (corp-wide): 58.7MM **Privately Held**
WEB: www.kccd.edu
SIC: 8331 Skill training center
PA: Kern Community College District
2100 Chester Ave
Bakersfield CA 93301
661 336-5100

(P-21959)
LINCOLN TRNING CTR RHBLTTION W
2643 Loma Ave, South El Monte (91733-1419)
PHONE...................................626 442-0621
Judith Angelo, *CEO*
David Nelson, *Vice Chairman*
Eric Brown, *Chairman*
Melissa Rus, *Program Mgr*
Judy Angelo, *Admin Sec*
EMP: 85 EST: 1964
SQ FT: 30,000
SALES: 21.7MM **Privately Held**
WEB: www.lincolntc.org
SIC: 8331 Vocational rehabilitation agency

(P-21960)
LOS ANGELES UNIFIED SCHOOL DST
Also Called: West Valley Occupational Ctr
6200 Winnetka Ave, Woodland Hills (91367-3826)
PHONE...................................818 346-3540
Candace Lee, *Principal*
EMP: 53

SALES (corp-wide): 9.3B **Privately Held**
WEB: www.laallcityband.com
SIC: 8211 8299 8331 Public elementary & secondary schools; educational service, nondegree granting: continuing educ.; job training & vocational rehabilitation services
PA: Los Angeles Unified School District
333 S Beaudry Ave Ste 209
Los Angeles CA 90017
213 241-1000

(P-21961)
MID-CITIES ASSOCIATION INC (PA)
Also Called: Hub-Limited Workshop
14208 Towne Ave, Los Angeles (90061-2653)
PHONE...................................310 537-4510
John Wagoner, *Exec Dir*
EMP: 60 EST: 1954
SALES (est): 7.2MM **Privately Held**
WEB: www.naidobrite.net
SIC: 8331 Sheltered workshop

(P-21962)
MOMENTUM WORK INC (PA)
Also Called: W O R K
5320 Carpinteria Ave G, Carpinteria (93013-2107)
PHONE...................................805 566-9000
Kathy Webb, *Exec Dir*
Pam Holcombe, *Director*
Maria Prince, *Director*
Ronica Smith, *Director*
Michael Craig, *Manager*
EMP: 60 EST: 1968
SQ FT: 2,000
SALES (est): 9.3MM **Privately Held**
WEB: www.momentum4work.org
SIC: 8331 Vocational rehabilitation agency; vocational training agency

(P-21963)
OPARC (PA)
Also Called: DIVERSIFIED INDUSTRIES
9029 Vernon Ave, Montclair (91763-2000)
PHONE...................................909 982-4090
Ronald P Wolff, *President*
Kam Banerjee, *Vice Chairman*
Nancy Dediemar, *Treasurer*
Sonia Borja, *Officer*
Andrea Wells, *Officer*
EMP: 50 EST: 1950
SQ FT: 350,000
SALES (est): 13.8MM **Privately Held**
WEB: www.oparc.org
SIC: 8331 8322 Job training & vocational rehabilitation services; individual & family services

(P-21964)
OWL EDUCATION AND TRAINING INC
2465 Campus Dr, Irvine (92612-1502)
PHONE...................................949 797-2000
Gregory J Burden, *President*
Stephen Seastrom, *Corp Secy*
EMP: 252 EST: 2005
SQ FT: 22,800
SALES (est): 1.1MM
SALES (corp-wide): 124.3MM **Privately Held**
WEB: www.owlcompanies.com
SIC: 8331 Job training & vocational rehabilitation services
PA: Owl Companies
2465 Campus Dr
Irvine CA 92612
949 797-2000

(P-21965)
PACIFIC ASIAN CNSRTIUM IN EMPL (PA)
Also Called: P A C E
1055 Wilshire Blvd # 147, Los Angeles (90017-2431)
PHONE...................................213 353-3982
Kerry N Doi, *Exec Dir*
Violeta Cartas-Ibarra, *Officer*
Jim Roman, *Officer*
Rachelle Arizmendi, *Vice Pres*
Michael Krebs, *Vice Pres*
EMP: 130 EST: 1976
SQ FT: 20,000

SALES: 28.4MM **Privately Held**
WEB: www.pacela.org
SIC: 8331 8322 7361 1521 Community service employment training program; individual & family services; labor contractors (employment agency); new construction, single-family houses

(P-21966)
SAN GABRIEL VLY TRAINING CTR (PA)
Also Called: PRODUCTION FACILITIES UN-LIMITE
400 S Covina Blvd, La Puente (91746-2212)
PHONE...................................626 330-3185
Randy Hyatt, *Exec Dir*
Mary Ryan Indenbaum, *President*
Robert Darragh, *Treasurer*
Shirley Roland, *Admin Sec*
EMP: 55 EST: 1962
SQ FT: 6,400
SALES: 5.8MM **Privately Held**
SIC: 8331 7389 Vocational rehabilitation agency; packaging & labeling services

(P-21967)
SEXY HAIR CONCEPTS LLC
21551 Prairie St, Chatsworth (91311-5831)
PHONE...................................818 435-0800
Karl H Pitsch,
Jeannene Stewart, *Regl Sales Mgr*
Mark Milner,
Alexis Wallsh,
David Yaeger,
◆ EMP: 20 EST: 2001
SALES (est): 12.3MM
SALES (corp-wide): 22.7B **Privately Held**
WEB: www.sexyhair.com
SIC: 5999 8331 3999 Hair care products; skill training center; hair & hair-based products
PA: Henkel Ag & Co. Kgaa
Henkelstr. 67
Dusseldorf NW 40589
211 797-0

(P-21968)
SPECIAL SERVICE FOR GROUPS INC (PA)
Also Called: SSG ADMINISTRATIVE OF-FICES
905 E 8th St, Los Angeles (90021-1848)
PHONE...................................213 368-1888
Herbert K Hatanaka, *CEO*
Antonio Gutierrez, *Officer*
Christopher Scott, *Officer*
Antonio Soria, *Officer*
Donna Wong, *Vice Pres*
EMP: 100 EST: 1952
SALES: 133.1MM **Privately Held**
WEB: www.ssg.org
SIC: 8331 8093 8399 Vocational rehabilitation agency; mental health clinic, outpatient; advocacy group

(P-21969)
SUCCESS STRATEGIES INST INC
Also Called: Tom Ferry Your Coach
6 Hutton Cntre Dr Ste 700, Santa Ana (92707)
PHONE...................................949 721-6808
Thomas Ferry, *President*
Ruby Sabile, *Executive Asst*
David Shanks, *Info Tech Dir*
Mark Le, *Info Tech Mgr*
David Goodman, *Software Dev*
EMP: 70 EST: 2005
SALES (est): 28.2MM **Privately Held**
WEB: www.tomferry.com
SIC: 8331 Job training & vocational rehabilitation services

(P-21970)
VALLEY LGHT CTR FOR SCIAL ADVN
Also Called: Valley Light Industries
5360 Irwindale Ave, Irwindale (91706-2086)
PHONE...................................626 337-6200
Newman Sheryl, *CEO*
Pamela Hayes, *President*
Julie Garcia, *Administration*
Penny Wiegand, *Director*

Johnny Camacho, *Case Mgr*
EMP: 150 EST: 1970
SQ FT: 14,220
SALES (est): 3.3MM **Privately Held**
WEB: www.valleylight.org
SIC: 8331 Job training & vocational rehabilitation services

(P-21971)
VALLEY RSRCE CTR FOR RTRDED IN (PA)
1285 N Santa Fe St, Hemet (92543-1823)
PHONE...................................951 766-8659
Lee Trisler, *CEO*
Gerhard Visagie, *Accountant*
Jenni Botha, *Human Resources*
Thomson Lintock, *Human Resources*
Darlene Noon, *Human Resources*
EMP: 50 EST: 1979
SQ FT: 80,000
SALES: 8.6MM **Privately Held**
WEB: www.weexceed.org
SIC: 8331 2389 Vocational training agency; apparel for handicapped

(P-21972)
VOCATIONAL IMPRV PROGRAM INC (PA)
9210 Rochester Ave, Rancho Cucamonga (91730-5521)
PHONE...................................909 483-5924
Wendy A Rogina, *CEO*
Christopher J McArdle, *Treasurer*
Rick Rogina, *Vice Pres*
Kenny Solano, *Business Dir*
M Stephen Cho, *Admin Sec*
EMP: 90 EST: 1986
SQ FT: 23,000
SALES: 15.5MM **Privately Held**
WEB: www.vipsolutions.com
SIC: 8331 Vocational rehabilitation agency

(P-21973)
VOCATIONAL VISIONS
26041 Pala, Mission Viejo (92691-2705)
PHONE...................................949 837-7280
Joan McKinney, *CEO*
Kathryn Hebel, *Exec Dir*
EMP: 170
SQ FT: 17,000
SALES: 8.1MM **Privately Held**
WEB: www.vocationalvsions.org
SIC: 8331 Sheltered workshop

(P-21974)
VTC ENTERPRISES (PA)
2445 A St, Santa Maria (93455-1401)
P.O. Box 1187 (93456-1187)
PHONE...................................805 928-5000
Jason Telander, *CEO*
Dr Mark Malangko, *President*
Lisa Walker, *CFO*
Henry M Grennan, *Treasurer*
Crystal Smith, *Associate Dir*
EMP: 286 EST: 1962
SQ FT: 21,093
SALES: 10.8MM **Privately Held**
WEB: www.vtc-sm.org
SIC: 8331 Vocational rehabilitation agency

(P-21975)
WESTVIEW SERVICES INC
1515 W Cameron Ave # 310, West Covina (91790-2726)
PHONE...................................626 962-0956
Patricia Stock, *Manager*
EMP: 58
SALES (corp-wide): 15.8MM **Privately Held**
WEB: www.westviewservices.org
SIC: 8331 5999 Job training & vocational rehabilitation services; technical aids for the handicapped
PA: Westview Services, Inc
10522 Katella Ave
Anaheim CA 92804
714 517-6606

(P-21976)
WESTVIEW SERVICES INC
Also Called: Westview Vocational Services
27576 Commerce Center Dr # 1, Temecula (92590-2571)
PHONE...................................951 699-0047
Mary Radecki, *Director*
EMP: 58

SALES (corp-wide): 15.8MM **Privately Held**
WEB: www.westviewservices.org
SIC: **8331** 8322 Vocational rehabilitation agency; social services for the handicapped
PA: Westview Services, Inc
10522 Katella Ave
Anaheim CA 92804
714 517-6606

(P-21977)
WESTVIEW SERVICES INC
Also Called: Westveiw Vo Ser
9776 Katella Ave, Anaheim (92804-6417)
PHONE.................................714 530-2703
Carol Cooper, *Manager*
Vanesa Ibarra, *Department Mgr*
Annmarie Desantiago, *Software Dev*
EMP: 58
SALES (corp-wide): 15.8MM **Privately Held**
WEB: www.westviewservices.org
SIC: **8331** 8249 Vocational rehabilitation agency; vocational schools
PA: Westview Services, Inc
10522 Katella Ave
Anaheim CA 92804
714 517-6606

(P-21978)
WESTVIEW SERVICES INC
Also Called: Westview Vocational Services
1655 S Euclid St Ste A, Anaheim (92802-2400)
PHONE.................................714 635-2444
Greg Gann, *CEO*
EMP: 58
SQ FT: 5,952
SALES (corp-wide): 15.8MM **Privately Held**
WEB: www.westviewservices.org
SIC: **8331** Vocational rehabilitation agency
PA: Westview Services, Inc
10522 Katella Ave
Anaheim CA 92804
714 517-6606

(P-21979)
WESTVIEW SERVICES INC
Also Called: Starlight Educational Center
9421 Edinger Ave, Westminster (92683-7426)
PHONE.................................714 418-2090
Lourdis Painter, *Principal*
EMP: 58
SQ FT: 3,775
SALES (corp-wide): 15.8MM **Privately Held**
WEB: www.westviewservices.org
SIC: **8331** 8244 Community service employment training program; business & secretarial schools
PA: Westview Services, Inc
10522 Katella Ave
Anaheim CA 92804
714 517-6606

8351 Child Day Care Svcs

(P-21980)
ADAMS LEARNING CENTER
Also Called: Adams Early Childhood Lrng Ctr
50800 Desert Club Dr, La Quinta (92253-2982)
PHONE.................................760 777-4260
Maria Moore, *Director*
Alejandra Bautista, *Teacher*
Joy Casaletti, *Teacher*
Anne Garcia, *Teacher*
Noriega Grace, *Teacher*
EMP: 50 EST: 1965
SALES (est): 511.9K **Privately Held**
SIC: **8351** Preschool center

(P-21981)
ADAT ARI EL
Also Called: Adat ARI El Day School
12020 Burbank Blvd, Valley Village (91607-2198)
PHONE.................................818 766-4992
Joanne Klein, *Exec Dir*
Herschel Bleefeld, *Comms Dir*
Eric Nicastro, *Exec Dir*
Robin Solomon, *CIO*

Kendra Silverstein, *Purch Agent*
EMP: 150 EST: 1938
SQ FT: 97,410
SALES (est): 21.9MM **Privately Held**
WEB: www.adatariel.org
SIC: **8211** 8661 8351 8299 Private elementary school; temples; Montessori child development center; religious school; religious goods

(P-21982)
ALLIES FOR EVERY CHILD INC
5721 W Slauson Ave # 200, Culver City (90230-6554)
PHONE.................................310 846-4100
Heather Carrigan, *CEO*
Richard Klein, *CFO*
Michelle Schafer, *Director*
EMP: 85 EST: 1987
SQ FT: 18,000
SALES (est): 9.6MM **Privately Held**
WEB: www.alliesforeverychild.org
SIC: **8351** 8322 Child day care services; child related social services

(P-21983)
ARBORLAND ENTERPRISES INC
Also Called: Arborland Mntssori Chld Acdemy
1700 W Valencia Dr, Fullerton (92833-3864)
PHONE.................................714 871-2311
Chen Sueling, *President*
Stan Chen, *Treasurer*
EMP: 55 EST: 1987
SQ FT: 1,417
SALES (est): 5.8MM **Privately Held**
WEB: www.arborland.com
SIC: **8211** 8351 8299 Private elementary school; preschool center; tutoring school

(P-21984)
BALDWIN PARK UNIFIED SCHL DST
Also Called: Baldwin Pk Unified Schl Dst Chl
13529 Francisquito Ave, Baldwin Park (91706-4834)
PHONE.................................626 337-2711
Russhell Martinez, *Director*
EMP: 72
SALES (corp-wide): 229.2MM **Privately Held**
WEB: www.bpusd.net
SIC: **8211** 8351 Public elementary & secondary schools; child day care services
PA: Baldwin Park Unified School District
3699 Holly Ave
Baldwin Park CA 91706
626 939-4000

(P-21985)
BEAUMONT UNFIED SCHL DST PUB F
Also Called: Community Day School
126 W Fifth St, Beaumont (92223-2142)
PHONE.................................951 845-6580
Douglas Walter, *Principal*
EMP: 476
SALES (corp-wide): 150.6MM **Privately Held**
WEB: www.beaumontusd.us
SIC: **8211** 8351 Public elementary & secondary schools; group day care center
PA: Beaumont Unified School District Public Facilities Corporation
350 W Brookside Ave
Cherry Valley CA 92223
951 845-1631

(P-21986)
BEL AIR PRESBYTERIAN CHURCH
Also Called: Presbyterian Church USA
16221 Mulholland Dr, Los Angeles (90049-1199)
PHONE.................................818 788-4200
Mark Brewer, *Pastor*
Sean Meade, *Vice Pres*
Michelle McMurtry, *Office Mgr*
Melissa Sique, *Executive Asst*
Angelo Duran, *Technical Staff*
EMP: 52 EST: 1956
SQ FT: 75,033

SALES (est): 12.2MM **Privately Held**
WEB: www.belairpres.org
SIC: **8661** 8351 Presbyterian Church; child day care services

(P-21987)
BERKELEY HALL SCHL FOUNDATION
Also Called: BERKELEY HALL SCHOOL
16000 Mulholland Dr, Los Angeles (90049-1196)
PHONE.................................310 476-6421
Caroline R Kuhn, *President*
Rick Larson, *Vice Chairman*
Lisa Lewis, *Executive*
Lisa Taylor, *Comms Mgr*
Tommi Johnson, *Human Resources*
EMP: 65 EST: 1911
SALES: 13.2MM **Privately Held**
WEB: www.berkeleyhall.org
SIC: **8211** 8351 Private elementary school; private junior high school; nursery school

(P-21988)
BETHANY BAPTIST SCHOOL
Also Called: Bethany Elementary & Pre Schl
2244 Clark Ave, Long Beach (90815-2521)
PHONE.................................562 985-0714
Bill Cook, *Principal*
J D Sarver, *Principal*
Frankie Fitchett, *Admin Sec*
Stacey Aldridge, *Teacher*
Nicole Cecil, *Teacher*
EMP: 70 EST: 1947
SALES (est): 3.5MM **Privately Held**
WEB: www.bethany.school
SIC: **8351** Preschool center

(P-21989)
BETHLHEM EVANG LTHRAN CH GRNAD
Also Called: Bethlhem Evang Lthern Pr-Schoo
12227 Balboa Blvd, Granada Hills (91344-1703)
PHONE.................................818 360-4777
Sue Akin, *Admin Sec*
EMP: 82 EST: 1964
SQ FT: 7,704
SALES (est): 517.1K **Privately Held**
WEB: www.bethlehemlutheran.net
SIC: **8351** 8661 Preschool center; Lutheran Church

(P-21990)
BLIND CHILDRENS LRNG CTR INC
18542 Vanderlip Ave Ste B, Santa Ana (92705-8201)
P.O. Box 25209 (92799-5209)
PHONE.................................714 573-8888
Kathy Buehler, *Exec Dir*
Hunter Johnson, *Senior VP*
Denise Grajek, *Admin Asst*
Rosa M Guijosa, *CIO*
Mindy Weinheimer, *Human Res Dir*
EMP: 94 EST: 1962
SQ FT: 18,824
SALES (est): 2.9MM **Privately Held**
WEB: www.beyondblindness.org
SIC: **8351** 8211 Child day care services; private special education school

(P-21991)
BRAWLEY UNION HIGH SCHOOL DIST (PA)
480 N Imperial Ave, Brawley (92227-1690)
PHONE.................................760 312-6068
Hasnik Danielian, *Superintendent*
Jenifer Layaye, *CFO*
Rusty Garcia, *Bd of Directors*
Cass Proo, *Executive*
Jessica Acedas, *Admin Sec*
EMP: 245 EST: 1908
SALES (est): 29.7MM **Privately Held**
WEB: www.brawleyhigh.org
SIC: **8211** 8351 High school, junior or senior; preschool center

(P-21992)
CAL POLY POMONA FOUNDATION INC
Also Called: Children Ctr At Cal Poly Pmona
3801 W Temple Ave # 116, Pomona (91768-2557)
PHONE.................................909 869-2284
Yvonne Bailey, *Manager*
Saccara Lim, *Executive Asst*
Francine Ramirez, *Administration*
EMP: 1376
SALES (corp-wide): 53.8MM **Privately Held**
WEB: www.cpp.edu
SIC: **8351** Child day care services
PA: Cal Poly Pomona Foundation, Inc.
3801 W Temple Ave Bldg 55
Pomona CA 91768
909 869-2950

(P-21993)
CALIFORNIA CHILDRENS ACADEMY
Also Called: Early Learning Center
233 N Breed St, Los Angeles (90033-2902)
PHONE.................................323 263-3846
Monica Barahona, *Director*
EMP: 144 **Privately Held**
WEB: www.californiachildrensacademy.org
SIC: **8351** Preschool center
PA: California Children's Academy
2701 N Main St
Los Angeles CA 90031

(P-21994)
CALVARY CHURCH SANTA ANA INC
1010 N Tustin Ave, Santa Ana (92705-3598)
PHONE.................................714 973-4800
Michael Welles, *Pastor*
Lois Chandler, *Executive Asst*
Karen Dornbach, *IT/INT Sup*
Eric Wakeling, *Pastor*
Dr D J Mitchell, *Sr Pastor*
EMP: 160 EST: 1932
SQ FT: 133,000
SALES (est): 11.4MM **Privately Held**
WEB: www.calvarylife.org
SIC: **8351** 8661 Nursery school; miscellaneous denomination church

(P-21995)
CANYON HILLS ASSEMBLY GOD CH
Also Called: Canyon Hill Preschool
7001 Auburn St, Bakersfield (93306-7213)
PHONE.................................661 871-1150
Wendell Ray Vinson, *Pastor*
Karina Galvan, *Admin Sec*
Kris Wattss, *Admin Asst*
Karl Hargestam, *Pastor*
Fern Segura, *Pastor*
EMP: 58 EST: 1958
SALES (est): 6.1MM **Privately Held**
WEB: www.canyonhills.com
SIC: **8661** 8351 Assembly of God Church; preschool center

(P-21996)
CHEF BOBO BRAND INC (PA)
419 N Hobart Blvd, Los Angeles (90004-1805)
PHONE.................................800 977-8912
Brian Park, *Principal*
EMP: 64 EST: 2016
SALES (est): 486.1K **Privately Held**
SIC: **8351** Group day care center

(P-21997)
CHILD CARE RESOURCE CENTER INC
Also Called: Volunteers America Head Start
454 S Kalisher St, San Fernando (91340-3535)
PHONE.................................818 837-0097
EMP: 214
SALES (corp-wide): 335.1MM **Privately Held**
WEB: www.ccrcca.org
SIC: **8351** Child day care services

PA: Child Care Resource Center, Inc.
20001 Prairie St
Chatsworth CA 91311
818 717-1000

(P-21998)
CHILD DEVELOPMENT INCORPORATED
Also Called: Turtle Rock Cdc
5151 Amalfi Dr, Irvine (92603-3443)
PHONE..............949 854-5060
Mindy Ho, *Director*
EMP: 406
SALES (corp-wide): 28MM **Privately Held**
WEB: www.catalystkids.org
SIC: 8351 Child day care services
PA: Child Development Incorporated
350 Woodview Ave
Morgan Hill CA 95037
408 556-7300

(P-21999)
CHILD EDUCATIONAL CENTER
Also Called: Cec
140 Foothill Blvd, La Canada (91011-3727)
PHONE..............818 354-3418
Elyssa Nelson, *Director*
Kayla Imhoff, *Corp Comm Staff*
Erinn Levin, *Director*
Sheryl Macphee, *Director*
EMP: 60 EST: 1979
SALES (est): 4.7MM **Privately Held**
WEB: www.ceconline.org
SIC: 8351 Preschool center

(P-22000)
CHILD LANE (PA)
2545 Pacific Ave, Long Beach (90806-3033)
PHONE..............562 427-8834
Dora Jazildo, *Exec Dir*
Dora Jacildo, *Exec Dir*
Maria Almeida, *General Mgr*
Roberta Ramirez, *Supervisor*
EMP: 114 EST: 1983
SALES (est): 11.6MM **Privately Held**
WEB: www.childlane.org
SIC: 8351 Preschool center

(P-22001)
CHILDRENS CHOICE INC
Also Called: Children's Choice Preschool
29028 Aloma Ave, Laguna Niguel (92677-1504)
PHONE..............949 495-5162
Christopher Lincoln, *Principal*
Cari Griesbach, *Exec Dir*
Hend Al-Ali, *Teacher*
Allison Duggan, *Teacher*
Lisa Schoenhoefer, *Teacher*
EMP: 56 EST: 1976
SQ FT: 10,000
SALES: 76.6K **Privately Held**
WEB: www.mcdowellschool.org
SIC: 8351 Preschool center

(P-22002)
CHILDRENS HOSPITAL ORANGE CNTY
500 Superior Ave, Newport Beach (92663-3657)
PHONE..............949 631-2062
EMP: 57
SALES (corp-wide): 992MM **Privately Held**
WEB: www.choc.org
SIC: 8351 Child day care services
PA: Children's Hospital Of Orange County
1201 W La Veta Ave
Orange CA 92868
714 997-3000

(P-22003)
CHRISTIAN ARCADIA SCHOOL
Also Called: Christian Schl Soc of Arcadia
1900 S Santa Anita Ave, Arcadia (91006-4607)
PHONE..............626 574-8229
Ryan Tungate, *President*
Greg Saltzer, *Treasurer*
Steve Blankenship, *Administration*
Josh Ambrose, *Teacher*
Jennifer Hearn, *Teacher*
EMP: 70 EST: 1945

SALES (est): 1.7MM **Privately Held**
SIC: 8211 8351 Private elementary school; private junior high school; preschool center

(P-22004)
CHRISTIAN BETHEL SCHOOL
3100 W Avenue K, Lancaster (93536-5403)
PHONE..............661 943-2224
Matt Connor, *Principal*
Shauna Konnerth, *Ch of Bd*
David Guess, *Technology*
Sherina Barker, *Teacher*
Victoria Bishop, *Teacher*
EMP: 53 EST: 1979
SALES (est): 3.1MM **Privately Held**
WEB: www.bethelchristian.net
SIC: 8211 8351 Private combined elementary & secondary school; preschool center

(P-22005)
CLAIRBOURN SCHOOL
8400 Huntington Dr, San Gabriel (91775-1154)
PHONE..............626 286-3108
Robert Nafie, *President*
Tara Edwards, *Teacher*
Rosemary Kiertzner, *Teacher*
Dannalou Machi, *Teacher*
Rebecca Messler, *Teacher*
EMP: 60 EST: 1926
SQ FT: 24,403
SALES (est): 6.5MM **Privately Held**
WEB: www.clairbourn.org
SIC: 8211 8351 Private elementary & secondary schools; child day care services

(P-22006)
COMMUNITY ACTION PRTNR SAN LUI (PA)
1030 Southwood Dr, San Luis Obispo (93401-5813)
PHONE..............805 544-4355
Anita Robinson, *Ch of Bd*
Frances I Coughlin, *President*
Jim Famalette, *COO*
Joan Limov, *CFO*
Rob Garcia, *Treasurer*
EMP: 72
SQ FT: 20,000
SALES: 79.1MM **Privately Held**
WEB: www.capslo.org
SIC: 8351 Head start center, except in conjunction with school

(P-22007)
COMMUNITY ACTION PRTNR SAN LUI
Also Called: Day Care Center
805a Fiero Ln Ste A, San Luis Obispo (93401-8700)
PHONE..............805 541-2272
Sheri Wilson, *Director*
EMP: 117
SALES (corp-wide): 93.2MM **Privately Held**
WEB: www.capslo.org
SIC: 8351 Head start center, except in conjunction with school
PA: Community Action Partnership Of San Luis Obispo County, Inc.
1030 Southwood Dr
San Luis Obispo CA 93401
805 544-4355

(P-22008)
COMPTON UNIFIED SCHOOL DST
Also Called: Child Development Center
411 N Tajauta Ave, Compton (90220-1755)
PHONE..............310 898-6008
Jean Gaston, *Director*
EMP: 72
SALES (corp-wide): 342.2MM **Privately Held**
WEB: www.compton.k12.ca.us
SIC: 8211 8351 Public elementary & secondary schools; child day care services
PA: Compton Unified School District
501 S Santa Fe Ave
Compton CA 90221
310 604-6508

(P-22009)
CROSSRADS CHRSTN SCHOLS CORONA
2380 Fullerton Ave, Corona (92881-3111)
PHONE..............951 278-3199
Dough Husen, *Superintendent*
Rebecca Carter, *Admin Asst*
Patty Santos, *Admin Asst*
Jackie Curtis, *Education*
EMP: 145 EST: 2001
SQ FT: 1,088
SALES (est): 5.5MM **Privately Held**
WEB: www.crossroadsschool.org
SIC: 8299 8211 8351 8699 Religious school; high school, junior or senior; preschool center; charitable organization

(P-22010)
EBEN-EZER CHLD DAY CARE CTR (PA)
Also Called: Kids First Learning Center
13232 Kagel Canyon St, Pacoima (91331-3926)
PHONE..............818 897-5427
Cynthia Saenz, *President*
Eloise Ortiz, *Principal*
Leslie Manuecci, *Administration*
EMP: 77 EST: 1996
SQ FT: 11,639
SALES (est): 3MM **Privately Held**
WEB: www.kids1st.org
SIC: 8351 Montessori child development center

(P-22011)
EGREMONT SCHOOLS INC
19850 Devonshire St, Chatsworth (91311-3598)
PHONE..............818 363-7803
Tina Struve, *Exec Dir*
Coleen Callahan, *Exec Dir*
Matthew Berandstetter, *Administration*
Helen Giambrone, *Administration*
David Burkhardt, *Bookkeeper*
EMP: 80 EST: 1936
SQ FT: 22,298
SALES (est): 1.8MM **Privately Held**
WEB: www.egremont.org
SIC: 8211 8351 Private elementary school; preschool center

(P-22012)
ENVIRONMENTS FOR LEARNING INC (PA)
Also Called: Montessori On The Lake
24291 Muirlands Blvd, Lake Forest (92630-3001)
PHONE..............949 855-5630
Sara Smith, *President*
Greta Isadora, *Teacher*
EMP: 65 EST: 1988
SALES (est): 2.6MM **Privately Held**
SIC: 8351 Montessori child development center; preparatory school; private combined elementary & secondary school

(P-22013)
FAIRPLEX CHILD DEVELOPMENT CTR
Also Called: SHERATON SUITES FAIRPLEX
1101 W Mckinley Ave, Pomona (91768-1650)
PHONE..............909 623-3899
Holly Reynolds, *Director*
EMP: 56 EST: 2001
SALES (est): 1.2MM
SALES (corp-wide): 66.3MM **Privately Held**
WEB: www.fairplex.com
SIC: 8351 Child day care services
PA: Los Angeles County Fair Association
1101 W Mckinley Ave
Pomona CA 91768
909 623-3111

(P-22014)
FAMILY CARE NETWORK INC (PA)
1255 Kendall Rd, San Luis Obispo (93401-8750)
PHONE..............805 503-6240
James Robert, *CEO*
Britney Page, *Partner*
Jonathan Nibbio, *COO*
Bobbie Boyer, *CFO*

Rolonda Nulton, *Admin Asst*
EMP: 71 EST: 1989
SQ FT: 2,600
SALES (est): 22.9MM **Privately Held**
WEB: www.fcni.org
SIC: 8351 Child day care services

(P-22015)
FIRST ASSMBLY OF GOD BKRSFIELD
Also Called: Stockdale Christian School
4901 California Ave, Bakersfield (93309-1111)
PHONE..............661 327-2227
Rev Steven Hunt, *Ch of Bd*
Rick Roper, *Treasurer*
Kevin Harrel, *Vice Ch Bd*
Bonnie Taylor, *Exec Dir*
Martha Salado, *Bookkeeper*
EMP: 97 EST: 1924
SQ FT: 60,000
SALES (est): 12MM **Privately Held**
WEB: www.bakersfield1st.com
SIC: 8661 8211 8351 Assembly of God Church; private junior high school; kindergarten; private elementary school; preschool center

(P-22016)
FIRST BAPTIST CHURCH POMONA (PA)
Also Called: First Baptist School
586 N Main St, Pomona (91768-3186)
PHONE..............909 629-5277
Glenn Gunderson, *Pastor*
Lisa Toney, *Pastor*
EMP: 53 EST: 1884
SALES (est): 4.4MM **Privately Held**
SIC: 8661 8211 8351 Baptist Church; high school, junior or senior; preschool center

(P-22017)
FOOTHILL CHILD DEV SVCS INC
16946 Sherman Way 100, Van Nuys (91406-3613)
PHONE..............818 353-3772
Mike Daldalyan, *CEO*
Emilia Broberg, *CEO*
Minas Daldalyan, *CFO*
Martiros Tngryan, *Admin Sec*
Ani Lalayan, *Supervisor*
EMP: 65 EST: 2005
SALES (est): 3.5MM **Privately Held**
WEB: www.foothillchild.com
SIC: 8351 Preschool center

(P-22018)
FSA ARLANZA CHILD DEV CTR (PA)
7801 Gramercy Pl, Riverside (92503-2557)
PHONE..............951 352-2810
Vianca Hernandez, *Manager*
EMP: 68 EST: 2006
SALES (est): 98.8K **Privately Held**
WEB: www.fsaca.org
SIC: 8351 Child day care services

(P-22019)
GROWING PLACE
401 Ashland Ave, Santa Monica (90405-4311)
PHONE..............310 399-7769
Ellen W Khokha, *Director*
Elaine Hochstrasser, *Office Mgr*
Teresa Lezak, *Teacher*
EMP: 67 EST: 1985
SALES: 3.3MM **Privately Held**
WEB: www.growingplace.org
SIC: 8351 Group day care center

(P-22020)
HOLLYWOOD SCHOOLHOUSE INC
1233 N Mccadden Pl, Los Angeles (90038-1214)
PHONE..............323 465-1320
Ilise Saye, *President*
Stephen Bloodworth, *President*
Tina Harris, *Principal*
Evelyn Moreira, *Admin Sec*
Virgess Way, *Admin Sec*
EMP: 50 EST: 1945

SALES (est): 8.4MM **Privately Held**
WEB: www.hshla.org
SIC: **8211** 8351 Elementary school; nursery school

(P-22021)
HUNG MANAGEMENT INC
Also Called: Hickory Tree School
21720 Madrona Ave, Torrance
(90503-7111)
PHONE..................................310 533-4830
Lisa Hung, *President*
EMP: 51 EST: 1979
SQ FT: 8,000
SALES (est): 3.7MM **Privately Held**
WEB: www.hickorytreeschool.com
SIC: **8351** 8211 Preschool center; private elementary school

(P-22022)
IMMANUEL BPTST CH OF SAN BRNRD
Also Called: Immanuel Baptist Day School
28355 Baseline St, Highland (92346-5008)
PHONE..................................909 862-6641
Rob Zinn, *Minister*
Andrew Preslar, *Maintence Staff*
Daniel Choi, *Minister*
Guillermo Fernandez, *Minister*
Ashley Culpepper, *Director*
EMP: 65 EST: 1953
SALES (est): 7.8MM **Privately Held**
WEB: www.ibchighland.org
SIC: **8351** 8661 Preschool center; Baptist Church

(P-22023)
IMPERIAL VALLEY FAMILY CARE (PA)
516 W Aten Rd Ste 2, Imperial
(92251-9805)
PHONE..................................760 355-7730
Kristal Swaim, *Principal*
EMP: 95 EST: 1995
SALES (est): 3.9MM **Privately Held**
WEB: www.ivfcmg.com
SIC: **8351** 8099 Group day care center; blood related health services

(P-22024)
INCLUSIVE EDCATN CMNTY PRTNR I
Also Called: Iecp
2323 Roosevelt Blvd Apt 3, Oxnard
(93035-4480)
PHONE..................................805 985-4808
Rick B Clemens, *President*
Rick Clemens, *President*
Elizabeth Davidson, *Analyst*
Cindy Salinas, *Hum Res Coord*
Sarah Van Aken, *Opers Mgr*
EMP: 300 EST: 2002
SALES (est): 11MM **Privately Held**
WEB: www.iecp.us
SIC: **8211** 8351 Specialty education; preschool center

(P-22025)
KERN COMMUNITY COLLEGE DST
Also Called: Cerro Corso Community College
3000 College Heights Blvd, Ridgecrest
(93555-9571)
PHONE..................................760 384-6100
Jill Board, *President*
Crystal Leffler, *Admin Sec*
Tammy Kinnan, *Admin Asst*
Angela Sellers, *Admin Asst*
Kristie Chavez, *Administration*
EMP: 73
SALES (corp-wide): 58.7MM **Privately Held**
WEB: www.kccd.edu
SIC: **8222** 8351 Community college; child day care services
PA: Kern Community College District
2100 Chester Ave
Bakersfield CA 93301
661 336-5100

(P-22026)
KIDS KLUB CARE CENTERS INC (PA)
Also Called: Kids Klub Pasadena
380 S Raymond Ave, Pasadena
(91105-2608)
PHONE..................................626 795-2501
Michael Wojciechowski, *President*
Bambi Wojciechowski, *Chairman*
Lauren Amezaga, *Director*
Debbie Rudman, *Regional*
EMP: 53 EST: 1995
SQ FT: 7,800
SALES (est): 5.4MM **Privately Held**
WEB: www.kidsklubcdc.com
SIC: **8351** Preschool center

(P-22027)
LEPORT EDUCATIONAL INST INC
Also Called: Leport Schools
1 Technology Dr Bldg A, Irvine
(92618-2350)
PHONE..................................914 374-8860
Ramandeep S Girn, *CEO*
Katie Little, *Admin Asst*
Annamaria Salzetti, *Business Mgr*
Daniela Becerra, *Teacher*
Serenity Fisher, *Teacher*
EMP: 255 EST: 2000
SALES (est): 24.8MM **Privately Held**
WEB: www.leportschools.com
SIC: **8351** Montessori child development center

(P-22028)
LITTLE PEOPLE PRE-SCHOOL
Also Called: Alta Loma Christian School
9974 19th St, Rancho Cucamonga
(91737-4234)
P.O. Box 8698 (91701-0698)
PHONE..................................909 989-2804
Irene Lopez, *Director*
Olivia Cleland, *Office Mgr*
Cheryl Louis, *Admin Sec*
Denae Salazar, *Admin Sec*
Jacob Acevedo, *Maintence Staff*
EMP: 54 EST: 1980
SALES (est): 5.1MM **Privately Held**
WEB: www.alchristian.com
SIC: **8351** Preschool center

(P-22029)
LITTLE SCHOLARS MONTESSORI
18706 Hatteras St, Tarzana (91356-1402)
PHONE..................................818 343-1794
Sarangi Weththasingha, *CEO*
Amal Weththasingha, *Admin Sec*
EMP: 50 EST: 2012
SQ FT: 4,000
SALES (est): 2.9MM **Privately Held**
WEB: www.littlescholarsmontessori.org
SIC: **8351** Child day care services; Montessori child development center; preschool center

(P-22030)
LONG BEACH DAY NURSERY
3965 N Bellflower Blvd, Long Beach
(90808-1902)
PHONE..................................562 421-1488
Margareth McMahon, *Director*
EMP: 55
SALES (corp-wide): 3.8MM **Privately Held**
WEB: www.lbdn.org
SIC: **8351** Preschool center
PA: Long Beach Day Nursery
1548 Chestnut Ave
Long Beach CA 90813
562 421-1488

(P-22031)
LOS ANGLES UNIVERSAL PRESCHOOL
Also Called: Child360
515 S Figueroa St Ste 900, Los Angeles
(90071-3309)
PHONE..................................213 416-1200
William Sperling, *CEO*
Elisa Santiago, *COO*
Elsa Luna, *CFO*
David Crippens, *Bd of Directors*
Claudia Sarmiento, *Comms Mgr*

EMP: 200 EST: 2004
SQ FT: 12,000
SALES: 76.2MM **Privately Held**
WEB: www.child360.org
SIC: **8351** Preschool center

(P-22032)
LYNWOOD UNIFIED SCHOOL DST
Also Called: Lindbergh Child Care Center
12120 Lindbergh Ave, Lynwood
(90262-4701)
PHONE..................................310 631-7308
Maria Noriega, *Director*
EMP: 88
SQ FT: 3,790
SALES (corp-wide): 215.4MM **Privately Held**
WEB: www.lynwood.k12.ca.us
SIC: **8211** 8351 Public elementary & secondary schools; child day care services
PA: Lynwood Unified School District
11321 Bullis Rd
Lynwood CA 90262
310 886-1600

(P-22033)
MARYVALE DAY CARE CENTER
Also Called: Maryvale Edcatn Fmly Rsrce Ctr
2502 Huntington Dr, Duarte (91010-2221)
PHONE..................................626 357-1514
Steve Gunther, *Director*
Juliann Curabba, *COO*
Jose Hermida, *Vice Pres*
Christina Moore, *Vice Pres*
Alie Rodriguez, *Admin Sec*
EMP: 109
SALES (corp-wide): 9MM **Privately Held**
WEB: www.maryvaleufsd.org
SIC: **8351** Preschool center
PA: Maryvale Day Care Center
1050 Maryvale Dr
Cheektowaga NY 14225
626 280-6511

(P-22034)
MEXICAN AMRCN OPRTNTY FNDATION
330 S Ford Blvd, Los Angeles
(90022-1806)
PHONE..................................323 264-4333
Maria Gallegoa, *Branch Mgr*
Marisela Munoz, *Clerk*
EMP: 59
SALES (corp-wide): 109.4MM **Privately Held**
WEB: www.maof.org
SIC: **5812** 8351 Mexican restaurant; child day care services
PA: Mexican American Opportunity Foundation
401 N Garfield Ave
Montebello CA 90640
323 890-9600

(P-22035)
MONICA ROS SCHOOL
783 Mcnell Rd, Ojai (93023-9316)
PHONE..................................805 646-8184
Susan Hardenvergh, *Principal*
Alice Meyer, *Principal*
Alice Fiore, *Technology*
Suzanne Feldman, *Director*
EMP: 52 EST: 1942
SQ FT: 7,500
SALES: 2.2MM **Privately Held**
WEB: www.monicaros.org
SIC: **8351** 8211 Nursery school; elementary school

(P-22036)
MONTE VISTA CHILD CARE CTR INC (PA)
13342 Victoria St, Rancho Cucamonga
(91739-2020)
PHONE..................................909 544-0040
David Hooyenga, *CEO*
EMP: 88 EST: 1976
SALES (est): 811.4K **Privately Held**
SIC: **8351** Group day care center

(P-22037)
MOUNTAIN VIEW CHILD CARE INC
Also Called: Totally Kids Spcalty Hlth Care
10716 La Tuna Canyon Rd, Sun Valley
(91352-2130)
PHONE..................................818 252-5863
Michelle Nydam, *Branch Mgr*
EMP: 150 **Privately Held**
WEB: www.totallykids.com
SIC: **8351** Child day care services
PA: Mountain View Child Care, Inc.
1720 Mountain View Ave
Loma Linda CA 92354

(P-22038)
MOUNTAIN VIEW ELMNTARY SCHL DS
Also Called: Mountain View Children'c Ctr
2109 Burkett Rd, El Monte (91733-4113)
PHONE..................................626 652-4250
Alma Gonzales, *Director*
EMP: 63
SALES (corp-wide): 105.2MM **Privately Held**
WEB: www.mtviewschools.com
SIC: **8211** 8351 Public elementary school; head start center, except in conjunction with school
PA: Mountain View Elementary School District
3320 Gilman Rd
El Monte CA 91732
626 652-4000

(P-22039)
MOUNTAIN VIEW MONTESSORI SCHL (PA)
4640 Granada Pl, Santa Barbara
(93110-1378)
PHONE..................................805 453-3197
Thushari Manjula Kandamby, *CEO*
EMP: 55 EST: 2014
SALES (est): 73.8K **Privately Held**
WEB: www.mountainviewmontessorischool.com
SIC: **8351** Montessori child development center

(P-22040)
MT CALVARY LTHRAN CHRCH-MSSURI
23300 Golden Springs Dr, Diamond Bar
(91765-2003)
PHONE..................................909 861-2740
Dennis Stueve, *Pastor*
Janina Gonzales, *Teacher*
Nacy Hobbs, *Teacher*
Julie Mawhorter, *Teacher*
Janine Shin, *Teacher*
EMP: 55 EST: 1965
SQ FT: 33,184
SALES (est): 5MM **Privately Held**
WEB: www.mcldb.org
SIC: **8211** 8661 8351 Private combined elementary & secondary school; Lutheran Church; child day care services

(P-22041)
MWLA INC
Also Called: TURNINGPOINT SCHOOL
8780 National Blvd, Culver City
(90232-2348)
PHONE..................................310 841-2505
Deborah Richman, *Principal*
Sam Widdoes, *Vice Pres*
Christine Sabihon, *Executive*
Courtney Baker, *Comms Dir*
Peter Boylan, *Office Mgr*
EMP: 54 EST: 1970
SQ FT: 50,000
SALES: 12.7MM **Privately Held**
WEB: www.turningpointschool.org
SIC: **8211** 8351 Private elementary school; child day care services

(P-22042)
NEWPORT MESA UNIFIED SCHL DST
Also Called: Harbor View Pre-School
900 Goldenrod Ave, Corona Del Mar
(92625-1503)
PHONE..................................949 515-6940
Todd Schmidt, *Principal*

Frederick Navarro, *Superintendent*
EMP: 69
SALES (corp-wide): 378.9MM **Privately Held**
WEB: www.web.nmusd.us
SIC: 8211 8351 Public elementary school; preschool center
PA: Newport Mesa Unified School District
2985 Bear St Ste A
Costa Mesa CA 92626
714 424-5000

(P-22043)
NURTURING TOTS INC
535 Avenue B A, Redondo Beach (90277-4827)
PHONE..................818 996-1602
Eugene Cobuzzi, *Owner*
Linda Cobuzzi, *President*
Debra Dinielli, *President*
Penny Raymer, *Office Mgr*
EMP: 60 **EST:** 2013
SALES (est): 1.3MM **Privately Held**
WEB: www.nurturingtots.com
SIC: 8351 Group day care center

(P-22044)
ONEGENERATION (PA)
Also Called: Onegenrtion Adult Dycare Chldc
17400 Victory Blvd, Van Nuys (91406-5349)
PHONE..................818 708-6625
Lawrence Gordon, *Exec Dir*
Angela Pennacchio, *Executive Asst*
Adam Tavitian, *Financial Analy*
Eduardo Benmaor, *Finance*
Judy Hamilton, *Finance*
EMP: 73 **EST:** 1978
SALES (est): 6MM **Privately Held**
WEB: www.onegeneration.org
SIC: 8351 8322 Child day care services; senior citizens' center or association

(P-22045)
ORANGE COUNTY HEAD START INC (PA)
2501 Pullman St, Santa Ana (92705-5515)
P.O. Box 9269, Fountain Valley (92728-9269)
PHONE..................714 241-8920
Colleen Versteeg, *Exec Dir*
Rose Alveraz, *Exec Dir*
Natalie Sarle, *Planning*
Loyal Sharp, *Finance Dir*
Michelle Couts, *Teacher*
EMP: 75 **EST:** 1965
SQ FT: 20,000
SALES (est): 38.8MM **Privately Held**
WEB: www.ochsinc.org
SIC: 8351 Head start center, except in conjunction with school

(P-22046)
PAGE PRIVATE SCHOOL
419 S Robertson Blvd, Beverly Hills (90211-3603)
PHONE..................323 272-3429
Janice Kim, *Principal*
Al Gonzalez, *Principal*
EMP: 81
SQ FT: 7,074
SALES (corp-wide): 4.8MM **Privately Held**
SIC: 8211 8351 Private elementary school; group day care center
PA: Page Private School
657 Victoria St
Costa Mesa CA 92627
949 515-1700

(P-22047)
PEOPLES CARE INC
12215 Telg Rd Ste 208, Santa Fe Springs (90670)
PHONE..................562 320-0174
Torres Cesaer, *Principal*
Conrado Nilo, *CFO*
Cristin Nicoletti, *Project Mgr*
Barbara Nguyen, *Director*
EMP: 132
SALES (corp-wide): 62.2MM **Privately Held**
WEB: www.peoplescare.com
SIC: 8351 Child day care services

PA: Peoples Care Inc.
13920 City Center Dr # 290
Chino Hills CA 91709
855 773-6753

(P-22048)
PLAZA DE LA RAZA CHILD DEV SVC (PA)
13300 Crssrds Pkwy N 44 440 N, La Puente (91746)
PHONE..................562 776-1301
Anthony Rendon, *Exec Dir*
Norayma Cabot, *Exec Dir*
Nneka Arinze, *Area Spvr*
Janelle Parker, *Teacher*
Rosalina Fine, *Director*
EMP: 72 **EST:** 1965
SALES (est): 20.5MM **Privately Held**
WEB: www.plazadelaraza.info
SIC: 8351 Head start center, except in conjunction with school

(P-22049)
PLAZA DE LA RAZA CHILD DEVELOP
225 N Avenue 25, Los Angeles (90031-1794)
PHONE..................323 224-1788
EMP: 71
SALES (corp-wide): 20.5MM **Privately Held**
WEB: www.plazadelaraza.info
SIC: 8351 Head start center, except in conjunction with school
PA: Plaza De La Raza Child Development Services, Inc.
13300 Crssrds Pkwy N 44 440 N
La Puente CA 91746
562 776-1301

(P-22050)
PLAZA DE LA RAZA CHILD DEVELOP
6411 Norwalk Blvd, Whittier (90606-1502)
PHONE..................562 695-1070
Adriana Gonzalez, *President*
EMP: 71
SALES (corp-wide): 20.5MM **Privately Held**
WEB: www.plazadelaraza.info
SIC: 8351 Head start center, except in conjunction with school
PA: Plaza De La Raza Child Development Services, Inc.
13300 Crssrds Pkwy N 44 440 N
La Puente CA 91746
562 776-1301

(P-22051)
PLYMOUTH CONGREGATIONAL CHURCH
Also Called: Plymouth Christian School
12058 Beverly Blvd, Whittier (90601-2948)
PHONE..................562 692-1228
Lisa Murray, *Administration*
Beverly Martin, *Principal*
Martha Alvarez, *Office Mgr*
Christina Carreon, *Teacher*
Angie Lampietti, *Teacher*
EMP: 53 **EST:** 1894
SQ FT: 36,204
SALES (est): 4.5MM **Privately Held**
WEB: www.plymouthchristianschool.org
SIC: 8351 Preschool center

(P-22052)
POLYTECHNIC SCHOOL
1030 E California Blvd, Pasadena (91106-4099)
PHONE..................626 792-2147
John W Bracker, *Headmaster*
Cynthia Crass, *Ch of Bd*
Ann Diederich, *Ch of Bd*
Wendy Munger, *President*
Dave Yamaoka, *COO*
EMP: 331 **EST:** 1907
SALES: 41.4MM **Privately Held**
WEB: www.polytechnic.org
SIC: 8211 8351 Kindergarten; private combined elementary & secondary school; preschool center

(P-22053)
PRESCHOOL SERVICES DEPARTMENT (PA)
662 S Tippecanoe Ave, San Bernardino (92415-0630)
PHONE..................909 383-2000
EMP: 83 **EST:** 2009
SALES (est): 668.4K **Privately Held**
WEB: www.sbcounty.gov
SIC: 8351 Preschool center

(P-22054)
PRESTIGE PRESCHOOLS INC (PA)
3795 La Crescenta Ave # 2, Glendale (91208-1057)
PHONE..................818 957-1170
Steven L Bush, *Principal*
EMP: 72 **EST:** 2008
SALES (est): 1.1MM **Privately Held**
WEB: www.prestigepreschoolacademy.com
SIC: 8351 Preschool center

(P-22055)
PRIME HEALTH CARE
Also Called: San Dimas Community Hospital
1350 W Covina Blvd, San Dimas (91773-3245)
PHONE..................909 394-2727
Prim Reddy, *Owner*
Carrie Chuck, *Treasurer*
Ravi Alla, *Vice Pres*
Will Conaway, *Vice Pres*
Marc Goldstone, *Vice Pres*
EMP: 266 **EST:** 2010
SALES (est): 30.5MM **Privately Held**
WEB: www.primehealthcare.com
SIC: 8351 8062 Child day care services; general medical & surgical hospitals

(P-22056)
RGBX INC
Also Called: Heritage Oak Prvate Elmntary S
16971 Imperial Hwy, Yorba Linda (92886-1663)
PHONE..................714 524-1350
Phyllis Cygan, *President*
Mac Gamse, *Principal*
Gregory Cygan, *Admin Sec*
Elizabeth Watkins, *Admin Sec*
Latrese Jackson, *Administration*
EMP: 74 **EST:** 1992
SQ FT: 22,000
SALES (est): 6.5MM **Privately Held**
WEB: www.heritageoak.org
SIC: 8351 8211 Preschool center; elementary school

(P-22057)
ROMAN CTHLIC DIOCESE OF ORANGE
Also Called: Saint Cecilia School
1311 Sycamore Ave, Tustin (92780-6276)
PHONE..................714 544-1533
Mary Alvarado, *Principal*
Wayne Adajar, *Assoc Pastor*
Bao Thai, *Pastor*
C Nguyen, *Teacher*
Juliana Gerace, *Director*
EMP: 175
SALES (corp-wide): 100.3MM **Privately Held**
WEB: www.rcbo.org
SIC: 8211 8351 Catholic combined elementary & secondary school; kindergarten; preschool center
PA: The Roman Catholic Diocese Of Orange
13280 Chapman Ave
Garden Grove CA 92840
714 282-3000

(P-22058)
SOUTHERN CALIFORNIA LRNG CORP
Also Called: Sylvan Learning Center
2970 Huntington Dr, San Marino (91108-2237)
PHONE..................818 639-9692
Todd Crabtree, *Principal*
EMP: 50 **EST:** 2005
SALES (est): 335.1K **Privately Held**
WEB: www.sylvanlearning.com
SIC: 8351 Child day care services

(P-22059)
ST MARKS EPISCOPAL CHURCH
330 E 16th St, Upland (91784-2050)
PHONE..................909 920-5565
Conrad White, *Pastor*
Jonathan T Glass, *President*
Emily Bell, *Pastor*
Karri Backer, *Headmaster*
Blane Abernathy, *Director*
EMP: 52 **EST:** 1911
SQ FT: 5,000
SALES (est): 4.9MM **Privately Held**
WEB: www.stmarks-upland.org
SIC: 8211 8351 8661 Private elementary school; preschool center; Episcopal Church

(P-22060)
ST TIMOTHY SCHOOL
10479 W Pico Blvd, Los Angeles (90064-2307)
PHONE..................310 474-1811
Iselda Richmond, *Principal*
Rita G Lapple, *Principal*
Lorraine Lowder, *Office Mgr*
Yolanda Garcia, *Business Mgr*
Ryan Benitez, *Teacher*
EMP: 68 **EST:** 1958
SALES (est): 5.8MM **Privately Held**
WEB: www.sttimothy.org
SIC: 8351 8211 Child day care services; Catholic elementary school

(P-22061)
START PACE HEAD
1541 Wilshire Blvd # 200 Los Angeles (90017-2211)
PHONE..................213 989-3222
Helen Goodman, *Principal*
Erika Paz, *Admin Asst*
Sherry Samuel, *Director*
EMP: 59 **EST:** 2000
SALES (est): 7.9MM **Privately Held**
WEB: www.pacela.org
SIC: 8351 Head start center, except in conjunction with school

(P-22062)
SUGAR SPICE EVRYTHING NICE INC (PA)
27000 Alicia Pkwy Ste E, Laguna Niguel (92677-3419)
PHONE..................949 307-8674
Victoria Emry, *CEO*
EMP: 60 **EST:** 2008
SALES (est): 130.8K **Privately Held**
SIC: 8351 Child day care services

(P-22063)
SUNDALE FNDTION FOR STDNTS CMN
Also Called: Sundale School
13990 Avenue 240, Tulare (93274-9563)
PHONE..................559 688-3419
Terri Rufert, *President*
Katie Biangone, *Executive Asst*
Shirley Wasnick, *Admin Sec*
Marty Robertson, *Comp Tech*
Linda Allen, *Teacher*
EMP: 117 **EST:** 1950
SALES (est): 3.2MM **Privately Held**
WEB: www.sundaleschool.com
SIC: 8351 Head start center, except in conjunction with school

(P-22064)
TEMPLE JDEA OF W SAN FRNNDO VL
Also Called: Temple Judea Nursery School
5429 Lindley Ave, Tarzana (91356-3703)
PHONE..................818 758-3800
Margie Ipp, *Director*
Richard Hoffman, *Exec Dir*
Tammy Lerman, *Executive Asst*
Orit Nazarian, *Admin Sec*
Emily Ferro, *Admin Asst*
EMP: 85 **Privately Held**
WEB: www.templejudea.com
SIC: 8351 8661 Child day care services; synagogue
PA: Temple Judea Of The West San Fernando Valley
5429 Lindley Ave
Tarzana CA 91356
818 758-3800

(P-22065)
THINK TOGETHER
202 E Airport Dr Ste 200, San Bernardino
(92408-3429)
PHONE.....................................909 723-1400
EMP: 512
SALES (corp-wide): 66.3MM **Privately Held**
WEB: www.thinktogether.org
SIC: 8351 Child day care services
PA: Think Together
2101 E 4th St Ste 200b
Santa Ana CA 92705
714 543-3807

(P-22066)
THINK TOGETHER
800 S Barranca Ave # 120, Covina
(91723-3680)
PHONE.....................................626 373-2311
Tom Lopez, *Branch Mgr*
Irene Bobadilla, *General Mgr*
EMP: 512
SALES (corp-wide): 66.3MM **Privately Held**
WEB: www.thinktogether.org
SIC: 8351 Child day care services
PA: Think Together
2101 E 4th St Ste 200b
Santa Ana CA 92705
714 543-3807

(P-22067)
THINK TOGETHER
22620 Goldencrest Dr # 104, Moreno Valley
(92553-9032)
PHONE.....................................951 571-9944
Tommy E Brewer, *Partner*
Irene Bobadilla, *General Mgr*
Stacy Galdamez, *General Mgr*
Fernando Reyes, *General Mgr*
Taylor Morris, *Senior Mgr*
EMP: 512
SALES (corp-wide): 66.3MM **Privately Held**
WEB: www.thinktogether.org
SIC: 8351 Child day care services
PA: Think Together
2101 E 4th St Ste 200b
Santa Ana CA 92705
714 543-3807

(P-22068)
TURTLE ROCK PRESCHOOL INC
1 Concordia, Irvine (92612-3202)
PHONE.....................................949 754-1685
Samy Adham, *President*
Sue Adham, *Vice Pres*
Jasmin De, *Asst Director*
Crystal McNamara, *Director*
EMP: 80 **EST:** 1978
SALES (est): 5.7MM **Privately Held**
WEB: www.turtlerockpreschool.com
SIC: 8351 Nursery school; preschool center

(P-22069)
TUTOR TIME LEARNING CTRS LLC
17150 Soledad Canyon Rd, Canyon Country (91387-3276)
PHONE.....................................866 930-7975
Mimi Haddad, *Manager*
EMP: 123 **Privately Held**
WEB: www.tutortime.com
SIC: 8351 8211 Group day care center; kindergarten
HQ: Tutor Time Learning Centers, Llc
21333 Haggerty Rd Ste 300
Novi MI 48375
248 697-9000

(P-22070)
TUTOR TIME LEARNING CTRS LLC
10420 Alta Loma Dr, Rancho Cucamonga
(91737-3847)
PHONE.....................................866 930-7975
Mona Kay, *Director*
EMP: 123 **Privately Held**
WEB: www.tutortime.com
SIC: 8351 8299 8211 Preschool center; educational service, nondegree granting: continuing educ.; kindergarten

HQ: Tutor Time Learning Centers, Llc
21333 Haggerty Rd Ste 300
Novi MI 48375
248 697-9000

(P-22071)
TUTOR TIME LEARNING CTRS LLC
5805 Corporate Ave, Cypress
(90630-4730)
PHONE.....................................714 484-1000
Jennifer Gardea, *Director*
EMP: 123 **Privately Held**
WEB: www.tutortime.com
SIC: 8351 Preschool center
HQ: Tutor Time Learning Centers, Llc
21333 Haggerty Rd Ste 300
Novi MI 48375
248 697-9000

(P-22072)
V I P TOTS INC
Also Called: VIP TOTS
41915 Acacia Ave, Hemet (92544-5001)
PHONE.....................................951 652-7611
R Thomas, *Exec Dir*
Marcia Nogrady, *Program Dir*
Debbie Haney, *Director*
EMP: 58 **EST:** 1979
SQ FT: 4,500
SALES: 1.6MM **Privately Held**
WEB: www.viptots.org
SIC: 8211 8351 School for physically handicapped; child day care services

(P-22073)
WEST VALLEY CHRISTIAN CHURCH
Also Called: West Valley Christian School
22450 Sherman Way, West Hills
(91307-2326)
PHONE.....................................818 884-4710
Glenn Kirby, *Pastor*
Dr Robert Lozano, *Administration*
Derek Swales, *Administration*
Dora Bessenbacher, *Finance Dir*
Kerri Moore, *Finance Dir*
EMP: 75 **EST:** 1976
SALES (est): 7.5MM **Privately Held**
WEB: www.westvalleychristianschool.com
SIC: 8661 8211 8351 Non-denominational church; private elementary & secondary schools; preschool center

(P-22074)
YESHIVATH TORATH EMETH ACADEMY (PA)
Also Called: Yeshiva Rav Isacsohn Academy
540 N La Brea Ave, Los Angeles
(90036-2016)
PHONE.....................................323 549-3170
Marc Chopp, *Administration*
Charles Abbott, *Ch of Bd*
Morris Weiss, *President*
Rabbi Berish Goldenberg, *Corp Secy*
EMP: 107 **EST:** 1957
SALES (est): 1.1MM **Privately Held**
WEB: www.yritea.org
SIC: 8351 8211 Preschool center; nursery school; elementary school

(P-22075)
YOUNG MNS CHRSTN ASSN MTRO LOS
Also Called: East Valley Family YMCA Dcc
5142 Tujunga Ave, North Hollywood
(91601-3742)
PHONE.....................................818 763-5126
Debbie Lozano, *Director*
EMP: 50
SQ FT: 11,260
SALES (corp-wide): 119.1MM **Privately Held**
WEB: www.ymcala.org
SIC: 8351 8322 Group day care center; youth center
PA: Young Men's Christian Association Of Metropolitan Los Angeles
625 S New Hampshire Ave
Los Angeles CA 90005
213 380-6448

8361 Residential Care

(P-22076)
ABTTC INC (DH)
Also Called: A Better Tomorrow Trtmnt Ctr
41640 Corning Pl Ste 104, Murrieta
(92562-7048)
PHONE.....................................951 837-2400
Jerrod Menz, *CEO*
James Fent, *President*
Paul Del Vacchio, *CFO*
EMP: 69 **EST:** 2004
SQ FT: 9,000
SALES (est): 14.6MM
SALES (corp-wide): 295.7MM **Publicly Held**
WEB: www.americanaddictioncenters.org
SIC: 8361 Rehabilitation center, residential: health care incidental

(P-22077)
ACTS FOR CHILDREN (PA)
Also Called: A C T S
18136 Jurupa Ave, Bloomington
(92316-3009)
P.O. Box 848, Colton (92324-0848)
PHONE.....................................909 877-5590
Ike Kerhulas, *President*
EMP: 55 **EST:** 1988
SALES (est): 608.9K **Privately Held**
SIC: 8361 Residential care

(P-22078)
AEGIS SENIOR COMMUNITIES LLC
Also Called: Aegis of Laguna Niguel
32170 Niguel Rd, Laguna Niguel
(92677-4264)
PHONE.....................................949 496-8080
Pamela Kerr, *Exec Dir*
Becky Spencer, *Info Tech Mgr*
Kelly Chong, *Hlthcr Dir*
EMP: 53
SALES (corp-wide): 137.2MM **Privately Held**
WEB: www.aegisliving.com
SIC: 8361 Residential care
PA: Senior Aegis Communities Llc
415 118th Ave Se
Bellevue WA 98005
866 688-5829

(P-22079)
ALLIANCE CHILDRENS SERVICES
Also Called: Mentor California
1001 Tower Way Ste 110, Bakersfield
(93309-1586)
PHONE.....................................661 863-0350
Andretta Stokes, *Manager*
Steve Cannon, *Director*
Megan Caragao, *Director*
EMP: 114
SALES (corp-wide): 4.8MM **Privately Held**
SIC: 8361 Home for the mentally handicapped; home for the physically handicapped
PA: Alliance Children's Services Inc
313 Congress St Fl 5
Boston MA 02210
617 790-4800

(P-22080)
ANGEL VIEW INC
Also Called: Angel View Rsale Str - Palm Sp
454 N Indian Canyon Dr, Palm Springs
(92262-6018)
P.O. Box 580021, North Palm Springs
(92258-0021)
PHONE.....................................760 322-2440
Tracy Powers, *General Mgr*
Joel Boucher, *Opers Staff*
Cleveland Hook, *Manager*
EMP: 53
SALES (corp-wide): 31MM **Privately Held**
WEB: www.angelview.org
SIC: 8361 Rehabilitation center, residential: health care incidental
PA: Angel View, Inc.
67625 E Palm Canyon Dr A1
Cathedral City CA 92234
760 329-6471

(P-22081)
ATRIA SENIOR LIVING INC
Also Called: Atria Park Pacific Palisades
15441 W Sunset Blvd, Pacific Palisades
(90272-3525)
PHONE.....................................310 573-9545
Elisa Brown, *Director*
Krav Maga, *Manager*
EMP: 60
SQ FT: 27,513
SALES (corp-wide): 3.8B **Publicly Held**
WEB: www.atriaseniorliving.com
SIC: 8361 Home for the aged
HQ: Atria Senior Living Inc.
300 E Market St Ste 100
Louisville KY 40202

(P-22082)
AVALON BY SEA AC LLC
32430 Pacific Coast Hwy, Malibu
(90265-2531)
PHONE.....................................310 457-9111
Margaret Giuffre,
EMP: 50 **EST:** 2017
SALES (est): 810.2K **Privately Held**
SIC: 8361 Residential care

(P-22083)
AVANTGARDE SENIOR LIVING
5645 Lindley Ave, Tarzana (91356-2557)
PHONE.....................................818 881-0055
Jason Adelman, *Principal*
EMP: 102 **EST:** 2010
SALES (est): 6.2MM **Privately Held**
WEB: www.avantgardeseniorliving.com
SIC: 8361 Home for the aged

(P-22084)
BANKERS MRTG RLTY ADVSORS SNTA
Also Called: Villa Alamar
45 E Alamar Ave, Santa Barbara
(93105-3403)
PHONE.....................................805 682-9345
Jackie Marston, *Administration*
EMP: 50
SALES (corp-wide): 6MM **Privately Held**
SIC: 8361 Residential care
PA: Bankers Mortgage Realty Advisors Of Santa Barbara, Inc.
4141 State St Ste E10
Santa Barbara CA 93110
805 692-2807

(P-22085)
BOYS REPUBLIC (PA)
Also Called: GIRLS REPUBLIC
1907 Boys Republic Dr, Chino Hills
(91709-5447)
PHONE.....................................909 902-6690
Dennis Slattery, *CEO*
Timothy J Kay, *President*
Robert Key, *Vice Pres*
Jeff Seymour, *Vice Pres*
Nadine Bosen, *Admin Sec*
EMP: 150 **EST:** 1907
SQ FT: 173,000
SALES (est): 20.5MM **Privately Held**
WEB: www.boysrepublic.org
SIC: 8361 Group foster home

(P-22086)
BRETHREN HILLCREST HOMES
2705 Mountain View Dr Ofc, La Verne
(91750-4398)
PHONE.....................................909 593-4917
Matthew Neeley, *President*
Elizabeth Ruan, *Records Dir*
Barbara Feliciano, *CFO*
Tom Hostetler, *Executive Asst*
Scott Frederick, *Data Proc Staff*
EMP: 230 **EST:** 1947
SQ FT: 34,000
SALES: 27.3MM **Privately Held**
WEB: www.livingathillcrest.org
SIC: 8361 8059 8051 Rest home, with health care incidental; nursing home, except skilled & intermediate care facility; extended care facility

(P-22087)
BRITTANY HOUSE LLC
5401 E Centralia St, Long Beach
(90808-1452)
PHONE.....................................562 421-4717

Colleen Rosatti, *Exec Dir*
Tisa Houston, *Office Mgr*
Mike Barron, *Director*
Eunice Poe, *Director*
EMP: 202 **EST:** 1989
SQ FT: 43,018
SALES (est): 28.7MM
SALES (corp-wide): 40.5MM **Privately Held**
WEB: www.activcareliving.com
SIC: 8361 Home for the aged
PA: Activcare Living, Inc.
10603 Rancho Bernardo Rd
San Diego CA 92127
858 565-4424

(P-22088)
CALIFORNIA FRIENDS HOMES
Also Called: QUAKER GARDENS
12151 Dale Ave, Stanton (90680-3889)
PHONE....................714 530-9100
Randy Brown, *CEO*
Gina Kolb, *Exec Dir*
Glenda Hementiza, *Managing Dir*
EMP: 315 **EST:** 1962
SQ FT: 10,000
SALES (est): 18.8MM **Privately Held**
WEB: www.rowntreegardens.org
SIC: 8361 8051 Home for the aged; convalescent home with continuous nursing care

(P-22089)
CARSON SENIOR ASSISTED LIVING
345 E Carson St, Carson (90745-2709)
PHONE....................310 830-4010
Fax: 310 830-0264
EMP: 75
SALES (est): 3.3MM **Privately Held**
SIC: 8361 Residential Care Services

(P-22090)
CASA-PACIFICA INC
Also Called: Freedom Properties
2200 W Acacia Ave Ofc, Hemet (92545-3737)
PHONE....................951 658-3369
Mary Ann Casino, *Director*
Anna Guerin, *Program Mgr*
Sarah Robles, *Program Mgr*
Lynne Gibbons, *Admin Mgr*
Matt Gillen, *Finance*
EMP: 251
SALES (corp-wide): 26.8MM **Privately Held**
WEB: www.casapacifica.org
SIC: 8361 8059 Geriatric residential care; rest home, with health care
PA: Casa-Pacifica, Inc
23442 El Toro Rd
San Juan Capistrano CA 92675
949 489-0430

(P-22091)
CASA-PACIFICA INC
Also Called: Freedom Properties Village
2400 W Acacia Ave, Hemet (92545-3743)
PHONE....................951 766-5116
Valeria Machain, *General Mgr*
Desiree Lindsay, *Records Dir*
Maricela Zambrano, *Records Dir*
Dorothy Nelson, *Executive*
Barbara Soto, *Office Mgr*
EMP: 251
SALES (corp-wide): 26.8MM **Privately Held**
WEB: www.casapacifica.org
SIC: 8361 8052 8051 6513 Home for the aged; intermediate care facilities; skilled nursing care facilities; apartment building operators
PA: Casa-Pacifica, Inc
23442 El Toro Rd
San Juan Capistrano CA 92675
949 489-0430

(P-22092)
CENTINELA VALLEY CARE CENTER
950 S Flower St, Inglewood (90301-4111)
PHONE....................310 674-3216
William A Nelson, *President*
Faye Sorianosos, *Nursing Dir*
EMP: 54 **EST:** 1993

SALES (est): 2.5MM **Privately Held**
WEB: www.centinelamed.com
SIC: 8361 8059 Home for the aged; convalescent home

(P-22093)
CLIFF VIEW TERRACE INC
Also Called: Mission Terrace
623 W Junipero St, Santa Barbara (93105-4213)
PHONE....................805 682-7443
Eve Murphy, *Manager*
EMP: 84
SALES (corp-wide): 11.7MM **Privately Held**
WEB: www.cliffviewterracesb.com
SIC: 8361 8051 Home for the aged; convalescent home with continuous nursing care
PA: Cliff View Terrace, Inc.
1020 Cliff Dr
Santa Barbara CA 93109
805 963-7556

(P-22094)
COMMUNITY ACTION PARTNR KERN
1611 1st St, Bakersfield (93304-2901)
PHONE....................661 336-5300
Aniko Matis, *Director*
EMP: 62
SALES (corp-wide): 63.1MM **Privately Held**
WEB: www.capk.org
SIC: 8361 Rehabilitation center, residential: health care incidental
PA: Community Action Partnership Of Kern
5005 Business Park N
Bakersfield CA 93309
661 336-5236

(P-22095)
CORECARE I I I
Also Called: Morningside of Fullerton
800 Morningside Dr, Fullerton (92835-3597)
PHONE....................714 256-8000
Carl Wilkins, *Administration*
EMP: 130 **EST:** 1989
SQ FT: 24,000
SALES (est): 13.7MM **Privately Held**
WEB: www.morningsideoffullerton.com
SIC: 8361 8052 Home for the aged; intermediate care facilities

(P-22096)
COUNSELING AND RESEARCH ASSOC (PA)
Also Called: MASADA HOMES
108 W Victoria St, Gardena (90248-3523)
P.O. Box 47001 (90247-6801)
PHONE....................310 715-2020
George Igi, *Exec Dir*
Bernard Smith, *COO*
Fay Ji, *CFO*
Linda Nakamura, *Psychologist*
Larry Fernandez, *Med Doctor*
EMP: 125 **EST:** 1966
SQ FT: 2,500
SALES (est): 19.6MM **Privately Held**
WEB: www.masadahomes.org
SIC: 8361 Children's home

(P-22097)
COVENANT HOUSE CALIFORNIA
Also Called: CHC
1325 N Western Ave, Los Angeles (90027-5615)
PHONE....................323 461-3131
Luz Juan, *CEO*
AMI Rowland, *COO*
David Weaver, *CFO*
Jillian Robinson, *Officer*
Alana Weinroth, *Officer*
EMP: 150 **EST:** 1986
SQ FT: 16,000
SALES (est): 20.4MM **Privately Held**
WEB: www.covenanthousecalifornia.org
SIC: 8361 Children's home

(P-22098)
CRI-HELP INC (PA)
Also Called: Cri Help Drug Rehabilitation
11027 Burbank Blvd, North Hollywood (91601-2431)
P.O. Box 899 (91603-0899)
PHONE....................818 985-8323
Jack Bernstein, *President*
Markus Sola, *Ch of Bd*
Anthony Edmonson, *Corp Secy*
Victoria Wyner, *Executive*
Kim Long, *Program Mgr*
EMP: 71
SQ FT: 40,000
SALES: 8MM **Privately Held**
WEB: www.cri-help.org
SIC: 8361 8069 Rehabilitation center, residential: health care incidental; drug addiction rehabilitation hospital

(P-22099)
DAVID AND MARGARET HOME INC
Also Called: David Margaret Youth Fmly Svcs
1350 3rd St, La Verne (91750-5299)
PHONE....................909 596-5921
Arun Tolia, *President*
Cindy Walkenbach, *President*
Timothy Evans, *Treasurer*
Michael Miller, *Officer*
Sabina Sullivan, *Vice Pres*
EMP: 240 **EST:** 1910
SQ FT: 40,000
SALES (est): 16.7MM **Privately Held**
WEB: www.davidandmargaret.org
SIC: 8361 8322 Home for the emotionally disturbed; individual & family services

(P-22100)
DREAM HOME CARE INC
20695 S Wstn Ave Ste 132, Torrance (90501)
PHONE....................562 595-9021
Cora Manalang, *CEO*
Reynaldo David, *COO*
Hazel Manalang, *CFO*
Maricris Ocampo, *Admin Asst*
EMP: 60 **EST:** 1994
SALES: 2.5MM **Privately Held**
SIC: 8361 Group foster home

(P-22101)
ELDER CARE ALLIANCE CAMARILLO
Also Called: ALMAVIA OF CAMARILLO
2500 Ponderosa Dr N, Camarillo (93010-2383)
PHONE....................510 769-2700
Jesse Jantzen, *CEO*
Kathleen Quinlan, *Director*
EMP: 75 **EST:** 1999
SALES (est): 6.3MM **Privately Held**
WEB: www.eldercarealliance.org
SIC: 8361 Home for the aged

(P-22102)
FIVE ACRES-THE BOYS & GIRLS &
760 Mountain View St, Altadena (91001-4996)
PHONE....................626 798-6793
Chanel W Boutakidis, *CEO*
Daniel Braun, *CFO*
Kim Warneke, *Officer*
Robert A Ketch, *Exec Dir*
Lizette Hooker, *Executive Asst*
EMP: 419 **EST:** 1888
SQ FT: 70,000
SALES (est): 32.8MM **Privately Held**
WEB: www.5acres.org
SIC: 8361 8322 8211 Children's home; public welfare center; public combined elementary & secondary school

(P-22103)
FLORENCE CRTTNTON SVCS ORNGE C
Also Called: CRITTENTON SERVICES FOR CHILDR
801 E Chapman Ave Ste 203, Fullerton (92831-3846)
P.O. Box 9 (92836-0009)
PHONE....................714 680-9000
Joyce Capelle, *CEO*
Ballesteros Chris, *Partner*

Mitzi Garciastein, *Partner*
Barbara Oropeza, *Partner*
Ana Eykel, *Vice Pres*
EMP: 320 **EST:** 1966
SALES: 37.6MM **Privately Held**
WEB: www.crittentonsocal.org
SIC: 8361 Residential care for children; home for the emotionally disturbed

(P-22104)
GOOD SHEPHERD LUTHERAN HM OF W (PA)
Also Called: Good Shepherd Communities
24800 Chrisanta Dr # 250, Mission Viejo (92691-4833)
PHONE....................559 791-2000
David Geske, *CEO*
EMP: 230 **EST:** 1952
SALES (est): 14.3MM **Privately Held**
WEB: www.grauranch.com
SIC: 8361 Residential care for the handicapped

(P-22105)
GOOD SHEPHERD LUTHERAN HM OF W
2949 Alamo St, Simi Valley (93063-2185)
PHONE....................805 526-2482
Brian Dietrich, *Principal*
EMP: 65
SALES (corp-wide): 14.3MM **Privately Held**
WEB: www.gsls-simi.com
SIC: 8361 8059 Residential care for the handicapped; personal care home, with health care
PA: Good Shepherd Lutheran Home Of The West
24800 Chrisanta Dr # 250
Mission Viejo CA 92691
559 791-2000

(P-22106)
HAMBURGER HOME (PA)
Also Called: AVIVA CENTER
7120 Franklin Ave, Los Angeles (90046-3002)
PHONE....................323 876-0550
Regina Bette, *President*
Usha Murthy, *CFO*
Penelope Leon, *Vice Pres*
Angela Miller, *Vice Pres*
Kim Peterson, *Vice Pres*
EMP: 90 **EST:** 1915
SQ FT: 25,000
SALES: 16.6MM **Privately Held**
WEB: www.aviva.org
SIC: 8361 Children's home

(P-22107)
HAMBURGER HOME
5900 Sepulvda Blvd # 104, Van Nuys (91411-2511)
PHONE....................818 980-3200
Jamerson Jeffrey, *Branch Mgr*
EMP: 80
SALES (corp-wide): 16.6MM **Privately Held**
WEB: www.aviva.org
SIC: 8361 Children's home
PA: Hamburger Home
7120 Franklin Ave
Los Angeles CA 90046
323 876-0550

(P-22108)
HARBOR HEALTH CARE INC
9461 Flower St, Bellflower (90706-5705)
PHONE....................562 866-7054
Cheryl Hutchins, *President*
Shantell Heard, *CIO*
EMP: 200 **EST:** 1999
SALES (est): 10MM **Privately Held**
WEB: www.harborhealthcare.org
SIC: 8361 Home for the mentally handicapped

(P-22109)
HATHAWY-SYCMRES CHILD FMLY SVC
840 N Avenue 66, Los Angeles (90042-1508)
PHONE....................323 257-9600
Jim Cheney, *Presiden*
Andie Gonzalez, *Vice Pres*

EMP: 163
SALES (corp-wide): 64.2MM **Privately Held**
WEB: www.hathaway-sycamores.org
SIC: 8361 8093 Home for the emotionally disturbed; mental health clinic, outpatient
PA: Hathaway-Sycamores Child And Family Services
100 W Walnut St Ste 375
Pasadena CA 91124
626 395-7100

(P-22110)
HATHAWY-SYCMRES CHILD FMLY SVC (PA)
100 W Walnut St Ste 375, Pasadena (91124-0001)
PHONE..................626 395-7100
Michael Galper, Ch of Bd
Sandra Tudor, Partner
William Martone, President
Gina Perez, Officer
Jeffrey Catania, Exec VP
EMP: 65 **EST:** 1920
SQ FT: 75,175
SALES (est): 64.2MM **Privately Held**
WEB: www.hathaway-sycamores.org
SIC: 8361 8093 Home for the emotionally disturbed; mental health clinic, outpatient

(P-22111)
HAYNES FAMILY PROGRAMS INC
Also Called: LEROY HAYNES CENTER
233 Baseline Rd, La Verne (91750-2353)
P.O. Box 400 (91750-0400)
PHONE..................909 593-2581
Daniel Maydeck, President
Tony Williams, CFO
Frank Linebaugh, Senior VP
Tom Chamberlain, MIS Mgr
Mike Hoffman, Accounting Mgr
EMP: 125 **EST:** 1946
SQ FT: 72,466
SALES: 26.6MM **Privately Held**
WEB: www.leroyhaynes.org
SIC: 8361 8211 8099 Boys' Towns; specialty education; medical services organization

(P-22112)
HEALTHVIEW INC (PA)
Also Called: Harbor View House
921 S Beacon St, San Pedro (90731-3740)
PHONE..................310 547-3341
Jeff Smith, CEO
Susan Major, Principal
EMP: 135 **EST:** 1965
SQ FT: 110,000
SALES: 5MM **Privately Held**
WEB: www.hvi.com
SIC: 8361 8052 Home for the mentally handicapped; home for the mentally retarded, with health care

(P-22113)
HILLSIDES
940 Avenue 64, Pasadena (91105-2711)
PHONE..................323 254-2274
Joseph M Costa, CEO
Amy Ley-Sanchez, COO
Ryan Herren; CFO
Elvira Contreras, Graphic Designe
Izabella Novikova, Asst Controller
EMP: 460 **EST:** 1913
SQ FT: 18,217
SALES: 51.1MM **Privately Held**
WEB: www.hillsides.org
SIC: 8361 Home for the emotionally disturbed

(P-22114)
HOLLENBECK PALMS
Also Called: HOLLENBECK HOME FOR THE AGED
24431 Lyons Ave Apt 336, Newhall (91321-2360)
PHONE..................323 263-6195
William G Heideman Jr, President
Morris Shockley, Vice Pres
Jean Shively, Chief Engr
Johnny Young, Controller
Chrys Nguyen, Human Res Dir
EMP: 170 **EST:** 1890

SALES: 18.3MM **Privately Held**
WEB: www.hollenbeckpalms.com
SIC: 8361 Home for the aged

(P-22115)
HOPE HSE FOR MLTPLE HNDCPPED I (PA)
Also Called: Schmitt House
4215 Peck Rd, El Monte (91732-2198)
PHONE..................626 443-1313
D Bernstein, Exec Dir
David Bernstein, Exec Dir
Mary Guardado, Admin Sec
Ookie Voong, Administration
Patty Fraijo, Comptroller
EMP: 100 **EST:** 1963
SQ FT: 15,000
SALES: 6.2MM **Privately Held**
WEB: www.hopehouse.org
SIC: 8361 Residential care for the handicapped; rest home, with health care incidental

(P-22116)
HUMANGOOD SOCAL
Also Called: Buena Vista Manor
802 Buena Vista St, Duarte (91010-1702)
PHONE..................626 359-8141
Judy Phornkein, Manager
EMP: 106
SALES (corp-wide): 25.9MM **Privately Held**
WEB: www.humangood.org
SIC: 8361 Home for the aged
HQ: Humangood Socal
516 Burchett St
Glendale CA 91203
818 247-0420

(P-22117)
INDEPENDENT OPTIONS INC
2625 Sherwood Ave, Fullerton (92831-1418)
PHONE..................714 738-4991
P Dennis Mattson, President
EMP: 99
SALES (corp-wide): 15.6MM **Privately Held**
WEB: www.independentoptions.org
SIC: 8361 8059 Home for the mentally handicapped; personal care home, with health care
PA: Independent Options, Inc.
391 Corporate Terrace Cir # 102
Corona CA 92879
951 279-2585

(P-22118)
J & L DAYCARE
Also Called: V.O.I.C.E.
24723 Rdlnds Blvd Ste A-C, Loma Linda (92354)
PHONE..................909 796-2656
Les Spoelstra, Owner
EMP: 61 **Privately Held**
SIC: 8361 Home for the mentally retarded
PA: J & L Daycare
415 Tennessee St Ste U
Redlands CA 92373

(P-22119)
J & L DAYCARE
Also Called: V O I C E
2985 W Lincoln St Ste 402, Banning (92220-3732)
PHONE..................951 849-1429
Lester Spoelstra, Owner
EMP: 61 **Privately Held**
SIC: 8361 8322 Home for the mentally retarded; adult day care center
PA: J & L Daycare
415 Tennessee St Ste U
Redlands CA 92373

(P-22120)
JEWISH HM FOR THE AGING ORNGE
Also Called: Heritage Pointe
27356 Bellogente, Mission Viejo (92691-6341)
PHONE..................949 364-9685
David Zarnow, Vice Pres
Brad Plose, President
Rena Loveless, Administration

Jacquelin Seybert, Info Tech Mgr
Patti Gardner, Director
EMP: 120 **EST:** 1969
SQ FT: 88,928
SALES (est): 10.5MM **Privately Held**
WEB: www.heritagepointe.org
SIC: 8361 Home for the aged

(P-22121)
LA HABRA VILLA
220 Newport Center Dr # 11, Newport Beach (92660-7506)
PHONE..................714 529-1697
David Tsoong, Partner
Herbert Tarlow MD, Partner
EMP: 54 **EST:** 1980
SQ FT: 100,000
SALES (est): 1.8MM **Privately Held**
WEB: www.apthomes4u.com
SIC: 8361 Home for the aged

(P-22122)
LAMP INC
Also Called: Lamp Community
2116 Arlington Ave Lbby, Los Angeles (90018-1365)
PHONE..................213 488-9559
Donna Gallup, CEO
Stuart Robinson, Officer
Kim Carson, Finance Dir
Dino Ferrare, Human Res Mgr
Patricia Lopez, Opers Staff
EMP: 110 **EST:** 1985
SQ FT: 4,500
SALES: 11.6MM **Privately Held**
WEB: www.lampcommunity.org
SIC: 8361 Residential care for the handicapped

(P-22123)
LE BLEU CHATEAU INC
Also Called: Bleu Chateau Assisted Living
1900 Grismer Ave, Burbank (91504-4405)
PHONE..................818 843-3141
Adam Zenou, President
Robert Rosenberg, Vice Pres
EMP: 50 **EST:** 1980
SALES (est): 3.3MM **Privately Held**
SIC: 8361 Home for the aged

(P-22124)
LEISURE CARE LLC
Also Called: Nohl Ranch Inn
380 S Anaheim Hills Rd, Anaheim (92807-4026)
PHONE..................714 974-1616
Wanda Reynolds, Branch Mgr
EMP: 124
SQ FT: 82,222
SALES (corp-wide): 175.2MM **Privately Held**
WEB: www.leisurecare.com
SIC: 8361 Home for the aged; skilled nursing care facilities
HQ: Leisure Care, Llc
999 3rd Ave Ste 4550
Seattle WA 98104
206 436-7827

(P-22125)
LITTLE PEOPLES
39514 Brookside Ave, Cherry Valley (92223-4602)
P.O. Box 248, Beaumont (92223-0248)
PHONE..................951 849-1959
EMP: 60
SALES: 2.8MM **Privately Held**
WEB: www.littlepeoples.com
SIC: 8361 Residential Care Services

(P-22126)
LOS ANGELES MISSION INC (PA)
6732 Brynhurst Ave Apt 3, Los Angeles (90043-4697)
P.O. Box 55900 (90055-0630)
PHONE..................213 629-1227
Herb Smith, President
Ivan Klassen, Partner
Steve Kennedy, CFO
EMP: 77 **EST:** 1977
SALES (est): 14MM **Privately Held**
WEB: www.losangelesmission.org
SIC: 8361 Home for destitute men & women; rehabilitation center, residential: health care incidental

(P-22127)
LOS ANGELES ORPHANS HOME SOC (HQ)
815 N El Centro Ave, Los Angeles (90038-3805)
PHONE..................323 463-2119
Darrell Evora, President
Alma Gomez, Administration
EMP: 192 **EST:** 1880
SQ FT: 45,000
SALES (est): 13.4MM
SALES (corp-wide): 105.5MM **Privately Held**
WEB: www.larchmontcharter.org
SIC: 8361 Residential care for children
PA: Uplift Family Services
251 Llewellyn Ave
Campbell CA 95008
408 379-3790

(P-22128)
LOS ANGELES RESIDENTIAL COMM F
29890 Bouquet Canyon Rd, Santa Clarita (91390-5111)
PHONE..................661 296-8636
Kathy Sturky, Exec Dir
Larry Sallows, CFO
Maureen Medeiros, Office Mgr
Rose Salgado, Administration
EMP: 85 **EST:** 1959
SQ FT: 5,000
SALES (est): 7.4MM **Privately Held**
SIC: 8361 8322 8051 Home for the mentally handicapped; individual & family services; skilled nursing care facilities

(P-22129)
MARYVALE
7600 Graves Ave, Rosemead (91770-3414)
P.O. Box 1039 (91770-1000)
PHONE..................626 280-6510
Steve Gunter, CEO
Renee Chan, Officer
Lorraine Varing, Executive Asst
Noreen Romanowski, Admin Sec
Elena Medina, Human Res Dir
EMP: 61 **EST:** 2011
SALES: 20.2MM **Privately Held**
WEB: www.maryvale.org
SIC: 8361 8322 Residential care for children; public welfare center

(P-22130)
MCKINLEY CHILDRENS CENTER INC (PA)
180 Via Verde Ste 200, San Dimas (91773-3993)
PHONE..................909 599-1227
Anil Vadatary, CEO
Michael Frazer, CFO
Chris Murray, Officer
Anil Vadaparty, Administration
Lacey Baptiste, Accountant
EMP: 190 **EST:** 1890
SALES (est): 31.1MM **Privately Held**
WEB: www.mckinleycc.org
SIC: 8361 8211 Boys' Towns; private elementary & secondary schools

(P-22131)
MERCEDES DIAZ HOMES INC
7239 Washington Ave # 100, Whittier (90602-1432)
PHONE..................562 945-4576
Mercedes Diaz, President
Ramon Diaz, Vice Pres
Maureen Brinkley, Program Dir
Lupe McClintock, Director
Rebeca Reyes, Director
EMP: 60 **EST:** 1980
SALES (est): 9.6MM **Privately Held**
WEB: www.mdhnetwork.com
SIC: 8361 Residential care

(P-22132)
MISSION HILLS SENIOR LIVING
34560 Bob Hope Dr, Rancho Mirage (92270-1727)
PHONE..................760 770-7737
Roland Gandy, Exec Dir
EMP: 62 **EST:** 2015

SALES (est): 2.6MM **Privately Held**
WEB: www.missionhillsseniorliving.com
SIC: 8361 Home for the aged

(P-22133)
MONTE VISTA GROVE HOMES
2889 San Pasqual St, Pasadena
(91107-5364)
PHONE..................626 796-6135
M Helen Baatz, *Exec Dir*
Meagan Swan, *Asst Admin*
Noelle Gonzales, *Admin Asst*
Barbara Stevens, *Accountant*
Kim Houser, *Controller*
EMP: 85 EST: 1924
SQ FT: 12,000
SALES (est): 9.2MM **Privately Held**
WEB: www.mvgh.org
SIC: 8361 Home for the aged

(P-22134)
NATIONAL MENTOR INC
Also Called: California Mentor
2131 Mars Ct, Bakersfield (93308-6830)
PHONE..................661 387-1000
EMP: 50
SALES (corp-wide): 1.6B **Privately Held**
SIC: 8361 Residential care
HQ: National Mentor, Inc.
313 Congress St Fl 5
Boston MA 02210
617 790-4800

(P-22135)
NATIONAL MENTOR HOLDINGS INC
Also Called: Horrigan Cole Enterprises
30033 Technology Dr, Murrieta
(92563-3520)
PHONE..................951 677-1453
Jennie Hurley, *Manager*
EMP: 231
SALES (corp-wide): 1.6B **Privately Held**
WEB: www.thementornetwork.com
SIC: 8361 Residential care
HQ: National Mentor Holdings, Inc.
313 Congress St Fl 5
Boston MA 02210
617 790-4800

(P-22136)
NEW VISTA HEALTH SERVICES INC
Also Called: Oak Park Manor
501 S College Ave, Claremont
(91711-5527)
PHONE..................909 626-0117
Robert Craig, *President*
EMP: 61 EST: 1991
SQ FT: 13,819
SALES (est): 4.2MM **Privately Held**
WEB: www.newvista.us
SIC: 8361 8059 Home for the aged; rest
home, with health care

(P-22137)
NINOS LATINO UNIDOS FSA
10016 Pioneer Blvd # 123, Santa Fe
Springs (90670-3245)
PHONE..................562 801-5454
EMP: 60
SALES: 6.8MM **Privately Held**
WEB: www.nlu.org
SIC: 8361 8322 Residential Care

(P-22138)
NURSECORE MANAGEMENT SVCS LLC
1010 S Broadway Ste A, Santa Maria
(93454-6600)
PHONE..................805 938-7660
Veronica Aburto, *Branch Mgr*
EMP: 398 **Privately Held**
WEB: www.nursecore.com
SIC: 8361 8082 8049 7361 Residential
care; home health care services; nurses
& other medical assistants; nurses' reg-
istry
PA: Nursecore Management Services, Llc
2201 Brookhollow Plaza Dr # 450
Arlington TX 76006

(P-22139)
OAKMONT OF ORANGE LLC
630 The City Dr S, Orange (92868-4926)
PHONE..................714 880-8624
Joseph G Lin, *CEO*
Gail Blessum, *Office Mgr*
Herbert Becher, *Director*
EMP: 50 EST: 2018
SALES (est): 1.5MM **Privately Held**
WEB: www.oakmontoforange.com
SIC: 8361 Residential care

(P-22140)
OLIVE CREST (PA)
2130 E 4th St Ste 200, Santa Ana
(92705-3818)
PHONE..................714 543-5437
Donald A Verleur, *CEO*
Patricia Barker, *Partner*
Rigoberto Galvan, *Partner*
Nicholas Morvan, *Partner*
Justin Laird, *CFO*
EMP: 300 EST: 1973
SQ FT: 40,000
SALES: 64.5MM **Privately Held**
WEB: www.olivecrest.org
SIC: 8361 8322 Home for the emotionally
disturbed; individual & family services

(P-22141)
PACIFIC LODGE YOUTH SVCS INC
Also Called: PACIFIC LODGE BOY'S HOME
4900 Serrania Ave, Woodland Hills
(91364-3301)
P.O. Box 308 (91365-0308)
PHONE..................818 347-1577
Leslie King, *Ch of Bd*
Lisa Alegria, *CEO*
Hazel Benavides, *Cust Mgr*
Sami Raboubi, *Director*
EMP: 110 EST: 1923
SQ FT: 22,634
SALES (est): 5K **Privately Held**
WEB: www.oyhfs.org
SIC: 8361 Residential care

(P-22142)
PASADENA CHLD TRAINING SOC
Also Called: Sycamores School
2933 El Nido Dr, Altadena (91001-4529)
PHONE..................626 798-0853
EMP: 180
SQ FT: 24,658
SALES (corp-wide): 9.6MM **Privately
Held**
WEB: www.hathaway-sycamores.org
SIC: 8361 8322 Residential Care Services
Individual/Family Services
PA: Pasadena Children's Training Society
100 W Walnut St Ste 375
Pasadena CA 91124
626 395-7100

(P-22143)
PEPPERMINT RIDGE (PA)
825 Magnolia Ave, Corona (92879-3129)
PHONE..................951 273-7320
Danette McCarnes, *Exec Dir*
EMP: 83 EST: 1965
SQ FT: 25,000
SALES (est): 8.2MM **Privately Held**
WEB: www.peppermintridge.org
SIC: 8361 8322 Home for the mentally
handicapped; individual & family services

(P-22144)
PHOENIX HOUSE ORANGE COUNTY
1207 E Fruit St, Santa Ana (92701-4296)
PHONE..................714 953-9373
Pouria Abbassi, *CEO*
Elena Ksendzov, *CFO*
Stephen Donowitz, *Vice Pres*
EMP: 133 EST: 2000
SALES (est): 1.8MM
SALES (corp-wide): 10.8MM **Privately
Held**
SIC: 8361 Rehabilitation center, residen-
tial: health care incidental
PA: Phoenix Houses Of California, Inc.
11600 Eldridge Ave
Sylmar CA 91342
818 896-1121

(P-22145)
PHOENIX HOUSES LOS ANGELES INC
11600 Eldridge Ave, Lake View Terrace
(91342-6506)
PHONE..................818 686-3000
Winifred Wechsler, *President*
EMP: 99 EST: 2000
SALES (est): 11.3MM
SALES (corp-wide): 10.8MM **Privately
Held**
SIC: 8361 Rehabilitation center, residen-
tial: health care incidental
PA: Phoenix Houses Of California, Inc.
11600 Eldridge Ave
Sylmar CA 91342
818 896-1121

(P-22146)
PROJECT INDEPENDENCE (PA)
3505 Cadillac Ave O103, Costa Mesa
(92626-1429)
PHONE..................714 549-3464
Debrah Marsteller, *Exec Dir*
Del Hart, *Treasurer*
Kathy Grunwald, *Controller*
Reginald Blanchard, *Manager*
Lynanne Finlen, *Manager*
EMP: 93 EST: 1977
SALES (est): 5.1MM **Privately Held**
WEB: www.proindependence.org
SIC: 8361 Home for the emotionally dis-
turbed; home for the mentally handi-
capped

(P-22147)
RANCHO SAN ANTONIO BOYS HM INC (PA)
21000 Plummer St, Chatsworth
(91311-4903)
PHONE..................818 882-6400
Aubree Sweeney, *Exec Dir*
Brother John Crowe, *CEO*
Nicholas Rizzo, *Finance Dir*
Troy McNair, *Human Resources*
Kevin Boyd, *Social Worker*
EMP: 100 EST: 1933
SALES (est): 19.8MM **Privately Held**
WEB: www.ranchosanantonio.org
SIC: 8361 Boys' Towns

(P-22148)
RCAN INC
Also Called: Diamond Terraces
600 E 11th St, Hanford (93230-4053)
PHONE..................559 585-8010
Jan Norman, *President*
Robert Norman, *Corp Secy*
EMP: 55 EST: 1996
SQ FT: 11,000
SALES (est): 2.7MM **Privately Held**
SIC: 8361 Home for the aged

(P-22149)
REGENCY PARK SENIOR LIVING INC
Also Called: Regency Park Oak Knoll
255 S Oak Knoll Ave, Pasadena
(91101-2992)
PHONE..................626 396-4911
Fax: 626 584-5719
EMP: 62
SALES (corp-wide): 10.6MM **Privately
Held**
SIC: 8361 Residential Care Services
PA: Regency Park Senior Living, Inc.
150 S Los Robles Ave # 480
Pasadena CA 91101
626 773-8800

(P-22150)
ROSEMARY CHILDRENS SERVICES (PA)
36 S Kinneloa Ave 200, Pasadena
(91107-3853)
PHONE..................626 844-3033
Greg Wessels, *Exec Dir*
Sungo Wang, *President*
Lynn Lu, *Vice Pres*
Veronica Fuentes, *Admin Sec*
Lesley Evangelista, *Finance Dir*
EMP: 101 EST: 1920
SQ FT: 9,000

SALES: 13.6MM **Privately Held**
WEB: www.rosemarychildren.org
SIC: 8361 Home for the emotionally dis-
turbed

(P-22151)
SAN CLEMENTE VILLAS BY SEA INC
660 Camino De Los Mares, San Clemente
(92673-1800)
PHONE..................949 489-3400
Paul J Brazeau,
Jan McAlister, *Exec Dir*
Maria Nemeth, *Sales Executive*
Esmeralda Lopez, *Mktg Dir*
Paul Brazeau, *Marketing Mgr*
EMP: 55 EST: 2000
SALES (est): 9.8MM **Privately Held**
WEB: www.sanclementevillas.com
SIC: 8361 Home for the aged

(P-22152)
SENIOR KEIRO HEALTH CARE
Also Called: Japanese Retirement Home
325 S Boyle Ave, Los Angeles
(90033-3812)
PHONE..................323 263-9651
Shawn Miyake, *CEO*
George Aratani, *President*
Rev David Shigekawa, *Treasurer*
Christina Tatsugawa, *Corp Comm Staff*
EMP: 51 EST: 1974
SQ FT: 50,000
SALES (est): 6.8MM **Privately Held**
WEB: www.keiro.org
SIC: 8361 Home for the aged

(P-22153)
SILVERADO SNIOR LVING HLDNGS
6400 Oak Cyn Ste 200, Irvine
(92618-5233)
PHONE..................949 240-7200
Loren B Shook, *CEO*
EMP: 4000 EST: 2010
SALES (est): 153.9MM **Privately Held**
WEB: www.silverado.com
SIC: 8361 Home for the aged

(P-22154)
SISTERS OF NZARETH LOS ANGELES
3333 Manning Ave, Los Angeles
(90064-4804)
PHONE..................310 839-2361
Margarette Brody, *Administration*
Christina Ceniceros, *Director*
EMP: 100 EST: 1935
SQ FT: 62,558
SALES (est): 6.9MM **Privately Held**
WEB: www.sistersofnazareth.com
SIC: 8361 Home for the aged

(P-22155)
SOLHEIM LUTHERAN HOME
2236 Merton Ave, Los Angeles
(90041-1915)
PHONE..................323 257-7518
James Graunke, *Principal*
Antonio Davila, *CFO*
Norma Heaton, *Exec Dir*
Sarah Keever, *Human Resources*
Dory Polo, *Nursing Dir*
EMP: 185 EST: 1923
SQ FT: 82,591
SALES: 14.6MM **Privately Held**
WEB: www.solheimlutheran.org
SIC: 8361 Home for the aged

(P-22156)
ST ANNES MATERNITY HOME
155 N Occidental Blvd, Los Angeles
(90026-4641)
PHONE..................213 381-2931
Tony Walker, *President*
Patrick Harris, *CFO*
Carmen Andreasen, *Officer*
Esperanza Evans, *Director*
Sarah Machat, *Director*
EMP: 158 EST: 1941
SQ FT: 100,000
SALES (est): 27.3MM **Privately Held**
WEB: www.stannes.org
SIC: 8361 Rehabilitation center, residen-
tial: health care incidental

(P-22157)
SUNNY ROSE GLEN LLC
29620 Bradley Rd, Sun City (92586-6521)
PHONE.............................951 679-3355
Karen Roper, *Exec Dir*
Mike Adams, *President*
EMP: 55 EST: 2017
SALES (est): 2.8MM **Privately Held**
WEB: www.sunnyroseglen.com
SIC: 8361 Home for the aged

(P-22158)
SUNRISE SENIOR LIVING MGT INC
Also Called: Claremont Pl Assisted Living
120 W San Jose Ave, Claremont
(91711-5294)
PHONE.............................909 447-5259
Nancy Halleck, *Exec Dir*
Lindsay Von Zabern, *Exec Dir*
EMP: 216
SQ FT: 4,900
SALES (corp-wide): 418.2MM **Privately Held**
WEB: www.sunriseseniorliving.com
SIC: 8361 8051 8082 Geriatric residential care; skilled nursing care facilities; home health care services
HQ: Sunrise Senior Living Management, Inc.
7902 Westpark Dr
Mc Lean VA 22102
703 273-7500

(P-22159)
TIERRA DEL SOL FOUNDATION (PA)
9919 Sunland Blvd, Sunland (91040-1599)
PHONE.............................818 352-1419
Steve Miller, *Exec Dir*
Maricela Castaneda, *Area Mgr*
Selene Morales, *Office Mgr*
Mirlo Tello, *Executive Asst*
Richard Barnes, *CIO*
EMP: 95
SQ FT: 20,000
SALES: 17.3MM **Privately Held**
WEB: www.tierradelsol.org
SIC: 8361 8211 8322 Home for the mentally handicapped; home for the physically handicapped; public special education school; individual & family services

(P-22160)
TRINITY YOUTH SERVICES (PA)
201 N Indian Hill Blvd # 201, Claremont
(91711-4668)
P.O. Box 1210 (91711-1210)
PHONE.............................909 825-5588
Cher Ofstedahl, *CEO*
Aris Alexandre, *President*
Nathan Mitakides, *President*
John Neiuber, *CEO*
Cher Leal, *COO*
EMP: 60 EST: 1965
SQ FT: 7,600
SALES: 22.9MM **Privately Held**
WEB: www.trinityys.org
SIC: 8361 Halfway home for delinquents & offenders

(P-22161)
VAGTHOLS RSDNTIAL CARE CTR INC
6537 Fountain Ave, Los Angeles
(90028-7824)
PHONE.............................323 464-6067
Amecita C Seisa, *President*
EMP: 161 EST: 1989
SQ FT: 2,400
SALES (est): 2.6MM **Privately Held**
WEB: www.vagthols.com
SIC: 8361 Home for the aged

(P-22162)
VASINDAS AROUND CLOCK CARE INC
Also Called: Around The Clock Home Care
5251 Office Park Dr # 403, Bakersfield
(93309-0695)
PHONE.............................661 395-5820
Mary Vasinda, *President*
John Vasinda, *Vice Pres*
Cassandra Ortiz, *Program Dir*
EMP: 50 EST: 1996

SALES (est): 11.1MM **Privately Held**
WEB: www.bakersfieldcare.com
SIC: 8361 Geriatric residential care

(P-22163)
VILLAGE AT NORTHRIDGE
9222 Corbin Ave, Northridge (91324-2409)
PHONE.............................818 514-4497
Cynthia Ramirez, *Human Res Dir*
EMP: 191 EST: 2008
SALES (est): 35MM
SALES (corp-wide): 170.2MM **Privately Held**
WEB: www.srgseniorliving.com
SIC: 8361 Home for the aged
PA: Senior Resource Group, Llc
500 Stevens Ave Ste 100
Solana Beach CA 92075
858 792-9300

(P-22164)
VILLAGE AT SHERMAN OAKS LLC
5450 Vesper Ave, Sherman Oaks
(91411-4221)
PHONE.............................818 994-7900
Michael Grust, *Mng Member*
Kevan Sidney, *Office Mgr*
Martin F Member,
EMP: 168 EST: 1970
SALES (est): 22.2MM
SALES (corp-wide): 170.2MM **Privately Held**
WEB: www.villageatshermanoaks.com
SIC: 8361 Home for the aged
HQ: Srg Holdings, Llc
500 Stevens Ave Ste 100
Solana Beach CA 92075
858 792-9300

(P-22165)
VISTA DEL MAR CHILD FMLY SVCS (PA)
3200 Motor Ave, Los Angeles
(90034-3740)
PHONE.............................310 836-1223
Roosevelena Wilson, *CEO*
Loren Montgomery, *Partner*
Claudia Garzel, *Officer*
James Gibson, *Officer*
Traci Levi, *Vice Pres*
EMP: 466 EST: 1908
SQ FT: 100,000
SALES: 41.7MM **Privately Held**
WEB: www.vistadelmar.org
SIC: 8211 8361 Elementary & secondary schools; home for the mentally handicapped; home for the mentally retarded

(P-22166)
WALDEN HOUSE INC
12423 Dahlia Ave, El Monte (91732-3611)
PHONE.............................626 258-0300
Grace Gerarto, *Manager*
EMP: 130
SALES (corp-wide): 22.7MM **Privately Held**
WEB: www.waldenhouse.org
SIC: 8361 Group foster home
PA: Walden House, Inc.
520 Townsend St
San Francisco CA 94103
415 554-1100

(P-22167)
WAYFINDER FAMILY SERVICES
1045 Bonita Ave, La Verne (91750-5109)
PHONE.............................909 305-1948
EMP: 50
SALES (corp-wide): 33.2MM **Privately Held**
WEB: www.wayfinderfamily.org
SIC: 8361 Residential care
PA: Wayfinder Family Services
5300 Angeles Vista Blvd
View Park CA 90043
323 295-4555

(P-22168)
WAYFINDER FAMILY SERVICES
1045 Bonita Ave, La Verne (91750-5109)
PHONE.............................909 305-1948
EMP: 50

SALES (corp-wide): 33.2MM **Privately Held**
WEB: www.wayfinderfamily.org
SIC: 8361 Residential care
PA: Wayfinder Family Services
5300 Angeles Vista Blvd
View Park CA 90043
323 295-4555

(P-22169)
WHITE RABBIT PARTNERS INC
9000 W Sunset Blvd, West Hollywood
(90069-5801)
PHONE.............................310 975-1450
Andrew William Spanswick, *CEO*
EMP: 150 EST: 2009
SALES (est): 5.6MM **Privately Held**
SIC: 8361 Residential care

8399 Social Services, NEC

(P-22170)
ASIAN PCF HLTH CARE VENTR INC (PA)
4216 Fountain Ave, Los Angeles
(90029-2256)
PHONE.............................323 644-3880
Kazue Shibata, *CEO*
Nardo Beltran, *CFO*
Lucia Mercado, *Bd of Directors*
Lorali Delos Reyes, *Principal*
John Hoh, *Med Doctor*
EMP: 130 EST: 1987
SQ FT: 1,800
SALES (est): 18.9MM **Privately Held**
WEB: www.aphcv.org
SIC: 8399 Health systems agency

(P-22171)
ASSOCIATED STUDENTS UCLA (PA)
Also Called: Asucla
308 Westwood Plz, Los Angeles
(90095-8355)
PHONE.............................310 794-8836
Pouria Abbassi, *Exec Dir*
Avanidhar Subrahmanyam, *Treasurer*
Richard Yamashita, *Treasurer*
Randy Jenkins, *Sr Corp Ofcr*
Tom Phelan, *Officer*
EMP: 500 EST: 1919
SQ FT: 200,000
SALES: 54.7MM **Privately Held**
WEB: www.asucla.ucla.edu
SIC: 8399 5942 Council for social agency; book stores

(P-22172)
ASSOCIATED STUDENTS UCLA
924 Westwood Blvd, Los Angeles
(90024-2910)
PHONE.............................310 794-0242
Roseanna P Malone, *Branch Mgr*
Carol Lemus, *Program Mgr*
Rebecca Bavolek, *Emerg Med Spec*
Jake Wilson, *Emerg Med Spec*
Richard Passmore, *Nurse*
EMP: 101
SALES (corp-wide): 54.7MM **Privately Held**
WEB: www.asucla.ucla.edu
SIC: 8399 Council for social agency
PA: Associated Students U.C.L.A.
308 Westwood Plz
Los Angeles CA 90095
310 794-8836

(P-22173)
BEACH CITIES HEALTH DISTRICT
1200 Del Amo St, Redondo Beach
(90277-3050)
PHONE.............................310 374-3426
Tom Bakaly, *Manager*
Monica Suua, *CFO*
Vish Chatterji, *Bd of Directors*
Michel Bennett, *Officer*
Tessa Garner, *Project Mgr*
EMP: 147 EST: 1955
SALES (est): 15.4MM **Privately Held**
WEB: www.bchd.org
SIC: 8399 Health systems agency

(P-22174)
BLIND CHILDRENS CENTER INC
4120 Marathon St, Los Angeles
(90029-3584)
PHONE.............................323 664-2153
Midge Horton, *Exec Dir*
Lena French, *President*
Jennifer Brown, *Vice Pres*
Fernanda Schmitt, *Education*
INA Zec, *Director*
EMP: 67 EST: 1938
SQ FT: 15,000
SALES (est): 1.7MM **Privately Held**
WEB: www.blindchildrenscenter.org
SIC: 8211 8399 8351 Specialty education; kindergarten; social service information exchange; nursery school

(P-22175)
CALIFORNIA ENDOWMENT (PA)
1000 N Alameda St, Los Angeles
(90012-1804)
PHONE.............................213 928-8800
Robert K Ross, *President*
Angel Zapata, *Vice Chairman*
Robert Alaniz, *President*
Dan C Deleon, *CFO*
Liron G Samara, *Treasurer*
EMP: 80 EST: 1995
SQ FT: 110,000
SALES (est): 37.9MM **Privately Held**
WEB: www.calendow.org
SIC: 8399 Fund raising organization, non-fee basis

(P-22176)
COMMUNITY ACTION COMM SNTA BRB (PA)
Also Called: C A C
5638 Hollister Ave # 230, Goleta
(93117-3474)
PHONE.............................805 964-8857
Fran Forman, *President*
Natalia Alarcon, *Program Mgr*
Alma Wilson, *Program Mgr*
Irene Mau, *Admin Sec*
Kimberly Maldonado, *Technician*
EMP: 50 EST: 1967
SALES: 22.4MM **Privately Held**
WEB: www.communifysb.org
SIC: 8399 Community action agency

(P-22177)
COMMUNITY ACTION PRTNSHIP SB C
Also Called: Capsbc
696 S Tippecanoe Ave, San Bernardino
(92408-2607)
PHONE.............................909 723-1500
Patricia L Nickols, *CEO*
Joanne Gilbert, *Ch of Bd*
Socorro Enriquez, *Vice Chairman*
Richard Schmidt, *CFO*
Ammie Hines, *Treasurer*
EMP: 88 EST: 1965
SALES (est): 24.2MM **Privately Held**
WEB: www.capsbc.org
SIC: 8399 8699 Community action agency; charitable organization

(P-22178)
COMMUNITY PARTNERS (PA)
1000 N Alameda St Ste 240, Los Angeles
(90012-1804)
PHONE.............................213 346-3200
Paul Vandeventer, *President*
Gary Erickson, *Ch of Bd*
Janet Elliott, *CFO*
Andrew Levey, *Vice Pres*
Eric V Ibarra, *Exec Dir*
EMP: 197 EST: 1990
SALES: 70.4MM **Privately Held**
WEB: www.communitypartners.org
SIC: 8399 Social service information exchange

(P-22179)
DESCANSO GARDENS GUILD INC
1418 Descanso Dr, La Canada
(91011-3102)
PHONE.............................818 952-4408
David Brown, *CEO*
Nadia Hagan, *Education*
Somer Sherwood-White, *Director*

PRODUCTS & SVCS

Susan Armstrong, *Manager*
Cris Martinez, *Manager*
EMP: 65 **EST:** 1960
SQ FT: 1,000
SALES (est): 9.4MM **Privately Held**
WEB: www.descansogardens.org
SIC: 5261 8399 Nurseries & garden centers; fund raising organization, non-fee basis

(P-22180)
DESERT AREA RESOURCES TRAINING
Also Called: Early Childhood Services
201 E Ridgecrest Blvd, Ridgecrest (93555-3919)
PHONE................760 375-8494
Fax: 760 375-1288
EMP: 70
SALES (est): 619.4K **Privately Held**
SIC: 8399 Social Services

(P-22181)
DVEAL CORPORATION
Also Called: D'Veal Family and Youth Svcs
2750 E Wshngtn Blvd # 230, Pasadena (91107-1448)
P.O. Box 40255 (91114-7255)
PHONE................626 296-8900
John McCall, *Exec Dir*
Ronald Mills, *COO*
David Gaffield, *CFO*
Adriana Bugarin, *Director*
Garey Thompson, *Manager*
EMP: 107 **EST:** 1996
SQ FT: 7,500
SALES (est): 8.1MM **Privately Held**
WEB: www.dveal.org
SIC: 8399 Community action agency

(P-22182)
EL SEGUNDO EDUCTL FOUNDATION
641 Sheldon St, El Segundo (90245-3036)
PHONE................310 615-2650
Duane Conover, *President*
Ashley Eveland, *Finance*
Geoff Yantz, *Superintendent*
EMP: 300
SALES: 2MM **Privately Held**
WEB: www.esedf.org
SIC: 8399 Fund raising organization, non-fee basis

(P-22183)
ESSENTIAL ACCESS HEALTH (PA)
Also Called: Cfhc
3600 Wilshire Blvd # 600, Los Angeles (90010-2603)
PHONE................213 386-5614
Julie Rabinovitz, *President*
Nomsa Khalfani, *Senior VP*
Brenda Flores, *Vice Pres*
Ron Frezieres, *Vice Pres*
Amy Moy, *Vice Pres*
EMP: 81 **EST:** 1968
SQ FT: 18,000
SALES: 28.7MM **Privately Held**
WEB: www.essentialaccess.org
SIC: 8399 8011 8099 Fund raising organization, non-fee basis; primary care medical clinic; medical services organization

(P-22184)
GREATER LOS ANGELES ZOO ASSN
Also Called: GLAZA
5333 Zoo Dr, Los Angeles (90027-1451)
PHONE................323 644-4200
Connie M Morgan, *President*
Jeb Bonner, *CFO*
Robert N Ruth, *Treasurer*
Kait Hilliard, *Vice Pres*
Eugenia Vasels, *Vice Pres*
EMP: 100 **EST:** 1963
SQ FT: 8,200
SALES: 17.9MM **Privately Held**
WEB: www.lazoo.org
SIC: 8399 7999 Fund raising organization, non-fee basis; concession operator

(P-22185)
HABITAT FOR HMNITY GRTER LOS A
8739 Artesia Blvd, Bellflower (90706-6330)
PHONE................310 323-4663
Erin Garrity Rank, *President*
Mark V Lue, *COO*
Mark Van Lue, *COO*
Gia Stokes, *CFO*
Francesca Dibrito, *Vice Pres*
EMP: 50
SALES: 23.9MM **Privately Held**
WEB: www.habitatla.org
SIC: 8399 Community development groups

(P-22186)
HARBOR AREA GANG ALTRNTVES PRG
309 W Opp St, Wilmington (90744-3412)
P.O. Box 408, San Pedro (90733-0408)
PHONE................310 519-7233
Juan Torres, *Exec Dir*
Larry Kurtz, *President*
Thomas E Boles, *Treasurer*
Michael Milton, *Vice Pres*
John Greenwood, *Principal*
EMP: 66 **EST:** 1985
SALES (est): 4.3MM **Privately Held**
WEB: www.gangfree.org
SIC: 8399 Community action agency

(P-22187)
HARBOR DVLPMNTAL DSBLTIES FNDT
Also Called: Harbor Regional Center
21231 Hawthorne Blvd, Torrance (90503-5501)
P.O. Box 2930 (90509-2930)
PHONE................310 540-1711
Judy Wada, *CFO*
Patricia Monico, *Exec Dir*
Liz Cohen-Zeboulon, *Program Mgr*
Leslie Estrada, *Program Mgr*
Pablo Ibanez, *Program Mgr*
EMP: 225 **EST:** 1977
SQ FT: 60,000
SALES: 260.1MM **Privately Held**
WEB: www.harborrc.org
SIC: 8399 Council for social agency

(P-22188)
HEALTH ADVOCATES LLC
21540 Plummer St Ste B, Chatsworth (91311-0888)
PHONE................818 995-9500
Al Leibovic, *Mng Member*
William Russell, *CFO*
Kyle Sherman, *Office Mgr*
Lorena Leslie, *Human Res Dir*
Nuria Morales, *Human Res Mgr*
EMP: 371 **EST:** 1997
SQ FT: 40,900
SALES (est): 29.1MM **Privately Held**
WEB: www.healthadvocates.com
SIC: 8399 Advocacy group

(P-22189)
HOSPITAL ASSN SOUTHERN CAL (PA)
Also Called: Hasc
515 S Figueroa St # 1300, Los Angeles (90071-3301)
PHONE................213 347-2002
Jim Barber, *CEO*
Roger Seaver, *Ch of Bd*
Isela Rivas, *President*
Scott Toomey, *CFO*
Martin Gallegos, *Senior VP*
EMP: 58 **EST:** 1923
SQ FT: 30,000
SALES (est): 19.1MM **Privately Held**
WEB: www.hasc.org
SIC: 8399 Advocacy group

(P-22190)
INTERNTNAL FNDTION FOR KREA UN
3435 Wilshire Blvd # 480, Los Angeles (90010-1901)
PHONE................213 550-2182
Willie Wang-Pyo Seung, *CEO*
EMP: 300
SALES: 664.4K **Privately Held**
WEB: www.ifkuusa.com
SIC: 8399 Advocacy group

(P-22191)
KCRW FOUNDATION INC
Also Called: KCRW FM RADIO
1900 Pico Blvd, Santa Monica (90405-1628)
PHONE................310 450-5183
Jennifer Ferro, *CEO*
Herbert Roney, *Treasurer*
Tom Wertheimer, *Treasurer*
Alex Couri, *Officer*
Warren Olney, *Social Dir*
EMP: 51 **EST:** 1981
SQ FT: 4,000
SALES: 21.7MM **Privately Held**
WEB: www.kcrw.com
SIC: 8399 Fund raising organization, non-fee basis

(P-22192)
KERN REGIONAL CENTER (PA)
3200 N Sillect Ave, Bakersfield (93308-6333)
P.O. Box 2536 (93303-2536)
PHONE................661 327-8531
Michal Clark, *Exec Dir*
Duane Law, *CEO*
Jerry Bowman, *CFO*
John Gusman, *CFO*
Sheryl Rodriguez, *Vice Pres*
EMP: 147 **EST:** 1971
SQ FT: 33,000
SALES (est): 201.3MM **Privately Held**
WEB: www.kernrc.org
SIC: 8399 Social service information exchange

(P-22193)
KEY MEDICAL GROUP INC
Also Called: Key Health Systems
3335 S Fairway St, Visalia (93277-7781)
PHONE................559 734-0388
Steve Beargeon, *CEO*
David Osbelt, *Nurse*
EMP: 56 **EST:** 1993
SALES (est): 946.8K **Privately Held**
WEB: www.keymedical.org
SIC: 8399 Health systems agency

(P-22194)
KEYSTONE NPS LLC (DH)
Also Called: Keystone Schools-Ramona
11980 Mount Vernon Ave, Grand Terrace (92313-5172)
PHONE................909 633-6354
Alfredo Alvarado, *Principal*
Don Whitfield, *CFO*
Martha Petrey, *Exec VP*
EMP: 100 **EST:** 1978
SALES (est): 30.2MM
SALES (corp-wide): 11.5B **Publicly Held**
SIC: 8399 Advocacy group
HQ: Children's Comprehensive Services, Inc.
3401 West End Ave Ste 400
Nashville TN 37203
615 250-0000

(P-22195)
KEYSTONE NPS LLC
9994 County Farm Rd, Riverside (92503-3518)
PHONE................951 785-0504
Holly Fields, *Branch Mgr*
EMP: 136
SALES (corp-wide): 11.5B **Publicly Held**
WEB: www.brightfuturesnps.com
SIC: 8399 8211 Advocacy group; private elementary & secondary schools
HQ: Keystone Nps Llc
11980 Mount Vernon Ave
Grand Terrace CA 92313
909 633-6354

(P-22196)
LONG BEACH CMNTY ACTION PARTNR
Also Called: Long Beach Cap
117 W Victoria St, Long Beach (90805-2162)
PHONE................562 216-4600
Darrick Simpson, *Exec Dir*
Janet McCarthy, *Ch of Bd*
Mary Sramek, *Treasurer*
Baty Amit, *Principal*
Darick Simpson, *Exec Dir*
EMP: 65 **EST:** 1979

SQ FT: 10,000
SALES: 6.1MM **Privately Held**
WEB: www.lbcap.org
SIC: 8399 Antipoverty board; community action agency

(P-22197)
LOS ANGELES EDUCATION PARTNR
1541 Wilshire Blvd # 200, Los Angeles (90017-2211)
PHONE................213 622-5237
Ellen Pais, *CEO*
Tina Demirdjian, *Partner*
Gustavo Morales, *Director*
Sara Noji, *Assistant*
EMP: 64 **EST:** 1984
SQ FT: 11,000
SALES (est): 6.8MM **Privately Held**
WEB: www.laep.org
SIC: 8399 Fund raising organization, non-fee basis

(P-22198)
LOS ANGELES LGBT CENTER (PA)
Also Called: L.A. GAY & LESBIAN CENTER
1625 Schrader Blvd, Los Angeles (90028-6213)
P.O. Box 2988 (90078-2988)
PHONE................323 993-7618
Lorri L Jean, *CEO*
Michael Holtzman, *CFC*
Mike Holtzman, *CFO*
Jim Key, *Chief Mktg Ofcr*
Matt Richter, *Social Dir*
EMP: 148 **EST:** 1972
SQ FT: 45,000
SALES: 140.4MM **Privately Held**
WEB: www.lalgbtcenter.org
SIC: 8399 Advocacy group

(P-22199)
LOS ANGLES CNTY MSEUM NTRAL HS (PA)
900 Exposition Blvd, Los Angeles (90007-4057)
PHONE................213 763-3466
Lori Bettison-Varga, *President*
Nooshin Nathan, *Officer*
Gretchen Baker, *Vice Pres*
Pamela Ashlund, *Train & Dev Mgr*
Egbert Gutierrez,
EMP: 210 **EST:** 1913
SQ FT: 450,000
SALES: 64.3MM **Privately Held**
WEB: www.nhm.org
SIC: 9111 8399 8412 County supervisors' & executives' offices; fund raising organization, non-fee basis; museums & art galleries

(P-22200)
LOS ANGLES FUND FOR PUB EDCATN (PA)
10250 Constellation Blvd, Los Angeles (90067-6200)
PHONE................310 912-3444
Daniel L Chang, *Exec Dir*
EMP: 79 **EST:** 2011
SALES (est): 369K **Privately Held**
WEB: www.lafund.org
SIC: 8399 Advocacy group

(P-22201)
LOS OSOS COMMUNITY SVCS DST
Also Called: LOS OSOS CSD
2122 9th St Ste 110, Los Osos (93402-3247)
P.O. Box 6064 (93412-6064)
PHONE................805 528-9370
Leonard Moothart, *President*
John Fouche, *Vice Pres*
Jose Acosta, *Admin Asst*
Chuck Cesena, *Director*
Steve Senet, *Director*
EMP: 50 **EST:** 1998
SALES (est): 3.2MM **Privately Held**
WEB: www.losososcsd.org
SIC: 8399 Community development groups

(P-22202)
MAGNOLIA EDUCTL RES FOUNDATION (PA)
Also Called: Magnolia Science Academy
250 E 1st St Ste 1500, Los Angeles
(90012-3831)
PHONE......................714 892-5066
Dr Suleyman Bahceci, *CEO*
Umit Yapanel, *Vice Chairman*
Mekan Muhammedov, *CFO*
Maria Huezo, *Office Mgr*
Marisol Lopez, *Office Mgr*
EMP: 193 **EST:** 1997
SALES: 51.3MM **Privately Held**
WEB: www.magnoliapublicschools.org
SIC: 8399 Fund raising organization, non-fee basis

(P-22203)
NEW ADVNCES FOR PPLE WITH DSBL
Also Called: Napd
4032 Jewett Ave, Bakersfield (93301-1114)
PHONE......................661 322-9735
Lou Lopez, *Branch Mgr*
Robert K Fallon, *Vice Pres*
Darla Benson, *Info Tech Mgr*
EMP: 91
SALES (corp-wide): 5.8MM **Privately Held**
WEB: www.napd-bak.org
SIC: 8399 Community development groups
PA: New Advances For People With Disabilities
2601 F St
Bakersfield CA 93301
661 395-1361

(P-22204)
NEW ADVNCES FOR PPLE WITH DSBL
Also Called: Center For Achievement Center
1120 21st St, Bakersfield (93301-4613)
PHONE......................661 327-0188
Linda Waninger, *Manager*
EMP: 91
SALES (corp-wide): 5.8MM **Privately Held**
WEB: www.napd-bak.org
SIC: 8399 Community development groups
PA: New Advances For People With Disabilities
2601 F St
Bakersfield CA 93301
661 395-1361

(P-22205)
ON THE RISE INC
305 E Buena Vista St, Barstow
(92311-2803)
P.O. Box 1169 (92312-1169)
PHONE......................760 964-7473
Kimberly Hammack, *Exec Dir*
Mike Parker, *Treasurer*
Jessica Sims, *Vice Pres*
Ashley Dunkin, *Admin Sec*
EMP: 63 **EST:** 2014
SALES (est): 5.5MM **Privately Held**
WEB: www.ontheriseinc.com
SIC: 8399 Health & welfare council

(P-22206)
ORTHALLIANCE INC
Also Called: Orthalliances
21535 Hawthorne Blvd # 20, Torrance
(90503-6604)
PHONE......................310 792-1300
Sam Westover, *President*
James C Wilson, *CFO*
W Summers, *Chairman*
Paul H Hayase, *Senior VP*
Randall Bennet,
EMP: 1700 **EST:** 1996
SQ FT: 4,200
SALES (est): 11.9MM **Privately Held**
WEB: www.orthalliance.com
SIC: 8399 8742 8741 Advocacy group; management consulting services; business management
PA: Orthosynetics, Inc.
3850 N Causeway Blvd # 800
Metairie LA 70002

(P-22207)
PENNY LANE CENTERS (PA)
15305 Rayen St, North Hills (91343-5117)
P.O. Box 2548 (91393-2548)
PHONE......................818 892-3423
Arthur Barr, *President*
Marisol Aguilar, *Partner*
Edie Sanchez, *Partner*
Wendy Carpenter, *Associate Dir*
Ivelise Markovits, *Exec Dir*
EMP: 275 **EST:** 1967
SQ FT: 7,000
SALES: 59.2MM **Privately Held**
WEB: www.pennylane.org
SIC: 8399 Social service information exchange

(P-22208)
PREMIER DISABILITY SVCS LLC
909 N Pacific Coast Hwy # 11, El Segundo
(90245-2724)
PHONE......................310 280-4000
Robert N Brisco, *Mng Member*
EMP: 99 **EST:** 2020
SALES (est): 1MM **Privately Held**
SIC: 8399 Advocacy group

(P-22209)
REACH OUT WEST END
1126 W Foothill Blvd # 150, Upland
(91786-3778)
PHONE......................909 982-8641
Diana Fox, *Director*
Teresa Fernandez, *Envir Svcs Dir*
Julie Martinez, *Director*
Julie Duarte, *Manager*
EMP: 60 **EST:** 1969
SQ FT: 12,232
SALES: 3.5MM **Privately Held**
WEB: www.we-reachout.org
SIC: 8399 Social change association

(P-22210)
SOUTH CNTL LOS ANGLES RGNAL CT (PA)
Also Called: SCLARC
2500 S Western Ave, Los Angeles
(90018-2609)
PHONE......................213 744-7000
Dexter Henderson, *CEO*
Roy Doronila, *COO*
Yewhala Hailemariam, *Information Mgr*
Georgina Mendoza, *Human Resources*
Sheila Armstrong, *Social Worker*
EMP: 223 **EST:** 1983
SQ FT: 110,470
SALES: 381.6MM **Privately Held**
WEB: www.sclarc.org
SIC: 8399 Health & welfare council

(P-22211)
SOUTHLAND INTEGRATED SVCS INC (PA)
Also Called: VIETNAMESE COMMUNITY OF ORANGE
1618 W 1st St, Santa Ana (92703-3614)
PHONE......................714 558-6009
Tricia Nguyen, *CEO*
Hung Nguyen, *Vice Chairman*
Olivia Nguyen, *Fmly & Gen Dent*
EMP: 68 **EST:** 1979
SALES (est): 7MM **Privately Held**
WEB: www.southlandintegrated.org
SIC: 8399 8322 8351 8011 Community development groups; senior citizens' center or association; social service center; preschool center; primary care medical clinic; mental health clinic, outpatient

(P-22212)
SPECIAL SERVICE FOR GROUPS INC
Also Called: Occupational Therapy Training
19401 S Vt Ave Ste A200, Torrance
(90502-4418)
PHONE......................310 323-6887
Sarah Bream, *Exec Dir*
Brian Hui, *Research*
Elizabeth Berger, *Director*
EMP: 131
SALES (corp-wide): 133.1MM **Privately Held**
WEB: www.ssg.org
SIC: 8399 8322 Community action agency; individual & family services

PA: Special Service For Groups, Inc.
905 E 8th St
Los Angeles CA 90021
213 368-1888

(P-22213)
SPECIAL SERVICE FOR GROUPS INC
520 S La Fyte Pk Pl 30, Los Angeles
(90057-1607)
PHONE......................213 553-1800
Herbert Hatanaka, *Branch Mgr*
Misael Ramos, *Officer*
EMP: 131
SALES (corp-wide): 133.1MM **Privately Held**
WEB: www.ssg.org
SIC: 8399 Community development groups
PA: Special Service For Groups, Inc.
905 E 8th St
Los Angeles CA 90021
213 368-1888

(P-22214)
UNITED WAY INC (PA)
Also Called: United Way Greater Los Angeles
1150 S Olive St Ste T-500, Los Angeles
(90015-2481)
PHONE......................213 808-6220
Caroline W Nahas, *Ch of Bd*
Mary Mack, *Ch of Bd*
Kimberly Smith, *Vice Chairman*
Elise Buik, *President*
Ray Chang, *Officer*
▲ **EMP:** 95 **EST:** 1962
SQ FT: 40,000
SALES: 46.7MM **Privately Held**
WEB: www.unitedwayla.org
SIC: 8399 Fund raising organization, non-fee basis; United Fund councils; health & welfare council

(P-22215)
WESTSIDE JEWISH CMNTY CTR INC (PA)
5870 W Olympic Blvd, Los Angeles
(90036-4657)
PHONE......................323 938-2531
Brian Greene, *Exec Dir*
Erin Goldstrom, *Marketing Staff*
ARI Cohen, *Director*
Oscar Yglesias, *Director*
EMP: 200 **EST:** 1932
SQ FT: 150,000
SALES (est): 3.7MM **Privately Held**
WEB: www.westsidejcc.org
SIC: 8399 8641 8322 Community development groups; civic social & fraternal associations; individual & family services

---

8412 Museums & Art Galleries

(P-22216)
ARMAND HMMER MSEUM OF ART CLTR
10899 Wilshire Blvd, Los Angeles
(90024-4343)
PHONE......................310 443-7000
Michael Rubel, *Director*
Steven A Olsen, *Treasurer*
Susan Edwards, *Associate Dir*
MO McGee, *Associate Dir*
Michael Monahan, *Associate Dir*
▲ **EMP:** 101 **EST:** 1989
SQ FT: 20,000
SALES: 36.6MM **Privately Held**
WEB: www.hammer.ucla.edu
SIC: 8412 Museum

(P-22217)
AUTRY MUSEUM OF AMERICAN WEST
4700 Western Heritage Way, Los Angeles
(90027-1462)
PHONE......................323 667-2000
Richard West, *Principal*
Fred Resendez, *Officer*
Robert Caragher, *Vice Pres*
Maren Dougherty, *Vice Pres*
Susan Harlow, *Vice Pres*
EMP: 140
SQ FT: 144,000

SALES (est): 33.9MM **Privately Held**
WEB: www.theautry.org
SIC: 8412 5947 5812 6512 Museum; gift shop; cafeteria; theater building, ownership & operation

(P-22218)
CALIFRNIA SCNCE CTR FOUNDATION
700 Exposition Park Dr, Los Angeles
(90037-1210)
PHONE......................213 744-2545
Jeffrey N Rudolph, *President*
Cynthia Pygin, *CFO*
Laurie Sowd, *Vice Pres*
Erica Guzman, *Accountant*
EMP: 260 **EST:** 1949
SALES: 28.6MM **Privately Held**
WEB: www.californiasciencecenter.org
SIC: 8412 7832 5947 Museum; motion picture theaters, except drive-in; gifts & novelties
HQ: California Natural Resources Agency
1416 9th St Ste 1311
Sacramento CA 95814

(P-22219)
CHARLES W BOWERS MUSEUM CORP
2002 N Main St, Santa Ana (92706-2731)
PHONE......................714 567-3600
Peter C Keller, *President*
Paul Dowdle, *Vice Pres*
Tom Reilly, *Principal*
Robert Ronus, *Admin Sec*
Emily Mahon, *Director*
▲ **EMP:** 72 **EST:** 1936
SALES (est): 4.7MM **Privately Held**
WEB: www.bowers.org
SIC: 8412 Museum

(P-22220)
DISCOVERY SCNCE CTR ORNGE CNTY
2500 N Main St, Santa Ana (92705-6600)
PHONE......................866 552-2823
Daniel Bolar, *Ch of Bd*
Joseph Adams, *President*
Brie Griset Smith, *Vice Pres*
Kafi Blumenfield, *Exec Dir*
Richard Matamoros, *Accountant*
▲ **EMP:** 135 **EST:** 1998
SALES: 7.5MM **Privately Held**
WEB: www.discoverycube.org
SIC: 8412 Museum

(P-22221)
EASTERN CALIFORNIA MUSEUM (PA)
155 N Grant St, Independence (93526)
PHONE......................760 878-0292
Margaret Mairs, *Ch of Bd*
Leah Kirk, *Treasurer*
Del Hubbs, *Vice Ch Bd*
Christian Ray, *Maintence Staff*
William Michaels, *Director*
EMP: 284 **EST:** 1928
SQ FT: 3,200
SALES (est): 3.2MM **Privately Held**
WEB: www.fecm.org
SIC: 8412 Museum

(P-22222)
HUNTINGTN LBRARY ART COLLCTNS
1151 Oxford Rd, San Marino (91108-1218)
PHONE......................626 405-2100
Robert F Erburu, *Ch of Bd*
Steve Koblik, *President*
Robert Skotheim, *President*
Alice Tsay, *President*
Larry Burik, *Vice Pres*
EMP: 380 **EST:** 1919
SALES (est): 34.4MM **Privately Held**
WEB: www.huntington.org
SIC: 8231 8412 8422 Public library; art gallery, noncommercial; botanical garden

(P-22223)
KIDSPACE A PRTICIPATORY MUSEUM
480 N Arroyo Blvd, Pasadena
(91103-3269)
PHONE......................626 449-9144

Jane Popovich, *President*
Mark McKinley, *Treasurer*
Chris Morphy, *Vice Pres*
Stephen H Baumann, *Exec Dir*
Nam Jack, *Admin Sec*
EMP: 83
SALES: 4.7MM **Privately Held**
WEB: www.kidspacemuseum.org
SIC: 8412 Museum

(P-22224)
LONG BCH MUSEUM ART FOUNDATION
2300 E Ocean Blvd, Long Beach
(90803-2442)
PHONE.....................562 439-2119
Ronald B Nelson, *Director*
Ron Nelson, *Exec Dir*
Alex Van Cuylenburg, *General Mgr*
Laurie Webb, *Admin Asst*
Suzanne Rivera, *Finance*
▲ **EMP:** 62
SQ FT: 24,000
SALES: 1.8MM **Privately Held**
WEB: www.lbma.org
SIC: 8412 Museum

(P-22225)
LOS ANGELES CNTY MSEUM OF ART
Also Called: Lacma
5905 Wilshire Blvd, Los Angeles
(90036-4504)
PHONE.....................323 857-6000
Michael Govan, *CEO*
Ann Rowland, *CFO*
Rachel Zelaya, *Officer*
Jane Burrell, *Senior VP*
John Bowsher, *Vice Pres*
▲ **EMP:** 86 **EST:** 2011
SALES (est): 5.5MM **Privately Held**
WEB: www.lacma.org
SIC: 8412 Museum

(P-22226)
MUSEUM ASSOCIATES
Also Called: LA COUNTY MUSEUM OF ART
5905 Wilshire Blvd, Los Angeles
(90036-4504)
PHONE.....................323 857-6172
Michael Gavin, *CEO*
Brianne Bear, *Partner*
Diana Vesga, *COO*
Ann Rowland, *CFO*
Mark Mitchell, *Officer*
EMP: 400 **EST:** 1938
SALES: 255.1MM **Privately Held**
WEB: www.lacma.org
SIC: 8412 Museum

(P-22227)
MUSEUM OF CONTEMPORARY ART (PA)
250 S Grand Ave, Los Angeles
(90012-3021)
PHONE.....................213 626-6222
Charles Young, *CEO*
Jeffrey Deitch, *CEO*
Michael Harrison, *CFO*
Grace KAO, *Executive Asst*
Marco K Braunschweiler, *Director*
▲ **EMP:** 150 **EST:** 1979
SQ FT: 100,000
SALES: 20.2MM **Privately Held**
WEB: www.moca.org
SIC: 8412 Museum

(P-22228)
MUSEUM OF LATIN AMERICAN ART
628 Alamitos Ave, Long Beach
(90802-1513)
PHONE.....................562 437-1689
Robert M Gumbiner, *Chairman*
Tim Degani, *Treasurer*
Mike Deovlet, *Corp Secy*
Wendy Celaya, *Vice Pres*
Todd Heustess, *Vice Pres*
▲ **EMP:** 50 **EST:** 1998
SQ FT: 30,000
SALES (est): 1.7MM **Privately Held**
WEB: www.molaa.org
SIC: 8412 Arts or science center; museum

(P-22229)
NATURAL HISTORY MUSEUM OF LOS
900 Exposition Blvd, Los Angeles
(90007-4057)
PHONE.....................213 763-3442
EMP: 300
SALES: 54MM **Privately Held**
SIC: 8412 Museum/Art Gallery

(P-22230)
NORTON SMON MSEUM ART AT PSDEN
411 W Colorado Blvd, Pasadena
(91105-1825)
PHONE.....................626 449-6840
Ronald H Dykhuizen, *Principal*
James Woodhead, *Partner*
Jennifer J Simon, *Ch of Bd*
Walter W Timoshuk, *Treasurer*
Jan Koester, *Officer*
▲ **EMP:** 100 **EST:** 1924
SQ FT: 70,000
SALES: 5.5MM **Privately Held**
WEB: www.nortonsimon.org
SIC: 8412 Museum

(P-22231)
PALM SPRINGS ART MUSEUM INC
101 N Museum Dr, Palm Springs
(92262-5659)
P.O. Box 2310 (92263-2310)
PHONE.....................760 322-4800
Donna Macmillan, *Ch of Bd*
Elizabeth Burke, *CFO*
Stanley Rosen, *Bd of Directors*
Gary Grace, *Trustee*
Rita Dane, *Officer*
▲ **EMP:** 96
SQ FT: 75,000
SALES: 12.5MM **Privately Held**
WEB: www.psmuseum.org
SIC: 8412 Museum

(P-22232)
RICHARD NIXON FOUNDATION
18001 Yorba Linda Blvd, Yorba Linda
(92886-3903)
PHONE.....................714 701-6832
Hugh Hewitt, *CEO*
James Byron, *Exec VP*
Mamta Dalal, *Principal*
John Taylor, *Exec Dir*
EMP: 76 **EST:** 1983
SQ FT: 52,000
SALES (est): 13.6K **Privately Held**
WEB: www.nixonlibrary.gov
SIC: 8231 8412 Libraries; museum

(P-22233)
RONALD RGAN PRSDNTIAL FNDTION
Also Called: Ronald Rgan Prsdntl Lib Fndt
40 Presidential Dr # 200, Simi Valley
(93065-0600)
PHONE.....................805 522-2977
Glenn Baker, *CFO*
Susie N Reagan, *Principal*
John Heubusch, *Exec Dir*
Meredith Stasa, *Program Mgr*
Katherine Hicks, *Executive Asst*
EMP: 70 **EST:** 1985
SQ FT: 225,000
SALES (est): 16.6MM **Privately Held**
WEB: www.reaganfoundation.org
SIC: 8412 8231 5947 8399 Museum;
public library; gifts & novelties; community
development groups

(P-22234)
SANTA BARBARA MUSEUM OF ART (PA)
Also Called: FINE ARTS MUSEUM
1130 State St, Santa Barbara
(93101-2746)
PHONE.....................805 963-4364
Larry J Feinberg, *CEO*
James Owen, *President*
Diane Wondolowski, *President*
Larry Feinberg, *CEO*
James Hutchinson, *CFO*
▲ **EMP:** 60 **EST:** 1939
SQ FT: 50,000

SALES: 12.2MM **Privately Held**
WEB: www.sbma.net
SIC: 8412 Museum

(P-22235)
SANTA BRBARA MSEUM NTRAL HSTOR
2559 Puesta Del Sol, Santa Barbara
(93105-2936)
PHONE.....................805 682-4711
Luke Swetland, *CEO*
Palmer Jackson Jr, *President*
Diane Wondolowski, *CFO*
Diane Wondoloski, *CFO*
Melissa Baffa, *Officer*
EMP: 95
SALES: 7.8MM **Privately Held**
WEB: www.sbnature.org
SIC: 8412 Museum

(P-22236)
SKIRBALL CULTURAL CENTER
2701 N Sepulveda Blvd, Los Angeles
(90049-6833)
PHONE.....................310 440-4500
Uri D Herscher, *President*
Leslie K Johnson, *Exec VP*
Gail Acosta, *Admin Asst*
Carolina Huerto, *Associate*
▲ **EMP:** 150 **EST:** 1995
SQ FT: 65,000
SALES: 26.4MM **Privately Held**
WEB: www.skirball.org
SIC: 8412 Museum

8422 Arboreta, Botanical & Zoological Gardens

(P-22237)
AQUARIUM OF PACIFIC (PA)
100 Aquarium Way, Long Beach
(90802-8126)
PHONE.....................562 590-3100
Jerry R Schubel, *President*
Anthony Brown, *CFO*
Cecile Fisher, *Vice Pres*
Perry Hampton, *Vice Pres*
Kathryn Nirschl, *Vice Pres*
▲ **EMP:** 220 **EST:** 1997
SQ FT: 10,000
SALES: 46.1MM **Privately Held**
WEB: www.aquariumofpacific.org
SIC: 8422 Aquarium

(P-22238)
LIVING DESERT
47900 Portola Ave, Palm Desert
(92260-6156)
PHONE.....................760 346-5694
Allen Monroe, *CEO*
Terrie Correll, *COO*
Amy Crabb, *Officer*
Eileen Gill, *Officer*
Kippy Laflame, *Officer*
EMP: 124 **EST:** 1970
SQ FT: 1,700
SALES: 23.9MM **Privately Held**
WEB: www.livingdesert.org
SIC: 8422 5947 Aquariums & zoological
gardens; gift shop

(P-22239)
LOS ANGLES ARBRTUM FNDTION INC
301 N Baldwin Ave, Arcadia (91007-2697)
PHONE.....................626 821-3222
Richard Schulhof, *CEO*
Jennifer Williams, *Principal*
EMP: 65 **EST:** 1948
SALES: 6.3MM **Privately Held**
WEB: www.arboretum.org
SIC: 8422 Arboretum

(P-22240)
RANCHO SANTA ANA BOTANIC GRDN
Also Called: CALIFORNIA BOTANIC GAR-
DEN
1500 N College Ave, Claremont
(91711-3157)
PHONE.....................909 625-8767
Lucinda McDade, *Exec Dir*
Peter Evans, *CFO*

Richard Grant, *Chairman*
Sonja Evensen, *Vice Pres*
Clement Hamilton, *Exec Dir*
EMP: 75 **EST:** 1927
SQ FT: 30,000
SALES: 3.6MM **Privately Held**
WEB: www.calbg.org
SIC: 8422 Botanical garden

(P-22241)
SANTA BRBARA ZLGCAL FOUNDATION
500 Ninos Dr, Santa Barbara (93103-3759)
PHONE.....................805 962-1673
Yul Vanek, *CEO*
Fred Clough, *President*
Nancy McToldridge, *COO*
Carol Bedford, *CFO*
Eldon Shiffman, *Treasurer*
▲ **EMP:** 130 **EST:** 1961
SQ FT: 1,200
SALES: 11.6MM **Privately Held**
WEB: www.sbzoo.org
SIC: 8422 Zoological garden, noncommer-
cial

8611 Business Associations

(P-22242)
ALL STATE ASSOCIATION INC
11487 San Fernando Rd, San Fernando
(91340-3406)
PHONE.....................877 425-2558
Steve Avetyan, *CEO*
Alfred Megrabyan, *President*
Armen Karibyan, *COO*
EMP: 250 **EST:** 2003
SALES (est): 14.9MM **Privately Held**
SIC: 8611 Trade associations

(P-22243)
CALIFORNIA ASSN REALTORS INC (PA)
525 S Virgil Ave, Los Angeles
(90020-1403)
PHONE.....................213 739-8200
Joel S Singer, *CEO*
Lefrancis Arnold, *CEO*
Joel S Singer, *CEO*
Don Flyn, *CFO*
Jennifer Branchini, *Treasurer*
EMP: 110 **EST:** 1907
SQ FT: 52,000
SALES: 45.5MM **Privately Held**
WEB: www.car.org
SIC: 8611 8742 Real Estate Board; real
estate consultant

(P-22244)
CALIFRNIA REALTORS MRTG NETWRK
Also Called: California Real Estate
525 S Virgil Ave, Los Angeles
(90020-1403)
PHONE.....................213 739-8200
Joel Singer, *President*
Don Flymn, *CFO*
EMP: 85 **EST:** 1996
SQ FT: 52,000
SALES (est): 2.9MM
SALES (corp-wide): 45.5MM **Privately
Held**
WEB: www.car.org
SIC: 8611 Real Estate Board
PA: California Association Of Realtors, Inc.
525 S Virgil Ave
Los Angeles CA 90020
213 739-8200

(P-22245)
CITY OF BRAWLEY (PA)
400 Main St, Brawley (92227-2434)
PHONE.....................760 344-8941
Rayan Kelley, *Mayor*
Blanca Lara, *Officer*
Gordon Gaste, *Administration*
Thomas Ray, *Agent*
EMP: 69
SQ FT: 6,000
SALES: 17.9MM **Privately Held**
WEB: www.brawley-ca.gov
SIC: 9111 8611 Mayors' offices; ; city &
town managers' offices; business associ-
ations

(P-22246)
CITY OF CULVER CITY
Also Called: Transportation Department
4343 Duquesne Ave, Culver City
(90232-2944)
PHONE...................310 253-6525
Steven Cunningham, *Manager*
EMP: 60
SALES (corp-wide): 137.2MM **Privately Held**
WEB: www.culvercity.org
SIC: 9111 8611 Executive offices, state & local; business associations
PA: City Of Culver City
9770 Culver Blvd
Culver City CA 90232
310 253-5640

(P-22247)
CITY ORANGE POLICE ASSN INC
1107 N Batavia St, Orange (92867-4615)
P.O. Box 906 (92856-6906)
PHONE...................714 457-5340
John Mancini, *President*
EMP: 216
SALES: 390.1K **Privately Held**
WEB: www.copa33.org
SIC: 8611 Business associations

(P-22248)
IAPMO RESEARCH AND TESTING INC (HQ)
5001 E Philadelphia St, Ontario
(91761-2816)
PHONE...................909 472-4100
G P Russ Chaney, *Exec Dir*
Ken Wijaya, *Exec VP*
Tina Donda, *Vice Pres*
Tony Zhou, *Vice Pres*
Russ Chaney, *Executive*
▲ **EMP:** 57 **EST:** 1994
SALES: 42.3MM
SALES (corp-wide): 8.8MM **Privately Held**
WEB: www.iapmo.org
SIC: 8611 Contractors' association
PA: International Association Of Plumbing And Mechanical Officials, A Non-Profit Corporation
4755 E Philadelphia St
Ontario CA 91761
909 472-4100

(P-22249)
INSTITUTE OF ELEC ELEC ENGNERS
Also Called: Ieee Computer Society
10662 Los Vaqueros Cir, Los Alamitos
(90720-2513)
P.O. Box 3014 (90720-1314)
PHONE...................714 821-8380
Linda Ashworth, *Administration*
Brookes Little, *Program Mgr*
Michelle Phon, *Program Mgr*
Anabell St Vincent, *Database Admin*
Katherine Mansfield, *Marketing Staff*
EMP: 85
SALES (corp-wide): 563.2MM **Privately Held**
WEB: www.ieee.org
SIC: 8611 Trade associations
PA: The Institute Of Electrical And Electronics Engineers Incorporated
445 Hoes Ln
Piscataway NJ 08854
212 419-7900

(P-22250)
INTERNTNAL ASSN PLBG MECH OFFC (PA)
Also Called: Iapmo
4755 E Philadelphia St, Ontario
(91761-2810)
PHONE...................909 472-4100
GP Russ Chaney, *CEO*
David Gans, *President*
Gary Hile, *Corp Secy*
Richard Beck, *Vice Pres*
Andy Ho, *Vice Pres*
▲ **EMP:** 296 **EST:** 1926
SQ FT: 65,000
SALES (est): 8.8MM **Privately Held**
WEB: www.iapmo.org
SIC: 8611 Contractors' association

(P-22251)
LOS ANGLES AREA CHMBER CMMERCE
350 S Bixel St, Los Angeles (90017-1418)
PHONE...................213 580-7500
Maria S Salinas, *President*
Gary Toebben, *President*
David Eads, *COO*
Glendy Valenzuela, *COO*
Benjamin Stilp, *CFO*
EMP: 85 **EST:** 2009
SALES (est): 7.3MM **Privately Held**
WEB: www.lachamber.com
SIC: 8611 Chamber of Commerce

(P-22252)
MENS APPAREL GUILD IN CAL INC
Also Called: Magic International
2901 28th St Ste 100, Santa Monica
(90405-2975)
PHONE...................310 857-7500
Joe Loggia, *President*
Jeff Stevenson, *Exec Dir*
Mike Ausec, *Sales Staff*
Arielle Mandell, *Mktg Coord*
Ana Uribe, *Accounts Exec*
EMP: 206 **EST:** 1932
SALES (est): 3.1MM
SALES (corp-wide): 1.3B **Privately Held**
WEB: www.epay.advanstar.com
SIC: 8611 Manufacturers' institute
HQ: Advanstar Communications Inc.
2501 Colorado Ave Ste 280
Santa Monica CA 90404
310 857-7500

(P-22253)
MERCY HOUSE LIVING CENTERS
Also Called: Mercy Hse Trnstnal Living Ctrs
807 N Garfield St, Santa Ana (92701-3821)
P.O. Box 1905 (92702-1905)
PHONE...................714 836-7188
Larry Haynes, *Exec Dir*
Jerome Karcher, *Ch of Bd*
Austin Drissen, *Program Mgr*
Elizabeth Andrade, *Opers Dir*
James Brooks, *Program Dir*
EMP: 170 **EST:** 1988
SQ FT: 19,000
SALES (est): 14.4MM **Privately Held**
WEB: www.mercyhouse.net
SIC: 8611 Community affairs & services

(P-22254)
PACIFIC HSPTLIST ASSOC A MED C
361 Hospital Rd Ste 521, Newport Beach
(92663-3526)
PHONE...................949 610-7245
Weston Chandler, *President*
EMP: 55 **EST:** 2000
SALES (est): 3.4MM **Privately Held**
WEB: www.pacifichospitalists.com
SIC: 8611 8699 Business associations; membership organizations

(P-22255)
RUBIDOUX COMMUNITY SVCS DST
3590 Rubidoux Blvd, Riverside
(92509-4525)
P.O. Box 3098 (92519-3098)
PHONE...................951 684-7580
Jeffrey Sims, *General Mgr*
Steven Appel, *General Mgr*
Claudia Rodriguez, *Accountant*
Dan Ballow, *Pastor*
EMP: 60 **EST:** 1952
SQ FT: 7,200
SALES (est): 5.8MM **Privately Held**
WEB: www.rcsd.org
SIC: 8611 Public utility association

(P-22256)
SAN BRNRDNO CNTY RET MED TR
157 W 5th St, San Bernardino
(92415-0225)
PHONE...................909 387-6053
John Deveaux, *CEO*
EMP: 71 **EST:** 2010

SALES (est): 1.2MM **Privately Held**
WEB: www.sbcounty.gov
SIC: 8611 Business associations

(P-22257)
SATICOY LEMON ASSOCIATION
600 E 3rd St, Oxnard (93030-6001)
P.O. Box 46, Santa Paula (93061-0046)
PHONE...................805 654-6543
Kevin Colvard, *Plant Mgr*
David Coert, *Manager*
EMP: 113
SALES (corp-wide): 26.6MM **Privately Held**
WEB: www.saticoylemon.com
SIC: 8611 Growers' associations
PA: Saticoy Lemon Association
103 N Peck Rd
Santa Paula CA 93060
805 654-6500

(P-22258)
SISTERS OF SOUL SOS YUTH FMLY
937 Via Lata Ste 400, Colton (92324-3958)
PHONE...................909 533-4889
Angela Beal, *CEO*
EMP: 55 **EST:** 1997
SQ FT: 2,800
SALES (est): 141.1K **Privately Held**
WEB: www.sosyouthandfamily.com
SIC: 8611 8322 Community affairs & services; general counseling services

(P-22259)
SOUTHERN CALIFORNIA GOLF ASSN (PA)
3740 Cahuenga Blvd, North Hollywood
(91604-3502)
P.O. Box 7186 (91615-0186)
PHONE...................818 980-3630
Ken Bien, *President*
Keenan Barber, *Treasurer*
Al Frank, *Vice Pres*
Tom Lindgren, *Principal*
Kevin Heaney, *Exec Dir*
EMP: 58 **EST:** 1899
SQ FT: 15,000
SALES (est): 1.7MM **Privately Held**
SIC: 8611 7992 Trade associations; public golf courses

(P-22260)
SOUTHLAND RGONAL ASSN REALTORS (PA)
7232 Balboa Blvd, Van Nuys (91406-2701)
PHONE...................818 786-2110
James Link, *Exec VP*
Steve White, *President*
Tim Johnson, *COO*
Chuck Nickerson, *Vice Pres*
Brian Paul, *Vice Pres*
EMP: 71 **EST:** 1957
SQ FT: 25,000
SALES (est): 10MM **Privately Held**
WEB: www.srar.com
SIC: 8611 Real Estate Board

(P-22261)
SPECIALTY EQUIPMENT MKT ASSN (PA)
Also Called: Sema
1575 Valley Vista Dr, Diamond Bar
(91765-3914)
PHONE...................909 396-0289
Christopher J Kersting, *CEO*
George Afremow, *Vice Pres*
Ira Gabriel, *Vice Pres*
Tom Gattuso, *Vice Pres*
Warren Kosikov, *Vice Pres*
EMP: 70
SQ FT: 23,000
SALES (est): 40.5MM **Privately Held**
WEB: www.sema.org
SIC: 8611 Trade associations

(P-22262)
UNITED AGRIBUSINESS LEAGUE (PA)
Also Called: U A L
54 Corporate Park, Irvine (92606-5105)
PHONE...................800 223-4590
William C Goodrich, *President*
Kirti Mutatkar, *CFO*
Clare M Einsmann, *Exec VP*

Terry Garza, *Administration*
Tomlyn Diep, *Analyst*
EMP: 50
SQ FT: 14,099
SALES (est): 45.2MM **Privately Held**
WEB: www.unitedag.org
SIC: 8611 Trade associations

(P-22263)
WESTERN GROWERS ASSOCIATION (PA)
Also Called: W G A
15525 Sand Canyon Ave, Irvine
(92618-3114)
P.O. Box 57089 (92619-7089)
PHONE...................949 863-1000
Tom A Nassif, *CEO*
Steve Patricio, *Ch of Bd*
Patricia Garner, *Treasurer*
Matt McInerney, *Exec VP*
Dave Puglia, *Senior VP*
EMP: 150 **EST:** 1926
SQ FT: 35,000
SALES (est): 57.8MM **Privately Held**
WEB: www.wga.com
SIC: 8611 8111 Growers' associations; legal services

8621 Professional Membership Organizations

(P-22264)
ACADEMY MPIC ARTS & SCIENCES (PA)
8949 Wilshire Blvd, Beverly Hills
(90211-1907)
PHONE...................310 247-3000
Dawn Hudson, *CEO*
Andrew Horn, *CFO*
Andy Horn, *CFO*
Shawn Finnie, *Exec VP*
Fernando Garcia, *Exec VP*
EMP: 100 **EST:** 1927
SQ FT: 35,000
SALES (est): 158.3MM **Privately Held**
WEB: www.oscars.org
SIC: 8621 7819 8611 Professional membership organizations; services allied to motion pictures; business associations

(P-22265)
AMERICAN SOC CINEMATOGRAPHERS
Also Called: ASC
1782 N Orange Dr, Los Angeles
(90028-4307)
PHONE...................323 969-4333
Victor J Kemper, *Assistant VP*
Richard Crudo, *President*
Holly Lowzik, *Admin Asst*
Shawnte Howard, *Accountant*
Sonja Pierce, *Advt Staff*
EMP: 14 **EST:** 1919
SQ FT: 8,500
SALES (est): 2.4MM **Privately Held**
WEB: www.theasc.com
SIC: 8621 7812 2721 7822 Professional membership organizations; motion picture & video production; periodicals; motion picture distribution; magazine stand

(P-22266)
CAPITAL INVSTMNTS VNTURES CORP (PA)
Also Called: Civco
30151 Tomas, Rcho STA Marg
(92688-2125)
PHONE...................949 858-0647
Drew Richardson, *President*
Brian Cronin, *Ch of Bd*
Gary Prenovost, *CFO*
Dave Freygang, *Managing Dir*
Marjorie Kelso, *Human Resources*
EMP: 195 **EST:** 1975
SQ FT: 95,000
SALES (est): 54.8MM **Privately Held**
WEB: www.padi.com
SIC: 8621 4724 Professional membership organizations; travel agencies

---

(P-22267)
CONCORDE CAREER COLLEGES INC
12412 Victory Blvd, North Hollywood (91606-3134)
PHONE...................818 766-8151
Carmen Bowen, *Director*
Darlene Montes, *Instructor*
Jill Massey, *Program Dir*
Jeff Hegardt, *Director*
Melody Villa, *Representative*
EMP: 60
SQ FT: 5,500
SALES (corp-wide): 75.6MM Privately Held
WEB: www.concorde.edu
SIC: 8249 8621 Medical & dental assistant school; professional membership organizations
PA: Concorde Career Colleges, Inc.
5800 Foxridge Dr Ste 500
Shawnee Mission KS 66202
913 831-9977

(P-22268)
COOPERTIVE AMRCN PHYSICANS INC (PA)
Also Called: Cap-Mpt
333 S Hope St Fl 8, Los Angeles (90071-3001)
PHONE...................213 473-8600
James Weidner, *CEO*
Cindy Belcher, *COO*
John Donaldson, *CFO*
Hammon P Acuna, *Senior VP*
Nancy Brusegaard Johnson, *Senior VP*
EMP: 100 EST: 1975
SALES (est): 33.4MM Privately Held
WEB: www.capphysicians.com
SIC: 8621 Medical field-related associations

(P-22269)
EMPIRECARE HEALTH ASSOC INC
3401 Lemon St, Riverside (92501-2861)
PHONE...................951 686-8202
Barry Port, *President*
Soon Burnam, *Treasurer*
Beverly B Wittekind, *Admin Sec*
Christopher R Christensen, *Director*
EMP: 72 EST: 2008
SALES (est): 6.5MM
SALES (corp-wide): 2.4B Publicly Held
WEB: www.ensigngroup.net
SIC: 8621 Health association
PA: The Ensign Group Inc
29222 Rncho Viejo Rd Ste 1
San Juan Capistrano CA 92675
949 487-9500

(P-22270)
GLEN BEVERLY LABORATORIES INC (PA)
Also Called: Inc J-Network
7777 Center Ave Ste 500, Huntington Beach (92647-3099)
PHONE...................714 848-5777
Akira Kodama, *CEO*
Mitsuhiro Eguchi, *Vice Pres*
Jackie Yashiro, *Office Mgr*
EMP: 56 EST: 2013
SALES (est): 10.5MM Privately Held
WEB: www.bglen.com
SIC: 8621 Professional membership organizations

(P-22271)
JEWISH FAMILY SVC LOS ANGELES (PA)
Also Called: JEWISH FREE LOAN ASSOCIATION
330 N Fairfax Ave, Los Angeles (90036-2109)
PHONE...................323 761-8800
Paul Castro, *CEO*
Tran Maggard, *CFO*
Todd Sosna, *Vice Pres*
Adina Karmon, *Loan*
Rebecca Marcus, *Loan*
EMP: 50 EST: 1918
SALES (est): 45.4MM Privately Held
WEB: www.jfsla.org
SIC: 8621 Professional membership organizations

(P-22272)
LOS ANGELES COUNTY BAR ASSN (PA)
Also Called: Los Angeles Lawyer Magazine
200 S Spring St, Los Angeles (90012-3710)
P.O. Box 55020 (90055-2020)
PHONE...................213 627-2727
Paul R Kiesel, *President*
James P Drummy, *Bd of Directors*
Kevin Mahoney, *Bd of Directors*
Sally Suchil, *Exec Dir*
Henry Martinez, *General Mgr*
▲ EMP: 85 EST: 1878
SALES (est): 12.4MM Privately Held
WEB: www.lacba.org
SIC: 8621 Bar association

(P-22273)
ORANGE CNTY HLTH AUTH A PUB AG
505 City Pkwy W, Orange (92868-2924)
PHONE...................714 246-8500
Richard Chambers, *CEO*
Michael Schrader, *CEO*
Ladan Khamseh, *COO*
Nancy Huang, *CFO*
Kim Cunningham, *Officer*
EMP: 432 EST: 1994
SQ FT: 200,000
SALES (est): 92.6MM Privately Held
WEB: www.caloptima.org
SIC: 8621 Professional membership organizations

(P-22274)
ORANGE COUNTY HEALTH CARE AGCY
405 W 5th St Ste 700, Santa Ana (92701-4534)
PHONE...................714 568-5683
Jenny Qian, *Principal*
Michael Rogers, *Admin Mgr*
Susanna Ganey, *Admin Sec*
Maggie Rawlins, *Admin Asst*
Julie Low, *Controller*
EMP: 99 EST: 2014
SALES (est): 10.3MM Privately Held
WEB: www.ochealthinfo.com
SIC: 8621 Health association

(P-22275)
PADI AMERICAS INC
30151 Tomas, Rcho STA Marg (92688-2125)
P.O. Box 7005 (92688-7005)
PHONE...................949 858-7234
Drew Richardson, *Principal*
Carlos Sanchez, *Receiver*
Christian Nimsky, *Senior VP*
Shane Blaser, *Vice Pres*
Stefanie Lee, *Vice Pres*
◆ EMP: 200 EST: 1967
SQ FT: 96,000
SALES (est): 45.5MM
SALES (corp-wide): 54.8MM Privately Held
WEB: www.padi.com
SIC: 8621 Education & teacher association
HQ: Padi Holdco, Inc.
30151 Tomas
Rcho Sta Marg CA 92688
949 858-7234

(P-22276)
POMONA COMMUNITY HEALTH CENTER
Also Called: Parktree Community Health Ctr
1450 E Holt Ave, Pomona (91767-5822)
PHONE...................909 630-7927
Ellen Silver, *CEO*
EMP: 60
SALES (est): 11.3MM Privately Held
WEB: www.parktreehc.org
SIC: 8621 Health association

(P-22277)
REGAL MEDICAL GROUP INC (PA)
Also Called: Heritage California Aco
8510 Balboa Blvd Ste 275, Northridge (91325-5809)
PHONE...................818 654-3400
Richard N Merkin, *CEO*
Daniel Frank, *COO*

Katie Franklin, *Vice Pres*
Girard Jacquet, *Risk Mgmt Dir*
Natacha Cave, *Principal*
EMP: 122 EST: 1986
SALES (est): 66.8MM Privately Held
SIC: 8621 Medical field-related associations

(P-22278)
ROCK BLUE ☉
601 Foothill Rd, Ojai (93023-1765)
PHONE...................703 314-0208
Peter Macy, *President*
Chris Fahlin, *COO*
Miles Crisp, *CFO*
Satish Menon, *Vice Pres*
Richard Noth, *Vice Pres*
EMP: 75 EST: 2021
SALES (est): 445.6K Privately Held
SIC: 8621 Professional membership organizations

(P-22279)
ST BALDRICKS FOUNDATION INC (PA)
1333 S Mayflower Ave # 40, Monrovia (91016-4066)
PHONE...................626 792-8247
Charles M Chamness, *Ch of Bd*
Katherine Lugar, *Ch of Bd*
Jennifer McCabe, *Officer*
Becky Weaver, *Officer*
Kathleen Ruddy, *Exec Dir*
EMP: 58 EST: 2004
SALES (est): 26.3MM Privately Held
WEB: www.stbaldricks.org
SIC: 8621 Health association

(P-22280)
ST VNCENT SNIOR CTZEN NTRTN P (PA)
Also Called: ST. VINCENT MEALS ON WHEELS
2303 Miramar St, Los Angeles (90057-2109)
PHONE...................213 484-7775
Veronica Dover, *CEO*
EMP: 96 EST: 1980
SALES (est): 10.5MM Privately Held
WEB: www.svmow.org
SIC: 8621 Professional membership organizations

(P-22281)
STATE BAR OF CALIFORNIA
845 S Figueroa St, Los Angeles (90017-2515)
PHONE...................213 765-1520
Eric Perez, *Chief Engr*
Cathy Molina, *Director*
EMP: 92
SALES (corp-wide): 119.6MM Privately Held
WEB: www.calbar.ca.gov
SIC: 8621 Bar association
PA: State Bar Of California
180 Howard St Fl Grnd
San Francisco CA 94105
415 538-2000

(P-22282)
STATE BAR OF CALIFORNIA
755 Santa Rosa St Ste 310, San Luis Obispo (93401-4805)
PHONE...................805 544-7551
EMP: 92
SALES (corp-wide): 119.6MM Privately Held
WEB: www.calbar.ca.gov
SIC: 8621 Bar association
PA: State Bar Of California
180 Howard St Fl Grnd
San Francisco CA 94105
415 538-2000

(P-22283)
TRI-COUNTIES ASSOCIATION F
1234 Fairway Dr A, Santa Maria (93455-1406)
PHONE...................805 922-4640
EMP: 55
SALES (corp-wide): 352.8MM Privately Held
WEB: www.tri-counties.org
SIC: 8621 Professional membership organizations

PA: Tri-Counties Association For The Developmentally Disabled, Inc.
520 E Montecito St
Santa Barbara CA 93103
805 962-7881

(P-22284)
TRUCK UNDERWRITERS ASSOCIATION (DH)
4680 Wilshire Blvd, Los Angeles (90010-3807)
PHONE...................323 932-3200
Leonard H Gelfand, *President*
Gerald Faulwell, *Vice Pres*
Martin Feinstein, *Vice Pres*
Jason Katz, *Vice Pres*
John Lynch, *Vice Pres*
EMP: 1767 EST: 1935
SALES (est): 55.7MM
SALES (corp-wide): 59.9B Privately Held
WEB: www.farmers.com
SIC: 8621 Professional membership organizations
HQ: Farmers Group, Inc.
6301 Owensmouth Ave
Woodland Hills CA 91367
323 932-3200

8631 Labor Unions & Similar Organizations

(P-22285)
AMERICAN FDRTION MSCANS LCAL 4
Also Called: American Fdrtion of Mscans of
3220 Winona Ave, Burbank (91504-2544)
PHONE...................323 462-2161
John Acosta, *President*
Gary Lasley, *Treasurer*
Rick Baptist, *Vice Pres*
Marisol Rhodes, *Vice Pres*
Diane Lauerman, *Administration*
EMP: 140 EST: 1897
SALES (est): 11.4MM
SALES (corp-wide): 14.1MM Privately Held
WEB: www.afm47.org
SIC: 8631 Labor union
PA: American Federation Of Musicians Of The United States & Canada (Inc)
1501 Broadway Fl 9
New York NY 10036
212 869-1330

(P-22286)
ART DRCTORS GILD ITSE LCAL 876
11969 Ventura Blvd # 200, Studio City (91604-2630)
PHONE...................818 762-9995
Mimi Gramatky, *President*
Cate Bangs, *Treasurer*
Cat Smith, *Treasurer*
Jim Wallis, *Vice Pres*
Chuck Parker, *Exec Dir*
EMP: 55 EST: 1937
SQ FT: 19,040
SALES (est): 10.1MM Privately Held
WEB: www.adg.org
SIC: 8631 Labor unions & similar labor organizations

(P-22287)
ASSOCIATIONS OF UNITED NURSES (PA)
Also Called: UNAC/UHCP
955 Overland Ct Ste 150, San Dimas (91773-1740)
PHONE...................909 599-8622
Ken Deitz, *President*
Jettie Deden-Castillo, *Treasurer*
Denise Duncan, *Vice Pres*
Charmaine Morales, *Admin Sec*
EMP: 63 EST: 1972
SALES (est): 4.2MM Privately Held
WEB: www.unacuhcp.org
SIC: 8631 Employees' association

(P-22288)
CENTER FOR CRGIVER ADVANCEMENT
2910 Beverly Blvd, Los Angeles (90057-1012)
PHONE...................................866 888-8213
Kent Wong, *Bd of Directors*
Corinne Eldridge, *Exec Dir*
Sarah Gonzaga, *Admin Asst*
Annie Lee-Houang, *Opers Staff*
Julia A Hernandez, *Education*
EMP: 120 **EST:** 1999
SALES (est): 9.9MM **Privately Held**
WEB: www.advancecaregivers.org
SIC: 8631 Labor union

(P-22289)
COUNTY OF LOS ANGELES
Also Called: Carson Gang Diversion Team
21356 Avalon Blvd, Carson (90745-2213)
PHONE...................................310 847-4018
EMP: 226 **Privately Held**
SIC: 8631 Labor Organization
PA: County Of Los Angeles
500 W Temple St Ste 375
Los Angeles CA 90012
213 974-1101

(P-22290)
HOSPITAL SVC EMPLYEES UN LCAL
Also Called: Service Employee Union
5480 Ferguson Dr, Commerce (90022-5119)
PHONE...................................323 734-8399
Dave Reagan, *President*
Carrie Budahn, *Graphic Designe*
EMP: 84 **EST:** 1948
SQ FT: 10,000
SALES (est): 580K **Privately Held**
WEB: www.seiu-uhw.org
SIC: 8631 Labor union

(P-22291)
INTERNTIONAL UN OPER ENGINEERS
Local 12
150 Corson St, Pasadena (91103-3839)
P.O. Box 7109 (91109-7209)
PHONE...................................626 792-2519
William C Waggoner, *Manager*
Tammy Caley, *Admin Asst*
Todd Bischoff, *Director*
Bob Wilds, *Director*
John Stevens, *Representative*
EMP: 50
SQ FT: 32,534
SALES (corp-wide): 52.1MM **Privately Held**
WEB: www.oefi.org
SIC: 8631 Labor union
PA: International Union Of Operating Engineers
1121 L St Ste 401
Sacramento CA 95814
916 444-6880

(P-22292)
INTERNTIONAL UN OPER ENGINEERS
Also Called: Local 12
1647 W Lugonia Ave, Redlands (92374-2048)
PHONE...................................909 307-8700
Ron Sikroski, *Manager*
EMP: 595
SALES (corp-wide): 52.1MM **Privately Held**
WEB: www.oefi.org
SIC: 8631 Labor union
PA: International Union Of Operating Engineers
1121 L St Ste 401
Sacramento CA 95814
916 444-6880

(P-22293)
LOS ANGLES CNTY EMPLOYEES ASSN
Also Called: Service Employee Intl Un
1545 Wilshire Blvd, Los Angeles (90017-4501)
PHONE...................................213 368-8660
Annelle Grajeda, *President*
Kathleen Austria, *Treasurer*

Bob Schoonover, *Vice Pres*
Annette Jeffrief, *Admin Sec*
Michael Green, *Regional*
EMP: 68 **EST:** 1950
SQ FT: 40,000
SALES (est): 12.7MM **Privately Held**
WEB: www.seiu721.org
SIC: 8631 Labor union

(P-22294)
RIVERSIDE SHERIFFS ASSOCIATION
21810 Cactus Ave, March ARB (92518-3010)
PHONE...................................951 653-5152
Robert Masson, *President*
Randy Thomas, *Treasurer*
Julie Kelley, *Executive Asst*
Brandon Arias, *Admin Sec*
Christina Hurtado, *Administration*
EMP: 51 **EST:** 1968
SQ FT: 10,000
SALES (est): 15.9MM **Privately Held**
WEB: www.rcdsa.org
SIC: 8631 6411 Labor union; insurance agents, brokers & service

(P-22295)
SAG-AFTRA FOUNDATION
5757 Wilshire Blvd Ph 1, Los Angeles (90036-3681)
PHONE...................................323 549-6708
Cyd Wilson, *Exec Dir*
Rochelle Rose, *Prgrmr*
Justus Hepburn, *Technician*
Anne Reburn, *Technician*
Franz Reynold, *Project Dir*
EMP: 50 **EST:** 1985
SALES (est): 5.2MM **Privately Held**
WEB: www.sagaftra.foundation
SIC: 8631 Labor union

(P-22296)
SEIU LOCAL 2015
2910 Beverly Blvd, Los Angeles (90057-1012)
PHONE...................................213 985-0384
Laphonza Butler, *President*
Crystal Miller, *President*
Dereck Smith, *COO*
Leticia Acosta, *Administration*
Carla Zaldivar, *Administration*
EMP: 210 **EST:** 2015
SALES (est): 76.9MM **Privately Held**
WEB: www.seiu2015.org
SIC: 8631 Labor union

(P-22297)
SEIU LOCAL 721
1545 Wilshire Blvd # 100, Los Angeles (90017-4510)
PHONE...................................213 368-8660
Annelle Grajeda, *Owner*
Lillian Cabral, *Treasurer*
Linda Dent, *Vice Pres*
EMP: 109 **EST:** 2007
SALES (est): 142.2K **Privately Held**
WEB: www.seiu721.org
SIC: 8631 Labor union

(P-22298)
SEIU UNITED SERVICE WORKERS W (PA)
Also Called: Seiu-Usww
828 W Washington Blvd, Los Angeles (90015-3310)
PHONE...................................213 284-7705
David Huerta, *President*
Alejandra Valles, *Corp Secy*
Kawana Anderson, *Principal*
Melissa Chadburn, *Principal*
Alfredo Fletes, *Principal*
EMP: 59 **EST:** 2012
SALES (est): 4.6MM **Privately Held**
WEB: www.seiu-usww.org
SIC: 8631 Labor union

(P-22299)
SOUTHWEST CRPNTERS TRNING FUND
533 S Fremont Ave, Los Angeles (90071-1712)
PHONE...................................213 386-8590
Matt Dunphy, *Administration*
Rosa Rodriguez, *Office Admin*

Cecile Standridge, *Admin Asst*
John Sartor, *Info Tech Mgr*
Rosylyn Luong, *Auditor*
EMP: 81 **EST:** 2012
SALES (est): 30.5MM **Privately Held**
WEB: www.swctf.org
SIC: 8631 Labor union

(P-22300)
SOUTHWEST RGNAL CNCIL CRPNTERS (PA)
533 S Fremont Ave Fl 10, Los Angeles (90071-1712)
PHONE...................................213 385-1457
Daniel Langford, *CEO*
Pedro Rodriguez, *President*
Frank Hawk, *Vice Pres*
Stephen Araiza, *Director*
Barry Jenkins, *Director*
EMP: 50 **EST:** 1920
SQ FT: 4,000
SALES (est): 25MM **Privately Held**
WEB: www.swcarpenters.org
SIC: 8631 Labor union

(P-22301)
SOUTHWEST RGNAL CNCIL CRPNTERS
15881 Valley View Ct, Sylmar (91342-3579)
PHONE...................................818 364-9303
Douglas McCarron, *President*
EMP: 83
SQ FT: 59,250
SALES (corp-wide): 25MM **Privately Held**
WEB: www.swcarpenters.org
SIC: 8631 Labor union
PA: Southwest Regional Council Of Carpenters
533 S Fremont Ave Fl 10
Los Angeles CA 90071
213 385-1457

(P-22302)
TEMPORARY STAFFING UNION
19800 Macarthur Blvd, Irvine (92612-2421)
PHONE...................................714 728-5186
Veronica Lake, *CEO*
Fe Santos, *President*
EMP: 4000
SQ FT: 1,500
SALES (est): 100K **Privately Held**
SIC: 8631 Labor union

(P-22303)
UNITED FARM WORKERS AMERICA (PA)
29700 Wdford Tehachapi Rd, Keene (93531)
P.O. Box 62 (93531-0062)
PHONE...................................661 822-5571
Arturo Rodriguez, *President*
Liz Villarino, *CFO*
Tanis Ybarra, *Corp Secy*
Irv Hershenbaum, *Vice Pres*
EMP: 110
SQ FT: 5,000
SALES: 7.2MM **Privately Held**
WEB: www.ufw.org
SIC: 8631 Labor union

(P-22304)
UNITED FOOD & COMMERCL WORKERS (PA)
8530 Stanton Ave, Buena Park (90620-3930)
P.O. Box 5004 (90622-5004)
PHONE...................................714 995-4601
Greg Conger, *President*
Andrea Zinder, *Treasurer*
George Landers, *Exec Dir*
Dave Wallauch, *Administration*
Shawn Ashe, *IT/INT Sup*
EMP: 61 **EST:** 1936
SQ FT: 45,000
SALES (est): 14MM **Privately Held**
WEB: www.ufcw324.org
SIC: 8631 Labor union

(P-22305)
UNITED FOOD AND COMMERCIAL (PA)
Also Called: Ufcw Local 770
630 Shatto Pl Ste 300, Los Angeles (90005-1372)
P.O. Box 770 (90078-0770)
PHONE...................................213 487-7070
Ricardo F Icaza, *President*
Paul Edwards, *CFO*
Kathy Finn, *Treasurer*
Rodney Diamond, *Corp Secy*
Danny Garcia, *Vice Pres*
EMP: 60 **EST:** 1937
SALES (est): 17.1MM **Privately Held**
WEB: www.ufcw770.org
SIC: 8631 Labor union

(P-22306)
UNITED TEACHERS-LOS ANGELES
Also Called: U T L A
3303 Wilshire Blvd Fl 10, Los Angeles (90010-1794)
PHONE...................................213 487-5560
Aj Duffy, *President*
David Goldburg, *Treasurer*
Joshua Pechthalt, *Vice Pres*
Ana Valencia, *Vice Pres*
Betty Forrester, *Admin Sec*
EMP: 72
SQ FT: 144,000
SALES: 40.9MM **Privately Held**
WEB: www.utla.net
SIC: 8631 Labor union

(P-22307)
WRITERS GUILD AMERICA WEST INC
7000 W 3rd St, Los Angeles (90048-4321)
PHONE...................................323 951-4000
David Young, *CEO*
Gregg Mitchell, *COO*
Theresa F Savino, *COO*
Aaron Mendelsohn, *Treasurer*
Elias Davis, *Corp Secy*
EMP: 160 **EST:** 1954
SQ FT: 67,000
SALES: 41.7MM **Privately Held**
WEB: www.wga.org
SIC: 8631 Labor union

8641 Civic, Social & Fraternal Associations

(P-22308)
21515 HAWTHORNE OWNER LLC
21535 Hawthorne Blvd # 10, Torrance (90503-6604)
PHONE...................................310 406-3730
Jon Muller,
Margaret Powell,
Jenny Blanchart, *Director*
EMP: 100 **EST:** 2014
SALES (est): 7.1MM **Privately Held**
WEB: www.ezerwilliamsonlaw.com
SIC: 8641 Dwelling-related associations

(P-22309)
AFRICAN WOMEN RISING
801 Cold Springs Rd, Santa Barbara (93108-1016)
PHONE...................................415 278-1784
Linda Cole, *CEO*
EMP: 200 **EST:** 2007
SALES (est): 567.7K **Privately Held**
WEB: www.africanwomenrising.org
SIC: 8641 Civic social & fraternal associations

(P-22310)
ARTHRTIS FUNDATION PCF REG INC
800 W 6th St Ste 1250, Los Angeles (90017-2721)
PHONE...................................323 954-5760
EMP: 50
SALES (est): 12.5MM **Privately Held**
SIC: 8641 Civic/Social Association

PRODUCTS & SVCS

(P-22311)
ASSOCTED STDNTS CAL STATE UNIV
Also Called: A S I
1212 N Bellflower Blvd # 22, Long Beach (90815-4148)
PHONE....................................562 985-4994
Richard Haller, *Exec Dir*
Adriana Andrade, *Treasurer*
EMP: 60 EST: 1956
SQ FT: 184,000
SALES: 16.8MM **Privately Held**
WEB: www.asicsulb.org
SIC: 8641 University club

(P-22312)
BEAR VALLEY SPRINGS ASSN
29541 Rollingoak Dr, Tehachapi (93561-7133)
PHONE....................................661 821-5537
Todd Lander, *President*
Terry Quinn, *President*
Larry Thompson, *Treasurer*
Tim Hawkins, *Vice Pres*
James Panek,
EMP: 200 EST: 1970
SQ FT: 2,000
SALES: 7.1MM **Privately Held**
WEB:
www.bearvalleysprings.wordpress.com
SIC: 8641 Homeowners' association

(P-22313)
BOYS GIRLS CLB HUNTINGTON VLY (PA)
16582 Brookhurst St, Fountain Valley (92708-2353)
PHONE....................................714 531-2582
Tanya Hoxsie, *President*
Ryan Brenes, *Program Dir*
Eddie Marquez, *Program Dir*
Diana Martinez, *Program Dir*
Alejandra Morales, *Program Dir*
EMP: 89
SALES: 11.7MM **Privately Held**
WEB: www.bgchv.com
SIC: 8641 Youth organizations

(P-22314)
BOYS GIRLS CLUBS OF KERN CNTY
Also Called: BOY'S & GIRL'S CLUB OF BAKERSF
801 Niles St, Bakersfield (93305-4419)
PHONE....................................661 325-3730
Zane Smith, *Exec Dir*
Ed Kuhn, *President*
Murry Tragish, *President*
Craig Stickler, *Treasurer*
Bill Campbell, *Vice Pres*
EMP: 100 EST: 1971
SALES: 9.2MM **Privately Held**
WEB: www.bgclubsofkerncounty.org
SIC: 8641 8322 Boy Scout organization; individual & family services

(P-22315)
BOYS GRLS CLB MRPARK SIMI VLY (PA)
2850 Lemon Dr, Simi Valley (93063-2193)
PHONE....................................805 527-4437
W Scott Mosher, *CEO*
Janice Parvin, *President*
Ken Simons, *CFO*
Scott Mosher, *Exec Dir*
Lori Nowaski, *Admin Sec*
EMP: 50 EST: 1985
SALES (est): 851.5K **Privately Held**
WEB: www.bgcmoorpark.org
SIC: 8641 Youth organizations

(P-22316)
BOYS GRLS CLB SNTA MONICA INC
Also Called: BOYS & GIRLS CLUBS OF SANTA MO
1220 Lincoln Blvd, Santa Monica (90401-1704)
PHONE....................................310 361-8500
Aaron Young, *Director*
Nina Kiefer, *Executive*
Virginia Kato, *General Mgr*
Yesenia Mendoza, *Finance*
Kevin Kirk, *Instructor*
EMP: 83 EST: 1943

SQ FT: 6,000
SALES: 3MM **Privately Held**
WEB: www.smbgc.org
SIC: 8641 7997 Youth organizations; membership sports & recreation clubs

(P-22317)
BOYS GRLS CLUBS CNTL ORNGE CAS (PA)
17701 Cowan Ste 110, Irvine (92614-6061)
PHONE....................................714 543-5540
Robert Santana, *CEO*
Travis Whitten, *Officer*
John Brewster, *Exec Dir*
Jesse Barrios, *Accounting Mgr*
Erica Aguirre, *Opers Staff*
EMP: 57 EST: 1957
SQ FT: 15,150
SALES (est): 53.7K **Privately Held**
WEB: www.boysandgirlsclub.com
SIC: 8641 Youth organizations; recreation association

(P-22318)
BOYS GRLS CLUBS GRTER CNEJO VL (PA)
1 Dole Dr Ste 3331, Westlake Village (91362-7300)
PHONE....................................818 706-0905
Crystal Naone, *CEO*
Mark Elswick, *President*
Joseph Cisneros, *Executive Asst*
Jennifer Wissusik, *Opers Staff*
Hazciel Vidrio, *Program Dir*
EMP: 56 EST: 2003
SALES (est): 4.9MM **Privately Held**
WEB: www.bgcconejo.org
SIC: 8641 Youth organizations

(P-22319)
BOYS GRLS CLUBS GRTER OXNARD P (PA)
1900 W 5th St, Oxnard (93030-6596)
PHONE....................................805 815-4959
Tim Blaylock, *Manager*
Andrew Franco, *Tech/Comp Coord*
Yolanda Montez, *Manager*
EMP: 81 EST: 1953
SALES (est): 3.9MM **Privately Held**
WEB: www.bgcop.org
SIC: 8641 Boy Scout organization; youth organizations

(P-22320)
BOYS GRLS CLUBS OF LOS ANGELES (PA)
Also Called: Boys & Girls Club of San Pedro
1200 S Cabrillo Ave, San Pedro (90731-4011)
PHONE....................................310 833-1322
Mike Lansing, *Branch Mgr*
Dominique Marino, *Volunteer Dir*
Robert Nizich, *President*
Dennis Lane, *Treasurer*
Josepth Rich, *Vice Pres*
EMP: 65 EST: 1939
SQ FT: 26,083
SALES (est): 7.7MM **Privately Held**
WEB: www.bgclaharbor.org
SIC: 8641 Youth organizations

(P-22321)
BUDDHIST TZU CHI FOUNDATION (PA)
1100 S Valley Center Ave, San Dimas (91773-3728)
PHONE....................................909 447-7799
Han Kuei Huang, *CEO*
Debra Boudreaux, *CEO*
Austin Tsao, *Exec VP*
Yuru Chou, *Administration*
Grace Chen, *Pub Rel Staff*
◆ EMP: 78 EST: 2005
SALES (est): 18.8MM **Privately Held**
WEB: www.tzuchi.us
SIC: 8641 Civic social & fraternal associations

(P-22322)
CALIFORNIA CLUB
538 S Flower St, Los Angeles (90071-2548)
PHONE....................................213 622-1391
Robert C Baker, *CEO*
Shanta Abeyratne, *Asst Controller*

Emerson Mark, *Controller*
Dindo Galanto, *Marketing Staff*
Jann McCord, *Director*
EMP: 185
SALES: 16.2MM **Privately Held**
WEB: www.californiaclub.org
SIC: 8641 7041 Business persons club; bars & restaurants, members only; residence club, organization

(P-22323)
CANYON LK PROPERTY OWNERS ASSN
31512 Railroad Canyon Rd, Canyon Lake (92587-9400)
PHONE....................................951 244-6841
Carl Armburst, *President*
Marty Gibson, *Treasurer*
Tom Nathan, *Vice Pres*
Chris Poland, *Vice Pres*
Clint Warrell, *General Mgr*
EMP: 84 EST: 1968
SQ FT: 18,000
SALES (est): 15.2MM **Privately Held**
WEB: www.canyonlakepoa.com
SIC: 8641 Homeowners' association

(P-22324)
CENTER CLUB
650 Town Center Dr Ste G, Costa Mesa (92626-7059)
PHONE....................................714 662-3414
Shahin Vosough, *Office Mgr*
Melody Thomas, *Corp Comm Staff*
EMP: 88 EST: 1982
SQ FT: 18,000
SALES (est): 1.2MM
SALES (corp-wide): 1B **Privately Held**
WEB: www.center-club.com
SIC: 5812 8641 Eating places; civic social & fraternal associations; business persons club
HQ: Clubcorp Usa, Inc.
3030 Lyndon B Johnson Fwy
Dallas TX 75234
972 243-6191

(P-22325)
CHANNEL ISLNDS YUNG MNS CHRSTN
301 W Figueroa St, Santa Barbara (93101-3632)
PHONE....................................805 963-8775
Teri Bradford Rouse, *Branch Mgr*
EMP: 88
SALES (corp-wide): 18.6MM **Privately Held**
WEB: www.ciymca.org
SIC: 8641 Youth organizations
PA: Channel Islands Young Men's Christian Association
105 E Carrillo St
Santa Barbara CA 93101
805 569-1103

(P-22326)
CHANNEL ISLNDS YUNG MNS CHRSTN
Also Called: Lompoc Family YMCA
201 W College Ave, Lompoc (93436-4415)
PHONE....................................805 736-3483
Dan Powell, *Branch Mgr*
EMP: 88
SALES (corp-wide): 18.6MM **Privately Held**
WEB: www.ciymca.org
SIC: 8641 7991 8351 7032 Youth organizations; physical fitness facilities; child day care services; youth camps; individual & family services
PA: Channel Islands Young Men's Christian Association
105 E Carrillo St
Santa Barbara CA 93101
805 569-1103

(P-22327)
CHANNEL ISLNDS YUNG MNS CHRSTN
Also Called: Camarillo Family YMCA
3111 Village Park Dr, Camarillo (93012)
PHONE....................................805 484-0423
Marge Castellano, *Director*
Michelle Jackson, *Office Mgr*
EMP: 88

SALES (corp-wide): 18.6MM **Privately Held**
WEB: www.ciymca.org
SIC: 8641 7991 8351 7032 Youth organizations; physical fitness facilities; child day care services; youth camps; individual & family services
PA: Channel Islands Young Men's Christian Association
105 E Carrillo St
Santa Barbara CA 93101
805 569-1103

(P-22328)
CHANNEL ISLNDS YUNG MNS CHRSTN
Also Called: Santa Barbara Family YMCA
36 Hitchcock Way, Santa Barbara (93105-3102)
PHONE....................................805 687-7727
Tim Hardy, *Branch Mgr*
Amy Bailey, *Exec Dir*
Paige Harris, *Dept Chairman*
Channing Hogue, *Director*
EMP: 88
SALES (corp-wide): 18.6MM **Privately Held**
WEB: www.ciymca.org
SIC: 8641 7991 8351 7032 Youth organizations; physical fitness facilities; child day care services; youth camps; individual & family services
PA: Channel Islands Young Men's Christian Association
105 E Carrillo St
Santa Barbara CA 93101
805 569-1103

(P-22329)
CHANNEL ISLNDS YUNG MNS CHRSTN
Also Called: Montecito Family YMCA
591 Santa Rosa Ln, Santa Barbara (93108-2145)
PHONE....................................805 969-3288
Yvonne Rubio, *Director*
EMP: 88
SALES (corp-wide): 18.6MM **Privately Held**
WEB: www.ciymca.org
SIC: 8641 7991 8351 7032 Youth organizations; physical fitness facilities; child day care services; youth camps; individual & family services
PA: Channel Islands Young Men's Christian Association
105 E Carrillo St
Santa Barbara CA 93101
805 569-1103

(P-22330)
CHANNEL ISLNDS YUNG MNS CHRSTN
Also Called: Ventura Family YMCA
3760 Telegraph Rd, Ventura (93003-3421)
PHONE....................................805 484-0423
Sarah Abrams, *Director*
Mike Yamasaki, *Exec Dir*
Jose Marin, *Accountant*
Amy Bailey, *Marketing Staff*
Allyson Walker, *Instructor*
EMP: 88
SALES (corp-wide): 18.6MM **Privately Held**
WEB: www.ciymca.org
SIC: 8641 7991 8351 7032 Youth organizations; physical fitness facilities; child day care services; youth camps; individual & family services
PA: Channel Islands Young Men's Christian Association
105 E Carrillo St
Santa Barbara CA 93101
805 569-1103

(P-22331)
CHANNEL ISLNDS YUNG MNS CHRSTN
Also Called: Stuart C. Gildred Family YMCA
900 N Refugio Rd, Santa Ynez (93460-9314)
PHONE....................................805 686-2037
Paula Parisotto, *Branch Mgr*
Marcus Kocmur, *Vice Chairman*
Damon D Brink, *Treasurer*

Ayres Mitchell, *Marketing Staff*
EMP: 88
SALES (corp-wide): 18.6MM **Privately Held**
WEB: www.ciymca.org
SIC: 8641 7991 8351 7032 Youth organizations; physical fitness facilities; child day care services; youth camps; individual & family services
PA: Channel Islands Young Men's Christian Association
105 E Carrillo St
Santa Barbara CA 93101
805 569-1103

(P-22332)
CODING SCHOOL
12438 Landale St, Studio City
(91604-1220)
PHONE..................424 339-3977
Kiera Peltz, *CEO*
EMP: 70 **EST:** 2014
SALES (est): 1.5MM **Privately Held**
WEB: www.codeconnects.org
SIC: 8641 Civic social & fraternal associations

(P-22333)
CRENSHAW YMCA
3820 Santa Rosalia Dr, Los Angeles
(90008-2516)
PHONE..................323 290-9113
EMP: 70
SALES: 2MM **Privately Held**
SIC: 8641 7991 8351 7032 Civic/Social Association Physical Fitness Faclty Child Day Care Services Sport/Recreation Camp Individual/Family Svcs

(P-22334)
CRESCENTA-CANADA YMCA (PA)
Also Called: YMCA CRESCENTA-CANADA
1930 Foothill Blvd, La Canada
(91011-1933)
PHONE..................818 790-0123
Larry Hall, *CEO*
Ken Gorvetzian, *Ch of Bd*
Tina Vincent, *Branch Mgr*
Hillary Schenk, *Director*
EMP: 150 **EST:** 1953
SALES (est): 115.6K **Privately Held**
WEB: www.ymcafoothills.org
SIC: 8641 7991 8351 7032 Youth organizations; physical fitness facilities; child day care services; youth camps; individual & family services

(P-22335)
CRESCENTA-CANADA YMCA
Also Called: Learning Tree Pre-School
6840 Foothill Blvd, Tujunga (91042-2711)
PHONE..................818 352-3255
Kathi Brink, *Branch Mgr*
EMP: 130
SALES (corp-wide): 115.6K **Privately Held**
WEB: www.ymcafoothills.org
SIC: 8641 7991 8351 7032 Youth organizations; physical fitness facilities; child day care services; youth camps; individual & family services
PA: Crescenta-Canada Ymca
1930 Foothill Blvd
La Canada CA 91011
818 790-0123

(P-22336)
DS LAKESHORE LP
200 Baker St Ste 100, Costa Mesa
(92626-4551)
PHONE..................916 286-5231
Patrick S Donahue, *Partner*
Trina Perales, *Partner*
EMP: 99 **EST:** 2019
SALES (est): 221.8K **Privately Held**
SIC: 8641 Civic social & fraternal associations

(P-22337)
EXCEPTIONAL CHLD FOUNDATION
11124 Fairbanks Way, Culver City
(90230-4945)
PHONE..................310 915-6606
Scott Bowling, *Branch Mgr*

EMP: 132
SALES (corp-wide): 26.7MM **Privately Held**
WEB: www.ecf.net
SIC: 8641 Civic social & fraternal associations
PA: Exceptional Children's Foundation
5350 Machado Ln
Culver City CA 90230
310 204-3300

(P-22338)
FRIENDLY VLY RECRTL ASSN INC
Also Called: Friendly Village Cmnty Assn
19345 Avenue Of The Oaks, Santa Clarita
(91321-1406)
PHONE..................661 252-3223
Debbie Makaryk, *Manager*
Ruth Gauthier, *President*
Linda Raktke, *Manager*
EMP: 50 **EST:** 1966
SQ FT: 1,500
SALES (est): 2.3MM **Privately Held**
WEB: www.friendlyvalleycountryclubwebsite.com
SIC: 8641 Homeowners' association

(P-22339)
GIRL SCUTS GREATER LOS ANGELES (PA)
1150 S Olive St Fl 6, Los Angeles
(90015-2846)
PHONE..................626 677-2265
Lise Luttgens, *CEO*
Sylvia Rosenberger, *COO*
Christa Weddle, *Director*
EMP: 114
SALES: 20.9MM **Privately Held**
WEB: www.girlscoutsla.org
SIC: 8641 Girl Scout organization

(P-22340)
GREATER LOS ANGLES AREA CNCIL (PA)
2333 Scout Way, Los Angeles
(90026-4912)
PHONE..................213 413-4400
Cash Sutton, *President*
EMP: 92 **EST:** 1935
SALES (est): 8.3MM **Privately Held**
WEB: www.glaacbsa.org
SIC: 8641 Boy Scout organization

(P-22341)
HENTREL GREATHOUSE FOUNDATION
127 S 1st Ave, Barstow (92311-2827)
PHONE..................302 513-4056
David Taylor, *President*
EMP: 68 **EST:** 2015
SQ FT: 15,000
SALES (est): 729.5K **Privately Held**
SIC: 8641 Civic social & fraternal associations

(P-22342)
JEWISH CMNTY FNDN OF (PA)
6505 Wilshire Blvd, Los Angeles
(90048-4906)
PHONE..................323 761-8700
Richard V Sandler, *Ch of Bd*
J Sanderson, *President*
Jack Klein, *COO*
Ivan Wolkind, *COO*
Leslie E Bider, *Chairman*
EMP: 150
SQ FT: 100,000
SALES: 47.7MM **Privately Held**
WEB: www.jewishla.org
SIC: 8641 8661 Community membership club; religious organizations

(P-22343)
JONATHAN CLUB (PA)
545 S Figueroa St, Los Angeles
(90071-1793)
PHONE..................213 624-0881
Gregory J Dumas, *President*
Randolph P Sinnott, *CEO*
Emma Ivester, *CFO*
Susan Brown, *Treasurer*
Tim Dillon, *Vice Pres*
EMP: 200
SQ FT: 230,276

SALES: 39.4MM **Privately Held**
WEB: www.jc.org
SIC: 8641 Social club, membership

(P-22344)
LAKE FREST NO II MSTR HMWNERS
Also Called: Sun & Sail Club
24752 Toledo Ln, Lake Forest
(92630-2318)
PHONE..................949 586-0860
Sonny Morper, *President*
Jim Richert, *President*
Ted Brackez, *Principal*
Terri Graham, *Principal*
Ken Hedge, *Principal*
EMP: 80 **EST:** 1971
SQ FT: 9,000
SALES: 4.3MM **Privately Held**
WEB: www.liveinlakeforest.com
SIC: 8641 Homeowners' association

(P-22345)
LAKE MISSION VIEJO ASSOCIATION
22555 Olympiad Rd, Mission Viejo
(92692-1118)
PHONE..................949 770-1313
Fred Mellenbruch, *President*
Sid Wittenberg, *Treasurer*
Jane Chadburn, *Vice Pres*
Sen Jeff Miklaus, *Vice Pres*
Wayne Dunn, *Admin Sec*
EMP: 90
SQ FT: 7,400
SALES: 7.7MM **Privately Held**
WEB: www.lmvyc.org
SIC: 8641 Homeowners' association

(P-22346)
LOS ANGELES UNIFIED SCHOOL DST
Also Called: YWCA of La-Burbank Blvd
12215 Albers St, North Hollywood
(91607-2011)
PHONE..................818 763-6497
Melissa Nabong, *Manager*
EMP: 53
SALES (corp-wide): 9.3B **Privately Held**
WEB: www.laallcityband.com
SIC: 8211 8641 Public elementary & secondary schools; civic social & fraternal associations
PA: Los Angeles Unified School District
333 S Beaudry Ave Ste 209
Los Angeles CA 90017
213 241-1000

(P-22347)
MEMORIALCARE MED FOUNDATION (PA)
17360 Brookhurst St, Fountain Valley
(92708-3720)
PHONE..................714 389-5353
Sherry Sherman, *Purchasing*
Arden Whittaker, *Quality Imp Dir*
To-Van Vu, *Analyst*
Laura Hunt, *Research Analys*
Timothy Chen, *Director*
EMP: 122 **EST:** 2011
SALES: 524.9MM **Privately Held**
WEB: www.memorialcare.org
SIC: 8641 Civic social & fraternal associations

(P-22348)
MIDNIGHT MISSION (PA)
601 S San Pedro St, Los Angeles
(90014-2415)
PHONE..................213 624-9258
Michael Arnold, *CEO*
Larry Adamson, *President*
Donald Hold, *COO*
Arpit Jain, *CFO*
Glenn D Woody, *CFO*
EMP: 69 **EST:** 1926
SQ FT: 11,550
SALES (est): 6.5MM **Privately Held**
WEB: www.midnightmission.org
SIC: 8641 8322 Veterans' organization; senior citizens' center or association

(P-22349)
MILKEN FAMILY FOUNDATION
1250 4th St Fl 1, Santa Monica
(90401-1418)
PHONE..................310 570-4800
Lowell J Milken, *President*
Susan Fox, *CFO*
Gregory Milken, *Trustee*
Mariano Guzm'n, *Trustee*
Gary Panas, *Vice Pres*
EMP: 200 **EST:** 1986
SALES (est): 27.8MM **Privately Held**
WEB: www.mff.org
SIC: 8641 Civic social & fraternal associations

(P-22350)
MOORE FOUNDATIONS INC
7046 Darby Ave, Reseda (91335-4401)
PHONE..................818 698-4737
Ryan Moore, *CEO*
EMP: 50 **EST:** 2017
SALES (est): 3.4MM **Privately Held**
WEB: www.moorefoundationsinc.com
SIC: 8641 Civic social & fraternal associations

(P-22351)
MORNINGSIDE COMMUNITY ASSN
82 Mayfair Dr, Rancho Mirage
(92270-2562)
PHONE..................760 328-3323
M Abdelnour, *General Mgr*
Charles Meeks, *Security Dir*
Michelle Abdelnour, *General Mgr*
Cecilia Sanchez, *Controller*
EMP: 73 **EST:** 1983
SQ FT: 3,500
SALES (est): 4.9MM **Privately Held**
WEB: www.morningsideca.com
SIC: 8641 Homeowners' association

(P-22352)
MRCA FIRE DIVISION
1670 Las Virgenes Cyn Rd, Calabasas
(91302-1920)
PHONE..................818 880-4752
Ken Nelson, *COO*
Jakub Slovacek, *Officer*
EMP: 50 **EST:** 2016
SALES (est): 792.5K **Privately Held**
SIC: 8641 Environmental protection organization

(P-22353)
ORANGE CNTY CNCIL BOY SCUTS AM (PA)
2 Irvine Park Rd, Orange (92869-1000)
PHONE..................714 546-4990
Les Baron, *President*
Robert Neal, *Ch of Bd*
Jeffrie A Herrmann, *President*
Larry Behm, *Principal*
Thomas Hartmann, *Exec Dir*
EMP: 65 **EST:** 1910
SALES (est): 10.1MM **Privately Held**
WEB: www.ocbsa.org
SIC: 8641 Boy Scout organization

(P-22354)
PALM DESERT GREENS ASSOCIATION
73750 Country Club Dr, Palm Desert
(92260-8663)
PHONE..................760 346-8005
Roberta Hollingsworth, *General Mgr*
Ken Dobson, *President*
Mal Sinclair, *Treasurer*
Roberta Reynolds, *General Mgr*
Barbara Houcek, *Human Res Mgr*
EMP: 75 **EST:** 1971
SQ FT: 12,400
SALES: 7.4MM **Privately Held**
WEB: www.pdgcc.com
SIC: 8641 Homeowners' association

(P-22355)
PALM DESERT RESORTER ASSN
77333 Country Club Dr B, Palm Desert
(92211-9231)
P.O. Box 12765 (92255-2765)
PHONE..................760 345-1954
Edwin Kraus, *President*

Christina Villarreal, *Manager*
EMP: 66 **EST:** 1980
SQ FT: 900
SALES (est): 2.6MM **Privately Held**
WEB: www.pdrhoa.org
SIC: 8641 Homeowners' association

(P-22356)
PHOENIX CLUB INC
Also Called: German Association Orange
Cnty
1340 S Sanderson Ave, Anaheim
(92806-5629)
PHONE..........................714 224-0194
Walter Bretthauer, *President*
EMP: 60 **EST:** 1961
SALES (est): 2.7MM **Privately Held**
WEB: www.thephoenixclub.com
SIC: 5812 8641 American restaurant; fra-
ternal associations

(P-22357)
PRO-YOUTH
Also Called: Pro-Youth Heart
505 N Court St, Visalia (93291-4912)
P.O. Box 387 (93279-0387)
PHONE..........................559 374-2030
Daryn Davis, *CEO*
Teresa Ramos, *Executive Asst*
Judy Gibson, *Human Resources*
Lou Fernandez, *Opers Dir*
Linda Brighton, *Director*
EMP: 260 **EST:** 1993
SQ FT: 1,400
SALES: 11.5MM **Privately Held**
WEB: www.proyouthexpandedlearning.org
SIC: 8641 Youth organizations

(P-22358)
PTA CA CNGRESS OF PARNTS PALM
5025 Palm Dr, La Canada (91011-1518)
PHONE..........................818 952-8360
Karen Hurley, *Principal*
Melissa Mazin, *President*
Kerry Russell, *Admin Sec*
EMP: 70
SALES: 144.1K **Privately Held**
WEB: www.palmcrestpta.membership-
toolkit.com
SIC: 8211 8641 Elementary school; par-
ent-teachers' association

(P-22359)
PTA CALIFORNIA CONGRESS OF PAR
Also Called: Annie R Mitchell Elementary
2121 E Laura Ave, Visalia (93292-1407)
PHONE..........................559 622-3195
Loreta Bryant, *Principal*
EMP: 50 **EST:** 2013
SALES: 180.2K **Privately Held**
SIC: 8641 Parent-teachers' association

(P-22360)
PTAC RAIL RANCH ELEM SCHOOL
25030 Via Santee, Murrieta (92563-5020)
PHONE..........................951 696-1404
Hunter Wethers, *Principal*
EMP: 60
SALES: 22.8K **Privately Held**
WEB: www.murrieta.k12.ca.us
SIC: 8641 Parent-teachers' association

(P-22361)
PUBLIC HLTH FNDATION ENTPS INC (PA)
Also Called: Heluna Health
13300 Crssrds Pkwy N, City of Industry
(91746)
PHONE..........................800 201-7320
Blain Cutler, *President*
Eric Ramanathan, *Ch of Bd*
Devecchio Finley, *Vice Chairman*
Gerald D Jensen, *President*
Michael R Gomez, *CEO*
EMP: 1071 **EST:** 1968
SQ FT: 25,000 **Privately Held**
WEB: www.helunahealth.org
SIC: 8641 Civic social & fraternal associa-
tions

(P-22362)
RECREATIONAL ASSN CORCORAN
Also Called: RAC
900 Dairy Ave, Corcoran (93212-2114)
P.O. Box 176 (93212-0176)
PHONE..........................559 992-5171
S S Brown, *Exec Dir*
Jim Razor, *President*
EMP: 63 **EST:** 2015
SALES (est): 1.8MM **Privately Held**
WEB: www.cityofcorcoran.com
SIC: 8641 8699 Recreation association;
charitable organization

(P-22363)
ROSARY ACADEMY PARENT COUNCIL
1340 N Acacia Ave, Fullerton (92831-1202)
PHONE..........................714 879-6302
Patty Weller, *President*
Kathryn Hennigan, *Principal*
Debbie Simonton, *Dept Chairman*
Tracy Drummer, *Finance Asst*
Jill Christensen, *Teacher*
EMP: 56 **EST:** 1968
SALES (est): 3.5MM **Privately Held**
WEB: www.rosaryacademy.org
SIC: 8641 Parent-teachers' association

(P-22364)
SAN LUIS OBISPO COUNTY YMCA
5785 Los Ranchos Rd, San Luis Obispo
(93401-8247)
PHONE..........................805 544-7225
Mike Robertson, *Director*
Dee Steele, *Personnel Assit*
Rachel Cementina, *Director*
EMP: 72
SALES (corp-wide): 2.5MM **Privately
Held**
WEB: www.sloymca.org
SIC: 8641 7991 8351 7032 Youth organi-
zations; physical fitness facilities; child
day care services; youth camps; individ-
ual & family services
PA: San Luis Obispo County Ymca Inc
1020 Southwood Dr
San Luis Obispo CA 93401
805 543-8235

(P-22365)
SANTA MONICA FAMILY YMCA
1332 6th St, Santa Monica (90401-1604)
P.O. Box 1160 (90406-1160)
PHONE..........................310 451-7387
Tara Pomposini, *Director*
Pam Andrews, *Associate*
EMP: 53 **EST:** 1901
SQ FT: 157,000
SALES (est): 4.3MM **Privately Held**
WEB: www.ymcasm.org
SIC: 8641 8351 8322 Youth organiza-
tions; child day care services; individual &
family services

(P-22366)
SANTA MRIA VLY YUNG MNS CHRSTN
Also Called: YMCA
3400 Skyway Dr, Santa Maria
(93455-2504)
PHONE..........................805 937-8521
Shannon Seifert, *Exec Dir*
Dave Wright, *Treasurer*
Kevin James, *Admin Sec*
Diana Borjas, *Facilities Dir*
Chris Kiser, *Facilities Dir*
EMP: 120 **EST:** 1980
SQ FT: 22,000
SALES (est): 3.8MM **Privately Held**
WEB: www.smvymca.org
SIC: 8641 7991 8351 7032 Youth organi-
zations; physical fitness facilities; child
day care services; youth camps; individ-
ual & family services

(P-22367)
SAVICE INC
30052 Tomas, Rcho STA Marg
(92688-2127)
PHONE..........................949 888-2444
Phu Hoang, *Principal*
EMP: 98

SALES (est): 71K **Privately Held**
SIC: 8641 Civic social & fraternal associations

(P-22368)
SIGNAL HEALTH POLICE DEPT
2745 Walnut Ave, Signal Hill (90755-1831)
PHONE..........................562 989-7200
Christopher Nunley, *Chief*
EMP: 50 **EST:** 2011
SALES (est): 45.5K **Privately Held**
WEB: www.cityofsignalhill.org
SIC: 8641 Civic social & fraternal associa-
tions

(P-22369)
SILVER LAKES ASSOCIATION
Also Called: Homeowners Association
15273 Orchard Hill Ln, Helendale
(92342-7824)
P.O. Box 179 (92342-0179)
PHONE..........................760 245-1606
Michael Bennett, *General Mgr*
Susan Bellani, *General Mgr*
Westly Campbell, *Opers Mgr*
Darcey Irvine, *Director*
Kerriann Dershem, *Manager*
EMP: 90 **EST:** 1976
SQ FT: 3,000
SALES (est): 5MM **Privately Held**
WEB: www.silverlakesassociation.com
SIC: 8641 Homeowners' association

(P-22370)
SUN CITY PALM DSERT CMNTY ASSN (PA)
Also Called: Palm Desert Community Assn
38180 Del Webb Blvd, Palm Desert
(92211-1256)
PHONE..........................760 200-2100
Helen McEnerney, *President*
Flor Limon, *Human Res Mgr*
Vanessa Schussler, *Opers Staff*
Erik Stacklie, *Director*
EMP: 80 **EST:** 1992
SQ FT: 4,000
SALES (est): 16.7MM **Privately Held**
WEB: www.scpdca.com
SIC: 8641 7992 7997 Dwelling-related as-
sociations; public golf courses; country
club, membership

(P-22371)
TEMECULA VLY UNIFIED SCHL DST
Also Called: Pauba Valley Elem. School
33125 Regina Dr, Temecula (92592-1473)
PHONE..........................951 302-5140
Kelli Sutherlands, *Principal*
Kelli Sunderland, *Administration*
Elena Barrios, *Teacher*
Angela Claybaugh, *Teacher*
Sandy Coward, *Teacher*
EMP: 70
SALES (corp-wide): 345.7MM **Privately
Held**
WEB: www.tvusd.k12.ca.us
SIC: 8211 8641 Public elementary school;
parent-teachers' association
PA: Temecula Valley Unified School District
School Facilities Corporation
31350 Rancho Vista Rd
Temecula CA 92592
951 676-2661

(P-22372)
TUSTIN MEMORIAL ACADEMY
Also Called: Tustin Memorial Academy Pto
12712 Browning Ave, Santa Ana
(92705-3465)
PHONE..........................714 730-7546
EMP: 82
SALES (corp-wide): 317.3MM **Privately
Held**
WEB: www.ocorganicgardenblog.com
SIC: 8641 Parent-teachers' association
HQ: Tustin Memorial Academy
12712 Browning Ave
Santa Ana CA 92705

(P-22373)
UNITED BYS GRLS CLUBS SNTA BRB
Also Called: Boys & Girls Club
5701 Hollister Ave, Goleta (93117-3420)
P.O. Box 1485, Santa Barbara (93102-
1485)
PHONE..........................805 967-1612
Sal Rodriguez, *Exec Dir*
Priscilla Hernandez, *Vice Pres*
Tina Ballue, *Director*
Chelsea Lincoln, *Director*
Jose Marquez, *Director*
EMP: 71
SALES (corp-wide): 3.7MM **Privately
Held**
WEB: www.unitedbg.org
SIC: 8641 8351 Bars & restaurants, mem-
bers only; community membership club;
youth organizations; child day care serv-
ices
PA: United Boys And Girls Clubs Of Santa
Barbara County
1124 Castillo St
Santa Barbara CA 93101
805 681-1315

(P-22374)
VALLEY HUNT CLUB
520 S Orange Grove Blvd, Pasadena
(91105-1799)
PHONE..........................626 793-7134
David Mole, *CEO*
Donald F Crumrine, *COO*
Kathleen Santos, *Comms Dir*
Bill Roemer, *Controller*
Dave Gieselman, *Purch Dir*
EMP: 85 **EST:** 1888
SQ FT: 40,000
SALES: 8.8MM **Privately Held**
WEB: www.valleyhuntclub.com
SIC: 8641 Social club membership

(P-22375)
WEST END YUNG MNS CHRISTN ASSN
Also Called: Ontario/Montclair YMCA
1257 E D St, Ontario (91764-4329)
P.O. Box 3220 (91760-0922)
PHONE..........................909 477-2780
Dianna Lee-Mitchell, *Director*
EMP: 115 **Privately Held**
WEB: www.weymca.org
SIC: 8641 7991 8351 7032 Youth organi-
zations; physical fitness facilities; child
day care services; youth camps; individ-
ual & family services
PA: West End Young Men's Christian Asso-
ciation Inc
1150 E Foothill Blvd
Upland CA 91786
909 481-0722

(P-22376)
WEST END YUNG MNS CHRISTN ASSN
Also Called: Chino Valley YMCA
5665 Edison Ave, Chino (91710-9051)
PHONE..........................909 597-7445
Deb Anderson, *Director*
EMP: 115 **Privately Held**
WEB: www.weymca.org
SIC: 8641 7991 8351 7032 Youth organi-
zations; physical fitness facilities; child
day care services; youth camps; individ-
ual & family services
PA: West End Young Men's Christian Asso-
ciation Inc
1150 E Foothill Blvd
Upland CA 91786
909 481-0722

(P-22377)
WOMENSHELTER OF LONG BEACH
Also Called: RESOURCE CENTER
4201 Long Beach Blvd # 102, Long Beach
(90807-2010)
P.O. Box 17098 (90807-7098)
PHONE..........................562 437-7233
Virginia Corbett, *Founder*
Kristi Fischer, *Principal*
Mary Mitchell, *Exec Dir*
EMP: 50 **EST:** 1902
SQ FT: 5,000

SALES: 1.9MM **Privately Held**
WEB: www.womenshelterlb.org
SIC: 8641 Civic associations; youth organizations

(P-22378)
WOODBRIDGE VILLAGE ASSOCIATION
31 Creek Rd, Irvine (92604-4793)
PHONE..................949 786-1800
Kevin Chudy, *Exec Dir*
Bertha Rivera, *Admin Sec*
Matt Nawabi, *Accountant*
Santiago Arteaga, *Maint Spvr*
Anne Sheldon,
EMP: 65 **EST:** 1976
SQ FT: 15,000
SALES (est): 11.4MM **Privately Held**
WEB: www.account.wva.org
SIC: 8641 Homeowners' association

(P-22379)
WORLD MVIE AWRDS ORGNZTION WMA
9171 Wilshire Blvd 500a, Beverly Hills (90210-5530)
PHONE..................833 375-5857
Lily Alphonsis, *CEO*
Royal Vincent, *CFO*
EMP: 99 **EST:** 2018
SALES (est): 452.6K **Privately Held**
WEB: www.worldmovieawards.org
SIC: 8641 Civic social & fraternal associations

(P-22380)
YMCA OF EAST VALLEY (PA)
500 E Citrus Ave, Redlands (92373-5285)
PHONE..................909 798-9622
Darwin Barnett, *CEO*
Ken Stein, *CEO*
Kevin Pearson, *COO*
Doug Thorne, *CFO*
Perry Mecate, *Vice Pres*
EMP: 125 **EST:** 1887
SQ FT: 100,000
SALES: 14.5MM **Privately Held**
WEB: www.ymcaeastvalley.org
SIC: 8641 Youth organizations

(P-22381)
YMCA OF EAST VALLEY
Also Called: YMCA Camp Edwards
42842 Jenks Lake Rd E, Angelus Oaks (92305-9769)
P.O. Box 277 (92305-0277)
PHONE..................909 794-1702
Loren Werner, *Director*
EMP: 77
SALES (corp-wide): 14.5MM **Privately Held**
WEB: www.ymcaeastvalley.org
SIC: 8641 7991 8351 7032 Youth organizations; physical fitness facilities; child day care services; youth camps; individual & family services
PA: Ymca Of The East Valley
500 E Citrus Ave
Redlands CA 92373
909 798-9622

(P-22382)
YMCA OF EAST VALLEY
Also Called: San Bernardino Family YMCA
808 E 21st St, San Bernardino (92404-4874)
PHONE..................909 881-9622
Bill Blank, *Director*
EMP: 77
SALES (corp-wide): 14.5MM **Privately Held**
WEB: www.ymcaeastvalley.org
SIC: 8641 7991 8351 7032 Youth organizations; physical fitness facilities; child day care services; youth camps; individual & family services
PA: Ymca Of The East Valley
500 E Citrus Ave
Redlands CA 92373
909 798-9622

(P-22383)
YMCA OF EAST VALLEY
Also Called: Young Mens Christn Assocation
7793 Central Ave, Highland (92346-4106)
PHONE..................909 425-9622

Ursula Walsh, *Branch Mgr*
Karli Maxfield, *Mktg Dir*
Damon Needelman, *Director*
Roshelle Ogden, *Director*
EMP: 77
SALES (corp-wide): 14.5MM **Privately Held**
WEB: www.ymcaeastvalley.org
SIC: 8641 7991 8351 7032 Youth organizations; physical fitness facilities; child day care services; youth camps; individual & family services
PA: Ymca Of The East Valley
500 E Citrus Ave
Redlands CA 92373
909 798-9622

(P-22384)
YOUNG MENS CHRISTIAN ASSOCIAT
Also Called: Downtown Community Dev YMCA
525 E 7th St, Long Beach (90813-4559)
PHONE..................562 624-2376
EMP: 99
SALES: 3.3MM **Privately Held**
SIC: 8641 7991 8351 7032 Civic/Social Association Physical Fitness Faclty Child Day Care Services Sport/Recreation Camp Individual/Family Svcs

(P-22385)
YOUNG MNS CHRSTN ASSN BRBANK C (PA)
Also Called: YMCA
321 E Magnolia Blvd, Burbank (91502-1132)
PHONE..................818 845-8551
JC Holt, *CEO*
Robert Rodriguez, *Marketing Staff*
Susan Sebastian, *Marketing Staff*
Naeiri Didarlou, *Instructor*
Nidia Reyes, *Instructor*
EMP: 100 **EST:** 1924
SQ FT: 47,000
SALES (est): 5.9MM **Privately Held**
WEB: www.burbankymca.org
SIC: 8641 7991 8351 7032 Youth organizations; physical fitness facilities; child day care services; youth camps; individual & family services

(P-22386)
YOUNG MNS CHRSTN ASSN MTRO LOS (PA)
Also Called: YMCA
625 S New Hampshire Ave, Los Angeles (90005-1342)
PHONE..................213 380-6448
Alan Hostrup, *President*
W J Ellison, *Ch of Bd*
Dan Cooper, *CFO*
Daniel Levin, *CFO*
Dana Lipman, *Officer*
EMP: 70 **EST:** 1887
SQ FT: 16,000
SALES: 119.1MM **Privately Held**
WEB: www.ymcala.org
SIC: 8641 Youth organizations

(P-22387)
YOUNG MNS CHRSTN ASSN OF GLNDA
Also Called: GLENDALE YMCA SWIM SCHOOL
140 N Louise St, Glendale (91206-4226)
PHONE..................818 484-8256
Tom Tyler, *CEO*
Cidinha Agamy, *Personnel*
Jose Sanchez, *Facilities Dir*
Catherine Gharapetian, *Director*
Norberto Montalvan, *Director*
EMP: 86 **EST:** 1924
SQ FT: 15,000
SALES (est): 4.9MM **Privately Held**
WEB: www.glendaleymca.org
SIC: 8641 Youth organizations

(P-22388)
YOUNG MNS CHRSTN ASSN STHAST V
Also Called: Simi YMCA Elementary Site
2925 Fletcher St, Simi Valley (93065-5270)
PHONE..................805 520-6775
Leann Olsen, *Branch Mgr*

EMP: 50
SALES (corp-wide): 10.2MM **Privately Held**
WEB: www.sevymca.org
SIC: 8641 8322 7999 Youth organizations; youth center; recreation center
PA: Young Men's Christian Association Of Southeast Ventura County
31105 E Thusand Oaks Blvd
Thousand Oaks CA 91362
805 497-3081

(P-22389)
YOUNG MNS CHRSTN ASSN STHAST V
Also Called: YMCA Simi Valley Family
828 Gibson Ave, Simi Valley (93065-5665)
PHONE..................805 527-5730
Kelly Stimac, *Manager*
Tori Dziedziak, *Director*
EMP: 50
SALES (corp-wide): 10.2MM **Privately Held**
WEB: www.sevymca.org
SIC: 8641 7991 8351 7032 Youth organizations; physical fitness facilities; child day care services; youth camps; individual & family services
PA: Young Men's Christian Association Of Southeast Ventura County
31105 E Thusand Oaks Blvd
Thousand Oaks CA 91362
805 497-3081

(P-22390)
YOUNG MNS CHRSTN ASSN STHAST V
4031 N Moorpark Rd, Thousand Oaks (91360-2660)
PHONE..................805 523-7613
Kelly Dulek, *Director*
Peter Penna, *Risk Mgmt Dir*
Annie Dyess, *Exec Dir*
Danielle Glezer, *Office Mgr*
Canaan Stanley,
EMP: 50
SALES (corp-wide): 10.2MM **Privately Held**
WEB: www.sevymca.org
SIC: 8641 7997 8351 Youth organizations; membership sports & recreation clubs; child day care services
PA: Young Men's Christian Association Of Southeast Ventura County
31105 E Thusand Oaks Blvd
Thousand Oaks CA 91362
805 497-3081

(P-22391)
YOUNG WNS CHRSTN ASSN GRTER LO
Also Called: YWCA
2501 W Vernon Ave, Los Angeles (90008-3927)
PHONE..................323 295-4280
Jozella Reed, *Administration*
Hanan Johnson, *Manager*
EMP: 91
SALES (corp-wide): 29.3MM **Privately Held**
WEB: www.ywcagla.org
SIC: 8641 Youth organizations
PA: Young Women's Christian Association Of Greater Los Angeles, California
1020 S Olive St Fl 7
Los Angeles CA 90015
213 365-2991

(P-22392)
YOUNG WNS CHRSTN ASSN GRTER LO
Also Called: Angeles Mesa YWCA Chldren Lrng
2519 W Vernon Ave, Los Angeles (90008-3927)
PHONE..................323 295-4288
Hertistine Taylor, *Director*
Paulino Raguindin, *Accountant*
May Chen Tham, *Manager*
EMP: 91
SALES (corp-wide): 29.3MM **Privately Held**
WEB: www.ywcagla.org
SIC: 8641 8351 Youth organizations; child day care services

PA: Young Women's Christian Association Of Greater Los Angeles, California
1020 S Olive St Fl 7
Los Angeles CA 90015
213 365-2991

8651 Political Organizations

(P-22393)
COUNTY OF ORANGE
Also Called: Registrar of Voters
1300 S Grand Ave Ste C, Santa Ana (92705-4402)
P.O. Box 11298 (92711-1298)
PHONE..................714 567-7422
Neal Kelly, *Director*
Matt Eimers, *Supervisor*
EMP: 50
SALES (corp-wide): 4.3B **Privately Held**
WEB: www.ocgov.com
SIC: 8651 9199 Political campaign organization; general government administration;
PA: County Of Orange
333 W Santa Ana Blvd
Santa Ana CA 92701
714 834-6200

8699 Membership Organizations, NEC

(P-22394)
AGUA CLNTE BAND CHILLA INDIANS (PA)
5401 Dinah Shore Dr, Palm Springs (92264-5970)
PHONE..................760 699-6800
Jeff L Grubbe, *Chairman*
Vincent Gonzales III, *Corp Secy*
Larry N Olinger, *Principal*
Stone Robin, *Exec Dir*
Rebecca Mejia, *Admin Asst*
EMP: 661 **EST:** 1988
SALES (est): 194.2MM **Privately Held**
WEB: www.aguacaliente.org
SIC: 8699 6552 7999 Reading rooms & other cultural organizations; subdividers & developers; tour & guide services

(P-22395)
ALLBRIGHT GROUP LA LLC
8474 Melrose Pl, Los Angeles (90069-5308)
PHONE..................310 402-3570
Azzi Kashani,
EMP: 50 **EST:** 2018
SALES (est): 410.2K **Privately Held**
SIC: 8699 Membership organizations

(P-22396)
AUTOMOBILE CLUB SOUTHERN CAL
Also Called: AAA - Auto CLB Southern Cal
6787 Carnelian St Ste A, Rancho Cucamonga (91701-4564)
PHONE..................909 477-8600
EMP: 70
SALES (corp-wide): 1B **Privately Held**
WEB: www.ace.aaa.com
SIC: 8699 Automobile owners' association
PA: Automobile Club Of Southern California
2601 S Figueroa St
Los Angeles CA 90007
213 741-3686

(P-22397)
AUTOMOBILE CLUB SOUTHERN CAL
25125 Madison Ave 101a, Murrieta (92562-8969)
PHONE..................951 304-3077
Brian McClendon, *Branch Mgr*
Hanson Gregory, *Comp Spec*
Vanessa Marie, *Business Mgr*
Cocotis Randa, *Analyst*
McGinty Sean, *Opers Mgr*
EMP: 70
SALES (corp-wide): 1B **Privately Held**
WEB: www.ace.aaa.com
SIC: 8699 Automobile owners' association

PRODUCTS & SVCS

PA: Automobile Club Of Southern California
2601 S Figueroa St
Los Angeles CA 90007
213 741-3686

(P-22398)
AUTOMOBILE CLUB SOUTHERN CAL
Also Called: A A A Automobile Club So Cal
13331 Jamboree Rd, Irvine (92602)
P.O. Box 11763, Santa Ana (92711-1763)
PHONE...................714 973-1211
Sid Munger, *Manager*
EMP: 70
SALES (corp-wide): 1B **Privately Held**
WEB: www.ace.aaa.com
SIC: 8699 Automobile owners' association
PA: Automobile Club Of Southern California
2601 S Figueroa St
Los Angeles CA 90007
213 741-3686

(P-22399)
AUTOMOBILE CLUB SOUTHERN CAL
Also Called: AAA
15503 Ventura Blvd # 150, Encino
(91436-3115)
PHONE...................818 997-6230
Jim Okun, *Branch Mgr*
Michael Gray,
EMP: 70
SALES (corp-wide): 1B **Privately Held**
WEB: www.ace.aaa.com
SIC: 8699 4724 6331 Automobile owners' association; travel agencies; fire, marine & casualty insurance
PA: Automobile Club Of Southern California
2601 S Figueroa St
Los Angeles CA 90007
213 741-3686

(P-22400)
AUTOMOBILE CLUB SOUTHERN CAL
3712 State St, Santa Barbara
(93105-3135)
PHONE...................805 682-5811
Nancy Alexander, *Branch Mgr*
Jamil Green,
Gianna Sayre, *Agent*
EMP: 70
SALES (corp-wide): 1B **Privately Held**
WEB: www.ace.aaa.com
SIC: 8699 Automobile owners' association
PA: Automobile Club Of Southern California
2601 S Figueroa St
Los Angeles CA 90007
213 741-3686

(P-22401)
AUTOMOBILE CLUB SOUTHERN CAL
Also Called: A A A
27889 Baseline St, Highland (92346-3325)
PHONE...................909 381-2211
Ross Corner, *Branch Mgr*
EMP: 70
SQ FT: 14,894
SALES (corp-wide): 1B **Privately Held**
WEB: www.ace.aaa.com
SIC: 8699 Automobile owners' association
PA: Automobile Club Of Southern California
2601 S Figueroa St
Los Angeles CA 90007
213 741-3686

(P-22402)
AUTOMOBILE CLUB SOUTHERN CAL
Also Called: AAA
1445 Calle Joaquin, San Luis Obispo
(93405-7203)
PHONE...................805 543-6454
Darlene Lair, *Branch Mgr*
Brian Farrell, *Broker*
EMP: 70
SALES (corp-wide): 1B **Privately Held**
WEB: www.ace.aaa.com
SIC: 8699 Automobile owners' association
PA: Automobile Club Of Southern California
2601 S Figueroa St
Los Angeles CA 90007
213 741-3686

(P-22403)
AUTOMOBILE CLUB SOUTHERN CAL
Also Called: AAA
100 E Wilbur Rd, Thousand Oaks
(91360-5564)
P.O. Box 1046 (91358-0046)
PHONE...................805 497-0911
Chris Davis, *Branch Mgr*
EMP: 70
SALES (corp-wide): 1B **Privately Held**
WEB: www.ace.aaa.com
SIC: 8699 Automobile owners' association
PA: Automobile Club Of Southern California
2601 S Figueroa St
Los Angeles CA 90007
213 741-3686

(P-22404)
AUTOMOBILE CLUB SOUTHERN CAL
Also Called: AAA
23001 Hawthorne Blvd, Torrance
(90505-3702)
P.O. Box 4298 (90510-4298)
PHONE...................310 325-3111
Bud Hudson, *Branch Mgr*
Gloria Gutierrez, *Admin Sec*
Melissa Coburn, *Agent*
EMP: 70
SQ FT: 34,720
SALES (corp-wide): 1B **Privately Held**
WEB: www.ace.aaa.com
SIC: 8699 Automobile owners' association
PA: Automobile Club Of Southern California
2601 S Figueroa St
Los Angeles CA 90007
213 741-3686

(P-22405)
AUTOMOBILE CLUB SOUTHERN CAL
Also Called: AAA
1501 S Victoria Ave, Ventura (93003-6539)
P.O. Box 3618 (93006-3618)
PHONE...................805 644-7171
Sigmund Grant, *Manager*
EMP: 70
SALES (corp-wide): 1B **Privately Held**
WEB: www.ace.aaa.com
SIC: 8699 4724 6331 Automobile owners' association; travel agencies; fire, marine & casualty insurance
PA: Automobile Club Of Southern California
2601 S Figueroa St
Los Angeles CA 90007
213 741-3686

(P-22406)
AUTOMOBILE CLUB SOUTHERN CAL
Also Called: AAA
420 N Euclid St, Anaheim (92801-5505)
PHONE...................714 774-2392
Conny Kuhm, *Manager*
EMP: 70
SALES (corp-wide): 1B **Privately Held**
WEB: www.ace.aaa.com
SIC: 8699 Automobile owners' association
PA: Automobile Club Of Southern California
2601 S Figueroa St
Los Angeles CA 90007
213 741-3686

(P-22407)
AUTOMOBILE CLUB SOUTHERN CAL
Also Called: AAA
1301s S Grand Ave, Glendora
(91740-5040)
PHONE...................626 963-8531
Connie Stelzer, *Manager*
Natalie Baudino, *Agent*
Perez Glendy, *Agent*
EMP: 70
SQ FT: 8,261
SALES (corp-wide): 1B **Privately Held**
WEB: www.ace.aaa.com
SIC: 8699 Automobile owners' association
PA: Automobile Club Of Southern California
2601 S Figueroa St
Los Angeles CA 90007
213 741-3686

(P-22408)
AUTOMOBILE CLUB SOUTHERN CAL
Also Called: AAA
401 E Main St Ste 101, Alhambra
(91801-3920)
P.O. Box 533, San Gabriel (91778-0533)
PHONE...................626 289-4491
Diana Price, *Branch Mgr*
EMP: 70
SALES (corp-wide): 1B **Privately Held**
WEB: www.ace.aaa.com
SIC: 8699 Automobile owners' association
PA: Automobile Club Of Southern California
2601 S Figueroa St
Los Angeles CA 90007
213 741-3686

(P-22409)
AUTOMOBILE CLUB SOUTHERN CAL
Also Called: AAA
1330 Industrial Park Ave, Redlands
(92374-2825)
PHONE...................909 793-3357
Jan Scearce, *Manager*
EMP: 70
SQ FT: 11,216
SALES (corp-wide): 1B **Privately Held**
WEB: www.ace.aaa.com
SIC: 8699 Automobile owners' association
PA: Automobile Club Of Southern California
2601 S Figueroa St
Los Angeles CA 90007
213 741-3686

(P-22410)
AUTOMOBILE CLUB SOUTHERN CAL
Also Called: AAA
1500 Commercial Way, Bakersfield
(93309-0625)
PHONE...................661 327-4661
Jeff Goldsmith, *Branch Mgr*
Paul Polacek, *Branch Mgr*
Annette Mojica, *Agent*
EMP: 70
SALES (corp-wide): 1B **Privately Held**
WEB: www.ace.aaa.com
SIC: 8699 Automobile owners' association
PA: Automobile Club Of Southern California
2601 S Figueroa St
Los Angeles CA 90007
213 741-3686

(P-22411)
AUTOMOBILE CLUB SOUTHERN CAL
Also Called: A A A Automobile Club
420 E Huntington Dr, Arcadia (91006-3748)
PHONE...................626 445-6687
Deborah Dario, *Branch Mgr*
Gina Dizon, *Financial Analy*
EMP: 70
SQ FT: 24,374
SALES (corp-wide): 1B **Privately Held**
WEB: www.ace.aaa.com
SIC: 8699 Automobile owners' association
PA: Automobile Club Of Southern California
2601 S Figueroa St
Los Angeles CA 90007
213 741-3686

(P-22412)
AUTOMOBILE CLUB SOUTHERN CAL
Also Called: AAA
5500 E Santa Ana Cyn Rd, Anaheim
(92807-3154)
PHONE...................714 921-2850
Louisa Solis, *Branch Mgr*
Crystal Bessant,
EMP: 70
SQ FT: 32,639
SALES (corp-wide): 1B **Privately Held**
WEB: www.ace.aaa.com
SIC: 8699 Automobile owners' association
PA: Automobile Club Of Southern California
2601 S Figueroa St
Los Angeles CA 90007
213 741-3686

(P-22413)
AUTOMOBILE CLUB SOUTHERN CAL
Also Called: AAA
9440 Reseda Blvd, Northridge
(91324-6014)
PHONE...................818 993-1616
Poonam Ravdjee, *Sales Staff*
Sylvia Andrews, *Agent*
EMP: 70
SQ FT: 15,624
SALES (corp-wide): 1B **Privately Held**
WEB: www.ace.aaa.com
SIC: 8699 Automobile owners' association
PA: Automobile Club Of Southern California
2601 S Figueroa St
Los Angeles CA 90007
213 741-3686

(P-22414)
AUTOMOBILE CLUB SOUTHERN CAL
Also Called: AAA
8223 Firestone Blvd, Downey
(90241-4809)
PHONE...................562 904-5970
Mirtha Rodriguez, *Branch Mgr*
EMP: 70
SALES (corp-wide): 1B **Privately Held**
WEB: www.ace.aaa.com
SIC: 8699 Automobile owners' association
PA: Automobile Club Of Southern California
2601 S Figueroa St
Los Angeles CA 90007
213 741-3686

(P-22415)
AUTOMOBILE CLUB SOUTHERN CAL
Also Called: A A A Automobile Club So Cal
300 S Farrell Dr, Palm Springs
(92262-7906)
PHONE...................760 320-1121
Joe Casaletti, *Branch Mgr*
EMP: 70
SALES (corp-wide): B **Privately Held**
WEB: www.ace.aaa.com
SIC: 8699 Automobile owners' association
PA: Automobile Club Of Southern California
2601 S Figueroa St
Los Angeles CA 90007
213 741-3686

(P-22416)
AUTOMOBILE CLUB SOUTHERN CAL
Also Called: AAA
700 S Aviation Blvd, Manhattan Beach
(90266-7106)
PHONE...................310 376-0521
John Dm, *Manager*
Sherry Major, *Agent*
EMP: 70
SQ FT: 7,815
SALES (corp-wide): 1B **Privately Held**
WEB: www.ace.aaa.com
SIC: 8699 Automobile owners' association
PA: Automobile Club Of Southern California
2601 S Figueroa St
Los Angeles CA 90007
213 741-3686

(P-22417)
AUTOMOBILE CLUB SOUTHERN CAL
Also Called: A A A Automobile Club So Cal
801 E Union St, Pasadena (91101-1885)
PHONE...................626 795-0601
Teresa Martinez, *Manager*
EMP: 70
SQ FT: 12,326
SALES (corp-wide): 1B **Privately Held**
WEB: www.ace.aaa.com
SIC: 8699 Automobile owners' association
PA: Automobile Club Of Southern California
2601 S Figueroa St
Los Angeles CA 90007
213 741-3686

(P-22418)
AUTOMOBILE CLUB SOUTHERN CAL
3880 Birch St, Newport Beach
(92660-2669)
PHONE...................................949 476-8880
Cindy Kitchens, *Manager*
David Stacy, *Supervisor*
EMP: 70
SQ FT: 14,794
SALES (corp-wide): 1B **Privately Held**
WEB: www.ace.aaa.com
SIC: 8699 Automobile owners' association
PA: Automobile Club Of Southern California
2601 S Figueroa St
Los Angeles CA 90007
213 741-3686

(P-22419)
AUTOMOBILE CLUB SOUTHERN CAL
Also Called: AAA
2112 Montrose Ave, Montrose
(91020-1508)
PHONE...................................818 249-3971
Freidie Forrest, *Manager*
Janine Goodsell, *Agent*
EMP: 70
SALES (corp-wide): 1B **Privately Held**
WEB: www.ace.aaa.com
SIC: 8699 Automobile owners' association
PA: Automobile Club Of Southern California
2601 S Figueroa St
Los Angeles CA 90007
213 741-3686

(P-22420)
AUTOMOBILE CLUB SOUTHERN CAL
Also Called: AAA
1405 N Montebello Blvd, Montebello
(90640-2584)
PHONE...................................323 725-6545
Lisa Taylor, *Branch Mgr*
EMP: 70
SALES (corp-wide): 1B **Privately Held**
WEB: www.ace.aaa.com
SIC: 8699 Automobile owners' association
PA: Automobile Club Of Southern California
2601 S Figueroa St
Los Angeles CA 90007
213 741-3686

(P-22421)
AUTOMOBILE CLUB SOUTHERN CAL
Also Called: AAA
1234 Commerce Center Dr, Lancaster
(93534-5841)
PHONE...................................661 948-7661
Sheril Watkins, *Branch Mgr*
EMP: 70
SALES (corp-wide): 1B **Privately Held**
WEB: www.ace.aaa.com
SIC: 8699 Automobile owners' association
PA: Automobile Club Of Southern California
2601 S Figueroa St
Los Angeles CA 90007
213 741-3686

(P-22422)
AUTOMOBILE CLUB SOUTHERN CAL
Also Called: AAA
16160 Beach Blvd, Huntington Beach
(92647-3805)
P.O. Box 1370 (92647-1370)
PHONE...................................714 848-2227
Jerald Kuhn, *Branch Mgr*
EMP: 70
SQ FT: 10,927
SALES (corp-wide): 1B **Privately Held**
WEB: www.ace.aaa.com
SIC: 8699 Automobile owners' association
PA: Automobile Club Of Southern California
2601 S Figueroa St
Los Angeles CA 90007
213 741-3686

(P-22423)
AUTOMOBILE CLUB SOUTHERN CAL
Also Called: AAA
22708 Victory Blvd, Woodland Hills
(91367-1697)
PHONE...................................818 883-2660
Glenn Lumley, *Branch Mgr*
EMP: 70
SQ FT: 15,624
SALES (corp-wide): 1B **Privately Held**
WEB: www.ace.aaa.com
SIC: 8699 4724 6331 Automobile owners'
association; travel agencies; fire, marine
& casualty insurance
PA: Automobile Club Of Southern California
2601 S Figueroa St
Los Angeles CA 90007
213 741-3686

(P-22424)
AUTOMOBILE CLUB SOUTHERN CAL
Also Called: A A A Automobile Club So Cal
1234 Centinela Ave, Inglewood
(90302-1138)
PHONE...................................310 673-5170
Lola Nix, *Branch Mgr*
EMP: 70
SQ FT: 11,228
SALES (corp-wide): 1B **Privately Held**
WEB: www.ace.aaa.com
SIC: 8699 Automobile owners' association
PA: Automobile Club Of Southern California
2601 S Figueroa St
Los Angeles CA 90007
213 741-3686

(P-22425)
AUTOMOBILE CLUB SOUTHERN CAL
Also Called: AAA
16041 Whittier Blvd, Whittier (90603-2526)
P.O. Box 4766 (90607-4766)
PHONE...................................562 698-3721
Velia Garcia, *Manager*
EMP: 70
SALES (corp-wide): 1B **Privately Held**
WEB: www.ace.aaa.com
SIC: 8699 4724 6331 Automobile owners'
association; travel agencies; fire, marine
& casualty insurance
PA: Automobile Club Of Southern California
2601 S Figueroa St
Los Angeles CA 90007
213 741-3686

(P-22426)
AUTOMOBILE CLUB SOUTHERN CAL
3700 Central Ave, Riverside (92506-2421)
P.O. Box 2217 (92516-2217)
PHONE...................................951 684-4250
Richard Meyer, *Branch Mgr*
Rebecca Holguin,
Mark Petersen, *Manager*
EMP: 70
SALES (corp-wide): 1B **Privately Held**
WEB: www.ace.aaa.com
SIC: 8699 Automobile owners' association
PA: Automobile Club Of Southern California
2601 S Figueroa St
Los Angeles CA 90007
213 741-3686

(P-22427)
AUTOMOBILE CLUB SOUTHERN CAL
Also Called: AAA
5402 Philadelphia St A, Chino
(91710-2488)
P.O. Box 1846 (91708-1846)
PHONE...................................909 591-9451
Tim Irwin, *Manager*
EMP: 70
SALES (corp-wide): 1B **Privately Held**
WEB: www.ace.aaa.com
SIC: 8699 Automobile owners' association
PA: Automobile Club Of Southern California
2601 S Figueroa St
Los Angeles CA 90007
213 741-3686

(P-22428)
AUTOMOBILE CLUB SOUTHERN CAL
Also Called: A A A Automobile Club So Cal
1450 N Harbor Blvd, Fullerton
(92835-4106)
PHONE...................................714 871-2333
Jennifer Thomson, *Manager*
Evelyn Amimoto, *Agent*
EMP: 70
SALES (corp-wide): 1B **Privately Held**
WEB: www.ace.aaa.com
SIC: 8699 Automobile owners' association
PA: Automobile Club Of Southern California
2601 S Figueroa St
Los Angeles CA 90007
213 741-3686

(P-22429)
AUTOMOBILE CLUB SOUTHERN CAL
Also Called: AAA
638 Cmino De Los Mres Ste, San Clemente
(92673)
PHONE...................................949 489-5572
Cindy Colter, *Branch Mgr*
EMP: 70
SALES (corp-wide): 1B **Privately Held**
WEB: www.ace.aaa.com
SIC: 8699 Automobile owners' association
PA: Automobile Club Of Southern California
2601 S Figueroa St
Los Angeles CA 90007
213 741-3686

(P-22430)
AUTOMOBILE CLUB SOUTHERN CAL
Also Called: AAA
2033b S Broadway, Santa Maria
(93454-7809)
P.O. Box 1308 (93456-1308)
PHONE...................................805 922-5731
Keith Pierce, *Manager*
EMP: 70
SALES (corp-wide): 1B **Privately Held**
WEB: www.ace.aaa.com
SIC: 8699 Automobile owners' association
PA: Automobile Club Of Southern California
2601 S Figueroa St
Los Angeles CA 90007
213 741-3686

(P-22431)
AUTOMOBILE CLUB SOUTHERN CAL
Also Called: A A A Automobile Club So Cal
23770 Valencia Blvd # 100, Valencia
(91355-2185)
PHONE...................................661 259-6222
Kelly Clark, *Branch Mgr*
Chad Hourigan, *Vice Pres*
Scott Derryberry, *Manager*
EMP: 70
SALES (corp-wide): 1B **Privately Held**
WEB: www.ace.aaa.com
SIC: 8699 Automobile owners' association
PA: Automobile Club Of Southern California
2601 S Figueroa St
Los Angeles CA 90007
213 741-3686

(P-22432)
AUTOMOBILE CLUB SOUTHERN CAL
Also Called: A A A Automobile Club So Cal
25181 Paseo De Alicia, Laguna Hills
(92653-4614)
PHONE...................................949 951-1400
Cindy Raymond, *Manager*
Heather Felix, *Regional Mgr*
Sonya Hanson, *Sales Staff*
EMP: 70
SQ FT: 13,948
SALES (corp-wide): 1B **Privately Held**
WEB: www.ace.aaa.com
SIC: 8699 Automobile owners' association
PA: Automobile Club Of Southern California
2601 S Figueroa St
Los Angeles CA 90007
213 741-3686

(P-22433)
AUTOMOBILE CLUB SOUTHERN CAL
Also Called: AAA
12490 Amargosa Rd, Victorville
(92392-5469)
PHONE...................................760 245-6666
Joel Mehler, *Manager*
EMP: 70
SQ FT: 7,950
SALES (corp-wide): 1B **Privately Held**
WEB: www.ace.aaa.com
SIC: 8699 4724 6331 Automobile owners'
association; travel agencies; fire, marine
& casualty insurance
PA: Automobile Club Of Southern California
2601 S Figueroa St
Los Angeles CA 90007
213 741-3686

(P-22434)
AUTOMOBILE CLUB SOUTHERN CAL
Also Called: A A A Automobile Club So Cal
450 W Stetson Ave, Hemet (92543-7328)
PHONE...................................951 652-6202
EMP: 70
SALES (corp-wide): 1B **Privately Held**
WEB: www.ace.aaa.com
SIC: 8699 Automobile owners' association
PA: Automobile Club Of Southern California
2601 S Figueroa St
Los Angeles CA 90007
213 741-3686

(P-22435)
AUTOMOBILE CLUB SOUTHERN CAL
2488 Foothill Blvd Ste A, La Verne
(91750-3062)
PHONE...................................909 392-1444
Bob Barron, *Manager*
EMP: 70
SALES (corp-wide): 1B **Privately Held**
WEB: www.ace.aaa.com
SIC: 8699 Automobile owners' association
PA: Automobile Club Of Southern California
2601 S Figueroa St
Los Angeles CA 90007
213 741-3686

(P-22436)
AUTOMOBILE CLUB SOUTHERN CAL
2730 Santa Monica Blvd, Santa Monica
(90404-2408)
PHONE...................................310 453-1909
Vasile Dejeu, *Manager*
Bethanne Smith, *Bd of Directors*
Malek Khouri, *Vice Pres*
Jeff Zacek, *Vice Pres*
Belinda Hardy, *Admin Asst*
EMP: 70
SQ FT: 10,000
SALES (corp-wide): 1B **Privately Held**
WEB: www.ace.aaa.com
SIC: 8699 Automobile owners' association
PA: Automobile Club Of Southern California
2601 S Figueroa St
Los Angeles CA 90007
213 741-3686

(P-22437)
AUTOMOBILE CLUB SOUTHERN CAL
19201 Bear Valley Rd C, Apple Valley
(92308-2704)
PHONE...................................760 247-4110
EMP: 70
SALES (corp-wide): 1B **Privately Held**
WEB: www.ace.aaa.com
SIC: 8699 Automobile owners' association
PA: Automobile Club Of Southern California
2601 S Figueroa St
Los Angeles CA 90007
213 741-3686

(P-22438)
AUTOMOBILE CLUB SOUTHERN CAL
1170 El Camino Ave, Corona (92879-1761)
PHONE...................................951 808-9624
EMP: 70

SALES (corp-wide): 1B **Privately Held**
WEB: www.ace.aaa.com
SIC: **8699** Automobile owners' association
PA: Automobile Club Of Southern California
2601 S Figueroa St
Los Angeles CA 90007
213 741-3686

(P-22439)
AUTOMOBILE CLUB SOUTHERN CAL
675 N H St, Lompoc (93436-4518)
PHONE.................................805 735-2731
Ani Ivin, *Regional Mgr*
EMP: 70
SALES (corp-wide): 1B **Privately Held**
WEB: www.ace.aaa.com
SIC: **8699** Automobile owners' association
PA: Automobile Club Of Southern California
2601 S Figueroa St
Los Angeles CA 90007
213 741-3686

(P-22440)
AUTOMOBILE CLUB SOUTHERN CAL
4228 S Mooney Blvd, Visalia (93277-9143)
PHONE.................................559 732-8045
Linda Sommer, *Manager*
EMP: 70
SALES (corp-wide): 1B **Privately Held**
WEB: www.ace.aaa.com
SIC: **8699** Automobile owners' association
PA: Automobile Club Of Southern California
2601 S Figueroa St
Los Angeles CA 90007
213 741-3686

(P-22441)
AUTOMOBILE CLUB SOUTHERN CAL
1111 W Alameda Ave, Burbank (91506-2847)
PHONE.................................818 843-2833
Chuck Forest, *Manager*
Lloyd Benedetti, *VP Finance*
EMP: 70
SALES (corp-wide): 1B **Privately Held**
WEB: www.ace.aaa.com
SIC: **8699** Automobile owners' association
PA: Automobile Club Of Southern California
2601 S Figueroa St
Los Angeles CA 90007
213 741-3686

(P-22442)
AUTOMOBILE CLUB SOUTHERN CAL
Also Called: A A A Automobile Club So Cal
4800 Airport Plaza Dr # 100, Long Beach (90815-1274)
PHONE.................................562 425-8350
Susan Dabinett, *Manager*
EMP: 70
SQ FT: 7,200
SALES (corp-wide): 1B **Privately Held**
WEB: www.ace.aaa.com
SIC: **8699** Automobile owners' association
PA: Automobile Club Of Southern California
2601 S Figueroa St
Los Angeles CA 90007
213 741-3686

(P-22443)
AUTOMOBILE CLUB SOUTHERN CAL
Also Called: A A A Automobile Club So Cal
1233 E Broadway, Glendale (91205-1407)
PHONE.................................818 240-2200
Sherry Abbot, *Branch Mgr*
Angela Hovhannisyan, *Sales Staff*
EMP: 70
SQ FT: 11,760
SALES (corp-wide): 1B **Privately Held**
WEB: www.ace.aaa.com
SIC: **8699** Automobile owners' association
PA: Automobile Club Of Southern California
2601 S Figueroa St
Los Angeles CA 90007
213 741-3686

(P-22444)
AUTOMOBILE CLUB SOUTHERN CAL
Also Called: AAA
18642 Gridley Rd, Artesia (90701-5441)
PHONE.................................562 924-6636
Diane Ruiz, *Branch Mgr*
Mike Aguirre, *Prgrmr*
Ben Lai, *Technical Staff*
Rob Wade, *Manager*
EMP: 70
SQ FT: 12,960
SALES (corp-wide): 1B **Privately Held**
WEB: www.ace.aaa.com
SIC: **8699** Automobile owners' association
PA: Automobile Club Of Southern California
2601 S Figueroa St
Los Angeles CA 90007
213 741-3686

(P-22445)
AUTOMOBILE CLUB SOUTHERN CAL
Also Called: AAA
8761 Santa Monica Blvd, West Hollywood (90069-4538)
PHONE.................................323 525-0018
Randy Miller, *Manager*
Judith Phillips, *Executive*
Sean Harris, *Manager*
Susan Malone, *Manager*
Fowler Tenia, *Agent*
EMP: 70
SALES (corp-wide): 1B **Privately Held**
WEB: www.ace.aaa.com
SIC: **8699** Automobile owners' association
PA: Automobile Club Of Southern California
2601 S Figueroa St
Los Angeles CA 90007
213 741-3686

(P-22446)
BOYS GRLS CLUBS GRDN GROVE INC (PA)
10540 Chapman Ave, Garden Grove (92840-3101)
PHONE.................................714 530-0430
Mark Surmanian, *CEO*
Jenna Ceballos, *Vice Pres*
Charles Osgood, *Supervisor*
EMP: 229 EST: 1952
SQ FT: 12,000
SALES (est): 11.5MM **Privately Held**
WEB: www.bgcgg.org
SIC: **8299 8699** Educational services; charitable organization

(P-22447)
BRISTOL HOSPICE FOUNDATION CAL (PA)
Also Called: Optimal Hospice Care
1227 Chester Ave Ste A, Bakersfield (93301-5453)
PHONE.................................661 410-3000
Ann Smart, *Director*
Stacey Harris, *Vice Pres*
Deborah Brazie, *Branch Mgr*
Vega Joe, *Office Mgr*
Dawn Knox, *Executive Asst*
EMP: 76 EST: 1979
SALES (est): 170.2K **Privately Held**
WEB: www.bristolhospicefoundationca.org
SIC: **8699** Charitable organization

(P-22448)
CAMPBELL CENTER
6512 San Fernando Rd, Glendale (91201-2109)
PHONE.................................818 242-2434
Nancy Niebrugge, *Exec Dir*
Lola Abrehamian, *President*
Rita Hopkins, *CEO*
David Fields, *Exec Dir*
Claudia Sandoval, *Manager*
EMP: 50 EST: 1954
SALES (est): 2.5MM **Privately Held**
WEB: www.thecampbell.org
SIC: **8699** Charitable organization

(P-22449)
CHRIST-CENTERED MINISTRIES
Also Called: RESTORATION SOBER LIVING HOMES
742 N La Brea Ave, Inglewood (90302-2204)
P.O. Box 4153 (90309-4153)
PHONE.................................310 528-4538
Troy Vaughn, *CEO*
Darlene Vaughn, *COO*
EMP: 50 EST: 1998
SALES (est): 9.6MM **Privately Held**
WEB: www.christcenteredministries.org
SIC: **8661 8699** Churches, temples & shrines; charitable organization

(P-22450)
COUNTY OF RIVERSIDE DEPARTMENT (PA)
4065 County Circle Dr, Riverside (92503-3410)
P.O. Box 7600 (92513-7600)
PHONE.................................951 358-5000
Susan Harrington, *Director*
Sandy Saldana, *Admin Sec*
Socorro Manzanilla, *Administration*
Roberto Renedo, *Technician*
Jeff Johnson, *Deputy Dir*
EMP: 90 EST: 2004
SALES (est): 10.6MM **Privately Held**
WEB: www.rivco-diseasecontrol.org
SIC: **8699** Charitable organization

(P-22451)
GIRLS ROCK SB
1522b Eucalyptus Hill Rd, Santa Barbara (93103-2811)
PHONE.................................805 861-8128
Jen Baron, *Exec Dir*
Kelsey Maloney, *Administration*
EMP: 70 EST: 2013
SALES (est): 330K **Privately Held**
WEB: www.girlsrocksb.org
SIC: **8699 8299** Charitable organization; music school

(P-22452)
HEMET UNIFIED SCHOOL DISTRICT
Also Called: Santa Fe Middle School
985 N Cawston Ave, Hemet (92545-1551)
P.O. Box 881 (92546-0881)
PHONE.................................951 765-6287
Todd Biggert, *Principal*
Elizabeth Jay, *Treasurer*
Rita Bivens, *Admin Sec*
Roxanne Estavillo, *Admin Sec*
Heather Garcia, *Admin Sec*
EMP: 80
SALES (corp-wide): 341.2MM **Privately Held**
WEB: www.hemetusd.org
SIC: **8211 8699** Public elementary & secondary schools; personal interest organization
PA: Hemet Unified School District
1791 W Acacia Ave
Hemet CA 92545
951 765-5100

(P-22453)
INLAND EMPIRE CHAPTER-ASSN OF
4200 Concours Ste 360, Ontario (91764-4982)
PHONE.................................512 478-9000
EMP: 82
SALES: 4.1K **Privately Held**
SIC: **8699** Membership Organization

(P-22454)
KAISER FOUNDATION HOSPITALS
Also Called: Kaiser Permanente
3699 Wilshire Blvd, Los Angeles (90010-2718)
PHONE.................................213 351-3550
Aida Ratevosian, *Auditor*
EMP: 78
SALES (corp-wide): 30.5B **Privately Held**
WEB: www.kaisercenter.com
SIC: **8699 8062** Charitable organization; general medical & surgical hospitals

HQ: Kaiser Foundation Hospitals Inc
1 Kaiser Plz
Oakland CA 94612
510 271-6611

(P-22455)
LOS ANGELES MEM COLISEUM COMM
Also Called: La Sports Arena
3911 S Figueroa St, Los Angeles (90037-1207)
PHONE.................................213 747-7111
Don Knabe, *President*
Gregory Hellmold, *CFO*
John Sandbrook, *Administration*
EMP: 500 EST: 1923
SQ FT: 2,000
SALES: 1.5K **Privately Held**
WEB: www.lacoliseum.com
SIC: **8699** Athletic organizations

(P-22456)
LOS ANGELES WAVES NETBALL CLUB
2059 Artesia Blvd Apt 81, Torrance (90504-3023)
PHONE.................................310 346-7211
La Verne Patane, *Treasurer*
EMP: 50 EST: 2009
SALES (est): 5K **Privately Held**
WEB: www.losangelesnetball.org
SIC: **8699** Membership organizations

(P-22457)
MARAVILLA FOUNDATION (PA)
5729 Union Pacific Ave, Commerce (90022-5134)
PHONE.................................323 721-4162
Alex M Sotomayor, *CEO*
Tristen Sotomayor, *CCO*
George Ross, *CFO*
Deo Tinana, *CFO*
Paul Lopez, *Chairman*
EMP: 151 EST: 1967
SQ FT: 30,000
SALES (est): 10.8MM **Privately Held**
WEB: www.maravilla.org
SIC: **8699** Charitable organization

(P-22458)
ORGANZTION AMRCN KDALY EDCTORS
10801 National Blvd # 590, Los Angeles (90064-4139)
PHONE.................................310 441-3555
Roger D Chittum Esq, *Principal*
Kevin Pearson, *Vice Pres*
Renee Higgins, *Director*
EMP: 50
SALES: 755.1K **Privately Held**
WEB: www.oake.org
SIC: **8699** Charitable organization

(P-22459)
PASADENA HUMANE SOCIETY
361 S Raymond Ave, Pasadena (91105-2687)
PHONE.................................626 792-7151
Steven R Mc Nall, *President*
Chris Briffett, *Volunteer Dir*
Kristina Lamas, *Vice Pres*
Ricky Whitman, *Vice Pres*
Jonathan Budisanroso, *Information Mgr*
EMP: 70
SQ FT: 26,000
SALES: 14.1MM **Privately Held**
WEB: www.pasadenahumane.org
SIC: **8699 0752** Animal humane society; animal specialty services

(P-22460)
RESCUE MISSION ALLIANCE (PA)
Also Called: MISSION BARGAIN CENTER
315 N A St, Oxnard (93030-4901)
P.O. Box 5545 (93031-5545)
PHONE.................................805 487-1234
Gary Gray, *President*
David Chittenden, *CFO*
Jim Ownes, *Chairman*
Andy Stay, *Treasurer*
Uel Leite, *Bd of Directors*
EMP: 77
SQ FT: 30,000

SALES: 30.3MM **Privately Held**
WEB: www.erescuemission.org
SIC: 8699 Charitable organization

(P-22461)
SERVE PEOPLE INC
1206 E 17th St Ste 101, Santa Ana
(92701-2641)
PHONE..................714 352-2911
Dimitri Sirakoff, *Principal*
Rocio Nunez-Magdaleno, *Info Tech Mgr*
Scott McQueen, *Physician Asst*
EMP: 61 EST: 2009
SALES (est): 9.2MM **Privately Held**
WEB: www.serve-the-people.com
SIC: 8699 Charitable organization

(P-22462)
SOCIETY OF ST VNCENT DE PAUL C (PA)
Also Called: ST VINCENT DE PAUL SOCI-
ETY OF
210 N Avenue 21, Los Angeles
(90031-1713)
PHONE..................323 226-9645
David Garcia, *Exec Dir*
Susana Santana, *Exec Dir*
Renee Fishman, *Human Res Dir*
Isidro Casas, *Asst Director*
EMP: 77
SQ FT: 108,000
SALES: 13.1MM **Privately Held**
WEB: www.svdpla.org
SIC: 8699 Charitable organization

(P-22463)
SOROPTMIST INTL HUNTINGTON BCH
212 Utica Ave, Huntington Beach
(92648-2804)
PHONE..................714 271-9305
Terry Rose, *Partner*
EMP: 50 EST: 2017
SALES: 42.5K **Privately Held**
WEB: www.soroptimisthuntingtonbeach.org
SIC: 8699 Charitable organization

(P-22464)
ST VINCENT DE PAUL VLG INC
Also Called: Joan Kroc Center
28225 Driza, Mission Viejo (92692-1305)
PHONE..................619 233-8500
Richard Swain, *Principal*
EMP: 63 **Privately Held**
WEB: www.my.neighbor.org
SIC: 8699 Charitable organization
PA: St. Vincent De Paul Village, Inc.
1501 Imperial Ave
San Diego CA 92101

(P-22465)
TORRANCE AMATEUR RDO ASSN INC
Also Called: Tara
2162 248th St, Lomita (90717-1608)
PHONE..................310 245-0989
Charles Galbasin, *Principal*
Kenneth Edwards, *Principal*
Bruce Fauver, *Principal*
Shelly Fauver, *Principal*
Kathleen Galbasin, *Principal*
EMP: 50 EST: 2016
SALES (est): 771.2K **Privately Held**
SIC: 8699 Membership organizations

(P-22466)
USA TRAVEL SERVICES LLC
714 Washington Blvd, Marina Del Rey
(90292-5543)
PHONE..................207 899-8803
Julian Brand,
EMP: 800 EST: 2016
SALES (est): 1MM **Privately Held**
SIC: 8699 Travel club

(P-22467)
VANGUARD UNIV SOUTHERN CAL
55 Fair Dr, Costa Mesa (92626-6520)
PHONE..................714 556-3610
Michael Beals, *CEO*
Jonathan Moralez, *Officer*
Kim Johnson, *Vice Pres*
David Alford, *Executive*

Celina Camarillo, *Executive Asst*
EMP: 200 EST: 1921
SQ FT: 420,000
SALES: 49.2MM **Privately Held**
WEB: www.vanguard.edu
SIC: 8221 8699 College, except junior;
charitable organization

(P-22468)
VICTORIA PLACE COMMUNITY ASSN
195 N Euclid Ave, Upland (91786-6055)
PHONE..................909 981-4131
John Melcher, *President*
EMP: 75 EST: 2008
SALES (est): 1.8MM **Privately Held**
SIC: 8699 Membership organizations

(P-22469)
VISION TO LEARN
12100 Wilshire Blvd # 1275, Los Angeles
(90025-7143)
PHONE..................800 485-9196
Ann Hollister, *President*
John Kim, *COO*
Gaye Williams, *Exec Dir*
Valerie Tran,
EMP: 50 EST: 2017
SALES: 11.2MM **Privately Held**
WEB: www.visiontolearn.org
SIC: 8699 8399 Charitable organization;
advocacy group

(P-22470)
WILDLIFE WAYSTATION
14831 Lttle Tjunga Cyn Rd, Sylmar
(91342-5906)
PHONE..................818 899-5201
Martine Colette, *President*
Peggy Summers, *Admin Sec*
Bill Knight, *IT/INT Sup*
Rebecca Walser,
Martine D Colette, *Manager*
EMP: 50 EST: 1969
SQ FT: 800
SALES (est): 3MM **Privately Held**
WEB: www.wildlifewaystation.org
SIC: 8699 Animal humane society

(P-22471)
WORLD VISION INTERNATIONAL (HQ)
800 W Chestnut Ave, Monrovia
(91016-3198)
P.O. Box 9716, Federal Way WA (98063-
9716)
PHONE..................626 303-8811
Andrew Morley, *Officer*
Valdir Steuernagel, *Ch of Bd*
Kevin Jenkins, *President*
Nicola Coulson, *Executive Asst*
Carmen Miller, *Executive Asst*
▼ EMP: 196 EST: 1977
SQ FT: 94,000
SALES (est): 47MM
SALES (corp-wide): 1.2B **Privately Held**
WEB: www.wvi.org
SIC: 8699 Charitable organization
PA: World Vision Inc.
34834 Weyerhaeuser Way S
Federal Way WA 98001
888 511-6548

8711 Engineering Services

(P-22472)
ABS CONSULTING INC
Also Called: ABS Group
300 Commerce Ste 150, Irvine
(92602-1302)
PHONE..................714 734-4242
Doug Frazier, *CEO*
Peter Yanev, *President*
Jim Johnson, *COO*
George Reitter, *CFO*
Steve Arendt, *Vice Pres*
EMP: 100 EST: 1970
SALES (est): 10.6MM
SALES (corp-wide): 564.3MM **Privately Held**
WEB: www.abs-group.com
SIC: 8711 8742 Consulting engineer;
management consulting services

HQ: Abs Group Of Companies, Inc.
1701 City Plaza Dr
Spring TX 77389

(P-22473)
ACCUNEX INC
Also Called: Accurate Electronics
20700 Lassen St, Chatsworth
(91311-4507)
PHONE..................818 882-5858
Farid Jadali, *President*
Roxana Coronado, *Vice Pres*
Sergio Martinez, *QC Mgr*
Ash Hazrati, *Mfg Staff*
▲ EMP: 50 EST: 1998
SQ FT: 25,000
SALES (est): 11.6MM **Privately Held**
WEB: www.accurate-elec.com
SIC: 8711 3679 Engineering services;
electronic circuits

(P-22474)
ACL CONSTRUCTION COMPANY INC
207 W State St, Ontario (91762-4360)
P.O. Box 1929, Chino Hills (91709-0065)
PHONE..................909 391-4477
Jonathan Jordan, *President*
Tim Jordan, *Project Mgr*
EMP: 50 EST: 1982
SQ FT: 800 **Privately Held**
WEB: www.aclrails.com
SIC: 8711 Engineering services

(P-22475)
ADAMS/STRTER CVIL ENGNERS INC
16755 Von Karman Ave # 1, Irvine
(92606-4930)
PHONE..................949 474-2330
Jan A Adams, *President*
Sue Zarrin, *COO*
Randal Streeter, *Vice Pres*
Nick Streeter-Pe, *Vice Pres*
Eduardo Cerda, *Design Engr*
EMP: 57 EST: 1981
SALES (est): 6.9MM **Privately Held**
WEB: www.adams-streeter.com
SIC: 8711 Civil engineering

(P-22476)
ADAPTIVE ENGRG FABRICATION INC
1921 Petra Ln, Placentia (92870-6749)
PHONE..................714 854-1300
Chuck Nadolski, *CEO*
Richard Buschini, *Vice Pres*
Rod Learned, *Project Engr*
Nitin Patel, *Engineer*
EMP: 16 EST: 1996
SQ FT: 15,500
SALES (est): 4.2MM **Privately Held**
WEB: www.aef-inc.com
SIC: 8711 3599 Engineering services; ma-
chine & other job shop work

(P-22477)
ADKISON ENGINEERS INC
Also Called: Adkan Engineers
6879 Airport Dr, Riverside (92504-1903)
PHONE..................951 688-0241
Ed Adkison, *President*
Jerry Snell, *Exec VP*
Chrissa Leach, *Vice Pres*
Yasmir Quintero, *Administration*
Leandra Hosfield, *Technician*
EMP: 52 EST: 1993
SALES (est): 11MM **Privately Held**
WEB: www.adkan.com
SIC: 8711 8713 Civil engineering; survey-
ing services

(P-22478)
ADVANTEDGE TECHNOLOGY INC
271 Market St Ste 15, Port Hueneme
(93041-3219)
PHONE..................805 488-0405
Tim Edward Huggins, *CEO*
Tim Huggins, *Exec Dir*
Kevin Bradley, *Program Mgr*
Bruce Underwood, *Info Tech Dir*
David Benham, *Senior Engr*
EMP: 60

SQ FT: 2,000
SALES (est): 14.3MM **Privately Held**
WEB: www.advantedgetechnology.com
SIC: 8711 Engineering services

(P-22479)
AECOM C&E INC
Also Called: Aecom Environment
1220 Avenida Acaso, Camarillo
(93012-8750)
PHONE..................805 388-3775
EMP: 100
SALES (corp-wide): 13.2B **Publicly Held**
WEB: www.townofchelmsford.us
SIC: 8711 Engineering Services, Nsk
HQ: Aecom C&E, Inc
250 Apollo Dr
Chelmsford MA 01824
978 905-2100

(P-22480)
AECOM E&C HOLDINGS INC (DH)
1999 Avenue Of The Stars, Los Angeles
(90067-6022)
PHONE..................213 593-8000
Robert W Zaist, *CEO*
Gary V Jandegian, *President*
H Thomas Hicks, *CFO*
Judy L Rodgers, *Treasurer*
Joseph Masters, *Vice Pres*
EMP: 79 EST: 2009
SALES (est): 1.5B
SALES (corp-wide): 13.2B **Publicly Held**
WEB: www.aecom.com
SIC: 8711 1611 1629 1623 Consulting
engineer; general contractor, highway &
street construction; dams, waterways,
docks & other marine construction;
pipeline construction; industrial buildings,
new construction; bridge construction
HQ: Urs Holdings, Inc.
600 Montgomery St Fl 25
San Francisco CA 94111
415 774-2700

(P-22481)
AECOM GLOBAL II LLC (HQ)
300 S Grand Ave Ste 900, Los Angeles
(90071-3135)
PHONE..................213 593-8100
Michael Burke, *Mng Member*
Tommy Bell, *President*
Rick L Randall, *President*
Joe Zahora, *Project Mgr*
Rich Beyak, *Sr Project Mgr*
◆ EMP: 65 EST: 1976
SALES (est): 3.1B
SALES (corp-wide): 13.2B **Publicly Held**
WEB: www.aecom.com
SIC: 8711 8712 8741 Engineering serv-
ices; consulting engineer; architectural
engineering; construction management
PA: Aecom
13355 Noel Rd Ste 400
Dallas TX 75240
972 788-1000

(P-22482)
ALBERT A WEBB ASSOCIATES (PA)
3788 Mccray St, Riverside (92506-2927)
PHONE..................951 686-1070
A Hubert Webb, *Chairman*
Matt Webb, *President*
Margaret Ewing, *CFO*
Todd R Smith, *CFO*
Scott Webb, *CFO*
EMP: 127 EST: 1949
SQ FT: 20,000
SALES (est): 32.5MM **Privately Held**
WEB: www.webbassociates.com
SIC: 8711 Civil engineering

(P-22483)
AMERESCO SOLAR LLC
42175 Zevo Dr, Temecula (92590-2503)
PHONE..................888 967-6527
EMP: 85 **Publicly Held**
WEB: www.ameresco.com
SIC: 8711 Energy conservation engineer-
ing
HQ: Ameresco Solar Llc
111 Speen St Ste 410
Framingham MA 01701
508 661-2200

PRODUCTS & SVCS

(P-22484)
AMERICAN GNC CORPORATION
888 E Easy St, Simi Valley (93065-1812)
PHONE..................................805 582-0582
Dr Ching-Fang Lin, *President*
Emily Melgarejo, *General Mgr*
EMP: 50 EST: 1986
SQ FT: 30,000
SALES (est): 4.6MM **Privately Held**
WEB: www.americangnc.com
SIC: 8711 Engineering services

(P-22485)
AMERICAN TECHNICAL SVCS INC
20384 Via Mantua, Porter Ranch
(91326-4441)
PHONE..................................951 372-9664
Alen Petrossian, *President*
Jerry Amaro, *Tech/Comp Coord*
Samuel Marrujo, *Software Dev*
Jeannie Montini, *Manager*
EMP: 70 EST: 2004
SQ FT: 2,040
SALES (est): 6.7MM **Privately Held**
WEB: www.atspage.com
SIC: 8711 Consulting engineer

(P-22486)
AMG HUNTINGTON BEACH LLC
Also Called: Notthoff Engineering
5416 Argosy Ave, Huntington Beach
(92649-1039)
PHONE..................................714 894-9802
Kelly Kaller, *CEO*
David L Patterson, *CEO*
J Ross Feeney, *COO*
Robert Taylor, *Exec VP*
Kelley Kaller, *Vice Pres*
EMP: 50 EST: 2011
SALES (est): 10.2MM **Privately Held**
WEB: www.amg-mfg.com
SIC: 8711 Engineering services
HQ: Aerospace Manufacturing Group Inc
5401 Business Dr
Huntington Beach CA 92649
714 894-9802

(P-22487)
AMP DISPLAY INC (PA)
9856 6th St, Rancho Cucamonga
(91730-5714)
PHONE..................................909 980-1310
Jason Young, *President*
Diana Beckman, *Marketing Staff*
EMP: 21 EST: 1999
SQ FT: 12,000
SALES (est): 3.4MM **Privately Held**
WEB: www.ampdisplay.com
SIC: 8711 3679 Engineering services; liq-
uid crystal displays (LCD)

(P-22488)
ANALEX CORPORATION
Vndnburg A Frce Bldg 840, Lompoc
(93438)
P.O. Box 640 (93438-0640)
PHONE..................................805 605-3898
Larry Stalter, *Manager*
EMP: 120
SALES (corp-wide): 1.8B **Privately Held**
SIC: 8711 7371 Aviation &/or aeronautical
engineering; chemical engineering; cus-
tom computer programming services;
computer software development
HQ: Analex Corporation
3076 Centreville Rd # 200
Herndon VA 20171
703 880-2800

(P-22489)
APEX MACHINE WORKS INC
2118 Wilshire Blvd # 258, Santa Monica
(90403-5704)
PHONE..................................310 393-5987
EMP: 100
SALES (est): 3.3MM **Privately Held**
SIC: 8711 Engineering Services

(P-22490)
APPLIED COMPANIES
28020 Avenue Stanford, Santa Clarita
(91355-1105)
P.O. Box 802078 (91380-2078)
PHONE..................................661 257-0090
Mary Elizabeth Klinger, *CEO*

Joseph Klinger, *Vice Pres*
Nayeem Khawaja, *Program Mgr*
Andrea Fleming, *Executive Asst*
Yeva Kadoyan, *Design Engr*
EMP: 50 EST: 1962
SQ FT: 58,000
SALES (est): 13.7MM **Privately Held**
WEB: www.appliedcompanies.net
SIC: 8711 3585 3443 3621 Mechanical
engineering; ice making machinery; cylin-
ders, pressure: metal plate; motors &
generators

(P-22491)
ARIA GROUP INCORPORATED
17395 Daimler St, Irvine (92614-5510)
PHONE..................................949 475-2915
Clive Hawkins, *President*
EMP: 70 EST: 1995
SQ FT: 45,489
SALES (est): 9.9MM **Privately Held**
WEB: www.aria-group.com
SIC: 8711 Consulting engineer

(P-22492)
ARKHAM TECHNOLOGY LIMITED (PA)
2525 Main St Ste 250, Irvine (92614-6683)
P.O. Box 4066 (92616-4066)
PHONE..................................949 585-0404
Otaway McGee Thomas IV, *CEO*
Ayumi Kobayashi, *Manager*
EMP: 14 EST: 1998
SALES (est): 2.2MM **Privately Held**
WEB: www.arkhamtechnology.com
SIC: 8711 5045 5065 8731 Consulting
engineer; mainframe computers; disk
drives; security control equipment & sys-
tems; commercial physical research;
radio & TV communications equipment

(P-22493)
ARMADA ENGINEERING LLC
21305 Itasca St, Chatsworth (91311-4929)
PHONE..................................818 280-5138
Ryan Bosman, *Engineer*
EMP: 15 EST: 2011
SALES (est): 867.5K **Privately Held**
WEB: www.armada-engineering.com
SIC: 8711 3799 Engineering services; off-
road automobiles, except recreational ve-
hicles

(P-22494)
ARQ LLC (PA)
3002 Dow Ave Ste 524, Tustin
(92780-7250)
PHONE..................................888 384-0971
Kunal Hinduja, *Mng Member*
Kamal Sadarangani, *Vice Pres*
Jawan Salman, *Vice Pres*
Bob Danner, *Project Mgr*
Maher Kirmiz, *Project Mgr*
EMP: 84 EST: 2008
SALES (est): 9.9MM **Privately Held**
WEB: www.arqwireless.com
SIC: 8711 Electrical or electronic engineer-
ing

(P-22495)
ARUP NORTH AMERICA LIMITED
12777 W Jefferson Blvd # 300, Los Angeles
(90066-7034)
PHONE..................................310 578-4182
Tony Panossian, *Branch Mgr*
Megan Knapp, *Administration*
Farbod Mehr, *CIO*
Paris Borovilos, *Engineer*
Haley Francis, *Engineer*
EMP: 322
SALES (corp-wide): 26.1MM **Privately Held**
WEB: www.arup.com
SIC: 8711 Consulting engineer
HQ: Arup North America Limited
560 Mission St Fl 7
San Francisco CA 94105

(P-22496)
ASHLEY & VANCE ENGINEERING INC
1413 Monterey St, San Luis Obispo
(93401-2913)
PHONE..................................805 545-0010
Truitt Vance, *Principal*

Charles R Ashley Jr, *Vice Pres*
Jon George, *Technology*
Michael Iannelli, *Project Engr*
Andrew Martin, *Project Engr*
EMP: 54 EST: 2008
SALES (est): 4.8MM **Privately Held**
WEB: www.ashleyvance.com
SIC: 8711 Structural engineering

(P-22497)
ATHICON
6310 San Vicente Blvd, Los Angeles
(90048-5426)
PHONE..................................213 454-0662
Victoria Lozada, *Manager*
EMP: 50 EST: 2017
SALES (est): 1.2MM **Privately Held**
SIC: 8711 Engineering services

(P-22498)
BAS ENGINEERING INC
11899 8th St, Rancho Cucamonga
(91730-5501)
PHONE..................................909 484-2575
Ajesh Bhakta, *Principal*
EMP: 16 EST: 2012
SALES (est): 1.8MM **Privately Held**
WEB:
www.basengineering.thebluebook.com
SIC: 8711 3312 Engineering services;
blast furnaces & steel mills

(P-22499)
BEACON WEST ENERGY GROUP LLC
1145 Eugenia Pl Ste 101, Carpinteria
(93013-1970)
PHONE..................................805 816-2790
Larry Huskins, *Mng Member*
Brian O 'neill, *Contract Mgr*
Christer Peltonen,
Keith Wenal,
Michael Wracher,
EMP: 55 EST: 2017
SQ FT: 5,000
SALES (est): 3MM **Privately Held**
WEB: www.beacon-west.com
SIC: 8711 Engineering services

(P-22500)
BINOPTICS LLC
977 S Meridian Ave, Alhambra
(91803-1250)
PHONE..................................607 257-3200
Norman Kwong, *Branch Mgr*
EMP: 107 **Publicly Held**
SIC: 8711 Engineering services
HQ: Binoptics, Llc
9 Brown Rd
Ithaca NY 14850
607 257-3200

(P-22501)
BKF ENGINEERS/AGS
4675 Macarthur Ct Ste 400, Newport Beach
(92660-8834)
PHONE..................................949 526-8400
Isaac Kontorovsky, *Branch Mgr*
EMP: 95
SALES (corp-wide): 72.8MM **Privately Held**
WEB: www.bkf.com
SIC: 8711 Civil engineering
PA: Bkf Engineers
255 Shoreline Dr Ste 200
Redwood City CA 94065
650 482-6300

(P-22502)
BOYLE ENGINEERING CORPORATION
999 W Town And Country Rd, Orange
(92868-4713)
P.O. Box 7350, Newport Beach (92658-
7350)
PHONE..................................714 543-5274
EMP: 80
SALES (corp-wide): 8.3B **Publicly Held**
SIC: 8711 8712 Eng & Architectural Serv-
ice
HQ: Boyle Engineering Corporation
999 W Town And Country Rd
Orange CA 92868
949 476-3300

(P-22503)
BRINDERSON LP (DH)
18841 S Broadwick St, Compton
(90220-6429)
PHONE..................................714 466-7100
Gary Wilson, *Principal*
Bob Lawvey, *Program Mgr*
Elizabeth Marcotte, *Administration*
Lily Dinh, *Technology*
Josie Gensaya, *Engineer*
EMP: 150 EST: 1993
SALES (est): 292.8MM
SALES (corp-wide): 1.2B **Privately Held**
WEB: www.aegion.com
SIC: 8711 1629 Engineering services;
dams, waterways, docks & other marine
construction
HQ: Aegion Corporation
17988 Edison Ave
Chesterfield MO 63005
636 530-8000

(P-22504)
BRINDERSON LP
19000 Macarthur Blvd # 800, Irvine
(92612-1461)
PHONE..................................714 466-7100
EMP: 60
SALES (est): 2.5MM
SALES (corp-wide): 1.3B **Publicly Held**
SIC: 8711 Engineering Services
HQ: Energy & Mining Holding Company Llc
17988 Edison Ave
Chesterfield MO
636 530-8000

(P-22505)
BURNS & MCDONNELL INC
140 S State College Blvd, Brea
(92821-5850)
PHONE..................................714 256-1595
Ken Gerling, *Branch Mgr*
James OH, *Department Mgr*
Poonam Joshi, *Project Mgr*
Garrick Herbert, *Manager*
Debra Klobuchar, *Assistant*
EMP: 80
SALES (corp-wide): 1.2B **Privately Held**
WEB: www.burnsmcc.com
SIC: 8711 Consulting engineer
PA: Burns & Mcdonnell, Inc.
9400 Ward Pkwy
Kansas City MO 64114
816 333-9400

(P-22506)
BUTLER AMERICA LLC (HQ)
3820 State St Ste B, Santa Barbara
(93105-3182)
PHONE..................................805 880-1965
Christine Ciocca, *President*
Robert Olson, *CEO*
Stephen Morrison, *CFO*
Bharani A Kroll, *Vice Pres*
James Elsner, *Vice Pres*
EMP: 903 EST: 2011
SQ FT: 160,000
SALES (est): 54.6MM
SALES (corp-wide): 81.8MM **Privately Held**
WEB: www.butler.com
SIC: 8711 8748 7361 Engineering serv-
ices; telecommunications consultant;
labor contractors (employment agency)
PA: Butler America Holdings, Inc.
3820 State St Ste B
Santa Barbara CA 93105
805 880-1978

(P-22507)
C D LYON CONSTRUCTION INC (PA)
380 W Stanley Ave, Ventura (93001-1350)
P.O. Box 1456 (93002-1456)
PHONE..................................805 653-0173
Christopher D Lyon, *CEO*
Debra C Lyon, *Corp Secy*
Chuck Ludaescher, *Manager*
EMP: 80
SALES (est): 21.2MM **Privately Held**
WEB: www.cdlyon.com
SIC: 8711 Petroleum engineering

(P-22508)
CALIFORNIA MFG TECH CONSULTING
Also Called: CMTC
690 Knox St Ste 200, Torrance (90502-1323)
PHONE..................................310 263-3060
James Watson, *CEO*
Bill Doxakis, *Partner*
Patrick Billiter, *CFO*
Jack Buren, *CFO*
Liezl Lao, *Vice Pres*
EMP: 74 **EST:** 1994
SQ FT: 10,000
SALES (est): 32.3MM **Privately Held**
WEB: www.cmtc.com
SIC: 8711 8742 Consulting engineer; marketing consulting services

(P-22509)
CALIFORNIA SEMICONDUCTOR TECH
Also Called: Calsemi
429 Santa Monica Blvd, Santa Monica (90401-3401)
PHONE..................................310 579-2939
Antonio Garcia, *CEO*
Jose Luis Lopez, *CFO*
EMP: 120 **EST:** 2013
SALES (est): 160MM **Privately Held**
WEB: www.calsemi-tech.com
SIC: 8711 Engineering services

(P-22510)
CALNETIX INC (PA)
Also Called: Calnetix Technologies
16323 Shoemaker Ave, Cerritos (90703-2244)
PHONE..................................562 293-1660
Vatche Artinian, *President*
Dennis Strouse, *COO*
Ian Hart, *CFO*
Herman Artinian, *Vice Pres*
Edgel Del, *Vice Pres*
▲ **EMP:** 53 **EST:** 1998
SQ FT: 68,000
SALES (est): 113.4MM **Privately Held**
WEB: www.calnetix.com
SIC: 8711 Engineering services

(P-22511)
CAPITAL ENGINEERING LLC
2830 Temple Ave, Long Beach (90806-2213)
PHONE..................................562 612-1302
EMP: 407
SALES (corp-wide): 7.1B **Privately Held**
SIC: 8711 Consulting engineer
HQ: Capital Engineering Llc
436 Creamery Way Ste H100
Exton PA 19341
219 791-1984

(P-22512)
CBM CONSULTING INC
1411 W 190th St Ste 525, Gardena (90248-4357)
PHONE..................................310 329-0102
Blake Mitchell, *President*
Paul Buckley P, *Sr Project Mgr*
Ruben Felix Jr, *Manager*
EMP: 69 **EST:** 1989
SQ FT: 4,850
SALES (est): 563.2K
SALES (corp-wide): 21.4MM **Privately Held**
WEB: www.cbmconsulting.com
SIC: 8711 Civil engineering
PA: Koa Corporation
1100 Corp Ctr Dr Ste 201
Monterey Park CA 91754
323 260-4703

(P-22513)
CDM CONSTRUCTORS INC
9220 Cleveland Ave # 100, Rancho Cucamonga (91730-8560)
PHONE..................................909 579-3500
Joyce Jackson, *Branch Mgr*
Gae Walters, *Director*
EMP: 90
SALES (corp-wide): 1.2B **Privately Held**
WEB: www.cdmsmith.com
SIC: 8711 Consulting engineer

HQ: Cdm Constructors Inc.
75 State St Ste 701
Boston MA 02109

(P-22514)
CELESTICA LLC
8840 Flower Rd Ste 110, Rancho Cucamonga (91730-4474)
PHONE..................................909 201-3995
EMP: 395
SALES (corp-wide): 55MM **Privately Held**
WEB: www.celestica.com
SIC: 8711 Engineering services
PA: Celestica Llc
280 Campillo St Ste G
Calexico CA 92231
760 357-4880

(P-22515)
CONCEPT TECHNOLOGY INC (PA)
895 Dove St Fl 3, Newport Beach (92660-2941)
PHONE..................................949 854-7047
Mahesh P Badani, *President*
Jonatan Chacin, *Analyst*
Luke Iannello, *Manager*
▲ **EMP:** 426 **EST:** 1981
SALES (est): 21.7MM **Privately Held**
WEB: www.concepttechnology.com
SIC: 8711 3599 8742 3825 Consulting engineer; machine shop, jobbing & repair; management information systems consultant; radio frequency measuring equipment

(P-22516)
CONCEPT TECHNOLOGY INC
2941 W Macarthur Blvd # 136, Santa Ana (92704-6952)
PHONE..................................949 851-6550
EMP: 64
SALES (corp-wide): 21.7MM **Privately Held**
WEB: www.concepttechnology.com
SIC: 8711 Consulting engineer
PA: Concept Technology, Inc.
895 Dove St Fl 3
Newport Beach CA 92660
949 854-7047

(P-22517)
CONTINENTAL GRAPHICS CORP
Also Called: Continental Data Graphics
4000 N Lakewood Blvd, Long Beach (90808-1700)
PHONE..................................714 503-4200
Steve Meade, *Manager*
Cathy Barnard, *Vice Pres*
Jose Madrid, *Vice Pres*
Jesse Weissman, *Administration*
Earl Nason, *Software Engr*
EMP: 73
SALES (corp-wide): 58.1B **Publicly Held**
WEB: www.cdgnow.com
SIC: 8711 Consulting engineer
HQ: Continental Graphics Corporation
4060 N Lakewood Blvd
Long Beach CA 90808
714 503-4200

(P-22518)
COOPER ENGINEERING INC
114 Business Center Dr, Corona (92878-3224)
PHONE..................................951 736-6135
Howard Cooper Jr, *Principal*
EMP: 50 **EST:** 2019
SALES (est): 2.6MM **Privately Held**
WEB: www.cooperconcrete.net
SIC: 8711 Consulting engineer

(P-22519)
CORA CONSTRUCTORS INC
Also Called: General Contractor
75140 Saint Charles Pl A, Palm Desert (92211-9044)
PHONE..................................760 674-3201
Dennis Stockton, *CEO*
EMP: 50 **EST:** 2004
SQ FT: 2,500
SALES (est): 8.7MM **Privately Held**
WEB: www.coraconstructors.com
SIC: 8711 Building construction consultant

(P-22520)
CUMMING MANAGEMENT GROUP INC
523 W 6th St Ste 1001, Los Angeles (90014-1210)
PHONE..................................951 216-6443
Alastair Burns, *President*
Toby Meier, *Vice Pres*
Eric Simmons, *Vice Pres*
Ryan Zuehlke, *Associate Dir*
Halli Bovia, *Program Mgr*
EMP: 72
SALES (corp-wide): 191.1MM **Privately Held**
WEB: www.cumming-group.com
SIC: 8711 8741 Engineering services; management services
PA: Cumming Management Group, Inc.
25220 Hancock Ave Ste 440
Murrieta CA 92562
858 485-6765

(P-22521)
CUMMING MANAGEMENT GROUP INC
27455 Tierra Alta Way A, Temecula (92590-3498)
PHONE..................................951 252-8555
Sarah Smedley, *Manager*
Christine Jennison, *Manager*
Christa Garcia, *Transportation*
EMP: 72
SALES (corp-wide): 191.1MM **Privately Held**
SIC: 8711 8741 Building construction consultant; construction management
PA: Cumming Management Group, Inc.
25220 Hancock Ave Ste 440
Murrieta CA 92562
858 485-6765

(P-22522)
CURTISS-WRGHT CNTRLS ELCTRNIC
28965 Avenue Penn, Santa Clarita (91355-4185)
PHONE..................................661 257-4430
Val Zarov, *Branch Mgr*
EMP: 194
SALES (corp-wide): 2.3B **Publicly Held**
WEB: www.curtisswright.com
SIC: 8711 Engineering services
HQ: Curtiss-Wright Controls Electronic Systems, Inc.
28965 Avenue Penn
Santa Clarita CA 91355
661 702-1494

(P-22523)
CURTISS-WRGHT CNTRLS ELCTRNIC (DH)
Also Called: Curtiss-Wrght Cntrls Elctrnc
28965 Avenue Penn, Santa Clarita (91355-4185)
PHONE..................................661 702-1494
Thomas P Quinly, *CEO*
David Dietz, *President*
Sara Franke, *Manager*
EMP: 172 **EST:** 1985
SQ FT: 18,700
SALES (est): 50.1MM
SALES (corp-wide): 2.3B **Publicly Held**
WEB: www.curtisswright.com
SIC: 8711 8731 3769 3625 Consulting engineer; commercial physical research; guided missile & space vehicle parts & auxiliary equipment; relays & industrial controls
HQ: Curtiss-Wright Controls, Inc.
15801 Brixham Hill Ave # 200
Charlotte NC 28277
704 869-4600

(P-22524)
CURTISS-WRGHT CNTRLS INTGRTED (DH)
Also Called: Avionics & Electronics
28965 Avenue Penn, Valencia (91355-4185)
PHONE..................................661 257-4430
Thomas Quinly, *CEO*
John Kuperhand, *President*
Tony Sozutek, *Treasurer*
Anabele Cloud, *Admin Sec*
EMP: 69 **EST:** 1978

SQ FT: 27,000
SALES (est): 21.3MM
SALES (corp-wide): 2.3B **Publicly Held**
WEB: www.curtisswrightds.com
SIC: 8711 Engineering services
HQ: Curtiss-Wright Controls, Inc.
15801 Brixham Hill Ave # 200
Charlotte NC 28277
704 869-4600

(P-22525)
CURTISS-WRGHT FLOW CTRL SVC LL (HQ)
Also Called: Anatec International, Inc.
2950 E Birch St, Brea (92821-6246)
PHONE..................................949 498-3350
Blaine Curtis, *President*
Tammy Holden, *Vice Pres*
EMP: 60 **EST:** 1979
SQ FT: 12,000
SALES (est): 28.3MM
SALES (corp-wide): 2.3B **Publicly Held**
WEB: www.cwnuclear.com
SIC: 8711 Consulting engineer
PA: Curtiss-Wright Corporation
130 Harbour Place Dr # 300
Davidson NC 28036
704 869-4600

(P-22526)
DCS CORPORATION
137 W Drummond Ave Ste C, Ridgecrest (93555-3583)
PHONE..................................760 384-5600
Charles Faris, *Branch Mgr*
Weadon Alice, *Vice Pres*
Amy Kirby, *Vice Pres*
Bill Nelson, *Vice Pres*
Don Read, *Vice Pres*
EMP: 62
SALES (corp-wide): 196.6MM **Privately Held**
WEB: www.dcscorp.com
SIC: 8711 Consulting engineer
PA: Dcs Corporation
6609 Metro Pk Dr Ste 500
Alexandria VA 22310
571 227-6000

(P-22527)
DELCAN CORPORATION
2201 Dupont Dr Ste 200, Irvine (92612-7511)
PHONE..................................714 562-5725
Daniel Lukasik, *Manager*
Steven Worley, *Area Mgr*
Lucy Doloiras, *Admin Asst*
Carole Cleary, *Sr Software Eng*
Rosalyn Wilson, *Info Tech Dir*
EMP: 120
SALES (corp-wide): 3.9B **Publicly Held**
WEB: www.delcaninc.com
SIC: 8711 Civil engineering
HQ: Delcan Corporation
650 E Algonquin Rd # 400
Schaumburg IL 60173

(P-22528)
DEPLOYABLE SPACE SYSTEMS INC
Also Called: D S S
153 Castilian Dr, Goleta (93117-3025)
PHONE..................................805 722-8090
Brian Spence, *President*
Steve White, *Vice Pres*
Mark Douglas, *Technical Staff*
Peter Lacorte, *Engineer*
Kai Staal, *Engineer*
EMP: 50 **EST:** 2008
SQ FT: 3,000
SALES (est): 9.3MM **Privately Held**
WEB: www.dss-space.com
SIC: 8711 Structural engineering

(P-22529)
DESIGNWORKS/USA INC (HQ)
2201 Corporate Center Dr, Newbury Park (91320-1421)
PHONE..................................805 499-9590
Laurenz Schaffer, *President*
Adrian Van Hooydonk, *Executive*
Desalis Andre, *Creative Dir*
Andre Desalis, *Creative Dir*
Molly Evans, *Creative Dir*
EMP: 77 **EST:** 1971

SQ FT: 78,000
SALES (est): 12.6MM
SALES (corp-wide): 117B **Privately Held**
WEB: www.bmwgroupdesignworks.com
SIC: 8711 Designing: ship, boat, machine
& product
PA: Bayerische Motoren Werke Ag
Petuelring 130
Munchen BY 80788
893 820-

(P-22530)
DEVELOPMENT RESOURCE CONS INC (PA)
160 S Old Springs Rd # 210, Anaheim
(92808-1260)
PHONE..................714 685-6860
Lawrence Gates, *President*
Brian Anderson, *Vice Pres*
Lena Starbird, *Info Tech Mgr*
Wayne Pena, *Project Mgr*
Homer Maniago, *Project Engr*
EMP: 90 EST: 1997
SQ FT: 12,000
SALES (est): 12.4MM **Privately Held**
SIC: 8711 Civil engineering

(P-22531)
DEX CORPORATION
Also Called: Data Exchange
3600 Via Pescador, Camarillo
(93012-5051)
PHONE..................805 388-1711
Sheldon Malchiconfqs, *CEO*
EMP: 150 EST: 2015
SQ FT: 100,000
SALES (est): 8.1MM **Privately Held**
WEB: www.dex.com
SIC: 8711 5065 Engineering services;
electronic parts

(P-22532)
DIVERGENT TECHNOLOGIES INC
Also Called: Divergent 3d
19601 Hamilton Ave, Torrance
(90502-1309)
PHONE..................310 339-1186
Kevin Czinger, *President*
Kira Khodskaya, *CFO*
Jinbo Chen, *Vice Pres*
Tonio Martinez, *Vice Pres*
Roland Martin, *VP Business*
EMP: 97 EST: 2014
SALES (est): 15.7MM **Privately Held**
WEB: www.divergent3d.com
SIC: 8711 Mechanical engineering

(P-22533)
DIVERSIFIED PRJ SVCS INTL INC (PA)
5351 Olive Dr Ste 100, Bakersfield
(93308-2926)
PHONE..................661 371-2800
Robert Chambers, *President*
Christina Bottoms, *Vice Pres*
Mark Allen, *Division Mgr*
Ashley Dugan, *Admin Asst*
Joseph Liberal, *Technician*
EMP: 86 EST: 2007
SALES (est): 15.6MM **Privately Held**
WEB: www.dpsiinc.com
SIC: 8711 Consulting engineer

(P-22534)
DMS FACILITY SERVICES LLC
2861 E Coronado St, Anaheim
(92806-2504)
PHONE..................949 975-1366
Richard E Dotts, *Branch Mgr*
Jeffrey Magann, *General Mgr*
Jose Huerta, *Technician*
EMP: 748 **Privately Held**
WEB: www.dmsfacilityservices.com
SIC: 8711 Engineering services
PA: Dms Facility Services, Llc
1040 Arroyo Dr
South Pasadena CA 91030

(P-22535)
DZYNE TECHNOLOGIES INC
11 Vanderbilt, Irvine (92618-2011)
PHONE..................703 454-0704
Thomas Strat, *CEO*

David Sammons, *CFO*
Larry Reding, *Engineer*
Adam Thurn, *Engineer*
EMP: 50 EST: 2013
SALES (est): 5.6MM **Privately Held**
WEB: www.dzynetech.com
SIC: 8711 Mechanical engineering; avia-
tion &/or aeronautical engineering

(P-22536)
E2 MANAGETECH INC (HQ)
26741 Portola Pkwy, Foothill Ranch
(92610-1743)
PHONE..................281 407-0820
Vijay Gudivaka, *CEO*
Chad Morris, *COO*
Glenn Mayer Pe, *CFO*
Mike Mitchell, *Principal*
Abbey Hesser, *Technical Staff*
EMP: 63 EST: 2008
SALES (est): 11.8MM
SALES (corp-wide): 10.9MM **Privately Held**
WEB: www.arcadis.com
SIC: 8711 8741 Consulting engineer;
management services
PA: Arcadis N.V.
Gustav Mahlerplein 97 103
Amsterdam
884 261-261

(P-22537)
EARTH SYSTEMS SOUTHWEST (HQ)
79811 Country Club Dr B, Bermuda Dunes
(92203-1290)
PHONE..................760 345-1588
Mark Spykerman, *President*
Jerol Brown, *Corp Secy*
Scot Stormo, *Senior VP*
Mark Houghton, *Vice Pres*
Lutz Kunze, *Vice Pres*
EMP: 59 EST: 1998
SQ FT: 6,750
SALES (est): 8.5MM
SALES (corp-wide): 21.7MM **Privately Held**
WEB: www.earthsystems.com
SIC: 8711 8734 8748 7389 Consulting
engineer; testing laboratories; soil analy-
sis; environmental consultant; building in-
spection service
PA: Earth Systems, Inc.
720 Aerovista Pl Ste A
San Luis Obispo CA 93401
805 781-0112

(P-22538)
EFS WEST
28472 Constellation Rd, Valencia
(91355-5081)
PHONE..................661 705-8200
Arthur Babcock, *CEO*
Robert Golden, *President*
Dante Jumanan, *Vice Pres*
Tom Soper, *Vice Pres*
Cesar SA Ntiago, *Manager*
EMP: 50 EST: 2003
SQ FT: 41,000
SALES (est): 9.4MM **Privately Held**
WEB: www.efswest.com
SIC: 8711 Engineering services

(P-22539)
EICHLEAY INC
5555 Garden Grove Blvd # 300, Westmin-
ster (92683-8230)
PHONE..................562 256-8600
Lori M Lofstrom, *Branch Mgr*
Samar H Adranly, *Senior VP*
Dee Honea, *Admin Sec*
Srilatha Gollapalli, *Project Mgr*
Jose Gantes, *Project Engr*
EMP: 149 **Privately Held**
WEB: www.eichleay.com
SIC: 8711 Consulting engineer
PA: Eichleay, Inc.
1390 Willow Pass Rd # 60
Concord CA 94520

(P-22540)
ELECTROSONIC INC (DH)
3320 N San Fernando Blvd, Burbank
(91504-2530)
PHONE..................818 333-3600

James Bowie, *President*
Scott Meyer, *CFO*
Nico Ahlstrom, *Managing Dir*
David Mitchell, *Admin Sec*
Martin Wasley, *Prgrmr*
◆ EMP: 70 EST: 1972
SALES (est): 115.8MM
SALES (corp-wide): 101.1MM **Privately Held**
WEB: www.electrosonic.com
SIC: 8711 7359 7812 Engineering serv-
ices; audio-visual equipment & supply
rental; audio-visual program production
HQ: Electrosonic Limited
Hawley Mill
Dartford DA2 7
132 222-2211

(P-22541)
ELITE ENGINEERING CONTRS INC
16619 S Broadway, Gardena (90248-2715)
PHONE..................310 465-8333
Brian Perazzolo, *CEO*
Jason M Metoyer, *Principal*
Todd Patterson, *Project Mgr*
Omar Vinas, *Opers Mgr*
EMP: 20 EST: 2017
SALES (est): 2.1MM **Privately Held**
WEB: www.eliteengineering.net
SIC: 8711 1771 1081 Engineering serv-
ices; stucco, gunite & grouting contrac-
tors; metal mining exploration &
development services

(P-22542)
EMBEE PROCESSING LLC
Also Called: Embee Plating
2158 S Hathaway St, Santa Ana
(92705-5249)
PHONE..................714 546-9842
Michael Coburn, *CEO*
Derek Watson, *Managing Prtnr*
Scott Chrisman, *CFO*
Leslie Zimmer, *Vice Pres*
Jeannie Roehrig, *Planning Mgr*
▲ EMP: 385 EST: 1947
SQ FT: 100,000
SALES (est): 32.8MM **Privately Held**
WEB: www.embee.com
SIC: 8711 3398 3479 8734 Aviation &/or
aeronautical engineering; shot peening
(treating steel to reduce fatigue); coating
of metals & formed products; metallurgi-
cal testing laboratory

(P-22543)
ENGLEKIRK INSTITUTIONAL INC (PA)
888 S Figueroa St Ste 180, Los Angeles
(90017-5307)
PHONE..................323 733-2640
Tom Sabol, *President*
EMP: 50 EST: 1979
SQ FT: 12,000
SALES (est): 3.6MM **Privately Held**
SIC: 8711 Structural engineering

(P-22544)
ENGLEKIRK STRUCTURAL ENGINEERS (PA)
888 S Figueroa St # 1800, Los Angeles
(90017-5449)
PHONE..................323 733-6673
Tom Sabol, *President*
Christopher Rosien, *CFO*
Prayut Patel, *Design Engr*
Karl Edwards, *Director*
EMP: 50 EST: 1998
SALES (est): 10.5MM **Privately Held**
WEB: www.englekirk.com
SIC: 8711 Consulting engineer

(P-22545)
EONTORK POWER INC
13427 Virginia Ave, Whittier (90605-3645)
PHONE..................888 959-1311
Erika Aldama, *President*
EMP: 50 EST: 2018
SALES (est): 4.6MM **Privately Held**
WEB: www.eontorkpower.com
SIC: 8711 Engineering services

(P-22546)
ES ENGINEERING SERVICES LLC
1 Park Plz Ste 1000, Irvine (92614-8507)
PHONE..................949 988-3500
Travis Hicks, *Project Engr*
EMP: 85 EST: 2015
SALES (est): 5MM
SALES (corp-wide): 328.2MM **Publicly Held**
WEB: www.montrose-env.com
SIC: 8711 8748 Engineering services; sys-
tems analysis & engineering consulting
services
PA: Montrose Environmental Group, Inc.
1 Park Plz Ste 1000
Irvine CA 92614
949 988-3500

(P-22547)
FARADAY&FUTURE INC
Also Called: Faraday & Future
18455 S Figueroa St, Gardena
(90248-4503)
PHONE..................424 276-7616
Carstein Breitfield, *CEO*
Carsten Breitfeld, *CEO*
Zvi Wang, *CFO*
Alan Cherry, *Vice Pres*
Jeff Risher, *Vice Pres*
EMP: 1111 EST: 2014
SALES (est): 121.3MM
SALES (corp-wide): 248.1MM **Publicly Held**
WEB: www.ff.com
SIC: 8711 7389 6282 Engineering serv-
ices; design, commercial & industrial; in-
vestment advisory service
PA: Faraday Future Intelligent Electric Inc.
18455 S Figueroa St
Gardena CA 90248
424 276-7616

(P-22548)
FIRE PROTECTION GROUP AMER INC
3712 W Jefferson Blvd, Los Angeles
(90016-4208)
P.O. Box 180520 (90018-9682)
PHONE..................323 732-4200
George Saadian, *President*
Louise Tchaman, *Corp Secy*
EMP: 40 EST: 1985
SQ FT: 20,000
SALES (est): 4.5MM **Privately Held**
WEB: www.firesprinkler.com
SIC: 8711 1711 3569 1731 Fire protec-
tion engineering; fire sprinkler system in-
stallation; firefighting apparatus & related
equipment; fire detection & burglar alarm
systems specialization

(P-22549)
FLINT ENERGY SERVICES INC
1999 Avenue Of The Stars # 2, Los Angeles
(90067-6022)
PHONE..................213 593-8000
EMP: 77
SALES (corp-wide): 13.2B **Publicly Held**
WEB: www.aecom.com
SIC: 8711 Engineering services
HQ: Flint Energy Services Inc.
7595 E Technology Way # 200
Denver CO 80237
918 294-3030

(P-22550)
FLUOR CORPORATION
Also Called: Trs Staffing Solutions
3 Polaris Way, Aliso Viejo (92656-5338)
PHONE..................949 349-2000
Tim Kirk, *Principal*
Stephen Hull, *Treasurer*
Lawrence N Fisher, *Vice Pres*
Brad Friesen, *Vice Pres*
Reid Pannill, *Exec Dir*
EMP: 99
SALES (corp-wide): 15.6B **Publicly Held**
WEB: www.fluor.com
SIC: 8711 7363 Engineering services;
help supply services
PA: Fluor Corporation
6700 Las Colinas Blvd
Irving TX 75039
469 398-7000

(P-22551)
**FLUOR DANIEL EURASIA INC
(DH)**
1 Fluor Daniel Dr, Aliso Viejo (92698-1000)
PHONE..................................949 349-2000
Alan Beckman, *CEO*
S T Hall, *Treasurer*
Robert Lief, *Director*
EMP: 1004 EST: 1999
SALES (est): 6.8MM
SALES (corp-wide): 15.6B Publicly Held
WEB: www.fluor.com
SIC: 8711 1541 1629 8742 Engineering
services; industrial buildings, new con-
struction; industrial plant construction;
maintenance management consultant;
strip mining, bituminous
HQ: Fluor Enterprises, Inc.
6700 Las Colinas Blvd
Irving TX 75039
469 398-7000

(P-22552)
**FLUOR PLANT SERVICES INTL
INC**
Also Called: Fluor Daniel
1 Enterprise, Aliso Viejo (92656-2606)
PHONE..................................949 349-2000
D Michael Steuert, *CFO*
Richard Carano, *Vice Pres*
Matt Stennes, *Exec Dir*
John Viggiano, *Exec Dir*
Ronald Albright, *Branch Mgr*
EMP: 100 EST: 1900
SALES (est): 26.7MM
SALES (corp-wide): 15.6B Publicly Held
WEB: www.fluor.com
SIC: 8711 Engineering services
PA: Fluor Corporation
6700 Las Colinas Blvd
Irving TX 75039
469 398-7000

(P-22553)
FLUORAMEC LLC (HQ)
1 Enterprise, Aliso Viejo (92656-2606)
PHONE..................................949 349-2000
Michelle Bell, *Director*
▼ **EMP: 50 EST: 2003**
SALES (est): 29MM
SALES (corp-wide): 15.6B Publicly Held
WEB: www.fluor.com
SIC: 8711 Engineering services
PA: Fluor Corporation
6700 Las Colinas Blvd
Irving TX 75039
469 398-7000

(P-22554)
FLUXERGY INC (PA)
30 Fairbanks, Irvine (92618-1623)
PHONE..................................949 305-4201
Tej Patel, *President*
Jonathan Tu, *CFO*
Ryan Revilla, *Vice Pres*
Charlotte Varela, *Office Mgr*
Shrin Kuo, *Director*
EMP: 65 EST: 2013
SALES (est): 10.2MM Privately Held
WEB: www.fluxergy.com
SIC: 8711 3841 Mechanical engineering;
diagnostic apparatus, medical

(P-22555)
FORTEL TRAFFIC INC
5310 E Hunter Ave, Anaheim (92807-2053)
PHONE..................................714 701-9800
Emery B Dyer, *President*
Kari Laitinen, *General Mgr*
Jayne M Dyer, *Admin Sec*
Laurie Casper, *Administration*
Thomas Frantz, *Engineer*
▼ **EMP: 17 EST: 1995**
SQ FT: 14,000
SALES (est): 3.2MM Privately Held
WEB: www.vcalm.com
SIC: 8711 3669 Consulting engineer; traf-
fic signals, electric

(P-22556)
FREAR CONSULTING INC
907 Buena Vista Apt A, San Clemente
(92672-5009)
PHONE..................................307 237-6060
David M Frear, *President*

Staci Pope, *Office Mgr*
EMP: 60 EST: 2004
SALES (est): 1.9MM Privately Held
WEB: www.frearconsulting.com
SIC: 8711 Consulting engineer

(P-22557)
FRICTION MATERIALS LLC
2525 W 190th St, Torrance (90504-6002)
PHONE..................................248 362-3600
Andre Bezuszka, *Mng Member*
EMP: 132 EST: 2002
SALES (est): 8.8MM
SALES (corp-wide): 3B Privately Held
SIC: 8711 Engineering services
PA: Garrett Motion Inc.
47548 Halyard Dr
Plymouth MI 48170
734 359-5901

(P-22558)
FTI CONSULTING INC
350 S Grand Ave Ste 3000, Los Angeles
(90071-3424)
PHONE..................................213 689-1200
Stewart Kahn, *President*
Shannon Bales, *Managing Dir*
Katherine Kim, *Managing Dir*
Alan Ruffier, *Managing Dir*
Kevin REA, *Managing Dir*
EMP: 80
SALES (corp-wide): 2.4B Publicly Held
WEB: www.fticonsulting.com
SIC: 8711 8748 8742 Consulting engi-
neer; business consulting; management
consulting services
PA: Fti Consulting, Inc.
555 12th St Nw Ste 3
Washington DC 20004
202 312-9100

(P-22559)
**FUSCOE ENGINEERING INC
(PA)**
16795 Von Karman Ave # 100, Irvine
(92606-4974)
PHONE..................................949 474-1960
Patrick Fuscoe, *President*
Sarah Johnson, *Technician*
Julian Blevins, *Project Mgr*
John Gilmour, *Project Mgr*
Carolina Gonzalez, *Project Mgr*
EMP: 85 EST: 1992
SQ FT: 16,000
SALES (est): 20.6MM Privately Held
WEB: www.fuscoe.com
SIC: 8711 Civil engineering

(P-22560)
**GARRETT J GENTRY GEN
ENGRG INC**
1297 W 9th St, Upland (91786-5706)
PHONE..................................909 693-3391
Garrett J Gentry, *President*
Bryan Copping, *Admin Sec*
Richard Barnes, *Project Mgr*
David Niederhauser, *Project Mgr*
Jim Zheng, *Project Mgr*
EMP: 100 EST: 2013
SALES (est): 30MM Privately Held
WEB: www.gjgentry.com
SIC: 8711 Acoustical engineering

(P-22561)
**GLOBAL SOLUTIONS
INTEGRATION**
Also Called: Gsico
26632 Towne Centre Dr # 300, Foothill
Ranch (92610-2813)
PHONE..................................949 307-1849
Cel Esmundi, *President*
EMP: 75 EST: 2016
SQ FT: 3,000
SALES (est): 4.6MM Privately Held
WEB: www.gsico.net
SIC: 8711 Engineering services

(P-22562)
GRADIENT ENGINEERS INC
Also Called: Leighton & Associates
17781 Cowan Ste 140, Irvine (92614-6009)
PHONE..................................949 477-0555
Terry Brennan, *Chairman*
Kris Lutton, *President*
Tom Mills, *Vice Pres*

EMP: 194 EST: 1996
SALES (est): 523.8K
**SALES (corp-wide): 25.6MM Privately
Held**
WEB: www.leightongroup.com
SIC: 8711 8744 Consulting engineer;
PA: Leighton Group, Inc.
17781 Cowan
Irvine CA 92614
949 477-4040

(P-22563)
GROUP ROSSIGNOL USA INC
Also Called: Felt Bicycles
30161 Avnida De Las Bnder, Rancho Santa
Margari (92688)
PHONE..................................949 452-9050
Bob Thomson, *Creative Dir*
Ty Buckenberger, *Design Engr*
Mark Rushmann, *Sales Staff*
EMP: 65
**SALES (corp-wide): 177.9K Privately
Held**
WEB: www.rossignol.com
SIC: 5941 8711 Bicycle & bicycle parts;
engineering services
HQ: Group Rossignol Usa, Inc.
1413 Center Dr
Park City UT 84098
435 252-3300

(P-22564)
GROWIT LLC
1157 Cliff Ave, Fillmore (93015-9604)
PHONE..................................949 305-4004
David Gurrola,
Leslie Davidson, *Manager*
Alyssa Otto, *Manager*
Matt Nebo, *Accounts Mgr*
EMP: 21 EST: 2007
SALES (est): 1.3MM Privately Held
WEB: www.forecast3d.com
SIC: 8711 2869 Engineering services; per-
fumes, flavorings & food additives

(P-22565)
**HAPPOLD HOLDINGS (NA) INC
(DH)**
800 Wilshire Blvd # 1600, Los Angeles
(90017-2604)
PHONE..................................310 945-4800
David Herd, *Managing Prtnr*
Al Fisher, *Director*
Adrian Palmer, *Director*
Andy Pottinger, *Director*
Craig Schwitter, *Director*
EMP: 50 EST: 2007
SALES (est): 13.9MM
**SALES (corp-wide): 259.3MM Privately
Held**
WEB: www.burohappold.com
SIC: 8711 Consulting engineer
HQ: Buro Happold Limited
Lower Bristol Road
Bath
122 532-0600

(P-22566)
**HERNANDEZ KROONE AND
ASSOC INC**
Also Called: Hka
234 E Drake Dr, San Bernardino
(92408-2224)
PHONE..................................909 884-3222
Ann Hernandez, *President*
Richard Hernandez, *Vice Pres*
Wendy McLlroy, *Principal*
John Hernandez, *Engineer*
Juan Rodriguez, *Accountant*
EMP: 51 EST: 1987
SQ FT: 6,000
SALES (est): 3.7MM Privately Held
WEB: www.hkagroup.com
SIC: 8711 8713 Civil engineering; survey-
ing services

(P-22567)
HNTB CORPORATION
601 W 5th St Ste 1000, Los Angeles
(90071-2028)
PHONE..................................213 403-1000
Lanson Nichols, *Vice Pres*
David Tiberi, *Vice Pres*
Susan Shaffer, *Admin Asst*
Teresa Miller, *Administration*
Elisabeth Suh, *Planning*

EMP: 56
SALES (corp-wide): 1.2B Privately Held
WEB: www.hntb.com
SIC: 8711 Consulting engineer
HQ: Hntb Corporation
715 Kirk Dr
Kansas City MO 64105
816 472-1201

(P-22568)
HNTB CORPORATION
6 Hutton Cntre Dr Ste 500, Santa Ana
(92707)
PHONE..................................714 460-1600
Andres Ocon, *Branch Mgr*
Craig Denson, *CFO*
Mark Ramsey, *Assoc VP*
Megan Monticone, *Project Mgr*
Michael Hernandez, *Engineer*
EMP: 51
SALES (corp-wide): 1.2B Privately Held
WEB: www.hntb.com
SIC: 8711 Consulting engineer
HQ: Hntb Corporation
715 Kirk Dr
Kansas City MO 64105
816 472-1201

(P-22569)
**HNTB GERWICK WATER
SOLUTIONS**
200 Sandpointe Ave, Santa Ana
(92707-5751)
PHONE..................................714 460-1600
EMP: 150
SALES (est): 3.7MM Privately Held
SIC: 8711 8712 Engineering Services,
Nsk

(P-22570)
HOLMES & NARVER INC (HQ)
999 W Town And Country Rd, Orange
(92868-4713)
P.O. Box 6240 (92863-6240)
PHONE..................................714 567-2400
Danny Seal, *CEO*
Raymond Landy, *President*
Dennis Deslatte, *CFO*
Tina Clugston, *Principal*
EMP: 250 EST: 1933
SQ FT: 100,000
SALES (est): 38.8MM
SALES (corp-wide): 13.2B Publicly Held
WEB: www.aecom.com
SIC: 8711 8742 8741 1542 Engineering
services; training & development consult-
ant; construction management; nonresi-
dential construction
PA: Aecom
13355 Noel Rd Ste 400
Dallas TX 75240
972 788-1000

(P-22571)
**HUNSAKER & ASSOC IRVINE
INC**
2900 Adams St Ste A15, Riverside
(92504-4337)
PHONE..................................951 352-7200
Brad Hay, *Branch Mgr*
John Michler, *Partner*
Pam Karmann, *Office Mgr*
James Maeding, *Planning*
Marisela Avena, *Design Engr*
EMP: 300
**SALES (corp-wide): 54MM Privately
Held**
WEB: www.hnagi.com
SIC: 8711 Civil engineering
PA: Hunsaker & Associates Irvine, Inc.
3 Hughes
Irvine CA 92618
949 583-1010

(P-22572)
**HUNSAKER & ASSOC IRVINE
INC (PA)**
3 Hughes, Irvine (92618-2021)
PHONE..................................949 583-1010
Richard Hunsaker, *CEO*
Douglas Snyder, *President*
Chris Kembrell, *CFO*
Chuck Cater, *Vice Pres*
Stephen Hunsaker, *Vice Pres*
EMP: 100 EST: 1976
SQ FT: 27,000

SALES (est): 54MM **Privately Held**
WEB: www.hnagi.com
SIC: 8711 8713 Civil engineering; surveying services

(P-22573)
HYUNDAI AMER TECHNICAL CTR INC
Also Called: Kia Design Center America
101 Peters Canyon Rd, Irvine
(92606-1790)
PHONE.....................734 337-2500
EMP: 69 **Privately Held**
WEB: www.hatci.com
SIC: 8711 8734 Designing: ship, boat, machine & product; automobile proving & testing ground
HQ: Hyundai America Technical Center Incorporated
6800 Geddes Rd
Ypsilanti MI 48198
734 337-2500

(P-22574)
IBI GROUP A CALIFORNIA PARTNR
Also Called: Ibi Group, Los Angeles
1001 Wilshire Blvd # 100, Los Angeles
(90017-2820)
PHONE.....................213 769-0011
Scott Stewart, CEO
EMP: 52
SALES (corp-wide): 345.8MM **Privately Held**
WEB: www.ibigroup.com
SIC: 8711 Engineering services
HQ: Ibi Group, A California Partnership
18401 Von Karman Ave
Irvine CA 92612
949 833-5588

(P-22575)
IMI CCI
Also Called: IMI Critical Engineering
22591 Avenida Empresa, Rcho STA Marg
(92688-2003)
PHONE.....................949 858-1877
C M Merrimon, President
Jorge Barcelo, Principal
Christian Lekavich, Design Engr
Shaun Lindley, Sales Staff
Mark Hollerbach, Director
EMP: 28 **EST:** 2016
SALES (est): 3.3MM **Privately Held**
WEB: www.imi-critical.com
SIC: 8711 3592 3999 Mechanical engineering; valves; atomizers; toiletry

(P-22576)
INNOVATIVE ENGRG SYSTEMS INC (PA)
Also Called: Ies Engineering
8800 Crippen St, Bakersfield (93311-9686)
P.O. Box 20610 (93390-0610)
PHONE.....................661 381-7800
David Wolfer, President
Steve Johnson, Division Mgr
Jordan Stockton, Division Mgr
Eric Powers, Administration
Darren Thorpe, Technician
EMP: 100 **EST:** 2002
SQ FT: 20,000
SALES (est): 26.3MM **Privately Held**
WEB: www.agilitechgroup.com
SIC: 8711 1731 Consulting engineer; electrical work

(P-22577)
INSIGHT ENVMTL ENGRG CNSTR INC (PA)
2749 Saturn St, Brea (92821-6705)
PHONE.....................714 678-6700
Aqeel Mohammad, President
Tina Woodside, CFO
Charles Duckworth, Exec VP
Tasawwar Ali, Vice Pres
Asrar Faheem, Vice Pres
EMP: 53 **EST:** 2004
SQ FT: 5,000 **Privately Held**
WEB: www.ieeci.com
SIC: 8711 8741 Consulting engineer; construction management

(P-22578)
INSPIRIA INC (PA)
Also Called: Audiovisions
140 Technology Dr Ste 100, Irvine
(92618-2427)
PHONE.....................949 206-0606
Mark Hoffenberg, President
Terence Murray, Vice Pres
Ted Taylor, Vice Pres
Bob Walpert, Executive
Katie Forester, Office Mgr
EMP: 64 **EST:** 1989
SALES (est): 11.7MM **Privately Held**
SIC: 8711 Electrical or electronic engineering

(P-22579)
INTERACT PMTI INC (DH)
260 Maple Ct Ste 210, Ventura
(93003-3566)
PHONE.....................805 658-5600
Tom Kennedy, President
Michelle Pasini, Project Dir
Jeff Hall, Project Mgr
Val Lerma, Engineer
Allen Scoging, Engineer
EMP: 54 **EST:** 1999
SQ FT: 6,000
SALES (est): 14.4MM **Publicly Held**
WEB: www.interactprojects.com
SIC: 8711 Consulting engineer
HQ: Acteon Group Limited
Ferry Road
Norwich NR1 1
160 322-7019

(P-22580)
INTERNTONAL STRL ENGINEERS INC
Also Called: I S E
11926 S La Cienega Blvd, Hawthorne
(90250-3463)
P.O. Box 836 (90251-0836)
PHONE.....................310 643-7310
Bengt Mossberg, President
Laurent Stoeckli, Project Mgr
EMP: 21 **EST:** 1970
SALES (est): 894.4K **Privately Held**
WEB: www.i-s-e.com
SIC: 8711 7371 7372 Consulting engineer; computer software development; prepackaged software

(P-22581)
IQA SOLUTIONS INC
4089 E Conant St, Long Beach
(90808-1777)
PHONE.....................562 420-1000
Mohsem H Hashemi, CEO
Andrew Stasio, Vice Pres
Paul Szabo, Department Mgr
Patricia Sandoval, Administration
Shamim Naderi, CIO
EMP: 62 **EST:** 2003
SQ FT: 8,500
SALES (est): 6.8MM **Privately Held**
WEB: www.iqasolutions.com
SIC: 8711 Consulting engineer

(P-22582)
JACOBS ATCS FEMA A JOINT VENTR
155 N Lake Ave Fl 5, Pasadena
(91101-1849)
PHONE.....................571 218-1115
Ed Pogreba, Vice Pres
EMP: 99 **EST:** 2017
SALES (est): 1.5MM **Privately Held**
SIC: 8711 8712 8748 8741 Consulting engineer; architectural services; business consulting; management services

(P-22583)
JACOBS CIVIL INC
1500 Hughes Way Ste B400, Long Beach
(90810-1882)
PHONE.....................310 847-2500
EMP: 229
SALES (corp-wide): 13.5B **Publicly Held**
SIC: 8711 Consulting engineer
HQ: Jacobs Civil Inc.
501 N Broadway Ste 185
Saint Louis MO

(P-22584)
JACOBS ENGINEERING COMPANY
1111 S Arroyo Pkwy, Pasadena
(91105-3254)
P.O. Box 7084 (91109-7084)
PHONE.....................626 449-2171
Noel G Watson, CEO
C L Martin, President
Supranee Degraw, Project Mgr
Clinton Jackson, Project Mgr
Britney Meshke, Agent
EMP: 4000 **EST:** 1989
SALES (est): 118.3MM
SALES (corp-wide): 13.5B **Publicly Held**
WEB: www.jacobs.com
SIC: 8711 1629 Engineering services; chemical plant & refinery construction
PA: Jacobs Engineering Group Inc.
1999 Bryan St 1200
Dallas TX 75201
214 583-8500

(P-22585)
JACOBS ENGINEERING GROUP INC
1111 S Arroyo Pkwy, Pasadena
(91105-3254)
P.O. Box 7084 (91109-7084)
PHONE.....................626 578-3500
Candace Hartley, Officer
Naomi McClain, Division VP
George Kunberger Jr, Exec VP
Andrew Berryman, Vice Pres
Jim McGrath, Vice Pres
EMP: 89
SALES (corp-wide): 13.5B **Publicly Held**
WEB: www.jacobs.com
SIC: 8711 Consulting engineer
PA: Jacobs Engineering Group Inc.
1999 Bryan St Ste 1200
Dallas TX 75201
214 583-8500

(P-22586)
JACOBS ENGINEERING INC (HQ)
155 N Lake Ave, Pasadena (91101-1849)
P.O. Box 7084 (91109-7084)
PHONE.....................626 578-3500
Craig L Martin, CEO
James Moran, Vice Chairman
Patrick Hill, Exec VP
Lorie Simpson, Senior VP
Martin Ahmad, Vice Pres
EMP: 2518 **EST:** 1971
SALES (est): 193.8MM
SALES (corp-wide): 13.5B **Publicly Held**
WEB: www.jacobs.com
SIC: 8711 Consulting engineer
PA: Jacobs Engineering Group Inc.
1999 Bryan St Ste 1200
Dallas TX 75201
214 583-8500

(P-22587)
JACOBS INTERNATIONAL LTD INC
155 N Lake Ave Ste 800, Pasadena
(91101-1857)
P.O. Box 7084 (91109-7084)
PHONE.....................626 578-3500
Craig Martin, President
John W Prosser Jr, Treasurer
Keith Ackley, Vice Pres
Rick Bourn, Vice Pres
Vinayak Pai, Vice Pres
EMP: 300 **EST:** 2002
SQ FT: 120,000
SALES (est): 68.4MM
SALES (corp-wide): 13.5B **Publicly Held**
WEB: www.jacobs.com
SIC: 8711 Consulting engineer
PA: Jacobs Engineering Group Inc.
1999 Bryan St Ste 1200
Dallas TX 75201
214 583-8500

(P-22588)
JACOBS PROJECT MANAGEMENT CO
2600 Michelson Dr Ste 500, Irvine
(92612-6506)
PHONE.....................949 224-7695
Les Steinberger, Manager

Frank Joyce, Contract Mgr
EMP: 99 **EST:** 2008
SALES (est): 9.7MM
SALES (corp-wide): 13.5B **Publicly Held**
WEB: www.jacobs.com
SIC: 8711 Consulting engineer
PA: Jacobs Engineering Group Inc.
1999 Bryan St Ste 1200
Dallas TX 75201
214 583-8500

(P-22589)
JBA CONSULTING ENGINEERS INC
163 Technology Dr Ste 100, Irvine
(92618-2486)
PHONE.....................949 419-3030
Ed Butera, Manager
Piyush Patel, Sr Project Mgr
EMP: 60
SALES (corp-wide): 659.3MM **Publicly Held**
WEB: www.nv5.com
SIC: 8711 Mechanical engineering; electrical or electronic engineering; consulting engineer
HQ: J.B.A. Consulting Engineers, Inc.
5155 W Patrick Ln
Las Vegas NV 89118
702 362-9200

(P-22590)
JOHN A MARTIN & ASSOCIATES INC
950 S Grand Ave Ste 400, Los Angeles
(90015-4202)
PHONE.....................213 483-6490
Kurt Clandening, President
EMP: 68
SALES (est): 12.4MM **Privately Held**
WEB: www.johnmartin.com
SIC: 8711 Consulting engineer

(P-22591)
JSL TECHNOLOGIES INC
1451 N Rice Ave Ste A, Oxnard
(93030-7991)
PHONE.....................805 985-7700
Joseph T Black III, President
Joe Black, Vice Pres
Ben Fujikawa, Vice Pres
Brian Kozlowski, Vice Pres
Jed Williams, Vice Pres
EMP: 290
SQ FT: 22,155
SALES (est): 28MM **Privately Held**
WEB: www.jsltechinc.com
SIC: 8711 Consulting engineer

(P-22592)
JT3 LLC
190 S Wolfe Ave Bldg 1260, Edwards
(93524-6501)
PHONE.....................661 277-4900
James Tedeschi, Manager
EMP: 176
SALES (corp-wide): 150MM **Privately Held**
SIC: 8711 Engineering services
PA: Jt3, L.L.C.
821 Grier Dr
Las Vegas NV 89119
704 492-2181

(P-22593)
K&B ELECTRIC LLC
Also Called: K&B Engineering
290 Corporate Terrace Cir # 200, Corona
(92879-6033)
PHONE.....................951 808-9501
Sandee Gibbs, Mng Member
Trey Gibbs,
EMP: 158 **EST:** 2011
SALES (est): 12.8MM **Privately Held**
WEB: www.kbeng.net
SIC: 8711 Engineering services

(P-22594)
K&B ENGINEERING
290 Corporate Terrace Cir, Corona
(92879-6033)
PHONE.....................951 808-9501
Trey Gibbs, Owner
Don Donato, Project Mgr
Jose Ochoa, Technology
Luis Garcia, Manager

EMP: 200 EST: 2007
SALES (est): 19.3MM **Privately Held**
SIC: 8711 Consulting engineer

(P-22595)
KAL KRSHNAN CNSULTING SVCS INC
Also Called: Kkcs
800 S Figueroa St # 1210, Los Angeles (90017-2521)
PHONE.....................213 488-0900
Ronald Anderson, *Manager*
Robert Badger, *Assoc VP*
David McCrossan, *Vice Pres*
Steven Friedlander, *Project Mgr*
Brandi Cagnolatti, *Human Resources*
EMP: 78
SALES (corp-wide): 9.2MM **Privately Held**
WEB: www.kkcsworld.com
SIC: 8711 Consulting engineer
PA: Kal Krishnan Consulting Services, Inc.
800 S Figueroa St # 1210
Los Angeles CA 90017
510 893-3500

(P-22596)
KINEMETRICS INC (DH)
222 Vista Ave, Pasadena (91107-3295)
PHONE.....................626 795-2220
Tadashi Jimbo, *CEO*
Michelle Harrington, *Treasurer*
Melvin Lund, *Exec VP*
Ogie Kuraica, *Vice Pres*
Ian Standley, *Vice Pres*
EMP: 59 **EST:** 1969
SQ FT: 50,000
SALES (est): 25.8MM **Privately Held**
WEB: www.kinemetrics.com
SIC: 8711 3829 Engineering services; seismographs

(P-22597)
KPFF INC
Also Called: K P F F Consulting Engineers
700 S Flower St Ste 2100, Los Angeles (90017-4208)
PHONE.....................310 665-1536
John Gavan, *Manager*
Mauricio Giron, *Administration*
Johnathan Duong, *Design Engr*
Tonissen Alan, *Project Mgr*
David McGraw, *Engineer*
EMP: 114
SALES (corp-wide): 218.3MM **Privately Held**
WEB: www.kpff.com
SIC: 8711 Consulting engineer
PA: Kpff, Inc.
1601 5th Ave Ste 1600
Seattle WA 98101
206 622-5822

(P-22598)
KSI ENGINEERING INC
6205 District Blvd, Bakersfield (93313-2141)
PHONE.....................661 617-1700
Kevin Small, *President*
Glenda Sue Small, *Corp Secy*
EMP: 53 **EST:** 1991
SQ FT: 7,000
SALES (est): 2.8MM **Privately Held**
WEB: www.ksilp.com
SIC: 8711 Electrical or electronic engineering

(P-22599)
L3 TECHNOLOGIES INC
Also Called: Maripro
7414 Hollister Ave, Goleta (93117-2583)
PHONE.....................805 683-3881
Robin Barker, *General Mgr*
Williaml Hall, *Engineer*
Mark Altshuler, *Director*
Joseph Shively, *Manager*
EMP: 90
SALES (corp-wide): 18.1B **Publicly Held**
WEB: www.l3harris.com
SIC: 8711 Marine engineering
HQ: L3 Technologies, Inc.
600 3rd Ave Fl 34
New York NY 10016
321 727-9100

(P-22600)
LEE & RO INC (PA)
1199 Fullerton Rd, City of Industry (91748-1232)
PHONE.....................626 912-3391
Myong Ro, *CEO*
Gregory Holmes, *CFO*
Jay Jung, *Vice Pres*
Kelly Mardorf, *Vice Pres*
Dhiru Patel, *Vice Pres*
EMP: 50 **EST:** 1979
SQ FT: 19,000
SALES: 9.8MM **Privately Held**
WEB: www.lee-ro.com
SIC: 8711 Civil engineering; mechanical engineering; sanitary engineers

(P-22601)
LINQUEST CORPORATION (PA)
5140 W Goldleaf Cir # 40, Los Angeles (90056-1299)
PHONE.....................323 924-1600
Timothy Dills, *President*
Greg Young, *COO*
Matthew Klein, *CFO*
Silvia Van Dusen, *Officer*
Kent Wilcher, *Officer*
EMP: 200
SQ FT: 20,000
SALES (est): 106.2MM **Privately Held**
WEB: www.linquest.com
SIC: 8711 Aviation &/or aeronautical engineering

(P-22602)
LOS ANGELES ENGINEERING INC
633 N Barranca Ave, Covina (91723-1229)
PHONE.....................626 869-1400
Henry Angus O'Brien, *President*
Aaron O'Brien, *COO*
Beth Ballard, *CFO*
Hallquist Pops, *Vice Pres*
Chuck Houston, *Safety Dir*
EMP: 110 **EST:** 1987
SQ FT: 33,000
SALES: 38.7MM **Privately Held**
WEB: www.laeng.net
SIC: 8711 1622 Construction & civil engineering; bridge, tunnel & elevated highway

(P-22603)
MANGAN INC (PA)
3901 Via Oro Ave, Long Beach (90810-1800)
PHONE.....................310 835-8080
Richard D Mangan, *Principal*
Amin Solehjou, *CEO*
Bimmy Dhanapala, *CFO*
Russell Seward, *CFO*
Mary Kelly, *Administration*
EMP: 90 **EST:** 1991
SQ FT: 15,000
SALES (est): 50MM **Privately Held**
WEB: www.manganinc.com
SIC: 8711 Consulting engineer

(P-22604)
MARTIN ASSOCIATES GROUP INC (PA)
Also Called: Martin, John A & Associates
950 S Grand Ave Fl 4, Los Angeles (90015-1436)
PHONE.....................213 483-6490
John A Martin, *Senior Partner*
Barry Schindler, *Vice Pres*
Richard Lawrence, *Project Mgr*
Kim Pacheco, *Project Mgr*
Shane SE, *Project Engr*
EMP: 63 **EST:** 1961
SQ FT: 70,000
SALES (est): 84.1MM **Privately Held**
WEB: www.johnmartin.com
SIC: 8711 Consulting engineer

(P-22605)
MARVIN ENGINEERING CO INC (PA)
Also Called: Marvin Group, The
261 W Beach Ave, Inglewood (90302-2904)
PHONE.....................310 674-5030
Gerald M Friedman, *CEO*
Howard Gussman, *President*
Wade Morse, *COO*
Leon Tsimmerman, *CFO*
Bryan Deblois, *Vice Pres*
▲ **EMP:** 580 **EST:** 1963
SQ FT: 300,000
SALES (est): 149.5MM **Privately Held**
WEB: www.marvingroup.com
SIC: 8711 Consulting engineer

(P-22606)
MAXAR SPACE ROBOTICS LLC (DH)
Also Called: Ssl Robotics LLC
1250 Lincoln Ave Ste 100, Pasadena (91103-2466)
PHONE.....................626 296-1373
Daniel Friedmann,
Chris Thayer, *Vice Pres*
Nick Zello, *Vice Pres*
Mohammad Manki, *Principal*
Irma Franco, *Sr Project Mgr*
EMP: 50 **EST:** 2012
SALES (corp-wide): 1.7B **Publicly Held**
WEB: www.maxar.com
SIC: 8711 8731 Aviation &/or aeronautical engineering; commercial physical research
HQ: Maxar Technologies Ltd
200 Burrard St Suite 1570
Vancouver BC V6C 3
604 974-5275

(P-22607)
MAXAR SPACE ROBOTICS LLC
1250 Lincoln Ave Ste 100, Pasadena (91103-2466)
PHONE.....................626 296-1373
Mohammad Manki, *Branch Mgr*
Jim Lee, *Vice Pres*
Chris Thayer, *Vice Pres*
Christopher Caporaletti, *General Mgr*
Dan Drury, *Administration*
EMP: 65
SALES (corp-wide): 1.7B **Publicly Held**
WEB: www.maxar.com
SIC: 8711 8731 Aviation &/or aeronautical engineering; commercial physical research
HQ: Maxar Space Robotics Llc
1250 Lincoln Ave Ste 100
Pasadena CA 91103
626 296-1373

(P-22608)
MDS CONSULTING (PA)
17320 Red Hill Ave # 350, Irvine (92614-5644)
PHONE.....................949 251-8821
Stanley C Morse, *Chairman*
Jerry R Schultz, *Co-Owner*
Jenny Richard, *Executive Asst*
Leo Pacis, *Project Mgr*
Mario Aoigan, *Project Engr*
EMP: 71 **EST:** 1976
SQ FT: 8,837
SALES (est): 8.4MM **Privately Held**
WEB: www.mdsconsulting.net
SIC: 8711 Civil engineering

(P-22609)
MESA ASSOCIATES INC
3670 W Temple Ave Ste 152, Pomona (91768-2588)
PHONE.....................909 979-6609
Brad Hoy, *Branch Mgr*
EMP: 156 **Privately Held**
WEB: www.mesainc.com
SIC: 8711 8712 Consulting engineer; architectural services
PA: Mesa Associates, Inc.
480 Production Ave
Madison AL 35758

(P-22610)
MICHAEL BAKER INTL INC
3536 Concours Ste 110, Ontario (91764-5586)
PHONE.....................909 974-4900
Ron Craig, *Manager*
Jason Stiller, *Project Mgr*
Joe Gonzalez, *Manager*
EMP: 56

SALES (corp-wide): 592.9MM **Privately Held**
WEB: www.mbakerintl.com
SIC: 8711 Civil engineering
HQ: Baker Michael International Inc
5 Hutton Cntre Dr Ste 500
Santa Ana CA 92707
949 472-3505

(P-22611)
MICHAEL BAKER INTL INC
75410 Gerald Ford Dr # 100, Palm Desert (92211-3501)
PHONE.....................760 346-7481
Bob Ross, *Vice Pres*
Mike Sutton, *Vice Pres*
EMP: 56
SALES (corp-wide): 592.9MM **Privately Held**
WEB: www.mbakerintl.com
SIC: 8711 Civil engineering
HQ: Baker Michael International Inc
5 Hutton Cntre Dr Ste 500
Santa Ana CA 92707
949 472-3505

(P-22612)
MICHAEL BAKER INTL INC
40810 County Center Dr # 100, Temecula (92591-6053)
PHONE.....................951 676-8042
William Green, *Vice Pres*
Tom Ryan, *Vice Pres*
EMP: 56
SALES (corp-wide): 592.9MM **Privately Held**
WEB: www.mbakerintl.com
SIC: 8711 8713 Civil engineering; surveying services
HQ: Baker Michael International Inc
5 Hutton Cntre Dr Ste 500
Santa Ana CA 92707
949 472-3505

(P-22613)
MICHAEL BAKER INTL INC
Also Called: Rbf Associates
5051 Verdugo Way Ste 300, Camarillo (93012-8683)
PHONE.....................805 383-3373
Darin Johnson, *Manager*
EMP: 56
SALES (corp-wide): 592.9MM **Privately Held**
WEB: www.mbakerintl.com
SIC: 8711 8713 Civil engineering; surveying services
HQ: Baker Michael International Inc
5 Hutton Cntre Dr Ste 500
Santa Ana CA 92707
949 472-3505

(P-22614)
MICROWAVE APPLICATIONS GROUP
Also Called: M A G
3030 Industrial Pkwy, Santa Maria (93455-1881)
PHONE.....................805 928-5711
Steven Van Dyke, *CEO*
Robin Hopp, *Vice Pres*
Tom Janzen, *Vice Pres*
Scott McKechnie, *Vice Pres*
Edmund George, *Technician*
EMP: 20 **EST:** 1969
SQ FT: 22,000
SALES (est): 3.9MM **Privately Held**
WEB: www.magsmx.com
SIC: 8711 3679 Engineering services; microwave components

(P-22615)
MNS ENGINEERS INC (PA)
201 N Calle Cesar Chavez, Santa Barbara (93103-3256)
PHONE.....................805 692-6921
James A Salvito, *CEO*
Shawn Kowalewski, *President*
Mark E Reinhardt, *CFO*
Gregory A Chelini, *Vice Pres*
Jeffrey L Edwards, *Vice Pres*
EMP: 94 **EST:** 1962
SQ FT: 7,000

PRODUCTS & SVCS

SALES (est): 17MM Privately Held
WEB: www.mnsengineers.com
SIC: 8711 8713 Civil engineering; survey-
ing services

(P-22616)
MOBILENET SERVICES INC (PA)
18 Morgan Ste 200, Irvine (92618-2074)
PHONE..................949 951-4444
Richard Grant, *President*
Eugene Powell, *Vice Pres*
Alicia Arroyo, *Technical Mgr*
Sundara Narasimhan, *Engineer*
Harish Pillai, *Engineer*
EMP: 180 **EST:** 2002
SQ FT: 17,500
SALES (est): 38MM Privately Held
WEB: www.mobilenet.net
SIC: 8711 4813 Engineering services;
telephone communication, except radio

(P-22617)
MOFFATT & NICHOL
555 Anton Blvd Ste 400, Costa Mesa
(92626-7667)
PHONE..................657 261-2699
Eric Nichol, *CEO*
EMP: 70
**SALES (corp-wide): 126.3MM Privately
Held**
WEB: www.moffattnichol.com
SIC: 8711 Structural engineering
PA: Moffatt & Nichol
4225 E Conant St Ste 101
Long Beach CA 90808
562 590-6500

(P-22618)
MSM INDUSTRIES INC
12660 Magnolia Ave, Riverside
(92503-4636)
PHONE..................951 735-0834
Darryl Clare, *President*
Craig Sparling, *Treasurer*
Carl Maas, *Admin Sec*
Peter Taylor, *Director*
EMP: 31 **EST:** 2002
SALES (est): 11.1MM Privately Held
WEB: www.msm-ind.com
SIC: 8711 2891 2515 Engineering serv-
ices; epoxy adhesives; mattresses, con-
taining felt, foam rubber, urethane, etc.

(P-22619)
MWH AMERICAS INC
437 2nd St, Solvang (93463-2763)
PHONE..................805 683-2409
EMP: 77
SALES (corp-wide): 1.5B Privately Held
SIC: 8711 Engineering Srvcs
HQ: Mwh Americas, Inc.
370 Interlocken Blvd
Broomfield CO 80021
303 410-4000

(P-22620)
NATIONAL SECURITY TECH LLC
5520 Ekwill St Ste B, Goleta (93111-2335)
PHONE..................805 681-2432
EMP: 545
**SALES (corp-wide): 414MM Privately
Held**
WEB: www.nnss.gov
SIC: 8711 1629 Civil engineering; indus-
trial plant construction
PA: National Security Technologies, Llc
2621 Losee Rd
North Las Vegas NV 89030
702 295-1000

(P-22621)
NATIONAL TELECONSULTANTS INC
550 N Brand Blvd Fl 17, Glendale
(91203-1944)
PHONE..................818 265-4400
Eliot P Graham, *Mng Member*
Chuck Phelan, *Managing Prtnr*
Peter Adamiak, *President*
Rich Hill, *President*
Michael Hicken, *CFO*
EMP: 108 **EST:** 1981
SQ FT: 35,400

SALES (est): 27.6MM Privately Held
WEB: www.ntc.com
SIC: 8711 Electrical or electronic engineer-
ing

(P-22622)
NAVAIR WD
1 Admin Cir, Ridgecrest (93555-6104)
PHONE..................760 939-1970
Victor Saucedo, *Officer*
Diane Balderson, *Executive*
Melissa Alton, *Program Mgr*
Richard Calabria, *Program Mgr*
Bob Dodge, *Program Mgr*
EMP: 66 **EST:** 2010
SALES (est): 4.4MM Privately Held
WEB: www.navair.navy.mil
SIC: 8711 Engineering services

(P-22623)
ONCORE MANUFACTURING LLC (HQ)
Also Called: Neo Tech
9340 Owensmouth Ave, Chatsworth
(91311-6915)
PHONE..................818 734-6500
Sudesh Arora, *President*
Kunal Sharma, *COO*
Laura Siegal, *CFO*
John Lowrey,
David Lane, *CTO*
▲ **EMP:** 700 **EST:** 2001
SALES (est): 146.2MM
SALES (corp-wide): 1.1B Privately Held
WEB: www.neotech.com
SIC: 8711 3672 Electrical or electronic en-
gineering; printed circuit boards
PA: Natel Engineering Company, Llc
9340 Owensmouth Ave
Chatsworth CA 91311
818 495-8617

(P-22624)
ONQUEST HEATERS INC (HQ)
180 E Arrow Hwy, San Dimas
(91773-3336)
PHONE..................909 451-0499
David Baker, *President*
▲ **EMP:** 119 **EST:** 2002
SQ FT: 20,000
SALES (est): 2.2MM Publicly Held
WEB: www.primoriscorp.com
SIC: 8711 Consulting engineer

(P-22625)
OPTIMUM INC (PA)
17890 Valley Blvd, Bloomington
(92316-1981)
PHONE..................909 990-0767
Ivan Iordanov Atanassov, *CEO*
Christopher Giordano, *Vice Pres*
EMP: 108 **EST:** 1997
SALES (est): 11.5MM Privately Held
WEB: www.optimuminc.org
SIC: 8711 1623 Engineering services; un-
derground utilities contractor

(P-22626)
P & D CONSULTANTS INC (HQ)
999 W Town And Country Rd, Orange
(92868-4713)
P.O. Box 5367 (92863-5367)
PHONE..................714 835-4447
John L Kinley, *President*
EMP: 50 **EST:** 1969
SQ FT: 23,000
SALES (est): 14.9MM
SALES (corp-wide): 13.2B Publicly Held
WEB: www.aecom.com
SIC: 8711 8742 Civil engineering; plan-
ning consultant
PA: Aecom
13355 Noel Rd Ste 400
Dallas TX 75240
972 788-1000

(P-22627)
PACIFIC ADVNCED CVIL ENGRG INC (PA)
17520 Newhope St Ste 200, Fountain Val-
ley (92708-8206)
PHONE..................714 481-7300
Mark E Krebs, *President*
Andy Komor, *Vice Pres*
Bruce Phillips, *Vice Pres*
Sonny Sim, *Vice Pres*

Gary Tolosa, *Vice Pres*
EMP: 71 **EST:** 1987
SQ FT: 18,254 **Privately Held**
WEB: www.pacewater.com
SIC: 8711 Civil engineering

(P-22628)
PACIFIC HYDROTECH CORPORATION
314 E 3rd St, Perris (92570-2225)
PHONE..................951 943-8803
J Kirk Harns, *President*
Kris Bertuco, *Vice Pres*
Sean Finnegan, *Vice Pres*
Joselito Guintu, *Vice Pres*
Dale McKay, *Vice Pres*
EMP: 135 **EST:** 1987
SQ FT: 1,500
SALES (est): 65.7MM Privately Held
WEB: www.pachydro.com
SIC: 8711 Construction & civil engineering

(P-22629)
PACIFICA SERVICES INC
106 S Mentor Ave Ste 200, Pasadena
(91106-2931)
PHONE..................626 405-0131
Ernest M Camacho, *President*
Stephen Caropino, *CFO*
Toby Bautista, *Officer*
EMP: 84 **EST:** 1979
SQ FT: 15,000
SALES (est): 11.2MM Privately Held
WEB: www.pacificaservices.com
SIC: 8711 7629 8741 Civil engineering;
electronic equipment repair; construction
management

(P-22630)
PANASONIC AVIONICS CORPORATION (DH)
26200 Enterprise Way, Lake Forest
(92630-8400)
PHONE..................949 672-2000
John Moritz, *CEO*
David Chung, *Treasurer*
Mark Jennings, *Exec VP*
Bob Dick, *Vice Pres*
Jonathan Moritz, *Vice Pres*
▲ **EMP:** 400 **EST:** 1990
SQ FT: 20,000
SALES (est): 925.1MM Privately Held
WEB: www.panasonic.aero
SIC: 8711 3728 Aviation &/or aeronautical
engineering; aircraft parts & equipment
HQ: Panasonic Corporation Of North Amer-
ica
2 Riverfront Plz Ste 200
Newark NJ 07102
201 348-7000

(P-22631)
PARSONS ENGRG SCIENCE INC (DH)
100 W Walnut St, Pasadena (91124-0001)
P.O. Box 88954, Chicago IL (60695-1954)
PHONE..................626 440-2000
Charles Harrington, *CEO*
Mary Ann Hopkins, *President*
Curtis A Bower, *Exec VP*
Nicholas L Presecan, *Senior VP*
Gary L Stone, *Senior VP*
EMP: 500 **EST:** 1946
SALES (est): 599.7MM
SALES (corp-wide): 3.9B Publicly Held
WEB: www.parsons.com
SIC: 8711 Consulting engineer
HQ: Parsons Government Services Inc.
5875 Trinity Pkwy Ste 230
Centreville VA 20120
703 988-8500

(P-22632)
PARSONS GOVERNMENT SVCS INC (HQ)
25531 Cmmrcntre Dr Ste 12, Lake Forest
(92630)
PHONE..................949 768-8161
Charles L Harrington, *CEO*
Sophie Odonnell, *Vice Pres*
David Schreiman, *VP Finance*
Cindy Marinkovich, *Controller*
Jody L Chiaro, *VP Human Res*
EMP: 53 **EST:** 1979

SALES (est): 116.3MM
SALES (corp-wide): 3.9B Publicly Held
WEB: www.parsons.com
SIC: 8711 Consulting engineer
PA: The Parsons Corporation
5875 Trinity Pkwy Ste 300
Centreville VA 20120
703 988-8500

(P-22633)
PARSONS SERVICES COMPANY
100 W Walnut St, Pasadena (91124-0001)
PHONE..................626 440-2000
Geoge L Ball, *Principal*
George Ball, *CFO*
Debra Fiori, *Officer*
Jennifer Frank, *Manager*
EMP: 797 **EST:** 1977
SALES (est): 40.6MM Privately Held
WEB: www.parsons.com
SIC: 8711 Construction & civil engineering

(P-22634)
PARSONS WTR INFRASTRUCTURE INC
100 W Walnut St, Pasadena (91124-0001)
PHONE..................626 440-7000
Virginia Grebbien, *CEC*
Anthony F Leketa, *President*
Christian Alexander, *Accounts Mgr*
EMP: 76 **EST:** 2003
SQ FT: 1,220,000
SALES (est): 5MM
SALES (corp-wide): 3.9B Publicly Held
WEB: www.parsons.com
SIC: 8711 Consulting engineer
PA: The Parsons Corporation
5875 Trinity Pkwy Ste 300
Centreville VA 20120
703 988-8500

(P-22635)
PARTNER ASSESSMENT CORPORATION (PA)
Also Called: Partner Engineering & Science
2154 Torrance Blvd # 200, Torrance
(90501-2609)
PHONE..................800 419-4923
Joseph P Derhake, *CEO*
Dillon Deloss, *Partner*
Dominic Juego, *Partner*
Dana Derhake, *Shareholder*
Mike Giuliano, *Admin Dir*
EMP: 135 **EST:** 2006
SQ FT: 10,000
SALES (est): 68.7MM Privately Held
WEB: www.partneresi.com
SIC: 8711 Consulting engineer

(P-22636)
PETRA GEOTECHNICAL INC (PA)
3198 Arprt Loop D Ste A2, Costa Mesa
(92626)
PHONE..................714 549-8921
Siamak Jafoudi, *President*
Alan Pace, *Vice Pres*
Darrel Roberts, *Project Mgr*
Stuart Allen Bell, *Director*
Kristen Scott, *Director*
EMP: 56 **EST:** 1988
SQ FT: 10,000
SALES (est): 6.1MM Privately Held
WEB: www.petra-inc.com
SIC: 8711 Consulting engineer

(P-22637)
PHG ENGINEERING SERVICES LLC
900 E Katella Ave Ste F, Orange
(92867-5059)
PHONE..................714 283-8288
Francis L Price,
Steve Kosto, *Engineer*
EMP: 100 **EST:** 2017
SALES (est): 6MM Privately Held
WEB: www.phcengineeringllc.com
SIC: 8711 Engineering services

(P-22638)
PHOENIX ENGINEERING TECH LLC
17117 Leal Ave, Cerritos (90703-1337)
PHONE..................714 918-0630
Vasu Ayithi,

Kadambari Ayithi,
EMP: 65 **EST:** 2017
SALES (est): 1.5MM **Privately Held**
WEB: www.phoenix-engineering.com
SIC: 8711 Engineering services

(P-22639)
PRESCIENCE CORPORATION
125 Columbia Ste A, Aliso Viejo
(92656-4157)
PHONE.................................949 600-8631
Khanh Tran, *CEO*
Elmo Delos-Santos, *President*
Benjamin Lim, *Bd of Directors*
Mina Seo, *Accounting Mgr*
William Doran, *Manager*
EMP: 52 **EST:** 2011
SALES (est): 3.1MM **Privately Held**
WEB: www.prescience.online
SIC: 8711 Civil engineering

(P-22640)
PTSI MANAGED SERVICES INC
100 W Walnut St, Pasadena (91124-0001)
PHONE.................................626 440-3118
Mary Ann Hopkins, *President*
EMP: 99 **EST:** 1983
SALES (est): 15.3MM
SALES (corp-wide): 3.9B **Publicly Held**
WEB: www.parsons.com
SIC: 8711 Engineering services
PA: The Parsons Corporation
5875 Trinity Pkwy Ste 300
Centreville VA 20120
703 988-8500

(P-22641)
QUAD KNOPF INC (PA)
901 E Main St, Visalia (93292-6546)
P.O. Box 3699 (93278-3699)
PHONE.................................559 733-0440
Michael Knopf, *President*
Janel Freeman, *CFO*
Amber Adams, *Vice Pres*
Jeffery S Cowart, *Branch Mgr*
Ernie Escobedo, *Branch Mgr*
EMP: 50 **EST:** 1972
SQ FT: 12,000
SALES (est): 16.9MM **Privately Held**
WEB: www.qkinc.com
SIC: 8711 8712 Civil engineering; consult-
ing engineer; architectural services

(P-22642)
R AND L LOPEZ ASSOCIATES INC (PA)
Also Called: Lopez & Associates Engineers
3649 Tyler Ave, El Monte (91731-2505)
PHONE.................................626 330-5296
Lourdes P Lopez, *President*
Remberto Lopez, *Vice Pres*
EMP: 80 **EST:** 1979
SQ FT: 2,700
SALES (est): 4.5MM **Privately Held**
SIC: 8711 Consulting engineer

(P-22643)
R M A GROUP (PA)
Also Called: RMA Group
12130 Santa Margarita Ct, Rancho Cuca-
monga (91730-6138)
PHONE.................................909 980-6096
Edward Duane Lyon, *Chairman*
Ed Lyon, *President*
Sue Lyon, *Corp Secy*
Marta Landaverde, *Officer*
Brian Haber, *Area Mgr*
EMP: 89 **EST:** 1970
SQ FT: 9,600
SALES (est): 24.1MM **Privately Held**
WEB: www.rmacompanies.com
SIC: 8711 Engineering services

(P-22644)
RAILPROS INC (PA)
15265 Alton Pkwy Ste 140, Irvine
(92618-2605)
PHONE.................................714 734-8765
Eric Hankinson, *President*
John Yarbrough, *President*
Stuart Hall, *CFO*
Jason Barton, *Vice Pres*
Rick Bellew, *Vice Pres*
EMP: 139 **EST:** 2000
SQ FT: 1,200

SALES (est): 23.1MM **Privately Held**
WEB: www.railpros.com
SIC: 8711 Civil engineering

(P-22645)
RECON REFRACTORY & CNSTR INC
3914 Cherry Ave Ste B, Long Beach
(90807-3738)
P.O. Box 93120 (90809-3120)
PHONE.................................562 988-7981
EMP: 50 **Privately Held**
WEB: www.recon-inc.com
SIC: 8711 3297 1522 Engineering Serv-
ices Mfg Nonclay Refractories Residential
Construction
PA: Recon Refractory & Construction, Inc.
10741 Los Alamitos Blvd
Los Alamitos CA 90720

(P-22646)
REZEK EQUIPMENT
970 Reece St, San Bernardino
(92411-2346)
PHONE.................................909 885-6221
Ronald Rezek Jr, *Owner*
EMP: 32 **EST:** 1980
SQ FT: 74,000
SALES (est): 531.7K **Privately Held**
WEB: www.ronrezek.com
SIC: 8711 3648 Civil engineering; lighting
equipment

(P-22647)
ROBERT CONSL ENGLEKIRK STRCTRL (PA)
2116 Arlington Ave Lbby, Los Angeles
(90018-1365)
PHONE.................................323 733-6673
Robert E Englekirk, *President*
Solveig Jensen, *Treasurer*
EMP: 55 **EST:** 1969
SQ FT: 12,000
SALES (est): 1.8MM **Privately Held**
SIC: 8711 Structural engineering

(P-22648)
RWC ENTERPRISES INC
Also Called: Professional Construction Svcs
9130 Santa Anita Ave, Rancho Cucamonga
(91730-6143)
PHONE.................................909 373-4100
Robert William Casey, *CEO*
Lori Casey, *Admin Sec*
Frank Heaton, *Project Mgr*
Jeff Hager, *Supervisor*
EMP: 50 **EST:** 1975
SQ FT: 16,000
SALES (est): 10MM **Privately Held**
WEB: www.pecs.biz
SIC: 8711 0781 Civil engineering; land-
scape counseling services

(P-22649)
SAALEX CORP (PA)
Also Called: Saalex Solutions
811 Camarillo Springs Rd A, Camarillo
(93012-9465)
PHONE.................................805 482-1070
Travis Mack, *President*
Arthur Glaab, *Officer*
Stephen Andersen, *Exec VP*
Kelly Nguyen, *Program Mgr*
Jeffrey Heath, *Admin Asst*
EMP: 245 **EST:** 1999
SQ FT: 7,000 **Privately Held**
WEB: www.saalex.com
SIC: 8711 7379 Consulting engineer; com-
puter related consulting services

(P-22650)
SAGE ASSOCIATES INC (PA)
2361 Campus Dr Ste 111, Irvine
(92612-1463)
PHONE.................................949 724-9600
Richard Tasker, *Owner*
Peter Carpenter, *COO*
Kathleen Ross, *Assoc VP*
Donna Baker, *Exec VP*
Kenneth Caldwell, *Exec VP*
EMP: 77 **EST:** 2008
SALES (est): 5.6MM **Privately Held**
WEB: www.sage-associates.com
SIC: 8711 Building construction consultant

(P-22651)
SAIFUL/BQUET CNSLTING STRL ENG (PA)
155 N Lake Ave Fl 6, Pasadena
(91101-1849)
PHONE.................................626 304-2616
Saiful Islam, *CEO*
Tom Bouquet, *CFO*
Helen Yoon, *Vice Pres*
Andrea Hammer, *Executive Asst*
Y K Low, *Admin Sec*
EMP: 53 **EST:** 1997
SQ FT: 25,000
SALES (est): 11.3MM **Privately Held**
WEB: www.saifulbouquet.com
SIC: 8711 Structural engineering

(P-22652)
SCICON TECHNOLOGIES CORP (PA)
27525 Nwhll Rnch Rd Ste 2, Valencia
(91355-4003)
PHONE.................................661 295-8630
Thomas J Bulger, *President*
Brad Bulger, *Executive*
Marie Bulger, *Admin Sec*
Mitch Greenwood, *Info Tech Mgr*
Carol Rhodes, *Purchasing*
▲ **EMP:** 50 **EST:** 1989
SQ FT: 25,000
SALES (est): 10.5MM **Privately Held**
WEB: www.scicontech.com
SIC: 8711 3999 Mechanical engineering;
models, except toy

(P-22653)
SEQUOIA CONSULTANTS INC (PA)
361 W Grove Ave, Orange (92865-3205)
PHONE.................................714 974-6316
Priyanga C Desilva, *CEO*
Leo Santamaria, *Project Mgr*
Ruben Jimenez, *Manager*
Thao Ninh, *Manager*
EMP: 84 **EST:** 2005
SQ FT: 10,500
SALES (est): 13MM **Privately Held**
WEB: www.sequoiacon.com
SIC: 8711 8742 8071 Engineering serv-
ices; quality assurance consultant; testing
laboratories

(P-22654)
SIA ENGINEERING (USA) INC
7001 W Imperial Hwy, Los Angeles
(90045-6313)
PHONE.................................310 693-7108
Cheng Hian Tan, *CEO*
Chiuyen Tseng, *CFO*
EMP: 51 **EST:** 2008
SALES (est): 6.2MM **Privately Held**
SIC: 8711 Consulting engineer

(P-22655)
SONIC INDUSTRIES INC
Also Called: Airframer R
20030 Normandie Ave, Torrance
(90502-1210)
PHONE.................................310 532-8382
Jamie King, *CEO*
▲ **EMP:** 150 **EST:** 1966
SQ FT: 65,000
SALES (est): 23.5MM
SALES (corp-wide): 608.9MM **Publicly Held**
WEB: www.sargentaerospace.com
SIC: 8711 7699 Machine tool design; avia-
tion propeller & blade repair
HQ: Roller Bearing Company Of America,
Inc.
102 Willenbrock Rd
Oxford CT 06478
203 267-7001

(P-22656)
SPEARMAN AEROSPACE INC
9215 Greenleaf Ave, Santa Fe Springs
(90670-3028)
PHONE.................................714 523-4751
Urio Zanetti, *President*
EMP: 25 **EST:** 2013
SALES: 6.9MM **Privately Held**
WEB: www.spearmanaerospace.com
SIC: 8711 3721 Aviation &/or aeronautical
engineering; aircraft

(P-22657)
SPEC SERVICES INC
10540 Talbert Ave 100e, Fountain Valley
(92708-6051)
PHONE.................................714 963-8077
Kim R Henry, *President*
Chris Smart, *COO*
Dan Letcher, *CFO*
Chuck Lake, *Vice Pres*
Long Pham, *Department Mgr*
EMP: 290 **EST:** 1981
SQ FT: 16,000
SALES (est): 50.5MM **Privately Held**
WEB: www.specservices.com
SIC: 8711 Consulting engineer

(P-22658)
SPIRAL TECHNOLOGY INC
229 E Avenue K8 Ste 105, Lancaster
(93535-4517)
PHONE.................................661 723-3148
Archie L Moore, *President*
Steve McCarter, *Ch of Bd*
Daniel Hare, *COO*
Eugene Savage, *Engineer*
Bill Hubbard, *Contract Mgr*
EMP: 56 **EST:** 2000
SQ FT: 4,984
SALES (est): 9.1MM **Privately Held**
WEB: www.spiraltechinc.com
SIC: 8711 Industrial engineers

(P-22659)
SSC CONSTRUCTION INC
4195 Chino Hills Pkwy, Chino Hills
(91709-2618)
PHONE.................................951 278-1177
Gregory E Larkin, *CEO*
Neil Nehmens, *Senior VP*
EMP: 53 **EST:** 1999
SALES (est): 8.7MM **Privately Held**
WEB: www.sscconstruction.net
SIC: 8711 Engineering services

(P-22660)
STANTEC CONSULTING SVCS INC
300 N Lake Ave Ste 400, Pasadena
(91101-4169)
PHONE.................................626 796-9141
Paul Boulos, *Branch Mgr*
Lori Van Dermark, *Agent*
EMP: 79
SALES (corp-wide): 3.6B **Privately Held**
WEB: www.stantec.com
SIC: 8711 Engineering services
HQ: Stantec Consulting Services Inc.
475 5th Ave Fl 12
New York NY 10017
212 352-5160

(P-22661)
STEVEN ENGINEERING INC
2398 Railroad St, Corona (92878-5410)
PHONE.................................650 588-9200
Bonnie A Walter, *CEO*
EMP: 50
SALES (corp-wide): 72.4MM **Privately Held**
WEB: www.stevenengineering.com
SIC: 8711 Consulting engineer
PA: Steven Engineering Inc
230 Ryan Way
South San Francisco CA 94080
650 588-9200

(P-22662)
STURGEON SON GRADING & PAV INC
Also Called: Sturgeon Services Intl
6516 Cat Canyon Rd, Santa Maria
(93454-9605)
PHONE.................................805 938-0618
Fax: 805 938-0894
EMP: 114
SALES (corp-wide): 56.7MM **Privately Held**
SIC: 8711 1794 Engineering Services Ex-
cavation Contractor
PA: Sturgeon & Son Grading & Paving, Inc.
3511 Gilmore Ave
Bakersfield CA 93308
661 322-4408

P R O D U C T S & S V C S

(P-22663)
SUMARIA SYSTEMS INC
105 13th St, Vandenberg Afb (93437-5209)
PHONE.....................................805 606-4973
EMP: 75
SALES (corp-wide): 87.7MM Privately Held
WEB: www.sumariasystems.com
SIC: 8711 Consulting engineer
PA: Sumaria Systems, Llc
    99 Rosewood Dr Ste 140
    Danvers MA 01923
    978 739-4200

(P-22664)
SYSTEMS APPLICATION & TECH INC
Also Called: Sa-Tech
1000 Town Center Dr # 110, Oxnard (93036-1100)
P.O. Box 25, Port Hueneme (93044-0025)
PHONE.....................................805 487-7373
Geoff Dezavala, Senior VP
Arthur J Gregg, Adv Board Mem
Aj Jothiraj, Principal
Wade Vanderwerff, Program Mgr
Cecil Jones, CIO
EMP: 80 Privately Held
WEB: www.sa-techinc.com
SIC: 8711 Consulting engineer
PA: Systems Application & Technologies, Inc.
    1101 Merc Ln Ste 200
    Largo MD 20774

(P-22665)
TECHNICAL AMERICA INC
301 N Smith Ave, Corona (92878-3242)
PHONE.....................................951 272-9540
Jing Xie, CEO
EMP: 55 EST: 2016
SALES (est): 4.8MM Privately Held
WEB: www.technicalamericainc.com
SIC: 8711 Engineering services

(P-22666)
TECHNIP STONE WBSTER PRCESS TE
555 W Arrow Hwy, Claremont (91711-4805)
PHONE.....................................909 447-3600
Gary Keyser, Manager
Stuart Millar, Senior VP
Nicolas Siwertz, Senior VP
Cecile Jolibois, VP Bus Dvlpt
Poornima Sharma, Managing Dir
EMP: 98
SALES (corp-wide): 489.9MM Privately Held
SIC: 8711 Chemical engineering
HQ: Technip Stone & Webster Process Technology, Inc.
    11740 Katy Fwy Ste 100
    Houston TX 77079
    281 870-1111

(P-22667)
TETRA TECH INC (PA)
3475 E Foothill Blvd, Pasadena (91107-6024)
PHONE.....................................626 351-4664
Dan L Batrack, Ch of Bd
Leslie L Shoemaker, President
Steven M Burdick, CFO
Craig L Christensen, Senior VP
Richard A Lemmon, Senior VP
EMP: 200 EST: 1966
SALES (est): 2.9B Publicly Held
WEB: www.tetratech.com
SIC: 8711 Engineering services; civil engineering; consulting engineer

(P-22668)
TETRA TECH INC
17885 Von Karman Ave # 500, Irvine (92614-5227)
PHONE.....................................949 263-0846
Jack Chicca, Branch Mgr
EMP: 85
SALES (corp-wide): 2.9B Publicly Held
WEB: www.tetratech.com
SIC: 8711 Consulting engineer

PA: Tetra Tech, Inc.
    3475 E Foothill Blvd
    Pasadena CA 91107
    626 351-4664

(P-22669)
TETRA TECH BAS INC (HQ)
Also Called: B A S
21700 Copley Dr Ste 200, Diamond Bar (91765-2219)
PHONE.....................................909 860-7777
Bryan A Stirrat, President
Ira Snyder, CFO
Jeanne Stirrat, Admin Sec
Kelly McGregor, Engineer
Jose A Velez, Manager
EMP: 65 EST: 1985
SALES (est): 10.5MM
SALES (corp-wide): 2.9B Publicly Held
WEB: www.tetratech.com
SIC: 8711 Civil engineering; pollution control engineering
PA: Tetra Tech, Inc.
    3475 E Foothill Blvd
    Pasadena CA 91107
    626 351-4664

(P-22670)
TETRA TECH HOLDING LLC (HQ)
3475 E Foothill Blvd, Pasadena (91107-6024)
PHONE.....................................626 351-4664
Dan L Batrack, Principal
EMP: 377 EST: 2012
SALES (est): 6.2MM
SALES (corp-wide): 2.9B Publicly Held
WEB: www.tetratech.com
SIC: 8711 Civil engineering
PA: Tetra Tech, Inc.
    3475 E Foothill Blvd
    Pasadena CA 91107
    626 351-4664

(P-22671)
TETRA TECH INTERNATIONAL INC (HQ)
3475 E Foothill Blvd, Pasadena (91107-6024)
PHONE.....................................626 351-4664
Dan L Batrack, President
EMP: 97 EST: 2006
SQ FT: 10,000
SALES (est): 1.3MM
SALES (corp-wide): 2.9B Publicly Held
WEB: www.tetratech.com
SIC: 8711 Consulting engineer
PA: Tetra Tech, Inc.
    3475 E Foothill Blvd
    Pasadena CA 91107
    626 351-4664

(P-22672)
TETRA TECH NUS INC
3475 E Foothill Blvd, Pasadena (91107-6024)
PHONE.....................................412 921-7090
Dan L Batrack, CEO
Steven M Burdick, Exec VP
John Trepanowski, Vice Pres
Ronald Chu, Principal
Janet Mandel, Director
▲ EMP: 195 EST: 1960
SALES (est): 5.4MM
SALES (corp-wide): 2.9B Publicly Held
WEB: www.tetratech.com
SIC: 8711 Consulting engineer
PA: Tetra Tech, Inc.
    3475 E Foothill Blvd
    Pasadena CA 91107
    626 351-4664

(P-22673)
THERMAL ENGRG INTL USA INC (HQ)
18000 Studebaker Rd # 400, Cerritos (90703-2691)
PHONE.....................................323 726-0641
Kenneth Murakoshi, CEO
Brian Antonini, President
William Farris, President
Andrew Finizio, President
Thomas Richardson, President
◆ EMP: 70 EST: 1919
SQ FT: 18,000

SALES (est): 38.2MM
SALES (corp-wide): 493.1MM Privately Held
WEB: www.babcockpower.com
SIC: 8711 3443 Professional engineer; air coolers, metal plate
PA: Babcock Power Inc.
    222 Rosewood Dr Fl 3
    Danvers MA 01923
    978 646-3300

(P-22674)
THORPE TECHNOLOGIES INC (DH)
449 W Allen Ave Ste 119, San Dimas (91773-1453)
PHONE.....................................562 903-8230
John E Allen, President
Thomas A Carpenter, Corp Secy
Gary Newby, Vice Pres
Robert Jenkins, Project Mgr
EMP: 25 EST: 1988
SQ FT: 7,000
SALES (est): 16.8MM
SALES (corp-wide): 38.4MM Privately Held
WEB: www.thorpetech.com
SIC: 8711 3567 Engineering services; industrial furnaces & ovens

(P-22675)
TJ CROSS ENGINEERS INC
200 New Stine Rd Ste 270, Bakersfield (93309-2658)
PHONE.....................................661 831-8782
Timothy Couch, Principal
Kent Halley, Principal
Stuart Heisler, Principal
Chuck Soderstrom, Principal
Lisa Wong, Principal
EMP: 89 EST: 1990
SQ FT: 22,000
SALES (est): 4.5MM
SALES (corp-wide): 3.9B Publicly Held
WEB: www.parsons.com
SIC: 8711 Consulting engineer
PA: The Parsons Corporation
    5875 Trinity Pkwy Ste 300
    Centreville VA 20120
    703 988-8500

(P-22676)
TMX ENGINEERING LLC
2141 S Standard Ave, Santa Ana (92707-3034)
PHONE.....................................714 641-5884
Eric Clack,
Kira Felix, Human Resources
EMP: 70 EST: 2018
SALES (est): 4MM Privately Held
WEB: www.tmxengineering.com
SIC: 8711 Engineering services

(P-22677)
TOYON RESEARCH CORPORATION (PA)
6800 Cortona Dr, Goleta (93117-3139)
PHONE.....................................805 968-6787
Tim Halsey,
Kevin Sullivan, President
Paul Castleberg, Vice Pres
Michael Grace, Vice Pres
Chuck Nardo, Vice Pres
EMP: 203 EST: 1980
SQ FT: 16,000
SALES (est): 34.4MM Privately Held
WEB: www.toyon.com
SIC: 8711 7371 Electrical or electronic engineering; custom computer programming services

(P-22678)
TRANSTECH ENGINEERS INC (PA)
13367 Benson Ave, Chino (91710-5246)
PHONE.....................................909 595-8599
Allen Cayir, President
Sybil Cayir, Corp Secy
Amy Chan, Technician
Bryant De La Torre, Technician
Matt Sert, Human Res Mgr
EMP: 88 EST: 1989
SQ FT: 10,000
SALES (est): 10.2MM Privately Held
WEB: www.transtech.org
SIC: 8711 Civil engineering

(P-22679)
TRUST AUTOMATION INC
125 Venture Dr Ste 110, San Luis Obispo (93401-9103)
PHONE.....................................805 544-0761
Ty Safreno, CEO
Brett Keegan, COO
Trudie Safreno, CFO
Chuck Kass, Exec VP
Dave Rennie, Vice Pres
▲ EMP: 65 EST: 1990
SQ FT: 100,000
SALES (est): 25.2MM Privately Held
WEB: www.trustautomation.com
SIC: 8711 3812 3731 3621 Machine tool design; antennas; radar or communications; submersible marine robots, manned or unmanned; generators for gas-electric or oil-electric vehicles; automation & robotics consultant

(P-22680)
UCI CONSTRUCTION INC
3900 Fruitvale Ave, Bakersfield (93308-5114)
PHONE.....................................661 587-0192
David Krugh, Branch Mgr
Leslie Green, Admin Asst
Jessica Weatherford, Administration
Mark Clifton, Manager
Mike Hackney, Manager
EMP: 98
SALES (corp-wide): 46.4MM Privately Held
WEB: www.uciconstruction.com
SIC: 8711 Professional engineer
PA: U.C.I. Construction, Inc.
    167 Grobric Ct
    Fairfield CA 94534
    925 370-9808

(P-22681)
UNDERWATER SYSTEMS INC
10603 Progress Way, Cypress (90630-4713)
PHONE.....................................714 229-9268
Taner Bayrak, President
EMP: 18 EST: 1988
SQ FT: 6,000
SALES (est): 1MM Privately Held
WEB: www.underwatersystems.com
SIC: 8711 3825 3678 3812 Engineering services; instruments to measure electricity; electronic connectors; search & navigation equipment; current-carrying wiring devices

(P-22682)
UNITED INDUSTRIES GROUP INC
Also Called: U I G
11 Rancho Cir, Lake Forest (92630-8324)
P.O. Box 8009, Newport Beach (92658-8009)
PHONE.....................................949 759-3200
James P Mansour, President
Lisa Harker, COO
John Mansell, Vice Pres
John Mensell, Vice Pres
Arthur Yanovskiy, Project Mgr
EMP: 26 EST: 1969
SQ FT: 10,000
SALES (est): 5.6MM Privately Held
WEB: www.unitedind.com
SIC: 8711 3589 Engineering services; water treatment equipment, industrial

(P-22683)
URS GROUP INC
6721 Sycamore Canyon Blvd, Riverside (92507-0751)
PHONE.....................................951 571-2220
Garin Yamato, Branch Mgr
EMP: 90
SALES (corp-wide): 13.2B Publicly Held
WEB: www.aeccm.com
SIC: 8711 Engineering services
HQ: Urs Group, Inc.
    300 S Grand Ave Ste 900
    Los Angeles CA 90071
    213 593-8000

(P-22684)
URS GROUP INC
300 S Grand Ave Ste 1100, Los Angeles
(90071-3173)
PHONE..................................213 996-2200
Paul Ryan, *Manager*
Nagaraju Suram, *Project Leader*
EMP: 90
SALES (corp-wide): 13.2B **Publicly Held**
WEB: www.aecom.com
SIC: 8711 8712 8741 Consulting engi-
neer; architectural engineering; construc-
tion management
HQ: Urs Group, Inc.
300 S Grand Ave Ste 900
Los Angeles CA 90071
213 593-8000

(P-22685)
URS GROUP INC
915 Wilshire Blvd Ste 700, Los Angeles
(90017-3436)
P.O. Box 116183, Atlanta GA (30368-6183)
PHONE..................................213 996-2200
Shahram Bahbagu, *Branch Mgr*
William Cleveland, *Program Mgr*
EMP: 90
SALES (corp-wide): 13.2B **Publicly Held**
WEB: www.aecom.com
SIC: 8711 Engineering services
HQ: Urs Group, Inc.
300 S Grand Ave Ste 900
Los Angeles CA 90071
213 593-8000

(P-22686)
URS GROUP INC
3995 Via Oro Ave, Long Beach
(90810-1869)
PHONE..................................562 420-2933
Wilfrido Simbol, *Branch Mgr*
EMP: 90
SALES (corp-wide): 13.2B **Publicly Held**
WEB: www.aecom.com
SIC: 8711 8712 Structural engineering; ar-
chitectural engineering
HQ: Urs Group, Inc.
300 S Grand Ave Ste 900
Los Angeles CA 90071
213 593-8000

(P-22687)
URS RESOURCES LLC (DH)
999 W Town And Country Rd, Orange
(92868-4713)
PHONE..................................626 331-0359
Thomas W Bishop,
EMP: 50 EST: 2006
SQ FT: 5,400
SALES (est): 15.1MM
SALES (corp-wide): 13.2B **Publicly Held**
WEB: www.aecom.com
SIC: 8711 1795 Engineering services;
demolition, buildings & other structures
HQ: Aecom Global Ii, Llc
300 S Grand Ave Ste 900
Los Angeles CA 90071
213 593-8100

(P-22688)
**VAN DORPE CHOU ASSOCIATES
INC**
Also Called: VCA Engineering
1845 W Orangewood Ave # 210, Orange
(92868-2051)
PHONE..................................714 978-9780
Daniel T Van Dorpe, *President*
Neil Evans, *Shareholder*
Margaret Van Dorpe, *Corp Secy*
Mark Van Gaale, *Vice Pres*
David Briski, *Info Tech Mgr*
EMP: 50 EST: 1979
SQ FT: 3,000
SALES (est): 5.1MM **Privately Held**
WEB: www.vcaengineers.com
SIC: 8711 Consulting engineer; structural
engineering

(P-22689)
VANGUARD SPACE TECH INC
Also Called: Alliance Spacesystems
4398 Corporate Center Dr, Los Alamitos
(90720-2537)
PHONE..................................858 587-4210
Frank Belknap, *CEO*
Ronald Miller, *CFO*

John Richer, *Exec VP*
David Kang, *Vice Pres*
Carl Sloan, *Vice Pres*
EMP: 101 EST: 1994
SQ FT: 50,000
SALES: 13.8MM
SALES (corp-wide): 62.7MM **Privately
Held**
WEB: www.solaerotech.com
SIC: 8711 Aviation &/or aeronautical engi-
neering
PA: Solaero Technologies Corp.
10420 Res Rd Se Bldg 1
Albuquerque NM 87123
505 332-5000

(P-22690)
VCA CODE GROUP
1845 W Orangewood Ave # 210, Orange
(92868-2051)
PHONE..................................714 363-4700
Dan Van Dope, *President*
Bob Chou, *Vice Pres*
Wayne Alldredge, *Associate Dir*
Kathy Ibarra, *Administration*
Glen Folland, *Project Mgr*
EMP: 50 EST: 2005
SALES (est): 4.5MM **Privately Held**
WEB: www.vca-green.com
SIC: 8711 Consulting engineer

(P-22691)
VELOCITEL RF INC
2415 Campus Dr Ste 200, Irvine
(92612-8530)
PHONE..................................949 809-4999
EMP: 200
SALES (est): 6.1MM
SALES (corp-wide): 648MM **Privately
Held**
SIC: 8711 Radio Frequency Engineering
For Telecommunications Industry
PA: Velocitel, Inc.
1033 Skokie Blvd Ste 320
Northbrook IL 27616
224 757-0001

(P-22692)
**VELOCITY AROSPC - EDN AVI
INC**
6720 Valjean Ave, Van Nuys (91406-5818)
PHONE..................................818 988-8826
Dale Gebel, *President*
Nishan Bostanian, *General Mgr*
EMP: 15 EST: 2014
SQ FT: 16,000
SALES (est): 293.1K **Privately Held**
WEB: www.ednaviation.com
SIC: 8711 3625 Aviation &/or aeronautical
engineering; industrial controls: push but-
ton, selector switches, pilot

(P-22693)
**VOLLMER-GRAY ENGRG LABS
INC**
2421 N Palm Dr, Signal Hill (90755-4006)
PHONE..................................562 427-8435
Gerry Zamiski, *President*
Paul Guthorn, *Vice Pres*
Beth Molinar, *Office Admin*
Richard Matson, *Technician*
Mohammad Atarod, *Engineer*
EMP: 54 EST: 1970
SQ FT: 4,000
SALES (est): 7.5MM **Privately Held**
WEB: www.vglabs.com
SIC: 8711 Mechanical engineering; con-
sulting engineer

(P-22694)
VSA AND ASSOCIATES INC
Also Called: Health Care Resource Group
6571 Altura Blvd Ste 100, Buena Park
(90620-1020)
PHONE..................................562 698-2468
Mahabir S Atwal, *President*
Kris English, *CFO*
Vicky Sumnogum, *Vice Pres*
Bruce Griffitts, *VP Bus Dvlpt*
Michael Mitama, *CIO*
EMP: 61 EST: 1987
SQ FT: 12,000
SALES (est): 5.4MM **Privately Held**
WEB: www.hcrg.com
SIC: 8711 8742 Acoustical engineering;
business planning & organizing services

(P-22695)
WESTWIND ENGINEERING INC
625 Esplanade Unit 70, Redondo Beach
(90277-4150)
PHONE..................................310 831-3454
Mary Anne Graves, *CEO*
Carl Graves, *Founder*
Maricela Delacruz, *Office Mgr*
Stephanie Sundius, *Engineer*
Raymond Liccini, *Consultant*
EMP: 150 EST: 1992
SQ FT: 2,400
SALES (est): 13MM **Privately Held**
WEB: www.westwind111.com
SIC: 8711 7363 Engineering services;
temporary help service

(P-22696)
WESTWIND ENGINEERING INC
553 N Pcf Coastte B179 B, Redondo Beach
(90277)
PHONE..................................310 831-3454
EMP: 70
SALES (est): 2.7MM **Privately Held**
SIC: 8711 Engineering Firm

(P-22697)
WILLDAN ENGINEERING
650 E Hospitality Ln # 250, San Bernardino
(92408-3535)
PHONE..................................909 386-0200
Ron Espalin, *Branch Mgr*
EMP: 57
SALES (corp-wide): 390.9MM **Publicly
Held**
WEB: www.willdan.com
SIC: 8711 8742 Civil engineering; busi-
ness planning & organizing services
HQ: Willdan Engineering
2401 E Katella Ave # 300
Anaheim CA 92806
714 978-8200

(P-22698)
WILLDAN ENGINEERING
13191 Crssrads Pkwy N Ste, City of Indus-
try (91746)
PHONE..................................562 908-6200
William Pagett, *Branch Mgr*
Barrientos Susie, *Technology*
EMP: 57
SALES (corp-wide): 390.9MM **Publicly
Held**
WEB: www.willdan.com
SIC: 8711 Civil engineering
HQ: Willdan Engineering
2401 E Katella Ave # 300
Anaheim CA 92806
714 978-8200

(P-22699)
WILLDAN ENGINEERING
374 Poli St Ste 101, Ventura (93001-2605)
PHONE..................................805 653-6597
Roxanne Hughes, *Branch Mgr*
EMP: 57
SALES (corp-wide): 390.9MM **Publicly
Held**
WEB: www.willdan.com
SIC: 8711 8742 Civil engineering; busi-
ness planning & organizing services
HQ: Willdan Engineering
2401 E Katella Ave # 300
Anaheim CA 92806
714 978-8200

(P-22700)
WILLDAN GROUP INC (PA)
2401 E Katella Ave # 300, Anaheim
(92806-5909)
PHONE..................................800 424-9144
Thomas D Brisbin, *Ch of Bd*
Michael A Bieber, *President*
Daniel Chow, *COO*
Creighton Early, *CFO*
Mohammed Shahidehpour, *Bd of Directors*
EMP: 123 EST: 1964
SQ FT: 18,000
SALES: 390.9MM **Publicly Held**
WEB: www.willdan.com
SIC: 8711 8748 Civil engineering; consult-
ing engineer; urban planning & consulting
services

(P-22701)
WSP USA INC
1100 W Town And Cntry 2, Orange
(92868-4600)
PHONE..................................714 973-4880
Charline Talmer, *General Mgr*
Gregory A Kelly, *President*
Michael Harris-Gifford, *Technical Staff*
Long Victoria, *Accountant*
Laura Hogan, *Human Res Mgr*
EMP: 100
SALES (corp-wide): 6.7B **Privately Held**
WEB: www.wsp.com
SIC: 8711 Consulting engineer
HQ: Wsp Usa Inc.
1 Penn Plz Fl 2250w34t
New York NY 10119
212 465-5000

(P-22702)
**WYLE SERVICES
CORPORATION (DH)**
1960 E Grand Ave Ste 900, El Segundo
(90245-5092)
PHONE..................................310 563-6800
George Melton, *President*
John Jordan, *President*
Dana Dorsey, *CFO*
Natasha Wagoner, *Officer*
Roger Wiederkehr, *Senior VP*
EMP: 3330 EST: 2003
SALES (est): 103.3MM **Publicly Held**
WEB: www.kbr.com
SIC: 8711 7371 Engineering services;
computer software development
HQ: Wyle Inc.
601 Jefferson St Ste 3452
Houston TX 77002
713 753-3834

(P-22703)
XLR8 SERVICES INC
1020 Calle Negocio Ste A, San Clemente
(92673-4226)
PHONE..................................949 498-9578
Jason Powell, *President*
Adrian Aldaz, *Program Mgr*
Linda Curtiss, *Program Mgr*
EMP: 22 EST: 2013
SALES (est): 5MM **Privately Held**
WEB: www.xlr8ems.com
SIC: 8711 3825 3829 Electrical or elec-
tronic engineering; digital test equipment,
electronic & electrical circuits; test equip-
ment for electronic & electrical circuits;
geophysical or meteorological electronic
equipment

(P-22704)
XORAIL INC
430 N Vineyard Ave # 220, Ontario
(91764-5494)
PHONE..................................904 443-0083
James Mayer, *Owner*
EMP: 119 **Publicly Held**
WEB: www.wabteccorp.com
SIC: 8711 7389 Engineering services;
drafting service, except temporary help
HQ: Xorail, Inc.
5011 Gate Pkwy 100-400
Jacksonville FL 32256

8712 Architectural Services

(P-22705)
5 DESIGN INC
Also Called: 5design
1024 N Orange Dr Ste 215, Los Angeles
(90038-2348)
PHONE..................................323 308-3558
Stan Hathaway, *President*
Michael Ellis, *Treasurer*
Arthur Benedetti Jr, *Vice Pres*
Mila Salahuddin, *Comms Mgr*
Tim Magill, *Admin Sec*
EMP: 76 EST: 2005
SALES (est): 15.1MM **Privately Held**
WEB: www.5plusdesign.com
SIC: 8712 Architectural engineering

(P-22706)
**AECOM MGT SVCS GLOBL
CORP (HQ)**
300 S Grand Ave Ste 900, Los Angeles
(90071-3135)
PHONE....................213 593-8000
Eric Chen, *President*
Catherine Hibbard, *Technician*
Joshua Shackelford, *Project Mgr*
John Hamilton, *Technology*
Paul Johanson, *Sr Project Mgr*
EMP: 428 **EST:** 1994
SALES (est): 35MM
SALES (corp-wide): 13.2B **Publicly Held**
WEB: www.aecom.com
SIC: 8712 8711 Architectural services; en-
gineering services
PA: Aecom
13355 Noel Rd Ste 400
Dallas TX 75240
972 788-1000

(P-22707)
AECOM SERVICES INC (HQ)
300 S Grand Ave Ste 900, Los Angeles
(90071-3135)
PHONE....................213 593-8000
Michael S Burke, *CEO*
Raymond Landy, *President*
Jane Chmielinski, *COO*
Deborah Klem, *CFO*
Dennis Deslatte, *Treasurer*
EMP: 250 **EST:** 1946
SALES (est): 2.1B
SALES (corp-wide): 13.2B **Publicly Held**
WEB: www.aecom.com
SIC: 8712 8741 8711 Architectural serv-
ices; management services; engineering
services
PA: Aecom
13355 Noel Rd Ste 400
Dallas TX 75240
972 788-1000

(P-22708)
ALTOON PARTNERS LLP (PA)
Also Called: Altoon Porter
617 W 7th St Ste 400, Los Angeles
(90017-3889)
PHONE....................213 225-1900
Ronald A Altoon, *Partner*
James Auld, *Partner*
Gary Dempster, *Partner*
William Sebring, *Partner*
Leslie Young, *Partner*
EMP: 69 **EST:** 1984
SQ FT: 20,000
SALES (est): 8MM **Privately Held**
WEB: www.stirarchitecture.com
SIC: 8712 Architectural engineering

(P-22709)
AMERICAN GENERAL DESIGN
388 Cordova St Ste 280, Pasadena
(91101-5839)
PHONE....................626 304-0800
Patrick Chraghchian, *President*
EMP: 50 **EST:** 2006
SALES (est): 3.1MM **Privately Held**
SIC: 8712 Architectural services

(P-22710)
AO SCIENCE + TECHNOLOGY
144 N Orange St, Orange (92866-1413)
PHONE....................714 639-9860
Jack Selman, *Senior Partner*
RC Alley III, *Partner*
Jim Dietze, *Partner*
Darrel Hebenstreit, *Partner*
Hugh Rose, *Partner*
EMP: 200 **EST:** 1973
SQ FT: 10,000
SALES (est): 37.4MM **Privately Held**
WEB: www.aoarchitects.com
SIC: 8712 Architectural engineering

(P-22711)
**BASSENIAN/LAGONI
ARCHITECTS**
2031 Orchard Dr Ste 100, Newport Beach
(92660-0753)
PHONE....................949 553-9100
Aram Bassenian, *CEO*
Carl Lagoni, *President*
Lee R Rogaliner, *CFO*

Lee Rogaliner, *CFO*
Hans Anderle, *Assoc VP*
EMP: 65 **EST:** 1979
SQ FT: 22,800
SALES (est): 10.7MM **Privately Held**
WEB: www.bassenianlagoni.com
SIC: 8712 Architectural engineering

(P-22712)
CALLISONRTKL INC
818 W 7th St Ste 300, Los Angeles
(90017-3426)
PHONE....................213 627-7373
EMP: 140
SALES (corp-wide): 2.5B **Privately Held**
SIC: 8712 Architectural Services
HQ: Callisonrtkl Inc
901 S Bond St
Baltimore MD 21231
410 528-8600

(P-22713)
DLR GROUP INC (HQ)
700 Suth Flwr St Fl 22 Flr 22, Los Angeles
(90017)
PHONE....................213 800-9400
Adrian O Cohen, *President*
Dennis Wiederholt, *Treasurer*
Jon P Anderson, *Vice Pres*
Jon Anderson, *Vice Pres*
Brian Arial, *Vice Pres*
EMP: 140 **EST:** 1997
SALES (est): 16.2MM
SALES (corp-wide): 268.7MM **Privately
Held**
WEB: www.dlrgroup.com
SIC: 8712 8711 Architectural engineering;
engineering services; mechanical engi-
neering
PA: Dlr Holding Company
6457 Frances St Ste 200
Omaha NE
402 393-4100

(P-22714)
DLR GROUP INC
Also Called: Wwcot Architects
4280 Latham St Ste H, Riverside
(92501-1737)
PHONE....................951 682-0470
Pam Touschner, *Branch Mgr*
EMP: 53
SALES (corp-wide): 268.7MM **Privately
Held**
WEB: www.dlrgroup.com
SIC: 8712 7389 Architectural services; in-
terior design services
HQ: Dlr Group Inc.
6457 Frances St Ste 200
Omaha NE 68106
216 522-1350

(P-22715)
GEHRY PARTNERS LLP
12541 Beatrice St, Los Angeles
(90066-7001)
PHONE....................310 482-3000
Frank Gehry, *Partner*
Brian Aamoth, *Partner*
John Bowers, *Partner*
Anand Devarajan, *Partner*
Morri Freeman, *Partner*
EMP: 130 **EST:** 2001
SQ FT: 12,100
SALES (est): 21.6MM **Privately Held**
WEB: www.foga.com
SIC: 8712 Architectural services

(P-22716)
GKK CORPORATION (PA)
Also Called: Gkkworks
2355 Main St Ste 220, Irvine (92614-4251)
PHONE....................949 250-1500
Praful Kulkarni, *President*
David Hunt, *Vice Pres*
Phillip Vogt, *Principal*
Leslie Long, *Office Mgr*
Becca Chikes, *Administration*
EMP: 85 **EST:** 1991
SQ FT: 11,000
SALES (est): 117.5MM **Privately Held**
SIC: 8712 8711 Architectural engineering;
building construction consultant

(P-22717)
GKK WORKS (HQ)
Also Called: Gkkworks Cannon Design
2875 Michelle, Irvine (92606-1021)
PHONE....................949 250-1500
Bradley Lukanic, *CEO*
Rob Good, *Project Dir*
Christina Gutierrez, *Project Mgr*
Liliana Lederman, *Project Mgr*
Vincent Petito, *Prdtn Mgr*
EMP: 74 **EST:** 2005
SALES (est): 10.4MM
SALES (corp-wide): 162.5MM **Privately
Held**
WEB: www.cannondesign.com
SIC: 8712 7389 Architectural engineering;
interior design services
PA: The Cannon Corporation
50 Fountain Plz Ste 200
Buffalo NY 14202
716 773-6800

(P-22718)
GRUEN ASSOCIATES INC
Also Called: Gruen Assoc Archtects Planners
6330 San Vicente Blvd # 200, Los Angeles
(90048-5441)
PHONE....................323 937-4270
Ki Suh Park, *Partner*
Michael A Enomoto, *Partner*
Larry Schlossberg, *Partner*
Michael Enomoto, *Managing Prtnr*
Orlando Gonzalez, *Planning*
EMP: 75 **EST:** 1947
SQ FT: 14,000
SALES (est): 10.6MM **Privately Held**
WEB: www.gruenassociates.com
SIC: 8712 Architectural engineering

(P-22719)
HAWKINS BROWN USA INC
8500 Steller Dr Ste 1, Culver City
(90232-2453)
PHONE....................310 600-2695
Matthew Ollier, *Principal*
Harbinder Birdi, *Partner*
Morag Morrison, *Partner*
Hazel York, *Managing Prtnr*
EMP: 276 **EST:** 2017
SALES (est): 7.5MM **Privately Held**
SIC: 8712 Architectural engineering

(P-22720)
HFS CONCEPTS 4 INC
3229 E Spring St Ste 330, Long Beach
(90806-2486)
PHONE....................562 424-1720
John Mamer, *President*
Bill Legg, *Vice Pres*
Susan Prann, *Creative Dir*
Jeannette Hurley, *Admin Asst*
Lori Dematteo, *Project Mgr*
EMP: 50 **EST:** 1977
SQ FT: 11,000
SALES (est): 7.9MM **Privately Held**
WEB: www.thehfsgroup.com
SIC: 8712 7389 Architectural services; in-
terior designer

(P-22721)
HMC GROUP (HQ)
Also Called: HMC Architects
3546 Concours, Ontario (91764-5584)
PHONE....................909 989-9979
Brian Staton, *CEO*
Mitch Carp, *Senior VP*
Ricardo Chaidez, *Software Dev*
Kathleen Stanton, *Corp Comm Staff*
▲ **EMP:** 165 **EST:** 1941
SQ FT: 58,000
SALES (est): 31.8MM
SALES (corp-wide): 57.5MM **Privately
Held**
WEB: www.hmcarchitects.com
SIC: 8712 Architectural engineering
PA: Hmc Holdings, Inc.
3546 Concours
Ontario CA 91764
909 989-9979

(P-22722)
HMC GROUP
2930 Inland Empire Blvd # 100, Ontario
(91764-4802)
PHONE....................909 980-8058
EMP: 56

SALES (corp-wide): 51.8MM **Privately
Held**
WEB: www.hmcarchitects.com
SIC: 8712 Architectural Services
HQ: Hmc Group
3546 Concours
Ontario CA 91764
909 989-9979

(P-22723)
JEFFREY ROME & ASSOCIATES
1715 Port Charles Pl, Newport Beach
(92660-5319)
PHONE....................949 760-3929
Jeffery Rome, *President*
Harold Crouch, *Project Mgr*
Manny Figueroa, *Project Mgr*
Randal Williams, *Project Mgr*
Andy MAI, *Finance*
EMP: 60 **EST:** 1991
SALES (est): 6.9MM **Privately Held**
WEB: www.jeffreyromeassociates.com
SIC: 8712 Architectural engineering

(P-22724)
JOHNSON FAIN INC
1201 N Broadway, Los Angeles
(90012-1407)
PHONE....................323 224-6000
William H Fain Jr, *Co-President*
R Scott Johnson, *Co-President*
Sherry Miller, *Admin Sec*
Tom Brakefield, *Technology*
Mark Owen, *Sales Staff*
EMP: 80 **EST:** 1950
SQ FT: 26,000
SALES (est): 9.2MM **Privately Held**
WEB: www.johnsonfain.com
SIC: 8712 7389 Architectural engineering;
interior design services

(P-22725)
KAA DESIGN GROUP INC
12921 W Washington Blvd, Los Angeles
(90066-5121)
PHONE....................310 821-1400
Grant Kirkpatrick, *President*
Joyce Lopez, *Office Mgr*
Meghan Beckmann, *Sr Associate*
John Margolis, *Sr Project Mgr*
Dan Murphy, *Sr Project Mgr*
EMP: 53 **EST:** 1987
SALES (est): 5.4MM **Privately Held**
WEB: www.kaadesigngroup.com
SIC: 8712 Architectural engineering

(P-22726)
KFA LLP
3573 Hayden Ave, Culver City
(90232-2412)
PHONE....................310 399-7975
Jonathan Watts, *Partner*
John Arnold, *Partner*
Lise Bornstein, *Partner*
Barbara Flammang, *Partner*
Wade Killefer, *Partner*
EMP: 58 **EST:** 2015
SALES (est): 807.7K **Privately Held**
WEB: www.kfalosangeles.com
SIC: 8712 Architectural engineering

(P-22727)
KTGY GROUP INC (PA)
17911 Von Karman Ave # 2, Irvine
(92614-6209)
PHONE....................949 851-2133
Tricia Esser, *CEC*
Stan Braden, *President*
Monica Cantu, *Executive*
Joe Hirsch, *Business Dir*
Axel Stoltz, *Exec Dir*
EMP: 70 **EST:** 1991
SQ FT: 21,000
SALES (est): 29.2MM **Privately Held**
WEB: www.ktgy.com
SIC: 8712 Architectural engineering

(P-22728)
LEE BURKHART LIU INC
5510 Lincoln Blvd Ste 250, Playa Vista
(90094-3008)
PHONE....................310 829-2249
Kenneth Lee, *President*
Erich Burkart, *Principal*
Ken Liu, *Principal*
EMP: 75 **EST:** 1986

SQ FT: 11,000
SALES (est): 5MM **Privately Held**
SIC: 8712 Architectural engineering

(P-22729)
LPA INC (PA)
5301 California Ave # 100, Irvine
(92617-3224)
PHONE..................................949 261-1001
Wendy Rogers, *CEO*
Dan Heinfeld, *President*
Charles Pruitt, *CFO*
Robert Kupper, *Exec VP*
James Kelly, *Vice Pres*
◆ **EMP:** 180 **EST:** 1971
SQ FT: 33,700
SALES (est): 36.6MM **Privately Held**
WEB: www.lpadesignstudios.com
SIC: 8712 8711 0781 Architectural engi-
neering; engineering services; landscape
counseling & planning

(P-22730)
M ARTHUR GENSLER JR ASSOC INC
Also Called: Gensler and Associates
500 S Figueroa St, Los Angeles
(90071-1705)
PHONE..................................213 927-3600
Rob Jernigan, *Branch Mgr*
Kathleen Oconnor, *Executive*
Barbara Bouza, *Managing Dir*
Vic Froglia, *Project Mgr*
Jim Young, *Project Mgr*
EMP: 249
SALES (corp-wide): 1.2B **Privately Held**
WEB: www.gensler.com
SIC: 8712 7389 Architectural engineering;
design, commercial & industrial
PA: M. Arthur Gensler Jr. & Associates, Inc.
45 Fremont St Ste 1500
San Francisco CA 94105
415 433-3700

(P-22731)
MARMOL RDZNER AN ARCHTCTRAL CO
12210 Nebraska Ave, Los Angeles
(90025-3620)
PHONE..................................310 826-6222
Ron Radziner, *CEO*
Leo Marmol, *President*
Todd Jerry, *COO*
Kristy Estrada, *Executive*
Colton Cross, *Project Mgr*
EMP: 70 **EST:** 1989
SQ FT: 6,500
SALES (est): 12MM **Privately Held**
WEB: www.marmol-radziner.com
SIC: 8712 1521 1542 Architectural engi-
neering; general remodeling, single-family
houses; new construction, single-family
houses; commercial & office building, new
construction; commercial & office build-
ings, renovation & repair

(P-22732)
MARTIN AC PARTNERS INC
444 S Flower St Ste 1200, Los Angeles
(90071-2977)
PHONE..................................213 683-1900
Robert Newsom, *President*
Christopher C Martin, *CEO*
David C Martin, *Principal*
Serena Chuatrakul, *Accountant*
Izabela Dimitrova, *Director*
EMP: 116 **EST:** 1906
SALES (est): 12.6MM **Privately Held**
WEB: www.acmartin.com
SIC: 8712 Architectural services

(P-22733)
MORPHOSIS ARCHITECTS
3440 Wesley St, Culver City (90232-2328)
PHONE..................................310 453-2247
Thom Mayne, *President*
Blythe Allison Mayne, *Vice Pres*
Robin Williams, *Project Dir*
Michael Duenas, *Technology*
Sung Lim, *Director*
EMP: 62 **EST:** 1975
SQ FT: 10,000
SALES (est): 8.8MM **Privately Held**
WEB: www.morphosis.net
SIC: 8712 Architectural engineering

(P-22734)
MVE + PARTNERS INC (PA)
1900 Main St Ste 800, Irvine (92614-7318)
PHONE..................................949 809-3388
Carl F McLarand, *CEO*
Raymond Albanesi, *Partner*
Tim Beuchat, *Partner*
Lori Ichisaka, *Partner*
Paul Kearney, *Partner*
EMP: 58 **EST:** 1975
SQ FT: 22,000
SALES (est): 12.6MM **Privately Held**
WEB: www.mve-architects.com
SIC: 8712 Architectural engineering

(P-22735)
NEWMAN GARRISON + PARTNERS INC
3100 Bristol St Ste 400, Costa Mesa
(92626-7333)
PHONE..................................949 756-0818
Kevin Newman, *Chairman*
Donald J Meeks, *President*
Yulis Ayton, *Project Mgr*
Ben Chiu, *Project Mgr*
Bruce Hargens, *Sr Project Mgr*
EMP: 70 **EST:** 1974
SQ FT: 7,000
SALES (est): 7.2MM **Privately Held**
WEB: www.nggpartners.com
SIC: 8712 Architectural engineering

(P-22736)
OEL/HHH INC
1833 Victory Blvd, Glendale (91201-2557)
PHONE..................................818 246-6050
Fax: 818 240-0430
EMP: 80 **EST:** 1978
SQ FT: 20,000
SALES (est): 4.5MM **Privately Held**
WEB: www.lhaarchitects.com
SIC: 8712 Architectural Services

(P-22737)
RACHLIN ARCHITECTS INC
8640 National Blvd, Culver City
(90232-2419)
PHONE..................................310 204-3400
Michael Rachlin, *President*
Michael Curto, *Principal*
Jennifer Puronen, *Principal*
Paul Dragescu, *Project Mgr*
Rudy Monico, *Project Mgr*
EMP: 60 **EST:** 1982
SQ FT: 4,000
SALES (est): 3.2MM **Privately Held**
WEB: www.rachlinarchitects.com
SIC: 8712 7389 Architectural engineering;
interior designer

(P-22738)
RBB ARCHITECTS INC (PA)
10980 Wilshire Blvd, Los Angeles
(90024-3944)
PHONE..................................310 479-1473
Joseph A Balbona, *CEO*
Deneys Purcell, *President*
Kevin Boots, *Senior VP*
Arthur E Border, *Senior VP*
Rebecca Phipps, *Project Mgr*
EMP: 54
SQ FT: 15,837
SALES (est): 9.1MM **Privately Held**
WEB: www.rbbinc.com
SIC: 8712 Architectural engineering

(P-22739)
RDC-S111 INC (PA)
Also Called: Perkowitz & Ruth Architects
245 E 3rd St, Long Beach (90802-3141)
PHONE..................................562 628-8000
Bradley Williams, *CEO*
Ian Denny, *CFO*
Jackson Thilenius, *Senior VP*
Steven J Ruth, *Vice Pres*
Brian Wolfe, *Admin Sec*
EMP: 141 **EST:** 1979
SALES (est): 28.6MM **Privately Held**
WEB: www.rdcollaborative.com
SIC: 8712 Architectural engineering

(P-22740)
RO ROCKET DESIGN INC (PA)
1031 W Mnchstr Blvd, Inglewood
(90301-1509)
PHONE..................................213 784-0014

Jason Ro, *CEO*
Zac Rockett, *Principal*
EMP: 51 **EST:** 2011
SALES (est): 1.7MM **Privately Held**
WEB: www.rorockettdesign.com
SIC: 8712 Architectural engineering

(P-22741)
RRM DESIGN GROUP (PA)
3765 S Higuera St Ste 102, San Luis
Obispo (93401-1577)
PHONE..................................805 439-0442
Victor Montgomery, *Ch of Bd*
John Wilbanks, *President*
Randy Russom, *Treasurer*
Keith Gurnee, *Senior VP*
Erik P Justesen, *Principal*
EMP: 99
SQ FT: 23,000
SALES (est): 17.8MM **Privately Held**
WEB: www.rrmdesign.com
SIC: 8712 Architectural engineering

(P-22742)
SHLEMMER ALGAZE ASSOCIATES (PA)
Also Called: Saa
6083 Bristol Pkwy, Culver City
(90230-6601)
PHONE..................................310 215-3991
Nelson Algaze, *Principal*
Maureen Hunter, *Administration*
Chris Messina, *Info Tech Dir*
Ly Chea, *Technical Staff*
Winson Ly, *Analyst*
EMP: 68 **EST:** 2005
SALES (est): 13.6MM **Privately Held**
SIC: 8712 7389 Architectural engineering;
interior design services

(P-22743)
STANTEC ARCHITECTURE INC
38 Technology Dr Ste 100, Irvine
(92618-5312)
PHONE..................................949 923-6000
Eric Nielsen, *Vice Pres*
Todd Watson, *Executive*
Michelle Clark, *Administration*
Arthur Maytorena, *Administration*
Wes Johnson, *Project Mgr*
EMP: 214
SALES (corp-wide): 3.6B **Privately Held**
WEB: www.stantec.com
SIC: 8712 8711 4111 Architectural serv-
ices; engineering services; local & subur-
ban transit
HQ: Stantec Architecture Inc.
224 S Michigan Ave # 1400
Chicago IL 60604
336 714-7413

(P-22744)
STANTEC ARCHITECTURE INC
300 N Lake Ave Ste 400, Pasadena
(91101-4169)
PHONE..................................626 796-9141
Simon Bluestone, *Branch Mgr*
John Hanula, *CIO*
EMP: 88
SALES (corp-wide): 3.6B **Privately Held**
WEB: www.stantec.com
SIC: 8712 Architectural services
HQ: Stantec Architecture Inc.
224 S Michigan Ave # 1400
Chicago IL 60604
336 714-7413

(P-22745)
STANTEC CONSULTING SVCS INC
38 Technology Dr Ste 100, Irvine
(92618-5312)
PHONE..................................949 923-6000
Bob Gomes, *Branch Mgr*
Chris Workman, *Administration*
Wally Spak, *Network Mgr*
Jeff Wilkerson, *Project Mgr*
Jeff Crawford, *Marketing Staff*
EMP: 117
SALES (corp-wide): 3.6B **Privately Held**
WEB: www.stantec.com
SIC: 8712 8711 Architectural services; en-
gineering services

HQ: Stantec Consulting Services Inc.
475 5th Ave Fl 12
New York NY 10017
212 352-5160

(P-22746)
STEINBERG HART (PA)
Also Called: Steinberg Architects
818 W 7th St Ste 1100, Los Angeles
(90017-3461)
PHONE..................................408 295-5446
David Hart, *President*
Katia McClain, *Managing Prtnr*
Robert Steinberg, *Ch of Bd*
Hong Chen, *COO*
Isaac Zamora, *CFO*
EMP: 74 **EST:** 1953
SQ FT: 14,000
SALES (est): 14.6MM **Privately Held**
WEB: www.steinberghart.com
SIC: 8712 Architectural engineering

(P-22747)
STV ARCHITECTS INC
1055 W 7th St Ste 3150, Los Angeles
(90017-2556)
PHONE..................................213 482-9444
Wagih Andraos, *Manager*
EMP: 175
SALES (corp-wide): 261MM **Privately
Held**
WEB: www.stvinc.com
SIC: 8712 8742 8711 Architectural engi-
neering; transportation consultant; con-
sulting engineer
HQ: Stv Architects Inc
205 W Welsh Dr
Douglassville PA 19518
610 385-8200

(P-22748)
TAYLOR & ASSOC ARCHITECTS INC (PA)
Also Called: Taylor Design
17850 Fitch, Irvine (92614-6002)
PHONE..................................949 574-1325
Linda Taylor, *Ch of Bd*
D Randy Regier, *President*
Gary Davidson, *Corp Secy*
Leslie Martinez, *Administration*
Bill O 'rourke, *CIO*
EMP: 72 **EST:** 1979
SQ FT: 12,000
SALES (est): 10.5MM **Privately Held**
WEB: www.wearetaylor.com
SIC: 8712 Architectural engineering

(P-22749)
TCA ARCHITECTS INC (PA)
18821 Bardeen Ave, Irvine (92612-1520)
PHONE..................................949 862-0270
Thomas P Cox, *President*
Aram C Chahbazian, *President*
Harry Steinway, *CFO*
Larry Scott, *Senior VP*
Heidi Mather, *Vice Pres*
EMP: 52 **EST:** 1992
SALES (est): 12.1MM **Privately Held**
WEB: www.tca-arch.com
SIC: 8712 Architectural engineering

(P-22750)
WARE MALCOMB (PA)
10 Edelman, Irvine (92618-4312)
PHONE..................................949 660-9128
Kenneth Wink, *CEO*
Jay Todisco, *President*
Tobin Sloane, *CFO*
Lawrence R Armstrong, *Chairman*
Matthew Brady, *Exec VP*
▲ **EMP:** 137 **EST:** 1972
SQ FT: 22,000
SALES: 90.3MM **Privately Held**
WEB: www.waremalcomb.com
SIC: 8712 7336 8711 7389 Architectural
engineering; commercial art & graphic de-
sign; civil engineering; interior design
services; design, commercial & industrial

(P-22751)
WEAVER AND TIDWELL LLP
1230 Rosecrans Ave # 510, Manhattan
Beach (90266-2477)
PHONE..................................310 382-5380
EMP: 54

SALES (corp-wide): 88.8MM **Privately Held**
WEB: www.weaver.com
SIC: 8712 Architectural engineering
PA: Weaver And Tidwell, L.L.P.
   2821 W 7th St Ste 700
   Fort Worth TX 76107
   817 332-7905

(P-22752)
WILLIAM HZMLHLCH ARCHTECTS INC
680 Nwport Ctr Dr Ste 300, Newport Beach (92660)
PHONE..................................949 250-0607
William Hezmalhalch, *CEO*
Rick Aiken, *Vice Pres*
Dinna Mize, *Vice Pres*
Amber Roberts, *Administration*
Denise J Ashton, *Planning*
EMP: 75
SALES (est): 12.6MM **Privately Held**
WEB: www.whainc.com
SIC: 8712 Architectural engineering

(P-22753)
ZIMMER GNSUL FRSCA ARCHTCTS LL
Also Called: Zimmer Gnsul Frsca Partnr Amer
515 S Flower St Ste 3700, Los Angeles (90071-2221)
PHONE..................................213 617-1901
Rachel Morris, *Manager*
Jihyon Kim, *Partner*
Aida Knur, *Partner*
Peter Van Der Meulen, *Partner*
Brett Meyer, *Partner*
EMP: 118
SALES (corp-wide): 41.5MM **Privately Held**
SIC: 8712 7389 Architectural engineering; interior designer
PA: Zimmer Gunsul Frasca Architects Llp
   1223 Sw Washington St # 200
   Portland OR 97205
   503 224-3860

8713 Surveying Services

(P-22754)
CANNON CORPORATION (PA)
1050 Southwood Dr, San Luis Obispo (93401-5813)
PHONE..................................805 544-7407
Michael F Cannon, *CEO*
John Evans, *Vice Pres*
Daniel Hutchinson, *Vice Pres*
Donna Martin, *Admin Asst*
Jonathon Fulkerson, *Info Tech Mgr*
EMP: 60 EST: 1975
SQ FT: 4,200
SALES (est): 18.9MM **Privately Held**
WEB: www.cannoncorp.us
SIC: 8713 8711 1611 Surveying services; civil engineering; highway & street construction

(P-22755)
PSOMAS (PA)
555 S Flower St Ste 4300, Los Angeles (90071-2405)
PHONE..................................213 223-1400
Ryan McLean, *President*
Ross W Barker, *Vice Pres*
Brett Barnett, *Vice Pres*
Jeff Chess, *Vice Pres*
Matthew Clark, *Vice Pres*
EMP: 125 EST: 1946
SQ FT: 30,000
SALES (est): 67.8MM **Privately Held**
WEB: www.psomas.com
SIC: 8713 8711 Surveying services; engineering services

(P-22756)
STANTEC ENERGY & RESOURCES INC (HQ)
5500 Ming Ave Ste 410, Bakersfield (93309-4631)
PHONE..................................661 396-3770
Robert Gomes, *President*
Richard Allen, *COO*
Daniel Lefaivre, *Treasurer*
Kirk Morrison, *Exec VP*

Paul Alpern, *Senior VP*
EMP: 182 EST: 2015
SALES (est): 31.9MM **Privately Held**
SIC: 8713 Surveying services
PA: Mustang Acquisition Holdings Inc.
   475 5th Ave Fl 12
   New York NY 10017
   301 220-1861

8721 Accounting, Auditing & Bookkeeping Svcs

(P-22757)
ACCRETIVE SOLUTIONS INC (HQ)
17101 Armstrong Ave # 100, Irvine (92614-5742)
PHONE..................................312 994-4600
Kerry Barrett, *CEO*
Jonathan Rosenthal, *Ch of Bd*
Joann Lilek, *CFO*
Richard A Moran, *Vice Ch Bd*
Mike Reinecke, *Exec VP*
EMP: 1000 EST: 1983
SALES (est): 63.5MM **Publicly Held**
WEB: www.rgp.com
SIC: 8721 Accounting, auditing & bookkeeping

(P-22758)
ADAME INSURANCE SERVICES INC
430 W Holt Ave Ste A, Pomona (91768-3612)
PHONE..................................909 620-7098
Valente Adame, *President*
EMP: 50 EST: 2006
SALES (est): 1.1MM **Privately Held**
SIC: 8721 Accounting, auditing & bookkeeping

(P-22759)
AMERICAN TAX SOLUTIONS
1055 W 7th St Ste 1600, Los Angeles (90017-2535)
PHONE..................................323 306-7032
Tyler Bennett, *Administration*
Geoff Plourde, *Vice Pres*
EMP: 50
SALES: 6MM **Privately Held**
WEB: www.atsco.tax
SIC: 8721 Accounting services, except auditing

(P-22760)
BARTLETT PRINGLE & WOLF LLP
1123 Chapala St Ste 300, Santa Barbara (93101-3163)
PHONE..................................805 963-7811
Robert Maloy, *General Ptnr*
Colleen Roberts, *Admin Asst*
Daniel Garcia, *Accountant*
Tyler Moore, *Accountant*
Jodie Nakajima, *Accountant*
EMP: 50 EST: 1966
SALES (est): 6.5MM **Privately Held**
WEB: www.bpw.com
SIC: 8721 Certified public accountant

(P-22761)
BMS PARENT INC (PA)
1220 Dewey Way Ste F, Upland (91786-1101)
PHONE..................................909 981-2341
John Wallace, *CEO*
Barbara Gillet, *Vice Pres*
EMP: 68 EST: 1997
SQ FT: 9,000
SALES (est): 5.8MM **Privately Held**
SIC: 8721 5045 Billing & bookkeeping service; computer software

(P-22762)
BRAULT
Also Called: Emergency Groups' Office
180 Via Verde Ste 100, San Dimas (91773-3993)
PHONE..................................626 447-0296
Andrea Brault, *President*
Genise Burgess, *COO*
Sharon Casey Cassell, *CFO*
James Blakeman, *Senior VP*

Bob Acker, *Vice Pres*
EMP: 200 EST: 2015
SALES (est): 10.2MM **Privately Held**
WEB: www.brault.us
SIC: 8721 Billing & bookkeeping service

(P-22763)
BROWN ARMSTRONG ACCNTANCY CORP
Also Called: Brown Armstrong Cpas
4200 Truxtun Ave Ste 300, Bakersfield (93309-0668)
PHONE..................................661 324-4971
Andrew J Paulden, *President*
Steve Starbuck, *Partner*
Christina Thornburgh, *Treasurer*
Benjamin P Reyes, *Corp Secy*
Christina M Thornburgh, *Corp Secy*
EMP: 65 EST: 1974
SQ FT: 30,000
SALES (est): 9.9MM **Privately Held**
WEB: www.bacpas.com
SIC: 8721 Certified public accountant

(P-22764)
CACHET FINANCIAL SERVICES
175 S Lake Ave Unit 200, Pasadena (91101-2629)
PHONE..................................626 578-9400
Aberash Asfaw, *President*
Alden Blowers, *President*
Sean Hardy, *Regional Mgr*
Marcus Acosta, *Regl Sales Mgr*
David Taub, *Sales Staff*
EMP: 80 EST: 2001
SALES (est): 6MM
SALES (corp-wide): 10.4MM **Privately Held**
WEB: www.cachetservices.com
SIC: 8721 Payroll accounting service
PA: Financial Business Group Holdings
   1932 E Deere Ave Ste 200
   Santa Ana CA 92705
   949 225-3000

(P-22765)
CALIFORNIA BUSINESS BUREAU INC (PA)
Also Called: Medical Billing Services
1711 S Mountain Ave, Monrovia (91016-4256)
P.O. Box 5010 (91017-7110)
PHONE..................................626 303-1515
Michael J Sigal, *President*
Jane Barnes, *VP Admin*
Brian Bonham, *Info Tech Mgr*
Antoinette Dominguez, *Technology*
EMP: 132
SQ FT: 24,000
SALES (est): 12.4MM **Privately Held**
WEB: www.cbbinc.com
SIC: 8721 Billing & bookkeeping service

(P-22766)
CALIFORNIA STATE UNIV LONG BCH
Also Called: Bursar's Office
1250 N Bellflower Blvd Bh155, Long Beach (90840-0004)
PHONE..................................562 985-1764
Randy Nielson, *Supervisor*
EMP: 117 **Privately Held**
WEB: www.csulb.edu
SIC: 8721 8221 9411 Accounting, auditing & bookkeeping; university; administration of educational programs
HQ: California State University, Long Beach
   1250 N Bellflower Blvd
   Long Beach CA 90840
   562 985-4111

(P-22767)
CAST & CREW PAYROLL LLC (PA)
Also Called: Cast and Crew Entrmt Svcs
2300 W Empire Ave Ste 500, Burbank (91504-5399)
PHONE..................................818 848-6022
Eric Belcher, *President*
Shardell Cavaliere, *President*
Shelly Mellott, *President*
Sally Knutson, *CFO*
Lee David, *Vice Pres*
EMP: 195 EST: 1976
SQ FT: 12,000

SALES (est): 52.6MM **Privately Held**
WEB: www.pslnet.com
SIC: 8721 Payroll accounting service

(P-22768)
CERIDIAN TAX SERVICE INC
17390 Brookhurst St, Fountain Valley (92708-3720)
P.O. Box 20805 (92728-0805)
PHONE..................................714 963-1311
Webster Hill, *General Mgr*
Bryan Odenwald, *Trust Officer*
Adam Masters, *Executive*
Jiming Liu, *Sr Software Eng*
Claudia Rohm, *Business Anlyst*
EMP: 300 EST: 1998
SQ FT: 130,000
SALES (est): 20.3MM
SALES (corp-wide): 842.5MM **Publicly Held**
WEB: www.ceridian.com
SIC: 8721 Payroll accounting service
PA: Ceridian Hcm Holding Inc.
   3311 E Old Shakopee Rd
   Minneapolis MN 55425
   952 853-8100

(P-22769)
CERTIFIED FRNSIC LN ADTORS LLC (PA)
Also Called: CA Oak Entps Bus Type Mktg
13101 W Wash Blvd Ste 444, Los Angeles (90066-5100)
PHONE..................................310 432-6304
Andrew P Lehman, *Mng Member*
Falisha J Lehman,
EMP: 130 EST: 2009
SALES (est): 8MM **Privately Held**
WEB: www.trollishly.com
SIC: 8721 Auditing services

(P-22770)
CITRIN COOPERMAN & COMPANY LLP
21650 Oxnard St, Woodland Hills (91367-4901)
PHONE..................................818 783-0570
EMP: 50
SALES (corp-wide): 63.3MM **Privately Held**
WEB: www.citrincooperman.com
SIC: 8721 Certified public accountant
PA: Citrin Cooperman & Company, Llp
   529 5th Ave Fl 2
   New York NY 10017
   212 697-1000

(P-22771)
CITY OF LOS ANGELES
Harbor Dept- Port Los Angeles
425 S Palos Verdes St, San Pedro (90731-3309)
P.O. Box 151 (90733-0151)
PHONE..................................310 732-3734
Geraldine Knatz, *Exec Dir*
William Beauford, *Officer*
William Chamberlain, *Officer*
Jerilyn L Pez Mendoza, *Vice Pres*
Lori Sanchez, *Administration*
EMP: 650 **Privately Held**
WEB: www.lacity.org
SIC: 9621 8721 Water vessels & port regulating agencies; accounting services, except auditing
PA: City Of Los Angeles
   200 N Spring St Ste 303
   Los Angeles CA 90012
   213 978-0600

(P-22772)
CLIFTONLARSONALLEN LLP
2210 E Route 66 Ste 100, Glendora (91740-4676)
PHONE..................................626 857-7300
Harriet Balderas, *Director*
Lindsey McClure, *Director*
Suhrab Hatef, *Manager*
Bradley Meyer, *Manager*
Renee Bollier, *Associate*
EMP: 55
SALES (corp-wide): 755.1MM **Privately Held**
WEB: www.blogs.claconnect.com
SIC: 8721 Certified public accountant

PA: Cliftonlarsonallen Llp
220 S 6th St Ste 300
Minneapolis MN 55402
612 376-4500

(P-22773)
CLIFTONLARSONALLEN LLP
Also Called: Nsbn
1925 Century Park E Fl 16, Los Angeles
(90067-2701)
PHONE..................310 273-2501
Sharon Altman, *CPA*
EMP: 91
SALES (corp-wide): 755.1MM **Privately Held**
WEB: www.blogs.claconnect.com
SIC: 8721 Accounting services, except auditing
PA: Cliftonlarsonallen Llp
220 S 6th St Ste 300
Minneapolis MN 55402
612 376-4500

(P-22774)
COMPUTERIZED MGT SVCS INC
Also Called: CMS
4100 Guardian St Ste 205, Simi Valley
(93063-6721)
P.O. Box 190 (93062-0190)
PHONE..................805 522-5940
J Daryl Favale, *President*
Robb Charlton, *Vice Pres*
Brett Clunis, *Vice Pres*
Rosie Gomes, *Patnt Acct Dir*
Jimitria Smith, *Division Mgr*
EMP: 100 **EST:** 1985
SQ FT: 7,500
SALES (est): 6.6MM
SALES (corp-wide): 49.4MM **Privately Held**
WEB: www.cmsmanagement.net
SIC: 8721 Billing & bookkeeping service
PA: Xifin, Inc.
12225 El Camino Real
San Diego CA 92130
858 793-5700

(P-22775)
COUNTY OF LOS ANGELES
Also Called: Internal Services Department
1100 N Eastern Ave, Los Angeles
(90063-3200)
PHONE..................323 267-2136
Scott Minnix, *Director*
EMP: 1800
SALES (corp-wide): 25.2B **Privately Held**
WEB: www.lacounty.gov
SIC: 8721 Accounting, auditing & bookkeeping
PA: County Of Los Angeles
500 W Temple St Ste 437
Los Angeles CA 90012
213 974-1101

(P-22776)
DELOITTE & TOUCHE LLP
555 W 5th St Ste 2700, Los Angeles
(90013-1024)
PHONE..................213 688-0800
Byron David, *Branch Mgr*
David N Bowen, *Partner*
Niloo Bedrood, *Managing Dir*
Wing Yee, *Managing Dir*
Maxim Noronha, *Info Tech Mgr*
EMP: 1000
SALES (corp-wide): 768.6K **Privately Held**
WEB: www.deloitte.com
SIC: 8721 Accounting services, except auditing
HQ: Deloitte & Touche Llp
30 Rockefeller Plz # 4350
New York NY 10112
212 492-4000

(P-22777)
DELOITTE & TOUCHE LLP
555 W 5th St Ste 2700, Los Angeles
(90013-1024)
PHONE..................213 688-0800
EMP: 244
SALES (corp-wide): 12.3B **Privately Held**
SIC: 8721 Accounting/Auditing/Bookkeeping

HQ: Deloitte & Touche Llp
30 Rockefeller Plz # 4350
New York NY 10112
212 492-4000

(P-22778)
EGO INC
Also Called: Emergency Groups Office
180 Via Verde Ste 100, San Dimas
(91773-3993)
PHONE..................626 447-0296
Andrea Brault, *President*
Del Brault, *President*
Jane Brault, *Treasurer*
James Blakeman, *Senior VP*
Edward Estrada, *MIS Mgr*
EMP: 150 **EST:** 1990
SQ FT: 8,500
SALES (est): 13.3MM **Privately Held**
WEB: www.brault.us
SIC: 8721 Billing & bookkeeping service

(P-22779)
EIDE BAILLY LLP
10681 Fthill Blvd Ste 300, Rancho Cucamonga (91730)
PHONE..................909 466-4410
Dave Stende, *Managing Prtnr*
EMP: 300
SALES (corp-wide): 339.7MM **Privately Held**
WEB: www.eidebailly.com
SIC: 8721 Certified public accountant
PA: Eide Bailly Llp
4310 17th Ave S
Fargo ND 58103
701 239-8500

(P-22780)
ENTERTAINMENT PARTNERS INC (PA)
2950 N Hollywood Way # 200, Burbank
(91505-1072)
PHONE..................818 955-6000
Mark Goldstein, *CEO*
George Vaughan, *CFO*
Carol Mills, *Bd of Directors*
Chris Bradley, *Officer*
Anita Geller, *Sr Exec VP*
EMP: 295 **EST:** 1992
SQ FT: 38,000
SALES (est): 70.3MM **Privately Held**
WEB: www.ep.com
SIC: 8721 Payroll accounting service

(P-22781)
ERNST & YOUNG LLP
Also Called: Ey
725 S Figueroa St Ste 200, Los Angeles
(90017-5403)
PHONE..................213 977-3200
Jeff Kaufman, *Manager*
Kevin Thoeng, *Technology*
Arun Ponnusamy, *Technical Staff*
Sarah Liang, *Accountant*
Andrew Mokhov, *CPA*
EMP: 1000
SALES (corp-wide): 1.2B **Privately Held**
WEB: www.ey.com
SIC: 8721 8742 7291 Certified public accountant; auditing services; business consultant; management information systems consultant; tax return preparation services
PA: Ernst & Young Llp
1 Manhattan West Fl 6
New York NY 10001
703 747-0049

(P-22782)
ERNST & YOUNG LLP
Also Called: Ey
18101 Von Karman Ave # 1000, Irvine
(92612-0164)
PHONE..................949 794-2300
Linda Minx, *Office Mgr*
Chris Abston, *Partner*
Kathy Dagestino, *Partner*
Mike Denning, *Partner*
John F Fritz, *Partner*
EMP: 450
SALES (corp-wide): 1.2B **Privately Held**
WEB: www.ey.com
SIC: 8721 8742 Certified public accountant; auditing services; business consultant; management information systems consultant

HQ: Deloitte & Touche Llp
30 Rockefeller Plz # 4350
New York NY 10112
212 492-4000

PA: Ernst & Young Llp
1 Manhattan West Fl 6
New York NY 10001
703 747-0049

(P-22783)
FAST PAY PARTNERS LLC (HQ)
8201 Beverly Blvd Ste 600, Los Angeles
(90048-4542)
PHONE..................310 651-9200
Jed Simon, *CEO*
Secil Baysal, *President*
David Frogel, *Officer*
Michael McGuire, *Exec VP*
Aaron Weinstein, *Exec VP*
EMP: 58 **EST:** 2009
SALES (est): 6.1MM
SALES (corp-wide): 165.8MM **Privately Held**
WEB: www.gofastpay.com
SIC: 8721 Accounting, auditing & bookkeeping
PA: Avidxchange, Inc.
1210 Avid Xchange Ln
Charlotte NC 28206
704 971-8160

(P-22784)
FILM PAYROLL SERVICES INC (PA)
Also Called: Quantos Payroll
500 S Sepulveda Blvd Fl 4, Los Angeles
(90049-3550)
PHONE..................310 440-9600
Gregory Pickert, *CEO*
Amy Lafay, *Office Mgr*
Norman Marcus, *Administration*
Ricardo Carvalho, *Prgrmr*
Roger Jones, *Analyst*
EMP: 100 **EST:** 1978
SQ FT: 5,000
SALES (est): 16.2MM **Privately Held**
WEB: www.mediaservices.com
SIC: 8721 Payroll accounting service

(P-22785)
FINEMAN WEST AND CO LLP
801 S Figueroa St # 1000, Los Angeles
(90017-5508)
PHONE..................213 688-9898
Gary Fineman, *Partner*
Jeffrey Hyldahl, *Partner*
Donald Levy, *Partner*
Richard Swartz, *Partner*
Harold West, *Partner*
EMP: 53 **EST:** 1960
SALES (est): 6.5MM **Privately Held**
WEB: www.everynumbertellsastory.co
SIC: 8721 Certified public accountant

(P-22786)
GREEN HASSON & JANKS LLP
700 S Flower St Ste 3300, Los Angeles
(90017-4221)
PHONE..................310 873-1600
Leon Janks, *Partner*
William Cline, *CFO*
Sutton David, *Managing Dir*
Andrew Holoubek, *Managing Dir*
Mark Kawauchi, *Managing Dir*
EMP: 120 **EST:** 1953
SALES (est): 23.6MM **Privately Held**
WEB: www.ghjadvisors.com
SIC: 8721 Certified public accountant

(P-22787)
GURSEY SCHNEIDER & CO LLC (PA)
1888 Century Park E # 900, Los Angeles
(90067-1702)
PHONE..................310 552-0960
Stephan H Wasserman,
Navneet Bal, *Executive Asst*
Marie Peterson, *Executive Asst*
Rudy Fuentes, *Admin Asst*
Andrea Murray, *Admin Asst*
EMP: 118 **EST:** 1964
SQ FT: 12,000
SALES (est): 23.6MM **Privately Held**
WEB: www.gursey.com
SIC: 8721 Certified public accountant

PA: Ernst & Young Llp
1 Manhattan West Fl 6
New York NY 10001
703 747-0049

(P-22788)
GYL DECAUWER LLP
Also Called: Matt Gyl Decauwer
4120 Concours Ste 100, Ontario
(91764-4999)
PHONE..................909 948-9990
Steven Williams, *Partner*
Dennis Deacauwer, *Partner*
Joseph Romero, *Partner*
John Lerias, *Managing Prtnr*
Sylvia Vargas, *Director*
EMP: 63 **EST:** 1980
SQ FT: 6,500
SALES (est): 5.6MM **Privately Held**
WEB: www.gylcpa.com
SIC: 8721 Certified public accountant

(P-22789)
HMWC CPAS & BUSINESS ADVISORS
Also Called: Yosemite Capital Mangagement
5120 Birch St Ste 100, Newport Beach
(92660-2182)
PHONE..................714 505-9000
Steven Williams, *President*
Gerald Herter, *Partner*
Steve Williams, *Managing Prtnr*
Marie F Alvarez, *Executive Asst*
Debra Leon, *Executive Asst*
EMP: 57 **EST:** 1972
SALES (est): 10.8MM **Privately Held**
WEB: www.eidebailly.com
SIC: 8721 Certified public accountant

(P-22790)
HOLTHOUSE CARLIN VAN TRIGT LLP (PA)
Also Called: H C V T
11444 W Olympic Blvd # 11, Los Angeles
(90064-1500)
PHONE..................310 566-1900
Philip Holthouse, *Managing Prtnr*
David Bierhorst, *Partner*
James Carlin, *Partner*
Blake Christian, *Partner*
Greg Hutchins, *Partner*
EMP: 110 **EST:** 1991
SALES (est): 36.2MM **Privately Held**
WEB: www.hcvt.com
SIC: 8721 Certified public accountant

(P-22791)
HUTCHINSON & BLOODGOOD LLP (PA)
550 N Brand Blvd Fl 14, Glendale
(91203-1952)
P.O. Box 1917 (91209-1917)
PHONE..................818 637-5000
Richard Preciado, *Managing Prtnr*
Michael Benneian, *Partner*
Gary Carruthers, *Partner*
Kenneth Chappell, *Partner*
Jenny Chen, *Partner*
EMP: 59 **EST:** 1922
SALES (est): 43.1K **Privately Held**
WEB: www.hbllp.com
SIC: 8721 Certified public accountant

(P-22792)
I L S WEST INC
17501 17th St Ste 100, Tustin
(92780-7924)
PHONE..................714 505-7530
EMP: 50
SALES (est): 1.5MM **Privately Held**
SIC: 8721 Accounting/Auditing/Bookkeeping

(P-22793)
INFINEON TECH AMERICAS CORP
Interntnal Rctfr/Ccunting Dept
222 Kansas St, El Segundo (90245-4315)
PHONE..................310 726-8000
Michael McGee, *Manager*
Craig Colpo, *Treasurer*
Tak-Kei Chan, *Senior VP*
Bill Bivens, *Vice Pres*
Tak Chan, *Vice Pres*
EMP: 699
SALES (corp-wide): 10.1B **Privately Held**
WEB: www.infineon.com
SIC: 8721 3674 Accounting, auditing & bookkeeping; semiconductors & related devices

HQ: Infineon Technologies Americas Corp.
101 N Pacific Coast Hwy
El Segundo CA 90245
310 726-8200

(P-22794)
INFOSEND INC (PA)
4240 E La Palma Ave, Anaheim
(92807-1816)
PHONE..................................714 993-2690
Mahmood Rezai, *President*
Rusteen Rezai, *COO*
Vedat Aral, *IT/INT Sup*
Sevki Piskinsoy, *IT/INT Sup*
Josue Martinez, *Technology*
EMP: 67 EST: 1997
SALES (est): 18.2MM Privately Held
WEB: www.secure.infosend.com
SIC: 8721 7338 2732 2741 Billing &
bookkeeping service; stenographic serv-
ices; pamphlets: printing only, not pub-
lished on site; business service
newsletters: publishing & printing; pre-
sorted mail service; electronic mail

(P-22795)
JS HELD LLC
4667 Macarthur Blvd # 400, Newport Beach
(92660-1817)
PHONE..................................949 390-7647
EMP: 99
SALES (corp-wide): 200MM Privately
Held
SIC: 8721 Calculating & statistical service
PA: J.S. Held Llc
50 Jericho Quadrangle # 117
Jericho NY 11753
516 621-2900

(P-22796)
KBKG INC
225 S Lake Ave Ste 400, Pasadena
(91101-3010)
PHONE..................................626 449-4225
Gregory A Kniss, *CEO*
Harry Sahi, *Engineer*
Jason Melillo, *Auditor*
Lisa Arangua, *Human Res Mgr*
Evelyn Fernandez, *Senior Mgr*
EMP: 57 EST: 2001
SALES (est): 11.3MM Privately Held
WEB: www.kbkg.com
SIC: 8721 Certified public accountant

(P-22797)
**KELLOGG ANDLSON
ACCNTANCY CORP (PA)**
21700 Oxnard St Ste 800, Woodland Hills
(91367-7500)
PHONE..................................818 971-5100
Christian Payne, *CEO*
James F Walters, *President*
William Wall, *Vice Pres*
Dolores Priddy, *Administration*
Lee Forman, *Consultant*
EMP: 60 EST: 1939
SALES (est): 9.7MM Privately Held
SIC: 8721 Certified public accountant

(P-22798)
KPMG LLP
4464 Jasmine Ave, Culver City
(90232-3429)
PHONE..................................703 286-8175
Daniel Smith, *Manager*
Gregory Jay, *Partner*
George Mack, *Associate Dir*
David Mesinger, *Exec Dir*
Andrea Roces, *Admin Asst*
EMP: 99
SALES (corp-wide): 1.3B Privately Held
WEB: www.kpmg.us
SIC: 8721 Certified public accountant
PA: Kpmg Llp
345 Park Ave
New York NY 10154
212 758-9700

(P-22799)
KROST (PA)
Also Called: Krost Bumgarten Kniss Guerrero
225 S Lake Ave Ste 400, Pasadena
(91101-3010)
PHONE..................................626 449-4225
Richard B Krost, *CEO*
Gregory Kniss, *President*

Mara Garcia, *Auditor*
Aric Wong,
Stacey Korman, *Director*
EMP: 180 EST: 1936
SALES (est): 13.7MM Privately Held
WEB: www.krostcpas.com
SIC: 8721 Accounting services, except au-
diting; certified public accountant

(P-22800)
KUBRA AMERICA WEST INC
14105 S Normandie Ave # 2, Gardena
(90249-2620)
PHONE..................................310 756-1717
Rick Watkin, *President*
Brian Silva, *General Mgr*
Travis Pearson, *Software Engr*
EMP: 59 EST: 2000
SQ FT: 10,000
SALES (est): 4.7MM
SALES (corp-wide): 97.3MM Privately
Held
WEB: www.kubra.com
SIC: 8721 Billing & bookkeeping service
PA: Clairvest Group Inc.
22 St Clair Ave E Ste 1700
Toronto ON M4T 2
416 925-9270

(P-22801)
**LANCE SOLL & LUNGHARD
LLP**
203 N Brea Blvd Ste 203 # 203, Brea
(92821-4056)
PHONE..................................714 672-0022
Ronald Stumpf, *President*
Edward J Leiber, *Treasurer*
Gregory N Lewis, *Vice Pres*
Yen Nguyen, *Principal*
Sherry Radmore, *Admin Sec*
EMP: 100 EST: 1968
SQ FT: 7,000
SALES (est): 5.5MM Privately Held
SIC: 8721 Certified public accountant

(P-22802)
LLP MOSS ADAMS
21700 Oxnard St Ste 300, Woodland Hills
(91367-7561)
PHONE..................................818 577-1822
Gidget Furness, *COO*
Bob Terada, *Office Mgr*
Brad Daley, *Opers Staff*
EMP: 67
SALES (corp-wide): 317.2MM Privately
Held
WEB: www.mossadams.com
SIC: 8721 Certified public accountant
PA: Moss Adams Llp
999 3rd Ave Ste 2800
Seattle WA 98104
206 302-6800

(P-22803)
LLP MOSS ADAMS
10960 Wilshire Blvd # 1100, Los Angeles
(90024-3714)
PHONE..................................310 477-0450
Rod Green, *Partner*
Elizabeth Powell, *Executive Asst*
Vartan Deranteriassian, *IT/INT Sup*
Derek Allen, *Technology*
Stephen De Rosa, *Auditing Mgr*
EMP: 150
SALES (corp-wide): 317.2MM Privately
Held
WEB: www.mossadams.com
SIC: 8721 Certified public accountant
PA: Moss Adams Llp
999 3rd Ave Ste 2800
Seattle WA 98104
206 302-6800

(P-22804)
LLP MOSS ADAMS
2040 Main St Ste 900, Irvine (92614-8213)
PHONE..................................949 221-4000
Roger Weninger, *Branch Mgr*
James Parr, *Vice Pres*
Mary Case, *CIO*
Cindy Sui, *Analyst*
Michelle Mastrocola, *Accountant*
EMP: 67

SALES (corp-wide): 317.2MM Privately
Held
WEB: www.mossadams.com
SIC: 8721 Certified public accountant
PA: Moss Adams Llp
999 3rd Ave Ste 2800
Seattle WA 98104
206 302-6800

(P-22805)
MEDCOR GROUP INC
Also Called: Medcor Revenue Services
725 W Twn Cntry Rd # 300, Orange
(92868-4707)
PHONE..................................714 221-8511
Jonathan Gerber, *Principal*
Jason Gerber, *Principal*
Rocio Gonzalez, *Principal*
Chelci Schroeder, *Principal*
Jessica Temple, *Principal*
EMP: 55 EST: 2017
SALES (est): 1.2MM Privately Held
WEB: www.medcorinc.com
SIC: 8721 Accounting, auditing & book-
keeping

(P-22806)
NASIF HICKS HARRIS & CO LLP
Also Called: Harris, Jeffery P
104 W Anapamu St Ste B, Santa Barbara
(93101-3126)
PHONE..................................805 966-1521
William Nasif, *Partner*
Tom W Burk, *Partner*
Jeffrey Hicks, *Partner*
Steven Hicks, *Partner*
Jody D Holehouse, *Partner*
EMP: 60 EST: 1988
SQ FT: 2,400
SALES (est): 3.9MM Privately Held
WEB: www.nhhco.com
SIC: 8721 Certified public accountant

(P-22807)
**PEHL FUTZ FUTZ TGRDEN
ACCNTNTS**
Also Called: Foutz, Michael B
1045 E Morton Pl, Hemet (92543-4537)
P.O. Box 1045 (92546-1045)
PHONE..................................951 658-3277
Michael Foutz, *President*
Todd Foutz, *Managing Prtnr*
EMP: 61 EST: 1955
SQ FT: 5,000
SALES (est): 1.2MM Privately Held
SIC: 8721 Certified public accountant

(P-22808)
**PHYSICIAN SUPPORT SYSTEMS
INC (DH)**
1131 W 6th St Ste 300, Ontario
(91762-1118)
PHONE..................................717 653-5340
Douglas Estock, *President*
EMP: 400 EST: 1991
SALES (est): 29.6MM
SALES (corp-wide): 238.2B Publicly
Held
WEB: www.pssbilling.com
SIC: 8721 Billing & bookkeeping service
HQ: Ndchealth Corporation
1564 Northeast Expy Ne
Brookhaven GA 30329
404 728-2000

(P-22809)
PHYSICIANS CHOICE LLC
21860 Burbank Blvd # 120, Woodland Hills
(91367-6477)
P.O. Box 4419 (91365-4419)
PHONE..................................818 340-9988
John D Uphold,
Jonathan Sturm, *COO*
Greer Contreras, *Vice Pres*
Karen Gagnon, *Vice Pres*
Michelle Reckleff, *Accountant*
EMP: 80 EST: 1999
SQ FT: 10,000
SALES (est): 4.8MM Privately Held
WEB: www.physchoice.com
SIC: 8721 Billing & bookkeeping service

(P-22810)
QBI LLC (PA)
Also Called: Qualified Benefits
21031 Ventura Blvd # 1200, Woodland Hills
(91364-2203)
PHONE..................................818 594-4900
Nicholas H Stonnington, *Mng Member*
Maricela Fabian, *Administration*
Matt Furniss, *Sales Staff*
Taylor Johnson, *Sales Staff*
Valerie McClendon, *Sales Staff*
EMP: 78 EST: 2008
WEB: www.futureplan.com
SIC: 8721 6411 Payroll accounting serv-
ice; pension & retirement plan consultants

(P-22811)
**QUALITY REIMBURSEMENT
SERVICES**
150 N Santa Anita Ave, Arcadia
(91006-3113)
PHONE..................................626 445-5092
James C Ravindran, *Principal*
Dayani Ratnavira, *Admin Asst*
Michael Appadurai, *Sr Consultant*
Efren Junio, *Sr Consultant*
Russell Kramer, *Director*
EMP: 78 EST: 1988
SALES (est): 4.2MM Privately Held
WEB: www.qualityreimbursement.com
SIC: 8721 Auditing services

(P-22812)
SEMA INC (PA)
Also Called: Cell Business Equipment
4 Mason Ste A, Irvine (92618-2554)
PHONE..................................949 830-1400
Tarek Abdulhafiz, *President*
Matt Lackie, *Vice Pres*
Todd Milligan, *Executive*
Mac Sakai, *Executive*
Gerry Lennon, *Branch Mgr*
▲ EMP: 150 EST: 1993
SQ FT: 18,000
SALES (est): 34.7MM Privately Held
WEB: www.cbesolutions.com
SIC: 8721 5044 Accounting, auditing &
bookkeeping; photocopy machines

(P-22813)
SINGERLEWAK LLP (PA)
10960 Wilshire Blvd Fl 7, Los Angeles
(90024-3710)
PHONE..................................310 477-3924
Jim Pitrat, *Managing Prtnr*
Marc Abrams, *Partner*
Sally Aubury, *Partner*
Mark Cook, *Partner*
David Free, *Partner*
◆ EMP: 120 EST: 1959
SQ FT: 24,000
SALES (est): 48.4MM Privately Held
WEB: www.singerlewak.com
SIC: 8721 8742 Certified public account-
ant; business consultant

(P-22814)
**SOREN MCADAM
CHRISTIANSON LLP**
2068 Orange Tree Ln # 100, Redlands
(92374-4555)
P.O. Box 8010 (92375-1210)
PHONE..................................909 798-2222
James L Soren, *Partner*
Gary Christianson, *Partner*
Doug McAdam, *Partner*
Kirk Stitt, *Partner*
David Tuttle, *Partner*
EMP: 59 EST: 1979
SQ FT: 14,000
SALES (est): 6.8MM Privately Held
WEB: www.sorenmcadam.com
SIC: 8721 Certified public accountant

(P-22815)
**SQUAR MLNER PTRSON
MRNDA WLLMS (PA)**
Also Called: Squar Milner
18500 Von Karman Ave # 10, Irvine
(92612-0504)
PHONE..................................949 222-2999
Steve Milner, *Managing Prtnr*
Steven Blatt, *Partner*
Scott Burack, *Partner*
Ray Hermansor, *Partner*

Stan Luker, *Partner*
EMP: 160 EST: 1983
SQ FT: 11,500
SALES (est): 45.8MM **Privately Held**
SIC: 8721 Certified public accountant

(P-22816)
TEAM COMPANIES LLC (PA)
Also Called: Team Services
901 W Alameda Ave Ste 100, Burbank
(91506-2849)
PHONE..................................818 558-3261
Justin Kramer, *CEO*
Geoffrey Matus, *Ch of Bd*
An De Vooght, *CFO*
Ashley Wilson, *Officer*
Sara Castrellon, *Vice Pres*
EMP: 90 **EST:** 1992
SQ FT: 20,000
SALES (est): 20.2MM **Privately Held**
WEB: www.theteamcompanies.com
SIC: 8721 Payroll accounting service

(P-22817)
TEAMAN RAMIREZ & SMITH INC
4201 Brockton Ave Ste 100, Riverside
(92501-3431)
PHONE..................................951 274-9500
Richard Teaman, *President*
V C Smith Jr, *CEO*
Brenda Angulo, *Accountant*
John Brinkmann, *Accountant*
Jilly Humbert, *Accountant*
EMP: 54 **EST:** 1971
SQ FT: 5,200
SALES (est): 10.3MM **Privately Held**
WEB: www.trscpas.com
SIC: 8721 Certified public accountant

(P-22818)
UNIVERSITY CALIFORNIA IRVINE
Also Called: UCI Division Plastic Surgery
200 S Manchester Ave # 400, Orange
(92868-3220)
PHONE..................................714 456-6655
Gregory Evans, *Branch Mgr*
EMP: 60 **Privately Held**
WEB: www.uci.edu
SIC: 8721 8221 9411 Accounting, auditing
& bookkeeping; university; administration
of educational programs
HQ: University Of California, Irvine
510 Aldrich Hall
Irvine CA 92697
949 824-5011

(P-22819)
WHITE ZUCKERMAN WARSAVSKY LUNA (PA)
15490 Ventura Blvd # 300, Sherman Oaks
(91403-3016)
PHONE..................................818 981-4226
Paul J White, *Partner*
Jackie Adams-Ings, *Senior Partner*
Luna Barbara, *Senior Partner*
Andrew L Hunt, *Senior Partner*
Jackie Ings, *Senior Partner*
EMP: 65 **EST:** 1972
SALES (est): 12.9MM **Privately Held**
WEB: www.wzwlh.com
SIC: 8721 Certified public accountant

(P-22820)
WINDES INC (PA)
3780 Kilroy Arprt Way, Long Beach
(90806-2457)
P.O. Box 87 (90801-0087)
PHONE..................................562 435-1191
John L Dicarlo, *CEO*
Donald L Allen, *Partner*
Allen L Basso, *Partner*
Jim Jimenez, *Partner*
Robin K Massingale, *Partner*
EMP: 100 **EST:** 1926
SQ FT: 26,560
SALES (est): 27.1MM **Privately Held**
WEB: www.windes.com
SIC: 8721 Certified public accountant

8731 Commercial Physical & Biological Research

(P-22821)
ACCELIOT INC
16601 Gothard St Ste E, Huntington Beach
(92647-4479)
PHONE..................................657 845-4250
Shawn Manesh, *CEO*
EMP: 15 **EST:** 2019
SALES (est): 15MM **Privately Held**
SIC: 8731 7372 Computer (hardware) de-
velopment; application computer software

(P-22822)
ALPHA SOURCE INC
10940 Wilshire Blvd # 15, Los Angeles
(90024-3915)
PHONE..................................424 270-9600
Howard Lewin, *President*
Vionnta Rivers, *Officer*
EMP: 52 **EST:** 2000
SQ FT: 40,000
SALES (est): 5.5MM **Privately Held**
WEB: www.alphasource.com
SIC: 8731 Commercial physical research

(P-22823)
ALTOR BIOSCIENCE LLC
9920 Jefferson Blvd, Culver City
(90232-3506)
PHONE..................................954 443-8600
Hing Wong,
Rick Greene, *CFO*
Jin-An Jiao, *Vice Pres*
Amy Rock, *Vice Pres*
Maria Villacorta, *Vice Pres*
EMP: 65 **EST:** 2002
SQ FT: 25,000
SALES (est): 9.1MM **Privately Held**
WEB: www.immunitybio.com
SIC: 8731 Biotechnical research, commer-
cial

(P-22824)
AMT DATASOUTH CORP (PA)
Also Called: A M T
803 Camarillo Springs Rd D, Camarillo
(93012-9460)
PHONE..................................805 388-5799
Joseph E Eichberger, *Ch of Bd*
Chris Biggers, *Vice Pres*
James Nolan, *Vice Pres*
◆ **EMP:** 20 **EST:** 1982
SALES (est): 11MM **Privately Held**
WEB: www.amtdatasouth.com
SIC: 8731 5045 7379 3577 Computer
(hardware) development; printers, com-
puter; computer related maintenance
services; computer peripheral equipment

(P-22825)
APPLIED RESEARCH ASSOC INC
10833 Valley View St # 420, Cypress
(90630-5045)
PHONE..................................505 881-8074
Robert H Sues, *Branch Mgr*
EMP: 99
SALES (corp-wide): 271.2MM **Privately Held**
WEB: www.ara.com
SIC: 8731 Commercial physical research
PA: Applied Research Associates, Inc.
4300 San Mateo Blvd Ne
Albuquerque NM 87110
505 883-3636

(P-22826)
ATK SPACE SYSTEMS LLC
370 N Halstead St, Pasadena
(91107-3122)
PHONE..................................626 351-0205
Joe Tellegrino, *Manager*
Lee Cardenas, *Manager*
EMP: 66 **Publicly Held**
WEB: www.northropgrumman.com
SIC: 8731 3826 8711 Commercial physi-
cal research; engineering laboratory, ex-
cept testing; instruments measuring
thermal properties; engineering services

HQ: Atk Space Systems Llc
6033 Bandini Blvd
Commerce CA 90040
323 722-0222

(P-22827)
AVERY CORP
207 N Goode Ave Fl 6, Glendale
(91203-1364)
PHONE..................................626 304-2000
Dean Scarborough, *President*
David Maxson, *Director*
EMP: 200 **EST:** 1968
SALES (est): 16.1MM
SALES (corp-wide): 6.9B **Publicly Held**
SIC: 8731 Biological research
PA: Avery Dennison Corporation
207 N Goode Ave
Glendale CA 91203
626 304-2000

(P-22828)
AVICENA LLC (PA)
117 E Colo Blvd Ste 510, Pasadena
(91105)
PHONE..................................626 344-9665
Sean Brady, *Mng Member*
EMP: 55 **EST:** 2014
SALES (est): 7.2MM **Privately Held**
WEB: www.avicenaheart.com
SIC: 8731 Biotechnical research, commer-
cial

(P-22829)
AXONICS INC
26 Technology Dr, Irvine (92618-2380)
PHONE..................................949 396-6322
Michael H Carrel, *Ch of Bd*
Danny L Dearen, *President*
Raymond W Cohen, *CEO*
Rinda Sama, *COO*
Robert McNamara, *Bd of Directors*
EMP: 72 **EST:** 2013
SQ FT: 25,548
SALES (est): 111.5MM **Privately Held**
WEB: www.axonics.com
SIC: 8731 Biotechnical research, commer-
cial; commercial physical research; com-
mercial research laboratory

(P-22830)
BIOCATALYTICS INC
129 N Hill Ave Ste 103, Pasadena
(91106-1961)
PHONE..................................626 585-9797
James D Rozzell, *President*
EMP: 63 **EST:** 1996
SQ FT: 10,000
SALES (est): 603.6K
SALES (corp-wide): 69MM **Publicly Held**
WEB: www.codexis.com
SIC: 8731 Biotechnical research, commer-
cial
PA: Codexis, Inc.
200 Penobscot Dr
Redwood City CA 94063
650 421-8100

(P-22831)
BIOSCREEN TESTING SERVICES INC (PA)
3904 Del Amo Blvd Ste 801, Torrance
(90503-2183)
PHONE..................................310 214-0043
Bradford L Rope, *President*
Ranil M Fernando, *Vice Pres*
EMP: 59 **EST:** 1985
SQ FT: 20,000
SALES (est): 23.1MM **Privately Held**
WEB: www.bioscreen.com
SIC: 8731 8734 Commercial physical re-
search; testing laboratories

(P-22832)
BIOSPACE INC
Also Called: Inbody
13850 Cerritos Corprt Dr C, Cerritos
(90703-2467)
PHONE..................................323 932-6503
Ki Chul Cha, *President*
Hak Hee Yun, *CEO*
Calvin Lee, *Regional Mgr*
Dan Park, *Natl Sales Mgr*
Daniel Park, *Sales Dir*
▲ **EMP:** 86 **EST:** 2000

SQ FT: 35,319
SALES (est): 18.6MM **Privately Held**
WEB: www.biospace.com
SIC: 8731 3821 Energy research; calibra-
tion tapes for physical testing machines
PA: Shenzhen Longgang District Baolong
Kangxing Fruit Firm
No.419-420, Chishi Gang Xiaoqu
Tongfu Road, Longxin Community, B
Shenzhen

(P-22833)
CLINDATRIX
1 Ada Ste 250, Irvine (92618-5340)
PHONE..................................949 428-6600
Louise Murphy, *President*
Brian Murphy, *CFO*
Reena Solanki, *Project Mgr*
Ned Whittemore, *Director*
Dennis Derosia, *Contractor*
EMP: 51 **EST:** 2003
SALES (est): 6.8MM **Privately Held**
WEB: www.clindatrix.com
SIC: 8731 Biotechnical research, commer-
cial

(P-22834)
DISNEY RESEARCH PITTSBURGH
532 Paula Ave, Glendale (91201-2328)
PHONE..................................412 623-1800
Jessica K Hodgins, *Lab Dir*
EMP: 142 **EST:** 2011
SALES (est): 1.6MM
SALES (corp-wide): 65.3B **Publicly Held**
WEB: www.disneyimaginations.com
SIC: 8731 Commercial research laboratory
HQ: Walt Disney Imagineering Research &
Development, Inc.
1401 Flower St
Glendale CA 91201
818 544-6500

(P-22835)
DUPONT DISPLAYS INC
600 Ward Dr Ste C, Santa Barbara
(93111-2300)
PHONE..................................805 562-5400
Steve Quindlen, *Branch Mgr*
James Tremel, *Engineer*
EMP: 135
SALES (corp-wide): 14.2B **Publicly Held**
WEB: www.dupont.com
SIC: 8731 Commercial physical research
HQ: Dupont Displays, Inc.
974 Centre Rd
Wilmington DE 19805

(P-22836)
E-SCEPTRE INC
16800 Gale Ave, City of Industry
(91745-1804)
PHONE..................................888 350-8989
Stephen Liu, *President*
Steven Liu, *CEO*
Richard Gallegos, *Exec VP*
EMP: 55 **EST:** 2001
SQ FT: 80,000
SALES (est): 1MM **Privately Held**
WEB: www.sceptre.com
SIC: 8731 Computer (hardware) develop-
ment
PA: Sceptre Industries, Inc.
16800 Gale Ave
City Of Industry CA 91745

(P-22837)
ENVIRONMENTAL SCIENCE ASSOC
Also Called: Envriontional Science Assoc
80 S Lake Ave Ste 570, Pasadena
(91101-2597)
PHONE..................................626 204-6170
EMP: 94
SALES (corp-wide): 80K **Privately Held**
WEB: www.esassoc.com
SIC: 8731 Environmental research
PA: Environmental Science Associates
550 Kearny St Ste 800
San Francisco CA 94108
415 896-5900

PRODUCTS & SVCS

(P-22838)
ENVIRONMENTAL SCIENCE ASSOC
Also Called: ESA
626 Wilshire Blvd # 1100, Los Angeles
(90017-2934)
PHONE..................213 599-4300
Melissa Gross, *Manager*
EMP: 94
SALES (corp-wide): 80K **Privately Held**
WEB: www.esassoc.com
SIC: 8731 8748 Environmental research;
environmental consultant
PA: Environmental Science Associates
550 Kearny St Ste 800
San Francisco CA 94108
415 896-5900

(P-22839)
F6S NETWORK LIMITED
16935 Encino Hills Dr, Encino
(91436-4007)
PHONE..................619 818-4363
Sean Kane, *CEO*
EMP: 80 EST: 2020
SALES (est): 877.4K **Privately Held**
SIC: 8731 Commercial physical research

(P-22840)
FIT ELECTRONICS INC (HQ)
Also Called: Foxconn Electronics
121 Theory Ste 200, Irvine (92617-3204)
PHONE..................949 270-8500
Mike Unger, *President*
Ralph Gillespie, *CEO*
Eriq Chin, *Accountant*
Jade Nguyen, *Production*
Brook Chang, *Manager*
▲ EMP: 53 EST: 1997
SALES (est): 26MM **Privately Held**
WEB: www.foxconn.com
SIC: 8731 5065 Electronic research; elec-
tronic parts

(P-22841)
GENTEX CORPORATION
Also Called: Western Operations
9859 7th St, Rancho Cucamonga
(91730-5244)
PHONE..................909 481-7667
Robert McCay, *Vice Pres*
John Zenkavich, *Program Mgr*
Steve Laterza, *General Mgr*
Chelsea Demeglio, *Executive Asst*
Jonathan Creamer, *CIO*
EMP: 90
SALES (corp-wide): 97.6MM **Privately
Held**
WEB: www.gentexcorp.com
SIC: 8731 3845 3841 Commercial re-
search laboratory; biological research;
electromedical equipment; surgical &
medical instruments
PA: Gentex Corporation
324 Main St
Simpson PA 18407
570 282-3550

(P-22842)
INTEGRATION INNOVATION INC
Also Called: I3
18374 Phantom St, Victorville
(92394-7976)
PHONE..................256 513-5179
Walter Strankman, *CEO*
EMP: 50
SALES (corp-wide): 126.3MM **Privately
Held**
WEB: www.i3-corps.com
SIC: 8731 Commercial physical research
PA: Integration Innovation, Inc.
689 Discovery Dr Nw # 500
Huntsville AL 35806
256 513-5179

(P-22843)
INTEGRIUM LLC (PA)
Also Called: Integrex Innovations
14351 Myford Rd Ste A, Tustin
(92780-7038)
PHONE..................714 541-5591
David Smith MD,
Michael Loftus, *Exec Dir*
Debbie Mason, *Human Resources*
Joel M Neutel, *Med Doctor*
David H Smith, *Med Doctor*

▼ EMP: 107 EST: 1998
SQ FT: 40,000
SALES (est): 13.4MM **Privately Held**
WEB: www.integrium.com
SIC: 8731 8742 Medical research, com-
mercial; industry specialist consultants

(P-22844)
INVASIX INC
Also Called: Inmode Aesthetic Solutions
17 Hughes, Irvine (92618-1902)
PHONE..................855 418-5306
Moshe Mizrahy, *CEO*
Shakil Lakhani, *President*
Yair Malca, *CFO*
Yang Phan, *Vice Pres*
Douglas Mitchell, *Controller*
EMP: 99 EST: 2008
SALES (est): 12.9MM **Privately Held**
WEB: www.inmodemd.com
SIC: 8731 5047 Medical research, com-
mercial; electro-medical equipment

(P-22845)
ISOTIS ORTHOBIOLOGICS INC
2 Goodyear Ste A, Irvine (92618-2052)
PHONE..................949 595-8710
Keith Valentine, *CEO*
Peter J Arduini, *President*
Andre Verwei, *CFO*
Christian S Schade, *Exec VP*
Nancy Toledo, *Principal*
▲ EMP: 150 EST: 1990
SALES (est): 22.6MM **Privately Held**
WEB: www.isotis.com
SIC: 8731 5047 Biotechnical research,
commercial; surgical equipment & sup-
plies
HQ: Isotis International Sarl
C/O Fidulem Sa
Lausanne VD 1005
216 132-501

(P-22846)
KITE PHARMA INC (HQ)
2400 Broadway Ste 100, Santa Monica
(90404-3058)
PHONE..................310 824-9999
Christi Shaw, *CEO*
Robin L Washington, *President*
Richard L Wang, *CEO*
Devvon Hinds, *Ch Credit Ofcr*
Stacey Boals, *Officer*
EMP: 146 EST: 2009
SQ FT: 20,000
SALES: 22.1MM
SALES (corp-wide): 24.6B **Publicly Held**
WEB: www.kitepharma.com
SIC: 8731 2836 Biotechnical research,
commercial; biological products, except
diagnostic
PA: Gilead Sciences, Inc.
333 Lakeside Dr
Foster City CA 94404
650 574-3000

(P-22847)
LEIDOS INC
Saic
590 W Central Ave Ste I, Brea
(92821-3019)
PHONE..................714 257-6400
Fax: 714 257-9886
EMP: 93
SALES (corp-wide): 7B **Publicly Held**
SIC: 8731 Research Institute
HQ: Leidos, Inc.
11951 Freedom Dr Ste 500
Reston VA 20190
571 526-6000

(P-22848)
**LIFE TECH CLNICAL SVCS LAB
INC (DH)**
405 N Wilmington Ave, Compton
(90220-1936)
PHONE..................866 522-1585
Vance Vanie, *President*
Sean George, *COO*
Becky Scott, *CFO*
Dietrich Stephan, *Security Dir*
Vijay Viswanathan, *Manager*
EMP: 50 EST: 2006

SALES (est): 994.6K
SALES (corp-wide): 32.2B **Publicly Held**
WEB: www.navigenics.com
SIC: 8731 Medical research, commercial
HQ: Life Technologies Corporation
5781 Van Allen Way
Carlsbad CA 92008
760 603-7200

(P-22849)
MARTINSOUND INC
Also Called: Martinsound Recording Studios
1151 W Valley Blvd, Alhambra
(91803-2440)
PHONE..................626 281-3555
Joe Martinson, *President*
Richard Greenhalgh, *Vice Pres*
▲ EMP: 17 EST: 1971
SQ FT: 24,000
SALES (est): 1.6MM **Privately Held**
WEB: www.martinsound.com
SIC: 8731 7389 3823 3663 Commercial
research laboratory; recording studio,
noncommercial records; industrial instrm-
nts msrmnt display/control process vari-
able; radio & TV communications
equipment; household audio & video
equipment; switchgear & switchboard apparatus

(P-22850)
**MEMORIAL HEALTHTEC
LABRATORIES**
9920 Talbert Ave, Fountain Valley
(92708-5153)
PHONE..................714 962-4677
Marcia Manker, *Manager*
Seema Inayatullah, *COO*
Carl Kildoo, *Vice Pres*
Cindy Callaghan, *Radiology Dir*
Stan Hill, *Business Dir*
EMP: 1365 **Privately Held**
WEB: www.memorialcare.org
SIC: 8731 Commercial physical research
HQ: Memorial Healthtec Labratories Inc
2865 Atlantic Ave Ste 203
Long Beach CA 90806

(P-22851)
MERCEDES-BENZ RE
4031 Via Oro Ave, Long Beach
(90810-1458)
PHONE..................310 547-6086
John Espeleta, *Branch Mgr*
Felix Purkl, *Engineer*
Johannes Schmalzriedt, *Relations*
EMP: 50
SALES (corp-wide): 182.4B **Privately
Held**
WEB: www.mbrdna.com
SIC: 8731 Commercial physical research
HQ: Mercedes-Benz Research & Develop-
ment North America, Inc.
309 N Pastoria Ave
Sunnyvale CA 94085

(P-22852)
MYST THERAPEUTICS INC
570 Westwood Plz Bldg 114, Los Angeles
(90095-8352)
PHONE..................415 516-8450
Sammy Farah, *CEO*
EMP: 54 EST: 2019
SALES (est): 1.7MM
SALES (corp-wide): 5.2MM **Privately
Held**
WEB: www.myst-tx.com
SIC: 8731 Medical research, commercial
PA: Turnstone Biologics Corp.
920 Broadway Fl 16
New York NY 10010
347 897-5988

(P-22853)
NANTCELL INC
9920 Jefferson Blvd, Culver City
(90232-3506)
PHONE..................562 397-3639
Richard Adcock, *CEO*
Sam Ross, *Associate Dir*
Kristina Ruppenkamp, *Associate Dir*
Yun Han, *Controller*
Michael McNamara, *Senior Mgr*
EMP: 64 EST: 2014

SALES (est): 226.4K **Publicly Held**
WEB: www.immunitybio.com
SIC: 8731 Biological research
PA: Immunitybio, Inc.
3530 John Hopkins Ct
San Diego CA 92121

(P-22854)
NEOTERYX LLC
421 Amapola Ave, Torrance (90501-1423)
PHONE..................310 787-8747
Farajollah F Mahjoor,
Stuart Kushon, *Officer*
Yibo Guo, *Research*
James Rudge, *Technical Staff*
Grace Kuo, *Finance Mgr*
EMP: 34 EST: 2014
SALES (est): 4.4MM **Privately Held**
WEB: www.neoteryx.com
SIC: 8731 2834 Biotechnical research,
commercial; pharmaceutical preparations

(P-22855)
**NORTHROP GRUMMAN
SYSTEMS CORP**
Also Called: Defense Systems Sector
5500 Canoga Ave 31, Woodland Hills
(91367-6621)
PHONE..................818 676-1321
Jim Post, *Branch Mgr*
Alice Reed, *Principal*
Michael Putnam, *Info Tech Mgr*
EMP: 176 **Publicly Held**
SIC: 8731 Commercial physical research
HQ: Northrop Grumman Systems Corpora-
tion
2980 Fairview Park Dr
Falls Church VA 22042
703 280-2900

(P-22856)
ONE LAMBDA INC (HQ)
22801 Roscoe Blvd, West Hills
(91304-3200)
PHONE..................747 494-1000
Seth H Hoogasian, *CEO*
George M Ayoub, *President*
James Keegan, *CFO*
Don Arii, *Vice Pres*
Emiko Terasaki, *Admin Sec*
EMP: 316 EST: 1984
SQ FT: 53,000
SALES (est): 35.7MM
SALES (corp-wide): 32.2B **Publicly Held**
WEB: www.thermofisher.com
SIC: 8731 Biotechnical research, commer-
cial
PA: Thermo Fisher Scientific Inc.
168 3rd Ave
Waltham MA 02451
781 622-1000

(P-22857)
**OPTO-KNOWLEDGE SYSTEMS
INC**
Also Called: Optoknowledge
19805 Hamilton Ave, Torrance
(90502-1341)
PHONE..................310 756-0520
Christopher Holmes Parker, *Principal*
Dorene Bloomer *Officer*
Linda Papermaster, *Executive*
Ilana Gat, *Principal*
Joel Gat, *Principal*
EMP: 29 EST: 1991
SQ FT: 14,000
SALES (est): 5.7MM **Privately Held**
WEB: www.optoknowledge.com
SIC: 8731 3827 Engineering laboratory,
except testing; optical instruments &
lenses

(P-22858)
PANACEA INC
14905 Parmnt Blvd Ste H, Paramount
(90723)
PHONE..................562 860-2869
Hsin Chou, *Branch Mgr*
EMP: 68
SALES (corp wide): 9.2MM **Privately
Held**
WEB: www.panaceaservices.org
SIC: 8731 Commercial physical research

PA: Panacea, Inc.
3152 N Mllbrook Ave Ste D
Fresno CA 93703

(P-22859)
QNAP INC
168 University Pkwy, Pomona
(91768-4300)
PHONE..........................909 598-6933
Ming-CHI Chang, *President*
Ken Cheah, *Bd of Directors*
Craig Reid, *Technical Mgr*
Albert Shan, *Technical Mgr*
Even Lo, *Web Dvlpr*
EMP: 58 EST: 2009
SALES (est): 12.9MM **Privately Held**
WEB: www.qnap.com
SIC: 8731 Biotechnical research, commercial
PA: Qnap Systems, Inc.
2f-5f, 22, Zhongxing Rd.,
New Taipei City TAP 22161

(P-22860)
RADNOTI GLASS TECHNOLOGY INC
541 E Edna Pl, Covina (91723-1311)
PHONE..........................626 357-8827
Desmond Radnoti Jr, *President*
Weasoo Rhee Radnoti, *Treasurer*
Donna Owen, *Office Mgr*
EMP: 17 EST: 1970
SQ FT: 5,400
SALES (est): 687.4K **Privately Held**
WEB: www.radnoti.com
SIC: 8731 3841 3826 Medical research, commercial; surgical & medical instruments; analytical instruments

(P-22861)
SCIENCE 37 HOLDINGS INC (PA)
600 Crprate Pinte Ste 320, Culver City
(90230)
PHONE..........................984 377-3737
David Coman, *CEO*
Mike Zaranek, *CFO*
Steven Geffon, *Ch Credit Ofcr*
Jonathan Cotliar, *Chief Mktg Ofcr*
Christine Pellizzari,
EMP: 644 EST: 2019 **Publicly Held**
WEB: www.lifesciacquisition.com
SIC: 8731 8733 Biotechnical research, commercial; commercial research laboratory; medical research, commercial; medical research

(P-22862)
SCIENTFIC APPLCTONS RES ASSOC (PA)
Also Called: SARA
6300 Gateway Dr, Cypress (90630-4844)
PHONE..........................714 224-4410
Parviz Parhami, *CEO*
James Wes, *President*
Bob McCord, *CFO*
Michael Zintl, *Program Mgr*
John Robinson, *Admin Sec*
EMP: 58 EST: 1989
SQ FT: 43,000
SALES (est): 57MM **Privately Held**
WEB: www.sara.com
SIC: 8731 Commercial physical research

(P-22863)
SEMINIS INC (DH)
2700 Camino Del Sol, Oxnard
(93030-7967)
PHONE..........................805 485-7317
Bruno Ferrari, *President*
Eugenio N Solorzano, *President*
Charles E Green, *Senior VP*
Oscar J Velasco, *Senior VP*
Enrique Lopez, *Vice Pres*
◆ EMP: 300 EST: 1995
SALES (est): 121.3MM
SALES (corp-wide): 48.9B **Privately Held**
WEB: www.vegetables.bayer.com
SIC: 8731 8742 2099 Agricultural research; productivity improvement consultant; food preparations

HQ: Monsanto Company
800 N Lindbergh Blvd
Saint Louis MO 63167
314 694-1000

(P-22864)
SOFIE BIOSCIENCES INC (PA)
160 Briston Pkwy Ste 200, Culver City
(90230)
PHONE..........................310 215-3159
Patrick W Phelps, *CEO*
Michael Phelps, *Ch of Bd*
Bob Balch, *Vice Pres*
Harry Jeffreys, *Vice Pres*
Nam Vu, *Vice Pres*
EMP: 135 EST: 2009
SQ FT: 3,500
SALES (est): 118.3MM **Privately Held**
WEB: www.sofie.com
SIC: 8731 Biotechnical research, commercial

(P-22865)
TAE LIFE SCIENCES US LLC
19571 Pauling, Foothill Ranch
(92610-2619)
PHONE..........................949 344-6112
Bruce Bauer, *Mng Member*
Anna Theriault,
EMP: 90 EST: 2017
SALES (est): 3.4MM **Privately Held**
WEB: www.taelifesciences.com
SIC: 8731 Biotechnical research, commercial

(P-22866)
TAE TECHNOLOGIES INC (PA)
19631 Pauling, Foothill Ranch
(92610-2607)
P.O. Box 7010, Rcho STA Marg (92688-7010)
PHONE..........................949 830-2117
Michl Binderbauer, *CEO*
Mark J Lewis, *President*
Rich Barth, *Vice Pres*
Mark Lewis, *Vice Pres*
Kurt Knapp, *Design Engr*
EMP: 155 EST: 2002
SALES (est): 54MM **Privately Held**
WEB: www.tae.com
SIC: 8731 Energy research

(P-22867)
TELEDYNE SCENTIFIC IMAGING LLC
5212 Verdugo Way, Camarillo
(93012-8662)
PHONE..........................805 373-4979
James Beletic, *President*
Kadri Vural, *Vice Pres*
Roxanne S Austin, *CIO*
Myung-Jun Choe, *Technical Staff*
Emil Hanna, *Engineer*
EMP: 53
SQ FT: 54,295
SALES (corp-wide): 3B **Publicly Held**
SIC: 8731 Commercial physical research
HQ: Teledyne Scientific & Imaging, Llc
1049 Camino Dos Rios
Thousand Oaks CA 91360

(P-22868)
TELEDYNE SCENTIFIC IMAGING LLC (HQ)
Also Called: Teledyne Scientific Company
1049 Camino Dos Rios, Thousand Oaks
(91360-2362)
PHONE..........................805 373-4545
Robert Mehrabian,
James Beletic, *President*
Berinder Brar, *President*
Aldo Pichelli, *President*
Roxanne Austin, *Bd of Directors*
EMP: 125 EST: 1962
SQ FT: 161,000
SALES (est): 34.4MM
SALES (corp-wide): 3B **Publicly Held**
WEB: www.teledyne.com
SIC: 8731 8732 8733 Commercial physical research; commercial nonphysical research; noncommercial research organizations

PA: Teledyne Technologies Inc
1049 Camino Dos Rios
Thousand Oaks CA 91360
805 373-4545

(P-22869)
TRUESDAIL LABORATORIES INC
3337 Michelson Dr, Irvine (92612-1699)
PHONE..........................714 730-6239
Ed Wilson, *CEO*
John Hill, *President*
Brian K Service, *Chairman*
Norman Hester, *Officer*
Clif McLellan, *Vice Pres*
EMP: 50 EST: 1931
SQ FT: 40,000
SALES (est): 4.8MM **Privately Held**
WEB: www.truesdail.com
SIC: 8731 8734 1711 Commercial physical research; water testing laboratory; plumbing contractors

(P-22870)
UNIVERSITY CALIFORNIA IRVINE
Also Called: Henry Samueli School Engrg
2220 Engineering Gateway, Irvine
(92697-0001)
PHONE..........................949 824-2819
Dr GP LI, *Director*
Amita Amte, *Info Tech Mgr*
Gonzalo Navajas, *Professor*
Breanna Hale, *Asst Director*
EMP: 60 **Privately Held**
WEB: www.uci.edu
SIC: 8731 8221 9411 Electronic research; university; administration of educational programs;
HQ: University Of California, Irvine
510 Aldrich Hall
Irvine CA 92697
949 824-5011

(P-22871)
VENTURE DESIGN SERVICES INC (PA)
1051 S East St, Anaheim (92805-5749)
PHONE..........................714 765-3740
Wong Ngit Liong, *Chairman*
Tan Kian Seng, *President*
E H SOO, *CEO*
Soin Sign, *Treasurer*
Lee Ghai Keen, *Exec VP*
EMP: 107 EST: 2003
SQ FT: 60,000
SALES (est): 12.7MM **Privately Held**
SIC: 8731 Commercial physical research

(P-22872)
ZYMO RESEARCH CORPORATION (PA)
17062 Murphy Ave, Irvine (92614-5914)
PHONE..........................949 679-1190
Xiyu Jia MD, *President*
LI Zhang, *Shareholder*
Angela Kim, *Admin Sec*
Tan Nguyen, *Asst Admin*
Michael Foss, *Project Mgr*
▲ EMP: 51 EST: 1994
SQ FT: 10,000
SALES (est): 29.8MM **Privately Held**
WEB: www.zymoresearch.com
SIC: 8731 Biotechnical research, commercial; medical research, commercial

8732 Commercial Economic, Sociological & Educational Research

(P-22873)
ADDED VALUE LLC (HQ)
3400 Cahuenga Blvd W B, Los Angeles
(90068-1376)
PHONE..........................323 254-4326
Meggy Taylor, *President*
Ruth Moss, *Exec VP*
Dennis Stefani, *Exec VP*
Marc Agostini, *Senior Mgr*
Francesca Simon-Millar, *Manager*
EMP: 177 EST: 1975
SQ FT: 9,800

SALES (est): 25.9MM
SALES (corp-wide): 151.4MM **Privately Held**
WEB: www.kantar.com
SIC: 8732 Market analysis or research
PA: Kantar Llc
175 Greenwich St Fl 35
New York NY 10007
212 548-7200

(P-22874)
ADVANCED SCNTIFIC CONCEPTS INC
Also Called: ASC
135 E Ortega St, Santa Barbara
(93101-1674)
PHONE..........................805 966-3331
Roger Stettner, *CEO*
Howard Bailey, *Vice Pres*
Thomas E Laux, *Vice Pres*
Simon Bill, *Electrical Engi*
Rosario Terrazas, *Human Res Mgr*
EMP: 57 EST: 1987
SQ FT: 8,000
SALES (est): 7.9MM **Privately Held**
WEB: www.asc3d.com
SIC: 8732 Research services, except laboratory

(P-22875)
BOVITZ INC
16133 Ventura Blvd # 820, Encino
(91436-2409)
PHONE..........................818 806-0800
Gregory L Bovitz, *President*
Jen Belcastro, *Vice Pres*
Cara Bovitz, *Vice Pres*
Mike Browning, *Vice Pres*
Debbie Kreger, *Vice Pres*
EMP: 51 EST: 2003
SALES (est): 6.7MM **Privately Held**
WEB: www.bovitzinc.com
SIC: 8732 Market analysis or research

(P-22876)
CHASE GROUP LLC
Also Called: Simi Vly Care & Rehabilitation
5270 E Los Angeles Ave, Simi Valley
(93063-4137)
PHONE..........................805 522-9155
Phil Chase, *Manager*
Maria Curiel, *Office Mgr*
Floyd Rhoades, *Administration*
EMP: 295 **Privately Held**
SIC: 8732 8742 Research services, except laboratory; management consulting services
PA: The Chase Group Llc
3075 E Thousand Oaks Blvd
Thousand Oaks CA 91362

(P-22877)
CORNERSTONE RESEARCH INC
555 W 5th St Ste 3800, Los Angeles
(90013-3016)
PHONE..........................213 553-2500
Richard Dalbeck, *Vice Pres*
Maria Rivas, *Administration*
Saniya Anand, *Analyst*
Marcelo Han, *Senior Mgr*
EMP: 73
SALES (corp-wide): 84MM **Privately Held**
WEB: www.cornerstone.com
SIC: 8732 Market analysis, business & economic research
PA: Cornerstone Research, Inc.
1000 El Camino Real # 250
Menlo Park CA 94025
650 853-1660

(P-22878)
DAVIS RESEARCH LLC
26610 Agoura Rd Ste 240, Calabasas
(91302-3857)
PHONE..........................818 591-2408
William A Davis III, *Mng Member*
Ali Asghar, *Research*
Robert Davis,
Jason Kerns, *Director*
Jesse Zamora, *Supervisor*
EMP: 150 EST: 1970

SALES (est): 14MM **Privately Held**
WEB: www.davisresearch.com
SIC: 8732 Market analysis or research

(P-22879)
DISQO INC
Also Called: Survey Junkie
400 N Brand Blvd Ste 600, Glendale
(91203-2359)
PHONE....................818 237-2186
Armen Adjemian, *CEO*
Jean-Philippe Durrios, *COO*
Stephen Jepson, *Exec VP*
Dan Campbell, *Vice Pres*
Rafi Kurkdjian, *Vice Pres*
EMP: 60 EST: 2018
SALES (est): 4MM **Privately Held**
WEB: www.disqo.com
SIC: 8732 7375 Market analysis or research; on-line data base information retrieval

(P-22880)
FKC INTERNATIONAL INC (PA)
21015 Pathfinder Rd # 140, Diamond Bar
(91765-4002)
PHONE....................909 869-9000
Fang Zhao, *CEO*
Jake Wang, *Marketing Mgr*
Rainine Yu, *Marketing Staff*
▲ EMP: 74 EST: 2003
SALES (est): 6.7MM **Privately Held**
WEB: www.efkcn.com
SIC: 5999 8732 Auction rooms (general merchandise); commercial nonphysical research

(P-22881)
GFK ETILIZE INC (DH)
18662 Macarthur Blvd # 20, Irvine
(92612-1202)
PHONE....................888 608-1212
Azhar Hameed, *President*
James Snell, *Opers Staff*
Lloyd Wood, *Marketing Mgr*
Shujaat Ameer, *Client Mgr*
Salman Halim, *Manager*
EMP: 83 EST: 2000
SQ FT: 4,000
SALES (est): 7.6MM
SALES (corp-wide): 536.6K **Privately Held**
WEB: www.etilize.com
SIC: 8732 Market analysis or research
HQ: Gfk North America Holding Gmbh
Sophie-Germain-Str. 3-5
Nurnberg BY
911 395-0

(P-22882)
HANLEY WOOD MKT INTELLIGENCE (HQ)
Also Called: Metrostudy
555 Anton Blvd Ste 950, Costa Mesa
(92626-7811)
PHONE....................714 540-8500
Chris Veator, *President*
Karen Meyers, *Managing Prtnr*
Kurt Nelson, *Vice Pres*
EMP: 55 EST: 1985
SALES (est): 11.1MM
SALES (corp-wide): 179MM **Privately Held**
WEB: www.builderonline.com
SIC: 8732 Market analysis or research
PA: Hw Holdco, Llc
1 Thomas Cir Nw Ste 600
Washington DC 20005
202 452-0800

(P-22883)
HI LLC
Also Called: Kernel
10361 Jefferson Blvd, Culver City
(90232-3511)
PHONE....................757 655-4113
Bryan Johnson, *Mng Member*
EMP: 90 EST: 2016
SQ FT: 3,500
SALES (est): 4.2MM **Privately Held**
SIC: 8732 Business research service

(P-22884)
HIGH DSERT PRTNR IN ACDMIC EXC
Also Called: NORTON SCIENCE AND LANGUAGE AC
17500 Mana Rd, Apple Valley
(92307-2181)
PHONE....................760 946-5414
Lisa Lamb, *CEO*
Larri Curtis, *CFO*
Linda Locke, *Executive*
Teresa Dowd, *Executive Asst*
Nancy Dust, *Admin Sec*
EMP: 350 EST: 1992
SQ FT: 35,000
SALES: 31.1MM **Privately Held**
WEB: www.lewiscenter.org
SIC: 8732 Commercial nonphysical research

(P-22885)
HRL LABORATORIES LLC
Also Called: Hughes Research Laboratories
3011 Malibu Canyon Rd, Malibu
(90265-4797)
PHONE....................310 317-5000
Penrose Albright, *President*
Mary Yesui, *COO*
Roger Gronwald, *CFO*
David Chow, *Officer*
Gary Lawrence, *Officer*
◆ EMP: 647 EST: 1997
SQ FT: 250,000
SALES (est): 282.3MM **Privately Held**
WEB: www.hrl.com
SIC: 8732 Commercial sociological & educational research

(P-22886)
IBISWORLD INC (DH)
11755 Wilshire Blvd # 1100, Los Angeles
(90025-1549)
PHONE....................800 330-3772
EMP: 81
SALES (est): 16.3MM **Privately Held**
WEB: www.ibisworld.com
SIC: 8732 Commercial Nonphysical Research

(P-22887)
INFORMA RESEARCH SERVICES INC (HQ)
26565 Agoura Rd Ste 300, Calabasas
(91302-1942)
PHONE....................818 880-8877
Michael E Adler, *President*
Kristen Mooney, *Partner*
Charles A Miwa, *COO*
Lori Jomsky, *Vice Pres*
Brian Richards, *Vice Pres*
EMP: 193 EST: 1993
SQ FT: 16,000
SALES (corp-wide): 2.2B **Privately Held**
WEB:
www.financialintelligence.informa.com
SIC: 8732 Market analysis or research
PA: Informa Plc
The Blue Fin Building
London SE1 0
207 017-5000

(P-22888)
INTERVIEWING SERVICE AMER LLC (PA)
Also Called: ISA
15400 Sherman Way Ste 400, Van Nuys
(91406-4211)
PHONE....................818 989-1044
Michael Halberstam, *Chairman*
Tony Kretzmer, *President*
Jacqueline Rosales, *COO*
Vicky Agalsoff, *Vice Pres*
John Fitzpatrick, *Vice Pres*
EMP: 250 EST: 1982
SQ FT: 20,000
SALES (est): 25MM **Privately Held**
WEB: www.isacorp.com
SIC: 8732 Market analysis or research

(P-22889)
IPSOS OTX CORPORATION (HQ)
300 Crprate Pinte Ste 500, Culver City
(90230)
PHONE....................310 736-3400
Shelley Zalis, *CEO*
Jeff Dean, *CFO*
Lauren Demar, *Officer*
Marissa Kins, *Project Mgr*
Ryan Mitchell, *Research*
EMP: 210 EST: 2003
SALES (est): 31.2MM
SALES (corp-wide): 453.5K **Privately Held**
WEB: www.ipsosotx.com
SIC: 8732 Market analysis or research
PA: Ipsos
35 Rue Du Val De Marne
Paris 75013
141 989-000

(P-22890)
IQVIA INC (DH)
Also Called: SK&a
2601 Main St Ste 650, Irvine (92614-4228)
PHONE....................949 476-2167
David Escalante Jr, *President*
Al M Cosentino, *CFO*
Albert Chang, *Principal*
Jaqueline Aguilera, *Director*
EMP: 87 EST: 1984
SQ FT: 12,000
SALES (est): 8.7MM
SALES (corp-wide): 8MM **Privately Held**
WEB: www.onekeydata.com
SIC: 8732 Market analysis or research

(P-22891)
JD POWER
30870 Russell Ranch Rd # 100, Westlake Village (91362-7372)
PHONE....................805 418-8000
Keith Webster, *Vice Pres*
Geoffrey Mortimer-Lamb, *Vice Pres*
Troy Snyder, *Vice Pres*
Chris Sutton, *Vice Pres*
Lenny Sims, *VP Bus Dvlpt*
EMP: 280 **Privately Held**
WEB: www.jdpower.com
SIC: 8732 Market analysis or research
HQ: J.D. Power
320 E Big Beaver Rd # 500
Troy MI 48083
248 680-6200

(P-22892)
LIEBERMAN RES WORLDWIDE LLC (PA)
Also Called: Lrw Group
1900 Avenue Of The Stars, Los Angeles
(90067-4301)
PHONE....................310 553-0550
David Sackman, *CEO*
Arnold Fishman, *Ch of Bd*
Stephanie Sutton, *CEO*
Cathy Lindquist, *CFO*
Jeremy Sack, *Exec VP*
EMP: 140 EST: 1973
SQ FT: 24,560
SALES (est): 91.2MM **Privately Held**
WEB: www.lrwonline.com
SIC: 8732 Market analysis or research

(P-22893)
MEYERS RESEARCH LLC (PA)
4000 Macarthur Blvd # 400, Newport Beach
(92660-2543)
PHONE....................714 619-7800
Jeff Meyers, *CEO*
Michelle L Wolkoys, *CFO*
Hamin Balaporia, *Exec VP*
Amy Dudley, *Exec VP*
Lorry Lynn, *Exec VP*
EMP: 124 EST: 2012
SALES (est): 17.5MM **Privately Held**
WEB: www.zondahome.com
SIC: 8732 Business research service

(P-22894)
NATIONAL RESEARCH GROUP INC
6255 W Sunset Blvd Fl 19, Los Angeles
(90028-7420)
PHONE....................323 817-2000
Jon Penn, *CEO*
Jeff Hall, *Exec VP*
James McNamara, *Exec VP*
Becky Wu, *Exec VP*
Ray Ydoyaga, *Exec VP*
EMP: 400 EST: 1977

SALES (est): 22.7K
SALES (corp-wide): 199. K **Privately Held**
WEB: www.stagwellgroup.com
SIC: 8732 Market analysis or research
PA: The Stagwell Group Lc
1808 Eye St Nw Ste 300
Washington DC 20006
917 765-2638

(P-22895)
NIELSEN AUDIO INC
6080 Center Dr Fl 6, Los Angeles
(90045-9209)
PHONE....................310 824-5906
George Bradey, *Manage*
Stephanie Brown, *Controller*
David Rice, *Manager*
Melanie Morris, *Account Dir*
EMP: 76
SALES (corp-wide): 3.3B **Privately Held**
WEB: www.nielsen.com
SIC: 8732 Market analysis or research
HQ: Nielsen Audio, Inc.
7000 Columbia Gateway Dr # 200
Columbia MD 210=6
410 312-8000

(P-22896)
PROSEARCH STRATEGIES LLC
3250 Wilshire Blvd # 301, Los Angeles
(90010-1577)
PHONE....................877 447-7291
Julia Kim Hasenzahl, *CEO*
Dan Kinney, *Vice Pres*
David Maciel, *Software Dev*
Cory Noonan, *Software Dev*
Brett Woodlief, *Software Dev*
EMP: 113 EST: 2005
SALES (est): 17.8MM **Privately Held**
WEB: www.prosearchstrategies.com
SIC: 8732 Research services, except laboratory

(P-22897)
QY RESEARCH INC
17890 Castleton St, City of Industry
(91748-1756)
PHONE....................626 295-2442
Song Chunming, *President*
Diao Hongwei, *Vice Pres*
Zhang Dong, *Director*
EMP: 61 EST: 2016
SALES (est): 2.5MM **Privately Held**
WEB: www.qyresearchglobal.com
SIC: 8732 Market analysis or research

(P-22898)
TOSHIBA EDUCATION CENTER
9740 Irvine Blvd, Irvine (92618-1651)
PHONE....................949 583-3000
Ted Flati, *Principal*
EMP: 165 EST: 2008
SALES (est): 1.3MM **Privately Held**
WEB: www.us.medical.canon
SIC: 8732 Educational research
HQ: Canon Medical Systems Usa, Inc.
2441 Michelle Dr
Tustin CA 92780
714 730-5000

(P-22899)
XDBS CORPORATION
Also Called: Xdbsb2b
3501 Jack Northrop Ave, Hawthorne
(90250-4433)
PHONE....................844 932-7356
Julie Strong, *CEC*
Kenny Waribam, *COO*
Imran Shaikh, *CFO*
Kartik Anand, *Chairman*
Nigel Wright, *Vice Pres*
EMP: 63 EST: 2012
SQ FT: 4,000
SALES (est): 1. MM **Privately Held**
WEB: www.xdbscorp.com
SIC: 8732 7389 5963 8742 Survey service: marketing, location, etc.; telemarketing services; direct sales, telemarketing; sales (including sales management) consultant

8733 Noncommercial Research Organizations

(P-22900)
BRENTWOOD BMDICAL RES INST INC
11301 Wilshire Blvd # 1, Los Angeles (90073-1003)
P.O. Box 25027 (90025-0027)
PHONE..........................310 312-1554
Kenneth Hickman, *CEO*
Thoyd Ellis, *CFO*
EMP: 130 **EST:** 1988
SQ FT: 1,500
SALES: 4.8MM **Privately Held**
WEB: www.brentwoodresearch.org
SIC: 8733 Medical research

(P-22901)
CALIFORNIA INSTITUTE TECH
Also Called: Jet Propulsion Laboratory
4800 Oak Grove Dr, Pasadena (91109-8001)
PHONE..........................818 354-9154
Michael Watkins, *Director*
Karen Piggee, *Principal*
EMP: 6000
SALES (corp-wide): 3.3B **Privately Held**
WEB: www.caltech.edu
SIC: 8733 Research institute
PA: California Institute Of Technology
1200 E California Blvd
Pasadena CA 91125
626 395-6811

(P-22902)
CARNEGIE INSTITUTION WASH
Also Called: Observatories of The Carnegie
813 Santa Barbara St, Pasadena (91101-1232)
PHONE..........................626 577-1122
Wendy L Freedman, *Director*
Beverly Fink, *Executive Asst*
Susan Cortinas, *Administration*
Erica Clark, *Planning*
Theo Van De Sande, *CIO*
EMP: 100
SQ FT: 24,075
SALES (corp-wide): 73.9MM **Privately Held**
WEB: www.carnegiescience.edu
SIC: 8733 7999 Scientific research agency; observation tower operation
PA: Carnegie Institution Of Washington
5251 Broad Branch Rd Nw
Washington DC 20015
202 387-6400

(P-22903)
CATHOLIC CHRTIES LOS ANGLES IN (PA)
1531 James M Wood Blvd, Los Angeles (90015-1112)
P.O. Box 15095 (90015-0095)
PHONE..........................213 251-3400
Monsignor G Cox, *Exec Dir*
James E Bathker, *CFO*
Ronald Lopez, *CFO*
Lelend Ratleff, *Human Res Dir*
Demetris Jones, *HR Admin*
EMP: 247 **EST:** 1919
SQ FT: 18,000
SALES: 57.6MM **Privately Held**
WEB: www.catholiccharitiesla.org
SIC: 8733 8322 Noncommercial research organizations; individual & family services

(P-22904)
CELERA CORPORATION (HQ)
33608 Ortega Hwy, San Juan Capistrano (92675-2042)
PHONE..........................510 749-4200
Kathy Ordoez, *CEO*
Mathew J Budoff, *Co-Owner*
H R Superko MD, *Officer*
Paul Arata, *Senior VP*
Tim Sharpe, *Vice Pres*
EMP: 482 **EST:** 1997
SQ FT: 48,000
SALES (est): 96.6MM
SALES (corp-wide): 9.4B **Publicly Held**
WEB: www.questdiagnostics.com
SIC: 8733 8731 Scientific research agency; commercial physical research

PA: Quest Diagnostics Incorporated
500 Plaza Dr Ste G
Secaucus NJ 07094
973 520-2700

(P-22905)
CENTER FOR CIVIC EDUCATION (PA)
5115 Douglas Fir Rd Ste J, Calabasas (91302-2590)
PHONE..........................818 591-9321
Christopher R Riano, *Exec Dir*
Jim Heredia, *Officer*
Margaret S Branson, *Associate Dir*
John Hale, *Associate Dir*
Markj Molli, *Associate Dir*
EMP: 60 **EST:** 1980
SQ FT: 16,000
SALES: 2MM **Privately Held**
WEB: www.civiced.org
SIC: 8733 8748 Educational research agency; educational consultant

(P-22906)
CHILDRENS INST LOS ANGELES (PA)
2121 W Temple St, Los Angeles (90026-4915)
PHONE..........................213 385-5100
Bradley Myslinski, *President*
Helen Contreras, *Partner*
Eugene Straub, *Treasurer*
Catherine Atack, *Vice Pres*
Martine Singer, *Vice Pres*
EMP: 150 **EST:** 2011
SALES: 392K **Privately Held**
WEB: www.childrensinstitute.org
SIC: 8733 Noncommercial research organizations

(P-22907)
DXTERITY DIAGNOSTICS INC (PA)
19500 S Rancho Way # 116, Compton (90220-6012)
PHONE..........................310 537-7857
Dr Bob Terbrueggen, *CEO*
Jim Healy, *CFO*
Brett Swansiger, *Officer*
Shelley Arnold, *Vice Pres*
Bill Coty, *Vice Pres*
EMP: 31 **EST:** 2006
SQ FT: 14,000
SALES (est): 8.7MM **Privately Held**
WEB: www.dxterity.com
SIC: 8733 8071 2835 Medical research; medical laboratories; in vitro & in vivo diagnostic substances

(P-22908)
ENERGY BERKELEY OFFICE US DEPT
Also Called: Lawrence Berkeley National Lab
555 W Imperial Hwy, Brea (92821-4802)
PHONE..........................510 486-7089
EMP: 135 **Publicly Held**
WEB: www.es.net
SIC: 8733 9611 Noncommercial research organizations; energy development & conservation agency, government
HQ: United States Department Of Energy Berkeley Office
1 Cyclotron Rd
Berkeley CA 94720
510 486-5784

(P-22909)
HUNTINGTON MED RES INSTITUTES
734 Fairmount Ave, Pasadena (91105-3104)
PHONE..........................626 397-5804
EMP: 60
SALES (est): 3.5MM
SALES (corp-wide): 15.5MM **Privately Held**
SIC: 8733 Noncommercial Research Organization
PA: Huntington Medical Research Institutes
686 S Fair Oaks Ave
Pasadena CA 91105
626 795-4343

(P-22910)
INDEGENE INC (DH)
4500 Park Granada Ste 2, Calabasas (91302-1663)
PHONE..........................732 750-2901
Manish Gupta, *CEO*
Rajesh Nair, *President*
Sanjay Virmani, *Exec VP*
Deepti Venkatesh, *Manager*
EMP: 50 **EST:** 1999
SALES (est): 18.9MM **Privately Held**
WEB: www.indegene.com
SIC: 8733 Medical research

(P-22911)
JWCH INSTITUTE INC
6912 Ajax Ave, Bell (90201-4057)
PHONE..........................323 562-5813
Annabel Munoz, *Manager*
EMP: 162
SALES (corp-wide): 86.3MM **Privately Held**
WEB: www.jwchinstitute.org
SIC: 8733 Noncommercial research organizations
PA: Jwch Institute, Inc.
5650 Jillson St
Commerce CA 90040
323 477-1171

(P-22912)
JWCH INSTITUTE INC
12360 Firestone Blvd, Norwalk (90650-4324)
PHONE..........................562 281-0306
Oyamendan Itohan, *COO*
Tom Grode, *Bd of Directors*
Jincy Jacob, *Family Practiti*
Nancy Choi, *Psychologist*
Jack Barbour, *Psychiatry*
EMP: 162
SALES (corp-wide): 86.3MM **Privately Held**
WEB: www.jwchinstitute.org
SIC: 8733 Noncommercial research organizations
PA: Jwch Institute, Inc.
5650 Jillson St
Commerce CA 90040
323 477-1171

(P-22913)
LAS CMBRES OBSRVTORY GLOBL TLS
6740 Cortona Dr Ste 102, Goleta (93117-5575)
PHONE..........................805 880-1600
Wayne Rosing, *President*
Dorothy Largay, *Treasurer*
Michael Falarsky, *Exec VP*
Nan Brooks, *Executive Asst*
David Douglass, *Sr Software Eng*
EMP: 50 **EST:** 1993
SQ FT: 37,795
SALES: 6.1MM **Privately Held**
WEB: www.lco.global
SIC: 8733 Scientific research agency

(P-22914)
MILKEN INSTITUTE
1250 4th St, Santa Monica (90401-1366)
PHONE..........................310 570-4600
Michael L Klowden, *CEO*
Michael Milken, *Ch of Bd*
Richard Ditizio, *President*
John Hunter, *CFO*
Rajiv Ahuja, *Associate Dir*
▲ **EMP:** 50 **EST:** 1989
SALES (est): 133.6MM **Privately Held**
WEB: www.milkeninstitute.org
SIC: 8733 Economic research, noncommercial

(P-22915)
MIND RESEARCH INSTITUTE
Also Called: Music Intlgnce Neuro Dev Inst
5281 California Ave # 300, Irvine (92617-3219)
PHONE..........................949 345-8700
Brett Woudenberg, *CEO*
Gabrielle Abutom, *Partner*
Brian Molitor, *Partner*
Jim Sidick, *Partner*
Karin Wu, *Partner*
EMP: 160 **EST:** 2000

SALES: 26.5MM **Privately Held**
WEB: www.mindresearch.org
SIC: 8733 Medical research

(P-22916)
NANTCELL INC
2040 E Mariposa Ave, El Segundo (90245-5027)
PHONE..........................310 883-1300
Patrick Soon-Shiong, *CEO*
Robert Murdock, *Vice Pres*
Bridget Klotz, *Program Mgr*
Juliet Hong, *Planning*
Linda Hondroulis, *Opers Staff*
EMP: 106 **EST:** 2014
SALES (est): 5.9MM
SALES (corp-wide): 158.2K **Publicly Held**
WEB: www.nantworks.com
SIC: 8733 Bacteriological research
PA: Nantworks, Llc
9920 Jefferson Blvd
Culver City CA 90232
310 883-1300

(P-22917)
RANCHO RESEARCH INSTITUTE
Also Called: Rri
7601 Imperial Hwy, Downey (90242-3456)
P.O. Box 3500 (90242-3500)
PHONE..........................562 401-8111
Julia Laplount, *CEO*
Yaga Szlachcic, *President*
Ana Santos, *Officer*
Valery Eberly, *Research*
Jeff Rankin, *Engineer*
EMP: 175 **EST:** 1956
SQ FT: 15,000
SALES (est): 6.8MM **Privately Held**
WEB: www.ranchoresearch.org
SIC: 8733 Educational research agency

(P-22918)
RIVERSIDE RESEARCH INSTITUTE
3333 W Coast Hwy Ste 101, Newport Beach (92663-4039)
PHONE..........................949 631-0107
Rosemary Ellis, *Director*
EMP: 61
SALES (corp-wide): 116MM **Privately Held**
WEB: www.riversideresearch.org
SIC: 8733 8092 Research institute; kidney dialysis centers
PA: Riverside Research Institute
156 William St Fl 9
New York NY 10038
212 563-4545

(P-22919)
SAINT JOHNS CANCER INSTITUTE
2200 Santa Monica Blvd, Santa Monica (90404-2312)
PHONE..........................310 449-5253
Michael Ricks, *CEO*
Patrick Wayne, *Ch of Bd*
Gary Grubbs, *COO*
EMP: 51 **EST:** 1991
SQ FT: 57,000
SALES (est): 5.9MM **Privately Held**
WEB: www.jwciauxiliary.com
SIC: 8733 Research institute

(P-22920)
SCOREUSA INSTITUTE
Also Called: Sgp.id11
528 19th St, Huntington Beach (92648-3814)
PHONE..........................714 909-0688
Shaun Harris, *Principal*
EMP: 51 **EST:** 2001
SALES (est): 1.6MM **Privately Held**
SIC: 8733 Noncommercial research organizations

(P-22921)
SOUTHERN CAL INST FOR RES EDCA
Also Called: S C I R E
5901 E 7th St 151, Long Beach (90822-5201)
P.O. Box 15298 (90815-0298)
PHONE..........................562 826-8139

PRODUCTS & SVCS

Timothy R Morgan, *President*
Moti Kashyap MD, *Treasurer*
EMP: 80 **EST:** 1989
SALES (est): 6MM **Privately Held**
WEB: www.scire-lb.org
SIC: 8733 Medical research

(P-22922)
SRI INTERNATIONAL
4111 Broad St Ste 220, San Luis Obispo
(93401-8743)
PHONE...................................805 542-9330
EMP: 142
SALES (corp-wide): 550MM **Privately Held**
SIC: 8733 Scientific Research
PA: Sri International
　　333 Ravenswood Ave
　　Menlo Park CA 94025
　　650 859-2000

(P-22923)
UNIVERSITY CAL LOS ANGELES
Tanms Engineering Research Ctr
Ucla Boelter Hall 420 Wes, Los Angeles
(90095-0001)
PHONE...................................310 825-7852
EMP: 200 **Privately Held**
WEB: www.ucla.edu
SIC: 8221 8733 9411 University; noncom-
mercial research organizations; adminis-
tration of educational programs;
HQ: University Of California, Los Angeles
　　405 Hilgard Ave
　　Los Angeles CA 90095

(P-22924)
VITAL RESEARCH LLC
6380 Wilshire Blvd # 170, Los Angeles
(90048-5003)
PHONE...................................323 951-1670
Harold N Urman,
Christina Anaya, *Admin Asst*
Albert Cheng, *Technology*
Gwen Uman,
EMP: 56 **EST:** 1982
SQ FT: 1,600
SALES (est): 5MM **Privately Held**
WEB: www.vitalresearch.com
SIC: 8733 7361 8732 Noncommercial re-
search organizations; employment agen-
cies; market analysis or research

(P-22925)
WCCT GLOBAL INC (PA)
5630 Cerritos Ave, Cypress (90630-4738)
PHONE...................................714 668-1500
Gregory Hanson, *CEO*
Bill Taaffe, *CEO*
Jon Rojas, *COO*
Josh Trenton, *Exec VP*
Bill Van Nostrand, *Exec VP*
EMP: 182 **EST:** 2005
SALES (est): 24.6MM **Privately Held**
WEB: www.wcct.com
SIC: 8733 8731 8721 Research institute;
biological research; biotechnical research,
commercial; calculating & statistical serv-
ice

(P-22926)
X PRIZE FOUNDATION INC
800 Crprate Pinte Ste 350, Culver City
(90230)
PHONE...................................310 741-4880
Robert Weiss, *President*
Ahmer Inam, *Partner*
Paul Rappoport, *COO*
Gil Elbaz, *Bd of Directors*
Anna Lewis, *Officer*
EMP: 50 **EST:** 1998
SQ FT: 17,705
SALES: 39.4MM **Privately Held**
WEB: www.xprize.org
SIC: 8733 Noncommercial research organ-
izations

8734 Testing Laboratories

(P-22927)
**AIRCRAFT XRAY
LABORATORIES INC**
5216 Pacific Blvd, Huntington Park
(90255-2595)
PHONE...................................323 587-4141
Gary G Newton, *CEO*
Justin Guzman, *President*
James Newton, *Vice Pres*
Jim Newton, *Vice Pres*
Sandi Spelic, *Principal*
EMP: 80 **EST:** 1938
SQ FT: 60,000
SALES (est): 7.5MM **Privately Held**
WEB: www.aircraftxray.com
SIC: 8734 7384 3471 Testing laborato-
ries; photograph developing & retouching;
plating & polishing

(P-22928)
ALCON VISION LLC
20521 Lake Forest Dr, Lake Forest
(92630-7741)
PHONE...................................949 505-6890
Ruben Garcia, *Supervisor*
EMP: 259
SALES (corp-wide): 6.8B **Privately Held**
WEB: www.alcon.com
SIC: 8734 Testing laboratories
HQ: Alcon Vision, Llc
　　6201 South Fwy
　　Fort Worth TX 76134
　　817 293-0450

(P-22929)
ALS GROUP USA CORP
Also Called: Bioscreen Testing Services
3904 Del Amo Blvd Ste 801, Torrance
(90503-2183)
PHONE...................................310 214-0043
Ranil Fernando, *General Mgr*
EMP: 70 **Privately Held**
SIC: 8734 8731 Testing laboratories;
commercial physical research
HQ: Als Group Usa, Corp.
　　10450 Stncliff Rd Ste 210
　　Houston TX 77099
　　281 530-5656

(P-22930)
**ATLAS TESTING
LABORATORIES INC**
9820 6th St, Rancho Cucamonga
(91730-5714)
PHONE...................................909 373-4130
H Leo Norton, *President*
Jerry Espeseth, *General Mgr*
EMP: 50
SQ FT: 25,000
SALES: 7.2MM **Privately Held**
WEB: www.atlastesting.com
SIC: 8734 Metallurgical testing laboratory

(P-22931)
B C LABORATORIES INC
4100 Atlas Ct, Bakersfield (93308-4510)
PHONE...................................661 327-4911
Carolyn I Jackson, *President*
Richard Eglin, *Shareholder*
Rich Eglin, *Vice Pres*
Stuart Buttram, *Lab Dir*
Mark Ellis, *Business Dir*
EMP: 93 **EST:** 1949
SQ FT: 18,000
SALES (est): 13.9MM
SALES (corp-wide): 64.8MM **Privately
Held**
WEB: www.bclabs.com
SIC: 8734 Water testing laboratory
HQ: Pace Analytical Services, Llc
　　1800 Elm St Se
　　Minneapolis MN 55414

(P-22932)
BABCOCK LABORATORIES INC
Also Called: E. S. Babcock & Sons
6100 Quail Valley Ct, Riverside
(92507-0704)
P.O. Box 432 (92502-0432)
PHONE...................................951 653-3351
Allison Mackenzie, *CEO*

Brad Meadows, *Vice Pres*
Roan McRae, *Business Dir*
Tami Kearns, *Admin Asst*
Kayelani Deener, *Project Mgr*
EMP: 70 **EST:** 1978
SQ FT: 20,000
SALES (est): 13.8MM **Privately Held**
WEB: www.babcocklabs.com
SIC: 8734 Water testing laboratory

(P-22933)
BTC LABORATORIES INC
1868 Palma Dr, Ventura (93003-6300)
PHONE...................................805 656-6074
Tom Williams, *President*
EMP: 99 **EST:** 1959
SALES (est): 1.4MM
SALES (corp-wide): 247.4MM **Privately
Held**
WEB: www.ceotesd.com
SIC: 8734 Testing laboratories
HQ: U.S. Laboratories Inc.
　　4400 140th Ave N Ste 230
　　Clearwater FL 33762

(P-22934)
**CALIFORNIA LAB SCIENCES
LLC**
Also Called: West Pacific Medical Lab
10200 Pioneer Blvd # 500, Santa Fe
Springs (90670-6000)
PHONE...................................562 758-6900
William McDonald,
EMP: 300 **EST:** 2009
SALES (est): 14.6MM **Privately Held**
WEB: www.westpaclab.com
SIC: 8734 Testing laboratories

(P-22935)
**COLOR DESIGN LABORATORY
INC (PA)**
Also Called: Color Design Labs
19151 Parthenia St Ste H, Northridge
(91324-5126)
PHONE...................................818 341-5100
Gilberto Amparo, *CEO*
Maria Amparo, *President*
Maria Gonzalez, *COO*
▲ **EMP:** 100 **EST:** 2010
SQ FT: 9,000
SALES (est): 5.6MM **Privately Held**
WEB: www.colordesignlaboratory.com
SIC: 8734 Testing laboratories

(P-22936)
**CONSUMER SAFETY
ANALYTICS LLC**
Also Called: Cannasafe
7027 Hayvenhurst Ave, Van Nuys
(91406-3802)
PHONE...................................818 922-2416
Aaron Riley, *Principal*
Antonio Frazier, *Principal*
Bosco Ramirez, *Principal*
EMP: 99 **EST:** 2017
SALES (est): 5.4MM **Privately Held**
SIC: 8734 Testing laboratories

(P-22937)
CRITERION LABS INC
10907 Magnolia Blvd, North Hollywood
(91601-3904)
P.O. Box 700190, San Jose (95170-0190)
PHONE...................................818 506-8332
Glenn H Hanson, *President*
Phil Castor, *CFO*
Jim Colton, *Treasurer*
Arnold Collins, *Vice Pres*
Terry Lindon, *Vice Pres*
▲ **EMP:** 62 **EST:** 1985
SQ FT: 7,200
SALES (est): 7.6MM **Privately Held**
WEB: www.criterionlabs.com
SIC: 8734 Product testing laboratory,
safety or performance

(P-22938)
DICKSON TESTING CO INC (DH)
11126 Palmer Ave, South Gate
(90280-7492)
PHONE...................................562 862-8378
Robert Lyddon, *President*
Jim Scanell, *Vice Pres*
EMP: 80 **EST:** 1970

SQ FT: 40,000
SALES (est): 19.4MM
SALES (corp-wide): 245.5B **Publicly
Held**
WEB: www.dicksontesting.com
SIC: 8734 Metallurgical testing laboratory
HQ: Precision Castparts Corp.
　　4650 Sw Mcdam Ave Ste 300
　　Portland OR 97239
　　503 946-4800

(P-22939)
ELEMENT MATERIALS (DH)
15062 Bolsa Chica St, Huntington Beach
(92649-1023)
PHONE...................................714 892-1961
Charles Noall, *President*
Eelco Niermeijer, *CFO*
Pete Regan, *Chairman*
Jeff Joyce, *Exec VP*
Jo Wetz, *Exec VP*
▲ **EMP:** 80 **EST:** 1997
SQ FT: 4,500
SALES (est): 51.3MM
SALES (corp-wide): 732.6MM **Privately
Held**
WEB: www.element.com
SIC: 8734 Metallurgical testing laboratory
HQ: Element Materials Technology Group
　　Us Holdings Inc.
　　15062 Bolsa Chica St
　　Huntington Beach CA 92649
　　714 892-1961

(P-22940)
ELEMENT MTRLS TECH HB INC
Also Called: Element Rancho Dominguez
18100 S Wilmington Ave, Compton
(90220-5909)
PHONE...................................310 632-8500
Chuck Gee, *General Mgr*
Jo Wetz, *CFO*
Juan Gonzalez, *Opers Mgr*
Victor Ratinoff, *Opers Mgr*
EMP: 86
SALES (corp-wide): 782.6MM **Privately
Held**
WEB: www.element.com
SIC: 8734 Metallurgical testing laboratory
HQ: Element Materials Technology Hunting-
　　ton Beach Llc
　　15062 Bolsa Chica St
　　Huntington Beach CA 92649
　　714 892-1961

(P-22941)
ELLISON INSTITUTE LLC
12414 Exposition Blvd, Los Angeles
(90064-1016)
PHONE...................................513 403-2628
Paul Marinelli, *CEO*
Jason Bowman, *COO*
EMP: 80 **EST:** 2019
SALES (est): 5.7MM **Privately Held**
WEB: www.eitm.org
SIC: 8734 Testing laboratories

(P-22942)
EMAX LABORATORIES INC
3051 Fujita St, Torrance (90505-4004)
PHONE...................................310 618-8889
Caspar J Pang, *CEO*
Kam P Yee, *President*
Richard Beauvil, *Officer*
Sing C Pang, *Admin Sec*
Sing Pang, *Admin Sec*
EMP: 50 **EST:** 1996
SALES (est): 10.6MM **Privately Held**
WEB: www.emaxlabs.com
SIC: 8734 8748 8731 Pollution testing;
environmental consultant; environmental
research

(P-22943)
**EUROFINS EAG ENGRG
SCIENCE LLC**
15 Morgan, Irvine (92618-2005)
PHONE...................................949 521-6200
Jon Gergen, *Manager*
Winfield Scott, *Info Tech Dir*
EMP: 50
SALES (corp-wide): 367.9K **Privately
Held**
WEB: www.eag.com
SIC: 8734 Product testing laboratories

HQ: Eurofins Eag Engineering Science, Llc
2710 Walsh Ave
Santa Clara CA 95051
408 588-0050

(P-22944)
EUROFINS EATON ANALYTICAL LLC (DH)
750 Royal Oaks Dr Ste 100, Monrovia (91016-6359)
PHONE..................................626 386-1100
Wilson Hershey, *Chairman*
Bosco Ramirez, *President*
William Lipps, *Officer*
Andrew Eaton, *Vice Pres*
Fred Haley, *Lab Dir*
EMP: 69 EST: 2012
SALES (est): 25.1MM
SALES (corp-wide): 367.9K **Privately Held**
WEB: www.eurofinsus.com
SIC: 8734 Testing laboratories
HQ: Eurofins Lancaster Laboratories, Inc.
2425 New Holland Pike
Lancaster PA 17601
717 656-2300

(P-22945)
FORENSIC ANALYTICAL SPC INC
20535 Belshaw Ave, Carson (90746-3505)
PHONE..................................310 763-2374
Bruce White, *Principal*
EMP: 94
SALES (corp-wide): 11.1MM **Privately Held**
WEB: www.forensicanalytical.com
SIC: 8734 8748 8731 8071 Forensic laboratory; environmental consultant; commercial physical research; medical laboratories; air pollution measuring service
PA: Forensic Analytical Specialties Incorporated
3777 Depot Rd Ste 409
Hayward CA 94545
510 887-8828

(P-22946)
HAMPTON TDDER TCHNCAL SVCS INC
4571 State St, Montclair (91763-6129)
P.O. Box 2338 (91763-0838)
PHONE..................................909 628-1256
Matthew C Tedder Sr, *President*
Samantha Vanscoy, *Technology*
EMP: 19 EST: 1972
SQ FT: 20,000 **Privately Held**
SIC: 8734 1731 1623 8711 Testing laboratories; electrical work; electric power line construction; engineering services; transformers, except electric

(P-22947)
HEIDER INSPECTION GROUP
Also Called: Consolidated Engineering Labs
14457 Meridian Pkwy, Riverside (92518-3007)
PHONE..................................909 673-0292
Gary Cappa, *President*
Tracy Hooper, *Administration*
EMP: 740 EST: 2015
SALES (est): 593.2K
SALES (corp-wide): 533.8MM **Privately Held**
WEB: www.oneatlas.com
SIC: 8734 Testing laboratories
PA: Atlas Technical Consultants Llc
13215 Bee Cave Pkwy B230
Austin TX 78738
866 858-4499

(P-22948)
HEMET UNIFIED SCHOOL DISTRICT
Also Called: Nutrition Services
2075 W Acacia Ave, Hemet (92545-3746)
PHONE..................................951 765-5100
Kathy Anderson, *Branch Mgr*
EMP: 80
SALES (corp-wide): 341.2MM **Privately Held**
WEB: www.hemetusd.org
SIC: 8211 8734 Public elementary & secondary schools; testing laboratories

PA: Hemet Unified School District
1791 W Acacia Ave
Hemet CA 92545
951 765-5100

(P-22949)
HYUNDAI AMER TECHNICAL CTR INC
Also Called: Hyundai America/Tech Center
12610 Eastend Ave, Chino (91710-3006)
PHONE..................................909 627-3525
Scott Kin, *Manager*
Ryan Miller, *Engineer*
EMP: 69
SQ FT: 19,620 **Privately Held**
WEB: www.hatci.com
SIC: 8734 8711 Product testing laboratories; mechanical engineering
HQ: Hyundai America Technical Center Incorporated
6800 Geddes Rd
Ypsilanti MI 48198
734 337-2500

(P-22950)
IRIS LLC
3800 N Mission Rd, Los Angeles (90031-3138)
PHONE..................................424 331-5441
Albert Banoun, *President*
EMP: 50 EST: 2019
SALES (est): 1.7MM **Privately Held**
WEB: www.irislabsolutions.com
SIC: 8734 Testing laboratories

(P-22951)
IRVINE PHARMACEUTICAL SVCS INC
5270 California Ave # 200, Irvine (92617-3231)
PHONE..................................949 439-6677
Assad Kazeminy, *CEO*
William Stowell, *CFO*
Aryo Nikopour, *Vice Pres*
Anita Jain, *Human Resources*
Wendy Ho, *Supervisor*
▲ EMP: 51 EST: 1988
SALES (est): 11.3MM **Privately Held**
WEB: www.aveciapharma.com
SIC: 8734 Testing laboratories

(P-22952)
MICHELSON LABORATORIES INC (PA)
6280 Chalet Dr, Commerce (90040-3761)
PHONE..................................562 928-0553
Grant Michelson, *President*
Jack E Michelson, *CEO*
Aaron Kaiser, *Vice Pres*
Eva Vasco, *Administration*
Benjamin Garcia, *Info Tech Mgr*
EMP: 67 EST: 1970
SQ FT: 20,000
SALES (est): 11.4MM **Privately Held**
WEB: www.michelsonlab.com
SIC: 8734 Food testing service

(P-22953)
MIRION TECHNOLOGIES GDS INC (HQ)
Also Called: Global Dosimetry Solutions
2652 Mcgaw Ave, Irvine (92614-5840)
PHONE..................................949 419-1000
Thomas Logan, *CEO*
Sander Perle, *President*
James Hippel, *CFO*
Jack Pacheco, *CFO*
Antony Besso, *Exec VP*
EMP: 125 EST: 2003
SALES (est): 86.7MM **Privately Held**
WEB: www.mirion.com
SIC: 8734 Radiation dosimetry laboratory

(P-22954)
NANTOMICS LLC (PA)
9920 Jefferson Blvd, Culver City (90232-3506)
PHONE..................................310 883-1300
Patrick Soon-Shiong, *CEO*
Mark Lindey, *CIO*
John Yanarella, *Software Engr*
Paul Woodard, *Research*
Kevin Givechian, *Analyst*
EMP: 55 EST: 2012

SALES (est): 6.7MM **Privately Held**
WEB: www.nantomics.com
SIC: 8734 8071 Testing laboratories; testing laboratories

(P-22955)
NATIONAL GENETICS INSTITUTE
2440 S Sepulveda Blvd # 235, Los Angeles (90064-1748)
PHONE..................................310 996-6610
Mike Aicher, *CEO*
Geri Cox, *Director*
EMP: 200 EST: 1991
SQ FT: 35,000
SALES (est): 10.7MM **Publicly Held**
WEB: www.plasma.labcorp.com
SIC: 8734 Testing laboratories
PA: Laboratory Corporation Of America Holdings
358 S Main St
Burlington NC 27215

(P-22956)
NORTH AMERCN SCIENCE ASSOC INC
N A M S A
9 Morgan, Irvine (92618-2005)
PHONE..................................949 951-3110
Dennis Nivens, *Vice Pres*
Michael Brookman, *CIO*
David Getz, *Programmer Anys*
Christopher Demorett, *Research*
Pamela Vaughan, *Research*
EMP: 60
SQ FT: 40,000
SALES (corp-wide): 102.4MM **Privately Held**
WEB: www.namsa.com
SIC: 8734 8071 8999 Testing laboratories; medical laboratories; chemical consultant
PA: North American Science Associates, Llc
6750 Wales Rd
Northwood OH 43619
419 666-9455

(P-22957)
OILFIELD ENVMTL COMPLIANCE INC (PA)
Also Called: O E C
307 Roemer Way Ste 300, Santa Maria (93454-1105)
PHONE..................................805 922-4772
Stefanie Haynes, *CEO*
Carrie McCrillis, *Officer*
Julius Carstens, *Vice Pres*
Meredith Sprister, *General Mgr*
Pete Alcocer, *Opers Staff*
EMP: 52 EST: 1999
SQ FT: 1,667
SALES (est): 9.8MM **Privately Held**
WEB: www.oecusa.com
SIC: 8734 Testing laboratories

(P-22958)
SHOGUN LABS INC (PA)
340 S Lemon Ave 1085, Walnut (91789-2706)
PHONE..................................206 679-1302
Damien Edward Kan, *Administration*
Sanal Panicker, *Partner*
Greg Beldam, *Vice Pres*
Scott Goci, *Software Engr*
Klaus Kohut, *Software Engr*
EMP: 57 EST: 2015
SALES (est): 9.1MM **Privately Held**
WEB: www.getshogun.com
SIC: 8734 Testing laboratories

(P-22959)
TANDEX TEST LABS INC
15849 Business Center Dr, Irwindale (91706-2053)
PHONE..................................626 962-7166
Brian Peale, *President*
Charles T Goolsby, *Vice Pres*
EMP: 49 EST: 1980
SQ FT: 15,000
SALES (est): 9.3MM **Privately Held**
WEB: www.tandexlabs.com
SIC: 8734 3674 Testing laboratories; hybrid integrated circuits

(P-22960)
TWINING INC (PA)
Also Called: Twining Laboratories
2883 E Spring St Ste 300, Long Beach (90806-6847)
PHONE..................................562 426-3355
Edward Butch M Twining Jr, *CEO*
Brian Kramer, *President*
Bob Hathaway, *CFO*
Talin Astourian, *Vice Pres*
Richard S Hazen, *Vice Pres*
EMP: 133 EST: 1959
SQ FT: 13,600
SALES (est): 22.1MM **Privately Held**
WEB: www.twininginc.com
SIC: 8734 Testing laboratories

(P-22961)
WESTPAC LABS INC
10200 Pioneer Blvd # 500, Santa Fe Springs (90670-6000)
PHONE..................................562 906-5227
Phillip Chen, *CEO*
EMP: 452
SALES (est): 53MM **Privately Held**
WEB: www.westpaclab.com
SIC: 8734 8071 Testing laboratories; pathological laboratory

(P-22962)
WORKSITE LABS INC
1890 E Miraloma Ave Ste D, Placentia (92870-6746)
PHONE..................................657 444-9146
Gary Frazier, *CEO*
EMP: 100 EST: 2020
SALES (est): 3.1MM **Privately Held**
SIC: 8734 Testing laboratories

8741 Management Services

(P-22963)
360 HEALTH PLAN INC
Also Called: 360 Clinic
13800 Arizona St Ste 104, Westminster (92683-3951)
PHONE..................................800 446-8888
Vince Pien, *CEO*
Mike Lee, *COO*
David Ngo, *CFO*
EMP: 200 EST: 2020
SALES (est): 5.8MM **Privately Held**
WEB: www.360clinic.md
SIC: 8741 Hospital management

(P-22964)
360 SUPPORT SERVICES
306 S Myrtle Ave, Monrovia (91016-2849)
P.O. Box 801238, Santa Clarita (91380-1238)
PHONE..................................866 360-6468
Kelly Martinez, *CEO*
Renee Fields, *COO*
Ola Ostlund, *Admin Sec*
EMP: 72 EST: 2016
SALES (est): 1.4MM **Privately Held**
WEB: www.360sgroup.com
SIC: 8741 7349 Nursing & personal care facility management; building cleaning service

(P-22965)
ACEPEX MANAGEMENT CORPORATION
13401 Yorba Ave, Chino (91710-5055)
PHONE..................................909 591-1999
EMP: 306
SALES (corp-wide): 37.5MM **Privately Held**
SIC: 8741 Management Services
PA: Acepex Management Corporation
10643 Mills Ave
Montclair CA 92821
909 625-6900

(P-22966)
ADVANCED BIOSERVICES LLC (PA)
19255 Vanowen St, Reseda (91335-5070)
PHONE..................................818 342-0100
Anna Kane,
EMP: 65 EST: 2004
SALES (est): 7MM **Privately Held**
SIC: 8741 Administrative management

(P-22967)
ADVANCED MEDICAL MGT INC
5000 Arprt Plz Dr Ste 150, Long Beach
(90815)
PHONE..................562 766-2000
Stephen Hegstrom, *CEO*
Kathy Hegstrom, *President*
Paul Pew, *Exec VP*
Courtney Plank, *Human Res Mgr*
EMP: 60 **EST:** 1982
SALES (est): 13.6MM **Privately Held**
WEB: www.amm.cc
SIC: 8741 8721 Hospital management;
nursing & personal care facility manage-
ment; accounting, auditing & bookkeeping

(P-22968)
AEG MANAGEMENT LACC LLC
Also Called: Los Angeles Convention Center
1201 S Figueroa St, Los Angeles
(90015-1308)
PHONE..................213 741-1151
Brad Gessner, *Senior VP*
Estella Flores, *Bd of Directors*
Estella M Flores, *Bd of Directors*
Keith Hilsgen, *Vice Pres*
Carisa Malanum, *Vice Pres*
EMP: 220 **EST:** 2013
SALES (est): 44.8MM
SALES (corp-wide): 153.5MM **Privately
Held**
WEB: www.lacclink.com
SIC: 8741 Business management
PA: Aeg Facilities, Llc
800 W Olympic Blvd # 305
Los Angeles CA 90015
213 763-7700

(P-22969)
AJIT HEALTHCARE INC
316 S Westlake Ave, Los Angeles
(90057-2906)
PHONE..................213 484-0510
Jasvant N Modi, *President*
EMP: 80 **EST:** 2004
SALES (est): 5MM **Privately Held**
SIC: 8741 Nursing & personal care facility
management

(P-22970)
ALDERWOOD GROUP LLC (PA)
42184 Moonridge Way 1, Big Bear Lake
(92315-2274)
P.O. Box 1987 (92315-1987)
PHONE..................909 866-6445
Thomas Johnson, *CEO*
Andrew Hall, *Vice Pres*
Stephanie Thompson, *Vice Pres*
Michael Knight, *Information Mgr*
Yesenia Bravo,
EMP: 70 **EST:** 1999
SALES (est): 6.4MM **Privately Held**
WEB: www.alderwoodgroup.com
SIC: 8741 Hotel or motel management

(P-22971)
**ALLIANCE FUNDING GROUP
(PA)**
Also Called: Alliance Capital Markets
17542 17th St Ste 200, Tustin
(92780-1960)
PHONE..................800 978-8817
Brijesh Ashok Patel, *President*
Shawn M Donohue, *Vice Pres*
Vishal V Masani, *Vice Pres*
EMP: 60 **EST:** 1998
SALES (est): 23.3MM **Privately Held**
WEB: www.afg.com
SIC: 8741 Financial management for busi-
ness

(P-22972)
**ALLZONE MANAGEMENT SVCS
INC**
Also Called: Allzone Management Solutions
3700 Wilshire Blvd # 979, Los Angeles
(90010-3088)
PHONE..................213 291-8879
Jonathan Rodrigues, *President*
Peter Brown, *Assoc VP*
Mg Suresh, *Assoc VP*
EMP: 500 **EST:** 2011
SALES (est): 12.9MM **Privately Held**
WEB: www.allzonems.com
SIC: 8741 Management services

(P-22973)
**ALTURA MANAGEMENT
SERVICES LLC**
1401 N Montebello Blvd, Montebello
(90640-2584)
PHONE..................323 768-2898
Jose Esparza, *CFO*
Darren McLathlan, *Vice Pres*
EMP: 375 **EST:** 2015
SALES (est): 6.5MM **Privately Held**
SIC: 8741 Management services

(P-22974)
**AMERICAN INTGRTED
RSOURCES INC**
2341 N Pacific St, Orange (92865-2601)
PHONE..................714 921-4100
Thomas C Stevens, *CEO*
John Georgagi, *Exec VP*
Gerald Adkerson, *Vice Pres*
Megan Duffy-Rigsby, *General Mgr*
Manish Patel, *General Mgr*
EMP: 80 **EST:** 2013
SALES (est): 10.3MM **Privately Held**
WEB: www.american-integrated.com
SIC: 8741 Construction management

(P-22975)
**AMERICAN MZHOU DNGPO
GROUP INC**
4520 Maine Ave, Baldwin Park
(91706-2671)
PHONE..................626 820-9239
Gang Wang, *CEO*
EMP: 100 **EST:** 2012
SALES (est): 10.2MM **Privately Held**
SIC: 8741 Restaurant management

(P-22976)
**ANTINOS MANAGEMENT
AMERICA INC (PA)**
2150 Colorado Ave, Santa Monica
(90404-3567)
PHONE..................310 453-8506
Nadeshiko Nakahara, *General Mgr*
EMP: 99 **EST:** 2008
SALES (est): 221.1K **Privately Held**
SIC: 8741 Management services

(P-22977)
**APOLLO MEDICAL HOLDINGS
INC (PA)**
Also Called: Apollomed
1668 S Garfield Ave Fl 2, Alhambra
(91801-5400)
PHONE..................626 282-0288
Brandon Sim, *Co-CEO*
Kenneth Sim, *Ch of Bd*
Thomas S Lam, *President*
Eric Chin, *CFO*
Albert Young, *Officer*
EMP: 72 **EST:** 1985
SQ FT: 35,000
SALES (est): 687.1MM **Publicly Held**
WEB: www.apollomed.net
SIC: 8741 8011 Hospital management;
health maintenance organization

(P-22978)
APPLECARE MEDICAL MGT LLC
18 Centerpointe Dr # 100, La Palma
(90623-1028)
P.O. Box 6014, Artesia (90702-6014)
PHONE..................714 443-4507
Vinod Jivrajka, *Principal*
Sean Igarta, *Info Tech Dir*
EMP: 108 **EST:** 2010
SALES (est): 15MM
SALES (corp-wide): 257.1B **Publicly
Held**
WEB: www.applecaremedical.com
SIC: 8741 Nursing & personal care facility
management
PA: Unitedhealth Group Incorporated
9900 Bren Rd E Ste 300w
Minnetonka MN 55343
952 936-1300

(P-22979)
**ARTIST SILVA MANAGEMENT
LLC (PA)**
722 Seward St, Los Angeles (90038-3504)
PHONE..................323 856-8222
John Silva,

Gary Gersh,
Michael Meisel, *Manager*
EMP: 102 **EST:** 1999
SALES (est): 8MM **Privately Held**
WEB: www.sammusicbiz.com
SIC: 8741 Business management

(P-22980)
**ASSET ATHENE MANAGEMENT
L P (HQ)**
2121 Rosecrans Ave # 5300, El Segundo
(90245-4750)
PHONE..................310 698-4444
James R Belardi, *CEO*
Jeff Boland, *Exec VP*
Robert Graham, *Exec VP*
James Hassett, *Exec VP*
Angelo Lombardo, *Senior VP*
EMP: 64 **EST:** 2014
SALES (est): 18.4MM **Publicly Held**
WEB: www.apollo.com
SIC: 8741 Financial management for busi-
ness

(P-22981)
**ATLAS FRANCHISE
MANAGEMENT INC**
17752 Sky Park Cir # 235, Irvine
(92614-6419)
PHONE..................949 239-1760
James Chung, *President*
EMP: 100 **EST:** 2013
SALES (est): 5.6MM
SALES (corp-wide): 8.9MM **Privately
Held**
WEB: www.t-mobile.com
SIC: 8741 Management services
PA: Atlas Inc.
100 N Citrus St Ste 300
West Covina CA 91791
626 671-0495

(P-22982)
**AWI MANAGEMENT
CORPORATION**
1800 E Lakeshore Dr, Lake Elsinore
(92530-4469)
PHONE..................951 674-8200
Angelica Chaidez, *Branch Mgr*
EMP: 241
SALES (corp-wide): 41.1MM **Privately
Held**
WEB: www.awimc.com
SIC: 8741 Business management
PA: Awi Management Corporation
120 Center St
Auburn CA 95603
530 745-6170

(P-22983)
**BARNETT CUSTOMER
MANAGEMENT**
3111 N Tustin St, Orange (92865-1750)
PHONE..................714 747-7908
Timothy Barnett, *President*
EMP: 50 **EST:** 2017
SALES (est): 1.3MM **Privately Held**
SIC: 8741 Management services

(P-22984)
**BEECH STREET CORPORATION
(DH)**
25550 Commercentre Dr # 200, Lake For-
est (92630-8893)
PHONE..................949 672-1000
William Fickling Jr, *Chairman*
William Hale, *President*
Jon Bird, *CFO*
Rick Markus, *Exec VP*
Norm Werthwein, *Senior VP*
EMP: 350 **EST:** 1951
SQ FT: 60,000
SALES (est): 50.1MM
SALES (corp-wide): 5B **Publicly Held**
WEB: www.beechstreet.com
SIC: 8741 Administrative management
HQ: Concentra Operating Corporation
5080 Spectrum Dr Ste 500w
Addison TX 75001
972 364-8000

(P-22985)
BELLWETHER ASSET MGT INC
200 N Pcf Cast Hwy Ste 14, El Segundo
(90245)
PHONE..................310 525-3022
Dennis Grzeskowiak, *CEO*
David Chalison, *Vice Pres*
Mitch Magoshi, *Vice Pres*
Omar Vargas, *Vice Pres*
Patrick Lesch, *Analyst*
EMP: 74 **EST:** 2013
SALES (est): 5.5MM **Privately Held**
WEB: www.bellwetheram.com
SIC: 8741 Financial management for busi-
ness

(P-22986)
BERNARDS INC
555 1st St, San Fernando (91340-3051)
PHONE..................818 898-1521
Jeff Bernards, *CEO*
Doug Bernards, *CEO*
Greg Simons, *Exec VP*
Gail Pascua, *Vice Pres*
Sal Nol, *Executive*
EMP: 60 **EST:** 2009
SALES (est): 2.8MM **Privately Held**
WEB: www.bernards.com
SIC: 8741 1542 Construction manage-
ment; commercial & office building con-
tractors

(P-22987)
**BEVERLY HEALTH CARE CORP
(PA)**
5445 Everglades St, Ventura (93003-6523)
PHONE..................805 642-1736
Carol Tradeway, *Director*
Rose Taylor-Calhoun *CEO*
Philip Drescher, *Principal*
Harry Maynard, *Principal*
Gary Wolfe, *Principal*
EMP: 50 **EST:** 1994
SQ FT: 85,000
SALES (est): 25MM **Privately Held**
SIC: 8741 Management services

(P-22988)
**BJS RESTAURANT OPERATIONS
CO**
7755 Center Ave Ste 300, Huntington
Beach (92647-3084)
PHONE..................714 500-2440
EMP: 132 **EST:** 2017
SALES (est): 1.4MM
SALES (corp-wide): 1.1B **Publicly Held**
WEB: www.bjsrestaurants.com
SIC: 8741 Restaurant management
PA: Bj's Restaurants, Inc.
7755 Center Ave Ste 300
Huntington Beach CA 92647
714 500-2400

(P-22989)
**BON APPETIT MANAGEMENT
CO**
1200 Getty Center Dr, Los Angeles
(90049-1657)
PHONE..................310 440-6052
Lori Flashner, *Vice Pres*
Haydee Gutierrez, *Manager*
EMP: 132
SALES (corp-wide): 26B **Privately Held**
WEB: www.eatlowcarbon.org
SIC: 8741 Management services
HQ: Bon Appetit Management Co.
201 Rdwood Shres Pkwy Ste
Redwood City CA 94065
650 798-8000

(P-22990)
**BON APPETIT MANAGEMENT
CO**
1050 N Mills Ave, Claremont (91711-3908)
PHONE..................909 607-2788
EMP: 132
SALES (corp-wide): 26B **Privately Held**
WEB: www.eatlowcarbon.org
SIC: 8741 Management services
HQ: Bon Appetit Management Co.
201 Rdwood Shres Pkwy Ste
Redwood City CA 94065
650 798-8000

(P-22991)
BON APPETIT MANAGEMENT CO
Also Called: Getty Center
1200 Getty Center Dr # 100, Los Angeles (90049-1657)
PHONE..................310 440-6209
Javier Ramirez, *Manager*
EMP: 132
SALES (corp-wide): 26B **Privately Held**
WEB: www.eatlowcarbon.org
SIC: 8741 Restaurant management
HQ: Bon Appetit Management Co.
201 Rdwood Shres Pkwy Ste
Redwood City CA 94065
650 798-8000

(P-22992)
BRET BOYLAN PROPERTY MGT
Also Called: Bret Boylan
35 N Alboni Pl Apt 409, Long Beach (90802-5438)
P.O. Box 14690 (90853-4690)
PHONE..................562 437-7886
EMP: 50
SQ FT: 300
SALES (est): 2MM **Privately Held**
SIC: 8741 Management Services

(P-22993)
BUFFALO SPOT MGT GROUP LLC
7245 Garden Grove Blvd, Garden Grove (92841-4216)
PHONE..................949 354-0884
Ivan Flores, *Mng Member*
EMP: 110 **EST:** 2016
SALES (est): 10.6MM **Privately Held**
WEB: www.thebuffalospotfranchise.com
SIC: 8741 Restaurant management

(P-22994)
BUTIER ENGINEERING INC
17822 17th St Ste 404, Tustin (92780-2154)
PHONE..................714 832-7222
Mark M Butier, *President*
Brent Morgheim, *Project Mgr*
Paul McDonnell, *Senior Mgr*
EMP: 56 **EST:** 1976
SQ FT: 1,500
SALES (est): 5.7MM **Privately Held**
WEB: www.butier.com
SIC: 8741 Construction management

(P-22995)
C C H S INC
Also Called: Courtyard Care Center
1880 Dawson Ave, Signal Hill (90755-5913)
PHONE..................562 494-5188
Julie Javier, *Administration*
Kay Alvarez, *Records Dir*
Spencer Olsen, *Treasurer*
Sally Ocampo, *Office Mgr*
Corona Flores-Moore, *Nursing Dir*
EMP: 53 **EST:** 1993
SALES (est): 3.5MM **Privately Held**
WEB: www.courtyardcarecenter.com
SIC: 8741 8052 8051 Management services; intermediate care facilities; skilled nursing care facilities

(P-22996)
CAL STATE LA UNIV AUX SVCS INC
Also Called: UAS
5151 State University Dr Ge314, Los Angeles (90032-4226)
PHONE..................323 343-2531
Tariq Marji, *Exec Dir*
▲ **EMP:** 600 **EST:** 1954
SQ FT: 108,000
SALES: 39MM **Privately Held**
WEB: www.calstatela.edu
SIC: 8741 5942 5651 5812 Business management; financial management for business; college book stores; unisex clothing stores; cafeteria

(P-22997)
CAMARILLO HEALTHCARE CENTER
205 Granada St, Camarillo (93010-7715)
PHONE..................805 482-9805

Erica Olsen, *Administration*
Angie Chavz, *Administration*
Brett Watson, *Administration*
EMP: 60 **EST:** 2007
SALES (est): 5.4MM
SALES (corp-wide): 2.4B **Publicly Held**
WEB: www.camarillohealthcare.com
SIC: 8741 Nursing & personal care facility management
PA: The Ensign Group Inc
29222 Rncho Vejo Rd Ste 1
San Juan Capistrano CA 92675
949 487-9500

(P-22998)
CAMERON ENERGY SERVICES CORP
4040 Capitol Ave, City of Industry (90601-1735)
PHONE..................562 321-9183
Steve Gassen, *President*
Hinda Gharbi, *Director*
Scott Osterling, *Director*
EMP: 68 **EST:** 2019
SALES (est): 6MM **Privately Held**
SIC: 8741 Management services

(P-22999)
CBS TELEVISION DISTRIBUTION
Also Called: CBS Enterprises
2450 Colo Ave Ste 500e, Santa Monica (90404)
PHONE..................310 264-3300
Paul Franklin, *President*
Katina Uribe, *Executive Asst*
Zach Rossi, *Engineer*
Erik Barlow, *Analyst*
Astra Austin, *Producer*
EMP: 69 **EST:** 2010
SQ FT: 20,000
SALES (est): 22.7MM **Privately Held**
WEB: www.cbstvd.com
SIC: 8741 Management services

(P-23000)
CHAN FAMILY PARTNERSHIP LP
801 S Grand Ave Apt 1811, Los Angeles (90017-4673)
PHONE..................626 322-7132
Ann Chan, *Partner*
EMP: 100 **EST:** 2017
SALES (est): 3MM **Privately Held**
SIC: 8741 Restaurant management

(P-23001)
CHARTER MGMT LLC
9660 Haven Ave Ste 203, Rancho Cucamonga (91730-5897)
PHONE..................909 644-4965
Fred Frank, *President*
EMP: 56 **EST:** 2018
SALES (est): 1.2MM **Privately Held**
SIC: 8741 Management services

(P-23002)
CHOOSING INDEPENDENCE INC
7615 Louise Ave, Northridge (91325-4523)
PHONE..................818 257-0323
Christian Richards Jr, *CEO*
EMP: 53 **EST:** 2009
SQ FT: 3,500
SALES (est): 1.7MM **Privately Held**
SIC: 8741 Nursing & personal care facility management

(P-23003)
CITY OF MENIFEE
29844 Haun Rd, Menifee (92586-6539)
PHONE..................951 672-6777
Robert Johnson, *Manager*
Mandy Stephens, *City Mgr*
Carlos Geronimo, *Engineer*
Wendy Preece, *Accounting Mgr*
Daniel Alvarado, *Human Res Dir*
EMP: 90
SALES: 88.7MM **Privately Held**
WEB: www.cityofmenifee.us
SIC: 8741 Personnel management

(P-23004)
CITY OF REDLANDS (PA)
35 Cajon St, Redlands (92373-4746)
P.O. Box 3005 (92373-1505)
PHONE..................909 798-7531
Jon Harrison,

Tina Kundig, *CFO*
Mike Reynolds, *CFO*
Patty Baker, *Admin Asst*
Monica Duran, *Admin Asst*
EMP: 98
SQ FT: 200,000
SALES: 85.4MM **Privately Held**
WEB: www.cityofredlands.org
SIC: 8741 Office management

(P-23005)
COHEN ASSET MANAGEMENT INC (PA)
1900 Avenue Of The Stars # 500, Los Angeles (90067-4301)
P.O. Box 24710 (90024-0710)
PHONE..................310 860-0598
Bradley S Cohen, *CEO*
Jason Haas, *COO*
Brandon Delf, *Ch Invest Ofcr*
Doreen Raigosa, *Exec VP*
Shelley Kodera, *Vice Pres*
EMP: 88 **EST:** 1997
SALES (est): 10.3MM **Privately Held**
WEB: www.cohenasset.com
SIC: 8741 Financial management for business

(P-23006)
COLLECTIVE MGT GROUP LLC
8383 Wilshire Blvd # 1050, Beverly Hills (90211-2425)
PHONE..................323 655-8585
Michael Green, *CEO*
Jordan Toplitzky, *CFO*
Jordan Berliant,
Gary Binkow,
Reza Izad,
EMP: 206 **EST:** 1999
SQ FT: 15,000
SALES (est): 8.9MM **Privately Held**
SIC: 8741 Management services

(P-23007)
COUNTRY VILLA SERVICE CORP (PA)
Also Called: Country Villa Health Services
2400 E Katella Ave # 800, Anaheim (92806-5945)
PHONE..................310 574-3733
Stephen Reissman, *CEO*
Rita Becerra, *Records Dir*
Imelda Gil, *Records Dir*
Connie Mooneyham, *Records Dir*
Radel Pare, *Records Dir*
EMP: 80 **EST:** 1972
SQ FT: 24,000
SALES (est): 78.2MM **Privately Held**
SIC: 8741 Nursing & personal care facility management; hospital management

(P-23008)
COUNTRY VILLA SERVICE CORP
3533 Motor Ave, Los Angeles (90034-4806)
PHONE..................310 574-3733
EMP: 110
SALES (corp-wide): 125.3MM **Privately Held**
SIC: 8741 Management Services
PA: Country Villa Service Corp.
2400 E Katella Ave # 800
Anaheim CA 92806
310 574-3733

(P-23009)
CUMMING - LLC
25220 Hancock Ave Ste 440, Murrieta (92562-0903)
PHONE..................951 252-8555
James Finlay Cumming, *Mng Member*
Alison Allen, *Controller*
EMP: 54 **EST:** 1997
SALES (est): 4.3MM **Privately Held**
WEB: www.cumming-group.com
SIC: 8741 Construction management

(P-23010)
CUMMING MANAGEMENT GROUP INC
27207 Puerta Real, Mission Viejo (92691-7316)
PHONE..................949 900-0440
EMP: 72

SALES (corp-wide): 191.1MM **Privately Held**
SIC: 8741 Construction management
PA: Cumming Management Group, Inc.
25220 Hancock Ave Ste 440
Murrieta CA 92562
858 485-6765

(P-23011)
CUMMING MANAGEMENT GROUP INC
25220 Hancock Ave Ste 440, Murrieta (92562-0903)
PHONE..................415 748-3095
Finlay Cumming, *CEO*
EMP: 72
SALES (corp-wide): 191.1MM **Privately Held**
SIC: 8741 Construction management
PA: Cumming Management Group, Inc.
25220 Hancock Ave Ste 440
Murrieta CA 92562
858 485-6765

(P-23012)
D I F GROUP INC
Also Called: Manufacture
1942 E 46th St, Vernon (90058-2004)
PHONE..................323 231-8800
Angie Kim, *CEO*
EMP: 23 **EST:** 2010
SALES (est): 1.5MM **Privately Held**
SIC: 8741 3161 Management services; clothing & apparel carrying cases

(P-23013)
D7 LLC ✪
Also Called: Dawson D7, LLC
200 Spectrum Center Dr # 12, Irvine (92618-5003)
PHONE..................808 630-9169
Dawna Smith,
EMP: 61 **EST:** 2021
SALES (est): 1.5MM **Privately Held**
SIC: 8741 Construction management

(P-23014)
DAICEL AMERICA HOLDINGS INC
21515 Hawthorne Blvd, Torrance (90503-6501)
PHONE..................480 798-6737
Kenichi Tanaka, *Branch Mgr*
Shu Sasada, *Finance*
EMP: 338 **EST:** 2012
WEB: www.daicelchemtech.com
SIC: 8741 Administrative management
HQ: Daicel America Holdings, Inc.
1 Parker Plz
Fort Lee NJ 07024
201 461-4466

(P-23015)
DENCO OF TEXAS INC (HQ)
Also Called: J'S 7570
8152 Painter Ave, Whittier (90602-3100)
PHONE..................562 777-2249
Gurbax R Marwah, *President*
EMP: 165 **EST:** 2000
SALES: 457.2K
SALES (corp-wide): 28.5MM **Privately Held**
WEB: www.dencofamily.com
SIC: 8741 Restaurant management
PA: Denco Enterprises, Inc.
15051 Leffingwell Rd # 201
Whittier CA 90604
562 777-2249

(P-23016)
DHS CONSULTING LLC
1820 E 1st St Ste 410, Santa Ana (92705-8311)
PHONE..................714 276-1135
Sudhir Damle, *President*
Eric Slaasted, *Senior VP*
Gary Cooley, *Vice Pres*
Hemalata Damle, *Vice Pres*
Lata Damle, *Vice Pres*
EMP: 140 **EST:** 2012
SQ FT: 6,000
SALES (est): 13.9MM
SALES (corp-wide): 36.2MM **Privately Held**
WEB: www.anseradvisory.com
SIC: 8741 Construction management

PA: Anser Advisory, Llc
2677 N Main St Ste 400
Santa Ana CA 92705
310 351-8907

(P-23017)
DIGITAL MEDIA MANAGEMENT INC
5670 Wilshire Blvd Fl 11, Los Angeles (90036-5627)
PHONE....................323 378-6505
Luigi Picarazzi, *Mng Member*
Adam Reynolds, *Vice Pres*
Brittany Rice, *Associate Dir*
Robbie Salapuddin, *Associate Dir*
Shelby Fox, *Comms Dir*
EMP: 65 **EST:** 2011
SALES (est): 7.4MM **Privately Held**
WEB: www.digitalmediamanagement.com
SIC: 8741 Management services

(P-23018)
DIGNITY HLTH MGT SVCS ORGNZTIO
4550 Cal Ave Bkrsfeld Ca, Glendale (91203)
PHONE....................661 716-7100
Michael Myers,
EMP: 50 **EST:** 2016
SALES (est): 2.6MM **Privately Held**
SIC: 8741 Management services

(P-23019)
EDDIE VS WILDFISH NEWPORT BCH (PA)
1370 Bison Ave, Newport Beach (92660-9071)
PHONE....................949 720-9925
Damon Hovannisian, *General Mgr*
Guenevere Wolfe, *General Mgr*
EMP: 92 **EST:** 2005
SALES (est): 4MM **Privately Held**
SIC: 8741 Business management

(P-23020)
EL CAMINO MANAGEMENT COMPANY
136 El Camino Dr, Beverly Hills (90212-2705)
P.O. Box 5275 (90209-5275)
PHONE....................310 276-3154
Richard B Rapozo, *President*
Mary A Masucci, *CFO*
Mary Masucci, *CFO*
Timothy M Doheny, *Vice Pres*
Mary A Masucci, *Vice Pres*
EMP: 62 **EST:** 1945
SQ FT: 1,100
SALES (est): 2.4MM **Privately Held**
WEB: www.151elcamino.com
SIC: 8741 Management services

(P-23021)
EPIC MANAGEMENT LP (PA)
1615 Orange Tree Ln, Redlands (92374-2804)
P.O. Box 19020, San Bernardino (92423-9020)
PHONE....................909 799-1818
John D Goodman, *CEO*
Jennifer Swartz, *CEO*
Lucy Adame, *Officer*
Fred Hollaus, *Officer*
Lisa Smith, *Officer*
EMP: 100 **EST:** 1995
SALES (est): 55.7MM **Privately Held**
WEB: www.epicmanagementlp.com
SIC: 8741 Nursing & personal care facility management

(P-23022)
ETHOS MANAGEMENT INC
560 W Main St, Alhambra (91801-3374)
PHONE....................626 456-3669
Nhac Vy Ngo, *CEO*
EMP: 50 **EST:** 2014
SALES (est): 1.7MM **Privately Held**
SIC: 8741 Management services

(P-23023)
EUREKA RESTAURANT GROUP LLC (PA)
12101 Crenshaw Blvd, Hawthorne (90250-3369)
PHONE....................310 331-8233

Justin Nedelman, *CEO*
Dawn Hernandez, *Vice Pres*
Gina Cariaga, *General Mgr*
Justin Christensen, *General Mgr*
Steve Farmer, *General Mgr*
EMP: 309 **EST:** 2014
SALES (est): 89.4MM **Privately Held**
WEB: www.eurekarestaurantgroup.com
SIC: 5812 8741 Fast-food restaurant, independent; restaurant management

(P-23024)
EVOLUTION HOSPITALITY LLC (HQ)
1211 Puerta Del Sol # 170, San Clemente (92673-6353)
PHONE....................949 325-1350
John Murphy, *President*
William Loughran, *COO*
Romie Mushtaq, *Officer*
Matt Raine, *Exec VP*
Christopher Conrad, *Vice Pres*
EMP: 2549 **EST:** 2010
SALES (est): 82.5MM
SALES (corp-wide): 802.5MM **Privately Held**
WEB: www.evolutionhospitality.com
SIC: 8741 7011 Hotel or motel management; hotels & motels
PA: Aimbridge Hospitality, Llc
5301 Headquarters Dr
Plano TX 75024
972 952-0200

(P-23025)
FINANCIAL GROUP INC
1991 Country Pl, Ojai (93023-4190)
PHONE....................805 646-7974
EMP: 136
SALES (corp-wide): 1.3B **Publicly Held**
WEB: www.securian.com
SIC: 8741 Management services
HQ: The Financial Group Inc
2555 Severn Ave Ste 100
Metairie LA 70002
504 456-0101

(P-23026)
FIRSTSERVICE RESIDENTIAL
3415 S Sepulveda Blvd # 720, Los Angeles (90034-6983)
PHONE....................213 213-0886
Gregg Evangelho, *Branch Mgr*
Amy Mathieson, *Vice Pres*
Danielle Graham, *Executive Asst*
Jose Orozco, *CIO*
Felecia Chambers, *Marketing Staff*
EMP: 72
SALES (corp-wide): 2.4B **Privately Held**
WEB: www.fsresidential.com
SIC: 8741 6531 Business management; real estate managers
HQ: Firstservice Residential
15241 Laguna Canyon Rd
Irvine CA 92618
949 448-6000

(P-23027)
FIRSTSERVICE RESIDENTIAL
43100 Cook St Ste 103, Palm Desert (92211-3124)
PHONE....................760 834-2480
Daniel Farrar, *Branch Mgr*
Wendy Coyne, *Manager*
EMP: 72
SALES (corp-wide): 2.4B **Privately Held**
WEB: www.fsresidential.com
SIC: 8741 6531 Business management; real estate managers
HQ: Firstservice Residential
15241 Laguna Canyon Rd
Irvine CA 92618
949 448-6000

(P-23028)
FRONT LINE MGT GROUP INC
1100 Glendon Ave Ste 2000, Los Angeles (90024-3524)
PHONE....................310 209-3100
Irving Azoff, *President*
EMP: 99 **EST:** 2004
SALES (est): 4.2MM **Publicly Held**
SIC: 8741 Management services

HQ: Flmg Holdings Corp.
9348 Civic Center Dr
Beverly Hills CA 90210
310 867-7000

(P-23029)
FUJITEC AMERICA INC
12170 Mora Dr Ste 1, Santa Fe Springs (90670-7339)
PHONE....................310 464-8270
Timothy Mooney, *Sales/Mktg Mgr*
Sean McMannis, *Manager*
EMP: 95 **Privately Held**
WEB: www.fujitecamerica.com
SIC: 8741 1796 Business management; elevator installation & conversion
HQ: Fujitec America Inc
7258 Innovation Way
Mason OH 45040
513 755-6100

(P-23030)
GHP MANAGEMENT CORPORATION
270 N Canon Dr, Beverly Hills (90210-5323)
PHONE....................310 432-1441
Geoffrey H Palmer, *Branch Mgr*
Uriel Luna, *Controller*
Laura Cruz, *Supervisor*
EMP: 253
SALES (corp-wide): 25.3MM **Privately Held**
WEB: www.ghpmgmt.com
SIC: 8741 Business management
PA: Ghp Management Corporation
1082 W 7th St
Los Angeles CA 90017
213 213-0190

(P-23031)
GONZALEZ MANAGEMENT CO INC
10147 San Fernando Rd, Pacoima (91331-2617)
PHONE....................818 485-0596
Luis Gonzalez, *President*
EMP: 65 **EST:** 2004
SQ FT: 20,000
SALES (est): 3.4MM **Privately Held**
SIC: 8741 Management services

(P-23032)
GREENWOOD HALL INC
6230 Wilshire Blvd # 136, Los Angeles (90048-5126)
PHONE....................310 905-8300
John Hall, *Ch of Bd*
Bill Bradfield, *CEO*
EMP: 111
SALES (est): 7.5MM **Privately Held**
WEB:
www.answerneteducationservices.com
SIC: 8299 8741 8742 7374 Educational services; management services; management consulting services; data processing service; prepackaged software

(P-23033)
GRIMMWAY ENTERPRISES INC
Grimmway Fresh Processing
14141 Di Giorgio Rd, Arvin (93203-9518)
P.O. Box 81498, Bakersfield (93380-1498)
PHONE....................661 854-6200
Jeff Meger, *President*
EMP: 194
SALES (corp-wide): 1.8B **Privately Held**
WEB: www.grimmway.com
SIC: 8741 2099 2037 Management services; food preparations; frozen fruits & vegetables
PA: Grimmway Enterprises, Inc.
14141 Di Giorgio Rd
Arvin CA 93203
800 301-3101

(P-23034)
GUADALUPE UNION SCHOOL DST (PA)
4465 9th St, Guadalupe (93434-1436)
P.O. Box 788 (93434-0788)
PHONE....................805 343-2114
Ed Cora, *Superintendent*
Jeffrey Alvarez, *Principal*
Celia Ramos, *Principal*

Sharon V Gundy, *Administration*
Becky Bendele, *Technician*
EMP: 114
SALES: 19.3MM **Privately Held**
WEB: www.guadusd.org
SIC: 8211 8741 Public elementary school; management services

(P-23035)
HAMMES COMPANY
2 Park Plz Ste 600, Irvine (92614-3517)
PHONE....................949 705-0900
Jim Kobayashi, *Branch Mgr*
EMP: 52 **Privately Held**
WEB: www.hammesco.com
SIC: 8741 Hospital management
PA: Hammes Company
1400 N Water St 500
Milwaukee WI 53202

(P-23036)
HARBOR-UCLA MED FOUNDATION INC (PA)
Also Called: Harbor Ucla Med Foundation
21840 Normandie Ave Ste 1, Torrance (90502-2047)
PHONE....................310 222-5015
Chester Choi, *CEO*
EMP: 100 **EST:** 1967
SQ FT: 45,000
SALES (est): 4.1MM **Privately Held**
WEB: www.harborucladocs.org
SIC: 8741 Hospital management

(P-23037)
HARDLOOP LLC
12301 Wilshire Blvd # 512, Los Angeles (90025-1053)
PHONE....................310 892-4284
Lawrence Genen, *CEO*
EMP: 50 **EST:** 2016
SALES (est): 3.5MM **Privately Held**
SIC: 8741 8011 Hospital management; psychiatric clinic

(P-23038)
HOTCHKIS WILEY CAPITL MGT LLC (PA)
725 S Figueroa St # 3900, Los Angeles (90017-5439)
PHONE....................213 430-1000
George Davis,
Chris Bartolone, *Technology*
Douglas Campbel, *Analyst*
Gail Bardin,
Michael Baxter,
EMP: 143 **EST:** 1980
SQ FT: 12,000
SALES (est): 24.1MM **Privately Held**
WEB: www.hwcm.com
SIC: 8741 6211 Financial management for business; security brokers & dealers

(P-23039)
IKEA PURCHASING SVCS US INC
600 N San Fernando Blvd, Burbank (91502-1021)
PHONE....................818 841-3500
Chris Maynard, *Manager*
EMP: 114
SALES (corp-wide): 120.1K **Privately Held**
WEB: www.ikea.com
SIC: 8741 8721 5712 Administrative management; accounting, auditing & bookkeeping; furniture stores
HQ: Ikea Purchasing Services (Us) Inc.
7810 Katy Fwy
Houston TX 77024

(P-23040)
INVESTORS CAPITAL MGT GROUP
Also Called: Cuisine Partners USA
10390 Santa Monica Blvd, Los Angeles (90025-5058)
PHONE....................310 553-5175
EMP: 277
SQ FT: 7,800
SALES (est): 11MM **Privately Held**
SIC: 8741 Restaurant Management Real Estate Investment Commercial Leasing

(P-23041)
JC RESORTS LLC
Also Called: Surf Sand Hotel
1555 S Coast Hwy, Laguna Beach
(92651-3226)
PHONE....................949 376-2779
Blaise Bartell, *Branch Mgr*
Amy McLimore, *Sales Staff*
Andrew Alicea, *Director*
Joanna Bear, *Director*
EMP: 486 **Privately Held**
WEB: www.jcresorts.com
SIC: 8741 5813 5812 7011 Hotel or
motel management; drinking places; eat-
ing places; hotels
PA: Jc Resorts Llc
533 Coast Blvd S
La Jolla CA 92037

(P-23042)
JIPC MANAGEMENT INC
Also Called: John's Incredible Pizza Co
22342 Avnida Empresa Ste, Rancho Santa
Margari (92688)
PHONE....................949 916-2000
John M Parlet, *President*
Natalie Cervantes, *Admin Asst*
Alice Louie, *Admin Asst*
EMP: 1000 EST: 1998
SALES (est): 36MM **Privately Held**
WEB: www.johnspizza.com
SIC: 8741 Restaurant management

(P-23043)
JPL MANAGEMENT LLC
6427 W Sunset Blvd 101, Los Angeles
(90028-7314)
PHONE....................310 844-3662
Julian Ledesma, *CEO*
EMP: 72 EST: 2018
SALES (est): 2.7MM **Privately Held**
SIC: 8741 8748 Management services;
business consulting

(P-23044)
**JUVENILE JUSTICE DIVISION
CAL**
Also Called: Ventura Yuth Crrctional Fcilty
3100 Wright Rd, Camarillo (93010-8307)
PHONE....................805 485-7951
Vivian Craford, *Superintendent*
Gary Collins, *Principal*
EMP: 190 **Privately Held**
SIC: 8741 9223 Office management;
house of correction, government
HQ: Juvenile Justice Division, California
1515 S St Ste 502s
Sacramento CA 95811

(P-23045)
KEIRO SERVICES
Also Called: Keiro Senior Health Care
420 E 3rd St Ste 1000, Los Angeles
(90013-1648)
PHONE....................213 873-5700
Shawn Miyake, *CEO*
Julie Naito, *Executive Asst*
Lance Maemori, *Chf Purch Ofc*
Audrey Lee-Sung, *Director*
Lauren Yoshiyama, *Associate*
EMP: 500 EST: 1984
SQ FT: 26,000
SALES: 1MM **Privately Held**
SIC: 8741 Nursing & personal care facility
management

(P-23046)
KINTETSU ENTERPRISES
328 E 1st St, Los Angeles (90012-3902)
PHONE....................213 687-2000
EMP: 90
SALES: 5MM
SALES (corp-wide): 11.4B **Privately Held**
WEB: www.miyakoinn.com
SIC: 8741 6531 Management Services
Real Estate Agent/Manager
PA: Kintetsu Group Holdings Co., Ltd.
6-1-55, Uehonmachi, Tennoji-Ku
Osaka OSK 543-0
667 753-355

(P-23047)
LA 1000 SANTA FE LLC
1000 S Santa Fe Ave, Los Angeles
(90021-1741)
PHONE....................213 205-1000
Byron Icute,
EMP: 210 EST: 2019
SALES (est): 6MM **Privately Held**
SIC: 8741 Hotel or motel management

(P-23048)
**LAKESIDE MEDICAL
ASSOCIATES (PA)**
8510 Balboa Blvd Ste 150, Northridge
(91325-5810)
PHONE....................818 637-2000
Richard N Merkin, *President*
April David, *Sr Project Mgr*
EMP: 139 EST: 1993
SALES (est): 3.2MM **Privately Held**
SIC: 8741 Management services

(P-23049)
LAKESIDE SYSTEMS INC
Also Called: Lakeside Medical Systems
8510 Balboa Blvd Ste 150, Northridge
(91325-5810)
PHONE....................866 654-3471
Richard Merkin, *CEO*
Kenneth B Epstein, *Med Doctor*
EMP: 700 EST: 1991
SQ FT: 20,000
SALES (est): 23.5MM
SALES (corp-wide): 38.3MM **Privately
Held**
WEB: www.heritageprovidernetwork.com
SIC: 8741 8742 6411 Management serv-
ices; management consulting services; in-
surance agents, brokers & service
PA: Heritage Provider Network Inc
8510 Balboa Blvd Ste 285
Northridge CA 91325
818 654-3461

(P-23050)
**LEGACY PRTNERS
RESIDENTIAL INC**
5141 California Ave # 100, Irvine
(92617-3060)
PHONE....................949 930-6600
Deborah Dodd, *Branch Mgr*
Erik Hansen, *Manager*
EMP: 328
SALES (corp-wide): 49.6MM **Privately
Held**
WEB: www.legacypartners.com
SIC: 8741 Management services
PA: Legacy Partners Residential, Inc.
950 Tower Ln Ste 900
Foster City CA 94404
650 571-2250

(P-23051)
LEXXIOM INC
99 N San Antonio Ave # 3, Upland
(91786-4575)
PHONE....................909 581-7313
Robert Lemelin, *President*
Brian Lemelin, *COO*
Leo Lemelin, *CFO*
John Lemelin, *Opers Staff*
EMP: 360 EST: 2000
SALES (est): 13.5MM **Privately Held**
WEB: www.lexxiom.com
SIC: 8741 Administrative management

(P-23052)
**LIGHTHOUSE PROPERTY MGT
INC (PA)**
15332 Antioch St 540, Pacific Palisades
(90272-3603)
PHONE....................210 340-7072
Gary Leshgold, *President*
Laurie Dennis, *Finance*
Richard Santilena, *Marketing Staff*
Andrea Hittle, *Manager*
EMP: 86 EST: 1999
SALES (est): 5MM **Privately Held**
WEB: www.lighthousepropertymanage-
ment.com
SIC: 8741 Management services

(P-23053)
**LIVINGSTON MEM VNA HLTH
CORP**
Also Called: Livingston Mem Vsting Nrse Ass
1996 Eastman Ave Ste 101, Ventura
(93003-5768)
PHONE....................805 642-0239
Lanyard K Dial MD, *President*
Charles Hair MD, *Ch of Bd*
Judy Hecox, *President*
Jeffrey Paul, *Treasurer*
Julie Gisler,
EMP: 292 EST: 1947
SQ FT: 12,600
SALES (est): 16.6MM **Privately Held**
WEB: www.lmvna.org
SIC: 8741 8082 Hospital management;
nursing & personal care facility manage-
ment; home health care services

(P-23054)
LOS ANGELES RAMS LLC
Also Called: La Rams Football Club
10271 W Pico Blvd, Los Angeles
(90064-2606)
P.O. Box 69216, West Hollywood (90069-
0216)
PHONE....................310 277-4700
John Shaw, *Principal*
Marissa Daly, *Vice Pres*
Marty Turman, *Vice Pres*
Lexi Vonderlieth, *Vice Pres*
Ted Monago, *Admin Sec*
EMP: 81
SALES (corp-wide): 63.3MM **Privately
Held**
WEB: www.therams.com
SIC: 8741 7941 Administrative manage-
ment; football club
PA: The Los Angeles Rams Llc
29899 Agoura Rd
Agoura Hills CA 91301
314 982-7267

(P-23055)
**LOS ANGELES UNIFIED
SCHOOL DST**
1406 S Highland Ave, Los Angeles
(90019-4221)
PHONE....................323 549-2018
Geoffrey Smith, *Director*
Michael Pena, *Technician*
Steve Burkenheim, *Supervisor*
EMP: 53
SALES (corp-wide): 9.3B **Privately Held**
WEB: www.laallcityband.com
SIC: 8211 8741 Public elementary & sec-
ondary schools; management services
PA: Los Angeles Unified School District
333 S Beaudry Ave Ste 209
Los Angeles CA 90017
213 241-1000

(P-23056)
**LOWE ENTERPRISES RLTY
SVCS INC (HQ)**
11777 San Vicente Blvd, Los Angeles
(90049-5011)
PHONE....................310 820-6661
Robert J Lowe, *President*
Peter R O'Keeffe, *Senior VP*
Bobbi Newell, *Vice Pres*
Peter R O 'keeffe, *Vice Pres*
EMP: 396 EST: 1974
SQ FT: 12,000
SALES (est): 5.3MM
SALES (corp-wide): 935.4MM **Privately
Held**
WEB: www.lowe-re.com
SIC: 8741 6531 Financial management for
business; real estate managers
PA: Lowe Enterprises, Inc.
11777 San Vicente Blvd # 900
Los Angeles CA 90049
310 820-6661

(P-23057)
**LZ MANAGEMENT GROUP LLC
(PA)**
3680 Wilshire Blvd # 206, Los Angeles
(90010-2707)
PHONE....................213 383-4800
Peter Lee, *Mng Member*
MEI Xi Zhang,
EMP: 55 EST: 2016

SALES (est): 16.3MM **Privately Held**
SIC: 8741 Management services

(P-23058)
**MAGGZ ADULT BUDDY CARE
LLC**
5850 Canoga Ave, Woodland Hills
(91367-6505)
PHONE....................818 396-3338
Amia Delaney, *CEO*
EMP: 50 EST: 2008
SALES (est): 1.6MM **Privately Held**
WEB: www.maggzbuddycare.com
SIC: 8741 Nursing & personal care facility
management

(P-23059)
**MASSACHUSETTS ELECTRIC
COMPANY**
1925 Wright Ave Ste C, La Verne
(91750-5847)
PHONE....................909 962-6001
EMP: 80
SALES (corp-wide): 20.8B **Privately Held**
SIC: 8741 Construction management
HQ: Massachusetts Electric Company
40 Sylvan Rd
Waltham MA 02451
781 907-1000

(P-23060)
MEDICAL NETWORK INC
Also Called: MBC Systems
1809 E Dyer Rd Ste 311, Santa Ana
(92705-5740)
PHONE....................949 863-0022
David Conrad, *President*
Davin Huch, *Info Tech Mgr*
Erica Weinstein-Galve, *Opers Staff*
Kimmie Le, *Director*
Tammy Poliquin, *Manager*
EMP: 80 EST: 1993
SQ FT: 3,500
SALES (est): 9.9MM **Privately Held**
WEB: www.mbcsystems.com
SIC: 8741 Hospital management; nursing
& personal care facility management

(P-23061)
**MENIFEE UNION SCHOOL
DISTRICT (PA)**
29775 Haun Rd, Sun City (92586-6540)
PHONE....................951 672-1851
Pam Gillette, *Director*
Rosemeri Rund, *Admin Sec*
Jeff McKaughan, *Network Enginr*
Regina Hanson, *Business Mgr*
Maria Carpenter, *Personnel*
EMP: 71 EST: 1951
SALES: 135.4MM **Privately Held**
SIC: 8211 8741 Public elementary & sec-
ondary schools; management services

(P-23062)
**MENTOR MDIA USA SUP CHAIN
MGT**
865 S Washington Ave, San Bernardino
(92408-2237)
PHONE....................909 930-0800
Kok Khoon Lim, *CEO*
Lizeth Villa, *Program Mgr*
Leslie Pantaleon, *Finance Asst*
Amy Tang, *Accountant*
Gregory Puetz, *Manager*
▲ EMP: 80 EST: 2008
SALES (est): 27.1MM
SALES (corp-wide): 7.3B **Privately Held**
WEB: www.mentormedia.com
SIC: 8741 8742 Business management;
business planning & organizing services
HQ: Mentor Media Ltd
47 Jalan Buroh
Singapore 61949

(P-23063)
MGT INDUSTRIES INC
19034 S Vermont Ave, Gardena
(90248-4412)
PHONE....................310 324-3152
EMP: 79
SALES (corp-wide): 25.4K **Privately Held**
WEB: www.mgtind.com
SIC: 8741 Management Services

PRODUCTS & SVCS

PA: Mgt Industries, Inc.
13889 S Figueroa St
Los Angeles CA 90061
310 516-5900

(P-23064)
MIG MANAGEMENT SERVICES LLC
660 Newport Center Dr, Newport Beach (92660-6401)
PHONE............949 474-5800
Paul Merage
EMP: 80 **EST:** 2010
SALES (est): 11.8MM
SALES (corp-wide): 38.6MM **Privately Held**
WEB: www.migcap.com
SIC: 8741 Management services
PA: Mig Capital, Llc
660 Newport Center Dr # 450
Newport Beach CA 92660
949 474-5800

(P-23065)
MIKE ROVNER CONSTRUCTION INC
22600 Lambert St, Lake Forest (92630-6201)
PHONE............949 458-1562
Mike Rovner, *Branch Mgr*
EMP: 126 **Privately Held**
WEB: www.rovnerconstruction.com
SIC: 8741 1522 1521 Construction management; residential construction; single-family housing construction
PA: Mike Rovner Construction, Inc.
5400 Tech Cir
Moorpark CA 93021

(P-23066)
MIMG MEDICAL MANAGEMENT LLC
26522 La Alameda Ste 120, Mission Viejo (92691-6330)
PHONE............949 282-1600
EMP: 60
SQ FT: 1,800
SALES (est): 2.6MM **Privately Held**
SIC: 8741 Medical Office Management

(P-23067)
MONTAGE HOTELS & RESORTS LLC
Also Called: Montage Laguna Beach
30801 Coast Hwy, Laguna Beach (92651-4221)
PHONE............949 715-6000
Alan Fuerstman, *CEO*
Bill Blaypool, *Vice Pres*
Becky Hinton, *Admin Sec*
Jamie Oakley, *Sales Mgr*
Mauricio Souza, *Director*
EMP: 600
SALES (corp-wide): 110.6MM **Privately Held**
WEB: www.montagehotels.com
SIC: 8741 7011 5813 5812 Hotel or motel management; hotels; drinking places; eating places
PA: Montage Hotels & Resorts, Llc
3 Ada Ste 100
Irvine CA 92618
949 715-5002

(P-23068)
MORGNER TECHNOLOGY MANAGEMENT
Also Called: Morgner Construction MGT
1880 Century Park E # 1402, Los Angeles (90067-1630)
PHONE............323 900-0030
Monique Morgner, *CEO*
Andrea D'Alfonso, *COO*
Chris Josefowski, *VP Engrg*
Andrew Dalfonso, *Project Mgr*
Walter Contreras, *VP Opers*
EMP: 68 **EST:** 1992
SALES (est): 5MM **Privately Held**
WEB: www.morgnerco.com
SIC: 8741 Construction management

(P-23069)
MTC FINANCIAL INC
Also Called: Trustee Corps
17100 Gillette Ave, Irvine (92614-5603)
PHONE............949 252-8300
Rande Johnsen, *CEO*
Alan Burton, *President*
Cathe Cole-Sherburn, *Vice Pres*
Victor Hutchins, *Vice Pres*
Robert Ruelas, *Vice Pres*
EMP: 78 **EST:** 1992
SALES (est): 18.3MM **Privately Held**
WEB: www.trusteecorps.com
SIC: 8741 Management services

(P-23070)
NAVIGANT CYMETRIX CORPORATION
1515 W 190th St Ste 350, Gardena (90248-4910)
PHONE............424 201-6300
Jeff Macdonald, *Branch Mgr*
Karen Ladika, *Principal*
EMP: 74 **Privately Held**
WEB: www.navigantcymetrix.com
SIC: 8741 Management services
HQ: Navigant Cymetrix Corporation
1 Park Plz Ste 1050
Irvine CA 92614
714 361-6800

(P-23071)
NAVIGATORS MANAGEMENT CO INC
19100 Von Karman Ave, Irvine (92612-1539)
PHONE............949 255-4860
EMP: 60 **Publicly Held**
SIC: 8741 Management services
HQ: Navigators Management Company, Inc.
6 International Dr # 100
Port Chester NY 10573
412 995-2255

(P-23072)
NELSON BROS PROPERTY MGT INC
Also Called: Nelson Brothers Property MGT
16b Journey Ste 200, Aliso Viejo (92656-3317)
PHONE............949 916-7300
Patrick Nelson, *President*
Jacob Benitez, *Vice Pres*
Rachelle Dow, *Vice Pres*
Carly Shepherd, *Vice Pres*
Paris Watson, *Vice Pres*
EMP: 134 **EST:** 2007
SALES (est): 6.5MM **Privately Held**
WEB: www.nelson-brothers.com
SIC: 8741 Management services

(P-23073)
NETWORK MANAGEMENT GROUP INC (PA)
1100 S Flower St Ste 3110, Los Angeles (90015-2287)
PHONE............323 263-2632
John Park, *President*
EMP: 160 **EST:** 1997
SQ FT: 2,039
SALES (est): 9.1MM **Privately Held**
SIC: 8741 8742 Business management; management consulting services

(P-23074)
NETWORK MEDICAL MANAGEMENT INC
1668 S Grfeld Ave Ste 100, Alhambra (91801)
PHONE............626 282-0288
Thomas Lam MD, *Co-CEO*
Gary Augusta, *President*
Hing Ang, *COO*
Mihir Shah, *CFO*
Warren Hosseinion MD, *Co-CEO*
EMP: 130 **EST:** 1994
SQ FT: 14,000
SALES (est): 15MM **Publicly Held**
WEB:
www.networkmedicalmanagement.com
SIC: 8741 Hospital management; nursing & personal care facility management

PA: Apollo Medical Holdings, Inc.
1668 S Garfield Ave Fl 2
Alhambra CA 91801

(P-23075)
NORTH AMERICAN CLIENT SVCS INC (PA)
25910 Acero Ste 350, Mission Viejo (92691-7908)
PHONE............949 240-2423
John L Sorensen, *Ch of Bd*
Timothy J Paulsen, *CEO*
Tim Paulson, *CFO*
Donald G Laws, *Chairman*
Victor Lundquist, *Officer*
▲ **EMP:** 175 **EST:** 1989
SALES (est): 48.3MM **Privately Held**
WEB: www.nahci.com
SIC: 8741 Nursing & personal care facility management

(P-23076)
NORTH AMERICAN MED MGT CAL INC (DH)
3281 E Guasti Rd Fl 7, Ontario (91761-7622)
PHONE............909 605-8000
Richard A Shinto MD, *CEO*
Glen Marconcini, *Exec VP*
Trisha L Daniels, *Vice Pres*
Don Thompson, *Vice Pres*
Mollie Van Hofwegen, *Executive Asst*
EMP: 75 **EST:** 1995
SALES (est): 16.4MM **Privately Held**
WEB: www.nammcal.com
SIC: 8741 Nursing & personal care facility management

(P-23077)
OAKWOOD WORLDWIDE LLC (DH)
1 World Trade Ctr # 2400, Long Beach (90831-2400)
PHONE............877 902-0832
Christopher Ahearn, *CEO*
Mandeep Singh, *COO*
Justin Pateman, *CFO*
Rebecca Tann, *Senior VP*
Rick Villarreal, *Senior VP*
EMP: 151 **EST:** 2014
SALES (est): 29.9MM **Privately Held**
WEB: www.oakwood.com
SIC: 8741 6411 Business management; insurance agents, brokers & service

(P-23078)
ONNI PROPERTIES LLC
Also Called: Level Furnished Living
888 S Olive St, Los Angeles (90014-3006)
PHONE............213 568-0278
Javier Sepeda, *General Mgr*
Colin Daley, *Exec Dir*
Julia Oletskaya, *Opers Staff*
Kaitlynn Nelson, *Agent*
Felipe Velez, *Agent*
EMP: 206
SALES (corp-wide): 40MM **Privately Held**
WEB: www.onni.com
SIC: 8741 Business management
PA: Onni Properties Llc
5055 N 32nd St
Phoenix AZ 85018
602 595-4810

(P-23079)
ONTRAPORT INC
2040 Alameda Padre Serra, Santa Barbara (93103-1760)
PHONE............805 568-1424
Landon Ray, *CEO*
Lena Requist, *COO*
Angela Fornelli, *Vice Pres*
Casey Hill, *Executive*
Laura Casanova, *Creative Dir*
EMP: 122 **EST:** 2012
SQ FT: 35,000
SALES (est): 18.8MM **Privately Held**
WEB: www.ontraport.com
SIC: 8741 Business management

(P-23080)
OREQ CORPORATION
Also Called: Pool Pals Division
42306 Remington Ave, Temecula (92590-2512)
PHONE............951 296-5076
Jess L Hetzner, *CEO*
Megan Lohre, *COO*
Ron Hetzner, *Exec VP*
Sandra Estrella, *Analyst*
Eric Richardson, *Purch Mgr*
▲ **EMP:** 82 **EST:** 1999
SALES (est): 12.7MM **Privately Held**
WEB: www.oreqcorp.com
SIC: 8741 5941 5091 Business management; water sport equipment; spa equipment & supplies

(P-23081)
OWEN GROUP LIMITED PARTNERSHIP (HQ)
Also Called: Owen Design Group
600 N Rosemead Blvd # 205, Pasadena (91107-2153)
PHONE............800 600-6936
Michael Chegini, *President*
Richard Henrickson, *Vice Pres*
Sholeh Noori, *Admin Sec*
Nader Namdar, *Engineer*
Desirae Walton, *Client Mgr*
EMP: 61 **EST:** 2003
SQ FT: 7,000
SALES (est): 12.3MM
SALES (corp-wide): 247.4MM **Privately Held**
WEB: www.owengroup.com
SIC: 8741 8712 8711 8742 Construction management; architectural services; engineering services; management consulting services
PA: Bureau Veritas
40 52 Immeuble Newtime
Neuilly Sur Seine 92200
155 230-200

(P-23082)
PACIFIC GARDENS MED CTR LLC
21530 Pioneer Blvd, Hawaiian Gardens (90716-2608)
PHONE............562 860-0401
Gurpreet Singh,
EMP: 250 **EST:** 2017
SALES (est): 21.6MM **Privately Held**
SIC: 8741 Hospital management

(P-23083)
PACIFIC LIFE FUND ADVISORS LLC
Pacific Asset Management
700 Newport Center Dr, Newport Beach (92660-6307)
PHONE............949 260-9000
Rex Olson, *Principal*
Michael Marzouk, *Managing Dir*
Karen Martin, *Opers Staff*
Scott Goldberg, *Director*
Claudia Flores, *Associate*
EMP: 554
SALES (corp-wide): 12.8B **Privately Held**
SIC: 8741 Financial management for business
HQ: Pacific Life Fund Advisors Llc
700 Newport Center Dr
Newport Beach CA 92660

(P-23084)
PACIFIC VENTURES LTD
Also Called: Jacmar Companies, The
2200 W Valley Blvd, Alhambra (91803-1928)
PHONE............626 576-0737
William H Tilley, *CEO*
Jim Dalpozzo, *President*
Randy Hill, *Exec VP*
EMP: 250 **EST:** 1976
SQ FT: 20,000
SALES (est): 6.6MM **Privately Held**
SIC: 8741 6722 Restaurant management; management investment, open-end

(P-23085)
PAMA MANAGEMENT CO
123 N Inez St Ste 16, Hemet (92543-4169)
PHONE..................................951 929-0340
EMP: 50
SALES (est): 2.4MM **Privately Held**
SIC: 8741 Management Services

(P-23086)
PARSONS CONSTRUCTORS INC
100 W Walnut St, Pasadena (91124-0001)
PHONE..................................626 440-2000
Chuck Harrington, *CEO*
Daryl Anderson, *CFO*
Thomas Peterson, *Treasurer*
Thomas E Barron, *Exec VP*
Virginia Grebbien, *Exec VP*
EMP: 1573 EST: 1978
SALES: 6.7MM
SALES (corp-wide): 3.9B **Publicly Held**
WEB: www.parsons.com
SIC: 8741 8711 Management services;
engineering services
PA: The Parsons Corporation
5875 Trinity Pkwy Ste 300
Centreville VA 20120
703 988-8500

(P-23087)
PATHWAY CAPITAL MANAGEMENT LP (PA)
18575 Jamboree Rd Ste 700, Irvine
(92612-2546)
PHONE..................................949 622-1000
Milt M Best,
Vincent Dee, *COO*
Curt Gerlach, *CFO*
Ben Dreyer, *Senior VP*
Adam A Belkairous, *Vice Pres*
EMP: 99 EST: 2003
SQ FT: 13,302
SALES (est): 21.4MM **Privately Held**
WEB:
www.pathwaycapitalmanagement.com
SIC: 8741 6282 Financial management for
business; investment advice

(P-23088)
PIPELINE GROUP LLC
2850 Redhill Ave Ste 110, Santa Ana
(92705-5537)
PHONE..................................949 296-8375
David Sundling, *CEO*
Raju Patel, *Admin Sec*
Deepak Khillare, *Sr Software Eng*
Chris Texter, *Consultant*
EMP: 199 EST: 2011
SALES (est): 1.1MM
SALES (corp-wide): 43.9MM **Privately Held**
WEB: www.prometheusgroup.com
SIC: 8741 Management services
HQ: Pegasus Sub-Intermediate Corp
1 Letterman Dr Bldg C
San Francisco CA 94129
919 378-2215

(P-23089)
PRIMARY PROVIDER MGT CO INC (PA)
Also Called: Ppmc
2115 Compton Ave Ste 301, Corona
(92881-7272)
PHONE..................................951 280-7700
Robert Dukes, *CEO*
Maureen B Tyson, *President*
Sara Williams, *Exec Dir*
Michael Gann, *Finance*
Ranji Somaweera, *Controller*
EMP: 90 EST: 1983
SQ FT: 23,500
SALES (est): 16MM **Privately Held**
SIC: 8741 Business management

(P-23090)
PROACTIVE RISK MANAGEMENT INC
22617 Hawthorne Blvd, Torrance
(90505-2510)
PHONE..................................213 840-8856
Benoit Grenier, *CEO*
Marielle Morin, *Director*
EMP: 100 EST: 2014

SALES (est): 15MM **Privately Held**
WEB: www.parminc.com
SIC: 8741 Business management

(P-23091)
PROFESSIONAL COMMUNITY MGT CAL
Also Called: Pcm
23081 Via Campo Verde, Aliso Viejo
(92656)
PHONE..................................949 380-0725
Richard Lee, *Branch Mgr*
EMP: 159
SALES (corp-wide): 51.5MM **Privately Held**
WEB: www.pcminternet.com
SIC: 8741 6519 Business management;
real property lessors
PA: Professional Community Management
Of California, Inc.
27051 Twne Cntre Dr Ste 2
Foothill Ranch CA 92610
800 369-7260

(P-23092)
PROSPECT MEDICAL GROUP INC (HQ)
1920 E 17th St Ste 200, Santa Ana
(92705-8626)
PHONE..................................714 796-5900
Jacob Y Terner MD, *President*
Mitchell Lew, *CEO*
Mike Heather, *CFO*
Stewart Kahn, *Admin Sec*
EMP: 350 EST: 1986
SQ FT: 2,420
SALES (est): 48.2MM
SALES (corp-wide): 3.4B **Privately Held**
WEB: www.prospectmedical.com
SIC: 8741 Hospital management; nursing
& personal care facility management
PA: Prospect Medical Holdings, Inc.
3415 S Sepulveda Blvd # 9
Los Angeles CA 90034
310 943-4500

(P-23093)
PROSPECT MEDICAL SYSTEMS INC (HQ)
Also Called: Genesis Health Care
600 City Pkwy W Ste 800, Orange
(92868-2948)
PHONE..................................714 667-8156
Mitchell Lew MD, *CEO*
Brice Keyser, *Surgery Dir*
Maria Salalac, *Technology*
Caryn Loomis, *Human Resources*
Mayo Steigler, *Director*
EMP: 179 EST: 1996
SALES (est): 28.5MM
SALES (corp-wide): 3.4B **Privately Held**
WEB: www.prospectmedical.com
SIC: 8741 Hospital management; nursing
& personal care facility management
PA: Prospect Medical Holdings, Inc.
3415 S Sepulveda Blvd # 9
Los Angeles CA 90034
310 943-4500

(P-23094)
PROVIDENT FINANCIAL MANAGEMENT
3130 Wilshire Blvd # 600, Santa Monica
(90403-2349)
P.O. Box 4084 (90411-4084)
PHONE..................................310 282-0477
Ivan Axelrod, *Managing Prtnr*
Barry Siegel, *Partner*
Rosa Grimes, *Business Mgr*
Nastaran Biglari, *Accountant*
Morgan Reid, *Bookkeeper*
EMP: 95 EST: 1981
SQ FT: 34,000
SALES (est): 2.6MM **Privately Held**
WEB: www.providentfm.com
SIC: 8741 Financial management for business

(P-23095)
QIC US MANAGEMENT INC (HQ)
222 N Pacific Coast Hwy, El Segundo
(90245-5648)
PHONE..................................310 955-1670
Damien Frawley, *CEO*
David Clarke, *Officer*

John Alderson, *Vice Pres*
Stacey Paluf, *Vice Pres*
Nicholas Pribuss, *Vice Pres*
EMP: 114 EST: 2012
SALES (est): 25.9MM **Privately Held**
WEB: www.qic.com.au
SIC: 8741 Business management

(P-23096)
RAYMOND GROUP (PA)
Also Called: Orange Cnty George M Raymond N
520 W Walnut Ave, Orange (92868-5008)
PHONE..................................714 771-7670
Travis Winsor, *CEO*
James Watson, *President*
Tom Obrien, *Treasurer*
Mary Raymond, *Corp Secy*
Kendra Eilers, *Vice Pres*
EMP: 95 EST: 1955
SQ FT: 20,000
SALES (est): 36.9MM **Privately Held**
WEB: www.raymondgroup.com
SIC: 8741 Construction management

(P-23097)
RED DOG MANAGEMENT INC (PA)
Also Called: Lucky Dog AG Services
2240 A St, Santa Maria (93455-1008)
P.O. Box 6808 (93456-6808)
PHONE..................................805 925-1414
Gregory James France, *CEO*
EMP: 111 EST: 2004
SALES (est): 2MM **Privately Held**
WEB: www.reddogmgmnt.com
SIC: 8741 Management services

(P-23098)
RELOCITY INC
10250 Constellation Blvd, Los Angeles
(90067-6200)
PHONE..................................323 207-9160
Klaus Siegmann, *CEO*
EMP: 120 EST: 2016
SQ FT: 800
SALES (est): 17.4MM **Privately Held**
WEB: www.relocity.com
SIC: 8741 Management services

(P-23099)
RENOVO SOLUTIONS LLC
4 Executive Cir Ste 185, Irvine
(92614-6791)
PHONE..................................714 599-7969
Sandy Morford, *CEO*
Haresh Saitiani, *COO*
Fernando Castorena, *CFO*
Don Carson, *Exec VP*
Donald K Carson, *Vice Pres*
EMP: 300 EST: 2009
SQ FT: 5,400
SALES (est): 73MM **Privately Held**
WEB: www.renovo1.com
SIC: 8741 Hospital management

(P-23100)
RHS CORP
Also Called: Redlands Community Hospital
350 Terracina Blvd, Redlands
(92373-4850)
PHONE..................................909 335-5500
James R Holmes, *President*
Tony Lerner, *Vice Pres*
James Agee, *Urology*
Bruce Meyer, *Med Doctor*
EMP: 1450 EST: 1985
SQ FT: 265.000
SALES (est): 416.6K **Privately Held**
WEB: www.redlandshospital.org
SIC: 8741 Hospital management

(P-23101)
RIALTO UNIFIED SCHOOL DISTRICT
Also Called: Maintnc/Pration/Transportation
625 W Rialto Ave, Rialto (92376-5749)
PHONE..................................909 820-7864
Karl Carlson, *Manager*
EMP: 67
SALES (corp-wide): 381.1MM **Privately Held**
WEB: www.rialto-ca.schoolloop.com
SIC: 8211 8741 7349 Public elementary &
secondary schools; management services; building maintenance services

PA: Rialto Unified School District
182 E Walnut Ave
Rialto CA 92376
909 820-7700

(P-23102)
ROCKPORT ADM SVCS LLC (PA)
Also Called: Rockport Healthcare Services
5900 Wilshire Blvd # 1600, Los Angeles
(90036-5016)
PHONE..................................323 330-6500
Vincent S Hambright, *CEO*
Brad Gibson, *CFO*
Michael Wasserman, *Chief Mktg Ofcr*
Janet Stone, *Vice Pres*
Rene Swoc, *Vice Pres*
EMP: 75 EST: 2010
SALES (est): 32.2MM **Privately Held**
SIC: 8741 Administrative management

(P-23103)
SAGA KAPITAL GROUP INC
108 Saybrook, Irvine (92620-7307)
PHONE..................................714 294-4132
Ashish Kapoor, *CEO*
EMP: 75 EST: 2019
SALES (est): 5.2MM **Privately Held**
WEB: www.sagakgi.com
SIC: 8741 Business management

(P-23104)
SANCTUS LLC
Also Called: Shift Digital
250 Broadway St, Laguna Beach
(92651-1807)
PHONE..................................248 594-2396
Michael Romano, *President*
Bianca Golani, *Program Mgr*
Justin Jaroh, *Business Anlyst*
Evan Kneisel, *Technical Staff*
Kristine Walker, *Technical Staff*
EMP: 140 **Privately Held**
WEB: www.shiftdigital.com
SIC: 8741 Management services
PA: Sanctus Llc
348 E Maple Rd
Birmingham MI 48009

(P-23105)
SANTA CLRITA HLTH CARE ASSN IN (PA)
23845 Mcbean Pkwy, Santa Clarita
(91355-2001)
PHONE..................................661 253-8000
Roger Seaver, *President*
Paul Salomon, *COO*
C R Hudson, *CFO*
James D Hicken, *Treasurer*
John Barstis, *Admin Sec*
EMP: 65 EST: 1975
SQ FT: 130,000
SALES (est): 50.5MM **Privately Held**
WEB: www.henrymayo.com
SIC: 8741 Hospital management; nursing
& personal care facility management

(P-23106)
SEABREEZE MANAGEMENT CO INC (PA)
26840 Aliso Viejo Pkwy, Aliso Viejo
(92656-2624)
PHONE..................................949 855-1800
Isaiah S Henry, *CEO*
Karen Inman, *President*
Brandon Tryon, *Exec VP*
Robert Curran, *Vice Pres*
Eron Kaylor, *Vice Pres*
EMP: 69 EST: 1987
SQ FT: 22,000
SALES (est): 32.8MM **Privately Held**
WEB: www.seabreezemgmt.com
SIC: 8741 Management services

(P-23107)
SIERRA CORPORATE MGT INC (PA)
320 N Park Vista St, Anaheim
(92806-3722)
PHONE..................................714 575-5130
Abraham Arrigopti, *Principal*
Clark Kessia, *Regional Mgr*
Sunny Kwon, *Regional Mgr*
Ericka Rodriguez, *Regional Mgr*
Manuel Salinas, *Regional Mgr*

EMP: 61 EST: 2003
SALES (est): 5MM **Privately Held**
WEB:
www.sierracorporatemanagement.com
SIC: 8741 Management services

(P-23108)
SIGMA FACTION INC
31681 Riverside Dr, Lake Elsinore
(92530-7815)
PHONE..................................951 416-0961
Andrew James, *Principal*
Juan Gonzalez, *Principal*
EMP: 50 EST: 2020
SALES (est): 1.3MM **Privately Held**
SIC: 8741 Management services

(P-23109)
SMILE BRANDS GROUP INC (PA)
Also Called: Bright Now Dental
100 Spectrum Center Dr # 100, Irvine
(92618-4963)
PHONE..................................714 668-1300
Steven C Bilt, *CEO*
Stan Andrakowicz, *President*
Judy Burke, *President*
Alan J Acierno, *COO*
Bradley Schmidt, *CFO*
EMP: 90 EST: 1978
SQ FT: 15,000
SALES (est): 335MM **Privately Held**
WEB: www.smilebrands.com
SIC: 8741 8021 Management services;
dental clinics & offices

(P-23110)
SMITH BROADCASTING GROUP INC (PA)
2315 Red Rose Way, Santa Barbara
(93109-1259)
PHONE..................................805 965-0400
Debrah Egar, *Exec Sec*
David A Fitz, *Vice Pres*
EMP: 165 EST: 1985
SALES (est): 15.2MM **Privately Held**
SIC: 8741 8742 Business management;
management consulting services

(P-23111)
SMITH BROTHERS RESTAURANT INC
100 Corson St Lbby, Pasadena
(91103-3854)
PHONE..................................626 577-2400
Robert Smith, *President*
Greg Smith, *Admin Sec*
EMP: 55 EST: 1997
SALES (est): 3.3MM **Privately Held**
WEB: www.smithbrothersrestaurants.com
SIC: 8741 8742 8721 Restaurant man-
agement; management consulting serv-
ices; accounting, auditing & bookkeeping

(P-23112)
SNF MANAGEMENT
9200 W Sunset Blvd # 700, West Holly-
wood (90069-3502)
PHONE..................................310 385-1090
Lee Samson, *President*
Ken Cess, *Shareholder*
Zev Tyner, *Director*
EMP: 79 EST: 2010
SALES (est): 13MM **Privately Held**
WEB: www.windsorcares.com
SIC: 8741 Management services

(P-23113)
SOUTH COAST PLAZA SECURITY
695 Town Center Dr Ste 50, Costa Mesa
(92626-1924)
PHONE..................................714 435-2180
Craig Farrow, *Manager*
Curtis Cienfuegos, *Security Mgr*
EMP: 120 EST: 1989
SALES (est): 2.9MM **Privately Held**
WEB: www.southcoastplaza.com
SIC: 8741 Management services

(P-23114)
SOUTHERN CALIFORNIA EDISON CO
Also Called: N Trans/Sub Regional Office
28250 Gateway Village Dr, Valencia
(91355-1177)
PHONE..................................661 607-0207
EMP: 121
SALES (corp-wide): 13.5B **Publicly Held**
WEB: www.sce.com
SIC: 8741 Business management
HQ: Southern California Edison Company
2244 Walnut Grove Ave
Rosemead CA 91770
626 302-1212

(P-23115)
SOUTHERN IMPLANTS INC
5 Holland Ste 209, Irvine (92618-2576)
PHONE..................................949 273-8505
Michael Kehoe, *President*
Michael Nealon, *CFO*
Sue Odendaal, *Sales Mgr*
EMP: 125 EST: 2007
SALES (est): 5.2MM **Privately Held**
WEB: www.southernimplantsinc.com
SIC: 8741 Management services

(P-23116)
SPEARMINT RHINO CMPNIES WRLDWI
1875 Tandem, Norco (92860-3606)
PHONE..................................951 371-3788
Dyanna Gray, *CEO*
Kathy Vercher, *President*
Dena Hernandez, *CFO*
Andrew Boyd, *Vice Pres*
Kathy McDonald, *Vice Pres*
EMP: 91 EST: 1996
SQ FT: 5,000
SALES (est): 11MM **Privately Held**
WEB: www.spearmintrhino.com
SIC: 8741 Business management

(P-23117)
STAN TASHMAN & ASSOCIATES INC
8675 Wash Blvd Ste 203, Culver City
(90232-7486)
PHONE..................................310 460-7600
Richard Tashman, *CEO*
Stan Tashman, *CFO*
Tyler Olson, *Exec VP*
Ty Olson, *Vice Pres*
Megha Gore, *Administration*
EMP: 69 EST: 1961
SQ FT: 14,000
SALES (est): 6.4MM **Privately Held**
WEB: www.tashman.com
SIC: 8741 Management services

(P-23118)
SUNAMERICA INVESTMENTS INC (DH)
1 Sun America Ctr Fl 37, Los Angeles
(90067-6100)
PHONE..................................310 772-6000
Eli Broad, *President*
EMP: 80 EST: 1978
SQ FT: 76,000
SALES (est): 42.4MM
SALES (corp-wide): 43.7B **Publicly Held**
WEB: www.lifeandretirement.aig.com
SIC: 8741 6211 6282 7311 Administrative
management; financial management for
business; security brokers & dealers; in-
vestment advisory service; advertising
agencies
HQ: Sunamerica Inc.
1 Sun America Ctr Fl 38
Los Angeles CA 90067
310 772-6000

(P-23119)
SYLMARK INC (PA)
Also Called: Sylmark Group
7821 Orion Ave Ste 200, Van Nuys
(91406-2032)
PHONE..................................818 217-2000
Peter Spiegel, *President*
Mark Funk, *CFO*
Steven Ober, *Vice Pres*
EMP: 90 EST: 1998

SALES (est): 20.3MM **Privately Held**
WEB: www.sylmark.com
SIC: 8741 Management services

(P-23120)
SYNTIRO HEALTHCARE SERVICES (PA)
Also Called: Physician Weblink MGT Svcs
7 Technology Dr, Irvine (92618-2302)
PHONE..................................949 923-3438
Breaux Castleman, *CEO*
William S Bernstein, *Partner*
Richard Greene, *CFO*
EMP: 86 EST: 1995
SALES (est): 14MM **Privately Held**
SIC: 8741 Hospital management; nursing
& personal care facility management

(P-23121)
TCT MOBILE INC
25 Edelman Ste 200, Irvine (92618-4359)
PHONE..................................949 892-2990
Xin Zhang, *President*
Juanjuan Feng, *CFO*
Qian Wen, *Admin Sec*
EMP: 100 EST: 2008
SALES (est): 16.7MM **Privately Held**
WEB: www.us.alcatelmobile.com
SIC: 8741 8711 7389 8721 Management
services; engineering services; financial
services; accounting, auditing & book-
keeping
HQ: Tcl Communication Technology Hold-
ings Limited
C/O: Conyers Trust Company (Cay-
man) Limited
George Town GR CAYMAN

(P-23122)
TEAM GROUP LLC
4076 Flat Rock Dr, Riverside (92505-5858)
PHONE..................................951 688-8593
EMP: 79 EST: 2018
SALES (est): 1.7MM
SALES (corp-wide): 6.7MM **Privately Held**
WEB: www.teamcorpint.com
SIC: 8741 Management services
PA: Total Educational Activity Model Corp
4076 Flat Rock Dr
Riverside CA 92505
951 977-9690

(P-23123)
TELACU CONSTRUCTION MGT INC
604 N Eckhoff St, Orange (92868-1019)
PHONE..................................714 541-2390
EMP: 50
SALES (est): 1.3MM **Privately Held**
SIC: 8741 Management Services, Nsk

(P-23124)
TOFASCO OF AMERICA INC (PA)
1661 Fairplex Dr, La Verne (91750-5871)
PHONE..................................909 392-8282
Edward Zheng, *President*
Stephen Chan, *CFO*
Chan Stephen, *CFO*
Eric Deininger, *Vice Pres*
Xiu Jun Liang, *Vice Pres*
▲ EMP: 58 EST: 1993
SQ FT: 160,554
SALES (est): 9MM **Privately Held**
WEB: www.tofasco.com
SIC: 8741 Financial management for busi-
ness

(P-23125)
TRADESMEN INTERNATIONAL LLC
16880 Valley View Ave, La Mirada
(90638-5825)
PHONE..................................949 588-3280
Jason Hammer, *Branch Mgr*
EMP: 60 **Privately Held**
WEB: www.tradesmeninternational.com
SIC: 8741 7361 Construction manage-
ment; employment agencies
PA: Tradesmen International, Llc
9760 Shepard Rd
Macedonia OH 44056

(P-23126)
TRANSCOSMOS ONMICONNECT LLC
879 W 190th St Ste 1050, Gardena
(90248-4224)
PHONE..................................310 630-0072
Shinichi Nagakura,
EMP: 100 EST: 2019
SALES (est): 10.1MM
SALES (corp-wide): 23.3MM **Privately
Held**
WEB: www.transcosmos.net
SIC: 8741 Management services
PA: Trans Cosmos America, Inc.
879 W 190th St Ste 410
Gardena CA 90248
310 630-0072

(P-23127)
TRICOM MANAGEMENT INC
Also Called: United Owners Services
4025 E La Palma Ave # 10, Anaheim
(92807-1734)
PHONE..................................714 630-2029
Woody Cary, *President*
Joz Zavlyn, *Business Mgr*
Kim Searcy, *Human Res Mgr*
Dina Fischer, *Human Resources*
Jamie Orrell, *Opers Staff*
EMP: 200 EST: 1979
SQ FT: 9,000
SALES (est): 17.1MM **Privately Held**
WEB: www.tricommanagement.com
SIC: 8741 7389 Management services;
time-share condominium exchange

(P-23128)
TRILAR MANAGEMENT GROUP
1025 S Gilbert St, Hemet (92543-7090)
PHONE..................................951 925-2021
Susan A York, *Branch Mgr*
EMP: 124
SALES (corp-wide): 13.7MM **Privately
Held**
WEB: www.trilar.com
SIC: 8741 Business management
PA: Trilar Management Group
2101 Cmino Vida Rble Ste
Carlsbad CA 92011
760 603-3205

(P-23129)
TROON GOLF LLC
Also Called: Indian Wells Golf Resort
44500 Indian Wells Ln, Indian Wells
(92210-8746)
PHONE..................................760 346-4653
Rich Carter, *General Mgr*
Steven Rosen, *General Mgr*
Andy Lindloff, *Superintendent*
EMP: 130 **Privately Held**
WEB: www.troon.com
SIC: 8741 7997 Management services;
country club, membership
PA: Troon Golf, L.L.C.
15044 N Scottsdale Rd
Scottsdale AZ 85254

(P-23130)
TWENTY4SEVEN HOTELS CORP
520 Newport Center Dr # 520, Newport
Beach (92660-7320)
PHONE..................................949 734-6400
David Wani, *CEO*
Drew Hardy, *President*
Samuel Grant, *Vice Pres*
Kelly Dickson, *General Mgr*
Ryan Murray, *General Mgr*
EMP: 500 EST: 2002
SQ FT: 15,000
SALES (est): 25.7MM **Privately Held**
WEB: www.247hotels.com
SIC: 8741 Hotel or motel management

(P-23131)
U S MANAGERS REALTY INC
2101 Rosecrans Ave # 5252, El Segundo
(90245-4749)
PHONE..................................310 607-0003
John Kusmiersky, *President*
Jack G Baker, *Admin Sec*
EMP: 57 EST: 1974
SQ FT: 6,000

SALES (est): 1MM **Privately Held**
SIC: 8741 6531 Management services;
real estate agents & managers

(P-23132)
UNITED PARADYNE CORPORATION
P.O. Box 5368 (93150-5368)
PHONE................................805 734-2359
Randy Cobb, *Manager*
EMP: 51 **Privately Held**
WEB: www.unitedparadyne.com
SIC: 8741 Management services
PA: United Paradyne Corporation
340 James Way Ste 230
Pismo Beach CA

(P-23133)
UNITED PARADYNE CORPORATION
Utah & 10th St Bldg 7525, Lompoc (93437)
P.O. Box 5398 (93437-0398)
PHONE................................805 734-4734
George Kennedy, *General Mgr*
EMP: 51 **Privately Held**
WEB: www.unitedparadyne.com
SIC: 8741 Industrial management
PA: United Paradyne Corporation
340 James Way Ste 230
Pismo Beach CA

(P-23134)
URM TECHNOLOGIES INC
28486 Wstnghuse Pl Ste 13, Valencia
(91355)
PHONE................................661 705-0500
William Quiros, *CEO*
Christina Ciccone, *Accounts Exec*
EMP: 50 EST: 2018
SALES (est): 7.1MM **Privately Held**
WEB: www.urmcorp.com
SIC: 8741 Management services

(P-23135)
VENTURA MEDICAL MANAGEMENT LLC
2601 E Main St, Ventura (93003-2801)
PHONE................................805 477-6220
Jim Malone,
Deborah Carlson MD,
Kent Coleman PHD,
John Pritchard MD,
EMP: 325 EST: 2002
SALES (est): 13.7MM **Privately Held**
WEB: www.ventura.org
SIC: 8741 Hospital management

(P-23136)
VPM MANAGEMENT INC
2400 Main St Ste 201, Irvine (92614-6271)
PHONE................................949 863-1500
Philip H McNamee, *CEO*
Mark Ellis,
Steve Tomlin,
Scott J Barker, *Mng Member*
EMP: 150 EST: 1997
SALES (est): 15.7MM **Privately Held**
WEB: www.vpmmanagement.com
SIC: 8741 Management services

(P-23137)
WARNER BROS DISTRIBUTING INC (DH)
4000 Warner Blvd, Burbank (91522-0002)
PHONE................................818 954-6000
Jeffrey Robinov, *CEO*
Dan Fellman, *President*
Connie Minnett, *Senior VP*
Deborah Gold, *Vice Pres*
Lynn Whitney, *Vice Pres*
EMP: 433 EST: 2003
SALES (est): 92.1MM
SALES (corp-wide): 171.7B **Publicly Held**
WEB: www.warnerbros.com
SIC: 8741 7829 Management services;
motion picture distribution services

(P-23138)
WESTERN MEDICAL MANAGEMENT LLC
3333 Michelson Dr Ste 735, Irvine
(92612-7679)
PHONE................................949 260-6575
EMP: 50
SALES (est): 3.9MM **Privately Held**
WEB: www.1wmm.com
SIC: 8741 Management Services

(P-23139)
WESTERN NATIONAL CONTRACTORS
8 Executive Cir, Irvine (92614-6746)
PHONE................................949 862-6200
Michael Hayde, *CEO*
Jeffrey R Scott, *CFO*
Randy Avery, *Vice Pres*
John Townsend, *Vice Pres*
Larry Johnson, *Director*
EMP: 88 EST: 2004
SALES (est): 14.1MM **Privately Held**
WEB: www.wng.com
SIC: 8741 Construction management

(P-23140)
WESTREC PROPERTIES INC
16633 Ventura Blvd Fl 6, Encino
(91436-1826)
PHONE................................818 907-0400
Michael M Sachs, *President*
EMP: 475 EST: 1990
SALES (est): 1.1MM **Privately Held**
SIC: 8741 Administrative management
PA: Westrec Financial, Inc.
16633 Ventura Blvd Fl 6
Encino CA

(P-23141)
WOLVERINE INTRMDATE HLDG II CO (PA)
360 N Crescent Dr Bldg S, Beverly Hills
(90210-2529)
PHONE................................310 712-1850
Heather McLeod, *Production*
Haydee Lopez, *Sales Staff*
EMP: 280 EST: 2019
SALES (est): 1.7B **Privately Held**
SIC: 8741 5072 Management services;
hardware

(P-23142)
WORLDSTAGE INC (PA)
1111 Bell Ave Ste A, Tustin (92780-6463)
PHONE................................714 508-1858
Gary Standard, *CEO*
Josh Weisberg, *President*
Stan Jacobs, *CFO*
Rodney Miller, *CFO*
Gregg Whitaker, *CFO*
EMP: 58 EST: 2007
SALES (est): 54.5MM **Privately Held**
WEB: www.worldstage.com
SIC: 8741 Business management

(P-23143)
XPERIENCE RESTAURANT GROUP (PA)
11065 Knott Ave Ste A, Cypress
(90630-5149)
PHONE................................562 346-1200
EMP: 51 EST: 2019
SALES (est): 30.5MM **Privately Held**
WEB: www.xperiencerg.com
SIC: 8741 Restaurant management

(P-23144)
ZA MANAGEMENT
250 N Robertson Blvd # 10, Beverly Hills
(90211-1788)
PHONE................................310 271-2200
Alexander Zaks, *CEO*
EMP: 90 EST: 2001
SALES (est): 1.6MM **Privately Held**
SIC: 8741 Management services

8742 Management Consulting Services

(P-23145)
656 LOS ANGELES STREET LLC
719 S Los Angeles St # 368, Los Angeles
(90014-2124)
PHONE................................949 900-6160
EMP: 50 EST: 2014
SALES (est): 1.2MM **Privately Held**
SIC: 8742 Business consultant

(P-23146)
ABACUS WEALTH PARTNERS LLC (PA)
429 Santa Monica Blvd # 500, Santa Monica (90401-3443)
PHONE................................707 829-6190
Brent Kessel,
Jamie Marsh, *Officer*
Lara Lamb, *Planning*
Spencer Sherman,
Brooke Mease, *Art Dir*
EMP: 52 EST: 1989
SALES (est): 5.1MM **Privately Held**
WEB: www.abacuswealth.com
SIC: 8742 Financial consultant

(P-23147)
ADVANTAGE SALES & MKTG INC (DH)
Also Called: Advantage Solutions
15310 Barranca Pkwy # 100, Irvine
(92618-2236)
PHONE................................949 797-2900
Tanya Domier, *CEO*
Beverly Blake, *Partner*
Abigail Cox, *Partner*
Chris Cuello, *President*
Brian Stevens, *COO*
▲ EMP: 250 EST: 2010
SQ FT: 48,000
SALES (est): 1.5B
SALES (corp-wide): 4.7B **Publicly Held**
WEB: www.advantagesolutions.net
SIC: 8742 Business consultant
HQ: Advantage Solutions Inc.
18100 Von Karman Ave # 1
Irvine CA 92612
949 797-2900

(P-23148)
AGR GROUP INC
13902 Harbor Blvd Ste 2c, Garden Grove
(92843-4013)
PHONE................................714 245-7151
EMP: 750
SQ FT: 15,500
SALES: 16MM **Privately Held**
WEB: www.agrgroupinc.com
SIC: 8742 Management Consulting Services

(P-23149)
AKASH MANAGEMENT LLC
716 Corporate Center Dr # 200, Pomona
(91768-2652)
PHONE................................805 672-2889
David Buffington,
Amir Siddiqi,
EMP: 1000 EST: 2014
SALES (est): 57.2MM **Privately Held**
SIC: 8742 Management consulting services

(P-23150)
ALAN B WHITSON COMPANY INC
1507 W Alton Ave, Santa Ana
(92704-7219)
P.O. Box 9229 (92728)
PHONE................................949 955-1200
Alan B Whitson, *President*
EMP: 750 EST: 1990
SQ FT: 18,000
SALES (est): 6.3MM **Privately Held**
SIC: 8742 1389 5411 Corporation organizing; servicing oil & gas wells; convenience stores, chain

(P-23151)
ALLIED TRADING GROUP INC
8966 Mason Ave, Chatsworth
(91311-6107)
PHONE................................818 576-9277
EMP: 20
SALES (est): 1.2MM **Privately Held**
SIC: 8742 3559 Management Consulting Services Mfg Misc Industry Machinery

(P-23152)
ALTEGRA HEALTH
3415 S Sepulveda Blvd # 900, Los Angeles
(90034-6981)
PHONE................................310 776-4001
EMP: 99
SALES (est): 6.6MM **Privately Held**
SIC: 8742 Management Consulting Services

(P-23153)
ALVAREZ MRSAL BUS CNSLTING LLC
2029 Century Park E, Los Angeles
(90067-2901)
PHONE................................310 975-2600
Dora Alverez, *Principal*
EMP: 214
SALES (corp-wide): 1.2B **Privately Held**
WEB: www.alvarezandmarsal.com
SIC: 8742 Management consulting services
PA: Alvarez & Marsal Corporate Performance Improvement, Llc
600 Madison Ave Fl 8
New York NY 10022
212 759-4433

(P-23154)
AMCO FOODS INC
601 E Glenoaks Blvd # 108, Glendale
(91207-1760)
PHONE................................818 247-4716
Bobken Amirian, *President*
Brian Polthow, *CFO*
Nick Amirian, *Corp Secy*
Nareg Amirian, *Principal*
EMP: 475 EST: 1999
SALES (est): 14MM **Privately Held**
SIC: 8742 Business consultant

(P-23155)
AMGREEN SOLUTIONS INC
1367 Venice Blvd Fl 2, Los Angeles
(90006-5519)
PHONE................................213 388-5647
Changhwan Ko, *President*
Nick Guillen, *Director*
EMP: 50 EST: 2010 **Privately Held**
WEB: www.amgreensolutions.com
SIC: 8742 7389 Management engineering; water softener service

(P-23156)
ANDERSON KAYNE INV MGT INC (PA)
1800 Avenue Of The Stars # 200, Los Angeles (90067-4204)
PHONE................................310 556-2721
Richard Kayne, *Ch of Bd*
John Anderson, *CEO*
Paul Stapleton, *Treasurer*
Frank Lee, *Officer*
Brian Lessans, *Vice Pres*
EMP: 55 EST: 1993
SQ FT: 20,000
SALES (est): 59.5MM **Privately Held**
WEB: www.kayne.com
SIC: 8742 6211 6726 6282 Financial consultant; investment firm, general brokerage; investment offices; investment advice

(P-23157)
ANDERSONPENNA PARTNERS INC (HQ)
3737 Birch St Ste 250, Newport Beach
(92660-2682)
PHONE................................949 428-1500
Lisa Penna, *President*
Angelique M Lucero, *CFO*
David R Anderson, *Exec VP*
Angelique Lucero, *Info Tech Mgr*
Teresa Kelley, *Project Mgr*
EMP: 71 EST: 2005

SALES (est): 8.7MM
SALES (corp-wide): 11.5MM **Privately Held**
WEB: www.ardurra.com
SIC: 8742 8711 Transportation consultant; engineering services
PA: Ardurra Group Holdings Llc
3012 26th St
Metairie LA 70002
504 454-3866

(P-23158)
ANSER ADVISORY LLC (PA)
2677 N Main St Ste 400, Santa Ana
(92705-6627)
PHONE.................................310 351-8907
Bryan Carruthers, *CEO*
Gary Cooley, *Officer*
Melanie Estes, *Officer*
Roger Miramontes, *Vice Pres*
Gerardo Quintero, *Vice Pres*
EMP: 56 **EST:** 2018
SALES (est): 36.2MM **Privately Held**
WEB: www.anseradvisory.com
SIC: 8742 Management consulting services

(P-23159)
ANTHOS GROUP INC
705 N Douglas St, El Segundo
(90245-2830)
PHONE.................................888 778-2986
Shan Umer, *President*
EMP: 25 **EST:** 2019
SALES (est): 1.5MM **Privately Held**
WEB: www.theanthos.com
SIC: 8742 5047 2834 6111 Manufacturing management consultant; medical equipment & supplies; pharmaceutical preparations; Export/Import Bank; pharmaceutical manufacturing plant construction

(P-23160)
APA INCORPORATED
405 S Beverly Dr, Beverly Hills
(90212-4416)
P.O. Box 45 (90213-0045)
PHONE.................................310 888-4200
Kat Cafeler, *President*
Brian Dow, *Bd of Directors*
Ralph Berge, *Vice Pres*
Andy Weltman, *Managing Dir*
Ashley Van Nuck, *Administration*
EMP: 51 **EST:** 2008
SALES (est): 4.3MM **Privately Held**
WEB: www.apa-agency.com
SIC: 8742 Business consultant

(P-23161)
APN BUSINESS RESOURCES INC
21418 Osborne St, Canoga Park
(91304-1520)
PHONE.................................818 717-9980
Michael Noori, *CEO*
Kos Noori, *Info Tech Dir*
Julio Arreyguy, *Info Tech Mgr*
EMP: 85 **EST:** 2011
SALES (est): 15MM **Privately Held**
SIC: 8742 8748 Business planning & organizing services; business consulting

(P-23162)
AVASANT LLC (PA)
1960 E Grand Ave Ste 1050, El Segundo
(90245-5096)
PHONE.................................310 643-3030
Kevin Parikh, *Mng Member*
Bob Randolph, *Senior Partner*
Carlos Hernandez, *Partner*
Swapnil Bhatnagar, *Research*
Stacey Rogers, *Marketing Staff*
EMP: 99 **EST:** 2006
SQ FT: 6,000
SALES (est): 16.7MM **Privately Held**
WEB: www.avasant.com
SIC: 8742 Marketing consulting services

(P-23163)
AVENIDA PARTNERS LLC (PA)
130 Nwport Ctr Dr Ste 220, Newport Beach
(92660)
PHONE.................................949 734-7810
Robert D May, *Mng Member*
Robert May, *Managing Prtnr*

Robin Craig, *Vice Pres*
Michael R Murphy, *Vice Pres*
Rob Muirhead, *Project Mgr*
EMP: 60 **EST:** 2007
SALES (est): 6.2MM **Privately Held**
WEB: www.avenidapartners.com
SIC: 8742 Real estate consultant

(P-23164)
AVETA HEALTH SOLUTION INC
3990 Concours Ste 500, Ontario
(91764-7983)
PHONE.................................909 605-8000
Tim O'Rourke, *President*
Marcia Anderson, *COO*
Rod St Clair, *Officer*
Carol Hairston, *Vice Pres*
EMP: 1014 **EST:** 2010
SALES (est): 506.8K **Privately Held**
SIC: 8742 Hospital & health services consultant
PA: Innovacare Services Company Llc
44 S Broadway Lbby 1
White Plains NY 10601

(P-23165)
AXIS UNLIMITED INC
13373 Lilyrose St, Eastvale (92880-0755)
PHONE.................................714 476-1341
Angelo Narvaez, *President*
EMP: 100
SQ FT: 2,800
SALES (est): 1MM **Privately Held**
SIC: 8742 Marketing consulting services

(P-23166)
BAMKO LLC (HQ)
Also Called: Bamko Promotional Items
11620 Wilshire Blvd # 610, Los Angeles
(90025-1267)
PHONE.................................310 470-5859
Philip Koosed, *CEO*
Jake Himelstein, *President*
Asim Khan, *Executive*
Kj Summers, *Business Dir*
Devin Rigg, *Business Mgr*
EMP: 80 **EST:** 2016
SALES (est): 54.5MM
SALES (corp-wide): 526.7MM **Publicly Held**
WEB: www.bamko.net
SIC: 8742 7336 Merchandising consultant; package design
PA: Superior Group Of Companies, Inc.
10055 Seminole Blvd
Seminole FL 33772
727 397-9611

(P-23167)
BARSTOW HEALTHCARE MGT INC (DH)
555 S 7th Ave, Barstow (92311-3043)
PHONE.................................831 319-4194
Alfred Lumsdaine, *Vice Pres*
W Larry Cash, *CEO*
EMP: 50 **EST:** 1995
SALES (est): 1.3MM
SALES (corp-wide): 1.6B **Privately Held**
WEB: www.mccormickbarstow.com
SIC: 8742 8099 Management consulting services; medical services organization

(P-23168)
BASKETBALL MARKETING CO INC
Also Called: and 1
101 Enterprise Ste 100, Aliso Viejo
(92656-2604)
PHONE.................................610 249-2255
Kevin Wulff, *President*
▲ **EMP:** 79 **EST:** 2006
SALES (est): 2.7MM
SALES (corp-wide): 2.1B **Publicly Held**
SIC: 8742 Management consulting services
HQ: American Sporting Goods Corp
101 Enterprise Ste 200
Aliso Viejo CA 92656
949 267-2800

(P-23169)
BEACON RESOURCES LLC
17300 Red Hill Ave, Irvine (92614-5643)
PHONE.................................949 955-1773
Colleen Freeman,

Katie McGovern, *Human Resources*
Mike Kelly,
Valerie Rodriguez, *Director*
Colette Alcott, *Manager*
EMP: 173 **EST:** 2010
SALES (est): 3.5MM
SALES (corp-wide): 153.3MM **Privately Held**
WEB: www.hirewithbeacon.com
SIC: 8742 Business planning & organizing services
HQ: David M. Lewis Company, Llc
20750 Ventura Blvd # 300
Woodland Hills CA 91364

(P-23170)
BEATING WALL STREET INC (PA)
20121 Ventura Blvd # 305, Woodland Hills
(91364-2559)
PHONE.................................818 332-9696
Hamed Khorsand, *President*
EMP: 230 **EST:** 2000
SALES (est): 9.9MM **Privately Held**
WEB: www.bwsfinancial.com
SIC: 8742 Financial consultant

(P-23171)
BECKETT ENTERPRISE
Also Called: Selu College
900 Kincaid Ave K8, Inglewood
(90302-2021)
PHONE.................................310 686-3817
Tyesha Beckett, *CEO*
EMP: 50 **EST:** 2017
SALES (est): 1.3MM **Privately Held**
SIC: 8742 Corporation organizing

(P-23172)
BLACKSTONE CONSULTING INC (PA)
11726 San Vicente Blvd # 550, Los Angeles
(90049-5089)
PHONE.................................310 826-4389
Ronald Joseph Blackstone, *President*
Bruce Marquardt, *Vice Pres*
Alejandra Ordaz, *Administration*
Jasmine Sandoval, *Administration*
Amira McCullough, *Asst Controller*
EMP: 461 **EST:** 1991
SQ FT: 1,500
SALES (est): 37.5MM **Privately Held**
WEB: www.blackstone-consulting.com
SIC: 8742 Management consulting services

(P-23173)
BLX GROUP LLC (PA)
777 S Figueroa St Ste 800, Los Angeles
(90017-5804)
PHONE.................................213 612-2200
Jeff Smith, *Director*
Christi McKnight, *Associate Dir*
Glen Casterline, *Managing Dir*
Jeff Higgins, *Managing Dir*
Greg Rowan, *Managing Dir*
EMP: 51 **EST:** 2000
SALES (est): 6.4MM **Privately Held**
WEB: www.blxgroup.com
SIC: 8742 Financial consultant

(P-23174)
BON APPETIT MANAGEMENT CO
1259 E Colton Ave, Redlands
(92374-3755)
PHONE.................................909 748-8970
Bret Martin, *General Mgr*
EMP: 132
SALES (corp-wide): 26B **Privately Held**
WEB: www.eatlowcarbon.org
SIC: 8742 Administrative services consultant
HQ: Bon Appetit Management Co.
201 Rdwood Shres Pkwy Ste
Redwood City CA 94065
650 798-8000

(P-23175)
BRANDED GROUP INC
Also Called: Facilities MGT & Coml RPS Svcs
222 S Harbor Blvd Ste 500, Anaheim
(92805-3712)
PHONE.................................323 940-1444

Mike Kurland, *CEO*
Jerry Jonathan Thomas, *President*
Andra Bereznay, *Vice Pres*
Kiira Esposito, *Vice Pres*
Josh Hawthorne, *Software Engr*
EMP: 107 **EST:** 2014
SQ FT: 13,372
SALES (est): 11.8MM **Privately Held**
WEB: www.branded-group.com
SIC: 8742 8741 Maintenance management consultant; construction management

(P-23176)
BRANDREP LLC
2850 Redhill Ave Ste 100, Santa Ana
(92705-5532)
PHONE.................................800 405-7119
Banir Ganatra,
Nathan Gibson, *Vice Pres*
Bobby Omari, *Exec Dir*
Haley Sauter, *Sales Associate*
Aubryanne Cook, *Marketing Staff*
EMP: 50 **EST:** 2013
SALES (est): 8.8MM **Privately Held**
WEB: www.brandrep.com
SIC: 8742 Marketing consulting services

(P-23177)
BRIDGWTER CONSULTING GROUP INC
18881 Von Karman Ave # 1, Irvine
(92612-1500)
PHONE.................................949 535-1755
Mark Montgomery, *President*
Ramon Gonzalez, *Vice Pres*
Richard Nyden, *Manager*
EMP: 90 **EST:** 2015
SQ FT: 1,600
SALES (est): 13.5MM **Privately Held**
WEB: www.bridgewcc.com
SIC: 8742 7379 Management consulting services;

(P-23178)
BROKER SOLUTONS INC
800 N Haven Ave Ste 330, Ontario
(91764-4976)
PHONE.................................909 458-0718
Brett Reichel, *Branch Mgr*
EMP: 69 **Privately Held**
WEB: www.newamericanfunding.com
SIC: 8742 6162 Financial consultant; bond & mortgage companies
PA: Broker Solutions, Inc.
14511 Myford Rd Ste 100
Tustin CA 92780

(P-23179)
BROKER SOLUTIONS INC (PA)
Also Called: New American Funding
14511 Myford Rd Ste 100, Tustin
(92780-7057)
PHONE.................................800 450-2010
Rick Arvielo, *CEO*
Patricia Arvielo, *President*
Christy Bunce, *COO*
Scott Frommert, *CFO*
Deborah Rust, *Officer*
EMP: 650 **EST:** 2002
SALES (est): 533.5MM **Privately Held**
WEB: www.newamericanfunding.com
SIC: 8742 6162 Financial consultant; bond & mortgage companies

(P-23180)
BROWN AND STREZA LLP
40 Pacifica Ste 1500, Irvine (92618-7496)
PHONE.................................949 453-2900
Richard Streza, *President*
David Brown, *Vice Pres*
Martha Demarco, *Executive Asst*
Dawn Alewine, *Admin Sec*
Victoria Hypolite, *Admin Asst*
EMP: 60 **EST:** 1979
SQ FT: 1,000
SALES (est): 8.9MM **Privately Held**
WEB: www.brownandstreza.com
SIC: 8742 8111 Business planning & organizing services; general practice attorney, lawyer

(P-23181)
CAERUS MARKETING GROUP LLC
17875 Von Karman Ave # 200, Irvine (92614-6273)
PHONE.................................877 627-2509
Matt Miller, *President*
Jodee Essensa, *Controller*
EMP: 70 EST: 2013
SALES (est): 25MM **Privately Held**
SIC: 8742 Marketing consulting services

(P-23182)
CARPE DATA (PA)
735 State St Ste 600, Santa Barbara (93101-7065)
PHONE.................................877 342-2773
James Arthur Taylor, *Owner*
Bryan Babineau, *CFO*
Jim Andrews, *Vice Pres*
Jennifer St James, *Director*
Adam Tashman, *Director*
EMP: 86 EST: 2017
SALES (est): 1.6MM **Privately Held**
WEB: www.carpe.io
SIC: 8742 General management consultant

(P-23183)
CBRE CONSULTING INC
Also Called: Sedway Group
355 S Grand Ave Ste 1200, Los Angeles (90071-1560)
PHONE.................................213 613-3750
Lynn Sedway, *CEO*
Lawrence Van Der Bogart, *CFO*
Allon Shapiro, *Vice Pres*
Valerija Beares, *Executive*
Jan Bottcher, *Administration*
EMP: 52 EST: 1978
SQ FT: 5,000
SALES (est): 3.8MM **Publicly Held**
WEB: www.cbre.com
SIC: 8742 Real estate consultant
HQ: Cbre, Inc.
    400 S Hope St Ste 2500
    Los Angeles CA 90071
    213 613-3333

(P-23184)
CBRE GLOBL VALUE INVESTORS LLC
3501 Jamboree Rd Ste 100, Newport Beach (92660-2940)
PHONE.................................949 725-8500
Steven Swerdlow, *Principal*
Jeff Oesterblad, *Vice Pres*
Carla Santi, *Technical Staff*
Stephen Buric, *Financial Analy*
Trevor Breaux, *Analyst*
EMP: 75 **Publicly Held**
WEB: www.cbreim.com
SIC: 8742 6531 Management consulting services; real estate agent, commercial
HQ: Cbre Global Value Investors, Llc
    601 S Figueroa St Ste 49
    Los Angeles CA 90017
    213 683-4200

(P-23185)
CBRE SERVICES INC
400 S Hope St Ste 2500, Los Angeles (90071-1993)
PHONE.................................213 613-3333
Robert Sulentic, *CEO*
Robert Stillman, *Vice Chairman*
Anthony Gange, *Exec VP*
Zane Brown, *Vice Pres*
Debbie Fan, *Vice Pres*
EMP: 70 EST: 1989
SALES (est): 15MM **Publicly Held**
WEB: www.cbre.us
SIC: 8742 6531 Real estate consultant; real estate agent, commercial
PA: Cbre Group, Inc.
    2100 Mckinney Ave Fl 12
    Dallas TX 75201

(P-23186)
CENTERFIELD MEDIA HOLDINGS LLC (PA)
12130 Millennium Ste 500, Los Angeles (90094-2946)
PHONE.................................310 341-4420

Brett Cravatt, *Co-President*
Jason Cohen, *Co-President*
Brad Green, *Exec VP*
Matt Payne, *Vice Pres*
Erik Estrada, *Software Dev*
EMP: 269 EST: 2010
SALES (est): 60.5MM **Privately Held**
WEB: www.centerfield.com
SIC: 8742 Marketing consulting services

(P-23187)
CHAPMAN UNIVERSITY
Also Called: Chapman Academic Center
39115 Trade Center Dr # 203, Palmdale (93551-3649)
PHONE.................................661 267-2001
Jerry Witte, *Sales/Mktg Mgr*
Adam James, *Technician*
Wenzhao LI, *Research*
Dirk Cross, *Accountant*
Cindy Nelson, *Recruiter*
EMP: 95
SALES (corp-wide): 461.3MM **Privately Held**
WEB: www.chapman.edu
SIC: 8221 8742 College, except junior; training & development consultant
PA: Chapman University
    1 University Dr
    Orange CA 92866
    714 997-6815

(P-23188)
CHASE GROUP LLC
Also Called: Center At Parkwest, The
6740 Wilbur Ave, Reseda (91335-5179)
PHONE.................................818 708-3533
Phil Chase, *Branch Mgr*
EMP: 295 **Privately Held**
SIC: 8742 8049 Management consulting services; nurses & other medical assistants
PA: The Chase Group Llc
    3075 E Thousand Oaks Blvd
    Thousand Oaks CA 91362

(P-23189)
CHINA MANUFACTURING NETWRK LLC
Also Called: Global Manufacturing Network
17891 Sky Park Cir Ste K, Irvine (92614-2400)
PHONE.................................949 756-0015
Everette Phillips,
Benjamin Yeung, *Engineer*
Albert F Tien,
▲ EMP: 16 EST: 2003
SQ FT: 2,000
SALES (est): 681.4K **Privately Held**
WEB: www.sourceglobally.com
SIC: 8742 5065 3444 3544 Business planning & organizing services; electronic parts & equipment; housings for business machines, sheet metal; dies & die holders for metal cutting, forming, die casting

(P-23190)
CITY NATIONAL ASSET MGT INC
400 N Roxbury Dr, Beverly Hills (90210-5021)
PHONE.................................310 888-6441
Richard Weiss, *President*
Kevin Laporte, *Vice Pres*
Paul Stowell, *Vice Pres*
Gabe Eisner, *Consultant*
EMP: 74 EST: 2001
SALES (est): 5.3MM
SALES (corp-wide): 31.1B **Privately Held**
WEB: www.cnb.com
SIC: 8742 Financial consultant
HQ: City National Bank
    555 S Flower St Ste 2500
    Los Angeles CA 90071
    310 888-6000

(P-23191)
CITY OF OXNARD (PA)
Also Called: Oxnard City Hall
300 W 3rd St, Oxnard (93030-5729)
PHONE.................................805 385-7803
Dr Thomas E Holden, *Mayor*
Phillip Molina, *Treasurer*
Christina Galindo, *Officer*
Christina Prado, *Officer*
Juanita Suarez, *Officer*

▲ EMP: 150 EST: 1903
SQ FT: 11,000
SALES (est): 209MM **Privately Held**
WEB: www.visitoxnard.com
SIC: 8742 Industrial & labor consulting services

(P-23192)
COCKRAM CONSTRUCTION INC (HQ)
605 8th St, San Fernando (91340-1400)
PHONE.................................818 650-0999
David Judd, *President*
Malcolm W Batten, *President*
Robert Sirgiovanni, *Vice Pres*
Louis E Sciuto, *Admin Sec*
Joshua Lushch, *Accountant*
EMP: 113 EST: 2000
SALES (est): 18.8MM **Privately Held**
WEB: www.cockram.com
SIC: 8742 8741 1541 Construction project management consultant; construction management; food products manufacturing or packing plant construction

(P-23193)
COHEN BROWN MGT GROUP INC (PA)
438 Amapola Ave 110, Torrance (90501-6221)
PHONE.................................310 966-1001
Martin L Cohen, *CEO*
Edward G Brown, *President*
James W Bywater, *Exec VP*
Cohen Herbst, *Vice Pres*
G Martin, *Vice Pres*
EMP: 63 EST: 1979
SALES (est): 8.6MM **Privately Held**
WEB: www.cohenbrown.com
SIC: 8742 Training & development consultant

(P-23194)
COMMONWEALTH EQUITY SVCS LLC
Also Called: Commonwealth Financial Network
20 Corporate Park Ste 150, Irvine (92606-5183)
PHONE.................................949 336-6440
Karen Caporaso, *Principal*
EMP: 51
SALES (corp-wide): 411.8K **Privately Held**
WEB: www.commonwealth.com
SIC: 8742 Financial consultant
PA: Commonwealth Equity Services, Llc
    29 Sawyer Rd Ste 2
    Waltham MA 02453
    781 736-7980

(P-23195)
COMPSPEC INC
801 N Brand Blvd Ste 650, Glendale (91203-1271)
PHONE.................................818 551-4200
Nabil Haddad, *President*
Shelly Murph, *Vice Pres*
Gabriel Cordero, *Info Tech Mgr*
Monica Peinado, *Info Tech Mgr*
Shelle Mitchell, *Director*
EMP: 53 EST: 1989
SALES (est): 4.7MM **Privately Held**
WEB: www.compspec.com
SIC: 8742 7299 Hospital & health services consultant; debt counseling or adjustment service, individuals

(P-23196)
CONCRETE WEST CONSTRUCTION INC
1733 S Douglass Rd Ste I, Anaheim (92806-6034)
PHONE.................................949 448-9940
Amber Zamora, *President*
EMP: 18 EST: 2017
SALES (est): 4MM **Privately Held**
WEB: www.concretewest.com
SIC: 8742 1389 1542 5051 Construction project management consultant; construction, repair & dismantling services; non-residential construction; forms, concrete construction (steel)

(P-23197)
CORONAL ENERGY LLC (PA)
301 N Lake Ave Ste 202, Pasadena (91101-5127)
PHONE.................................855 267-6625
Jonathan D Jaffrey, *Ch of Bd*
Edwin F Feo, *President*
Gregory Bohan, *CFO*
Philip R Leiber, *CFO*
Jamie Evans, *Exec VP*
EMP: 92 EST: 2014
SALES (est): 6.7MM **Privately Held**
WEB: www.coronalenergy.com
SIC: 8742 1711 Management consulting services; solar energy contractor

(P-23198)
CPE HR INC
9000 W Sunset Blvd # 900, West Hollywood (90069-5801)
PHONE.................................310 270-9800
Harold Walt, *CEO*
Faith Branvold, *President*
Grace Drulias, *CFO*
Carl Barragato, *Vice Pres*
Walt Robinson, *Vice Pres*
EMP: 90 EST: 1982
SALES (est): 9.2MM **Privately Held**
WEB: www.cpehr.com
SIC: 8742 Human resource consulting services

(P-23199)
CREATIVE CHANNEL SERVICES LLC (HQ)
Also Called: C C S
6601 Center Dr W Ste 400, Los Angeles (90045-1577)
PHONE.................................310 482-6500
Andy Restivo, *CEO*
Michael Butler, *CFO*
Hanoz Gandhi, *Officer*
George Plumb, *Exec VP*
Elizabeth Taylor-Fredo, *Regional Mgr*
EMP: 554 EST: 1995
SALES (est): 87.6MM
SALES (corp-wide): 13.1B **Publicly Held**
WEB: www.omnicomgroup.com
SIC: 8742 Marketing consulting services
PA: Omnicom Group Inc.
    280 Park Ave Fl 31w
    New York NY 10017
    212 415-3600

(P-23200)
CROWN GOLF PROPERTIES LP
Also Called: Tustin Ranch Golf Club
12442 Tustin Ranch Rd, Tustin (92782-1000)
PHONE.................................714 730-1611
Steve Plummer, *Manager*
Brent Boznanski, *General Mgr*
Ashley Jeynes, *Sales Staff*
Lisa Krivchuk, *Sales Staff*
Renee Morris, *Sales Staff*
EMP: 59
SALES (corp-wide): 92.1MM **Privately Held**
WEB: www.tustinranchgolf.com
SIC: 8742 7997 7992 Business consultant; membership sports & recreation clubs; public golf courses
PA: Crown Golf Properties, Lp
    222 N La Salle St # 2000
    Chicago IL 60601
    312 395-7701

(P-23201)
CROWNE COLD STORAGE LLC
786 Road 188, Delano (93215-9508)
PHONE.................................661 725-6458
EMP: 50 EST: 2014
SALES (est): 1.3MM **Privately Held**
SIC: 8742 Business consultant

(P-23202)
CUMMING CORPORATION
25220 Hancock Ave Ste 440, Murrieta (92562-0903)
PHONE.................................951 200-7860
Finlay Cumming, *CEO*
Peter Heald, *President*
Michael Jensen, *COO*
Brian Ruttencutter, *CFO*
Marty Breen, *Vice Pres*
EMP: 60 EST: 2007

SALES (est): 8MM **Privately Held**
WEB: www.cumming-group.com
SIC: 8742 Industry specialist consultants

(P-23203)
CUSTOMIZED DIST SVCS INC
3355 E Cedar St, Ontario (91761-7632)
PHONE....................909 947-0084
Mark Tuttle, *Branch Mgr*
Melinda Wright, *Cust Mgr*
EMP: 81
SALES (corp-wide): 65MM **Privately Held**
WEB: www.cdslogistics.com
SIC: 8742 7319 8741 Transportation consultant; distribution of advertising material or sample services; management services
PA: Customized Distribution Services, Inc.
20 Harry Shupe Blvd
Wharton NJ 07885
973 366-5090

(P-23204)
CYDCOR LLC (PA)
29899 Agoura Rd Ste 100, Agoura Hills (91301-2493)
PHONE....................805 277-5500
Gary Polson, *President*
Jim Majeski, *President*
Vera Quinn, *COO*
Ron Nathanson, *CFO*
Christine Noche, *Officer*
EMP: 78 EST: 1994
SALES (est): 32.1MM **Privately Held**
WEB: www.cydcor.com
SIC: 8742 Marketing consulting services

(P-23205)
DCW SERVICES LLC ✪
20500 Denker Ave, Torrance (90501-1645)
PHONE....................310 324-3147
Henry Mandil,
EMP: 75 EST: 2021
SALES (est): 1MM **Privately Held**
SIC: 8742 Distribution channels consultant

(P-23206)
DIAGNOSTIC HEALTH CORPORATION
Also Called: Diagnostic Health Los Angeles
6801 Park Ter, Los Angeles (90045-1543)
PHONE....................310 665-7180
Janet Bateman, *Principal*
EMP: 159
SALES (corp-wide): 1.8B **Privately Held**
SIC: 8742 Hospital & health services consultant
HQ: Diagnostic Health Corporation
22 Inverness Pkwy Ste 425
Birmingham AL 35242

(P-23207)
DIVERSIFIED WATERSCAPES INC
27324 Camn Capistrano # 213, Laguna Niguel (92677-1118)
PHONE....................949 582-5414
Patrick Simmsgeiger, *President*
Maria Angel, *CFO*
Sarah Clarke, *Office Mgr*
EMP: 15 EST: 1988
SQ FT: 2,000
SALES (est): 3MM **Privately Held**
WEB: www.dwiwater.com
SIC: 8742 2842 Maintenance management consultant; cleaning or polishing preparations

(P-23208)
DOWLING ADVISORY GROUP
3579 E Foothill Blvd # 651, Pasadena (91107-3119)
PHONE....................626 319-1369
James Dowling, *Owner*
Brian Y Lopez, *Director*
EMP: 100 EST: 2010
SALES (est): 1MM **Privately Held**
WEB: www.dowlingadvisorygroup.com
SIC: 8742 Business consultant

(P-23209)
DUFF & PHELPS LLC
350 S Grand Ave Ste 3100, Los Angeles (90071-3420)
PHONE....................213 270-2300
EMP: 67
SALES (corp-wide): 97.4MM **Privately Held**
SIC: 8742 Management Consulting Services
HQ: Duff & Phelps, Llc
55 E 52nd St Fl 31
New York NY 10055
212 871-6777

(P-23210)
EGON ZEHNDER INTERNATIONAL
350 S Grand Ave Ste 3580, Los Angeles (90071-3456)
PHONE....................213 337-1500
A Daniel Meiland, *CEO*
Elaine Yew, *Senior Partner*
Greig T Schneider, *Partner*
Marc Normandin, *Managing Prtnr*
Gizem Weggemans, *Officer*
EMP: 374 EST: 1987
SQ FT: 4,300
SALES (est): 1.6MM
SALES (corp-wide): 80.4MM **Privately Held**
WEB: www.egonzehnder.com
SIC: 8742 7361 Personnel management consultant; executive placement
HQ: Egon Zehnder International Inc.
520 Madison Ave Fl 23
New York NY 10022
212 519-6000

(P-23211)
ELECTRIC POWER GROUP LLC
251 S Lake Ave Ste 300, Pasadena (91101-3055)
PHONE....................626 685-2015
Vikram Budhraja,
Krish Narendra, *COO*
Frank Carrera, *Vice Pres*
Mahesh Shamaiah, *Sr Software Eng*
Harpreet Singh, *Software Dev*
EMP: 26 EST: 1999
SALES: 4.3MM **Privately Held**
WEB: www.electricpowergroup.com
SIC: 8742 7372 Management consulting services; prepackaged software

(P-23212)
ENBIO CORP
150 E Olive Ave Ste 114, Burbank (91502-1849)
PHONE....................818 953-9976
Arthur Zenian, *CEO*
Irving Flores, *Admin Asst*
Florence Price-Barrett, *Administration*
Jeremy Chung, *Opers Mgr*
Paul Kuykendall, *Senior Mgr*
◆ EMP: 142 EST: 2008
SQ FT: 1,500
SALES (est): 11.7MM **Privately Held**
WEB: www.enbiocorp.com
SIC: 8742 Hospital & health services consultant

(P-23213)
EXULT INC
121 Innovation Dr Ste 200, Irvine (92617-3094)
P.O. Box 6300, Newport Beach (92658-6300)
PHONE....................949 856-8800
James C Madden, *Ch of Bd*
Jim Aselta, *Partner*
Kevin Campbell, *President*
John Adams, *CFO*
Brian Irion, *Bd of Directors*
EMP: 2424 EST: 1998
SQ FT: 22,000
SALES (est): 108.8MM
SALES (corp-wide): 2.3B **Privately Held**
WEB: www.exult.net
SIC: 8742 Human resource consulting services
HQ: Alight (Us), Llc
200 E Randolph St Ll3
Chicago IL 60601
312 381-1000

(P-23214)
FDSI LOGISTICS LLC
27680 Avenue Mentry 2, Valencia (91355-1200)
PHONE....................818 971-3300
David Kolchins, *Vice Pres*
Dee Weller, *Marketing Staff*
John Hudson, *Director*
EMP: 75 EST: 2000
SALES (est): 24.5MM
SALES (corp-wide): 152.9B **Publicly Held**
WEB: www.fdsi.com
SIC: 8742 4731 Transportation consultant; freight transportation arrangement
PA: Cardinal Health, Inc.
7000 Cardinal Pl
Dublin OH 43017
614 757-5000

(P-23215)
FINANCIAL TECH SLTONS INTL INC
Also Called: Ftsi
406 E Huntington Dr # 100, Monrovia (91016-3638)
PHONE....................818 241-9571
Susan Baird Napier, *President*
EMP: 101 EST: 2000
SALES (est): 20.8MM **Privately Held**
WEB: www.ftsius.com
SIC: 8742 Banking & finance consultant

(P-23216)
FIRST AMRCN MRTG SOLUTIONS LLC
1 First American Way, Santa Ana (92707-5913)
PHONE....................714 250-3046
Kenneth D Degiorgio, *Manager*
David Chadwick, *Vice Pres*
Janice Letcher, *Opers Staff*
Todd Sleight, *Opers Staff*
Eva Osborne, *Sales Staff*
EMP: 57 EST: 2012
SALES (est): 5.4MM **Privately Held**
WEB: www.firstam.com
SIC: 8742 Management consulting services

(P-23217)
FIRST CAPITOL CONSULTING INC
3530 Wilshire Blvd # 1460, Los Angeles (90010-2334)
PHONE....................213 382-1115
Robert Sheen, *President*
Mark Dwyer, *Vice Pres*
Joanna H Kim, *General Counsel*
EMP: 73 EST: 1999
SALES (est): 19.5MM **Privately Held**
WEB: www.trusaic.com
SIC: 8742 Management consulting services

(P-23218)
FISHERIES RESOURCE VLNTR CORPS
109 Stanford Ln, Seal Beach (90740-2533)
PHONE....................562 596-9261
Thomas J Walsh, *President*
EMP: 113 EST: 2011
SALES (est): 1.9MM **Privately Held**
WEB: www.frvc.net
SIC: 8742 Business planning & organizing services

(P-23219)
FOOD MANAGEMENT ASSOCIATES INC
22349 La Palma Ave # 115, Yorba Linda (92887-3810)
PHONE....................714 694-2828
Richard Warmolts, *President*
Laura Warmolts, *Vice Pres*
Darlene Riego, *Sales Executive*
EMP: 50 EST: 2004
SQ FT: 1,800
SALES (est): 4.8MM **Privately Held**
WEB: www.foodmgt.com
SIC: 8742 Business consultant

(P-23220)
FOUNDATION LEAD GROUP LLC
Also Called: Doctor Genius
16800 Aston Ste 270, Irvine (92606-4839)
PHONE....................877 477-2311
Christopher M Lopez, *Mng Member*
Maurice Bishop, *Graphic Designe*
Amber Arden, *Marketing Staff*
Joseph Alcaraz,
EMP: 66 EST: 2009
SALES (est): 6MM **Privately Held**
SIC: 8742 Marketing consulting services

(P-23221)
FOUNDATION PROPERTY MGT INC (HQ)
Also Called: F P M
911 N Studebaker Rd # 100, Long Beach (90815-4980)
PHONE....................562 257-5100
Laverne R Joseph, *CEO*
Frank Rossello, *CFO*
Robert Amberg, *Vice Pres*
Stuart Hartman, *Vice Pres*
Deborah Stouff, *Admin Sec*
EMP: 50 EST: 1981
SQ FT: 24,000
SALES (est): 17.4MM
SALES (corp-wide): 38.7MM **Privately Held**
WEB: www.rhf.org
SIC: 8742 Management consulting services
PA: Retirement Housing Foundation Inc
911 N Studebaker Rd # 100
Long Beach CA 90815
562 257-5100

(P-23222)
FREIGHT MANAGEMENT INC
Also Called: F M I
2900 E La Palma Ave, Anaheim (92806-2616)
PHONE....................714 632-1440
Robert J Walters, *President*
Heidi Calamusa, *Vice Pres*
Sue Harkey, *Vice Pres*
Tim Ponder, *Vice Pres*
Dwayne Phillips, *Info Tech Dir*
EMP: 53 EST: 1987
SQ FT: 9,000
SALES (est): 11.8MM **Privately Held**
WEB: www.freightmgt.com
SIC: 8742 Transportation consultant

(P-23223)
GANZ USA LLC
16525 Sherman Way Ste C5, Van Nuys (91406-3753)
PHONE....................818 901-0077
Marilyn Smith, *Branch Mgr*
Richelle Beesinger, *Sales Staff*
Roberta Tuso, *Sales Staff*
Melissa Rogers, *Manager*
EMP: 59 **Privately Held**
WEB: www.ganz.com
SIC: 8742 5199 Management consulting services; gifts & novelties
HQ: Ganz U.S.A., Llc
3855 Shallowford Rd # 220
Marietta GA 30062

(P-23224)
GAVIN DE BECKER & ASSOC GP LLC
350 N Glendale Ave # 517, Glendale (91206-3794)
PHONE....................818 505-0177
Gavin De Becker, *Mng Member*
Joshua Dessalines, *Exec VP*
Michael La Fever, *Exec VP*
Jeffrey Marquart, *Exec VP*
Gary Howlin, *Senior VP*
EMP: 180 EST: 1979
SQ FT: 1,600
SALES (est): 35.7MM **Privately Held**
WEB: www.gdbc.com
SIC: 8742 Business consultant

(P-23225)
GLOBAL RISK MGT SOLUTIONS LLC
5271 California Ave # 290, Irvine (92617-3222)
PHONE...............................949 759-8500
Gerard Smith, *Mng Member*
EMP: 100 EST: 2013
SALES (est): 6.9MM **Privately Held**
WEB: www.globalrms.com
SIC: 8742 General management consultant

(P-23226)
GOETZMAN GROUP INC (PA)
21333 Oxnard St Ste 200, Woodland Hills (91367-5194)
PHONE...............................818 595-1112
Greg Goetzman, *President*
James Lee, *Consultant*
EMP: 75 EST: 1998
SALES (est): 7.8MM **Privately Held**
WEB: www.goetzmangroup.com
SIC: 8742 8721 Management consulting services; accounting, auditing & bookkeeping

(P-23227)
GPS FLYERS
527 Prospect Ave, Hermosa Beach (90254-4940)
PHONE...............................951 588-7777
Patrick Antrim, *Owner*
EMP: 51 EST: 2014
SQ FT: 3,000
SALES (est): 1.1MM **Privately Held**
WEB: www.gpsflyers.com
SIC: 8742 Marketing consulting services

(P-23228)
GREENHOUSE AGENCY INC
18195 Mcdurmott E Ste A, Irvine (92614-4787)
PHONE...............................949 752-7542
Sean Roche, *Managing Prtnr*
Thomas Barker, *Senior VP*
Richard Barnes, *CIO*
Jessica Parsley, *Mktg Dir*
Stacye Hill, *Manager*
EMP: 58 EST: 2012
SALES (est): 6MM **Privately Held**
WEB: www.greenhouseagency.com
SIC: 8742 Marketing consulting services

(P-23229)
GREENSPIRE LLC
Also Called: Greenspire Construction
515 S Flower St Ste 1800, Los Angeles (90071-2231)
PHONE...............................310 477-7686
David Murray, *CEO*
Andy Baker, *President*
Robert Beihl, *CFO*
Lindsie Garrison, *Human Res Dir*
EMP: 50 EST: 2016
SALES (est): 8.7MM **Privately Held**
WEB: www.greenspire.com
SIC: 8742 7389 Marketing consulting services;

(P-23230)
GUTHY-RENKER LLC (PA)
Also Called: Proactiv
100 N Pcf Cast Hwy Ste 16, El Segundo (90245)
P.O. Box 13670, Palm Desert (92255-3670)
PHONE...............................760 773-9022
Greg Renker, *Chairman*
Bill Guthy, *Chairman*
Dirk Van De Bunt, *Exec VP*
Eric Deutsch, *Vice Pres*
Kendra Elliott, *Vice Pres*
◆ EMP: 60 EST: 1988
SQ FT: 15,000
SALES (est): 138.7MM **Privately Held**
WEB: www.guthy-renker.com
SIC: 5999 8742 Cosmetics; marketing consulting services

(P-23231)
GYM CONSULTING INC
Also Called: My Gym Enterprises
15300 Ventura Blvd # 414, Sherman Oaks (91403-3103)
PHONE...............................818 907-6966

Cory Bertisch, *President*
Mike Chalovich, *COO*
Jamie Bertisch, *CFO*
Mae Perez, *Officer*
Gene Barr, *Senior VP*
EMP: 90 EST: 1994
SQ FT: 2,400
SALES (est): 10.6MM **Privately Held**
WEB: www.mygym.com
SIC: 8742 Marketing consulting services; franchising consultant

(P-23232)
HATCHBEAUTY AGENCY LLC (PA)
10951 W Pico Blvd Ste 300, Los Angeles (90064-2188)
PHONE...............................310 396-7070
Tracy Holland, *Mng Member*
Ann Deno, *Vice Pres*
Silpa Vincent, *Administration*
Aaron Hermosura, *Technical Mgr*
Erika Anderson, *Graphic Designe*
◆ EMP: 30 EST: 2008
SQ FT: 5,400
SALES (est): 14.8MM **Privately Held**
WEB: www.hatchbeautybrands.com
SIC: 8742 2844 5122 Marketing consulting services; toilet preparations; cosmetics, perfumes & hair products

(P-23233)
HAWKE MEDIA VENTURES LLC
1714 16th St, Santa Monica (90404-4402)
PHONE...............................310 451-7295
Erik Huberman, *CEO*
Mike Banuelos, *Vice Pres*
Matt Osias, *Vice Pres*
Logan Schiff, *Associate Dir*
Scott Poniewaz, *Business Dir*
EMP: 75 EST: 2013
SALES (est): 10.2MM **Privately Held**
WEB: www.hawkemedia.com
SIC: 8742 Marketing consulting services

(P-23234)
HEALTHCARE FINANCE DIRECT LLC
1707 Eye St Ste 300, Bakersfield (93301-5208)
PHONE...............................661 616-4400
Tyler Johnson, *CEO*
Eric Powers, *President*
Mark Weighall, *CFO*
Ron Johnson, *CTO*
Sylvia Arnoldus, *Software Dev*
EMP: 84 EST: 2009
SALES (est): 7.1MM **Privately Held**
WEB: www.healthcarefinancedirect.com
SIC: 8742 Financial consultant

(P-23235)
HITCHCOCK AUTOMOTIVE RESOURCES
17110 Gale Ave, City of Industry (91745-1809)
P.O. Box 8610 (91748-0610)
PHONE...............................626 839-8400
Fritz Hitchcock, *Ch of Bd*
Barry Wasserman, *CFO*
Rico Guerrero, *Finance Mgr*
Hiro Sayama, *Sales Mgr*
Lisa Barcelona, *Manager*
EMP: 63 EST: 1990
SQ FT: 70,000
SALES (est): 5.3MM **Privately Held**
WEB: www.phford.com
SIC: 8742 Business consultant

(P-23236)
HR MOBILE SERVICES INC
1850 S Central St, Visalia (93277-4418)
PHONE...............................559 625-2322
Ken Hernandez, *President*
Justina Hernandez, *Vice Pres*
Dayana Quezada, *Litigation*
Raquel Medina, *Manager*
EMP: 55 EST: 2006
SALES (est): 5.1MM **Privately Held**
WEB: www.hrmobileservices.com
SIC: 8742 Human resource consulting services

(P-23237)
HR&A ADVISORS INC
700 S Flower St Ste 2995, Los Angeles (90017-4217)
PHONE...............................310 581-0900
George Bogakos, *Branch Mgr*
Jamie Dang, *COO*
Alex Stokes, *Principal*
Zachary Russell, *Admin Asst*
Roxanna Torhan, *Accounting Mgr*
EMP: 75 **Privately Held**
WEB: www.hraadvisors.com
SIC: 8742 Business consultant
PA: Hr&A Advisors, Inc.
99 Hudson St Rm 3l
New York NY 10013

(P-23238)
HYKSO INC ✪
Also Called: Fightcamp
936 W 17th St, Costa Mesa (92627-4403)
PHONE...............................213 785-3372
EMP: 60 EST: 2021
SALES (est): 5MM **Privately Held**
SIC: 8742 Business consultant

(P-23239)
IAUTOMATION INC
Also Called: Ia-Robotics
41633 Eastman Dr, Murrieta (92562-7054)
PHONE...............................951 304-2222
Saksit Suetrong, *CEO*
EMP: 13 EST: 2012
SALES (est): 2.8MM **Privately Held**
WEB: www.ia-robotics.com
SIC: 8742 3549 Automation & robotics consultant; assembly machines, including robotic

(P-23240)
ICF JONES & STOKES INC
1 Ada Ste 100, Irvine (92618-5339)
PHONE...............................949 333-6600
David Freytag, *Manager*
EMP: 77
SALES (corp-wide): 1.4B **Publicly Held**
WEB: www.icf.com
SIC: 8742 8748 Business consultant; business consulting
HQ: Icf Jones & Stokes, Inc
9300 Lee Hwy
Fairfax VA 22031
703 934-3000

(P-23241)
IMPACT RADIUS INC (HQ)
223 E De La Guerra St, Santa Barbara (93101-2206)
PHONE...............................805 324-6021
David A Yovanno, *CEO*
Scott Brazin, *Chief Mktg Ofcr*
Wade Crang, *Vice Pres*
Stan Rosenberg, *Vice Pres*
Tijs Van Santen, *Vice Pres*
EMP: 59 EST: 2007
SQ FT: 8,000
SALES (est): 20.5MM **Privately Held**
WEB: www.impact.com
SIC: 8742 Marketing consulting services

(P-23242)
INFORMATION FORECAST INC
Also Called: Infocast
22144 Clarendon St # 280, Woodland Hills (91367-6321)
PHONE...............................818 888-4445
Bill Meyer, *President*
John M Clerici, *Partner*
Frank M Rapoport, *Partner*
Carin Ralph, *Corp Secy*
Robert De Santiago, *Producer*
EMP: 30 EST: 1986
SALES (est): 0 **Privately Held**
WEB: www.infocastinc.com
SIC: 8742 2721 Public utilities consultant; human resource consulting services; marketing consulting services; productivity improvement consultant; magazines: publishing only, not printed on site

(P-23243)
INFOSPAN
31878 Del Obispo St, San Juan Capistrano (92675-3223)
PHONE...............................949 260-9990

Farooq Bajwa, *President*
John Olson, *Treasurer*
Dan Johnson, *Vice Pres*
P Kyle Moody, *Vice Pres*
Rizwan Uraizee, *Vice Pres*
EMP: 750 EST: 2003
SQ FT: 8,000
SALES (est): 9.4MM **Privately Held**
WEB: www.infospaninc.com
SIC: 8742 Management consulting services

(P-23244)
INTERNTNAL CRTIVE MGT PRTNERS (PA)
Also Called: ICM Partners
10250 Constellation Blvd, Los Angeles (90067-6200)
PHONE...............................310 550-4000
EMP: 59 EST: 1983
SALES (est): 1.3MM **Privately Held**
WEB: www.icmpartners.com
SIC: 8742 General management consultant

(P-23245)
INTERSTATE ELECTRONICS CORP
Also Called: Human Resources
708 E Vermont Ave, Anaheim (92805-5611)
PHONE...............................714 758-0500
EMP: 57
SALES (corp-wide): 18.1B **Publicly Held**
SIC: 8742 Human resource consulting services
HQ: Interstate Electronics Corporation
602 E Vermont Ave
Anaheim CA 92805
714 758-0500

(P-23246)
ISYS SOLUTIONS INC
2601 Saturn St Ste 302, Brea (92821-6702)
PHONE...............................714 521-7656
Chris Loumakis, *CEO*
Lisa Archibald, *Vice Pres*
Lorika Loumakis, *Vice Pres*
Kerry Hennessy, *Executive*
Darin Cyr, *Business Dir*
EMP: 69 EST: 1997
SALES (est): 9.4MM **Privately Held**
WEB: www.isyscm.com
SIC: 8742 Hospital & health services consultant

(P-23247)
JACK NADEL INC (PA)
Also Called: Jack Nadel International
8701 Bellanca Ave, Los Angeles (90045-4411)
P.O. Box 8342, Pasadena (91109-8342)
PHONE...............................310 815-2600
Jack Nadel, *Chairman*
Sarah Kliewer, *Partner*
Craig Nadel, *CEO*
Marco Icardo, *CFO*
Robert Kritzler, *CFO*
◆ EMP: 70 EST: 1953
SQ FT: 30,000
SALES (est): 68.8MM **Privately Held**
WEB: www.nadel.com
SIC: 8742 5199 Marketing consulting services; advertising specialties

(P-23248)
JACOBUS CONSULTING INC
15375 Barranca Pkwy B202, Irvine (92618-2213)
P.O. Box 50127 (92619-0127)
PHONE...............................949 727-0720
Sandra Jacobs, *President*
Arizdelsy Vega, *Executive Asst*
Alan Hall, *Technology*
Dave Boucher, *Director*
EMP: 50 EST: 2007
SQ FT: 1,800
SALES (est): 7.2MM **Privately Held**
WEB: www.jacobusconsulting.com
SIC: 8742 Hospital & health services consultant

(P-23249)
JC PROMOTIONS INC
Also Called: Bauman Curry & Co
5601 W Slauson Ave # 168, Culver City
(90230-6582)
P.O. Box 2200 (90231-2200)
PHONE................................310 870-1183
Janet Curry, *President*
Edward Curry, *Principal*
Ridgley Curry, *Principal*
EMP: 15 **EST:** 1989
SQ FT: 3,500
SALES (est): 1.2MM **Privately Held**
WEB: www.baumancurry.com
SIC: 8742 8748 8999 3993 Marketing
consulting services; communications con-
sulting; advertising copy writing; advertis-
ing artwork; advertising agencies

(P-23250)
JIMS STEEL SUPPLY LLC
3530 Buck Owens Blvd, Bakersfield
(93308-4920)
P.O. Box 191 (93302-0191)
PHONE................................661 324-6514
Greg Boylan,
Karen Rohrbach, *Purch Agent*
Charles Feliscian, *Opers Staff*
Daron Hobson, *Sales Staff*
Jeff Rohrbach, *Manager*
EMP: 50
SALES (est): 15MM **Privately Held**
WEB: www.jimssteelsupply.com
SIC: 8742 Business consultant

(P-23251)
JNR INC
19900 Macarthur Blvd # 700, Irvine
(92612-8416)
PHONE................................949 476-2788
James Jalet III, *CEO*
Desiree Barto, *CEO*
Luann Jalet, *COO*
Greg Moody, *CFO*
Derek Dressler, *Exec VP*
EMP: 60
SQ FT: 15,000
SALES (est): 12.2MM **Privately Held**
WEB: www.jnrcorp.com
SIC: 8742 7389 4724 Incentive or award
program consultant; convention & show
services; tourist agency arranging trans-
port, lodging & car rental

(P-23252)
KINGS GARDEN LLC
Also Called: Kings Garden Royal Deliveries
3540 N Anza Rd, Palm Springs
(92262-1606)
PHONE................................760 275-4969
Lauri Kibby, *Mng Member*
Michael King, *Mng Member*
EMP: 180 **EST:** 2018
SALES (est): 7.1MM **Privately Held**
SIC: 8742 Marketing consulting services

(P-23253)
KPC GROUP INC (PA)
9 Kpc Pkwy 301, Corona (92879-7102)
PHONE................................951 782-8812
Michael O'Brien, *President*
Bill Thomas, *Exec VP*
John Petty, *Vice Pres*
EMP: 79 **EST:** 2006
SALES (est): 22.8MM **Privately Held**
WEB: www.thekpcgroup.com
SIC: 8742 Financial consultant

(P-23254)
KVC GROUP LLC
1551 N Tustin Ave Ste 550, Santa Ana
(92705-8637)
PHONE................................855 438-0377
Kim Vo, *Mng Member*
EMP: 75 **EST:** 2018
SALES (est): 3.3MM **Privately Held**
WEB: www.corporatefinancialiability.com
SIC: 8742 Marketing consulting services

(P-23255)
LABMED PARTNERS
5000 Birch St, Newport Beach
(92660-2127)
PHONE................................949 242-9925
EMP: 50

SALES (est): 1.3MM **Privately Held**
SIC: 8742 Management Consulting Services

(P-23256)
LBA INC
Also Called: Lba Realty
3347 Michelson Dr Ste 210, Irvine
(92612-0687)
PHONE................................949 833-0400
Perry Schonfeid, *Branch Mgr*
EMP: 73 **Privately Held**
WEB: www.lbarealty.com
SIC: 8742 Real estate consultant
PA: Lba Inc.
3347 Michelson Dr Ste 200
Irvine CA 92612

(P-23257)
LD HOLDINGS GROUP LLC (HQ)
26642 Towne Centre Dr, Foothill Ranch
(92610-2808)
PHONE................................888 337-6888
Unknown Hsieh, *Principal*
EMP: 50 **EST:** 2019
SALES (est): 986.9MM
SALES (corp-wide): 4.4B **Publicly Held**
WEB: www.loandepot.com
SIC: 8742 Business consultant
PA: Loandepot, Inc.
26642 Towne Centre Dr
Foothill Ranch CA 92610
888 337-6888

(P-23258)
LEAF COMMERCIAL CAPITAL INC
1100 W Town And Country R, Orange
(92868-4684)
PHONE................................866 219-7924
Rich Vohra, *Vice Pres*
Gene Cummins, *Executive*
EMP: 50 **Publicly Held**
WEB: www.leafnow.com
SIC: 8742 Financial consultant
HQ: Leaf Commercial Capital, Inc.
2005 Market St Fl 14
Philadelphia PA 19103
800 819-5556

(P-23259)
LEEKILPATRICK MANAGEMENT INC
Also Called: Management Success
324 S Myrtle Ave, Monrovia (91016-2849)
PHONE................................818 500-9631
Bill Kilpatrick, *President*
Brandon Molander, *Business Anlyst*
EMP: 60 **EST:** 1993
SQ FT: 18,200
SALES (est): 9.5MM **Privately Held**
WEB: www.driveshops.com
SIC: 8742 7538 Business consultant; gen-
eral automotive repair shops

(P-23260)
LEK CONSULTING LLC
1100 Glendon Ave Ste 2100, Los Angeles
(90024-3592)
PHONE................................310 209-9800
Sherice Lenons, *Manager*
Stephen Matthews, *Partner*
Jeffery Baxter, *Vice Pres*
Bill Frack, *Vice Pres*
Dan Schechter, *Vice Pres*
EMP: 50
SALES (corp-wide): 484.5MM **Privately Held**
WEB: www.lek.com
SIC: 8742 8748 Business consultant; busi-
ness consulting
HQ: L.E.K. Consulting, Llc
75 State St Ste 1901
Boston MA 02109

(P-23261)
LEVITY ENTERTAINMENT GROUP LLC
Also Called: L E G
6701 Center Dr W Fl 11, Los Angeles
(90045-1535)
PHONE................................310 417-4861
Robert Hartmann, *Mng Member*

Francesco Pace, *Vice Pres*
Marko Velazquez, *Vice Pres*
Ruth Pasillas, *Admin Asst*
Lenise Strong, *Project Mgr*
EMP: 50 **EST:** 2009
SALES (est): 13.3MM **Privately Held**
WEB: www.levitylive.com
SIC: 8742 Personnel management consult-
ant

(P-23262)
LIFEWORKS (US) LTD
27715 Jefferson Ave # 103, Temecula
(92590-2660)
PHONE................................888 577-3784
Muhammad Iftekhar, *Analyst*
Andrew Zur,
David Gruber, *Legal Staff*
EMP: 78
SALES (corp-wide): 747.4MM **Privately Held**
WEB: www.lifeworks.com
SIC: 8742 Human resource consulting
services
HQ: Lifeworks (Us) Ltd.
115 Perimeter Center Pl N
Atlanta GA 30346

(P-23263)
LINEA SOLUTIONS INC
10940 Wilshire Blvd, Los Angeles
(90024-3915)
PHONE................................310 443-4191
Akio Tagawa, *President*
Nicole Naddy, *Associate*
EMP: 61 **EST:** 1999
SALES (est): 5.1MM **Privately Held**
WEB: www.lineasolutions.com
SIC: 8742 Business consultant

(P-23264)
M E NOLLKAMPER INC (PA)
940 Manor Way, Corona (92882-7979)
PHONE................................951 737-9300
Milton Nollkamper, *President*
EMP: 50 **EST:** 1980
SALES (est): 2.7MM **Privately Held**
WEB: www.menoll.com
SIC: 8742 8711 Public utilities consultant;
consulting engineer

(P-23265)
M F SALTA CO INC (PA)
Also Called: Atlas Advertising
20 Executive Park Ste 150, Irvine
(92614-4732)
PHONE................................562 421-2512
Mike Salta, *President*
James Smith, *Treasurer*
EMP: 70 **EST:** 1959
SALES (est): 2.1MM **Privately Held**
SIC: 8742 Management consulting serv-
ices

(P-23266)
MAINLINE SALES INC (PA)
659 E Ball Rd, Anaheim (92805-5910)
PHONE................................714 300-0641
John Cristy, *CEO*
Carri Eshnaur, *Admin Asst*
Jeremy Lloyd, *Opers Staff*
Marc Peeples, *Regl Sales Mgr*
Michael Dennehy, *Sales Associate*
EMP: 67 **EST:** 2008
SALES (est): 10.6MM **Privately Held**
WEB: www.mlsalesinc.com
SIC: 8742 Sales (including sales manage-
ment) consultant

(P-23267)
MANAGEMENT TRUST ASSN INC
12607 Hiddencreek Way R, Cerritos
(90703-2146)
PHONE................................562 926-3372
Christie Alviso, *Administration*
EMP: 186 **Privately Held**
WEB: www.managementtrust.com
SIC: 8742 8741 Management consulting
services; business management
PA: The Management Trust Association Inc
15661 Red Hill Ave # 201
Tustin CA 92780

(P-23268)
MARCUS BUCKINGHAM COMPANY LLC
8350 Wilshire Blvd # 200, Beverly Hills
(90211-2348)
PHONE................................323 302-9810
Marcus Buckingham, *CEO*
Christian Gomez, *President*
EMP: 60 **EST:** 2005
SALES (est): 17.7MM
SALES (corp-wide): 14.5B **Publicly Held**
WEB: www.dev-mwb.tmoc.com
SIC: 8742 Training & development consult-
ant
PA: Automatic Data Processing, Inc.
1 Adp Blvd Ste 1 # 1
Roseland NJ 07068
973 974-5000

(P-23269)
MATT CONSTRUCTION CORPORATION (PA)
9814 Norwalk Blvd Ste 100, Santa Fe
Springs (90670-2997)
PHONE................................562 903-2277
Paul J Matt, *CEO*
Steve F Matt, *President*
Jennifer Halstead, *COO*
Neil Matt, *Treasurer*
Alan B Matt, *Corp Sec*
EMP: 124 **EST:** 1991
SQ FT: 21,000
SALES (est): 38.5MM **Privately Held**
WEB: www.mattconstruction.com
SIC: 8742 Construction project manage-
ment consultant

(P-23270)
MEDICAL SPC MANAGERS INC
Also Called: Medical Specialty Billing
1 City Blvd W Ste 1100, Orange
(92868-3647)
PHONE................................714 571-5000
Matt Haberman, *CEO*
Barry Haberman, *President*
Uri Klugman, *CFO*
Zachary Saltzman, *Officer*
Randy Brooks, *Vice Pres*
EMP: 115 **EST:** 1990
SQ FT: 29,000
SALES (est): 17.7MM **Privately Held**
WEB: www.msmhealth.com
SIC: 8742 8721 Hospital & health services
consultant; billing & bookkeeping service

(P-23271)
METROSTUDY INC
Also Called: Zonda Intelligence
4000 Macarthur Blvd # 400, Newport Beach
(92660-2543)
PHONE................................714 619-7800
Jeff Meyers, *CEO*
Diana Stewart, *Controller*
Karen Bennett,
Dorothy Dominguez,
Erin Ramirez, *Senior Mgr*
EMP: 184 **EST:** 2013
SALES (est): 50MM **Privately Held**
WEB: www.zondahome.com
SIC: 8742 7379 Real estate consultant;
computer related consulting services

(P-23272)
MF SERVICES COMPANY LLC (HQ)
4350 Von Karman Ave # 400, Newport
Beach (92660-2007)
PHONE................................949 474-5800
Paul Merage, *Mng Member*
Richard Merage,
EMP: 60 **EST:** 2005
SALES (est): 16MM
SALES (corp-wide): 38.6MM **Privately Held**
WEB: www.migcap.com
SIC: 8742 Financial consultant
PA: Mig Capital, Llc
660 Newport Center Dr # 450
Newport Beach CA 92660
949 474-5800

(P-23273)
MGID INC (PA)
1149 3rd St Ste 210, Santa Monica
(90403-7201)
PHONE....................424 322-8059
Ben Artikov, *Accountant*
James Song, *President*
Roman Bazar, *IT/INT Sup*
Samanta Jefferson, *Marketing Staff*
Igor Kozak, *Manager*
EMP: 95 EST: 2011
SALES (est): 3.6MM **Privately Held**
WEB: www.mgid.com
SIC: 8742 Marketing consulting services

(P-23274)
MICHAELSON CONNOR & BOUL (PA)
5312 Bolsa Ave, Huntington Beach
(92649-1051)
PHONE....................714 230-3600
Joan Heid, *President*
Firmin Boul, *Corp Secy*
Michael Ryan, *Vice Pres*
Kerry Neterer, *Exec Dir*
Ralph Muniz, *Accounting Mgr*
EMP: 100 EST: 1994
SQ FT: 12,500
SALES (est): 12.9MM **Privately Held**
WEB: www.mcbreo.com
SIC: 8742 Real estate consultant

(P-23275)
MOMENTFEED INC
3415 S Sepulveda Blvd # 1100, Los Angeles (90034-7090)
PHONE....................310 853-3336
Nick Hedges, *CEO*
Ed Cluss, *Partner*
Ed Shaughnessy, *CFO*
Robert Blatt, *Chairman*
Jim D'Arcangelo, *Chief Mktg Ofcr*
EMP: 79 EST: 2010
SALES (est): 11.2MM **Privately Held**
WEB: www.momentfeed.com
SIC: 8742 Marketing consulting services

(P-23276)
MORRIS & WILLNER PARTNERS
Also Called: Mw Partners
2151 Michelson Dr Ste 185, Irvine
(92612-1368)
PHONE....................949 705-0682
Divya Pyreddy, *CEO*
Michael Willner, *Managing Prtnr*
Keith Lippert, *Vice Pres*
Jeff Skarvan, *Vice Pres*
Jeffrey Skarvan, *Vice Pres*
EMP: 100 EST: 2010
SALES (est): 7.1MM **Privately Held**
WEB: www.mwpartners.net
SIC: 8742 Management consulting services

(P-23277)
MUTH MACHINE WORKS
4510 Rutile St, Riverside (92509-2649)
PHONE....................951 685-1521
Dwayne Gleason, *Manager*
EMP: 80
SALES (corp-wide): 52.2MM **Privately Held**
SIC: 8742 Manufacturing management consultant
HQ: Muth Machine Works
8042 Katella Ave
Stanton CA 90680

(P-23278)
MV MEDICAL MANAGEMENT
1860 Colo Blvd Ste 200, Los Angeles
(90041)
PHONE....................323 257-7637
Eva Vargas, *President*
Daniel E Vargas Jr, *COO*
Alma Moreno, *Treasurer*
Evy Vargas, *Admin Sec*
EMP: 60 EST: 1996
SQ FT: 7,400
SALES (est): 9.8MM **Privately Held**
WEB: www.mvmedical.com
SIC: 8742 Marketing consulting services

(P-23279)
NAMM CALIFORNIA (PA)
3990 Concours Ste 500, Ontario
(91764-7983)
PHONE....................909 605-8058
Leigh Hutchins, *Principal*
Doug Loop, *Assoc VP*
Vicki Medlen, *Assoc VP*
Trisha L Daniels, *Vice Pres*
Vera Grodzen, *Vice Pres*
EMP: 65 EST: 2010
SALES (est): 10.7MM **Privately Held**
WEB: www.nammcal.com
SIC: 8742 Hospital & health services consultant

(P-23280)
NATIONAL TOUR INTGRTED RSRCES
23141 Arroyo Vis Ste 100, Rcho STA Marg (92688-2613)
PHONE....................949 215-6330
Johnny R Capels, *President*
EMP: 23 EST: 2009
SQ FT: 6,000
SALES (est): 2MM **Privately Held**
WEB: www.nationaltourintegrated.com
SIC: 8742 3448 Marketing consulting services; prefabricated metal buildings

(P-23281)
NBC CONSULTING INC
Also Called: Pacific Health and Welness
2110 Artesia Blvd Ste 323, Redondo Beach (90278-3073)
PHONE....................310 798-5000
Neal M Bychek, *President*
Robin Bychek, *CFO*
EMP: 100 EST: 2004
SALES (est): 1MM **Privately Held**
WEB: www.phaws.com
SIC: 8742 Hospital & health services consultant

(P-23282)
NCOMPASS INTERNATIONAL LLC
12101 Crenshaw Blvd # 800, Hawthorne
(90250-3458)
PHONE....................323 785-1700
Donna Direnzo Graves, *President*
Kae Erickson, *COO*
Michaela McCoy, *Vice Pres*
Bethany Adam, *Graphic Designe*
Austin Noble, *Graphic Designe*
EMP: 138 EST: 2003
SALES (est): 24.5MM **Privately Held**
WEB: www.ncompassinternational.com
SIC: 8742 Marketing consulting services

(P-23283)
NEARDATA INC
Also Called: Neardata Systems
4502 Dyer St Ste 103, La Crescenta
(91214-2854)
PHONE....................818 249-2469
Samuel S Chilingurian, *President*
Samuel Chilinguirian, *COO*
Sam Chillingurian, *COO*
EMP: 76 EST: 2005
SQ FT: 5,600
SALES (est): 7.5MM **Privately Held**
WEB: www.neardata.net
SIC: 8742 7371 Management consulting services; computer software development

(P-23284)
NIUSOURCE INC
14266 Euclid Ave, Chino (91710-8803)
PHONE....................909 631-2895
Jie Lin, *CEO*
Michael Chan, *Officer*
Linda Lin, *General Mgr*
EMP: 17 EST: 2014
SALES (est): 2.3MM **Privately Held**
WEB: www.niusource.com
SIC: 8742 2834 Food & beverage consultant; chlorination tablets & kits (water purification)

(P-23285)
NORTH HIGHLAND COMPANY LLC
4640 Lankershim Blvd # 30, North Hollywood (91602-1841)
PHONE....................818 509-5100
John Depoma, *Branch Mgr*
Angi Fisher, *Manager*
EMP: 109 **Privately Held**
WEB: www.northhighland.com
SIC: 8742 Business consultant
PA: The North Highland Company Llc
3333 Piedmont Rd Ne # 1000
Atlanta GA 30305

(P-23286)
NVE INC (PA)
700 N San Vicnte Blvd, West Hollywood
(90069-5060)
PHONE....................323 512-8400
Brett Nathan Hyman, *CEO*
Sean Anglin, *Prdtn Mgr*
Melanie Miron, *Production*
Sarah Zimmerman, *Production*
Lilit Nurse-Kalachyan, *Art Dir*
EMP: 99 EST: 2005
SALES (est): 10.4MM **Privately Held**
WEB: www.experiencenve.com
SIC: 8742 Marketing consulting services; business planning & organizing services

(P-23287)
OM FOOD SEJAL ENTERPRISES INC
449 W Allen Ave Ste 111, San Dimas
(91773-1483)
PHONE....................626 712-3138
Pete J Patel, *CEO*
EMP: 52 EST: 2012
SALES (est): 1.8MM **Privately Held**
WEB: www.mysubwaysubs.com
SIC: 8742 Restaurant & food services consultants

(P-23288)
ONYX GLOBAL HR LLC (PA)
110 Pine Ave Ste 920, Long Beach
(90802-4455)
P.O. Box 5673, Orange (92863-5673)
PHONE....................866 715-4806
Douglas R Bender Sr,
Barbara Sullivan,
Pierre Towns,
Mark Wilcher,
EMP: 64 EST: 2008
SQ FT: 1,000 **Privately Held**
WEB: www.onyxglobalhr.com
SIC: 8742 Human resource consulting services

(P-23289)
OPERAM INC
1041 N Formosa Ave 500, West Hollywood
(90046-6703)
PHONE....................855 673-7261
Johnny Wong, *Principal*
Sara Kabani, *Office Mgr*
Jerry Sommerville, *CIO*
Marc Pierson, *Accountant*
Samuel Hafer, *Opers Staff*
EMP: 84 EST: 2015
SQ FT: 23,000
SALES (est): 9.4MM **Privately Held**
WEB: www.operam.com
SIC: 8742 Marketing consulting services

(P-23290)
ORANGE COAST WNS MED GROUP INC
24411 Health Center Dr # 200, Laguna Hills
(92653-3651)
PHONE....................949 829-5500
Dennis Martin, *President*
EMP: 85
SALES (corp-wide): 16.1MM **Privately Held**
WEB: www.ocwmg.com
SIC: 8742 8011 Hospital & health services consultant; pediatrician
PA: Orange Coast Women's Medical Group, Inc.
24411 Health Center Dr # 200
Laguna Hills CA 92653
949 829-5500

(P-23291)
P H S MANAGEMENT GROUP (PA)
721 N Eckhoff St, Orange (92868-1005)
PHONE....................714 547-7551
Kevin O Lewand, *President*
EMP: 50 EST: 1978
SALES (est): 1.5MM **Privately Held**
SIC: 8742 Hospital & health services consultant

(P-23292)
PANDORA MARKETING LLC
Also Called: Timeshare Compliance
26970 Aliso Viejo Pkwy # 150, Aliso Viejo
(92656-2683)
PHONE....................800 705-6856
William Wilson,
Irene Dasalla, *Vice Pres*
EMP: 75 EST: 2016
SALES (est): 10.4MM **Privately Held**
WEB: www.timesharecompliance.com
SIC: 8742 Marketing consulting services

(P-23293)
PARA SEMPRE INC ✪
11322 Idaho Ave Ste 202, Los Angeles
(90025-3170)
P.O. Box 45, Santa Monica (90406-0045)
PHONE....................310 444-0555
Tahj Zeekvrotzkii, *CEO*
EMP: 74 EST: 2021
SALES (est): 1MM **Privately Held**
SIC: 8742 Management consulting services

(P-23294)
PARTNERS IN LEADERSHIP LLC (HQ)
27555 Ynez Rd Ste 200, Temecula
(92591-4677)
PHONE....................951 694-5596
Gordon Treadway, *CEO*
Jeff McMullin, *Senior Partner*
Marcus Nicolls, *Senior Partner*
Brad Starr, *Senior Partner*
Brad Burton, *Partner*
▲ EMP: 94 EST: 2004
SALES (est): 31MM **Privately Held**
WEB: www.culture.io
SIC: 8742 Business consultant
PA: Partners In Leadership Intermediate Holdings Llc
27555 Ynez Rd
Temecula CA 92591
951 506-6878

(P-23295)
PENSINMARK RTIREMENT GROUP LLC
24 E Cota St Ste 200, Santa Barbara
(93101-1665)
PHONE....................805 456-6260
Troy G Hammond, *Mng Member*
Tony Black, *Partner*
Jeffrey Seymour, *Managing Prtnr*
Barry Toole, *Officer*
Jennifer Tanck, *Exec VP*
EMP: 55 EST: 2008
SALES (est): 4.7MM **Privately Held**
WEB: www.pensionmark.com
SIC: 8742 Financial consultant

(P-23296)
PHENOMENON MKTG & ENTRMT LLC (PA)
5900 Wilshire Blvd Fl 28, Los Angeles
(90036-5013)
PHONE....................323 648-4000
Krishnan Menon, *CEO*
Jackie Aronson, *Officer*
Linda Knight, *Officer*
Brittney McDonald, *Business Dir*
Kayla Lee, *Business Mgr*
EMP: 60 EST: 2006
SQ FT: 15,289
SALES (est): 16.2MM **Privately Held**
WEB: www.phenomenon.com
SIC: 8742 Marketing consulting services

(P-23297)
POSTALIO INC
75 Higuera St Ste 240, San Luis Obispo
(93401-5425)
PHONE....................408 616-9284

Erik Kostelnik, *CEO*
EMP: 16 **EST:** 2019
SALES (est): 2.1MM **Privately Held**
WEB: www.postal.io
SIC: 8742 5734 7372 Marketing consulting services; software, business & non-game; business oriented computer software

(P-23298)
POWERSOURCE TALENT LLC
12655 W Jefferson Blvd, Los Angeles (90066-7008)
PHONE..................424 835-0878
Lisa Tran McKee, *CEO*
Mike Bassignani, *Partner*
EMP: 101 **EST:** 2017
SALES (est): 3.4MM **Privately Held**
WEB: www.powersourcetalent.com
SIC: 8742 Management consulting services

(P-23299)
PRIMUS GROUP INC (PA)
Also Called: Primus Labs
2810 Industrial Pkwy, Santa Maria (93455-1812)
PHONE..................805 922-0055
Robert F Stovicek, *Principal*
Mike Sullivan, *CFO*
Rob Pearson, *Vice Pres*
Brian Mansfield, *Business Dir*
Debra Ritorto, *Office Mgr*
EMP: 50 **EST:** 1987
SQ FT: 12,000
SALES (est): 24.2MM **Privately Held**
WEB: www.primuslabs.com
SIC: 8742 8734 8731 Food & beverage consultant; food testing service; commercial physical research

(P-23300)
PRO SAFETY & RESCUE INC
3701 Pegasus Dr Ste 124, Bakersfield (93308-6843)
PHONE..................888 269-5095
Sarah Pierce, *President*
Jesse Pierce, *Vice Pres*
Jessie Pierce, *Admin Sec*
EMP: 70 **EST:** 2014
SQ FT: 6,900
SALES (est): 5.8MM **Privately Held**
WEB: www.prosafetyandrescue.com
SIC: 8742 8999 Training & development consultant; search & rescue service

(P-23301)
PROMO SHOP INC (PA)
5420 Mcconnell Ave, Los Angeles (90066-7037)
PHONE..................310 821-1780
Guillermo Kahan, *President*
Robert Golden, *CFO*
Kris Robinson, *Officer*
Matthew Mason, *Vice Pres*
Caren Aardema, *Executive*
◆ **EMP:** 55 **EST:** 1998
SALES: 39.6MM **Privately Held**
WEB: www.promoshopinc.com
SIC: 8742 Marketing consulting services

(P-23302)
PROMOTE MEDIA LP
8484 Wilshire Blvd # 630, Beverly Hills (90211-3227)
PHONE..................323 433-7950
Jeffrey Essebag, *CEO*
EMP: 60 **EST:** 2017
SALES (est): 2.6MM **Privately Held**
WEB: www.promoteroi.com
SIC: 8742 Marketing consulting services

(P-23303)
PUBLIC AGENCY RESOURCES
2125 E Katella Ave # 200, Anaheim (92806-6072)
PHONE..................714 940-6300
Richard Kopecky, *President*
EMP: 77 **EST:** 2005
SALES (est): 441.5K
SALES (corp-wide): 390.9MM **Publicly Held**
WEB: www.willdan.com
SIC: 8742 Business planning & organizing services

PA: Willdan Group, Inc.
2401 E Katella Ave # 300
Anaheim CA 92806
800 424-9144

(P-23304)
QUINTILE WEALTH MANAGEMENT LLC
11150 Santa Monica Blvd # 400, Los Angeles (90025-3380)
PHONE..................310 806-4000
Robert Francais,
Kenneth Anderson,
Marc Primiani,
Robert Wagman,
EMP: 50 **EST:** 2002
SQ FT: 8,000
SALES (est): 1.8MM **Privately Held**
WEB: www.aspiriant.com
SIC: 8742 Financial consultant

(P-23305)
RALIS SERVICES CORP
1 City Blvd W Ste 600, Orange (92868-3639)
PHONE..................844 347-2547
Delbert O Meeks, *CEO*
Mike Chiang, *Admin Sec*
Nathan Aila, *Senior Engr*
Bridgette Moore, *Analyst*
Bryan Pinkham, *Analyst*
EMP: 150 **EST:** 2014
SALES (est): 6MM **Privately Held**
WEB: www.ralisservices.com
SIC: 8742 7371 8721 Human resource consulting services; marketing consulting services; business planning & organizing services; custom computer programming services; accounting services, except auditing

(P-23306)
RALPH BRENNAN REST GROUP LLC
Also Called: Red Fish Grill
1590 S Disneyland Dr, Anaheim (92802-2319)
PHONE..................714 776-5200
Kiki Lungquist, *Branch Mgr*
Duarte Bruno, *Executive*
EMP: 79 **Privately Held**
WEB: www.neworleans-food.com
SIC: 8742 Restaurant & food services consultants
PA: The Ralph Brennan Restaurant Group Llc
550 Bienville St
New Orleans LA 70130

(P-23307)
RED PEAK GROUP LLC
23975 Park Sorrento # 410, Calabasas (91302-4031)
PHONE..................818 222-7762
Michael Birkin, *CEO*
EMP: 90 **EST:** 2009
SALES (est): 2.4MM **Privately Held**
SIC: 8742 Marketing consulting services

(P-23308)
RENEW HEALTH GROUP LLC
107 W Lemon Ave, Monrovia (91016-2809)
PHONE..................310 625-2838
Crystal Solorzano, *CEO*
Cheryl Petterson, *Vice Pres*
Donald Bruhns, *Director*
EMP: 50 **EST:** 2016
SALES (est): 5.1MM **Privately Held**
WEB: www.renewhg.com
SIC: 8742 Hospital & health services consultant

(P-23309)
RESOURCES CONNECTION INC (PA)
17101 Armstrong Ave # 100, Irvine (92614-5742)
PHONE..................714 430-6400
Kate W Duchene, *President*
Donald B Murray, *Ch of Bd*
Timothy Brackney, *COO*
Jennifer Ryu, *CFO*
Michelle Stone, *Chairman*
EMP: 732 **EST:** 1996

SQ FT: 56,200
SALES (est): 629.5MM **Publicly Held**
WEB: www.rgp.com
SIC: 8742 7389 8721 Business consultant; business planning & organizing services; financial services; legal & tax services; accounting, auditing & bookkeeping; auditing services

(P-23310)
RMD GROUP INC
2311 E South St, Long Beach (90805-4424)
PHONE..................562 866-9288
Ralph Holguin, *President*
Eli Saiz, *General Mgr*
Leslie Castellanos, *Controller*
Katia Pena, *Account Dir*
EMP: 300 **EST:** 2008
SALES (est): 20.2MM **Privately Held**
WEB: www.rmdgroupinc.com
SIC: 8742 Marketing consulting services

(P-23311)
RMI UTILITY SERVICES INC
2323 E Vernon Ave, Vernon (90058-1608)
PHONE..................323 589-9498
John S Forman, *Director*
EMP: 59 **EST:** 1989
SQ FT: 20,000
SALES (est): 1.2MM **Privately Held**
WEB: www.guidehouse.com
SIC: 8742 Business consultant
HQ: Guidehouse Inc.
2941 Frview Pk Dr Ste 501
Falls Church VA 22042
571 633-1711

(P-23312)
ROSSIER PARK SCHOOL
Also Called: Rossier Park School
7100 Knott Ave, Buena Park (90620-1314)
PHONE..................714 562-0441
Maria Wagner, *Director*
Maria Chappelear, *Exec Dir*
Joan Bogaty, *Administration*
Jamie Linan, *Teacher*
Martha Teran, *Supervisor*
EMP: 53 **EST:** 1993
SALES (est): 3.2MM **Privately Held**
SIC: 8299 8742 Educational services; hospital & health services consultant

(P-23313)
RUBY CREEK RESOURCES INC
11835 W Olympic Blvd, Los Angeles (90064-5001)
PHONE..................212 671-0404
Robert Slavik, *CEO*
EMP: 50 **EST:** 2006
SALES (est): 2.4MM **Privately Held**
WEB: www.rubycreekgold.com
SIC: 8742 Business planning & organizing services

(P-23314)
S E O P INC
1621 Alton Pkwy Ste 150, Irvine (92606-4875)
PHONE..................949 682-7906
Gary Hagins, *CEO*
Rhonda Spears, *President*
Kyra Herrick, *Manager*
Abram Serrano, *Manager*
Joshua Wyrick, *Consultant*
EMP: 150 **EST:** 2001
SALES (est): 13.8MM **Privately Held**
WEB: www.seop.com
SIC: 8742 Marketing consulting services

(P-23315)
SABAN BRANDS LLC (HQ)
10100 Santa Monica Blvd # 500, Los Angeles (90067-4003)
PHONE..................310 557-5230
Elie Dekel, *President*
Jack Sorensen, *President*
Janet Scardino, *COO*
William Kehoe, *CFO*
Rami S Yanni, *Vice Pres*
EMP: 88 **EST:** 2010
SQ FT: 605,000

SALES (est): 16.5MM
SALES (corp-wide): 42.9MM **Privately Held**
WEB: www.saban.com
SIC: 8742 General management consultant
PA: Global Reach 18, Inc.
10100 Santa Monica Blvd # 900
Los Angeles CA 90067
310 203-5850

(P-23316)
SAVIYNT INC (PA)
1301 E El Segundo Blvd El Segundo (90245-4303)
PHONE..................310 641-1664
Amit Saha, *CEO*
Darren Martin, *Partner*
Scott Plutko, *Partner*
Rishma Shariff, *Partner*
Paul Zolfaghari, *Bd of Directors*
EMP: 122 **EST:** 2011
SQ FT: 10,000
SALES (est): 34.5MM **Privately Held**
WEB: www.saviynt.com
SIC: 8742 Business consultant

(P-23317)
SCORPION DESIGN LLC
27750 Entertainment Dr, Valencia (91355-1091)
PHONE..................661 702-0100
Daniel Street, *CEO*
Raj Ramanan, *COO*
Eric Reuveni, *COO*
Corey Quinn, *Chief Mktg Ofcr*
Mikel Chertudi, *Officer*
EMP: 565 **EST:** 2003
SQ FT: 100,000
SALES (est): 117.7MM **Privately Held**
WEB: www.scorpion.co
SIC: 8742 Marketing consulting services

(P-23318)
SEARCH AGENCY INC (DH)
801 N Brand Blvd Ste 1020, Glendale (91203-1279)
PHONE..................310 873-5700
David Hughes, *CEO*
Joy Musry, *Admin Sec*
EMP: 89 **EST:** 2003
SALES (est): 16.8MM
SALES (corp-wide): 199.1K **Privately Held**
WEB: www.forwardpmx.com
SIC: 8742 Marketing consulting services
HQ: Forwardpmx Group Llc
1 World Trade Ctr Fl 63
New York NY 10007
212 387-0300

(P-23319)
SEEK CAPITAL LLC
6420 Wilshire Blvd # 500, Los Angeles (90048-5562)
PHONE..................855 978-6106
Roy Ferman, *CEO*
Mary Ann Dacaney, *Partner*
Michael Freeman, *Senior VP*
David Halverson, *Vice Pres*
Ryan Kelly, *VP Bus Dvlpt*
EMP: 75 **EST:** 2014
SALES (est): 5.7MM **Privately Held**
WEB: www.seekcapital.com
SIC: 8742 Management consulting services

(P-23320)
SERVICE BENEFITS LLC
8201 Beverly Blvd Ste 302, West Hollywood (90048-4542)
PHONE..................312 576-2247
Carlos Cruz, *Mng Member*
EMP: 57 **EST:** 2020
SALES (est): 1.3MM **Privately Held**
SIC: 8742 Human resource consulting services

(P-23321)
SHELL OIL COMPANY
511 N Brookhurst St, Anaheim (92801-5231)
P.O. Box 4848 (92803-4848)
PHONE..................714 991-9200
Roger Underwood, *Branch Mgr*
EMP: 125

SALES (corp-wide): 180.5B **Privately Held**
WEB: www.shell.com
SIC: 8742 Industry specialist consultants
HQ: Shell Oil Company
150 N Dairy Ashford Rd
Houston TX 77079
713 241-6161

(P-23322)
SIERRA SYSTEMS INC (PA)
222 N Pacific Coast Hwy # 1310, El Segundo (90245-5644)
PHONE...................................310 536-6288
Calvin Yonker, *President*
Patricia Kaiser, *COO*
Brian Fees, *CFO*
Chad Helton, *Consultant*
EMP: 139 **EST:** 1980
SALES (est): 12.1MM **Privately Held**
SIC: 8742 Management consulting services

(P-23323)
SITESTUFF YARDI SYSTEMS I (PA)
430 S Fairview Ave, Goleta (93117-3637)
PHONE...................................805 966-3666
Steven Sewell, *Principal*
Samuel Giles, *Software Engr*
Steven Eilat, *Project Mgr*
David Fletcher, *Technical Staff*
Jessica Flores, *Technical Staff*
EMP: 195 **EST:** 2010
SALES (est): 32.4MM **Privately Held**
WEB: www.yardi.com
SIC: 8742 Real estate consultant

(P-23324)
SITRICK BRINCKO GROUP LLC
1840 Century Park E # 800, Los Angeles (90067-2101)
PHONE...................................310 788-2850
EMP: 60
SALES (est): 3.6MM **Publicly Held**
SIC: 8742 8743 Management Consulting Services
PA: Resources Connection, Inc.
17101 Armstrong Ave # 100
Irvine CA 92614

(P-23325)
SKYNET USA ASSET MGT INC
17011 Beach Blvd Fl 9th, Huntington Beach (92647-5946)
PHONE...................................702 969-5599
Johnny Thanh Hong, *CEO*
EMP: 50 **EST:** 2017
SALES (est): 1.2MM **Privately Held**
SIC: 8742 Financial consultant

(P-23326)
SMART CIRCLE INTERNATIONAL LLC (PA)
Also Called: Smart Circle, The
4490 Von Karman Ave, Newport Beach (92660-2008)
PHONE...................................949 587-9207
Michael Meryash, *CEO*
George Graffy, *President*
Jigna Patel, *COO*
Paul Sunny, *CFO*
James Stone, *Vice Pres*
EMP: 90 **EST:** 2007
SQ FT: 10,700
SALES (est): 327.1MM **Privately Held**
WEB: www.smartcircle.com
SIC: 8742 Marketing consulting services

(P-23327)
SMITH-EMERY COMPANY (PA)
781 E Washington Blvd, Los Angeles (90021-3091)
PHONE...................................213 745-5312
James Partridge, *Ch of Bd*
James E Partridge, *Ch of Bd*
Beth Power, *Business Dir*
William Partridge, *Project Mgr*
Janeth Quintero, *Director*
▲ **EMP:** 168 **EST:** 1904
SQ FT: 35,000
SALES (est): 26.8MM **Privately Held**
WEB: www.smithemery.com
SIC: 8742 Construction project management consultant

(P-23328)
SOCIALCOM INC
Also Called: Audiencex
13468 Beach Ave, Marina Del Rey (90292-5624)
PHONE...................................310 289-4477
Reeve Benaron, *CEO*
Shane Taylor, *Partner*
Brian Katz, *Officer*
Lauren Hutton, *Vice Pres*
Tiffany Kim, *Finance*
EMP: 75 **EST:** 2013
SALES (est): 6.2MM **Privately Held**
WEB: www.audiencex.com
SIC: 8742 Marketing consulting services

(P-23329)
SODEXO MANAGEMENT INC
450 World Way, Los Angeles (90045-5812)
PHONE...................................310 646-3738
EMP: 414
SALES (corp-wide): 158.5MM **Privately Held**
WEB: www.sodexo.com
SIC: 8742 Food & beverage consultant
HQ: Sodexo Management Inc.
9801 Washingtonian Blvd
Gaithersburg MD 20878

(P-23330)
SOUTH COAST WATER DISTRICT
34152 Del Obispo St, Dana Point (92629-2916)
P.O. Box 30205, Laguna Beach (92607-0205)
PHONE...................................949 499-4555
Mark Dunber, *Manager*
Joe McDivitt, *Officer*
Jillian Van Orden, *Admin Asst*
Tom Madeo, *Senior Engr*
Brian Huber, *Manager*
EMP: 56
SALES (corp-wide): 35.7MM **Privately Held**
WEB: www.scwd.org
SIC: 8742 Public utilities consultant
PA: South Coast Water District
31592 West St
Laguna Beach CA 92651
949 499-4555

(P-23331)
SPINLAUNCH INC
4350 E Conant St, Long Beach (90808-1868)
PHONE...................................650 516-7746
Jonathan Yaney, *President*
Stephen Hobart, *Vice Pres*
Chris Weals, *Accounting Mgr*
Ralph Monserrat, *Director*
Sean Rivkin, *Director*
EMP: 99 **EST:** 2015
SALES (est): 10.7MM **Privately Held**
WEB: www.spinlaunch.com
SIC: 8742 Business consultant

(P-23332)
SPRINTRAY INC
2705 Media Center Dr 2, Los Angeles (90065-1700)
PHONE...................................800 914-8004
Amir Mansouri, *CEO*
Erich Kreidler, *President*
Arun Subramony, *CFO*
Ed Cohen, *Officer*
John Cox, *Officer*
EMP: 200 **EST:** 2017
SALES (est): 13.8MM **Privately Held**
WEB: www.sprintray.com
SIC: 8742 Management consulting services

(P-23333)
SQA SERVICES INC
425 Via Corta Ste 203, Palos Verdes Estates (90274-1358)
P.O. Box 5220, Pls Vrds Pnsl (90274-9672)
PHONE...................................800 333-6180
James C McKay, *CEO*
J Michael McKay, *President*
Ricky Smith, *Officer*
Gerard Pearce, *Vice Pres*
Stephanie Rankin, *Office Mgr*
EMP: 267 **EST:** 1995

SQ FT: 8,000
SALES (est): 26.7MM **Privately Held**
WEB: www.sqaservices.com
SIC: 8742 Quality assurance consultant

(P-23334)
ST MARYS MEDICAL CENTER
1050 Linden Ave, Long Beach (90813-3321)
PHONE...................................562 491-9230
Suzan Konel, *Branch Mgr*
EMP: 1928
SALES (corp-wide): 17.6B **Publicly Held**
WEB: www.stmarysmc.com
SIC: 8742 Hospital & health services consultant
HQ: St. Mary's Medical Center, Inc.
901 45th St
Mangonia Park FL 33407
561 844-6300

(P-23335)
STONE CANYON INDS HOLDINGS LLC (PA)
1875 Century Park E # 320, Los Angeles (90067-2253)
PHONE...................................424 316-2061
James Fordyce, *CEO*
Michael Neumann, *President*
Michael C Salvator, *COO*
Adam Cohn, *Co-CEO*
EMP: 25 **EST:** 2018
SALES (est): 701.2MM **Privately Held**
WEB: www.scihinc.com
SIC: 8742 2899 Industrial consultant; heat treating salts

(P-23336)
SULLIVNCRTSMNROE INSUR SVCS LL (PA)
Also Called: Nationwide
1920 Main St Ste 600, Irvine (92614-7226)
P.O. Box 19763 (92623-9763)
PHONE...................................800 427-3253
John Monroe, *CEO*
Bill Curtis, *Managing Prtnr*
David Kummer, *President*
Mark Eckenweiler, *CFO*
Carol Jenkins, *Officer*
EMP: 103 **EST:** 1987
SQ FT: 22,000
SALES (est): 38.3MM **Privately Held**
WEB: www.sullivancurtismonroe.com
SIC: 8742 6411 Management consulting services; insurance brokers

(P-23337)
SUN PACIFIC MARKETING COOP INC
33502 Lerdo Hwy, Bakersfield (93308-9438)
PHONE...................................213 612-9957
Berne H Evans III, *Branch Mgr*
EMP: 395
SALES (corp-wide): 336MM **Privately Held**
WEB: www.sunpacific.com
SIC: 8742 Marketing consulting services
PA: Sun Pacific Marketing Cooperative, Inc.
1095 E Green St
Pasadena CA 91106
213 612-9957

(P-23338)
SYSTEM1 LLC (PA)
4235 Redwood Ave, Los Angeles (90066-5605)
PHONE...................................310 256-4882
Ian Weingarten, *CEO*
Paul Filsinger, *President*
Beth Sestanovich, *COO*
Jennie Telehowski, *Vice Pres*
Scott Birnbaum, *General Mgr*
EMP: 107 **EST:** 2017
SALES (est): 26.6MM **Privately Held**
WEB: www.system1.com
SIC: 8742 Marketing consulting services

(P-23339)
TECHNICAL MICRO CONS INC (PA)
Also Called: Technology Management Concepts
807 N Park View Dr # 150, El Segundo (90245-4932)
PHONE...................................310 559-3982
Jennifer Harris, *President*
EMP: 24 **EST:** 1985
SQ FT: 3,000
SALES (est): 4MM **Privately Held**
WEB: www.aboutttmc.com
SIC: 8742 7372 5734 Management information systems consultant; prepackaged software; software, business & non-game

(P-23340)
TECOLOTE RESEARCH INC
2120 E Grand Ave Ste 200, El Segundo (90245-5024)
PHONE...................................310 640-4700
James Takayesu, *President*
Lee Atkins, *Manager*
Charles Delio, *Consultant*
EMP: 53
SALES (corp-wide): 70.2MM **Privately Held**
WEB: www.tecolote.com
SIC: 8742 8731 Management consulting services; commercial physical research
PA: Tecolote Research, Inc.
420 S Fairview Ave # 201
Goleta CA 93117
805 571-6366

(P-23341)
TECOLOTE RESEARCH INC
Also Called: Santa Barbara Group
5266 Hollister Ave # 301, Santa Barbara (93111-2089)
PHONE...................................805 964-6963
James Suttle, *Branch Mgr*
John Bielecki, *Principal*
Ayesha Roorok, *Technical Mgr*
Emily Bower, *Prgrmr*
Andrew Polk, *Prgrmr*
EMP: 53
SALES (corp-wide): 70.2MM **Privately Held**
WEB: www.tecolote.com
SIC: 8742 Marketing consulting services
PA: Tecolote Research, Inc.
420 S Fairview Ave # 201
Goleta CA 93117
805 571-6366

(P-23342)
TECOLOTE RESEARCH INC
Also Called: Software Products & Svcs Group
5383 Hollister Ave # 100, Santa Barbara (93111-2304)
PHONE...................................805 964-6963
James Takayesu, *President*
EMP: 53
SALES (corp-wide): 70.2MM **Privately Held**
WEB: www.tecolote.com
SIC: 8742 8731 Management consulting services; commercial physical research
PA: Tecolote Research, Inc.
420 S Fairview Ave # 201
Goleta CA 93117
805 571-6366

(P-23343)
TELECOM LEASE ADVISORS LLC (DH)
4640 Admiralty Way # 1030, Marina Del Rey (90292-6621)
PHONE...................................877 418-5238
Jarred D Saba, *Mng Member*
Seth Evenson, *COO*
Yariel Chiong, *Vice Pres*
Rob Korman, *Vice Pres*
Kira Vance, *Surgery Dir*
EMP: 50 **EST:** 2008
SALES (est): 9.6MM **Publicly Held**
WEB: www.leaseadvisors.com
SIC: 8742 8748 Banking & finance consultant; construction project management consultant; site location consultant; telecommunications consultant; systems analysis & engineering consulting services

HQ: Insite Wireless Group, Llc
10 Presidential Way # 101
Woburn MA 01801
703 535-3009

(P-23344)
TELESECTOR RESOURCES GROUP INC
Also Called: Verizon
5010 Azusa Canyon Rd, Baldwin Park
(91706-1830)
PHONE..................626 813-4538
Nancy Cano, *Manager*
EMP: 363
SALES (corp-wide): 128.2B **Publicly Held**
SIC: 8742 Management consulting services
HQ: Telesector Resources Group, Inc.
140 West St
New York NY 10007
212 395-1000

(P-23345)
TELESTAR INTERNATIONAL CORP
Also Called: Telestar Material
5536 Balboa Blvd, Encino (91316-1505)
PHONE..................909 598-3636
Frank Liu, *President*
Karen Liu, *Corp Secy*
Charlie Fu, *Senior VP*
EMP: 46 **EST:** 1976
SALES (est): 3.6MM **Privately Held**
WEB: www.telestarcorporation.com
SIC: 8742 3663 Marketing consulting services; management information systems consultant; antennas, transmitting & communications

(P-23346)
THIEL CAPITAL LLC (PA)
9200 W Sunset Blvd # 1110, West Hollywood (90069-3616)
PHONE..................323 990-2030
Peter Thiel,
Justin Truscott, *CFO*
Timothy Voris, *Officer*
Hanna Leeke, *Office Mgr*
Ashton Rank, *Executive Asst*
EMP: 50 **EST:** 1996
SALES (est): 6.6MM **Privately Held**
WEB: www.thielcapital.com
SIC: 8742 Financial consultant

(P-23347)
TINSON LLC
450 N Brand Blvd, Glendale (91203-2347)
PHONE..................901 494-6405
EMP: 50 **EST:** 2019
SALES (est): 1.3MM **Privately Held**
SIC: 8742 Business consultant

(P-23348)
TOM PONTON INDUSTRIES INC
22901 Savi Ranch Pkwy, Yorba Linda
(92887-4615)
PHONE..................714 998-9073
Martin H Ponton, *President*
Karen Pettifer, *Corp Secy*
Carl Pino, *Vice Pres*
Jay Poulter, *Manager*
EMP: 19 **EST:** 1972
SALES (est): 18MM **Privately Held**
WEB: www.pontonind.com
SIC: 8742 3823 Industrial consultant; absorption analyzers: infrared, X-ray, etc.: industrial

(P-23349)
TOTAL RECON SOLUTIONS INC
27 Oakbrook, Trabuco Canyon
(92679-4741)
PHONE..................949 584-8417
Santiago Rydelski, *CEO*
EMP: 90 **EST:** 2011
SALES (est): 3.7MM **Privately Held**
SIC: 8742 Management consulting services

(P-23350)
TRACE3 LLC (HQ)
7565 Irvine Center Dr # 20, Irvine
(92618-4918)
PHONE..................949 333-2300
Rich Fennessy, *CEO*

Kelly Frazee, *Partner*
Jesse Janssen, *Partner*
Tyler Beecher, *Ch of Bd*
Kevin Manzo, *CFO*
EMP: 81 **EST:** 2001
SQ FT: 10,000
SALES (est): 212.5MM **Privately Held**
WEB: www.trace3.com
SIC: 8742 Sales (including sales management) consultant
PA: Escape Velocity Holdings, Inc.
7565 Irvine Center Dr # 20
Irvine CA 92618
949 333-2381

(P-23351)
TRANSPACIFIC FINANCIAL INC (PA)
185 W Chestnut Ave, Monrovia
(91016-3429)
PHONE..................626 447-7888
Philip Hu, *President*
Tracy Tung, *Partner*
Michael Fang, *Officer*
Yvonne Tung, *Exec VP*
Hans Wang, *Vice Pres*
EMP: 58 **EST:** 2009
SALES (est): 5MM **Privately Held**
WEB: www.transpacificagency.com
SIC: 8742 6311 Financial consultant; life insurance

(P-23352)
TRIDANT SOLUTIONS INC
453 N Lake Ave, Pasadena (91101-1215)
PHONE..................310 292-7382
Annette Palazuelos, *CEO*
Tristan Murcia, *Director*
Christopher Levens, *Manager*
EMP: 61 **EST:** 2005
SALES (est): 4.9MM **Privately Held**
WEB: www.tridantsolutions.com
SIC: 8742 8748 8741 7389 Hospital & health services consultant; financial consultant; business consulting; management services; financial management for business; inventory stocking service; hazardous waste collection & disposal; graphic arts & related design

(P-23353)
TRINAMIX INC (PA)
35 Amoret Dr, Irvine (92602-0770)
PHONE..................408 507-3583
Amit Sharma, *CEO*
Molly Chakraborty, *President*
Sandeep Goyal, *CFO*
EMP: 262 **EST:** 2008
SALES (est): 15.2MM **Privately Held**
WEB: www.trinamix.com
SIC: 8742 7379 7361 Management consulting services; computer related consulting services; labor contractors (employment agency)

(P-23354)
TRIVISTA BUSINESS GROUP INC (PA)
18565 Jamboree Rd Ste 350, Irvine
(92612-2566)
PHONE..................949 218-4830
Timothy Ristoff, *President*
Joe Ruiz, *CFO*
Ted Ristoff, *Chairman*
George Atkinson, *Senior VP*
Stuart Lowe, *Senior VP*
EMP: 109 **EST:** 2008
SALES (est): 11.5MM **Privately Held**
WEB: www.trivista.com
SIC: 8742 Business consultant

(P-23355)
TRUOG-RYDING COMPANY INC
2659 Townsgate Rd Ste 101, Westlake Village (91361-2797)
PHONE..................805 371-9222
David Ryding, *President*
David Jockisch, *Vice Pres*
Irene Ryding, *Vice Pres*
Danielle Sesock, *Business Dir*
Brianne Galik, *Administration*
EMP: 66 **EST:** 1975
SQ FT: 3,200

SALES (est): 11.3MM **Privately Held**
WEB: www.trco.com
SIC: 8742 6411 Administrative services consultant; pension & retirement plan consultants

(P-23356)
TUNNELWORKS SERVICES INC (PA)
13502 Whittier Blvd Ste H, Whittier
(90605-1944)
PHONE..................562 201-4036
William Duarte Jr, *President*
Nicole Valdez, *Principal*
EMP: 91 **EST:** 2009
SALES (est): 1MM **Privately Held**
SIC: 8742 Business consultant

(P-23357)
UC ADVANTAGE INC
92 Argonaut Ste 200, Aliso Viejo
(92656-4121)
PHONE..................949 540-3403
Jason Hynek, *CEO*
Valerie Chitty, *Analyst*
EMP: 50 **EST:** 2010
SALES (est): 3.4MM **Privately Held**
WEB: www.ucadvantage.net
SIC: 8742 Business consultant

(P-23358)
VAYAN MARKETING GROUP LLC
10877 Wilshire Blvd Fl 12, Los Angeles
(90024-4332)
PHONE..................310 943-4990
Jesse Lo RE,
Laura Kall,
Michael Medema,
Brad Morrison,
EMP: 50 **EST:** 2004
SQ FT: 7,000
SALES (est): 6.5MM
SALES (corp-wide): 40.5MM **Privately Held**
WEB: www.tritonpacific.com
SIC: 8742 Marketing consulting services
PA: Triton Pacific Capital Partners, Llc
6701 Center Dr W Ste 1400
Los Angeles CA 90045
310 943-4990

(P-23359)
VENDOR SURVEILLANCE CORP
2525 Main St Ste 100, Irvine (92614-6678)
PHONE..................949 833-2111
Bernard J Fallon, *Ch of Bd*
Brenda Delong, *Administration*
Andre Wright, *Controller*
EMP: 130 **EST:** 1976
SALES (est): 2.5MM
SALES (corp-wide): 13.6MM **Privately Held**
WEB: www.verifyglobal.com
SIC: 8742 Quality assurance consultant
PA: Verify, Inc.
2525 Main St Ste 100
Irvine CA 92614
949 833-2111

(P-23360)
VERIFI INC
8391 Beverly Blvd Ste 310, Los Angeles
(90048-2633)
P.O. Box 310 (90078-0310)
PHONE..................323 655-5789
Matthew G Katz, *CEO*
Sara Craven, *COO*
Ronald B Cushey, *CFO*
Hitesh Anand,
Tony Wootton, *Risk Mgmt Dir*
EMP: 65
SALES (est): 14.1MM **Publicly Held**
WEB: www.verifi.com
SIC: 8742 Quality assurance consultant
PA: Visa Inc.
900 Metro Center Blvd
Foster City CA 94404

(P-23361)
VIVA AMERICA MARKETING INC (PA)
1239 Victoria St, Costa Mesa (92627-3933)
PHONE..................949 645-6100

David Fan, *President*
Henry Wang, *Administration*
Elijah Fan, *Associate*
▲ **EMP:** 67 **EST:** 2002
SALES (est): 1.1MM **Privately Held**
SIC: 8742 Marketing consulting services

(P-23362)
WARNER FOOD MANAGEMENT CO INC
4917 Genesta Ave, Encino (91316-3438)
PHONE..................818 285-2160
Sudesh Sood, *President*
Terry Herrick, *Admin Sec*
Terry O'Herrick, *Admin Sec*
EMP: 125 **EST:** 1989
SQ FT: 2,000
SALES (est): 8.6MM **Privately Held**
SIC: 5812 8742 Fast-food restaurant, chain; restaurant & food services consultants

(P-23363)
WASSERMAN MEDIA GROUP LLC (PA)
10900 Wilshire Blvd Fl 2, Los Angeles
(90024-6548)
PHONE..................310 407-0200
Casey Wasserman, *Mng Member*
Marc Murphy, *President*
Tim Chadwick, *COO*
Dean Christopher, *CFO*
Christopher Armstrong, *Exec VP*
EMP: 115 **EST:** 2003
SQ FT: 40,000
SALES (est): 128.1MM **Privately Held**
WEB: www.teamwass.com
SIC: 8742 Marketing consulting services

(P-23364)
WELLMADE INC
Also Called: Polagram
800 E 12th St, Los Angeles (90021-2198)
PHONE..................213 221-1123
Jin Kim, *President*
Elizabeth Rubio, *Sales Mgr*
EMP: 100 **EST:** 2018
SALES (est): 1.9MM **Privately Held**
SIC: 8742 Business consultant

(P-23365)
WEST COAST AVIATION SVCS LLC (PA)
Also Called: West Coast Charters
19711 Campus Dr Ste 200, Santa Ana
(92707-5203)
PHONE..................949 852-8340
Gary Standell, *President*
Laura Trenerry, *Vice Pres*
Art Muro, *General Mgr*
Michael Griba, *IT/INT Sup*
Gary Bushouse, *Sales Staff*
EMP: 50 **EST:** 1987
SQ FT: 2,000
SALES (est): 13.1MM **Privately Held**
WEB: www.wcas.aero
SIC: 8742 5088 Industry specialist consultants; aircraft & parts

(P-23366)
WESTERN HEALTH RESOURCES
440 Greenfield Ave Ste B, Hanford
(93230-3568)
PHONE..................559 537-2860
Sandy Delarosa, *Director*
EMP: 50
SALES (corp-wide): 57MM **Privately Held**
SIC: 8742 Hospital & health services consultant
PA: Western Health Resources
2100 Douglas Blvd
Roseville CA
916 781-2000

(P-23367)
WILSHIRE ADVISORS LLC (PA)
1299 Ocean Ave Ste 700, Santa Monica
(90401-1061)
PHONE..................310 451-3051
Dennis A Tito, *CEO*
John C Hindman, *President*
Andrew Junkin, *President*
Michael Wauters, *CFO*

Benkai Bouey, *Officer*
EMP: 210 **EST:** 1972
SQ FT: 57,530
SALES (est): 42MM **Privately Held**
WEB: www.wilshire.com
SIC: 8742 Financial consultant

(P-23368)
WPROMOTE LLC (PA)
2100 E Grand Ave Fl 1, El Segundo
(90245-5150)
PHONE.................................310 421-4844
Michael Mothner, *President*
Gabriel Peralta, *Partner*
Paul Rappoport, *President*
Michael Block, *COO*
Michael Stone, *Officer*
EMP: 219 **EST:** 2004
SALES (est): 82.8MM **Privately Held**
WEB: www.wpromote.com
SIC: 8742 Marketing consulting services

(P-23369)
YMARKETING LLC
4000 Macarthur Blvd # 350, Newport Beach
(92660-2517)
PHONE.................................714 545-2550
Ryan Lash, *CEO*
Brian Yun, *COO*
Jennifer Jee, *Officer*
Kate Brueck, *Supervisor*
EMP: 70 **EST:** 2007
SALES (est): 10.2MM
SALES (corp-wide): 134.6MM **Privately Held**
WEB: www.mergeworld.com
SIC: 8742 Marketing consulting services
HQ: The Sandbox Group Llc
1 E Wacker Dr Ste 3200
Chicago IL 60601
312 803-1900

(P-23370)
YOUNG & RUBICAM LLC
1735 Irvine Center Dr, Irvine (92618)
PHONE.................................949 224-6300
David Murphy, *President*
Patricia Anastos, *Exec VP*
Peter Rentschler, *Exec VP*
Pamela Jackson, *Senior VP*
Don Longfellow, *Senior VP*
EMP: 300
SALES (corp-wide): 15.9B **Privately Held**
WEB: www.vmlyr.com
SIC: 8742 Marketing consulting services
HQ: Young & Rubicam Llc
3 Columbus Cir Frnt 3 # 3
New York NY 10019
212 210-3000

(P-23371)
YOUR PRACTICE ONLINE LLC
(PA)
4590 Macarthur Blvd # 500, Newport Beach
(92660-2030)
PHONE.................................877 388-8569
Dr Prem Lobo, *Mng Member*
Holly Edmonds, *Vice Pres*
Clifford Misquith, *Opers Staff*
Holly Olds, *Marketing Staff*
EMP: 69 **EST:** 2004 **Privately Held**
WEB: www.yourpracticeonline.net
SIC: 8742 Marketing consulting services

(P-23372)
ZENSHO USA CORPORATION
27261 Las Ramblas Ste 240, Mission Viejo
(92691-6468)
PHONE.................................760 585-8455
Masaaki Terada, *CEO*
Yasu Nori Hiraguchi, *President*
▲ **EMP:** 4000 **EST:** 2004
SQ FT: 1,500
SALES (est): 47MM **Privately Held**
WEB: www.zensho.co.jp
SIC: 8742 Franchising consultant
PA: Zensho Holdings Co., Ltd.
2-18-1, Konan
Minato-Ku TKY 108-0

(P-23373)
ZIPRECRUITER INC
604 Arizona Ave, Santa Monica
(90401-1610)
PHONE.................................877 252-1062

Ian Siegel, *Ch of Bd*
Jeff Zwelling, *COO*
David Travers, *CFO*
Qasim Saifee, *Chief Mktg Ofcr*
Renata Dionello, *Officer*
EMP: 840 **EST:** 2010
SQ FT: 60,000
SALES (est): 418.1MM **Privately Held**
WEB: www.ziprecruiter.com
SIC: 8742 7371 Human resource consult-
ing services; custom computer program-
ming services

8743 Public Relations Svcs

(P-23374)
BEHR PROCESS SALES
COMPANY
3000 S Main St Apt 84e, Santa Ana
(92707-4225)
P.O. Box 1287 (92702-1287)
PHONE.................................714 545-7101
Kevin Jaffe, *Partner*
John V Croul, *Partner*
Scott Richards, *Vice Pres*
EMP: 32 **EST:** 1969
SQ FT: 54,000
SALES (est): 6.4MM **Privately Held**
WEB: www.behr.com
SIC: 8743 2851 5198 Sales promotion;
varnishes; paints & paint additives; stains:
varnish, oil or wax; lacquer: bases, dopes,
thinner; paints, varnishes & supplies

(P-23375)
BNI ENTERPRISES INC
Also Called: B N I
545 College Commerce Way, Upland
(91786-4377)
PHONE.................................909 305-1818
Ivan Misner, *Chairman*
Karen Ellis, *Vice Pres*
Sandy Donovan, *Exec Dir*
Michael Gallagher, *Exec Dir*
Stephen Hand, *Exec Dir*
EMP: 600 **EST:** 1985
SQ FT: 33,000
SALES (est): 73.5MM **Privately Held**
WEB: www.bni.com
SIC: 8743 Promotion service

(P-23376)
BRAND AMP LLC
1945 Placentia Ave Ste C, Costa Mesa
(92627-6274)
PHONE.................................949 438-1060
Todd Brooks, *Mng Member*
Luke Davison, *Producer*
Mike Iwamasa, *Marketing Staff*
Danielle Grado, *Pub Rel Staff*
Bradley Hartman, *Pub Rel Staff*
EMP: 74 **EST:** 2012
SQ FT: 16,059
SALES (est): 7.7MM **Privately Held**
WEB: www.thebrandamp.com
SIC: 8743 8742 Public relations & public-
ity; marketing consulting services

(P-23377)
BWR AN OGLVY PUB RLTONS
WRLDW (DH)
9100 Wlshire Blvd Ste 500, Los Angeles
(90036)
PHONE.................................310 550-7776
Paul A Baker, *President*
David Chapman, *Exec VP*
Larry Winokur, *Vice Pres*
Nanci Ryder, *Admin Sec*
Victoria Geis, *Human Resources*
EMP: 50 **EST:** 1979
SALES (est): 7.3MM
SALES (corp-wide): 15.9B **Privately Held**
WEB: www.ogilvy.com
SIC: 8743 Public relations & publicity
HQ: Ogilvy Public Relations Worldwide Llc
636 11th Ave
New York NY 10036
212 880-5200

(P-23378)
BWR PUBLIC RELATIONS
Also Called: Baker Winokur Ryder
9100 Wilshire Blvd # 500, Beverly Hills
(90212-3415)
PHONE.................................310 248-6100
Larry Winokur, *President*
Neal Cohen, *Officer*
Eric Green, *Vice Pres*
Michael Moses, *Vice Pres*
Lauren Peteroy, *Executive*
EMP: 59 **EST:** 2011
SALES (est): 9.6MM **Privately Held**
SIC: 8743 Public relations & publicity

(P-23379)
CALIBRE INTERNATIONAL LLC
(PA)
Also Called: High Caliber Line
6250 N Irwindale Ave, Irwindale
(91702-3208)
PHONE.................................626 969-4660
Daniel Oas,
Kenan Ozcan, *CFO*
Catherine Oas,
Joey Vogliardo,
Freddy Garcia, *Representative*
◆ **EMP:** 120 **EST:** 1998
SQ FT: 100,000
SALES (est): 28MM **Privately Held**
WEB: www.highcaliberline.com
SIC: 8743 2759 Promotion service; pro-
motional printing

(P-23380)
CATALINA EVENTS INC
2605 184th St, Redondo Beach
(90278-4508)
PHONE.................................310 925-6986
John Ellis, *CEO*
EMP: 50 **EST:** 2013
SALES (est): 1.3MM **Privately Held**
SIC: 8743 Promotion service

(P-23381)
MAGIC WORKFORCE
SOLUTIONS LLC
9100 Wilsh Blvd Ste 700e, Beverly Hills
(90212)
PHONE.................................310 246-6153
Earvin Johnson, *CEO*
Eric Holoman, *President*
Kawanna Brown, *COO*
EMP: 2079 **EST:** 2007
SALES (est): 594.8K
SALES (corp-wide): 75.7MM **Privately Held**
WEB: www.magicjohnson.com
SIC: 8743 Promotion service
PA: Magic Johnson Enterprises, Inc.
9100 Wilshire Blvd 700e
Beverly Hills CA 90212
310 247-2033

(P-23382)
MURPHY OBRIEN INC
407 N Maple Dr Ste 1, Beverly Hills
(90210-4274)
PHONE.................................310 453-2539
Karen Murphy O'Brien, *CEO*
Brett O'Brien, *Managing Prtnr*
Emily Warner, *Vice Pres*
Nicole Allison, *Executive*
Niki Jensen, *Executive*
EMP: 55 **EST:** 1989
SALES (est): 9.1MM **Privately Held**
WEB: www.murphyobrien.com
SIC: 8743 Public relations & publicity

(P-23383)
PIEPER AND ASSOCIATES INC
19823 Hamilton Ave, Torrance
(90502-1341)
PHONE.................................310 515-5600
Jeff Pieper, *President*
Nicki McVoy, *Creative Dir*
Jeanne E Pieper, *Admin Sec*
Cathy Jordan, *Prdtn Mgr*
Cathy Jordan-Digney, *Prdtn Mgr*
▲ **EMP:** 54 **EST:** 1976
SQ FT: 12,000
SALES (est): 4.7MM **Privately Held**
SIC: 8743 Sales promotion

(P-23384)
PMK-BNC INC (PA)
1840 Century Park E # 1400, Los Angeles
(90067-2115)
PHONE.................................310 854-0455
EMP: 80
SQ FT: 4,000
SALES (est): 20.5MM **Privately Held**
WEB: www.rogersandcowanpmk.com
SIC: 8743 Public Relations Services, Nsk

(P-23385)
PMK-BNC INC
8687 Melrose Ave Fl 8th, Los Angeles
(90069-5746)
PHONE.................................310 854-4800
EMP: 50 **Privately Held**
WEB: www.rogersandcowanpmk.com
SIC: 8743 Public Relations Services
PA: Pmk-Bnc, Inc.
1840 Century Park E # 1400
Los Angeles CA 90067

(P-23386)
ROGERS & COWAN INC (HQ)
8687 Melrose Ave Ste 7, Los Angeles
(90069-5721)
PHONE.................................310 854-8100
Mark Owens, *CEO*
Dennis Dembia, *President*
Michael Donkis, *President*
Lindsay Galin, *President*
Marian Koltai-Levine, *President*
EMP: 72 **EST:** 2007
SALES (est): 14.1MM
SALES (corp-wide): 9B **Publicly Held**
WEB: www.rogersandcowanpmk.com
SIC: 8743 Public relations & publicity
PA: The Interpublic Group Of Companies
Inc
909 3rd Ave
New York NY 10022
212 704-1200

8744 Facilities Support Mgmt
Svcs

(P-23387)
ACEPEX MANAGEMENT
CORPORATION
2707 Saturn St, Brea (92821-6705)
PHONE.................................909 625-6900
Henry C Rhee, *CEO*
Monica Goldsborough, *Office Admin*
Nancy Escobar, *Executive Asst*
Drew Hansen, *Administration*
Helen Ward, *Project Mgr*
EMP: 150 **EST:** 1989
SALES (est): 22.8MM **Privately Held**
WEB: www.acepex.com
SIC: 8744 Base maintenance (providing
personnel on continuing basis)

(P-23388)
ADVANCED CLEANUP TECH INC
Also Called: Acti
230 E C St, Wilmington (90744-6612)
PHONE.................................310 763-1423
Ruben Garcia, *CEO*
Beatriz Esparza, *Business Mgr*
Lonnie McBee, *Contract Mgr*
Dave See, *Manager*
EMP: 260 **EST:** 1992
SALES (est): 15.6MM **Privately Held**
WEB: www.actihazmat.com
SIC: 8744

(P-23389)
AMERIKO INC (PA)
Also Called: Ameriko Industries
980 S Arroyo Pkwy Ste 240, Pasadena
(91105-3928)
PHONE.................................626 795-7988
Chase C Rhee, *President*
Socorro Rhee, *Executive*
Gilbert Rhee, *Manager*
EMP: 178 **EST:** 1972
SQ FT: 5,000
SALES (est): 9.8MM **Privately Held**
WEB: www.ameriko.com
SIC: 8744 7349 Facilities support serv-
ices; building maintenance services

PRODUCTS & SVCS

(P-23390)
AMERITAC INC (PA)
24 Toscana Way W, Rancho Mirage
(92270-1978)
P.O. Box 2550 (92270-1088)
PHONE...................................925 989-2942
Isiah Harris, *President*
Lawrence Stevens, *Vice Pres*
EMP: 80 EST: 1994
SQ FT: 2,024
SALES: 5.3MM Privately Held
WEB: www.ameritac.net
SIC: 8744 Base maintenance (providing
personnel on continuing basis)

(P-23391)
**ARGUS MANAGEMENT
COMPANY LLC**
Also Called: Argus Medical Management
5150 E Pcf Cast Hwy Ste 5, Long Beach
(90804)
PHONE...................................562 299-5200
Robert C Boullon,
Patty Durna, *Regional Mgr*
Manuel Gonzalez, *Regional Mgr*
Barry Allswang,
Peter Ferrera,
EMP: 300 EST: 1995
SQ FT: 2,500
SALES (est): 23MM Privately Held
WEB: www.argusmso.com
SIC: 8744 Facilities support services

(P-23392)
HENRY CALL INC
Clark & Arguello Bldg 861, Vandenberg Afb
(93437)
PHONE...................................805 734-2762
Robert Clark, *Manager*
William Makynen, *President*
EMP: 148 Privately Held
WEB: www.callhenry.com
SIC: 8744 7371 8742 Base maintenance
(providing personnel on continuing basis);
computer software development; man-
agement consulting services
PA: Call Henry Inc
1425 Chaffee Dr Ste 4
Titusville FL 32780

(P-23393)
INDYNE INC
1036 California Blvd # 11013, Vandenberg
Afb (93437-6202)
PHONE...................................805 606-7225
Kenneth A Cinal, *Branch Mgr*
David Miller, *Principal*
Jerome Johnson, *Analyst*
EMP: 227
SALES (corp-wide): 117MM Privately
Held
WEB: www.indyneinc.com
SIC: 8744 Base maintenance (providing
personnel on continuing basis)
PA: Indyne, Inc.
46561 Expedition Dr 100
Lexington Park MD 20653
703 903-6900

(P-23394)
INNOVATIVE CNSTR SOLUTIONS
575 Anton Blvd Ste 850, Costa Mesa
(92626-7023)
PHONE...................................714 893-6366
Hirad Emadi, *President*
Greg Sherman, *Vice Pres*
John R White, *Vice Pres*
Justin Gough, *Executive*
Brian Laurin, *Executive*
EMP: 105 EST: 1999
SQ FT: 2,000
SALES (est): 24MM Privately Held
WEB: www.icsinc.tv
SIC: 8744 1795 ; demolition, buildings &
other structures

(P-23395)
**MILITARY CALIFORNIA
DEPARTMENT**
Also Called: CA Arng 115th Rsg
11300 Lexington Dr # 100, Los Alamitos
(90720-5002)
PHONE...................................562 795-2065
CHI Huynh, *Branch Mgr*

EMP: 500 Privately Held
WEB: www.ngac.org
SIC: 8744 Facilities support services
HQ: Department Of Military California
9800 Goethe Rd 10
Sacramento CA 95827

(P-23396)
**PONDER ENVIRONMENTAL
SVCS INC**
19484 Broken Ct, Shafter (93263-3146)
PHONE...................................661 589-7771
Curtis Fox, *Manager*
Summer Smith, *Office Mgr*
Brandon McMaster, *Project Mgr*
EMP: 25
SALES (corp-wide): 16.1MM Privately
Held
WEB:
www.ponderenvironmentalservices.com
SIC: 8744 4959 2899 ; environmental
cleanup services; fuel tank or engine
cleaning chemicals
PA: Ponder Environmental Services, Inc.
4563 E 2nd St
Benicia CA 94510
707 748-7775

(P-23397)
**US FACILITY SOLUTIONS LLC
(PA)**
Also Called: Facilities Support Services
17541 17th St Ste 200, Tustin
(92780-1984)
PHONE...................................888 904-7900
Chris Dabek, *CEO*
EMP: 65 EST: 2001
SALES (est): 5.2MM Privately Held
WEB: www.usfacilitysolutions.com
SIC: 8744 1711 1731 1721 Facilities sup-
port services; plumbing, heating, air-con-
ditioning contractors; electrical work;
painting & paper hanging

(P-23398)
WEST COAST STORM INC (PA)
9701 Wilshire Blvd # 1000, Beverly Hills
(90212-2020)
PHONE...................................909 890-5700
Michelle Padilla, *President*
Renata Salo, *CFO*
Rafael Padilla, *Vice Pres*
EMP: 50 EST: 2005
SQ FT: 48,000
SALES (est): 6.7MM Privately Held
WEB: www.wcstorm.com
SIC: 8744

(P-23399)
WORKCARE INC
300 S Harbor Blvd Ste 600, Anaheim
(92805-3718)
PHONE...................................714 978-7488
Peter P Greaney, *CEO*
Barry Fager, *CFO*
Bill Nixon, *CFO*
William E Nixon, *CFO*
Mason D Harrell III, *Officer*
EMP: 181 EST: 1997
SQ FT: 11,000
SALES (est): 25.8MM Privately Held
WEB: www.workcare.com
SIC: 8744 8011 Facilities support services;
offices & clinics of medical doctors

8748 Business Consulting
Svcs, NEC

(P-23400)
**AAA GLOBAL CONSULTING
LLC (PA)**
32002 Camino Del Cielo, Trabuco Canyon
(92679-3439)
PHONE...................................949 201-6204
Mina Abdelmalek, *Principal*
EMP: 54 EST: 2015
SALES (est): 396.7K Privately Held
SIC: 8748 Business consulting

(P-23401)
**ADVANCED CORPORATE SVCS
INC**
Also Called: ACS Cloud Partners
2416 Amsler St, Torrance (90505-5302)
PHONE...................................310 937-6848
Eric A Asquino, *President*
Jean Cinq-Mars, *Opers Staff*
Nathan Szczesiul, *Manager*
EMP: 20 EST: 2002
SQ FT: 1,500
SALES (est): 5MM Privately Held
WEB: www.acscp.com
SIC: 8748 7372 Telecommunications con-
sultant; application computer software

(P-23402)
AECOM GLOBAL II LLC
915 Wilshire Blvd Ste 800, Los Angeles
(90017-3488)
PHONE...................................213 996-2200
EMP: 200
SALES (corp-wide): 13.2B Publicly Held
WEB: www.aecom.com
SIC: 8748 Business Consulting Services
Insurance Agent/Broker
HQ: Aecom Global Ii, Llc
1999 Avenue Of The Stars
Los Angeles CA 90071
213 593-8100

(P-23403)
**AECOM TECHNICAL SERVICES
INC (HQ)**
300 S Grand Ave Ste 900, Los Angeles
(90071-3135)
PHONE...................................213 593-8000
Timothy H Keener, *CEO*
Andrew Bui, *Treasurer*
John Sykes, *Vice Pres*
Kevin Underwood, *Vice Pres*
Daryle Fontenot, *Project Mgr*
▲ EMP: 100 EST: 1970
SQ FT: 43,000
SALES (est): 1.1B
SALES (corp-wide): 13.2B Publicly Held
WEB: www.aecom.com
SIC: 8748 4953 8742 8711 Environmen-
tal consultant; refuse systems; industry
specialist consultants; engineering serv-
ices
PA: Aecom
13355 Noel Rd Ste 400
Dallas TX 75240
972 788-1000

(P-23404)
AECOM USA INC
515 S Figueroa St Ste 400, Los Angeles
(90071-3323)
PHONE...................................213 330-7200
EMP: 105
SALES (corp-wide): 13.2B Publicly Held
WEB: www.aecom.com
SIC: 8748 Business consulting
HQ: Aecom Usa, Inc.
605 3rd Ave
New York NY 10158
212 973-2900

(P-23405)
AECOM USA INC
300 S Grand Ave Ste 900, Los Angeles
(90071-3135)
PHONE...................................213 593-8000
Frederick Werner, *Branch Mgr*
EMP: 105
SALES (corp-wide): 13.2B Publicly Held
WEB: www.aecom.com
SIC: 8748 Business consulting
HQ: Aecom Usa, Inc.
605 3rd Ave
New York NY 10158
212 973-2900

(P-23406)
AECOM USA INC
999 W Town And Country Rd, Orange
(92868-4713)
PHONE...................................714 567-2501
Bruce Toro, *Manager*
EMP: 105
SALES (corp-wide): 13.2B Publicly Held
WEB: www.aecom.com
SIC: 8748 Business consulting

HQ: Aecom Usa, Inc.
605 3rd Ave
New York NY 10158
212 973-2900

(P-23407)
ALIANTEL INC
1940 W Corporate Way, Anaheim
(92801-5373)
PHONE...................................714 829-1650
Suresh Sachdeva, *CEO*
John Kelly, *Principal*
EMP: 90 EST: 1996
SALES (est): 12.9MM Privately Held
SIC: 8748 7389 Telecommunications con-
sultant; telephone services

(P-23408)
**ALL-CITY MANAGEMENT SVCS
INC (PA)**
10440 Pioneer Blvd Ste 5, Santa Fe
Springs (90670-8238)
PHONE...................................310 202-8284
Baron Farwell, *CEO*
Ronald Farwell, *CFO*
Ron Farwell, *Admin Sec*
Alan Stone, *Opers Mgr*
EMP: 1688 EST: 1985
SQ FT: 3,500
SALES (est): 63.7MM Privately Held
WEB: www.thecrossingguardcompany.com
SIC: 8748 Traffic consultant

(P-23409)
**ALLIANT INSURANCE SERVICES
INC (PA)**
Also Called: Nationwide
1301 Dove St Ste 200, Newport Beach
(92660-2436)
P.O. Box 6450 (92658-6450)
PHONE...................................949 756-0271
Thomas Corbett, *Ch of Bd*
Greg Zimmer, *President*
Jerold Hall, *COO*
Ilene Anders, *CFO*
Robert J Bothwell, *Exec VP*
EMP: 170 EST: 1925
SQ FT: 45,000
SALES (est): 1.1B Privately Held
WEB: www.alliant.com
SIC: 8748 6411 Business consulting; in-
surance agents

(P-23410)
ALLIED INDUSTRIES INC (PA)
Also Called: Allied Environmental Services
21650 Oxnard St Ste 500, Woodland Hills
(91367-4911)
PHONE...................................800 605-5323
Ernesto Gutierrez, *President*
Fernando Gutierrez, *COO*
EMP: 150 EST: 1993
SQ FT: 11,000
SALES (est): 37.4MM Privately Held
WEB: www.alliedlead.com
SIC: 8748 Environmental consultant

(P-23411)
AMATEL INC (PA)
1017 S Mountain Ave, Monrovia
(91016-3642)
PHONE...................................323 801-0199
Joe Nwankwo, *President*
EMP: 64 EST: 1993
SQ FT: 5,500
SALES (est): 11.5MM Privately Held
WEB: www.sobenma.com
SIC: 8748 8711 Telecommunications con-
sultant; engineering services

(P-23412)
AMBREEN ENTERPRISES INC
20370 Via Badalona, Yorba Linda
(92887-3136)
PHONE...................................909 620-1339
EMP: 80 EST: 2011
SALES (est): 157.4K Privately Held
SIC: 8748 Business Consulting Services

(P-23413)
AMERICAN JUSTICE SOLUTIONS INC
Also Called: Correctivesolutions
25910 Acero Ste 100, Mission Viejo
(92691-2777)
PHONE.....................949 369-6210
Mats Jonsson, *CEO*
Karen Boyd, *Vice Pres*
Kristy Silguero, *Vice Pres*
Beverly Stikeleather, *Accounting Mgr*
Karl Jonsson, *General Counsel*
EMP: 70 **EST:** 2014
SQ FT: 20,000
SALES (est): 5.3MM **Privately Held**
WEB: www.correctivesolutions.org
SIC: 8299 8748 Educational service, non-degree granting: continuing educ.; educational consultant

(P-23414)
ANKURA CONSULTING GROUP LLC
633 W 5th St Fl 28, Los Angeles
(90071-3502)
PHONE.....................213 223-2109
Shannon Nolan, *Principal*
Kathryn Sturgis-Bright, *Director*
Beau Towers, *Director*
Kenneth Macdonald, *Consultant*
Eleena Rieger, *Associate*
EMP: 200
SALES (corp-wide): 110MM **Privately Held**
WEB: www.ankura.com
SIC: 8748 Business consulting
HQ: Ankura Consulting Group, Llc
    485 Lexington Ave Fl 10
    New York NY 10017
    212 818-1555

(P-23415)
ARMANI TRADE LLC
21255 Burbank Blvd, Woodland Hills
(91367-6610)
PHONE.....................310 849-0067
Nader Abdollahi, *CEO*
EMP: 50 **EST:** 2018
SALES (est): 3.6MM **Privately Held**
WEB: www.armanitrade.com
SIC: 8748 Testing services

(P-23416)
B & L CONSULTING LLC
164 N 2nd Ave 9, Upland (91786-6001)
PHONE.....................682 238-6994
Bayandre Lewis, *Mng Member*
EMP: 63 **EST:** 1995
SQ FT: 5,000
SALES (est): 5.2MM **Privately Held**
SIC: 8748 Business consulting

(P-23417)
BC2 ENVIRONMENTAL LLC
1150 W Trenton Ave, Orange (92867-3536)
PHONE.....................714 744-2990
Kurt Samuelson,
Scott Traub,
EMP: 54 **EST:** 2018
SALES (est): 4.5MM **Privately Held**
WEB: www.bc2env.com
SIC: 8748 Environmental consultant

(P-23418)
BEYONDSOFT CONSULTING INC
19009 S Laurel Park Rd # 6, Compton
(90220-6054)
PHONE.....................310 532-2822
Maria Pena, *Manager*
EMP: 120 **Privately Held**
WEB: www.beyondsoft.com
SIC: 8748 Business consulting
HQ: Beyondsoft Consulting, Inc.
    3025 112th Ave Ne Ste 200
    Bellevue WA 98004
    425 332-4520

(P-23419)
BNY MELLON NATIONAL ASSN
10250 Constellation Blvd # 2710, Los Angeles (90067-6200)
PHONE.....................310 551-7600
Tiffany L Barbara, *Director*
Paul Benson, *Managing Dir*

Merryll McElwain, *Director*
EMP: 66
SALES (corp-wide): 15.8B **Publicly Held**
WEB: www.bnymellon.com
SIC: 8748 Business consulting
HQ: Bny Mellon, National Association
    1 Mellon Center Ste 3831
    Pittsburgh PA 15258
    412 234-5000

(P-23420)
BOCA MESA INCORPORATED
3130 Skyway Dr Ste 701, Santa Maria
(93455-1800)
PHONE.....................805 934-9470
EMP: 69
SALES (est): 4.7MM **Privately Held**
SIC: 8748 7349 Business Consulting Services

(P-23421)
BON SUISSE INC
392 W Walnut Ave, Fullerton (92832-2351)
PHONE.....................714 578-0001
EMP: 13 **Privately Held**
WEB: www.bonsuisse.com
SIC: 8748 5149 2052 Agricultural consultant; bakery products: cones, ice cream
PA: Bon Suisse Inc.
    11860 Cmnty Rd Ste 100
    Poway CA 92064

(P-23422)
CAL SOUTHERN ASSN GOVERNMENTS (PA)
Also Called: S C A G
900 Wilshire Blvd # 1700, Los Angeles
(90017-4701)
PHONE.....................213 236-1800
Hasan Ikhrata, *Exec Dir*
Basil Panas, *CFO*
Rongsheng Luo, *Program Mgr*
Thupten Dorjee, *Administration*
Sarah Jepson, *Planning*
EMP: 116 **EST:** 1965
SQ FT: 50,000
SALES (est): 40MM **Privately Held**
WEB: www.scag.ca.gov
SIC: 8748 Urban planning & consulting services

(P-23423)
CALIFORNIA COML INV GROUP INC
Also Called: Ccig
4530 E Thousand Oaks Blvd, Westlake Village (91362-3894)
PHONE.....................805 495-8400
Gary Collett, *President*
Danielle Hastie, *Exec VP*
Kim Siegert, *Exec VP*
Louis Mellman, *Vice Pres*
Rochelle Sabo, *Vice Pres*
EMP: 50 **EST:** 2006
SALES (est): 7.1MM **Privately Held**
WEB: www.ccinvest.com
SIC: 8748 Urban planning & consulting services

(P-23424)
CALIFORNIA PSYCHCARE INC
Also Called: CALIFORNIA PSYCHCARE,INC
25411 Cabot Rd Ste 206, Laguna Hills
(92653-5525)
PHONE.....................833 227-3454
EMP: 50
SALES (corp-wide): 11.7MM **Privately Held**
WEB: www.jamesgeorge.me
SIC: 8748 Educational consultant
PA: California Psychcare, Inc
    9201 Oakdale Ave Ste 101
    Chatsworth CA 91311
    818 401-0661

(P-23425)
CAPITAL OVERSIGHT INC (PA)
2118 Wilshire Blvd, Santa Monica
(90403-5704)
PHONE.....................310 453-8000
Dayne Williams, *CEO*
Matthew Denti, *Vice Pres*
Kenneth Mays, *Vice Pres*
Tamara Stewart, *Vice Pres*
Patricia Sewell, *Admin Sec*

EMP: 65 **EST:** 2002
SQ FT: 11,000
SALES (est): 7.7MM **Privately Held**
WEB: www.capitaloversight.com
SIC: 8748 7323 7389 7299 Business consulting; credit clearinghouse; ; personal financial services

(P-23426)
CDS COLD
10035 Painter Ave, Santa Fe Springs
(90670-3015)
PHONE.....................562 777-9969
Dan Nagel, *President*
Mitchell Patton, *CFO*
Colton Nagel, *Sales Staff*
April Gaspar, *Supervisor*
Lucy Cardenas, *Clerk*
EMP: 50 **EST:** 2004
SQ FT: 40,000
SALES (est): 3.3MM **Privately Held**
WEB: www.cdscold.com
SIC: 8748 Business consulting

(P-23427)
CDSNET LLC
Also Called: Fmsinfoserv
6053 W Century Blvd, Los Angeles
(90045-6430)
PHONE.....................310 981-9500
Michael Griffus, *President*
Francis G Homan, *CFO*
Helmut Bredow, *Project Mgr*
Omar Deleon, *Manager*
EMP: 598 **EST:** 2006
SALES (est): 2.4MM
SALES (corp-wide): 4.2MM **Privately Held**
WEB: www.keolisna.com
SIC: 8748 Business consulting
HQ: Keolis Transit America, Inc.
    6053 W Century Blvd # 900
    Los Angeles CA 90045

(P-23428)
CEMTEK ENVIRONMENTAL INC
3041 Orange Ave, Santa Ana (92707-4247)
PHONE.....................714 437-7100
Tyron Smith, *CEO*
Randy Thompson, *Vice Pres*
Ken Korzun, *Project Mgr*
Keith Crabbe, *Engineer*
Dan Oquendo, *Engineer*
EMP: 50 **EST:** 2003
SQ FT: 15,500
SALES (est): 22.9MM **Privately Held**
WEB: www.cemteks.com
SIC: 8748 Environmental consultant

(P-23429)
CITY OF NORCO
Also Called: Successor Agency To The Norco
2870 Clark Ave, Norco (92860-1903)
PHONE.....................951 270-5617
Greg Newton, *Mayor*
EMP: 100
SALES (corp-wide): 33.2MM **Privately Held**
WEB: www.norco.ca.us
SIC: 8748 Urban planning & consulting services
PA: City Of Norco
    2870 Clark Ave
    Norco CA 92860
    951 270-5617

(P-23430)
COMMUNITY REDEVELOPMENT AGENCY (PA)
Also Called: C R A
448 S Hill St Ste 1200, Los Angeles
(90013-1153)
PHONE.....................213 977-1600
Cecilia V Estolano, *Administration*
Christine Essel, *CEO*
Craig Bullock, *Officer*
Estevan Valenzuela, *Principal*
Sylvia Amaya, *General Mgr*
EMP: 165
SQ FT: 80,000
SALES: 68.8MM **Privately Held**
WEB: www.crala.org
SIC: 8748 Urban planning & consulting services

(P-23431)
DAVINA DOUTHARD INC
Also Called: Polishing The Professional
400 Crprate Pinte Ste 300, Culver City
(90230)
PHONE.....................310 540-5120
Davina Douthard, *CEO*
Lorraine Brown, *Admin Asst*
EMP: 15 **EST:** 1991
SQ FT: 1,600
SALES (est): 1.9MM **Privately Held**
WEB: www.polishingtheprofessional.com
SIC: 8748 8743 7361 2721 Business consulting; public relations services; employment agencies; magazines: publishing only, not printed on site; convention & show services

(P-23432)
DISRUPTIVE VISIONS LLC
23456 Madero Ste 210, Mission Viejo
(92691-2783)
PHONE.....................949 502-3800
Marc Anthony, *Mng Member*
Gary Arnett, *CFO*
EMP: 60 **EST:** 2016
SALES (est): 1.1MM **Privately Held**
WEB: www.disruptivevisions.com
SIC: 8748 Telecommunications consultant

(P-23433)
ECONOMIC DEV CORP LOS ANGLES C
Also Called: Laedc
444 S Flower St Ste 3700, Los Angeles
(90071-2972)
PHONE.....................213 622-4300
William C Allen, *President*
Jill Yoshimi, *President*
David A Flaks, *COO*
Susan D Stel, *CFO*
Nhien Lasky, *Treasurer*
EMP: 50 **EST:** 1981
SQ FT: 18,000
SALES (est): 7.3MM **Privately Held**
WEB: www.wtca-lalb.org
SIC: 8748 Economic consultant

(P-23434)
EDGE MORTGAGE ADVISORY CO LLC
2125 E Katella Ave # 350, Anaheim
(92806-6072)
PHONE.....................714 564-5800
Robin Auerbach, *President*
Dean Holbein, *Officer*
Doug Speaker, *Senior VP*
Didi Parks, *Vice Pres*
Lorie Boutboul, *Hum Res Coord*
EMP: 88 **EST:** 2009
SALES (est): 13MM **Privately Held**
WEB: www.edgemac.com
SIC: 8748 Business consulting

(P-23435)
EL CAPITAN ENVIRONMENTAL SVCS
11080 Tuxford St, Sun Valley (91352-2630)
PHONE.....................818 768-9222
Al Maurad, *President*
Harry Boyajian, *Vice Pres*
Mark Fator, *Sr Project Mgr*
EMP: 53 **EST:** 1991
SQ FT: 2,400
SALES (est): 3.3MM **Privately Held**
WEB: www.elcapitanenvironmental.com
SIC: 8748 Environmental consultant

(P-23436)
EMILY GRENE CORP
190 E Arrow Hwy Ste H, San Dimas
(91773-3314)
PHONE.....................855 463-6459
Burke Ewers, *CEO*
Ben Drake, *Director*
Adrienne Ewers, *Director*
EMP: 50 **EST:** 2012
SALES (est): 3.9MM **Privately Held**
WEB: www.emilygrene.com
SIC: 8748 1731 Energy conservation consultant; electrical work; general electrical contractor

PRODUCTS & SVCS

(P-23437)
ENVENT CORPORATION (PA)
3220 E 29th St, Long Beach (90806-2321)
PHONE...................................562 997-9465
Steve Sellinger, *President*
Daniel Paik, *CFO*
Willie Lule, *Area Mgr*
JD Jaeger, *General Mgr*
Keith Hurley, *Technician*
EMP: 94 **EST:** 1992
SQ FT: 6,400
SALES (est): 36MM **Privately Held**
WEB: www.enventcorporation.com
SIC: 8748 Environmental consultant

(P-23438)
**ENVIRONMENTAL
RESOLUTIONS INC**
Also Called: Cardno Eri
25371 Cmmrcntre Dr Ste 25, Lake Forest
(92630)
PHONE...................................949 457-8950
Steve M Zigan, *CEO*
Robert L Kroeger, *Vice Pres*
Courtney Marsden, *Admin Sec*
Mike Madden, *Info Tech Mgr*
Sushil Silva, *Engineer*
EMP: 300 **EST:** 1989
SQ FT: 14,100
SALES (est): 23.7MM **Privately Held**
WEB: www.cardno.com
SIC: 8748 8744 Environmental consultant;
HQ: Cardno Usa, Inc.
   8310 S Valley Hwy Ste 300
   Englewood CO 80112

(P-23439)
ETONIEN LLC (PA)
222 N Pacific Coast Hwy # 1507, El Se-
gundo (90245-5644)
PHONE...................................310 321-5800
Joseph E Davis, *CEO*
Lawrence Greaves,
James Floyd, *Director*
EMP: 68 **EST:** 2008
SQ FT: 5,000
SALES (est): 5.3MM **Privately Held**
WEB: www.etonien.com
SIC: 8748 Business consulting

(P-23440)
FAITH COM INC (PA)
Also Called: Fci Management
13850 Cerritos Corprt Dr D, Cerritos
(90703-2467)
PHONE...................................562 719-9300
Patricia Watts, *President*
Donald Gregg, *COO*
EMP: 58 **EST:** 1998
SQ FT: 7,000
SALES (est): 10.4MM **Privately Held**
SIC: 8748 Energy conservation consultant

(P-23441)
**FAME ASSISTANCE
CORPORATION**
2270 S Harvard Blvd, Los Angeles
(90018-2142)
PHONE...................................323 373-7720
Denise Hunter, *President*
EMP: 75 **EST:** 1988
SQ FT: 33,748
SALES (est): 2.1MM **Privately Held**
WEB: www.famecorporations.org
SIC: 8748 Business consulting

(P-23442)
**FOX TRANSPORTATION INC
(PA)**
8610 Helms Ave, Rancho Cucamonga
(91730-4520)
P.O. Box 3119 (91729-3119)
PHONE...................................909 291-4646
Michael K Fox, *CEO*
Mary Anne Fox, *Shareholder*
Chad Shearer, *President*
Mary Fox, *CFO*
David Langrehr, *Senior VP*
EMP: 59 **EST:** 2003
SALES (est): 15.7MM **Privately Held**
WEB: www.foxtransportationinc.com
SIC: 8748 4213 Business consulting;
   trucking, except local

(P-23443)
GABE INC
300 Spectrum Center Dr # 40, Irvine
(92618-4925)
P.O. Box 8675, Newport Beach (92658-
8675)
PHONE...................................949 679-2727
Gabe Gabriel, *Ch of Bd*
Sassine Shahine, *President*
Dorene Gabriel, *Treasurer*
EMP: 58 **EST:** 1985
SQ FT: 1,000
SALES (est): 6.3MM **Privately Held**
WEB: www.gabeinc.com
SIC: 8748 Business consulting

(P-23444)
**GEBBS HEALTHCARE
SOLUTIONS (HQ)**
600 Corporate Pointe # 1200, Culver City
(90230-7626)
PHONE...................................201 227-0088
Milind Godbole, *CEO*
Deepesh Rana, *Assoc VP*
Gabe Stein, *Exec VP*
Denise Cawley, *Senior VP*
Pooja Mehendale, *Vice Pres*
EMP: 220 **EST:** 2008
SALES (est): 62MM **Privately Held**
WEB: www.gebbs.com
SIC: 8748 Business consulting

(P-23445)
GEOLOGICS CORPORATION
25375 Orch Vlg Rd Ste 102, Valencia
(91355-3000)
PHONE...................................661 259-5767
Fernando Arroyo, *Manager*
Dick Brewer, *Vice Pres*
Kurt Brewer, *Exec Dir*
Bob Abril, *Program Mgr*
Fred Busch, *Division Mgr*
EMP: 273 **Privately Held**
WEB: www.geologics.com
SIC: 8748 8711 7379 Systems analysis &
   engineering consulting services; consult-
   ing engineer; computer related consulting
   services
PA: Geologics Corporation
   5500 Cherokee Ave Ste 400
   Alexandria VA 22312

(P-23446)
**GOLDEN WEST PARTNERS INC
(PA)**
Also Called: Golden West Casino
200 Spectrum Center Dr # 1250, Irvine
(92618-5003)
PHONE...................................949 477-3090
Franklin R Elfend, *President*
Bob Patty, *Vice Pres*
Chris Hein, *Manager*
EMP: 290 **EST:** 1994
SALES (est): 8.2MM **Privately Held**
SIC: 8748 Business consulting

(P-23447)
**HEATH CONSULTANTS
INCORPORATED**
9473 Slauson Ave, Pico Rivera
(90660-4747)
PHONE...................................562 942-0315
Jeffrey Tuttle, *Branch Mgr*
EMP: 157
SALES (corp-wide): 235.2MM **Privately
Held**
WEB: www.heathus.com
SIC: 8748 Business consulting
PA: Heath Consultants Incorporated
   9030 W Monroe Rd
   Houston TX 77061
   713 844-1300

(P-23448)
HERE FILMS
10990 Wilshire Blvd, Los Angeles
(90024-3913)
PHONE...................................310 806-4288
EMP: 50
SALES (est): 1.2MM **Privately Held**
SIC: 8748 Business Consulting, Nec, Nsk

(P-23449)
**HIGHER GROUND EDUCATION
INC (PA)**
10 Orchard Ste 200, Lake Forest
(92630-8309)
PHONE...................................949 836-9401
Ramandeep Grin, *CEO*
Ramandeep Girn, *CEO*
Guy Barnett, *Vice Pres*
Matt Bateman, *Vice Pres*
Steven Gaudino, *Vice Pres*
EMP: 272 **EST:** 2016
SALES (est): 40.5MM **Privately Held**
WEB: www.tohigherground.com
SIC: 8748 8299 Business consulting; edu-
   cational services

(P-23450)
HJI GROUP CORPORATION (PA)
5 Rochelle, Newport Coast (92657-0107)
PHONE...................................714 557-8800
Hong Jiang, *President*
Guangwei Huang, *Vice Pres*
James Qin, *General Mgr*
EMP: 59 **EST:** 1992
SALES (est): 1.7MM **Privately Held**
WEB: www.hjigroup.com
SIC: 8748 8711 8741 4111 Energy con-
   servation consultant; environmental con-
   sultant; mechanical engineering; civil
   engineering; construction management;
   subway operation

(P-23451)
**IACCESS TECHNOLOGIES INC
(PA)**
1251 E Dyer Rd Ste 160, Santa Ana
(92705-5655)
P.O. Box 53545, Irvine (92619-3545)
PHONE...................................714 922-9158
Hasan I Ramlaoui, *CEO*
Neil Duong, *General Mgr*
Brendan Cheng, *Software Engr*
Christine Ostrowski, *Engineer*
Eric Reichard, *Engineer*
EMP: 54 **EST:** 2003
SQ FT: 20,000
SALES (est): 10.7MM **Privately Held**
WEB: www.iaccesstech.com
SIC: 8748 3812 3699 3728 Business
   consulting; aircraft/aerospace flight instru-
   ments & guidance systems; flight simula-
   tors (training aids), electronic; refueling
   equipment for use in flight, airplane

(P-23452)
IBASET INC (PA)
27442 Portola Pkwy # 300, Foothill Ranch
(92610-2822)
PHONE...................................949 598-5200
Ladeira Poonian, *Ch of Bd*
Naveen Poonian, *CEO*
Elizabeth Conley, *CFO*
Daniel De Haas, *CFO*
Scott Baril, *Officer*
EMP: 96 **EST:** 2015
SQ FT: 28,000
SALES (est): 11MM **Privately Held**
WEB: www.ibaset.com
SIC: 8748 7371 7372 Business consult-
   ing; custom computer programming serv-
   ices; application computer software

(P-23453)
**INSTITUTE FOR MLTCLTRAL
CNSLIN (PA)**
3580 Wilshire Blvd # 200, Los Angeles
(90010-2501)
PHONE...................................213 381-1239
Tara Pir, *CEO*
Leland Keel, *Human Res Mgr*
Gil Morquecho, *Supervisor*
EMP: 54 **EST:** 1990
SALES: 7.9MM **Privately Held**
WEB: www.imces.org
SIC: 8748 Educational consultant

(P-23454)
**INTRINSIK ENVMTL SCIENCES
INC**
1608 Pacific Ave Ste 201, Venice
(90291-5112)
PHONE...................................310 392-6462
EMP: 67

SALES (corp-wide): 3.5MM **Privately
Held**
SIC: 8748 Environmental Consulting Serv-
   ices
PA: Intrinsik Environmental Sciences Inc
   6605 Hurontario St Suite 605
   Mississauga ON
   905 364-7800

(P-23455)
**IRVINE TECHNOLOGY
CORPORATION**
2850 Redhill Ave Ste 230, Santa Ana
(92705-5550)
PHONE...................................714 445-2624
Nicole McMackin, *President*
Kevin Orlando, *CFO*
Nicole Ortiz, *Vice Pres*
Janet Thornby, *Vice Pres*
Michael Rose, *Admin Sec*
EMP: 160 **EST:** 2000
SALES (est): 19MM **Privately Held**
WEB: www.irvinetechcorp.com
SIC: 8748 7363 7371 7379 Business
   consulting; temporary help service; soft-
   ware programming applications; computer
   related consulting services

(P-23456)
IVY ENTERPRISES INC
5564 E 61st St, Commerce (90040-3406)
PHONE...................................323 887-8661
Jane Kim, *Manager*
EMP: 440 **Privately Held**
WEB: www.myivyusa.com
SIC: 8748 Business consulting
HQ: Ivy Enterprises, Inc.
   25 Harbor Park Dr
   Port Washington NY 11050

(P-23457)
**JAG PROFESSIONAL SERVICES
INC**
2008 Walnut Ave, Manhattan Beach
(90266-2841)
P.O. Box 3007, El Segundo (90245-8107)
PHONE...................................310 945-5648
Judith Hinkley, *CEO*
EMP: 126 **EST:** 2001
SQ FT: 1,000 **Privately Held**
WEB: www.jagprof.com
SIC: 8748 Business consulting

(P-23458)
**JRW RESEARCH &
CONSULTING INC**
1055 E Colo Blvd Ste 310, Pasadena
(91106)
PHONE...................................877 579-1031
Joshua Ungerecht, *CEO*
Warren Thomas, *President*
Susana Dryden, *COO*
EMP: 50 **EST:** 2007
SALES (est): 1.5MM **Privately Held**
WEB: www.jrw.com
SIC: 8748 Business consulting

(P-23459)
JULIO GONZALEZ
1417 S Fairfax Ave Apt 4, Los Angeles
(90019-3736)
PHONE...................................310 310-4055
Julio Gonzalez, *Owner*
EMP: 99
SALES (est): 950K **Privately Held**
SIC: 8748 Business consulting

(P-23460)
KARMAN TOPCO LP (PA)
18100 Von Karman Ave # 1000, Irvine
(92612-0169)
PHONE...................................949 797-2900
Robert Fischer, *Vice Pres*
Maria Weathersby, *Recruiter*
Brittany Moore, *Supervisor*
EMP: 1206 **EST:** 2014
SALES (est): 4.7B **Publicly Held**
SIC: 8748 Business consulting

(P-23461)
KINGDOM ENTITIES LLC (PA)
Also Called: Kingdom Elixir
32401 Calle Perfecto, San Juan Capistrano (92675-4773)
PHONE..................................949 325-9240
Ryan Botsch, *Mng Member*
EMP: 65 EST: 2014
SALES (est): 3.4MM **Privately Held**
WEB: www.illuminent.com
SIC: 8748 Business consulting

(P-23462)
LAGUNA BLANCA SCHOOL (PA)
4125 Paloma Dr, Santa Barbara (93110-2146)
PHONE..................................805 687-2461
Sue Smith, *Manager*
Rose Steeber, *Ch of Bd*
Jack Stein, *Creative Dir*
Tina Braniff, *Principal*
Alexandra Goodman, *Admin Asst*
EMP: 94 EST: 1933
SQ FT: 24,857
SALES: 15.1MM **Privately Held**
WEB: www.lagunablanca.org
SIC: 8211 8748 Private elementary & secondary schools; business consulting

(P-23463)
LAND DESIGN CONSULTANTS INC
2700 E Fthill Blvd Ste 20, Pasadena (91107)
PHONE..................................626 578-7000
Robert Sims, *President*
Larry Mar, *CFO*
Steve Hunter, *Vice Pres*
EMP: 70 EST: 1992 **Privately Held**
WEB: www.ldcla.com
SIC: 8748 8711 8713 Urban planning & consulting services; environmental consultant; civil engineering; surveying services

(P-23464)
LANDMARK GLOBAL INC
27 W Anapamu St, Santa Barbara (93101-3107)
PHONE..................................805 720-5874
EMP: 69
SALES (corp-wide): 2.6B **Privately Held**
WEB: www.landmarkglobal.com
SIC: 8748 Business consulting
HQ: Landmark Global, Inc.
506 Chapala St
Santa Barbara CA 93101
805 679-5029

(P-23465)
LEAF COMMUNICATIONS INC
1000 Calle Cordillera, San Clemente (92673-6235)
PHONE..................................949 388-0192
Frederick Dan Leaf, *President*
Melissa Acosta, *Vice Pres*
Lisa Leaf, *Vice Pres*
EMP: 64 EST: 2016
SALES (est): 5.7MM **Privately Held**
WEB: www.leafcomm.com
SIC: 8748 1623 Communications consulting; transmitting tower (telecommunication) construction

(P-23466)
LEIGHTON AND ASSOCIATES INC (PA)
17781 Cowan, Irvine (92614-6009)
PHONE..................................949 250-1421
Terry Brennan, *President*
Robert Riha, *COO*
Bruce Clark, *Vice Pres*
Carl Kim, *Vice Pres*
Chris Lutton, *Vice Pres*
EMP: 70 EST: 1960
SQ FT: 30,000
SALES (est): 15.2MM **Privately Held**
WEB: www.leightongroup.com
SIC: 8748 8711 Environmental consultant; engineering services

(P-23467)
LEVEL FOUR BUSINESS MGT LLC
11812 San Vicente Blvd # 400, Los Angeles (90049-6625)
PHONE..................................310 914-1600
Mark Friedman, *Mng Member*
Mark Cattalini, *Business Mgr*
Jeremy Marcus, *Business Mgr*
John Rigney, *Business Mgr*
Melina Schroeder, *Business Mgr*
EMP: 50 EST: 2007
SALES (est): 5.3MM **Privately Held**
WEB: www.levelfourllc.com
SIC: 8748 Business consulting

(P-23468)
LOS ANGELES UNIFIED SCHOOL DST
Also Called: Los Angels Unified School Dst
1208 Magnolia Ave, Gardena (90247-4399)
PHONE..................................310 354-3417
Linda Delcueto, *Superintendent*
Anna Estevez, *Director*
Elizabeth Kaley, *Director*
Michael Romero, *Superintendent*
EMP: 53
SALES (corp-wide): 9.3B **Privately Held**
WEB: www.laallcityband.com
SIC: 8211 8748 Public elementary & secondary schools; school for the retarded; educational consultant
PA: Los Angeles Unified School District
333 S Beaudry Ave Ste 209
Los Angeles CA 90017
213 241-1000

(P-23469)
LOS ANGELES UNIFIED SCHOOL DST
Also Called: Los Angeles Board of Education
333 S Beaudry Ave Fl 29, Los Angeles (90017-5106)
P.O. Box 513307 (90051-1307)
PHONE..................................323 265-1898
EMP: 53
SALES (corp-wide): 9.3B **Privately Held**
WEB: www.laallcityband.com
SIC: 8211 8748 Public elementary & secondary schools; educational consultant
PA: Los Angeles Unified School District
333 S Beaudry Ave Ste 209
Los Angeles CA 90017
213 241-1000

(P-23470)
LOS ANGELES UNIFIED SCHOOL DST
Also Called: Granada Hills Sr High School
10535 Zelzah Ave, Granada Hills (91344-5902)
PHONE..................................818 360-2361
Brian Bauer, *Principal*
Ann Falotico, *Principal*
EMP: 53
SALES (corp-wide): 9.3B **Privately Held**
WEB: www.laallcityband.com
SIC: 8211 8748 Elementary & secondary schools; business consulting
PA: Los Angeles Unified School District
333 S Beaudry Ave Ste 209
Los Angeles CA 90017
213 241-1000

(P-23471)
LSA ASSOCIATES INC (PA)
Also Called: L S A
20 Executive Park Ste 200, Irvine (92614-4739)
PHONE..................................949 553-0666
Les Card, *CEO*
Rob McCann, *President*
James Baum, *CFO*
Rosie Evans, *Vice Pres*
Marco Perez, *Regional Mgr*
EMP: 110 EST: 1974
SQ FT: 22,000
SALES (est): 39.1MM **Privately Held**
WEB: www.lsa.net
SIC: 8748 Environmental consultant

(P-23472)
LUSIVE DECOR
Also Called: Luxe Light and Home
3400 Medford St, Los Angeles (90063-2530)
PHONE..................................323 227-9207
Jason Kai Cooper, *CEO*
Sally Cooper, *Marketing Staff*
John Carbajal, *Manager*
Mike McLafferty, *Manager*
Nathan Bignell, *Assistant*
EMP: 55 EST: 2006
SALES (est): 13.3MM **Privately Held**
WEB: www.lusive.com
SIC: 8748 3646 Lighting consultant; ceiling systems, luminous

(P-23473)
MIDNIGHT SUN ENTERPRISES INC
Also Called: Spearmint Rhino Gentlemens CLB
19900 Normandie Ave, Torrance (90502-1113)
PHONE..................................310 532-2427
Kathy Vercher, *Principal*
EMP: 86 EST: 2008
SALES (est): 5.8MM **Privately Held**
SIC: 8748 Business consulting

(P-23474)
MIRAMED GLOBAL SERVICES INC
Also Called: On Call Consulting
199 E Thsand Oaks Blvd, Thousand Oaks (91360)
PHONE..................................805 277-1017
Donna Perry, *Vice Pres*
EMP: 107 EST: 2012
WEB: www.miramedgs.com
SIC: 8748 Business consulting
PA: Miramed Global Services, Inc.
255 W Michigan Ave
Jackson MI 49201

(P-23475)
MONTROSE ENVMTL GROUP INC (PA)
1 Park Plz Ste 1000, Irvine (92614-8507)
PHONE..................................949 988-3500
Vijay Manthripragada, *President*
Richard E Perlman, *Ch of Bd*
Joshua W Lemaire, *COO*
Allan Dicks, *CFO*
Peter Zemek, *Senior VP*
EMP: 274 EST: 2012
SALES (est): 328.2MM **Publicly Held**
WEB: www.montrose-env.com
SIC: 8748 Environmental consultant

(P-23476)
MONTROSE MSRMNTS ANALYTICS LLC (HQ)
1 Park Plz Ste 1000, Irvine (92614-8507)
PHONE..................................949 988-3500
Steve Eckard, *Senior VP*
EMP: 50 EST: 2018
SALES (est): 26.5MM
SALES (corp-wide): 328.2MM **Publicly Held**
WEB: www.montrose-env.com
SIC: 8748 Environmental consultant
PA: Montrose Environmental Group, Inc.
1 Park Plz Ste 1000
Irvine CA 92614
949 988-3500

(P-23477)
MONTROSE WATER AND SUSTAINABIL
Also Called: Mwss
1 Park Plz Ste 1000, Irvine (92614-8507)
PHONE..................................949 988-3500
Vijay Manthripragada, *President*
Allan Dicks, *Treasurer*
Jose Revuelta, *Vice Pres*
Nasym Afsari, *Admin Sec*
EMP: 90 EST: 2019
SALES (est): 9.2MM
SALES (corp-wide): 328.2MM **Publicly Held**
WEB: www.montrose-env.com
SIC: 8748 8744 Environmental consultant;

PA: Montrose Environmental Group, Inc.
1 Park Plz Ste 1000
Irvine CA 92614
949 988-3500

(P-23478)
MOUNTAIN TOP COMM SVCS LLC
1902 Orange Tree Ln # 14, Redlands (92374-2888)
PHONE..................................909 798-4400
Diodore Pesquera,
David Carranza, *Engineer*
Joseph Jacobson,
Justin Mata,
EMP: 50 EST: 2011
SQ FT: 4,025
SALES (est): 3.2MM **Privately Held**
WEB: www.box826.bluehost.com
SIC: 8748 Telecommunications consultant

(P-23479)
N2W ENGINEERING INC
3240 El Cmino Real Ste 15, Irvine (92602)
P.O. Box 60472 (92602-6015)
PHONE..................................714 716-1711
Niu Jinghui, *President*
Aleyda Marquez, *Vice Pres*
Dane Nygaard, *Project Mgr*
Nestor Ruiz, *Project Mgr*
Jeff Lippert, *Plant Supt*
EMP: 60 EST: 1996
SQ FT: 2,300
SALES (est): 22.5MM **Privately Held**
SIC: 8748 Environmental consultant

(P-23480)
NATIONAL SAFETY SERVICES
3400 Avenue Of The Arts F214, Costa Mesa (92626-1927)
PHONE..................................714 679-9118
Charles Hudson, *President*
EMP: 50 EST: 2015
SALES (est): 2.7MM **Privately Held**
WEB: www.nsrsi.com
SIC: 8748 8999 Safety training service; search & rescue service

(P-23481)
NEWBOOK INTERNATIONAL INC
3680 Wilshire Blvd P04, Los Angeles (90010-2707)
PHONE..................................310 855-3773
Bradley Illich, *President*
EMP: 55 EST: 2018
SALES (est): 2.2MM **Privately Held**
SIC: 8748 Business consulting

(P-23482)
NMS DATA INC
Also Called: Neilson Marketing Services
23172 Plaza Pointe Dr # 205, Laguna Hills (92653-1477)
PHONE..................................949 472-2700
Lawrence Neilson, *CEO*
Jeffrey Neilson, *President*
Jolie Eritano, *Accountant*
Jeannette Nickell, *Train & Dev Mgr*
Paul Neilson, *VP Sales*
EMP: 50 EST: 2006
SQ FT: 9,500
SALES (est): 5MM **Privately Held**
WEB: www.programbusiness.com
SIC: 8748 Business consulting

(P-23483)
NO WORLD BORDERS (PA)
620 Newport Center Dr, Newport Beach (92660-6420)
PHONE..................................949 718-4427
Michael F Arrigo, *Managing Prtnr*
Martha Bradt, *Vice Pres*
EMP: 61 EST: 2000
SQ FT: 12,000
SALES (est): 5.9MM **Privately Held**
WEB: www.noworldborders.com
SIC: 8748 8742 Business consulting; hospital & health services consultant

(P-23484)
NORTH LA COUNTY REGIONAL CTR (PA)
9200 Oakdale Ave Ste 100, Chatsworth (91311-6505)
PHONE....................................818 778-1900
George Stevens, *Director*
Kim Rolfes, *CFO*
Fay Shapiro, *Office Mgr*
Mike Rahmani, *Social Worker*
Elizabeth Walters, *Social Worker*
EMP: 280 **EST:** 1974
SQ FT: 57,000
SALES: 572.5MM **Privately Held**
WEB: www.nlacrc.org
SIC: 8748 Test development & evaluation service

(P-23485)
NORTHROP GRUMMAN SYSTEMS CORP
Defense Systems Sector
1 Space Park Blvd, Redondo Beach (90278-1071)
PHONE....................................855 737-8364
Jack Distaso, *Branch Mgr*
Alice Reed, *Principal*
Felipe Rico, *Electrical Engi*
Todd Sebastian, *Engineer*
EMP: 140
SQ FT: 500,000 **Publicly Held**
WEB: www.northropgrumman.com
SIC: 8748 Systems analysis & engineering consulting services
HQ: Northrop Grumman Systems Corporation
2980 Fairview Park Dr
Falls Church VA 22042
703 280-2900

(P-23486)
OCEAN PARK COMMUNITY CENTER
Turning Point
1447 16th St, Santa Monica (90404-2715)
PHONE....................................310 828-6717
Patricia Bauman, *Director*
EMP: 95
SALES (corp-wide): 68MM **Privately Held**
WEB: www.thepeopleconcern.org
SIC: 8748 Urban planning & consulting services
PA: The People Concern
2116 Arlington Ave # 100
Los Angeles CA 90018
323 334-9000

(P-23487)
ONLINE LAND PLANNING LLC
Also Called: Professnal Svcs - Archtectural
856 Avenue B, Redondo Beach (90277-4835)
PHONE....................................310 594-7782
Frederick Abelson, *CEO*
Annette Roe, *Officer*
EMP: 50 **EST:** 2008
SALES (est): 1.5MM **Privately Held**
WEB: www.onlinelandplanning.com
SIC: 8748 0781 8399 8712 Urban planning & consulting services; industrial development planning; landscape architects; regional planning organization; architectural services; transportation consultant

(P-23488)
OPENPOPCOM INC (PA)
12539 Carson St, Hawaiian Gardens (90716-1607)
PHONE....................................714 249-7044
Sun Jong Baek, *President*
EMP: 75 **EST:** 1999
SALES (est): 4.8MM **Privately Held**
WEB: www.openpop.com
SIC: 8748 Telecommunications consultant

(P-23489)
P8GE CONSULTING INC
Also Called: Fame Hardwood Floors
8406 Beverly Blvd, Los Angeles (90048-3402)
PHONE....................................310 666-2301
Pedram Youav Nazarian, *CEO*
EMP: 50 **EST:** 2004
SQ FT: 1,500

SALES (est): 5.4MM **Privately Held**
WEB: www.famehardwood.com
SIC: 8748 Business consulting

(P-23490)
PALM VALLEY SCHOOL
35525 Da Vall Dr, Rancho Mirage (92270-1822)
PHONE....................................760 328-0861
Robert Graves, *Principal*
Ana Bernstein, *Ch of Bd*
Grahm Hookey, *Principal*
Kate Agoglia, *Teacher*
Maxine Bernstein, *Teacher*
EMP: 65 **EST:** 1958
SALES: 7.4MM **Privately Held**
WEB: www.pvs.org
SIC: 8211 8748 Private elementary & secondary schools; business consulting

(P-23491)
PARAGON PARTNERS LTD (PA)
5660 Katella Ave Ste 100, Cypress (90630-5058)
PHONE....................................714 379-3376
Neilia A La Valle, *President*
Joel Sewell, *Vice Pres*
Cindy Gomez, *Exec Dir*
Allen Armstrong, *Regional Mgr*
Pam Samms, *Regional Mgr*
EMP: 65 **EST:** 1993
SQ FT: 10,000
SALES (est): 18.4MM **Privately Held**
WEB: www.paragon-partners.com
SIC: 8748 Business consulting

(P-23492)
PATRIOT COMMUNICATIONS LLC (PA)
Also Called: Benefit Resources Group
3415 S Sepulveda Blvd # 8, Los Angeles (90034-6060)
PHONE....................................888 833-4711
Doug Livingston,
Kyra Gagnon, *CFO*
Steve Berger, *Vice Pres*
Dio King, *Software Engr*
Vassilka Lazarova, *Network Enginr*
EMP: 53 **EST:** 1990
SQ FT: 15,000
SALES (est): 8.4MM **Privately Held**
WEB: www.patriotllc.com
SIC: 8748 Telecommunications consultant

(P-23493)
PEARCE SERVICES LLC (HQ)
1222 Vine St Ste 301, Paso Robles (93446-2333)
P.O. Box 1708 (93447-1708)
PHONE....................................805 467-2528
Bret Forster, *CEO*
Benjamin Krick, *President*
Kristin Osborn, *CFO*
Matt Gillette, *Exec VP*
Kullen Burk, *Vice Pres*
EMP: 50 **EST:** 1998
SQ FT: 2,800
SALES (est): 240MM
SALES (corp-wide): 488.1MM **Privately Held**
WEB: www.pearce-services.com
SIC: 8748 1731 Telecommunications consultant; energy management controls
PA: New Mountain Partners V, L.P.
1633 Broadway Fl 48
New York NY 10019
212 720-0300

(P-23494)
PEOPLES SELF-HELP HOUSING CORP
Also Called: Los Adobes De Maria
1026 W Boone St, Santa Maria (93458-5499)
PHONE....................................805 349-9341
John Fowler, *Director*
Rick Gulino, *Director*
EMP: 65
SALES (corp-wide): 17.4MM **Privately Held**
WEB: www.pshhc.org
SIC: 8748 Urban planning & consulting services

PA: Peoples' Self-Help Housing Corporation
3533 Empleo St
San Luis Obispo CA 93401
805 781-3088

(P-23495)
PRIME FOCUS TECHNOLOGIES INC
2255 N Ontario St Ste 230, Burbank (91504-3195)
PHONE....................................310 895-9550
Ramki Sankaranarayanan, *CEO*
Patrick McDonald-King, *President*
Raghunath Mohanrao, *COO*
Amer Saleem, *Vice Pres*
Atul Saxena, *Vice Pres*
EMP: 62 **EST:** 2013
SALES (est): 9.9MM **Privately Held**
WEB: www.primefocustechnologies.com
SIC: 8748 Business consulting
HQ: Prime Focus Technologies Limited
Plot No 63 True North,
Mumbai MH 40009

(P-23496)
PROFIT RECOVERY PARTNERS LLC
Also Called: P R P
1600 Sunflower Ave # 100, Costa Mesa (92626-1544)
PHONE....................................949 851-2777
Donald Steiner, *President*
Jeremy Linehan, *President*
Marty Bozarth, *COO*
Paul J Bottiaux, *CFO*
Edward Lyon, *CFO*
EMP: 75 **EST:** 1997
SALES (est): 11.7MM **Privately Held**
WEB: www.prpllc.com
SIC: 8748 Business consulting

(P-23497)
PS ARTS
Also Called: Crossroads Cmnty Foundation
2947 S Sepulveda Blvd, Los Angeles (90064-3912)
PHONE....................................310 586-1017
Kristin Paglia, *Exec Dir*
Amy Shario, *Exec Dir*
Allison Schaub, *Manager*
EMP: 50 **EST:** 1991
SALES: 4.1MM **Privately Held**
WEB: www.psarts.org
SIC: 8748 Educational consultant

(P-23498)
QMERIT ELECTRIFICATION LLC (PA)
2 Venture Ste 550, Irvine (92618-7406)
PHONE....................................888 272-0090
Tracy Price, *Mng Member*
Jon Holland,
EMP: 119 **EST:** 2020
SALES (est): 4.6MM **Privately Held**
WEB: www.qmerit.com
SIC: 8748 Energy conservation consultant

(P-23499)
RESTOR-TECH CNSTR CNSLTING INC (PA)
9125 Long Beach Blvd, South Gate (90280-2811)
PHONE....................................323 249-2277
Eduardo Hernandez, *Principal*
Gaby Vargas, *Office Mgr*
EMP: 54 **EST:** 2018
SALES (est): 729.4K **Privately Held**
WEB: www.restortech.com
SIC: 8748 Business consulting

(P-23500)
RIGHT ANGLE SOLUTIONS INC
6315 Pedley Rd, Jurupa Valley (92509-6007)
P.O. Box 965, Mira Loma (91752-0965)
PHONE....................................951 934-3081
Duane Eric Cook, *CEO*
EMP: 25 **EST:** 2009

SALES (est): 4.9MM **Privately Held**
WEB: www.rightanglesolutionsinc.com
SIC: 8748 1711 3569 4959 Environmental consultant; plumbing contractors; filters & strainers, pipeline; environmental cleanup services; facilities support services

(P-23501)
RINCON CONSULTANTS INC
1530 Monterey St Ste D, San Luis Obispo (93401-2969)
PHONE....................................805 547-0900
John Rickenvach, *Manager*
EMP: 238 **Privately Held**
WEB: www.rinconconsultants.com
SIC: 8748 Environmental consultant
PA: Rincon Consultants, Inc.
180 N Ashwood Ave
Ventura CA 93003

(P-23502)
RIVERSIDE COUNTY OFF EDUCATN
1055 E Vista Chino, Palm Springs (92262-3207)
PHONE....................................760 320-8266
Fax: 760 320-9689
EMP: 105
SALES (corp-wide): 211.3MM **Privately Held**
SIC: 9199 8748 General Government Business Consulting Services
PA: Riverside County Office Of Education
3939 13th St
Riverside CA 92501
951 826-6530

(P-23503)
ROBIN SINGH EDUCTL SVCS INC
Also Called: Testmasters
8383 Wilshire Blvd # 810, Beverly Hills (90211-2425)
PHONE....................................310 460-7199
Robin Singh, *CEO*
Naim Sharon, *Exec VP*
Cabrera Jorge, *Technology*
Kamille Chiong, *Opers Mgr*
Hannah Rosson, *Marketing Staff*
EMP: 72 **EST:** 2002
SALES (est): 4.5MM **Privately Held**
SIC: 8748 8299 Testing services; tutoring school

(P-23504)
ROSE INTERNATIONAL INC
17701 Cowan Ste 230, Irvine (92614-6840)
PHONE....................................636 812-4000
Ashley Votaw, *Associate Dir*
Brendan Thomas, *Business Anlyst*
Amit Bishnoi, *Tech Recruiter*
Ayush Goyal, *Tech Recruiter*
Amanda Hague, *Technology*
EMP: 107 **Privately Held**
WEB: www.roseint.com
SIC: 8748 7371 7363 7361 Systems engineering consultant, ex. computer or professional; computer software development; help supply services; employment agencies
PA: Rose International, Inc.
16305 Swingley Ridge Rd # 350
Chesterfield MO 63017

(P-23505)
ROUGHAN ASSOCIATES AT LINC
465 N Halstead St Ste 120, Pasadena (91107-3144)
PHONE....................................626 351-0991
Jan Roughan, *President*
EMP: 50 **EST:** 2017
SALES (est): 2.1MM **Privately Held**
WEB: www.linc.biz
SIC: 8748 Business consulting

(P-23506)
SANAN INC
Also Called: Panini Kabob Grill
8505 Irvine Center Dr, Irvine (92618-4298)
PHONE....................................949 679-9200
EMP: 50 **EST:** 2004

SALES (est): 2.1MM **Privately Held**
SIC: 8748 Business consulting

(P-23507)
SECURITY 20/20 INC
Also Called: Security Pro USA
8543 Venice Blvd, Los Angeles
(90034-2548)
PHONE..............................310 475-7780
Amnon Even, *CEO*
Galia Even, *President*
Hunter Solsona, *Exec VP*
Al Even, *Info Tech Mgr*
Cindy Perez, *Sales Staff*
EMP: 15 **EST:** 1986
SQ FT: 2,600
SALES (est): 4.7MM **Privately Held**
WEB: www.securityprousa.com
SIC: 5999 8748 3482 3812 Safety sup-
plies & equipment; safety training service;
small arms ammunition; radar systems &
equipment

(P-23508)
SIERRA MONOLITHICS INC (HQ)
103 W Torrance Blvd, Redondo Beach
(90277-3633)
PHONE..............................310 698-1000
Charles Harper, *CEO*
Javed Patel, *President*
Trevor Roots, *CFO*
Derek Obata, *Exec VP*
David Rowe, *CTO*
EMP: 53 **EST:** 1986
SQ FT: 15,000
SALES (est): 10.8MM
SALES (corp-wide): 595.1MM **Publicly
Held**
WEB: www.semtech.com
SIC: 8748 8731 3812 Communications
consulting; electronic research; radar sys-
tems & equipment
PA: Semtech Corporation
200 Flynn Rd
Camarillo CA 93012
805 498-2111

(P-23509)
SITESERVER INC
4514 Ish Dr, Simi Valley (93063-7666)
PHONE..............................805 579-7831
Mark McDonald, *President*
Matt Hayford, *Engineer*
Elysa McDonald,
Andrew O'Brien,
EMP: 21 **EST:** 2005
SQ FT: 4,000
SALES (est): 1MM **Privately Held**
WEB: www.siteserver.com
SIC: 8748 3674 Business consulting; hy-
brid integrated circuits

(P-23510)
SLALOM LLC
300 Spectrum Center Dr # 1500, Irvine
(92618-3095)
PHONE..............................949 450-1100
EMP: 113 **Privately Held**
WEB: www.slalom.com
SIC: 8748 Business consulting
PA: Slalom, Llc
821 2nd Ave Ste 1900
Seattle WA 98104

(P-23511)
SOUTH COAST AIR QULTY MGT DST (PA)
Also Called: A Q M D
21865 Copley Dr, Diamond Bar
(91765-4178)
P.O. Box 4940 (91765-0940)
PHONE..............................909 396-2000
Raymond E Robinson, *CEO*
Marcia Crane, *President*
Rebecca Garcia, *President*
Michael O'Kelly, *Officer*
Barry R Wallerstein, *Exec Dir*
EMP: 720 **EST:** 1955
SQ FT: 350
SALES: 457.5MM **Privately Held**
WEB: www.aqmd.gov
SIC: 8748 Environmental consultant

(P-23512)
SUCCETTI GROUP INC
5020 Campus Dr, Newport Beach
(92660-2120)
PHONE..............................949 335-2292
Ryan Michael Succetti, *CEO*
EMP: 50 **EST:** 2012
SALES (est): 1.9MM **Privately Held**
SIC: 8748 Business consulting

(P-23513)
SUNRUN INSTALLATION SVCS INC
13012 Saticoy St Ste 1, North Hollywood
(91605-3513)
PHONE..............................818 255-5462
Winnowski Paul, *Branch Mgr*
EMP: 216 **Publicly Held**
SIC: 8748 5999 5211 1711 Energy conservation consultant; alcoholic beverage
making equipment & supplies; energy
conservation products; solar energy contractor
HQ: Sunrun Installation Services Inc.
775 Fiero Ln Ste 200
San Luis Obispo CA 93401
415 580-6900

(P-23514)
SYSTEMS EXPERIENCE INC
6033 W Century Blvd # 820, Los Angeles
(90045-6424)
PHONE..............................310 215-9000
Richard L Jivery, *President*
Vince Rangel, *Vice Pres*
EMP: 65 **EST:** 1979
SQ FT: 3,600
SALES (est): 4.4MM **Privately Held**
WEB: www.systemsexperience.com
SIC: 8748 Business consulting

(P-23515)
T-FORCE INC (PA)
4695 Macarthur Ct, Newport Beach
(92660-1882)
PHONE..............................949 208-1527
Raid Al-Khawaldeh, *President*
EMP: 98 **EST:** 2004
SALES (est): 8.1MM **Privately Held**
WEB: www.tforcelogistics.com
SIC: 8748 7379 Telecommunications con-
sultant;

(P-23516)
TEMPEST TELECOM SOLUTIONS LLC (PA)
136 W Canon Perdido St # 100, Santa Bar-
bara (93101-3242)
PHONE..............................805 879-4800
Jessica Firestone, *CEO*
Dan Firestone, *COO*
Julie Lubin, *CFO*
Richard Smith, *Vice Pres*
Arielle Stetson, *Office Mgr*
EMP: 60 **EST:** 2005
SQ FT: 9,000
SALES (est): 24.6MM **Privately Held**
WEB: www.tempesttelecom.com
SIC: 8748 Systems analysis & engineering
consulting services; telecommunications
consultant

(P-23517)
TOTAL EDUCATION SOLUTIONS INC (PA)
625 Fair Oaks Ave Ste 300, South
Pasadena (91030-5805)
PHONE..............................323 341-5580
Nancy Lavelle, *President*
Piero Stillitano, *CFO*
Jeanne Bauer, *CIO*
Jeremiah Clark, *Info Tech Mgr*
Aaron San Juan, *Web Dvlpr*
EMP: 50
SALES (est): 39.5MM **Privately Held**
WEB: www.tesidea.com
SIC: 8748 Educational consultant

(P-23518)
TRC COMPANIES INC
2820 Pegasus Dr, Bakersfield
(93308-6847)
PHONE..............................661 837-0022
EMP: 50

SALES (corp-wide): 693.7MM **Privately
Held**
WEB: www.trccompanies.com
SIC: 8748 Business Consulting Services
PA: Trc Companies, Inc.
21 Griffin Rd N
Windsor CT 06095
860 298-9692

(P-23519)
TRC SOLUTIONS INC (HQ)
Also Called: Alton Geoscience
9685 Research Dr Ste 100, Irvine
(92618-4657)
PHONE..............................949 753-0101
Christopher P Vincze, *Ch of Bd*
Thomas W Bennet Jr, *CFO*
John Cowdery, *Principal*
Martin H Dodd, *Principal*
Ed Wiegele, *Principal*
EMP: 125 **EST:** 1981
SQ FT: 47,000
SALES (est): 29.4MM
SALES (corp-wide): 711.8MM **Privately
Held**
WEB: www.trccompanies.com
SIC: 8748 8711 Environmental consultant;
engineering services
PA: Trc Companies, L.L.C.
21 Griffin Rd N
Windsor CT 06095
860 298-9692

(P-23520)
TULE RIVER ECONOMIC DEV
Also Called: Tredc
31071 Highway 190, Porterville
(93257-9168)
PHONE..............................559 781-4271
Dennis Ickes, *CEO*
Kellie Carrillo, *Principal*
William Hayter, *Principal*
Isacc Manuel, *Principal*
Novalie Harry, *Executive Asst*
EMP: 80 **EST:** 2001
SALES (est): 96K **Privately Held**
WEB: www.tulereredc.com
SIC: 8748 8711 Economic consultant; con-
sulting engineer

(P-23521)
URBAN FUTURES INC
17821 17th St Ste 245, Tustin
(92780-2173)
PHONE..............................714 283-9334
Michael Busch, *CEO*
Wingsee Fox, *Managing Dir*
Jim Morris, *Managing Dir*
Timothy Fryndendall, *Analyst*
Kathleen Robles, *Sr Project Mgr*
EMP: 69 **EST:** 1972
SALES (est): 5.7MM **Privately Held**
WEB: www.urbanfuturesinc.com
SIC: 8748 Urban planning & consulting
services

(P-23522)
VENTEGRA INC A CAL BENEFT CORP
450 N Brand Blvd Ste 600, Glendale
(91203-2349)
PHONE..............................858 551-8111
Robert Taketomo, *President*
Mariana Ritchie, *Vice Pres*
Mike Gannon, *Director*
Don Schoenly, *Director*
Michele Yoon, *Director*
EMP: 85 **EST:** 2004
SALES (est): 4.7MM **Privately Held**
WEB: www.ventegra.com
SIC: 8748 Business consulting

(P-23523)
VINCULUMS SERVICES LLC
10 Pasteur Ste 100, Irvine (92618-3823)
PHONE..............................949 783-3552
Paul Foster, *CEO*
Brian Woodward, *COO*
Norm Alexander, *CFO*
Paula Shaffer, *Program Mgr*
Isabel Lightbourn, *Executive Asst*
EMP: 220 **EST:** 2005
SQ FT: 8,000

SALES (est): 32.7MM
SALES (corp-wide): 517.1MM **Privately
Held**
WEB: www.qualtekservices.com
SIC: 8748 Telecommunications consultant
PA: Qualtek, Llc
475 Sentry Pkwy E # 1000
Blue Bell PA 19422
484 804-4500

(P-23524)
VOLT TELECOM GROUP INC
Also Called: Volt Telecom Group
218 Helicopter Cir, Corona (92878-5031)
PHONE..............................951 493-8900
Frank D'Alessio, *CEO*
Kingsley H Nelson, *Principal*
EMP: 260
SALES (corp-wide): 822MM **Publicly
Held**
WEB: www.volt.com
SIC: 8748 Telecommunications consultant
HQ: Volt Telecommunications Group, Inc.
560 Lexington Ave
New York NY 10022
212 704-2400

(P-23525)
W CORPORATION
Also Called: Vantage Company
1643 W Orange Grove Ave, Orange
(92868-1116)
PHONE..............................714 532-8800
EMP: 100 ,
SALES (est): 24.5MM **Privately Held**
WEB: www.vantagecompany.com
SIC: 8748 1542 1522 Business Consult-
ing Services Nonresidential Construction
Residential Construction

(P-23526)
WARNER BROS CONSUMER PDTS INC (DH)
4001 W Olive Ave, Burbank (91505-4272)
PHONE..............................818 954-7980
Brad Globe, *President*
Dan Romanelli, *President*
Randy Blotky, *Senior VP*
Ana De Castro, *Senior VP*
John Louie, *Vice Pres*
▲ **EMP:** 112 **EST:** 2003
SALES (est): 26.8MM
SALES (corp-wide): 171.7B **Publicly
Held**
WEB: www.warnerbros.com
SIC: 8748 5961 Business consulting; nov-
elty merchandise, mail order
HQ: Warner Bros. Entertainment Inc.
4000 Warner Blvd
Burbank CA 91522
818 954-6000

(P-23527)
WATERTALENT LLC
10877 Wilshire Blvd # 708, Los Angeles
(90024-4364)
PHONE..............................424 832-7217
Tyler Reifert, *President*
David Sibelman, *COO*
Jason Anish, *Administration*
EMP: 50 **EST:** 2016
SALES (est): 2.6MM **Privately Held**
WEB: www.watertalent.net
SIC: 8748 Environmental consultant

(P-23528)
WTP AMERICA LLC (HQ)
Also Called: Wt Partnership
520 Broadway Ste 200, Santa Monica
(90401-2470)
PHONE..............................310 356-4636
Adam Shaw, *Exec VP*
Darren Blyth, *Exec VP*
Bridey Best, *Vice Pres*
Paul Mackintosh, *Vice Pres*
Shannon Percy, *Vice Pres*
EMP: 54 **EST:** 2015
SALES (est): 12.8MM **Privately Held**
WEB: www.wtpartnership.co
SIC: 8748 8742 7389 Business consult-
ing; management consulting services;
construction project management consult-
ant; estimating service, construction

PRODUCTS & SVCS

(P-23529)
YUCAIPA COMPANIES LLC (PA)
9130 W Sunset Blvd, Los Angeles
(90069-3110)
PHONE..............................310 789-7200
Ronald W Burkle, *Mng Member*
Scott Stedman,
EMP: 150 EST: 1986
SALES (est): 247.9MM **Privately Held**
WEB: www.yucaipaco.com
SIC: 8748 6719 6726 Business consulting; investment holding companies, except banks; investment offices

8999 Services Not Elsewhere Classified

(P-23530)
ARTISTS GUILD OF AMERICA
Also Called: Art Mate
13225 S Western Ave, Gardena
(90249-1923)
PHONE..............................310 532-3331
Shozo Osawa, *President*
Iris Ornelas, *Office Mgr*
EMP: 16 EST: 1978
SQ FT: 25,000
SALES (est): 1MM **Privately Held**
WEB: www.artistsguildofamerica.com
SIC: 8999 3952 Artist; artists' materials, except pencils & leads

(P-23531)
DATA TRACE INFO SVCS LLC (HQ)
4 First American Way, Santa Ana
(92707-5913)
PHONE..............................714 250-6700
Mike Henney Sr,
Mark Johnson, *Vice Pres*
Christine Esguerra, *Analyst*
Donna Schopper, *Client Mgr*
EMP: 100 EST: 2000
SALES (est): 16.8MM **Publicly Held**
WEB: www.datatracetitle.com
SIC: 8999 Information bureau

(P-23532)
ENGEO INCORPORATED
29025 Avenue Penn, Valencia
(91355-5426)
PHONE..............................661 257-4004
Uri Eliahu, *President*
EMP: 105
SALES (corp-wide): 38.5MM **Privately Held**
WEB: www.engeo.com
SIC: 8999 8711 Earth science services; engineering services
PA: Engeo Incorporated
2010 Crow Canyon Pl # 250
San Ramon CA 94583
925 866-9000

(P-23533)
ESSENSE
Also Called: Maxus USA
6300 Wilshire Blvd # 720, Los Angeles
(90048-5204)
PHONE..............................323 202-4650
EMP: 618 EST: 2015
SALES (est): 566.4K
SALES (corp-wide): 15.9B **Privately Held**
WEB: www.shopping-bag-delivery.com
SIC: 8999 Communication services
HQ: Maxus Communications Llc
498 Fashion Ave
New York NY 10018
212 297-8300

(P-23534)
GEOLOGIC ASSOCIATES INC
1831 Commercenter E, San Bernardino
(92408-3405)
PHONE..............................909 383-8728
Sarah Battelle, *Vice Pres*
Lori Bartlett, *Vice Pres*
Stacy Baird, *Manager*
Bryan Fritzler, *Manager*
EMP: 67 **Privately Held**
WEB: www.geo-logic.com
SIC: 8999 7373 Geological consultant; systems integration services

PA: Geologic Associates, Inc.
2777 E Guasti Rd Ste 1
Ontario CA 91761

(P-23535)
HEALTHCARE SERVICES GROUP INC
5199 E Pacific Coast Hwy # 402, Long Beach (90804-3309)
PHONE..............................562 494-7939
Mike Hammond, *Principal*
EMP: 742
SALES (corp-wide): 1.7B **Publicly Held**
WEB: www.hcsgcorp.com
SIC: 8999 Artists & artists' studios
PA: Healthcare Services Group Inc
3220 Tillman Dr Ste 300
Bensalem PA 19020
215 639-4274

(P-23536)
MGM AND UA SERVICES COMPANY
245 N Beverly Dr, Beverly Hills
(90210-5319)
PHONE..............................310 449-3000
Gary Barber, *President*
Chris Brearton, *COO*
Ted Lim, *Senior VP*
Michael Katzer, *Exec Dir*
Chantel Rusher, *Production*
EMP: 560 EST: 1994
SALES (est): 61.4MM
SALES (corp-wide): 1.1B **Privately Held**
WEB: www.mgm.com
SIC: 8999 Artists & artists' studios
HQ: Metro-Goldwyn-Mayer, Inc.
245 N Beverly Dr
Beverly Hills CA 90210

(P-23537)
OPTIMA NETWORK SERVICES INC (DH)
15345 Frfeld Rnch Rd Ste, Chino Hills
(91709)
PHONE..............................305 599-1800
Robert E Apple, *CEO*
Michael Mosel, *President*
EMP: 75 EST: 2004
SQ FT: 6,475
SALES (est): 10.6MM
SALES (corp-wide): 6.3B **Publicly Held**
WEB: www.mastecnetworksolutions.com
SIC: 8999 Communication services
HQ: Mastec North America, Inc.
800 S Douglas Rd Ste 1200
Coral Gables FL 33134
305 599-1800

(P-23538)
ORACLE CORP
17901 Von Karman Ave # 800, Irvine
(92614-5241)
PHONE..............................650 506-7000
EMP: 567
SALES (est): 27.1MM **Privately Held**
SIC: 8999 Services-Misc

(P-23539)
ORANGEPEOPLE LLC
300 Spectrum Center Dr # 40, Irvine
(92618-4925)
PHONE..............................949 535-1308
Raghav Putrevu, *President*
Kasey Rajan, *Tech Recruiter*
Jenny Alex, *Manager*
Loreen Aoki, *Manager*
Carole Logvin, *Manager*
EMP: 76 EST: 2004
SQ FT: 8,000
SALES (est): 9.6MM **Privately Held**
WEB: www.orangepeople.com
SIC: 8999 7374 7371 8742 Cloud seeding; data processing service; computer software development; construction project management consultant

(P-23540)
PACE LITHOGRAPHERS INC
Also Called: Pace Marketing Communications
18030 Cortney Ct, City of Industry
(91748-1202)
PHONE..............................626 913-2108

Robert Bennitt, *President*
Carl Bennitt Jr, *Vice Pres*
Randy Marquis, *Info Tech Dir*
Mark Hoch, *Production*
EMP: 35 EST: 1970
SQ FT: 27,000
SALES (est): 5.4MM **Privately Held**
WEB: www.engagepace.com
SIC: 8999 2752 Communication services; commercial printing, lithographic

(P-23541)
RIVERSIDE CNTY FLOOD CTRL WTR
1995 Market St, Riverside (92501-1719)
PHONE..............................951 955-1200
Jason Uhley, *Principal*
Joe Barcenas, *Technician*
Stuart McKibbin, *Engineer*
Robert Meals, *Engineer*
Cassandra Sanchez, *Engineer*
EMP: 210 EST: 1945
SALES (est): 87MM **Privately Held**
WEB: www.rcflood.org
SIC: 8999 Natural resource preservation service

(P-23542)
RUBIO ARTS CORPORATION
1313 S Harbor Blvd, Anaheim
(92802-2309)
PHONE..............................407 849-1643
David Johnson, *Branch Mgr*
EMP: 111
SALES (corp-wide): 2.5MM **Privately Held**
SIC: 8999 Artist
PA: Rubio Arts Corporation
8100 Chancellor Dr # 100
Orlando FL 32809
407 849-1643

(P-23543)
WESTAMERICA COMMUNICATIONS INC
26012 Atlantic Ocean Dr, Lake Forest
(92630-8843)
PHONE..............................949 340-8942
Douglas Grant, *CEO*
Tralton Bellings, *CFO*
Mike Milota, *Vice Pres*
Ken Dunn, *Info Tech Dir*
Lynnette Carpenter, *Project Mgr*
EMP: 93 EST: 1975
SALES (est): 9.9MM **Privately Held**
WEB: www.mywestamerica.com
SIC: 8999 Communication services

(P-23544)
WORLEY FIELD SERVICES INC
2422 E 223rd St, Carson (90810-1617)
PHONE..............................310 816-8939
Michael Serrano, *Manager*
EMP: 64 **Privately Held**
SIC: 8999 Artists & artists' studios
HQ: Worley Field Services, Inc.
5995 Rogerdale Rd
Houston TX 77072
832 351-6000

(P-23545)
X WEAPON SECURITY
297 Country Club Dr, Simi Valley
(93065-6632)
P.O. Box 940835 (93094-0835)
PHONE..............................818 818-9950
Mish Marie, *CEO*
Sayed Sadat, *President*
EMP: 80 EST: 2018
SALES (est): 3.5MM **Privately Held**
WEB: www.weaponxsecurity.com
SIC: 8999 1731 7381 Personal services; safety & security specialization; security guard service

ALPHABETIC SECTION

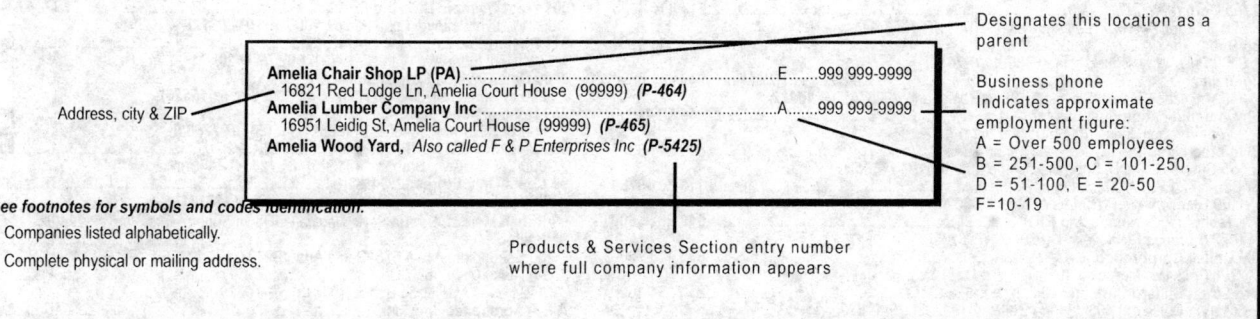

Amelia Chair Shop LP (PA) .... E 999 999-9999
16821 Red Lodge Ln, Amelia Court House (99999) ***(P-464)***
Amelia Lumber Company Inc .... A 999 999-9999
16951 Leidig St, Amelia Court House (99999) ***(P-465)***
Amelia Wood Yard, *Also called F & P Enterprises Inc* ***(P-5425)***

Address, city & ZIP

Designates this location as a parent

Business phone

Indicates approximate employment figure:
A = Over 500 employees
B = 251-500, C = 101-250,
D = 51-100, E = 20-50
F=10-19

Products & Services Section entry number where full company information appears

See footnotes for symbols and codes identification.

- Companies listed alphabetically.
- Complete physical or mailing address.

1-800 Dentist, Los Angeles *Also called Futuredontics Inc* ***(P-20178)***
10 Day Parts Inc .... E 951 279-4810
235 Citation Cir Corona (92878) ***(P-5539)***
10 Gauge Sheet Metal Inc .... F 909 208-4525
1101 Endeavor Dr Upland (91786) ***(P-6768)***
10-8 Retrofit Inc .... F 909 986-5551
415 W Main St Ontario (91762) ***(P-18812)***
101 Apparel Inc .... F 714 454-8988
1802 N Glassell St Orange (92865) ***(P-2754)***
101 Vertical Fabrication Inc .... D 909 428-6000
10255 Beech Ave Fontana (92335) ***(P-13543)***
10632 Bolsa Avenue LP .... D 949 673-1221
500 Nwport Ctr Dr Ste 200 Newport Beach (92660) ***(P-15715)***
1115 Bakersfield Mhrc, Bakersfield *Also called Crestwood Behavioral Hlth Inc* ***(P-21764)***
1135 N Leisure Ct Inc .... D 714 772-1353
1135 N Leisure Ct Anaheim (92801) ***(P-20236)***
116 Angwin Mhrc, Bakersfield *Also called Crestwood Behavioral Hlth Inc* ***(P-19777)***
117 Global LLC (PA) .... F **949 570-1552**
32861 Camn Capistrano San Juan Capistrano (92675) ***(P-18423)***
1170 Lompoc Mhrc, Lompoc *Also called Crestwood Behavioral Hlth Inc* ***(P-20307)***
1221 Ocean Ave Apartments, Santa Monica *Also called Irvine APT Communities LP* ***(P-15731)***
123 Home Care, Los Angeles *Also called Confido LLC* ***(P-21155)***
123ewireless, Rcho STA Marg *Also called Sarco Inc* ***(P-13772)***
1260 Bb Property LLC .... B 805 969-2261
1260 Channel Dr Santa Barbara (93108) ***(P-16305)***
1334 Partners LP .... D 310 546-5656
1330 Park View Ave Manhattan Beach (90266) ***(P-19526)***
1370 Realty Corp .... E 818 817-0092
14545 Friar St Shrmano Van Nuys (91411) ***(P-15762)***
14 Cannons Brewing Company Inc .... F 818 652-6971
31125 Via Colinas Ste 907 Westlake Village (91362) ***(P-2135)***
17400 Inc .... D 626 913-1800
17400 Chestnut St City of Industry (91748) ***(P-12104)***
18 Media Inc (PA) .... F **650 324-1818**
200 N Pcf Cast Hwy Ste 11 El Segundo (90245) ***(P-4047)***
180 Snacks Inc .... E 714 238-1192
1151 N Armando St Anaheim (92806) ***(P-2109)***
180la LLC .... C 310 382-1400
12555 W Jefferson Blvd # 200 Los Angeles (90066) ***(P-16988)***
1855 S Hbr Blvd Drv Hldngs LLC .... C 714 750-1811
1855 S Harbor Blvd Anaheim (92802) ***(P-16306)***
1928 Jewelry Company, Burbank *Also called Mel Bernie and Company Inc* ***(P-14135)***
1integer LLC .... E 424 320-2977
1999 Avenue Of The Stars Los Angeles (90067) ***(P-17533)***
1perfectchoice .... F 909 594-8855
21908 Valley Blvd Walnut (91789) ***(P-3719)***
1st Century Builders Inc .... F 818 254-7183
5737 Kanan Rd Agoura Hills (91301) ***(P-588)***
1st Class Event Services, Long Beach *Also called Cloudstaff LLC* ***(P-17407)***
1st Team Real Estate, Tustin *Also called First Team RE - Orange Cnty* ***(P-15864)***
20/20 Mobile Corp (PA) .... D **951 354-8100**
10050 Magnolia Ave Riverside (92503) ***(P-12588)***
20/20 Plumbing & Heating Inc (PA) .... C **951 396-2020**
7343 Orangewood Dr Ste B Riverside (92504) ***(P-1011)***
2006 Sage Publications .... F 805 499-0721
2455 Teller Rd Thousand Oaks (91320) ***(P-4117)***
20th Century Fox Studio, Los Angeles *Also called Fox Net Inc* ***(P-19126)***
2100 Freedom Inc (HQ) .... D **714 796-7000**
625 N Grand Ave Santa Ana (92701) ***(P-3941)***
2100 Trust LLC (PA) .... C **877 469-7344**
625 N Grand Ave Santa Ana (92701) ***(P-16171)***
211 LA COUNTY, San Gabriel *Also called Informtion Rfrral Fdrtion of L* ***(P-16959)***
21515 Hawthorne Owner LLC .... D 310 406-3730
21535 Hawthorne Blvd # 10 Torrance (90503) ***(P-22308)***
21seeds Inc .... F 310 415-8605
8605 Santa Monica Blvd West Hollywood (90069) ***(P-2163)***
21st Century Insurance, Woodland Hills *Also called 21st Century Life Insurance Co* ***(P-15524)***
21st Century Lf & Hlth Co Inc (PA) .... C **818 887-4436**
21600 Oxnard St Ste 1500 Woodland Hills (91367) ***(P-15373)***
21st Century Life Insurance Co (HQ) .... A **877 310-5687**
6301 Owensmouth Ave # 700 Woodland Hills (91367) ***(P-15524)***
220 Laboratories LLC (HQ) .... C **951 683-2912**
2375 3rd St Riverside (92507) ***(P-4986)***
2253 Apparel LLC (PA) .... D **323 837-9800**
1708 Aeros Way Montebello (90640) ***(P-14325)***
2310 Catalina LLC .... D 818 696-2040
1507 Western Ave Glendale (91201) ***(P-18424)***
23627 Calabasas Road LLC .... D 818 222-5300
23627 Calabasas Rd Calabasas (91302) ***(P-16307)***
24 Hour Home Care, El Segundo *Also called 24hr Homecare LLC* ***(P-21116)***
24-7 Caregivers Registry Inc .... C 800 687-8066
6800 Owensmouth Ave # 420 Canoga Park (91303) ***(P-21114)***
24-Hour Med Staffing Svcs LLC .... C 909 895-8960
21700 Copley Dr Ste 270 Diamond Bar (91765) ***(P-17385)***
24/7 Studio Equipment Inc .... E 818 840-8247
3111 N Kenwood St Burbank (91505) ***(P-9247)***
24hr Homecare LLC (PA) .... A **310 906-3683**
300 N Pacific Coast Hwy # 1065 El Segundo (90245) ***(P-21115)***
24hr Homecare LLC .... C 310 375-5353
200 N Pcf Cast Hwy Ste 30 El Segundo (90245) ***(P-21116)***
24hr Homecare LLC .... D 310 258-9525
5901 Green Valley Cir Culver City (90230) ***(P-21117)***
24hr Homecare LLC .... D 818 385-0227
17141 Ventura Blvd # 205 Encino (91316) ***(P-21118)***
24hr Homecare LLC .... D 714 881-4245
1440 N Harbor Blvd # 715 Fullerton (92835) ***(P-21119)***
24hr Homecare LLC .... D 949 607-8115
16485 Laguna Canyon Rd # 110 Irvine (92618) ***(P-21120)***
24hr Homecare LLC .... D 805 988-2205
2401 E Gonzales Rd # 170 Oxnard (93036) ***(P-21121)***
24hr Homecare LLC .... D 310 375-5353
21311 Hawthorne Blvd # 101 Torrance (90503) ***(P-21122)***
29 Palms Enterprises Corp .... A 760 775-5566
46200 Harrison Pl Coachella (92236) ***(P-19629)***
29 Palms Inn .... D 760 367-3505
73950 Inn Ave Twentynine Palms (92277) ***(P-16308)***
2h Construction Inc .... D 562 424-5567
2653 Walnut Ave Signal Hill (90755) ***(P-728)***
2nd Gen Productions Inc .... E 800 877-6282
400 El Sobrante Rd Corona (92879) ***(P-4950)***
2nd Location, SW Eye Care, Bakersfield *Also called Gregory A Stainer MD Facs* ***(P-19834)***
3 - D Polymers .... F 310 324-7694
13026 S Normandie Ave Gardena (90249) ***(P-5362)***
3 Point Distribution LLC .... E 949 266-2700
170 Technology Dr Irvine (92618) ***(P-2793)***
3-D Precision Machine Inc .... E 951 296-5449
42132 Remington Ave Temecula (92590) ***(P-10208)***
3-V Fastener Co Inc .... D 949 888-7700
630 E Lambert Rd Brea (92821) ***(P-7053)***
3067 Orange Avenue LLC .... D 714 827-2440
3067 W Orange Ave Anaheim (92804) ***(P-20237)***
313 Acquisition LLC .... A 801 234-6374
1111 Citrus St Ste 1 Riverside (92507) ***(P-18363)***
32 North Brewing Co LLC (PA) .... F **619 363-2622**
2238 N Glassell St Ste E Orange (92865) ***(P-2136)***
360 Clinic, Westminster *Also called 360 Health Plan Inc* ***(P-22963)***
360 Health Plan Inc .... C 800 446-8888
13800 Arizona St Ste 104 Westminster (92683) ***(P-22963)***
360 Support Services .... D 866 360-6468
306 S Myrtle Ave Monrovia (91016) ***(P-22964)***
360zebra, City of Industry *Also called Gels Logistics Inc* ***(P-12460)***
365 Delivery Inc .... D 818 815-5005
440 E Huntington Dr # 300 Arcadia (91006) ***(P-11945)***
365 Printing Inc .... F 714 752-6990
14747 Artesia Blvd Ste 3a La Mirada (90638) ***(P-4220)***
3650 Industry Avenue LLC .... F 949 509-5000
100 Bayview Cir Ste 310 Newport Beach (92660) ***(P-7957)***
3ality Digital LLC (PA) .... D **818 970-7756**
895 N Todd Ave Azusa (91702) ***(P-19087)***
3ality Technica, Azusa *Also called 3ality Digital LLC* ***(P-19087)***
3bd Holdings Inc (PA) .... E **323 524-0541**
717 Mateo St Los Angeles (90021) ***(P-17769)***
3becom Inc (PA) .... F **818 726-0007**
2400 Lincoln Ave Ste 216 Altadena (91001) ***(P-17770)***
3blackdot, Los Angeles *Also called 3bd Holdings Inc* ***(P-17769)***
3d Machine Co Inc .... E 714 777-8985
4790 E Wesley Dr Anaheim (92807) ***(P-8449)***

© Mergent Inc. 1-800-342-5647

3d/International Inc.....C.....661 250-2020
20724 Cntre Pnte Pkwy Uni Santa Clarita (91350) ***(P-4951)***
3dna Corp (PA).....**D.....213 394-4623**
520 S Grand Ave Fl 2 Los Angeles (90071) ***(P-17534)***
3g Rebar Inc.....F.....661 588-0294
6400 Price Way Bakersfield (93308) ***(P-7012)***
3gen Inc.....F.....949 481-6384
31521 Rncho Vejo Rd Ste 1 San Juan Capistrano (92675) ***(P-10922)***
3h Communication Systems Inc.....E.....949 529-1583
3 Winterbranch Irvine (92604) ***(P-12621)***
3i Infotech Inc.....F.....805 544-8327
555 Chorro St Ste B San Luis Obispo (93405) ***(P-17535)***
3l Capital I LP (PA).....**D.....310 801-3789**
1100 Glendon Ave Ph 1 Los Angeles (90024) ***(P-16152)***
3M Technical Ceramics Inc (HQ).....**A.....949 862-9600**
1922 Barranca Pkwy Irvine (92606) ***(P-6175)***
3M Unitek Corporation.....B.....626 445-7960
2724 Peck Rd Monrovia (91016) ***(P-11158)***
3rd Street Billiard Club Inc.....D.....310 434-1000
3111 Via Dolce Apt 403 Marina Del Rey (90292) ***(P-19630)***
3s Sign Services Inc.....E.....714 683-1120
1320 N Red Gum St Anaheim (92806) ***(P-11517)***
3y Power Technology Inc.....F.....949 450-0152
80 Bunsen Irvine (92618) ***(P-9668)***
4 Earth Farms LLC (PA).....**B.....323 201-5800**
5555 E Olympic Blvd Commerce (90022) ***(P-14610)***
4 Gen Digital.....F.....714 486-1150
3540 Cadillac Ave Costa Mesa (92626) ***(P-4221)***
4 Over LLC (HQ).....**C.....818 246-1170**
5900 San Fernando Rd D Glendale (91202) ***(P-4470)***
4 Over LLC.....F.....818 246-1170
1225 Los Angeles St Glendale (91204) ***(P-4471)***
4 What Its Worth Inc (PA).....**D.....323 728-4503**
5815 Smithway St Commerce (90040) ***(P-2794)***
4 Wheel Parts Performance Ctrs, Compton *Also called Tap Worldwide LLC* ***(P-13098)***
412280 Inc (HQ).....**D.....209 545-1111**
5990 Sepulvda Blvd # 600 Van Nuys (91411) ***(P-14427)***
417 Stockton St LLC.....D.....323 327-9656
1180 S Beverly Dr Ste 508 Los Angeles (90035) ***(P-16309)***
48forty Solutions.....F.....951 682-3095
2641 Hall Ave Riverside (92509) ***(P-17771)***
4as Trucking.....E.....424 308-9563
20604 Belshaw Ave Carson (90746) ***(P-11946)***
4excelsior, Anaheim *Also called Excelsior Nutrition Inc* ***(P-4746)***
4g Wireless Inc (PA).....**C.....949 748-6100**
8871 Research Dr Irvine (92618) ***(P-12589)***
4inkjets, Long Beach *Also called Ld Products Inc* ***(P-3760)***
4medica Inc (PA).....**D.....310 695-3300**
13160 Mindanao Way # 350 Marina Del Rey (90292) ***(P-18078)***
5 Arches LLC.....D.....949 387-8092
19800 Macarthur Blvd Irvine (92612) ***(P-15234)***
5 Day Business Forms Mfg Inc (PA).....**D.....213 623-3577**
2910 E La Cresta Ave Anaheim (92806) ***(P-14189)***
5 Day Business Forms Mfg Inc.....D.....714 632-8674
2921 E La Cresta Ave Anaheim (92806) ***(P-14190)***
5 Design Inc.....D.....323 308-3558
1024 N Orange Dr Ste 215 Los Angeles (90038) ***(P-22705)***
5 Star Job Source.....D.....562 788-7391
12025 Garfield Ave South Gate (90280) ***(P-17386)***
5.11 Tactical Series, Irvine *Also called 511 Inc* ***(P-2609)***
51 Minds Entertainment LLC.....D.....818 643-8200
5200 Lankershim Blvd # 200 North Hollywood (91601) ***(P-19341)***
511 Inc (HQ).....**B.....949 800-1511**
1360 Reynolds Ave Ste 101 Irvine (92614) ***(P-2609)***
550 Flower St Operations LLC.....C.....213 892-8080
550 S Flower St Los Angeles (90071) ***(P-16310)***
5525 E Pacific Coast Hwy Inc.....D.....323 669-9090
2016 Riverside Dr Los Angeles (90039) ***(P-16226)***
5800 Sunset Productions Inc.....F.....323 460-3987
5800 W Sunset Blvd Los Angeles (90028) ***(P-3942)***
5design, Los Angeles *Also called 5 Design Inc* ***(P-22705)***
5h Sheet Metal Fabrication Inc.....F.....714 633-7544
1826 W Business Center Dr Orange (92867) ***(P-6769)***
603 N La Cienega Boulevard LLC.....D.....310 855-9955
603 N La Cienega Blvd West Hollywood (90069) ***(P-18425)***
6417 Selma Hotel LLC.....C.....323 844-6417
6417 Selma Ave Los Angeles (90028) ***(P-16311)***
6480 Corporation.....F.....818 765-9670
7230 Coldwater Canyon Ave North Hollywood (91605) ***(P-4472)***
6500 Hllister Ave Partners LLC.....D.....805 722-1362
6500 Hollister Ave Goleta (93117) ***(P-15655)***
656 Los Angeles Street LLC.....E.....949 900-6160
719 S Los Angeles St # 368 Los Angeles (90014) ***(P-23145)***
6th Street Partners LLC.....F.....213 377-5277
3950 W 6th St Apt 201 Los Angeles (90020) ***(P-3720)***
7 Diamonds Clothing, Tustin *Also called M & S Trading Inc* ***(P-14341)***
7 Up / R C Bottling Co, Vernon *Also called American Bottling Company* ***(P-2253)***
716 Management Inc.....D.....818 471-4956
3900 W Alameda Ave # 120 Burbank (91505) ***(P-654)***
72andsunny Midco LLC.....A.....310 215-9009
12101 Bluff Creek Dr Playa Vista (90094) ***(P-16989)***
75s Corp.....E.....323 234-7708
800 E 62nd St Los Angeles (90001) ***(P-14106)***
7th Standard Ranch Company.....B.....661 399-0416
33374 Lerdo Hwy Bakersfield (93308) ***(P-39)***
860, Shameless, Hot Wire, Los Angeles *Also called JT Design Studio Inc* ***(P-2960)***
88rising Inc.....E.....626 372-7387
5735 Melrose Ave Los Angeles (90038) ***(P-19088)***

8th Street Enterprise Inc.....D.....213 622-9287
777 S Central Ave Los Angeles (90021) ***(P-14552)***
901 West Olympic Blvd Ltd Prtn.....C.....347 992-5707
901 W Olympic Blvd Los Angeles (90015) ***(P-16312)***
911 Restoration Entps Inc (PA).....**C.....8*8 373-4880**
7721 Densmore Ave Van Nuys (91406) ***(P-1629)***
9200 Data Devices Corporation.....E.....3*0 494-1794
9200 W Sunset Blvd West Hollywood (90069) ***(P-15525)***
939 Holdings Inc.....D.....818 525-5000
2600 W Olive Ave Ste 800 Burbank (91505) ***(P-12683)***
939 Investment LLC (PA).....**C.....818 525-5000**
2600 W Olive Ave Burbank (91505) ***(P-12684)***
99 Cents Only Stores LLC (HQ).....**B.....323 980-8145**
4000 Union Pacific Ave Commerce (90023) ***(P-12181)***
99 Ranch Market, Buena Park *Also called Tawa Supermarket Inc* ***(P-1940)***
9edge Inc.....E.....657 229-3343
200 Sandpointe Ave # 575 Santa Ana (92707) ***(P-17536)***
A & A Aerospace Inc.....F.....562 901-6803
1442 Hayes Ave Long Beach (90813) ***(P-10229)***
A & A Aerospace Inc.....F.....562 901-6803
1987 W 16th St Long Beach (90813) ***(P-10230)***
A & A Electronic Assembly, San Fernando *Also called Signature Tech Group Inc* ***(P-9781)***
A & A Fabrication & Polsg Corp.....F.....562 696-0441
12031 Philadelphia St Whittier (90601) ***(P-6577)***
A & A Jewelry Tools Findings.....F.....213 627-8004
319 W 6th St Los Angeles (90014) ***(P-11621)***
A & A Machine & Dev Co Inc.....F.....310 532-7706
16625 Gramercy Pl Gardena (90247) ***(P-8450)***
A & A Ready Mix Concrete, Newport Beach *Also called Lebata Inc* ***(P-6098)***
A & A Ready Mixed Concrete Inc (PA).....**E.....949 253-2800**
4621 Teller Ave Ste 130 Newport Beach (92660) ***(P-6065)***
A & B Aerospace Inc.....E.....626 334-2976
612 S Ayon Ave Azusa (91702) ***(P-8451)***
A & B Brush Mfg Corp.....E.....626 303-8856
1150 3 Ranch Rd Duarte (91010) ***(P-11506)***
A & D Precision Mfg Inc.....E.....714 779-2714
4751 E Hunter Ave Anaheim (92807) ***(P-8452)***
A & G Instr Svc Clibration Inc.....F.....714 630-7400
1227 N Tustin Ave Anaheim (92807) ***(P-7436)***
A & H Communications Inc.....C.....949 250-4555
15 Chrysler Irvine (92618) ***(P-931)***
A & H Engineering & Mfg Inc.....E.....562 623-9717
17109 Edwards Rd Cerritos (90703) ***(P-8453)***
A & H Tool Engineering, Cerritos *Also called A & H Engineering & Mfg Inc* ***(P-8453)***
A & I Color Laboratory, Burbank *Also called Jake Hey Incorporated* ***(P-18409)***
A & J Industries Inc.....F.....310 216-2170
1430 240th St Harbor City (90710) ***(P-3373)***
A & J Manufacturing, Harbor City *Also called A & J Industries Inc* ***(P-3373)***
A & J Manufacturing Company.....E.....714 544-9570
70 Icon Foothill Ranch (92610) ***(P-7116)***
A & L Engineering, Hawthorne *Also called Acuna Dionisio Able* ***(P-8468)***
A & M Electronics Inc.....E.....661 257-3680
25018 Avenue Kearny Valencia (91355) ***(P-9369)***
A & M Engineering Inc.....D.....626 813-2020
15854 Salvatiera St Irwindale (91706) ***(P-8454)***
A & M Sculpture Lighting, Los Angeles *Also called A & M Sculptured Metals LLC* ***(P-6770)***
A & M Sculptured Metals LLC.....E.....323 263-2221
1781 N Indiana St Los Angeles (90063) ***(P-6770)***
A & P Towing-Metropro Rd Svcs, Costa Mesa *Also called Metropro Road Services Inc* ***(P-18938)***
A & R Electric, Fullerton *Also called Swinford Electric Inc* ***(P-1324)***
A & R Engineering Co Inc.....D.....310 603-9060
1053 E Bedmar St Carson (90746) ***(P-8455)***
A & R Powder Coating Inc.....F.....714 630-0709
1198 N Grove St Ste B Anaheim (92806) ***(P-7333)***
A & R Wholesale Distrs Inc.....D.....714 777-7742
1765 W Penhall Way Anaheim (92801) ***(P-14553)***
A & S Metal Recycling Inc (PA).....**D.....213 623-9443**
2261 E 15th St Los Angeles (90021) ***(P-11947)***
A & S Mold and Die Corp.....D.....818 341-5393
9705 Eton Ave Chatsworth (91311) ***(P-5540)***
A & S Technologies, Northridge *Also called Ikano Communications Inc* ***(P-18096)***
A A A, Highland *Also called Automobile Club Southern Cal* ***(P-22401)***
A A A Automobile Club, Arcadia *Also called Automobile Club Southern Cal* ***(P-22411)***
A A A Automobile Club So Cal, Los Angeles *Also called Automobile Club Southern Cal* ***(P-15540)***
A A A Automobile Club So Cal, Irvine *Also called Automobile Club Southern Cal* ***(P-22398)***
A A A Automobile Club So Cal, Palm Springs *Also called Automobile Club Southern Cal* ***(P-22415)***
A A A Automobile Club So Cal, Pasadena *Also called Automobile Club Southern Cal* ***(P-22417)***
A A A Automobile Club So Cal, Inglewood *Also called Automobile Club Southern Cal* ***(P-22424)***
A A A Automobile Club So Cal, Fullerton *Also called Automobile Club Southern Cal* ***(P-22428)***
A A A Automobile Club So Cal, Valencia *Also called Automobile Club Southern Cal* ***(P-22431)***
A A A Automobile Club So Cal, Laguna Hills *Also called Automobile Club Southern Cal* ***(P-22432)***
A A A Automobile Club So Cal, Hemet *Also called Automobile Club Southern Cal* ***(P-22434)***
A A A Automobile Club So Cal, Long Beach *Also called Automobile Club Southern Cal* ***(P-22442)***
A A A Automobile Club So Cal, Glendale *Also called Automobile Club Southern Cal* ***(P-22443)***
A A A Couriers, Los Angeles *Also called Classic Couriers Inc* ***(P-12125)***

A A A Packing and Shipping Inc..........E.......626 310-7787
2000 E 49th St Vernon (90058) *(P-11948)*
A A C N, Aliso Viejo *Also called American Assn Crtcal Care Nrse (P-21937)*
A A Cater Truck Mfg Co Inc..........E.......323 233-2343
750 E Slauson Ave Los Angeles (90011) *(P-3523)*
A A Construction, Rialto *Also called Arnett Construction Inc (P-1591)*
A A E Aerospace & Coml Tech, Huntington Beach *Also called American Automated Engrg Inc (P-10530)*
A A Gonzalez Inc..........D.......818 367-2242
13264 Ralston Ave Sylmar (91342) *(P-1358)*
A A P, Gardena *Also called American Aircraft Products Inc (P-6782)*
A and G Inc (HQ)..........**A.......714 765-0400**
11296 Harrel St Jurupa Valley (91752) *(P-2795)*
A and M Ornamental Iron & Wldg..........F.......951 734-6730
1611 Railroad St Corona (92878) *(P-6945)*
A and M Welding Inc..........E.......310 329-2700
16935 S Broadway Gardena (90248) *(P-18965)*
A B, Sylmar *Also called Advanced Bionics LLC (P-11081)*
A B C Plastic Fabrication,, Chatsworth *Also called A B C Plastics Inc (P-5446)*
A B C Plastics Inc..........F.......818 775-0065
9132 De Soto Ave Chatsworth (91311) *(P-5446)*
A B C Restaurant Equipment Co, South El Monte *Also called Master Enterprises Inc (P-6868)*
A B C Unified School District..........D.......562 865-1676
11865 178th St Artesia (90701) *(P-17208)*
A B P Inc..........F.......310 532-9400
15608 New Century Dr Gardena (90248) *(P-14907)*
A B S, Signal Hill *Also called Applied Business Software Inc (P-17787)*
A B S, City of Industry *Also called Magnell Associate Inc (P-13413)*
A B S Auto Auctions, Corona *Also called Auto Buyline Systems Inc (P-13020)*
A Better Tomorrow Trtmnt Ctr, Murrieta *Also called Abttc Inc (P-22076)*
A Buchalter Professional Corp (PA)..........**C.......213 891-0700**
1000 Wilshire Blvd # 150 Los Angeles (90017) *(P-21499)*
A C D, Santa Ana *Also called Acd LLC (P-6723)*
A C G, Laguna Hills *Also called American Capital Group Inc (P-15160)*
A C I Communications, Calabasas *Also called Able Cable Inc (P-18950)*
A C M, Santa Ana *Also called Advanced Clnroom McRclean Corp (P-17212)*
A C N, City of Industry *Also called America Chung Nam LLC (P-14108)*
A C Plating, Bakersfield *Also called U M S Inc (P-7325)*
A C T, Fountain Valley *Also called Advanced Charging Tech Inc (P-8970)*
A C T, Hawthorne *Also called All Cartage Transportation Inc (P-12105)*
A C T, Ontario *Also called Aerospace and Coml Tooling Inc (P-8480)*
A C T S, Bloomington *Also called Acts For Children (P-22077)*
A C U Precision Sheet Metal, Perris *Also called American Coffee Urn Mfg Co Inc (P-6783)*
A C W, Los Angeles *Also called Alcoholism Center For Women (P-21710)*
A Caregiver LLC..........E.......951 676-4190
31520 Rr Cyn Rd Ste A Canyon Lake (92587) *(P-21123)*
A Cdg Boeing Company..........E.......562 608-2000
4060 N Lakewood Blvd Long Beach (90808) *(P-10231)*
A Commom Thread, Los Angeles *Also called Dda Holdings Inc (P-2938)*
A Community of Friends..........D.......213 480-0809
3701 Wilshire Blvd # 700 Los Angeles (90010) *(P-15716)*
A Cori Partnership..........E.......818 368-2802
10626 Balboa Blvd Granada Hills (91344) *(P-20549)*
A D S, Los Angeles *Also called Advanced Digital Services Inc (P-19091)*
A D S Environmental Srvs, Huntington Beach *Also called ADS LLC (P-10673)*
A D S Gold Inc..........F.......714 632-1888
3843 E Eagle Dr Anaheim (92807) *(P-6289)*
A Dentons Innovation Wirthlin, Los Angeles *Also called Dentons US LLP (P-21547)*
A Development Stage Company, Beverly Hills *Also called Stratos Renewables Corporation (P-5149)*
A Division Acorn Engrg Co, City of Industry *Also called Whitehall Manufacturing Inc (P-11154)*
A Division Continental Can Co, Santa Ana *Also called Altium Packaging LP (P-5487)*
A F C, Rancho Dominguez *Also called Advanced Fresh Concepts Corp (P-16201)*
A F E Industries Inc (PA)..........**F.......562 944-6889**
13233 Barton Cir Whittier (90605) *(P-4473)*
A Fab, Lake Forest *Also called American Deburring Inc (P-8495)*
A Filml Inc..........D.......213 977-8600
6255 W Sunset Blvd Fl 12 Los Angeles (90028) *(P-19216)*
A G Hacienda Incorporated..........B.......661 792-2418
32794 Sherwood Ave Mc Farland (93250) *(P-11949)*
A G I, Riverside *Also called Aleph Group Inc (P-10929)*
A Good Sign & Graphics Co..........F.......714 444-4466
2110 S Susan St Santa Ana (92704) *(P-11518)*
A Growing Concern Landscapes..........D.......714 843-5137
17382 Gothard St Huntington Beach (92647) *(P-231)*
A H Machine Inc..........E.......310 672-0016
214 N Cedar Ave Inglewood (90301) *(P-8456)*
A H Plating, Valencia *Also called Sunvair Overhaul Inc (P-10424)*
A Its Laugh Productions Inc..........D.......818 848-8787
914 N Victory Blvd Burbank (91502) *(P-19089)*
A J Fasteners Inc..........E.......714 630-1556
2800 E Miraloma Ave Anaheim (92806) *(P-7054)*
A J Parent Company Inc (PA)..........**D.......714 521-1100**
6910 Aragon Cir Ste 6 Buena Park (90620) *(P-18426)*
A J R Trucking Inc..........D.......562 989-9555
435 E Weber Ave Compton (90222) *(P-11950)*
A L S Industries Inc..........D.......310 532-9262
1942 Artesia Blvd Torrance (90504) *(P-14090)*
A Lighting By Design, Anaheim *Also called Albd Electric and Cable (P-1211)*
A Lot To Say Inc..........E.......877 366-8448
1541 S Vineyard Ave Ontario (91761) *(P-3186)*
A M Cabinets Inc (PA)..........**D.......310 532-1919**
239 E Gardena Blvd Gardena (90248) *(P-3575)*
A M I Encn-Trzana Rgnal Med Ce, Tarzana *Also called AMI-Hti Trzana Encino Jint Vnt (P-20673)*
A M I/Coast Magnetics Inc..........E.......323 936-6188
5333 W Washington Blvd Los Angeles (90016) *(P-9618)*
A M Ortega Construction Inc..........D.......951 360-1352
58 Kellogg St Ventura (93001) *(P-589)*
A M Ortega Construction Inc..........D.......951 360-1352
224 N Sherman Ave Corona (92882) *(P-1203)*
A M R, Riverside *Also called American Med Rspnse Amblnce Sv (P-11849)*
A M S Partnership (PA)..........**D.......310 312-6698**
1517 S Sepulveda Blvd Los Angeles (90025) *(P-16045)*
A M T, Camarillo *Also called Amt Datasouth Corp (P-22824)*
A N Tool & Die..........F.......626 795-3238
518 S Fair Oaks Ave Pasadena (91105) *(P-7772)*
A P Express Worldwide, Irwindale *Also called AP Express LLC (P-12422)*
A P R Consulting Inc..........B.......714 544-3696
17852 17th St Ste 206 Tustin (92780) *(P-18154)*
A P R Inc..........C.......805 379-3400
100 E Thsnd Oaks Blvd Thousand Oaks (91360) *(P-17483)*
A P S, Santa Clarita *Also called Applied Polytech Systems Inc (P-3428)*
A P Seedorff & Company Inc..........F.......714 252-5330
1338 N Knollwood Cir Anaheim (92801) *(P-8940)*
A Plus Cabinets Inc..........F.......760 322-5262
83930 Dr Carreon Blvd Indio (92201) *(P-3303)*
A Plus Custom Metal Supply Inc..........F.......951 736-7900
1891 1st St Norco (92860) *(P-1472)*
A Plus Custom Shtmtl & Sup, Norco *Also called A Plus Custom Metal Supply Inc (P-1472)*
A Plus International Inc (PA)..........**D.......909 591-5168**
5138 Eucalyptus Ave Chino (91710) *(P-13469)*
A Plus Label Inc..........E.......714 229-9811
3215 W Warner Ave Santa Ana (92704) *(P-3921)*
A Plus Senior Care Inc..........E.......909 989-2563
4701 Arrow Hwy Montclair (91763) *(P-21706)*
A Q M D, Diamond Bar *Also called South Coast Air Qulty MGT Dst (P-23511)*
A Q Pharmaceuticals Inc..........E.......714 903-1000
11555 Monarch St Ste C Garden Grove (92841) *(P-4771)*
A Quality In Home Care, Banning *Also called Porto Inc (P-21871)*
A R C O, La Palma *Also called Atlantic Richfield Company (P-418)*
A R Electronics Inc..........E.......760 343-1200
31290 Plantation Dr Thousand Palms (92276) *(P-9669)*
A R O Service, Anaheim *Also called Aircraft Repair & Overhaul Svc (P-12338)*
A R P, Ventura *Also called Automotive Racing Products Inc (P-6500)*
A R P, Santa Paula *Also called Automotive Racing Products Inc (P-6501)*
A Royal Wolf Portable Stor Inc..........E.......310 719-1048
400 E Compton Blvd Gardena (90248) *(P-13967)*
A Rudin Inc (PA)..........**D.......323 589-5547**
6062 Alcoa Ave Vernon (90058) *(P-3494)*
A Rudin Designs, Vernon *Also called A Rudin Inc (P-3494)*
A S A Engineering Inc..........F.......949 460-9911
8 Hammond Ste 105 Irvine (92618) *(P-8144)*
A S G Corporation..........F.......213 748-6361
1361 Newton St Los Angeles (90021) *(P-11622)*
A S I, Long Beach *Also called Assocted Stdnts Cal State Univ (P-22311)*
A S I, North Hollywood *Also called Asi Semiconductor Inc (P-9484)*
A S I, North Hollywood *Also called Advanced Semiconductor Inc (P-9475)*
A S I American, Corona *Also called Spangler Industries Inc (P-5413)*
A S P, Irvine *Also called Advanced Sterlization (P-10925)*
A Shoc Beverage LLC..........E.......949 490-1612
844 Production Pl Newport Beach (92663) *(P-1962)*
A T A, Paso Robles *Also called Applied Technologies Assoc Inc (P-10869)*
A T Parker Inc (PA)..........**E.......818 755-1700**
10866 Chandler Blvd North Hollywood (91601) *(P-9845)*
A T S, Burbank *Also called Accratronics Seals Corporation (P-9670)*
A T T, Orange *Also called Air Tube Transfer Systems Inc (P-7683)*
A Terrycable California Corp..........E.......760 244-9351
17376 Eucalyptus St Hesperia (92345) *(P-10002)*
A Thread Ahead Inc..........E.......818 837-1984
1925 1st St San Fernando (91340) *(P-18427)*
A Transportation, Tarzana *Also called Airey Enterprises LLC (P-14050)*
A V Nursing Care Center, Lancaster *Also called Antelope Vly Retirement HM Inc (P-20552)*
A V Poles and Lighting Inc..........E.......661 945-2731
43827 Division St Lancaster (93535) *(P-9076)*
A W Chang Corporation (PA)..........**E.......310 764-2000**
6945 Atlantic Ave Long Beach (90805) *(P-14300)*
A Yafa Pen Company..........E.......818 704-8888
21306 Gault St Canoga Park (91303) *(P-14191)*
A&A Fulfillment Center, Vernon *Also called A&A Global Imports LLC (P-5541)*
A&A Global Imports LLC..........E.......888 315-2453
3389 E 50th St Vernon (90058) *(P-5541)*
A&A Jewelry Supply, Los Angeles *Also called Adfa Incorporated (P-7336)*
A&A Jewelry Tools & Supplies, Los Angeles *Also called A & A Jewelry Tools Findings (P-11621)*
A&A Plating, Riverside *Also called Arturo Campos (P-7216)*
A&R Tarpaulins Inc..........E.......909 829-4444
16246 Valley Blvd Fontana (92335) *(P-3132)*
A&W Precision Machining Inc..........F.......310 527-7242
16320 S Main St Gardena (90248) *(P-8457)*
A-1 Building & Fence Mtls Inc..........E.......562 693-4853
2210 Chico Ave South El Monte (91733) *(P-1630)*
A-1 Delivery Co..........D.......909 444-1220
1777 S Vintage Ave Ontario (91761) *(P-11951)*
A-1 Electric Service Co Inc..........E.......310 204-1077
4204 Sepulveda Blvd Culver City (90230) *(P-1204)*

ALPHABETIC

Employee Codes: A=Over 500 employees, B=251-500
C=101-250, D=51-100, E=20-50 F=10-19
2022 Southern California Business
Directory and Buyers Guide
© Mergent Inc. 1-800-342-5647
1039

A-1 Engraving Co Inc...E...562 861-2216
8225 Phlox St Downey (90241) ***(P-7334)***
A-1 Enterprises Inc...E...714 630-3390
2831 E La Cresta Ave Anaheim (92806) ***(P-1631)***
A-1 Estrn-Home-Made Pickle Inc...F...323 223-1141
1832 Johnston St Los Angeles (90031) ***(P-1885)***
A-1 Event & Party Rentals...D...626 967-0500
251 E Front St Covina (91723) ***(P-16941)***
A-1 Fence, Anaheim *Also called A-1 Enterprises Inc* ***(P-1631)***
A-1 Grit Co, Riverside *Also called Newman Bros California Inc* ***(P-3274)***
A-1 Hospice Care Inc...D...818 237-2700
217 E Alameda Ave Ste 306 Burbank (91502) ***(P-20518)***
A-1 Metal Products Inc...E...323 721-3334
2707 Supply Ave Commerce (90040) ***(P-6771)***
A-1 Party Rentals, Covina *Also called Cwf Inc* ***(P-17344)***
A-1 Pomona Linen, Paramount *Also called Braun Linen Service* ***(P-16847)***
A-1 Steel Fence Company, South El Monte *Also called A-1 Building & Fence Mtls Inc* ***(P-1630)***
A-A Mortgage Opportunities LP (PA)...B...**888 469-0810**
1 Baxter Way Westlake Village (91362) ***(P-15169)***
A-Able Inc (PA)...D...**323 658-5779**
17801 Ventura Blvd Encino (91316) ***(P-17196)***
A-Avis HM Svcs Plbg Htg AC Inc...D...909 825-3600
600 E Valley Blvd Colton (92324) ***(P-1012)***
A-Aztec Rents & Sells Inc (PA)...C...**310 347-3010**
2665 Columbia St Torrance (90503) ***(P-3133)***
A-C Electric Company (PA)...E...**661 410-0000**
2921 Hanger Way Bakersfield (93308) ***(P-1205)***
A-C Electric Company...D...559 732-4733
1035 W Murray Ave Visalia (93291) ***(P-1206)***
A-Check America Inc (PA)...C...**951 750-1501**
1501 Research Park Dr Riverside (92507) ***(P-17119)***
A-Check America, Member Act 1, Riverside *Also called A-Check America Inc* ***(P-17119)***
A-G Sod Farms Inc...D...951 687-7581
2900 Adams St Ste C120 Riverside (92504) ***(P-72)***
A-Info Inc...E...949 346-7326
60 Tesla Irvine (92618) ***(P-10232)***
A-LINE MESSENGER SERVICE, Chatsworth *Also called M & N Consulting Inc* ***(P-12141)***
A-List, Vernon *Also called Just For Wraps Inc* ***(P-2961)***
A-Mark Precious Metals Inc (PA)...C...**310 587-1477**
2121 Rosecrans Ave # 6300 El Segundo (90245) ***(P-14125)***
A-Throne Co Inc...D...562 981-1197
1850 E 33rd St Long Beach (90807) ***(P-17324)***
A-W Engineering Company Inc...E...562 945-1041
8528 Dice Rd Santa Fe Springs (90670) ***(P-7117)***
A-Z Bus Sales Inc (PA)...D...**951 781-7188**
1900 S Riverside Ave Colton (92324) ***(P-13016)***
A-Z Bussales, Colton *Also called A-Z Emissions Solutions Inc* ***(P-9846)***
A-Z Emissions Solutions Inc...E...951 781-1856
1900 S Riverside Ave Colton (92324) ***(P-9846)***
A-Z Industries Div, Los Angeles *Also called Aero Shade Co Inc* ***(P-3704)***
A-Z Mfg Inc...E...714 444-4446
3101 W Segerstrom Ave Santa Ana (92704) ***(P-8458)***
A.B.S. By Allen Schwartz, Encino *Also called ABs Clothing Collection Inc* ***(P-2913)***
A.I.M. Services, Los Angeles *Also called Aiminsight Solutions Inc* ***(P-18158)***
A.J. Metal Manufacturing, Corona *Also called Aqua Performance Inc* ***(P-14073)***
A.M. Ortega Construction, Corona *Also called A M Ortega Construction Inc* ***(P-1203)***
A/C Folding Gates Inc...F...909 629-3026
1374 E 9th St Pomona (91766) ***(P-6946)***
A/D Enterprises, Fountain Valley *Also called Adrienne Designs LLC* ***(P-11306)***
A1 Carton Co, Los Angeles *Also called Best Box Company Inc* ***(P-3786)***
A1 Event & Party Rentals, Covina *Also called A-1 Event & Party Rentals* ***(P-16941)***
Aa Leasing, Los Angeles *Also called Vahe Enterprises Inc* ***(P-10000)***
AAA, Encino *Also called Automobile Club Southern Cal* ***(P-22399)***
AAA, San Luis Obispo *Also called Automobile Club Southern Cal* ***(P-22402)***
AAA, Thousand Oaks *Also called Automobile Club Southern Cal* ***(P-22403)***
AAA, Torrance *Also called Automobile Club Southern Cal* ***(P-22404)***
AAA, Ventura *Also called Automobile Club Southern Cal* ***(P-22405)***
AAA, Anaheim *Also called Automobile Club Southern Cal* ***(P-22406)***
AAA, Glendora *Also called Automobile Club Southern Cal* ***(P-22407)***
AAA, Alhambra *Also called Automobile Club Southern Cal* ***(P-22408)***
AAA, Redlands *Also called Automobile Club Southern Cal* ***(P-22409)***
AAA, Bakersfield *Also called Automobile Club Southern Cal* ***(P-22410)***
AAA, Anaheim *Also called Automobile Club Southern Cal* ***(P-22412)***
AAA, Northridge *Also called Automobile Club Southern Cal* ***(P-22413)***
AAA, Downey *Also called Automobile Club Southern Cal* ***(P-22414)***
AAA, Manhattan Beach *Also called Automobile Club Southern Cal* ***(P-22416)***
AAA, Montrose *Also called Automobile Club Southern Cal* ***(P-22419)***
AAA, Montebello *Also called Automobile Club Southern Cal* ***(P-22420)***
AAA, Lancaster *Also called Automobile Club Southern Cal* ***(P-22421)***
AAA, Huntington Beach *Also called Automobile Club Southern Cal* ***(P-22422)***
AAA, Woodland Hills *Also called Automobile Club Southern Cal* ***(P-22423)***
AAA, Whittier *Also called Automobile Club Southern Cal* ***(P-22425)***
AAA, Chino *Also called Automobile Club Southern Cal* ***(P-22427)***
AAA, San Clemente *Also called Automobile Club Southern Cal* ***(P-22429)***
AAA, Santa Maria *Also called Automobile Club Southern Cal* ***(P-22430)***
AAA, Victorville *Also called Automobile Club Southern Cal* ***(P-22433)***
AAA, Artesia *Also called Automobile Club Southern Cal* ***(P-22444)***
AAA, West Hollywood *Also called Automobile Club Southern Cal* ***(P-22445)***
AAA - Auto CLB Southern Cal, Rancho Cucamonga *Also called Automobile Club Southern Cal* ***(P-22396)***
AAA Auto Club, Costa Mesa *Also called Automobile Club Southern Cal* ***(P-15543)***
AAA Elctrcal Cmmunications Inc (PA)...C...**800 892-4784**
25007 Anza Dr Valencia (91355) ***(P-1207)***
AAA Electric Motor Sales & Svc (PA)...F...**213 749-2367**
1346 Venice Blvd Los Angeles (90006) ***(P-13607)***
AAA Flag & Banner Mfg Co Inc (PA)...C...**310 836-3200**
8937 National Blvd Los Angeles (90034) ***(P-3187)***
AAA Global Consulting LLC (PA)...D...**949 201-6204**
32002 Camino Del Cielo Trabuco Canyon (92679) ***(P-23400)***
AAA Imaging & Supplies Inc...E...714 431-0570
2313 S Susan St Santa Ana (92704) ***(P-13340)***
AAA Imaging Solutions, Santa Ana *Also called AAA Imaging & Supplies Inc* ***(P-13340)***
AAA Network Solutions Inc...D...714 484-2711
8401 Page St Buena Park (90621) ***(P-1208)***
AAA Pallet, Mentone *Also called Power Pt Inc* ***(P-7716)***
AAA Pallet Recycling & Mfg Inc...E...951 681-7748
23120 Oleander Ave Perris (92570) ***(P-3380)***
AAA Plating & Inspection Inc...D...323 979-8930
424 E Dixon St Compton (90222) ***(P-7195)***
AAA Property Services, Valencia *Also called AAA Elctrcal Cmmunications Inc* ***(P-1207)***
AAA Restoration Inc...E...951 471-5828
29850 2nd St Lake Elsinore (92532) ***(P-1632)***
AAA Stamping Inc...F...909 947-4151
1630 Shearwater St Ontario (91761) ***(P-7118)***
AAC, Irvine *Also called American Audio Component Inc* ***(P-9673)***
Aadlen Bros Auto Wrecking Inc (PA)...D...**323 875-1400**
11590 Tuxford St Sun Valley (91352) ***(P-14107)***
AAF Steel Structural, Lake Elsinore *Also called Afakori Inc* ***(P-6583)***
Aahs Enterprises Inc...F...323 838-9130
6600 Telegraph Rd Commerce (90040) ***(P-11519)***
Aahs Graphics Signs & Engrv, Commerce *Also called Aahs Enterprises Inc* ***(P-11519)***
Aakaa Inc (PA)...F...**213 221-7086**
1100 S San Pedro St C08 Los Angeles (90015) ***(P-2909)***
AAM, Anaheim *Also called Anaheim Arena Management LLC* ***(P-19405)***
Aamcom LLC...E...310 318-8100
800 N Pacific Coast Hwy Redondo Beach (90277) ***(P-12622)***
Aamp of America...E...805 338-6800
2500 E Francis St Ontario (91761) ***(P-9847)***
Aap Division, Inglewood *Also called Engineered Magnetics Inc* ***(P-8975)***
Aard Industries Inc...E...951 296-0844
42075 Avenida Alvarado Temecula (92590) ***(P-7480)***
Aard Spring & Stamping, Temecula *Also called Aard Industries Inc* ***(P-7480)***
Aardvark Clay & Supplies Inc (PA)...E...**714 541-4157**
1400 E Pomona St Santa Ana (92705) ***(P-11465)***
Aaren Laboratories LLC...F...909 906-5400
1040 S Vintage Ave Ste A Ontario (91761) ***(P-10821)***
Aaren Scientific Inc (HQ)...C...**909 937-1033**
1040 S Vintage Ave Ste A Ontario (91761) ***(P-10822)***
Aaron Corporation...C...323 235-5959
2645 Industry Way Lynwood (90262) ***(P-2910)***
Aaron Group, The, Chatsworth *Also called Aaron Thomas & Associates Inc* ***(P-17127)***
Aaron Thomas & Associates Inc...E...818 727-9040
21344 Superior St Chatsworth (91311) ***(P-17127)***
Aaron Thomas Company Inc (PA)...C...**714 894-4468**
7421 Chapman Ave Garden Grove (92841) ***(P-18428)***
Aatech...F...909 854-3200
6666 Box Springs Blvd Riverside (92507) ***(P-8360)***
AB Mauri Food Inc...E...562 483-4619
12604 Hiddencreek Way A Cerritos (90703) ***(P-2384)***
AB&r Inc...E...323 727-0007
5849 Smithway St Commerce (90040) ***(P-2911)***
Abacus Business Capital Inc...E...909 594-8080
738 Epperson Dr City of Industry (91748) ***(P-14447)***
Abacus Powder Coating...E...626 443-7556
1829 Tyler Ave South El Monte (91733) ***(P-7335)***
Abacus Wealth Partners LLC (PA)...D...**707 829-6190**
429 Santa Monica Blvd # 500 Santa Monica (90401) ***(P-23146)***
Abad Foam Inc...E...714 994-2223
6560 Caballero Blvd Buena Park (90620) ***(P-5482)***
Abalquiga, Los Angeles *Also called La Princesita Tortilleria Inc* ***(P-2468)***
ABB Enterprise Software Inc...E...213 743-4819
4600 Colorado Blvd Los Angeles (90039) ***(P-9471)***
ABB Inc...D...714 630-4111
741 E Ball Rd Anaheim (92805) ***(P-8860)***
Abba Roller LLC (HQ)...F...**909 947-1244**
1351 E Philadelphia St Ontario (91761) ***(P-5363)***
Abbey-Properties LLC (PA)...D...**562 435-2100**
12447 Lewis St Ste 203 Garden Grove (92840) ***(P-15656)***
Abbott...F...949 769-5018
2375 Morse Ave Irvine (92614) ***(P-4772)***
Abbott Technologies Inc...E...818 504-0644
8203 Vineland Ave Sun Valley (91352) ***(P-8861)***
Abbott Vascular Inc...E...951 941-2400
26531 Ynez Rd Temecula (92591) ***(P-4773)***
ABC - Clio Inc (PA)...C...**805 968-1911**
147 Castilian Dr Goleta (93117) ***(P-4118)***
ABC Bus Inc...D...714 444-5888
1485 Dale Way Costa Mesa (92626) ***(P-13017)***
ABC Cable Networks Group (HQ)...C...**818 460-7477**
500 S Buena Vista St Burbank (91521) ***(P-12685)***
ABC Custom Wood Shutters Inc...E...949 595-0300
20561 Pascal Way Lake Forest (92630) ***(P-3227)***
ABC Family Worldwide Inc (HQ)...B...**818 560-1000**
500 S Buena Vista St Burbank (91521) ***(P-19090)***
ABC Imaging of Washington...F...949 419-3728
17240 Red Hill Ave Irvine (92614) ***(P-4474)***
ABC Imaging of Washington...F...562 375-7280
13573 Larwin Cir Santa Fe Springs (90670) ***(P-4475)***
ABC Precision Sheet Metal Inc...F...951 741-6667
13378 Monte Vista Ave Chino (91710) ***(P-6772)***

Mergent e-mail: customerrelations@mergent.com
1040
2022 Southern California Business Directory and Buyers Guide
(P-0000) Products & Services Section entry number
(PA)=Parent Co (HQ)=Headquarters (DH)=Div Headquarters

ABC School Equipment Inc ... D ... 951 817-2200
1451 E 6th St Corona (92879) ***(P-13532)***

ABC Sheet Metal, Anaheim *Also called Steeldyne Industries* ***(P-6918)***

ABC Signature Studios Inc ... D ... 818 569-7500
500 S Buena Vista St Burbank (91521) ***(P-12708)***

ABC Sun Control LLC ... F ... 818 982-6989
7241 Ethel Ave North Hollywood (91605) ***(P-3134)***

ABC Valencia, Corona *Also called Amerisourcebergen Drug Corp* ***(P-14233)***

ABC-Clio, Goleta *Also called ABC - Clio Inc* ***(P-4118)***

Abco Insulation, Azusa *Also called Oj Insulation LP* ***(P-1388)***

Abel Automatics LLC ... E ... 805 388-3721
165 N Aviador St Camarillo (93010) ***(P-7028)***

Abel Reels, Camarillo *Also called Abel Automatics LLC* ***(P-7028)***

Aben Machine Products Inc ... F ... 818 960-4502
9550 Owensmouth Ave Chatsworth (91311) ***(P-8459)***

Aberdeen, Santa Fe Springs *Also called Source Code LLC* ***(P-8176)***

Abex Display Systems Inc (PA) ... **C ... 800 537-0231**
355 Parkside Dr San Fernando (91340) ***(P-3781)***

Abex Exhibit Systems, San Fernando *Also called Abex Display Systems Inc* ***(P-3781)***

ABF Prints Inc ... E ... 909 875-7163
102 N Riverside Ave Rialto (92376) ***(P-4476)***

ABG Communications, Yorba Linda *Also called Luce Communications LLC* ***(P-5229)***

ABI Attorneys Service Inc (PA) ... **D ... 909 793-0613**
2015 W Park Ave Redlands (92373) ***(P-17143)***

ABI Document Support Services, Cerritos *Also called Edco Health Info Solution* ***(P-18511)***

ABI Document Support Svcs LLC ... D ... 909 793-0613
10459 Mountain View Ave E Loma Linda (92354) ***(P-18429)***

ABI VIP Attorney Service, Redlands *Also called ABI Attorneys Service Inc* ***(P-17143)***

Abianca Khanna LLC ... F ... 833 225-7527
8504 Firestone Blvd Downey (90241) ***(P-14766)***

Abilities Recovery Center Inc ... D ... 310 488-1122
909 N Beverly Glen Blvd Los Angeles (90077) ***(P-21269)***

Ability Counts Inc (PA) ... **D ... 951 734-6595**
775 Trademark Cir Ste 101 Corona (92879) ***(P-21934)***

Abisco Products Co ... E ... 562 906-9330
5925 E Washington Blvd Commerce (90040) ***(P-4606)***

Abl Space Systems Company ... D ... 424 321-5049
224 Oregon St El Segundo (90245) ***(P-10512)***

Able, Azusa *Also called California Pediatric Fmly Svcs* ***(P-21727)***

Able Building Maintenance, Santa Ana *Also called Crown Building Maintenance Co* ***(P-17234)***

Able Cable Inc (PA) ... **C ... 818 223-3600**
5115 Douglas Fir Rd Ste A Calabasas (91302) ***(P-18950)***

Able Card Corporation, Irwindale *Also called Million Corporation* ***(P-4545)***

Able Design and Fabrication, Rancho Dominguez *Also called Adf Incorporated* ***(P-6948)***

Able Engineering Services, Los Angeles *Also called Crown Energy Services Inc* ***(P-17235)***

Able Industrial Products Inc (PA) ... **E ... 909 930-1585**
2006 S Baker Ave Ontario (91761) ***(P-5326)***

Able Industries Inc ... D ... 559 651-8150
8929 W Goshen Ave Visalia (93291) ***(P-21935)***

Able Iron Works ... E ... 909 397-5300
222 Hershey St Pomona (91767) ***(P-6578)***

Able Microsystems Corporation ... E ... 626 723-7777
2021 Las Lomitas Dr Hacienda Heights (91745) ***(P-18016)***

Able Rise Limited Corp ... E ... 626 416-5680
11100 Valley Blvd Ste 306 El Monte (91731) ***(P-18430)***

Able Sheet Metal Inc (PA) ... **E ... 323 269-2181**
614 N Ford Blvd Los Angeles (90022) ***(P-6773)***

Able Software Inc ... F ... 949 274-8321
20251 Sw Acacia St # 220 Newport Beach (92660) ***(P-17772)***

Able Wire Edm Inc ... F ... 714 255-1967
440 Atlas St Ste A Brea (92821) ***(P-8460)***

ABM Elctrcal Ltg Solutions Inc (HQ) ... **E ... 866 226-2838**
14201 Franklin Ave Tustin (92780) ***(P-17209)***

ABM Janitorial Services Inc ... D ... 559 651-1612
1335 N Plaza Dr Ste C Visalia (93291) ***(P-17210)***

ABM Onsite Services Inc ... A ... 949 863-9100
3337 Michelson Dr Ste Cn7 Irvine (92612) ***(P-18237)***

Abode Communities LLC ... C ... 213 629-2702
1149 S Hill St Fl 7 Los Angeles (90015) ***(P-15763)***

Above & Beyond Balloons Inc ... E ... 949 586-8470
16661 Jamboree Rd Irvine (92606) ***(P-11623)***

Above and Beyond, Irvine *Also called Above & Beyond Balloons Inc* ***(P-11623)***

Abrasive Finishing Co ... F ... 310 323-7175
14920 S Main St Gardena (90248) ***(P-6424)***

Abraxis Bioscience LLC (HQ) ... **C ... 800 564-0216**
11755 Wilshire Blvd Fl 20 Los Angeles (90025) ***(P-4774)***

Abraxis Health Inc (PA) ... **D ... 310 883-1300**
11755 Wilshire Blvd Los Angeles (90025) ***(P-21369)***

Abrazar Inc ... D ... 714 893-3581
7101 Wyoming St Westminster (92683) ***(P-21707)***

Abrazar Elderly Assistance, Westminster *Also called Abrazar Inc* ***(P-21707)***

Abrisa Glass & Coating, Santa Paula *Also called Abrisa Industrial Glass Inc* ***(P-10823)***

Abrisa Industrial Glass Inc (HQ) ... **D ... 805 525-4902**
200 Hallock Dr Santa Paula (93060) ***(P-10823)***

Abrisa Technologies ... E ... 805 525-4902
200 Hallock Dr Santa Paula (93060) ***(P-10824)***

ABS By Allen Schwartz, Encino *Also called Aquarius Rags LLC* ***(P-2877)***

ABS By Allen Schwartz LLC (HQ) ... **C ... 213 895-4400**
15821 Ventura Blvd # 270 Encino (91436) ***(P-2912)***

ABs Clothing Collection Inc ... F ... 213 895-4400
15821 Ventura Blvd # 270 Encino (91436) ***(P-2913)***

ABS Consulting Inc ... D ... 714 734-4242
300 Commerce Ste 150 Irvine (92602) ***(P-22472)***

ABS Group, Irvine *Also called ABS Consulting Inc* ***(P-22472)***

Absolute EDM ... F ... 951 694-5601
43153 Business Park Dr Temecula (92590) ***(P-8461)***

Absolute Graphic Tech USA Inc ... E ... 909 597-1133
235 Jason Ct Corona (92879) ***(P-8941)***

Absolute Machining Inc ... F ... 818 709-7367
20622 Superior St Unit 4 Chatsworth (91311) ***(P-6579)***

Absolute Packaging Inc ... E ... 714 630-3020
1201 N Miller St Anaheim (92806) ***(P-3845)***

Absolute Pro Music, Los Angeles *Also called Absolute Usa Inc* ***(P-9154)***

Absolute Screenprint Inc ... C ... 714 529-2120
333 Cliffwood Park St Brea (92821) ***(P-3166)***

Absolute Sign Inc ... F ... 562 592-5838
10655 Humbolt St Los Alamitos (90720) ***(P-11520)***

Absolute Technologies, Anaheim *Also called D & D Gear Incorporated* ***(P-10306)***

Absolute Twing - Hllnbeck Div ... E ... 323 225-9294
4760 Valley Blvd Los Angeles (90032) ***(P-18919)***

Absolute Usa Inc ... E ... 213 744-0044
1800 E Washington Blvd Los Angeles (90021) ***(P-9154)***

ABSTINATE LIVING CENTERS, San Pedro *Also called Fred Browns Recovery Svcs Inc* ***(P-18520)***

Abtech Incorporated ... D ... 714 550-9961
3420 W Fordham Ave Santa Ana (92704) ***(P-3673)***

Abttc Inc (HQ) ... **D ... 951 837-2400**
41640 Corning Pl Ste 104 Murrieta (92562) ***(P-22076)***

AC Hotel Beverly Hills, Los Angeles *Also called Candleberry Properties LP* ***(P-16366)***

AC Products Inc ... E ... 714 630-7311
9930 Painter Ave Whittier (90605) ***(P-5176)***

AC Pumping Unit Repair Inc ... F ... 562 492-1300
2625 Dawson Ave Signal Hill (90755) ***(P-474)***

AC&a Enterprises LLC (HQ) ... **C ... 949 716-3511**
25671 Commercentre Dr Lake Forest (92630) ***(P-10209)***

Acacia Technologies Inc (HQ) ... **D ... 949 480-8300**
520 Nwport Cntr Dr 12th F Flr 12 Newport Beach (92660) ***(P-16199)***

Academic Cap & Gown, Chatsworth *Also called Academic Ch Choir Gwns Mfg Inc* ***(P-3064)***

Academic Ch Choir Gwns Mfg Inc ... E ... 818 886-8697
20644 Superior St Chatsworth (91311) ***(P-3064)***

Academy Awning Inc ... E ... 800 422-9646
1501 Beach St Montebello (90640) ***(P-3149)***

Academy Foundation (HQ) ... **E ... 310 247-3000**
8949 Wilshire Blvd Beverly Hills (90211) ***(P-19217)***

Academy Mpic Arts & Sciences (PA) ... **D ... 310 247-3000**
8949 Wilshire Blvd Beverly Hills (90211) ***(P-22264)***

Academy of Cosmetology, Santa Barbara *Also called Santa Brbara Cmnty College Dst* ***(P-16917)***

Academy Swim Club ... D ... 661 702-8585
28079 Smyth Dr Valencia (91355) ***(P-19527)***

Acapulco Mexican Restaurants, Montclair *Also called Acapulco Restaurants Inc* ***(P-8324)***

Acapulco Mxican Rest Y Cantina, Moreno Valley *Also called Acapulco Restaurants Inc* ***(P-16942)***

Acapulco Restaurants Inc ... D ... 951 653-8809
12625 Frederick St Ste T Moreno Valley (92553) ***(P-16942)***

Acapulco Restaurants Inc ... D ... 909 621-3955
9405 Monte Vista Ave Montclair (91763) ***(P-8324)***

ACC Precision Inc ... F ... 805 278-9801
321 Hearst Dr Oxnard (93030) ***(P-8462)***

Accelerated Envmtl Svcs Inc ... D ... 661 765-4003
23601 Taft Hwy Bakersfield (93311) ***(P-17211)***

Accelerated Memory Prod Inc ... E ... 714 460-9800
1317 E Edinger Ave Santa Ana (92705) ***(P-9472)***

Acceliot Inc ... F ... 657 845-4250
16601 Gothard St Ste E Huntington Beach (92647) ***(P-22821)***

Accelon Inc ... E ... 925 216-5735
19075 Wells Dr Tarzana (91356) ***(P-17387)***

Accent Awnings, Santa Ana *Also called Accent Industries Inc* ***(P-6686)***

Accent Industries Inc (PA) ... **E ... 714 708-1389**
1600 E Saint Gertrude Pl Santa Ana (92705) ***(P-6686)***

Accent Plastics Inc (HQ) ... **D ... 951 273-7777**
13948 Mountain Ave Chino (91710) ***(P-5542)***

Accentcare HM Hlth El Cntro In ... C ... 760 352-4022
2344 S 2nd St Ste A El Centro (92243) ***(P-21124)***

Accentcare Home Hlth Yuma Inc ... B ... 909 605-7000
1455 Auto Center Dr # 200 Ontario (91761) ***(P-21125)***

Accepted Co ... F ... 310 815-9553
2229 S Canfield Ave Los Angeles (90034) ***(P-4147)***

Access Business Group LLC ... C ... 808 422-9482
12825 Leffingwell Ave Santa Fe Springs (90670) ***(P-14767)***

Access Business Group LLC ... C ... 714 562-6200
5600 Beach Blvd Buena Park (90621) ***(P-14768)***

Access Business Group LLC ... C ... 714 562-7914
5609 River Way Buena Park (90621) ***(P-14769)***

Access Control Security Inc (PA) ... **D ... 714 835-3800**
21049 Devonshire St # 211 Chatsworth (91311) ***(P-18238)***

Access Dental Centers, Orange *Also called Access Dental Plan* ***(P-20168)***

Access Dental Plan (PA) ... **D ... 916 922-5000**
530 S Main St Ste 100 Orange (92868) ***(P-20168)***

Access Finance Inc ... E ... 310 826-4000
3415 S Sepulveda Blvd # 400 Los Angeles (90034) ***(P-18431)***

Access Info Holdings LLC ... C ... 909 459-1417
12135 Davis St Moreno Valley (92557) ***(P-12265)***

Access Logistics, Santa Fe Springs *Also called Access Business Group LLC* ***(P-14767)***

Access Marketing, San Luis Obispo *Also called ITW Global Tire Repair Inc* ***(P-5303)***

Access Networks Inc (PA) ... **D ... 310 453-1800**
28482 Constellation Rd Valencia (91355) ***(P-18155)***

Access Pacific Inc ... E ... 626 792-0616
2835 Sierra Grande St Pasadena (91107) ***(P-729)***

ACCESS PARATRANSIT, El Monte *Also called Access Services* ***(P-11801)***

Access Services ... D ... 213 270-6000
3449 Santa Anita Ave El Monte (91731) ***(P-11801)***

Accessory Power, Westlake Village *Also called AP Global Inc* ***(P-13701)***

Employee Codes: A=Over 500 employees, B=251-500
C=101-250, D=51-100, E=20-50 F=10-19
2022 Southern California Business
Directory and Buyers Guide
© Mergent Inc. 1-800-342-5647
1041

Acclaim Lighting LLC ....F....323 213-4626
6122 S Eastern Ave Commerce (90040) *(P-9077)*
Acclaimed Trucking Corp (PA) ....F....**805 577-7611**
1106 El Monte Dr Simi Valley (93065) *(P-7701)*
Acclarent Inc ....B....650 687-5888
31 Technology Dr Ste 200 Irvine (92618) *(P-10923)*
Acco Engineered Systems Inc ....F....661 631-1975
3121 N Sillect Ave # 104 Bakersfield (93308) *(P-8325)*
Acco Engineered Systems Inc ....E....323 201-0931
6446 E Washington Blvd Commerce (90040) *(P-18432)*
Accolade Pharma USA ....E....626 279-9699
13260 Temple Ave City of Industry (91746) *(P-4775)*
Accor Corp ....C....310 278-5444
8555 Beverly Blvd Los Angeles (90048) *(P-16313)*
Accountble Hlth Cre IPA A Prof ....C....562 435-3333
2525 Cherry Ave Ste 225 Signal Hill (90755) *(P-21370)*
Accounts Payable Dept, Fountain Valley *Also called Orange County Water District (P-12911)*
Accratronics Seals Corporation ....D....818 843-1500
2211 Kenmere Ave Burbank (91504) *(P-9670)*
Accredited Nursing Care, Pasadena *Also called Accredited Nursing Services (P-20238)*
Accredited Nursing Care, Woodland Hills *Also called Dunn & Berger Inc (P-21160)*
Accredited Nursing Care, Costa Mesa *Also called Accredited Nursing Services (P-21126)*
Accredited Nursing Services ....C....626 573-1234
80 S Lake Ave Ste 630 Pasadena (91101) *(P-20238)*
Accredited Nursing Services ....C....714 973-1234
950 S Coast Dr Ste 215 Costa Mesa (92626) *(P-21126)*
Accretive Solutions Inc (HQ) ....A....**312 994-4600**
17101 Armstrong Ave # 100 Irvine (92614) *(P-22757)*
ACCU, Glendora *Also called Americas Christian Credit Un (P-15058)*
Accu-Blend Corporation ....F....626 334-7744
364 Malbert St Perris (92570) *(P-5247)*
Accu-Grinding Inc ....F....818 768-4497
8518 Glencrest Dr Sun Valley (91352) *(P-7844)*
Accu-Sembly Inc ....D....626 357-3447
1835 Huntington Dr Duarte (91010) *(P-9370)*
Accu-Tek, Ontario *Also called Excel Industries Inc (P-7145)*
Accudyne Engineering & Eqp, Bell *Also called West Coast-Accudyne Inc (P-7769)*
Accumedical USA Inc ....F....714 929-1020
3545 Harbor Gtwy S # 103 Costa Mesa (92626) *(P-10924)*
Accunex Inc ....E....818 882-5858
20700 Lassen St Chatsworth (91311) *(P-22473)*
Accurate Background LLC (PA) ....B....**800 784-3911**
7515 Irvine Center Dr Irvine (92618) *(P-18117)*
Accurate Circuit Engrg Inc ....D....714 546-2162
3019 Kilson Dr Santa Ana (92707) *(P-9371)*
Accurate Courier Services Inc ....D....310 481-3937
11022 Santa Monica Blvd # 360 Los Angeles (90025) *(P-11952)*
Accurate Delivery Systems Inc ....D....951 823-8870
173 Resource Dr Bloomington (92316) *(P-11953)*
Accurate Double Disc Grinding, Pacoima *Also called Westcoast Grinding Corporation (P-8849)*
Accurate Electronics, Chatsworth *Also called Accunex Inc (P-22473)*
Accurate Engineering Inc ....E....818 768-3919
8710 Telfair Ave Sun Valley (91352) *(P-9372)*
Accurate Grinding and Mfg Corp ....E....951 479-0909
807 E Parkridge Ave Corona (92879) *(P-10210)*
Accurate Laminated Pdts Inc ....E....714 632-2773
1826 Dawns Way Fullerton (92831) *(P-3674)*
Accurate Manufacturing Company, Glendale *Also called McCoppin Enterprises (P-8682)*
Accurate Metal Products Inc ....F....951 360-3594
4276 Campbell St Riverside (92509) *(P-6580)*
Accurate Plating Company ....E....323 268-8567
2811 Alcazar St Los Angeles (90033) *(P-7196)*
Accurate Prfmce Machining Inc ....E....714 434-7811
2255 S Grand Ave Santa Ana (92705) *(P-8463)*
Accurate Screen Processing ....F....818 957-3965
3538 Foothill Blvd La Crescenta (91214) *(P-3167)*
Accurate Staging Mfg Inc (PA) ....F....**310 324-1040**
13900 S Figueroa St Los Angeles (90061) *(P-11624)*
Accurate Steel Treating Inc ....E....562 927-6528
10008 Miller Way South Gate (90280) *(P-6425)*
Accurate Technology, Anaheim *Also called Gledhill/Lyons Inc (P-10337)*
Accuride International Inc (PA) ....E....**562 903-0200**
12311 Shoemaker Ave Santa Fe Springs (90670) *(P-6494)*
Accutherm Air Heating & Coolg, Garden Grove *Also called Accutherm Refrigeraton Inc (P-1013)*
Accutherm Refrigeraton Inc ....D....714 766-7800
11264 Monarch St Ste A Garden Grove (92841) *(P-1013)*
Accuturn Corporation ....E....951 656-6621
7189 Old 215 Frontage Rd Moreno Valley (92553) *(P-10558)*
Acd LLC (HQ) ....C....**949 261-7533**
2321 Pullman St Santa Ana (92705) *(P-6723)*
Ace, Anaheim *Also called Anaheim Custom Extruders Inc (P-5563)*
Ace, Santa Ana *Also called Accurate Circuit Engrg Inc (P-9371)*
Ace Air Manufacturing ....F....310 323-7246
1430 W 135th St Gardena (90249) *(P-10233)*
Ace Attrney Svc Inc A Cal Corp (PA) ....D....**213 623-3979**
811 Wilshire Blvd Ste 900 Los Angeles (90017) *(P-18433)*
Ace Beverage Co ....C....323 266-6238
550 S Mission Rd Los Angeles (90033) *(P-14817)*
Ace Calendering Entps Inc (PA) ....F....**909 937-1901**
1311 S Wanamaker Ave Ontario (91761) *(P-5364)*
Ace Cash Express, Riverside *Also called Populus Financial Group Inc (P-15131)*
Ace Clearwater Enterprises Inc (PA) ....D....**310 323-2140**
19815 Magellan Dr Torrance (90502) *(P-10234)*
Ace Clearwater Enterprises Inc ....E....310 538-5380
1614 Kona Dr Compton (90220) *(P-7773)*
Ace Commercial Inc ....E....562 946-6664
10310 Pioneer Blvd Ste 1 Santa Fe Springs (90670) *(P-4222)*
Ace Direct ....E....760 969-5500
948 S Vella Rd Palm Springs (92264) *(P-17128)*
Ace Duraflo Pipe Restoration, Santa Ana *Also called Pipe Restoration Inc (P-1117)*
Ace Hardware, Baldwin Park *Also called Nichols Lumber & Hardware Co (P-13278)*
Ace Hardware, Exeter *Also called Exeter Mercantile Company (P-7611)*
Ace Hardware, Santa Ana *Also called Murrays Hardware (P-6711)*
Ace Hardware, Blythe *Also called Inland Builders Supply Inc (P-13217)*
Ace Heaters LLC ....E....951 738-2230
130 Klug Cir Corona (92878) *(P-8326)*
Ace Holdings Inc ....F....213 972-2100
650 S Hill St Ste 510 Los Angeles (90014) *(P-11305)*
Ace Hotel & Swim Club ....D....760 325-9900
701 E Palm Canyon Dr Palm Springs (92264) *(P-16314)*
Ace Hydraulic Sales & Svc Inc ....F....661 327-0571
2901 Gibson St Bakersfield (93308) *(P-13880)*
Ace Industrial Supply Inc (PA) ....C....**818 252-1981**
7535 N San Fernando Rd Burbank (91505) *(P-590)*
Ace Iron Inc ....E....510 324-3300
929 Howard St Marina Del Rey (90292) *(P-6947)*
Ace Machine Shop Inc ....D....310 608-2277
11200 Wright Rd Lynwood (90262) *(P-8464)*
Ace Parking Management Inc ....D....310 575-3192
11500 W Olympic Blvd Los Angeles (90064) *(P-18756)*
Ace Parking Management Inc ....D....949 769-3696
18150 Von Karman Ave A Irvine (92612) *(P-18757)*
Ace Parking Management Inc ....D....310 393-9863
1221 Ocean Ave Santa Monica (90401) *(P-18758)*
Ace Parking Management Inc ....D....310 645-6025
6200 W 98th St Los Angeles (90045) *(P-18759)*
Ace Parking Management Inc ....D....714 845-8000
21500 Pacific Coast Hwy Huntington Beach (92648) *(P-18760)*
Ace Parking Management Inc ....D....949 724-0963
610 Newport Center Dr # 50 Newport Beach (92660) *(P-18761)*
Ace Parking Management Inc ....D....562 437-6700
332 W Broadway Long Beach (90802) *(P-18762)*
Ace Printing, Palm Springs *Also called Ace Direct (P-17128)*
Ace Sushi, Torrance *Also called Asiana Cuisine Enterprises Inc (P-2393)*
Acepex Management Corporation ....B....909 591-1999
13401 Yorba Ave Chino (91710) *(P-22965)*
Acepex Management Corporation ....C....909 625-6900
2707 Saturn St Brea (92821) *(P-23387)*
Acg Ecopack, Ontario *Also called Advanced Color Graphics (P-4223)*
Ach Mechanical Contractors Inc ....D....909 307-2850
411 Business Center Ct Redlands (92373) *(P-1014)*
Achem Industry America Inc (PA) ....E....**562 802-0998**
4250 N Harbor Blvd Fullerton (92835) *(P-13968)*
Aci International (PA) ....D....**310 889-3400**
844 Moraga Dr Los Angeles (90049) *(P-14428)*
Acker Stone Industries Inc (HQ) ....E....**951 674-0047**
13296 Temescal Canyon Rd Corona (92883) *(P-6014)*
Ackley Metal Products Inc ....E....714 979-7431
1311 E Saint Gertrude Pl B Santa Ana (92705) *(P-8465)*
ACI Construction Company Inc ....E....909 391-4477
207 W State St Ontario (91762) *(P-22474)*
Acm Technologies Inc (PA) ....D....**951 738-9898**
2535 Research Dr Corona (92882) *(P-13350)*
Acme Auto Headlining, Long Beach *Also called Acme Headlining Co (P-10003)*
Acme Castings Inc ....E....323 583-3129
6009 Santa Fe Ave Huntington Park (90255) *(P-6403)*
Acme Communications Inc (PA) ....D....**714 245-9499**
4790 Irvine Blvd Ste 105 Irvine (92620) *(P-12709)*
Acme Cryogenics Inc ....E....805 981-4500
531 Sandy Cir Oxnard (93036) *(P-7958)*
Acme Divac Industries, Newport Beach *Also called C&H Hydraulics Inc (P-10290)*
Acme Headlining Co ....D....562 432-0281
550 W 16th St Long Beach (90813) *(P-10003)*
Acme Metals, Gardena *Also called Jayem Enterprises Inc (P-13571)*
Acme Portable Machines Inc ....E....626 610-1888
1330 Mountain View Cir Azusa (91702) *(P-8145)*
Acme Screw Products ....E....323 581-8611
7950 S Alameda St Huntington Park (90255) *(P-7013)*
Acme Staffing, El Centro *Also called I N C Builders Inc (P-17495)*
Acme United Corporation ....E....714 557-2001
630 Young St Santa Ana (92705) *(P-3746)*
Acme Vial & Glass Co ....E....805 239-2666
1601 Commerce Way Paso Robles (93446) *(P-5926)*
Acom Solutions Inc (PA) ....E....**562 424-7899**
2850 E 29th St Long Beach (90806) *(P-17537)*
Acorn Engineering Company (PA) ....A....**800 488-8999**
15125 Proctor Ave City of Industry (91746) *(P-6985)*
Acorn Newspaper Inc ....E....818 706-0266
30423 Canwood St Ste 108 Agoura Hills (91301) *(P-3943)*
Acorn Paper Products Co., Los Angeles *Also called Oak Paper Products Co Inc (P-14217)*
Acorn Vac, Chino *Also called Acornvac Inc (P-6550)*
Acorn-Gencon Plastics LLC ....D....909 591-8461
13818 Oaks Ave Chino (91710) *(P-5543)*
Acornvac Inc ....E....909 902-1141
13818 Oaks Ave Chino (91710) *(P-6550)*
Acosolar Inc ....F....626 575-8822
4120 Valley Blvd Ste A Walnut (91789) *(P-1015)*
Acosta Inc ....C....714 988-1500
480 Apollo St Ste C Brea (92821) *(P-14448)*
Acosta Sales & Marketing, Brea *Also called Acosta Inc (P-14448)*
Acousticfab LLC (HQ) ....D....**661 257-2242**
28150 Industry Dr Valencia (91355) *(P-7453)*

Mergent e-mail: customerrelations@mergent.com
1042
2022 Southern California Business Directory and Buyers Guide
(P-0000) Products & Services Section entry number
(PA)=Parent Co (HQ)=Headquarters (DH)=Div Headquarters

Acp Noxtat Inc....E....714 547-5477
1112 E Washington Ave Santa Ana (92701) ***(P-4675)***
Acpt, Huntington Beach *Also called Advanced Cmpsite Pdts Tech Inc* ***(P-5546)***
Acratech Inc....F....909 392-7522
2502 Supply St Pomona (91767) ***(P-8466)***
Acrl, Chatsworth *Also called Advanced Cosmetic RES Labs Inc* ***(P-11626)***
Acro-Spec Grinding Co Inc....F....951 736-1199
4134 Indus Way Riverside (92503) ***(P-8467)***
Acroamatics Inc....F....805 967-9909
125 Cremona Dr Ste 130 Goleta (93117) ***(P-9248)***
Acromil LLC (HQ)....C....626 964-2522
18421 Railroad St City of Industry (91748) ***(P-10235)***
Acromil LLC....D....951 808-9929
1168 Sherborn St Corona (92879) ***(P-10236)***
Acromil Corporation (PA)....C....626 964-2522
18421 Railroad St City of Industry (91748) ***(P-10237)***
Acrontos Manufacturing Inc....E....714 850-9133
1641 E Saint Gertrude Pl Santa Ana (92705) ***(P-7119)***
Acrylic Distribution Corp....E....818 767-8448
8501 Lankershim Blvd Sun Valley (91352) ***(P-3564)***
Acrylicore Inc....F....310 515-4846
15902 S Broadway Gardena (90248) ***(P-5447)***
ACS, Los Angeles *Also called Authorized Cellular Service* ***(P-18952)***
ACS Cloud Partners, Torrance *Also called Advanced Corporate Svcs Inc* ***(P-23401)***
ACS Communications Inc....D....310 767-2145
680 Knox St Ste 150 Torrance (90502) ***(P-1209)***
Acsco Products Inc....E....818 953-2240
313 N Lake St Burbank (91502) ***(P-10004)***
Acss, Beaumont *Also called Anderson Chrnesky Strl Stl Inc* ***(P-6587)***
Act 1 Group Inc (PA)....D....310 750-3400
1999 W 190th St Torrance (90504) ***(P-17388)***
Act Fulfillment Inc (PA)....C....909 930-9083
3155 Universe Dr Jurupa Valley (91752) ***(P-12182)***
Act Inc Dmand Kontrols Systems, Costa Mesa *Also called Advanced Conservation Technolo* ***(P-6567)***
Actavis LLC....D....909 270-1400
311 Bonnie Cir Corona (92878) ***(P-4776)***
Acti, Wilmington *Also called Advanced Cleanup Tech Inc* ***(P-23388)***
Acti Corporation Inc....E....949 753-0352
3 Jenner Ste 160 Irvine (92618) ***(P-9155)***
Action Bag & Cover Inc....D....714 965-7777
18401 Mount Langley St Fountain Valley (92708) ***(P-3124)***
Action Crash Parts, Santa Fe Springs *Also called Global Trade Alliance Inc* ***(P-13060)***
Action Embroidery Corp (PA)....C....909 983-1359
1315 Brooks St Ontario (91762) ***(P-3188)***
Action Enterprises Inc....F....714 978-0333
1911 S Westside Dr Anaheim (92805) ***(P-5544)***
Action Gypsum Supply West LP (PA)....D....909 993-5655
13940 Magnolia Ave Chino (91710) ***(P-14144)***
Action Home Health Care Inc....E....310 659-9930
6300 Wilshire Blvd # 710 Los Angeles (90048) ***(P-21127)***
Action Innovations Inc....F....714 978-0333
1911 S Westside Dr Anaheim (92805) ***(P-5545)***
Action Messenger Service, Los Angeles *Also called Peach Inc* ***(P-12145)***
Action Mold and Tool Co, Anaheim *Also called Action Innovations Inc* ***(P-5545)***
Action Plastics, Santa Ana *Also called Smiths Action Plastic Inc* ***(P-5536)***
Action Property Management Inc (PA)....D....949 450-0202
2603 Main St Ste 500 Irvine (92614) ***(P-15754)***
Action Response Team Inc....F....909 585-9019
114 Stony Creek Rd Big Bear Lake (92315) ***(P-10776)***
Action Roofing, Santa Barbara *Also called JM Roofing Company Inc* ***(P-1491)***
Action Sales, Monterey Park *Also called JC Foodservice Inc* ***(P-13461)***
Action Stamping Inc....E....626 914-7466
517 S Glendora Ave Glendora (91741) ***(P-7120)***
Actionmold, Anaheim *Also called Action Enterprises Inc* ***(P-5544)***
Actionpac Scales & Automation, Oxnard *Also called Coastal Cnting Indus Scale Inc* ***(P-7849)***
Active Plating Inc....E....714 547-0356
1411 E Pomona St Santa Ana (92705) ***(P-7197)***
Active Window Products....D....323 245-5185
5431 W San Fernando Rd Los Angeles (90039) ***(P-6687)***
Activeapparel Inc (PA)....F....951 361-0060
11076 Venture Dr Jurupa Valley (91752) ***(P-2796)***
Activision Blizzard Inc (PA)....B....310 255-2000
3100 Ocean Park Blvd Santa Monica (90405) ***(P-17773)***
Activision Blizzard Inc....D....949 955-1380
3 Blizzard Irvine (92618) ***(P-17774)***
Actron Manufacturing Inc....D....951 371-0885
1841 Railroad St Corona (92878) ***(P-6495)***
Acts For Children (PA)....D....909 877-5590
18136 Jurupa Ave Bloomington (92316) ***(P-22077)***
Acuant Inc (HQ)....C....213 867-2621
6080 Center Dr Ste 850 Los Angeles (90045) ***(P-17775)***
Acufast Aircraft Products Inc....E....818 365-7077
12445 Gladstone Ave Sylmar (91342) ***(P-10238)***
Acuna Dionisio Able....F....310 978-4741
12629 Prairie Ave Hawthorne (90250) ***(P-8468)***
Acuprint, Los Angeles *Also called Ink & Color Inc* ***(P-4329)***
Acura Client Services, Torrance *Also called American Honda Motor Co Inc* ***(P-10457)***
Acura Spa Systems Inc....F....951 684-6667
2954 Rubidoux Blvd Riverside (92509) ***(P-8441)***
Acx Intermodal Inc....C....310 241-6229
920 E Pacific Coast Hwy Wilmington (90744) ***(P-14851)***
Ad Art Company, Vernon *Also called RJ Acquisition Corp* ***(P-4568)***
AD Receivables Corp (PA)....D....323 296-8787
5457 Crenshaw Blvd Los Angeles (90043) ***(P-1016)***
Ad/S Companies, Corona *Also called Architectural Design Signs Inc* ***(P-11523)***
Adam Nutrition, A Division Ivc, Jurupa Valley *Also called International Vitamin Corp* ***(P-4831)***
Adamation, Hacienda Heights *Also called Barhena Inc* ***(P-8368)***
Adame Insurance Services Inc....E....909 620-7098
430 W Holt Ave Ste A Pomona (91768) ***(P-22758)***
Adams and Barnes Inc....D....626 358-1858
433 W Foothill Blvd Monrovia (91016) ***(P-15764)***
Adams and Brooks Inc....D....213 392-8700
4345 Hallmark Pkwy San Bernardino (92407) ***(P-2081)***
Adams Business Media, Palm Springs *Also called Adams Trade Press LP* ***(P-4048)***
Adams Comm & Engrg Tech Inc....C....301 861-5000
1875 Century Park E # 1130 Los Angeles (90067) ***(P-18156)***
Adams Early Childhood Lrng Ctr, La Quinta *Also called Adams Learning Center* ***(P-21980)***
Adams Learning Center....E....760 777-4260
50800 Desert Club Dr La Quinta (92253) ***(P-21980)***
Adams Rite Aerospace, Fullerton *Also called Zmp Aquisition Corporation* ***(P-8969)***
Adams Rite Aerospace Inc (HQ)....C....714 278-6500
4141 N Palm St Fullerton (92835) ***(P-10239)***
Adams Steel, Anaheim *Also called Self Serve Auto Dismantlers* ***(P-12979)***
Adams Trade Press LP (PA)....E....760 318-7000
420 S Palm Canyon Dr Palm Springs (92262) ***(P-4048)***
Adams/Strter Cvil Engneers Inc....D....949 474-2330
16755 Von Karman Ave # 1 Irvine (92606) ***(P-22475)***
Adapt Automation Inc....E....714 662-4454
1661 Palm St Ste A Santa Ana (92701) ***(P-7898)***
Adaptiv I/S, Walnut *Also called Adaptive Inc* ***(P-17776)***
Adaptive Inc (PA)....E....631 760-6577
340 S Lemon Ave Walnut (91789) ***(P-17776)***
Adaptive Aerospace Corporation....E....661 300-0616
501 Bailey Ave Tehachapi (93561) ***(P-10240)***
Adaptive Digital Systems Inc....E....949 955-3116
20322 Sw Acacia St # 200 Newport Beach (92660) ***(P-9249)***
Adaptive Engrg Fabrication Inc....F....714 854-1300
1921 Petra Ln Placentia (92870) ***(P-22476)***
Adaptive Shelters LLC....E....949 923-5444
427 E 17th St Ste F268 Costa Mesa (92627) ***(P-3426)***
Adaptive Tech Group Inc....E....562 424-1100
1635 E Burnett St Signal Hill (90755) ***(P-9156)***
Adat ARI El....C....818 766-4992
12020 Burbank Blvd Valley Village (91607) ***(P-21981)***
Adat ARI El Day School, Valley Village *Also called Adat ARI El* ***(P-21981)***
ADB Industries....B....310 679-9193
1400 Manhattan Ave Fullerton (92831) ***(P-6426)***
ADC Aerospace, Buena Park *Also called Alloy Die Casting Co* ***(P-6362)***
Adco Container Company....E....818 998-2565
9959 Canoga Ave Chatsworth (91311) ***(P-13969)***
Adco Products Inc....E....937 339-6267
23091 Mill Creek Dr Laguna Hills (92653) ***(P-9671)***
Adcolony Inc....D....650 625-1262
11400 W Olympic Blvd # 1200 Los Angeles (90064) ***(P-17538)***
Adcom Interactive Media Inc....D....800 296-7104
21200 Oxnard St 429 Woodland Hills (91367) ***(P-18157)***
Adconion Media Inc (PA)....C....310 382-5521
3301 Exposition Blvd Fl 1 Santa Monica (90404) ***(P-16990)***
Adconion Media Group, Santa Monica *Also called Adconion Media Inc* ***(P-16990)***
Adcraft Products Co Inc....E....714 776-1230
1230 S Sherman St Anaheim (92805) ***(P-4477)***
Add-On Computer Peripheral Inc....C....949 546-8200
15775 Gateway Cir Tustin (92780) ***(P-8232)***
Addaday Inc....F....805 300-3331
12304 Santa Monica Blvd # 214 Los Angeles (90025) ***(P-11397)***
Added Value LLC (HQ)....C....323 254-4326
3400 Cahuenga Blvd W B Los Angeles (90068) ***(P-22873)***
Addice Inc (PA)....D....626 617-7779
19977 Harrison Ave City of Industry (91789) ***(P-8233)***
Adding Technology Inc (PA)....F....805 252-6971
27 W Anapamu St Santa Barbara (93101) ***(P-17777)***
Addink Turf, Riverside *Also called A-G Sod Farms Inc* ***(P-72)***
Adel Park LLC....F....213 321-2030
1432 Edinger Ave Ste 120 Tustin (92780) ***(P-7633)***
Adelanto Elementary School Dst....E....760 530-7680
14350 Bellflower St Adelanto (92301) ***(P-2385)***
Adelman Broadcasting Inc....D....760 371-1700
731 Balsam St Ridgecrest (93555) ***(P-12686)***
Adenna LLC....F....909 510-6999
2151 Michelson Dr Ste 260 Irvine (92612) ***(P-11078)***
Adept Builder LLC....E....949 933-2785
285 Imperial Hwy Ste 201 Fullerton (92835) ***(P-15717)***
Adept Fasteners Inc (PA)....C....661 257-6600
27949 Hancock Pkwy Valencia (91355) ***(P-13789)***
Aderans Hair Goods Inc (HQ)....E....818 428-1626
9135 Independence Ave Chatsworth (91311) ***(P-14301)***
Adesa International LLC....E....909 321-8240
1440 S Vineyard Ave Ontario (91761) ***(P-1844)***
Adesso Inc....C....909 839-2929
20659 Valley Blvd Walnut (91789) ***(P-13371)***
Adex Electronics Inc....F....949 597-1772
3 Watson Irvine (92618) ***(P-9473)***
Adex Medical Inc....F....951 653-9122
6101 Quail Valley Ct D Riverside (92507) ***(P-11079)***
Adexa Inc (PA)....E....310 642-2100
5777 W Century Blvd # 1100 Los Angeles (90045) ***(P-17778)***
Adf Incorporated....E....310 669-9700
1550 W Mahalo Pl Rancho Dominguez (90220) ***(P-6948)***
Adfa Incorporated....E....213 627-8004
319 W 6th St Los Angeles (90014) ***(P-7336)***
ADI, Compton *Also called American Dawn Inc* ***(P-2718)***
ADI, San Bernardino *Also called Aviation & Defense Inc* ***(P-12341)***
ADI, Valencia *Also called Aerospace Dynamics Intl Inc* ***(P-10250)***
Adir Restaurants Corp (PA)....B....213 201-2990
1625 W Olympic Blvd # 1020 Los Angeles (90015) ***(P-16200)***

ALPHABETIC

Employee Codes: A=Over 500 employees, B=251-500
C=101-250, D=51-100, E=20-50 F=10-19
2022 Southern California Business
Directory and Buyers Guide
© Mergent Inc. 1-800-342-5647
1043

Adj Products LLC (PA) ... **C** ... **323 582-2650**
6122 S Eastern Ave Commerce (90040) ***(P-13608)***
Adkan Engineers, Riverside *Also called Adkison Engineers Inc* ***(P-22477)***
Adkison Engineers Inc ... D ... 951 688-0241
6879 Airport Dr Riverside (92504) ***(P-22477)***
ADM Works LLC ... E ... 714 245-0536
1343 E Wilshire Ave Santa Ana (92705) ***(P-6382)***
Admedia, Woodland Hills *Also called Adcom Interactive Media Inc* ***(P-18157)***
Administrative Svcs Coop Inc ... C ... 310 715-1968
1515 W 190th St Ste 200 Gardena (90248) ***(P-11900)***
Adminsure Inc ... C ... 909 718-1200
3380 Shelby St Ontario (91764) ***(P-15526)***
Admiral Hospice Care Inc ... D ... 562 429-1500
4010 Watson Plaza Dr # 120 Lakewood (90712) ***(P-20519)***
Adnet Media, Los Angeles *Also called Xbiz* ***(P-4114)***
Adonis Inc ... E ... 951 432-3960
475 N Sheridan St Corona (92878) ***(P-4987)***
Adopt-A-Beach, Costa Mesa *Also called Adopt-A-Highway Maintenance* ***(P-852)***
Adopt-A-Highway Maintenance ... C ... 800 200-0003
3158 Red Hill Ave Ste 200 Costa Mesa (92626) ***(P-852)***
ADP, Irvine *Also called Automatic Data Processing Inc* ***(P-18079)***
ADP, San Dimas *Also called Automatic Data Processing Inc* ***(P-18080)***
Adrianas Insurance LLC ... D ... 909 291-4040
9445 Charles Smith Ave Rancho Cucamonga (91730) ***(P-15527)***
Adrianas Insurance Svcs Inc (PA) ... **C** ... **909 291-4040**
9445 Charles Smith Ave Rancho Cucamonga (91730) ***(P-15528)***
Adrienne Designs LLC ... F ... 714 558-1209
17150 Newhope St Ste 514 Fountain Valley (92708) ***(P-11306)***
ADS, Bloomington *Also called Accurate Delivery Systems Inc* ***(P-11953)***
ADS Construction Inc ... D ... 805 310-6788
2321 Eastbury Way Santa Maria (93455) ***(P-1359)***
ADS LLC ... F ... 714 379-9778
15205 Springdale St Huntington Beach (92649) ***(P-10673)***
ADS Techonlogy, Walnut *Also called Adesso Inc* ***(P-13371)***
Adtech Optics, City of Industry *Also called Adtech Photonics Inc* ***(P-9474)***
Adtech Photonics Inc ... E ... 626 956-1000
18007 Cortney Ct City of Industry (91748) ***(P-9474)***
Adult Video News, Chatsworth *Also called Avn Media Network Inc* ***(P-4120)***
Advance Adapters Inc ... E ... 805 238-7000
4320 Aerotech Center Way Paso Robles (93446) ***(P-10005)***
Advance Adapters LLC ... E ... 805 238-7000
4320 Aerotech Center Way Paso Robles (93446) ***(P-10006)***
Advance Aqua Tanks, Los Angeles *Also called Alan Lem & Co Inc* ***(P-5945)***
Advance Architectural, Fountain Valley *Also called Advanced Architectural Frames* ***(P-6689)***
Advance Beverage Co Inc ... D ... 661 833-3783
5200 District Blvd Bakersfield (93313) ***(P-14818)***
Advance Disposal Company, Hesperia *Also called Best Way Disposal Co Inc* ***(P-12930)***
Advance Overhead Door Inc ... E ... 818 781-5590
15829 Stagg St Van Nuys (91406) ***(P-6688)***
Advance Paper Box Company ... C ... 323 750-2550
6100 S Gramercy Pl Los Angeles (90047) ***(P-3782)***
Advance Pipe Bending & Fabg Co, Huntington Park *Also called B F McGilla Inc* ***(P-7528)***
Advance Powder Coatings LLC ... F ... 909 543-0014
169 W Mindanao St Bloomington (92316) ***(P-7337)***
Advance Storage Products, Huntington Beach *Also called JCM Industries Inc* ***(P-3687)***
Advanced Aerospace ... F ... 714 265-6200
10781 Forbes Ave Garden Grove (92843) ***(P-8327)***
Advanced Aircraft Seal, Riverside *Also called Sphere Alliance Inc* ***(P-4720)***
Advanced Ambltory Srgery Ctr L ... E ... 909 557-1700
1901 W Lugonia Ave # 100 Redlands (92374) ***(P-19684)***
Advanced Architectural Frames ... E ... 424 209-6018
17102 Newhope St Fountain Valley (92708) ***(P-6689)***
Advanced Arm Dynamics (PA) ... **E** ... **310 372-3050**
123 W Torrance Blvd # 203 Redondo Beach (90277) ***(P-11080)***
Advanced Bionics LLC ... E ... 310 819-4004
26081 Avenue Hall Valencia (91355) ***(P-11213)***
Advanced Bionics LLC (HQ) ... **B** ... **661 362-1400**
12740 San Fernando Rd Sylmar (91342) ***(P-11081)***
Advanced Bionics Corporation (HQ) ... **A** ... **661 362-1400**
28515 Westinghouse Pl Valencia (91355) ***(P-11082)***
Advanced Bioservices LLC (PA) ... **D** ... **818 342-0100**
19255 Vanowen St Reseda (91335) ***(P-22966)***
Advanced Building Systems Inc ... E ... 818 652-4252
11905 Regentview Ave Downey (90241) ***(P-11625)***
Advanced Cable Technologies ... E ... 818 262-6484
13400 Saticoy St Ste 30 North Hollywood (91605) ***(P-932)***
Advanced Ceramic Technology ... F ... 714 538-2524
803 W Angus Ave Orange (92868) ***(P-8469)***
Advanced Charging Tech Inc ... E ... 877 228-5922
17260 Newhope St Fountain Valley (92708) ***(P-8970)***
Advanced Chemical Technology ... E ... 800 527-9607
3540 E 26th St Vernon (90058) ***(P-4649)***
Advanced Circuits Inc ... F ... 818 345-1993
17067 Cantara St Van Nuys (91406) ***(P-9373)***
Advanced Cleanup Tech Inc ... B ... 310 763-1423
230 E C St Wilmington (90744) ***(P-23388)***
Advanced Clnroom McRclean Corp ... C ... 714 751-1152
3250 S Susan St Ste A Santa Ana (92704) ***(P-17212)***
Advanced Clutch Technology Inc ... E ... 661 940-7555
206 E Avenue K4 Lancaster (93535) ***(P-10007)***
Advanced Cmbstn Prcess Cntrls ... F ... 661 615-1193
1648 Art St Bakersfield (93312) ***(P-19019)***
Advanced Cmpsite Pdts Tech Inc ... E ... 714 895-5544
15602 Chemical Ln Huntington Beach (92649) ***(P-5546)***
Advanced Color Graphics ... D ... 909 930-1500
1921 S Business Pkwy Ontario (91761) ***(P-4223)***
Advanced Conservation Technolo ... F ... 714 668-1200
3176 Pullman St Ste 119 Costa Mesa (92626) ***(P-6567)***
Advanced Corporate Svcs Inc ... E ... 310 937-6848
2416 Amsler St Torrance (90505) ***(P-23401)***
Advanced Cosmetic RES Labs Inc ... E ... 818 709-9945
20550 Prairie St Chatsworth (91311) ***(P-11626)***
Advanced Cutting Tools Inc ... E ... 714 342-9376
17741 Metzler Ln Huntington Beach (92647) ***(P-6473)***
Advanced Digital Services Inc (PA) ... **D** ... **323 962-8585**
948 N Cahuenga Blvd Los Angeles (90038) ***(P-19091)***
Advanced Electronic Solutions, Irvine *Also called Patric Communications Inc* ***(P-1292)***
Advanced Engine Management Inc, Hawthorne *Also called Nmsp Inc* ***(P-10109)***
Advanced Engrg Mlding Tech Inc ... E ... 888 264-0392
6510 Box Springs Blvd B Riverside (92507) ***(P-5547)***
Advanced Equipment Corporation (PA) ... **E** ... **714 635-5350**
2401 W Commonwealth Ave Fullerton (92833) ***(P-3675)***
Advanced Erosion Services ... F ... 951 929-8780
175 N Cawston Ave Ste 170 Hemet (92545) ***(P-5268)***
Advanced Flow Engineering Inc (PA) ... **D** ... **951 493-7155**
252 Granite St Corona (92879) ***(P-10008)***
Advanced Foam Inc ... E ... 310 515-0728
1745 W 134th St Gardena (90249) ***(P-5483)***
Advanced Fresh Cncpts Frnchise ... E ... 310 604-3200
19205 S Laurel Park Rd Rancho Dominguez (90220) ***(P-2344)***
Advanced Fresh Concepts Corp (PA) ... **D** ... **310 604-3630**
19205 S Laurel Park Rd Rancho Dominguez (90220) ***(P-16201)***
Advanced Global Tech Group ... E ... 714 281-8020
8015 E Treeview Ct Anaheim (92808) ***(P-9646)***
Advanced Grund Systems Engrg L (HQ) ... **E** ... **562 906-9300**
10805 Painter Ave Santa Fe Springs (90670) ***(P-10211)***
Advanced H2o, Ontario *Also called Advanced Refreshment LLC* ***(P-2248)***
Advanced Image Direct, Fullerton *Also called Real Estate Image Inc* ***(P-17140)***
Advanced Image Direct LLC ... E ... 714 502-3900
1415 S Acacia Ave Fullerton (92831) ***(P-17129)***
Advanced Industrial Cmpt Inc (PA) ... **D** ... **909 895-8989**
21808 Garcia Ln City of Industry (91789) ***(P-13372)***
Advanced Industrial Services, Bakersfield *Also called CL Knox Inc* ***(P-492)***
Advanced Industrial Svcs Cal, Paramount *Also called Advanced Industrial Svcs Inc* ***(P-1165)***
Advanced Industrial Svcs Inc ... D ... 562 940-8305
7831 Alondra Blvd Paramount (90723) ***(P-1165)***
Advanced Innvtive Rcovery Tech, Lake Forest *Also called Pura Naturals Inc* ***(P-5065)***
Advanced Innvtive Rcvery Tech (PA) ... **F** ... **949 273-8100**
23615 El Toro Rd Ste 207 Lake Forest (92630) ***(P-3539)***
Advanced Innvtive Rcvery Tech ... E ... 949 273-8100
3401 Space Center Ct # 811 Jurupa Valley (91752) ***(P-3540)***
Advanced Instruments, Pomona *Also called Analytical Industries Inc* ***(P-10676)***
Advanced Keyboard Tech Inc ... F ... 805 237-2055
2501 Golden Hill Rd # 200 Paso Robles (93446) ***(P-8146)***
Advanced Manufacturing Tech ... A ... 714 238-1488
3140a E Coronado St Anaheim (92806) ***(P-9848)***
Advanced Materials Inc (HQ) ... **F** ... **310 537-5444**
20211 S Susana Rd Compton (90221) ***(P-5484)***
Advanced Medical MGT Inc ... D ... 562 766-2000
5000 Arprt Plz Dr Ste 150 Long Beach (90815) ***(P-22967)***
Advanced Medical Reviews LLC ... D ... 310 575-0900
600 Crprate Pinte Ste 300 Culver City (90230) ***(P-17484)***
Advanced Metal Mfg Inc ... E ... 805 322-4161
49 Strathearn Pl Simi Valley (93065) ***(P-6774)***
Advanced Micro Instruments Inc ... E ... 714 848-5533
225 Paularino Ave Costa Mesa (92626) ***(P-10777)***
Advanced Mktg Print & Mail, Corona *Also called Inland Mailing Services Inc* ***(P-4335)***
Advanced Mnlythic Ceramics Inc ... D ... 818 364-9800
15191 Bledsoe St Sylmar (91342) ***(P-13697)***
Advanced Mobility Inc ... F ... 818 780-1788
7720 Sepulveda Blvd Van Nuys (91405) ***(P-11627)***
Advanced Motion Controls, Camarillo *Also called Barta-Schoenewald Inc* ***(P-8909)***
Advanced Mp Technology LLC (HQ) ... **C** ... **800 492-3113**
27271 Las Ramblas Ste 300 Mission Viejo (92691) ***(P-13698)***
Advanced Mtls Joining Corp (PA) ... **E** ... **626 449-2696**
2858 E Walnut St Pasadena (91107) ***(P-10241)***
Advanced Office, Irvine *Also called Integrus LLC* ***(P-13359)***
Advanced Office Services, Irvine *Also called Offiserve Inc* ***(P-13365)***
Advanced Orthpdic Slutions Inc ... E ... 310 533-9966
3203 Kashiwa St Torrance (90505) ***(P-11083)***
Advanced Pattern & Mold Inc ... F ... 909 930-3444
1720 S Balboa Ave Ontario (91761) ***(P-6280)***
Advanced Photonix, Camarillo *Also called OSI Optoelectronics Inc* ***(P-9554)***
Advanced Phrm Svcs Inc ... F ... 714 903-1006
11555 Monarch St Ste B Garden Grove (92841) ***(P-14231)***
Advanced Plastics Corporation ... F ... 626 286-7163
1855 Rose Ave San Marino (91108) ***(P-5548)***
Advanced Precision Inc ... F ... 909 591-4244
13445 Yorba Ave Chino (91710) ***(P-6581)***
Advanced Process Services Inc ... E ... 323 278-6530
4350 E Washington Blvd Commerce (90023) ***(P-7437)***
Advanced Products, Costa Mesa *Also called Pro-Lite Inc* ***(P-11583)***
Advanced Prof Imging Med Group (PA) ... **C** ... **714 995-5400**
6905 Oslo Cir Ste F Buena Park (90621) ***(P-19685)***
Advanced Protection Inds LLC ... D ... 800 662-1711
25341 Commercentre Dr Lake Forest (92630) ***(P-18364)***
Advanced Publishing Tech Inc ... F ... 818 557-3035
1105 N Hollywood Way Burbank (91505) ***(P-4148)***
Advanced Realtime Systems Inc ... F ... 760 636-0444
110 Conejo Cir Palm Desert (92260) ***(P-17539)***
Advanced Refreshment LLC (HQ) ... **C** ... **425 746-8100**
2560 E Philadelphia St Ontario (91761) ***(P-2248)***
Advanced Scntific Concepts Inc ... D ... 805 966-3331
135 E Ortega St Santa Barbara (93101) ***(P-22874)***
Advanced Sealing (HQ) ... **D** ... **562 802-7782**
15500 Blackburn Ave Norwalk (90650) ***(P-5327)***

Advanced Semiconductor Inc ....D....818 982-1200
7525 Ethel Ave Ste I North Hollywood (91605) ***(P-9475)***
Advanced Spectral Tech Inc ....F....805 527-7657
74 W Cochran St Ste A Simi Valley (93065) ***(P-10825)***
Advanced Sterlization (HQ) ....**C....800 595-0200**
33 Technology Dr Irvine (92618) ***(P-10925)***
Advanced Structural Tech Inc ....C....805 204-9133
950 Richmond Ave Oxnard (93030) ***(P-7081)***
Advanced Tech Plating ....F....714 630-7093
1061 N Grove St Anaheim (92806) ***(P-7198)***
Advanced Technology Co, Pasadena *Also called Advanced Mtls Joining Corp* ***(P-10241)***
Advanced Thermal Sciences Corp ....E....714 688-4200
3355 E La Palma Ave Anaheim (92806) ***(P-9476)***
Advanced Uv Inc (PA) ....**E....562 407-0299**
16350 Manning Way Cerritos (90703) ***(P-8361)***
Advanced Vehicle Mfg Inc (PA) ....**F....866 622-8628**
892 W 10th St Azusa (91702) ***(P-6496)***
Advanced Vision Science Inc ....E....805 683-3851
5743 Thornwood Dr Goleta (93117) ***(P-11244)***
Advanced Vsual Image Dsign LLC ....E....951 279-2138
229 N Sherman Ave Irvine (92614) ***(P-4224)***
Advancedware Corporation ....F....949 609-1240
13844 Alton Pkwy Ste 136 Irvine (92618) ***(P-17540)***
Advanex Americas Inc (HQ) ....**C....714 995-4519**
5780 Cerritos Ave Cypress (90630) ***(P-7481)***
Advanstar Communications Inc ....F....310 857-7500
2901 28th St Ste 100 Santa Monica (90405) ***(P-18434)***
Advanstar Communications Inc ....F....818 593-5000
6200 Canoga Ave Fl 3 Woodland Hills (91367) ***(P-4049)***
Advantage Adhesives Inc ....E....909 204-4990
8345 White Oak Ave Rancho Cucamonga (91730) ***(P-5177)***
Advantage Backhoes, Blue Jay *Also called Travis Snyder* ***(P-7654)***
Advantage Bridal, Gardena *Also called Advantage Products Group LLC* ***(P-3189)***
Advantage Chemical LLC ....E....951 225-4631
27375 Via Industria Temecula (92590) ***(P-14770)***
Advantage Custom Fixtures, Los Angeles *Also called American Furniture Systems Inc* ***(P-3604)***
Advantage Engrg & Chemistry, Santa Ana *Also called AEC Group Inc* ***(P-10010)***
Advantage Ford Lincoln Mercury ....D....626 305-9188
1031 Central Ave Duarte (91010) ***(P-18782)***
Advantage Mailing LLC (PA) ....**C....714 538-3881**
1600 N Kraemer Blvd Anaheim (92806) ***(P-17130)***
Advantage Mailing Service, Anaheim *Also called Advantage Mailing LLC* ***(P-17130)***
Advantage Manufacturing Inc ....E....714 505-1166
616 S Santa Fe St Santa Ana (92705) ***(P-13609)***
Advantage Media Services Inc ....D....661 705-7588
28220 Industry Dr Valencia (91355) ***(P-12183)***
Advantage Media Services Inc (PA) ....**C....661 775-0611**
29010 Commerce Center Dr Valencia (91355) ***(P-12554)***
Advantage Plumbing Group Inc ....D....714 898-6020
3331 Orangewood Ave Los Alamitos (90720) ***(P-1017)***
Advantage Pntg Solutions Inc ....D....951 739-9204
14734 Yorba Ct Chino (91710) ***(P-1166)***
Advantage Produce Inc ....E....213 627-2777
1511 Bay St Los Angeles (90021) ***(P-14611)***
Advantage Products Group LLC ....E....310 371-2060
15620 S Figueroa St Gardena (90248) ***(P-3189)***
Advantage Sales & Mktg Inc (HQ) ....**C....949 797-2900**
15310 Barranca Pkwy # 100 Irvine (92618) ***(P-23147)***
Advantage Solutions, Irvine *Also called Advantage Sales & Mktg Inc* ***(P-23147)***
Advantage Solutions Inc (HQ) ....**A....949 797-2900**
18100 Von Karman Ave # 1 Irvine (92612) ***(P-16991)***
Advantage Systems Inc ....F....949 250-0260
34 Executive Park Ste 100 Irvine (92614) ***(P-17541)***
Advantage-Crown Sls & Mktg LLC (HQ) ....**A....714 780-3000**
1400 S Douglass Rd # 200 Anaheim (92806) ***(P-14449)***
Advantedge Technology Inc ....D....805 488-0405
271 Market St Ste 15 Port Hueneme (93041) ***(P-22478)***
Advantest Test Solutions Inc (HQ) ....**D....949 523-6900**
4 Goodyear Irvine (92618) ***(P-9477)***
Advanti Racing Usa LLC (HQ) ....**F....951 272-5930**
10721 Business Dr Ste 1 Fontana (92337) ***(P-10009)***
Advent Resources Inc ....D....310 241-1500
235 W 7th St San Pedro (90731) ***(P-17542)***
Advent Securities Investments (PA) ....**E....562 920-5467**
9631 Alondra Blvd Ste 202 Bellflower (90706) ***(P-15261)***
Adventist Health Bakersfield, Bakersfield *Also called San Joaquin Community Hospital* ***(P-20932)***
Adventist Health Cmnty. Care, Dinuba *Also called Adventist Health System* ***(P-19686)***
Adventist Health Homecare Svcs, Glendale *Also called Glendale Adventist Medical Ctr* ***(P-21167)***
Adventist Health Job Care, Dinuba *Also called Adventist Hlth Systm/West Corp* ***(P-20653)***
Adventist Health Med Tehachapi (PA) ....**C....661 750-4848**
305 S Robinson St Tehachapi (93561) ***(P-20643)***
Adventist Health System ....A....559 595-9890
250 W El Monte Way Dinuba (93618) ***(P-19686)***
Adventist Health System/West ....D....949 499-7175
31872 Coast Hwy Laguna Beach (92651) ***(P-20644)***
Adventist Health System/West ....D....661 869-6700
1040 7th St Wasco (93280) ***(P-20645)***
Adventist Health System/West ....D....559 537-0305
1524 W Lacey Blvd Ste 102 Hanford (93230) ***(P-20646)***
Adventist Health System/West ....D....661 763-5131
501 6th St Taft (93268) ***(P-20647)***
Adventist Health System/West ....D....805 955-7000
301 Science Dr Ste 150 Moorpark (93021) ***(P-20648)***
Adventist Health System/West ....D....559 537-2510
470 Greenfield Ave Hanford (93230) ***(P-20649)***
Adventist Health Tulare ....B....559 688-0821
869 N Cherry St Tulare (93274) ***(P-20650)***
Adventist Hlth Cmnty Care-Taft, Taft *Also called Adventist Health System/West* ***(P-20647)***
Adventist Hlth Med Foundation, Glendale *Also called Adventist Hlth Systm/West Corp* ***(P-20656)***
Adventist Hlth Systm/West Corp ....D....559 386-5200
337 E Kings St Avenal (93204) ***(P-20651)***
Adventist Hlth Systm/West Corp ....D....323 646-2858
3191 Casitas Ave Ste 216 Los Angeles (90039) ***(P-20652)***
Adventist Hlth Systm/West Corp ....D....559 591-1906
444 W El Monte Way Dinuba (93618) ***(P-20653)***
Adventist Hlth Systm/West Corp ....D....888 443-2273
1025 N Douty St Hanford (93230) ***(P-20654)***
Adventist Hlth Systm/West Corp ....D....559 528-6966
41696 Road 128 Orosi (93647) ***(P-20655)***
Adventist Hlth Systm/West Corp ....D....818 409-8540
381 Merrill Ave Glendale (91206) ***(P-20656)***
Adventist Hlth Systm/West Corp ....D....559 591-3342
1451 E El Monte Way Dinuba (93618) ***(P-20657)***
Adventist Hlth Systm/West Corp ....D....559 386-5364
216 E Fresno St Avenal (93204) ***(P-20658)***
Adventist Hlth Systm/West Corp ....D....559 992-2800
1212 Hanna Ave Corcoran (93212) ***(P-20659)***
Adventist Hlth Systm/West Corp ....D....559 924-7711
810 E D St Lemoore (93245) ***(P-20660)***
Adventist Hlth Systm/West Corp ....D....818 409-8050
1509 Wilson Ter Glendale (91206) ***(P-20661)***
Adventist Med Center-Hanford (HQ) ....**E....559 582-9000**
115 Mall Dr Hanford (93230) ***(P-20662)***
Adventist Med Center-Hanford ....B....559 537-1377
125 Mall Dr Hanford (93230) ***(P-20663)***
Adventist Media Center Inc (PA) ....**C....805 955-7777**
11291 Pierce St Riverside (92505) ***(P-19300)***
Adventure City Inc ....D....714 821-3311
1238 S Beach Blvd Anaheim (92804) ***(P-19631)***
Adventureplex ....E....310 546-7708
1701 Marine Ave Manhattan Beach (90266) ***(P-19437)***
Advertising Consultants Inc (PA) ....**E....310 233-2750**
330 Golden Shore Ste 410 Long Beach (90802) ***(P-17093)***
Advexure LLC ....F....920 917-9566
2288 Westwood Blvd # 100 Los Angeles (90064) ***(P-10242)***
Advisorsquare, Culver City *Also called Liveoffice LLC* ***(P-17906)***
Advocacy For Rspect Chice - Lo (PA) ....**D....562 597-7716**
4519 E Stearns St Long Beach (90815) ***(P-21936)***
Adwest Technologies Inc (HQ) ....**E....714 632-8595**
4222 E La Palma Ave Anaheim (92807) ***(P-8038)***
AEC Group Inc ....F....714 444-1395
3600 W Carriage Dr Santa Ana (92704) ***(P-10010)***
Aecom C&E Inc ....D....805 388-3775
1220 Avenida Acaso Camarillo (93012) ***(P-22479)***
Aecom E&C Holdings Inc (HQ) ....**D....213 593-8000**
1999 Avenue Of The Stars Los Angeles (90067) ***(P-22480)***
Aecom Environment, Camarillo *Also called Aecom C&E Inc* ***(P-22479)***
Aecom Global II LLC (HQ) ....**D....213 593-8100**
300 S Grand Ave Ste 900 Los Angeles (90071) ***(P-22481)***
Aecom Global II LLC ....C....213 996-2200
915 Wilshire Blvd Ste 800 Los Angeles (90017) ***(P-23402)***
Aecom MGT Svcs Globl Corp (HQ) ....**B....213 593-8000**
300 S Grand Ave Ste 900 Los Angeles (90071) ***(P-22706)***
Aecom Services Inc (HQ) ....**C....213 593-8000**
300 S Grand Ave Ste 900 Los Angeles (90071) ***(P-22707)***
Aecom Technical Services Inc (HQ) ....**D....213 593-8000**
300 S Grand Ave Ste 900 Los Angeles (90071) ***(P-23403)***
Aecom Usa Inc ....C....213 330-7200
515 S Figueroa St Ste 400 Los Angeles (90071) ***(P-23404)***
Aecom Usa Inc ....C....213 593-8000
300 S Grand Ave Ste 900 Los Angeles (90071) ***(P-23405)***
Aecom Usa Inc ....C....714 567-2501
999 W Town And Country Rd Orange (92868) ***(P-23406)***
Aee Solar Inc (HQ) ....**E....800 777-6609**
775 Fiero Ln Ste 200 San Luis Obispo (93401) ***(P-13610)***
AEG Management Lacc LLC ....C....213 741-1151
1201 S Figueroa St Los Angeles (90015) ***(P-22968)***
AEG Presents LLC (HQ) ....**C....323 930-5700**
425 W 11th St Los Angeles (90015) ***(P-19301)***
AEG Worldwide, Los Angeles *Also called Anschutz Entrmt Group Inc* ***(P-19343)***
Aegean Stoneworks Inc ....D....800 762-9089
880 N Eckhoff St Orange (92868) ***(P-18435)***
Aegis Ambulance Service Inc (PA) ....**D....626 685-9410**
1907 Border Ave Torrance (90501) ***(P-11847)***
Aegis Medical Systems, Bakersfield *Also called Nationwide Medical Group Inc* ***(P-21048)***
Aegis of Granada Hills, Granada Hills *Also called Aegis Senior Communities LLC* ***(P-21129)***
Aegis of Laguna Niguel, Laguna Niguel *Also called Aegis Senior Communities LLC* ***(P-22078)***
Aegis of Ventura, Ventura *Also called Aegis Senior Communities LLC* ***(P-21128)***
Aegis SEC & Investigations Inc ....C....310 838-2787
10866 Wash Blvd Ste 308 Culver City (90232) ***(P-18239)***
Aegis Senior Communities LLC ....C....805 650-1114
4964 Telegraph Rd Ventura (93003) ***(P-21128)***
Aegis Senior Communities LLC ....D....949 496-8080
32170 Niguel Rd Laguna Niguel (92677) ***(P-22078)***
Aegis Senior Communities LLC ....C....818 363-3373
10801 Lindley Ave Granada Hills (91344) ***(P-21129)***
Aem Corporation, Camarillo *Also called Applied Engineering MGT Corp* ***(P-17551)***
Aer Technologies Inc ....B....714 871-7357
650 Columbia St Brea (92821) ***(P-19020)***
Aera Energy LLC, Bakersfield *Also called Aera Energy Services Company* ***(P-421)***

ALPHABETIC

Employee Codes: A=Over 500 employees, B=251-500
C=101-250, D=51-100, E=20-50 F=10-19
2022 Southern California Business
Directory and Buyers Guide
© Mergent Inc. 1-800-342-5647
1045

Aera Energy LLC.....D.....661 427-9717
1800 School Canyon Rd Ventura (93001) ***(P-14799)***

Aera Energy LLC.....D.....661 334-3100
19590 7th Standard Rd Mc Kittrick (93251) ***(P-385)***

Aera Energy Services Company (HQ).....**A.....661 665-5000**
10000 Ming Ave Bakersfield (93311) ***(P-421)***

Aera Energy Services Company.....E.....661 665-4400
59231 Main Camp Rd Mc Kittrick (93251) ***(P-422)***

Aera Energy Services Company.....E.....661 665-3200
29235 Highway 33 Maricopa (93252) ***(P-423)***

Aera Energy South Midway, Maricopa *Also called Aera Energy Services Company* ***(P-423)***

Aercap Global Aviation Trust (HQ).....**C.....310 788-1999**
10250 Constellation Blvd Los Angeles (90067) ***(P-17325)***

Aercap Los Angeles, Los Angeles *Also called Aercap US Global Aviation LLC* ***(P-10175)***

Aercap US Global Aviation LLC (HQ).....**D.....310 788-1999**
10250 Constellation Blvd Los Angeles (90067) ***(P-10175)***

Aero Automatic Sprinkler Co.....E.....951 273-1889
170 N Maple St Corona (92878) ***(P-1018)***

Aero Bending Company.....D.....661 948-2363
560 Auto Center Dr Ste A Palmdale (93551) ***(P-6775)***

Aero Chip Inc.....E.....562 404-6300
13563 Freeway Dr Santa Fe Springs (90670) ***(P-8470)***

Aero Chip Intgrted Systems Inc.....F.....310 329-8600
13565 Freeway Dr Santa Fe Springs (90670) ***(P-10559)***

Aero Classics Inc.....E.....909 596-1630
1677 Curtiss Ct La Verne (91750) ***(P-7959)***

Aero Dynamic Machining Inc.....D.....714 379-1073
11841 Monarch St Garden Grove (92841) ***(P-8471)***

Aero Engineering Inc.....F.....714 879-6200
1020 E Elm Ave Fullerton (92831) ***(P-8472)***

Aero Engrg & Mfg Co Cal LLC.....E.....661 295-0875
28217 Avenue Crocker Valencia (91355) ***(P-10243)***

Aero Industries LLC.....B.....805 688-6734
139 Industrial Way Buellton (93427) ***(P-8473)***

Aero Mechanism Precision Inc.....E.....818 886-1855
21700 Marilla St Chatsworth (91311) ***(P-8474)***

Aero Mfg & Pltg Co LLC.....E.....818 241-2844
927 Thompson Ave Glendale (91201) ***(P-7199)***

Aero Pacific Corporation.....D.....714 961-9200
20445 E Walnut Dr N Walnut (91789) ***(P-10244)***

Aero Pacific Mfg, Garden Grove *Also called Arch Precision Components* ***(P-10275)***

Aero Performance, Corona *Also called Irwin Aviation Inc* ***(P-10359)***

Aero Port Services Inc (PA).....**A.....310 623-8230**
216 W Florence Ave Inglewood (90301) ***(P-18365)***

Aero Powder Coating Inc.....E.....323 264-6405
710 Monterey Pass Rd Monterey Park (91754) ***(P-7338)***

Aero Precision Engineering.....E.....310 642-9747
11300 Hindry Ave Los Angeles (90045) ***(P-6776)***

Aero Products Co., Los Angeles *Also called Coating Specialties Inc* ***(P-10301)***

Aero Sense Inc.....F.....661 257-1608
26074 Avenue Hall Ste 18 Valencia (91355) ***(P-10245)***

Aero Shade Co Inc (PA).....**E.....323 938-2314**
8404 W 3rd St Los Angeles (90048) ***(P-3704)***

Aero Worx, Torrance *Also called Aeroworx Inc* ***(P-19021)***

Aero-Clssics Heat Trnsf Pdts I.....F.....909 596-1630
1677 Curtiss Ct La Verne (91750) ***(P-6724)***

Aero-Craft Hydraulics Inc.....E.....951 736-4690
392 N Smith Ave Corona (92878) ***(P-10246)***

Aero-Electric Connector Inc (PA).....**B.....310 618-3737**
2280 W 208th St Torrance (90501) ***(P-9025)***

Aero-k.....E.....626 350-5125
10764 Lower Azusa Rd El Monte (91731) ***(P-8475)***

Aero-Mechanical Engrg Inc.....F.....323 682-0961
6475 E Pcf Cast Hwy Ste 1 Long Beach (90803) ***(P-8476)***

Aero-Nasch Aviation Inc.....F.....818 786-5480
6849 Hayvenhurst Ave Van Nuys (91406) ***(P-10247)***

Aeroantenna Technology Inc.....C.....818 993-3842
20732 Lassen St Chatsworth (91311) ***(P-10560)***

Aerocraft Heat Treating Co Inc.....D.....562 674-2400
15701 Minnesota Ave Paramount (90723) ***(P-6427)***

Aerodynamic Engineering Inc.....E.....714 891-2651
15495 Graham St Huntington Beach (92649) ***(P-8477)***

Aerodynamic Plating Co.....E.....310 329-7959
13620 S Saint Andrews Pl Gardena (90249) ***(P-7200)***

Aerodyne Prcsion Machining Inc.....E.....714 891-1311
5471 Argosy Ave Huntington Beach (92649) ***(P-8478)***

Aerofab Corporation.....F.....714 635-0902
4001 E Leaverton Ct Anaheim (92807) ***(P-6582)***

Aerofit LLC.....C.....714 521-5060
1425 S Acacia Ave Fullerton (92831) ***(P-7526)***

Aeroflex Incorporated.....D.....800 843-1553
15375 Barranca Pkwy F10 Irvine (92618) ***(P-9478)***

Aerofoam Industries Inc.....D.....951 245-4429
31855 Corydon St Lake Elsinore (92530) ***(P-3618)***

Aerojet Rcketdyne Holdings Inc (PA).....**D.....310 252-8100**
222 N Pcf Cast Hwy Ste 50 El Segundo (90245) ***(P-10561)***

Aerojet Rocketdyne De Inc (HQ).....**A.....818 586-1000**
8900 De Soto Ave Canoga Park (91304) ***(P-5123)***

Aerojet Rocketdyne De Inc.....C.....818 586-1000
9001 Lurline Ave Chatsworth (91311) ***(P-5124)***

Aeroliant Manufacturing Inc.....E.....310 257-1903
1613 Lockness Pl Torrance (90501) ***(P-8479)***

Aeromovel, Westlake Village *Also called Xenel International USA* ***(P-16117)***

Aeroshear Aviation Svcs Inc (PA).....**E.....818 779-1650**
7701 Woodley Ave 200 Van Nuys (91406) ***(P-10248)***

Aerospace and Coml Tooling Inc.....F.....909 930-5780
1866 S Lake Pl Ontario (91761) ***(P-8480)***

Aerospace Driven Tech Inc.....F.....949 553-1606
2807 Catherine Way Santa Ana (92705) ***(P-10249)***

Aerospace Dynamics Intl Inc (HQ).....**B.....661 257-3535**
25540 Rye Canyon Rd Valencia (91355) ***(P-10250)***

Aerospace Engineering LLC.....C.....714 996-8178
2632 Saturn St Brea (92821) ***(P-10251)***

Aerospace Engrg Support Corp.....E.....310 297-4050
645 Hawaii St El Segundo (90245) ***(P-10252)***

Aerospace Fasteners Group, Santa Ana *Also called SPS Technologies LLC* ***(P-11501)***

Aerospace Parts Holdings Inc.....A.....949 877-3630
3150 E Miraloma Ave Anaheim (92806) ***(P-10253)***

Aerospace Service & Controls.....F.....818 833-0088
28402 Livingston Ave Valencia (91355) ***(P-10254)***

Aerospace Systems, Redondo Beach *Also called Northrop Grumman Systems Corp* ***(P-10198)***

Aerospace Systems Strctres LLC.....F.....626 965-1630
423 Berry Way Brea (92821) ***(P-10255)***

Aerospace Tool Grinding.....E.....562 802-3339
14020 Shoemaker Ave Norwalk (90650) ***(P-7720)***

Aerospace Welding Inc.....F.....310 914-0324
2035 Granville Ave Los Angeles (90025) ***(P-18966)***

Aerotec Alloys Inc.....E.....562 809-1378
10632 Alondra Blvd Norwalk (90650) ***(P-6361)***

Aerotech News and Review Inc (PA).....**E.....661 945-5634**
220 E Avenue K4 Ste 4 Lancaster (93535) ***(P-4050)***

Aerotech Precision Machining.....F.....661 802-7185
42541 6th St E Ste 17 Lancaster (93535) ***(P-8481)***

Aerotransporte De Carge Union.....B.....310 649-0069
5625 W Imperial Hwy Los Angeles (90045) ***(P-12300)***

Aeroturbine LLC (HQ).....**C.....305 406-3090**
10250 Constellation Blvd Los Angeles (90067) ***(P-17326)***

Aeroturbine, Inc., Los Angeles *Also called Aeroturbine LLC* ***(P-17326)***

Aerounion, Los Angeles *Also called Aerotransporte De Carge Union* ***(P-12300)***

Aeroworx Inc.....E.....310 891-0300
2565 W 237th St Torrance (90505) ***(P-19021)***

AES Alamitos LLC.....D.....562 493-7891
690 N Studebaker Rd Long Beach (90803) ***(P-12795)***

AES Heavy Equipment Rental Inc.....D.....213 892-9720
10880 Wilshire Blvd Los Angeles (90024) ***(P-17327)***

AES Huntington Beach LLC.....E.....714 374-1476
21730 Newland St Huntington Beach (92646) ***(P-12796)***

AES NDT.....E.....310 947-6755
1821 W 213th St Ste L Torrance (90501) ***(P-10867)***

Aetco Inc.....F.....909 593-2521
2825 Metropolitan Pl Pomona (91767) ***(P-3435)***

Aetna Dental of California.....C.....860 273-5677
21215 Burbank Blvd Fl 6 Woodland Hills (91367) ***(P-15356)***

AF Technology LLC.....E.....310 361-5710
12130 Millennium 3-154 Playa Vista (90094) ***(P-17543)***

Afakori Inc.....E.....949 859-4277
29390 Hunco Way Lake Elsinore (92530) ***(P-6583)***

Afc Distribution Corp.....C.....310 604-3630
19205 S Laurel Park Rd Rancho Dominguez (90220) ***(P-14450)***

Afc Trading & Wholesale Inc.....E.....323 223-7738
4738 Valley Blvd Los Angeles (90032) ***(P-14451)***

Afcfc, Rancho Dominguez *Also called Advanced Fresh Cncpts Frnchise* ***(P-2344)***

Afco, Gardena *Also called Abrasive Finishing Co* ***(P-6424)***

Afco, Alhambra *Also called Alhambra Foundry Company Ltd* ***(P-6256)***

Afco, Huntington Park *Also called Aircraft Foundry Co Inc* ***(P-6383)***

Afe Power, Corona *Also called Advanced Flow Engineering Inc* ***(P-10008)***

Afex, Woodland Hills *Also called Associated Foreign Exch Inc* ***(P-15121)***

Affiliated Communications Inc.....C.....805 447-2101
3601 Calle Tecate Camarillo (93012) ***(P-18436)***

Affinity Group, Ventura *Also called Agi Holding Corp* ***(P-19528)***

Affluent Living Publication, Anaheim *Also called Affluent Target Marketing Inc* ***(P-4051)***

Affluent Target Marketing Inc.....F.....714 446-6280
3855 E La Palma Ave # 250 Anaheim (92807) ***(P-4051)***

Affordable Plas & Packg Inc.....F.....909 972-1944
739 E Francis St Ontario (91761) ***(P-4676)***

Afk Furniture, Rcho STA Marg *Also called Art For Kids Inc* ***(P-3438)***

Afm & Sg-Ftra Intllctual Prprt.....D.....818 255-7980
4705 Laurel Canyon Blvd # 40 Valley Village (91607) ***(P-18437)***

AFP Advanced Food Products LLC.....E.....559 627-2070
1211 E Noble Ave Visalia (93292) ***(P-1845)***

AFP Advanced Food Products LLC.....C.....559 651-1737
900 N Plaza Dr Visalia (93291) ***(P-1829)***

Afr Apparel International Inc.....D.....818 773-5000
19401 Business Center Dr Northridge (91324) ***(P-3012)***

African Women Rising.....C.....415 278-1784
801 Cold Springs Rd Santa Barbara (93108) ***(P-22309)***

Afrix Telecom LLC.....D.....323 359-8683
722 N Lucia Ave B Redondo Beach (90277) ***(P-12623)***

Aft Corporation.....F.....310 576-1007
1815 Centinela Ave Unit C Santa Monica (90404) ***(P-4628)***

Aftco Mfg Co Inc.....D.....877 489-4278
2400 S Garnsey St Santa Ana (92707) ***(P-11398)***

After-Party2 Inc.....D.....805 563-3800
1120 Mark Ave Carpinteria (93013) ***(P-17328)***

After-Party2 Inc (HQ).....**C.....310 202-0011**
901 W Hillcrest Blvd Inglewood (90301) ***(P-17329)***

Aftermarket Services.....F.....610 251-1000
28150 Industry Dr Valencia (91355) ***(P-10256)***

Aftershock La Studios Inc.....D.....650 450-9660
3633 Lenawee Ave Ste 100 Los Angeles (90016) ***(P-17544)***

AG Adriano Goldschmied Inc (PA).....**D.....323 357-1111**
2741 Seminole Ave South Gate (90280) ***(P-2767)***

AG Air Conditioning & Htg Inc.....E.....818 988-5388
14620 Keswick St Van Nuys (91405) ***(P-1019)***

AG Heating and AC, Van Nuys *Also called AG Air Conditioning & Htg Inc* ***(P-1019)***

AG Jeans, South Gate *Also called AG Adriano Goldschmied Inc* ***(P-2767)***

AG Laboratory Consulting.......F.......805 739-5333
2255 S Brdwy Ste 12 Santa Maria (93454) *(P-10778)*
AG Machining Inc.......D.......805 531-9555
609 Science Dr Moorpark (93021) *(P-6584)*
AG Millworks, Ventura *Also called Art Glass Etc Inc (P-3232)*
AG Rx (PA).......**D.......805 487-0696**
751 S Rose Ave Oxnard (93030) *(P-14852)*
AG Spray Equipment Inc.......F.......661 391-9081
4618 Saco Rd Bakersfield (93308) *(P-7602)*
Ag-Weld Inc.......E.......661 758-3061
1236 G St Wasco (93280) *(P-18967)*
Ag-Wise Enterprises Inc (PA).......**C.......661 325-1567**
5100 California Ave # 209 Bakersfield (93309) *(P-220)*
AGA Precision Systems Inc.......E.......714 540-3163
122 E Dyer Rd Santa Ana (92707) *(P-8482)*
Age Incorporated.......E.......562 483-7300
14831 Spring Ave Santa Fe Springs (90670) *(P-8888)*
Agency For Performing Arts Inc.......D.......310 888-4200
405 S Beverly Dr Ste 500 Beverly Hills (90212) *(P-19302)*
Agency For Performing Arts Inc (PA).......**D.......310 557-9049**
405 S Beverly Dr Ste 500 Beverly Hills (90212) *(P-19303)*
Agencycom LLC.......B.......415 817-3800
5353 Grosvenor Blvd Los Angeles (90066) *(P-17779)*
Agendia Inc.......C.......949 540-6300
22 Morgan Irvine (92618) *(P-21270)*
Agent Franchise LLC.......C.......949 930-5025
9518 9th St Ste C2 Rancho Cucamonga (91730) *(P-15374)*
Agents West Inc.......E.......949 614-0293
6 Hughes Ste 210 Irvine (92618) *(P-9849)*
Aggregate West Coast, Thermal *Also called West Coast Aggregate Supply (P-576)*
Aggressive Engineering Corp.......F.......714 995-8313
1235 N Knollwood Cir Anaheim (92801) *(P-13881)*
Agi General Contracting, Stanton *Also called Art Gautreau Inc (P-739)*
Agi Holding Corp (HQ).......**A.......805 667-4100**
2575 Vista Del Mar Dr Ventura (93001) *(P-19528)*
Agia Affinity, Carpinteria *Also called AGIA Inc (P-15529)*
AGIA Inc (PA).......**C.......805 566-9191**
1155 Eugenia Pl Carpinteria (93013) *(P-15529)*
Agile Sourcing Partners Inc.......C.......951 279-4154
2385 Railroad St Corona (92878) *(P-12876)*
Agile Technologies Inc.......E.......949 454-8030
2 Orion Aliso Viejo (92656) *(P-9479)*
Agileone, Torrance *Also called Act 1 Group Inc (P-17388)*
Agility Fuel Systems LLC (HQ).......**C.......949 236-5520**
1815 Carnegie Ave Santa Ana (92705) *(P-10011)*
Agility Holdings Inc (HQ).......**D.......714 617-6300**
310 Commerce Ste 250 Irvine (92602) *(P-12417)*
Agility Logistics, Irvine *Also called Agility Holdings Inc (P-12417)*
Agility Powertrain Systems LLC (HQ).......**B.......949 236-5520**
3335 Susan St Ste 100 Costa Mesa (92626) *(P-13040)*
Agilon Health Management Inc.......A.......562 256-3800
1 World Trade Ctr Ste 200 Long Beach (90831) *(P-21371)*
Aging & Adult Services, Victorville *Also called County of San Bernardino (P-21761)*
Agl, Temecula *Also called Artificial Grass Liquidators (P-11633)*
Agnaldos Welding Inc.......F.......559 752-4254
828 S Burnett Rd Tipton (93272) *(P-18968)*
Agoura Health Products LLC (PA).......**D.......800 852-0477**
9465 Wilshire Blvd # 300 Beverly Hills (90212) *(P-14232)*
Agoura Hills Renaissance Hotel, Agoura Hills *Also called Davidson Hotel Partners Lp (P-16404)*
AGR Group Inc.......A.......714 245-7151
13902 Harbor Blvd Ste 2c Garden Grove (92843) *(P-23148)*
Agre Dcp Palm Sprng Tenant LLC (PA).......**C.......760 327-8311**
1600 N Palm Spgs Palm Springs (92262) *(P-16315)*
Agri-Cel Inc.......E.......661 792-2107
401 Road 192 Delano (93215) *(P-5485)*
Agri-Empire.......C.......951 654-7311
630 W 7th St San Jacinto (92583) *(P-14612)*
Agri-Link Plastics Inc.......E.......559 564-2889
296 E Wutchumna Ave Woodlake (93286) *(P-5549)*
Agrifrost LLC.......E.......805 485-2519
4324 E Vineyard Ave Oxnard (93036) *(P-23)*
Agritec International Ltd.......E.......626 812-7200
5820 Martin Rd Irwindale (91706) *(P-14145)*
Agron Inc.......D.......310 473-7223
2440 S Sepulveda Blvd # 201 Los Angeles (90064) *(P-3023)*
Agse, Santa Fe Springs *Also called Advanced Grund Systems Engrg L (P-10211)*
Agstar Services Inc (PA).......**F.......661 303-5556**
13947 Santa Fe Ct Bakersfield (93314) *(P-5550)*
Agt, Corona *Also called Absolute Graphic Tech USA Inc (P-8941)*
Agua Caliente Casino & Resort, Rancho Mirage *Also called Agua Clnte Band Chilla Indians (P-16316)*
Agua Caliente Development Auth.......D.......760 699-6800
5401 Dinah Shore Dr Palm Springs (92264) *(P-15765)*
Agua Clnte Band Chilla Indians.......A.......760 321-2000
32250 Bob Hope Dr Rancho Mirage (92270) *(P-16316)*
Agua Clnte Band Chilla Indians (PA).......**A.......760 699-6800**
5401 Dinah Shore Dr Palm Springs (92264) *(P-22394)*
Agua Dulce Vineyards LLC.......E.......661 268-7402
9640 Sierra Hwy Agua Dulce (91390) *(P-2164)*
Aguila Financial, La Mirada *Also called Groupex Financial Corporation (P-15329)*
Aguilar Williams Inc.......F.......562 693-2736
7635 Baldwin Pl Whittier (90602) *(P-7201)*
Agusa.......E.......559 924-4785
1055 S 19th Ave Lemoore (93245) *(P-2386)*
Ahf-Ducommun Incorporated (HQ).......**C.......310 380-5390**
268 E Gardena Blvd Gardena (90248) *(P-10257)*
Ahg Inc.......B.......703 596-0111
340 S Lemon Ave 6633 Walnut (91789) *(P-16933)*
Ahi Investment Inc (HQ).......**E.......818 979-0030**
675 Glenoaks Blvd San Fernando (91340) *(P-14908)*
Ahm Gemch Inc.......C.......626 579-7777
1701 Santa Anita Ave El Monte (91733) *(P-20664)*
Ahmc, Anaheim *Also called Anaheim Regional Medical Ctr (P-20677)*
Ahmc Garfield Medical Ctr LP.......C.......626 573-2222
525 N Garfield Ave Monterey Park (91754) *(P-20239)*
Ahmc Healthcare Inc.......A.......626 248-3452
506 W Valley Blvd Ste 300 San Gabriel (91776) *(P-21372)*
Ahmc Healthcare Inc (PA).......**C.......626 943-7526**
506 W Valley Blvd Ste 300 San Gabriel (91776) *(P-20665)*
Ahmc Healthcare Inc.......A.......626 579-7777
1701 Santa Anita Ave South El Monte (91733) *(P-20666)*
Ahmc Inc.......D.......626 570-1606
100 S Raymond Ave Alhambra (91801) *(P-19687)*
Ahmc Whittier Hosp Med Ctr LP.......A.......562 945-3561
9080 Colima Rd Whittier (90605) *(P-20667)*
Ahr Signs Incorporated.......F.......323 255-1102
3400 N San Fernando Rd Los Angeles (90065) *(P-11521)*
Ahtineb Nvels Photos By Design.......F.......442 327-9234
473 Ecarnegie Dr Ste 200 San Bernardino (92408) *(P-17157)*
Ahtna-CDM JV.......E.......714 824-3470
3200 El Cmino Real Ste 24 Irvine (92602) *(P-686)*
Ahw, Long Beach *Also called Aircraft Hardware West (P-14049)*
AI Foods Corporation.......E.......323 222-0827
1700 N Soto St Los Angeles (90033) *(P-14590)*
AIA Holdings Inc (PA).......**D.......818 222-4999**
26560 Agoura Rd Ste 100 Calabasas (91302) *(P-18438)*
Aic Inc USA, City of Industry *Also called Advanced Industrial Cmpt Inc (P-13372)*
Aicco Inc (HQ).......**D.......714 481-3215**
3 Hutton Cntre Dr Ste 630 Santa Ana (92707) *(P-15136)*
AID FOR AIDS, Los Angeles *Also called Alliance For Housing & Healing (P-20520)*
Aids Project La, Los Angeles *Also called Aids Project Los Angeles (P-21708)*
Aids Project Los Angeles (PA).......**D.......213 201-1600**
611 S Kingsley Dr Los Angeles (90005) *(P-21708)*
Aids Svcs Fndation Orange Cnty.......D.......949 809-5700
17982 Sky Park Cir Ste J Irvine (92614) *(P-21709)*
AIDS WALK ORANGE COUNTY, Irvine *Also called Aids Svcs Fndation Orange Cnty (P-21709)*
Aii Beauty, Commerce *Also called American Intl Inds Inc (P-4988)*
Aiminsight Solutions Inc.......F.......310 313-0047
4127 Berryman Ave Los Angeles (90066) *(P-18158)*
Aims360, Playa Vista *Also called AF Technology LLC (P-17543)*
Air Blast Inc.......E.......626 576-0144
2050 Pepper St Alhambra (91801) *(P-8039)*
Air Cleaning Systems Inc.......F.......909 620-7114
3633 Pomona Blvd Pomona (91768) *(P-8040)*
Air Combat Systems, Palmdale *Also called Northrop Grumman Systems Corp (P-10197)*
Air Components Inc.......E.......909 980-8224
10235 Indiana Ct Rancho Cucamonga (91730) *(P-10258)*
Air Control Systems Inc.......E.......909 786-4230
1940 S Grove Ave Ontario (91761) *(P-1020)*
Air Craftors Engineering Inc.......F.......909 900-0635
4040 Cheyenne Ct Chino (91710) *(P-8483)*
Air Fayre USA Inc.......C.......310 808-1061
1720 W 135th St Gardena (90249) *(P-2387)*
Air Flow Research Heads Inc.......E.......661 257-8124
28611 Industry Dr Valencia (91355) *(P-10012)*
Air Force Village West Inc.......B.......951 697-2000
17050 Arnold Dr Riverside (92518) *(P-20240)*
Air Frame Mfg & Supply Co Inc.......E.......661 257-7728
26135 Technology Dr Valencia (91355) *(P-14048)*
Air Lease Corp (PA).......**D.......818 387-8924**
7520 Hayvenhurst Ave Van Nuys (91406) *(P-17330)*
Air Lease Corporation (PA).......**C.......310 553-0555**
2000 Avenue Of The Stars 1000n Los Angeles (90067) *(P-17331)*
Air Liquide Electronics US LP.......A.......310 549-7079
1502 W Anaheim St Wilmington (90744) *(P-4637)*
Air New Zealand Limited.......D.......310 648-7000
222 N Pacific Coast Hwy # 90 El Segundo (90245) *(P-12301)*
Air Products and Chemicals Inc.......F.......310 212-2800
3700 W 190th St Torrance (90504) *(P-5248)*
Air Pure, Cerritos *Also called Eco-Air Products Inc (P-13841)*
Air Rutter International LLC.......E.......855 359-2576
3501 N Lakewood Blvd Long Beach (90808) *(P-12334)*
Air Source Industries.......E.......562 426-4017
3976 Cherry Ave Long Beach (90807) *(P-4638)*
Air Treatment Corporation (PA).......**D.......909 869-7975**
640 N Puente St Brea (92821) *(P-13839)*
Air Tube Transfer Systems Inc.......E.......714 363-0700
715 N Cypress St Orange (92867) *(P-7683)*
Air-Sea Forwarders Inc (PA).......**D.......310 216-1616**
9009 S La Cienega Blvd Inglewood (90301) *(P-12418)*
Air-TEC, Carson *Also called Clay Dunn Enterprises Inc (P-1046)*
Air-Vol Block Inc.......E.......805 543-1314
1 Suburban Rd San Luis Obispo (93401) *(P-6008)*
Airborne Components, Carson *Also called Stanford Mu Corporation (P-10536)*
Airborne Systems N Amer CA Inc.......C.......714 662-1400
3100 W Segerstrom Ave Santa Ana (92704) *(P-3190)*
Airborne Technologies Inc.......D.......805 389-3700
999 Avenida Acaso Camarillo (93012) *(P-10259)*
Aircoat Inc.......E.......310 527-2258
13405 S Broadway Los Angeles (90061) *(P-7339)*
Aircraft Foundry Co Inc.......E.......323 587-3171
5316 Pacific Blvd Huntington Park (90255) *(P-6383)*
Aircraft Hardware West.......E.......562 961-9324
2180 Temple Ave Long Beach (90804) *(P-14049)*

ALPHABETIC

Employee Codes: A=Over 500 employees, B=251-500
C=101-250, D=51-100, E=20-50 F=10-19
2022 Southern California Business
Directory and Buyers Guide
© Mergent Inc. 1-800-342-5647
1047

Aircraft Hinge Inc E 661 257-3434
28338 Constellation Rd # 970 Santa Clarita (91355) *(P-10260)*

Aircraft Repair & Overhaul Svc (PA) E **714 630-9494**
1186 N Grove St Anaheim (92806) *(P-12338)*

Aircraft Spruce Speciality Co, Corona *Also called Irwin International Inc (P-14057)*

Aircraft Stamping Company Inc F 323 283-1239
1285 Paseo Alicia San Dimas (91773) *(P-6777)*

Aircraft Xray Laboratories Inc D 323 587-4141
5216 Pacific Blvd Huntington Park (90255) *(P-22927)*

Airdraulics Inc E 818 982-1400
13261 Saticoy St North Hollywood (91605) *(P-18889)*

Airdyne Refrigeration, Cerritos *Also called Refrigerator Manufacturers LLC (P-8348)*

Airdyne Refrigeration, Cerritos *Also called ARI Industries Inc (P-8329)*

Aire-Rite AC & Rfrgn Inc D 714 895-2338
15122 Bolsa Chica St Huntington Beach (92649) *(P-1021)*

Airemasters Air Conditioning, Santa Fe Springs *Also called Scorpio Enterprises (P-1134)*

Airespring Inc D 818 786-8990
7800 Woodley Ave Van Nuys (91406) *(P-12624)*

Airex, Anaheim *Also called Emitcon Inc (P-10737)*

Airey Enterprises LLC C 818 530-3362
5530 Corbin Ave Ste 325 Tarzana (91356) *(P-14050)*

Airframer R, Torrance *Also called Sonic Industries Inc (P-22655)*

Airgas Safety Inc F 562 699-5239
2355 Workman Mill Rd City of Industry (90601) *(P-13882)*

Airgas Specialty Products Inc D 951 353-2390
6270 Wilderness Ave Riverside (92504) *(P-14771)*

Airo Industries Company E 818 838-1008
429 Jessie St San Fernando (91340) *(P-3619)*

Airport Connection Inc C 805 389-8196
95 Dawson Dr Camarillo (93012) *(P-11802)*

Airport Honda, Los Angeles *Also called Noarus Investments Inc (P-18858)*

Airport Marina Ford, Los Angeles *Also called Fox Hills Auto Inc (P-18831)*

Airports Cmrllo Oxnard Arprt I, Oxnard *Also called County of Ventura (P-12354)*

Airstream of Orange County, Midway City *Also called Lin Consulting LLC (P-10543)*

Airtech Advanced Mtls Group, Huntington Beach *Also called Airtech International Inc (P-10261)*

Airtech International Inc (PA) C **714 899-8100**
5700 Skylab Rd Huntington Beach (92647) *(P-10261)*

Ais Construction Company D 805 928-9467
7015 Vista Rincon Dr Ventura (93001) *(P-730)*

Aisin World Corp of America B 310 326-8681
19801 S Vermont Ave Torrance (90502) *(P-10013)*

Aisling Industries, Calexico *Also called Creation Tech Calexico Inc (P-9396)*

AITA Clutch Inc E 323 585-4140
960 S Santa Fe Ave Compton (90221) *(P-10014)*

Aitech Defense Systems Inc E 818 700-2000
19756 Prairie St Chatsworth (91311) *(P-9850)*

Aitech Rugged Group Inc (PA) E **818 700-2000**
19756 Prairie St Chatsworth (91311) *(P-9851)*

AJ Kirkwood & Associates Inc B 714 505-1977
4300 N Harbor Blvd Fullerton (92835) *(P-1210)*

AJ Sons Inc F 949 497-1741
2975 Laguna Canyon Rd Laguna Beach (92651) *(P-1913)*

Aj Special Coatings Inc F 760 646-2813
17881 Bangor Ave Hesperia (92345) *(P-7340)*

Ajax Forge Company (PA) F **323 582-6307**
1956 E 48th St Vernon (90058) *(P-7082)*

Ajg Inc E 323 346-0171
7220 E Slauson Ave Commerce (90040) *(P-3053)*

Ajinomoto Foods North Amer Inc C 909 477-4700
4200 Concours Ste 100 Ontario (91764) *(P-1914)*

Ajinomoto Foods North Amer Inc (HQ) D **909 477-4700**
4200 Concours Ste 100 Ontario (91764) *(P-1915)*

Ajit Healthcare Inc D 213 484-0510
316 S Westlake Ave Los Angeles (90057) *(P-22969)*

Ajr Trucking Inc C 562 989-9555
435 E Weber Ave Compton (90222) *(P-11954)*

AK Constructors Inc D 951 280-0269
1751 Jenks Dr Corona (92878) *(P-731)*

AK Darcy, Costa Mesa *Also called Darcy AK Corporation (P-8568)*

AK Electrical Services, Corona *Also called AK Constructors Inc (P-731)*

AK Industries, Compton *Also called Allan Kidd (P-9026)*

Akash Management LLC A 805 672-2889
716 Corporate Center Dr # 200 Pomona (91768) *(P-23149)*

Akerman LLP D 213 688-9500
601 W 5th St Ste 300 Los Angeles (90071) *(P-21500)*

Akh Company Inc C 818 691-1978
7120 Laurel Canyon Blvd North Hollywood (91605) *(P-18890)*

Akh Company Inc D 909 748-5016
1647 W Rdlands Blvd Ste C Redlands (92373) *(P-18891)*

Akh Company Inc D 951 924-5356
23316 Sunnymead Blvd Moreno Valley (92553) *(P-13111)*

Akiwa Technology Inc F 562 407-2782
13021 Arctic Cir Santa Fe Springs (90670) *(P-8186)*

Akm Fire Inc F 818 343-8208
18322 Oxnard St Tarzana (91356) *(P-8111)*

Akra Plastic Products Inc E 909 930-1999
1504 E Cedar St Ontario (91761) *(P-5551)*

Akt, Paso Robles *Also called Advanced Keyboard Tech Inc (P-8146)*

Akua Behavioral Health Inc (PA) C **949 777-2283**
20271 Sw Birch St Ste 200 Newport Beach (92660) *(P-21030)*

Akua Mind & Body, Newport Beach *Also called Akua Behavioral Health Inc (P-21030)*

Al Asher & Sons Inc E 800 896-2480
5301 Valley Blvd Los Angeles (90032) *(P-17304)*

Al Fakhory Trading LLC (PA) F **323 728-8840**
13047 Lakeland Rd Santa Fe Springs (90670) *(P-13155)*

Al Industries, Santa Ana *Also called Acrontos Manufacturing Inc (P-7119)*

Al Johnson Company, Camarillo *Also called Gc International Inc (P-9218)*

Al-Mag Heat Treat F 626 442-8570
9735 Alpaca St South El Monte (91733) *(P-6428)*

Alabama Metal Industries Corp D 909 350-9280
11093 Beech Ave Fontana (92337) *(P-6949)*

Alabbasi, Perris *Also called Mamco Inc (P-899)*

Alaco Ladder Company, Chino *Also called B E & P Enterprises LLC (P-3439)*

Alaco Ladder Company E 909 591-7561
5167 G St Chino (91710) *(P-3436)*

Alakor Healthcare LLC C 626 408-9800
323 S Heliotrope Ave Monrovia (91016) *(P-20668)*

Alameda Construction Svcs Inc E 310 635-3277
2528 E 125th St Compton (90222) *(P-567)*

Alamitos Blmont Rhblttion Hosp, Long Beach *Also called Alamitos-Belmont Rehab Inc (P-20241)*

Alamitos Intermediate School, Garden Grove *Also called Garden Grove Unified Schl Dst (P-4130)*

Alamitos W Convalescent Hosp, Los Alamitos *Also called Katella Properties (P-20384)*

Alamitos-Belmont Rehab Inc C 562 434-8421
3901 E 4th St Long Beach (90814) *(P-20241)*

Alan B Whitson Company Inc A 949 955-1200
1507 W Alton Ave Santa Ana (92704) *(P-23150)*

Alan Gordon Enterprises Inc E 323 466-3561
5625 Melrose Ave Los Angeles (90038) *(P-19218)*

Alan Johnson Prfmce Engrg Inc E 305 922-1202
1097 Foxen Canyon Rd Santa Maria (93454) *(P-9932)*

Alan Lem & Co Inc E 310 538-4282
515 W 130th St Los Angeles (90061) *(P-5945)*

Alan Pre-Fab Building Corp F 310 538-0333
17817 Evelyn Ave Gardena (90248) *(P-3427)*

Alan Smith Pool Plastering Inc D 714 628-9494
227 W Carleton Ave Orange (92867) *(P-1360)*

Alard Machine Products, Gardena *Also called GT Precision Inc (P-7037)*

Alarin Aircraft Hinge Inc E 323 725-1666
6231 Randolph St Commerce (90040) *(P-6497)*

Alaska Diesel Electric C 626 934-6211
425 S Hacienda Blvd City of Industry (91745) *(P-18892)*

Alatus Aerosystems, Brea *Also called Aerospace Systems Strctres LLC (P-10255)*

Alatus Aerosystems (PA) A **610 965-1630**
423 Berry Way Brea (92821) *(P-10262)*

Alatus Aerosystems D 714 732-0559
423 Berry Way Brea (92821) *(P-10263)*

Alatus Aerosystems D 626 498-7376
423 Berry Way Brea (92821) *(P-10264)*

Albd Electric and Cable D 949 440-1216
995 E Discovery Ln Anaheim (92801) *(P-1211)*

Albers Dairy Equipment. Inc, Chino *Also called Albers Mfg Co Inc (P-7603)*

Albers Mfg Co Inc (PA) E **909 597-5537**
14323 Albers Way Chino (91710) *(P-7603)*

Albert & Mackenzie LLP (PA) C **818 575-9876**
28216 Dorothy Dr Ste 200 Agoura Hills (91301) *(P-21501)*

Albert A Webb Associates (PA) C **951 686-1070**
3788 Mccray St Riverside (92506) *(P-22482)*

Albert's Organics - West, Vernon *Also called Alberts Organics Inc (P-14452)*

Alberts Organics Inc D 323 587-6367
3268 E Vernon Ave Vernon (90058) *(P-14452)*

Albertsons - Savon 6153, Torrance *Also called New Albertsons Inc (P-18420)*

Albertsons 6376, Ridgecrest *Also called Albertsons LLC (P-1979)*

Albertsons 6514, Riverside *Also called Albertsons LLC (P-1978)*

Albertsons 6798, Lake Elsinore *Also called Albertsons LLC (P-2055)*

Albertsons Brea Dist Ctr, Brea *Also called Albertsons LLC (P-12184)*

Albertsons LLC C 951 656-6603
8938 Trautwein Rd Ste A Riverside (92508) *(P-1978)*

Albertsons LLC C 951 245-4461
30901 Riverside Dr Lake Elsinore (92530) *(P-2055)*

Albertsons LLC A 714 990-8200
200 N Puente St Brea (92821) *(P-12184)*

Albertsons LLC C 760 446-2544
1301 N Norma St Ridgecrest (93555) *(P-1979)*

Albion Knitting Mills Inc F 213 624-7740
2152 Sacramento St Los Angeles (90021) *(P-2914)*

Alcast Mfg Inc (PA) E **310 542-3581**
7355 E Slauson Ave Commerce (90040) *(P-6384)*

Alcast Mfg Inc E 310 542-3581
2910 Fisk Ln Redondo Beach (90278) *(P-6373)*

Alcatraz Brewing Company, Orange *Also called Tavistock Restaurants LLC (P-2156)*

Alco Designs, Gardena *Also called Vege-Mist Inc (P-8355)*

Alco Engrg & Tooling Corp E 714 556-6060
3001 Oak St Santa Ana (92707) *(P-8484)*

Alco Manufacturing Inc F 714 549-5007
207 E Alton Ave Santa Ana (92707) *(P-7774)*

Alco Metal Fab, Santa Ana *Also called Alco Engrg & Tooling Corp (P-3484)*

Alco Plating Corp (PA) E **213 749-7561**
1400 Long Beach Ave Los Angeles (90021) *(P-7202)*

Alco Service, Los Angeles *Also called Automatic Leasing Inc (P-13681)*

Alco Tech Inc E 818 503-9209
12750 Raymer St Unit 2 North Hollywood (91605) *(P-7121)*

Alcoa Fastening Systems D 909 483-2333
11711 Arrow Rte Rancho Cucamonga (91730) *(P-11493)*

Alcoholism Center For Women E 213 381-8500
1147 S Alvarado St Los Angeles (90006) *(P-21710)*

Alcon Lensx Inc (HQ) C **949 753-1393**
15800 Alton Pkwy Irvine (92618) *(P-10926)*

Alcon Manufacturing Ltd (PA) C **949 753-1393**
15800 Alton Pkwy Irvine (92618) *(P-4777)*

Alcon Surgical, Irvine *Also called Alcon Vision LLC (P-10928)*

Mergent e-mail: customerrelations@mergent.com
1048
2022 Southern California Business Directory and Buyers Guide
(P-0000) Products & Services Section entry number
(PA)=Parent Co (HQ)=Headquarters (DH)=Div Headquarters

Alcon Vision LLC C 949 753-6218
24514 Sunshine Dr Laguna Niguel (92677) *(P-10927)*
Alcon Vision LLC B 949 505-6890
20521 Lake Forest Dr Lake Forest (92630) *(P-22928)*
Alcon Vision LLC A 949 753-6488
15800 Alton Pkwy Irvine (92618) *(P-10928)*
Alcone Marketing Group Inc (HQ) **D 949 595-5322**
4 Studebaker Irvine (92618) *(P-16992)*
Alcorn Fence Company (PA) **D 818 983-0650**
9901 Glenoaks Blvd Sun Valley (91352) *(P-1633)*
Alcott Ctr For Mntal Hlth Svcs C 310 785-2121
1433 S Robertson Blvd Los Angeles (90035) *(P-21271)*
Alder & Co LLC F 661 326-0320
412 Wallace St Bakersfield (93307) *(P-3460)*
Alderwood Group LLC (PA) **D 909 866-6445**
42184 Moonridge Way 1 Big Bear Lake (92315) *(P-22970)*
Aldo Fragale E 310 324-0050
17813 S Main St Ste 111 Gardena (90248) *(P-8485)*
Aldoc Inc D 714 836-8477
910 E Orangefair Ln Anaheim (92801) *(P-1022)*
Aldon Ter Convalsent Hosptial, Los Angeles *Also called Longwood Management Corp (P-20604)*
Ale USA Inc A 818 878-4816
26801 Agoura Rd Calabasas (91301) *(P-9250)*
Alectro Inc F 909 590-9521
6770 Central Ave Ste B Riverside (92504) *(P-8862)*
Aleeda Wetsuits, Huntington Beach *Also called Sgt Boardriders Inc (P-5410)*
Alegacy Fdsrvice Pdts Group In D 562 320-3100
12683 Corral Pl Santa Fe Springs (90670) *(P-3721)*
Alejandro Medina, San Bernardino *Also called Medina Concrete Construction (P-1540)*
Aleksandar Inc F 310 516-7700
1542 W 130th St Gardena (90249) *(P-1424)*
Alene Le DDS MS Inc (PA) **D 626 332-6291**
511 E 1st St Ste C Tustin (92780) *(P-20169)*
Aleph Group Inc E 951 213-4815
1900 E Alessndro Blvd # 105 Riverside (92508) *(P-9933)*
Aleph Group Inc F 951 213-4815
6920 Sycamore Canyon Blvd Riverside (92507) *(P-10929)*
Alere San Diego Inc F 909 482-0840
829 Towne Center Dr Pomona (91767) *(P-4917)*
Alerion Aviation, Long Beach *Also called Air Rutter International LLC (P-12334)*
Alert Communications, Camarillo *Also called Affiliated Communications Inc (P-18436)*
Alert Insulation Company Inc D 626 961-9113
15913 Old Valley Blvd A La Puente (91744) *(P-1361)*
Alert Plating Company E 818 771-9304
9939 Glenoaks Blvd Sun Valley (91352) *(P-7203)*
Alex A Khadavi MD Inc E 818 528-2500
16260 Ventura Blvd # 140 Encino (91436) *(P-19688)*
Alex Velvet Inc F 323 255-6900
3334 Eagle Rock Blvd Los Angeles (90065) *(P-11307)*
Alexander Becker Carpets, Los Angeles *Also called Becker Interiors Ltd (P-13159)*
Alexander Henry Fabrics Inc E 818 562-8200
1550 Flower St Glendale (91201) *(P-14302)*
Alexander's Grand Salon & Spa, Anaheim *Also called Alexanders Grand Salon (P-16895)*
Alexanders Grand Salon D 714 282-6438
5579 E Santa Ana Cyn Rd Anaheim (92807) *(P-16895)*
Alexis Oil Company, Corona *Also called Dal Chem Inc (P-14795)*
Alexs Tile Works Inc E 805 967-5308
208b N Calle Cesar Chavez Santa Barbara (93103) *(P-1410)*
Alflex, Compton *Also called Southwire Inc (P-6302)*
Alfred Domaine F 805 541-9463
7525 Orcutt Rd San Luis Obispo (93401) *(P-2165)*
Alfred Louie Incorporated F 661 831-2520
4501 Shepard St Bakersfield (93313) *(P-2388)*
Alfred Music Group Inc (PA) **C 818 891-5999**
16320 Roscoe Blvd Ste 100 Van Nuys (91406) *(P-4119)*
Alger International, Los Angeles *Also called Alger-Triton Inc (P-9056)*
Alger Precision Machining LLC C 909 986-4591
724 S Bon View Ave Ontario (91761) *(P-7029)*
Alger-Triton Inc E 310 229-9500
5600 W Jefferson Blvd Los Angeles (90016) *(P-9056)*
Algos Inc A Medical Corp (PA) **D 626 696-1400**
224 N Fair Oaks Ave Pasadena (91103) *(P-21272)*
Alhambra Foundry Company Ltd E 626 289-4294
1147 S Meridian Ave Alhambra (91803) *(P-6256)*
Alhambra Hospital Med Ctr LP C 626 570-1606
100 S Raymond Ave Alhambra (91801) *(P-20669)*
Alhambra Hospital Medical Ctr, Alhambra *Also called Alhambra Hospital Med Ctr LP (P-20669)*
Ali & Jay, Vernon *Also called Bailey 44 LLC (P-2836)*
Aliantel Inc D 714 829-1650
1940 W Corporate Way Anaheim (92801) *(P-23407)*
Alice G Fink-Painter, Santa Fe Springs *Also called Spec Tool Company (P-10422)*
Align Aerospace LLC (PA) **B 818 727-7800**
9401 De Soto Ave Chatsworth (91311) *(P-10265)*
Alignmed Inc F 866 987-5433
1936 E Deere Ave Ste 115 Santa Ana (92705) *(P-11084)*
Alignment Health Plan D 323 728-7232
1100 W Town & Country Orange (92868) *(P-15386)*
Alignment Healthcare Inc A 844 310-2247
1100 W Twn Cntry Rd Orange (92868) *(P-15387)*
Alignment Healthcare USA LLC (PA) **D 844 310-2247**
1100 W Twn Cntry Rd Orange (92868) *(P-21373)*
Alin Party Supply Co E 951 682-7441
6493 Magnolia Ave Riverside (92506) *(P-18439)*
Alisal Guest Ranch, Solvang *Also called Alisal Properties (P-16816)*
Alisal Properties (PA) **C 805 688-6411**
1054 Alisal Rd Solvang (93463) *(P-16816)*

Aliso Air Conditioning & Htg, Rancho Santa Margari *Also called Jct Company LLC (P-1086)*
Aliso Viejo Medical Offices, Aliso Viejo *Also called Kaiser Foundation Hospitals (P-19860)*
Aliso Viejo Stadium Cinemas 10, Aliso Viejo *Also called Edwards Theatres Circuit Inc (P-19275)*
Alj, Camarillo *Also called Gc International Inc (P-6396)*
All About Printing, Canoga Park *Also called Barrys Printing Inc (P-4236)*
All About Produce Inc C 805 543-9000
712 Fiero Ln Ste 30 San Luis Obispo (93401) *(P-14613)*
All Access Apparel Inc (PA) **C 323 889-4300**
1515 Gage Rd Montebello (90640) *(P-3027)*
All Access Stging Prdctons Inc (PA) **D 310 784-2464**
1320 Storm Pkwy Torrance (90501) *(P-9121)*
All American Agrigate, Corona *Also called All American Asphalt (P-853)*
All American Asphalt (PA) **D 951 736-7600**
400 E 6th St Corona (92879) *(P-853)*
All American Asphalt D 951 736-7617
1776 All American Way Corona (92879) *(P-854)*
All American Asphalt D 818 361-6141
11549 Bradley Ave San Fernando (91340) *(P-855)*
All American Asphalt D 951 736-7617
1776 All American Way Corona (92879) *(P-856)*
All American Cabinetry Inc E 818 376-0500
13901 Saticoy St Van Nuys (91402) *(P-3636)*
All American Decorative Con, Irvine *Also called Home Franchise Concepts LLC (P-1530)*
All American Fabricators, Vernon *Also called Donald O Smith Company (P-13804)*
All American Frame & Bedg Corp F 323 773-7415
4641 Ardine St Cudahy (90201) *(P-3524)*
All American Pipe Bending, Santa Ana *Also called Saf-T-Co Supply (P-9053)*
All American Racers Inc C 714 557-2116
2334 S Broadway Santa Ana (92707) *(P-10480)*
All American Sterile Coat, Van Nuys *Also called All American Cabinetry Inc (P-3636)*
All Amrcan Injction Mlding Svc, Temecula *Also called TST Molding LLC (P-5845)*
All Care Home Health Provider D 818 241-2473
1218 E Broadway Glendale (91205) *(P-21130)*
All Care Medical Group Inc D 408 278-3550
31 Crescent St Huntington Park (90255) *(P-19689)*
All Cartage Transportation Inc (PA) **D 310 970-0600**
12621 Chadron Ave Hawthorne (90250) *(P-12105)*
All Counties, Santa Ana *Also called Larry Mthvin Installations Inc (P-13332)*
All Counties Courier Inc C 714 599-9300
1642 Kaiser Ave Irvine (92614) *(P-12123)*
All Diameter Grinding Inc E 714 744-1200
725 N Main St Orange (92868) *(P-8486)*
All For Hlth Hlth For All Inc (PA) **C 818 409-3020**
519 E Broadway Glendale (91205) *(P-19690)*
All Health Services Corp (PA) **D 559 583-9101**
11104 Bonneyview Ln Hanford (93230) *(P-17389)*
All Integrated Solutions LLC F 951 817-3328
2900 Palisades Dr Corona (92878) *(P-11399)*
All Manufacturers Inc C 951 280-4200
1831 Commerce St Ste 101 Corona (92878) *(P-10930)*
All Metals Proc San Diego Inc C 714 828-8238
8401 Standustrial St Stanton (90680) *(P-7204)*
All Mtals Proc Orange Cnty LLC C 714 828-8238
8401 Standustrial St Stanton (90680) *(P-7205)*
All New Stamping Co C 626 443-8813
10801 Lower Azusa Rd El Monte (91731) *(P-7122)*
All Nuts and Snacks Inc F 818 367-5902
12910 San Fernando Rd Sylmar (91342) *(P-14554)*
All Power Manufacturing Co E 562 802-2640
13141 Molette St Santa Fe Springs (90670) *(P-10266)*
All Racks Solutions, Los Angeles *Also called Vescio Enterprises Inc (P-13960)*
ALl Roofg Mtls Long Bch Inc D 805 656-6319
1435 Walter St Ventura (93003) *(P-13323)*
ALl Roofg Mtls Long Bch Inc D 562 595-7377
3100 Orange Ave Long Beach (90755) *(P-13324)*
All Seasons Framing Corp E 714 634-2324
1022 Fuller St Santa Ana (92701) *(P-1425)*
All Spec Welding Solutions F 909 794-4828
10406 Enterprise St Rancho Cucamonga (91730) *(P-18969)*
All Star Precision E 909 944-8373
8739 Lion St Rancho Cucamonga (91730) *(P-8487)*
All State Association Inc C 877 425-2558
11487 San Fernando Rd San Fernando (91340) *(P-22242)*
All Strong Industry (usa) Inc (PA) **E 909 598-6494**
326 Paseo Tesoro Walnut (91789) *(P-3705)*
All Technology Machine, Irvine *Also called Lubrication Scientifics Inc (P-7450)*
All Tmperatures Controlled Inc D 818 882-1478
9720 Topanga Canyon Pl Chatsworth (91311) *(P-1023)*
All Valley Washer Service Inc D 818 787-1100
15008 Delano St Van Nuys (91411) *(P-16871)*
All Wall Inc D 760 600-5108
46150 Commerce St Ste 102 Indio (92201) *(P-1362)*
All West Plastics Inc E 714 894-9922
5451 Argosy Ave Huntington Beach (92649) *(P-5443)*
All Year Roofing Inc D 310 851-9440
16828 S Broadway Gardena (90248) *(P-1473)*
All's Well Healthcare Staffing, Glendale *Also called Alls Well Inc (P-17390)*
All-American Mfg Co F 323 581-6293
2201 E 51st St Vernon (90058) *(P-6551)*
All-City Management Svcs Inc (PA) **A 310 202-8284**
10440 Pioneer Blvd Ste 5 Santa Fe Springs (90670) *(P-23408)*
All-In Prdctons Csino Rntals L D 866 875-8628
7222 Garden Grove Blvd Westminster (92683) *(P-17332)*
All-Power Plastcs Div Dial, Los Angeles *Also called Dial Industries Inc (P-5626)*
All-Rite Leasing Company Inc B 714 957-1822
950 S Coast Dr Ste 110 Costa Mesa (92626) *(P-17213)*

ALPHABETIC

All-Star Lettering Inc ....E 562 404-5995
9419 Ann St Santa Fe Springs (90670) ***(P-4478)***
All-Ways Metal Inc ....E 310 217-1177
401 E Alondra Blvd Gardena (90248) ***(P-6778)***
All3media America LLC (HQ) ....D **424 732-6600**
6060 Center Dr Ste 400 Los Angeles (90045) ***(P-19092)***
All4-Pcb (north America) Inc ....F 866 734-9403
345 Mira Loma Ave Glendale (91204) ***(P-8488)***
Allagash Industries Inc ....F 212 246-5757
1656 Sargent Pl Los Angeles (90026) ***(P-11628)***
Allan Aircraft Supply Co LLC ....E 818 765-4992
11643 Vanowen St North Hollywood (91605) ***(P-7469)***
Allan Company, Baldwin Park *Also called Cedarwood-Young Company* ***(P-12937)***
Allan Company, Baldwin Park *Also called Cedarwood-Young Company* ***(P-14112)***
Allan Kidd ....E 310 762-1600
3115 E Las Hermanas St Compton (90221) ***(P-9026)***
Allaquaria LLC ....D 310 645-1107
5420 W 104th St Los Angeles (90045) ***(P-14909)***
Allblack Co Inc ....E 562 946-2955
13090 Park St Santa Fe Springs (90670) ***(P-7206)***
Allbright Group La LLC ....E 310 402-3570
8474 Melrose Pl Los Angeles (90069) ***(P-22395)***
Alldigital Holdings Inc ....F 949 250-7340
1405 Warner Ave Ste A Tustin (92780) ***(P-17780)***
Allegretto Vineyard Resort, Paso Robles *Also called Ayres - Paso Robles LP* ***(P-16332)***
Allegro Pacific Corporation ....F 323 724-0101
7250 Oxford Way Commerce (90040) ***(P-5905)***
Allen Development Partners LLC (PA) ....D **559 732-5425**
125 Sbridge 100 Visalia (93291) ***(P-16046)***
Allen Gwynn Chevrolet Inc ....D 818 240-0000
1400 S Brand Blvd Glendale (91204) ***(P-18747)***
Allen Lund Company LLC (HQ) ....D **818 790-8412**
4529 Angeles Crest Hwy La Canada Flintridge (91011) ***(P-12419)***
Allen Lund Corporation (PA) ....E **818 790-8412**
4529 Angeles Crest Hwy La Canada Flintridge (91011) ***(P-12420)***
Allen Media LLC (HQ) ....C **310 277-3500**
1925 Century Park E Fl 10 Los Angeles (90067) ***(P-19342)***
Allen Mold Inc ....F 714 538-6517
1100 W Katella Ave Ste N Orange (92867) ***(P-5552)***
Allen Mtkins Leck Gmble Mllory (PA) ....C **213 622-5555**
865 S Figueroa St # 2800 Los Angeles (90017) ***(P-21502)***
Allen United Inc ....F 562 944-5650
12711 Imperial Hwy Santa Fe Springs (90670) ***(P-5553)***
Allen/Clark Cadillac ....D 626 966-7441
2700 E Garvey Ave S West Covina (91791) ***(P-18920)***
Allergan Sales LLC (HQ) ....A **862 261-7000**
2525 Dupont Dr Irvine (92612) ***(P-4778)***
Allergan Spclty Thrpeutics Inc ....A 714 246-4500
2525 Dupont Dr Irvine (92612) ***(P-4779)***
Allergan Usa Inc ....A 714 427-1900
18581 Teller Ave Irvine (92612) ***(P-4780)***
Allergy & Asthma Assoc Cal ....D 949 364-2900
27800 Med Ctr Rd Ste 244 Mission Viejo (92691) ***(P-19691)***
Allesandro Automatic Inc ....F 323 663-8253
1146 N Central Ave Glendale (91202) ***(P-8489)***
Allfast Fastening Systems LLC ....D 626 968-9388
15200 Don Julian Rd City of Industry (91745) ***(P-13790)***
Allhealth ....F 213 538-0762
515 S Figueroa St # 1300 Los Angeles (90071) ***(P-8147)***
Alliance Apparel Inc ....E 323 888-8900
3422 Garfield Ave Commerce (90040) ***(P-2834)***
Alliance Capital Markets, Tustin *Also called Alliance Funding Group* ***(P-22971)***
Alliance Chemical & Envmtl ....F 805 385-3330
1721 Ives Ave Oxnard (93033) ***(P-7207)***
Alliance Childrens Services ....C 661 863-0350
1001 Tower Way Ste 110 Bakersfield (93309) ***(P-22079)***
Alliance Construction, Costa Mesa *Also called Empire Leasing Inc* ***(P-1434)***
Alliance Finishing and Mfg, Oxnard *Also called Alliance Chemical & Envmtl* ***(P-7207)***
Alliance For Housing & Healing (PA) ....D **323 344-4885**
825 Colorado Blvd Ste 100 Los Angeles (90041) ***(P-20520)***
Alliance Funding Group (PA) ....D **800 978-8817**
17542 17th St Ste 200 Tustin (92780) ***(P-22971)***
Alliance Ground Intl LLC ....C 310 646-2446
6181 W Imperial Hwy Los Angeles (90045) ***(P-12339)***
Alliance Healthcare Svcs Inc (HQ) ....C **949 242-5300**
18201 Von Karman Ave # 6 Irvine (92612) ***(P-21058)***
Alliance Medical Products Inc (HQ) ....C **949 768-4690**
9342 Jeronimo Rd Irvine (92618) ***(P-10931)***
Alliance Metal Products Inc ....C 818 709-1204
20844 Plummer St Chatsworth (91311) ***(P-6779)***
Alliance Nrsing Rhbltation Ctr, El Monte *Also called Georgia Atkison Snf LLC* ***(P-20358)***
Alliance Oncology LLC (HQ) ....E **949 242-5345**
100 Bayview Cir Ste 400 Newport Beach (92660) ***(P-19692)***
Alliance Protection Service ....E 760 347-3747
45130 Golf Center Pkwy A Indio (92201) ***(P-732)***
Alliance Ready Mix Inc (PA) ....D **805 343-0360**
915 Sheridan Rd Arroyo Grande (93420) ***(P-6066)***
Alliance Residential LLC ....C 818 841-2441
1200 W Riverside Dr Ofc Burbank (91506) ***(P-15657)***
Alliance Spacesystems, Los Alamitos *Also called Vanguard Space Tech Inc* ***(P-22689)***
Alliance Spacesystems LLC ....C 714 226-1400
4398 Corporate Center Dr Los Alamitos (90720) ***(P-8936)***
Alliance Title, Glendale *Also called Wfg National Title Insur Co* ***(P-15513)***
Alliant Asset MGT Co LLC (PA) ....D **818 668-2805**
21600 Oxnard St Ste 1200 Woodland Hills (91367) ***(P-15766)***
Alliant Insurance Services Inc (PA) ....C **949 756-0271**
1301 Dove St Ste 200 Newport Beach (92660) ***(P-23409)***
Alliant Tchsystems Oprtons LLC ....E 818 887-8185
21250 Califa St Woodland Hills (91367) ***(P-10562)***
Alliant Tchsystems Oprtons LLC ....B 818 887-8195
9401 Corbin Ave Northridge (91324) ***(P-10563)***
Alliant Tchsystems Oprtons LLC ....E 818 887-8195
9401 Corbin Ave Northridge (91324) ***(P-10564)***
Allianz Asset MGT Amer LLC (HQ) ....D **949 219-2200**
650 Newport Center Dr Newport Beach (92660) ***(P-16119)***
Allianz Globl Corp & Specialty, Burbank *Also called Allianz Underwriters Insur Co* ***(P-15464)***
Allianz Globl Invstors Amer LP (HQ) ....D **310 549-0729**
104 E 213th St Carson (90745) ***(P-16246)***
Allianz Globl Invstors Cpitl L ....D 949 219-2200
680 Nwport Ctr Dr Ste 250 Newport Beach (92660) ***(P-16120)***
Allianz Globl Risks US Insur (HQ) ....C **818 260-7500**
2350 W Empire Ave Burbank (91504) ***(P-15463)***
Allianz Insurance Company, Burbank *Also called Allianz Globl Risks US Insur* ***(P-15463)***
Allianz Underwriters Insur Co ....D 818 260-7500
2350 W Empire Ave Ste 200 Burbank (91504) ***(P-15464)***
Allied Artists International, City of Industry *Also called Allied Entertainment Group Inc* ***(P-19093)***
Allied Avocados & Citrus Inc ....D 805 625-7155
1203 S Sespe St Fillmore (93015) ***(P-160)***
Allied Bio Medical, Ventura *Also called Implantech Associates Inc* ***(P-11114)***
Allied Company Holdings Inc (PA) ....B **818 493-6400**
13235 Golden State Rd Sylmar (91342) ***(P-14819)***
Allied Components Intl ....E 949 356-1780
19671 Descartes Foothill Ranch (92610) ***(P-9619)***
Allied Construction Services ....E 951 405-3193
4740 Green Rver Rd Ste 10 Corona (92878) ***(P-591)***
Allied Digital Services LLC (HQ) ....C **310 431-2375**
680 Knox St Ste 200 Torrance (90502) ***(P-18138)***
Allied Electronic Services Inc ....E 714 245-2500
1342 E Borchard Ave Santa Ana (92705) ***(P-9374)***
Allied Entertainment Group Inc (PA) ....B **626 330-0600**
273 W Allen Ave City of Industry (91746) ***(P-19093)***
Allied Environmental Services, Woodland Hills *Also called Allied Industries Inc* ***(P-23410)***
Allied Farming Company, Exeter *Also called Sun Pacific Farming Coop Inc* ***(P-229)***
Allied Guard Services Inc (PA) ....D **424 227-9912**
110 S La Brea Ave Ste 425 Inglewood (90301) ***(P-18240)***
Allied Harbor Aerospace Fas, Corona *Also called All Manufacturers Inc* ***(P-10930)***
Allied High Tech Products Inc ....D 310 635-2466
2376 E Pacifica Pl Rancho Dominguez (90220) ***(P-13970)***
Allied Industries Inc (PA) ....C **800 605-5323**
21650 Oxnard St Ste 500 Woodland Hills (91367) ***(P-23410)***
Allied International LLC (PA) ....E **818 364-2333**
28955 Avenue Sherman Valencia (91355) ***(P-13791)***
Allied Litho Products, Los Angeles *Also called Allied Pressroom Products Inc* ***(P-11466)***
Allied Lube Inc ....D 949 651-8814
3087 Edinger Ave Tustin (92780) ***(P-18813)***
Allied Mdular Bldg Systems Inc (PA) ....E **714 516-1188**
642 W Nicolas Ave Orange (92868) ***(P-6986)***
Allied Mechanical Products, Ontario *Also called Tower Mechanical Products Inc* ***(P-10649)***
Allied Mechanical Products, Ontario *Also called Tower Industries Inc* ***(P-8823)***
Allied Merchandising Industry, Corona *Also called Core-Mark Intrrlted Cmpnies In* ***(P-14923)***
Allied Plumbing & Fire Supply, Sun Valley *Also called Plumbingandfire Inc* ***(P-13835)***
Allied Pressroom Products Inc ....F 323 266-6250
3546 Emery St Los Angeles (90023) ***(P-11466)***
Allied Prof Nursing Care Inc ....D 909 949-1066
2345 W Fthlls Blvd Ste 14 Upland (91786) ***(P-21131)***
Allied Protection Services Inc ....C 310 330-8314
19164 Van Ness Ave Torrance (90501) ***(P-18241)***
Allied Refrigeration Inc (PA) ....D **562 595-5301**
2300 E 28th St Signal Hill (90755) ***(P-13840)***
Allied Signal Aerospace, Torrance *Also called Alliedsignal Arospc Svc Corp* ***(P-6411)***
Allied Steel Co Inc ....D 951 241-7000
1027 Palmyrita Ave Riverside (92507) ***(P-1564)***
Allied Trading Group Inc ....E 818 576-9277
8966 Mason Ave Chatsworth (91311) ***(P-23151)***
Allied Universal, Santa Ana *Also called Universal Services America LP* ***(P-18354)***
Allied Universal Event Svcs, Fullerton *Also called Staff Pro Inc* ***(P-18402)***
Allied Universal Security Svcs, Santa Ana *Also called Universal Protection Svc LP* ***(P-18351)***
Allied West Paper Corp ....D 909 349-0710
11101 Etiwanda Ave # 100 Fontana (92337) ***(P-3747)***
Allied Wheel Components Inc ....E 714 893-4160
12300 Edison Way Garden Grove (92841) ***(P-10015)***
Alliedsignal Arospc Svc Corp (HQ) ....D **310 323-9500**
2525 W 190th St Torrance (90504) ***(P-6411)***
Allies For Every Child Inc ....D 310 846-4100
5721 W Slauson Ave # 200 Culver City (90230) ***(P-21982)***
Allison-Kaufman Co ....E 818 373-5100
7640 Haskell Ave Van Nuys (91406) ***(P-11308)***
Allman Products Inc ....E 818 715-0093
21251 Deering Ct Canoga Park (91304) ***(P-5486)***
Allmark Inc (PA) ....D **909 989-7556**
10070 Arrow Rte Rancho Cucamonga (91730) ***(P-15767)***
Alloy Die Casting Co ....C 714 521-9800
6550 Caballero Blvd Buena Park (90620) ***(P-6362)***
Alloy Machining and Honing Inc ....E 323 726-8248
2808 Supply Ave Commerce (90040) ***(P-8490)***
Alloy Machining Services Inc ....F 323 725-2545
2808 Supply Ave Commerce (90040) ***(P-8491)***
Alloy Processing, Compton *Also called Kens Spray Equipment Inc* ***(P-7380)***
Alls Well Inc (PA) ....D **818 240-8688**
327 W Broadway Glendale (91204) ***(P-17390)***
Allsale Electric Inc ....D 818 715-0181
9261 Jordan Ave Chatsworth (91311) ***(P-13611)***
Allstar Home Services, Rancho Cucamonga *Also called Infinity Svc Group Inc A Cal C* ***(P-1084)***

Allstar Microelectronics Inc ....F....949 546-0888
30191 Avendia De Las Rancho Santa Margari (92688) ***(P-8187)***
Allstarshop.com, Rancho Santa Margari *Also called Allstar Microelectronics Inc* ***(P-8187)***
Allstate, Corona *Also called Acm Technologies Inc* ***(P-13350)***
Allstate Communications, Agoura Hills *Also called Allstate Technologies Inc* ***(P-12625)***
Allstate Floral Inc ....C....562 926-2989
15928 Commerce Way Cerritos (90703) ***(P-15530)***
Allstate Imaging Inc (PA) ....**D....818 678-4550**
21621 Nordhoff St Chatsworth (91311) ***(P-13351)***
Allstate Technologies Inc (PA) ....**D....818 889-7600**
5699 Kanan Rd Ste 455 Agoura Hills (91301) ***(P-12625)***
Alltec Integrated Mfg Inc ....E....805 595-3500
2240 S Thornburg St Santa Maria (93455) ***(P-5554)***
Alltech Industries Inc ....E....323 450-2168
301 E Pomona Blvd Monterey Park (91755) ***(P-1212)***
Alltek Company U S A Inc ....E....714 375-9785
18281 Gothard St Ste 102 Huntington Beach (92648) ***(P-13883)***
Alltrade Tools LLC ....E....310 522-9008
6122 Katella Ave Cypress (90630) ***(P-13792)***
Allure Medical Staffing Inc ....D....888 310-1020
23152 Verdugo Dr Ste 120 Laguna Hills (92653) ***(P-21374)***
Ally Enterprises ....E....661 412-9933
5001 E Commercecenter Dr # 260 Bakersfield (93309) ***(P-475)***
Allzone Management Solutions, Los Angeles *Also called Allzone Management Svcs Inc* ***(P-22972)***
Allzone Management Svcs Inc ....B....213 291-8879
3700 Wilshire Blvd # 979 Los Angeles (90010) ***(P-22972)***
Almack Liners Inc ....E....818 718-5878
9541 Cozycroft Ave Chatsworth (91311) ***(P-2876)***
Almatron Electronics Inc ....E....714 557-6000
644 Young St Santa Ana (92705) ***(P-9375)***
ALMAVIA OF CAMARILLO, Camarillo *Also called Elder Care Alliance Camarillo* ***(P-22101)***
Almore Dye House Inc ....E....818 506-5444
6850 Tujunga Ave North Hollywood (91605) ***(P-2668)***
Alna Envelope Company Inc ....F....323 235-3161
1567 E 25th St Los Angeles (90011) ***(P-4465)***
Aloft Ontario-Rancho Cucamonga ....D....909 484-2018
10480 4th St Rancho Cucamonga (91730) ***(P-16317)***
Alorica Inc (PA) ....**D....949 527-4600**
5161 California Ave # 100 Irvine (92617) ***(P-18440)***
Alpargatas Usa Inc ....E....646 277-7171
513 Boccaccio Ave Venice (90291) ***(P-5878)***
Alpase, Chino *Also called Tst Inc* ***(P-6297)***
Alpena Sausage Inc ....F....818 505-9482
5329 Craner Ave North Hollywood (91601) ***(P-1726)***
ALPERT JEWISH COMMUNITY CENTRE, Long Beach *Also called Jewish Community Ctr Long Bch* ***(P-21820)***
Alpha Aviation Components Inc (PA) ....**E....818 894-8801**
16772 Schoenborn St North Hills (91343) ***(P-8492)***
Alpha Corporation of Tennessee ....C....951 657-5161
19991 Seaton Ave Perris (92570) ***(P-4677)***
Alpha Dental of Utah Inc ....E....562 467-7759
12898 Towne Center Dr Cerritos (90703) ***(P-11159)***
Alpha Dyno Nobel ....F....661 824-1356
1682 Sabovich St Bldg A Mojave (93501) ***(P-5200)***
Alpha Explosives, Mojave *Also called Alpha Dyno Nobel* ***(P-5200)***
Alpha Grinding Inc ....F....562 803-1509
12402 Benedict Ave Downey (90242) ***(P-8493)***
Alpha Imaging Technology ....F....626 330-0808
16453 Old Valley Blvd City of Industry (91744) ***(P-13470)***
Alpha Laser ....F....951 582-0285
1801 Railroad St Corona (92878) ***(P-9852)***
Alpha Materials Inc ....E....951 788-5150
6170 20th St Riverside (92509) ***(P-6067)***
Alpha Omega Cmpt Ntwrk Svcs In ....F....714 962-3129
20042 Beach Blvd Ste 202 Huntington Beach (92648) ***(P-18141)***
Alpha Omega Swiss Inc ....F....714 692-8009
23305 La Palma Ave Yorba Linda (92887) ***(P-7030)***
Alpha Polishing Corporation (PA) ....**D....323 263-7593**
1313 Mirasol St Los Angeles (90023) ***(P-7208)***
Alpha Printing & Graphics Inc ....E....626 851-9800
12758 Schabarum Ave Irwindale (91706) ***(P-4225)***
Alpha Productions Incorporated ....F....310 559-1364
5830 W Jefferson Blvd # 1 Los Angeles (90016) ***(P-6780)***
Alpha Products Inc ....E....805 981-8666
351 Irving Dr Oxnard (93030) ***(P-9647)***
Alpha Professional Resources, Thousand Oaks *Also called A P R Inc* ***(P-17483)***
Alpha Soft Support LLC ....D....857 219-5505
8605 Santa Monica Blvd West Hollywood (90069) ***(P-17545)***
Alpha Source Inc ....D....424 270-9600
10940 Wilshire Blvd # 15 Los Angeles (90024) ***(P-22822)***
Alpha Star Corporation ....E....562 961-7827
2601 Main St Ste 660 Irvine (92614) ***(P-17781)***
Alpha-Owens Corning, Perris *Also called Alpha Corporation of Tennessee* ***(P-4677)***
Alphaeon Corporation (HQ) ....**D....949 284-4555**
17901 Von Karman Ave # 150 Irvine (92614) ***(P-13471)***
Alphalogix Inc ....F....714 901-1456
5811 Mcfadden Ave Huntington Beach (92649) ***(P-9833)***
Alpine Camp Conference Ctr Inc ....D....909 337-6287
415 Clubhouse Dr Blue Jay (92317) ***(P-19632)***
Alpine Carpets, Culver City *Also called Alpine Interiors Corporation* ***(P-13156)***
Alpine Electronics America Inc (HQ) ....**C....310 326-8000**
2150 195th St Torrance (90501) ***(P-13680)***
Alpine Inn Restaurant, Torrance *Also called Alpine Village* ***(P-15658)***
Alpine Interiors Corporation (PA) ....**E....310 390-7639**
3961 Sepulveda Blvd # 205 Culver City (90230) ***(P-13156)***
Alpine Village ....C....310 327-4384
833 Torrance Blvd Ste 1a Torrance (90502) ***(P-15658)***
Alpinestars USA ....D....310 891-0222
2780 W 237th St Torrance (90505) ***(P-2835)***
Alquest Technologies Inc ....D....909 592-8708
1760 Yeager Ave La Verne (91750) ***(P-18142)***
Als Garden Art Inc (PA) ....**B....909 424-0221**
311 W Citrus St Colton (92324) ***(P-6176)***
Als Group Inc ....E....909 622-7555
1788 W 2nd St Pomona (91766) ***(P-13793)***
Als Group Usa Corp ....D....310 214-0043
3904 Del Amo Blvd Ste 801 Torrance (90503) ***(P-22929)***
Alsana, Thousand Oaks *Also called Castlewood Treatment Ctr LLC* ***(P-21283)***
Alstom Signaling Operation LLC ....C....951 343-9699
7337 Central Ave Riverside (92504) ***(P-12562)***
Alston & Bird LLP ....D....213 576-1000
333 S Hope St Ste 1600 Los Angeles (90071) ***(P-21503)***
Alston & Bird LLP ....D....202 239-3673
2815 Townsgate Rd Ste 200 Westlake Village (91361) ***(P-21504)***
Alston Tascom Inc ....F....909 517-3660
5171 Edison Ave Ste C Chino (91710) ***(P-9226)***
Alstyle AP & Activewear MGT Co (HQ) ....**A....714 765-0400**
1501 E Cerritos Ave Anaheim (92805) ***(P-14361)***
Alstyle Apparel, Jurupa Valley *Also called A and G Inc* ***(P-2795)***
Alstyle Apparel LLC ....A....714 765-0400
1501 E Cerritos Ave Anaheim (92805) ***(P-2556)***
Alta Advanced Technologies Inc ....E....909 983-2973
760 E Sunkist St Ontario (91761) ***(P-4928)***
Alta California Med Group Inc ....D....805 578-9622
2925 Sycamore Dr Ste 204 Simi Valley (93065) ***(P-19693)***
Alta Finish & Stair Inc ....D....951 496-0117
12625 Frederick St I529 Moreno Valley (92553) ***(P-1426)***
Alta Healthcare System LLC (HQ) ....**C....323 267-0477**
4081 E Olympic Blvd Los Angeles (90023) ***(P-20670)***
Alta Hllywood Cmnty Hosp Van N ....A....818 787-1511
14433 Emelita St Van Nuys (91401) ***(P-21012)***
Alta Hospitals System LLC ....A....714 619-7700
14662 Newport Ave Tustin (92780) ***(P-20671)***
Alta Hospitals System LLC (HQ) ....**E....310 943-4500**
3415 S Sepulveda Blvd # 900 Los Angeles (90034) ***(P-20672)***
Alta Loma Christian School, Rancho Cucamonga *Also called Little People Pre-School* ***(P-22028)***
Alta Med Health Services, El Monte *Also called Altamed Health Services Corp* ***(P-21382)***
ALTA ONE FCU, Ridgecrest *Also called Altaone Federal Credit Union* ***(P-15056)***
Alta Properties Inc ....B....805 683-1431
879 Ward Dr Santa Barbara (93111) ***(P-9853)***
Alta Properties Inc ....C....805 683-2575
869 Ward Dr Santa Barbara (93111) ***(P-10741)***
Alta Properties Inc ....B....805 690-5382
879 Ward Dr Santa Barbara (93111) ***(P-9854)***
Alta Properties Inc ....C....805 967-0171
839 Ward Dr Santa Barbara (93111) ***(P-5997)***
Alta Properties Inc (PA) ....**C....805 967-0171**
879 Ward Dr Santa Barbara (93111) ***(P-5998)***
Alta Verdugo Consulting Inc ....D....323 257-5715
4170 Verdugo Rd Los Angeles (90065) ***(P-20521)***
Alta Vista Country Club LLC ....D....714 524-1591
777 Alta Vista St Placentia (92870) ***(P-19529)***
Alta Vista Credit Union ....D....909 809-3838
2025 N Riverside Ave Rialto (92377) ***(P-15105)***
Alta Vista Healthcare and Well ....C....951 688-8200
9020 Garfield St Riverside (92503) ***(P-19694)***
Alta-Dena Certified Dairy LLC ....C....805 685-8328
123 Aero Camino Goleta (93117) ***(P-1830)***
Alta-Dena Certified Dairy LLC (HQ) ....**B....626 964-6401**
17637 E Valley Blvd City of Industry (91744) ***(P-130)***
Altadena Town and Country Club ....D....626 345-9088
2290 Country Club Dr Altadena (91001) ***(P-19530)***
Altair Lighting, Compton *Also called Jimway Inc* ***(P-9136)***
Altamed Adhc Golden Age, Lynwood *Also called Altamed Health Services Corp* ***(P-19696)***
Altamed Health Services Corp ....C....562 923-9414
12130 Paramount Blvd Downey (90242) ***(P-19695)***
Altamed Health Services Corp ....C....310 632-0415
3820 Mrtin Lther King Jr Lynwood (90262) ***(P-19696)***
Altamed Health Services Corp ....C....323 980-4466
5427 Whittier Blvd Los Angeles (90022) ***(P-19697)***
Altamed Health Services Corp ....D....714 919-0280
1515 S Broadway Ste A Santa Ana (92707) ***(P-21375)***
Altamed Health Services Corp ....C....714 635-0593
1325 N Anaheim Blvd 101 Anaheim (92801) ***(P-19698)***
Altamed Health Services Corp ....C....323 277-7678
6330 Rugby Ave Ste 200 Huntington Park (90255) ***(P-19699)***
Altamed Health Services Corp ....E....626 214-1480
535 S 2nd Ave Covina (91723) ***(P-15375)***
Altamed Health Services Corp ....C....323 276-0267
268 Bloom St Los Angeles (90012) ***(P-19700)***
Altamed Health Services Corp ....D....323 889-7847
10454 Valley Blvd El Monte (91731) ***(P-21376)***
Altamed Health Services Corp (PA) ....**C....323 725-8751**
2040 Camfield Ave Commerce (90040) ***(P-19701)***
Altamed Health Services Corp ....C....323 374-6848
1776 E Century Blvd Los Angeles (90002) ***(P-19702)***
Altamed Health Services Corp ....D....323 562-6700
8627 Atlantic Ave South Gate (90280) ***(P-21377)***
Altamed Health Services Corp ....D....323 307-0400
3945 Whittier Blvd Los Angeles (90023) ***(P-21378)***
Altamed Health Services Corp ....D....323 890-8767
5255 Pomona Blvd Ste 11 Los Angeles (90022) ***(P-21379)***
Altamed Health Services Corp ....D....562 949-8717
9436 Slauson Ave Pico Rivera (90660) ***(P-21380)***

Altamed Health Services Corp ......C......323 728-0411
5425 Pomona Blvd Los Angeles (90022) ***(P-19703)***

Altamed Health Services Corp ......D......562 595-8040
711 E Wardlow Rd Ste 203 Long Beach (90807) ***(P-21381)***

Altamed Health Services Corp ......C......323 269-0421
2219 E 1st St Los Angeles (90033) ***(P-19704)***

Altamed Health Services Corp ......D......626 453-8466
10418 Valley Blvd Ste B El Monte (91731) ***(P-21382)***

Altamed Ltc Trnsp Dept, Los Angeles *Also called Altamed Health Services Corp* ***(P-21379)***

Altamed Med & Dntl Group Bell, South Gate *Also called Altamed Health Services Corp* ***(P-21377)***

Altamed Med Dntl Grp Whttier W, Los Angeles *Also called Altamed Health Services Corp* ***(P-21378)***

Altametrics Hosting LLC ......C......800 676-1281
3191 Red Hill Ave Ste 100 Costa Mesa (92626) ***(P-13373)***

Altaone Federal Credit Union (PA) ......**C......760 371-7000**
701 S China Lake Blvd Ridgecrest (93555) ***(P-15056)***

Altec Products Inc (PA) ......**D......949 727-1248**
23422 Mill Creek Dr # 225 Laguna Hills (92653) ***(P-18441)***

Altegra Health ......D......310 776-4001
3415 S Sepulveda Blvd # 900 Los Angeles (90034) ***(P-23152)***

Alteryx Inc (PA) ......**E......888 836-4274**
3345 Michelson Dr Ste 400 Irvine (92612) ***(P-18017)***

Altinex Inc ......E......714 990-0877
500 S Jefferson St Placentia (92870) ***(P-9251)***

Altium Holdings LLC ......B......951 340-9390
12165 Madera Way Riverside (92503) ***(P-5555)***

Altium Packaging ......D......626 856-2100
4516 Azusa Canyon Rd Irwindale (91706) ***(P-5556)***

Altium Packaging LLC ......F......888 425-7343
1070 Samuelson St City of Industry (91748) ***(P-5557)***

Altium Packaging LLC ......F......714 241-6640
1217 E Saint Gertrude Pl Santa Ana (92707) ***(P-5558)***

Altium Packaging LLC ......F......310 952-8736
1500 E 223rd St Carson (90745) ***(P-5473)***

Altium Packaging LP ......C......714 241-6640
1217 E Saint Gertrude Pl Santa Ana (92707) ***(P-5487)***

Altium Packaging LP ......C......909 590-7334
14312 Central Ave Chino (91710) ***(P-5559)***

Altmans Products LLC (HQ) ......**E......310 559-4093**
7136 Kittyhawk Ave Apt 4 Los Angeles (90045) ***(P-6546)***

Alto Lucero Transitional Care, Santa Barbara *Also called Compass Health Inc* ***(P-20285)***

Alton Geoscience, Irvine *Also called TRC Solutions Inc* ***(P-23519)***

Alton Irvine Inc ......D......949 428-4141
2052 Alton Pkwy Irvine (92606) ***(P-13125)***

Alton/Sand Canyon Medical Offs, Irvine *Also called Kaiser Foundation Hospitals* ***(P-15402)***

Altoon Partners LLP (PA) ......**D......213 225-1900**
617 W 7th St Ste 400 Los Angeles (90017) ***(P-22708)***

Altoon Porter, Los Angeles *Also called Altoon Partners LLP* ***(P-22708)***

Altor Bioscience LLC ......D......954 443-8600
9920 Jefferson Blvd Culver City (90232) ***(P-22823)***

Altour International Inc ......D......818 464-9200
21800 Burbank Blvd # 120 Woodland Hills (91367) ***(P-12378)***

Altour International Inc (PA) ......**D......310 571-6000**
12100 W Olympic Blvd # 300 Los Angeles (90064) ***(P-12379)***

Altour International Inc ......D......310 571-6000
10635 Santa Monica Blvd # 200 Los Angeles (90025) ***(P-12380)***

Altour Travel Master, Los Angeles *Also called Altour International Inc* ***(P-12380)***

Altra Inc (PA) ......**D......310 348-7244**
5757 W Century Blvd # 70 Los Angeles (90045) ***(P-5125)***

Altro Usa Inc ......D......562 944-8292
12648 Clark St Santa Fe Springs (90670) ***(P-11618)***

Altura Centers For Health ......D......559 686-9097
1201 N Cherry St Tulare (93274) ***(P-19705)***

Altura Comm Solutions LLC (HQ) ......**D......714 948-8400**
1540 S Lewis St Anaheim (92805) ***(P-13699)***

Altura Credit Union (PA) ......**D......888 883-7228**
2847 Campus Pkwy Riverside (92507) ***(P-15106)***

Altura Holdings LLC (HQ) ......**D......714 948-8400**
1335 S Acacia Ave Fullerton (92831) ***(P-16121)***

Altura Management Services LLC ......B......323 768-2898
1401 N Montebello Blvd Montebello (90640) ***(P-22973)***

Alum-A-Coat, El Monte *Also called Santoshi Corporation* ***(P-7310)***

Alum-Alloy Co Inc ......E......909 986-0410
603 S Hope Ave Ontario (91761) ***(P-7102)***

Alumin-Art Plating Co Inc ......F......909 983-1866
803 W State St Ontario (91762) ***(P-7209)***

Aluminum Casting Company, Ontario *Also called Employee Owned PCF Cast Pdts I* ***(P-6394)***

Aluminum Die Casting Co Inc ......D......951 681-3900
10775 San Sevaine Way Jurupa Valley (91752) ***(P-6363)***

Aluminum Precision Pdts Inc (PA) ......**A......714 546-8125**
3333 W Warner Ave Santa Ana (92704) ***(P-13544)***

Aluminum Precision Pdts Inc ......C......805 488-4401
1001 Mcwane Blvd Oxnard (93033) ***(P-13545)***

Aluminum Technology Inc ......F......909 946-3697
1455 Columbia Ave Riverside (92507) ***(P-3706)***

Aluminum Tube Railings, Pomona *Also called Atr Technologies Incorporated* ***(P-6951)***

Alumistar Inc ......E......562 633-6673
520 S Palmetto Ave Ontario (91762) ***(P-6385)***

Aluratek Inc ......E......949 468-2046
15241 Barranca Pkwy Irvine (92618) ***(P-9157)***

Alva Manufacturing Inc ......E......714 237-0925
236 E Orangethorpe Ave Placentia (92870) ***(P-10267)***

Alvarado Manufacturing Co Inc ......D......909 591-8431
12660 Colony Ct Chino (91710) ***(P-10868)***

Alvarez Mrsal Bus Cnslting LLC ......C......310 975-2600
2029 Century Park E Los Angeles (90067) ***(P-23153)***

Always Best, City of Industry *Also called Rongcheng Trading LLC* ***(P-14606)***

Always Best Care Desert Cities, Indian Wells *Also called Bjz LLC* ***(P-21138)***

Always Right Home Care, Northridge *Also called Tiffany Homecare Inc* ***(P-21223)***

Alyn Industries Inc ......D......818 988-7696
16028 Arminta St Van Nuys (91406) ***(P-9672)***

Alzheimers Greater Los Angeles ......D......323 938-3379
4221 Wilshire Blvd # 400 Los Angeles (90010) ***(P-21711)***

AM Machining Inc ......E......714 367-0830
7422 Walnut Ave Buena Park (90620) ***(P-14051)***

Am-PM Printing Inc ......F......909 599-0811
163 W Bonita Ave San Dimas (91773) ***(P-4226)***

Am-TEC Security, Chino *Also called Am-TEC Total Security Inc* ***(P-18366)***

Am-TEC Total Security Inc (PA) ......**D......909 573-4678**
4075 Schaefer Ave Chino (91710) ***(P-18366)***

Am-Tek Engineering Inc ......F......909 673-1633
1180 E Francis St Ste C Ontario (91761) ***(P-8494)***

Am-Touch Dental, Valencia *Also called American Med & Hosp Sup Co Inc* ***(P-13472)***

Am/PM Mini Market, La Palma *Also called Prestige Stations Inc* ***(P-18941)***

Am/PM Mini Market, Piru *Also called Tesoro Refining & Mktg Co LLC* ***(P-14811)***

AMA Plastics (PA) ......**C......951 734-5600**
1100 Citrus St Riverside (92507) ***(P-5560)***

Amada America Inc (HQ) ......**D......714 739-2111**
7025 Firestone Blvd Buena Park (90621) ***(P-13884)***

Amada Enterprises Inc ......C......323 757-1881
12619 Avalon Blvd Los Angeles (90061) ***(P-20242)***

Amada North America Inc (HQ) ......**B......714 739-2111**
7025 Firestone Blvd Buena Park (90621) ***(P-13885)***

Amada Weld Tech Inc (HQ) ......**C......626 303-5676**
1820 S Myrtle Ave Monrovia (91016) ***(P-7888)***

Amag Technology Inc (HQ) ......**E......310 518-2380**
2205 W 126th St Ste B Hawthorne (90250) ***(P-8234)***

Amanecer Cmnty Counseling Svc ......D......213 481-7464
1200 Wilshire Blvd # 200 Los Angeles (90017) ***(P-21273)***

Amanet, Canoga Park *Also called American Mfg Netwrk Inc* ***(P-8496)***

Amaretto Orchards LLC ......E......661 399-9697
32331 Famoso Woody Rd Mc Farland (93250) ***(P-11629)***

Amarillo Wind Machine LLC ......F......559 592-4256
20513 Avenue 256 Exeter (93221) ***(P-7604)***

Amark Industries Inc (PA) ......**E......951 654-7351**
600 W Esplanade Ave San Jacinto (92583) ***(P-8083)***

Amass Brands Inc ......E......619 204-2560
927 S Santa Fe Ave Los Angeles (90021) ***(P-4737)***

Amatel Inc (PA) ......**D......323 801-0199**
1017 S Mountain Ave Monrovia (91016) ***(P-23411)***

Amawaterways LLC (PA) ......**C......800 626-0126**
4500 Park Granada 200 Calabasas (91302) ***(P-12381)***

Amays Bakery & Noodle Co Inc (PA) ......**D......213 626-2713**
837 E Commercial St Los Angeles (90012) ***(P-2056)***

Amazing Steel, Montclair *Also called Mitchell Fabrication* ***(P-6640)***

Amazing Steel Company ......E......909 590-0393
4564 Mission Blvd Montclair (91763) ***(P-6585)***

Ambay Circuits Inc ......E......818 786-8241
16117 Leadwell St Van Nuys (91406) ***(P-9376)***

Amber Steel Co., Rialto *Also called H Wayne Lewis Inc* ***(P-7021)***

Amberwood Convalescent Hosp ......D......323 254-3407
6071 York Blvd Los Angeles (90042) ***(P-20550)***

Ambiance Apparel, Los Angeles *Also called Ambiance USA Inc* ***(P-2917)***

Ambiance Transportation LLC ......D......818 955-5757
6901 San Fernando Rd Glendale (91201) ***(P-12563)***

Ambiance USA Inc ......E......213 765-9600
930 Towne Ave Los Angeles (90021) ***(P-2915)***

Ambiance USA Inc ......E......323 587-0007
2465 E 23rd St Los Angeles (90058) ***(P-2916)***

Ambiance USA Inc (PA) ......**D......323 587-0007**
930 Towne Ave Los Angeles (90021) ***(P-2917)***

Ambreen Enterprises Inc ......D......909 620-1339
20370 Via Badalona Yorba Linda (92887) ***(P-23412)***

Ambrit Engineering Corporation ......D......714 557-1074
2640 Halladay St Santa Ana (92705) ***(P-7775)***

Ambrit Industries Inc ......E......818 243-1224
432 Magnolia Ave Glendale (91204) ***(P-7753)***

Ambry Genetics Corporation (HQ) ......**D......949 900-5500**
1 Enterprise Aliso Viejo (92656) ***(P-21059)***

Ambulnz Co LLC ......D......877 311-5555
1907 Border Ave Torrance (90501) ***(P-16092)***

Ambulnz Health LLC (PA) ......**B......877 311-5555**
1907 Border Ave Torrance (90501) ***(P-18118)***

Ambuserve Inc ......C......310 644-0500
15105 S Broadway Gardena (90248) ***(P-11848)***

AMC, Stanton *Also called All Metals Proc San Diego Inc* ***(P-7204)***

AMC, Pasadena *Also called American Multi-Cinema Inc* ***(P-19269)***

AMC, Huntington Beach *Also called House Seven Gables RE Inc* ***(P-15884)***

AMC, Sylmar *Also called Advanced Mnlythic Ceramics Inc* ***(P-13697)***

AMC Machining Inc ......E......805 238-5452
1540 Commerce Way Paso Robles (93446) ***(P-7014)***

AMC&, Los Angeles *Also called Anderson McPharlin Conners LLP* ***(P-21505)***

Amco Foods Inc ......B......818 247-4716
601 E Glenoaks Blvd # 108 Glendale (91207) ***(P-23154)***

Amcom Food Service, City of Industry *Also called Klm Management Company* ***(P-14542)***

Amcor Flexibles LLC ......A......323 721-6777
5416 Union Pacific Ave Commerce (90022) ***(P-3848)***

Amcor Industries Inc ......E......323 585-2852
2011 E 49th St Vernon (90058) ***(P-10016)***

AMD International Tech LLC ......E......909 985-8300
1725 S Campus Ave Ontario (91761) ***(P-6781)***

Amdal In-Home Care Inc (PA) ......**E......559 686-6611**
147 N K St Tulare (93274) ***(P-21132)***

Mergent e-mail: customerrelations@mergent.com
1052
2022 Southern California Business Directory and Buyers Guide
(P-0000) Products & Services Section entry number
(PA)=Parent Co (HQ)=Headquarters (DH)=Div Headquarters

ALPHABETIC SECTION American Homes 4 Rent

AME-Gyu Co Ltd ....A....310 214-9572
20000 Mariner Ave Ste 500 Torrance (90503) ***(P-16093)***
Amen Clinics Inc A Med Corp (PA) ....**D....888 564-2700**
3150 Bristol St Ste 400 Costa Mesa (92626) ***(P-19706)***
Amerasia Furn Cmpnnts Mfg Impr ....E....310 638-0570
2772 Norton Ave Lynwood (90262) ***(P-3495)***
Amerdale Industries Inc ....D....714 521-3800
14750 Northam St La Mirada (90638) ***(P-13157)***
Ameresco Solar LLC ....D....888 967-6527
42175 Zevo Dr Temecula (92590) ***(P-22483)***
Amerex Company, Riverside *Also called Nsa Holdings Inc* ***(P-5732)***
Amergence Technology Inc ....E....909 859-8400
295 Brea Canyon Rd Walnut (91789) ***(P-7960)***
Ameri-Fax, Orange *Also called Positive Concepts Inc* ***(P-3933)***
Ameri-Kleen ....C....805 546-0706
1023 E Grand Ave Arroyo Grande (93420) ***(P-17214)***
Ameri-Kleen Building Services, Arroyo Grande *Also called Ameri-Kleen* ***(P-17214)***
America Chung Nam LLC (HQ) ....**C....909 839-8383**
1163 Fairway Dr Fl 3 City of Industry (91789) ***(P-14108)***
America Metal Mfg Resources ....E....909 620-4500
1989 W Holt Ave Pomona (91768) ***(P-10212)***
America West Airlines Inc ....D....949 852-5471
18601 Airport Way Ste 238 Santa Ana (92707) ***(P-12302)***
America Wood Finishes Inc ....E....323 232-8256
728 E 59th St Los Angeles (90001) ***(P-5087)***
American Air, Visalia *Also called American Incorporated* ***(P-733)***
American Aircraft Products Inc ....D....310 532-7434
15411 S Broadway Gardena (90248) ***(P-6782)***
American Airlines Inc ....C....213 935-6045
7000 World Way W Los Angeles (90045) ***(P-12303)***
American Airlines/Eagle, Long Beach *Also called Piedmont Airlines Inc* ***(P-12312)***
American AP Dyg & Finshg Inc ....E....310 644-4001
747 Warehouse St Los Angeles (90021) ***(P-2610)***
American Apparel, Los Angeles *Also called App Winddown LLC* ***(P-3066)***
American Apparel ACC Inc (PA) ....**E....626 350-3828**
10160 Olney St El Monte (91731) ***(P-5561)***
American Apparel Retail Inc (HQ) ....**D....213 488-0226**
747 Warehouse St Los Angeles (90021) ***(P-2557)***
American Arium ....E....949 623-7090
17791 Fitch Irvine (92614) ***(P-9480)***
American Asphalt South Inc ....D....909 427-8276
19792 El Rivino Rd Riverside (92509) ***(P-857)***
American Assn Crtcal Care Nrse ....C....949 362-2000
27071 Aliso Creek Rd Aliso Viejo (92656) ***(P-21937)***
American Audio Component Inc ....E....909 596-3788
20 Fairbanks Ste 198 Irvine (92618) ***(P-9673)***
American Automated Engrg Inc ....D....714 898-9951
5382 Argosy Ave Huntington Beach (92649) ***(P-10530)***
American Bath Factory, Corona *Also called Le Elegant Bath Inc* ***(P-5534)***
American Beef Packers Inc ....C....909 628-4888
13677 Yorba Ave Chino (91710) ***(P-210)***
American Best Car Parts, Anaheim *Also called American Fabrication Corp* ***(P-10017)***
American Bicycle Security Co, Santa Paula *Also called Turtle Storage Ltd* ***(P-3699)***
American Board Assembly Inc ....C....805 523-0274
5456 Endeavour Ct Moorpark (93021) ***(P-9377)***
American Bolt & Screw Mfg Corp (PA) ....**D....909 390-0522**
600 S Wanamaker Ave Ontario (91761) ***(P-13971)***
American Bottling Company ....F....951 341-7500
1188 Mt Vernon Ave Riverside (92507) ***(P-2249)***
American Bottling Company ....F....661 323-7921
230 E 18th St Bakersfield (93305) ***(P-2250)***
American Bottling Company ....F....818 898-1471
1166 Arroyo St San Fernando (91340) ***(P-2251)***
American Bottling Company ....F....805 928-1001
618 Hanson Way Santa Maria (93458) ***(P-2252)***
American Bottling Company ....F....323 268-7779
3220 E 26th St Vernon (90058) ***(P-2253)***
American Brass & Alum Fndry Co ....E....800 545-9988
2060 Garfield Ave Commerce (90040) ***(P-6552)***
American Building Jantr Inc (PA) ....**D....562 986-4474**
5527 South St Lakewood (90713) ***(P-211)***
American Building Supply Inc ....D....909 879-8700
120 S Cedar Ave Rialto (92376) ***(P-13199)***
American Business Bank ....D....909 919-2040
3633 Inland Empire Blvd Ontario (91764) ***(P-15009)***
American Business Bank ....D....310 808-1200
970 W 190th St Ste 301 Torrance (90502) ***(P-15010)***
American Cabinet Works ....E....310 715-6815
13518 S Normandie Ave Gardena (90249) ***(P-3228)***
American Capacitor Corporation ....E....626 814-4444
5367 3rd St Irwindale (91706) ***(P-9609)***
American Capital Group Inc ....D....949 271-5800
23382 Mill Creek Dr # 115 Laguna Hills (92653) ***(P-15160)***
American Casuals, Torrance *Also called Pmp Products Inc* ***(P-5895)***
American Cinemas Group Inc (PA) ....**C....760 597-5777**
1180 Nevada St Ste 100 Redlands (92374) ***(P-19268)***
American Circuit Tech Inc (PA) ....**E....714 777-2480**
5330 E Hunter Ave Anaheim (92807) ***(P-9378)***
American Cmpus Communities Inc ....D....949 854-0900
62600 Arroyo Dr Irvine (92617) ***(P-16810)***
American Coffee Urn Mfg Co Inc ....F....951 943-1495
5178 Western Way Perris (92571) ***(P-6783)***
American Compaction Eqp Inc ....E....949 661-2921
29380 Hunco Way Lake Elsinore (92530) ***(P-7634)***
American Companies, Pico Rivera *Also called Three Sons Inc* ***(P-14608)***
American Consumer Products LLC ....E....323 289-6610
2833 Leonis Blvd Ste 102 Vernon (90058) ***(P-5210)***
American Contractors Inc ....D....714 282-5700
404 W Blueridge Ave Orange (92865) ***(P-1024)***
American Contrs Indemnity Co (HQ) ....**C....213 330-1309**
801 S Figueroa St Ste 700 Los Angeles (90017) ***(P-15494)***
American Cooling Tower Inc (PA) ....**F....714 898-2436**
3130 W Harvard St Santa Ana (92704) ***(P-19022)***
American Copak Corporation ....C....818 576-1000
9175 Eton Ave Chatsworth (91311) ***(P-18442)***
American Corporate SEC Inc (PA) ....**B....562 216-7440**
1 World Trade Ctr # 1240 Long Beach (90831) ***(P-18242)***
American Cover Design 26 Inc ....F....323 582-8666
2131 E 52nd St Vernon (90058) ***(P-2681)***
American Crclation Innovations, Long Beach *Also called Advertising Consultants Inc* ***(P-17093)***
American Data Vault Inc ....F....559 686-2838
21346 Road 140 Tulare (93274) ***(P-6015)***
American Dawn Inc (PA) ....**D....800 821-2221**
401 W Artesia Blvd Compton (90220) ***(P-2718)***
American De Rosa Lamparts LLC ....D....800 777-4440
10650 4th St Rancho Cucamonga (91730) ***(P-687)***
American Deburring Inc ....E....949 457-9790
20742 Linear Ln Lake Forest (92630) ***(P-8495)***
American Designs, Los Angeles *Also called Kesmor Associates* ***(P-11319)***
American Development Corp (PA) ....**D....562 989-3730**
3605 Long Beach Blvd # 41 Long Beach (90807) ***(P-15768)***
American Die Casting Inc ....E....909 356-7768
14576 Fontlee Ln Fontana (92335) ***(P-6374)***
American Dj Group of Companies, Commerce *Also called D J American Supply Inc* ***(P-14150)***
American Eagle Protective Svcs, Inglewood *Also called American Egle Prtctive Svcs In* ***(P-18243)***
American Egle Prtctive Svcs In ....D....310 412-0019
425 W Kelso St Inglewood (90301) ***(P-18243)***
American Elc Components Inc ....F....323 771-4888
4901 Fruitland Ave Vernon (90058) ***(P-18951)***
American Electric Supply Inc (PA) ....**D....951 734-7910**
361 S Maple St Corona (92878) ***(P-13612)***
American Electronics, Carson *Also called Ducommun Labarge Tech Inc* ***(P-10318)***
American Elements, Los Angeles *Also called Merelex Corporation* ***(P-4662)***
American Etching & Mfg ....E....323 875-3910
13730 Desmond St Pacoima (91331) ***(P-7341)***
American Eye Institute ....D....310 652-1396
8635 W 3rd St Ste 390 Los Angeles (90048) ***(P-19707)***
American Fabrication, Bakersfield *Also called Russell Fabrication Corp* ***(P-7543)***
American Fabrication Corp (PA) ....**D....714 632-1709**
2891 E Via Martens Anaheim (92806) ***(P-10017)***
American Fdrtion Mscans Lcal 4 ....C....323 462-2161
3220 Winona Ave Burbank (91504) ***(P-22285)***
American Fdrtion of Mscans of, Burbank *Also called American Fdrtion Mscans Lcal 4* ***(P-22285)***
American Filter Company, Azusa *Also called Water Filter Exchange Inc* ***(P-8143)***
American Financial Network Inc (PA) ....**C....909 606-3905**
10 Pointe Dr Ste 330 Brea (92821) ***(P-15170)***
American Fine Arts Foundry LLC ....F....818 848-7593
2520 N Ontario St Ste A Burbank (91504) ***(P-6404)***
American First Credit Union (PA) ....**D....562 691-1112**
6 Pointe Dr Ste 400 Brea (92821) ***(P-15057)***
American Fish and Seafood, Los Angeles *Also called Prospect Enterprises Inc* ***(P-14579)***
American Fleet & Ret Graphics ....E....909 937-7570
2091 Del Rio Way Ontario (91761) ***(P-11522)***
American Foam & Packaging, Gardena *Also called Amfoam Inc* ***(P-5488)***
American Foam Fiber & Sups Inc (PA) ....**D....626 969-7268**
255 S 7th Ave Ste A City of Industry (91746) ***(P-2719)***
American Fruits & Flavors LLC (HQ) ....**C....818 899-9574**
10725 Sutter Ave Pacoima (91331) ***(P-2306)***
American Fruits & Flavors LLC ....E....818 899-9574
12950 Pierce St Pacoima (91331) ***(P-2307)***
American Fruits & Flavors LLC ....E....323 264-7791
1547 Knowles Ave Los Angeles (90063) ***(P-2308)***
American Funds Distrs Inc (HQ) ....**C....213 486-9200**
333 S Hope St Ste Levb Los Angeles (90071) ***(P-16122)***
American Furniture Systems Inc ....E....626 457-9900
14105 Avalon Blvd Los Angeles (90061) ***(P-3604)***
American Future Tech Corp ....C....888 462-3899
529 Baldwin Park Blvd City of Industry (91746) ***(P-13374)***
American General Design ....E....626 304-0800
388 Cordova St Ste 280 Pasadena (91101) ***(P-22709)***
American GNC Corporation ....E....805 582-0582
888 E Easy St Simi Valley (93065) ***(P-22484)***
American Golf Construction, Canoga Park *Also called American Landscape Inc* ***(P-232)***
American Golf Corporation ....D....702 431-2191
68311 Paseo Real Cathedral City (92234) ***(P-19531)***
American Graphic Board Inc ....E....323 721-0585
5880 E Slauson Ave Commerce (90040) ***(P-3748)***
American Grip Inc ....E....818 768-8922
8468 Kewen Ave Sun Valley (91352) ***(P-9122)***
American Guard Services Inc (PA) ....**B....310 645-6200**
1125 W 190th St Gardena (90248) ***(P-18244)***
American Health Connection ....A....424 226-0420
8484 Wilshire Blvd # 501 Beverly Hills (90211) ***(P-18443)***
American Health Services LLC ....D....661 254-6630
26460 Summit Cir Santa Clarita (91350) ***(P-19708)***
American Healthcare Reit Inc (PA) ....**D....949 270-9200**
18191 Von Karman Ave # 300 Irvine (92612) ***(P-16227)***
American Historic Inns Inc ....F....949 499-8070
249 Forest Ave Laguna Beach (92651) ***(P-4149)***
American Hmes 4 Rent MGT Hldng ....D....805 413-5300
23975 Park Sorrento # 300 Calabasas (91302) ***(P-16228)***
American Homes 4 Rent (PA) ....**C....805 413-5300**
23975 Park Sorrento # 300 Calabasas (91302) ***(P-16229)***

ALPHABETIC

Employee Codes: A=Over 500 employees, B=251-500
C=101-250, D=51-100, E=20-50 F=10-19
2022 Southern California Business
Directory and Buyers Guide
© Mergent Inc. 1-800-342-5647
1053

American Honda Finance Corp (HQ) ....C.......**310 972-2239**
1919 Torrance Blvd Torrance (90501) ***(P-15137)***
American Honda Motor Co Inc (HQ) ....A.......**310 783-2000**
1919 Torrance Blvd Torrance (90501) ***(P-13018)***
American Honda Motor Co Inc..F.......800 382-2238
1919 Torrance Blvd Torrance (90501) ***(P-10457)***
American Household Company, Los Angeles *Also called Housewares International Inc* ***(P-5667)***
American HX Auto Trade Inc ....D.......909 484-1010
4845 Via Del Cerro Yorba Linda (92887) ***(P-9934)***
American Imaging MGT Inc..A.......847 310-0366
505 N Brand Blvd Ste 900 Glendale (91203) ***(P-15376)***
American Imex, Irvine *Also called J F Fong Inc* ***(P-10997)***
American Incorporated..B.......805 597-6545
3450 Sacramento Dr San Luis Obispo (93401) ***(P-1025)***
American Incorporated (PA) ....B.......**559 651-1776**
1345 N American St Visalia (93291) ***(P-733)***
American Indian Health & Svcs..E.......805 681-7356
4141 State St Ste B11 Santa Barbara (93110) ***(P-21383)***
American International Inds, Commerce *Also called Glamour Industries Co* ***(P-14244)***
American Intgrted Rsources Inc ....D.......714 921-4100
2341 N Pacific St Orange (92865) ***(P-22974)***
American Intl Inds Inc..A.......323 728-2999
2220 Gaspar Ave Commerce (90040) ***(P-4988)***
American Justice Solutions Inc..D.......949 369-6210
25910 Acero Ste 100 Mission Viejo (92691) ***(P-23413)***
American Kal Enterprises Inc (PA)..D.......**626 338-7308**
4265 Puente Ave Baldwin Park (91706) ***(P-13794)***
American Lab and Systems, Los Angeles *Also called Mjw Inc* ***(P-8017)***
American Landscape Inc ....C.......818 999-2041
7013 Owensmouth Ave Canoga Park (91303) ***(P-232)***
American Landscape MGT Inc..D.......805 647-5077
1607 Los Angeles Ave I Ventura (93004) ***(P-290)***
American Landscape MGT Inc (PA) ....C.......**818 999-2041**
7013 Owensmouth Ave Canoga Park (91303) ***(P-233)***
American Liberty Capital Corp ....C.......949 623-0288
19000 Macarthur Blvd # 400 Irvine (92612) ***(P-15235)***
American Liberty Funding, Irvine *Also called American Liberty Capital Corp* ***(P-15235)***
American Mailing & Prtg Svc, Anaheim *Also called Sharon Havriluk* ***(P-4612)***
American Maple Inc ....F.......310 515-8881
14020 S Western Ave Gardena (90249) ***(P-11400)***
American Marble & Granite Co (PA) ....F.......**323 268-7979**
4084 Whittier Blvd Los Angeles (90023) ***(P-6133)***
American Marble & Onyx Coinc ....E.......323 776-0900
10321 S La Cienega Blvd Los Angeles (90045) ***(P-6134)***
American Med & Hosp Sup Co Inc..E.......661 294-1213
28703 Industry Dr Valencia (91355) ***(P-13472)***
American Med O & P Clinic Inc..E.......818 281-5747
4955 Van Nuys Blvd Sherman Oaks (91403) ***(P-11085)***
American Med Rspnse Amblnce Sv (HQ)..A.......**303 495-1217**
879 Marlborough Ave Riverside (92507) ***(P-11849)***
American Med Rspnse Inland Emp (HQ)..D.......**951 782-5200**
879 Marlborough Ave Riverside (92507) ***(P-11850)***
American Medical Response Inc..C.......760 883-5000
1111 Montalvo Way Palm Springs (92262) ***(P-11851)***
American Medical Tech Inc..D.......949 553-0359
17595 Cartwright Rd Irvine (92614) ***(P-13473)***
American Medical Technologies, Irvine *Also called Gordian Medical Inc* ***(P-13490)***
American Metal, Pomona *Also called America Metal Mfg Resources* ***(P-10212)***
American Metal & Paint Inc..F.......818 882-6333
9030 Owensmouth Ave Canoga Park (91304) ***(P-6586)***
American Metal Bearing Company..E.......714 892-5527
7191 Acacia Ave Garden Grove (92841) ***(P-8026)***
American Mfg Netwrk Inc ....F.......818 786-1113
7001 Eton Ave Canoga Park (91303) ***(P-8496)***
American Multi-Cinema Inc..E.......626 585-8900
42 Miller Aly Pasadena (91103) ***(P-19269)***
American Multimedia TV USA ....D.......626 466-1038
530 S Lake Ave Unit 368 Pasadena (91101) ***(P-12710)***
American Mutual Fund..C.......213 486-9200
333 S Hope St Fl 51 Los Angeles (90071) ***(P-16123)***
American Mzhou Dngpo Group Inc..D.......626 820-9239
4520 Maine Ave Baldwin Park (91706) ***(P-22975)***
American Nail Plate Ltg Inc ....D.......909 982-1807
9044 Del Mar Ave Montclair (91763) ***(P-9057)***
American National Mfg Inc..C.......951 273-7888
252 Mariah Cir Corona (92879) ***(P-3541)***
American Naturals Company LLC..E.......323 201-6891
3737 Longridge Ave Sherman Oaks (91423) ***(P-2389)***
American Nuts Imprt-Export Inc..E.......818 364-8855
12950 San Fernando Rd Sylmar (91342) ***(P-14555)***
American Paper & Plastics LLC ....C.......626 444-0000
550 S 7th Ave City of Industry (91746) ***(P-14910)***
American Paper & Provisions, City of Industry *Also called American Paper & Plastics LLC* ***(P-14910)***
American PCF Prtrs College Inc..E.......949 250-3212
675 N Main St Orange (92868) ***(P-4227)***
American Plant Services Inc (PA)..E.......**562 630-1773**
6242 N Paramount Blvd Long Beach (90805) ***(P-6187)***
American Plastic Card Co ....F.......818 784-4224
21550 Oxnard St Ste 300 Woodland Hills (91367) ***(P-5562)***
American Plastic Products Inc..D.......818 504-1073
9243 Glenoaks Blvd Sun Valley (91352) ***(P-7776)***
American Pneumatic Tools Inc ....F.......562 204-1555
1000 S Grand Ave Santa Ana (92705) ***(P-7754)***
American Power SEC Svc Inc..D.......866 974-9994
1451 Rimpau Ave Ste 207 Corona (92879) ***(P-18245)***
American Power Solutions Inc ....E.......714 626-0300
14355 Industry Cir La Mirada (90638) ***(P-9123)***

American Prcision Grinding Mch ....F.......626 357-6610
456 Gerona Ave San Gabriel (91775) ***(P-8497)***
American Precision Hydraulics..E.......714 903-8610
5601 Research Dr Huntington Beach (92649) ***(P-7755)***
American Precision Sheet Metal, Chatsworth *Also called Keith E Archambeau Sr Inc* ***(P-6861)***
American Premier Corp..E.......909 923-7070
1531 S Carlos Ave Ontario (91761) ***(P-11401)***
American Printing & Design Ltd..F.......310 287-0460
14622 Ventura Blvd # 102 Sherman Oaks (91403) ***(P-4228)***
American Printworks, Vernon *Also called P&Y T-Shrts Silk Screening Inc* ***(P-7910)***
American Private Duty Inc..D.......818 386-6358
13111 Ventura Blvd # 100 Studio City (91604) ***(P-21133)***
American Prof Ambulance Corp ....D.......818 996-2200
16945 Sherman Way Van Nuys (91406) ***(P-11852)***
American Protection Group Inc (PA) ....C.......**818 279-2433**
8551 Vesper Ave Panorama City (91402) ***(P-18246)***
American Prtctive Svcs Invstgt..C.......626 705-8600
12471 Balsam Rd Victorville (92395) ***(P-18247)***
American Quality Tools Inc..E.......951 280-4700
12650 Magnolia Ave Ste B Riverside (92503) ***(P-7845)***
American Quilting Company Inc ....E.......323 233-2500
1540 Calzona St Los Angeles (90023) ***(P-3150)***
American Range Corporation..C.......818 897-0808
13592 Desmond St Pacoima (91331) ***(P-6784)***
American Ready Mix Inc..F.......760 446-4556
1141 W Graaf Ave Ridgecrest (93555) ***(P-6068)***
American Realty Advisors ....D.......818 545-1152
515 S Flower St Ste 4900 Los Angeles (90071) ***(P-16230)***
American Red Cross Los Angles (PA)..C.......**310 445-9900**
1320 Newton St Los Angeles (90021) ***(P-21712)***
American Relays Inc..E.......562 926-2837
43 Gingerwood Irvine (92603) ***(P-8942)***
American Reliance Inc..E.......626 443-6818
789 N Fair Oaks Ave Pasadena (91103) ***(P-8148)***
American Reprographics Co LLC ....D.......626 289-5021
616 Monterey Pass Rd Monterey Park (91754) ***(P-17144)***
American Retirement Corp ....C.......310 399-3227
2107 Ocean Ave Santa Monica (90405) ***(P-20243)***
American Roof Tools, Monterey Park *Also called Oakcroft Associates Inc* ***(P-13865)***
American Rotary Broom Co Inc..E.......909 629-9117
688 New York Dr Pomona (91768) ***(P-11507)***
American Sanitary Supply Inc..D.......714 632-3010
3800 E Miraloma Ave Anaheim (92806) ***(P-14032)***
American Scale Co Inc ....E.......800 773-7225
21326 E Arrow Hwy Covina (91724) ***(P-13375)***
American Scence Tech As T Corp..D.......310 773-1978
2372 Morse Ave Ste 571 Irvine (92614) ***(P-10176)***
American Scopes, Irvine *Also called Iscope Corp* ***(P-10843)***
American Security Force Inc ....D.......323 722-8585
5400 E Olympic Blvd # 225 Commerce (90022) ***(P-18248)***
American Security Products Co..C.......951 685-9680
11925 Pacific Ave Fontana (92337) ***(P-7548)***
American Single Sheets, Redlands *Also called Continental Datalabel Inc* ***(P-3925)***
American Soc Cinematographers ....F.......323 969-4333
1782 N Orange Dr Los Angeles (90028) ***(P-22265)***
American Soc Cmpsers Athors Pb ....E.......323 883-1000
7920 W Sunset Blvd # 300 Los Angeles (90046) ***(P-4150)***
American Soccer Company Inc (PA)..B.......**310 830-6161**
726 E Anaheim St Wilmington (90744) ***(P-2797)***
American Solar Advantage Inc ....E.......877 765-2388
13348 Monte Vista Ave Chino (91710) ***(P-9481)***
American Solar LLC..E.......323 250-1307
8484 Wilshire Blvd Beverly Hills (90211) ***(P-6568)***
American Spring Inc..F.......310 324-2181
321 W 135th St Los Angeles (90061) ***(P-7461)***
American States Water Company (PA) ....A.......**909 394-3600**
630 E Foothill Blvd San Dimas (91773) ***(P-12879)***
American Stream Solar Inc ....E.......888 919-6636
1149 W 190th St Gardena (90248) ***(P-16943)***
American Supply, Ontario *Also called Castillo Maritess* ***(P-3136)***
American System Publications ....E.......323 259-1867
3018 Carmel St Los Angeles (90065) ***(P-4151)***
American Tax Solutions..E.......323 306-7032
1055 W 7th St Ste 1600 Los Angeles (90017) ***(P-22759)***
American Technical Svcs Inc ....C.......951 372-9664
20384 Via Mantua Porter Ranch (91326) ***(P-22485)***
American Textile Maint Co..D.......213 749-4433
1705 Hooper Ave Los Angeles (90021) ***(P-16840)***
American Textile Maint Co..D.......562 438-7656
3001 E Anaheim St Long Beach (90804) ***(P-16841)***
American Textile Maint Co..D.......562 438-1126
3001 E Anaheim St Long Beach (90804) ***(P-16842)***
American Textile Maint Co..D.......951 684-4940
4459 Brockton Ave Riverside (92501) ***(P-16843)***
American Textile Maint Co..D.......323 735-1661
1664 W Washington Blvd Los Angeles (90007) ***(P-16844)***
American Textile Maint Co..C.......562 424-1607
2201 E Carson St Long Beach (90807) ***(P-16882)***
American Tire Depot, Vernon *Also called Atv Inc* ***(P-18814)***
American Tooth Industries ....D.......805 487-9868
1200 Stellar Dr Oxnard (93033) ***(P-13474)***
American Trading Intl Inc..D.......310 445-2000
3415 S Sepulveda Blvd # 6 Los Angeles (90034) ***(P-14556)***
American Transportation Co LLC ....D.......818 660-2343
635 W Colo St Ste 108a Glendale (91204) ***(P-12564)***
American Travel Solutions LLC..D.......818 359-6514
27509 Agoura Rd Ste 100 Agoura Hills (91301) ***(P-12382)***

American Trnsp Systems ......E......562 531-8000
3133 E South St Long Beach (90805) ***(P-11908)***

American Two-Way, North Hollywood *Also called Emergency Technologies Inc* ***(P-18375)***

American Ultraviolet West Inc ......E......310 784-2930
23555 Telo Ave Torrance (90505) ***(P-7684)***

American Untd HM Care Crp-Priv, Studio City *Also called American Private Duty Inc* ***(P-21133)***

American Vanguard Corporation (PA) ......**C......949 260-1200**
4695 Macarthur Ct Newport Beach (92660) ***(P-5165)***

American Vision Windows Inc ......C......805 582-1833
2125 N Madera Rd Ste A Simi Valley (93065) ***(P-19023)***

American West Worldwide Ex Inc (PA) ......**D......800 788-4534**
51 Zaca Ln Ste 120 San Luis Obispo (93401) ***(P-12106)***

American Window Covering Inc ......F......714 879-3880
825 Williamson Ave Fullerton (92832) ***(P-16875)***

American Wire Inc ......F......909 884-9990
784 S Lugo Ave San Bernardino (92408) ***(P-7494)***

American Wire Sales, Rancho Dominguez *Also called Standard Wire & Cable Co* ***(P-6357)***

American Wrecking Inc ......D......626 350-8303
2459 Lee Ave South El Monte (91733) ***(P-1609)***

American Zabin Intl Inc ......E......213 746-3770
3933 S Hill St Los Angeles (90037) ***(P-4479)***

American Zettler Inc (HQ) ......**E......949 831-5000**
75 Columbia Aliso Viejo (92656) ***(P-13700)***

American Zinc Enterprises, Walnut *Also called Sea Shield Marine Products* ***(P-6371)***

Americantours Intl LLC (HQ) ......**C......310 641-9953**
6053 W Century Blvd # 70 Los Angeles (90045) ***(P-12383)***

Americare Ambulance Service, Huntington Beach *Also called Americare Medservices Inc* ***(P-11853)***

Americare Medservices Inc ......D......310 632-1141
6524 Fremont Cir Huntington Beach (92648) ***(P-11853)***

Americas Christian Credit Un (PA) ......**D......626 208-5400**
2100 E Route 66 Ste 100 Glendora (91740) ***(P-15058)***

Americas Gold Inc ......E......213 688-4904
650 S Hill St Ste 224 Los Angeles (90014) ***(P-11309)***

Americas Gold - Amrcas Damonds, Los Angeles *Also called Americas Gold Inc* ***(P-11309)***

Americas Moneyline Inc ......E......800 247-6663
27081 Aliso Creek Rd # 20 Aliso Viejo (92656) ***(P-15236)***

Americas Printer.com, Buena Park *Also called A J Parent Company Inc* ***(P-18426)***

Americawear, Commerce *Also called RDD Enterprises Inc* ***(P-2747)***

Americh Corporation (PA) ......**C......818 982-1711**
13222 Saticoy St North Hollywood (91605) ***(P-11086)***

Americhip Inc (PA) ......**E......310 323-3697**
19032 S Vermont Ave Gardena (90248) ***(P-4229)***

Americo Builders LLC ......E......714 430-7730
1511 E Orangethorpe Ave Fullerton (92831) ***(P-592)***

Americon ......F......805 987-0412
900 Flynn Rd Camarillo (93012) ***(P-3576)***

Americor Funding Inc ......C......866 333-8686
18200 Von Karman Ave # 600 Irvine (92612) ***(P-16944)***

Ameriflex Inc ......D......951 737-5557
2390 Railroad St Corona (92878) ***(P-7527)***

Amerifoods Trading Company LLC (HQ) ......**A......323 869-7500**
600 Citadel Dr Commerce (90040) ***(P-14453)***

Amerihome Inc ......A......888 469-0810
1 Baxter Way Ste 300 Westlake Village (91362) ***(P-15171)***

Amerihome Mortgage Company LLC ......A......888 469-0810
1 Baxter Way Ste 300 Westlake Village (91362) ***(P-15262)***

Ameriko Inc (PA) ......**C......626 795-7988**
980 S Arroyo Pkwy Ste 240 Pasadena (91105) ***(P-23389)***

Ameriko Industries, Pasadena *Also called Ameriko Inc* ***(P-23389)***

Ameripark LLC ......B......949 279-7525
17165 Von Karman Ave # 110 Irvine (92614) ***(P-18763)***

Ameripec Inc ......C......714 690-9191
6965 Aragon Cir Buena Park (90620) ***(P-2254)***

Ameripharma, Orange *Also called Harpers Pharmacy Inc* ***(P-4829)***

Ameripride Services Inc ......C......661 324-7941
335 Washington St Bakersfield (93307) ***(P-16845)***

Ameripride Unifom Svcs, Bakersfield *Also called Ameripride Services Inc* ***(P-16845)***

Amerisourcebergen Drug Corp ......C......951 371-2000
1851 California Ave Corona (92881) ***(P-14233)***

Amerit Fleet Solutions Inc ......A......909 357-0100
15325 Manila St Fontana (92337) ***(P-18921)***

Ameritac Inc (PA) ......**D......925 989-2942**
24 Toscana Way W Rancho Mirage (92270) ***(P-23390)***

Ameritex International, Los Angeles *Also called Amtex California Inc* ***(P-3091)***

Ameritrans Express Inc ......F......818 201-0524
15130 Ventura Blvd # 313 Sherman Oaks (91403) ***(P-12421)***

Ameron International Corp ......C......425 258-2616
1020 B St Fillmore (93015) ***(P-6016)***

Ameron International Corp ......D......805 524-0223
1020 B St Fillmore (93015) ***(P-6017)***

Ameru, Los Angeles *Also called Romar Group Inc* ***(P-2760)***

Ames Construction Inc ......C......951 356-1275
391 N Main St Ste 302 Corona (92878) ***(P-1427)***

Ames Industrial, Los Angeles *Also called Ames Rubber Mfg Co Inc* ***(P-5365)***

Ames Rubber Mfg Co Inc ......E......818 240-9313
4516 Brazil St Los Angeles (90039) ***(P-5365)***

Ametek Aerospace ......F......949 473-6754
17072 Daimler St Irvine (92614) ***(P-10674)***

Ametek Ameron LLC ......E......626 337-4640
4750 Littlejohn St Baldwin Park (91706) ***(P-10565)***

Ametek Ameron LLC (HQ) ......**D......626 856-0101**
4750 Littlejohn St Baldwin Park (91706) ***(P-10675)***

Ametek HCC, Rosemead *Also called Hermetic Seal Corporation* ***(P-9722)***

Ametek Intellipower, Orange *Also called Intellipower Inc* ***(P-13731)***

AMF Pharma LLC ......F......909 930-9599
1909 S Campus Ave Ontario (91761) ***(P-4781)***

AMF Support Surfaces Inc (HQ) ......**C......951 549-6800**
1691 N Delilah St Corona (92879) ***(P-3542)***

Amfoam Inc (PA) ......**D......310 327-4003**
15110 S Broadway Gardena (90248) ***(P-5488)***

AMG Construction Group ......D......800 310-2609
1103 W Gardena Blvd # 201 Gardena (90248) ***(P-858)***

AMG Employee Management Inc ......F......323 254-7448
3235 N San Fernando Rd 1d Los Angeles (90065) ***(P-11300)***

AMG Huntington Beach LLC ......E......714 894-9802
5416 Argosy Ave Huntington Beach (92649) ***(P-22486)***

AMG Torrance LLC (HQ) ......**D......310 515-2584**
5401 Business Dr Huntington Beach (92649) ***(P-10268)***

Amgen Distribution Inc ......D......760 989-4424
1244 Valley View Rd # 119 Glendale (91202) ***(P-12010)***

Amgen Inc (PA) ......**A......805 447-1000**
1 Amgen Center Dr Thousand Oaks (91320) ***(P-4929)***

Amgen Manufacturing Limited ......D......787 656-2000
1 Amgen Center Dr Newbury Park (91320) ***(P-11630)***

Amgen USA Inc (HQ) ......**D......805 447-1000**
1 Amgen Center Dr Thousand Oaks (91320) ***(P-4782)***

Amgraph, Ontario *Also called American Fleet & Ret Graphics* ***(P-11522)***

Amgreen Solar & Electric Inc ......E......213 388-5647
1367 Venice Blvd Los Angeles (90006) ***(P-1026)***

Amgreen Solutions Inc ......E......213 388-5647
1367 Venice Blvd Fl 2 Los Angeles (90006) ***(P-23155)***

AMI, Costa Mesa *Also called Advanced Micro Instruments Inc* ***(P-10777)***

AMI-Hti Trzana Encino Jint Vnt ......C......818 881-0800
18321 Clark St Tarzana (91356) ***(P-20673)***

Amiad Filtration Systems, Oxnard *Also called Amiad USA Inc* ***(P-8362)***

Amiad USA Inc ......E......805 988-3323
1251 Maulhardt Ave Oxnard (93030) ***(P-8362)***

Amico - Diamond Perforated, Visalia *Also called Diamond Perforated Metals Inc* ***(P-7142)***

Amico Fontana, Fontana *Also called Alabama Metal Industries Corp* ***(P-6949)***

Aminco International USA Inc ......D......949 457-3261
20571 Crescent Bay Dr Lake Forest (92630) ***(P-11310)***

Amiri, Los Angeles *Also called Atelier Luxury Group LLC* ***(P-3168)***

Amisub of California Inc (HQ) ......**A......818 881-0800**
18321 Clark St Tarzana (91356) ***(P-20674)***

Amity Foundation, Los Angeles *Also called Epidaurus* ***(P-16177)***

Amity Washer & Stamping Co ......F......562 941-1259
10926 Painter Ave Santa Fe Springs (90670) ***(P-7123)***

Amk Foodservices Inc ......C......805 544-7600
830 Capitolio Way San Luis Obispo (93401) ***(P-14454)***

Amko Service Company ......D......760 246-3600
17909 Adelanto Rd Adelanto (92301) ***(P-19024)***

AMO Usa Inc ......C......714 247-8200
1700 E Saint Andrew Pl Santa Ana (92705) ***(P-10932)***

Amoretti, Oxnard *Also called Noushig Inc* ***(P-2025)***

Amos Art Studio, Northridge *Also called Emanuel Morez Inc* ***(P-3470)***

AMP, Santa Ana *Also called Accelerated Memory Prod Inc* ***(P-9472)***

AMP Display Inc (PA) ......**E......909 980-1310**
9856 6th St Rancho Cucamonga (91730) ***(P-22487)***

AMP Plus Inc ......D......323 231-2600
2042 E Vernon Ave Vernon (90058) ***(P-9113)***

AMP Research, Tustin *Also called Lund Motion Products Inc* ***(P-10095)***

Ampam Parks Mechanical Inc ......A......310 835-1532
17036 Avalon Blvd Carson (90746) ***(P-1027)***

Ampco Contracting Inc ......C......949 955-2255
1420 S Allec St Anaheim (92805) ***(P-13004)***

Ampersand Contract Signing Grp, Los Angeles *Also called Ahr Signs Incorporated* ***(P-11521)***

Ampersand Publishing LLC (PA) ......**E......805 564-5200**
715 Anacapa St Santa Barbara (93101) ***(P-3944)***

Amphastar Pharmaceuticals Inc (PA) ......**C......909 980-9484**
11570 6th St Rancho Cucamonga (91730) ***(P-4783)***

Amphenol Nelson-Dunn Tech Inc (HQ) ......**E......714 249-7700**
17707 Valley View Ave Cerritos (90703) ***(P-13886)***

Amphion, Rancho Cucamonga *Also called Executive Safe and SEC Corp* ***(P-7557)***

Amplifier Technologies Inc ......E......323 278-0001
1749 Chapin Rd Montebello (90640) ***(P-9252)***

AMpm Maintenance Corporation ......E......424 230-1300
1010 E 14th St Los Angeles (90021) ***(P-2720)***

Ampronix Inc ......D......949 273-8000
15 Whatney Irvine (92618) ***(P-13475)***

Amrapur Overseas Incorporated (PA) ......**E......714 893-8808**
1560 E 6th St Ste 101 Corona (92879) ***(P-2721)***

Amrel, Pasadena *Also called American Reliance Inc* ***(P-8148)***

Amrep Inc (HQ) ......**C......909 923-0430**
1555 S Cucamonga Ave Ontario (91761) ***(P-4952)***

Amrep Manufacturing Co LLC ......B......877 468-9278
1555 S Cucamonga Ave Ontario (91761) ***(P-7961)***

Amrex Electrotherapy Equipment, Paramount *Also called Amrex-Zetron Inc* ***(P-9855)***

Amrex-Zetron Inc ......E......310 527-6868
7034 Jackson St Paramount (90723) ***(P-9855)***

Amro Fabricating Corporation ......E......951 842-6140
17101 Heacock St Moreno Valley (92551) ***(P-10269)***

Amro Fabricating Corporation (PA) ......**C......626 579-2200**
1430 Amro Way South El Monte (91733) ***(P-10270)***

AMS - Exotic LLC ......D......213 612-5888
720 S Alameda St Los Angeles (90021) ***(P-14614)***

AMS American Mech Svcs MD Inc ......C......714 888-6820
2116 E Walnut Ave Fullerton (92831) ***(P-1028)***

AMS Fulfillement, Valencia *Also called Advantage Media Services Inc* ***(P-12554)***

AMS Fulfillment, Valencia *Also called Advantage Media Services Inc* ***(P-12183)***

Amsafe Bridport, Anaheim *Also called Bridport Erie Aviation Inc* ***(P-19025)***

Amsco US Inc ......C......562 630-0333
15341 Texaco Ave Paramount (90723) ***(P-9674)***

Amscope, Irvine *Also called United Scope LLC (P-10864)*
Amsec, Fontana *Also called American Security Products Co (P-7548)*
Amsurg, Colton *Also called Premier Otptent Srgery Ctr Inc (P-20024)*
Amsurg, Glendale *Also called Glendale Eye Medical Group (P-19831)*
Amt Datasouth Corp (PA) ....E.......**805 388-5799**
803 Camarillo Springs Rd D Camarillo (93012) *(P-22824)*
Amtech Elevator Services, Los Angeles *Also called Pacific Coast Elevator Corp (P-19053)*
Amtex California Inc ....E.......323 859-2200
113 S Utah St Los Angeles (90033) *(P-3091)*
Amtrav, Agoura Hills *Also called American Travel Solutions LLC (P-12382)*
Amtrend Corporation ....D.......714 630-2070
1458 Manhattan Ave Fullerton (92831) *(P-3637)*
Amtv USA, Pasadena *Also called American Multimedia TV USA (P-12710)*
Amvac Chemical Corporation (HQ) ....E.......**323 264-3910**
4695 Macarthur Ct # 1200 Newport Beach (92660) *(P-5166)*
Amwear USA Inc ....E.......800 858-6755
250 Benjamin Dr Corona (92879) *(P-2740)*
Amwest Funding Corp ....D.......714 831-3333
6 Pointe Dr Ste 300 Brea (92821) *(P-15149)*
Amwins Access Insur Svcs LLC (HQ) ....D.......**310 683-0469**
435 N Pcf Cast Hwy Ste 2 Redondo Beach (90277) *(P-15531)*
Amwins Connect Insur Svcs LLC ....D.......714 460-5153
2677 N Main St Ste 800 Santa Ana (92705) *(P-15523)*
Amwins Insurance Brkg Cal LLC (HQ) ....D.......**818 772-1774**
21550 Oxnard St Ste 1100 Woodland Hills (91367) *(P-15532)*
An Open Check, Costa Mesa *Also called North American Acceptance Corp (P-15147)*
Ana Nacapa Surgical Associates, Ventura *Also called Ventura County Medical Center (P-20137)*
Ana Trading Corp USA (HQ) ....D.......**310 542-2500**
3625 Del Amo Blvd Ste 300 Torrance (90503) *(P-13887)*
Anabella Hotel The, Anaheim *Also called Fjs Inc (P-16445)*
Anabelle Hotel Inc ....D.......818 845-7800
2011 W Olive Ave Burbank (91506) *(P-16318)*
Anabolic Incorporated ....E.......949 863-0340
17802 Gillette Ave Irvine (92614) *(P-4784)*
Anabolic Laboratories Inc ....E.......949 863-0340
26021 Commercentre Dr Lake Forest (92630) *(P-4785)*
Anacapa Boatyard, Newport Beach *Also called Anacapa Marine Services (P-10458)*
Anacapa Marine Services (PA) ....F.......**805 985-1818**
151 Shipyard Way Ste 5 Newport Beach (92663) *(P-10458)*
Anaco Inc ....C.......951 372-2732
1001 El Camino Ave Corona (92879) *(P-8102)*
Anacom General Corporation ....E.......714 774-8484
1240 S Claudina St Anaheim (92805) *(P-9158)*
Anacom Medtek, Anaheim *Also called Anacom General Corporation (P-9158)*
Anadite Cal Restoration Tr ....C.......562 861-2205
10647 Garfield Ave South Gate (90280) *(P-7210)*
Anaheim - 1855 S Hbr Blvd Owne ....D.......714 750-1811
1855 S Harbor Blvd Anaheim (92802) *(P-16319)*
Anaheim Arena Management LLC ....A.......714 704-2400
2695 E Katella Ave Anaheim (92806) *(P-19405)*
Anaheim Automation Inc ....E.......714 992-6990
4985 E Landon Dr Anaheim (92807) *(P-8943)*
Anaheim Ca LLC ....D.......714 634-4500
100 The City Dr S Orange (92868) *(P-16320)*
Anaheim Crest Nursing Center, Anaheim *Also called 3067 Orange Avenue LLC (P-20237)*
Anaheim Custom Extruders Inc ....E.......714 693-8508
1360 N Mccan St Anaheim (92806) *(P-5563)*
Anaheim Ducks Hockey Club LLC (PA) ....C.......**714 940-2900**
2695 E Katella Ave Anaheim (92806) *(P-19406)*
Anaheim General Hospital, Los Angeles *Also called Pacific Health Corporation (P-20878)*
Anaheim Global Medical Center ....A.......714 533-6220
1025 S Anaheim Blvd Anaheim (92805) *(P-20675)*
Anaheim Harbor Medical Group (PA) ....E.......**714 533-4511**
710 N Euclid St Anaheim (92801) *(P-19709)*
Anaheim Healthcare Center LLC ....D.......714 816-0540
501 S Beach Blvd Anaheim (92804) *(P-20244)*
Anaheim Hills Auto Body Inc ....D.......714 632-8266
3500 E La Palma Ave Anaheim (92806) *(P-18783)*
Anaheim Hills Medical Offices, Anaheim *Also called Kaiser Foundation Hospitals (P-19886)*
Anaheim Hotel LLC ....C.......714 750-1811
1855 S Harbor Blvd Anaheim (92802) *(P-16321)*
Anaheim Hotel, The, Anaheim *Also called Anaheim Plaza Hotel Inc (P-16324)*
Anaheim Kraemer Medical Offs, Anaheim *Also called Kaiser Foundation Hospitals (P-19888)*
Anaheim Majestic Garden Hotel, Anaheim *Also called Ken Real Estate Lease Ltd (P-16522)*
Anaheim Marriott Suites ....D.......714 750-1000
12015 Harbor Blvd Garden Grove (92840) *(P-16322)*
Anaheim Park Hotel ....C.......714 992-1700
222 W Houston Ave Fullerton (92832) *(P-16323)*
Anaheim Plaza Hotel Inc ....C.......714 772-5900
1700 S Harbor Blvd Anaheim (92802) *(P-16324)*
Anaheim Precision Mfg, Orange *Also called APM Manufacturing (P-10272)*
Anaheim Regional Medical Ctr ....C.......714 774-1450
1111 W La Palma Ave Anaheim (92801) *(P-20676)*
Anaheim Regional Medical Ctr ....C.......714 999-3847
1211 W La Palma Ave Anaheim (92801) *(P-20677)*
Anaheim Regional Medical Ctr (PA) ....A.......**714 774-1450**
1111 W La Palma Ave Anaheim (92801) *(P-21031)*
Anaheim V A Clinic, Anaheim *Also called Veterans Health Administration (P-20151)*
Anaheim Wire Products Inc ....E.......714 563-8300
1009 E Vermont Ave Anaheim (92805) *(P-7495)*
Anaheim/Orange Cnty Visitor Bu (PA) ....D.......**714 765-8888**
2099 S State College Blvd Anaheim (92806) *(P-18444)*
Anajet LLC ....E.......714 662-3200
1100 Valencia Ave Tustin (92780) *(P-7916)*
Analex Corporation ....C.......805 605-3898
Vndnburg A Frce Bldg 840 Lompoc (93438) *(P-22488)*
Analytic Endodontics, Orange *Also called Sybron Dental Specialties Inc (P-11197)*
Analytical Industries Inc ....E.......909 392-6900
2855 Metropolitan Pl Pomona (91767) *(P-10676)*
Analytik Jena US LLC (HQ) ....D.......**909 946-3197**
2066 W 11th St Upland (91786) *(P-10779)*
Anamex Corporation (PA) ....E.......**714 779-7055**
250 S Peralta Way Anaheim (92807) *(P-17546)*
Anaplex Corporation ....E.......714 522-4481
15547 Garfield Ave Paramount (90723) *(P-7211)*
Anas Iron Supply Inc ....F.......626 401-0483
1322 Santa Anita Ave South El Monte (91733) *(P-1565)*
Anasys Instruments Corp (PA) ....F.......**805 730-3310**
325 Chapala St Santa Barbara (93101) *(P-10780)*
Anatase Products, Tehachapi *Also called Henway Inc (P-11497)*
Anatec International, Inc., Brea *Also called Curtiss-Wrght Flow Ctrl Svc LL (P-22525)*
Anatesco Inc ....F.......661 399-6990
128 Bedford Way Bakersfield (93308) *(P-476)*
Anatex Enterprises Inc ....E.......818 908-1888
15929 Arminta St Van Nuys (91406) *(P-14091)*
Anaya Brothers Cutting LLC ....D.......323 582-5758
3130 Leonis Blvd Vernon (90058) *(P-3065)*
Ancca Corporation ....D.......949 553-0084
7 Goddard Irvine (92618) *(P-1363)*
Anchor Blue, Corona *Also called Hub Distributing Inc (P-14380)*
Anchor Loans LP ....C.......310 395-0010
1 Baxter Way 220 Westlake Village (91362) *(P-15172)*
Anchor Nationwide Loans, Westlake Village *Also called Anchor Loans LP (P-15172)*
Anchor-41 Construction LLC ....F.......559 740-7776
9301 W Airport Dr Ste A Visalia (93277) *(P-734)*
Anchore Inc ....E.......805 456-8981
800 Presidio Ave Ste B Santa Barbara (93101) *(P-17547)*
Anchored Prints Inc ....E.......714 929-9317
635 N Eckhoff St Ste Q Orange (92868) *(P-4230)*
Anco International Inc ....E.......909 887-2521
19851 Cajon Blvd San Bernardino (92407) *(P-7470)*
Ancon Marine ....D.......760 348-9606
6496 Brandt Rd Calipatria (92233) *(P-1634)*
Ancon Marine LLC ....D.......562 326-5900
2735 Rose Ave Signal Hill (90755) *(P-11955)*
Ancra International LLC ....E.......626 765-4818
601 S Vincent Ave Azusa (91702) *(P-7702)*
Ancra International LLC (HQ) ....C.......**626 765-4800**
601 S Vincent Ave Azusa (91702) *(P-7703)*
and 1, Aliso Viejo *Also called Basketball Marketing Co Inc (P-23168)*
and Syndicated Productions Inc ....D.......818 308-5200
3500 W Olive Ave Ste 1000 Burbank (91505) *(P-19094)*
Andanov Music, Burbank *Also called Hollywood Records Inc (P-9220)*
Andari Fashion Inc ....C.......626 575-2759
9626 Telstar Ave El Monte (91731) *(P-2798)*
Andaz West Hollywood ....D.......323 656-1234
8401 W Sunset Blvd Los Angeles (90069) *(P-16325)*
Anderco Inc ....E.......714 446-9508
540 Airpark Dr Fullerton (92833) *(P-3229)*
Andersen Industries Inc ....E.......760 246-8766
17079 Muskrat Ave Adelanto (92301) *(P-10163)*
Andersen Tax LLC ....D.......949 885-4550
3200 Park Center Dr # 1200 Costa Mesa (92626) *(P-16934)*
Andersen Tax LLC ....D.......213 593-2300
400 Suth Hope St Ste 2000 Los Angeles (90071) *(P-16935)*
Anderson & Howard Electric Inc ....C.......949 250-4555
15 Chrysler Irvine (92618) *(P-1213)*
Anderson Air Conditioning LP ....D.......714 998-6850
2100 E Walnut Ave Fullerton (92831) *(P-1029)*
Anderson Assoc Staffing Corp (PA) ....C.......**323 930-3170**
8200 Wilshire Blvd # 200 Beverly Hills (90211) *(P-17485)*
Anderson Bat Company LLC ....D.......714 524-7500
236 E Orangethorpe Ave Placentia (92870) *(P-11402)*
Anderson Burton Cnstr Inc (PA) ....D.......**805 481-5096**
121 Nevada St Arroyo Grande (93420) *(P-735)*
Anderson Chrnesky Strl Stl Inc ....D.......951 769-5700
353 Risco Cir Beaumont (92223) *(P-6587)*
Anderson Hay & Grain Co Inc ....D.......509 925-9818
915 E Colon St Wilmington (90744) *(P-14853)*
Anderson Howard, Irvine *Also called Anderson & Howard Electric Inc (P-1213)*
Anderson Kayne Capital ....B.......800 231-7414
1800 Avenue Of The Los Angeles (90067) *(P-15316)*
Anderson Kayne Inv MGT Inc (PA) ....D.......**310 556-2721**
1800 Avenue Of The Stars # 200 Los Angeles (90067) *(P-23156)*
Anderson McPharlin Conners LLP (PA) ....D.......**213 688-0080**
707 Wilshire Blvd # 4000 Los Angeles (90017) *(P-21505)*
Anderson Rubbish Disposal, Simi Valley *Also called Sea/Sue Inc (P-12978)*
Anderson Trophy Company, North Hollywood *Also called Pnk Enterprises Inc (P-7567)*
Andersonpenna Partners Inc (HQ) ....D.......**949 428-1500**
3737 Birch St Ste 250 Newport Beach (92660) *(P-23157)*
Andresen Digital Pre-Press, Santa Monica *Also called Aft Corporation (P-4628)*
Andrew Alexander Inc ....D.......323 752-0066
1306 S Alameda St Compton (90221) *(P-5867)*
Andrew L Youngquist Cnstr Inc ....D.......949 862-5611
3187 Red Hill Ave Ste 200 Costa Mesa (92626) *(P-736)*
Andrew Lauren Company Inc ....C.......949 861-4222
15225 Alton Pkwy Unit 300 Irvine (92618) *(P-18445)*
Andrew LLC ....F.......909 270-9356
17058 Lagos Dr Chino Hills (91709) *(P-1941)*
Andrews International Inc ....C.......818 260-9586
455 N Moss St Burbank (91502) *(P-18249)*
Andrews International Inc ....C.......310 575-4844
11601 Wilshire Blvd # 50 Los Angeles (90025) *(P-18250)*
Andrews International Inc (PA) ....A.......**818 487-4060**
455 N Moss St Burbank (91502) *(P-18251)*

Mergent e-mail: customerrelations@mergent.com
1056
2022 Southern California Business Directory and Buyers Guide
(P-0000) Products & Services Section entry number
(PA)=Parent Co (HQ)=Headquarters (DH)=Div Headquarters

Andrews Powder Coating Inc ....E....818 700-1030
10138 Canoga Ave Chatsworth (91311) *(P-7342)*
Androp Packaging Inc ....E....909 605-8842
4400 E Francis St Ontario (91761) *(P-3783)*
Anduril Industries Inc (PA) ....C....949 891-1607
2722 Michelson Dr Ste 150 Irvine (92612) *(P-10566)*
Andwin Corporation (PA) ....D....818 999-2828
167 W Cochran St Simi Valley (93065) *(P-14203)*
Andwin Scientific, Simi Valley *Also called Andwin Corporation (P-14203)*
Anello Corporation ....E....714 546-0561
111 E Garry Ave Santa Ana (92707) *(P-10933)*
Anemostat Inc ....E....310 835-7500
1220 E Watson Center Rd Carson (90745) *(P-13200)*
Anemostat Door Products Inc ....F....310 835-7500
1220 E Watson Center Rd Carson (90745) *(P-6690)*
Anemostat Products, Carson *Also called Mestek Inc (P-8345)*
Anesthsia Med Group Snta Brbar, Santa Barbara *Also called Anesthsia Med Group Snta Brbar (P-19710)*
Anesthsia Med Group Snta Brbar ....D....805 682-7751
514 W Pueblo St Fl 2 Santa Barbara (93105) *(P-19710)*
Anfinson Lumber Sales Inc (PA) ....D....951 681-4707
13041 Union Ave Fontana (92337) *(P-13201)*
Angel Lift Inc ....F....310 871-6115
10662 Mina St Whittier (90605) *(P-7704)*
Angel Manufacturing, Los Angeles *Also called Angels Garments (P-2799)*
Angel View Inc ....D....760 322-2440
454 N Indian Canyon Dr Palm Springs (92262) *(P-22080)*
Angel View Rsale Str - Palm Sp, Palm Springs *Also called Angel View Inc (P-22080)*
Angeles Clinic & RES Inst Inc ....D....310 582-7900
11818 Wilshire Blvd Los Angeles (90025) *(P-19711)*
Angeles Contractor Inc (PA) ....D....714 523-1021
783 Phillips Rowland Heights (91748) *(P-688)*
Angeles Mesa YWCA Chldren Lrng, Los Angeles *Also called Young Wns Chrstn Assn Grter Lo (P-22392)*
Angeles Park Communities Ltd ....C....310 277-4900
10301 W Pico Blvd Los Angeles (90064) *(P-15769)*
Angell & Giroux Inc ....D....323 269-8596
2727 Alcazar St Los Angeles (90033) *(P-3605)*
Angels Baseball LP (PA) ....A....714 940-2000
2000 E Gene Autry Way Anaheim (92806) *(P-19407)*
Angels Garments ....F....213 748-0581
525 E 12th St Ste 107 Los Angeles (90015) *(P-2799)*
Angels Hand Hospice Care Inc (PA) ....D....818 782-2516
2501 W Burbank Blvd # 310 Burbank (91505) *(P-20522)*
Angels In Motion LLC ....D....909 590-9102
4091 Riverside Dr Ste 111 Chino (91710) *(P-21134)*
Angels Nursing Center, Los Angeles *Also called Gva Enterprises Inc (P-20369)*
Angelus Aluminum Foundry Co ....E....323 268-0145
3479 E Pico Blvd Los Angeles (90023) *(P-6386)*
Angelus Block Co Inc (PA) ....E....714 637-8594
11374 Tuxford St Sun Valley (91352) *(P-6009)*
Angelus Sheet Metal & Plbg Sup, Los Angeles *Also called Angelus Sheet Metal Mfg Inc (P-6785)*
Angelus Sheet Metal Mfg Inc ....F....323 221-4191
1355 Carroll Ave Los Angeles (90026) *(P-6785)*
Angelus Shtmtl & Plbg Sup Inc ....F....323 221-4191
1355 Carroll Ave Los Angeles (90026) *(P-13822)*
Angelus Western Ppr Fibers Inc ....D....213 623-9221
2474 Porter St Los Angeles (90021) *(P-14109)*
Anheuser-Busch LLC ....C....949 263-9270
18952 Macarthur Blvd Irvine (92612) *(P-14820)*
Aniise Skin Care, Los Angeles *Also called Global Sales Inc (P-5025)*
Anillo Industries Inc (PA) ....E....714 637-7000
2090 N Glassell St Orange (92865) *(P-7055)*
Animal Health & Sanitary Sup, Riverside *Also called Health Tech Prof Pdts Inc (P-199)*
Animal Services Dept, Los Angeles *Also called City of Los Angeles (P-212)*
Animal Specialty Group ....D....818 244-7977
4641 Colorado Blvd Los Angeles (90039) *(P-197)*
Anitas Mexican Foods Corp (PA) ....B....909 884-8706
3454 N Mike Daley Dr San Bernardino (92407) *(P-2359)*
Anitsa Inc ....C....213 237-0533
6032 Shull St Bell Gardens (90201) *(P-16835)*
Anjana Software Solutions Inc ....D....805 583-0121
1445 E Los Angeles Ave 301t Simi Valley (93065) *(P-17548)*
Ankura Consulting Group LLC ....C....213 223-2109
633 W 5th St Fl 28 Los Angeles (90071) *(P-23414)*
Anmar Precision Components Inc ....E....818 764-0901
7424 Greenbush Ave North Hollywood (91605) *(P-10271)*
Anna Corporation ....E....951 736-6037
2078 2nd St Norco (92860) *(P-1167)*
Annandale Golf Club ....C....626 796-6125
1 N San Rafael Ave Pasadena (91105) *(P-19532)*
Annenberg Fndtion Tr At Snnyln (PA) ....C....760 202-2222
37977 Bob Hope Dr Rancho Mirage (92270) *(P-16172)*
Annex Pro Inc ....E....800 682-6639
4100 W Alameda Ave Fl 3 Burbank (91505) *(P-17782)*
Annie R Mitchell Elementary, Visalia *Also called Pta California Congress of Par (P-22359)*
Anning-Johnson Company ....E....626 369-7131
13250 Temple Ave City of Industry (91746) *(P-1364)*
Anns Trading Company Inc ....E....323 585-4702
5333 S Downey Rd Vernon (90058) *(P-14911)*
Anochem Coatings ....F....949 322-3280
4525 W 1st St Ste B Santa Ana (92703) *(P-7343)*
Anodizing Industries Inc ....E....323 227-4916
5222 Alhambra Ave Los Angeles (90032) *(P-7212)*
Anodyne Inc ....E....714 549-3321
2230 S Susan St Santa Ana (92704) *(P-7213)*
Anonymous Content LLC (PA) ....D....310 558-6000
3532 Hayden Ave Culver City (90232) *(P-19095)*
Anoroc Precision Shtmtl Inc ....E....310 515-6015
19122 S Santa Fe Ave Compton (90221) *(P-6786)*
Anp Lighting, Montclair *Also called American Nail Plate Ltg Inc (P-9057)*
Anre Technologies Inc ....C....818 627-5433
741 W Woodbury Rd Altadena (91001) *(P-17549)*
Ansar Gallery Inc ....C....949 220-0000
2505 El Camino Rd Tustin (92782) *(P-14455)*
Anschutz Entrtmt Group Inc (HQ) ....D....213 763-7700
800 W Olympic Blvd # 305 Los Angeles (90015) *(P-19343)*
Anschutz Film Group ....A....310 887-1000
1888 Century Park E # 1400 Los Angeles (90067) *(P-1365)*
Anschutz Film Group LLC (HQ) ....E....310 887-1000
1888 Century Park E # 1400 Los Angeles (90067) *(P-11267)*
Anschutz Sthern Cal Spt Cmplex ....C....310 630-2000
18400 Avalon Blvd Ste 100 Carson (90746) *(P-19408)*
Ansell Sndel Med Solutions LLC ....E....818 534-2500
9301 Oakdale Ave Ste 300 Chatsworth (91311) *(P-11087)*
Anser Advisory LLC (PA) ....D....310 351-8907
2677 N Main St Ste 400 Santa Ana (92705) *(P-23158)*
Ansett Arcft Spares & Svcs Inc (PA) ....D....818 362-1100
12675 Encinitas Ave Sylmar (91342) *(P-14052)*
Ansira Partners Inc ....D....818 461-6100
5000 Van Nuys Blvd Sherman Oaks (91403) *(P-18446)*
Answer Financial Inc (HQ) ....C....818 644-4000
15910 Ventura Blvd Fl 6 Encino (91436) *(P-18447)*
Antaeus Fashions Group Inc ....E....626 452-0797
2400 Chico Ave South El Monte (91733) *(P-2800)*
Antaira Technologies LLC (PA) ....E....714 386-7036
780 Challenger St Brea (92821) *(P-9331)*
Antaky Quilting Company, Los Angeles *Also called American Quilting Company Inc (P-3150)*
Antcom Corporation ....E....310 782-1076
367 Van Ness Way Ste 602 Torrance (90501) *(P-9253)*
Antelope Valley Health Center, Lancaster *Also called County of Los Angeles (P-21294)*
Antelope Valley Healthcare Dst, Lancaster *Also called Antelope Valley Hospital Inc (P-20678)*
Antelope Valley Hlth Care Dst, Lancaster *Also called Antelope Valley Hospital Inc (P-20680)*
Antelope Valley Home Care, Lancaster *Also called Antelope Valley Hospital Inc (P-20679)*
Antelope Valley Hospital, Lancaster *Also called Kaiser Foundation Hospitals (P-20810)*
Antelope Valley Hospital Inc ....D....661 726-6180
1600 W Avenue J Lancaster (93534) *(P-19712)*
Antelope Valley Hospital Inc (PA) ....A....661 949-5000
1600 W Avenue J Lancaster (93534) *(P-20678)*
Antelope Valley Hospital Inc ....C....661 949-5936
44335 Lowtree Ave Lancaster (93534) *(P-20679)*
Antelope Valley Hospital Inc ....C....661 949-5000
44335 Lowtree Ave Lancaster (93534) *(P-20680)*
Antelope Valley Hospital Inc ....C....661 726-6050
44105 15th St W Ste 100 Lancaster (93534) *(P-20681)*
Antelope Valley Hospital Inc ....C....661 949-5938
44335 Lowtree Ave Lancaster (93534) *(P-20682)*
Antelope Valley Lincoln, Lancaster *Also called Johnson Ford (P-18844)*
Antelope Valley Newspapers Inc ....E....661 940-1000
44939 10th St W Lancaster (93534) *(P-3945)*
Antelope Valley Press, Lancaster *Also called Antelope Valley Newspapers Inc (P-3945)*
Antelope Valley Surgery Ctr LP ....E....661 947-4600
44301 Lorimer Ave Lancaster (93534) *(P-19713)*
Antelope Vly Cntry CLB Imprv ....C....661 947-3142
39800 Country Club Dr Palmdale (93551) *(P-19533)*
Antelope Vly Convalecent Hosp, Lancaster *Also called Antelope Vly Retirement HM Inc (P-20551)*
Antelope Vly Dom Vlnce Council (PA) ....C....661 949-1916
1150 W Avenue I Lancaster (93534) *(P-21713)*
Antelope Vly Rcycl Dspsal Fclt ....D....661 945-5944
1200 W City Ranch Rd Palmdale (93551) *(P-12925)*
Antelope Vly Retirement HM Inc ....C....661 949-5584
44523 15th St W Lancaster (93534) *(P-20245)*
Antelope Vly Retirement HM Inc ....C....661 948-7501
44445 15th St W Lancaster (93534) *(P-20551)*
Antelope Vly Retirement HM Inc ....C....661 949-5524
44567 15th St W Lancaster (93534) *(P-20552)*
Antelope Vly Retirement Manor, Lancaster *Also called Antelope Vly Retirement HM Inc (P-20245)*
Antelope Vly Schl Trnsp Agcy ....C....661 952-3106
670 W Avenue L8 Lancaster (93534) *(P-11917)*
Antenna Works, Long Beach *Also called Metra Electronics Corporation (P-10102)*
Antex Knitting Mills, Los Angeles *Also called Tenenblatt Corporation (P-2648)*
Antex Knitting Mills, Los Angeles *Also called Matchmaster Dyg & Finshg Inc (P-2676)*
Antex Knitting Mills, Los Angeles *Also called Guru Knits Inc (P-2845)*
Anthony Inc (HQ) ....A....818 365-9451
12391 Montero Ave Sylmar (91342) *(P-8328)*
Anthony California Inc (PA) ....E....909 627-0351
14485 Monte Vista Ave Chino (91710) *(P-9058)*
Anthony Electric, Santa Fe Springs *Also called RGA Electric Inc (P-1308)*
Anthony International, Sylmar *Also called Anthony Inc (P-8328)*
Anthony Vineyards Inc ....D....760 391-5488
52 301 Enterprise Way Coachella (92236) *(P-40)*
Anthony Vineyards Inc (PA) ....E....661 858-6211
5512 Valpredo Ave Bakersfield (93307) *(P-41)*
Anthony Welded Products Inc (PA) ....E....661 721-7211
1447 S Lexington St Delano (93215) *(P-7705)*
Anthos Group Inc ....E....888 778-2986
705 N Douglas St El Segundo (90245) *(P-23159)*
Antigen Discovery, Irvine *Also called Immport Therapeutics Inc (P-11208)*
Antinos Management America Inc (PA) ....D....310 453-8506
2150 Colorado Ave Santa Monica (90404) *(P-22976)*

ALPHABETIC

Employee Codes: A=Over 500 employees, B=251-500
C=101-250, D=51-100, E=20-50 F=10-19
2022 Southern California Business
Directory and Buyers Guide
© Mergent Inc. 1-800-342-5647
1057

Antique Apparatus Company, Torrance *Also called Rock-Ola Manufacturing Corp* ***(P-9190)***
Antique Designs, Inglewood *Also called Glp Designs Inc* ***(P-3730)***
Antique Designs Ltd Inc....E....310 671-5400
916 W Hyde Park Blvd Inglewood (90302) ***(P-3577)***
Antis Roofg Waterproofing LLC....D....949 461-9222
2649 Campus Dr Irvine (92612) ***(P-1635)***
Anton Paar Usa Inc....E....310 775-2196
2824 Columbia St Torrance (90503) ***(P-15659)***
Anup Inc....D....760 921-2300
600 W Donlon St Blythe (92225) ***(P-16326)***
Anura Plastic Engineerign....E....626 814-9684
5050 Rivergrade Rd Baldwin Park (91706) ***(P-5564)***
Anvil Cases Inc....C....626 968-4100
1242 E Edna Pl Unit B Covina (91724) ***(P-5888)***
Anvil Iron, Gardena *Also called Anvil Steel Corporation* ***(P-1566)***
Anvil Steel Corporation....D....310 329-5811
134 W 168th St Gardena (90248) ***(P-1566)***
Anwright Corporation....E....818 896-2465
10225 Glenoaks Blvd Pacoima (91331) ***(P-7031)***
Anza A Calabasas Hotel, The, Calabasas *Also called 23627 Calabasas Road LLC* ***(P-16307)***
Anza Management Company (PA)....C....949 645-1422
2280 University Dr Newport Beach (92660) ***(P-15770)***
Ao Science + Technology....C....714 639-9860
144 N Orange St Orange (92866) ***(P-22710)***
Aoc LLC....D....951 657-5161
19991 Seaton Ave Perris (92570) ***(P-2705)***
AOC California Plant, Perris *Also called Aoc LLC* ***(P-2705)***
Aoclsc Inc....C....813 248-1988
8015 Paramount Blvd Pico Rivera (90660) ***(P-5287)***
Aoclsc Inc....E....562 776-4000
3365 E Slauson Ave Vernon (90058) ***(P-5288)***
Aocusa, Pico Rivera *Also called Aoclsc Inc* ***(P-5287)***
Aocusa, Vernon *Also called Aoclsc Inc* ***(P-5288)***
AON/Albert G Ruben Insur Svcs (HQ)....D....310 234-6800
10880 Wilshire Blvd # 700 Los Angeles (90024) ***(P-15533)***
Aos, Torrance *Also called Advanced Orthpdic Slutions Inc* ***(P-11083)***
Aot Electronics Inc....F....949 600-6335
2 Argos Laguna Niguel (92677) ***(P-8235)***
AP Express LLC (PA)....D....562 236-2250
5301a Rivergrade Rd Irwindale (91706) ***(P-12422)***
AP Global Inc....D....818 707-3167
2326 Townsgate Rd Westlake Village (91361) ***(P-13701)***
AP Parpro Inc (PA)....C....714 545-8886
2700 S Fairview St Santa Ana (92704) ***(P-18448)***
APA Incorporated....D....310 888-4200
405 S Beverly Dr Beverly Hills (90212) ***(P-23160)***
APC-Lsma Dsmc (HQ)....C....626 282-0288
1668 S Garfield Ave Fl 2 Alhambra (91801) ***(P-21384)***
Apct Anaheim, Orange *Also called Cirtech Inc* ***(P-18480)***
Apeiro Technologies, Irvine *Also called It Division Inc* ***(P-17645)***
Aperto Property Management Inc....C....626 965-1961
17351 Main St La Puente (91744) ***(P-15718)***
Aperto Property Management Inc (PA)....C....949 873-4200
2 Venture Ste 525 Irvine (92618) ***(P-15759)***
Apex Communications Inc (HQ)....F....818 379-8400
21700 Oxnard St Ste 1060 Woodland Hills (91367) ***(P-17783)***
Apex Computer Systems Inc....D....562 926-6820
13875 Cerritos Corprt Dr A Cerritos (90703) ***(P-18143)***
Apex Container Services, Commerce *Also called Apex Drum Company Inc* ***(P-3413)***
Apex Conveyor Corp....E....951 304-7808
27455 Bostik Ct Temecula (92590) ***(P-7685)***
Apex Conveyor Systems Inc....F....951 304-7808
27455 Bostik Ct Temecula (92590) ***(P-7686)***
Apex Design Technology, Anaheim *Also called Apex Technology Holdings Inc* ***(P-10567)***
Apex Drum Company Inc....F....323 721-8994
6226 Ferguson Dr Commerce (90022) ***(P-3413)***
Apex Holding Co....D....818 876-0161
23901 Calabasas Rd # 2090 Calabasas (91302) ***(P-14800)***
Apex Logistics Intl Inc (PA)....D....310 665-0288
18554 S Susana Rd Compton (90221) ***(P-12423)***
Apex Machine Works Inc....D....310 393-5987
2118 Wilshire Blvd # 258 Santa Monica (90403) ***(P-22489)***
Apex Parks Group LLC....D....210 341-6663
27061 Aliso Creek Rd # 100 Aliso Viejo (92656) ***(P-19633)***
Apex Technology Holdings Inc....A....321 270-3630
2850 E Coronado St Anaheim (92806) ***(P-10567)***
Apex USA, Compton *Also called Apex Logistics Intl Inc* ***(P-12423)***
Apffels Coffee Inc....D....562 309-0400
12115 Pacific St Santa Fe Springs (90670) ***(P-2351)***
Apg, Panorama City *Also called American Protection Group Inc* ***(P-18246)***
Apic Corporation....D....310 642-7975
5800 Uplander Way Culver City (90230) ***(P-9482)***
Apla Health & Wellness....D....213 201-1600
611 S Kingsley Dr Los Angeles (90005) ***(P-19714)***
Aplasticbag.com, Riverside *Also called Plasticbagsonsalecom Inc* ***(P-14226)***
APM Manufacturing (HQ)....C....714 453-0100
1738 N Neville St Orange (92865) ***(P-10272)***
APM Terminals Pacific LLC....B....310 221-4000
2500 Navy Way Pier 400 San Pedro (90731) ***(P-12424)***
APM Terminals Pacific LLC (HQ)....C....704 571-2768
2500 Navy Way San Pedro (90731) ***(P-12285)***
APn Business Resources Inc....D....818 717-9980
21418 Osborne St Canoga Park (91304) ***(P-23161)***
Apogee Electronics Corporation....E....310 584-9394
1715 Berkeley St Santa Monica (90404) ***(P-9159)***
Apogee Manufacturing....F....661 467-0440
28231 Avenue Crocker # 90 Valencia (91355) ***(P-8498)***

Apollo Couriers Inc (PA)....D....310 337-0377
1039 W Hillcrest Blvd Inglewood (90301) ***(P-12124)***
Apollo Electric....D....714 256-8414
330 N Basse Ln Brea (92821) ***(P-1214)***
Apollo Instruments Inc....F....949 756-3111
55 Peters Canyon Rd Irvine (92606) ***(P-10826)***
Apollo Medical Holdings Inc (PA)....D....626 282-0288
1668 S Garfield Ave Fl 2 Alhambra (91801) ***(P-22977)***
Apollo Metal Spinning Co Inc....F....562 634-5141
15315 Illinois Ave Paramount (90723) ***(P-7111)***
Apollo Printing & Graphics, Anaheim *Also called Tajen Graphics Inc* ***(P-4432)***
Apollo Technologies Inc....E....949 888-0573
31441 Snta Margarita Pkwy Rcho STA Marg (92688) ***(P-5211)***
Apollo Wood Recovery Inc....F....909 371-9510
7225 Edison Ave Ontario (91762) ***(P-3437)***
Apollomed, Alhambra *Also called Apollo Medical Holdings Inc* ***(P-22977)***
Apollotek International Inc....E....800 787-1244
1702 Mcgaw Ave Irvine (92614) ***(P-5212)***
Apotheka Systems Inc....E....844 777-4455
14040 Panay Way Marina Del Rey (90292) ***(P-17784)***
App Wholesale LLC....B....323 980-8315
3686 E Olympic Blvd Los Angeles (90023) ***(P-14669)***
App Winddown LLC (HQ)....F....213 488-0226
747 Warehouse St Los Angeles (90021) ***(P-3066)***
Apparel House USA, Gardena *Also called Stanzino Inc* ***(P-2590)***
Apparel News Group....E....213 327-1002
110 E 9th St Ste A777 Los Angeles (90079) ***(P-4052)***
Apparel Newsgroup, The, Los Angeles *Also called Mnm Corporation* ***(P-4086)***
Apparel Prod Svcs Globl LLC....E....818 700-3700
8954 Lurline Ave Chatsworth (91311) ***(P-2918)***
Apperson Inc (PA)....D....562 356-3333
17315 Studebaker Rd # 209 Cerritos (90703) ***(P-4597)***
Appetize Technologies Inc....C....877 559-4225
6601 Center Dr W Ste 700 Los Angeles (90045) ***(P-17785)***
Appfolio Inc (PA)....A....805 364-6093
50 Castilian Dr Ste 101 Goleta (93117) ***(P-17786)***
Apple Farm Collections-Slo Inc (PA)....B....805 544-2040
2015 Monterey St San Luis Obispo (93401) ***(P-16327)***
Apple One Employment, Glendale *Also called Howroyd-Wright Emplymnt Agcy* ***(P-17428)***
Apple Paper Converting Inc....E....714 632-3195
3800 E Miraloma Ave Anaheim (92806) ***(P-3922)***
Apple Store Glendale Galleria, Glendale *Also called Glendale Associates Ltd* ***(P-15670)***
Apple Tree International Corp....E....626 679-7025
10700 Business Dr Fontana (92337) ***(P-8149)***
Apple Valley Care Center, Apple Valley *Also called Front Prch Cmmnties Svcs - Cas* ***(P-20347)***
Applecare Medical MGT LLC....C....714 443-4507
18 Centerpointe Dr # 100 La Palma (90623) ***(P-22978)***
Appleone Employment Services, Glendale *Also called Howroyd-Wright Emplymnt Agcy* ***(P-17429)***
Applica Inc....F....818 565-0011
11651 Vanowen St North Hollywood (91605) ***(P-9254)***
Applied Business Software Inc....E....562 426-2188
2847 Gundry Ave Signal Hill (90755) ***(P-17787)***
Applied Cardiac Systems Inc....D....949 855-9366
1 Hughes Ste A Irvine (92618) ***(P-10934)***
Applied Circuit Solutions Inc....F....949 754-1545
3232 S Fairview St Santa Ana (92704) ***(P-9379)***
Applied Cmpsite Structures Inc (HQ)....C....714 990-6300
1195 Columbia St Brea (92821) ***(P-10273)***
Applied Coatings & Linings....E....626 280-6354
3224 Rosemead Blvd El Monte (91731) ***(P-7344)***
Applied Companies....E....661 257-0090
28020 Avenue Stanford Santa Clarita (91355) ***(P-22490)***
Applied Companies RE LLC....E....661 257-0090
28020 Avenue Stanford Valencia (91355) ***(P-15660)***
Applied Computer Solutions (HQ)....D....714 861-2200
15461 Springdale St Huntington Beach (92649) ***(P-17550)***
Applied Engineering MGT Corp....C....805 484-1909
760 Paseo Camarillo # 101 Camarillo (93010) ***(P-17551)***
Applied General Agency Inc (PA)....D....800 498-6880
1040 N Tustin Ave Anaheim (92807) ***(P-15534)***
Applied Instrument Tech Inc....E....909 204-3700
2121 Aviation Dr Upland (91786) ***(P-10781)***
Applied Manufacturing LLC....A....949 713-8000
22872 Avenida Empresa Rcho STA Marg (92688) ***(P-10935)***
Applied Medical Corporation (PA)....A....949 713-8000
22872 Avenida Empresa Rcho STA Marg (92688) ***(P-10936)***
Applied Medical Dist Corp....A....949 713-8000
22872 Avenida Empresa Rcho STA Marg (92688) ***(P-10937)***
Applied Medical Distribution, Rcho STA Marg *Also called Applied Medica Resources Corp* ***(P-10939)***
Applied Medical Resources, Rcho STA Marg *Also called Applied Medical Corporation* ***(P-10936)***
Applied Medical Resources....E....949 459-1042
30152 Esperanza Rcho STA Marg (92688) ***(P-10938)***
Applied Medical Resources Corp (HQ)....A....949 713-8000
22872 Avenida Empresa Rcho STA Marg (92688) ***(P-10939)***
Applied Natural Gas Fuels Inc....F....818 450-3659
31111 Agoura Rd Ste 208 Westlake Village (91361) ***(P-5126)***
Applied Orthopedic Design....F....805 481-3685
860 Oak Park Blvd Ste 101 Arroyo Grande (93420) ***(P-11088)***
Applied Polytech Systems Inc....E....818 504-9261
26000 Springbrook Ave # 102 Santa Clarita (91350) ***(P-3428)***
Applied Powdercoat Inc....E....805 981-1991
3101 Camino Del Sol Oxnard (93030) ***(P-7345)***
Applied Research Assoc Inc....D....505 881-8074
10833 Valley View St # 420 Cypress (90630) ***(P-22825)***

Mergent e-mail: customerrelations@mergent.com
1058
2022 Southern California Business Directory and Buyers Guide
(P-0000) Products & Services Section entry number
(PA)=Parent Co (HQ)=Headquarters (DH)=Div Headquarters

Applied Statistics & MGT Inc....E....951 699-4600
32848 Wolf Store Rd Ste A Temecula (92592) *(P-17788)*
Applied Technologies Assoc Inc (HQ)....**C....805 239-9100**
3025 Buena Vista Dr Paso Robles (93446) *(P-10869)*
Apponboard....F....707 933-7729
11620 Wilshire Blvd # 37 Los Angeles (90025) *(P-9211)*
Apprentice Jrnymen Trning Tr F....C....310 604-0892
7850 Haskell Ave Van Nuys (91406) *(P-21938)*
Approved Aeronautics LLC....E....951 200-3730
9130 Pulsar Ct Corona (92883) *(P-10274)*
Approved Networks LLC (PA)....**D....800 590-9535**
6 Orchard Ste 150 Lake Forest (92630) *(P-6177)*
Approved Optics, Lake Forest *Also called Approved Networks LLC (P-6177)*
APR Engineering Inc....E....562 983-3800
1812 W 9th St Long Beach (90813) *(P-10451)*
Apria Healthcare Group LLC (HQ)....**B....949 639-2000**
26220 Enterprise Ct Lake Forest (92630) *(P-21135)*
Apria Healthcare LLC (HQ)....**B....949 639-2000**
26220 Enterprise Ct Lake Forest (92630) *(P-17302)*
Apricot Designs Inc....D....626 966-3299
677 Arrow Grand Cir Covina (91722) *(P-10940)*
Apriso Corporation....C....562 951-8000
301 E Ocean Blvd Ste 1200 Long Beach (90802) *(P-17552)*
APS Global, Chatsworth *Also called Apparel Prod Svcs Globl LLC (P-2918)*
APT, Santa Ana *Also called American Pneumatic Tools Inc (P-7754)*
APT Electronics Inc....C....714 687-6760
241 N Crescent Way Anaheim (92801) *(P-9380)*
APT Manufacturing LLC....F....714 632-0040
2899 E Coronado St Ste E Anaheim (92806) *(P-7721)*
APT Metal Fabricators Inc....E....818 896-7478
11164 Bradley Ave Pacoima (91331) *(P-7124)*
Aptan Corp....E....213 748-5271
2000 S Main St Los Angeles (90007) *(P-2558)*
Aptco LLC (PA)....**D....661 792-2107**
31381 Pond Rd Bldg 2 Mc Farland (93250) *(P-4678)*
Apu Inc (PA)....**D....661 948-2880**
14939 Oxnard St Van Nuys (91411) *(P-13041)*
Apu Inc....D....818 508-7211
10452 Magnolia Blvd North Hollywood (91601) *(P-13042)*
Aputure Imaging Industries....F....626 295-6133
1715 N Gower St Los Angeles (90028) *(P-5930)*
APV Manufacturing & Engrg Co, Buena Park *Also called AM Machining Inc (P-14051)*
Apw Knox-Seeman Warehouse Inc (HQ)....**D....310 604-4373**
1073 E Artesia Blvd Carson (90746) *(P-13043)*
Aq Lighting Group Texas Inc....E....818 534-5300
28486 Wstnghuse Pl Ste 12 Santa Clarita (91355) *(P-13613)*
Aqua Blues, Los Angeles *Also called Shane Hunter LLC (P-3085)*
Aqua Mix Inc....E....951 256-3040
250 Benjamin Dr Corona (92879) *(P-4953)*
Aqua Performance Inc....E....951 340-2056
425 N Smith Ave Corona (92878) *(P-14073)*
Aqua Products Inc....F....714 670-0691
6351 Burnham Ave Ste B Buena Park (90621) *(P-8321)*
Aqua-Serv Engineers Inc (HQ)....**C....951 681-9696**
13560 Colombard Ct Fontana (92337) *(P-14772)*
Aquafine Corporation (HQ)....**D....661 257-4770**
29010 Avenue Paine Valencia (91355) *(P-8363)*
Aquahydrate Inc....D....310 559-5058
5870 W Jefferson Blvd D Los Angeles (90016) *(P-2255)*
Aquamar Inc....C....909 481-4700
10888 7th St Rancho Cucamonga (91730) *(P-2340)*
Aquamor LLC....D....951 541-9517
42188 Rio Nedo Temecula (92590) *(P-8364)*
Aquarian Coatings Corp....F....714 632-0230
2244 N Pacific St Orange (92865) *(P-7214)*
Aquarium of Pacific (PA)....**C....562 590-3100**
100 Aquarium Way Long Beach (90802) *(P-22237)*
Aquarius Rags LLC (PA)....**E....213 895-4400**
15821 Ventura Blvd # 270 Encino (91436) *(P-2877)*
Aquassage, Riverside *Also called Acura Spa Systems Inc (P-8441)*
Aquastar Pool Productions, Ventura *Also called Aquastar Pool Products Inc (P-8003)*
Aquastar Pool Products Inc....E....877 768-2717
2340 Palma Dr Ste 104 Ventura (93003) *(P-8003)*
Aquatec International Inc....D....949 225-2200
17422 Pullman St Irvine (92614) *(P-8004)*
Aquatec Water Systems, Irvine *Also called Aquatec International Inc (P-8004)*
Aquatic Co....C....714 993-1220
1700 N Delilah St Corona (92879) *(P-5528)*
Aquatic Co....C....714 993-1220
8101 E Kaiser Blvd # 200 Anaheim (92808) *(P-5529)*
Aquatic Industries Inc....E....800 877-2005
8101 E Kaiser Blvd # 200 Anaheim (92808) *(P-5530)*
Aqueos Corporation....D....805 676-4330
2550 Eastman Ave Ventura (93003) *(P-7665)*
Aqueos Corporation (PA)....**D....805 364-0570**
418 Chapala St Ste E Santa Barbara (93101) *(P-7666)*
Aqueous Technologies Corp....E....909 944-7771
1678 N Maple St Corona (92878) *(P-8365)*
Aquiesse, Moorpark *Also called Global Uxe Inc (P-11678)*
Aquirecorps Norwalk Auto Auctn....C....562 864-7464
12405 Rosecrans Ave Norwalk (90650) *(P-13019)*
AR Industries....F....626 332-8918
730 E Edna Pl Covina (91723) *(P-11631)*
AR Tech Aerospace, Fontana *Also called A&R Tarpaulins Inc (P-3132)*
Ar-Ce Inc....F....310 771-1960
141 E 162nd St Gardena (90248) *(P-11467)*
Araca Merchandise LP....D....818 743-5400
459 Park Ave San Fernando (91340) *(P-4480)*
Araco Enterprises LLC....B....818 767-0675
9189 De Garmo Ave Sun Valley (91352) *(P-12926)*
Aragon Construction Inc....D....909 621-2200
5440 Arrow Hwy Montclair (91763) *(P-737)*
Arakelian Enterprises Inc (PA)....**A....626 336-3636**
14048 Valley Blvd City of Industry (91746) *(P-12927)*
Aram Precision Tool & Die Inc....F....818 998-1000
9758 Cozycroft Ave Chatsworth (91311) *(P-8499)*
Aramark Facility Services LLC....C....213 740-8968
941 W 35th St Los Angeles (90007) *(P-17215)*
Aramark Healthcare Sprt Serv, Santa Maria *Also called Aramark Healthcare Support (P-21385)*
Aramark Healthcare Support....C....805 739-3000
1400 E Church St Santa Maria (93454) *(P-21385)*
Aramark Unf & Career AP LLC....D....818 973-3700
115 N First St Burbank (91502) *(P-16846)*
Aramark Unf & Career AP LLC (HQ)....**C....818 973-3700**
115 N First St Ste 203 Burbank (91502) *(P-16883)*
Aramark Uniform Mfg Co....F....800 999-8989
115 N First St Burbank (91502) *(P-11632)*
Aranda Tooling Inc....D....714 379-6565
13950 Yorba Ave Chino (91710) *(P-8500)*
Arandas Woodcraft Inc....E....310 538-9945
137 W 157th St Gardena (90248) *(P-3304)*
Ararat Convalescent Hospital, Los Angeles *Also called Ararat Home Los Angeles Inc (P-20554)*
Ararat Home Los Angeles Inc....C....818 837-1800
15099 Mission Hills Rd Mission Hills (91345) *(P-20553)*
Ararat Home Los Angeles Inc....C....323 256-8012
2373 Colorado Blvd Los Angeles (90041) *(P-20554)*
Ararat Nursing Facility, Mission Hills *Also called Ararat Home Los Angeles Inc (P-20553)*
ARB, Lake Forest *Also called Juniper Rock Corporation (P-564)*
Arb Inc (HQ)....**C....949 598-9242**
26000 Commercentre Dr Lake Forest (92630) *(P-933)*
Arbitech LLC....D....949 376-6650
64 Fairbanks Irvine (92618) *(P-13376)*
Arbiter Systems Incorporated (PA)....**E....805 237-3831**
1324 Vendels Cir Ste 121 Paso Robles (93446) *(P-10742)*
Arbo Box Inc....F....562 404-2726
2900 Supply Ave Commerce (90040) *(P-3374)*
Arbonne International LLC (HQ)....**E....949 770-2610**
9400 Jeronimo Rd Irvine (92618) *(P-4786)*
Arbor Glen Care Center, Glendora *Also called Ensign San Dimas LLC (P-20579)*
Arborland Enterprises Inc....D....714 871-2311
1700 W Valencia Dr Fullerton (92833) *(P-21983)*
Arborland Mntssori Chld Acdemy, Fullerton *Also called Arborland Enterprises Inc (P-21983)*
Arbormed Inc (PA)....**C....714 689-1500**
725 W Town And Country Rd Orange (92868) *(P-21386)*
ARC, Torrance *Also called Good Sports Plus Ltd (P-17629)*
ARC (PA)....**E....714 424-8500**
345 Clinton St Costa Mesa (92626) *(P-17145)*
ARC - Imperial Valley (PA)....**D....760 352-0180**
298 E Ross Ave El Centro (92243) *(P-21714)*
ARC - Imperial Valley....E....760 768-1944
340 E 1st St Calexico (92231) *(P-21274)*
ARC Imaging Resources, Monterey Park *Also called American Reprographics Co LLC (P-17144)*
ARC Los Angles Orange Counties (PA)....**D....562 803-1556**
12049 Woodruff Ave Downey (90241) *(P-21939)*
ARC Plastics Inc....E....562 802-3299
14010 Shoemaker Ave Norwalk (90650) *(P-5565)*
ARC Riverside....D....951 845-3385
702 E Eleventh St Beaumont (92223) *(P-21715)*
Arcadia Inc....E....310 665-0490
2323 Firestone Blvd South Gate (90280) *(P-6691)*
Arcadia Cabinetry LLC....F....909 550-0074
5467 Brooks St Montclair (91763) *(P-3305)*
Arcadia Contractors Inc....D....714 562-8200
5692 Fresca Dr La Palma (90623) *(P-3578)*
Arcadia Convalescent Hosp Inc (PA)....**C....626 445-2170**
1601 S Baldwin Ave Arcadia (91007) *(P-20555)*
Arcadia Convalescent Hosp Inc....D....818 352-4438
10158 Sunland Blvd Sunland (91040) *(P-20246)*
Arcadia Gardens MGT Corp....D....626 574-8571
720 W Camino Real Ave Arcadia (91007) *(P-20523)*
Arcadia Health Care Center, Arcadia *Also called Arcadia Convalescent Hosp Inc (P-20555)*
Arcadia Hotel Venture LP....D....626 445-8525
211 E Huntington Dr Arcadia (91006) *(P-16328)*
Arcadia Inc (PA)....**C....323 269-7300**
2301 E Vernon Ave Vernon (90058) *(P-6324)*
Arcadia Mri Centre, Arcadia *Also called Medical Imaging Partners LLC (P-19973)*
Arcadia Norcal, Vernon *Also called Arcadia Inc (P-6324)*
Arcadia Suites, Arcadia *Also called Springhill Suites LLC (P-16727)*
Arch Bay Holdings LLC....D....949 679-2400
327 W Maple Ave Monrovia (91016) *(P-16094)*
Arch Precision Components....E....714 961-9200
7100 Belgrave Ave Garden Grove (92841) *(P-10275)*
Arch Telecom Inc (PA)....**B....714 312-2724**
1940 W Corporate Way Anaheim (92801) *(P-12590)*
Arch-Rite Inc....E....714 630-9305
1062 N Armando St Anaheim (92806) *(P-3230)*
Archion, Glendora *Also called Postvision Inc (P-8211)*
Archipelago Inc....C....213 743-9200
1548 18th St Santa Monica (90404) *(P-4989)*
Archipelago Botanicals, Santa Monica *Also called Archipelago Inc (P-4989)*
Archipelago Lighting Inc....D....909 627-5333
4615 State St Montclair (91763) *(P-13614)*

ALPHABETIC

Employee Codes: A=Over 500 employees, B=251-500
C=101-250, D=51-100, E=20-50 F=10-19
2022 Southern California Business
Directory and Buyers Guide
© Mergent Inc. 1-800-342-5647
1059

Architctral Mllwk Snta Barbara.....E.....805 965-7011
8 N Nopal St Santa Barbara (93103) ***(P-3231)***
Architectural Coatings Inc.....E.....714 701-1360
1565 E Edinger Ave Santa Ana (92705) ***(P-1168)***
Architectural Design Signs Inc (PA).....D.....**951 278-0680**
1160 Railroad St Corona (92882) ***(P-11523)***
Architectural Doors Inc (PA).....D.....**714 898-3667**
17102 Newhope St Fountain Valley (92708) ***(P-13202)***
Architectural Enterprises Inc.....E.....323 268-4000
5821 Randolph St Commerce (90040) ***(P-6950)***
Architectural Shtmtl Contr, Temecula *Also called Pgc Construction Inc* ***(P-633)***
Architectural Window Shades.....D.....626 578-1936
9900 Gidley St El Monte (91731) ***(P-13158)***
Architectural Woodworking Co.....D.....626 570-4125
582 Monterey Pass Rd Monterey Park (91754) ***(P-3638)***
Archwood Mfg Group Inc.....F.....818 781-7673
15058 Delano St Van Nuys (91411) ***(P-560)***
Arclight Cinema Company.....D.....818 501-0753
15301 Ventura Blvd Bldg A Sherman Oaks (91403) ***(P-19270)***
Arclight Cinema Company.....C.....323 464-1465
120 N Robertson Blvd Fl 3 Los Angeles (90048) ***(P-19271)***
Arconic Fastening Systems, Carson *Also called Huck International Inc* ***(P-7067)***
Arconic Fastening Systems, Sylmar *Also called Valley-Todeco Inc* ***(P-7080)***
Arconic Fstening Systems Rings, Fontana *Also called Forged Metals Inc* ***(P-7086)***
Arconic Fstening Systems Rings, Sylmar *Also called JW Manufacturing Inc* ***(P-7069)***
Arcoro Holdings Corp.....F.....877 252-2168
27001 Agoura Rd Ste 280 Calabasas (91301) ***(P-17789)***
Arcs Commercial Mortgage Co LP (HQ).....C.....**818 676-3274**
26901 Agoura Rd Ste 200 Calabasas (91301) ***(P-15173)***
Arctic Glacier USA Inc.....C.....310 638-0321
17011 Central Ave Carson (90746) ***(P-2368)***
Arcules Inc.....D.....949 439-0053
17875 Von Karman Ave # 450 Irvine (92614) ***(P-17553)***
Arcutis Biotherapeutics Inc.....D.....805 418-5006
3027 Townsgate Rd Ste 300 Westlake Village (91361) ***(P-4787)***
Arden Engineering Inc (HQ).....E.....**949 877-3642**
3130 E Miraloma Ave Anaheim (92806) ***(P-10276)***
Arden Engineering Inc.....C.....714 998-6410
1878 N Main St Orange (92865) ***(P-10277)***
Arden Engineering Holdings Inc (HQ).....D.....**714 998-6410**
1878 N Main St Orange (92865) ***(P-10278)***
Arden/Paradise Manufacturing, Victorville *Also called Paradise Manufacturing Co Inc* ***(P-3143)***
Ardensel & Co Intl Inc.....F.....949 365-6943
30131 Town Center Dr # 298 Laguna Niguel (92677) ***(P-1809)***
Ardent Companies Inc.....D.....661 633-1465
4842 Airport Dr Bakersfield (93308) ***(P-1215)***
Ardent Mills LLC.....F.....951 201-1170
2020 E Steel Rd Colton (92324) ***(P-1942)***
Ardent Mills LLC.....F.....909 887-3407
19684 Cajon Blvd San Bernardino (92407) ***(P-1943)***
Ardwin Freight, Burbank *Also called Ardwin Inc* ***(P-12011)***
Ardwin Inc.....C.....818 767-7777
2940 N Hollywood Way Burbank (91505) ***(P-12011)***
Area Hsing Auth of The Cnty Vn (PA).....E.....**805 480-9991**
1400 W Hillcrest Dr Newbury Park (91320) ***(P-15771)***
Aremac Associates Inc.....E.....626 303-8795
2004 S Myrtle Ave Monrovia (91016) ***(P-8501)***
Aremac Heat Treating Inc.....E.....626 333-3898
330 S 9th Ave City of Industry (91746) ***(P-6429)***
Arena Painting Contractors Inc.....D.....310 316-2446
525 E Alondra Blvd Gardena (90248) ***(P-1169)***
Ares Investments Holdings LLC (HQ).....D.....**310 201-4100**
2000 Avenue Of The Stars # 12 Los Angeles (90067) ***(P-16247)***
Ares Management Corporation (PA).....B.....**310 201-4100**
2000 Avenue Of The Stars # 12 Los Angeles (90067) ***(P-16124)***
Ares Management LLC (HQ).....D.....**310 201-4100**
2000 Avenue Of The Stars # 12 Los Angeles (90067) ***(P-16125)***
Arete Associates (PA).....C.....**818 885-2200**
9301 Corbin Ave Ste 2000 Northridge (91324) ***(P-10568)***
Arevalo Tortilleria Inc.....E.....323 888-1711
3033 Supply Ave Commerce (90040) ***(P-2390)***
Arevalo Tortilleria Inc (PA).....D.....**323 888-1711**
1537 W Mines Ave Montebello (90640) ***(P-2391)***
Arga Cntrls A Unit Elctro Swtc, Rancho Cucamonga *Also called Electro Switch Corp* ***(P-9704)***
Arga Controls Inc.....F.....626 799-3314
10410 Trademark St Rancho Cucamonga (91730) ***(P-10677)***
Argent Management LLC (PA).....B.....**949 777-4000**
4131 S Main St Santa Ana (92707) ***(P-15772)***
Argent Management LLC.....D.....949 777-4070
4131 S Main St Santa Ana (92707) ***(P-15773)***
Argo Spring Mfg Co Inc.....D.....800 252-2740
13930 Shoemaker Ave Norwalk (90650) ***(P-7462)***
Argonaut.....E.....310 822-1629
5355 Mcconnell Ave Los Angeles (90066) ***(P-3946)***
Arguello Inc.....E.....805 567-1632
17100 Clle Mariposa Reina Goleta (93117) ***(P-440)***
Argus Contracting LLC (HQ).....D.....**562 422-7370**
11807 Smith Ave Santa Fe Springs (90670) ***(P-1366)***
Argus Management Company LLC.....B.....562 299-5200
5150 E Pcf Cast Hwy Ste 5 Long Beach (90804) ***(P-23391)***
Argus Medical Management, Long Beach *Also called Argus Management Company LLC* ***(P-23391)***
Argyle Precision, Orange *Also called ISI Detention Contg Group Inc* ***(P-8630)***
ARI Industries Inc.....D.....714 993-3700
17018 Edwards Rd Cerritos (90703) ***(P-8329)***
Aria Group Incorporated.....D.....949 475-2915
17395 Daimler St Irvine (92614) ***(P-22491)***
Arias Industries Inc.....E.....310 532-9737
275 Roswell Ave Long Beach (90803) ***(P-10018)***
Arias Pistons, Long Beach *Also called Arias Industries Inc* ***(P-10018)***
Aries 33 LLC.....E.....310 355-8330
3400 S Main St Los Angeles (90007) ***(P-2801)***
Ariston Hospitality Inc.....E.....626 458-8668
1124 Westminster Ave Alhambra (91803) ***(P-3722)***
Ariza Cheese Co Inc.....E.....562 630-4144
7602 Jackson St Paramount (90723) ***(P-1767)***
Arizona Channel Isla.....D.....480 788-0755
300 W 9th St Oxnard (93030) ***(P-19634)***
Arizona Pipeline Company (PA).....B.....**760 244-8212**
17372 Lilac St Hesperia (92345) ***(P-934)***
Arizona Pipeline Company.....C.....951 270-3100
1745 Sampson Ave Corona (92879) ***(P-935)***
Arizona Portland Cement, Glendora *Also called Calportland Company* ***(P-5975)***
Arizona Tile LLC.....D.....714 978-6403
1620 S Lewis St Anaheim (92805) ***(P-13292)***
Arjay's Window Fashions, Ventura *Also called Window Products Management Inc* ***(P-3300)***
Arjo Inc.....C.....714 412-1170
17502 Fabrica Way Cerritos (90703) ***(P-13476)***
Ark & Co, Los Angeles *Also called Bizz Inc* ***(P-14365)***
Ark Program, Lynwood *Also called Shields For Families* ***(P-21050)***
Arkebauer Properties, Irvine *Also called Western National Prpts LLC* ***(P-674)***
Arkema Coating Resins, Torrance *Also called Arkema Inc* ***(P-4634)***
Arkema Inc.....E.....310 214-5327
19206 Hawthorne Blvd Torrance (90503) ***(P-4634)***
Arkham Technology Limited (PA).....F.....**949 585-0404**
2525 Main St Ste 250 Irvine (92614) ***(P-22492)***
Arklin Brothers Hauling, Palmdale *Also called Antelope Vly Rcycl Dspsal Fclt* ***(P-12925)***
Arktura LLC (HQ).....E.....**310 532-1050**
18225 S Figueroa St Gardena (90248) ***(P-3565)***
Arlon Graphics LLC.....C.....714 985-6300
200 Boysenberry Ln Placentia (92870) ***(P-5426)***
Arlon LLC.....C.....714 540-2811
2811 S Harbor Blvd Santa Ana (92704) ***(P-5566)***
Armada Engineering LLC.....F.....818 280-5138
21305 Itasca St Chatsworth (91311) ***(P-22493)***
Armand Hmmer Mseum of Art Cltr.....C.....310 443-7000
10899 Wilshire Blvd Los Angeles (90024) ***(P-22216)***
Armani Trade LLC.....E.....310 849-0067
21255 Burbank Blvd Woodland Hills (91367) ***(P-23415)***
Armata Pharmaceuticals Inc (PA).....E.....**310 665-2928**
4503 Glencoe Ave Marina Del Rey (90292) ***(P-4930)***
Armc, Colton *Also called Arrowhead Regional Medical Ctr* ***(P-20683)***
Armed/Xctive Prtction Armed Un, Torrance *Also called Allied Protection Services Inc* ***(P-18241)***
Armen Living, Valencia *Also called Legacy Commercial Holdings Inc* ***(P-3476)***
Armenco Catrg Trck Mfg Co Inc.....E.....818 768-0400
11819 Vose St North Hollywood (91605) ***(P-9976)***
Arminak & Associates LLC.....D.....626 358-4804
4832 Azusa Canyon Rd A Irwindale (91706) ***(P-14912)***
Armorcast Products Company Inc.....E.....909 390-1365
500 S Dupont Ave Ontario (91761) ***(P-5567)***
Armored Group Inc.....E.....818 767-3030
11555 Cantara St North Hollywood (91605) ***(P-3375)***
Armored Transport Inc (HQ).....E.....**909 468-2229**
20325 E Walnut Dr N Walnut (91789) ***(P-18252)***
Armstrong Flooring Inc.....D.....323 562-7258
5037 Patata St South Gate (90280) ***(P-11619)***
Armtec Countermeasures Co (HQ).....C.....**760 398-0143**
85901 Avenue 53 Coachella (92236) ***(P-10569)***
Armtec Defense Products Co (HQ).....B.....**760 398-0143**
85901 Avenue 53 Coachella (92236) ***(P-7432)***
Arnaco Industrial Coatings.....E.....562 222-1022
8445 Warvale St Pico Rivera (90660) ***(P-7346)***
Arnel Commercial Properties (PA).....C.....**714 481-5023**
949 S Coast Dr Ste 600 Costa Mesa (92626) ***(P-15719)***
Arnel Development Company (PA).....D.....**714 481-5000**
949 S Coast Dr Ste 600 Costa Mesa (92626) ***(P-738)***
Arnett Construction Inc.....E.....909 421-7960
626 W 1st St Rialto (92376) ***(P-1591)***
Arnies Supply Service Ltd (PA).....E.....**323 263-1696**
1541 N Ditman Ave Los Angeles (90063) ***(P-3381)***
Arnold-Gonsalves Engrg Inc.....E.....909 465-1579
5731 Chino Ave Chino (91710) ***(P-8502)***
Aroma Spa & Sports LLC.....D.....213 387-2111
3680 Wilshire Blvd # 301 Los Angeles (90010) ***(P-19635)***
Aroma Wilshire Center, Los Angeles *Also called Hanil Development Inc* ***(P-16084)***
Aroma Wilshire Center, Los Angeles *Also called Aroma Spa & Sports LLC* ***(P-19635)***
Around The Clock Care, Bakersfield *Also called Vasinda Investments Inc* ***(P-17521)***
Around The Clock Home Care, Bakersfield *Also called Vasindas Around Clock Care Inc* ***(P-22162)***
Arq LLC (PA).....D.....**888 384-0971**
3002 Dow Ave Ste 524 Tustin (92780) ***(P-22494)***
Arriaga Usa Inc.....D.....818 764-1777
7127 Radford Ave North Hollywood (91605) ***(P-561)***
Arriaga Usa Inc (PA).....D.....**818 982-9559**
12000 Sherman Way North Hollywood (91605) ***(P-1411)***
Arrietta Incorporated.....E.....626 334-0302
429 N Azusa Ave Azusa (91702) ***(P-2392)***
Arrival Communications Inc (HQ).....D.....**661 716-2100**
1800 19th St Bakersfield (93301) ***(P-18449)***
Arrow Abrasive Company Inc.....E.....562 869-2282
12033 1/2 Regentview Ave Downey (90241) ***(P-6150)***

Arrow Disposal Services Inc....E....626 336-2255
14332 Valley Blvd La Puente (91746) *(P-12928)*
Arrow Engineering....E....626 960-2806
4946 Azusa Canyon Rd Irwindale (91706) *(P-8503)*
Arrow Screw Products Inc....E....805 928-2269
941 W Mccoy Ln Santa Maria (93455) *(P-8504)*
Arrow Staffing, Redlands *Also called Redlands Employment Services (P-17458)*
Arrow Transit Mix....E....661 945-7600
507 E Avenue L12 Lancaster (93535) *(P-6069)*
Arrow Truck Bodies & Eqp Inc....F....909 947-3991
1639 S Campus Ave Ontario (91761) *(P-9977)*
Arrowhead Brass & Plumbing LLC....D....323 221-9137
4900 Valley Blvd Los Angeles (90032) *(P-1030)*
Arrowhead Central Credit Union (PA)....B....866 212-4333
8686 Haven Ave Rancho Cucamonga (91730) *(P-15059)*
Arrowhead Country Club Golf Sp....D....909 882-1735
3433 Parkside Dr San Bernardino (92404) *(P-19534)*
ARROWHEAD COUNTRY CLUB PRO SHO, San Bernardino *Also called Arrowhead Country Club Golf Sp (P-19534)*
Arrowhead Ice, Torrance *Also called Southern California Ice Co (P-2374)*
Arrowhead Press Inc....E....626 358-1168
220 W Maple Ave Ste B Monrovia (91016) *(P-4231)*
Arrowhead Products Corporation....A....714 828-7770
4411 Katella Ave Los Alamitos (90720) *(P-10279)*
Arrowhead Regional Medical Ctr....A....909 580-1000
400 N Pepper Ave Colton (92324) *(P-20683)*
Arroyo Grande Care Center, Arroyo Grande *Also called Compass Health Inc (P-20288)*
Arroyo Holdings Inc (PA)....E....626 765-9340
898 N Fair Oaks Ave Pasadena (91103) *(P-6787)*
Arroyo Insurance Services Inc (PA)....D....626 799-9532
440 E Huntington Dr # 100 Arcadia (91006) *(P-15535)*
Arroyo Seco Medical Group (PA)....D....626 795-7556
301 S Fair Oaks Ave # 300 Pasadena (91105) *(P-19715)*
Arroyo Vista Family Health Ctr, Los Angeles *Also called Arroyo Vsta Fmly Hlth Fndation (P-19716)*
Arroyo Vsta Fmly Hlth Fndation....D....323 224-2188
2411 N Broadway Los Angeles (90031) *(P-19716)*
ARS, Burbank *Also called Hutchinson Arospc & Indust Inc (P-10345)*
ARS, Los Angeles *Also called Asian Rehabilitation Svc Inc (P-21941)*
ARS Enterprises (PA)....F....562 946-3505
15554 Minnesota Ave Paramount (90723) *(P-11089)*
Art & Logic Inc....D....818 500-1933
87 N Raymond Ave Pasadena (91103) *(P-18018)*
Art Bronze Inc....E....818 897-2222
11275 San Fernando Rd San Fernando (91340) *(P-6405)*
Art Drctors Gild Itse Lcal 876....D....818 762-9995
11969 Ventura Blvd # 200 Studio City (91604) *(P-22286)*
Art For Kids Inc....E....949 459-2800
23191 Arroyo Vis Rcho STA Marg (92688) *(P-3438)*
Art Gautreau Inc....E....714 934-8066
8210 Katella Ave Ste I Stanton (90680) *(P-739)*
Art Glass Etc Inc....E....805 644-4494
3111 Golf Course Dr Ventura (93003) *(P-3232)*
Art Mate, Gardena *Also called Artists Guild of America (P-23530)*
Art Mold Die Casting Inc....E....818 767-6464
11872 Sheldon St Sun Valley (91352) *(P-7777)*
Art Plates, Rancho Cucamonga *Also called Pitbull Gym Incorporated (P-5745)*
Artcrafters Cabinets....E....818 752-8960
5446 Cleon Ave North Hollywood (91601) *(P-3306)*
Arte De Mexico Inc (PA)....D....818 753-4559
1000 Chestnut St Burbank (91506) *(P-3606)*
Arte De Mexico Inc....D....818 753-4510
5506 Riverton Ave North Hollywood (91601) *(P-9078)*
Artech Industries Inc....E....951 276-3331
1966 Keats Dr Riverside (92501) *(P-9675)*
Artesia Christian Home Inc....C....562 865-5218
11614 183rd St Artesia (90701) *(P-20556)*
Artesia Sawdust Products Inc....E....909 947-5983
13434 S Ontario Ave Ontario (91761) *(P-3207)*
Arthrtis Fundation PCF Reg Inc....E....323 954-5760
800 W 6th St Ste 1250 Los Angeles (90017) *(P-22310)*
Arthur Dogswell LLC (PA)....E....888 559-8833
11301 W Olympic Blvd Los Angeles (90064) *(P-1955)*
Arthur Enterprises, Huntington Beach *Also called H & M Nursery Supply Corp (P-14860)*
Arthur J Gallagher & Co....D....559 733-1181
500 N Santa Fe St Visalia (93292) *(P-15536)*
Arthur J Gallagher & Co....D....800 217-9800
1825 Chicago Ave Ste 240 Riverside (92507) *(P-15537)*
Arthur J Gallagher Risk Mgmt....D....818 539-2300
505 N Brand Blvd Ste 600 Glendale (91203) *(P-15538)*
Arthur Loussararian MD, Mission Viejo *Also called Mission Internal Med Group Inc (P-19981)*
Arthurmade Plastics Inc....D....323 721-7325
2131 Garfield Ave Commerce (90040) *(P-5568)*
Artic Mechanical Inc (PA)....D....909 980-2539
10440 Trademark St Rancho Cucamonga (91730) *(P-1031)*
Artica & Arbox LLC....F....213 446-6272
9355 Wilshire Blvd # 300 Beverly Hills (90210) *(P-3067)*
Articouture Inc....E....626 336-7299
1265 S Johnson Dr City of Industry (91745) *(P-14326)*
Artificial Grass Liquidators....E....951 677-3377
42505 Rio Nedo Temecula (92590) *(P-11633)*
Artisan Entertainment Inc....A....310 449-9200
2700 Colorado Ave Ste 200 Santa Monica (90404) *(P-19096)*
Artisan Glass and Design Inc....D....714 542-0507
2665 W Woodland Dr Anaheim (92801) *(P-1636)*
Artisan House Inc....E....818 767-7476
8238 Lankershim Blvd North Hollywood (91605) *(P-7549)*
Artisan Nameplate Awards Corp....E....714 556-6222
2730 S Shannon St Santa Ana (92704) *(P-4481)*
Artisan Screen Printing Inc....C....626 815-2700
1055 W 5th St Azusa (91702) *(P-4482)*
Artisan Vehicle Systems Inc....D....805 402-6856
742 Pancho Rd Camarillo (93012) *(P-9935)*
Artist Silva Management LLC (PA)....C....323 856-8222
722 Seward St Los Angeles (90038) *(P-22979)*
Artistic Coverings Inc....E....562 404-9343
14135 Artesia Blvd Cerritos (90703) *(P-5489)*
Artistic Entrmt Svcs LLC....D....626 334-9388
120 N Aspan Ave Azusa (91702) *(P-19344)*
Artistic Maintenance Inc....D....949 733-8690
16092 Construction Cir E Irvine (92606) *(P-291)*
Artistic Plastics Inc....F....951 808-9700
725 E Harrison St Corona (92879) *(P-5569)*
Artistic Pltg & Met Finshg Inc....E....619 661-1691
2801 E Miraloma Ave Anaheim (92806) *(P-7215)*
Artistic Welding....D....310 515-4922
505 E Gardena Blvd Gardena (90248) *(P-6788)*
Artistry In Motion Inc....E....818 994-7388
19411 Londelius St Northridge (91324) *(P-3923)*
Artists Guild of America....F....310 532-3331
13225 S Western Ave Gardena (90249) *(P-23530)*
Artists Studio Gallery (PA)....D....310 265-2592
550 Deep Valley Dr # 327 Rllng HLS Est (90274) *(P-19636)*
Artiva USA Inc....E....562 298-8968
12866 Ann St Ste 1 Santa Fe Springs (90670) *(P-9059)*
Artiva USA Inc (PA)....E....909 628-1388
13901 Magnolia Ave Chino (91710) *(P-9060)*
Artlogic, Pasadena *Also called Art & Logic Inc (P-18018)*
Arto Brick / California Pavers....E....310 768-8500
15209 S Broadway Gardena (90248) *(P-5982)*
Arto Brick and Cal Pavers, Gardena *Also called Arto Brick / California Pavers (P-5982)*
Arts Custom Cabinets Inc....E....559 562-2766
897 E Tulare Rd Lindsay (93247) *(P-3461)*
Arts Elegance Inc....E....626 793-4794
154 W Bellevue Dr Pasadena (91105) *(P-11311)*
Artsons Manufacturing Company....E....323 773-3469
11121 Garfield Ave South Gate (90280) *(P-6188)*
Arturo Campos....F....951 300-2111
796 Palmyrita Ave Ste B Riverside (92507) *(P-7216)*
Arturo Gonzalez....F....818 837-7221
13409 Harding St San Fernando (91340) *(P-9381)*
Artwear Inc....E....310 217-1393
13621 S Main St Los Angeles (90061) *(P-14327)*
Arup North America Limited....B....310 578-4182
12777 W Jefferson Blvd # 300 Los Angeles (90066) *(P-22495)*
Arvato Services, Valencia *Also called Bertelsmann Inc (P-4121)*
Arvin-Edison Water Storage Dst (PA)....E....661 854-5573
20401 E Bear Mtn Blvd Arvin (93203) *(P-12880)*
Arvinyl Laminates LP....E....951 371-7800
233 N Sherman Ave Corona (92882) *(P-5427)*
Arxis Technology Inc....E....805 306-7890
2468 Tapo Canyon Rd Simi Valley (93063) *(P-17790)*
Arya Design Group, Los Angeles *Also called Arya Group Inc (P-593)*
Arya Group Inc....E....310 446-7000
10490 Santa Monica Blvd Los Angeles (90025) *(P-593)*
Arya Ice Cream Distrg Co Inc....D....323 234-2994
914 E 31st St Los Angeles (90011) *(P-14535)*
Arz Tech Inc....F....714 642-9954
1411 N Batavia St Ste 110 Orange (92867) *(P-5570)*
AS Match Dyeing Co Inc....C....323 277-0470
2522 E 37th St Vernon (90058) *(P-2655)*
Asa, Oxnard *Also called Advanced Structural Tech Inc (P-7081)*
Asa Power BDH Engrg & Cnstr, Chino *Also called American Solar Advantage Inc (P-9481)*
Asab Inc (HQ)....C....818 551-7300
500 N Brand Blvd Fl 3 Glendale (91203) *(P-17193)*
Asai, Glendale *Also called Passport Technology Usa Inc (P-19055)*
Asana Integrated Medical Group....D....888 212-7545
6200 Canoga Ave Ste 350 Woodland Hills (91367) *(P-21716)*
Asana Rcvery Alchol DRG Trtmnt, Costa Mesa *Also called Asana Recovery (P-21275)*
Asana Recovery....E....702 786-2396
1730 Pomona Ave Ste 3 Costa Mesa (92627) *(P-21275)*
Asbestos Instant Response Inc....D....323 733-0508
3517 W Washington Blvd Los Angeles (90018) *(P-1637)*
Asbury Environmental Services (PA)....D....310 886-3400
1300 S Santa Fe Ave Compton (90221) *(P-11956)*
Asbury Transportation Co....D....661 327-2271
2144 Mohawk St Bakersfield (93308) *(P-12012)*
ASC, Santa Barbara *Also called Advanced Scntific Concepts Inc (P-22874)*
ASC, Los Angeles *Also called American Soc Cinematographers (P-22265)*
ASC Group Inc....A....818 896-1101
12243 Branford St Sun Valley (91352) *(P-9483)*
ASC Process Systems Inc....C....818 833-0088
28402 Livingston Ave Valencia (91355) *(P-8084)*
ASC Process Systems Internati....F....818 833-0088
28402 Livingston Ave Valencia (91355) *(P-6725)*
Ascap, Los Angeles *Also called American Soc Cmpsers Athors Pb (P-4150)*
Ascension Constructors Inc (PA)....D....909 242-3106
7211 Haven Ave Alta Loma (91701) *(P-594)*
Ascent Aerospace....E....586 726-0500
1395 S Lyon St Santa Ana (92705) *(P-10570)*
Ascent Manufacturing LLC....E....714 540-6414
2545 W Via Palma Anaheim (92801) *(P-7125)*
Asco LP....C....877 208-4316
1749 Stergios Rd Calexico (92231) *(P-6726)*
Asco Power Services Inc....F....714 283-4000
120 S Chaparral Ct # 200 Anaheim (92808) *(P-9856)*

A L P H A B E T I C

Employee Codes: A=Over 500 employees, B=251-500
C=101-250, D=51-100, E=20-50 F=10-19
2022 Southern California Business
Directory and Buyers Guide
© Mergent Inc. 1-800-342-5647
1061

Asco Sintering Co ... E ... 323 725-3550
2750 Garfield Ave Commerce (90040) ***(P-6498)***

Ascot Hotel LP ... C ... 310 476-6411
170 N Church Ln Los Angeles (90049) ***(P-16329)***

Asdak International ... E ... 714 449-0733
1809 1/2 N Orngethorpe Pa Anaheim (92801) ***(P-6000)***

Aseptic Innovations Inc ... E ... 714 584-2110
4940 E Landon Dr Anaheim (92807) ***(P-5927)***

Aseptic Sltons USA Vntures LLC ... C ... 951 736-9230
484 Alcoa Cir Corona (92878) ***(P-2256)***

Aseptic Solutions USA-Corona, Corona *Also called Aseptic Sltons USA Vntures LLC* ***(P-2256)***

Aseptic Technology LLC ... C ... 714 694-0168
24855 Corbit Pl Yorba Linda (92887) ***(P-1858)***

Ash Holdings LLC ... D ... 909 793-2600
1620 W Fern Ave Redlands (92373) ***(P-20247)***

Ashford Trs Seven LLC (PA) ... C ... **760 776-4150**
74895 Frank Sinatra Dr Palm Desert (92211) ***(P-16330)***

Ashley & Vance Engineering Inc ... D ... 805 545-0010
1413 Monterey St San Luis Obispo (93401) ***(P-22496)***

Ashley Furniture, Ridgecrest *Also called Mpb Furniture Corporation* ***(P-3512)***

Ashley Furniture Homestore, Redlands *Also called Ashley Furniture Inds LLC* ***(P-13126)***

Ashley Furniture Inds LLC ... B ... 909 825-4900
2250 W Lugonia Ave Redlands (92374) ***(P-12185)***

Ashley Furniture Inds LLC ... B ... 800 240-3440
2250 W Lugonia Ave Redlands (92374) ***(P-13126)***

Ashtel Dental, Ontario *Also called Ashtel Studios Inc* ***(P-11205)***

Ashtel Studios Inc ... E ... 909 434-0911
1610 E Philadelphia St Ontario (91761) ***(P-11205)***

Ashunya Inc ... D ... 714 385-1900
642 N Eckhoff St Orange (92868) ***(P-17554)***

Asi Networks Inc ... F ... 800 251-1336
19331 E Walnut Dr N City of Industry (91748) ***(P-18159)***

Asi Semiconductor Inc ... E ... 818 982-1200
7525 Ethel Ave North Hollywood (91605) ***(P-9484)***

Asia Food Inc ... E ... 626 284-1328
566 Monterey Pass Rd Monterey Park (91754) ***(P-1705)***

Asia Plastics Inc ... E ... 626 448-8100
9347 Rush St South El Monte (91733) ***(P-3878)***

Asia-Pacific California Inc (PA) ... E ... **323 318-2254**
2121 W Mission Rd Ste 207 Alhambra (91803) ***(P-3947)***

Asia-Pacific California Inc ... E ... 626 281-8500
923 E Valley Blvd Ste 203 San Gabriel (91776) ***(P-3948)***

Asian PCF Hlth Care Ventr Inc (PA) ... C ... **323 644-3880**
4216 Fountain Ave Los Angeles (90029) ***(P-22170)***

Asian Rehabilitation Svc Inc (PA) ... D ... **562 632-1141**
7009 Washington Ave Whittier (90602) ***(P-21940)***

Asian Rehabilitation Svc Inc ... C ... 213 680-3790
312 N Spring St Ste B30 Los Angeles (90012) ***(P-21941)***

Asian Youth Center ... D ... 626 309-0622
100 Clary Ave San Gabriel (91776) ***(P-21717)***

Asiana Cuisine Enterprises Inc ... A ... 310 327-2223
22771 S Wstn Ave Ste 100 Torrance (90501) ***(P-2393)***

Asics America Corporation (HQ) ... C ... **949 453-8888**
7755 Irvine Center Dr # 400 Irvine (92618) ***(P-14429)***

Asics Tiger, Irvine *Also called Asics America Corporation* ***(P-14429)***

Asig, Ontario *Also called Menzies Aviation (texas) Inc* ***(P-12362)***

Asistencia Villa, Redlands *Also called Redlands Cmnty Hosp Foundation* ***(P-20624)***

Asistencia Villa Rehab & Care, Redlands *Also called Silverscreen Healthcare Inc* ***(P-20627)***

Askgene Pharma Inc ... E ... 805 807-9868
5217 Verdugo Way Ste A Camarillo (93012) ***(P-4788)***

Asp Henry Holdings Inc ... A ... 310 955-9200
999 N Pcf Cast Hwy Ste 80 El Segundo (90245) ***(P-16095)***

ASPE Inc ... F ... 951 296-2595
42295 Avnida Alvrado Unit Temecula (92590) ***(P-4483)***

Aspect Ratio Inc (HQ) ... D ... **323 467-2121**
5161 Lankershim Blvd # 30 North Hollywood (91601) ***(P-19219)***

Aspen Brands Corporation ... F ... 702 946-9430
2959 Fairview Rd Costa Mesa (92626) ***(P-3462)***

Aspen Medical Products LLC ... D ... 949 681-0200
6481 Oak Cyn Irvine (92618) ***(P-10941)***

Aspen Surgery Center, Simi Valley *Also called Simi Vly Hosp & Hlth Care Svcs* ***(P-20940)***

Asphalt Fabric and Engrg Inc ... D ... 562 997-4129
2683 Lime Ave Signal Hill (90755) ***(P-11403)***

Asphalt Management Inc ... E ... 562 630-6811
7243 Somerset Blvd Paramount (90723) ***(P-1512)***

Aspire Bakeries LLC ... C ... 909 472-3500
1220 S Baker Ave Ontario (91761) ***(P-14670)***

Aspire Bakeries LLC ... D ... 949 261-7400
2350 Pullman St Santa Ana (92705) ***(P-14671)***

Aspire Bakeries LLC ... D ... 818 904-8230
15963 Strathern St Van Nuys (91406) ***(P-2057)***

Asrock America Inc ... E ... 909 590-8308
13848 Magnolia Ave Chino (91710) ***(P-9382)***

Assa Abloy ACC Door Cntrls Gro ... D ... 805 642-2600
4226 Transport St Ventura (93003) ***(P-6499)***

Assa Abloy Rsdential Group Inc (HQ) ... C ... **626 961-0413**
12801 Schabarum Ave Baldwin Park (91706) ***(P-13795)***

Assa Abloy Rsdential Group Inc ... A ... 626 369-4718
600 Balwin Park Blvd City of Industry (91746) ***(P-13796)***

Assembly Automation Industries ... E ... 626 303-2777
1849 Business Center Dr Duarte (91010) ***(P-7899)***

Asset Athene Management L P (HQ) ... D ... **310 698-4444**
2121 Rosecrans Ave # 5300 El Segundo (90245) ***(P-22980)***

Assi Security (PA) ... D ... **949 955-0244**
1370 Reynolds Ave Ste 201 Irvine (92614) ***(P-1216)***

ASSICIATED STUDENTS, San Luis Obispo *Also called Associated Students Inc* ***(P-21718)***

Assign Corporation ... C ... 818 247-7100
200 N Maryland Ave # 204 Glendale (91206) ***(P-18160)***

Assistance In Home Care, Garden Grove *Also called Our Watch* ***(P-21196)***

Assisted Home Care, Northridge *Also called Assisted Home Recovery Inc* ***(P-17391)***

Assisted Home Care, Thousand Oaks *Also called Staff Assistance Inc* ***(P-17468)***

Assisted Home Recovery Inc (PA) ... C ... **818 894-8117**
8550 Balboa Blvd Lbby Northridge (91325) ***(P-17391)***

Assisted Home Recovery Inc ... D ... 626 915-5595
1900 W Garvey Ave S # 210 West Covina (91790) ***(P-21136)***

Assisvis Inc ... F ... 909 528-2031
10780 Mulberry Ave Fontana (92337) ***(P-5465)***

Associated Bond, Calabasas *Also called AIA Holdings Inc* ***(P-18438)***

Associated Desert Newspaper (HQ) ... E ... **760 337-3400**
205 N 8th St El Centro (92243) ***(P-3949)***

Associated Desert Shoppers Inc (HQ) ... D ... **760 346-1729**
73400 Highway 111 Palm Desert (92260) ***(P-4152)***

Associated Electrics Inc ... E ... 949 544-7500
21062 Bake Pkwy Ste 100 Lake Forest (92630) ***(P-11366)***

Associated Engineering Company, Lake Forest *Also called Berry-Perussi Inc* ***(P-7127)***

Associated Entrmt Releasing (PA) ... E ... **323 556-5600**
4401 Wilshire Blvd Los Angeles (90010) ***(P-19097)***

Associated Foreign Exch Inc (HQ) ... D ... **888 307-2339**
21045 Califa St Woodland Hills (91367) ***(P-15121)***

Associated Group, Los Angeles *Also called Assocted Ldscp Dsplay Group In* ***(P-18450)***

Associated Intl Insur Co, Woodland Hills *Also called Markel Corp* ***(P-15591)***

Associated Microbreweries Inc ... D ... 714 546-2739
901 S Coast Dr Ste A Costa Mesa (92626) ***(P-2137)***

Associated Plating Company ... E ... 562 946-5525
9636 Ann St Santa Fe Springs (90670) ***(P-7217)***

Associated Ready Mix Con Inc ... E ... 818 504-3100
8946 Bradley Ave Sun Valley (91352) ***(P-6070)***

Associated Ready Mix Con Inc ... C ... 805 485-4155
392 S Del Norte Blvd Oxnard (93030) ***(P-859)***

Associated Ready Mix Con Inc (PA) ... E ... **949 253-2800**
4621 Teller Ave Ste 130 Newport Beach (92660) ***(P-6071)***

Associated Ready Mix Concrete, Baldwin Park *Also called Standard Concrete Products Inc* ***(P-6118)***

Associated Students Inc (PA) ... D ... **805 756-1281**
University Un Bldg 65 San Luis Obispo (93407) ***(P-21718)***

Associated Students UCLA (PA) ... B ... **310 794-8836**
308 Westwood Plz Los Angeles (90095) ***(P-22171)***

Associated Students UCLA ... C ... 310 794-0242
924 Westwood Blvd Los Angeles (90024) ***(P-22172)***

Associated Students UCLA ... C ... 310 825-9451
650 Chrles Yung Dr S Rm 2 Los Angeles (90095) ***(P-19717)***

Associated Students UCLA ... C ... 310 206-8282
11000 Kinross Ave Ave # 245 Los Angeles (90095) ***(P-17160)***

Associated Students UCLA ... C ... 310 825-2787
308 Westwood Plz Ste 118 Los Angeles (90095) ***(P-3950)***

Associated Television Intl, Los Angeles *Also called Associated Entrmt Releasing* ***(P-19097)***

Associates First Capital Corp ... C ... 818 248-7055
3634 5th Ave Glendale (91214) ***(P-15138)***

Associates First Capital Corp ... C ... 805 487-9825
519 S C St Oxnard (93030) ***(P-15139)***

Associates Insectary ... D ... 805 933-1301
1400 E Santa Paula St Santa Paula (93060) ***(P-17197)***

Associations of United Nurses (PA) ... D ... **909 599-8622**
955 Overland Ct Ste 150 San Dimas (91773) ***(P-22287)***

Assocted Fgn Exch Holdings Inc (PA) ... D ... **818 386-2702**
21045 Califa St Woodland Hills (91367) ***(P-15122)***

Assocted Ldscp Dsplay Group In ... D ... 714 558-6100
1005 Mateo St Los Angeles (90021) ***(P-18450)***

Assocted Stdnts Cal State Univ ... D ... 562 985-4994
1212 N Bellflower Blvd # 22 Long Beach (90815) ***(P-22311)***

Assocted Wire Rope Rigging Inc ... E ... 310 448-5444
910 Mahar Ave Wilmington (90744) ***(P-2711)***

Assoluto Inc ... F ... 213 748-1116
215 S Santa Fe Ave Apt 5 Los Angeles (90012) ***(P-2919)***

AST Enzymes ... F ... 800 608-1688
4880 Murrieta St Chino (91710) ***(P-5127)***

AST Sportswear Inc (PA) ... B ... **714 223-2030**
2701 E Imperial Hwy Brea (92821) ***(P-3028)***

Astella, Jurupa Valley *Also called March Products Inc* ***(P-11711)***

Astoria Convalescent Hospital ... D ... 818 367-5881
14040 Astoria St Sylmar (91342) ***(P-20248)***

Astoria Nursing & Rehab Center, Sylmar *Also called Astoria Convalescent Hospital* ***(P-20248)***

Astourian Jewelry Mfg Inc ... F ... 213 683-0436
635 S Hill St Ste 407 Los Angeles (90014) ***(P-11312)***

Astra Communications Inc ... E ... 818 859-7305
1101 Chestnut St Burbank (91506) ***(P-9255)***

Astro Aluminum Treating Co ... D ... 562 923-4344
11040 Palmer Ave South Gate (90280) ***(P-6430)***

Astro Chrome and Polsg Corp ... E ... 818 781-1463
8136 Lankershim Blvd North Hollywood (91605) ***(P-7218)***

Astro Display Company Inc ... E ... 909 605-2875
4247 E Airport Dr Ontario (91761) ***(P-11524)***

Astro Haven Enterprises Inc ... F ... 949 215-3777
555 Anton Blvd Ste 150 Costa Mesa (92626) ***(P-10870)***

Astro Machine Co Inc ... F ... 310 679-8291
3734 W 139th St Hawthorne (90250) ***(P-8505)***

Astro News, Lancaster *Also called Aerotech News and Review Inc* ***(P-4050)***

Astro Packaging, Anaheim *Also called Reliable Packaging Systems Inc* ***(P-5194)***

Astro Seal Inc ... E ... 951 787-6670
827 Palmyrita Ave Ste B Riverside (92507) ***(P-9676)***

Astro-Tek Industries LLC ... D ... 714 238-0022
1198 N Kraemer Blvd Anaheim (92806) ***(P-10280)***

Astrochef LLC ... D ... 213 627-9860
1111 Mateo St Los Angeles (90021) ***(P-1916)***

Mergent e-mail: customerrelations@mergent.com
1062
2022 Southern California Business Directory and Buyers Guide
(P-0000) Products & Services Section entry number
(PA)=Parent Co (HQ)=Headquarters (DH)=Div Headquarters

Astrofoam Molding Company Inc F 805 482-7276
4117 Calle Tesoro Camarillo (93012) *(P-5571)*
Astrologie California, Commerce *Also called Ajg Inc (P-3053)*
Astron Corporation E 949 458-7277
9 Autry Irvine (92618) *(P-9620)*
Astronic C 949 454-1180
2 Orion Aliso Viejo (92656) *(P-9383)*
Astronics Company, Pasadena *Also called Sabrin Corporation (P-10406)*
Astronics Test Systems Inc (HQ) C **800 722-2528**
4 Goodyear Irvine (92618) *(P-10743)*
Astrophysics Inc (PA) C **909 598-5488**
21481 Ferrero City of Industry (91789) *(P-11206)*
Asturies Manufacturing Co Inc E 951 270-1766
310 Cessna Cir Corona (92878) *(P-10281)*
Asucla, Los Angeles *Also called Associated Students UCLA (P-22171)*
Asucla Publications, Los Angeles *Also called Associated Students UCLA (P-3950)*
Asv Wines Inc (PA) F **661 792-3159**
1998 Road 152 Delano (93215) *(P-2166)*
Asylum, The, Glendale *Also called Global Asylum Incorporated (P-19129)*
At Battery Company Inc E 661 775-2020
28381 Constellation Rd Valencia (91355) *(P-13615)*
At Work, Tustin *Also called B2 Services Llc (P-17393)*
AT&T Corp B 714 284-2878
Rm 620 Anaheim (92805) *(P-12591)*
AT&T Corp D 949 622-8240
17675 Harvard Ave Ste B Irvine (92614) *(P-12592)*
AT&T Corp D 310 659-7600
998 S Robertson Blvd # 103 Los Angeles (90035) *(P-12593)*
AT&T Corp C 303 596-8431
2260 E Imperial Hwy El Segundo (90245) *(P-12626)*
At-Tech Staffing Services Inc (PA) D **818 240-8688**
327 W Broadway Glendale (91204) *(P-17392)*
Ata-Boy F 323 644-0117
3171 Los Feliz Blvd # 205 Los Angeles (90039) *(P-11634)*
Atascadero State Hospital, Atascadero *Also called State Hospitals Cal Dept (P-21029)*
Atbatt.com, Valencia *Also called At Battery Company Inc (P-13615)*
Atchesons Express Inc E 714 808-9199
1590 S Archibald Ave Ontario (91761) *(P-11957)*
Atco Rubber Products Inc E 951 788-4345
3080 12th St Riverside (92507) *(P-6727)*
Atd Corporation C 909 481-6210
5100 Ontario Mills Pkwy Ontario (91764) *(P-13112)*
Atelier Ace LLC E 503 546-6836
3191 Casitas Ave Ste 116 Los Angeles (90039) *(P-17161)*
Atelier Luxury Group LLC E 310 751-2444
1330 Channing St Los Angeles (90021) *(P-3168)*
Aten Technology Inc D 949 428-1111
15365 Barranca Pkwy Irvine (92618) *(P-8236)*
Atg - Designing Mobility Inc (HQ) E **562 921-0258**
11075 Knott Ave Ste B Cypress (90630) *(P-13477)*
Athanor Group Inc F 909 467-1205
921 E California St Ontario (91761) *(P-7032)*
Athas Capital Group Inc D 877 877-1477
27001 Agoura Rd Ste 200 Agoura Hills (91301) *(P-15174)*
Athena Pick Your Fit, Tustin *Also called Raj Manufacturing Inc (P-15963)*
Athens Disposal Company Inc (PA) B **626 336-3636**
14048 Valley Blvd La Puente (91746) *(P-12929)*
Athens Environmental Services, Sun Valley *Also called Araco Enterprises LLC (P-12926)*
Athens Services, City of Industry *Also called Arakelian Enterprises Inc (P-12927)*
Atherton Baptist Homes C 626 863-1710
214 S Atlantic Blvd Alhambra (91801) *(P-20249)*
Athicon E 213 454-0662
6310 San Vicente Blvd Los Angeles (90048) *(P-22497)*
Athletic Schlarship Connection E 909 705-5875
3920 Cinnamon Ct Bakersfield (93309) *(P-16173)*
ATI Forged Products, Irvine *Also called Chen-Tech Industries Inc (P-10961)*
ATI Restoration LLC (PA) C **714 283-9990**
3360 E La Palma Ave Anaheim (92806) *(P-1638)*
ATI Solutions Inc (PA) F **818 772-7900**
18425 Napa St Northridge (91325) *(P-9332)*
ATI Windows, Riverside *Also called Nevada Window Supply Inc (P-3273)*
ATI Windows, Riverside *Also called San Joaquin Window Inc (P-6718)*
Atk Audiotek D 661 705-3700
28238 Avenue Crocker Valencia (91355) *(P-1217)*
Atk Services, Valencia *Also called Atk Audiotek (P-1217)*
Atk Space Systems LLC D 626 351-0205
370 N Halstead St Pasadena (91107) *(P-22826)*
Atk Space Systems LLC (HQ) E **323 722-0222**
6033 Bandini Blvd Commerce (90040) *(P-10571)*
Atk Space Systems LLC D 805 685-2262
600 Pine Ave Goleta (93117) *(P-10572)*
Atk Space Systems LLC D 310 343-3799
1960 E Grand Ave Ste 1150 El Segundo (90245) *(P-10573)*
Atkinson Andelson Loya, Cerritos *Also called Atkinson Andlson Loya Ruud Rom (P-21506)*
Atkinson Andlson Loya Ruud Rom (PA) C **562 653-3200**
12800 Center Court Dr S # 300 Cerritos (90703) *(P-21506)*
Atkinson Construction Inc B 303 410-2540
18201 Von Karman Ave # 800 Irvine (92612) *(P-860)*
Atlantc-Pcfic Proc Systems Inc (PA) C **714 241-1402**
18350 Mount Langley St # 20 Fountain Valley (92708) *(P-18451)*
Atlantic Aviation Holding Corp D 310 396-6770
2828 Donald Douglas Loop Santa Monica (90405) *(P-12340)*
Atlantic Box & Carton Company, Pico Rivera *Also called Jkv Inc (P-3814)*
Atlantic Mem Healthcare Assoc (PA) D **562 424-8101**
2750 Atlantic Ave Long Beach (90806) *(P-20250)*
Atlantic Mem Healthcare Ctr, Long Beach *Also called Atlantic Mem Healthcare Assoc (P-20250)*
Atlantic Representations Inc E 562 903-9550
10018 Santa Fe Springs Rd Santa Fe Springs (90670) *(P-3525)*
Atlantic Richfield Company (HQ) A **800 333-3991**
4 Centerpointe Dr Ste 200 La Palma (90623) *(P-418)*
Atlantis Computing Inc E 650 917-9471
900 Glenneyre St Laguna Beach (92651) *(P-17791)*
Atlantis Enterprises Inc E 818 712-0572
8100 Remmet Ave Ste 1 Canoga Park (91304) *(P-14913)*
Atlas Advertising, Irvine *Also called M F Salta Co Inc (P-23265)*
Atlas Carpet Mills Inc C 323 724-7930
3201 S Susan St Santa Ana (92704) *(P-2682)*
Atlas Construction Supply Inc E 714 441-9500
7550 Stage Rd Buena Park (90621) *(P-13293)*
Atlas Copco Mafi-Trench Co LLC (HQ) C **805 352-0112**
3037 Industrial Pkwy Santa Maria (93455) *(P-8041)*
Atlas Database Software Corp (PA) C **818 340-7080**
26679 Agoura Rd Ste 200 Calabasas (91302) *(P-17555)*
Atlas Development, Calabasas *Also called Atlas Database Software Corp (P-17555)*
Atlas Digital LLC (PA) D **323 762-2626**
170 S Flower St Burbank (91502) *(P-19098)*
Atlas Entertainment Inc E 310 786-4900
9200 W Sunset Blvd Ste 10 West Hollywood (90069) *(P-19099)*
Atlas Foam Products F 818 837-3626
12836 Arroyo St Sylmar (91342) *(P-5490)*
Atlas Franchise Management Inc D 949 239-1760
17752 Sky Park Cir # 235 Irvine (92614) *(P-22981)*
Atlas Galvanizing LLC E 323 587-6247
2639 Leonis Blvd Vernon (90058) *(P-7347)*
Atlas Hospitality Group D 949 622-3400
1901 Main St Ste 175 Irvine (92614) *(P-15774)*
Atlas Magnetics Inc E 714 632-9718
1121 N Kraemer Pl Anaheim (92806) *(P-9677)*
Atlas Match LLC D 714 993-3328
1337 Limerick Dr Placentia (92870) *(P-11635)*
Atlas Mover Services, Rancho Dominguez *Also called Mover Services Inc (P-1676)*
Atlas Pacific Corporation (PA) E **909 421-1200**
2803 Industrial Dr Bloomington (92316) *(P-14110)*
Atlas Sheet Metal Inc F 949 600-8787
19 Musick Irvine (92618) *(P-6789)*
Atlas Spring Mfgcorp E 310 532-6200
10635 Santa Monica Blvd Los Angeles (90025) *(P-7482)*
Atlas Survival Shelters LLC E 323 727-7084
7407 Telegraph Rd Montebello (90640) *(P-3526)*
Atlas Testing Laboratories Inc E 909 373-4130
9820 6th St Rancho Cucamonga (91730) *(P-22930)*
Atlas/Eastern Van Lines, Pomona *Also called W Why W Enterprises Inc (P-12121)*
Atm Consultants, Claremont *Also called Atmc Incorporated (P-1218)*
Atm Fly-Ware, Signal Hill *Also called Adaptive Tech Group Inc (P-9156)*
Atmc Incorporated (PA) D **909 390-0470**
725 W Baseline Rd Claremont (91711) *(P-1218)*
Atmospheric-Greenscreen, Los Angeles *Also called Greenscreen (P-260)*
Atmpartmart.com, Westlake Village *Also called Cash Convenience Inds LLC (P-19029)*
Atomica Corp C 805 681-2807
75 Robin Hill Rd Goleta (93117) *(P-9485)*
Atr Sales Inc E 714 432-8411
110 E Garry Ave Santa Ana (92707) *(P-8103)*
Atr Technologies Incorporated F 909 399-9724
805 Towne Center Dr Pomona (91767) *(P-6951)*
Atra International Traders Inc F 562 864-3885
3301 Leonis Blvd Vernon (90058) *(P-3849)*
Atra-Flex, Santa Ana *Also called Atr Sales Inc (P-8103)*
Atria Park Pacific Palisades, Pacific Palisades *Also called Atria Senior Living Inc (P-22081)*
Atria Senior Living Inc D 310 573-9545
15441 W Sunset Blvd Pacific Palisades (90272) *(P-22081)*
Atrium Door & Win Co Ariz Inc C 714 693-0601
5455 E La Palma Ave Ste A Anaheim (92807) *(P-13203)*
Atrium Hotel, Irvine *Also called Golden Hotels Ltd Partnership (P-16456)*
Ats, Long Beach *Also called American Trnsp Systems (P-11908)*
Ats International, Los Angeles *Also called Parts Out Inc (P-9827)*
Ats Systems, Rcho STA Marg *Also called Ats Workholding Llc (P-7846)*
Ats Tool Inc D 949 888-1744
30222 Esperanza Rcho STA Marg (92688) *(P-7778)*
Ats Workholding, Rcho STA Marg *Also called Ats Tool Inc (P-7778)*
Ats Workholding Llc D 800 321-1833
30222 Esperanza Rcho STA Marg (92688) *(P-7846)*
Attn Inc C 323 413-2878
729 Seward St Los Angeles (90038) *(P-17078)*
Attom Data Solutions LLC (PA) D **949 502-8300**
505 Technology Dr Ste 100 Irvine (92618) *(P-15775)*
Attorney Recovery Systems Inc (PA) D **818 774-1420**
18757 Burbank Blvd # 225 Tarzana (91356) *(P-17104)*
Atv Inc (PA) D **562 977-8565**
4490 Ayers Ave Vernon (90058) *(P-18814)*
Aubrey Industries F 626 261-4242
750 W Golden Grove Way Covina (91722) *(P-9079)*
Auburn Tile Inc E 909 984-2841
545 W Main St Ontario (91762) *(P-6018)*
Auctioncom Inc C 800 499-6199
1 Mauchly Ste 27 Irvine (92618) *(P-15776)*
Auctioncom LLC (PA) A **949 859-2777**
1 Mauchly Irvine (92618) *(P-15777)*
Audience Inc F 323 413-2370
5670 Wilshire Blvd # 100 Los Angeles (90036) *(P-4153)*
Audiencex, Marina Del Rey *Also called Socialcom Inc (P-23328)*
Audio Images, Tustin *Also called Henrys Adio Vsual Slutions Inc (P-9178)*
Audio Video Color Corporation (PA) B **424 213-7500**
17707 S Santa Fe Ave E Rncho Dmngz (90221) *(P-3850)*

A L P H A B E T I C

Employee Codes: A=Over 500 employees, B=251-500 C=101-250, D=51-100, E=20-50 F=10-19
2022 Southern California Business Directory and Buyers Guide
© Mergent Inc. 1-800-342-5647
1063

Audio Visual Headquarters (HQ)......E......**310 603-0652**
16320 Arthur St Cerritos (90703) ***(P-17333)***
Audiolink, Thousand Palms *Also called A R Electronics Inc* ***(P-9669)***
Audionics System Inc......F......818 345-9599
21541 Nordhoff St Ste C Chatsworth (91311) ***(P-9160)***
Audioquest, Irvine *Also called Quest Group* ***(P-14176)***
Audiovisions, Irvine *Also called Inspiria Inc* ***(P-22578)***
Auditboard Inc (PA)......E......**877 769-5444**
12900 Park Plaza Dr # 200 Cerritos (90703) ***(P-17556)***
Audrey 3plus1, Vernon *Also called Three Plus One Inc* ***(P-2871)***
Auger Industries Inc......F......714 577-9350
390 E Crowther Ave Placentia (92870) ***(P-8506)***
Augora Hills 8 Cinema Center, Agoura Hills *Also called Weststar Cinemas Inc* ***(P-19293)***
August Accessories, Thousand Oaks *Also called August Hat Company Inc* ***(P-3024)***
August Hat Company Inc (PA)......E......**805 983-4651**
2021 Calle Yucca Thousand Oaks (91360) ***(P-3024)***
Augustine Casino, Coachella *Also called Augustine Gaming MGT Corp* ***(P-17557)***
Augustine Gaming MGT Corp......D......760 391-9500
84001 Avenue 54 Coachella (92236) ***(P-17557)***
Ault Global Holdings Inc (PA)......E......**949 444-5464**
201 Shipyard Way Ste E Newport Beach (92663) ***(P-9678)***
Aurident Inc......E......714 870-1851
610 S State College Blvd Fullerton (92831) ***(P-11160)***
Auritec Pharmaceuticals Inc......F......424 272-9501
2285 E Foothill Blvd Pasadena (91107) ***(P-4789)***
Aurora Bhvioral Healthcare LLC (HQ)......E......**951 549-8032**
4238 Green River Rd Corona (92878) ***(P-21013)***
Aurora Casting & Engrg Inc......D......805 933-2761
1790 E Lemonwood Dr Santa Paula (93060) ***(P-13546)***
Aurora Las Encinas LLC......C......626 795-9901
2900 E Del Mar Blvd Pasadena (91107) ***(P-21014)***
Aurora Las Encinas Hospital, Pasadena *Also called Aurora Las Encinas LLC* ***(P-21014)***
Aurora World Inc......C......562 205-1222
8820 Mercury Ln Pico Rivera (90660) ***(P-14092)***
Austin Dialysis Centers LP (HQ)......E......**310 536-2400**
601 Hawaii St El Segundo (90245) ***(P-21233)***
Austin Pang Glv Mfg USA Corp (HQ)......E......**562 777-0088**
17343 Freedom Way City of Industry (91748) ***(P-14146)***
Aut Inc......F......909 393-9961
3925 Schaefer Ave Chino (91710) ***(P-3951)***
Authority of Housing (PA)......D......**805 736-3423**
815 W Ocean Ave Lompoc (93436) ***(P-15778)***
Authority Tax Services LLC......D......213 486-5135
777 S Figueroa St # 1900 Los Angeles (90017) ***(P-18452)***
Authorized Cellular Service......D......310 466-4144
8808 S Sepulveda Blvd Los Angeles (90045) ***(P-18952)***
Auto Buyline Systems Inc (PA)......E......**951 271-8999**
341 Corporate Terrace Cir Corona (92879) ***(P-13020)***
Auto Club Enterprises (PA)......A......**714 850-5111**
3333 Fairview Rd Msa451 Costa Mesa (92626) ***(P-15377)***
Auto Club Enterprises......C......310 914-8500
8761 Santa Monica Blvd West Hollywood (90069) ***(P-15378)***
Auto Club Enterprises......C......714 885-2376
3333 Fairview Rd Costa Mesa (92626) ***(P-4053)***
Auto Club Speedway, Fontana *Also called California Speedway Corp* ***(P-19429)***
Auto Doctor, Temecula *Also called Thompson Magnetics Inc* ***(P-9796)***
Auto Edge Solutions, Pacoima *Also called Moc Products Company Inc* ***(P-5234)***
Auto Gallery (PA)......D......**818 884-4411**
5711 Van Nuys Blvd Van Nuys (91401) ***(P-18893)***
Auto Insurance Specialists LLC (HQ)......C......**562 345-6247**
17785 Center Court Dr N # 110 Cerritos (90703) ***(P-15539)***
Auto Parts Unlimited, North Hollywood *Also called Apu Inc* ***(P-13042)***
Auto Parts Warehouse Inc (PA)......E......**800 913-6119**
16941 Keegan Ave Carson (90746) ***(P-13044)***
Auto Pride, Anaheim *Also called Cal-State Auto Parts Inc* ***(P-13049)***
Auto Supply Company, Los Angeles *Also called Stanley M Scher Inc* ***(P-13097)***
Auto Trend Products, Vernon *Also called Punch Press Products Inc* ***(P-7828)***
Auto-Chlor System Wash Inc......F......818 376-0940
16141 Hart St Van Nuys (91406) ***(P-4954)***
Autobahn Construction Inc......F......714 769-7025
933 N Batavia St Ste A Orange (92867) ***(P-7635)***
Autocrib Inc......C......714 274-0400
2882 Dow Ave Tustin (92780) ***(P-18453)***
Autoflow Products Co......F......310 515-2866
15915 S San Pedro St Gardena (90248) ***(P-10678)***
Autograph Vespera On Ocean, Pismo Beach *Also called Pismo Beach Ht Investments LLC* ***(P-16632)***
Autogravity Corporation......D......949 392-8777
15495 Sand Canyon Ave # 100 Irvine (92618) ***(P-15140)***
Automate Parking Inc......D......310 674-3396
8405 Pershing Dr Ste 301 Playa Del Rey (90293) ***(P-18764)***
Automatic Data Processing Inc......C......949 751-0360
3972 Barranca Pkwy J610 Irvine (92606) ***(P-18079)***
Automatic Data Processing Inc......C......800 225-5237
400 W Covina Blvd San Dimas (91773) ***(P-18080)***
Automatic Leasing Inc (PA)......B......**213 746-4117**
445 S Figueroa St Los Angeles (90071) ***(P-13681)***
Automation Electronics, Chatsworth *Also called RJA Industries Inc* ***(P-9772)***
Automation Plating, Glendale *Also called Aero Mfg & Pltg Co LLC* ***(P-7199)***
Automation Plating Corporation......E......323 245-4951
927 Thompson Ave Glendale (91201) ***(P-7219)***
Automation Printing Co (PA)......E......**213 488-1230**
1230 Long Beach Ave Los Angeles (90021) ***(P-4623)***
Automation Tech - Low Voltage, Anaheim *Also called ABB Inc* ***(P-8860)***
Automation West Inc......E......714 556-7381
1605 E Saint Gertrude Pl Santa Ana (92705) ***(P-8507)***

Automax Styling Inc......E......951 530-1876
16833 Krameria Ave Riverside (92504) ***(P-10019)***
Automobile Club Southern Cal......D......909 477-8600
6787 Carnelian St Ste A Rancho Cucamonga (91701) ***(P-22396)***
Automobile Club Southern Cal......D......951 304-3077
25125 Madison Ave 101a Murrieta (92562) ***(P-22397)***
Automobile Club Southern Cal (PA)......C......**213 741-3686**
2601 S Figueroa St Los Angeles (90007) ***(P-15540)***
Automobile Club Southern Cal......D......714 973-1211
13331 Jamboree Rd Irvine (92602) ***(P-22398)***
Automobile Club Southern Cal......D......818 997-6230
15503 Ventura Blvd # 150 Encino (91436) ***(P-22399)***
Automobile Club Southern Cal......D......805 682-5811
3712 State St Santa Barbara (93105) ***(P-22400)***
Automobile Club Southern Cal......D......909 381-2211
27889 Baseline St Highland (92346) ***(P-22401)***
Automobile Club Southern Cal......D......213 741-3686
33323 Fairview R Ste Msa Costa Mesa (92626) ***(P-15541)***
Automobile Club Southern Cal......D......805 543-6454
1445 Calle Joaquin San Luis Obispo (93405) ***(P-22402)***
Automobile Club Southern Cal......D......805 497-0911
100 E Wilbur Rd Thousand Oaks (91360) ***(P-22403)***
Automobile Club Southern Cal......D......310 325-3111
23001 Hawthorne Blvd Torrance (90505) ***(P-22404)***
Automobile Club Southern Cal......D......805 644-7171
1501 S Victoria Ave Ventura (93003) ***(P-22405)***
Automobile Club Southern Cal......D......714 774-2392
420 N Euclid St Anaheim (92801) ***(P-22406)***
Automobile Club Southern Cal......D......626 963-8531
1301s S Grand Ave Glendora (91740) ***(P-22407)***
Automobile Club Southern Cal......D......626 289-4491
401 E Main St Ste 101 Alhambra (91801) ***(P-22408)***
Automobile Club Southern Cal......D......909 793-3357
1330 Industrial Park Ave Redlands (92374) ***(P-22409)***
Automobile Club Southern Cal......D......661 327-4661
1500 Commercial Way Bakersfield (93309) ***(P-22410)***
Automobile Club Southern Cal......D......626 445-6687
420 E Huntington Dr Arcadia (91006) ***(P-22411)***
Automobile Club Southern Cal......D......714 921-2850
5500 E Santa Ana Cyn Rd Anaheim (92807) ***(P-22412)***
Automobile Club Southern Cal......D......818 993-1616
9440 Reseda Blvd Northridge (91324) ***(P-22413)***
Automobile Club Southern Cal......D......562 904-5970
8223 Firestone Blvd Downey (90241) ***(P-22414)***
Automobile Club Southern Cal......D......760 320-1121
300 S Farrell Dr Palm Springs (92262) ***(P-22415)***
Automobile Club Southern Cal......D......310 376-0521
700 S Aviation Blvd Manhattan Beach (90266) ***(P-22416)***
Automobile Club Southern Cal......D......626 795-0601
801 E Union St Pasadena (91101) ***(P-22417)***
Automobile Club Southern Cal......D......949 476-8880
3880 Birch St Newport Beach (92660) ***(P-22418)***
Automobile Club Southern Cal......D......818 249-3971
2112 Montrose Ave Montrose (91020) ***(P-22419)***
Automobile Club Southern Cal......D......323 725-6545
1405 N Montebello Blvd Montebello (90640) ***(P-22420)***
Automobile Club Southern Cal......D......661 948-7661
1234 Commerce Center Dr Lancaster (93534) ***(P-22421)***
Automobile Club Southern Cal......D......714 848-2227
16160 Beach Blvd Huntington Beach (92647) ***(P-22422)***
Automobile Club Southern Cal......D......818 883-2660
22708 Victory Blvd Woodland Hills (91367) ***(P-22423)***
Automobile Club Southern Cal......D......310 673-5170
1234 Centinela Ave Inglewood (90302) ***(P-22424)***
Automobile Club Southern Cal......D......562 698-3721
16041 Whittier Blvd Whittier (90603) ***(P-22425)***
Automobile Club Southern Cal......D......951 684-4250
3700 Central Ave Riverside (92506) ***(P-22426)***
Automobile Club Southern Cal......D......909 591-9451
5402 Philadelphia St A Chino (91710) ***(P-22427)***
Automobile Club Southern Cal......D......714 871-2333
1450 N Harbor Blvd Fullerton (92835) ***(P-22428)***
Automobile Club Southern Cal......D......949 489-5572
638 Cmino De Los Mres Ste San Clemente (92673) ***(P-22429)***
Automobile Club Southern Cal......D......805 922-5731
2033b S Broadway Santa Maria (93454) ***(P-22430)***
Automobile Club Southern Cal......D......661 259-6222
23770 Valencia Blvd # 100 Valencia (91355) ***(P-22431)***
Automobile Club Southern Cal......D......949 951-1400
25181 Paseo De Alicia Laguna Hills (92653) ***(P-22432)***
Automobile Club Southern Cal......D......760 245-6666
12490 Amargosa Rd Victorville (92392) ***(P-22433)***
Automobile Club Southern Cal......D......626 442-0944
3534 Peck Rd El Monte (91731) ***(P-15542)***
Automobile Club Southern Cal......D......951 652-6202
450 W Stetson Ave Hemet (92543) ***(P-22434)***
Automobile Club Southern Cal......C......714 885-1343
3333 Fairview Rd Costa Mesa (92626) ***(P-15543)***
Automobile Club Southern Cal......D......909 392-1444
2488 Foothill Blvd Ste A La Verne (91750) ***(P-22435)***
Automobile Club Southern Cal......D......310 453-1909
2730 Santa Monica Blvd Santa Monica (90404) ***(P-22436)***
Automobile Club Southern Cal......D......760 247-4110
19201 Bear Valley Rd C Apple Valley (92308) ***(P-22437)***
Automobile Club Southern Cal......D......951 808-9624
1170 El Camino Ave Corona (92879) ***(P-22438)***
Automobile Club Southern Cal......D......909 980-0233
10540 Fthill Blvd Ste 100 Rancho Cucamonga (91730) ***(P-15544)***
Automobile Club Southern Cal......D......805 735-2731
675 N H St Lompoc (93436) ***(P-22439)***

ALPHABETIC SECTION — Ax II Inc

Automobile Club Southern Cal ... D ... 559 732-8045
4228 S Mooney Blvd Visalia (93277) *(P-22440)*

Automobile Club Southern Cal ... D ... 818 843-2833
1111 W Alameda Ave Burbank (91506) *(P-22441)*

Automobile Club Southern Cal ... D ... 562 425-8350
4800 Airport Plaza Dr # 100 Long Beach (90815) *(P-22442)*

Automobile Club Southern Cal ... D ... 818 240-2200
1233 E Broadway Glendale (91205) *(P-22443)*

Automobile Club Southern Cal ... D ... 562 924-6636
18642 Gridley Rd Artesia (90701) *(P-22444)*

Automobile Club Southern Cal ... D ... 323 525-0018
8761 Santa Monica Blvd West Hollywood (90069) *(P-22445)*

Automoco LLC ... E ... 707 544-4761
9142 Independence Ave Chatsworth (91311) *(P-10020)*

Automotive Aftermarket Inc ... D ... 310 793-0046
15912 Hawthorne Blvd Lawndale (90260) *(P-13045)*

Automotive Lease Guide Alg Inc ... B ... 424 258-8026
120 Broadway Ste 200 Santa Monica (90401) *(P-4154)*

Automotive Racing Products Inc (PA) ... **D ... 805 339-2200**
1863 Eastman Ave Ventura (93003) *(P-6500)*

Automotive Racing Products Inc ... E ... 805 525-1497
1760 E Lemonwood Dr Santa Paula (93060) *(P-6501)*

Automotive Tstg & Dev Svcs Inc (PA) ... **C ... 909 390-1100**
400 Etiwanda Ave Ontario (91761) *(P-18922)*

Automted Cntrls Technical Svcs, Bakersfield *Also called A-C Electric Company (P-1205)*

Auton Motorized Systems, Valencia *Also called Virgil Walker Inc (P-6680)*

Auton Motorized Systems, Valencia *Also called Virgil Walker Inc (P-9615)*

Autonation Ford Valencia, Valencia *Also called Magic Acquisition Corp (P-18852)*

Autonomous Medical Devices Inc (PA) ... **E ... 424 331-0900**
10604 S La Cienega Blvd Inglewood (90304) *(P-10782)*

Autotechbizcom Inc ... F ... 949 245-7033
23551 Commerce Center Dr I Laguna Hills (92653) *(P-7962)*

Autozone Inc ... D ... 310 525-2333
1361 W 190th St Gardena (90248) *(P-13046)*

Autry Museum of American West ... C ... 323 667-2000
4700 Western Heritage Way Los Angeles (90027) *(P-22217)*

Auxilary of Mssion Hosp Mssion ... A ... 949 364-1400
27700 Medical Center Rd Mission Viejo (92691) *(P-20684)*

Ava Enterprises Inc ... E ... 805 988-0192
3451 Lunar Ct Oxnard (93030) *(P-13682)*

Ava James, Los Angeles *Also called C-Quest Inc (P-2839)*

Avalon Apparel LLC (PA) ... **C ... 323 581-3511**
2520 W 6th St Los Angeles (90057) *(P-2878)*

Avalon At Penasquitos Hills, Irvine *Also called Avalonbay Communities Inc (P-15779)*

Avalon Building Maint Inc (PA) ... **C ... 714 693-2407**
3148 E La Palma Ave Ste A Anaheim (92806) *(P-17216)*

Avalon By Sea AC LLC ... E ... 310 457-9111
32430 Pacific Coast Hwy Malibu (90265) *(P-22082)*

Avalon Communications, Torrance *Also called Technology Training Corp (P-18687)*

Avalon Communications, Hawthorne *Also called Technology Training Corp (P-4435)*

Avalon Hotel, Beverly Hills *Also called Honeymoon Real Estate LP (P-16490)*

Avalon Mfg Co Incoirporated ... F ... 951 340-0280
509 Bateman Cir Corona (92878) *(P-7927)*

Avalon Shutters Inc ... C ... 909 937-4900
3407 N Perris Blvd Perris (92571) *(P-3233)*

Avalon Transportation Co, Culver City *Also called Virgin Fish Inc (P-11896)*

Avalonbay Communities Inc ... E ... 949 955-6200
2050 Main St Ste 1200 Irvine (92614) *(P-15779)*

Avanir Pharmaceuticals Inc (HQ) ... **B ... 949 389-6700**
30 Enterprise Ste 200 Aliso Viejo (92656) *(P-4790)*

Avanquest North America LLC (HQ) ... **D ... 818 591-9600**
23801 Calabasas Rd # 2005 Calabasas (91302) *(P-17558)*

Avante Health Solutions, San Clemente *Also called Pacific Medical Group Inc (P-13507)*

Avantec Manufacturing Inc ... E ... 714 532-6197
1811 N Case St Orange (92865) *(P-9384)*

Avantgarde Senior Living ... C ... 818 881-0055
5645 Lindley Ave Tarzana (91356) *(P-22083)*

Avantra Financial, Arcadia *Also called Avantra Real Estate Services (P-15780)*

Avantra Real Estate Services ... E ... 626 357-7028
148 E Fthill Blvd Ste 100 Arcadia (91006) *(P-15780)*

Avantus Aerospace Inc (HQ) ... **C ... 661 295-8620**
29101 The Old Rd Valencia (91355) *(P-10282)*

Avantus Aerospace Inc ... E ... 562 633-6626
14957 Gwenchris Ct Paramount (90723) *(P-6502)*

Avanzato Technology Corp ... E ... 312 509-0506
5335 Mcconnell Ave Los Angeles (90066) *(P-7963)*

Avasant LLC (PA) ... **D ... 310 643-3030**
1960 E Grand Ave Ste 1050 El Segundo (90245) *(P-23162)*

Avatar Machine LLC ... E ... 714 434-2737
18100 Mount Washington St Fountain Valley (92708) *(P-8508)*

Avatar Technology Inc ... E ... 909 598-7696
339 Cheryl Ln City of Industry (91789) *(P-13377)*

Avca Fixture System Inc ... F ... 562 693-3214
6203 Southwind Dr Whittier (90601) *(P-3676)*

Avco Financial, Glendale *Also called Associates First Capital Corp (P-15138)*

Avco Financial, Oxnard *Also called Associates First Capital Corp (P-15139)*

Avcorp Cmpsite Fabrication Inc ... B ... 310 970-5658
1600 W 135th St Gardena (90249) *(P-10283)*

Avd, Newport Beach *Also called American Vanguard Corporation (P-5165)*

Ave Jewelry Design Mfg, North Hollywood *Also called Ave Jewelry Inc (P-11313)*

Ave Jewelry Inc ... F ... 213 488-0097
13127 Ebell St North Hollywood (91605) *(P-11313)*

Avendren Building Systems Inc ... F ... 909 806-0938
3660 Placentia Ln Riverside (92501) *(P-740)*

Avenida Partners LLC (PA) ... **D ... 949 734-7810**
130 Nwport Ctr Dr Ste 220 Newport Beach (92660) *(P-23163)*

Avente Inc ... E ... 844 385-1556
200 Spectrum Dr Ste 300 Irvine (92618) *(P-18161)*

Avenue Lighting ... F ... 800 798-0409
9000 Fullbright Ave Chatsworth (91311) *(P-5931)*

Avenue of Arts Wyndham Hotel, Costa Mesa *Also called Rosanna Inc (P-16671)*

Aveox Inc ... E ... 805 915-0200
2265 Ward Ave Ste A Simi Valley (93065) *(P-8971)*

Averitt Express Inc ... D ... 310 970-9520
3133 W 131st St Hawthorne (90250) *(P-12013)*

Avery Corp ... C ... 626 304-2000
207 N Goode Ave Fl 6 Glendale (91203) *(P-22827)*

Avery Dennison Corporation (PA) ... **A ... 626 304-2000**
207 N Goode Ave Glendale (91203) *(P-3863)*

Avery Dennison Corporation ... B ... 714 674-8500
50 Pointe Dr Brea (92821) *(P-3864)*

Avery Dennison Corporation ... C ... 626 304-2000
2900 Bradley St Pasadena (91107) *(P-3865)*

Avery Dennison Foundation ... E ... 626 304-2000
207 N Goode Ave Ste 500 Glendale (91203) *(P-3866)*

Avery Group Inc ... B ... 310 217-1070
8941 Dalton Ave Los Angeles (90047) *(P-17217)*

Avery Products Corporation (HQ) ... **A ... 714 675-8500**
50 Pointe Dr Brea (92821) *(P-3913)*

Avet Industries Inc ... F ... 818 576-9895
9687 Topanga Canyon Pl Chatsworth (91311) *(P-11404)*

Avet Reels, Chatsworth *Also called Avet Industries Inc (P-11404)*

Aveta Health Solution Inc ... A ... 909 605-8000
3990 Concours Ste 500 Ontario (91764) *(P-23164)*

Aveva Software LLC (HQ) ... **B ... 949 727-3200**
26561 Rancho Pkwy S Lake Forest (92630) *(P-18019)*

Aviation & Defense Inc ... C ... 909 382-3487
255 S Leland Norton Way San Bernardino (92408) *(P-12341)*

Aviation Equipment Processing, Costa Mesa *Also called Flare Group (P-10327)*

Aviation Maintenance Group Inc ... D ... 714 469-0515
8352 Kimball Ave Hngr 3 Chino (91708) *(P-12342)*

Aviation Repair Solutions Inc ... F ... 562 437-2825
1480 Canal Ave Long Beach (90813) *(P-12343)*

Avibank Mfg Inc (HQ) ... **C ... 818 392-2100**
11500 Sherman Way North Hollywood (91605) *(P-10284)*

Avibank Mfg Inc ... D ... 661 257-2329
25323 Rye Canyon Rd Valencia (91355) *(P-6503)*

Avicena LLC (PA) ... **D ... 626 344-9665**
117 E Colo Blvd Ste 510 Pasadena (91105) *(P-22828)*

Avid Bioservices Inc (PA) ... **C ... 714 508-6000**
2642 Michelle Dr Ste 200 Tustin (92780) *(P-4791)*

Avid Idntification Systems Inc (PA) ... **D ... 951 371-7505**
3185 Hamner Ave Norco (92860) *(P-9486)*

Avid Ink, Irvine *Also called Advanced Vsual Image Dsign LLC (P-4224)*

Avid Technology Inc ... C ... 818 779-7860
14007 Runnymede St Van Nuys (91405) *(P-11268)*

Avidex Industries LLC ... D ... 949 428-6333
20382 Hermana Cir Lake Forest (92630) *(P-18162)*

Avient Colorants USA LLC ... C ... 909 606-1325
14355 Ramona Ave Chino (91710) *(P-5128)*

Avilas Garden Art (PA) ... **D ... 909 350-4546**
14608 Merrill Ave Fontana (92335) *(P-6019)*

Avion Graphics Inc ... E ... 949 472-0438
27192 Burbank Foothill Ranch (92610) *(P-4232)*

Avion Tl Mfg Machining Ctr Inc ... F ... 661 257-2915
29035 The Old Rd Valencia (91355) *(P-8509)*

Avionics & Electronics, Valencia *Also called Curtiss-Wrght Cntrls Intgrted (P-22524)*

Avis Roto Die Co ... E ... 323 255-7070
1560 N San Fernando Rd Los Angeles (90065) *(P-7779)*

Avison Yung - Southern Cal Ltd (HQ) ... **D ... 424 265-9200**
10940 Wilshire Blvd # 2100 Los Angeles (90024) *(P-15781)*

Avita Medical Americas LLC ... D ... 661 367-9170
28159 Ave Stnford Ste 220 Valencia (91355) *(P-13478)*

AVIVA CENTER, Los Angeles *Also called Hamburger Home (P-22106)*

Aviva Family & Childrens Svcs (PA) ... **D ... 323 876-0550**
1701 Camino Palmero St Los Angeles (90046) *(P-21719)*

Avn Media Network Inc ... E ... 818 718-5788
9400 Penfield Ave Chatsworth (91311) *(P-4120)*

Avongard Products USA Ltd ... E ... 310 319-2300
12855 Runway Rd Apt 1208 Playa Vista (90094) *(P-19220)*

AVX Filters Corporation ... D ... 818 767-6770
11144 Penrose St Ste 7 Sun Valley (91352) *(P-8112)*

AW Die Engraving Inc ... E ... 714 521-7910
8550 Roland St Buena Park (90621) *(P-7780)*

Aw Industries Inc ... F ... 909 629-1500
1810 S Reservoir St Pomona (91766) *(P-3463)*

Awake Inc ... E ... 818 365-9361
10711 Walker St Cypress (90630) *(P-2879)*

Award Packaging Spc Corp ... E ... 323 727-1200
12855 Midway Pl Cerritos (90703) *(P-3784)*

Aware Products Inc ... E ... 818 206-6700
9250 Mason Ave Chatsworth (91311) *(P-4990)*

Aware Products LLC ... C ... 818 206-6700
9250 Mason Ave Chatsworth (91311) *(P-4991)*

Awesome Office Inc ... D ... 310 845-7733
3415 S Sepulveda Blvd # 1100 Los Angeles (90034) *(P-14557)*

Awesome Products Inc (PA) ... **C ... 714 562-8873**
6370 Altura Blvd Buena Park (90620) *(P-4955)*

AWH Burbank Hotel LLC ... D ... 813 843-6000
2500 N Hollywood Way Burbank (91505) *(P-16331)*

AWI Management Corporation ... C ... 951 674-8200
1800 E Lakeshore Dr Lake Elsinore (92530) *(P-22982)*

AWR, San Dimas *Also called Golden State Water Company (P-12892)*

Awr, San Dimas *Also called American States Water Company (P-12879)*

Ax II Inc ... F ... 310 292-6523
13921 S Figueroa St Los Angeles (90061) *(P-2615)*

ALPHABETIC

Employee Codes: A=Over 500 employees, B=251-500 C=101-250, D=51-100, E=20-50 F=10-19
2022 Southern California Business Directory and Buyers Guide
© Mergent Inc. 1-800-342-5647
1065

Axaio Industries LLC.....E.....323 504-1074
538 S Oxford Ave Apt 302 Los Angeles (90020) ***(P-12627)***
Axelacare Holdings Inc.....A.....714 522-8802
12604 Hiddencreek Way C Cerritos (90703) ***(P-21137)***
Axent Corporation Limited.....F.....949 900-4349
3 Musick Irvine (92618) ***(P-3902)***
Axent USA, Irvine *Also called Axent Corporation Limited* ***(P-3902)***
Axeon Water Technologies.....D.....760 723-5417
40980 County Center Dr # 110 Temecula (92591) ***(P-8366)***
Axia Technologies Inc.....E.....855 376-2942
4183 State St Santa Barbara (93110) ***(P-17792)***
Axia Technologies Inc.....E.....855 376-2942
4183 State St Santa Barbara (93110) ***(P-17793)***
Axiamed, Santa Barbara *Also called Axia Technologies Inc* ***(P-17792)***
Axiom Designs & Printing, Glendale *Also called Axiomprint Inc* ***(P-4233)***
Axiom Label & Packaging, Compton *Also called Resource Label Group LLC* ***(P-4468)***
Axiom Materials Inc.....E.....949 623-4400
2320 Pullman St Santa Ana (92705) ***(P-5178)***
Axiom Memory Solutions Inc.....D.....949 581-1450
16 Goodyear Ste 120 Irvine (92618) ***(P-13378)***
Axiomprint Inc.....F.....747 888-7777
513 State St Glendale (91203) ***(P-4233)***
Axis, Culver City *Also called Rick Solomon Enterprises Inc* ***(P-14347)***
Axis Construction Inc.....D.....818 545-9292
901 S Glendale Ave # 200 Glendale (91205) ***(P-741)***
Axis Unlimited Inc.....D.....714 476-1341
13373 Lilyrose St Eastvale (92880) ***(P-23165)***
Axles Now, Anaheim *Also called Friedl Corporation* ***(P-10062)***
Axminster Medical Group Inc (PA).....**D.....310 670-3255**
8540 S Sepulveda Blvd # 818 Los Angeles (90045) ***(P-19718)***
Axon Networks Inc.....D.....949 310-4429
15420 Laguna Canyon Rd # 15 Irvine (92618) ***(P-17559)***
Axonics Inc.....D.....949 396-6322
26 Technology Dr Irvine (92618) ***(P-22829)***
Axxcelera Brdband Wireless Inc (HQ).....**D.....805 968-9621**
82 Coromar Dr Santa Barbara (93117) ***(P-12594)***
Axxion USA Inc.....F.....213 622-3717
8323 Canford St Pico Rivera (90660) ***(P-5491)***
Axxis Corporation.....E.....951 436-9921
1535 Nandina Ave Perris (92571) ***(P-8510)***
Ayc, San Gabriel *Also called Asian Youth Center* ***(P-21717)***
Aylesva Inc.....C.....562 688-0592
14537 Garfield Ave Paramount (90723) ***(P-14430)***
Ayo Foods LLC.....E.....661 345-5457
927 Main St Delano (93215) ***(P-1831)***
Ayres - Paso Robles LP.....C.....714 850-0409
2700 Buena Vista Dr Paso Robles (93446) ***(P-16332)***
Ayres Group (PA).....**B.....714 540-6060**
355 Bristol St Costa Mesa (92626) ***(P-16333)***
Ayres Hotel Barstow, Barstow *Also called Country Side Inn Ontario LP* ***(P-16390)***
Ayzenberg Group Inc.....D.....626 584-4070
49 E Walnut St Pasadena (91103) ***(P-16993)***
AZ Displays Inc.....E.....949 831-5000
75 Columbia Aliso Viejo (92656) ***(P-9679)***
AZ Gems Inc (PA).....**F.....909 206-3384**
405 Missouri Ct Redlands (92373) ***(P-14672)***
AZ Manufacturing, Santa Ana *Also called A-Z Mfg Inc* ***(P-8458)***
Az-Iz Case Co, Pico Rivera *Also called Procases Inc* ***(P-3379)***
Azachorok Contract Svcs LLC.....F.....661 951-6566
320 Grand Cypress Ave # 502 Palmdale (93551) ***(P-6790)***
Azimc Investments Inc.....C.....818 678-1200
8901 Canoga Ave Canoga Park (91304) ***(P-13047)***
Azimuth Electronics Inc.....F.....949 492-6481
2605 S El Camino Real San Clemente (92672) ***(P-10744)***
Azitex Knitting Mills, Los Angeles *Also called Azitex Trading Corp* ***(P-2651)***
Azitex Trading Corp.....D.....213 745-7072
1850 E 15th St Los Angeles (90021) ***(P-2651)***
Aztec Tents, Torrance *Also called A-Aztec Rents & Sells Inc* ***(P-3133)***
Azteca Jeans Inc.....E.....323 758-7721
6600 Avalon Blvd Los Angeles (90003) ***(P-2920)***
Azteca Landscape (PA).....**C.....909 673-0889**
1525 E Ontario Ave # 101 Corona (92881) ***(P-292)***
Aztecs Telecom Inc.....D.....714 373-1560
1353 Walker Ln Corona (92879) ***(P-18454)***
Aztek Incorporated.....E.....949 770-8406
13765 Alton Pkwy Ste F Irvine (92618) ***(P-18020)***
Azure Microdynamics Inc.....D.....949 699-3344
19652 Descartes Foothill Ranch (92610) ***(P-8511)***
Azusa Engineering Inc.....F.....626 966-4071
1542 W Industrial Park St Covina (91722) ***(P-10021)***
B & B Battery (usa) Inc (PA).....**F.....323 278-1900**
6415 Randolph St Commerce (90040) ***(P-9816)***
B & B Doors and Windows Inc.....F.....818 837-8480
11455 Ilex Ave San Fernando (91340) ***(P-6692)***
B & B Jewelry Mfg, Los Angeles *Also called Nationwide Jewelry Mfrs Inc* ***(P-11325)***
B & B Nurseries Inc.....C.....951 352-8383
9505 Cleveland Ave Riverside (92503) ***(P-14876)***
B & B Pipe and Tool Co (PA).....**E.....562 424-0704**
3035 Walnut Ave Long Beach (90807) ***(P-477)***
B & B Pipe and Tool Co.....E.....661 323-8208
2301 Parker Ln Bakersfield (93308) ***(P-8512)***
B & B Plastics Inc.....E.....909 829-3606
1892 W Casmalia St Rialto (92377) ***(P-4679)***
B & B Plastics Recyclers Inc (PA).....**C.....909 829-3606**
3040 N Locust Ave Rialto (92377) ***(P-14111)***
B & B Red-I-Mix Concrete Inc.....F.....626 359-8371
590 Live Oak Ave Baldwin Park (91706) ***(P-6072)***
B & B Refractories Inc.....E.....562 946-4535
12121 Los Nietos Rd Santa Fe Springs (90670) ***(P-5987)***
B & B Services, Baldwin Park *Also called B & B Red-I-Mix Concrete Inc* ***(P-6072)***
B & B Specialties Inc (PA).....**D.....714 985-3000**
4321 E La Palma Ave Anaheim (92807) ***(P-6504)***
B & B Specialties Inc.....D.....714 985-3075
4321 E La Palma Ave Anaheim (92807) ***(P-13797)***
B & B Specialty Metals, Bakersfield *Also called B & B Surplus Inc* ***(P-13547)***
B & B Surplus Inc (PA).....**D.....661 589-0381**
7020 Rosedale Hwy Bakersfield (93308) ***(P-13547)***
B & C Industries, Anaheim *Also called B & Cawnings Inc* ***(P-6791)***
B & C Plating Co.....F.....323 263-6757
1507 S Sunol Dr Los Angeles (90023) ***(P-7220)***
B & Cawnings Inc.....E.....714 632-3303
3082 E Miraloma Ave Anaheim (92806) ***(P-6791)***
B & E Convalescent Center Inc (PA).....**D.....562 923-9449**
11627 Telg Rd Ste 200 Santa Fe Springs (90670) ***(P-20557)***
B & E Enterprises.....F.....714 630-3731
1380 N Mccan St Anaheim (92806) ***(P-10481)***
B & E Manufacturing Co Inc.....E.....714 898-2269
12151 Monarch St Garden Grove (92841) ***(P-10285)***
B & G House of Printing, Gardena *Also called Matsuda House Printing Inc* ***(P-4358)***
B & G Millworks.....F.....562 944-4599
12522 Lakeland Rd Santa Fe Springs (90670) ***(P-3234)***
B & H Signs Inc.....F.....626 359-6643
926 S Primrose Ave Monrovia (91016) ***(P-11525)***
B & L Casing Service LLC.....F.....661 589-9080
21054 Kratzmeyer Rd Bakersfield (93314) ***(P-478)***
B & L Consulting LLC.....D.....682 238-6994
164 N 2nd Ave 9 Upland (91786) ***(P-23416)***
B & M Contractors Inc.....D.....805 581-5480
4473 Cochran St Simi Valley (93063) ***(P-1513)***
B & M Racing & Prfmce Pdts, Chatsworth *Also called Automoco LLC* ***(P-10020)***
B & R Mold Inc.....E.....805 526-8665
4564 E Los Angeles Ave C Simi Valley (93063) ***(P-7781)***
B & S Food Products.....F.....323 263-6728
20268 Pase Del Prado Walnut (91789) ***(P-14456)***
B & S Plastics Inc.....A.....805 981-0262
2200 Sturgis Rd Oxnard (93030) ***(P-5572)***
B & W Precision Inc.....F.....714 447-0971
1260 Pioneer St Ste A Brea (92821) ***(P-8513)***
B & W Tile Co Inc (PA).....**E.....310 538-9579**
14600 S Western Ave Gardena (90249) ***(P-5984)***
B & W Tile Manufacturing, Gardena *Also called B & W Tile Co Inc* ***(P-5984)***
B A S, Diamond Bar *Also called Tetra Tech Bas Inc* ***(P-22669)***
B and Z Printing Inc.....E.....714 892-2000
1300 E Wakeham Ave B Santa Ana (92705) ***(P-4234)***
B B & B, Palmdale *Also called Bowlero Corp* ***(P-19392)***
B B Blu, Los Angeles *Also called Treivush Industries* ***(P-3006)***
B B C, Long Beach *Also called Belmont Brewing Company Inc* ***(P-2138)***
B B G Management Group (PA).....**E.....909 797-9581**
12164 California St Yucaipa (92399) ***(P-14558)***
B Boston & Associates Inc (PA).....**C.....323 264-3915**
4871 S Santa Fe Ave Vernon (90058) ***(P-14362)***
B Braun Medical Inc.....A.....610 691-5400
2525 Mcgaw Ave Irvine (92614) ***(P-10942)***
B C Laboratories Inc.....D.....661 327-4911
4100 Atlas Ct Bakersfield (93308) ***(P-22931)***
B C S, Canoga Park *Also called Buyers Consultation Svc Inc* ***(P-13706)***
B C T, Laguna Hills *Also called Raintree Business Products Inc* ***(P-4415)***
B D L, Brea *Also called Belt Drives Ltd* ***(P-10483)***
B Dazzle Inc.....F.....310 374-3000
500 Meyer Ln Redondo Beach (90278) ***(P-11367)***
B E & P Enterprises LLC (PA).....**E.....909 591-7561**
5167 G St Chino (91710) ***(P-3439)***
B E B E, Los Angeles *Also called Bebe Studio Inc* ***(P-2924)***
B E M R, Bakersfield *Also called Bakersfield Elc Mtr Repr Inc* ***(P-19006)***
B F, Riverside *Also called Brenner-Fiedler & Assoc Inc* ***(P-10873)***
B F I Labels, Yorba Linda *Also called Beckers Fabrication Inc* ***(P-3867)***
B F McGilla Inc.....E.....323 581-8288
2020 E Slauson Ave Huntington Park (90255) ***(P-7528)***
B J Bindery Inc.....D.....714 835-7342
833 S Grand Ave Santa Ana (92705) ***(P-4617)***
B Jacqueline and Assoc Inc.....D.....626 844-1400
1192 N Lake Ave Pasadena (91104) ***(P-17560)***
B L S Limousine Service, Los Angeles *Also called Bls Lmsine Svc Los Angeles Inc* ***(P-11855)***
B M W of Riverside, Riverside *Also called David A Campbell Corporation* ***(P-18822)***
B N I, Upland *Also called Bni Enterprises Inc* ***(P-23375)***
B O A Inc.....E.....714 256-8960
580 W Lambert Rd Ste L Brea (92821) ***(P-2802)***
B P John Hauling, Murrieta *Also called B P John Recycle Inc* ***(P-3208)***
B P John Recycle Inc.....F.....951 696-1144
38875 Avenida La Cresta Murrieta (92562) ***(P-3208)***
B P W, Santa Fe Springs *Also called Brown-Pacific Inc* ***(P-6189)***
B Riley Retail Solutions LLC.....D.....818 884-3737
30870 Russell Ranch Rd Westlake Village (91362) ***(P-18455)***
B S A Partners.....D.....714 523-2800
14419 Firestone Blvd La Mirada (90638) ***(P-16334)***
B S K T Inc.....F.....818 349-1566
8447 Canoga Ave Canoga Park (91304) ***(P-8514)***
B Stephen Cooperage Inc.....F.....909 591-2929
10746 Vernon Ave Ontario (91762) ***(P-6471)***
B T I, City of Industry *Also called Battery Technology Inc* ***(P-9807)***
B T I Aerospace & Electronics, Chino *Also called Bti Aerospace & Electronics* ***(P-8532)***
B W F, Bakersfield *Also called Bwf Banducci Inc* ***(P-5153)***
B W I, Anaheim *Also called Bud Wil Inc* ***(P-5494)***

Mergent e-mail: customerrelations@mergent.com
1066
2022 Southern California Business Directory and Buyers Guide
(P-0000) Products & Services Section entry number
(PA)=Parent Co (HQ)=Headquarters (DH)=Div Headquarters

B W Implement Co ....E....661 764-5254
288 W Front St Buttonwillow (93206) *(P-7605)*
B&A Health Products Co, Brea *Also called Lifebloom Corporation (P-4847)*
B&B Hardware Inc ....F....805 683-6700
5370 Hollister Ave Ste 2 Santa Barbara (93111) *(P-7056)*
B&B Industrial Services Inc (PA) ....B....**909 428-3167**
14549 Manzanita Dr Fontana (92335) *(P-1341)*
B&B Manufacturing Co (PA) ....C....**661 257-2161**
27940 Beale Ct Santa Clarita (91355) *(P-8515)*
B&B Pallet Company, Whittier *Also called Bruce Iversen (P-3382)*
B&B Spring Co, Cerritos *Also called Clio Inc (P-7485)*
B&D Investment Partners Inc (PA) ....E....**661 255-0955**
20950 Centre Pointe Pkwy Santa Clarita (91350) *(P-4956)*
B&D Litho California Inc ....F....909 390-0903
325 N Ponderosa Ave Ontario (91761) *(P-4235)*
B&G Machine Shop, Bakersfield *Also called McCain & Mccain Inc (P-8681)*
B&K Precision Corporation (PA) ....E....**714 921-9095**
22820 Savi Ranch Pkwy Yorba Linda (92887) *(P-10745)*
B&W Custom Restaurant Eqp Inc ....E....714 578-0332
541 E Jamie Ave La Habra (90631) *(P-8367)*
B/E Aerospace Inc ....D....951 278-4563
350 W Rincon St Corona (92878) *(P-10286)*
B2 Services Llc ....D....714 363-3481
17291 Irvine Blvd Ste 258 Tustin (92780) *(P-17393)*
B2b Payroll Services, Cypress *Also called B2b Staffing Services Inc (P-17486)*
B2b Staffing Services Inc ....B....714 243-4104
4501 Cerritos Ave Ste 201 Cypress (90630) *(P-17486)*
Ba Holdings Inc (HQ) ....E....**951 684-5110**
3016 Kansas Ave Bldg 1 Riverside (92507) *(P-6728)*
Baatz Enterprises Inc ....F....323 660-4866
2223 W San Bernardino Rd West Covina (91790) *(P-9936)*
Bab Hydraulics, Fontana *Also called Bab Steering Hydraulics (P-10022)*
Bab Steering Hydraulics (PA) ....E....**208 573-4502**
14554 Whittram Ave Fontana (92335) *(P-10022)*
Babcock Enterprises Inc ....E....805 736-1455
5175 E Highway 246 Lompoc (93436) *(P-42)*
Babcock Laboratories Inc ....D....951 653-3351
6100 Quail Valley Ct Riverside (92507) *(P-22932)*
Babcock Vineyards, Lompoc *Also called Babcock Enterprises Inc (P-42)*
Baby Guess Inc ....D....213 765-3100
1444 S Alameda St Los Angeles (90021) *(P-3039)*
Baby Trend Inc (HQ) ....D....**909 773-0018**
1607 S Campus Ave Ontario (91761) *(P-14363)*
Babyfirst Americas LLC ....D....310 442-9853
10390 Santa Monica Blvd Los Angeles (90025) *(P-17561)*
Babylon Security Services Inc ....D....818 766-8122
6032 One Half Vneland Ave North Hollywood (91606) *(P-18253)*
Bace Manufacturing Inc (HQ) ....A....**714 630-6002**
3125 E Coronado St Anaheim (92806) *(P-5573)*
Bachem Americas Inc (HQ) ....C....**310 784-4440**
3132 Kashiwa St Torrance (90505) *(P-4931)*
Bachem Bioscience Inc ....E....310 784-7322
3132 Kashiwa St Torrance (90505) *(P-4932)*
Bachem California, Torrance *Also called Bachem Americas Inc (P-4931)*
Back Support Systems Inc ....F....760 329-1472
67688 San Andreas St Desert Hot Springs (92240) *(P-5492)*
Backstage Equipment Inc ....F....818 504-6026
8052 Lankershim Blvd North Hollywood (91605) *(P-7015)*
Backstage Studio Equip, North Hollywood *Also called Backstage Equipment Inc (P-7015)*
Bad Robot Productions Inc ....D....310 664-3456
1221 Olympic Blvd Santa Monica (90404) *(P-19256)*
Badalian Enterprises Inc ....D....714 635-4082
1540 S Harbor Blvd Anaheim (92802) *(P-16335)*
Bae Systems Controls Inc ....F....323 642-5000
5140 W Goldleaf Cir G100 Los Angeles (90056) *(P-7579)*
Baf Industries (PA) ....E....**714 258-8055**
1451 Edinger Ave Ste F Tustin (92780) *(P-4957)*
Bagcraftpapercon I LLC ....D....626 961-6766
515 Turnbull Canyon Rd City of Industry (91745) *(P-3894)*
Baghouse and Indus Shtmtl Svcs, Corona *Also called MS Industrial Shtmtl Inc (P-1498)*
Bagmasters, Corona *Also called CTA Manufacturing Inc (P-3126)*
Baguette World, Los Angeles *Also called Kobi Katz Inc (P-11320)*
Baier Marine Company Inc ....E....800 455-3917
2920 Airway Ave Costa Mesa (92626) *(P-6505)*
Bailey 44 LLC ....E....213 228-1930
4700 S Boyle Ave Vernon (90058) *(P-2836)*
Bailey Industries Inc ....F....949 461-0807
25256 Terreno Dr Mission Viejo (92691) *(P-10287)*
Bailey, Rollin C MD, Lompoc *Also called Valley Med Group Lompoc Inc (P-20999)*
Bait Inc (PA) ....E....**909 595-1712**
2753 S Dmnd Bar Blvd B Diamond Bar (91765) *(P-13702)*
Bake R Us Inc ....E....310 630-5873
13400 S Western Ave Gardena (90249) *(P-1980)*
Bakell LLC ....D....800 292-2137
24723 Redlands Blvd Ste F Loma Linda (92354) *(P-689)*
Bakemark USA LLC (PA) ....A....**562 949-1054**
7351 Crider Ave Pico Rivera (90660) *(P-1950)*
Baker & Hostetler LLP ....D....310 820-8800
11601 Wilshire Blvd Fl 14 Los Angeles (90025) *(P-21507)*
Baker & Hostetler LLP ....D....714 754-6600
600 Anton Blvd Ste 900 Costa Mesa (92626) *(P-21508)*
Baker & McKenzie LLP ....C....310 201-4728
10250 Constellation Blvd Los Angeles (90067) *(P-21509)*
Baker Commodities Inc (PA) ....C....**323 268-2801**
4020 Bandini Blvd Vernon (90058) *(P-2122)*
Baker Commodities Inc ....E....559 686-4797
7480 Hanford Armona Rd Hanford (93230) *(P-2123)*
Baker Commodities Inc ....E....323 318-8260
3001 Sierra Pine Ave Vernon (90058) *(P-2124)*
Baker Coupling Company Inc ....E....323 583-3444
2929 S Santa Fe Ave Vernon (90058) *(P-7529)*
Baker Winokur Ryder, Beverly Hills *Also called Bwr Public Relations (P-23378)*
Bakers Kneaded LLC ....E....213 321-9952
148 W 132nd St Ste D Los Angeles (90061) *(P-1981)*
Bakersfeld Assn For Rtrded Ctz ....C....661 834-2272
2240 S Union Ave Bakersfield (93307) *(P-21942)*
Bakersfeld Bhvral Hlthcare Hos ....C....661 398-1800
5201 White Ln Bakersfield (93309) *(P-21015)*
Bakersfeld Cmnty Bsed Otptent, Bakersfield *Also called Veterans Health Administration (P-20152)*
Bakersfeld Hlthcare Wllness CN ....D....661 872-2121
2211 Mount Vernon Ave Bakersfield (93306) *(P-20558)*
Bakersfield Country Club ....D....661 871-4000
4200 Country Club Dr Bakersfield (93306) *(P-19535)*
Bakersfield District Office, Bakersfield *Also called State Compensation Insur Fund (P-15481)*
Bakersfield Elc Mtr Repr Inc ....D....661 327-3583
121 W Sumner St Bakersfield (93301) *(P-19006)*
Bakersfield Family Medical Ctr, Bakersfield *Also called Heritage Medical Group Inc (P-19843)*
Bakersfield Healthcare ....D....661 872-2121
2211 Mount Vernon Ave Bakersfield (93306) *(P-20251)*
Bakersfield Heart Hospital, Bakersfield *Also called Heart Hospital of Bk LLC (P-20784)*
Bakersfield Inn Inc ....C....661 323-1900
801 Truxtun Ave Bakersfield (93301) *(P-16336)*
Bakersfield Machine Co Inc ....D....661 709-1992
5605 N Chester Ave Ext Bakersfield (93308) *(P-8516)*
Bakersfield Mazda, Bakersfield *Also called Cjm Automotive Group Inc (P-18819)*
Bakersfield Memorial Hospital ....A....661 327-1792
420 34th St Bakersfield (93301) *(P-20685)*
Bakersfield News Observer, Bakersfield *Also called Observer Group Newspaper (P-4019)*
Bakersfield Respite Homecare, Bakersfield *Also called Maxim Healthcare Services Inc (P-17503)*
Bakersfield Vet Center, Bakersfield *Also called Veterans Health Administration (P-20154)*
Bakersfield Westwind Corp ....C....661 327-2121
1810 Westwind Dr Bakersfield (93301) *(P-15782)*
Bakery Depot Inc ....F....323 261-8388
4489 Bandini Blvd Vernon (90058) *(P-1982)*
Bakery Ex Southern Cal LLC ....D....714 446-9470
1910 W Malvern Ave Fullerton (92833) *(P-14673)*
Bakkavor Foods Usa Inc (HQ) ....B....**704 522-1977**
18201 Central Ave Carson (90746) *(P-14674)*
Bal Seal Engineering LLC (HQ) ....B....**949 460-2100**
19650 Pauling Foothill Ranch (92610) *(P-7483)*
Balaji Trading Inc ....D....909 444-7999
4850 Eucalyptus Ave Chino (91710) *(P-9227)*
Balance Foods Inc ....E....323 838-5555
5743 Smithway St Ste 103 Commerce (90040) *(P-14559)*
Balboa Bay Club Inc (HQ) ....B....**949 645-5000**
1221 W Coast Hwy Ste 145 Newport Beach (92663) *(P-19536)*
Balboa Bay Club and Resort, Newport Beach *Also called International Bay Clubs LLC (P-19570)*
Balboa Capital Corporation (PA) ....C....**949 756-0800**
575 Anton Blvd Ste 1200 Costa Mesa (92626) *(P-15150)*
Balboa Plaza Admin Offices, Granada Hills *Also called Kaiser Foundation Hospitals (P-19902)*
Balboa Water Group LLC (HQ) ....B....**714 384-0384**
3030 Airway Ave Ste B Costa Mesa (92626) *(P-8944)*
Balboa Yacht Club ....E....949 673-3515
1801 Bayside Dr Corona Del Mar (92625) *(P-19537)*
Balda C Brewer Inc (HQ) ....C....**714 630-6810**
4501 E Wall St Ontario (91761) *(P-5574)*
Baldwin Brass, Foothill Ranch *Also called Baldwin Hardware Corporation (P-6506)*
Baldwin Construction, Chino *Also called Jpm Industries Inc (P-615)*
Baldwin Hardware Corporation (HQ) ....A....**949 672-4000**
19701 Da Vinci Foothill Ranch (92610) *(P-6506)*
Baldwin Hospitality LLC ....D....626 446-2988
14635 Bldwin Pk Towne Ctr Baldwin Park (91706) *(P-16337)*
Baldwin Hospitality LLC ....D....626 962-6000
14635 Baldwin Ave Baldwin Park (91706) *(P-16338)*
Baldwin Park Unified Schl Dst ....D....626 337-2711
13529 Francisquito Ave Baldwin Park (91706) *(P-21984)*
Baldwin Pk Unfied Schl Dst Chl, Baldwin Park *Also called Baldwin Park Unified Schl Dst (P-21984)*
Bali Construction Inc ....D....626 442-8003
9852 Joe Vargas Way South El Monte (91733) *(P-936)*
Balita Media Inc ....F....818 552-4503
2629 Foothill Blvd La Crescenta (91214) *(P-3952)*
Ball of Cotton Inc ....F....323 888-9448
6400 E Wash Blvd Unit 10 Commerce (90040) *(P-2626)*
Ball TEC, Los Angeles *Also called Micro Surface Engr Inc (P-6460)*
Ballard & Tighe Publishers, Brea *Also called Educational Ideas Incorporated (P-4128)*
Ballard Inn Inc ....D....805 688-7770
2436 Baseline Ave Solvang (93463) *(P-16339)*
Ballard Rehabilitation Hosp, San Bernardino *Also called Robert Ballard Rehab Hospital (P-20232)*
Ballard Spahr LLP ....D....424 204-4400
2029 Century Park E # 800 Los Angeles (90067) *(P-21510)*
Balmoral Funds LLC (PA) ....A....**310 473-3065**
11150 Santa Monica Blvd Los Angeles (90025) *(P-15317)*
Balt Usa LLC ....D....949 788-1443
29 Parker Ste 100 Irvine (92618) *(P-13479)*
Baltazar Construction Inc ....E....626 339-8620
236 E Arrow Hwy Covina (91722) *(P-1514)*

ALPHABETIC

Employee Codes: A=Over 500 employees, B=251-500
C=101-250, D=51-100, E=20-50 F=10-19
2022 Southern California Business
Directory and Buyers Guide
© Mergent Inc. 1-800-342-5647
1067

Baltic Ltvian Unvrsal Elec LLC......E......818 879-5200
5706 Corsa Ave Ste 102 Westlake Village (91362) *(P-9161)*
Bambeck Systems Inc (PA)......F......**949 250-3100**
1921 Carnegie Ave Ste 3a Santa Ana (92705) *(P-10679)*
Bamko LLC (HQ)......D......**310 470-5859**
11620 Wilshire Blvd # 610 Los Angeles (90025) *(P-23166)*
Bamko Promotional Items, Los Angeles *Also called Bamko LLC* *(P-23166)*
Bana Home Loan Servicing......A......213 345-7975
31303 Agoura Rd Westlake Village (91361) *(P-14989)*
Banamex USA Bancorp (HQ)......C......**310 203-3440**
787 W 5th St Los Angeles (90071) *(P-16091)*
Bananafish Productions Inc......F......714 956-2129
1536 W Embassy St Anaheim (92802) *(P-5946)*
Banc California National Assn (HQ)......D......**877 770-2262**
3 Macarthur Pl Santa Ana (92707) *(P-14990)*
Banc California National Assn......E......310 286-0710
10100 Santa Monica Blvd Los Angeles (90067) *(P-14991)*
Banc of California Inc (PA)......C......**855 361-2262**
3 Macarthur Pl Ste 100 Santa Ana (92707) *(P-14992)*
Bandag Licensing Corporation......D......562 531-3880
2500 E Thompson St Long Beach (90805) *(P-5366)*
Bandai America Incorporated (HQ)......D......**714 816-9751**
2120 Park Pl Ste 120 El Segundo (90245) *(P-11368)*
Bandel Mfg Inc......E......818 246-7493
4459 Alger St Los Angeles (90039) *(P-7126)*
Bandy Manufacturing LLC......D......818 846-9020
3420 N San Fernando Blvd Burbank (91504) *(P-10288)*
Bangkit (usa) Inc......D......626 672-0888
10511 Valley Blvd El Monte (91731) *(P-14192)*
Bank C Plating Co, Los Angeles *Also called We Five-R Corporation* *(P-7331)*
Bank of Hope (HQ)......C......**213 639-1700**
3200 Wilshire Blvd # 1400 Los Angeles (90010) *(P-14993)*
Bank of New York Trust of Cal (HQ)......C......**213 630-6327**
700 S Flower St Ste 340 Los Angeles (90017) *(P-15118)*
Bank of Sierra (HQ)......C......**559 782-4300**
90 N Main St Porterville (93257) *(P-15011)*
Bankcard Services, Torrance *Also called Credit Card Services Inc* *(P-18497)*
Bankcard Services (PA)......C......**213 365-1122**
21281 S Western Ave Torrance (90501) *(P-18456)*
Bankcard USA Merchant Srvc......D......818 597-7000
5701 Lindero Canyon Rd Westlake Village (91362) *(P-18457)*
Bankers Investment Group Inc......C......714 618-1736
12341 Lewis St Apt 26 Garden Grove (92840) *(P-15175)*
Bankers Mrtg Rlty Advsors Snta......E......805 682-9345
45 E Alamar Ave Santa Barbara (93105) *(P-22084)*
Bankruptcy Management Cons, El Segundo *Also called BMC Group Inc* *(P-21519)*
Banks Pest Control......C......661 323-7858
7440 District Blvd Ste A Bakersfield (93313) *(P-17198)*
Banks Power Products, Azusa *Also called Gale Banks Engineering* *(P-7595)*
Banner Solutions, Anaheim *Also called Mid-West Wholesale Hardware Co* *(P-6526)*
Banzai......F......310 231-7292
2229 Barry Ave Los Angeles (90064) *(P-14093)*
Banzai Foods LLC......F......714 200-9933
10937 El Coco Cir Fountain Valley (92708) *(P-2394)*
Bapko Metal Inc......D......714 639-9380
180 S Anita Dr Orange (92868) *(P-1567)*
Bar Bakers LLC......D......562 719-0300
10711 Bloomfield St Los Alamitos (90720) *(P-14675)*
Bar Hrbor Apartments Anchorage, Los Angeles *Also called E & S Ring Management Corp* *(P-15842)*
Bar None Inc......F......714 259-8450
1302 Santa Fe Dr Tustin (92780) *(P-2241)*
Bar-S Foods Co......D......323 589-3600
4919 Alcoa Ave Vernon (90058) *(P-1727)*
Bar-S Foods Co. Los Angeles, Vernon *Also called Bar-S Foods Co* *(P-1727)*
Barber-Webb Company Inc (PA)......E......**541 488-4821**
3833 Medford St Los Angeles (90063) *(P-5575)*
Barbour & Floyd Medical Assoc, Lynwood *Also called South Cntl Hlth Rhbltion Prgr* *(P-21342)*
Barclays USA Inc......D......310 829-9539
1620 26th St Ste 2000n Santa Monica (90404) *(P-15046)*
Barco Uniforms Inc......C......310 323-7315
350 W Rosecrans Ave Gardena (90248) *(P-2741)*
Bardex Corporation (PA)......D......**805 964-7747**
6338 Lindmar Dr Goleta (93117) *(P-13888)*
Bare Nothings Inc (PA)......E......**714 848-8532**
17705 Sampson Ln Huntington Beach (92647) *(P-2921)*
Barfresh, Los Angeles *Also called Smoothie Inc* *(P-1910)*
Barfresh Corporation Inc......F......303 502-5233
3600 Wilshire Blvd # 1720 Los Angeles (90010) *(P-2257)*
Bargain Mart Classifieds, North Hollywood *Also called Hughes Price & Sharp Inc* *(P-3993)*
Bargain Rent-A-Car......C......562 865-7447
18800 Studebaker Rd Cerritos (90703) *(P-13021)*
Barhena Inc......E......888 383-8800
1085 Bixby Dr Hacienda Heights (91745) *(P-8368)*
Barkens Hardchrome Inc......E......310 632-2000
239 E Greenleaf Blvd Compton (90220) *(P-7964)*
Barksdale Inc (HQ)......C......**323 583-6243**
3211 Fruitland Ave Vernon (90058) *(P-10871)*
Barlow Group (PA)......C......**213 250-4200**
2000 Stadium Way Los Angeles (90026) *(P-21032)*
Barlow Respiratory Hospital (PA)......C......**213 250-4200**
2000 Stadium Way Los Angeles (90026) *(P-21033)*
Barlow Respiratory Hospital......E......562 698-0811
12401 Washington Blvd Whittier (90602) *(P-21034)*
Barlow Respitory Hospital, Los Angeles *Also called Barlow Group* *(P-21032)*
Barnes & Thornburg LLP......C......310 284-3880
2029 Century Park E # 300 Los Angeles (90067) *(P-21511)*
Barnes Plastics Inc......E......310 329-6301
18903 Anelo Ave Gardena (90248) *(P-5576)*
Barnett Customer Management......E......714 747-7908
3111 N Tustin St Orange (92865) *(P-22983)*
Barnett Performance Products, Ventura *Also called Barnett Tool & Engineering* *(P-10482)*
Barnett Tool & Engineering......D......805 642-9435
2238 Palma Dr Ventura (93003) *(P-10482)*
Barns and Buildings Inc......F......951 678-4571
23100 Wildomar Trl Wildomar (92595) *(P-6987)*
Baron & Baron, Huntington Beach *Also called License Frame Inc* *(P-7381)*
Baronhr LLC......D......909 517-3800
13085 Central Ave Ste 4 Chino (91710) *(P-17394)*
Barr Engineering Inc......D......562 944-1722
12612 Clark St Santa Fe Springs (90670) *(P-1032)*
Barr, Ronald J MD /UCI Med Gro, Orange *Also called University California Irvine* *(P-20126)*
Barranca Medical Offices, Irvine *Also called Kaiser Foundation Hospitals* *(P-20800)*
Barrett Business Services Inc......A......909 890-3633
862 E Hospitality Ln San Bernardino (92408) *(P-17395)*
Barrett Business Services Inc......A......805 987-0331
815 Camarillo Springs Rd C Camarillo (93012) *(P-17396)*
Barrot Corporation......E......949 852-1640
1881 Kaiser Ave Irvine (92614) *(P-7782)*
Barry Avenue Plating Co Inc......D......310 478-0078
2210 Barry Ave Los Angeles (90064) *(P-7221)*
Barry Controls Aerospace, Burbank *Also called Hutchinson Arospc & Indust Inc* *(P-5382)*
Barry's Boot Camp, Los Angeles *Also called Barrys Bootcamp LLC* *(P-19438)*
Barrys Bootcamp Holdings LLC......B......270 535-5005
7373 Beverly Blvd Los Angeles (90036) *(P-14074)*
Barrys Bootcamp LLC (PA)......B......**323 452-0037**
7373 Beverly Blvd Los Angeles (90036) *(P-19438)*
Barrys Printing Inc......E......818 998-8600
9005 Eton Ave Ste D Canoga Park (91304) *(P-4236)*
Barrys Security Services Inc (PA)......C......**951 789-7575**
16739 Van Buren Blvd Riverside (92504) *(P-18254)*
Barrys Security Services Inc......C......562 493-7007
5480 Katella Ave Ste 203 Los Alamitos (90720) *(P-18255)*
BARSTOW COMMUNITY HOSPITAL, Barstow *Also called Hospital of Barstow Inc* *(P-20794)*
Barstow Healthcare MGT Inc (HQ)......E......**831 319-4194**
555 S 7th Ave Barstow (92311) *(P-23167)*
Barta-Schoenewald Inc (PA)......C......**805 389-1935**
3805 Calle Tecate Camarillo (93012) *(P-8909)*
Bartco Lighting Inc......D......714 230-3200
5761 Research Dr Huntington Beach (92649) *(P-13616)*
Bartholomew Barry & Associates......D......818 543-4000
701 N Brand Blvd Ste 800 Glendale (91203) *(P-21512)*
Bartlett Pringle & Wolf LLP......E......805 963-7811
1123 Chapala St Ste 300 Santa Barbara (93101) *(P-22760)*
Barto Signal Petroleum Inc......F......949 631-8066
1041 W 18th St Ste A101 Costa Mesa (92627) *(P-479)*
Barton Perreira LLC......E......949 305-5360
459 Wald Irvine (92618) *(P-11245)*
Barzillai Manufacturing Co Inc......F......909 947-4200
1410 S Cucamonga Ave Ontario (91761) *(P-6792)*
Bas Engineering Inc......F......909 484-2575
11899 8th St Rancho Cucamonga (91730) *(P-22498)*
Basaw Manufacturing Inc (PA)......E......**818 765-6650**
11323 Hartland St North Hollywood (91605) *(P-3376)*
Base Lite Corporation......E......909 444-2776
12260 Eastend Ave Chino (91710) *(P-9061)*
Baselite, Chino *Also called Base Lite Corporation* *(P-9061)*
Basic Business Forms Inc......E......805 278-4551
561 Kinetic Dr Ste A Oxnard (93030) *(P-4484)*
Basic Electronics Inc......E......714 530-2400
11371 Monarch St Garden Grove (92841) *(P-9680)*
Basic Energy Services Inc......E......661 588-3800
6710 Stewart Way Bakersfield (93308) *(P-480)*
Basic Industries Intl Inc......C......951 226-1500
10850 Wilshire Blvd Los Angeles (90024) *(P-6729)*
Basin Marine Inc......E......949 673-0360
829 Harbor Island Dr A Newport Beach (92660) *(P-10459)*
Basin Marine Shipyard, Newport Beach *Also called Basin Marine Inc* *(P-10459)*
Basis Worldwide......E......424 261-2354
1557 7th St Santa Monica (90401) *(P-16994)*
Basket Basics, Carson *Also called Kole Imports* *(P-14944)*
Basketball Marketing Co Inc......D......610 249-2255
101 Enterprise Ste 100 Aliso Viejo (92656) *(P-23168)*
Basmat Inc (PA)......D......**310 325-2063**
1531 240th St Harbor City (90710) *(P-6793)*
Bassani Exhaust, Anaheim *Also called Bassani Manufacturing* *(P-7530)*
Bassani Manufacturing......E......714 630-1821
2900 E La Jolla St Anaheim (92806) *(P-7530)*
Bassenian/Lagoni Architects......D......949 553-9100
2031 Orchard Dr Ste 100 Newport Beach (92660) *(P-22711)*
Basso Distributing Coinc......D......805 656-1946
2505 Pleasant Valley Rd Camarillo (93012) *(P-14821)*
Batchmaster Software, Irvine *Also called Eworkplace Manufacturing Inc* *(P-13397)*
Baton Lock & Hardware Co Inc......E......714 265-3636
14275 Commerce Dr Garden Grove (92843) *(P-6507)*
Baton Security, Garden Grove *Also called Baton Lock & Hardware Co Inc* *(P-6507)*
Battery Agency, Hollywood *Also called Battery Marketing Inc* *(P-16995)*
Battery Marketing Inc......D......323 467-7267
6515 W Sunset Blvd # 200 Hollywood (90028) *(P-16995)*
Battery Technology Inc (PA)......D......**626 336-6878**
16651 E Johnson Dr City of Industry (91745) *(P-9807)*
Battery-Biz Inc......D......800 848-6782
1380 Flynn Rd Camarillo (93012) *(P-9820)*
Bau Furniture Mfg Inc (PA)......E......**949 643-2729**
21 Kelly Ln Ladera Ranch (92694) *(P-3464)*

Bauman Curry & Co, Culver City *Also called JC Promotions Inc* ***(P-23249)***

Baumann Engineering ..... D 909 621-4181
212 S Cambridge Ave Claremont (91711) ***(P-8517)***

Bausch & Lomb Incorporated ..... D 949 788-6000
50 Technology Dr Irvine (92618) ***(P-4792)***

Bausch & Lomb Incorporated ..... C 949 788-6000
15273 Alton Pkwy Ste 100 Irvine (92618) ***(P-11246)***

Bausch & Lomb Surgical Div, Irvine *Also called Eyeonics Inc* ***(P-11253)***

Bausman and Company Inc (PA) ..... **C** **909 947-0139**
1500 Crafton Ave Bldg 124 Mentone (92359) ***(P-3579)***

Baxalta Incorporated ..... B 818 240-5600
4501 Colorado Blvd Los Angeles (90039) ***(P-4793)***

Baxalta US Inc ..... C 805 498-8664
1700 Rancho Conejo Blvd Thousand Oaks (91320) ***(P-10943)***

Baxalta US Inc ..... B 949 474-6301
17511 Armstrong Ave Irvine (92614) ***(P-18458)***

Baxco Pharmaceutical Inc ..... F 626 610-7088
2393 Bateman Ave Duarte (91010) ***(P-4794)***

Baxstra Inc ..... E 323 770-4171
1224 W 132nd St Gardena (90247) ***(P-3214)***

Baxter Healthcare Corporation ..... C 949 474-6301
17511 Armstrong Ave Irvine (92614) ***(P-10944)***

Baxter International Inc ..... F 818 550-4500
550 N Brand Blvd Fl 14 Glendale (91203) ***(P-4795)***

Baxter Medication Delivery, Irvine *Also called Baxter Healthcare Corporation* ***(P-10944)***

Bay Area Community Med Group, Los Angeles *Also called Santa Monica Bay Physicians He* ***(P-20059)***

Bay Cities Container Corp (PA) ..... **C** **562 948-3751**
5138 Industry Ave Pico Rivera (90660) ***(P-3785)***

Bay Cities Italian Bakery Inc ..... F 310 608-1881
1120 W Mahalo Pl Compton (90220) ***(P-1983)***

Bay Cities Metal Products, Gardena *Also called Bay Cities Tin Shop Inc* ***(P-6794)***

Bay Cities Tin Shop Inc ..... E 310 660-0351
301 E Alondra Blvd Gardena (90248) ***(P-6794)***

Bay Citis Surgery Centre L P ..... D 310 784-2710
23500 Madison St Torrance (90505) ***(P-19719)***

Bay Ornamental Iron Inc ..... E 949 548-1015
757 Newton Way Costa Mesa (92627) ***(P-6952)***

Bay Valley Mortgage, Garden Grove *Also called Pacific Bay Lending Group* ***(P-15247)***

Bayco Financial Corporation (PA) ..... **D** **310 378-8181**
24050 Madison St Ste 101 Torrance (90505) ***(P-15783)***

Bayless Engineering Inc ..... C 661 257-3373
26140 Avenue Hall Valencia (91355) ***(P-8518)***

Bayless Engineering & Mfg, Valencia *Also called Bayless Engineering Inc* ***(P-8518)***

Baymarr Constructors Inc ..... C 661 395-1676
6950 Mcdivitt Dr Bakersfield (93313) ***(P-1515)***

Bayshore Healthcare Inc ..... C 805 544-5100
3033 Augusta St San Luis Obispo (93401) ***(P-20252)***

Bayside Care Center, Morro Bay *Also called Compass Health Inc* ***(P-20287)***

Bayside Medical Center, Hawthorne *Also called Honda Stephan T MD Inc* ***(P-19845)***

Baywa R.E.renewable Energy, Irvine *Also called Baywa RE Solar Projects LLC* ***(P-9487)***

Baywa RE Solar Projects LLC (HQ) ..... **F** **949 398-3915**
18575 Jamboree Rd Ste 850 Irvine (92612) ***(P-9487)***

Bazic Product, El Monte *Also called Bangkit (usa) Inc* ***(P-14192)***

Bazz Houston Co, Garden Grove *Also called Houston Bazz Co* ***(P-7151)***

Bb Co Inc ..... E 213 550-1158
1753 E 21st St Los Angeles (90058) ***(P-2922)***

BB&k, Riverside *Also called Best Best & Krieger LLP* ***(P-21514)***

Bbe Sound Inc (PA) ..... **E** **714 897-6766**
2548 Fender Ave Ste G Fullerton (92831) ***(P-11340)***

Bbk Performance Inc ..... D 951 296-1771
27427 Bostik Ct Temecula (92590) ***(P-13048)***

Bbk Specialties Inc ..... F 661 255-2857
24147 Del Monte Dr # 297 Valencia (91355) ***(P-5991)***

Bbsi Camarillo, Camarillo *Also called Barrett Business Services Inc* ***(P-17396)***

Bbva USA ..... C 951 279-7071
195 W Ontario Ave Corona (92882) ***(P-15012)***

Bbva USA ..... C 951 672-4829
27851 Bradley Rd Ste 125 Sun City (92586) ***(P-14994)***

Bbva USA ..... C 760 325-2021
420 S Palm Canyon Dr Palm Springs (92262) ***(P-15050)***

Bc Rentals LLC (HQ) ..... **D** **714 974-1190**
638 W Southern Ave Orange (92865) ***(P-13889)***

Bc Traffic Specialist, Orange *Also called Bc Rentals LLC* ***(P-13889)***

Bc Tree Service Inc ..... E 805 649-6875
4288 Quatal Canyon Rd Maricopa (93252) ***(P-353)***

Bc2 Environmental, Orange *Also called Beks Acquisition Inc* ***(P-1559)***

Bc2 Environmental LLC ..... D 714 744-2990
1150 W Trenton Ave Orange (92867) ***(P-23417)***

Bcbg Max Azria Group LLC ..... D 323 589-2224
2761 Fruitland Ave Vernon (90058) ***(P-14364)***

Bcd Food Inc ..... F 310 323-1200
13507 S Normandie Ave Gardena (90249) ***(P-2395)***

Bcd Industries Corp ..... F 760 927-8988
24298 Via Vargas Dr Moreno Valley (92553) ***(P-11636)***

Bcd Tofu House, Los Angeles *Also called Wilshire Kingsley Inc* ***(P-15713)***

Bci Inc ..... E 626 579-4234
1822 Belcroft Ave South El Monte (91733) ***(P-8519)***

Bcp Systems Inc ..... D 714 202-3900
1560 S Sinclair St Anaheim (92806) ***(P-18144)***

Bdc Epoxy Systems Inc ..... E 562 944-6177
12903 Sunshine Ave Santa Fe Springs (90670) ***(P-4680)***

Bdeebz Investment Inc (PA) ..... **D** **909 646-9498**
16414 Foothill Blvd Fontana (92335) ***(P-16248)***

Bdfco Inc ..... D 714 228-2900
1926 Kauai Dr Costa Mesa (92626) ***(P-9333)***

Bdo Capital Advisors LLC ..... C 310 557-0300
1888 Century Park E Los Angeles (90067) ***(P-15318)***

BDR Industries Inc ..... E 818 341-2112
9700 Owensmouth Ave Lbby Chatsworth (91311) ***(P-8237)***

BDR Industries Inc (PA) ..... **D** **661 940-8554**
820 E Avenue L12 Lancaster (93535) ***(P-12751)***

BDS Marketing LLC (HQ) ..... **B** **949 472-6700**
9750 Irvine Blvd Ste 101 Irvine (92618) ***(P-16996)***

BDS Natural Products Inc (PA) ..... **E** **310 518-2227**
14824 S Main St Gardena (90248) ***(P-2396)***

BDS Solutions Group LLC (HQ) ..... **E** **949 472-6700**
10 Holland Irvine (92618) ***(P-16997)***

Be Beauty, Garden Grove *Also called Cali Chem Inc* ***(P-4997)***

Be Bop Clothing ..... B 323 846-0121
5833 Avalon Blvd Los Angeles (90003) ***(P-2923)***

Beach Cities Health District ..... C 310 374-3426
1200 Del Amo St Redondo Beach (90277) ***(P-22173)***

Beach Cities Memory Care Cmnty, Redondo Beach *Also called Silverado Senior Living Inc* ***(P-20465)***

Beach Club ..... D 310 395-3254
201 Palisades Beach Rd Santa Monica (90402) ***(P-19538)***

Beach Front Property MGT Inc (PA) ..... **D** **562 981-7777**
1212 Long Beach Blvd Long Beach (90813) ***(P-15784)***

Beach Mtl Prtners A Cal Ltd PR ..... D 800 755-0222
28 W Cabrillo Blvd Santa Barbara (93101) ***(P-16340)***

Beach Paving Inc ..... E 714 978-2414
749 N Poplar St Orange (92868) ***(P-1516)***

Beach Reporter, Rllng HLS Est *Also called National Media Inc* ***(P-4011)***

Beach Reporter, The, Hermosa Beach *Also called National Media Inc* ***(P-4012)***

Beachbody LLC (HQ) ..... **B** **310 883-9000**
3301 Exposition Blvd Fl 3 Santa Monica (90404) ***(P-17079)***

Beachfront Properties, Long Beach *Also called Beach Front Property MGT Inc* ***(P-15784)***

Beachside Nursing Center, Huntington Beach *Also called Sea Breeze Health Care Inc* ***(P-20460)***

Beachwood Post-Acute & Rehab, Santa Monica *Also called Cantaloupe Holdings LLC* ***(P-20568)***

Beacon Concrete Inc ..... E 323 889-7775
1597 S Bluff Rd Montebello (90640) ***(P-6073)***

Beacon Healthcare Services ..... D 949 650-9750
1501 E 16th St Newport Beach (92663) ***(P-21276)***

Beacon Manufacturing Inc ..... E 714 529-0980
1000 Beacon St Brea (92821) ***(P-4738)***

Beacon Resources LLC ..... C 949 955-1773
17300 Red Hill Ave Irvine (92614) ***(P-23169)***

Beacon Roofing Supply Inc ..... D 818 768-4661
8501 Telfair Ave Sun Valley (91352) ***(P-13972)***

Beacon West Energy Group LLC ..... D 805 816-2790
1145 Eugenia Pl Ste 101 Carpinteria (93013) ***(P-22499)***

Beador Construction Co Inc ..... D 951 674-7352
26320 Lester Cir Corona (92883) ***(P-861)***

Bear Creek Golf & Country Club, Murrieta *Also called Bear Creek Golf Club Inc* ***(P-19539)***

Bear Creek Golf Club Inc ..... D 951 677-8621
22640 Bear Creek Dr N Murrieta (92562) ***(P-19539)***

Bear Nash Productions ..... D 310 428-5167
521 E Sycamore Ave El Segundo (90245) ***(P-19221)***

Bear State Water Heating LLC ..... F 951 269-3753
43234 Bus Pk Dr Ste 105 Temecula (92590) ***(P-10662)***

Bear Valley Springs Assn ..... C 661 821-5537
29541 Rollingoak Dr Tehachapi (93561) ***(P-22312)***

Bear Vly Cmnty Healthcare Dst (PA) ..... **C** **909 866-6501**
41870 Garstin Dr Big Bear Lake (92315) ***(P-20686)***

Beard Seats, Newport Beach *Also called Redart Corporation* ***(P-3631)***

Bearing Engineers Inc (PA) ..... **D** **949 586-7442**
27 Argonaut Aliso Viejo (92656) ***(P-13973)***

Bearing Inspection Inc (HQ) ..... **C** **714 484-9373**
4422 Corp Ctr Dr Los Alamitos (90720) ***(P-13974)***

Bearsaver, Ontario *Also called Compumeric Engineering Inc* ***(P-6810)***

Beating Wall Street Inc (PA) ..... **C** **818 332-9696**
20121 Ventura Blvd # 305 Woodland Hills (91364) ***(P-23170)***

Beats By Dr. Dre, Culver City *Also called Beats Electronics LLC* ***(P-9681)***

Beats By Dre, Culver City *Also called Beats Electronics LLC* ***(P-9162)***

Beats Electronics LLC (PA) ..... **F** **424 268-3055**
8600 Hayden Pl Culver City (90232) ***(P-9681)***

Beats Electronics LLC ..... B 424 326-4679
8600 Hayden Pl Culver City (90232) ***(P-9162)***

Beauchamp Distributing Company ..... D 310 639-5320
1911 S Santa Fe Ave Compton (90221) ***(P-14822)***

Beaumont Juice Inc ..... D 951 769-7171
550 B St Beaumont (92223) ***(P-1859)***

Beaumont Unfied Schl Dst Pub F ..... B 951 845-6580
126 W Fifth St Beaumont (92223) ***(P-21985)***

Beautiful Group LLC (PA) ..... **C** **310 299-4100**
9720 Wilshire Blvd Fl 6 Beverly Hills (90212) ***(P-16896)***

Beautologie MGT Group Inc ..... E 661 327-3800
4850 Commerce Dr Bakersfield (93309) ***(P-19720)***

Beauty & Health International ..... E 714 903-9730
7541 Anthony Ave Garden Grove (92841) ***(P-4796)***

Beauty 21 Cosmetics Inc ..... C 909 945-2220
2021 S Archibald Ave Ontario (91761) ***(P-14234)***

Beauty Barrage LLC ..... C 949 771-3399
4340 Von Karman Ave # 200 Newport Beach (92660) ***(P-16897)***

Beauty Counter LLC ..... D 310 828-0111
1733 Ocean Ave Ste 400 Santa Monica (90401) ***(P-16898)***

Beauty Tent Inc ..... E 323 717-7131
1131 N Kenmore Ave Apt 6 Los Angeles (90029) ***(P-11637)***

Beautycounter, Santa Monica *Also called Beauty Counter LLC* ***(P-16898)***

Beautycounter, Santa Monica *Also called Counter Brands LLC* ***(P-14238)***

Beaver Medical Clinic, Highland *Also called Beaver Medical Group LP* ***(P-19722)***

Beaver Medical Clinic Inc (PA) ..... **C** **909 793-3311**
1615 Orange Tree Ln Redlands (92374) ***(P-19721)***

Employee Codes: A=Over 500 employees, B=251-500
C=101-250, D=51-100, E=20-50 F=10-19

2022 Southern California Business
Directory and Buyers Guide

© Mergent Inc. 1-800-342-5647

1069

Beaver Medical Group LP (HQ) ... C ... **909 425-3321**
7000 Boulder Ave Highland (92346) ***(P-19722)***
Bebe Studio Inc ... C ... 213 362-2323
10250 Santa Monica Blvd # 6 Los Angeles (90067) ***(P-2924)***
Bechler Cams Inc ... F ... 714 774-5150
1313 S State College Pkwy Anaheim (92806) ***(P-8520)***
Becho Inc ... D ... 818 362-8391
15901 Olden St Sylmar (91342) ***(P-862)***
Becker Automotive Design USA, Oxnard *Also called Becker Automotive Designs Inc* ***(P-9937)***
Becker Automotive Designs Inc ... E ... 805 487-5227
1711 Ives Ave Oxnard (93033) ***(P-9937)***
Becker Interiors Ltd ... F ... 323 469-1938
5552 Hollywood Blvd Los Angeles (90028) ***(P-13159)***
Becker Specialty Corporation ... E ... 909 356-1095
15310 Arrow Blvd Fontana (92335) ***(P-9621)***
Beckers Fabrication Inc ... E ... 714 692-1600
22465 La Palma Ave Yorba Linda (92887) ***(P-3867)***
Beckett Enterprise ... E ... 310 686-3817
900 Kincaid Ave K8 Inglewood (90302) ***(P-23171)***
Beckman Coulter Inc ... D ... 909 597-3967
15989 Cypress Ave Chino (91708) ***(P-10783)***
Beckman Coulter Inc ... C ... 818 970-2161
250 S Kraemer Blvd Brea (92821) ***(P-10945)***
Beckman Industries ... F ... 805 375-3003
701 Del Nrte Blvd Ste 205 Oxnard (93030) ***(P-11494)***
Beckman Instruments Inc ... D ... 714 871-4848
2500 N Harbor Blvd Fullerton (92835) ***(P-10784)***
Beckman RES Inst of The Cy Hop ... C ... 626 359-8111
1500 Duarte Rd Duarte (91010) ***(P-19723)***
Beckmen Vineyards ... E ... 805 688-8664
2670 Ontiveros Rd Los Olivos (93441) ***(P-43)***
Beco Dairy Automation Inc ... F ... 559 582-2566
9955 9 1/4 Ave Hanford (93230) ***(P-13875)***
Bed Time Originals, El Segundo *Also called Lambs & Ivy Inc* ***(P-3106)***
Bedard Machine Inc ... F ... 714 990-4846
141 Viking Ave Brea (92821) ***(P-8521)***
Bedford Surgical Center Inc ... D ... 310 271-6996
436 N Bedford Dr Ste 305 Beverly Hills (90210) ***(P-21060)***
Bedrock Company ... D ... 951 273-1931
2970 Myers St Riverside (92503) ***(P-1517)***
Bedrosian Tile & Stone, Anaheim *Also called Paragon Industries Inc* ***(P-13312)***
Bedrosian's Tile & Marble, Bakersfield *Also called Paragon Industries Inc* ***(P-13311)***
Bee Darlin Inc (PA) ... D ... **213 749-2116**
1875 E 22nd St Los Angeles (90058) ***(P-2880)***
Bee Darlin and Be Smart, Los Angeles *Also called Bee Darlin Inc* ***(P-2880)***
Bee Wire & Cable Inc ... E ... 909 923-5800
2850 E Spruce St Ontario (91761) ***(P-6342)***
Beech Street Corporation (HQ) ... B ... **949 672-1000**
25550 Commercentre Dr # 200 Lake Forest (92630) ***(P-22984)***
Beef Jerky Factory, Colton *Also called Hawa Corporation* ***(P-1734)***
Beemak Plastics LLC ... D ... 800 421-4393
16711 Knott Ave La Mirada (90638) ***(P-5577)***
Beemak-Idl Display Products, La Mirada *Also called Beemak Plastics LLC* ***(P-5577)***
Bega North America Inc ... D ... 805 684-0533
1000 Bega Way Carpinteria (93013) ***(P-9124)***
Begroup (PA) ... D ... **818 638-4563**
516 Burchett St Glendale (91203) ***(P-20559)***
Behavior Frontiers LLC ... D ... 310 856-0800
18726 S Wstn Ave Ste 408 Gardena (90248) ***(P-20208)***
Behavior One Atism Sltions LLC ... D ... 657 294-5113
3002 Dow Ave Ste 206 Tustin (92780) ***(P-21277)***
Behavioral Health, Lancaster *Also called Kaiser Foundation Hospitals* ***(P-19905)***
Behavioral Health Services Inc (PA) ... E ... **310 679-9031**
15519 Crenshaw Blvd Gardena (90249) ***(P-21720)***
Behavioral Health Works Inc ... D ... 800 249-1266
1301 E Orangewood Ave Anaheim (92805) ***(P-21278)***
Behavioral Learning Center Inc ... D ... 661 254-7086
13400 Rverside Dr Ste 209 Sherman Oaks (91423) ***(P-21721)***
Behavioral Medicine Center, Redlands *Also called Loma Linda University Med Ctr* ***(P-20839)***
Behavoral Autism Therapies LLC (PA) ... C ... **909 483-5000**
2930 Inland Empire Blvd Ontario (91764) ***(P-21722)***
Behr Holdings Corporation (HQ) ... D ... **714 545-7101**
3400 W Segerstrom Ave Santa Ana (92704) ***(P-5088)***
Behr Paint Company, Santa Ana *Also called Behr Process Corporation* ***(P-5089)***
Behr Paint Corp., Santa Ana *Also called Behr Sales Inc* ***(P-5090)***
Behr Process Corporation (HQ) ... A ... **714 545-7101**
1801 E Saint Andrew Pl Santa Ana (92705) ***(P-5089)***
Behr Process Sales Company ... E ... 714 545-7101
3000 S Main St Apt 84e Santa Ana (92707) ***(P-23374)***
Behr Sales Inc (HQ) ... B ... **714 545-7101**
3400 W Segerstrom Ave Santa Ana (92704) ***(P-5090)***
Behringer Harvard Wilshire Blv ... D ... 310 475-8711
10740 Wilshire Blvd Los Angeles (90024) ***(P-16341)***
BEI Industrial Encoders, Thousand Oaks *Also called Sensata Technologies Inc* ***(P-8301)***
BEI Industrial Encoders, Thousand Oaks *Also called Carros Sensors Systems Co LLC* ***(P-10876)***
BEI North America LLC (HQ) ... C ... **805 716-0642**
1461 Lawrence Dr Thousand Oaks (91320) ***(P-10872)***
Beitler & Associates Inc (PA) ... E ... **310 820-2955**
825 S Barrington Ave Los Angeles (90049) ***(P-15785)***
Beitler Commercial Realty Svcs, Los Angeles *Also called Beitler & Associates Inc* ***(P-15785)***
Bejac Corporation (PA) ... D ... **714 528-6224**
569 S Van Buren St Placentia (92870) ***(P-13890)***
Bekins Moving & Storage, Santa Fe Springs *Also called Bekins Moving Solutions Inc* ***(P-12107)***
Bekins Moving Solutions Inc (PA) ... D ... **562 356-9460**
12610 Shoemaker Ave Santa Fe Springs (90670) ***(P-12107)***
Beks Acquisition Inc ... E ... 714 744-2990
1150 W Trenton Ave Orange (92867) ***(P-1559)***
Bel Air Inv Advisors LLC (HQ) ... D ... **310 229-1500**
1999 Avenue Of The Stars # 3200 Los Angeles (90067) ***(P-15319)***
Bel Air Presbyterian Church ... D ... 818 788-4200
16221 Mulholland Dr Los Angeles (90049) ***(P-21986)***
Bel Esprit Builders Inc ... E ... 949 709-3500
23112 Alcalde Dr Ste A Laguna Hills (92653) ***(P-742)***
Bel Vino LLC ... F ... 951 676-6414
33515 Rancho Cal Rd Temecula (92591) ***(P-2167)***
Bel-Air Bay Club Ltd ... C ... 310 230-4700
16801 Pacific Coast Hwy Pacific Palisades (90272) ***(P-19540)***
Bel-Air Cases, Ontario *Also called California Quality Plas Inc* ***(P-5596)***
Bel-Air Country Club ... C ... 310 472-9563
10768 Bellagio Rd Los Angeles (90077) ***(P-19541)***
Bel-Air Machining Co ... F ... 714 953-6616
151 E Columbine Ave Santa Ana (92707) ***(P-8522)***
Belagio Enterprises Inc ... E ... 323 731-6934
3737 Ross St Vernon (90058) ***(P-2559)***
Belco Packaging Systems Inc ... E ... 626 357-9566
910 S Mountain Ave Monrovia (91016) ***(P-8063)***
Belden Inc ... A ... 310 639-9473
1048 E Burgrove St Carson (90746) ***(P-6343)***
Belding Golf Bag Company, The, Oxnard *Also called Illah Sports Inc A Corporation* ***(P-11429)***
Belinda, Vernon *Also called New Pride Corporation* ***(P-14404)***
Belkin Inc ... C ... 800 223-5546
12045 Waterfront Dr Playa Vista (90094) ***(P-9163)***
Belkin Components, Playa Vista *Also called Belkin International Inc* ***(P-8238)***
Belkin International Inc (HQ) ... B ... **310 751-5100**
12045 Waterfront Dr Playa Vista (90094) ***(P-8238)***
Bell Bros Steel Inc ... E ... 951 784-0903
1510 Palmyrita Ave Riverside (92507) ***(P-6588)***
Bell Computer, Pomona *Also called Bell Technologies Inc* ***(P-13379)***
Bell Foundry Co (PA) ... D ... **323 564-5701**
5310 Southern Ave South Gate (90280) ***(P-11405)***
Bell Gardens Bicycle Club Inc ... A ... 562 806-4646
888 Bicycle Casino Dr Bell Gardens (90201) ***(P-19637)***
Bell Pipe & Supply Co ... E ... 714 772-3200
215 E Ball Rd Anaheim (92805) ***(P-13975)***
Bell Powder Coating Inc ... F ... 805 658-2233
4747 Mcgrath St Ventura (93003) ***(P-7348)***
Bell Technologies Inc ... F ... 909 598-1006
187 Pacific St Pomona (91768) ***(P-13379)***
Bell Villa Care Associates LLC ... D ... 562 925-4252
9028 Rose St Bellflower (90706) ***(P-20253)***
Bella Collina San Clemente ... D ... 949 498-6604
200 Avenida La Pata San Clemente (92673) ***(P-19542)***
Bella Terra Carwash, Huntington Beach *Also called Russell Fisher Partnership* ***(P-18916)***
Bella Vsta Trnstional Care Ctr, San Luis Obispo *Also called Bayshore Healthcare Inc* ***(P-20252)***
Bellacanvas, Commerce *Also called Color Image Apparel Inc* ***(P-3029)***
Bellami Hair LLC ... C ... 844 235-5264
21123 Nordhoff St Chatsworth (91311) ***(P-16899)***
Bellflower Dental Group, Bellflower *Also called Peter Wylan DDS* ***(P-20194)***
Bellis Steel Company Inc (PA) ... E ... **818 886-5601**
8740 Vanalden Ave Northridge (91324) ***(P-1568)***
Bellows Mfg & RES Inc ... E ... 818 838-1333
864 Arroyo St San Fernando (91340) ***(P-6589)***
Bellrock Media Inc (PA) ... E ... **310 315-2727**
11500 W Olympic Blvd # 400 Los Angeles (90064) ***(P-17562)***
Bellwether Asset MGT Inc ... D ... 310 525-3022
200 N Pcf Cast Hwy Ste 14 El Segundo (90245) ***(P-22985)***
Bellzi Inc ... F ... 888 317-1502
5575 Daniels St Chino (91710) ***(P-11357)***
Belmond El Encanto, Santa Barbara *Also called El Encanto Inc* ***(P-16431)***
Belmont Athletic Club ... D ... 562 438-3816
4918 E 2nd St Long Beach (90803) ***(P-19543)***
Belmont Brewing Company Inc ... E ... 562 433-3891
25 39th Pl Long Beach (90803) ***(P-2138)***
Belport Company Inc (PA) ... F ... **805 484-1051**
4825 Calle Alto Camarillo (93012) ***(P-11161)***
Belt Drives Ltd ... E ... 714 693-1313
505 W Lambert Rd Brea (92821) ***(P-10483)***
Belvedere Hotel Partnership ... B ... 310 551-2888
9882 Santa Monica Blvd Beverly Hills (90212) ***(P-16342)***
Belvedere Partnership ... B ... 310 551-2888
9882 Santa Monica Blvd Beverly Hills (90212) ***(P-16343)***
Bemco Inc (PA) ... E ... **805 583-4970**
2255 Union Pl Simi Valley (93065) ***(P-10785)***
Bemus Landscape Inc ... B ... 714 557-7910
1225 Puerta Del Sol # 500 San Clemente (92673) ***(P-988)***
Ben Bennett Inc (PA) ... C ... **949 209-9712**
3419 Via Lido 646 Newport Beach (92663) ***(P-20560)***
Ben Bollinger Productions Inc ... D ... 909 626-3296
455 W Foothill Blvd Claremont (91711) ***(P-19304)***
Ben Clymers Body Sp Perris Inc ... F ... 800 338-5872
12203 Magnolia Ave Riverside (92503) ***(P-9938)***
Ben Group Inc ... F ... 310 342-1500
14724 Ventura Blvd # 1200 Sherman Oaks (91403) ***(P-17794)***
Ben Myerson Candy Co Inc (PA) ... B ... **800 331-2829**
6550 E Washington Blvd Commerce (90040) ***(P-14838)***
Bench 2 Bench Technologies, Fullerton *Also called Winonics Inc* ***(P-9469)***
Benchmark Elec Mfg Sltons Mrpa ... A ... 805 532-2800
200 Science Dr Moorpark (93021) ***(P-9385)***
Benchmark Engineering Div of, Santa Fe Springs *Also called K Metal Products Inc* ***(P-7503)***
Benchmark Secure Technology, Santa Ana *Also called Secure Comm Systems Inc* ***(P-9315)***
Bend-Tek Inc ... D ... 714 210-8966
2205 S Yale St Santa Ana (92704) ***(P-6795)***

Mergent e-mail: customerrelations@mergent.com
1070
2022 Southern California Business Directory and Buyers Guide
(P-0000) Products & Services Section entry number
(PA)=Parent Co (HQ)=Headquarters (DH)=Div Headquarters

Bender Ccp Inc (PA) ....D....**707 745-9970**
2150 E 37th St Vernon Vernon (90058) *(P-8523)*
Bender US, Vernon *Also called Bender Ccp Inc (P-8523)*
Bendick Precision Inc ....E....626 445-0217
56 La Porte St Arcadia (91006) *(P-8524)*
Bendpak Inc (PA) ....C....**805 933-9970**
1645 E Lemonwood Dr Santa Paula (93060) *(P-7965)*
Beneficial AG Services, Ontario *Also called Circle Green Inc (P-5131)*
BENEFIT PROGRAMS ADMINISTRATIO, City of Industry *Also called Management Applied Prgrm Inc (P-18099)*
Benefit Resources Group, Los Angeles *Also called Patriot Communications LLC (P-23492)*
Benefit Software Incorporated ....F....805 679-6200
212 Cottage Grove Ave A Santa Barbara (93101) *(P-17795)*
Benefitvision Inc ....D....818 348-3100
5550 Topanga Canyon Blvd # 180 Woodland Hills (91367) *(P-21943)*
Benettis Italia Inc ....E....310 537-8036
3037 E Maria St Compton (90221) *(P-13127)*
Benevolence Food Products LLC ....E....888 832-3738
2761 Saturn St Ste D Brea (92821) *(P-2397)*
Benevolence Health Center (PA) ....D....**323 732-0100**
1010 Crenshaw Blvd # 100 Torrance (90501) *(P-21387)*
Benevolence Industries Inc ....E....310 800-7963
3533 W Pico Blvd Los Angeles (90019) *(P-21723)*
Benjamin Moore Authorized Ret, Corona *Also called Ganahl Lumber Company (P-3250)*
Benjamin Moore Authorized Ret, Buena Park *Also called Ganahl Lumber Company (P-13209)*
Benjamin Moore Authorized Ret, Los Alamitos *Also called Ganahl Lumber Company (P-13210)*
Benjamin Moore Authorized Ret, Lake Forest *Also called Ganahl Lumber Company (P-13211)*
Bennett Entps A Cal Ldscp Cntg ....D....310 534-3543
25889 Belle Porte Ave Harbor City (90710) *(P-234)*
Bennett Landscape, Harbor City *Also called Bennett Entps A Cal Ldscp Cntg (P-234)*
Bennett's Honey Farm, Fillmore *Also called Honey Bennetts Farm Inc (P-2450)*
Bennion Deville Fine Homes Inc ....B....760 674-3452
74850 Us Highway 111 Indian Wells (92210) *(P-15786)*
Benq America Corp (HQ) ....D....**714 559-4900**
3200 Park Center Dr # 150 Costa Mesa (92626) *(P-13380)*
Bens Asphalt Inc ....E....714 540-1700
2200 S Yale St Santa Ana (92704) *(P-17218)*
Bens Asphalt & Maint Co Inc ....D....951 248-1103
2537 Rubidoux Blvd Riverside (92509) *(P-863)*
Bent Manufacturing Co Bdaa Inc ....F....714 842-0600
15442 Chemical Ln Huntington Beach (92649) *(P-5578)*
Bentley Mills Inc (PA) ....C....**626 333-4585**
14641 Don Julian Rd City of Industry (91746) *(P-2683)*
Bentley-Simonson Inc ....E....805 650-2794
1746 S Victoria Ave Ste F Ventura (93003) *(P-386)*
Bento Box Entertainment LLC ....B....818 333-7700
5161 Lankershim Blvd North Hollywood (91601) *(P-19100)*
Benz - One Complete Operation, Tehachapi *Also called Pjbs Holdings Inc (P-12965)*
Beonca Machine Inc ....F....909 392-9991
1680 Curtiss Ct La Verne (91750) *(P-8525)*
Bep (lp) I LLC ....F....213 225-5900
515 Suth Flwr St Ste 4800 Los Angeles (90071) *(P-387)*
Beranek LLC ....E....310 328-9094
2340 W 205th St Torrance (90501) *(P-8526)*
Berg Lacquer Co (PA) ....D....**323 261-8114**
3150 E Pico Blvd Los Angeles (90023) *(P-14905)*
Bergandi Machinery Company, Ontario *Also called Bmci Inc (P-7900)*
Bergelectric Corp ....D....951 520-0851
13375 Estelle St Corona (92879) *(P-1219)*
Bergelectric Corp ....D....818 991-8600
5142 Clareton Dr Ste 140 Agoura Hills (91301) *(P-1220)*
Bergelectric Corp ....D....949 250-7005
15776 Gateway Cir Tustin (92780) *(P-1221)*
Berger Kahn A Law Corporation (PA) ....D....**949 474-1880**
1 Park Plz Ste 340 Irvine (92614) *(P-21513)*
Berglund & Johnson Law Office, Woodland Hills *Also called Law Offices Berglund & Johnson (P-21606)*
Bergman Kprs LLC (PA) ....C....**714 924-7000**
2850 Saturn St Ste 100 Brea (92821) *(P-743)*
Bergsen Inc ....E....562 236-9787
12241 Florence Ave Santa Fe Springs (90670) *(P-13548)*
Bericap LLC ....D....905 634-2248
1671 Champagne Ave Ste B Ontario (91761) *(P-5579)*
Berkeley E Convalescent Hosp, Santa Monica *Also called Berkeley E Convalescent Hosp (P-20561)*
Berkeley E Convalescent Hosp ....C....310 829-5377
2021 Arizona Ave Santa Monica (90404) *(P-20561)*
Berkeley Hall Schl Foundation ....D....310 476-6421
16000 Mulholland Dr Los Angeles (90049) *(P-21987)*
BERKELEY HALL SCHOOL, Los Angeles *Also called Berkeley Hall Schl Foundation (P-21987)*
Berkshire Hathaway Home Servic ....C....310 230-3700
881 Alma Real Dr Pacific Palisades (90272) *(P-21724)*
Berkshire Hthway HM Svcs CA Rp (PA) ....D....**562 860-2625**
18000 Studebaker Rd # 600 Cerritos (90703) *(P-15787)*
Berkshire Hthway Hmsrvces Trot, Lancaster *Also called V Troth Inc (P-16027)*
Bermingham Cntrls Inc A Cal Co (PA) ....E....**562 860-0463**
11144 Business Cir Cerritos (90703) *(P-7438)*
Bermuda Dunes Country Club ....E....760 360-2481
42765 Adams St Bermuda Dunes (92203) *(P-19544)*
Bernardi Financial Inc ....E....323 581-1900
459 S Peck Dr Beverly Hills (90212) *(P-2742)*
Bernardi of California, Beverly Hills *Also called Bernardi Financial Inc (P-2742)*
Bernards Builders Inc ....B....818 898-1521
555 1st St San Fernando (91340) *(P-655)*
Bernards Inc ....D....818 898-1521
555 1st St San Fernando (91340) *(P-22986)*
Bernel Inc ....C....714 778-6070
501 W Southern Ave Orange (92865) *(P-1033)*
Bernell Hydraulics Inc (PA) ....E....**909 899-1751**
8810 Etiwanda Ave Rancho Cucamonga (91739) *(P-8442)*
Berney-Karp Inc ....D....323 260-7122
3350 E 26th St Vernon (90058) *(P-6001)*
Bernhardt and Bernhardt Inc ....E....714 544-0708
14771 Myford Rd Ste D Tustin (92780) *(P-7722)*
Berns Bros Inc ....F....562 437-0471
1250 W 17th St Long Beach (90813) *(P-8527)*
Berri Pro Inc ....F....781 929-8288
929 Colorado Ave Santa Monica (90401) *(P-2309)*
Berro Management ....D....562 432-3444
3950 Parmnt Blvd Ste 115 Lakewood (90712) *(P-15788)*
Berry Global Inc ....C....909 465-9055
14000 Monte Vista Ave Chino (91710) *(P-5580)*
Berry Petroleum Company LLC ....F....661 255-6066
25121 Sierra Hwy Newhall (91321) *(P-388)*
Berry Petroleum Company LLC ....F....661 769-8820
28700 Hovey Hills Rd Taft (93268) *(P-389)*
Berry Petroleum Company LLC (HQ) ....C....**661 616-3900**
11117 River Run Blvd Bakersfield (93311) *(P-390)*
Berry-Perussi Inc ....E....949 461-7000
25131 Arctic Ocean Dr Lake Forest (92630) *(P-7127)*
Bershtel Enterprises LLC (PA) ....C....**626 301-9214**
2745 Huntington Dr Duarte (91010) *(P-18459)*
Bert-Co. of Ontario CA, Ontario *Also called Edelmann Usa Inc (P-11546)*
Bertelsmann Inc ....A....661 702-2700
29011 Commerce Center Dr Valencia (91355) *(P-4121)*
Beryl Lockhart Enterprises, Sun Valley *Also called Ble Inc (P-424)*
Besser Company, Compton *Also called Concrete Mold Corporation (P-7792)*
Best Best & Krieger LLP (PA) ....C....**951 686-1450**
3390 University Ave # 500 Riverside (92501) *(P-21514)*
Best Best & Krieger LLP ....E....949 263-2600
18101 Von Karman Ave # 1000 Irvine (92612) *(P-21515)*
Best Box Company Inc ....E....323 589-6088
8011 Beach St Los Angeles (90001) *(P-3786)*
Best Buy Imports, Vernon *Also called Makabi 26 Inc (P-5703)*
Best Cheer Stone Inc (PA) ....E....**714 399-1588**
3190 E Miraloma Ave Anaheim (92806) *(P-13294)*
Best Data Products Inc ....D....818 534-1414
21541 Blythe St Canoga Park (91304) *(P-8239)*
Best Financial, The, Signal Hill *Also called First American Team Realty Inc (P-15856)*
Best Formulations ....F....626 912-9998
938 Radecki Ct City of Industry (91748) *(P-5213)*
Best Formulations Inc ....C....626 912-9998
17758 Rowland St City of Industry (91748) *(P-2398)*
Best Friends By Sheri, Commerce *Also called Sentiments Inc (P-11752)*
Best Ink and Thread, Ontario *Also called Medrano Raymundo (P-2703)*
Best Interiors Inc (PA) ....C....**714 490-7999**
2100 E Via Burton Anaheim (92806) *(P-1367)*
Best Life and Health Insur Co ....D....949 253-4080
17701 Mitchell N Irvine (92614) *(P-15357)*
Best Limousines & Trnsp Inc (PA) ....D....**714 375-9128**
2701 S Birch St Santa Ana (92707) *(P-11854)*
Best Office Products, Murrieta *Also called Bop Inc (P-4238)*
Best Opportunities, Apple Valley *Also called BEST Opportunities Inc (P-21944)*
BEST Opportunities Inc ....C....760 628-0111
22450 Headquarters Ave Apple Valley (92307) *(P-21944)*
Best Overnight Express, Irwindale *Also called Best Overnite Express Inc (P-12014)*
Best Overnite Express Inc (PA) ....D....**626 256-6340**
406 Live Oak Ave Irwindale (91706) *(P-12014)*
Best Pack Packaging Systems, Ontario *Also called Future Commodities Intl Inc (P-8069)*
Best Quality Furniture Mfg Inc ....F....909 230-6440
5400 E Francis St Ontario (91761) *(P-13128)*
Best Roll-Up Door Inc ....E....562 802-2233
13202 Arctic Cir Santa Fe Springs (90670) *(P-6693)*
Best Signs Inc (PA) ....E....**760 320-3042**
1550 S Gene Autry Trl Palm Springs (92264) *(P-18460)*
Best Way Disposal Co Inc ....D....760 244-9773
17105 Mesa St Hesperia (92345) *(P-12930)*
Best Way Marble, Los Angeles *Also called Best-Way Marble & Tile Co Inc (P-6135)*
Best Western, North Hollywood *Also called Mikado Hotels Inc (P-16569)*
Best Western, San Simeon *Also called Cavalier Inn Incorporated (P-16371)*
Best Western, Lone Pine *Also called Frontier Motel Inc (P-16450)*
Best Western, Santa Barbara *Also called Encina Pepper Tree Joint Ventr (P-16433)*
Best Western, Los Angeles *Also called Tripadvisor LLC (P-16758)*
Best Western, San Luis Obispo *Also called Royal Oak Motor Hotel (P-16673)*
Best Western, Anaheim *Also called George Drumheller Properties (P-16453)*
Best Western, Costa Mesa *Also called Newport Mesa Inn LLC (P-16582)*
Best Western, Victorville *Also called L & S Investment Co Inc (P-16531)*
Best Western, Bakersfield *Also called Salimar Inc (P-16686)*
Best Western, Carpinteria *Also called Carpinteria Motor Inn Inc (P-16368)*
Best Western, Santa Barbara *Also called Encina Pepper Tree Joint Ventr (P-16434)*
Best Western Golden Sails Ht, Torrance *Also called Long Beach Golden Sails Inc (P-16544)*
Best Western Porterville Inn ....D....559 781-7411
350 Montgomery Ave Porterville (93257) *(P-16344)*
Best Western Stovalls Inn (PA) ....D....**714 956-4430**
1110 W Katella Ave Anaheim (92802) *(P-16345)*
Best Western Sunset Plaza Ht, West Hollywood *Also called Sunset Plaza Hotel (P-16739)*
Best Wstn Black Oak Mtr Lodge, Paso Robles *Also called Black Oaks Inc (P-16354)*

ALPHABETIC

Employee Codes: A=Over 500 employees, B=251-500 C=101-250, D=51-100, E=20-50 F=10-19
2022 Southern California Business Directory and Buyers Guide
© Mergent Inc. 1-800-342-5647
1071

Best Wstn Bshp Hlday Spa Lodge ....D....760 873-3543
1025 N Main St Bishop (93514) ***(P-16346)***

Best Wstn Capistrano Inn LLC ....D....949 493-5661
27174 Ortega Hwy San Juan Capistrano (92675) ***(P-16347)***

Best- In- West ....E....909 947-6507
2279 Eagle Glen Pkwy # 1 Corona (92883) ***(P-3151)***

Best-In-West Emblem Co, Corona *Also called Best- In- West* ***(P-3151)***

Best-Way Distributing Co, Sylmar *Also called Allied Company Holdings Inc* ***(P-14819)***

Best-Way Marble & Tile Co Inc ....E....323 266-6794
5037 Telegraph Rd Los Angeles (90022) ***(P-6135)***

Bestest International ....E....714 974-8837
181 W Orangethorpe Ave C Placentia (92870) ***(P-10680)***

Bestest Medical, Placentia *Also called Bestest International* ***(P-10680)***

Bestforms Inc ....E....805 388-0503
1135 Avenida Acaso Camarillo (93012) ***(P-4598)***

Bestitcom Inc (PA) ....D....**602 667-5613**
1464 Madera Rd Simi Valley (93065) ***(P-18163)***

Bestonlinecabinets ....E....626 589-6827
5100 Walnut Grove Ave San Gabriel (91776) ***(P-3307)***

Bestway International Group ....F....562 921-7100
14797 Carmenita Rd Norwalk (90650) ***(P-7349)***

Bestway Powder, Norwalk *Also called Bestway International Group* ***(P-7349)***

Bestway Recycling Company Inc (PA) ....D....**323 588-8157**
1032 Industrial St Pomona (91766) ***(P-12931)***

Bestway Sandwiches Inc (PA) ....C....**818 361-1800**
1530 1st St San Fernando (91340) ***(P-1984)***

Bet Tzedek ....D....323 939-0506
3250 Wilshire Blvd Fl 13 Los Angeles (90010) ***(P-21516)***

Beta Bionics Inc ....E....949 297-6635
11 Hughes Irvine (92618) ***(P-11214)***

Beta Offshore, Long Beach *Also called Beta Operating Company LLC* ***(P-391)***

Beta Operating Company LLC ....D....562 628-1526
111 W Ocean Blvd Long Beach (90802) ***(P-391)***

Bethany Baptist School ....D....562 985-0714
2244 Clark Ave Long Beach (90815) ***(P-21988)***

Bethany Elementary & Pre Schl, Long Beach *Also called Bethany Baptist School* ***(P-21988)***

Bethebeast Inc ....E....424 206-1081
3738 W 181st St Torrance (90504) ***(P-17796)***

Bethlehem Construction Inc ....D....661 758-1001
425 J St Wasco (93280) ***(P-690)***

Bethlhem Evang Lthern Pr-Schoo, Granada Hills *Also called Bethlhem Evang Lthran Ch Grnad* ***(P-21989)***

Bethlhem Evang Lthran Ch Grnad ....D....818 360-4777
12227 Balboa Blvd Granada Hills (91344) ***(P-21989)***

Betria Interactive LLC ....E....949 273-0920
26170 Enterprise Way Lake Forest (92630) ***(P-12344)***

Better Bar Manufacturing LLC ....E....951 525-3111
6975 Arlington Ave Riverside (92503) ***(P-1782)***

Better Beverages Inc (PA) ....D....**562 924-8321**
10624 Midway Ave Cerritos (90703) ***(P-2310)***

Better Mens Clothes, Los Angeles *Also called Hirsh Inc* ***(P-508)***

Better Nutritionals LLC (PA) ....A....**310 356-9019**
3390 Hrseless Carriage Dr Norco (92860) ***(P-1783)***

Better Nutritionals LLC ....E....310 356-9019
17120 S Figueroa St Ste B Gardena (90248) ***(P-1784)***

Betty Ford Center (HQ) ....C....**760 773-4100**
39000 Bob Hope Dr Rancho Mirage (92270) ***(P-21279)***

Beu Industries Inc ....F....310 885-9626
2937 E Maria St E Rncho Dmngz (90221) ***(P-3851)***

Beverly Bay Inc (PA) ....F....**818 852-2408**
P.O. Box 8078 Porter Ranch (91327) ***(P-3191)***

Beverly Center, Los Angeles *Also called La Cienega Associates* ***(P-15905)***

Beverly Community Hosp Assn (PA) ....A....**323 726-1222**
309 W Beverly Blvd Montebello (90640) ***(P-20687)***

Beverly Health Care Corp (PA) ....E....**805 642-1736**
5445 Everglades St Ventura (93003) ***(P-22987)***

Beverly Hillcrest Oil Corp ....F....949 598-7300
27241 Burbank El Toro (92610) ***(P-392)***

Beverly Hills BMW, Los Angeles *Also called FAA Beverly Hills Inc* ***(P-18826)***

Beverly Hills Courier Inc ....E....310 278-1322
499 N Canon Dr Ste 100 Beverly Hills (90210) ***(P-3953)***

Beverly Hills Escrow A Cal ....D....310 273-9850
118 S Beverly Dr Ste 222 Beverly Hills (90212) ***(P-15789)***

Beverly Hills Hotel, Beverly Hills *Also called Sajahtera Inc* ***(P-16685)***

Beverly Hills Luxury Hotel LLC ....B....310 274-9999
1801 Century Park E # 1200 Los Angeles (90067) ***(P-16348)***

Beverly Hills Luxury Interiors, Los Angeles *Also called Kenneth Brdwick Intr Dsgns Inc* ***(P-18562)***

Beverly Hills Plaza Hotel, Los Angeles *Also called Donald T Sterling Corporation* ***(P-16416)***

Beverly Hills Teddy Bear Co (PA) ....D....**661 257-0750**
12725 Encinitas Ave Sylmar (91342) ***(P-14094)***

Beverly Hlls Onclogy Med Group ....D....310 432-8900
8900 Wilshire Blvd Beverly Hills (90211) ***(P-21035)***

Beverly Holdings Inc ....C....310 274-7777
9876 Wilshire Blvd Beverly Hills (90210) ***(P-16349)***

BEVERLY HOSPITAL, Montebello *Also called Beverly Community Hosp Assn* ***(P-20687)***

Beverly Pl Memory Care Cmnty, Los Angeles *Also called Silverado Senior Living Inc* ***(P-20475)***

Beverly Radiology, Reseda *Also called Northridge Diagnostic Center* ***(P-20005)***

Beverly Sunstone Hills LLC ....D....310 228-4100
1177 S Beverly Dr Los Angeles (90035) ***(P-16350)***

Beverly West Health Care Inc ....D....323 938-2451
1020 S Fairfax Ave Los Angeles (90019) ***(P-20254)***

Bey-Berk International (PA) ....E....**818 773-7534**
9145 Deering Ave Chatsworth (91311) ***(P-7550)***

Beyond Limits Inc (PA) ....C....**818 643-2344**
400 N Brand Blvd Ste 700 Glendale (91203) ***(P-18164)***

Beyond Meat Inc (PA) ....E....**866 756-4112**
119 Standard St El Segundo (90245) ***(P-1917)***

Beyond Meat Inc ....E....310 567-3323
1325 E El Segundo Blvd El Segundo (90245) ***(P-1918)***

Beyond Meat and Company, Anaheim *Also called Caballero & Sons Inc* ***(P-15313)***

Beyond Yoga, Culver City *Also called I AM Beyond LLC* ***(P-2952)***

Beyondgreen Btech Inc DBA Bynd ....F....800 983-7221
1202 E Wakeham Ave Santa Ana (92705) ***(P-4485)***

Beyondsoft Consulting Inc ....C....310 532-2822
19009 S Laurel Park Rd # 6 Compton (90220) ***(P-23418)***

BF Suma Pharmaceuticals Inc ....F....626 285-8366
5077 Walnut Grove Ave San Gabriel (91776) ***(P-4797)***

Bgk Equities Inc (HQ) ....D....**505 982-2184**
2000 Avenue Of The Stars Los Angeles (90067) ***(P-15790)***

BH Centro Internacional LLC ....D....310 820-8888
11111 Santa Monica Blvd Los Angeles (90025) ***(P-15661)***

Bhc Alhambra Hospital Inc ....D....626 286-1191
4619 Rosemead Blvd Rosemead (91770) ***(P-20688)***

Bhc Alhambra Hospital Inc ....B....626 286-1191
4619 Rosemead Blvd Rosemead (91770) ***(P-21388)***

BHC Industries Inc ....E....310 632-2000
239 E Greenleaf Blvd Compton (90220) ***(P-7222)***

Bhk Inc ....F....909 983-2973
760 E Sunkist St Ontario (91761) ***(P-9018)***

Bhtb, Sylmar *Also called Beverly Hills Teddy Bear Co* ***(P-14094)***

Bi-Search International Inc ....D....714 258-4500
17550 Gillette Ave Irvine (92614) ***(P-9682)***

Bibi Products Co, Carson *Also called Jobar International Inc* ***(P-14942)***

Bicara Ltd ....B....310 316-6222
318 Avenue I Ste 65 Redondo Beach (90277) ***(P-14591)***

Bicycle Casino LP ....A....562 806-4646
888 Bicycle Casino Dr Bell Gardens (90201) ***(P-16351)***

Bicycle Club Casino, Bell Gardens *Also called Bell Gardens Bicycle Club Inc* ***(P-19637)***

Bicycle Hotel and Casino, Bell Gardens *Also called Bicycle Casino LP* ***(P-16351)***

Bidart Bros (PA) ....C....**661 832-2447**
4805 Centennial Plaza Way # 100 Bakersfield (93312) ***(P-127)***

Bidart Bros Land & Development, Bakersfield *Also called Bidart Bros* ***(P-127)***

Bielski Services Inc ....D....714 630-2316
1200 N Lance Ln Anaheim (92806) ***(P-17219)***

Bielski Window & Masonry Clng., Anaheim *Also called Bielski Services Inc* ***(P-17219)***

BIENVENIDOS COMMUNITY HEALTH C, Los Angeles *Also called Via Care Cmnty Hlth Ctr Inc* ***(P-20155)***

Big 5 Electronics Inc ....E....562 941-4669
13452 Alondra Blvd Cerritos (90703) ***(P-9164)***

Big Bear Bowling Barn Inc ....E....909 878-2695
40625 Big Bear Blvd Big Bear Lake (92315) ***(P-1639)***

Big Bear Grizzly & Big Bear Lf, Big Bear Lake *Also called Hi-Desert Publishing Company* ***(P-3989)***

Big Bear Lake Resort Assn Inc ....E....909 866-6190
630 Bartlett Rd Big Bear Lake (92315) ***(P-16352)***

Big Canyon Country Club ....C....949 644-5404
1 Big Canyon Dr Newport Beach (92660) ***(P-19545)***

Big Chill ....F....310 441-0643
10850 W Olympic Blvd Los Angeles (90064) ***(P-1810)***

Big Dog Sportswear, Los Angeles *Also called Walking Company Holdings Inc* ***(P-14359)***

Big Five Electronics, Cerritos *Also called Big 5 Electronics Inc* ***(P-9164)***

Big Front Uniforms, Los Angeles *Also called Bunkerhill Indus Group Inc* ***(P-2776)***

Big Heart Pet Brands ....C....310 519-3791
24700 Main St Carson (90745) ***(P-1860)***

Big Lgue Dreams Consulting LLC ....D....619 846-8855
2155 Trumble Rd Perris (92571) ***(P-19409)***

Big Lgue Dreams Consulting LLC ....D....760 324-5600
33700 Date Palm Dr Cathedral City (92234) ***(P-16817)***

Big Lgue Dreams Consulting LLC ....D....626 839-1100
2100 S Azusa Ave West Covina (91792) ***(P-19410)***

Big Nickel, Palm Desert *Also called Daniels Inc* ***(P-4166)***

Big Star, South Gate *Also called Koos Manufacturing Inc* ***(P-18567)***

Big Studio Inc ....F....562 989-2444
1247 E Hill St Long Beach (90755) ***(P-2656)***

Big Tree Furniture & Inds Inc (PA) ....E....**310 894-7500**
760 S Vail Ave Montebello (90640) ***(P-3465)***

Big Tree Sales Inc ....F....626 672-0048
10401 Rush St South El Monte (91733) ***(P-14095)***

Big3 Basketball LLC ....D....213 417-2013
644 S Figueroa St Los Angeles (90017) ***(P-19411)***

Bigfogg Inc (PA) ....F....**951 587-2460**
30818 Wealth St Murrieta (92563) ***(P-8330)***

Bigge Group ....C....714 523-4092
14511 Industry Cir La Mirada (90638) ***(P-1640)***

Biggest Lser Ftnes Rdge Malibu, Malibu *Also called Fitness Ridge Malibu LLC* ***(P-16444)***

Bighorn Golf Club Charities ....C....760 773-2468
255 Palowet Dr Palm Desert (92260) ***(P-19546)***

Bigrentz Inc (PA) ....D....**855 999-5438**
1063 Mcgaw Ave Ste 200 Irvine (92614) ***(P-17305)***

Bigrentz.com, Irvine *Also called Bigrentz Inc* ***(P-17305)***

Bijan, Beverly Hills *Also called Fashion World Incorporated* ***(P-14332)***

Bijan Rad Inc ....F....818 902-1606
16125 Cantlay St Van Nuys (91406) ***(P-7966)***

Bijou Healthcare Inc ....D....949 487-9500
29222 Rncho Vejo Rd Ste 1 San Juan Capistrano (92675) ***(P-20255)***

Bikeexchange Inc ....F....949 344-2616
21 Spectrum Pointe Dr # 101 Lake Forest (92630) ***(P-18165)***

Bill & Daves Ldscp Maint Inc ....E....951 943-6455
32750 Keller Rd Winchester (92596) ***(P-235)***

Bill Williams Welding Co ....D....562 432-5421
1735 Santa Fe Ave Long Beach (90813) ***(P-18970)***

Billabong, Huntington Beach *Also called Boardriders Inc* ***(P-2803)***

Mergent e-mail: customerrelations@mergent.com
1072
2022 Southern California Business Directory and Buyers Guide
(P-0000) Products & Services Section entry number
(PA)=Parent Co (HQ)=Headquarters (DH)=Div Headquarters

Bills Pipes Inc .... F 951 371-1329
226 N Maple St Corona (92878) *(P-10484)*

Billy Blues, Commerce *Also called AB&r Inc (P-2911)*

Bilt-Well Roofing & Mtl Co, Los Angeles *Also called Sbb Roofing Inc (P-1505)*

Bimbo Bakeries Usa Inc .... F 323 720-6099
480 S Vail Ave Montebello (90640) *(P-1985)*

Bimeda Inc .... E 626 815-1680
5539 Ayon Ave Irwindale (91706) *(P-4798)*

Binder Metal Products Inc .... D 800 233-0896
14909 S Broadway Gardena (90248) *(P-7128)*

Binex Line Corp (PA) .... D 310 416-8600
19515 S Vermont Ave Torrance (90502) *(P-12325)*

Bingo Publishers Incorporated .... F 949 581-5410
24881 Alicia Pkwy Ste E Laguna Hills (92653) *(P-4155)*

Binoptics LLC .... C 607 257-3200
977 S Meridian Ave Alhambra (91803) *(P-22500)*

Bio Creative Enterprises .... F 714 352-3600
350 Kalmus Dr Costa Mesa (92626) *(P-4992)*

Bio Creative Labs, Costa Mesa *Also called Bio Creative Enterprises (P-4992)*

Bio Cybernetics International .... F 909 447-7050
2701 Kimball Ave Pomona (91767) *(P-11090)*

Bio-Med Services Inc .... D 909 235-4400
3300 E Guasti Rd Ontario (91761) *(P-20689)*

Bio-Medical Devices Inc .... E 949 752-9642
17171 Daimler St Irvine (92614) *(P-10946)*

Bio-Medical Devices Intl Inc .... E 800 443-3842
17171 Daimler St Irvine (92614) *(P-10947)*

Bio-Medics Inc .... C 909 883-9501
371 W Highland Ave San Bernardino (92405) *(P-21389)*

Bio-Nutritional RES Group Inc (PA) .... C 714 427-6990
6 Morgan Ste 100 Irvine (92618) *(P-1785)*

Bio-Reigns Inc .... E 949 922-2032
1451 Edinger Ave Ste D Tustin (92780) *(P-11638)*

Bio2, Westminster *Also called Biolargo Inc (P-4650)*

Biocatalytics Inc .... D 626 585-9797
129 N Hill Ave Ste 103 Pasadena (91106) *(P-22830)*

Biodot Inc (HQ) .... D 949 440-3685
2852 Alton Pkwy Irvine (92606) *(P-10681)*

Biolargo Inc (PA) .... F 949 643-9540
14921 Chestnut St Westminster (92683) *(P-4650)*

Biolase Inc .... D 949 361-1200
4225 Prado Rd Ste 102 Corona (92878) *(P-11162)*

Biolase Inc (PA) .... C 949 361-1200
27042 Twne Cntre Dr Ste 2 Lake Forest (92610) *(P-11163)*

Biomat Usa Inc (HQ) .... E 323 225-2221
2410 Lillyvale Ave Los Angeles (90032) *(P-21390)*

Biomechanical Services Inc .... E 714 990-5932
20509 Earlgate St Walnut (91789) *(P-11091)*

Biomed Instruments Inc .... E 714 459-5716
1511 Alto Ln Fullerton (92831) *(P-11215)*

Biomerica Inc (PA) .... D 949 645-2111
17571 Von Karman Ave Irvine (92614) *(P-4918)*

Bioness Inc .... C 661 362-4850
25103 Rye Canyon Loop Valencia (91355) *(P-11216)*

Bionime USA Corporation .... E 909 781-6969
1450 E Spruce St Ste B Ontario (91761) *(P-13480)*

Biopac Systems Inc .... E 805 685-0066
42 Aero Camino Goleta (93117) *(P-10786)*

Bioplate Inc .... E 310 815-2100
570 S Melrose St Placentia (92870) *(P-10948)*

Biorad Inc .... E 949 598-1200
9500 Jeronimo Rd Irvine (92618) *(P-10787)*

Bioray Inc .... F 949 305-7454
10 Mason Ste B Irvine (92618) *(P-1786)*

Bioriginal Food & Science .... E 949 622-9030
1851 Kaiser Ave Irvine (92614) *(P-1787)*

Biorx Laboratories, Commerce *Also called Biorx Pharmaceuticals Inc (P-4799)*

Biorx Pharmaceuticals Inc .... E 323 725-3100
6465 Corvette St Commerce (90040) *(P-4799)*

Bioscreen Testing Services, Torrance *Also called Als Group Usa Corp (P-22929)*

Bioscreen Testing Services Inc (PA) .... D 310 214-0043
3904 Del Amo Blvd Ste 801 Torrance (90503) *(P-22831)*

Bioseal .... E 714 528-4695
167 W Orangethorpe Ave Placentia (92870) *(P-10949)*

Biosense Webster Inc (HQ) .... C 909 839-8500
31 Technology Dr Ste 200 Irvine (92618) *(P-11217)*

Biospace Inc .... D 323 932-6503
13850 Cerritos Corprt Dr C Cerritos (90703) *(P-22832)*

Biosynthetic Technologies LLC (HQ) .... F 949 390-5910
2 Park Plz Ste 200 Irvine (92614) *(P-7928)*

Biosys Healthcare, Yorba Linda *Also called Viasys Respiratory Care Inc (P-11077)*

Biovail Technologies Ltd .... D 703 995-2400
1 Enterprise Aliso Viejo (92656) *(P-4800)*

Birch Street Systems LLC 949 567-7100
1301 Dove St Ste 300 Newport Beach (92660) *(P-18081)*

Birchstreet, Newport Beach *Also called Birch Street Systems LLC (P-18081)*

Birchwood Lighting Inc .... E 714 550-7118
3340 E La Palma Ave Anaheim (92806) *(P-9125)*

Bird Mrlla Bxer Wlpert Nssim .... D 310 201-2100
1875 Century Park E Fl 23 Los Angeles (90067) *(P-21517)*

Bird B Gone LLC (PA) .... F 949 472-3122
1921 E Edinger Ave Santa Ana (92705) *(P-5444)*

Bird Marella, Los Angeles *Also called Bird Mrlla Bxer Wlpert Nssim (P-21517)*

Bird Rides Inc .... D 866 205-2442
2501 Colorado Ave Santa Monica (90404) *(P-17563)*

Bird Rides Inc (PA) .... B 866 205-2442
406 Broadway Ste 369 Santa Monica (90401) *(P-17564)*

Birnam Wood Golf Club (PA) .... C 805 969-2223
1941 E Valley Rd Santa Barbara (93108) *(P-19547)*

Bis Computer Solutions Inc (PA) .... E 818 248-4282
5500 Alta Canyada Rd La Canada Flintridge (91011) *(P-17565)*

Biscomerica Corp .... B 909 877-5997
565 W Slover Ave Rialto (92377) *(P-2058)*

Bishop Inc (PA) .... D 714 628-1208
1928 W Business Center Dr Orange (92867) *(P-1474)*

Bishop Care Center .... D 760 872-1000
151 Pioneer Ln Bishop (93514) *(P-20256)*

Bishop Paiute Gaming Corp .... C 760 872-6005
2742 N Sierra Hwy Bishop (93514) *(P-16353)*

Bison Engineering Company Inc .... F 562 408-1525
15535 Texaco Ave Paramount (90723) *(P-8528)*

Bit Group Usa Inc (PA) .... D 949 238-1200
6 Thomas Ste 100 Irvine (92618) *(P-10950)*

Bit Medtech, Irvine *Also called Bit Group Usa Inc (P-10950)*

Bitfone Corporation (PA) .... E 949 234-7000
32451 Golden Lantern # 301 Laguna Niguel (92677) *(P-17566)*

Bitmax LLC (PA) .... E 323 978-7878
6255 W Sunset Blvd # 1515 Los Angeles (90028) *(P-9334)*

Bitvore Corp .... E 866 869-5151
15300 Barranca Pkwy # 150 Irvine (92618) *(P-17797)*

Bivar Inc .... E 949 951-8808
4 Thomas Irvine (92618) *(P-9683)*

Bixby Knolls Prtg & Graphics, Fullerton *Also called Fullerton Printing Inc (P-4300)*

Bixolon America Inc .... E 858 764-4580
13705 Cimarron Ave Gardena (90249) *(P-8240)*

Bizz Inc (PA) .... D 323 235-5450
170 E Jefferson Blvd Los Angeles (90011) *(P-14365)*

Bjb Enterprises Inc .... E 714 734-8450
14791 Franklin Ave Tustin (92780) *(P-4681)*

BJs Restaurant Operations Co .... C 714 500-2440
7755 Center Ave Ste 300 Huntington Beach (92647) *(P-22988)*

Bjz LLC .... C 760 851-0740
45150 Club Dr Indian Wells (92210) *(P-21138)*

Bk Sems Usa Inc .... F 949 390-7120
4 Executive Park Ste 270 Irvine (92614) *(P-3440)*

BK Signs Inc .... E 626 334-5600
1028 W Kirkwall Rd Azusa (91702) *(P-11526)*

Bkf Engineers/Ags .... C 949 526-8400
4675 Macarthur Ct Ste 400 Newport Beach (92660) *(P-22501)*

BKK Corporation (PA) .... D 626 965-0911
2210 S Azusa Ave West Covina (91792) *(P-12932)*

BKM Diablo 227 LLC .... D 602 688-6409
1701 Quail St Ste 100 Newport Beach (92660) *(P-15791)*

BKM Office Environments Inc (PA) .... F 805 339-6388
816 Via Alondra Camarillo (93012) *(P-1641)*

Black & Decker (us) Inc .... E 562 925-7551
9020 Alondra Blvd Bellflower (90706) *(P-7879)*

Black & Decker Corporation .... F 909 390-5548
3949 E Guasti Rd Ste A Ontario (91761) *(P-7880)*

Black Box Network Services, Los Angeles *Also called Scottel Voice & Data Inc (P-18956)*

Black Diamond Blade Company (PA) .... E 800 949-9014
234 E O St Colton (92324) *(P-7636)*

Black Dot Wireless LLC .... D 949 502-3800
23456 Madero Ste 210 Mission Viejo (92691) *(P-12595)*

Black Drop Coffee Inc .... F 323 742-5666
225 W Fairview Ave San Gabriel (91776) *(P-2352)*

Black Egle Pllet Logistics Inc (PA) .... E 951 332-6315
9651 Bellegrave Ave Riverside (92509) *(P-13204)*

Black Gold Golf Club .... D 714 961-0060
1 Black Gold Dr Yorba Linda (92886) *(P-19476)*

Black Gold Pump & Supply Inc .... F 323 298-0077
2459 Lewis Ave Signal Hill (90755) *(P-481)*

Black Jack Farms, Santa Maria *Also called Blackjack Frms De La Csta Cntl (P-101)*

Black Knght RE Data Sltons LLC (HQ) .... A 626 808-9000
121 Theory Ste 100 Irvine (92617) *(P-15792)*

Black Knight Data & Analytics, Irvine *Also called Black Knght RE Data Sltons LLC (P-15792)*

Black Knight Infoserv LLC .... C 904 854-5100
2500 Redhill Ave Ste 100 Santa Ana (92705) *(P-18082)*

Black Media News, Winnetka *Also called Life Media Inc (P-4080)*

Black N Gold, Paramount *Also called Kum Kang Trading USAinC (P-5040)*

Black Oaks Inc .... D 805 238-2392
1135 24th St Paso Robles (93446) *(P-16354)*

Black Oxide Industries Inc .... E 714 870-9610
1745 N Orangethorpe Park Anaheim (92801) *(P-7223)*

Black Series Campers, City of Industry *Also called Blackseries Campers Inc (P-10164)*

Blackburn Alton Invstments LLC .... E 714 731-2000
700 E Alton Ave Santa Ana (92705) *(P-4486)*

Blackcoffee Fabricators Inc .... F 909 974-4499
777 W Mill St San Bernardino (92410) *(P-11527)*

Blackcoffee Sign Fabricators, San Bernardino *Also called Blackcoffee Fabricators Inc (P-11527)*

Blackjack Frms De La Csta Cntl .... C 805 347-1333
2385 A St Santa Maria (93455) *(P-101)*

Blackline Inc .... B 818 223-9008
21300 Victory Blvd Fl 12 Woodland Hills (91367) *(P-17798)*

Blackline Systems Inc (HQ) .... D 877 777-7750
21300 Victory Blvd Fl 12 Woodland Hills (91367) *(P-17799)*

Blackseries Campers Inc .... E 833 822-6737
19501 E Walnut Dr S City of Industry (91748) *(P-10164)*

Blackstone Consulting Inc (PA) .... B 310 826-4389
11726 San Vicente Blvd # 550 Los Angeles (90049) *(P-23172)*

Blaga Precision Inc .... E 714 891-9509
11650 Seaboard Cir Stanton (90680) *(P-8529)*

Blairs Metal Polsg Pltg Co Inc .... E 562 860-7106
17760 Crusader Ave Cerritos (90703) *(P-7224)*

Blake H Brown Inc (HQ) .... D 310 764-0110
1300 W Artesia Blvd Compton (90220) *(P-13891)*

Employee Codes: A=Over 500 employees, B=251-500
C=101-250, D=51-100, E=20-50 F=10-19

2022 Southern California Business
Directory and Buyers Guide

© Mergent Inc. 1-800-342-5647

1073

Blake Sign Company Inc E 714 891-5682
11661 Seaboard Cir Stanton (90680) ***(P-11528)***

Blankstylcom Vision Sport Mtrs, Irvine *Also called Cnm Marketing Inc* ***(P-4496)***

Blastco Texas Inc D 562 869-0200
11905 Regentview Ave Downey (90241) ***(P-1170)***

Blavity Inc E 818 669-9162
600 Wilshire Blvd # 1650 Los Angeles (90017) ***(P-4156)***

Blaze Fast Fire'd Pizza, Pasadena *Also called Blaze Pizza LLC* ***(P-16202)***

Blaze Pizza LLC (PA) D **626 584-5880**
35 N Lake Ave Ste 710 Pasadena (91101) ***(P-16202)***

Blaze Solutions Inc D 415 964-5689
4590 Macarthur Blvd # 500 Newport Beach (92660) ***(P-17567)***

Blazing Industrial Steel Inc E 951 360-8340
9040 Jurupa Rd Riverside (92509) ***(P-6590)***

Blc Residential Care Inc D 310 722-7541
1455 W 112th St Los Angeles (90047) ***(P-21725)***

Blc Wc Inc (PA) C **562 926-1452**
13260 Moore St Cerritos (90703) ***(P-4487)***

Ble Inc E 818 504-9577
11360 Goss St Sun Valley (91352) ***(P-424)***

Bleeker Brothers Inc1 F 310 639-4367
10868 Drury Ln Lynwood (90262) ***(P-6796)***

Bleeker Manufacturing Inc E 800 421-1107
2721 W Coast Hwy Newport Beach (92663) ***(P-11639)***

Blend Inc D 650 550-4810
415 Kearny St Los Angeles (90041) ***(P-15176)***

Bleu Chateau Assisted Living, Burbank *Also called Le Bleu Chateau Inc* ***(P-22123)***

Blh Construction Company C 818 905-3837
20750 Ventura Blvd # 155 Woodland Hills (91364) ***(P-656)***

Blind Childrens Center Inc D 323 664-2153
4120 Marathon St Los Angeles (90029) ***(P-22174)***

Blind Childrens Lrng Ctr Inc D 714 573-8888
18542 Vanderlip Ave Ste B Santa Ana (92705) ***(P-21990)***

Blind Decker Productions Inc (PA) D **310 264-4247**
8621 Hayden Pl Culver City (90232) ***(P-19101)***

Blind Squirrel Games Inc E 714 460-0860
7545 Irvine Center Dr # 150 Irvine (92618) ***(P-17800)***

Bliss World LLC D 323 500-0921
6250 Hollywood Blvd Fl 4 Los Angeles (90028) ***(P-19439)***

Blitzz Technology Inc E 949 380-7709
53 Parker Irvine (92618) ***(P-9256)***

Blizzard Entertainment Inc (HQ) D **949 955-1380**
1 Blizzard Irvine (92618) ***(P-17801)***

Blk International LLC E 424 282-3443
26565 Agoura Rd Ste 205 Calabasas (91302) ***(P-2258)***

Block At Orange, The, Orange *Also called Orange City Mills Ltd Partnr* ***(P-15687)***

Block Tops Inc (PA) E **714 978-5080**
1321 S Sunkist St Anaheim (92806) ***(P-3639)***

Blockade Medical, Irvine *Also called Balt Usa LLC* ***(P-13479)***

Blois Construction Inc C 805 485-0011
3201 Sturgis Rd Oxnard (93030) ***(P-937)***

Blood Bnk San Brnrdino Rvrside (HQ) C **909 885-6503**
384 W Orange Show Rd San Bernardino (92408) ***(P-21391)***

Blooddiamond.gallery, Los Angeles *Also called Sovereign Arts Met Finshg LLC* ***(P-7313)***

Bloom Hergott Diemer Cook LLC D 310 859-6800
9665 Wilshire Blvd # 500 Beverly Hills (90212) ***(P-21518)***

Bloom, Jacob A, Beverly Hills *Also called Bloom Hergott Diemer Cook LLC* ***(P-21518)***

Bloomers Metal Stampings Inc E 661 257-2955
28615 Braxton Ave Valencia (91355) ***(P-7129)***

Bloomfield Bakers A 626 610-2253
10711 Bloomfield St Los Alamitos (90720) ***(P-2059)***

Blow Molded Products, Riverside *Also called Plastic Technologies Inc* ***(P-5755)***

Blower-Dempsay Corporation (PA) C **714 481-3800**
4042 W Garry Ave Santa Ana (92704) ***(P-14914)***

Blower-Dempsay Corporation E 714 547-9266
4044 W Garry Ave Santa Ana (92704) ***(P-3787)***

Bls Lmsine Svc Los Angeles Inc B 323 644-7166
2860 Fletcher Dr Los Angeles (90039) ***(P-11855)***

BLT & Associates Inc C 323 860-4000
6430 W Sunset Blvd # 800 Los Angeles (90028) ***(P-17162)***

Bltee LLC E 213 802-1736
7101 Telegraph Rd Montebello (90640) ***(P-2837)***

Blu Digital Group Inc D 818 294-7695
2233 N Ontario St 130 Burbank (91504) ***(P-17568)***

Blu Heaven, Commerce *Also called Alliance Apparel Inc* ***(P-2834)***

Blue Bay Industries, Encino *Also called Sayari Shahrzad* ***(P-14349)***

Blue Blush Clothing Inc (PA) F **323 923-2895**
2021 E 49th St Vernon (90058) ***(P-2925)***

Blue California Company, Rcho STA Marg *Also called Phyto Tech Corp* ***(P-4874)***

Blue Chip Mayflower, Hawthorne *Also called Blue Chip Moving and Stor Inc* ***(P-12015)***

Blue Chip Moving and Stor Inc D 323 463-6888
13525 Crenshaw Blvd Hawthorne (90250) ***(P-12015)***

Blue Chip Stamps Inc A 626 585-6700
301 E Colo Blvd Ste 300 Pasadena (91101) ***(P-13549)***

Blue Circle Corp F 562 531-2711
7520 Monroe St Paramount (90723) ***(P-7057)***

Blue Cross Beauty Products Inc F 818 896-8681
557 Jessie St San Fernando (91340) ***(P-4993)***

Blue Cross of California (HQ) D **805 557-6050**
21215 Burbank Blvd Woodland Hills (91367) ***(P-15388)***

Blue Desert International Inc D 951 273-7575
510 N Sheridan St Ste A Corona (92878) ***(P-8369)***

Blue Diamond Materials, Brea *Also called Sully-Miller Contracting Co* ***(P-918)***

Blue Lagoon Textile Inc E 213 590-4545
317 N Palm Dr Apt 4d Beverly Hills (90210) ***(P-18461)***

Blue Marble Game Co, Altadena *Also called Blue Marble Rehab Inc* ***(P-17802)***

Blue Marble Rehab Inc F 626 296-6400
2400 Lincoln Ave Altadena (91001) ***(P-17802)***

Blue Microphone, Westlake Village *Also called Baltic Ltvian Unvrsal Elec LLC* ***(P-9161)***

Blue Microphones LLC F 818 879-5200
5706 Corsa Ave Ste 102 Westlake Village (91362) ***(P-9165)***

Blue Ocean Marine LLC (PA) E **805 658-2628**
2060 Knoll Dr Ste 100 Ventura (93003) ***(P-12297)***

Blue Pacific Flavors Inc E 626 934-0099
1354 Marion Ct City of Industry (91745) ***(P-2311)***

Blue Planet International Inc E 323 526-9999
1526 E Washington Blvd Los Angeles (90021) ***(P-14366)***

Blue Ribbon Cont & Display Inc F 562 944-1217
11106 Shoemaker Ave Santa Fe Springs (90670) ***(P-3788)***

Blue Ribbon Draperies Inc E 805 983-4848
5109 Walker St Ventura (93003) ***(P-3092)***

Blue Shield of California, El Segundo *Also called California Physicians Service* ***(P-15390)***

Blue Shield of California, Ontario *Also called California Physicians Service* ***(P-15391)***

Blue Shield of California, Woodland Hills *Also called California Physicians Service* ***(P-15392)***

Blue Sky Natural Beverage Co F 800 426-7367
1 Monster Way Corona (92879) ***(P-2259)***

Blue Sphere Inc E 714 953-7555
10869 Portal Dr Los Alamitos (90720) ***(P-2743)***

Blue-White Industries Ltd (PA) D **714 893-8529**
5300 Business Dr Huntington Beach (92649) ***(P-10735)***

Bluebeam Inc (PA) C **626 788-4100**
443 S Raymond Ave Pasadena (91105) ***(P-17569)***

Bluebridge Prof Svcs Inc D 909 625-6151
420 W Baseline Rd Ste D Claremont (91711) ***(P-21139)***

Bluefield Associates Inc E 909 476-6027
14900 Hilton Dr Fontana (92336) ***(P-4994)***

Bluemark Inc C 323 230-0770
27909 Hancock Pkwy Valencia (91355) ***(P-14915)***

Bluescope Buildings N Amer Inc C 559 651-5300
7440 W Doe Ave Visalia (93291) ***(P-6988)***

Bluestone Medical Inc F 949 338-3723
2807 Villa Way Newport Beach (92663) ***(P-10951)***

BLUEWATER WEAR, Santa Ana *Also called Aftco Mfg Co Inc* ***(P-11398)***

Bluewave Technologies E 949 500-4652
2901 W Coast Hwy Ste 200 Newport Beach (92663) ***(P-1222)***

Blufocus, Burbank *Also called Blu Digital Group Inc* ***(P-17568)***

Blumenthal Distributing Inc (PA) C **909 930-2000**
1901 S Archibald Ave Ontario (91761) ***(P-13129)***

Bluprint Clothing Corp D 323 780-4347
6013 Randolph St Commerce (90040) ***(P-2838)***

Blur Studio Inc D 424 258-3145
3960 Ince Blvd Culver City (90232) ***(P-17570)***

Blx Group Inc D 760 776-6622
71534 Sahara Rd Rancho Mirage (92270) ***(P-73)***

Blx Group LLC D 213 612-2400
777 S Figueroa St # 3200 Los Angeles (90017) ***(P-15320)***

Blx Group LLC (PA) D **213 612-2200**
777 S Figueroa St Ste 800 Los Angeles (90017) ***(P-23173)***

Blyth/Wndsor Cntry Pk Hlthcare D 310 385-1090
3232 E Artesia Blvd Long Beach (90805) ***(P-20524)***

Blythe Energy Inc F 760 922-9950
385 N Buck Blvd Blythe (92225) ***(P-419)***

Blytheco Inc (PA) E **949 583-9500**
23161 Mill Creek Dr # 200 Laguna Hills (92653) ***(P-18166)***

Bmb 1 LLC D 951 741-0663
495 E Rincon St Ste 211 Corona (92879) ***(P-20562)***

BMC E 310 321-5555
300 Continental Blvd # 570 El Segundo (90245) ***(P-17803)***

BMC Group Inc D 310 321-5555
300 N Cntntl Blvd Ste 570 El Segundo (90245) ***(P-21519)***

BMC Industries, Bakersfield *Also called Bakersfield Machine Co Inc* ***(P-8516)***

Bmci Inc E 951 361-8000
1689 S Parco Ave Ontario (91761) ***(P-7900)***

Bmi, Temecula *Also called Bomatic Inc* ***(P-5582)***

Bmp, Glendale *Also called Bunim-Murray Productions* ***(P-19105)***

Bms Healthcare Inc C 562 942-7019
8925 Mines Ave Pico Rivera (90660) ***(P-21392)***

Bms Investments LLC F 714 376-2535
12626 Hackberry Ln Moreno Valley (92553) ***(P-4801)***

Bms Parent Inc (PA) D **909 981-2341**
1220 Dewey Way Ste F Upland (91786) ***(P-22761)***

BMW of Palm Springs F 760 324-7071
3737 E Palm Canyon Dr Palm Springs (92264) ***(P-3215)***

Bni Enterprises Inc A 909 305-1818
545 College Commerce Way Upland (91786) ***(P-23375)***

Bnk Petroleum (us) Inc E 805 484-3613
3623 Old Conejo Rd # 207 Newbury Park (91320) ***(P-441)***

Bnl Technologies Inc E 310 320-7272
20525 Manhattan Pl Torrance (90501) ***(P-8188)***

Bnn, Los Angeles *Also called Breitbart News Network LLC* ***(P-17080)***

Bnrg, Irvine *Also called Bio-Nutritional RES Group Inc* ***(P-1785)***

Bnsf Railway Company D 714 348-5810
18982 Oriente Dr Yorba Linda (92886) ***(P-11794)***

Bny Mellon National Assn C 877 420-6377
1600 Nwport Ctr Dr Ste 20 Newport Beach (92660) ***(P-15013)***

Bny Mellon National Assn D 310 551-7600
10250 Constellation Blvd # 2710 Los Angeles (90067) ***(P-23419)***

Boardhouse, Gardena *Also called L&F Wood LLC* ***(P-3261)***

Boardriders Inc (HQ) A **714 889-5404**
5600 Argosy Ave Ste 100 Huntington Beach (92649) ***(P-2803)***

Boardwalk Solutions, Gardena *Also called Ocean Direct LLC* ***(P-2348)***

Boatyard-Channel Islands, The, Oxnard *Also called Tbyci LLC* ***(P-10472)***

Boaventure Brewing Co E 213 236-0802
404 S Figueroa St 418a Los Angeles (90071) ***(P-2139)***

Bob Hope Health Center, Woodland Hills *Also called Motion Picture and TV Fund* ***(P-20866)***

Mergent e-mail: customerrelations@mergent.com
1074
2022 Southern California Business
Directory and Buyers Guide
(P-0000) Products & Services Section entry number
(PA)=Parent Co (HQ)=Headquarters (DH)=Div Headquarters

Bob Hubbard Horse Trnsp Inc (PA)..................................E......951 369-3770
3730 S Riverside Ave Colton (92324) *(P-11958)*

Bob Martin Co, South El Monte *Also called Robert P Martin Company (P-6232)*

Bobbi Boss, Cerritos *Also called Midway International Inc (P-14952)*

Bobco Metals LLC...D......213 748-5171
2000 S Alameda St Vernon (90058) *(P-13550)*

Boca Mesa Incorporated..D......805 934-9470
3130 Skyway Dr Ste 701 Santa Maria (93455) *(P-23420)*

Bocchi Laboratories, Santa Clarita *Also called Shadow Holdings LLC (P-5068)*

Bock Machine Company Inc...F......909 947-7250
2141 S Parco Ave Ontario (91761) *(P-8530)*

Body Flex Sports, Walnut *Also called Hupa International Inc (P-11425)*

Body Glove International LLC.......................................F......310 374-3441
6255 W Sunset Blvd # 650 Hollywood (90028) *(P-2804)*

Bodycote Thermal Proc Inc..E......310 604-8000
515 W Apra St Ste A Rancho Dominguez (90220) *(P-6431)*

Bodycote Thermal Proc Inc..D......323 583-1231
3370 Benedict Way Huntington Park (90255) *(P-7225)*

Bodycote Usa Inc...A......323 264-0111
2900 S Sunol Dr Vernon (90058) *(P-6432)*

Bodycote W Cast Anlytcal Svc I.....................................E......562 948-2225
9840 Alburtis Ave Santa Fe Springs (90670) *(P-6433)*

Boeing Coml Satellite Svcs Inc (HQ)................................E......**310 335-6682**
900 N Pacific Coast Hwy El Segundo (90245) *(P-9257)*

Boeing Company..B......714 896-3311
14441 Astronautics Ln Huntington Beach (92647) *(P-10513)*

Boeing Company..F......805 606-6340
Slc 2 Bldg 1628 San Luis Obispo (93401) *(P-12345)*

Boeing Company..A......562 496-1000
4000 N Lakewood Blvd Long Beach (90808) *(P-10177)*

Boeing Company..A......562 593-5511
4060 N Lakewood Blvd Long Beach (90808) *(P-10178)*

Boeing Company, The, El Segundo *Also called Boeing Stllite Systems Intl In (P-14053)*

Boeing Comsatcom Services Inc (HQ)................................D......**310 335-6682**
900 N Pacific Coast Hwy El Segundo (90245) *(P-10179)*

Boeing Encore Interiors LLC..E......949 559-0930
5511 Skylab Rd Huntington Beach (92647) *(P-10289)*

Boeing Intllctual Prprty Lcnsi.......................................B......562 797-2020
14441 Astronautics Ln Huntington Beach (92647) *(P-10180)*

Boeing Satellite Systems...D......310 364-5088
2060 E Imperial Hwy Fl 1 El Segundo (90245) *(P-10574)*

Boeing Satellite Systems Inc.......................................A......310 568-2735
2300 E Imperial Hwy El Segundo (90245) *(P-10181)*

Boeing Satellite Systems Inc (HQ).................................E......310 791-7450
900 N Pacific Coast Hwy El Segundo (90245) *(P-9258)*

Boeing Stllite Systems Intl In (HQ).................................E......**310 364-4000**
2260 E Imperial Hwy El Segundo (90245) *(P-14053)*

Boething Treeland Farms Inc (PA)...................................D......**818 883-1222**
23475 Long Valley Rd Woodland Hills (91367) *(P-365)*

Boething Treeland Nursery Co.......................................D......818 883-1222
23475 Long Valley Rd Woodland Hills (91367) *(P-12016)*

Bogart Construction Inc..D......949 453-1400
9980 Irvine Center Dr # 200 Irvine (92618) *(P-744)*

Bogh Engineering Inc..D......951 845-5130
401 W Fourth St Beaumont (92223) *(P-1518)*

Boiling Point Rest S CA Inc...B......626 551-5181
13668 Valley Blvd Unit C2 City of Industry (91746) *(P-17397)*

Boise Cascade Company...C......951 343-3000
7145 Arlington Ave Riverside (92503) *(P-13205)*

Bojer Inc..E......626 334-1711
177 S Peckham Rd Azusa (91702) *(P-3096)*

Bolero Inds Inc A Cal Corp..E......562 693-3000
11850 Burke St Santa Fe Springs (90670) *(P-5581)*

Bolero Plastics, Santa Fe Springs *Also called Bolero Inds Inc A Cal Corp (P-5581)*

Bolide International, San Dimas *Also called Bolide Technology Group Inc (P-18367)*

Bolide Technology Group Inc.......................................D......909 305-8889
468 S San Dimas Ave San Dimas (91773) *(P-18367)*

Bollingers Candelight Pavilion, Claremont *Also called Ben Bollinger Productions Inc (P-19304)*

Bolsa Medical Group, Westminster *Also called Co D L Pham MD (P-19755)*

Bolthouse Farms..A......661 366-7205
3200 E Brundage Ln Bakersfield (93304) *(P-11)*

Bolthouse Investment Company......................................F......661 366-7209
7200 E Brundage Ln Bakersfield (93307) *(P-12)*

Bomark Inc...E......626 968-1666
601 S 6th Ave La Puente (91746) *(P-5201)*

Bomatic Inc (HQ)...E......**909 947-3900**
43225 Business Park Dr Temecula (92590) *(P-5582)*

Bomatic Inc...D......909 947-3900
2181 E Francis St Ontario (91761) *(P-5583)*

Bomel Construction Co Inc (PA).....................................D......**714 921-1660**
96 Corporate Park Ste 100 Irvine (92606) *(P-745)*

Bomel Construction Co Inc...D......909 923-3319
939 E Francis St Ontario (91761) *(P-746)*

Bon Appetit Management Co..C......310 440-6052
1200 Getty Center Dr Los Angeles (90049) *(P-22989)*

Bon Appetit Management Co..C......909 607-2788
1050 N Mills Ave Claremont (91711) *(P-22990)*

Bon Appetit Management Co..C......909 748-8970
1259 E Colton Ave Redlands (92374) *(P-23174)*

Bon Appetit Management Co..C......310 440-6209
1200 Getty Center Dr # 100 Los Angeles (90049) *(P-22991)*

Bon Suisse Inc...F......714 578-0001
392 W Walnut Ave Fullerton (92832) *(P-23421)*

Bonanza Plumbing Inc (PA)...D......**951 360-8262**
2259 Hamner Ave Norco (92860) *(P-1034)*

Bonanza Productions Inc..A......818 954-4212
4000 Warner Blvd Burbank (91522) *(P-19345)*

Bonaventure Brewing Co, Los Angeles *Also called Boaventure Brewing Co (P-2139)*

Bonded Fiberloft Inc...B......323 726-7820
2748 Tanager Ave Commerce (90040) *(P-2560)*

Boneso Brothers Cnstr Inc..D......805 227-4450
2758 Concrete Ct Paso Robles (93446) *(P-1035)*

Bonne Brdges Mller Okefe Nchol (PA)...............................D......213 480-1900
355 S Grand Ave Ste 1750 Los Angeles (90071) *(P-21520)*

Bonnie Brae Cnvlscent Hosp Inc (PA)...............................D......213 483-8144
420 S Bonnie Brae St Los Angeles (90057) *(P-20563)*

Book Binders, Pico Rivera *Also called Kater-Crafts Incorporated (P-4618)*

Boom Industrial Inc..D......909 495-3555
167 University Pkwy Pomona (91768) *(P-7967)*

Boom-Boom Jeans, Los Angeles *Also called Blue Planet International Inc (P-14366)*

Boomers, Newport Beach *Also called Festival Fun Parks LLC (P-19648)*

Boone Printing & Graphics Inc......................................D......805 683-2349
70 S Kellogg Ave Ste 8 Goleta (93117) *(P-4237)*

Booth Mitchel & Strange LLP..D......805 400-0703
979 Osos St Ste C1 San Luis Obispo (93401) *(P-21521)*

Boozak Inc..E......951 245-6045
508 Chaney St Ste A Lake Elsinore (92530) *(P-6797)*

Bop Inc..F......909 598-5776
23575 Underwood Cir Murrieta (92562) *(P-4238)*

Boral Building Products, Irvine *Also called Boral Roofing LLC (P-1475)*

Boral Roofing LLC (HQ)...E......**949 756-1605**
7575 Irvine Center Dr # 100 Irvine (92618) *(P-1475)*

Borbon Incorporated..C......714 994-0170
2560 W Woodland Dr Anaheim (92801) *(P-1171)*

Border Valley Trading Ltd..D......760 344-6700
604 Mead Rd Brawley (92227) *(P-14854)*

Border Valley Trading Ltd..D......760 344-6700
604 Mead Rd Brawley (92227) *(P-14855)*

Bore-Max, El Monte *Also called GAI Manufacturing Co LLC (P-7678)*

Borges Rock Product, Sun Valley *Also called Over & Over Ready Mix Inc (P-6046)*

Borin Manufacturing Inc...E......310 822-1000
5741 Buckingham Pkwy B Culver City (90230) *(P-6730)*

Borrmann Metal Center (HQ)..D......**818 846-7171**
110 W Olive Ave Burbank (91502) *(P-13551)*

Boskovich Farms Inc (PA)...C......**805 487-2299**
711 Diaz Ave Oxnard (93030) *(P-161)*

Boskovich Fresh Cut LLC...C......805 487-2299
711 Diaz Ave Oxnard (93030) *(P-14615)*

Bosman Dairy LLC..C......559 752-7018
6802 Avenue 120 A Tipton (93272) *(P-131)*

Boss, Commerce *Also called Norstar Office Products Inc (P-3593)*

Boss Audio Systems, Oxnard *Also called Boss International LLC (P-9166)*

Boss Audio Systems, Oxnard *Also called Ava Enterprises Inc (P-13682)*

Boss International LLC (PA)..D......**805 988-0192**
3451 Lunar Ct Oxnard (93030) *(P-9166)*

Boss Litho Inc...E......626 912-7088
2380 Peck Rd City of Industry (90601) *(P-4239)*

Boston Scientific - Valencia, Valencia *Also called Boston Scientific Corporation (P-10952)*

Boston Scientific Corporation......................................E......800 678-2575
25155 Rye Canyon Loop Valencia (91355) *(P-10952)*

Boston Scntfic Nrmdlation Corp (HQ)...............................B......661 949-4310
25155 Rye Canyon Loop Valencia (91355) *(P-11092)*

Boswell Properties Inc..A......626 583-3000
101 W Walnut St Pasadena (91103) *(P-150)*

Bot Travel & Staffing..D......323 272-4911
5900 Wilshire Blvd # 243 Los Angeles (90036) *(P-17398)*

Botanas Mexico Inc...F......626 279-1512
11122 Rush St South El Monte (91733) *(P-2399)*

Botanx LLC..E......714 854-1601
3357 E Miraloma Ave # 156 Anaheim (92806) *(P-4995)*

Bottle Coatings, Sun Valley *Also called Sundial Powder Coatings Inc (P-7418)*

Bottlemate Inc (PA)..E......**323 887-9009**
2095 Leo Ave Commerce (90040) *(P-5584)*

Bottling Group LLC...D......951 697-3200
6659 Sycamore Canyon Blvd Riverside (92507) *(P-2260)*

Boudraux Prcsion McHining Corp.....................................E......714 894-4523
11762 Western Ave Ste G Stanton (90680) *(P-8531)*

Boudreau Pipeline Corporation......................................B......951 493-6780
463 N Smith Ave Corona (92878) *(P-938)*

Boulevard Labs Inc..D......323 310-2093
1041 N Formosa Ave Bldg W West Hollywood (90046) *(P-17571)*

Bouqs Company...D......888 320-2687
4094 Glencoe Ave Marina Del Rey (90292) *(P-14877)*

Bourget Bros Building Mtls Inc (PA)................................E......**310 450-6556**
1636 11th St Santa Monica (90404) *(P-13976)*

Bourget Flagstone Co, Santa Monica *Also called Bourget Bros Building Mtls Inc (P-13976)*

Bourns Inc (PA)...C......**951 781-5500**
1200 Columbia Ave Riverside (92507) *(P-9622)*

Bourns APL Corp (HQ)..D......**951 781-5500**
1200 Columbia Ave Riverside (92507) *(P-9623)*

Bovitz Inc...D......818 806-0800
16133 Ventura Blvd # 820 Encino (91436) *(P-22875)*

Bowers & Kelly Products Inc.......................................E......714 630-1285
4572 E Eisenhower Cir Anaheim (92807) *(P-5493)*

Bowie Enterprises..D......559 732-2988
1920 S Mooney Blvd Visalia (93277) *(P-18907)*

Bowlero Corp...D......626 339-1286
1060 W San Bernardino Rd Covina (91722) *(P-19387)*

Bowlero Corp...D......626 960-3636
675 S Glendora Ave West Covina (91790) *(P-19388)*

Bowlero Corp...D......951 924-6008
24666 Sunnymead Blvd Moreno Valley (92553) *(P-19389)*

Bowlero Corp...D......909 946-7006
451 W Foothill Blvd Upland (91786) *(P-19390)*

Bowlero Corp...D......951 734-8410
1800 Hamner Ave Norco (92860) *(P-19391)*

Employee Codes: A=Over 500 employees, B=251-500
C=101-250, D=51-100, E=20-50 F=10-19

2022 Southern California Business
Directory and Buyers Guide

© Mergent Inc. 1-800-342-5647

1075

Bowlero Corp ... D ... 661 274-2878
38241 30th St E Palmdale (93550) *(P-19392)*

Bowlero Corp ... D ... 909 945-9392
7930 Haven Ave Ste 101 Rancho Cucamonga (91730) *(P-19393)*

Bowlero Corp ... D ... 951 698-2202
40440 California Oaks Rd Murrieta (92562) *(P-19394)*

Bowlero Corp ... D ... 909 822-9900
17238 Foothill Blvd Fontana (92335) *(P-19395)*

Bowman Pipeline Contractors, Bakersfield *Also called Southwest Contractors (P-972)*

Bowman Plating Co Inc ... C ... 310 639-4343
2631 E 126th St Compton (90222) *(P-7226)*

Bowsmith Inc (PA) ... D ... **559 592-9485**
131 2nd St Exeter (93221) *(P-16884)*

Boxes R Us Inc ... D ... 626 820-5410
15051 Don Julian Rd City of Industry (91746) *(P-3789)*

Boxunion Santa Monica LLC (PA) ... D ... **310 882-5508**
1755 Ocean Ave Santa Monica (90401) *(P-19440)*

BOY'S & GIRL'S CLUB OF BAKERSF, Bakersfield *Also called Boys Girls Clubs of Kern Cnty (P-22314)*

Boyd & Associates ... C ... 714 835-5423
3151 Airway Ave Ste K105 Costa Mesa (92626) *(P-18256)*

Boyd & Boyd Industries (PA) ... F ... **661 631-8400**
3500 Chester Ave Bakersfield (93301) *(P-8064)*

Boyd and Associates ... D ... 805 988-8298
445 E Esplanade Dr # 210 Oxnard (93036) *(P-18257)*

Boyd and Associates (PA) ... C ... **818 752-1888**
2191 E Thompson Blvd Ventura (93001) *(P-18258)*

Boyd Construction, Yorba Linda *Also called Boyd Corporation (P-6591)*

Boyd Corporation (PA) ... C ... **714 533-2375**
5832 Ohio St Yorba Linda (92886) *(P-6591)*

Boyd Dental Corporation (PA) ... D ... **909 384-1111**
599 Inland Center Dr # 110 San Bernardino (92408) *(P-20170)*

Boyd Flotation Inc ... E ... 314 997-5222
7551 Cherry Ave Fontana (92336) *(P-3543)*

Boyd Specialties LLC ... D ... 909 219-5120
1016 E Cooley Dr Ste N Colton (92324) *(P-1728)*

Boyd Specialty Sleep, Fontana *Also called Boyd Flotation Inc (P-3543)*

Boyle Engineering Corporation ... D ... 714 543-5274
999 W Town And Country Rd Orange (92868) *(P-22502)*

Boys & Girls Club, Goleta *Also called United Bys Grls Clubs Snta BRB (P-22373)*

Boys & Girls Club of San Pedro, San Pedro *Also called Boys Grls Clubs of Los Angles (P-22320)*

BOYS & GIRLS CLUBS OF SANTA MO, Santa Monica *Also called Boys Grls CLB Snta Monica Inc (P-22316)*

Boys and Girls Club ... E ... 818 225-8406
22450 Mulholland Hwy Calabasas (91302) *(P-19548)*

Boys Girls CLB Huntington Vly (PA) ... D ... **714 531-2582**
16582 Brookhurst St Fountain Valley (92708) *(P-22313)*

Boys Girls Clubs of Kern Cnty ... D ... 661 325-3730
801 Niles St Bakersfield (93305) *(P-22314)*

Boys Grls CLB Mrpark Simi Vly (PA) ... E ... **805 527-4437**
2850 Lemon Dr Simi Valley (93063) *(P-22315)*

Boys Grls CLB Snta Monica Inc ... D ... 310 361-8500
1220 Lincoln Blvd Santa Monica (90401) *(P-22316)*

Boys Grls Clubs Cntl Ornge Cas (PA) ... D ... **714 543-5540**
17701 Cowan Ste 110 Irvine (92614) *(P-22317)*

Boys Grls Clubs Grdn Grove Inc (PA) ... C ... **714 530-0430**
10540 Chapman Ave Garden Grove (92840) *(P-22446)*

Boys Grls Clubs Grter Cnejo Vl (PA) ... D ... **818 706-0905**
1 Dole Dr Ste 3331 Westlake Village (91362) *(P-22318)*

Boys Grls Clubs Grter Oxnard P (PA) ... D ... **805 815-4959**
1900 W 5th St Oxnard (93030) *(P-22319)*

Boys Grls Clubs of Los Angles (PA) ... D ... **310 833-1322**
1200 S Cabrillo Ave San Pedro (90731) *(P-22320)*

Boys Republic (PA) ... C ... **909 902-6690**
1907 Boys Republic Dr Chino Hills (91709) *(P-22085)*

BP Communications Inc (PA) ... C ... **626 912-0600**
1600 N Broadway Ste 900 Santa Ana (92706) *(P-12628)*

BP Industries Incorporated ... D ... 909 481-0227
5300 E Concours St Ontario (91764) *(P-13160)*

Bpi Records, Commerce *Also called Bridge Publications Inc (P-4122)*

Bpo Management Services Inc (HQ) ... C ... **714 974-2670**
8175 E Kaiser Blvd 100 Anaheim (92808) *(P-17804)*

Bpo Management Services Inc (PA) ... D ... **714 972-2670**
8175 E Kaiser Blvd 100 Anaheim (92808) *(P-17572)*

Bps Supply Group (PA) ... D ... **661 589-9141**
3301 Zachary Ave Shafter (93263) *(P-13552)*

Bps Tactical Inc ... F ... 909 794-2435
2165 E Colton Ave Mentone (92359) *(P-2755)*

BQE Software Inc ... D ... 310 602-4020
3825 Del Amo Blvd Trrance Torrance Torrance (90503) *(P-17805)*

BR Building Resources Co ... C ... 626 963-4880
2247 Lindsay Way Glendora (91740) *(P-747)*

Brad Rambo & Associates Inc (PA) ... D ... **949 366-9911**
1341 Calle Avanzado San Clemente (92673) *(P-14328)*

Bradco Environmental, Redlands *Also called Bradco Industrial Corporation (P-370)*

Bradco Industrial Corporation ... F ... 888 272-3261
1671 Sessums Dr Redlands (92374) *(P-370)*

Braden Court LLC ... F ... 714 288-3936
1517 W Braden Ct Orange (92868) *(P-5367)*

Bradfield Manufacturing Inc ... F ... 714 543-8348
2633 E Mardi Gras Ave Anaheim (92806) *(P-6953)*

Bradford Soap Mexico Inc ... B ... 760 768-4539
1778 Zinetta Rd Ste G Calexico (92231) *(P-4940)*

Bradley Manufacturing Co Inc ... E ... 562 923-5556
9130 Firestone Blvd Downey (90241) *(P-5585)*

Bradley's Plastic Bag Co, Downey *Also called Bradley Manufacturing Co Inc (P-5585)*

Bradshaw Home, Rancho Cucamonga *Also called Bradshaw International Inc (P-13161)*

Bradshaw International Inc (HQ) ... B ... **909 476-3884**
9409 Buffalo Ave Rancho Cucamonga (91730) *(P-13161)*

Brady Vorwerck Rydr & Cspno (PA) ... D ... **480 456-9888**
19200 Von Karman Ave Irvine (92612) *(P-21522)*

Braemar Country Club Inc ... C ... 323 873-6880
4001 Reseda Blvd Tarzana (91356) *(P-19549)*

Bragel International Inc ... E ... 909 598-8808
3383 Pomona Blvd Pomona (91768) *(P-3020)*

Bragg Crane & Rigging, Long Beach *Also called Bragg Investment Company Inc (P-17306)*

Bragg Investment Company Inc (PA) ... B ... **562 984-2400**
6251 N Paramount Blvd Long Beach (90805) *(P-17306)*

Braille Institute America Inc (PA) ... C ... **323 663-1111**
741 N Vermont Ave Los Angeles (90029) *(P-21726)*

Braille Signs Inc ... E ... 949 797-1570
1815 E Wilshire Ave # 901 Santa Ana (92705) *(P-11529)*

Brainchip Inc (HQ) ... F ... **949 330-6750**
65 Enterprise Ste 325 Aliso Viejo (92656) *(P-17806)*

Brains Out Media Inc ... F ... 818 296-1036
2629 Foothill Blvd # 111 La Crescenta (91214) *(P-17807)*

Brand Amp LLC ... D ... 949 438-1060
1945 Placentia Ave Ste C Costa Mesa (92627) *(P-23376)*

Brand Flower Farms Inc (PA) ... C ... **805 684-5531**
5300 Foothill Rd Carpinteria (93013) *(P-14878)*

Branded Entrmt Netwrk Inc (PA) ... C ... **310 342-1500**
15250 Ventura Blvd # 300 Sherman Oaks (91403) *(P-17158)*

Branded Group Inc ... C ... 323 940-1444
222 S Harbor Blvd Ste 500 Anaheim (92805) *(P-23175)*

Brandify, Anaheim *Also called Where 2 Get It Inc (P-18236)*

Brandnew Industries Inc ... F ... 805 964-8251
375 Pine Ave Ste 22 Santa Barbara (93117) *(P-11471)*

Brandrep LLC ... E ... 800 405-7119
2850 Redhill Ave Ste 100 Santa Ana (92705) *(P-23176)*

Brands Republic Inc ... E ... 302 401-1195
10333 Rush St South El Monte (91733) *(P-9000)*

Brandt Cattle, Calipatria *Also called Brandt Co Inc (P-123)*

Brandt Co Inc ... D ... 760 348-2295
7015 Brandt Rd Calipatria (92233) *(P-123)*

Brandywine Communications ... D ... 714 755-1050
1609 E Mcfadden Ave Ste B Santa Ana (92705) *(P-13703)*

Brandywine Communications (PA) ... F ... **714 755-1050**
1153 Warner Ave Tustin (92780) *(P-13704)*

Branlyn Prominence Inc ... C ... 760 843-5655
13334 Amargosa Rd Victorville (92392) *(P-21140)*

Branlyn Prominence Inc (PA) ... D ... **909 476-9030**
9213 Archibald Ave Rancho Cucamonga (91730) *(P-21141)*

Branvid Ltd Inc ... E ... 714 630-0661
4920 E La Palma Ave Anaheim (92807) *(P-17334)*

Brass Unique Inc ... E ... 626 444-8977
9948 Hayward Way South El Monte (91733) *(P-6592)*

Brasscraft Corona, Corona *Also called Brasscraft Manufacturing Co (P-7471)*

Brasscraft Manufacturing Co ... E ... 951 735-4375
215 N Smith Ave Corona (92878) *(P-7471)*

Brasstech Inc (HQ) ... B ... **949 417-5207**
2001 Carnegie Ave Santa Ana (92705) *(P-6553)*

Braswell Ivy Retreat, Mentone *Also called Braswlls Mdterranean Grdns Inc (P-20257)*

Braswells Chateau Villa, San Bernardino *Also called Braswlls Mdterranean Grdns Inc (P-20259)*

Braswells Yucaipa Leisre Manor, Yucaipa *Also called Braswlls Mdterranean Grdns Inc (P-20260)*

Braswlls Mdterranean Grdns Inc ... D ... 909 794-1189
2278 Nice Ave Mentone (92359) *(P-20257)*

Braswlls Mdterranean Grdns Inc ... D ... 909 793-0433
620 E Highland Ave Redlands (92374) *(P-20258)*

Braswlls Mdterranean Grdns Inc ... D ... 909 793-0433
620 E Highland Ave San Bernardino (92404) *(P-20259)*

Braswlls Mdterranean Grdns Inc ... D ... 909 797-1314
32195 Avenue E Yucaipa (92399) *(P-20260)*

Braswlls Mdterranean Grdns Inc ... D ... 909 795-2421
13542 2nd St Yucaipa (92399) *(P-20261)*

Braswlls Mdterranean Grdns Inc ... D ... 909 795-2476
35253 Avenue H Yucaipa (92399) *(P-20262)*

Braswlls Ycipa Vly Cnvlscent H, Yucaipa *Also called Braswlls Mdterranean Grdns Inc (P-20262)*

Brault ... C ... 626 447-0296
180 Via Verde Ste 100 San Dimas (91773) *(P-22762)*

Braun Electric Company Inc (HQ) ... E ... **661 633-1451**
3000 E Belle Ter Bakersfield (93307) *(P-1223)*

Braun Linen Service (PA) ... C ... **909 623-2678**
16514 Garfield Ave Paramount (90723) *(P-16847)*

Braun Linen Service ... E ... 909 623-2678
396 La Mesa St Pomona (91766) *(P-16836)*

Braun Linen Service Inc ... E ... 310 719-8661
738 E Turmont St Carson (90746) *(P-16848)*

Brava, Pomona *Also called Bragel International Inc (P-3020)*

Bravo Sign & Design Inc ... F ... 714 284-0500
520 S Central Park Ave E Anaheim (92802) *(P-1642)*

Bravo Sports (HQ) ... D ... **562 484-5100**
12801 Carmenita Rd Santa Fe Springs (90670) *(P-11406)*

Bravo Support, Commerce *Also called S Bravo Systems Inc (P-6751)*

Bravo Tech Inc ... E ... 714 230-8333
14600 Industry Cir La Mirada (90638) *(P-12596)*

Brawley Union High School Dist (PA) ... C ... **760 312-6068**
480 N Imperial Ave Brawley (92227) *(P-21991)*

Braxton Caribbean Mfg Co Inc ... D ... 714 508-3570
2641 Walnut Ave Tustin (92780) *(P-7130)*

Brazeau Thoroughbred Farms LP ... E ... 951 201-2278
30500 State St Hemet (92543) *(P-7606)*

Brazil Minerals Inc F 213 590-2500
155 N Lake Ave Ste 800 Pasadena (91101) *(P-584)*

BRC Imagination Arts Inc (PA) **D 818 841-8084**
2711 Winona Ave Burbank (91504) *(P-19102)*

Brea Canon Oil Co Inc F 310 326-4002
23903 Normandie Ave Harbor City (90710) *(P-393)*

Bread Los Angeles F 323 201-3953
1527 Beach St Montebello (90640) *(P-2060)*

Break Media, Beverly Hills *Also called Nextpoint Inc (P-12659)*

Breakaway Press Inc E 818 727-7388
9620 Topanga Canyon Pl A Chatsworth (91311) *(P-4240)*

Breast Care Center of Orange (PA) **D 714 541-0101**
230 S Main St Ste 100 Orange (92868) *(P-19724)*

Breathe La Lhc LLC E 212 989-9332
8060 Melrose Ave Fl 3 Los Angeles (90046) *(P-21393)*

Breathe La Lhc LLC D 800 929-5904
8060 Melrose Ave Fl 3 Los Angeles (90046) *(P-21394)*

Breathe Life Healing Centers, Los Angeles *Also called Breathe La Lhc LLC (P-21393)*

Breathe Technologies Inc E 949 988-7700
15091 Bake Pkwy Irvine (92618) *(P-11093)*

Brecks Electric Motors Inc F 559 651-1475
30510 Road 68 Visalia (93291) *(P-19007)*

Breeders Choice Pet Foods LLC E 626 334-9301
16321 Arrow Hwy Irwindale (91706) *(P-14676)*

Breeze Air Conditioning LLC D 760 346-0855
75145 Saint Charles Pl A Palm Desert (92211) *(P-1036)*

Breitbart News Network LLC D 424 371-0585
149 S Barrington Ste 735 Los Angeles (90049) *(P-17080)*

Breitburn Energy Holdings LLC F 213 225-5900
707 Wilshire Blvd # 4600 Los Angeles (90017) *(P-442)*

Breitburn GP LLC F 213 225-5900
707 Wilshire Blvd # 4600 Los Angeles (90017) *(P-394)*

Bremer Whyte Brown Omeara, Newport Beach *Also called Bremer Whyte Brown Omeara LLP (P-21523)*

Bremer Whyte Brown Omeara LLP (PA) **E 949 221-1000**
20320 Sw Birch St Ste 200 Newport Beach (92660) *(P-21523)*

Bremik International Inc D 310 715-6622
14403 S Main St Gardena (90248) *(P-4157)*

Bremik Press, Gardena *Also called Bremik International Inc (P-4157)*

Brenner-Fiedler & Assoc Inc (PA) **E 562 404-2721**
4059 Flat Rock Dr Riverside (92505) *(P-10873)*

Brenntag Pacific Inc (HQ) **C 562 903-9626**
10747 Patterson Pl Santa Fe Springs (90670) *(P-14773)*

Brent-Wood Products Inc E 800 400-7335
777 E Rosecrans Ave Los Angeles (90059) *(P-3441)*

Brentwood Appliances Inc E 323 266-4600
3088 E 46th St Vernon (90058) *(P-9013)*

Brentwood Bmdical RES Inst Inc C 310 312-1554
11301 Wilshire Blvd # 1 Los Angeles (90073) *(P-22900)*

Brentwood Builders, Burbank *Also called 716 Management Inc (P-654)*

Brentwood Country Club C 310 451-8011
590 S Burlingame Ave Los Angeles (90049) *(P-19550)*

Brentwood Health Care Center, Santa Monica *Also called Coastal Health Care Inc (P-20283)*

Brentwood Home LLC (PA) **C 562 949-3759**
701 Burning Tree Rd Ste A Fullerton (92833) *(P-3544)*

Brentwood Medical Tech Corp D 800 624-8950
1125 W 190th St Gardena (90248) *(P-13481)*

Brentwood Originals Inc (PA) **C 925 202-9290**
20639 S Fordyce Ave Carson (90810) *(P-3097)*

Brer Affiliates LLC (HQ) **C 949 794-7900**
18500 Von Karman Ave # 4 Irvine (92612) *(P-16203)*

Bret Boylan, Long Beach *Also called Bret Boylan Property Mgt (P-22992)*

Bret Boylan Property Mgt E 562 437-7886
35 N Alboni Pl Apt 409 Long Beach (90802) *(P-22992)*

Brethren Inc E 714 836-4800
1170 E Fruit St Santa Ana (92701) *(P-14147)*

Brethren Hillcrest Homes C 909 593-4917
2705 Mountain View Dr Ofc La Verne (91750) *(P-22086)*

Breville Usa Inc E 310 755-3000
19400 S Western Ave Torrance (90501) *(P-13162)*

Briarcrest Nursing Center Inc D 562 927-2641
5648 Gotham St Bell (90201) *(P-20263)*

Brica Inc (HQ) **D 818 893-5000**
7835 Gloria Ave Van Nuys (91406) *(P-14916)*

Brice Tool & Stamping F 714 630-6400
1170 N Van Horne Way Anaheim (92806) *(P-7131)*

Brickley Construction Co Inc E 909 888-2010
957 Reece St San Bernardino (92411) *(P-1643)*

Brickley Environmental, San Bernardino *Also called Brickley Construction Co Inc (P-1643)*

Bridge Metals, Los Angeles *Also called Zia Aamir (P-6685)*

Bridge Publications Inc (PA) **E 323 888-6200**
5600 E Olympic Blvd Commerce (90022) *(P-4122)*

Bridgeport Products Inc E 949 348-8800
26895 Aliso Creek Rd Aliso Viejo (92656) *(P-5889)*

Bridges At Sn Pdro Pnnsla Hspt D 310 514-5359
1300 W 7th St Fl 4 San Pedro (90732) *(P-21280)*

Bridgestone Americas D 909 770-8523
14521 Hawthorne Ave Fontana (92335) *(P-18809)*

Bridgestone Hosepower LLC F 562 699-9500
2865 Pellissier Pl City of Industry (90601) *(P-13977)*

Bridgestone Living LLC D 949 487-9500
27101 Puerta Real Ste 450 Mission Viejo (92691) *(P-20264)*

Bridgford Foods Corporation (HQ) **B 714 526-5533**
1308 N Patt St Anaheim (92801) *(P-1951)*

Bridgford Marketing Company (HQ) **D 714 526-5533**
1308 N Patt St Anaheim (92801) *(P-14592)*

Bridgwter Consulting Group Inc D 949 535-1755
18881 Von Karman Ave # 1 Irvine (92612) *(P-23177)*

Bridlewood Winery LLC E 805 688-9000
3555 Roblar Ave Santa Ynez (93460) *(P-2168)*

Bridport Erie Aviation Inc D 714 634-8801
2220 E Cerritos Ave Anaheim (92806) *(P-19025)*

Brierwood Terrace Ventura Inc (HQ) **D 805 642-4101**
4904 Telegraph Rd Ventura (93003) *(P-20564)*

Briggs Electric Inc (PA) **D 714 544-2500**
14381 Franklin Ave Tustin (92780) *(P-1224)*

Bright Care Home Health Inc (PA) **D 626 285-9698**
3925 Rosemead Blvd 205a Rosemead (91770) *(P-21142)*

Bright Event Rentals LLC (PA) **C 310 202-0011**
1640 W 190th St Ste A Torrance (90501) *(P-17335)*

Bright Expectations Inc E 951 360-2070
8175 Limonite Ave Ste C Riverside (92509) *(P-21143)*

Bright Foods LLC F 708 263-7771
777 S Alameda St Ste 220 Los Angeles (90021) *(P-2110)*

Bright Glow Candle Company Inc (PA) **E 909 469-4733**
110 Erie St Pomona (91768) *(P-11640)*

Bright Health Physicians (PA) **C 562 947-8478**
15725 Whittier Blvd # 500 Whittier (90603) *(P-19725)*

Bright Now Dental, Irvine *Also called Smile Brands Group Inc (P-23109)*

Bright Shark Powder Coating F 909 591-1385
4530 Schaefer Ave Chino (91710) *(P-7350)*

Brighton Convalescent Center D 626 798-9124
1836 N Fair Oaks Ave Pasadena (91103) *(P-20565)*

Brightside Scientific Inc F 626 453-6436
3029 E South St Ste A Long Beach (90805) *(P-10653)*

Brightstar Care NW San Frnndo, Northridge *Also called Sfv LLC (P-21211)*

Brightstar Health, Riverside *Also called Smart Choice Investments Inc (P-17466)*

Brightview Companies LLC (HQ) **C 818 223-8500**
27001 Agoura Rd Ste 350 Calabasas (91301) *(P-989)*

Brightview Golf Maint Inc C 805 968-6400
405 Glen Annie Rd Santa Barbara (93117) *(P-236)*

Brightview Golf Maint Inc (HQ) **D 818 223-8500**
27001 Agoura Rd Ste 350 Agoura Hills (91301) *(P-237)*

Brightview Landscape Dev Inc (HQ) **E 818 223-8500**
27001 Agoura Rd Ste 350 Calabasas (91301) *(P-238)*

Brightview Landscape Dev Inc D 818 838-4700
13691 Vaughn St San Fernando (91340) *(P-1037)*

Brightview Landscape Dev Inc D 714 546-7975
8 Hughes Ste 125 Irvine (92618) *(P-1038)*

Brightview Landscape Svcs Inc C 951 684-2730
715 W La Cadena Dr Riverside (92501) *(P-239)*

Brightview Landscape Svcs Inc C 714 215-7423
1900 S Lewis St Anaheim (92805) *(P-240)*

Brightview Landscape Svcs Inc C 714 546-7843
32202 Paseo Adelanto San Juan Capistrano (92675) *(P-241)*

Brightview Landscape Svcs Inc C 310 829-4707
47 Plateau Aliso Viejo (92656) *(P-242)*

Brightview Landscape Svcs Inc C 909 946-3196
8726 Calabash Ave Fontana (92335) *(P-243)*

Brightview Landscape Svcs Inc C 714 546-7843
1960 S Yale St Santa Ana (92704) *(P-244)*

Brightview Landscape Svcs Inc C 714 939-6600
17846 Van Buren Blvd Riverside (92508) *(P-245)*

Brightview Landscape Svcs Inc C 805 642-9300
2064 Eastman Ave Ste 104 Ventura (93003) *(P-246)*

Brightview Landscape Svcs Inc C 949 480-4187
1 University Dr Aliso Viejo (92656) *(P-247)*

Brightview Landscape Svcs Inc C 310 327-8700
17813 S Main St Ste 105 Gardena (90248) *(P-248)*

Brightview Tree Company D 818 951-5500
9500 Foothill Blvd Sunland (91040) *(P-366)*

Brightview Tree Company D 714 546-7975
3200 W Telegraph Rd Fillmore (93015) *(P-367)*

Brightview Tree Company D 760 955-2560
P.O. Box 1611 Apple Valley (92307) *(P-249)*

Brightwater Medical Inc F 951 290-3410
42580 Rio Nedo Temecula (92590) *(P-10953)*

Briles Aerospace Inc D 310 701-2087
1559 W 135th St Gardena (90249) *(P-7058)*

Brilliant AV, Costa Mesa *Also called Walin Group Inc (P-8141)*

Brilliant Imaging Group Inc F 626 333-1868
1206 John Reed Ct City of Industry (91745) *(P-13892)*

Brilliant Solutions, Irvine *Also called Meguiars Inc (P-4971)*

Brillstein Entrmt Partners LLC (PA) **D 310 205-5100**
9150 Wilshire Blvd # 350 Beverly Hills (90212) *(P-19103)*

Brillstein Grey Entertainment, Beverly Hills *Also called Brillstein Entrmt Partners LLC (P-19103)*

Brimad Enterprises Inc E 951 354-8187
2900 Adams St Ste B16 Riverside (92504) *(P-17075)*

Brinderson LP (HQ) **C 714 466-7100**
18841 S Broadwick St Compton (90220) *(P-22503)*

Brinderson LP D 714 466-7100
19000 Macarthur Blvd # 800 Irvine (92612) *(P-22504)*

Brinks Incorporated C 714 903-9272
7191 Patterson Dr Garden Grove (92841) *(P-18259)*

Brio Water Technology Inc E 800 781-1680
768 Turnbull Canyon Rd Hacienda Heights (91745) *(P-13851)*

Brisam Lax (de) LLC D 310 649-5151
9901 S La Cienega Blvd Los Angeles (90045) *(P-16355)*

Bristol Farms (HQ) **D 310 233-4700**
915 E 230th St Carson (90745) *(P-2400)*

Bristol Hospice Foundation Cal D 562 494-7687
3200 E 19th St Signal Hill (90755) *(P-20525)*

Bristol Hospice Foundation Cal (PA) **D 661 410-3000**
1227 Chester Ave Ste A Bakersfield (93301) *(P-22447)*

Bristol Hospice Foundation Cal D 661 716-4000
1675 Chester Ave Ste 401 Bakersfield (93301) *(P-20526)*

ALPHABETIC

Employee Codes: A=Over 500 employees, B=251-500
C=101-250, D=51-100, E=20-50 F=10-19
2022 Southern California Business
Directory and Buyers Guide
© Mergent Inc. 1-800-342-5647
1077

Bristol Omega Inc ....E....909 794-6862
9441 Opal Ave Ste 2 Mentone (92359) ***(P-3640)***

Bristolite, Santa Ana *Also called Sundown Liquidating Corp* ***(P-5923)***

Brite Plating Co Inc ....F....323 263-7593
1313 Mirasol St Los Angeles (90023) ***(P-7227)***

Brite Vue Div, Visalia *Also called Kawneer Company Inc* ***(P-6970)***

Brite-Lite Neon Corp ....F....818 763-4798
17242 Goya St Granada Hills (91344) ***(P-11530)***

Briteworks Inc ....D....626 337-0099
620 N Commercial Ave Covina (91723) ***(P-17220)***

Brithinee Electric ....D....909 825-7971
620 S Rancho Ave Colton (92324) ***(P-13617)***

Brittany House LLC ....C....562 421-4717
5401 E Centralia St Long Beach (90808) ***(P-22087)***

Brittney House ....D....562 421-4717
5401 E Centralia St Long Beach (90808) ***(P-21144)***

Britz Fertilizers Inc ....D....559 582-0942
12498 11th Ave Hanford (93230) ***(P-7607)***

Brixen & Sons Inc ....E....714 566-1444
2100 S Fairview St Santa Ana (92704) ***(P-4488)***

Brk Group LLC ....E....562 949-4394
6415 Bandini Blvd Commerce (90040) ***(P-2722)***

Brm Manufacturing, Los Angeles *Also called Brush Research Mfg Co* ***(P-11508)***

Broadata Communications Inc ....D....310 530-1416
2545 W 237th St Ste K Torrance (90505) ***(P-6344)***

Broadley-James Corporation ....D....949 829-5555
19 Thomas Irvine (92618) ***(P-10788)***

Broadreach Capitl Partners LLC ....A....310 691-5760
6430 W Sunset Blvd # 504 Los Angeles (90028) ***(P-16249)***

Broadspire Inc ....D....213 785-8043
19425 Soledad Canyon Rd # 34 Santa Clarita (91351) ***(P-12629)***

Broadstreet Power, Van Nuys *Also called Broadstreet Solar Inc* ***(P-1039)***

Broadstreet Solar Inc ....E....818 206-1464
16112 Hart St Van Nuys (91406) ***(P-1039)***

Broadway AC Htg & Shtmtl ....E....818 781-1477
7855 Burnet Ave Van Nuys (91405) ***(P-6798)***

Broadway Auto Parts, Santa Ana *Also called United Syatt America Corp* ***(P-13103)***

Broadway Manor Care Center, Glendale *Also called Longwood Management Corp* ***(P-20602)***

Broadway Sheet Metal, Van Nuys *Also called Broadway AC Htg & Shtmtl* ***(P-6798)***

Brochure Holders 4u, Santa Ana *Also called Clear-Ad Inc* ***(P-5607)***

Brodie Construction & Recycl, Indio *Also called Brodie Holdings Inc* ***(P-1428)***

Brodie Holdings Inc ....E....760 775-3744
83256 Indio Blvd Indio (92201) ***(P-1428)***

Brokaw Nursery LLC ....D....805 647-2262
5501 Elizabeth Rd Ventura (93004) ***(P-74)***

Broker Solutions Inc ....D....818 235-0640
19300 Rinaldi St Ste M Porter Ranch (91326) ***(P-15151)***

Broker Solutions Inc ....D....800 450-2010
233 Milford Dr Corona Del Mar (92625) ***(P-15177)***

Broker Solutions Inc ....D....951 637-2300
11820 Pierce St Riverside (92505) ***(P-18462)***

Broker Solutions Inc ....D....909 458-0718
800 N Haven Ave Ste 330 Ontario (91764) ***(P-23178)***

Broker Solutions Inc (PA) ....**A....800 450-2010**
14511 Myford Rd Ste 100 Tustin (92780) ***(P-23179)***

Broma Applicators LLC ....E....760 351-0101
322 W J St Brawley (92227) ***(P-14856)***

Bromack, Los Angeles *Also called LA Cabinet & Millwork Inc* ***(P-3656)***

Bromwell Company (PA) ....**E....800 683-2626**
8605 Santa Monica Blvd Los Angeles (90069) ***(P-5995)***

Bronze-Way Plating Corporation (PA) ....**E....323 266-6933**
3301 E 14th St Los Angeles (90023) ***(P-7228)***

Brook & Whittle Limited ....E....714 634-3466
1177 N Grove St Anaheim (92806) ***(P-4489)***

Brookdale Brea ....E....714 706-9968
285 W Central Ave Brea (92821) ***(P-20265)***

Brooker Associates ....D....949 559-4877
16372 Cnstr Cir E 5 Irvine (92618) ***(P-354)***

Brookfeld Sthland Holdings LLC ....C....714 427-6868
3200 Park Center Dr # 1000 Costa Mesa (92626) ***(P-595)***

Brookfield Residential, Costa Mesa *Also called Brookfeld Sthland Holdings LLC* ***(P-595)***

Brooksamerica Mortgage Corp ....E....714 429-4500
2 Ada Ste 100 Irvine (92618) ***(P-15178)***

Brookside Golf Course, Pasadena *Also called City of Pasadena* ***(P-19477)***

Brothers Desserts, Santa Ana *Also called Brothers Intl Desserts* ***(P-1811)***

Brothers Intl Desserts (PA) ....**C....949 655-0080**
3400 W Segerstrom Ave Santa Ana (92704) ***(P-1811)***

Brothers Machine & Tool Inc ....E....951 361-9454
11095 Inland Ave Jurupa Valley (91752) ***(P-7756)***

Brothers Machine & Tool Inc (PA) ....**F....951 361-2909**
11098 Inland Ave Jurupa Valley (91752) ***(P-7757)***

Brothers of Industry Inc ....F....805 628-3545
3891 N Ventura Ave Ste B1 Ventura (93001) ***(P-11641)***

Brotman Medical Center Inc ....B....310 836-7000
3828 Delmas Ter Culver City (90232) ***(P-20690)***

Brouwerij West ....F....908 391-2599
110 E 22nd St San Pedro (90731) ***(P-2140)***

Brower Hale, Laguna Hills *Also called Valley Insurance Service Inc* ***(P-15643)***

Brown and Streza LLP ....D....949 453-2900
40 Pacifica Ste 1500 Irvine (92618) ***(P-23180)***

Brown Armstrong Accntancy Corp ....D....661 324-4971
4200 Truxtun Ave Ste 300 Bakersfield (93309) ***(P-22763)***

Brown Armstrong Cpas, Bakersfield *Also called Brown Armstrong Accntancy Corp* ***(P-22763)***

Brown Hnycutt Truss Systems In ....E....760 244-8887
16775 Smoke Tree St Hesperia (92345) ***(P-3356)***

Brown-Pacific Inc ....E....562 921-3471
13639 Bora Dr Santa Fe Springs (90670) ***(P-6189)***

Brownco Construction Co Inc ....D....714 935-9600
1000 E Katella Ave Anaheim (92805) ***(P-596)***

Browning Apartments ....E....213 252-8847
1104 Browning Blvd Los Angeles (90037) ***(P-15720)***

Browntrout Publishers Inc (PA) ....**E....424 290-6122**
201 Continental Blvd # 200 El Segundo (90245) ***(P-4158)***

Brownwood Furniture Inc ....C....909 945-5613
9805 6th St Ste 104 Rancho Cucamonga (91730) ***(P-3466)***

Bruce Iversen ....F....310 537-4168
11734 Grande Vista Dr Whittier (90601) ***(P-3382)***

Bruck Lighting Systems, Irvine *Also called Ledra Brands Inc* ***(P-13176)***

Bruckheimer, Jerry Films, Santa Monica *Also called Jerry Bruckheimer Inc* ***(P-19137)***

Brud Inc ....F....310 806-2283
837 N Spring St Ste 101 Los Angeles (90012) ***(P-4159)***

Bruin Biometrics LLC ....F....310 268-9494
10877 Wilshire Blvd # 1600 Los Angeles (90024) ***(P-10954)***

Brunswick Cal Oaks Bowl, Murrieta *Also called Bowlero Corp* ***(P-19394)***

Brunswick Classic Lanes, Norco *Also called Bowlero Corp* ***(P-19391)***

Brunswick Covino Lanes, Covina *Also called Bowlero Corp* ***(P-19387)***

Brunswick Deer Creks Lnes 213, Rancho Cucamonga *Also called Bowlero Corp* ***(P-19393)***

Brunswick Foothill Lanes, Fontana *Also called Bowlero Corp* ***(P-19395)***

Brunswick Moreno Valley Lanes, Moreno Valley *Also called Bowlero Corp* ***(P-19389)***

Brunton Enterprises Inc ....C....562 945-0013
8815 Sorensen Ave Santa Fe Springs (90670) ***(P-6593)***

Brusco Tug & Barge Inc ....C....805 986-1600
170 E Port Hueneme Rd Port Hueneme (93041) ***(P-12295)***

Brush Research Mfg Co ....C....323 261-2193
4642 Floral Dr Los Angeles (90022) ***(P-11508)***

Bryan Press Inc ....F....626 961-9257
1011 S Stimson Ave City of Industry (91745) ***(P-4241)***

Bryant Fuel Systems LLC ....E....661 334-5462
1300 32nd St Bakersfield (93301) ***(P-6731)***

Bryant Ranch Prepack ....E....818 764-7225
1919 N Victory Pl Burbank (91504) ***(P-14235)***

Bryant Rubber Corp (PA) ....**E....310 530-2530**
1580 W Carson St Long Beach (90810) ***(P-5328)***

Bryant Rubber Corp ....C....310 530-2530
1083 W 251st St Bellflower (90706) ***(P-5329)***

Brybradan Inc ....F....323 230-8604
3016 N Alameda St Compton (90222) ***(P-11642)***

Brymax Construction Svcs Inc ....D....949 200-9619
7436 Lorge Cir Huntington Beach (92647) ***(P-1040)***

Bsh Home Appliances Corp (HQ) ....**C....949 440-7100**
1901 Main St Ste 600 Irvine (92614) ***(P-18953)***

BSI Financial Services, Irvine *Also called Servis One Inc* ***(P-15253)***

Bsnap LLC ....D....657 269-4410
4 Hutton Centre Dr Fl 10 Santa Ana (92707) ***(P-15179)***

Bsst LLC ....C....626 593-4500
5462 Irwindale Ave Ste A Irwindale (91706) ***(P-10023)***

BT Americas Inc ....D....646 487-7400
2160 E Grand Ave El Segundo (90245) ***(P-13705)***

BT Baking ....F....213 880-9828
8702 Valley Blvd Rosemead (91770) ***(P-1986)***

BT Infonet, El Segundo *Also called Infonet Services Corporation* ***(P-12651)***

BT Screw Products, Los Angeles *Also called Crellin Machine Company* ***(P-7034)***

Btc Laboratories Inc ....D....805 656-6074
1868 Palma Dr Ventura (93003) ***(P-22933)***

Bti Aerospace & Electronics ....E....909 465-1569
13546 Vintage Pl Chino (91710) ***(P-8532)***

Bti Wireless, La Mirada *Also called Bravo Tech Inc* ***(P-12596)***

Btrade LLC ....E....818 334-4433
701 N Brand Blvd Ste 205 Glendale (91203) ***(P-17808)***

Bu LLC ....F....951 277-7470
9073 Pulsar Ct Ste A Corona (92883) ***(P-2141)***

Bu Ru LLC ....F....424 316-2878
826 E 3rd St Los Angeles (90013) ***(P-2926)***

Buchanan Street Partners LP ....D....949 721-1414
3501 Jamboree Rd Ste 4200 Newport Beach (92660) ***(P-15793)***

Buchbinder, Jay Industries, Compton *Also called Jbi LLC* ***(P-3529)***

Buckeye Check Cashing Inc ....D....909 792-8816
1615 W Redlands Blvd Redlands (92373) ***(P-15123)***

Bucy Die Casting ....F....818 843-5044
4122 W Burbank Blvd Burbank (91505) ***(P-7783)***

Bud Wil Inc ....E....714 630-1242
3224 E Radcliffe Ave Anaheim (92806) ***(P-5494)***

Buddhist Tzu CHI Foundation (PA) ....**D....909 447-7799**
1100 S Valley Center Ave San Dimas (91773) ***(P-22321)***

Buddy Bar Casting LLC ....C....562 861-9664
10801 Sessler St South Gate (90280) ***(P-6387)***

Budget Blinds LLC (HQ) ....**D....949 404-1100**
19000 Macarthur Blvd # 100 Irvine (92612) ***(P-18463)***

Budget Electrical Contrs Inc ....C....909 381-2646
25051 5th St San Bernardino (92410) ***(P-1225)***

Budget Industrial Unf Sup Inc ....D....310 532-7550
1702 W 134th St Gardena (90249) ***(P-16849)***

Buds Cotton Inc ....E....714 223-7800
1240 N Fee Ana St Anaheim (92807) ***(P-4996)***

Budway Enterprises Inc (PA) ....**D....909 463-0500**
13600 Napa St Fontana (92335) ***(P-12017)***

Budway Trucking & Warehousing, Fontana *Also called Budway Enterprises Inc* ***(P-12017)***

Buena Park Medical Group Inc (PA) ....**E....714 994-5290**
6301 Beach Blvd Ste 101 Buena Park (90621) ***(P-19726)***

Buena Park Tool & Engrg Inc ....F....714 843-6215
7661 Windfield Dr Huntington Beach (92647) ***(P-8533)***

Buena Ventura Care Center Inc (PA) ....**D....323 268-0106**
1016 S Record Ave Los Angeles (90023) ***(P-20266)***

Buena Ventura Care Center Inc ....D....818 247-4476
1505 Colby Dr Glendale (91205) ***(P-20566)***

Buena Vista Care Center, Santa Barbara *Also called Covenant Care California LLC* ***(P-20300)***
Buena Vista Food Products Inc (HQ) ....C....626 815-8859
823 W 8th St Azusa (91702) ***(P-14677)***
Buena Vista International Inc (HQ) ....E....818 560-1000
500 S Buena Vista St Burbank (91521) ***(P-19257)***
Buena Vista International Inc ....C....818 295-5200
350 S Buena Vista St Burbank (91521) ***(P-19104)***
Buena Vista Manor, Duarte *Also called Humangood Socal* ***(P-22116)***
Buena Vista Television (HQ) ....C....818 560-1878
500 S Buena Vista St Burbank (91521) ***(P-18406)***
Buena Vista TV Advg Sls, Burbank *Also called Buena Vista Television* ***(P-18406)***
Buenaventura 6, Ventura *Also called Weststar Cinemas Inc* ***(P-19292)***
Buenaventura Medical Group (PA) ....C....805 477-6000
888 S Hill Rd Ventura (93003) ***(P-19727)***
Buenaventura Medical Group ....D....805 477-6220
2601 E Main St Ste 104 Ventura (93003) ***(P-19728)***
Buff and Shine Mfg Inc ....E....310 886-5111
2139 E Del Amo Blvd Rancho Dominguez (90220) ***(P-6151)***
Buffalo Spot MGT Group LLC ....C....949 354-0884
7245 Garden Grove Blvd Garden Grove (92841) ***(P-22993)***
Buffalo Wild Wings, Beverly Hills *Also called BW Hotel LLC* ***(P-16361)***
Builders Fence Company Inc (PA) ....E....818 768-5500
8937 San Fernando Rd Sun Valley (91352) ***(P-13206)***
Building Elctronic Contrls Inc (PA) ....E....909 305-1600
2246 Lindsay Way Glendora (91740) ***(P-1226)***
Buildit Engineering Co Inc ....F....818 244-6666
3074 N Lima St Burbank (91504) ***(P-6304)***
Buk Optics Inc ....E....714 384-9620
3600 W Moore Ave Santa Ana (92704) ***(P-10827)***
Bulk Transportation (PA) ....D....909 594-2855
415 S Lemon Ave Walnut (91789) ***(P-12018)***
Bumble Bee Plastics Inc ....F....562 903-0833
10140 Shoemaker Ave Santa Fe Springs (90670) ***(P-5586)***
Bungalow 16 Entertainment LLC ....E....310 226-7870
8113 Melrose Ave Los Angeles (90046) ***(P-14126)***
Bunim-Murray Productions ....C....818 756-5100
1015 Grandview Ave Glendale (91201) ***(P-19105)***
Bunker Corp (PA) ....D....949 361-3935
1131 Via Callejon San Clemente (92673) ***(P-10024)***
Bunkerhill Indus Group Inc ....F....323 227-4222
4535 Huntington Dr S Los Angeles (90032) ***(P-2776)***
Bunzl Distribution Cal LLC (HQ) ....D....714 688-1900
3310 E Miraloma Ave Anaheim (92806) ***(P-14204)***
Bunzl Retail Services LLC ....D....909 476-2457
8449 Milliken Ave Ste 102 Rancho Cucamonga (91730) ***(P-14205)***
Burbank Airport Mariott Hotel, Burbank *Also called PHF II Burbank LLC* ***(P-16628)***
Burbank Dental Laboratory Inc ....C....818 841-2256
2101 Floyd St Burbank (91504) ***(P-21103)***
Burbank Emrgncy Med Group Inc ....D....818 506-5778
501 S Buena Vista St Burbank (91505) ***(P-19729)***
Burbank Leader, Glendale *Also called California Community News LLC* ***(P-3954)***
Burbank Partners LLC ....D....818 263-8704
15433 Ventura Blvd Sherman Oaks (91403) ***(P-16356)***
Burbank Plating Service Corp ....F....818 899-1157
13561 Desmond St Pacoima (91331) ***(P-7229)***
Burbank Steel Treating Inc ....E....818 842-0975
415 S Varney St Burbank (91502) ***(P-6434)***
Burbank Water & Power, Burbank *Also called City of Burbank* ***(P-12869)***
Burke Display Systems Inc ....F....949 248-0091
55 S Peak Laguna Niguel (92677) ***(P-3677)***
Burke Williams & Sorensen LLP (PA) ....D....213 236-0600
444 S Flower St Ste 2400 Los Angeles (90071) ***(P-21524)***
Burkshine Enterprises Inc (PA) ....D....661 399-4321
6404 Sierra Hills Ct Bakersfield (93308) ***(P-16900)***
Burlingame Industries Inc (PA) ....D....909 355-7000
3546 N Riverside Ave Rialto (92377) ***(P-16829)***
Burlingame Industries Inc ....D....909 887-7038
277 Lytle Creek Rd Lytle Creek (92358) ***(P-16830)***
Burlingame Industries Inc ....D....909 355-7000
2352 N Locust Ave Rialto (92377) ***(P-6178)***
Burlington Convalescent Hosp (PA) ....D....213 381-5585
845 S Burlington Ave Los Angeles (90057) ***(P-20267)***
Burlington Convalescent Hosp ....C....323 295-7737
3737 Don Felipe Dr Los Angeles (90008) ***(P-20268)***
Burlington Engineering Inc ....F....714 921-4045
220 W Grove Ave Orange (92865) ***(P-7230)***
Burlington Northern, Yorba Linda *Also called Bnsf Railway Company* ***(P-11794)***
Burnaby Intl Tech Corp ....D....888 930-2090
20955 Pathfinder Rd # 100 Diamond Bar (91765) ***(P-13618)***
Burnett & Son Meat Co Inc ....D....626 357-2165
1420 S Myrtle Ave Monrovia (91016) ***(P-1706)***
Burnett Fine Foods, Monrovia *Also called Burnett & Son Meat Co Inc* ***(P-1706)***
Burning Torch Inc ....E....323 733-7700
1738 Cordova St Los Angeles (90007) ***(P-2927)***
Burns & McDonnell Inc ....D....714 256-1595
140 S State College Blvd Brea (92821) ***(P-22505)***
Burns Environmental Services ....E....818 446-9869
19360 Rinaldi St Ste 381 Northridge (91326) ***(P-4958)***
Burrtec Waste Industries Inc (HQ) ....C....909 429-4200
9890 Cherry Ave Fontana (92335) ***(P-12933)***
Bursar's Office, Long Beach *Also called California State Univ Long Bch* ***(P-22766)***
Burt L Howe & Associates ....D....714 701-9180
5415 E La Palma Ave Anaheim (92807) ***(P-21525)***
Burtch Construction, Bakersfield *Also called Burtch Trucking Inc* ***(P-864)***
Burtch Trucking Inc ....D....661 399-1736
18815 Highway 65 Bakersfield (93308) ***(P-864)***
Burton James Inc ....D....626 961-7221
428 Turnbull Canyon Rd City of Industry (91745) ***(P-3496)***
Burton Way Hotels LLC ....D....310 273-2222
300 S Doheny Dr Los Angeles (90048) ***(P-16357)***
Burton Way Htels Ltd A Cal Ltd (PA) ....E....310 552-6623
2029 Century Park E # 2200 Los Angeles (90067) ***(P-16358)***
Burton-Way House Ltd A CA ....C....805 214-8075
2 Dole Dr Westlake Village (91362) ***(P-16359)***
Burton-Way House Ltd A CA ....C....310 273-2222
300 S Doheny Dr Los Angeles (90048) ***(P-16360)***
Burtree Inc ....E....818 786-4276
13513 Sherman Way Van Nuys (91405) ***(P-8534)***
Bus Services Corporation ....E....562 231-1770
6801 Suva St Bell Gardens (90201) ***(P-10025)***
Busa Servicing Inc (HQ) ....C....310 203-3400
787 W 5th St Los Angeles (90071) ***(P-15014)***
Bushman Products, Torrance *Also called Momentum Management LLC* ***(P-5394)***
Bushnell Industries Inc ....E....559 651-9039
7449 Avenue 304 Visalia (93291) ***(P-4959)***
Bushnell Ribbon Corporation ....E....562 948-1410
300 W Brookdale Pl Fullerton (92832) ***(P-11474)***
Business Department, Murrieta *Also called Southwest Healthcare Sys Aux* ***(P-20952)***
Business Information Systems, La Canada Flintridge *Also called Bis Computer Solutions Inc* ***(P-17565)***
Business Office, Irvine *Also called St Joseph Hospital of Orange* ***(P-20963)***
Buster and Punch Inc ....E....818 392-3827
10844 Burbank Blvd North Hollywood (91601) ***(P-13163)***
Buswest LLC (HQ) ....D....310 984-3900
21107 Chico St Carson (90745) ***(P-11905)***
Busy Bee LLC ....C....951 404-9900
36798 Pictor Ave Murrieta (92563) ***(P-17199)***
Busy Bee Tooling, Ontario *Also called Philips Tool & Die Inc* ***(P-7823)***
Butier Engineering Inc ....D....714 832-7222
17822 17th St Ste 404 Tustin (92780) ***(P-22994)***
Butler Inc ....F....310 323-3114
2140 S Dupont Dr Anaheim (92806) ***(P-7059)***
Butler America LLC (HQ) ....A....805 880-1965
3820 State St Ste B Santa Barbara (93105) ***(P-22506)***
Butler America Holdings Inc ....C....951 563-0020
12625 Frederick St Ste E2 Moreno Valley (92553) ***(P-17399)***
Butler America Holdings Inc (PA) ....C....805 880-1978
3820 State St Ste B Santa Barbara (93105) ***(P-17400)***
Butler America Holdings Inc ....C....909 417-3660
8647 Haven Ave Ste 100 Rancho Cucamonga (91730) ***(P-17401)***
Butler Home Products LLC ....C....909 476-3884
9409 Buffalo Ave Rancho Cucamonga (91730) ***(P-11509)***
Butler International Inc (PA) ....C....805 882-2200
3820 State St Ste A Santa Barbara (93105) ***(P-17402)***
Butler Manufacturing, Visalia *Also called Bluescope Buildings N Amer Inc* ***(P-6988)***
Butler Service Group Inc (HQ) ....D....201 891-5312
3820 State St Ste A Santa Barbara (93105) ***(P-17487)***
Buttonwillow Warehouse Co Inc (HQ) ....D....661 695-6500
3430 Unicorn Rd Bakersfield (93308) ***(P-14857)***
Buttonwood Farm Winery Inc ....F....805 688-3032
1500 Alamo Pintado Rd Solvang (93463) ***(P-2169)***
Buy Fresh Produce Inc ....D....323 796-0127
6636 E 26th St Commerce (90040) ***(P-14616)***
Buy Insta Slim Inc ....F....949 263-2301
17831 Sky Park Cir Ste C Irvine (92614) ***(P-2777)***
Buyers Consultation Svc Inc (PA) ....D....818 341-4820
8735 Remmet Ave Canoga Park (91304) ***(P-13706)***
BV General Inc ....C....323 651-0043
619 N Fairfax Ave Los Angeles (90036) ***(P-20567)***
BV Wilms, Indio *Also called M F G Eurotec Inc* ***(P-3477)***
Bvs Entertainment Inc (HQ) ....E....818 460-6917
500 S Buena Vista St Burbank (91521) ***(P-19106)***
BW Hotel LLC ....A....310 275-5200
9500 Wilshire Blvd Beverly Hills (90212) ***(P-16361)***
Bwf Banducci Inc ....F....661 302-6625
321 Industrial St Bakersfield (93307) ***(P-5153)***
Bwr An Oglvy Pub Rltons Wrldw (HQ) ....E....310 550-7776
9100 Wlshire Blvd Ste 500 Los Angeles (90036) ***(P-23377)***
Bwr Public Relations ....D....310 248-6100
9100 Wilshire Blvd # 500 Beverly Hills (90212) ***(P-23378)***
By The Blue Sea LLC ....B....310 458-0030
1 Pico Blvd Santa Monica (90405) ***(P-16362)***
Byd Energy LLC ....E....661 949-2918
1800 S Figueroa St Los Angeles (90015) ***(P-9821)***
Byd Motors LLC (HQ) ....E....213 748-3980
1800 S Figueroa St Los Angeles (90015) ***(P-10026)***
Byer California ....D....323 780-7615
1201 Rio Vista Ave Los Angeles (90023) ***(P-2627)***
Byrd Harvest Inc ....D....805 343-1608
192 Guadalupe St Guadalupe (93434) ***(P-151)***
Byrd Produce, Guadalupe *Also called Byrd Harvest Inc* ***(P-151)***
Byrnes & Kiefer Co ....D....714 554-4000
501 Airpark Dr Fullerton (92833) ***(P-2312)***
Byrnes W J & Co of Los Angeles ....D....310 615-2325
615 N Nash St El Segundo (90245) ***(P-12425)***
Bz Upland Bowl, Upland *Also called Bowlero Corp* ***(P-19390)***
C & A Transducers Inc ....F....714 554-9188
14329 Commerce Dr Garden Grove (92843) ***(P-9684)***
C & B Delivery Services ....D....909 623-4708
230 Diamond St Laguna Beach (92651) ***(P-12186)***
C & C Boats Inc ....E....714 969-0900
2124 Main St Ste 145 Huntington Beach (92648) ***(P-12298)***
C & C Die Engraving ....E....562 944-3399
12510 Mccann Dr Santa Fe Springs (90670) ***(P-8535)***
C & C Signs, Long Beach *Also called Canzone and Company* ***(P-11532)***
C & D Precision Components Inc ....E....626 799-7109
969 S Raymond Ave Pasadena (91105) ***(P-8536)***

ALPHABETIC

Employee Codes: A=Over 500 employees, B=251-500
C=101-250, D=51-100, E=20-50 F=10-19
2022 Southern California Business
Directory and Buyers Guide
© Mergent Inc. 1-800-342-5647
1079

C & F Foods Inc ... B ... 626 723-1000
12400 Wilshire Blvd # 1180 Los Angeles (90025) ***(P-2401)***
C & G Mercury Plastics, Sylmar *Also called C & G Plastics* ***(P-5587)***
C & G Plastics ... E ... 818 837-3773
12729 Foothill Blvd Sylmar (91342) ***(P-5587)***
C & H Letterpress Inc ... F ... 714 438-1350
3400 W Castor St Santa Ana (92704) ***(P-4242)***
C & H Meat Company, Vernon *Also called Eastland Corporation* ***(P-14593)***
C & H Testing Service Inc (PA) ... **E ... 661 589-4030**
6224 Price Way Bakersfield (93308) ***(P-482)***
C & J Industries, Santa Fe Springs *Also called Custom Steel Fabrication Inc* ***(P-6611)***
C & J Metal Prducts, Paramount *Also called Jeffrey Fabrication LLC* ***(P-6857)***
C & J Metal Products Inc ... E ... 562 634-3101
6323 Alondra Blvd Paramount (90723) ***(P-6799)***
C & L Graphics Inc ... F ... 818 785-8310
6825 Valjean Ave Van Nuys (91406) ***(P-4243)***
C & L Refrigeration Corp ... C ... 800 901-4822
4111 N Palm St Fullerton (92835) ***(P-1041)***
C & M Spring Engrg Co Inc ... E ... 909 597-2030
5244 Las Flores Dr Chino (91710) ***(P-7484)***
C & M Wood Industries ... E ... 760 949-3292
17229 Lemon St Ste D Hesperia (92345) ***(P-3707)***
C & R Extrusions ... F ... 626 642-0244
2618 River Ave Rosemead (91770) ***(P-5428)***
C & R Molds Inc ... E ... 805 658-7098
2737 Palma Dr Ventura (93003) ***(P-5588)***
C & S Assembly Inc ... D ... 866 779-8939
1150 N Armando St Anaheim (92806) ***(P-9685)***
C & S Plastics ... F ... 818 896-2489
12621 Foothill Blvd Sylmar (91342) ***(P-5589)***
C A A, Los Angeles *Also called Creative Artsts Agcy Hldngs LL* ***(P-19308)***
C A Buchen Corp ... E ... 818 767-5408
9231 Glenoaks Blvd Sun Valley (91352) ***(P-6594)***
C A C, Goleta *Also called Community Action Comm Snta BRB* ***(P-22176)***
C A L M, Santa Barbara *Also called Child Abuse Lstening Mediation* ***(P-21736)***
C A Rasmussen Inc (PA) ... **E ... 661 367-9040**
28548 Livingston Ave Valencia (91355) ***(P-990)***
C A Schroeder Inc (PA) ... **E ... 818 365-9561**
1318 1st St San Fernando (91340) ***(P-6169)***
C B Coast Newport Properties ... A ... 949 644-1600
840 Nwport Ctr Dr Ste 100 Newport Beach (92660) ***(P-15794)***
C B Richard Ellis Inc (HQ) ... **C ... 818 737-1200**
8521 Fallbrook Ave # 150 West Hills (91304) ***(P-16250)***
C B Sheets Inc ... E ... 562 921-1223
13901 Carmenita Rd Santa Fe Springs (90670) ***(P-3790)***
C Brent Peeke DDS Inc (PA) ... **D ... 951 845-4685**
264 N Hghland Sprng Ave S Banning (92220) ***(P-20171)***
C Brewer Company, Ontario *Also called Balda C Brewer Inc* ***(P-5574)***
C C Graber Co ... E ... 909 983-1761
315 E 4th St Ontario (91764) ***(P-68)***
C C H S Inc ... D ... 562 494-5188
1880 Dawson Ave Signal Hill (90755) ***(P-22995)***
C C I, Orange *Also called Coastal Component Inds Inc* ***(P-9694)***
C C I ... E ... 910 616-7426
22591 Avenida Empresa Rcho STA Marg (92688) ***(P-7439)***
C C I Redlands Inc ... E ... 909 307-6500
721 Nevada St Ste 308 Redlands (92373) ***(P-10485)***
C C M D Inc ... E ... 310 673-5532
700 Centinela Ave Inglewood (90302) ***(P-7231)***
C C S, Los Angeles *Also called Creative Channel Services LLC* ***(P-23199)***
C D C, Costa Mesa *Also called Creative Design Consultants* ***(P-18496)***
C D Lyon Construction Inc (PA) ... **D ... 805 653-0173**
380 W Stanley Ave Ventura (93001) ***(P-22507)***
C D R, Oxnard *Also called Child Dev Rsrces of Vntura CNT* ***(P-21739)***
C D R Enterprises Inc ... D ... 661 940-0344
42302 8th St E Lancaster (93535) ***(P-1368)***
C D S, Canyon Country *Also called Commercial Display Systems LLC* ***(P-8332)***
C D Video, Santa Ana *Also called CD Video Manufacturing Inc* ***(P-9834)***
C E D, Orange *Also called County Whl Elc Co Los Angeles* ***(P-13621)***
C E T, Gardena *Also called Charles E Thomas Company Inc* ***(P-751)***
C F I, Los Angeles *Also called Commodity Forwarders Inc* ***(P-12438)***
C F W Research & Dev Co ... F ... 805 489-8750
338 S 4th St Grover Beach (93433) ***(P-6298)***
C F X, Carson *Also called City Fashion Express Inc* ***(P-12435)***
C G Motor Sports Inc ... F ... 909 628-1440
5150 Eucalyptus Ave Ste A Chino (91710) ***(P-5590)***
C I Container Line, Monterey Park *Also called Carmichael International Svc* ***(P-12429)***
C I Design, Lake Forest *Also called Commercial Indus Design Co Inc* ***(P-13382)***
C I G A, Glendale *Also called Califrnia Insur Guarantee Assn* ***(P-15547)***
C J Foods, Los Angeles *Also called CJ America Inc* ***(P-14682)***
C J Instruments Inc ... E ... 818 996-4131
P.O. Box 570430 Tarzana (91357) ***(P-10874)***
C J Ritchie Farms ... D ... 559 625-1114
11878 Avenue 328 Visalia (93291) ***(P-1)***
C L A, Van Nuys *Also called Clay Lacy Aviation Inc* ***(P-12349)***
C L E, Downey *Also called Can Lines Engineering Inc* ***(P-8065)***
C M Automotive Systems Inc (PA) ... **E ... 909 869-7912**
120 Commerce Way Walnut (91789) ***(P-8032)***
C M C, Ontario *Also called California Mfg Cabinetry Inc* ***(P-3641)***
C M G Inc ... E ... 323 780-8250
801 S Figueroa St Los Angeles (90017) ***(P-2928)***
C M I, Corona *Also called Corona Magnetics Inc* ***(P-9626)***
C Magazine, Santa Monica *Also called C Publishing LLC* ***(P-4160)***
C MBA Rn Inc ... D ... 661 395-1700
4801 Truxtun Ave Bakersfield (93309) ***(P-21145)***
C N C Machining Inc ... E ... 805 681-8855
510 S Fairview Ave Goleta (93117) ***(P-8537)***
C P Construction Co Inc ... E ... 909 981-1091
105 N Loma Pl Upland (91786) ***(P-939)***
C P I, Chatsworth *Also called Chatsworth Products Inc* ***(P-7551)***
C P S Express (HQ) ... **D ... 951 685-1041**
3401 Space Center Ct 711a Jurupa Valley (91752) ***(P-11959)***
C Preme Limited LLC ... F ... 310 355-0498
1250 E 223rd St Carson (90745) ***(P-11407)***
C Publishing LLC ... E ... 310 393-3800
1543 7th St Fl 2 Santa Monica (90401) ***(P-4160)***
C R A, Los Angeles *Also called Community Redevelopment Agency* ***(P-23430)***
C R Laurence Co Inc (HQ) ... **B ... 323 588-1281**
2503 E Vernon Ave Vernon (90058) ***(P-10027)***
C R M, Newport Beach *Also called Crm Co LLC* ***(P-5356)***
C R W Distributors Inc ... F ... 310 463-4577
1223 Wilshire Blvd # 153 Santa Monica (90403) ***(P-1729)***
C S C, Northridge *Also called Contemporary Services Corp* ***(P-18265)***
C S Dash Cover Inc ... F ... 562 790-8300
14020 Paramount Blvd Paramount (90723) ***(P-3169)***
C S I, Santa Ana *Also called Color Science Inc* ***(P-5121)***
C S I, Santa Fe Springs *Also called Csi Electrical Contractors Inc* ***(P-1240)***
C S S, Bakersfield *Also called Construction Specialty Svc Inc* ***(P-945)***
C S T, Thousand Oaks *Also called Custom Sensors & Tech Inc* ***(P-9699)***
C S Transport Inc ... D ... 760 666-5661
425 E Heber Rd Ste 200 Heber (92249) ***(P-11960)***
C Sanders Emblems LP ... F ... 800 336-7467
26370 Diamond Pl Unit 506 Santa Clarita (91350) ***(P-14917)***
C T I, Rancho Cucamonga *Also called Collection Technology Inc* ***(P-17107)***
C T L Printing Inds Inc ... E ... 714 635-2980
1741 W Lincoln Ave Ste A Anaheim (92801) ***(P-4490)***
C W Cole & Company Inc ... E ... 626 443-2473
2560 Rosemead Blvd South El Monte (91733) ***(P-9080)***
C W Driver Incorporated (PA) ... **D ... 626 351-8800**
468 N Rosemead Blvd Pasadena (91107) ***(P-748)***
C W Hotels Ltd ... C ... 310 395-9700
1740 Ocean Ave Santa Monica (90401) ***(P-16363)***
C&C Jewelry Mfg Inc ... D ... 213 623-6800
323 W 8th St Fl 4 Los Angeles (90014) ***(P-14127)***
C&C Metal Form & Tooling Inc ... F ... 562 861-9554
10654 Garfield Ave South Gate (90280) ***(P-7132)***
C&F Wire Products, Stanton *Also called Stecher Enterprises Inc* ***(P-7492)***
C&H Hydraulics Inc ... E ... 949 646-6230
1585 Monrovia Ave Newport Beach (92663) ***(P-10290)***
C&H Metal Products, Ontario *Also called Daaze Inc* ***(P-6815)***
C&J Well Services LLC ... A ... 661 589-5220
3752 Allen Rd Bakersfield (93314) ***(P-483)***
C&M Industries ... F ... 626 391-5102
4506 Maine Ave Ste D Baldwin Park (91706) ***(P-11643)***
C&O Manufacturing Company Inc ... D ... 562 692-7525
9640 Beverly Rd Pico Rivera (90660) ***(P-6800)***
C&R Maintance, Oxnard *Also called HE Julien & Associates Inc* ***(P-309)***
C&R Systems Inc (PA) ... **E ... 951 270-0255**
1835 Capital St Corona (92878) ***(P-1227)***
C&W Facility Services Inc ... C ... 805 267-7123
3011 Townsgate Rd Ste 410 Westlake Village (91361) ***(P-17221)***
C-Air International Inc ... D ... 310 695-3400
9841 Arprt Blvd Ste 1400 Los Angeles (90045) ***(P-12426)***
C-Cure, Ontario *Also called Western States Wholesale Inc* ***(P-6013)***
C-G Systems Inc ... E ... 714 632-8882
1470 N Hundley St Anaheim (92806) ***(P-1228)***
C-Guy Industries Inc (PA) ... **F ... 714 587-9575**
19611 Trident Ln Huntington Beach (92646) ***(P-11644)***
C-Pak Industries Inc ... E ... 909 880-6017
4925 Hallmark Pkwy San Bernardino (92407) ***(P-5591)***
C-Preme, Carson *Also called C Preme Limited LLC* ***(P-11407)***
C-Quest Inc ... E ... 323 980-1400
1439 S Herbert Ave Los Angeles (90023) ***(P-2839)***
C-Thru Sunrooms, Ontario *Also called Stell Industries Inc* ***(P-7008)***
C.E.G. Construction, Pico Rivera *Also called Chalmers Corporation* ***(P-692)***
C2 Imaging, Costa Mesa *Also called Crisp Enterprises Inc* ***(P-17147)***
C2 Publishing, Costa Mesa *Also called Chet Cooper* ***(P-4058)***
C4 Litho LLC ... F ... 714 259-1073
27020 Daisy Cir Yorba Linda (92887) ***(P-4244)***
Ca Inc ... D ... 310 670-6500
6100 Center Dr Ste 700 Los Angeles (90045) ***(P-18021)***
CA Arng 115th Rsg, Los Alamitos *Also called Military California Department* ***(P-23395)***
CA Department Development Svc, Cathedral City *Also called Developmental Svcs Cal Dept* ***(P-21420)***
CA Landscape and Design, Upland *Also called California Ldscp & Design Inc* ***(P-295)***
CA Oak Entps Bus Type Mktg, Los Angeles *Also called Certified Frnsic Lr Adtors LLC* ***(P-22769)***
CA Signs, Pacoima *Also called California Signs Inc* ***(P-11531)***
CA Station Management Inc ... C ... 909 245-6251
3200 E Guasti Rd Ste 100 Ontario (91761) ***(P-940)***
Ca'del Sole, Toluca Lake *Also called Tre Venezie Inc* ***(P-16981)***
Ca-WA Corp ... F ... 909 868-0630
1360 W 1st St Pomona (91766) ***(P-5368)***
Ca937 Afjrotc ... D ... 818 394-3600
12431 Roscoe Blvd Ste 300 Sun Valley (91352) ***(P-11645)***
Caa Sports LLC (HQ) ... **D ... 424 288-2000**
2000 Avenue Of The Stars # 100 Los Angeles (90067) ***(P-19412)***
Caballero & Sons Inc ... E ... 562 368-1644
5753 E Snta Ana Cyn Rd St Anaheim (92807) ***(P-15313)***
Cabazon Band Mission Indians ... A ... 760 342-5000
84245 Indio Springs Dr Indio (92203) ***(P-16364)***

Cabe Brothers D 562 595-7411
2895 Long Beach Blvd Long Beach (90806) ***(P-18815)***
Cabe Toyota, Long Beach *Also called Cabe Brothers* ***(P-18815)***
Cabinet & Millwork Installers, Agua Dulce *Also called Door & Hardware Installers Inc* ***(P-3245)***
Cabinet Factory Outlet F 714 635-9080
1141 W Katella Ave Orange (92867) ***(P-3308)***
Cabinet Home, El Monte *Also called Home Paradise LLC* ***(P-7150)***
Cabinet Master & Son Inc (PA) **F 323 727-9717**
5429 Via Corona St Los Angeles (90022) ***(P-3309)***
Cabinets 2000 LLC C 562 868-0909
11100 Firestone Blvd Norwalk (90650) ***(P-3310)***
Cabinets R US E 562 483-6886
1240 N Fee Ana St Anaheim (92807) ***(P-3311)***
Cable Aml Inc (PA) **F 310 222-5599**
2271 W 205th St Ste 101 Torrance (90501) ***(P-9259)***
Cable Devices Incorporated (HQ) **C 714 554-4370**
3008 S Croddy Way Santa Ana (92704) ***(P-8241)***
Cable Exchange, Santa Ana *Also called Cable Devices Incorporated* ***(P-8241)***
Cableco E 562 942-8076
13100 Firestone Blvd Santa Fe Springs (90670) ***(P-2712)***
Cabrac Inc E 818 834-0177
13250 Paxton St Pacoima (91331) ***(P-7133)***
Cabrillo Crdolgy Med Group Inc D 805 983-0922
2241 Wankel Way Ste C Oxnard (93030) ***(P-19730)***
Cac Inc E 949 587-3328
20322 Windrow Dr Ste 100 Lake Forest (92630) ***(P-9686)***
Cac Fabrication Inc F 818 882-2626
9710 Owensmouth Ave Ste C Chatsworth (91311) ***(P-6595)***
Cachcach, Santa Ana *Also called Funny-Bunny Inc* ***(P-2810)***
Cachet Financial Services D 626 578-9400
175 S Lake Ave Unit 200 Pasadena (91101) ***(P-22764)***
Cacho Landscape Maint Co Inc E 818 365-0773
711 Truman St San Fernando (91340) ***(P-293)***
Cacique Inc C 626 961-3399
14923 Proctor Ave La Puente (91746) ***(P-14536)***
Cacique Cheese, Monrovia *Also called Cacique Foods LLC* ***(P-1768)***
Cacique Foods LLC (PA) **C 626 961-3399**
800 Royal Oaks Dr Ste 200 Monrovia (91016) ***(P-1768)***
Caco-Pacific Corporation (PA) **C 626 331-3361**
813 N Cummings Rd Covina (91724) ***(P-7784)***
Cad Works Inc E 626 336-5491
16366 E Valley Blvd La Puente (91744) ***(P-8538)***
Cadence Aerospace, Anaheim *Also called Aerospace Parts Holdings Inc* ***(P-10253)***
Cadence Aerospace LLC (PA) **E 949 877-3630**
3150 E Miraloma Ave Anaheim (92806) ***(P-10291)***
Cadence Aerospace LLC E 425 353-0405
3130 E Miraloma Ave Anaheim (92806) ***(P-10292)***
Cadence Design Systems Inc E 949 788-6080
7505 Irvine Center Dr # 250 Irvine (92618) ***(P-17809)***
Cadence Gourmet LLC E 951 444-9269
155 Klug Cir Corona (92878) ***(P-2402)***
Cadence Gourmet Involve Foods, Corona *Also called Cadence Gourmet LLC* ***(P-2402)***
Cadillac Motor Div Area C 805 373-9575
30930 Russell Ranch Rd Westlake Village (91362) ***(P-9939)***
Cadillac Plating Inc E 714 639-0342
1147 W Struck Ave Orange (92867) ***(P-7232)***
Cadnchev Inc D 562 944-6422
13603 Foster Rd Santa Fe Springs (90670) ***(P-13123)***
Cadogan Tate Fine Art Lgstics (PA) **D 562 206-0191**
5233 Alcoa Ave Vernon (90058) ***(P-12108)***
Caduceus Physcans Med Group A D 714 646-8000
18200 Yorba Linda Blvd # 401 Yorba Linda (92886) ***(P-19731)***
Caer Inc E 415 879-9864
8070 Melrose Ave Los Angeles (90046) ***(P-1846)***
Caerus Marketing Group LLC D 877 627-2509
17875 Von Karman Ave # 200 Irvine (92614) ***(P-23181)***
Caesar and Seider Insur Svcs (PA) **D 805 682-2571**
40 E Alamar Ave Ste 4 Santa Barbara (93105) ***(P-15545)***
Caesar Hardware Intl Ltd E 800 306-3829
4985 Hallmark Pkwy San Bernardino (92407) ***(P-6508)***
Cafe Champagne, Temecula *Also called Thornton Winery* ***(P-2230)***
Cafvina Coffee & Tea, Orange *Also called Quoc Viet Foods* ***(P-14728)***
Cageco Inc E 800 605-4859
16225 Beaver Rd Adelanto (92301) ***(P-7608)***
Cahuilla Creek Casino, Anza *Also called Cahuilla Creek Rest & Casino* ***(P-19638)***
Cahuilla Creek Rest & Casino C 951 763-1200
52702 Us Highway 371 Anza (92539) ***(P-19638)***
Cai, Corona *Also called Combustion Associates Inc* ***(P-12797)***
Cai, Orange *Also called Califrnia Anlytical Instrs Inc* ***(P-10682)***
Cai Company, Brea *Also called California Automobile Insur Co* ***(P-15465)***
Caine & Weiner Company Inc (PA) **D 818 226-6000**
5805 Sepulvda Blvd # 400 Van Nuys (91411) ***(P-17105)***
Caitac Garment Processing Inc B 310 217-9888
14725 S Broadway Gardena (90248) ***(P-2657)***
Cake Collection LLC E 310 479-7783
2221 Barry Ave Fl 1 Los Angeles (90064) ***(P-14678)***
Cal Coast Acidizing Co D 805 934-2411
6226 Dominion Rd Santa Maria (93454) ***(P-484)***
Cal Coast Acidizing Service, Santa Maria *Also called Cal Coast Acidizing Co* ***(P-484)***
Cal Coffee Shop, Lakewood *Also called Nationwide Theatres Corp* ***(P-19404)***
Cal Empire Engineering Inc E 626 915-8030
628 E Edna Pl Covina (91723) ***(P-1610)***
Cal Flex, San Fernando *Also called California Flex Corporation* ***(P-5594)***
Cal Lift Inc D 562 566-1400
13027 Crossroads Pkwy S La Puente (91746) ***(P-13893)***
Cal Micro, Ontario *Also called Ruuhwa Dann and Associates Inc* ***(P-12972)***
Cal Mutual Inc D 888 700-4650
34077 Temecula Creek Rd Temecula (92592) ***(P-15180)***
Cal Pac Sheet Metal Inc E 714 979-2733
2720 S Main St Ste B Santa Ana (92707) ***(P-6801)***
Cal Pacific Dyeing & Finishing F 310 327-3792
233 E Gardena Blvd Gardena (90248) ***(P-2669)***
Cal Partitions Inc E 310 539-1911
23814 President Ave Harbor City (90710) ***(P-3678)***
Cal Pipe Manufacturing Inc (PA) **E 562 803-4388**
12160 Woodruff Ave Downey (90241) ***(P-7531)***
Cal Plate (PA) **D 562 403-3000**
17110 Jersey Ave Artesia (90701) ***(P-7917)***
Cal Poly Pomona Foundation Inc A 909 869-2284
3801 W Temple Ave # 116 Pomona (91768) ***(P-21992)***
Cal Portland Cement Co E 909 423-0436
695 S Rancho Ave Colton (92324) ***(P-6074)***
Cal Precision Inc F 951 273-9901
1720 S Bon View Ave Ontario (91761) ***(P-8539)***
Cal Quake Construction Inc E 323 931-2969
636 N Formosa Ave Los Angeles (90036) ***(P-485)***
Cal Select Builders Inc D 714 694-0203
23253 La Palma Ave Yorba Linda (92887) ***(P-749)***
Cal Simba Inc (PA) **E 805 240-1177**
1283 Flynn Rd Camarillo (93012) ***(P-11334)***
Cal Southern Assn Governments (PA) **C 213 236-1800**
900 Wilshire Blvd # 1700 Los Angeles (90017) ***(P-23422)***
Cal Southern Braiding Inc D 562 927-5531
7450 Scout Ave Bell Gardens (90201) ***(P-9687)***
Cal Southern Components Inc F 760 949-5144
9927 C Ave Hesperia (92345) ***(P-3357)***
Cal Southern Graphics Corp (PA) **D 310 559-3600**
8432 Steller Dr Culver City (90232) ***(P-4245)***
Cal Southern Packg Eqp Inc F 909 598-3198
4102 Valley Blvd Walnut (91789) ***(P-13894)***
Cal Southern Presbt Homes D 818 247-0420
516 Burchett St Glendale (91203) ***(P-15721)***
Cal Southern Services D 626 281-5942
419 Mcgroarty St San Gabriel (91776) ***(P-16850)***
Cal Southern United Food C 714 220-2297
6425 Katella Ave Cypress (90630) ***(P-15514)***
Cal Spas, Pomona *Also called California Acrylic Inds Inc* ***(P-11646)***
Cal Springs LLC D 562 943-5599
6250 N Irwindale Ave Irwindale (91702) ***(P-4491)***
Cal State La Univ Aux Svcs Inc A 323 343-2531
5151 State University Dr Ge314 Los Angeles (90032) ***(P-22996)***
Cal State Rubber, Santa Fe Springs *Also called Duro Roller Company Inc* ***(P-5373)***
Cal State Site Services E 800 499-5757
4518 Industrial St Simi Valley (93063) ***(P-6220)***
Cal Tape & Label, Anaheim *Also called C T L Printing Inds Inc* ***(P-4490)***
Cal Tech Emplyees Fderal Cr Un (PA) **D 818 952-4444**
528 Foothill Blvd La Canada Flintridge (91011) ***(P-15060)***
Cal Tech Precision Inc D 714 992-4130
1830 N Lemon St Anaheim (92801) ***(P-10293)***
Cal Treehouse Almonds LLC (PA) **C 559 757-5020**
6914 Road 160 Earlimart (93219) ***(P-2111)***
Cal Trend Automotive Products, Santa Ana *Also called Cal Trends Accessories LLC* ***(P-3192)***
Cal Trends Accessories LLC E 714 708-5115
2121 S Anne St Santa Ana (92704) ***(P-3192)***
Cal West Designs, Santa Fe Springs *Also called K S Designs Inc* ***(P-11564)***
Cal West Underground Inc D 951 371-6775
951 6th St Norco (92860) ***(P-991)***
Cal-Aurum Industries E 714 898-0996
15632 Container Ln Huntington Beach (92649) ***(P-7233)***
Cal-Coast Pkg & Crating Inc E 310 518-7215
2040 E 220th St Carson (90810) ***(P-3377)***
Cal-Draulics, Corona *Also called Johnson Caldraul Inc* ***(P-10361)***
Cal-India Foods International E 909 613-1660
13591 Yorba Ave Chino (91710) ***(P-5129)***
Cal-June Inc (PA) **D 323 877-4164**
5238 Vineland Ave North Hollywood (91601) ***(P-6509)***
Cal-Med Ambulance, South El Monte *Also called California Med Response Inc* ***(P-11856)***
Cal-Mold Incorporated E 951 361-6400
3900 Hamner Ave Eastvale (91752) ***(P-5592)***
Cal-Monarch, Corona *Also called California Wire Products Corp* ***(P-7496)***
Cal-Organic Farms, Lamont *Also called Grimmway Enterprises Inc* ***(P-14637)***
Cal-Pac Chemical Co Inc F 323 585-2178
6231 Maywood Ave Huntington Park (90255) ***(P-4651)***
Cal-Sensors Inc (PA) **E 707 303-3837**
1260 Calle Suerte Camarillo (93012) ***(P-10575)***
Cal-State Auto Parts Inc (PA) **C 714 630-5950**
1361 N Red Gum St Anaheim (92806) ***(P-13049)***
Cal-Tron Corporation E 760 873-8491
2290 Dixon Ln Bishop (93514) ***(P-5593)***
Cal-Tron Plating Inc E 562 945-1181
11919 Rivera Rd Santa Fe Springs (90670) ***(P-7234)***
Cal-West Nurseries Inc C 951 270-0667
138 North Dr Norco (92860) ***(P-294)***
Cal/Pac Pntngs Ctngs Acqstion D 714 628-1514
608 N Eckhoff St Orange (92868) ***(P-1172)***
Cala Action Inc E 213 272-9759
2440 Troy Ave South El Monte (91733) ***(P-2561)***
Calabasas Country Club, Calabasas *Also called Knight-Calabasas LLC* ***(P-19573)***
Calabasas Memory Care Cmnty, Calabasas *Also called Silverado Senior Living Inc* ***(P-20474)***
Calabasas Tms Center E 805 261-0824
2950 Sycamore Dr Simi Valley (93065) ***(P-6190)***

Employee Codes: A=Over 500 employees, B=251-500 C=101-250, D=51-100, E=20-50 F=10-19
2022 Southern California Business Directory and Buyers Guide
© Mergent Inc. 1-800-342-5647
1081

Calamp Corp (PA).....B.....949 600-5600
15635 Alton Pkwy Ste 250 Irvine (92618) *(P-9260)*

Calance, Anaheim *Also called Partners Information Tech (P-18209)*

Calatlantic Group Inc.....D.....310 821-9843
13200 Fiji Way Marina Del Rey (90292) *(P-597)*

Calavo Foods, Santa Paula *Also called Calavo Growers Inc (P-12555)*

Calavo Growers Inc (PA).....A.....805 525-1245
1141 Cummings Rd Ste A Santa Paula (93060) *(P-2403)*

Calavo Growers Inc.....D.....805 525-5511
15765 W Telegraph Rd Santa Paula (93060) *(P-12555)*

Calbond, Downey *Also called Calpipe Industries LLC (P-13555)*

Calcareous Vineyard LLC.....F.....805 239-0289
3430 Peachy Canyon Rd Paso Robles (93446) *(P-2170)*

Calcon Steel Construction Inc.....F.....310 768-8094
1226 W 196th St Torrance (90502) *(P-6596)*

Calcraft Company, Rialto *Also called Calcraft Corporation (P-6597)*

Calcraft Corporation.....F.....909 879-2900
1426 S Willow Ave Rialto (92376) *(P-6597)*

Caldera Medical Inc.....D.....818 879-6555
4360 Park Terrace Dr # 140 Westlake Village (91361) *(P-10955)*

Calderon Drywall Contrs Inc (PA).....D.....714 900-1863
2085 N Nordic St Orange (92865) *(P-1644)*

Caldesso LLC.....D.....909 888-2882
439 S Stoddard Ave San Bernardino (92401) *(P-8085)*

Caldigit Inc.....F.....714 572-6668
1941 E Miraloma Ave Ste B Placentia (92870) *(P-8189)*

Caldyn, Los Angeles *Also called California Dynamics Corp (P-10875)*

Caleb Technology Corporation.....F.....310 257-4780
2905 Lomita Blvd Torrance (90505) *(P-9808)*

Calenergy LLC.....B.....402 231-1527
7030 Gentry Rd Calipatria (92233) *(P-1229)*

Calex Engineering Inc.....D.....661 254-1866
23651 Pine St Newhall (91321) *(P-1592)*

Calex Engineering Co., Newhall *Also called Calex Engineering Inc (P-1592)*

Calgren Renewable Fuels, Pixley *Also called Gfp Ethanol LLC (P-5137)*

Calhoun & Poxon Company Inc.....F.....323 225-2328
5330 Alhambra Ave Los Angeles (90032) *(P-8889)*

Cali Chem Inc.....E.....714 265-3740
14271 Corporate Dr Ste B Garden Grove (92843) *(P-4997)*

Cali Food Company Inc.....E.....714 821-8630
8258 Saigon Pl Garden Grove (92844) *(P-1847)*

Cali Framing Supplies LLC.....E.....818 899-7777
20450 Plummer St Chatsworth (91311) *(P-19026)*

Cali-Fame Los Angeles Inc.....D.....310 747-5263
20934 S Santa Fe Ave Carson (90810) *(P-3025)*

Caliber Bodyworks Texas Inc.....D.....714 665-3905
5 Auto Center Dr Tustin (92782) *(P-18784)*

Caliber Collision Centers, Tustin *Also called Caliber Bodyworks Texas Inc (P-18784)*

Caliber Holdings Corporation.....D.....323 913-4000
3020 Riverside Dr Los Angeles (90039) *(P-18785)*

Caliber Sealing Solutions Inc (PA).....F.....949 461-0555
2780 Palisades Dr Corona (92882) *(P-5330)*

Calibre International LLC (PA).....C.....626 969-4660
6250 N Irwindale Ave Irwindale (91702) *(P-23379)*

Calico Brands Inc.....E.....909 930-5000
2055 S Haven Ave Ontario (91761) *(P-14918)*

Calico Building Services Inc.....C.....949 380-8707
15550 Rockfield Blvd C Irvine (92618) *(P-17222)*

Calidad Inc.....E.....909 947-3937
1730 S Balboa Ave Ontario (91761) *(P-6388)*

Calient Technologies Inc (PA).....E.....805 695-4800
25 Castilian Dr Goleta (93117) *(P-9228)*

Caliente Farms, Delano *Also called M Caratan Disc Inc (P-49)*

Califia Farms LLC (PA).....E.....213 694-4667
1321 Palmetto St Los Angeles (90013) *(P-14537)*

California Access Scaffold LLC.....D.....310 324-3388
331 Vineland Ave City of Industry (91746) *(P-1645)*

California Acrylic Inds Inc (HQ).....B.....909 623-8781
1462 E 9th St Pomona (91766) *(P-11646)*

California Acti, Irvine *Also called Acti Corporation Inc (P-9155)*

California Air Conveying Corp.....F.....562 531-4570
16260 Minnesota Ave Paramount (90723) *(P-1622)*

California Amforge Corporation.....C.....626 334-4931
750 N Vernon Ave Azusa (91702) *(P-6191)*

California Apparel News, Los Angeles *Also called Apparel News Group (P-4052)*

California Art Products Co, North Hollywood *Also called Capco/Psa (P-5599)*

California Assn Realtors Inc (PA).....C.....213 739-8200
525 S Virgil Ave Los Angeles (90020) *(P-22243)*

California Automobile Insur Co (HQ).....D.....714 232-8669
555 W Imperial Hwy Brea (92821) *(P-15465)*

California Basic, Santa Fe Springs *Also called Mias Fashion Mfg Co Inc (P-14400)*

California Bio-Productex Inc.....E.....559 582-5308
13220 Crown Ave Hanford (93230) *(P-5130)*

CALIFORNIA BOTANIC GARDEN, Claremont *Also called Rancho Santa Ana Botanic Grdn (P-22240)*

California Box II.....E.....909 944-9202
8949 Toronto Ave Rancho Cucamonga (91730) *(P-3791)*

California Broadcast Ctr LLC.....C.....310 233-2425
3800 Via Oro Ave Long Beach (90810) *(P-12752)*

California Business Bureau Inc (PA).....C.....626 303-1515
1711 S Mountain Ave Monrovia (91016) *(P-22765)*

California Candy, South El Monte *Also called California Snack Foods Inc (P-2082)*

California Carbon Company Inc.....E.....562 436-1962
2825 E Grant St Wilmington (90744) *(P-4652)*

California Cartage Company Inc.....D.....888 537-1432
2902 E Val Verde Ct Compton (90221) *(P-12187)*

California Cascade Fontana, Fontana *Also called Fontana Wood Treating Inc (P-3432)*

California Chemical, Costa Mesa *Also called Durrani Investments Corp (P-14778)*

California Childrens Academy.....C.....323 263-3846
233 N Breed St Los Angeles (90033) *(P-21993)*

California Choice, Orange *Also called Choic Admini Insur Servi (P-15550)*

California Churros Corporation.....C.....909 370-4777
751 Via Lata Colton (92324) *(P-1987)*

California Classics, Santa Clarita *Also called California Millworks Corp (P-3236)*

California Closet Co O (PA).....C.....714 899-4905
5921 Skylab Rd Huntington Beach (92647) *(P-1646)*

California Club.....C.....213 622-1391
538 S Flower St Los Angeles (90071) *(P-22322)*

California Cmnty Foundation (PA).....D.....213 413-4130
221 S Figueroa St Ste 400 Los Angeles (90012) *(P-16165)*

California Combining Corp.....E.....323 589-5727
5607 S Santa Fe Ave Vernon (90058) *(P-2706)*

California Coml Inv Group Inc.....E.....805 495-8400
4530 E Thousand Oaks Blvd Westlake Village (91362) *(P-23423)*

California Commerce Club Inc.....A.....323 721-2100
6131 Telegraph Rd Commerce (90040) *(P-16365)*

California Community News LLC.....D.....818 843-8700
221 N Brand Blvd Fl 2 Glendale (91203) *(P-3954)*

California Community News LLC (HQ).....B.....626 388-1017
2000 E 8th St Los Angeles (90021) *(P-3955)*

California Composite Cont Corp.....F.....951 940-9343
22770 Perry St Perris (92570) *(P-3833)*

California Composite Container, Perris *Also called Green Products Packaging Corp (P-3836)*

California Composites MGT Inc.....E.....714 258-0405
1935 E Occidental St Santa Ana (92705) *(P-10294)*

California Concrete Rdymx Inc (PA).....E.....714 401-4382
2715 E Mayfair Ave Orange (92867) *(P-6075)*

California Convalescent Center, Los Angeles *Also called Bonnie Brae Cnvlscent Hosp Inc (P-20563)*

California Convalescent Hosp.....D.....305 682-1355
2225 De La Vina St Santa Barbara (93105) *(P-20269)*

California Costume Int'l, Los Angeles *Also called Califrnia Cstume Cllctions Inc (P-3068)*

California Country Club.....D.....626 333-4571
1509 Workman Mill Rd City of Industry (90601) *(P-19551)*

California Credit Union (PA).....C.....818 291-6700
701 N Brand Blvd Fl 7 Glendale (91203) *(P-15107)*

California Credits Group LLC.....E.....626 584-9800
87 N Raymond Ave Ste 526 Pasadena (91103) *(P-18464)*

California Cryobank LLC (PA).....D.....310 496-5691
11915 La Grange Ave Los Angeles (90025) *(P-21395)*

California Cstm Frt & Flavors, Irwindale *Also called Califrnia Cstm Frits Flvors In (P-2313)*

California Dairies Inc (PA).....D.....559 625-2200
2000 N Plaza Dr Visalia (93291) *(P-1832)*

California Dairies Inc.....C.....559 752-5200
11894 Avenue 120 Pixley (93256) *(P-14538)*

California Dairy Distributors (PA).....D.....661 948-0829
43861 Sierra Hwy Lancaster (93534) *(P-14539)*

California Decor.....F.....310 603-9944
541 E Pine St Compton (90222) *(P-3235)*

California Department Trnsp.....D.....562 692-0823
1940 Workman Mill Rd Whittier (90601) *(P-865)*

California Department Trnsp.....D.....805 922-1987
2201 S Thornburg St Santa Maria (93455) *(P-866)*

California Department Trnsp.....D.....805 434-1812
640 N Main St Templeton (93465) *(P-867)*

California Department Trnsp.....D.....760 352-1129
1607 Adams Ave El Centro (92243) *(P-868)*

California Dept of Pub Hlth.....D.....714 567-2906
681 S Parker St Ste 200 Orange (92868) *(P-20270)*

California Die Casting Inc.....E.....909 947-9947
1820 S Grove Ave Ontario (91761) *(P-6375)*

California Digital Inc (PA).....D.....310 217-0500
6 Saddleback Rd Rolling Hills (90274) *(P-8242)*

California Dynamics Corp (PA).....E.....323 223-3882
5572 Alhambra Ave Los Angeles (90032) *(P-10875)*

CALIFORNIA DYNASTY, Los Angeles *Also called MGT Industries Inc (P-2973)*

California Economizer.....E.....714 898-9963
5622 Engineer Dr Huntington Beach (92649) *(P-8945)*

California Electric Supply, Anaheim *Also called Ced Anaheim 018 (P-9859)*

California Endowment (PA).....D.....213 928-8800
1000 N Alameda St Los Angeles (90012) *(P-22175)*

California Exotic Novlt LLC.....D.....909 606-1950
1455 E Francis St Ontario (91761) *(P-11647)*

California Expanded Met Pdts (PA).....D.....626 369-3564
13191 Crssrads Pkwy N Ste City of Industry (91746) *(P-6802)*

California Fair Plan Assn.....D.....213 487-0111
725 S Figueroa St # 3900 Los Angeles (90017) *(P-15546)*

California Faucets Inc.....E.....657 400-1639
5231 Argosy Ave Huntington Beach (92649) *(P-6554)*

California Faucets Inc (PA).....E.....714 890-0450
5271 Argosy Ave Huntington Beach (92649) *(P-6555)*

California Field Ironwrkrs, San Bernardino *Also called Iron Workers Local 433 (P-16178)*

California Flex Corporation (PA).....D.....818 361-1169
1318 1st St San Fernando (91340) *(P-5594)*

California Flexrake Corp.....E.....626 443-4026
9620 Gidley St Temple City (91780) *(P-6474)*

California Friends Homes.....B.....714 530-9100
12151 Dale Ave Stanton (90680) *(P-22088)*

California Gasket and Rbr Corp (PA).....E.....310 323-4250
533 W Collins Ave Orange (92867) *(P-5369)*

California Gate Entry Systems, Anaheim *Also called C-G Systems Inc (P-1228)*

California Glass & Mirror Div, Santa Ana *Also called Twed-Dells Inc (P-5971)*

California Heart Associates.....D.....714 546-2238
18111 Brookhurst St # 5100 Fountain Valley (92708) *(P-19732)*

California Hydroforming Co Inc.....F.....626 912-0036
850 Lawson St City of Industry (91748) *(P-6803)*

California Imaging Nework, Los Angeles *Also called Oaks Diagnostics Inc* ***(P-20008)***
California Institute Tech ....A....818 354-9154
4800 Oak Grove Dr Pasadena (91109) ***(P-22901)***
California Insulated Wire & ....D....818 569-4930
3050 N California St Burbank (91504) ***(P-6345)***
California Interfill Inc ....F....951 351-2619
8178 Mar Vista Ct Riverside (92504) ***(P-4998)***
California Internet LP (PA) ....**D....805 225-4638**
251 Camarillo Ranch Rd Camarillo (93012) ***(P-12630)***
California Lab Sciences LLC ....B....562 758-6900
10200 Pioneer Blvd # 500 Santa Fe Springs (90670) ***(P-22934)***
California Ldscp & Design Inc ....C....909 949-1601
273 N Benson Ave Upland (91786) ***(P-295)***
California Linen Service, Pasadena *Also called Dy-Dee Service Pasadena Inc* ***(P-16889)***
California Machine Specialties, Chino *Also called Young Machine Inc* ***(P-8858)***
California Med Response Inc ....D....562 968-1818
1557 Santa Anita Ave South El Monte (91733) ***(P-11856)***
California Mentor, Bakersfield *Also called National Mentor Inc* ***(P-22134)***
California Metal & Supply Inc ....F....800 707-6061
10230 Freeman Ave Santa Fe Springs (90670) ***(P-6732)***
California Metal Processing Co ....E....323 753-2247
1518 W Slauson Ave # 1530 Los Angeles (90047) ***(P-7235)***
California Mfg Cabinetry Inc ....F....909 930-3632
1474 E Francis St Ontario (91761) ***(P-3641)***
California Mfg Tech Consulting ....D....310 263-3060
690 Knox St Ste 200 Torrance (90502) ***(P-22508)***
California Millworks Corp ....E....661 294-2345
27772 Avenue Scott Santa Clarita (91355) ***(P-3236)***
California Offset Printers Inc ....D....818 291-1100
5075 Brooks St Montclair (91763) ***(P-4246)***
California Overnight, Anaheim *Also called Express Messenger Systems Inc* ***(P-12129)***
California Pak Intl Inc ....E....310 223-2500
1700 S Wilmington Ave Compton (90220) ***(P-8863)***
California Pav Grading Co Inc ....D....323 372-5920
3253 Verdugo Rd Los Angeles (90065) ***(P-869)***
California Pediatric Fmly Svcs ....D....626 812-0055
326 E Foothill Blvd Azusa (91702) ***(P-21727)***
California Physicians Service ....D....661 631-2277
2020 17th St Bakersfield (93301) ***(P-15389)***
California Physicians Service ....D....310 744-2668
100 N Pacific Coast Hwy # 20 El Segundo (90245) ***(P-15390)***
California Physicians Service ....D....909 974-5201
3401 Centre Lake Dr # 400 Ontario (91761) ***(P-15391)***
California Physicians Service ....D....818 598-8000
6300 Canoga Ave Ste A Woodland Hills (91367) ***(P-15392)***
California Plasteck, Ontario *Also called Paramount Panels Inc* ***(P-5738)***
California Plastic Cntrs Inc ....F....562 423-3900
2210 E Artesia Blvd Long Beach (90805) ***(P-5595)***
California Plastics, Downey *Also called Abianca Khanna LLC* ***(P-14766)***
California Plastics, Riverside *Also called Altium Holdings LLC* ***(P-5555)***
California Plastix Inc ....E....909 629-8288
1319 E 3rd St Pomona (91766) ***(P-3879)***
California Pools, Coachella *Also called Teserra* ***(P-1694)***
California Portland Cement, Mojave *Also called Calportland Company* ***(P-5974)***
California Poultry, Los Angeles *Also called Western Supreme Inc* ***(P-1764)***
California Premium Incentives, Lake Forest *Also called Aminco International USA Inc* ***(P-11310)***
California Prtg Solutions Inc ....E....909 307-2032
1950 W Park Ave Redlands (92373) ***(P-4247)***
California Psychcare Inc ....E....833 227-3454
25411 Cabot Rd Ste 206 Laguna Hills (92653) ***(P-23424)***
California Psychcare Inc (PA) ....**D....818 401-0661**
9201 Oakdale Ave Ste 101 Chatsworth (91311) ***(P-20209)***
CALIFORNIA PSYCHCARE,INC, Laguna Hills *Also called California Psychcare Inc* ***(P-23424)***
California Quality Plas Inc ....E....909 930-5667
2104 S Cucamonga Ave Ontario (91761) ***(P-5596)***
California Rain Company Inc ....D....213 623-6061
1213 E 14th St Los Angeles (90021) ***(P-14367)***
California Ramp Works Inc ....F....909 949-1601
273 N Benson Ave Upland (91786) ***(P-6989)***
California Real Estate, Los Angeles *Also called Califrnia Realtors Mrtg Netwrk* ***(P-22244)***
California Reamer Company Inc ....F....562 946-6377
12747 Los Nietos Rd Santa Fe Springs (90670) ***(P-7847)***
California Redwood Products, Colton *Also called Frank Kams & Associates Inc* ***(P-3414)***
California Resources Corp (PA) ....**C....888 848-4754**
27200 Tourney Rd Ste 200 Santa Clarita (91355) ***(P-395)***
California Resources Prod Corp ....D....805 483-8017
3450 E 5th St Oxnard (93033) ***(P-396)***
California Resources Prod Corp ....E....661 869-8000
4900 W Lokern Rd Mc Kittrick (93251) ***(P-397)***
California Resources Prod Corp (HQ) ....**C....661 869-8000**
27200 Tourney Rd Ste 200 Santa Clarita (91355) ***(P-398)***
California Respiratory Care ....D....818 379-9999
16055 Ventura Blvd # 715 Encino (91436) ***(P-5214)***
California Restaurant Sup Co ....E....213 581-5100
4665 E 49th St Vernon (90058) ***(P-14457)***
California Ribbon Carbn Co Inc ....D....323 724-9100
10914 Thienes Ave South El Monte (91733) ***(P-11475)***
California Safety Agency ....E....866 996-6990
8932 Katella Ave Ste 108 Anaheim (92804) ***(P-18260)***
California Screw Products Corp ....D....562 633-6626
14957 Gwenchris Ct Paramount (90723) ***(P-6510)***
California Semiconductor Tech ....C....310 579-2939
429 Santa Monica Blvd Santa Monica (90401) ***(P-22509)***
California Shirt Printer Inc ....D....714 898-9946
12221 Monarch St Garden Grove (92841) ***(P-14329)***
California Signs Inc ....E....818 899-1888
10280 Glenoaks Blvd Pacoima (91331) ***(P-11531)***
California Silica Products LLC (PA) ....**E....760 885-5358**
1420 S Bon View Ave Ontario (91761) ***(P-4653)***
California Silica Products LLC ....E....909 947-0028
12808 Rancho Rd Adelanto (92301) ***(P-4654)***
California Silver-Agriculture ....E....559 562-3795
831 Ash Ave Lindsay (93247) ***(P-371)***
California Skateparks ....C....909 949-1601
285 N Benson Ave Upland (91786) ***(P-250)***
California Snack Foods Inc ....E....626 444-4508
2131 Tyler Ave South El Monte (91733) ***(P-2082)***
California Specialty Farms, Los Angeles *Also called Worldwide Specialties Inc* ***(P-2548)***
California Speedway Corp ....E....909 429-5000
9300 Cherry Ave Fontana (92335) ***(P-19429)***
California State Univ Long Bch ....C....562 985-1764
1250 N Bellflower Blvd Bh155 Long Beach (90840) ***(P-22766)***
California Steel and Tube ....C....626 968-5511
16049 Stephens St City of Industry (91745) ***(P-13553)***
California Steel Inds Inc (PA) ....**A....909 350-6300**
14000 San Bernardino Ave Fontana (92335) ***(P-6192)***
California Steel Inds Inc ....E....909 350-6300
1 California Steel Way Fontana (92335) ***(P-6193)***
California Steel Products Inc ....F....310 603-5645
10851 Drury Ln Lyhwood (90262) ***(P-7016)***
California Steel Services Inc ....E....909 796-2222
1212 S Mountain View Ave San Bernardino (92408) ***(P-13554)***
California Strl Concepts Inc ....D....661 257-6903
28358 Constellation Rd # 660 Valencia (91355) ***(P-750)***
California Sulphur Company ....E....562 437-0768
2250 E Pacific Coast Hwy Wilmington (90744) ***(P-4655)***
California Supertrucks Inc ....E....951 656-2903
14385 Veterans Way Moreno Valley (92553) ***(P-9978)***
California Supply Inc (PA) ....**D....310 532-2500**
491 E Compton Blvd Gardena (90248) ***(P-14206)***
California Ticketscom Inc (HQ) ....**C....714 327-5400**
555 Anton Blvd Fl 11 Costa Mesa (92626) ***(P-19305)***
California Title Company (PA) ....**D....949 582-8709**
28202 Cabot Rd Ste 625 Laguna Niguel (92677) ***(P-16037)***
California Tool & Die, Azusa *Also called Mc William & Son Inc* ***(P-7163)***
California Traffic Control ....D....562 595-7575
3333 Cherry Ave Long Beach (90807) ***(P-18465)***
California Traffic Ctrl Svcs, Long Beach *Also called California Traffic Control* ***(P-18465)***
California Trusframe LLC (HQ) ....**A....951 350-4880**
25220 Hancock Ave Ste 350 Murrieta (92562) ***(P-3358)***
California Truss Company (PA) ....**C....951 657-7491**
23665 Cajalco Rd Perris (92570) ***(P-3359)***
California Waste Services LLC ....C....310 538-5998
621 W 152nd St Gardena (90247) ***(P-12934)***
California Watercress Inc (PA) ....**D....805 524-4808**
550 E Telegraph Rd Fillmore (93015) ***(P-13)***
California Wire Products Corp ....E....951 371-7730
1316 Railroad St Corona (92882) ***(P-7496)***
California Woodworking Inc ....E....805 982-9090
1726 Ives Ave Oxnard (93033) ***(P-3312)***
Califrnia Anlytical Instrs Inc ....D....714 974-5560
1312 W Grove Ave Orange (92865) ***(P-10682)***
Califrnia Auto Dalers Exch LLC ....B....714 996-2400
1320 N Tustin Ave Anaheim (92807) ***(P-13022)***
Califrnia Citrus Producers Inc ....D....559 562-5169
525 E Lindmore St Lindsay (93247) ***(P-1895)***
Califrnia Clnic Plstic Surgery (PA) ....**D....626 817-0818**
100 E California Blvd Pasadena (91105) ***(P-19733)***
Califrnia Cstm Frits Flvors In (PA) ....**E....626 736-4130**
15800 Tapia St Irwindale (91706) ***(P-2313)***
Califrnia Cstume Cllctions Inc (PA) ....**B....323 262-8383**
210 S Anderson St Los Angeles (90033) ***(P-3068)***
Califrnia Dluxe Wndows Inds In (PA) ....**E....818 349-5566**
20735 Superior St Chatsworth (91311) ***(P-3237)***
Califrnia Dsgners Chice Cstm C ....E....805 987-5820
547 Constitution Ave F Camarillo (93012) ***(P-3313)***
Califrnia Elctrmechanical Repr ....F....818 840-9211
606 W Doran St Glendale (91203) ***(P-19027)***
Califrnia Frnsic Med Group Inc ....D....805 654-3343
800 S Victoria Ave Ventura (93009) ***(P-21396)***
Califrnia Grnhse Frm II Ltd PR ....D....949 715-3987
17712 Adobe Rd Bakersfield (93307) ***(P-18466)***
Califrnia Hosp Med Ctr Fndtion ....A....213 748-2411
1401 S Grand Ave Los Angeles (90015) ***(P-20691)***
Califrnia Indus Rfrgn Mchs Inc ....F....951 361-0040
3197 Cornerstone Dr Eastvale (91752) ***(P-8331)***
Califrnia Insur Guarantee Assn ....C....818 844-4300
101 N Brand Blvd Ste 600 Glendale (91203) ***(P-15547)***
Califrnia Intermodal Assoc Inc (PA) ....**E....323 562-7788**
6666 E Washington Blvd Commerce (90040) ***(P-12019)***
Califrnia Nrsing Rhbltion Ctr, Palm Springs *Also called Califrnia Nrsing Rhbltion Ctr* ***(P-20271)***
Califrnia Nrsing Rhbltion Ctr ....D....760 325-2937
2299 N Indian Ave Palm Springs (92262) ***(P-20271)***
Califrnia Nwspapers Ltd Partnr (HQ) ....**B....626 962-8811**
605 E Huntington Dr # 100 Monrovia (91016) ***(P-3956)***
Califrnia Nwspapers Ltd Partnr ....C....909 987-6397
3200 E Guasti Rd Ste 100 Ontario (91761) ***(P-3957)***
Califrnia Nwspapers Ltd Partnr ....C....909 793-3221
19 E Citrus Ave Ste 102 Redlands (92373) ***(P-3958)***
Califrnia Prcast Stone Mfg Inc ....F....951 657-7913
1796 Karen Ct Hemet (92545) ***(P-6020)***
Califrnia Rcrtion Instllations, Corona *Also called Playmax Surfacing Inc* ***(P-5398)***
Califrnia Realtors Mrtg Netwrk ....D....213 739-8200
525 S Virgil Ave Los Angeles (90020) ***(P-22244)***
Califrnia Rhblitation Inst LLC ....D....424 363-1003
2070 Century Park E Los Angeles (90067) ***(P-20692)***

ALPHABETIC

Employee Codes: A=Over 500 employees, B=251-500
C=101-250, D=51-100, E=20-50 F=10-19
2022 Southern California Business
Directory and Buyers Guide
© Mergent Inc. 1-800-342-5647
1083

Califrnia Rsrces Elk Hills LLC B 661 412-0000
27200 Tourney Rd Ste 200 Santa Clarita (91355) ***(P-443)***

Califrnia Scnce Ctr Foundation B 213 744-2545
700 Exposition Park Dr Los Angeles (90037) ***(P-22218)***

Califrnia State Univ Chnnel Is D 805 437-2670
45 Rincon Dr Unit 104a Camarillo (93012) ***(P-8864)***

Califrnia Trade Converters Inc E 818 899-1455
9816 Variel Ave Chatsworth (91311) ***(P-3772)***

Calimesa Operations LLC C 909 795-2421
13542 2nd St Yucaipa (92399) ***(P-20272)***

Calimesa Post Acute, Yucaipa *Also called Calimesa Operations LLC* ***(P-20272)***

Calimex Deli E 323 261-7271
711 1/2 S Kern Ave Los Angeles (90022) ***(P-1988)***

Calimmune Inc F 310 806-6240
129 N Hill Ave Ste 105 Pasadena (91106) ***(P-4802)***

Calipaso Winery LLC F 805 226-9296
4230 Buena Vista Dr Paso Robles (93446) ***(P-2171)***

Calko Transport Company Inc D 310 816-0602
720 E Watson Center Rd Carson (90745) ***(P-12109)***

Call & Jensen APC E 949 717-3000
610 Nwport Ctr Dr Ste 700 Newport Beach (92660) ***(P-21526)***

Call To Action Partners Llc C 310 996-7200
11601 Wilshire Blvd Fl 23 Los Angeles (90025) ***(P-16251)***

Callan Advertising Company, Burbank *Also called S Callan Company Inc* ***(P-17053)***

Callaway Vineyard & Winery D 951 676-4001
32720 Rancho Cal Rd Temecula (92591) ***(P-2172)***

Calleguas Municipal Water Dict D 805 526-9323
2100 E Olsen Rd Thousand Oaks (91360) ***(P-12881)***

Callfire Inc D 213 221-2289
1410 2nd St Ste 200 Santa Monica (90401) ***(P-17573)***

Callisonrtkl Inc C 213 627-7373
818 W 7th St Ste 300 Los Angeles (90017) ***(P-22712)***

Calmat Co (HQ) **C 818 553-8821**
500 N Brand Blvd Ste 500 # 500 Glendale (91203) ***(P-5269)***

Calmat Co E 661 858-2673
16101 Hwy 156 Maricopa (93252) ***(P-563)***

Calmation Incorporated E 805 520-2515
2222 Shasta Way Simi Valley (93065) ***(P-13895)***

Calmet Inc (PA) **C 323 721-8120**
7202 Petterson Ln Paramount (90723) ***(P-12935)***

Calmet Services Inc D 562 259-1239
7202 Petterson Ln Paramount (90723) ***(P-12936)***

Calmex Engineering Inc D 909 546-1311
2764 S Vista Ave Bloomington (92316) ***(P-1519)***

Calmex Fireplace Eqp Mfg Inc E 716 645-2901
13629 Talc St Santa Fe Springs (90670) ***(P-6511)***

Calmex Fireplace Equip Mfg, Santa Fe Springs *Also called Calmex Fireplace Eqp Mfg Inc* ***(P-6511)***

Calmont Engrg & Elec Corp (PA) **E 714 549-0336**
420 E Alton Ave Santa Ana (92707) ***(P-6346)***

Calmont Wire & Cable, Santa Ana *Also called Calmont Engrg & Elec Corp* ***(P-6346)***

Calmut Industrial Asphalt, Glendale *Also called Huntmix Inc* ***(P-5273)***

Calnetix Inc (PA) **D 562 293-1660**
16323 Shoemaker Ave Cerritos (90703) ***(P-22510)***

Calnetix Technologies, Cerritos *Also called Calnetix Inc* ***(P-22510)***

Calnetix Technologies LLC (HQ) **E 562 293-1660**
16323 Shoemaker Ave Cerritos (90703) ***(P-8910)***

Calor Apparel Group Intl Corp E 949 548-9095
884 W 16th St Newport Beach (92663) ***(P-3013)***

Calpaco Papers Inc (PA) **C 323 767-2800**
3155 Universe Dr Jurupa Valley (91752) ***(P-3924)***

Calpak Usa Inc E 310 937-7335
13748 Prairie Ave Hawthorne (90250) ***(P-9386)***

Calpi Inc E 661 589-5648
7141 Downing Ave Bakersfield (93308) ***(P-486)***

Calpipe Industries LLC E 562 803-4388
923 Calpipe Rd Santa Paula (93060) ***(P-6194)***

Calpipe Industries LLC (HQ) **D 562 803-4388**
12160 Woodruff Ave Downey (90241) ***(P-13555)***

Calpipe Security Bollards, Downey *Also called Cal Pipe Manufacturing Inc* ***(P-7531)***

Calportland, Colton *Also called Cal Portland Cement Co* ***(P-6074)***

Calportland D 760 343-3403
2025 E Financial Way Glendora (91741) ***(P-568)***

Calportland Company C 661 824-2401
9350 Oak Creek Rd Mojave (93501) ***(P-5974)***

Calportland Company (HQ) **D 626 852-6200**
2025 E Financial Way Glendora (91741) ***(P-5975)***

Calrad Electronics Inc E 323 465-2131
819 N Highland Ave Los Angeles (90038) ***(P-13707)***

Calsemi, Santa Monica *Also called California Semiconductor Tech* ***(P-22509)***

Calstar Systems Group Inc E 818 922-2000
6345 Balboa Blvd Ste 105 Encino (91316) ***(P-9857)***

Calstrip Industries Inc (PA) **E 323 726-1345**
3030 Dulles Dr Jurupa Valley (91752) ***(P-6242)***

Calstrip Steel Corporation (HQ) **D 323 838-2097**
3030 Dulles Dr Jurupa Valley (91752) ***(P-6435)***

CALTECH EFCU, La Canada Flintridge *Also called Cal Tech Emplyees Fderal Cr Un* ***(P-15060)***

Caltrans, Santa Maria *Also called California Department Trnsp* ***(P-866)***

Caltrans, Templeton *Also called California Department Trnsp* ***(P-867)***

Caltrans Eastern Reg Rd Maint, Whittier *Also called California Department Trnsp* ***(P-865)***

Calvary Church Santa Ana Inc C 714 973-4800
1010 N Tustin Ave Santa Ana (92705) ***(P-21994)***

Calwax LLC (HQ) **E 626 969-4334**
16511 Knott Ave La Mirada (90638) ***(P-14774)***

Calwest Galvanizing Corp E 310 549-2200
2226 E Dominguez St Carson (90810) ***(P-7351)***

CAM, Fullerton *Also called Consolidated Aerospace Mfg LLC* ***(P-10578)***

CAM Services, Torrance *Also called Common Area Maint Svcs Inc* ***(P-17231)***

Camarillo Family YMCA, Camarillo *Also called Channel Islnds Yung MNS Chrstn* ***(P-22327)***

Camarillo Healthcare Center D 805 482-9805
205 Granada St Camarillo (93010) ***(P-22997)***

Cambium Business Group Inc (PA) **C 714 670-1171**
6950 Noritsu Ave Buena Park (90620) ***(P-13130)***

Cambria Pines Lodge, Cambria *Also called Pacific Cambria Inc* ***(P-16605)***

Cambria Winery, Santa Maria *Also called Jackson Family Wines Inc* ***(P-2197)***

Cambridge Equities LP E 858 350-2300
9922 Jefferson Blvd Culver City (90232) ***(P-4933)***

Cambridge Sierra Holdings LLC B 909 370-4411
1350 Reche Canyon Rd Colton (92324) ***(P-20273)***

Cambro Manufacturing Company (PA) **B 714 848-1555**
5801 Skylab Rd Huntington Beach (92647) ***(P-5597)***

Camden Center Inc C 844 422-6336
10780 Santa Monica Blvd Los Angeles (90025) ***(P-21281)***

Camden Development Inc C 949 427-4674
27261 Las Ramblas Mission Viejo (92691) ***(P-15795)***

Camden Solar LLC E 940 398-3915
18575 Jamboree Rd Ste 850 Irvine (92612) ***(P-9488)***

Camellia Gardens Care Center, Pasadena *Also called Camellia Gardens Care Ctr* ***(P-20274)***

Camellia Gardens Care Ctr D 626 798-6777
1920 N Fair Oaks Ave Pasadena (91103) ***(P-20274)***

Cameo Technologies Inc E 949 672-7000
20511 Lake Forest Dr Lake Forest (92630) ***(P-8190)***

Camera Ready Cars, Fountain Valley *Also called Gaffoglio Fmly Mtlcrafters Inc* ***(P-5953)***

Cameron Energy Services Corp D 562 321-9183
4040 Capitol Ave City of Industry (90601) ***(P-22998)***

Cameron Metal Cutting, Santa Ana *Also called Automation West Inc* ***(P-8507)***

Cameron Surface Systems, Bakersfield *Also called Cameron West Coast Inc* ***(P-13857)***

Cameron Technologies Us LLC E 562 222-8440
4040 Capitol Ave Whittier (90601) ***(P-10683)***

Cameron Welding Supply (PA) **E 714 530-9353**
11061 Dale Ave Stanton (90680) ***(P-18971)***

Cameron West Coast Inc D 661 837-4980
4315 Yeager Way Bakersfield (93313) ***(P-13857)***

Cameron's Measurement Systems, Whittier *Also called Cameron Technologies Us LLC* ***(P-10683)***

Camfil Farr Inc F 973 616-7300
3625 Del Amo Blvd Ste 260 Torrance (90503) ***(P-8042)***

Camino Real Foods Inc (PA) **C 323 585-6599**
2638 E Vernon Ave Vernon (90058) ***(P-2404)***

Camino Real Kitchens, Vernon *Also called Camino Real Foods Inc* ***(P-2404)***

Camisasca Automotive Mfg Inc E 949 452-0195
20341 Hermana Cir Lake Forest (92630) ***(P-7134)***

Camisasca Automotive Mfg Inc (PA) **E 949 452-0195**
20352 Hermana Cir Lake Forest (92630) ***(P-7135)***

Camland Inc F 805 485-9242
3152 Canopy Dr Camarillo (93012) ***(P-18972)***

Camlever Inc E 909 629-9669
954 S East End Ave Pomona (91766) ***(P-7637)***

Camp Franchise Systems LLC (PA) **D 909 325-6011**
14738 Pipeline Ave Ste A Chino Hills (91709) ***(P-16818)***

Camp Smidgemore Inc (HQ) **E 323 634-0333**
3641 10th Ave Los Angeles (90018) ***(P-2929)***

Camp Transformation Center, Chino Hills *Also called Camp Franchise Systems LLC* ***(P-16818)***

Campagna, Los Olivos *Also called Pagliei Collection Inc* ***(P-11489)***

Campbell Center E 818 242-2434
6512 San Fernando Rd Glendale (91201) ***(P-22448)***

Campbell Construction, Chino *Also called Campbell Painting Inc* ***(P-1173)***

Campbell Engineering Inc E 949 859-3306
20412 Barents Sea Cir Lake Forest (92630) ***(P-7848)***

Campbell Painting Inc D 919 591-4300
14175 Telephone Ave Ste M Chino (91710) ***(P-1173)***

Camper Packaging LLC F 562 239-6167
13208 Arctic Cir Santa Fe Springs (90670) ***(P-1788)***

Campus By The Sea, Avalon *Also called Intervrsity Chrstn Fllwshp/Usa* ***(P-16823)***

Camstar International Inc D 909 931-2540
939 W 9th St Upland (91786) ***(P-13798)***

Camtech, Irvine *Also called Computer Assisted Mfg Tech LLC* ***(P-8561)***

Can Lines Engineering Inc (PA) **D 562 861-2996**
9839 Downey Norwalk Rd Downey (90241) ***(P-8065)***

Canadas Finest Foods Inc D 951 296-1040
26090 Ynez Rd Temecula (92591) ***(P-1896)***

Canady Manufacturing Co Inc F 818 365-9181
500 5th St San Fernando (91340) ***(P-8540)***

Candle Crafters, Moorpark *Also called Globaluxe Inc* ***(P-11679)***

Candleberry Properties LP E 323 852-7000
6399 Wilshire Blvd Los Angeles (90048) ***(P-16366)***

Candlewick-Porterville, Porterville *Also called Tdg Operations LLC* ***(P-2702)***

Candy Cane Inn, Anaheim *Also called Cinderella Motel* ***(P-16382)***

Canfab, Corona *Also called Cannon Fabrication Inc* ***(P-1476)***

Canine Caviar Pet Foods Inc E 714 223-1800
4131 Tigris Way Riverside (92503) ***(P-1963)***

Canine Caviar Pet Foods De Inc F 714 223-1800
4131 Tigris Way Riverside (92503) ***(P-1956)***

Cannalogic F 619 458-0775
5404 Whitsett Ave 219 Valley Village (91607) ***(P-11648)***

Cannasafe, Van Nuys *Also called Consumer Safety Analytics LLC* ***(P-22936)***

Cannasafe, Van Nuys *Also called Csa Silicon Valley LLC* ***(P-21065)***

Canndescent F 877 778-9587
3905 State St Santa Barbara (93105) ***(P-4803)***

Cannon Cochran MGT Svcs Inc D 949 474-6500
18881 Von Karman Ave # 380 Irvine (92612) ***(P-15548)***

Cannon Corporation (PA) **D 805 544-7407**
1050 Southwood Dr San Luis Obispo (93401) ***(P-22754)***

Cannon Fabrication Inc......D......951 278-1830
182 Granite St Ste 101 Corona (92879) ***(P-1476)***
Cannon Gasket Inc......E......909 355-1547
7784 Edison Ave Fontana (92336) ***(P-5331)***
Canoga Perkins Corporation (HQ)......**D......818 718-6300**
20600 Prairie St Chatsworth (91311) ***(P-9335)***
Canon Medical Systems USA Inc (HQ)......**B......714 730-5000**
2441 Michelle Dr Tustin (92780) ***(P-13482)***
Canon Recruiting Group LLC......B......661 252-7400
27651 Lincoln Pl Ste 250 Santa Clarita (91387) ***(P-17488)***
Canon Solutions America Inc......E......844 443-4636
6435 Ventura Blvd Ste C00 Ventura (93003) ***(P-13352)***
Canon USA Inc......B......949 753-4000
15955 Alton Pkwy Irvine (92618) ***(P-13341)***
Canoo Inc (PA)......**C......424 271-2144**
19951 Mariner Ave Torrance (90503) ***(P-10028)***
Canopy Energy, Van Nuys *Also called Energy Enterprises USA Inc* ***(P-1062)***
Cantaloupe Holdings LLC......D......310 451-9706
1340 15th St Santa Monica (90404) ***(P-20568)***
Canteen Vending, Garden Grove *Also called Compass Group Usa Inc* ***(P-17338)***
Canterbury Designs Inc......E......323 936-7111
6195 Maywood Ave Huntington Park (90255) ***(P-6954)***
Canterbury International, Huntington Park *Also called Canterbury Designs Inc* ***(P-6954)***
Canterbury, The, Pls Vrds Pnsl *Also called Episcopal Communities & Servic* ***(P-20336)***
Canton Food Co Inc......C......213 688-7707
750 S Alameda St Los Angeles (90021) ***(P-14458)***
Canvas Worldwide LLC......C......424 303-4300
12015 Bluff Creek Dr Los Angeles (90094) ***(P-17081)***
Canyon Composites Incorporated......E......714 991-8181
1548 N Gemini Pl Anaheim (92801) ***(P-10295)***
Canyon Country Medical Offices, Santa Clarita *Also called Kaiser Foundation Hospitals* ***(P-19918)***
Canyon Crest Country Club Inc......D......951 274-7900
975 Country Club Dr Riverside (92506) ***(P-19552)***
Canyon Crest Mental Hlth Offs, Riverside *Also called Kaiser Foundation Hospitals* ***(P-19915)***
Canyon Engineering Pdts Inc......D......661 294-0084
28909 Avenue Williams Valencia (91355) ***(P-10296)***
Canyon Hill Preschool, Bakersfield *Also called Canyon Hills Assembly God Ch* ***(P-21995)***
Canyon Hills Assembly God Ch......D......661 871-1150
7001 Auburn St Bakersfield (93306) ***(P-21995)***
Canyon Lk Property Owners Assn......D......951 244-6841
31512 Railroad Canyon Rd Canyon Lake (92587) ***(P-22323)***
Canyon Oaks Nursing and Rehab......D......818 887-7050
22029 Saticoy St Canoga Park (91303) ***(P-20569)***
Canyon Partners Incorporated (HQ)......**D......310 272-1000**
2000 Ave Of The Sts Fl 11 Los Angeles (90067) ***(P-15263)***
Canyon Plastics Inc......D......800 350-6325
28455 Livingston Ave Valencia (91355) ***(P-5598)***
Canyon Ridge Hospital Inc......A......909 590-3700
5353 G St Chino (91710) ***(P-21016)***
Canyon Steel Fabricators Inc......E......951 683-2352
8314 Sultana Ave Fontana (92335) ***(P-6598)***
Canyon Tire Sales Inc (PA)......**D......951 603-0615**
10064 Dawson Canyon Rd A Corona (92883) ***(P-13113)***
Canzone and Company......F......714 537-8175
1345 W Cowles St Long Beach (90813) ***(P-11532)***
Cap Diagnostics LLC......D......714 966-1221
17661 Cowan Irvine (92614) ***(P-21061)***
Cap-Mpt, Los Angeles *Also called Coopertive Amrcn Physcians Inc* ***(P-22268)***
Cap-Mpt (PA)......**C......213 473-8600**
333 S Hope St Fl 8 Los Angeles (90071) ***(P-15495)***
Capable Transport Inc......D......310 697-0198
3528 Torrance Blvd # 220 Torrance (90503) ***(P-12427)***
Capax Technologies Inc......E......661 257-7666
24842 Avenue Tibbitts Valencia (91355) ***(P-8972)***
Capc Adult Services, Whittier *Also called Whittier Union High Schl Dist* ***(P-21929)***
Capco Unlimited......F......714 257-0154
591 Apollo St Brea (92821) ***(P-6458)***
Capco/Psa......E......818 762-4276
11125 Vanowen St North Hollywood (91605) ***(P-5599)***
Cape Robbin Inc......E......626 810-8080
1943 W Mission Blvd Pomona (91766) ***(P-14431)***
Capistrano Dispatch......F......949 388-7700
34932 Calle Del Sol Ste B Capistrano Beach (92624) ***(P-3959)***
Capistrano Labs Inc......E......949 492-0390
150 Calle Iglesia Ste B San Clemente (92672) ***(P-10956)***
Capistrano Volkswagen, San Juan Capistrano *Also called Mission Volkswagen Inc* ***(P-18857)***
Capital Brands LLC (HQ)......**E......310 996-7200**
11601 Wilshire Blvd # 360 Los Angeles (90025) ***(P-14679)***
Capital Brands Dist LLC (PA)......**D......310 996-7200**
11601 Wilshire Blvd # 360 Los Angeles (90025) ***(P-9001)***
Capital Commercial Property, Culver City *Also called Property Management Assoc Inc* ***(P-15961)***
Capital Cooking Equipment Inc......E......562 903-1168
1025 E Bedmar St Carson (90746) ***(P-6569)***
Capital Drywall LP......C......909 599-6818
333 S Grand Ave Ste 4070 Los Angeles (90071) ***(P-1369)***
Capital Engineering LLC......B......562 612-1302
2830 Temple Ave Long Beach (90806) ***(P-22511)***
Capital Group Companies Inc (PA)......**A......213 486-9200**
333 S Hope St Fl 55 Los Angeles (90071) ***(P-15321)***
Capital Group, The, Los Angeles *Also called Capital Group Companies Inc* ***(P-15321)***
Capital Guardian Trust Company (HQ)......**D......213 486-9200**
333 S Hope St Fl 52 Los Angeles (90071) ***(P-16174)***
Capital Invstmnts Vntures Corp (PA)......**C......949 858-0647**
30151 Tomas Rcho STA Marg (92688) ***(P-22266)***
Capital Kingz LLC......E......888 470-4114
3415 S Sepulveda Blvd # 1 Los Angeles (90034) ***(P-15796)***

Capital Mortgage Services, Ventura *Also called E&S Financial Group Inc* ***(P-15240)***
Capital Network Funding Svcs, Los Angeles *Also called Capnet Financial Services Inc* ***(P-15161)***
Capital Oversight Inc (PA)......**D......310 453-8000**
2118 Wilshire Blvd Santa Monica (90403) ***(P-23425)***
Capital Prvate Clent Svcs Fnds......D......949 975-5000
6455 Irvine Center Dr Irvine (92618) ***(P-16126)***
Capital Ready Mix Inc......E......818 771-1122
11311 Pendleton St Sun Valley (91352) ***(P-6076)***
Capital Research and MGT Co (HQ)......**B......213 486-9200**
333 S Hope St Fl 55 Los Angeles (90071) ***(P-15322)***
Capitol Machine Co, Santa Ana *Also called M & W Machine Corporation* ***(P-8670)***
Capitol Steel Fabricators Inc......E......323 721-5460
3565 Greenwood Ave Commerce (90040) ***(P-6599)***
Caplugs, Rancho Dominguez *Also called Protective Industries Inc* ***(P-5783)***
Caplugs......F......310 537-2300
18704 S Ferris Pl Rancho Dominguez (90220) ***(P-5600)***
Capna Fabrication......E......888 416-6777
16501 Ventura Blvd # 400 Encino (91436) ***(P-7929)***
Capna Systems, Encino *Also called Capna Fabrication* ***(P-7929)***
Capnet Financial Services Inc (PA)......**D......877 980-0558**
11901 Santa Monica Blvd Los Angeles (90025) ***(P-15161)***
Capri Tools, Pomona *Also called Als Group Inc* ***(P-13793)***
Capricor Therapeutics Inc (PA)......**F......310 358-3200**
8840 Wilshire Blvd Fl 2 Beverly Hills (90211) ***(P-4804)***
Capsa Solutions LLC......E......800 437-6633
14000 S Broadway Los Angeles (90061) ***(P-8191)***
Capsbc, San Bernardino *Also called Community Action Prtnship Sb C* ***(P-22177)***
Capstone Green Energy Corp (PA)......**C......818 734-5300**
16640 Stagg St Van Nuys (91406) ***(P-7580)***
Capstone Logistics LLC......A......770 414-1929
12661 Aldi Pl Moreno Valley (92555) ***(P-12565)***
Capsule Manufacturing Inc......D......949 245-4151
1399 N Miller St Anaheim (92806) ***(P-487)***
Capsule Mfg, Anaheim *Also called Capsule Manufacturing Inc* ***(P-487)***
Captek Holdings LLC......E......562 921-9511
16218 Arthur St Cerritos (90703) ***(P-1789)***
Captek Midco Inc (HQ)......**C......562 921-9511**
16218 Arthur St Cerritos (90703) ***(P-2125)***
Captek Pharma, La Mirada *Also called Captek Softgel Intl Inc* ***(P-4805)***
Captek Softgel Intl Inc......C......657 325-0412
14535 Industry Cir La Mirada (90638) ***(P-4805)***
Captek Softgel Intl Inc (HQ)......**B......562 921-9511**
16218 Arthur St Cerritos (90703) ***(P-4806)***
Captivate Brands Usa Inc......F......949 229-8927
25541 Arctic Ocean Dr Lake Forest (92630) ***(P-8987)***
Captive Ocean Reef Entps Inc (PA)......**D......714 543-4100**
1011 S Linwood Ave Santa Ana (92705) ***(P-8113)***
Captive-Aire Systems Inc......E......714 957-1500
2915 Red Hill Ave C106 Costa Mesa (92626) ***(P-6804)***
Captive-Aire Systems Inc......E......310 876-8505
1123 Washington Ave Santa Monica (90403) ***(P-6805)***
Captive-Aire Systems Inc......E......951 231-5102
2510 Cloudcrest Way Riverside (92507) ***(P-6806)***
Car Wash Partners Inc......B......661 377-1020
2619 Mount Vernon Ave Bakersfield (93306) ***(P-18908)***
Car Wash Partners Inc......D......661 231-3689
5375 Olive Dr Bakersfield (93308) ***(P-18909)***
Cara Communications Corp......E......310 442-5600
12233 W Olympic Blvd # 170 Los Angeles (90064) ***(P-19107)***
Caraustar Cstm Packg Group Inc......D......323 724-5989
6001 S Eastern Ave Commerce (90040) ***(P-3834)***
Caraustar Custom Packg Group, Commerce *Also called Caraustar Cstm Packg Group Inc* ***(P-3834)***
Caravan Canopy Intl Inc......E......714 367-3000
17512 Studebaker Rd Cerritos (90703) ***(P-3135)***
Carberry LLC (HQ)......**E......800 564-0842**
17130 Muskrat Ave Ste B Adelanto (92301) ***(P-11649)***
Carbide Saw and Tool Inc......F......909 884-9956
336 S Waterman Ave Ste P San Bernardino (92408) ***(P-19028)***
Carbon 38 Inc......D......888 723-5838
10000 Wash Blvd Ste 800 Culver City (90232) ***(P-18467)***
Carbon California Company LLC......F......805 933-1901
270 Quail Ct Ste 201 Santa Paula (93060) ***(P-399)***
Carbro Company, Lawndale *Also called Curry Company LLC* ***(P-7852)***
Card Scanning Solutions, Los Angeles *Also called Acuant Inc* ***(P-17775)***
Cardenas Enterprises Inc......F......323 588-0137
339 W Norman Ave Arcadia (91007) ***(P-3679)***
Cardenas Markets LLC......C......909 947-4824
2929 S Vineyard Ave Ontario (91761) ***(P-1919)***
Cardenas Markets LLC......C......909 923-7426
1621 E Francis St Ontario (91761) ***(P-1920)***
Cardflex Inc......D......714 361-1900
2900 Bristol St Ste F Costa Mesa (92626) ***(P-18468)***
Cardiac Noninvasive Laboratory, Los Angeles *Also called Cedars-Sinai Medical Center* ***(P-19740)***
Cardiac Unit, Anaheim *Also called Anaheim Regional Medical Ctr* ***(P-20676)***
Cardic Machine Products Inc......F......310 884-3400
17000 Keegan Ave Carson (90746) ***(P-8541)***
Cardiff Transportation, Palm Desert *Also called Gary Cardiff Enterprises Inc* ***(P-11869)***
Cardigan Road Productions......F......310 289-1442
1999 Ave Of The Sts 110 Los Angeles (90067) ***(P-9688)***
Cardinal C G, Moreno Valley *Also called Cardinal Glass Industries Inc* ***(P-5916)***
Cardinal Cg Company, Los Angeles *Also called Cardinal Glass Industries Inc* ***(P-5947)***
Cardinal Glass Industries Inc......E......951 485-9007
24100 Cardinal Ave Moreno Valley (92551) ***(P-5916)***

Employee Codes: A=Over 500 employees, B=251-500
C=101-250, D=51-100, E=20-50 F=10-19
2022 Southern California Business Directory and Buyers Guide
© Mergent Inc. 1-800-342-5647
1085

Cardinal Glass Industries Inc ....E....323 319-0070
1125 E Lanzit Ave Los Angeles (90059) ***(P-5947)***
Cardinal Health Inc ....D....951 360-2199
1100 Bird Center Dr Palm Springs (92262) ***(P-13483)***
Cardinal Paint and Powder Inc ....D....626 937-6767
15010 Don Julian Rd City of Industry (91746) ***(P-5091)***
Cardinal Transportation, Gardena *Also called First Student Inc* ***(P-11934)***
Cardiology Department, Los Angeles *Also called Usc Care Medical Group Inc* ***(P-20994)***
Cardlogix ....F....949 380-1312
16 Hughes Ste 100 Irvine (92618) ***(P-8243)***
Cardno Eri, Lake Forest *Also called Environmental Resolutions Inc* ***(P-23438)***
Cardona Manufacturing Corp ....E....818 841-8358
1869 N Victory Pl Burbank (91504) ***(P-10297)***
Cardservice International Inc ....D....714 773-1778
1538 W Commonwealth Ave Fullerton (92833) ***(P-18469)***
Cardservice International Inc (HQ) ....**B....805 648-1425**
5898 Condor Dr 220 Moorpark (93021) ***(P-18470)***
Care 1st Health Plan (PA) ....**C....323 889-6638**
601 Potrero Grande Dr # 2 Monterey Park (91755) ***(P-21397)***
Care Stffing Professionals Inc ....D....909 906-2060
2151 E Cnvntion Ctr Way S Ontario (91764) ***(P-21146)***
Care Tech Inc ....E....909 882-2965
4280 Cypress Dr San Bernardino (92407) ***(P-20275)***
Carecar Inc ....E....949 287-8349
120 Newport Center Dr Newport Beach (92660) ***(P-11857)***
Career Dev Inst For Excptnal I ....E....951 337-3678
1470 Marsh Way Riverside (92501) ***(P-16047)***
Career Engagement Group LLC ....D....212 235-1470
30025 Alicia Pkwy Laguna Niguel (92677) ***(P-17574)***
Career Group Inc (PA) ....**A....310 277-8188**
10100 Santa Monica Blvd # 900 Los Angeles (90067) ***(P-17403)***
Career Strategies Tmpry Inc ....D....213 385-0440
719 N Victory Blvd Burbank (91502) ***(P-17404)***
Career Tech Circuit Services, Chatsworth *Also called Circuit Services Llc* ***(P-9391)***
Carefree Communities Inc ....C....805 498-2612
1251 Old Conejo Rd Newbury Park (91320) ***(P-15756)***
Carefusion 202 Inc (HQ) ....**C....800 231-2466**
22745 Savi Ranch Pkwy Yorba Linda (92887) ***(P-10957)***
Carefusion 207 Inc ....B....760 778-7200
1100 Bird Center Dr Palm Springs (92262) ***(P-10958)***
Careismatic Brands Inc (PA) ....**C....818 671-2100**
9800 De Soto Ave Chatsworth (91311) ***(P-5876)***
Caremark Rx Inc ....D....909 887-7951
2150 N Waterman Ave # 200 San Bernardino (92404) ***(P-19734)***
Caremark Rx Inc ....D....909 822-1164
1851 N Riverside Ave Rialto (92376) ***(P-19735)***
Caremark Rx Inc ....D....760 948-6606
15576 Main St Hesperia (92345) ***(P-19736)***
Caremore Health Plan (HQ) ....**C....562 622-2950**
12900 Park Plaza Dr # 150 Cerritos (90703) ***(P-19737)***
Caremore Insurance Services, Cerritos *Also called Caremore Health Plan* ***(P-19737)***
Careonsite Inc (PA) ....**E....562 437-0831**
1250 Pacific Ave Long Beach (90813) ***(P-19738)***
Caretex Inc ....F....323 567-5074
4581 Firestone Blvd South Gate (90280) ***(P-5120)***
Careworks Health Services ....D....949 859-4700
5151 Oceanus Dr Ste 102 Huntington Beach (92649) ***(P-21728)***
Cargill Incorporated ....E....323 588-2274
566 N Gilbert St Fullerton (92833) ***(P-2128)***
Cargill Flour Milling Division, San Bernardino *Also called Ardent Mills LLC* ***(P-1943)***
Cargill Meat Solutions Corp ....B....562 345-5240
13034 Excelsior Dr Norwalk (90650) ***(P-1707)***
Cargill Meat Solutions Corp ....B....909 476-3120
10602 N Trademark Pkwy # 500 Rancho Cucamonga (91730) ***(P-1708)***
Cargo Service Center, Los Angeles *Also called Swissport Cargo Services LP* ***(P-12370)***
Cargo Solution Brokerage Inc ....C....909 350-1644
14587 Valley Blvd Fontana (92335) ***(P-11961)***
Cargo Solution Express Inc (PA) ....**C....909 350-1644**
14587 Valley Blvd 89 Fontana (92335) ***(P-12020)***
Cargomatic Inc ....D....866 513-2343
211 E Ocean Blvd Ste 350 Long Beach (90802) ***(P-12428)***
Caribbean Coffee Company Inc ....E....805 692-2200
495 Pine Ave Ste A Goleta (93117) ***(P-1947)***
Carl Zeiss Meditec Prod LLC ....D....877 644-4657
1040 S Vintage Ave Ste A Ontario (91761) ***(P-10828)***
Carl Zeiss Meditec,, Ontario *Also called Aaren Scientific Inc* ***(P-10822)***
Carley (PA) ....**B....310 325-8474**
1502 W 228th St Torrance (90501) ***(P-5932)***
Carli Suspension Inc ....D....951 403-6570
596 Crane St Lake Elsinore (92530) ***(P-18894)***
Carlisle Interconnect, El Segundo *Also called Tri-Star Electronics Intl Inc* ***(P-13783)***
Carlos Shower Doors Inc ....E....661 204-6689
300 Kentucky St Bakersfield (93305) ***(P-5948)***
Carlson Arts LLC ....F....818 767-1500
11230 Peoria St Sun Valley (91352) ***(P-7017)***
Carlyle Group Inc (PA) ....**B....310 550-8656**
9073 Nemo St Ste 100 West Hollywood (90069) ***(P-15797)***
Carmi Flavors, Commerce *Also called Carmi Flvr & Fragrance Co Inc* ***(P-2314)***
Carmi Flvr & Fragrance Co Inc (PA) ....**E....323 888-9240**
6030 Scott Way Commerce (90040) ***(P-2314)***
Carmichael International Svc (HQ) ....**D....213 353-0800**
1200 Corp Ctr Dr Ste 200 Monterey Park (91754) ***(P-12429)***
Carnegie Institution Wash ....D....626 577-1122
813 Santa Barbara St Pasadena (91101) ***(P-22902)***
Carnegie Mortgage LLC ....B....949 379-7000
15480 Laguna Canyon Rd # 100 Irvine (92618) ***(P-15237)***
Carneros Energy Inc ....F....661 616-5600
4550 California Ave # 720 Bakersfield (93309) ***(P-400)***
Carnevale & Lohr Inc ....E....562 927-8311
6521 Clara St Bell Gardens (90201) ***(P-6136)***
Carol Anderson Inc (PA) ....**E....310 638-3333**
18700 S Laurel Park Rd Rancho Dominguez (90220) ***(P-2881)***
Carol Anderson By Invitation, Rancho Dominguez *Also called Carol Anderson Inc* ***(P-2881)***
Carol Electric Company Inc ....D....562 431-1870
3822 Cerritos Ave Los Alamitos (90720) ***(P-1230)***
Carol Wior Inc ....E....562 927-0052
7533 Garfield Ave Bell (90201) ***(P-2930)***
Carolina Lquid Chmistries Corp ....F....336 722-8910
510 W Central Ave Ste C Brea (92821) ***(P-10959)***
Carolyn E Wylie Ctr For Chldre ....D....951 683-5193
4164 Brockton Ave Riverside (92501) ***(P-21729)***
Carousel USA, Fontana *Also called JE Thomson & Company LLC* ***(P-7712)***
Carpe Data (PA) ....**D....877 342-2773**
735 State St Ste 600 Santa Barbara (93101) ***(P-23182)***
Carpenters Southwest ADM Corp (PA) ....**D....213 386-8590**
533 S Fremont Ave Los Angeles (90071) ***(P-16367)***
Carpenters Southwest ADM Corp ....C....805 688-5581
376 Ave Of The Flags Buellton (93427) ***(P-16945)***
Carpet Care By Tri-Star, Northridge *Also called Tri - Star Win Coverings Inc* ***(P-13190)***
Carpet USA Ltd (PA) ....**D....310 390-8570**
9310 S La Cienega Blvd Inglewood (90301) ***(P-13164)***
Carpet Wagon-Glendale Inc (PA) ....**F....818 937-9545**
3614 San Fernando Rd Glendale (91204) ***(P-3314)***
Carpinteria Motor Inn Inc ....E....805 684-0473
4558 Carpinteria Ave Carpinteria (93013) ***(P-16368)***
Carquest Auto Parts, Brawley *Also called Shank Kretz Mch Auto Parts Inc* ***(P-13088)***
Carr Corporation (PA) ....**E....310 587-1113**
1547 11th St Santa Monica (90401) ***(P-11207)***
Carr Management Inc ....D....951 277-4800
22324 Temescal Canyon Rd Corona (92883) ***(P-5601)***
Carrara Marble Co Amer Inc (PA) ....**D....626 961-6010**
15939 Phoenix Dr City of Industry (91745) ***(P-13295)***
Carrierx LLC (PA) ....**D....562 437-1411**
4300 E Pacific Coast Hwy Long Beach (90804) ***(P-17575)***
Carrillos Tortilleria Inc (PA) ....**F....818 365-1636**
1242 Pico St San Fernando (91340) ***(P-2405)***
Carrington Mrtg Holdings LLC ....C....888 267-0584
1600 S Douglass Rd # 110 Anaheim (92806) ***(P-15181)***
Carroll Fulmer Logistics Corp ....B....626 435-9940
13773 Algranti Ave Sylmar (91342) ***(P-12430)***
Carroll Klly Trtter Frnzen A L (PA) ....**D....562 432-5855**
111 W Ocean Blvd Fl 14 Long Beach (90802) ***(P-21527)***
Carros Americas Inc ....C....805 267-7176
2945 Townsgate Rd Ste 200 Westlake Village (91361) ***(P-9689)***
Carros Sensors Systems Co LLC (HQ) ....**C....805 968-0782**
1461 Lawrence Dr Thousand Oaks (91320) ***(P-10876)***
Carryout Bags LLC (PA) ....**D....626 279-7000**
550 S 7th Ave City of Industry (91746) ***(P-3852)***
Carryoutsupplies.com, Walnut *Also called Swc Group Inc* ***(P-3843)***
Carson Gang Diversion Team, Carson *Also called County of Los Angeles* ***(P-22289)***
Carson Industries Division, Riverside *Also called Oldcastle Infrastructure Inc* ***(P-6045)***
Carson Kurtzman Consultants (HQ) ....**C....310 823-9000**
2335 Alaska Ave El Segundo (90245) ***(P-21528)***
Carson Medical Offices, Gardena *Also called Kaiser Foundation Hospitals* ***(P-19901)***
Carson Operating Company LLC ....D....310 830-9200
2 Civic Plaza Dr Carson (90745) ***(P-16369)***
Carson Senior Assisted Living, Carson *Also called Secrom Inc* ***(P-20626)***
Carson Senior Assisted Living ....D....310 830-4010
345 E Carson St Carson (90745) ***(P-22089)***
Carson Trailer Inc (PA) ....**D....310 835-0876**
14831 S Maple Ave Gardena (90248) ***(P-10538)***
Carson Trailer Sales, Gardena *Also called Carson Trailer Inc* ***(P-10538)***
Cartel Industries LLC ....E....949 474-3200
17152 Armstrong Ave Irvine (92614) ***(P-6807)***
Cartel Marketing Inc ....C....818 483-1130
5230 Las Virgenes Rd # 25 Calabasas (91302) ***(P-15549)***
Carter Fire Protection Inc ....E....805 648-5906
1229 N Ventura Ave Ventura (93001) ***(P-14033)***
Carter Holt Harvey Holdings ....E....951 272-8180
1230 Railroad St Corona (92882) ***(P-6195)***
Carter Plating Inc ....E....818 842-1325
1842 N Keystone St Burbank (91504) ***(P-7236)***
Carter Pump & Machine Inc ....E....661 393-8620
635 G St Wasco (93280) ***(P-8542)***
Carton Design, Pico Rivera *Also called CD Container Inc* ***(P-3792)***
Carttronics LLC (HQ) ....**E....888 696-2278**
90 Icon Foothill Ranch (92610) ***(P-9858)***
Cartwright Termite & Pest Ctrl ....E....760 771-6091
51360 Calle Guatemala La Quinta (92253) ***(P-17200)***
Caruso MGT Ltd A Cal Ltd Prtnr (PA) ....**D....323 900-8100**
101 The Grove Dr Los Angeles (90036) ***(P-15798)***
Cas Medical Systems Inc (HQ) ....**F....203 488-6056**
1 Edwards Way Irvine (92614) ***(P-10960)***
Casa Clina Cmprhnsive Otptent ....D....909 596-7733
255 E Bonita Ave Pomona (91767) ***(P-21282)***
Casa Clina Ctrs For Rhbltation, Pomona *Also called Casa Colina Hospita and Cente* ***(P-20693)***
Casa Clina Hosp Ctrs For Hlthc ....C....760 248-6245
11981 Midway Ave Lucerne Valley (92356) ***(P-21730)***
Casa Colina Inc (PA) ....**A....909 596-7733**
255 E Bonita Ave Pomona (91767) ***(P-21731)***
CASA COLINA HOSPITAL AND CENTE, Pomona *Also called Casa Coline Inc* ***(P-21731)***
Casa Colina Hospital and Cente ....C....626 334-8735
910 E Alosta Ave Azusa (91702) ***(P-20210)***
Casa Colina Hospital and Cente (HQ) ....**B....909 596-7733**
255 E Bonita Ave Pomona (91767) ***(P-20693)***

Casa De Hermandad (PA)....E....**310 477-8272**
1639 11th St Santa Monica (90404) ***(P-11408)***
Casa Dorinda, Santa Barbara *Also called Montecito Retirement Assn* ***(P-20419)***
Casa Herrera Inc (PA)....C....**909 392-3930**
2655 Pine St Pomona (91767) ***(P-7930)***
Casa Pcfica Ctrs For Chldren F (PA)....C....**805 482-3260**
1722 S Lewis Rd Camarillo (93012) ***(P-21732)***
Casa Serena Apts, Bakersfield *Also called Gsf Properties Inc* ***(P-15878)***
Casa-Pacifica Inc....B....951 658-3369
2200 W Acacia Ave Ofc Hemet (92545) ***(P-22090)***
Casa-Pacifica Inc....B....951 766-5116
2400 W Acacia Ave Hemet (92545) ***(P-22091)***
Casanova Pndrill Pblicidad Inc (PA)....D....**949 474-5001**
275 Mccormick Ave Ste 1a Costa Mesa (92626) ***(P-16998)***
Cascade Optical Coating Inc....F....714 543-9777
1225 E Hunter Ave Santa Ana (92705) ***(P-10829)***
Cascade Pump Company....D....562 946-1414
10107 Norwalk Blvd Santa Fe Springs (90670) ***(P-8005)***
Casco Mfg, San Fernando *Also called C A Schroeder Inc* ***(P-6169)***
Case Automation Corporation....F....951 493-6666
208 Jason Ct Corona (92879) ***(P-7687)***
Case Club, Anaheim *Also called Foam Plastics & Rbr Pdts Corp* ***(P-5505)***
Case Paper Company....F....626 358-8450
9168 Hermosa Ave Unit 100 Rancho Cucamonga (91730) ***(P-14207)***
Case World Co....F....626 330-1000
301 S Doubleday Ave Ontario (91761) ***(P-5906)***
Casecentral Inc (HQ)....D....**415 989-2300**
1055 E Colo Blvd Ste 400 Pasadena (91106) ***(P-18471)***
Casecentral.com, Pasadena *Also called Casecentral Inc* ***(P-18471)***
Casestack LLC (HQ)....D....**310 473-8885**
3000 Ocean Park Blvd Santa Monica (90405) ***(P-12188)***
Casestack, Inc., Santa Monica *Also called Casestack LLC* ***(P-12188)***
Casewise Systems Inc (HQ)....D....**424 284-4101**
9465 Wilshire Blvd # 300 Beverly Hills (90212) ***(P-13381)***
Caseworx Inc....E....909 799-8550
1130 Research Dr Redlands (92374) ***(P-3580)***
Casey Company (PA)....C....**562 436-9685**
180 E Ocean Blvd Ste 1010 Long Beach (90802) ***(P-14801)***
Cash Convenience Inds LLC....F....805 381-0806
733 Lakefield Rd Ste Aa Westlake Village (91361) ***(P-19029)***
Cash It Here, Santa Ana *Also called Continental Currency Svcs Inc* ***(P-15125)***
Cashcall Inc....A....949 752-4600
1 City Blvd W Ste 102 Orange (92868) ***(P-15141)***
Casing Specialties Inc....E....661 399-5522
12454 Snow Rd Bakersfield (93314) ***(P-488)***
Casino Morongo....D....951 849-3080
49500 Seminole Dr Cabazon (92230) ***(P-19516)***
Casino Table Rentals, Westminster *Also called All-In Prdctons Csino Rntals L* ***(P-17332)***
Casita Michi, Irvine *Also called Michelle Barrionuevo-Mazzini* ***(P-11716)***
Casitas Care Center, Granada Hills *Also called A Cori Partnership* ***(P-20549)***
Caspian Commercial Plbg Inc....D....818 649-2500
711 Ivy St Glendale (91204) ***(P-1042)***
Cast & Crew Payroll LLC (PA)....C....**818 848-6022**
2300 W Empire Ave Ste 500 Burbank (91504) ***(P-22767)***
Cast and Crew Entrmt Svcs, Burbank *Also called Cast & Crew Payroll LLC* ***(P-22767)***
Cast Partner....F....323 876-9000
4658 W Washington Blvd Los Angeles (90016) ***(P-6412)***
Cast Parts Inc (HQ)....C....**909 595-2252**
4200 Valley Blvd Walnut (91789) ***(P-6263)***
Cast Parts Inc....C....626 937-3444
16800 Chestnut St City of Industry (91748) ***(P-6264)***
Cast-Rite Corporation....D....310 532-2080
515 E Airline Way Gardena (90248) ***(P-7785)***
Cast-Rite International Inc (PA)....D....**310 532-2080**
515 E Airline Way Gardena (90248) ***(P-6413)***
Castaic Brick, Castaic *Also called Clay Castaic Manufacturing Co* ***(P-5983)***
Castaic Lake RV Park Inc....F....661 257-3340
31540 Ridge Route Rd Castaic (91384) ***(P-3418)***
Castaic R V Park, Castaic *Also called Castaic Lake RV Park Inc* ***(P-3418)***
Castaic Truck Stop Inc....E....661 295-1374
31611 Castaic Rd Castaic (91384) ***(P-5249)***
Castaway Restaurant, The, Burbank *Also called Specialty Restaurants Corp* ***(P-16977)***
Caster Technology Corp (PA)....F....**714 893-6886**
11552 Markon Dr Garden Grove (92841) ***(P-13556)***
Castillo Maritess....F....949 216-0468
1490 S Vineyard Ave Ste G Ontario (91761) ***(P-3136)***
Castle Importing Inc....F....909 428-9200
14550 Miller Ave Fontana (92336) ***(P-1769)***
Castle Inn Inc....D....855 214-3079
1734 S Harbor Blvd Anaheim (92802) ***(P-16370)***
Castle Peak Resources LLC....E....805 535-2000
1000 Town Center Dr Fl 6 Oxnard (93036) ***(P-20276)***
Castle Press....F....800 794-0858
1128 N Gilbert St Anaheim (92801) ***(P-4624)***
Castle Rock Farming and Trnspt....D....661 721-1058
501 Richgrove Dr Richgrove (93261) ***(P-152)***
Castle Rock Vineyards, Richgrove *Also called Castle Rock Farming and Trnspt* ***(P-152)***
Castle Rock Vineyards, Delano *Also called Castlerock Farms LLC* ***(P-2173)***
Castlebrook Barns, Fontana *Also called Jocer Enterprises Inc* ***(P-775)***
Castlerock Farms LLC....E....661 721-1933
501 Richgrove Dr Delano (93215) ***(P-2173)***
Castlewood Treatment Ctr LLC (PA)....D....**805 273-5217**
2545 W Hillcrest Dr # 20 Thousand Oaks (91320) ***(P-21283)***
Caston Inc....D....909 381-1619
354 S Allen St San Bernardino (92408) ***(P-1370)***
Castoro Cellars (PA)....F....**805 467-2002**
1315 N Bethel Rd Templeton (93465) ***(P-2174)***
Casual Iq, Los Angeles *Also called Global Wide Media Inc* ***(P-17016)***
Casualway Home & Garden, Oxnard *Also called Casualway Usa LLC* ***(P-3527)***
Casualway Usa LLC....D....805 660-7408
1623 Lola Way Oxnard (93030) ***(P-3527)***
CAT Exteriors Inc....E....714 985-6906
1290 N Hancock St Ste 102 Anaheim (92807) ***(P-1477)***
Catalina Canyon Resort, Avalon *Also called Pacific Catalina Hotel Inc* ***(P-16606)***
Catalina Carpet Mills Inc (PA)....D....**562 926-5811**
14418 Best Ave Santa Fe Springs (90670) ***(P-2684)***
Catalina Channel Express Inc (HQ)....C....**310 519-7971**
385 E Swinford St San Pedro (90731) ***(P-12280)***
Catalina Channel Express Inc....D....310 510-1212
95 Berth San Pedro (90731) ***(P-12281)***
Catalina Channel Express Inc....D....562 435-8686
320 Golden Shore Lbby Long Beach (90802) ***(P-12286)***
Catalina Cylinders Inc (PA)....D....**714 890-0999**
7300 Anaconda Ave Garden Grove (92841) ***(P-6733)***
Catalina Events Inc....E....310 925-6986
2605 184th St Redondo Beach (90278) ***(P-23380)***
Catalina Express, San Pedro *Also called Catalina Channel Express Inc* ***(P-12281)***
Catalina Express, Long Beach *Also called Catalina Channel Express Inc* ***(P-12286)***
Catalina Express Cruises, San Pedro *Also called Catalina Channel Express Inc* ***(P-12280)***
Catalina Home, Santa Fe Springs *Also called Catalina Carpet Mills Inc* ***(P-2684)***
Catalina Pacific Concrete....E....310 532-4600
19030 Normandie Ave Torrance (90502) ***(P-6077)***
Catalina Spas, Murrieta *Also called Vortex Whirlpool Systems Inc* ***(P-5538)***
Catalina Yachts Inc (PA)....E....**818 884-7700**
2259 Ward Ave Simi Valley (93065) ***(P-10460)***
Catalyst Development Corp....E....760 228-9653
56925 Yucca Trl Yucca Valley (92284) ***(P-17810)***
Catalytic Solutions Inc (HQ)....D....**805 486-4649**
1700 Fiske Pl Oxnard (93033) ***(P-10663)***
Catame Inc (PA)....E....**213 749-2610**
1930 Long Beach Ave Los Angeles (90058) ***(P-11495)***
Catapult Communications Corp (HQ)....D....**818 871-1800**
26601 Agoura Rd Calabasas (91302) ***(P-17811)***
Catawba County Schools, Camarillo *Also called Microsemi Communications Inc* ***(P-9541)***
Cater Line , The, City of Industry *Also called CH Image Inc* ***(P-4249)***
Cater Tots Too, Santa Ana *Also called DAd Investments* ***(P-2416)***
Caterpillar Authorized Dealer, Riverside *Also called Johnson Machinery Co* ***(P-13863)***
Caterpillar Authorized Dealer, City of Industry *Also called Quinn Shepherd Machinery* ***(P-13871)***
Caterpillar Authorized Dealer, Corcoran *Also called Quinn Company* ***(P-13866)***
Caterpillar Authorized Dealer, Bakersfield *Also called Quinn Company* ***(P-13868)***
Caterpillar Authorized Dealer, Oxnard *Also called Quinn Company* ***(P-13869)***
Caterpillar Authorized Dealer, Santa Maria *Also called Quinn Company* ***(P-13870)***
Caterpillar Authorized Dealer, Pomona *Also called Quinn Company* ***(P-7616)***
Cathay Bank (HQ)....C....**626 279-3698**
777 N Broadway Los Angeles (90012) ***(P-15015)***
Cathay General Bancorp (PA)....D....**213 625-4700**
777 N Broadway Los Angeles (90012) ***(P-15016)***
Catholic Charities of La Inc....E....818 883-6015
21600 Hart St Canoga Park (91303) ***(P-21733)***
Catholic Chrties Los Angles In (PA)....C....**213 251-3400**
1531 James M Wood Blvd Los Angeles (90015) ***(P-22903)***
Catholic Chrties Snta Clara CN....D....805 643-4694
303 N Ventura Ave Ste A Ventura (93001) ***(P-21734)***
Catholic Family Life Ins 991, Mission Viejo *Also called Catholic Family Life Insurance* ***(P-15358)***
Catholic Family Life Insurance....E....949 472-2284
27001 La Paz Rd Ste 412 Mission Viejo (92691) ***(P-15358)***
Catholic Resource Center, West Covina *Also called Saint Jseph Communications Inc* ***(P-19174)***
Catholic Social Services, Visalia *Also called Diocese Fresno Education Corp* ***(P-21770)***
Cathy Ireland Home, Chino *Also called Omnia Leather Motion Inc* ***(P-3110)***
Cats U S A Pest Control, North Hollywood *Also called Cats USA Inc* ***(P-17201)***
Cats USA Inc....D....818 506-1000
5683 Whitnall Hwy North Hollywood (91601) ***(P-17201)***
Cattaneo Bros Inc....E....805 543-7188
769 Caudill St San Luis Obispo (93401) ***(P-1730)***
Cattrac Construction Inc....D....909 355-1146
15030 Slover Ave Fontana (92337) ***(P-992)***
Caulipower LLC....E....844 422-8544
16200 Ventura Blvd # 400 Encino (91436) ***(P-1921)***
Causeforce Inc (PA)....D....**323 654-9255**
12301 Wilshire Blvd # 430 Los Angeles (90025) ***(P-18472)***
Causeway Capital MGT LLC....C....310 231-6100
11111 Santa Monica Blvd # 1500 Los Angeles (90025) ***(P-16127)***
Cavalier Inn Incorporated....D....805 927-6444
250 San Simeon Ave Ste 4c San Simeon (93452) ***(P-16371)***
Cavalier Inn Inc....D....805 927-4688
9415 Hearst Dr San Simeon (93452) ***(P-16372)***
Cavalier Oceanfront Resort, San Simeon *Also called Cavalier Inn Inc* ***(P-16372)***
Cavallo & Cavallo Inc....F....909 428-6994
14955 Hilton Dr Fontana (92336) ***(P-8543)***
Cavanaugh Machine Works Inc....E....562 437-1126
1540 Santa Fe Ave Long Beach (90813) ***(P-8544)***
Caviar Express Inc....F....818 956-1566
820 Thompson Ave Glendale (91201) ***(P-4161)***
Cavins Oil Well Tools, Signal Hill *Also called Dawson Enterprises* ***(P-7667)***
Cavotec Dabico US Inc....E....714 947-0005
5665 Corporate Ave Cypress (90630) ***(P-10298)***
Cavotec Inet, Cypress *Also called Cavotec US Holdings Inc* ***(P-7660)***
Cavotec Inet US Inc....D....714 947-0005
5665 Corporate Ave Cypress (90630) ***(P-7638)***
Cavotec US Holdings Inc (HQ)....E....**714 545-7900**
5665 Corporate Ave Cypress (90630) ***(P-7660)***

ALPHABETIC

Employee Codes: A=Over 500 employees, B=251-500
C=101-250, D=51-100, E=20-50 F=10-19
2022 Southern California Business
Directory and Buyers Guide
© Mergent Inc. 1-800-342-5647
1087

CAW Cowie Inc (PA)......E......**212 396-9007**
7 Ginger Root Ln Rancho Palos Verdes (90275) ***(P-18473)***
CB Performance Products, Farmersville *Also called Claudes Buggies Inc* ***(P-13052)***
CB Richard Ellis, Los Angeles *Also called Cbre Inc* ***(P-15800)***
CB Richard Ellis Strgc Prtners......D......213 683-4200
515 S Flower St Los Angeles (90071) ***(P-15662)***
Cbabr Inc (PA)......D......**951 640-7056**
31620 Rr Cyn Rd Ste A Canyon Lake (92587) ***(P-15799)***
Cbdfx, Chatsworth *Also called Newhere Inc* ***(P-4860)***
Cbj LP......E......818 676-1750
21550 Oxnard St Woodland Hills (91367) ***(P-4054)***
Cbj LP......E......323 549-5225
11150 Santa Monica Blvd Los Angeles (90025) ***(P-4055)***
Cbj LP......E......949 833-8373
18500 Von Karman Ave # 150 Irvine (92612) ***(P-4056)***
Cbm Consulting Inc......D......310 329-0102
1411 W 190th St Ste 525 Gardena (90248) ***(P-22512)***
Cbol Corporation......C......818 704-8200
19850 Plummer St Chatsworth (91311) ***(P-13708)***
Cbr Electric Inc......C......949 455-0331
22 Rancho Cir Lake Forest (92630) ***(P-1231)***
Cbre Inc (HQ)......C......**213 613-3333**
400 S Hope St Ste 2500 Los Angeles (90071) ***(P-15800)***
Cbre Consulting Inc......D......213 613-3750
355 S Grand Ave Ste 1200 Los Angeles (90071) ***(P-23183)***
Cbre Global Investors Inc (HQ)......C......**213 683-4200**
601 S Figueroa St Ste 49 Los Angeles (90017) ***(P-15801)***
Cbre Globl Value Investors LLC (HQ)......C......**213 683-4200**
601 S Figueroa St Ste 49 Los Angeles (90017) ***(P-15802)***
Cbre Globl Value Investors LLC......D......949 725-8500
3501 Jamboree Rd Ste 100 Newport Beach (92660) ***(P-23184)***
Cbre Holdings LLC (HQ)......D......**213 613-3333**
400 S Hope St Ste 2500 Los Angeles (90071) ***(P-15803)***
Cbre Services Inc......D......213 613-3333
400 S Hope St Ste 2500 Los Angeles (90071) ***(P-23185)***
Cbrite Inc......E......805 722-1121
421 Pine Ave Goleta (93117) ***(P-10684)***
CBS, Los Angeles *Also called Entercom Media Corp* ***(P-12688)***
CBS, Colton *Also called Entercom Media Corp* ***(P-12689)***
CBS Enterprises, Santa Monica *Also called CBS Television Distribution* ***(P-22999)***
CBS Fasteners Inc......E......714 779-6368
1345 N Brasher St Anaheim (92807) ***(P-7060)***
CBS Network News, Los Angeles *Also called Merlot Film Productions Inc* ***(P-19148)***
CBS Paramount Television, Los Angeles *Also called CBS Studios Inc* ***(P-19108)***
CBS Studio Center, Studio City *Also called Radford Studio Center Inc* ***(P-19330)***
CBS Studios Inc (HQ)......B......**323 634-3519**
6100 Wilshire Blvd # 1000 Los Angeles (90048) ***(P-19108)***
CBS Television Distribution......D......310 264-3300
2450 Colo Ave Ste 500e Santa Monica (90404) ***(P-22999)***
CC Wellness LLC (PA)......D......**661 714-0841**
29000 Hancock Pkwy Valencia (91355) ***(P-14236)***
CCC Property Holdings LLC......C......310 609-1957
500 S Alameda St Compton (90221) ***(P-16096)***
Cccc Growth Fund LLC......D......626 441-8770
899 El Centro St South Pasadena (91030) ***(P-16252)***
Ccd, Los Angeles *Also called I T I Electro-Optic Corp* ***(P-10701)***
Ccd, Anaheim *Also called Craftsman Cutting Dies Inc* ***(P-6475)***
Ccf China Operating Corp......E......818 871-3000
26901 Malibu Hills Rd Calabasas Hills (91301) ***(P-1989)***
Ccf International LLC......F......818 871-3000
26901 Malibu Hills Rd Calabasas (91301) ***(P-1990)***
CCI, Vernon *Also called Cherokee Chemical Co Inc* ***(P-14777)***
CCI, Redlands *Also called C C I Redlands Inc* ***(P-10485)***
CCI Industries Inc (PA)......E......**714 662-3879**
350 Fischer Ave Ste A Costa Mesa (92626) ***(P-5602)***
Ccig, Westlake Village *Also called California Coml Inv Group Inc* ***(P-23423)***
CCL Label (delaware) Inc......C......909 608-2260
576 College Commerce Way Upland (91786) ***(P-4492)***
CCL Tube Inc (HQ)......C......**310 635-4444**
2250 E 220th St Carson (90810) ***(P-5603)***
Ccmsi, Irvine *Also called Cannon Cochran MGT Svcs Inc* ***(P-15548)***
CCS Industries Inc......F......559 786-8489
4125 W Noble Ave Visalia (93277) ***(P-11650)***
CCS Los Angeles Janitorial LLC (HQ)......E......**818 455-4551**
16514 Arminta St Van Nuys (91406) ***(P-17223)***
CCS Los Angeles Janitorial LLC......A......714 966-5600
10540 Talbert Ave 300w Fountain Valley (92708) ***(P-17224)***
Ccts, Santa Ana *Also called Satellite Management Co* ***(P-15994)***
CD, Culver City *Also called Charles David of California* ***(P-14432)***
CD Alexander LLC......E......949 250-3306
2802 Willis St Santa Ana (92705) ***(P-8244)***
CD Container Inc......D......562 948-1910
7343 Paramount Blvd Pico Rivera (90660) ***(P-3792)***
CD Video Manufacturing Inc......D......714 265-0770
12650 Westminster Ave Santa Ana (92706) ***(P-9834)***
Cdeq Inc......F......818 767-5143
9421 Telfair Ave Sun Valley (91352) ***(P-5933)***
CDI, Irvine *Also called Concept Development Llc* ***(P-9394)***
CDI, Reseda *Also called Child Development Institute* ***(P-21740)***
CDI Torque Products, City of Industry *Also called Consolidated Devices Inc* ***(P-9695)***
CDK Global Inc......D......714 426-4800
1100 W Town And Country R Orange (92868) ***(P-15323)***
CDM Company Inc......E......949 644-2820
12 Corporate Plaza Dr # 200 Newport Beach (92660) ***(P-11651)***
CDM Constructors Inc......D......909 579-3500
9220 Cleveland Ave # 100 Rancho Cucamonga (91730) ***(P-22513)***
CDM Corp......F......818 787-4002
7922 Haskell Ave Van Nuys (91406) ***(P-4999)***
Cdnetworks Inc (HQ)......D......**408 228-3379**
1550 Valley Vista Dr # 110 Diamond Bar (91765) ***(P-12631)***
Cdr Graphics Inc (PA)......E......**310 474-7600**
1207 E Washington Blvd Los Angeles (90021) ***(P-4248)***
Cds California LLC......F......818 766-5000
3330 Chnga Blvd W Ste 200 Los Angeles (90068) ***(P-11269)***
Cds Cold......E......562 777-9969
10035 Painter Ave Santa Fe Springs (90670) ***(P-23426)***
CDS Moving Equipment Inc (PA)......D......**310 631-1100**
375 W Manville St Rancho Dominguez (90220) ***(P-13896)***
Cdsnet LLC......A......310 981-9500
6053 W Century Blvd Los Angeles (90045) ***(P-23427)***
Cdsrvs LLC......D......714 912-8353
840 W Grove Ave Orange (92865) ***(P-19030)***
Cdti Advanced Materials Inc (PA)......E......**805 639-9458**
1641 Fiske Pl Oxnard (93033) ***(P-4656)***
Cdw, Anaheim *Also called Consolidated Design West Inc* ***(P-17166)***
CE Allencompany Inc......E......562 989-6100
2109 Gundry Ave Long Beach (90755) ***(P-993)***
Ce Nut & Bolt, Santa Fe Springs *Also called Coop Engineering Inc* ***(P-8563)***
Cebe Co, Paramount *Also called Robert W Wiesmantel* ***(P-8772)***
Cec, La Canada *Also called Child Educational Center* ***(P-21999)***
Cecal Enterprises Inc......E......949 380-7100
26081 Merit Cir Ste 106 Laguna Hills (92653) ***(P-1569)***
CECILLA GONZALEZ DE AL HOYA CA, Los Angeles *Also called White Memoria Medical Center* ***(P-21010)***
Ceco, Oxnard *Also called Component Equipment Coinc* ***(P-9649)***
Ced Anaheim 018......F......714 956-5156
1304 S Allec St Anaheim (92805) ***(P-9859)***
Cedar Holdings LLC......D......909 862-0611
7534 Palm Ave Highland (92346) ***(P-20277)***
Cedar House Rehabilitation Ctr, Bloomington *Also called Social Science Service Center* ***(P-21053)***
Cedar Mountain Post Acute, Yucaipa *Also called Cedar Operations LLC* ***(P-20278)***
Cedar Operations LLC......C......909 790-2273
11970 4th St Yucaipa (92399) ***(P-20278)***
Cedar Sinai Medical Group, Beverly Hills *Also called Medical Group Bverly Hills Inc* ***(P-19972)***
Cedarlane Natural Foods Inc (PA)......D......**310 886-7720**
1135 E Artesia Blvd Carson (90746) ***(P-2406)***
Cedarlane Natural Foods Inc......A......310 527-7833
717 E Artesia Blvd Carson (90746) ***(P-1922)***
Cedars Surgical Research Ctr, West Hollywood *Also called Cedars-Sinai Medical Center* ***(P-20695)***
Cedars- Sinai Medical Group, Los Angeles *Also called Core Medical Group Inc* ***(P-21401)***
Cedars-Sinai Home Care, Los Angeles *Also called Cedars-Sinai Medical Center* ***(P-20704)***
Cedars-Sinai Medical Center......B......310 824-3664
8635 W 3rd St Ste 1195 Los Angeles (90048) ***(P-20694)***
Cedars-Sinai Medical Center......B......310 855-7701
8700 Beverly Blvd 4018 West Hollywood (90048) ***(P-20695)***
Cedars-Sinai Medical Center......D......800 233-2771
8700 Beverly Blvd West Hollywood (90048) ***(P-19739)***
Cedars-Sinai Medical Center......B......310 423-5468
8797 Beverly Blvd Ste 220 West Hollywood (90048) ***(P-20696)***
Cedars-Sinai Medical Center......B......310 423-6451
8727 W 3rd St Los Angeles (90048) ***(P-20697)***
Cedars-Sinai Medical Center......B......310 423-8965
8723 Alden Dr Los Angeles (90048) ***(P-20698)***
Cedars-Sinai Medical Center......B......310 423-5841
8700 Beverly Blvd # 8211 West Hollywood (90048) ***(P-20699)***
Cedars-Sinai Medical Center......C......310 423-3849
127 S San Vicente Blvd # 3417 Los Angeles (90048) ***(P-19740)***
Cedars-Sinai Medical Center......B......310 423-5147
8700 Beverly Blvd # 2216 West Hollywood (90048) ***(P-20700)***
Cedars-Sinai Medical Center......B......310 423-9310
310 N San Vicente Blvd West Hollywood (90048) ***(P-20701)***
Cedars-Sinai Medical Center......B......310 967-1884
99 N La Cienega Blvd Me Beverly Hills (90211) ***(P-20702)***
Cedars-Sinai Medical Center......B......310 385-3326
200 N Robertson Blvd Beverly Hills (90211) ***(P-20703)***
Cedars-Sinai Medical Center......B......310 423-3277
8635 W 3rd St Ste 1165w Los Angeles (90048) ***(P-20704)***
Cedars-Sinai Medical Center......B......310 423-9520
444 S San Vicente Blvd # 1001 Los Angeles (90048) ***(P-20705)***
Cedars-Sinai Medical Center......C......323 866-8483
8631 W 3rd St Ste 730 Los Angeles (90048) ***(P-19741)***
Cedars-Sinai Medical Center......B......310 967-1900
4100 W 190th St Torrance (90504) ***(P-20706)***
Cedars-Sinai Medical Center......B......310 385-3400
250 N Robertson Blvd # 101 Beverly Hills (90211) ***(P-20707)***
Cedars-Sinai Medical Center......B......310 423-8780
8700 Beverly Blvd # 1103 West Hollywood (90048) ***(P-20708)***
Cedars-Snai Imging Med Group A......D......310 423-8000
8700 Beverly Blvd West Hollywood (90048) ***(P-20709)***
Cedarwood-Young Company (PA)......C......**626 962-4047**
14620 Joanbridge St Baldwin Park (91706) ***(P-12937)***
Cedarwood-Young Company......D......626 962-4047
14618 Arrow Hwy Baldwin Park (91706) ***(P-14112)***
Cee Baileys Aircraft Plastics, Montebello *Also called Desser Tire & Rubber Co LLC* ***(P-14055)***
Cee Baileys Aircraft Plastics......F......323 721-4900
6900 W Acco St Montebello (90640) ***(P-10486)***
Cee Jay Research & Sales LLC......F......626 815-1530
920 W 10th St Azusa (91702) ***(P-4493)***
Cee Sportswear......F......323 726-8158
6409 Gayhart St Commerce (90040) ***(P-2931)***

Mergent e-mail: customerrelations@mergent.com
1088
2022 Southern California Business Directory and Buyers Guide
(P-0000) Products & Services Section entry number
(PA)=Parent Co (HQ)=Headquarters (DH)=Div Headquarters

Celebrity Casinos Inc ....B....310 631-3838
123 E Artesia Blvd Compton (90220) ***(P-16373)***
Celebrity Pink, Montebello *Also called 2253 Apparel LLC* ***(P-14325)***
Celera Corporation (HQ) ....**B....510 749-4200**
33608 Ortega Hwy San Juan Capistrano (92675) ***(P-22904)***
Celesco Transducer Products ....F....818 701-2701
20630 Plummer St Chatsworth (91311) ***(P-9690)***
Celestial Lighting, Santa Fe Springs *Also called Shimada Enterprises Inc* ***(P-9146)***
Celestica Aerospace Tech Corp ....C....512 310-7540
895 S Rockefeller Ave Ontario (91761) ***(P-9387)***
Celestica LLC ....B....909 201-3995
8840 Flower Rd Ste 110 Rancho Cucamonga (91730) ***(P-22514)***
Celestica-Aerospace, Ontario *Also called Celestica Aerospace Tech Corp* ***(P-9387)***
Celestron Acquisition LLC ....D....310 328-9560
2835 Columbia St Torrance (90503) ***(P-10830)***
Celestron International ....E....310 328-9560
2835 Columbia St Torrance (90503) ***(P-10831)***
Celex Solutions, Brea *Also called Contract Services Group Inc* ***(P-17232)***
Cell Business Equipment, Irvine *Also called Sema Inc* ***(P-22812)***
Cellco Partnership ....D....818 344-3366
18471 Ventura Blvd Tarzana (91356) ***(P-12597)***
Cellco Partnership ....D....310 603-0101
237 E Compton Blvd Compton (90220) ***(P-12598)***
Cellco Partnership ....D....818 500-7779
1023 E Colorado St Glendale (91205) ***(P-12599)***
Cellco Partnership ....D....661 765-5397
407 Kern St Taft (93268) ***(P-12600)***
Cellco Partnership ....D....951 205-4170
20 City Blvd W Orange (92868) ***(P-12601)***
Cellco Partnership ....D....323 662-0009
2921 Los Feliz Blvd Los Angeles (90039) ***(P-12602)***
Cellco Partnership ....D....562 244-8814
11902 Gem St Norwalk (90650) ***(P-12603)***
Cellco Partnership ....D....949 488-9990
638 Cmino De Los Mres Ste San Clemente (92673) ***(P-12604)***
Cello Jeans, Commerce *Also called Hidden Jeans Inc* ***(P-2574)***
Cellu-Con Inc ....E....559 568-0190
19994 Meredith Dr Strathmore (93267) ***(P-5167)***
Celmol Inc ....D....714 259-1000
1611 E Saint Andrew Pl Santa Ana (92705) ***(P-14919)***
Cemco, City of Industry *Also called California Expanded Met Pdts* ***(P-6802)***
Cemcoat Inc ....E....323 733-0125
4928 W Jefferson Blvd Los Angeles (90016) ***(P-7237)***
Cemex Cement Inc ....B....626 969-1747
1201 W Gladstone St Azusa (91702) ***(P-13296)***
Cemex Cement Inc ....C....760 381-7616
25220 Black Mtn Quar Rd Apple Valley (92307) ***(P-6078)***
Cemex Cnstr Mtls PCF LLC ....F....909 335-3105
8203 Alabama Ave Highland (92346) ***(P-6079)***
Cemex Cnstr Mtls PCF LLC ....F....909 355-8754
13200 Santa Ana Ave Fontana (92337) ***(P-6080)***
Cemex Construction Mtls Inc (HQ) ....**E....909 974-5500**
3990 Concourse Ste 200 Ontario (91764) ***(P-13297)***
Cemex Materials LLC ....D....951 277-2420
23200 Temescal Canyon Rd Corona (92883) ***(P-6081)***
Cemex Materials LLC ....D....909 825-1500
1201 S La Cadena Dr Colton (92324) ***(P-6082)***
Cemex USA Inc ....C....909 798-1144
8731 Orange St Redlands (92374) ***(P-6083)***
Cemex USA Inc ....F....909 974-5500
4120 Jurupa St Ste 202 Ontario (91761) ***(P-6084)***
Cemtek Environmental Inc ....E....714 437-7100
3041 Orange Ave Santa Ana (92707) ***(P-23428)***
Cemtrol Inc ....F....714 666-6606
3035 E La Jolla St Anaheim (92806) ***(P-8150)***
Cencal Health, Santa Barbara *Also called Santa Barbara San Luis Obispo* ***(P-15383)***
Cencal Machine Company ....F....661 392-7831
19444 Colombo St Bakersfield (93308) ***(P-8545)***
Centech Group Inc ....E....661 275-5688
2 Draco Dr Bldg 8352 Edwards (93524) ***(P-18474)***
Centene Chwp ....C....760 482-5593
1699 W Main St El Centro (92243) ***(P-15393)***
Centent Company ....F....714 979-6491
3879 S Main St Santa Ana (92707) ***(P-8151)***
Center At Parkwest, The, Reseda *Also called Chase Group Llc* ***(P-23188)***
Center Automotive Inc ....D....818 907-9995
5201 Van Nuys Blvd Sherman Oaks (91401) ***(P-13023)***
Center B M W, Sherman Oaks *Also called Center Automotive Inc* ***(P-13023)***
Center Club ....D....714 662-3414
650 Town Center Dr Ste G Costa Mesa (92626) ***(P-22324)***
Center For Achievement Center, Bakersfield *Also called New Advnces For Pple With Dsbl* ***(P-22204)***
Center For Atism Rlted Dsrders (PA) ....**C....818 345-2345**
21600 Oxnard St Ste 1800 Woodland Hills (91367) ***(P-20211)***
Center For Autism & ....E....949 203-8872
106 Discovery Irvine (92618) ***(P-21284)***
Center For Civic Education (PA) ....**D....818 591-9321**
5115 Douglas Fir Rd Ste J Calabasas (91302) ***(P-22905)***
Center For Crgiver Advancement ....C....866 888-8213
2910 Beverly Blvd Los Angeles (90057) ***(P-22288)***
Center Line Performance Wheels, Newport Beach *Also called Center Line Wheel Corporation* ***(P-10029)***
Center Line Wheel Corporation ....E....562 921-9637
23 Corporate Plaza Dr # 150 Newport Beach (92660) ***(P-10029)***
Center Thtre Group Los Angeles (PA) ....**C....213 972-7344**
601 W Temple St Los Angeles (90012) ***(P-19306)***
Centerfield Media, Los Angeles *Also called Qology Direct LLC* ***(P-18646)***
Centerfield Media Holdings LLC (PA) ....**B....310 341-4420**
12130 Millennium Ste 500 Los Angeles (90094) ***(P-23186)***
Centerline Mortgage Capitl Inc ....D....949 221-6685
18300 Von Karman Ave # 6 Irvine (92612) ***(P-16253)***
Centerline Wood Products ....D....760 246-4530
10007 Yucca Rd Adelanto (92301) ***(P-14148)***
Centerpoint Mfg Co Inc ....E....818 842-2147
2625 N San Fernando Blvd Burbank (91504) ***(P-8546)***
Centinela Consulting Group Inc ....F....310 674-2115
720 E Florence Ave Inglewood (90301) ***(P-6021)***
Centinela Frman Rgonal Med Ctr, Marina Del Rey *Also called Cfhs Holdings Inc* ***(P-20710)***
Centinela Frman Rgonal Med Ctr, Marina Del Rey *Also called Cfhs Holdings Inc* ***(P-20711)***
Centinela Frman Rgonal Med Ctr, Inglewood *Also called Cfhs Holdings Inc* ***(P-20713)***
Centinela Hospital Medical Ctr, Inglewood *Also called Prime Healthcare Centinela LLC* ***(P-20902)***
Centinela Skld Nrng Wlns Cntr, Inglewood *Also called West Cntinela Vly Care Ctr Inc* ***(P-20505)***
Centinela Valley Care Center ....D....310 674-3216
950 S Flower St Inglewood (90301) ***(P-22092)***
Centon Electronics Inc (PA) ....**D....949 855-9111**
27 Journey Ste 100 Aliso Viejo (92656) ***(P-8192)***
Centra Freight Services Inc ....D....310 568-8810
5140 W 104th St Inglewood (90304) ***(P-12431)***
Central Blower Co ....E....626 330-3182
211 S 7th Ave City of Industry (91746) ***(P-8043)***
Central Bsin Mncpl Wtr Dst Fin ....D....323 201-5500
6252 Telegraph Rd Commerce (90040) ***(P-12882)***
Central California Baking Co ....C....559 592-2270
701 Industrial Dr Ca Exeter (93221) ***(P-1991)***
Central California Cnstr Inc ....E....661 978-8230
7221 Downing Ave Bakersfield (93308) ***(P-489)***
Central California Power ....E....661 589-2870
19487 Broken Ct Shafter (93263) ***(P-18816)***
Central Cardiology Med Clinic ....C....661 395-0000
2901 Sillect Ave Ste 100 Bakersfield (93308) ***(P-19742)***
Central Cast Pthlogy Cons Inc (HQ) ....**D....805 541-6033**
3701 S Higuera St San Luis Obispo (93401) ***(P-21062)***
Central Coast Agriculture Inc (PA) ....**D....805 694-8594**
8701 Santa Rosa Rd Buellton (93427) ***(P-102)***
Central Coast Distributing LLC ....D....805 922-2108
815 S Blosser Rd Santa Maria (93458) ***(P-14823)***
Central Coast Management, Ventura *Also called Pierpont Inn Inc* ***(P-16630)***
Central Coast Pathology Lab, Bakersfield *Also called Physicians Automated Lab Inc* ***(P-21084)***
Central Coast Printing, San Luis Obispo *Also called David B Anderson* ***(P-4272)***
Central Coast Seafoods ....C....805 462-3474
5495 Traffic Way Atascadero (93422) ***(P-14568)***
Central Coast Wine Services, Santa Maria *Also called Central Coast Wine Warehouse* ***(P-2175)***
Central Coast Wine Warehouse (PA) ....**E....805 928-9210**
2717 Aviation Way Ste 101 Santa Maria (93455) ***(P-2175)***
Central Envmtl Training Ctr, Bakersfield *Also called Kern Cmnty Cllege Dst Fndation* ***(P-21958)***
Central Garden Distribution, Santa Fe Springs *Also called Excel Garden Products* ***(P-14858)***
Central Health Plan Cal Inc ....C....626 938-7120
1540 Bridgegate Dr Diamond Bar (91765) ***(P-21147)***
Central KY Dialysis Ctrs LLC (HQ) ....**E....310 536-2400**
601 Hawaii St El Segundo (90245) ***(P-21234)***
Central Medical Offices, Bakersfield *Also called Kaiser Foundation Hospitals* ***(P-19887)***
Central Orange County Svc Ctr, Santa Ana *Also called Southern California Edison Co* ***(P-12839)***
Central Purchasing LLC (HQ) ....**B....800 444-3353**
3491 Mission Oaks Blvd Camarillo (93012) ***(P-13978)***
Central Roofing Company, Gardena *Also called Claud Townsley Inc* ***(P-1478)***
Central Tent, Santa Clarita *Also called Frametent Inc* ***(P-3139)***
Central Valley Almond Assn ....D....661 792-2171
12655 Garzoli Ave Mc Farland (93250) ***(P-162)***
Central Valley Family Health, Avenal *Also called Adventist Hlth Systm/West Corp* ***(P-20658)***
Central Valley Meat Co Inc (PA) ....**C....559 583-9624**
10431 8 3/4 Ave Hanford (93230) ***(P-1709)***
Central Vly Fmly Halthcorcoran, Corcoran *Also called Adventist Hlth Systm/West Corp* ***(P-20659)***
Central Vly Fmly Health-Dinuba, Dinuba *Also called Adventist Hlth Systm/West Corp* ***(P-20657)***
Central Vly Fmly Hlth-Lmoore E, Lemoore *Also called Adventist Hlth Systm/West Corp* ***(P-20660)***
Central Vly Regional Ctr Inc ....C....559 738-2200
5441 W Cypress Ave Visalia (93277) ***(P-21285)***
Centralize Leasing Corp ....D....949 252-2000
18301 Von Karman Ave # 1 Irvine (92612) ***(P-15162)***
Centre For Neuro Skills (PA) ....**B....661 872-3408**
5215 Ashe Rd Bakersfield (93313) ***(P-21286)***
Centrescapes Inc ....D....909 392-3303
165 Gentry St Pomona (91767) ***(P-296)***
Centric Brands Inc ....E....951 797-5077
48650 Seminole Dr Ste 170 Cabazon (92230) ***(P-2562)***
Centric Brands Inc ....E....323 837-3700
1500 Cotner Ave Ste 1 Los Angeles (90025) ***(P-2563)***
Centric Brands LLC ....D....323 837-3700
5900 Triumph St Commerce (90040) ***(P-691)***
Centric Parts, City of Industry *Also called Cwd LLC* ***(P-9941)***
Centric Parts, Carson *Also called Cwd LLC* ***(P-10039)***
Centron Industries Inc ....E....310 324-6443
441 W Victoria St Gardena (90248) ***(P-9261)***
Centurion Group, The, Los Angeles *Also called Mulholland SEC & Patrol Inc* ***(P-18298)***

ALPHABETIC

Employee Codes: A=Over 500 employees, B=251-500 C=101-250, D=51-100, E=20-50 F=10-19
2022 Southern California Business Directory and Buyers Guide
© Mergent Inc. 1-800-342-5647
1089

Centurion Security Svcs Inc (PA).....D.....**949 474-0444**
20102 Sw Cypress St Newport Beach (92660) ***(P-18261)***

Century 21, Victorville *Also called Fairway Realty Inc* ***(P-15853)***

Century 21, Monrovia *Also called Adams and Barnes Inc* ***(P-15764)***

Century 21, Redlands *Also called Lois Lauer Realty* ***(P-15912)***

Century 21, West Covina *Also called Impact Realty Inc* ***(P-15889)***

Century 21, Visalia *Also called Jordan - Link & Company* ***(P-15898)***

Century 21, Hesperia *Also called Hannaknapp Realty Inc* ***(P-15879)***

Century 21 A Better Svc Rlty.....D.....562 806-1000
5831 Firestone Blvd Ste J South Gate (90280) ***(P-15804)***

Century 21 Crest.....D.....818 248-9100
4005 Foothill Blvd La Crescenta (91214) ***(P-15805)***

Century 21 Exclusive Realtors.....C.....310 373-5252
22831 Hawthorne Blvd Torrance (90505) ***(P-15806)***

Century 21 Hill Top Realtors, Simi Valley *Also called First & La Realty Corp* ***(P-15854)***

Century 21 Landmark Properties.....E.....562 422-0911
1650 Ximeno Ave Ste 120 Long Beach (90804) ***(P-15807)***

Century 21 Ludecke Inc (PA).....D.....**626 445-0123**
34 E Foothill Blvd Arcadia (91006) ***(P-15808)***

Century 21 Masters (PA).....D.....**909 595-6697**
1169 Fairway Dr Ste 100 Walnut (91789) ***(P-15809)***

Century 21 Superstars (PA).....D.....**949 888-1950**
22342 Avend Emprs S 155 Rancho Santa Margari (92688) ***(P-15810)***

Century 8, North Hollywood *Also called Century Theatres Inc* ***(P-19295)***

Century American Aluminum Inc.....E.....909 390-2384
1001 S Doubleday Ave Ontario (91761) ***(P-6305)***

Century Bankcard Services.....D.....818 700-3100
25129 The Old Rd Ste 222 Stevenson Ranch (91381) ***(P-18475)***

Century Blinds Inc.....D.....951 734-3762
300 S Promenade Ave Corona (92879) ***(P-3708)***

Century Downtown 10, Ventura *Also called Century Theatres Inc* ***(P-19294)***

Century Electronics, Newbury Park *Also called Perillo Industries Inc* ***(P-13762)***

Century Hlth Staffing Svcs Inc.....C.....661 322-0606
1701 Westwind Dr Ste 101 Bakersfield (93301) ***(P-17405)***

Century National, Westlake Village *Also called Kramer-Wilson Company Inc* ***(P-15468)***

Century National Properties (PA).....D.....**818 760-0880**
12200 Sylvan St Ste 250 North Hollywood (91606) ***(P-16374)***

Century Pacific Realty Corp.....C.....310 729-9922
9401 Wilshire Blvd # 1250 Beverly Hills (90212) ***(P-16048)***

Century Pallets, Lynwood *Also called Roger R Caruso Enterprises Inc* ***(P-3406)***

Century Parts Inc.....F.....310 328-0281
913 W 223rd St Torrance (90502) ***(P-8547)***

Century Pk Capitl Partners LLC (PA).....C.....**310 867-2210**
2101 Rosecrans Ave # 4275 El Segundo (90245) ***(P-16153)***

Century Precision Engrg Inc.....E.....310 538-0015
2141 W 139th St Gardena (90249) ***(P-8548)***

Century Properties Owners Assn.....E.....310 272-8580
1 W Century Dr Los Angeles (90067) ***(P-15811)***

Century Publishing.....F.....951 849-4586
218 N Murray St Banning (92220) ***(P-4494)***

Century Rubber Company Inc.....F.....661 366-7009
719 Rooster Dr Bakersfield (93307) ***(P-5370)***

Century Skill Care.....D.....310 672-1012
301 Centinela Ave Inglewood (90302) ***(P-20279)***

Century Skilled Nursing Care, Inglewood *Also called Century Skill Care* ***(P-20279)***

Century Snacks LLC.....B.....323 278-9578
5560 E Slauson Ave Commerce (90040) ***(P-14560)***

Century Spring, Commerce *Also called Matthew Warren Inc* ***(P-7466)***

Century Theatres Inc.....C.....805 641-6555
555 E Main St Ventura (93001) ***(P-19294)***

Century Theatres Inc.....C.....818 508-1943
12827 Victory Blvd North Hollywood (91606) ***(P-19295)***

Century West BMW.....D.....818 432-5800
4245 Lankershim Blvd North Hollywood (91602) ***(P-18817)***

Century West Plumbing, Westlake Village *Also called Sdg Enterprises* ***(P-1135)***

Century Wilshire Hotel, Culver City *Also called Century Wilshire Inc* ***(P-16375)***

Century Wilshire Inc.....D.....310 558-9400
9400 Culver Blvd Culver City (90232) ***(P-16375)***

Century Wire & Cable Inc.....D.....800 999-5566
7400 E Slauson Ave Commerce (90040) ***(P-6347)***

Century, The, Los Angeles *Also called Century Properties Owners Assn* ***(P-15811)***

Century-National Insurance Co (HQ).....B.....**818 760-0880**
16650 Sherman Way Van Nuys (91406) ***(P-15359)***

Cenveo Worldwide Limited.....B.....626 369-4921
705 Baldwin Park Blvd City of Industry (91746) ***(P-14193)***

Cera Inc.....E.....626 814-2688
14180 Live Oak Ave Ste I Baldwin Park (91706) ***(P-10654)***

Ceramic Decorating Company Inc.....E.....323 268-5135
4651 Sheila St Commerce (90040) ***(P-18476)***

Ceramic Tile Art Inc.....D.....818 767-9088
11601 Pendleton St Sun Valley (91352) ***(P-1412)***

Ceratizit Los Angeles LLC.....D.....310 464-8050
1401 W Walnut St Rancho Dominguez (90220) ***(P-7723)***

Cerenzia Foods Inc.....D.....909 989-4000
8585 White Oak Ave Rancho Cucamonga (91730) ***(P-14459)***

Ceridian Tax Service Inc.....B.....714 963-1311
17390 Brookhurst St Fountain Valley (92708) ***(P-22768)***

Cerritos Ctr For Prfrmg Arts, Cerritos *Also called City of Cerritos* ***(P-19307)***

Cerritos Medical Office Bldg, Cerritos *Also called Kaiser Foundation Hospitals* ***(P-19892)***

Cerritos Reference Labs Inc.....D.....562 865-3609
3848 Del Amo Blvd Ste 303 Torrance (90503) ***(P-21063)***

Cerro Corso Community College, Ridgecrest *Also called Kern Community College Dst* ***(P-22025)***

Certainteed Corona Inc.....C.....951 272-1300
235 Radio Rd Corona (92879) ***(P-5604)***

Certance LLC (HQ).....B.....**949 856-7800**
141 Innovation Dr Irvine (92617) ***(P-8193)***

Certemy Inc.....F.....866 907-4088
14876 Raymer St Ste 200 Van Nuys (91405) ***(P-17812)***

Certified Aviation Svcs LLC.....D.....310 338-1224
5720 Avion Dr Los Angeles (90045) ***(P-12346)***

Certified Distribution Svcs, Santa Fe Springs *Also called Contract Transportation Sys Co* ***(P-5094)***

Certified Enameling Inc (PA).....D.....**323 264-4403**
3342 Emery St Los Angeles (90023) ***(P-7352)***

Certified Frnsic Ln Adtors LLC (PA).....C.....**310 432-6304**
13101 W Wash Blvd Ste 444 Los Angeles (90066) ***(P-22769)***

Certified Frt Logistics Inc (PA).....C.....**800 592-5906**
1344 White Ct Santa Maria (93458) ***(P-12021)***

Certified Steel Treating Corp.....E.....323 583-8711
2454 E 58th St Vernon (90058) ***(P-7238)***

Certified Thermoplastics Inc.....E.....661 222-3006
26381 Ferry Ct Santa Clarita (91350) ***(P-5605)***

Certified Thermoplastics LLC, Santa Clarita *Also called Certified Thermoplastics Inc* ***(P-5605)***

Certified Trnsp Svcs Inc.....D.....714 835-8676
1038 N Custer St Santa Ana (92701) ***(P-11909)***

Certified Wtr Dmage Rstrtion E.....E.....800 417-1776
5319 University Dr Irvine (92612) ***(P-17225)***

Certifix Inc.....F.....714 496-3850
1950 W Corporate Way Anaheim (92801) ***(P-11652)***

Certifix Live Scan, Anaheim *Also called Certifix Inc* ***(P-11652)***

Certis USA LLC.....E.....661 758-8471
720 5th St Wasco (93280) ***(P-5168)***

Cerwin Vega & Diamond Audio, Los Angeles *Also called Cv & Da Holdings Inc* ***(P-18786)***

Cetera Financial Group Inc (PA).....D.....**866 489-3100**
200 N Pacific Coast Hwy # 11 El Segundo (90245) ***(P-18477)***

Ceva Logistics LLC.....B.....310 223-6500
19600 S Western Ave Torrance (90501) ***(P-12432)***

Ceva Logistics US Inc.....D.....310 972-5500
19600 S Western Ave Torrance (90501) ***(P-12433)***

Cevians LLC.....D.....714 619-5135
3128 Red Hill Ave Costa Mesa (92626) ***(P-5917)***

CF, Van Nuys *Also called Consolidated Fabricators Corp* ***(P-6738)***

CF Valencia Arcis LLC.....D.....661 254-4401
27330 Tourney Rd Valencia (91355) ***(P-19553)***

CF&b Manufacturing Inc.....E.....714 744-8361
1405 N Manzanita St Orange (92867) ***(P-3880)***

Cfbtel.....F.....949 381-2525
3151 Airway Ave Ste B2 Costa Mesa (92626) ***(P-9229)***

Cfhc, Los Angeles *Also called Essential Access Health* ***(P-22183)***

Cfhs Holdings Inc.....B.....310 823-8911
4650 Lincoln Blvd Marina Del Rey (90292) ***(P-20710)***

Cfhs Holdings Inc.....B.....310 448-7800
4640 Admiralty Way # 650 Marina Del Rey (90292) ***(P-20711)***

Cfhs Holdings Inc (HQ).....A.....**310 823-8911**
4650 Lincoln Blvd Marina Del Rey (90292) ***(P-20712)***

Cfhs Holdings Inc.....B.....310 673-4660
555 E Hardy St Inglewood (90301) ***(P-20713)***

CFI Holdings Corp.....D.....909 595-2252
4200 Valley Blvd Pomona (91765) ***(P-6265)***

Cforia Software Inc.....E.....818 871-9687
4333 Park Terrace Dr # 201 Westlake Village (91361) ***(P-17813)***

Cfp Designs Inc.....D.....661 903-8940
3001 Petrol Rd Bakersfield (93308) ***(P-1043)***

Cfp Fire Protection Inc.....D.....949 727-3277
153 Technology Dr Ste 200 Irvine (92618) ***(P-1044)***

Cfr Rinkens LLC (PA).....D.....**310 639-7725**
15501 Texaco Ave Paramount (90723) ***(P-12434)***

CFS Income Tax, Simi Valley *Also called CFS Tax Software* ***(P-17814)***

CFS Tax Software.....E.....805 522-1157
1445 E Los Angeles Ave # 214 Simi Valley (93065) ***(P-17814)***

Cfw Precision Metal Components, Grover Beach *Also called C F W Research & Dev Co* ***(P-6298)***

Cg Oncology Inc.....E.....949 409-3700
400 Spectrum Center Dr # 20 Irvine (92618) ***(P-4807)***

CGB, Gardena *Also called Pulp Studio Incorporated* ***(P-17184)***

Cgm Inc.....E.....818 609-7088
19611 Ventura Blvd # 211 Tarzana (91356) ***(P-11335)***

Cgm Findings, Tarzana *Also called Cgm Inc* ***(P-11335)***

Cgnfm, Valencia *Also called Creatons Grdn Ntral Fd Mkts In* ***(P-4742)***

Cgp Holdings LLC.....D.....760 764-1300
2 Gill Station Coastal Rd Little Lake (93542) ***(P-13009)***

Cgpc America Corporation.....E.....951 332-4100
1181 California Ave # 235 Corona (92881) ***(P-4682)***

Cgr/Thompson Industries Inc.....D.....714 678-4200
7155 Fenwick Ln Westminster (92683) ***(P-8865)***

Cgtech (HQ).....E.....**949 753-1050**
9000 Research Dr Irvine (92618) ***(P-18022)***

Cgtech Vericut, Irvine *Also called Cgtech* ***(P-18022)***

CH Image Inc.....E.....626 336-6063
15350 Valley Blvd City of Industry (91746) ***(P-4249)***

CH Laboratories Inc (PA).....E.....**310 516-8273**
1243 W 130th St Gardena (90247) ***(P-4808)***

CH Morris Co Inc.....E.....909 829-4481
8539 Nuevo Ave Fontana (92335) ***(P-13050)***

Cha Health Systems Inc (PA).....A.....**213 487-3211**
3731 Wilshire Blvd # 850 Los Angeles (90010) ***(P-19743)***

Cha Hollywood Medical Ctr LP (HQ).....A.....**213 413-3000**
1300 N Vermont Ave Los Angeles (90027) ***(P-20714)***

Cha La Mirada LLC.....C.....714 739-8500
14299 Firestone Blvd La Mirada (90638) ***(P-16376)***

Cha Renetative Medicine, Los Angeles *Also called Cha Health Systems Inc* ***(P-19743)***

Chad Industries Incorporated.....E.....714 938-0080
1565 S Sinclair St Anaheim (92806) ***(P-8114)***

Mergent e-mail: customerrelations@mergent.com
1090
2022 Southern California Business
Directory and Buyers Guide
(P-0000) Products & Services Section entry number
(PA)=Parent Co (HQ)=Headquarters (DH)=Div Headquarters

Challenge Graphics Inc...E...818 892-0123
7661 Densmore Ave Ste 3 Van Nuys (91406) ***(P-4250)***
Challenge Publications Inc...F...818 700-6868
21835 Nordhoff St Chatsworth (91311) ***(P-4057)***
Challenger Ornamental Ir Works...F...818 507-7030
437 W Palmer Ave Glendale (91204) ***(P-6955)***
Chalmers Corporation...D...562 948-4850
7901 Crossway Dr Pico Rivera (90660) ***(P-692)***
Chambers & Chambers Inc...F...818 995-6961
14011 Ventura Blvd 210e Sherman Oaks (91423) ***(P-2176)***
Chambers Chmbers Wine Mrchants, Sherman Oaks *Also called Chambers & Chambers Inc* ***(P-2176)***
Chameleon Beverage Company Inc (PA)...**D...323 724-8223**
6444 E 26th St Commerce (90040) ***(P-2261)***
Chamisal Vineyards LLC...F...866 808-9463
7525 Orcutt Rd San Luis Obispo (93401) ***(P-2177)***
Champion Chemical Co Cal Inc...E...562 945-1456
8319 Greenleaf Ave Whittier (90602) ***(P-14775)***
Champion Electric Inc...D...951 276-9619
3950 Garner Rd Riverside (92501) ***(P-1232)***
Champion Newspapers, Chino *Also called Champion Pblications Chino Inc* ***(P-3960)***
Champion Pblications Chino Inc...F...909 628-5501
13179 9th St Chino (91710) ***(P-3960)***
Champion-Arrowhead LLC...E...323 221-9137
5147 Alhambra Ave Los Angeles (90032) ***(P-6556)***
Champions Bowling & Embroidery...F...714 968-5033
3058 Capri Ln Costa Mesa (92626) ***(P-19396)***
Champions Choice Inc...F...714 635-4491
1910 E Via Burton Anaheim (92806) ***(P-5289)***
Chamson Management Inc...D...714 751-2400
7 Hutton Centre Dr Santa Ana (92707) ***(P-16377)***
Chan Family Partnership LP...D...626 322-7132
801 S Grand Ave Apt 1811 Los Angeles (90017) ***(P-23000)***
Chancellor Hlth Care Cal I Inc (PA)...**D...909 796-0235**
25383 Cole St Loma Linda (92354) ***(P-20570)***
Chandler Aggregates Inc (PA)...**E...951 277-1341**
24867 Maitri Rd Corona (92883) ***(P-562)***
Chandlers Plos Vrdes Sand Grav...F...310 784-2900
26311 Palos Verdes Dr E Rllng HLS Est (90274) ***(P-569)***
Change Home Mortgage, Irvine *Also called Change Lending LLC* ***(P-15182)***
Change Lending LLC (PA)...**D...949 423-6814**
16845 Von Karman Ave # 2 Irvine (92606) ***(P-15182)***
Channel 9 Australia Inc (HQ)...**D...323 461-3853**
6255 W Sunset Blvd # 1500 Los Angeles (90028) ***(P-12711)***
Channel Electric Supply, Oxnard *Also called Dieners Electric Inc* ***(P-1243)***
Channel Islnds Opt-Mchncal Eng...F...805 644-2153
1595 Walter St Ste 1 Ventura (93003) ***(P-8549)***
Channel Islnds Vgtble Frms Inc (PA)...**D...805 984-1910**
595 Victoria Ave Oxnard (93030) ***(P-99)***
Channel Islnds Yung MNS Chrstn...D...805 963-8775
301 W Figueroa St Santa Barbara (93101) ***(P-22325)***
Channel Islnds Yung MNS Chrstn...D...805 736-3483
201 W College Ave Lompoc (93436) ***(P-22326)***
Channel Islnds Yung MNS Chrstn...D...805 484-0423
3111 Village Park Dr Camarillo (93012) ***(P-22327)***
Channel Islnds Yung MNS Chrstn...D...805 687-7727
36 Hitchcock Way Santa Barbara (93105) ***(P-22328)***
Channel Islnds Yung MNS Chrstn...D...805 969-3288
591 Santa Rosa Ln Santa Barbara (93108) ***(P-22329)***
Channel Islnds Yung MNS Chrstn...D...805 484-0423
3760 Telegraph Rd Ventura (93003) ***(P-22330)***
Channel Islnds Yung MNS Chrstn...D...805 686-2037
900 N Refugio Rd Santa Ynez (93460) ***(P-22331)***
Channel Technologies Group, Santa Barbara *Also called International Tranducer Corp* ***(P-10759)***
Channel Vision Technology, Laguna Hills *Also called Djh Enterprises* ***(P-9267)***
Channell Commercial Corp (PA)...**D...951 719-2600**
33380 Zeiders Rd Ste 101 Menifee (92584) ***(P-9230)***
CHAP, Pasadena *Also called Community Hlth Alance Pasadena* ***(P-20726)***
Chapala Iron & Manufacturing...E...805 654-9803
1301 Callens Rd Ventura (93003) ***(P-6196)***
Chaparral, Ontario *Also called Kls Doors LLC* ***(P-3259)***
Chaparral Construction Corp...D...805 647-8606
2101 Ventura Blvd Oxnard (93036) ***(P-870)***
Chaparral Motorsports, San Bernardino *Also called Ocelot Engineering Inc* ***(P-13076)***
Chapman Academic Center, Palmdale *Also called Chapman University* ***(P-23187)***
Chapman Designs Inc...E...562 698-4600
11203 Shoemaker Ave Santa Fe Springs (90670) ***(P-3209)***
Chapman Engineering Corp...E...714 542-1942
2321 Cape Cod Way Santa Ana (92703) ***(P-8550)***
CHAPMAN FAMILY HEALTH, Orange *Also called Chapman Global Medical Center* ***(P-20715)***
Chapman Global Medical Center...B...714 633-0011
2601 E Chapman Ave Orange (92869) ***(P-20715)***
Chapman Golf Development LLC...D...760 564-8723
78505 Avenue 52 La Quinta (92253) ***(P-19554)***
Chapman Hbr Sklled Nrsing Care...D...714 971-5517
12232 Chapman Ave Garden Grove (92840) ***(P-20280)***
Chapman House Inc...C...714 288-6100
1412 E Chapman Ave Orange (92866) ***(P-21036)***
Chapman University...D...661 267-2001
39115 Trade Center Dr # 203 Palmdale (93551) ***(P-23187)***
Chapmn-Hrbor Sklled Nrsing Ctr, Garden Grove *Also called Chapman Hbr Sklled Nrsing Care* ***(P-20280)***
Chapmn-Wlters Intrcoastal Corp...F...949 448-9940
141 Via Lampara Rcho STA Marg (92688) ***(P-11409)***
Chapmn/Lnard Stdio Eqp Cnada I (PA)...**C...323 877-5309**
12950 Raymer St North Hollywood (91605) ***(P-19222)***
Charades, Walnut *Also called Diamond Collection LLC* ***(P-3074)***
Charades LLC (PA)...**C...626 435-0077**
20579 Valley Blvd Walnut (91789) ***(P-3069)***
Chargers Football Company LLC (PA)...**D...619 280-2121**
3333 Susan St Costa Mesa (92626) ***(P-19413)***
Chargetek Inc...F...805 444-7792
409 Calle San Pablo # 104 Camarillo (93012) ***(P-8973)***
Chariot Travelware, Ontario *Also called Damao Luggage Intl Inc* ***(P-14151)***
Charles & Cynthia Eberly Inc...D...323 937-6468
8383 Wilshire Blvd # 906 Beverly Hills (90211) ***(P-15722)***
Charles C Manger III MD Inc...D...949 951-4641
23161 Moulton Pkwy Laguna Hills (92653) ***(P-19744)***
Charles C Regan Inc...D...951 735-8100
216 N Smith Ave Corona (92878) ***(P-871)***
Charles David of California (PA)...**D...310 348-5050**
5731 Buckingham Pkwy Culver City (90230) ***(P-14432)***
Charles Dunn RE Svcs Inc (PA)...**D...213 270-6200**
800 W 6th St Ste 600 Los Angeles (90017) ***(P-15812)***
Charles E Thomas Company Inc (PA)...**D...310 323-6730**
13701 Alma Ave Gardena (90249) ***(P-751)***
Charles Gemeiner Cabinets...F...323 299-8696
3225 Exposition Pl Los Angeles (90018) ***(P-3238)***
Charles Komar & Sons Inc...B...951 934-1377
11850 Riverside Dr Jurupa Valley (91752) ***(P-3014)***
Charles Meisner Inc...E...909 946-8216
201 Sierra Pl Ste A Upland (91786) ***(P-7786)***
Charles Pnkow Bldrs Ltd A Cal (PA)...**E...626 304-1190**
199 S Los Robles Ave # 3 Pasadena (91101) ***(P-752)***
Charles Ting...C...310 828-5517
2815 Santa Monica Blvd Santa Monica (90404) ***(P-16378)***
Charles W Bowers Museum Corp...D...714 567-3600
2002 N Main St Santa Ana (92706) ***(P-22219)***
CHARLIE JADE, Los Angeles *Also called Fortune Swimwear LLC* ***(P-2633)***
Charman Manufacturing Inc...F...213 489-7000
5681 S Downey Rd Vernon (90058) ***(P-6245)***
Charming Hawaii, Walnut *Also called New Origins Accessories Inc* ***(P-11488)***
Charmshin Group Inc (PA)...**F...949 331-0301**
9039 Bolsa Ave Ste 309 Westminster (92683) ***(P-13331)***
Chartec LLC...D...661 281-4000
1600 Mill Rock Way Bakersfield (93311) ***(P-18167)***
Charter Bhvral Hlth Sys S C/Ch...C...626 966-1632
1161 E Covina Blvd Covina (91724) ***(P-21017)***
Charter Hospice Colton LLC...C...909 825-2969
1007 E Cooley Dr Ste 100 Colton (92324) ***(P-20527)***
Charter Mgmt LLC...D...909 644-4965
9660 Haven Ave Ste 203 Rancho Cucamonga (91730) ***(P-23001)***
Charter Oak Hospital, Covina *Also called Charter Bhvral Hlth Sys S C/Ch* ***(P-21017)***
Chase Bros Dairy, Ventura *Also called Hailwood Inc* ***(P-15672)***
Chase Care Center Inc...D...323 935-8490
1101 Crenshaw Blvd Los Angeles (90019) ***(P-20571)***
Chase Group Llc...B...818 708-3533
6740 Wilbur Ave Reseda (91335) ***(P-23188)***
Chase Group Llc...B...805 522-9155
5270 E Los Angeles Ave Simi Valley (93063) ***(P-22876)***
Chase-Durer Ltd (PA)...**F...310 550-7280**
8455 Ftn Ave Unit 515 West Hollywood (90069) ***(P-11301)***
Chatham Mdr LLC...E...310 301-2000
4200 Admiralty Way Marina Del Rey (90292) ***(P-16379)***
Chatham Rigg LLC...E...714 591-4000
11931 Harbor Blvd Garden Grove (92840) ***(P-16049)***
Chatsworth Park Hlth Care Ctr, Chatsworth *Also called Cpcc Inc* ***(P-20575)***
Chatsworth Products Inc (PA)...**E...818 735-6100**
9353 Winnetka Ave Chatsworth (91311) ***(P-7551)***
Chauhan Industries Inc...F...805 484-1616
32 Wood Rd Ste A Camarillo (93010) ***(P-10299)***
Chavers Gasket Corporation...E...949 472-8118
23325 Del Lago Dr Laguna Hills (92653) ***(P-5332)***
CHC, Los Angeles *Also called Covenant House California* ***(P-22097)***
CHE Precision Inc...E...805 499-8885
2586 Calcite Cir Newbury Park (91320) ***(P-8551)***
Check It Out, Los Angeles *Also called Nexxen Apparel Inc* ***(P-2976)***
Checkworks Inc...D...626 333-1444
315 Cloverleaf Dr Ste J Baldwin Park (91706) ***(P-4607)***
Cheek Machine Corp...E...714 279-9486
1312 S Allec St Anaheim (92805) ***(P-8552)***
Cheesecake Factory Inc (PA)...**A...818 871-3000**
26901 Malibu Hills Rd Calabasas Hills (91301) ***(P-1992)***
CHEESECAKE FACTORY, THE, Calabasas Hills *Also called Cheesecake Factory Inc* ***(P-1992)***
Chef Bobo Brand Inc (PA)...**D...800 977-8912**
419 N Hobart Blvd Los Angeles (90004) ***(P-21996)***
Chef Merito Inc (PA)...**D...818 787-0100**
7915 Sepulveda Blvd Van Nuys (91405) ***(P-2407)***
Chefmaster...E...714 554-4000
501 Airpark Dr Fullerton (92833) ***(P-2408)***
Chefs Toys LLC (HQ)...**C...508 399-2400**
18430 Pacific St Fountain Valley (92708) ***(P-13453)***
Chefs Warehouse West Coast LLC (HQ)...**D...626 465-4200**
16633 Gale Ave City of Industry (91745) ***(P-14460)***
Chem Arrow Corp...E...626 358-2255
13643 Live Oak Ln Irwindale (91706) ***(P-5290)***
Chem-Mark of Orange County, Cerritos *Also called Better Beverages Inc* ***(P-2310)***
Chemat Technology Inc...E...818 727-9786
9036 Winnetka Ave Northridge (91324) ***(P-10655)***
Chemat Vision, Northridge *Also called Chemat Technology Inc* ***(P-10655)***
Chemco Products Company, Paramount *Also called LMC Enterprises* ***(P-4968)***
Chemeor Inc...E...626 966-3808
727 Arrow Grand Cir Covina (91722) ***(P-4983)***

ALPHABETIC

Employee Codes: A=Over 500 employees, B=251-500 C=101-250, D=51-100, E=20-50 F=10-19
2022 Southern California Business Directory and Buyers Guide
© Mergent Inc. 1-800-342-5647
1091

Chemical Methods Assoc LLC (HQ)..................E......**714 898-8781**
12700 Knott St Garden Grove (92841) ***(P-8370)***

Chemical Waste Management Inc..................D......559 386-9711
35251 Old Skyline Rd Kettleman City (93239) ***(P-12938)***

Chemseal, Pacoima *Also called Flamemaster Corporation* ***(P-5221)***

Chemsil Silicones Inc..................E......818 700-0302
21900 Marilla St Chatsworth (91311) ***(P-14776)***

Chemtec Chemical Company, Chatsworth *Also called Vijall Inc* ***(P-14794)***

Chemtool Incorporated..................C......661 823-7190
1300 Goodrick Dr Tehachapi (93561) ***(P-5291)***

Chemtrans, Gardena *Also called Radford Alexander Corporation* ***(P-11988)***

Chemtrol, Santa Barbara *Also called Santa Barbara Control Systems* ***(P-10721)***

Chen & Huang Partners LP..................D......714 557-8700
1400 S Bristol St Santa Ana (92704) ***(P-16380)***

Chen Dvid MD Dgnstc Med Group..................D......626 288-8029
208 N Garfield Ave Monterey Park (91754) ***(P-19745)***

Chen-Tech Industries Inc (HQ)..................E......**949 855-6716**
9 Wrigley Irvine (92618) ***(P-10961)***

Chenbro Micom (usa) Inc..................E......909 937-0100
2800 Jurupa St Ontario (91761) ***(P-8194)***

Cheque Guard Inc..................D......818 563-9335
512 S Verdugo Dr Burbank (91502) ***(P-17576)***

Cherokee Chemical Co Inc (PA)..................E......**323 265-1112**
3540 E 26th St Vernon (90058) ***(P-14777)***

Cherokee Uniform, Chatsworth *Also called Careismatic Brands Inc* ***(P-5876)***

Cherokee Uniforms, Chatsworth *Also called Strategic Distribution L P* ***(P-2791)***

Cherry City Electric, City of Industry *Also called Morrow-Meadows Corporation* ***(P-1283)***

Chester Avenue Medical Offices, Bakersfield *Also called Kaiser Foundation Hospitals* ***(P-19889)***

Chester Avenue Medical Offs II, Bakersfield *Also called Kaiser Foundation Hospitals* ***(P-19890)***

Chet Cooper..................F......949 854-8700
1001 W 17th St Costa Mesa (92627) ***(P-4058)***

Chevelle Classics Parts & ACC, Seal Beach *Also called Original Parts Group Inc* ***(P-7112)***

Chevron, Torrance *Also called Madrona Carwash Inc* ***(P-18915)***

Chevron Corporation..................A......310 615-5000
324 W El Segundo Blvd El Segundo (90245) ***(P-401)***

Chevron Mining Inc..................C......760 856-7625
67750 Bailey Rd Mountain Pass (92366) ***(P-380)***

Chevys Fresh Mex Restaurant, Burbank *Also called Chevys Restaurants LLC* ***(P-16946)***

Chevys Restaurants LLC..................D......818 846-6999
701 N San Fernando Blvd Burbank (91502) ***(P-16946)***

Chez Bon Guest Home, Long Beach *Also called Viacare Inc* ***(P-20638)***

CHG Security Inc..................E......562 284-6260
16431 Grayville Dr La Mirada (90638) ***(P-18262)***

Chhp Holdings II LLC (HQ)..................B......**323 583-1931**
2623 E Slauson Ave Huntington Park (90255) ***(P-20716)***

Chhp Management LLC..................D......323 583-1931
2623 E Slauson Ave Huntington Park (90255) ***(P-20717)***

CHi Doors Holdings Inc..................C......909 605-1508
4495 E Wall St Ste 103 Ontario (91761) ***(P-1429)***

CHI Overhead Doors, Ontario *Also called CHi Doors Holdings Inc* ***(P-1429)***

Chicago Brothers, Vernon *Also called Overhill Farms Inc* ***(P-2504)***

Chicago Title Company (HQ)..................D......**213 488-4375**
725 S Figueroa St Ste 200 Los Angeles (90017) ***(P-15497)***

Chicago Title Insurance Co (HQ)..................C......**805 565-6900**
4050 Calle Real Santa Barbara (93110) ***(P-15498)***

Chick N Skin LLC..................F......626 759-2925
913 S Charlotte Ave San Gabriel (91776) ***(P-2360)***

Chick Publications Inc..................E......909 987-0771
8780 Archibald Ave Rancho Cucamonga (91730) ***(P-4123)***

Chicken of Sea International, El Segundo *Also called Tri-Union Seafoods LLC* ***(P-14588)***

Chief Engineering Co, Lake Elsinore *Also called Chief Trnsp & Engrg Contrs Inc* ***(P-872)***

Chief Neon Sign Co Inc..................F......310 327-1317
15027 S Maple Ave Gardena (90248) ***(P-11533)***

Chief Trnsp & Engrg Contrs Inc..................D......951 258-6607
4056 Tamarind Rdg Lake Elsinore (92530) ***(P-872)***

Child & Family Center..................C......661 259-9439
21545 Centre Pointe Pkwy Santa Clarita (91350) ***(P-21735)***

Child Abuse Lstening Mediation..................E......805 965-2376
1236 Chapala St Santa Barbara (93101) ***(P-21736)***

Child and Family Guidance Ctr (PA)..................C......**818 739-5140**
9650 Zelzah Ave Northridge (91325) ***(P-21287)***

Child Care Resource Center Inc (PA)..................C......**818 717-1000**
20001 Prairie St Chatsworth (91311) ***(P-21737)***

Child Care Resource Center Inc..................C......661 723-3246
250 Grand Cypress Ave # 601 Palmdale (93551) ***(P-21738)***

Child Care Resource Center Inc..................C......818 837-0097
454 S Kalisher St San Fernando (91340) ***(P-21997)***

Child Dev Rsrces of Vntura CNT (PA)..................C......**805 485-7878**
221 Ventura Blvd Oxnard (93036) ***(P-21739)***

Child Development Center, Compton *Also called Compton Unified School Dst* ***(P-22008)***

Child Development Incorporated..................C......714 842-4064
17341 Jacquelyn Ln Huntington Beach (92647) ***(P-15813)***

Child Development Incorporated..................B......949 854-5060
5151 Amalfi Dr Irvine (92603) ***(P-21998)***

Child Development Institute..................D......818 888-4559
18050 Vanowen St Reseda (91335) ***(P-21740)***

Child Educational Center..................D......818 354-3418
140 Foothill Blvd La Canada (91011) ***(P-21999)***

Child Lane (PA)..................C......**562 427-8834**
2545 Pacific Ave Long Beach (90806) ***(P-22000)***

Child360, Los Angeles *Also called Los Angles Universal Preschool* ***(P-22031)***

Childhelp Inc..................D......909 335-1164
1955 Hunts Ln Ste 200 San Bernardino (92408) ***(P-21741)***

Childhelp Foster Family, San Bernardino *Also called Childhelp Inc* ***(P-21741)***

Childnet Youth & Fmly Svcs Inc (PA)..................C......**562 498-5500**
4155 Outer Traffic Cir Long Beach (90804) ***(P-21742)***

Children Ctr At Cal Poly Pmona, Pomona *Also called Cal Poly Pomona Foundation Inc* ***(P-21992)***

Children's Choice Preschool, Laguna Niguel *Also called Childrens Choice Inc* ***(P-22001)***

Childrens Bureau Southern Cal (PA)..................C......**213 342-0100**
1910 Magnolia Ave Los Angeles (90007) ***(P-21743)***

Childrens Choice Inc..................D......949 495-5162
29028 Aloma Ave Laguna Niguel (92677) ***(P-22001)***

Childrens Clnic Srving Chldren..................B......562 264-4638
701 E 28th St Ste 200 Long Beach (90806) ***(P-19746)***

Childrens Health Center..................D......310 825-0867
200 Ucla Med Ctr Plz 265 Los Angeles (90095) ***(P-19747)***

Childrens Healthcare Cal..................B......714 997-3000
455 S Main St Orange (92868) ***(P-19748)***

Childrens Healthcare Cal (PA)..................A......**714 997-3000**
1201 W La Veta Ave Orange (92868) ***(P-21037)***

Childrens Hosp Los Angles Med (PA)..................D......**323 361-2336**
6430 W Sunset Blvd # 600 Los Angeles (90028) ***(P-20718)***

CHILDRENS HOSPITAL LOS ANGELES, Los Angeles *Also called Childrens Hosp Los Angles Med* ***(P-20718)***

Childrens Hospital Los Angeles (PA)..................A......**323 660-2450**
4650 W Sunset Blvd Los Angeles (90027) ***(P-21038)***

Childrens Hospital Los Angeles..................B......323 361-2751
4661 W Sunset Blvd Los Angeles (90027) ***(P-20719)***

Childrens Hospital Orange Cnty (PA)..................A......**714 997-3000**
1201 W La Veta Ave Orange (92868) ***(P-20720)***

Childrens Hospital Orange Cnty..................C......949 365-2416
455 S Main St Orange (92868) ***(P-20721)***

Childrens Hospital Orange Cnty..................D......949 631-2062
500 Superior Ave Newport Beach (92663) ***(P-22002)***

Childrens Hospital Orange Cnty..................C......949 387-2586
980 Roosevelt Irvine (92620) ***(P-20722)***

Childrens Hunger Fund (PA)..................D......**818 979-7100**
13931 Balboa Blvd Sylmar (91342) ***(P-21744)***

Childrens Inst Los Angeles..................A......213 383-2765
679 S New Hampshire Ave Los Angeles (90005) ***(P-21745)***

Childrens Inst Los Angeles (PA)..................C......**213 385-5100**
2121 W Temple St Los Angeles (90026) ***(P-22906)***

Childrens Institute Inc (PA)..................C......**213 385-5100**
2121 W Temple St Los Angeles (90026) ***(P-21746)***

Childrens Law Center Cal (PA)..................C......**323 980-8700**
101 Centre Plaza Dr Monterey Park (91754) ***(P-21529)***

Chili's, Santa Maria *Also called Impo International LLC* ***(P-5880)***

Chilicon Power LLC (PA)..................E......**310 800-1396**
15415 W Sunset Blvd # 102 Pacific Palisades (90272) ***(P-10746)***

Chimney Products Inc..................F......818 272-2011
11011 Glenoaks Blvd Pacoima (91331) ***(P-17226)***

China Airlines Ltd..................D......310 484-1818
5651 W 96th St Los Angeles (90045) ***(P-12304)***

China Airlines Ltd (HQ)..................B......**310 646-4233**
11201 Aviation Blvd Los Angeles (90045) ***(P-12305)***

China Manufacturing Netwrk LLC..................F......949 756-0015
17891 Sky Park Cir Ste K Irvine (92614) ***(P-23189)***

China Master USA Entrmt Co..................E......626 810-9372
17890 Castleton St # 230 City of Industry (91748) ***(P-6179)***

China Mfg Solutions USA LLC (PA)..................D......**562 537-8788**
5199 E Pacific Coast Hwy Long Beach (90804) ***(P-8997)***

China Pac Sheet Metal Mfg, Los Angeles *Also called China Pacific Inc* ***(P-753)***

China Pacific Inc..................F......323 222-9580
1777 N Main St Los Angeles (90031) ***(P-753)***

China Pearl, Pacoima *Also called CPI Luxury Group* ***(P-14128)***

China Press, The, Alhambra *Also called Asia-Pacific California Inc* ***(P-3947)***

Chinatown Service Center (PA)..................C......**213 808-1701**
767 N Hill St Ste 400 Los Angeles (90012) ***(P-21945)***

Chinese Consumer Yellow Pages, Rosemead *Also called Chinese Overseas Mktg Svc Corp* ***(P-4162)***

Chinese La Daily News, El Monte *Also called LA Web Inc* ***(P-1187)***

Chinese Laundry Inc..................E......310 945-3299
3485 S La Cienega Blvd Los Angeles (90016) ***(P-14433)***

Chinese Laundry Shoes, Los Angeles *Also called Chinese Laundry Inc* ***(P-14433)***

Chinese Overseas Mktg Svc Corp (PA)..................D......**626 280-8588**
3940 Rosemead Blvd Rosemead (91770) ***(P-4162)***

Chinese-La Daily News, El Monte *Also called LAweb Offset Printing Inc* ***(P-4535)***

Chinesefn, San Gabriel *Also called Chineseinvestorscom Inc* ***(P-18478)***

Chineseinvestorscom Inc (PA)..................D......**626 589-2468**
227 W Valley Blvd 208a San Gabriel (91776) ***(P-18478)***

Chino Ice Service..................E......909 628-2105
3640 Francis Ave Chino (91710) ***(P-2369)***

Chino Medical Group Inc..................D......909 591-6446
5475 Walnut Ave Chino (91710) ***(P-19749)***

Chino Mfg & Repair Inc..................F......909 628-0519
13563 12th St Chino (91710) ***(P-18895)***

Chino Valley Medical Center, Chino *Also called Veritas Health Services Inc* ***(P-21002)***

Chino Valley YMCA, Chino *Also called West End Yung MNS Christn Assn* ***(P-22376)***

Chino-Pacific Warehouse Corp (PA)..................D......**909 545-8100**
3601 Jurupa St Ontario (91761) ***(P-12189)***

Chip-Makers Tooling Supply Inc..................F......562 698-5840
7352 Whittier Ave Whittier (90602) ***(P-7787)***

Chipmasters Manufacturing Inc (PA)..................F......**626 804-8178**
798 N Coney Ave Azusa (91702) ***(P-8553)***

Chipton-Ross Inc..................D......310 414-7800
420 Culver Blvd Playa Del Rey (90293) ***(P-10182)***

Chiro Inc (PA)..................B......**909 879-1160**
2260 S Vista Ave Bloomington (92316) ***(P-14034)***

Chk America, Santa Barbara *Also called Cook Hammond and Kell Inc* ***(P-18492)***

CHOC, Orange *Also called Childrens Hospital Orange Cnty* ***(P-20720)***

CHOC CHILDREN'S, Orange *Also called Childrens Healthcare Cal* ***(P-21037)***

Choc Mission, Orange *Also called Childrens Hospital Orange Cnty* ***(P-20721)***

Chocolates and Health, Fontana *Also called Vitawest Nutraceuticals Inc* ***(P-1807)***

Choic Admini Insur Servi ....B....714 542-4200
721 S Parker St Ste 200 Orange (92868) ***(P-15550)***

Choice Internet, Irvine *Also called Cie Digital Labs LLC* ***(P-17094)***

Choice Lithographics, Buena Park *Also called Cyu Lithographics Inc* ***(P-4271)***

Choicepoint, Irvine *Also called Lexisnexis Risk Assets Inc* ***(P-15588)***

Chol Enterprises Inc ....E....310 516-1328
12831 S Figueroa St Los Angeles (90061) ***(P-10300)***

Choon Inc (PA) ....**E....213 225-2500**
1443 E 4th St Los Angeles (90033) ***(P-2882)***

Choose Manufacturing Co LLC ....E....714 327-1698
24 Passion Flower Irvine (92618) ***(P-9388)***

Choosing Independence Inc ....D....818 257-0323
7615 Louise Ave Northridge (91325) ***(P-23002)***

Choura Events ....D....310 320-6200
540 Hawaii Ave Torrance (90503) ***(P-17336)***

Choura Venue Services ....D....562 426-0555
4101 E Willow St Long Beach (90815) ***(P-16947)***

Choura Vnue Svcs At Carson Ctr, Long Beach *Also called Choura Venue Services* ***(P-16947)***

Chownow Inc ....D....888 707-2469
12181 Bluff Creek Dr Playa Vista (90094) ***(P-17815)***

Christ-Centered Ministries ....E....310 528-4538
742 N La Brea Ave Inglewood (90302) ***(P-22449)***

Christian Arcadia School ....D....626 574-8229
1900 S Santa Anita Ave Arcadia (91006) ***(P-22003)***

Christian Atascadero Home ....D....805 466-0281
611 Hollyhock Ln Templeton (93465) ***(P-20281)***

Christian Bethel School ....D....661 943-2224
3100 W Avenue K Lancaster (93536) ***(P-22004)***

Christian Community Credit Un (PA) ....**D....626 915-7551**
255 N Lone Hill Ave San Dimas (91773) ***(P-15108)***

Christian Hartland Association ....D....559 337-2349
57611 Eshom Valley Dr # 1 Badger (93603) ***(P-16819)***

Christian Schl Soc of Arcadia, Arcadia *Also called Christian Arcadia School* ***(P-22003)***

Christie Dgtal Systems USA Inc (HQ) ....**C....714 236-8610**
10550 Camden Dr Cypress (90630) ***(P-13342)***

Christie Digital Systems Inc (HQ) ....**C....714 236-8610**
10550 Camden Dr Cypress (90630) ***(P-11270)***

Christie Medical Holdings Inc ....E....714 236-8610
10550 Camden Dr Cypress (90630) ***(P-11218)***

Christine Alexander Inc ....E....213 488-1114
110 E 9th St Ste B336 Los Angeles (90079) ***(P-3152)***

Christmas Bonus Fund of The Pl ....D....213 385-6161
501 Shatto Pl Fl 5 Los Angeles (90020) ***(P-16175)***

Christys Edtorial Film Sup Inc ....D....818 845-1755
3625 W Pacific Ave Burbank (91505) ***(P-13343)***

Chroma Systems ....D....714 557-8480
3201 S Susan St Santa Ana (92704) ***(P-16879)***

Chroma Systems Solutions Inc (HQ) ....**D....949 297-4848**
19772 Pauling Foothill Ranch (92610) ***(P-10747)***

Chromadex Corporation (PA) ....**E....949 419-0288**
10005 Muirlands Blvd G Irvine (92618) ***(P-4739)***

Chromal Plating & Grinding, Los Angeles *Also called Chromal Plating Company* ***(P-7239)***

Chromal Plating Company ....E....323 222-0119
1748 Workman St Los Angeles (90031) ***(P-7239)***

Chromatic Inc Lithographers ....E....818 242-5785
127 Concord St Glendale (91203) ***(P-4251)***

Chromcraft Rvngton Douglas Ind (PA) ....**E....909 930-9891**
1011 S Grove Ave Ontario (91761) ***(P-3497)***

Chrome Hearts LLC (PA) ....**E....323 957-7544**
921 N Mansfield Ave Los Angeles (90038) ***(P-3054)***

Chrome River Technology ....E....888 781-0088
5757 Wilshire Blvd # 270 Los Angeles (90036) ***(P-17816)***

Chromologic LLC ....E....626 381-9974
1225 S Shamrock Ave Monrovia (91016) ***(P-10962)***

Chronicle Technology Inc ....F....949 651-8968
3972 Barranca Pkwy Irvine (92606) ***(P-9489)***

Chronomite Laboratories Inc ....E....310 534-2300
17451 Hurley St City of Industry (91744) ***(P-10664)***

Chrysler West Coast Bus Ctr, Irvine *Also called FCA US LLC* ***(P-10058)***

Chua & Sons Co Inc ....E....323 588-8044
3300 E 50th St Vernon (90058) ***(P-2616)***

Chuaolson Enterprises Inc ....E....714 630-4751
1274 N Grove St Anaheim (92806) ***(P-13799)***

Chubb, Los Angeles *Also called Pacific Indemnity Company* ***(P-15607)***

Chubby Gorilla Inc (PA) ....**E....844 365-5218**
4320 N Harbor Blvd Fullerton (92835) ***(P-5606)***

Chulada Inc ....F....818 841-6536
640 S Flower St Burbank (91502) ***(P-4740)***

Chulada Spices Herbs & Snacks, Burbank *Also called Chulada Inc* ***(P-4740)***

Chumash Casino Resort (HQ) ....**C....805 686-0855**
3400 E Highway 246 Santa Ynez (93460) ***(P-19639)***

Chup Corporation ....F....949 455-0676
2990 Airway Ave Ste A Costa Mesa (92626) ***(P-4252)***

Church & Larsen Inc ....C....626 303-8741
16103 Avenida Padilla Irwindale (91702) ***(P-1371)***

Churchill Management Corp ....E....877 937-7110
5900 Wilshire Blvd # 400 Los Angeles (90036) ***(P-15324)***

Churm Publishing Inc (PA) ....**E....714 796-7000**
1451 Quail St Ste 201 Newport Beach (92660) ***(P-3961)***

Chus Packaging Supplies Inc ....E....562 944-6411
10011 Santa Fe Springs Rd Santa Fe Springs (90670) ***(P-14920)***

Chuze Fitness, Rancho Cucamonga *Also called Rachas Inc* ***(P-19465)***

Chuze Fitness, Anaheim *Also called Rachas Inc* ***(P-19466)***

Ciao Wireless Inc ....D....805 389-3224
4000 Via Pescador Camarillo (93012) ***(P-9691)***

Ciasons Industrial Inc ....E....714 259-0838
1615 Boyd St Santa Ana (92705) ***(P-5333)***

Ciba Insurance Svcs Cal Inc (PA) ....**D....818 638-8525**
655 N Central Ave # 2100 Glendale (91203) ***(P-15551)***

Cibaria International Inc ....E....951 823-8490
705 Columbia Ave Riverside (92507) ***(P-14680)***

Cicileo Landscapes Inc ....E....805 967-3939
4565 Hollister Ave Santa Barbara (93110) ***(P-251)***

Cicoil LLC ....D....661 295-1295
24960 Avenue Tibbitts Valencia (91355) ***(P-13709)***

Cicon Engineering Inc (PA) ....**C....818 909-6060**
6633 Odessa Ave Van Nuys (91406) ***(P-9692)***

Cid Management, Westlake Village *Also called Comprhnsive Indus Dsblity MGT* ***(P-21399)***

Cie Digital Labs LLC ....D....949 381-6200
19600 Fairchild Ste 350 Irvine (92612) ***(P-17094)***

Cigna Behavioral Health of Cal ....B....800 753-0540
450 N Brand Blvd Ste 500 Glendale (91203) ***(P-15394)***

Cigna Healthcare Cal Inc (HQ) ....**B....818 500-6262**
400 N Brand Blvd Ste 400 # 400 Glendale (91203) ***(P-15395)***

Cilajet LLC ....E....310 320-8000
16425 Ishida Ave Gardena (90248) ***(P-4960)***

Cim, Compton *Also called Circle Industrial Mfg Corp* ***(P-7758)***

Cim Group LP (PA) ....**C....323 860-4900**
4700 Wilshire Blvd Ste 1 Los Angeles (90010) ***(P-16381)***

Cim Services, Compton *Also called Circle Industrial Mfg Corp* ***(P-8086)***

Cimatron Gibbs LLC ....D....805 523-0004
323 Science Dr Moorpark (93021) ***(P-17577)***

Cimc Intermodal Equipment LLC (HQ) ....**D....562 904-8600**
10530 Sessler St South Gate (90280) ***(P-10165)***

Cimc Reefer Trailer Inc (PA) ....**C....951 218-1414**
22101 Alessandro Blvd Moreno Valley (92553) ***(P-7706)***

Cinderella Motel ....D....559 432-0118
1747 S Harbor Blvd Anaheim (92802) ***(P-16382)***

Cinema Secrets Inc ....D....818 846-0579
6639 Odessa Ave Van Nuys (91406) ***(P-3070)***

Cingular Wireless, Lake Elsinore *Also called United Wireless Inc* ***(P-12615)***

Cinnabar ....C....818 842-8190
4571 Electronics Pl Los Angeles (90039) ***(P-17163)***

Cinnabar California Inc ....D....818 842-8190
4571 Electronics Pl Los Angeles (90039) ***(P-17164)***

Cintas Corporation ....D....714 646-2550
4320 E Miraloma Ave Anaheim (92807) ***(P-18479)***

Cintas Fire, Anaheim *Also called Cintas Corporation* ***(P-18479)***

Cintas Sales Corporation ....D....714 957-2852
2618 Oak St Santa Ana (92707) ***(P-16851)***

Cinton Inc ....E....714 961-8808
620 Richfield Rd Placentia (92870) ***(P-3868)***

Ciphertex LLC ....F....818 773-8989
9301 Jordan Ave Ste 105a Chatsworth (91311) ***(P-8245)***

Ciphertex Data Security, Chatsworth *Also called Ciphertex LLC* ***(P-8245)***

Circle Green Inc ....F....909 930-0200
8271 Chino Ave Ontario (91761) ***(P-5131)***

Circle Industrial Mfg Corp (PA) ....**E....310 638-5101**
1613 W El Segundo Blvd Compton (90222) ***(P-8086)***

Circle Industrial Mfg Corp ....F....310 638-5101
2727 N Slater Ave Compton (90222) ***(P-7758)***

Circle Produce Co Inc ....E....760 357-5454
2420 M L King St Ste A Calexico (92231) ***(P-14617)***

Circle Racing Wheels Inc (PA) ....**F....800 959-2100**
14955 Don Julian Rd City of Industry (91746) ***(P-10030)***

Circle W Enterprises Inc ....E....661 257-2400
27737 Avenue Hopkins Valencia (91355) ***(P-7497)***

Circor Aerospace Inc (HQ) ....**C....951 270-6200**
2301 Wardlow Cir Corona (92878) ***(P-7440)***

Circor Instrmentation Tech Inc ....F....951 270-6200
2301 Wardlow Cir Corona (92878) ***(P-7454)***

Circuit Automation Inc ....F....714 763-4180
32052 Sea Island Dr Dana Point (92629) ***(P-9389)***

Circuit Express Inc ....E....805 581-2172
67 W Easy St Ste 129 Simi Valley (93065) ***(P-9390)***

Circuit Services Llc ....E....818 701-5391
9134 Independence Ave Chatsworth (91311) ***(P-9391)***

Circulating Air Inc (PA) ....**D....818 764-0530**
7337 Varna Ave North Hollywood (91605) ***(P-1045)***

Ciri - Stroup Inc ....B....949 488-3104
25135 Park Lantern Dana Point (92629) ***(P-16948)***

Cirrus Asset Management Inc (PA) ....**B....818 222-4840**
20720 Ventura Blvd # 300 Woodland Hills (91364) ***(P-15814)***

Cirrus Enterprises LLC ....D....310 204-6159
18027 Bishop Ave Carson (90746) ***(P-14753)***

Cirrus Health II LP ....C....949 855-0562
24331 El Toro Rd Ste 150 Laguna Hills (92637) ***(P-19750)***

Cirtech Inc ....E....714 921-0860
250 E Emerson Ave Orange (92865) ***(P-18480)***

Cisco & Brothers Designs, Commerce *Also called Cisco Bros Corp* ***(P-3498)***

Cisco Bros Corp (PA) ....**C....323 778-8612**
5340 Harbor St Commerce (90040) ***(P-3498)***

Ciscos Shop Inc ....F....657 230-9158
2911 E Miraloma Ave # 17 Anaheim (92806) ***(P-6557)***

CIT Bank NA (HQ) ....**D....626 859-5400**
75 N Fair Oaks Ave Ste C Pasadena (91103) ***(P-14995)***

Citibank FSB ....C....562 999-3453
1 World Trade Ctr Ste 100 Long Beach (90831) ***(P-14996)***

Citifinancial Credit Company ....C....626 712-8780
2655 Del Vista Dr City of Industry (91745) ***(P-15142)***

Citigroup Inc ....D....949 726-5124
3996 Barranca Pkwy # 130 Irvine (92606) ***(P-14997)***

Citistaff Solutions Inc (PA) ....**C....310 763-1636**
1865 E 4th St Ontario (91764) ***(P-17406)***

ALPHABETIC

Employee Codes: A=Over 500 employees, B=251-500
C=101-250, D=51-100, E=20-50 F=10-19

2022 Southern California Business Directory and Buyers Guide

© Mergent Inc. 1-800-342-5647
1093

Citivest Inc ....D....949 474-0440
4340 Von Karman Ave # 110 Newport Beach (92660) ***(P-15815)***
Citizens Business Bank (HQ) ....C....**909 980-4030**
701 N Haven Ave Ste 280 Ontario (91764) ***(P-15017)***
Citizens Choice Health Plan, Orange *Also called Alignment Health Plan* ***(P-15386)***
Citizens of Humanity LLC (PA) ....C....**323 923-1240**
5715 Bickett St Huntington Park (90255) ***(P-2932)***
Citizship Immigration Svcs US ....C....626 448-0135
9251 Garvey Ave Ste M El Monte (91733) ***(P-21530)***
Citizship Immigration Svcs US ....D....805 588-7002
113 N I St Lompoc (93436) ***(P-21531)***
Citrin Cooperman & Company LLP ....E....818 783-0570
21650 Oxnard St Woodland Hills (91367) ***(P-22770)***
Citrix Systems Inc ....F....800 424-8749
7414 Hollister Ave Goleta Los Angeles (90074) ***(P-17817)***
Citrus Ford, Ontario *Also called Citrus Motors Ontario Inc* ***(P-18818)***
Citrus Motors Ontario Inc (PA) ....C....**909 390-0930**
1375 S Woodruff Way Ontario (91761) ***(P-18818)***
Citrus North Venture LLC ....D....256 428-2000
6591 Collins Dr Ste E11 Moorpark (93021) ***(P-16383)***
Citrus Vly Hlth Care Partners, Glendora *Also called Emanate Health* ***(P-20763)***
Citrus Vly Hlth Partners Inc ....A....626 962-4011
1115 S Sunset Ave West Covina (91790) ***(P-20723)***
Citrus Vly Hlth Partners Inc ....B....626 732-3100
1325 N Grand Ave Ste 300 Covina (91724) ***(P-21398)***
Citrusbyte LLC ....E....888 969-2983
21550 Oxnard St Ste 300 Woodland Hills (91367) ***(P-17578)***
City Bean Inc ....F....323 734-0828
5051 W Jefferson Blvd Los Angeles (90016) ***(P-14681)***
City Crane, Bakersfield *Also called Dunbar Electric Sign Company* ***(P-11543)***
City Dinuba Ambulance Service, Dinuba *Also called City of Dinuba* ***(P-11858)***
City Fashion Express Inc ....D....310 223-1010
2888 E El Presidio St Carson (90810) ***(P-12435)***
City Fibers Inc (PA) ....D....**323 583-1013**
2500 S Santa Fe Ave Vernon (90058) ***(P-14113)***
City Hanford Public Imprv Corp ....D....559 585-2550
900 S 10th Ave Hanford (93230) ***(P-941)***
City Hope National Medical Ctr ....A....626 256-4673
1500 Duarte Rd Duarte (91010) ***(P-20724)***
City Moving Inc ....C....888 794-8808
6319 Colfax Ave North Hollywood (91606) ***(P-12110)***
City National Asset MGT Inc ....D....310 888-6441
400 N Roxbury Dr Beverly Hills (90210) ***(P-23190)***
City National Bank (HQ) ....B....**310 888-6000**
555 S Flower St Ste 2500 Los Angeles (90071) ***(P-14998)***
City National Securities Inc ....C....310 888-6393
400 N Roxbury Dr Ste 400 # 400 Beverly Hills (90210) ***(P-14999)***
City News Group Inc ....F....909 370-1200
22797 Barton Rd Grand Terrace (92313) ***(P-3962)***
City of Brawley (PA) ....D....**760 344-8941**
400 Main St Brawley (92227) ***(P-22245)***
City of Burbank ....B....818 238-3550
164 W Magnolia Blvd Burbank (91502) ***(P-12869)***
City of Cerritos ....C....562 916-8500
18125 Bloomfield Ave Cerritos (90703) ***(P-19307)***
City of Culver City ....D....310 253-6525
4343 Duquesne Ave Culver City (90232) ***(P-22246)***
City of Culver City ....E....310 253-6510
4343 Duquesne Ave Culver City (90232) ***(P-11903)***
City of Delano ....E....661 721-3352
1107 Lytle Ave Delano (93215) ***(P-8371)***
City of Dinuba ....D....559 595-9999
496 E Tulare St Dinuba (93618) ***(P-11858)***
City of Fountain Valley ....E....714 593-4441
10200 Slater Ave Fountain Valley (92708) ***(P-942)***
City of Gardena ....D....310 324-1475
13999 S Western Ave Gardena (90249) ***(P-11803)***
City of Industry, Chino *Also called Balaji Trading Inc* ***(P-9227)***
City of Lemoore ....E....559 924-6744
711 W Cinnamon Dr Lemoore (93245) ***(P-12939)***
City of Long Beach ....D....562 570-2600
4100 E Don Douglas Dr Fl Flr 2 Long Beach (90808) ***(P-12347)***
City of Los Angeles ....C....213 473-7511
3201 Lacy St Los Angeles (90031) ***(P-212)***
City of Los Angeles ....A....310 732-3734
425 S Palos Verdes St San Pedro (90731) ***(P-22771)***
City of Menifee ....D....951 672-6777
29844 Haun Rd Menifee (92586) ***(P-23003)***
City of Norco ....D....951 270-5617
2870 Clark Ave Norco (92860) ***(P-23429)***
City of Oxnard (PA) ....C....**805 385-7803**
300 W 3rd St Oxnard (93030) ***(P-23191)***
City of Pasadena ....D....626 543-4708
1133 Rosemont Ave Pasadena (91103) ***(P-19477)***
City of Redlands (PA) ....D....**909 798-7531**
35 Cajon St Redlands (92373) ***(P-23004)***
City of Riverside ....E....951 351-6140
5950 Acorn St Riverside (92504) ***(P-8372)***
City of Torrance ....D....310 784-7950
3301 Airport Dr Torrance (90505) ***(P-12348)***
City of Visalia ....C....559 713-4100
425 E Oak Ave Ste 301 Visalia (93291) ***(P-11804)***
City Orange Police Assn Inc ....C....714 457-5340
1107 N Batavia St Orange (92867) ***(P-22247)***
City Paper Box Co ....F....323 231-5990
652 E 61st St Los Angeles (90001) ***(P-3793)***
City Service Contracting Inc (PA) ....D....**714 632-6610**
920 Lawrence St Placentia (92870) ***(P-873)***
City Service Paving, Placentia *Also called City Service Contracting Inc* ***(P-873)***

City Snta Mnica Wtr Trtmnt Pla, Los Angeles *Also called Santa Monica City of* ***(P-8411)***
City Tile & Stone Tile Inc ....D....818 994-0100
14720 Keswick St Van Nuys (91405) ***(P-1413)***
City Triangles, Los Angeles *Also called Jodi Kristopher LLC* ***(P-2889)***
City Ventures LLC (PA) ....B....**949 258-7555**
3121 Michelson Dr Ste 150 Irvine (92612) ***(P-15816)***
City Wide Aquatics (PA) ....D....**323 906-7953**
3900 Chevy Chase Dr Los Angeles (90039) ***(P-19640)***
City Wire Cloth, Fontana *Also called Daniel Gerard Worldwide Inc* ***(P-13562)***
Cityfreighter Inc (PA) ....E....**805 455-1440**
414 Olive St Santa Barbara (93101) ***(P-10031)***
Citysearch (HQ) ....D....**310 360-4555**
8833 W Sunset Blvd # 101 West Hollywood (90069) ***(P-17082)***
Ciuti International Inc ....F....909 484-1414
8790 Rochester Ave Ste A Rancho Cucamonga (91730) ***(P-2129)***
Civco, Rcho STA Marg *Also called Capital Invstmnts Vntures Corp* ***(P-22266)***
Civic Center News Inc ....F....213 481-1448
1264 W 1st St Los Angeles (90026) ***(P-3963)***
CJ America, La Palma *Also called CJ Foods Inc* ***(P-2409)***
CJ America Inc (HQ) ....D....**213 427-5566**
5700 Wilshire Blvd # 540 Los Angeles (90036) ***(P-14682)***
CJ Berry Well Services MGT LLC ....A....661 589-5220
3752 Allen Rd Bakersfield (93314) ***(P-490)***
CJ Enterprises ....F....714 898-8558
11530 Western Ave Stanton (90680) ***(P-7788)***
CJ Foods Inc (HQ) ....E....**714 367-7200**
4 Centerpointe Dr Ste 100 La Palma (90623) ***(P-2409)***
CJ Foods Manufacturing Corp ....E....714 888-3500
500 S State College Blvd Fullerton (92831) ***(P-2410)***
CJ Foods Mfg Beaumont Corp ....E....951 916-9300
415 Nicholas Rd Beaumont (92223) ***(P-11653)***
CJ Foods USA Inc ....C....213 427-5566
5700 Wilshire Blvd # 550 Los Angeles (90036) ***(P-2361)***
CJ Logistics America LLC ....C....909 363-4354
1895 Marigold Ave Redlands (92374) ***(P-12022)***
CJ Logistics America LLC ....C....540 377-2302
5690 Industrial Pkwy San Bernardino (92407) ***(P-12436)***
CJ Logistics America LLC ....C....909 605-7233
12350 Philadelphia Ave Eastvale (91752) ***(P-11962)***
CJ Precision Industries Inc ....E....562 426-3708
2817 Cherry Ave Signal Hill (90755) ***(P-8554)***
CJ Seto Support Services LLC (PA) ....D....**805 644-1214**
2300 Knoll Dr Ste G Ventura (93003) ***(P-18168)***
CJ Wilson BMW Mtcyc Murrieta, Murrieta *Also called Wilson Cycles Sports Corp* ***(P-10510)***
CJd Construction Svcs Inc ....E....626 335-1116
416 S Vermont Ave Glendora (91741) ***(P-491)***
Cji Process Systems Inc ....D....562 777-0614
12000 Clark St Santa Fe Springs (90670) ***(P-6734)***
CJJ Farming Inc ....E....805 739-1723
125 W Mill St Santa Maria (93458) ***(P-24)***
Cjm Automotive Group Inc ....D....661 832-3000
3101 Cattle Dr Bakersfield (93313) ***(P-18819)***
CK Franchising Inc (HQ) ....B....**800 498-8144**
1 Park Plz Ste 300 Irvine (92614) ***(P-21148)***
CK Steel Inc ....F....310 638-0855
19826 S Alameda St Compton (90221) ***(P-6600)***
CK Technologies Inc (PA) ....E....**805 987-4801**
3629 Vista Mercado Camarillo (93012) ***(P-10685)***
Ckcc Inc ....E....213 629-0939
1017 San Julian St Los Angeles (90015) ***(P-3170)***
Ckd Industries Inc ....F....714 871-5600
501 E Jamie Ave La Habra (90631) ***(P-7136)***
Ckkm Inc (PA) ....E....**951 371-8484**
265 Radio Rd Corona (92879) ***(P-13557)***
Ckt, Camarillo *Also called CK Technologies Inc* ***(P-10685)***
CL Knox Inc ....D....661 837-0477
34933 Imperial Ave Bakersfield (93308) ***(P-492)***
Claims Management Service, Santa Ana *Also called State Compensation Insur Fund* ***(P-15482)***
Clairbourn School ....D....626 286-3108
8400 Huntington Dr San Gabriel (91775) ***(P-22005)***
Clairmont Camera Inc (PA) ....D....**818 761-4440**
15411 Mulholland Dr Los Angeles (90077) ***(P-17337)***
Clamshell Buildings, Oxnard *Also called Clamshell Structures Inc* ***(P-6990)***
Clamshell Structures Inc ....F....805 988-1340
300 Graves Ave Ste B Oxnard (93030) ***(P-6990)***
Clara Bldwin Stcker HM For Wme ....E....626 962-7151
527 S Valinda Ave West Covina (91790) ***(P-20282)***
Clare Matrix (PA) ....D....**310 314-6200**
2644 30th St Ste 100 Santa Monica (90405) ***(P-21039)***
Claremont Club, The, Claremont *Also called Claremont Tennis Club* ***(P-19555)***
Claremont Courier Inc ....F....909 621-4761
114 Olive St Claremont (91711) ***(P-3964)***
Claremont Inst For The Study O (PA) ....F....**909 981-2200**
1317 W Fthill Blvd Ste 12 Upland (91786) ***(P-4495)***
CLAREMONT INSTITUTE, THE, Upland *Also called Claremont Inst For The Study O* ***(P-4495)***
Claremont Manor, Claremont *Also called Front Prch Cmmnties Svcs - Cas* ***(P-20586)***
Claremont Pl Assisted Living, Claremont *Also called Sunrise Senior Living MGT Inc* ***(P-22158)***
Claremont Tennis Club ....C....909 625-9515
1777 Monte Vista Ave Claremont (91711) ***(P-19555)***
Clarendon Specialty Fas Inc ....D....714 842-2603
16761 Burke Ln Huntington Beach (92647) ***(P-13800)***
Clariant Corporation ....E....909 825-1793
926 S 8th St Colton (92324) ***(P-3869)***
Clarient Inc (HQ) ....B....**949 445-7300**
31 Columbia Aliso Viejo (92656) ***(P-10963)***
Clarient Diagnostic Services, Aliso Viejo *Also called Clarient Inc* ***(P-10963)***

Clarion Construction Inc....E....909 598-4060
21067 Commerce Point Dr Walnut (91789) ***(P-754)***
Clarion Hotel, El Centro *Also called Mahavir Hospitality LLC* ***(P-16552)***
Clarion Hotel, Anaheim *Also called Comfort California Inc* ***(P-16387)***
Clariphy Communications Inc (HQ)....C....**949 861-3074**
7585 Irvine Center Dr # 100 Irvine (92618) ***(P-9490)***
Clark & Trevithick A Prof Corp....D....213 629-5700
800 Wilshire Blvd # 1200 Los Angeles (90017) ***(P-21532)***
Clark - Pacific Corporation....E....626 962-8751
131 Los Angeles St Irwindale (91706) ***(P-6022)***
Clark - Pacific Corporation....E....626 962-8755
9367 Holly Rd Adelanto (92301) ***(P-6023)***
Clark - Pacific Corporation....E....909 823-1433
13592 Slover Ave Fontana (92337) ***(P-6024)***
Clark Cnstr Group - Cal Inc....B....714 754-0764
18201 Von Karman Ave # 800 Irvine (92612) ***(P-693)***
Clark Cnstr Group - Cal LP....B....714 429-9779
18201 Von Karman Ave # 800 Irvine (92612) ***(P-755)***
Clark Plumbing Co, Van Nuys *Also called Valley Clark Plbg & Htg Co Inc* ***(P-1160)***
Clarkdietrich Building Systems, Riverside *Also called Clarkwestern Dietrich Building* ***(P-6808)***
Clarkwestern Dietrich Building....F....951 360-3500
6510 General Rd Riverside (92509) ***(P-6808)***
Claro Pool Services Inc....D....760 341-3377
42161 Beacon Hl Palm Desert (92211) ***(P-18481)***
Clarte Lighting, Covina *Also called Aubrey Industries* ***(P-9079)***
Clary Corporation....E....626 359-4486
150 E Huntington Dr Monrovia (91016) ***(P-9693)***
Classe Party Rentals, Rancho Cucamonga *Also called Sunn America Inc* ***(P-17378)***
Classic, Torrance *Also called I C Class Components Corp* ***(P-13728)***
Classic Bath Designs Inc....E....818 767-1144
11544 Sheldon St Sun Valley (91352) ***(P-3315)***
Classic Camaro Inc....C....714 847-6887
18460 Gothard St Huntington Beach (92648) ***(P-13051)***
Classic Collision Center 2, Los Angeles *Also called Caliber Holdings Corporation* ***(P-18785)***
Classic Concepts Inc (PA)....F....**323 266-8993**
4505 Bandini Blvd Vernon (90058) ***(P-13165)***
Classic Containers Inc....B....909 930-3610
1700 S Hellman Ave Ontario (91761) ***(P-5474)***
Classic Cosmetics Inc (PA)....C....**818 773-9042**
9530 De Soto Ave Chatsworth (91311) ***(P-5000)***
Classic Couriers Inc (PA)....D....**323 461-3741**
1601 N El Centro Ave Los Angeles (90028) ***(P-12125)***
Classic Distrg & Bev Group Inc....B....626 934-3700
120 Puente Ave City of Industry (91746) ***(P-14824)***
Classic Firebird, Huntington Beach *Also called Classic Camaro Inc* ***(P-13051)***
Classic Home, Vernon *Also called Classic Concepts Inc* ***(P-13165)***
Classic Installs Inc....D....951 678-9906
22475 Baxter Rd Wildomar (92595) ***(P-1623)***
Classic Litho & Design Inc....E....310 224-5200
340 Maple Ave Torrance (90503) ***(P-4253)***
Classic Party Rentals, Los Angeles *Also called CP Opco LLC* ***(P-17339)***
Classic Party Rentals, Inglewood *Also called CP Opco LLC* ***(P-16952)***
Classic Party Rentals, Inglewood *Also called After-Party2 Inc* ***(P-17329)***
Classic Party Rentals, Los Angeles *Also called CP Opco LLC* ***(P-17340)***
Classic Party Rentals, Carpinteria *Also called CP Opco LLC* ***(P-17341)***
Classic Party Rentals, Santa Ana *Also called CP Opco LLC* ***(P-17342)***
Classic Slipcover Inc....F....323 583-0804
4300 District Blvd Vernon (90058) ***(P-3098)***
Classic Tees Inc....F....626 607-0255
4915 Walnut Grove Ave San Gabriel (91776) ***(P-2933)***
Classic Tile & Mosaic Inc (PA)....D....**310 538-9605**
14463 S Broadway Gardena (90248) ***(P-13298)***
Classic Wire Cut Company Inc....C....661 257-0558
28210 Constellation Rd Valencia (91355) ***(P-8555)***
Classical Silk Inc (PA)....D....**213 488-0909**
2016 E 15th St Los Angeles (90021) ***(P-17165)***
Claud Townsley Inc....D....310 527-6770
555 W 182nd St Gardena (90248) ***(P-1478)***
Claudes Buggies Inc....E....559 733-8222
1715 N Farmersville Blvd Farmersville (93223) ***(P-13052)***
Clay Castaic Manufacturing Co....F....661 259-3066
32201 Castaic Lake Dr Castaic (91384) ***(P-5983)***
Clay Corona Company (PA)....E....**951 277-2667**
22079 Knabe Rd Corona (92883) ***(P-756)***
Clay Designs Inc....F....562 432-3991
6435 Green Valley Cir # 1 Culver City (90230) ***(P-6002)***
Clay Dunn Enterprises Inc....C....310 549-1698
1606 E Carson St Carson (90745) ***(P-1046)***
Clay Lacy Aviation Inc (PA)....B....**818 989-2900**
7435 Valjean Ave Van Nuys (91406) ***(P-12349)***
Clay Laguna Co (HQ)....D....**626 330-0631**
14400 Lomitas Ave City of Industry (91746) ***(P-6165)***
Clayton Industries, City of Industry *Also called Clayton Manufacturing Company* ***(P-8115)***
Clayton Manufacturing Company (PA)....C....**626 443-9381**
17477 Hurley St City of Industry (91744) ***(P-8115)***
Clayton Manufacturing Inc (HQ)....D....**626 443-9381**
17477 Hurley St City of Industry (91744) ***(P-8116)***
CLC Work Gear, South Gate *Also called Custom Leathercraft Mfg LLC* ***(P-5912)***
Clean America Inc....F....562 694-5990
1400 Pioneer St Brea (92821) ***(P-9860)***
Clean Cut Technologies, Anaheim *Also called Oliver Healthcare Packaging Co* ***(P-13924)***
Clean Energy....A....949 437-1000
4675 Macarthur Ct Ste 800 Newport Beach (92660) ***(P-12865)***
Clean Energy Fuels Corp (PA)....C....**949 437-1000**
4675 Macarthur Ct Ste 800 Newport Beach (92660) ***(P-12874)***
Clean Harbors Buttonwillow LLC....D....661 762-6200
2500 W Lokern Rd Buttonwillow (93206) ***(P-12940)***
Clean Hrbors Es Indus Svcs Inc....E....562 436-0636
118 Pier S Ave Long Beach (90802) ***(P-1647)***
Clean Water Technology Inc (HQ)....E....**310 380-4648**
13008 S Western Ave Gardena (90249) ***(P-8373)***
Clean Wave Management Inc....F....949 488-2922
1291 Puerta Del Sol San Clemente (92673) ***(P-10183)***
Clean Wave Management Inc....E....949 361-5356
1291 Puerta Del Sol San Clemente (92673) ***(P-8027)***
Cleaning For King Inc....C....559 733-3856
720 E Center Ave Ste A Visalia (93292) ***(P-17227)***
Cleanroom Film & Bags, Orange *Also called CF&b Manufacturing Inc* ***(P-3880)***
Cleanstreet LLC....C....800 225-7316
1937 W 169th St Gardena (90247) ***(P-13005)***
Cleantech Environmental, Irwindale *Also called Agritec International Ltd* ***(P-14145)***
Cleantek Electric Inc....E....424 400-3315
403 W 21st St San Pedro (90731) ***(P-1233)***
Clear Channel Radio Sales, Los Angeles *Also called Katz Millennium Sls & Mktg Inc* ***(P-9281)***
Clear Group Inc....D....603 325-5600
408 N Avalon Blvd Los Angeles (90074) ***(P-16384)***
Clear Image Printing Inc....E....818 547-4684
12744 San Fernando Rd # 200 Sylmar (91342) ***(P-4254)***
Clear Water Corporation Inc....F....818 765-8293
7848 San Fernando Rd B Sun Valley (91352) ***(P-8374)***
Clear-Ad Inc....E....877 899-1002
2410 W 3rd St Santa Ana (92703) ***(P-5607)***
Clearflow Inc (PA)....E....**714 916-5010**
16 Technology Dr Ste 150 Irvine (92618) ***(P-10964)***
Clearlake Capital Group LP (PA)....B....**310 400-8800**
233 Wilshire Blvd Ste 800 Santa Monica (90401) ***(P-16128)***
Clearlake Capital Partners....A....310 400-8800
233 Wilshire Blvd Ste 800 Santa Monica (90401) ***(P-17818)***
Clearpath Lending....C....949 502-3577
15635 Alton Pkwy Ste 300 Irvine (92618) ***(P-15238)***
Clearpathgps LLC....E....805 979-3442
3463 State St 494 Santa Barbara (93105) ***(P-9648)***
Clearview Capital LLC....A....310 806-9555
12100 Wilshire Blvd # 800 Los Angeles (90025) ***(P-16254)***
Clearview Orthopedic Dev LLC....F....949 752-7885
15550 Rockfield Blvd D Irvine (92618) ***(P-10965)***
Cleatech LLC....E....714 754-6668
2106 N Glassell St Orange (92865) ***(P-10656)***
Clegg Industries Inc....C....310 225-3800
19032 S Vermont Ave Gardena (90248) ***(P-11534)***
Clegg Promo, Gardena *Also called Clegg Industries Inc* ***(P-11534)***
Clementine Ht & Suites Anaheim, Anaheim *Also called Holiday Garden SF Corp* ***(P-16483)***
Clemson Distribution Inc (PA)....E....**909 595-2770**
20722 Currier Rd City of Industry (91789) ***(P-14540)***
Cleveland Wrecking Company (HQ)....D....**626 967-4287**
999 W Town And Country Rd Orange (92868) ***(P-1611)***
Cli, Indio *Also called Commercial Lighting Inds Inc* ***(P-13619)***
Clickbrand, Newport Beach *Also called Saritasa LLC* ***(P-18108)***
Cliff View Terrace Inc....D....805 682-7443
623 W Junipero St Santa Barbara (93105) ***(P-22093)***
Cliffdale Manufacturing LLC....C....818 341-3344
20409 Prairie St Chatsworth (91311) ***(P-10531)***
Cliffs Resort LLC....E....805 773-5000
2757 Shell Beach Rd Pismo Beach (93449) ***(P-16949)***
Cliftonlarsonallen LLP....D....626 857-7300
2210 E Route 66 Ste 100 Glendora (91740) ***(P-22772)***
Cliftonlarsonallen LLP....D....310 273-2501
1925 Century Park E Fl 16 Los Angeles (90067) ***(P-22773)***
Clima-Tech Inc....D....909 613-5513
1820 Town And Country Dr Norco (92860) ***(P-18945)***
Clinch-On Cornerbead Company, Orange *Also called Continuous Coating Corp* ***(P-7243)***
Clindatrix....D....949 428-6600
1 Ada Ste 250 Irvine (92618) ***(P-22833)***
Clinic Inc....D....323 730-1920
3834 S Western Ave Los Angeles (90062) ***(P-19751)***
Clinica Msr Oscar A Romero (PA)....D....**213 989-7700**
123 S Alvarado St Los Angeles (90057) ***(P-19752)***
Clinica Sierra Vista (PA)....D....**661 635-3050**
1430 Truxtun Ave Ste 400 Bakersfield (93301) ***(P-19753)***
Clinical Translational RES Ctr, Los Angeles *Also called Cedars-Sinai Medical Center* ***(P-20698)***
Clinicas De Slud Del Peblo Inc (PA)....D....**760 344-9951**
852 Danenberg Dr El Centro (92243) ***(P-19754)***
Clinics On Demand Inc....D....310 709-7355
11000 Wilshire Blvd Los Angeles (90024) ***(P-21149)***
Clio Inc....E....562 926-3724
12981 166th St Cerritos (90703) ***(P-7485)***
Clipper Windpower PLC....A....805 690-3275
6305 Carpinteria Ave # 300 Carpinteria (93013) ***(P-7581)***
Clique Brands Inc (PA)....E....**310 623-6916**
750 N San Vicnte Blvd West Hollywood (90069) ***(P-4059)***
Clm Group Inc....E....818 349-2549
20730 Dearborn St Chatsworth (91311) ***(P-5001)***
Clorox Manufacturing Company....D....909 307-2756
2300 W San Bernardino Ave Redlands (92374) ***(P-4961)***
Closet Factory Inc (PA)....D....**310 516-7000**
12800 S Broadway Los Angeles (90061) ***(P-1648)***
Closet World Inc....D....626 855-0846
14438 Don Julian Rd City of Industry (91746) ***(P-1430)***
Closet World Inc....C....800 576-7717
320 S 6th Ave City of Industry (91746) ***(P-1649)***
Closet World Inc....C....714 890-5860
13272 Garden Grove Blvd Garden Grove (92843) ***(P-1650)***
Closet World, The, City of Industry *Also called Home Organizers Inc* ***(P-1440)***

ALPHABETIC

Employee Codes: A=Over 500 employees, B=251-500 C=101-250, D=51-100, E=20-50 F=10-19
2022 Southern California Business Directory and Buyers Guide
© Mergent Inc. 1-800-342-5647
1095

Closetmaid LLC E 909 590-4444
5150 Edison Ave Ste C Chino (91710) ***(P-7498)***
Closets By Design Inc E 562 699-9945
3860 Capitol Ave City of Industry (90601) ***(P-3642)***
Closingmark Fincl Group LLC (HQ) **D 949 833-3600**
4695 Macarthur Ct Fl 8 Newport Beach (92660) ***(P-15183)***
Clothing Illustrated Inc (PA) **E 213 403-9950**
2030 E 15th St Los Angeles (90021) ***(P-2934)***
Clothng/Pparel/Uniform/ppe Mfg, Vernon *Also called David Grment Ctng Fsing Svc In* ***(P-2937)***
Cloud Automation Division, Aliso Viejo *Also called Quest Software Inc* ***(P-17968)***
Cloud B Inc E 310 781-3833
150 W Walnut St Ste 100 Gardena (90248) ***(P-11358)***
Cloud Company (PA) **E 805 549-8093**
4855 Morabito Pl San Luis Obispo (93401) ***(P-8117)***
Cloud Creations Inc D 800 951-7651
790 E Colorado Blvd Fl 9 Pasadena (91101) ***(P-18169)***
Cloud Management Suite, Aliso Viejo *Also called Syxsense Inc* ***(P-17728)***
Cloud Nine Comforts, Los Angeles *Also called Universal Cushion Company Inc* ***(P-3122)***
Cloudburst Inc F 805 986-4125
707 E Hueneme Rd Oxnard (93033) ***(P-8044)***
Cloudcover Iot Inc E 888 511-2022
14 Goodyear Ste 125b Irvine (92618) ***(P-17819)***
Cloudradiant Corp (PA) **C 408 256-1527**
12 Fuchsia Lake Forest (92630) ***(P-14921)***
Cloudstaff LLC C 888 551-5339
26895 Aliso Creek Rd B-2 Aliso Viejo (92656) ***(P-16950)***
Cloudstaff LLC (PA) **B 888 551-5339**
1165 E San Antonio Dr Long Beach (90807) ***(P-17407)***
Cloudvirga Inc D 949 799-2643
5291 California Ave # 300 Irvine (92617) ***(P-17820)***
Clougherty Packing LLC (HQ) **B 323 583-4621**
3049 E Vernon Ave Vernon (90058) ***(P-1710)***
Clover Imaging Group LLC E 760 357-9277
315 Weakley St Bldg 3 Calexico (92231) ***(P-11271)***
Clover Imaging Group LLC B 815 431-8100
9414 Eton Ave Chatsworth (91311) ***(P-13979)***
Cls Landscape Management Inc B 909 628-3005
4329 State St Ste B Montclair (91763) ***(P-355)***
Cls Trnsprttion Los Angles LLC (HQ) **C 310 414-8189**
600 S Allied Way El Segundo (90245) ***(P-11859)***
Club Assist North America Inc (HQ) **D 213 388-4333**
888 W 6th St Ste 300 Los Angeles (90017) ***(P-13053)***
Club Speed LLC E 951 817-7073
400 Spectrum Center Dr # 1900 Irvine (92618) ***(P-17821)***
Clutter Inc (PA) **C 800 805-4023**
3526 Hayden Ave Culver City (90232) ***(P-16951)***
Clw Foods LLC F 323 432-4600
3425 E Vernon Ave Vernon (90058) ***(P-2411)***
CM Brewing Technologies LLC F 888 391-9990
13681 Newport Ave Ste 8 Tustin (92780) ***(P-8375)***
CM Construction Services Inc (PA) **E 559 735-9556**
8300 W Doe Ave Visalia (93291) ***(P-757)***
CM Laundry LLC D 310 436-6170
14919 S Figueroa St Gardena (90248) ***(P-16888)***
CM Machine Inc F 951 654-6019
560 S Grand Ave San Jacinto (92582) ***(P-8556)***
CM School Supply Inc F 714 680-6681
1025 E Orangethorpe Ave Anaheim (92801) ***(P-11369)***
CMA Dish Machines, Garden Grove *Also called Chemical Methods Assoc LLC* ***(P-8370)***
Cmac Cnstr Refinery & Pipeline, Long Beach *Also called Cmac Construction Company* ***(P-943)***
Cmac Construction Company D 562 435-5611
1450 Santa Fe Ave Long Beach (90813) ***(P-943)***
Cmb Laboratory, Cypress *Also called Consoldted Med Bo-Analysis Inc* ***(P-21064)***
CMC Rebar West D 909 713-1130
5425 Industrial Pkwy San Bernardino (92407) ***(P-13558)***
CMC Rebar West C 714 692-7082
10840 Norwalk Blvd Santa Fe Springs (90670) ***(P-694)***
CMC Rescue Inc D 805 562-9120
6740 Cortona Dr Goleta (93117) ***(P-14149)***
CMC Steel California, Rancho Cucamonga *Also called Tamco* ***(P-6215)***
CMC Steel Us LLC F 909 646-7827
12459 Arrow Rte Rancho Cucamonga (91739) ***(P-7018)***
Cmf Inc D 714 637-2409
1317 W Grove Ave Orange (92865) ***(P-1479)***
CMH Records Inc E 323 663-8098
2898 Rowena Ave Ste 201 Los Angeles (90039) ***(P-9212)***
CMI, Irvine *Also called Cooper Microelectronics Inc* ***(P-9495)***
CMI, San Clemente *Also called Composite Manufacturing Inc* ***(P-10966)***
Cmp Display Systems Inc D 805 499-3642
23301 Wilmington Ave Carson (90745) ***(P-5608)***
Cmp Industries LLC (PA) **E 518 434-3147**
18150 Rowland St City of Industry (91748) ***(P-11164)***
Cmre Financial Services Inc B 714 528-3200
3075 E Imperial Hwy # 200 Brea (92821) ***(P-17106)***
CMS, Simi Valley *Also called Computerized Mgt Svcs Inc* ***(P-22774)***
CMS, Mission Viejo *Also called Community Merch Solutions LLC* ***(P-8313)***
CMS Circuit Solutions Inc E 951 698-4452
41549 Cherry St Murrieta (92562) ***(P-9392)***
Cmt Sheet Metal F 949 679-9868
22732 Granite Way Ste C Laguna Hills (92653) ***(P-6735)***
CMTC, Torrance *Also called California Mfg Tech Consulting* ***(P-22508)***
CN Publishing Group, Irvine *Also called Cycle News Inc* ***(P-3967)***
Cnc Industries Inc F 909 445-0300
4965 Brooks St Montclair (91763) ***(P-8557)***
Cnc Worldwide Inc (PA) **D 310 670-7121**
12217 Rosecrans Ave Norwalk (90650) ***(P-12437)***
Cnet Express C 949 357-5475
15134 Indiana Ave Apt 38 Paramount (90723) ***(P-11963)***
Cni Mfg Inc E 626 962-6646
15627 Arrow Hwy Irwindale (91706) ***(P-8558)***
Cni Thl Propco Fe LLC D 661 325-9700
5101 California Ave Bakersfield (93309) ***(P-16385)***
Cnm Marketing Inc F 866 792-5265
2569 Mccabe Way Ste 210 Irvine (92614) ***(P-4496)***
CNT Acquisition Corp (HQ) **B 949 380-6100**
1 Enterprise Aliso Viejo (92656) ***(P-9491)***
Co D L Pham MD E 714 531-2091
10362 Bolsa Ave Ste 110 Westminster (92683) ***(P-19755)***
Co-Op Network, Rancho Cucamonga *Also called CU Cooperative Systems Inc* ***(F-15110)***
Co-Optimum, Sherman Oaks *Also called Ansira Partners Inc* ***(P-18446)***
Co-West Commodities, San Bernardino *Also called Park West Enterprises Inc* ***(F-2127)***
Coach Inc F 949 365-0771
3333 Bristol St Ste 2883 Costa Mesa (92626) ***(P-5899)***
Coach Inc F 805 496-9933
434 W Hillcrest Dr Thousand Oaks (91360) ***(P-5900)***
Coach Usa Inc D 626 357-7912
5640 Peck Rd Arcadia (91006) ***(P-11910)***
Coach Yard, Pasadena *Also called Original Whistle Stop Inc* ***(P-11388)***
Coachella Valley Water Dst, Palm Desert *Also called Coachlla Vly Wtr Dst Pub Fclti* ***(P-12883)***
Coachella Vly Rescue Mission D 760 347-3512
82873 Via Venecia Indio (92201) ***(P-21747)***
Coachlla Vly Wtr Dst Pub Fclti (PA) **C 760 398-2651**
75515 Hovley Ln E Palm Desert (92211) ***(P-12883)***
Coachlla Vly Wtr Dst Pub Fclti C 760 398-2651
75 525 Hovley Ln Palm Desert (92260) ***(P-12884)***
Coachworks Holdings Inc F 951 684-9585
1863 Service Ct Riverside (92507) ***(P-9940)***
Coalition For Family Harmony D 805 983-6014
1030 N Ventura Rd Oxnard (93030) ***(P-21748)***
Coalition Technologies LLC E 310 905-8268
445 S Figueroa St # 3100 Los Angeles (90071) ***(P-17579)***
Coast 2 Coast Cables LLC E 714 666-1062
3162 E La Palma Ave Ste D Anaheim (92806) ***(P-6348)***
Coast Aerospace Mfg Inc E 714 893-8066
950 Richfield Rd Placentia (92870) ***(P-7789)***
Coast Air Supply Co Inc F 310 472-5612
26501 Summit Cir Santa Clarita (91350) ***(P-9027)***
Coast Aluminum Inc (PA) **C 562 946-6061**
10628 Fulton Wells Ave Santa Fe Springs (90670) ***(P-13559)***
Coast Composites LLC (PA) **B 949 455-0665**
5 Burroughs Irvine (92618) ***(P-8559)***
Coast Custom Cable, Carson *Also called Belden Inc* ***(P-6343)***
Coast Cutters Co F 626 444-2965
105 N 9th Ave Upland (91786) ***(P-6197)***
Coast Flagstone Co D 310 829-4010
1810 Colorado Ave Santa Monica (90404) ***(P-6137)***
Coast Heat Treating Co F 323 263-6944
1767 Industrial Way Los Angeles (90023) ***(P-6436)***
Coast Iron & Steel Co E 562 946-4421
12300 Lakeland Rd Santa Fe Springs (90670) ***(P-1570)***
Coast Plastics Inc (PA) **F 626 812-9174**
936 E Francis St Ontario (91761) ***(P-14754)***
Coast Plaza Hospital, Norwalk *Also called Cph Hospital Management LLC* ***(P-20742)***
Coast Plz Dctors Hosp A Cal Lt (HQ) **B 562 868-3751**
13100 Studebaker Rd Norwalk (90650) ***(P-20725)***
Coast Produce Company (PA) **C 213 955-4900**
1791 Bay St Los Angeles (90021) ***(P-14618)***
Coast Rock Products Inc E 805 925-2505
1625 E Donovan Rd Santa Maria (93454) ***(P-13299)***
Coast Sheet Metal Inc E 949 645-2224
990 W 17th St Costa Mesa (92627) ***(P-6809)***
Coast Sign Display, Anaheim *Also called Coast Sign Incorporated* ***(P-11535)***
Coast Sign Incorporated C 714 520-9144
1500 W Embassy St Anaheim (92802) ***(P-11535)***
Coast To Coast Bus Eqp Inc (PA) **D 949 457-7300**
8 Vanderbilt Ste 200 Irvine (92618) ***(P-13353)***
Coast To Coast Circuits Inc (PA) **E 714 891-9441**
5331 Mcfadden Ave Huntington Beach (92649) ***(P-9393)***
Coast To Coast Cmpt Pdts Inc C 805 244-9500
4277 Valley Fair St Simi Valley (93063) ***(P-18023)***
Coast To Coast Met Finshg Corp E 626 282-2122
401 S Raymond Ave Alhambra (91803) ***(P-7240)***
Coast To Coast Mfg LLC F 909 798-5024
430 Nevada St Redlands (92373) ***(P-5609)***
Coast Valley Moving & Stor Inc D 949 361-7500
1111 Via Callejon San Clemente (92673) ***(P-12023)***
Coast/A C M, Torrance *Also called Coast/Dvnced Chip Mgnetics Inc* ***(P-9624)***
Coast/Dvnced Chip Mgnetics Inc F 310 370-8188
4225 Spencer St Torrance (90503) ***(P-9624)***
Coast2coast Public Safety LLC E 833 262-7877
1733 S Douglass Rd Ste H Anaheim (92806) ***(P-18368)***
Coastal Alliance Holdings Inc C 562 370-1000
1650 Ximeno Ave Ste 120 Long Beach (90804) ***(P-15817)***
Coastal Building Services Inc B 714 775-2855
1433 W Central Park Ave N Anaheim (92802) ***(P-17228)***
Coastal Closeouts Inc D 323 589-7900
100 Oceangate Ste 1200 Long Beach (90802) ***(P-18482)***
Coastal Cmnty Senior Care LLC C 562 596-4884
5500 E Atherton St # 216 Long Beach (90815) ***(P-21150)***
Coastal Cnting Indus Scale Inc E 805 487-0403
1621 Fiske Pl Oxnard (93033) ***(P-7849)***
Coastal Cocktails Inc E 949 250-3129
18011 Mitchell S Ste B Irvine (92614) ***(P-2262)***
Coastal Community Hospital, Santa Ana *Also called Health Resources Corp* ***(P-20782)***

Mergent e-mail: customerrelations@mergent.com
1096
2022 Southern California Business Directory and Buyers Guide
(P-0000) Products & Services Section entry number
(PA)=Parent Co (HQ)=Headquarters (DH)=Div Headquarters

Coastal Component Inds Inc ....E 714 685-6677
133 E Bristol Ln Orange (92865) ***(P-9694)***

Coastal Connections ....E 805 644-5051
2085 Sperry Ave Ste B Ventura (93003) ***(P-9231)***

Coastal Container Inc ....E 562 801-4595
8455 Loch Lomond Dr Pico Rivera (90660) ***(P-3794)***

Coastal Doors ....F 562 665-5585
21818 S Wilmington Ave Carson (90810) ***(P-6694)***

Coastal Enterprises, Fountain Valley *Also called Joy Products California Inc* ***(P-11472)***

Coastal Enterprises ....E 714 771-4969
1925 W Collins Ave Orange (92867) ***(P-4683)***

Coastal Grading and Excavating ....E 805 445-6433
756 Calle Plano Camarillo (93012) ***(P-1593)***

Coastal Harvesting Inc ....B 805 525-6250
503 S Palm Ave Santa Paula (93060) ***(P-214)***

Coastal Health Care Inc ....D 310 828-5596
1321 Franklin St Santa Monica (90404) ***(P-20283)***

Coastal Intl Holdings LLC ....C 714 635-1200
2832 Walnut Ave Ste B Tustin (92780) ***(P-18483)***

Coastal Products Company Inc ....E 661 323-0487
2157 Mohawk St Bakersfield (93308) ***(P-8006)***

Coastal Rdtion Onclogy Med Gro ....D 805 494-4483
1240 S Westlake Blvd # 1 Westlake Village (91361) ***(P-19756)***

Coastal Tag & Label Inc ....D 562 946-4318
13233 Barton Cir Whittier (90605) ***(P-4497)***

Coastal The, Sherman Oaks *Also called Coastal Tile Inc* ***(P-1414)***

Coastal Tile Inc ....D 818 988-6134
13226 Moorpark St Apt 104 Sherman Oaks (91423) ***(P-1414)***

Coastal View Halthcare Ctr LLC ....D 805 642-4101
4904 Telegraph Rd Ventura (93003) ***(P-20572)***

Coasthills Credit Union (PA) ....**D 805 733-7600**
1075 E Betteravia Rd Santa Maria (93454) ***(P-15109)***

Coastline Cnstr & Awng Co Inc ....D 714 891-9798
5742 Research Dr Huntington Beach (92649) ***(P-598)***

Coastline High Prfmce Ctngs Lt ....F 714 372-3263
7181 Orangewood Ave Garden Grove (92841) ***(P-9262)***

Coastline Metal Finishing Corp ....D 714 895-9099
7061 Patterson Dr Garden Grove (92841) ***(P-7241)***

Coastwide Tag & Label Co Inc ....E 323 721-1501
7647 Industry Ave Pico Rivera (90660) ***(P-4498)***

Coated Fabrics Company (HQ) ....**F 562 298-1300**
12658 Cisneros Ln Santa Fe Springs (90670) ***(P-14755)***

Coating Specialties Inc ....F 310 639-6900
815 E Rosecrans Ave Los Angeles (90059) ***(P-10301)***

Coatings By Sandberg Inc ....F 714 538-0888
856 N Commerce St Orange (92867) ***(P-7353)***

Coatings Hub, Commerce *Also called H-D Specialty Groups Inc* ***(P-7370)***

Coatings Resource, Huntington Beach *Also called Laird Coatings Corporation* ***(P-5100)***

Cobalt Construction Company ....D 805 577-6222
2259 Ward Ave Ste 200 Simi Valley (93065) ***(P-657)***

Cobel Technologies Inc ....F 626 332-2100
822 N Grand Ave Covina (91724) ***(P-8890)***

Cobham Exeter Inc ....E 714 841-4976
17831 Jamestown Ln Huntington Beach (92647) ***(P-9263)***

Cobham Trivec-Avant Inc., Huntington Beach *Also called Cobham Exeter Inc* ***(P-9263)***

Coc Inc, Los Angeles *Also called Colon Manufacturing Inc* ***(P-2840)***

Coca-Cola, Santa Maria *Also called Tognazzini Beverage Service* ***(P-2301)***

Coca-Cola Company ....D 909 975-5200
1650 S Vintage Ave Ontario (91761) ***(P-2315)***

Cockram Construction Inc (HQ) ....**C 818 650-0999**
605 8th St San Fernando (91340) ***(P-23192)***

Cod USA Inc ....E 949 381-7367
25954 Commercentre Dr Lake Forest (92630) ***(P-3620)***

Coda Automotive Inc ....E 310 820-3611
12101 W Olympic Blvd Los Angeles (90064) ***(P-10032)***

Coda Automotive Inc ....E 949 830-7000
14 Auto Center Dr Irvine (92618) ***(P-10033)***

Coda Energy Holdings LLC ....E 626 775-3900
111 N Artsakh Ave Ste 300 Glendale (91206) ***(P-9861)***

Codan US Corporation ....C 714 430-1300
3501 S Harbor Blvd # 100 Santa Ana (92704) ***(P-5610)***

Codazen Inc ....D 949 916-6266
60 Bunsen Irvine (92618) ***(P-17580)***

Code-In-Motion LLC ....F 949 361-2633
1307 Calle Avanzado San Clemente (92673) ***(P-8118)***

Coding School ....D 424 339-3977
12438 Landale St Studio City (91604) ***(P-22332)***

Cody Cylinder Service LLC ....E 951 786-3650
1393 Dodson Way Ste A Riverside (92507) ***(P-8560)***

Codysales Inc ....F 951 786-3650
1393 Dodson Way Ste A Riverside (92507) ***(P-8007)***

Coffee Bean & Tea Leaf, The, Los Angeles *Also called International Coffee & Tea LLC* ***(P-16209)***

Cofiroute Usa LLC ....C 949 754-0198
200 Spectrum Center Dr # 16 Irvine (92618) ***(P-12561)***

Cognito Company Inc ....E 661 588-8085
34935 Flyover Ct Bakersfield (93308) ***(P-10034)***

Cohen Asset Management Inc (PA) ....**D 310 860-0598**
1900 Avenue Of The Stars # 500 Los Angeles (90067) ***(P-23005)***

Cohen Brown MGT Group Inc (PA) ....**D 310 966-1001**
438 Amapola Ave 110 Torrance (90501) ***(P-23193)***

Coi Rubber Products Inc ....B 626 965-9966
19255 San Jose Ave Unit D City of Industry (91748) ***(P-4730)***

Coil Winding Specialist Inc ....F 714 279-9010
353 W Grove Ave Orange (92865) ***(P-9625)***

Coilwscom Inc ....E 714 279-9010
353 W Grove Ave Orange (92865) ***(P-14749)***

Coinmach Corporation (PA) ....**D 818 637-4300**
3628 San Fernando Rd Glendale (91204) ***(P-16872)***

Colbi Technologies Inc ....E 714 505-9544
12841 Newport Ave Tustin (92780) ***(P-4163)***

Colbrit Manufacturing Co Inc ....E 818 709-3608
9666 Owensmouth Ave Ste G Chatsworth (91311) ***(P-7790)***

Cold Canyon Land Fill Inc ....E 805 549-8332
2268 Carpenter Canyon Rd San Luis Obispo (93401) ***(P-12941)***

Cold Steel Inc (PA) ....**F 805 650-8481**
6060 Nicolle St Ventura (93003) ***(P-6472)***

Coldwell Banker, Canyon Lake *Also called Cbabr Inc* ***(P-15799)***

Coldwell Banker, Bakersfield *Also called Bakersfield Westwind Corp* ***(P-15782)***

Coldwell Banker, Bakersfield *Also called Preferred Brokers Inc* ***(P-15954)***

Coldwell Banker Coastl Aliance, Long Beach *Also called Coastal Alliance Holdings Inc* ***(P-15817)***

Coldwell Banker Hartwig Co, Lancaster *Also called Hartwig Realty Inc* ***(P-15880)***

Coldwell Banker Home Source ....D 760 684-8100
15500 W Sand St Ste 2 Victorville (92392) ***(P-15818)***

Coldwell Banker Residential (HQ) ....**D 949 837-5700**
27742 Vista Del Lago # 1 Mission Viejo (92692) ***(P-15819)***

Coldwell Bankers Residential (PA) ....**D 818 575-2660**
604 Lindero Canyon Rd Agoura Hills (91377) ***(P-15820)***

Coldwell Bnkr Rsdntial Rfrral, Newport Beach *Also called C B Coast Newport Properties* ***(P-15794)***

Coldwell Bnkr Rsdntial Rfrral (HQ) ....**B 949 367-1800**
27271 Las Ramblas Mission Viejo (92691) ***(P-15821)***

Coldwell Bnkr Rsdntial Rfrral ....A 949 673-8700
201 Marine Ave Newport Beach (92662) ***(P-15822)***

Cole Instrument Corp ....D 714 556-3100
2650 S Croddy Way Santa Ana (92704) ***(P-8911)***

Cole Lighting, South El Monte *Also called C W Cole & Company Inc* ***(P-9080)***

Cole, Norman Anne, Anaheim *Also called House Seven Gables RE Inc* ***(P-15885)***

Colepro Inc ....F 714 488-0996
7351 Heil Ave Ste B Huntington Beach (92647) ***(P-3216)***

Colich & Sons, Gardena *Also called Colich Sons* ***(P-944)***

Colich Sons ....D 323 770-2920
547 W 140th St Gardena (90248) ***(P-944)***

Colimatic Usa Inc ....F 949 600-6440
1792 Kaiser Ave Irvine (92614) ***(P-8066)***

Colin Cowie Lifestyle, Rancho Palos Verdes *Also called CAW Cowie Inc* ***(P-18473)***

Collab Inc ....D 310 991-0062
155 W Wash Blvd Ste 417 Los Angeles (90015) ***(P-16999)***

Collection Technology Inc ....D 800 743-4284
10801 6th St Ste 200 Rancho Cucamonga (91730) ***(P-17107)***

Collective Digital Studio, LLC, Beverly Hills *Also called Studio 71 LP* ***(P-17090)***

Collective MGT Group LLC ....C 323 655-8585
8383 Wilshire Blvd # 1050 Beverly Hills (90211) ***(P-23006)***

Collectors Universe Inc (PA) ....**B 949 567-1234**
1610 E Saint Andrew Pl Santa Ana (92705) ***(P-19031)***

College Hospital Inc (PA) ....**B 562 924-9581**
10802 College Pl Cerritos (90703) ***(P-21018)***

College Hospital Cerritos, Cerritos *Also called College Hospital Inc* ***(P-21018)***

College Park Realty Inc (PA) ....**D 562 594-6753**
10791 Los Alamitos Blvd Los Alamitos (90720) ***(P-15823)***

College Vsta Convalescent Hosp, Los Angeles *Also called Notellage Corporation* ***(P-20618)***

College Works Painting, Irvine *Also called Cwpnc Inc* ***(P-1175)***

Collicutt Energy Services Inc ....E 562 944-4413
12349 Hawkins St Santa Fe Springs (90670) ***(P-6558)***

Collins Cllins Muir Stwart LLP ....E 626 243-1100
790 E Colo Blvd Ste 600 Pasadena (91101) ***(P-21533)***

Collins Company, Chino *Also called Warren Collins and Assoc Inc* ***(P-1008)***

Colon Manufacturing Inc (PA) ....**F 213 749-6149**
1100 S San Pedro St Los Angeles (90015) ***(P-2840)***

Colonel Lee's Enterprises, Vernon *Also called T & T Foods Inc* ***(P-1856)***

Colonial Care Center, Long Beach *Also called Longwood Management Corp* ***(P-20607)***

Colonial Gardens Nursing Home, Pico Rivera *Also called Rivera Sanitarium Inc* ***(P-20447)***

Colonial Home Textiles, Corona *Also called Amrapur Overseas Incorporated* ***(P-2721)***

Colonial Mnor Cnvalescent Hosp, West Covina *Also called Wicoro Inc* ***(P-20641)***

Colony Capital LLC (PA) ....**A 310 282-8820**
2450 Broadway Ste 600 Santa Monica (90404) ***(P-16255)***

Colony Management, Santa Monica *Also called Colony Capital LLC* ***(P-16255)***

Colony Palms Hotel LLC ....D 760 969-1800
572 N Indian Canyon Dr Palm Springs (92262) ***(P-16386)***

Color Inc ....E 818 240-1350
1600 Flower St Glendale (91201) ***(P-4255)***

Color Ad Inc ....E 310 632-5500
18601 S Santa Fe Ave Compton (90221) ***(P-17000)***

Color By Deluxe, Burbank *Also called Deluxe Laboratories Inc* ***(P-19226)***

Color Concepts, Canoga Park *Also called Rte Enterprises Inc* ***(P-1197)***

Color Depot Inc ....F 818 500-9033
512 State St Glendale (91203) ***(P-4499)***

Color Design Laboratory Inc ....E 818 341-8200
21329 Nordhoff St Chatsworth (91311) ***(P-18484)***

Color Design Laboratory Inc (PA) ....**D 818 341-5100**
19151 Parthenia St Ste H Northridge (91324) ***(P-22935)***

Color Design Labs, Northridge *Also called Color Design Laboratory Inc* ***(P-22935)***

Color Digit, Costa Mesa *Also called Chup Corporation* ***(P-4252)***

Color Fx Inc ....F 877 763-7671
8000 Haskell Ave Van Nuys (91406) ***(P-4500)***

Color Image Apparel Inc (PA) ....**E 855 793-3100**
6670 Flotilla St Commerce (90040) ***(P-3029)***

Color Laser R&D, Chatsworth *Also called Clover Imaging Group LLC* ***(P-13979)***

Color ME Cotton, Los Angeles *Also called Jd/Cmc Inc* ***(P-2958)***

Color Science Inc ....E 714 434-1033
1230 E Glenwood Pl Santa Ana (92707) ***(P-5121)***

Color Service Inc ....F 323 283-4793
40 E Verdugo Ave Burbank (91502) ***(P-4256)***

Employee Codes: A=Over 500 employees, B=251-500
C=101-250, D=51-100, E=20-50 F=10-19
2022 Southern California Business
Directory and Buyers Guide
© Mergent Inc. 1-800-342-5647
1097

Color Spot Nurseries Inc.....D.....310 549-7470
321 W Sepulveda Blvd Carson (90745) *(P-14879)*

Color Tech Commercial Printing, Lake Forest *Also called Universal Printing Svcs Inc* *(P-4446)*

Color-TEC Indus Finshg Inc.....F.....818 897-2669
11231 Ilex Ave Pacoima (91331) *(P-7354)*

Colorado River Adventures Inc (PA).....C.....760 663-3737
2715 Parker Dam Rd Earp (92242) *(P-16831)*

Colorado River Medical Center, Needles *Also called Community Hlthcare Partner Inc* *(P-19759)*

Colorama Wholesale Nursery, Azusa *Also called Richard Wilson Wellington* *(P-94)*

Colorcom Inc.....D.....323 246-4640
2437 S Eastern Ave Commerce (90040) *(P-4257)*

Colorfast Dye & Print Hse Inc.....F.....323 581-1656
5075 Pacific Blvd Vernon (90058) *(P-4258)*

Colorfx Inc.....E.....818 767-7671
11050 Randall St Sun Valley (91352) *(P-4259)*

Colorgraphics, Los Angeles *Also called Madisn/Grham Clor Graphics Inc* *(P-4363)*

Colormax Industries Inc (PA).....E.....213 748-6600
1627 Paloma St Los Angeles (90021) *(P-2564)*

Colornet Press, Van Nuys *Also called Niknejad Inc* *(P-4380)*

Colortech Label Inc.....F.....714 999-5545
1230 S Sherman St Anaheim (92805) *(P-4501)*

Colosseum Athletics Corp.....D.....310 667-8341
2400 S Wilmington Ave Compton (90220) *(P-14330)*

Colton Truck Terminal Garage, Colton *Also called Erf Enterprises Inc* *(P-9986)*

Columbia Aluminum Products LLC.....D.....323 728-7361
1150 W Rincon St Corona (92878) *(P-6601)*

Columbia Fabricating Co Inc.....E.....818 247-4220
5079 Gloria Ave Encino (91436) *(P-6956)*

Columbia Pictures Inds Inc (HQ).....C.....310 244-4000
10202 Washington Blvd Culver City (90232) *(P-19109)*

Columbia Products Co, Irvine *Also called Columbia Sanitary Products Inc* *(P-6559)*

Columbia Sanitary Products Inc.....E.....949 474-0777
1622 Browning Irvine (92606) *(P-6559)*

Columbia Screw Products Inc.....E.....714 549-1171
3403 S Main St Unit B Santa Ana (92707) *(P-7033)*

Columbia Showcase & Cab Co Inc.....C.....818 765-9710
11034 Sherman Way Ste A Sun Valley (91352) *(P-3643)*

Columbia Spclty A Trstar Indus, Long Beach *Also called Tristar Industrial LLC* *(P-14028)*

Columbia Steel Inc.....D.....909 874-8840
2175 N Linden Ave Rialto (92377) *(P-6602)*

Comac America Corporation.....F.....760 616-9614
4350 Von Karman Ave # 400 Newport Beach (92660) *(P-10184)*

Comak Trading Inc A Cal Corp.....D.....323 261-3404
2550 S Soto St Vernon (90058) *(P-14368)*

Comav LLC (PA).....C.....760 523-5100
18499 Phantom St Ste 17 Victorville (92394) *(P-14054)*

Comav Technical Services LLC.....C.....760 530-2400
18438 Readiness St Victorville (92394) *(P-12350)*

Combimatrix Corporation (HQ).....D.....949 753-0624
310 Goddard Ste 150 Irvine (92618) *(P-10789)*

Combustion Associates Inc.....E.....951 272-6999
555 Monica Cir Corona (92878) *(P-12797)*

Comcast Corporation.....D.....909 890-0886
1205 S Dupont Ave Ontario (91761) *(P-12753)*

Comchoice, El Segundo *Also called Scenewise Inc* *(P-9838)*

Comco Inc.....E.....818 333-8500
2151 N Lincoln St Burbank (91504) *(P-8376)*

Come Land Inc (PA).....B.....818 567-2455
1419 N San Fernando Blvd Burbank (91504) *(P-17229)*

Come Land Maint Svc Co Inc.....A.....818 567-2455
1419 N San Fernando Blvd # 250 Burbank (91504) *(P-17230)*

Come Land Maintenance Company, Burbank *Also called Come Land Inc* *(P-17229)*

Comedy Club Oxnard LLC.....D.....805 535-5400
591 Collection Blvd Oxnard (93036) *(P-19556)*

Comet Electric Inc.....C.....818 340-0965
21625 Prairie St Chatsworth (91311) *(P-1234)*

Comet Medical, Ventura *Also called Peter Brasseler Holdings LLC* *(P-13510)*

Comfort Bedding Mfg Inc.....F.....310 667-7720
11680 Wright Rd Lynwood (90262) *(P-3099)*

Comfort California Inc.....C.....714 750-3131
616 W Convention Way Anaheim (92802) *(P-16387)*

Comfort Care Hospice Inc.....D.....818 501-3129
5170 Sepulveda Blvd # 290 Sherman Oaks (91403) *(P-21040)*

Comfort Industries Inc.....E.....562 692-8288
12266 Rooks Rd Whittier (90601) *(P-2611)*

Comfort Inn, Santa Monica *Also called Charles Ting* *(P-16378)*

Comfort Keepers, Irvine *Also called CK Franchising Inc* *(P-21148)*

Comfort Keepers, Claremont *Also called Bluebridge Prof Svcs Inc* *(P-21139)*

Comfort Keepers (PA).....C.....951 696-2710
29970 Tech Dr Ste 213 Murrieta (92563) *(P-21151)*

Comfort Suites Sequoia Area, Visalia *Also called Equitable Hotels* *(P-16435)*

Command Gard Srvces Wsa Srvces, Gardena *Also called United Facility Solutions Inc* *(P-18348)*

Command Guard Services, Torrance *Also called Resource Collection Inc* *(P-17281)*

Command Packaging LLC (HQ).....C.....323 980-0918
3840 E 26th St Vernon (90058) *(P-14922)*

Commander Boats.....F.....951 273-0100
4020 Tyler St Riverside (92503) *(P-10461)*

Commander Boats-Mira Loma Mar, Riverside *Also called Commander Boats* *(P-10461)*

Commander Packaging West Inc.....E.....714 921-9350
602 S Rockefeller Ave D Ontario (91761) *(P-3795)*

Commerce, Commerce *Also called Alarin Aircraft Hinge Inc* *(P-6497)*

Commerce Casino, Commerce *Also called California Commerce Club Inc* *(P-16365)*

Commerce Home Mortgage LLC.....D.....949 769-3526
32 Discovery Ste 160 Irvine (92618) *(P-15184)*

Commerce Velocity LLC.....E.....949 756-8950
1 Technology Dr Ste J725 Irvine (92618) *(P-17822)*

Commercial and Security Labels, Valencia *Also called Quadriga USA Enterprises Inc* *(P-3937)*

Commercial Casting Co, Fontana *Also called Hartman Industries* *(P-13569)*

Commercial Cleaning Services, Van Nuys *Also called CCS Los Angeles Janitorial LLC* *(P-17223)*

Commercial Coating Company Inc.....D.....323 256-1331
2809 W Avenue 37 Los Angeles (90065) *(P-874)*

Commercial Cooling, City of Industry *Also called Par Engineering Inc* *(P-1116)*

Commercial Crrers Insur Agcy I.....C.....562 404-4900
4 Centerpointe Dr Ste 300 La Palma (90623) *(P-15552)*

Commercial Cstm Sting Uphl Inc.....D.....714 850-0520
12601 Western Ave Garden Grove (92841) *(P-3723)*

Commercial Display Systems LLC.....E.....818 361-8160
17341 Sierra Hwy Canyon Country (91351) *(P-8332)*

Commercial Door Company Inc.....D.....714 529-2179
1374 E 9th St Pomona (91766) *(P-1431)*

Commercial Electronics Pho, Newport Beach *Also called Macom Technology Solutions Inc* *(P-9288)*

Commercial Grinding Co Inc.....D.....562 531-9970
6829 Walthall Way Paramount (90723) *(P-18485)*

Commercial Indus Design Co Inc.....D.....949 273-6199
20372 N Sea Cir Lake Forest (92630) *(P-13382)*

Commercial Intr Resources Inc.....D.....562 926-5885
6077 Rickenbacker Rd Commerce (90040) *(P-3499)*

Commercial Inv MGT Group, Los Angeles *Also called Cim Group LP* *(P-16381)*

Commercial Lbr & Pallet Co Inc (PA).....C.....626 968-0631
135 Long Ln City of Industry (91746) *(P-3383)*

Commercial Lighting Inds Inc.....D.....800 755-0155
81161 Indio Blvd Indio (92201) *(P-13619)*

Commercial Metal Forming Inc.....D.....714 532-6321
341 W Collins Ave Orange (92867) *(P-6736)*

Commercial Paving, Los Angeles *Also called Commercial Coating Company Inc* *(P-874)*

Commercial Prgrm Systems Inc (PA).....C.....818 308-8560
4400 Cldwtr Cyn Ave Studio City (91604) *(P-18170)*

Commercial Property Management (PA).....D.....213 739-2000
3251 W 6th St Ste 109 Los Angeles (90020) *(P-15824)*

Commercial Protective Svcs Inc.....A.....310 515-5290
3400 E Airport Way Long Beach (90806) *(P-18263)*

Commercial Roofing Systems Inc.....D.....626 359-5354
11735 Goldring Rd Arcadia (91006) *(P-1480)*

Commercial Shtmtl Works Inc.....E.....213 748-7321
1800 S San Pedro St Los Angeles (90015) *(P-6603)*

Commercial Truck Eqp Co LLC.....D.....562 803-4466
12351 Bellflower Blvd Downey (90242) *(P-9979)*

Commission Junction LLC (HQ).....D.....805 730-8000
530 E Montecito St Santa Barbara (93103) *(P-17581)*

Commodity Forwarders Inc (HQ).....C.....310 348-8855
11101 S La Cienega Blvd Los Angeles (90045) *(P-12438)*

Commodity Resource Envmtl Inc.....E.....661 824-2416
11847 United St Mojave (93501) *(P-6285)*

Commodity Rsource Enviromental, Mojave *Also called Commodity Resource Envmtl Inc* *(P-6285)*

Commodity Sales Co.....C.....323 980-5463
517 S Clarence St Los Angeles (90033) *(P-1756)*

Common Area Maint Svcs Inc (PA).....D.....310 390-3552
21811 S Western Ave Torrance (90501) *(P-17231)*

Common Collabs LLC.....E.....714 519-3245
1820 E Walnut Ave Fullerton (92831) *(P-2316)*

Commons At Calabasas, The, Los Angeles *Also called Caruso MGT Ltd A Cal Ltd Prtnr* *(P-15798)*

Commonwealth Equity Svcs LLC.....D.....949 336-6440
20 Corporate Park Ste 150 Irvine (92606) *(P-23194)*

Commonwealth Financial Network, Irvine *Also called Commonwealth Equity Svcs LLC* *(P-23194)*

Commonwealth Land Title Insur.....C.....800 432-0706
4100 Nwport Pl Dr Ste 120 Newport Beach (92660) *(P-15499)*

Commonwealth Land Title Insur.....C.....949 460-4500
6 Executive Cir Ste 100 Irvine (92614) *(P-15500)*

Commonwealth Land Title Insur.....C.....951 296-6289
41637 Margarita Rd # 101 Temecula (92591) *(P-15501)*

Communication Tech Svcs LLC.....B.....508 382-2700
1590 S Milliken Ave Ste H Ontario (91761) *(P-1235)*

Communications Supply Corp.....C.....714 670-7711
6251 Knott Ave Buena Park (90620) *(P-12781)*

Community Access Ntwrk Non Prf (PA).....E.....951 279-1333
2275 S Main St Ste 201 Corona (92882) *(P-21749)*

Community Action Comm Snta BRB (PA).....E.....805 964-8857
5638 Hollister Ave # 230 Goleta (93117) *(P-22176)*

Community Action Partnership.....D.....805 541-4122
3970 Short St San Luis Obispo (93401) *(P-21750)*

Community Action Partnership.....D.....805 489-4026
1152 E Grand Ave Arroyo Grande (93420) *(P-21534)*

Community Action Partnr Kern.....D.....661 871-6055
3000 Sterling Rd Bakersfield (93306) *(P-21751)*

Community Action Partnr Kern (PA).....E.....661 336-5236
5005 Business Park N Bakersfield (93309) *(P-21752)*

Community Action Partnr Kern.....D.....661 336-5300
1611 1st St Bakersfield (93304) *(P-22094)*

Community Action Prtnr Ornge C.....C.....714 897-6670
11870 Monarch St Garden Grove (92841) *(P-21753)*

Community Action Prtnr San Lui (PA).....D.....805 544-4355
1030 Southwood Dr San Luis Obispo (93401) *(P-22006)*

Community Action Prtnr San Lui.....C.....805 541-2272
805a Fiero Ln Ste A San Luis Obispo (93401) *(P-22007)*

Community Action Prtnr San Lui.....C.....805 544-2478
705 Grand Ave San Luis Obispo (93401) *(P-21288)*

Mergent e-mail: customerrelations@mergent.com
1098
2022 Southern California Business Directory and Buyers Guide
(P-0000) Products & Services Section entry number
(PA)=Parent Co (HQ)=Headquarters (DH)=Div Headquarters

ALPHABETIC SECTION Compuvac Industries Inc

Community Action Prtnship Sb C.......D.......909 723-1500
696 S Tippecanoe Ave San Bernardino (92408) *(P-22177)*
Community Adviser Newspaper, Banning *Also called Century Publishing (P-4494)*
Community Care Licensing, Riverside *Also called Social Services Cal Dept (P-21889)*
Community Care On Palm, Riverside *Also called South Coast Health Wellness (P-20478)*
Community Care Rhblitation Ctr, Newport Beach *Also called Ben Bennett Inc (P-20560)*
Community Close-Up Westminster.......D.......714 704-5811
1771 S Lewis St Anaheim (92805) *(P-3965)*
Community Cnvlscent Hosp Mntcl, Montclair *Also called US Skillserve Inc (P-20493)*
Community College Foundation.......E.......213 427-6910
3530 Wilshire Blvd # 610 Los Angeles (90010) *(P-21754)*
Community Day School, Beaumont *Also called Beaumont Unfied Schl Dst Pub F (P-21985)*
Community Family Guidance Ctr (PA).......D.......**562 865-6444**
10929 South St Ste 208b Cerritos (90703) *(P-21289)*
Community Health Center, Bakersfield *Also called Omni Family Health (P-20011)*
Community Health Systems Inc.......C.......951 571-2300
21801 Alessandro Blvd Moreno Valley (92553) *(P-19757)*
Community Hlth Alance Pasadena (PA).......D.......**626 398-6300**
1855 N Fair Oaks Ave Pasadena (91103) *(P-20726)*
Community Hlth Ctrs of Cntl CA (PA).......C.......**805 929-3211**
150 Tejas Pl Nipomo (93444) *(P-19758)*
Community Hlthcare Partner Inc.......D.......760 326-4531
1401 Bailey Ave Needles (92363) *(P-19759)*
Community Hosp Huntington Pk, Huntington Park *Also called Chhp Holdings II LLC (P-20716)*
Community Hosp Huntington Pk, Huntington Park *Also called Chhp Management LLC (P-20717)*
Community Hosp San Bernardino (HQ).......B.......**909 887-6333**
1805 Medical Center Dr San Bernardino (92411) *(P-20727)*
Community Hospital Long Beach.......A.......562 494-0600
1760 Termino Ave Ste 105 Long Beach (90804) *(P-20728)*
Community Manufacturing Inc.......F.......323 720-8811
5880 E Slauson Ave 2nd Commerce (90040) *(P-7639)*
Community Media Corporation (PA).......D.......**714 220-0292**
5119 Ball Rd Cypress (90630) *(P-3966)*
Community Mem Hosp San Bnvntur.......D.......805 652-5072
147 N Brent St Ventura (93003) *(P-20729)*
Community Memorial Health Sys (PA).......A.......**805 652-5011**
147 N Brent St Ventura (93003) *(P-20730)*
Community Memorial Health Sys.......C.......805 646-1401
1306 Maricopa Hwy Ojai (93023) *(P-20731)*
Community Memorial Hospital, Ventura *Also called Community Memorial Health Sys (P-20730)*
Community Merch Solutions LLC.......E.......877 956-9258
27201 Puerta Real Ste 120 Mission Viejo (92691) *(P-8313)*
Community Orthpd Med Group Prt.......D.......949 348-4000
26401 Crown Valley Pkwy Mission Viejo (92691) *(P-19760)*
Community Partners (PA).......C.......**213 346-3200**
1000 N Alameda St Ste 240 Los Angeles (90012) *(P-22178)*
Community Patrol.......D.......657 247-4744
1420 E Edinger Ave # 213 Santa Ana (92705) *(P-18264)*
Community Redevelopment Agency (PA).......C.......**213 977-1600**
448 S Hill St Ste 1200 Los Angeles (90013) *(P-23430)*
Community Seniorserv Inc.......D.......714 558-1216
1101 S Grand Ave Ste K Santa Ana (92705) *(P-21152)*
Community Support Options Inc.......C.......661 758-5331
1401 Poso Dr Wasco (93280) *(P-21755)*
Community Therapies Baby Steps, Santa Clarita *Also called Community Therapies LLC (P-20212)*
Community Therapies LLC.......E.......661 945-7878
19040 Soledad Canyon Rd # 25 Santa Clarita (91351) *(P-20212)*
Community Transit Services, El Monte *Also called First Student Inc (P-11806)*
Compaction American, Lake Elsinore *Also called American Compaction Eqp Inc (P-7634)*
Company of Motion LLC.......F.......805 963-1996
121 E Mason St Ste A Santa Barbara (93101) *(P-11272)*
Compart Engineering Inc (HQ).......D.......**909 947-6688**
1730 E Philadelphia St Ontario (91761) *(P-13710)*
Compas Health, Templeton *Also called Compass Health Inc (P-20284)*
Compass Bank, Corona *Also called Bbva USA (P-15012)*
Compass Bank, Sun City *Also called Bbva USA (P-14994)*
Compass Flooring, Santa Fe Springs *Also called Altro Usa Inc (P-11618)*
Compass Group Usa Inc.......C.......714 899-2520
12640 Knott St Garden Grove (92841) *(P-17338)*
Compass Health Inc.......C.......805 434-3035
290 Heather Ct Templeton (93465) *(P-20284)*
Compass Health Inc.......C.......805 687-6651
3880 Via Lucero Santa Barbara (93110) *(P-20285)*
Compass Health Inc.......C.......805 543-0210
1425 Woodside Dr San Luis Obispo (93401) *(P-20286)*
Compass Health Inc.......C.......805 772-7372
1405 Teresa Dr Morro Bay (93442) *(P-20287)*
Compass Health Inc.......C.......805 489-8137
1212 Farroll Ave Arroyo Grande (93420) *(P-20288)*
Compass Health Inc.......C.......805 466-9254
10805 El Camino Real Atascadero (93422) *(P-20289)*
Compass Transportation Inc.......D.......310 834-4530
11591 Martha Ann Dr Los Alamitos (90720) *(P-12566)*
Compass Water Solutions Inc (PA).......E.......**949 222-5777**
15542 Mosher Ave Tustin (92780) *(P-8377)*
Compatico Inc.......E.......616 940-1772
1901 S Archibald Ave Ontario (91761) *(P-3644)*
Competent Care HM Hlth Nursing, Costa Mesa *Also called Competent Care Inc (P-21153)*
Competent Care Inc.......D.......714 545-4818
2900 Bristol St Ste D107 Costa Mesa (92626) *(P-21153)*
Compex Legal Services Inc (PA).......C.......**310 782-1801**
325 Maple Ave Torrance (90503) *(P-21535)*
Complete Aquatic Systems, Gardena *Also called Wally & Pat Enterprises (P-11792)*
Complete Clothing Company (PA).......E.......**323 277-1470**
4950 E 49th St Vernon (90058) *(P-2883)*
Complete Coach Works (HQ).......B.......**951 682-2557**
1863 Service Ct Riverside (92507) *(P-18923)*
Complete Food Service Inc.......D.......951 685-8490
3815 Wabash Dr Jurupa Valley (91752) *(P-14683)*
Complete Garment Inc.......E.......323 846-3731
2101 E 38th St Vernon (90058) *(P-2628)*
Complete Landscape Care Inc.......D.......562 946-4441
13316 Leffingwell Rd Whittier (90605) *(P-297)*
Complete Logistics Company.......C.......909 427-9800
15895 Valley Blvd 200 Fontana (92335) *(P-12024)*
Complete Metal Fabrication Inc.......F.......760 353-0260
596 E Main St El Centro (92243) *(P-6604)*
Complete Office California Inc.......D.......714 880-1222
12724 Moore St Cerritos (90703) *(P-13131)*
Completely Fresh Foods Inc.......C.......323 722-9136
4401 S Downey Rd Vernon (90058) *(P-14684)*
Completes Plus, Lawndale *Also called Automotive Aftermarket Inc (P-13045)*
Compliance Poster, Monrovia *Also called Global Compliance Inc (P-4174)*
Complyright Dist Svcs Inc.......E.......805 981-0992
3451 Jupiter Ct Oxnard (93030) *(P-4599)*
Component Equipment Coinc.......E.......805 988-8004
3050 Camino Del Sol Oxnard (93030) *(P-9649)*
Composite Manufacturing Inc.......E.......949 361-7580
970 Calle Amanecer Ste D San Clemente (92673) *(P-10966)*
Composites Horizons LLC (HQ).......C.......**626 331-0861**
1629 W Industrial Park St Covina (91722) *(P-10302)*
Composites One LLC.......F.......562 906-0173
11917 Altamar Pl Santa Fe Springs (90670) *(P-14756)*
Comppartners Inc.......E.......949 253-3111
333 City Blvd W Ste 1500 Orange (92868) *(P-21154)*
Comprehensive Autism Ctr Inc (PA).......D.......**951 813-4034**
40485 Mrreta Hot Sprng Rd Murrieta (92563) *(P-20213)*
Comprehensive Cmnty Hlth Ctr.......E.......323 344-4144
5059 York Blvd Los Angeles (90042) *(P-19761)*
Comprehensive Dist Svcs Inc.......C.......310 523-1546
18726 S Wstn Ave Ste 300 Gardena (90248) *(P-12567)*
Comprhnsive Crdvsclar Spcalist (PA).......F.......**626 281-8663**
220 S 1st St Ste 101 Alhambra (91801) *(P-4809)*
Comprhnsive Indus Dsblity MGT.......D.......866 301-6568
2555 Townsgate Rd Ste 125 Westlake Village (91361) *(P-21399)*
Compspec Inc.......D.......818 551-4200
801 N Brand Blvd Ste 650 Glendale (91203) *(P-23195)*
Compton Family Mhc Fsp, Compton *Also called County of Los Angeles (P-21403)*
Compton Service Center, Compton *Also called Southern California Edison Co (P-12844)*
COMPTON TRAINING CENTER, Van Nuys *Also called Apprentice Jrnymen Trning Tr F (P-21938)*
Compton Unified School Dst.......D.......310 898-6470
1104 E 148th St Compton (90220) *(P-21756)*
Compton Unified School Dst.......D.......310 898-6008
411 N Tajauta Ave Compton (90220) *(P-22008)*
Compton Unified School Dst.......D.......310 639-4321
2600 N Central Ave Compton (90222) *(P-18486)*
Compu Aire Inc.......C.......562 945-8971
8167 Byron Rd Whittier (90606) *(P-8333)*
Compucase Corporation.......A.......626 336-6588
16720 Chestnut St Ste C City of Industry (91748) *(P-8195)*
Compugroup Medical Inc.......E.......949 789-0500
25 B Tech Dr Ste 200 Irvine (92618) *(P-17823)*
Compulink Business Systems Inc (PA).......C.......**805 446-2050**
1100 Business Center Cir Newbury Park (91320) *(P-17824)*
Compulink Healthcare Solutions, Newbury Park *Also called Compulink Business Systems Inc (P-17824)*
Compulink Management Ctr Inc (PA).......C.......**562 988-1688**
3545 Long Beach Blvd Long Beach (90807) *(P-17582)*
Compulocks Brands Inc.......F.......562 201-2913
9115 Dice Rd Ste 18 Santa Fe Springs (90670) *(P-9862)*
Compumeric Engineering Inc.......E.......909 605-7666
1390 S Milliken Ave Ontario (91761) *(P-6810)*
Computational Sensors Corp.......E.......805 962-1175
1042 Via Los Padres Santa Barbara (93111) *(P-10576)*
Computational Systems Inc.......C.......661 832-5306
4301 Resnik Ct Bakersfield (93313) *(P-10686)*
Computed Tool & Engrg Inc.......E.......714 630-3911
2910 E Ricker Way Anaheim (92806) *(P-7791)*
Computer Assisted Mfg Tech LLC.......E.......949 263-8911
8710-8750 Research Dr Irvine (92618) *(P-8561)*
Computer EMB Specialists.......E.......949 852-8888
17312 Gillette Ave Irvine (92614) *(P-18487)*
Computer Metal Products Corp.......D.......805 520-6966
370 E Easy St Simi Valley (93065) *(P-6811)*
Computer Service Company.......E.......951 738-1444
210 N Delilah St Corona (92879) *(P-9336)*
Computer-Nozzles, Irwindale *Also called Cni Mfg Inc (P-8558)*
Computerized Mgt Svcs Inc.......D.......805 522-5940
4100 Guardian St Ste 205 Simi Valley (93063) *(P-22774)*
Computershare Inc.......A.......800 522-6645
2335 Alaska Ave El Segundo (90245) *(P-15355)*
Computerworks Technologies, Burbank *Also called Global Service Resources Inc (P-17626)*
Computrition Inc (HQ).......D.......**818 961-3999**
8521 Fllbrook Ave Ste 100 Canoga Park (91304) *(P-17583)*
Computrus Inc.......E.......951 245-9103
250 Klug Cir Corona (92878) *(P-6737)*
Computrzed Vhcl Rgstration Inc (HQ).......E.......**800 386-1746**
1100 W Twn Cntry Rd Orange (92868) *(P-18024)*
Compuvac Industries Inc.......F.......949 574-5085
18381 Mount Langley St Fountain Valley (92708) *(P-8033)*

A L P H A B E T I C

Employee Codes: A=Over 500 employees, B=251-500
C=101-250, D=51-100, E=20-50 F=10-19
2022 Southern California Business
Directory and Buyers Guide
© Mergent Inc. 1-800-342-5647
1099

Comstock Crosser Assoc Dev Inc ....E.......310 546-5781
321 12th St Ste 200 Manhattan Beach (90266) ***(P-16050)***

Comstock Homes, Manhattan Beach *Also called Comstock Crosser Assoc Dev Inc* ***(P-16050)***

Con-Tech Plastics, Brea *Also called Ramtec Associates Inc* ***(P-5788)***

Con-Way, Blythe *Also called Xpo Logistics Freight Inc* ***(P-12101)***

Concept, Walnut *Also called King Audio Inc* ***(P-13688)***

Concept Development Llc ....E.......949 623-8000
1881 Langley Ave Irvine (92614) ***(P-9394)***

Concept Packaging Group, Ontario *Also called Southland Container Corp* ***(P-3828)***

Concept Studio Inc ....F.......949 759-0606
3195 Red Hill Ave Ste G Costa Mesa (92626) ***(P-5985)***

Concept Technology Inc (PA) ....B.......**949 854-7047**
895 Dove St Fl 3 Newport Beach (92660) ***(P-22515)***

Concept Technology Inc ....D.......949 851-6550
2941 W Macarthur Blvd # 136 Santa Ana (92704) ***(P-22516)***

Concepts & Wood, Huntington Park *Also called Plycraft Industries Inc* ***(P-3353)***

Concert Golf Partners LLC ....A.......949 715-0602
1 Coastal Oak Newport Coast (92657) ***(P-19478)***

Conco Cement Co, Fontana *Also called Gonsalves & Santucci Inc* ***(P-1526)***

Concord Document Services Inc (PA) ....D.......**213 745-3175**
1321 W 12th St Los Angeles (90015) ***(P-17146)***

Concord Foods Inc (PA) ....D.......**909 975-2000**
4601 E Guasti Rd Ontario (91761) ***(P-14461)***

Concordance Healthcare, Long Beach *Also called Mkr Medical Supply Inc* ***(P-13501)***

Concorde Career Colleges Inc ....D.......818 766-8151
12412 Victory Blvd North Hollywood (91606) ***(P-22267)***

Concorde-New Horizons Corp ....D.......310 820-6733
11600 San Vicente Blvd Los Angeles (90049) ***(P-19110)***

Concorse Ht At Los Angles Arpr, Los Angeles *Also called Humnit Hotel At Lax LLC* ***(P-16495)***

Concourse Bowling Center, Anaheim *Also called Concourse Recreation Center* ***(P-19397)***

Concourse Recreation Center (PA) ....D.......**714 666-2695**
3364 E La Palma Ave Anaheim (92806) ***(P-19397)***

Concrete Holding Co Cal Inc ....A.......818 788-4228
15821 Ventura Blvd # 475 Encino (91436) ***(P-6085)***

Concrete Mold Corporation ....D.......310 537-5171
2121 E Del Amo Blvd Compton (90220) ***(P-7792)***

Concrete Tie Industries Inc (PA) ....D.......**310 628-2328**
130 E Oris St Compton (90222) ***(P-13300)***

Concrete West Construction Inc ....F.......949 448-9940
1733 S Douglass Rd Ste I Anaheim (92806) ***(P-23196)***

Concurrent Holdings LLC ....A.......310 473-3065
11150 Santa Monica Blvd # 8 Los Angeles (90025) ***(P-8974)***

Condition Monitoring Svcs Inc ....E.......888 359-3277
855 San Ysidro Ln Nipomo (93444) ***(P-10790)***

Condor Outdoor Products Inc (PA) ....E.......**626 358-3270**
5268 Rivergrade Rd Baldwin Park (91706) ***(P-11410)***

Condor Pacific Industries Inc (PA) ....E.......**818 889-2150**
905 Rancho Conejo Blvd Newbury Park (91320) ***(P-10577)***

Condor Productions LLC ....D.......310 449-3000
245 N Beverly Dr Beverly Hills (90210) ***(P-19223)***

Conductive, Rcho STA Marg *Also called Standard Cable Usa Inc* ***(P-7514)***

Conduent Wkrs Cmpnstion Hldngs (HQ) ....E.......**860 678-7877**
17838 Gillette Ave Irvine (92614) ***(P-21400)***

Conejo Pacific Technologies ....D.......805 498-5315
1560 Newbury Rd Ste 1 Newbury Park (91320) ***(P-695)***

Conesco Industries, Riverside *Also called Doka USA Ltd* ***(P-6821)***

Conestoga Hotel ....D.......714 535-0300
1240 S Walnut St Anaheim (92802) ***(P-16388)***

Conesys Inc (PA) ....B.......**310 618-3737**
2280 W 208th St Torrance (90501) ***(P-13711)***

Conexant Systems Inc ....F.......949 483-5714
1901 Main St Ste 300 Irvine (92614) ***(P-9492)***

Conexant Systems LLC (HQ) ....B.......**949 483-4600**
1901 Main St Ste 300 Irvine (92614) ***(P-9493)***

Conexant Systems Worldwide Inc ....E.......949 483-4600
4000 Macarthur Blvd Newport Beach (92660) ***(P-9494)***

Conexis Bnfits Admnstrators LP (HQ) ....C.......**714 835-5006**
721 S Parker St Ste 300 Orange (92868) ***(P-15553)***

Confido LLC ....A.......310 361-8558
3407 W 6th St Ste 709 Los Angeles (90020) ***(P-21155)***

Confie Seguros Inc (HQ) ....C.......**714 252-2500**
7711 Center Ave Ste 200 Huntington Beach (92647) ***(P-15554)***

Confie Seguros Holdings II Co (PA) ....C.......**714 252-2500**
7711 Center Ave Ste 200 Huntington Beach (92647) ***(P-15555)***

Confie Seguros Texas Inc (HQ) ....D.......**714 252-2649**
7711 Center Ave Ste 200 Huntington Beach (92647) ***(P-15556)***

Congaree Health Holdings LLC ....D.......949 487-9500
29222 Rncho Vejo Rd Ste 1 San Juan Capistrano (92675) ***(P-20290)***

Conglas, Bakersfield *Also called Consolidated Fibrgls Pdts Co* ***(P-6170)***

Conico Coro Inc (HQ) ....D.......**805 373-1880**
4520 E Thsand Oaks Blvd S Westlake Village (91362) ***(P-18910)***

Conico Roro Inc (HQ) ....E.......**818 716-1238**
4520 E Thsand Oaks Blvd S Westlake Village (91362) ***(P-18911)***

Conley's Mfg & Sales, Montclair *Also called John L Conley Inc* ***(P-6999)***

Connect Computers, Anaheim *Also called General Procurement Inc* ***(P-13402)***

Connect Systems Inc ....E.......805 642-7184
1802 Eastman Ave Ste 116 Ventura (93003) ***(P-9264)***

Connectall LLC ....E.......800 913-7457
177 E Colo Blvd Ste 200 Pasadena (91105) ***(P-18025)***

Connectec Company Inc (PA) ....D.......**949 252-1077**
1701 Reynolds Ave Irvine (92614) ***(P-9028)***

Connectpoint Inc ....E.......805 682-8900
175 Cremona Dr Ste 160 Goleta (93117) ***(P-17825)***

Connectpro, Walnut *Also called Gemtek Technology Inc* ***(P-13400)***

Connell Processing Inc ....E.......818 845-7661
3094 N Avon St Burbank (91504) ***(P-7242)***

Connelly Machine Works ....E.......714 558-6855
420 N Terminal St Santa Ana (92701) ***(P-8562)***

Connexity Inc (HQ) ....C.......**310 571-1235**
2120 Colorado Ave Ste 400 Santa Monica (90404) ***(P-12632)***

Conquer Nation Inc ....C.......310 562-8000
5525 S Soto St Vernon (90058) ***(P-3071)***

Conroy & Knowlton Inc ....E.......323 665-5288
320 S Montebello Blvd Montebello (90640) ***(P-5611)***

Conroy's Florist, Canyon Country *Also called M & M Florists Inc* ***(P-14040)***

Consejosano Inc ....D.......855 735-6726
5200 Lankershim Blvd # 31 North Hollywood (91601) ***(P-18488)***

Consensus Cloud Solutions Inc ....B.......323 860-9200
700 S Flower St Fl 15 Los Angeles (90017) ***(P-17826)***

Conservation Corps Long Beach ....C.......562 986-1249
340 Nieto Ave Long Beach (90814) ***(P-21946)***

Consilio LLC ....C.......626 921-1600
605 E Huntington Dr # 211 Monrovia (91016) ***(P-21536)***

Consoldted Fire Protection LLC (HQ) ....A.......**949 727-3277**
153 Technology Dr Ste 200 Irvine (92618) ***(P-18489)***

Consoldted Med Bo-Analysis Inc (PA) ....D.......**714 657-7369**
10700 Walker St Cypress (90630) ***(P-21064)***

Consolidated Aerospace Mfg LLC ....E.......714 989-2802
630 E Lambert Rd Brea (92821) ***(P-6512)***

Consolidated Aerospace Mfg LLC (HQ) ....C.......**714 989-2797**
1425 S Acacia Ave Fullerton (92831) ***(P-10578)***

Consolidated Aircraft Coatings, Riverside *Also called Poly-Fiber Inc* ***(P-5107)***

Consolidated Color Corporation ....E.......562 420-7714
12316 Carson St Hawaiian Gardens (90716) ***(P-5092)***

Consolidated Design West, Pomona *Also called Western Converting Spc Inc* ***(P-4593)***

Consolidated Design West Inc ....E.......714 999-1476
1345 S Lewis St Anaheim (92805) ***(P-17166)***

Consolidated Devices Inc (HQ) ....E.......**626 965-0668**
19220 San Jose Ave City of Industry (91748) ***(P-9695)***

Consolidated Engineering Labs, Riverside *Also called Heider Inspection Group* ***(P-22947)***

Consolidated Fabricators Corp (PA) ....C.......**818 901-1005**
14620 Arminta St Van Nuys (91402) ***(P-6738)***

Consolidated Fibrgls Pdts Co ....D.......661 323-6026
3801 Standard St Bakersfield (93308) ***(P-6170)***

Consolidated Foundries, Pomona *Also called CFI Holdings Corp* ***(P-6265)***

Consolidated Foundries Inc ....C.......323 773-2363
8333 Wilcox Ave Cudahy (90201) ***(P-6389)***

Consolidated Plastics Corp (PA) ....E.......**909 393-8222**
14954 La Palma Dr Chino (91710) ***(P-14757)***

Consolidated Svc Distrs Inc ....D.......908 687-5800
777 S Central Ave Los Angeles (90021) ***(P-14561)***

Consolidated Trading Co Amer, Cerritos *Also called Ctcoa LLC* ***(P-10305)***

Consteel Industrial Inc ....E.......562 806-4575
15435 Woodcrest Dr Whittier (90604) ***(P-6605)***

Constellation Homebuilder (HQ) ....E.......**714 768-6100**
888 S Dsnyland Dr Ste 430 Tustin (92780) ***(P-18171)***

Constrction Instllton Mint Gr, Anaheim *Also called Kesa Incorporated* ***(P-18391)***

Construction Specialty Svc Inc ....D.......661 864-7573
4550 Buck Owens Blvd Bakersfield (93308) ***(P-945)***

Consumer Attrney Mktg Group LL (PA) ....D.......**800 200-2264**
21051 Warner Center Ln # 25 Woodland Hills (91367) ***(P-17001)***

Consumer Loan Dept, Tustin *Also called Schoolsfirst Federal Credit Un* ***(P-15087)***

Consumer Safety Analytics LLC ....D.......818 922-2416
7027 Hayvenhurst Ave Van Nuys (91406) ***(P-22936)***

Container Options ....F.......909 478-0045
1493 E San Bernardino Ave San Bernardino (92408) ***(P-5612)***

Contec Microelectronics USA ....D.......949 250-4025
17811 Gillette Ave Fl 1 Irvine (92614) ***(P-13383)***

Contec USA, Irvine *Also called Contec Microelectronics USA* ***(P-13383)***

Contech Engnered Solutions Inc ....D.......714 281-7883
950 S Coast Dr Ste 145 Costa Mesa (92626) ***(P-6246)***

Contemporary Bath.com, City of Industry *Also called Tonusa LLC* ***(P-3342***

Contemporary Services Corp (PA) ....A.......**818 885-5150**
17101 Superior St Northridge (91325) ***(P-18265)***

Contessa Premium Foods, Vernon *Also called F I O Imports Inc* ***(P-2431)***

Contex Inc ....F.......818 788-5836
4505 Van Nuys Blvd Van Nuys (91403) ***(P-11247)***

Contex Inc Contact Lenses, Van Nuys *Also called Contex Inc* ***(P-11247)***

Contiki Holidays, Cypress *Also called Contiki US Holdings Inc* ***(P-12404)***

Contiki US Holdings Inc ....D.......714 935-0808
5551 Katella Ave Cypress (90630) ***(P-12404)***

Continental Acrylics, Compton *Also called Plaskolite West LLC* ***(P-4708)***

Continental Agency Inc (PA) ....D.......**909 595-8884**
1768 W 2nd St Pomona (91766) ***(P-12439)***

Continental Bdr Specialty Corp (PA) ....C.......**310 324-8227**
407 W Compton Blvd Gardena (90248) ***(P-4608)***

Continental Coatings Inc ....F.......909 355-1200
10938 Beech Ave Fontana (92337) ***(P-5093)***

Continental Colorcraft, Monterey Park *Also called Graphic Color Systems Inc* ***(P-4306)***

Continental Currency Svcs Inc (HQ) ....E.......**714 569-0300**
1108 E 17th St Santa Ana (92701) ***(P-15124)***

Continental Currency Svcs Inc (PA) ....D.......**714 569-0300**
1108 E 17th St Santa Ana (92701) ***(P-15125)***

Continental Data Graphics, Rancho Cucamonga *Also called Continental Graphics Corp* ***(P-4261)***

Continental Data Graphics, Long Beach *Also called Continental Graphics Corp* ***(P-17167)***

Continental Data Graphics, Long Beach *Also called Continental Graphics Corp* ***(P-22517)***

Continental Data Graphics, El Segundo *Also called Continental Graphics Corp* ***(P-4262)***

Continental Datalabel Inc ....F.......909 307-3600
211 Business Center Ct Redlands (92373) ***(P-3925)***

Continental Dialysis Ctr Inc (HQ) ....E.......**310 536-2400**
601 Hawaii St El Segundo (90245) ***(P-21235)***

Continental Dntl Ceramics Inc ... E ... 310 618-8821
1873 Western Way Torrance (90501) *(P-21104)*

Continental Exch Solutions Inc ... D ... 562 345-2100
7001 Village Dr Ste 200 Buena Park (90621) *(P-18490)*

Continental Exch Solutions Inc (HQ) ... **A ... 714 522-7044**
6565 Knott Ave Buena Park (90620) *(P-15126)*

Continental Forge Company (PA) ... **D ... 310 603-1014**
412 E El Segundo Blvd Compton (90222) *(P-7083)*

Continental Graphics Corp ... D ... 714 827-1752
4060 N Lakewood Blvd 8015fl Long Beach (90808) *(P-4260)*

Continental Graphics Corp ... D ... 909 758-9800
9302 Pttsbrgh Ave Ste 100 Rancho Cucamonga (91730) *(P-4261)*

Continental Graphics Corp (HQ) ... **C ... 714 503-4200**
4060 N Lakewood Blvd Long Beach (90808) *(P-17167)*

Continental Graphics Corp ... D ... 714 503-4200
4000 N Lakewood Blvd Long Beach (90808) *(P-22517)*

Continental Graphics Corp ... D ... 310 662-2307
222 N Pacific Coast Hwy # 300 El Segundo (90245) *(P-4262)*

Continental Heat Treating Inc ... D ... 562 944-8808
10643 Norwalk Blvd Santa Fe Springs (90670) *(P-6437)*

Continental Industries, Anaheim *Also called International West Inc (P-6855)*

Continental Machine Tool Co, Santa Ana *Also called Supreme Abrasives (P-6158)*

Continental Marketing Svc Inc ... F ... 626 626-8888
15381 Proctor Ave City of Industry (91745) *(P-3125)*

Continental Sales Co., Los Angeles *Also called Val-Pro Inc (P-14661)*

Continental Signs Inc ... F ... 714 894-2011
7541 Santa Rita Cir Ste D Stanton (90680) *(P-11536)*

Continental Vitamin Co Inc ... D ... 323 581-0176
4510 S Boyle Ave Vernon (90058) *(P-4810)*

Continential Data Graphics, Long Beach *Also called Continental Graphics Corp (P-4260)*

Continntal Advncej Ldar Sltons ... D ... 805 318-2072
6307 Crpinteria Ave Ste A Santa Barbara (93103) *(P-10035)*

Continuous Coating Corp (PA) ... **D ... 714 637-4642**
520 W Grove Ave Orange (92865) *(P-7243)*

Contour Engineering Inc ... F ... 562 630-0250
2344 Pullman St Santa Ana (92705) *(P-10303)*

Contra Costa Electric Inc ... C ... 661 322-4036
3208 Landco Dr Bakersfield (93308) *(P-1236)*

Contract Labeling Service Inc ... E ... 909 937-0344
13885 Ramona Ave Chino (91710) *(P-18491)*

Contract Resources, Commerce *Also called Commercial Intr Resources Inc (P-3499)*

Contract Services Group Inc ... C ... 714 582-1800
480 Capricorn St Brea (92821) *(P-17232)*

Contract Transportation Sys Co ... E ... 562 696-3262
12500 Slauson Ave Ste B2 Santa Fe Springs (90670) *(P-5094)*

Contractor, Inglewood *Also called L and W Developers LLC (P-16055)*

Contractor, Anaheim *Also called Sunset Signs and Printing Inc (P-11607)*

Contractor Access, Ontario *Also called Ez-Flo International Inc (P-13826)*

Contractors Cargo Company, Compton *Also called CCC Property Holdings LLC (P-16096)*

Contractors Cargo Company (PA) ... **D ... 310 609-1957**
500 S Alameda St Compton (90221) *(P-12025)*

Contractors Flrg Svc Cal Inc ... C ... 714 556-6100
300 E Dyer Rd Santa Ana (92707) *(P-13166)*

Contractors Glass Company, San Luis Obispo *Also called Mid Coast Suppliers Inc (P-13336)*

Contractors Rigging & Erectors, Compton *Also called Contractors Cargo Company (P-12025)*

Contrband Ctrl Specialists Inc ... E ... 661 322-3363
26 H St Bakersfield (93304) *(P-5215)*

Control AC Svc Corp ... D ... 714 777-8600
5200 E La Palma Ave Anaheim (92807) *(P-1047)*

Control Components Inc (HQ) ... **B ... 949 858-1877**
22591 Avenida Empresa Rcho STA Marg (92688) *(P-7441)*

Control Switches Intl Inc ... E ... 562 498-7331
2425 Mira Mar Ave Long Beach (90815) *(P-8946)*

Controlmyspa, Costa Mesa *Also called Balboa Water Group LLC (P-8944)*

Convaid Products LLC ... D ... 310 618-0111
2830 California St Torrance (90503) *(P-13484)*

Converging Systems Inc ... F ... 310 544-2628
32420 Nautilus Dr Ste 100 Pls Vrds Pnsl (90275) *(P-8246)*

Converse Inc ... D ... 310 451-0314
1437-39 3rd St Promenade Santa Monica (90401) *(P-14434)*

Conversion Devices Inc ... F ... 714 898-6551
15481 Electronic Ln Ste D Huntington Beach (92649) *(P-11219)*

Conversion Technology Co Inc (PA) ... **E ... 805 378-0033**
5360 N Commerce Ave Moorpark (93021) *(P-11468)*

Conversionpoint Holdings Inc ... D ... 888 706-6764
840 Nwport Cntr Dr Ste 45 Newport Beach (92660) *(P-17827)*

Conveyor Concepts, Los Angeles *Also called Machine Building Spc Inc (P-7943)*

Conveyor Mfg & Svc Inc ... F ... 909 621-0406
771 Marylind Ave Claremont (91711) *(P-7688)*

Conveyor Service & Electric ... E ... 562 777-1221
9550 Ann St Santa Fe Springs (90670) *(P-7689)*

Convoy Technologies LLC ... F ... 949 680-9400
3300 Irvine Ave Ste 300 Newport Beach (92660) *(P-9167)*

Cook Hammond and Kell Inc ... F ... 805 682-8900
115 S La Cumbre Ln # 201 Santa Barbara (93105) *(P-18492)*

Cook and Cook Incorporated ... E ... 714 680-6669
1000 E Elm Ave Fullerton (92831) *(P-6739)*

Cook Induction Heating Co Inc ... E ... 323 560-1327
4925 Slauson Ave Maywood (90270) *(P-6438)*

Cook King, La Mirada *Also called Stainless Stl Fabricators Inc (P-13943)*

Cookingcom Inc ... C ... 310 664-1283
1960 E Grand Ave Ste 60 El Segundo (90245) *(P-13454)*

Cooksey Tlen Gage Dffy Woog A (PA) ... **D ... 714 431-1100**
535 Anton Blvd Fl 10 Costa Mesa (92626) *(P-21537)*

Cool Curtain CCI, Costa Mesa *Also called CCI Industries Inc (P-5602)*

Cool Things, Santa Ana *Also called Ecoolthing Corp (P-7555)*

Cool-Pak LLC ... D ... 805 981-2434
401 N Rice Ave Oxnard (93030) *(P-5613)*

Coolhaus, Culver City *Also called Farchitecture Bb LLC (P-1817)*

Cooljet Systems, Brea *Also called Mkt Innovations (P-8702)*

Coolsys Inc (HQ) ... **B ... 714 510-9577**
145 S State College Blvd Brea (92821) *(P-18946)*

Coolsys Coml Indus Sltions Inc (HQ) ... **A ... 714 510-9609**
145 S State College Blvd Brea (92821) *(P-1048)*

Cooltec Refrigeration Corp ... E ... 909 865-2229
1250 E Franklin Ave B Pomona (91766) *(P-8334)*

Coolwater Generating Station, Daggett *Also called NRG California South LP (P-12811)*

Cooner Sales Company LLC (PA) ... **F ... 818 882-8311**
9265 Owensmouth Ave Chatsworth (91311) *(P-13560)*

Cooner Wire Company, Chatsworth *Also called Cooner Sales Company LLC (P-13560)*

Coop Engineering Inc ... E ... 562 944-0171
12930 Lakeland Rd Santa Fe Springs (90670) *(P-8563)*

Cooper & Brain Inc ... E ... 310 834-4411
655 E D St Wilmington (90744) *(P-402)*

Cooper Engineering Inc ... E ... 951 736-6135
114 Business Center Dr Corona (92878) *(P-22518)*

Cooper Interconnect Inc (HQ) ... **D ... 805 484-0543**
750 W Ventura Blvd Camarillo (93010) *(P-9029)*

Cooper Microelectronics Inc ... E ... 949 553-8352
1671 Reynolds Ave Irvine (92614) *(P-9495)*

Coopertive Amrcn Physcians Inc (PA) ... **D ... 213 473-8600**
333 S Hope St Fl 8 Los Angeles (90071) *(P-22268)*

Coordinated Companies, Wilmington *Also called Coordnted Wire Rope Rgging Inc (P-2713)*

Coordnted Wire Rope Rgging Inc (HQ) ... **E ... 310 834-8535**
1707 E Anaheim St Wilmington (90744) *(P-2713)*

Coorstek Inc ... D ... 805 644-5583
4544 Mcgrath St Ventura (93003) *(P-7850)*

Cop Communications, Montclair *Also called California Offset Printers Inc (P-4246)*

Copan Diagnostics Inc ... C ... 951 696-6957
26055 Jefferson Ave Murrieta (92562) *(P-14237)*

Copier Source Inc ... C ... 909 890-4040
650 E Hospitality Ln # 500 San Bernardino (92408) *(P-13354)*

Copp Industrial Mfg Inc ... E ... 909 593-7448
2837 Metropolitan Pl Pomona (91767) *(P-6812)*

Coppel Corporation ... D ... 760 357-3707
503 Scaroni Ave Calexico (92231) *(P-13132)*

Coppersmith Global Logistics, El Segundo *Also called L E Coppersmith Inc (P-12477)*

Copy Solutions Inc ... E ... 323 307-0900
919 S Fremont Ave Ste 398 Alhambra (91803) *(P-4263)*

Cor Medica Technology (PA) ... **E ... 949 353-4554**
188 Technology Dr Ste F Irvine (92618) *(P-19762)*

Cora Constructors Inc ... E ... 760 674-3201
75140 Saint Charles Pl A Palm Desert (92211) *(P-22519)*

Corbell Products, Bloomington *Also called Westco Industries Inc (P-6683)*

Corbell Products Inc (PA) ... **E ... 909 574-9139**
14650 Hawthorne Ave Fontana (92335) *(P-6606)*

Corbett Canyon Vineyards ... F ... 805 782-9463
2195 Corbett Canyon Rd Arroyo Grande (93420) *(P-2178)*

Corbin Foods, Santa Ana *Also called Corbin-Hill Inc (P-1993)*

Corbin-Hill Inc ... F ... 714 966-6695
2961 W Macarthur Blvd # 1 Santa Ana (92704) *(P-1993)*

Corbis Images LLC (PA) ... **F ... 323 602-5700**
6060 Center Dr Ste 1000 Los Angeles (90045) *(P-16893)*

Corcoran Irrigation District ... D ... 559 992-5165
1150 6 1/2 Ave Corcoran (93212) *(P-13010)*

Corcoran Sawtelle Rosprim Inc ... E ... 559 992-2117
542 Otis Ave Corcoran (93212) *(P-6607)*

Corday Productions Inc (PA) ... **E ... 818 295-2821**
3400 W Olive Ave Ste 170 Burbank (91505) *(P-19111)*

Cordelia Lighting Inc ... C ... 310 886-3490
20101 S Santa Fe Ave Compton (90221) *(P-13620)*

Cordoba Corporation ... D ... 213 895-0224
1401 N Broadway Los Angeles (90012) *(P-18026)*

Cordova Industries, Sylmar *Also called International Academy of Fin (P-5139)*

Cordovan & Grey Ltd ... E ... 562 699-8300
4826 Gregg Rd Pico Rivera (90660) *(P-2768)*

Core Bts Inc ... C ... 818 766-2400
5250 Lankershim Blvd # 62 North Hollywood (91601) *(P-18027)*

Core Medical Group Inc ... D ... 310 967-1884
8635 W 3rd St Ste 1 Los Angeles (90048) *(P-21401)*

Core Monrovia LLC ... C ... 626 357-5211
700 W Huntington Dr Monrovia (91016) *(P-16389)*

Core Nutrition LLC ... E ... 310 640-0500
1222 E Grand Ave Ste 102 El Segundo (90245) *(P-14685)*

Core Realty Holdings LLC (PA) ... **D ... 949 863-1031**
1600 Dove St Ste 450 Newport Beach (92660) *(P-16231)*

Core Realty Holdings MGT Inc ... D ... 949 863-1031
1600 Dove St Ste 450 Newport Beach (92660) *(P-15825)*

Core-Mark Intrrlted Cmpnies In (HQ) ... **E ... 951 272-4790**
311 Reed Cir Corona (92879) *(P-14923)*

Corecare I I I ... C ... 714 256-8000
800 Morningside Dr Fullerton (92835) *(P-22095)*

Corecare V A Cal Ltd Partnr ... C ... 714 256-1000
2525 Brea Blvd Fullerton (92835) *(P-20291)*

Corelis Inc ... E ... 562 926-6727
13100 Alondra Blvd # 102 Cerritos (90703) *(P-9696)*

Corelogic Inc ... E ... 714 250-6400
40 Pacifica Ste 900 Irvine (92618) *(P-15826)*

Corelogic Credco LLC (HQ) ... **C ... 800 255-0792**
40 Pacifica Ste 900 Irvine (92618) *(P-17120)*

Coresite LLC ... D ... 213 327-1231
624 S Grand Ave Ste 1800 Los Angeles (90017) *(P-16232)*

Coreslab Structures La Inc ... C ... 951 943-9119
150 W Placentia Ave Perris (92571) *(P-6025)*

Employee Codes: A=Over 500 employees, B=251-500
C=101-250, D=51-100, E=20-50 F=10-19
2022 Southern California Business
Directory and Buyers Guide
© Mergent Inc. 1-800-342-5647
1101

Coretex Products Inc (PA).....F.....**661 834-6805**
1850 Sunnyside Ct Bakersfield (93308) ***(P-5002)***

Corey Nursery Co Inc (PA).....D.....**909 621-6886**
1650 Monte Vista Ave Claremont (91711) ***(P-14880)***

Corinthian Group, Ontario *Also called Surveillance Systems Group Inc* ***(P-18343)***

Corn Maiden Foods Inc.....D.....310 784-0400
24201 Frampton Ave Harbor City (90710) ***(P-1848)***

Cornell Ptrson Arospc Tech LLC.....F.....714 656-5376
167 Del Mar Ave Costa Mesa (92627) ***(P-9395)***

Corner Products Company.....D.....949 231-5000
15774 Gateway Cir Tustin (92780) ***(P-13712)***

Cornerstone Display Group Inc.....E.....661 705-1700
28606 Livingston Ave Valencia (91355) ***(P-11537)***

Cornerstone Ondemand Inc (PA).....A.....**310 752-0200**
1601 Cloverf Blvd 620s Santa Monica (90404) ***(P-17828)***

Cornerstone Ondmand Globl Oprt (HQ).....B.....**310 752-0200**
1601 Cloverf Blvd Ste 60 Santa Monica (90404) ***(P-21947)***

Cornerstone Research Inc.....D.....213 553-2500
555 W 5th St Ste 3800 Los Angeles (90013) ***(P-22877)***

Corningware Corelle & More, Riverside *Also called Snapware Corporation* ***(P-5823)***

Cornucopia Tool & Plastics Inc.....E.....805 238-7660
448 Sherwood Rd Paso Robles (93446) ***(P-5614)***

Corona - Cllege Hts Ornge Lmon.....B.....951 359-6451
8000 Lincoln Ave Riverside (92504) ***(P-163)***

Corona Clipper Inc.....D.....951 737-6515
22440 Temescal Canyon Rd # 102 Corona (92883) ***(P-13801)***

Corona Magnetics Inc.....C.....951 735-7558
201 Corporate Terrace St Corona (92879) ***(P-9626)***

Corona Medical Offices, Corona *Also called Kaiser Foundation Hospitals* ***(P-16185)***

Corona Millworks Company (PA).....C.....**909 606-3288**
5572 Edison Ave Chino (91710) ***(P-3316)***

Corona Regional Med Ctr Hosp, Corona *Also called Uhs-Corona Inc* ***(P-20987)***

Corona Rgnal Med Ctr Rhbltion, Corona *Also called Uhs-Corona Inc* ***(P-21359)***

Corona Tools, Corona *Also called Corona Clipper Inc* ***(P-13801)***

Coronado Manufacturing Inc.....E.....818 768-5010
8991 Glenoaks Blvd Sun Valley (91352) ***(P-10304)***

Coronado Stone Products, Fontana *Also called Creative Stone Mfg Inc* ***(P-6026)***

Coronal Energy LLC (PA).....D.....**855 267-6625**
301 N Lake Ave Ste 202 Pasadena (91101) ***(P-23197)***

Coronal Lost Hills LLC (PA).....D.....**855 267-6625**
301 N Lake Ave Ste 202 Pasadena (91101) ***(P-1049)***

Coronet Concrete Products Inc (PA).....E.....**760 398-2441**
83801 Avenue 45 Indio (92201) ***(P-6086)***

Coronet Lighting, Gardena *Also called Dasol Inc* ***(P-9019)***

Corp., R.g Barry, Fontana *Also called DSV Solutions LLC* ***(P-12448)***

Corpinfo Services, Santa Monica *Also called K-Micro Inc* ***(P-13411)***

Corporate Alnce Strategies Inc.....C.....877 777-7487
3410 La Sierra Ave F244 Riverside (92503) ***(P-18369)***

Corporate Graphics & Printing.....F.....805 529-5333
335 Science Dr Moorpark (93021) ***(P-4264)***

Corporate Image Maintenance, Santa Ana *Also called Gamboa Service Inc* ***(P-17244)***

Corporate Impressions La Inc.....E.....818 761-9295
10742 Burbank Blvd North Hollywood (91601) ***(P-4502)***

Corprint Incorporated.....F.....818 839-5316
4235 Mission Oaks Blvd Camarillo (93010) ***(P-4503)***

Corptax LLC.....D.....818 316-2400
21550 Oxnard St Ste 700 Woodland Hills (91367) ***(P-17584)***

Correa Pallet Inc (PA).....E.....**559 757-1790**
13036 Avenue 76 Pixley (93256) ***(P-3384)***

Correctivesolutions, Mission Viejo *Also called American Justice Solutions Inc* ***(P-23413)***

Corridor Capital LLC (PA).....C.....**310 442-7000**
12400 Wilshire Blvd # 645 Los Angeles (90025) ***(P-16256)***

Corridor Recycling Inc.....D.....310 835-3849
22500 S Alameda St Long Beach (90810) ***(P-12942)***

Corru Kraft Buena Pk Div 5058, Buena Park *Also called Orora North America* ***(P-14220)***

Corru-Kraft IV.....F.....714 773-0124
1911 E Rosslynn Ave Fullerton (92831) ***(P-3796)***

Corsair Elec Connectors Inc.....C.....949 833-0273
17100 Murphy Ave Irvine (92614) ***(P-9650)***

Corsican Furniture, Gardena *Also called Victor Martin Inc* ***(P-3537)***

Corte Custom Case, San Jacinto *Also called Wallace Wood Products* ***(P-3671)***

Cortez Pallets Service Inc (PA).....F.....**626 961-9891**
14739 Proctor Ave La Puente (91746) ***(P-3385)***

Corwin Press Inc (HQ).....C.....**805 499-9734**
2455 Teller Rd Newbury Park (91320) ***(P-4124)***

Cosasco Inc.....D.....562 949-0123
11841 Smith Ave Santa Fe Springs (90670) ***(P-10687)***

Cosco Agencies Los Angeles Inc (HQ).....D.....**213 689-6700**
588 Harbor Scenic Way Long Beach (90802) ***(P-12440)***

Cosco Home & Office Products, Ontario *Also called Dorel Juvenile Group Inc* ***(P-5630)***

Cosemi Technologies Inc (HQ).....F.....**949 623-9816**
1370 Reynolds Ave Ste 100 Irvine (92614) ***(P-9496)***

Cosmetic Enterprises Ltd.....F.....818 896-5355
12848 Pierce St Pacoima (91331) ***(P-5003)***

Cosmetic Group Usa Inc.....C.....818 767-2889
8430 Tujunga Ave Sun Valley (91352) ***(P-5004)***

Cosmetic Specialties Intl LLC.....C.....805 487-6698
550 E 3rd St Oxnard (93030) ***(P-5615)***

Cosmic Plastics Inc (PA).....E.....**661 257-3274**
28410 Industry Dr Valencia (91355) ***(P-4684)***

Cosmo - Pharm Inc.....F.....818 764-0246
11751 Vose St Ste 53 North Hollywood (91605) ***(P-4741)***

Cosmo Beauty Lab & Mfg, San Dimas *Also called Cosmobeauti Labs & Mfg Inc* ***(P-5006)***

Cosmo Fiber Corporation (PA).....E.....**626 256-6098**
1802 Santo Domingo Ave Duarte (91010) ***(P-4504)***

Cosmo International Corp.....D.....310 271-1100
9200 W Sunset Blvd # 401 West Hollywood (90069) ***(P-5005)***

Cosmo International Fragrances, West Hollywood *Also called Cosmo International Corp* ***(P-5005)***

Cosmo Products LLC.....E.....888 784-3108
5431 Brooks St Montclair (91763) ***(P-9002)***

Cosmo Textiles Inc.....D.....562 220-1177
13984 Orange Ave Paramount (90723) ***(P-2649)***

Cosmobeauti Labs & Mfg Inc.....F.....909 971-9832
480 E Arrow Hwy San Dimas (91773) ***(P-5006)***

Cosmodyne LLC.....E.....562 795-5990
3010 Old Ranch Pkwy # 300 Seal Beach (90740) ***(P-7968)***

Cosmos Food Co Inc.....E.....323 221-9142
16015 Phoenix Dr City of Industry (91745) ***(P-2412)***

Coso Operating Company LLC.....D.....760 764-1300
2 Gill Station Coso Rd Little Lake (93542) ***(P-12798)***

Cosrich Group Inc.....E.....818 686-2500
12243 Branford St Sun Valley (91352) ***(P-5007)***

Cost Saver Tours.....E.....714 935-2569
5551 Katella Ave Anaheim (92805) ***(P-12405)***

Costa Mesa Country Club, Costa Mesa *Also called Mesa Verde Partners* ***(P-19500)***

Costco Wholesale Corporation.....B.....951 361-3606
11600 Riverside Dr Ste A Jurupa Valley (91752) ***(P-12190)***

Costco Wholesale Corporation.....C.....909 823-8270
16505 Sierra Lakes Pkwy Fontana (92336) ***(P-14924)***

Costco Wholesale Corporation.....C.....323 890-1904
1345 N Montebello Blvd Montebello (90640) ***(P-13114)***

Costco Wholesale Depot, Jurupa Valley *Also called Costco Wholesale Corporation* ***(P-12190)***

Cosway Company Inc.....E.....310 527-9135
14805 S Maple Ave Gardena (90248) ***(P-5008)***

Cosway Company Inc (PA).....E.....**310 900-4100**
20633 S Fordyce Ave Carson (90810) ***(P-5009)***

Coto De Caza Golf Club Inc.....C.....949 766-7886
25291 Vista Del Verde Trabuco Canyon (92679) ***(P-19414)***

Cots Journal Magazine, San Clemente *Also called R T C Group* ***(P-4102)***

Cott Technologies Inc.....F.....626 961-3399
14923 Proctor Ave La Puente (91746) ***(P-7532)***

Cottage Childrens Medical Ctr, Santa Barbara *Also called Santa Brbara Cttage Hosp Fndti* ***(P-20934)***

Cottage Health.....D.....805 541-9113
1035 Peach St Ste 203 San Luis Obispo (93401) ***(P-20732)***

Cottage Health.....D.....805 688-6432
2050 Viborg Rd Solvang (93463) ***(P-20733)***

Cottage Health System, Santa Barbara *Also called Goleta Valley Cottage Hosp Aux* ***(P-20779)***

Cottage Health System.....D.....805 967-3411
351 S Patterson Ave Goleta (93111) ***(P-20734)***

Cottage Rehabilitation Hosp.....E.....805 569-8999
2415 De La Vina St Santa Barbara (93105) ***(P-20735)***

Cotterman Company, Bakersfield *Also called Material Control Inc* ***(P-7564)***

Cotton Generation Inc.....F.....323 581-8555
6051 Maywood Ave Huntington Park (90255) ***(P-3030)***

Cotton Knits Trading.....E.....310 884-9600
3097 E Ana St Compton (90221) ***(P-2652)***

Cotton Tale Designs Inc.....F.....714 435-9558
16291 Sierra Ridge Way Hacienda Heights (91745) ***(P-3100)***

Cottrell Paul Enterprises LLC (PA).....C.....**661 212-2357**
16654 Soledad Canyon Rd # 23 Santa Clarita (91387) ***(P-18266)***

Cotty On, Vernon *Also called Cottyon Inc* ***(P-2565)***

Cottyon Inc.....E.....323 589-1563
2202 E Anderson St Vernon (90058) ***(P-2565)***

Cougar Biotechnology Inc.....D.....310 943-8040
10990 Wilshire Blvd # 1200 Los Angeles (90024) ***(P-4811)***

Council of Orange County of St (PA).....D.....**949 653-2900**
1505 E 17th St Ste 109 Santa Ana (92705) ***(P-21948)***

Council On Aging - Sthern Cal.....D.....714 479-0107
2 Executive Cir Ste 175 Irvine (92614) ***(P-21757)***

Council Program Serv & Admin, Santa Ana *Also called Council of Orange County of St* ***(P-21948)***

Counseling and Research Assoc (PA).....C.....**310 715-2020**
108 W Victoria St Gardena (90248) ***(P-22096)***

Counter Brands LLC (PA).....D.....**888 988-9108**
1733 Ocean Ave Santa Monica (90401) ***(P-14238)***

Countertop Factory (PA).....F.....**562 903-4080**
2740 E Coronado St Anaheim (92806) ***(P-3431)***

Country Archer Jerky, San Bernardino *Also called S&E Gourmet Cuts Inc* ***(P-14565)***

Country Floral Supply Inc (PA).....D.....**805 520-8026**
3802 Weatherly Cir Westlake Village (91361) ***(P-14881)***

Country Furnishings, Westlake Village *Also called Country Floral Supply Inc* ***(P-14881)***

Country Garden Ldscp & Maint, Anaheim *Also called G C Landscape Inc* ***(P-306)***

Country House.....E.....714 505-8988
2852 Walnut Ave Ste C1 Tustin (92780) ***(P-2083)***

Country Oaks Care Center Inc.....D.....805 922-6657
830 E Chapel St Santa Maria (93454) ***(P-20292)***

Country Plastics Inc.....F.....559 597-2556
32501 Road 228 Woodlake (93286) ***(P-5616)***

Country Side Inn Ontario LP.....D.....909 390-7778
2812 Lenwood Rd Barstow (92311) ***(P-16390)***

Country Villa Health Services, Anaheim *Also called Country Villa Service Corp* ***(P-23007)***

Country Villa Nursing Ctr Inc.....C.....213 484-9730
340 S Alvarado St Los Angeles (90057) ***(P-20293)***

Country Villa Rancho.....C.....760 340-0053
39950 Vista Del Sol Rancho Mirage (92270) ***(P-21758)***

Country Villa Service Corp.....D.....562 598-2477
3000 N Gate Rd Seal Beach (90740) ***(P-21759)***

Country Villa Service Corp (PA).....D.....**310 574-3733**
2400 E Katella Ave # 800 Anaheim (92806) ***(P-23007)***

Country Villa Service Corp.....C.....818 246-5516
1208 S Central Ave Glendale (91204) ***(P-20294)***

Mergent e-mail: customerrelations@mergent.com
1102
2022 Southern California Business Directory and Buyers Guide
(P-0000) Products & Services Section entry number
(PA)=Parent Co (HQ)=Headquarters (DH)=Div Headquarters

Country Villa Service Corp C 626 285-2165
112 E Broadway San Gabriel (91776) ***(P-20573)***
Country Villa Service Corp C 626 445-2421
400 W Huntington Dr Arcadia (91007) ***(P-20295)***
Country Villa Service Corp C 310 574-3733
3533 Motor Ave Los Angeles (90034) ***(P-23008)***
Country Villa Service Corp C 310 537-2500
3611 E Imperial Hwy Lynwood (90262) ***(P-20296)***
Country Villa Terrace (PA) **D 323 653-3980**
6050 W Pico Blvd Los Angeles (90035) ***(P-20574)***
Country Vlla Convalescent Hosp, Los Angeles *Also called Country Villa Terrace* ***(P-20574)***
Country Vlla Mar Vsta Nrsing C, Los Angeles *Also called Rrt Enterprises LP* ***(P-20454)***
Country Vlla Nrsing Rhbltion, Los Angeles *Also called Country Villa Nursing Ctr Inc* ***(P-20293)***
Country Vlla Wstwood Nrsing Ct, Los Angeles *Also called Westwood Healthcare Center LP* ***(P-20509)***
Country Weave, Santa Ana *Also called Newport Plastic Inc* ***(P-5727)***
Countrywide Home Loans Inc A 818 550-8700
801 N Brand Blvd Ste 750 Glendale (91203) ***(P-15185)***
COUNTY CARE COVELECEST HOSPITA, Templeton *Also called Christian Atascadero Home* ***(P-20281)***
County Clothing Company, Irvine *Also called Snowmass Apparel Inc* ***(P-14417)***
County General Hospital, San Luis Obispo *Also called County of San Luis Obispo* ***(P-20741)***
County of Kern A 661 326-2054
1700 Mount Vernon Ave Bakersfield (93306) ***(P-20736)***
County of Los Angeles D 310 354-2300
711 Del Amo Blvd Torrance (90502) ***(P-19763)***
County of Los Angeles C 818 896-5271
12653 Osborne St Ste 8 Pacoima (91331) ***(P-12351)***
County of Los Angeles D 626 280-8225
8640 Rush St Rosemead (91770) ***(P-19479)***
County of Los Angeles D 818 837-6969
1212 Pico St San Fernando (91340) ***(P-19764)***
County of Los Angeles D 661 223-8700
30500 Arrastre Canyon Rd Acton (93510) ***(P-21041)***
County of Los Angeles D 213 739-2360
600 S Commwl Ave Fl 2 Flr 2 Los Angeles (90005) ***(P-21402)***
County of Los Angeles C 213 974-0515
320 W Temple St Fl 9 Los Angeles (90012) ***(P-18119)***
County of Los Angeles D 310 885-2100
546 W Compton Blvd Compton (90220) ***(P-21403)***
County of Los Angeles C 310 222-2401
1000 W Carson St Fl 8 Flr 8 Palos Verdes Peninsu (90274) ***(P-20737)***
County of Los Angeles D 562 401-7088
7601 Imperial Hwy Downey (90242) ***(P-21290)***
County of Los Angeles D 213 974-7284
515 E 6th St Los Angeles (90021) ***(P-21042)***
County of Los Angeles C 310 668-4545
12025 Wilmington Ave Los Angeles (90059) ***(P-20738)***
County of Los Angeles D 818 717-4644
20151 Nordhoff St Chatsworth (91311) ***(P-21404)***
County of Los Angeles D 323 897-6187
5850 S Main St Los Angeles (90003) ***(P-21291)***
County of Los Angeles D 213 744-3919
2829 S Grand Ave Los Angeles (90007) ***(P-19765)***
County of Los Angeles D 626 968-3711
15930 Central Ave Ste 100 La Puente (91744) ***(P-19766)***
County of Los Angeles D 310 668-6845
921 E Compton Blvd Compton (90221) ***(P-21405)***
County of Los Angeles D 626 229-3825
532 E Colorado Blvd Fl 8 Pasadena (91101) ***(P-21406)***
County of Los Angeles D 323 226-3373
1200 N State St Rm 3250 Los Angeles (90089) ***(P-19767)***
County of Los Angeles D 310 257-4989
1403 Lomita Blvd Harbor City (90710) ***(P-19768)***
County of Los Angeles A 323 267-2136
1100 N Eastern Ave Los Angeles (90063) ***(P-22775)***
County of Los Angeles D 562 429-9711
3101 Carson St Lakewood (90712) ***(P-19480)***
County of Los Angeles D 323 769-7800
5205 Melrose Ave Los Angeles (90038) ***(P-21292)***
County of Los Angeles D 909 231-0549
1875 Fairplex Dr Pomona (91768) ***(P-19481)***
County of Los Angeles C 661 974-7700
42011 4th St W Ste 3530 Lancaster (93534) ***(P-21538)***
County of Los Angeles D 323 226-3468
1240 N Mission Rd Los Angeles (90033) ***(P-21043)***
County of Los Angeles F 626 968-3312
14959 Proctor Ave La Puente (91746) ***(P-7640)***
County of Los Angeles F 310 456-8014
3637 Winter Canyon Rd Malibu (90265) ***(P-7641)***
County of Los Angeles C 818 890-5777
12605 Osborne St Pacoima (91331) ***(P-12352)***
County of Los Angeles D 213 351-7800
3530 Wilshire Blvd Fl 9 Los Angeles (90010) ***(P-21407)***
County of Los Angeles A 562 940-4324
1100 N Eastern Ave Los Angeles (90063) ***(P-17585)***
County of Los Angeles C 323 226-6021
1100 N Mission Rd Rm 236 Los Angeles (90033) ***(P-20739)***
County of Los Angeles D 562 945-2581
9402 Greenleaf Ave Whittier (90605) ***(P-11918)***
County of Los Angeles D 562 861-0316
5525 Imperial Hwy South Gate (90280) ***(P-21408)***
County of Los Angeles D 310 549-4953
1235 Figueroa Pl Wilmington (90744) ***(P-19482)***
County of Los Angeles D 562 402-0688
17707 Studebaker Rd Artesia (90703) ***(P-21293)***
County of Los Angeles D 562 804-8111
10005 E Flower Ave Bellflower (90706) ***(P-19769)***
County of Los Angeles D 323 730-3507
3834 S Western Ave Los Angeles (90062) ***(P-19770)***
County of Los Angeles D 310 518-8800
1325 Broad Ave Wilmington (90744) ***(P-19771)***
County of Los Angeles D 818 896-1903
13300 Van Nuys Blvd Pacoima (91331) ***(P-19772)***
County of Los Angeles B 626 458-4000
900 S Fremont Ave Alhambra (91803) ***(P-12885)***
County of Los Angeles D 626 969-7885
150 N Azusa Ave Azusa (91702) ***(P-19773)***
County of Los Angeles D 818 995-1170
16821 Burbank Blvd Ste 4 Encino (91436) ***(P-19483)***
County of Los Angeles D 323 226-7131
1900 Zonal Ave Los Angeles (90033) ***(P-19774)***
County of Los Angeles D 661 524-2005
335 E Avenue K6 Ste B Lancaster (93535) ***(P-21294)***
County of Los Angeles D 661 223-8700
38200 Lake Hughes Rd Castaic (91384) ***(P-21044)***
County of Los Angeles D 562 599-9200
2600 Redondo Ave 3 Long Beach (90806) ***(P-19775)***
County of Los Angeles C 213 473-6100
450 Bauchet St Los Angeles (90012) ***(P-20740)***
County of Los Angeles C 213 974-4561
441 Bauchet St Los Angeles (90012) ***(P-12568)***
County of Los Angeles C 310 847-4018
21356 Avalon Blvd Carson (90745) ***(P-22289)***
County of Orange E 714 567-7444
1300 S Grand Ave Ste B Santa Ana (92705) ***(P-4505)***
County of Orange C 949 252-5006
3160 Airway Ave Costa Mesa (92626) ***(P-12353)***
County of Orange E 714 567-7422
1300 S Grand Ave Ste C Santa Ana (92705) ***(P-22393)***
County of Orange D 714 796-8200
901 W Civic Center Dr # 200 Santa Ana (92703) ***(P-21539)***
County of Orange D 714 834-6021
405 W 5th St Ofc Santa Ana (92701) ***(P-20528)***
County of Riverside C 951 955-6000
4075 Main St Riverside (92501) ***(P-21540)***
County of Riverside D 951 955-5659
2001 Iowa Ave Ste 218 Riverside (92507) ***(P-21760)***
County of Riverside C 951 763-5611
56560 State Hwy 371 Anza (92539) ***(P-21409)***
County of Riverside Department (PA) **D 951 358-5000**
4065 County Circle Dr Riverside (92503) ***(P-22450)***
County of San Bernardino D 760 843-5100
17270 Bear Valley Rd # 108 Victorville (92395) ***(P-21761)***
County of San Luis Obispo C 805 781-4753
2180 Johnson Ave San Luis Obispo (93401) ***(P-20741)***
County of Ventura C 805 654-2561
800 S Victoria Ave Ventura (93009) ***(P-21762)***
County of Ventura D 805 388-4274
2889 W 5th St Oxnard (93030) ***(P-12354)***
County of Ventura D 805 388-4274
555 Airport Way Ste D Camarillo (93010) ***(P-12355)***
County of Ventura C 805 983-1332
2800 Wright Rd Camarillo (93010) ***(P-21763)***
County Snttion Dst No 2 Los An (PA) **A 562 699-7411**
1955 Workman Mill Rd Whittier (90601) ***(P-13006)***
County Ventura Human Resources, Ventura *Also called County of Ventura* ***(P-21762)***
County Whl Elc Co Los Angeles D 714 633-3801
560 N Main St Orange (92868) ***(P-13621)***
Countywide Childrens Case MGT, Los Angeles *Also called County of Los Angeles* ***(P-21402)***
Courtcall LLC (PA) **D 310 342-0888**
2158 W 190th St Torrance (90504) ***(P-21541)***
Courthuse Tours-Docent Council, Santa Barbara *Also called Santa Barbara City of* ***(P-12409)***
Courtney Inc (PA) **D 949 222-2050**
16781 Millikan Ave Irvine (92606) ***(P-1651)***
Courtside Cellars LLC F 805 467-2882
2425 Mission St San Miguel (93451) ***(P-2179)***
Courtside Cellars LLC (PA) **E 805 782-0500**
4910 Edna Rd San Luis Obispo (93401) ***(P-2180)***
Courtyard & Residence Inn La, Los Angeles *Also called 901 West Olympic Blvd Ltd Prtn* ***(P-16312)***
Courtyard By Marriott, Sherman Oaks *Also called Burbank Partners LLC* ***(P-16356)***
Courtyard By Marriott, Palm Desert *Also called Ashford Trs Seven LLC* ***(P-16330)***
Courtyard By Marriott, Baldwin Park *Also called Baldwin Hospitality LLC* ***(P-16337)***
Courtyard By Marriott, Pasadena *Also called Rt Pasad Hotel Partners LP* ***(P-16675)***
Courtyard By Marriott, Baldwin Park *Also called Baldwin Hospitality LLC* ***(P-16338)***
Courtyard By Marriott, Monrovia *Also called Core Monrovia LLC* ***(P-16389)***
Courtyard By Marriott, Torrance *Also called Courtyard Management Corp* ***(P-16394)***
Courtyard By Marriott, Hacienda Heights *Also called Courtyard Management Corp* ***(P-16395)***
Courtyard By Marriott D 562 435-8511
500 E 1st St Long Beach (90802) ***(P-16391)***
Courtyard By Marriott Irvine, Irvine *Also called Courtyard Management Corp* ***(P-16393)***
Courtyard By Marriott/Lax D 310 981-2350
6161 W Century Blvd Los Angeles (90045) ***(P-16392)***
Courtyard By Mrrott Los Angles, Monrovia *Also called Sage Hospitality Resources LLC* ***(P-16682)***
Courtyard Care Center, Signal Hill *Also called C C H S Inc* ***(P-22995)***
Courtyard Management Corp D 949 453-1033
7955 Irvine Center Dr Irvine (92618) ***(P-16393)***
Courtyard Management Corp D 310 533-8000
2633 Sepulveda Blvd Torrance (90505) ***(P-16394)***
Courtyard Management Corp D 626 965-1700
1905 S Azusa Ave Hacienda Heights (91745) ***(P-16395)***
Courtyard Oxnard D 805 988-3600
600 E Esplanade Dr Oxnard (93036) ***(P-16396)***

ALPHABETIC

Employee Codes: A=Over 500 employees, B=251-500
C=101-250, D=51-100, E=20-50 F=10-19
2022 Southern California Business
Directory and Buyers Guide
© Mergent Inc. 1-800-342-5647
1103

Courtyard Paso Robles, Paso Robles *Also called Lvp Cy Paso Robles LLC* ***(P-16548)***

Cousins Foods LLC ....E....818 767-3842
2021 1st St San Fernando (91340) ***(P-1886)***

Covanta Long Bch Rnwble Enrgy ....C....562 436-0636
118 Pier S Ave Long Beach (90802) ***(P-12943)***

Cove Electric Inc ....D....760 568-9924
77971 Wildcat Dr Ste F Palm Desert (92211) ***(P-1237)***

Cove Four-Slide Stamping Corp (PA) ....**D....516 379-4232**
355 S Hale Ave Fullerton (92831) ***(P-7499)***

Cove West Division, Fullerton *Also called Cove Four-Slide Stamping Corp* ***(P-7499)***

Covenant Care California LLC ....D....562 427-7493
2725 Pacific Ave Long Beach (90806) ***(P-20297)***

Covenant Care California LLC ....D....805 488-3696
5225 S J St Oxnard (93033) ***(P-20298)***

Covenant Care California LLC ....D....323 589-5941
6425 Miles Ave Huntington Park (90255) ***(P-20299)***

Covenant Care California LLC ....D....805 964-4871
160 S Patterson Ave Santa Barbara (93111) ***(P-20300)***

Covenant Care California LLC (HQ) ....**E....949 349-1200**
120 Vantis Dr Ste 200 Aliso Viejo (92656) ***(P-20301)***

Covenant Care California LLC ....D....714 554-9700
1929 N Fairview St Santa Ana (92706) ***(P-20302)***

Covenant Care Dubuque LLC ....D....949 349-1200
120 Vantis Dr Ste 200 Aliso Viejo (92656) ***(P-20303)***

Covenant House California ....C....323 461-3131
1325 N Western Ave Los Angeles (90027) ***(P-22097)***

Covenant Rtirement Communities ....D....805 687-0701
2550 Treasure Dr Santa Barbara (93105) ***(P-20304)***

Covenant Transport Inc ....A....909 469-0130
1300 E Franklin Ave Pomona (91766) ***(P-12026)***

Coventry Court Health Center ....C....714 636-2800
2040 S Euclid St Anaheim (92802) ***(P-20305)***

Coverance Insur Solutions Inc (PA) ....**D....231 218-6100**
100 W Broadway Ste 3000 Long Beach (90802) ***(P-15557)***

Coveris, Hanford *Also called Hood Packaging Corporation* ***(P-14937)***

Coverking, Anaheim *Also called Shrin LLC* ***(P-13089)***

Covert Iron Works ....F....323 560-2792
7821 Otis S Ave Huntington Park (90255) ***(P-6261)***

Covid Clinic Inc ....D....877 219-8378
18800 Delaware St Ste 800 Huntington Beach (92648) ***(P-19776)***

Covidien, Costa Mesa *Also called Newport Medical Instrs Inc* ***(P-11034)***

Covina Rehabilitation Center ....C....626 967-3874
261 W Badillo St Covina (91723) ***(P-20306)***

Covina Service Center, San Dimas *Also called Southern California Edison Co* ***(P-12852)***

Cowan Precision Grinding Inc ....D....818 361-3512
12864 Foothill Blvd Sylmar (91342) ***(P-18493)***

Coway Usa Inc ....E....213 486-1600
4221 Wilshire Blvd # 308 Los Angeles (90010) ***(P-8045)***

Cowboy Direct Response ....E....714 824-3780
130 E Alton Ave Santa Ana (92707) ***(P-11538)***

Cox Castle & Nicholson LLP (PA) ....**C....310 284-2200**
2029 Century Park E # 2100 Los Angeles (90067) ***(P-21542)***

Cox Castle, Los Angeles *Also called Cox Castle & Nicholson LLP* ***(P-21542)***

Cox Petroleum Transport, Bakersfield *Also called HF Cox Inc* ***(P-12053)***

Cox Petroleum Transport, Cudahy *Also called HF Cox Inc* ***(P-11974)***

Coy Industries Inc ....D....310 603-2970
2970 E Maria St E Rncho Dmngz (90221) ***(P-6813)***

Coyle Reproductions Inc (PA) ....**C....866 269-5373**
2850 Orbiter St Brea (92821) ***(P-4265)***

Coyne Companies LLC ....F....760 353-1016
2351 S 4th St El Centro (92243) ***(P-4164)***

Cozzia USA LLC (HQ) ....**F....626 667-2272**
861 S Oak Park Rd Covina (91724) ***(P-9863)***

CP Auto Products Inc ....E....323 266-3850
3901 Medford St Los Angeles (90063) ***(P-7244)***

CP Opco LLC ....D....209 524-1966
333 S Grand Ave Ste 4070 Los Angeles (90071) ***(P-17339)***

CP Opco LLC (HQ) ....**A....310 966-4900**
901 W Hillcrest Blvd A Inglewood (90301) ***(P-16952)***

CP Opco LLC ....D....310 966-4900
11766 Wilshire Blvd # 380 Los Angeles (90025) ***(P-17340)***

CP Opco LLC ....D....805 566-3566
1120 Mark Ave Carpinteria (93013) ***(P-17341)***

CP Opco LLC ....D....714 540-6111
3101 S Harbor Blvd Santa Ana (92704) ***(P-17342)***

CP Technologies, Tustin *Also called Corner Products Company* ***(P-13712)***

Cp-Carrillo Inc ....E....949 567-9000
17401 Armstrong Ave Irvine (92614) ***(P-8431)***

Cp-Carrillo Inc (HQ) ....**C....949 567-9000**
1902 Mcgaw Ave Irvine (92614) ***(P-8432)***

CPC Fabrication Inc ....E....714 549-2426
2904 Oak St Santa Ana (92707) ***(P-6814)***

CPC Services Inc ....E....626 852-6200
2025 E Fincl Way Ste 200 Glendora (91741) ***(P-6087)***

Cpcc Inc ....D....818 882-3200
10610 Owensmouth Ave Chatsworth (91311) ***(P-20575)***

Cpd Industries ....E....909 465-5596
4665 State St Montclair (91763) ***(P-5495)***

Cpe Hr Inc ....D....310 270-9800
9000 W Sunset Blvd # 900 West Hollywood (90069) ***(P-23198)***

Cph Hospital Management LLC ....A....562 838-3751
13100 Studebaker Rd Norwalk (90650) ***(P-20742)***

Cph Monarch Hotel LLC ....A....949 234-3200
1 Monarch Beach Resort Dana Point (92629) ***(P-16397)***

CPI Advanced Inc ....F....909 597-5533
14708 Central Ave Chino (91710) ***(P-8866)***

CPI Luxury Group ....D....818 249-9888
10220 Norris Ave Pacoima (91331) ***(P-14128)***

CPI Malibu Division ....D....805 383-1829
3623 Old Conejo Rd # 205 Newbury Park (91320) ***(P-9265)***

Cpl Holdings LLC ....C....310 348-6800
12181 Bluff Creek Dr 25 Playa Vista (90094) ***(P-16097)***

Cpo Commerce LLC ....D....626 585-3600
251 S Lake Ave Ste 400 Pasadena (91101) ***(P-13802)***

Cpp Cudahy, Cudahy *Also called Consolidated Foundries Inc* ***(P-6389)***

Cpp Ind ....E....909 595-2252
16800 Chestnut St City of Industry (91748) ***(P-10579)***

Cpp-Azusa, Azusa *Also called Magparts* ***(P-6399)***

Cpp-City of Industry, City of Industry *Also called Cast Parts Inc* ***(P-6264)***

Cpp-Pomona, Walnut *Also called Cast Parts Inc* ***(P-6263)***

Cppg Inc ....E....714 572-3662
3905 E Miraloma Ave Anaheim (92806) ***(P-18494)***

CPS, Studio City *Also called Commercial Prgrm Systems Inc* ***(P-18170)***

CPS Receivables Five LLC ....D....949 753-6800
19500 Jamboree Rd Irvine (92612) ***(P-17108)***

CPS Security, Long Beach *Also called Commercial Protective Svcs Inc* ***(P-18263)***

CPS Security Solutions Inc (PA) ....**A....310 818-1030**
3400 E Airport Way Long Beach (90806) ***(P-18267)***

Cr & A Custom, Los Angeles *Also called CR & A Custom Apparel Inc* ***(P-4506)***

CR & A Custom Apparel Inc ....E....213 749-4440
312 W Pico Blvd Los Angeles (90015) ***(P-4506)***

Cr Print, Westlake Village *Also called Earth Print Inc* ***(P-4286)***

Craftech EDM Corporation ....C....714 630-8117
2941 E La Jolla St Anaheim (92806) ***(P-5617)***

Craftech Metal Forming Inc ....E....951 940-6444
24100 Water Ave Ste B Perris (92570) ***(P-6608)***

Crafters Companion ....E....714 630-2444
2750 E Regal Park Dr Anaheim (92806) ***(P-11370)***

Craftsman Cutting Dies Inc (PA) ....**E....714 776-8995**
2273 E Via Burton Anaheim (92806) ***(P-6475)***

Craftsman Lath and Plaster Inc ....B....951 685-9922
8325 63rd St Riverside (92509) ***(P-1432)***

Craftsman Unity LLC ....C....714 776-8995
2273 E Via Burton Anaheim (92806) ***(P-6476)***

Crafttech, Anaheim *Also called Craftech EDM Corporation* ***(P-5617)***

Craig Kackert Design Tech, Simi Valley *Also called Jaxx Manufacturing Inc* ***(P-9735)***

Craig Manufacturing Company (PA) ....**D....323 726-7355**
8129 Slauson Ave Montebello (90640) ***(P-10036)***

Craig Tools Inc ....E....310 322-0614
142 Lomita St El Segundo (90245) ***(P-7851)***

Cramer Painting Inc ....E....909 397-5770
4080 Mission Blvd Montclair (91763) ***(P-1174)***

Crane Aerospace Inc ....E....818 526-2600
3000 Winona Ave Burbank (91504) ***(P-10580)***

Crane Co ....C....562 426-2531
3201 Walnut Ave Long Beach (90755) ***(P-7455)***

Craneveyor Corp (PA) ....**D....626 442-1524**
1524 Potrero Ave El Monte (91733) ***(P-7697)***

Craneveyor Midwest Corp ....E....909 627-6801
13730 Central Ave Chino (91710) ***(P-6957)***

Craniofacial Department, Loma Linda *Also called Loma Linda University Med Ctr* ***(P-20836)***

Crate Modular Inc ....D....310 405-0829
3025 E Dominguez St Carson (90810) ***(P-6991)***

Crave Foods Inc ....E....562 900-7272
2043 Imperial St Los Angeles (90021) ***(P-2413)***

Crawford Associates ....E....760 922-6804
2635 E Chanslor Way Blythe (92225) ***(P-1520)***

CRC Health Corporate ....A....714 542-3581
2101 E 1st St Santa Ana (92705) ***(P-21295)***

CRC Health Group Inc ....D....951 784-8010
1021 W La Cadena Dr Riverside (92501) ***(P-21296)***

CRC Services LLC ....F....888 848-4754
27200 Tourney Rd Ste 200 Santa Clarita (91355) ***(P-444)***

Crd Mfg Inc ....E....714 871-3300
615 Fee Ana St Placentia (92870) ***(P-6513)***

Crdn of Southern La County, Long Beach *Also called Foasberg Laundry and Clrs Inc* ***(P-16852)***

Creamer Printing Co ....F....310 671-9491
1413 N La Brea Ave Inglewood (90302) ***(P-4266)***

Create Music Group Inc ....D....310 623-0696
1320 N Wilton Pl Los Angeles (90028) ***(P-18495)***

Creation Tech Calexico Inc (HQ) ....**E....760 336-8543**
1778 Zinetta Rd Ste A Calexico (92231) ***(P-9396)***

Creative Accents ....E....760 373-1222
6294 Curtis Pl California City (93505) ***(P-2685)***

Creative Age Publications Inc ....E....818 782-7328
15975 High Knoll Rd Encino (91436) ***(P-4060)***

Creative Artsts Agcy Hldngs LL (PA) ....**A....424 288-2000**
2000 Avenue Of The Stars Los Angeles (90067) ***(P-19308)***

Creative Automation, Sun Valley *Also called Jack J Engel Manufacturing Inc* ***(P-9877)***

Creative Channel Services LLC (HQ) ....**A....310 482-6500**
6601 Center Dr W Ste 400 Los Angeles (90045) ***(P-23199)***

Creative Circle LLC (HQ) ....**D....323 930-2333**
5900 Wilshire Blvd # 1100 Los Angeles (90036) ***(P-17408)***

Creative Costuming Designs Inc ....E....714 895-0982
15402 Electronic Ln Huntington Beach (92649) ***(P-2566)***

Creative Design Consultants (PA) ....**D....714 641-4868**
2915 Red Hill Ave G201 Costa Mesa (92626) ***(P-18496)***

Creative Dgtal Systems Intgrti ....F....805 364-0555
670 E Easy St Simi Valley (93065) ***(P-17586)***

Creative Essences Inc ....E....310 638-9277
15320 Cornet St Santa Fe Springs (90670) ***(P-2317)***

Creative Graphic Services, Santa Clarita *Also called Living Way Industries Inc* ***(P-4361)***

Creative Impressions Inc ....E....714 521-4441
7697 9th St Buena Park (90621) ***(P-5429)***

Creative Industry Handbooks, Toluca Lake *Also called Gmm Inc* ***(P-4175)***

Mergent e-mail: customerrelations@mergent.com
1104
2022 Southern California Business Directory and Buyers Guide
(P-0000) Products & Services Section entry number
(PA)=Parent Co (HQ)=Headquarters (DH)=Div Headquarters

Creative Inflatables, South El Monte *Also called Promotonal Design Concepts Inc* ***(P-5401)***
Creative Intelligence Inc......F......323 936-9009
4988 Venice Blvd Los Angeles (90019) ***(P-17168)***
Creative Machine Technology, Corona *Also called Cremach Tech Inc* ***(P-7724)***
Creative Maintenance Systems......D......949 852-2871
1340 Reynolds Ave Ste 111 Irvine (92614) ***(P-17233)***
Creative Outdoor Advertising, Riverside *Also called Brimad Enterprises Inc* ***(P-17075)***
Creative Outdoor Distrs USA, Lake Forest *Also called Cod USA Inc* ***(P-3620)***
Creative Park Productions LLC......B......818 622-3702
100 Universal City Plz Universal City (91608) ***(P-19112)***
Creative Pathways Inc......E......310 530-1965
20815 Higgins Ct Torrance (90501) ***(P-7889)***
Creative Press LLC (PA)......D......**714 774-5060**
1350 S Caldwell Cir Anaheim (92805) ***(P-4267)***
Creative Stone Mfg Inc (PA)......C......**909 357-8295**
11191 Calabash Ave Fontana (92337) ***(P-6026)***
Creative Teaching Press Inc (PA)......D......**714 799-2100**
6262 Katella Ave Cypress (90630) ***(P-4125)***
Creative Technology Group Inc (HQ)......D......**818 779-2400**
14000 Arminta St Panorama City (91402) ***(P-17343)***
Creatons Grdn Ntral Fd Mkts In......F......661 877-4280
24849 Anza Dr Valencia (91355) ***(P-4742)***
Credible Labs Inc......D......650 866-5861
2121 Avenue Of The Stars # 25 Los Angeles (90067) ***(P-13384)***
Credit Card Services Inc (PA)......D......**213 365-1122**
21281 S Western Ave Torrance (90501) ***(P-18497)***
Credit Monkey LLC......D......877 701-7307
8484 Wilshire Blvd # 515 Beverly Hills (90211) ***(P-17121)***
Credit Repair, Beverly Hills *Also called Credit Monkey LLC* ***(P-17121)***
Credit Union Southern Cal (PA)......C......**562 698-8326**
8028 Greenleaf Ave Whittier (90602) ***(P-15061)***
Creditors Adjustment Bur Inc......D......818 990-4800
14226 Ventura Blvd Sherman Oaks (91423) ***(P-17109)***
Crellin Machine Company......E......323 225-8101
114 W Elmyra St Los Angeles (90012) ***(P-7034)***
Cremach Tech Inc (PA)......C......**951 735-3194**
369 Meyer Cir Corona (92879) ***(P-7724)***
Crenshaw Chrstn Ctr Ch Los Ang (PA)......B......**323 758-3777**
7901 S Vermont Ave Los Angeles (90044) ***(P-19113)***
Crenshaw Die and Mfg Corp......D......949 475-5505
7432 Prince Dr Huntington Beach (92647) ***(P-7793)***
Crenshaw Nursing, Los Angeles *Also called Longwood Management Corp* ***(P-20408)***
Crenshaw YMCA......D......323 290-9113
3820 Santa Rosalia Dr Los Angeles (90008) ***(P-22333)***
Cresa Partners Los Angeles Inc......E......310 207-1700
11726 San Vicente Blvd Los Angeles (90049) ***(P-15827)***
Crescent Inc......E......714 992-6030
1196 N Osprey Cir Anaheim (92807) ***(P-4268)***
Crescent Capital Bdc Inc (PA)......C......**310 235-5971**
11100 Santa Monica Blvd # 2000 Los Angeles (90025) ***(P-16257)***
Crescent Capital Group LP (HQ)......C......**310 235-5900**
11100 Santa Monica Blvd Los Angeles (90025) ***(P-15325)***
Crescent Healthcare Inc......D......949 646-2267
1640 Newport Blvd Ste 435 Costa Mesa (92627) ***(P-21156)***
Crescent Healthcare Inc......D......562 347-2800
11980 Telg Rd Ste 102 Santa Fe Springs (90670) ***(P-21157)***
Crescent Healthcare Inc (HQ)......C......**714 520-6300**
11980 Telg Rd Ste 100 Santa Fe Springs (90670) ***(P-21158)***
Crescent Healthcare Inc......D......562 347-2900
11980 Telg Rd Ste 100 Santa Fe Springs (90670) ***(P-21159)***
Crescent Hotel......D......310 247-0505
403 N Crescent Dr Beverly Hills (90210) ***(P-16398)***
Crescenta-Canada YMCA (PA)......C......**818 790-0123**
1930 Foothill Blvd La Canada (91011) ***(P-22334)***
Crescenta-Canada YMCA......C......818 352-3255
6840 Foothill Blvd Tujunga (91042) ***(P-22335)***
Cresco Manufacturing Inc......E......714 525-2326
1614 N Orangethorpe Way Anaheim (92801) ***(P-8564)***
Crescomfg.com, Anaheim *Also called Cresco Manufacturing Inc* ***(P-8564)***
Crest Chevrolet, San Bernardino *Also called Harbill Inc* ***(P-13028)***
Crest Coating Inc......D......714 635-7090
1361 S Allec St Anaheim (92805) ***(P-7355)***
Crest Digital, Laguna Beach *Also called National Film Laboratories* ***(P-19241)***
Crest Financial Corporation (HQ)......D......**562 733-6500**
12641 166th St Cerritos (90703) ***(P-15558)***
Crest R E O & Relocation, La Crescenta *Also called EAM Enterprises Inc* ***(P-15844)***
Crest Steel Corporation......D......310 830-2651
6580 General Rd Riverside (92509) ***(P-13561)***
Crestec Los Angeles, Long Beach *Also called Crestec Usa Inc* ***(P-4269)***
Crestec Usa Inc......E......310 327-9000
2410 Mira Mar Ave Long Beach (90815) ***(P-4269)***
Crestline Hotels & Resorts Inc (HQ)......C......**213 629-1200**
120 S Los Angeles St 11 Los Angeles (90012) ***(P-16399)***
Crestmont Capital LLC......C......949 537-3882
1422 Edinger Ave Ste 210 Tustin (92780) ***(P-16258)***
Crestone LLC......F......323 588-8857
2511 S Alameda St Vernon (90058) ***(P-3031)***
Crestview Cadillac, West Covina *Also called Allen/Clark Cadillac* ***(P-18920)***
Crestview Landscape Inc......D......818 962-7771
13915 Saticoy St Panorama City (91402) ***(P-252)***
Crestwood Behavioral Hlth Inc......D......805 308-8720
303 S C St Lompoc (93436) ***(P-20307)***
Crestwood Behavioral Hlth Inc......D......661 363-8127
6700 Eucalyptus Dr Ste A Bakersfield (93306) ***(P-21764)***
Crestwood Behavioral Hlth Inc......A......661 363-0124
6700 Eucalyptus Dr Ste A Bakersfield (93306) ***(P-19777)***
Creu LLC......E......909 483-4888
12750 Baltic Ct Rancho Cucamonga (91739) ***(P-5618)***
Crew Inc......D......310 608-6860
19618 S Susana Rd Compton (90221) ***(P-1594)***
Crew Knitwear LLC (PA)......C......**323 526-3888**
660 S Myers St Los Angeles (90023) ***(P-2935)***
Crh Management, Newport Beach *Also called Core Realty Holdings MGT Inc* ***(P-15825)***
Cri Help Drug Rehabilitation, North Hollywood *Also called Cri-Help Inc* ***(P-22098)***
Cri Sub 1 (HQ)......E......**310 537-1657**
1715 S Anderson Ave Compton (90220) ***(P-3581)***
Cri-Help Inc (PA)......D......**818 985-8323**
11027 Burbank Blvd North Hollywood (91601) ***(P-22098)***
Crimson Resource Management, Bakersfield *Also called Delta Trading LP* ***(P-5270)***
Crisp California Walnuts, Stratford *Also called Crisp Warehouse Inc* ***(P-164)***
Crisp Enterprises Inc (PA)......D......**714 668-5955**
3180 Pullman St Costa Mesa (92626) ***(P-17147)***
Crisp Warehouse Inc......E......559 947-9221
20500 Main St Stratford (93266) ***(P-164)***
Crissair Inc......C......661 367-3300
28909 Avenue Williams Valencia (91355) ***(P-8443)***
Cristek Interconnects Inc (HQ)......C......**714 696-5200**
5395 E Hunter Ave Anaheim (92807) ***(P-9651)***
Critchfeld Mech Inc Sthern Cal......D......949 390-2900
15391 Springdale St Huntington Beach (92649) ***(P-1050)***
Criterion Automation Inc......F......951 683-2400
1722 Production Cir Riverside (92509) ***(P-6247)***
Criterion Labs Inc......D......818 506-8332
10907 Magnolia Blvd North Hollywood (91601) ***(P-22937)***
Criterion Supply Inc......F......562 222-2382
6985 Arlington Ave Ste P Riverside (92503) ***(P-2686)***
Criterion Supply Inc......F......562 222-2382
13006 Saticoy St Ste 4 North Hollywood (91605) ***(P-2687)***
Critical Io LLC......F......949 553-2200
36 Executive Park Ste 150 Irvine (92614) ***(P-8247)***
Criticalpoint Capital LLC......D......909 987-9533
9433 Hyssop Dr Rancho Cucamonga (91730) ***(P-4731)***
CRITTENTON SERVICES FOR CHILDR, Fullerton *Also called Florence Crttnton Svcs Ornge C* ***(P-22103)***
Crl, Vernon *Also called C R Laurence Co Inc* ***(P-10027)***
Crm Co LLC (PA)......E......**949 263-9100**
1301 Dove St Ste 940 Newport Beach (92660) ***(P-5356)***
Crmls Inc......C......909 859-2040
15325 Frfeld Rnch Rd Ste Chino Hills (91709) ***(P-15663)***
Crockett Graphics Inc (PA)......D......**805 987-8577**
980 Avenida Acaso Camarillo (93012) ***(P-3797)***
Crome Gallery, North Hollywood *Also called Alco Tech Inc* ***(P-7121)***
Crookshanks Sales Co......E......559 992-5077
2375 Dairy Ave Corcoran (93212) ***(P-6088)***
Crosby Fruit Products, Fontana *Also called Refresco Beverages US Inc* ***(P-1874)***
Crosno Construction Inc......E......805 343-7437
819 Sheridan Rd Arroyo Grande (93420) ***(P-6609)***
Crossfield Products Corp (PA)......E......**310 886-9100**
3000 E Harcourt St Compton (90221) ***(P-4685)***
Crossing Guard Company......C......310 202-8284
10440 Pioneer Blvd Ste 5 Santa Fe Springs (90670) ***(P-18268)***
Crossport Mocean......F......949 646-1701
1611 Babcock St Newport Beach (92663) ***(P-2744)***
Crossrads Adult Day Hlth Care, Rancho Cucamonga *Also called Horrigan Enterprises Inc* ***(P-21805)***
Crossrads Chrstn Schols Corona......C......951 278-3199
2380 Fullerton Ave Corona (92881) ***(P-22009)***
Crossroads Cmnty Foundation, Los Angeles *Also called PS Arts* ***(P-23497)***
Crossroads Eqp Lease & Fin LLC......D......909 291-6400
9385 Haven Ave Rancho Cucamonga (91730) ***(P-13455)***
Crossroads Medical Offices, City of Industry *Also called Kaiser Foundation Hospitals* ***(P-19895)***
Crossroads Software Inc......F......714 990-6433
210 W Birch St Ste 207 Brea (92821) ***(P-17829)***
Crosstown Elec & Data Inc......D......626 813-6693
5454 Diaz St Baldwin Park (91706) ***(P-1238)***
Crothall Services Group......A......714 562-9275
14710 Northam St La Mirada (90638) ***(P-19032)***
Crowley Marine Services Inc......B......310 732-6500
86 Berth San Pedro (90731) ***(P-12441)***
Crown Building Maintenance Co......B......714 434-9494
3300 W Macarthur Blvd Santa Ana (92704) ***(P-17234)***
Crown Carton Company Inc......E......323 582-3053
1820 E 48th Pl Vernon (90058) ***(P-3798)***
Crown Citrus Company Inc......F......760 344-1930
551 W Main St Brawley (92227) ***(P-1897)***
Crown Contracting Inc......E......760 203-4613
7311 Hopi Trl Yucca Valley (92284) ***(P-599)***
Crown Discount Tools, Sylmar *Also called TMW Corporation* ***(P-10432)***
Crown Drilling Services Inc......F......661 479-0710
5300 Woodmere Dr Ste 101 Bakersfield (93313) ***(P-425)***
Crown Energy Services Inc......A......213 765-7800
2601 S Fgroa St Bldg Fl 1 Los Angeles (90007) ***(P-17235)***
Crown Equipment Corporation......D......310 952-6600
4061 Via Oro Ave Long Beach (90810) ***(P-7707)***
Crown Facility Solutions......E......657 266-0821
3617 W Macarthur Blvd Santa Ana (92704) ***(P-17236)***
Crown Fence Co......D......562 864-5177
12118 Bloomfield Ave Santa Fe Springs (90670) ***(P-1652)***
Crown Golf Properties LP......D......714 730-1611
12442 Tustin Ranch Rd Tustin (92782) ***(P-23200)***
Crown Lift Trucks, Long Beach *Also called Crown Equipment Corporation* ***(P-7707)***
Crown Limousine L.A., Hawthorne *Also called Crown Transportation Inc* ***(P-11860)***
Crown Media Holdings Inc (HQ)......C......**888 390-7474**
12700 Ventura Blvd # 100 Studio City (91604) ***(P-12754)***

Employee Codes: A=Over 500 employees, B=251-500
C=101-250, D=51-100, E=20-50 F=10-19
2022 Southern California Business
Directory and Buyers Guide
© Mergent Inc. 1-800-342-5647
1105

Crown Media United States LLC (HQ)....D....**818 755-2400**
12700 Ventura Blvd # 100 Studio City (91604) ***(P-12712)***
Crown Pallet Company Inc....F....626 937-6565
15151 Salt Lake Ave La Puente (91746) ***(P-3386)***
Crown Paper Converting Inc....E....909 923-5226
1380 S Bon View Ave Ontario (91761) ***(P-3749)***
Crown Pavers Inc....F....323 636-3365
2434 W Valley Blvd Ste C Alhambra (91803) ***(P-7642)***
Crown Plaza La Harbor Hotel, San Pedro *Also called Spf Capital Real Estate LLC* ***(P-16724)***
Crown Plaza Los Angeles, Los Angeles *Also called Ihg Management (maryland) LLC* ***(P-16501)***
Crown Plz Ht At Cmmerce Casino....D....323 728-3600
6121 Telegraph Rd Commerce (90040) ***(P-16400)***
Crown Poly Inc....F....323 583-4570
5701 S Boyle Ave Vernon (90058) ***(P-3881)***
Crown Poly Inc....C....323 268-1298
5700 Bickett St Huntington Park (90255) ***(P-3882)***
Crown Printers, San Bernardino *Also called Shorett Printing Inc* ***(P-4573)***
Crown Surgery Med Group Inc (PA)....D....**951 973-7290**
25470 Med Ctr Dr Ste 203 Murrieta (92562) ***(P-19778)***
Crown Technical Systems (PA)....C....**951 332-4170**
13470 Philadelphia Ave Fontana (92337) ***(P-8891)***
Crown Transportation Inc....D....310 737-0888
13543 Prairie Ave Hawthorne (90250) ***(P-11860)***
Crown Vly Precision Machining, Irwindale *Also called Sinecera Inc* ***(P-18668)***
Crowne Cold Storage LLC....E....661 725-6458
786 Road 188 Delano (93215) ***(P-23201)***
Crowne Plaza, Los Angeles *Also called Sonesta Los Angles Arprt Lax L* ***(P-16719)***
Crowne Plaza Ventura Beach, Ventura *Also called Ventura Hsptality Partners LLC* ***(P-16771)***
Crowne Plz Ht Commerce Casino, Commerce *Also called Crown Plz Ht At Cmmerce Casino* ***(P-16400)***
Crowner Sheet Metal Pdts Inc....E....626 960-4971
14346 Arrow Hwy Baldwin Park (91706) ***(P-1481)***
Crowntonka California Inc....E....909 230-6720
6514 E 26th St Commerce (90040) ***(P-8335)***
Crp Centinela LP....D....901 821-4117
6161 W Centinela Ave Culver City (90230) ***(P-16401)***
CRST International Inc....C....909 829-1313
10641 Calabash Ave Fontana (92337) ***(P-12027)***
Crucial Power Products....E....323 721-5017
14000 S Broadway Los Angeles (90061) ***(P-9697)***
Crum & Forster, Los Angeles *Also called United States Fire Insur Co* ***(P-15641)***
Crumbl Cookies....D....949 519-0791
23702 El Toro Rd Ste B Lake Forest (92630) ***(P-2061)***
Crunch LLC....D....951 327-0202
19867 Prairie St Ste 200 Chatsworth (91311) ***(P-19441)***
Crunch LLC....D....719 301-1760
19867 Prairie St Ste 200 Chatsworth (91311) ***(P-19442)***
Crunch Fitness, Chatsworth *Also called Crunch LLC* ***(P-19442)***
Crunch Fitness....D....805 522-5454
19867 Prairie St Ste 200 Chatsworth (91311) ***(P-19443)***
Crusader Insurance Company....D....818 591-9800
26050 Mureau Rd Calabasas (91302) ***(P-15466)***
Crush Master Grinding Corp....E....909 595-2249
755 Penarth Ave Walnut (91789) ***(P-8565)***
Cruz Modular Inc (PA)....D....**714 283-2890**
249 W Baywood Ave Ste B Orange (92865) ***(P-12111)***
Cryogenic Experts, Oxnard *Also called Acme Cryogenics Inc* ***(P-7958)***
Cryogenic Industries Inc....C....951 677-2060
25720 Jefferson Ave Murrieta (92562) ***(P-9003)***
Cryomax USA Inc (HQ)....F....**626 330-3388**
127 N California Ave B City of Industry (91744) ***(P-12191)***
Cryoport Systems LLC (HQ)....F....**949 540-7204**
19000 Macarthur Blvd # 80 Irvine (92612) ***(P-7969)***
Cryoport Systems, Inc., Irvine *Also called Cryoport Systems LLC* ***(P-7969)***
Cryostar USA, Whittier *Also called Messer LLC* ***(P-4642)***
Cryostar USA LLC....D....562 903-1290
13117 Meyer Rd Whittier (90605) ***(P-8008)***
Cryoworks Inc....D....951 360-0920
3309 Grapevine St Jurupa Valley (91752) ***(P-7533)***
Cryst Mark Inc A Swan Techno C....E....818 240-7520
613 Justin Ave Glendale (91201) ***(P-7970)***
Crystal Art of Florida, Vernon *Also called Rggd Inc* ***(P-14177)***
Crystal Cal Lab Inc....E....714 991-1580
3981 E Miraloma Ave Anaheim (92806) ***(P-9698)***
Crystal Casino & Hotel, Compton *Also called Celebrity Casinos Inc* ***(P-16373)***
Crystal Castle, Pomona *Also called Golden Grove Trading Inc* ***(P-4521)***
Crystal Cathedral Ministries (PA)....C....**714 622-2900**
12901 Lewis St Garden Grove (92840) ***(P-19114)***
Crystal Craft, La Verne *Also called P F Plastics Inc* ***(P-3570)***
Crystal Engineering Corp....E....805 595-5477
708 Fiero Ln Ste 9 San Luis Obispo (93401) ***(P-10688)***
Crystal Form, Santa Fe Springs *Also called Coated Fabrics Company* ***(P-14755)***
Crystal Geyser Water Company....E....661 323-6296
1233 E California Ave Bakersfield (93307) ***(P-2263)***
Crystal Geyser Water Company....E....661 321-0896
2351 E Brundage Ln Ste A Bakersfield (93307) ***(P-2264)***
Crystal Lighting Corp....F....562 944-0223
13182 Flores St Santa Fe Springs (90670) ***(P-9081)***
Crystal Mark, Glendale *Also called Cryst Mark Inc A Swan Techno C* ***(P-7970)***
Crystal Organic Farms LLC....A....661 845-5200
6900 Mountain View Rd Bakersfield (93307) ***(P-103)***
Crystal Stairs Inc (PA)....B....**323 299-8998**
5110 W Goldleaf Cir # 150 Los Angeles (90056) ***(P-21765)***
Crystal Tex Shoehorn, Downey *Also called Van Grace Quality Injection* ***(P-5856)***
Crystal Tip, Irvine *Also called Westside Resources Inc* ***(P-11203)***

Crystal Tips Holdings....E....800 544-3939
8850 Research Dr Irvine (92618) ***(P-5357)***
Crystaliner Corp....F....949 548-0292
1626 Placentia Ave Costa Mesa (92627) ***(P-10462)***
Cs Electronics, Irvine *Also called Cs Systems Inc* ***(P-8248)***
Cs Manfacturing Indus Svcs Inc (PA)....F....**760 390-7746**
619 Paulin Ave Ste 105 Calexico (92231) ***(P-9652)***
Cs Systems Inc....E....949 475-9100
16781 Noyes Ave Irvine (92606) ***(P-8248)***
Csa Silicon Valley LLC....D....818 922-2416
7027 Hayvenhurst Ave Van Nuys (91406) ***(P-21065)***
CSB Industries Corp....F....626 964-4058
268 Benton Ct Walnut (91789) ***(P-6406)***
CSC Auto Salv Dismantling Inc....D....818 532-4624
12207 Branford St Sun Valley (91352) ***(P-12442)***
CSC Ranch, Corcoran *Also called Crookshanks Sales Co* ***(P-6088)***
Cscu, Santa Maria *Also called Coasthills Credit Union* ***(P-15109)***
Csi, Santa Clarita *Also called Custom Suppression Inc* ***(P-9627)***
Csi, Fullerton *Also called Cardservice International Inc* ***(P-18469)***
Csi Electrical Contractors Inc....B....661 723-0869
41769 11th St W Ste B Palmdale (93551) ***(P-1239)***
Csi Electrical Contractors Inc (HQ)....C....**562 946-0700**
10623 Fulton Wells Ave Santa Fe Springs (90670) ***(P-1240)***
CSM Metal Fabricating & Engrg, Los Angeles *Also called Commercial Shtmtl Works Inc* ***(P-6603)***
CSX Corporation....C....626 336-1377
14863 Clark Ave Hacienda Heights (91745) ***(P-11795)***
CT Commodities Inc....D....559 757-3996
217 W Terra Bella Ave Pixley (93256) ***(P-15314)***
CTA Fixtures Inc....D....909 390-6744
5721 Santa Ana St Ste B Ontario (91761) ***(P-3680)***
CTA Manufacturing Inc....E....951 280-2400
1160 California Ave Corona (92881) ***(P-3126)***
Ctac Research 60901, Irwindale *Also called Southern California Edison Co* ***(P-12856)***
Ctbla Inc....D....323 276-1933
1740 Albion St Los Angeles (90031) ***(P-9980)***
Ctc Global Corporation (PA)....C....**949 428-8500**
2026 Mcgaw Ave Irvine (92614) ***(P-9030)***
Ctc Group Inc (HQ)....C....**310 540-0500**
21333 Hawthorne Blvd Torrance (90503) ***(P-16402)***
Ctcoa LLC....E....562 407-5375
16818 Marquardt Ave Cerritos (90703) ***(P-10305)***
Ctd Machines Inc....F....213 689-4455
7355 E Slauson Ave Commerce (90040) ***(P-7725)***
Ctek Inc....E....310 241-2973
2425 Golden Hill Rd # 106 Paso Robles (93446) ***(P-12782)***
Ctf, Murrieta *Also called California Trusframe LLC* ***(P-3358)***
Ctg, Santa Barbara *Also called Alta Properties Inc* ***(P-5998)***
Ctm, Gardena *Also called Classic Tile & Mosaic Inc* ***(P-13298)***
Ctour Holiday LLC....B....323 261-8811
222 E Huntington Dr # 221 Monrovia (91016) ***(P-19641)***
Ctp Solutions, Agoura Hills *Also called Schachtel Corporation* ***(P-4419)***
CTS Cement Manufacturing Corp (PA)....E....**714 379-8260**
12442 Knott St Garden Grove (92841) ***(P-5179)***
CTS Cement Manufacturing Corp....F....310 472-4004
2077 Linda Flora Dr Los Angeles (90077) ***(P-5180)***
CU Cooperative Systems Inc (PA)....B....**909 948-2500**
9692 Haven Ave Rancho Cucamonga (91730) ***(P-15110)***
CU Direct Corporation (PA)....C....**909 481-2300**
2855 E Guasti Rd Ste 500 Ontario (91761) ***(P-17587)***
CU Vehicles LLC....D....818 885-1226
20131 Prairie St B Chatsworth (91311) ***(P-18748)***
Cucamonga Valley Water Dst....D....909 987-2591
10440 Ashford St Rancho Cucamonga (91730) ***(P-12886)***
Cudahy Medical Offices, Cudahy *Also called Kaiser Foundation Hospitals* ***(P-20812)***
Cudc, Ontario *Also called CU Direct Corporation* ***(P-17587)***
Cuddly Toys....F....323 980-0572
1833 N Eastern Ave Los Angeles (90032) ***(P-11359)***
Cudoform Inc....F....805 617-0818
802 Calle Plano Camarillo (93012) ***(P-7137)***
Cuevas Mattress Inc....F....310 631-8382
3504 E Olympic Blvd Los Angeles (90023) ***(P-3545)***
Cuisine Partners USA, Los Angeles *Also called Investors Capital MGT Group* ***(P-23040)***
Cuiti International, Rancho Cucamonga *Also called Ciuti International Inc* ***(P-2129)***
Culinary Brands Inc (PA)....C....**626 289-3000**
3280 E 44th St Vernon (90058) ***(P-1923)***
Culinary International LLC (PA)....C....**626 289-3000**
3280 E 44th St Vernon (90058) ***(P-2414)***
Culinary Services America Inc....E....323 965-7582
6404 Wilshire Blvd # 500 Los Angeles (90048) ***(P-17489)***
Culinary Staffing of America (PA)....D....**559 741-1314**
2950 S Mooney Blvd Ste G Visalia (93277) ***(P-17490)***
Culinary Staffing Service, Los Angeles *Also called Culinary Services America Inc* ***(P-17489)***
Culligan, Oxnard *Also called Harris Water Conditioning Inc* ***(P-18538)***
Cult/Cvlt LLC....F....714 435-2858
1555 E Saint Gertrude Pl Santa Ana (92705) ***(P-10487)***
Culture AMP Inc (HQ)....E....**415 326-8453**
16501 Ventura Blvd # 400 Encino (91436) ***(P-17830)***
Culver City Bus Lines Municipal, Culver City *Also called City of Culver City* ***(P-11903)***
Culver West Health Center LLC....D....310 390-9506
4035 Grand View Blvd Los Angeles (90066) ***(P-20576)***
Cumming - LLC....D....951 252-8555
25220 Hancock Ave Ste 440 Murrieta (92562) ***(P-23009)***
Cumming Corporation....D....951 200-7860
25220 Hancock Ave Ste 440 Murrieta (92562) ***(P-23202)***
Cumming Management Group Inc....D....949 900-0440
27207 Puerta Real Mission Viejo (92691) ***(P-23010)***

Mergent e-mail: customerrelations@mergent.com
1106
2022 Southern California Business Directory and Buyers Guide
(P-0000) Products & Services Section entry number
(PA)=Parent Co (HQ)=Headquarters (DH)=Div Headquarters

ALPHABETIC SECTION Cw Industries

Cumming Management Group Inc ....D.......415 748-3095
25220 Hancock Ave Ste 440 Murrieta (92562) ***(P-23011)***

Cumming Management Group Inc ....D.......951 216-6443
523 W 6th St Ste 1001 Los Angeles (90014) ***(P-22520)***

Cumming Management Group Inc ....D.......951 252-8555
27455 Tierra Alta Way A Temecula (92590) ***(P-22521)***

Cummings Resources LLC ....E.......951 248-1130
330 W Citrus St Colton (92324) ***(P-11539)***

Cummings Resources LLC ....E.......951 248-1130
1495 Columbia Ave Riverside (92507) ***(P-11540)***

Cummings Transportation, Shafter *Also called Cummings Vacuum Service Inc* ***(P-493)***

Cummings Vacuum Service Inc ....D.......661 746-1786
19605 Broken Ct Shafter (93263) ***(P-493)***

Cummins Aerospace, Anaheim *Also called Yeager Manufacturing Corp* ***(P-10446)***

Cummins Pacific LLC ....F.......866 934-4373
9520 Stewart And Gray Rd Downey (90241) ***(P-7591)***

Cummins Pacific LLC ....F.......909 877-0433
3061 S Riverside Ave Bloomington (92316) ***(P-7592)***

Cummins Pacific LLC ....E.......661 325-9404
4601 E Brundage Ln Bakersfield (93307) ***(P-10037)***

Cummins Pacific LLC ....F.......323 728-8111
1105 S Greenwood Ave Montebello (90640) ***(P-13897)***

Cummins Pacific LLC (HQ) ....D.......949 253-6000
1939 Deere Ave Irvine (92606) ***(P-7593)***

Cummins Pacific LLC ....F.......805 644-7281
3958 Transport St Ventura (93003) ***(P-7594)***

Curation Foods Inc (HQ) ....D.......800 454-1355
2811 Airpark Dr Santa Maria (93455) ***(P-2415)***

Curative-Korva LLC ....D.......424 645-7575
430 S Cataract Ave San Dimas (91773) ***(P-21066)***

Cure Apparel Llc ....F.......562 927-7460
3338 S Malt Ave Commerce (90040) ***(P-2841)***

Curlin Medical Inc (HQ) ....D.......714 897-9301
15662 Commerce Ln Huntington Beach (92649) ***(P-8009)***

Curran Engineering Company Inc ....E.......800 643-6353
28727 Industry Dr Valencia (91355) ***(P-6958)***

Currency Capital LLC ....D.......310 571-9600
12100 Wilshire Blvd # 1800 Los Angeles (90025) ***(P-18498)***

Currie Acquisitions LLC ....F.......805 915-4900
3850 Royal Ave Ste A Simi Valley (93063) ***(P-10488)***

Currie Enterprises ....E.......714 528-6957
382 N Smith Ave Corona (92878) ***(P-10038)***

Currie Technologies, Simi Valley *Also called Currie Acquisitions LLC* ***(P-10488)***

Curry Company LLC ....E.......310 643-8400
15724 Condon Ave Lawndale (90260) ***(P-7852)***

Curtco Media Group ....E.......310 589-7700
29160 Heathercliff Rd # 1 Malibu (90265) ***(P-4061)***

Curtco Robb Media LLC (PA) ....E.......310 589-7700
29160 Heathercliff Rd # 1 Malibu (90265) ***(P-4062)***

Curtis 1000 Los Angeles, Ontario *Also called Taylor Print Vsual Imprssons I* ***(P-14199)***

Curtis Industries, Visalia *Also called Powers Holdings Inc* ***(P-9764)***

Curtis Winery, Los Olivos *Also called Firestone Vineyard LP* ***(P-2184)***

Curtiss-Wrght Cntrls Elctrnic, Santa Clarita *Also called Curtiss-Wrght Cntrls Elctrnic* ***(P-22523)***

Curtiss-Wrght Cntrls Elctrnic ....C.......661 257-4430
28965 Avenue Penn Santa Clarita (91355) ***(P-22522)***

Curtiss-Wrght Cntrls Elctrnic (HQ) ....C.......661 702-1494
28965 Avenue Penn Santa Clarita (91355) ***(P-22523)***

Curtiss-Wrght Cntrls Intgrted (HQ) ....D.......661 257-4430
28965 Avenue Penn Valencia (91355) ***(P-22524)***

Curtiss-Wrght Flow Ctrl Svc LL (HQ) ....D.......949 498-3350
2950 E Birch St Brea (92821) ***(P-22525)***

Curtiss-Wright Flow Control ....C.......626 851-3100
28965 Avenue Penn Valencia (91355) ***(P-7442)***

Curvature LLC (HQ) ....B.......800 230-6638
859 Ward Dr 200 Santa Barbara (93111) ***(P-13385)***

Cushman & Wakefield Cal Inc ....A.......714 591-0451
7281 Garden Grove Blvd G Garden Grove (92841) ***(P-15828)***

Cushman & Wakefield Cal Inc ....A.......805 322-7244
770 Paseo Camarillo 315 Camarillo (93010) ***(P-15829)***

Cushman & Wakefield Cal Inc ....A.......909 980-3781
901 Via Piemonte Ste 200 Ontario (91764) ***(P-15830)***

Cushman & Wakefield Cal Inc ....A.......310 556-1805
10250 Constellation Blvd # 2200 Los Angeles (90067) ***(P-15831)***

Cushman & Wakefield Cal Inc ....A.......562 276-1400
3780 Kilroy Arprt Way Long Beach (90806) ***(P-15832)***

Cushman & Wakefield Cal Inc ....A.......949 474-4004
18111 Von Karman Ave # 1000 Irvine (92612) ***(P-15833)***

Cushman & Wakefield California, Garden Grove *Also called Cushman & Wakefield Cal Inc* ***(P-15828)***

Cushman Winery Corporation ....E.......805 688-9339
6905 Foxen Canyon Rd Los Olivos (93441) ***(P-14839)***

Custom Alloy Light Metals, City of Industry *Also called Custom Alloy Sales Inc* ***(P-6290)***

Custom Alloy Sales Inc (PA) ....F.......626 369-3641
13181 Crssrads Pkwy N Ste City of Industry (91746) ***(P-6290)***

Custom Autosound Mfg Inc ....E.......714 535-1091
1030 Williamson Ave Fullerton (92833) ***(P-9168)***

Custom Aviation Supply, Chatsworth *Also called Custom Control Sensors LLC* ***(P-8892)***

Custom Building Products LLC (HQ) ....D.......800 272-8786
7711 Center Ave Ste 500 Huntington Beach (92647) ***(P-5181)***

Custom Business Solutions Inc (PA) ....D.......949 380-7674
1 Studebaker Irvine (92618) ***(P-13355)***

Custom Characters Inc ....F.......818 507-5940
621 Thompson Ave Glendale (91201) ***(P-3072)***

Custom Chemical Formulators, Santa Fe Springs *Also called Morgan Gallacher Inc* ***(P-4972)***

Custom Control Sensors Inc ....E.......818 341-4610
21111 Plummer St Chatsworth (91311) ***(P-8947)***

Custom Control Sensors LLC (PA) ....B.......818 341-4610
21111 Plummer St Chatsworth (91311) ***(P-8892)***

Custom Control Sensors Intl ....E.......818 341-4610
21111 Plummer St Chatsworth (91311) ***(P-8893)***

Custom Cooler Inc (HQ) ....D.......909 592-1111
420 E Arrow Hwy San Dimas (91773) ***(P-13852)***

Custom Design Iron Works Inc ....F.......818 700-9182
9182 Kelvin Ave Chatsworth (91311) ***(P-6376)***

Custom Displays Inc ....F.......323 770-8074
411 W 157th St Gardena (90248) ***(P-3645)***

Custom Enamelers Inc ....E.......714 540-7884
18340 Mount Baldy Cir Fountain Valley (92708) ***(P-7356)***

Custom Fibreglass Mfg Co ....C.......562 432-5454
1711 Harbor Ave Long Beach (90813) ***(P-10539)***

Custom Foods, Santa Fe Springs *Also called J & J Processing Inc* ***(P-2330)***

Custom Glass Fabricators Inc ....F.......562 529-2300
15521 Vermont Ave Paramount (90723) ***(P-5371)***

Custom Goods LLC ....D.......310 241-6700
907 E 236th St Carson (90745) ***(P-12192)***

Custom Goods LLC ....D.......310 241-6700
809 E 236th St Carson (90745) ***(P-12193)***

Custom Goods LLC (PA) ....E.......310 241-6700
1035 E Watson Center Rd Carson (90745) ***(P-12194)***

Custom Hardtops, Long Beach *Also called Custom Fibreglass Mfg Co* ***(P-10539)***

Custom Hardware Mfg Inc ....E.......714 547-7440
2112 E 4th St Ste 228g Santa Ana (92705) ***(P-6514)***

Custom Hotel, Los Angeles *Also called Playa Proper Jv LLC* ***(P-16634)***

Custom Hotel LLC ....A.......310 645-0400
8639 Lincoln Blvd Los Angeles (90045) ***(P-16403)***

Custom Industries Inc ....E.......714 779-9101
1371 N Miller St Anaheim (92806) ***(P-5949)***

Custom Ingredients Inc (PA) ....E.......949 276-7994
160 Calle Iglesia Ste 102 San Clemente (92672) ***(P-2318)***

Custom Iron Corporation ....E.......949 939-4379
26895 Aliso Creek Rd Aliso Viejo (92656) ***(P-6610)***

Custom Iron Design (PA) ....F.......310 537-5936
522 E Banning St Compton (90222) ***(P-6959)***

Custom Laminators Inc ....F.......714 778-0895
1350 S Claudina St Anaheim (92805) ***(P-5448)***

Custom Lawn Services, Ventura *Also called American Landscape MGT Inc* ***(P-290)***

Custom Lawn Services, Canoga Park *Also called American Landscape MGT Inc* ***(P-233)***

Custom Leathercraft Mfg LLC (HQ) ....E.......323 752-2221
10240 Alameda St South Gate (90280) ***(P-5912)***

Custom Lithograph ....F.......323 778-7751
7006 Stanford Ave Los Angeles (90001) ***(P-4270)***

Custom Metal Fabricators, Orange *Also called Cmf Inc* ***(P-1479)***

Custom Metal Finishing Corp ....E.......310 532-5075
17804 S Western Ave Gardena (90248) ***(P-7971)***

Custom Molded Devices, Simi Valley *Also called Poly-Tainer Inc* ***(P-5480)***

Custom Pack Inc ....F.......714 534-2201
11621 Cardinal Cir Garden Grove (92843) ***(P-5928)***

Custom Packaging Design, Montclair *Also called Cpd Industries* ***(P-5495)***

Custom Pipe & Fabrication Inc (HQ) ....D.......800 553-3058
10560 Fern Ave Stanton (90680) ***(P-7534)***

Custom Printing, Oxnard *Also called Pinegrove Industries Inc* ***(P-4391)***

Custom Quality Door & Trim Inc ....E.......951 278-0066
1116 Bradford Cir Corona (92882) ***(P-3239)***

Custom Quilting Inc ....E.......714 731-7271
2832 Walnut Ave Ste D Tustin (92780) ***(P-3101)***

Custom Sensors & Tech Inc (HQ) ....A.......805 716-0322
1461 Lawrence Dr Thousand Oaks (91320) ***(P-9699)***

Custom Service Systems, Riverside *Also called Ghossain & Truelock Entps Inc* ***(P-17246)***

Custom Steel Fabrication Inc ....F.......562 907-2777
11966 Rivera Rd Santa Fe Springs (90670) ***(P-6611)***

Custom Suppression Inc ....F.......818 718-1040
26470 Ruether Ave Ste 106 Santa Clarita (91350) ***(P-9627)***

Custom Upholstered Furn Inc ....F.......323 731-3033
5000 W Jefferson Blvd Los Angeles (90016) ***(P-3500)***

Customer Loan Depot, Foothill Ranch *Also called Loandepotcom LLC* ***(P-15213)***

Customfab Inc ....C.......714 891-9119
7345 Orangewood Ave Garden Grove (92841) ***(P-5868)***

Customized Dist Svcs Inc ....D.......909 947-0084
3355 E Cedar St Ontario (91761) ***(P-23203)***

Customline Professional ....B.......714 996-1333
567 S Melrose St Placentia (92870) ***(P-17169)***

Cut N Clean Greens, Oxnard *Also called San Miguel Produce Inc* ***(P-18)***

Cutting Edge Creative LLC ....D.......562 907-7007
9944 Flower St Bellflower (90706) ***(P-3681)***

Cutting Edge Supply, Colton *Also called Black Diamond Blade Company* ***(P-7636)***

Cv & Da Holdings Inc (PA) ....D.......213 261-4161
3761 S Hill St Los Angeles (90007) ***(P-18786)***

Cv of Riverside, Riverside *Also called CV Wndows Dors Riverside Inc* ***(P-5950)***

CV Wndows Dors Riverside Inc ....F.......951 784-8766
6676 Lance Dr Riverside (92507) ***(P-5950)***

Cvb Financial Corp (PA) ....D.......909 980-4030
701 N Haven Ave Ste 350 Ontario (91764) ***(P-15018)***

Cvc Specialties, Vernon *Also called Continental Vitamin Co Inc* ***(P-4810)***

Cvc Technologies Inc ....E.......909 355-0311
10861 Business Dr Fontana (92337) ***(P-8067)***

Cvr, Orange *Also called CDK Global Inc* ***(P-15323)***

Cvr, Orange *Also called Computrzed Vhcl Rgstration Inc* ***(P-18024)***

Cvr Nitrogen LP (HQ) ....D.......310 571-9800
10877 Wilshire Blvd Fl 10 Los Angeles (90024) ***(P-5154)***

Cvrm, Indio *Also called Coachella Vly Rescue Mission* ***(P-21747)***

CVS Health Corporation ....D.......714 578-4601
777 S Harbor Blvd E-163 La Habra (90631) ***(P-12195)***

Cw Industries ....E.......562 432-5421
1735 Santa Fe Ave Long Beach (90813) ***(P-6612)***

ALPHABETIC

Employee Codes: A=Over 500 employees, B=251-500
C=101-250, D=51-100, E=20-50 F=10-19
2022 Southern California Business
Directory and Buyers Guide
© Mergent Inc. 1-800-342-5647
1107

Cw Industries Inc... D ... 661 399-5422
761 Majors Ct Bakersfield (93308) ***(P-14129)***
Cw Industries Inc (PA)... E ... **562 432-5421**
1735 Santa Fe Ave Long Beach (90813) ***(P-18973)***
Cw Network LLC (PA)... C ... **818 977-2500**
3300 W Olive Ave Fl 3 Burbank (91505) ***(P-12713)***
CWC Acquisition, Orange *Also called Cleveland Wrecking Company* ***(P-1611)***
Cwd LLC... D ... 626 961-5775
14528 Bonelli St City of Industry (91746) ***(P-9941)***
Cwd LLC (HQ)... E ... **310 218-1082**
21046 Figueroa St Ste B Carson (90745) ***(P-10039)***
Cwdre, Irvine *Also called Certified Wtr Dmage Rstrtion E* ***(P-17225)***
Cwf Inc... D ... 626 967-0500
251 E Front St Covina (91723) ***(P-17344)***
Cwic, Rcho STA Marg *Also called Chapmn-Wlters Intrcoastal Corp* ***(P-11409)***
Cwp Cabinets Inc... C ... 760 246-4530
10007 Yucca Rd Adelanto (92301) ***(P-1433)***
Cwpnc Inc... D ... 714 564-7904
1682 Langley Ave Irvine (92614) ***(P-1175)***
Cws, Orange *Also called Coil Winding Specialist Inc* ***(P-9625)***
Cws International, Orange *Also called Coilwscom Inc* ***(P-14749)***
CWT, Gardena *Also called Clean Water Technology Inc* ***(P-8373)***
Cwtv, Burbank *Also called Cw Network LLC* ***(P-12713)***
Cyber Medical Imaging Inc... E ... 888 937-9729
11300 W Olympic Blvd Los Angeles (90064) ***(P-11165)***
Cybercoders Inc... C ... 949 885-5151
6591 Irvine Center Dr # 200 Irvine (92618) ***(P-17409)***
Cybercopy Inc (PA)... E ... **310 736-1001**
2766 S La Cienega Blvd Los Angeles (90034) ***(P-17148)***
Cyberdefender Corporation... E ... 323 449-0774
617 W 7th St Fl 10 Los Angeles (90017) ***(P-17588)***
Cybernet Manufacturing Inc... A ... 949 600-8000
5 Holland Ste 201 Irvine (92618) ***(P-8152)***
Cyberpolicy Inc... C ... 877 626-9991
19584 Pine Valley Ave Porter Ranch (91326) ***(P-15559)***
Cyberscientific, Irvine *Also called Cybercoders Inc* ***(P-17409)***
Cybertech, Pomona *Also called Bio Cybernetics International* ***(P-11090)***
Cybertouch, Newbury Park *Also called Transparent Devices Inc* ***(P-8307)***
Cybrex Consulting Inc... D ... 513 999-2109
4470 W Sunset Blvd # 961 Los Angeles (90027) ***(P-17831)***
Cycle News Inc (PA)... E ... **949 863-7082**
17771 Mitchell N Irvine (92614) ***(P-3967)***
Cydcor LLC (PA)... D ... **805 277-5500**
29899 Agoura Rd Ste 100 Agoura Hills (91301) ***(P-23204)***
Cydwoq Inc... E ... 818 848-8307
2102 Kenmere Ave Burbank (91504) ***(P-5873)***
Cygal Art Deco Inc... F ... 424 288-4011
8687 Melrose Ave Ste B300 West Hollywood (90069) ***(P-3582)***
Cygnet Stampng & Fabrictng Inc... E ... 818 240-7574
916 Western Ave Glendale (91201) ***(P-7138)***
Cygnet Stampng & Fabrictng Inc (PA)... E ... **818 240-7574**
613 Justin Ave Glendale (91201) ***(P-7139)***
Cyi Pins Ltd... F ... 626 600-9017
6211 Sierra Ave Ste 147 Fontana (92336) ***(P-7061)***
Cynergy Prof Systems LLC... E ... 800 776-7978
23187 La Cadena Dr # 102 Laguna Hills (92653) ***(P-13713)***
Cypress Creek Holdings LLC... D ... 310 581-6299
3250 Ocean Park Blvd # 355 Santa Monica (90405) ***(P-12799)***
Cypress Creek Renewables LLC (PA)... C ... **310 581-6299**
3250 Ocean Park Blvd # 355 Santa Monica (90405) ***(P-12800)***
Cypress Manufacturing LLC... F ... 818 477-2777
25620 Rye Canyon Rd Ste B Valencia (91355) ***(P-5619)***
Cytec Aerospace Mtls CA Inc... C ... 714 899-0400
851 W 18th St Costa Mesa (92627) ***(P-2707)***
Cytec Engineered Materials, Costa Mesa *Also called Cytec Aerospace Mtls CA Inc* ***(P-2707)***
Cytec Engineered Materials Inc... E ... 714 632-8444
1191 N Hawk Cir Anaheim (92807) ***(P-4686)***
Cytec Engineered Materials Inc... C ... 714 630-9400
645 N Cypress St Orange (92867) ***(P-5216)***
Cytec Engineered Materials Inc... C ... 714 632-1174
1440 N Kraemer Blvd Anaheim (92806) ***(P-6390)***
Cytydel Plastics Inc... F ... 310 523-2884
17813 S Main St Ste 117 Gardena (90248) ***(P-5620)***
Cyu Lithographics Inc... E ... 888 878-9898
6951 Oran Cir Buena Park (90621) ***(P-4271)***
Czinger Vehicles, Los Angeles *Also called Czv Inc* ***(P-9942)***
Cznd Inc... D ... 323 378-6505
8444 Wilshire Blvd Fl 5 Beverly Hills (90211) ***(P-19346)***
Czv Inc... E ... 424 603-1450
2395 Silver Lake Blvd # 8 Los Angeles (90039) ***(P-9942)***
D & D Cremations Service, Vernon *Also called D & D Services Inc* ***(P-2126)***
D & D Gear Incorporated... C ... 714 692-6570
4890 E La Palma Ave Anaheim (92807) ***(P-10306)***
D & D Services Inc... E ... 323 261-4176
4105 Bandini Blvd Vernon (90058) ***(P-2126)***
D & D Technologies USA Inc... E ... 949 852-5140
17531 Metzler Ln Huntington Beach (92647) ***(P-6221)***
D & D Wholesale Distrs Inc... D ... 626 333-2111
777 Baldwin Park Blvd City of Industry (91746) ***(P-14619)***
D & G Manufacturing, Signal Hill *Also called Flex-Mate Inc* ***(P-6479)***
D & K Concrete Co, Fontana *Also called Dennie Manning Concrete Inc* ***(P-6089)***
D & M Plastics, San Dimas *Also called Han Rigid Plastics Corp USA* ***(P-5510)***
D & M Steel Inc... E ... 818 896-2070
13020 Pierce St Pacoima (91331) ***(P-6613)***
D & S Custom Plating Inc... F ... 714 537-5411
11552 Anabel Ave Garden Grove (92843) ***(P-10040)***
D & S Industries Inc... F ... 714 779-8074
4515 E Eisenhower Cir Anaheim (92807) ***(P-10307)***
D & S Media Group Inc... F ... 714 881-4700
16808 Armstrong Ave Ste 2 Irvine (92606) ***(P-4063)***
D - Link, Irvine *Also called D-Link Systems Incorporated* ***(P-13386)***
D A C, Carpinteria *Also called Dac International Inc* ***(P-7727)***
D and J Marketing Inc... E ... 310 538-1583
580 W 184th St Gardena (90248) ***(P-3171)***
D B Specialty Farms, Santa Maria *Also called Darensberries LLC* ***(P-25)***
D C H California Motors Inc... D ... 805 988-7900
1631 Auto Center Dr Oxnard (93036) ***(P-18820)***
D C N Wireless, Woodland Hills *Also called Digital Communications Network* ***(P-12505)***
D C S, Brea *Also called Diversfied Cmmnctions Svcs Inc* ***(P-12633)***
D C Shower Doors Inc... C ... 66- 257-1177
26121 Avenue Hall Valencia (91355) ***(P-12028)***
D D N, Chatsworth *Also called Datadirect Networks Inc* ***(P-8196)***
D D Office Products Inc... F ... 323 582-3400
5025 Hampton St Vernon (90058) ***(P-3750)***
D D Wire Co Inc (PA)... E ... **626 442-0459**
4335 Temple City Blvd Temple City (91780) ***(P-6614)***
D E I, Chino Hills *Also called Dynamic Enterprises Inc* ***(P-8576)***
D E X, Camarillo *Also called Data Exchange Corporation* ***(P-13388)***
D F Stauffer Biscuit Co Inc... E ... 7-4 546-6855
4041 W Garry Ave Santa Ana (92704) ***(P-2062)***
D G A, Los Angeles *Also called Directors Guild America Inc* ***(P-19228)***
D G A Machine Shop Inc... F ... 951 354-2113
5825 Ordway St Riverside (92504) ***(P-8566)***
D G A Mch Sp Blnchard Grinding, Riverside *Also called D G A Machine Shop Inc* ***(P-8566)***
D G Associates, Ventura *Also called Douglas Maxim Inc* ***(P-13302)***
D G Industries... F ... 714 990-3787
226 Viking Ave Brea (92821) ***(P-7726)***
D G X, E Rncho Dmngz *Also called Dependable Global Express Inc* ***(P-12444)***
D Hauptman Co Inc... F ... 323 734-2507
4856 W Jefferson Blvd Los Angeles (90016) ***(P-11411)***
D I F Group Inc... E ... 323 231-8800
1942 E 46th St Vernon (90058) ***(P-23012)***
D J American Supply Inc... C ... 323 582-2650
6122 S Eastern Ave Commerce (90040) ***(P-14150)***
D K Environmental, Vernon *Also called Demenno/Kerdoon Holdings* ***(P-5292)***
D K Fortune & Associates Inc... C ... 310 391-7266
5240 Sepulveda Blvd Culver City (90230) ***(P-20577)***
D L B Pallets (PA)... F ... **951 360-9896**
4510 Rutile St Riverside (92509) ***(P-3387)***
D Longo Inc... B ... 626 580-6000
3534 Peck Rd El Monte (91731) ***(P-18821)***
D M Camp & Sons (PA)... D ... **661 399-5511**
4520 E Merced Ave Bakersfield (93308) ***(P-104)***
D Mills Grnding Machining Inc... C ... 951 697-6847
6131 Quail Valley Ct Riverside (92507) ***(P-8567)***
D P I, Porterville *Also called Distributors Processing Inc* ***(P-2320)***
D P S Inc... C ... 714 564-7900
1682 Langley Ave Irvine (92614) ***(P-1176)***
D R X, Los Angeles *Also called Destinationrx Inc* ***(P-17595)***
D S S, Goleta *Also called Deployable Space Systems Inc* ***(P-22528)***
D S T Macdonald, Valencia *Also called Whi Solutions Inc* ***(P-13452)***
D V S Mdia Srvces/Intelestream, Burbank *Also called Dvs Media Services* ***(P-17149)***
D W I, Chino *Also called Diamond Wipes Intl Inc* ***(P-5013)***
D W Mack Co Inc... E ... 626 969-1817
900 W 8th St Azusa (91702) ***(P-5334)***
D X Communications Inc... E ... 323 256-3000
8160 Van Nuys Blvd Panorama City (91402) ***(P-9266)***
D&A Endeavors Inc... D ... 310 390-7540
8484 Wilshire Blvd # 605 Beverly Hills (90211) ***(P-1653)***
D&A Metal Fabrication Inc... F ... 818 780-8231
16129 Runnymede St Van Nuys (91406) ***(P-6615)***
D'Andrea Graphics, Cypress *Also called DAndrea Graphic Corportion* ***(P-1170)***
D'Veal Family and Youth Svcs, Pasadena *Also called DVeal Corporation* ***(P-22181)***
D-1280-X Inc... F ... 310 835-6909
126 N Marine Ave Wilmington (90744) ***(P-5250)***
D-Link Systems Incorporated... C ... 714 885-6000
14420 Myford Rd Ste 100 Irvine (92606) ***(P-13386)***
D-Mac Inc... E ... 714 808-3918
1105 E Discovery Ln Anaheim (92801) ***(P-3419)***
D-Tech Optoelectronics Inc... E ... 626 956-1100
18062 Rowland St City of Industry (91748) ***(P-9337)***
D.F. Industries, Chino *Also called Dick Farrell Industries Inc* ***(P-8088)***
D/K Mechanical Contractors Inc... D ... 714 970-0180
3870 E Eagle Dr Anaheim (92807) ***(P-1051)***
D3 Go, Encino *Also called D3publisher of America Inc* ***(P-17832)***
D3publisher of America Inc... D ... 310 268-0820
15910 Ventura Blvd # 800 Encino (91436) ***(P-17832)***
D7 LLC... D ... 808 630-9169
200 Spectrum Center Dr # 12 Irvine (92618) ***(P-23013)***
Da-Ly Glass Corp... E ... 323 589-5461
1193 W 2nd St Pomona (91766) ***(P-5951)***
Daart Engineering Company Inc... D ... 909 888-8696
4100 Garner Rd Riverside (92501) ***(P-1052)***
Daaze Inc... F ... 626 442-4961
1714 S Grove Ave Ste B Ontario (91761) ***(P-6815)***
Dac International Inc... E ... 805 684-8307
6390 Rose Ln Carpinteria (93013) ***(P-7727)***
Dacor (HQ)... D ... **626 799-1000**
14425 Clark Ave City of Industry (91745) ***(P-8988)***
DAd Investments... E ... 714 751-8500
2929 Halladay St Santa Ana (92705) ***(P-2416)***
DAd Investments... E ... 310 627-6316
16 Medlar Irvine (92618) ***(P-2417)***
Dadee Manufacturing LLC... E ... 602 276-4390
911 N Poinsettia St Santa Ana (92701) ***(P-9981)***

Mergent e-mail: customerrelations@mergent.com
1108
2022 Southern California Business Directory and Buyers Guide
(P-0000) Products & Services Section entry number
(PA)=Parent Co (HQ)=Headquarters (DH)=Div Headquarters

Dae Shin Usa Inc.....D.....714 578-8900
610 N Gilbert St Fullerton (92833) *(P-2595)*

Daicel America Holdings Inc.....B.....480 798-6737
21515 Hawthorne Blvd Torrance (90503) *(P-23014)*

Dailey & Associates.....D.....323 490-3847
8687 Melrose Ave Ste 100 West Hollywood (90069) *(P-17002)*

Daily Doses LLC (PA).....**E.....858 220-0076**
1130 S Shenandoah St Los Angeles (90035) *(P-3968)*

Daily Journal Corporation (PA).....**C.....213 229-5300**
915 E 1st St Los Angeles (90012) *(P-3969)*

Daily Manufacturing, San Bernardino *Also called Ten Days Manufacturing (P-14023)*

Daily News, Valencia *Also called Medianews Group Inc (P-4009)*

Daily Sports Seoul Usa Inc.....F.....213 487-9331
3550 Wilshire Blvd # 1912 Los Angeles (90010) *(P-3970)*

Dailylook Inc.....D.....888 888-6645
2445 E 12th St Ste B Los Angeles (90021) *(P-18499)*

Dailymedia Inc (PA).....**F.....541 821-5207**
8 E Figueroa St Ste 220 Santa Barbara (93101) *(P-3971)*

Dairy Farmers America Inc.....C.....805 653-0042
4375 N Ventura Ave Ventura (93001) *(P-1833)*

Dairy Queen.....E.....909 422-1501
1407 E Washington St Colton (92324) *(P-1812)*

Daisy Publishing Company Inc.....D.....661 295-1910
25233 Anza Dr Santa Clarita (91355) *(P-4064)*

Daisy Scout Publishing.....F.....714 630-6611
1200 N Barsten Way Anaheim (92806) *(P-4165)*

Daiwa Corporation.....D.....562 375-6800
11137 Warland Dr Cypress (90630) *(P-14075)*

Daiwa Golf Company Division, Cypress *Also called Daiwa Corporation (P-14075)*

Dako North America Inc.....D.....805 566-3037
6392 Via Real Carpinteria (93013) *(P-18500)*

Dakota Drilling & Concrete Inc.....E.....818 833-4654
2235 Statham Blvd Oxnard (93033) *(P-1521)*

Dal Chem Inc.....D.....951 279-9830
219 Glider Cir Corona (92878) *(P-14795)*

Dal-Tile Corporation.....F.....818 780-1301
16300 Stagg St Van Nuys (91406) *(P-13301)*

Dale Tiffany, La Mirada *Also called Amerdale Industries Inc (P-13157)*

Dallas-Fort Wrth Nephrology LP (HQ).....**E.....310 536-2400**
601 Hawaii St El Segundo (90245) *(P-21236)*

Daltile, Van Nuys *Also called Dal-Tile Corporation (P-13301)*

Dalton Trucking Inc (PA).....**C.....909 823-0663**
13560 Whittram Ave Fontana (92335) *(P-12196)*

Damac, Costa Mesa *Also called Bdfco Inc (P-9333)*

Damao Luggage Intl Inc.....A.....909 923-6531
1909 S Vineyard Ave Ontario (91761) *(P-14151)*

Damco USA Inc.....C.....951 360-4940
11900 Riverside Dr Jurupa Valley (91752) *(P-12273)*

Dameron Alloy Foundries (PA).....**D.....310 631-5165**
6330 Gateway Dr Ste B Cypress (90630) *(P-6275)*

Damo Clothing Company, Los Angeles *Also called Damo Textile Inc (P-14369)*

Damo Textile Inc.....E.....213 741-1323
12121 Wilshire Blvd # 1120 Los Angeles (90025) *(P-14369)*

Dan Copp Crushing Corp.....F.....714 777-6400
22765 Savi Ranch Pkwy E Yorba Linda (92887) *(P-570)*

Dan Freitas Electric.....D.....559 686-9572
983 E Levin Ave Tulare (93274) *(P-1241)*

Dan Gurneys All Amercn Racers, Santa Ana *Also called All American Racers Inc (P-10480)*

Dan Luna Inc.....F.....949 859-3631
23400 Peralta Dr Ste I Laguna Hills (92653) *(P-3240)*

Dan Tudor & Sons (PA).....**D.....661 792-2933**
11081 Zachary Ave Delano (93215) *(P-44)*

Dana Capital Group Inc (PA).....**D.....949 789-0200**
8001 Irvine Center Dr Irvine (92618) *(P-15239)*

Dana Creath Designs Ltd.....E.....714 662-0111
3030 Kilson Dr Santa Ana (92707) *(P-9126)*

Dana Innovations.....D.....949 492-7777
991 Calle Amanecer San Clemente (92673) *(P-9169)*

Dana Wharf Sportfishing, Dana Point *Also called San Clemente Sportfishing Inc (P-19667)*

Danchuk Manufacturing Inc.....D.....714 540-4363
3201 S Standard Ave Santa Ana (92705) *(P-10041)*

Danco Anodizing Inc (PA).....**E.....626 445-3303**
44 La Porte St Arcadia (91006) *(P-7245)*

Danco Anodizing Inc.....C.....909 923-0562
1750 E Monticello Ct Ontario (91761) *(P-7246)*

Danco Metal Surfacing, Arcadia *Also called Danco Anodizing Inc (P-7245)*

Danco Valve Company.....E.....562 925-2588
15230 Lakewood Blvd Bellflower (90706) *(P-7443)*

DAndrea Graphic Corportion.....D.....310 642-0260
6100 Gateway Dr Cypress (90630) *(P-17170)*

Dandy Don's Gourmet Ice Cream, San Fernando *Also called Don Whittemore Corp (P-1815)*

Dane Elec Corp USA (HQ).....**E.....949 450-2900**
17520 Von Karman Ave Irvine (92614) *(P-13387)*

Danell Bros Inc.....D.....559 582-1251
8265 Hanford Armona Rd Hanford (93230) *(P-153)*

Danell Custom Harvesting LLC.....C.....559 582-1251
8265 Hanford Armona Rd Hanford (93230) *(P-154)*

Dang Tha.....F.....714 898-0989
13050 Hoover St Westminster (92683) *(P-3621)*

Daniel Gerard Worldwide Inc.....D.....951 361-1111
13055 Jurupa Ave Fontana (92337) *(P-13562)*

Daniel J Edelman Inc.....D.....323 857-9100
5900 Wilshire Blvd # 2400 Los Angeles (90036) *(P-17083)*

Daniels Inc (PA).....**E.....801 621-3355**
74745 Leslie Ave Palm Desert (92260) *(P-4166)*

Danish Care Center, Atascadero *Also called Compass Health Inc (P-20289)*

Danne Montague-King Co (PA).....**E.....562 944-0230**
10420 Pioneer Blvd Santa Fe Springs (90670) *(P-14239)*

Danning Gill Damnd Kollitz LLP.....D.....310 277-0077
1901 Avenue Of The Stars # 450 Los Angeles (90067) *(P-21543)*

Danny Ryan Precision Contg Inc.....D.....949 642-6664
1818 N Orangethorpe Park Anaheim (92801) *(P-1612)*

Danone Us LLC.....C.....949 474-9670
3500 Barranca Pkwy # 240 Irvine (92606) *(P-1813)*

Danrich Welding Co Inc.....E.....562 634-4811
7001 Jackson St Paramount (90723) *(P-6816)*

Danville Materials LLC.....E.....714 399-0334
4020 E Leaverton Ct Anaheim (92807) *(P-11166)*

Danza Del Sol Winery Inc.....E.....951 302-6363
39050 De Portola Rd Temecula (92592) *(P-2181)*

Daqri LLC (HQ).....**D.....213 375-8830**
1201 W 5th St Ste T800 Los Angeles (90017) *(P-17589)*

Dar-Ken Inc.....E.....760 246-4010
10515 Rancho Rd Adelanto (92301) *(P-5335)*

Darbo Manufacturing Company.....E.....714 529-7693
363 Glenoaks St Brea (92821) *(P-2936)*

Darco Construction, Stanton *Also called Denver D Darling Inc (P-696)*

Darcy AK Corporation.....F.....949 650-5566
1760 Monrovia Ave Ste A22 Costa Mesa (92627) *(P-8568)*

Dardanella Electric Corp.....D.....818 445-5009
150 N Santa Anita Ave # 220 Arcadia (91006) *(P-13622)*

Darensberries LLC.....C.....805 937-8000
714 S Blosser Rd Santa Maria (93458) *(P-25)*

Darfield Industries Inc (PA).....**F.....818 247-8350**
4626 Sperry St Los Angeles (90039) *(P-6306)*

Daring Foods Inc (PA).....**C.....855 862-5825**
3505 Helms Ave Culver City (90232) *(P-14523)*

Darius E Lin MD Inc.....D.....215 601-6899
15 Blessing Irvine (92612) *(P-19779)*

Darly Filtration Inc (PA).....**E.....909 591-7999**
14225 Telephone Ave Chino (91710) *(P-13980)*

DART, Ridgecrest *Also called Desert Area Resources Training (P-17237)*

Dart Container Corp California (PA).....**B.....951 735-8115**
150 S Maple Ctr Corona (92880) *(P-5496)*

Dart Entities, Commerce *Also called Dart Transportation Svc A Corp (P-18734)*

Dart Entities, Commerce *Also called Dart International A Corp (P-12197)*

Dart International A Corp (HQ).....**C.....323 264-8746**
1430 S Eastman Ave Commerce (90023) *(P-12197)*

Dart Transportation Svc A Corp (PA).....**C.....323 981-8205**
1430 S Eastman Ave Ste 1 Commerce (90023) *(P-18734)*

Dart Warehouse Corporation (HQ).....**B.....323 264-1011**
1430 S Eastman Ave Ste 1 Commerce (90023) *(P-12198)*

Daryls Pet Shop.....F.....909 793-1788
208 E State St Redlands (92373) *(P-11654)*

Dasco Engineering Corp.....C.....310 326-2277
24747 Crenshaw Blvd Torrance (90505) *(P-10308)*

Dasol Inc.....C.....310 327-6700
16210 S Avalon Blvd Gardena (90248) *(P-9019)*

Data Aire Inc (HQ).....**C.....800 347-2473**
230 W Blueridge Ave Orange (92865) *(P-8336)*

Data Circle Inc.....F.....949 260-6569
3333 Michelson Dr Ste 735 Irvine (92612) *(P-9497)*

Data Exchange, Camarillo *Also called Dex Corporation (P-22531)*

Data Exchange Corporation (PA).....**B.....805 388-1711**
3600 Via Pescador Camarillo (93012) *(P-13388)*

Data Lights Rigging LLC.....E.....818 786-0536
7508 Tyrone Ave Van Nuys (91405) *(P-8894)*

Data Linkage Software Inc.....F.....310 781-3056
2421 W 205th St Ste D207 Torrance (90501) *(P-17833)*

Data Processing Design Inc.....F.....714 695-1000
1409 Glenneyre St Ste B Laguna Beach (92651) *(P-17590)*

Data Solder Inc.....F.....714 429-9866
2915 Kilson Dr Santa Ana (92707) *(P-9031)*

Data Trace Info Svcs LLC (HQ).....**D.....714 250-6700**
4 First American Way Santa Ana (92707) *(P-23531)*

Database Marketing Group Inc.....D.....714 727-0800
300 Commerce Ste 200 Irvine (92602) *(P-17131)*

Database Works Inc.....F.....714 203-8800
500 S Kraemer Blvd # 110 Brea (92821) *(P-17834)*

Databyte Technology Inc (PA).....**E.....626 305-0500**
2300 Peck Rd City of Industry (90601) *(P-13683)*

Datadirect Networks Inc (PA).....**C.....818 700-7600**
9351 Deering Ave Chatsworth (91311) *(P-8196)*

Datallegro Inc.....D.....949 680-3000
85 Enterprise Ste 200 Aliso Viejo (92656) *(P-13389)*

Datametrics Corporation.....E.....805 577-9710
25 E Easy St Simi Valley (93065) *(P-8249)*

Datatronics Romoland Inc.....D.....951 928-7700
28151 Us Highway 74 Menifee (92585) *(P-8867)*

Datazeo Inc.....F.....805 461-3458
8655 Morro Rd Ste C Atascadero (93422) *(P-17835)*

Dauntless Industries Inc.....E.....626 966-4494
806 N Grand Ave Covina (91724) *(P-7794)*

Dauntless Molds, Covina *Also called Dauntless Industries Inc (P-7794)*

Davalan Fresh, Los Angeles *Also called Davalan Sales Inc (P-14620)*

Davalan Sales Inc.....C.....213 623-2500
1601 E Olympic Blvd # 325 Los Angeles (90021) *(P-14620)*

Davco Enterprises Inc.....F.....714 432-0600
3301 W Segerstrom Ave Santa Ana (92704) *(P-5182)*

Dave Williams Plbg & Elec Inc.....C.....760 296-1397
75140 Saint Charles Pl C Palm Desert (92211) *(P-1053)*

Dave's Donuts & Baking Co, Gardena *Also called Bake R Us Inc (P-1980)*

Davenport International Corp.....F.....818 765-6400
7230 Coldwater Canyon Ave North Hollywood (91605) *(P-9170)*

David & Goliath LLC.....C.....310 445-5200
909 N Pacific Coast Hwy # 700 El Segundo (90245) *(P-17003)*

ALPHABETIC

David A Campbell Corporation C 951 785-4444
3060 Adams St Riverside (92504) *(P-18822)*

David and Margaret Home Inc C 909 596-5921
1350 3rd St La Verne (91750) *(P-22099)*

David B Anderson E 805 489-0661
174 Suburban Rd Ste 100 San Luis Obispo (93401) *(P-4272)*

David C Han DDS A Prof Corp (PA) **D 661 254-1924**
41253 12th St W Ste B Palmdale (93551) *(P-20172)*

David Engineering & Mfg, Corona *Also called David Engineering & Mfg Inc (P-7140)*

David Engineering & Mfg Inc E 951 735-5200
1230 Quarry St Corona (92879) *(P-7140)*

David Grment Ctng Fsing Svc In E 323 216-1574
5008 S Boyle Ave Vernon (90058) *(P-2937)*

David H Fell & Co Inc (PA) **E 323 722-9992**
6009 Bandini Blvd Los Angeles (90040) *(P-6291)*

David Haid E 323 752-8096
8619 Crocker St Los Angeles (90003) *(P-3724)*

David Kopf Instruments E 818 352-3274
7324 Elmo St Tujunga (91042) *(P-10967)*

David L Manwarren Corp E 909 989-5883
9146 9th St Rancho Cucamonga (91730) *(P-758)*

David Levy Co Inc E 562 404-9998
12753 Moore St Cerritos (90703) *(P-13714)*

David Margaret Youth Fmly Svcs, La Verne *Also called David and Margaret Home Inc (P-22099)*

David Ollis Landscape Dev Inc E 909 307-1911
450 Kansas St Ste 104 Redlands (92373) *(P-298)*

David Oppenheimer and Co I LLC D 909 631-2600
15345 Frfeld Rnch Rd Ste Chino Hills (91709) *(P-14462)*

David Oppenheimer and Co I LLC D 559 636-7700
317 W Main St Visalia (93291) *(P-14463)*

David Oppenheimer and Co I LLC D 310 900-7140
1071 E 233rd St 2 Carson (90745) *(P-14464)*

David S Boyer MD Inc D 818 754-2090
12840 Rverside Dr Ste 402 North Hollywood (91607) *(P-19780)*

David S Tsai DDS Inc (PA) **F 626 358-9136**
400 Hillcrest Blvd Arcadia (91006) *(P-4812)*

David Shield Security Inc D 310 849-4950
23945 Calabasas Rd # 108 Calabasas (91302) *(P-18269)*

David Wilson's Villa Ford, Orange *Also called Villa Ford Inc (P-18807)*

David-Kleis II LLC D 951 845-3125
1665 E Eighth St Beaumont (92223) *(P-21410)*

Davidson Enterprises Inc E 661 325-2145
3223 Brittan St Bakersfield (93308) *(P-1654)*

Davidson Hotel Partners Lp A 818 707-1220
30100 Agoura Rd Agoura Hills (91301) *(P-16404)*

Davidson Optronics Inc E 626 962-5181
9087 Arrow Rte Ste 180 Rancho Cucamonga (91730) *(P-10877)*

Davidsons AC & Htg Inc E 909 885-2703
495 S Sierra Way San Bernardino (92408) *(P-1054)*

Davidsons AC Htg & Sh, San Bernardino *Also called Davidsons AC & Htg Inc (P-1054)*

Davina Douthard Inc F 310 540-5120
400 Crprate Pinte Ste 300 Culver City (90230) *(P-23431)*

Davinci Schools E 310 725-5800
201 N Douglas St El Segundo (90245) *(P-18501)*

Davis Research LLC C 818 591-2408
26610 Agoura Rd Ste 240 Calabasas (91302) *(P-22878)*

Davis Wire Corporation (HQ) **C 626 969-7651**
5555 Irwindale Ave Irwindale (91706) *(P-6222)*

Davis Wright Tremaine LLP D 213 633-6800
865 S Figueroa St # 2400 Los Angeles (90017) *(P-21544)*

Daviselen Advertising Inc (PA) **C 213 688-7000**
865 S Figueroa St # 1200 Los Angeles (90017) *(P-17004)*

Davita - Riverside LLC (HQ) **E 310 536-2400**
601 Hawaii St El Segundo (90245) *(P-21237)*

Davita Hesperia Dialysis Ctr, Hesperia *Also called Davita Inc (P-21238)*

Davita Hesperia Dialysis Ctr, Hesperia *Also called Total Renal Care Inc (P-21267)*

Davita Inc C 310 536-2406
14135 Main St Ste 501 Hesperia (92345) *(P-21238)*

Davita Inc B 949 930-4400
15271 Laguna Canyon Rd Irvine (92618) *(P-21239)*

Davita Magan Management Inc (HQ) **C 626 331-6411**
420 W Rowland St Covina (91723) *(P-19781)*

Davita Medical Management LLC D 562 923-4911
8311 Florence Ave Downey (90240) *(P-21411)*

Davita Medical Management LLC D 562 432-5661
1081 Long Beach Blvd # 10 Long Beach (90813) *(P-21412)*

Davita Medical Management LLC D 714 995-1000
1236 N Magnolia Ave Anaheim (92801) *(P-21413)*

Davita Medical Management LLC D 714 968-0068
19066 Magnolia St Huntington Beach (92646) *(P-21414)*

Davita Medical Management LLC D 714 835-8501
901 W Civic Center Dr # 120 Santa Ana (92703) *(P-21415)*

Davita Medical Management LLC D 626 309-7600
9810 Las Tunas Dr Temple City (91780) *(P-19782)*

Davita Medical Management LLC D 714 252-1135
4281 Katella Ave Ste 220 Los Alamitos (90720) *(P-19783)*

Davita Medical Management LLC D 818 226-3666
7301 Med Ctr Dr Ste 500 West Hills (91307) *(P-21416)*

Davita Medical Management LLC D 562 304-2100
3932 Long Beach Blvd Long Beach (90807) *(P-19784)*

Davita Medical Management LLC D 310 783-5567
2160 W 190th St Torrance (90504) *(P-21417)*

Davita Medical Management LLC D 562 420-1338
6226 E Spring St Ste 100 Long Beach (90815) *(P-19785)*

Davita Medical Management LLC D 562 429-2473
4910 Airport Plaza Dr Long Beach (90815) *(P-21418)*

Davita Medical Management LLC D 562 988-7000
2600 Redondo Ave Ste 405 Long Beach (90806) *(P-19786)*

Davita Medical Management LLC D 310 316-0811
502 Torrance Blvd Redondo Beach (90277) *(P-19787)*

Davita Medical Management LLC D 323 720-1144
2601 Via Campo Montebello (90640) *(P-19788)*

Davita Medical Management LLC D 626 444-0333
3144 Santa Anita Ave # 2 El Monte (91733) *(P-19789)*

Davita Medical Management LLC D 562 426-3333
2699 Atlantic Ave Long Beach (90806) *(P-19790)*

Davita Medical Management LLC (HQ) **A 310 354-4200**
2175 Park Pl El Segundo (90245) *(P-19791)*

Davita Medical Management LLC D 626 358-0269
931 Buena Vista St # 405 Duarte (91010) *(P-19792)*

Davita Medical Management LLC D 714 964-6229
3501 S Harbor Blvd Santa Ana (92704) *(P-21419)*

Dawn Food Products Inc C 714 258-1223
15601 Mosher Ave Tustin (92780) *(P-1994)*

Dawson & Dawson Staffing Inc (PA) **D 949 421-3966**
26522 La Alameda Ste 110 Mission Viejo (92691) *(P-17410)*

Dawson D7, LLC, Irvine *Also called D7 LLC (P-23013)*

Dawson Enterprises (PA) **E 562 424-8564**
2853 Cherry Ave Signal Hill (90755) *(P-7667)*

Day Care Center, San Luis Obispo *Also called Community Action Prtnr San Lui (P-22007)*

Day Star Educational Center, Fullerton *Also called Westview Services Inc (P-21928)*

Day Star Industries F 562 926-8800
13727 Excelsior Dr Santa Fe Springs (90670) *(P-3241)*

Daylight Transport LLC (PA) **D 310 507-8200**
1501 Hughes Way Ste 200 Long Beach (90810) *(P-12029)*

Days Inn, Glendale *Also called JP Allen Extended Stay (P-16516)*

Days Inn, Los Angeles *Also called Hollywood Partnership (P-16489)*

Daytec Center LLC F 760 995-3515
17469 Lemon St Hesperia (92345) *(P-10489)*

Daytona Surfise, North Hollywood *Also called Century National Properties (P-15374)*

Daz Inc F 949 724-8800
2500 White Rd Ste B Irvine (92614) *(P-8895)*

Daz Systems LLC B 310 640-1300
1003 E 4th Pl Ste 800 Los Angeles (90013) *(P-17591)*

Db Building Fasteners, Ontario *Also called DB Building Fasteners Inc (P-7019)*

DB Building Fasteners Inc (PA) **F 909 581-6740**
5555 E Gibralter Ontario (91764) *(P-7019)*

Db Studios Inc E 949 833-0100
17032 Murphy Ave Irvine (92614) *(P-11655)*

DBC Printing Incorporated F 805 988-8855
220 Bernoulli Cir Oxnard (93030) *(P-4273)*

Dbv Inc (PA) **C 323 857-5577**
314 N Vista St Los Angeles (90036) *(P-4813)*

DC Partners Inc (PA) **E 714 558-9444**
19329 Bryant St Northridge (91324) *(P-6391)*

DC Shoes Inc (HQ) **C 714 889-4206**
5600 Argosy Ave Ste 100 Huntington Beach (92649) *(P-2805)*

Dc-001 Inc F 833 526-5332
10541 Calle Lee Ste 125 Los Alamitos (90720) *(P-10581)*

DCH Acura of Temecula D 877 847-9532
26705 Ynez Rd Temecula (92591) *(P-18896)*

DCH Gardena Honda C 310 515-5700
15541 S Western Ave Gardena (90249) *(P-18823)*

DCI Hollow Metal On Demand, Fontana *Also called Door Components Inc (P-6695)*

Dcl, Ontario *Also called Discopylabs (P-9214)*

Dcli, Huntington Beach *Also called Direct Chassislink Inc (P-17345)*

Dcor LLC (PA) **C 805 535-2000**
1000 Town Center Dr Fl 6 Oxnard (93036) *(P-445)*

DCS Corporation D 760 384-5600
137 W Drummond Ave Ste C Ridgecrest (93555) *(P-22526)*

Dct, Fontana *Also called Desert Coastal Transport Inc (P-12033)*

Dcw Services LLC D 310 324-3147
20500 Denker Ave Torrance (90501) *(P-23205)*

Dcx-Chol Enterprises Inc (PA) **D 310 516-1692**
12831 S Figueroa St Los Angeles (90061) *(P-9360)*

Dcx-Chol Enterprises Inc E 310 516-1692
12831 S Figueroa St Los Angeles (90061) *(P-9361)*

Dcx-Chol Enterprises Inc E 562 927-5531
7450 Scout Ave Bell (90201) *(P-9700)*

Dcx-Chol Enterprises Inc F 310 516-1692
12831 S Figueroa St Los Angeles (90061) *(P-9362)*

Dcx-Chol Enterprises Inc E 310 525-1205
12831 S Figueroa St Los Angeles (90061) *(P-9363)*

Dda Holdings Inc E 213 624-5200
834 S Broadway Ste 600 Los Angeles (90014) *(P-2938)*

De Berns Company, Long Beach *Also called Berns Bros Inc (P-8527)*

De Castro W Chdrow Mndler Glck D 310 478-2541
10960 Wilshire Blvd # 14 Los Angeles (90024) *(P-21545)*

De La Cruz Products, Paramount *Also called Dlc Laboratories Inc (P-4816)*

De La Mare Engineering Inc E 818 365-9208
1908 1st St San Fernando (91340) *(P-19224)*

De La Torre Ldscp & Maint Corp D 951 549-3525
656 Paseo Grande Corona (92882) *(P-299)*

De Larshe Cabinetry LLC E 909 627-2757
2000 S Reservoir St Pomona (91766) *(P-3242)*

De Leon Entps Elec Spclist Inc E 818 252-6690
11934 Allegheny St Sun Valley (91352) *(P-9397)*

De Menno-Kerdoon Trading Co (HQ) **C 310 537-7100**
2000 N Alameda St Compton (90222) *(P-5251)*

De Nora Water Technologies LLC F 310 618-9700
1230 Rosecrans Ave # 300 Manhattan Beach (90266) *(P-8378)*

De Novo Software LLC E 213 814-1240
207 N Sierra Madre Blvd # 1 Pasadena (91107) *(P-17836)*

De Vries International Inc (PA) **D 949 252-1212**
17671 Armstrong Ave Irvine (92614) *(P-494)*

Mergent e-mail: customerrelations@mergent.com
1110
2022 Southern California Business Directory and Buyers Guide
(P-0000) Products & Services Section entry number
(PA)=Parent Co (HQ)=Headquarters (DH)=Div Headquarters

De Well Container Shipping Inc ......D......310 735-8600
5553 Bandini Blvd Unit A Bell (90201) *(P-12443)*
Dealership Auto Dtail Rstrtons, Monrovia *Also called Executive Auto Reconditioning (P-18914)*
Dealersocket Inc (PA) ......D......**949 900-0300**
100 Avenida La Pata San Clemente (92673) *(P-17592)*
Dealsaday Inc ......F......626 964-4266
1819 Floradale Ave South El Monte (91733) *(P-8197)*
Deamco Corporation ......E......323 890-1190
6520 E Washington Blvd Commerce (90040) *(P-7690)*
Dean Distributors Inc ......E......323 587-8147
5015 Hallmark Pkwy San Bernardino (92407) *(P-2418)*
Dean Goodman Inc ......D......714 229-8999
10833 Valley View St # 240 Cypress (90630) *(P-15834)*
Dean L Davis MD ......E......661 632-5000
2215 Truxtun Ave Bakersfield (93301) *(P-21766)*
Deanco Healthcare LLC ......A......818 787-2222
14850 Roscoe Blvd Panorama City (91402) *(P-20743)*
Deans Certified Welding Inc ......F......951 676-0242
27645 Commerce Center Dr Temecula (92590) *(P-18974)*
Dear John American Classic, Arcadia *Also called Dear John Denim Inc (P-2567)*
Dear John Denim Inc ......F......626 350-5100
12318 Lower Azusa Rd Arcadia (91006) *(P-2567)*
Deardorff Family Farm, Oxnard *Also called Deardorff-Jackson Co (P-14621)*
Deardorff-Jackson Co ......E......805 487-7801
400 Lombard St Oxnard (93030) *(P-14621)*
Debisys Inc (PA) ......D......**949 699-1401**
27442 Portola Pkwy # 150 Foothill Ranch (92610) *(P-15127)*
Debmar/Mercury LLC ......E......310 393-6000
2700 Colorado Ave Santa Monica (90404) *(P-19115)*
Debtmerica LLC ......D......714 389-4200
3100 S Harbor Blvd # 250 Santa Ana (92704) *(P-16953)*
Debtmerica Relief, Santa Ana *Also called Debtmerica LLC (P-16953)*
Dec, Santa Ana *Also called Dynasty Electronic Company LLC (P-9399)*
Dec Fabricators Inc ......F......562 403-3626
16916 Gridley Pl Cerritos (90703) *(P-7552)*
Deca International Corp ......E......714 367-5900
10700 Norwalk Blvd Santa Fe Springs (90670) *(P-10582)*
Decco Graphics Inc ......E......310 534-2861
24411 Frampton Ave Harbor City (90710) *(P-7141)*
Decco US Post-Harvest Inc (HQ) ......E......**800 221-0925**
1713 S California Ave Monrovia (91016) *(P-5169)*
Deccofelt Corporation ......E......626 963-8511
555 S Vermont Ave Glendora (91741) *(P-2723)*
Decision Ready Solutions Inc ......E......949 400-1126
400 Spectrum Center Dr # 2050 Irvine (92618) *(P-15186)*
Decisionpoint Systems Intl Inc (HQ) ......E......**949 465-0065**
8697 Research Dr Irvine (92618) *(P-18028)*
DECKERS BRANDS, Goleta *Also called Deckers Outdoor Corporation (P-3073)*
Deckers Outdoor Corporation (PA) ......A......**805 967-7611**
250 Coromar Dr Goleta (93117) *(P-3073)*
Deco, Arcadia *Also called Dardanella Electric Corp (P-13622)*
Deco Enterprises Inc ......D......323 726-2575
2917 Vail Ave Commerce (90040) *(P-9082)*
Deco Lighting, Commerce *Also called Deco Enterprises Inc (P-9082)*
Decorative Woods Lbr & Molding, Irvine *Also called Decwood Inc (P-13207)*
Decorators Rug Warehouse Inc (PA) ......D......**310 638-8300**
1810 Loma Vista Dr Beverly Hills (90210) *(P-2688)*
Decore-Ative Spc NC LLC (PA) ......A......**626 254-9191**
2772 Peck Rd Monrovia (91016) *(P-3243)*
Decore-Ative Spc NC LLC ......C......626 960-7731
4414 Azusa Canyon Rd Irwindale (91706) *(P-3244)*
Decra Roofing Systems Inc (HQ) ......D......**951 272-8180**
1230 Railroad St Corona (92882) *(P-6817)*
Decron Properties Corp (PA) ......C......**323 556-6600**
6222 Wilshire Blvd # 400 Los Angeles (90048) *(P-15835)*
Decton Inc (PA) ......C......**949 851-0111**
15635 Alton Pkwy Ste 475 Irvine (92618) *(P-17411)*
Decton Trade Solutions, Irvine *Also called Decton Inc (P-17411)*
Decurion Corporation (PA) ......D......**310 659-9432**
120 N Robertson Blvd Fl 3 Los Angeles (90048) *(P-19272)*
Decwood Inc ......E......949 588-9663
3 Oldfield Irvine (92618) *(P-13207)*
Dedicated Dental Systems Inc ......D......661 397-5513
9800 S La Cnga Blvd Inglewood (90301) *(P-20173)*
Dedicated Fleet Systems Inc (PA) ......D......**909 590-8209**
1350 Philadelphia St Pomona (91766) *(P-11964)*
Dedicated Media Inc (PA) ......D......**310 524-9400**
1221 Hermosa Ave Ste 210 Hermosa Beach (90254) *(P-17005)*
Dee Engineering Inc ......E......909 947-5616
1893 S Lake Pl Ontario (91761) *(P-10042)*
Defense Systems Sector, Woodland Hills *Also called Northrop Grumman Systems Corp (P-22855)*
Defined Cntrbtion Tr Fund For ......D......213 385-6161
501 Shatto Pl Ste 500 Los Angeles (90020) *(P-16176)*
Definitive Media Corp (PA) ......E......**714 305-5900**
155 El Camino Real Ste B Tustin (92780) *(P-17837)*
Defoe Furniture For Kids Inc ......F......909 947-4459
910 S Grove Ave Ontario (91761) *(P-3622)*
Degenerate Sound Inc (PA) ......D......**818 385-1933**
16000 Ventura Blvd Encino (91436) *(P-1242)*
Deiny Automotive Inc ......F......818 362-5865
13040 Bradley Ave Sylmar (91342) *(P-9943)*
Dekra-Lite Industries Inc ......D......714 436-0705
3102 W Alton Ave Santa Ana (92704) *(P-18502)*
Del AMO Construction ......D......310 378-6203
23840 Madison St Torrance (90505) *(P-759)*
Del AMO Grdns Cnvalescent Hosp, Torrance *Also called Del AMO Grdns Cnvlscent Hosp S (P-20308)*
Del AMO Grdns Cnvlscent Hosp S ......D......310 378-4233
22419 Kent Ave Torrance (90505) *(P-20308)*
Del AMO Hospital Inc ......B......310 530-1151
23700 Camino Del Sol Torrance (90505) *(P-21297)*
Del Mar Convalescent Hospital, Santa Ana *Also called Gibralter Convalescent Hosp (P-20592)*
Del Mar Die Casting Co, Gardena *Also called Del Mar Industries (P-6377)*
Del Mar Industries (PA) ......D......**323 321-0600**
12901 S Western Ave Gardena (90249) *(P-6377)*
Del Mar Industries ......E......310 327-2634
12901 S Western Ave Gardena (90249) *(P-6378)*
Del Mar Seafoods Inc ......C......805 850-0421
1449 Spinnaker Dr Ventura (93001) *(P-14569)*
Del Real LLC (PA) ......C......**951 681-0395**
11041 Inland Ave Jurupa Valley (91752) *(P-1924)*
Del Real Foods, Jurupa Valley *Also called Del Real LLC (P-1924)*
Del Rey Yacht Club ......D......310 823-4664
13900 Palawan Way Marina Del Rey (90292) *(P-19557)*
Del Rio Convalescent, Bell Gardens *Also called Del Rio Sanitarium Inc (P-20309)*
Del Rio Sanitarium Inc ......C......562 927-6586
7002 Gage Ave Bell Gardens (90201) *(P-20309)*
Del Rosa Villa Inc ......D......909 885-3261
2018 Del Rosa Ave San Bernardino (92404) *(P-20310)*
Del Taco Restaurants Inc (PA) ......C......**949 462-9300**
25521 Commercentre Dr # 200 Lake Forest (92630) *(P-16204)*
Del West Engineering Inc (PA) ......C......**661 295-5700**
28128 Livingston Ave Valencia (91355) *(P-10043)*
Del West USA, Valencia *Also called Del West Engineering Inc (P-10043)*
Delafield Corporation (PA) ......C......**626 303-0740**
1520 Flower Ave Duarte (91010) *(P-8569)*
Delafield Fluid Technology, Duarte *Also called Delafield Corporation (P-8569)*
Delafoil Holdings Inc (PA) ......B......**949 752-4580**
18500 Von Karman Ave # 450 Irvine (92612) *(P-6818)*
Delamo Manufacturing Inc ......D......323 936-3566
7171 Telegraph Rd Montebello (90640) *(P-5621)*
Delaney Manufacturing Inc (PA) ......E......**661 587-6681**
6810 Downing Ave Bakersfield (93308) *(P-11656)*
Delano Dst Sklled Nrsing Fclty, Delano *Also called North Kern S Tulare Hosp Dst (P-20870)*
Delano Dst Sklled Nrsing Fclty ......D......661 720-2100
1509 Tokay St Delano (93215) *(P-20311)*
Delano Growers Grape Products ......D......661 725-3255
32351 Bassett Ave Delano (93215) *(P-2319)*
Delano Waste Water Treatment, Delano *Also called City of Delano (P-8371)*
Delaware Systems Technology, San Bernardino *Also called Systems Technology Inc (P-8078)*
Delcan Corporation ......C......714 562-5725
2201 Dupont Dr Ste 200 Irvine (92612) *(P-22527)*
Delfin Design & Mfg Inc ......E......949 888-4644
15672 Producer Ln Huntington Beach (92649) *(P-5622)*
Delgado Brothers LLC ......E......323 233-9793
647 E 59th St Los Angeles (90001) *(P-3442)*
Delicate Productions Inc (PA) ......D......**415 484-1174**
874 Verdulera St Camarillo (93010) *(P-19309)*
Deliver-It, Anaheim *Also called Di Overnite LLC (P-12127)*
Delivery Zone LLC ......F......323 780-0888
120 S Anderson St Los Angeles (90033) *(P-2419)*
Della Robbia Inc ......E......951 372-9199
796 E Harrison St Corona (92879) *(P-3546)*
Dellarise, Pasadena *Also called Pak Group LLC (P-2071)*
Dellarobbia Inc (PA) ......E......**949 251-9532**
119 Waterworks Way Irvine (92618) *(P-3501)*
Delmart Farms Inc ......D......661 746-2148
30988 Riverside Cntrl Vly Shafter (93263) *(P-45)*
Delnorte Rgnal Rcycl Trnsf Stn (PA) ......D......**805 278-8200**
111 S Del Norte Blvd Oxnard (93030) *(P-12944)*
Deloitte & Touche LLP ......A......213 688-0800
555 W 5th St Ste 2700 Los Angeles (90013) *(P-22776)*
Deloitte & Touche LLP ......C......213 688-0800
555 W 5th St Ste 2700 Los Angeles (90013) *(P-22777)*
Delori Foods, City of Industry *Also called Delori-Nutifood Products Inc (P-2420)*
Delori-Nutifood Products Inc ......E......626 965-3006
17043 Green Dr City of Industry (91745) *(P-2420)*
Delphi Control Systems Inc ......F......909 593-8099
2806 Metropolitan Pl Pomona (91767) *(P-10689)*
Delphi Display Systems Inc ......D......714 825-3400
3550 Hyland Ave Costa Mesa (92626) *(P-8250)*
Delphic Enterprises Inc ......D......661 254-2000
23026 Soledad Canyon Rd Santa Clarita (91350) *(P-198)*
Delt Industries Inc ......F......805 579-0213
90 W Easy St Ste 2 Simi Valley (93065) *(P-6414)*
Delta Computer Consulting ......C......310 541-9440
25550 Hawthorne Blvd # 106 Torrance (90505) *(P-18172)*
Delta Creative Inc ......C......800 423-4135
2690 Pellissier Pl City of Industry (90601) *(P-14096)*
Delta D V H Circuits Inc ......F......818 786-8241
16117 Leadwell St Van Nuys (91406) *(P-9398)*
Delta Dvh Circuits, Van Nuys *Also called Ambay Circuits Inc (P-9376)*
Delta Fabrication Inc ......D......818 407-4000
9600 De Soto Ave Chatsworth (91311) *(P-6819)*
Delta Floral Distributors Inc ......C......323 751-8116
6810 West Blvd Los Angeles (90043) *(P-14882)*
Delta Galil USA Inc ......D......949 296-0380
16912 Von Karman Ave Irvine (92606) *(P-14370)*
Delta Hi-Tech ......C......818 407-4000
9600 De Soto Ave Chatsworth (91311) *(P-8570)*
Delta Nrsing Rhabilitation Ctr, Visalia *Also called Delta Nrsing Rhblttion Hosp In (P-20312)*

ALPHABETIC

Employee Codes: A=Over 500 employees, B=251-500 C=101-250, D=51-100, E=20-50 F=10-19
2022 Southern California Business Directory and Buyers Guide
© Mergent Inc. 1-800-342-5647
1111

Delta Nrsing Rhblttion Hosp In....E....559 625-4003
514 N Bridge St Visalia (93291) ***(P-20312)***

Delta Pacific Activewear Inc....D....714 871-9281
331 S Hale Ave Fullerton (92831) ***(P-2629)***

Delta Packaging Products, Los Angeles *Also called E & S Paper Co* ***(P-14208)***

Delta Plastics, Glendale *Also called Califrnia Elctrmechanical Repr* ***(P-19027)***

Delta Printing Solutions Inc....C....661 257-0584
28210 Avenue Stanford Valencia (91355) ***(P-4274)***

Delta Scientific Corporation (PA)....**C....661 575-1100**
40355 Delta Ln Palmdale (93551) ***(P-18370)***

Delta Stag Manufacturing....E....562 904-6444
1818 E Rosslynn Ave Fullerton (92831) ***(P-9982)***

Delta T Thermal Solutions....F....800 928-5828
8323 Loch Lomond Dr Pico Rivera (90660) ***(P-8087)***

Delta Tau Data Systems Inc Cal (HQ)....**C....818 998-2095**
9200 Oakdale Ave Fl 9 Chatsworth (91311) ***(P-8119)***

Delta Tech Industries LLC....E....909 673-1900
1901 S Vineyard Ave Ontario (91761) ***(P-9114)***

Delta Trading LP....E....661 834-5560
17731 Millux Rd Bakersfield (93311) ***(P-5270)***

Delta-Stag Truck Body, Fullerton *Also called Delta Stag Manufacturing* ***(P-9982)***

Deltronic Corporation....D....714 545-5800
3900 W Segerstrom Ave Santa Ana (92704) ***(P-10832)***

Deluxe Auto Carriers Inc....D....909 746-0900
4788 Brookhollow Cir Jurupa Valley (92509) ***(P-11965)***

Deluxe Check Printers, Lancaster *Also called Deluxe Corporation* ***(P-4609)***

Deluxe Corporation....B....661 942-1144
42933 Business Ctr Pkwy Lancaster (93535) ***(P-4609)***

Deluxe Digital Studios, Burbank *Also called Deluxe Media Inc* ***(P-19227)***

Deluxe Entertainment Svcs Inc....D....323 960-7303
2400 W Empire Ave Burbank (91504) ***(P-19225)***

Deluxe Entrmt Svcs Group Inc (PA)....**D....818 565-3600**
2400 W Empire Ave Ste 200 Burbank (91504) ***(P-19347)***

Deluxe Laboratories Inc (HQ)....**A....323 462-6171**
2400 W Empire Ave Ste 400 Burbank (91504) ***(P-19226)***

Deluxe Media Inc (PA)....**A....818 565-3697**
2400 W Empire Ave Ste 400 Burbank (91504) ***(P-19227)***

Deluxe Nms Inc....C....310 760-8500
4499 Glencoe Ave Marina Del Rey (90292) ***(P-19258)***

Demaria Electric Inc....E....310 549-4980
7048 Marcelle St Paramount (90723) ***(P-19008)***

Demaria Electric Motor Svcs, Paramount *Also called Demaria Electric Inc* ***(P-19008)***

Demenno Kerdoon....E....310 537-7100
2000 N Alameda St Compton (90222) ***(P-446)***

Demenno-Kerdoon, South Gate *Also called Demenno/Kerdoon Holdings* ***(P-5293)***

Demenno/Kerdoon Holdings....F....323 268-3387
3650 E 26th St Vernon (90058) ***(P-5292)***

Demenno/Kerdoon Holdings (HQ)....**D....562 231-1550**
9302 Garfield Ave South Gate (90280) ***(P-5293)***

Demler Armstrong & Rowland LLP....E....562 597-0029
4500 E Pcf Cast Hwy Ste 4 Long Beach (90804) ***(P-21546)***

Demo Deluxe, Yorba Linda *Also called IMG* ***(P-18546)***

Demoldco Plastics Inc....E....714 577-9391
3931 E Miraloma Ave Anaheim (92806) ***(P-5623)***

Den-Mat Corporation (HQ)....**B....805 922-8491**
236 S Broadway St Orcutt (93455) ***(P-5010)***

Den-Mat Corporation....C....800 445-0345
21515 Vanowen St Ste 200 Canoga Park (91303) ***(P-5011)***

Denco of Texas Inc (HQ)....**C....562 777-2249**
8152 Painter Ave Whittier (90602) ***(P-23015)***

Dendreon Pharmaceuticals Inc....F....562 253-3931
1700 Saturn Way Seal Beach (90740) ***(P-4814)***

Dendreon Pharmaceuticals LLC (HQ)....**E....562 252-7500**
1700 Saturn Way Seal Beach (90740) ***(P-4815)***

Denken Solutions Inc....C....949 630-5263
9170 Irvine Center Dr # 200 Irvine (92618) ***(P-17593)***

Denmac Industries Inc....E....562 634-2714
7616 Rosecrans Ave Paramount (90723) ***(P-7357)***

Dennie Manning Concrete Inc....F....909 823-7521
15815 Arrow Blvd Fontana (92335) ***(P-6089)***

Dennis & Leen, Los Angeles *Also called EC Group Inc* ***(P-13134)***

Dennis Allen Associates (PA)....**D....805 884-8777**
201 N Milpas St Santa Barbara (93103) ***(P-600)***

Dennis Bolton Enterprises Inc....E....818 982-1800
7285 Coldwater Canyon Ave North Hollywood (91605) ***(P-4275)***

Dennis Foland Inc (PA)....**D....909 930-9900**
1500 S Hellman Ave Ontario (91761) ***(P-14152)***

Dennis M McCoy & Sons Inc....D....818 874-3872
32107 Lindero Canyon Rd # 212 Westlake Village (91361) ***(P-875)***

Dennison Inc....E....626 965-8917
17901 Railroad St City of Industry (91748) ***(P-6960)***

Denovo Dental Inc....E....626 480-0182
5130 Commerce Dr Baldwin Park (91706) ***(P-11167)***

Denso Pdts & Svcs Americas Inc (HQ)....**B....310 834-6352**
3900 Via Oro Ave Long Beach (90810) ***(P-13054)***

Denso Pdts & Svcs Americas Inc....C....951 698-3379
41673 Corning Pl Murrieta (92562) ***(P-10044)***

Dental Imaging Tech Corp....A....714 516-7868
1717 W Collins Ave Orange (92867) ***(P-20174)***

Dentalville, Bell *Also called Leonid M Glsman DDS A Dntl Cor* ***(P-20186)***

Dentons US LLP....C....213 623-9300
601 S Figueroa St # 2500 Los Angeles (90017) ***(P-21547)***

Denttio Inc....F....323 254-1000
116 N Maryland Ave # 125 Glendale (91206) ***(P-11168)***

Denver D Darling Inc....D....714 761-8299
8402 Katella Ave Stanton (90680) ***(P-696)***

Department of Army....D....760 380-3114
390 N Loop Rd Fort Irwin (92310) ***(P-20744)***

Department of Health, Los Angeles *Also called County of Los Angeles* ***(P-21407)***

Department of Health Services, Los Angeles *Also called County of Los Angeles* ***(P-21043)***

Department of Mental Health, Los Angeles *Also called County of Los Angeles* ***(P-18119)***

Department of Public Works, Alhambra *Also called County of Los Angeles* ***(P-12885)***

Dependable Dodge Inc....E....818 883-9060
21415 Roscoe Blvd Canoga Park (91304) ***(P-18787)***

Dependable Global Express Inc (PA)....**C....310 537-2000**
19201 S Susana Rd E Rncho Dmngz (90221) ***(P-12444)***

Dependable Highway Express Inc....D....909 923-0065
1351 S Campus Ave Ontario (91761) ***(P-12030)***

Dependable Highway Express Inc....D....310 522-4111
800 E 230th St Carson (90745) ***(P-12031)***

Dependable Highway Express Inc (PA)....**B....323 526-2200**
2555 E Olympic Blvd Los Angeles (90023) ***(P-12032)***

Dependable Logistics Services, Los Angeles *Also called Dependable Highway Express Inc* ***(P-12032)***

Dependble Incontinence Sup Inc....E....626 812-0044
590 S Vincent Ave Azusa (91702) ***(P-3903)***

Deployable Space Systems Inc....E....805 722-8090
153 Castilian Dr Goleta (93117) ***(P-22528)***

Depo Auto Parts, Fontana *Also called Maxzone Vehicle Lighting Corp* ***(P-13072)***

Depot, Porterville *Also called Tharp Truck Rental Inc* ***(P-19078)***

Dept of Recreation Parks Cy La, Los Angeles *Also called City Wide Aquatics* ***(P-19640)***

Derek and Constance Lee Corp (PA)....**D....909 595-8831**
19355 San Jose Ave City of Industry (91748) ***(P-1731)***

Derm Cosmetic Labs Inc (PA)....**E....714 562-8873**
6370 Altura Blvd Buena Park (90620) ***(P-14240)***

Derma E, Simi Valley *Also called Stearns Corporation* ***(P-5072)***

Dermal Group, The, Carson *Also called Dermalogica LLC* ***(P-5012)***

Dermalogica LLC (HQ)....**C....310 900-4000**
1535 Beachey Pl Carson (90746) ***(P-5012)***

Descanso Gardens Guild Inc....D....818 952-4408
1418 Descanso Dr La Canada (91011) ***(P-22179)***

Deschner Corporation....E....714 557-1261
3211 W Harvard St Santa Ana (92704) ***(P-8120)***

Desco Manufacturing Company (PA)....**F....949 858-7400**
23031 Arroyo Vis Ste A Rcho STA Marg (92688) ***(P-8571)***

Desert Aids Project (PA)....**D....760 323-2118**
1695 N Sunrise Way # 101 Palm Springs (92262) ***(P-21767)***

Desert Air Conditioning Inc....E....760 323-3383
590 S Williams Rd Palm Springs (92264) ***(P-1482)***

Desert Area Resources Training (PA)....**D....760 375-9787**
201 E Ridgecrest Blvd Ridgecrest (93555) ***(P-17237)***

Desert Area Resources Training....D....760 375-8494
201 E Ridgecrest Blvd Ridgecrest (93555) ***(P-22180)***

Desert Block Co Inc....E....661 824-2624
11374 Tuxford St Sun Valley (91352) ***(P-5271)***

Desert Brand, City of Industry *Also called Hill Brothers Chemical Company* ***(P-4635)***

Desert Cardiology Cons Med G, Rancho Mirage *Also called Desert Crdlgy Cons Med Group I* ***(P-19793)***

Desert Cities Dialysis, Victorville *Also called Jamboor Medical Corporation* ***(P-21250)***

Desert Coastal Transport Inc (PA)....**D....909 357-3395**
10686 Banana Ave Fontana (92337) ***(P-12033)***

Desert Crdlgy Cons Med Group I....D....760 346-0642
39000 Bob Hope Dr Rancho Mirage (92270) ***(P-19793)***

Desert Falls Country Club Inc....D....760 340-5646
1111 Desert Falls Pkwy Palm Desert (92211) ***(P-19558)***

Desert Grafics, Palm Springs *Also called Desert Publications Inc* ***(P-4065)***

Desert Haven Enterprises Inc....A....661 948-8402
43437 Copeland Cir Lancaster (93535) ***(P-300)***

Desert Heart Physicians Inc....D....760 325-1203
1180 N Indian Canyon Dr Palm Springs (92262) ***(P-19794)***

Desert Horizons Country Club, Indian Wells *Also called Dhccnp* ***(P-19560)***

Desert Hot Springs Spa Hotel, Desert Hot Springs *Also called Whatever It Takes Inc* ***(P-16786)***

Desert Hot Springs Spa Hotel, Desert Hot Springs *Also called Desert Hot Sprng Real Prpts In* ***(P-15664)***

Desert Hot Sprng Real Prpts In....D....760 329-6000
10805 Palm Dr Desert Hot Springs (92240) ***(P-15664)***

Desert Inn & Suites, Anaheim *Also called SAI Management Co Inc* ***(P-16634)***

Desert Knlls Convalescent Hosp, Victorville *Also called Knolls Convalescent Hosp Inc* ***(P-20388)***

Desert Mechanical Inc....F....702 873-7333
15870 Olden St Sylmar (91342) ***(P-1055)***

Desert Medical Group Inc (PA)....**C....760 320-8814**
275 N El Cielo Rd D-402 Palm Springs (92262) ***(P-19795)***

Desert Mountain Fics, Victorville *Also called Victor Cmnty Support Svcs Inc* ***(P-21364)***

Desert Oasis Healthcare, Palm Springs *Also called Desert Medical Group Inc* ***(P-19795)***

Desert Orthpd Ctr A Med Group (PA)....**D....760 568-2684**
39000 Bob Hope Dr Ste W30 Rancho Mirage (92270) ***(P-19796)***

Desert Prncess HM Owners CLB I....E....760 322-1655
28555 Landau Blvd Cathedral City (92234) ***(P-19559)***

Desert Publications Inc (PA)....**E....760 325-2333**
303 N Indian Canyon Dr Palm Springs (92262) ***(P-4065)***

Desert Radiology Medical Group....D....760 778-5900
1150 N Indian Canyon Dr Palm Springs (92262) ***(P-19797)***

Desert Recreation District (PA)....**D....760 347-3484**
45305 Oasis St Indio (92201) ***(P-19642)***

Desert Redi Mix, Indio *Also called Coronet Concrete Products Inc* ***(P-6086)***

Desert Regional Med Ctr Inc....D....760 771-6158
47647 Caleo Bay Dr # 260 La Quinta (92253) ***(P-20745)***

Desert Regional Med Ctr Inc (HQ)....**A....760 323-6511**
1150 N Indian Canyon Dr Palm Springs (92262) ***(P-20746)***

Desert Regional Med Ctr Inc....D....760 416-4613
1180 N Indian Canyon Dr Palm Springs (92262) ***(P-20747)***

Desert Resort Management....D....760 831-0172
42635 Melanie Pl Ste 103 Palm Desert (92211) ***(P-15836)***

Mergent e-mail: customerrelations@mergent.com
1112
2022 Southern California Business Directory and Buyers Guide
(P-0000) Products & Services Section entry number
(PA)=Parent Co (HQ)=Headquarters (DH)=Div Headquarters

Desert Rose Golf Course, Cathedral City *Also called American Golf Corporation* **(P-19531)**
Desert Shades Inc...F...323 731-5000
2928 Leonis Blvd Vernon (90058) **(P-11657)**
Desert Sun Publishing Co (HQ)...**C...760 322-8889**
750 N Gene Autry Trl Palm Springs (92262) **(P-3972)**
Desert Sun Science Center, The, Idyllwild *Also called Guided Discoveries Inc* **(P-16821)**
Desert Sun The, Palm Springs *Also called Desert Sun Publishing Co* **(P-3972)**
Desert Trils Prpratory Academy, Adelanto *Also called Adelanto Elementary School Dst* **(P-2385)**
Desert Valley Date Inc...E...760 398-0999
86740 Industrial Way Coachella (92236) **(P-165)**
Desert Valley Date LLC...D...760 398-0999
86740 Industrial Way Coachella (92236) **(P-14686)**
Desert Valley Hospital Inc (HQ)...**C...760 241-8000**
16850 Bear Valley Rd Victorville (92395) **(P-20748)**
DESERT VALLEY INDUSTRIES, Palm Desert *Also called Desertarc* **(P-21768)**
Desert Valley Med Group Inc (PA)...**B...760 241-8000**
16850 Bear Valley Rd Victorville (92395) **(P-19798)**
Desert Water Agency Fing Corp...D...760 323-4971
1200 S Gene Autry Trl Palm Springs (92264) **(P-12887)**
Desert Willow Golf Course, Palm Desert *Also called Desert Willow Golf Resort Inc* **(P-19484)**
Desert Willow Golf Resort Inc...C...760 346-0015
38995 Desert Willow Dr Palm Desert (92260) **(P-19484)**
Desertarc...B...760 346-1611
73255 Country Club Dr Palm Desert (92260) **(P-21768)**
Desiccare Inc...E...909 444-8272
3400 Pomona Blvd Pomona (91768) **(P-6166)**
Design Catapult Manufacturing...F...949 522-6789
17331 Newhope St Fountain Valley (92708) **(P-10968)**
Design Collection Inc...D...323 277-9200
2209 S Santa Fe Ave Los Angeles (90058) **(P-14303)**
Design Form Inc...E...714 952-3700
8250 Electric Ave Stanton (90680) **(P-6740)**
Design Masonry Inc...D...661 252-2784
20703 Santa Clara St Canyon Country (91351) **(P-1342)**
Design People...C...800 969-5799
1700 E Walnut Ave Ste 400 El Segundo (90245) **(P-18083)**
Design Polymerics, Santa Ana *Also called Davco Enterprises Inc* **(P-5182)**
Design Printing, Los Angeles *Also called Red Brick Corporation* **(P-4417)**
Design Science Inc...E...562 432-2920
444 W Ocean Blvd Ste 800 Long Beach (90802) **(P-17594)**
Design Shapes In Steel Inc...E...626 579-2032
10315 Rush St South El Monte (91733) **(P-6198)**
Design Todays Inc (PA)...**E...213 745-3091**
11707 Cetona Way Porter Ranch (91326) **(P-2939)**
Design West Technologies Inc...D...714 731-0201
2701 Dow Ave Tustin (92780) **(P-5624)**
Designed Metal Connections Inc (HQ)...**B...310 323-6200**
14800 S Figueroa St Gardena (90248) **(P-10309)**
Designer Fashion Door, Temecula *Also called Designer Sash and Door Sys Inc* **(P-5625)**
Designer Imports Intl Inc...E...323 753-5448
6931 Stanford Ave Los Angeles (90001) **(P-13133)**
Designer Sash and Door Sys Inc...E...951 657-4179
45899 Via Tornado Temecula (92590) **(P-5625)**
Designory Inc (HQ)...**C...562 624-0200**
211 E Ocean Blvd Ste 100 Long Beach (90802) **(P-17171)**
Designworks/Usa Inc (HQ)...**D...805 499-9590**
2201 Corporate Center Dr Newbury Park (91320) **(P-22529)**
Deskmakers Inc...E...323 264-2260
6525 Flotilla St Commerce (90040) **(P-3583)**
Desmond Mail Delivery Service...D...323 262-1085
4600 Worth St Los Angeles (90063) **(P-11966)**
Desser Holding Company LLC (HQ)...**E...323 721-4900**
6900 W Acco St Montebello (90640) **(P-16098)**
Desser Tire & Rubber Co LLC...E...323 837-1497
6900 W Acco St Montebello (90640) **(P-14055)**
Desser Tire & Rubber Co., Montebello *Also called Desser Holding Company LLC* **(P-16098)**
Destination Residences LLC...C...760 346-4647
45750 San Luis Rey Ave Palm Desert (92260) **(P-16405)**
Destinationrx Inc (HQ)...**D...800 379-9060**
600 Wilshire Blvd # 1100 Los Angeles (90017) **(P-17595)**
Detectors Incorporated...F...714 982-5350
1800 E Miraloma Ave Ste A Placentia (92870) **(P-9338)**
Detoronics Corp...E...626 579-7130
13071 Rosecrans Ave Santa Fe Springs (90670) **(P-9653)**
Deutsch La Inc...D...310 862-3000
12901 W Jefferson Blvd Los Angeles (90066) **(P-17006)**
Deutsche Bank National Tr Co (HQ)...**D...310 788-6200**
1999 Avenue Of The Stars Los Angeles (90067) **(P-15133)**
Deutsche Bank National Tr Co...D...714 247-6054
1761 E Saint Andrew Pl Santa Ana (92705) **(P-15119)**
Deva, Tustin *Also called Distribution Electrnics Vlued* **(P-9864)**
Developers Surety Indemnity Co, Irvine *Also called Insco Insurance Services Inc* **(P-15583)**
Developers Surety Indemnity Co (HQ)...**D...949 263-3300**
17771 Cowan Ste 100 Irvine (92614) **(P-15496)**
Developlus Inc...C...951 738-8595
1575 Magnolia Ave Corona (92879) **(P-11658)**
DEVELOPMENT DISABILITIES CENTE, Santa Ana *Also called Regional Ctr Orange Cnty Inc* **(P-21877)**
Development Resource Cons Inc (PA)...**D...714 685-6860**
160 S Old Springs Rd # 210 Anaheim (92808) **(P-22530)**
Development Services, Lancaster *Also called Lancaster Cmnty Svcs Fndtion I* **(P-18851)**
Developmental Svcs Cal Dept...A...559 782-2222
26501 Avenue 140 Porterville (93257) **(P-20313)**
Developmental Svcs Cal Dept...A...760 770-6248
696 Ramon Cathedral City (92234) **(P-21420)**
Developmental Svcs Cal Dept...B...714 957-5151
2501 Harbor Blvd Costa Mesa (92626) **(P-21949)**

Deveraux Specialties LLC (PA)...**F...818 837-3700**
12835 Arroyo St Sylmar (91342) **(P-14241)**
Devereux California Center, Goleta *Also called Devereux Foundation* **(P-21298)**
Devereux Foundation...D...805 968-2525
7055 Seaway Dr Goleta (93117) **(P-21298)**
Devereux Foundation...D...805 968-2525
6980 Falberg Way Goleta (93117) **(P-21299)**
Devoll Rubber Mfg Group, Victorville *Also called Devoll Rubber Mfg Group Inc* **(P-5372)**
Devoll Rubber Mfg Group Inc...F...760 246-0142
18626 Phantom St Victorville (92394) **(P-5372)**
Devorss & Co...F...805 322-9010
553 Constitution Ave Camarillo (93012) **(P-14870)**
Devorss Publications, Camarillo *Also called Devorss & Co* **(P-14870)**
Dewalt Service Center 148, Bellflower *Also called Black & Decker (us) Inc* **(P-7879)**
Dewitt Stern Group Inc...C...818 933-2700
5990 Sepulvda Blvd # 550 Van Nuys (91411) **(P-15560)**
Dex Corporation...C...805 388-1711
3600 Via Pescador Camarillo (93012) **(P-22531)**
Dex-O-Tex Division, Compton *Also called Crossfield Products Corp* **(P-4685)**
Dext Company, Santa Monica *Also called Reconserve Inc* **(P-1974)**
Dext Company of Maryland (HQ)...**E...310 458-1574**
2811 Wilshire Blvd # 410 Santa Monica (90403) **(P-1964)**
Dexyp, Glendale *Also called Yellowpagescom LLC* **(P-18731)**
Dezario Shoe Company, North Hollywood *Also called Meco-Nag Corporation* **(P-5881)**
Dfa Dairy Brands Fluid LLC...B...800 395-7004
17851 Railroad St City of Industry (91748) **(P-14541)**
Dfds International Corporation...D...310 414-1516
898 N Pacific Coast Hwy # 6 El Segundo (90245) **(P-12445)**
Dfds Transport US, El Segundo *Also called Dfds International Corporation* **(P-12445)**
Dfndr Armor, Camarillo *Also called Engense Inc* **(P-6200)**
Dfs Flooring Inc (PA)...**D...818 374-5200**
15651 Saticoy St Van Nuys (91406) **(P-1466)**
Dfusion Software Inc...E...323 617-5577
5900 Wilshire Blvd # 2550 Los Angeles (90036) **(P-17596)**
Dg Engineering Corp (PA)...**E...818 364-9024**
13326 Ralston Ave Sylmar (91342) **(P-10583)**
Dg Holdings Inc...F...714 891-9300
2367 W La Palma Ave Anaheim (92801) **(P-10045)**
DG Performance Spc Inc...D...714 961-8850
4100 E La Palma Ave Anaheim (92807) **(P-10549)**
Dg-Displays LLC...E...877 358-5976
355 Parkside Dr San Fernando (91340) **(P-11541)**
Dg2 Worldwide Group LLC...E...310 809-0899
12655 W Jefferson Blvd Los Angeles (90066) **(P-17007)**
Dggr Packaging Crating & Foam, Anaheim *Also called JDC Development Group Inc* **(P-3415)**
Dgwb Inc...D...714 881-2300
217 N Main St Ste 200 Santa Ana (92701) **(P-17008)**
Dgwb Advg & Communications, Santa Ana *Also called Dgwb Inc* **(P-17008)**
DH Caster International Inc...F...909 930-6400
2260 S Haven Ave Ste C Ontario (91761) **(P-13803)**
Dharma Ventures Group Inc (PA)...**B...661 294-4200**
24700 Ave Rockefeller Valencia (91355) **(P-16099)**
Dhb Delivery LLC...D...626 588-7562
1134 N Chestnut Ln Azusa (91702) **(P-12126)**
Dhccnp...D...760 340-4646
44900 Desert Horizons Dr Indian Wells (92210) **(P-19560)**
Dhe, Ontario *Also called Dependable Highway Express Inc* **(P-12030)**
Dhl Supply Chain, Fontana *Also called Exel Inc* **(P-12203)**
DHm International Corp...F...323 263-3888
901 Monterey Pass Rd Monterey Park (91754) **(P-2940)**
Dhs Consulting LLC...C...714 276-1135
1820 E 1st St Ste 410 Santa Ana (92705) **(P-23016)**
Dhv Industries Inc...D...661 392-8948
3451 Pegasus Dr Bakersfield (93308) **(P-13981)**
Dhx-Dependable Hawaiian Ex Inc (PA)...**C...310 537-2000**
19201 S Susana Rd Compton (90221) **(P-12446)**
Di Overnite LLC...D...877 997-7447
1900 S State College Blvd Anaheim (92806) **(P-12127)**
Diack 1 Inc...E...626 961-2491
19437 Windrose Dr Rowland Heights (91748) **(P-6325)**
Diagnostic Health Corporation...C...310 665-7180
6801 Park Ter Los Angeles (90045) **(P-23206)**
Diagnostic Health Los Angeles, Los Angeles *Also called Diagnostic Health Corporation* **(P-23206)**
Diagnostic Labs & Rdlgy, Burbank *Also called Kan-Di-Ki LLC* **(P-21073)**
Diagnostic Reagents, Los Angeles *Also called James Stewart* **(P-4834)**
Diagnostic Solutions Intl LLC...F...909 930-3600
2580 E Philadelphia St C Ontario (91761) **(P-10310)**
Diagnstic Intrvntnal Srgcal CT...D...310 574-0400
13160 Mindanao Way # 150 Marina Del Rey (90292) **(P-19799)**
Dial Communications, Camarillo *Also called Dial Security Inc* **(P-18371)**
Dial Global Digital, Culver City *Also called Triton Media Group LLC* **(P-12707)**
Dial Industries Inc...D...323 263-6878
3616 Noakes St Los Angeles (90023) **(P-5626)**
Dial Precision Inc...D...760 947-3557
17235 Darwin Ave Hesperia (92345) **(P-8572)**
Dial Security Inc (PA)...**C...805 389-6700**
760 W Ventura Blvd Camarillo (93010) **(P-18371)**
Diality Inc...F...949 916-5851
181 Technology Dr Ste 150 Irvine (92618) **(P-10969)**
Dialysis North Atlanta LLC (HQ)...**E...310 536-2400**
601 Hawaii St El Segundo (90245) **(P-21240)**
Diamodent Inc...E...888 281-8850
1580 N Harmony Cir Anaheim (92807) **(P-11169)**
Diamon Fusion Intl Inc...F...949 388-8000
9361 Irvine Blvd Irvine (92618) **(P-5217)**

Employee Codes: A=Over 500 employees, B=251-500
C=101-250, D=51-100, E=20-50 F=10-19
2022 Southern California Business
Directory and Buyers Guide
© Mergent Inc. 1-800-342-5647
1113

Diamond Bar Medical Offices, Diamond Bar *Also called Kaiser Foundation Hospitals* ***(P-19897)***

Diamond Baseball Company Inc ....E....800 366-2999
1880 E Saint Andrew Pl Santa Ana (92705) ***(P-11412)***

Diamond Collection LLC ....E....626 435-0077
20579 Valley Blvd Walnut (91789) ***(P-3074)***

Diamond Crystal Brands Inc ....E....559 651-7782
8700 W Doe Ave Visalia (93291) ***(P-2421)***

Diamond Crystal Brands-Hormel, Visalia *Also called Diamond Crystal Brands Inc* ***(P-2421)***

Diamond Gloves ....E....714 667-0506
1100 S Linwood Ave Ste A Santa Ana (92705) ***(P-11094)***

Diamond Goldenwest Corporation (PA) ....**C....714 542-9000**
15732 Tustin Village Way Tustin (92780) ***(P-14130)***

Diamond Ground Products Inc ....E....805 498-3837
2651 Lavery Ct Newbury Park (91320) ***(P-7890)***

Diamond K2 ....E....310 539-6116
23911 Garnier St Ste C Torrance (90505) ***(P-6492)***

Diamond Mattress Company Inc (PA) ....**D....310 638-0363**
3112 E Las Hermanas St Compton (90221) ***(P-3547)***

Diamond Mattress Nf, Compton *Also called Diamond Mattress Company Inc* ***(P-3547)***

Diamond Multimedia, Canoga Park *Also called Best Data Products Inc* ***(P-8239)***

Diamond Peo LLC ....C....714 728-5186
27442 Calle Arroyo Ste A San Juan Capistrano (92675) ***(P-17412)***

Diamond Perforated Metals Inc ....D....559 651-1889
7300 W Sunnyview Ave Visalia (93291) ***(P-7142)***

Diamond Resorts LLC ....D....760 866-1800
2800 S Palm Canyon Dr Palm Springs (92264) ***(P-16406)***

Diamond Ridge Corporation ....C....909 949-0605
121 S Mountain Ave Upland (91786) ***(P-15837)***

Diamond Sports, Santa Ana *Also called Diamond Baseball Company Inc* ***(P-11412)***

Diamond Terraces, Hanford *Also called Rcan Inc* ***(P-22148)***

Diamond Vly Hlth Holdings LLC ....D....949 487-9500
29222 Rncho Vejo Rd Ste 1 San Juan Capistrano (92675) ***(P-20314)***

Diamond W Floorcovering, City of Industry *Also called W Diamond Supply Co* ***(P-13198)***

Diamond Wipes Intl Inc (PA) ....**D....909 230-9888**
4651 Schaefer Ave Chino (91710) ***(P-5013)***

Diamonds By Design, Los Angeles *Also called Stardust Diamond Corp* ***(P-11339)***

Diamotec Inc ....F....310 539-4994
22104 S Vt Ave Ste 104 Torrance (90502) ***(P-7853)***

Diana Did-It Designs Inc ....E....970 226-5062
20579 Valley Blvd Walnut (91789) ***(P-3075)***

Dianas Mexican Food Pdts Inc (PA) ....**E....562 926-5802**
16330 Pioneer Blvd Norwalk (90650) ***(P-2422)***

Dianas Mexican Food Pdts Inc ....D....310 834-4886
300 E Sepulveda Blvd Carson (90745) ***(P-2423)***

Dianas Mexican Food Pdts Inc ....E....626 444-0555
2905 Durfee Ave El Monte (91732) ***(P-2424)***

Diani Building Corp (PA) ....**D....805 925-9533**
351 N Blosser Rd Santa Maria (93458) ***(P-760)***

Diasorin Molecular LLC ....C....562 240-6500
11331 Valley View St Cypress (90630) ***(P-4919)***

Diatomaceous Earth.com, Santa Barbara *Also called Esperer Webstores LLC* ***(P-1790)***

Diaz Plastering Inc ....D....661 244-8228
4900 California Ave 210b Bakersfield (93309) ***(P-1372)***

Dicaperl Corporation (HQ) ....**D....610 667-6640**
23705 Crenshaw Blvd # 10 Torrance (90505) ***(P-585)***

Dick Dewese Chevrolet Inc ....C....909 793-2681
800 Alabama St Redlands (92374) ***(P-18824)***

Dick Farrell Industries Inc ....F....909 613-9424
5071 Lindsay Ct Chino (91710) ***(P-8088)***

Dick Howells Hole Drlg Svc Inc ....E....562 633-9898
2579 E 67th St Long Beach (90805) ***(P-426)***

Dickeys Barbecue Pit, Tustin *Also called Dickeys Barbecue Rest Inc* ***(P-1861)***

Dickeys Barbecue Rest Inc ....E....714 602-3874
17245 17th St Tustin (92780) ***(P-1861)***

Dickson Testing Co Inc (HQ) ....**D....562 862-8378**
11126 Palmer Ave South Gate (90280) ***(P-22938)***

DIDI HIRSCH COMMUNITY MENTAL H, Culver City *Also called Didi Hirsch Psychiatric Svc* ***(P-21769)***

Didi Hirsch Psychiatric Svc (PA) ....**C....310 390-6612**
4760 Sepulveda Blvd Culver City (90230) ***(P-21769)***

Die Cast Model Madness ....F....626 791-0364
743 N Mentor Ave Pasadena (91104) ***(P-7795)***

Die Craft Stamping Inc ....F....562 944-2395
10132 Norwalk Blvd Santa Fe Springs (90670) ***(P-7472)***

Die Shop ....F....562 630-4400
7302 Adams St Paramount (90723) ***(P-7796)***

Dieners Electric Inc ....D....805 988-1515
167 Lambert St Oxnard (93036) ***(P-1243)***

Dietzgen Corporation ....E....951 278-3259
1522 E Bentley Dr Corona (92879) ***(P-3926)***

Digestive Care Consultants ....D....310 375-1246
23451 Madison St Ste 290 Torrance (90505) ***(P-19800)***

Digital Communications Network (PA) ....**D....818 227-3333**
6300 Canoga Ave Ste 1625 Woodland Hills (91367) ***(P-12605)***

Digital Domain 30 Inc (PA) ....**B....310 314-2800**
12641 Beatrice St Los Angeles (90066) ***(P-19116)***

Digital Film Labs, Los Angeles *Also called Point360* ***(P-19245)***

Digital Insight Corporation ....D....818 879-1010
5601 Lindero Canyon Rd # 100 Westlake Village (91362) ***(P-18120)***

Digital Label Solutions LLC ....E....714 982-5000
22745 Old Canal Rd Yorba Linda (92887) ***(P-3927)***

Digital Map Products Inc ....D....949 333-5111
5201 California Ave # 200 Irvine (92617) ***(P-12783)***

Digital Media Management Inc ....D....323 378-6505
5670 Wilshire Blvd Fl 11 Los Angeles (90036) ***(P-23017)***

Digital Periph Solutions Inc ....E....714 998-3440
160 S Old Springs Rd # 22 Anaheim (92808) ***(P-9171)***

Digital Printing Systems Inc (PA) ....**D....626 815-1888**
2350 Panorama Ter Los Angeles (90039) ***(P-4276)***

Digital Publisher, Tustin *Also called Medium Large LLC* ***(P-19147)***

Digital Rdlgic Imging Assoc In ....D....949 499-1311
29122 Rncho Vejo Rd Ste 1 San Juan Capistrano (92675) ***(P-19801)***

Digital Room Holdings Inc (PA) ....**C....310 575-4440**
8000 Haskell Ave Van Nuys (91406) ***(P-4507)***

Digital Sherpas, Culver City *Also called Wongdoody Inc* ***(P-17071)***

Digital Signal Power Mfg, Ontario *Also called Dspm Inc* ***(P-9628)***

Digital Surgery Systems Inc ....E....805 978-5400
125 Cremona Dr 110 Goleta (93117) ***(P-10970)***

Digitran, Rancho Cucamonga *Also called Electro Switch Corp* ***(P-8896)***

Dignity Health ....B....805 739-3000
1400 E Church St Santa Maria (93454) ***(P-20749)***

Dignity Health ....B....805 988-2868
200 Oceangate Long Beach (90802) ***(P-20750)***

Dignity Health ....E....818 993-4054
18460 Roscoe Blvd Northridge (91325) ***(P-20751)***

Dignity Health ....A....818 885-8500
18300 Roscoe Blvd Northridge (91325) ***(P-20752)***

Dignity Health ....C....805 389-5800
2309 Antonio Ave Camarillo (93010) ***(P-20753)***

Dignity Health ....A....805 988-2500
1600 N Rose Ave Oxnard (93030) ***(P-20754)***

Dignity Health Med Foundation ....D....805 981-6101
2901 N Ventura Rd Ste 100 Oxnard (93036) ***(P-20755)***

Dignity Hlth MGT Svcs Orgnztio ....E....661 716-7100
4550 Cal Ave Bkrsfeld Ca Glendale (91203) ***(P-23018)***

Dilbeck Inc (PA) ....**D....818 790-6774**
1030 Foothill Blvd La Canada (91011) ***(P-15838)***

Dilbeck Inc ....E....805 379-1880
850 Hampshire Rd Ste A Westlake Village (91361) ***(P-15839)***

Dilbeck Realtors, La Canada *Also called Dilbeck Inc* ***(P-15838)***

Dilbeck Realtors, Westlake Village *Also called Dilbeck Inc* ***(P-15839)***

Dilco Industrial Inc ....F....714 998-5266
205 E Bristol Ln Orange (92865) ***(P-7908)***

Dillon Aircraft Deburring Inc ....F....818 768-0801
11771 Sheldon St Sun Valley (91352) ***(P-7247)***

Dillon Companies Inc ....C....951 352-8353
4250 Van Buren Blvd Riverside (92503) ***(P-1995)***

Dimar Enterprises Inc ....C....949 492-1100
26021 Pala Ste 150 Mission Viejo (92691) ***(P-17238)***

Dimensions In Screen Printing, Irvine *Also called Tomorrows Lock Inc* ***(P-2661)***

Dimic Steel Tech Inc ....E....909 946-6767
145 N 8th Ave Upland (91786) ***(P-6820)***

Dinasty Security Services ....E....310 507-7848
640 S Ford Blvd Los Angeles (90022) ***(P-18270)***

Dincloud Inc ....D....310 929-1101
27520 Hawthorne Blvd # 185 Rllng HLS Est (90274) ***(P-17838)***

Dine Brands Global Inc (PA) ....**B....818 240-6055**
450 N Brand Blvd Glendale (91203) ***(P-16205)***

Dinsmore & Associates Inc ....F....714 641-7111
1681 Kettering Irvine (92614) ***(P-5430)***

Diocese Fresno Education Corp ....D....559 734-1572
1638 N Dinuba Blvd Visalia (93291) ***(P-21770)***

Dip Braze Inc ....E....818 768-1555
9131 De Garmo Ave Sun Valley (91352) ***(P-18975)***

Diplomat Packaging, Sylmar *Also called Winning Performance Pdts Inc* ***(P-18728)***

Direct Chassislink Inc ....C....657 216-5846
7777 Center Ave Ste 325 Huntington Beach (92647) ***(P-17345)***

Direct Chemicals, Huntington Beach *Also called Home & Body Company* ***(P-4964)***

Direct Delivery Center, Ontario *Also called Sears Roebuck and Co* ***(P-19066)***

Direct Drive Systems Inc ....D....714 872-5500
621 Burning Tree Rd Fullerton (92833) ***(P-8912)***

Direct Edge Media Inc (PA) ....**F....714 221-8686**
2900 E White Star Ave Anaheim (92806) ***(P-4508)***

Direct Edge Screenworks Inc ....E....714 579-3686
1221 N Lakeview Ave Anaheim (92807) ***(P-4277)***

Direct Partners Inc (HQ) ....**D....310 482-4200**
12777 W Jefferson Blvd Los Angeles (90066) ***(P-17009)***

Direct Wheel Inc ....F....909 390-2824
1000 E Garvey Ave Monterey Park (91755) ***(P-10046)***

Directcnnect Lgal Slutions Inc ....E....888 685-7771
9431 Hven Ave Ste 100-280 Rancho Cucamonga (91730) ***(P-21548)***

Directline Motor Express Inc ....B....213 266-2670
2720 E 26th St Vernon (90058) ***(P-12034)***

Directors Guild America Inc (PA) ....**C....310 289-2000**
7920 W Sunset Blvd Los Angeles (90046) ***(P-19228)***

Directv Inc ....B....888 388-4249
2230 E Imperial Hwy El Segundo (90245) ***(P-12755)***

Directv Enterprises LLC ....A....310 535-5000
2230 E Imperial Hwy El Segundo (90245) ***(P-12756)***

Directv Group Holdings LLC ....C....760 375-8300
140 Station Ave Ridgecrest (93555) ***(P-12757)***

Directv Group Holdings LLC ....C....805 207-6675
360 Cortez Cir Camarillo (93012) ***(P-12758)***

Directv Group Holdings LLC ....C....661 632-6562
715 E Avenue L8 Ste 101 Lancaster (93535) ***(P-12759)***

Directv Group Holdings LLC (HQ) ....**C....310 964-5000**
2260 E Imperial Hwy El Segundo (90245) ***(P-12606)***

Directv Group Inc (HQ) ....**C....310 964-5000**
2260 E Imperial Hwy El Segundo (90245) ***(P-12760)***

Directv Holdings LLC (HQ) ....**A....310 964-5000**
2230 E Imperial Hwy El Segundo (90245) ***(P-12761)***

Directv International Inc (HQ) ....**C....310 964-6460**
2230 E Imperial Hwy Fl 10 El Segundo (90245) ***(P-12762)***

Directv Sports Network LLC (HQ) ....**D....310 964-5000**
2230 E Imperial Hwy El Segundo (90245) ***(P-12763)***

Dis, Azusa *Also called Dependble Incontinence Sup Inc* ***(P-3903)***

Mergent e-mail: customerrelations@mergent.com
1114

2022 Southern California Business Directory and Buyers Guide

(P-0000) Products & Services Section entry number
(PA)=Parent Co (HQ)=Headquarters (DH)=Div Headquarters

Disability Rights California..........D.......213 213-8000
350 S Bixel St Los Angeles (90017) ***(P-21549)***
Disaster Rstrtion Prfssnals In..........D.......310 301-8030
1517 W 130th St Gardena (90249) ***(P-601)***
Disc Replicator Inc..........F.......909 385-0118
21137 Commerce Point Dr Walnut (91789) ***(P-9213)***
Disco Print Whl 46 Sup Cmpnies..........F.......949 261-8457
1891 Alton Pkwy Ste A Irvine (92606) ***(P-18029)***
Discopylabs..........F.......909 390-3800
4455 E Philadelphia St Ontario (91761) ***(P-9214)***
Discount Tire Center 025, North Hollywood *Also called Akh Company Inc* ***(P-18890)***
Discount Tire Center 038, Redlands *Also called Akh Company Inc* ***(P-18891)***
Discount Tire Center 077, Moreno Valley *Also called Akh Company Inc* ***(P-13111)***
Discounted Wheel Warehouse, Fullerton *Also called Wheel and Tire Club Inc* ***(P-6218)***
Discovery Communications Inc (PA)..........**C.......310 975-5906**
10100 Santa Monica Blvd Los Angeles (90067) ***(P-12784)***
Discovery Plz Med & Admin Offs, Bakersfield *Also called Kaiser Foundation Hospitals* ***(P-19891)***
Discovery Scnce Ctr Ornge Cnty..........C.......866 552-2823
2500 N Main St Santa Ana (92705) ***(P-22220)***
Dish Network Corporation..........D.......909 381-4767
396 Orange Show Ln San Bernardino (92408) ***(P-12764)***
Dish Network Corporation..........D.......818 334-8740
1297 N Verdugo Rd Glendale (91206) ***(P-12765)***
Dish Network Corporation..........D.......714 424-0503
2602 Halladay St Santa Ana (92705) ***(P-12766)***
Disk Faktory, Tustin *Also called Innovative Diversfd Tech Inc* ***(P-8205)***
Disney Book Group LLC (HQ)..........**D.......818 560-1000**
500 S Buena Vista St Burbank (91521) ***(P-4126)***
Disney Enterprises Inc (HQ)..........**A.......818 560-1000**
500 S Buena Vista St Burbank (91521) ***(P-12687)***
Disney Enterprises Inc..........A.......714 778-6600
1150 W Magic Way Anaheim (92802) ***(P-16407)***
Disney Enterprises Inc..........D.......407 397-6000
1313 S Harbor Blvd Anaheim (92802) ***(P-19117)***
Disney Financial Services, Burbank *Also called Twdc Enterprises 18 Corp* ***(P-12747)***
Disney Incorporated (HQ)..........**C.......818 560-1000**
500 S Buena Vista St Burbank (91521) ***(P-19118)***
Disney Interactive Studios Inc..........B.......818 560-1000
601 Circle Seven Dr Glendale (91201) ***(P-17597)***
Disney Interactive Studios Inc..........B.......818 553-5000
681 W Buena Vista St Burbank (91521) ***(P-17598)***
Disney Online..........D.......818 553-7200
500 S Buena Vista St Burbank (91521) ***(P-12714)***
Disney Publishing Worldwide (HQ)..........**D.......212 633-4400**
500 S Buena Vista St Burbank (91521) ***(P-4066)***
Disney Regional Entrtmt Inc (HQ)..........**C.......818 560-1000**
500 S Buena Vista St Burbank (91521) ***(P-19643)***
Disney Research Pittsburgh..........C.......412 623-1800
532 Paula Ave Glendale (91201) ***(P-22834)***
Disney Worldwide Services Inc..........D.......818 560-1250
589 Paula Ave Glendale (91201) ***(P-18173)***
Disneyland Hotel, Anaheim *Also called Wco Hotels Inc* ***(P-16779)***
Disneyland International..........A.......714 956-6746
1580 S Disneyland Dr Anaheim (92802) ***(P-16408)***
Disneyland International (HQ)..........**C.......714 781-4565**
1313 S Harbor Blvd Anaheim (92802) ***(P-19517)***
Disneyland Resort (HQ)..........**C.......714 781-4000**
1313 S Harbor Blvd Anaheim (92802) ***(P-16409)***
Disneyland Resort..........B.......714 781-7560
1020 W Ball Rd Anaheim (92802) ***(P-12556)***
Disneys Grnd Clifornian Ht Spa, Anaheim *Also called Wco Hotels Inc* ***(P-16780)***
Disorderly Kids, Los Angeles *Also called Avalon Apparel LLC* ***(P-2878)***
Dispatch Commodity Trucking, Fontana *Also called Dispatch Transportation LLC* ***(P-17346)***
Dispatch Transportation LLC..........E.......909 355-5531
14032 Santa Ana Ave Fontana (92337) ***(P-17346)***
Dispatch Trucking LLC (PA)..........**D.......909 355-5531**
14032 Santa Ana Ave Fontana (92337) ***(P-12447)***
Display Fabrication Group Inc..........E.......714 373-2100
1231 N Miller St Ste 100 Anaheim (92806) ***(P-3193)***
Displays & Holders, Anaheim *Also called Hippo Corporation* ***(P-14936)***
Disposable Chafing Equipment, Whittier *Also called Swiss Park Banquet Center* ***(P-9012)***
Disposable Waste System, Santa Ana *Also called Jwc Environmental Inc* ***(P-8390)***
Disqo Inc..........D.......818 237-2186
400 N Brand Blvd Ste 600 Glendale (91203) ***(P-22879)***
Disruptive Visions LLC..........D.......949 502-3800
23456 Madero Ste 210 Mission Viejo (92691) ***(P-23432)***
Distillery Tech Inc..........C.......310 776-6234
1914 Huntington Ln A Redondo Beach (90278) ***(P-17599)***
Distinct Indulgence Inc..........E.......818 546-1700
5018 Lante St Baldwin Park (91706) ***(P-1996)***
Distinctive Inds Texas Inc..........E.......323 889-5766
9419 Ann St Santa Fe Springs (90670) ***(P-3055)***
Distinctive Inds Texas Inc..........E.......512 491-3500
10618 Shoemaker Ave Santa Fe Springs (90670) ***(P-3056)***
Distinctive Industries..........B.......800 421-9777
10618 Shoemaker Ave Santa Fe Springs (90670) ***(P-3172)***
Distribution, Ontario *Also called Index Fasteners Inc* ***(P-13991)***
Distribution Alternatives Inc..........D.......909 673-1000
1990 S Cucamonga Ave Ontario (91761) ***(P-12199)***
Distribution Alternatives Inc..........D.......909 746-5600
10621 6th St Rancho Cucamonga (91730) ***(P-12200)***
Distribution Alternatives Inc..........C.......909 770-8900
1979 Renaissance Pkwy Rialto (92376) ***(P-14242)***
Distribution Cente, Calexico *Also called Clover Imaging Group LLC* ***(P-11271)***
Distribution Electrnics Vlued..........E.......714 368-1717
2651 Dow Ave Tustin (92780) ***(P-9864)***
Distributors Processing Inc..........F.......559 781-0297
17656 Avenue 168 Porterville (93257) ***(P-2320)***
District Attorney, Lancaster *Also called County of Los Angeles* ***(P-21538)***
District Attorney, Santa Ana *Also called County of Orange* ***(P-21539)***
District Attorney's Office, Riverside *Also called County of Riverside* ***(P-21760)***
District Service, Pasadena *Also called Pasadena Unified School Dst* ***(P-17271)***
Dita Inc (PA)..........**E.......949 599-2700**
1787 Pomona Rd Corona (92878) ***(P-11248)***
Dita Eyewear, Corona *Also called Dita Inc* ***(P-11248)***
Ditec Co..........F.......805 566-7800
1019 Mark Ave Carpinteria (93013) ***(P-10971)***
Ditec Mfg., Carpinteria *Also called Ditec Co* ***(P-10971)***
Divergent 3d, Torrance *Also called Divergent Technologies Inc* ***(P-22532)***
Divergent Technologies Inc..........D.......310 339-1186
19601 Hamilton Ave Torrance (90502) ***(P-22532)***
Diverscape Inc..........D.......951 245-1686
21730 Bundy Canyon Rd Wildomar (92595) ***(P-301)***
Diverse Journeys Inc (PA)..........**D.......310 643-7403**
525 S Douglas St Ste 210 El Segundo (90245) ***(P-21771)***
Diverse Optics Inc..........E.......909 593-9330
10339 Dorset St Rancho Cucamonga (91730) ***(P-5627)***
Diversfied Cmmnctions Svcs Inc..........D.......714 888-2284
1260 Pioneer St Brea (92821) ***(P-12633)***
Diversfied Mrcury Cmmnctons LL..........D.......508 598-3569
11620 Wilshire Blvd Los Angeles (90025) ***(P-17095)***
Diversfied Mtllrgical Svcs Inc..........E.......714 895-7777
12101 Industry St Garden Grove (92841) ***(P-6439)***
Diversfied Tchncal Systems Inc (HQ)..........**E.......562 493-0158**
1720 Apollo Ct Seal Beach (90740) ***(P-10748)***
Diversified Coatings Linings..........E.......909 591-6366
4810 Cheyenne Way Chino (91710) ***(P-1522)***
DIVERSIFIED INDUSTRIES, Montclair *Also called Oparc* ***(P-21963)***
Diversified Landscape Co, Wildomar *Also called Diverscape Inc* ***(P-301)***
Diversified Logistic Svcs Inc..........E.......562 941-3600
13033 Telegraph Rd Santa Fe Springs (90670) ***(P-12557)***
Diversified Metal Works, Orange *Also called Rika Corporation* ***(P-1581)***
Diversified Mfg Tech Inc..........F.......714 577-7000
149 Via Trevizio Corona (92879) ***(P-7797)***
Diversified Minerals Inc..........E.......805 247-1069
1100 Mountain View Ave F Oxnard (93030) ***(P-6090)***
Diversified Packaging Inc..........F.......714 850-9316
2221 S Anne St Santa Ana (92704) ***(P-5497)***
Diversified Printers Inc..........D.......714 994-3400
12834 Maxwell Dr Tustin (92782) ***(P-4167)***
Diversified Prj Svcs Intl Inc (PA)..........**D.......661 371-2800**
5351 Olive Dr Ste 100 Bakersfield (93308) ***(P-22533)***
Diversified Silicone, Santa Fe Springs *Also called Rogers Corporation* ***(P-5406)***
Diversified Utility Svcs Inc..........B.......661 325-3212
3105 Unicorn Rd Bakersfield (93308) ***(P-946)***
Diversified Waterscapes Inc..........F.......949 582-5414
27324 Camn Capistrano # 213 Laguna Niguel (92677) ***(P-23207)***
Diversity Bus Solutions Inc..........C.......909 395-0243
2515 S Euclid Ave Ontario (91762) ***(P-17413)***
Divine Foods Inc..........E.......800 440-6476
16752 Millikan Ave Irvine (92606) ***(P-2084)***
Divine Pasta Company, Burbank *Also called Palermo Family LP* ***(P-2507)***
Divine Pasta Company..........F.......818 559-7440
550 Ceres Ave Los Angeles (90013) ***(P-2425)***
Divinity Recovery..........E.......866 757-0474
20301 Ventura Blvd # 121 Woodland Hills (91364) ***(P-21772)***
Division 1, Los Angeles *Also called Los Angles Cnty Mtro Trnsp Aut* ***(P-11819)***
Division 7, Venice *Also called Los Angles Cnty Mtro Trnsp Aut* ***(P-11827)***
Dix Metals Inc..........D.......714 677-0777
14801 Able Ln Ste 101 Huntington Beach (92647) ***(P-13563)***
Dixieline Lumber Company LLC..........A.......951 224-8491
2625 Durahart St Riverside (92507) ***(P-3360)***
Dixon Hard Chrome, Sun Valley *Also called Florence International Co Inc* ***(P-7260)***
DJ John Park MD Inc (PA)..........**D.......714 326-7715**
180 Nwport Ctr Dr Ste 170 Newport Beach (92660) ***(P-20756)***
Djh Enterprises..........E.......714 424-6500
23011 Moulton Pkwy Ste B6 Laguna Hills (92653) ***(P-9267)***
Dji Service LLC..........F.......818 235-0788
17301 Edwards Rd Cerritos (90703) ***(P-10311)***
Dji Technology Inc..........E.......818 235-0789
17301 Edwards Rd Cerritos (90703) ***(P-11273)***
DJM Suspension, Gardena *Also called D and J Marketing Inc* ***(P-3171)***
Djont Operations LLC..........C.......310 640-3600
1440 E Imperial Ave El Segundo (90245) ***(P-16410)***
Djont/Jpm Hsptlity Lsg Spe LLC..........D.......805 984-2500
2101 Mandalay Beach Rd Oxnard (93035) ***(P-16411)***
Djont/Jpm Hsptlity Lsg Spe LLC..........D.......310 451-0676
120 Colorado Ave Santa Monica (90401) ***(P-16412)***
DK Amans Valve & Supply, Long Beach *Also called DK Valve & Supply Inc* ***(P-19033)***
DK Valve & Supply Inc..........E.......562 529-8400
2385 E Artesia Blvd Long Beach (90805) ***(P-19033)***
Dkn Hotel LLC (PA)..........**B.......714 427-4320**
42 Corporate Park Ste 200 Irvine (92606) ***(P-16413)***
Dkp Designs Inc..........F.......310 322-6000
110 Maryland St El Segundo (90245) ***(P-11659)***
Dl Imaging, Santa Ana *Also called Dekra-Lite Industries Inc* ***(P-18502)***
DL Long Landscaping Inc..........D.......909 628-5531
5475 G St Chino (91710) ***(P-253)***
Dlb Fire Protection, Bakersfield *Also called Cfp Designs Inc* ***(P-1043)***
Dlc, Cerritos *Also called David Levy Co Inc* ***(P-13714)***
Dlc Laboratories Inc..........F.......562 602-2184
7008 Marcelle St Paramount (90723) ***(P-4816)***

ALPHABETIC

Employee Codes: A=Over 500 employees, B=251-500
C=101-250, D=51-100, E=20-50 F=10-19
2022 Southern California Business
Directory and Buyers Guide
© Mergent Inc. 1-800-342-5647
1115

Dlh Davinci LLC .... D 818 703-5100
22135 Roscoe Blvd Ste 101 West Hills (91304) ***(P-21105)***

Dlr Group Inc (HQ) .... C **213 800-9400**
700 Suth Flwr St Fl 22 Flr 22 Los Angeles (90017) ***(P-22713)***

Dlr Group Inc .... D 951 682-0470
4280 Latham St Ste H Riverside (92501) ***(P-22714)***

Dlt Growers Inc .... E 909 947-8198
13131 S Bon View Ave Ontario (91761) ***(P-75)***

Dm Collective Inc .... F 323 923-2400
4536 District Blvd Vernon (90058) ***(P-2630)***

Dm Software Inc .... E 714 953-2653
1842 Park Skyline Rd Santa Ana (92705) ***(P-17839)***

Dma Claims Management Inc (PA) .... C **323 342-6800**
330 N Brand Blvd Ste 230 Glendale (91203) ***(P-15561)***

Dma Claims Services, Glendale *Also called Dma Claims Management Inc* ***(P-15561)***

Dma Greencare Contracting Inc .... E 714 630-9470
950 N Tustin Ave Ste 118 Anaheim (92807) ***(P-302)***

DMC, Simi Valley *Also called Datametrics Corporation* ***(P-8249)***

DMC Power Inc (PA) .... D **310 323-1616**
623 E Artesia Blvd Carson (90746) ***(P-9032)***

Dmf Inc .... D 323 934-7779
1118 E 223rd St Carson (90745) ***(P-9062)***

Dmf Lighting, Carson *Also called Dmf Inc* ***(P-9062)***

Dmi, Sylmar *Also called Desert Mechanical Inc* ***(P-1055)***

Dmi Ready Mix, Oxnard *Also called Diversified Minerals Inc* ***(P-6090)***

Dmk, Santa Fe Springs *Also called Danne Montague-King Co* ***(P-14239)***

DMS Facility Services Inc .... A 949 975-1366
2861 E Coronado St Anaheim (92806) ***(P-17239)***

DMS Facility Services LLC .... A 949 975-1366
2861 E Coronado St Anaheim (92806) ***(P-22534)***

DMS-Bkl Drywall & Intr Systems .... E 415 508-4968
2900 E Belle Ter Unit A Bakersfield (93307) ***(P-1373)***

Dmt, Corona *Also called Diversified Mfg Tech Inc* ***(P-7797)***

Dmz Studio Inc (PA) .... F **805 640-9240**
1211 Maricopa Hwy Ste 250 Ojai (93023) ***(P-4127)***

Dna Health Inst Cyrogenic Div, Ventura *Also called Dna Health Institute Llc* ***(P-5132)***

Dna Health Institute Llc .... F 805 654-9363
4562 Westinghouse St B Ventura (93003) ***(P-5132)***

Dna Specialty Inc .... D 310 767-4070
200 W Artesia Blvd Compton (90220) ***(P-13055)***

DNam Apparel Industries LLC .... E 323 859-0114
4938 Triggs St Commerce (90022) ***(P-2941)***

DNC Prks Rsorts At Sequoia Inc .... D 559 565-4070
64740 Wuksachi Way Seq Natl Pk (93262) ***(P-16414)***

Dneg North America Inc (PA) .... D **323 461-7887**
5750 Hannum Ave Ste 100 Culver City (90230) ***(P-19229)***

Dnf Controls, Northridge *Also called Universal Ctrl Solutions Corp* ***(P-8965)***

Dng Fashion .... F 917 747-3158
3209 S Main St Los Angeles (90007) ***(P-11660)***

Dnick24 Academy .... E 310 904-4545
3054 E Via Corvina Ontario (91764) ***(P-18503)***

Do It American Mfg Company LLC .... F 951 254-9204
137 Vander St Corona (92878) ***(P-7553)***

Do It Best, Pasadena *Also called George L Throop Co* ***(P-6035)***

Do It Center, Simi Valley *Also called Lumber City Corp* ***(P-83)***

Do It Center, Westlake Village *Also called Lumber City Corp* ***(P-13276)***

Do It Right Products LLC (PA) .... E **661 722-9664**
44321 62nd St W Lancaster (93536) ***(P-6027)***

Docircle Inc .... E 415 484-4221
2544 W Woodland Dr Anaheim (92801) ***(P-12634)***

Dockside Machine & Ship Repair, Wilmington *Also called Marine Technical Services Inc* ***(P-18586)***

Dockum Research Laboratory Inc .... F 626 794-1821
844 E Mariposa St Altadena (91001) ***(P-11170)***

Docmagic Inc .... D 800 649-1362
1800 W 213th St Torrance (90501) ***(P-18504)***

Doctor Genius, Irvine *Also called Foundation Lead Group LLC* ***(P-23220)***

Doctors Hospital Riverside LLC (PA) .... E **951 354-7404**
3865 Jackson St Riverside (92503) ***(P-20757)***

Doctors Hospital W Covina Inc .... C 626 338-8481
725 S Orange Ave West Covina (91790) ***(P-20758)***

Documedia Group (PA) .... F **949 567-9930**
2082 Bus Ctr Dr Ste 257 Irvine (92612) ***(P-4278)***

Document Systems, Torrance *Also called Docmagic Inc* ***(P-18504)***

Documotion Research Inc .... F 714 662-3800
2020 S Eastwood Ave Santa Ana (92705) ***(P-4279)***

Docupace Technologies LLC .... C 310 445-7722
11766 Wilshire Blvd # 1120 Los Angeles (90025) ***(P-17600)***

Docupak Inc .... E 714 670-7944
17515 Valley View Ave Cerritos (90703) ***(P-4610)***

DOE & Ingalls Cal Oper LLC .... E 951 801-7175
1060 Citrus St Riverside (92507) ***(P-10791)***

Doi Venture, Rancho Cucamonga *Also called Davidson Optronics Inc* ***(P-10877)***

Doing Good Works .... F 949 354-0400
12 Mauchly Ste B Irvine (92618) ***(P-4509)***

Doka USA Ltd .... F 951 509-0023
6901 Central Ave Riverside (92504) ***(P-6821)***

Dolby Theatre, Los Angeles *Also called Theatredreams La/Chi L P* ***(P-19334)***

Dolce Dolci LLC .... F 818 343-8400
16745 Saticoy St Ste 112 Van Nuys (91406) ***(P-1814)***

Dole Citrus .... C 818 879-6600
1 Dole Dr Westlake Village (91362) ***(P-14622)***

Dole Food Company Inc (HQ) .... A **818 874-4000**
1 Dole Dr Westlake Village (91362) ***(P-69)***

Dole Holding Company LLC .... A 818 879-6600
1 Dole Dr Westlake Village (91362) ***(P-70)***

Dole Packaged Foods LLC (HQ) .... A **805 601-5500**
3059 Townsgate Rd Westlake Village (91361) ***(P-1898)***

Doll House Footwear, City of Industry *Also called J P Original Corp* ***(P-14440)***

Dollar Shave Club Inc (HQ) .... B **310 975-8528**
13335 Maxella Ave Marina Del Rey (90292) ***(P-7728)***

Dolores Canning Co Inc .... E 323 263-9155
1020 N Eastern Ave Los Angeles (90063) ***(P-1849)***

Dolphin Bay Hotel & Residences, Shell Beach *Also called Dolphin Bay Ht & Residence Inc* ***(P-16415)***

Dolphin Bay Ht & Residence Inc .... D 805 773-4300
2727 Shell Beach Rd Shell Beach (93449) ***(P-16415)***

Dolphin Hkg Ltd (PA) .... D **310 215-3356**
1125 W Hillcrest Blvd Inglewood (90301) ***(P-14925)***

Dolphin Imaging Systems LLC .... C 818 435-1368
9200 Oakdale Ave Chatsworth (91311) ***(P-17601)***

Dolphin International, Inglewood *Also called Dolphin Hkg Ltd* ***(P-14925)***

Dolphin Medical Inc (HQ) .... D **800 448-6506**
12525 Chadron Ave Hawthorne (90250) ***(P-11220)***

Dolphin Spas Inc .... F 626 334-0099
701 W Foothill Blvd Azusa (91702) ***(P-11661)***

Dolstra Automatic Products .... F 714 894-2062
14441 Edwards St Westminster (92683) ***(P-8573)***

Dominguez Firm Inc .... D 213 388-7788
3250 Wilshire Blvd # 2200 Los Angeles (90010) ***(P-21550)***

Dominion Corporation .... D 310 477-3041
11355 W Olympic Blvd # 210 Los Angeles (90064) ***(P-15187)***

Dominion Mortgage, Los Angeles *Also called Dominion Corporation* ***(P-15187)***

Domino Plastics Mfg Inc .... E 661 396-3744
601 Gateway Ct Bakersfield (93307) ***(P-5628)***

Domino Realty Management Co .... D 714 556-0466
3700 S Plaza Dr Ofc Santa Ana (92704) ***(P-15723)***

Dominos Pizza LLC .... C 909 390-1990
301 S Rockefeller Ave Ontario (91761) ***(P-12266)***

Domo Company LLC (PA) .... E **626 407-0015**
15925 Canary Ave La Mirada (90638) ***(P-17840)***

Don Alderson Associates Inc .... E 310 837-5141
3327 La Cienega Pl Los Angeles (90016) ***(P-3566)***

Don Brandel Plumbing Inc .... E 562 408-0400
15100 Texaco Ave Paramount (90723) ***(P-1056)***

Don Lee Farms, Inglewood *Also called Goodman Food Products Inc* ***(P-2446)***

Don Miguel Foods, Orange *Also called Don Miguel Mexican Foods Inc* ***(P-1925)***

Don Miguel Mexican Foods Inc (HQ) .... E **714 385-4500**
333 S Anita Dr Ste 1000 Orange (92868) ***(P-1925)***

Don Whittemore Corp .... F 818 994-0111
501 Library St San Fernando (91340) ***(P-1815)***

Donahue Schrber Rlty Group Inc (PA) .... D **714 545-1400**
200 Baker St Ste 100 Costa Mesa (92626) ***(P-15840)***

Donahue Schriber Rlty Group LP (PA) .... D **714 545-1400**
200 Baker St Ste 100 Costa Mesa (92626) ***(P-15665)***

Donald J Schefflers Cnstr, Azusa *Also called Heidi Corporation* ***(P-1529)***

Donald O Smith Company .... F 323 685-5011
5420 S Santa Fe Ave Vernon (90058) ***(P-13804)***

Donald T Sterling Corporation .... D 310 275-5575
10300 Wilshire Blvd Los Angeles (90024) ***(P-16416)***

Donco & Sons Inc .... E 714 779-0099
2871 E Blue Star St Anaheim (92806) ***(P-1244)***

Donco Associates & Sons, Anaheim *Also called Donco & Sons Inc* ***(P-1244)***

Dongsuk Park DDS Inc .... D 714 734-0900
14 Crestwood Irvine (92620) ***(P-20175)***

Donoco Industries Inc .... E 714 893-7889
5642 Research Dr Ste B Huntington Beach (92649) ***(P-5934)***

Donovan Aluminum Racing Engine, Torrance *Also called Donovan Engineering Corp* ***(P-10047)***

Donovan Engineering Corp .... F 310 320-3772
2305 Border Ave Torrance (90501) ***(P-10047)***

Dool Fna Inc .... C 562 483-4100
16624 Edwards Rd Cerritos (90703) ***(P-2596)***

Door & Hardware Installers Inc .... E 661 298-9383
14300 Davenport Rd Ste 1a Agua Dulce (91390) ***(P-3245)***

Door Components Inc .... C 909 770-5700
7980 Redwood Ave Fontana (92336) ***(P-6695)***

Door Doctor, Anaheim *Also called R & S Overhead Door of So Cal* ***(P-6716)***

Door Service Company .... F 760 320-0788
680 S Williams Rd Palm Springs (92264) ***(P-6223)***

Doorking Inc (PA) .... C **310 645-0023**
120 S Glasgow Ave Inglewood (90301) ***(P-9865)***

Dorado Pkg, North Hollywood *Also called Corporate Impressions La Inc* ***(P-4502)***

Dorco Electronics Inc .... F 562 623-1133
13540 Larwin Cir Santa Fe Springs (90670) ***(P-3835)***

Dorco Fiberglass Products, Santa Fe Springs *Also called Dorco Electronics Inc* ***(P-3835)***

Dorel Home Furnishings Inc .... C 909 390-5705
5400 Shea Center Dr Ontario (91761) ***(P-3467)***

Dorel Juvenile Group Inc .... E 909 428-0295
9950 Calabash Ave Fontana (92335) ***(P-5629)***

Dorel Juvenile Group Inc .... E 909 390-5705
5400 Shea Center Dr Ontario (91761) ***(P-5630)***

Doremi Cinema LLC .... F 818 562-1101
1020 Chestnut St Burbank (91506) ***(P-11274)***

Doringer Manufacturing Co Inc .... F 310 366-7766
13400 Estrella Ave Gardena (90248) ***(P-7729)***

Dosa Inc .... E 213 627-3672
850 S Broadway Ste 700 Los Angeles (90014) ***(P-2942)***

Dose Medical Corporation .... F 949 367-9600
229 Avenida Fabricante San Clemente (92672) ***(P-10972)***

DOT Blue Safes Corporation .... E 909 445-8888
2707 N Garey Ave Pomona (91767) ***(P-7554)***

DOT Copy Inc .... D 818 341-6666
9655 De Soto Ave Chatsworth (91311) ***(P-4280)***

DOT Corp (PA) .... E **714 708-5800**
2525 Pullman St Santa Ana (92705) ***(P-4281)***

Mergent e-mail: customerrelations@mergent.com
1116
2022 Southern California Business Directory and Buyers Guide
(P-0000) Products & Services Section entry number
(PA)=Parent Co (HQ)=Headquarters (DH)=Div Headquarters

DOT Corp...E.......714 708-5960
1801 S Standard Ave Santa Ana (92707) ***(P-4282)***
DOT Fulfillment The, Santa Ana *Also called DOT Corp* ***(P-4281)***
DOT Graphics, Chatsworth *Also called DOT Copy Inc* ***(P-4280)***
DOT Printer Inc (PA)...D.......949 474-1100
2424 Mcgaw Ave Irvine (92614) ***(P-4283)***
Double Eagle Trnsp Corp...C.......760 956-3770
12135 Scarbrough Ct Oak Hills (92344) ***(P-12035)***
Double Inks, La Crescenta *Also called Pro Media Merchants* ***(P-4407)***
Double K Industries, Chatsworth *Also called Invelop Inc* ***(P-7612)***
Double K Industries Inc...F.......818 772-2887
9711 Mason Ave Chatsworth (91311) ***(P-7609)***
Double Zero Inc (PA)...E.......323 846-1400
2011 E 49th St Vernon (90058) ***(P-14371)***
Double Zero Aougenoire, Vernon *Also called Double Zero Inc* ***(P-14371)***
Doubleco Incorporated...D.......909 481-0799
9444 9th St Rancho Cucamonga (91730) ***(P-7062)***
Doubleline Capital LP...C.......213 633-8200
333 S Grand Ave Fl 18 Los Angeles (90071) ***(P-18505)***
Doubletree By Hilton Carson, Carson *Also called Carson Operating Company LLC* ***(P-16369)***
Doubletree Hotel, Commerce *Also called W2005 Wyn Hotels LP* ***(P-16776)***
Doubletree Hotel, Santa Ana *Also called Chamson Management Inc* ***(P-16377)***
Doubletree Hotel, Irvine *Also called Spectrum Hotel Group LLC* ***(P-16723)***
Doubletree Hotel, Anaheim *Also called Doubltree Suites By Hilton LLC* ***(P-16419)***
Doubletree Hotel, Santa Barbara *Also called Fess Prker-Red Lion Gen Partnr* ***(P-16442)***
Doubletree Hotel, Torrance *Also called Ctc Group Inc* ***(P-16402)***
Doubletree Hotel, San Pedro *Also called San Pedro Ownership Inc* ***(P-16688)***
Doubletree Hotel...D.......323 722-8800
888 Montebello Blvd Rosemead (91770) ***(P-16417)***
Doubletree Suites Doheny, Dana Point *Also called Ergs Aim Hotel Realty LLC* ***(P-16436)***
Doubltree By Hlton Ht Monrovia...C.......626 357-1900
924 W Huntington Dr Monrovia (91016) ***(P-16418)***
Doubltree By Hlton Ontrio Arpr, Ontario *Also called Dt Ontrio Ht Prtners Lssee LLC* ***(P-16420)***
Doubltree Ht Anhim-Orange Cnty, Orange *Also called Anaheim Ca LLC* ***(P-16320)***
Doubltree Los Angeles Westside, Culver City *Also called Crp Centinela LP* ***(P-16401)***
Doubltree Palm Sprng Golf Rsor, Cathedral City *Also called T Alliance One - Palm Sprng LLC* ***(P-19674)***
Doubltree Stes By Hlton Snta M, Santa Monica *Also called Santa Monica Hotel Owner LLC* ***(P-16692)***
Doubltree Suites By Hilton LLC...C.......714 750-3000
2085 S Harbor Blvd Anaheim (92802) ***(P-16419)***
Doug Deleo Welding Inc...F.......559 562-3700
249 N Ashland Ave Lindsay (93247) ***(P-18976)***
Doug Mockett & Company Inc...E.......310 318-2491
1915 Abalone Ave Torrance (90501) ***(P-3468)***
Doughpro, Perris *Also called Stearns Product Dev Corp* ***(P-8140)***
Douglas Casual Living, Ontario *Also called Chromcraft Rvngton Douglas Ind* ***(P-3497)***
Douglas Emmett Builders...D.......310 255-7800
1299 Ocean Ave Ste 1000 Santa Monica (90401) ***(P-16233)***
Douglas Fir Holdings LLC...C.......714 842-5551
8382 Newman Ave Huntington Beach (92647) ***(P-20315)***
Douglas Maxim Inc...E.......805 648-7761
1726 N Ventura Ave Ste A Ventura (93001) ***(P-13302)***
Douglas Steel Supply Inc (PA)...D.......323 587-7676
4804 Laurel Canyon Blvd Valley Village (91607) ***(P-13564)***
DOUGLAS STEEL SUPPLY CO., Valley Village *Also called Douglas Steel Supply Inc* ***(P-13564)***
Douglas Technologies Group Inc (PA)...E.......760 758-5560
42092 Winchester Rd Ste B Temecula (92590) ***(P-10048)***
Douglas Wheel, Temecula *Also called Douglas Technologies Group Inc* ***(P-10048)***
Douglass Truck Bodies Inc...E.......661 327-0258
231 21st St Bakersfield (93301) ***(P-9983)***
Doval Industries Inc...D.......323 226-0335
3961 N Mission Rd Los Angeles (90031) ***(P-6515)***
Doval Industries Co, Los Angeles *Also called Doval Industries Inc* ***(P-6515)***
Dow Chemical Co Foundation...C.......909 476-4127
11266 Jersey Blvd Rancho Cucamonga (91730) ***(P-4687)***
Dow Hydraulic Systems Inc...D.......909 596-6602
2895 Metropolitan Pl Pomona (91767) ***(P-8574)***
Dow-Elco Inc...E.......323 723-1288
1313 W Olympic Blvd Montebello (90640) ***(P-8868)***
Dow-Key Microwave Corporation...C.......805 650-0260
4822 Mcgrath St Ventura (93003) ***(P-8948)***
Dowdys Sales and Services Inc...F.......559 688-6973
15185 Avenue 224 Tulare (93274) ***(P-7610)***
Dowell Aluminum Foundry Inc...E.......323 877-9645
11342 Hartland St North Hollywood (91605) ***(P-6392)***
Dowling Advisory Group...D.......626 319-1369
3579 E Foothill Blvd # 651 Pasadena (91107) ***(P-23208)***
Downey Care Center, Downey *Also called Ensign Group Inc* ***(P-20328)***
Downey Community Health Center...C.......562 862-6506
8425 Iowa St Downey (90241) ***(P-20316)***
Downey Grinding Co...E.......562 803-5556
12323 Bellflower Blvd Downey (90242) ***(P-7730)***
Downey Orthopedic Med Group, Manhattan Beach *Also called Southwestern Orthpd Med Corp* ***(P-20094)***
Downey Regional Medical Center, Downey *Also called Pih Health Hospital - Whitti* ***(P-20892)***
Downhole Stabilization Inc...E.......661 631-1044
3515 Thomas Way Bakersfield (93308) ***(P-7668)***
Downs Equipment Rentals Inc (PA)...D.......661 615-6119
4800 Saco Rd Bakersfield (93308) ***(P-17307)***
Downtown Community Dev YMCA, Long Beach *Also called Young Mens Christian Associat* ***(P-22384)***
Dozuki...E.......805 464-0573
1330 Monterey St San Luis Obispo (93401) ***(P-17841)***
DP Technology LLC (HQ)...D.......805 388-6000
1150 Avenida Acaso Camarillo (93012) ***(P-17602)***
Dpa Components International, Simi Valley *Also called Dpa Labs Inc* ***(P-9498)***
Dpa Labs Inc...E.......805 581-9200
2251 Ward Ave Simi Valley (93065) ***(P-9498)***
DPI Labs Inc...E.......909 392-5777
1350 Arrow Hwy La Verne (91750) ***(P-10312)***
Dpi Specialty Foods West Inc (HQ)...A.......909 975-1019
601 S Rockefeller Ave Ontario (91761) ***(P-14465)***
Dpr Construction A Gen Partnr...C.......626 463-1265
88 W Colo Blvd Ste 301 Pasadena (91105) ***(P-761)***
Dr Harold Katz LLC...F.......323 993-8320
5802 Willoughby Ave Los Angeles (90038) ***(P-5014)***
Dr Pepper Snapple Group, Riverside *Also called American Bottling Company* ***(P-2249)***
DR Radon Boatbuilding Inc...F.......805 692-2170
67 Depot Rd Goleta (93117) ***(P-10463)***
Dr Smoothie Brands Inc...F.......714 449-9787
1730 Raymer Ave Fullerton (92833) ***(P-2321)***
Dr Smoothie Enterprises...E.......714 449-9787
1730 Raymer Ave Fullerton (92833) ***(P-2322)***
Dr Squatch Inc...E.......704 989-9024
4065 Glencoe Ave Apt 300b Marina Del Rey (90292) ***(P-5015)***
Dr. Fresh, La Palma *Also called Ranir LLC* ***(P-11192)***
Draco Broadcast Inc...E.......818 736-5788
2000 N Lincoln St Burbank (91504) ***(P-9268)***
Dragon Alliance Inc...D.......760 931-4900
971 Calle Amanecer San Clemente (92673) ***(P-11249)***
Dragon Herbs, Los Angeles *Also called Ron Teeguarden Enterprises Inc* ***(P-4762)***
Dranse Technology Inc...F.......323 908-8554
8605 Santa Monica Blvd # 795 West Hollywood (90069) ***(P-9269)***
Drapery Affair, Ventura *Also called Blue Ribbon Draperies Inc* ***(P-3092)***
Drcollins Inc...E.......888 583-6048
26229 Enterprise Ct Lake Forest (92630) ***(P-11171)***
Dream Hollywood, Los Angeles *Also called 6417 Selma Hotel LLC* ***(P-16311)***
Dream Home Care Inc...D.......562 595-9021
20695 S Wstn Ave Ste 132 Torrance (90501) ***(P-22100)***
Dream River, Vernon *Also called Shason Inc* ***(P-14319)***
Dreamgear LLC...E.......310 222-5522
20001 S Western Ave Torrance (90501) ***(P-11371)***
Dreamhost.com, Los Angeles *Also called New Dream Network LLC* ***(P-12658)***
Dreamworks Animation Pubg LLC...A.......818 695-5000
1000 Flower St Glendale (91201) ***(P-19119)***
Dreamworks Knitting, Santa Ana *Also called Nutrade Inc* ***(P-2583)***
Drees Wood Products Inc...E.......562 633-7337
14020 Orange Ave Paramount (90723) ***(P-3246)***
Drees Wood Products Inc (PA)...E.......562 633-7337
14003 Orange Ave Paramount (90723) ***(P-3317)***
Dreier's Nursing Care Center, Glendale *Also called Ksm Healthcare Inc* ***(P-20390)***
Dretloh Aircraft Supply Inc (PA)...F.......714 632-6982
2830 E La Cresta Ave Anaheim (92806) ***(P-10313)***
Drew Chain Security Corp...D.......626 457-8626
55 S Raymond Ave Ste 303 Alhambra (91801) ***(P-18271)***
Drew Child Dev Corp Inc (PA)...C.......323 249-2950
1770 E 118th St Los Angeles (90059) ***(P-21773)***
Dreyers Grand Ice Cream Inc...C.......909 444-2253
351 Cheryl Ln City of Industry (91789) ***(P-1816)***
Driftwood Dairy Holding Corp...F.......626 444-9591
10724 Lower Azusa Rd El Monte (91731) ***(P-2426)***
Drill Cool Systems Inc (PA)...F.......661 633-2665
627 Williams St Bakersfield (93305) ***(P-13898)***
Drillmec Inc (HQ)...E.......281 885-0777
8140 Rosecrans Ave Paramount (90723) ***(P-447)***
Drinks Holdings Inc (PA)...D.......310 441-8400
10900 Wilshire Blvd # 1600 Los Angeles (90024) ***(P-14840)***
Drissi Advertising Inc (PA)...D.......323 466-4700
6721 Romaine St Los Angeles (90038) ***(P-17096)***
Drivenbi LLC...D.......626 795-2088
1606 Camino Lindo South Pasadena (91030) ***(P-17603)***
Driver Spg LLC...E.......855 300-4774
468 N Rosemead Blvd Pasadena (91107) ***(P-18506)***
Drop Lot Services, San Juan Capistrano *Also called Merit Logistics LLC* ***(P-12580)***
Dropship Vendor Group LLC...E.......424 391-6943
9469 Opal Ave Ste 6 Mentone (92359) ***(P-3469)***
Dropzone Waterpark...C.......951 210-1600
2165 Trumble Rd Perris (92571) ***(P-19644)***
Drs Ntwork Imaging Systems LLC...D.......714 220-3800
10600 Valley View St Cypress (90630) ***(P-9499)***
Drybar Holdings LLC (PA)...B.......310 776-6330
125 Technology Dr Ste 150 Irvine (92618) ***(P-16901)***
Drymaster, Mission Viejo *Also called Dimar Enterprises Inc* ***(P-17238)***
Drywired Defense LLC...F.......310 684-3891
9606 Santa Monica Blvd # 4 Beverly Hills (90210) ***(P-7358)***
Ds Lakeshore LP, Costa Mesa *Also called Donahue Schriber Rlty Group LP* ***(P-15665)***
Ds Lakeshore LP...D.......916 286-5231
200 Baker St Ste 100 Costa Mesa (92626) ***(P-22336)***
DSA Signage...F.......877 305-4911
16961 Central Ave Carson (90746) ***(P-11542)***
Dsca, Long Beach *Also called Denso Pdts & Svcs Americas Inc* ***(P-13054)***
Dsd Trucking Inc (PA)...D.......310 338-3395
2411 Santa Fe Ave Redondo Beach (90278) ***(P-12356)***
DSI Logistics LLC (PA)...D.......800 335-6557
675 Placentia Ave Ste 325 Brea (92821) ***(P-12569)***
Dsj Printing Inc...F.......310 828-8051
1703 Stewart St Santa Monica (90404) ***(P-4284)***

Employee Codes: A=Over 500 employees, B=251-500
C=101-250, D=51-100, E=20-50 F=10-19
2022 Southern California Business
Directory and Buyers Guide
© Mergent Inc. 1-800-342-5647
1117

DSM&t Co Inc .... C 909 357-7960
10609 Business Dr Fontana (92337) ***(P-9822)***

Dsp Winner Inc .... F 858 336-9471
1641 W Main St Ste 222 Alhambra (91801) ***(P-8989)***

Dspm Inc .... E 714 970-2304
1921 S Quaker Ridge Pl Ontario (91761) ***(P-9628)***

Dss, Calabasas *Also called David Shield Security Inc* ***(P-18269)***

Dss Networks Inc .... F 949 981-3473
24462 Redlen St Lake Forest (92630) ***(P-8251)***

DSV Solutions LLC .... C 909 349-6100
13230 San Bernardino Ave Fontana (92335) ***(P-12448)***

DSV Solutions LLC .... C 909 390-4563
1670 Etiwanda Ave Ste A Ontario (91761) ***(P-12449)***

DSV Solutions LLC .... C 714 630-0110
3454 E Miraloma Ave Anaheim (92806) ***(P-12450)***

Dsy Educational Corporation .... E 805 684-8111
525 Maple St Carpinteria (93013) ***(P-3194)***

Dt Club Hotel Santa Ana, Santa Ana *Also called Jhc Investment Inc* ***(P-16513)***

DT Mattson Enterprises Inc .... E 951 849-9781
201 W Lincoln St Banning (92220) ***(P-11372)***

Dt Ontrio Ht Prtners Lssee LLC .... B 909 937-0900
222 N Vineyard Ave Ontario (91764) ***(P-16420)***

Dti Services Inc (PA) .... D 213 670-1100
601 S Figueroa St # 4300 Los Angeles (90017) ***(P-18174)***

Dtrs Santa Monica LLC .... B 310 458-6700
1700 Ocean Ave Santa Monica (90401) ***(P-16421)***

Dts Inc (HQ) .... C 818 436-1000
5220 Las Virgenes Rd Calabasas (91302) ***(P-19230)***

Dts LLC .... E 818 436-1000
5220 Las Virgenes Rd Calabasas (91302) ***(P-9172)***

Dtv Network Systems Inc (PA) .... C 800 531-5000
2230 E Imperial Hwy El Segundo (90245) ***(P-12767)***

Dtwusa, Hacienda Heights *Also called Brio Water Technology Inc* ***(P-13851)***

Dtz, Westlake Village *Also called C&W Facility Services Inc* ***(P-17221)***

Dual Diagnosis Trtmnt Ctr Inc (PA) .... B 949 276-5553
1211 Puerta Del Sol # 200 San Clemente (92673) ***(P-21300)***

Duarte Manor, Los Angeles *Also called Emp III Inc* ***(P-16259)***

Dubnoff Ctr For Child Devl & (PA) .... D 818 755-4950
10526 Dubnoff Way North Hollywood (91606) ***(P-21301)***

Duclos Lenses Inc .... F 818 773-0600
20222 Bahama St Chatsworth (91311) ***(P-19034)***

Ducommun Aerostructures Inc (HQ) .... B 310 380-5390
268 E Gardena Blvd Gardena (90248) ***(P-10213)***

Ducommun Aerostructures Inc .... E 626 358-3211
801 Royal Oaks Dr Monrovia (91016) ***(P-10314)***

Ducommun Aerostructures Inc .... C 760 246-4191
4001 El Mirage Rd Adelanto (92301) ***(P-10315)***

Ducommun Aerostructures Inc .... C 714 637-4401
1885 N Batavia St Orange (92865) ***(P-10214)***

Ducommun Aerostructures Inc .... C 310 513-7200
23301 Wilmington Ave Carson (90745) ***(P-10316)***

Ducommun Arostructures-Gardena, Gardena *Also called Ahf-Ducommun Incorporated* ***(P-10257)***

Ducommun Incorporated (PA) .... B 657 335-3665
200 Sandpointe Ave # 700 Santa Ana (92707) ***(P-10317)***

Ducommun Incorporated .... E 626 812-9666
1321 Mountain View Cir Azusa (91702) ***(P-9629)***

Ducommun Labarge Tech Inc (HQ) .... C 310 513-7200
23301 Wilmington Ave Carson (90745) ***(P-10318)***

Dudes Brewing Company .... E 424 271-2915
1840 W 208th St Somis (93066) ***(P-2142)***

Duff & Phelps LLC .... D 213 270-2300
350 S Grand Ave Ste 3100 Los Angeles (90071) ***(P-23209)***

Duggan & Associates Inc .... D 323 965-1502
1442 W 135th St Gardena (90249) ***(P-1177)***

Duke Energy Corporation .... C 949 727-7434
8001 Irvine Center Dr Irvine (92618) ***(P-12801)***

Duke Pacific Inc .... D 909 591-0191
13950 Monte Vista Ave Chino (91710) ***(P-1483)***

Dukes Research and Mfg Inc .... E 818 998-9811
9060 Winnetka Ave Northridge (91324) ***(P-10319)***

Dulcinea Farms, Los Angeles *Also called Pacific Trellis Fruit LLC* ***(P-14646)***

Dun & Brdstreet Emrging Bsnsse (HQ) .... C 310 456-8271
22761 Pacific Coast Hwy Malibu (90265) ***(P-18507)***

Dunbar Electric Sign Company .... E 661 323-2600
4020 Rosedale Hwy Bakersfield (93308) ***(P-11543)***

Duncan Bolt Co .... F 909 581-6740
5555 E Gibralter Ontario (91764) ***(P-7063)***

Duncan Carter Corporation (PA) .... D 805 964-9749
5427 Hollister Ave Santa Barbara (93111) ***(P-11341)***

Duncan McIntosh Company Inc (PA) .... E 949 660-6150
18475 Bandilier Cir Fountain Valley (92708) ***(P-4067)***

Dunham Metal Processing Co .... E 714 532-5551
936 N Parker St Orange (92867) ***(P-7248)***

Dunkel Bros. Machinery Moving, La Mirada *Also called MEI Rigging & Crating LLC* ***(P-7989)***

Dunn & Berger Inc .... B 818 986-1234
5955 De Soto Ave Ste 160 Woodland Hills (91367) ***(P-21160)***

Dunn-Dwrds Pints Wallcoverings, Vernon *Also called Dunn-Edwards Corporation* ***(P-5095)***

Dunn-Edwards Corporation (HQ) .... C 888 337-2468
4885 E 52nd Pl Vernon (90058) ***(P-5095)***

Dunstan Enterprises Inc .... F 562 630-6292
11821 Slauson Ave Santa Fe Springs (90670) ***(P-8575)***

Dunweizer Machine Inc .... F 562 698-7787
8338 Allport Ave Santa Fe Springs (90670) ***(P-6741)***

Dunweizer Mch & Fabrication, Santa Fe Springs *Also called Dunweizer Machine Inc* ***(P-6741)***

Duplo USA Corporation (PA) .... D 949 752-8222
3050 Daimler St Santa Ana (92705) ***(P-13356)***

Dupont Displays Inc .... C 805 562-5400
600 Ward Dr Ste C Santa Barbara (93111) ***(P-22835)***

Dupree Inc .... E 909 597-4889
14395 Ramona Ave Chino (91710) ***(P-7064)***

Dur-Red Products .... E 323 771-9000
4900 Cecilia St Cudahy (90201) ***(P-6822)***

Dura Coat Products Inc (PA) .... D 951 341-6500
5361 Via Ricardo Riverside (92509) ***(P-7359)***

Dura Freight Lines, Walnut *Also called Patina Freight Inc* ***(P-12228)***

Dura Plastic Products Inc (HQ) .... D 951 845-3161
533 E Third St Beaumont (92223) ***(P-5631)***

Dura Technologies Inc .... C 909 877-8477
2720 S Willow Ave Ste A Bloomington (92316) ***(P-5096)***

Durabag Company Inc .... D 714 259-8811
1432 Santa Fe Dr Tustin (92780) ***(P-3883)***

Durable Coating Inc .... F 805 299-8850
28716 Garnet Canyon Dr Santa Clarita (91390) ***(P-7360)***

Duracold Refrigeration Mfg LLC .... E 626 358-1710
1551 S Primrose Ave Monrovia (91016) ***(P-6992)***

Duralum Products Inc .... F 951 736-4500
4001 Greystone Dr Ontario (91761) ***(P-6326)***

Duramar Interior Surfaces, Irvine *Also called Daz Inc* ***(P-8895)***

Duramax Building Products, Montebello *Also called US Polymers Inc* ***(P-5852)***

Durango Foods, Bell *Also called Flores Brothers Inc* ***(P-2433)***

Duray, Downey *Also called J F Duncan Industries Inc* ***(P-8387)***

Durham School Services L P .... C 310 767-5820
723 S Alameda St Compton (90220) ***(P-11919)***

Durham School Services L P .... C 562 408-1206
8555 Flower Ave Paramount (90723) ***(P-11920)***

Durham School Services L P .... C 818 880-4257
4029 Las Virgenes Rd Calabasas (91302) ***(P-11921)***

Durham School Services L P .... C 909 899-1809
12999 Victoria St Rancho Cucamonga (91739) ***(P-11922)***

Durham School Services L P .... C 805 483-6076
3151 W 5th St Ste A Oxnard (93030) ***(P-11923)***

Durham School Services L P .... C 714 542-8989
2818 W 5th St Santa Ana (92703) ***(P-11942)***

Durham School Services L P .... C 626 573-3769
2713 River Ave Rosemead (91770) ***(P-11924)***

Durham School Services L P .... C 949 376-0376
2003 Laguna Canyon Rd Laguna Beach (92651) ***(P-11925)***

Durkan Patterned Carpets Inc .... C 310 838-2898
3633 Lenawee Ave 120 Los Angeles (90016) ***(P-2689)***

Duro Corporation .... F 626 839-6541
17018 Evergreen Pl City of Industry (91745) ***(P-8990)***

Duro Roller Company Inc .... F 562 944-8856
13006 Park St Santa Fe Springs (90670) ***(P-5373)***

Duro-Flex Rubber Products Inc .... E 562 946-5533
13215 Lakeland Rd Santa Fe Springs (90670) ***(P-5374)***

Duro-Sense Corp .... F 310 533-6877
869 Sandhill Ave Carson (90746) ***(P-10690)***

Durrani Investments Corp .... E 424 292-3424
555 Anton Blvd Ste 150 Costa Mesa (92626) ***(P-14778)***

Durston Manufacturing Company .... F 909 593-1506
1395 Palomares St La Verne (91750) ***(P-6477)***

Duthie Electric Service Corp .... E 562 790-1772
2335 E Cherry Indus Cir Long Beach (90805) ***(P-18954)***

Duthie Power Services, Long Beach *Also called Duthie Electric Service Corp* ***(P-18954)***

Dutt Hospitality Group Inc .... D 760 340-1001
74900 Gerald Ford Dr Palm Desert (92211) ***(P-16422)***

Dutton Home Services LLC .... E 702 625-9104
997 Flower Glen St Simi Valley (93065) ***(P-1057)***

Dutton Plumbing, Simi Valley *Also called Dutton Home Services LLC* ***(P-1057)***

Dv Custom Farming LLC .... D 661 858-2888
2101 Mettler Frontage E Bakersfield (93307) ***(P-105)***

Dva Healthcare Tuscaloosa LLC (HQ) .... E 310 536-2400
601 Hawaii St El Segundo (90245) ***(P-21241)***

DVeal Corporation .... C 626 296-8900
2750 E Wshngtn Blvd # 230 Pasadena (91107) ***(P-22181)***

Dvele Inc .... E 909 796-2561
25525 Redlands Blvd Loma Linda (92354) ***(P-3420)***

Dvele Omega Corporation .... D 909 796-2561
25525 Redlands Blvd Loma Linda (92354) ***(P-3421)***

Dvs Media Services (PA) .... F 818 841-6750
2625 W Olive Ave Burbank (91505) ***(P-17149)***

Dw and Bb Consulting Inc .... D 818 896-9899
11381 Bradley Ave Pacoima (91331) ***(P-10532)***

DWA, Palm Springs *Also called Desert Water Agency Fing Corp* ***(P-128[illegible]7)***

Dwa Alminum Composites USA Inc .... E 818 998-1504
21100 Superior St Chatsworth (91311) ***(P-6393)***

Dwa Holdings LLC (HQ) .... D 818 695-5000
1000 Flower St Glendale (91201) ***(P-19120)***

Dwaynes Engineering & Cnstr .... F 661 762-7261
3559 Addie Ave Fellows (93224) ***(P-495)***

Dwi Enterprises .... E 714 842-2236
11081 Winners Cir Ste 100 Los Alamitos (90720) ***(P-9173)***

Dxterity Diagnostics Inc (PA) .... E 310 537-7857
19500 S Rancho Way # 116 Compton (90220) ***(P-22907)***

Dy-Dee Service Pasadena Inc .... D 626 792-6183
40 E California Blvd Pasadena (91105) ***(P-16889)***

Dynabee USA, Anaheim *Also called Dynaflex International* ***(P-11413)***

Dynabook Americas Inc (HQ) .... B 949 583-3000
5241 California Ave # 100 Irvine (92617) ***(P-8153)***

Dynacast LLC .... C 949 707-1211
25952 Commercentre Dr Lake Forest (92630) ***(P-6379)***

Dynaflex International .... E 714 630-0909
1144 N Grove St Anaheim (92806) ***(P-11413)***

Dynaflex Products (PA) .... D 323 724-1555
6466 Gayhart St Commerce (90040) ***(P-9984)***

Dynalloy Inc.....E.....714 436-1206
1562 Reynolds Ave Irvine (92614) *(P-9701)*
Dynamation Research, Los Angeles *Also called Gali Corporation (P-10333)*
Dynamation Research Inc.....F.....909 864-2310
2301 Pontius Ave Los Angeles (90064) *(P-10320)*
Dynamet Incorporated.....E.....714 375-3150
16052 Beach Blvd Ste 221 Huntington Beach (92647) *(P-6331)*
Dynamex Corporation.....D.....310 329-0399
155 E Albertoni St Carson (90746) *(P-2714)*
Dynamic Auto Images Inc.....B.....714 771-3400
2860 Michelle Ste 140 Irvine (92606) *(P-18912)*
Dynamic Chiropractic, Huntington Beach *Also called Maxwell Petersen Associates (P-4085)*
Dynamic Collections, Temecula *Also called Dynamic Designs Inc (P-5016)*
Dynamic Cooking Systems Inc.....A.....714 372-7000
695 Town Center Dr # 180 Costa Mesa (92626) *(P-8379)*
Dynamic Denim Corporation.....F.....323 232-2524
5609 Mckinley Ave Los Angeles (90011) *(P-2568)*
Dynamic Designs Inc.....F.....951 302-1344
42259 Rio Nedo Temecula (92590) *(P-5016)*
Dynamic Detail, Irvine *Also called Dynamic Auto Images Inc (P-18912)*
Dynamic Dezign.....E.....562 735-3060
32 S Broadway Los Angeles (90012) *(P-17172)*
Dynamic Enterprises Inc.....E.....562 944-0271
2081 Rancho Hills Dr Chino Hills (91709) *(P-8576)*
Dynamic Fabrication Inc.....E.....714 662-2440
2615 S Hickory St Santa Ana (92707) *(P-10321)*
Dynamic Home Care Service Inc (PA).....D.....**818 981-4446**
14260 Ventura Blvd # 301 Sherman Oaks (91423) *(P-21161)*
Dynamic Sciences Intl Inc.....E.....818 226-6262
9400 Lurline Ave Unit B Chatsworth (91311) *(P-9270)*
Dynamic Woodworks Inc.....F.....562 483-8400
3509 Crooked Creek Dr Diamond Bar (91765) *(P-3247)*
Dynamic Worldwide West Inc (PA).....C.....**562 407-1000**
14141 Alondra Blvd Santa Fe Springs (90670) *(P-12451)*
Dynamics O&P, Los Angeles *Also called Dynamics Orthtics Prsthtics In (P-11095)*
Dynamics Orthtics Prsthtics In.....E.....213 383-9212
1830 W Olympic Blvd Ste 1 Los Angeles (90006) *(P-11095)*
Dynamite Sign Group Inc.....E.....562 595-7725
3080 E 29th St Long Beach (90806) *(P-11544)*
Dynamo Aviation Inc.....D.....818 785-9561
9601 Mason Ave A Chatsworth (91311) *(P-12357)*
Dynapro.....F.....626 898-4411
255 E Santa Clara St # 2 Arcadia (91006) *(P-7708)*
Dynapro Logistics, Arcadia *Also called Dynapro (P-7708)*
Dynasty Electronic Company LLC.....D.....714 550-1197
1790 E Mcfadden Ave # 10 Santa Ana (92705) *(P-9399)*
Dynasty Staffing Solutionsinc.....D.....909 727-3801
17255 Sycamore St Hesperia (92345) *(P-17414)*
Dynatrac Products Co Inc.....F.....714 596-4461
7392 Count Cir Huntington Beach (92647) *(P-10049)*
Dynomill Inc.....F.....626 454-1805
2018 Edwards Ave South El Monte (91733) *(P-8577)*
Dyntek Inc (PA).....C.....**949 271-6700**
5241 California Ave # 150 Irvine (92617) *(P-18175)*
Dytran Instruments Inc.....C.....818 700-7818
21592 Marilla St Chatsworth (91311) *(P-9702)*
Dz Trading Ltd.....D.....951 479-5700
12492 Feather Dr Eastvale (91752) *(P-14153)*
Dzyne Technologies Inc.....E.....703 454-0704
11 Vanderbilt Irvine (92618) *(P-22535)*
E & B Ntral Resources MGT Corp.....F.....661 766-2501
1848 Perkins Rd New Cuyama (93254) *(P-448)*
E & B Ntral Resources Mgt Corp (PA).....D.....**661 679-1714**
1608 Norris Rd Bakersfield (93308) *(P-449)*
E & C Fashion Inc.....B.....323 262-0099
1420 Esperanza St Los Angeles (90023) *(P-18508)*
E & L Electric.....F.....562 903-9272
12322 Los Nietos Rd Santa Fe Springs (90670) *(P-19009)*
E & R Glass Contractors Inc.....E.....909 624-1763
5369 Brooks St Montclair (91763) *(P-5952)*
E & S International Entps Inc (PA).....C.....**818 887-0700**
7801 Hayvenhurst Ave Van Nuys (91406) *(P-13684)*
E & S Paper Co.....E.....310 538-8700
14110 S Broadway Los Angeles (90061) *(P-14208)*
E & S Prcsion Shtmetal Mfg Inc.....E.....760 329-1607
19298 Mclane St North Palm Springs (92258) *(P-6823)*
E & S Ring Management Corp.....D.....310 821-4916
4600 Via Marina Apt 209 Marina Del Rey (90292) *(P-15841)*
E & S Ring Management Corp.....D.....310 337-5444
11050 Santa Monica Blvd # 2 Los Angeles (90025) *(P-15842)*
E & S Ring Management Corp.....D.....310 670-5983
6300 Green Valley Cir Culver City (90230) *(P-15843)*
E & T Foods Inc.....B.....760 843-7730
14827 Seventh St Victorville (92395) *(P-141)*
E A Shields Inc.....F.....661 325-5969
6613 Olympia Dr Bakersfield (93309) *(P-947)*
E Alko Inc.....E.....818 587-9700
8201 Woodley Ave Van Nuys (91406) *(P-11476)*
E and B Natural Resources.....D.....661 679-1700
1600 Norris Rd Bakersfield (93308) *(P-450)*
E and J Gallo, Santa Ynez *Also called Bridlewood Winery LLC (P-2168)*
E B Bradley Co (PA).....E.....**323 585-9917**
5602 Bickett St Vernon (90058) *(P-13805)*
E B Bradley Co.....E.....800 533-3030
10903 Vanowen St North Hollywood (91605) *(P-13806)*
E C R M C, El Centro *Also called El Centro Rgnal Med Ctr Fndtio (P-20761)*
E E Black Limited (HQ).....A.....**671 646-4861**
15901 Olden St Sylmar (91342) *(P-994)*
E Film Digital Labratories, Los Angeles *Also called Efilm LLC (P-19121)*
E H Summit Inc (PA).....D.....**310 476-6571**
11461 W Sunset Blvd Los Angeles (90049) *(P-16423)*
E J Harrison & Sons Inc.....C.....805 647-1414
1589 Lirio Ave Ventura (93004) *(P-12945)*
E J Lauren LLC.....E.....562 803-1113
9400 Hall Rd Downey (90241) *(P-3502)*
E L S, Los Angeles *Also called J C Entertainment Ltg Svcs Inc (P-19318)*
E M C, Moreno Valley *Also called Envirnmntal Mlding Cncepts LLC (P-5375)*
E M E Inc.....C.....310 639-1621
500 E Pine St Compton (90222) *(P-7249)*
E M S Trading Inc.....E.....909 581-7800
5161 Richton St Montclair (91763) *(P-14435)*
E M Tharp Inc (PA).....D.....**559 782-5800**
15243 Road 192 Porterville (93257) *(P-13024)*
E O C, Compton *Also called Cri Sub 1 (P-3581)*
E O C Health Services, San Luis Obispo *Also called Community Action Prtnr San Lui (P-21288)*
E O I, Walnut *Also called Excellence Opto Inc (P-9115)*
E P S Products, Palm Springs *Also called Xy Corp Inc (P-7770)*
E R C Company, E Rncho Dmngz *Also called Coy Industries Inc (P-6813)*
E R G Home Health Provider.....D.....562 403-1070
11700 South St Ste 200 Artesia (90701) *(P-21162)*
E R G International, Oxnard *Also called Ergonom Corporation (P-3727)*
E Sales, Garden Grove *Also called Elasco Inc (P-4689)*
E T Horn Company (PA).....D.....**714 523-8050**
16050 Canary Ave La Mirada (90638) *(P-14779)*
E V G, Anaheim *Also called Emergency Vehicle Group Inc (P-13025)*
E Vasquez Distributors Inc.....E.....805 487-8458
4524 E Pleasant Valley Rd Oxnard (93033) *(P-3388)*
E Z Buy E Z Sell Recycler Corp (HQ).....C.....**310 886-7808**
4954 Van Nuys Blvd Ste 20 Sherman Oaks (91403) *(P-3973)*
E Z Data Inc (HQ).....D.....**626 585-3505**
251 S Lake Ave Ste 200 Pasadena (91101) *(P-17604)*
E Z Lube No 54, Los Angeles *Also called EZ Lube LLC (P-18925)*
E Z Staffing Inc (PA).....B.....**818 845-2500**
200 N Maryland Ave # 303 Glendale (91206) *(P-17415)*
E&S Financial Group Inc.....D.....805 644-1621
3140 Telegraph Rd Ste A Ventura (93003) *(P-15240)*
E-Liq Cube Inc (PA).....F.....**562 537-9454**
13515 Alondra Blvd Santa Fe Springs (90670) *(P-11662)*
E-Scepter, City of Industry *Also called Sceptre Inc (P-9779)*
E-Sceptre Inc.....D.....888 350-8989
16800 Gale Ave City of Industry (91745) *(P-22836)*
E-Times Corporation Ltd.....B.....213 452-6720
601 S Figueroa St # 5000 Los Angeles (90017) *(P-18121)*
E-Z Lube 13, North Hollywood *Also called EZ Lube LLC (P-18929)*
E-Z Mix Inc (PA).....E.....**818 768-0568**
11450 Tuxford St Sun Valley (91352) *(P-3895)*
E-Z Up Directcom.....E.....909 426-0060
1900 2nd St Colton (92324) *(P-3137)*
E-Z-Hook Test Products Div, Arcadia *Also called Tektest Inc (P-9665)*
E. S. Babcock & Sons, Riverside *Also called Babcock Laboratories Inc (P-22932)*
E.V. Roberts, Carson *Also called Cirrus Enterprises LLC (P-14753)*
E2 Managetech Inc (HQ).....D.....**281 407-0820**
26741 Portola Pkwy Foothill Ranch (92610) *(P-22536)*
E4site Inc (PA).....F.....**714 242-5700**
6700 E Pacific Coast Hwy # 201 Long Beach (90803) *(P-17605)*
Ea Mobile Inc.....D.....310 754-7125
5510 Lincoln Blvd Los Angeles (90094) *(P-12607)*
EAC Intrnational Logistics Inc.....E.....877 668-7837
18945 San Jose Ave City of Industry (91748) *(P-12570)*
Eaco Corporation (PA).....D.....**714 876-2490**
5065 E Hunter Ave Anaheim (92807) *(P-13715)*
Eagle Access Ctrl Systems Inc.....E.....818 837-7900
12953 Foothill Blvd Sylmar (91342) *(P-8949)*
Eagle Dominion Energy Corp.....F.....805 272-9557
200 N Hayes Ave Oxnard (93030) *(P-451)*
Eagle Dominion Trust, Oxnard *Also called Eagle Dominion Energy Corp (P-451)*
Eagle Glen Country Club LLC.....D.....951 272-4653
1800 Eagle Glen Pkwy Corona (92883) *(P-19485)*
Eagle Glen Golf Club, Corona *Also called Eagle Glen Country Club LLC (P-19485)*
Eagle Graphics Inc (PA).....F.....**714 978-2200**
1430 W Katella Ave Orange (92867) *(P-4285)*
Eagle Labs LLC.....D.....909 481-0011
10201a Trademark St Ste A Rancho Cucamonga (91730) *(P-10973)*
Eagle Med Packg Sterilization, Paso Robles *Also called Eagle Med Pckg Strlization Inc (P-18509)*
Eagle Med Pckg Strlization Inc.....E.....805 238-7401
2921 Union Rd Ste A Paso Robles (93446) *(P-18509)*
Eagle Mountain Casino.....C.....559 788-6220
681 Suth Tule Rsrvtion Rd Porterville (93258) *(P-16424)*
Eagle Print Dynamics, Orange *Also called Eagle Graphics Inc (P-4285)*
Eagle Products - Plast Indust.....F.....909 465-1548
10811 Fremont Ave Ontario (91762) *(P-5632)*
Eagle Ridge Paper Ltd (HQ).....C.....**714 780-1799**
100 S Anaheim Blvd # 250 Anaheim (92805) *(P-3751)*
Eagle Roofing Products, Rialto *Also called Burlingame Industries Inc (P-16829)*
Eagle Roofing Products Co, Rialto *Also called Burlingame Industries Inc (P-6178)*
Eagle Roofing Products Fla LLC.....D.....909 822-6000
3546 N Riverside Ave Rialto (92377) *(P-5988)*
Eagle Security Services Inc.....C.....310 642-0656
12903 S Normandie Ave Gardena (90249) *(P-18272)*
Eagle Signs Inc.....F.....909 923-3034
1028 E Acacia St Ontario (91761) *(P-11545)*
Eagle Trs 1 LLC.....D.....657 439-0060
3100 E Frontera St Anaheim (92806) *(P-16425)*

A
L
P
H
A
B
E
T
I
C

Employee Codes: A=Over 500 employees, B=251-500
C=101-250, D=51-100, E=20-50 F=10-19
2022 Southern California Business
Directory and Buyers Guide
© Mergent Inc. 1-800-342-5647
1119

Eaglerider Finance LLC ....D....310 321-3191
11860 S La Cienega Blvd Hawthorne (90250) ***(P-18510)***
Eagleridge Paper CA, Anaheim *Also called Eagle Ridge Paper Ltd* ***(P-3751)***
Eagleware Manufacturing Co Inc ....E....562 320-3100
12683 Corral Pl Santa Fe Springs (90670) ***(P-7143)***
EAM Enterprises Inc (PA) ....D....**818 248-9100**
4005 Foothill Blvd La Crescenta (91214) ***(P-15844)***
Ear Charms Inc ....E....949 494-4147
1855 Laguna Canyon Rd Laguna Beach (92651) ***(P-11314)***
Ear Gear, Laguna Beach *Also called Ear Charms Inc* ***(P-11314)***
Earl Hays Press ....F....818 765-0700
10707 Sherman Way Sun Valley (91352) ***(P-4510)***
Early Childhood Services, Ridgecrest *Also called Desert Area Resources Training* ***(P-22180)***
Early Learning Center, Los Angeles *Also called California Childrens Academy* ***(P-21993)***
Earth Print Inc ....F....818 879-6050
31115 Via Colinas Ste 301 Westlake Village (91362) ***(P-4286)***
Earth Systems Southwest (HQ) ....D....**760 345-1588**
79811 Country Club Dr B Bermuda Dunes (92203) ***(P-22537)***
Earth Technology Corp USA ....C....213 593-8000
300 S Grand Ave Ste 900 Los Angeles (90071) ***(P-12946)***
Earthco, Santa Ana *Also called Morrison Landscape* ***(P-270)***
Earthcore Industries Inc ....F....805 484-7350
460 Calle San Pablo Ste D Camarillo (93012) ***(P-11663)***
Earthrise Nutritionals LLC (HQ) ....E....**949 623-0980**
2151 Michelson Dr Ste 262 Irvine (92612) ***(P-106)***
Earthrise Nutritionals LLC ....E....760 348-5027
113 E Hoober Rd Calipatria (92233) ***(P-2427)***
Earthscapes Landscape Inc ....E....714 936-7810
1420 S Allec St Anaheim (92805) ***(P-254)***
Earthwise Bag Company Inc ....F....818 847-2174
2819 Burton Ave Burbank (91504) ***(P-10584)***
Earthwise Packaging Inc ....F....714 602-2169
14281 Franklin Ave Tustin (92780) ***(P-9033)***
Eas Sensorsense Inc (PA) ....E....**818 763-9186**
13351 Riverside Dr Ste D Sherman Oaks (91423) ***(P-4511)***
East Lion Corporation ....E....626 912-1818
318 Brea Canyon Rd Walnut (91789) ***(P-14436)***
East Los Angeles Community Un (PA) ....E....**323 721-1655**
5400 E Olympic Blvd Fl 3 Commerce (90022) ***(P-15152)***
East Los Angeles Doctors Hosp, Los Angeles *Also called Eladh LP* ***(P-20762)***
East Los Angles Rmrkble Ctzens ....D....323 223-3079
3839 Selig Pl Los Angeles (90031) ***(P-21774)***
East Shore Garment Company LLC ....E....323 923-4454
2015 E 48th St Vernon (90058) ***(P-2569)***
East Valley Cmnty Hlth Ctr Inc (PA) ....D....**626 919-3402**
420 S Glendora Ave West Covina (91790) ***(P-21302)***
East Valley Family YMCA Dcc, North Hollywood *Also called Young MNS Chrstn Assn Mtro Los* ***(P-22075)***
East Valley Glendora Hosp LLC ....B....626 852-5000
150 W Route 66 Glendora (91740) ***(P-20759)***
East Valley Tourist Dev Auth ....A....760 342-5000
84245 Indio Springs Dr Indio (92203) ***(P-19645)***
East Valley Water District ....D....909 889-9501
31111 Greenspot Rd Highland (92346) ***(P-12888)***
East West Bancorp Inc (PA) ....B....**626 768-6000**
135 N Los Robles Ave Fl 7 Pasadena (91101) ***(P-15019)***
East West Bank (HQ) ....B....**626 768-6000**
135 N Los Robles Ave # 100 Pasadena (91101) ***(P-15020)***
East West Enterprises ....E....310 632-9933
20545 Belshaw Ave Carson (90746) ***(P-6224)***
East West Tea Company LLC ....C....310 275-9891
1616 Preuss Rd Los Angeles (90035) ***(P-1948)***
Easter Seals Southern Cal Inc ....D....909 981-4668
531 W 8th St Upland (91786) ***(P-21775)***
Eastern California Museum (PA) ....B....**760 878-0292**
155 N Grant St Independence (93526) ***(P-22221)***
Eastern Los Angeles RE (PA) ....C....**626 299-4700**
1000 S Fremont Ave # 40 Alhambra (91803) ***(P-21776)***
Eastern Municipal Water Dst (PA) ....B....**951 928-3777**
2270 Trumble Rd Perris (92572) ***(P-12889)***
Eastern Municipal Water Dst ....C....951 657-7469
19750 Evans Rd Perris (92571) ***(P-12890)***
Eastern Sierra Transit Auth ....E....760 872-1901
565 Airport Rd Bishop (93514) ***(P-11805)***
Eastern Star Homes California (PA) ....D....**714 986-2380**
16850 Bastanchury Rd Yorba Linda (92886) ***(P-21777)***
EASTERN STAR PROFESSIONAL BUIL, Yorba Linda *Also called Eastern Star Homes California* ***(P-21777)***
Easterncctv (usa) LLC ....C....626 961-8810
525 Parriott Pl W Hacienda Heights (91745) ***(P-9866)***
Eastland Corporation ....E....323 261-5388
3017 Bandini Blvd Vernon (90058) ***(P-14593)***
Eastman Music Company (PA) ....D....**909 868-1777**
2158 Pomona Blvd Pomona (91768) ***(P-14154)***
Eastmans Guitars, Pomona *Also called Eastman Music Company* ***(P-14154)***
Easton Baseball / Softball Inc ....F....800 632-7866
3500 Willow Ln Thousand Oaks (91361) ***(P-14076)***
Easton Diamond Sports LLC ....D....800 632-7866
3500 Willow Ln Thousand Oaks (91361) ***(P-14077)***
Eastwest Clothing Inc (PA) ....E....**323 980-1177**
40 E Verdugo Ave Burbank (91502) ***(P-2842)***
Eastwestproto Inc ....C....888 535-5728
1120 S Maple Ave Ste 200 Montebello (90640) ***(P-11861)***
Easy Ad Magazine, San Luis Obispo *Also called M G A Investment Co Inc* ***(P-4188)***
Easy Care Mso LLC ....C....562 676-9600
3900 Kilroy Airport Way Long Beach (90806) ***(P-21421)***
Easy Choice Health Plan Inc (HQ) ....D....**866 999-3945**
10803 Hope St Cypress (90630) ***(P-15379)***
Easy Flex, Santa Ana *Also called Easyflex Inc* ***(P-6199)***
Easy Fuel, Aliso Viejo *Also called Efuel LLC* ***(P-14802)***
Easy Reader Inc ....E....310 372-4611
832 Hermosa Ave Hermosa Beach (90254) ***(P-3974)***
Easyflex Inc ....E....888 577-8999
2700 N Main St Ste 800 Santa Ana (92705) ***(P-6199)***
Eat Like A Woman, Burbank *Also called Staness Jonekos Entps Inc* ***(P-2528)***
Eaton Aerospace LLC ....C....818 550-4200
2905 Winona Ave Burbank (91504) ***(P-10585)***
Eaton Aerospace LLC ....E....949 452-9500
9650 Jerpnimo Rd Irvine (92618) ***(P-10586)***
Eaton Aerospace LLC ....B....818 409-0200
4690 Colorado Blvd Los Angeles (90039) ***(P-13623)***
Eaton Electrical Inc ....E....951 685-5788
13201 Dahlia St Fontana (92337) ***(P-8950)***
EBA & M Corporation (PA) ....D....**714 668-8920**
3505 Cadillac Ave O201 Costa Mesa (92626) ***(P-15396)***
Ebatts.com, Camarillo *Also called Battery-Biz Inc* ***(P-9820)***
Ebc Inc (PA) ....D....**310 753-6407**
219 Manhattan Beach Blvd # 3 Manhattan Beach (90266) ***(P-602)***
Eben-Ezer Chld Day Care Ctr (PA) ....D....**818 897-5427**
13232 Kagel Canyon St Pacoima (91331) ***(P-22010)***
Ebs General Engineering Inc ....D....951 279-6869
1345 Quarry St Ste 101 Corona (92879) ***(P-876)***
Ebus Inc ....E....562 904-3474
9250 Washburn Rd Downey (90242) ***(P-9985)***
EC Group Inc (PA) ....D....**310 815-2700**
5960 Bowcroft St Los Angeles (90016) ***(P-13134)***
Eca, Brea *Also called Energy Cnvrsion Applctions Inc* ***(P-8869)***
Eca Medical Instruments (HQ) ....E....**805 376-2509**
1107 Tourmaline Dr Newbury Park (91320) ***(P-10974)***
Ecamsecure ....D....888 246-0556
3400 E Airport Way Long Beach (90806) ***(P-18372)***
ECB Corp (PA) ....D....**714 385-8900**
6400 Artesia Blvd Buena Park (90620) ***(P-1058)***
Ecc Capital Corporation (PA) ....A....**949 954-7060**
2600 E Coast Hwy Ste 250 Corona Del Mar (92625) ***(P-15188)***
ECCU, Brea *Also called Evangelical Christian Cr Un* ***(P-15113)***
Echelon Fine Printing, Vernon *Also called The Ligature Inc* ***(P-4437)***
Echo Bridge Home Entertainment, Los Angeles *Also called Platinum Disc LLC* ***(P-14174)***
Eci Fuel Systems, Upland *Also called Exhaust Center Inc* ***(P-6833)***
Eci Water Ski Products Inc ....E....951 940-9999
224 Malbert St Perris (92570) ***(P-11414)***
Eckert Zegler Isotope Pdts Inc ....E....661 309-1010
1800 N Keystone St Burbank (91504) ***(P-10878)***
Eckert Zegler Isotope Pdts Inc (HQ) ....E....**661 309-1010**
24937 Avenue Tibbitts Valencia (91355) ***(P-10879)***
Eckert Zegler Isotope Pdts Inc ....E....661 309-1010
1800 N Keystone St Burbank (91504) ***(P-10880)***
Ecko Print & Packaging, Ontario *Also called Ecko Products Group LLC* ***(P-3799)***
Ecko Products Group LLC ....E....909 628-5678
740 S Milliken Ave Ste C Ontario (91761) ***(P-3799)***
Eclectic Printing & Design LLC ....F....714 528-8040
1030 Ortega Way Ste A Placentia (92870) ***(P-4512)***
Eclipse Berry Farms LLC ....D....310 207-7879
11812 San Vicente Blvd # 250 Los Angeles (90049) ***(P-26)***
Eclipse Prtg & Graphics LLC ....E....909 390-2452
4462 E Airport Dr Ontario (91761) ***(P-4287)***
Ecliptek Inc ....F....714 433-1200
24422 Avnida De La Crlota Carlota Laguna Hills (92653) ***(P-9703)***
Eclypse International Corp (PA) ....F....**951 371-8008**
341 S Maple St Corona (92878) ***(P-10749)***
Ecmm Services Inc ....C....714 988-9388
1320 Valley Vista Dr # 204 Diamond Bar (91765) ***(P-11477)***
Eco Farms Avocados Inc (PA) ....D....**951 694-3013**
28790 Las Haciendas St Temecula (92590) ***(P-14623)***
Eco Farms Sales Inc (PA) ....E....**951 694-3013**
28790 Las Haciendas St Temecula (92590) ***(P-14624)***
Eco Farms Trdg Operations LLC ....C....951 676-4047
28790 Las Haciendas St Temecula (92590) ***(P-14625)***
Eco Services Operations Corp ....D....310 885-6719
20720 S Wilmington Ave Long Beach (90810) ***(P-4657)***
Eco-Air Products Inc ....F....562 801-0133
17122 Marquardt Ave Cerritos (90703) ***(P-13841)***
Ecola Services Inc ....D....818 920-7301
15314 Devonshire St Ste F Mission Hills (91345) ***(P-17202)***
Ecology Recycling Services LLC (PA) ....C....**562 921-9975**
13750 Imperial Hwy Santa Fe Springs (90670) ***(P-12947)***
Ecology Recycling Services LLC ....D....909 370-1318
785 E M St Colton (92324) ***(P-12948)***
Ecoly International Inc ....F....818 718-6982
5800 Bristol Pkwy Ste 700 Culver City (90230) ***(P-5017)***
Econ-O-Plate Inc ....F....310 342-5900
5731 W Slauson Ave # 175 Culver City (90230) ***(P-4288)***
Econo Air, Brea *Also called Mddr Inc* ***(P-1100)***
Econocold Refrigerators, Cerritos *Also called Refrigerator Manufacters Inc* ***(P-8999)***
Econolite Control Products Inc (PA) ....C....**714 630-3700**
1250 N Tustin Ave Anaheim (92807) ***(P-9339)***
Economic Dev Corp Los Angles C ....E....213 622-4300
444 S Flower St Ste 3700 Los Angeles (90071) ***(P-23433)***
Ecoolthing Corp ....E....714 368-4791
1321 E Saint Gertrude Pl Santa Ana (92705) ***(P-7555)***
Ecoplast Corporation Inc ....E....909 346-0450
13414 Slover Ave Fontana (92337) ***(P-5633)***
Ecosense Lighting Inc (PA) ....D....**855 632-6736**
837 N Spring St Ste 103 Los Angeles (90012) ***(P-13624)***
Ecotech Rfrgn & Hvac Inc ....D....888 833-8100
630 S Sunkist St Ste R Anaheim (92806) ***(P-1059)***

Mergent e-mail: customerrelations@mergent.com
1120
2022 Southern California Business Directory and Buyers Guide
(P-0000) Products & Services Section entry number
(PA)=Parent Co (HQ)=Headquarters DH)=Div Headquarters

Ecotech Services Inc......E......626 335-1500
2143 S Myrtle Ave Monrovia (91016) *(P-255)*
Ecowise Inc......E......626 759-3997
13538 Excelsior Dr Unit B Santa Fe Springs (90670) *(P-4688)*
Ect News Network Inc......F......818 461-9700
16133 Ventura Blvd # 700 Encino (91436) *(P-4168)*
Ecw Technology Inc......F......310 373-0082
609 Deep Valley Dr Rllng HLS Est (90274) *(P-8046)*
Ed Hardy, Commerce *Also called DNam Apparel Industries LLC (P-2941)*
Ed Tucker Distributor Inc......E......800 347-1010
8505 W Doe Ave Visalia (93291) *(P-13056)*
Edco Die Inc......E......909 985-4417
2199 W Arrow Rte Upland (91786) *(P-7798)*
Edco Disposal Corporation (PA)......C......**619 287-7555**
2755 California Ave Signal Hill (90755) *(P-12949)*
Edco Health Info Solution......D......909 793-0613
17316 Edwards Rd Ste 280 Cerritos (90703) *(P-18511)*
Edco Plastics Inc......E......714 772-1986
2110 E Winston Rd Anaheim (92806) *(P-5634)*
Eddie VS Wildfish Newport Bch (PA)......D......**949 720-9925**
1370 Bison Ave Newport Beach (92660) *(P-23019)*
Eddies Perfume & Cosmtc Co Inc......F......818 341-1717
19859 Nordhoff St Northridge (91324) *(P-5018)*
Edelbrock Holdings Inc......C......310 781-2290
2301 Dominguez Way Torrance (90501) *(P-10050)*
Edelbrock Holdings Inc......C......951 654-6677
1380 S Buena Vista St San Jacinto (92583) *(P-10051)*
Edelman Public Relations, Los Angeles *Also called Daniel J Edelman Inc (P-17083)*
Edelmann Usa Inc (HQ)......F......**323 669-5700**
2150 S Parco Ave Ontario (91761) *(P-11546)*
Edeniq Inc (PA)......D......**559 302-1777**
6910 W Pershing Ct Visalia (93291) *(P-5133)*
Edessa Inc......E......909 823-1377
11027 Cherry Ave Fontana (92337) *(P-6028)*
Edey Door, Los Angeles *Also called Edey Manufacturing Co Inc (P-6696)*
Edey Manufacturing Co Inc......E......323 566-6151
2159 E 92nd St Los Angeles (90002) *(P-6696)*
Edge Mortgage Advisory Co LLC......D......714 564-5800
2125 E Katella Ave # 350 Anaheim (92806) *(P-23434)*
Edge Plastics Inc (PA)......E......**951 786-4750**
3016 Kansas Ave Bldg 3 Riverside (92507) *(P-5635)*
Edge Solutions Consulting Inc (PA)......D......**818 591-3500**
5126 Clareton Dr Ste 160 Agoura Hills (91301) *(P-8154)*
Edge Systems LLC......E......562 391-2052
3600 E Burnett St Long Beach (90815) *(P-12201)*
Edge Systems LLC (PA)......C......**800 603-4996**
2165 E Spring St Long Beach (90806) *(P-10975)*
Edgebrook Productions Inc......D......818 766-6789
10806 Ventura Blvd Studio City (91604) *(P-19231)*
Edgemine Inc......C......323 267-8222
1801 E 50th St Los Angeles (90058) *(P-14372)*
Edgewater Convalescent Hosp......D......562 434-0974
2625 E 4th St Long Beach (90814) *(P-20317)*
Edgewater Skilled Nursing Ctr, Long Beach *Also called Edgewater Convalescent Hosp (P-20317)*
Edgewood Press Inc......F......714 516-2455
1130 N Main St Orange (92867) *(P-4289)*
Edgeworth Integration LLC......D......805 915-0211
2360 Shasta Way Ste F Simi Valley (93065) *(P-18373)*
Edi Ideas, Fountain Valley *Also called Freightgate Inc (P-17862)*
Edie Lee, Commerce *Also called J Michelle of California (P-2673)*
Edinger Medical Group Inc......D......714 965-2500
18682 Beach Blvd Ste 150 Huntington Beach (92648) *(P-19802)*
Edison Capital......C......909 594-3789
18101 Von Karman Ave Irvine (92612) *(P-12802)*
Edison International (PA)......A......**626 302-2222**
2244 Walnut Grove Ave Rosemead (91770) *(P-12803)*
Edison Mission Energy (HQ)......B......**626 302-5778**
2244 Walnut Grove Ave Rosemead (91770) *(P-12804)*
Edison Mission Oper & Maint (HQ)......C......**626 302-5151**
3 Macarthur Pl Ste 100 Santa Ana (92707) *(P-12870)*
Edison Mssion Midwest Holdings......A......626 302-2222
2244 Walnut Grove Ave Rosemead (91770) *(P-12805)*
Edison Opto USA Corporation......F......909 284-9710
1809 Excise Ave Ste 201 Ontario (91761) *(P-9500)*
Edje-Enterprises......D......951 245-7070
520 Crane St Ste B Lake Elsinore (92530) *(P-1484)*
EDM Intrnational Logistics Inc......F......626 588-2299
7211 Haven Ave Ste E368 Alta Loma (91701) *(P-5498)*
EDM Performance Accessories, Brea *Also called Clean America Inc (P-9860)*
Edmund A Gray Co (PA)......C......**213 625-0376**
2277 E 15th St Los Angeles (90021) *(P-7535)*
Edmund Kim International Inc (PA)......E......**310 604-1100**
2880 E Ana St Compton (90221) *(P-2806)*
Edmunds Holding Company (PA)......A......**310 309-6300**
2401 Colorado Ave Santa Monica (90404) *(P-18122)*
Edmunds.com, Santa Monica *Also called Edmunds Holding Company (P-18122)*
Edmundscom Inc (HQ)......A......**310 309-6300**
2401 Colorado Ave Ste P1 Santa Monica (90404) *(P-17084)*
EDN Aviation Inc......E......818 988-8826
6720 Valjean Ave Van Nuys (91406) *(P-19035)*
Edris Plastics Mfg Inc......E......323 581-7000
4560 Pacific Blvd Vernon (90058) *(P-5636)*
Edro Engineering Inc (HQ)......D......**909 594-5751**
20500 Carrey Rd Walnut (91789) *(P-7799)*
Edro Specialty Steels Inc......F......800 368-3376
20500 Carrey Rd Walnut (91789) *(P-7800)*
Educational Employees Cr Un......D......559 587-4460
1460 W 7th St Hanford (93230) *(P-15111)*
Educational Emporium, Anaheim *Also called CM School Supply Inc (P-11369)*
Educational Ideas Incorporated......D......714 990-4332
471 Atlas St Brea (92821) *(P-4128)*
Educational Insights, Gardena *Also called Learning Resources Inc (P-11706)*
Edward G Chester Adult Center, Compton *Also called Compton Unified School Dst (P-21756)*
Edward Thomas Companies......C......714 782-7500
640 W Katella Ave Anaheim (92802) *(P-16426)*
Edward Thomas Hospitality Corp......B......310 458-0030
1 Pico Blvd Santa Monica (90405) *(P-16427)*
Edwards Assoc Cmmnications Inc (PA)......C......**805 658-2626**
2277 Knoll Dr Ste A Ventura (93003) *(P-3870)*
Edwards Cinemas University, Irvine *Also called Edwards Theatres Circuit Inc (P-19278)*
Edwards Label, Ventura *Also called Edwards Assoc Cmmnications Inc (P-3870)*
Edwards Lfesciences Foundation......F......949 250-2806
1 Edwards Way Irvine (92614) *(P-11096)*
Edwards Lfsciences Cardiaq LLC......D......949 387-2615
1 Edwards Way Irvine (92614) *(P-10976)*
Edwards Lfscnces Wrld Trade Co (HQ)......D......**949 250-2500**
1 Edwards Way Irvine (92614) *(P-11097)*
Edwards Lifesciences Corp (PA)......A......**949 250-2500**
1 Edwards Way Irvine (92614) *(P-11098)*
Edwards Lifesciences Corp PR......D......949 250-2500
1 Edwards Way Irvine (92614) *(P-11099)*
Edwards Lifesciences Fing LLC......D......949 250-3480
1 Edwards Way Irvine (92614) *(P-11664)*
Edwards Lifesciences LLC (HQ)......A......**949 250-2500**
1 Edwards Way Irvine (92614) *(P-19803)*
Edwards Lifesciences US Inc......C......949 250-2500
1 Edwards Way Irvine (92614) *(P-11221)*
Edwards Sheet Metal Supply Inc......E......818 785-8600
7810 Burnet Ave Van Nuys (91405) *(P-6824)*
Edwards Technologies Inc......C......310 536-7070
139 Maryland St El Segundo (90245) *(P-1245)*
Edwards Theatres Circuit Inc......C......714 428-0962
901 S Coast Dr Costa Mesa (92626) *(P-19273)*
Edwards Theatres Circuit Inc......C......949 582-4078
27741 Crown Valley Pkwy Mission Viejo (92691) *(P-19274)*
Edwards Theatres Circuit Inc......D......949 425-3838
26701 Aliso Creek Rd Aliso Viejo (92656) *(P-19275)*
Edwards Theatres Circuit Inc (HQ)......C......**949 640-4600**
300 Newport Center Dr Newport Beach (92660) *(P-19276)*
Edwards Theatres Circuit Inc......C......951 296-0144
40750 Winchester Rd Temecula (92591) *(P-19277)*
Edwards Theatres Circuit Inc......C......949 854-8811
4245 Campus Dr Irvine (92612) *(P-19278)*
Edwards Theatres Circuit Inc......C......805 347-1164
1521 S Bradley Rd Santa Maria (93454) *(P-19279)*
Edwards Vacuum LLC......D......626 532-5585
15326 Valley Blvd City of Industry (91746) *(P-13982)*
EE Pauley Plastic Extrusion......F......760 240-3737
17177 Navajo Rd Apple Valley (92307) *(P-5637)*
Eeco, Los Angeles *Also called Elevator Equipment Corporation (P-13899)*
Eema Industries Inc......E......323 904-0200
5461 W Jefferson Blvd Los Angeles (90016) *(P-9127)*
Eemus Manufacturing Corp......F......626 443-8841
16750 Pocono St La Puente (91744) *(P-7361)*
Eep Holdings LLC (PA)......B......**909 597-7861**
4626 Eucalyptus Ave Chino (91710) *(P-5638)*
Eeye Digital Security, Aliso Viejo *Also called Eeye Inc (P-17842)*
Eeye Inc (HQ)......D......**949 333-1900**
65 Enterprise Ste 100 Aliso Viejo (92656) *(P-17842)*
Efax Corporate, Los Angeles *Also called J2 Cloud Services LLC (P-12682)*
Efaxcom (HQ)......D......**323 817-3207**
6922 Hollywood Blvd Fl 5 Los Angeles (90028) *(P-8252)*
Efaxcom......E......805 692-0064
5385 Hollister Ave # 208 Santa Barbara (93111) *(P-8253)*
Effective Graphics NC Inc......E......310 323-2223
40 E Verdugo Ave Burbank (91502) *(P-4629)*
Efficient Pwr Conversion Corp (PA)......D......**310 615-0279**
909 N Pacific Coast Hwy El Segundo (90245) *(P-9501)*
Efilm LLC......C......323 463-7041
1144 N Las Palmas Ave Los Angeles (90038) *(P-19121)*
Efs West......E......661 705-8200
28472 Constellation Rd Valencia (91355) *(P-22538)*
Efuel LLC......D......949 330-7145
65 Enterprise Fl 3 Aliso Viejo (92656) *(P-14802)*
Egge Machine Company Inc (PA)......E......**562 945-3419**
8403 Allport Ave Santa Fe Springs (90670) *(P-13057)*
Eggleston Youth Centers Inc (PA)......D......**626 480-8107**
13001 Ramona Blvd Ste E Irwindale (91706) *(P-21778)*
Ego Inc......C......626 447-0296
180 Via Verde Ste 100 San Dimas (91773) *(P-22778)*
Egon Zehnder International......B......213 337-1500
350 S Grand Ave Ste 3580 Los Angeles (90071) *(P-23210)*
Egr Incorporated (HQ)......C......**909 923-7075**
4000 Greystone Dr Ontario (91761) *(P-10052)*
Egremont Schools Inc......D......818 363-7803
19850 Devonshire St Chatsworth (91311) *(P-22011)*
Egs Financial Care Inc (HQ)......B......**877 217-4423**
5 Park Plz Ste 1100 Irvine (92614) *(P-17110)*
Eharmony Inc (HQ)......C......**424 258-1199**
10900 Wilshire Blvd Fl 17 Los Angeles (90024) *(P-16954)*
Eharmony.com, Los Angeles *Also called Eharmony Inc (P-16954)*
Ehp Administrators, Chatsworth *Also called Electronic Health Plans Inc (P-21422)*
Ehy, Santa Barbara *Also called Evans Hardy & Young Inc (P-17011)*
Eibach Inc......D......951 256-8300
264 Mariah Cir Corona (92879) *(P-7463)*
Eibach Springs, Inc., Corona *Also called Eibach Inc (P-7463)*

Employee Codes: A=Over 500 employees, B=251-500
C=101-250, D=51-100, E=20-50 F=10-19
2022 Southern California Business
Directory and Buyers Guide
© Mergent Inc. 1-800-342-5647
1121

Eichleay Inc .... C 562 256-8600
  5555 Garden Grove Blvd # 300 Westminster (92683) *(P-22539)*
Eide Bailly LLP .... B 909 466-4410
  10681 Fthill Blvd Ste 300 Rancho Cucamonga (91730) *(P-22779)*
Eide Industries Inc .... D 562 402-8335
  16215 Piuma Ave Cerritos (90703) *(P-3138)*
EIDIM AV TECHNOLOGY, Buena Park *Also called Eidim Group Inc (P-9128)*
Eidim Group Inc .... F 562 777-1009
  6905 Oslo Cir Ste J Buena Park (90621) *(P-9128)*
Eie Electric, Costa Mesa *Also called Pmd Industries Inc (P-1297)*
Eight Point Trailer Corp .... E 909 357-9227
  14770 Slover Ave Fontana (92337) *(P-18897)*
Eight Star Equipment, El Centro *Also called Noblesse Oblige Inc (P-158)*
Eighty Eight, Los Angeles *Also called Ms Bubbles Inc (P-14403)*
Eighty One Enterprise Inc .... E 626 371-1980
  9401 Whitmore St El Monte (91731) *(P-14373)*
Eim Corporation .... E 805 963-2935
  315 Meigs Rd Santa Barbara (93109) *(P-17606)*
Einflatables, Cerritos *Also called Funtastic Factory Inc (P-8595)*
Einflatables, Buena Park *Also called Spn Investments Inc (P-11448)*
Einstein Noah Rest Group Inc .... C 714 847-4609
  16304 Beach Blvd Westminster (92683) *(P-1770)*
Eisel Enterprises Inc .... E 714 993-1706
  714 Fee Ana St Placentia (92870) *(P-6029)*
Eisenberg International Corp (PA) .... D 818 365-8161
  9128 Jordan Ave Chatsworth (91311) *(P-14331)*
Eisenberg Village, Reseda *Also called Los Angles Jewish HM For Aging (P-20410)*
EISENHOWER HEALTH, Rancho Mirage *Also called Eisenhower Medical Center (P-20760)*
Eisenhower Medical Center (PA) .... A 760 340-3911
  39000 Bob Hope Dr Rancho Mirage (92270) *(P-20760)*
EISNER PEDIATRIC & FAMILY MEDI, Los Angeles *Also called Pediatric & Family Medical Ctr (P-20020)*
Ejay Filtration Inc .... E 951 683-0805
  3036 Durahart St Riverside (92507) *(P-7500)*
Ejays Machine Co Inc .... E 714 879-0558
  1108 E Valencia Dr Fullerton (92831) *(P-8578)*
Ejl, Downey *Also called E J Lauren LLC (P-3502)*
Ekedal Concrete Inc .... D 949 729-8082
  19600 Fairchild Ste 123 Irvine (92612) *(P-1523)*
Ekran System Inc .... E 424 242-8838
  260 Nwport Ctr Dr Ste 425 Newport Beach (92660) *(P-17843)*
El & El Wood Products Corp (PA) .... C 909 591-0339
  6011 Schaefer Ave Chino (91710) *(P-3248)*
EL ARCA, Los Angeles *Also called East Los Angles Rmrkble Ctzens (P-21774)*
El Aviso Magazine .... E 323 586-9199
  4850 Gage Ave Bell (90201) *(P-14871)*
El Caballero Country Club .... C 818 654-3000
  18300 Tarzana Dr Tarzana (91356) *(P-19561)*
El Camino Management Company .... D 310 276-3154
  136 El Camino Dr Beverly Hills (90212) *(P-23020)*
El Capitan Canyon LLC .... D 805 685-3887
  11560 Calle Real Santa Barbara (93117) *(P-16832)*
El Capitan Environmental Svcs .... D 818 768-9222
  11080 Tuxford St Sun Valley (91352) *(P-23435)*
El Centro Hospitality LLC .... C 760 353-2600
  503 E Danenberg Dr El Centro (92243) *(P-16428)*
El Centro Hospitality 2 LLC .... C 760 370-3800
  3003 S Dogwood Rd El Centro (92243) *(P-16429)*
El Centro Rgnal Med Ctr Fndtio (PA) .... A 760 339-7100
  1415 Ross Ave El Centro (92243) *(P-20761)*
El Clasificado (PA) .... D 323 837-4095
  11205 Imperial Hwy Norwalk (90650) *(P-3975)*
El Clasificado .... D 323 278-5310
  1125 Goodrich Blvd Commerce (90022) *(P-4169)*
El Dorado Enterprises Inc .... A 310 719-9800
  1000 W Redondo Beach Blvd Gardena (90247) *(P-16430)*
El Dorado Mexican Food Pdts, Los Angeles *Also called Food-O-Mex Corporation (P-2434)*
El Encanto Healthcare & Rehab .... D 626 336-1274
  555 El Encanto Rd City of Industry (91745) *(P-20318)*
EL ENCANTO HOME HEALTH CARE, City of Industry *Also called El Encanto Healthcare & Rehab (P-20318)*
El Encanto Inc .... D 805 845-5800
  800 Alvarado Pl Santa Barbara (93103) *(P-16431)*
El Gallito Market Inc .... E 626 442-1190
  12242 Valley Blvd El Monte (91732) *(P-2428)*
El Guapo Spices Inc (PA) .... D 213 312-1300
  6200 E Slauson Ave Commerce (90040) *(P-14687)*
El Guapo Spices and Herbs Pkg, Commerce *Also called El Guapo Spices Inc (P-14687)*
El Indio Tortillas Fctry, Santa Ana *Also called El Indio Tortilleria (P-2429)*
El Indio Tortilleria .... F 714 542-3114
  1502 W 5th St Santa Ana (92703) *(P-2429)*
El Metate Inc .... C 949 646-9362
  817 W 19th St Costa Mesa (92627) *(P-1997)*
El Metate Market, Costa Mesa *Also called El Metate Inc (P-1997)*
El Monte Automotive Group Inc .... C 626 580-6200
  3530 Peck Rd El Monte (91731) *(P-18788)*
El Monte Convalescent Hospital .... D 626 442-1500
  4096 Easy St El Monte (91731) *(P-20319)*
El Monte Rents Inc (HQ) .... C 562 404-9300
  12818 Firestone Blvd Santa Fe Springs (90670) *(P-18755)*
El Monte Rv, Santa Fe Springs *Also called El Monte Rents Inc (P-18755)*
El Nido Family Centers (PA) .... C 818 830-3646
  10200 Sepulveda Blvd # 350 Mission Hills (91345) *(P-21779)*
El Pollo Loco, Cypress *Also called WKS Restaurant Corporation (P-16223)*
El Pollo Loco Holdings Inc (PA) .... C 714 599-5000
  3535 Harbor Blvd Ste 100 Costa Mesa (92626) *(P-16206)*

El Prado Golf Course LP .... D 909 597-1751
  6555 Pine Ave Chino (91708) *(P-19486)*
El Segundo Bread Bar LLC .... E 310 615-9898
  701 E El Segundo Blvd El Segundo (90245) *(P-1998)*
El Segundo Eductl Foundation .... B 310 615-2650
  641 Sheldon St El Segundo (90245) *(P-22182)*
El-Com Systems, Garden Grove *Also called Elrob Inc (P-13717)*
Eladh LP .... D 323 268-5514
  4060 Whittier Blvd Los Angeles (90023) *(P-20762)*
Elan Blanc, Palm Desert *Also called Equipment De Sport Usa Inc (P-3155)*
Elasco Inc .... D 714 373-4767
  11377 Markon Dr Garden Grove (92841) *(P-4689)*
Elasco Urethane Inc .... E 714 895-7031
  11377 Markon Dr Garden Grove (92841) *(P-4690)*
Elastpro Silicone Sheeting LLC .... F 562 348-2348
  13937 Rosecrans Ave Santa Fe Springs (90670) *(P-5134)*
Elation Lighting Inc .... D 323 582-3322
  6122 S Eastern Ave Commerce (90040) *(P-9129)*
Elation Professional, Commerce *Also called Elation Lighting Inc (P-9129)*
Elba Company, San Dimas *Also called Elba Jewelry Inc (P-11315)*
Elba Jewelry Inc .... F 909 394-5803
  910 N Amelia Ave San Dimas (91773) *(P-11315)*
Elco Lighting, Vernon *Also called AMP Plus Inc (P-9113)*
Elder Care Alliance Camarillo .... D 510 769-2700
  2500 Ponderosa Dr N Camarillo (93010) *(P-22101)*
Elder Statesman LLC (PA) .... F 310 920-4659
  2416 Hunter St Los Angeles (90021) *(P-13167)*
Eldorado Country Club .... C 760 346-8081
  46000 Fairway Dr Indian Wells (92210) *(P-19562)*
Eldorado National Cal Inc (HQ) .... B 951 727-9300
  9670 Galena St Riverside (92509) *(P-9944)*
Eldorado Stone LLC .... A 951 601-3838
  24100 Orange Ave Perris (92570) *(P-13303)*
Elecnor Inc (HQ) .... C 909 993-5470
  4331 Schaefer Ave Chino (91710) *(P-1060)*
Electra Craft, Westlake Village *Also called Toller Enterprises Inc (P-10473)*
Electrasem Corp .... D 951 371-6140
  372 Elizabeth Ln Corona (92878) *(P-10665)*
Electrcal Instrmnttion Cntrls, Bakersfield *Also called Mic (P-13918)*
Electric Designs, Gardena *Also called Gloria Lance Inc (P-2844)*
Electric Gate Store Inc .... C 818 361-6872
  15342 Chatsworth St Mission Hills (91345) *(P-9867)*
Electric Motor Works Inc .... E 661 327-4271
  803 Inyo St Bakersfield (93305) *(P-19010)*
Electric Motors, Santa Ana *Also called Advantage Manufacturing Inc (P-13609)*
Electric On Target Inc .... D 949 247-3842
  17691 Mitchell N Ste A Irvine (92614) *(P-1061)*
Electric Power Group LLC .... E 626 685-2015
  251 S Lake Ave Ste 300 Pasadena (91101) *(P-23211)*
Electric Sales Unlimited .... E 562 463-8300
  9023 Norwalk Blvd Santa Fe Springs (90670) *(P-13625)*
Electric Solidus LLC .... E 917 692-7764
  26565 Agoura Rd Ste 200 Calabasas (91302) *(P-4170)*
Electric Svc & Sup Co Pasadena .... D 626 795-8641
  2668 E Foothill Blvd Pasadena (91107) *(P-1246)*
Electric Visual Evolution LLC (PA) .... E 949 940-9125
  950 Calle Amanecer # 101 San Clemente (92673) *(P-11250)*
Electrical Products Division, Fontana *Also called Southwire Inc (P-6303)*
Electrical Products Rep, Irvine *Also called Agents West Inc (P-9849)*
Electrical Rebuilders Sls Inc (PA) .... D 323 249-7545
  7603 Willow Glen Rd Los Angeles (90046) *(P-9823)*
Electrical Systems, Corona *Also called Panel Shop Inc (P-8902)*
Electro Adapter Inc .... D 818 998-1198
  20640 Nordhoff St Chatsworth (91311) *(P-9034)*
Electro Kinetics Division, Simi Valley *Also called Pacific Scientific Company (P-10633)*
Electro Machine & Engrg Co, Compton *Also called E M E Inc (P-7249)*
Electro Optical Industries .... E 805 964-6701
  320 Storke Rd Ste 100 Goleta (93117) *(P-10833)*
Electro Rent Corporation (HQ) .... C 818 787-2100
  8511 Fllbrook Ave Ste 200 West Hills (91304) *(P-17347)*
Electro Switch Corp .... E 909 581-0855
  10410 Trademark St Rancho Cucamonga (91730) *(P-8896)*
Electro Switch Corp .... E 909 581-0855
  10410 Trademark St Rancho Cucamonga (91730) *(P-9704)*
Electro-Comm, Burbank *Also called Y B S Enterprises Inc (P-9246)*
Electro-Support Systems Corp .... D 951 676-2751
  27449 Colt Ct Temecula (92590) *(P-9705)*
Electro-Tech Machining Div, Long Beach *Also called Kbr Inc (P-8938)*
Electro-Tech Products Inc .... E 909 592-1434
  2001 E Gladstone St Ste A Glendora (91740) *(P-9706)*
Electro-Tech's, Corona *Also called R&M Deese Inc (P-11585)*
Electrocube Inc (PA) .... D 909 595-1821
  3366 Pomona Blvd Pomona (91768) *(P-9707)*
Electrode Technologies Inc .... E 714 549-3771
  3110 W Harvard St Ste 14 Santa Ana (92704) *(P-7250)*
Electrofilm Mfg Co LLC .... D 661 257-2242
  28150 Industry Dr Valencia (91355) *(P-7456)*
Electrolizing Inc .... E 213 749-7876
  1947 Hooper Ave Los Angeles (90011) *(P-7251)*
Electrolurgy Inc .... D 949 250-4494
  1121 Duryea Ave Irvine (92614) *(P-7252)*
Electromatic .... F 562 623-9993
  14025 Stage Rd Santa Fe Springs (90670) *(P-7253)*
Electron Beam Engineering Inc .... F 714 491-5990
  1425 S Allec St Anaheim (92805) *(P-18977)*
Electron Devices, Torrance *Also called Stellant Systems Inc (P-9368)*
Electron Plating III Inc .... E 714 554-2210
  13932 Enterprise Dr Garden Grove (92843) *(P-7254)*

ALPHABETIC SECTION
Embassy Suites, Lompoc

Electronic Auto Systems Inc ....F....626 280-3855
9855 Joe Vargas Way South El Monte (91733) *(P-9174)*

Electronic Chrome Grinding Inc ....E....562 946-6671
9128 Dice Rd Santa Fe Springs (90670) *(P-7255)*

Electronic Clearing House Inc (HQ) ....D....805 419-8700
730 Paseo Camarillo Camarillo (93010) *(P-17844)*

Electronic Commerce LLC ....D....800 770-5520
4100 Nwport Pl Dr Ste 500 Newport Beach (92660) *(P-15163)*

Electronic Hardware Limited (PA) ....E....818 982-6100
13257 Saticoy St North Hollywood (91605) *(P-13716)*

Electronic Health Plans Inc ....D....818 734-4700
9131 Oakdale Ave Ste 150 Chatsworth (91311) *(P-21422)*

Electronic Mfg, Torrance *Also called Reliable Circuits Mfg Inc (P-9447)*

Electronic Mfg Leaders & Qulty, Simi Valley *Also called Emlinq LLC (P-9400)*

Electronic Precision Spc Inc ....E....714 256-8950
545 Mercury Ln Brea (92821) *(P-7256)*

Electronic Services, Los Angeles *Also called Esi Inc (P-9505)*

Electronic Source Company, Van Nuys *Also called Alyn Industries Inc (P-9672)*

Electronic Stamping Corp ....F....310 639-2120
19920 S Alameda St Compton (90221) *(P-8897)*

Electronic Waveform Lab Inc ....E....714 843-0463
5702 Bolsa Ave Huntington Beach (92649) *(P-10977)*

Electrorack, Anaheim *Also called Ortronics Inc (P-6884)*

Electrosonic Inc (HQ) ....D....818 333-3600
3320 N San Fernando Blvd Burbank (91504) *(P-22540)*

Elegance Upholstery Inc ....F....562 698-2584
11803 Slauson Ave Unit A Ontario (91762) *(P-3725)*

Eleganza Tiles Inc (PA) ....D....714 224-1700
3125 E Coronado St Anaheim (92806) *(P-1415)*

Element Anheim Rsort Cnvntion, Anaheim *Also called Singod Investors Vi LLC (P-4669)*

Element Materials (HQ) ....D....714 892-1961
15062 Bolsa Chica St Huntington Beach (92649) *(P-22939)*

Element Mtrls Tech HB Inc ....D....310 632-8500
18100 S Wilmington Ave Compton (90220) *(P-22940)*

Element Rancho Dominguez, Compton *Also called Element Mtrls Tech HB Inc (P-22940)*

Elements Behavioral Health Inc (PA) ....C....562 741-6470
5000 Arprt Plz Dr Ste 100 Long Beach (90815) *(P-21303)*

Elements Food Group Inc ....D....909 983-2011
5560 Brooks St Montclair (91763) *(P-2063)*

Elena Villa Healthcare Center ....D....562 868-0591
13226 Studebaker Rd Norwalk (90650) *(P-20578)*

Elers Medical Usa Inc ....E....858 336-4900
21707 Hawthorne Blvd # 20 Torrance (90503) *(P-13485)*

Elesco ....E....714 673-6600
170 Mccormick Ave Costa Mesa (92626) *(P-13626)*

Elevate Inc ....F....949 276-5428
180 Avnida La Pata Ste 20 San Clemente (92673) *(P-17845)*

Elevated Resources Inc ....C....949 419-6632
3990 Westerly Pl Ste 270 Newport Beach (92660) *(P-18084)*

Elevator Equipment Corporation (PA) ....D....323 245-0147
4035 Goodwin Ave Los Angeles (90039) *(P-13899)*

Elevator Research & Mfg Co ....E....213 746-1914
1417 Elwood St Los Angeles (90021) *(P-7677)*

Elias Elliott Lampasi Fehn (PA) ....D....951 689-5031
7251 Magnolia Ave Riverside (92504) *(P-20176)*

Elijah Textiles Inc ....D....310 666-3443
1251 E Olympic Blvd Los Angeles (90021) *(P-13168)*

Elisid Magazine ....E....619 990-9999
1450 University Ave F168 Riverside (92507) *(P-4068)*

Elite, Culver City *Also called West Publishing Corporation (P-18074)*

Elite 4 Print Inc ....E....310 366-1344
851 E Walnut St Carson (90746) *(P-4290)*

Elite Airways LLC (PA) ....C....805 496-3334
4607 Lakeview Canyon Rd Westlake Village (91361) *(P-12413)*

Elite Anywhere Corp (PA) ....D....917 860-9247
82585 Showcase Pkwy A101 Indio (92203) *(P-12452)*

Elite Cabinetry Inc ....F....951 698-5050
25755 Jefferson Ave Murrieta (92562) *(P-3726)*

Elite Color Technologies Inc ....F....310 324-3040
851 E Walnut St Carson (90746) *(P-4513)*

Elite Craftsman (PA) ....C....562 989-3511
2763 Saint Louis Ave Long Beach (90755) *(P-17240)*

Elite Diagnostic Imaging LLC ....D....760 962-9866
17260 Bear Valley Rd # 109 Victorville (92395) *(P-19804)*

Elite Electric ....D....951 681-5811
9415 Bellegrave Ave Riverside (92509) *(P-1247)*

Elite Enfrcment SEC Sltons Inc (PA) ....C....866 354-8308
1290 N Hancock St Ste 101 Anaheim (92807) *(P-18273)*

Elite Engineering Contrs Inc ....E....310 465-8333
16619 S Broadway Gardena (90248) *(P-22541)*

Elite Global Solutions Inc ....F....949 709-4872
19732 Descartes Foothill Ranch (92610) *(P-4691)*

Elite Imaging, Victorville *Also called Elite Diagnostic Imaging LLC (P-19804)*

Elite Intractive Solutions Inc ....E....310 740-5426
1200 W 7th St Ste L1-180 Los Angeles (90017) *(P-18374)*

Elite Lighting ....C....323 888-1973
5424 E Slauson Ave Commerce (90040) *(P-9130)*

Elite Metal Finishing LLC (PA) ....D....805 983-4320
540 Spectrum Cir Oxnard (93030) *(P-7257)*

Elite Metal Finishing LLC ....E....805 983-4320
3430 Galaxy Pl Oxnard (93030) *(P-7258)*

Elite Mfg Corp ....C....888 354-8356
12143 Altamar Pl Santa Fe Springs (90670) *(P-3607)*

Elite Modern, Santa Fe Springs *Also called Elite Mfg Corp (P-3607)*

Elite Nursing Services Inc ....D....714 919-7898
1915 W Orangewood Ave # 110 Orange (92868) *(P-17416)*

Elite Screens Inc ....E....877 511-1211
12282 Knott St Garden Grove (92841) *(P-11275)*

Elite Sign Services Inc ....F....714 373-0220
15162 Goldenwest Cir Westminster (92683) *(P-11547)*

Elite Slides Inc ....D....310 537-4210
11220 Wright Rd Santa Ana (92706) *(P-3217)*

Elite Stone & Cabinet Inc ....F....909 629-6988
1655 E Mission Blvd Pomona (91766) *(P-3318)*

Elizabeth Glaser Pedia ....D....310 231-0400
16130 Ventura Blvd # 250 Encino (91436) *(P-21423)*

Elizabeth Shutters Inc ....E....909 825-1531
525 S Rancho Ave Colton (92324) *(P-6697)*

Elk Corporation of Texas ....C....661 391-3900
6200 Zerker Rd Shafter (93263) *(P-6030)*

Elk Hills Power LLC ....E....888 848-4754
27200 Tourney Rd Ste 315 Santa Clarita (91355) *(P-452)*

Elkay Plastics Co Inc (PA) ....D....323 722-7073
6000 Sheila St Commerce (90040) *(P-14758)*

Elkor Properties, Santa Monica *Also called Roscoe Real Estate Ltd Partnr (P-16672)*

Ellen Degeneres Show, The, Burbank *Also called Wad Productions Inc (P-19201)*

Ellens Silk Screening Inc ....E....626 441-4415
1500 Mission St South Pasadena (91030) *(P-17173)*

Ellie Mae Inc ....C....818 223-2000
24025 Park Sorrento # 210 Calabasas (91302) *(P-17607)*

Ellingson Inc ....E....714 773-1923
119 W Santa Fe Ave Fullerton (92832) *(P-8579)*

Ellis Building Contractors, Manhattan Beach *Also called Ebc Inc (P-602)*

Ellison Educational Eqp Inc (PA) ....D....949 598-8822
25862 Commercentre Dr Lake Forest (92630) *(P-7914)*

Ellison Institute LLC ....D....513 403-2628
12414 Exposition Blvd Los Angeles (90064) *(P-22941)*

Elljay Acoustics Inc ....D....714 961-1173
511 Cameron St Placentia (92870) *(P-1374)*

Ellsworth Trck Auto Machining ....F....714 761-2500
1167 N Knollwood Cir Anaheim (92801) *(P-13058)*

Elmco Sales Inc (PA) ....D....626 855-4831
15070 Proctor Ave City of Industry (91746) *(P-13823)*

Elmco Stewart, City of Industry *Also called Elmco/Duddy Inc (P-13824)*

Elmco/Duddy Inc (HQ) ....E....626 333-9942
15070 Proctor Ave City of Industry (91746) *(P-13824)*

Elmer F Karpe Inc ....E....661 847-4800
8501 Camino Media Ste 400 Bakersfield (93311) *(P-15845)*

Elotek Systems Inc (PA) ....E....949 366-4404
216 Avnida Fbrcnte Ste 11 San Clemente (92672) *(P-13390)*

Elro Manufacturing Company (PA) ....E....310 380-7444
400 W Walnut St Gardena (90248) *(P-11548)*

Elro Sign Company, Gardena *Also called Elro Manufacturing Company (P-11548)*

Elrob Inc ....D....714 230-6122
12691 Monarch St Garden Grove (92841) *(P-13717)*

Elsinore Vly Municpl Wtr Dst (PA) ....D....951 674-3146
31315 Chaney St Lake Elsinore (92530) *(P-12891)*

Elsinore Vly Municpl Wtr Dst ....D....951 245-0276
1800 E Lakeshore Dr Lake Elsinore (92530) *(P-12924)*

Elwin Inc ....E....714 752-6962
6910 8th St Buena Park (90620) *(P-3709)*

Elwyn Cal Rehabilitation Ctr, Fountain Valley *Also called Elwyn Pennsylvania and Del (P-21304)*

Elwyn Pennsylvania and Del ....D....714 557-6313
18325 Mount Baldy Cir Fountain Valley (92708) *(P-21304)*

Ely Co Inc ....E....310 539-5831
3046 Kashiwa St Torrance (90505) *(P-8580)*

Elysium Ceramics, Anaheim *Also called Elysium Tiles Inc (P-5986)*

Elysium Jennings LLC ....C....661 679-1700
1600 Norris Rd Bakersfield (93308) *(P-427)*

Elysium Tiles Inc ....F....714 991-7885
1160 N Anaheim Blvd Anaheim (92801) *(P-5986)*

Elysium West LLC ....E....661 679-1700
1600 Norris Rd Bakersfield (93308) *(P-496)*

Ema, City of Industry *Also called Engineering Model Assoc Inc (P-5641)*

Emac Assembly Corp ....F....818 882-2999
21615 Parthenia St Canoga Park (91304) *(P-9708)*

Emak Worldwide Inc (PA) ....D....310 633-9311
1727 Berkeley St Santa Monica (90404) *(P-17010)*

Emanate Health ....C....626 912-5282
1722 Desire Ave Ste 206 Rowland Heights (91748) *(P-19805)*

Emanate Health ....A....626 857-3477
427 W Carroll Ave Glendora (91741) *(P-20763)*

Emanate Health Medical Center (PA) ....A....626 962-4011
1115 S Sunset Ave West Covina (91790) *(P-20764)*

Emanate Health Medical Center ....A....626 858-8515
140 W College St Covina (91723) *(P-20765)*

Emanate Health Medical Center ....A....626 963-8411
1115 S Sunset Ave West Covina (91790) *(P-20766)*

Emanate Health Medical Center ....A....626 331-7331
210 W San Bernardino Rd Covina (91723) *(P-20767)*

Emanate Health Medical Group (PA) ....A....626 331-7331
210 W San Bernardino Rd Covina (91723) *(P-20768)*

Emanate Hlth Intr-Cmmnity Hosp, Covina *Also called Emanate Health Medical Group (P-20768)*

Emanuel Morez Inc ....F....818 780-2787
8754 Yolanda Ave Northridge (91324) *(P-3470)*

Emax Laboratories Inc ....E....310 618-8889
3051 Fujita St Torrance (90505) *(P-22942)*

Emazing Lights LLC ....E....626 628-6482
240 S Loara St Anaheim (92802) *(P-9131)*

Embassy Stes - Mndlay Bch Rsor, Oxnard *Also called Djont/Jpm Hsptlity Lsg Spe LLC (P-16411)*

Embassy Suites, El Segundo *Also called NBC Suite Hotel (P-16576)*

Embassy Suites, Downey *Also called Sanwa Jutaku Co Ltd (P-16694)*

Embassy Suites, Lompoc *Also called Windsor Capital Group Inc (P-16790)*

ALPHABETIC

Employee Codes: A=Over 500 employees, B=251-500
C=101-250, D=51-100, E=20-50 F=10-19
2022 Southern California Business
Directory and Buyers Guide
© Mergent Inc. 1-800-342-5647
1123

Embassy Suites, Brea *Also called Windsor Capital Group Inc (P-16795)*
Embassy Suites, Temecula *Also called Windsor Capital Group Inc (P-16796)*
Embassy Suites, Santa Ana *Also called Windsor Capital Group Inc (P-16800)*
Embassy Suites - Lax Airport S, El Segundo *Also called Djont Operations LLC (P-16410)*
Embassy Suites Arcadia, Arcadia *Also called Arcadia Hotel Venture LP (P-16328)*
Embassy Suites Arcadia, Santa Monica *Also called Windsor Capital Group Inc (P-16792)*
Embassy Suites Brea, Brea *Also called Park Hotels & Resorts Inc (P-16620)*
Embassy Suites El Paso, Santa Monica *Also called Windsor Capital Group Inc (P-16798)*
Embassy Suites Lompoc, Santa Monica *Also called Windsor Capital Group Inc (P-16793)*
Embedded Systems Inc....E....805 624-6030
2250a Union Pl Simi Valley (93065) ***(P-8951)***
Embee Performance LLC....E....714 540-1354
2100 Ritchey St Santa Ana (92705) ***(P-14780)***
Embee Plating, Santa Ana *Also called Embee Processing LLC (P-22542)*
Embee Powder Coating, Santa Ana *Also called Embee Performance LLC (P-14780)*
Embee Processing LLC....B....714 546-9842
2158 S Hathaway St Santa Ana (92705) ***(P-22542)***
Ember Technologies Inc....E....520 400-9337
880 Hampshire Rd Westlake Village (91361) ***(P-5639)***
Embroidertex West Ltd (PA)....F....**213 749-4319**
435 E 16th St Los Angeles (90015) ***(P-3153)***
Embroidery One Corp....F....213 572-0280
1359 Channing St Los Angeles (90021) ***(P-3154)***
Emcare Inc....D....805 564-5097
3916 State St 200 Santa Barbara (93105) ***(P-17417)***
Emcor Group Inc....E....949 475-6020
2 Cromwell Irvine (92618) ***(P-10736)***
Emcor Services Mesa Energy, Irvine *Also called Mesa Energy Systems Inc (P-1102)*
Emcore Corporation (PA)....C....**626 293-3400**
2015 Chestnut St Alhambra (91803) ***(P-9502)***
Emcore Corporation....C....626 293-3400
2015 Chestnut St Alhambra (91803) ***(P-9503)***
Eme Fan & Motor, Brea *Also called Sunon Inc (P-8054)*
Emerald Acquisition LLC....D....714 891-8752
6381 Industry Way Westminster (92683) ***(P-877)***
Emerald Expositions, LLC, San Juan Capistrano *Also called Emerald X LLC (P-18513)*
Emerald Health Services, El Segundo *Also called Tempus LLC (P-17474)*
Emerald Holding Inc (PA)....C....**949 226-5700**
31910 Del Obispo St # 200 San Juan Capistrano (92675) ***(P-18512)***
Emerald Landscape Services Inc....D....714 844-2200
26415 Summit Cir Santa Clarita (91350) ***(P-303)***
Emerald Paving Company, Westminster *Also called Emerald Acquisition LLC (P-877)*
Emerald Trans Los Angeles LLC....E....323 277-2500
5756 Alba St Los Angeles (90058) ***(P-12950)***
Emerald X LLC (HQ)....C....**949 226-5700**
31910 Del Obispo St # 20 San Juan Capistrano (92675) ***(P-18513)***
Emercon Construction Inc (PA)....E....**714 630-9615**
125 E Bristol Ln Orange (92865) ***(P-603)***
Emergency Ambulance Service....D....714 990-1331
3200 E Birch St Ste A Brea (92821) ***(P-11862)***
Emergency Groups Office, San Dimas *Also called Ego Inc (P-22778)*
Emergency Groups' Office, San Dimas *Also called Brault (P-22762)*
Emergency Reporting Systems, El Monte *Also called ERs SEC Alarm Systems Inc (P-13627)*
Emergency Technologies Inc....D....818 765-4421
7345 Varna Ave North Hollywood (91605) ***(P-18375)***
Emergency Vehicle Group Inc....E....714 238-0110
2883 E Coronado St Ste A Anaheim (92806) ***(P-13025)***
Emergent Group Inc (HQ)....D....**818 394-2800**
10939 Pendleton St Sun Valley (91352) ***(P-11100)***
Emergent Medical Associates (PA)....C....**310 379-2134**
111 N Sepulveda Blvd # 210 Manhattan Beach (90266) ***(P-19806)***
Emergncy Mdcine Spclist Ornge....C....714 543-8911
1310 W Stewart Dr Ste 212 Orange (92868) ***(P-17491)***
Emerik Hotel Corp....C....213 748-1291
1020 S Figueroa St Los Angeles (90015) ***(P-16432)***
Emeritus At Casa Glendale, Glendale *Also called Emeritus Corporation (P-20323)*
Emeritus At San Dimas, San Dimas *Also called Emeritus Corporation (P-20320)*
Emeritus At Villa Colima, Walnut *Also called Emeritus Corporation (P-20324)*
Emeritus Corporation....C....909 394-0304
1740 S San Dimas Ave San Dimas (91773) ***(P-20320)***
Emeritus Corporation....C....951 744-9861
1001 N Lyon Ave Hemet (92545) ***(P-20321)***
Emeritus Corporation....C....714 639-3590
142 S Prospect St Orange (92869) ***(P-20322)***
Emeritus Corporation....C....818 246-7457
426 Piedmont Ave Glendale (91206) ***(P-20323)***
Emeritus Corporation....C....909 595-5030
19850 Colima Rd Walnut (91789) ***(P-20324)***
Emeritus Corporation....C....909 420-0153
22325 Barton Rd Grand Terrace (92313) ***(P-20325)***
Emery Financial Inc (PA)....D....**949 219-0640**
625 Kings Rd Newport Beach (92663) ***(P-15241)***
Emet Lending Group Inc....D....714 933-9800
2601 Saturn St Ste 200 Brea (92821) ***(P-15189)***
EMI Solutions Inc....F....949 206-9960
13805 Alton Pkwy Ste B Irvine (92618) ***(P-9709)***
EMI-Jay Inc....F....888 779-9733
16060 Ventura Blvd # 110 Encino (91436) ***(P-16955)***
Emida Technologies, Foothill Ranch *Also called Debisys Inc (P-15127)*
Emily Grene Corp....E....855 463-6459
190 E Arrow Hwy Ste H San Dimas (91773) ***(P-23436)***
Emily's Classic Beauty Salon, Long Beach *Also called La Rutan (P-11704)*
Emission Methods Inc....E....909 605-6800
1307 S Wanamaker Ave Ontario (91761) ***(P-10881)***
Emitcon Inc....F....714 632-8595
1175 N Van Horne Way Anaheim (92806) ***(P-10737)***
Emling LLC....C....805 409-4807
2125 N Madera Rd Ste C Simi Valley (93065) ***(P-9400)***
Emmis Publishing Corporation....D....323 301-0100
5900 Wilshire Blvd # 1000 Los Angeles (90036) ***(P-14872)***
Emp Connectors Inc....E....310 533-6799
2280 W 208th St Torrance (90501) ***(P-9035)***
Emp III Inc....D....323 231-4174
1755 Mrtn Lthr Kng Jr Blv Los Angeles (90058) ***(P-16259)***
Empcc Inc....C....714 564-7900
1682 Langley Ave Fl 2 Irvine (92614) ***(P-1178)***
Empi Inc....D....714 446-9606
301 E Orangethorpe Ave Anaheim (92801) ***(P-13059)***
Empire Building Services Inc....D....714 836-7700
1570 E Edinger Ave Ste D Santa Ana (92705) ***(P-17241)***
Empire Cls Wrldwide Chffred Sv, El Segundo *Also called Cls Trnsprttion Los Angles LLC (P-11859)*
Empire Community Painting, Irvine *Also called Empcc Inc (P-1178)*
Empire Community Painting, Irvine *Also called D P S Inc (P-1176)*
Empire Container Corporation....D....310 537-8190
1161 E Walnut St Carson (90746) ***(P-3800)***
Empire Demolition Inc....D....909 393-8300
1623 Leeson Ln Corona (92879) ***(P-1613)***
Empire Enterprises Inc (PA)....F....**818 784-8918**
4264 Fulton Ave Ste 1 Studio City (91604) ***(P-13135)***
Empire Leasing Inc....D....949 646-7400
2045 Placentia Ave Ste A Costa Mesa (92627) ***(P-1434)***
Empire Med Transportations LLC....D....951 530-8420
1433 W Linden St Ste M Riverside (92507) ***(P-12453)***
Empire Oil Co....A....909 877-0226
2756 S Riverside Ave Bloomington (92316) ***(P-14803)***
Empire Pre-Cast Inc....E....951 609-1590
19473 Grand Ave Lake Elsinore (92530) ***(P-6031)***
Empire Sheet Metal Inc....E....909 923-2927
1215 S Bon View Ave Ontario (91761) ***(P-6825)***
Empire Transportation....B....562 529-2676
8800 Park St Bellflower (90706) ***(P-11906)***
Empirecare Health Assoc Inc....D....951 686-8202
3401 Lemon St Riverside (92501) ***(P-22269)***
Employbridge LLC (HQ)....C....**805 882-2200**
301 Mentor Dr 210 Santa Barbara (93111) ***(P-17418)***
Employee Benefits Security ADM....D....626 229-1000
1055 E Colo Blvd Ste 200 Pasadena (91106) ***(P-15515)***
Employee Owned PCF Cast Pdts I....F....562 633-6673
520 S Palmetto Ave Ontario (91762) ***(P-6394)***
Employees Benefit ADM & MGT, Costa Mesa *Also called EBA & M Corporation (P-15396)*
Employers Compensation Insur (HQ)....C....**818 549-4600**
500 N Brand Blvd Ste 800 Glendale (91203) ***(P-15562)***
Employment Intake Training Ctr, Los Angeles *Also called Swissport Usa Inc (P-12371)*
Employnet Inc....C....909 458-0961
123 E 9th St Ste 103 Upland (91786) ***(P-17419)***
Empower Our Youth....D....323 203-5436
6767 W Sunset Blvd 8-188 Los Angeles (90028) ***(P-16166)***
Empower Rf Systems Inc (PA)....D....**310 412-8100**
316 W Florence Ave Inglewood (90301) ***(P-9271)***
Empower Software Tech LLC....F....951 672-6257
28999 Old Town Front St # 203 Temecula (92590) ***(P-17846)***
Emser International LLC (PA)....D....**323 650-2000**
8431 Santa Monica Blvd Los Angeles (90069) ***(P-13304)***
Emser Tile LLC....D....909 974-1600
5300 Shea Center Dr Ontario (91761) ***(P-1416)***
Emsoc, Orange *Also called Emergncy Mdcine Spclist Ornge (P-17491)*
Emtek Products, Baldwin Park *Also called Assa Abloy Rsdential Group Inc (P-13795)*
En Pointe Technologies Sls LLC....C....310 337-6151
200 N Pacific Coast Hwy El Segundo (90245) ***(P-13391)***
Ena Intouch, Three, Vernon *Also called Lenovati Inc (P-14392)*
Enaba-Kbw USA, Chino *Also called CPI Advanced Inc (P-8866)*
Enas Media Inc....E....626 962-1115
1316 Michillinda Ave Arcadia (91006) ***(P-9215)***
Enbio Corp....C....818 953-9976
150 E Olive Ave Ste 114 Burbank (91502) ***(P-23212)***
Enbiz International, Lake Forest *Also called Cloudradiant Corp (P-14921)*
Encina Pepper Tree Joint Ventr (PA)....D....**805 687-5511**
3850 State St Santa Barbara (93105) ***(P-16433)***
Encina Pepper Tree Joint Ventr....D....805 682-7277
2220 Bath St Santa Barbara (93105) ***(P-16434)***
Encino Center Car Wash Inc....E....818 788-6300
16300 Ventura Blvd Encino (91436) ***(P-18913)***
Encino Drmtology Laser Med Ctr, Encino *Also called Alex A Khadavi MD Inc (P-19688)*
Encino Financial Center, Encino *Also called Lowe Enterprises Rlty Svcs Inc (P-15914)*
Encino Trzana Regional Med Ctr....B....818 995-5000
16237 Ventura Blvd Encino (91436) ***(P-20769)***
Enclarity Inc....A....949 797-7160
16815 Von Karman Ave # 1 Irvine (92606) ***(P-18085)***
Encompass Dgtal Mdia Group Inc (PA)....C....**323 344-4500**
15260 Ventura Blvd # 680 Sherman Oaks (91403) ***(P-12715)***
Encore Cases Inc....E....818 768-8803
5260 Vineland Ave North Hollywood (91601) ***(P-5890)***
Encore Image Inc....E....909 986-4632
303 W Main St Ontario (91762) ***(P-11549)***
Encore Image Group Inc (PA)....D....**310 534-7500**
1445 Sepulveda Blvd Torrance (90501) ***(P-11550)***
Encore Plastics, Huntington Beach *Also called Donoco Industries Inc (P-5934)*
Encore Seats Inc....E....949 559-0930
5511 Skylab Rd Huntington Beach (92647) ***(P-10322)***
Encore Tex Inc, Huntington Park *Also called Kuk Rim USA Inc (P-2700)*
Encorr Sheets LLC....D....626 523-4661
5171 E Francis St Ontario (91761) ***(P-3928)***

Mergent e-mail: customerrelations@mergent.com
1124
2022 Southern California Business Directory and Buyers Guide
(P-0000) Products & Services Section entry number
(PA)=Parent Co (HQ)=Headquarters (DH)=Div Headquarters

Encrypted Access Corporation......E......714 371-4125
1730 Redhill Ave Irvine (92697) *(P-8254)*
Endeavor Group Holdings Inc (PA)......D......310 285-9000
9601 Wilshire Blvd Beverly Hills (90210) *(P-19415)*
Enderle Fuel Injection......E......805 526-3838
1830 Voyager Ave Simi Valley (93063) *(P-10053)*
Enderle Vault Co, Inglewood *Also called Centinela Consulting Group Inc (P-6021)*
Endodent Inc......E......626 359-5715
851 Meridian St Duarte (91010) *(P-11172)*
Endologix Inc (PA)......B......949 595-7200
2 Musick Irvine (92618) *(P-10978)*
Endologix Canada LLC......D......949 595-7200
2 Musick Irvine (92618) *(P-10979)*
Endotec Inc......E......714 681-6306
14525 Valley View Ave H Santa Fe Springs (90670) *(P-11101)*
Endpak Packaging Inc......D......562 801-0281
9101 Perkins St Pico Rivera (90660) *(P-3896)*
Endress & Hauser Conducta Inc......E......800 835-5474
4123 E La Palma Ave Anaheim (92807) *(P-10792)*
Endress + Hauser Inc......F......714 577-5600
4123 E La Palma Ave # 20 Anaheim (92807) *(P-10691)*
Endresshauser Conducta, Anaheim *Also called Endress & Hauser Conducta Inc (P-10792)*
Endresshouser Conducta, Anaheim *Also called Endress + Hauser Inc (P-10691)*
Endura Healthcare Inc......D......949 487-9500
29222 Rncho Vejo Rd Ste 1 San Juan Capistrano (92675) *(P-20326)*
Endura Steel Inc (HQ)......F......760 244-9325
17671 Bear Valley Rd Hesperia (92345) *(P-13565)*
Enduratex, Corona *Also called Cgpc America Corporation (P-4682)*
Endurequest Corporation......E......559 783-9220
1813 Thunderbolt Dr Porterville (93257) *(P-5640)*
Ener-Core Power Inc (HQ)......F......949 428-3300
30100 Town Center Dr O Laguna Niguel (92677) *(P-7582)*
Ener-Tech Metals Inc......D......562 529-5034
7815 Somerset Blvd Paramount (90723) *(P-6276)*
Energent Corporation......F......949 885-0365
1831 Carnegie Ave Santa Ana (92705) *(P-7583)*
Energent Corporation......F......949 885-0365
2321 Pullman St Santa Ana (92705) *(P-7584)*
Energetic Lighting, Chino *Also called Yankon Industries Inc (P-9112)*
Energy Berkeley Office US Dept......C......510 486-7089
555 W Imperial Hwy Brea (92821) *(P-22908)*
Energy Cnvrsion Applctions Inc......F......714 256-2166
582 Explorer St Brea (92821) *(P-8869)*
Energy Enterprises USA Inc (PA)......D......424 339-0005
6842 Van Nuys Blvd # 800 Van Nuys (91405) *(P-1062)*
Energy Link Indus Svcs Inc......E......661 765-4444
11439 S Enos Ln Bakersfield (93311) *(P-8581)*
Energy Suspension, San Clemente *Also called Bunker Corp (P-10024)*
Enerpath Services Inc......D......909 335-1699
1758 Orange Tree Ln Redlands (92374) *(P-1248)*
Enerpro Inc......E......805 683-2114
99 Aero Camino Goleta (93117) *(P-13718)*
Enervee Corporation......D......650 996-7048
1746 Abbot Kinney Blvd Venice (90291) *(P-18086)*
Enevate Corporation......D......949 243-0399
101 Theory Ste 200 Irvine (92617) *(P-9809)*
Engel & Gray Inc......E......805 925-2771
745 W Betteravia Rd Ste A Santa Maria (93455) *(P-497)*
Engense Inc......F......805 484-8317
2255 Pleasant Valley Rd G Camarillo (93012) *(P-6200)*
Engeo Incorporated......C......661 257-4004
29025 Avenue Penn Valencia (91355) *(P-23532)*
Engineered Application LLC......F......323 585-2894
4727 E 49th St Vernon (90058) *(P-7362)*
Engineered Food Systems......E......714 921-9913
2490 Anselmo Dr Corona (92879) *(P-8380)*
Engineered Lighting Products, El Monte *Also called R W Swarens Associates Inc (P-9101)*
Engineered Magnetics Inc......E......310 649-9000
10524 S La Cienega Blvd Inglewood (90304) *(P-8975)*
Engineered Products By Lee Ltd......F......818 352-3322
10444 Mcvine Ave Sunland (91040) *(P-8582)*
Engineered Well Svc Intl Inc......F......866 913-6283
3120 Standard St Bakersfield (93308) *(P-498)*
Engineering Jk Aerospace & Def......E......714 499-9092
23231 La Palma Ave Yorba Linda (92887) *(P-10323)*
Engineering Materials Co Inc......F......562 436-0063
2055 W Cowles St Long Beach (90813) *(P-11496)*
Engineering Model Assoc Inc (PA)......E......626 912-7011
1020 Wallace Way City of Industry (91748) *(P-5641)*
Englekirk Institutional Inc (PA)......E......323 733-2640
888 S Figueroa St Ste 180 Los Angeles (90017) *(P-22543)*
Englekirk Structural Engineers (PA)......E......323 733-6673
888 S Figueroa St # 1800 Los Angeles (90017) *(P-22544)*
Englewood Marketing Group LLC......D......909 875-3649
127 W Jurupa Ave Ste 1 Bloomington (92316) *(P-12454)*
Engstrom Lipscomb and Lack A (PA)......D......310 552-3800
10100 Santa Monica Blvd # 1200 Los Angeles (90067) *(P-21551)*
Enhance America Inc......E......951 361-3000
3463 Grapevine St Jurupa Valley (91752) *(P-11551)*
Enhanced Vision Systems Inc (HQ)......D......800 440-9476
15301 Springdale St Huntington Beach (92649) *(P-10834)*
Enjoy Food, Colton *Also called Saab Enterprises Inc (P-1750)*
Enki Health and RES Systems......D......626 961-8971
160 S 7th Ave La Puente (91746) *(P-19807)*
Enki Health Care, La Puente *Also called Enki Health and RES Systems (P-19807)*
Enlink Geoenergy Services Inc......E......424 242-1200
2630 Homestead Pl Rancho Dominguez (90220) *(P-8337)*
Enova Solutions Inc......F......661 327-2405
3553 Landco Dr Ste B Bakersfield (93308) *(P-5218)*

Enpower Innovation, City of Industry *Also called PC Club Inc (P-13425)*
Ens Security, Hacienda Heights *Also called Easterncctv (usa) LLC (P-9866)*
ENSIGN, Mission Viejo *Also called Pennant Healthcare Inc (P-20440)*
Ensign Group Inc......D......949 642-0387
340 Victoria St Costa Mesa (92627) *(P-20327)*
Ensign Group Inc......D......562 923-9301
13007 Paramount Blvd Downey (90242) *(P-20328)*
Ensign Group Inc......D......818 893-6385
9541 Van Nuys Blvd Panorama City (91402) *(P-20329)*
Ensign Group Inc......D......562 947-7817
10426 Bogardus Ave Whittier (90603) *(P-20330)*
Ensign Group Inc......D......626 607-2400
4800 Delta Ave Rosemead (91770) *(P-20331)*
Ensign Palm I LLC......C......760 323-2638
2990 E Ramon Rd Palm Springs (92264) *(P-20332)*
Ensign San Dimas LLC......C......626 963-7531
1033 E Arrow Hwy Glendora (91740) *(P-20579)*
Ensign Services Inc......D......949 487-9500
29222 Rncho Vejo Rd Ste 1 San Juan Capistrano (92675) *(P-20333)*
Ensign Southland LLC......B......949 487-9500
29222 Rncho Vejo Rd Ste 1 San Juan Capistrano (92675) *(P-20334)*
Ensign US Drlg Cal Inc (HQ)......C......661 589-0111
7001 Charity Ave Bakersfield (93308) *(P-7731)*
Ensign Whittier East LLC......C......562 947-7817
10426 Bogardus Ave Whittier (90603) *(P-20335)*
Ensign-Bickford Arospc Def Co......E......805 292-4000
14370 White Sage Rd Moorpark (93021) *(P-10587)*
Entech Instruments Inc......D......805 527-5939
2207 Agate Ct Simi Valley (93065) *(P-10793)*
Entegris Gp Inc......C......805 541-9299
4175 Santa Fe Rd San Luis Obispo (93401) *(P-8121)*
Entercom Media Corp......D......323 930-7317
5670 Wilshire Blvd # 200 Los Angeles (90036) *(P-12688)*
Entercom Media Corp......D......909 825-9525
900 E Washington St # 315 Colton (92324) *(P-12689)*
Enterprise Bank & Trust......C......562 345-9092
17785 Center Court Dr N # 750 Cerritos (90703) *(P-15021)*
Enterprise Portable Welding......F......760 328-6316
68548 Iroquois St Cathedral City (92234) *(P-11102)*
Enterprise Rnt—car Los Angeles (HQ)......D......657 221-4400
333 City Blvd W Ste 1000 Orange (92868) *(P-18739)*
Enterprise Security Inc (PA)......D......714 630-9100
22860 Savi Ranch Pkwy Yorba Linda (92887) *(P-18376)*
Enterprise Security Solutions, Yorba Linda *Also called Enterprise Security Inc (P-18376)*
Enterprises Industries Inc......C......818 989-6103
7500 Tyrone Ave Van Nuys (91405) *(P-7144)*
Entertainment Partners Inc (PA)......B......818 955-6000
2950 N Hollywood Way # 200 Burbank (91505) *(P-22780)*
Entertinment Studios Media Inc (PA)......D......310 277-3500
1925 Century Park E # 1025 Los Angeles (90067) *(P-19348)*
Entertnment Stdios Mtion Pctre......E......310 277-3500
1925 Century Park E Fl 10 Los Angeles (90067) *(P-19349)*
Entitlement LLC......E......224 336-2669
1236 Euclid St Santa Monica (90404) *(P-19350)*
Entravsion Communications Corp......D......323 900-6100
5700 Wilshire Blvd # 250 Los Angeles (90036) *(P-12716)*
Entravsion Communications Corp......D......760 836-0466
72920 Parkview Dr Palm Desert (92260) *(P-12717)*
Entravsion Communications Corp (PA)......B......310 447-3870
2425 Olympic Blvd Ste 600 Santa Monica (90404) *(P-12718)*
Entrepeneur Magazine, Irvine *Also called Entrepreneur Media Inc (P-4069)*
Entrepreneur Media Inc (PA)......D......949 261-2325
18061 Fitch Irvine (92614) *(P-4069)*
Entrepreneurial Capital Corp......C......949 809-3900
4100 Nwport Pl Dr Ste 400 Newport Beach (92660) *(P-15666)*
Envelopments Inc......E......714 569-3300
13091 Sandhurst Pl Santa Ana (92705) *(P-3752)*
Envent Corporation (PA)......D......562 997-9465
3220 E 29th St Long Beach (90806) *(P-23437)*
Envion LLC......D......818 217-2500
14724 Ventura Blvd Fl 200 Sherman Oaks (91403) *(P-8047)*
Envirnmntal Mlding Cncepts LLC......F......951 214-6596
14050 Day St Moreno Valley (92553) *(P-5375)*
Enviro Safety Products, Visalia *Also called Guardian Safety and Supply LLC (P-14934)*
Enviro-Intercept Inc......F......818 982-6063
7327 Varna Ave Unit 5 North Hollywood (91605) *(P-8338)*
Envirogenics Systems Company......D......818 573-9220
9255 Telstar Ave El Monte (91731) *(P-995)*
Enviroguard, Montclair *Also called Expo Power Systems Inc (P-13628)*
Envirokinetics Inc (PA)......F......909 621-7599
101 S Milliken Ave Ontario (91761) *(P-7972)*
Environment Control, Visalia *Also called Tim Hofer Inc (P-17290)*
Environmental Construction Inc......D......818 449-8920
21550 Oxnard St Ste 1060 Woodland Hills (91367) *(P-762)*
Environmental Industries, Fillmore *Also called Brightview Tree Company (P-367)*
Environmental Resolutions Inc......B......949 457-8950
25371 Cmmrcntre Dr Ste 25 Lake Forest (92630) *(P-23438)*
Environmental Science Assoc......D......626 204-6170
80 S Lake Ave Ste 570 Pasadena (91101) *(P-22837)*
Environmental Science Assoc......D......213 599-4300
626 Wilshire Blvd # 1100 Los Angeles (90017) *(P-22838)*
Environments For Learning Inc (PA)......D......949 855-5630
24291 Muirlands Blvd Lake Forest (92630) *(P-22012)*
Envise (HQ)......D......800 613-6240
12131 Western Ave Garden Grove (92841) *(P-1063)*
Envise......D......714 901-5800
12131 Western Ave Garden Grove (92841) *(P-1064)*
Envision Computer Design, City of Industry *Also called Brilliant Imaging Group Inc (P-13892)*

ALPHABETIC

Envista Holdings Corporation (PA) ....A....714 817-7000
200 S Kraemer Blvd Bldg E Brea (92821) *(P-11173)*
Envrionmental Science Assoc, Pasadena *Also called Environmental Science Assoc (P-22837)*
Envveno Medical Corporation ....F....949 261-2900
70 Doppler Irvine (92618) *(P-10980)*
Eon Innovative Technology Inc ....D....213 381-0061
10645 W Vanowen St Burbank (91505) *(P-18377)*
Eon Reality Inc (PA) ....C....949 460-2000
18 Technology Dr Ste 110 Irvine (92618) *(P-13392)*
Eonstar Ledlight Corp ....C....626 693-8084
18835 San Jose Ave City of Industry (91748) *(P-18514)*
Eontork Power Inc ....E....888 959-1311
13427 Virginia Ave Whittier (90605) *(P-22545)*
Eos Estate Winery ....E....805 239-2562
2300 Airport Rd Paso Robles (93446) *(P-2182)*
Eoy, Los Angeles *Also called Empower Our Youth (P-16166)*
Ep Holdings Inc ....E....949 713-4600
30442 Esperanza Rcho STA Marg (92688) *(P-8198)*
Ep Memory, Rcho STA Marg *Also called Ep Holdings Inc (P-8198)*
Epe Industries Usa Inc (HQ) ....F....800 315-0336
17835 Newhope St Ste G Fountain Valley (92708) *(P-5499)*
Epe USA, Fountain Valley *Also called Epe Industries Usa Inc (P-5499)*
Ephesoft Inc (PA) ....D....949 335-5335
8707 Research Dr Irvine (92618) *(P-13393)*
Epic Management LP (PA) ....D....909 799-1818
1615 Orange Tree Ln Redlands (92374) *(P-23021)*
Epic Sheet Metal Inc ....F....714 679-5917
1720 Industrial Ave Norco (92860) *(P-6826)*
Epic Technologies LLC (HQ) ....C....818 495-8617
9340 Owensmouth Ave Chatsworth (91311) *(P-9232)*
Epica Medical Innovations LLC ....E....949 238-6323
901 Calle Amanecer # 150 San Clemente (92673) *(P-10981)*
Epicuren Discovery ....D....949 588-5807
31 Journey Ste 100 Aliso Viejo (92656) *(P-4920)*
Epidaurus ....B....213 743-9075
3745 S Grand Ave Los Angeles (90007) *(P-16177)*
Epilogue and Arrested, Los Angeles *Also called Rhapsody Clothing Inc (P-2989)*
Epirus Inc ....E....310 620-8678
12831 Weber Way Hawthorne (90250) *(P-17847)*
Episcopal Communities & Servic ....D....310 544-2204
5801 Crestridge Rd Pls Vrds Pnsl (90275) *(P-20336)*
Epitome Enterprises LLC ....D....909 625-4728
821 Mary Pl Claremont (91711) *(P-17608)*
Eplica Inc ....C....562 977-4300
17785 Center Court Dr N Cerritos (90703) *(P-17420)*
Epmar Corporation ....E....562 946-8781
13210 Barton Cir Whittier (90605) *(P-5097)*
Epoca Yocool, South Gate *Also called Win Soon Inc (P-1841)*
Epochcom LLC ....C....310 664-5700
3110 Main St Ste 220 Santa Monica (90405) *(P-18087)*
Eppink of California Inc ....E....562 633-1275
11900 Center St South Gate (90280) *(P-1435)*
Eps Corporate Holdings Inc ....D....714 635-3131
1235 S Lewis St Anaheim (92805) *(P-13825)*
Eps Corporate Holdings Inc (HQ) ....C....310 204-7238
3100 Dnald Dglas Loop Hng Santa Monica (90405) *(P-7536)*
Epsilon Electronics Inc (PA) ....D....323 722-3333
1550 S Maple Ave Montebello (90640) *(P-13685)*
Epsilon Plastics Inc ....D....310 609-1320
3100 E Harcourt St Compton (90221) *(P-14926)*
Epson Accessories Inc ....D....562 981-3840
3840 Kilroy Airport Way Long Beach (90806) *(P-13394)*
Epson America Inc (HQ) ....A....800 463-7766
3131 Katella Ave Los Alamitos (90720) *(P-8255)*
Epson Electronics America Inc (HQ) ....E....408 922-0200
3131 Katella Ave Los Alamitos (90720) *(P-9504)*
Epstein Becker & Green PC ....D....310 556-8861
1875 Century Park E # 500 Los Angeles (90067) *(P-21552)*
Eptronics Inc ....F....310 536-0700
19210 S Vermont Ave C Gardena (90248) *(P-9083)*
Epworth Morehouse Cowles, Chino *Also called Morehouse-Cowles LLC (P-7991)*
Eqh Limited Inc ....F....310 736-4130
5440 Mcconnell Ave Los Angeles (90066) *(P-6478)*
Equator LLC (HQ) ....C....310 469-9500
6060 Center Dr Ste 500 Los Angeles (90045) *(P-17609)*
Equator Business Solutions, Los Angeles *Also called Equator LLC (P-17609)*
Equimine Inc ....F....877 437-8464
26457 Rancho Pkwy S Lake Forest (92630) *(P-17848)*
Equinox Fitness Club, Irvine *Also called Equinox-76th Street Inc (P-19448)*
Equinox Fitness Club, Rllng HLS Est *Also called Equinox-76th Street Inc (P-19449)*
Equinox Fitness Club, Los Angeles *Also called Equinox-76th Street Inc (P-19450)*
Equinox-76th Street Inc ....D....310 727-9543
5400 W Rosecrans Ave Up Hawthorne (90250) *(P-19444)*
Equinox-76th Street Inc ....D....323 471-0130
1550 Vine St Hollywood (90028) *(P-19445)*
Equinox-76th Street Inc ....D....805 367-3925
112 S Lakeview Canyon Rd Westlake Village (91362) *(P-19446)*
Equinox-76th Street Inc ....D....310 479-5200
1835 S Sepulveda Blvd Los Angeles (90025) *(P-19447)*
Equinox-76th Street Inc ....D....949 296-1700
19540 Jamboree Rd Irvine (92612) *(P-19448)*
Equinox-76th Street Inc ....D....949 975-8400
1980 Main St Fl 4 Irvine (92614) *(P-20214)*
Equinox-76th Street Inc ....D....310 697-1016
550 Deep Valley Dr Rllng HLS Est (90274) *(P-19449)*
Equinox-76th Street Inc ....D....310 552-0420
10250 Santa Monica Blvd Los Angeles (90067) *(P-19450)*

Equipment & Tool Institute, Irvine *Also called Innova Electronics Corporation (P-10081)*
Equipment De Sport Usa Inc ....F....760 772-5544
39301 Badger St Ste 500 Palm Desert (92211) *(P-3155)*
Equipment Depot Inc ....C....562 949-1000
12393 Slauson Ave Whittier (90606) *(P-13900)*
Equipment Design & Mfg Inc ....D....909 594-2229
119 Explorer St Pomona (91768) *(P-6827)*
Equitable Hotels ....D....559 738-1700
210 E Acequia Ave Visalia (93291) *(P-16435)*
Equity Marketing, Santa Monica *Also called Emak Worldwide Inc (P-17010)*
Equity Title Company (HQ) ....D....818 291-4400
801 N Brand Blvd Ste 400 Glendale (91203) *(P-16038)*
Equus Products Inc ....E....714 424-6779
17352 Von Karman Ave Irvine (92614) *(P-10750)*
ERA Products Inc ....F....310 324-4908
1130 Benedict Canyon Dr Beverly Hills (90210) *(P-3623)*
Erba Organics, Chatsworth *Also called Erbaviva Inc (P-4743)*
Erbaviva Inc ....E....818 998-7112
19831 Nordhoff Pl Ste 116 Chatsworth (91311) *(P-4743)*
Erdle Perforating Co Inc ....F....559 651-1889
7300 W Sunnyview Ave Visalia (93291) *(P-499)*
Erf Enterprises Inc ....F....909 825-4080
863 E Valley Blvd Colton (92324) *(P-9986)*
Erg International, Oxnard *Also called Ergonom Corporation (P-3728)*
Ergo Baby Carrier Inc (HQ) ....F....213 283-2090
617 W 7th St Fl 10 Los Angeles (90017) *(P-11373)*
Ergomotion Inc ....D....805 979-9400
6790 Navigator Way Goleta (93117) *(P-13136)*
Ergonom Corporation (PA) ....D....805 981-9978
361 Bernoulli Cir Oxnard (93030) *(P-3727)*
Ergonom Corporation ....D....805 981-9978
390 Lombard St Oxnard (93030) *(P-3728)*
Ergononmic Comfort Design Inc ....F....951 277-1558
9140 Stellar Ct Ste B Corona (92883) *(P-3608)*
Ergs Aim Hotel Realty LLC ....D....949 661-1100
34402 Pacific Coast Hwy Dana Point (92624) *(P-16436)*
Erika Records Inc ....E....714 228-5420
6300 Caballero Blvd Buena Park (90620) *(P-9216)*
Eriks North America Inc ....D....562 802-7782
15500 Blackburn Ave Norwalk (90650) *(P-5336)*
Erlanger Distribution Ctr Inc ....E....951 784-5147
797 Palmyrita Ave Riverside (92507) *(P-12202)*
Erlanger Sales, Riverside *Also called Erlanger Distribution Ctr Inc (P-12202)*
Ermm Corporation ....F....310 635-0524
5415 Mrtin Lther King Jr Lynwood (90262) *(P-10166)*
Ernest Packaging (PA) ....C....800 233-7788
5777 Smithway St Commerce (90040) *(P-14927)*
Ernest Paper, Commerce *Also called Ernest Packaging (P-14927)*
Ernst & Young LLP ....A....213 977-3200
725 S Figueroa St Ste 200 Los Angeles (90017) *(P-22781)*
Ernst & Young LLP ....B....949 794-2300
18101 Von Karman Ave # 1000 Irvine (92612) *(P-22782)*
Ernst Mfg, Bakersfield *Also called Triple E Manufacturing (P-7954)*
Eros Stx Global Corporation ....A....818 524-7000
3900 W Alameda Ave Fl 32 Burbank (91505) *(P-19297)*
Erp Integrated Solutions LLC ....D....562 425-7800
1501 Hughes Way Ste 320 Long Beach (90810) *(P-17610)*
Erp Power LLC (PA) ....F....805 517-1300
893 Patriot Dr Ste E Moorpark (93021) *(P-10751)*
ERs SEC Alarm Systems Inc ....D....626 579-2525
4538 Santa Anita Ave El Monte (91731) *(P-13627)*
Erwin Street Medical Offices, Woodland Hills *Also called Kaiser Foundation Hospitals (P-20814)*
Es Engineering Services LLC ....D....949 988-3500
1 Park Plz Ste 1000 Irvine (92614) *(P-22546)*
ES Kluft & Company Inc (PA) ....C....909 373-4211
11096 Jersey Blvd Ste 101 Rancho Cucamonga (91730) *(P-3548)*
ESA, Los Angeles *Also called Environmental Science Assoc (P-22838)*
Esaloncom LLC ....C....866 550-2424
1910 E Maple Ave El Segundo (90245) *(P-16902)*
Esc, Compton *Also called Electronic Stamping Corp (P-8897)*
Escape Communications Inc ....F....310 997-1300
2790 Skypark Dr Ste 203 Torrance (90505) *(P-9272)*
Esco Industries Inc ....F....951 782-2130
1755 Iowa Ave Bldg A Riverside (92507) *(P-7084)*
Esco Technologies Inc ....E....805 604-3875
501 Del Norte Blvd Oxnard (93030) *(P-9340)*
Ese, El Segundo *Also called Mod-Electronics Inc (P-11302)*
Ese, Los Angeles *Also called ESE Electronics Inc (P-14781)*
ESE Electronics Inc ....E....213 614-0102
1111 S Central Ave Los Angeles (90021) *(P-14781)*
Esi Inc ....E....310 670-4974
5710 W Manchester Ave Los Angeles (90045) *(P-9505)*
Esi Motion, Simi Valley *Also called Embedded Systems Inc (P-8951)*
Esl Gaming America Inc ....E....818 861-7315
1212 Chestnut St Burbank (91506) *(P-19351)*
Esl Power Systems Inc ....D....800 922-4188
2800 Palisades Dr Corona (92878) *(P-9036)*
ESM Aerospace Inc ....E....818 841-3653
1203 W Isabel St Burbank (91506) *(P-6828)*
Esm Plastics Inc ....F....909 591-7658
13575 Yorba Ave Chino (91710) *(P-8583)*
Esmart Massage Inc ....F....657 341-0360
339 N Berry St Brea (92821) *(P-9004)*
Esolar Inc (HQ) ....D....818 303-9500
900 Glenneyre St Laguna Beach (92651) *(P-996)*
ESP Computer Services Inc (PA) ....D....818 487-4500
12444 Victory Blvd Fl 4 North Hollywood (91606) *(P-18088)*

ESP Group Ltd ....D....626 301-0280
2397 Bateman Ave Duarte (91010) ***(P-14374)***
Espana Metal Craft Inc ....F....818 988-4988
7600 Ventura Canyon Ave Van Nuys (91402) ***(P-6829)***
Esparza Enterprises Inc ....C....760 344-2031
251 W Main St Ste G&F Brawley (92227) ***(P-221)***
Esparza Enterprises Inc (PA) ....**A....661 831-0002**
3851 Fruitvale Ave Bakersfield (93308) ***(P-17492)***
Esparza Enterprises Inc ....B....661 831-0002
3851 Fruitvale Ave A Bakersfield (93308) ***(P-17421)***
Esparza Enterprises Inc ....B....760 398-0349
51335 Harrison St Ste 112 Coachella (92236) ***(P-17422)***
Esparza Enterprises Inc ....B....661 631-0347
222 S Union Ave Bakersfield (93307) ***(P-17423)***
Esparza Enterprises Inc ....A....661 631-0347
500 Workman St Bakersfield (93307) ***(P-12036)***
Especial T Hvac Shtmtl Fttngs ....E....909 869-9150
1239 E Franklin Ave Pomona (91766) ***(P-13842)***
Esperer Holdings Inc (PA) ....**F....805 880-4220**
3820 State St Santa Barbara (93105) ***(P-6292)***
Esperer Webstores LLC ....F....805 880-1900
3820 State St Ste B Santa Barbara (93105) ***(P-1790)***
Esprit, Camarillo *Also called DP Technology LLC* ***(P-17602)***
Esquivel Designs LLC (PA) ....**D....714 670-2200**
7372 Walnut Ave Ste U Buena Park (90620) ***(P-14437)***
Esri International LLC ....E....909 793-2853
380 New York St Redlands (92373) ***(P-13395)***
Ess LLC ....D....888 303-6424
5227 Dantes View Dr Agoura Hills (91301) ***(P-1065)***
Essco, Pasadena *Also called Electric Svc & Sup Co Pasadena* ***(P-1246)***
Essendant Co ....D....626 961-0011
918 S Stimson Ave City of Industry (91745) ***(P-14194)***
Essense ....A....323 202-4650
6300 Wilshire Blvd # 720 Los Angeles (90048) ***(P-23533)***
Essential Access Health (PA) ....**D....213 386-5614**
3600 Wilshire Blvd # 600 Los Angeles (90010) ***(P-22183)***
Essential Pharmaceutical Corp ....E....909 623-4565
1906 W Holt Ave Pomona (91768) ***(P-4817)***
Essex Electronics Inc ....E....805 684-7601
1130 Mark Ave Carpinteria (93013) ***(P-9506)***
Essex Properties LLC ....D....949 798-8100
18012 Sky Park Cir # 200 Irvine (92614) ***(P-15846)***
Essex Property Trust Inc ....E....323 461-9346
1234 Larrabee St West Hollywood (90069) ***(P-15724)***
Esslinger Engineering Inc ....E....909 539-0544
5946 Freedom Dr Chino (91710) ***(P-10054)***
Estam, Los Angeles *Also called Orbita Corp* ***(P-3050)***
Estes Express Lines ....D....714 994-3770
14727 Alondra Blvd La Mirada (90638) ***(P-12037)***
Estes Express Lines ....D....909 427-9850
10736 Cherry Ave Fontana (92337) ***(P-12038)***
Estes Express Lines ....D....626 333-9090
13327 Temple Ave City of Industry (91746) ***(P-12039)***
Estes Express Lines ....D....818 504-4155
9120 San Fernando Rd Sun Valley (91352) ***(P-12040)***
Estes Express Lines ....D....805 922-8206
945 Noble Way Santa Maria (93454) ***(P-12041)***
Estes Express Lines ....D....310 549-7306
1531 Blinn Ave Wilmington (90744) ***(P-12042)***
Estrella Inc ....C....562 925-6418
1340 Highland Ave 12 Duarte (91010) ***(P-20337)***
Estrella Communications Inc ....D....818 260-5700
3000 W Alameda Ave Burbank (91523) ***(P-12719)***
Estrella Media Inc ....D....818 729-5316
1845 W Empire Ave Burbank (91504) ***(P-12690)***
Esys Energy Control Company ....D....661 833-1902
4520 Stine Rd Ste 7 Bakersfield (93313) ***(P-1249)***
Et Whitehall Seascape LLC ....C....310 581-5533
1910 Ocean Way Santa Monica (90405) ***(P-16437)***
Eta Compute Inc ....E....805 379-5121
340 N Westlake Blvd # 115 Westlake Village (91362) ***(P-10752)***
Etairos Consulting ....E....844 219-7027
6711 Studio Pl Riverside (92509) ***(P-18176)***
Etap, Irvine *Also called Operation Technology Inc* ***(P-17684)***
Etchandy Farms LLC ....D....805 983-4700
4324 E Vineyard Ave Oxnard (93036) ***(P-27)***
Etchegaray Farms LLC ....E....661 393-0920
32324 Famoso Rd Mc Farland (93250) ***(P-129)***
Eternal Star Corporation ....E....310 768-1945
17813 S Main St Ste 101 Gardena (90248) ***(P-3914)***
Eternity Floors, Pacoima *Also called LA Hardwood Flooring Inc* ***(P-3220)***
Etherwan Systems Inc ....D....714 779-3800
2301 E Winston Rd Anaheim (92806) ***(P-18177)***
Ethically Made Goods Inc ....F....213 683-1123
1613 Santee St Los Angeles (90015) ***(P-2943)***
Ethicon Inc ....B....949 581-5799
33 Technology Dr Irvine (92618) ***(P-11103)***
Ethos Management Inc ....E....626 456-3669
560 W Main St Alhambra (91801) ***(P-23022)***
Ethosenergy Field Services LLC (HQ) ....**E....310 639-3523**
10455 Slusher Dr Bldg 12 Santa Fe Springs (90670) ***(P-500)***
Eti B Si Professional, Commerce *Also called Eti Sound Systems Inc* ***(P-9175)***
Eti Partners IV LLC ....E....949 273-4990
901 Wshngton Blvd Ste 208 Marina Del Rey (90292) ***(P-9401)***
Eti Sound Systems Inc ....E....323 835-6660
5300 Harbor St Commerce (90040) ***(P-9175)***
Eti Systems ....D....310 684-3664
1800 Century Park E # 600 Los Angeles (90067) ***(P-10692)***
Etiwanda Power Plant, Rancho Cucamonga *Also called NRG California South LP* ***(P-12810)***
Etnies, Lake Forest *Also called Sole Technology Inc* ***(P-5887)***
Etonien LLC (PA) ....**D....310 321-5800**
222 N Pacific Coast Hwy # 1507 El Segundo (90245) ***(P-23439)***
Etrade 24 Inc ....E....818 712-0574
20524 Ventura Blvd # 102 Woodland Hills (91364) ***(P-2724)***
Ets Express LLC (HQ) ....**E....805 278-7771**
420 Lombard St Oxnard (93030) ***(P-7363)***
Eturns Inc ....E....949 265-2626
19700 Fairchild Ste 290 Irvine (92612) ***(P-17849)***
Eubanks Engineering Co (PA) ....**E....909 483-2456**
1921 S Quaker Ridge Pl Ontario (91761) ***(P-7901)***
Euclid Parking, Porterville *Also called Exeter Packers Inc* ***(P-168)***
Eugenios Sheet Metal Inc ....E....909 923-2002
2151 Maple Privado Ontario (91761) ***(P-6830)***
Eurasia Power LLC ....E....805 383-1234
4022 Cmino Ranchero Ste D Camarillo (93012) ***(P-13719)***
Eureka Restaurant Group LLC (PA) ....**B....310 331-8233**
12101 Crenshaw Blvd Hawthorne (90250) ***(P-23023)***
Eurmax Canopy Inc ....F....626 279-1622
9460 Telstar Ave Ste 2 El Monte (91731) ***(P-6831)***
Euro Bello USA ....E....213 446-2818
10660 Wilshire Blvd Los Angeles (90024) ***(P-3057)***
Eurocraft Archtectural Met Inc ....E....323 771-1323
5619 Watcher St Bell Gardens (90201) ***(P-6961)***
Eurofins Eag Engrg Science LLC ....E....949 521-6200
15 Morgan Irvine (92618) ***(P-22943)***
Eurofins Eaton Analytical LLC (HQ) ....**D....626 386-1100**
750 Royal Oaks Dr Ste 100 Monrovia (91016) ***(P-22944)***
Euroline Steel Windows ....E....877 590-2741
22600 Savi Ranch Pkwy E Yorba Linda (92887) ***(P-6698)***
Euroline Steel Windows & Doors, Yorba Linda *Also called Euroline Steel Windows* ***(P-6698)***
European Ht Invstors I I A Cal (PA) ....**E....949 474-7368**
2532 Dupont Dr Irvine (92612) ***(P-16438)***
Eurotec Seating, La Habra *Also called Orbo Corporation* ***(P-3629)***
Eurton Electric Company Inc ....E....562 946-4477
9920 Painter Ave Santa Fe Springs (90670) ***(P-19011)***
Ev Connect Inc ....D....310 751-7997
615 N Nash St Ste 203 El Segundo (90245) ***(P-1250)***
Ev Infrastructure LLC ....E....714 908-5266
1690 Scenic Ave Costa Mesa (92626) ***(P-1251)***
Ev Ray Inc ....E....818 346-5381
6400 Variel Ave Woodland Hills (91367) ***(P-13169)***
Ev3 Neurovascular, Irvine *Also called Micro Therapeutics Inc* ***(P-11023)***
Eva Franco Inc ....F....213 746-4776
1704 Hooper Ave Los Angeles (90021) ***(P-2902)***
Evangelical Christian Cr Un ....C....714 671-5700
955 W Imperial Hwy # 100 Brea (92821) ***(P-15112)***
Evangelical Christian Cr Un (PA) ....**C....714 671-5700**
955 W Imperial Hwy # 100 Brea (92821) ***(P-15113)***
Evans Hardy & Young Inc ....E....805 963-5841
829 De La Vina St Ste 100 Santa Barbara (93101) ***(P-17011)***
Evans Hydro Inc ....E....310 608-5801
18128 S Santa Fe Ave Compton (90221) ***(P-19036)***
Evans Industries Inc ....E....626 912-1688
17915 Railroad St City of Industry (91748) ***(P-7556)***
Evans Manufacturing Inc (PA) ....**C....714 379-6100**
7422 Chapman Ave Garden Grove (92841) ***(P-11552)***
Evans Walker Enterprises ....E....951 784-7223
2304 Fleetwood Dr Riverside (92509) ***(P-10055)***
Evans, Walker Racing, Riverside *Also called Evans Walker Enterprises* ***(P-10055)***
Eve Hair Inc (PA) ....**E....562 377-1020**
3935 Paramount Blvd Lakewood (90712) ***(P-14928)***
Eveg Inc ....E....844 221-3359
16540 Aston Irvine (92606) ***(P-17611)***
Eventure Interactive Inc ....F....855 986-5669
3420 Bristol St Fl 6 Costa Mesa (92626) ***(P-17850)***
Ever Increasing Faith Ministry, Los Angeles *Also called Crenshaw Chrstn Ctr Ch Los Ang* ***(P-19113)***
Ever Win International Corp ....E....626 810-8218
17579 Railroad St City of Industry (91748) ***(P-13720)***
Everbrands Inc ....E....855 595-2999
401 N Oak St Inglewood (90302) ***(P-5019)***
Everbridge Inc (PA) ....**C....818 230-9700**
155 N Lake Ave Ste 100 Pasadena (91101) ***(P-17851)***
Everest Group Usa Inc ....E....909 923-1818
2030 S Carlos Ave Ontario (91761) ***(P-2725)***
Everest Sonoma Management LLC ....D....213 272-0088
520 Newport Center Dr # 2 Newport Beach (92660) ***(P-16439)***
Everfilt, Jurupa Valley *Also called Puri Tech Inc* ***(P-8406)***
Everfocus Electronics Corp (HQ) ....**E....626 844-8888**
324 W Blueridge Ave Orange (92865) ***(P-13721)***
Evergreen Alliance Golf Ltd LP ....D....805 495-6421
299 S Moorpark Rd Thousand Oaks (91361) ***(P-19487)***
Evergreen Alliance Golf Ltd LP ....D....805 650-1794
3750 Olivas Park Dr Ventura (93001) ***(P-19488)***
Evergreen At Lakeport LLC ....D....661 871-3133
6212 Tudor Way Bakersfield (93306) ***(P-20338)***
Evergreen Chemicals USA LLC ....F....626 821-9236
1700 Lee Ave Arcadia (91006) ***(P-5135)***
Evergreen Environmental Svcs, Gardena *Also called Evergreen Oil Inc* ***(P-5295)***
Evergreen Fullerton Healthcare, Fullerton *Also called Fullerton Hlthcare Wllness CNT* ***(P-20348)***
Evergreen Health Care LLC ....A....661 854-4475
323 Campus Dr Arvin (93203) ***(P-20339)***
Evergreen Healthcare Center, Bakersfield *Also called Evergreen At Lakeport LLC* ***(P-20338)***
Evergreen Holdings Inc (PA) ....**E....949 757-7770**
18952 Macarthur Blvd # 410 Irvine (92612) ***(P-5294)***
Evergreen Hospice Care Inc (PA) ....**C....562 865-9006**
17215 Studebaker Rd # 100 Cerritos (90703) ***(P-21163)***

Employee Codes: A=Over 500 employees, B=251-500
C=101-250, D=51-100, E=20-50 F=10-19
2022 Southern California Business
Directory and Buyers Guide
© Mergent Inc. 1-800-342-5647
1127

Evergreen Industries Inc D 323 583-1331
2300 E 49th St Vernon (90058) ***(P-10657)***

Evergreen Licensing LLC F 844 270-2700
5737 Kanan Rd Ste 344 Agoura Hills (91301) ***(P-4744)***

Evergreen Lighting, Pomona *Also called Yawitz Inc* ***(P-9075)***

Evergreen Oil Inc (HQ) C **949 757-7770**
18025 S Broadway Gardena (90248) ***(P-5295)***

Evergreen Realty, Irvine *Also called Evr Lending Inc* ***(P-15848)***

Evergreen Scientific, Vernon *Also called Evergreen Industries Inc* ***(P-10657)***

Evergreen Solar Services, Agoura Hills *Also called Ess LLC* ***(P-1065)***

Everidge Inc D 909 605-6419
8886 White Oak Ave Rancho Cucamonga (91730) ***(P-8339)***

Everleigh, Huntington Park *Also called J Heyri Inc* ***(P-2848)***

Everpac C 951 774-3274
1499 Palmyrita Ave Riverside (92507) ***(P-13858)***

Everpark Inc C 310 987-6922
3470 Wilshire Blvd # 940 Los Angeles (90010) ***(P-18765)***

Everport Terminal Services Inc (PA) D **310 221-0220**
389 Terminal Island Way San Pedro (90731) ***(P-12287)***

Everson Spice Company Inc E 562 595-4785
2667 Gundry Ave Long Beach (90755) ***(P-2430)***

Everspring Chemical Inc F 310 707-1600
11577 W Olympic Blvd Los Angeles (90064) ***(P-5219)***

Everytable Pbc (PA) D **917 319-6156**
1101 W 23rd St Los Angeles (90007) ***(P-155)***

Evga Corporation (PA) E **714 528-4500**
408 Saturn St Brea (92821) ***(P-13396)***

Evgo Services LLC C 310 954-2900
11835 W Olympic Blvd 900e Los Angeles (90064) ***(P-18924)***

Evo Manufacturing Inc F 714 879-8913
20420 S Susana Rd Carson (90810) ***(P-11665)***

Evocative Inc D 888 365-2656
600 W 7th St Ste 510 Los Angeles (90017) ***(P-17852)***

Evolectric Incorporated F 714 260-7022
2330 E Artesia Blvd Long Beach (90805) ***(P-6516)***

Evolife Scientific Llc E 888 750-0310
1452 E 33rd St Signal Hill (90755) ***(P-4745)***

Evolus Inc (PA) C **949 284-4555**
520 Nwport Ctr Dr Ste 120 Newport Beach (92660) ***(P-4818)***

Evolution Design Lab Inc E 626 960-8388
150 S Los Robles Ave # 1 Pasadena (91101) ***(P-5879)***

Evolution Film & Tape Inc D 818 260-0300
3310 W Vanowen St Burbank (91505) ***(P-19122)***

Evolution Fresh Inc C 800 794-9986
11655 Jersey Blvd Ste A Rancho Cucamonga (91730) ***(P-14626)***

Evolution Hospitality LLC (HQ) A **949 325-1350**
1211 Puerta Del Sol # 170 San Clemente (92673) ***(P-23024)***

Evolution Juice, Rancho Cucamonga *Also called Evolution Fresh Inc* ***(P-14626)***

Evolution Media, Burbank *Also called Evolution Film & Tape Inc* ***(P-19122)***

Evolution Robotics Inc D 626 993-3300
1055 E Colo Blvd Ste 320 Pasadena (91106) ***(P-17853)***

Evolve Dental Technologies Inc E 949 713-0909
5 Vanderbilt Irvine (92618) ***(P-11174)***

Evolve Media Holdings LLC (PA) C **310 449-1890**
11390 W Olympic Blvd # 450 Los Angeles (90064) ***(P-17012)***

Evoq Properties Inc D 213 988-8890
1318 E 7th St Ste 200 Los Angeles (90021) ***(P-15847)***

Evox Productions LLC (PA) D **310 605-1400**
2363 E Pacifica Pl 305 Compton (90220) ***(P-17612)***

Evr Lending Inc (PA) D **949 753-7888**
9901 Irvine Center Dr Irvine (92618) ***(P-15848)***

Ew Corprtion Indus Fabricators (PA) D **760 337-0020**
1002 E Main St El Centro (92243) ***(P-6616)***

Eworkplace Manufacturing Inc C 949 583-1646
9861 Irvine Center Dr Irvine (92618) ***(P-13397)***

Exactax Inc (PA) D **714 284-4802**
1100 E Orngthrp Ave # 100 Anaheim (92801) ***(P-16936)***

Exactuals LLC F 310 689-7491
1100 Glendon Ave Fl 17 Los Angeles (90024) ***(P-17854)***

Exam Room Supply LLC F 805 298-3631
2419 Hrbour Blvd Unit 126 Ventura (93001) ***(P-11222)***

Excalibur International, Long Beach *Also called A W Chang Corporation* ***(P-14300)***

Excalibur Well Services Corp C 661 589-5338
22034 Rosedale Hwy Bakersfield (93314) ***(P-428)***

Excavo LLC F 310 823-7670
13428 Maxella Ave Ste 409 Marina Del Rey (90292) ***(P-3218)***

Excel Auto Transporting Towing, Jurupa Valley *Also called Deluxe Auto Carriers Inc* ***(P-11965)***

Excel Bridge Manufacturing Co., Santa Fe Springs *Also called Excel Sheet Metal Inc* ***(P-6832)***

Excel Cabinets Inc E 951 279-4545
225 Jason Ct Corona (92879) ***(P-3319)***

Excel Construction Svcs Inc (PA) D **714 680-9200**
1950 Raymer Ave Fullerton (92833) ***(P-697)***

Excel Contractors Inc D 661 942-6944
348 E Avenue K8 Ste B Lancaster (93535) ***(P-604)***

Excel Garden Products (HQ) B **562 567-2000**
10708 Norwalk Blvd Santa Fe Springs (90670) ***(P-14858)***

Excel Industries Inc E 909 947-4867
1601 Fremont Ct Ontario (91761) ***(P-7145)***

Excel Landscape Inc C 951 735-9650
710 Rimpau Ave Ste 108 Corona (92879) ***(P-304)***

Excel Paving Co, Long Beach *Also called Palp Inc* ***(P-905)***

Excel Picture Frames Inc E 323 231-0244
647 E 59th St Los Angeles (90001) ***(P-19037)***

Excel Scientific LLC E 760 246-4545
18350 George Blvd Victorville (92394) ***(P-13533)***

Excel Sheet Metal Inc (PA) D **562 944-0701**
12001 Shoemaker Ave Santa Fe Springs (90670) ***(P-6832)***

Excelity E 818 767-1000
11127 Dora St Sun Valley (91352) ***(P-6415)***

Excellence Opto Inc (PA) E **909 468-0550**
21858 Garcia Ln Walnut (91789) ***(P-9115)***

Excellent In-Home Care Inc D 818 755-4900
22041 Clarendon St 100 Woodland Hills (91367) ***(P-21164)***

Excelline Food Products LLC E 818 701-7710
833 N Hollywood Way Burbank (91505) ***(P-1926)***

Excello Circuits Inc E 714 993-0560
1924 Nancita Cir Placentia (92870) ***(P-9402)***

Excellon Acquisition LLC (HQ) E **310 668-7700**
20001 S Rancho Way Compton (90220) ***(P-7973)***

Excellon Automation Co, Compton *Also called Excellon Acquisition LLC* ***(P-7973)***

Excelpro Inc (PA) E **323 415-8544**
1630 Amapola Ave Torrance (90501) ***(P-1771)***

Excelsior Capital Partners LLC (PA) C **949 566-8110**
4695 Macarthur Ct Ste 370 Newport Beach (92660) ***(P-15849)***

Excelsior Nutrition Inc E 657 999-5188
1206 N Miller St Unit D Anaheim (92806) ***(P-4746)***

Exceptional Chld Foundation C 310 915-6606
11124 Fairbanks Way Culver City (90230) ***(P-22337)***

Exceptional Chld Foundation (PA) C **310 204-3300**
5350 Machado Ln Culver City (90230) ***(P-21950)***

Exceptional Chld Foundation C 213 748-3556
1430 Venice Blvd Los Angeles (90006) ***(P-21951)***

Exchangrght Nlp 3 Mstr Lssee L (PA) D **855 317-4448**
1055 E Colo Blvd Ste 310 Pasadena (91106) ***(P-16260)***

Exclusive Powder Coatings Inc E 661 294-9812
24922 Anza Dr Ste C Valencia (91355) ***(P-7364)***

Executive Auto Reconditioning E 626 416-3322
522 E Duarte Rd Monrovia (91016) ***(P-18914)***

Executive Network Entps Inc A 310 457-8822
1224 21st St Apt E Santa Monica (90404) ***(P-11863)***

Executive Network Entps Inc (PA) D **310 447-2759**
13440 Beach Ave Marina Del Rey (90292) ***(P-11864)***

Executive Personnel Services B 714 310-9506
1526 Brookhollow Dr # 83 Santa Ana (92705) ***(P-17424)***

Executive Safe and SEC Corp E 909 947-7020
10722 Edison Ct Rancho Cucamonga (91730) ***(P-7557)***

Exel Inc E 909 350-6976
9211 Kaiser Way Fontana (92335) ***(P-12203)***

Exemplis LLC E 714 995-4800
6280 Artesia Blvd Buena Park (90620) ***(P-3609)***

Exemplis LLC E 714 898-5500
6280 Artesia Blvd Buena Park (90620) ***(P-3610)***

Exemplis LLC (PA) E **714 995-4800**
6415 Katella Ave Cypress (90630) ***(P-3611)***

Exer Holding Company LLC E 818 287-0894
15503 Ventura Blvd Encino (91436) ***(P-19808)***

Exeter Engineering Inc D 559 592-3161
109 W Pine St Exeter (93221) ***(P-166)***

Exeter Mercantile Company F 559 592-2121
258 E Pine St Exeter (93221) ***(P-7611)***

Exeter Packers Inc (PA) C **559 592-5168**
1250 E Myer Ave Exeter (93221) ***(P-167)***

Exeter Packers Inc D 626 993-6245
1095 E Green St Pasadena (91106) ***(P-62)***

Exeter Packers Inc C 661 399-0416
33374 Lerdo Hwy Bakersfield (93308) ***(P-12173)***

Exeter Packers Inc C 559 784-8820
23744 Avenue 181 Porterville (93257) ***(P-168)***

Exeter Specialties F 559 592-5999
301 N G St Exeter (93221) ***(P-1899)***

Exeter-Ivanhoe Citrus Assn D 559 592-3141
901 Rocky Hill Dr Exeter (93221) ***(P-169)***

Exhart Envmtl Systems Inc (PA) F **818 576-9628**
20364 Plummer St Chatsworth (91311) ***(P-11666)***

Exhaust Center Inc F 951 685-8602
1794 W 11th St Upland (91786) ***(P-6833)***

Exhaust Gas Technologies Inc F 909 548-8100
15642 Dupont Ave Ste B Chino (91710) ***(P-10056)***

Exhaust Tech, Commerce *Also called Dynaflex Products* ***(P-9984)***

Exigent Sensors LLC E 949 439-1321
11441 Markon Dr Garden Grove (92841) ***(P-9341)***

Exodus Recovery Inc (PA) C **310 945-3350**
9808 Venice Blvd Ste 700 Culver City (90232) ***(P-21305)***

Exodus Recovery Ctr At Brotman (PA) D **310 253-9494**
3828 Delmas Ter Culver City (90232) ***(P-21045)***

Expak Logistics, Los Angeles *Also called Kxp Carrier Services LLC* ***(P-12140)***

Expeditors Intl Wash Inc B 310 343-6200
19701 Hamilton Ave Torrance (90502) ***(P-12455)***

Experea Healthcare LLC D 949 716-3071
27 Spectrum Pointe Dr # 30 Lake Forest (92630) ***(P-13486)***

Experian Corporation C 714 830-7000
475 Anton Blvd Santa Ana (92704) ***(P-17122)***

Experian Holdings Inc (HQ) C **714 830-7000**
475 Anton Blvd Costa Mesa (92626) ***(P-17123)***

Experian Info Solutions Inc (HQ) A **714 830-7000**
475 Anton Blvd Costa Mesa (92626) ***(P-17124)***

Experian Mktg Solutions LLC A 714 830-7000
475 Anton Blvd Costa Mesa (92626) ***(P-17125)***

Experience 1 Inc (HQ) D **949 475-3752**
5000 Birch St Ste 300 Newport Beach (92660) ***(P-15502)***

Expert Assembly Services Inc E 714 258-8880
14312 Chambers Rd Ste B Tustin (92780) ***(P-9403)***

Expert Ems, Tustin *Also called Expert Assembly Services Inc* ***(P-9403)***

Expert Pharmaceutical LLC F 626 581-4008
1136 Samuelson St City of Industry (91748) ***(P-4819)***

Mergent e-mail: customerrelations@mergent.com
1128

2022 Southern California Business
Directory and Buyers Guide

(P-0000) Products & Services Section entry number
(PA)=Parent Co (HQ)=Headquarters (DH)=Div Headquarters

Experts Exch Exprts-Xchangecom, Atascadero *Also called Experts Exchange LLC* ***(P-18178)***
Experts Exchange LLC....D....805 787-0603
7301 Morro Rd Ste 105a Atascadero (93422) ***(P-18178)***
Exploremypc....E....877 497-1650
1968 S Coast Hwy 402 Laguna Beach (92651) ***(P-17174)***
Expo Dyeing & Finishing Inc....C....714 220-9583
1365 N Knollwood Cir Anaheim (92801) ***(P-2670)***
Expo Power Systems Inc....E....800 506-9884
5534 Olive St Montclair (91763) ***(P-13628)***
Expo-3 International Inc....E....714 379-8383
12350 Edison Way 60 Garden Grove (92841) ***(P-11553)***
Express Chipping....F....562 789-8058
418 Goetz Ave Santa Ana (92707) ***(P-4171)***
Express Container Inc....E....909 798-3857
560 Iowa St Redlands (92373) ***(P-3801)***
Express Contractors Inc....D....951 360-6500
11625 Industry Ave Fontana (92337) ***(P-16880)***
Express Group Inc (PA)....**D....310 474-5999**
10801 National Blvd # 104 Los Angeles (90064) ***(P-12128)***
Express Imaging Services Inc....D....888 846-8804
1805 W 208th St Ste 202 Torrance (90501) ***(P-12267)***
Express Lens Lab Inc....F....714 545-1024
17150 Newhope St Ste 305 Fountain Valley (92708) ***(P-11251)***
Express Manufacturing Inc (PA)....**B....714 979-2228**
3519 W Warner Ave Santa Ana (92704) ***(P-9710)***
Express Messenger Systems Inc....D....949 235-1400
1240 S Allec St Anaheim (92805) ***(P-12129)***
Express Messenger Systems Inc....D....800 488-2829
914 W Boone St Santa Maria (93458) ***(P-12130)***
Express Messenger Systems Inc....D....818 504-9043
11085 Olinda St Sun Valley (91352) ***(P-12131)***
Express Messenger Systems Inc....D....800 359-2959
375 W Apra St Compton (90220) ***(P-12132)***
Express Messenger Systems Inc....D....804 334-5000
9774 Calabash Ave Fontana (92335) ***(P-12133)***
Express Network, Los Angeles *Also called Legal Support Network LLC* ***(P-18575)***
Express Pipe & Supply Co LLC (HQ)....**D....310 204-7238**
1235 S Lewis St Santa Monica (90404) ***(P-7537)***
Express Sheet Metal Product....E....562 925-9340
10131 Flora Vista St Bellflower (90706) ***(P-6834)***
Express Systems & Engrg Inc....F....951 461-1500
41357 Date St Murrieta (92562) ***(P-5642)***
Expressions Home Gallery, Santa Monica *Also called Express Pipe & Supply Co LLC* ***(P-7537)***
Exquisite Corporation....F....626 856-0200
5000 Rivergrade Rd Baldwin Park (91706) ***(P-5020)***
Exquisite Mfg & Filling Serv, Baldwin Park *Also called Exquisite Corporation* ***(P-5020)***
Extended Care Hosp Westminster....C....714 891-2769
206 Hospital Cir Westminster (92683) ***(P-20340)***
Extensions Plus Inc....E....818 881-5611
5428 Reseda Blvd Tarzana (91356) ***(P-14035)***
Exterran Inc....D....626 455-0739
3449 Santa Anita Ave El Monte (91731) ***(P-17308)***
Extra Express (cerritos) Inc....E....714 985-6000
20405 Business Pkwy Walnut (91789) ***(P-12456)***
Extreme Group Holdings LLC....E....310 899-3200
1531 14th St Santa Monica (90404) ***(P-9217)***
Extreme Production Music, Santa Monica *Also called Extreme Group Holdings LLC* ***(P-9217)***
Extron Electronics, Anaheim *Also called Rgb Systems Inc* ***(P-8297)***
Extrude Hone Abrsive Flow McHn, Paramount *Also called Extrude Hone Deburring Svc Inc* ***(P-8584)***
Extrude Hone Deburring Svc Inc....E....562 531-2976
8800 Somerset Blvd Paramount (90723) ***(P-8584)***
Extrumed Inc (HQ)....**D....951 547-7400**
547 Trm Cir Corona (92879) ***(P-5643)***
Exult Inc....A....949 856-8800
121 Innovation Dr Ste 200 Irvine (92617) ***(P-23213)***
Exxel Outdoors Inc....C....626 369-7278
343 Baldwin Park Blvd City of Industry (91746) ***(P-3195)***
Ey, Los Angeles *Also called Ernst & Young LLP* ***(P-22781)***
Ey, Irvine *Also called Ernst & Young LLP* ***(P-22782)***
Eye Physcans Long Bch A Med Gr....D....562 421-2757
2925 Palo Verde Ave Long Beach (90815) ***(P-19809)***
Eyebrain Medical Inc (PA)....**F....949 339-5157**
3188 Airway Ave Ste F Costa Mesa (92626) ***(P-11252)***
Eyeonics Inc....E....949 788-6000
15273 Alton Pkwy Ste 100 Irvine (92618) ***(P-11253)***
Eyeshadow, Los Angeles *Also called Stony Apparel Corp* ***(P-2999)***
EZ Lube LLC....D....323 930-9389
201 S La Brea Ave Los Angeles (90036) ***(P-18925)***
EZ Lube LLC....D....310 821-2517
13421 Washington Blvd Marina Del Rey (90292) ***(P-18926)***
EZ Lube LLC....D....909 920-0476
1460 E Foothill Blvd Upland (91786) ***(P-18927)***
EZ Lube LLC....D....951 766-1996
532 W Florida Ave Hemet (92543) ***(P-5296)***
EZ Lube LLC....D....310 791-8480
24043 Hawthorne Blvd Torrance (90505) ***(P-18825)***
EZ Lube LLC....D....310 479-4704
11827 Santa Monica Blvd Los Angeles (90025) ***(P-18928)***
EZ Lube LLC....D....818 761-5696
10800 Riverside Dr North Hollywood (91602) ***(P-18929)***
EZ Lube LLC....D....818 610-8866
21000 Ventura Blvd Woodland Hills (91364) ***(P-18930)***
EZ Lube LLC....D....714 871-9980
4002 N Harbor Blvd Fullerton (92835) ***(P-18931)***
EZ Lube LLC....D....714 966-1647
3599 Harbor Blvd Costa Mesa (92626) ***(P-18932)***
EZ Lube- Costco, Marina Del Rey *Also called EZ Lube LLC* ***(P-18926)***
EZ Texting, Santa Monica *Also called Callfire Inc* ***(P-17573)***
EZ Up Factory Store, Colton *Also called E-Z Up Directcom* ***(P-3137)***
Ez-Flo International Inc (PA)....**E....909 947-5256**
2750 E Mission Blvd Ontario (91761) ***(P-13826)***
Ezaki Glico USA Corporation....F....949 251-0144
18022 Cowan Ste 110 Irvine (92614) ***(P-2085)***
Ezcaretech Usa Inc....B....424 558-3191
21081 S Wstn Ave Ste 130 Torrance (90501) ***(P-18515)***
Ezekiel, Irvine *Also called 3 Point Distribution LLC* ***(P-2793)***
Ezviz Inc....C....855 693-9849
908 Canada Ct City of Industry (91748) ***(P-18378)***
F & A Federal Credit Union....D....213 268-1226
2625 Corporate Pl Monterey Park (91754) ***(P-15062)***
F & D Flores Enterprises Inc....E....909 975-4853
761 E Francis St Ontario (91761) ***(P-10882)***
F & E Arcft Mint Los Angles LL....B....310 338-0063
531 Main St El Segundo (90245) ***(P-12358)***
F & L Tls Precision Machining, Corona *Also called F & L Tools Corporation* ***(P-10324)***
F & L Tools Corporation....F....951 279-1555
245 Jason Ct Corona (92879) ***(P-10324)***
F & Sfabrics, Los Angeles *Also called Southland Home Fabrics Inc* ***(P-3164)***
F &L Machine Inc....F....818 899-6738
10490 Ilex Ave Pacoima (91331) ***(P-8585)***
F C I, Anaheim *Also called Fci Lender Services Inc* ***(P-17111)***
F E E, Rcho STA Marg *Also called Fakouri Electrical Engrg Inc* ***(P-18145)***
F G S Packing Services, Exeter *Also called Fruit Growers Supply Company* ***(P-3804)***
F Gavina & Sons Inc....B....323 582-0671
2700 Fruitland Ave Vernon (90058) ***(P-2353)***
F I N, Granada Hills *Also called Financial Info Netwrk Inc* ***(P-17615)***
F I O Imports Inc....C....323 263-5100
5980 Alcoa Ave Vernon (90058) ***(P-2431)***
F I T, Compton *Also called Fastener Innovation Tech Inc* ***(P-7035)***
F J & J Corporation....F....505 452-1700
6938 Shadygrove St Tujunga (91042) ***(P-19232)***
F M H, Irvine *Also called Fmh Aerospace Corp* ***(P-10329)***
F M I, Santa Ana *Also called Flexible Manufacturing LLC* ***(P-9654)***
F M I, Anaheim *Also called Freight Management Inc* ***(P-23222)***
F M Tarbell Co....D....714 772-8990
321 S State College Blvd Anaheim (92806) ***(P-15850)***
F M Tarbell Co (HQ)....**C....714 972-0988**
1403 N Tustin Ave Ste 380 Santa Ana (92705) ***(P-15851)***
F M Tarbell Co....E....760 346-7405
73700 El Paseo Palm Desert (92260) ***(P-15852)***
F O X, Los Angeles *Also called Fox Sports Inc* ***(P-12724)***
F P I, Shafter *Also called Farm Pump & Irrigation Co Inc* ***(P-13901)***
F P M, Long Beach *Also called Foundation Property MGT Inc* ***(P-23221)***
F R T International Inc....D....310 329-5700
14439 S Avalon Blvd Gardena (90248) ***(P-12204)***
F R T International Inc....D....909 390-4892
2825 Jurupa St Ontario (91761) ***(P-12457)***
F R T International Inc (PA)....**D....310 604-8208**
1700 N Alameda St Compton (90222) ***(P-12205)***
F T B & Son Inc....E....714 891-8003
11551 Markon Dr Garden Grove (92841) ***(P-6835)***
F T I, Long Beach *Also called Fundamental Tech Intl Inc* ***(P-10695)***
F&M Bank, Long Beach *Also called Farmers Merchants Bnk Long Bch* ***(P-15022)***
F-J-E Inc....E....562 437-7466
546 W Esther St Long Beach (90813) ***(P-3646)***
F6s Network Limited....D....619 818-4363
16935 Encino Hills Dr Encino (91436) ***(P-22839)***
FAA Beverly Hills Inc....D....323 801-1430
5070 Wilshire Blvd Los Angeles (90036) ***(P-18826)***
Faac....E....800 221-8278
357 S Acacia Ave Unit 357 # 357 Fullerton (92831) ***(P-9868)***
Fab Four Corp....F....714 901-5300
15392 Vermont St Westminster (92683) ***(P-10057)***
Fab Services West Inc....D....909 350-7500
10007 Elm Ave Fontana (92335) ***(P-7020)***
Fabco Steel Fabrication Inc....E....909 350-1535
14688 San Bernardino Ave Fontana (92335) ***(P-6617)***
Faber Enterprises Inc....C....310 323-6200
14800 S Figueroa St Gardena (90248) ***(P-7457)***
Fabnet, Anaheim *Also called Fabrication Network Inc* ***(P-6836)***
Fabrica Fine Carpet, Santa Ana *Also called Fabrica International Inc* ***(P-2690)***
Fabrica International Inc....C....949 261-7181
3201 S Susan St Santa Ana (92704) ***(P-2690)***
Fabricast Inc (PA)....**E....626 443-3247**
2517 Seaman Ave South El Monte (91733) ***(P-9711)***
Fabricated Components Corp....C....714 974-8590
130 W Bristol Ln Orange (92865) ***(P-9404)***
Fabrication Network Inc....F....714 393-5282
5410 E La Palma Ave Anaheim (92807) ***(P-6836)***
Fabricmate Systems Inc....E....805 642-7470
2781 Golf Course Dr A Ventura (93003) ***(P-2597)***
Fabritex Inc....F....213 747-1417
2301 E 7th St Ste D102 Los Angeles (90023) ***(P-2598)***
Fabtex Inc....C....714 538-0877
1202 W Struck Ave Orange (92867) ***(P-2599)***
Fabtronic Inc....E....626 962-3293
5026 Calmview Ave Baldwin Park (91706) ***(P-6837)***
Fabulous & Company LLC....E....818 261-7242
19553 Enadia Way Reseda (91335) ***(P-16903)***
Facey Medical Foundation (PA)....**C....818 365-9531**
15451 San Frnndo Mssion B Mission Hills (91345) ***(P-19810)***
Facey Medical Foundation....C....818 837-5677
11211 Sepulveda Blvd Mission Hills (91345) ***(P-21424)***

ALPHABETIC

Employee Codes: A=Over 500 employees, B=251-500
C=101-250, D=51-100, E=20-50 F=10-19
2022 Southern California Business
Directory and Buyers Guide
© Mergent Inc. 1-800-342-5647
1129

Facey Medical Foundation ... C ... 661 250-5225
17909 Soledad Canyon Rd Santa Clarita (91387) ***(P-21425)***
Facey Medical Foundation ... C ... 661 513-2100
27924 Seco Canyon Rd Santa Clarita (91350) ***(P-19811)***
Facey Medical Foundation ... C ... 818 365-9531
11165 Sepulveda Blvd Mission Hills (91345) ***(P-19812)***
Facey Medical Foundation ... C ... 626 576-0800
1237 E Main St San Gabriel (91776) ***(P-21426)***
Facey Medical Group, Santa Clarita *Also called Facey Medical Foundation* ***(P-21425)***
Facey Medical Group PC (HQ) ... C ... 818 365-9531
11333 Sepulveda Blvd Mission Hills (91345) ***(P-19813)***
Facilitec West, Covina *Also called Stavros Enterprises Inc* ***(P-19070)***
Facilities MGT & Coml RPS Svcs, Anaheim *Also called Branded Group Inc* ***(P-23175)***
Facilities Support Services, Tustin *Also called US Facility Solutions LLC* ***(P-23397)***
Facility Makers Inc ... E ... 714 544-1702
345 W Freedom Ave Orange (92865) ***(P-6838)***
Facility Shield Intl Inc ... E ... 909 923-1800
2950 E Philadelphia St Ontario (91761) ***(P-13629)***
Facility Solutions Group Inc ... D ... 714 993-3966
801 Richfield Rd Placentia (92870) ***(P-13630)***
Facilty, Eastvale *Also called Orange County Water District* ***(P-12910)***
Fact Foundation ... B ... 818 729-8105
303 N Glenoaks Blvd Burbank (91502) ***(P-18516)***
Facter Direct Ltd ... B ... 323 634-1999
4751 Wilshire Blvd # 140 Los Angeles (90010) ***(P-18517)***
Factory One Studio Inc ... D ... 323 752-1670
6700 Avalon Blvd Ste 101 Los Angeles (90003) ***(P-2570)***
Factory Showroom Exchange, Los Angeles *Also called Sofa U Love LLC* ***(P-3517)***
Fahetas LLC ... D ... 949 280-1983
1419 N Tustin St Ste A Orange (92867) ***(P-17613)***
Fair Price Carpets, Riverside *Also called Fairprice Enterprises Inc* ***(P-6138)***
Faircom Inc ... D ... 626 820-9900
951 Lawson St City of Industry (91748) ***(P-9507)***
Fairfeld Inn By Mrrott Ltd Prt ... D ... 714 772-6777
1460 S Harbor Blvd Anaheim (92802) ***(P-16440)***
Fairfield Inn, El Segundo *Also called Rubicon B Hacienda LLC* ***(P-16676)***
Fairfield Inn, Mission Viejo *Also called Leader Hospitality LP* ***(P-16539)***
Fairfield Inn, El Centro *Also called El Centro Hospitality LLC* ***(P-16428)***
Fairhaven Mem Pk & Mortuary, Santa Ana *Also called R A F LP* ***(P-16926)***
Fairmont Designs, Buena Park *Also called Cambium Business Group Inc* ***(P-13130)***
Fairmont Miramar Hotel, Santa Monica *Also called Ocean Avenue LLC* ***(P-16590)***
Fairplex Child Development Ctr ... D ... 909 623-3899
1101 W Mckinley Ave Pomona (91768) ***(P-22013)***
Fairplex Enterprises Inc ... D ... 909 623-3111
1101 W Mckinley Ave Pomona (91768) ***(P-19646)***
Fairplex Rv Park, Pomona *Also called Los Angeles County Fair Assn* ***(P-19654)***
Fairprice Enterprises Inc ... D ... 951 684-8578
1070 Center St Riverside (92507) ***(P-6138)***
Fairview Developmental Center, Costa Mesa *Also called State Hospitals Cal Dept* ***(P-21027)***
Fairview Developmental Center, Costa Mesa *Also called Developmental Svcs Cal Dept* ***(P-21949)***
Fairview Mtm Pharma Inc ... F ... 714 881-0012
1002 N Fairview St Santa Ana (92703) ***(P-4820)***
Fairway Import-Export Inc ... E ... 262 788-7313
2130 E Gladwick St Rancho Dominguez (90220) ***(P-11415)***
Fairway Injection Molds Inc ... D ... 909 595-2201
20109 Paseo Del Prado Walnut (91789) ***(P-5644)***
Fairway Realty Inc (PA) ... D ... 760 245-3471
14281 Seventh St Victorville (92395) ***(P-15853)***
Fairwinds-West Hills, West Hills *Also called Leisure Care LLC* ***(P-20535)***
Faith Com Inc (PA) ... D ... 562 719-9300
13850 Cerritos Corprt Dr D Cerritos (90703) ***(P-23440)***
Faith Electric LLC ... C ... 909 767-2682
1980 Orange Tree Ln # 106 Redlands (92374) ***(P-1252)***
Faith Quality Auto Body Inc ... D ... 951 698-8215
41130 Nick Ln Murrieta (92562) ***(P-18789)***
Fakouri Electrical Engrg Inc ... D ... 949 888-2400
30001 Comercio Rcho STA Marg (92688) ***(P-18145)***
Falck Mobile Health Corp ... D ... 323 720-1578
212 S Atl Blvd Ste 102 Los Angeles (90022) ***(P-11865)***
Falck Mobile Health Corp ... D ... 714 828-7750
8932 Katella Ave Ste 201 Anaheim (92804) ***(P-11866)***
Falcon Abrasive Mfg Inc ... E ... 909 598-3078
5490 Brooks St Montclair (91763) ***(P-6152)***
Falcon Aerospace Holdings LLC ... A ... 661 775-7200
27727 Avenue Scott Valencia (91355) ***(P-14056)***
Falcon Auto Repair, Gardena *Also called Raymak Automotive Inc* ***(P-18865)***
Falcon Automotive Inc ... F ... 714 569-1085
1305 E Wakeham Ave Santa Ana (92705) ***(P-3196)***
Falcon Electric, Baldwin Park *Also called Yutaka Electric Intl Inc* ***(P-8985)***
Falcon Electric Inc ... F ... 626 962-7770
5116 Azusa Canyon Rd Baldwin Park (91706) ***(P-8870)***
Falcon Waterfree Tech LLC (HQ) ... E ... 310 209-7250
2255 Barry Ave Los Angeles (90064) ***(P-5376)***
Falken Tire, Rancho Cucamonga *Also called Sumitomo Rubber North Amer Inc* ***(P-13120)***
Falken Tire Holdings Inc ... D ... 800 723-2553
8656 Haven Ave Rancho Cucamonga (91730) ***(P-13115)***
Falken Tires, Rancho Cucamonga *Also called Falken Tire Holdings Inc* ***(P-13115)***
Falkner Winery Inc ... D ... 951 676-6741
40620 Calle Contento Temecula (92591) ***(P-2183)***
Falkor Partners LLC ... E ... 714 721-8772
333 Mccormick Ave Costa Mesa (92626) ***(P-9508)***
Fallbrook Bonsall Village News, Temecula *Also called Villlage News Inc* ***(P-4042)***
Falltech, Compton *Also called Andrew Alexander Inc* ***(P-5867)***
Fam LLC (PA) ... C ... 323 888-7755
5553-B Bandini Blvd Bell (90201) ***(P-2612)***
Fam Brands, Bell *Also called Fam LLC* ***(P-2612)***
Fam Ppe LLC ... C ... 323 888-7755
5553-B Bandini Blvd B Bell (90201) ***(P-14155)***
Fama Holdings LLC ... F ... 323 581-5888
4510 Loma Vista Ave Vernon (90058) ***(P-16890)***
Fame Assistance Corporation ... D ... 323 373-7720
2270 S Harvard Blvd Los Angeles (90018) ***(P-23441)***
Fame Hardwood Floors, Los Angeles *Also called P8ge Consulting Inc* ***(P-23489)***
Fame Systems Inc ... E ... 805 485-0808
301 Hearst Dr Oxnard (93030) ***(P-17242)***
Families Chice HM Care Svcs In ... D ... 909 303-9377
545 N Mountain Ave # 209 Upland (91786) ***(P-21780)***
Family Assistance Program ... D ... 760 843-0701
15075 Seventh St Victorville (92395) ***(P-21781)***
Family Asssment Cnsling Edcat ... D ... 714 447-9024
1651 E 4th St Ste 128 Santa Ana (92701) ***(P-21782)***
Family Care Network Inc (PA) ... D ... 805 503-6240
1255 Kendall Rd San Luis Obispo (93401) ***(P-22014)***
Family Care Specialists, Montebello *Also called Fcs Medical Corporation* ***(P-19822)***
Family Circle Inc ... D ... 805 385-4180
2100 Outlet Center Dr # 380 Oxnard (93036) ***(P-21783)***
Family Health Center, Pomona *Also called Premiere Medical Group* ***(P-20025)***
Family Health Program, Long Beach *Also called Davita Medical Management LLC* ***(P-21418)***
Family Healthcare Network ... C ... 559 734-1939
501 N Bridge St Visalia (93291) ***(P-19814)***
Family Healthcare Network ... C ... 559 781-7242
1137 W Poplar Ave Porterville (93257) ***(P-19815)***
Family Healthcare Network ... C ... 559 741-4500
400 E Oak Ave Visalia (93291) ***(P-19816)***
Family Healthcare Network ... C ... 559 737-4700
801 W Center Ave Visalia (93291) ***(P-19817)***
Family Healthcare Network ... C ... 559 582-2013
250 W 5th St Hanford (93230) ***(P-19818)***
Family Healthcare Network ... C ... 559 798-1877
33025 159th Rd Ivanhoe (93235) ***(P-19819)***
Family Hospice Ltd ... C ... 818 571-2870
9253 Reseda Blvd Northridge (91324) ***(P-20529)***
Family Industries LLC ... F ... 619 306-1035
1700 N Spring St Los Angeles (90012) ***(P-11667)***
Family Plg Assoc Med Group (PA) ... D ... 213 738-7283
3050 E Airport Way Long Beach (90806) ***(P-19820)***
Family Service Association ... D ... 951 653-8109
21801 Alessandro Blvd Moreno Valley (92553) ***(P-21784)***
Family Service Association ... D ... 951 672-9673
29995 Evans Rd Sun City (92586) ***(P-21785)***
Family Services Tulare County ... D ... 559 732-1970
815 W Oak Ave Visalia (93291) ***(P-21786)***
Family Svc Agcy Snta Brbara CN ... D ... 805 965-1001
123 W Gutierrez St Santa Barbara (93101) ***(P-21787)***
Family Tree Produce Inc ... C ... 714 693-5688
5510 E La Palma Ave Anaheim (92807) ***(P-14627)***
Family Urgent Care Center, Anaheim *Also called Anaheim Harbor Medical Group* ***(P-19709)***
FAMILY, ADULT AND CHILD THERAP, Los Angeles *Also called Focus On All Child Thrpies Inc* ***(P-20582)***
Famoso Nut, Mc Farland *Also called Amaretto Orchards LLC* ***(P-11629)***
Famous Vineyards LLC ... D ... 661 392-5000
20715 Ave 8 Richgrove (93261) ***(P-14628)***
Fan Fave Inc ... E ... 909 975-4999
10329 Dorset St Rancho Cucamonga (91730) ***(P-11554)***
Fanboys Window Factory Inc (PA) ... E ... 626 280-8787
10750 Saint Louis Dr El Monte (91731) ***(P-6699)***
Fanfave, Rancho Cucamonga *Also called Fan Fave Inc* ***(P-11554)***
Fang Inc ... D ... 714 898-7785
12235 Beach Blvd Ste 20h Stanton (90680) ***(P-19821)***
Fantasia Distribution Inc ... F ... 714 817-8300
1566 W Embassy St Anaheim (92802) ***(P-2555)***
Fantasia Hookah Tobacco, Anaheim *Also called Fantasia Distribution Inc* ***(P-2555)***
Fantastic Fawn, Vernon *Also called Incremento Inc* ***(P-14382)***
Fantastic Sams, Upland *Also called Welch Management Corporation* ***(P-16920)***
Fantasy Activewear Inc (PA) ... C ... 213 705-4111
5383 Alcoa Ave Vernon (90058) ***(P-2631)***
Fantasy Dyeing & Finishing Inc ... E ... 323 983-9988
5383 Alcoa Ave Vernon (90058) ***(P-2632)***
Fantasy Manufacturing, Vernon *Also called Fantasy Activewear Inc* ***(P-2631)***
Fantasy Springs Resort Casino, Indio *Also called East Valley Tourist Dev Auth* ***(P-19645)***
Fantom Drives, Torrance *Also called Bnl Technologies Inc* ***(P-8188)***
Fanuc America Corporation ... D ... 949 595-2700
25951 Commercentre Dr Lake Forest (92630) ***(P-7974)***
Fanuc Robotics West, Lake Forest *Also called Fanuc America Corporation* ***(P-7974)***
Far East Broadcasting Co Inc ... D ... 562 947-4651
15700 Imperial Hwy La Mirada (90638) ***(P-12691)***
Far East Landscape & Maint Inc ... D ... 800 887-3227
6201 1/2 Van Nuys Blvd Van Nuys (91401) ***(P-305)***
Far Out Toys Inc ... E ... 310 480-7554
300 N Pcf Cast Hwy Ste 10 El Segundo (90245) ***(P-11360)***
Far West Inc ... D ... 559 627-1241
4444 W Meadow Ave Visalia (93277) ***(P-20341)***
Far West Inc ... D ... 323 564-7761
8455 State St South Gate (90280) ***(P-20342)***
Far West Inc ... D ... 559 733-0901
4525 W Tulare Ave Visalia (93277) ***(P-20580)***
Far West Inc ... D ... 909 884-4781
467 E Gilbert St San Bernardino (92404) ***(P-20343)***
Far West Meats, Highland *Also called Raemica Inc* ***(P-1747)***
Far West Technology Inc ... F ... 805 964-3615
330 S Kellogg Ave Goleta (93117) ***(P-10883)***
Faraday & Future, Gardena *Also called FARaday&future Inc* ***(P-22547)***

Mergent e-mail: customerrelations@mergent.com
1130
2022 Southern California Business Directory and Buyers Guide
(P-0000) Products & Services Section entry number
(PA)=Parent Co (HQ)=Headquarters (DH)=Div Headquarters

Faraday Fture Intllgent Elc In (PA) ....D....**424 276-7616**
18455 S Figueroa St Gardena (90248) ***(P-9945)***
FAraday&future Inc....A....424 276-7616
18455 S Figueroa St Gardena (90248) ***(P-22547)***
Farbod Parvinjah DMD Inc (PA)....D....**805 583-5589**
4128 Whitsett Ave Apt 111 Studio City (91604) ***(P-20177)***
Farbotech Color Inc....F....909 596-9330
1630 Yeager Ave La Verne (91750) ***(P-5202)***
Farchitecture Bb LLC....E....917 701-2777
8588 Washington Blvd Culver City (90232) ***(P-1817)***
Farley Interlocking Pav Stones, Palm Desert *Also called Farley Paving Stone Co Inc* ***(P-6032)***
Farley Machine Inc....E....661 397-4987
7800 Davin Park Dr Bakersfield (93308) ***(P-7669)***
Farley Paving Stone Co Inc....D....760 773-3960
75135 Sheryl Ave Ste A Palm Desert (92211) ***(P-6032)***
Farm Credit West....D....661 399-7360
19628 Industry Parkway Dr Bakersfield (93308) ***(P-15164)***
Farm Pump & Irrigation Co Inc (PA)....D....**661 589-6901**
535 N Shafter Ave Shafter (93263) ***(P-13901)***
Farm Street Designs Inc....E....562 985-0026
2520 Mira Mar Ave Long Beach (90815) ***(P-14841)***
Farmdale Creamery Inc....D....909 888-4938
1049 W Base Line St San Bernardino (92411) ***(P-1834)***
Farmers Fincl Solutions LLC (PA)....D....**818 584-0200**
30801 Agoura Rd Agoura Hills (91301) ***(P-15563)***
Farmers Group Inc (HQ)....A....**323 932-3200**
6301 Owensmouth Ave Woodland Hills (91367) ***(P-15564)***
Farmers Group Inc....A....805 583-7400
6303 Owensmouth Ave Fl 1 Woodland Hills (91367) ***(P-15565)***
Farmers Insur Group Fdral Cr U (PA)....D....**323 209-6000**
2255 N Ontario St Ste 320 Burbank (91504) ***(P-15063)***
Farmers Insurance, Agoura Hills *Also called Farmers Fincl Solutions LLC* ***(P-15563)***
Farmers Insurance, Woodland Hills *Also called Farmers Group Inc* ***(P-15564)***
Farmers Insurance, Woodland Hills *Also called Farmers Group Inc* ***(P-15565)***
Farmers Insurance Exchange (HQ)....A....**888 327-6335**
6301 Owensmouth Ave # 750 Woodland Hills (91367) ***(P-15566)***
Farmers Insurance Exchange....B....559 594-4149
411 E Pine St Ste A Exeter (93221) ***(P-15567)***
Farmers Merchants Bnk Long Bch (HQ)....C....**562 437-0011**
302 Pine Ave Long Beach (90802) ***(P-15022)***
Farmers W Flowers & Bouquets, Carpinteria *Also called Brand Flower Farms Inc* ***(P-14878)***
Farrar Grinding Company....E....323 678-4879
347 E Beach Ave Inglewood (90302) ***(P-10325)***
Farrell Brothers Holding Corp....F....714 630-3417
1137 N Armando St Anaheim (92806) ***(P-8586)***
Farsi Jewelry Mfg Co Inc....F....213 624-0043
631 Suth Olive St Ste 565 Los Angeles (90014) ***(P-11316)***
Farstone Technology Inc....C....949 336-4321
184 Technology Dr Ste 205 Irvine (92618) ***(P-9835)***
Farwest Corrosion Control Co (PA)....D....**310 532-9524**
12029 Regentview Ave Downey (90241) ***(P-1655)***
Fashion World Incorporated....C....310 273-6544
420 N Rodeo Dr Beverly Hills (90210) ***(P-14332)***
Fashiongo.com, Los Angeles *Also called Nhn Global Inc* ***(P-14406)***
Fast Deer Bus Chrtr Incrprtion....D....323 201-8988
8105 Slauson Ave Montebello (90640) ***(P-11911)***
Fast Lane Container Services, Wilmington *Also called Fast Lane Transportation Inc* ***(P-12043)***
Fast Lane Transportation Inc (PA)....D....**562 435-3000**
2400 E Pacific Coast Hwy Wilmington (90744) ***(P-12043)***
Fast Pay Partners LLC (HQ)....D....**310 651-9200**
8201 Beverly Blvd Ste 600 Los Angeles (90048) ***(P-22783)***
Fast Sportswear Inc....F....323 720-1078
6400 E Washington Blvd Commerce (90040) ***(P-2944)***
Fast Undercar, Ventura *Also called Parts Authority LLC* ***(P-13078)***
Fastclick Inc....B....805 689-9839
530 E Montecito St Santa Barbara (93103) ***(P-17097)***
Fastclick.com, Santa Barbara *Also called Fastclick Inc* ***(P-17097)***
Fastech, Buena Park *Also called Fueling and Service Tech Inc* ***(P-13902)***
Fastener Innovation Tech Inc....D....310 538-1111
19300 S Susana Rd Compton (90221) ***(P-7035)***
Fastener Technology Corp....C....818 764-6467
7415 Fulton Ave North Hollywood (91605) ***(P-13983)***
Fasthouse Inc....F....661 775-5963
28757 Industry Dr Valencia (91355) ***(P-11416)***
Fastxchange Inc....E....310 827-2445
4640 Admiralty Way # 710 Marina Del Rey (90292) ***(P-18030)***
Faust Printing Inc....F....909 980-1577
8656 Utica Ave Ste 100 Rancho Cucamonga (91730) ***(P-4291)***
Fax Star, Costa Mesa *Also called S E P E Inc* ***(P-8174)***
Fay's Foods, North Hollywood *Also called Fayes Foods Inc* ***(P-2432)***
Fayes Foods Inc....E....818 508-8392
10650 Burbank Blvd North Hollywood (91601) ***(P-2432)***
Faze Clan Inc....D....818 538-5204
7288 Mulholland Dr Los Angeles (90068) ***(P-19647)***
FBproductions Inc....F....818 773-9337
12722 Rverside Dr Ste 204 Valley Village (91607) ***(P-4292)***
Fc Management Services....E....805 499-0050
2001 Anchor Ct Ste B Newbury Park (91320) ***(P-7975)***
FCA US LLC....F....949 450-5111
7700 Irvine Center Dr # 40 Irvine (92618) ***(P-10058)***
Fci Lender Services Inc....C....800 931-2424
8180 E Kaiser Blvd Anaheim (92808) ***(P-17111)***
Fci Management, Cerritos *Also called Faith Com Inc* ***(P-23440)***
FCkingston Co....E....310 326-8287
23201 Normandie Ave Torrance (90501) ***(P-7444)***
Fcp Inc (PA)....D....**951 678-4571**
23100 Wildomar Trl Wildomar (92595) ***(P-6993)***
Fcp Inc....F....805 684-1117
4125 Market St Ste 14 Ventura (93003) ***(P-6994)***
Fcpp, Anaheim *Also called First Choice Physcn Partners* ***(P-19823)***
Fcs Medical Corporation....D....323 728-3955
815 Washington Blvd Montebello (90640) ***(P-19822)***
Fcti Inc (PA)....D....**310 405-0022**
11766 Wilshire Blvd # 30 Los Angeles (90025) ***(P-15128)***
Fd, Newbury Park *Also called Follmer Development Inc* ***(P-4639)***
FDS Manufacturing Company (PA)....D....**909 591-1733**
2200 S Reservoir St Pomona (91766) ***(P-3929)***
FDS Manufacturing Company Svcs, Pomona *Also called Federated Diversified Sls Inc* ***(P-3853)***
Fdsi Logistics LLC....D....818 971-3300
27680 Avenue Mentry 2 Valencia (91355) ***(P-23214)***
Fear of God LLC (PA)....E....**213 235-7985**
3940 Lrl Cyn Blvd Ste 42 Studio City (91604) ***(P-2807)***
Featherock Inc (PA)....F....**818 882-3888**
20219 Bahama St Chatsworth (91311) ***(P-586)***
FEC Fture Contrs Engineers Inc....D....949 328-9758
184 Technology Dr Ste 205 Irvine (92618) ***(P-878)***
Federal Custom Cable LLC....E....949 851-3114
1891 Alton Pkwy Ste A Irvine (92606) ***(P-13722)***
Federal Express Corporation....D....800 463-3339
3333 S Grand Ave Los Angeles (90007) ***(P-12326)***
Federal Express Corporation....B....800 463-3339
7000 Barranca Pkwy Irvine (92618) ***(P-18518)***
Federal Express Corporation....D....909 390-3237
2060 S Wineville Ave B Ontario (91761) ***(P-12327)***
Federal Express Corporation....C....800 463-3339
2451 N Palm Dr Long Beach (90755) ***(P-12328)***
Federal Express Corporation....C....949 862-4500
2601 Main St Ste 1000 Irvine (92614) ***(P-12306)***
Federal Express Corporation....C....562 522-4014
1 World Trade Ctr Ste 191 Long Beach (90831) ***(P-12329)***
Federal Home Loan Mrtg Corp....C....213 337-4200
444 S Flower St Fl 44 Los Angeles (90071) ***(P-15190)***
Federal Industries Inc....F....310 297-4040
645 Hawaii St El Segundo (90245) ***(P-7473)***
Federal Manufacturing Corp....E....818 341-9825
9825 De Soto Ave Chatsworth (91311) ***(P-7065)***
Federal Rsrve Bnk San Frncisco....A....213 683-2300
950 S Grand Ave Los Angeles (90015) ***(P-14988)***
Federated Diversified Sls Inc....D....909 591-1733
2200 S Reservoir St Pomona (91766) ***(P-3853)***
Fedex, Los Angeles *Also called Federal Express Corporation* ***(P-12326)***
Fedex, Irvine *Also called Federal Express Corporation* ***(P-18518)***
Fedex, Ontario *Also called Federal Express Corporation* ***(P-12327)***
Fedex, Long Beach *Also called Federal Express Corporation* ***(P-12328)***
Fedex, Irvine *Also called Federal Express Corporation* ***(P-12306)***
Fedex, Long Beach *Also called Federal Express Corporation* ***(P-12329)***
Fedex Freight Corporation....C....323 269-9800
4500 Bandini Blvd Vernon (90058) ***(P-12044)***
Fedex Freight West Inc....B....909 357-3555
11153 Mulberry Ave Fontana (92337) ***(P-12045)***
Fedex Office & Print Svcs Inc....E....714 892-1452
15951 Goldenwest St Huntington Beach (92647) ***(P-17150)***
Fedex Office & Print Svcs Inc....D....562 942-1953
8642 Whittier Blvd Pico Rivera (90660) ***(P-12134)***
Fedex Smartpost Inc....D....323 888-8879
5560 Ferguson Dr Commerce (90022) ***(P-12135)***
Feedonomics LLC, Woodland Hills *Also called Legacy Epoch LLC* ***(P-1971)***
Feemster Co Inc....F....909 621-9772
119 Yale Ave Claremont (91711) ***(P-1999)***
Fei Enterprises Inc....E....323 937-0856
633 S La Brea Ave Los Angeles (90036) ***(P-1253)***
Fei-Zyfer Inc (HQ)....B....**714 933-4000**
7321 Lincoln Way Garden Grove (92841) ***(P-9273)***
Feihe International Inc (PA)....A....**626 757-8885**
2275 Huntington Dr # 278 San Marino (91108) ***(P-1791)***
Feit Electric Company Inc (PA)....C....**562 463-2852**
4901 Gregg Rd Pico Rivera (90660) ***(P-9063)***
Felbro Inc....C....323 263-8686
3666 E Olympic Blvd Los Angeles (90023) ***(P-3682)***
Felbro Food Products Inc....E....323 936-5266
5700 W Adams Blvd Los Angeles (90016) ***(P-2323)***
Felcor Lax Lessee LLC....E....310 640-3600
1440 E Imperial Ave El Segundo (90245) ***(P-16441)***
Felix Chevrolet LP (PA)....C....**213 748-6141**
714 W Olympic Blvd Ste 11 Los Angeles (90015) ***(P-18827)***
Felix Tool & Engineering....F....830 947-4601
14535 Bessemer St Van Nuys (91411) ***(P-7801)***
Felt Bicycles, Rancho Santa Margari *Also called Group Rossignol Usa Inc* ***(P-22563)***
Fema Electronics Corporation....E....714 825-0140
22 Corporate Park Irvine (92606) ***(P-9712)***
Fencecorp Inc (HQ)....C....**951 686-3170**
18440 Van Buren Blvd Riverside (92508) ***(P-1656)***
Fenceworks Inc (PA)....C....**951 788-5620**
870 Main St Riverside (92501) ***(P-1657)***
Fenchem Inc (HQ)....E....**909 597-8880**
15308 El Prado Rd Bldg 8 Chino (91710) ***(P-1792)***
Fender Digital LLC (HQ)....D....**323 462-2198**
1575 N Gower St Ste 170 Los Angeles (90028) ***(P-17614)***
Fender Musical Instrs Corp....A....480 596-9690
311 Cessna Cir Corona (92878) ***(P-11342)***
Fenderscape Inc....C....562 988-2228
1446 E Hill St Signal Hill (90755) ***(P-256)***

ALPHABETIC

Employee Codes: A=Over 500 employees, B=251-500
C=101-250, D=51-100, E=20-50 F=10-19
2022 Southern California Business Directory and Buyers Guide
© Mergent Inc. 1-800-342-5647
1131

Fenico Precision Castings Inc.....D.....562 634-5000
7805 Madison St Paramount (90723) *(P-6416)*
Fenix Marine Services Ltd (HQ).....E.....**310 548-8877**
614 Terminal Way San Pedro (90731) *(P-17348)*
Fennel Inc.....D.....951 284-2020
1169 Sherborn St Corona (92879) *(P-1436)*
Ferco, Laguna Hills *Also called Fossil Energy Research Corp (P-18519)*
Ferco Color Inc.....E.....909 930-0773
5498 Vine St Chino (91710) *(P-4692)*
Ferco Plastic Products, Chino *Also called Ferco Color Inc (P-4692)*
Fergadis Enterprises, Bell *Also called Perrin Bernard Supowitz LLC (P-14224)*
Ferguson Co.....F.....562 428-3300
6226 Cherry Ave Long Beach (90805) *(P-8340)*
Ferguson Fire Fabrication Inc (HQ).....D.....**909 517-3085**
2750 S Towne Ave Pomona (91766) *(P-13827)*
Fermented Sciences Inc.....E.....818 427-8442
3200 Golf Course Dr Ventura (93003) *(P-2143)*
Fern Oaks Frms A Cal Gen Prtnr.....E.....559 684-8220
17001 Avenue 160 Porterville (93257) *(P-132)*
Ferra Aerospace Inc.....E.....918 787-2220
940 E Orngthrp Ave Ste A Anaheim (92801) *(P-10326)*
Ferraco Inc (HQ).....E.....**562 988-2414**
2933 Long Beach Blvd Long Beach (90806) *(P-11104)*
Ferrante Paul Cstm Lmps & Shds, West Hollywood *Also called Paul Ferrante Inc (P-11730)*
Ferreira Service Inc (PA).....D.....**925 831-9330**
1811 Tortuga St Acton (93510) *(P-1066)*
Ferruzzo & Ferruzzo LLP.....D.....949 608-6900
3737 Birch St Ste 400 Newport Beach (92660) *(P-21553)*
Fess Prker-Red Lion Gen Partnr.....C.....805 564-4333
633 E Cabrillo Blvd Santa Barbara (93103) *(P-16442)*
Festival Fun Parks LLC.....C.....954 921-1411
4590 Macarthur Blvd # 400 Newport Beach (92660) *(P-19648)*
Festival of Arts Laguna Beach.....D.....949 494-1145
650 Laguna Canyon Rd Laguna Beach (92651) *(P-19649)*
Fetish Group Inc (PA).....E.....**323 587-7873**
1013 S Los Angeles St # 700 Los Angeles (90015) *(P-2808)*
Fff Enterprises Inc (PA).....B.....**951 296-2500**
44000 Winchester Rd Temecula (92590) *(P-14243)*
FFI, Irvine *Also called First Foundation Inc (P-15024)*
Ffna, Foothill Ranch *Also called Frontech N Fujitsu Amer Inc (P-8314)*
Fgr 1 LLC.....E.....800 653-3517
3191 Red Hill Ave Ste 100 Costa Mesa (92626) *(P-17855)*
Fgs-Wi LLC.....E.....909 467-8300
5401 Jurupa St Ontario (91761) *(P-4293)*
Fh & Hf-Torrance I LLC.....C.....310 320-4130
22617 S Vermont Ave Torrance (90502) *(P-20344)*
Fh Packaging, Eastvale *Also called Wolfgang Enterprise Inc (P-18729)*
Fht Printing, Fullerton *Also called Advanced Image Direct LLC (P-17129)*
FI, El Segundo *Also called Federal Industries Inc (P-7473)*
Fiber Care Baths Inc.....B.....760 246-0019
9832 Yucca Rd Ste A Adelanto (92301) *(P-5531)*
Fiber Optic Technologies, Torrance *Also called ACS Communications Inc (P-1209)*
Fiberoptic Systems Inc.....E.....805 579-6600
60 Moreland Rd Ste A Simi Valley (93065) *(P-6349)*
Fibreform Electronics Inc.....E.....714 898-9641
5341 Argosy Ave Huntington Beach (92649) *(P-8587)*
Fibreform Precision Machining, Huntington Beach *Also called Fibreform Electronics Inc (P-8587)*
Fidelity Nat Title Insur Co NY.....A.....805 370-1400
950 Hampshire Rd Westlake Village (91361) *(P-16039)*
Fidelity Security Services Inc.....D.....661 295-5007
25133 Avenue Tibbitts H Valencia (91355) *(P-18274)*
Field Foundation.....F.....562 921-3567
15306 Carmenita Rd Santa Fe Springs (90670) *(P-501)*
Field Manufacturing Corp (PA).....E.....**310 781-9292**
1751 Torrance Blvd Ste H Torrance (90501) *(P-3683)*
Field Time Target Training LLC.....E.....714 677-2841
8230 Electric Ave Stanton (90680) *(P-7427)*
Fieldcentrix Inc.....F.....949 784-5000
24001 Mrlnds Blvd Spc 125 Lake Forest (92630) *(P-17856)*
Fieldstone Communities Inc (PA).....C.....**949 790-5400**
16 Technology Dr Ste 125 Irvine (92618) *(P-676)*
Fierrito Metal Stamping.....F.....818 362-6136
12358 San Fernando Rd Sylmar (91342) *(P-8588)*
Fiesta Concession, Vernon *Also called Mahar Manufacturing Corp (P-11361)*
Fiesta Fashion Co Inc (PA).....E.....**213 748-5775**
1100 Wall St Ste 106 Los Angeles (90015) *(P-14375)*
Fiesta Ford Inc.....C.....760 775-7777
79015 Avenue 40 Indio (92203) *(P-18828)*
Fiesta Ford Lincoln-Mercury, Indio *Also called Fiesta Ford Inc (P-18828)*
Fiesta Mexican Foods Inc.....E.....760 344-3580
979 G St Brawley (92227) *(P-2000)*
Fifty Five Foundry, The, Manhattan Beach *Also called The Fifty Five Foundry Inc (P-17733)*
Fightcamp, Costa Mesa *Also called Hykso Inc (P-23238)*
Figs Inc.....C.....424 300-8330
2834 Colorado Ave Ste 100 Santa Monica (90404) *(P-2778)*
Figure 8, Torrance *Also called Nothing To Wear Inc (P-2863)*
Filanity Corporation.....D.....714 475-3521
17011 Beach Bvld Ste 1440 Huntington Beach (92647) *(P-12635)*
Fillmore Convalescent Ctr LLC.....D.....805 524-0083
118 B St Fillmore (93015) *(P-20581)*
Film Payroll Services Inc (PA).....D.....**310 440-9600**
500 S Sepulveda Blvd Fl 4 Los Angeles (90049) *(P-22784)*
Film Roman Llc.....C.....818 748-4000
6320 Canoga Ave Woodland Hills (91367) *(P-19123)*
FILML.A, Los Angeles *Also called A Filml Inc (P-19216)*
Filmtools Inc (PA).....E.....**323 467-1116**
1015 N Hollywood Way Burbank (91505) *(P-13344)*
Filtec, Torrance *Also called Industrial Dynamics Co Ltd (P-7982)*
Filter Pump Industries, Sun Valley *Also called Penguin Pumps Incorporated (P-8018)*
Filtration Technology Group, Cerritos *Also called Ftg Inc (P-10063)*
Filtronics Inc.....F.....714 630-5040
16872 Hale Ave Ste B Irvine (92606) *(P-8381)*
Filyn Corporation.....C.....714 632-0225
2950 E La Jolla St Anaheim (92806) *(P-11867)*
Final Film.....D.....323 467-0700
3620 W Valhalla Dr Burbank (91505) *(P-17175)*
Final Finish Inc.....F.....562 777-7774
10910 Norwalk Blvd Santa Fe Springs (90670) *(P-2663)*
Final Touch Apparel Inc.....F.....323 484-9621
4801 Pacific Blvd Vernon (90058) *(P-14376)*
Finan Group, North Hollywood *Also called Financial Group Inc (P-15568)*
Finance America LLC (HQ).....C.....**949 440-1000**
1901 Main St Ste 150 Irvine (92614) *(P-15191)*
Finance America Mortgage LLC.....D.....562 478-4664
13200 Crssrads Pkwy N Ste City of Industry (91746) *(P-15192)*
Finance America Mortgage LLC.....D.....661 775-6253
23734 Valencia Blvd Valencia (91355) *(P-15193)*
Finance America Mortgage LLC.....D.....2-5 591-0222
680 E Colo Blvd Ste 230 Pasadena (91101) *(P-15194)*
Finance Express LLC (HQ).....D.....**949 635-5892**
30071 Tomas Ste 250 Rcho STA Marg (92688) *(P-18031)*
Financial Credit Network Inc (PA).....D.....**559 733-7550**
1300 W Main St Visalia (93291) *(P-17112)*
Financial Group Inc.....C.....805 646-7974
1991 Country Pl Ojai (93023) *(P-23025)*
Financial Group Inc.....C.....818 308-8527
12432 Oxnard St North Hollywood (91606) *(P-15568)*
Financial Info Netwrk Inc.....E.....818 782-0331
11164 Bertrand Ave Granada Hills (91344) *(P-17615)*
Financial Partners Credit Un (PA).....D.....**562 904-3000**
7800 Imperial Hwy Downey (90242) *(P-15064)*
Financial Statement Svcs Inc (PA).....C.....**714 436-3326**
3300 S Fairview St Santa Ana (92704) *(P-17132)*
Financial Tech Sltons Intl Inc.....C.....818 241-9571
406 E Huntington Dr # 100 Monrovia (91016) *(P-23215)*
Finch Tree Surgery Inc.....D.....626 287-9838
841 E Mission Rd San Gabriel (91776) *(P-356)*
FINE ARTS MUSEUM, Santa Barbara *Also called Santa Barbara Museum of Ar (P-22234)*
Fine Ptch Elctrnic Assmbly LLC.....E.....626 337-2800
5106 Azusa Canyon Rd Irwindale (91706) *(P-9405)*
Fine Quality Metal Finshg Inc.....F.....562 983-7425
1640 Daisy Ave Long Beach (90813) *(P-7259)*
Fineline Architectural Mllwk, Costa Mesa *Also called Fineline Woodworking Inc (P-3249)*
Fineline Circuits & Technology.....E.....714 529-2942
594 Apollo St Ste A Brea (92821) *(P-9406)*
Fineline Woodworking Inc.....D.....714 540-5468
1139 Baker St Costa Mesa (92626) *(P-3249)*
Fineman West and Co LLP.....D.....213 688-9898
801 S Figueroa St # 1000 Los Angeles (90017) *(P-22785)*
Finis LLC.....D.....949 250-4929
3347 Michelson Dr Ste 100 Irvine (92612) *(P-8256)*
Finnco Services Incorporated.....D.....909 355-0707
8241 Beech Ave Fontana (92335) *(P-17349)*
Finntech Inc.....F.....310 323-0790
1930 W 169th St Gardena (90247) *(P-8589)*
Fiore Stone Inc.....E.....909 424-0221
1814 Commercenter W Ste E San Bernardino (92408) *(P-6033)*
Firan Tech Group USA Corp (HQ).....C.....**818 407-4024**
20750 Marilla St Chatsworth (91311) *(P-10588)*
Fire & Gas Detection Tech Inc.....F.....714 671-8500
4222 E La Palma Ave Anaheim (92807) *(P-9342)*
Fire and Safety Elec Inc.....F.....714 850-1320
3160 Pullman St Costa Mesa (92626) *(P-8952)*
Fire Department Station 29, Anza *Also called County of Riverside (P-21409)*
Fire Insurance Exchange (PA).....A.....**323 932-3200**
6301 Owensmouth Ave Woodland Hills (91367) *(P-15569)*
Fire Protection Group Amer Inc.....E.....323 732-4200
3712 W Jefferson Blvd Los Angeles (90016) *(P-22548)*
Fire Safe Systems Inc.....D.....310 542-0585
1312 Kingsdale Ave Redondo Beach (90278) *(P-1067)*
Fire Safety First, Santa Ana *Also called Brethren Inc (P-14147)*
Fire Sprinkler Systems Inc (PA).....D.....**800 915-3473**
705 E Harrison St Ste 200 Corona (92879) *(P-1068)*
Fire Windows and Doors, Redlands *Also called Coast To Coast Mfg LLC (P-5609)*
Fireblast Global Inc.....E.....951 277-8319
545 Monica Cir Corona (92878) *(P-8122)*
Firebrand Media LLC.....E.....949 715-4100
580 Broadway St Ste 301 Laguna Beach (92651) *(P-4294)*
Firefighter Cancer Support Ntw.....E.....866 994-3276
3460 Fletcher Ave El Monte (91731) *(P-21788)*
Firefighter Gas Safety Pdts, Santa Ana *Also called Little Firefighter Corporation (P-7449)*
Firefighters First Credit Un (PA).....C.....**323 254-1700**
815 Colorado Blvd Los Angeles (90041) *(P-15065)*
Firequick Products Inc.....E.....760 371-4279
1137 Red Rock Inyokern Rd Inyokern (93527) *(P-8123)*
Firequick Products Inc.....F.....760 377-5766
1137 Red Rock Inyokern Rd Inyokern (93527) *(P-5220)*
Firestone, Ontario *Also called Ramona Auto Services Inc (P-18864)*
Firestone Vineyard LP.....D.....805 688-3940
5000 Zaca Station Rd Los Olivos (93441) *(P-2184)*
Firestone Walker Inc (PA).....B.....**805 225-5911**
1400 Ramada Dr Paso Robles (93446) *(P-2144)*
Firestone Walker Brewing Co, Paso Robles *Also called Firestone Walker Inc (P-2144)*
Firma Plastic Co Inc.....B.....323 567-7767
9309 Rayo Ave South Gate (90280) *(P-14114)*

Mergent e-mail: customerrelations@mergent.com
1132
2022 Southern California Business Directory and Buyers Guide
(P-0000) Products & Services Section entry number
(PA)=Parent Co (HQ)=Headquarters (DH)=Div Headquarters

Firmenich ....D 714 535-2871
424 S Atchison St Anaheim (92805) *(P-5136)*

First & La Realty Corp (PA) ....D 805 581-0021
1301 E Los Angeles Ave Simi Valley (93065) *(P-15854)*

First 5 La ....D 213 482-9487
750 N Alameda St Ste 300 Los Angeles (90012) *(P-21789)*

First Amercn Prof RE Svcs Inc (HQ) ....C 714 250-1400
200 Commerce Irvine (92602) *(P-15855)*

First Amercn Specialty Insur (HQ) ....C 949 474-7500
4 First American Way Santa Ana (92707) *(P-15467)*

First American Financial Corp (PA) ....A 714 250-3000
1 First American Way Santa Ana (92707) *(P-15503)*

First American Mortgage Svcs ....B 714 250-4210
3 First American Way Santa Ana (92707) *(P-15504)*

First American Team Realty Inc (PA) ....C 562 427-7765
2501 Cherry Ave Ste 100 Signal Hill (90755) *(P-15856)*

First American Title Company ....A 714 250-3109
1 First American Way Santa Ana (92707) *(P-16040)*

First American Title Insur Co (HQ) ....D 800 854-3643
1 First American Way Santa Ana (92707) *(P-15505)*

First American Trust Company (HQ) ....D 714 560-7856
5 First American Way Santa Ana (92707) *(P-15326)*

First Amrcn Mrtg Solutions LLC ....D 714 250-3046
1 First American Way Santa Ana (92707) *(P-23216)*

First Amrcn Mrtg Solutions LLC (HQ) ....C 800 333-4510
3 First American Way Santa Ana (92707) *(P-15242)*

First Amrcn Prprty Insur Cslty ....D 949 474-7500
114 E 5th St Santa Ana (92701) *(P-15570)*

First Assmbly of God Bkrsfield ....D 661 327-2227
4901 California Ave Bakersfield (93309) *(P-22015)*

First Avenue Inc ....D 626 856-2076
5105 Heintz St Baldwin Park (91706) *(P-1485)*

First Bank and Trust ....D 562 595-8775
4040 Atlantic Ave Long Beach (90807) *(P-15000)*

First Baptist Church Pomona (PA) ....D 909 629-5277
586 N Main St Pomona (91768) *(P-22016)*

First Baptist School, Pomona *Also called First Baptist Church Pomona* *(P-22016)*

First Capitol Consulting Inc ....D 213 382-1115
3530 Wilshire Blvd # 1460 Los Angeles (90010) *(P-23217)*

First Choice Bank ....D 213 617-0082
888 W 6th St Ste 550 Los Angeles (90017) *(P-15023)*

First Choice Physcn Partners (HQ) ....E 714 428-2311
1400 S Douglass Rd # 250 Anaheim (92806) *(P-19823)*

First City Credit Union (PA) ....E 213 482-3477
717 W Temple St Ste 400 Los Angeles (90012) *(P-15066)*

First Class Foods, Hawthorne *Also called Firstclass Foods - Trojan Inc* *(P-1711)*

First Energy Services Inc ....E 661 387-1972
1031 Carrier Parkway Ave Bakersfield (93308) *(P-502)*

First Entertainment Credit Un (PA) ....D 323 851-3673
6735 Forest Lawn Dr # 100 Los Angeles (90068) *(P-15067)*

First Finish Inc ....E 310 631-6717
11126 Wright Rd Lynwood (90262) *(P-2571)*

First Fire Systems Inc (PA) ....D 310 559-0900
5947 Burchard Ave Los Angeles (90034) *(P-1254)*

First Foundation Advisors (HQ) ....D 949 202-4100
18101 Von Karman Ave # 700 Irvine (92612) *(P-15327)*

First Foundation Consulting, Irvine *Also called First Foundation Advisors* *(P-15327)*

First Foundation Inc (PA) ....C 949 202-4160
18101 Von Karman Ave # 7 Irvine (92612) *(P-15024)*

First Group Holdings Inc ....D 855 910-5626
700 N Brand Blvd Ste 200 Glendale (91203) *(P-16261)*

First Group of America, Santa Maria *Also called First Transit* *(P-11807)*

First Hotels International Inc ....D 909 884-9364
295 N E St San Bernardino (92401) *(P-16443)*

First Interstate Services Inc ....B 818 638-3435
635 W Colo St Ste 108a Glendale (91204) *(P-18379)*

First Legal Network ....E 213 250-1111
1517 Beverly Blvd Los Angeles (90026) *(P-10753)*

First Legal Support Svcs LLC (PA) ....D 213 250-1111
1517 Beverly Blvd Los Angeles (90026) *(P-21554)*

First Press, North Hollywood *Also called 6480 Corporation* *(P-4472)*

First Quadrant LP (PA) ....D 626 795-8220
800 E Colo Blvd Ste 900 Pasadena (91101) *(P-16129)*

First Reprographic, Los Angeles *Also called Lasr Inc* *(P-17151)*

First Republic Bank ....D 213 239-8883
888 S Figueroa St Ste 100 Los Angeles (90017) *(P-15025)*

First Republic Bank ....D 818 263-8798
16300 Ventura Blvd Fl 1 Encino (91436) *(P-15026)*

First Republic Bank ....D 310 712-1888
1888 Century Park E # 200 Los Angeles (90067) *(P-15047)*

First Republic Bank ....D 818 752-4777
12070 Ventura Blvd Studio City (91604) *(P-15027)*

First Republic Bank ....D 424 408-6088
601 N Sepulveda Blvd Manhattan Beach (90266) *(P-15028)*

First Student Inc ....C 855 870-8747
5127 Heintz St Baldwin Park (91706) *(P-11926)*

First Student Inc ....C 855 870-8747
16332 Construction Cir W Irvine (92606) *(P-11927)*

First Student Inc ....C 951 736-3234
300 S Buena Vista Ave Corona (92882) *(P-11943)*

First Student Inc ....C 909 383-1640
234 S I St San Bernardino (92410) *(P-11928)*

First Student Inc ....C 760 320-4659
5006 E Calle San Raphael Palm Springs (92264) *(P-11929)*

First Student Inc ....B 626 448-9446
4337 Rowland Ave El Monte (91731) *(P-11806)*

First Student Inc ....D 818 707-2082
5320 Derry Ave Ste O Agoura Hills (91301) *(P-11930)*

First Student Inc ....C 714 850-7578
3401 W Castor St Santa Ana (92704) *(P-11931)*

First Student Inc ....C 760 256-2333
320 W Mountain View St Barstow (92311) *(P-11932)*

First Student Inc ....C 818 896-0333
11233 San Fernando Rd San Fernando (91340) *(P-11933)*

First Student Inc ....A 310 769-2400
14800 S Avalon Blvd Gardena (90248) *(P-11934)*

First Team RE - Orange Cnty ....D 714 223-2143
18180 Yorba Linda Blvd # 501 Yorba Linda (92886) *(P-15857)*

First Team RE - Orange Cnty ....C 562 596-9911
12501 Seal Beach Blvd # 1 Seal Beach (90740) *(P-15858)*

First Team RE - Orange Cnty ....C 949 759-5747
4 Corporate Plaza Dr # 100 Newport Beach (92660) *(P-15859)*

First Team RE - Orange Cnty (PA) ....C 888 236-1943
108 Pacifica Ste 300 Irvine (92618) *(P-15860)*

First Team RE - Orange Cnty ....C 951 270-2800
200 S Main St Ste 100 Corona (92882) *(P-15861)*

First Team RE - Orange Cnty ....C 562 346-5088
42 64th Pl Long Beach (90803) *(P-15862)*

First Team RE - Orange Cnty ....C 949 240-7979
32451 Golden Lantern # 21 Laguna Niguel (92677) *(P-15863)*

First Team RE - Orange Cnty ....C 714 544-5456
17240 17th St Tustin (92780) *(P-15864)*

First Team RE - Orange Cnty ....C 714 974-9191
8028 E Santa Ana Cyn Rd Anaheim (92808) *(P-15865)*

First Team RE - Orange Cnty ....C 949 389-0004
26711 Aliso Creek Rd Aliso Viejo (92656) *(P-15866)*

First Team Walk-In Realty, Irvine *Also called First Team RE - Orange Cnty* *(P-15860)*

First Transit ....D 805 925-5254
1303 Fairway Dr Santa Maria (93455) *(P-11807)*

First Transit Inc ....D 310 515-8270
2400 E Dominguez St Long Beach (90810) *(P-11808)*

First Transit Inc ....C 949 857-7211
6671 Marine Way Irvine (92618) *(P-11809)*

First Transit Inc ....C 805 544-2730
29 Prado Rd San Luis Obispo (93401) *(P-11810)*

Firstclass Foods - Trojan Inc ....C 310 676-2500
12500 Inglewood Ave Hawthorne (90250) *(P-1711)*

Firstmed Ambulance Svcs Inc ....D 818 982-8333
8630 Tamarack Ave Sun Valley (91352) *(P-11868)*

Firstservice Residential ....D 213 213-0886
3415 S Sepulveda Blvd # 720 Los Angeles (90034) *(P-23026)*

Firstservice Residential ....D 760 834-2480
43100 Cook St Ste 103 Palm Desert (92211) *(P-23027)*

Firstservice Residential (HQ) ....C 949 448-6000
15241 Laguna Canyon Rd Irvine (92618) *(P-15867)*

Firstsight Vision Services Inc (HQ) ....E 909 920-5008
1202 Monte Vista Ave # 17 Upland (91786) *(P-20205)*

Firstsrvice Rsidential Cal Inc (HQ) ....D 909 981-4131
9130 Anaheim Pl Ste 110 Rancho Cucamonga (91730) *(P-15868)*

Firth Rixson Inc ....E 909 483-2200
11711 Arrow Rte Rancho Cucamonga (91730) *(P-7085)*

Fischer Cstm Cmmunications Inc (PA) ....E 310 303-3300
19220 Normandie Ave B Torrance (90502) *(P-10754)*

Fischer Inc ....D 909 881-2910
1372 W 26th St San Bernardino (92405) *(P-1069)*

Fischer Mold Incorporated ....D 951 279-1140
393 Meyer Cir Corona (92879) *(P-5645)*

Fiserv Inc ....D 818 226-4400
8413 Fallbrook Ave West Hills (91304) *(P-18089)*

Fish Bowl, Los Angeles *Also called Second Generation Inc* *(P-2992)*

Fish House Partners One LLC ....D 323 460-4170
5955 Melrose Ave Los Angeles (90038) *(P-16262)*

Fishel Company ....C 714 668-9268
647 Young St Santa Ana (92705) *(P-948)*

Fisher & Paykel, Costa Mesa *Also called Dynamic Cooking Systems Inc* *(P-8379)*

Fisher & Paykel Appliances Inc (HQ) ....C 949 790-8900
695 Town Center Dr # 180 Costa Mesa (92626) *(P-9014)*

Fisher & Paykel Healthcare Inc ....C 949 453-4000
173 Technology Dr Ste 100 Irvine (92618) *(P-13487)*

Fisher Manufacturing Co (PA) ....E 559 685-5200
1900 S O St Tulare (93274) *(P-6560)*

Fisher Printing Inc (PA) ....C 714 998-9200
2257 N Pacific St Orange (92865) *(P-4295)*

Fisher Ranch LLC ....D 760 922-4151
10610 Ice Plant Rd Blythe (92225) *(P-170)*

Fisheries Resource Vlntr Corps ....C 562 596-9261
109 Stanford Ln Seal Beach (90740) *(P-23218)*

Fishermans Pride Prcessors Inc ....B 323 232-1980
4510 S Alameda St Vernon (90058) *(P-2345)*

Fisk Electric Company ....C 818 884-1166
15870 Olden St Sylmar (91342) *(P-1255)*

Fisker Auto & Tech Group LLC ....C 714 723-3247
3080 Airway Ave Costa Mesa (92626) *(P-9946)*

Fisker Group Inc (HQ) ....D 833 434-7537
1888 Rosecrans Ave # 1000 Manhattan Beach (90266) *(P-9947)*

Fisker Inc (PA) ....E 833 434-7537
1888 Rosecrans Ave # 1000 Manhattan Beach (90266) *(P-9948)*

Fit Electronics Inc (HQ) ....D 949 270-8500
121 Theory Ste 200 Irvine (92617) *(P-22840)*

Fit-Line Inc ....E 714 549-9091
2901 S Tech Center Dr Santa Ana (92705) *(P-5646)*

Fit-Line Global, Santa Ana *Also called Fit-Line Inc* *(P-5646)*

Fitness Ridge Malibu LLC ....D 818 874-1300
277 Latigo Canyon Rd Malibu (90265) *(P-16444)*

Fittings That Fit Inc ....F 909 248-2808
4628 Mission Blvd Montclair (91763) *(P-7501)*

Fitzgerald Formliners, Santa Ana *Also called Prime Forming & Cnstr Sups Inc* *(P-6052)*

Five Acres-The Boys & Girls & ....B 626 798-6793
760 Mountain View St Altadena (91001) *(P-22102)*

ALPHABETIC

Employee Codes: A=Over 500 employees, B=251-500
C=101-250, D=51-100, E=20-50 F=10-19
2022 Southern California Business
Directory and Buyers Guide
© Mergent Inc. 1-800-342-5647
1133

Five Point Holdings LLC (PA) ....C.......**949 349-1000**
15131 Alton Pkwy Ste 400 Irvine (92618) ***(P-15869)***

Five Star Food Containers Inc ....D.......626 437-6219
250 Eastgate Rd Barstow (92311) ***(P-5500)***

Five Star Gourmet Foods Inc ....A.......909 390-0032
3880 Ebony St Ontario (91761) ***(P-1927)***

Five Star Juice, Torrance *Also called La Ejuice LLC* ***(P-14904)***

Five Star Plastering Inc ....D.......949 683-5091
23022 La Cadena Dr # 200 Laguna Hills (92653) ***(P-1375)***

Five Star Transportation Inc ....E.......310 348-0820
8703 La Tijera Blvd # 102 Los Angeles (90045) ***(P-12414)***

Five Ten, Redlands *Also called Stone Age Equipment Inc* ***(P-14446)***

Fixd Construction Co., Claremont *Also called Nhs Western Division Inc* ***(P-625)***

Fjs Inc ....C.......714 905-1050
888 S Disneyland Dr # 400 Anaheim (92802) ***(P-16445)***

Fkc International Inc (PA) ....D.......**909 869-9000**
21015 Pathfinder Rd # 140 Diamond Bar (91765) ***(P-22880)***

Flagstone Healthcare South LLC ....D.......949 487-9500
29222 Rncho Vejo Rd Ste 1 San Juan Capistrano (92675) ***(P-20345)***

Flame and Wax Inc ....E.......949 752-4000
2900 Mccabe Way Irvine (92614) ***(P-11668)***

Flame Broiler Inc (PA) ....C.......**714 549-2870**
1538 E Warner Ave Ste E Santa Ana (92705) ***(P-16207)***

Flamemaster Corporation ....E.......818 890-1401
13576 Desmond St Pacoima (91331) ***(P-5221)***

Flannigans Merchandising Inc ....F.......818 785-7428
15803 Stagg St Van Nuys (91406) ***(P-4514)***

Flap Happy Inc ....F.......310 453-3527
2857 E 11th St Los Angeles (90023) ***(P-3040)***

Flare Group ....E.......714 850-2080
1571 Macarthur Blvd Costa Mesa (92626) ***(P-10327)***

Flash Code Solutions LLC ....F.......800 633-7467
4727 Wilshire Blvd # 302 Los Angeles (90010) ***(P-17857)***

Flash Point Graphix, Burbank *Also called Final Film* ***(P-17175)***

Flat Planet Inc ....E.......310 392-0683
618 Hampton Dr Venice (90291) ***(P-7976)***

Flat White Economy Inv USA LLC ....C.......949 344-5013
5151 Cal Ave Ste 100 Costa Mesa (92626) ***(P-12951)***

Flatiron Electric Group Inc ....E.......714 228-9631
15335 Fairfield Ranch Rd # 200 Chino Hills (91709) ***(P-1256)***

Flatiron West Inc ....C.......909 597-8413
16341 Chino Corona Rd Chino (91708) ***(P-927)***

Flaunt Magazine ....F.......323 836-1044
1418 N Highland Ave Los Angeles (90028) ***(P-4070)***

Flavor Factory Inc ....F.......951 273-9877
2058 2nd St Norco (92860) ***(P-2324)***

Flavor House Inc ....E.......760 246-9131
16378 Koala Rd Adelanto (92301) ***(P-2325)***

Flavors Division, Los Angeles *Also called American Fruits & Flavors LLC* ***(P-2308)***

Flawless Vape Whl & Dist Inc ....D.......714 406-2933
1021 E Orangethorpe Ave Anaheim (92801) ***(P-14902)***

Fleet Management Solutions Inc ....E.......800 500-6009
310 Commerce Ste 100 Irvine (92602) ***(P-9274)***

Fleet Mangement Solutions, Irvine *Also called Teletrac Inc* ***(P-12790)***

Fleetwood Continental Inc ....D.......310 609-1477
19451 S Susana Rd Compton (90221) ***(P-6407)***

Fleetwood Enterprises Inc (HQ) ....A.......**951 354-3000**
1351 Pomona Rd Ste 230 Corona (92882) ***(P-10550)***

Fleetwood Homes, Riverside *Also called Fleetwood Motor Homes-Califinc* ***(P-10173)***

Fleetwood Homes, Riverside *Also called Fleetwood Motor Homes-Califinc* ***(P-19038)***

Fleetwood Homes California Inc (HQ) ....B.......**951 351-2494**
7007 Jurupa Ave Riverside (92504) ***(P-3422)***

Fleetwood Homes of Florida (HQ) ....B.......**909 261-4274**
3125 Myers St Riverside (92503) ***(P-3423)***

Fleetwood Homes of Kentucky (HQ) ....D.......**800 688-1745**
1351 Pomona Rd Ste 230 Corona (92882) ***(P-3424)***

Fleetwood Homes of PA (HQ) ....D.......**717 367-8222**
1351 Pomona Rd Ste 230 Corona (92882) ***(P-3425)***

Fleetwood Motor Homes-Califinc (HQ) ....B.......**951 354-3000**
3125 Myers St Riverside (92503) ***(P-10173)***

Fleetwood Motor Homes-Califinc ....C.......951 274-2000
2350 Fleetwood Dr Riverside (92509) ***(P-19038)***

Fleetwood Travel Trlrs Ind Inc (HQ) ....D.......**951 354-3000**
3125 Myers St Riverside (92503) ***(P-10540)***

Fleetwood Travel Trlrs of MD (HQ) ....D.......**951 351-3500**
3125 Myers St Riverside (92503) ***(P-10541)***

Fleis Chmanns Vinegar, Cerritos *Also called AB Mauri Food Inc* ***(P-2384)***

Fleming Metal Fabricators ....E.......323 723-8203
2810 Tanager Ave Commerce (90040) ***(P-9987)***

Fletcher Bldg Holdings USA Inc (HQ) ....D.......**951 272-8180**
1230 Railroad St Corona (92882) ***(P-6839)***

Fletcher Coating Co ....E.......714 637-4763
426 W Fletcher Ave Orange (92865) ***(P-7365)***

Flex Company (PA) ....E.......**424 209-2711**
318 Lincoln Blvd Ste 200 Venice (90291) ***(P-5377)***

Flex Trim Industries Inc (PA) ....D.......**909 748-6578**
210 E Citrus Ave Redlands (92373) ***(P-6700)***

Flex-Mate Inc ....F.......562 426-7169
1855 E 29th St Ste E Signal Hill (90755) ***(P-6479)***

Flexco Inc ....E.......562 927-2525
6855 Suva St Bell Gardens (90201) ***(P-10328)***

Flexfirm Holdings LLC ....F.......323 283-1173
2300 Chico Ave El Monte (91733) ***(P-2708)***

Flexi-Liner, Chino *Also called Liner Technologies Inc* ***(P-5698)***

Flexible Manufacturing LLC ....D.......714 259-7996
1719 S Grand Ave Santa Ana (92705) ***(P-9654)***

Flexible Video Systems, Marina Del Rey *Also called Sewer Rodding Equipment Co* ***(P-8412)***

Flexicare Incorporated ....D.......949 450-9999
15281 Barranca Pkwy Ste D Irvine (92618) ***(P-13488)***

Flexline Inc ....E.......562 921-4141
15405 Cornet St Santa Fe Springs (90670) ***(P-4630)***

Flexogenix Group Inc (PA) ....D.......**213 622-6010**
1000 S Hope St Ste 101 Los Angeles (90015) ***(P-20770)***

Flexpoint Funding Corporation (PA) ....C.......**949 250-4466**
30 Executive Park Ste 200 Irvine (92614) ***(P-15243)***

Flexy Foam, Chino *Also called Inter-Packing Inc* ***(P-5512)***

Flight Centre Usa Inc ....D.......310 458-3310
888 W 6th St Ste 110 Los Angeles (90017) ***(P-12384)***

Flight Line Products LLC ....D.......661 775-8366
28732 Witherspoon Pkwy Valencia (91355) ***(P-1658)***

Flight Microwave Corporation ....E.......310 607-9819
410 S Douglas St El Segundo (90245) ***(P-7977)***

Flightpath3d, Lake Forest *Also called Betria Interactive LLC* ***(P-12344)***

Flint Energy Services Inc ....D.......213 593-8000
1999 Avenue Of The Stars # 2 Los Angeles (90067) ***(P-22549)***

Flir Commercial Systems Inc (HQ) ....B.......**805 964-9797**
6769 Hollister Ave Goleta (93117) ***(P-10794)***

Flir Elctr-Ptcal Comp Bus Unit, Ventura *Also called Flir Eoc LLC* ***(P-10795)***

Flir Eoc LLC ....E.......805 642-4645
2223 Eastman Ave Ste B Ventura (93003) ***(P-10795)***

Flir Motion Ctrl Systems Inc ....D.......650 692-3900
6769 Hollister Ave Goleta (93117) ***(P-7978)***

Flo-CHI, Los Angeles *Also called Lindsey & Sons* ***(P-18578)***

Flo-Kem, Compton *Also called LMC Enterprises* ***(P-4969)***

Flo-Mac Inc ....E.......323 583-8751
1846 E 60th St Los Angeles (90001) ***(P-7538)***

Flood Ranch Company ....E.......805 937-3616
6600 Foxen Canyon Rd Santa Maria (93454) ***(P-2185)***

Floor Covering Soft ....E.......626 683-9188
221 E Walnut St Ste 110 Pasadena (91101) ***(P-17858)***

Flora Beauty Inc ....D.......213 374-0448
1608 Nogales St D02 Rowland Heights (91748) ***(P-14036)***

Flora Gold LLC ....F.......949 252-1122
3165 Red Hill Ave Costa Mesa (92626) ***(P-11669)***

Floral Gift HM Decor Intl Inc ....E.......818 849-8832
3200 Golf Course Dr Ste B Ventura (93003) ***(P-76)***

Florence Crttnton Svcs Ornge C ....B.......714 680-9000
801 E Chapman Ave Ste 203 Fullerton (92831) ***(P-22103)***

Florence Filter Corporation ....D.......310 637-1137
530 W Manville St Compton (90220) ***(P-13843)***

Florence International Co Inc ....E.......818 767-9650
11645 Pendleton St Sun Valley (91352) ***(P-7260)***

Florence Macaroni Company ....F.......310 548-5942
1312 W 2nd St San Pedro (90732) ***(P-2375)***

Flores Brothers Inc ....F.......562 806-9128
7777 Scout Ave Bell (90201) ***(P-2433)***

Floride Products LLC (PA) ....E.......**323 201-4363**
2867 Vail Ave Commerce (90040) ***(P-4658)***

Flow Dynamics Inc ....F.......909 930-5522
1215 E Acacia St Ste 104 Ontario (91761) ***(P-6201)***

Flow Sports Inc ....E.......949 361-5260
1011 Calle Sombra San Clemente (92673) ***(P-11417)***

Flowline Inc ....E.......562 598-3015
10500 Humbolt St Los Alamitos (90720) ***(P-10884)***

Flowline Liquid Intelligence, Los Alamitos *Also called Flowline Inc* ***(P-10884)***

Flowmetrics Inc ....F.......818 407-3420
9201 Independence Ave Chatsworth (91311) ***(P-10693)***

Flowserve Corporation ....B.......323 584-1890
2300 E Vernon Ave Stop 76 Vernon (90058) ***(P-8010)***

Floyd Skeren & Kelly LLP (PA) ....D.......**818 206-9222**
101 Moody Ct Ste 200 Thousand Oaks (91360) ***(P-21555)***

Fluid Line Technology Corp ....E.......818 998-8848
9362 Eton Ave Ste A Chatsworth (91311) ***(P-10982)***

Fluid Power Ctrl Systems Inc ....F.......714 525-3727
1400 E Valencia Dr Fullerton (92831) ***(P-10694)***

Fluidmaster Inc (PA) ....C.......**949 728-2000**
30800 Rancho Viejo Rd San Juan Capistrano (92675) ***(P-5647)***

Fluids Manufacturing Inc ....C.......818 264-4657
11941 Vose St North Hollywood (91605) ***(P-14750)***

Fluidstance, Santa Barbara *Also called Company of Motion LLC* ***(P-11272)***

Fluor Corporation ....D.......949 349-2000
3 Polaris Way Aliso Viejo (92656) ***(P-22550)***

Fluor Daniel, Aliso Viejo *Also called Fluor Plant Services Intl Inc* ***(P-22552)***

Fluor Daniel Construction Co (HQ) ....B.......**949 349-2000**
3 Polaris Way Aliso Viejo (92656) ***(P-928)***

Fluor Daniel Eurasia Inc (HQ) ....A.......**949 349-2000**
1 Fluor Daniel Dr Aliso Viejo (92698) ***(P-22551)***

Fluor Fltron Blfour Btty Drgdo ....D.......949 420-5000
5901 W Century Blvd Los Angeles (90045) ***(P-12571)***

Fluor Industrial Services Inc ....C.......949 439-2000
1 Enterprise Aliso Viejo (92656) ***(P-17243)***

Fluor Plant Services Intl Inc ....D.......949 349-2000
1 Enterprise Aliso Viejo (92656) ***(P-22552)***

Fluoramec LLC (HQ) ....E.......**949 349-2000**
1 Enterprise Aliso Viejo (92656) ***(P-22553)***

Fluorescent Supply Co Inc ....E.......909 948-8878
9120 Center Ave Rancho Cucamonga (91730) ***(P-9084)***

Fluxergy Inc (PA) ....D.......**949 305-4201**
30 Fairbanks Irvine (92618) ***(P-22554)***

Flw Inc ....D.......714 751-7512
5672 Bolsa Ave Huntington Beach (92649) ***(P-13686)***

Flying Colors, Walnut *Also called Jakks Pacific Inc* ***(P-11379)***

Flying Embers Brewing Co ....D.......781 856-3648
3200 Golf Course Dr Ventura (93003) ***(P-14842)***

Flying Machine Factory, Compton *Also called Fmf Racing* ***(P-10490)***

Flynn Signs and Graphics Inc ....E.......562 498-6655
1345 Coronado Ave Long Beach (90804) ***(P-11555)***

Flynn Signs and Letters, Long Beach *Also called Flynn Signs and Graphics Inc* ***(P-11555)***

Flynt, Larry Publishing, Beverly Hills *Also called L F P Inc* ***(P-4077)***
Flyr Inc.......D.......415 841-3597
3205 Pico Blvd Santa Monica (90405) ***(P-18090)***
FMC Financial Group (PA).......**D.......949 225-9369**
4675 Macarthur Ct # 1250 Newport Beach (92660) ***(P-15571)***
FMC Metals, Los Angeles *Also called 75s Corp* ***(P-14106)***
Fmf Racing.......C.......310 631-4363
18033 S Santa Fe Ave Compton (90221) ***(P-10490)***
Fmh Aerospace Corp.......D.......714 751-1000
17072 Daimler St Irvine (92614) ***(P-10329)***
FMI International West 2, San Pedro *Also called Toll Global Fwdg Scs USA Inc* ***(P-12539)***
Fmsinfoserv, Los Angeles *Also called Cdsnet LLC* ***(P-23427)***
FN Logistics Llc.......D.......213 625-5900
12588 Florence Ave Santa Fe Springs (90670) ***(P-12112)***
Fnc Medical Corporation.......E.......805 644-7576
6000 Leland St Ventura (93003) ***(P-5021)***
Fns Inc (PA).......**D.......661 615-2300**
1545 Francisco St Torrance (90501) ***(P-12458)***
Fntech.......E.......714 429-7833
3000 W Segerstrom Ave Santa Ana (92704) ***(P-9132)***
Foam Co, The, Van Nuys *Also called Grht Inc* ***(P-14933)***
Foam Concepts Inc.......E.......714 693-1037
4729 E Wesley Dr Anaheim (92807) ***(P-5501)***
Foam Depot, City of Industry *Also called American Foam Fiber & Sups Inc* ***(P-2719)***
Foam Factory Inc.......E.......310 603-9808
17515 S Santa Fe Ave Compton (90221) ***(P-5502)***
Foam Molders and Specialties (PA).......**D.......562 924-7757**
11110 Business Cir Cerritos (90703) ***(P-5503)***
Foam Molders and Specialties.......E.......562 924-7757
20004 State Rd Cerritos (90703) ***(P-5504)***
Foam Plastics & Rbr Pdts Corp.......F.......714 779-0990
4765 E Bryson St Anaheim (92807) ***(P-5505)***
Foam Specialties, Cerritos *Also called Foam Molders and Specialties* ***(P-5503)***
Foam-Craft Inc.......C.......714 459-9971
2441 Cypress Way Fullerton (92831) ***(P-5506)***
Foamex LP.......C.......323 774-5600
19201 S Reyes Ave Compton (90221) ***(P-12206)***
Foampro Manufacturing, Irvine *Also called Foampro Mfg Inc* ***(P-11510)***
Foampro Mfg Inc.......D.......949 252-0112
1781 Langley Ave Irvine (92614) ***(P-11510)***
Foasberg Laundry and Clrs Inc (PA).......**D.......562 426-7345**
640 E Wardlow Rd Long Beach (90807) ***(P-16852)***
Focu Vision Clinic, Beaumont *Also called Focus Vsion Clnic Optmetry Inc* ***(P-20206)***
Focus 360 Inc.......D.......949 234-0008
27721 La Paz Rd Ste B Laguna Niguel (92677) ***(P-17616)***
Focus Diagnostics Inc.......B.......714 220-1900
11331 Valley View St # 150 Cypress (90630) ***(P-21067)***
Focus Health, Aliso Viejo *Also called Rehabfocus Home Health Inc* ***(P-21207)***
Focus Healthcare Holdings Inc (HQ).......**E.......949 349-1200**
27071 Aliso Creek Rd # 100 Aliso Viejo (92656) ***(P-21427)***
Focus Industries Inc.......D.......949 830-1350
25301 Commercentre Dr Lake Forest (92630) ***(P-9085)***
Focus Landscape, Lake Forest *Also called Focus Industries Inc* ***(P-9085)***
Focus Line LLC.......F.......818 517-5171
160 Delfern Dr Los Angeles (90077) ***(P-9133)***
Focus On All Child Thrpies Inc.......D.......310 475-9620
1880 Century Park E # 512 Los Angeles (90067) ***(P-20582)***
Focus Technologies Holding Co.......E.......800 838-4548
10703 Progress Way Cypress (90630) ***(P-21068)***
Focus Vsion Clnic Optmetry Inc (PA).......**D.......951 845-4749**
1668 E Second St Ste B Beaumont (92223) ***(P-20206)***
Foilflex Products Inc.......F.......661 702-0775
25636 Avenue Stanford Valencia (91355) ***(P-4515)***
Fold-A-Goal, Los Angeles *Also called D Hauptman Co Inc* ***(P-11411)***
Foldimate Inc.......E.......805 876-4418
879 White Pine Ct Oak Park (91377) ***(P-9005)***
Folding Cartons, Camarillo *Also called Crockett Graphics Inc* ***(P-3797)***
Foley Bezek & Komoroske, Santa Barbara *Also called Foley Bezek Behle & Curtis LLP* ***(P-21556)***
Foley Bezek Behle & Curtis LLP.......D.......805 962-9495
15 W Carrillo St Santa Barbara (93101) ***(P-21556)***
Foley OK Electric Inc.......D.......818 962-8555
5459 Diaz St Irwindale (91706) ***(P-1257)***
Follmer Development Inc.......E.......805 498-4531
840 Tourmaline Dr Newbury Park (91320) ***(P-4639)***
Fonco Creative Services.......E.......415 254-5460
1310 N San Fernando Rd Los Angeles (90065) ***(P-19124)***
Fonco Studios, Los Angeles *Also called Fonco Creative Services* ***(P-19124)***
Fonegear LLC.......F.......909 627-7999
13953 Ramona Ave Chino (91710) ***(P-9233)***
Fontal Controls Inc.......E.......818 833-1127
12725 Encinitas Ave Sylmar (91342) ***(P-8590)***
Fontana Foundry Corporation.......E.......909 822-6128
8306 Cherry Ave Fontana (92335) ***(P-6395)***
Fontana Mental Health Offices, Fontana *Also called Kaiser Foundation Hospitals* ***(P-19900)***
Fontana Paper Mills Inc.......D.......909 823-4100
13733 Valley Blvd Fontana (92335) ***(P-5279)***
Fontana Resources At Work.......C.......909 428-3833
8608 Live Oak Ave Fontana (92335) ***(P-21952)***
Fontana Water Company, El Monte *Also called San Gabriel Valley Water Co* ***(P-12915)***
Fontana Wood Treating Inc.......F.......909 357-2136
8395 Sultana Ave Fontana (92335) ***(P-3432)***
Food & Bev Innovations LLC.......F.......888 491-3772
1801 Century Park E # 1420 Los Angeles (90067) ***(P-7931)***
Food 4 Less, Riverside *Also called Dillon Companies Inc* ***(P-1995)***
Food For Life Baking Co Inc (PA).......**D.......951 273-3031**
2991 Doherty St Corona (92879) ***(P-2001)***
Food Machinery Sales Inc.......D.......559 651-2339
7020 W Sunnyview Ave Visalia (93291) ***(P-8068)***
Food Management Associates Inc.......E.......714 694-2828
22349 La Palma Ave # 115 Yorba Linda (92887) ***(P-23219)***
Food Pharma, Santa Fe Springs *Also called Food Technology and Design LLC* ***(P-2086)***
Food Processing Equipment Co, Santa Fe Springs *Also called FPec Corporation A Cal Corp* ***(P-7934)***
Food Sales West Inc (PA).......**D.......714 966-2900**
235 Baker St Costa Mesa (92626) ***(P-14466)***
Food Technology and Design LLC.......E.......562 944-7821
10012 Painter Ave Santa Fe Springs (90670) ***(P-2086)***
Food-O-Mex Corporation.......F.......323 225-1737
2928 N Main St Los Angeles (90031) ***(P-2434)***
Foodbeast Inc.......F.......949 344-2634
220 E 4th St Ste 202 Santa Ana (92701) ***(P-4172)***
Foodology LLC.......D.......818 252-1888
8920 Norris Ave Sun Valley (91352) ***(P-2435)***
Foods and Produce, Buena Park *Also called Walong Marketing Inc* ***(P-14747)***
Foodtools Consolidated Inc (PA).......**E.......805 962-8383**
315 Laguna St Santa Barbara (93101) ***(P-7932)***
Foot In Motion Inc.......F.......312 752-0990
2239 Business Way Riverside (92501) ***(P-11105)***
Foote Axle & Forge LLC.......E.......323 268-4151
250 W Duarte Rd Ste A Monrovia (91016) ***(P-10059)***
Foothill / Estrn Trnsp Crrdor.......D.......949 754-3400
125 Pacifica Ste 100 Irvine (92618) ***(P-879)***
Foothill Child Dev Svcs Inc.......D.......818 353-3772
16946 Sherman Way 100 Van Nuys (91406) ***(P-22017)***
Foothill Eye Surgical Center, Glendora *Also called Mark Kislinger MD Inc* ***(P-19971)***
Foothill Group Inc (HQ).......**C.......310 453-7300**
1800 Century Park E # 1100 Los Angeles (90067) ***(P-15001)***
Foothill Hsptl-Mrris L Jhnston (PA).......**D.......626 857-3145**
250 S Grand Ave Glendora (91741) ***(P-20771)***
Foothill Packing Inc.......B.......805 925-7900
2255 S Broadway Santa Maria (93454) ***(P-14467)***
FOOTHILL PRESBYTERIAN HOSPITAL, Glendora *Also called Foothill Hsptl-Mrris L Jhnston* ***(P-20771)***
Foothill Ranch Medical Offices, Foothill Ranch *Also called Kaiser Foundation Hospitals* ***(P-19899)***
Foothill Regional Medical Ctr, Tustin *Also called Alta Hospitals System LLC* ***(P-20671)***
Foothill Transit West Covina, Arcadia *Also called Coach Usa Inc* ***(P-11910)***
Foothills Advertiser, Exeter *Also called Foothills Sun-Gazette* ***(P-3976)***
Foothills Sun-Gazette.......F.......559 592-3171
120 N E St Exeter (93221) ***(P-3976)***
For Cali Productions LLC (HQ).......**C.......323 956-9508**
5808 W Sunset Blvd Los Angeles (90028) ***(P-19233)***
For Cali Productions LLC.......D.......323 956-9500
5555 Melrose Ave Bldg 213 Los Angeles (90038) ***(P-19234)***
Forbes Industries Div.......C.......909 923-4559
1933 E Locust St Ontario (91761) ***(P-3729)***
Ford Wlker Haggerty Behar LLP (PA).......**D.......562 983-2500**
1 World Trade Ctr Ste 270 Long Beach (90831) ***(P-21557)***
Ford Motor Land Dev Corp.......B.......949 242-6606
3 Glen Bell Way Ste 100 Irvine (92618) ***(P-15667)***
Ford of Santa Monica Inc.......D.......310 451-1588
1230 Santa Monica Blvd Santa Monica (90404) ***(P-13026)***
Ford of Simi Valley Inc.......D.......805 583-0333
2440 1st St Simi Valley (93065) ***(P-18829)***
Fordon Grind Industries, Torrance *Also called Aeroliant Manufacturing Inc* ***(P-8479)***
Foremay Inc (PA).......**E.......408 228-3468**
225 S Lake Ave Ste 300 Pasadena (91101) ***(P-17617)***
Foremost Fresh Direct LLC (PA).......**E.......559 735-3100**
4747 S Mooney Blvd Visalia (93277) ***(P-14629)***
Foremost Spring & Mfg, Santa Fe Springs *Also called Foremost Spring Company Inc* ***(P-7486)***
Foremost Spring Company Inc.......F.......562 923-0791
11876 Burke St Santa Fe Springs (90670) ***(P-7486)***
Forensic Analytical Spc Inc.......D.......310 763-2374
20535 Belshaw Ave Carson (90746) ***(P-22945)***
Forensic Toxicology Associates, Chatsworth *Also called Pacific Toxicology Labs* ***(P-21082)***
Foreseeson Custom Displays Inc (PA).......**E.......714 300-0540**
2210 E Winston Rd Anaheim (92806) ***(P-8257)***
Forespar, Rcho STA Marg *Also called Light Composite Corporation* ***(P-6524)***
Forest Hlls Invstors Mmber LLC (HQ).......**D.......818 808-0600**
15301 Ventura Blvd B570 Sherman Oaks (91403) ***(P-15870)***
Forest Lawn Co.......C.......818 241-4151
1712 S Glendale Ave Glendale (91205) ***(P-16082)***
Forest Lawn Mem Parks Mortuary, Glendale *Also called Forest Lawn Memorial-Park Assn* ***(P-16083)***
Forest Lawn Memorial-Park Assn (PA).......**B.......323 254-3131**
1712 S Glendale Ave Glendale (91205) ***(P-16083)***
Forest Lawn Mortuary (HQ).......**B.......323 254-3131**
1712 S Glendale Ave Glendale (91205) ***(P-16922)***
Forever Link International Inc.......E.......877 839-9899
888 S Azusa Ave City of Industry (91748) ***(P-14438)***
Forged Metals Inc.......C.......909 350-9260
10685 Beech Ave Fontana (92337) ***(P-7086)***
Forgiato Inc.......D.......747 271-7151
11915 Wicks St Sun Valley (91352) ***(P-10060)***
Form Grind Corporation.......E.......949 858-7000
30062 Aventura Rcho STA Marg (92688) ***(P-8591)***
Form Products, Rcho STA Marg *Also called Form Grind Corporation* ***(P-8591)***
Formative, Los Angeles *Also called Smartest Edu Inc* ***(P-17985)***
Forme Life Retail LLC.......E.......703 577-9585
942 N Laurel Ave Los Angeles (90046) ***(P-14078)***
Forming Specialties Inc.......E.......310 639-1122
1309 W Walnut Pkwy Compton (90220) ***(P-10330)***

ALPHABETIC

Employee Codes: A=Over 500 employees, B=251-500
C=101-250, D=51-100, E=20-50 F=10-19
2022 Southern California Business
Directory and Buyers Guide
© Mergent Inc. 1-800-342-5647
1135

Formology Lab Inc.....F.....424 452-0377
9174 Deering Ave Chatsworth (91311) ***(P-5022)***
Formosa Meat Company Inc.....E.....909 987-0470
10646 Fulton Ct Rancho Cucamonga (91730) ***(P-1732)***
Forms and Surfaces Inc.....D.....805 684-8626
6395 Cindy Ln Carpinteria (93013) ***(P-6962)***
Forms and Surfaces Company LLC.....C.....805 684-8626
6395 Cindy Ln Carpinteria (93013) ***(P-6034)***
Formsolver Inc.....F.....323 664-7888
3041 N North Coolidge Ave Los Angeles (90039) ***(P-3443)***
Formula Consultants Inc.....F.....714 778-0123
222 S Harbor Blvd Ste 650 Anaheim (92805) ***(P-17618)***
Forrest Machining Inc., Valencia *Also called Forrest Machining Llc* ***(P-10331)***
Forrest Machining Llc.....C.....661 257-0231
27756 Avenue Mentry Valencia (91355) ***(P-10331)***
Forrester Eastland Corporation.....E.....310 784-2464
1320 Storm Pkwy Torrance (90501) ***(P-11670)***
Fort Hill Construction (PA).....D.....**323 656-7425**
12711 Ventura Blvd # 390 Studio City (91604) ***(P-605)***
Fortanasce & Associates, Murrieta *Also called McHael G Fortansce Physcl Thra* ***(P-20226)***
Forte Biosciences Inc (PA).....E.....**310 618-6994**
1124 W Crson St Mrl Bldg Torrance (90502) ***(P-4821)***
Fortel Traffic Inc.....F.....714 701-9800
5310 E Hunter Ave Anaheim (92807) ***(P-22555)***
Forterra Pipe & Precast LLC.....E.....661 746-3527
30781 San Diego St Shafter (93263) ***(P-6840)***
Fortiss LLC.....D.....323 415-4900
1100 S Flower St Ste 3100 Los Angeles (90015) ***(P-19650)***
Fortner Eng & Mfg Inc.....E.....818 240-7740
918 Thompson Ave Glendale (91201) ***(P-8592)***
Fortress Inc.....E.....909 593-8600
1721 Wright Ave La Verne (91750) ***(P-3584)***
Fortress Holding Group LLC.....D.....714 202-8710
5500 E Snta Ana Cyn Rd St Anaheim (92807) ***(P-16100)***
Fortress Resources LLC (HQ).....C.....**562 633-9951**
24200 Main St Carson (90745) ***(P-18830)***
Fortron/Source Corporation (PA).....D.....**949 766-9240**
23181 Antonio Pkwy Rcho STA Marg (92688) ***(P-8871)***
Fortuna Enterprises LP.....B.....310 410-4000
5711 W Century Blvd Los Angeles (90045) ***(P-16446)***
Fortune Avenue Foods Inc.....D.....909 930-5989
2117 Pointe Ave Ontario (91761) ***(P-14468)***
Fortune Casuals LLC (PA).....D.....**310 733-2100**
10119 Jefferson Blvd Culver City (90232) ***(P-2843)***
Fortune Dynamic Inc.....D.....909 979-8318
21923 Ferrero City of Industry (91789) ***(P-14439)***
Fortune Swimwear LLC (HQ).....E.....**310 733-2130**
2340 E Olympic Blvd Ste A Los Angeles (90021) ***(P-2633)***
Forty-Niner Shops Inc.....A.....562 985-5093
6049 E 7th St Long Beach (90840) ***(P-16811)***
Foss Maritime Co Inc.....D.....562 435-0171
Berth 35 Pier D Long Beach (90802) ***(P-12274)***
Fossil Energy Research Corp.....F.....949 859-4466
23342 S Pointe Dr Ste C Laguna Hills (92653) ***(P-18519)***
Foster Farms LLC.....E.....559 793-5501
770 N Plano St Porterville (93257) ***(P-139)***
Foster Planing Mill Co.....F.....323 759-9156
1258 W 58th St Los Angeles (90037) ***(P-3444)***
Foster Poultry Farms.....C.....559 457-6509
4107 Ave 360 Traver (93673) ***(P-14859)***
Foster Poultry Farms.....B.....559 793-5501
770 N Plano St Porterville (93257) ***(P-1757)***
Foster Poultry Farms.....B.....310 223-1499
1805 N Santa Fe Ave Compton (90221) ***(P-1758)***
Foster Print, Santa Ana *Also called Blackburn Alton Invstments LLC* ***(P-4486)***
Foster Printing Company Inc.....D.....714 731-2000
700 E Alton Ave Santa Ana (92705) ***(P-4296)***
Foster Sand & Gravel, Corona *Also called Werner Corporation* ***(P-6127)***
Fotis and Son Imports Inc.....E.....714 894-9022
15451 Electronic Ln Huntington Beach (92649) ***(P-7933)***
Foto Kem Film & Video, Burbank *Also called Foto-Kem Industries Inc* ***(P-19235)***
Foto-Kem Industries Inc (PA).....B.....**818 846-3102**
2801 W Alameda Ave Burbank (91505) ***(P-19235)***
Foundation 9 Entertainment Inc (PA).....C.....**949 698-1500**
30211 A De Las Bandera200 Rancho Santa Margari (92688) ***(P-17859)***
Foundation Ai, Tustin *Also called Foundation Inc* ***(P-17860)***
Foundation Building Mtls Inc (HQ).....A.....**714 380-3127**
2520 Redhill Ave Santa Ana (92705) ***(P-13208)***
Foundation For Dance Education.....D.....909 482-1590
9061 Central Ave Montclair (91763) ***(P-19298)***
Foundation Inc.....E.....310 294-8955
17632 Irvine Blvd Ste 225 Tustin (92780) ***(P-17860)***
Foundation Laboratory, Pomona *Also called Latara Enterprise Inc* ***(P-21074)***
Foundation Lead Group LLC.....D.....877 477-2311
16800 Aston Ste 270 Irvine (92606) ***(P-23220)***
Foundation Pile Inc.....D.....909 350-1584
8375 Almeria Ave Fontana (92335) ***(P-997)***
Foundation Property MGT Inc (HQ).....E.....**562 257-5100**
911 N Studebaker Rd # 100 Long Beach (90815) ***(P-23221)***
Foundry Service & Supplies Inc.....E.....909 284-5000
2029 S Parco Ave Ontario (91761) ***(P-6180)***
Foundstone Inc.....E.....949 297-5600
27201 Puerta Real Ste 400 Mission Viejo (92691) ***(P-17861)***
Foundtion For Erly Chldhood Ed (PA).....C.....**626 572-5107**
3450 E Sierra Madre Blvd Pasadena (91107) ***(P-21790)***
Fountain View Cnvalescent Hosp, Los Angeles *Also called Genesis Healthcare LLC* ***(P-20590)***
Fountain Vly Rgnal Hosp Med CT.....A.....714 966-7200
17100 Euclid St Fountain Valley (92708) ***(P-20772)***
Fountainhead Industries.....E.....310 248-2444
700 N San Vicente Blvd G910 West Hollywood (90069) ***(P-11671)***
Fountains At The Carlotta, The, Palm Desert *Also called Watermark Rtrment Cmmnties Inc* ***(P-20503)***
Four Pnts By Shrton La Intl Ar, Los Angeles *Also called Irp Lax Hotel LLC* ***(P-16508)***
Four Points Bakersfield, Bakersfield *Also called Cni Thl Propco Fe LLC* ***(P-16385)***
Four Points By Sheraton.....D.....310 645-4600
9750 Airport Blvd Los Angeles (90045) ***(P-16447)***
Four Points Sheraton Lax, Los Angeles *Also called Lax Hotel Ventures LLC* ***(P-16537)***
Four Seasons Building Products.....F.....714 522-7852
6450 Caballero Blvd Buena Park (90620) ***(P-6995)***
Four Seasons Hotel, Westlake Village *Also called Burton-Way House Ltd A CA* ***(P-16359)***
Four Seasons Hotel, Los Angeles *Also called Burton-Way House Ltd A CA* ***(P-16360)***
Four Seasons Hotel, Los Angeles *Also called Burton Way Htels Ltd A Cal Ltd* ***(P-16358)***
Four Seasons Hotels Limited, Los Angeles *Also called Burton Way Hotels LLC* ***(P-16357)***
Four Seasons Hummus Inc.....F.....305 409-0449
11030 Randall St Sun Valley (91352) ***(P-2436)***
Four Seasons Landscaping, Van Nuys *Also called S G D Enterprises* ***(P-340)***
Four Seasons Rest Eqp Inc.....E.....951 278-9100
412 Jenks Cir Corona (92878) ***(P-6841)***
Four Seasons Surgery Centers.....F.....909 933-6576
1211 W 6th St Ontario (91762) ***(P-19824)***
Four Seasons Westlake.....D.....818 575-3000
2 Dole Dr Westlake Village (91362) ***(P-16448)***
Four Ssons Rsort Santa Barbara, Santa Barbara *Also called 1260 Bb Property LLC* ***(P-16305)***
Four Star Chemical, Vernon *Also called Starco Enterprises Inc* ***(P-7995)***
Four Star Distribution.....D.....949 369-4420
206 Calle Conchita San Clemente (92672) ***(P-5308)***
Four Wheel Parts Wholesalers, Compton *Also called Transamerican Dissolution LLC* ***(P-13101)***
Fourbro Inc.....F.....714 277-3858
13772 A Better Way Garden Grove (92843) ***(P-2809)***
Foursquare International, Los Angeles *Also called Interntnal Ch of Frsqare Gospl* ***(P-15674)***
Fourthfloor Fashion Talent, Los Angeles *Also called Career Group Inc* ***(P-17403)***
Foutz, Michael B, Hemet *Also called Pehl Futz Futz Tgrden Accntnts* ***(P-22807)***
Fovell Enterprises Inc.....E.....951 734-6275
1852 Pomona Rd Corona (92878) ***(P-11556)***
Fowlie Enterprises Inc.....E.....805 583-2800
1143 Fern Oaks Dr Santa Paula (93060) ***(P-2064)***
Fox Inc (HQ).....A.....**310 369-1000**
2121 Avenue Of The Stars Los Angeles (90067) ***(P-12720)***
Fox Animation Studios Inc.....C.....323 857-8800
5700 Wilshire Blvd # 325 Los Angeles (90036) ***(P-19125)***
Fox Baseball Holdings Inc.....A.....323 224-1500
1000 Vin Scully Ave Los Angeles (90090) ***(P-19416)***
Fox Broadcasting Company LLC (HQ).....C.....**310 369-1000**
10201 W Pico Blvd Bldg 10 Los Angeles (90064) ***(P-12721)***
Fox Electronics, Laguna Hills *Also called Fox Enterprises LLC* ***(P-9713)***
Fox Enterprises LLC (HQ).....E.....**239 693-0099**
24422 Avnida De La Crlota Carlota Laguna Hills (92653) ***(P-9713)***
Fox Entertainment Television, Los Angeles *Also called Fox Television Stations Inc* ***(P-12726)***
Fox Family Channel, Burbank *Also called International Fmly Entrmt Inc* ***(P-12772)***
Fox Films Entertainment, Los Angeles *Also called Twentieth Cntury Fox Film Corp* ***(P-19190)***
Fox Head Inc (PA).....C.....**408 776-8800**
16752 Armstrong Ave Irvine (92606) ***(P-14333)***
Fox Hills Auto Inc (PA).....C.....**310 649-3673**
5880 W Centinela Ave Los Angeles (90045) ***(P-18831)***
Fox Hills Industries.....E.....714 893-1940
5831 Research Dr Huntington Beach (92649) ***(P-6257)***
FOX INTERACTIVE, Los Angeles *Also called Twentieth Cntury Fox Intl Corp* ***(P-19263)***
Fox Intrntonal Channels US Inc (HQ).....D.....**310 369-8759**
10201 W Pico Blvd Los Angeles (90064) ***(P-12722)***
Fox Landing, Avalon *Also called Guided Discoveries Inc* ***(P-16822)***
Fox Luggage Inc.....D.....323 588-1688
221 N Orange Ave City of Industry (91744) ***(P-14156)***
Fox Net Inc.....A.....310 369-1000
10201 W Pico Blvd Los Angeles (90064) ***(P-19126)***
Fox Network Center, Los Angeles *Also called Fox Networks Group Inc* ***(P-12723)***
Fox Networks Group Inc (HQ).....C.....**310 369-1000**
10201 W Pico Blvd Bldg 10 Los Angeles (90064) ***(P-12723)***
Fox Printing Company Inc (PA).....F.....**818 768-6110**
18017 Chatsworth St Granada Hills (91344) ***(P-4297)***
Fox Racing, Irvine *Also called Fox Head Inc* ***(P-14333)***
Fox Rent A Car Inc.....D.....310 342-5155
325 Baker St Costa Mesa (92626) ***(P-18740)***
Fox Rent A Car Inc (HQ).....E.....**310 342-5155**
5500 W Century Blvd Los Angeles (90045) ***(P-18741)***
Fox Sports Inc (HQ).....C.....**310 369-1000**
10201 W Pico Blvd Los Angeles (90064) ***(P-12724)***
Fox Sports Productions Inc.....D.....310 369-1000
10201 W Pico Blvd Los Angeles (90064) ***(P-12725)***
Fox Television Stations Inc (HQ).....B.....**310 584-2000**
1999 S Bundy Dr Los Angeles (90025) ***(P-12726)***
Fox Transportation Inc (PA).....D.....**909 291-4646**
8610 Helms Ave Rancho Cucamonga (91730) ***(P-23442)***
Fox US Productions 27 Inc.....C.....310 727-2550
1600 Rosecrans Ave 5a Manhattan Beach (90266) ***(P-12727)***
Foxconn Electronics, Irvine *Also called Fit Electronics Inc* ***(P-22840)***
Foxen Vineyard Inc.....E.....805 937-4251
7600 Foxen Canyon Rd Santa Maria (93454) ***(P-2186)***
Foxlink International Inc (HQ).....E.....**714 256-1777**
3010 Saturn St Ste 200 Brea (92821) ***(P-9037)***
Foxlink World Circuit Tech.....E.....714 256-0877
925 W Lambert Rd Ste C Brea (92821) ***(P-9407)***

Foxnext Games LLC (PA)......C......424 222-5889
12121 Bluff Creek Dr # 400 Playa Vista (90094) *(P-17619)*
Fpc Graphics Inc......E......951 686-0232
2682 Market St Riverside (92501) *(P-4298)*
FPec Corporation A Cal Corp (PA)......F......562 802-3727
13623 Pumice St Santa Fe Springs (90670) *(P-7934)*
Fpg Oc Inc......E......714 692-2950
24855 Corbit Pl Ste B Yorba Linda (92887) *(P-2326)*
Fpk Investigaions, Valencia *Also called Fpk Security Inc (P-18275)*
Fpk Security Inc......B......661 702-9091
28348 Constellation Rd # 880 Valencia (91355) *(P-18275)*
Fpl LLC......D......805 643-6144
550 San Jon Rd Ventura (93001) *(P-16449)*
Fr-Industries Inc (HQ)......E......817 645-4366
1701 Lombard St Ste 200 Oxnard (93030) *(P-14157)*
Fragomen Del Rey Bernse......D......949 660-3504
18401 Von Karman Ave # 255 Irvine (92612) *(P-21558)*
Fragrant Jewels LLC......E......888 443-5049
807 Mateo St Los Angeles (90021) *(P-11672)*
Fralock, Valencia *Also called Lockwood Industries LLC (P-9532)*
Framatic Company, Los Angeles *Also called Formsolver Inc (P-3443)*
Frameless Hardware Company LLC......E......888 295-4531
4361 Firestone Blvd South Gate (90280) *(P-6517)*
Frametent Inc......E......661 290-3375
26480 Summit Cir Santa Clarita (91350) *(P-3139)*
Framing Fabrics International, Los Angeles *Also called Frm-Usa LLC (P-7525)*
Franchise Services Inc (PA)......E......949 348-5400
26722 Plaza Mission Viejo (92691) *(P-4299)*
Franco American Corporation......F......323 268-2345
1051 Monterey Pass Rd Monterey Park (91754) *(P-6163)*
Franco American Textile, Monterey Park *Also called Franco American Corporation (P-6163)*
Frandzel Share Robins Bloom Lc......D......323 852-1000
1000 Wilshire Blvd # 190 Los Angeles (90017) *(P-21559)*
FRANK D LANTERMAN REGIONAL CEN, Los Angeles *Also called Los Angles Cnty Dvlpmntal Svcs (P-21451)*
Frank Kams & Associates Inc......F......909 382-0047
242 W Hanna St Colton (92324) *(P-3414)*
Frank Russell Inc......F......661 324-5575
341 Pacific Ave Shafter (93263) *(P-8593)*
Frank S Smith Masonry Inc......D......909 468-0525
2830 Pomona Blvd Pomona (91768) *(P-1343)*
Frank Schipper Construction Co......E......805 963-4359
610 E Cota St Santa Barbara (93103) *(P-763)*
Frank Stubbs Co Inc......E......805 278-4300
1830 Eastman Ave Oxnard (93030) *(P-11106)*
Frankies Bikinis LLC......E......323 354-4133
4030 Del Rey Ave Venice (90292) *(P-3041)*
Franklin Renfro......F......909 984-5500
525 Brooks St Ontario (91762) *(P-7502)*
Franz Family Bakeries, Los Angeles *Also called United States Bakery (P-2039)*
Frasco Inc (PA)......D......818 848-3888
215 W Alameda Ave Ste 105 Burbank (91502) *(P-18276)*
Frasco Investigative Services, Burbank *Also called Frasco Inc (P-18276)*
Fraud Fighters Inc......E......800 576-6116
2600 Michelson Dr Ste 160 Irvine (92612) *(P-18277)*
Frazier Aviation Inc......E......818 898-1998
445 N Fox St San Fernando (91340) *(P-10332)*
Frear Consulting Inc......D......307 237-6060
907 Buena Vista Apt A San Clemente (92672) *(P-22556)*
Fred Browns Recovery Svcs Inc......D......310 519-8723
270 W 14th St San Pedro (90731) *(P-18520)*
Fred Leeds Properties......E......310 826-2466
3860 Crenshaw Blvd # 201 Los Angeles (90008) *(P-15871)*
Freddie Mac, Los Angeles *Also called Federal Home Loan Mrtg Corp (P-15190)*
FREDERICKA MANOR CARE CENTER, Glendale *Also called Front Prch Cmmnties Svcs - Cas (P-20585)*
FREDERICKA MANOR CARE CENTER, Glendale *Also called Front Prch Cmmnties Oprting Gr (P-20583)*
Free Conferencing Corporation......C......562 437-1411
4300 E Pacific Coast Hwy Long Beach (90804) *(P-12636)*
Freeconferencecall.com, Long Beach *Also called Free Conferencing Corporation (P-12636)*
Freedom Communications Inc......E......949 454-7300
22481 Aspan St El Toro (92630) *(P-3977)*
Freedom Designs Inc......C......805 582-0077
2241 N Madera Rd Simi Valley (93065) *(P-11107)*
Freedom Finishing, Los Angeles *Also called Freedom Wood Finishing Inc (P-2671)*
Freedom Forever, Temecula *Also called Freedom Solar Services (P-1071)*
Freedom Forever LLC......C......888 557-6431
43445 Bus Pk Dr Ste 104 Temecula (92590) *(P-1070)*
Freedom Newspapers Inc......F......714 796-7000
729 N Grand Ave Santa Ana (92701) *(P-3978)*
Freedom Painting Inc......E......562 696-0785
8822 Calmada Ave Whittier (90605) *(P-1179)*
Freedom Photonics LLC......E......805 967-4900
41 Aero Camino Santa Barbara (93117) *(P-9869)*
Freedom Properties, Hemet *Also called Casa-Pacifica Inc (P-22090)*
Freedom Properties Village, Hemet *Also called Casa-Pacifica Inc (P-22091)*
Freedom Properties-Hemet LLC......C......949 489-0430
27122 Paseo Espada Ste 1b San Juan Capistrano (92675) *(P-15668)*
Freedom Solar Services......C......888 557-6431
43445 Bus Pk Dr Ste 110 Temecula (92590) *(P-1071)*
Freedom Village Healthcare Ctr......C......949 472-4733
23442 El Toro Rd Bldg 2 Lake Forest (92630) *(P-20346)*
Freedom Wood Finishing Inc......F......213 534-6620
600 Wilshire Blvd # 1200 Los Angeles (90017) *(P-2671)*
Freeman Freeman & Smiley (PA)......D......310 398-6100
1888 Century Park E Fl 19 Los Angeles (90067) *(P-21560)*
Freeman Expositions LLC......C......714 254-3400
2170 S Towne Centre Pl Anaheim (92806) *(P-18521)*
Freeman Freeman & Smiley LLP, Los Angeles *Also called Freeman Freeman & Smiley (P-21560)*
Freestyle, Costa Mesa *Also called Sunburst Products Inc (P-11303)*
Freestyle Filmworks LLC......F......818 660-2888
1518 Talmadge St Los Angeles (90027) *(P-11276)*
Freestyle Sales Co Ltd Partnr......D......323 660-3460
12231 Florence Ave Santa Fe Springs (90670) *(P-13345)*
Freeway Insurance, Huntington Beach *Also called Confie Seguros Inc (P-15554)*
Freeway Insurance (PA)......C......714 252-2500
7711 Center Ave Ste 200 Huntington Beach (92647) *(P-15572)*
Freight Management Inc......D......714 632-1440
2900 E La Palma Ave Anaheim (92806) *(P-23222)*
Freightgate Inc......E......714 799-2833
10055 Slater Ave Ste 231 Fountain Valley (92708) *(P-17862)*
Fremantle Media, Burbank *Also called Prdctions N Fremantle Amer Inc (P-19328)*
Fremarc Designs, City of Industry *Also called Fremarc Industries Inc (P-3471)*
Fremarc Industries Inc (PA)......D......626 965-0802
18810 San Jose Ave City of Industry (91748) *(P-3471)*
French Hospital Medical Center (HQ)......B......805 543-5353
1911 Johnson Ave San Luis Obispo (93401) *(P-20773)*
French Tradition (PA)......F......310 719-9977
2413 Moreton St Torrance (90505) *(P-3472)*
Fresenius Med Care San Juan CP......D......949 240-0221
31001 Rncho Vejo Rd Ste 1 San Juan Capistrano (92675) *(P-21242)*
Fresh & Ready, San Fernando *Also called Lehman Foods Inc (P-2474)*
Fresh & Ready Foods LLC (PA)......D......818 837-7600
1145 Arroyo St Ste B San Fernando (91340) *(P-2437)*
Fresh Air Environmental Svcs......D......323 913-1965
10675 Rush St South El Monte (91733) *(P-1659)*
Fresh Grill LLC......C......714 444-2126
111 E Garry Ave Santa Ana (92707) *(P-18522)*
Fresh Griller, Costa Mesa *Also called Fgr 1 LLC (P-17855)*
Fresh Innovations LLC......E......805 483-2265
908 E 3rd St Oxnard (93030) *(P-2370)*
Fresh Packing Corporation......E......213 612-0136
4333 S Maywood Ave Vernon (90058) *(P-1850)*
Fresh Start Bakeries, Ontario *Also called Aspire Bakeries LLC (P-14670)*
Fresh Venture Farms LLC......D......805 754-4449
1181 S Wolff Rd Oxnard (93033) *(P-14)*
Fresh Venture Foods LLC......C......805 928-3374
1205 Craig Dr Santa Maria (93458) *(P-7935)*
Freshlunches Inc......E......818 885-1718
19431 Business Center Dr Northridge (91324) *(P-21791)*
Freshpoint Southern Cal Inc......C......626 855-1400
155 N Orange Ave City of Industry (91744) *(P-14630)*
Freshpoint Southern California, City of Industry *Also called Freshpoint Southern Cal Inc (P-14630)*
Freshrealm LLC (PA)......F......800 264-1297
34 N Palm St Ste 100 Ventura (93001) *(P-2438)*
Freshway Farms LLC......C......805 349-7170
2165 W Main St Santa Maria (93458) *(P-28)*
Freudenberg Medical LLC......C......626 814-9684
5050 Rivergrade Rd Baldwin Park (91706) *(P-10983)*
Freudenberg Medical LLC (HQ)......C......805 684-3304
1110 Mark Ave Carpinteria (93013) *(P-11108)*
Freudenberg-Nok General Partnr......C......714 834-0602
2041 E Wilshire Ave Santa Ana (92705) *(P-5337)*
Freund Baking, Commerce *Also called Oakhurst Industries Inc (P-2026)*
Frick Paper Company......C......323 726-8200
2164 N Batavia St Orange (92865) *(P-14209)*
Friction Materials LLC......C......248 362-3600
2525 W 190th St Torrance (90504) *(P-22557)*
Friday Flier, Canyon Lake *Also called Golding Publications (P-4625)*
Friedas Inc......D......714 826-6100
4465 Corporate Center Dr Los Alamitos (90720) *(P-14631)*
Friedas Specialty Produce, Los Alamitos *Also called Friedas Inc (P-14631)*
Friedl Axle Corporation......E......714 944-5749
2430 N Glassell St Ste Q Orange (92865) *(P-10061)*
Friedl Corporation......E......714 443-0122
1291 N Patt St Anaheim (92801) *(P-10062)*
Friedman Professional Mgt Co......D......714 842-1426
17752 Beach Blvd Side Huntington Beach (92647) *(P-19825)*
Friendly Hlls Cntry CLB Fndtio......C......562 698-0331
8500 Villaverde Dr Whittier (90605) *(P-19563)*
Friendly Village Cmnty Assn, Santa Clarita *Also called Friendly Vly Recrtl Assn Inc (P-22338)*
Friendly Vly Recrtl Assn Inc......E......661 252-3223
19345 Avenue Of The Oaks Santa Clarita (91321) *(P-22338)*
Friends Group Express Inc......D......909 346-6814
14520 Village Dr Apt 1013 Fontana (92337) *(P-12046)*
Friends of Cultural Center Inc......D......760 346-6505
73000 Fred Waring Dr Palm Desert (92260) *(P-19310)*
Frisco Baking Company Inc......C......323 225-6111
621 W Avenue 26 Los Angeles (90065) *(P-2002)*
Frito-Lay North America Inc......B......909 941-6214
9535 Archibald Ave Rancho Cucamonga (91730) *(P-14562)*
Frize Corporation......D......800 834-2127
16605 Gale Ave City of Industry (91745) *(P-698)*
Frm-Usa LLC......F......323 469-9006
6001 Santa Monica Blvd Los Angeles (90038) *(P-7525)*
Front Edge Technology Inc......E......626 856-8979
13455 Brooks Dr Ste A Baldwin Park (91706) *(P-9810)*
Front Line MGT Group Inc......D......310 209-3100
1100 Glendon Ave Ste 2000 Los Angeles (90024) *(P-23028)*
Front Porch Communities......D......909 626-3490
621 W Bonita Ave Claremont (91711) *(P-21428)*

ALPHABETIC

Employee Codes: A=Over 500 employees, B=251-500 C=101-250, D=51-100, E=20-50 F=10-19
2022 Southern California Business Directory and Buyers Guide
© Mergent Inc. 1-800-342-5647
1137

Front Prch Cmmnties Oprting Gr ... C ... 800 233-3709
800 N Brand Blvd Fl 19 Glendale (91203) ***(P-20583)***

Front Prch Cmmnties Svcs - Cas ... C ... 714 776-7150
1401 W Ball Rd Anaheim (92802) ***(P-20584)***

Front Prch Cmmnties Svcs - Cas (PA) ... **D ... 818 729-8100**
800 N Brand Blvd Fl 19 Glendale (91203) ***(P-20585)***

Front Prch Cmmnties Svcs - Cas ... C ... 909 626-1227
650 Harrison Ave Claremont (91711) ***(P-20586)***

Front Prch Cmmnties Svcs - Cas ... C ... 805 687-0793
3775 Modoc Rd Santa Barbara (93105) ***(P-20587)***

Front Prch Cmmnties Svcs - Cas ... D ... 626 570-5293
303 N Glenoaks Blvd # 100 Burbank (91502) ***(P-20588)***

Front Prch Cmmnties Svcs - Cas ... C ... 562 868-9761
11701 Studebaker Rd Norwalk (90650) ***(P-20589)***

Front Prch Cmmnties Svcs - Cas ... C ... 760 240-5051
11959 Apple Valley Rd Apple Valley (92308) ***(P-20347)***

Frontech N Fujitsu Amer Inc (HQ) ... **C ... 949 855-5500**
27121 Twne Cntre Dr Ste 1 Foothill Ranch (92610) ***(P-8314)***

Frontera Solutions Inc ... F ... 714 368-1631
1913 E 17th St Ste 210 Santa Ana (92705) ***(P-8937)***

Frontier California Inc ... B ... 760 342-0500
83793 Dr Carreon Blvd Indio (92201) ***(P-12637)***

Frontier California Inc ... B ... 805 925-0000
200 W Church St Santa Maria (93458) ***(P-12638)***

Frontier California Inc ... B ... 818 365-0542
510 Park Ave San Fernando (91340) ***(P-12639)***

Frontier California Inc ... B ... 760 872-0812
350 Lagoon St Bishop (93514) ***(P-12640)***

Frontier California Inc ... B ... 714 375-6713
7352 Slater Ave Huntington Beach (92647) ***(P-12641)***

Frontier California Inc ... B ... 805 372-6000
112 S Lakeview Canyon Rd Westlake Village (91362) ***(P-13723)***

Frontier California Inc ... B ... 805 372-6000
1 Wellpoint Way Westlake Village (91362) ***(P-12642)***

Frontier Communities, Ontario *Also called Shii LLC* ***(P-15998)***

Frontier Electronics Corp ... F ... 805 522-9998
667 Cochran St Simi Valley (93065) ***(P-9630)***

Frontier Engrg & Mfg Tech Inc ... E ... 562 606-2655
800 W 16th St Long Beach (90813) ***(P-8594)***

Frontier Logistics Services, Gardena *Also called F R T International Inc* ***(P-12204)***

Frontier Logistics Services, Ontario *Also called F R T International Inc* ***(P-12457)***

Frontier Logistics Services, Compton *Also called F R T International Inc* ***(P-12205)***

Frontier Mechanical Inc ... D ... 661 589-6203
6309 Seven Seas Ave Bakersfield (93308) ***(P-1072)***

Frontier Motel Inc ... D ... 760 876-5571
1008 S Main St Lone Pine (93545) ***(P-16450)***

Frontier Plumbing, Bakersfield *Also called Frontier Mechanical Inc* ***(P-1072)***

Frontier Technologies, Long Beach *Also called Frontier Engrg & Mfg Tech Inc* ***(P-8594)***

Frontiers Magazine, Los Angeles *Also called Frontiers Media LLC* ***(P-4173)***

Frontiers Media LLC ... E ... 323 930-3220
5657 Wilshire Blvd # 470 Los Angeles (90036) ***(P-4173)***

Frozen Bean Inc ... E ... 855 837-6936
9238 Bally Ct Rancho Cucamonga (91730) ***(P-2327)***

Frsport.com, Huntington Beach *Also called Sound Investment Group* ***(P-13091)***

Fruit Growers Supply Company (PA) ... **E ... 888 997-4855**
27770 N Entrmt Dr Fl 3 Flr 3 Valencia (91355) ***(P-3802)***

Fruit Growers Supply Company ... E ... 559 783-6383
934 W Scranton Ave Porterville (93257) ***(P-3803)***

Fruit Growers Supply Company ... E ... 559 592-6550
674 E Myer Ave Exeter (93221) ***(P-3804)***

Fry Reglet Corporation (PA) ... **D ... 800 237-9773**
14013 Marquardt Ave Santa Fe Springs (90670) ***(P-6307)***

Fs - Precision Tech Co LLC ... D ... 310 638-0595
3025 E Victoria St Compton (90221) ***(P-6417)***

FS Commercial Landscape Inc (PA) ... **D ... 951 360-7070**
5151 Pedley Rd Riverside (92509) ***(P-257)***

FS&k, Thousand Oaks *Also called Floyd Skeren & Kelly LLP* ***(P-21555)***

FSA Arlanza Child Dev Ctr (PA) ... **D ... 951 352-2810**
7801 Gramercy Pl Riverside (92503) ***(P-22018)***

Fsc, Rancho Cucamonga *Also called Fluorescent Supply Co Inc* ***(P-9084)***

Fscc, Santa Barbara *Also called Frank Schipper Construction Co* ***(P-763)***

FSI Coating Technologies Inc ... E ... 949 540-1140
45 Parker Ste 100 Irvine (92618) ***(P-5098)***

FSI Energy Services, Ontario *Also called Facility Shield Intl Inc* ***(P-13629)***

Fssi, Santa Ana *Also called Financial Statement Svcs Inc* ***(P-17132)***

Fst Sand & Gravel Inc ... E ... 951 277-8440
21780 Temescal Canyon Rd Corona (92883) ***(P-13305)***

Ft Textiles, Orange *Also called Fabtex Inc* ***(P-2599)***

Ft USA, Ontario *Also called Inqbrands Inc* ***(P-18188)***

Ft3 Tactical, Stanton *Also called Field Time Target Training LLC* ***(P-7427)***

Ftdi West Inc ... D ... 909 473-1111
3375 Enterprise Dr Bloomington (92316) ***(P-12207)***

Ftg Inc (PA) ... **F ... 562 865-9200**
12750 Center Court Dr S # 280 Cerritos (90703) ***(P-10063)***

Ftg Aerospace Inc (HQ) ... **E ... 818 407-4024**
20740 Marilla St Chatsworth (91311) ***(P-6380)***

Ftg Circuits Inc (HQ) ... **D ... 818 407-4024**
20750 Marilla St Chatsworth (91311) ***(P-9408)***

Fti Consulting Inc ... D ... 213 689-1200
350 S Grand Ave Ste 3000 Los Angeles (90071) ***(P-22558)***

Ftp Productions LLC (PA) ... **C ... 818 560-2977**
500 S Buena Vista St Burbank (91521) ***(P-19127)***

Ftsi, Monrovia *Also called Financial Tech Sltons Intl Inc* ***(P-23215)***

Fuel Cycle Inc (PA) ... **D ... 323 556-5400**
11859 Wilshire Blvd # 400 Los Angeles (90025) ***(P-17620)***

Fuel Injection Engineering Co ... F ... 949 360-0909
22892 Glenwood Dr Aliso Viejo (92656) ***(P-10064)***

Fuel50, Laguna Niguel *Also called Career Engagement Group LLC* ***(P-17574)***

Fuel50 Inc ... D ... 833 344-1103
30025 Alicia Pkwy 20-23 Laguna Niguel (92677) ***(P-17621)***

Fueling and Service Tech Inc ... D ... 714 523-0194
7050 Village Dr Ste D Buena Park (90621) ***(P-13902)***

Fugro Roadware Inc ... D ... 949 536-5175
17752 Sky Park Cir Irvine (92614) ***(P-18933)***

Fuji Food Products Inc (PA) ... **D ... 562 404-2590**
14420 Bloomfield Ave Santa Fe Springs (90670) ***(P-2439)***

Fuji Natural Foods Inc (HQ) ... **D ... 909 947-1008**
13500 S Hamner Ave Ontario (91761) ***(P-2440)***

Fujifilm Irvine Scientific Inc (HQ) ... **E ... 949 261-7800**
1830 E Warner Ave Santa Ana (92705) ***(P-4934)***

Fujitec America Inc ... D ... 310 464-8270
12170 Mora Dr Ste 1 Santa Fe Springs (90670) ***(P-23029)***

Fujitsu Glovia Inc (HQ) ... **C ... 310 563-7000**
200 Continental Blvd Fl 3 El Segundo (90245) ***(P-17622)***

Fulcrum Microsystems Inc ... D ... 818 871-8100
26630 Agoura Rd Calabasas (91302) ***(P-9509)***

Fulghum Fibres Inc (HQ) ... **F ... 706 651-1000**
333 S Grand Ave Ste 4100 Los Angeles (90071) ***(P-3210)***

Fulham Co Inc ... E ... 323 779-2980
12705 S Van Ness Ave Hawthorne (90250) ***(P-8872)***

Full Circle Distribution, Huntington Beach *Also called Madrid Pro Designs Inc* ***(P-14084)***

Fullerton College Bookstore, Fullerton *Also called North Ornge Cnty Cmnty Cllege* ***(P-13422)***

Fullerton Hlthcare Wllness CNT ... C ... 714 992-5701
2222 N Harbor Blvd Fullerton (92835) ***(P-20348)***

Fullerton Orthpd Srgery Med Gr ... D ... 714 879-0050
680 Langsdorf Dr Fullerton (92831) ***(P-19826)***

Fullerton Printing Inc ... F ... 714 870-7500
315 N Lemon St Fullerton (92832) ***(P-4300)***

Fullmer Construction ... C ... 909 947-9467
1725 S Grove Ave Ontario (91761) ***(P-699)***

Fullscreen Inc (HQ) ... **C ... 310 202-3333**
12180 Millennium Playa Vista (90094) ***(P-17013)***

Fulltone Musical Products Inc ... F ... 310 204-0155
11018 Washington Blvd Culver City (90232) ***(P-11343)***

Fulwider and Patton LLP ... D ... 310 824-5555
111 W Ocean Blvd Long Beach (90802) ***(P-21561)***

Fume-A-Pest & Termite Control, Encino *Also called A-Able Inc* ***(P-17196)***

Fun Flex, Big Bear Lake *Also called Big Bear Bowling Barn Inc* ***(P-1639)***

Fun Properties Inc (PA) ... **D ... 310 787-4500**
2645 Maricopa St Torrance (90503) ***(P-6480)***

Funai Corporation Inc (HQ) ... **E ... 201 806-7635**
12489 Lakeland Rd Santa Fe Springs (90670) ***(P-9176)***

Fundamental Tech Intl Inc ... E ... 562 595-0661
2900 E 29th St Long Beach (90806) ***(P-10695)***

Fundamntal Chrstn Endavors Inc ... D ... 760 257-3503
49191 Cherokee Rd Newberry Springs (92365) ***(P-16820)***

Fungs Village Inc ... E ... 323 881-1600
5339 E Washington Blvd Commerce (90040) ***(P-2376)***

Funimation Entertainment, Culver City *Also called Funimation Global Group LLC* ***(P-19128)***

Funimation Global Group LLC (HQ) ... **C ... 972 355-7300**
10202 Washington Blvd Culver City (90232) ***(P-19128)***

Funny or Die Inc ... E ... 650 461-3929
1013 N Orange Dr Los Angeles (90038) ***(P-18179)***

Funny-Bunny Inc (PA) ... **D ... 714 957-1114**
1513b E Saint Gertrude Pl Santa Ana (92705) ***(P-2810)***

Funtastic Factory Inc ... F ... 562 777-1140
19703 Meadows Cir Cerritos (90703) ***(P-8595)***

Fur Accents LLC ... F ... 714 403-5286
349 W Grove Ave Orange (92865) ***(P-3048)***

Furnace Creek Ranch & Inn, Death Valley *Also called Xanterra Parks & Resorts Inc* ***(P-16807)***

Furnace Pros, Orange *Also called Lochaber Cornwall Inc* ***(P-8095)***

Furniture America Cal Inc (PA) ... **D ... 909 718-7276**
19605 E Walnut Dr N City of Industry (91789) ***(P-13137)***

Furniture America California, City of Industry *Also called Furniture America Cal Inc* ***(P-13137)***

Furniture Solutions Inc ... E ... 714 666-0424
1347 N Blue Gum St Anaheim (92806) ***(P-3585)***

Furniture Technics Inc ... E ... 562 802-0261
2900 Supply Ave Commerce (90040) ***(P-3473)***

Furniture Techniques, Commerce *Also called Furniture Technics Inc* ***(P-3473)***

Furniture Technologies Inc ... E ... 760 246-9180
17227 Columbus St Adelanto (92301) ***(P-3219)***

Furniture Trnsp Systems Inc ... C ... 909 869-1200
3100 Pomona Blvd Pomona (91768) ***(P-12459)***

Furst, Los Angeles *Also called Lf Sportswear Inc* ***(P-2855)***

Fuscoe Engineering Inc (PA) ... **D ... 949 474-1960**
16795 Von Karman Ave # 100 Irvine (92606) ***(P-22559)***

Fuse LLC (HQ) ... **C ... 323 256-8900**
700 N Central Ave Ste 600 Glendale (91203) ***(P-18523)***

Fuse Media, Glendale *Also called Fuse LLC* ***(P-18523)***

Fusefx LLC ... B ... 818 237-5052
14823 Califa St Van Nuys (91411) ***(P-19236)***

Fusion Finish LLC (PA) ... **E ... 562 773-5303**
19200 S Reyes Ave Compton (90221) ***(P-7366)***

Fusion Sign & Design Inc (PA) ... **C ... 877 477-8777**
680 Columbia Ave Riverside (92507) ***(P-11557)***

Futek Advanced Sensor Tech Inc ... C ... 949 465-0900
10 Thomas Irvine (92618) ***(P-10696)***

Future Commodities Intl Inc ... E ... 909 987-4258
1425 S Campus Ave Ontario (91761) ***(P-8069)***

Future Foam Inc ... E ... 714 871-2344
2451 Cypress Way Fullerton (92831) ***(P-5507)***

Future Foam Inc ... C ... 714 459-9971
2441 Cypress Way Fullerton (92831) ***(P-5508)***

Mergent e-mail: customerrelations@mergent.com
1138
2022 Southern California Business Directory and Buyers Guide
(P-0000) Products & Services Section entry number
(PA)=Parent Co (HQ)=Headquarters (DH)=Div Headquarters

Future Health Company ....E....424 244-2221
4404 Chaumont Rd Woodland Hills (91364) *(P-14377)*
Future Tech Metals Inc ....E....951 781-4801
719 Palmyrita Ave Riverside (92507) *(P-8596)*
Futuredontics Inc (HQ) ....**C....310 215-6400**
11209 National Blvd # 409 Los Angeles (90064) *(P-20178)*
Futureflite Inc ....E....818 653-2145
806 Calle Plano Camarillo (93012) *(P-3624)*
Futurestitch Inc ....F....760 707-2003
144 Avenida Serra San Clemente (92672) *(P-2634)*
Fx Networks LLC ....C....310 369-1000
10201 W Pico Blvd Bldg 10 Los Angeles (90064) *(P-12768)*
Fxc Corporation ....D....714 557-8032
3050 Red Hill Ave Costa Mesa (92626) *(P-3197)*
Fxc Corporation (PA) ....**E....714 556-7400**
3050 Red Hill Ave Costa Mesa (92626) *(P-6518)*
Fxp Technologies, Brea *Also called S&B Industry Inc (P-5809)*
Fyeo Apparel Inc ....E....213 278-0435
757 E 14th Pl Los Angeles (90021) *(P-21429)*
Fziomed Inc (PA) ....**E....805 546-0610**
231 Bonetti Dr San Luis Obispo (93401) *(P-10984)*
G & G Door Products Inc ....E....714 228-2008
7600 Stage Rd Buena Park (90621) *(P-6701)*
G & G Quality Case Co Inc ....D....323 233-2482
2025 E 25th St Vernon (90058) *(P-5891)*
G & H Precision Inc ....F....818 982-3873
11950 Vose St North Hollywood (91605) *(P-8597)*
G & I Industries, Baldwin Park *Also called G & I Islas Industries Inc (P-7936)*
G & I Islas Industries Inc (PA) ....**E....626 960-5020**
12860 Schabarum Ave Baldwin Park (91706) *(P-7936)*
G & L Musical Instruments, Fullerton *Also called Bbe Sound Inc (P-11340)*
G & P Group Inc ....F....323 268-2686
13842 Bettencourt St Cerritos (90703) *(P-2112)*
G A Systems, Orange *Also called SA Serving Lines Inc (P-6906)*
G A Systems Inc ....E....714 848-7529
226 W Carleton Ave Orange (92867) *(P-8382)*
G B Remanufacturing Inc ....D....562 272-7333
2040 E Cherry Indus Cir Long Beach (90805) *(P-5648)*
G Brothers Construction Inc ....E....714 590-3070
7070 Patterson Dr Garden Grove (92841) *(P-1376)*
G C Landscape Inc ....E....714 535-5640
6465 Wayazpa Blvd 3110 Anaheim (92805) *(P-306)*
G C Pallets Inc ....E....909 357-8515
5490 26th St Riverside (92509) *(P-3389)*
G C S, Torrance *Also called Global Comm Semiconductors LLC (P-9510)*
G E Shell Core Co ....E....323 773-4242
8346 Salt Lake Ave Cudahy (90201) *(P-7802)*
G F Cole Corporation (PA) ....**E....310 320-0601**
21735 S Western Ave Torrance (90501) *(P-5338)*
G F I, Vernon *Also called Good Fellas Industries Inc (P-1662)*
G Girl Clothing, Vernon *Also called LAT LLC (P-2967)*
G K Tool Corp ....D....626 338-7300
4265 Puente Ave Baldwin Park (91706) *(P-13807)*
G Kagan and Sons Inc (PA) ....**E....323 583-1400**
3957 S Hill St Los Angeles (90037) *(P-2572)*
G M I, Anaheim *Also called Gear Manufacturing Inc (P-10334)*
G M S, Rancho Cucamonga *Also called General Micro Systems Inc (P-13401)*
G O Pallets Inc ....F....909 823-4663
15642 Slover Ave Fontana (92337) *(P-3390)*
G P H Medical Services, Beverly Hills *Also called GPh Medical & Legal Services (P-20364)*
G P Manufacturing Inc ....F....714 974-0288
541 W Briardale Ave Orange (92865) *(P-8598)*
G P Resources, Compton *Also called General Petroleum Corporation (P-14804)*
G P S, Taft *Also called General Production Svc Cal Inc (P-949)*
G Powell Electric ....E....909 865-2291
1020 Price Ave Pomona (91767) *(P-19012)*
G Printing Inc ....E....818 246-1156
1815 Ayers Way Burbank (91501) *(P-4516)*
G R C, Chatsworth *Also called General Ribbon Corp (P-11478)*
G S C Ball, Commerce *Also called Grocers Specialty Company (P-14470)*
G S N, Santa Monica *Also called Game Show Network Music LLC (P-12769)*
G S T, Cerritos *Also called Golden Star Technology Inc (P-18147)*
G T C, Whittier *Also called General Transistor Corporation (P-13724)*
G T Water Products Inc ....F....805 529-2900
5239 N Commerce Ave Moorpark (93021) *(P-6561)*
G W Maintenance Inc (PA) ....**D....714 541-2211**
1101 E 6th St Santa Ana (92701) *(P-13984)*
G W Murphy Cnstr Co Inc ....C....818 362-8391
15901 Olden St Sylmar (91342) *(P-764)*
G W Surfaces (PA) ....**D....805 642-5004**
2432 Palma Dr Ventura (93003) *(P-1660)*
G&A Apparel Group ....E....323 234-1746
3610 S Broadway Los Angeles (90007) *(P-3173)*
G&A Bias Les, Los Angeles *Also called G&A Apparel Group (P-3173)*
G-2 Graphic Service Inc ....D....818 623-3100
5510 Cleon Ave North Hollywood (91601) *(P-4517)*
G-M Enterprises, Corona *Also called Jhawar Industries LLC (P-8092)*
G3 Group La Inc (PA) ....**D....323 848-4186**
2500 Townsgate Rd Thousand Oaks (91361) *(P-765)*
G4s Government Services, Anaheim *Also called G4s Justice Services LLC (P-18380)*
G4s Justice Services LLC ....D....800 589-6003
1290 N Hancock St Ste 103 Anaheim (92807) *(P-18380)*
GA Services LLC ....E....949 752-6515
1681 Kettering Irvine (92614) *(P-18180)*
Gabe Inc ....D....949 679-2727
300 Spectrum Center Dr # 40 Irvine (92618) *(P-23443)*
Gable House Inc ....D....310 378-2265
22501 Hawthorne Blvd Torrance (90505) *(P-19398)*
Gable House Bowl, Torrance *Also called Gable House Inc (P-19398)*
Gabriel Container (PA) ....**C....562 699-1051**
8844 Millergrove Dr Santa Fe Springs (90670) *(P-3805)*
Gac Brokerage Inc (PA) ....**D....714 846-2732**
4792 Tiara Dr Apt 101 Huntington Beach (92649) *(P-16451)*
Gachupin Enterprises LLC ....F....714 375-4111
5671 Engineer Dr Huntington Beach (92649) *(P-4518)*
GAF Materials, Shafter *Also called Standard Industries Inc (P-13329)*
Gaffoglio Fmly Mtlcrafters Inc (PA) ....**C....714 444-2000**
11161 Slater Ave Fountain Valley (92708) *(P-5953)*
Gail Materials Inc ....E....951 667-6106
10060 Dawson Canyon Rd Corona (92883) *(P-571)*
Gainey Ceramics Inc ....E....909 596-4464
1200 Arrow Hwy La Verne (91750) *(P-6003)*
Gainey Vineyard ....E....805 688-0558
3950 E Highway 246 Santa Ynez (93460) *(P-2187)*
Gaju Market Corporation ....C....213 382-9444
450 S Western Ave Los Angeles (90020) *(P-14929)*
GAI Manufacturing Co LLC ....F....626 443-8616
3380 Gilman Rd El Monte (91732) *(P-7678)*
Gala Deluxe Corporation (PA) ....**E....626 283-4804**
979 S Meridian Ave Alhambra (91803) *(P-4301)*
Galactic Co LLC (HQ) ....**B....661 824-6600**
16555 Spceship Landing Wa Mojave (93501) *(P-10514)*
Galassos Bakery (PA) ....**C....951 360-1211**
10820 San Sevaine Way Jurupa Valley (91752) *(P-14688)*
Galaxy Bearing Company, Valencia *Also called Galaxy Die and Engineering Inc (P-6408)*
Galaxy Brazing Co Inc ....E....562 946-9039
10015 Freeman Ave Santa Fe Springs (90670) *(P-18978)*
Galaxy Die and Engineering Inc ....E....661 775-9301
24910 Avenue Tibbitts Valencia (91355) *(P-6408)*
Galaxy Enterprises Inc ....E....323 728-3980
5411 Sheila St Commerce (90040) *(P-11673)*
Galaxy Medical, Commerce *Also called Galaxy Enterprises Inc (P-11673)*
Gale Banks Engineering ....C....626 969-9600
546 S Duggan Ave Azusa (91702) *(P-7595)*
Gale/Triangle, San Pedro *Also called Performance Team LLC (P-12230)*
Gale/Triangle Inc (PA) ....**D....562 741-1300**
12816 Shoemaker Ave Santa Fe Springs (90670) *(P-11967)*
Gali Corporation ....E....310 477-1224
2301 Pontius Ave Los Angeles (90064) *(P-10333)*
Galileo Technologies Corp ....D....626 447-3100
11800 Clark St Arcadia (91006) *(P-403)*
Galkos Construction Inc (PA) ....**C....714 373-8545**
15262 Pipeline Ln Huntington Beach (92649) *(P-16956)*
Gallagher Pediatric Therapy, Fullerton *Also called Therapy For Kids Inc (P-21354)*
Gallagher Rental Inc ....E....714 690-1559
15701 Heron Ave La Mirada (90638) *(P-9134)*
Galleher LLC (PA) ....**C....562 944-8885**
9303 Greenleaf Ave Santa Fe Springs (90670) *(P-13170)*
Gallup & Stribling Orchids LLC ....E....805 684-1998
3450 Via Real Carpinteria (93013) *(P-14883)*
Gallup and Stribling Holdings, Carpinteria *Also called Gallup & Stribling Orchids LLC (P-14883)*
Galpin Ford, North Hills *Also called Galpin Motors Inc (P-18832)*
Galpin Motors Inc (PA) ....**B....818 787-3800**
15505 Roscoe Blvd North Hills (91343) *(P-18832)*
Galtech Computer Corporation ....E....805 376-1060
501 Flynn Rd Camarillo (93012) *(P-3586)*
Galtech International, Camarillo *Also called Galtech Computer Corporation (P-3586)*
Gama Contracting Services Inc ....C....626 442-7200
1835 Floradale Ave South El Monte (91733) *(P-13859)*
Gamboa Service Inc ....D....714 966-5325
2116 S Wright St Santa Ana (92705) *(P-17244)*
Gambol Industries Inc ....E....562 901-2470
1825 W Pier D St Long Beach (90802) *(P-10464)*
Game Show Network Music LLC (HQ) ....**B....310 255-6800**
2150 Colorado Ave Ste 100 Santa Monica (90404) *(P-12769)*
Gamebreaker Inc (PA) ....**E....818 224-7424**
31324 Via Colinas Ste 102 Westlake Village (91362) *(P-11418)*
Gamecloud Studios Inc ....E....951 677-2345
30111 Tech Dr Ste 110 Murrieta (92563) *(P-17863)*
Gamemine LLC ....E....310 310-3105
2341 Wilson Ave Venice (90291) *(P-17864)*
Gamma, Vernon *Also called Rotax Incorporated (P-2990)*
Gamma Aerospace LLC ....E....310 532-4480
1415 W 178th St Gardena (90248) *(P-8599)*
Gammil Services, Baldwin Park *Also called Gammill Electric Inc (P-1258)*
Gammill Electric Inc ....F....626 812-4515
16224 Arrow Hwy Baldwin Park (91706) *(P-1258)*
Gan Limited ....B....702 964-5777
400 Spectrum Center Dr # 19 Irvine (92618) *(P-17623)*
Ganahl Lumber Company ....D....951 278-4000
150 W Blaine St Corona (92878) *(P-3250)*
Ganahl Lumber Company ....D....714 522-2864
6586 Beach Blvd Buena Park (90621) *(P-13209)*
Ganahl Lumber Company ....D....562 346-2100
10742 Los Alamitos Blvd Los Alamitos (90720) *(P-13210)*
Ganahl Lumber Company ....D....949 830-3600
23132 Orange Ave Lake Forest (92630) *(P-13211)*
Gander Publishing Inc ....E....805 541-5523
450 Front St Avila Beach (93424) *(P-4129)*
Gang Tyre Ramer & Brown Inc ....E....310 777-7158
132 S Rodeo Dr Ste 306 Beverly Hills (90212) *(P-21562)*
Gannett Stllite Info Ntwrk LLC ....E....310 846-5870
6060 Center Dr Los Angeles (90045) *(P-3979)*

ALPHABETIC

Employee Codes: A=Over 500 employees, B=251-500
C=101-250, D=51-100, E=20-50 F=10-19
2022 Southern California Business
Directory and Buyers Guide
© Mergent Inc. 1-800-342-5647
1139

Gano Excel (usa) Inc ....D......626 338-8081
  15439 Dupont Ave Chino (91710) *(P-14689)*
Gans Ink and Supply Co Inc (PA) ....E......**323 264-2200**
  1441 Boyd St Los Angeles (90033) *(P-5203)*
Ganz USA LLC ....D......323 629-9871
  307 S Sadler Ave 1d Los Angeles (90022) *(P-14930)*
Ganz USA LLC ....D......818 901-0077
  16525 Sherman Way Ste C5 Van Nuys (91406) *(P-23223)*
Gaps, Port Hueneme *Also called Global Auto Proc Svcs Inc (P-18934)*
Gar Bennett LLC ....E......559 582-9336
  955 S Commerce Way Lemoore (93245) *(P-1073)*
Gar Enterprises (PA) ....D......**626 574-1175**
  418 E Live Oak Ave Arcadia (91006) *(P-13398)*
Gar Enterprises ....E......909 985-4575
  1396 W 9th St Upland (91786) *(P-9714)*
Garage Equipment Supply Inc ....F......805 530-0027
  16000 Ventura Blvd # 1000 Encino (91436) *(P-7979)*
Garage Team Mazda, Costa Mesa *Also called Team Garage LLC (P-17061)*
Garagecoatings.com, Anaheim *Also called Versatile Building Pdts LLC (P-1461)*
Garcia Roofing Inc ....E......661 325-5736
  201 Mount Vernon Ave Bakersfield (93307) *(P-1486)*
Gard Inc ....E......714 738-5891
  524 E Walnut Ave Fullerton (92832) *(P-6842)*
Garda CL West Inc (HQ) ....B......**213 383-3611**
  1612 W Pico Blvd Los Angeles (90015) *(P-18278)*
Garden Crest Cnvlscent Hosp In ....D......323 663-8281
  909 Lucile Ave Los Angeles (90026) *(P-20349)*
Garden Crest Rtrment Residence, Los Angeles *Also called Garden Crest Cnvlscent Hosp In (P-20349)*
Garden Grove Advanced Imaging ....C......310 445-2800
  1510 Cotner Ave Los Angeles (90025) *(P-19827)*
GARDEN GROVE HOSPITAL, Garden Grove *Also called Kenneth Corp (P-20824)*
Garden Grove Medical Investors (HQ) ....D......**714 534-1041**
  12332 Garden Grove Blvd Garden Grove (92843) *(P-20350)*
Garden Grove Post Acute, Garden Grove *Also called In Garden Grove Cnvlscent Hosp (P-20598)*
Garden Grove Rehabilitation, Garden Grove *Also called Garden Grove Medical Investors (P-20350)*
Garden Grove Unified Schl Dst ....D......714 663-6101
  12381 Dale St Garden Grove (92841) *(P-4130)*
Garden Grove Unified Schl Dst ....D......714 663-6185
  8211 Lampson Ave Garden Grove (92841) *(P-17245)*
Garden Medical Offices, Downey *Also called Kaiser Foundation Hospitals (P-19898)*
Garden Pals Inc ....E......909 605-0200
  21753 Birch Hill Dr Diamond Bar (91765) *(P-6481)*
Garden View Inc ....E......626 303-4043
  417 E Huntington Dr Monrovia (91016) *(P-258)*
Garden View Care Center Inc ....E......626 962-7095
  14475 Garden View Ln Baldwin Park (91706) *(P-20351)*
Gardena Convalescent Center, Santa Fe Springs *Also called B & E Convalescent Center Inc (P-20557)*
Gardena Flores 310 323-4570
  14165 Purche Ave Gardena (90249) *(P-20352)*
Gardena Hospital LP ....A......310 532-4200
  1145 W Redondo Beach Blvd Gardena (90247) *(P-20774)*
Gardena Medical Offices, Gardena *Also called Kaiser Foundation Hospitals (P-20813)*
Gardena Municipal Bus Lines, Gardena *Also called City of Gardena (P-11803)*
Gardena Retirement Center Inc ....D......310 327-4091
  14741 S Vermont Ave Gardena (90247) *(P-20353)*
Gardena Textile Inc ....E......310 327-5060
  245 W 135th St Los Angeles (90061) *(P-2635)*
Gardena Valley News Inc ....E......310 329-6351
  15005 S Vermont Ave Gardena (90247) *(P-3980)*
Gardner Systems Inc ....F......714 668-9018
  3321 S Yale St Santa Ana (92704) *(P-10658)*
Gardner Trucking Inc (HQ) ....B......**909 563-5606**
  1219 E Elm St Ontario (91761) *(P-12047)*
Garfield Imaging Center Inc 626 572-0912
  555 N Garfield Ave Monterey Park (91754) *(P-19828)*
Garhauer Marine Corporation ....E......909 985-9993
  1062 W 9th St Upland (91786) *(P-6519)*
Garlic Company ....C......661 393-4212
  18602 Zerker Rd Shafter (93263) *(P-6)*
Garmin International Inc ....D......909 444-5000
  135 S State College Blvd # 110 Brea (92821) *(P-10589)*
Garmon Corporation ....C......951 296-6308
  27461 Via Industria Temecula (92590) *(P-11674)*
Garner Holt Productions Inc ....E......909 799-3030
  1255 Research Dr Redlands (92374) *(P-8155)*
Garrett J Gentry Gen Engrg Inc ....D......909 693-3391
  1297 W 9th St Upland (91786) *(P-22560)*
Garrett Precision Inc ....F......949 855-9710
  25082 La Suen Rd Laguna Hills (92653) *(P-8600)*
Garrett Transportation I Inc (HQ) ....C......**973 455-2000**
  2525 W 190th St Torrance (90504) *(P-10215)*
Garris Plastering, Orange *Also called Padilla Construction Company (P-1393)*
Garrison Family Med Group Inc ....D......661 947-7100
  41210 11th St W Ste K Palmdale (93551) *(P-19829)*
Garrison Manufacturing Inc ....E......714 549-4880
  3320 S Yale St Santa Ana (92704) *(P-10065)*
Gary Bale Redi-Mix Con Inc ....D......949 786-9441
  16131 Construction Cir W Irvine (92606) *(P-6091)*
Gary Cardiff Enterprises Inc ....D......760 568-1403
  75255 Sheryl Ave Palm Desert (92211) *(P-11869)*
Gary Siposs Inc ....F......714 557-3830
  633 Young St Santa Ana (92705) *(P-3871)*
Gary Steel Division, Santa Fe Springs *Also called Kloeckner Metals Corporation (P-13575)*
Gary's of California, Granada Hills *Also called Garys Leather Inc (P-5907)*

Garys Leather Inc ....F......818 831-9977
  12644 Bradford Pl Granada Hills (91344) *(P-5907)*
GAS COMPANY, THE, Los Angeles *Also called Southern California Gas Co (P-12866)*
Gasket Manufacturing Co ....E......310 217-5600
  8427 Secura Way Santa Fe Springs (90670) *(P-5339)*
Gasket Manufacturing Engrg Inc ....F......310 217-5600
  8427 Secura Way Santa Fe Springs (90670) *(P-7146)*
Gasketfab Division, Torrance *Also called Industrial Gasket and Sup Co (P-5342)*
Gat - Arln Ground Support Inc ....D......818 847-9127
  2627 N Hollywood Way Burbank (91505) *(P-12415)*
Gate City Beverage Distrs (PA) ....B......909 799-0281
  2505 Steele Rd San Bernardino (92408) *(P-14825)*
Gate Three Healthcare LLC ....C......949 770-3348
  24962 Calle Aragon Laguna Hills (92637) *(P-20354)*
Gatehouse Media LLC ....E......760 241-7744
  13891 Park Ave Victorville (92392) *(P-3981)*
Gatehouse Msi LLC ....E......562 623-3000
  15511 Carmenita Rd Santa Fe Springs (90670) *(P-1437)*
Gatekeeper Systems Inc (PA) 949 268-1414
  90 Icon Foothill Ranch (92610) *(P-9870)*
Gateway Inc (HQ) ....C......**949 471-7000**
  7565 Irvine Center Dr # 150 Irvine (92618) *(P-8156)*
Gateway Hardware, Inyokern *Also called Herbert Rizzardini (P-1967)*
Gateway Home Realty, Brea *Also called American Financial Network Inc (P-15174)*
Gateway Manufacturing LLC ....E......949 471-7000
  7565 Irvine Center Dr Irvine (92618) *(P-8224)*
Gateway Post Acute, Porterville *Also called Valley Careidence Opco LLC (P-20494)*
Gateway US Retail Inc ....D......949 471-7000
  7565 Irvine Center Dr Irvine (92618) *(P-8157)*
Gateways Hosp Mental Hlth Ctr ....D......323 644-2026
  340 N Madison Ave Los Angeles (90004) *(P-20775)*
Gateways Hosp Mental Hlth Ctr (PA) 323 644-2000
  1891 Effie St Los Angeles (90026) *(P-21019)*
Gavia, Vernon *Also called F Gavina & Sons Inc (P-2353)*
Gavial Engineering & Mfg, Santa Maria *Also called Gavial Holdings Inc (P-9715)*
Gavial Engineering & Mfg Inc ....E......805 614-0060
  1435 W Mccoy Ln Santa Maria (93455) *(P-9409)*
Gavial Holdings Inc (PA) ....F......805 614-0060
  1435 W Mccoy Ln Santa Maria (93455) *(P-9715)*
Gavin De Becker & Assoc GP Inc ....C......818 505-0177
  350 N Glendale Ave # 517 Glendale (91206) *(P-23224)*
Gaylord's Meat Co, Fullerton *Also called Gaylords HRI Meats (P-1712)*
Gaylords HRI Meats ....F......714 526-2278
  1100 E Ash Ave Ste C Fullerton (92831) *(P-1712)*
Gaze USA Inc ....E......213 622-0022
  1665 Mateo St Los Angeles (90021) *(P-2945)*
Gaze USA Inc ....F......213 622-0022
  1665 Mateo St Los Angeles (90021) *(P-2884)*
Gazette Newspapers Inc ....E......562 433-2000
  5225 E 2nd St Long Beach (90803) *(P-3982)*
Gbc Concrete Masnry Cnstr Inc ....C......951 245-2355
  561 Birch St Lake Elsinore (92530) *(P-1344)*
GBF Enterprises Inc ....E......714 979-7131
  2709 Halladay St Santa Ana (92705) *(P-8601)*
Gbl Systems Corporation ....E......805 987-4345
  760 Paseo Camarillo # 401 Camarillo (93010) *(P-18032)*
Gbm, Alhambra *Also called Gracing Brand Management Inc (P-3042)*
GBS Financial Corp ....D......310 937-0073
  904 Manhattan Ave Ste 3 Manhattan Beach (90266) *(P-18524)*
GBS Linens Inc (PA) ....D......**714 778-6448**
  305 N Muller St Anaheim (92801) *(P-16853)*
GBS Party Linens, Anaheim *Also called GBS Linens Inc (P-16853)*
GBT Inc ....C......626 854-9338
  17358 Railroad St City of Industry (91748) *(P-13399)*
Gc Aero Inc ....F......310 539-7600
  21143 Hawthorne Blvd # 13 Torrance (90503) *(P-6570)*
Gc International Inc (PA) ....E......**805 389-4631**
  4671 Calle Carga Camarillo (93012) *(P-6396)*
Gc International Inc ....F......805 389-4631
  4671 Calle Carga Camarillo (93012) *(P-9218)*
Gc Technology LLC (PA) ....F......310 633-5095
  1223 Wilshire Blvd 425 Santa Monica (90403) *(P-9275)*
Gcg Corporation ....E......818 247-8508
  608 Ruberta Ave Glendale (91201) *(P-7261)*
Gcg Precision Metal Finishing, Glendale *Also called Gcg Corporation (P-7261)*
GCI Construction Inc ....E......714 957-0233
  1031 Calle Recodo Ste D San Clemente (92673) *(P-880)*
Gcl W, Los Angeles *Also called Garda CL West Inc (P-18278)*
Gcn Supply LLC ....E......909 643-4603
  9070 Bridgeport Pl Rancho Cucamonga (91730) *(P-6996)*
GCR Tires & Service 185, Fontana *Also called Bridgestone Americas (P-18809)*
GD Heil Inc ....C......714 687-9100
  1031 Segovia Cir Placentia (92870) *(P-1614)*
Gdr Group Inc ....D......949 453-8818
  3 Park Plz Ste 1700 Irvine (92614) *(P-18181)*
GE Wind Energy LLC (HQ) ....B......**661 822-6835**
  13000 Jameson Rd Tehachapi (93561) *(P-7585)*
GE Wind Energy LLC ....D......661 823-6423
  13681 Chantico Rd Tehachapi (93561) *(P-7586)*
Gear Manufacturing Inc ....E......714 792-2895
  3701 E Miraloma Ave Anaheim (92806) *(P-10334)*
Gear Technology, Rancho Cucamonga *Also called Marino Enterprises Inc (P-10372)*
Gearment Inc ....D......323 822-9999
  14801 Able Ln Ste 102 Huntington Beach (92647) *(P-2672)*
Geartech Services Inc ....F......323 309-7861
  1640 N Dillon St Los Angeles (90026) *(P-8602)*
Geary Pacific Corporation ....E......626 513-0273
  16037 E Foothill Blvd Irwindale (91702) *(P-13828)*

Geary Pacific Supply, Irwindale *Also called Geary Pacific Corporation* (P-13828)
Gebbs Healthcare Solutions (HQ) .... C 201 227-0088
  600 Corporate Pointe # 1200 Culver City (90230) (P-23444)
Gebbs Software Intl Inc .... D 201 227-0088
  4640 Admiralty Way Fl 9 Marina Del Rey (90292) (P-18182)
Gebe Electronic Services Inc .... F 323 731-2439
  4112 W Jefferson Blvd Los Angeles (90016) (P-7367)
Gedney Foods Company .... C 952 448-2612
  12243 Branford St Sun Valley (91352) (P-1887)
Geek Squad Inc .... D 562 402-1555
  12989 Park Plaza Dr Cerritos (90703) (P-18183)
Geeriraj Inc .... E 760 244-6149
  7042 Santa Fe Ave E A1 Hesperia (92345) (P-9410)
Gehr Development New York LLC, Commerce *Also called Gehr Hospitality New York LLC* (P-15669)
Gehr Group, Commerce *Also called Gehr Industries Inc* (P-6350)
Gehr Group Inc (PA) .... C 323 728-5558
  7400 E Slauson Ave Commerce (90040) (P-16452)
Gehr Hospitality LLC (HQ) .... D 323 728-5558
  1999 Avenue Of The Stars Los Angeles (90067) (P-15264)
Gehr Hospitality New York LLC (HQ) .... D 323 728-5558
  7400 E Slauson Ave Commerce (90040) (P-15669)
Gehr Industries Inc (HQ) .... C 323 728-5558
  7400 E Slauson Ave Commerce (90040) (P-6350)
Gehry Partners LLP .... C 310 482-3000
  12541 Beatrice St Los Angeles (90066) (P-22715)
Gehry Technologies Inc (HQ) .... D 310 862-1200
  12181 Bluff Creek Dr # 200 Playa Vista (90094) (P-17624)
Geiger Plastics Inc .... E 310 327-9926
  16150 S Maple Ave A Gardena (90248) (P-5649)
Gelfand Rennert & Feldman LLP (PA) .... E 310 553-1707
  1880 Century Park E # 1600 Los Angeles (90067) (P-18525)
Gels Logistics Inc .... D 909 610-2277
  20275 Business Pkwy City of Industry (91789) (P-12460)
Gelsons Markets .... E 310 306-3192
  13455 Maxella Ave Marina Del Rey (90292) (P-2003)
Geltman Industries, Vernon *Also called Rezex Corporation* (P-2679)
Gem, Palmdale *Also called Golden Empire Mortgage Inc* (P-15198)
Gem Box of West .... E 213 748-4875
  2430 S Hill St Los Angeles (90007) (P-3806)
Gem Mobile Treatment Svcs Inc (HQ) .... C 562 595-7075
  2525 Cherry Ave Ste 105 Signal Hill (90755) (P-10666)
Gem Trans Care, Pasadena *Also called Gem Transitional Care Center* (P-20355)
Gem Transitional Care Center .... E 626 737-0560
  716 S Fair Oaks Ave Pasadena (91105) (P-20355)
Gemalto Cogent Inc (HQ) .... B 626 325-9600
  2964 Bradley St Pasadena (91107) (P-18033)
Gemco Display and Str Fixs LLC (PA) .... E 800 262-1126
  2640 E Del Amo Blvd Compton (90221) (P-13456)
Gemcon Inc .... F 818 767-0892
  7660 San Fernando Rd Sun Valley (91352) (P-1259)
Gemdale USA Corporation (HQ) .... D 626 381-9709
  680 E Colo Blvd Ste 300 Pasadena (91101) (P-15872)
Gemini Aluminum Corporation .... E 909 595-7403
  3255 Pomona Blvd Pomona (91768) (P-6308)
Gemini Construction and SEC Co, Sun Valley *Also called Gemcon Inc* (P-1259)
Gemini Film & Bag Inc (PA) .... E 323 582-0901
  3574 Fruitland Ave Maywood (90270) (P-5650)
Gemini GEL Llc 323 651-0513
  8365 Melrose Ave Los Angeles (90069) (P-4631)
Gemini Industries Inc .... D 949 250-4011
  2311 Pullman St Santa Ana (92705) (P-6293)
Gemini Mfg & Engrg Inc .... E 714 999-0010
  1020 E Vermont Ave Anaheim (92805) (P-7803)
Gemini Moving Specialists, Toluca Lake *Also called James B Branch Inc* (P-11978)
Gemini Plastics, Maywood *Also called Gemini Film & Bag Inc* (P-5650)
Gemmm Corp (PA) .... D 805 496-0555
  2860 E Thousand Oaks Blvd Thousand Oaks (91362) (P-15873)
Gems of Fruit Co, Placentia *Also called Packers Food Products Inc* (P-1907)
Gemsa Enterprises LLC .... E 714 521-1736
  14370 Gannet St La Mirada (90638) (P-2130)
Gemsa Oils, La Mirada *Also called Gemsa Enterprises LLC* (P-2130)
Gemtech Inds Good Earth Mfg .... E 714 848-2517
  2737 S Garnsey St Santa Ana (92707) (P-7368)
Gemtech International, Santa Ana *Also called Gemtech Inds Good Earth Mfg* (P-7368)
Gemtek Technology Inc .... F 909 444-9288
  20525 Paseo Del Prado Walnut (91789) (P-13400)
Gene Wtson Cnstr A Cal Ltd Prt .... E 661 763-5254
  10312 Skiles Dr Bakersfield (93311) (P-503)
Genea Energy Partners Inc .... D 714 694-0536
  19100 Von Karman Ave # 550 Irvine (92612) (P-18034)
Genequity Mortgage Inc .... D 310 540-1550
  3848 W Carson St Torrance (90503) (P-15265)
General Acute Care Hospital, Downey *Also called Pih Health Hospital - Downey* (P-20891)
General Acute Care Hospital, Los Angeles *Also called Pih Health Good Samaritan Hosp* (P-20890)
General Acute Care Hospital, Whittier *Also called Pih Health Whittier Hospital* (P-20893)
General Atomic Aeron .... C 760 388-8208
  73 El Mirage Airport Rd B Adelanto (92301) (P-10185)
General Carbon Company .... E 323 588-9291
  7542 Maie Ave Los Angeles (90001) (P-4659)
General Coatings Corporation .... E 909 204-4150
  9349 Feron Blvd Rancho Cucamonga (91730) (P-1180)
General Coatings Corporation .... D 858 587-1277
  600 W Freedom Ave Orange (92865) (P-1181)
General Coatings Manufact .... F 562 802-8834
  14722 Spring Ave Santa Fe Springs (90670) (P-11675)

General Container .... D 714 562-8700
  235 Radio Rd Corona (92879) (P-3807)
GENERAL CONTRACTOR, Duarte *Also called Png Builders* (P-665)
General Contractor, Anaheim *Also called Pinner Construction Co Inc* (P-810)
General Contractor, Palm Desert *Also called Cora Constructors Inc* (P-22519)
General Contractor, Irvine *Also called Uprite Construction Corp* (P-725)
General Electric Company .... E 760 530-5200
  18000 Phantom St Victorville (92394) (P-10186)
General Electric Company .... E 951 360-2400
  11600 Philadelphia Ave Mira Loma (91752) (P-9086)
General Engineering Contractor, Bloomington *Also called Vance Corporation* (P-926)
General Engineering Wstn Inc (PA) .... D 714 630-3200
  1140 N Red Gum St Anaheim (92806) (P-1074)
General Fire Control .... F 323 260-7015
  828 S Alma Ave Los Angeles (90023) (P-10835)
General Forming Corporation .... E 310 326-0624
  640 Alaska Ave Torrance (90503) (P-6843)
General Grinding & Mfg Co LLC .... E 562 921-7033
  15100 Valley View Ave La Mirada (90638) (P-8438)
General Industrial Repair .... E 323 278-0873
  7417 E Slauson Ave Commerce (90040) (P-8603)
General Lgstics Systems US Inc .... C 559 651-1850
  827 N American St Visalia (93291) (P-12136)
General Lgstics Systems US Inc .... C 951 677-3972
  24305 Prielipp Rd Wildomar (92595) (P-11968)
General Lgstics Systems US Inc .... C 562 577-6037
  12300 Bell Ranch Dr Santa Fe Springs (90670) (P-11969)
General Linear Systems Inc .... F 714 994-4822
  4332 Artesia Ave Fullerton (92833) (P-9631)
General Micro Systems Inc (PA) .... D 909 980-4863
  8358 Maple Pl Rancho Cucamonga (91730) (P-13401)
General Mills Inc .... E 310 605-6108
  1055 Sandhill Ave Carson (90746) (P-1835)
General Monitors Inc (HQ) .... C 949 581-4464
  26776 Simpatica Cir Lake Forest (92630) (P-9343)
General Motors LLC .... D 818 752-6619
  5350 Biloxi Ave North Hollywood (91601) (P-18790)
General Motors LLC .... D 951 361-6302
  11900 Cabernet Dr Dr1 Fontana (92337) (P-12208)
General Motors LLC .... F 313 556-5000
  3050 Lomita Blvd Bldg Ste Torrance (90505) (P-9949)
General Networks Corporation .... D 818 249-1962
  3524 Ocean View Blvd Glendale (91208) (P-18184)
General Petroleum Corporation (HQ) .... C 562 983-7300
  19501 S Santa Fe Ave Compton (90221) (P-14804)
General Photonics Corp .... D 909 590-5473
  14351 Pipeline Ave Chino (91710) (P-9234)
General Plating, Los Angeles *Also called Alpha Polishing Corporation* (P-7208)
General Power Systems Inc .... E 714 956-9321
  955 E Ball Rd Anaheim (92805) (P-9716)
General Procurement Inc (PA) .... C 949 679-7960
  1964 W Corporate Way Anaheim (92801) (P-13402)
General Produce, Vernon *Also called V & L Produce Inc* (P-14660)
General Production Services .... E 818 365-4211
  670 Arroyo St San Fernando (91340) (P-8604)
General Production Svc Cal Inc .... C 661 765-5330
  1333 Kern St Taft (93268) (P-949)
General Restaurant Equipment, Los Angeles *Also called South China Sheet Metal Inc* (P-1144)
General Ribbon Corp .... B 818 709-1234
  5775 E Los Angles Ave Ste Chatsworth (91311) (P-11478)
General Sealants .... C 626 961-0211
  300 Turnbull Canyon Rd City of Industry (91745) (P-5183)
General Steel Fabricators Inc .... E 818 897-1300
  12179 Branford St Ste B Sun Valley (91352) (P-6618)
General Tool Inc .... D 949 261-2322
  2025 Alton Pkwy Irvine (92606) (P-13985)
General Transistor Corporation (PA) .... E 310 578-7344
  12449 Putnam St Whittier (90602) (P-13724)
General Underground .... E 714 632-8646
  701 W Grove Ave Orange (92865) (P-1075)
General Veneer Mfg Co .... E 323 564-2661
  8652 Otis St South Gate (90280) (P-3350)
General Wax & Candle Co, North Hollywood *Also called General Wax Co Inc* (P-11676)
General Wax Co Inc (PA) .... D 818 765-5800
  6863 Beck Ave North Hollywood (91605) (P-11676)
Generation Construction Inc .... C 909 923-2077
  15650 El Prado Rd Chino (91710) (P-606)
Generational Properties Inc .... B 323 583-3163
  3141 E 44th St Vernon (90058) (P-12209)
Generis Holdings LP (PA) .... E 661 366-7209
  7200 E Brundage Ln Bakersfield (93307) (P-15)
Genesis 2000, La Puente *Also called Genesis Tc Inc* (P-3503)
Genesis Computer Systems Inc .... E 714 632-3648
  4055 E La Palma Ave Ste C Anaheim (92807) (P-13403)
Genesis Group Sftwr Developers .... E 714 630-4297
  16027 Brookhurst St Ste G Fountain Valley (92708) (P-17865)
Genesis Health Care, Orange *Also called Prospect Medical Systems Inc* (P-23093)
Genesis Healthcare LLC .... C 310 370-3594
  20900 Earl St Ste 100 Torrance (90503) (P-20356)
Genesis Healthcare LLC .... C 805 922-3558
  425 Barcellus Ave Santa Maria (93454) (P-20357)
Genesis Healthcare LLC .... C 323 461-9961
  5310 Fountain Ave Los Angeles (90029) (P-20590)
Genesis Supreme Rv Inc (PA) .... E 951 337-0254
  23129 Cajalco Rd Perris (92570) (P-10551)
Genesis Tc Inc .... F 626 968-4455
  524 Hofgaarden St La Puente (91744) (P-3503)

Employee Codes: A=Over 500 employees, B=251-500
C=101-250, D=51-100, E=20-50 F=10-19

2022 Southern California Business
Directory and Buyers Guide

© Mergent Inc. 1-800-342-5647

1141

Genesis Tech Partners LLC...C.......800 950-2647
21540 Plummer St Ste A Chatsworth (91311) ***(P-19039)***
Genesys Solutions, Newport Beach *Also called Bluewave Technologies* ***(P-1222)***
Genex (HQ)...C.......**424 672-9500**
800 Corporate Pointe # 100 Culver City (90230) ***(P-17625)***
Genius Products Inc...C.......310 453-1222
3301 Expo Blvd Ste 100 Santa Monica (90404) ***(P-14158)***
Genius Products Nt Inc...C.......510 671-0219
556 N Dmnd Bar Blvd Ste 1 Diamond Bar (91765) ***(P-2265)***
Genpact Mortgage Services Inc (HQ)...D.......**949 417-5131**
15420 Laguna Canyon Rd Irvine (92618) ***(P-15195)***
Gensia Sicor Inc (HQ)...A.......**949 455-4700**
19 Hughes Irvine (92618) ***(P-4822)***
Gensler and Associates, Los Angeles *Also called M Arthur Gensler Jr Assoc Inc* ***(P-22730)***
Gentekk Industries LLC (PA)...E.......**714 985-9280**
534 E Lambert Rd Brea (92821) ***(P-11677)***
Genter Capital LLC (PA)...D.......**310 477-6543**
11601 Wilshire Blvd Ph Los Angeles (90025) ***(P-15328)***
Gentex Corporation...D.......909 481-7667
9859 7th St Rancho Cucamonga (91730) ***(P-22841)***
Gentiva Health Services Inc...D.......805 549-0801
3220 S Higuera St Ste 101 San Luis Obispo (93401) ***(P-21165)***
Gentiva Home Health Care, San Luis Obispo *Also called Gentiva Health Services Inc* ***(P-21165)***
Gentiva Hospice...C.......661 324-1232
5001 E Cmmrccnter Dr Ste Bakersfield (93309) ***(P-21166)***
Gentle Dental Service Corp (HQ)...D.......**800 277-1112**
9800 S La Cnga Blvd Fl 2 Inglewood (90301) ***(P-20179)***
Gentle Giant Studios Inc...D.......818 504-3555
7511 N San Fernando Rd Burbank (91505) ***(P-18526)***
Gentry Golf Maintenance...E.......714 630-3541
14893 Ball Rd Anaheim (92806) ***(P-11419)***
Gentry Magazine, El Segundo *Also called 18 Media Inc* ***(P-4047)***
Genuine Parts Distributors, Ontario *Also called Tracy Industries Inc* ***(P-7600)***
Geo Drilling Fluids Inc (PA)...E.......**661 325-5919**
1431 Union Ave Bakersfield (93305) ***(P-14782)***
Geo Guidance Drilling Svcs Inc (PA)...E.......**661 833-9999**
200 Old Yard Dr Bakersfield (93307) ***(P-429)***
Geo Labels Inc...F.......909 923-6832
1180 E Francis St Ste G Ontario (91761) ***(P-4519)***
Geo Plastics...E.......323 277-8106
2200 E 52nd St Vernon (90058) ***(P-5651)***
Geodis Usa Inc...D.......310 518-6467
2255 E 220th St Carson (90810) ***(P-12461)***
Geodis Wilson Usa Inc...B.......310 507-6300
2155 E 220th St Long Beach (90810) ***(P-12462)***
Geolabs Westlake Village, Westlake Village *Also called R & R Services Corporation* ***(P-5404)***
Geolinks, Camarillo *Also called California Internet LP* ***(P-12630)***
Geologic Associates Inc...D.......909 383-8728
1831 Commercenter E San Bernardino (92408) ***(P-23534)***
Geologics Corporation...B.......661 259-5767
25375 Orch Vlg Rd Ste 102 Valencia (91355) ***(P-23445)***
Georg Fischer Harvel LLC...E.......661 396-0653
7001 Schirra Ct Bakersfield (93313) ***(P-5466)***
Georg Fischer LLC (HQ)...D.......**714 731-8800**
9271 Jeronimo Rd Irvine (92618) ***(P-13566)***
Georg Fischer Piping, Irvine *Also called Georg Fischer LLC* ***(P-13566)***
Georg Fischer Signet LLC...D.......626 571-2770
5462 Irwindale Ave Ste A Baldwin Park (91706) ***(P-10697)***
George Brazil Plbg Htg & AC, Culver City *Also called Orange County Services Inc* ***(P-1112)***
George Chevrolet...D.......562 925-2500
17000 Lakewood Blvd Bellflower (90706) ***(P-18749)***
George Coriaty...E.......562 698-7513
7240 Greenleaf Ave Whittier (90602) ***(P-4302)***
George Drumheller Properties...D.......714 779-0252
5710 E La Palma Ave Anaheim (92807) ***(P-16453)***
George Fischer Inc (HQ)...B.......**626 571-2770**
5462 Irwindale Ave Ste A Baldwin Park (91706) ***(P-8605)***
George Industries...B.......323 264-6660
4116 Whiteside St Los Angeles (90063) ***(P-7262)***
George J Savin Jr, Granada Hills *Also called Savin & Bursk Law Offices of* ***(P-21673)***
George Jue Mfg Co Inc...D.......562 634-8181
8140 Rosecrans Ave Paramount (90723) ***(P-7881)***
George L Throop Co...E.......626 796-0285
444 N Fair Oaks Ave Pasadena (91103) ***(P-6035)***
George M Rajacich MD PC...E.......818 787-2020
14914 Sherman Way Van Nuys (91405) ***(P-19830)***
George Oliveri Hair Design (PA)...D.......**562 421-4744**
3019 N Los Cytes Diagonal Long Beach (90808) ***(P-16904)***
George Oliveri Salon, Long Beach *Also called George Oliveri Hair Design* ***(P-16904)***
George P Johnson Company...E.......310 965-4300
18500 Crenshaw Blvd Torrance (90504) ***(P-11558)***
George T Hall Co Inc (PA)...E.......**909 825-9751**
1605 E Gene Autry Way Anaheim (92805) ***(P-13844)***
George Verhoeven Grain Inc (PA)...F.......**909 605-1531**
5355 E Airport Dr Ontario (91761) ***(P-1965)***
Georgia Atkison Snf LLC...D.......626 444-2535
3825 Durfee Ave El Monte (91732) ***(P-20358)***
Georgia Pacific Holdings Inc...A.......626 926-1474
13208 Hadley St Apt 1 Whittier (90601) ***(P-3904)***
Georgia-Pacific LLC...B.......562 861-6226
9206 Santa Fe Springs Rd Santa Fe Springs (90670) ***(P-14210)***
Georgian Hotel...D.......310 395-9945
1415 Ocean Ave Santa Monica (90401) ***(P-16454)***
Gerald Michael Ltd...E.......562 921-9611
1852 Carnegie Ave Santa Ana (92705) ***(P-14334)***
Gerard Roof Products LLC (HQ)...D.......**714 529-0407**
721 Monroe Way Placentia (92870) ***(P-6844)***
Gerard Roofing Technologies, Placentia *Also called Gerard Roof Products LLC* ***(P-6844)***
Gerdau Ameristeel, Rancho Cucamonga *Also called CMC Steel Us LLC* ***(P-7018)***
Gerhardt Gear Co Inc...E.......818 842-6700
133 E Santa Anita Ave Burbank (91502) ***(P-10066)***
Geri-Care Inc...D.......310 320-0961
21521 S Vermont Ave Torrance (90502) ***(P-20359)***
Geri-Care II Inc...C.......310 328-0812
22035 S Vermont Ave Torrance (90502) ***(P-20591)***
German Association Orange Cnty, Anaheim *Also called Phoenix Club Inc* ***(P-22356)***
German Knife Inc...F.......310 900-1081
4184 E Conant St Long Beach (90808) ***(P-7732)***
Gersh Agency Inc (PA)...D.......**310 274-6611**
9465 Wilshire Blvd Fl 6 Beverly Hills (90212) ***(P-19311)***
Ges, Huntington Beach *Also called Global Exprnce Specialists Inc* ***(P-18529)***
Ges US (new England) Inc...C.......973 459-4434
1051 S East St Anaheim (92805) ***(P-9717)***
Get...F.......562 989-5400
2030 W 17th St Long Beach (90813) ***(P-8383)***
Get Heal Inc...D.......310 528-4957
528 Palisades Dr Ste 176 Pacific Palisades (90272) ***(P-17493)***
Get-A-Lift Handicap Bus Trnsp, Bakersfield *Also called Golden Empire Transit District* ***(P-11811)***
Getac Inc...D.......949 681-2900
15495 Sand Canyon Ave # 300 Irvine (92618) ***(P-13404)***
Getmedlegal, San Dimas *Also called Legal Solutions Holdings Inc* ***(P-21608)***
Getty Center, Los Angeles *Also called Bon Appetit Management Co* ***(P-22991)***
Gff Inc...D.......323 232-6255
145 Willow Ave City of Industry (91746) ***(P-1888)***
Gfk Etilize Inc (HQ)...D.......**888 608-1212**
18662 Macarthur Blvd # 20 Irvine (92612) ***(P-22881)***
Gfmi Aerospace & Defense Inc...E.......714 361-4444
17375 Mount Herrmann St Fountain Valley (92708) ***(P-10335)***
Gfn North America Corp (HQ)...E.......**626 584-9722**
260 S Los Robles Ave # 217 Pasadena (91101) ***(P-17350)***
Gfp Ethanol LLC...E.......559 757-3850
11704 Road 120 Pixley (93256) ***(P-5137)***
Ggg Demolition Inc (PA)...D.......**714 699-9350**
1130 W Trenton Ave Orange (92867) ***(P-766)***
Ggis Insurance Services Inc...C.......818 553-2110
600 N Brand Blvd Ste 300 Glendale (91203) ***(P-15573)***
Ggsdi, Fountain Valley *Also called Genesis Group Sftwr Developers* ***(P-17865)***
Ggwh LLC...E.......310 786-1700
9440 Santa Monica Blvd Beverly Hills (90210) ***(P-16455)***
Gh Bass, Chatsworth *Also called Piege Co* ***(P-14345)***
Gh Group Inc...C.......562 264-5078
3645 Long Beach Blvd Long Beach (90807) ***(P-16101)***
Ghc of Lompoc LLC...D.......805 735-4010
1428 W North Ave Lompoc (93436) ***(P-21306)***
Ghossain & Truelock Entps Inc...E.......951 781-9345
783 Palmyrita Ave Ste A Riverside (92507) ***(P-17246)***
Ghost Management Group LLC...C.......949 870-1400
41 Discovery Irvine (92618) ***(P-17085)***
Ghp Management Corporation...B.......310 432-1441
270 N Canon Dr Beverly Hills (90210) ***(P-23030)***
Gl Industries...D.......805 522-2150
195 W Los Angeles Ave Simi Valley (93065) ***(P-12952)***
Giant Inland Empire Rv Ctr Inc (PA)...C.......**909 981-0444**
9150 Benson Ave Montclair (91763) ***(P-18833)***
Giant Rv, Montclair *Also called Giant Inland Empire Rv Ctr Inc* ***(P-18833)***
Giant Sportz Paintball Park, Bellflower *Also called Hollywood Sports Park LLC* ***(P-18545)***
Giant Steps Trning Prgrams Inc...D.......323 733-6401
2228 Crenshaw Blvd Los Angeles (90016) ***(P-21953)***
Giant Teddy, Anaheim *Also called Raykorvay Inc* ***(P-11364)***
Gibbel Bros Inc...E.......323 875-1367
11145 Tuxford St Sun Valley (91352) ***(P-6092)***
Gibbs Giden Locher...D.......310 552-3400
1880 Century Park E # 1200 Los Angeles (90067) ***(P-21563)***
Gibbs & Associates, Moorpark *Also called Cimatron Gibbs LLC* ***(P-17577)***
Gibbs International Inc (PA)...D.......**805 485-0551**
2201 Ventura Blvd Oxnard (93036) ***(P-18834)***
Gibbs International Truck Ctrs, Oxnard *Also called Gibbs International Inc* ***(P-18834)***
Gibraltar, Jurupa Valley *Also called Pacific Award Metals Inc* ***(P-13326)***
Gibraltar Plastic Pdts Corp...E.......818 365-9318
12885 Foothill Blvd Sylmar (91342) ***(P-5652)***
Gibralter Convalescent Hosp (PA)...D.......**714 550-5380**
600 E Washington Ave Santa Ana (92701) ***(P-20592)***
Gibralter Convalescent Hosp...D.......626 443-9425
2720 Nevada Ave El Monte (91733) ***(P-20593)***
Gibson Dunn & Crutcher LLP (PA)...B.......**213 229-7000**
333 S Grand Ave Ste 4600 Los Angeles (90071) ***(P-21564)***
Gibson and Schaefer Inc (PA)...E.......**619 352-3535**
1126 Rock Wood Rd Heber (92249) ***(P-6093)***
Gibson Exhaust Systems, Corona *Also called Gibson Performance Corporation* ***(P-10067)***
Gibson Overseas Inc...A.......323 832-8900
2410 Yates Ave Commerce (90040) ***(P-13171)***
Gibson Performance Corporation...D.......951 372-1220
1270 Webb Cir Corona (92879) ***(P-10067)***
Giddens Industries Inc (HQ)...C.......**425 353-0405**
3130 E Miraloma Ave Anaheim (92806) ***(P-10336)***
Giddyup Group Inc...D.......800 828-2785
20 N Oak St Ste B Ventura (93001) ***(P-17014)***
Gifting Group LLC...D.......951 296-0310
42210 Zevo Dr Temecula (92590) ***(P-14931)***
GIGABYTE TECHNOLOGY CO, City of Industry *Also called GBT Inc* ***(P-13399)***
Gigamem LLC...F.......949 461-9999
9 Spectrum Pointe Dr Lake Forest (92630) ***(P-8199)***
Gigastone America, Irvine *Also called Dane Elec Corp USA* ***(P-13387)***

Mergent e-mail: customerrelations@mergent.com
1142
2022 Southern California Business Directory and Buyers Guide
(P-0000) Products & Services Section entry number
(PA)=Parent Co (HQ)=Headquarters (DH)=Div Headquarters

Gigatera Communications ......D 714 515-1100
1818 E Orangethorpe Ave Fullerton (92831) *(P-9718)*

Gigavac LLC (HQ) ......**F 805 684-8401**
6382 Rose Ln Carpinteria (93013) *(P-8953)*

Gilbert Klly Crwley Jnnett LLP (PA) ......**D 213 615-7000**
550 S Hope St Ste 2200 Los Angeles (90071) *(P-21565)*

Gilchrist & Rutter Prof Corp ......E 310 393-4000
1299 Ocean Ave Ste 900 Santa Monica (90401) *(P-21566)*

Gildan USA Inc ......E 909 485-1475
28200 Highway 189 Lake Arrowhead (92352) *(P-2620)*

Gilead Palo Alto Inc ......E 909 394-4000
550 Cliffside Dr San Dimas (91773) *(P-4823)*

Gilead Sciences Inc ......D 650 522-2771
1800 Wheeler St La Verne (91750) *(P-4824)*

Gilead Scientist, San Dimas *Also called Gilead Palo Alto Inc (P-4823)*

Gill Corporation (PA) ......**C 626 443-6094**
4056 Easy St El Monte (91731) *(P-5653)*

Gillette Citrus Company ......D 559 626-4236
10175 S Anchor Ave Dinuba (93618) *(P-171)*

Gilliam & Sons Inc ......E 661 589-0913
9831 Rosedale Hwy Bakersfield (93312) *(P-1595)*

Gills Onions LLC ......D 805 240-1983
1051 Pacific Ave Oxnard (93030) *(P-14632)*

Gils Distributing Service ......C 213 627-0539
718 E 8th St Los Angeles (90021) *(P-17098)*

Gin'l Fabrics, Los Angeles *Also called Ax II Inc (P-2615)*

Gina B Ltd ......F 310 366-7926
1601 W 134th St Gardena (90249) *(P-13172)*

Gina B Showroom, Gardena *Also called Gina B Ltd (P-13172)*

Ginger Golden Products Inc ......F 323 838-1070
5860 Bandini Blvd Commerce (90040) *(P-1889)*

Gingi Pak, Camarillo *Also called Belport Company Inc (P-11161)*

Gino Corporation ......E 323 234-7979
555 E Jefferson Blvd Los Angeles (90011) *(P-2756)*

Ginza Collection Design Inc ......E 562 531-1116
6015 Obispo Ave Long Beach (90805) *(P-2885)*

Giovanni Cosmetics Inc ......D 310 952-9960
2064 E University Dr Rancho Dominguez (90220) *(P-5023)*

Giovanni Hair Care & Cosmetics, Rancho Dominguez *Also called Giovanni Cosmetics Inc (P-5023)*

Gipson Hffman Pncone A Prof Co ......D 310 556-4660
1901 Avenue Of The Stars Los Angeles (90067) *(P-21567)*

Girard Food Service, City of Industry *Also called Gff Inc (P-1888)*

Girardi Keese (PA) ......**D 213 977-0211**
1126 Wilshire Blvd Los Angeles (90017) *(P-21568)*

Girl Scuts Greater Los Angeles (PA) ......**C 626 677-2265**
1150 S Olive St Fl 6 Los Angeles (90015) *(P-22339)*

GIRLS REPUBLIC, Chino Hills *Also called Boys Republic (P-22085)*

Girls Rock Sb ......D 805 861-8128
1522b Eucalyptus Hill Rd Santa Barbara (93103) *(P-22451)*

Giroux Glass Inc (PA) ......**C 213 747-7406**
850 W Wash Blvd Ste 200 Los Angeles (90015) *(P-1586)*

Giuliano's Bakery, Carson *Also called Giuliano-Pagano Corporation (P-2004)*

Giuliano-Pagano Corporation ......D 310 537-7700
1264 E Walnut St Carson (90746) *(P-2004)*

Giumarra Bros Fruit Co Inc (PA) ......**D 213 627-2900**
1601 E Olympic Blvd # 408 Los Angeles (90021) *(P-14633)*

Giumarra International Berry, Los Angeles *Also called Giumarra Bros Fruit Co Inc (P-14633)*

Giumarra Vineyards Corporation ......C 661 395-7071
11220 Edison Hwy Bakersfield (93307) *(P-46)*

Giumarra Vineyards Corporation (PA) ......**B 661 395-7000**
11220 Edison Hwy Edison (93220) *(P-47)*

Given Imaging Los Angeles LLC ......C 310 641-8492
5860 Uplander Way Culver City (90230) *(P-11223)*

Giving Keys Inc ......E 213 935-8791
836 Traction Ave Los Angeles (90013) *(P-11317)*

Gizmac Accessories LLC ......F 310 320-5563
4025 Spencer St Ste 102 Torrance (90503) *(P-8258)*

GK Management Co Inc (PA) ......**C 310 204-2050**
5150 Overland Ave Culver City (90230) *(P-15874)*

Gkk Corporation (PA) ......**D 949 250-1500**
2355 Main St Ste 220 Irvine (92614) *(P-22716)*

Gkk Works (HQ) ......**D 949 250-1500**
2875 Michelle Irvine (92606) *(P-22717)*

Gkkworks, Irvine *Also called Gkk Corporation (P-22716)*

Gkkworks Cannon Design, Irvine *Also called Gkk Works (P-22717)*

GKN Aerospace ......E 714 653-7531
12242 Western Ave Garden Grove (92841) *(P-10187)*

GKN Aerospace Camarillo Inc ......F 805 383-6684
3030 Redhll Ave Santa Ana (92705) *(P-6845)*

GKN Arspace Trnsprncy Systems (HQ) ......**B 714 893-7531**
12122 Western Ave Garden Grove (92841) *(P-5654)*

Gky Dental Arts Inc (PA) ......**D 310 214-8007**
4212 Artesia Blvd Torrance (90504) *(P-21106)*

GL Nemirow Inc ......D 818 562-9433
2550 N Hollywood Way # 5 Burbank (91505) *(P-17015)*

GL Ventura Inc ......E 818 890-1886
12595 Foothill Blvd Sylmar (91342) *(P-6139)*

GL Woodworking Inc ......D 949 515-2192
14341 Franklin Ave Tustin (92780) *(P-3445)*

Gla Agricultural Elec Inc ......E 805 541-3758
3563 Sueldo St Ste D San Luis Obispo (93401) *(P-10885)*

Glacial Garden Inc (PA) ......**D 714 502-9029**
3975 Pixie Ave Lakewood (90712) *(P-19651)*

Glacial Garden Skating Arena, Lakewood *Also called Glacial Garden Inc (P-19651)*

Glacier Design Systems Inc (PA) ......**F 714 897-2337**
5405 Production Dr Huntington Beach (92649) *(P-2145)*

Glacier Foods Division, Westlake Village *Also called Dole Packaged Foods LLC (P-1898)*

Glad-A-Way Gardens Inc ......C 805 938-0569
2669 E Clark Ave Santa Maria (93455) *(P-77)*

Gladding, McBean, South Gate *Also called Pabco Clay Products LLC (P-13309)*

Gladstones Inc ......F 562 432-8588
330 S Pine Ave Long Beach (90802) *(P-2341)*

Glam and Glits Nail Design Inc ......D 661 393-4800
8700 Swigert Ct Unit 209 Bakersfield (93311) *(P-5024)*

Glamour Industries Co (PA) ......**B 323 728-2999**
2220 Gaspar Ave Commerce (90040) *(P-14244)*

Glamour Industries Co ......D 213 687-8600
100 Wilshire Blvd Ste 700 Santa Monica (90401) *(P-14037)*

Glare Technology Usa Inc ......C 909 437-6999
30898 Wealth St Murrieta (92563) *(P-18527)*

Glas Werk Inc ......E 949 766-1296
29710 Avnida De Las Bnder Rancho Santa Margari (92688) *(P-5935)*

Glaser Weil Fink Jacobs (PA) ......**C 310 553-3000**
10250 Constellation Blvd # 1900 Los Angeles (90067) *(P-21569)*

Glaspro, Santa Fe Springs *Also called GP Merger Sub Inc (P-5956)*

Glass Fabrication and Dist, Stanton *Also called Newport Industrial Glass Inc (P-5965)*

Glass House Group, Long Beach *Also called Gh Group Inc (P-16101)*

Glassplax ......F 951 677-4800
26605 Madison Ave Murrieta (92562) *(P-5954)*

Glasswerks Group, South Gate *Also called Glasswerks La Inc (P-5955)*

Glasswerks La Inc (HQ) ......**B 888 789-7810**
8600 Rheem Ave South Gate (90280) *(P-5955)*

Glastar Corporation ......E 818 341-0301
8425 Canoga Ave Canoga Park (91304) *(P-7980)*

Glaukos Corporation (PA) ......**C 949 367-9600**
229 Avenida Fabricante San Clemente (92672) *(P-10985)*

GLAZA, Los Angeles *Also called Greater Los Angeles Zoo Assn (P-22184)*

Glazier, Anaheim *Also called Artisan Glass and Design Inc (P-1636)*

Gledhill/Lyons Inc ......E 714 502-0274
1521 N Placentia Ave Anaheim (92806) *(P-10337)*

Glen Annie Golf Club ......D 805 968-6400
405 Glen Annie Rd Goleta (93117) *(P-19489)*

Glen Beverly Laboratories Inc (PA) ......**D 714 848-5777**
7777 Center Ave Ste 500 Huntington Beach (92647) *(P-22270)*

Glen Ivy Hot Springs ......C 714 990-2090
1001 Brea Mall Brea (92821) *(P-16957)*

Glen Park Retirement Hotel ......D 818 769-6626
5527 Laurel Canyon Blvd North Hollywood (91607) *(P-20530)*

Glen-Mac Swiss Co ......E 310 978-4555
12848 Weber Way Hawthorne (90250) *(P-9655)*

Glenco Manufacturing Company ......E 909 984-3348
707 S Hope Ave Ontario (91761) *(P-7036)*

Glendale Adventist Medical Ctr ......E 818 409-8379
281 Harvey Dr Unit B Glendale (91206) *(P-21167)*

Glendale Adventist Medical Ctr (HQ) ......**A 818 409-8000**
1509 Wilson Ter Glendale (91206) *(P-20776)*

Glendale Associates Ltd ......D 818 246-6737
100 W Broadway Ste 100 # 100 Glendale (91210) *(P-15670)*

Glendale Eye Medical Group (PA) ......**D 818 956-1010**
607 N Central Ave Ste 203 Glendale (91203) *(P-19831)*

Glendale Medical Offices, Glendale *Also called Kaiser Foundation Hospitals (P-19936)*

Glendale Mem Hosp & Hlth Ctr ......D 818 502-1900
1420 S Central Ave Glendale (91204) *(P-20777)*

Glendale Orange St Med Offs, Glendale *Also called Kaiser Foundation Hospitals (P-19903)*

GLENDALE YMCA SWIM SCHOOL, Glendale *Also called Young MNS Chrstn Assn of Glnda (P-22387)*

Glendora Chevrolet, Glendora *Also called Martin Automotive Inc (P-18853)*

Glendora Country Club ......D 626 335-4051
2400 Country Club Dr Glendora (91741) *(P-19564)*

Glendora Oaks Bhvral Hlth Hosp, Glendora *Also called East Valley Glendora Hosp LLC (P-20759)*

Glenoaks Convalescent Hospital ......D 818 240-4300
409 W Glenoaks Blvd Glendale (91202) *(P-20778)*

Glenoaks Food Inc ......E 818 768-9091
11030 Randall St Sun Valley (91352) *(P-1759)*

Glentek Inc ......D 310 322-3026
208 Standard St El Segundo (90245) *(P-8913)*

Glentrans, Glendale *Also called Hemodialysis Inc (P-21246)*

Glenwood Care Center, Oxnard *Also called Glenwood Corporation (P-20360)*

Glenwood Corporation ......D 805 983-0305
1300 N C St Oxnard (93030) *(P-20360)*

Gless Ranch Inc (PA) ......**E 951 780-8458**
18541 Van Buren Blvd Riverside (92508) *(P-222)*

Glidewell Laboratories, Newport Beach *Also called James R Gldwell Dntl Crmics In (P-21107)*

Global Aerospace Tech Corp ......E 818 407-5600
25109 Rye Canyon Loop Valencia (91355) *(P-10338)*

Global Aerostructures ......F 909 987-4888
10291 Trademark St Ste C Rancho Cucamonga (91730) *(P-10339)*

Global Agri-Trade ......E 562 320-8550
15500 S Avalon Blvd Rancho Dominguez (90220) *(P-2121)*

Global Asylum Incorporated ......E 323 850-1214
440 W Los Feliz Rd Glendale (91204) *(P-19129)*

Global Auto Proc Svcs Inc (PA) ......**D 805 382-9601**
567 W Channel Islands Blv Port Hueneme (93041) *(P-18934)*

Global Billiard Mfg Co Inc ......F 310 764-5000
1141 Sandhill Ave Carson (90746) *(P-11420)*

Global Building Services Inc (PA) ......**A 800 675-6643**
27433 Tourney Rd Ste 280 Valencia (91355) *(P-17247)*

Global Casuals Inc ......D 310 817-2828
18505 S Broadway Gardena (90248) *(P-2811)*

Global Comm Semiconductors LLC (HQ) ......**F 310 530-7274**
23155 Kashiwa Ct Torrance (90505) *(P-9510)*

ALPHABETIC

Employee Codes: A=Over 500 employees, B=251-500
C=101-250, D=51-100, E=20-50 F=10-19

2022 Southern California Business
Directory and Buyers Guide

© Mergent Inc. 1-800-342-5647
1143

Global Communications Network, Santa Monica *Also called Paradigm Communications Corp* ***(P-12663)***

Global Compliance Inc..........E.......626 303-6855
438 W Chestnut Ave Ste A Monrovia (91016) ***(P-4174)***

Global Debt Management Llc (PA)..........**D.......949 825-7800**
18881 Von Karman Ave # 1500 Irvine (92612) ***(P-18528)***

Global Dosimetry Solutions, Irvine *Also called Mirion Technologies Gds Inc* ***(P-22953)***

Global Edge LLC..........E.......888 315-2692
5230 Las Virgenes Rd # 265 Calabasas (91302) ***(P-17866)***

Global Elastomeric Pdts Inc..........D.......661 831-5380
5551 District Blvd Bakersfield (93313) ***(P-7670)***

Global Electronics Intl, Rancho Cucamonga *Also called Mercury United Electronics Inc* ***(P-9748)***

Global Emergency Road Svc LLC..........E.......818 518-1166
9908 San Fernando Rd Pacoima (91331) ***(P-11870)***

Global Entertainment Inds Inc..........D.......818 567-0000
2948 N Ontario St Burbank (91504) ***(P-1661)***

Global Environmental Pdts Inc..........D.......909 713-1600
5405 Industrial Pkwy San Bernardino (92407) ***(P-9950)***

Global Exprnce Specialists Inc..........C.......619 498-6300
18504 Beach Blvd Unit 511 Huntington Beach (92648) ***(P-18529)***

Global Garments, Los Angeles *Also called Design Collection Inc* ***(P-14303)***

Global Innovation Partner, Los Angeles *Also called Cbre Globl Value Investors LLC* ***(P-15802)***

Global Language Solutions LLC..........D.......949 798-1400
19800 Macarthur Blvd # 750 Irvine (92612) ***(P-18530)***

Global Link Sourcing Inc..........D.......951 698-1977
41690 Corporate Center Ct Murrieta (92562) ***(P-3854)***

Global Locate Inc..........D.......949 926-5000
5300 California Ave Irvine (92617) ***(P-9511)***

Global Mail Inc..........C.......310 735-0800
921 W Artesia Blvd Compton (90220) ***(P-12463)***

Global Manufacturing Network, Irvine *Also called China Manufacturing Netwrk LLC* ***(P-23189)***

Global Metal Solutions Inc..........E.......949 872-2995
2150 Mcgaw Ave Irvine (92614) ***(P-7263)***

Global Mfg Solutions LLC..........E.......562 356-3222
2100 E Valencia Dr Ste D Fullerton (92831) ***(P-6351)***

Global Packaging, La Habra *Also called Uvw Inc* ***(P-5854)***

Global Paper Solutions Inc..........E.......714 687-6102
100 S Anaheim Blvd # 250 Anaheim (92805) ***(P-3753)***

Global Paratransit Inc..........B.......310 715-7550
400 W Compton Blvd Gardena (90248) ***(P-11871)***

Global Pcci (gpc) (PA)..........**C.......757 637-9000**
2465 Campus Dr Ste 100 Irvine (92612) ***(P-7147)***

Global Plastics Inc..........C.......951 657-5466
145 Malbert St Perris (92570) ***(P-14115)***

Global Reach 18 Inc (PA)..........**D.......310 203-5850**
10100 Santa Monica Blvd # 900 Los Angeles (90067) ***(P-16154)***

Global Rental Co Inc..........C.......909 469-5160
1253 Price Ave Pomona (91767) ***(P-17309)***

Global Risk MGT Solutions LLC..........D.......949 759-8500
5271 California Ave # 290 Irvine (92617) ***(P-23225)***

Global Sales Inc..........E.......310 474-7700
1732 Westwood Blvd Los Angeles (90024) ***(P-5025)***

Global Service Resources Inc..........D.......800 679-7658
711 S Victory Blvd Burbank (91502) ***(P-17626)***

Global Solutions Integration..........D.......949 307-1849
26632 Towne Centre Dr # 300 Foothill Ranch (92610) ***(P-22561)***

Global Sweeping Solutions, San Bernardino *Also called Global Environmental Pdts Inc* ***(P-9950)***

Global Trade Alliance Inc..........C.......562 944-6422
13642 Orden Dr Santa Fe Springs (90670) ***(P-13060)***

Global Truss America LLC..........D.......323 415-6225
4295 Charter St Vernon (90058) ***(P-6309)***

Global Uxe Inc..........E.......805 583-4600
405 Science Dr Moorpark (93021) ***(P-11678)***

Global Vision Holdings Inc..........F.......949 281-6438
19200 Von Karman Ave 6 Irvine (92612) ***(P-2441)***

Global Wave Group..........F.......949 916-9800
26970 Aliso Viejo Pkwy # 250 Aliso Viejo (92656) ***(P-17867)***

Global Wide Media Inc (PA)..........**D.......805 267-7000**
11766 Wilshire Blvd # 1400 Los Angeles (90025) ***(P-17016)***

Globalux Lighting LLC..........F.......909 591-7506
773 S Benson Ave Ontario (91762) ***(P-9064)***

Globaluxe Inc..........E.......805 583-4600
405 Science Dr Moorpark (93021) ***(P-11679)***

Globalvision Systems Inc..........F.......888 227-7967
9401 Oakdale Ave Ste 100 Chatsworth (91311) ***(P-8200)***

Globe Iron Foundry Inc..........D.......323 723-8983
5649 Randolph St Commerce (90040) ***(P-6258)***

Globe Plastics, Chino *Also called PRC Composites LLC* ***(P-5771)***

Globe Shoes, El Segundo *Also called Osata Enterprises Inc* ***(P-14443)***

Globe Tire & Motor Sports, Los Angeles *Also called Globe Tire & Motorsports Corp* ***(P-13116)***

Globe Tire & Motorsports Corp..........D.......310 836-0804
2450 S La Cienega Blvd Los Angeles (90034) ***(P-13116)***

Globecast America Incorporated (HQ)..........**B.......310 845-3900**
10525 Washington Blvd Culver City (90232) ***(P-12770)***

Gloria Lance Inc (PA)..........**D.......310 767-4400**
15616 S Broadway Gardena (90248) ***(P-2844)***

Glory Global Solutions Inc..........D.......714 897-7545
11135 Knott Ave Ste C Cypress (90630) ***(P-17627)***

Gloves In A Bottle Inc..........E.......818 248-9980
3720 Park Pl Montrose (91020) ***(P-14245)***

Glovis America Inc (HQ)..........**C.......714 435-2960**
17305 Von Karman Ave # 200 Irvine (92614) ***(P-12464)***

Glp Designs Inc..........F.......310 652-6800
916 W Hyde Park Blvd Inglewood (90302) ***(P-3730)***

Gluten Free Foods Mfg LLC (PA)..........**D.......909 323-8230**
5010 Eucalyptus Ave Chino (91710) ***(P-2442)***

GM Windows & Doors Inc..........F.......323 771-0348
4303 Santa Ana St Huntington Park (90255) ***(P-3251)***

Gmh Inc..........E.......805 485-1410
561 Kinetic Dr Ste A Oxnard (93030) ***(P-18947)***

Gmm Inc..........F.......818 752-3200
10152 Riverside Dr Toluca Lake (91602) ***(P-4175)***

Gmp Laboratories America Inc..........D.......714 630-2467
2931 E La Jolla St Anaheim (92806) ***(P-4825)***

Gmp Nutrition Enterprises Inc..........F.......909 628-8889
13653 Central Ave Chino (91710) ***(P-4826)***

Gms Elevator Services Inc..........E.......909 599-3904
401 Borrego Ct San Dimas (91773) ***(P-7679)***

Gms Landscapes Inc..........D.......805 402-3925
207 Camino Leon Camarillo (93012) ***(P-6562)***

Gms Molds (PA)..........**E.......310 684-1168**
729 E 223rd St Carson (90745) ***(P-7804)***

Gmto Corporation..........D.......626 204-0500
465 N Halstead St Ste 250 Pasadena (91107) ***(P-10836)***

Go Get Em Inc..........D.......702 985-5637
45248 Trevor Ave Lancaster (93534) ***(P-18381)***

Go Rhino, Brea *Also called Iddea California LLC* ***(P-10078)***

Go Sales.us, West Covina *Also called Ola Nation LLC* ***(P-2894)***

Go-Staff Inc..........C.......657 242-9350
240 W Lincoln Ave Anaheim (92805) ***(P-17425)***

Go2zero Strategies LLC..........F.......626 840-1850
6625 N Calle Eva Miranda Irwindale (91702) ***(P-3743)***

Godigital Media Group LLC..........D.......310 853-7940
3103 S La Cienega Blvd Los Angeles (90016) ***(P-12785)***

Goeppner Industries Inc..........E.......310 784-2800
22924 Lockness Ave Torrance (90501) ***(P-8606)***

Goetzman Group Inc (PA)..........**D.......818 595-1112**
21333 Oxnard St Ste 200 Woodland Hills (91367) ***(P-23226)***

Goglanian Bakeries Inc (HQ)..........**B.......714 338-1145**
3401 W Segerstrom Ave Santa Ana (92704) ***(P-14690)***

Goguardian, El Segundo *Also called Liminex Inc* ***(P-17653)***

Gohz Inc..........E.......800 603-1219
23555 Golden Springs Dr K1 Diamond Bar (91765) ***(P-8914)***

Gold Coast Bakeries, Santa Ana *Also called Gold Coast Baking Company Inc* ***(P-2005)***

Gold Coast Baking Company Inc (PA)..........**C.......714 545-2253**
1590 E Saint Gertrude Pl Santa Ana (92705) ***(P-2005)***

Gold Coast Broadcasting, Ventura *Also called Kkzz 1590* ***(P-12697)***

Gold Coast Farms Inc..........D.......805 928-2727
123 N Depot St Santa Maria (93458) ***(P-16)***

Gold Coast Health Plan, Camarillo *Also called Ventura County Medi-Cal Manage* ***(P-21495)***

Gold Coast Ingredients Inc..........D.......323 724-8935
2429 Yates Ave Commerce (90040) ***(P-2443)***

Gold Coast Tours, Brea *Also called Hot Dogger Tours Inc* ***(P-11912)***

Gold Crest Industries Inc..........E.......909 930-9069
1018 E Acacia St Ontario (91761) ***(P-3127)***

Gold Metropolitan Media (PA)..........**E.......818 348-1913**
16000 Blythe St Van Nuys (91406) ***(P-3198)***

Gold Parent LP..........A.......310 954-0444
11111 Santa Monica Blvd Los Angeles (90025) ***(P-15266)***

Gold Prospectors Assn Amer, Murrieta *Also called Old Prospectors Assn Amer LLC* ***(P-4088)***

Gold Star Foods Inc (HQ)..........**C.......909 843-9600**
3781 E Airport Dr Ontario (91761) ***(P-2444)***

Gold Store Inc..........F.......805 495-5464
2539 E Thousand Oaks Blvd Thousand Oaks (91362) ***(P-11318)***

Gold Venture Inc..........C.......909 623-1810
1050 S State College Blvd Fullerton (92831) ***(P-5509)***

Gold's Gym, West Hollywood *Also called Rsg Group USA Inc* ***(P-16110)***

Gold/Gold/Gold Inc..........E.......323 845-9746
4605 Lankershim Blvd North Hollywood (91602) ***(P-14131)***

Golda & I Chocolatiers Inc..........D.......949 660-9581
23052 Alicia Pkwy Ste H Mission Viejo (92692) ***(P-14691)***

Goldak Inc..........E.......818 240-2666
15835 Monte St Ste 104 Sylmar (91342) ***(P-10590)***

Goldberg and Solovy Foods Inc, Vernon *Also called Palisades Ranch Inc* ***(P-14485)***

Golden Applexx Co Inc..........E.......909 594-9788
19805 Harrison Ave Walnut (91789) ***(P-4520)***

Golden Brands, Huntington Beach *Also called Harbor Distributing LLC* ***(P-14827)***

Golden Color Printing Inc..........E.......626 455-0850
9353 Rush St South El Monte (91733) ***(P-4303)***

Golden Cross Care Inc..........D.......626 791-1948
1450 N Fair Oaks Ave Pasadena (91103) ***(P-20361)***

Golden Cross Health Care, Pasadena *Also called Golden Cross Care Inc* ***(P-20361)***

Golden Empire Con Pdts Inc..........D.......661 833-4490
8261 Mccutchen Rd Bakersfield (93311) ***(P-1524)***

Golden Empire Mortgage Inc (PA)..........**D.......661 328-1600**
1200 Discovery Dr Ste 300 Bakersfield (93309) ***(P-15196)***

Golden Empire Mortgage Inc (PA)..........**D.......661 328-1600**
2130 Chester Ave Bakersfield (93301) ***(P-15197)***

Golden Empire Mortgage Inc..........B.......661 949-3388
41331 12th St W Ste 102 Palmdale (93551) ***(P-15198)***

Golden Empire Transit District (PA)..........**C.......661 869-2438**
1830 Golden State Ave Bakersfield (93301) ***(P-11811)***

Golden Five Consulting, Simi Valley *Also called Golden Five LLC* ***(P-17628)***

Golden Five LLC..........E.......323 489-8001
3045 Auburn Ct Simi Valley (93063) ***(P-17628)***

Golden Fleece Designs..........F.......323 849-1901
441 S Victory Blvd Burbank (91502) ***(P-3140)***

Golden Gate Hosiery Inc..........F.......909 464-0805
14095 Laurelwood Pl Chino (91710) ***(P-2621)***

Golden Gate Steel Inc F 310 638-0855
19826 S Alameda St Compton (90221) *(P-6619)*
Golden Grove Trading Inc F 909 718-8000
468 S Humane Way Pomona (91766) *(P-4521)*
Golden Hotels Ltd Partnership C 949 833-2770
18700 Macarthur Blvd Irvine (92612) *(P-16456)*
Golden International A 213 628-1388
424 S Los Angeles St # 2 Los Angeles (90013) *(P-16263)*
Golden Island Jerky Co Inc (HQ) **E 844 362-3222**
10646 Fulton Ct Rancho Cucamonga (91730) *(P-1733)*
Golden Kraft Inc B 562 926-8888
15500 Valley View Ave La Mirada (90638) *(P-3930)*
Golden Mattress Co Inc D 323 887-1888
11680 Wright Rd Lynwood (90262) *(P-3549)*
Golden Pacific, Pomona *Also called Travelers Choice Travelware (P-5898)*
Golden Pacific Seafoods Inc E 714 589-8888
700 S Raymond Ave Fullerton (92831) *(P-7937)*
Golden Peterbilt, Porterville *Also called E M Tharp Inc (P-13024)*
Golden Queen Mining Co LLC C 661 824-4300
2818 Silver Queen Rd Mojave (93501) *(P-374)*
Golden Rain Foundation C 562 493-9581
1661 Golden Rain Rd Seal Beach (90740) *(P-19832)*
Golden Specialty Foods LLC E 562 802-2537
14605 Best Ave Norwalk (90650) *(P-2445)*
Golden Star Technology Inc E 951 778-8930
1215 Columbia Ave Ste C3 Riverside (92507) *(P-18146)*
Golden Star Technology Inc (PA) **D 562 345-8700**
12881 166th St Cerritos (90703) *(P-18147)*
Golden State Care Center, Baldwin Park *Also called Golden State Habilitation Conv (P-20362)*
Golden State Drilling Inc D 661 589-0730
3500 Fruitvale Ave Bakersfield (93308) *(P-430)*
Golden State Engineering Inc C 562 634-3125
15338 Garfield Ave Paramount (90723) *(P-7902)*
Golden State Fence Co., Riverside *Also called Fenceworks Inc (P-1657)*
Golden State Foods Corp (PA) **E 949 247-8000**
18301 Von Karman Ave # 1 Irvine (92612) *(P-2328)*
Golden State Foods Corp B 626 465-7500
640 S 6th Ave City of Industry (91746) *(P-1928)*
Golden State Grating Inc F 909 854-2489
8224 Goldmine Ave Fontana (92335) *(P-6963)*
Golden State Habilitation Conv (PA) **C 626 962-3274**
1758 Big Dalton Ave Baldwin Park (91706) *(P-20362)*
Golden State Health Ctrs Inc (PA) **C 818 385-3200**
13347 Ventura Blvd Sherman Oaks (91423) *(P-20363)*
Golden State Health Ctrs Inc C 310 451-9706
1340 15th St Santa Monica (90404) *(P-20594)*
Golden State Holdg Group Corp (PA) **A 909 860-7668**
23624 Falcons View Dr Diamond Bar (91765) *(P-12275)*
Golden State Medical Sup Inc C 805 477-9866
5187 Camino Ruiz Camarillo (93012) *(P-13489)*
Golden State Medical Supply D 805 477-8966
5247 Camino Ruiz Camarillo (93012) *(P-14159)*
Golden State Mutl Lf Insur Co (PA) **D 713 526-4361**
1999 W Adams Blvd Los Angeles (90018) *(P-15360)*
Golden State Prvders A Med Cor (PA) **D 805 523-8250**
865 Patriot Dr Moorpark (93021) *(P-21430)*
Golden State Water Company (HQ) **C 909 394-3600**
630 E Foothill Blvd San Dimas (91773) *(P-12892)*
Golden Supreme Inc E 562 903-1063
12304 Mccann Dr Santa Fe Springs (90670) *(P-11680)*
Golden Temple, Los Angeles *Also called East West Tea Company LLC (P-1948)*
Golden Valley Dairy Products C 559 687-1188
1025 E Bardsley Ave Tulare (93274) *(P-1772)*
Golden West Casino, Irvine *Also called Golden West Partners Inc (P-23446)*
Golden West Custom WD Shutters E 949 951-0600
20561 Pascal Way Lake Forest (92630) *(P-14160)*
Golden West Food Group Inc (PA) **E 888 807-3663**
4401 S Downey Rd Vernon (90058) *(P-1713)*
Golden West K-9, Pacoima *Also called Golden West Security (P-18279)*
Golden West Machine Inc E 562 903-1111
9930 Jordan Cir Santa Fe Springs (90670) *(P-8607)*
Golden West Packg Group LLC (PA) **B 888 501-5893**
15400 Don Julian Rd City of Industry (91745) *(P-3808)*
Golden West Partners Inc (PA) **B 949 477-3090**
200 Spectrum Center Dr # 1250 Irvine (92618) *(P-23446)*
Golden West Security C 818 897-5965
12502 Van Nuys Blvd Ste 2 Pacoima (91331) *(P-18279)*
Golden West Shutters, Lake Forest *Also called ABC Custom Wood Shutters Inc (P-3227)*
Golden West Technology D 714 738-3775
1180 E Valencia Dr Fullerton (92831) *(P-9411)*
Golden West Trading Inc C 323 581-3663
4401 S Downey Rd Vernon (90058) *(P-14594)*
Goldencorr Sheets LLC C 626 369-6446
13890 Nelson Ave City of Industry (91746) *(P-3809)*
Goldenwood Truss Corporation D 805 659-2520
11032 Nardo St Ventura (93004) *(P-3361)*
Golding Publications F 951 244-1966
31558 Railroad Canyon Rd Canyon Lake (92587) *(P-4625)*
Goldman Global Greenfield Inc F 323 589-3444
2025 E 48th St Vernon (90058) *(P-5655)*
Goldman Sachs & Co LLC C 310 407-5700
2121 Avenue Of The Stars # 2600 Los Angeles (90067) *(P-15267)*
Goldrich & Kest Industries LLC (PA) **A 310 204-2050**
5150 Overland Ave Culver City (90230) *(P-16051)*
Goldrichkest (PA) **C 310 204-2050**
5150 Overland Ave Culver City (90230) *(P-16052)*
Goldsign, Huntington Park *Also called Citizens of Humanity LLC (P-2932)*
Goldsmith Construction Co Inc E 562 595-5975
2683 Lime Ave Signal Hill (90755) *(P-1525)*
Goldstar, Irvine *Also called Spireon Inc (P-17721)*
Goldstar Asphalt Products, Perris *Also called Npg Inc (P-5275)*
Goldstar Asphalt Products Inc E 951 940-1610
1354 Jet Way Perris (92571) *(P-5272)*
Goleta Valley Cottage Hosp Aux B 805 681-6468
351 S Patterson Ave Santa Barbara (93111) *(P-20779)*
Golf Apparel Brands Inc E 310 327-5188
404 Fordyce Rd Los Angeles (90049) *(P-2946)*
Golf Buddy, Santa Fe Springs *Also called Deca International Corp (P-10582)*
Golf Design Inc F 714 899-4040
10523 Humbolt St Los Alamitos (90720) *(P-11421)*
Golf Design USA, Los Alamitos *Also called Golf Design Inc (P-11421)*
Golf Investment LLC (PA) **D 949 498-6604**
200 Avenida La Pata San Clemente (92673) *(P-19565)*
Golf Pro Shop, Riverside *Also called Canyon Crest Country Club Inc (P-19552)*
Golfsmith Intl Holdings E 760 202-1023
72700 Dinah Shore Dr # 200 Palm Desert (92211) *(P-14079)*
Gomen Furniture Mfg Inc E 310 635-4894
11612 Wright Rd Lynwood (90262) *(P-3504)*
Gonsalves & Santucci Inc B 909 350-0474
13052 Dahlia St Fontana (92337) *(P-1526)*
Gonzalez Feliciano F 909 236-1372
1583 E Grand Ave Pomona (91766) *(P-3252)*
Gonzalez Kitchen Supplies Inc (PA) **F 909 460-0581**
959 W State St Ste F Ontario (91762) *(P-7148)*
Gonzalez Management Co Inc D 818 485-0596
10147 San Fernando Rd Pacoima (91331) *(P-23031)*
Gooch and Housego Cal LLC D 805 529-3324
5390 Kazuko Ct Moorpark (93021) *(P-10837)*
Good American LLC (PA) **E 213 357-5100**
3125 S La Cienega Blvd Los Angeles (90016) *(P-2947)*
Good Culture LLC E 949 545-9945
1621 Alton Pkwy Ste 250 Irvine (92606) *(P-1836)*
Good Fellas Industries Inc D 323 924-9495
4400 Bandini Blvd Vernon (90058) *(P-1662)*
Good Neighbor Pharmacy, Encino *Also called Zelzah Pharmacy Inc (P-4916)*
Good Samaritan Hospital Aux C 213 977-2121
1225 Wilshire Blvd Los Angeles (90017) *(P-19833)*
Good Samaritan Shelter D 805 346-8185
245 Inger Dr Ste 103b Santa Maria (93454) *(P-21792)*
Good Shepherd Communities, Mission Viejo *Also called Good Shepherd Lutheran Hm of W (P-22104)*
Good Shepherd Lutheran Hm of W (PA) **C 559 791-2000**
24800 Chrisanta Dr # 250 Mission Viejo (92691) *(P-22104)*
Good Shepherd Lutheran HM of W D 805 526-2482
2949 Alamo St Simi Valley (93063) *(P-22105)*
Good Smrtan Hosp A Cal Ltd Prt B 661 903-9555
901 Olive Dr Bakersfield (93308) *(P-20780)*
Good Sports Plus Ltd B 310 671-4400
370 Amapola Ave Ste 208 Torrance (90501) *(P-17629)*
Good Trading Co E 951 688-2495
4085 Flat Rock Dr Riverside (92505) *(P-18531)*
Good Worldwide LLC E 323 206-6495
6380 Wilshire Blvd # 1500 Los Angeles (90048) *(P-4176)*
Good-West Rubber Corp (PA) **C 909 987-1774**
9615 Feron Blvd Rancho Cucamonga (91730) *(P-5378)*
Gooden Center D 626 356-0078
191 N El Molino Ave Pasadena (91101) *(P-21046)*
Goodix Technology Inc F 858 554-0352
133 Technology Dr Ste 200 Irvine (92618) *(P-8259)*
Goodman Food Products Inc (PA) **C 310 674-3180**
200 E Beach Ave Fl 1 Inglewood (90302) *(P-2446)*
Goodman Manufacturing Co LP B 760 955-7770
15024 Anacapa Rd Victorville (92392) *(P-8341)*
Goodman North America LLC D 714 680-7460
2001 E Orangethorpe Ave Fullerton (92831) *(P-3754)*
Goodman North America LLC (PA) **D 949 407-0100**
18201 Von Karman Ave # 1 Irvine (92612) *(P-15875)*
Goodnight Industries Inc F 818 988-2801
15035 Califa St Van Nuys (91411) *(P-11681)*
Goodrich Corporation C 714 984-1461
2727 E Imperial Hwy Brea (92821) *(P-10340)*
Goodridge Usa Inc (HQ) **D 310 533-1924**
529 Van Ness Ave Torrance (90501) *(P-13061)*
Goodrx Inc (PA) **F 855 268-2822**
2701 Olympic Blvd A Santa Monica (90404) *(P-17868)*
Goodrx Holdings Inc (PA) **C 855 268-2822**
2701 Olympic Blvd Santa Monica (90404) *(P-18091)*
Goodwest Linings & Coatings, Rancho Cucamonga *Also called Goodwest Rubber Linings Inc (P-5379)*
Goodwest Rubber Linings Inc E 888 499-0085
8814 Industrial Ln Rancho Cucamonga (91730) *(P-5379)*
Goodwill Central Coast C 805 544-0542
880 Industrial Way San Luis Obispo (93401) *(P-21793)*
Goodwill Inds Orange Cnty Cal C 714 754-7808
2910 W Garry Ave Santa Ana (92704) *(P-21954)*
Goodwill Inds Orange Cnty Cal D 714 881-3986
5880 Edinger Ave Huntington Beach (92649) *(P-21955)*
Goodwill Inds San Luis Obispo, San Luis Obispo *Also called Goodwill Central Coast (P-21793)*
Goodwill Inds Southern Cal (PA) **A 323 223-1211**
342 N San Fernando Rd Los Angeles (90031) *(P-21956)*
Goodwill Srving The Pple Sther (PA) **D 562 435-3411**
800 W Pacific Coast Hwy Long Beach (90806) *(P-18532)*
Goodwin Ammonia Company (PA) **F 714 894-0531**
12102 Industry St Garden Grove (92841) *(P-4941)*

ALPHABETIC

Employee Codes: A=Over 500 employees, B=251-500
C=101-250, D=51-100, E=20-50 F=10-19

2022 Southern California Business
Directory and Buyers Guide

© Mergent Inc. 1-800-342-5647
1145

Goodwin Ammonia Company.....D.....714 894-0531
12361 Monarch St Garden Grove (92841) *(P-4942)*

Goodyear Rbr Co Southern Cal, Rancho Cucamonga *Also called Good-West Rubber Corp (P-5378)*

Google Fiber Inc (HQ).....D.....**650 253-0000**
35018 Avenue D Yucaipa (92399) *(P-12643)*

Google International LLC (HQ).....A.....**650 253-0000**
35018 Avenue D Yucaipa (92399) *(P-12644)*

Gordian Medical Inc.....B.....714 556-0200
17595 Cartwright Rd Irvine (92614) *(P-13490)*

Gordon Brush Mfg Co Inc (PA).....E.....**323 724-7777**
3737 Capitol Ave City of Industry (90601) *(P-11511)*

Gordon Edelstein & Krepack, Los Angeles *Also called Gordon Edlstein Krpack Grant F (P-21570)*

Gordon Edlstein Krpack Grant F.....E.....213 739-7000
3580 Wilshire Blvd # 180 Los Angeles (90010) *(P-21570)*

Gordon Laboratories Inc.....C.....310 327-5240
751 E Artesia Blvd Carson (90746) *(P-5026)*

Gores Group LLC (PA).....D.....**310 209-3010**
9800 Wilshire Blvd Beverly Hills (90212) *(P-15268)*

Gores Radio Holdings LLC.....D.....310 209-3010
10877 Wilshire Blvd Fl 18 Los Angeles (90024) *(P-9871)*

Gores URS Holdings Corp (PA).....A.....**310 209-3010**
10877 Wilshire Blvd Fl 18 Los Angeles (90024) *(P-12048)*

Gorilla Automotive Products, Vernon *Also called Amcor Industries Inc (P-10016)*

Gorlitz Sewer & Drain Inc.....E.....562 944-3060
10132 Norwalk Blvd Santa Fe Springs (90670) *(P-8384)*

Gorlitz Sewer and Drain, Santa Fe Springs *Also called Die Craft Stamping Inc (P-7472)*

Gosch Ford Lincoln Mercury, Hemet *Also called Jack Gosch Ford Inc (P-18842)*

Gospel Recordings.....F.....951 719-1650
41823 Enterprise Cir N # 200 Temecula (92590) *(P-9219)*

Gothic Ground Management, Santa Clarita *Also called Gothic Landscaping Inc (P-307)*

Gothic Grounds Mgmt, Valencia *Also called Gothic Landscaping Inc (P-259)*

Gothic Landscaping Inc (PA).....C.....**661 678-1400**
27413 Tourney Rd Santa Clarita (91355) *(P-307)*

Gothic Landscaping Inc.....D.....661 257-5085
27413 Tourney Rd Ste 200 Valencia (91355) *(P-259)*

Gotprint.....F.....877 922-7374
7651 N San Fernando Rd Burbank (91505) *(P-4304)*

Gottstein Contracting Corp.....D.....661 322-8934
4114 Armour Ave Bakersfield (93308) *(P-13860)*

Gould & Bass Company Inc.....E.....909 623-6793
1431 W 2nd St Pomona (91766) *(P-10755)*

Gould Welding Inc.....F.....805 489-9353
3725 Alisos Rd Arroyo Grande (93420) *(P-18979)*

Goulds Pumps.....F.....562 949-2113
3951 Capitol Ave City of Industry (90601) *(P-8011)*

Gourmet Coffee Warehouse Inc (PA).....E.....**323 871-8930**
920 N Formosa Ave Los Angeles (90046) *(P-2354)*

Gourmet Foods Inc (PA).....C.....**310 632-3300**
2910 E Harcourt St Compton (90221) *(P-14469)*

Gourmet India Food Company LLC.....D.....562 698-9763
12220 Rivera Rd Ste A Whittier (90606) *(P-14692)*

Gourmet Specialties Inc.....D.....323 587-1734
2120 E 25th St Vernon (90058) *(P-14634)*

Gourmet Trading Company, Redondo Beach *Also called Nzg Specialties Inc (P-14483)*

Governmentjobscom Inc.....C.....310 426-6304
300 Continental Blvd # 565 El Segundo (90245) *(P-17869)*

GP Color Imaging Group, North Hollywood *Also called Wes Go Inc (P-4592)*

GP Electric, Pomona *Also called G Powell Electric (P-19012)*

GP Machining Inc.....E.....805 686-0852
94 Commerce Dr Buellton (93427) *(P-8608)*

GP Merger Sub Inc.....D.....562 946-7722
9401 Ann St Santa Fe Springs (90670) *(P-5956)*

GPA Printing CA LLC.....F.....818 618-1500
9655 De Soto Ave Chatsworth (91311) *(P-4305)*

GPde Slva Spces Incrporation (PA).....E.....**562 407-2643**
8531 Loch Lomond Dr Pico Rivera (90660) *(P-2447)*

GPh Medical & Legal Services (PA).....C.....**213 207-2700**
468 N Camden Dr Beverly Hills (90210) *(P-20364)*

Gpi Ca-Niii Inc.....D.....626 305-3000
1434 Buena Vista St Duarte (91010) *(P-18835)*

Gps Associates Inc.....E.....949 408-3162
1803 Carnegie Ave Santa Ana (92705) *(P-4962)*

Gps Flyers.....D.....951 588-7777
527 Prospect Ave Hermosa Beach (90254) *(P-23227)*

Gps Painting Wallcovering Inc.....C.....714 730-8904
1307 E Saint Gertrude Pl C Santa Ana (92705) *(P-1182)*

Gqr, Marina Del Rey *Also called Wynden Stark LLC (P-17481)*

Gr8 Care Inc.....D.....626 337-7229
14518 Los Angeles St Baldwin Park (91706) *(P-20365)*

Graber Olive House, Ontario *Also called C C Graber Co (P-68)*

Grabit Interactive Inc.....E.....844 472-2488
14724 Ventura Blvd Sherman Oaks (91403) *(P-17086)*

Grace Communications Inc (PA).....E.....**213 628-4384**
210 S Spring St Los Angeles (90012) *(P-3983)*

Grace In La, City of Industry *Also called Gracing Inc (P-2769)*

Grace Machine Co Inc.....F.....323 771-6215
4540 Cecilia St Cudahy (90201) *(P-8609)*

Grace To You (PA).....D.....**661 295-5777**
28001 Harrison Pkwy Valencia (91355) *(P-12692)*

Grace To You Radio Ministries, Valencia *Also called Grace To You (P-12692)*

Graceful Snscnce Adult Day HLT.....F.....310 538-5808
120 W El Segundo Blvd Los Angeles (90061) *(P-21794)*

Graceland Hospice Care, Orange *Also called Sherman Oaks Hspice Care Group (P-20543)*

Gracing Brand Management Inc.....B.....626 297-2472
1108 W Vly Blvb Ste 660 Alhambra (91803) *(P-3042)*

Gracing Inc.....E.....626 269-6818
17003 Evergreen Pl City of Industry (91745) *(P-2769)*

Graco Childrens Products Inc.....C.....770 418-7200
17182 Nevada St Victorville (92394) *(P-3528)*

Grade A Sign LLC.....E.....310 652-9700
529 N La Cienega Blvd # 300 West Hollywood (90048) *(P-11559)*

Gradient Engineers Inc.....C.....949 477-0555
17781 Cowan Ste 140 Irvine (92614) *(P-22562)*

Graffiti Shield Inc.....F.....714 575-1100
2940 E Le Palma Ave Ste D Anaheim (92806) *(P-5431)*

Graham Lee Associates Inc.....F.....323 581-8203
8674 Atlantic Ave South Gate (90280) *(P-3587)*

Graham Packaging Co Europe LLC.....C.....909 989-5367
11555 Arrow Rte Rancho Cucamonga (91730) *(P-5475)*

Graham Webb International Inc (HQ).....D.....**760 918-3600**
6109 De Soto Ave Woodland Hills (91367) *(P-5027)*

Gramic Enterprises Inc.....F.....714 329-8627
21770 Deveron Cv Yorba Linda (92887) *(P-2146)*

Gramicci Comfort Engineered, Agoura Hills *Also called Sole Survivor Corporation (P-2994)*

Granada Hills Care Center, Granada Hills *Also called In Granada Hlls Cnvlscent Hosp (P-20378)*

Granada Hills Sr High School, Granada Hills *Also called Los Angeles Unified School Dst (P-23470)*

Granatelli Motor Sports Inc.....E.....805 486-6644
1000 Yarnell Pl Oxnard (93033) *(P-10068)*

Granath & Granath Inc.....E.....310 327-5740
1930 W Rosecrans Ave Gardena (90249) *(P-7264)*

Grancell Village, Reseda *Also called Los Angles Jewish HM For Aging (P-20409)*

Grand Avenue Hlth Holdings LLC.....D.....949 487-9500
29222 Rncho Vejo Rd Ste 1 San Juan Capistrano (92675) *(P-20366)*

Grand Casino On Main Inc.....F.....310 253-9066
3826 Main St Culver City (90232) *(P-2006)*

Grand Fusion Housewares LLC (PA).....E.....**888 614-7263**
12 Partridge Irvine (92604) *(P-5656)*

Grand General Accessories LLC.....E.....310 631-2589
1965 E Vista Bella Way Rancho Dominguez (90220) *(P-8873)*

Grand Prix Performance, Costa Mesa *Also called Grand Prix Road Trends Inc (P-6202)*

Grand Prix Road Trends Inc (PA).....F.....**949 645-7022**
1718 Newport Blvd Costa Mesa (92627) *(P-6202)*

Grand Terrace Care Center (PA).....D.....**909 825-5221**
12000 Mount Vernon Ave Grand Terrace (92313) *(P-20367)*

Grand Textile, Cerritos *Also called Dool Fna Inc (P-2596)*

Grand View Geranium Grdns Inc.....D.....310 217-0490
18307 Central Ave Carson (90746) *(P-78)*

Grand Vista Hotel, Simi Valley *Also called Simi West Inc (P-16711)*

Grand-Way Fabri-Graphic Inc.....F.....818 206-8560
22550 Lamplight Pl Santa Clarita (91350) *(P-7369)*

Grandall Distributing Co Inc.....E.....818 242-6640
321 El Bonito Ave Glendale (91204) *(P-18533)*

Grandcare Health Services LLC (PA).....C.....**866 554-2447**
3452 E Fthill Blvd Ste 70 Pasadena (91107) *(P-21168)*

Grandis Metals Intl Corp.....F.....949 459-2621
29752 Ave De Las Bndra Rcho STA Marg (92688) *(P-6332)*

Grandis Titanium, Rcho STA Marg *Also called Grandis Metals Intl Corp (P-6332)*

Grandma Lucys LLC.....F.....949 206-8547
30432 Esperanza Rcho STA Marg (92688) *(P-1957)*

Grani Installation Inc (PA).....D.....**714 898-0441**
5411 Commercial Dr Huntington Beach (92649) *(P-767)*

Granite Construction Company.....B.....760 775-7500
38000 Monroe St Indio (92203) *(P-881)*

Granite Construction Company.....C.....805 964-9951
5335 Debbie Rd Santa Barbara (93111) *(P-882)*

Granite Software Inc.....F.....818 252-1950
7590 N Glenoaks Blvd # 102 Burbank (91504) *(P-17870)*

Granitize Products Inc.....D.....562 923-5438
11022 Vulcan St South Gate (90280) *(P-4963)*

Granlund Candies, Yucaipa *Also called B B G Management Group (P-14558)*

Grant & Weber (PA).....C.....**818 878-7700**
26610 Agoura Rd Ste 209 Calabasas (91302) *(P-17113)*

Grant & Weber Travel, Calabasas *Also called Grant & Weber (P-17113)*

Grant Construction Inc.....C.....661 588-4586
7702 Meany Ave Ste 103 Bakersfield (93308) *(P-1438)*

Grant Piston Rings, Anaheim *Also called Rtr Industries LLC (P-8436)*

Grant, Richard S, Los Angeles *Also called Wolf Rfkin Shpiro Schlman Rbk (P-21697)*

Grants Custom Cabinets.....C.....805 466-9680
7310 Kingsbury Rd Templeton (93465) *(P-607)*

Grapefruit Blvd Invstments Inc.....F.....310 575-1175
10866 Wilshire Blvd # 225 Los Angeles (90024) *(P-4747)*

Grapheex, Simi Valley *Also called Pars Publishing Corp (P-4387)*

Graphic Color Systems Inc.....D.....323 283-3000
1166 W Garvey Ave Monterey Park (91754) *(P-4306)*

Graphic Design Services Inc.....E.....562 282-8000
1059 West Rd La Habra Heights (90631) *(P-17176)*

Graphic Film Group LLC (PA).....F.....**310 887-6330**
1901 Avenue Of The Stars Los Angeles (90067) *(P-4071)*

Graphic Ink Corp.....E.....714 901-2805
5382 Industrial Dr Huntington Beach (92649) *(P-17177)*

Graphic Ink and Graphic Ink, Huntington Beach *Also called Graphic Ink Corp (P-17177)*

Graphic Packaging Intl LLC.....C.....559 651-3535
1600 Kelsey Rd Visalia (93291) *(P-14932)*

Graphic Prints Inc.....E.....310 870-1239
904 Silver Spur Rd # 415 Rllng HLS Est (90274) *(P-3174)*

Graphic Research Inc.....E.....818 886-7340
9334 Mason Ave Chatsworth (91311) *(P-9412)*

Graphic Trends Incorporated.....E.....562 531-2339
7301 Adams St Paramount (90723) *(P-4522)*

Graphic Visions Inc.....E.....818 845-8393
7119 Fair Ave North Hollywood (91605) *(P-4307)*

Graphics United, Covina *Also called Shift Calendars Inc* ***(P-4422)***
Graphiq LLC......C......805 335-2433
101a Innovation Pl Santa Barbara (93108) ***(P-4177)***
Graphtec America Inc (HQ)......**E......949 770-6010**
17462 Armstrong Ave Irvine (92614) ***(P-10698)***
Grasshopper House Partners LLC......C......310 589-2880
6428 Meadows Ct Malibu (90265) ***(P-21307)***
Grating Pacific Inc (PA)......**E......562 598-4314**
3651 Sausalito St Los Alamitos (90720) ***(P-6620)***
Graybar Electric Company Inc......C......909 451-4300
1370 Valley Vista Dr # 100 Diamond Bar (91765) ***(P-13631)***
Graycon Inc......E......626 961-9640
232 S 8th Ave City of Industry (91746) ***(P-1076)***
Grayd-A Prcsion Met Fbricators......E......562 944-8951
13233 Florence Ave Santa Fe Springs (90670) ***(P-6846)***
Graypay LLC......F......818 387-6735
6345 Balboa Blvd Ste 115 Encino (91316) ***(P-17871)***
Grayson Service Inc......E......661 589-5444
1845 Greeley Rd Bakersfield (93314) ***(P-504)***
Great Amercn Seafood Import Co, Carson *Also called Southwind Foods LLC* ***(P-14585)***
Great American Packaging......E......323 582-2247
4361 S Soto St Vernon (90058) ***(P-3884)***
Great Amrcn Logistics Dist Inc......D......800 381-4527
13565 Larwin Cir Santa Fe Springs (90670) ***(P-12113)***
Great Atlantic News LLC......C......770 863-9000
1575 N Main St Orange (92867) ***(P-14873)***
Great Clips, Bakersfield *Also called Burkshine Enterprises Inc* ***(P-16900)***
Great Eastern Entertainment Co......E......310 638-5058
610 W Carob St Compton (90220) ***(P-4178)***
Great Northern Corporation......E......951 361-4770
12075 Cabernet Dr Fontana (92337) ***(P-3855)***
Great Pacific Elbow Company......E......909 606-5551
13900 Sycamore Way Chino (91710) ***(P-6847)***
Great River Food, City of Industry *Also called Derek and Constance Lee Corp* ***(P-1731)***
Great Scott Tree Service Inc (PA)......**C......714 826-1750**
10761 Court Ave Stanton (90680) ***(P-357)***
Great Western Distributing Svc, Los Angeles *Also called Gils Distributing Service* ***(P-17098)***
Great Western Grinding Inc......F......714 890-6592
15292 Bolsa Chica St Huntington Beach (92649) ***(P-18534)***
Great Western Litho, Van Nuys *Also called Investment Enterprises Inc* ***(P-4530)***
Great Western Packaging LLC......D......818 464-3800
8230-8240 Haskell Ave Van Nuys (91406) ***(P-4523)***
Greater Alarm Company Inc (HQ)......**D......949 474-0555**
3750 Schaufele Ave # 200 Long Beach (90808) ***(P-18382)***
Greater El Monte Cmnty Hosp, El Monte *Also called Ahm Gemch Inc* ***(P-20664)***
Greater Las Vegas Dialysis LLC (HQ)......**E......310 536-2400**
601 Hawaii St El Segundo (90245) ***(P-21243)***
Greater Los Angeles Zoo Assn......D......323 644-4200
5333 Zoo Dr Los Angeles (90027) ***(P-22184)***
Greater Los Angles Area Cncil (PA)......**D......213 413-4400**
2333 Scout Way Los Angeles (90026) ***(P-22340)***
Greater Los Angles Vtrans RES......D......310 312-1554
11301 Wilshire Blvd # 1 Los Angeles (90073) ***(P-16167)***
Greater Valley Medical Group (PA)......**D......818 838-4500**
11600 Indian Hills Rd # 300 Mission Hills (91345) ***(P-21308)***
Greater Valley Medical Group......C......818 781-7097
14600 Sherman Way Ste 300 Van Nuys (91405) ***(P-21309)***
Grech Motors LLC (PA)......**E......951 688-8347**
6915 Arlington Ave Riverside (92504) ***(P-19013)***
Green Acres Lodge, Rosemead *Also called Longwood Management Corp* ***(P-20406)***
Green Convergence (PA)......**D......661 294-9495**
28476 Westinghouse Pl Valencia (91355) ***(P-13829)***
Green Dot Corporation (PA)......**A......626 765-2000**
3465 E Foothill Blvd Pasadena (91107) ***(P-15143)***
Green Energy Innovations, Buena Park *Also called Sfadia Inc* ***(P-1316)***
Green Equity Investors IV LP (PA)......**A......310 954-0444**
11111 Santa Monica Blvd Los Angeles (90025) ***(P-16264)***
Green Farms California LLC (PA)......**C......213 747-4411**
2652 Long Beach Ave Ste 2 Los Angeles (90058) ***(P-14635)***
Green Hasson & Janks LLP......C......310 873-1600
700 S Flower St Ste 3300 Los Angeles (90017) ***(P-22786)***
Green Hills Software LLC (HQ)......**C......805 965-6044**
30 W Sola St Santa Barbara (93101) ***(P-17872)***
Green Line Rail Eqp Maint, Lawndale *Also called Los Angles Cnty Mtro Trnsp Aut* ***(P-11816)***
Green Products Packaging Corp......F......951 940-9343
22770 Perry St Perris (92570) ***(P-3836)***
Green River Golf Corporation......D......714 970-8411
5215 Green River Rd Corona (92878) ***(P-19490)***
Green River Golf Course, Corona *Also called Green River Golf Corporation* ***(P-19490)***
Green Spot Packaging Inc......E......909 625-8771
100 S Cambridge Ave Claremont (91711) ***(P-2266)***
Green Thumb International Inc......C......661 259-1071
23734 Newhall Ave Newhall (91321) ***(P-14884)***
Green Thumb International Inc......D......818 340-6400
21812 Sherman Way Canoga Park (91303) ***(P-14885)***
Green Thumb Nurseries, Newhall *Also called Green Thumb International Inc* ***(P-14884)***
Green Thumb Produce Inc......C......951 849-4711
2648 W Ramsey St Banning (92220) ***(P-14636)***
Green Tomato Grill, Orange *Also called Fahetas LLC* ***(P-17613)***
Green Valley Foods Product......F......760 964-1105
25684 Community Blvd Barstow (92311) ***(P-1773)***
Green Worldwide Shipping LLC......D......310 988-1550
5777 W Century Blvd # 1285 Los Angeles (90045) ***(P-12465)***
Green's Metal Cutoff, Santa Fe Springs *Also called Dunstan Enterprises Inc* ***(P-8575)***
Greenball Corp (PA)......**E......714 782-3060**
222 S Harbor Blvd Ste 700 Anaheim (92805) ***(P-13117)***
Greenberg Glsker Flds Clman Mc......C......310 553-3610
2049 Century Park E # 2600 Los Angeles (90067) ***(P-21571)***
Greenberg Traurig LLP......D......310 586-7708
1840 Century Park E # 1900 Los Angeles (90067) ***(P-21572)***
Greenbrier Rail, San Bernardino *Also called Meridian Rail Acquisition* ***(P-12579)***
Greenbrier Rail Services, San Bernardino *Also called Gunderson Rail Services LLC* ***(P-12572)***
Greenfields Outdoor Fitnes Inc......F......888 315-9037
2617 W Woodland Dr Anaheim (92801) ***(P-11422)***
Greengro Technologies Inc (PA)......**E......714 367-6538**
1676 W Lincoln Ave Anaheim (92801) ***(P-17873)***
Greenheart Farms Inc......B......805 481-2234
902 Zenon Way Arroyo Grande (93420) ***(P-107)***
Greenhouse Agency Inc......D......949 752-7542
18195 Mcdurmott E Ste A Irvine (92614) ***(P-23228)***
Greenjacket, Foothill Ranch *Also called Hubbell Power Systems Inc* ***(P-13634)***
Greenkraft Inc......F......714 545-7777
2530 S Birch St Santa Ana (92707) ***(P-9951)***
Greenlots, Los Angeles *Also called Zeco Systems Inc* ***(P-14798)***
Greenlots, Los Angeles *Also called Shell New Energies US LLC* ***(P-17712)***
Greenpath Recovery Recycl Svcs, Colton *Also called Greenpath Recovery West Inc* ***(P-14116)***
Greenpath Recovery West Inc......D......909 954-0686
330 W Citrus St Ste 250 Colton (92324) ***(P-14116)***
Greenpower Motor Company Inc......E......909 308-0960
8885 Haven Ave Ste 150 Rancho Cucamonga (91730) ***(P-9952)***
Greens Group Inc......C......949 829-4902
8815 Research Dr Ste 100 Irvine (92618) ***(P-16457)***
Greenscreen......E......310 837-0526
725 S Figueroa St # 1825 Los Angeles (90017) ***(P-260)***
Greenshine New Energy LLC......D......949 609-9636
23661 Birtcher Dr Lake Forest (92630) ***(P-9135)***
Greensoft Technology Inc......C......323 254-5961
155 S El Molino Ave # 100 Pasadena (91101) ***(P-18092)***
Greenspire LLC......E......310 477-7686
515 S Flower St Ste 1800 Los Angeles (90071) ***(P-23229)***
Greenspire Construction, Los Angeles *Also called Greenspire LLC* ***(P-23229)***
Greenwave Reality Inc......E......714 805-9283
15420 Laguna Canyon Rd # 15 Irvine (92618) ***(P-18035)***
Greenwave Systems, Irvine *Also called Greenwave Reality Inc* ***(P-18035)***
Greenwood Hall Inc......C......310 905-8300
6230 Wilshire Blvd # 136 Los Angeles (90048) ***(P-23032)***
Greers Bnner A Bakersfield Inc......D......661 322-5858
4115 Buck Owens Blvd Bakersfield (93308) ***(P-1077)***
Grefco Dicaperl, Torrance *Also called Dicaperl Corporation* ***(P-585)***
Greg Ian Islands Inc......E......626 355-0019
123b E Montecito Ave B Sierra Madre (91024) ***(P-3647)***
Gregg Drilling LLC......C......562 427-6899
2726 Walnut Ave Signal Hill (90755) ***(P-1560)***
Gregg Drilling & Testing Inc (PA)......**D......562 427-6899**
2726 Walnut Ave Signal Hill (90755) ***(P-1663)***
Gregg Electric Inc......C......909 983-1794
608 W Emporia St Ontario (91762) ***(P-1260)***
Gregg Hammork Enterprizes Inc......E......949 586-7902
23002 Alicia Pkwy Mission Viejo (92692) ***(P-404)***
Gregg's Mission Viejo Mobile, Mission Viejo *Also called Gregg Hammork Enterprizes Inc* ***(P-404)***
Gregory A Stainer MD Facs......D......661 393-2331
215 China Grade Loop Bakersfield (93308) ***(P-19834)***
Gregory Consulting Inc (PA)......**C......805 642-0111**
6350 Leland St Ventura (93003) ***(P-18836)***
Gregory W Peterson DDS (PA)......**D......626 354-4223**
25260 La Paz Rd Ste I Laguna Hills (92653) ***(P-20180)***
Greif Bros Corp......E......909 941-4570
3042 Inland Empire Blvd Ontario (91764) ***(P-3837)***
Greka Inc......F......805 347-8700
1791 Sinton Rd Santa Maria (93458) ***(P-382)***
Greka Integrated Inc (PA)......**C......805 347-8700**
1700 Sinton Rd Santa Maria (93458) ***(P-453)***
Greneker Furniture......F......323 263-9000
3110 E 12th St Los Angeles (90023) ***(P-3648)***
Greneker Solutions, Los Angeles *Also called Pacific Manufacturing MGT Inc* ***(P-3690)***
Grenfield Consulting......E......310 286-0200
1801 Century Park E Fl 23 Los Angeles (90067) ***(P-454)***
Gresham Savage Nolan & Tilden (PA)......**E......619 794-0050**
550 E Hospitality Ln # 300 San Bernardino (92408) ***(P-21573)***
Grey Studio Inc......F......323 780-8111
629 S Clarence St Los Angeles (90023) ***(P-2573)***
Greystar Management Svcs LP......B......818 596-2180
6320 Canoga Ave Ste 1512 Woodland Hills (91367) ***(P-15876)***
Greystar Management Svcs LP......B......949 705-0010
620 Nwport Ctr Dr Fl 15 Flr 15 Newport Beach (92660) ***(P-15877)***
Grfco Inc......D......951 657-8887
4517 Wade Ave Perris (92571) ***(P-950)***
Grht Inc......D......323 873-6393
14818 Raymer St Van Nuys (91405) ***(P-14933)***
Grico Precision Inc......F......626 963-0368
128 S Valencia Ave Ste A Glendora (91741) ***(P-8610)***
Griff Industries Inc......F......661 728-0111
4515 Runway Dr Lancaster (93536) ***(P-5657)***
Griffin Capital Holdings Corp......D......310 469-6100
1520 E Grand Ave El Segundo (90245) ***(P-16265)***
Griffith Company (PA)......**D......714 984-5500**
3050 E Birch St Brea (92821) ***(P-883)***
Griffith Company......B......661 392-6640
1128 Carrier Parkway Ave Bakersfield (93308) ***(P-884)***
Griffith Company......D......562 929-1128
12200 Bloomfield Ave Santa Fe Springs (90670) ***(P-885)***
Griffith Park Healthcare Ctr, Glendale *Also called Griffith Pk Rhbltation Ctr LLC* ***(P-20368)***

ALPHABETIC

Employee Codes: A=Over 500 employees, B=251-500
C=101-250, D=51-100, E=20-50 F=10-19
2022 Southern California Business Directory and Buyers Guide
© Mergent Inc. 1-800-342-5647
1147

Griffith Pk Rhbltation Ctr LLC ....D....818 845-8507
201 Allen Ave Glendale (91201) ***(P-20368)***

Grifols Biologicals LLC (HQ) ....B....**323 225-2221**
5555 Valley Blvd Los Angeles (90032) ***(P-4935)***

Grifols Diagnstc Solutions Inc (HQ) ....A....**323 225-2221**
2410 Lillyvale Ave Los Angeles (90032) ***(P-21069)***

Grifols Shared Svcs N Amer Inc (HQ) ....A....**323 225-2221**
2410 Lillyvale Ave Los Angeles (90032) ***(P-14246)***

Grifols Usa LLC ....B....626 435-2600
13111 Temple Ave City of Industry (91746) ***(P-13491)***

Grifols Wrldwide Oprtons USA I ....D....626 435-2600
13111 Temple Ave City of Industry (91746) ***(P-21431)***

Grimmway Enterprises Inc ....B....661 854-6240
12020 Malaga Rd Arvin (93203) ***(P-700)***

Grimmway Enterprises Inc ....C....760 344-0204
2171 W Bannister Rd Brawley (92227) ***(P-18837)***

Grimmway Enterprises Inc ....C....661 393-3320
6101 Zerker Rd Shafter (93263) ***(P-172)***

Grimmway Enterprises Inc ....C....661 854-6200
14141 Di Giorgio Rd Arvin (93203) ***(P-23033)***

Grimmway Enterprises Inc ....C....661 854-6250
830 Sycamore Rd Arvin (93203) ***(P-173)***

Grimmway Enterprises Inc ....C....661 854-6200
11412 Malaga Rd Arvin (93203) ***(P-174)***

Grimmway Enterprises Inc ....C....661 845-5200
6900 Mountain View Rd Bakersfield (93307) ***(P-175)***

Grimmway Enterprises Inc ....C....661 399-0844
6301 Zerker Rd Shafter (93263) ***(P-108)***

Grimmway Enterprises Inc ....C....661 845-3758
12000 Main St Lamont (93241) ***(P-14637)***

Grimmway Farms, Arvin *Also called Grimmway Enterprises Inc* ***(P-174)***

Grimmway Farms, Bakersfield *Also called Grimmway Enterprises Inc* ***(P-175)***

Grimmway Frozen Foods, Arvin *Also called Grimmway Enterprises Inc* ***(P-173)***

Gripp, Temecula *Also called Bbk Performance Inc* ***(P-13048)***

Griswold Controls LLC (PA) ....D....**949 559-6000**
1700 Barranca Pkwy Irvine (92606) ***(P-7474)***

Griswold Pump Company ....E....909 422-1700
22069 Van Buren St Grand Terrace (92313) ***(P-8012)***

Grit Management LLC ....D....949 220-7765
864 W 16th St Newport Beach (92663) ***(P-19451)***

Gritcycle, Newport Beach *Also called Grit Management LLC* ***(P-19451)***

Griton Industries Inc (PA) ....F....**714 554-8875**
10821 Capital Ave Garden Grove (92843) ***(P-6153)***

Gro-Power Inc ....E....909 393-3744
15065 Telephone Ave Chino (91710) ***(P-5155)***

Grocers Specialty Company (HQ) ....E....**323 264-5200**
5200 Sheila St Commerce (90040) ***(P-14470)***

Grolink Plant Company Inc (PA) ....C....**805 984-7958**
4107 W Gonzales Rd Oxnard (93036) ***(P-14886)***

Grosslight Insurance Inc ....D....310 473-9611
6200 Canoga Ave Ste 325 Woodland Hills (91367) ***(P-15574)***

Grosvenor Inv MGT US Inc ....D....310 265-0297
2308 Chelsea Rd Palos Verdes Estates (90274) ***(P-15575)***

Grosvenor Visalia Associates ....E....559 651-5000
9000 W Airport Dr Visalia (93277) ***(P-16458)***

Ground Hog Inc ....E....909 478-5700
1470 Victoria Ct San Bernardino (92408) ***(P-7643)***

Ground Maintenance Services, Thousand Oaks *Also called Kevin Persons Inc* ***(P-263)***

Groundwork Coffee Company, Los Angeles *Also called Gourmet Coffee Warehouse Inc* ***(P-2354)***

Groundwork Coffee Roasters LLC ....C....818 506-6020
5457 Cleon Ave North Hollywood (91601) ***(P-2355)***

Groundwork Open Source Inc ....D....415 992-4500
23332 Mill Creek Dr # 155 Laguna Hills (92653) ***(P-18123)***

Group Five, Whittier *Also called Russ Bassett Corp* ***(P-3487)***

Group Rossignol Usa Inc ....D....949 452-9050
30161 Avnida De Las Bnder Rancho Santa Margari (92688) ***(P-22563)***

Groupex Financial Corporation (HQ) ....B....**714 690-8321**
14849 Firestone Blvd Fl 1 Flr 1 La Mirada (90638) ***(P-15329)***

Grove Diagnstc Imaging Ctr Inc ....A....909 982-8638
8805 Haven Ave Ste 120 Rancho Cucamonga (91730) ***(P-19835)***

Grove Diagnstc Imaging Ctr Inc (HQ) ....E....**909 982-8638**
8283 Grove Ave Ste 101 Rancho Cucamonga (91730) ***(P-19836)***

Grove Lumber & Bldg Sups Inc (PA) ....C....**909 947-0277**
1300 S Campus Ave Ontario (91761) ***(P-13212)***

Grover Manufacturing, South El Monte *Also called Grover Smith Mfg Corp* ***(P-8013)***

Grover Products Co ....D....323 263-9981
3424 E Olympic Blvd Los Angeles (90023) ***(P-10069)***

Grover Smith Mfg Corp ....E....323 724-3444
9717 Factorial Way South El Monte (91733) ***(P-8013)***

Grow Brains System Inc ....E....310 428-6445
2324 Ocean Park Blvd D Santa Monica (90405) ***(P-11374)***

Grow More Inc ....D....310 515-1700
15600 New Century Dr Gardena (90248) ***(P-5170)***

Growest Inc (PA) ....F....**951 638-1000**
1660 Chicago Ave Ste M11 Riverside (92507) ***(P-2188)***

Growest Development, Riverside *Also called Growest Inc* ***(P-2188)***

Growing Place ....D....310 399-7769
401 Ashland Ave Santa Monica (90405) ***(P-22019)***

Growit LLC ....E....949 305-4004
1157 Cliff Ave Fillmore (93015) ***(P-22564)***

Gruber Systems Inc ....E....661 257-0464
29071 The Old Rd Valencia (91355) ***(P-7805)***

Gruen Assoc Archtects Planners, Los Angeles *Also called Gruen Associates Inc* ***(P-22718)***

Gruen Associates Inc ....D....323 937-4270
6330 San Vicente Blvd # 200 Los Angeles (90048) ***(P-22718)***

Grunion Gazette, Long Beach *Also called Gazette Newspapers Inc* ***(P-3982)***

Grupo Deco California Corp (HQ) ....D....**562 634-8990**
8545 Rosecrans Ave Paramount (90723) ***(P-16923)***

Grupoex, La Mirada *Also called Mejico Express Inc* ***(P-12330)***

Gs Brothers Inc (PA) ....C....**310 833-1369**
20331 Main St Carson (90745) ***(P-308)***

Gs Promo Inc (PA) ....E....**626 223-4755**
20829 Valley Blvd Walnut (91789) ***(P-7558)***

Gsa Des Plaines LLC ....D....310 557-5100
10100 Santa Monica Blvd # 2600 Los Angeles (90067) ***(P-16266)***

Gsa Design Inc ....E....818 241-2558
4551 San Fernando Rd # 102 Glendale (91204) ***(P-18535)***

Gscm Ventures Inc ....E....818 303-2600
12924 Pierce St Pacoima (91331) ***(P-5028)***

Gsf Properties Inc ....D....661 834-1498
5051 Ming Ave Apt 69 Bakersfield (93309) ***(P-15878)***

Gsico, Foothill Ranch *Also called Global Solutions Integration* ***(P-22561)***

Gsl Tech Inc ....F....877 572-9617
3134 Maxson Rd El Monte (91732) ***(P-1793)***

Gsms Inc (PA) ....D....**805 477-9866**
5187 Camino Ruiz Camarillo (93012) ***(P-4827)***

Gsp Metal Finishing Inc ....E....818 744-1328
16520 S Figueroa St Gardena (90248) ***(P-7265)***

GSP Precision Inc ....E....818 845-2212
650 Town Center Dr # 950 Costa Mesa (92626) ***(P-8611)***

Gst Inc ....D....949 510-1142
3419 Via Lido Ste 164 Newport Beach (92663) ***(P-8201)***

Gst Industries Inc ....E....818 350-1900
9060 Winnetka Ave Northridge (91324) ***(P-10341)***

Gt Diamond, Irvine *Also called General Tool Inc* ***(P-13985)***

GT Precision Inc ....C....310 323-4374
1629 W 132nd St Gardena (90249) ***(P-7037)***

GT Styling Corp ....E....714 644-9214
2830 E Via Martens Anaheim (92806) ***(P-5658)***

GTM Management Company Inc ....E....562 988-0449
3930b Cherry Ave Long Beach (90807) ***(P-998)***

Gtran Inc (PA) ....E....**805 445-4500**
829 Flynn Rd Camarillo (93012) ***(P-9719)***

Gts Living Foods LLC ....A....323 581-7787
4415 Bandini Blvd Vernon (90058) ***(P-2267)***

Gtt International Inc ....E....951 788-8729
1615 Eastridge Ave Riverside (92507) ***(P-13173)***

Guadalupe Cooling Company Inc ....D....805 343-2331
2040 Guadalupe Rd Guadalupe (93434) ***(P-176)***

Guadalupe Union School Dst (PA) ....C....**805 343-2114**
4465 9th St Guadalupe (93434) ***(P-23034)***

Guarachi Wine Partners Inc ....D....818 225-5100
22837 Ventura Blvd # 300 Woodland Hills (91364) ***(P-14843)***

Guaranteed Rate Inc ....C....424 354-5344
230 Commerce Ste 200 Irvine (92602) ***(P-15199)***

Guaranteed Rate Inc ....C....805 550-6933
1065 Higuera St Ste 100 San Luis Obispo (93401) ***(P-15200)***

Guard Systems District 1, Monterey Park *Also called Guard-Systems Inc* ***(P-18281)***

Guard-Systems Inc ....A....909 947-5400
1910 S Archibald Ave M2 Ontario (91761) ***(P-18280)***

Guard-Systems Inc ....A....323 881-6715
1190 Monterey Pass Rd Monterey Park (91754) ***(P-18281)***

Guardian Fire & Safety, Visalia *Also called Guardian Fire Service Inc* ***(P-1078)***

Guardian Fire Service Inc ....E....559 651-0919
8248 W Doe Ave Visalia (93291) ***(P-1078)***

Guardian General Insur Svcs, Glendale *Also called Ggis Insurance Services Inc* ***(P-15573)***

Guardian Health Care Svcs Inc ....E....714 377-7767
16561 Graham St Huntington Beach (92649) ***(P-21795)***

Guardian Life Insur Co of Amer ....D....626 792-1935
975 San Pasqual St Pasadena (91106) ***(P-15361)***

Guardian Life Insur Co of Amer ....D....213 624-2002
510 W 6th St Ste 815 Los Angeles (90014) ***(P-15362)***

Guardian Safety and Supply LLC ....D....559 651-0919
8248 W Doe Ave Visalia (93291) ***(P-14934)***

Guardnow Inc ....E....877 482-7366
18663 Ventura Blvd # 217 Tarzana (91356) ***(P-18282)***

Guardsmark LLC ....D....310 522-9603
1225 W 190th St Ste 280 Gardena (90248) ***(P-18283)***

Guardsmark LLC (HQ) ....D....**714 619-9700**
1551 N Tustin Ave Ste 650 Santa Ana (92705) ***(P-18284)***

Guardsmark LLC ....C....661 325-5906
5300 Lennox Ave Ste 102 Bakersfield (93309) ***(P-18285)***

Guelaguetza, Los Angeles *Also called Pbf & E LLC* ***(P-2335)***

Guess Inc (PA) ....A....**213 765-3100**
1444 S Alameda St Los Angeles (90021) ***(P-3015)***

Guesty Inc ....C....415 244-0277
340 S Lemon Ave Walnut (91789) ***(P-16459)***

Guggenheim Prtners Inv MGT LLC ....D....310 576-1270
100 Wilshire Blvd Fl 5 Santa Monica (90401) ***(P-16130)***

Guhring Inc ....E....714 841-3582
15581 Computer Ln Huntington Beach (92649) ***(P-7854)***

Guidance Software Inc (HQ) ....C....**626 229-9191**
1055 E Colo Blvd Ste 400 Pasadena (91106) ***(P-17874)***

Guidance Software Inc ....E....626 229-9199
215 N Marengo Ave Ste 250 Pasadena (91101) ***(P-17875)***

Guidance Solutions Inc ....E....310 754-4000
4134 Del Rey Ave Marina Del Rey (90292) ***(P-18124)***

Guided Discoveries Inc ....D....951 659-6062
26800 Saunders Meadows Rd Idyllwild (92549) ***(P-16821)***

Guided Discoveries Inc ....D....310 510-1622
1 Toyon Bay Rd Avalon (90704) ***(P-16822)***

Guinn Corporation ....D....661 325-6109
6533 Rosedale Hwy Bakersfield (93308) ***(P-1596)***

Gulf Enterprises, Chatsworth *Also called Mercury Magnetics Inc* ***(P-9634)***

Mergent e-mail: customerrelations@mergent.com
1148
2022 Southern California Business Directory and Buyers Guide
(P-0000) Products & Services Section entry number
(PA)=Parent Co (HQ)=Headquarters (DH)=Div Headquarters

Gulf Streams......E......562 420-1818
4150 E Donald Douglas Dr Long Beach (90808) ***(P-10188)***
Gulf- California Broadcast Co......D......760 773-0342
31276 Dunham Way Thousand Palms (92276) ***(P-12728)***
Gulfstream Aerospace Corp GA......A......562 907-9300
9818 Mina Ave Whittier (90605) ***(P-10189)***
Gulfstream Aerospace Corp GA......E......805 236-5755
16644 Roscoe Blvd Van Nuys (91406) ***(P-10190)***
Gulfstream Aerospace Corp GA......A......562 420-1818
4150 E Donald Douglas Dr Long Beach (90808) ***(P-10191)***
Gumbiner Savett Inc......D......310 828-9798
1723 Cloverfield Blvd Santa Monica (90404) ***(P-15671)***
Gumbiner Svett Fnkel Fnglson R, Santa Monica *Also called Gumbiner Savett Inc* ***(P-15671)***
Gumgum Sports Inc......E......310 400-0396
1314 7th St Fl 4 Santa Monica (90401) ***(P-17876)***
Gund Company Inc......F......909 890-9300
4701 E Airport Dr Ontario (91761) ***(P-9050)***
Gunderson Rail Services LLC......D......909 478-0541
1475 Cooley Ct San Bernardino (92408) ***(P-12572)***
Gundlach Plbg & Shtmtl Co Ltd......D......661 327-3052
4415 Foster Ave Bakersfield (93308) ***(P-1079)***
Gundlach Plumbing AC & Htg, Bakersfield *Also called Gundlach Plbg & Shtmtl Co Ltd* ***(P-1079)***
Gundrill Tech Inc......F......562 946-9355
10030 Greenleaf Ave Santa Fe Springs (90670) ***(P-8612)***
Gundry MD, Beverly Hills *Also called Agoura Health Products LLC* ***(P-14232)***
Gursey Schneider & Co LLC (PA)......**C......310 552-0960**
1888 Century Park E # 900 Los Angeles (90067) ***(P-22787)***
Guru Denim LLC (HQ)......**C......323 266-3072**
500 W 190th St Ste 300 Gardena (90248) ***(P-14378)***
Guru Knits Inc......D......323 235-9424
225 W 38th St Los Angeles (90037) ***(P-2845)***
Gurucul Solutions LLC......E......213 291-6888
222 N Pcf Cast Hwy Ste 13 El Segundo (90245) ***(P-17877)***
Guthy-Renker Direct, Santa Monica *Also called Guthy-Renker LLC* ***(P-14161)***
Guthy-Renker LLC (PA)......**D......760 773-9022**
100 N Pcf Cast Hwy Ste 16 El Segundo (90245) ***(P-23230)***
Guthy-Renker LLC......D......310 581-6250
3340 Ocean Park Blvd Fl 2 Santa Monica (90405) ***(P-14161)***
Guy Yocom Construction Inc (PA)......**A......951 284-3456**
3299 Horseless Carriage R Norco (92860) ***(P-1527)***
Guys Patio Inc......E......844 968-7485
2907 Oak St Santa Ana (92707) ***(P-18963)***
Gva Enterprises Inc (PA)......**D......213 484-0510**
316 S Westlake Ave Los Angeles (90057) ***(P-20369)***
Gvs Italy......D......424 382-4343
8616 La Tijera Blvd Los Angeles (90045) ***(P-13567)***
Gwla Acquisition Corp (PA)......**C......323 789-7800**
8600 Rheem Ave South Gate (90280) ***(P-5918)***
Gxo Logistics Supply Chain Inc......A......336 309-6201
3520 S Cactus Ave Bloomington (92316) ***(P-12210)***
Gxo Logistics Supply Chain Inc......D......951 512-1201
2163 S Riverside Ave Colton (92324) ***(P-12211)***
Gyl Decauwer LLP......D......909 948-9990
4120 Concours Ste 100 Ontario (91764) ***(P-22788)***
Gym Consulting Inc......D......818 907-6966
15300 Ventura Blvd # 414 Sherman Oaks (91403) ***(P-23231)***
Gynecologic Oncology Assoc, Newport Beach *Also called Micha-Rettenmaier Partnership* ***(P-19977)***
Gypsy 05 Inc......E......323 265-2700
3200 Union Pacific Ave Los Angeles (90023) ***(P-2948)***
H & A Transmissions Inc......E......909 941-9020
8727 Rochester Ave Rancho Cucamonga (91730) ***(P-18811)***
H & C Headwear Inc (PA)......**D......310 324-5263**
17145 Margay Ave Carson (90746) ***(P-14335)***
H & H Agency Inc (PA)......**C......949 260-8840**
1403 N Tustin Ave Ste 280 Santa Ana (92705) ***(P-15576)***
H & H Manufacturing, Pomona *Also called Holland & Herring Mfg Inc* ***(P-8621)***
H & H Nail Products Inc......F......818 902-9995
7011 Hayvenhurst Ave D Van Nuys (91406) ***(P-14247)***
H & H Specialties Inc......E......626 575-0776
14850 Don Julian Rd Ste B City of Industry (91746) ***(P-11682)***
H & H Transportation LLC......D......951 817-2300
300 El Sobrante Rd Corona (92879) ***(P-12049)***
H & H Truck Terminal, Victorville *Also called Hartwick & Hand Inc* ***(P-11972)***
H & L Tooth Company (PA)......**D......323 721-5146**
1540 S Greenwood Ave Montebello (90640) ***(P-7644)***
H & M Nursery Supply Corp......F......714 898-1311
5181 Argosy Ave Huntington Beach (92649) ***(P-14860)***
H & N Fish Co., Vernon *Also called H & N Foods International Inc* ***(P-14570)***
H & N Foods International Inc (HQ)......**C......323 586-9300**
5580 S Alameda St Vernon (90058) ***(P-14570)***
H A I, Placentia *Also called Hai Advnced Mtl Spcialists Inc* ***(P-7371)***
H and H Drug Stores Inc (PA)......**D......818 956-6691**
3604 San Fernando Rd Glendale (91204) ***(P-13492)***
H and H Drug Stores Inc......D......909 890-9700
114 E Airport Dr San Bernardino (92408) ***(P-13493)***
H B A, Santa Monica *Also called Hirsch Bedner Associates* ***(P-18543)***
H C I, Riverside *Also called Hci Inc* ***(P-951)***
H C Olsen Cnstr Co Inc......D......626 359-8900
710 Los Angeles Ave Monrovia (91016) ***(P-701)***
H C V T, Los Angeles *Also called Holthouse Carlin Van Trigt LLP* ***(P-22790)***
H Co Computer Products (PA)......**E......949 833-3222**
16812 Hale Ave Irvine (92606) ***(P-8202)***
H D G Associates......B......805 963-0744
1111 E Cabrillo Blvd Santa Barbara (93103) ***(P-16460)***
H Fam Engineering Inc......F......909 930-5678
2131 S Hellman Ave Ste F Ontario (91761) ***(P-8613)***
H G Group Inc......B......805 486-6463
4225 Saviers Rd Oxnard (93033) ***(P-16937)***
H J Harkins Company Inc......E......805 929-1333
1400 W Grand Ave Ste F Grover Beach (93433) ***(P-4828)***
H J S Graphics......F......818 782-5490
3533 Old Conejo Rd # 104 Newbury Park (91320) ***(P-4308)***
H L Moe Co Inc (PA)......**C......818 572-2100**
526 Commercial St Glendale (91203) ***(P-1080)***
H M F, Anaheim *Also called Hitech Metal Fabrication Corp* ***(P-6621)***
H M H Emergency Medical Group......D......626 397-5106
100 W California Blvd Pasadena (91105) ***(P-17494)***
H Rauvel Inc......C......562 989-3333
501 W Walnut St Compton (90220) ***(P-12050)***
H Rauvel Inc (PA)......**D......310 604-0060**
1710 E Sepulveda Blvd Carson (90745) ***(P-12212)***
H Roberts Construction......D......562 590-4825
2165 W Gaylord St Long Beach (90813) ***(P-6997)***
H T V, Studio City *Also called High Technology Video Inc* ***(P-19131)***
H V I, Huntington Beach *Also called Huntington Valley Inds Inc* ***(P-13989)***
H W Hunter Inc (PA)......**D......661 948-8411**
1130 Auto Mall Dr Lancaster (93534) ***(P-18838)***
H Wayne Lewis Inc......E......909 874-2213
312 S Willow Ave Rialto (92376) ***(P-7021)***
H&S Energy LLC (HQ)......**B......714 761-5426**
2860 N Santiago Blvd Orange (92867) ***(P-18536)***
H-D Specialty Groups Inc......F......323 516-6186
5913 E Washington Blvd Commerce (90040) ***(P-7370)***
H.U.M.A.N. Healthy Vending, Culver City *Also called Nutrition Without Borders LLC* ***(P-8322)***
H2 Environmental......F......909 628-0369
13122 6th St Chino (91710) ***(P-6164)***
H2 Home Collection Inc......E......714 916-9513
505 21st St Huntington Beach (92648) ***(P-3102)***
H2 Wellness Incorporated......E......310 362-1888
15414 Milldale Dr Los Angeles (90077) ***(P-17878)***
H2scan Corporation......E......661 775-9575
27215 Turnberry Ln Unit A Valencia (91355) ***(P-10886)***
H2w......F......800 578-3088
20630 Superior St Chatsworth (91311) ***(P-14162)***
H2w Technologies Inc......F......661 291-1620
26380 Ferry Ct Santa Clarita (91350) ***(P-8954)***
Haaker Equipment Company (PA)......**D......909 598-2706**
2070 N White Ave La Verne (91750) ***(P-13027)***
Haas Factory Outlet, Anaheim *Also called Machining Time Savers Inc* ***(P-13912)***
Haberfelde Ford (PA)......**C......661 328-3600**
2001 Oak St Bakersfield (93301) ***(P-18839)***
Haberfelde Ford......D......661 837-6400
5300 Gasoline Alley Dr Bakersfield (93313) ***(P-18840)***
Habit Homes, Bellflower *Also called Kevin White* ***(P-3999)***
Habitat For Hmnity Grter Los A......E......310 323-4663
8739 Artesia Blvd Bellflower (90706) ***(P-22185)***
Hacienda Golf Club......D......562 694-1081
718 East Rd La Habra Heights (90631) ***(P-19566)***
Hacienda Health Care, Hanford *Also called Hacienda Rhbltion Hlth Care C* ***(P-20370)***
Hacienda Rhbltion Hlth Care C......C......559 582-9221
361 E Grangeville Blvd Hanford (93230) ***(P-20370)***
Hackney Electric Inc (PA)......**D......949 264-4000**
23286 Arroyo Vis Rcho STA Marg (92688) ***(P-1261)***
Hacsb, Lompoc *Also called Authority of Housing* ***(P-15778)***
Haddads Fine Arts Inc......E......714 996-2100
3855 E Miraloma Ave Anaheim (92806) ***(P-5204)***
Hadley Fruit Orchards Inc (PA)......**E......951 849-5255**
48980 Seminole Dr Cabazon (92230) ***(P-1882)***
Hadsell & Stormer Attorneys, Pasadena *Also called Hadsell Strmer Keny Rchrdson R* ***(P-21574)***
Hadsell Strmer Keny Rchrdson R......D......626 585-9600
128 N Fair Oaks Ave Fl 2 Pasadena (91103) ***(P-21574)***
Haemo Stat Acute Services, Van Nuys *Also called Haemo-Stat Inc* ***(P-21244)***
Haemo-Stat Inc (HQ)......**D......818 908-0371**
7247 Hayvenhurst Ave A1 Van Nuys (91406) ***(P-21244)***
Haemonetics Manufacturing Inc (HQ)......**C......626 339-7388**
1630 W Industrial Park St Covina (91722) ***(P-10986)***
Hagen-Renaker Inc (PA)......**D......909 599-2341**
914 W Cienega Ave San Dimas (91773) ***(P-6004)***
Hager Mfg Inc......E......714 522-8870
14610 Industry Cir La Mirada (90638) ***(P-10342)***
Hai Advnced Mtl Spcialists Inc......F......714 414-0575
1688 Sierra Madre Cir Placentia (92870) ***(P-7371)***
Haight Brown & Bonesteel LLP (PA)......**D......213 542-8000**
555 S Flwr St Frty Ffth F Forty Los Angeles (90071) ***(P-21575)***
Hailwood Inc......F......805 487-4981
5755 Valentine Rd Ste 203 Ventura (93003) ***(P-15672)***
Haimetal Duct Inc......E......818 768-2315
625 Arroyo St San Fernando (91340) ***(P-6848)***
Hain Celestial Group Inc......C......323 859-0553
5630 Rickenbacker Rd Bell (90201) ***(P-5029)***
Hair Perfect International......D......626 304-9286
135 W California Blvd Pasadena (91105) ***(P-16905)***
Haircutters......D......562 690-2217
1230 W Imperial Hwy Ste A La Habra (90631) ***(P-16921)***
Hakes Sash & Door Inc......C......951 674-2414
31945 Corydon St Lake Elsinore (92530) ***(P-1439)***
Hal Hays Construction Inc (PA)......**C......951 788-0703**
4181 Latham St Riverside (92501) ***(P-702)***
Halcyon Microelectronics Inc......E......626 814-4688
5467 2nd St Irwindale (91706) ***(P-9512)***
Haldeman Inc......E......323 726-7011
2937 Tanager Ave Commerce (90040) ***(P-1081)***
Haldex Brake Products Corp......F......909 974-1200
291 Kettering Dr Ontario (91761) ***(P-10070)***

Hale Corporation ... D ... 626 358-4523
513 S Myrtle Ave Ste A Monrovia (91016) *(P-608)*
Halex Corporation (HQ) ... E ... **909 629-6219**
4200 Santa Ana St Ste A Ontario (91761) *(P-6482)*
Haley Bros, Riverside *Also called T M Cobb Company (P-3293)*
Haley Bros Inc (HQ) ... C ... **714 670-2112**
6291 Orangethorpe Ave Buena Park (90620) *(P-3253)*
Haley Indus Ctings Linings Inc ... E ... 323 588-8086
2919 Tanager Ave Commerce (90040) *(P-7372)*
Hall Ambulance Service Inc ... E ... 760 762-6402
12500 Boron Ave Boron (93516) *(P-11872)*
Hall Ambulance Service Inc ... D ... 661 322-8741
2001 O St O Bakersfield (93301) *(P-11873)*
Hall Ambulance Service Inc (PA) ... D ... **661 322-8741**
1001 21st St Bakersfield (93301) *(P-11874)*
Hall Associates Racg Pdts Inc ... F ... 310 326-4111
23104 Normandie Ave Torrance (90502) *(P-10552)*
Hall Letter Shop Inc ... F ... 661 327-3228
5200 Rosedale Hwy Bakersfield (93308) *(P-4309)*
Hall Research Technologies LLC (PA) ... F ... **714 641-6607**
1163 Warner Ave Tustin (92780) *(P-8260)*
Hallett Boats LLC ... F ... 626 969-8844
180 S Irwindale Ave Azusa (91702) *(P-10465)*
Halley Olsen Murphy Mem Chapel, Lancaster *Also called SE Acqstion Lncaster Cal Inc (P-16929)*
Hallmark Channel, Studio City *Also called Crown Media United States LLC (P-12712)*
Hallmark Labs LLC ... C ... 424 210-3600
3130 Wilshire Blvd # 400 Santa Monica (90403) *(P-4179)*
Hallmark Lighting LLC ... D ... 818 885-5010
1945 S Tubeway Ave Commerce (90040) *(P-9087)*
Hallmark Metals Inc ... E ... 626 335-1263
600 W Foothill Blvd Glendora (91741) *(P-6849)*
Hallmark Southwest, Loma Linda *Also called Dvele Omega Corporation (P-3421)*
Halo Unlimted Inc ... D ... 714 692-2270
1867 California Ave # 101 Corona (92881) *(P-21432)*
Halsteel Inc (HQ) ... C ... **909 937-1001**
4190 Santa Ana St Ste A Ontario (91761) *(P-6225)*
Halter Properties LLC ... E ... 805 226-9455
8910 Adelaida Rd Paso Robles (93446) *(P-2189)*
Halter Ranch Vineyard, Paso Robles *Also called Halter Properties LLC (P-2189)*
Halter Winery LLC ... E ... 805 226-9455
8910 Adelaida Rd Paso Robles (93446) *(P-2190)*
HAM Brokerage ... D ... 909 659-5392
325 W Hospitality Ln # 102 San Bernardino (92408) *(P-12466)*
Hamblin's Auto & Body Shop, Riverside *Also called Hamblins Bdy Pnt Frame Sp Inc (P-18841)*
Hamblins Bdy Pnt Frame Sp Inc ... D ... 951 689-8440
7590 Cypress Ave Riverside (92503) *(P-18841)*
Hamburger Home ... D ... 213 637-5000
3701 Wilshire Blvd # 900 Los Angeles (90010) *(P-609)*
Hamburger Home (PA) ... D ... **323 876-0550**
7120 Franklin Ave Los Angeles (90046) *(P-22106)*
Hamburger Home ... D ... 818 980-3200
5900 Sepulvda Blvd # 104 Van Nuys (91411) *(P-22107)*
Hamilton Brwart Insur Agcy LLC ... D ... 909 920-3250
1282 W Arrow Hwy Upland (91786) *(P-15577)*
Hamilton Iron Works, Torrance *Also called Calcon Steel Construction Inc (P-6596)*
Hamilton Metalcraft Inc ... E ... 626 795-4811
848 N Fair Oaks Ave Pasadena (91103) *(P-6850)*
Hamilton Sundstrand Corp ... C ... 909 593-5300
960 Overland Ct San Dimas (91773) *(P-10796)*
Hamilton Sundstrand Spc Systms ... D ... 909 288-5300
960 Overland Ct San Dimas (91773) *(P-10887)*
Hamilton Technology Corp ... F ... 310 217-1191
14900 S Figueroa St Gardena (90248) *(P-9088)*
Hammer Collection Inc ... E ... 310 515-0276
14427 S Main St Gardena (90248) *(P-3505)*
Hammerhead Industries Inc ... E ... 805 658-9922
5720 Nicolle St Ventura (93003) *(P-5659)*
Hammes Company ... D ... 949 705-0900
2 Park Plz Ste 600 Irvine (92614) *(P-23035)*
Hammitt Inc ... D ... 310 292-5200
2101 Pacific Coast Hwy Hermosa Beach (90254) *(P-5892)*
Hammond Power Solutions Inc ... D ... 310 537-4690
17715 S Susana Rd Compton (90221) *(P-13632)*
Hamo Constraction ... E ... 818 415-3334
3650 Altura Ave La Crescenta (91214) *(P-505)*
Hampton Fitness Products Ltd ... F ... 805 339-9733
1913 Portola Rd Ventura (93003) *(P-11423)*
Hampton Inn, Bakersfield *Also called Prime Hospitality Services LLC (P-16641)*
Hampton Inn, Arcadia *Also called Heprand Hospitality Inc (P-16471)*
Hampton Inn, Foothill Ranch *Also called Stonebridge Rlty Advisors Inc (P-16733)*
Hampton Inn, Camarillo *Also called Summit Hotel Trs 111 LLC (P-16736)*
Hampton Inn, Garden Grove *Also called Harbor Suites LLC (P-16463)*
Hampton Inn, Palm Desert *Also called Dutt Hospitality Group Inc (P-16422)*
Hampton Inn, Santa Clarita *Also called Valencia Hotel Ltd Partnership (P-16769)*
Hampton Inn, Buena Park *Also called Posadas Usa Inc (P-16639)*
Hampton Inn (PA) ... D ... **559 732-3900**
4747 W Noble Ave Visalia (93277) *(P-16461)*
Hampton Products Intl Corp (PA) ... D ... **949 472-4256**
50 Icon Foothill Ranch (92610) *(P-13808)*
Hampton Tdder Tchncal Svcs Inc ... F ... 909 628-1256
4571 State St Montclair (91763) *(P-22946)*
Hamrock Inc ... C ... 562 944-0255
12400 Wilshire Blvd # 1180 Los Angeles (90025) *(P-6226)*
Han Rigid Plastics Corp USA ... F ... 909 394-5832
980 W Cienega Ave San Dimas (91773) *(P-5510)*
Hana Commercial Finance Inc ... D ... 213 240-1234
1000 Wilshire Blvd # 2000 Los Angeles (90017) *(P-15153)*
Hana Financial Inc (PA) ... D ... **213 240-1234**
1000 Wilshire Blvd # 2000 Los Angeles (90017) *(P-17351)*
Hancor Inc ... E ... 661 366-1520
140 Vineland Rd Bakersfield (93307) *(P-5467)*
Hand and Nail Harmony, Brea *Also called Nail Alliance - North Amer Inc (P-16909)*
Hand Piece Parts and Products ... E ... 714 997-4331
707 W Angus Ave Orange (92868) *(P-11175)*
Handbill Printers LP ... E ... 951 547-5910
820 E Parkridge Ave Corona (92879) *(P-4310)*
Handelman, Steven Studios, Santa Barbara *Also called Steven Handelman Studios (P-6262)*
Handels Homemade Ice Cream ... E ... 909 989-7065
6403 Haven Ave Rancho Cucamonga (91737) *(P-14693)*
Handford Community Center, Hanford *Also called Adventist Health System/West (P-20649)*
Hanford Community Hospital (HQ) ... A ... **559 582-9000**
115 Mall Dr Hanford (93230) *(P-20781)*
Hanford Community Medical Ctr, Hanford *Also called Hanford Community Hospital (P-20781)*
Hanford Hotels Inc ... C ... 714 557-3000
3131 Bristol St Costa Mesa (92626) *(P-16462)*
Hanford Sentinel Inc ... B ... 559 582-0471
300 W 6th St Hanford (93230) *(P-3984)*
Hanford Truck Repair & Parts, Hanford *Also called Danell Bros Inc (P-153)*
Hang-UPS Unlimited, Santa Monica *Also called Magna-Pole Products Inc (P-3638)*
Hanger Inc ... E ... 818 563-9590
201 S Buena Vista St Burbank (91505) *(P-11109)*
Hanger Clinic, Burbank *Also called Hanger Inc (P-11109)*
Hanger, The, Vernon *Also called Hawthorne Distribution Inc (P-11110)*
Hanil Development Inc ... E ... 213 387-0111
3680 Wilshire Blvd B01 Los Angeles (90010) *(P-16084)*
Hanin Federal Credit Union (PA) ... E ... **213 368-9000**
3700 Wilshire Blvd # 104 Los Angeles (90010) *(P-15068)*
HANJIN GLOBAL LOGISTICS, Carson *Also called Hanjin Transportation Co Ltd (P-12467)*
Hanjin Shipping Co Ltd ... A ... 201 291-4600
301 Hanjin Rd Long Beach (90802) *(P-12299)*
Hanjin Transportation Co Ltd ... D ... 310 522-5030
1111 E Watson Center Rd Ua Carson (90745) *(P-12467)*
Hank's Electrical Supplies, Costa Mesa *Also called PH Corporation (P-13659)*
Hankey Group, Los Angeles *Also called Nowcom LLC (P-18204)*
Hanks Inc ... D ... 909 350-8365
13866 Slover Ave Fontana (92337) *(P-11970)*
Hankyu Hanshin Express USA Inc (HQ) ... E ... **630 285-7100**
1561 Beachey Pl Carson (90746) *(P-12468)*
Hanley Welding, Hawthorne *Also called Marleon Inc (P-18989)*
Hanley Wood Mkt Intelligence (HQ) ... D ... **714 540-8500**
555 Anton Blvd Ste 950 Costa Mesa (92626) *(P-22882)*
Hanmar LLC (PA) ... D ... **818 890-2802**
11441 Bradley Ave Pacoima (91331) *(P-7149)*
Hanmi Bank (HQ) ... B ... **213 382-2200**
3660 Wilshire Blvd Ph A Los Angeles (90010) *(P-15029)*
Hanna Fuji Sushi, Santa Fe Springs *Also called Nikko Enterprise Corporation (P-2347)*
Hannah Industries Inc ... F ... 714 939-7873
401 S Santa Fe St Santa Ana (92705) *(P-8385)*
Hannaknapp Realty Inc ... E ... 760 244-8557
15311 Bear Valley Rd # 1 Hesperia (92345) *(P-15879)*
Hannam Chain Super 1 Market, Los Angeles *Also called Hannam Chain USA Inc (P-13457)*
Hannam Chain USA Inc (PA) ... C ... **213 382-2922**
2740 W Olympic Blvd Los Angeles (90006) *(P-13457)*
Hannan Products Corp (PA) ... F ... **951 735-1587**
220 N Smith Ave Corona (92878) *(P-8070)*
Hannemann Fiberglass Inc ... F ... 626 969-7317
1132 W Kirkwall Rd Azusa (91702) *(P-10071)*
Hannibal Industries Inc (HQ) ... C ... **323 513-1200**
3851 S Santa Fe Ave Vernon (90058) *(P-6248)*
Hannibal Material Handling Inc ... C ... 323 587-4060
2230 E 38th St Vernon (90058) *(P-3684)*
Hanover Builders Inc ... E ... 818 706-2279
141 Duesenberg Dr Ste 6 Westlake Village (91362) *(P-610)*
Hansai Inc ... F ... 714 539-3311
13012 Moore St Cerritos (90703) *(P-506)*
Hansen Engineering Co ... F ... 310 534-3870
24050 Frampton Ave Harbor City (90710) *(P-10343)*
Hansen Equipment Company LLC ... E ... 559 992-3111
7124 Whitley Ave Corcoran (93212) *(P-223)*
Hansen Ranches ... D ... 559 992-3111
7124 Whitley Ave Corcoran (93212) *(P-109)*
Hansens Welding Inc ... E ... 310 329-6888
358 W 168th St Gardena (90248) *(P-18980)*
Hanson Aggrgtes Md-Pacific Inc ... E ... 805 967-2371
50 S Kellogg Ave Goleta (93117) *(P-11971)*
Hanson Distributing Company (PA) ... C ... **626 224-9800**
975 W 8th St Azusa (91702) *(P-13062)*
Hanson Distributing Company ... D ... 626 839-4026
19154 San Jose Ave Rowland Heights (91748) *(P-14163)*
Hanson Distributing Company ... D ... 559 802-1198
7940 W Doe Ave Visalia (93291) *(P-13063)*
Hanson Lab Solutions Inc ... E ... 805 498-3121
747 Calle Plano Camarillo (93012) *(P-10659)*
Hanson Tank, Los Angeles *Also called Roy E Hanson Jr Mfg (P-6750)*
Hanson Truss Inc ... B ... 909 591-9256
13950 Yorba Ave Chino (91710) *(P-3362)*
Hanwha Q Cells America Inc ... C ... 949 748-5996
400 Spectrum Center Dr # 14 Irvine (92618) *(P-9513)*
Hapag-Lloyd (america) LLC ... D ... 562 435-0771
555 E Ocean Blvd Ste 300 Long Beach (90802) *(P-12469)*
Happold Holdings (na) Inc (HQ) ... E ... **310 945-4800**
800 Wilshire Blvd # 1600 Los Angeles (90017) *(P-22565)*

Happy Cells Inc ....F.......818 528-5080
15911 Arminta St Van Nuys (91406) ***(P-2268)***
Happy Jump Inc ....F.......818 886-3991
9749 Independence Ave Chatsworth (91311) ***(P-19652)***
Happy Money, Costa Mesa *Also called Payoff Inc* ***(P-15148)***
Happy Planner, The, Fountain Valley *Also called ME & My Big Ideas LLC* ***(P-14097)***
Haralambos Beverage Co ....B.......562 347-4300
26717 Palmetto Ave Redlands (92374) ***(P-14826)***
Harbill Inc ....D.......909 883-8833
909 W 21st St San Bernardino (92405) ***(P-13028)***
Harbor Area Gang Altrntves Prg ....D.......310 519-7233
309 W Opp St Wilmington (90744) ***(P-22186)***
Harbor Building Services ....D.......310 320-2966
2761 Plaza Del Amo # 901 Torrance (90503) ***(P-17248)***
Harbor Community Clinic ....D.......310 547-0202
593 W 6th St San Pedro (90731) ***(P-21310)***
Harbor Corporate Park, Santa Ana *Also called Kaiser Foundation Hospitals* ***(P-19917)***
Harbor Diesel and Eqp Inc ....D.......562 591-5665
537 W Anaheim St Long Beach (90813) ***(P-13903)***
Harbor Distributing LLC (HQ) ....C.......714 933-2400**
5901 Bolsa Ave Huntington Beach (92647) ***(P-14827)***
Harbor Distributing LLC ....D.......310 538-5483
16407 S Main St Gardena (90248) ***(P-14828)***
Harbor Distributing Co, Gardena *Also called Harbor Distributing LLC* ***(P-14828)***
Harbor Dvlpmntal Dsblties Fndt ....C.......310 540-1711
21231 Hawthorne Blvd Torrance (90503) ***(P-22187)***
Harbor Freight Tools, Camarillo *Also called Central Purchasing LLC* ***(P-13978)***
Harbor Furniture Mfg Inc (PA) ....E.......323 636-1201**
12508 Center St South Gate (90280) ***(P-3506)***
Harbor Glen Care Center ....B.......626 963-7531
1033 E Arrow Hwy Glendora (91740) ***(P-20371)***
Harbor Green Grain LP ....E.......310 991-8089
13181 Crssroads Pkwy N City of Industry (91746) ***(P-1966)***
Harbor Health Care Inc ....C.......562 866-7054
9461 Flower St Bellflower (90706) ***(P-22108)***
Harbor Health Systems LLC ....D.......949 273-7020
3501 Jamboree Rd Ste 540 Newport Beach (92660) ***(P-21433)***
Harbor House, South Gate *Also called Harbor Furniture Mfg Inc* ***(P-3506)***
Harbor Industrial Services ....D.......310 522-1193
211 N Marine Ave Wilmington (90744) ***(P-17310)***
Harbor Pipe and Steel Inc ....C.......951 369-3990
1495 Columbia Ave Bldg 10 Riverside (92507) ***(P-13568)***
Harbor Post Accute Care Center, Torrance *Also called Geri-Care Inc* ***(P-20359)***
Harbor Regional Center, Torrance *Also called Harbor Dvlpmntal Dsblties Fndt* ***(P-22187)***
Harbor Seal Incorporated ....F.......626 305-5754
909 S Myrtle Ave Monrovia (91016) ***(P-5340)***
Harbor Suites LLC ....E.......714 703-8800
11747 Harbor Blvd Garden Grove (92840) ***(P-16463)***
Harbor Truck Bodies Inc ....D.......714 996-0411
255 Voyager Ave Brea (92821) ***(P-9988)***
Harbor Truck Body, Brea *Also called Harbor Truck Bodies Inc* ***(P-9988)***
Harbor Ucla Med Foundation, Torrance *Also called Harbor-Ucla Med Foundation Inc* ***(P-23036)***
Harbor Ucla Medical Center, Harbor City *Also called County of Los Angeles* ***(P-19768)***
Harbor View House, San Pedro *Also called Healthview Inc* ***(P-22112)***
Harbor View Inn, Santa Barbara *Also called Beach Mtl Prtners A Cal Ltd PR* ***(P-16340)***
Harbor View Pre-School, Corona Del Mar *Also called Newport Mesa Unified Schl Dst* ***(P-22042)***
Harbor-Ucla Med Foundation Inc ....B.......310 533-0413
21602 S Vermont Ave Torrance (90502) ***(P-21245)***
Harbor-Ucla Med Foundation Inc (PA) ....D.......310 222-5015**
21840 Normandie Ave Ste 1 Torrance (90502) ***(P-23036)***
Hard Candy LLC ....E.......949 515-3923
833 W 16th St Newport Beach (92663) ***(P-14248)***
Hard Rock Hotel Palm Springs, Palm Springs *Also called Kittridge Hotels & Resorts LLC* ***(P-16526)***
Hard Tail, Santa Monica *Also called Richard Cantrell* ***(P-14413)***
Hardcore Racing Components LLC ....F.......661 294-5032
27717 Avenue Scott Valencia (91355) ***(P-11375)***
Hardesty LLC (PA) ....E.......949 407-6625**
19800 Macarthur Blvd # 820 Irvine (92612) ***(P-17426)***
Harding Containers Intl Inc ....E.......310 549-7272
4000 Santa Fe Ave Long Beach (90810) ***(P-3391)***
Hardloop LLC ....E.......310 892-4284
12301 Wilshire Blvd # 512 Los Angeles (90025) ***(P-23037)***
Hardrock Tile & Marble Inc ....D.......714 282-1766
23151 Verdugo Dr Ste 111 Laguna Hills (92653) ***(P-1345)***
Hardware Imports Inc ....F.......909 595-6201
161 Commerce Way Walnut (91789) ***(P-9989)***
Hardware Specialties, Ontario *Also called F & D Flores Enterprises Inc* ***(P-10882)***
Hardy & Harper Inc ....E.......714 444-1851
32 Rancho Cir Lake Forest (92630) ***(P-886)***
Hardy Diagnostics (PA) ....B.......805 346-2766**
1430 W Mccoy Ln Santa Maria (93455) ***(P-13494)***
Hardy Frames Inc ....D.......951 245-9525
250 Klug Cir Corona (92878) ***(P-6203)***
Hardy Window Company (PA) ....C.......714 996-1807**
1639 E Miraloma Ave Placentia (92870) ***(P-13213)***
Harel General Contractors Inc ....E.......310 558-8304
6015 Washington Blvd Culver City (90232) ***(P-768)***
Haringa Inc (PA) ....D.......800 499-9991**
14422 Best Ave Santa Fe Springs (90670) ***(P-18537)***
Harkham Industries Inc (PA) ....E.......323 586-4600**
857 S San Pedro St # 300 Los Angeles (90014) ***(P-2846)***
Harman Envelopes, North Hollywood *Also called Harman Press Inc* ***(P-4311)***
Harman Press Inc ....E.......818 432-0570
6840 Vineland Ave North Hollywood (91605) ***(P-4311)***
Harman Professional Inc (HQ) ....B.......818 893-8411**
8500 Balboa Blvd Northridge (91329) ***(P-9177)***
Harman-Kardon Incorporated ....B.......818 841-4600
8500 Balboa Blvd Northridge (91329) ***(P-13687)***
Harmony Cellars ....F.......805 927-1625
3255 Harmony Valley Rd Harmony (93435) ***(P-2191)***
Harmony Kids, San Fernando *Also called Newco International Inc* ***(P-3481)***
Harper & Two Inc (PA) ....F.......562 424-3030**
2937 Cherry Ave Signal Hill (90755) ***(P-9720)***
Harpers Pharmacy Inc ....C.......877 778-3773
132 S Anita Dr Ste 210 Orange (92868) ***(P-4829)***
Harpo Entertainment Group, West Hollywood *Also called Harpo Productions Inc* ***(P-19130)***
Harpo Inc ....D.......312 633-1000
1041 N Formosa Ave West Hollywood (90046) ***(P-19312)***
Harpo Productions Inc ....C.......312 633-1000
1041 N Formosa Ave West Hollywood (90046) ***(P-19130)***
Harpo Studios, West Hollywood *Also called Harpo Inc* ***(P-19312)***
Harrell Holdings (PA) ....C.......661 322-5627**
1707 Eye St Ste 102 Bakersfield (93301) ***(P-3985)***
Harrington Industrial Plas LLC (PA) ....D.......909 597-8641**
14480 Yorba Ave Chino (91710) ***(P-13830)***
Harris & Ruth Painting Contg (PA) ....D.......626 960-4004**
28408 Lorna Ave West Covina (91790) ***(P-1183)***
Harris Construction Inc ....F.......310 246-0188
174 N Wetherly Dr Beverly Hills (90211) ***(P-4312)***
Harris Freeman & Co Inc (PA) ....B.......714 765-7525**
3110 E Miraloma Ave Anaheim (92806) ***(P-14694)***
Harris Industries Inc (PA) ....E.......714 898-8048**
5181 Argosy Ave Huntington Beach (92649) ***(P-3872)***
Harris L Woods Elec Contr ....D.......562 945-8751
9214 Norwalk Blvd Santa Fe Springs (90670) ***(P-1262)***
Harris Organs Inc ....E.......562 693-3442
7047 Comstock Ave Whittier (90602) ***(P-11344)***
Harris Spice Company Inc ....E.......714 507-1919
3110 E Miraloma Ave Anaheim (92806) ***(P-2448)***
Harris Stockwell (PA) ....E.......310 277-6669**
3580 Wilshire Blvd Fl 19 Los Angeles (90010) ***(P-21576)***
Harris Tea Company, Anaheim *Also called Harris Freeman & Co Inc* ***(P-14694)***
Harris Water Conditioning Inc ....D.......805 656-4411
1025 S Rose Ave Oxnard (93030) ***(P-18538)***
Harris' Precision Products, Whittier *Also called Harris Organs Inc* ***(P-11344)***
Harris, Jeffery P, Santa Barbara *Also called Nasif Hicks Harris & Co LLP* ***(P-22806)***
Harrison Beverage Inc ....F.......626 757-1159
726 Arabian Ln Walnut (91789) ***(P-1818)***
Harrison Group, Walnut *Also called Harrison Beverage Inc* ***(P-1818)***
Harrison, E J & Sons Recycling, Ventura *Also called E J Harrison & Sons Inc* ***(P-12945)***
Harry's Auto Collision, Los Angeles *Also called Harrys Auto Body Inc* ***(P-18791)***
Harrys Auto Body Inc ....D.......323 933-4600
1013 S La Brea Ave Los Angeles (90019) ***(P-18791)***
Harrys Dye and Wash Inc ....E.......714 446-0300
1015 E Orangethorpe Ave Anaheim (92801) ***(P-2658)***
Hart King A Professional Corp ....D.......714 432-8700
4 Hutton Cntre Dr Ste 900 Santa Ana (92707) ***(P-21577)***
Hart Sales LLC ....F.......650 532-9200
74959 Jasmine Way Indian Wells (92210) ***(P-7903)***
Harters Surfaces ....F.......818 899-9917
12612 Osborne St 14 Pacoima (91331) ***(P-5449)***
Hartford Great Health Corp (PA) ....D.......626 321-1915**
8832 Glendon Way Rosemead (91770) ***(P-16464)***
Hartland Christian Camp, Badger *Also called Christian Hartland Association* ***(P-16819)***
Hartley Company ....E.......949 646-9643
1987 Placentia Ave Costa Mesa (92627) ***(P-11464)***
Hartley-Racon, Costa Mesa *Also called Hartley Company* ***(P-11464)***
Hartman Industries ....D.......909 428-0114
14933 Whittram Ave Fontana (92335) ***(P-13569)***
Hartman Slicer Div, Rancho Dominguez *Also called United Bakery Equipment Co Inc* ***(P-8079)***
Hartmark Cab Design & Mfg Inc ....E.......909 591-9153
3575 Grapevine St Jurupa Valley (91752) ***(P-1664)***
Hartwell Corporation (HQ) ....C.......714 993-4200**
900 Richfield Rd Placentia (92870) ***(P-6520)***
Hartwick & Hand Inc (PA) ....D.......760 245-1666**
16953 N D St Victorville (92394) ***(P-11972)***
Hartwig Realty Inc (PA) ....D.......661 948-8424**
43912 20th St W Lancaster (93534) ***(P-15880)***
Hartzell Aerospace, Valencia *Also called Electrofilm Mfg Co LLC* ***(P-7456)***
Harvard Card Systems, City of Industry *Also called Harvard Label LLC* ***(P-3755)***
Harvard Grand Inv Inc A Cal ....D.......310 513-7560
2 Civic Plaza Dr Carson (90745) ***(P-16267)***
Harvard Label LLC ....C.......626 333-8881
111 Baldwin Park Blvd City of Industry (91746) ***(P-3755)***
Harvest Container Company ....E.......559 562-1394
24476 Road 216 Lindsay (93247) ***(P-3810)***
Harvest Farms Inc ....D.......661 945-3636
45000 Yucca Ave Lancaster (93534) ***(P-1929)***
Harvest Landscape Entps Inc (PA) ....C.......714 693-8100**
2339 N Batavia St Orange (92865) ***(P-261)***
Harvest Landscape Maintenance, Orange *Also called Harvest Landscape Entps Inc* ***(P-261)***
Harvest Management Sub LLC ....A.......805 543-0187
1299 Briarwood Dr San Luis Obispo (93401) ***(P-15725)***
Harvest Sensations LLC ....E.......305 591-8173
3030 E Washington Blvd Los Angeles (90023) ***(P-14638)***
Harvest Small Business Fin LLC ....D.......949 446-8683
24422 Avnida De Crlota St Laguna Hills (92653) ***(P-15201)***
Harveys Industries Inc ....D.......714 277-4700
724 N Poinsettia St Santa Ana (92701) ***(P-14379)***
Harwil Precision Products ....E.......805 988-6800
541 Kinetic Dr Oxnard (93030) ***(P-9721)***

ALPHABETIC

Employee Codes: A=Over 500 employees, B=251-500 C=101-250, D=51-100, E=20-50 F=10-19
2022 Southern California Business Directory and Buyers Guide
© Mergent Inc. 1-800-342-5647
1151

Hasc, Los Angeles *Also called Hospital Assn Southern Cal* ***(P-22189)***

Hasco, Placentia *Also called Hartwell Corporation* ***(P-6520)***

Haskel International LLC (HQ).....C.....**818 843-4000**
100 E Graham Pl Burbank (91502) ***(P-8014)***

Haskon, Div of, Brea *Also called Kirkhill Inc* ***(P-5346)***

Hassen Development Corporation.....D.....626 967-7374
1932 E Garvey Ave S West Covina (91791) ***(P-658)***

Hatchbeauty Agency LLC (PA).....E.....**310 396-7070**
10951 W Pico Blvd Ste 300 Los Angeles (90064) ***(P-23232)***

Hatchbeauty Products LLC (PA).....D.....**310 396-7070**
10951 W Pico Blvd Ste 300 Los Angeles (90064) ***(P-14249)***

Hathaway Children and Family, Pacoima *Also called Hathawy-Sycmres Child Fmly Svc* ***(P-21796)***

Hathaway LLC.....E.....661 393-2004
4205 Atlas Ct Bakersfield (93308) ***(P-405)***

Hathawy-Sycmres Child Fmly Svc.....C.....626 395-7100
12502 Van Nuys Blvd Ste 1 Pacoima (91331) ***(P-21796)***

Hathawy-Sycmres Child Fmly Svc.....C.....323 257-9600
840 N Avenue 66 Los Angeles (90042) ***(P-22109)***

Hathawy-Sycmres Child Fmly Svc.....C.....323 733-0322
3741 Stocker St Ste 101 View Park (90008) ***(P-21797)***

Hathawy-Sycmres Child Fmly Svc (PA).....D.....**626 395-7100**
100 W Walnut St Ste 375 Pasadena (91124) ***(P-22110)***

Haulaway Storage Cntrs Inc.....B.....800 826-9040
11292 Western Ave Stanton (90680) ***(P-12213)***

Haus Laboratories, El Segundo *Also called Hlb90067 Inc* ***(P-5030)***

Hav Holdings & Subsidiaries, Sun Valley *Also called Hollywood Film Company* ***(P-11279)***

Havaianas, Venice *Also called Alpargatas Usa Inc* ***(P-5878)***

Havana Graphic Center Inc.....E.....818 841-3774
9250 Independence Ave # 109 Chatsworth (91311) ***(P-4313)***

Havasu Landing Casino (PA).....D.....**760 858-5380**
1 Main St Needles (92363) ***(P-16465)***

Haven Hills Inc.....D.....818 887-7481
7112 Owensmouth Ave Canoga Park (91303) ***(P-21798)***

Hawa Corporation (PA).....F.....**909 825-8882**
125 E Laurel St Colton (92324) ***(P-1734)***

Hawaiian Gardens Casino.....A.....562 860-5887
11871 Carson St Hawaiian Gardens (90716) ***(P-16466)***

Hawaiian Hotels & Resorts Inc.....C.....805 480-0052
2830 Borchard Rd Newbury Park (91320) ***(P-16467)***

Hawk Transportation Inc.....D.....800 709-4295
15238 Arrow Blvd Fontana (92335) ***(P-12051)***

Hawke Media Ventures LLC.....D.....310 451-7295
1714 16th St Santa Monica (90404) ***(P-23233)***

Hawker Pacific Aerospace.....B.....818 765-6201
11240 Sherman Way Sun Valley (91352) ***(P-19040)***

Hawkins Brown USA Inc.....B.....310 600-2695
8500 Steller Dr Ste 1 Culver City (90232) ***(P-22719)***

Haworth Inc.....F.....310 854-7633
144 N Robertson Blvd # 202 West Hollywood (90048) ***(P-3612)***

Hawthorne Distribution Ctr Inc.....E.....213 431-6101
6099 Malburg Way Vernon (90058) ***(P-12137)***

Hawthorne Distribution Inc.....F.....323 238-7738
6099 Malburg Way Vernon (90058) ***(P-11110)***

Hawthorne Lowe's, Hawthorne *Also called Lowes Home Centers LLC* ***(P-13238)***

Hay Kuhn Inc.....E.....760 353-0124
1880 Jeffrey Rd El Centro (92243) ***(P-14935)***

Hayday Farms Inc.....D.....760 922-4713
15500 S Commercial St Blythe (92225) ***(P-7)***

Hayden Industrial Products, San Bernardino *Also called Hayden Products LLC* ***(P-6742)***

Hayden Products LLC.....D.....951 736-2600
1393 E San Bernardino Ave San Bernardino (92408) ***(P-6742)***

Hayes Protective Services Inc.....C.....323 755-2282
2930 W Imperial Hwy 200b Inglewood (90303) ***(P-18286)***

Hayes Welding Inc (PA).....D.....**760 246-4878**
12522 Violet Rd Adelanto (92301) ***(P-18981)***

Hayhoe Construction Corp.....D.....714 508-2400
17821 17th St Ste 150 Tustin (92780) ***(P-769)***

Haymarket Worldwide Inc.....D.....949 417-6700
17030 Red Hill Ave Irvine (92614) ***(P-4072)***

Haynes Building Service LLC.....C.....626 359-6100
16027 Arrow Hwy Ste I Baldwin Park (91706) ***(P-17249)***

Haynes Family Programs Inc.....C.....909 593-2581
233 Baseline Rd La Verne (91750) ***(P-22111)***

Haynes Publications, Newbury Park *Also called Odcombe Press (nashville)* ***(P-4382)***

Hazel Clothes, Vernon *Also called Crestone LLC* ***(P-3031)***

Hazelrigg Claims MGT Svcs Inc (HQ).....D.....**909 606-6373**
15345 Frfeld Rnch Rd Ste Chino (91710) ***(P-15578)***

Hazens Investment LLC.....B.....310 642-1111
6101 W Century Blvd Los Angeles (90045) ***(P-16468)***

Hazmat Chemical Storage Inc (PA).....F.....**714 480-1290**
13681 Newport Ave Ste 8 Tustin (92780) ***(P-6998)***

Hazmat Tsdf Inc (PA).....D.....**909 873-4141**
180 W Monte Ave Rialto (92376) ***(P-12953)***

HB Parkco Construction Inc (PA).....B.....**714 567-4752**
24795 State Highway 74 Perris (92570) ***(P-1528)***

HB Products LLC.....E.....714 799-6967
5671 Engineer Dr Huntington Beach (92649) ***(P-4524)***

Hba Incorporated.....D.....714 635-8602
512 E Vermont Ave Anaheim (92805) ***(P-1346)***

Hba International, Santa Monica *Also called Hirsch/Bedner Intl Inc* ***(P-18544)***

Hbc Solutions Holdings LLC.....E.....321 727-9100
10877 Wilshire Blvd Fl 18 Los Angeles (90024) ***(P-9276)***

HBO, Santa Monica *Also called Home Box Office Inc* ***(P-12771)***

HC Brill.....E.....909 825-7343
2111 W Valley Blvd Colton (92324) ***(P-2077)***

HCA HEALTHCARE, Thousand Oaks *Also called Los Robles Regional Med Ctr* ***(P-20854)***

HCC Industries Leasing Inc (HQ).....F.....**626 443-8933**
4232 Temple City Blvd Rosemead (91770) ***(P-10699)***

HCC Surety Group, Los Angeles *Also called American Contrs Indemnity Co* ***(P-15494)***

Hchd.....F.....909 923-8889
1175 S Grove Ave Ste 104 Ontario (91761) ***(P-9953)***

Hci Inc (HQ).....B.....**951 520-4200**
6830 Airport Dr Riverside (92504) ***(P-951)***

Hco Holding I Corporation (HQ).....D.....**323 583-5000**
999 N Pacific Coast Hwy # 80 El Segundo (90245) ***(P-16102)***

Hco Holding II Corporation.....A.....310 955-9200
999 N Pacific Coast Hwy El Segundo (90245) ***(P-5280)***

Hct Packaging Inc (PA).....C.....**310 260-7680**
2800 28th St Ste 240 Santa Monica (90405) ***(P-18539)***

Hd Industries, Long Beach *Also called Harbor Diesel and Eqp Inc* ***(P-13903)***

Hd Supply Facilities Maint Ltd.....D.....909 594-3843
21651 Baker Pkwy City of Industry (91789) ***(P-17352)***

Hd Window Fashions Inc (HQ).....B.....**213 749-6333**
1818 Oak St Los Angeles (90015) ***(P-3710)***

HE Julien & Associates Inc.....E.....805 488-8342
2275 E Hueneme Rd Oxnard (93033) ***(P-309)***

Headmaster Inc (PA).....E.....**714 556-5244**
3000 S Croddy Way Santa Ana (92704) ***(P-3026)***

Headquarters, Los Angeles *Also called Nationwide Legal LLC* ***(P-21643)***

Headwaters Construction Inc.....E.....714 523-1530
16005 Phoebe Ave La Mirada (90638) ***(P-5976)***

Headwinds.....F.....626 359-8044
805 W Hillcrest Blvd Monrovia (91016) ***(P-10491)***

Health Advocates (PA).....D.....**818 995-9500**
13412 Ventura Blvd # 300 Sherman Oaks (91423) ***(P-21578)***

Health Advocates LLC.....B.....818 995-9500
21540 Plummer St Ste B Chatsworth (91311) ***(P-22188)***

Health and Happiness H&H Inc.....F.....619 330-6030
10000 Wash Blvd Fl 6 Culver City (90232) ***(P-1794)***

Health Care Investments Inc.....C.....310 323-3194
1140 W Rosecrans Ave Gardena (90247) ***(P-20372)***

Health Care Partners, Long Beach *Also called Davita Medical Management LLC* ***(P-19785)***

Health Care Provider Labs Inc.....D.....626 813-3800
14411 Palmrose Ave Baldwin Park (91706) ***(P-21070)***

Health Care Resource Group, Buena Park *Also called Vsa and Associates Inc* ***(P-22694)***

Health Data Vision Inc (PA).....D.....**866 969-3222**
425 W Broadway Ste 100 Glendale (91204) ***(P-18093)***

Health Department, Torrance *Also called County of Los Angeles* ***(P-19763)***

Health Dept, Los Angeles *Also called County of Los Angeles* ***(P-21291)***

Health Educatn Psychiatry Offs, Los Angeles *Also called Kaiser Foundation Hospitals* ***(P-21317)***

Health Fitness America, Irvine *Also called Equinox-76th Street Inc* ***(P-20214)***

Health Net LLC (HQ).....C.....**818 676-6000**
21650 Oxnard St Fl 25 Woodland Hills (91367) ***(P-15397)***

Health Net LLC.....C.....661 321-3904
6013 Niles St Bakersfield (93306) ***(P-15398)***

Health Net LLC.....C.....818 676-5000
21281 Burbank Blvd Woodland Hills (91367) ***(P-15399)***

Health Resources Corp.....B.....714 754-5454
2701 S Bristol St Santa Ana (92704) ***(P-20782)***

Health Service Alliance.....D.....909 464-9675
13193 Central Ave Ste 100 Chino (91710) ***(P-21434)***

Health Services Dept, Palos Verdes Peninsu *Also called County of Los Angeles* ***(P-20737)***

Health Services Dept, Los Angeles *Also called County of Los Angeles* ***(P-20739)***

Health Services, Dept of, Acton *Also called County of Los Angeles* ***(P-21041)***

Health Services, Dept of, Downey *Also called County of Los Angeles* ***(P-21290)***

Health Services, Dept of, Los Angeles *Also called County of Los Angeles* ***(P-20738)***

Health Services, Dept of, La Puente *Also called County of Los Angeles* ***(P-19766)***

Health Services, Dept of, Los Angeles *Also called County of Los Angeles* ***(P-19767)***

Health Services, Dept of, Los Angeles *Also called County of Los Angeles* ***(P-21292)***

Health Services, Dept of, Bellflower *Also called County of Los Angeles* ***(P-19769)***

Health Services, Dept of, Los Angeles *Also called County of Los Angeles* ***(P-19770)***

Health Services, Dept of, Wilmington *Also called County of Los Angeles* ***(P-19771)***

Health Services, Dept of, Azusa *Also called County of Los Angeles* ***(P-19773)***

Health Services, Dept of, Los Angeles *Also called County of Los Angeles* ***(P-19774)***

Health Services, Dept of, Castaic *Also called County of Los Angeles* ***(P-21044)***

Health Smart Clinic, Long Beach *Also called Healthsmart Pacific Inc* ***(P-19838)***

Health South Tustin Rehab Hosp.....C.....714 832-9200
14851 Yorba St Tustin (92780) ***(P-21799)***

Health System Medical Network, Beverly Hills *Also called Cedars-Sinai Medical Center* ***(P-20707)***

Health Tech Prof Pdts Inc.....F.....800 424-7536
11614 Sterling Ave Riverside (92503) ***(P-199)***

Health-Ade LLC (HQ).....F.....**844 337-6368**
24325 Crenshaw Blvd Torrance (90505) ***(P-1862)***

Healthcare, Los Angeles *Also called Breathe La Lhc LLC* ***(P-21394)***

Healthcare Ctr of Downey LLC.....C.....562 869-0978
12023 Lakewood Blvd Downey (90242) ***(P-20373)***

Healthcare Finance Direct LLC.....D.....661 616-4400
1707 Eye St Ste 300 Bakersfield (93301) ***(P-23234)***

Healthcare Partners, Van Nuys *Also called Greater Valley Medical Group* ***(P-21309)***

Healthcare Partners Med Group, Long Beach *Also called Davita Medical Management LLC* ***(P-19784)***

Healthcare Partners Med Group, Torrance *Also called Davita Medical Management LLC* ***(P-21417)***

Healthcare Partners Med Group, Montebello *Also called Davita Medical Management LLC* ***(P-19788)***

Healthcare Partners Med Group, El Monte *Also called Davita Medical Management LLC* ***(P-19789)***

Mergent e-mail: customerrelations@mergent.com
1152
2022 Southern California Business Directory and Buyers Guide
(P-0000) Products & Services Section entry number
(PA)=Parent Co (HQ)=Headquarters (DH)=Div Headquarters

Healthcare Partners Med Group, El Segundo *Also called Davita Medical Management LLC* ***(P-19791)***
Healthcare Services Group Inc....A....562 494-7939
5199 E Pacific Coast Hwy # 402 Long Beach (90804) ***(P-23535)***
Healthcare Synergy Inc....D....714 229-8700
5555 Corporate Ave Cypress (90630) ***(P-17630)***
Healthcompare Insur Svcs Inc (HQ)....D....714 542-4200
721 S Parker St Orange (92868) ***(P-15579)***
Healthpointe Medical Group Inc (PA)....D....714 956-2663
16702 Valley View Ave La Mirada (90638) ***(P-19837)***
Healthquest Laboratories Inc (PA)....D....714 418-5867
18023 Sky Park Cir # 66 Irvine (92614) ***(P-21071)***
Healthsmart Management Service....D....714 947-8600
10855 Bus Ctr Dr Ste C Cypress (90630) ***(P-15580)***
Healthsmart Pacific Inc (PA)....A....562 595-1911
5150 E Pacific Cst Hwy # 200 Long Beach (90804) ***(P-20783)***
Healthsmart Pacific Inc....B....562 595-1911
2683 Pacific Ave Long Beach (90806) ***(P-19838)***
HealthSouth, Oxnard *Also called N S C Channel Islands Inc* ***(P-19990)***
Healthview Inc (PA)....C....310 547-3341
921 S Beacon St San Pedro (90731) ***(P-22112)***
Healthy Medical Solutions Inc....D....818 974-1980
5943 Rhodes Ave Valley Village (91607) ***(P-21435)***
Health Sanitation Services, Santa Maria *Also called Valley Garbage Rubbish Co Inc* ***(P-12988)***
Heart Center A Medical Corp....D....661 324-4100
5020 Commerce Dr Bakersfield (93309) ***(P-19839)***
Heart Hospital of Bk LLC....B....661 316-6000
3001 Sillect Ave Bakersfield (93308) ***(P-20784)***
Heart Rate Inc....E....714 850-9716
1411 E Wilshire Ave Santa Ana (92705) ***(P-11424)***
Heartland Express Inc Iowa....A....319 626-3600
10131 Redwood Ave Fontana (92335) ***(P-12052)***
Heartland Payment Systems Inc....D....760 324-0133
510 Cerritos Way Cathedral City (92234) ***(P-18540)***
Hearts Delight....E....805 648-7123
4035 N Ventura Ave Ventura (93001) ***(P-2949)***
Heat Transfer Pdts Group LLC....C....909 786-3669
1933 S Vineyard Ave Ontario (91761) ***(P-13845)***
Heater Designs Inc....E....909 421-0971
2211 S Vista Ave Bloomington (92316) ***(P-8089)***
Heath Consultants Incorporated....C....562 942-0315
9473 Slauson Ave Pico Rivera (90660) ***(P-23447)***
Heather By Bordeaux Inc....E....213 622-0555
5983 Malburg Way Vernon (90058) ***(P-2950)***
Heaven or Las Vegas, Van Nuys *Also called Kimball Nelson Inc* ***(P-11701)***
Heavy Civil - Gen Engrg Cnstr, Chatsworth *Also called Maloof Naman Builders Inc* ***(P-13864)***
Heavy Duty Trucking, Irvine *Also called HIC Corporation* ***(P-4073)***
Heavy Load Transfer LLC....D....310 816-0260
18735 S Ferris Pl Rancho Dominguez (90220) ***(P-11973)***
Hec Inc....B....818 879-7414
30961 Agoura Rd Ste 311 Westlake Village (91361) ***(P-13725)***
Hedman Hedders, Whittier *Also called Hedman Manufacturing* ***(P-10072)***
Hedman Manufacturing (PA)....E....562 204-1031
12438 Putnam St Whittier (90602) ***(P-10072)***
Heeger Inc....F....323 728-5108
2431 Strozier Ave South El Monte (91733) ***(P-8915)***
HEI Hospitality LLC....C....818 887-4800
21850 Oxnard St Woodland Hills (91367) ***(P-16469)***
HEI Long Beach LLC....C....562 983-3400
701 W Ocean Blvd Long Beach (90831) ***(P-16470)***
Heider Inspection Group....A....909 673-0292
14457 Meridian Pkwy Riverside (92518) ***(P-22947)***
Heidi Corporation....D....626 333-6317
727 N Vernon Ave Azusa (91702) ***(P-1529)***
Heights Insurance Group Inc (PA)....D....626 333-1111
2048 S Hacienda Blvd Hacienda Heights (91745) ***(P-15581)***
Heinaman Contract Glazing Inc (PA)....E....949 587-0266
26981 Vista Ter Ste E Lake Forest (92630) ***(P-1665)***
Hel Mar Mfg LLC (PA)....E....805 278-9099
3000 Paseo Mercado Oxnard (93036) ***(P-11683)***
Helens Place Inc....E....909 981-5715
893 W 9th St Upland (91786) ***(P-4314)***
Helfer Enterprises....E....714 557-2733
3030 Oak St Santa Ana (92707) ***(P-8614)***
Helfer Tool Co, Santa Ana *Also called Helfer Enterprises* ***(P-8614)***
Helica Biosystems Inc....F....714 578-7830
3310 W Macarthur Blvd Santa Ana (92704) ***(P-4921)***
Helical Products, Santa Maria *Also called Matthew Warren Inc* ***(P-7465)***
Helicopter Tech Co Ltd Partnr....E....310 523-2750
12902 S Broadway Los Angeles (90061) ***(P-10344)***
Helix Electric Inc....C....562 941-7200
13100 Alondra Blvd # 108 Cerritos (90703) ***(P-1263)***
Helix Medical, Carpinteria *Also called Freudenberg Medical LLC* ***(P-11108)***
Helix Medical....F....805 576-5458
1009 Cindy Ln Carpinteria (93013) ***(P-11111)***
Helix Semiconductors (PA)....D....949 748-6057
9980 Irvine Center Dr Irvine (92618) ***(P-9514)***
Hellman Properties LLC....E....562 431-6022
711 First St Seal Beach (90740) ***(P-406)***
Hello Bello, Pacific Palisades *Also called Unconditional Love Inc* ***(P-14425)***
Helloworld Travel Svcs USA Inc....D....310 535-1000
6510 E Spring St Long Beach (90815) ***(P-12385)***
Hellwig Products Company Inc....E....559 734-7451
16237 Avenue 296 Visalia (93292) ***(P-10073)***
Helmet House LLC (PA)....C....800 421-7247
26855 Malibu Hills Rd Calabasas Hills (91301) ***(P-14336)***

Help Children World Foundation....B....818 706-9848
26500 Agoura Rd Ste 657 Calabasas (91302) ***(P-21800)***
Help Group West (PA)....C....818 781-0360
13130 Burbank Blvd Sherman Oaks (91401) ***(P-21311)***
Help Hospitalized Veterans (PA)....D....951 926-4500
36585 Penfield Ln Winchester (92596) ***(P-21801)***
Help Unlmted Personnel Svc Inc....A....805 962-4646
3202 E Ojai Ave Ojai (93023) ***(P-21169)***
Helpline Youth Counseling Inc (PA)....E....562 273-0722
14181 Telegraph Rd Whittier (90604) ***(P-21802)***
Heluna Health, City of Industry *Also called Public Hlth Fndation Entps Inc* ***(P-22361)***
Hely & Weber Orthopedic, Santa Paula *Also called Weber Orthopedic LP* ***(P-11153)***
Hemacare Corporation (HQ)....D....877 310-0717
8500 Balboa Blvd Ste 130 Northridge (91325) ***(P-21436)***
Hemar & Rousso Attys At Law, Encino *Also called Hemar Rousso & Heald L L P* ***(P-21579)***
Hemar Rousso & Heald L L P....E....818 501-3800
15910 Ventura Blvd # 1201 Encino (91436) ***(P-21579)***
Hemet Ready Mix, Hemet *Also called Superior Ready Mix Concrete LP* ***(P-6122)***
Hemet Unified School District....D....951 765-5100
2075 W Acacia Ave Hemet (92545) ***(P-22948)***
Hemet Unified School District....D....951 765-6287
985 N Cawston Ave Hemet (92545) ***(P-22452)***
Hemilane Inc....F....424 277-1134
909 E El Segundo Blvd El Segundo (90245) ***(P-2242)***
Hemisphere Design & Mfg LLC....F....661 294-9500
28895 Industry Dr Valencia (91355) ***(P-3649)***
Hemme Hay & Feed Inc....D....661 942-7880
43719 Sierra Hwy Lancaster (93534) ***(P-14861)***
Hemme Hay Feed, Lancaster *Also called Hemme Hay & Feed Inc* ***(P-14861)***
Hemocue Inc....D....800 881-1611
250 S Kraemer Blvd # 250 Brea (92821) ***(P-13495)***
Hemocue America, Brea *Also called Hemocue Inc* ***(P-13495)***
Hemodialysis Inc (PA)....E....818 500-8736
710 W Wilson Ave Glendale (91203) ***(P-21246)***
Hemodialysis Inc....E....626 792-0548
806 S Fair Oaks Ave Pasadena (91105) ***(P-10987)***
Hemodialysis Inc....C....818 365-6961
14901 Rinaldi St Ste 100 Mission Hills (91345) ***(P-21247)***
Hemosure Inc....E....888 436-6787
5358 Irwindale Ave Baldwin Park (91706) ***(P-5222)***
Henkel Chemical Management LLC....C....888 943-6535
14000 Jamboree Rd Irvine (92606) ***(P-5184)***
Henkel Electronic Mtls LLC, Irvine *Also called Henkel Chemical Management LLC* ***(P-5184)***
Henkel US Operations Corp....C....310 764-4600
20021 S Susana Rd Compton (90221) ***(P-4984)***
Henkels & McCoy Inc....B....909 517-3011
2840 Ficus St Pomona (91766) ***(P-952)***
Hennis Enterprises Inc....E....805 477-0257
2646 Palma Dr Ste 430 Ventura (93003) ***(P-4693)***
Henry C Cox II and John L West....D....951 360-2090
5700 Club House Dr Riverside (92509) ***(P-19491)***
Henry Call Inc....C....805 734-2762
Clark & Arguello Bldg 861 Vandenberg Afb (93437) ***(P-23392)***
Henry Company LLC (HQ)....D....310 955-9200
999 N Pcf Cast Hwy Ste 80 El Segundo (90245) ***(P-5281)***
Henry Mayo Newhall Mem Hosp....D....661 253-8112
23845 Mcbean Pkwy Valencia (91355) ***(P-19840)***
Henry Mayo Newhall Mem Hosp (PA)....A....661 253-8000
23845 Mcbean Pkwy Valencia (91355) ***(P-20785)***
Henry Mayo Nwhall Mem Hlth Fnd....D....661 253-8000
23845 Mcbean Pkwy Santa Clarita (91355) ***(P-20786)***
Henry Mayo Nwhall Mem Hlth Fnd....A....661 253-8000
23845 Mcbean Pkwy Valencia (91355) ***(P-20787)***
Henry Samueli School Engrg, Irvine *Also called University California Irvine* ***(P-22870)***
Henrymayo Newhall Mem Hosp, Valencia *Also called Henry Mayo Nwhall Mem Hlth Fnd* ***(P-20787)***
Henrys Adio Vsual Slutions Inc....E....714 258-7238
1582 Parkway Loop Ste F Tustin (92780) ***(P-9178)***
Henrys Metal Polishing Inc....F....323 263-9701
9856 Rush St South El Monte (91733) ***(P-7266)***
Henson Recording Studio, Los Angeles *Also called Jim Henson Company Inc* ***(P-19138)***
Hentrel Greathouse Foundation....D....302 513-4056
127 S 1st Ave Barstow (92311) ***(P-22341)***
Henway Inc....F....661 822-6873
1314 Goodrick Dr Tehachapi (93561) ***(P-11497)***
Heppner Hardwoods Inc....D....626 969-7983
555 W Danlee St Azusa (91702) ***(P-13214)***
Heprand Hospitality Inc....D....626 574-5600
311 E Huntington Dr Arcadia (91006) ***(P-16471)***
Hera Technologies LLC....E....951 751-6191
1590 S Milliken Ave Ste D Ontario (91761) ***(P-8615)***
Heraeus Prcous Mtls N Amer LLC (HQ)....C....562 921-7464
15524 Carmenita Rd Santa Fe Springs (90670) ***(P-6294)***
Herald Christian Health Center....D....626 286-8700
1661 Hanover Rd Ste 103 City of Industry (91748) ***(P-19841)***
Herald Christian Health Center (PA)....D....626 286-8700
3401 Aero Jet Ave El Monte (91731) ***(P-19842)***
Herb Thyme Farm Inc....D....603 542-3690
7909 Crossway Dr Pico Rivera (90660) ***(P-8)***
Herbal Science Intl Inc....F....626 333-9998
655 S 6th Ave 208 La Puente (91746) ***(P-4748)***
Herbalife Manufacturing LLC....D....949 457-0951
20481 Crescent Bay Dr Lake Forest (92630) ***(P-2329)***
Herbert Malarkey Roofing Co....D....562 806-8000
9301 Garfield Ave South Gate (90280) ***(P-1487)***
Herbert Rizzardini....F....760 377-4571
6259 Highway 178 Inyokern (93527) ***(P-1967)***
Herca Construction Services, Perris *Also called Herca Telecomm Services Inc* ***(P-13861)***

Employee Codes: A=Over 500 employees, B=251-500
C=101-250, D=51-100, E=20-50 F=10-19
2022 Southern California Business
Directory and Buyers Guide
© Mergent Inc. 1-800-342-5647
1153

ALPHABETIC

Herca Telecomm Services Inc D 951 940-5941
18610 Beck St Perris (92570) *(P-13861)*
Here Films E 310 806-4288
10990 Wilshire Blvd Los Angeles (90024) *(P-23448)*
Heritage Auctions Inc D 310 300-8390
9478 W Olympic Blvd Beverly Hills (90212) *(P-18541)*
Heritage Cabinet Co Inc F 818 786-4900
21740 Marilla St Chatsworth (91311) *(P-3650)*
Heritage California Aco, Northridge *Also called Regal Medical Group Inc (P-22277)*
Heritage Container Inc D 951 360-1900
4777 Felspar St Riverside (92509) *(P-3811)*
Heritage Distributing Company E 626 333-9526
425 S 9th Ave City of Industry (91746) *(P-1795)*
Heritage Distributing Company (PA) E **323 838-1225**
5743 Smithway St Ste 105 Commerce (90040) *(P-1837)*
Heritage Equipment Company D 661 587-2250
29341 Kimberlina Rd Wasco (93280) *(P-13458)*
Heritage Farms LLC (PA) D **442 283-5145**
2309 E Us Highway 98 Holtville (92250) *(P-110)*
Heritage Gardens Hlth Care Ctr, Loma Linda *Also called Heritage Health Care Inc (P-20374)*
Heritage Golf Group LLC C 949 369-6226
990 Avenida Talega San Clemente (92673) *(P-19492)*
Heritage Golf Group LLC C 661 254-4401
27330 Tourney Rd Valencia (91355) *(P-19493)*
Heritage Health Care, Lancaster *Also called High Dsert Med Corp A Med Grou (P-19844)*
Heritage Health Care Inc C 909 796-0216
25271 Barton Rd Loma Linda (92354) *(P-20374)*
Heritage Leather Company Inc E 323 983-0420
4011 E 52nd St Maywood (90270) *(P-5869)*
Heritage Medical Group C 760 956-1286
12370 Hesperia Rd Ste 6 Victorville (92395) *(P-21437)*
Heritage Medical Group Inc (PA) C **661 327-4411**
4580 California Ave Bakersfield (93309) *(P-19843)*
Heritage Oak Prvate Elmntary S, Yorba Linda *Also called Rgbx Inc (P-22056)*
Heritage Palms Golf Club, Indio *Also called Heritage Palms Hoa (P-19494)*
Heritage Palms Hoa D 760 772-7334
44291 Heritage Palms Dr S Indio (92201) *(P-19494)*
Heritage Paper Co (HQ) D **714 540-9737**
2400 S Grand Ave Santa Ana (92705) *(P-3812)*
Heritage Pointe, Mission Viejo *Also called Jewish HM For The Aging Ornge (P-22120)*
Heritage Security Services, Temecula *Also called Richman Management Corporation (P-18317)*
Herman Engineering & Mfg Inc F 909 483-1631
4501 E Airport Dr Ste B Ontario (91761) *(P-5660)*
Herman Weissker Inc (HQ) B **951 826-8800**
1645 Brown Ave Riverside (92509) *(P-953)*
Hermetic Seal Corporation (HQ) C **626 443-8931**
4232 Temple City Blvd Rosemead (91770) *(P-9722)*
Hernandez Kroone and Assoc Inc D 909 884-3222
234 E Drake Dr San Bernardino (92408) *(P-22566)*
Hertz Claim Management Corp D 626 296-4760
2923 Bradley St Ste 190 Pasadena (91107) *(P-18742)*
Hertz Entertainment Services, Burbank *Also called 24/7 Studio Equipment Inc (P-9247)*
Hertz Investment Group LLC (PA) C **310 584-8000**
21860 Burbank Blvd # 300 Woodland Hills (91367) *(P-15881)*
Herzog Contracting Corp C 562 595-7414
3760 Kilroy Arprt Way # 120 Long Beach (90806) *(P-999)*
Herzog Wine Cellars, Oxnard *Also called Royal Wine Corporation (P-2218)*
Hesperia Holding Inc D 760 244-8787
9780 E Ave Hesperia (92345) *(P-3363)*
Hesperia Unified School Dst E 760 948-1051
11176 G Ave Hesperia (92345) *(P-2449)*
Hesperia Usd Food Service, Hesperia *Also called Hesperia Unified School Dst (P-2449)*
Hestan Commercial Corporation C 714 869-2380
3375 E La Palma Ave Anaheim (92806) *(P-9015)*
Hewitt Industries, Anaheim *Also called Dg Holdings Inc (P-10045)*
Hewitt Industries Los Angeles E 714 891-9300
1455 Crenshaw Blvd # 290 Torrance (90501) *(P-10700)*
Hexagon Agility Inc F 949 236-5520
3335 Susan St Ste 100 Costa Mesa (92626) *(P-420)*
Hexpol Compounding CA Inc D 626 961-0311
491 Wilson Way City of Industry (91744) *(P-5380)*
HF Cox Inc (PA) D **661 366-3236**
118 Cox Transport Way Bakersfield (93307) *(P-12053)*
HF Cox Inc B 323 587-2359
8330 Atlantic Ave Cudahy (90201) *(P-11974)*
Hf Group Inc (PA) E **310 605-0755**
203 W Artesia Blvd Compton (90220) *(P-11277)*
Hff Securities LP (PA) D **310 407-2100**
1999 Avenue Of The Stars # 1200 Los Angeles (90067) *(P-15269)*
HFS Concepts 4 Inc E 562 424-1720
3229 E Spring St Ste 330 Long Beach (90806) *(P-22720)*
Hg Graphic & Printing F 323 412-3866
4217 Gage Ave Bell (90201) *(P-4315)*
Hg Insights Inc D 805 880-1100
1 N Calle Cesar Chavez # 1 Santa Barbara (93103) *(P-18542)*
Hgc Holdings Inc F 323 567-2226
3303 Mrtin Lther King Jr Lynwood (90262) *(P-2087)*
Hgt, Ontario *Also called Hub Group Trucking Inc (P-11977)*
HHC Ha Trs Inc E 714 750-4321
777 W Convention Way Anaheim (92802) *(P-16472)*
HHC Trs Portsmouth LLC D 760 322-6000
888 E Tahquitz Canyon Way Palm Springs (92262) *(P-16473)*
HHS Communications Inc D 909 230-5170
2042 S Grove Ave Ontario (91761) *(P-1264)*
HHS Construction LLC (HQ) C **909 393-3322**
2042 S Grove Ave Ontario (91761) *(P-770)*

HI Anaheim LLC D 714 533-1500
100 W Katella Ave Anaheim (92802) *(P-16474)*
HI LLC D 757 355-4113
10361 Jefferson Blvd Culver City (90232) *(P-22883)*
HI Perfrmnce Elc Vhcl Systems E 909 923-1973
620 S Magnolia Ave Ste B Ontario (91762) *(P-8916)*
HI Rel Connectors Inc B 909 626-1820
760 Wharton Dr Claremont (91711) *(P-9038)*
HI Tech Heat Treating Inc F 310 532-3705
331 W 168th St Gardena (90248) *(P-6440)*
HI Temp Forming Co F 714 529-6556
315 Arden Ave Ste 28 Glendale (91203) *(P-8616)*
Hi-Craft Metal Products E 310 323-6949
606 W 184th St Gardena (90248) *(P-6851)*
Hi-Desert Publishing Company E 909 795-8145
35154 Yucaipa Blvd Yucaipa (92399) *(P-3986)*
Hi-Desert Publishing Company E 909 336-3555
28200 Highway 189 O-1 Lake Arrowhead (92352) *(P-3987)*
Hi-Desert Publishing Company (HQ) D **760 365-3315**
56445 29 Palms Hwy Yucca Valley (92284) *(P-3988)*
Hi-Desert Publishing Company E 909 866-3456
42007 Fox Farm Rd Ste 3b Big Bear Lake (92315) *(P-3989)*
Hi-Grade Materials Co D 661 533-3100
6500 E Avenue T Littlerock (93543) *(P-6094)*
Hi-Lite Manufacturing Co Inc D 909 465-1999
13450 Monte Vista Ave Chino (91710) *(P-9089)*
Hi-Plas, Jurupa Valley *Also called Highland Plastics Inc (P-5663)*
Hi-Precision Grinding, Santa Ana *Also called Deltronic Corporation (P-10832)*
Hi-Rel Plastics & Molding Corp E 951 354-0258
7575 Jurupa Ave Riverside (92504) *(P-5661)*
Hi-Shear Corporation (HQ) A **310 784-4025**
2600 Skypark Dr Torrance (90505) *(P-7066)*
Hi-TEC Sports Usa, Inc., Van Nuys *Also called 412280 Inc (P-14427)*
Hi-Tech Engineering, Camarillo *Also called Hte Acquisition LLC (P-8623)*
Hi-Tech Iron Works, Commerce *Also called Architectural Enterprises Inc (P-6950)*
Hi-Tech Labels Incorporated (PA) E **714 670-2150**
8530 Roland St Buena Park (90621) *(P-8617)*
Hi-Tech Products, Buena Park *Also called Hi-Tech Labels Incorporated (P-8617)*
Hi-Temp Insulation Inc B 805 484-2774
4700 Calle Alto Camarillo (93012) *(P-1377)*
Hi-Torque Publications, Santa Clarita *Also called Daisy Publishing Company Inc (P-4064)*
Hiatus, Los Angeles *Also called Crew Knitwear LLC (P-2935)*
Hibernia Woolen Mills, Manhattan Beach *Also called Stanton Carpet Corp (P-2696)*
HIC Corporation (PA) F **949 261-1636**
38 Executive Park Ste 300 Irvine (92614) *(P-4073)*
Hickory Tree School, Torrance *Also called Hung Management Inc (P-22021)*
Hidden Jeans Inc E 213 746-4223
7210 Dominion Cir Commerce (90040) *(P-2574)*
Hidden Villa Ranch Produce Inc B 714 680-3447
310 N Harbor Blvd Ste 205 Fullerton (92832) *(P-14547)*
Hideaway C 760 777-7400
80440 Hideaway Club Ct La Quinta (92253) *(P-16833)*
Hideaway Club A 760 777-7400
80440 Hideaway Club Ct La Quinta (92253) *(P-19567)*
High Caliber Line, Irwindale *Also called Calibre International LLC (P-23379)*
High Desert, Victorville *Also called Southern California Edison Co (P-12855)*
High Dsert Med Corp A Med Grou (PA) C **661 945-5984**
43839 15th St W Lancaster (93534) *(P-19844)*
High Dsert Prtnr In Acdmic Exc B 760 946-5414
17500 Mana Rd Apple Valley (92307) *(P-22884)*
High End Seating Solutions LLC E 714 259-0177
1919 E Occidental St Santa Ana (92705) *(P-10492)*
High Five Inc F 714 847-2200
625 Fee Ana St Placentia (92870) *(P-4316)*
High Performance Logistics LLC D 702 300-4880
7227 Central Ave Riverside (92504) *(P-11975)*
High Plains Ranch LLC (PA) C **559 583-1277**
2911 Hanford Armona Rd Hanford (93230) *(P-133)*
High Rise Gdies Rest Group Inc (PA) C **310 772-0726**
1875 Century Park E Ste A Los Angeles (90067) *(P-16208)*
High Sierra Plastics F 760 873-5600
375 Joe Smith Rd Bishop (93514) *(P-5662)*
High Sierra Truss Company Inc F 559 688-6611
1201 S K St Tulare (93274) *(P-3364)*
High Tech Coatings Inc F 714 547-2122
1724 S Santa Fe St Santa Ana (92705) *(P-7373)*
High Tech Machine Shop S-Corp F 909 356-5437
15149 Boyle Ave Fontana (92337) *(P-7596)*
High Tech Pet Products D 805 644-1797
2111 Portola Rd A Ventura (93003) *(P-11684)*
High Technology Video Inc D 323 969-8822
10900 Ventura Blvd Studio City (91604) *(P-19131)*
High Tide and Green Grass Inc E 805 981-8722
2401 W Vineyard Ave Oxnard (93036) *(P-19495)*
High Valley Lodge, Sunland *Also called P R N Convalescent Hospital (P-20430)*
High-End Knitwear Inc E 323 582-6061
1100 S Hope St Ph 202 Los Angeles (90015) *(P-2636)*
High-Light Electric Inc D 951 352-9646
1460 E Cooley Dr Ste 100 Colton (92324) *(P-1265)*
High-Tech Coatings, Santa Ana *Also called High Tech Coatings Inc (P-7373)*
Higher Ground Education Inc (PA) B **949 836-9401**
10 Orchard Ste 200 Lake Forest (92630) *(P-23449)*
Highland Lumber Sales Inc D 714 778-2293
300 E Santa Ana St Anaheim (92805) *(P-13215)*
Highland Palms Healthcare Ctr, Highland *Also called Cedar Holdings LLC (P-20277)*
Highland Pk Sklled Nrsing Wlln D 323 254-6125
5125 Monte Vista St Los Angeles (90042) *(P-20375)*

Highland Plastics Inc ....C....951 360-9587
3650 Dulles Dr Jurupa Valley (91752) ***(P-5663)***
Hightower Metal Products ....D....714 637-7000
2090 N Glassell St Orange (92865) ***(P-7806)***
Hightower Metals, Orange *Also called Hightower Plating & Mfg Co* ***(P-7267)***
Hightower Plating & Mfg Co ....E....714 637-9110
2090 N Glassell St Orange (92865) ***(P-7267)***
Hikvision USA Inc (HQ) ....**C....909 895-0400**
18639 Railroad St City of Industry (91748) ***(P-18383)***
Hilborn Fuel Injection Company, Aliso Viejo *Also called Fuel Injection Engineering Co* ***(P-10064)***
Hill Brothers Chemical Company (PA) ....**C....714 998-8800**
3000 E Birch St Ste 108 Brea (92821) ***(P-14783)***
Hill Brothers Chemical Company ....F....626 333-2251
15017 Clark Ave City of Industry (91745) ***(P-4635)***
Hill Cress Home, San Bernardino *Also called Care Tech Inc* ***(P-20275)***
Hill Farrer & Burrill ....D....213 620-0460
300 S Grand Ave Ste 3700 Los Angeles (90071) ***(P-21580)***
Hill Marine Products LLC ....F....714 855-2986
2683 Halladay St Santa Ana (92705) ***(P-8618)***
Hillcrest Contracting Inc ....D....951 273-9600
1467 Circle City Dr Corona (92879) ***(P-887)***
Hillcrest Country Club ....C....310 553-8911
10000 W Pico Blvd Los Angeles (90064) ***(P-19568)***
Hilliard Bruce Vineyards LLC (PA) ....**F....805 736-5366**
2097 Vineyard View Ln Lompoc (93436) ***(P-2192)***
Hillquest SEC Patrol Svcs Inc ....E....213 213-9763
8383 Wilshire Blvd # 800 Beverly Hills (90211) ***(P-18384)***
Hillquest Security Services, Beverly Hills *Also called Hillquest SEC Patrol Svcs Inc* ***(P-18384)***
Hills Wldg & Engrg Contr Inc ....D....661 746-5400
22038 Stockdale Hwy Bakersfield (93314) ***(P-507)***
Hillsdale Group LP ....C....818 623-2170
12750 Riverside Dr North Hollywood (91607) ***(P-20595)***
Hillside Capital Inc ....C....650 367-2011
6222 Fallbrook Ave Woodland Hills (91367) ***(P-9277)***
HILLSIDE ENTERPRISES - AR & C, Long Beach *Also called Advocacy For Rspect Chice - Lo* ***(P-21936)***
Hillside House ....D....805 687-0788
1235 Veronica Springs Rd Santa Barbara (93105) ***(P-20531)***
Hillside Mem Pk & Mortuary, Los Angeles *Also called Temple Israel of Hollywood* ***(P-16932)***
Hillside Wines & Spirits LLC ....F....424 268-5168
15751 Tapia St Irwindale (91706) ***(P-2193)***
Hillsides ....B....323 254-2274
940 Avenue 64 Pasadena (91105) ***(P-22113)***
Hillview Mental Health Ctr Inc ....D....818 896-1161
12450 Van Nuys Blvd Ste 2 Pacoima (91331) ***(P-21312)***
Hilton, Anaheim *Also called Makar Anaheim LLC* ***(P-16554)***
Hilton, Beverly Hills *Also called Park Hotels & Resorts Inc* ***(P-16621)***
Hilton, Long Beach *Also called Merritt Hospitality LLC* ***(P-16564)***
Hilton, Orange *Also called Hit Portfolio II Trs LLC* ***(P-16482)***
Hilton, Oxnard *Also called T M Mian & Associates Inc* ***(P-16750)***
Hilton, Huntington Beach *Also called Waterfront Hotel LLC* ***(P-16778)***
Hilton, Los Angeles *Also called Fortuna Enterprises LP* ***(P-16446)***
Hilton Anaheim, Anaheim *Also called HHC Ha Trs Inc* ***(P-16472)***
Hilton Garden Inn ....D....323 876-8600
2005 N Highland Ave Los Angeles (90068) ***(P-16475)***
Hilton Garden Inn Calabasas, Calabasas *Also called T M Mian & Associates Inc* ***(P-16749)***
Hilton Garden Inn Fontana, Fontana *Also called Sierra Hotel Group LLC* ***(P-16709)***
Hilton Grdn Inn Marina Del Rey, Marina Del Rey *Also called Chatham Mdr LLC* ***(P-16379)***
Hilton Hotel, San Gabriel *Also called Landwin Hospitality LLC* ***(P-16534)***
Hilton Hotels, Long Beach *Also called HEI Long Beach LLC* ***(P-16470)***
Hilton Inns Inc (HQ) ....**A....310 278-4321**
9336 Civic Center Dr Beverly Hills (90210) ***(P-16476)***
Hilton Los Angeles Culver City, Culver City *Also called Woodbine Lgacy/Playa Owner LLC* ***(P-16803)***
Hilton Los Angles Universal Cy ....C....818 506-2500
555 Unversal Hollywood Dr Universal City (91608) ***(P-16477)***
Hilton Los Angls/Nversal Cy Ht, Universal City *Also called Sun Hill Properties Inc* ***(P-16738)***
Hilton Port Los Angls-San Pdro, San Pedro *Also called Meristar San Pedro Hilton LLC* ***(P-16563)***
Hilton Resort In Palm Spring, Palm Springs *Also called Walters Family Partnership* ***(P-16777)***
Hilton Resort Palm Springs ....C....760 320-6868
400 E Tahquitz Canyon Way Palm Springs (92262) ***(P-16478)***
Hilton Universal Hotel ....D....818 506-2500
555 Unversal Hollywood Dr Universal City (91608) ***(P-16479)***
Hilton Woodland Hills & Towers ....C....818 595-1000
6360 Canoga Ave Woodland Hills (91367) ***(P-16480)***
Hilz Cable Assemblies Inc ....F....951 245-0499
31889 Corydon St Ste 110 Lake Elsinore (92530) ***(P-10888)***
Himco National Inc ....F....323 231-9104
120 E 33rd St Los Angeles (90011) ***(P-1266)***
Himco Security Products, Los Angeles *Also called Himco National Inc* ***(P-1266)***
Hines Growers Inc ....B....800 554-4065
27368 Via Industria # 201 Temecula (92590) ***(P-79)***
Hino Motors Mfg USA Inc ....D....951 727-0286
4550 Wineville Ave Jurupa Valley (91752) ***(P-13064)***
Hinoichi Tofu, Garden Grove *Also called House Foods America Corp* ***(P-2451)***
Hippo Corporation ....F....714 229-9152
2535 W Via Palma Anaheim (92801) ***(P-14936)***
Hirel Connectors, Claremont *Also called HI Rel Connectors Inc* ***(P-9038)***
Hirsch Bedner Associates (PA) ....**C....310 829-9087**
3216 Nebraska Ave Santa Monica (90404) ***(P-18543)***
Hirsch Electronics LLC ....D....949 250-8888
1900 Carnegie Ave Ste B Santa Ana (92705) ***(P-13726)***
Hirsch/Bedner Intl Inc (PA) ....**D....310 829-9087**
3216 Nebraska Ave Santa Monica (90404) ***(P-18544)***
Hirsh Inc ....E....213 622-9441
860 S Los Angeles St # 900 Los Angeles (90014) ***(P-508)***
Hirsh Industries-Mexicali Div ....F....515 299-3200
1778 Zinetta Rd Ste A Calexico (92231) ***(P-11685)***
His Industries Inc ....E....949 383-4308
1202 W Shelley Ct Orange (92868) ***(P-8071)***
His Intl Tours NY Inc (HQ) ....**D....213 624-0777**
404 S Figueroa St Ste 500 Los Angeles (90071) ***(P-12386)***
His Life Woodworks ....E....310 756-0170
15107 S Main St Gardena (90248) ***(P-3254)***
Hisham's Towing, Gardena *Also called Jabi Enterprises Inc* ***(P-18935)***
Historic Mission Inn Corp ....B....951 784-0300
3649 Mission Inn Ave Riverside (92501) ***(P-16481)***
Hit Portfolio II Trs LLC ....D....714 938-1111
400 N State College Blvd Orange (92868) ***(P-16482)***
Hitachi Astemo Ohio Mfg Inc ....D....951 340-0702
1235 Graphite Dr Corona (92881) ***(P-10074)***
Hitachi Automotive Systems ....D....310 212-0200
6200 Gateway Dr Cypress (90630) ***(P-8917)***
Hitachi Solutions America Ltd (HQ) ....**E....949 242-1300**
100 Spectrum Center Dr # 350 Irvine (92618) ***(P-13405)***
Hitchcock Automotive Resources ....D....626 839-8400
17110 Gale Ave City of Industry (91745) ***(P-23235)***
Hitech Metal Fabrication Corp ....D....714 635-3505
1705 S Claudina Way Anaheim (92805) ***(P-6621)***
Hitech Plastics and Molds, Valencia *Also called Cypress Manufacturing LLC* ***(P-5619)***
Hitex Dyeing & Finishing Inc ....E....626 363-0160
355 Vineland Ave City of Industry (91746) ***(P-3199)***
Hiti Digital America Inc ....E....909 594-0099
20803 Valley Blvd Ste 110 Walnut (91789) ***(P-11278)***
Hits Magazine Inc (PA) ....**D....323 946-7600**
6906 Hollywood Blvd Fl 2 Los Angeles (90028) ***(P-14874)***
Hitt Companies ....E....714 979-1405
3231 W Macarthur Blvd Santa Ana (92704) ***(P-5381)***
Hitt Contracting Inc ....B....424 326-1042
3733 Motor Ave Ste 200 Los Angeles (90034) ***(P-771)***
Hitt Marking Devices I D Tech, Santa Ana *Also called Hitt Companies* ***(P-5381)***
Hixson Metal Finishing ....C....800 900-9798
829 Production Pl Newport Beach (92663) ***(P-7268)***
Hizco Truck Body, Los Angeles *Also called A A Cater Truck Mfg Co Inc* ***(P-3523)***
Hj Construction Inc ....E....805 534-1617
2320 Clark Valley Rd San Luis Obispo (93402) ***(P-954)***
Hji Group Corporation (PA) ....**D....714 557-8800**
5 Rochelle Newport Coast (92657) ***(P-23450)***
HK Aerspace Krkhill Arcft Prts ....D....818 559-9783
3098 N California St Burbank (91504) ***(P-13986)***
HK Canning Inc (PA) ....**E....805 652-1392**
130 N Garden St Ventura (93001) ***(P-1863)***
Hka, San Bernardino *Also called Hernandez Kroone and Assoc Inc* ***(P-22566)***
Hkf Inc (PA) ....**D....323 225-1318**
5983 Smithway St Commerce (90040) ***(P-13846)***
Hlb90067 Inc (PA) ....**F....626 689-8614**
2008 Park Pl Ste E El Segundo (90245) ***(P-5030)***
HMC Architects, Ontario *Also called HMC Group* ***(P-22721)***
HMC Group (HQ) ....**C....909 989-9979**
3546 Concours Ontario (91764) ***(P-22721)***
HMC Group ....D....909 980-8058
2930 Inland Empire Blvd # 100 Ontario (91764) ***(P-22722)***
HMcompany ....E....805 650-2651
4464 Mcgrath St Ste 111 Ventura (93003) ***(P-8619)***
Hmi Associates Inc ....C....818 887-6800
6800 Owensmouth Ave # 330 Canoga Park (91303) ***(P-18287)***
Hmm Construction Inc ....E....805 377-1402
3541 Old Conejo Rd Newbury Park (91320) ***(P-611)***
Hmr Building Systems LLC ....D....951 749-4700
620 Newport Center Dr # 12 Newport Beach (92660) ***(P-3211)***
Hmwc Cpas & Business Advisors ....D....714 505-9000
5120 Birch St Ste 100 Newport Beach (92660) ***(P-22789)***
Hnc Parent Inc (PA) ....**D....310 955-9200**
999 N Pacific Coast Hwy # 80 El Segundo (90245) ***(P-5282)***
Hnh Motorsports ....F....805 487-0505
350 S C St Oxnard (93030) ***(P-10075)***
Hntb Corporation ....D....213 403-1000
601 W 5th St Ste 1000 Los Angeles (90071) ***(P-22567)***
Hntb Corporation ....D....714 460-1600
6 Hutton Cntre Dr Ste 500 Santa Ana (92707) ***(P-22568)***
Hntb Gerwick Water Solutions ....C....714 460-1600
200 Sandpointe Ave Santa Ana (92707) ***(P-22569)***
Hoag Family Cancer Institute (PA) ....**D....949 722-6237**
1 Hoag Dr Bldg 41 Newport Beach (92663) ***(P-20788)***
Hoag Hospital Foundation (HQ) ....**E....949 764-7217**
330 Placentia Ave Ste 100 Newport Beach (92663) ***(P-20789)***
Hoag Memorial Hospital Presbt (PA) ....**A....949 764-4624**
1 Hoag Dr Newport Beach (92663) ***(P-20790)***
Hoag Orthopedic Institute LLC ....D....949 764-8690
16250 Sand Canyon Ave Irvine (92618) ***(P-20791)***
Hob Entertainment LLC ....D....714 778-2583
1350 Disneyland Dr Anaheim (92802) ***(P-19352)***
Hob Entertainment LLC ....D....323 848-5100
8430 W Sunset Blvd West Hollywood (90069) ***(P-19353)***
Hob Entertainment LLC (HQ) ....**C....323 769-4600**
7060 Hollywood Blvd Los Angeles (90028) ***(P-19354)***
Hochiki America Corporation ....C....714 522-2246
7051 Village Dr Ste 100 Buena Park (90621) ***(P-13633)***
Hoefner Corporation ....E....626 443-3258
9722 Rush St South El Monte (91733) ***(P-8620)***

ALPHABETIC

Hoffman Farms, Tulare *Also called Nielsens Creamery (P-135)*
Hoffman Hospice of The Valley ....D....661 410-1010
4325 Buena Vista Rd Bakersfield (93311) *(P-20532)*
Hoffman Magnetics Inc ....E....818 717-5095
19528 Ventura Blvd Tarzana (91356) *(P-9836)*
Hoffman Plastic Compounds Inc ....D....323 636-3346
16616 Garfield Ave Paramount (90723) *(P-4694)*
Hoffy, Vernon *Also called Square H Brands Inc (P-1752)*
Hog Inc ....F....626 279-5275
9519 Rush St Ste A South El Monte (91733) *(P-17178)*
Hogan Co Inc ....E....909 421-0245
2741 S Lilac Ave Bloomington (92316) *(P-6227)*
Hogan Lovells US LLP ....D....310 785-4600
1999 Avenue Of The Stars Los Angeles (90067) *(P-21581)*
Hogue Inc ....D....805 239-1440
550 Linne Rd Paso Robles (93446) *(P-19041)*
Hoke Outdoor Advertising Inc ....F....714 637-3610
1955 N Main St Orange (92865) *(P-11560)*
Holbrook Construction Inc ....D....714 523-1150
9814 Norwalk Blvd Ste 200 Santa Fe Springs (90670) *(P-772)*
Holden Industrial Inc ....E....909 919-5505
280 S Lemon Ave Unit 1608 Walnut (91788) *(P-8261)*
Holiday Garden SF Corp ....D....714 533-3555
1700 S Clementine St Anaheim (92802) *(P-16483)*
Holiday Inn, Los Angeles *Also called Packard Realty Inc (P-16615)*
Holiday Inn, Victorville *Also called Victorvlle Trsure Holdings LLC (P-16772)*
Holiday Inn, Santa Barbara *Also called S B Hotel Partners (P-16679)*
Holiday Inn, Costa Mesa *Also called Jds Hospitality Group (P-16512)*
Holiday Inn, Burbank *Also called JP Allen Extended Stay (P-16515)*
Holiday Inn, Los Angeles *Also called W&J Business Ventures LLC (P-16775)*
Holiday Inn, Los Angeles *Also called Brisam Lax (de) LLC (P-16355)*
Holiday Inn, North Hollywood *Also called Rio Vista Development Co Inc (P-16663)*
Holiday Inn, Anaheim *Also called Conestoga Hotel (P-16388)*
Holiday Inn, Santa Ana *Also called S W K Properties LLC (P-16680)*
Holiday Inn, Beverly Hills *Also called Ggwh LLC (P-16455)*
Holiday Inn, Los Angeles *Also called Seattle Arprt Hospitality LLC (P-16700)*
Holiday Inn, Long Beach *Also called Yhb Long Beach LLC (P-16809)*
Holiday Inn, Bakersfield *Also called Newport Hospitality Group Inc (P-16580)*
Holiday Inn, Grover Beach *Also called Oak Parks Inns Inc (P-16588)*
Holiday Inn, Lawndale *Also called Knr Devco (P-16528)*
Holiday Inn, Laguna Hills *Also called Laguna Hills Hotel Dev Ventr (P-16532)*
Holiday Inn, Torrance *Also called V Todays Inc (P-16766)*
Holiday Inn, Ontario *Also called Ontario Hospitality Properties (P-16597)*
Holiday Inn, Visalia *Also called Grosvenor Visalia Associates (P-16458)*
Holiday Inn, Palmdale *Also called Palmdale Resort Inc (P-16619)*
Holiday Inn, North Hollywood *Also called Marcus Hotels Inc (P-16555)*
Holiday Inn, Buena Park *Also called Uniwell Corporation (P-16762)*
Holiday Inn, San Gabriel *Also called R C L Lodging Systems Inc (P-16648)*
Holiday Inn, Diamond Bar *Also called Oak Creek LP (P-16587)*
Holiday Inn, Lebec *Also called Six Continents Hotels Inc (P-16713)*
Holiday Inn, Santa Maria *Also called Santa Maria Hotel Corp (P-16690)*
Holiday Inn, Los Angeles *Also called Remington Hotel Corporation (P-16659)*
Holiday Inn, Ontario *Also called Prime Hospitality LLC (P-16640)*
Holiday Inn ....E....714 748-7777
1915 S Manchester Ave Anaheim (92802) *(P-16484)*
Holiday Inn Anheim - Rsort Are, Anaheim *Also called Holiday Inn (P-16484)*
Holiday Inn Ex Anheim Main Gat ....D....714 772-7755
435 W Katella Ave Anaheim (92802) *(P-16485)*
Holiday Inn Ex Ht & Suites LLC ....D....760 253-9200
2700 Lenwood Rd Barstow (92311) *(P-16486)*
Holiday Inn Express ....C....805 584-6006
2550 Erringer Rd Simi Valley (93065) *(P-16487)*
Holiday Inn Express ....D....323 726-1111
705 San Gabriel Blvd Rosemead (91770) *(P-16488)*
Holiday Inn La Mirada, La Mirada *Also called Cha La Mirada LLC (P-16376)*
Holiday Inn Resort At Lodge, Big Bear Lake *Also called Pacific Snow Valley Resort LLC (P-16613)*
Holiday Manor Care Center, Upland *Also called Sela Healthcare Inc (P-20462)*
Holiday Manor Care Center, Canoga Park *Also called Sela Healthcare Inc (P-20463)*
Holiday Tree Farms Inc ....C....323 276-1900
329 Van Norman Rd Montebello (90640) *(P-368)*
Holland & Herring Mfg Inc ....E....909 469-4700
661 E Monterey Ave Pomona (91767) *(P-8621)*
Holland Construction ....D....562 285-5300
5000 E Spring St Ste 500 Long Beach (90815) *(P-612)*
HOLLENBECK HOME FOR THE AGED, Newhall *Also called Hollenbeck Palms (P-22114)*
Hollenbeck Palms ....C....323 263-6195
24431 Lyons Ave Apt 336 Newhall (91321) *(P-22114)*
Holliday Inn Express, Bishop *Also called Snk Lodging Inc (P-16717)*
Holliday Rock Trucking Inc ....D....888 273-2200
2300 W Base Line St San Bernardino (92410) *(P-6095)*
Holliday Trucking Inc (PA) ....**D....909 982-1553**
1401 N Benson Ave Upland (91786) *(P-6096)*
Hollingshead Management, Los Angeles *Also called Proland Property Managment LLC (P-15960)*
Hollywood Bed Spring Mfg Inc (PA) ....**D....323 887-9500**
5959 Corvette St Commerce (90040) *(P-6521)*
Hollywood Bowl, Los Angeles *Also called Los Angeles Philharmonic Assn (P-19365)*
Hollywood Cmnty Hosp Hollywood, Los Angeles *Also called Hollywood Cmnty Hosp Med Ctr I (P-20792)*
Hollywood Cmnty Hosp Med Ctr I ....C....323 462-2271
6245 De Longpre Ave Los Angeles (90028) *(P-20792)*
Hollywood Film Company ....F....818 683-1130
9265 Borden Ave Sun Valley (91352) *(P-11279)*
Hollywood Hookah Lounge Inc ....F....323 469-4622
6512 Hollywood Blvd Los Angeles (90028) *(P-11686)*
Hollywood Lamp & Shade Co ....E....323 585-3999
2928 Leonis Blvd Vernon (90058) *(P-9020)*
Hollywood Medical Center LP ....A....213 413-3000
1300 N Vermont Ave Los Angeles (90027) *(P-20793)*
Hollywood Partnership ....D....323 463-7171
5410 Hollywood Blvd Los Angeles (90027) *(P-16489)*
Hollywood Presbyterian Med Ctr, Los Angeles *Also called Hollywood Medical Center LP (P-20793)*
Hollywood Presbyterian Med Ctr, Los Angeles *Also called Cha Hollywood Medical Ctr LP (P-20714)*
Hollywood Records Inc ....E....818 560-5670
500 S Buena Vista St Burbank (91521) *(P-9220)*
Hollywood Reporter ....E....323 525-2000
6715 W Sunset Blvd Los Angeles (90028) *(P-3990)*
Hollywood Reporter ....E....323 525-2150
100 N Crescent Dr Gl-1 Beverly Hills (90210) *(P-3991)*
Hollywood Reporter LLC ....E....323 525-2000
100 N Crescent Dr Gl-1 Beverly Hills (90210) *(P-3992)*
Hollywood Rntals Prod Svcs LLC (PA) ....**D....818 407-7800**
5300 Melrose Ave Los Angeles (90038) *(P-19237)*
Hollywood Roosevelt Hotel, Los Angeles *Also called Roosevelt Hotel LLC (P-16670)*
Hollywood Schoolhouse Inc ....E....323 465-1320
1233 N Mccadden Pl Los Angeles (90038) *(P-22020)*
Hollywood Software Inc ....E....818 205-2121
5000 Van Nuys Blvd # 460 Van Nuys (91403) *(P-17879)*
Hollywood Sports Park LLC ....D....562 867-9600
9030 Somerset Blvd Bellflower (90706) *(P-18545)*
Holman Family Counseling Inc (PA) ....**D....818 704-1444**
8511 Fllbrook Ave Ste 400 West Hills (91304) *(P-20215)*
Holman Group, The, West Hills *Also called Holman Family Counseling Inc (P-20215)*
Holmes & Narver Inc (HQ) ....**C....714 567-2400**
999 W Town And Country Rd Orange (92868) *(P-22570)*
Holmes Body Shop-Alhambra ....D....626 282-6173
1130 E Main St Alhambra (91801) *(P-18792)*
Holmes Body Shop-Alhambra Inc (PA) ....**D....626 795-6447**
466 Foothill Blvd La Canada Flintridge (91011) *(P-18793)*
Holt Integrated Circuits, Mission Viejo *Also called W G Holt Inc (P-9604)*
Holthouse Carlin Van Trigt LLP (PA) ....**C....310 566-1900**
11444 W Olympic Blvd # 11 Los Angeles (90064) *(P-22790)*
Holy Cross Renal Center, Mission Hills *Also called Hemodialysis Inc (P-21247)*
Home & Body Company (PA) ....**E....714 842-8000**
5800 Skylab Rd Huntington Beach (92647) *(P-4964)*
Home Box Office Inc ....D....310 382-3000
2500 Broadway Ste 400 Santa Monica (90404) *(P-12771)*
Home Comfort USA, Anaheim *Also called Ken Starr Inc (P-1089)*
Home Deco Corp (PA) ....**D....818 669-5287**
11116 Tuxford St Sun Valley (91352) *(P-13216)*
Home Decor Wholesaler, City of Industry *Also called Pacific Heritg HM Fashion Inc (P-13183)*
Home Depot USA Inc ....C....818 716-9141
6345 Variel Ave Woodland Hills (91367) *(P-17353)*
Home Depot USA Inc ....C....818 887-7083
22855 Victory Blvd Canoga Park (91307) *(P-17354)*
Home Depot, The, Woodland Hills *Also called Home Depot USA Inc (P-17353)*
Home Depot, The, Canoga Park *Also called Home Depot USA Inc (P-17354)*
Home Entertainment Div, Los Angeles *Also called Fox Inc (P-12720)*
Home Express Delivery Svc LLC ....A....949 715-9844
230 Diamond St Laguna Beach (92651) *(P-12470)*
Home Franchise Concepts LLC (PA) ....**D....949 404-1100**
19000 Macarthur Blvd # 100 Irvine (92612) *(P-1530)*
Home Health Care Dept, Pacific Palisades *Also called Luxe Homecare Inc (P-21189)*
Home Instead Senior Care, Long Beach *Also called Coastal Cmnty Senior Care LLC (P-21150)*
Home Instead Senior Care, Los Angeles *Also called Tender Home Healthcare Inc (P-21221)*
Home Instead Senior Care, Victorville *Also called Branlyn Prominence Inc (P-21140)*
Home Instead Senior Care, Rancho Cucamonga *Also called Branlyn Prominence Inc (P-21141)*
Home Junction Inc ....D....858 777-9533
1 Venture Ste 300 Irvine (92618) *(P-17631)*
Home Mag, The, Irvine *Also called D & S Media Group Inc (P-4063)*
Home Organizers Inc ....A....562 699-9945
3860 Capitol Ave City of Industry (90601) *(P-1440)*
Home Paradise LLC ....F....626 284-9999
10932 Klingerman St Ste C El Monte (91733) *(P-7150)*
Home-Flex, Valencia *Also called Valencia Pipe Company (P-5472)*
Home2 Sites By Hilton Temecula, Temecula *Also called Temecula Hhc Hotel Dev LP (P-16752)*
Homeboy Bakery, Los Angeles *Also called Homeboy Industries (P-21803)*
Homeboy Industries (PA) ....**B....323 526-1254**
130 Bruno St Los Angeles (90012) *(P-21803)*
Homebridge Financial Svcs Inc ....A....818 981-0606
15301 Ventura Blvd Sherman Oaks (91403) *(P-15244)*
Homefacts Management LLC ....F....949 502-8300
1 Venture Ste 300 Irvine (92618) *(P-4180)*
Homefacts.com, Irvine *Also called Homefacts Management LLC (P-4180)*
Homeless Care, North Hollywood *Also called Northeast Valley Health Corp (P-20001)*
Homeowners Association, Helendale *Also called Silver Lakes Association (P-22369)*
HOMES OF HOPE, West Covina *Also called West Covina Foster Family Agcy (P-15648)*
Homewatch Caregivers, Los Angeles *Also called South Bay Senior Services Inc (P-21213)*
Homewood Stes By Hlton Aliso V, Aliso Viejo *Also called Summit Hotel Trs 129 LLC (P-16737)*

Mergent e-mail: customerrelations@mergent.com
1156
2022 Southern California Business Directory and Buyers Guide
(P-0000) Products & Services Section entry number
(PA)=Parent Co (HQ)=Headquarters (DH)=Div Headquarters

Homewood Suites, Palm Desert *Also called Palm Desert Hospitality LLC* ***(P-16616)***
Honav Usa Inc ....F....858 634-0617
3030 W Warner Ave Santa Ana (92704) ***(P-9179)***
Honda Stephan T MD Inc ....D....323 757-2118
2301 W El Segundo Blvd Hawthorne (90250) ***(P-19845)***
Honda World Westminster ....C....714 890-8900
13600 Beach Blvd Westminster (92683) ***(P-18898)***
Honest Company Inc (PA) ....C....310 917-9199
12130 Millennium Ste 500 Los Angeles (90094) ***(P-3016)***
Honey Bennetts Farm Inc (PA) ....E....805 521-1375
3176 Honey Ln Fillmore (93015) ***(P-2450)***
Honey Isabells Inc ....E....800 708-8485
539 N Glenoaks Blvd # 207 Burbank (91502) ***(P-140)***
Honey Punch, Los Angeles *Also called Klk Forte Industry Inc* ***(P-2963)***
Honey Punch Inc (PA) ....F....323 800-3812
1535 Rio Vista Ave Los Angeles (90023) ***(P-2951)***
Honey Science LLC ....C....949 795-1695
963 E 4th St Ste 100 Los Angeles (90013) ***(P-17632)***
Honeybee Health Inc (PA) ....C....310 559-5903
3515 Helms Ave Culver City (90232) ***(P-21438)***
Honeybee Robotics Ltd ....E....303 774-7613
2408 Lincoln Ave Altadena (91001) ***(P-8124)***
Honeybee Robotics Ltd ....E....510 207-4555
398 W Washington Blvd Pasadena (91103) ***(P-8125)***
Honeymoon Real Estate LP ....D....310 277-5221
9400 W Olympic Blvd Beverly Hills (90212) ***(P-16490)***
Honeyville Inc ....D....909 980-9500
11600 Dayton Dr Rancho Cucamonga (91730) ***(P-12171)***
Honeyville Grain Inc ....E....909 243-1050
9175 Milliken Ave Rancho Cucamonga (91730) ***(P-1944)***
Honeywell Authorized Dealer, Santa Fe Springs *Also called Western Allied Corporation* ***(P-1162)***
Honeywell Authorized Dealer, Palm Springs *Also called Desert Air Conditioning Inc* ***(P-1482)***
Honeywell Authorized Dealer, Chatsworth *Also called All Tmperatures Controlled Inc* ***(P-1023)***
Honeywell Authorized Dealer, North Hollywood *Also called Circulating Air Inc* ***(P-1045)***
Honeywell Authorized Dealer, Santa Clarita *Also called Tri-Signal Integration Inc* ***(P-1330)***
Honeywell Authorized Dealer, Corona *Also called LDI Mechanical Inc* ***(P-1093)***
Honeywell Authorized Dealer, Riverside *Also called 20/20 Plumbing & Heating Inc* ***(P-1011)***
Honeywell Authorized Dealer, Fullerton *Also called C & L Refrigeration Corp* ***(P-1041)***
Honeywell Authorized Dealer, Bakersfield *Also called Greers Bnner A Bakersfield Inc* ***(P-1077)***
Honeywell Authorized Dealer, Corona *Also called Multi Mechanical Inc* ***(P-1105)***
Honeywell Authorized Dealer, Paramount *Also called Reliable Energy Management Inc* ***(P-1128)***
Honeywell International Inc ....A....310 323-9500
2525 W 190th St Torrance (90504) ***(P-10216)***
Hong Kong & Shanghai Banking ....D....213 626-2460
770 Wilshire Blvd Ste 800 Los Angeles (90017) ***(P-15117)***
Hong Kong Bank, Los Angeles *Also called Hong Kong & Shanghai Banking* ***(P-15117)***
Hongfa America Inc ....E....714 669-2888
20381 Hermana Cir Lake Forest (92630) ***(P-8955)***
Hongray USA Medical Pdts Inc ....E....909 590-1611
2235 E Francis St Ontario (91761) ***(P-11112)***
Honk Technologies Inc ....C....800 979-3162
2251 Barry Ave Los Angeles (90064) ***(P-18094)***
Honor Plastics, Pomona *Also called Performance Engineered Pdts* ***(P-5742)***
Hood Container Corporation ....F....818 848-1648
801 S Main St Ste 101 Burbank (91506) ***(P-11687)***
Hood Manufacturing Inc ....D....714 979-7681
2621 S Birch St Santa Ana (92707) ***(P-5664)***
Hood Packaging Corporation ....C....559 585-2040
10801 Iona Ave Hanford (93230) ***(P-14937)***
Hook It Up ....F....714 600-0100
1513 S Grand Ave Santa Ana (92705) ***(P-2549)***
Hoosier Inc ....D....951 272-3070
1152 California Ave Corona (92881) ***(P-5665)***
Hoover Treated Wood Pdts Inc ....F....661 833-0429
5601 District Blvd Bakersfield (93313) ***(P-3433)***
Hoover Treated Wood Pdts Plant, Bakersfield *Also called Hoover Treated Wood Pdts Inc* ***(P-3433)***
Hope Bancorp Inc (PA) ....D....213 639-1700
3200 Wilshire Blvd # 1400 Los Angeles (90010) ***(P-15002)***
Hope Family Wines (PA) ....E....805 238-4112
1585 Live Oak Rd Paso Robles (93446) ***(P-2194)***
Hope Hse For Mltple Hndcpped I (PA) ....D....626 443-1313
4215 Peck Rd El Monte (91732) ***(P-22115)***
Hope of Valley Rescue Mission ....D....818 392-0020
11076 Norris Ave Fl 2 Pacoima (91331) ***(P-21804)***
Hope Plastic Co Inc ....E....818 769-5560
5353 Strohm Ave North Hollywood (91601) ***(P-5666)***
Horiba Americas Holding Inc (HQ) ....A....949 250-4811
9755 Research Dr Irvine (92618) ***(P-10797)***
Horiba Automotive Test Systems, Irvine *Also called Horiba Instruments Inc* ***(P-10798)***
Horiba Instruments Inc (HQ) ....C....949 250-4811
9755 Research Dr Irvine (92618) ***(P-10798)***
Horizon Communication Tech Inc (PA) ....D....714 982-3900
16441 Scientific Ste 200 Irvine (92618) ***(P-12786)***
Horizon Media Inc ....B....310 282-0909
1888 Century Park E # 700 Los Angeles (90067) ***(P-17017)***
Horizon Personnel Services (PA) ....C....714 912-7500
770 The Cy Dr S Ste 2000 Orange (92868) ***(P-17427)***
Horizon Solar Power, Hemet *Also called Lpsh Holdings Inc* ***(P-1097)***
Horizon Solar Power, Hemet *Also called Lpsh Holdings Inc* ***(P-1098)***
Horizon Well Logging Inc ....E....805 733-0972
711 Saint Andrews Way Lompoc (93436) ***(P-509)***

Hormel Foods Corp Svcs LLC ....E....949 753-5350
2 Venture Ste 250 Irvine (92618) ***(P-1735)***
Hornblower Cruisers and Events, Newport Beach *Also called Hornblower Yachts LLC* ***(P-12389)***
Hornblower Dining Yachts, Marina Del Rey *Also called Hornblower Yachts LLC* ***(P-12282)***
Hornblower Yachts LLC ....D....562 901-3420
100 Aquarium Way Long Beach (90802) ***(P-12387)***
Hornblower Yachts LLC ....D....310 301-9900
13755 Fiji Way Marina Del Rey (90292) ***(P-12388)***
Hornblower Yachts LLC ....D....310 301-6000
13755 Fiji Way Marina Del Rey (90292) ***(P-12282)***
Hornblower Yachts LLC ....D....949 650-2412
2527 W Coast Hwy Newport Beach (92663) ***(P-12389)***
Horrigan Cole Enterprises, Murrieta *Also called National Mentor Holdings Inc* ***(P-22135)***
Horrigan Enterprises Inc ....C....909 481-9663
7945 Cartilla Ave Rancho Cucamonga (91730) ***(P-21805)***
Horsemen Inc ....D....714 847-4243
16911 Algonquin St Huntington Beach (92649) ***(P-18288)***
Hose Power USA, City of Industry *Also called Bridgestone Hosepower LLC* ***(P-13977)***
Hospice Family, Northridge *Also called Family Hospice Ltd* ***(P-20529)***
Hospice Prgram Rdlnds Cmnty Ho, Redlands *Also called Hospice Redland Community Hosp* ***(P-21170)***
Hospice Redland Community Hosp ....D....909 335-5643
350 Terracina Blvd Redlands (92373) ***(P-21170)***
Hospice Touch Inc (PA) ....D....714 327-1936
3070 Bristol St Ste 100 Costa Mesa (92626) ***(P-21171)***
Hospital, Yucaipa *Also called Braswlls Mdterranean Grdns Inc* ***(P-20261)***
Hospital Assn Southern Cal (PA) ....D....213 347-2002
515 S Figueroa St # 1300 Los Angeles (90071) ***(P-22189)***
Hospital of Barstow Inc (HQ) ....C....760 256-1761
820 E Mountain View St Barstow (92311) ***(P-20794)***
Hospital Svc Emplyees Un Lcal ....D....323 734-8399
5480 Ferguson Dr Commerce (90022) ***(P-22290)***
Hospitalist Corp Inland Empire ....D....909 398-1550
840 Towne Center Dr Pomona (91767) ***(P-20795)***
Hospitality Sleep Systems Inc ....F....909 387-9779
107 E Rialto Ave San Bernardino (92408) ***(P-3550)***
Hospitality Wood Products Inc ....F....562 806-5564
7206 E Gage Ave Commerce (90040) ***(P-3255)***
Host Hotels & Resorts LP ....D....760 341-2211
74855 Country Club Dr Palm Desert (92260) ***(P-16491)***
Hot Dogger Tours Inc ....C....714 988-4088
105 Gemini Ave Brea (92821) ***(P-11912)***
Hot Shoppe Designs Inc ....F....949 487-2828
1323 Calle Avanzado San Clemente (92673) ***(P-2812)***
Hot Topic Inc (HQ) ....A....626 839-4681
18305 San Jose Ave City of Industry (91748) ***(P-2779)***
Hotchkis Wiley Capitl MGT LLC (PA) ....C....213 430-1000
725 S Figueroa St # 3900 Los Angeles (90017) ***(P-23038)***
Hotel Angeleno, Los Angeles *Also called Ascot Hotel LP* ***(P-16329)***
Hotel Associates Palm Springs, La Quinta *Also called Msr Desert Resort LP* ***(P-16574)***
Hotel Bel-Air, Los Angeles *Also called Kava Holdings Inc* ***(P-16521)***
Hotel Bel-Air ....B....310 472-1211
701 Stone Canyon Rd Los Angeles (90077) ***(P-16492)***
Hotel Casa Del Mar, Santa Monica *Also called Et Whitehall Seascape LLC* ***(P-16437)***
Hotel Company, El Segundo *Also called Uhg Lax Prop Llc* ***(P-16760)***
Hotel Fullerton Anaheim, The, Fullerton *Also called Huoyen International Inc* ***(P-16496)***
Hotel Hanford, The, Costa Mesa *Also called Hanford Hotels Inc* ***(P-16462)***
Hotel Indigo Los Angles Dwntwn, Los Angeles *Also called Metropolis Hotel MGT LLC* ***(P-16567)***
Hotel June, The, Los Angeles *Also called Custom Hotel LLC* ***(P-16403)***
Hotel Marmonte, Santa Barbara *Also called H D G Associates* ***(P-16460)***
Hotel Maya, Long Beach *Also called Queensbay Hotel LLC* ***(P-16646)***
Hotel Menage, Anaheim *Also called Newport Hotel Capital LLC* ***(P-16581)***
Hotel On Huntington Beach, Huntington Beach *Also called R C Hotels Inc* ***(P-16647)***
Hotel Pacific Garden ....D....310 532-5200
1625 W Redondo Beach Blvd Gardena (90247) ***(P-16493)***
Hotel Palomar, Los Angeles *Also called Behringer Harvard Wilshire Blv* ***(P-16341)***
Hotel Portofino, Redondo Beach *Also called Portofino Hotel Partners LP* ***(P-16636)***
Hotlix (PA) ....E....805 473-0596
966 Griffin St Grover Beach (93433) ***(P-2088)***
Hotlix Candy, Grover Beach *Also called Hotlix* ***(P-2088)***
Houalla Enterprises Ltd ....D....949 515-4350
2610 Avon St Newport Beach (92663) ***(P-773)***
Houchin Blood Services (PA) ....D....661 323-4222
11515 Bolthouse Dr Bakersfield (93311) ***(P-21439)***
Houchin Blood Services ....D....661 327-8541
11515 Bolthouse Dr Bakersfield (93311) ***(P-21440)***
Houchin Community Blood Bank ....D....661 323-4222
11515 Bolthouse Dr Bakersfield (93311) ***(P-21441)***
Houdini Inc (PA) ....D....714 525-0325
4225 N Palm St Fullerton (92835) ***(P-14938)***
Houdini Inc ....C....714 228-4406
6311 Knott Ave Buena Park (90620) ***(P-12214)***
Houlihan Lokey Inc (PA) ....B....310 788-5200
10250 Constellation Blvd Los Angeles (90067) ***(P-15330)***
House Blues Houston Rest Corp ....C....310 867-7000
9348 Civic Center Dr Beverly Hills (90210) ***(P-19355)***
House Blues Orlando Rest Corp ....C....310 867-7000
9348 Civic Center Dr Beverly Hills (90210) ***(P-19356)***
House Ear Clinic Inc (PA) ....D....213 483-9930
2100 W 3rd St Ste 111 Los Angeles (90057) ***(P-19846)***
House Foods America Corp (HQ) ....B....714 901-4350
7351 Orangewood Ave Garden Grove (92841) ***(P-2451)***
House of Blues, Los Angeles *Also called Hob Entertainment LLC* ***(P-19354)***

ALPHABETIC

Employee Codes: A=Over 500 employees, B=251-500
C=101-250, D=51-100, E=20-50 F=10-19
2022 Southern California Business Directory and Buyers Guide
© Mergent Inc. 1-800-342-5647
1157

House of Blues Concerts Inc (HQ) ....C.......**323 769-4977**
6255 W Sunset Blvd Fl 16 Los Angeles (90028) ***(P-19357)***
House of Graphics, South El Monte *Also called Hog Inc* ***(P-17178)***
House of Lashes ....F.......714 515-4162
1565 Mcgaw Ave Ste C Irvine (92614) ***(P-11688)***
House of Printing Inc ....E.......626 793-7034
3336 E Colorado Blvd Pasadena (91107) ***(P-4317)***
House of Uhuru, Los Angeles *Also called Watts Health Foundation Inc* ***(P-21057)***
House of Uniforms, Chatsworth *Also called Warrens Department Store Inc* ***(P-2753)***
House Seven Gables RE Inc ....D.......714 500-3300
19440 Goldenwest St Huntington Beach (92648) ***(P-15882)***
House Seven Gables RE Inc ....D.......714 974-7000
5481 E Santa Ana Cyn Dr Anaheim (92807) ***(P-15883)***
House Seven Gables RE Inc ....D.......714 754-6262
16872 Bolsa Chica St # 1 Huntington Beach (92649) ***(P-15884)***
House Seven Gables RE Inc ....D.......714 282-0306
5753 E Santa Ana Canyon P Anaheim (92807) ***(P-15885)***
Housewares International Inc ....E.......323 581-3000
1933 S Broadway Ste 867 Los Angeles (90007) ***(P-5667)***
Houston Bazz Co ....D.......714 898-2666
12700 Western Ave Garden Grove (92841) ***(P-7151)***
Houston Cheesecake Fctry Corp ....E.......818 871-3000
26901 Malibu Hills Rd Calabasas Hills (91301) ***(P-2007)***
Houston Fearless 76, Compton *Also called Hf Group Inc* ***(P-11277)***
Houston Kidney Center/Total R (HQ) ....E.......**310 536-2400**
601 Hawaii St El Segundo (90245) ***(P-21248)***
Houston Ontic Inc ....E.......818 678-6555
20400 Plummer St Chatsworth (91311) ***(P-8622)***
Houweling Nurseries Oxnard Inc ....B.......805 271-5105
645 Laguna Rd Camarillo (93012) ***(P-14471)***
Houweling's Tomatoes, Camarillo *Also called Houweling Nurseries Oxnard Inc* ***(P-14471)***
Howard CDM ....E.......562 427-4124
3750 Long Beach Blvd Long Beach (90807) ***(P-613)***
Howard Construction, Long Beach *Also called Howard CDM* ***(P-613)***
Howard Contracting Inc ....E.......562 596-2969
12354 Carson St Hawaiian Gardens (90716) ***(P-1597)***
Howard Johnson, Anaheim *Also called Northwest Hotel Corporation* ***(P-16585)***
Howard Roofing Company Inc ....D.......909 622-5598
245 N Mountain View Ave Pomona (91767) ***(P-1488)***
Howe Construction Co, Anaheim *Also called Burt L Howe & Associates* ***(P-21525)***
Howell Drilling, Long Beach *Also called Dick Howells Hole Drlg Svc Inc* ***(P-426)***
Howmet Aerospace Inc ....B.......212 836-2674
3016 Lomita Blvd Torrance (90505) ***(P-6281)***
Howmet Aerospace Inc ....C.......323 728-3901
1550 Gage Rd Montebello (90640) ***(P-6299)***
Howmet Corporation ....C.......310 847-8152
900 E Watson Center Rd Carson (90745) ***(P-6266)***
Howmet Fastening Systems, Simi Valley *Also called Howmet Globl Fstning Systems I* ***(P-13988)***
Howmet Globl Fstning Systems I ....D.......310 784-0700
3000 Lomita Blvd Torrance (90505) ***(P-13987)***
Howmet Globl Fstning Systems I (HQ) ....C.......**805 426-2270**
3990a Heritage Oak Ct Simi Valley (93063) ***(P-13988)***
Howmet Globl Fstning Systems I ....D.......714 871-1550
800 S State College Blvd Fullerton (92831) ***(P-6267)***
Howroyd-Wright Emplymnt Agcy (HQ) ....C.......**818 240-8688**
327 W Broadway Glendale (91204) ***(P-17428)***
Howroyd-Wright Emplymnt Agcy ....C.......818 240-8688
325 W Broadway Glendale (91204) ***(P-17429)***
Hoya Holdings Inc ....D.......626 739-5200
425 E Huntington Dr Monrovia (91016) ***(P-10838)***
Hoya Surgical Optics Inc ....E.......909 680-3900
15335 Frfeld Rnch Rd Ste Chino Hills (91709) ***(P-10988)***
Hoyt Roofs Inc ....E.......714 773-1820
1809 N Orangethorpe Park Anaheim (92801) ***(P-1489)***
Hoyu America Co ....D.......714 230-3000
6265 Phyllis Dr Cypress (90630) ***(P-14250)***
HP Communications Inc (PA) ....C.......**951 572-1200**
13341 Temescal Canyon Rd Corona (92883) ***(P-955)***
HP Core Co Inc ....E.......323 582-1688
1264 Indian Springs Dr Glendora (91741) ***(P-7771)***
HP It Services Incorporated ....E.......714 844-7737
1506 W Flower Ave Fullerton (92833) ***(P-8262)***
Hpi Cylinders, Santa Fe Springs *Also called Hydraulic Pneumatic Inc* ***(P-8439)***
Hpp Food Services, Wilmington *Also called Icpk Corporation* ***(P-14473)***
Hps Mechanical Inc (PA) ....C.......**661 397-2121**
3100 E Belle Ter Bakersfield (93307) ***(P-1082)***
Hps Performance Products ....F.......626 747-9200
15332 Valley Blvd City of Industry (91746) ***(P-5320)***
Hpv Technologies Inc ....F.......949 476-7000
3030 Orange Ave Santa Ana (92707) ***(P-9180)***
Hr Cloud Inc (PA) ....D.......**510 909-1993**
222 N Pcf Cast Hwy Ste 20 El Segundo (90245) ***(P-17880)***
Hr Mobile Services Inc ....D.......559 625-2322
1850 S Central St Visalia (93277) ***(P-23236)***
HR&a Advisors Inc ....D.......310 581-0900
700 S Flower St Ste 2995 Los Angeles (90017) ***(P-23237)***
Hrc Fertility, Pasadena *Also called Huntington Reprodctve Ctr Inc* ***(P-19850)***
Hrd Aero Systems Inc (PA) ....C.......**661 295-0670**
25555 Avenue Stanford Valencia (91355) ***(P-19042)***
Hrk Pet Food Products Inc ....E.......818 897-2521
12924 Pierce St Pacoima (91331) ***(P-1968)***
Hrl Laboratories LLC ....A.......310 317-5000
3011 Malibu Canyon Rd Malibu (90265) ***(P-22885)***
Hronis Inc A California Corp (PA) ....C.......**661 725-2503**
10443 Hronis Rd Delano (93215) ***(P-63)***
Hsa Bell Gardens Laup, Bell *Also called Human Services Association* ***(P-21807)***
Hsb Holdings Inc ....E.......951 214-6590
14050 Day St Moreno Valley (92553) ***(P-5302)***
Hsiao & Montano Inc ....E.......626 588-2528
809 W Santa Anita Ave San Gabriel (91776) ***(P-5893)***
Hsssi, San Dimas *Also called Hamilton Sundstrand Spc Systms* ***(P-10887)***
Hst Lessee South Coast LP ....D.......714 540-2500
686 Anton Blvd Costa Mesa (92626) ***(P-16494)***
Ht Multinational Inc ....E.......626 964-2686
12851 Reservoir St Apt A Chino (91710) ***(P-10076)***
Hte Acquisition LLC ....E.......805 987-5449
4610 Calle Quetzal Camarillo (93012) ***(P-8623)***
Htec Group Inc (PA) ....A.......**213 785-7824**
10250 Constellation Blvd Los Angeles (90067) ***(P-17633)***
Htl Manufacturing Div, Simi Valley *Also called Meggitt Safety Systems Inc* ***(P-10330)***
Htpghnl, Ontario *Also called Heat Transfer Pdts Group LLC* ***(P-13845)***
Hts Division, Lake Elsinore *Also called Mercury Metal Die & Ltr Co Inc* ***(P-7387)***
Hua Xing Pcba Limited ....E.......310 626-7575
Carlow Rd Torrance (90505) ***(P-9413)***
Huang Qi ....F.......626 442-6808
4700 Miller Dr Ste H Temple City (91780) ***(P-2886)***
Hub Construction Spc Inc (HQ) ....E.......**909 889-0161**
379 S I St San Bernardino (92410) ***(P-17355)***
Hub Construction Sups & Eqp, San Bernardino *Also called Hub Construction Spc Inc* ***(P-17355)***
Hub Distributing Inc (HQ) ....B.......**951 340-3149**
1260 Corona Pointe Ct Corona (92879) ***(P-14380)***
Hub Group Trucking Inc ....B.......909 770-8950
13867 Valley Blvd Fontana (92335) ***(P-11976)***
Hub Group Trucking Inc ....C.......951 693-9813
3801 E Guasti Rd Ontario (91761) ***(P-11977)***
Hub-Limited Workshop, Los Angeles *Also called Mid-Cities Association Inc* ***(P-21961)***
Hubbell Power Systems Inc ....D.......949 305-3311
27151 Burbank Foothill Ranch (92610) ***(P-13634)***
Huck International Inc ....C.......310 830-8200
900 E Watson Center Rd Carson (90745) ***(P-7067)***
HUD Industries ....F.......310 327-7110
2104 W Rosecrans Ave Gardena (90249) ***(P-7938)***
Hudson H Clude Cmplete Hlth Ct, Los Angeles *Also called County of Los Angeles* ***(P-19765)***
Hudson Pacific Properties Inc (PA) ....C.......**310 445-5700**
11601 Wilshire Blvd # 600 Los Angeles (90025) ***(P-16234)***
Hudson Pacific Properties LP (HQ) ....B.......**310 445-5700**
11601 Wilshire Blvd # 600 Los Angeles (90025) ***(P-16235)***
Hudson Valve Co Inc ....E.......661 831-6208
5630 District Blvd # 108 Bakersfield (93313) ***(P-7445)***
Hueston Hennigan LLP ....D.......213 788-4340
523 W 6th St Ste 400 Los Angeles (90014) ***(P-21582)***
Huf Worldwide LLC ....C.......323 264-8656
420 Boyd St Ste 400 Los Angeles (90013) ***(P-12645)***
Hufcor Airwall Since 1900, Long Beach *Also called Hufcor California Inc* ***(P-3685)***
Hufcor California Inc (HQ) ....D.......**562 634-3116**
2380 E Artesia Blvd Long Beach (90805) ***(P-3685)***
Hughes Bros Aircrafters Inc ....E.......323 773-4541
11010 Garfield Pl South Gate (90280) ***(P-7807)***
Hughes Price & Sharp Inc ....F.......865 675-6278
5200 Lankershim Blvd # 85 North Hollywood (91601) ***(P-3993)***
Hughes Research Laboratories, Malibu *Also called Hrl Laboratories LLC* ***(P-22885)***
Huhtamaki Inc ....D.......323 269-0151
4209 Noakes St Commerce (90023) ***(P-5511)***
Hula Post Productions Inc ....D.......818 954-0200
1111 S Victory Blvd Burbank (91502) ***(P-19132)***
Hulk Construction ....D.......714 701-9458
4352 Lakeview Ave Yorba Linda (92886) ***(P-1615)***
Hulsey Contracting Inc ....E.......951 549-3665
1740 Howard Pl Redlands (92373) ***(P-13862)***
Hulu LLC ....D.......888 631-4858
12312 W Olympic Boulev Los Angeles (90064) ***(P-12646)***
Hulu LLC (HQ) ....A.......**310 571-4700**
2500 Broadway Ste 200 Santa Monica (90404) ***(P-12647)***
Human Designs Prosthetic (HQ) ....F.......**562 988-2414**
49 E Foothill Blvd Arcadia (91006) ***(P-11113)***
Human Dsgns Prsthtic Orthtic L, Long Beach *Also called Ferraco Inc* ***(P-11104)***
Human Options Inc ....E.......949 757-3635
1901 Newport Blvd Ste 240 Costa Mesa (92627) ***(P-21806)***
Human Resources, Anaheim *Also called Interstate Electronics Corp* ***(P-23245)***
Human Resources Department, Covina *Also called Emanate Health Medical Center* ***(P-20765)***
Human Services Association (PA) ....D.......**562 806-5400**
6800 Florence Ave Bell (90201) ***(P-21807)***
Human Touch LLC ....D.......562 426-8700
4600 E Conant St Long Beach (90808) ***(P-13138)***
Humangood Norcal ....D.......661 834-0620
1401 New Stine Rd Bakersfield (93309) ***(P-20596)***
Humangood Norcal ....D.......909 793-1233
900 Salem Dr Redlands (92373) ***(P-20597)***
Humangood Socal (HQ) ....D.......**818 247-0420**
516 Burchett St Glendale (91203) ***(P-15726)***
Humangood Socal ....C.......626 359-8141
802 Buena Vista St Duarte (91010) ***(P-22116)***
Hummus Guy, The, Torrance *Also called Thg Brands Inc* ***(P-2537)***
Humnit Hotel At Lax LLC ....D.......424 702-1234
6225 W Century Blvd Los Angeles (90045) ***(P-16495)***
Humphrey Gcpzzi Vtrnary Group ....D.......805 386-4291
4774 Donlon Rd Somis (93066) ***(P-200)***
Hung Management Inc ....D.......310 533-4830
21720 Madrona Ave Torrance (90503) ***(P-22021)***
Hungry Heart Media Inc ....C.......323 951-0010
5450 W Washington Blvd Los Angeles (90016) ***(P-19133)***
Hunnington Dialysis Center, Pasadena *Also called Hemodialysis Inc* ***(P-10987)***

Hunsaker & Assoc Irvine Inc ....B....951 352-7200
2900 Adams St Ste A15 Riverside (92504) *(P-22571)*
Hunsaker & Assoc Irvine Inc (PA) ....D....949 583-1010
3 Hughes Irvine (92618) *(P-22572)*
Hunt Ortmann Palffy Nieves ....E....626 440-5200
301 N Lake Ave Fl 7 Pasadena (91101) *(P-21583)*
Hunt Enterprises Inc ....C....310 325-1496
2270 Sepulveda Blvd # 50 Torrance (90501) *(P-15886)*
Hunter Dodge Chrysler Jeep Ram, Lancaster *Also called H W Hunter Inc (P-18838)*
Hunter Easterday Corporation ....C....714 238-3400
1475 N Hundley St Anaheim (92806) *(P-17250)*
Huntingtn Lbrary Art Collctns ....B....626 405-2100
1151 Oxford Rd San Marino (91108) *(P-22222)*
Huntington Ambltry Surg Ctr ....E....626 229-8999
625 S Fair Oaks Ave Pasadena (91105) *(P-19847)*
Huntington Bch Cnvlscent Hosp ....D....949 487-9500
29222 Rncho Vejo Rd Ste 1 San Juan Capistrano (92675) *(P-20376)*
Huntington Bch Senior Hsing LP ....C....714 842-4006
18765 Florida St Huntington Beach (92648) *(P-15727)*
Huntington Beach Ford, Huntington Beach *Also called York Enterprises South Inc (P-18888)*
Huntington Beach Hospital, Huntington Beach *Also called Prime Hlthcare Hntngton Bch LL (P-20904)*
Huntington Beach Machining, Huntington Beach *Also called Madsen Products Incorporated (P-8673)*
Huntington Beach Medical Offs, Huntington Beach *Also called Kaiser Foundation Hospitals (P-16180)*
Huntington Care LLC ....C....877 405-6990
3452 E Fthill Blvd Ste 76 Pasadena (91107) *(P-21172)*
Huntington Extended Care Ctr, Pasadena *Also called Pasadena Hospital Assn Ltd (P-20436)*
Huntington Gardens, Huntington Beach *Also called Huntington Bch Senior Hsing LP (P-15727)*
Huntington Home Care, Pasadena *Also called Huntington Care LLC (P-21172)*
Huntington Med Res Institutes ....D....626 397-5804
734 Fairmount Ave Pasadena (91105) *(P-22909)*
Huntington Medical Foundation ....D....626 795-4210
10 Congress St Ste 208 Pasadena (91105) *(P-19848)*
Huntington Medical Foundation ....C....626 792-3141
65 N Madison Ave Ste 800 Pasadena (91101) *(P-20796)*
Huntington Memorial Hospital, Pasadena *Also called Pasadena Hospital Assn Ltd (P-20435)*
Huntington Memory Care Cmnty, Alhambra *Also called Silverado Senior Living Inc (P-20473)*
Huntington Park Dialysis LLC ....D....323 585-7605
5942 Rugby Ave Huntington Park (90255) *(P-21249)*
Huntington Park Nursing Center, Huntington Park *Also called Covenant Care California LLC (P-20299)*
Huntington Radiology ....D....562 904-1111
11525 Brookshire Ave # 11 Downey (90241) *(P-19849)*
Huntington Reprodctve Ctr Inc (PA) ....E....626 204-9699
135 S Rosemead Blvd Pasadena (91107) *(P-19850)*
Huntington Valley Inds Inc ....F....714 892-0256
16752 Burke Ln Huntington Beach (92647) *(P-13989)*
Huntington Vly Healthcare Ctr, Huntington Beach *Also called Douglas Fir Holdings LLC (P-20315)*
Huntley Hotel Santa Monica Bch, Santa Monica *Also called Second Street Corporation (P-16701)*
Huntmix Inc ....C....818 548-5200
500 N Brand Blvd Ste 500 Glendale (91203) *(P-5273)*
Huntsman Advanced Materials AM ....C....818 265-7221
5121 W San Fernando Rd Los Angeles (90039) *(P-4695)*
Huoyen International Inc ....D....714 635-9000
1500 S Raymond Ave Fullerton (92831) *(P-16496)*
Hupa International Inc ....E....909 598-9876
21717 Ferrero Walnut (91789) *(P-11425)*
Hurley International LLC (PA) ....C....949 548-9375
3080 Bristol St Costa Mesa (92626) *(P-2813)*
Hurst International, Chatsworth *Also called Labeling Hurst Systems LLC (P-4532)*
Husky Injction Mlding Systems ....D....805 523-9593
5245 Maureen Ln Moorpark (93021) *(P-5668)*
Husky Injction Mlding Systems ....D....714 545-8200
3505 Cadillac Ave Ste N4 Costa Mesa (92626) *(P-5669)*
Hussmann Corporation ....B....909 590-4910
13770 Ramona Ave Chino (91710) *(P-8342)*
Hustler Casino, Gardena *Also called El Dorado Enterprises Inc (P-16430)*
Hutchinson & Bloodgood LLP (PA) ....D....818 637-5000
550 N Brand Blvd Fl 14 Glendale (91203) *(P-22791)*
Hutchinson Arospc & Indust Inc ....C....818 843-1000
4510 W Vanowen St Burbank (91505) *(P-10345)*
Hutchinson Arospc & Indust Inc ....C....818 843-1000
4510 W Vanowen St Burbank (91505) *(P-5382)*
Hutchinson Seal Corporation (HQ) ....A....248 375-4190
11634 Patton Rd Downey (90241) *(P-5341)*
Hutchison Corporation ....E....310 763-7991
6107 Obispo Ave Long Beach (90805) *(P-1378)*
Huxley Apartments, The, West Hollywood *Also called Essex Property Trust Inc (P-15724)*
Huy Fong Foods Inc ....E....626 286-8328
4800 Azusa Canyon Rd Irwindale (91706) *(P-1864)*
Hvac Installation and Repair, Los Angeles *Also called Precise Air Systems Inc (P-1122)*
Hvantage Technologies Inc ....D....818 661-6301
6700 Fllbrook Ave Ste 222 West Hills (91307) *(P-17634)*
Hwe Mechanical, Bakersfield *Also called Hills Wldg & Engrg Contr Inc (P-507)*
Hwmm (HQ) ....D....949 581-1144
7 Studebaker Irvine (92618) *(P-14337)*
Hy-Tech Tile Inc ....C....951 788-0550
1355 Palmyrita Ave Riverside (92507) *(P-1467)*
Hyatt Corporation ....B....312 750-1234
6225 W Century Blvd Los Angeles (90045) *(P-16497)*
Hyatt Corporation ....B....562 432-0161
200 S Pine Ave Long Beach (90802) *(P-16498)*
Hyatt Corporation ....B....949 729-1234
1107 Jamboree Rd Newport Beach (92660) *(P-16499)*
Hyatt Die Cast Engrg Corp - S ....E....714 622-2131
12250 Industry St Garden Grove (92841) *(P-6364)*
Hyatt Hotel, Long Beach *Also called Hyatt Corporation (P-16498)*
Hyatt Hotel, Newport Beach *Also called Hyatt Corporation (P-16499)*
Hyatt Hotel, Los Angeles *Also called Jwmcc Limited Partnership (P-16517)*
Hyatt Hotel, Westlake Village *Also called Sky Court USA Inc (P-16714)*
Hyatt Los Angeles Airport, Los Angeles *Also called Hyatt Corporation (P-16497)*
Hyatt Regency Century Plaza ....A....310 228-1234
2025 Avenue Of The Stars Los Angeles (90067) *(P-16500)*
Hyatt Rgency Suites Palm Sprng, Palm Springs *Also called Rbd Hotel Palm Springs LLC (P-16656)*
Hyatt Westlake, Westlake Village *Also called Swvp Westlake LLC (P-16746)*
Hybrid Promotions LLC (PA) ....B....714 952-3866
10711 Walker St Cypress (90630) *(P-14338)*
Hycor Biomedical LLC ....C....714 933-3000
7272 Chapman Ave Ste A Garden Grove (92841) *(P-10989)*
Hyde, Vernon *Also called Streets Ahead Inc (P-3062)*
Hyde Pk Convalescent Hosp Inc ....E....323 753-1354
6520 West Blvd Los Angeles (90043) *(P-20377)*
Hydra-Electric Company (PA) ....C....818 843-6211
3151 N Kenwood St Burbank (91505) *(P-8898)*
Hydrafacial Company, The, Long Beach *Also called Edge Systems LLC (P-12201)*
Hydrafacial Company, The, Long Beach *Also called Edge Systems LLC (P-10975)*
Hydraforce Incorporated ....F....951 689-3987
7383 Orangewood Dr Riverside (92504) *(P-8015)*
Hydraulic Pneumatic Inc ....F....562 926-1122
13766 Milroy Pl Santa Fe Springs (90670) *(P-8439)*
Hydraulic Shop Inc ....E....909 875-9336
2753 S Vista Ave Bloomington (92316) *(P-7709)*
Hydraulics International Inc (PA) ....B....818 998-1231
9201 Independence Ave Chatsworth (91311) *(P-10346)*
Hydraulics International Inc ....E....818 998-1231
20961 Knapp St Chatsworth (91311) *(P-10347)*
Hydraulx, Playa Vista *Also called Avongard Products USA Ltd (P-19220)*
Hydril Company ....D....661 588-9332
3237 Patton Way Bakersfield (93308) *(P-7671)*
Hydrite Chemical Co ....D....559 651-3450
1603 Clancy Ct Visalia (93291) *(P-14784)*
Hydro Extrusion Usa LLC ....B....626 964-3411
18111 Railroad St City of Industry (91748) *(P-6310)*
Hydro Quip, Corona *Also called Blue Desert International Inc (P-8369)*
Hydro Systems Inc (PA) ....D....661 775-0686
29132 Avenue Paine Valencia (91355) *(P-6547)*
Hydro Tek Systems Inc ....D....909 799-9222
2353 Almond Ave Redlands (92374) *(P-14038)*
Hydro-Aire Inc (HQ) ....B....818 526-2600
3000 Winona Ave Burbank (91504) *(P-10348)*
Hydro-Dig Inc ....D....714 772-9947
700 E Sycamore St Anaheim (92805) *(P-262)*
Hydro-Pressure Systems, North Hollywood *Also called Woods Maintenance Services Inc (P-1704)*
Hydrochempsc, Torrance *Also called PSC Industrial Outsourcing LP (P-19058)*
Hydrochempsc, Bakersfield *Also called PSC Industrial Outsourcing LP (P-541)*
Hydrodex LLC ....E....800 218-8813
31225 La Baya Dr Westlake Village (91362) *(P-8386)*
Hydroform USA Incorporated ....C....310 632-6353
2848 E 208th St Carson (90810) *(P-10349)*
Hydromach Inc ....E....818 341-0915
20400 Prairie St Chatsworth (91311) *(P-10533)*
Hygenia, Camarillo *Also called Medical Packaging Corporation (P-11123)*
Hygiena LLC (PA) ....B....805 388-2383
941 Avenida Acaso Camarillo (93012) *(P-4922)*
Hykso Inc ....D....213 785-3372
936 W 17th St Costa Mesa (92627) *(P-23238)*
Hyland's Homeopathic, Los Angeles *Also called Standard Homeopathic Company (P-4896)*
Hyper Ice Inc (PA) ....E....714 524-3742
525 Technology Dr Irvine (92618) *(P-11426)*
Hypercel Corporation ....D....661 310-1000
28385 Constellation Rd Valencia (91355) *(P-13727)*
Hyperice, Irvine *Also called Hyper Ice Inc (P-11426)*
Hyperion Books For Children, Burbank *Also called Disney Book Group LLC (P-4126)*
Hyperion Motors LLC ....E....714 363-5858
1032 W Taft Ave Orange (92865) *(P-8444)*
Hyperloop One, Los Angeles *Also called Hyperloop Technologies Inc (P-12573)*
Hyperloop Technologies Inc (PA) ....C....213 800-3270
2159 Bay St Los Angeles (90021) *(P-12573)*
Hyponex Corporation ....C....909 597-2811
12273 Brown Ave Jurupa Valley (92509) *(P-5156)*
Hyrecar Inc ....D....888 688-6769
355 S Grand Ave Ste 1650 Los Angeles (90071) *(P-11875)*
Hytech Processing, Inglewood *Also called C C M D Inc (P-7231)*
Hytron Mfg Co Inc ....E....714 903-6701
15582 Chemical Ln Huntington Beach (92649) *(P-8624)*
Hyundai Amer Technical Ctr Inc ....D....734 337-2500
101 Peters Canyon Rd Irvine (92606) *(P-22573)*
Hyundai Amer Technical Ctr Inc ....D....909 627-3525
12610 Eastend Ave Chino (91710) *(P-22949)*
Hyundai America/Tech Center, Chino *Also called Hyundai Amer Technical Ctr Inc (P-22949)*
Hyundai Capital America (HQ) ....B....714 965-3000
3161 Michelson Dr # 1900 Irvine (92612) *(P-15144)*
Hyundai Finance, Irvine *Also called Hyundai Capital America (P-15144)*

ALPHABETIC

Employee Codes: A=Over 500 employees, B=251-500
C=101-250, D=51-100, E=20-50 F=10-19
2022 Southern California Business Directory and Buyers Guide
© Mergent Inc. 1-800-342-5647
1159

Hyundai Motor America (HQ)....B....714 965-3000
10550 Talbert Ave Fountain Valley (92708) *(P-13029)*

I & I Deburring Inc....F....562 802-0058
14504 Carmenita Rd Ste A Norwalk (90650) *(P-7733)*

I & I Sports Supply Company (PA)....E....310 715-6800
19751 Figueroa St Carson (90745) *(P-11427)*

I A C, Irvine *Also called Irvine APT Communities LP (P-15734)*

I A D S, Palmdale *Also called Teletronics Technology Corp (P-10646)*

I AM Beyond LLC....F....310 882-6476
11248 Playa Ct Culver City (90230) *(P-2952)*

I and E Cabinets Inc....E....818 933-6480
14660 Raymer St Van Nuys (91405) *(P-3320)*

I B E, Sun Valley *Also called Industrial Battery Engrg Inc (P-9811)*

I Brands LLC....C....424 336-5216
2617 N Sepulveda Blvd Manhattan Beach (90266) *(P-13876)*

I C C, Fullerton *Also called Interntnal Cnnctors Cable Corp (P-9235)*

I C Class Components Corp (PA)....D....310 539-5500
23605 Telo Ave Torrance (90505) *(P-13728)*

I C I....F....213 749-3709
11693 San Vicente Blvd Los Angeles (90049) *(P-10756)*

I C M, Los Angeles *Also called International Creative Mgt Inc (P-19316)*

I C M, Los Angeles *Also called International Creative MGT Inc (P-19317)*

I C S, Ventura *Also called Instrument Control Services (P-510)*

I C U Security Inc....D....805 498-9620
2530 Calcite Cir Newbury Park (91320) *(P-18385)*

I CANN, Los Angeles *Also called Internet Corp For Assgned Nmes (P-18039)*

I Copy Inc....E....562 921-0202
11266 Monarch St Ste B Garden Grove (92841) *(P-8625)*

I D Brand LLC....E....949 422-7057
3185 Airway Ave Ste A Costa Mesa (92626) *(P-3175)*

I D C, Bakersfield *Also called Industrial Data Communications (P-13905)*

I D Property Corporation....C....213 625-0100
1001 Wilshire Blvd # 100 Los Angeles (90017) *(P-15887)*

I D W, Rancho Cucamonga *Also called Innovative Displayworks Inc (P-13459)*

I Hot Leads....D....714 960-8028
19671 Beach Blvd Ste 204 Huntington Beach (92648) *(P-18095)*

I I D, Imperial *Also called Imperial Irrigation District (P-12806)*

I L S West Inc....E....714 505-7530
17501 17th St Ste 100 Tustin (92780) *(P-22792)*

I M T, Sherman Oaks *Also called Investors MGT Tr RE Group Inc (P-15729)*

I N C Builders Inc....B....760 352-4200
1560 Ocotillo Dr Ste L El Centro (92243) *(P-17495)*

I N G, Compton *Also called Newport Apparel Corporation (P-14405)*

I O Interconnect Ltd (PA)....E....714 564-1111
1041 W 18th St Ste A101 Costa Mesa (92627) *(P-9656)*

I P, Chatsworth *Also called International Precision Inc (P-8627)*

I P E, Norco *Also called Industrial Process Eqp Inc (P-8091)*

I P Global, Van Nuys *Also called 911 Restoration Entps Inc (P-1629)*

I P I, Los Angeles *Also called Imperial Parking Inds Inc (P-18766)*

I P S, Mentone *Also called International Paving Svcs Inc (P-888)*

I S D, Los Angeles *Also called IDS Real Estate Group (P-15888)*

I S E, Hawthorne *Also called Interntonal Strl Engineers Inc (P-22580)*

I S G, Three Rivers *Also called Innovative Structural GL Inc (P-5958)*

I S W Inc....E....323 653-6453
8347 Beverly Blvd Los Angeles (90048) *(P-14304)*

I Source Technical Svcs Inc (PA)....F....949 453-1500
5 Rancho Cir Lake Forest (92630) *(P-9723)*

I T C, Buellton *Also called Infraredvision Technology Corp (P-9517)*

I T I Electro-Optic Corp (PA)....E....310 445-8900
11500 W Olympic Blvd Los Angeles (90064) *(P-10701)*

I T I Electro-Optic Corp....E....310 312-4526
1500 E Olympic Blvd # 400 Los Angeles (90021) *(P-10702)*

I T P, Burbank *Also called Information Tech Partners Inc (P-18187)*

I Transplant Enterprise Tech, Los Angeles *Also called Transplant Connect Inc (P-18000)*

I V C, Irvine *Also called International Vitamin Corp (P-4832)*

I-Coat Company LLC....E....562 941-9989
12020 Mora Dr Ste 2 Santa Fe Springs (90670) *(P-10839)*

I-Flow LLC....A....800 448-3569
43 Discovery Ste 100 Irvine (92618) *(P-10990)*

I.C.O.N. Salon, Woodland Hills *Also called ICON Line Inc (P-11689)*

I.V. League Medical, Camarillo *Also called Western Mfg & Distrg LLC (P-10509)*

I/O Controls Corporation (PA)....D....626 812-5353
1357 W Foothill Blvd Azusa (91702) *(P-8956)*

I/O Interconnect, Costa Mesa *Also called I O Interconnect Ltd (P-9656)*

I/O Magic Corporation....F....949 707-4800
4 Marconi Irvine (92618) *(P-8158)*

I/Omagic Corporation (PA)....E....949 707-4800
20512 Crescent Bay Dr Lake Forest (92630) *(P-8203)*

I2k LLC....E....626 969-7780
748 N Mckeever Ave Azusa (91702) *(P-19299)*

I3, Victorville *Also called Integration Innovation Inc (P-22842)*

I3 Enterprise Inc....F....626 272-9538
21912 Garcia Ln Walnut (91789) *(P-10077)*

Ia-Robotics, Murrieta *Also called Iautomation Inc (P-23239)*

Iaba, Los Angeles *Also called Institute For Applied Behavior (P-20219)*

Iaba, Camarillo *Also called Institute For Applied Bhvior A (P-20221)*

IAC Industries....E....714 990-8997
8175 E Brookdale Ln Anaheim (92807) *(P-3731)*

Iaccess Technologies Inc (PA)....D....714 922-9158
1251 E Dyer Rd Ste 160 Santa Ana (92705) *(P-23451)*

IaMplus LLC....D....323 210-3852
809 N Cahuenga Blvd Los Angeles (90038) *(P-8976)*

IaMplus Electronics Inc (PA)....E....323 210-3852
809 N Cahuenga Blvd Los Angeles (90038) *(P-17881)*

Iap West Inc....D....310 667-9720
20036 S Via Baron Rancho Dominguez (90220) *(P-13065)*

Iapmo, Ontario *Also called Interntnal Assn Plbg Mech Offc (P-22250)*

Iapmo Research and Testing Inc (HQ)....D....909 472-4100
5001 E Philadelphia St Ontario (91761) *(P-22248)*

Iautomation Inc....F....951 304-2222
41633 Eastman Dr Murrieta (92562) *(P-23239)*

Ibackup.com, Calabasas *Also called Idrive Inc (P-18185)*

Ibaset Inc (PA)....D....949 598-5200
27442 Portola Pkwy # 300 Foothill Ranch (92610) *(P-23452)*

Ibaset Federal Services LLC (PA)....D....949 598-5200
27442 Portola Pkwy # 300 Foothill Ranch (92610) *(P-17635)*

Ibe Digital, Garden Grove *Also called I Copy Inc (P-8625)*

Ibftech Inc....D....424 217-8010
343 Main St El Segundo (90245) *(P-17430)*

Ibg Holdings Inc....E....661 702-8680
24841 Avenue Tibbitts Valencia (91355) *(P-5031)*

Ibi Group A California Partnr....D....213 769-0011
1001 Wilshire Blvd # 100 Los Angeles (90017) *(P-22574)*

Ibi Group, Los Angeles, Los Angeles *Also called Ibi Group A California Partnr (P-22574)*

Ibisworld Inc (HQ)....C....310 496-6871
11755 Wilshire Blvd # 1100 Los Angeles (90025) *(P-4181)*

Ibisworld Inc (HQ)....D....800 330-3772
11755 Wilshire Blvd # 1100 Los Angeles (90025) *(P-22886)*

Ibitta Enterprises Inc....F....323 588-6300
4593 Firestone Blvd South Gate (90280) *(P-14472)*

IBM, Glendale *Also called International Bus Mchs Corp (P-8162)*

Ibuypower, City of Industry *Also called American Future Tech Corp (P-13374)*

ICC, Fontana *Also called Inland Cc Inc (P-1531)*

ICC Collision Centers 6 Inc....F....888 894-4079
3131 S Standard Ave Santa Ana (92705) *(P-9954)*

ICC Networking, Riverside *Also called Interntnal Communications Corp (P-18040)*

Ice Cream Way, The, Laguna Niguel *Also called Ardensel & Co Intl Inc (P-1809)*

Ice Man Inc....E....562 633-4423
8710 Park St Bellflower (90706) *(P-2371)*

Iced Out Gear, Chatsworth *Also called H2w (P-14162)*

Icf Jones & Stokes Inc....D....949 333-6600
1 Ada Ste 100 Irvine (92618) *(P-23240)*

ICI Architectural Millwork Inc....F....323 759-4993
14059 Garfield Ave Paramount (90723) *(P-3256)*

Icl Systems Inc (PA)....D....877 425-8725
19782 Macarthur Blvd # 260 Irvine (92612) *(P-18036)*

ICM Partners, Los Angeles *Also called Interntnal Crtive MGT Prtners (P-23244)*

ICON Line Inc....F....818 709-4266
20600 Ventura Blvd Ste C Woodland Hills (91364) *(P-11689)*

Icon Media Direct Inc (PA)....D....818 995-6400
5910 Lemona Ave Van Nuys (91411) *(P-17018)*

Icon Screen Printing, Orange *Also called Icon Screening Inc (P-4525)*

Icon Screening Inc....F....714 630-4266
1108 W Grove Ave Orange (92865) *(P-4525)*

Iconn Inc....E....800 286-6742
8909 Irvine Center Dr Irvine (92618) *(P-13635)*

Iconn Engineering LLC....E....714 696-8826
6882 Preakness Dr Huntington Beach (92648) *(P-7487)*

Iconn Technologies, Irvine *Also called Iconn Inc (P-13635)*

ICP West, Buena Park *Also called Interntional Color Posters Inc (P-4529)*

Icpk Corporation....D....310 830-8020
1130 W C St Wilmington (90744) *(P-14473)*

Icpu, Santa Ana *Also called Industrial Cpu Systems Intl (P-8160)*

Icsn Inc (PA)....F....951 687-2305
17565 Cedarwood Dr Riverside (92503) *(P-7022)*

Icu Medical Inc (PA)....A....949 366-2183
951 Calle Amanecer San Clemente (92673) *(P-10991)*

Icu Medical Sales Inc (HQ)....D....949 366-2183
951 Calle Amanecer San Clemente (92673) *(P-10992)*

ID Supply....E....714 728-6478
1970 Placentia Ave Costa Mesa (92627) *(P-4526)*

IDB Holdings Inc (HQ)....F....909 390-5624
601 S Rockefeller Ave Ontario (91761) *(P-1774)*

Iddea California LLC....F....714 257-7389
589 Apollo St Brea (92821) *(P-10078)*

Idea Tooling and Engrg Inc....D....310 608-7488
13915 S Main St Los Angeles (90061) *(P-7808)*

Ideal Fasteners Inc....E....714 630-7840
3850 E Miraloma Ave Anaheim (92806) *(P-13990)*

Ideal Graphics Inc....F....714 632-3398
580 S State College Blvd Fullerton (92831) *(P-4318)*

Ideal Pallet System Inc....F....714 847-9657
7422 Cedar Dr Huntington Beach (92647) *(P-3392)*

Ideal Printing Co Inc....E....626 964-2019
17855 Maclaren St City of Industry (91744) *(P-4319)*

Ideal Products Inc....E....951 727-8600
4501 Etiwanda Ave Jurupa Valley (91752) *(P-3651)*

Ideal Products LLC....E....818 217-2574
14724 Ventura Blvd Fl 200 Sherman Oaks (91403) *(P-16958)*

Ideal Program Services Inc....D....323 296-2255
3970 W Mrtn Lther King Jr Los Angeles (90008) *(P-21808)*

Ideal Transit Inc....E....626 448-2690
13404 Waco St Baldwin Park (91706) *(P-11812)*

Idealab (HQ)....D....626 356-3654
130 W Union St Pasadena (91103) *(P-16155)*

Idealab Holdings LLC (PA)....A....626 585-6900
130 W Union St Pasadena (91103) *(P-16268)*

Idemia America Corp....C....310 884-7900
3150 E Ana St Compton (90221) *(P-5670)*

Identigraphix Inc....E....909 468-4741
19866 Quiroz Ct Walnut (91789) *(P-17179)*

Identity Intlligence Group LLC ....C....626 522-7993
43454 Business Park Dr Temecula (92590) ***(P-18386)***
Ideon, Buena Park *Also called Exemplis LLC* ***(P-3610)***
Idiq, Temecula *Also called Identity Intlligence Group LLC* ***(P-18386)***
IDM, Santa Ana *Also called International Disc Mfr Inc* ***(P-9222)***
Idrive Inc ....D....818 594-5972
26115 Mureau Rd Ste A Calabasas (91302) ***(P-18185)***
IDS Inc ....D....866 297-5757
20300 Ventura Blvd # 200 Woodland Hills (91364) ***(P-12390)***
IDS Real Estate Group (PA) ....D....**213 627-9937**
515 S Figueroa St # 1600 Los Angeles (90071) ***(P-15888)***
IDS Technology, Woodland Hills *Also called IDS Inc* ***(P-12390)***
Idx Los Angeles LLC ....C....909 212-8333
5005 E Philadelphia St Ontario (91761) ***(P-3686)***
Ie Horticulture & Cultivation ....F....909 295-1446
56524 Sunset Dr Yucca Valley (92284) ***(P-5171)***
IEC, Commerce *Also called Interstate Electric Co Inc* ***(P-13460)***
IEC, Arleta *Also called International Envmtl Corp* ***(P-310)***
Iecp, Oxnard *Also called Inclusive Edcatn Cmnty Prtnr I* ***(P-22024)***
Iee, Van Nuys *Also called Industrial Elctrnic Engners In* ***(P-8264)***
Ieee Computer Society, Los Alamitos *Also called Institute of Elec Elec Engners* ***(P-22249)***
Iehp, Rancho Cucamonga *Also called Inland Empire Health Plan* ***(P-15380)***
IEPC Corp ....F....714 892-4443
15179 Springdale St Huntington Beach (92649) ***(P-17636)***
Ies Commercial Inc ....D....713 860-1500
1633 Maria St Burbank (91504) ***(P-1267)***
Ies Engineering, Bakersfield *Also called Innovative Engrg Systems Inc* ***(P-22576)***
If Live LLC (PA) ....D....**323 957-6868**
2254 S Sepulveda Blvd Los Angeles (90064) ***(P-19134)***
Ifco Systems North America Inc ....E....909 356-0697
14750 Miller Ave Fontana (92336) ***(P-3393)***
Ifco Systems Us LLC ....D....909 484-4332
8950 Rochester Ave # 150 Rancho Cucamonga (91730) ***(P-3394)***
Ifiber Optix Inc ....E....714 665-9796
14450 Chambers Rd Tustin (92780) ***(P-5936)***
Ifit Inc ....A....909 335-2888
2220 Almond Ave Redlands (92374) ***(P-11428)***
Ifncom Inc (PA) ....D....**213 452-1505**
13005 Artesia Blvd A10 Cerritos (90703) ***(P-12648)***
Igi, Sierra Madre *Also called Greg Ian Islands Inc* ***(P-3647)***
Ignify Inc (HQ) ....E....**562 219-2000**
200 Pine Ave Ste 400 Long Beach (90802) ***(P-18037)***
Ignify Consulting, Long Beach *Also called Ignify Inc* ***(P-18037)***
Ignite Health LLC (PA) ....D....**949 861-3200**
7535 Irvine Center Dr # 200 Irvine (92618) ***(P-17019)***
Ignited LLC (PA) ....C....**310 773-3100**
2150 Park Pl Ste 100 El Segundo (90245) ***(P-17020)***
Ignition Creative LLC ....D....310 315-6300
1201 W 5th St Ste T1100 Los Angeles (90017) ***(P-19135)***
IGS Molding LLC ....F....562 801-3522
5093 Walnut Grove Ave San Gabriel (91776) ***(P-5671)***
Iheartcommunications Inc ....D....661 942-1268
352 E Avenue K4 Lancaster (93535) ***(P-12693)***
Iheartraves LLC ....F....626 628-6482
250 S Glendora Ave West Covina (91790) ***(P-2847)***
Iherb LLC (PA) ....A....**951 616-3600**
22780 Hrley Knox Blvd Uni Perris (92570) ***(P-14251)***
Iherb House Brands, Perris *Also called Iherb LLC* ***(P-14251)***
Ihg, Yucaipa *Also called Inter-Continental Hotels Corp* ***(P-16505)***
Ihg Management (maryland) LLC ....E....310 642-7500
5985 W Century Blvd Los Angeles (90045) ***(P-16501)***
Ihr Grnbuck Rncho Ccmnga Ventr, Rancho Cucamonga *Also called Aloft Ontario-Rancho Cucamonga* ***(P-16317)***
Ii-VI Aerospace & Defense Inc ....D....714 247-7100
14192 Chambers Rd Tustin (92780) ***(P-10840)***
IJ Research Inc ....E....714 546-8522
2919 S Tech Center Dr Santa Ana (92705) ***(P-9724)***
Ikano Communications Inc (PA) ....D....**801 924-0900**
9221 Corbin Ave Ste 260 Northridge (91324) ***(P-18096)***
IKEA Purchasing Svcs US Inc ....C....818 841-3500
600 N San Fernando Blvd Burbank (91502) ***(P-23039)***
Ikhana Aircraft Services, Murrieta *Also called Ikhana Group LLC* ***(P-10350)***
Ikhana Group LLC ....C....951 600-0009
37260 Sky Canyon Dr # 20 Murrieta (92563) ***(P-10350)***
Ikonick LLC ....E....516 680-7765
705 W 9th St Apt 1404 Los Angeles (90015) ***(P-4320)***
IL Colore Inc (PA) ....D....**949 975-1325**
2082 Se Bristol St Ste 4 Newport Beach (92660) ***(P-1379)***
IL Fornaio (america) LLC ....C....714 752-7052
16932 Valley View Ave A La Mirada (90638) ***(P-14695)***
Ilco Industries Inc ....E....310 631-8655
1308 W Mahalo Pl Compton (90220) ***(P-7539)***
Illah Sports Inc A Corporation ....E....805 240-7790
1610 Fiske Pl Oxnard (93033) ***(P-11429)***
Illumnate Educatn Holdings Inc (PA) ....D....**949 656-3133**
6531 Irvine Center Dr # 10 Irvine (92618) ***(P-17882)***
Ilwu Federal Credit Union ....D....310 834-6411
3447 Atlantic Ave Long Beach (90807) ***(P-15069)***
Image 2000 Inc (PA) ....E....**818 781-2200**
26037 Huntington Ln Valencia (91355) ***(P-19043)***
Image Apparel For Business Inc ....E....714 541-5247
1618 E Edinger Ave Santa Ana (92705) ***(P-2780)***
Image Business Forms, El Segundo *Also called Ibftech Inc* ***(P-17430)***
Image Distribution Services ....F....909 599-7680
3191 W Temple Ave Ste 180 Pomona (91768) ***(P-4321)***
Image Distribution Services (PA) ....E....**949 754-9000**
19781 Pauling Foothill Ranch (92610) ***(P-4322)***
Image Entertainment Inc (HQ) ....D....**818 407-9100**
6320 Canoga Ave Ste 790 Woodland Hills (91367) ***(P-19259)***
Image IV Systems Inc (PA) ....D....**323 849-3049**
512 S Varney St Burbank (91502) ***(P-13357)***
Image Micro Spare Parts Inc ....E....562 776-9808
6301 Chalet Dr Commerce (90040) ***(P-8918)***
Image Options ....C....949 586-7665
80 Icon Foothill Ranch (92610) ***(P-17099)***
Image Printing Solutions, Foothill Ranch *Also called Image Distribution Services* ***(P-4322)***
Image Solutions Apparel Inc ....D....310 464-8991
19571 Magellan Dr Torrance (90502) ***(P-2781)***
Image Source, San Bernardino *Also called Copier Source Inc* ***(P-13354)***
Image Square Inc ....E....310 586-2333
1627 Stanford St Santa Monica (90404) ***(P-4323)***
Image Square Copy & Print, Santa Monica *Also called Image Square Inc* ***(P-4323)***
Image Transfer, Valencia *Also called D C Shower Doors Inc* ***(P-12028)***
Image X, Goleta *Also called Image-X Enterprises Inc* ***(P-17637)***
Image-X Enterprises Inc ....E....805 964-3535
6464 Hollister Ave Ste 7g Goleta (93117) ***(P-17637)***
Imagemover Inc ....F....818 485-8840
10051 Bradley Ave Pacoima (91331) ***(P-4324)***
Imagine This, Irvine *Also called Shye West Inc* ***(P-11594)***
Imaging Center, Anaheim *Also called Southern Cal Dgnstc Imging Inc* ***(P-20073)***
Imajean Nation Inc ....E....323 980-9000
3600 E Olympic Blvd Los Angeles (90023) ***(P-2575)***
Imax Corporation (HQ) ....B....**310 255-5559**
12582 Millennium Los Angeles (90094) ***(P-19280)***
Imax Theatre Marketing, Los Angeles *Also called Imax Corporation* ***(P-19280)***
IMC Networks Corp (PA) ....D....**949 465-3000**
25531 Commercentre Dr Lake Forest (92630) ***(P-8225)***
Imdex Technology Usa LLC ....E....805 540-2017
3474 Empresa Dr Ste 150 San Luis Obispo (93401) ***(P-10889)***
Imerys Filtration Minerals, Lompoc *Also called Imerys Minerals California Inc* ***(P-582)***
Imerys Minerals California Inc ....A....805 736-1221
2500 Miguelito Canyon Rd Lompoc (93436) ***(P-582)***
Imerys Minerals California Inc (HQ) ....D....**805 736-1221**
2500 San Miguelito Rd Lompoc (93436) ***(P-587)***
IMG (PA) ....E....**714 974-1700**
4560 Dorinda Rd Yorba Linda (92887) ***(P-18546)***
IMG Worldwide LLC (PA) ....C....**424 653-1900**
9601 Wilshire Blvd Beverly Hills (90210) ***(P-14381)***
Imhoff & Associates PC ....D....310 691-2200
12424 Wilshire Blvd # 770 Los Angeles (90025) ***(P-21584)***
IMI CCI, Rcho STA Marg *Also called Control Components Inc* ***(P-7441)***
IMI CCI ....E....949 858-1877
22591 Avenida Empresa Rcho STA Marg (92688) ***(P-22575)***
IMI Critical Engineering, Rcho STA Marg *Also called IMI CCI* ***(P-22575)***
Immanuel Baptist Day School, Highland *Also called Immanuel Bptst Ch of San Brnrd* ***(P-22022)***
Immanuel Bptst Ch of San Brnrd ....D....909 862-6641
28355 Baseline St Highland (92346) ***(P-22022)***
Immco, El Monte *Also called Industrial Machine & Mfg Co* ***(P-6622)***
Immedate Clinic Healthcare Inc (HQ) ....E....**949 487-9500**
27101 Puerta Real Ste 450 Mission Viejo (92691) ***(P-21173)***
Immediate Medical Care Center, Pls Vrds Pnsl *Also called Palos Vrdes Fmly Immdate Med C* ***(P-20883)***
Immortals LLC ....D....310 554-8267
11460 W Washington Blvd A Los Angeles (90066) ***(P-19417)***
Immport Therapeutics Inc ....E....949 679-4068
1 Technology Dr Ste E309 Irvine (92618) ***(P-11208)***
Immunalysis, Pomona *Also called Alere San Diego Inc* ***(P-4917)***
Imp International Inc (PA) ....E....**909 321-1000**
1905 S Lynx Ave Ontario (91761) ***(P-4749)***
Impac Funding Corporation (HQ) ....C....**949 475-3600**
19500 Jamboree Rd Irvine (92612) ***(P-15202)***
Impac International, Ontario *Also called New Greenscreen Incorporated* ***(P-3689)***
Impac Mortgage Corp ....B....949 475-3600
19500 Jamboree Rd Ste 100 Irvine (92612) ***(P-15203)***
Impac Mortgage Holdings Inc (PA) ....C....**949 475-3600**
19500 Jamboree Rd Ste 100 Irvine (92612) ***(P-15204)***
Impac Technologies Inc ....E....714 427-2000
3050 Red Hill Ave Costa Mesa (92626) ***(P-9278)***
Impact Bearing, San Clemente *Also called Clean Wave Management Inc* ***(P-10183)***
Impact Bearing, San Clemente *Also called Clean Wave Management Inc* ***(P-8027)***
Impact DRG Alcohol Trtmnt Ctr, Pasadena *Also called Principles Inc* ***(P-21329)***
Impact LLC ....E....714 546-6000
22521 Avenida Empresa # 107 Rcho STA Marg (92688) ***(P-9725)***
Impact Printing & Graphics ....E....909 614-1678
15150 Sierra Bonita Ln Chino (91710) ***(P-4325)***
Impact Radius Inc (HQ) ....D....**805 324-6021**
223 E De La Guerra St Santa Barbara (93101) ***(P-23241)***
Impact Realty Inc (PA) ....C....**626 331-4868**
3110 E Garvey Ave S West Covina (91791) ***(P-15889)***
Impact-O-Graph Devices, Chatsworth *Also called Iog Products LLC* ***(P-9523)***
Impax Automation LLC ....E....661 391-8210
2131 Saturn Ct Bakersfield (93308) ***(P-13904)***
Impco Technologies Inc (HQ) ....C....**714 656-1200**
3030 S Susan St Santa Ana (92704) ***(P-10079)***
Imperial Bag & Paper Co LLC ....D....800 834-6248
2825 Warner Ave Irvine (92606) ***(P-14211)***
Imperial Cal Products Inc ....E....714 990-9100
425 Apollo St Brea (92821) ***(P-7152)***
Imperial Capital Group LLC (PA) ....D....**310 246-3700**
2000 Avenue Of The Stars 900s Los Angeles (90067) ***(P-16269)***
Imperial Capital LLC (PA) ....D....**310 246-3700**
10100 Santa Monica Blvd # 2400 Los Angeles (90067) ***(P-15270)***
Imperial Care Center, Studio City *Also called Longwood Management Corp* ***(P-20605)***

Employee Codes: A=Over 500 employees, B=251-500
C=101-250, D=51-100, E=20-50 F=10-19
2022 Southern California Business
Directory and Buyers Guide
© Mergent Inc. 1-800-342-5647
1161

Imperial Cfs Inc .... E 310 768-8188
1000 Francisco St Torrance (90502) ***(P-12268)***
Imperial Convalescent, La Mirada *Also called Life Care Centers America Inc* ***(P-20396)***
Imperial Credit, Santa Ana *Also called Aicco Inc* ***(P-15136)***
Imperial Crest Healthcare Ctr, Hawthorne *Also called Longwood Management Corp* ***(P-20404)***
Imperial Dam, Winterhaven *Also called Imperial Irrigation District* ***(P-13012)***
Imperial Enterprises Inc .... E 818 886-5028
9666 Owensmouth Ave Ste A Chatsworth (91311) ***(P-5937)***
Imperial Hotel Group LLC .... E 949 474-7368
2532 Dupont Dr Irvine (92612) ***(P-18547)***
Imperial Irrgtion Dst Wtr Dept, Imperial *Also called Imperial Irrigation District* ***(P-13011)***
Imperial Irrigation District (PA) .... **A 800 303-7756**
333 E Barioni Blvd Imperial (92251) ***(P-12806)***
Imperial Irrigation District .... E 760 339-9220
333 E Barioni Blvd Imperial (92251) ***(P-13011)***
Imperial Irrigation District .... E 760 398-5811
81600 58th Ave La Quinta (92253) ***(P-12877)***
Imperial Irrigation District .... E 760 572-0392
2400 Imperial Rd Winterhaven (92283) ***(P-13012)***
Imperial Irrigation District .... E 760 339-9253
Bell Bldg El Centro (92243) ***(P-12871)***
Imperial Irrigation District .... E 760 339-9800
2151 W Adams Ave El Centro (92243) ***(P-12872)***
Imperial Marking Systems, Cerritos *Also called Blc Wc Inc* ***(P-4487)***
Imperial Mfg Co, Corona *Also called Spenuzza Inc* ***(P-8417)***
Imperial Parking Inds Inc (PA) .... **D 323 651-5588**
6404 Wilshire Blvd B Los Angeles (90048) ***(P-18766)***
Imperial Pipe & Supply, Shafter *Also called Bps Supply Group* ***(P-13552)***
Imperial Pipe Services LLC .... E 951 682-3307
12375 Brown Ave Riverside (92509) ***(P-6249)***
Imperial Pre Mix Company, Imperial *Also called Imperial Premix LLC* ***(P-1969)***
Imperial Premix LLC (PA) .... **F 760 355-7997**
422 E Barioni Blvd Imperial (92251) ***(P-1969)***
Imperial Printers (PA) .... **F 760 352-4374**
430 W Main St El Centro (92243) ***(P-4326)***
Imperial Printers Rocket Copy, El Centro *Also called Imperial Printers* ***(P-4326)***
Imperial Roof Truss Inc .... E 760 355-1809
701 E 2nd St Imperial (92251) ***(P-3365)***
Imperial Rubber Products Inc .... E 909 393-0528
5691 Gates St Chino (91710) ***(P-7918)***
Imperial Toy LLC (PA) .... **C 818 536-6500**
16641 Roscoe Pl North Hills (91343) ***(P-11376)***
Imperial Valley Family Care (PA) .... **D 760 355-7730**
516 W Aten Rd Ste 2 Imperial (92251) ***(P-22023)***
Imperial Valley Foods Inc .... B 760 203-1896
1961 Buchanan Ave Calexico (92231) ***(P-1900)***
Imperial Valley Press, El Centro *Also called Associated Desert Newspaper* ***(P-3949)***
Imperial Western Products Inc .... D 951 727-8950
4085 Bain St Jurupa Valley (91752) ***(P-14751)***
Imperials Sand Dunes, Brea *Also called Worldwide Envmtl Pdts Inc* ***(P-10732)***
Implant Direct Sybron Intl LLC (HQ) .... **F 818 444-3000**
22715 Savi Ranch Pkwy Yorba Linda (92887) ***(P-11176)***
Implant Direct Sybron Mfg LLC .... C 818 444-3300
3050 E Hillcrest Dr # 100 Westlake Village (91362) ***(P-11177)***
Implantech Associates Inc .... E 805 289-1665
6025 Nicolle St Ste B Ventura (93003) ***(P-11114)***
Impo International LLC .... E 805 922-7753
3510 Black Rd Santa Maria (93455) ***(P-5880)***
Import, Vernon *Also called Brentwood Appliances Inc* ***(P-9013)***
Import Collection (PA) .... **D 818 782-3060**
7885 Nelson Rd Panorama City (91402) ***(P-14939)***
Import Direct, Van Nuys *Also called E & S International Entps Inc* ***(P-13684)***
Importla LLC .... F 626 336-8118
1300 John Reed Ct Ste D City of Industry (91745) ***(P-3732)***
Impresa Aerospace LLC .... C 310 354-1200
344 W 157th St Gardena (90248) ***(P-10351)***
Impress Communications Inc .... D 818 701-8800
9320 Lurline Ave Chatsworth (91311) ***(P-4327)***
Impressions Vanity Company (PA) .... **D 844 881-0790**
1402 Morgan Cir Tustin (92780) ***(P-13636)***
Improv Tvs Inc (PA) .... **E 323 937-5030**
5455 Wilshire Blvd # 1812 Los Angeles (90036) ***(P-21585)***
Improvstnal Cmedy Traffic Schl, Los Angeles *Also called Improv Tvs Inc* ***(P-21585)***
Impulse Internet Services LLC .... D 805 456-5800
6144 Calle Real Ste 200 Goleta (93117) ***(P-12649)***
Imri, Aliso Viejo *Also called Information MGT Resources Inc* ***(P-18038)***
IMS, South El Monte *Also called Interntnal Mdction Systems Ltd* ***(P-4750)***
IMS, South El Monte *Also called Interntnal Mdction Systems Ltd* ***(P-4833)***
IMS Flightdeck LLC .... C 714 854-8600
2929 E Imperial Hwy # 170 Brea (92821) ***(P-13406)***
IMS Products Inc .... F 951 653-7720
6240 Box Springs Blvd E Riverside (92507) ***(P-10493)***
IMS-Ess, Temecula *Also called Electro-Support Systems Corp* ***(P-9705)***
IMT Analytical, Goleta *Also called Atomica Corp* ***(P-9485)***
IMT Capital LLC (PA) .... **C 818 784-4700**
15303 Ventura Blvd # 200 Sherman Oaks (91403) ***(P-16236)***
IMT-Stason Laboratories, Irvine *Also called Stason Pharmaceuticals Inc* ***(P-4897)***
In Garden Grove Cnvlscent Hosp .... D 714 638-9470
12882 Shackelford Ln Garden Grove (92841) ***(P-20598)***
In Granada Hlls Cnvlscent Hosp .... D 818 891-1745
16123 Chatsworth St Granada Hills (91344) ***(P-20378)***
In Home Comfort and Care Inc .... D 714 485-4120
17155 Newhope St Ste O Fountain Valley (92708) ***(P-21174)***
In House Custom Decals .... F 909 613-1403
2300 S Reservoir St # 308 Pomona (91766) ***(P-4527)***
In House Stickers, Pomona *Also called In House Custom Decals* ***(P-4527)***
In Oakwood Cnstr Rstrtion Svcs (HQ) .... **E 714 529-8300**
4955 E Hunter Ave Anaheim (92807) ***(P-614)***
In Win Development USA Inc .... E 909 348-0588
188 Brea Canyon Rd Walnut (91789) ***(P-8204)***
In-Roads Creative Programs .... D 909 989-9944
9057 Arrow Rte Ste 120 Rancho Cucamonga (91730) ***(P-21809)***
In-Roads Creative Programs .... D 909 947-9142
1951 E Saint Andrews Dr Ontario (91761) ***(P-21810)***
In-Roads Creative Programs (PA) .... **A 909 864-1551**
7955 Webster St Ste 7 Highland (92346) ***(P-21811)***
Inari Medical Inc .... C 877 927-4747
9 Parker Ste 100 Irvine (92618) ***(P-10993)***
Inbody, Cerritos *Also called Biospace Inc* ***(P-22832)***
Inbody Co Ltd .... E 323 932-6503
13850 Cerritos Corprt Dr Cerritos (90703) ***(P-11224)***
Inc J-Network, Huntington Beach *Also called Glen Beverly Laboratories Inc* ***(P-22270)***
Inc Polycarbon, Valencia *Also called Sgl Technic LLC* ***(P-6168)***
Inca One Corporation .... E 310 808-0001
1632 1/2 W 134th St Gardena (90249) ***(P-9610)***
Inca Pallets Supply Inc .... E 909 622-1414
1349 S East End Ave Pomona (91766) ***(P-3395)***
Inca Plastics Molding Co Inc .... E 909 923-3235
948 E Belmont St Ontario (91761) ***(P-5672)***
Inca Plastics Molding Co Inc .... F 760 246-8087
17129 Koala Rd Adelanto (92301) ***(P-5673)***
Incipio Group, Irvine *Also called Incipio Technologies Inc* ***(P-8263)***
Incipio Technologies Inc (PA) .... **E 949 250-4929**
3347 Michelson Dr Ste 100 Irvine (92612) ***(P-8263)***
Incipio, LLC, Irvine *Also called Finis LLC* ***(P-8256)***
Inclinator of California, San Fernando *Also called TL Shield & Associates Inc* ***(P-7681)***
Inclusion Services LLC .... C 562 945-2000
7255 Greenleaf Ave Ste 20 Whittier (90602) ***(P-21812)***
Inclusive Edcatn Cmnty Prtnr I .... B 805 985-4808
2323 Roosevelt Blvd Apt 3 Oxnard (93035) ***(P-22024)***
Incomnet Communications Corp .... D 949 251-8000
2801 Main St Irvine (92614) ***(P-12650)***
Incora, Valencia *Also called Wesco Aircraft Hardware Corp* ***(P-14071)***
Incremento Inc (PA) .... **D 213 624-7777**
2670 Leonis Blvd Vernon (90058) ***(P-14382)***
Indaba Group Inc (HQ) .... **E 805 964-3313**
6144 Calle Real Ste 200 Santa Barbara (93117) ***(P-17883)***
Indegene Inc (HQ) .... **E 732 750-2901**
4500 Park Granada Ste 2 Calabasas (91302) ***(P-22910)***
Indel Engineering Inc .... E 562 594-0995
6400 E Marina Dr Long Beach (90803) ***(P-10466)***
Indemnity Company California (HQ) .... **D 949 263-3300**
17771 Cowan Ste 100 Irvine (92614) ***(P-15582)***
Independant Book Publs Assn .... F 310 546-1818
1020 Manhattan Beach Blvd Manhattan Beach (90266) ***(P-4182)***
Independence At Home Iah, Long Beach *Also called Senior Care Action Ntwrk Fndti* ***(P-15453)***
Independent Electric Vehicles, Vernon *Also called Indiev Inc* ***(P-13030)***
Independent Forge Company .... E 714 997-7337
692 N Batavia St Orange (92868) ***(P-7087)***
Independent Options Inc .... D 714 738-4991
2625 Sherwood Ave Fullerton (92831) ***(P-22117)***
Independent Studio Svcs LLC .... D 818 951-5600
9545 Wentworth St Sunland (91040) ***(P-19313)***
Independent Trading Company, San Clemente *Also called Brad Rambo & Associates Inc* ***(P-14328)***
Indepndent Lving Ctr Kern Cnty .... D 661 325-1063
5251 Office Park Dr # 200 Bakersfield (93309) ***(P-21813)***
Indepndnt Asstd Lvng & Memory, Arcadia *Also called Arcadia Gardens MGT Corp* ***(P-20523)***
Index Fasteners Inc (PA) .... **E 909 923-5002**
945 E Grevillea Ct Ontario (91761) ***(P-13991)***
Index Fresh Inc (PA) .... **D 909 877-0999**
1250 Corona Pointe Ct # 40 Corona (92879) ***(P-14639)***
India Tea Importers, Commerce *Also called Interntional Tea Importers Inc* ***(P-2453)***
Indian Hills Country Club, Riverside *Also called Henry C Cox II and John L West* ***(P-19491)***
Indian Summer, Rancho Cucamonga *Also called Mizkan America Inc* ***(P-2187)***
Indian Wells Brewery, Inyokern *Also called Indian Wells Companies* ***(P-2147)***
Indian Wells Companies .... F 760 377-4290
2565 State Highway 14 Inyokern (93527) ***(P-2147)***
Indian Wells Country Club Inc .... D 760 345-2561
46000 Club Dr Indian Wells (92210) ***(P-19569)***
Indian Wells Golf Resort, Indian Wells *Also called Troon Golf LLC* ***(P-23129)***
Indian Wells Property LLC .... D 442 305-4500
45000 Indian Wells Ln Indian Wells (92210) ***(P-16502)***
Indian Wells Resort Hotel .... D 760 345-6466
76661 Us Highway 111 Indian Wells (92210) ***(P-16503)***
Indie Ridge Inc .... F 323 207-9181
4701 Arrow Hwy Montclair (91763) ***(P-7981)***
Indie Semiconductor Inc .... D 949 608-0854
32 Journey Aliso Viejo (92656) ***(P-9515)***
Indie Source .... E 424 200-2027
1933 S Broadway Los Angeles (90007) ***(P-2782)***
Indiev Inc .... D 323 703-5720
5001 S Soto St Vernon (90058) ***(P-13030)***
Indio Medical Offices, Indio *Also called Kaiser Foundation Hospitals* ***(P-19904)***
Indio Products Inc .... E 323 720-9117
5331 E Slauson Ave Commerce (90040) ***(P-5223)***
Indizen Optical Tech Amer LLC .... E 310 783-1533
2925 California St # 201 Torrance (90503) ***(P-17638)***
Indorama Vntres Sstnble Sltion .... E 951 727-8318
11591 Etiwanda Ave Fontana (92337) ***(P-4696)***
Indu-Electric North Amer Inc (PA) .... **E 310 578-2144**
27756 Avenue Hopkins Valencia (91355) ***(P-8104)***

Induction Technology Corp....E....760 246-7333
22060 Bear Valley Rd Apple Valley (92308) *(P-8090)*
Inductors Inc....E....949 623-2460
1740 W Collins Ave Orange (92867) *(P-13729)*
Induspac California Inc....F....909 390-4422
1550 Champagne Ave Ontario (91761) *(P-4697)*
Industrial Battery Engrg Inc....E....818 767-7067
9121 De Garmo Ave Sun Valley (91352) *(P-9811)*
Industrial Cont Svcs - CA LLC (HQ)....C....323 724-8507
1540 S Greenwood Ave Montebello (90640) *(P-13992)*
Industrial Cpu Syste....F....714 957-2815
111 W Dyer Rd Ste D Santa Ana (92707) *(P-8159)*
Industrial Cpu Systems Intl....F....714 957-2815
2225 S Grand Ave Santa Ana (92705) *(P-8160)*
Industrial Data Communications....E....661 589-4477
4000 Fruitvale Ave Ste 16 Bakersfield (93308) *(P-13905)*
Industrial Design Products Inc....E....909 468-0693
2700 Pomona Blvd Pomona (91768) *(P-7710)*
Industrial Dynamics Co Ltd (PA)....C....310 325-5633
3100 Fujita St Torrance (90505) *(P-7982)*
Industrial Elctrnic Engners In....D....818 787-0311
7723 Kester Ave Van Nuys (91405) *(P-8264)*
Industrial Gasket and Sup Co....E....310 530-1771
23018 Normandie Ave Torrance (90502) *(P-5342)*
Industrial Glass Products Inc....F....323 526-7125
4229 Union Pacific Ave Los Angeles (90023) *(P-5957)*
Industrial Insulations Inc (PA)....F....909 574-7433
10509 Business Dr Ste A Fontana (92337) *(P-9051)*
Industrial Machine & Mfg Co....E....626 444-0181
2626 Seaman Ave El Monte (91733) *(P-6622)*
Industrial Manufacturing Inc....F....562 941-5888
10110 Norwalk Blvd Santa Fe Springs (90670) *(P-6571)*
Industrial Media Inc....C....310 777-1940
6007 Sepulveda Blvd Van Nuys (91411) *(P-19238)*
Industrial Medical Group....D....661 327-2225
2501 G St Bakersfield (93301) *(P-19851)*
Industrial Medical Support Inc....A....877 878-9185
3320 E Airport Way Long Beach (90806) *(P-21442)*
Industrial Metal Finishing Inc....E....714 628-8808
1941 Petra Ln Placentia (92870) *(P-7269)*
Industrial Metal Supply Co, Sun Valley *Also called Norman Industrial Mtls Inc* ***(P-13580)***
Industrial Metal Supply Co, Irvine *Also called Norman Industrial Mtls Inc* ***(P-13581)***
Industrial Parts Depot LLC (HQ)....D....310 530-1900
23231 Normandie Ave Torrance (90501) *(P-13906)*
Industrial Printers California....F....714 545-8484
3012 S Croddy Way Santa Ana (92704) *(P-4632)*
Industrial Printing Group, Santa Ana *Also called Industrial Printers California* ***(P-4632)***
Industrial Process Eqp Inc....F....714 447-0171
1700 Industrial Ave Norco (92860) *(P-8091)*
Industrial Relations Cal Dept....D....714 558-4121
28 Civic Center Plz # 239 Santa Ana (92701) *(P-21814)*
Industrial Sprockets Gears Inc....E....323 233-7221
13650 Rosecrans Ave Santa Fe Springs (90670) *(P-8105)*
Industrial Stitchtech Inc....C....818 361-6319
520 Library St San Fernando (91340) *(P-18548)*
INDUSTRIAL SUPPORT SYSTEMS, Fontana *Also called Fontana Resources At Work* ***(P-21952)***
Industrial Tctnics Brings Corp (HQ)....C....310 537-3750
18301 S Santa Fe Ave E Rncho Dmngz (90221) *(P-8028)*
Industrial Tools Inc....E....805 483-1111
1111 S Rose Ave Oxnard (93033) *(P-7983)*
Industrial Tube Company LLC....D....661 295-4000
28150 Industry Dr Valencia (91355) *(P-7458)*
Industrial Valco Inc (PA)....E....310 635-0711
3135 E Ana St Compton (90221) *(P-13993)*
Industrial Wood Products Inc....F....909 625-1247
5123 Brooks St Montclair (91763) *(P-3396)*
Industrious Software Solution....F....310 672-8700
8901 S La Cnga Blvd # 202 Inglewood (90301) *(P-17884)*
Industrious Software Solutions, Inglewood *Also called Industrious Software Solution* ***(P-17884)***
Industry Color Printing Inc....F....626 961-2403
11642 Washington Blvd Whittier (90606) *(P-4328)*
Indyne Inc....C....805 606-7225
1036 California Blvd # 11013 Vandenberg Afb (93437) *(P-23393)*
Ineos Composites Us LLC....D....323 767-1300
6608 E 26th St Commerce (90040) *(P-14785)*
Inertech Supply Inc....D....626 282-2000
641 Monterey Pass Rd Monterey Park (91754) *(P-5343)*
Infab LLC....D....805 987-5255
1040 Avenida Acaso Camarillo (93012) *(P-11115)*
Infant Hring Scrning Spcalists, Corona *Also called Halo Unlimted Inc* ***(P-21432)***
Infineon Tech Americas Corp (HQ)....A....310 726-8200
101 N Pacific Coast Hwy El Segundo (90245) *(P-9516)*
Infineon Tech Americas Corp....A....951 375-6008
41915 Business Park Dr Temecula (92590) *(P-8265)*
Infineon Tech Americas Corp....A....310 726-8000
222 Kansas St El Segundo (90245) *(P-22793)*
Infinite Electronics Inc (HQ)....D....949 261-1920
17792 Fitch Irvine (92614) *(P-9726)*
Infinite Electronics Intl Inc (HQ)....B....949 261-1920
17792 Fitch Irvine (92614) *(P-9657)*
Infinite Engineering Inc....F....714 534-4688
13682 Newhope St Garden Grove (92843) *(P-8626)*
Infinite Home Health Inc....D....818 888-7772
22151 Ventura Blvd # 102 Woodland Hills (91364) *(P-21175)*
Infinite Optics Inc....E....714 557-2299
1712 Newport Cir Ste F Santa Ana (92705) *(P-10841)*
Infinite Technologies LLC....C....786 408-7995
1667 N Batavia St Orange (92867) *(P-17639)*
Infiniter, Diamond Bar *Also called Quarton Usa Inc* ***(P-9903)***
Infinity Aerospace Inc (PA)....E....818 998-9811
9060 Winnetka Ave Northridge (91324) *(P-10352)*
Infinity Broadcasting Corp Cal....D....323 936-5784
5670 Wilshire Blvd # 200 Los Angeles (90036) *(P-12694)*
Infinity Drywall Contg Inc....D....714 634-2255
225 S Loara St Anaheim (92802) *(P-1380)*
Infinity Kitchen Products Inc....F....562 806-5771
7750 Scout Ave Bell Gardens (90201) *(P-6852)*
Infinity Plumbing Designs Inc....B....951 737-4436
9182 Stellar Ct Corona (92883) *(P-1083)*
Infinity Stainless Products, Bell Gardens *Also called Infinity Kitchen Products Inc* ***(P-6852)***
Infinity Svc Group Inc A Cal C....D....909 466-6237
9155 Archibald Ave # 302 Rancho Cucamonga (91730) *(P-1084)*
Infinity Watch Corporation....E....626 289-9878
21078 Commerce Point Dr Walnut (91789) *(P-11561)*
Inflight Entrmt & Connectivity, Irvine *Also called Thales Avionics Inc* ***(P-10429)***
Inflight Warning Systems Inc....F....714 993-9394
3940 Prospect Ave Ste P Yorba Linda (92886) *(P-10353)*
Infocast, Woodland Hills *Also called Information Forecast Inc* ***(P-23242)***
Infogen Labs Inc....D....818 825-5024
18223 Charlton Ln Porter Ranch (91326) *(P-18186)*
Infokorea Inc....E....213 487-1580
626 S Kingsley Dr Los Angeles (90005) *(P-4074)*
Infonet Services Corporation (HQ)....A....310 335-2600
2160 E Grand Ave El Segundo (90245) *(P-12651)*
Inform Decisions Inc....F....949 709-5838
30162 Tomas 101 Rcho STA Marg (92688) *(P-17885)*
Inform Solution Incorporated....F....805 879-6000
201 Mentor Dr Santa Barbara (93111) *(P-17886)*
Informa Business Media Inc....E....949 252-1146
16815 Von Karman Ave # 150 Irvine (92606) *(P-4183)*
Informa Research Services Inc (HQ)....C....818 880-8877
26565 Agoura Rd Ste 300 Calabasas (91302) *(P-22887)*
Information Forecast Inc....E....818 888-4445
22144 Clarendon St # 280 Woodland Hills (91367) *(P-23242)*
Information MGT Resources Inc (PA)....C....949 215-8889
85 Argonaut Ste 215 Aliso Viejo (92656) *(P-18038)*
Information Systems, Orange *Also called St Joseph Hospital of Orange* ***(P-20961)***
Information Tech Partners Inc....D....800 789-7487
3003 N San Fernando Blvd Burbank (91504) *(P-18187)*
Informs, Anaheim *Also called Rush Business Forms Inc* ***(P-11589)***
Informtion Intgrtion Group Inc....E....818 956-3744
457 Palm Dr Ste 200 Glendale (91202) *(P-17887)*
Informtion Rfrral Fdrtion of L....D....626 350-1841
526 W Las Tunas Dr San Gabriel (91776) *(P-16959)*
Infosend Inc (PA)....D....714 993-2690
4240 E La Palma Ave Anaheim (92807) *(P-22794)*
Infospan....A....949 260-9990
31878 Del Obispo St San Juan Capistrano (92675) *(P-23243)*
Infrared Dynamics Inc....E....714 572-4050
3830 Prospect Ave Yorba Linda (92886) *(P-6572)*
Infraredvision Technology Corp....C....805 686-8848
140 Industrial Way Buellton (93427) *(P-9517)*
Infratab....F....805 986-8880
4347 Raytheon Rd Unit 6 Oxnard (93033) *(P-4936)*
Infusion Care, Long Beach *Also called Long Beach Medical Center* ***(P-20846)***
Ingalls Conveyors Inc....E....323 837-9900
1005 W Olympic Blvd Montebello (90640) *(P-7691)*
Ingenue Inc....D....323 726-8084
6114 Scott Way Commerce (90040) *(P-1760)*
Ingla Rubber Products, Bellflower *Also called Bryant Rubber Corp* ***(P-5329)***
Ingleside & Melvyn's, Palm Springs *Also called Ingleside Investors Spe LLC* ***(P-16504)***
Ingleside Investors Spe LLC....D....760 325-0046
200 W Ramon Rd Palm Springs (92264) *(P-16504)*
Inglewood Cmtry Mortuary Inc....D....310 412-6811
3801 W Manchester Blvd Inglewood (90305) *(P-16924)*
Inglewood Park Cemetery (PA)....C....310 412-6500
720 E Florence Ave Inglewood (90301) *(P-16085)*
Ingram Micro Inc (HQ)....A....714 566-1000
3351 Michelson Dr Ste 100 Irvine (92612) *(P-13407)*
Ingram Micro Management Co (HQ)....C....714 566-1000
3351 Michelson Dr Ste 100 Irvine (92612) *(P-13408)*
Ingredients By Nature LLC....E....909 230-6200
5555 Brooks St Montclair (91763) *(P-2452)*
Inhealth Technologies....E....800 477-5969
1110 Mark Ave Carpinteria (93013) *(P-11116)*
Inhealth Technology, Carpinteria *Also called Helix Medical* ***(P-11111)***
Inhouseit Inc....D....949 660-5655
400 Exchange Ste 100 Irvine (92602) *(P-18148)*
Initiative Media North America, Los Angeles *Also called Mediabrands Worldwide Inc* ***(P-17033)***
Injen Technology Company Ltd....E....909 839-0706
244 Pioneer Pl Pomona (91768) *(P-13847)*
Ink & Color Inc....E....310 280-6060
5920 Bowcroft St Los Angeles (90016) *(P-4329)*
Ink Direct....F....714 418-1999
17572 Griffin Ln Huntington Beach (92647) *(P-5205)*
Ink Fx Corporation....E....909 673-1950
2031 S Lynx Ave Ontario (91761) *(P-4528)*
Ink Makers Inc....F....323 728-7500
2121 Yates Ave Commerce (90040) *(P-5206)*
Ink Mill Corp., Glendale *Also called Ink Mill LLC* ***(P-5207)***
Ink Mill LLC....F....626 304-2000
207 N Goode Ave Fl 5 Glendale (91203) *(P-5207)*

ALPHABETIC

Employee Codes: A=Over 500 employees, B=251-500
C=101-250, D=51-100, E=20-50 F=10-19
2022 Southern California Business
Directory and Buyers Guide
© Mergent Inc. 1-800-342-5647
1163

Ink Spot Inc.....E.....626 338-4500
9737 Bell Ranch Dr Santa Fe Springs (90670) *(P-4330)*
Ink Spot Digital Printing LLC (PA).....**E.....562 777-1666**
9825 Bell Ranch Dr Santa Fe Springs (90670) *(P-4331)*
Ink Spots, Montclair *Also called Thomas Burt (P-4438)*
Inkgrabber.com, Moorpark *Also called Inkjetmadnesscom Inc (P-5208)*
Inkjetmadnesscom Inc.....F.....805 583-7755
882 Patriot Dr Ste G Moorpark (93021) *(P-5208)*
Inkovation Inc.....E.....800 465-4174
13659 Excelsior Dr Santa Fe Springs (90670) *(P-4332)*
Inkwright LLC.....E.....714 892-3300
5822 Research Dr Huntington Beach (92649) *(P-4333)*
Inland Bhavioral Hlth Svcs Inc (PA).....**D.....909 881-6146**
1963 N E St San Bernardino (92405) *(P-21443)*
Inland Builders Supply Inc.....E.....760 922-0361
1224 W Hobsonway Blythe (92225) *(P-13217)*
Inland Cc Inc.....C.....909 355-1318
13820 Slover Ave Fontana (92337) *(P-1531)*
Inland Chrstn HM Fundation Inc.....C.....909 395-9322
1950 S Mountain Ave Ofc Ontario (91762) *(P-20379)*
Inland Cnties Regional Ctr Inc (PA).....**A.....909 890-3000**
1365 S Waterman Ave San Bernardino (92408) *(P-21815)*
Inland Cold Storage, Bloomington *Also called Lineage Logistics Holdings LLC (P-12114)*
Inland Custom Manufacturing, Ontario *Also called Inland Signs Inc (P-11562)*
Inland Empire 66ers Bsbal CLB.....C.....909 888-9922
280 S E St San Bernardino (92401) *(P-19418)*
Inland Empire Chapter-Assn of.....D.....512 478-9000
4200 Concours Ste 360 Ontario (91764) *(P-22453)*
Inland Empire Cmnty Newspapers.....F.....909 381-9898
1809 Commercenter W San Bernardino (92408) *(P-3994)*
Inland Empire Drv Line Svc Inc (PA).....**F.....909 390-3030**
4035 E Guasti Rd Ste 301 Ontario (91761) *(P-10080)*
Inland Empire Foods Inc (PA).....**E.....951 682-8222**
5425 Wilson St Riverside (92509) *(P-1883)*
Inland Empire Health Plan (PA).....**A.....909 890-2000**
10801 6th St Ste 120 Rancho Cucamonga (91730) *(P-15380)*
Inland Empire Heart Institute, San Bernardino *Also called St Bernardine Med Ctr Aux Inc (P-20956)*
Inland Empire Magazine, Temecula *Also called Inland Empire Media Group Inc (P-4075)*
Inland Empire Media Group Inc.....E.....951 682-3026
36095 Monte De Oro Rd Temecula (92592) *(P-4075)*
Inland Empire RE Solutions.....D.....909 476-1000
8794 19th St Alta Loma (91701) *(P-15890)*
Inland Empire Therapy Provider (PA).....**D.....909 985-7905**
1150 N Mountain Ave # 214 Upland (91786) *(P-20216)*
Inland Empire Utlties Agcy A M (PA).....**D.....909 993-1600**
6075 Kimball Ave Chino (91708) *(P-12893)*
Inland Envelope Company.....D.....909 622-2016
150 N Park Ave Pomona (91768) *(P-3909)*
Inland Erosion Ctrl Svcs Inc.....D.....951 301-8334
42181 Avnida Alvrado Ste Temecula (92590) *(P-1598)*
Inland Eye Inst Med Group Inc (PA).....**D.....909 825-3425**
1900 E Washington St Colton (92324) *(P-19852)*
Inland Group, Anaheim *Also called Inland Litho LLC (P-4334)*
Inland Hlth Orgnztion of Sther (HQ).....**E.....909 335-7171**
1980 Orange Tree Ln # 200 Redlands (92374) *(P-20797)*
Inland Kenworth Inc (HQ).....**C.....909 823-9955**
9730 Cherry Ave Fontana (92335) *(P-13031)*
Inland Litho LLC.....D.....714 993-6000
4305 E La Palma Ave Anaheim (92807) *(P-4334)*
Inland Mailing Services Inc.....F.....951 371-6245
160 W Fthill Pkwy Ste 105 Corona (92882) *(P-4335)*
Inland Metal Trading Inc.....E.....833 396-0740
41187 Sandalwood Cir Murrieta (92562) *(P-6853)*
Inland Pacific Ballet, Montclair *Also called Foundation For Dance Education (P-19298)*
Inland Pacific Coatings Inc.....E.....909 822-0594
3556 Lytle Creek Rd Lytle Creek (92358) *(P-7374)*
Inland Powder Coating Corp.....C.....909 947-1122
1656 S Bon View Ave Ste F Ontario (91761) *(P-7375)*
INLAND REGIONAL CENTER, San Bernardino *Also called Inland Cnties Regional Ctr Inc (P-21815)*
Inland Signs Inc.....F.....909 923-0006
1715 S Bon View Ave Ontario (91761) *(P-11562)*
Inland Truss Inc (PA).....**D.....951 300-1758**
275 W Rider St Perris (92571) *(P-3366)*
Inland Valley Care & Rehab Ctr, Pomona *Also called Inland Valley Partners LLC (P-20217)*
Inland Valley Daily Bulletin, Monrovia *Also called Califrnia Nwspapers Ltd Partnr (P-3956)*
Inland Valley Daily Bulletin, Ontario *Also called Califrnia Nwspapers Ltd Partnr (P-3957)*
Inland Valley News Inc.....F.....909 949-3099
2009 Porter Field Way C Upland (91786) *(P-3995)*
Inland Valley Partners LLC.....C.....909 623-7100
250 W Artesia St Pomona (91768) *(P-20217)*
Inland Vly Rgional Med Ctr Inc.....B.....951 677-1111
36485 Inland Valley Dr Wildomar (92595) *(P-20798)*
Inline Plastics Inc.....E.....909 923-1033
1950 S Baker Ave Ontario (91761) *(P-5674)*
Inlog Inc.....D.....949 212-3867
6765 Westminster Blvd # 4 Westminster (92683) *(P-12471)*
Inmode Aesthetic Solutions, Irvine *Also called Invasix Inc (P-22844)*
Inmoment Research LLC.....D.....310 783-4300
20285 S Wstn Ave Ste 101 Torrance (90501) *(P-12406)*
Inn At Mssion San Juan Cpstran, San Juan Capistrano *Also called Marriott International Inc (P-16558)*
Inner Space Constructors Div, Long Beach *Also called Hutchison Corporation (P-1378)*
Inners Tasks LLC.....E.....951 225-9696
27708 Jefferson Ave # 201 Temecula (92590) *(P-8161)*
Innerspace Cases, North Hollywood *Also called Armored Group Inc (P-3375)*

Innocean Wrldwide Americas LLC (HQ).....**B.....714 861-5200**
180 5th St Ste 200 Huntington Beach (92648) *(P-17021)*
Innocor West LLC.....B.....909 307-3737
300-310 S Tippecanoe Ave San Bernardino (92408) *(P-5383)*
Innotec Group Inc.....F.....616 772-5959
61 Moreland Rd Simi Valley (93065) *(P-8977)*
Innov8v, Irvine *Also called Innovative Tech & Engrg Inc (P-8266)*
Innova Electronics Corporation.....E.....714 241-6800
17352 Von Karman Ave Irvine (92614) *(P-10081)*
Innovate Labs LLC.....F.....917 753-2673
556 S Fair Oaks Ave Ste 5 Pasadena (91105) *(P-17888)*
Innovated Solutions Inc.....F.....949 222-1088
7201 Garden Grove Blvd C Garden Grove (92841) *(P-7984)*
Innovations Building Svcs LLC.....D.....323 787-6068
402 S Orange Ave Apt D Monterey Park (91755) *(P-17251)*
Innovative Bedg Solutions Inc.....F.....714 994-2223
6560 Caballero Blvd Buena Park (90620) *(P-13174)*
Innovative Casework Mfg Inc.....E.....714 890-9100
12261 Industry St Garden Grove (92841) *(P-11690)*
Innovative Cnstr Solutions.....C.....714 893-6366
575 Anton Blvd Ste 850 Costa Mesa (92626) *(P-23394)*
Innovative Cosmetic Labs Inc.....F.....818 349-1121
9740 Cozycroft Ave Chatsworth (91311) *(P-5032)*
Innovative Displayworks Inc.....E.....909 447-8254
8825 Boston Pl Ste 100 Rancho Cucamonga (91730) *(P-13459)*
Innovative Diversfd Tech Inc.....E.....949 455-1701
18062 Irvine Blvd Ste 304 Tustin (92780) *(P-8205)*
Innovative Emergency Equipment, Riverside *Also called Innovtive Dsign Shtmtl Pdts In (P-6854)*
Innovative Emergency Equipment.....E.....951 222-2270
1616 Marlborough Ave Riverside (92507) *(P-19044)*
Innovative Engrg Systems Inc (PA).....**D.....661 381-7800**
8800 Crippen St Bakersfield (93311) *(P-22576)*
Innovative Integration Inc.....E.....305 520-3300
741 Flynn Rd Camarillo (93012) *(P-10703)*
Innovative Metal Designs Inc.....E.....714 799-6700
12691 Monarch St Garden Grove (92841) *(P-13066)*
Innovative Metal Inds Inc.....D.....909 796-6200
1330 Riverview Dr San Bernardino (92408) *(P-7023)*
Innovative Organics Inc.....E.....714 701-3900
4905 E Hunter Ave Anaheim (92807) *(P-5138)*
Innovative Plastics Inc.....E.....714 891-8800
5502 Buckingham Dr Huntington Beach (92649) *(P-5450)*
Innovative Power Inc.....F.....951 928-7700
P.O. Box 1580 Sun City (92585) *(P-8874)*
Innovative Produce Inc.....E.....805 349-2714
1615 W Main St Santa Maria (93458) *(P-111)*
Innovative Product Brands Inc.....E.....909 864-7477
7045 Palm Ave Highland (92346) *(P-10994)*
Innovative Skin Care, Burbank *Also called Science of Skincare LLC (P-14287)*
Innovative Stamping Inc.....E.....310 537-6996
2068 E Gladwick St Compton (90220) *(P-7153)*
Innovative Structural GL Inc.....D.....559 561-7000
40220 Pierce Dr Three Rivers (93271) *(P-5958)*
Innovative Systems, Compton *Also called Innovative Stamping Inc (P-7153)*
Innovative Tech & Engrg Inc.....E.....949 955-2501
2691 Richter Ave Ste 124 Irvine (92606) *(P-8266)*
Innovative Technologies Group.....F.....909 476-2555
10155 Sharon Cir Rancho Cucamonga (91730) *(P-5675)*
Innovativetek Inc.....F.....909 981-3401
1271 W 9th St Upland (91786) *(P-9872)*
Innovel Solutions Inc.....A.....909 605-1446
5691 E Philadelphia St # 2 Ontario (91761) *(P-12472)*
Innovent Inc (PA).....**F.....949 387-7725**
4667 Macarthur Blvd # 220 Newport Beach (92660) *(P-3756)*
Innovista Sensors, Westlake Village *Also called Carros Americas Inc (P-9689)*
Innovtive Artsts Tlent Ltrary (PA).....**D.....310 656-0400**
1505 10th St Santa Monica (90401) *(P-19314)*
Innovtive Dsign Shtmtl Pdts In.....F.....951 222-2270
616 Mrlbrugh Ave Unit S-1 Riverside (92507) *(P-6854)*
Inogen Inc (PA).....**C.....805 562-0500**
301 Coromar Dr Goleta (93117) *(P-10995)*
Inovativ Inc.....E.....626 969-5300
1500 W Mckinley St Azusa (91702) *(P-6282)*
Inovit Inc.....F.....626 444-4775
3630 Cypress Ave El Monte (91731) *(P-10082)*
Inpatient Consultants Fla Inc (HQ).....**C.....888 447-2362**
4605 Lankershim Blvd # 216 North Hollywood (91602) *(P-19853)*
Inphi International Pte Ltd.....E.....805 719-2300
112 S Lakeview Canyon Rd Westlake Village (91362) *(P-9518)*
Input 1 LLC.....C.....818 340-0030
6200 Canoga Ave Ste 400 Woodland Hills (91367) *(P-15154)*
Input/Output Technology Inc.....E.....661 257-1000
28415 Industry Dr Ste 520 Valencia (91355) *(P-8267)*
Inqbrands Inc.....D.....909 390-7788
1150 S Milliken Ave Ontario (91761) *(P-18188)*
Insco Dico Group , The, Irvine *Also called Developers Surety Indemnity Co (P-15496)*
Insco Insurance Services Inc (HQ).....**D.....949 263-3415**
17771 Cowan Ste 100 Irvine (92614) *(P-15583)*
Inseat Solutions LLC.....E.....562 447-1780
1871 Wright Ave La Verne (91750) *(P-9006)*
Insight Envmtl Engrg Cnstr Inc (PA).....**D.....714 678-6700**
2749 Saturn St Brea (92821) *(P-22577)*
Insight Hlth Svcs Hldings Corp (PA).....**C.....949 282-6000**
26250 Entp Ct Ste 100 Lake Forest (92630) *(P-21072)*
Insight Investments LLC (HQ).....**D.....714 939-2300**
611 Anton Blvd Ste 700 Costa Mesa (92626) *(P-18140)*
Insight Management Corporation (PA).....**E.....866 787-3588**
1130 E Clark Ave Santa Maria (93455) *(P-9221)*

Insight System Exchange, Santa Ana *Also called Limpus Prints Inc* ***(P-4538)***
Insignia/Esg Ht Partners Inc (HQ)..........B.......**310 765-2600**
11150 Santa Monica Blvd # 220 Los Angeles (90025) ***(P-15673)***
Insite Digestive Health Care..........D.......818 346-9911
7320 Woodlake Ave Ste 310 West Hills (91307) ***(P-19854)***
Insite Digestive Health Care..........D.......626 817-2900
225 W Broadway Ste 350 Glendale (91204) ***(P-19855)***
Insomniac Inc..........C.......323 874-7020
9441 W Olympic Blvd Beverly Hills (90212) ***(P-19358)***
Insomniac Games Inc (PA)..........B.......**818 729-2400**
2255 N Ontario St Ste 550 Burbank (91504) ***(P-11377)***
Insomniac Holdings LLC (HQ)..........C.......**323 874-7020**
9441 W Olympic Blvd Beverly Hills (90212) ***(P-19359)***
Insparation Inc..........E.......805 553-0820
11950 Hertz Ave Moorpark (93021) ***(P-5033)***
Inspectorate America Corp..........C.......800 424-0099
3401 Jack Northrop Ave Hawthorne (90250) ***(P-18549)***
Inspire Energy Holdings LLC..........C.......866 403-2620
3402 Pico Blvd Ste 300 Santa Monica (90405) ***(P-12807)***
Inspiria Inc (PA)..........D.......**949 206-0606**
140 Technology Dr Ste 100 Irvine (92618) ***(P-22578)***
Instacure Healing Products..........E.......818 222-9600
235 N Moorpark Rd # 2022 Thousand Oaks (91358) ***(P-4830)***
Instant Tuck Inc..........E.......310 955-8824
9663 Santa Monica Blvd Beverly Hills (90210) ***(P-3103)***
Instant Web LLC..........E.......562 658-2020
7300 Flores St Downey (90242) ***(P-4336)***
Instantfigure, Irvine *Also called Buy Insta Slim Inc* ***(P-2777)***
Institute Applied Bhvior Anlis, Tarzana *Also called Institute For Applied Behavior* ***(P-20220)***
Institute For Applied Behavior..........D.......818 341-1933
9221 Corbin Ave Northridge (91324) ***(P-20218)***
Institute For Applied Behavior (PA)..........C.......**310 649-0499**
5777 W Century Blvd # 675 Los Angeles (90045) ***(P-20219)***
Institute For Applied Behavior..........D.......818 881-1933
19510 Ventura Blvd # 204 Tarzana (91356) ***(P-20220)***
Institute For Applied Bhvior A..........D.......805 987-5886
2310 E Ponderosa Dr Ste 1 Camarillo (93010) ***(P-20221)***
Institute For Bhvoral Hlth Inc..........B.......909 289-1041
1905 Bus Ctr Dr S Ste 100 San Bernardino (92408) ***(P-21444)***
Institute For Mltcltral Cnslin (PA)..........D.......**213 381-1239**
3580 Wilshire Blvd # 200 Los Angeles (90010) ***(P-23453)***
Institute of Elec Elec Engners..........D.......714 821-8380
10662 Los Vaqueros Cir Los Alamitos (90720) ***(P-22249)***
Instrument Bearing Factory USA..........E.......818 989-5052
19360 Rinaldi St Northridge (91326) ***(P-7068)***
Instrument Control Services..........E.......805 642-1999
6085 King Dr Unit 100 Ventura (93003) ***(P-510)***
Instrumentation Tech Systems..........E.......818 886-2034
19360 Business Center Dr Northridge (91324) ***(P-8268)***
Instyler, Torrance *Also called Tre Milano LLC* ***(P-11784)***
Insua Graphics Incorporated..........E.......818 767-7007
9121 Glenoaks Blvd Sun Valley (91352) ***(P-4337)***
Insulectro (PA)..........D.......**949 587-3200**
20362 Windrow Dr Ste 100 Lake Forest (92630) ***(P-13730)***
Insulfab Inc..........E.......805 482-2751
4725 Calle Alto Camarillo (93012) ***(P-6171)***
Insultech LLC (PA)..........D.......**714 384-0506**
3530 W Garry Ave Santa Ana (92704) ***(P-5224)***
Insurance Inc Southern Cal..........D.......951 300-9333
3400 Central Ave Ste 220 Riverside (92506) ***(P-15584)***
Insure Express Insurance Svc, Calabasas *Also called Cartel Marketing Inc* ***(P-15549)***
Integra Devices, Irvine *Also called Xidas Inc* ***(P-9804)***
Integra Technologies Inc..........E.......310 606-0855
321 Coral Cir El Segundo (90245) ***(P-9519)***
Integral Aerospace LLC..........C.......949 250-3123
2040 E Dyer Rd Santa Ana (92705) ***(P-10354)***
Integral Engrg Fabrication Inc..........E.......626 369-0958
520 Hofgaarden St City of Industry (91744) ***(P-6623)***
Integrated Communications Inc..........E.......310 851-8066
208 N Broadway Santa Ana (92701) ***(P-4338)***
Integrated Data Services Inc (PA)..........D.......**310 647-3439**
2141 Rosecrans Ave # 2050 El Segundo (90245) ***(P-17640)***
Integrated Fire and Safety, Ventura *Also called Carter Fire Protection Inc* ***(P-14033)***
Integrated Food Service, Gardena *Also called Lets Do Lunch* ***(P-2475)***
Integrated Intermodal Svcs Inc..........D.......909 355-4100
8600 Banana Ave Fontana (92335) ***(P-18189)***
Integrated Magnetics, Culver City *Also called Magnet Sales & Mfg Co Inc* ***(P-5999)***
Integrated Magnetics Inc..........E.......310 391-7213
11250 Playa Ct Culver City (90230) ***(P-8919)***
Integrated Marketing Group LLC..........F.......714 771-2401
528 W Briardale Ave Orange (92865) ***(P-2576)***
Integrated Office Tech LLC (PA)..........D.......**562 236-9200**
12150 Mora Dr U2 Santa Fe Springs (90670) ***(P-13358)***
Integrated Parcel Network..........B.......714 278-6100
4373 Santa Anita Ave El Monte (91731) ***(P-12138)***
Integrated Polymer Inds Inc..........E.......949 788-1050
9741 Irvine Center Dr Irvine (92618) ***(P-7376)***
Integrated Polymer Solutions, Long Beach *Also called Sanders Inds Holdings Inc* ***(P-4715)***
Integrated Solutions, Garden Grove *Also called Innovated Solutions Inc* ***(P-7984)***
Integrated Tech Group Inc (PA)..........C.......**310 391-7213**
11250 Playa Ct Culver City (90230) ***(P-7559)***
Integrated Technical Services, Anaheim *Also called Interstate Electronics Corp* ***(P-10761)***
Integrated Voting Systems Inc..........E.......559 498-0281
496 S Uruapan Way Dinuba (93618) ***(P-18550)***
Integration Innovation Inc..........E.......256 513-5179
18374 Phantom St Victorville (92394) ***(P-22842)***
Integrex Innovations, Tustin *Also called Integrium LLC* ***(P-22843)***
Integrity Rebar Placers..........C.......951 696-6843
1345 Nandina Ave Perris (92571) ***(P-1571)***
Integrity Security Svcs LLC (HQ)..........F.......**805 965-6044**
30 W Sola St Santa Barbara (93101) ***(P-9873)***
Integrity Tires, Hemet *Also called S T Moll Inc* ***(P-18869)***
Integrium LLC (PA)..........C.......**714 541-5591**
14351 Myford Rd Ste A Tustin (92780) ***(P-22843)***
Integrted Healthcare Dlvry Sys, Whittier *Also called Pih Health Inc* ***(P-20889)***
Integrus LLC..........D.......714 547-9500
14370 Myford Rd Ste 100 Irvine (92606) ***(P-13359)***
Inteliglas Corporation..........E.......626 722-8881
685 E California Blvd Pasadena (91106) ***(P-5919)***
Intellective, Irvine *Also called Vegatek Corporation* ***(P-17750)***
Intellectyx Inc..........D.......720 256-7540
680 E Colo Blvd Ste 180 Pasadena (91101) ***(P-17889)***
Intelligent Cmpt Solutions Inc (PA)..........E.......**818 998-5805**
8968 Fullbright Ave Chatsworth (91311) ***(P-10757)***
Intelligent SCM LLC (PA)..........D.......**310 775-9195**
12900 Simms Ave Hawthorne (90250) ***(P-12473)***
Intellipower Inc..........D.......714 921-1580
1746 N Saint Thomas Cir Orange (92865) ***(P-13731)***
Intellisense Systems Inc..........C.......310 320-1827
21041 S Western Ave Torrance (90501) ***(P-10591)***
Intellitime Systems Corp..........D.......714 444-3020
1118 E 17th St Santa Ana (92701) ***(P-17641)***
Intense Lighting LLC..........D.......714 630-9877
3340 E La Palma Ave Anaheim (92806) ***(P-9090)***
Intepro America LP (PA)..........E.......**714 953-2686**
14662 Franklin Ave Ste E Tustin (92780) ***(P-10758)***
Inter Community Hospital, Covina *Also called Emanate Health Medical Center* ***(P-20767)***
Inter Con Systems, Pasadena *Also called Inter-Con Investigators Inc* ***(P-18289)***
Inter Valley Health Plan Inc..........D.......909 623-6333
300 S Park Ave Ste 300 # 300 Pomona (91766) ***(P-15400)***
Inter Valley Pool Supply Inc..........D.......626 969-5657
1415 E 3rd St Pomona (91766) ***(P-14080)***
Inter-Con Investigators Inc..........D.......626 535-2200
210 S De Lacey Ave Pasadena (91105) ***(P-18289)***
Inter-Con Security Systems Inc (PA)..........A.......**626 535-2200**
210 S De Lacey Ave Pasadena (91105) ***(P-18387)***
Inter-Continental Hotels Corp (HQ)..........B.......**770 604-5000**
35016 Avenue D Yucaipa (92399) ***(P-16505)***
Inter-Packing Inc..........F.......909 465-5555
12315 Colony Ave Chino (91710) ***(P-5512)***
Inter/Media Advertising, Woodland Hills *Also called Inter/Media Time Buying Corp* ***(P-17022)***
Inter/Media Time Buying Corp (PA)..........E.......**818 995-1455**
22120 Clarendon St # 300 Woodland Hills (91367) ***(P-17022)***
Interact Pmti Inc (HQ)..........D.......**805 658-5600**
260 Maple Ct Ste 210 Ventura (93003) ***(P-22579)***
Interact Theatre Co..........E.......818 765-8732
5215 Bakman Ave North Hollywood (91601) ***(P-19315)***
Interactive Media Holdings Inc (HQ)..........E.......**949 861-8888**
2722 Michelson Dr Ste 100 Irvine (92612) ***(P-17023)***
Interamerican Motor LLC (HQ)..........C.......**800 874-8925**
8901 Canoga Ave Canoga Park (91304) ***(P-13067)***
Interbase Corporation (PA)..........D.......**714 701-3600**
22485 La Palma Ave # 200 Yorba Linda (92887) ***(P-18190)***
Intercare Therapy Inc..........C.......323 866-1880
4221 Wilshire Blvd 300a Los Angeles (90010) ***(P-20222)***
Intercoastal Group, Los Angeles *Also called Intercoastal Property Svcs LLC* ***(P-15891)***
Intercoastal Property Svcs LLC (PA)..........C.......**310 277-0057**
1755 E Martin Lu Los Angeles (90058) ***(P-15891)***
Intercom, Los Angeles *Also called I C I* ***(P-10756)***
Intercommunity Care Centers..........C.......562 427-8915
2626 Grand Ave Long Beach (90815) ***(P-20380)***
Interconnect Solutions, Santa Ana *Also called Mx Electronics Mfg Inc* ***(P-6353)***
Interconnect Solutions Co LLC (PA)..........D.......**909 545-6140**
17595 Mount Herrmann St Fountain Valley (92708) ***(P-8978)***
Interconnect Solutions Co LLC..........C.......714 556-7007
17595 Mount Herrmann St Fountain Valley (92708) ***(P-9727)***
Interconnect Systems Intl LLC (HQ)..........D.......**805 482-2870**
741 Flynn Rd Camarillo (93012) ***(P-9520)***
Interconnect Systems, Inc., Camarillo *Also called Interconnect Systems Intl LLC* ***(P-9520)***
Interctive Dsplay Slutions Inc..........E.......949 727-1959
490 Wald Irvine (92618) ***(P-9728)***
Interdent Inc (HQ)..........D.......**310 765-2400**
9800 S La Cnga Blvd # 800 Inglewood (90301) ***(P-20181)***
Interdent Service Corporation..........C.......951 682-1720
3630 Central Ave Riverside (92506) ***(P-20182)***
Interdent Service Corporation (HQ)..........E.......**310 765-2400**
9800 S La Cnga Blvd # 800 Inglewood (90301) ***(P-20183)***
INTERFACE CHILDREN FAMILY SERV, Camarillo *Also called Interface Community* ***(P-21816)***
Interface Community (PA)..........D.......**805 485-6114**
4001 Mission Oaks Blvd Camarillo (93012) ***(P-21816)***
Interface Rehab Inc..........A.......714 646-8300
774 S Placentia Ave # 200 Placentia (92870) ***(P-20223)***
Interface Welding..........E.......310 323-4944
20722 Belshaw Ave Carson (90746) ***(P-19045)***
Interfaceflor LLC..........D.......213 741-2139
1111 S Grand Ave Ste 103 Los Angeles (90015) ***(P-2691)***
Intergro Rehab Service..........D.......714 901-4200
1922 N Broadway Santa Ana (92706) ***(P-20224)***
Interhealth Services Inc (HQ)..........C.......**562 698-0811**
12401 Washington Blvd Whittier (90602) ***(P-21176)***
Interim Services, Bakersfield *Also called C MBA Rn Inc* ***(P-21145)***
Interior Electric Incorporated..........D.......714 771-9098
747 N Main St Orange (92868) ***(P-1268)***
Interior Experts Gen Bldrs Inc..........D.......909 203-4922
4534 Carter Ct Chino (91710) ***(P-1381)***
Interior Logic Group Inc (HQ)..........A.......**800 959-8333**
10 Bunsen Irvine (92618) ***(P-18551)***

ALPHABETIC

Employee Codes: A=Over 500 employees, B=251-500
C=101-250, D=51-100, E=20-50 F=10-19
2022 Southern California Business
Directory and Buyers Guide
© Mergent Inc. 1-800-342-5647
1165

Interior Rmoval Specialist Inc ....C......323 357-6900
8990 Atlantic Ave South Gate (90280) ***(P-1616)***
Interlink Inc ....D......714 905-7700
3845 E Coronado St Anaheim (92807) ***(P-4339)***
Interlink Electronics Inc (PA) ....**D......805 484-8855**
1 Jenner Ste 200 Irvine (92618) ***(P-9729)***
Interlink Securities Corp ....D......818 992-6700
20750 Ventura Blvd # 300 Woodland Hills (91364) ***(P-15271)***
Interlog Construction, Anaheim *Also called Interlog Corporation* ***(P-9730)***
Interlog Corporation ....E......714 529-7808
1295 N Knollwood Cir Anaheim (92801) ***(P-9730)***
Intermed Video Tech Inc ....E......203 270-9100
38 Waterworks Way Irvine (92618) ***(P-9181)***
Intermountain Specialty Eqp, La Palma *Also called Isec Incorporated* ***(P-1443)***
Internal Revenue Service ....D......714 512-2818
2400 E Katella Ave # 800 Anaheim (92806) ***(P-16938)***
Internal Services, Los Angeles *Also called County of Los Angeles* ***(P-17585)***
Internal Services Department, Los Angeles *Also called County of Los Angeles* ***(P-22775)***
International Academy of Fin (PA) ....**E......818 361-7724**
13177 Foothill Blvd Sylmar (91342) ***(P-5139)***
International Baggyz, Los Angeles *Also called Krissy Op Shins USA Inc* ***(P-2817)***
International Bay Clubs LLC (PA) ....**C......949 645-5000**
1221 W Coast Hwy Ste 145 Newport Beach (92663) ***(P-19570)***
International Bus Mchs Corp ....A......818 553-8100
400 N Brand Blvd Fl 7 Glendale (91203) ***(P-8162)***
INTERNATIONAL CHILDREN'S CHARI, Calabasas *Also called Help Children World Foundation* ***(P-21800)***
International Coatings Co Inc (PA) ....**E......562 926-1010**
13929 166th St Cerritos (90703) ***(P-5185)***
International Coffee & Tea LLC (HQ) ....**D......310 237-2326**
5700 Wilshire Blvd # 120 Los Angeles (90036) ***(P-16209)***
International Creative Mgt Inc (HQ) ....**C......310 550-4000**
10250 Constellation Blvd Los Angeles (90067) ***(P-19316)***
International Creative MGT Inc ....E......310 550-4000
10250 Constellation Blvd Los Angeles (90067) ***(P-19317)***
International Daily News Inc (PA) ....**E......323 265-1317**
870 Monterey Pass Rd Monterey Park (91754) ***(P-3996)***
International Disc Mfr Inc ....F......714 210-1780
4906 W 1st St Santa Ana (92703) ***(P-9222)***
International E-Z Up Inc (PA) ....**D......800 457-4233**
1900 2nd St Norco (92860) ***(P-3141)***
International Envmtl Corp ....D......818 892-9341
13432 Wentworth St Arleta (91331) ***(P-310)***
International Fluid Power Amer, Temecula *Also called Normont Hydraulic Sls Svc Inc* ***(P-13923)***
International Fmly Entrmt Inc (HQ) ....**C......818 560-1000**
3800 W Alameda Ave Burbank (91505) ***(P-12772)***
International Immunology Corp ....E......951 677-5629
25549 Adams Ave Murrieta (92562) ***(P-4923)***
International Inst Los Angeles (PA) ....**D......323 224-3800**
3845 Selig Pl Los Angeles (90031) ***(P-21817)***
International Lease Fin Corp (HQ) ....**A......310 788-1999**
10250 Constellation Blvd Los Angeles (90067) ***(P-17356)***
International Marine Pdts Inc (HQ) ....**E......213 893-6123**
3020 E Washington Blvd Los Angeles (90023) ***(P-14571)***
International Medical Corps (PA) ....**D......310 826-7800**
12400 Wilshire Blvd # 1500 Los Angeles (90025) ***(P-21818)***
International Paper, Ontario *Also called New-Indy Containerboard LLC* ***(P-3763)***
International Paper, Visalia *Also called Graphic Packaging Intl LLC* ***(P-14932)***
International Paving Svcs Inc ....D......909 794-2101
1199 Opal Ave Mentone (92359) ***(P-888)***
International Port MGT Entp, Compton *Also called Ipme* ***(P-7560)***
International Precision Inc ....E......818 882-3933
9526 Vassar Ave Chatsworth (91311) ***(P-8627)***
International Processing Corp (HQ) ....**E......310 458-1574**
233 Wilshire Blvd Ste 310 Santa Monica (90401) ***(P-1970)***
International Prtg & Typsg Inc ....F......818 787-6804
14535 Hamlin St Van Nuys (91411) ***(P-4340)***
International Rectifier Corp (PA) ....**E......949 453-1008**
17885 Von Karman Ave # 100 Irvine (92614) ***(P-9521)***
International Research Labs, Moorpark *Also called Lifetech Resources LLC* ***(P-14256)***
International Rite-Way Pdts, Ontario *Also called AMD International Tech LLC* ***(P-6781)***
International Rubber Pdts Inc (HQ) ....**D......909 947-1244**
1035 Calle Amanecer San Clemente (92673) ***(P-5384)***
International Seal Company, Santa Ana *Also called Freudenberg-Nok General Partnr* ***(P-5337)***
International Sensor Tech ....E......949 452-9000
3 Whatney Ste 100 Irvine (92618) ***(P-10890)***
International Silicon Company ....E......929 291-0056
3972 Barranca Pkwy J210 Irvine (92606) ***(P-5140)***
International Silk, Los Angeles *Also called I S W Inc* ***(P-14304)***
International Tranducer Corp ....C......805 683-2575
869 Ward Dr Santa Barbara (93111) ***(P-10759)***
International Trnsp Svc LLC (PA) ....**C......562 435-7781**
1281 Pier G Way Long Beach (90802) ***(P-12288)***
International Vitamin Corp ....C......951 361-1120
11010 Hopkins St Ste B Jurupa Valley (91752) ***(P-4831)***
International Vitamin Corp (PA) ....**D......949 664-5500**
1 Park Plz Ste 800 Irvine (92614) ***(P-4832)***
International West Inc ....D......714 632-9190
1025 N Armando St Anaheim (92806) ***(P-6855)***
International Wind Inc (PA) ....**E......562 240-3963**
137 N Joy St Corona (92879) ***(P-10217)***
Internet Brands, El Segundo *Also called Mh Sub I LLC* ***(P-17035)***
Internet Corp For Assgned Nmes (PA) ....**C......310 823-9358**
12025 Waterfront Dr # 300 Los Angeles (90094) ***(P-18039)***
Internet Machines Corporation (PA) ....**D......818 575-2100**
30501 Agoura Rd Ste 203 Agoura Hills (91301) ***(P-8269)***

Interntional Color Posters Inc ....E......949 768-1005
8081 Orangethorpe Ave Buena Park (90621) ***(P-4529)***
Interntional Photo Plates Corp ....E......805 496-5031
2641 Townsgate Rd Ste 100 Westlake Village (91361) ***(P-7270)***
Interntional Tea Importers Inc (PA) ....**D......562 301-9600**
2140 Davie Ave Commerce (90040) ***(P-2453)***
Interntional Tech Systems Corp ....E......714 761-8886
10721 Walker St Cypress (90630) ***(P-13732)***
Interntional Un Oper Engineers ....E......626 792-2519
150 Corson St Pasadena (91103) ***(P-22291)***
Interntional Un Oper Engineers ....A......909 307-8700
1647 W Lugonia Ave Redlands (92374) ***(P-22292)***
Interntnal Assn Plbg Mech Offc (PA) ....**B......909 472-4100**
4755 E Philadelphia St Ontario (91761) ***(P-22250)***
Interntnal Ch of Frsqare Gospl (PA) ....**D......213 989-4234**
1910 W Sunset Blvd Los Angeles (90026) ***(P-15674)***
Interntnal Cnnctors Cable Corp ....C......883 275-4422
2100 E Valencia Dr Ste D Fullerton (92831) ***(P-9235)***
Interntnal Communications Corp ....E......951 934-0531
11801 Pierce St Fl 2 Riverside (92505) ***(P-18040)***
Interntnal Crtive MGT Prtners (PA) ....**D......310 550-4000**
10250 Constellation Blvd Los Angeles (90067) ***(P-23244)***
Interntnal Engrg PDT Cnsulting, Huntington Beach *Also called IEPC Corp* ***(P-17636)***
Interntnal Fndtion For Krea Un ....B......213 550-2182
3435 Wilshire Blvd # 480 Los Angeles (90010) ***(P-22190)***
Interntnal Litigation Svcs Inc ....E......838 313-4457
65 Enterprise Aliso Viejo (92656) ***(P-13360)***
Interntnal Mdction Systems Ltd ....F......626 459-5586
10642 El Poche St South El Monte (91733) ***(P-4750)***
Interntnal Mdction Systems Ltd ....A......626 442-6757
1886 Santa Anita Ave South El Monte (91733) ***(P-4833)***
Interntnal Plymr Solutions Inc ....E......949 458-3731
5 Studebaker Irvine (92618) ***(P-7446)***
Interntnal Pvment Slutions Inc ....E......909 794-2101
1209 Van Buren St Ste 3 Thermal (92274) ***(P-889)***
Interntonal Metallurgical Svcs ....F......310 645-7300
6371 Arizona Cir Los Angeles (90045) ***(P-6441)***
Interntonal Strl Engineers Inc ....E......310 643-7310
11926 S La Cienega Blvd Hawthorne (90250) ***(P-22580)***
Interntonal Super Sensors Corp ....F......909 590-5054
2300 S Reservoir St # 306 Pomona (91766) ***(P-10891)***
Interorbital Systems ....F......661 965-0771
1394 Barnes St Bldg 7 Mojave (93501) ***(P-6397)***
Interplastic, Ontario *Also called North American Composites Co* ***(P-4704)***
Interpore Cross Intl Inc (HQ) ....**D......949 453-3200**
181 Technology Dr Irvine (92618) ***(P-11117)***
Interpreting Services Intl LLC ....D......818 753-9181
700 N Brand Blvd Ste 950 Glendale (91203) ***(P-18552)***
Interscan Corporation ....E......805 823-8301
4590 Ish Dr Ste 110 Simi Valley (93063) ***(P-10738)***
Interspace Battery Inc (PA) ....**E......626 813-1234**
2009 W San Bernardino Rd West Covina (91790) ***(P-6333)***
Interstate Cabinet Inc ....E......951 736-0777
1631 Pomona Rd Ste B Corona (92878) ***(P-11691)***
Interstate Design Industry, Corona *Also called Interstate Cabinet Inc* ***(P-11691)***
Interstate Electric Co Inc (PA) ....**D......323 724-0420**
2240 Yates Ave Commerce (90040) ***(P-13460)***
Interstate Electronics Corp (HQ) ....**B......714 758-0500**
602 E Vermont Ave Anaheim (92805) ***(P-10760)***
Interstate Electronics Corp ....D......714 758-0500
708 E Vermont Ave Anaheim (92805) ***(P-23245)***
Interstate Electronics Corp ....D......714 758-0500
600 E Vermont Ave Anaheim (92805) ***(P-10761)***
Interstate Electronics Corp ....D......714 758-3395
604 E Vermont Ave Anaheim (92805) ***(P-9279)***
Interstate Electronics Corp ....D......714 758-0500
707a E Vermont Ave Anaheim (92805) ***(P-13733)***
Interstate Foods Inc ....C......310 635-0426
310 S Long Beach Blvd Compton (90221) ***(P-14548)***
Interstate Hotels Resorts Inc ....D......805 966-2285
901 E Cabrillo Blvd Santa Barbara (93103) ***(P-16506)***
Interstate Meat Co Inc ....E......323 838-9400
6114 Scott Way Commerce (90040) ***(P-7939)***
Interstate Mnroe McHy Sups Div, Huntington Beach *Also called Statco Engrg & Fabricators Inc* ***(P-13944)***
Interstate Rhbltation Svcs LLC ....C......818 244-5656
333 E Glenoaks Blvd # 204 Glendale (91207) ***(P-21313)***
Interstate Steel Center Co ....E......323 583-0855
7001 S Alameda St Los Angeles (90001) ***(P-6327)***
Interstate-Rim MGT Co LLC ....C......949 783-2500
3990 Westerly Pl Ste 120 Newport Beach (92660) ***(P-16507)***
Intertrade Aviation Corp ....F......714 895-3335
5722 Buckingham Dr Huntington Beach (92649) ***(P-10355)***
Intertrend Communications Inc ....D......562 733-1888
228 E Broadway Long Beach (90802) ***(P-17024)***
Interval House ....C......562 594-4555
6615 E Pcf Cast Hwy Ste 1 Long Beach (90803) ***(P-21819)***
Intervalley Pools, Pomona *Also called Inter Valley Pool Supply Inc* ***(P-14080)***
Intervest Property MGT Inc ....E......562 634-5672
5601 N Paramount Blvd Long Beach (90805) ***(P-15728)***
Interviewing Service Amer LLC (PA) ....**C......818 989-1044**
15400 Sherman Way Ste 400 Van Nuys (91406) ***(P-22888)***
Intervisual Books Inc ....F......302 636-5400
9800 S La Cienega Blvd Inglewood (90301) ***(P-4131)***
Intervrsity Chrstn Fllwshp/Usa ....B......310 510-0015
Gallager&Apos S Cv Avalon (90704) ***(P-16823)***
Intex Recreation Corp (PA) ....**B......310 549-5400**
4001 Via Oro Ave Ste 210 Long Beach (90810) ***(P-14081)***
Intimo Industry, Vernon *Also called Pjy Inc* ***(P-2585)***

Intouch Health, Goleta *Also called Intouch Technologies Inc* ***(P-17890)***

Intouch Technologies Inc (HQ)......B......**805 562-8686**
7402 Hollister Ave Goleta (93117) ***(P-17890)***

Intra Aerospace LLC......E......909 476-0343
10671 Civic Center Dr Rancho Cucamonga (91730) ***(P-8628)***

Intratek Computer Inc......C......949 334-4200
9950 Irvine Center Dr Irvine (92618) ***(P-18191)***

Intrepid Healthcare Svcs Inc, North Hollywood *Also called IPC Healthcare Inc* ***(P-19856)***

Intrepid Inv Bankers LLC......B......310 478-9000
11755 Wilshire Blvd # 2200 Los Angeles (90025) ***(P-16270)***

Intri-Plex Technologies Inc (HQ)......C......**805 683-3414**
751 S Kellogg Ave Goleta (93117) ***(P-8629)***

Intrinsik Envmtl Sciences Inc......D......310 392-6462
1608 Pacific Ave Ste 201 Venice (90291) ***(P-23454)***

Invapharm Inc......E......909 757-1818
1320 W Mission Blvd Ontario (91762) ***(P-15315)***

Invasix Inc......D......855 418-5306
17 Hughes Irvine (92618) ***(P-22844)***

Inveco Inc......E......949 378-3850
440 Fair Dr Ste 200 Costa Mesa (92626) ***(P-7271)***

Invelop Inc......E......818 772-2887
9711 Mason Ave Chatsworth (91311) ***(P-7612)***

Invenios LLC......D......805 962-3333
320 N Nopal St Santa Barbara (93103) ***(P-5959)***

Invenlux Corporation......F......626 277-4163
168 Mason Way Ste B5 City of Industry (91746) ***(P-9522)***

Invensys Climate Controls, Long Beach *Also called Schneider Elc Buildings LLC* ***(P-9910)***

Inveserve Corporation......D......626 458-3435
123 S Chapel Ave Alhambra (91801) ***(P-15892)***

Investlinc Group LLC (PA)......D......**310 997-0580**
1230 Rosecrans Ave # 600 Manhattan Beach (90266) ***(P-18553)***

Investlinc Group, The, Manhattan Beach *Also called Investlinc Group LLC* ***(P-18553)***

Investment Banking, Los Angeles *Also called J Alexander Investments Inc* ***(P-16156)***

Investment Enterprises Inc (PA)......E......**818 464-3800**
8230 Haskell Ave Ste 8240 Van Nuys (91406) ***(P-4530)***

Investment Tech Group Inc......C......310 216-6777
400 Crprate Pinte Ste 855 Culver City (90230) ***(P-15272)***

Investors Business Daily Inc (HQ)......C......**310 448-6000**
12655 Beatrice St Los Angeles (90066) ***(P-3997)***

Investors Capital MGT Group......B......310 553-5175
10390 Santa Monica Blvd Los Angeles (90025) ***(P-23040)***

Investors MGT Tr RE Group Inc (PA)......E......**818 784-4700**
15303 Ventura Blvd # 200 Sherman Oaks (91403) ***(P-15729)***

Invisble Prtection Systems Inc......E......213 254-0463
8847 S Halldale Ave Los Angeles (90047) ***(P-17891)***

Invision Networking LLC......C......949 309-3441
333 City Blvd W Ste 1700 Orange (92868) ***(P-17642)***

Invitation Homes Inc......D......805 372-2900
465 N Halstead St Ste 150 Pasadena (91107) ***(P-15675)***

Invoca Inc......D......855 977-3154
419 State St Santa Barbara (93101) ***(P-17643)***

Invotech Systems Inc......F......818 461-9800
20951 Burbank Blvd Ste B Woodland Hills (91367) ***(P-17892)***

Inwesco Incorporated (PA)......D......**626 334-7115**
746 N Coney Ave Azusa (91702) ***(P-6228)***

INX Prints Inc......D......949 660-9190
1802 Kettering Irvine (92614) ***(P-2664)***

Iog Products LLC......F......818 350-5070
9737 Lurline Ave Chatsworth (91311) ***(P-9523)***

Iogear, Irvine *Also called Aten Technology Inc* ***(P-8236)***

Iot Photochromics, Torrance *Also called Indizen Optical Tech Amer LLC* ***(P-17638)***

Iotec, Santa Fe Springs *Also called Integrated Office Tech LLC* ***(P-13358)***

Ip Access International......E......949 655-1000
31831 Camn Capistrano San Juan Capistrano (92675) ***(P-18192)***

Ip Corporation......E......323 757-1801
12335 S Van Ness Ave Hawthorne (90250) ***(P-4698)***

Ipayment Inc......D......213 387-1353
3325 Wilshire Blvd # 535 Los Angeles (90010) ***(P-18554)***

Ipayment Inc (HQ)......C......**212 802-7200**
30721 Russell Ranch Rd # 200 Westlake Village (91362) ***(P-18555)***

Ipayment Holdings Inc (HQ)......E......**310 436-5294**
30721 Russell Ranch Rd # 200 Westlake Village (91362) ***(P-18556)***

Ipb, Highland *Also called Innovative Product Brands Inc* ***(P-10994)***

IPC Cal Flex Inc......E......714 952-0373
13337 South St 307 Cerritos (90703) ***(P-9414)***

IPC Healthcare Inc (HQ)......A......**888 447-2362**
4605 Lankershim Blvd North Hollywood (91602) ***(P-19856)***

IPC of Florida, North Hollywood *Also called Inpatient Consultants Fla Inc* ***(P-19853)***

Ipd, Torrance *Also called Industrial Parts Depot LLC* ***(P-13906)***

Ipme......E......866 237-6302
19523 S Susana Rd Compton (90221) ***(P-7560)***

Ipolymer, Irvine *Also called Interntnal Plymr Solutions Inc* ***(P-7446)***

Ipr Software, Encino *Also called Ipressroom Inc* ***(P-17893)***

Ipressroom Inc......E......310 499-0544
16501 Ventura Blvd # 424 Encino (91436) ***(P-17893)***

Ips Corporation (PA)......C......**310 898-3300**
455 W Victoria St Compton (90220) ***(P-5186)***

Ips Industries Inc......D......562 623-2555
12641 166th St Cerritos (90703) ***(P-5676)***

Ipsos Otx Corporation (HQ)......C......**310 736-3400**
300 Crprate Pinte Ste 500 Culver City (90230) ***(P-22889)***

Ipt Holding Inc (PA)......D......**805 683-3414**
751 S Kellogg Ave Goleta (93117) ***(P-7154)***

Iqa Solutions Inc......D......562 420-1000
4089 E Conant St Long Beach (90808) ***(P-22581)***

Iqair North America Inc......E......877 715-4247
14351 Firestone Blvd La Mirada (90638) ***(P-8048)***

Iqd Frequency Products Inc......E......408 250-1435
592 N Tercero Cir Palm Springs (92262) ***(P-9731)***

Iqms LLC (HQ)......C......**805 227-1122**
2231 Wisteria Ln Paso Robles (93446) ***(P-17894)***

Iqvia Inc (HQ)......D......**949 476-2167**
2601 Main St Ste 650 Irvine (92614) ***(P-22890)***

Ircamera LLC......E......805 965-9650
30 S Calle Cesar Chavez Santa Barbara (93103) ***(P-10842)***

Irdeto Usa Inc (HQ)......B......**818 508-2333**
5250 Lankershim Blvd North Hollywood (91601) ***(P-18125)***

Irell & Manella LLP (PA)......B......**310 277-1010**
1800 Avenue Of The Stars # 900 Los Angeles (90067) ***(P-21586)***

Irell & Manella LLP......C......949 760-0991
840 Nwport Ctr Dr Ste 400 Newport Beach (92660) ***(P-21587)***

Iridium Technology Group (PA)......D......**626 839-7488**
17578 Rowland St City of Industry (91748) ***(P-14164)***

Iris LLC......E......424 331-5441
3800 N Mission Rd Los Angeles (90031) ***(P-22950)***

Irise (PA)......D......**800 556-0399**
2381 Rosecrans Ave # 100 El Segundo (90245) ***(P-17644)***

Irish Communication Company (HQ)......D......**626 288-6170**
2649 Stingle Ave Rosemead (91770) ***(P-956)***

Irish Construction (HQ)......C......**626 288-8530**
2641 River Ave Rosemead (91770) ***(P-957)***

Irish Farms Co Inc (PA)......E......**661 746-4392**
8711 Goldfinch Dr Bakersfield (93312) ***(P-215)***

Irish Interiors Inc (HQ)......C......**949 559-0930**
5511 Skylab Rd Ste 101 Huntington Beach (92647) ***(P-10356)***

Irish Interiors Holdings Inc......C......562 344-1700
5511 Skylab Rd Ste 101 Huntington Beach (92647) ***(P-10357)***

Irish Interiors Holdings Inc......E......949 559-0930
1729 Apollo Ct Seal Beach (90740) ***(P-10358)***

Irish International......C......949 559-0930
5511 Skylab Rd Huntington Beach (92647) ***(P-10218)***

Iron Beds of America, Los Angeles *Also called Wesley Allen Inc* ***(P-3538)***

Iron Grip Barbell Company Inc......D......714 850-6900
11377 Markon Dr Garden Grove (92841) ***(P-11430)***

Iron Mountain Info MGT LLC......D......818 848-9766
441 N Oak St Inglewood (90302) ***(P-12474)***

Iron Press Incorporated......F......714 426-8088
20201 Sw Birch St Ste 275 Newport Beach (92660) ***(P-4184)***

Iron Workers Local 433......E......909 884-5500
252 Hillcrest Ave San Bernardino (92408) ***(P-16178)***

Ironman Inc......E......818 341-0980
20555 Superior St Chatsworth (91311) ***(P-18982)***

Ironwood, Newberry Springs *Also called Fundamntal Chrstn Endavors Inc* ***(P-16820)***

Ironwood Electric Inc......E......714 630-2350
1239 N Tustin Ave Anaheim (92807) ***(P-9874)***

Ironwood Fabrication Inc......F......714 576-7320
215 Industry Ave La Habra (90631) ***(P-7088)***

IRONWORKERS UNION, Pasadena *Also called Ironwrker Emplyees Beneft Corp* ***(P-16179)***

Ironwrker Emplyees Beneft Corp......D......626 792-7337
131 N El Molino Ave # 330 Pasadena (91101) ***(P-16179)***

Irp, San Clemente *Also called International Rubber Pdts Inc* ***(P-5384)***

Irp Lax Hotel LLC......C......310 645-4600
9750 Airport Blvd Los Angeles (90045) ***(P-16508)***

Irriscape Construction Inc......D......951 694-6936
20182 Carancho Rd Temecula (92590) ***(P-311)***

Irrometer Company Inc......F......951 682-9505
1425 Palmyrita Ave Riverside (92507) ***(P-10892)***

Irvine APT Communities LP......C......714 937-8900
299 N State College Blvd Orange (92868) ***(P-15730)***

Irvine APT Communities LP......C......310 255-1221
1221 Ocean Ave Santa Monica (90401) ***(P-15731)***

Irvine APT Communities LP......C......949 854-4942
146 Berkeley Irvine (92612) ***(P-15732)***

Irvine APT Communities LP......C......714 537-8500
13212 Magnolia St Ofc Garden Grove (92844) ***(P-15733)***

Irvine APT Communities LP (HQ)......C......**949 720-5600**
110 Innovation Dr Irvine (92617) ***(P-15734)***

Irvine APT Communities LP......C......714 505-7181
100 Robinson Dr Tustin (92782) ***(P-15735)***

Irvine Company Office Property, Newport Beach *Also called Irvine Eastgate Office II LLC* ***(P-16237)***

Irvine Eastgate Office II LLC......A......949 720-2000
550 Newport Center Dr Newport Beach (92660) ***(P-16237)***

Irvine Electronics Inc......D......949 250-0315
1601 Alton Pkwy Ste A Irvine (92606) ***(P-9415)***

Irvine Medical Center, Orange *Also called University California Irvine* ***(P-20990)***

Irvine Pharmaceutical Svcs Inc......D......949 439-6677
5270 California Ave # 200 Irvine (92617) ***(P-22951)***

Irvine Ranch Water District (PA)......C......**949 453-5300**
15600 Sand Canyon Ave Irvine (92618) ***(P-12894)***

Irvine Ranch Water District......C......949 453-5300
3512 Michelson Dr Irvine (92612) ***(P-12895)***

Irvine Regional Hospital, Anaheim *Also called Tenet Healthsystem Medical Inc* ***(P-20974)***

Irvine Scientific, Santa Ana *Also called Fujifilm Irvine Scientific Inc* ***(P-4934)***

Irvine Sensors Corporation......E......714 444-8700
3000 Airway Ave Ste A1 Costa Mesa (92626) ***(P-9524)***

Irvine Technology Corporation......C......714 445-2624
2850 Redhill Ave Ste 230 Santa Ana (92705) ***(P-23455)***

Irwin Aviation Inc......E......951 372-9555
225 Airport Cir Corona (92878) ***(P-10359)***

Irwin International Inc (PA)......D......**951 372-9555**
225 Airport Cir Corona (92878) ***(P-14057)***

Irwindale 6000, Irwindale *Also called Southern California Edison Co* ***(P-12842)***

ISA, Van Nuys *Also called Interviewing Service Amer LLC* ***(P-22888)***

Isabel Garreton Inc (PA)......C......**310 833-7768**
770 Miraflores San Pedro (90731) ***(P-14383)***

Isabell's Honey Farm, Burbank *Also called Honey Isabells Inc* ***(P-140)***

Employee Codes: A=Over 500 employees, B=251-500
C=101-250, D=51-100, E=20-50 F=10-19
2022 Southern California Business Directory and Buyers Guide
© Mergent Inc. 1-800-342-5647
1167

Isabelle Handbags Inc ....E.......323 277-9888
3155 Bandini Blvd Unit A Vernon (90058) ***(P-5901)***
Iscope Corp ....F.......949 333-0001
14370 Myford Rd Ste 150 Irvine (92606) ***(P-10843)***
Isec Incorporated ....D.......714 761-5151
9381 Haven Ave Ste 101 Rancho Cucamonga (91730) ***(P-659)***
Isec Incorporated ....D.......714 761-5151
20 Centerpointe Dr # 140 La Palma (90623) ***(P-1441)***
Isec Incorporated ....D.......805 375-6957
2363 Teller Rd Ste 106 Newbury Park (91320) ***(P-1442)***
Isec Incorporated ....D.......714 761-5151
20 Centerpointe Dr # 140 La Palma (90623) ***(P-1443)***
ISI Detention Contg Group Inc ....D.......714 288-1770
577 N Batavia St Orange (92868) ***(P-8630)***
Isiqalo LLC ....B.......714 683-2820
5610 Daniels St Chino (91710) ***(P-2637)***
Island Brewing Co ....F.......805 745-8272
5049 6th St Carpinteria (93013) ***(P-2148)***
Island Pacific Supermarket, City of Industry *Also called Abacus Business Capital Inc* ***(P-14447)***
Island Packers Corporation ....D.......805 642-1393
1691 Spinnaker Dr 105b Ventura (93001) ***(P-12283)***
Island Powder Coating ....E.......626 279-2460
1830 Tyler Ave South El Monte (91733) ***(P-7377)***
Island Products, Buena Park *Also called Island Snacks Inc* ***(P-2089)***
Island Snacks Inc ....E.......714 994-1228
7650 Stage Rd Buena Park (90621) ***(P-2089)***
Isles Ranch Partners (PA) ....D.......**949 383-2354**
26 Corporate Plaza Dr # 200 Newport Beach (92660) ***(P-142)***
Isn Global Enterprises Inc ....F.......909 670-0601
678 S Indian Hill Blvd # 300 Claremont (91711) ***(P-18126)***
Isolutecom Inc (PA) ....E.......**805 498-6259**
9 Northam Ave Newbury Park (91320) ***(P-17895)***
Isotis Orthobiologics Inc ....C.......949 595-8710
2 Goodyear Ste A Irvine (92618) ***(P-22845)***
Isotope Products Lab, Valencia *Also called Eckert Zegler Isotope Pdts Inc* ***(P-10879)***
Isound, Torrance *Also called Dreamgear LLC* ***(P-11371)***
Isovac Engineering Inc ....E.......818 552-6200
614 Justin Ave Glendale (91201) ***(P-18557)***
Ispace Inc ....C.......310 563-3800
2381 Rosecrans Ave # 110 El Segundo (90245) ***(P-18193)***
Issac, Tustin *Also called Trellborg Sling Sltions US Inc* ***(P-11067)***
Istarusa Group ....E.......888 989-1189
727 Phillips Rowland Heights (91748) ***(P-8163)***
ISU Petasys Corp ....D.......818 833-5800
12930 Bradley Ave Sylmar (91342) ***(P-9416)***
Isuzu North America Corp (HQ) ....C.......**714 935-9300**
1400 S Douglass Rd # 100 Anaheim (92806) ***(P-13907)***
Isuzu Truck Services, Santa Ana *Also called Toms Truck Center Inc* ***(P-13037)***
Isys Solutions Inc ....D.......714 521-7656
2601 Saturn St Ste 302 Brea (92821) ***(P-23246)***
It Division Inc ....C.......678 648-2709
9170 Irvine Center Dr # 200 Irvine (92618) ***(P-17645)***
It Is Written, Riverside *Also called Adventist Media Center Inc* ***(P-19300)***
It's Delish, North Hollywood *Also called Mave Enterprises Inc* ***(P-2096)***
Italias Pizza Kitchen Ltd (PA) ....F.......**714 861-8178**
15554 Producer Ln Huntington Beach (92649) ***(P-1930)***
Itc Sftware Slutions Group LLC (PA) ....B.......**877 248-2774**
201 Sandpointe Ave # 305 Santa Ana (92707) ***(P-17896)***
Itcssg, Santa Ana *Also called Itc Sftware Slutions Group LLC* ***(P-17896)***
Itech Smart Home Inc ....F.......805 673-8414
1015 Concord Ave Ventura (93004) ***(P-9875)***
Itek Services Inc ....D.......949 770-4835
25501 Arctic Ocean Dr Lake Forest (92630) ***(P-18194)***
Iteris Inc (PA) ....B.......**949 270-9400**
1700 Carnegie Ave Ste 100 Santa Ana (92705) ***(P-9344)***
Itg, City of Industry *Also called Iridium Technology Group* ***(P-14164)***
Itochu Aviation Inc (HQ) ....E.......**310 640-2770**
222 N Pcf Cast Hwy Ste 22 El Segundo (90245) ***(P-14058)***
Its, Northridge *Also called Instrumentation Tech Systems* ***(P-8268)***
Its All About Cake Inc ....F.......949 240-7100
24921 Dana Pt Hbr D Ste B Dana Point (92629) ***(P-2008)***
Itsco, Cypress *Also called Interntional Tech Systems Corp* ***(P-13732)***
ITT Aerospace Controls LLC ....B.......661 295-4000
28150 Industry Dr Valencia (91355) ***(P-10360)***
ITT Cannon LLC ....C.......714 557-4700
56 Technology Dr Irvine (92618) ***(P-8957)***
ITT LLC ....D.......562 908-4144
3951 Capitol Ave City of Industry (90601) ***(P-8958)***
ITW Global Tire Repair Inc ....D.......805 489-0490
125 Venture Dr Ste 210 San Luis Obispo (93401) ***(P-5303)***
IV Inc ....D.......310 658-7374
1211 Westerly Ter Ste 300 Los Angeles (90026) ***(P-17646)***
Iv. Ai, Los Angeles *Also called IV Inc* ***(P-17646)***
Ivantis Inc (PA) ....C.......**949 600-9650**
201 Technology Dr Irvine (92618) ***(P-10996)***
Ivar's Displays, Ontario *Also called Ivars Display* ***(P-3652)***
Ivars Display (PA) ....C.......**909 923-2761**
2314 E Locust Ct Ontario (91761) ***(P-3652)***
Ivie McNeill Wyatt A Prof Law ....E.......213 489-0028
444 S Flower St Ste 1800 Los Angeles (90071) ***(P-21588)***
Ivy Enterprises Inc ....B.......323 887-8661
5564 E 61st St Commerce (90040) ***(P-23456)***
Iw Group (PA) ....D.......**213 262-6978**
6300 Wilshire Blvd # 215 Los Angeles (90048) ***(P-17025)***
Iwco Direct - Downey, Downey *Also called Instant Web LLC* ***(P-4336)***
Iwcus, Walnut *Also called Infinity Watch Corporation* ***(P-11561)***
Iwerks Entertainment Inc ....D.......661 678-1800
27509 Avenue Hopkins Santa Clarita (91355) ***(P-9876)***
Iworks Us Inc ....D.......323 278-8363
2501 S Malt Ave Commerce (90040) ***(P-9021)***
Iws Predictive Technologies, Yorba Linda *Also called Inflight Warning Systems Inc* ***(P-10353)***
Ixi Technology, Yorba Linda *Also called Mc2 Sabtech Holdings Inc* ***(P-8165)***
Ixia (HQ) ....A.......**818 871-1800**
26601 Agoura Rd Calabasas (91302) ***(P-10762)***
Ixos Software Inc (PA) ....D.......**949 784-8000**
8717 Research Dr Irvine (92618) ***(P-13409)***
Ixys Intgrted Crcits Div AV In ....C.......949 831-4622
145 Columbia Aliso Viejo (92656) ***(P-9525)***
Ixys Long Beach Inc (HQ) ....E.......**562 296-6584**
2500 Mira Mar Ave Long Beach (90815) ***(P-9526)***
Iyuno-Sdi Group, Los Angeles *Also called SDI Media USA Inc* ***(P-19176)***
J & F Design Inc ....D.......323 526-4444
2042 Garfield Ave Commerce (90040) ***(P-2953)***
J & F Machine Inc ....E.......714 527-3499
6401 Global Dr Cypress (90630) ***(P-8631)***
J & H Drilling Co Inc ....F.......714 994-0402
13124 Firestone Blvd Santa Fe Springs (90670) ***(P-431)***
J & H Production ....E.......323 261-6600
4481 S Santa Fe Ave Vernon (90058) ***(P-3176)***
J & J Co, Chatsworth *Also called J & J Products Inc* ***(P-7561)***
J & J Processing Inc ....E.......562 926-2333
14715 Anson Ave Santa Fe Springs (90670) ***(P-2330)***
J & J Products Inc ....F.......818 998-4250
9134 Independence Ave Chatsworth (91311) ***(P-7561)***
J & J Snack Foods Corp Cal (HQ) ....C.......**323 581-0171**
5353 S Downey Rd Vernon (90058) ***(P-2065)***
J & L Cstm Plstic Extrsons Inc ....E.......626 442-0711
1532 Santa Anita Ave South El Monte (91733) ***(P-5677)***
J & L Daycare ....D.......909 796-2656
24723 Rdlnds Blvd Ste A-C Loma Linda (92354) ***(P-22118)***
J & L Daycare ....D.......951 849-1429
2985 W Lincoln St Ste 402 Banning (92220) ***(P-22119)***
J & L Tank Co, Lynwood *Also called Ermm Corporation* ***(P-10166)***
J & L Vineyards ....D.......559 268-1627
1850 Ramada Dr Ste 3 Paso Robles (93446) ***(P-48)***
J & M Realty Company (PA) ....D.......**949 261-2727**
41 Corporate Park Ste 240 Irvine (92606) ***(P-15893)***
J & P Precision Deburring Inc ....F.......818 998-6079
9135 Alabama Ave Ste D Chatsworth (91311) ***(P-8632)***
J & R Concrete Products Inc ....E.......951 943-5855
440 W Markham St Perris (92571) ***(P-6036)***
J & R Machine Works ....E.......661 945-8826
45420 60th St W Lancaster (93536) ***(P-8633)***
J & S Inc ....E.......310 719-7144
229 E Gardena Blvd Gardena (90248) ***(P-8634)***
J & S Building Maintenance Inc ....E.......562 714-4033
7400 E Slauson Ave Ste 3w Commerce (90040) ***(P-17252)***
J & S Machine ....E.......562 945-6419
8112 Freestone Ave Santa Fe Springs (90670) ***(P-8635)***
J A Contracting Inc ....B.......559 733-4865
2209 W Tulare Ave Visalia (93277) ***(P-216)***
J A M, Monrovia *Also called Jam Fire Protection Inc* ***(P-18388)***
J Alexander Investments Inc (PA) ....E.......**213 687-8400**
922 S Barrington Ave A Los Angeles (90049) ***(P-16156)***
J and D Stl Fbrication Repr LP ....F.......805 928-9674
2360 Westgate Rd Santa Maria (93455) ***(P-18983)***
J and L Industries, El Segundo *Also called Aerospace Engrg Support Corp* ***(P-10252)***
J and S Machine, Santa Fe Springs *Also called J & S Machine* ***(P-8635)***
J B, Chatsworth *Also called J B Whl Roofg Bldg Sups Inc* ***(P-13325)***
J B A, Pasadena *Also called B Jacqueline and Assoc Inc* ***(P-17560)***
J B Hunt Transport Inc ....C.......909 466-5361
11559 Jersey Blvd Rancho Cucamonga (91730) ***(P-12054)***
J B J Distributing, Fullerton *Also called Veg-Land Inc* ***(P-12172)***
J B Tool Inc ....F.......714 993-7173
350 E Orngthrp Ave Ste 6 Placentia (92870) ***(P-8636)***
J B Whl Roofg Bldg Sups Inc (HQ) ....D.......**818 998-0440**
21524 Nordhoff St Chatsworth (91311) ***(P-13325)***
J B'S Private Label, Studio City *Also called JBs Private Label Inc* ***(P-2638)***
J B3d, Orange *Also called John Bishop Design Inc* ***(P-11563)***
J Bee NP Publishing Ltd ....F.......818 706-0266
30423 Canwood St Ste 108 Agoura Hills (91301) ***(P-4185)***
J C Entertainment Ltg Svcs Inc ....D.......818 252-7481
5435 W San Fernando Rd Los Angeles (90039) ***(P-19318)***
J C Ford Company (HQ) ....D.......**714 871-7361**
901 S Leslie St La Habra (90631) ***(P-7940)***
J C Industries Inc ....F.......805 389-4040
3977 Camino Ranchero Camarillo (93012) ***(P-11692)***
J C Precision, Rancho Cucamonga *Also called JCPM Inc* ***(P-8641)***
J C Rack Systems, Arcadia *Also called Cardenas Enterprises Inc* ***(P-3679)***
J C Sales, Vernon *Also called Shims Bargain Inc* ***(P-14975)***
J C Trimming Company Inc ....D.......323 235-4458
3800 S Hill St Los Angeles (90037) ***(P-2887)***
J D Diffenbaugh Inc ....D.......951 351-6865
6865 Airport Dr Riverside (92504) ***(P-774)***
J F Duncan Industries Inc (PA) ....D.......**562 862-4269**
9301 Stewart And Gray Rd Downey (90241) ***(P-8387)***
J F Fong Inc ....F.......949 553-8885
16520 Aston Irvine (92606) ***(P-10997)***
J F I, Los Angeles *Also called Jet Fleet International Corp* ***(P-16960)***
J F McCaughin Co ....F.......626 573-3000
2628 River Ave Rosemead (91770) ***(P-11469)***
J Filippi Vintage Co (PA) ....F.......**909 899-5755**
12467 Baseline Rd Rancho Cucamonga (91739) ***(P-2195)***

J Flying Manufacturing ... F ... 805 839-9229
11000 Brimhall Rd Ste E Bakersfield (93312) *(P-5358)*
J G Boswell Company ... D ... 559 992-2141
710 Bainum Ave Corcoran (93212) *(P-177)*
J G Boswell Company ... C ... 661 327-7721
21101 Bear Mountain Blvd Bakersfield (93311) *(P-2)*
J G Boswell Company ... D ... 559 992-5011
26073 Santa Fe Ave Corcoran (93212) *(P-128)*
J G Boswell Company ... C ... 559 992-5141
28001 S Dairy Ave Corcoran (93212) *(P-3)*
J G Construction, Chino *Also called June A Grothe Construction Inc (P-778)*
J Ginger Masonry LP (PA) ... B ... **951 688-5050**
8188 Lincoln Ave Ste 100 Riverside (92504) *(P-1347)*
J H Synder Co LLC ... D ... 323 857-5546
5757 Wilshire Blvd Ph 30 Los Angeles (90036) *(P-15894)*
J H Textiles Inc ... E ... 323 585-4124
2301 E 55th St Vernon (90058) *(P-2726)*
J Harris Indus Wtr Trtmnt Inc (PA) ... D ... **805 656-4411**
3151 Sturgis Rd Oxnard (93030) *(P-13831)*
J Hellman Frozen Foods Inc (PA) ... E ... **213 243-9105**
1601 E Olympic Blvd # 200 Los Angeles (90021) *(P-1901)*
J Heyri Inc ... E ... 323 588-1234
6900 S Alameda St Huntington Park (90255) *(P-2848)*
J I T Supply, Norco *Also called JIT Corporation (P-13736)*
J J Foil Company Inc ... E ... 714 998-9920
650 W Freedom Ave Orange (92865) *(P-3898)*
J K Star Corp ... D ... 310 538-0185
1123 N Stanford Ave Los Angeles (90059) *(P-2814)*
J L Cooper Electronics Inc ... E ... 310 322-9990
142 Arena St El Segundo (90245) *(P-9732)*
J L Fisher Inc ... D ... 818 846-8366
1000 W Isabel St Burbank (91506) *(P-17357)*
J L Industries, Commerce *Also called Samson Products Inc (P-3696)*
J L Shepherd and Assoc Inc ... E ... 818 898-2361
1010 Arroyo St San Fernando (91340) *(P-10893)*
J L Wingert Company ... D ... 714 379-5519
11800 Monarch St Garden Grove (92841) *(P-8388)*
J Lohr Winery Corporation ... E ... 805 239-8900
6169 Airport Rd Paso Robles (93446) *(P-2196)*
J M A R Precision Systems, Chatsworth *Also called Pacific Precision Labs Inc (P-10902)*
J M Carden Sprinkler Co Inc ... D ... 323 258-8300
2909 Fletcher Dr Los Angeles (90065) *(P-1085)*
J M V B Inc ... D ... 714 288-9797
12118 Severn Way Riverside (92503) *(P-1184)*
J Michelle of California ... F ... 323 585-8500
6409 Gayhart St Commerce (90040) *(P-2673)*
J Miller Co Inc ... E ... 818 837-0181
11537 Bradley Ave San Fernando (91340) *(P-5344)*
J P B Jewelry Box Co (PA) ... F ... **323 225-0500**
2428 Dallas St Los Angeles (90031) *(P-3653)*
J P H Consulting Inc (PA) ... E ... **323 934-5660**
1101 Crenshaw Blvd Los Angeles (90019) *(P-20381)*
J P H Consulting Inc ... D ... 323 934-5660
4515 Huntington Dr S Los Angeles (90032) *(P-20382)*
J P Original Corp (PA) ... D ... **626 839-4300**
19101 E Walnut Dr N City of Industry (91748) *(P-14440)*
J P Sportswear, Lynwood *Also called Aaron Corporation (P-2910)*
J P Turgeon & Sons Inc ... F ... 323 773-3105
7758 Scout Ave Bell (90201) *(P-7272)*
J Perez Associates Inc (PA) ... D ... **562 801-5397**
10833 Valley View St # 200 Cypress (90630) *(P-1666)*
J R C Industries Inc ... E ... 562 698-0171
11804 Wakeman St Santa Fe Springs (90670) *(P-3757)*
J R Industries, Westlake Village *Also called Jri Inc (P-13737)*
J R V Products Inc ... E ... 714 259-9772
1314 N Harbor Blvd # 302 Santa Ana (92703) *(P-9733)*
J Riley Distillery Inc ... F ... 909 792-0510
11855 Beverly Ct Loma Linda (92354) *(P-2243)*
J T Walker Industries Inc ... E ... 909 481-1909
9322 Hyssop Dr Rancho Cucamonga (91730) *(P-6702)*
J Talley Corporation (PA) ... D ... **951 654-2123**
989 W 7th St San Jacinto (92582) *(P-6964)*
J Tech Inc ... F ... 310 533-6700
548 Amapola Ave Torrance (90501) *(P-9039)*
J W Mrrott Los Angles L A Live ... C ... 213 765-8600
900 W Olympic Blvd Los Angeles (90015) *(P-16509)*
J&C Apparel ... E ... 323 490-8260
757 Towne Ave Unit B Los Angeles (90021) *(P-2770)*
J&E Private Security Corp ... D ... 909 594-1111
3227 Producer Way Ste 110 Pomona (91768) *(P-18290)*
J&G Berry Farms LLC ... C ... 831 750-9408
720 Rosemary Rd Santa Maria (93454) *(P-29)*
J&K Welding, Rancho Cucamonga *Also called Kathleen Brugger (P-18988)*
J&L Press Inc (PA) ... F ... **818 549-8344**
1218 W 163rd St Gardena (90247) *(P-4341)*
J&P Nutriceutical Services, Walnut *Also called Longstar Healthpro Inc (P-14705)*
J&R Taylor Brothers Assoc Inc ... D ... 626 334-9301
16321 Arrow Hwy Irwindale (91706) *(P-1958)*
J&S Goodwin Inc (HQ) ... C ... **714 956-4040**
5753 E Sta Ana Cyn G355 Anaheim (92807) *(P-7711)*
J&S Janitorial Services, Commerce *Also called J & S Building Maintenance Inc (P-17252)*
J&S Machine Works, Sylmar *Also called Kay & James Inc (P-8651)*
J'S 7570, Whittier *Also called Denco of Texas Inc (P-23015)*
J-M Manufacturing Company Inc (PA) ... C ... **800 621-4404**
5200 W Century Blvd Los Angeles (90045) *(P-7447)*
J-T E C H ... C ... 310 533-6700
548 Amapola Ave Torrance (90501) *(P-9658)*
J. Perez & Associates, Cypress *Also called J Perez Associates Inc (P-1666)*

J2 Cloud Services LLC (HQ) ... D ... **323 860-9200**
700 S Flower St Fl 15 Los Angeles (90017) *(P-12682)*
J2 Global Communications, Santa Barbara *Also called Efaxcom (P-8253)*
J5 Infrastructure Partners LLC ... D ... 949 299-5258
23 Mauchly Ste 110 Irvine (92618) *(P-12608)*
Jabi Enterprises Inc ... D ... 310 323-8436
14201 Halldale Ave Gardena (90249) *(P-18935)*
Jabil Chad Automation, Anaheim *Also called Jabil Inc (P-9417)*
Jabil Inc ... E ... 714 938-0080
1565 S Sinclair St Anaheim (92806) *(P-9417)*
Jack C Drees Grinding Co Inc ... F ... 818 764-8301
11815 Vose St B North Hollywood (91605) *(P-8637)*
Jack Engle & Co (PA) ... D ... **323 589-8111**
10556 Ilona Ave Los Angeles (90064) *(P-14117)*
Jack Gosch Ford Inc ... D ... 951 658-3181
150 Carriage Cir Hemet (92545) *(P-18842)*
Jack J Engel Manufacturing Inc ... E ... 818 767-6220
11641 Pendleton St Sun Valley (91352) *(P-9877)*
Jack Jones Trucking Inc ... D ... 909 456-2500
1090 E Belmont St Ontario (91761) *(P-12055)*
Jack Kramer Club ... E ... 310 326-4404
11 Montecillo Dr Rllng HLS Est (90274) *(P-19571)*
Jack Nadel Inc (PA) ... D ... **310 815-2600**
8701 Bellanca Ave Los Angeles (90045) *(P-23247)*
Jack Nadel International, Los Angeles *Also called Jack Nadel Inc (P-23247)*
Jack Parker Corp ... D ... 760 770-5000
4200 E Palm Canyon Dr Palm Springs (92264) *(P-16510)*
Jack Rubin & Sons Inc (PA) ... E ... **310 635-5407**
13103 S Alameda St Compton (90222) *(P-13570)*
Jack's Candy, Los Angeles *Also called 8th Street Enterprise Inc (P-14552)*
Jackandjillkidscom, Carson *Also called Jnj Operations LLC (P-11695)*
Jackoway Tyreman Wertheimer Au ... D ... 310 553-0305
1925 Century Park E Fl 2 Los Angeles (90067) *(P-21589)*
Jacks Candy, Los Angeles *Also called Consolidated Svc Distrs Inc (P-14561)*
JACKSAM CORP BLACKOUT, Newport Beach *Also called Jacksam Corporation (P-8072)*
Jacksam Corporation ... E ... 800 605-3580
4440 Von Karman Ave # 220 Newport Beach (92660) *(P-8072)*
Jackson Engineering Co Inc ... E ... 818 886-9567
9411 Winnetka Ave A Chatsworth (91311) *(P-8875)*
Jackson Family Wines Inc ... E ... 805 938-7300
5475 Chardonnay Ln Santa Maria (93454) *(P-2197)*
Jackson Shrub Supply Inc ... D ... 818 982-0100
11505 Vanowen St North Hollywood (91605) *(P-19239)*
Jackson Tidus A Law Corp (PA) ... D ... **949 752-8585**
2030 Main St Ste 1200 Irvine (92614) *(P-21590)*
Jacmar Companies, The, Alhambra *Also called Pacific Ventures Ltd (P-23084)*
Jaco Engineering ... E ... 714 991-1680
879 S East St Anaheim (92805) *(P-8638)*
Jacobellis, Burbank *Also called V J Provision Inc (P-1722)*
Jacobs Atcs Fema A Joint Ventr ... D ... 571 218-1115
155 N Lake Ave Fl 5 Pasadena (91101) *(P-22582)*
Jacobs Civil Inc ... C ... 310 847-2500
1500 Hughes Way Ste B400 Long Beach (90810) *(P-22583)*
Jacobs Engineering Company ... A ... 626 449-2171
1111 S Arroyo Pkwy Pasadena (91105) *(P-22584)*
Jacobs Engineering Group Inc ... D ... 626 578-3500
1111 S Arroyo Pkwy Pasadena (91105) *(P-22585)*
Jacobs Engineering Inc (HQ) ... A ... **626 578-3500**
155 N Lake Ave Pasadena (91101) *(P-22586)*
Jacobs International Ltd Inc ... B ... 626 578-3500
155 N Lake Ave Ste 800 Pasadena (91101) *(P-22587)*
Jacobs Project Management Co ... D ... 949 224-7695
2600 Michelson Dr Ste 500 Irvine (92612) *(P-22588)*
Jacobson Plastics Inc ... D ... 562 433-4911
1401 Freeman Ave Long Beach (90804) *(P-5678)*
Jacobsson Engrg Cnstr Inc ... D ... 760 345-8700
72310 Varner Rd Thousand Palms (92276) *(P-890)*
Jacobus Consulting Inc ... E ... 949 727-0720
15375 Barranca Pkwy B202 Irvine (92618) *(P-23248)*
Jacor Communications Company ... D ... 805 879-8300
414 E Cota St Santa Barbara (93101) *(P-12695)*
Jacuzzi Brands LLC (HQ) ... E ... **909 606-1416**
13925 City Center Dr # 200 Chino Hills (91709) *(P-11693)*
Jacuzzi Group Worldwide, Chino Hills *Also called Jacuzzi Brands LLC (P-11693)*
Jacuzzi Inc (HQ) ... C ... **909 606-7733**
14525 Monte Vista Ave Chino (91710) *(P-8389)*
Jacuzzi Outdoor Products, Chino *Also called Jacuzzi Inc (P-8389)*
Jacuzzi Products Co (HQ) ... C ... **909 606-1416**
13925 City Center Dr # 200 Chino Hills (91709) *(P-5532)*
Jacuzzi Products Co ... B ... 909 548-7732
14525 Monte Vista Ave Chino (91710) *(P-5533)*
Jada Group Inc ... D ... 626 810-8382
938 Hatcher Ave City of Industry (91748) *(P-11378)*
Jada Toys, City of Industry *Also called Jada Group Inc (P-11378)*
Jade Inc ... D ... 818 365-7137
11126 Sepulveda Blvd B Mission Hills (91345) *(P-1382)*
Jade Products, Brea *Also called Jade Range LLC (P-8991)*
Jade Range LLC ... C ... 714 961-2400
2650 Orbiter St Brea (92821) *(P-8991)*
Jae Electronics Inc (HQ) ... E ... **949 753-2600**
142 Technology Dr Ste 100 Irvine (92618) *(P-13734)*
Jaffa Precision Engrg Inc ... F ... 951 278-8797
12117 Madera Way Riverside (92503) *(P-8639)*
Jafra Cosmetics Intl Inc (HQ) ... C ... **805 449-3000**
2451 Townsgate Rd Westlake Village (91361) *(P-5034)*
Jag Professional Services Inc ... C ... 310 945-5648
2008 Walnut Ave Manhattan Beach (90266) *(P-23457)*

Employee Codes: A=Over 500 employees, B=251-500
C=101-250, D=51-100, E=20-50 F=10-19
2022 Southern California Business
Directory and Buyers Guide
© Mergent Inc. 1-800-342-5647
1169

Jaguar Energy LLC (PA) .... E **949 706-7060**
2404 Colony Plz Newport Beach (92660) *(P-511)*

Jaguar Mfg Cstm Wrought Ir, Bakersfield *Also called Jaguars Wrought Iron* *(P-6965)*

Jaguars Wrought Iron .... F 661 323-5015
300 Union Ave Bakersfield (93307) *(P-6965)*

Jake Hey Incorporated .... C 323 856-5280
257 S Lake St Burbank (91502) *(P-18409)*

Jakks Pacific Inc .... E 909 594-7771
21749 Baker Pkwy Walnut (91789) *(P-11379)*

Jakks Pacific Inc (PA) .... B **424 268-9444**
2951 28th St Santa Monica (90405) *(P-11380)*

Jakov Dulcich and Sons LLC .... C 661 792-6360
31956 Peterson Rd Mc Farland (93250) *(P-112)*

Jal Avionet USA (HQ) .... E **310 606-1000**
300 Continental Blvd # 190 El Segundo (90245) *(P-13410)*

Jaltrans Inc (HQ) .... C 310 215-7471
6041 W Imperial Hwy Los Angeles (90045) *(P-12335)*

Jam City Inc (PA) .... C 310 205-4800
3562 Eastham Dr Culver City (90232) *(P-17897)*

Jam Design Inc .... F 818 505-1680
5415 Cleon Ave North Hollywood (91601) *(P-11485)*

Jam Fire Protection Inc (PA) .... E **626 256-4400**
1930 S Myrtle Ave Monrovia (91016) *(P-18388)*

Jamac Steel Inc .... E 909 983-7592
1037 S Sultana Ave Ontario (91761) *(P-6624)*

Jamboor Medical Corporation .... D 760 241-8063
12675 Hesperia Rd Victorville (92395) *(P-21250)*

Jamboree Management, Laguna Hills *Also called Jamboree Realty Corp* *(P-15895)*

Jamboree Realty Corp (PA) .... C **949 380-0300**
22982 Mill Creek Dr Laguna Hills (92653) *(P-15895)*

James A Quaglino Inc .... D 805 543-0560
815 Fiero Ln San Luis Obispo (93401) *(P-1490)*

James B Branch Inc (PA) .... E **818 765-3521**
4367 Clybourn Ave Toluca Lake (91602) *(P-11978)*

James Fedor Masonry Inc .... D 760 772-3036
54859 Bodine Dr Thermal (92274) *(P-1348)*

James H Cowan & Associates Inc .... D 310 457-2574
5126 Clareton Dr Ste 200 Agoura Hills (91301) *(P-312)*

James Hardie Building Pdts Inc .... D 949 348-1800
26300 La Alameda Ste 400 Mission Viejo (92691) *(P-5977)*

James Hardie Trading Co Inc .... D 949 582-2378
26300 La Alameda Ste 400 Mission Viejo (92691) *(P-5283)*

James Jones Company .... A 909 418-2558
1470 S Vintage Ave Ontario (91761) *(P-7448)*

James Litho, Ontario *Also called Eclipse Prtg & Graphics LLC* *(P-4287)*

James Magna Ltd .... F 909 391-2025
8782 Lanyard Ct Rancho Cucamonga (91730) *(P-18899)*

James McMinn Inc .... D 909 514-1231
21834 Cactus Ave Riverside (92518) *(P-891)*

James Metals, Riverside *Also called Harbor Pipe and Steel Inc* *(P-13568)*

James R Gldwell Dntl Crmics In (PA) .... A **949 440-2600**
4141 Macarthur Blvd Newport Beach (92660) *(P-21107)*

James Stewart .... E 323 778-1687
8931 S Vermont Ave Los Angeles (90044) *(P-4834)*

James Tobin Cellars Inc .... E 805 239-2204
8950 Union Rd Paso Robles (93446) *(P-2198)*

Jan Pro Clg Systems Sthern Cal .... E 714 220-0500
2401 E Katella Ave # 525 Anaheim (92806) *(P-17253)*

Jan-Al Cases, Los Angeles *Also called Jan-Al Innerprizes Inc* *(P-5894)*

Jan-Al Innerprizes Inc .... E 323 260-7212
3339 Union Pacific Ave Los Angeles (90023) *(P-5894)*

Jan-Pro Cleaning Systems, Anaheim *Also called Jan Pro Clg Systems Sthern Cal* *(P-17253)*

Janel Glass Company Inc .... E 323 661-8621
2960 Marsh St Los Angeles (90039) *(P-5960)*

Janin .... C 323 564-0995
10031 Hunt Ave South Gate (90280) *(P-2954)*

Janitorial Equipment Svcs Inc .... D 951 205-8937
11752 Garden Grove Blvd Garden Grove (92843) *(P-17254)*

Jankovich Company (PA) .... D **310 547-3305**
307 W 22nd St San Pedro (90731) *(P-14796)*

Jano Graphics, Oxnard *Also called National Graphics LLC* *(P-4378)*

Jans Enterprises Corporation .... E 626 575-2000
4181 Temple City Blvd A El Monte (91731) *(P-14696)*

Jans Towing Inc (PA) .... C **626 334-1383**
1045 W Kirkwall Rd Azusa (91702) *(P-18936)*

Jansen Ornamental Supply Co .... E 626 442-0271
10926 Schmidt Rd El Monte (91733) *(P-6966)*

Jantek Electronics Inc .... F 626 350-4198
4820 Arden Dr Temple City (91780) *(P-9878)*

Janteq Corp (PA) .... E **949 215-2603**
9975 Toledo Way Ste 150 Irvine (92618) *(P-9280)*

Janus Et Cie (PA) .... C **310 601-2958**
12310 Greenstone Ave Santa Fe Springs (90670) *(P-13139)*

Japanese Retirement Home, Los Angeles *Also called Senior Keiro Health Care* *(P-22152)*

Jar Machine Fabrication Inc .... F 626 939-1111
1031 W Kirkwall Rd Azusa (91702) *(P-8640)*

Jariet Technologies Inc .... E 310 698-1001
103 W Torrance Blvd Redondo Beach (90277) *(P-10592)*

Jarrow Formulas Inc (PA) .... D **310 204-6936**
1824 S Robertson Blvd Los Angeles (90035) *(P-14252)*

Jarrow Industries Inc .... C 562 906-1919
12246 Hawkins St Santa Fe Springs (90670) *(P-4835)*

Jason Markk Inc (PA) .... E **213 687-7060**
329 E 2nd St Los Angeles (90012) *(P-4965)*

Jason Tool and Engineering Inc .... E 714 895-5067
7101 Honold Cir Garden Grove (92841) *(P-5679)*

Jason's Natural, Bell *Also called Hain Celestial Group Inc* *(P-5029)*

Jasper Electronics .... E 714 917-0749
1580 N Kellogg Dr Anaheim (92807) *(P-9734)*

Jax and Bones Inc .... E 626 363-9350
345 Cloverleaf Dr Baldwin Park (91706) *(P-11694)*

Jaxx Manufacturing Inc .... E 805 526-4979
1912 Angus Ave Simi Valley (93063) *(P-9735)*

Jay's Catering, Garden Grove *Also called Mastroianni Family Entps Ltd* *(P-16965)*

Jay-Cee Blouse Co Inc .... F 213 622-0116
823 Maple Ave Ste 200 Los Angeles (90014) *(P-2888)*

Jaya Apparel Group LLC .... E 714 904-9051
2760 Fruitland Ave Vernon (90058) *(P-2955)*

Jaya Apparel Group LLC .... E 323 584-3500
5175 S Soto St Vernon (90058) *(P-2956)*

Jaya Apparel Group LLC (PA) .... D 323 584-3500
5175 S Soto St Vernon (90058) *(P-2957)*

Jaybee Huntington LLC .... D 562 756-3124
44 Skyward Irvine (92620) *(P-16511)*

Jayco Interface Technology Inc .... E 951 738-2000
1351 Pico St Corona (92881) *(P-9736)*

Jayco/Mmi Inc .... E 951 738-2000
1351 Pico St Corona (92881) *(P-9737)*

Jayem Enterprises Inc .... D 310 329-2263
14930 S San Pedro St Gardena (90248) *(P-13571)*

Jayone Foods Inc .... E 562 633-7400
7212 Alondra Blvd Paramount (90723) *(P-2454)*

Jaz Distribution Inc .... F 714 521-3888
8485 Artesia Blvd Ste B Buena Park (90621) *(P-7089)*

Jaz Products, Santa Paula *Also called Westlake Engrg Roto Form* *(P-5864)*

Jazz Semiconductor, Newport Beach *Also called Newport Fab LLC* *(P-9549)*

JB Bostick Company Inc (PA) .... D **714 238-2121**
2870 E La Cresta Ave Anaheim (92806) *(P-892)*

JB Brananne Inc .... E 949 215-7704
6 Orchard Lake Forest (92630) *(P-5680)*

JB Dental Supply Co Inc (PA) .... C **310 202-8855**
17000 Kingsview Ave Carson (90746) *(P-13496)*

JB Plastics Inc .... E 714 541-8500
1921 E Edinger Ave Santa Ana (92705) *(P-5681)*

JBa Consulting Engineers Inc .... D 949 419-3030
163 Technology Dr Ste 100 Irvine (92618) *(P-22589)*

Jbb Inc .... E 888 538-9287
4900 E Hunter Ave Anaheim (92807) *(P-9879)*

Jbi LLC (PA) .... C **310 886-8034**
2650 E El Presidio St Long Beach (90810) *(P-3733)*

Jbi LLC .... E 310 537-2910
18521 S Santa Fe Ave Compton (90221) *(P-3529)*

Jbi Interiors, Long Beach *Also called Jbi LLC* *(P-3733)*

Jbs Case Ready, Riverside *Also called Swift Beef Company* *(P-1753)*

JBs Private Label Inc .... E 818 762-3736
4383 Irvine Ave Studio City (91604) *(P-2638)*

Jbsprotection, Redondo Beach *Also called Jones Bold Security Inc* *(P-18291)*

JBW Precision Inc .... E 805 499-1973
2650 Lavery Ct Newbury Park (91320) *(P-6856)*

JC Foodservice Inc (PA) .... D **626 299-3800**
415 S Atlantic Blvd Monterey Park (91754) *(P-13461)*

JC Ford, La Habra *Also called J C Ford Company* *(P-7940)*

JC Hanscom Inc .... E 562 789-9955
11830 Wakeman St Santa Fe Springs (90670) *(P-3351)*

JC Industries, Los Angeles *Also called J C Trimming Company Inc* *(P-2887)*

JC Majestic Real Estate LLC .... E 800 398-6879
6750 Clybourn Ave Apt 218 North Hollywood (91606) *(P-15896)*

JC Party Rentals Inc .... D 818 765-4819
11562 Vanowen St North Hollywood (91605) *(P-17358)*

JC Penney, Arcadia *Also called Penney Opco LLC* *(P-16911)*

JC Penney, Thousand Oaks *Also called Penney Opco LLC* *(P-16912)*

JC Penney 1505, West Covina *Also called Penney Opco LLC* *(P-16913)*

JC Promotions Inc .... F 310 870-1183
5601 W Slauson Ave # 168 Culver City (90230) *(P-23249)*

JC Resorts LLC .... B 949 376-2779
1555 S Coast Hwy Laguna Beach (92651) *(P-23041)*

JC Sales, Commerce *Also called Shims Bargain Inc* *(P-716)*

JC Supply & Manufacturing, Diamond Bar *Also called Simplex Supplies Inc* *(P-6662)*

JC Window Fashions Inc .... E 909 364-8888
2438 Peck Rd Whittier (90601) *(P-3711)*

Jc's Pie Pops, Chatsworth *Also called We The Pie People LLC* *(P-1827)*

Jci Jones Chemicals Inc .... F 310 523-1629
1401 Del Amo Blvd Torrance (90501) *(P-4636)*

Jcm Engineering Corp .... D 909 923-3730
2690 E Cedar St Ontario (91761) *(P-14059)*

JCM Industries Inc (PA) .... E **714 902-9000**
15302 Pipeline Ln Huntington Beach (92649) *(P-3687)*

JCP, Visalia *Also called Penney Opco LLC* *(P-16910)*

JCPM Inc .... E 909 484-9040
8576 Red Oak St Rancho Cucamonga (91730) *(P-8641)*

Jcr Aircraft Deburring LLC .... D 714 870-4427
221 Foundation Ave La Habra (90631) *(P-7273)*

Jcr Deburring, La Habra *Also called Jcr Aircraft Deburring LLC* *(P-7273)*

Jct Company LLC .... E 949 589-2021
29736 Avnida De Las Bnder Rancho Santa Margari (92688) *(P-1086)*

JD Business Solutions Inc .... E 805 962-8193
1351 Holiday Hill Rd Goleta (93117) *(P-4342)*

JD Power .... B 805 418-8000
30870 Russell Ranch Rd # 100 Westlake Village (91362) *(P-22891)*

JD Processing Inc .... E 714 972-8161
2220 Cape Cod Way Santa Ana (92703) *(P-7274)*

Jd/Cmc Inc .... E 818 767-2260
2834 E 11th St Los Angeles (90023) *(P-2958)*

JDC Development Group Inc .... F 714 575-1108
1321 N Blue Gum St Anaheim (92806) *(P-3415)*

Jdh Pacific Inc (PA) .... E **562 926-8088**
14821 Artesia Blvd La Mirada (90638) *(P-6259)*

2022 Southern California Business
Directory and Buyers Guide

(P-0000) Products & Services Section entry number
(PA)=Parent Co (HQ)=Headquarters (DH)=Div Headquarters

Jdi Distribution, Loma Linda *Also called Bakell LLC* ***(P-689)***
Jdr Engineering Cons Inc (PA)....C....**714 751-7084**
3122 Maple St Santa Ana (92707) ***(P-5682)***
Jds Hospitality Group....D....949 631-6000
2070 Newport Blvd Costa Mesa (92627) ***(P-16512)***
JE Thomson & Company LLC....F....626 334-7190
15206 Ceres Ave Fontana (92335) ***(P-7712)***
Jealous Devil LLC....D....800 446-0135
2629 Manhattan Ave # 214 Hermosa Beach (90254) ***(P-14940)***
Jeanne Jugan, A Residence, San Pedro *Also called Little Ssters of The Poor Los* ***(P-20401)***
Jeannine's Bakery, Santa Barbara *Also called Jeannines Bkg Co Santa Barbara* ***(P-2009)***
Jeannines Bkg Co Santa Barbara (PA)....F....**805 966-1717**
15 E Figueroa St Santa Barbara (93101) ***(P-2009)***
Jeb Holdings Corp (PA)....D....**951 659-2183**
54125 Maranatha Dr Idyllwild (92549) ***(P-13735)***
Jeb Holdings Corp....E....951 296-9900
42033 Rio Nedo Temecula (92590) ***(P-6352)***
Jeb-Phi Inc....E....562 861-0863
10417 Lakewood Blvd Downey (90241) ***(P-4343)***
Jedco Inc....E....949 699-2974
23529 Castle Rock Mission Viejo (92692) ***(P-10593)***
Jeep Chrysler Ddge Ram Ontario, Ontario *Also called Jeep Chrysler of Ontario* ***(P-18843)***
Jeep Chrysler of Ontario....D....909 390-9898
1202 Auto Center Dr Ontario (91761) ***(P-18843)***
Jeep Gear, Irvine *Also called Alcone Marketing Group Inc* ***(P-16992)***
Jeeva Corp....D....909 238-4073
750 E E St Unit B Ontario (91764) ***(P-1269)***
Jeff Carpenter Inc....D....951 657-5115
1380 W Oleander Ave Perris (92571) ***(P-1599)***
Jeffer Mngels Btlr Mtchell LLP (PA)....C....**310 203-8080**
1900 Avenue Of The Stars 7th Los Angeles (90067) ***(P-21591)***
Jeffrey Fabrication LLC....E....562 634-3101
6323 Alondra Blvd Paramount (90723) ***(P-6857)***
Jeffrey Rome & Associates....D....949 760-3929
1715 Port Charles Pl Newport Beach (92660) ***(P-22723)***
Jeffries Global Inc....D....888 255-3488
8484 Wilshire Blvd # 605 Beverly Hills (90211) ***(P-1667)***
Jejomi Designs Inc....F....323 584-4211
2626 Fruitland Ave Vernon (90058) ***(P-3058)***
Jelight Company Inc (PA)....D....**949 380-8774**
2 Mason Irvine (92618) ***(P-13637)***
Jellco Container Inc....D....714 666-2728
1151 N Tustin Ave Anaheim (92807) ***(P-3813)***
Jellypop, Pasadena *Also called Evolution Design Lab Inc* ***(P-5879)***
Jem Sportswear, Cypress *Also called Awake Inc* ***(P-2879)***
Jem Unlimited Iron, Anaheim *Also called Jorge Ulloa* ***(P-11697)***
Jenco Productions Inc (PA)....C....**909 381-9453**
401 S J St San Bernardino (92410) ***(P-18558)***
Jeneric/Pentron Incorporated (HQ)....C....**203 265-7397**
1717 W Collins Ave Orange (92867) ***(P-11178)***
Jennifer Meyer Inc (PA)....E....**310 446-0057**
8491 W Sunset Blvd # 475 West Hollywood (90069) ***(P-11486)***
Jennings Aeronautics LLC....E....805 544-0932
831 Buckley Rd San Luis Obispo (93401) ***(P-10594)***
Jensen Enterprises Inc....B....909 357-7264
14221 San Bernardino Ave Fontana (92335) ***(P-6037)***
Jensen Precast, Fontana *Also called Jensen Enterprises Inc* ***(P-6037)***
Jeopardy Productions Inc....C....310 244-8855
10202 Washington Blvd Culver City (90232) ***(P-19136)***
Jeremys Electric....F....818 249-5656
3009 Honolulu Ave La Crescenta (91214) ***(P-2010)***
Jeremywell International Inc....F....949 588-6888
14 Vanderbilt Irvine (92618) ***(P-8126)***
Jericho Foods, San Fernando *Also called Cousins Foods LLC* ***(P-1886)***
Jerry Bruckheimer Inc....D....310 664-6260
1631 10th St Santa Monica (90404) ***(P-19137)***
Jerry Leigh Entertainment AP, Panorama City *Also called Leigh Jerry California Inc* ***(P-14391)***
Jerry Melton & Sons Cnstr, Taft *Also called Jerry Melton & Sons Cnstr* ***(P-512)***
Jerry Melton & Sons Cnstr....D....661 765-5546
100 Jamison Ln Taft (93268) ***(P-512)***
JES Disc Grinding Inc....F....909 596-3823
2824 Metropolitan Pl Pomona (91767) ***(P-7378)***
Jesse Alexander Transport....D....760 669-0379
9338 Azurite Ave Hesperia (92344) ***(P-12574)***
Jessica Cosmetics Intl Inc....D....818 759-1050
13209 Saticoy St North Hollywood (91605) ***(P-14253)***
Jessica's Cosmetics, North Hollywood *Also called Jessica Cosmetics Intl Inc* ***(P-14253)***
Jessie & Jenna, Gardena *Also called Lily Bleu Inc* ***(P-14393)***
Jessie Lord Bakery LLC....E....310 533-6010
21100 S Western Ave Torrance (90501) ***(P-14697)***
Jesta Digital Entrmt Inc (HQ)....E....**323 648-4200**
15303 Ventura Blvd # 900 Sherman Oaks (91403) ***(P-17898)***
Jet Blue, Long Beach *Also called Jetblue Airways Inc* ***(P-12307)***
Jet Cutting Solutions Inc....E....909 948-2424
10853 Bell Ct Rancho Cucamonga (91730) ***(P-8642)***
Jet Delivery Inc (PA)....D....**800 716-7177**
2169 Wright Ave La Verne (91750) ***(P-12139)***
Jet Edge International LLC (PA)....D....**818 442-0096**
16700 Roscoe Blvd Hngr C Van Nuys (91406) ***(P-12359)***
Jet Fleet International Corp....E....310 440-3820
2370 Westwood Blvd Ste K Los Angeles (90064) ***(P-16960)***
Jet I, Fontana *Also called Jeti Inc* ***(P-18984)***
Jet Manufacturing Inc....D....951 736-9316
13445 Estelle St Corona (92879) ***(P-6858)***
Jet Performance Products Inc....E....714 848-5500
17491 Apex Cir Huntington Beach (92647) ***(P-9824)***
Jet Plastics (PA)....E....**323 268-6706**
941 N Eastern Ave Los Angeles (90063) ***(P-5683)***
Jet Propulsion Laboratory, Pasadena *Also called California Institute Tech* ***(P-22901)***
Jet Sets, North Hollywood *Also called M Gaw Inc* ***(P-1672)***
Jet Transmission, Huntington Beach *Also called Jet Performance Products Inc* ***(P-9824)***
Jet/Brella Inc....E....818 786-5480
6849 Hayvenhurst Ave Van Nuys (91406) ***(P-10219)***
Jetblue Airways Inc....C....562 394-4397
4100 E Donald Douglas Dr Long Beach (90808) ***(P-12307)***
Jetfax, Los Angeles *Also called Efaxcom* ***(P-8252)***
Jeti Inc (PA)....F....**909 357-2966**
14578 Hawthorne Ave Fontana (92335) ***(P-18984)***
Jetro Holdings LLC....C....213 516-0301
1611 E Washington Blvd Los Angeles (90021) ***(P-13462)***
Jetsuite Inc (PA)....C....**949 892-4300**
18952 Macarthur Blvd # 200 Irvine (92612) ***(P-12336)***
Jewel Date Company Inc....E....760 399-4474
48440 Prairie Dr Palm Desert (92260) ***(P-2090)***
Jewelers Security Products (PA)....F....**323 231-0600**
939 E 31st St Los Angeles (90011) ***(P-13994)***
Jewelers Touch....E....714 579-1616
2535 E Imperial Hwy Brea (92821) ***(P-11336)***
Jewelry Exchange, The, Tustin *Also called Diamond Goldenwest Corporation* ***(P-14130)***
Jewish Cmnty Fndn of (PA)....C....**323 761-8700**
6505 Wilshire Blvd Los Angeles (90048) ***(P-22342)***
Jewish Community Ctr Long Bch....C....562 426-7601
3801 E Willow St Long Beach (90815) ***(P-21820)***
Jewish Family and Chld Svc, Long Beach *Also called Jewish Fmly Chld Svc Long Bch-* ***(P-21826)***
Jewish Family Service of....D....818 988-7682
16439 Vanowen St Van Nuys (91406) ***(P-21821)***
Jewish Family Svc Los Angeles....D....323 937-5900
330 N Fairfax Ave Los Angeles (90036) ***(P-21822)***
Jewish Family Svc Los Angeles (PA)....E....**323 761-8800**
330 N Fairfax Ave Los Angeles (90036) ***(P-22271)***
Jewish Family Svc Los Angeles....D....818 984-0276
12821 Victory Blvd North Hollywood (91606) ***(P-21823)***
Jewish Family Svc Los Angeles....D....323 937-5900
330 N Fairfax Ave Los Angeles (90036) ***(P-21824)***
Jewish Family Svc Los Angeles....D....323 935-5303
4311 Wilshire Blvd Los Angeles (90010) ***(P-21825)***
Jewish Fmly Chld Svc Long Bch-....E....562 426-7601
3801 E Willow St Ste 217 Long Beach (90815) ***(P-21826)***
JEWISH FREE LOAN ASSOCIATION, Los Angeles *Also called Jewish Family Svc Los Angeles* ***(P-22271)***
Jewish HM For The Aging Ornge....C....949 364-9685
27356 Bellogente Mission Viejo (92691) ***(P-22120)***
Jewish Journal, The, Los Angeles *Also called Tribe Media Corp* ***(P-4039)***
Jewish Vocational Services (PA)....E....**323 761-8888**
6505 Wilshire Blvd # 200 Los Angeles (90048) ***(P-21957)***
Jezowski & Markel Contrs Inc....C....714 978-2222
749 N Poplar St Orange (92868) ***(P-1532)***
Jf Fixtures & Design, Long Beach *Also called F-J-E Inc* ***(P-3646)***
Jf Fixtures & Design LLC....F....562 437-7466
546 W Esther St Long Beach (90813) ***(P-18559)***
Jf Ready Mix Inc....F....626 818-1204
4038 N Woodgrove Ave Covina (91722) ***(P-6097)***
Jfc International Inc (HQ)....C....**323 721-6100**
7101 E Slauson Ave Commerce (90040) ***(P-14698)***
Jfc International Inc....C....323 721-6900
7101 E Slauson Ave Commerce (90040) ***(P-14699)***
Jfe Shoji America Holdings Inc (HQ)....D....**562 637-3500**
301 E Ocean Blvd Ste 1750 Long Beach (90802) ***(P-13572)***
Jff Uniforms, Torrance *Also called Just For Fun Inc* ***(P-2758)***
Jfp Company, Norco *Also called Anna Corporation* ***(P-1167)***
Jfp Painting....D....951 736-6037
2078 2nd St Norco (92860) ***(P-1185)***
JG Boswell Tomato - Kern LLC....E....661 764-9000
36889 Hwy 58 Buttonwillow (93206) ***(P-1865)***
JG Plastics Group LLC....E....714 751-4266
335 Fischer Ave Costa Mesa (92626) ***(P-5684)***
JGM Automotive Tooling Inc....E....714 895-7001
5355 Industrial Dr Huntington Beach (92649) ***(P-7985)***
Jh Biotech Inc (PA)....E....**805 650-8933**
4951 Olivas Park Dr Ventura (93003) ***(P-5164)***
JH Bryant Jr Inc (PA)....E....**310 532-1840**
17217 S Broadway Gardena (90248) ***(P-703)***
JH Snyder Company....E....323 857-5546
5757 Wilshire Blvd Ph 30 Los Angeles (90036) ***(P-16053)***
Jhawar Industries LLC....E....951 340-4646
525 Klug Cir Corona (92878) ***(P-8092)***
Jhc Investment Inc....D....714 751-2400
7 Hutton Centre Dr Santa Ana (92707) ***(P-16513)***
Jhp Produce Inc....D....213 627-1093
1601 E Olympic Blvd Ste 2 Los Angeles (90021) ***(P-14640)***
Jiffy Lube, Moreno Valley *Also called Bms Investments LLC* ***(P-4801)***
Jiffy Lube, Tustin *Also called Allied Lube Inc* ***(P-18813)***
Jilk Heavy Construction Inc....D....310 830-6323
500 S Kraemer Blvd # 380 Brea (92821) ***(P-1000)***
Jim Burke Ford, Bakersfield *Also called Haberfelde Ford* ***(P-18839)***
Jim Burke Ford, Bakersfield *Also called Haberfelde Ford* ***(P-18840)***
Jim Henson Company Inc (PA)....D....**323 856-6680**
1416 N La Brea Ave Los Angeles (90028) ***(P-19138)***
Jim ONeal Distributing Inc....E....805 426-3300
799 Camarillo Springs Rd Camarillo (93012) ***(P-10494)***
Jim's Machining, Camarillo *Also called Thiessen Products Inc* ***(P-8817)***
Jim-Buoy, North Hollywood *Also called Cal-June Inc* ***(P-6509)***

Employee Codes: A=Over 500 employees, B=251-500
C=101-250, D=51-100, E=20-50 F=10-19
2022 Southern California Business
Directory and Buyers Guide
© Mergent Inc. 1-800-342-5647
1171

Jimenes Food Inc ....E....562 602-2505
7046 Jackson St Paramount (90723) ***(P-2455)***

Jimenez Mexican Foods Inc ....E....951 351-0102
11010 Wells Ave Riverside (92505) ***(P-1851)***

Jimenez Nursery Inc ....D....805 684-7955
3800 Via Real Carpinteria (93013) ***(P-80)***

Jimenez Nursery and Landscapes, Carpinteria *Also called Jimenez Nursery Inc* ***(P-80)***

Jims Steel Supply LLC ....E....661 324-6514
3530 Buck Owens Blvd Bakersfield (93308) ***(P-23250)***

Jims Supply Co Inc (PA) ....**D....661 616-6977**
3500 Buck Owens Blvd Bakersfield (93308) ***(P-13573)***

Jimway Inc ....D....310 886-3718
20101 S Santa Fe Ave Compton (90221) ***(P-9136)***

Jinelle, Los Angeles *Also called Rose Genuine Inc* ***(P-3036)***

Jipc Management Inc ....A....949 916-2000
22342 Avnida Empresa Ste Rancho Santa Margari (92688) ***(P-23042)***

JIT Corporation ....D....805 238-5000
2790 Valley View Ave Norco (92860) ***(P-13736)***

JIT Manufacturing Inc ....E....805 238-5000
1610 Commerce Way Paso Robles (93446) ***(P-10998)***

Jit Video Game, Hacienda Heights *Also called Joy International Trading Inc* ***(P-11381)***

Jj Acquisitions LLC ....E....818 772-0100
8501 Fllbrook Ave Ste 370 West Hills (91304) ***(P-5385)***

Jj Fisher Construction Inc ....D....805 723-5220
261 W Dana St Ste 100 Nipomo (93444) ***(P-893)***

JJ Mac Intyre Co Inc (PA) ....**C....951 898-4300**
4160 Temescal Canyon Rd Corona (92883) ***(P-17114)***

Jk Imaging Ltd ....D....310 755-6848
17239 S Main St Gardena (90248) ***(P-13346)***

JKB Corporation ....E....562 905-3477
561 S Walnut St La Habra (90631) ***(P-1533)***

JKL Components Corporation ....E....818 896-0019
13343 Paxton St Pacoima (91331) ***(P-9116)***

Jkv Inc ....E....562 948-3000
8343 Loch Lomond Dr Pico Rivera (90660) ***(P-3814)***

Jl Design Enterprises Inc ....D....714 479-0240
1451 Edinger Ave Ste C Tustin (92780) ***(P-2757)***

Jl Racing.com, Tustin *Also called Jl Design Enterprises Inc* ***(P-2757)***

Jlcooper, El Segundo *Also called J L Cooper Electronics Inc* ***(P-9732)***

Jlg Industries Inc ....C....951 358-1915
7820 Lincoln Ave Riverside (92504) ***(P-7645)***

Jlg Serviceplus, Riverside *Also called Jlg Industries Inc* ***(P-7645)***

Jlm & Mag Associates Inc ....D....562 869-3343
9204 Lakewood Blvd Downey (90240) ***(P-16906)***

JM Eagle, Los Angeles *Also called J-M Manufacturing Company Inc* ***(P-7447)***

JM Eagle, Los Angeles *Also called Pw Eagle Inc* ***(P-5470)***

JM Huber Micropowders Inc ....E....714 994-7855
16024 Phoebe Ave La Mirada (90638) ***(P-4660)***

JM Roofing Company Inc ....D....805 966-3696
534 E Ortega St Santa Barbara (93103) ***(P-1491)***

Jmac Lending Inc ....D....949 390-2688
2510 Redhill Ave Santa Ana (92705) ***(P-15205)***

Jmbm, Los Angeles *Also called Jeffer Mngels Btlr Mtchell LLP* ***(P-21591)***

Jme Inc (PA) ....**D....201 896-8600**
527 Park Ave San Fernando (91340) ***(P-13638)***

Jmg Investments Inc ....D....818 519-0670
23041 Hatteras St Woodland Hills (91367) ***(P-16271)***

Jmg Machine Inc ....E....714 522-6221
17037 Industry Pl La Mirada (90638) ***(P-8643)***

Jmg Security Systems Inc ....D....714 545-8882
17150 Newhope St Ste 109 Fountain Valley (92708) ***(P-1270)***

JMI Steel Inc ....E....818 768-3955
8983 San Fernando Rd Sun Valley (91352) ***(P-6967)***

JMJ Enterprises Inc ....C....818 343-5151
5973 Reseda Blvd Tarzana (91356) ***(P-16961)***

JMJ Financial Group (PA) ....**E....949 340-6336**
26800 Aliso Viejo Pkwy # 200 Aliso Viejo (92656) ***(P-15206)***

Jml Textile Inc ....E....323 584-2323
5801 S 2nd St Vernon (90058) ***(P-2577)***

Jmp Electronics Inc ....E....714 730-2086
2685 Dow Ave Ste A1 Tustin (92780) ***(P-9418)***

Jnj Operations LLC ....E....855 525-6545
859 E Sepulveda Blvd Carson (90745) ***(P-11695)***

Jnr Inc ....D....949 476-2788
19900 Macarthur Blvd # 700 Irvine (92612) ***(P-23251)***

Jns Industries Inc ....F....909 923-8334
2322 S Vineyard Ave Ste C Ontario (91761) ***(P-8644)***

Jo's Candies, Torrance *Also called Manhattan Confectioners Inc* ***(P-2095)***

Joa Corporation (PA) ....**F....951 785-4411**
7254 Magnolia Ave Riverside (92504) ***(P-11118)***

Joan Baker Designs Inc ....E....949 498-1983
1130 Via Callejon San Clemente (92673) ***(P-14941)***

Joan Kroc Center, Mission Viejo *Also called St Vincent De Paul Vlg Inc* ***(P-22464)***

Joan Young Co Realtors, Westlake Village *Also called Young Realtors* ***(P-16036)***

Joanka Inc ....F....310 326-8940
25510 Frampton Ave Harbor City (90710) ***(P-6703)***

Job Options Incorporated ....A....909 890-4612
1110 S Washington Ave San Bernardino (92408) ***(P-16891)***

Job Shop Managers, Valencia *Also called Skm Industries Inc* ***(P-7182)***

Jobar International Inc ....D....310 222-8682
21022 Figueroa St Carson (90745) ***(P-14942)***

Jobsite Stud Welding ....F....855 885-7883
9445 Washburn Rd Downey (90242) ***(P-18985)***

Jocer Enterprises Inc ....E....909 822-0500
14600 Whittram Ave Fontana (92335) ***(P-775)***

Jodi Kristopher LLC (PA) ....**C....323 890-8000**
1950 Naomi Ave Los Angeles (90011) ***(P-2889)***

Jody of California, Los Angeles *Also called Private Brand Mdsg Corp* ***(P-2895)***

Joe Blasco Cosmetics, Palm Springs *Also called Joe Blasco Enterprises Inc* ***(P-11696)***

Joe Blasco Enterprises Inc ....E....323 467-4949
1285 N Valdivia Way A Palm Springs (92262) ***(P-11696)***

Joe Heger Farms LLC ....C....760 353-5111
1625 Drew Rd El Centro (92243) ***(P-113)***

Joe's Auto Parks, Los Angeles *Also called L and R Auto Parks Inc* ***(P-18767)***

Joe's Dsert Hlls Prmium Otlets, Cabazon *Also called Centric Brands Inc* ***(P-2562)***

Joe's Jeans, Los Angeles *Also called Centric Brands Inc* ***(P-2563)***

Joerns LLC (HQ) ....**C....800 966-6662**
19748 Dearborn St Chatsworth (91311) ***(P-13497)***

Joes Plastics, Vernon *Also called Joes Plastics Inc* ***(P-4699)***

Joes Plastics Inc ....E....323 771-8433
5725 District Blvd Vernon (90058) ***(P-4699)***

Joes Sweeping Inc ....D....562 929-4344
11914 Front St Norwalk (90650) ***(P-12954)***

Johanson Dielectrics Inc (HQ) ....**C....805 389-1166**
4001 Calle Tecate Camarillo (93012) ***(P-9611)***

Johanson Technology Inc ....C....805 389-1166
4001 Calle Tecate Camarillo (93012) ***(P-9612)***

Johasee Rebar Inc ....E....661 589-0972
26365 Earthmover Cir Corona (92883) ***(P-6625)***

John A Martin & Associates Inc ....D....213 483-6490
950 S Grand Ave Ste 400 Los Angeles (90015) ***(P-22590)***

John Bishop Design Inc ....E....714 744-2300
731 N Main St Orange (92868) ***(P-11563)***

John Chapman Inc ....E....661 212-5053
21648 Nutmeg Ln Santa Clarita (91350) ***(P-18560)***

John Currie Performance Group ....E....714 367-1580
1592 Jenks Dr Corona (92878) ***(P-7986)***

John Deere Authorized Dealer, City of Industry *Also called Valley Power Systems Inc* ***(P-13957)***

John Deere Authorized Dealer, Colton *Also called A-Z Bus Sales Inc* ***(P-13016)***

John Deere Authorized Dealer, Riverside *Also called Complete Coach Works* ***(P-18923)***

John Deere Authorized Dealer, Carson *Also called Buswest LLC* ***(P-11905)***

John F Kennedy Mem Hosp Aux ....A....760 347-6191
47111 Monroe St Indio (92201) ***(P-20799)***

John F Knnedy Mem Hosp Emrgncy, Indio *Also called John F Kennedy Mem Hosp Aux* ***(P-20799)***

John Hancock, Irvine *Also called Signature Rsrces Insur Fncl Sv* ***(P-15628)***

John Hancock Life Insur Co USA (HQ) ....**A....213 689-0813**
865 S Figueroa St # 3320 Los Angeles (90017) ***(P-15585)***

John Hancock Life Insur Co USA ....A....949 254-1440
5000 Birch St Ste 120 Newport Beach (92660) ***(P-15363)***

John Henry Foundation ....D....714 554-8906
403 N Susan St Santa Ana (92703) ***(P-21827)***

John J Ohara MD A Medical Corp ....D....310 316-7095
23456 Hawthorne Blvd # 300 Torrance (90505) ***(P-19857)***

John Jory Corporation (PA) ....**B....714 279-7901**
2180 N Glassell St Orange (92865) ***(P-1383)***

John Kenney Construction Inc ....D....805 884-1579
619 E Montecito St Santa Barbara (93103) ***(P-1534)***

John L Conley Inc ....D....909 627-0981
4344 Mission Blvd Montclair (91763) ***(P-6999)***

John List Corporation ....E....818 882-7848
9732 Cozycroft Ave Chatsworth (91311) ***(P-7885)***

John M Frank Construction Inc ....D....714 210-3600
913 E 4th St Santa Ana (92701) ***(P-776)***

John M Frank Service Group, Santa Ana *Also called John M Frank Construction Inc* ***(P-776)***

John M Phillips LLC ....E....661 327-3118
2800 Gibson St Bakersfield (93308) ***(P-513)***

John M Phillips Oil Field Eqp, Bakersfield *Also called John M Phillips LLC* ***(P-513)***

John S Carter Inc ....F....805 962-5889
1102 Highland Rd Santa Ynez (93460) ***(P-1668)***

John Stewart Company ....E....213 787-2700
888 S Figueroa St Ste 700 Los Angeles (90017) ***(P-15897)***

John Tillman Company, Compton *Also called Blake H Brown Inc* ***(P-13891)***

John Wayne Airport, Costa Mesa *Also called County of Orange* ***(P-12353)***

John's Incredible Pizza Co, Rancho Santa Margari *Also called Jipc Management Inc* ***(P-23042)***

Johnny Was ....F....310 656-0600
395 Santa Monica Pl # 124 Santa Monica (90401) ***(P-14384)***

Johnny Was (PA) ....**E....949 219-0557**
903 Newport Center Dr Newport Beach (92660) ***(P-14385)***

Johnny Was LLC (PA) ....**C....323 582-1005**
2423 E 23rd St Los Angeles (90058) ***(P-14386)***

Johnny Was Showroom, Los Angeles *Also called Jwc Studio Inc* ***(P-2890)***

Johnre Care LLC ....D....951 658-6374
461 E Johnston Ave Hemet (92543) ***(P-20383)***

Johnson & Johnson ....B....909 839-8650
15715 Arrow Hwy Irwindale (91706) ***(P-11119)***

Johnson & Johnson Vision, Santa Ana *Also called Johnson Jhnson Srgcal Vsion In* ***(P-11225)***

Johnson & Turner Painting Co ....E....714 828-8282
8241 Electric Ave Stanton (90680) ***(P-1186)***

Johnson Caldraul Inc ....E....951 340-1067
220 N Delilah St Ste 101 Corona (92879) ***(P-10361)***

Johnson Controls ....C....562 405-3817
12728 Shoemaker Ave Santa Fe Springs (90670) ***(P-18389)***

Johnson doc Enterprises ....E....818 764-1543
11933 Vose St North Hollywood (91605) ***(P-5685)***

Johnson Fain Inc ....D....323 224-6000
1201 N Broadway Los Angeles (90012) ***(P-22724)***

Johnson Ford (PA) ....**C....888 483-0454**
1155 Auto Mall Dr Lancaster (93534) ***(P-18844)***

Johnson Jhnson Srgcal Vsion In (HQ) ....**B....714 247-8200**
1700 E Saint Andrew Pl Santa Ana (92705) ***(P-11225)***

Mergent e-mail: customerrelations@mergent.com
1172
2022 Southern California Business Directory and Buyers Guide
(P-0000) Products & Services Section entry number
(PA)=Parent Co (HQ)=Headquarters (DH)=Div Headquarters

Johnson Laminating Coating Inc......D......310 635-4929
20631 Annalee Ave Carson (90746) ***(P-5451)***
Johnson Machinery Co (PA)......**C......951 686-4560**
800 E La Cadena Dr Riverside (92507) ***(P-13863)***
Johnson Manufacturing Inc......E......714 903-0393
15201 Connector Ln Huntington Beach (92649) ***(P-8645)***
Johnson Precision Products Inc......F......714 824-6971
1308 E Wakeham Ave Santa Ana (92705) ***(P-8646)***
Johnson Racing, Santa Maria *Also called Alan Johnson Prfmce Engrg Inc* ***(P-9932)***
Johnson Safety Inc......F......909 796-3385
3404 De Forest Cir Jurupa Valley (91752) ***(P-14165)***
Johnson Wilshire, City of Industry *Also called Austin Pang Glv Mfg USA Corp* ***(P-14146)***
Johnsons Orthopedic, Riverside *Also called Joa Corporation* ***(P-11118)***
Johnston Farms Fmly Ltd Partnr......D......661 366-3201
13031 E Packinghouse Rd Edison (93220) ***(P-64)***
Johnston Vacuum Tank Service, Taft *Also called Watkins Construction Co Inc* ***(P-985)***
Joico Laboratories Inc......D......626 321-4100
5800 Bristol Pkwy Culver City (90230) ***(P-5035)***
JOINT POWERS AGENCY, Irvine *Also called San Jquin Hlls Trnsp Crrdor AG* ***(P-912)***
Jolly Roger Games, Commerce *Also called Ultra Pro International LLC* ***(P-4614)***
Jolly Roger Inn, Anaheim *Also called Edward Thomas Companies* ***(P-16426)***
Jolyn Clothing Company LLC......E......714 794-2149
150 5th St Ste 100 Huntington Beach (92648) ***(P-2959)***
Jomar Industries Inc......E......323 770-0505
1500 W 139th St Gardena (90249) ***(P-18561)***
Jon Brooks Inc (PA)......**D......626 330-0631**
14400 Lomitas Ave City of Industry (91746) ***(P-6167)***
Jon Davler Inc......E......626 941-6558
9440 Gidley St Temple City (91780) ***(P-5036)***
Jon Steel Erectors Inc......E......909 799-0005
1431 S Gage St San Bernardino (92408) ***(P-18986)***
Jon-Lin Foods, Colton *Also called Jon-Lin Frozen Foods* ***(P-14524)***
Jon-Lin Frozen Foods (PA)......**C......909 825-8542**
1620 N 8th St Colton (92324) ***(P-14524)***
Jonathan Beach Club, Santa Monica *Also called Jonathan Club* ***(P-19572)***
Jonathan Club (PA)......**C......213 624-0881**
545 S Figueroa St Los Angeles (90071) ***(P-22343)***
Jonathan Club......D......310 393-9245
850 Palisades Beach Rd Santa Monica (90403) ***(P-19572)***
Jonathan Engnred Slutions Corp (HQ)......**E......714 665-4400**
250 Commerce Ste 100 Irvine (92602) ***(P-6522)***
Jonathan Louis International......D......323 770-3330
12919 S Figueroa St Los Angeles (90061) ***(P-3530)***
Jonathan Martin, Los Angeles *Also called Harkham Industries Inc* ***(P-2846)***
Jonbec Care Incorporated (PA)......**D......909 798-4003**
1711 Plum Ln Redlands (92374) ***(P-20533)***
Jondo Ltd (PA)......**D......714 279-2300**
22700 Savi Ranch Pkwy Yorba Linda (92887) ***(P-11280)***
Jonel Engineering......E......714 879-2360
500 E Walnut Ave Fullerton (92832) ***(P-8448)***
Jones Bold Security Inc......D......323 800-2542
1611 S Catalina Ave L50 Redondo Beach (90277) ***(P-18291)***
Jones Brothers Cnstr Corp (PA)......**D......310 470-1885**
1601 Cloverfield Blvd Santa Monica (90404) ***(P-777)***
Jones Covey Group, Rancho Cucamonga *Also called Jones/Covey Group Incorporated* ***(P-1669)***
Jones Day Limited Partnership......D......949 851-3939
3161 Michelson Dr Ste 800 Irvine (92612) ***(P-21592)***
Jones Iron Works......F......323 386-2368
2658 Griffith Park Blvd Los Angeles (90039) ***(P-6968)***
Jones/Covey Group Incorporated......D......888 972-7581
9595 Lucas Ranch Rd # 100 Rancho Cucamonga (91730) ***(P-1669)***
Jong S Yoon Dmd Inc (PA)......**D......213 383-0010**
520 S Virgil Ave Ste 101 Los Angeles (90020) ***(P-20184)***
Joni and Friends Foundation (PA)......**D......818 707-5664**
30009 Ladyface Ct Agoura (91301) ***(P-21828)***
Jonset Corporation......D......949 551-5151
16251 Construction Cir W Irvine (92606) ***(P-13007)***
Joong-Ang Daily News Cal Inc (HQ)......**C......213 368-2500**
690 Wilshire Pl Los Angeles (90005) ***(P-3998)***
Joong-Ang Daily News Cal Inc......D......213 487-2355
2880 W Olympic Blvd Ste 2 Los Angeles (90006) ***(P-21108)***
Joor Bros Metal Supply, Corona *Also called Joor Bros Welding Inc* ***(P-13574)***
Joor Bros Welding Inc......F......951 737-3950
2818 Garretson Ave Corona (92881) ***(P-13574)***
Jordan - Link & Company (PA)......**D......559 733-9696**
2009 W Feemster Ave Visalia (93277) ***(P-15898)***
Jordana Cosmetics LLC......D......310 730-4400
2035 E 49th St Vernon (90058) ***(P-14254)***
Jordano's Food Service, Santa Barbara *Also called Jordanos Inc* ***(P-14829)***
Jordanos Inc (PA)......**C......805 964-0611**
550 S Patterson Ave Santa Barbara (93111) ***(P-14829)***
Jorge Ulloa......F......714 630-0499
3162 E La Palma Ave Ste F Anaheim (92806) ***(P-11697)***
Jos Candies LLC......F......800 770-1946
2530 W 237th St Torrance (90505) ***(P-14563)***
Joseph C Sansone Company (PA)......**D......818 226-3400**
21300 Victory Blvd # 300 Woodland Hills (91367) ***(P-21593)***
Joseph Company Intl Inc......E......949 474-2200
1711 Langley Ave Irvine (92614) ***(P-6464)***
Joshua Tree Memorial Park......E......760 366-9210
6021 Twentynine Palms Hwy Joshua Tree (92252) ***(P-16086)***
Joslyn Sunbank Company LLC......B......805 238-2840
1740 Commerce Way Paso Robles (93446) ***(P-9659)***
Joy International Trading Inc......F......626 736-5987
2440 S Hcnda Blvd Ste 219 Hacienda Heights (91745) ***(P-11381)***
Joy Processed Foods Inc......F......562 435-1106
1330 Seabright Ave Long Beach (90813) ***(P-2456)***
Joy Products California Inc......E......714 437-7250
17281 Mount Wynne Cir Fountain Valley (92708) ***(P-11472)***
Joybird, Commerce *Also called Stitch Industries Inc* ***(P-3519)***
JP Allen Inc......B......818 841-4770
150 E Angeleno Ave Burbank (91502) ***(P-16514)***
JP Allen Extended Stay......E......818 841-4770
150 E Angeleno Ave Burbank (91502) ***(P-16515)***
JP Allen Extended Stay (PA)......**D......818 956-0202**
450 Pioneer Dr Glendale (91203) ***(P-16516)***
JP Crown House Dental Lab Inc (PA)......**D......714 323-8555**
6481 Orangethorpe Ave # 8 Buena Park (90620) ***(P-21109)***
JP Motorsports Inc......D......818 381-8313
11582 Sheldon St Sun Valley (91352) ***(P-12575)***
JP Products LLC......E......310 237-6237
2054 Davie Ave Commerce (90040) ***(P-3474)***
JP Weaver & Company......E......818 500-1740
941 Air Way Glendale (91201) ***(P-6181)***
Jpi Development Group Inc......D......951 973-7680
41205 Golden Gate Cir Murrieta (92562) ***(P-1087)***
Jpl Management LLC......D......310 844-3662
6427 W Sunset Blvd 101 Los Angeles (90028) ***(P-23043)***
Jpm Finishing Company, Hesperia *Also called Daytec Center LLC* ***(P-10489)***
Jpm Industries Inc......E......909 592-2292
13326 Elliot Ave Chino (91710) ***(P-615)***
JR Machine Company Inc......E......562 903-9477
13245 Florence Ave Santa Fe Springs (90670) ***(P-8647)***
Jr286 Inc (PA)......**F......877 464-5301**
20100 S Vermont Ave Torrance (90502) ***(P-11431)***
Jri Inc......E......818 706-2424
31280 La Baya Dr Westlake Village (91362) ***(P-13737)***
Jrw Research & Consulting Inc......E......877 579-1031
1055 E Colo Blvd Ste 310 Pasadena (91106) ***(P-23458)***
Js Apparel Inc......D......310 631-6333
1751 E Del Amo Blvd Carson (90746) ***(P-2815)***
JS Held LLC......D......949 390-7647
4667 Macarthur Blvd # 400 Newport Beach (92660) ***(P-22795)***
Jsl Foods Inc (PA)......**C......323 223-2484**
3550 Pasadena Ave Los Angeles (90031) ***(P-2457)***
Jsl Technologies Inc......B......805 985-7700
1451 N Rice Ave Ste A Oxnard (93030) ***(P-22591)***
Jsm Productions Inc......F......951 929-5771
537 E Florida Ave Hemet (92543) ***(P-4344)***
Jsn Industries Inc......D......949 458-0050
9700 Jeronimo Rd Irvine (92618) ***(P-5686)***
Jsn Packaging Products Inc......D......949 458-0050
9700 Jeronimo Rd Irvine (92618) ***(P-5445)***
Jsp, Los Angeles *Also called Jewelers Security Products* ***(P-13994)***
JT Design Studio Inc (PA)......**E......213 891-1500**
860 S Los Angeles St # 912 Los Angeles (90014) ***(P-2960)***
Jt Resources......C......661 367-6827
26372 Ruether Ave Santa Clarita (91350) ***(P-17431)***
JT Wimsatt Contg Co Inc (PA)......**B......661 775-8090**
28064 Avenue Stanford B Valencia (91355) ***(P-1535)***
Jt Windows Inc......E......818 709-7950
9261 Independence Ave Chatsworth (91311) ***(P-1444)***
Jt3 LLC......C......661 277-4900
190 S Wolfe Ave Bldg 1260 Edwards (93524) ***(P-22592)***
Jtb Americas Ltd (HQ)......**D......310 406-3121**
19700 Mariner Ave Torrance (90503) ***(P-12391)***
Jtb Supply Company Inc......D......714 639-9558
1030 N Batavia St Ste A Orange (92867) ***(P-9345)***
Jts Modular Inc......E......661 835-9270
7001 Mcdivitt Dr Ste B Bakersfield (93313) ***(P-7000)***
Ju-Ju-Be Intl LLC......E......877 258-5823
35 Argonaut Ste B2 Aliso Viejo (92656) ***(P-3128)***
Juanitas Foods......C......310 834-5339
645 N Eubank Ave Wilmington (90744) ***(P-1852)***
Judith Von Hopf Inc......E......909 481-1884
1525 W 13th St Ste H Upland (91786) ***(P-3654)***
Judy Ann, Culver City *Also called Fortune Casuals LLC* ***(P-2843)***
Judy O Productions Inc......E......323 938-8513
4858 W Pico Blvd Ste 331 Los Angeles (90019) ***(P-4132)***
Juengermann Inc......E......805 644-7165
1899 Palma Dr Ste A Ventura (93003) ***(P-7464)***
Juice Division, Pacoima *Also called American Fruits & Flavors LLC* ***(P-2306)***
Juicy Couture Inc......C......888 824-8826
1580 Jesse St Los Angeles (90021) ***(P-2600)***
Juicy Whip Inc......E......909 392-7500
1668 Curtiss Ct La Verne (91750) ***(P-7941)***
Jujube, Aliso Viejo *Also called Ju-Ju-Be Intl LLC* ***(P-3128)***
Jukin Media Inc (HQ)......**C......323 932-0960**
5764 W Jefferson Blvd Los Angeles (90016) ***(P-19319)***
Jules and Associates Inc......D......213 362-5600
515 S Figueroa St # 1900 Los Angeles (90071) ***(P-17359)***
Julio Gonzalez......D......310 310-4055
1417 S Fairfax Ave Apt 4 Los Angeles (90019) ***(P-23459)***
Julius Steve Construction Inc......E......949 369-7820
230 Calle Pintoresco San Clemente (92672) ***(P-704)***
Jump Start Juice Bar......F......949 754-3120
8001 Irvine Center Dr # 40 Irvine (92618) ***(P-1902)***
Jumpstart Games Inc......D......424 645-4311
830 S Pcf Cast Hwy Ste 20 El Segundo (90245) ***(P-17647)***
Jumpstart Juice, Irvine *Also called Jump Start Juice Bar* ***(P-1902)***
June A Grothe Construction Inc......D......909 993-9393
15632 El Prado Rd Chino (91710) ***(P-778)***
Jungle Jumps, Pacoima *Also called Twin Peak Industries Inc* ***(P-11454)***
Juniper Networks Inc......D......805 880-2000
6868 Cortona Dr Ste C Goleta (93117) ***(P-18041)***

ALPHABETIC

Employee Codes: A=Over 500 employees, B=251-500
C=101-250, D=51-100, E=20-50 F=10-19
2022 Southern California Business
Directory and Buyers Guide
© Mergent Inc. 1-800-342-5647
1173

Juniper Rock Corporation ....E....949 500-1797
26000 Commercentre Dr Lake Forest (92630) *(P-564)*
Juntee of California Inc ....E....213 742-0246
1031 S Broadway Rm 327 Los Angeles (90015) *(P-2849)*
Jupiter Holding I Corp (HQ) ....**E....909 606-1416**
13925 City Center Dr # 200 Chino Hills (91709) *(P-14082)*
Jurlique Hlistic Skin Care Inc (PA) ....E....914 998-8800
234 E Colo Blvd Ste 450 Pasadena (91101) *(P-19452)*
Jurupa Community Services Dst ....D....951 685-7073
11201 Harrel St Riverside (92509) *(P-12896)*
Jurupa Hills Post Acute, Riverside *Also called Mt Rubidouxidence Opco LLC (P-20422)*
Jurupa Unified School District ....D....951 222-7756
Riverside Ca 92509 Riverside (92509) *(P-18845)*
Just For Fun Inc ....E....310 320-1327
557 Van Ness Ave Torrance (90501) *(P-2758)*
Just For Wraps Inc (PA) ....C....213 239-0503
4871 S Santa Fe Ave Vernon (90058) *(P-2961)*
Just Off Melrose Inc ....E....714 533-4566
1196 Montalvo Way Palm Springs (92262) *(P-2066)*
Justenough Software Corp Inc (HQ) ....E....949 706-5400
15440 Laguna Canyon Rd # 100 Irvine (92618) *(P-17899)*
Justice Bros Dist Co Inc ....E....626 359-9174
2734 Huntington Dr Duarte (91010) *(P-4985)*
Justice Bros-J B Car Care Pdts, Duarte *Also called Justice Bros Dist Co Inc (P-4985)*
Justice Design Group LLC (PA) ....E....213 437-0102
500 S Grand Ave Ste 1100 Los Angeles (90071) *(P-13639)*
Justin Inc ....E....626 444-4516
2663 Lee Ave El Monte (91733) *(P-8876)*
Justin Vineyards & Winery LLC (HQ) ....**E....805 238-6932**
11680 Chimney Rock Rd Paso Robles (93446) *(P-2199)*
Justman Packaging & Display ....D....323 728-8888
5819 Telegraph Rd Commerce (90040) *(P-13463)*
Juvenile Justice Division Cal ....C....805 485-7951
3100 Wright Rd Camarillo (93010) *(P-23044)*
Jvac Inc ....D....559 584-5531
1073 Cadillac Ln Hanford (93230) *(P-18846)*
Jvckenwood USA Corporation (HQ) ....C....310 639-9000
2201 E Dominguez St Long Beach (90810) *(P-13738)*
Jvr Sheetmetal Fabrication Inc ....E....714 841-2464
7101 Patterson Dr Garden Grove (92841) *(P-10192)*
JVSLA, Los Angeles *Also called Jewish Vocational Services (P-21957)*
JW Manufacturing Inc ....E....805 498-4594
12989 Bradley Ave Sylmar (91342) *(P-7069)*
JW Marriott Le Merigot, Santa Monica *Also called C W Hotels Ltd (P-16363)*
JW Marrott Dsert Sprng Rsort S, Palm Desert *Also called Host Hotels & Resorts LP (P-16491)*
JW Molding Inc ....F....805 499-2682
2523 Calcite Cir Newbury Park (91320) *(P-7809)*
Jwc Carbide Inc ....F....714 540-8870
33700 Calle Vis Temecula (92592) *(P-7734)*
Jwc Environmental Inc ....D....714 662-5829
2600 S Garnsey St Santa Ana (92707) *(P-8390)*
Jwc Environmental Inc (HQ) ....**E....949 833-3888**
2850 Redhill Ave Ste 125 Santa Ana (92705) *(P-13908)*
Jwc Studio Inc (PA) ....E....323 231-8222
2423 E 23rd St Los Angeles (90058) *(P-2890)*
Jwch Institute Inc ....B....562 867-7999
14371 Clark Ave Bellflower (90706) *(P-21445)*
Jwch Institute Inc ....C....323 562-5813
6912 Ajax Ave Bell (90201) *(P-22911)*
Jwch Institute Inc ....C....562 281-0306
12360 Firestone Blvd Norwalk (90650) *(P-22912)*
Jwch Institute Inc ....C....310 223-1035
3591 E Imperial Hwy Lynwood (90262) *(P-21829)*
Jwch Medical Center, Lynwood *Also called Jwch Institute Inc (P-21829)*
JWdangelo Company Inc ....E....562 690-1000
601 S Harbor Blvd La Habra (90631) *(P-14039)*
Jwmcc Limited Partnership ....D....310 277-1234
2151 Avenue Of The Stars Los Angeles (90067) *(P-16517)*
Jxp Tech Inc ....F....714 723-0696
6950 Aragon Cir Ste 6 Buena Park (90620) *(P-13739)*
Jynormus LLC ....F....949 436-2112
19800 Macarthur Blvd 3 Irvine (92612) *(P-12652)*
K & D Contracting, Diamond Bar *Also called Dynamic Woodworks Inc (P-3247)*
K & D Graphics ....E....714 639-8900
1432 N Main St Ste C Orange (92867) *(P-3899)*
K & D Graphics Prtg & Packg, Orange *Also called K & D Graphics (P-3899)*
K & E Printing Ink, La Verne *Also called Farbotech Color Inc (P-5202)*
K & G Latirovian Inc (PA) ....E....818 319-2862
8277 Lankershim Blvd North Hollywood (91605) *(P-10083)*
K & J Wire Products Corp ....E....714 816-0360
1220 N Lance Ln Anaheim (92806) *(P-6969)*
K & M Meat Co, Vernon *Also called K & M Packing Co Inc (P-1714)*
K & M Packing Co Inc ....E....323 585-5318
2443 E 27th St Vernon (90058) *(P-1714)*
K & N Engineering Inc (PA) ....**A....951 826-4000**
1455 Citrus St Riverside (92507) *(P-10495)*
K & P Janitorial Services ....D....310 540-8878
412 S Pcf Cast Hwy Ste 20 Redondo Beach (90277) *(P-17255)*
K & S Air Conditioning Inc ....C....714 685-0077
143 E Meats Ave Orange (92865) *(P-1088)*
K & S Enterprises, Adelanto *Also called Dar-Ken Inc (P-5335)*
K & W Manufacturing Co Inc ....E....951 277-3300
23107 Temescal Canyon Rd Corona (92883) *(P-6523)*
K & Z Cabinet Co Inc ....D....909 947-3567
1450 S Grove Ave Ontario (91761) *(P-3321)*
K B I, Anaheim *Also called Kinsbursky Bros Supply Inc (P-14118)*
K C C, El Segundo *Also called Carson Kurtzman Consultants (P-21528)*

K C Hilites Inc ....E....928 635-2607
13637 Cimarron Ave Gardena (90249) *(P-9117)*
K C Restoration Co Inc ....E....310 280-0597
1514 W 130th St Gardena (90249) *(P-514)*
K C Welding Inc ....F....760 352-3832
1549 Dogwood Rd El Centro (92243) *(P-18987)*
K Ceniceros Community Center, Sun City *Also called Family Service Association (P-21785)*
K E, Irvine *Also called Kite Electric Inc (P-1272)*
K G S Electronics, Arcadia *Also called Gar Enterprises (P-13398)*
K Hovnanian, Irvine *Also called K Hovnanian Companies Cal Inc (P-616)*
K Hovnanian Companies Cal Inc (HQ) ....D....714 368-4500
400 Exchange Ste 200 Irvine (92602) *(P-616)*
K I S Computer Center, Hacienda Heights *Also called Able Microsystems Corporation (P-18016)*
K M I, Dana Point *Also called Kanstul Musical Instrs Inc (P-11345)*
K Metal Products Inc ....C....562 693-5425
11935 Baker Pl Santa Fe Springs (90670) *(P-7503)*
K P F F Consulting Engineers, Los Angeles *Also called Kpff Inc (P-22597)*
K S Designs Inc ....E....562 929-3973
9515 Sorensen Ave Santa Fe Springs (90670) *(P-11564)*
K S Fabrication & Machine Inc ....C....661 617-1700
6205 District Blvd Bakersfield (93313) *(P-958)*
K S I, Bakersfield *Also called KS Industries LP (P-960)*
K S Printing Inc ....F....951 268-5180
710 E Parkridge Ave # 105 Corona (92879) *(P-4345)*
K S S C - F M, Los Angeles *Also called Entravsion Communications Corp (P-12716)*
K Squared Metals, Lake Elsinore *Also called Boozak Inc (P-6797)*
K T Lucky Co Inc ....D....626 579-7272
10925 Schmidt Rd El Monte (91733) *(P-14700)*
K Too ....E....213 747-7766
800 E 12th St Ste 117 Los Angeles (90021) *(P-2850)*
K Wave 1079 ....D....714 918-6207
3000 W Macarthur Blvd # 50 Santa Ana (92704) *(P-12696)*
K&B Electric LLC ....C....951 808-9501
290 Corporate Terrace Cir # 200 Corona (92879) *(P-22593)*
K&B Engineering, Corona *Also called K&B Electric LLC (P-22593)*
K&B Engineering ....C....951 808-9501
290 Corporate Terrace Cir Corona (92879) *(P-22594)*
K&N, Riverside *Also called K & N Engineering Inc (P-10495)*
K&S, Orange *Also called K & S Air Conditioning Inc (P-1088)*
K-1 Packaging Group (PA) ....**C....626 964-9384**
17989 Arenth Ave City of Industry (91748) *(P-4346)*
K-Cal Group Inc (PA) ....**F....626 922-1103**
7171 Talasi Dr Corona Eastvale (92880) *(P-1819)*
K-Max Health Products Corp ....E....909 455-0158
1468 E Mission Blvd Pomona (91766) *(P-4836)*
K-Max Health Products Internat ....F....909 455-0158
1468 E Mission Blvd Pomona (91766) *(P-1796)*
K-Micro Inc ....D....310 442-3200
1618 Stanford St Santa Monica (90404) *(P-13411)*
K-P Engineering Corp ....E....714 545-7045
2126 S Lyon St Ste A Santa Ana (92705) *(P-8648)*
K-Swiss Inc (HQ) ....**B....323 675-2700**
523 W 6th St Ste 534 Los Angeles (90014) *(P-5309)*
K-Swiss Sales Corp ....D....818 706-5100
31248 Oak Crest Dr # 200 Westlake Village (91361) *(P-5310)*
K-Too, Los Angeles *Also called K Too (P-2850)*
K-Tops Plastic Mfg Inc ....E....626 575-9679
15051 Don Julian Rd City of Industry (91746) *(P-11698)*
K-V Engineering Inc ....D....714 229-9977
2411 W 1st St Santa Ana (92703) *(P-7735)*
K.G.S.electronics, Upland *Also called Gar Enterprises (P-9714)*
K2 Label & Printing Inc ....E....626 922-8108
633 Great Bend Dr Diamond Bar (91765) *(P-4347)*
K9 Ballistics Inc ....F....844 772-3125
708 Via Alondra Camarillo (93012) *(P-11699)*
Kaa Design Group Inc ....D....310 821-1400
12921 W Washington Blvd Los Angeles (90066) *(P-22725)*
Kabc-TV ....D....818 863-7171
500 Circle Seven Dr Glendale (91201) *(P-12729)*
Kace Entertainment Inc (PA) ....**D....310 372-2222**
2988 Columbia St Torrance (90503) *(P-19360)*
Kadan Consultants Incorporated ....F....562 988-1165
5662 Research Dr Huntington Beach (92649) *(P-8649)*
Kaden Cash LLC ....E....818 714-4665
15845 Jackson Dr Fontana (92336) *(P-19361)*
Kadenwood LLC ....F....949 287-6703
450 Nwport Ctr Dr Ste 550 Newport Beach (92660) *(P-4751)*
Kadenwood Per & Pet Care LLC ....E....949 287-6789
450 Nwport Ctr Dr Ste 550 Newport Beach (92660) *(P-1797)*
Kafco Sales Company ....E....323 588-7141
2300 E 37th St Vernon (90058) *(P-13909)*
Kafp, Foothill Ranch *Also called Kaiser Aluminum Fab Pdts LLC (P-6300)*
Kaga (usa) Inc ....E....714 540-2697
2620 S Susan St Santa Ana (92704) *(P-7155)*
Kagan Truck Center, Los Angeles *Also called G Kagan and Sons Inc (P-2572)*
Kahgo Truck Parts, North Hollywood *Also called K & G Latirovian Inc (P-10083)*
Kairos Manufacturing Inc ....F....805 544-2216
201 Bridge St San Luis Obispo (93401) *(P-11700)*
Kaiser Aluminum Corporation (PA) ....D....949 614-1740
27422 Portola Pkwy # 350 Foothill Ranch (92610) *(P-6283)*
Kaiser Aluminum Fab Pdts LLC (HQ) ....**A....949 614-1740**
27422 Portola Pkwy # 200 Foothill Ranch (92610) *(P-6300)*
Kaiser Fndtion Hlth Plan GA In ....C....951 270-1200
1850 California Ave Corona (92881) *(P-15401)*
Kaiser Foundation Health Plan, Lancaster *Also called Kaiser Foundation Hospitals (P-21446)*
Kaiser Foundation Health Plan, Pasadena *Also called Kaiser Foundation Hospitals (P-15406)*

Mergent e-mail: customerrelations@mergent.com
1174

2022 Southern California Business
Directory and Buyers Guide

(P-0000) Products & Services Section entry number
(PA)=Parent Co (HQ)=Headquarters (DH)=Div Headquarters

Kaiser Foundation Health Plan, Los Angeles *Also called Kaiser Foundation Hospitals* ***(P-15407)***

Kaiser Foundation Health Plan, Victorville *Also called Kaiser Foundation Hospitals* ***(P-15408)***

Kaiser Foundation Health Plan, Temecula *Also called Kaiser Foundation Hospitals* ***(P-15409)***

Kaiser Foundation Health Plan, Mission Hills *Also called Kaiser Foundation Hospitals* ***(P-15410)***

Kaiser Foundation Health Plan, Panorama City *Also called Kaiser Foundation Hospitals* ***(P-15411)***

Kaiser Foundation Health Plan, Los Angeles *Also called Kaiser Foundation Hospitals* ***(P-15412)***

Kaiser Foundation Health Plan, Anaheim *Also called Kaiser Foundation Hospitals* ***(P-15415)***

Kaiser Foundation Health Plan, Woodland Hills *Also called Kaiser Foundation Hospitals* ***(P-15418)***

Kaiser Foundation Health Plan, Ontario *Also called Kaiser Foundation Hospitals* ***(P-15419)***

Kaiser Foundation Health Plan, Ontario *Also called Kaiser Foundation Hospitals* ***(P-15420)***

Kaiser Foundation Health Plan, Palm Desert *Also called Kaiser Foundation Hospitals* ***(P-19942)***

Kaiser Foundation Health Plan, Ventura *Also called Kaiser Foundation Hospitals* ***(P-15421)***

Kaiser Foundation Health Plan, Santa Ana *Also called Kaiser Foundation Hospitals* ***(P-15422)***

Kaiser Foundation Health Plan, San Bernardino *Also called Kaiser Foundation Hospitals* ***(P-19943)***

Kaiser Foundation Health Plan, Carson *Also called Kaiser Foundation Hospitals* ***(P-15423)***

Kaiser Foundation Health Plan, Corona *Also called Kaiser Foundation Hospitals* ***(P-21447)***

Kaiser Foundation Health Plan, Chino *Also called Kaiser Foundation Hospitals* ***(P-15424)***

Kaiser Foundation Health Plan, West Covina *Also called Kaiser Foundation Hospitals* ***(P-15425)***

Kaiser Foundation Health Plan, Bellflower *Also called Kaiser Foundation Hospitals* ***(P-15426)***

Kaiser Foundation Health Plan, Palm Springs *Also called Kaiser Foundation Hospitals* ***(P-15427)***

Kaiser Foundation Health Plan, Torrance *Also called Kaiser Foundation Hospitals* ***(P-15428)***

Kaiser Foundation Health Plan, Thousand Oaks *Also called Kaiser Foundation Hospitals* ***(P-15429)***

Kaiser Foundation Health Plan, Simi Valley *Also called Kaiser Foundation Hospitals* ***(P-15430)***

Kaiser Foundation Health Plan, San Juan Capistrano *Also called Kaiser Foundation Hospitals* ***(P-15431)***

Kaiser Foundation Health Plan, Fontana *Also called Kaiser Foundation Hospitals* ***(P-15432)***

Kaiser Foundation Health Plan, Downey *Also called Kaiser Foundation Hospitals* ***(P-15433)***

Kaiser Foundation Health Plan, Inglewood *Also called Kaiser Foundation Hospitals* ***(P-15434)***

Kaiser Foundation Health Plan, North Hollywood *Also called Kaiser Foundation Hospitals* ***(P-15435)***

Kaiser Foundation Health Plan, Palm Desert *Also called Kaiser Foundation Hospitals* ***(P-15436)***

Kaiser Foundation Health Plan, Placentia *Also called Kaiser Foundation Hospitals* ***(P-15437)***

Kaiser Foundation Health Plan, Orange *Also called Kaiser Foundation Hospitals* ***(P-15438)***

Kaiser Foundation Hospitals..........C.......909 399-3700
5330 San Bernardino St Montclair (91763) ***(P-21314)***

Kaiser Foundation Hospitals..........C.......714 279-4675
411 N Lakeview Ave Anaheim (92807) ***(P-19858)***

Kaiser Foundation Hospitals..........A.......949 262-5780
6 Willard Irvine (92604) ***(P-20800)***

Kaiser Foundation Hospitals..........C.......310 922-8916
1011 Baldwin Park Blvd Baldwin Park (91706) ***(P-19859)***

Kaiser Foundation Hospitals..........C.......949 425-3150
24502 Pacific Park Dr Aliso Viejo (92656) ***(P-19860)***

Kaiser Foundation Hospitals..........C.......949 932-5000
6670 Alton Pkwy Irvine (92618) ***(P-15402)***

Kaiser Foundation Hospitals..........C.......310 325-5111
15446 S Western Ave Gardena (90249) ***(P-19861)***

Kaiser Foundation Hospitals..........C.......888 750-0036
3750 Grand Ave Chino (91710) ***(P-15403)***

Kaiser Foundation Hospitals..........A.......818 719-2000
5601 De Soto Ave Woodland Hills (91367) ***(P-20801)***

Kaiser Foundation Hospitals..........A.......951 353-4000
12620 Prescott Ave Tustin (92782) ***(P-20802)***

Kaiser Foundation Hospitals..........A.......661 412-6777
8800 Ming Ave Bakersfield (93311) ***(P-20803)***

Kaiser Foundation Hospitals..........C.......661 729-7250
1050 Commerce Center Dr Lancaster (93534) ***(P-21446)***

Kaiser Foundation Hospitals..........A.......661 726-2500
43112 15th St W Lancaster (93534) ***(P-20804)***

Kaiser Foundation Hospitals..........C.......805 582-0100
3900 Alamo St Simi Valley (93063) ***(P-19862)***

Kaiser Foundation Hospitals..........C.......714 741-3448
12100 Euclid St Garden Grove (92840) ***(P-19863)***

Kaiser Foundation Hospitals..........D.......714 841-7293
18081 Beach Blvd Huntington Beach (92648) ***(P-16180)***

Kaiser Foundation Hospitals..........D.......323 783-4011
4867 W Sunset Blvd Los Angeles (90027) ***(P-20805)***

Kaiser Foundation Hospitals..........D.......213 351-3550
3699 Wilshire Blvd Los Angeles (90010) ***(P-22454)***

Kaiser Foundation Hospitals..........C.......949 262-5760
6 Willard Irvine (92604) ***(P-19864)***

Kaiser Foundation Hospitals..........C.......818 719-2000
5601 De Soto Ave Woodland Hills (91367) ***(P-19865)***

Kaiser Foundation Hospitals..........A.......626 851-1011
1011 Baldwin Park Blvd Baldwin Park (91706) ***(P-15404)***

Kaiser Foundation Hospitals..........C.......213 217-4514
333 S Hope St Los Angeles (90071) ***(P-21315)***

Kaiser Foundation Hospitals..........A.......714 644-2000
3440 E La Palma Ave Anaheim (92806) ***(P-20806)***

Kaiser Foundation Hospitals..........B.......562 657-9000
9333 Imperial Hwy Downey (90242) ***(P-15405)***

Kaiser Foundation Hospitals..........C.......818 375-4023
13652 Cantara St Panorama City (91402) ***(P-19866)***

Kaiser Foundation Hospitals..........C.......323 783-7695
4950 W Sunset Blvd # 200 Los Angeles (90027) ***(P-19867)***

Kaiser Foundation Hospitals..........C.......949 932-2604
6650 Alton Pkwy Irvine (92618) ***(P-19868)***

Kaiser Foundation Hospitals..........C.......310 325-6542
2081 Palos Verdes Dr N Lomita (90717) ***(P-19869)***

Kaiser Foundation Hospitals..........E.......626 405-5000
393 E Walnut St Pasadena (91188) ***(P-15406)***

Kaiser Foundation Hospitals..........C.......323 783-8191
1515 N Vermont Ave Fl 1 Los Angeles (90027) ***(P-19870)***

Kaiser Foundation Hospitals..........C.......818 375-3475
8220 Woodman Ave Panorama City (91402) ***(P-19871)***

Kaiser Foundation Hospitals..........C.......951 898-7370
2055 Kellogg Ave Corona (92879) ***(P-19872)***

Kaiser Foundation Hospitals..........C.......626 405-2589
400 S Sepulveda Blvd Manhattan Beach (90266) ***(P-19873)***

Kaiser Foundation Hospitals..........A.......323 783-4011
4733 W Sunset Blvd Fl 2 Los Angeles (90027) ***(P-20807)***

Kaiser Foundation Hospitals..........C.......323 857-2000
6041 Cadillac Ave Los Angeles (90034) ***(P-19874)***

Kaiser Foundation Hospitals..........A.......909 394-2530
1255 W Arrow Hwy San Dimas (91773) ***(P-20808)***

Kaiser Foundation Hospitals..........C.......951 251-7300
14305 Meridian Pkwy March ARB (92518) ***(P-19875)***

Kaiser Foundation Hospitals..........C.......888 750-0036
1301 California St Redlands (92374) ***(P-19876)***

Kaiser Foundation Hospitals..........C.......714 672-5100
1900 E Lambert Rd Brea (92821) ***(P-19877)***

Kaiser Foundation Hospitals..........C.......951 353-3790
10800 Magnolia Ave Riverside (92505) ***(P-19878)***

Kaiser Foundation Hospitals..........C.......323 562-6400
7825 Atlantic Ave Cudahy (90201) ***(P-19879)***

Kaiser Foundation Hospitals..........C.......818 375-2369
13640 Roscoe Blvd Panorama City (91402) ***(P-19880)***

Kaiser Foundation Hospitals..........C.......323 857-2000
6041 Cadillac Ave Los Angeles (90034) ***(P-19881)***

Kaiser Foundation Hospitals..........C.......818 375-2000
13651 Willard St Panorama City (91402) ***(P-19882)***

Kaiser Foundation Hospitals..........C.......562 658-3441
10740 4th St Rancho Cucamonga (91730) ***(P-19883)***

Kaiser Foundation Hospitals..........D.......323 264-4310
3355 E 26th St Vernon (90058) ***(P-3322)***

Kaiser Foundation Hospitals..........C.......909 609-3800
17284 Slover Ave Fontana (92337) ***(P-19884)***

Kaiser Foundation Hospitals..........C.......800 954-8000
1550 W Manchester Ave Los Angeles (90047) ***(P-15407)***

Kaiser Foundation Hospitals..........C.......888 750-0036
14011 Park Ave Victorville (92392) ***(P-15408)***

Kaiser Foundation Hospitals..........C.......866 984-7483
27309 Madison Ave Temecula (92590) ***(P-15409)***

Kaiser Foundation Hospitals..........C.......888 778-5000
11001 Sepulveda Blvd Mission Hills (91345) ***(P-15410)***

Kaiser Foundation Hospitals..........C.......818 375-2028
8001 Ventura Canyon Ave Panorama City (91402) ***(P-15411)***

Kaiser Foundation Hospitals..........C.......800 954-8000
5620 Mesmer Ave Los Angeles (90230) ***(P-15412)***

Kaiser Foundation Hospitals..........B.......714 734-4500
17542 17th St Tustin (92780) ***(P-21177)***

Kaiser Foundation Hospitals..........C.......888 750-0036
10850 Arrow Rte Rancho Cucamonga (91730) ***(P-19885)***

Kaiser Foundation Hospitals..........C.......888 988-2800
5475 E La Palma Ave # 20 Anaheim (92807) ***(P-19886)***

Kaiser Foundation Hospitals..........C.......877 524-7373
3733 San Dimas St Bakersfield (93301) ***(P-19887)***

Kaiser Foundation Hospitals..........C.......888 988-2800
3460 E La Palma Ave Anaheim (92806) ***(P-19888)***

Kaiser Foundation Hospitals..........A.......661 395-3000
2615 Chester Ave Bakersfield (93301) ***(P-20809)***

Kaiser Foundation Hospitals..........C.......877 524-7373
2531 Chester Ave Bakersfield (93301) ***(P-19889)***

Kaiser Foundation Hospitals..........C.......661 337-7160
2620 Chester Ave Bakersfield (93301) ***(P-19890)***

Kaiser Foundation Hospitals..........C.......877 524-7373
1200 Discovery Dr Bakersfield (93309) ***(P-19891)***

Kaiser Foundation Hospitals..........C.......800 823-4040
10820 183rd St Cerritos (90703) ***(P-19892)***

Kaiser Foundation Hospitals..........C.......888 515-3500
2620 Las Posas Rd Camarillo (93010) ***(P-19893)***

Kaiser Foundation Hospitals..........C.......877 524-7373
8800 Ming Ave Bakersfield (93311) ***(P-19894)***

Kaiser Foundation Hospitals..........C.......562 463-4377
12801 Crssrads Pkwy S Ste City of Industry (91746) ***(P-19895)***

Kaiser Foundation Hospitals..........C.......800 823-4040
9449 Imperial Hwy Downey (90242) ***(P-19896)***

Kaiser Foundation Hospitals..........C.......800 780-1277
1336 Bridgegate Dr Diamond Bar (91765) ***(P-19897)***

Kaiser Foundation Hospitals..........C.......800 823-4040
9353 Imperial Hwy Downey (90242) ***(P-19898)***

Kaiser Foundation Hospitals..........C.......800 922-2000
26882 Towne Centre Dr # 1 Foothill Ranch (92610) ***(P-19899)***

Kaiser Foundation Hospitals..........C.......866 205-3595
9310 Sierra Ave Fontana (92335) ***(P-19900)***

Kaiser Foundation Hospitals..........C.......800 780-1230
18600 S Figueroa St Gardena (90248) ***(P-19901)***

Employee Codes: A=Over 500 employees, B=251-500
C=101-250, D=51-100, E=20-50 F=10-19
2022 Southern California Business
Directory and Buyers Guide
© Mergent Inc. 1-800-342-5647
1175

Kaiser Foundation Hospitals .... C 818 832-7200
10605 Balboa Blvd Ste 330 Granada Hills (91344) ***(P-19902)***

Kaiser Foundation Hospitals .... C 800 954-8000
501 N Orange St Glendale (91203) ***(P-19903)***

Kaiser Foundation Hospitals .... C 866 984-7483
46900 Monroe St Indio (92201) ***(P-19904)***

Kaiser Foundation Hospitals .... A 661 949-5000
1600 W Avenue J Lancaster (93534) ***(P-20810)***

Kaiser Foundation Hospitals .... C 626 931-3580
1813 N Hacienda Blvd La Puente (91744) ***(P-21251)***

Kaiser Foundation Hospitals .... C 661 951-0070
44444 20th St W Lancaster (93534) ***(P-19905)***

Kaiser Foundation Hospitals .... C 310 325-6542
2081 Palos Verdes Dr N Lomita (90717) ***(P-19906)***

Kaiser Foundation Hospitals .... C 424 251-7000
2040 Pacific Coast Hwy Lomita (90717) ***(P-21316)***

Kaiser Foundation Hospitals .... C 310 604-5700
3830 Mrtin Lther King Jr Lynwood (90262) ***(P-19907)***

Kaiser Foundation Hospitals .... C 888 778-5000
5250 Lankershim Blvd North Hollywood (91601) ***(P-19908)***

Kaiser Foundation Hospitals .... C 562 807-6100
12501 Imperial Hwy Ste 40 Norwalk (90650) ***(P-19909)***

Kaiser Foundation Hospitals .... C 909 724-5000
2295 S Vineyard Ave Ontario (91761) ***(P-19910)***

Kaiser Foundation Hospitals .... C 888 515-3500
2200 E Gonzales Rd Oxnard (93036) ***(P-19911)***

Kaiser Foundation Hospitals .... C 800 777-1256
73733 Fred Waring Dr # 1 Palm Desert (92260) ***(P-19912)***

Kaiser Foundation Hospitals .... C 805 988-6300
2103 E Gonzales Rd Oxnard (93036) ***(P-19913)***

Kaiser Foundation Hospitals .... A 866 984-7483
University Park Ctr Palm Desert (92211) ***(P-19914)***

Kaiser Foundation Hospitals .... C 951 248-4000
5225 Canyon Crest Dr # 10 Riverside (92507) ***(P-19915)***

Kaiser Foundation Hospitals .... C 866 984-7483
14305 Meridian Pkwy Riverside (92518) ***(P-19916)***

Kaiser Foundation Hospitals .... C 951 353-4670
10689 Magnolia Ave Riverside (92505) ***(P-20225)***

Kaiser Foundation Hospitals .... C 714 223-2606
3601 S Harbor Blvd Santa Ana (92704) ***(P-19917)***

Kaiser Foundation Hospitals .... C 888 778-5000
26415 Carl Boyer Dr Santa Clarita (91350) ***(P-19918)***

Kaiser Foundation Hospitals .... C 888 515-3500
145 Hodencamp Rd Thousand Oaks (91360) ***(P-19919)***

Kaiser Foundation Hospitals .... C 888 515-3500
322 E Thousand Oaks Blvd Thousand Oaks (91360) ***(P-19920)***

Kaiser Foundation Hospitals .... C 888 988-2800
2521 Michelle Dr Tustin (92780) ***(P-19921)***

Kaiser Foundation Hospitals .... C 817 372-8201
9521 Dalen St Downey (90242) ***(P-19922)***

Kaiser Foundation Hospitals .... C 714 562-3420
5 Centerpointe Dr La Palma (90623) ***(P-19923)***

Kaiser Foundation Hospitals .... C 714 830-6500
3401 S Harbor Blvd Santa Ana (92704) ***(P-19924)***

Kaiser Foundation Hospitals .... C 909 988-0379
10850 Arrow Rte Rancho Cucamonga (91730) ***(P-19925)***

Kaiser Foundation Hospitals .... C 310 915-5000
12001 W Washington Blvd Los Angeles (90066) ***(P-19926)***

Kaiser Foundation Hospitals .... C 310 325-5111
18600 S Figueroa St Gardena (90248) ***(P-19927)***

Kaiser Foundation Hospitals .... C 909 427-5521
5330 San Bernardino St Montclair (91763) ***(P-19928)***

Kaiser Foundation Hospitals .... D 323 881-5516
5119 Pomona Blvd Los Angeles (90022) ***(P-16181)***

Kaiser Foundation Hospitals .... C 310 325-5111
25825 Vermont Ave Harbor City (90710) ***(P-19929)***

Kaiser Foundation Hospitals .... C 877 524-7373
9000 Ming Ave Bakersfield (93311) ***(P-19930)***

Kaiser Foundation Hospitals .... C 323 783-8568
4733 W Sunset Blvd Los Angeles (90027) ***(P-15413)***

Kaiser Foundation Hospitals .... C 323 783-7955
1550 N Edgemont St Los Angeles (90027) ***(P-19931)***

Kaiser Foundation Hospitals .... C 909 427-5000
9961 Sierra Ave Fontana (92335) ***(P-19932)***

Kaiser Foundation Hospitals .... C 661 398-5011
3501 Stockdale Hwy Bakersfield (93309) ***(P-19933)***

Kaiser Foundation Hospitals .... C 951 352-0292
3951 Van Buren Blvd Riverside (92503) ***(P-19934)***

Kaiser Foundation Hospitals .... D 951 601-6174
12815 Heacock St Moreno Valley (92553) ***(P-16182)***

Kaiser Foundation Hospitals .... A 951 353-2000
36450 Inland Valley Dr # 2 Wildomar (92595) ***(P-20811)***

Kaiser Foundation Hospitals .... C 714 562-3420
5 Centerpointe Dr La Palma (90623) ***(P-19935)***

Kaiser Foundation Hospitals .... C 818 552-3000
444 W Glenoaks Blvd Glendale (91202) ***(P-19936)***

Kaiser Foundation Hospitals .... C 626 440-5639
3280 E Foothill Blvd Pasadena (91107) ***(P-19937)***

Kaiser Foundation Hospitals .... A 323 562-6400
7825 Atlantic Ave Cudahy (90201) ***(P-20812)***

Kaiser Foundation Hospitals .... C 866 319-4269
1249 S Sunset Ave West Covina (91790) ***(P-15414)***

Kaiser Foundation Hospitals .... A 310 517-2956
15446 S Western Ave Gardena (90249) ***(P-20813)***

Kaiser Foundation Hospitals .... A 818 592-3100
21263 Erwin St Woodland Hills (91367) ***(P-20814)***

Kaiser Foundation Hospitals .... C 310 325-5111
2521 Michelle Dr Tustin (92780) ***(P-19938)***

Kaiser Foundation Hospitals .... C 866 205-3595
325 W Hospitality Ln San Bernardino (92408) ***(P-19939)***

Kaiser Foundation Hospitals .... C 714 284-6634
1011 S East St Fl 1 Anaheim (92805) ***(P-15415)***

Kaiser Foundation Hospitals .... C 323 783-8306
1515 N Vermont Ave Fl 3 Los Angeles (90027) ***(P-19940)***

Kaiser Foundation Hospitals .... C 661 334-2020
5055 California Ave # 110 Bakersfield (93309) ***(P-15416)***

Kaiser Foundation Hospitals .... C 323 298-3300
5105 W Goldleaf Cir Los Angeles (90056) ***(P-21317)***

Kaiser Foundation Hospitals .... B 213 580-7200
765 W College St Los Angeles (90012) ***(P-21020)***

Kaiser Foundation Hospitals .... C 866 340-5974
12470 Whittier Blvd Whittier (90602) ***(P-15417)***

Kaiser Foundation Hospitals .... C 661 222-2323
27107 Tourney Rd Santa Clarita (91355) ***(P-19941)***

Kaiser Foundation Hospitals .... C 888 515-3500
21263 Erwin St Woodland Hills (91367) ***(P-15418)***

Kaiser Foundation Hospitals .... C 888 750-0036
2295 S Vineyard Ave Ontario (91761) ***(P-15419)***

Kaiser Foundation Hospitals .... C 866 205-3595
3330 Centre Lake Dr Ontario (91761) ***(P-15420)***

Kaiser Foundation Hospitals .... C 760 360-1475
42575 Washington St Palm Desert (92211) ***(P-19942)***

Kaiser Foundation Hospitals .... C 888 515-3500
888 S Hill Rd Ventura (93003) ***(P-15421)***

Kaiser Foundation Hospitals .... C 888 988-2800
3401 S Harbor Blvd Santa Ana (92704) ***(P-15422)***

Kaiser Foundation Hospitals .... C 888 750-0036
1717 Date Pike San Bernardino (92404) ***(P-19943)***

Kaiser Foundation Hospitals .... C 310 816-5440
23701 Main St Carson (90745) ***(P-15423)***

Kaiser Foundation Hospitals .... C 866 984-7483
2055 Kellogg Ave Corona (92879) ***(P-21447)***

Kaiser Foundation Hospitals .... C 888 750-0036
11911 Central Ave Chino (91710) ***(P-15424)***

Kaiser Foundation Hospitals .... C 626 856-3045
1539 W Garvey Ave N West Covina (91790) ***(P-15425)***

Kaiser Foundation Hospitals .... C 562 461-3084
9333 Rosecrans Ave Bellflower (90706) ***(P-15426)***

Kaiser Foundation Hospitals .... C 866 370-1942
1717 E Vista Chino Ste B2 Palm Springs (92262) ***(P-15427)***

Kaiser Foundation Hospitals .... C 800 780-1230
20790 Madrona Ave Torrance (90503) ***(P-15428)***

Kaiser Foundation Hospitals .... C 888 515-3500
365 E Hillcrest Dr Thousand Oaks (91360) ***(P-15429)***

Kaiser Foundation Hospitals .... C 888 515-3500
3900 Alamo St Simi Valley (93063) ***(P-15430)***

Kaiser Foundation Hospitals .... C 888 988-2800
30400 Camino Capistrano San Juan Capistrano (92675) ***(P-15431)***

Kaiser Foundation Hospitals .... C 909 427-3910
9961 Sierra Ave Fontana (92335) ***(P-15432)***

Kaiser Foundation Hospitals .... C 562 622-4190
12200 Bellflower Blvd Downey (90242) ***(P-15433)***

Kaiser Foundation Hospitals .... C 800 954-8000
110 N La Brea Ave Inglewood (90301) ***(P-15434)***

Kaiser Foundation Hospitals .... C 951 353-2000
10800 Magnolia Ave Riverside (92505) ***(P-19944)***

Kaiser Foundation Hospitals .... D 909 427-5521
789 E Cooley Dr Colton (92324) ***(P-16183)***

Kaiser Foundation Hospitals .... C 951 243-0811
27300 Iris Ave Moreno Valley (92555) ***(P-19945)***

Kaiser Foundation Hospitals .... C 818 503-7082
11666 Sherman Way North Hollywood (91605) ***(P-15435)***

Kaiser Foundation Hospitals .... C 310 419-3303
110 N La Brea Ave Inglewood (90301) ***(P-19946)***

Kaiser Foundation Hospitals .... B 626 440-5659
1055 E Colo Blvd Ste 100 Pasadena (91106) ***(P-20815)***

Kaiser Foundation Hospitals .... D 661 533-7500
4502 E Avenue S Palmdale (93552) ***(P-16184)***

Kaiser Foundation Hospitals .... C 303 404-4700
73733 Fred Waring Dr # 1 Palm Desert (92260) ***(P-15436)***

Kaiser Foundation Hospitals .... C 310 517-3400
25825 Vermont Ave Harbor City (90710) ***(P-19947)***

Kaiser Foundation Hospitals .... C 714 572-5700
1707 Barcelona Cir Placentia (92870) ***(P-15437)***

Kaiser Foundation Hospitals .... A 888 750-0036
250 W San Jose Ave Claremont (91711) ***(P-20816)***

Kaiser Foundation Hospitals .... C 310 513-6707
23621 Main St Carson (90745) ***(P-21318)***

Kaiser Foundation Hospitals .... C 888 988-2800
200 N Lewis St Fl 1 Orange (92868) ***(P-15438)***

Kaiser Foundation Hospitals .... D 866 984-7483
182 Granite St Corona (92879) ***(P-16185)***

Kaiser Foundation Hospitals .... D 949 932-5000
6640 Alton Pkwy Irvine (92618) ***(P-16186)***

Kaiser Foundation Hospitals .... C 714 967-4700
1900 E 4th St Santa Ana (92705) ***(P-15439)***

Kaiser Mental Health Center, Los Angeles *Also called Kaiser Foundation Hospitals* ***(P-21020)***

Kaiser Permanente, Chino *Also called Kaiser Foundation Hospitals* ***(P-15403)***

Kaiser Permanente, Woodland Hills *Also called Kaiser Foundation Hospitals* ***(P-20801)***

Kaiser Permanente, Tustin *Also called Kaiser Foundation Hospitals* ***(P-20802)***

Kaiser Permanente, Bakersfield *Also called Kaiser Foundation Hospitals* ***(P-20803)***

Kaiser Permanente, Lancaster *Also called Kaiser Foundation Hospitals* ***(P-20804)***

Kaiser Permanente, Garden Grove *Also called Kaiser Foundation Hospitals* ***(P-19863)***

Kaiser Permanente, Los Angeles *Also called Kaiser Foundation Hospitals* ***(P-20805)***

Kaiser Permanente, Los Angeles *Also called Kaiser Foundation Hospitals* ***(P-22454)***

Kaiser Permanente, Baldwin Park *Also called Kaiser Foundation Hospitals* ***(P-15404)***

Kaiser Permanente, Los Angeles *Also called Kaiser Foundation Hospitals* ***(P-21315)***

Kaiser Permanente, San Dimas *Also called Kaiser Foundation Hospitals* ***(P-20808)***

Mergent e-mail: customerrelations@mergent.com
1176

2022 Southern California Business
Directory and Buyers Guide

(P-0000) Products & Services Section entry number
(PA)=Parent Co (HQ)=Headquarters (DH)=Div Headquarters

ALPHABETIC SECTION
Kaweah Delta Health Care

Kaiser Permanente, Redlands *Also called Kaiser Foundation Hospitals* ***(P-19876)***
Kaiser Permanente, Brea *Also called Kaiser Foundation Hospitals* ***(P-19877)***
Kaiser Permanente, Pasadena *Also called Southern Cal Prmnnte Med Group* ***(P-15458)***
Kaiser Permanente, Panorama City *Also called Kaiser Foundation Hospitals* ***(P-19882)***
Kaiser Permanente, Santa Ana *Also called Kaiser Foundation Hospitals* ***(P-19924)***
Kaiser Permanente, Los Angeles *Also called Kaiser Foundation Hospitals* ***(P-19926)***
Kaiser Permanente, Los Angeles *Also called Kaiser Foundation Hospitals* ***(P-16181)***
Kaiser Permanente, Harbor City *Also called Kaiser Foundation Hospitals* ***(P-19929)***
Kaiser Permanente, Fontana *Also called Kaiser Foundation Hospitals* ***(P-19932)***
Kaiser Permanente, Riverside *Also called Kaiser Foundation Hospitals* ***(P-19934)***
Kaiser Permanente, West Covina *Also called Kaiser Foundation Hospitals* ***(P-15414)***
Kaiser Permanente, Los Angeles *Also called Kaiser Foundation Hospitals* ***(P-19940)***
Kaiser Permanente, Bakersfield *Also called Kaiser Foundation Hospitals* ***(P-15416)***
Kaiser Permanente, Whittier *Also called Kaiser Foundation Hospitals* ***(P-15417)***
Kaiser Permanente, Santa Clarita *Also called Kaiser Foundation Hospitals* ***(P-19941)***
Kaiser Permanente, Colton *Also called Kaiser Foundation Hospitals* ***(P-16183)***
Kaiser Permanente, Inglewood *Also called Kaiser Foundation Hospitals* ***(P-19946)***
Kaiser Permanente, Pasadena *Also called Kaiser Foundation Hospitals* ***(P-20815)***
Kaiser Permanente, Downey *Also called Southern Cal Prmnnte Med Group* ***(P-15461)***
Kaiser Permanente, Claremont *Also called Kaiser Foundation Hospitals* ***(P-20816)***
Kaiser Permanente, Carson *Also called Kaiser Foundation Hospitals* ***(P-21318)***
Kaiser Permanente, Santa Ana *Also called Kaiser Foundation Hospitals* ***(P-15439)***
Kaiser Permanente 24 Hour, Montclair *Also called Kaiser Foundation Hospitals* ***(P-19928)***
Kaiser Permanente Med Library, Los Angeles *Also called Kaiser Foundation Hospitals* ***(P-15413)***
Kaiser Permanente Member Svcs, Palm Desert *Also called Kaiser Foundation Hospitals* ***(P-19912)***
Kaiser Prmnente Downey Med Ctr, Downey *Also called Kaiser Foundation Hospitals* ***(P-15405)***
Kaiser Prmnnte Mreno Vly Med C, Moreno Valley *Also called Kaiser Foundation Hospitals* ***(P-19945)***
Kaiser Prmnnte Nat Fclties Svc, Vernon *Also called Kaiser Foundation Hospitals* ***(P-3322)***
Kaiser Prmnnte Ornge Cnty-Nhei, Anaheim *Also called Kaiser Foundation Hospitals* ***(P-20806)***
Kaiser Prmnnte Psadena Med Off, Pasadena *Also called Kaiser Foundation Hospitals* ***(P-19937)***
Kaiser Prmnnte Schl Anesthesia .... D 626 564-3016
100 S Los Robles Ave # 501 Pasadena (91101) ***(P-19948)***
Kaiser Prmnnte W Los Angles Me, Los Angeles *Also called Kaiser Foundation Hospitals* ***(P-19881)***
Kaiser Psychiatry Srvs Div, San Bernardino *Also called Kaiser Foundation Hospitals* ***(P-19939)***
Kajabi LLC .... E 855 452-5224
17100 Laguna Canyon Rd # 100 Irvine (92618) ***(P-18127)***
Kak Industry LLC .... E 805 981-4734
2241 Celsius Ave Oxnard (93030) ***(P-7428)***
Kakuichi America Inc .... D 310 539-1590
23540 Telo Ave Torrance (90505) ***(P-5468)***
Kal Krshnan Cnsulting Svcs Inc .... D 213 488-0900
800 S Figueroa St # 1210 Los Angeles (90017) ***(P-22595)***
Kal Plastics, Vernon *Also called Tom York Enterprises Inc* ***(P-5840)***
Kal Tool Co, Baldwin Park *Also called G K Tool Corp* ***(P-13807)***
Kal-Cameron Manufacturing Corp (HQ) .... **D** **626 338-7308**
4265 Puente Ave Baldwin Park (91706) ***(P-6483)***
Kaleidioscope Stadium Cinema, Mission Viejo *Also called Edwards Theatres Circuit Inc* ***(P-19274)***
Kalpana LLC .... C 213 624-0000
535 S Grand Ave Los Angeles (90071) ***(P-16518)***
Kaltec Electronics Inc (PA) .... **F** **813 888-9555**
16220 Bloomfield Ave Cerritos (90703) ***(P-11281)***
Kaltec Enterprises, Cerritos *Also called Kaltec Electronics Inc* ***(P-11281)***
Kalypsys Inc .... E 858 552-0674
333 S Grand Ave Ste 4070 Los Angeles (90071) ***(P-4837)***
Kam Sang Company Inc .... D 714 523-2800
14419 Firestone Blvd La Mirada (90638) ***(P-16519)***
Kama Sutra, Thousand Oaks *Also called Kamsut Incorporated* ***(P-5037)***
Kamali Print Division Samtex, Vernon *Also called Samtex Fabrics Inc* ***(P-12522)***
Kamiran Inc .... F 213 746-9161
1415 Maple Ave Ste 220 Los Angeles (90015) ***(P-2851)***
Kamm Industries Inc .... E 800 317-6253
43352 Business Park Dr Temecula (92590) ***(P-3177)***
Kamsut Incorporated .... E 805 495-7479
2151 Anchor Ct Thousand Oaks (91320) ***(P-5037)***
Kan-Di-Ki LLC (HQ) .... **A** **818 549-1880**
2820 N Ontario St Burbank (91504) ***(P-21073)***
Kana Pipeline Inc .... D 714 986-1400
12620 Magnolia Ave Riverside (92503) ***(P-959)***
Kanex .... E 714 332-1681
500 S Brea Blvd Unit B Brea (92821) ***(P-9880)***
Kanex Pro Inc .... F 714 332-1681
500 S Brea Blvd Unit B Brea (92821) ***(P-2715)***
Kaney Foods, San Luis Obispo *Also called Amk Foodservices Inc* ***(P-14454)***
Kang Family Partners LLC .... C 805 688-1000
555 Mcmurray Rd Buellton (93427) ***(P-16520)***
Kanstul Musical Instrs Inc .... E 714 563-1000
23772 Perth Bay Dana Point (92629) ***(P-11345)***
Kap Manufacturing Inc .... E 909 599-2525
327 W Allen Ave San Dimas (91773) ***(P-8650)***
Kap Medical .... E 951 340-4360
1395 Pico St Corona (92881) ***(P-10894)***
Kapstone Ontario .... F 909 390-0619
1790 Champagne Ave Ontario (91761) ***(P-3815)***
KAR Construction Inc .... D 909 988-5054
1306 Brooks St Ontario (91762) ***(P-617)***
Kar Ice Service Inc (PA) .... **F** **760 256-2648**
2521 Solar Way Barstow (92311) ***(P-2372)***
Karat Packaging Inc (PA) .... **D** **626 965-8882**
6185 Kimball Ave Chino (91708) ***(P-5687)***
Karbz Inc .... E 760 567-9953
77806 Flora Rd Ste E Palm Desert (92211) ***(P-10084)***
Karcher Environmental Inc (PA) .... **E** **714 385-1490**
2300 E Orangewood Ave Anaheim (92806) ***(P-1670)***
Karel Manufacturing, Calexico *Also called Lorenz Inc* ***(P-9889)***
Karen Kane Stores Inc (PA) .... **C** **323 588-0000**
2275 E 37th St Vernon (90058) ***(P-14387)***
Kargo Global Inc .... C 212 979-9000
1437 4th St Ste 200 Santa Monica (90401) ***(P-17087)***
Karl M Smith Inc .... F 559 992-4109
1204 Dairy Ave Corcoran (93212) ***(P-6859)***
Karl Storz Endscpy-America Inc .... D 508 248-9011
2151 E Grand Ave Ste 100 El Segundo (90245) ***(P-10999)***
Karl Storz Endscpy-America Inc (HQ) .... **B** **424 218-8100**
2151 E Grand Ave El Segundo (90245) ***(P-11000)***
Karl Storz Endscpy-America Inc .... D 800 964-5563
1 N Los Carneros Rd Goleta (93117) ***(P-11001)***
Karl Storz Imaging Inc .... E 805 968-5563
32 Aero Camino Goleta (93117) ***(P-11002)***
Karl Storz Imaging Inc (HQ) .... **B** **805 968-5563**
1 S Los Carneros Rd Goleta (93117) ***(P-10895)***
Karl's Sash & Doors, Huntington Beach *Also called Karls Custom Sash & Doors LLC* ***(P-3257)***
Karls Custom Sash & Doors LLC .... F 714 842-7877
18292 Gothard St Huntington Beach (92648) ***(P-3257)***
Karma Automotive LLC .... A 714 723-3247
9950 Jeronimo Rd Irvine (92618) ***(P-9955)***
Karman Topco LP (PA) .... **A** **949 797-2900**
18100 Von Karman Ave # 1000 Irvine (92612) ***(P-23460)***
Karoun Cheese, San Fernando *Also called Karoun Dairies Inc* ***(P-1775)***
Karoun Dairies Inc (PA) .... **E** **818 767-7000**
13023 Arroyo St San Fernando (91340) ***(P-1775)***
Karpe Real Estate Center, Bakersfield *Also called Elmer F Karpe Inc* ***(P-15845)***
Karrior Electric Vehicles Inc .... F 310 515-7600
570 W 184th St Gardena (90248) ***(P-7713)***
Karrior Indus Elc Vehicles, Gardena *Also called Karrior Electric Vehicles Inc* ***(P-7713)***
Kasdan Smnds Riley Vaughan LLP (PA) .... **D** **949 851-9000**
19900 Macarthur Blvd # 850 Irvine (92612) ***(P-21594)***
Kash Organization .... D 702 330-9215
81964 Camino Cantos Indio (92203) ***(P-16168)***
Kaslen Textiles LLC .... F 323 588-7700
2140 E 51st St Vernon (90058) ***(P-2709)***
Kastle Stair Inc (PA) .... **E** **714 596-2600**
7422 Mountjoy Dr Huntington Beach (92648) ***(P-3258)***
Katana Racing Inc (PA) .... **C** **562 340-6252**
4490 Ayers Ave Vernon (90058) ***(P-13068)***
Katana Racing Whl & Tire Distr, Vernon *Also called Katana Racing Inc* ***(P-13068)***
Kate Farms Inc .... C 805 845-2446
101 Innovation Pl Santa Barbara (93108) ***(P-2458)***
Kate Smrvlle Skin Hlth Experts, Beverly Hills *Also called Kate Somerville Skincare LLC* ***(P-4838)***
Kate Somerville Skincare LLC .... D 310 623-6822
5959 Randolph St Commerce (90040) ***(P-14255)***
Kate Somerville Skincare LLC (PA) .... **D** **323 655-7546**
144 S Beverly Dr Ste 500 Beverly Hills (90212) ***(P-4838)***
Katella Properties .... C 562 596-5561
3902 Katella Ave Los Alamitos (90720) ***(P-20384)***
Kater-Crafts Incorporated .... E 562 692-0665
4860 Gregg Rd Pico Rivera (90660) ***(P-4618)***
Kathleen Brugger .... E 909 226-1372
6815 Foxtail Ct Rancho Cucamonga (91739) ***(P-18988)***
Kathryn M Ireland Inc (PA) .... **C** **323 965-9888**
1750 W Adams Blvd Los Angeles (90018) ***(P-2578)***
Kathy Ireland Worldwide LLC .... E 310 557-2700
39 Princeton Dr Rancho Mirage (92270) ***(P-2852)***
Katten Muchin Rosenman LLP .... D 310 788-4498
515 S Flower St Los Angeles (90071) ***(P-21595)***
Katten Muchin Rosenman LLP .... D 310 788-4400
2029 Century Park E # 2600 Los Angeles (90067) ***(P-21596)***
Katz Millennium Sls & Mktg Inc .... C 323 966-5066
5700 Wilshire Blvd # 100 Los Angeles (90036) ***(P-9281)***
Katzirs Floor & HM Design Inc (PA) .... **E** **818 988-9663**
14959 Delano St Van Nuys (91411) ***(P-13175)***
Katzkin Leather Inc (PA) .... **C** **323 725-1243**
6868 W Acco St Montebello (90640) ***(P-14943)***
Kaufman & Broad, Los Angeles *Also called Kaufman and Broad Limited* ***(P-677)***
Kaufman and Broad Limited .... C 310 231-4000
10990 Wilshire Blvd Fl 7 Los Angeles (90024) ***(P-677)***
Kav America Ag Inc .... F 855 528-8721
422 Commercial Rd San Bernardino (92408) ***(P-2356)***
Kava Holdings Inc (HQ) .... **C** **310 472-1211**
701 Stone Canyon Rd Los Angeles (90077) ***(P-16521)***
Kavlico Corporation (HQ) .... **A** **805 523-2000**
1461 Lawrence Dr Thousand Oaks (91320) ***(P-9738)***
Kawai America Corporation (HQ) .... **E** **310 631-1771**
2055 E University Dr Compton (90220) ***(P-14166)***
Kawasaki Motors Corp USA (HQ) .... **B** **949 837-4683**
26972 Burbank Foothill Ranch (92610) ***(P-13069)***
Kaweah Container Inc (HQ) .... **D** **559 651-7846**
7101 Avenue 304 Visalia (93291) ***(P-3816)***
Kaweah Delta Health Care .... D 559 624-2854
101 S Floral St Visalia (93291) ***(P-21448)***

ALPHABETIC

Employee Codes: A=Over 500 employees, B=251-500
C=101-250, D=51-100, E=20-50 F=10-19
2022 Southern California Business
Directory and Buyers Guide
© Mergent Inc. 1-800-342-5647
1177

Kaweah Delta Health Care Dst.....C.....559 591-5513
355 Monte Vista Dr Dinuba (93618) *(P-20817)*
Kaweah Delta Health Care Dst.....C.....559 592-7128
1014 San Juan Ave Exeter (93221) *(P-20818)*
Kaweah Delta Health Care Dst.....C.....559 624-4800
1110 S Ben Maddox Way Visalia (93292) *(P-20819)*
Kaweah Delta Health Care Dst (PA).....A.....**559 624-2000**
400 W Mineral King Ave Visalia (93291) *(P-20820)*
Kaweah Delta Medical Center, Visalia *Also called Kaweah Delta Health Care Dst (P-20820)*
Kaweah Dlta Hlth Care Dst Gild.....D.....559 624-3300
1100 S Akers St Visalia (93277) *(P-21021)*
Kaweah Dlta Hlth Care Dst Gild.....C.....559 624-2000
400 W Mineral King Ave Visalia (93291) *(P-20821)*
Kawneer Company Inc.....C.....559 651-4000
7200 W Doe Ave Visalia (93291) *(P-6970)*
Kawneer Company Inc.....D.....951 410-4779
925 Marlborough Ave Riverside (92507) *(P-6704)*
Kay & James Inc.....D.....818 998-0357
14062 Balboa Blvd Sylmar (91342) *(P-8651)*
Kay and Associates Inc.....E.....559 410-0917
300 Reeves Blvd Lemoore (93246) *(P-10193)*
Kay Automotive Distrs Inc (PA).....E.....**818 781-6850**
14650 Calvert St Van Nuys (91411) *(P-13070)*
Kaydan Logistics LLC.....D.....951 961-9000
45562 Ponderosa Ct Temecula (92592) *(P-12576)*
Kaylas Cake Corporation.....E.....714 869-1522
1311 S Gilbert St Fullerton (92833) *(P-14701)*
Kayne Andrson Rdnick Inv MGT L.....D.....310 229-9260
1800 Avenue Of The Stars Los Angeles (90067) *(P-16131)*
Kayo Clothing Company, Lynwood *Also called Kayo of California (P-2903)*
Kayo of California (PA).....E.....**323 233-6107**
11854 Alameda St Lynwood (90262) *(P-2903)*
KB Delta Inc.....E.....310 530-1539
3340 Fujita St Torrance (90505) *(P-7156)*
KB Delta Comprsr Valve Parts, Torrance *Also called KB Delta Inc (P-7156)*
KB Home (PA).....D.....**310 231-4000**
10990 Wilshire Blvd Fl 7 Los Angeles (90024) *(P-678)*
KB Home Grater Los Angeles Inc (HQ).....D.....**310 231-4000**
10990 Wilshire Blvd # 700 Los Angeles (90024) *(P-618)*
KB Home Grater Los Angeles Inc.....C.....951 691-5300
36310 Inland Valley Dr Wildomar (92595) *(P-619)*
KB Sheetmetal Fabrication Inc.....E.....714 979-1780
17371 Mount Wynne Cir B Fountain Valley (92708) *(P-6860)*
Kba Engineering LLC.....D.....661 323-0487
2157 Mohawk St Bakersfield (93308) *(P-7672)*
Kbkg Inc.....D.....626 449-4225
225 S Lake Ave Ste 400 Pasadena (91101) *(P-22796)*
Kbl Group International Ltd.....E.....562 699-9995
9142 9150 Norwalk Blvd Santa Fe Springs (90670) *(P-14388)*
Kbl International, Santa Fe Springs *Also called Kbl Group International Ltd (P-14388)*
Kbr Inc.....E.....562 436-9281
2000 W Gaylord St Long Beach (90813) *(P-8938)*
Kc Exclusive Inc (PA).....D.....**213 749-0088**
1100 S San Pedro St M06 Los Angeles (90015) *(P-14389)*
Kc Pharmaceuticals Inc (PA).....D.....**909 598-9499**
3201 Producer Way Pomona (91768) *(P-4839)*
KC SERVICES, Anaheim *Also called Korean Community Services Inc (P-21047)*
Kca Electronics Inc.....C.....714 239-2433
223 N Crescent Way Anaheim (92801) *(P-9419)*
Kcal Insurance, Hacienda Heights *Also called Heights Insurance Group Inc (P-15581)*
KCAO, Hanford *Also called Kings Cmnty Action Orgnztion I (P-21831)*
Kcb Towers Inc.....D.....909 862-0322
27260 Meines St Highland (92346) *(P-1572)*
Kci Newport Inc.....F.....877 302-5302
15763 Ornelas St Baldwin Park (91706) *(P-3734)*
KCRW FM RADIO, Santa Monica *Also called Kcrw Foundation Inc (P-22191)*
Kcrw Foundation Inc.....D.....310 450-5183
1900 Pico Blvd Santa Monica (90405) *(P-22191)*
KCS West Inc.....D.....323 269-0020
250 E 1st St Ste 700 Los Angeles (90012) *(P-705)*
Kdc Inc (HQ).....B.....**714 828-7000**
4462 Corporate Center Dr Los Alamitos (90720) *(P-1271)*
Kdc Systems, Los Alamitos *Also called Kdc Inc (P-1271)*
Kdc-One, Chatsworth *Also called Thibiant International Inc (P-5073)*
Kdc/One Cosmetic Labs Amer Inc.....C.....818 998-3511
20245 Sunburst St Chatsworth (91311) *(P-5038)*
Kdg Construction Consulting, Glendale *Also called Kennard Development Group (P-660)*
KDI Elements.....D.....760 345-9933
79431 Country Club Dr Bermuda Dunes (92203) *(P-1417)*
Kds Donut Chinese Foods.....F.....949 588-1688
26761 Portola Pkwy Ste 2g Foothill Ranch (92610) *(P-2011)*
Kearn Alternative Care Inc (PA).....B.....**661 631-2036**
2029 21st St Bakersfield (93301) *(P-21178)*
Keating Dental Arts.....C.....949 955-2100
16881 Hale Ave Ste A Irvine (92606) *(P-21110)*
Kec Engineering.....C.....951 734-3010
200 N Sherman Ave Corona (92882) *(P-894)*
Kechika, Rcho STA Marg *Also called Point Conception Inc (P-2985)*
Keck Hospital of Usc.....B.....800 872-2273
1500 San Pablo St Los Angeles (90033) *(P-20822)*
Kedren Acute Psychtric Hosp Cm, Los Angeles *Also called Kedren Community Hlth Ctr Inc (P-21022)*
Kedren Community Hlth Ctr Inc.....C.....323 524-0634
3800 S Figueroa St Los Angeles (90037) *(P-21830)*
Kedren Community Hlth Ctr Inc (PA).....B.....**323 233-0425**
4211 Avalon Blvd Los Angeles (90011) *(P-21022)*
Keebler Company.....D.....714 228-1555
14000 183rd St La Palma (90623) *(P-2067)*
Keefe Plumbing Services, Glendale *Also called H L Moe Co Inc (P-1080)*
Keenan & Associates (HQ).....B.....**310 212-3344**
2355 Crenshaw Blvd # 200 Torrance (90501) *(P-15586)*
Keenan Farms Inc.....D.....559 945-1400
31510 Plymouth Ave Kettleman City (93239) *(P-56)*
Keenan Hpkins Sder Stwell Cntr (PA).....D.....**714 695-3670**
5109 E La Palma Ave Ste A Anaheim (92807) *(P-1384)*
Keesal Young Logan A Prof Corp (PA).....D.....**562 436-2000**
400 Oceangate Ste 1400 Long Beach (90802) *(P-21597)*
Keiro Nursing Home.....C.....323 276-5700
2221 Lincoln Park Ave Los Angeles (90031) *(P-20823)*
Keiro Senior Health Care, Los Angeles *Also called Keiro Services (P-23045)*
Keiro Services.....B.....213 873-5700
420 E 3rd St Ste 1000 Los Angeles (90013) *(P-23045)*
Keith E Archambeau Sr Inc.....E.....818 718-6110
20615 Plummer St Chatsworth (91311) *(P-6861)*
Kelco, Oxnard *Also called Kim Laube & Company Inc (P-5039)*
Kelco Sales & Engineering, Norwalk *Also called Polley Inc (P-8137)*
Kelcourt Plastics Inc (HQ).....D.....**949 361-0774**
1000 Calle Recodo San Clemente (92673) *(P-5688)*
Keller Classics Inc (PA).....E.....**805 524-1322**
19628 Country Oaks St Tehachapi (93561) *(P-2904)*
Keller Engineering Inc.....F.....310 326-6291
3203 Kashiwa St Torrance (90505) *(P-8652)*
Keller Lincoln Ford, Hanford *Also called Jvac Inc (P-18846)*
Keller Williams Realtors, Corona *Also called Pro Group Inc (P-15955)*
Keller Williams Realtors, Beverly Hills *Also called Keller Wllams Rlty Bvrly Hills (P-15899)*
Keller Wllams Rlty Bvrly Hills.....D.....310 432-6400
439 N Canon Dr Ste 300 Beverly Hills (90210) *(P-15899)*
Kelley Blue Book Co Inc (HQ).....D.....**949 770-7704**
195 Technology Dr Irvine (92618) *(P-4076)*
Kellogg Andlson Accntancy Corp (PA).....D.....**818 971-5100**
21700 Oxnard St Ste 800 Woodland Hills (91367) *(P-22797)*
Kellstrom Holding Corporation (PA).....D.....**561 222-7455**
100 N Pcf Cast Hwy Ste 19 El Segundo (90245) *(P-14060)*
Kelly & Thome.....F.....909 623-2559
228 San Lorenzo St Pomona (91766) *(P-8653)*
Kelly Paper Company (HQ).....E.....**909 859-8200**
12310 Slauson Ave Santa Fe Springs (90670) *(P-14187)*
Kelly Pneumatics Inc.....E.....800 704-7552
1611 Babcock St Newport Beach (92663) *(P-9881)*
Kelly Spicers Inc (HQ).....C.....**562 698-1199**
12310 Slauson Ave Santa Fe Springs (90670) *(P-14188)*
Kelly Spicers Packaging, Santa Fe Springs *Also called Kelly Spicers Inc (P-14188)*
Kelly Toys Holdings LLC.....D.....323 923-1300
4811 S Alameda St Vernon (90058) *(P-16103)*
Kelly-Wright Hardwoods Inc.....F.....714 632-9930
450 Delta Ave Brea (92821) *(P-13218)*
Kelmscott Communications LLC.....B.....949 475-1900
2485 Da Vinci Irvine (92614) *(P-4348)*
Kelpac Medical, San Clemente *Also called Kelcourt Plastics Inc (P-5688)*
Kemco, Ontario *Also called Kitchen Equipment Mfg Co Inc (P-7157)*
Kemp Bros Construction Inc.....E.....562 236-5000
10135 Geary Ave Santa Fe Springs (90670) *(P-706)*
Kemper Enterprises Inc.....E.....909 627-6191
13595 12th St Chino (91710) *(P-6484)*
Kemper Insurance, Visalia *Also called Mitchell Buckman Inc (P-15595)*
Kempton Machine Works Inc.....E.....714 990-0596
4070 E Leaverton Ct Anaheim (92807) *(P-7855)*
Ken Grody Ford, Buena Park *Also called Ted Ford Jones Inc (P-18878)*
Ken Grody Ford - Redlands, Redlands *Also called Ken Grody Redlands LLC (P-18847)*
Ken Grody Redlands LLC.....D.....909 793-3211
1121 W Colton Ave Redlands (92374) *(P-18847)*
Ken Hoffmann Inc.....E.....760 325-6012
345 Del Sol Rd Palm Springs (92262) *(P-7275)*
Ken Real Estate Lease Ltd.....D.....714 778-1700
900 S Disneyland Dr Anaheim (92802) *(P-16522)*
Ken Starr Inc.....D.....714 632-8789
1120 N Tustin Ave Anaheim (92807) *(P-1089)*
Kenai Drilling Limited.....C.....661 587-0117
2651 Patton Way Bakersfield (93308) *(P-1561)*
Kendon Industries LLC.....E.....714 630-7144
2990 E Miraloma Ave Anaheim (92806) *(P-10542)*
Kenlor Industries Inc.....F.....714 647-0770
1560 E Edinger Ave Ste A1 Santa Ana (92705) *(P-11003)*
Kennard Development Group.....D.....818 241-0800
1025 N Brand Blvd Ste 300 Glendale (91202) *(P-660)*
Kennedy Athletics, Carson *Also called Cali-Fame Los Angeles Inc (P-3025)*
Kennedy Care Center, Los Angeles *Also called BV General Inc (P-20567)*
Kennedy Engineered Pdts Inc.....E.....661 272-1147
38830 17th St E Palmdale (93550) *(P-10085)*
Kennedy Name Plate Co.....E.....323 585-0121
4501 Pacific Blvd Vernon (90058) *(P-7379)*
Kennedy-Wilson Inc (PA).....C.....**310 887-6400**
151 El Camino Dr Beverly Hills (90212) *(P-15900)*
Kenneth Brdwick Intr Dsgns Inc.....D.....310 274-9999
1615 Westwood Blvd # 202 Los Angeles (90024) *(P-18562)*
Kenneth Corp.....A.....714 537-5160
12601 Garden Grove Blvd Garden Grove (92843) *(P-20824)*
Kenneth Norris Cancer Hospital, Los Angeles *Also called Tenet Health Systems Norris (P-20971)*
Kenny The Printer, Orange *Also called American PCF Prtrs College Inc (P-4227)*
Kens Spray Equipment Inc (HQ).....C.....**310 635-9995**
1900 W Walnut St Compton (90220) *(P-7380)*
Kent Seafarms, Mecca *Also called Kent Seatech LLC (P-373)*
Kent Seatech LLC.....E.....760 396-2301
70775 Buchanan St Mecca (92254) *(P-373)*

Mergent e-mail: customerrelations@mergent.com
1178
2022 Southern California Business Directory and Buyers Guide
(P-0000) Products & Services Section entry number
(PA)=Parent Co (HQ)=Headquarters (DH)=Div Headquarters

Kentina, Temecula *Also called Sft Realty Galway Downs LLC* ***(P-15996)***
Kentmaster Mfg Co Inc (PA)......E......**626 359-8888**
1801 S Mountain Ave Monrovia (91016) ***(P-13910)***
Kenwalt Die Casting Company, Sun Valley *Also called Kenwalt Die Casting Corp* ***(P-6365)***
Kenwalt Die Casting Corp......E......818 768-5800
8719 Bradley Ave Sun Valley (91352) ***(P-6365)***
Keolis Transit America Inc......C......818 616-5254
14663 Keswick St Van Nuys (91405) ***(P-11813)***
Keolis Transit America Inc......D......661 341-3910
660 W Avenue L Lancaster (93534) ***(P-11814)***
Keolis Transit America Inc (HQ)......E......**310 981-9500**
6053 W Century Blvd # 900 Los Angeles (90045) ***(P-11876)***
Kepner Plas Fabricators Inc......E......310 325-3162
3131 Lomita Blvd Torrance (90505) ***(P-5689)***
Kerlan-Jobe Orthopedic Clinic (PA)......D......**310 665-7200**
6801 Park Ter Ste 500 Los Angeles (90045) ***(P-19949)***
Kern Cmnty Cllege Dst Fndation......D......661 336-5117
2100 Chester Ave Bakersfield (93301) ***(P-21958)***
Kern Community College Dst......D......760 384-6100
3000 College Heights Blvd Ridgecrest (93555) ***(P-22025)***
Kern County Hospital Authority (PA)......A......**661 326-2102**
1700 Mount Vernon Ave Bakersfield (93306) ***(P-20825)***
Kern Direct Marketing, Woodland Hills *Also called Kern Organization Inc* ***(P-17026)***
Kern Family Helathcare, Bakersfield *Also called Kern Health Systems Inc* ***(P-19950)***
Kern Federal Credit Union......D......661 327-9461
1717 Truxtun Ave Bakersfield (93301) ***(P-15070)***
Kern Health Systems Inc......D......661 664-5000
2900 Buck Owens Blvd Bakersfield (93308) ***(P-19950)***
Kern Organization Inc......D......818 703-8775
20955 Warner Center Ln Woodland Hills (91367) ***(P-17026)***
Kern Rdlgy Imaging Systems Inc (PA)......D......**661 326-9600**
2301 Bahamas Dr Bakersfield (93309) ***(P-19951)***
Kern Rdlgy Imaging Systems Inc......D......661 322-9958
4100 Truxtun Ave Ste 306 Bakersfield (93309) ***(P-19952)***
Kern Regional Center (PA)......C......**661 327-8531**
3200 N Sillect Ave Bakersfield (93308) ***(P-22192)***
Kern Ridge Growers LLC......B......661 854-3141
25429 Barbara St Arvin (93203) ***(P-178)***
Kern Schools Federal Credit Un, Delano *Also called Valley Strong Credit Union* ***(P-15098)***
Kern Security Corporation......D......661 363-6874
2701 Fruitvale Ave Bakersfield (93308) ***(P-18390)***
Kern Security Systems, Bakersfield *Also called Kern Security Corporation* ***(P-18390)***
Kern Steel Fabrication Inc (PA)......D......**661 327-9588**
627 Williams St Bakersfield (93305) ***(P-6626)***
Kern Valley Hosp Foundation (PA)......B......**760 379-2681**
6412 Laurel Ave Lake Isabella (93240) ***(P-20385)***
Kern Valley Sun, Lake Isabella *Also called Wick Communications Co* ***(P-4045)***
Kernel, Culver City *Also called Hl LLC* ***(P-22883)***
Kerning Data Systems Inc......F......818 882-8712
21628 Lassen St Chatsworth (91311) ***(P-7919)***
Kernridge Division, Mc Kittrick *Also called Aera Energy LLC* ***(P-385)***
Kerr Corporation (HQ)......C......**714 516-7400**
1717 W Collins Ave Orange (92867) ***(P-11179)***
Kerry Inc......E......760 396-2116
64405 Lincoln St Mecca (92254) ***(P-1798)***
Kerry Ingredients......F......323 430-9718
1916 S Tubeway Ave Commerce (90040) ***(P-2459)***
Kerv Interactive, Sherman Oaks *Also called Grabit Interactive Inc* ***(P-17086)***
Kesa Incorporated......E......714 956-2827
960 E Discovery Ln Anaheim (92801) ***(P-18391)***
Kesmor Associates......E......213 629-2300
610 S Broadway Ste 717 Los Angeles (90014) ***(P-11319)***
Kesq TV, Thousand Palms *Also called Gulf- California Broadcast Co* ***(P-12728)***
Ketab Corporation......E......310 477-7477
12701 Van Nuys Blvd Ste H Pacoima (91331) ***(P-4186)***
Kettenbach LP......E......877 532-2123
16052 Beach Blvd Ste 221 Huntington Beach (92647) ***(P-11180)***
Kevidko Inc......F......310 601-0060
9903 Santa Monica Blvd # 982 Beverly Hills (90212) ***(P-3758)***
Kevin Orthopedic, Riverside *Also called Foot In Motion Inc* ***(P-11105)***
Kevin Persons Inc......E......805 371-8746
2977 Los Feliz Dr Thousand Oaks (91362) ***(P-263)***
Kevin White......F......562 231-6642
9918 Ramona St Apt 1 Bellflower (90706) ***(P-3999)***
Kevita Inc (HQ)......D......**805 200-2250**
2220 Celsius Ave Ste A Oxnard (93030) ***(P-2269)***
Key Air Cnditioning Contrs Inc......D......562 941-2233
10905 Laurel Ave Santa Fe Springs (90670) ***(P-1090)***
Key Container, South Gate *Also called Liberty Container Company* ***(P-3817)***
Key Environmental Services, Los Angeles *Also called The Teecor Group Inc* ***(P-1695)***
Key Health Systems, Visalia *Also called Key Medical Group Inc* ***(P-22193)***
Key Material Handling Inc......F......805 520-6007
4790 Alamo St Simi Valley (93063) ***(P-7714)***
Key Medical Group Inc......D......559 734-0388
3335 S Fairway St Visalia (93277) ***(P-22193)***
Key-Bak, Ontario *Also called West Coast Chain Mfg Co* ***(P-9928)***
Keyes Lexus, Van Nuys *Also called Keylex Inc* ***(P-18849)***
Keyes Motors Inc (PA)......D......**818 782-0122**
5855 Van Nuys Blvd Van Nuys (91401) ***(P-18848)***
Keyes Toyota, Van Nuys *Also called Keyes Motors Inc* ***(P-18848)***
Keylex Inc (PA)......D......**818 379-4000**
5905 Van Nuys Blvd Van Nuys (91401) ***(P-18849)***
Keyline Sales Inc......E......562 904-3910
9768 Firestone Blvd Downey (90241) ***(P-13832)***
Keystone Automotive Warehouse......D......951 277-5237
15640 Cntu Gllano Rnch Rd Eastvale (91752) ***(P-13071)***
Keystone Ford Inc (PA)......C......**562 868-0825**
12000 Firestone Blvd Norwalk (90650) ***(P-18743)***
Keystone NPS LLC (HQ)......D......**909 633-6354**
11980 Mount Vernon Ave Grand Terrace (92313) ***(P-22194)***
Keystone NPS LLC......C......951 785-0504
9994 County Farm Rd Riverside (92503) ***(P-22195)***
Keystone PCF Property MGT Inc (PA)......D......**949 833-2600**
16775 Von Karman Ave # 100 Irvine (92606) ***(P-15901)***
Keystone Schools-Ramona, Grand Terrace *Also called Keystone NPS LLC* ***(P-22194)***
Keyt Television, Santa Barbara *Also called Smith Broadcasting Group Inc* ***(P-12741)***
Kf Fiberglass Inc (PA)......F......**562 869-1536**
8247 Phlox St Downey (90241) ***(P-10086)***
Kf Ontario Healthcare LLC......E......909 984-6713
1661 S Euclid Ave Ontario (91762) ***(P-20599)***
Kfa LLP......D......310 399-7975
3573 Hayden Ave Culver City (90232) ***(P-22726)***
KG Constrctons Sltions USA Inc (PA)......D......**800 295-9109**
7450 Greenbush Ave North Hollywood (91605) ***(P-620)***
Kh9100 LLC......F......818 972-2580
3073 N California St Burbank (91504) ***(P-11254)***
Kharon, Los Angeles *Also called 1nteger LLC* ***(P-17533)***
Kheir, Los Angeles *Also called Korean Hlth Edcatn Info RES CT* ***(P-21833)***
Khs & S Contractors, Anaheim *Also called Keenan Hpkins Sder Stwell Cntr* ***(P-1384)***
Khyber Foods Incorporated......F......714 879-0900
500 S Acacia Ave Fullerton (92831) ***(P-2460)***
Ki-P C USA Jeans Inc......D......310 234-8185
6738 Los Verdes Dr Apt 2 Rancho Palos Verdes (90275) ***(P-2771)***
Kia Design Center America, Irvine *Also called Hyundai Amer Technical Ctr Inc* ***(P-22573)***
Kiara Sky Professional Nails, Bakersfield *Also called Glam and Glits Nail Design Inc* ***(P-5024)***
Kidney Center Ventura Inc......D......805 433-7777
50 Moreland Rd Simi Valley (93065) ***(P-21252)***
Kidney Centers Michigan LLC (HQ)......E......**310 536-2400**
601 Hawaii St El Segundo (90245) ***(P-21253)***
Kidney Dialysis Center Verdugo, Simi Valley *Also called Kidney Center Ventura Inc* ***(P-21252)***
Kids First Learning Center, Pacoima *Also called Eben-Ezer Chld Day Care Ctr* ***(P-22010)***
Kids Healthy Foods LLC......E......949 260-4950
2030 Main St Ste 1300 Irvine (92614) ***(P-14702)***
Kids Klub Care Centers Inc (PA)......D......**626 795-2501**
380 S Raymond Ave Pasadena (91105) ***(P-22026)***
Kids Klub Pasadena, Pasadena *Also called Kids Klub Care Centers Inc* ***(P-22026)***
Kidspace A Prticipatory Museum......D......626 449-9144
480 N Arroyo Blvd Pasadena (91103) ***(P-22223)***
Kiewit Infrastructure West Co......C......562 946-1816
10704 Shoemaker Ave Santa Fe Springs (90670) ***(P-895)***
Kifuki USA Co Inc (HQ)......D......**626 334-8090**
15547 1st St Irwindale (91706) ***(P-1761)***
Kik Custom Products, Torrance *Also called Prestone Products Corporation* ***(P-5238)***
Kik Pool Additives Inc......C......909 390-9912
5160 E Airport Dr Ontario (91761) ***(P-5225)***
Kik-Socal Inc......A......562 946-6427
9028 Dice Rd Santa Fe Springs (90670) ***(P-4966)***
Kilgore Machine Company Inc......E......714 540-3659
2312 S Susan St Santa Ana (92704) ***(P-8654)***
Kilroy Realty LP (PA)......C......**310 481-8400**
12200 W Olympic Blvd # 200 Los Angeles (90064) ***(P-15902)***
Kilroy Realty Corporation (PA)......C......**310 481-8400**
12200 W Olympic Blvd # 200 Los Angeles (90064) ***(P-16238)***
Kim & Cami Productions Inc......E......323 584-1300
2950 Leonis Blvd Vernon (90058) ***(P-2962)***
Kim Bonjun Inc (PA)......E......**213 385-1258**
821 S Vermont Ave Los Angeles (90005) ***(P-11565)***
Kim Chong......E......323 581-4700
2105 E 25th St Los Angeles (90058) ***(P-18563)***
Kim Laube & Company Inc......E......805 240-1300
2221 Statham Blvd Oxnard (93033) ***(P-5039)***
Kim's Fence, Fullerton *Also called Kims Welding and Iron Works* ***(P-7090)***
Kimball Nelson Inc......F......310 636-0081
7740 Lemona Ave Van Nuys (91405) ***(P-11701)***
Kimberly Lighting, Vernon *Also called Hollywood Lamp & Shade Co* ***(P-9020)***
Kimberly Machine Inc......E......714 539-0151
12822 Joy St Garden Grove (92840) ***(P-8655)***
Kimco Services, Ontario *Also called Kimco Staffing Services Inc* ***(P-17433)***
Kimco Staffing Services Inc......A......310 622-1616
3415 S Sepulveda Blvd # 1100 Los Angeles (90034) ***(P-17432)***
Kimco Staffing Services Inc......A......909 390-9881
4295 Jurupa St Ste 107 Ontario (91761) ***(P-17433)***
Kimco Staffing Services Inc......A......951 686-3800
1770 Iowa Ave Ste 160 Riverside (92507) ***(P-17434)***
Kimco Staffing Solutions, Riverside *Also called Kimco Staffing Services Inc* ***(P-17434)***
Kimoa Broadcast TV Netwrk......F......213 364-9558
12222 Grfield Ave Apt 222 South Gate (90280) ***(P-18564)***
Kimoyo Productions, Burbank *Also called Ftp Productions LLC* ***(P-19127)***
Kimpton Hotel & Rest Group LLC......C......323 852-6000
6317 Wilshire Blvd Los Angeles (90048) ***(P-16523)***
Kims Welding and Iron Works......F......714 680-7700
2331 E Orangethorpe Ave Fullerton (92831) ***(P-7090)***
Kinamad, Camarillo *Also called VME Acquisition Corp* ***(P-11152)***
Kinamed Inc......E......805 384-2748
820 Flynn Rd Camarillo (93012) ***(P-11120)***
Kincaid Industries Inc......C......760 343-5457
31065 Plantation Dr Thousand Palms (92276) ***(P-1091)***
Kindeva Drug Delivery LP......B......818 341-1300
19901 Nordhoff St Northridge (91324) ***(P-4840)***
Kindred Healthcare LLC......D......760 241-7044
17290 Jasmine St Ste 104 Victorville (92395) ***(P-21179)***
Kindred Healthcare LLC......D......661 324-1232
5001 E Cmmrccnter Dr Ste Bakersfield (93309) ***(P-21180)***

A L P H A B E T I C

Employee Codes: A=Over 500 employees, B=251-500
C=101-250, D=51-100, E=20-50 F=10-19
2022 Southern California Business Directory and Buyers Guide
© Mergent Inc. 1-800-342-5647
1179

Kindred Healthcare LLC ... C ... 909 391-0333
550 N Monterey Ave Ontario (91764) ***(P-20826)***

Kindred Healthcare LLC ... D ... 909 890-1226
735 Carnegie Dr Ste 240 San Bernardino (92408) ***(P-21181)***

Kindred Healthcare LLC ... C ... 951 436-3535
2224 Medical Center Dr Perris (92571) ***(P-20827)***

Kindred Healthcare LLC ... C ... 714 564-7800
1901 College Ave Santa Ana (92706) ***(P-20828)***

Kindred Healthcare LLC ... C ... 805 544-4472
3220 S Higuera St San Luis Obispo (93401) ***(P-20386)***

Kindred Healthcare LLC ... C ... 562 531-3110
16453 Colorado Ave Paramount (90723) ***(P-20829)***

Kindred Hospital - Baldwin Pk, Baldwin Park *Also called Knd Development 52 LLC* ***(P-20830)***

Kindred Hospital - Rancho, Rancho Cucamonga *Also called Knd Development 55 LLC* ***(P-20831)***

Kindred Hospital La Mirada, La Mirada *Also called Southern Cal Spcialty Care Inc* ***(P-20949)***

Kindred Hospital La Mirata, West Covina *Also called Southern Cal Spcialty Care Inc* ***(P-20948)***

Kindred Hospital Paramount, Paramount *Also called Kindred Healthcare LLC* ***(P-20829)***

Kindred Hospital Santa Ana, Santa Ana *Also called Kindred Healthcare LLC* ***(P-20828)***

Kindred Hospital Santa Ana, Santa Ana *Also called Southern Cal Spcialty Care Inc* ***(P-20947)***

Kindred Litho Incorporated ... E ... 909 944-4015
10833 Bell Ct Rancho Cucamonga (91730) ***(P-4349)***

Kinecta Federal Credit Union (PA) ... **C ... 310 643-5400**
1440 Rosecrans Ave Manhattan Beach (90266) ***(P-15071)***

Kinemetrics Inc (HQ) ... **D ... 626 795-2220**
222 Vista Ave Pasadena (91107) ***(P-22596)***

King Hlmes Pterno Soriano LLP ... E ... 310 282-8989
1900 Avenue Of The Stars Los Angeles (90067) ***(P-21598)***

King Audio Inc ... F ... 626 968-8827
152 S Brent Cir Walnut (91789) ***(P-13688)***

King David Convalescent Hosp, Santa Monica *Also called Golden State Health Ctrs Inc* ***(P-20594)***

King Equipment LLC ... D ... 909 986-5300
1690 Ashley Way Colton (92324) ***(P-17311)***

King Ex Chinese Fd & Donut, North Hollywood *Also called King Express Inc* ***(P-2012)***

King Express Inc ... F ... 818 503-2772
12053 Vanowen St North Hollywood (91605) ***(P-2012)***

King Henrys Inc ... E ... 818 536-3692
29124 Hancock Pkwy 1 Valencia (91355) ***(P-2362)***

King Instrument Company Inc ... E ... 714 891-0008
12700 Pala Dr Garden Grove (92841) ***(P-10704)***

King Janitorial Equipment Svcs, Garden Grove *Also called Janitorial Equipment Svcs Inc* ***(P-17254)***

King Nutronics Corporation ... E ... 818 887-5460
6421 Independence Ave Woodland Hills (91367) ***(P-10705)***

King Plastics Inc ... D ... 714 997-7540
840 N Elm St Orange (92867) ***(P-5690)***

King Relocation Services, Santa Fe Springs *Also called Van King & Storage Inc* ***(P-12089)***

King Shock Technology Inc ... D ... 719 394-3754
12472 Edison Way Garden Grove (92841) ***(P-10087)***

King Supply Company LLC ... D ... 714 670-8980
6340 Valley View St Buena Park (90620) ***(P-1671)***

King Ventures ... C ... 805 544-4444
285 Bridge St San Luis Obispo (93401) ***(P-16054)***

King's Caps, Carson *Also called H & C Headwear Inc* ***(P-14335)***

Kingcom(us) LLC (HQ) ... **E ... 424 744-5697**
3100 Ocean Park Blvd Santa Monica (90405) ***(P-17900)***

Kingdom Elixir, San Juan Capistrano *Also called Kingdom Entities LLC* ***(P-23461)***

Kingdom Enterprise Films LLC ... E ... 818 963-2513
10812 Bothwell Rd Chatsworth (91311) ***(P-19139)***

Kingdom Entities LLC (PA) ... **D ... 949 325-9240**
32401 Calle Perfecto San Juan Capistrano (92675) ***(P-23461)***

Kingdom Matress Company, Commerce *Also called Kingdom Mattress Co Inc* ***(P-3551)***

Kingdom Mattress Co Inc ... E ... 562 630-5531
2425 S Malt Ave Commerce (90040) ***(P-3551)***

Kingdomway Usa LLC ... F ... 714 832-9700
2802 Dow Ave Tustin (92780) ***(P-4841)***

Kingman Industries Inc ... E ... 951 698-1812
26370 Beckman Ct Ste A Murrieta (92562) ***(P-4943)***

Kings Cabinet Systems ... F ... 559 584-9662
426 Park Ave Hanford (93230) ***(P-3588)***

Kings Cmnty Action Orgnztion I (PA) ... **D ... 559 582-4386**
1130 N 11th Ave Hanford (93230) ***(P-21831)***

Kings County Truck Lines (HQ) ... **C ... 559 686-2857**
754 S Blackstone St Tulare (93274) ***(P-12056)***

Kings Garden LLC ... C ... 760 275-4969
3540 N Anza Rd Palm Springs (92262) ***(P-23252)***

Kings Garden Royal Deliveries, Palm Springs *Also called Kings Garden LLC* ***(P-23252)***

Kings Hawaiian Bakery, Gardena *Also called Kings Hawaiian Bakery W Inc* ***(P-14525)***

Kings Hawaiian Bakery W Inc (HQ) ... **E ... 310 533-3250**
1411 W 190th St Gardena (90248) ***(P-14525)***

Kings Nrsing Rhabilitation Ctr, Hanford *Also called Kings Nrsing Rhblttion Hosp In* ***(P-20387)***

Kings Nrsing Rhblttion Hosp In ... E ... 559 582-4414
851 Leslie Ln Hanford (93230) ***(P-20387)***

Kings Rehabilitation Ctr Inc (PA) ... **D ... 559 582-9234**
490 E Hanford Armona Rd Hanford (93230) ***(P-21832)***

Kingseal Corporation ... F ... 562 944-3100
12681 Corral Pl Santa Fe Springs (90670) ***(P-5691)***

Kingsolver Inc ... F ... 562 945-7590
8417 Secura Way Santa Fe Springs (90670) ***(P-11512)***

Kingson Mold & Machine Inc ... E ... 714 871-0221
1350 Titan Way Brea (92821) ***(P-7810)***

Kingspan Light & Air LLC ... C ... 714 540-8950
401 Goetz Ave Santa Ana (92707) ***(P-1492)***

Kingston Digital Inc (HQ) ... **C ... 714 435-2600**
17600 Newhope St Fountain Valley (92708) ***(P-8270)***

Kingston Technology Corp (PA) ... **B ... 714 435-2600**
17600 Newhope St Fountain Valley (92708) ***(P-8271)***

Kingswood Capital MGT LP ... C ... 424 744-8238
11111 Santa Monica Blvd # 1700 Los Angeles (90025) ***(P-16157)***

Kingz & Kompany LLC ... E ... 888 274-8882
3415 S Sepulveda Blvd # 1 Los Angeles (90034) ***(P-15903)***

Kinkisharyo International LLC (HQ) ... **F ... 424 276-1803**
1960 E Grand Ave Ste 1210 El Segundo (90245) ***(P-10477)***

Kinsbursky Bros Supply Inc (PA) ... **D ... 714 738-8516**
125 E Commercial St Ste A Anaheim (92801) ***(P-14118)***

Kintetsu Enterprises ... D ... 213 687-2000
328 E 1st St Los Angeles (90012) ***(P-23046)***

Kintetsu Enterprises Co Amer, Torrance *Also called Kintetsu Enterprises Co Amer* ***(P-16524)***

Kintetsu Enterprises Co Amer (HQ) ... **C ... 310 782-9300**
21241 S Wstn Ave Ste 100 Torrance (90501) ***(P-16524)***

Kintetsu Enterprises Co Amer ... E ... 213 617-2000
328 E 1st St Los Angeles (90012) ***(P-16525)***

Kip Steel Inc ... E ... 714 461-1051
1650 Valley Ln Fullerton (92833) ***(P-6243)***

Kipe Molds Inc ... F ... 714 572-9576
340 E Crowther Ave Placentia (92870) ***(P-7811)***

Kirby Industries Inc ... F ... 714 437-0789
2109 S Lyon St Santa Ana (92705) ***(P-1418)***

Kirby Jeep-Eagle Suzuki, Ventura *Also called Kirby Oldsmobile* ***(P-18850)***

Kirby Oldsmobile ... D ... 805 644-2241
6424 Auto Center Dr Ventura (93003) ***(P-18850)***

Kirk API Containers ... E ... 323 278-5400
2131 Garfield Ave Commerce (90040) ***(P-5692)***

Kirk Containers, Commerce *Also called Arthurmade Plastics Inc* ***(P-5568)***

Kirkhill Aircraft Parts Co (PA) ... **C ... 714 223-5400**
3120 Enterprise St Brea (92821) ***(P-14061)***

Kirkhill Inc ... D ... 562 803-1117
12023 Woodruff Ave Downey (90241) ***(P-5386)***

Kirkhill Inc (HQ) ... **A ... 714 529-4901**
300 E Cypress St Brea (92821) ***(P-10362)***

Kirkhill Inc ... A ... 714 529-4901
300 E Cypress St Brea (92821) ***(P-5345)***

Kirkhill Inc ... A ... 714 529-4901
300 E Cypress St Brea (92821) ***(P-5346)***

Kirkhill Rubber Company ... D ... 562 803-1117
2500 E Thompson St Long Beach (90805) ***(P-5387)***

Kirschenman Enterprises Inc ... D ... 661 366-5736
10100 Digiorgio Rd Bakersfield (93307) ***(P-114)***

Kirschenman Enterprises Sls LP ... C ... 661 366-5736
12826 Edison Hwy Edison (93220) ***(P-18565)***

Kisca, Los Angeles *Also called Komarov Enterprises Inc* ***(P-2905)***

Kisco Senior Living LLC ... D ... 714 872-9785
1731 W Medical Center Dr Anaheim (92801) ***(P-15736)***

Kisco Senior Living LLC ... D ... 949 888-2250
21952 Buena Suerte Rcho STA Marg (92688) ***(P-15737)***

Kisco Senior Living LLC ... D ... 714 997-5355
620 S Glassell St Orange (92866) ***(P-15738)***

Kitara Media Corp (HQ) ... **E ... 201 539-2200**
2010 Main St Ste 900 Irvine (92614) ***(P-17027)***

Kitch Engineering Inc ... E ... 818 897-7133
12320 Montague St Pacoima (91331) ***(P-8656)***

Kitchen Cuts LLC ... D ... 323 560-7415
6045 District Blvd Maywood (90270) ***(P-1736)***

Kitchen Equipment Mfg Co Inc ... E ... 909 923-3153
2102 Maple Privado Ontario (91761) ***(P-7157)***

Kitchen Post Inc ... F ... 909 948-6768
8617 Baseline Rd Rancho Cucamonga (91730) ***(P-3323)***

Kitcor Corporation ... E ... 323 875-2820
9959 Glenoaks Blvd Sun Valley (91352) ***(P-7158)***

Kite Electric Inc ... C ... 949 380-7471
2 Thomas Irvine (92618) ***(P-1272)***

Kite Pharma Inc (HQ) ... **C ... 310 824-9999**
2400 Broadway Ste 100 Santa Monica (90404) ***(P-22846)***

Kitsinian Jewellers, Valencia *Also called SA Kitsinian Inc* ***(P-14138)***

Kitson Landscape MGT Inc ... C ... 805 681-9460
5787 Thornwood Dr Goleta (93117) ***(P-313)***

Kittrich Corporation (PA) ... **C ... 714 736-1000**
1585 W Mission Blvd Pomona (91766) ***(P-3712)***

Kittridge Hotels & Resorts LLC ... D ... 760 325-9676
150 S Indian Canyon Dr Palm Springs (92262) ***(P-16526)***

Kittyhawk Inc ... E ... 714 895-5024
11651 Monarch St Garden Grove (92841) ***(P-6442)***

Kittyhawk Products, Garden Grove *Also called Kpi Services Inc* ***(P-6444)***

Kittyhawk Products CA LLC ... E ... 714 895-5024
11651 Monarch St Garden Grove (92841) ***(P-6443)***

Kizure Hair Products & Irons, Compton *Also called Kizure Product Co Inc* ***(P-9007)***

Kizure Product Co Inc ... E ... 310 604-0058
1950 N Central Ave Compton (90222) ***(P-9007)***

Kkcs, Los Angeles *Also called Kal Krshnan Cnsulting Svcs Inc* ***(P-22595)***

Kkw Trucking Inc (PA) ... **C ... 909 869-1200**
3100 Pomona Blvd Pomona (91768) ***(P-12215)***

Kkzz 1590 ... E ... 805 289-1400
2284 S Victoria Ave 2g Ventura (93003) ***(P-12697)***

Kl Electronics Inc ... E ... 714 751-5611
3083 S Harbor Blvd Santa Ana (92704) ***(P-9420)***

KLA Corporation ... F ... 714 893-2474
15061 Beach Blvd Westminster (92683) ***(P-10763)***

Klassen Corporation (PA) ... **D ... 661 327-0875**
2021 Westwind Dr Bakersfield (93301) ***(P-779)***

Klax Radio Station, Los Angeles *Also called Spanish Brdcstg Sys of Cal* ***(P-12706)***

Kleen Maid Inc ... F ... 323 581-3000
11450 Sheldon St Sun Valley (91352) ***(P-3104)***

Klein Denatale Goldner Et Al (PA) ..... C 661 401-7755
4550 California Ave Fl 2 Bakersfield (93309) *(P-21599)*

Klein Dntale Gldner Cper Rsnli, Bakersfield *Also called Klein Denatale Goldner Et Al (P-21599)*

Kleverness Incorporated ..... F 213 559-2480
340 S Lemon Ave 2291 Walnut (91789) *(P-17901)*

Klink Citrus Association ..... C 559 798-1881
32921 Road 159 Ivanhoe (93235) *(P-179)*

Klink Citrus Exchange, Ivanhoe *Also called Klink Citrus Association (P-179)*

Klk Forte Industry Inc (PA) ..... E 323 415-9181
1535 Rio Vista Ave Los Angeles (90023) *(P-2963)*

Klm Laboratories Inc ..... D 661 295-2600
28280 Alta Vista Ave Valencia (91355) *(P-13498)*

Klm Management Company ..... D 626 330-3479
14120 Valley Blvd City of Industry (91746) *(P-14542)*

Klm Orthotic, Valencia *Also called Klm Laboratories Inc (P-13498)*

Kloeckner Metals Corporation ..... D 562 906-2020
9804 Norwalk Blvd Ste A Santa Fe Springs (90670) *(P-13575)*

Kloeckner Metals Corporation ..... D 559 688-7980
2000 S O St Tulare (93274) *(P-13576)*

Klooma Holdings Inc ..... E 305 747-3315
113 N San Vicente Blvd Beverly Hills (90211) *(P-17902)*

Kls Doors LLC (PA) ..... E 909 605-6468
501 Kettering Dr Ontario (91761) *(P-3259)*

Klune Industries Inc (HQ) ..... B 818 503-8100
7323 Coldwater Canyon Ave North Hollywood (91605) *(P-10363)*

Klx LLC ..... D 559 684-1037
1351 Charles Willard St Carson (90746) *(P-12057)*

Km Printing Production Inc ..... F 626 821-0008
218 Longden Ave Irwindale (91706) *(P-4350)*

Kmb Foods Inc (PA) ..... E 626 447-0545
1010 S Sierra Way San Bernardino (92408) *(P-1737)*

Kme Cnc Inc ..... F 714 345-5816
17200 Red Hill Ave Irvine (92614) *(P-7904)*

Kme Fire, Jurupa Valley *Also called Kovatch Mobile Equipment Corp (P-9956)*

Kmp Numatech Pacific, Pomona *Also called Numatech West (kmp) LLC (P-3822)*

KMW Communications, Fullerton *Also called Gigatera Communications (P-9718)*

Knd Development 52 LLC ..... D 626 388-2700
14148 Francisquito Ave Baldwin Park (91706) *(P-20830)*

Knd Development 55 LLC ..... D 909 581-6400
10841 White Oak Ave Rancho Cucamonga (91730) *(P-20831)*

Kng Brnds Inc DBA Pstola DBA D ..... E 323 588-6903
2211 E 27th St Vernon (90058) *(P-18566)*

Knight LLC (HQ) ..... D 949 595-4800
15340 Barranca Pkwy Irvine (92618) *(P-8127)*

Knight-Calabasas LLC (PA) ..... D 818 222-3200
4515 Park Entrada Calabasas (91302) *(P-19573)*

Knit Generation Group Inc ..... E 213 221-5081
3818 S Broadway Los Angeles (90037) *(P-2579)*

Knk Apparel Inc ..... F 310 768-3333
223 W Rosecrans Ave Gardena (90248) *(P-2783)*

Knobbe Martens Olson Bear LLP (PA) ..... B 949 760-0404
2040 Main St Fl 14 Irvine (92614) *(P-21600)*

Knolls Convalescent Hosp Inc (PA) ..... C 760 245-5361
16890 Green Tree Blvd Victorville (92395) *(P-20388)*

Knolls West Enterprise ..... C 760 245-0107
16890 Green Tree Blvd Victorville (92395) *(P-20389)*

Knolls West Residential Care, Victorville *Also called Knolls West Enterprise (P-20389)*

Knollwood Center, Riverside *Also called Knollwood Psychtric Hosp Chem (P-21023)*

Knollwood Psychtric Hosp Chem ..... D 951 275-8400
5900 Brockton Ave Riverside (92506) *(P-21023)*

Knorr-Bremse Evac LLC ..... E 410 875-0900
21136 S Wilmington Ave Long Beach (90810) *(P-11702)*

Knott's Berry Farm, Buena Park *Also called Knotts Berry Farm LLC (P-19518)*

Knott's Berry Farm Hotel, Buena Park *Also called Knotts Berry Farm LLC (P-16527)*

Knotts Berry Farm LLC (HQ) ..... B 714 827-1776
8039 Beach Blvd Buena Park (90620) *(P-19518)*

Knotts Berry Farm LLC ..... D 714 995-1111
7675 Crescent Ave Buena Park (90620) *(P-16527)*

Knr Devco ..... D 310 676-1111
14814 Hawthorne Blvd Lawndale (90260) *(P-16528)*

KOA Cctv, North Hollywood *Also called KOA Electronics Distribution (P-13740)*

KOA Electronics Distribution (PA) ..... D 818 255-6666
7306 Coldwater Canyon Ave North Hollywood (91605) *(P-13740)*

Kobelco Compressors Amer Inc ..... D 951 739-3030
301 N Smith Ave Corona (92878) *(P-8034)*

Kobelco Compressors Amer Inc (HQ) ..... B 951 739-3030
1450 W Rincon St Corona (92878) *(P-8035)*

Kobi Katz Inc ..... F 213 689-9505
801 S Flower St Fl 3 Los Angeles (90017) *(P-11320)*

Kobis Windows & Doors Mfg Inc ..... E 818 764-6400
7326 Laurel Canyon Blvd North Hollywood (91605) *(P-3324)*

Kodella LLC ..... C 786 408-7995
17922 Fitch Ste 200 Irvine (92614) *(P-18195)*

Koder Inc ..... E 415 906-4157
9541 Irvine Center Dr Irvine (92618) *(P-17648)*

Koeller Nbker Crlson Hluck LLP (PA) ..... D 949 864-3400
3 Park Plz Ste 1500 Irvine (92614) *(P-21601)*

Kofax Inc (PA) ..... B 949 783-1000
15211 Laguna Canyon Rd Irvine (92618) *(P-17649)*

Kofax Limited (HQ) ..... A 949 783-1000
15211 Laguna Canyon Rd Irvine (92618) *(P-17903)*

Kohls Corporation ..... B 909 382-4300
890 E Mill St San Bernardino (92408) *(P-12216)*

Kole Imports ..... D 310 834-0004
24600 Main St Carson (90745) *(P-14944)*

Kollmorgen Corporation ..... D 805 696-1236
33 S La Patera Ln Santa Barbara (93117) *(P-8920)*

Koltov Inc (PA) ..... E 805 764-0280
300 S Lewis Rd Ste A Camarillo (93012) *(P-5908)*

Komar Alliance LLC (PA) ..... D 323 890-3000
6900 Washington Blvd Montebello (90640) *(P-14305)*

Komar Apparel Supply, Los Angeles *Also called Mdc Interior Solutions LLC (P-3079)*

Komar Distribution Services, Jurupa Valley *Also called Charles Komar & Sons Inc (P-3014)*

Komarov Enterprises Inc ..... D 213 244-7000
10939 Venice Blvd Los Angeles (90034) *(P-2905)*

Kondaur Capital Corporation (PA) ..... C 714 352-2038
333 S Anita Dr Ste 400 Orange (92868) *(P-16272)*

Kone Inc ..... E 714 890-7080
11165 Knott Ave Ste B Cypress (90630) *(P-19046)*

Kong Veterinary Products ..... F 626 633-0077
16018 Adelante St Ste C Irwindale (91702) *(P-11004)*

Konica Mnlta Hlthcare Amrcas I, Aliso Viejo *Also called Ambry Genetics Corporation (P-21059)*

Konoike-Pacific California Inc (HQ) ..... D 310 518-1000
1420 Coil Ave Wilmington (90744) *(P-12174)*

Kool Blast Gas ..... F 949 420-9675
3059 Scholarship Irvine (92612) *(P-11005)*

Kool Star, Long Beach *Also called Three Star Rfrgn Engrg Inc (P-8350)*

Koolfog Inc (PA) ..... F 760 321-9203
31290 Plantation Dr Thousand Palms (92276) *(P-8343)*

Koos Manufacturing Inc ..... A 323 249-1000
2741 Seminole Ave South Gate (90280) *(P-18567)*

Kopy Kat Attorney Service, Brea *Also called V A Anderson Enterprises Inc (P-18715)*

Kopykake Enterprises Inc (PA) ..... F 310 373-8906
3699 W 240th St Torrance (90505) *(P-7159)*

Kor Realty Group LLC (PA) ..... D 323 930-3700
1212 S Flower St Fl 5 Los Angeles (90015) *(P-15904)*

Kor Shots Inc ..... E 805 351-0700
29160 Heathercliff Rd # 4273 Malibu (90264) *(P-1903)*

Kora Organics, Los Angeles *Also called Kora Us LLC (P-16907)*

Kora Us LLC (PA) ..... D 424 744-8903
1990 S Bundy Dr Ste 375 Los Angeles (90025) *(P-16907)*

Koral Activewear, Vernon *Also called Koral LLC (P-2816)*

Koral Industries LLC (PA) ..... D 323 585-5343
5124 Pacific Blvd Vernon (90058) *(P-2964)*

Koral LLC ..... E 323 391-1060
5124 Pacific Blvd Vernon (90058) *(P-2816)*

Koral Los Angeles, Vernon *Also called Koral Industries LLC (P-2964)*

Koram Insurance Center Inc ..... D 323 660-1000
3807 Wilshire Blvd # 400 Los Angeles (90010) *(P-15587)*

Korden Inc ..... D 909 988-8979
611 S Palmetto Ave Ontario (91762) *(P-3613)*

Kore1 Inc ..... D 949 706-6990
530 Technology Dr Ste 150 Irvine (92618) *(P-18196)*

Korea Daily, Los Angeles *Also called Joong-Ang Daily News Cal Inc (P-3998)*

Korean Air Lines Co Ltd ..... C 310 646-4866
380 World Way Ste S4 Los Angeles (90045) *(P-12308)*

Korean Airlines Co Ltd ..... C 310 410-2000
6101 W Imperial Hwy Los Angeles (90045) *(P-12309)*

Korean Airlines Co Ltd ..... D 213 484-1900
1813 Wilshire Blvd # 400 Los Angeles (90057) *(P-12310)*

Korean Arln Crgo Reservations, Los Angeles *Also called Korean Airlines Co Ltd (P-12309)*

Korean Community Services Inc ..... C 714 527-6561
451 W Lincoln Ave Ste 100 Anaheim (92805) *(P-21047)*

Korean Hlth Edcatn Info RES CT (PA) ..... D 213 427-4000
3727 W 6th St Ste 210 Los Angeles (90020) *(P-21833)*

Korean Television Enterprises ..... D 213 382-6700
625 S Kingsley Dr Los Angeles (90005) *(P-12730)*

Korn Ferry (PA) ..... C 310 552-1834
1900 Avenue Of The Stars # 2600 Los Angeles (90067) *(P-17435)*

Koros USA Inc ..... E 805 529-0825
610 Flinn Ave Moorpark (93021) *(P-11006)*

Kortz Gregg Dvm Dplomate Acvim, Los Angeles *Also called Animal Specialty Group (P-197)*

Kott Koatings Inc (PA) ..... F 949 770-5055
27161 Burbank El Toro (92610) *(P-16210)*

Kovatch Mobile Equipment Corp ..... E 951 685-1224
4725 Troy Ct Jurupa Valley (92509) *(P-9956)*

Kovel/Fuller LLC ..... D 310 841-4444
9925 Jefferson Blvd Culver City (90232) *(P-17028)*

KP Concrete & Steel Inc ..... F 909 461-4163
3835 E 9th St Pomona (91766) *(P-1536)*

Kpac, Wilmington *Also called Konoike-Pacific California Inc (P-12174)*

Kpc Group Inc (PA) ..... D 951 782-8812
9 Kpc Pkwy 301 Corona (92879) *(P-23253)*

Kpff Inc ..... C 310 665-1536
700 S Flower St Ste 2100 Los Angeles (90017) *(P-22597)*

Kpi Services Inc ..... E 714 895-5024
11651 Monarch St Garden Grove (92841) *(P-6444)*

Kpmg LLP ..... D 703 286-8175
4464 Jasmine Ave Culver City (90232) *(P-22798)*

Kpower Sup McRswitch Inverters, Irvine *Also called Zippy Usa Inc (P-13679)*

Kprs Construction Services Inc (PA) ..... D 714 672-0800
2850 Saturn St Ste 110 Brea (92821) *(P-780)*

Kpu Roofing ..... E 909 586-2531
1497 Freesia Way Beaumont (92223) *(P-1493)*

Kqsb Radio 990, Santa Barbara *Also called Jacor Communications Company (P-12695)*

Kradjian Importing Company Inc (PA) ..... D 818 502-1313
5018 San Fernando Rd Glendale (91204) *(P-14703)*

Kraft/Tech Inc ..... F 818 837-3520
661 Arroyo St San Fernando (91340) *(P-10496)*

Kraftwerks Prfmce Group LLC ..... F 951 808-9888
2050 5th St Norco (92860) *(P-10088)*

Kraj Radio, Ridgecrest *Also called Adelman Broadcasting Inc (P-12686)*

Kramer-Wilson Company Inc (PA) ..... C 818 760-0880
340 N Westlake Blvd # 210 Westlake Village (91362) *(P-15468)*

Employee Codes: A=Over 500 employees, B=251-500
C=101-250, D=51-100, E=20-50 F=10-19
2022 Southern California Business
Directory and Buyers Guide
© Mergent Inc. 1-800-342-5647
1181

Kratos Instruments LLC ....F....949 660-0666
2201 Alton Pkwy Irvine (92606) ***(P-10595)***

Kratos Pressure Products, Irvine *Also called Kratos Instruments LLC* ***(P-10595)***

KRC Orange, Orange *Also called Kisco Senior Living LLC* ***(P-15738)***

KRC Santa Margarita, Rcho STA Marg *Also called Kisco Senior Living LLC* ***(P-15737)***

Krca Television LLC (HQ) ....D....**818 563-5722**
1845 W Empire Ave Burbank (91504) ***(P-12731)***

Krca Tv-62, Burbank *Also called Krca Television LLC* ***(P-12731)***

Kretek International Inc (HQ) ....D....**805 531-8888**
5449 Endeavour Ct Moorpark (93021) ***(P-14903)***

Kretus Group Inc (PA) ....E....**714 738-6640**
1129 N Patt St Anaheim (92801) ***(P-13306)***

Kretus Inc ....F....714 694-2061
1055 W Struck Ave Orange (92867) ***(P-5099)***

Krg Technologies Inc ....B....661 257-9967
25000 Ave Stnford Ste 243 Valencia (91355) ***(P-17650)***

Krieger Speciality Products, Pico Rivera *Also called Metal Tite Products* ***(P-6709)***

Krikorian Premiere Theatre LLC ....D....714 826-7469
8290 La Palma Ave Buena Park (90620) ***(P-19281)***

Krikorian Premiere Theatre LLC ....D....562 205-3456
8540 Whittier Blvd Pico Rivera (90660) ***(P-19282)***

Krishnamurti Foundation Amer (PA) ....E....**805 646-2726**
134 Besant Rd Ojai (93023) ***(P-16169)***

Krissy Op Shins USA Inc ....F....213 747-2591
2408 S Broadway Los Angeles (90007) ***(P-2817)***

Kristie L Lin MD Inc (PA) ....D....**626 272-4408**
100 E California Blvd Pasadena (91105) ***(P-19953)***

Kritech Corporation (PA) ....F....**310 538-9940**
333 W 131st St Los Angeles (90061) ***(P-9739)***

Kroger Co ....B....859 630-6959
2201 S Wilmington Ave Compton (90220) ***(P-12217)***

Krost (PA) ....C....**626 449-4225**
225 S Lake Ave Ste 400 Pasadena (91101) ***(P-22799)***

Krost Bumgarten Kniss Guerrero, Pasadena *Also called Krost* ***(P-22799)***

Krth Radio 101 FM, Los Angeles *Also called Infinity Broadcasting Corp Cal* ***(P-12694)***

Kruse and Son Inc ....E....626 358-4536
235 Kruse Ave Monrovia (91016) ***(P-1738)***

Kryler Corp ....E....714 871-9611
1217 E Ash Ave Fullerton (92831) ***(P-7276)***

KS Electronics Inc ....E....909 869-8826
322 Paseo Sonrisa Walnut (91789) ***(P-9527)***

KS Engineering Inc ....F....562 483-7788
14948 Shoemaker Ave Santa Fe Springs (90670) ***(P-10364)***

KS Fabrication & Machine, Bakersfield *Also called K S Fabrication & Machine Inc* ***(P-958)***

KS Industries LP (PA) ....A....**661 617-1700**
6205 District Blvd Bakersfield (93313) ***(P-960)***

Ksby Communications LLC ....D....805 541-6666
1772 Calle Joaquin San Luis Obispo (93405) ***(P-12732)***

Ksfcu, Bakersfield *Also called Valley Strong Credit Union* ***(P-15099)***

Ksi Engineering Inc ....D....661 617-1700
6205 District Blvd Bakersfield (93313) ***(P-22598)***

Ksl II Mngement Operations LLC ....D....760 564-8000
18575 Jamboree Rd Ste 500 Irvine (92612) ***(P-16529)***

Ksl Media Inc ....C....212 468-3395
15910 Ventura Blvd # 900 Encino (91436) ***(P-17100)***

Ksm Healthcare Inc ....D....818 242-1183
1400 W Glenoaks Blvd Glendale (91201) ***(P-20390)***

Ksu Corporation ....F....951 409-7055
3 Emmy Ln Ladera Ranch (92694) ***(P-6627)***

KT Engineering Corporation ....F....310 537-3818
2016 E Vista Bella Way Rancho Dominguez (90220) ***(P-8657)***

KT&c USA, Burbank *Also called Eon Innovative Technology Inc* ***(P-18377)***

Ktc-Tu Corporation ....F....714 435-2600
17600 Newhope St Fountain Valley (92708) ***(P-9528)***

Ktgy Group Inc (PA) ....D....**949 851-2133**
17911 Von Karman Ave # 2 Irvine (92614) ***(P-22727)***

Kti Incorporated ....D....909 434-1888
3011 N Laurel Ave Rialto (92377) ***(P-6038)***

Kts Kitchens Inc ....C....310 764-0850
1065 E Walnut St Ste C Carson (90746) ***(P-2461)***

Kubic Marketing Inc (HQ) ....C....**310 297-1600**
225 S Aviation Blvd El Segundo (90245) ***(P-14083)***

Kubota Industrial Equipment ....D....817 756-1171
3401 Del Amo Blvd Torrance (90503) ***(P-13464)***

Kubra America West Inc ....D....310 756-1717
14105 S Normandie Ave # 2 Gardena (90249) ***(P-22800)***

Kui Co Inc ....E....949 369-7949
266 Calle Pintoresco San Clemente (92672) ***(P-3759)***

Kuk Rim USA Inc ....C....323 277-9256
7507 Roseberry Ave Huntington Park (90255) ***(P-2700)***

Kukdong Apparel America Inc ....E....562 403-0044
17100 Pioneer Blvd # 230 Artesia (90701) ***(P-18568)***

Kulicke & Soffa Industries, Santa Ana *Also called Kulicke Sffa Wedge Bonding Inc* ***(P-9882)***

Kulicke Sffa Wedge Bonding Inc ....C....949 660-0440
1821 E Dyer Rd Ste 200 Santa Ana (92705) ***(P-9882)***

Kum Kang Trading USAinC ....E....562 531-6111
6433 Alondra Blvd Paramount (90723) ***(P-5040)***

Kumar, Vinod MD Facc, Bakersfield *Also called Heart Center A Medical Corp* ***(P-19839)***

Kureiji Inc ....F....626 788-2657
1442 Chico Ave South El Monte (91733) ***(P-2853)***

Kurz Transfer Products LP ....E....951 738-9521
415 N Smith Ave Corona (92878) ***(P-11703)***

Kushco Holdings Inc (PA) ....D....**714 462-4603**
6261 Katella Ave Ste 250 Cypress (90630) ***(P-5693)***

Kushwood Chair Inc ....E....909 930-2100
1290 E Elm St Ontario (91761) ***(P-3589)***

Kuster Co Oil Well Services ....E....562 595-0661
2900 E 29th St Long Beach (90806) ***(P-432)***

Kuster Company, Long Beach *Also called Kuster Co Oil Well Services* ***(P-432)***

Kustom Kanopies Inc ....E....801 399-3400
210 Senior Cir Lompoc (93436) ***(P-707)***

Kut From The Kloth, City of Industry *Also called Swatfame Inc* ***(P-14420)***

Kvc Group LLC ....D....855 438-0377
1551 N Tustin Ave Ste 550 Santa Ana (92705) ***(P-23254)***

Kvcr, TV & FM, San Bernardino *Also called San Brnrdino Cmnty College Dst* ***(P-12705)***

Kvea-Tv-Channel 52, Burbank *Also called Estrella Communications Inc* ***(P-12719)***

KVP, Irwindale *Also called Kong Veterinary Products* ***(P-11004)***

Kvr Investment Group Inc ....D....818 896-1102
12113 Branford St Sun Valley (91352) ***(P-7987)***

Kw International Inc ....D....310 354-6944
1457 Glenn Curtiss St Carson (90746) ***(P-12475)***

Kw International Inc ....D....310 747-1380
18511 S Broadwick St Rancho Dominguez (90220) ***(P-12476)***

Kw International Inc ....D....213 703-6914
18724 S Broadwick St Rancho Dominguez (90220) ***(P-12269)***

Kwdz Manufacturing LLC (PA) ....D....**323 526-3526**
337 S Anderson St Los Angeles (90033) ***(P-3032)***

Kwikparts.com, Torrance *Also called Probe Racing Components Inc* ***(P-8434)***

Kwl Industrial Company ....E....714 847-3268
17925 Metzler Ln Huntington Beach (92647) ***(P-13911)***

Kworld (usa) Computer Inc ....E....626 581-0867
499 Nibus Ste D Brea (92821) ***(P-9282)***

Kxp Carrier Services LLC ....C....424 320-5300
11777 San Vicente Blvd Los Angeles (90049) ***(P-12140)***

Kya Services LLC ....E....714 659-6476
1800 E Mcfadden Ave Santa Ana (92705) ***(P-1468)***

Kymsta Corp ....F....213 380-8118
1506 W 12th St Los Angeles (90015) ***(P-2965)***

Kyocera Dcment Solutions W LLC ....C....800 996-9591
14101 Alton Pkwy Irvine (92618) ***(P-13361)***

Kyocera Medical Tech Inc ....E....909 557-2360
1200 California St # 210 Redlands (92374) ***(P-11121)***

Kyocera Sld Laser Inc (HQ) ....D....**805 696-6999**
485 Pine Ave Goleta (93117) ***(P-9883)***

Kyolic, Mission Viejo *Also called Wakunaga of America Co Ltd* ***(P-4911)***

Kyoto Grand Hotel and Gardens, Los Angeles *Also called Crestline Hotels & Resorts Inc* ***(P-16399)***

Kythera Biopharmaceuticals Inc (HQ) ....C....**818 587-4500**
30930 Russell Ranch Rd # 3 Westlake Village (91362) ***(P-4842)***

Kyue TV, Palm Desert *Also called Entravsion Communications Corp* ***(P-12717)***

L & A Care Corporation ....D....310 202-7693
5000 Overland Ave Ste 101 Culver City (90230) ***(P-20534)***

L & A Care Corporation (PA) ....D....**323 938-1155**
18107 Sherman Way Ste 100 Reseda (91335) ***(P-21182)***

L & A Plastics, Yorba Linda *Also called Loritz & Associates Inc* ***(P-5700)***

L & G Farming Co Inc ....E....805 928-1559
1141 Tama Ln Santa Maria (93455) ***(P-30)***

L & H Mold & Engineering Inc (PA) ....E....**909 930-1547**
140 Atlantic St Pomona (91768) ***(P-5694)***

L & H Molds, Pomona *Also called L & H Mold & Engineering Inc* ***(P-5694)***

L & L Custom Shutters Inc ....F....714 996-9539
3133 Yukon Ave Costa Mesa (92626) ***(P-3260)***

L & L Louvers Inc ....E....951 735-9300
12355 Doherty St Riverside (92503) ***(P-6705)***

L & L Nursery Supply Inc (HQ) ....C....**909 591-0461**
2552 Shenandoah Way San Bernardino (92407) ***(P-14862)***

L & M Machining Corporation ....D....714 414-0923
550 S Melrose St Placentia (92870) ***(P-9660)***

L & N Fixtures Inc ....E....626 442-4778
2214 Tyler Ave El Monte (91733) ***(P-3655)***

L & O Aliso Viejo LLC ....D....949 643-6700
50 Enterprise Aliso Viejo (92656) ***(P-16530)***

L & S Investment Co Inc ....D....760 245-3461
14173 Green Tree Blvd Victorville (92395) ***(P-16531)***

L & T Meat Co ....D....323 262-2815
3050 E 11th St Los Angeles (90023) ***(P-14595)***

L A Air Inc ....C....310 215-8245
5933 W Century Blvd 500 Los Angeles (90045) ***(P-12311)***

L A Cstm AP & Promotions Inc (PA) ....D....**562 595-1770**
2680 Temple Ave Long Beach (90806) ***(P-2818)***

L A Girl, Ontario *Also called Beauty 21 Cosmetics Inc* ***(P-14234)***

L A H S A, Los Angeles *Also called Los Angeles Homeless Svcs Auth* ***(P-21843)***

L A Japanese Daily News, Los Angeles *Also called Rafu Shimpo* ***(P-4025)***

L A Lighting, El Monte *Also called Los Angeles Ltg Mfg Co Inc* ***(P-13641)***

L A P F C U, Van Nuys *Also called Los Angeles Police Credit Un* ***(P-15114)***

L A Party Rents Inc ....D....818 989-4300
13520 Saticoy St Van Nuys (91402) ***(P-17360)***

L A Philharmonic, Los Angeles *Also called Los Angeles Philharmonic Assn* ***(P-19364)***

L A Press, Los Angeles *Also called LA Printing & Graphics Inc* ***(P-4352)***

L A Propoint Inc ....E....818 767-6800
10870 La Tuna Canyon Rd Sun Valley (91352) ***(P-7562)***

L A S A M Inc ....F....323 586-8717
3844 S Santa Fe Ave Vernon (90058) ***(P-3033)***

L A Sani-Felt Co ....F....323 233-5278
830 E 59th St Los Angeles (90001) ***(P-2727)***

L A Steel Craft Products (PA) ....E....**626 798-7401**
1975 Lincoln Ave Pasadena (91103) ***(P-11432)***

L and R Auto Parks Inc ....C....213 784-3018
707 Wilshire Blvd # 4700 Los Angeles (90017) ***(P-18767)***

L and W Developers LLC ....E....310 654-8428
1635 Centinela Ave Inglewood (90302) ***(P-16055)***

L Barrios and Associates Inc ....E....909 592-5893
302 E Fthill Blvd Ste 101 San Dimas (91773) ***(P-314)***

L C Miller Company ....E....323 268-3611
717 Monterey Pass Rd Monterey Park (91754) ***(P-8093)***

Mergent e-mail: customerrelations@mergent.com
1182
2022 Southern California Business Directory and Buyers Guide
(P-0000) Products & Services Section entry number
(PA)=Parent Co (HQ)=Headquarters (DH)=Div Headquarters

L C Pringle Sales Inc (PA) .... E 714 892-1524
12020 Western Ave Garden Grove (92841) *(P-3713)*
L E Cooke Co .... C 559 732-9146
26333 Road 140 Visalia (93292) *(P-81)*
L E Coppersmith Inc (PA) .... D 310 607-8000
525 S Douglas St Ste 100 El Segundo (90245) *(P-12477)*
L E G, Los Angeles *Also called Levity Entertainment Group LLC (P-23261)*
L F P Inc (PA) .... D 323 651-3525
8484 Wilshire Blvd # 900 Beverly Hills (90211) *(P-4077)*
L J R Grinding Corp .... F 310 532-7232
445 W 164th St Gardena (90248) *(P-8658)*
L J T Flowers Inc (PA) .... C 877 929-2476
2425 Bonita School Rd Nipomo (93444) *(P-14863)*
L M I, Ontario *Also called Larry Mthvin Installations Inc (P-5961)*
L M Scofield Company (HQ) .... E 323 720-3000
12767 Imperial Hwy Santa Fe Springs (90670) *(P-5226)*
L S A, Irvine *Also called Lsa Associates Inc (P-23471)*
L Space, Costa Mesa *Also called Lspace America LLC (P-2857)*
L T Litho & Printing Co .... F 949 466-8584
16811 Noyes Ave Irvine (92606) *(P-4351)*
L T S, City of Industry *Also called Lt Security Inc (P-13746)*
L T Seroge Inc .... F 951 354-7141
7400 Jurupa Ave Riverside (92504) *(P-9884)*
L Tech Network Services Inc .... D 562 222-1121
3424 Garfield Ave A Commerce (90040) *(P-1273)*
L W Lefort, Placentia *Also called Richfield Engineering Inc (P-6749)*
L Y A Group Inc .... E 213 683-1123
1317 S Grand Ave Los Angeles (90015) *(P-2966)*
L&D Farm Labor .... E 760 408-6311
53762 Sapphire Ln Coachella (92236) *(P-217)*
L&F Wood LLC .... F 310 400-5569
416 E Alondra Blvd Gardena (90248) *(P-3261)*
L&T Staffing Inc (PA) .... B 714 558-1821
950 W 17th St Ste E Santa Ana (92706) *(P-17436)*
L'Ermitage Hotel, Beverly Hills *Also called Raffles Lrmitage Beverly Hills (P-16653)*
L-3 Interstate Electronics, Anaheim *Also called Interstate Electronics Corp (P-10760)*
L-G Wood Products, Pomona *Also called De Larshe Cabinetry LLC (P-3242)*
L.A. Care Health Plan, Los Angeles *Also called Local Inttive Hlth Auth For Lo (P-15443)*
L.A. Cold Storage, Los Angeles *Also called Standard-Southern Corporation (P-12178)*
L.A. GAY & LESBIAN CENTER, Los Angeles *Also called Los Angeles Lgbt Center (P-22198)*
L.A. Inflight Service Company, Gardena *Also called World Svc Wst/La Inflght Svc L (P-12374)*
L.A. Sleeve, Santa Fe Springs *Also called Los Angeles Sleeve Co Inc (P-10093)*
L.A.cO., Whittier *Also called County Snttion Dst No 2 Los An (P-13006)*
L3 Technologies Inc .... C 818 833-2500
28022 Industry Dr Valencia (91355) *(P-10596)*
L3 Technologies Inc .... B 650 591-8411
3100 Lomita Blvd Torrance (90505) *(P-9283)*
L3 Technologies Inc .... C 714 758-4222
602 E Vermont Ave Anaheim (92805) *(P-9284)*
L3 Technologies Inc .... D 805 683-3881
7414 Hollister Ave Goleta (93117) *(P-22599)*
L3 Technologies Inc .... D 805 584-1717
200 W Los Angeles Ave Simi Valley (93065) *(P-9285)*
L3harris Technologies Inc .... B 818 901-2523
7821 Orion Ave Van Nuys (91406) *(P-10597)*
La 1000 Santa Fe LLC .... C 213 205-1000
1000 S Santa Fe Ave Los Angeles (90021) *(P-23047)*
La Aloe LLC .... E 888 968-2563
2301 E 7th St Ste A152 Los Angeles (90023) *(P-1904)*
La Apparel, Los Angeles *Also called Los Angeles Apparel Inc (P-3078)*
La Asccion Ncnal Pro Prsnas My .... D 213 202-5900
1452 W Temple St Ste 100 Los Angeles (90026) *(P-21834)*
La Asccion Ncnal Pro Prsnas My (PA) .... A 626 564-1988
234 E Colo Blvd Ste 300 Pasadena (91101) *(P-21835)*
La Barca Tortilleria Inc .... E 323 268-1744
3047 Whittier Blvd Los Angeles (90023) *(P-2462)*
La Bath Vanity Inc (PA) .... F 909 303-3323
1071 W 9th St Upland (91786) *(P-3325)*
La Bonita, Norwalk *Also called Dianas Mexican Food Pdts Inc (P-2422)*
La Bonne Vie Inc .... D 805 773-5003
2723 Shell Beach Rd Shell Beach (93449) *(P-19453)*
La Bottleworks Inc .... E 323 724-4076
1605 Beach St Montebello (90640) *(P-2270)*
La Boxing Franchise Corp .... C 714 668-0911
1241 E Dyer Rd Ste 100 Santa Ana (92705) *(P-19454)*
LA Brands LLC .... E 323 234-5070
4726 Loma Vista Ave Vernon (90058) *(P-14339)*
LA Cabinet & Millwork Inc .... E 323 227-5000
3005 Humboldt St Los Angeles (90031) *(P-3656)*
La Canada Flintridge Cntry CLB .... D 818 790-0611
5500 Godbey Dr La Canada (91011) *(P-19574)*
La Canada Unified School Dst .... D 818 952-8320
1100 Foothill Blvd La Canada (91011) *(P-11944)*
LA CAPITAL, Los Angeles *Also called Los Angeles Capital MGT LLC (P-16132)*
La Casa Mhrc, Long Beach *Also called Telecare Corporation (P-21353)*
La Chapalita Inc (PA) .... E 626 443-8556
1724 Chico Ave El Monte (91733) *(P-2463)*
La Chic, Vernon *Also called Rmla Inc (P-3044)*
La Cienega Associates .... D 310 854-0071
8500 Beverly Blvd Ste 501 Los Angeles (90048) *(P-15905)*
La Clippers LLC .... D 213 742-7500
1212 S Flower St Fl 5 Los Angeles (90015) *(P-19419)*
La Colonial Mexican Foods, Monterey Park *Also called La Colonial Tortilla Pdts Inc (P-2464)*
La Colonial Tortilla Pdts Inc .... C 626 289-3647
543 Monterey Pass Rd Monterey Park (91754) *(P-2464)*
LA COUNTY MUSEUM OF ART, Los Angeles *Also called Museum Associates (P-22226)*
La Cumbre Country Club .... D 805 687-2421
4015 Via Laguna Santa Barbara (93110) *(P-19575)*
La Dye & Print Inc .... E 310 327-3200
13416 Estrella Ave Gardena (90248) *(P-14390)*
La Ejuice LLC (PA) .... E 310 257-1198
22873 Lockness Ave Torrance (90501) *(P-14904)*
LA Envelope Incorporated .... E 323 838-9300
1053 S Vail Ave Montebello (90640) *(P-3910)*
La Espanola Meats Inc .... E 310 539-0455
25020 Doble Ave Harbor City (90710) *(P-1739)*
La Flora Del Sur, Los Angeles *Also called Walker Foods Inc (P-1880)*
La Follette Johnson De Haas (PA) .... C 213 426-3600
701 N Brand Blvd Ste 600 Glendale (91203) *(P-21602)*
La Fortaleza Inc .... D 323 261-1211
525 N Ford Blvd Los Angeles (90022) *(P-2465)*
LA Gauge Co Inc .... D 818 767-7193
7440 San Fernando Rd Sun Valley (91352) *(P-8659)*
LA Gem and Jewelry Design (PA) .... D 213 488-1290
659 S Broadway Fl 7 Los Angeles (90014) *(P-11321)*
La Gloria Flour Tortillas, Los Angeles *Also called La Gloria Foods Corp (P-2467)*
La Gloria Foods Corp (PA) .... D 323 262-0410
3455 E 1st St Los Angeles (90063) *(P-2466)*
La Gloria Foods Corp .... E 323 263-6755
3285 E Cesar E Chavez Ave Los Angeles (90063) *(P-2467)*
La Gloria Tortilleria, Los Angeles *Also called La Gloria Foods Corp (P-2466)*
La Habra Stucco, Riverside *Also called Parex Usa Inc (P-6186)*
La Habra Villa .... D 714 529-1697
220 Newport Center Dr # 11 Newport Beach (92660) *(P-22121)*
LA Hardwood Flooring Inc (PA) .... F 818 361-0099
9880 San Fernando Rd Pacoima (91331) *(P-3220)*
LA Hydro-Jet Rooter Svc Inc .... D 818 768-4225
10639 Wixom St Sun Valley (91352) *(P-19047)*
La Hydrojet, Sun Valley *Also called LA Hydro-Jet Rooter Svc Inc (P-19047)*
La Indiana Tamales Inc .... F 323 262-4682
1142 S Indiana St Los Angeles (90023) *(P-1853)*
La Installs Corporation (PA) .... E 909 923-7076
2949 S Vineyard Ave Ontario (91761) *(P-12577)*
La Jolla Group Inc (PA) .... C 949 428-2800
14350 Myford Rd Irvine (92606) *(P-18569)*
La Jolla Sport USA Inc (PA) .... D 949 428-2800
14350 Myford Rd Irvine (92606) *(P-14340)*
La La Land Production & Design .... E 323 406-9223
1701 S Santa Fe Ave Los Angeles (90021) *(P-5870)*
La Linen Inc .... E 213 745-4004
1760 E 15th St Los Angeles (90021) *(P-3105)*
La Live Properties LLC .... E 213 763-7700
800 W Olympic Blvd Ste 30 Los Angeles (90015) *(P-19320)*
La Mamba LLC .... E 323 526-3526
150 N Myers St Los Angeles (90033) *(P-2854)*
La Mancha Development, Los Angeles *Also called A M S Partnership (P-16045)*
La Mejor Restaurant, Farmersville *Also called Tortilleria La Mejor (P-2541)*
La Mesa Disposal, Signal Hill *Also called Edco Disposal Corporation (P-12949)*
La Mexicana LLC .... E 323 277-3660
10615 Ruchti Rd South Gate (90280) *(P-1931)*
La Mode, Los Angeles *Also called Golf Apparel Brands Inc (P-2946)*
La Mousse Desserts Inc .... E 310 478-6051
18211 S Broadway Gardena (90248) *(P-1932)*
La Opinion LP (HQ) .... D 213 891-9191
915 Wilshire Blvd Ste 915 # 915 Los Angeles (90017) *(P-4000)*
La Opinion LP .... B 213 896-2222
210 E Washington Blvd Los Angeles (90015) *(P-4001)*
La Palm Furnitures & ACC Inc (PA) .... D 310 217-2700
1650 W Artesia Blvd Gardena (90248) *(P-3156)*
La Palma Medical Offices, La Palma *Also called Kaiser Foundation Hospitals (P-19935)*
La Parent Magazine (PA) .... F 818 264-2222
5855 Topanga Canyon Blvd # 210 Woodland Hills (91367) *(P-4078)*
La Paz Products Inc .... F 714 990-0982
345 Oak Pl Brea (92821) *(P-2331)*
La Peer Health Systems, Beverly Hills *Also called La Peer Surgery Center LLC (P-19954)*
La Peer Surgery Center LLC .... D 310 360-9119
8920 Wilshire Blvd # 101 Beverly Hills (90211) *(P-19954)*
La Princesita Tortilleria Inc (PA) .... F 323 267-0673
3432 E Cesar E Chavez Ave Los Angeles (90063) *(P-2468)*
LA Printing & Graphics Inc .... E 310 527-4526
13951 S Main St Los Angeles (90061) *(P-4352)*
La Punte Prtneal Dialysis Unit, La Puente *Also called Kaiser Foundation Hospitals (P-21251)*
La Quinta Cliff House, La Quinta *Also called TS Enterprises Inc (P-4627)*
La Quinta Country Club .... D 760 564-4151
77750 Avenue 50 La Quinta (92253) *(P-19576)*
La Quinta Resort & Club, La Quinta *Also called Lqr Property LLC (P-16547)*
La Quinta Vacation Rental, Palm Springs *Also called Palm Springs Rental Agency Inc (P-16618)*
La Rams Football Club, Los Angeles *Also called Los Angeles Rams LLC (P-23054)*
La Rancherita Tortilleria Deli, Santa Ana *Also called MRS Foods Incorporated (P-2492)*
La Reina, Los Angeles *Also called Old Pueblo Ranch Inc (P-2498)*
La Rocks, Los Angeles *Also called LA Gem and Jewelry Design (P-11321)*
La Rocque Better Roofs Inc .... D 909 476-2699
9077 Arrow Rte Ste 100 Rancho Cucamonga (91730) *(P-1494)*
La Rosa De Mexico, Paramount *Also called Williamson Granados (P-2900)*
La Rose of California, Los Angeles *Also called Jay-Cee Blouse Co Inc (P-2888)*
La Rutan .... F 310 940-7956
6284 Long Beach Blvd Long Beach (90805) *(P-11704)*
La Sentinel Newspaper, Los Angeles *Also called Los Angeles Sentinel Inc (P-4004)*
La Sierra Promotions, Panorama City *Also called La Sierra Records Inc (P-14167)*
La Sierra Records Inc .... E 818 830-1919
8628 Van Nuys Blvd Panorama City (91402) *(P-14167)*

ALPHABETIC

Employee Codes: A=Over 500 employees, B=251-500 C=101-250, D=51-100, E=20-50 F=10-19
2022 Southern California Business Directory and Buyers Guide
© Mergent Inc. 1-800-342-5647
1183

LA Signal F 909 599-2201
155 N Eucla Ave La Puente (91744) ***(P-1274)***
La Spec Industries Inc F 323 588-8746
2315 E 52nd St Vernon (90058) ***(P-9091)***
LA Specialty Produce Co (PA) B **562 741-2200**
13527 Orden Dr Santa Fe Springs (90670) ***(P-14641)***
La Sports Arena, Los Angeles *Also called Los Angeles Mem Coliseum Comm* ***(P-22455)***
LA Sports Properties Inc C 213 742-7500
1212 S Flower St Fl 5 Los Angeles (90015) ***(P-19420)***
La Steel Services Inc E 951 393-2013
1180 Olympic Dr Ste 108 Corona (92881) ***(P-1573)***
La Strada Contracting Co F 949 680-4237
26247 Enterprise Ct Lake Forest (92630) ***(P-661)***
LA Supply Company LLC F 714 735-9053
13700 Rosecrans Ave Santa Fe Springs (90670) ***(P-5141)***
La Times E 213 237-2279
202 W 1st St Ste 500 Los Angeles (90012) ***(P-4002)***
La Tolteca Mexican Foods, Azusa *Also called Arrietta Incorporated* ***(P-2392)***
LA Triumph Inc E 562 404-7657
13336 Alondra Blvd Cerritos (90703) ***(P-2784)***
LA Turbine (HQ) D **661 294-8290**
28557 Industry Dr Valencia (91355) ***(P-7587)***
La Verne Nursery Inc D 805 521-0111
3653 Center St Piru (93040) ***(P-82)***
LA Web Inc E 626 453-8800
9639 Telstar Ave El Monte (91731) ***(P-1187)***
La Workout Inc C 805 482-8884
500 Paseo Camarillo Camarillo (93010) ***(P-19455)***
La Workout Camarillo West, Camarillo *Also called La Workout Inc* ***(P-19455)***
La Xpress Air & Heating Svcs D 310 856-9678
6400 E Wash Blvd Ste 121 Commerce (90040) ***(P-4187)***
La's Totally Awesome, Buena Park *Also called Awesome Products Inc* ***(P-4955)***
La6721 LLC F 323 484-4070
6721 Romaine St Los Angeles (90038) ***(P-11566)***
Laaco Ltd (PA) C **213 622-1254**
431 W 7th St Los Angeles (90014) ***(P-15760)***
Lab Clean Inc E 714 689-0063
3627 Briggeman Dr Los Alamitos (90720) ***(P-4967)***
Lab Ecx.com, Valencia *Also called Pharma Alliance Group Inc* ***(P-4871)***
Lab Support LLC (HQ) C **818 878-7900**
26745 Malibu Hills Rd Calabasas (91301) ***(P-17496)***
Lab, The, Burbank *Also called Kh9100 LLC* ***(P-11254)***
Labarge/Stc Inc A 281 207-1400
200 Sandpointe Ave # 700 Santa Ana (92707) ***(P-9529)***
Labaya Beachcomber LP E 805 278-6688
3101 Sturgis Rd Oxnard (93030) ***(P-18794)***
Label Impressions, Anaheim *Also called Brook & Whittle Limited* ***(P-4489)***
Label Shoppe, The, City of Industry *Also called Labels-R-Us Inc* ***(P-4533)***
Label Specialties Inc E 714 961-8074
704 Dunn Way Placentia (92870) ***(P-4531)***
Labeling Hurst Systems LLC F 818 701-0710
20747 Dearborn St Chatsworth (91311) ***(P-4532)***
Labels-R-Us Inc E 626 333-4001
1121 Fullerton Rd City of Industry (91748) ***(P-4533)***
Labeltex Mills Inc (PA) C **323 582-0228**
6100 Wilmington Ave Los Angeles (90001) ***(P-11498)***
Labeltronix LLC D 800 429-4321
2419 E Winston Rd Anaheim (92806) ***(P-4534)***
Labmed Partners E 949 242-9925
5000 Birch St Newport Beach (92660) ***(P-23255)***
Labonita Diana's Mexican Food, Carson *Also called Dianas Mexican Food Pdts Inc* ***(P-2423)***
Laboratory Specialist, La Palma *Also called Isec Incorporated* ***(P-1441)***
Labrucherie Produce LLC E 760 352-2170
1407 S La Brucherie Rd El Centro (92243) ***(P-2469)***
Lac & Usc Medical Center C 323 409-2345
2051 Marengo St Los Angeles (90033) ***(P-19955)***
LAC Motor Enterprises Inc D 626 329-1411
127 N Acacia St San Dimas (91773) ***(P-11979)***
Lacba Counsel For Justice D 951 489-2919
200 S Spring St Los Angeles (90012) ***(P-21836)***
Lacera, Pasadena *Also called Los Angles Cnty Emplyees Rtrme* ***(P-15516)***
Lacey Milling Company F 559 584-6634
217 W 5th St Ste 231 Hanford (93230) ***(P-1945)***
Laclede Inc E 310 605-4280
2103 E University Dr Rancho Dominguez (90220) ***(P-11181)***
Laclede Research Center, Rancho Dominguez *Also called Laclede Inc* ***(P-11181)***
Lacma, Los Angeles *Also called Los Angeles Cnty Mseum of Art* ***(P-22225)***
Lacmta, Los Angeles *Also called Los Angles Cnty Mtro Trnsp Aut* ***(P-11826)***
Ladwp, Independence *Also called Los Angeles Dept Wtr & Pwr* ***(P-12903)***
Ladwp, Los Angeles *Also called Los Angeles Dept Wtr & Pwr* ***(P-12904)***
Ladwp, Los Angeles *Also called Los Angeles Dept Wtr & Pwr* ***(P-12808)***
Ladybug Medical Supply, Chatsworth *Also called Loveis Corp* ***(P-11011)***
Laedc, Los Angeles *Also called Economic Dev Corp Los Angles C* ***(P-23433)***
Laetitia Vineyard & Winery Inc D 805 481-1772
453 Laetitia Vineyard Dr Arroyo Grande (93420) ***(P-2200)***
Laetitia Winery, Arroyo Grande *Also called Laetitia Vineyard & Winery Inc* ***(P-2200)***
Lafond Vineyard Inc F 805 962-9303
114 E Haley St Ste M Santa Barbara (93101) ***(P-2201)***
LAg and Associates LLC D 909 242-4394
1514 E Adams Park Dr Covina (91724) ***(P-18570)***
Lagun Engineering Solutions, Harbor City *Also called Republic Machinery Co Inc* ***(P-7742)***
Laguna Bch Golf Bnglow Vlg LLC E 949 499-2271
31106 Coast Hwy Laguna Beach (92651) ***(P-143)***
Laguna Beach Magazine, Laguna Beach *Also called Firebrand Media LLC* ***(P-4294)***
Laguna Blanca School (PA) D **805 687-2461**
4125 Paloma Dr Santa Barbara (93110) ***(P-23462)***
Laguna Clay Company, City of Industry *Also called Jon Brooks Inc* ***(P-6167)***
Laguna Cookie Company Inc D 714 546-6855
4041 W Garry Ave Santa Ana (92704) ***(P-2068)***
Laguna Fabrics, Vernon *Also called Roshan Trading Inc* ***(P-14318)***
Laguna Hills Hotel Dev Ventr D 949 586-5000
25205 La Paz Rd Laguna Hills (92653) ***(P-16532)***
Laguna Hills Surgery Center, Laguna Hills *Also called Cirrus Health II LP* ***(P-19750)***
Laguna Niguel Racquet Club, Laguna Niguel *Also called Spearman Clubs Inc* ***(P-19671)***
Laguna Playhouse (PA) C **949 497-2787**
606 Laguna Canyon Rd Laguna Beach (92651) ***(P-19321)***
Laguna Woods Village A 949 597-4267
24351 El Toro Rd Laguna Woods (92637) ***(P-15906)***
Laidlaw Education Services, Santa Ana *Also called First Student Inc* ***(P-11931)***
Laidlaw Educational Services, Palm Springs *Also called First Student Inc* ***(P-11929)***
Laird Coatings Corporation D 714 894-5252
15541 Commerce Ln Huntington Beach (92649) ***(P-5100)***
Laird Construction Co Inc D 909 989-5595
9460 Lucas Ranch Rd Rancho Cucamonga (91730) ***(P-896)***
Lake Arrwhead Rsort Oprtor Inc (HQ) C **909 336-1511**
27984 Hwy 189 Lake Arrowhead (92352) ***(P-16533)***
Lake Balboa Care Center, Van Nuys *Also called Van Nuys Care Center Inc* ***(P-20637)***
Lake Elsinore Hotel & Casino C 951 674-3101
20930 Malaga Rd Lake Elsinore (92530) ***(P-19653)***
Lake Elsinore Resort & Casino, Lake Elsinore *Also called Lake Elsinore Hotel & Casino* ***(P-19653)***
Lake Forest Nursing Center, Lake Forest *Also called Life Care Centers America Inc* ***(P-20395)***
Lake Frest No II Mstr Hmwners D 949 586-0860
24752 Toledo Ln Lake Forest (92630) ***(P-22344)***
Lake Hemet Municipal Water Dst (PA) D **951 658-3241**
26385 Fairview Ave Hemet (92544) ***(P-12897)***
Lake Mission Viejo Association D 949 770-1313
22555 Olympiad Rd Mission Viejo (92692) ***(P-22345)***
Lake Piru Marina, Valencia *Also called Pyramid Enterprises Inc* ***(P-19662)***
Lakenor Auto Salvage, Santa Fe Springs *Also called Cadnchev Inc* ***(P-13123)***
Lakes Country Club Assn Inc (PA) B **760 568-4321**
161 Old Ranch Rd Palm Desert (92211) ***(P-19577)***
Lakes Country Club, The, Palm Desert *Also called Lakes Country Club Assn Inc* ***(P-19577)***
Lakeshirts LLC E 805 239-1290
1400 Railroad St Ste 104 Paso Robles (93446) ***(P-3157)***
Lakeside Golf Club D 818 984-0601
4500 W Lakeside Dr Burbank (91505) ***(P-19496)***
Lakeside Medical Associates (PA) C **818 637-2000**
8510 Balboa Blvd Ste 150 Northridge (91325) ***(P-23048)***
Lakeside Medical Systems, Northridge *Also called Lakeside Systems Inc* ***(P-23049)***
Lakeside Systems Inc A 866 654-3471
8510 Balboa Blvd Ste 150 Northridge (91325) ***(P-23049)***
Lakeview Medical Offices, Anaheim *Also called Kaiser Foundation Hospitals* ***(P-19858)***
Lakewood Healthcare Center, Downey *Also called Healthcare Ctr of Downey LLC* ***(P-20373)***
Lakewood Park Health Ctr Inc (PA) B **562 869-0978**
12023 Lakewood Blvd Downey (90242) ***(P-18571)***
Lakewood Regional Med Ctr Inc A 562 531-2550
3700 South St Lakewood (90712) ***(P-20832)***
Lakewood Regional Medical Ctr, Lakewood *Also called Tenet Healthsystem Medical Inc* ***(P-20104)***
Lakewood Regional Medical Ctr, Lakewood *Also called Lakewood Regional Med Ctr Inc* ***(P-20832)***
Lakim Industries Incorporated (PA) E **310 637-8900**
389 Rood Rd Calexico (92231) ***(P-11513)***
Lakin Tire of Calif, Santa Fe Springs *Also called Lakin Tire West Incorporated* ***(P-13118)***
Lakin Tire West Incorporated (PA) C **562 802-2752**
15305 Spring Ave Santa Fe Springs (90670) ***(P-13118)***
Lambda Research Optics Inc D 714 327-0600
1695 Macarthur Blvd Costa Mesa (92626) ***(P-10799)***
Lambs & Ivy Inc D 310 322-3800
2042 E Maple Ave El Segundo (90245) ***(P-3106)***
Laminating Company of America, Lake Forest *Also called Tri-Star Laminates Inc* ***(P-9462)***
Laminating Company of America E 949 587-3300
20322 Windrow Dr Ste 100 Lake Forest (92630) ***(P-9421)***
Laminating Technologies, Anaheim *Also called Yti Enterprises Inc* ***(P-3459)***
Lamonicas Pizza Dough Intl E 323 263-0644
3706 E 26th St Vernon (90058) ***(P-14526)***
Lamonicas Pizza Dough Intl Inc (PA) D **310 208-5535**
1066 Gayley Ave Los Angeles (90024) ***(P-14527)***
Lamont Community Health Center, Bakersfield *Also called Clinica Sierra Vista* ***(P-19753)***
Lamp Inc C 213 488-9559
2116 Arlington Ave Lbby Los Angeles (90018) ***(P-22122)***
Lamp Community, Los Angeles *Also called Lamp Inc* ***(P-22122)***
Lamps Plus Inc F 805 642-9007
4723 Telephone Rd Ventura (93003) ***(P-9092)***
Lamsco West Inc D 661 295-8620
29101 The Old Rd Santa Clarita (91355) ***(P-5695)***
Lancaster Cmnty Svcs Fndtion I C 661 723-6230
46008 7th St W Lancaster (93534) ***(P-18851)***
Lancaster Crdlgy Med Group Inc (PA) D **661 726-3058**
43847 Heaton Ave Ste B Lancaster (93534) ***(P-19956)***
Lance Soll & Lunghard LLP D 714 672-0022
203 N Brea Blvd Ste 203 # 203 Brea (92821) ***(P-22801)***
Lance Rygg Dental Corp (PA) C **714 508-3600**
2860 Michelle Fl 2 Irvine (92606) ***(P-20185)***
Land Concern Ltd D 949 250-4822
1750 E Deere Ave Ste A Santa Ana (92705) ***(P-264)***
Land Design Consultants Inc D 626 578-7000
2700 E Fthill Blvd Ste 20 Pasadena (91107) ***(P-23463)***
Land Disposition Company, Irvine *Also called NRLL LLC* ***(P-16281)***
Land Forms Landscape Cnstr, Santa Ana *Also called Land Forms Landscape Cnstr Inc* ***(P-1092)***

Land Forms Lanscape Cnstr Inc.....E.....949 582-0877
1901 Carnegie Ave Ste 1e Santa Ana (92705) ***(P-1092)***
Land OLakes Inc.....D.....559 687-8287
400 S M St Tulare (93274) ***(P-1776)***
Landcare USA LLC.....C.....949 559-7771
216 N Clara St Santa Ana (92703) ***(P-265)***
Landcare USA LLC.....D.....805 520-9394
1196 Patricia Ave Simi Valley (93065) ***(P-315)***
Landcare USA LLC.....D.....951 320-1522
1616 Marlborough Ave S Riverside (92507) ***(P-316)***
Landcare USA LLC.....D.....714 936-9512
15606 Cornet St Santa Fe Springs (90670) ***(P-317)***
Landcare USA LLC.....D.....310 719-1008
1315 W 130th St Gardena (90247) ***(P-318)***
Landcare USA LLC.....D.....818 346-7552
7755 Deering Ave Canoga Park (91304) ***(P-319)***
Landforce Corporation.....C.....760 843-7839
17201 N D St Victorville (92394) ***(P-12058)***
Landmark Dividend LLC (PA).....**C.....323 306-2683**
400 Continental Blvd # 500 El Segundo (90245) ***(P-15907)***
Landmark Event Staffing.....A.....714 293-4248
4790 Irvine Blvd Ste 105 Irvine (92620) ***(P-18292)***
Landmark Global Inc (HQ).....**D.....805 679-5029**
506 Chapala St Santa Barbara (93101) ***(P-12478)***
Landmark Global Inc.....D.....805 720-5874
27 W Anapamu St Santa Barbara (93101) ***(P-23464)***
Landmark Health LLC (PA).....**B.....657 237-2450**
7755 Center Ave Ste 630 Huntington Beach (92647) ***(P-21183)***
Landmark Imaging LLC.....D.....310 914-7336
11620 Wilshire Blvd Fl 10 Los Angeles (90025) ***(P-19957)***
Landmark Medical Center, Pomona *Also called Landmark Medical Services Inc* ***(P-21024)***
Landmark Medical Services Inc.....D.....909 593-2585
2030 N Garey Ave Pomona (91767) ***(P-21024)***
Landmark Services Inc.....D.....714 547-6308
410 N Fairview St Santa Ana (92703) ***(P-17256)***
Landmark Theatres, West Hollywood *Also called Silver Cinemas Acquisition Co* ***(P-19289)***
Landor Associates, Irvine *Also called Young & Rubicam LLC* ***(P-17073)***
Landsberg La Valley Div 1027, Pacoima *Also called Orora North America* ***(P-14219)***
Landsberg Los Angeles Div 1001, Montebello *Also called Orora Packaging Solutions* ***(P-14222)***
Landsberg Orora, Buena Park *Also called Orora Packaging Solutions* ***(P-14221)***
Landscape Center, Riverside *Also called B & B Nurseries Inc* ***(P-14876)***
Landscape Communications Inc.....E.....714 979-5276
14771 Plaza Dr Ste A Tustin (92780) ***(P-4079)***
Landscape Contract National, Tustin *Also called Landscape Communications Inc* ***(P-4079)***
Landscape Contractor, Thousand Oaks *Also called Oak Ridge Landworks* ***(P-328)***
Landscape Development Inc.....C.....951 371-9370
1290 Carbide Dr Corona (92881) ***(P-320)***
Landscape Development Inc (PA).....**B.....661 295-1970**
28447 Witherspoon Pkwy Valencia (91355) ***(P-321)***
Landscape Pest Management, Anaheim *Also called Pest Options Inc* ***(P-17204)***
Landscape Support Services.....D.....818 475-0680
12610 Saticoy St S North Hollywood (91605) ***(P-322)***
Landsea Homes Corporation (HQ).....**D.....949 345-8080**
660 Nwport Ctr Dr Ste 300 Newport Beach (92660) ***(P-679)***
Landsea Homes US Corporation (HQ).....**D.....949 345-8080**
660 Nwport Ctr Dr Ste 300 Newport Beach (92660) ***(P-16056)***
Landslide Technologies Inc (HQ).....**C.....412 489-1705**
6922 Hollywood Blvd # 500 Los Angeles (90028) ***(P-17651)***
Landstar Global Logistics Inc.....D.....909 266-0096
2313 E Philadelphia St Ontario (91761) ***(P-12059)***
Landwin Hospitality LLC.....D.....626 270-2700
225 W Valley Blvd San Gabriel (91776) ***(P-16534)***
Lane & Kuschner Medical Group.....D.....310 858-0104
9001 Wilshire Blvd # 200 Beverly Hills (90211) ***(P-19958)***
Lane Winpak Inc (HQ).....**D.....909 386-1762**
1365 N Ayala Dr Rialto (92376) ***(P-14945)***
Laneaire.....F.....951 808-3658
1121 California Ave Corona (92881) ***(P-6862)***
Lange Precision Inc.....F.....714 870-5420
1106 E Elm Ave Fullerton (92831) ***(P-8660)***
Langers Juice Company Inc.....B.....626 336-3100
129 Stephen St City of Industry (91744) ***(P-1905)***
Langham Hotels International, Pasadena *Also called Langham Hotels Pacific Corp* ***(P-16535)***
Langham Hotels Pacific Corp.....D.....617 451-1900
1401 S Oak Knoll Ave Pasadena (91106) ***(P-16535)***
Langham Huntington Hotel & Spa, Pasadena *Also called Pacific Huntington Hotel Corp* ***(P-16609)***
Langlois, Laguna Beach *Also called AJ Sons Inc* ***(P-1913)***
Langlois Company.....E.....951 360-3900
10810 San Sevaine Way Jurupa Valley (91752) ***(P-1952)***
Langlois Flour Company, Jurupa Valley *Also called Langlois Company* ***(P-1952)***
Language Los Angeles, Burbank *Also called Eastwest Clothing Inc* ***(P-2842)***
Language Weaver Inc.....D.....310 437-7300
6060 Center Dr Ste 150 Los Angeles (90045) ***(P-17652)***
Lani, Irvine *Also called Loan Administration Netwrk Inc* ***(P-17437)***
Lanic Aerospace, Rancho Cucamonga *Also called Lanic Engineering Inc* ***(P-10365)***
Lanic Engineering Inc (PA).....**E.....877 763-0411**
12144 6th St Rancho Cucamonga (91730) ***(P-10365)***
Lanpar Inc.....F.....541 484-1962
1333 S Bon View Ave Ontario (91761) ***(P-3475)***
Lansair Corporation.....E.....661 294-9503
25228 Anza Dr Santa Clarita (91355) ***(P-8661)***
Lanstreetcom.....F.....626 964-2000
1216 John Reed Ct City of Industry (91745) ***(P-8226)***
Lantic Inc.....E.....949 830-9951
27081 Burbank Foothill Ranch (92610) ***(P-5696)***
Lantronix Inc (PA).....**B.....949 453-3990**
7535 Irvine Center Dr # 10 Irvine (92618) ***(P-8272)***
Lanty Inc.....C.....626 582-8001
9660 Flair Dr El Monte (91731) ***(P-2470)***
Lantz Security Systems Inc.....C.....805 496-5775
101 N Westlake Blvd # 20 Westlake Village (91362) ***(P-18293)***
Lantz Security Systems Inc (PA).....**D.....661 949-3565**
43440 Sahuayo St Lancaster (93535) ***(P-18294)***
Lantz Security Systems Inc.....C.....818 871-0193
4111 Las Virgenes Rd # 202 Calabasas (91302) ***(P-18392)***
Lanza Research International.....F.....310 393-5227
429 Santa Monica Blvd # 5 Santa Monica (90401) ***(P-5041)***
Lapco West LLC.....E.....562 348-4850
6901 Marlin Cir La Palma (90623) ***(P-10089)***
Laquer Urban Clfford Hodge LLP.....D.....626 449-1882
225 S Lake Ave Ste 200 Pasadena (91101) ***(P-21603)***
Largo Concrete Inc.....B.....909 981-7844
1690 W Foothill Blvd B Upland (91786) ***(P-1537)***
Larin Corp.....E.....909 464-0605
5651 Schaefer Ave Chino (91710) ***(P-6485)***
Laritech Inc.....C.....805 529-5000
5898 Condor Dr Moorpark (93021) ***(P-9422)***
Lark Engineering, Anaheim *Also called Secure Technology Company* ***(P-9452)***
LARK Industries Inc (HQ).....**C.....714 701-4200**
10 Bunsen Irvine (92618) ***(P-18572)***
Larry Jacinto Construction Inc.....D.....909 794-2151
9555 N Wabash Ave Redlands (92374) ***(P-897)***
Larry Jacinto Farming Inc.....D.....909 794-2276
9555 N Wabash Ave Redlands (92374) ***(P-224)***
Larry Mthvin Installations Inc.....D.....714 547-8021
210 S Center St Santa Ana (92703) ***(P-13332)***
Larry Mthvin Installations Inc (HQ).....**C.....909 563-1700**
501 Kettering Dr Ontario (91761) ***(P-5961)***
Larry Spun Products Inc.....E.....323 881-6300
1533 S Downey Rd Los Angeles (90023) ***(P-7160)***
Larsen Supply Co (PA).....**D.....562 698-0731**
12055 Slauson Ave Santa Fe Springs (90670) ***(P-13833)***
Larson Al Boat Shop.....D.....310 514-4100
1046 S Seaside Ave San Pedro (90731) ***(P-10452)***
Las Brisas, San Luis Obispo *Also called Harvest Management Sub LLC* ***(P-15725)***
Las Brisas Hotel, Palm Springs *Also called Robray Hotel Partnership LLP* ***(P-16669)***
Las Cmbres Obsrvtory Globl Tls.....E.....805 880-1600
6740 Cortona Dr Ste 102 Goleta (93117) ***(P-22913)***
Las Colinas.....F.....714 528-8100
600 S Jefferson St Ste M Placentia (92870) ***(P-8391)***
Las Flores Convalescent Hosp, Gardena *Also called Gardena Flores* ***(P-20352)***
Las Glondrinas Mexican Fd Pdts (PA).....**F.....949 240-3440**
27124 Paseo Espada # 803 San Juan Capistrano (92675) ***(P-2471)***
Las Islas Family Med Group PC.....D.....805 385-8662
325 W Chnnel Islands Blvd Oxnard (93033) ***(P-19959)***
Las Palmas Park, San Fernando *Also called San Fernando City of Inc* ***(P-21883)***
Las Posas Berry Farms LLC.....D.....805 483-1000
730 S A St Oxnard (93030) ***(P-31)***
Las Posas Country Club.....D.....805 482-4518
955 Fairway Dr Camarillo (93010) ***(P-19578)***
Las Posas Road Medical Offices, Camarillo *Also called Kaiser Foundation Hospitals* ***(P-19893)***
Las Vegas / LA Express Inc (PA).....**C.....909 972-3100**
1000 S Cucamonga Ave Ontario (91761) ***(P-12060)***
Las Virgenes Municipal Wtr Dst.....C.....818 251-2100
4232 Las Virgenes Rd Lbby Calabasas (91302) ***(P-12898)***
Lasalle Intl Hldings Group Inc.....F.....818 233-8000
9667 Owensmouth Ave Chatsworth (91311) ***(P-7673)***
Lasco, Santa Fe Springs *Also called Larsen Supply Co* ***(P-13833)***
Lasdos Victorias Candy Company, Rosemead *Also called Ldvc Inc* ***(P-2092)***
Laser Image Plus.....E.....714 556-5277
14751 Franklin Ave Ste B Tustin (92780) ***(P-18197)***
Laser Imaging International, Van Nuys *Also called E Alko Inc* ***(P-11476)***
Laser Industries Inc.....D.....714 532-3271
1351 Manhattan Ave Fullerton (92831) ***(P-8662)***
Laser Operations LLC.....E.....818 986-0000
15632 Roxford St Sylmar (91342) ***(P-9530)***
Laser Spectrum Inc.....E.....949 726-2978
15 Mira Mesa Rcho STA Marg (92688) ***(P-9885)***
Laser Spectrum Inc (PA).....**F.....949 551-8225**
4605 Barranca Pkwy 101g Irvine (92604) ***(P-9886)***
Laser Tech, Riverside *Also called L T Seroge Inc* ***(P-9884)***
Laseraway Medical Group Inc (PA).....**C.....888 252-7497**
9615 Brighton Way Ste 202 Beverly Hills (90210) ***(P-19960)***
Lasercare Technologies Inc (PA).....**E.....310 202-4200**
3375 Robertson Pl Los Angeles (90034) ***(P-11479)***
Laserfiche Document Imaging, Long Beach *Also called Compulink Management Ctr Inc* ***(P-17582)***
Lasergraphics Inc.....E.....949 753-8282
20 Ada Irvine (92618) ***(P-8273)***
Lasergraphics General Business, Irvine *Also called Lasergraphics Inc* ***(P-8273)***
Laserod Technologies LLC.....E.....310 328-5869
20312 Gramercy Pl Torrance (90501) ***(P-9887)***
Laspec Lighting, Vernon *Also called La Spec Industries Inc* ***(P-9091)***
Lasr Inc.....C.....877 591-9979
1517 Beverly Blvd Los Angeles (90026) ***(P-17151)***
Lassonde Pappas and Co Inc.....E.....909 923-4041
1755 E Acacia St Ontario (91761) ***(P-2472)***
LAT LLC.....E.....323 233-3017
2618 Fruitland Ave Vernon (90058) ***(P-2967)***
Latara Enterprise Inc (PA).....**C.....909 623-9301**
1716 W Holt Ave Pomona (91768) ***(P-21074)***
Latexco West, Santa Fe Springs *Also called Sleepcomp West LLC* ***(P-5521)***

ALPHABETIC

Employee Codes: A=Over 500 employees, B=251-500
C=101-250, D=51-100, E=20-50 F=10-19
2022 Southern California Business
Directory and Buyers Guide
© Mergent Inc. 1-800-342-5647
1185

Latham & Watkins LLP (PA) ... A ... **213 485-1234**
555 W 5th St Ste 300 Los Angeles (90013) ***(P-21604)***
Latino Film Inst Yuth Cnema PR ... D ... 626 222-9252
143 S Glendale Ave # 204 Glendale (91205) ***(P-19240)***
Latitudes Intl Fragrance Inc ... D ... 866 639-3999
10940 Wilshire Blvd # 23 Los Angeles (90024) ***(P-14946)***
Lats International, Los Angeles *Also called Los Angles Tmes Cmmnctions LLC* ***(P-4006)***
Launchpint Elc Prplsion Sltons ... E ... 805 683-9659
5735 Hollister Ave Ste B Goleta (93117) ***(P-10366)***
Launchpoint Eps, Goleta *Also called Launchpint Elc Prplsion Sltons* ***(P-10366)***
Laundry By Shelli Segal, Commerce *Also called LCI Laundry Inc* ***(P-2891)***
Lauras French Baking Co Inc ... F ... 323 585-5144
722 S Oxford Ave Apt 107 Los Angeles (90005) ***(P-2013)***
Lauras House ... D ... 949 361-3775
33 Journey Ste 150 Aliso Viejo (92656) ***(P-21837)***
Lauree LLC ... D ... 949 446-9900
25901 Commercentre Dr Lake Forest (92630) ***(P-18573)***
Laurence-Hovenier Inc ... C ... 951 736-2990
179 N Maple St Corona (92878) ***(P-1445)***
Laurus Construction Corp ... E ... 714 641-0318
3189 Red Hill Ave Ste D Costa Mesa (92626) ***(P-781)***
Lava Heat Italia ... F ... 310 559-1700
940 W Washington Blvd Los Angeles (90015) ***(P-8094)***
Lava Products Inc ... E ... 949 951-7191
3168 Airway Ave Costa Mesa (92626) ***(P-4353)***
Lavash Corporation of America ... E ... 323 663-5249
2835 Newell St Los Angeles (90039) ***(P-2014)***
Lavi Industries (PA) ... D ... **877 275-5284**
27810 Avenue Hopkins Valencia (91355) ***(P-6971)***
Law Offces Les Zeve A Prof Cor ... C ... 714 848-7920
30 Corporate Park Ste 450 Irvine (92606) ***(P-21605)***
Law Offices Berglund & Johnson (PA) ... D ... **951 276-4783**
21550 Oxnard St Ste 900 Woodland Hills (91367) ***(P-21606)***
Law Offices Juan J. Dominguez, Los Angeles *Also called Dominguez Firm Inc* ***(P-21550)***
Law School Financial Inc ... C ... 626 243-1800
175 S Lake Ave Unit 200 Pasadena (91101) ***(P-15134)***
Law School Loans, Pasadena *Also called Law School Financial Inc* ***(P-15134)***
Lawa Inc ... D ... 424 646-7770
7333 World Way W Los Angeles (90045) ***(P-12360)***
LAweb Offset Printing Inc ... E ... 626 454-2469
9639 Telstar Ave El Monte (91731) ***(P-4535)***
Lawrence Berkeley National Lab, Brea *Also called Energy Berkeley Office US Dept* ***(P-22908)***
Lawrence Equipment Leasing Inc (PA) ... C ... **626 442-2894**
2034 Peck Rd El Monte (91733) ***(P-7942)***
Lawrence Roll Up Doors Inc (PA) ... E ... **626 962-4163**
4525 Littlejohn St Baldwin Park (91706) ***(P-6706)***
Lawrence Welk Desert Oasis, Cathedral City *Also called Welk Resort Group Inc* ***(P-16783)***
Lawrys Restaurants II Inc ... C ... 323 664-0228
2980 Los Feliz Blvd Los Angeles (90039) ***(P-16962)***
Lawyers Title Company (HQ) ... E ... **818 767-0425**
7530 N Glenoaks Blvd Burbank (91504) ***(P-15506)***
Lawyers Title Escrow, Irvine *Also called Lawyers Title Insurance Corp* ***(P-15507)***
Lawyers Title Insurance Corp ... C ... 949 223-5575
16755 Von Karman Ave # 100 Irvine (92606) ***(P-15507)***
Lawyers Title Insurance Corp ... C ... 805 484-2701
2751 Park View Ct Oxnard (93036) ***(P-15508)***
Lawyers Title Insurance Corp ... C ... 949 223-5575
18551 Von Karman Ave # 100 Irvine (92612) ***(P-15509)***
Lax Hotel Investment Co Inc ... D ... 310 846-3200
10300 S La Cienega Blvd Inglewood (90304) ***(P-16536)***
Lax Hotel Ventures LLC ... E ... 310 645-4600
9750 Airport Blvd Los Angeles (90045) ***(P-16537)***
Lax In-Flite Services LLC ... F ... 310 677-9885
125 N Ash Ave Inglewood (90301) ***(P-9888)***
Lax-C Inc ... E ... 323 343-9000
1100 N Main St Los Angeles (90012) ***(P-14474)***
Layer Cake Bakery, Irvine *Also called Modaan Inc* ***(P-2021)***
Laymon Candy Co Inc ... E ... 909 825-4408
276 Commercial Rd San Bernardino (92408) ***(P-14564)***
Layne Laboratories Inc ... E ... 805 242-7918
4303 Huasna Rd Arroyo Grande (93420) ***(P-2728)***
Layton Printing & Mailing ... F ... 909 592-4419
1538 Arrow Hwy La Verne (91750) ***(P-4354)***
Lb Beadels LLC ... F ... 562 726-1700
70 Atlantic Ave Long Beach (90802) ***(P-2091)***
Lba Inc ... D ... 949 833-0400
3347 Michelson Dr Ste 210 Irvine (92612) ***(P-23256)***
Lba Realty, Irvine *Also called Lba Inc* ***(P-23256)***
Lba Realty LLC (PA) ... E ... **949 833-0400**
3347 Michelson Dr Ste 200 Irvine (92612) ***(P-15908)***
Lbi - USA, Chatsworth *Also called Lehrer Brllnprfktion Werks Inc* ***(P-5697)***
Lbi Media Holdings Inc (HQ) ... D ... **818 563-5722**
1845 W Empire Ave Burbank (91504) ***(P-12698)***
Lbs Financial Credit Union (PA) ... C ... **562 598-9007**
5505 Garden Grove Blvd # 500 Westminster (92683) ***(P-15135)***
Lca Promotions Inc ... E ... 818 773-9170
3073 Cicero Ct Simi Valley (93063) ***(P-4536)***
LCI Laundry Inc ... C ... 323 767-1900
5835 S Eastrn Ave Ste 100 Commerce (90040) ***(P-2891)***
Lcoa, Lake Forest *Also called Laminating Company of America* ***(P-9421)***
Lcptracker Inc ... E ... 714 669-0052
117 E Chapman Ave Orange (92866) ***(P-17904)***
Ld Acquisition Company 16 LLC ... D ... 310 294-8160
400 Continental Blvd # 500 El Segundo (90245) ***(P-16273)***
Ld Holdings Group LLC (HQ) ... E ... **888 337-6888**
26642 Towne Centre Dr Foothill Ranch (92610) ***(P-23257)***

Ld Products Inc ... C ... 888 321-2552
3700 Cover St Long Beach (90808) ***(P-3760)***
Ld Steel Inc ... F ... 213 632-8073
15517 Illinois Ave Paramount (90723) ***(P-6972)***
LDI Mechanical Inc (PA) ... B ... **951 340-9685**
1587 E Bentley Dr Corona (92879) ***(P-1093)***
LDI Operations LLC ... C ... 818 240-7500
450 N Brand Blvd Ste 900 Glendale (91203) ***(P-11705)***
Ldvc Inc ... F ... 626 448-4611
9606 Valley Blvd Rosemead (91770) ***(P-2092)***
Le Beau Thelen LLP ... D ... 661 325-8962
5001 E Commercecenter Dr Bakersfield (93309) ***(P-21607)***
Le Bleu Chateau Inc ... E ... 818 843-3141
1900 Grismer Ave Burbank (91504) ***(P-22123)***
Le Courier, Burbank *Also called Tidavater Inc* ***(P-18692)***
Le Elegant Bath Inc ... C ... 951 734-0238
13405 Estelle St Corona (92879) ***(P-5534)***
Le Montrose Hotel ... D ... 310 855-1115
900 Hammond St Apt 434 West Hollywood (90069) ***(P-16538)***
Le Montrose Suite Hotel, West Hollywood *Also called Le Montrose Hotel* ***(P-16538)***
Le Parc Suite Hotel, West Hollywood *Also called Ols Hotels & Resorts LLC* ***(P-16593)***
Le Parker Meridien Palm Sprng, Palm Springs *Also called Jack Parker Corp* ***(P-16510)***
Le Petit Sheet Metal Inc ... F ... 626 334-4415
720 N Georgia Ave Azusa (91702) ***(P-6863)***
Le Val of California Inc ... E ... 323 221-9116
3305 Pasadena Ave Los Angeles (90031) ***(P-18574)***
Le Vecke Corporation (PA) ... D ... **951 681-8600**
10810 Inland Ave Jurupa Valley (91752) ***(P-14830)***
Le Vecke Group, Jurupa Valley *Also called Le Vecke Corporation* ***(P-14830)***
Leach Grain & Milling Co Inc ... E ... 562 869-4451
8131 Pivot St Downey (90241) ***(P-14864)***
Leach International Corp (HQ) ... B ... **714 736-7537**
6900 Orangethorpe Ave A Buena Park (90620) ***(P-10367)***
Leader Drug Store, Torrance *Also called Little Company Mary Hospital* ***(P-20834)***
Leader Electronics (na) Inc ... E ... 714 435-0505
2901 S Harbor Blvd Santa Ana (92704) ***(P-9236)***
Leader Emergency Vehicles, South El Monte *Also called Leader Industries Inc* ***(P-11877)***
Leader Hospitality LP ... D ... 949 582-7100
26328 Oso Pkwy Mission Viejo (92691) ***(P-16539)***
Leader Industries Inc ... C ... 626 575-0880
10941 Weaver Ave South El Monte (91733) ***(P-11877)***
Leadingway Corporation (PA) ... F ... **949 509-6589**
4199 Campus Dr Ste 550 Irvine (92612) ***(P-18042)***
Leadingway Knowledge Systems, Irvine *Also called Leadingway Corporation* ***(P-18042)***
Leaf Commercial Capital Inc ... E ... 866 219-7924
1100 W Town And Country R Orange (92868) ***(P-23258)***
Leaf Communications Inc ... D ... 949 388-0192
1000 Calle Cordillera San Clemente (92673) ***(P-23465)***
Leaf Group Ltd (PA) ... B ... **310 656-6253**
1655 26th St Santa Monica (90404) ***(P-18097)***
Lean Supply Solutions Amer Inc (PA) ... D ... **844 310-5252**
26871 San Bernardino Ave Redlands (92374) ***(P-12218)***
Lear Capital Inc ... D ... 310 571-0190
1990 S Bundy Dr Ste 600 Los Angeles (90025) ***(P-15273)***
Learfield Communications LLC ... D ... 949 823-1729
5291 California Ave # 100 Irvine (92617) ***(P-12699)***
LEARN, Whittier *Also called Rio Hondo Education Consortium* ***(P-21878)***
Learning Resources Inc ... E ... 800 995-4436
152 W Walnut St Ste 201 Gardena (90248) ***(P-11706)***
Learning Tree Pre-School, Tujunga *Also called Crescenta-Canada YMCA* ***(P-22335)***
Leather In Chicago ... F ... 818 349-3456
11808 Turtle Springs Ln Porter Ranch (91326) ***(P-14947)***
Leather Pro Inc ... E ... 818 833-8822
12900 Bradley Ave Sylmar (91342) ***(P-5909)***
Leatherupcom (PA) ... F ... **213 763-6185**
955 Venice Blvd Los Angeles (90015) ***(P-2819)***
Leatt Corporation (PA) ... E ... **661 287-9258**
26475 Summit Cir Santa Clarita (91350) ***(P-11433)***
Lebata Inc ... E ... 949 253-2800
4621 Teller Ave Ste 130 Newport Beach (92660) ***(P-6098)***
Leda Corporation ... E ... 714 841-7821
7080 Kearny Dr Huntington Beach (92648) ***(P-10534)***
Leda Multimedia, Chino *Also called Shop4techcom* ***(P-8217)***
Ledconn Corp ... E ... 714 256-2111
301 Thor Pl Brea (92821) ***(P-9137)***
Ledesma & Meyer Cnstr Co Inc ... D ... 909 297-1100
9441 Haven Ave Rancho Cucamonga (91730) ***(P-782)***
Ledingedge Lighting Inc (PA) ... F ... **805 383-8493**
4682 Calle Bolero Ste A Camarillo (93012) ***(P-9093)***
Ledra Brands Inc ... C ... 714 259-9959
88 Maxwell Irvine (92618) ***(P-13176)***
Ledtronics Inc ... C ... 310 534-1505
23105 Kashiwa Ct Torrance (90505) ***(P-9531)***
Lee Burkhart Liu Inc ... D ... 310 829-2249
5510 Lincoln Blvd Ste 250 Playa Vista (90094) ***(P-22728)***
Lee & Assoc Coml RE Svcs Inc - (PA) ... E ... **949 727-1200**
7700 Irvine Center Dr # 60 Irvine (92618) ***(P-15909)***
Lee & Assoc Comm Real Est Svcs ... E ... 909 989-7771
3535 Inland Empire Blvd Ontario (91764) ***(P-15910)***
Lee & Assoc Rlty Group Nwport ... E ... 949 724-1000
100 Bayview Cir Ste 600 Newport Beach (92660) ***(P-15911)***
Lee & Associates Coml RE Svcs, Ontario *Also called Lee & Assoc Comm Real Est Svcs* ***(P-15910)***
Lee & Ro Inc (PA) ... E ... **626 912-3391**
1199 Fullerton Rd City of Industry (91748) ***(P-22600)***
Lee Kum Kee (usa) Foods Inc ... D ... 626 709-1888
14455 Don Julian Rd City of Industry (91746) ***(P-2473)***

Lee Kum Kee (usa) Inc (HQ)..E.......626 709-1888
14841 Don Julian Rd City of Industry (91746) *(P-14704)*
Lee Machine Products..F.......626 301-4105
2030 Central Ave Duarte (91010) *(P-7812)*
Lee Maxton Inc..F.......909 483-0688
10844 Edison Ct Rancho Cucamonga (91730) *(P-4355)*
Lee Pharmaceuticals..D.......626 442-3141
1434 Santa Anita Ave South El Monte (91733) *(P-5042)*
Lee Ray Sandblasting, Santa Fe Springs *Also called Cji Process Systems Inc (P-6734)*
Lee Thomas Inc (PA)..E.......310 532-7560
13800 S Figueroa St Los Angeles (90061) *(P-2968)*
LEE& Associates, Newport Beach *Also called Lee & Assoc Rlty Group Nwport (P-15911)*
Lee's Enterprise, Chatsworth *Also called Molnar Engineering Inc (P-8705)*
Lee's Kitchen, City of Industry *Also called Lee Kum Kee (usa) Inc (P-14704)*
Leed Electric Inc..C.......562 270-9500
13138 Arctic Cir Santa Fe Springs (90670) *(P-1275)*
Leekilpatrick Management Inc..D.......818 500-9631
324 S Myrtle Ave Monrovia (91016) *(P-23259)*
Leeper's Stair Products, Corona *Also called Leepers Wood Turning Co Inc (P-3262)*
Leepers Wood Turning Co Inc (PA)..E.......562 422-6525
341 Bonnie Cir Ste 104 Corona (92878) *(P-3262)*
Lees Maintenance Service Inc..B.......818 988-6644
14740 Keswick St Van Nuys (91405) *(P-17257)*
Leet Technology Inc..F.......877 238-4492
1427 S Robertson Blvd Los Angeles (90035) *(P-10090)*
Left Coast Brewing Company..F.......949 218-3961
1245 Puerta Del Sol San Clemente (92673) *(P-2149)*
Leftbank Art, La Mirada *Also called Outlook Resources Inc (P-3162)*
Legacy Commercial Holdings Inc..E.......818 767-6626
28939 Avenue Williams Valencia (91355) *(P-3476)*
Legacy Epoch LLC (HQ)..D.......844 673-7305
21011 Warner Center Ln A Woodland Hills (91367) *(P-1971)*
Legacy Farms LLC..C.......714 736-1800
1765 W Penhall Way Anaheim (92801) *(P-14642)*
Legacy Frames..D.......310 537-4210
11220 Wright Rd Lynwood (90262) *(P-13741)*
Legacy Healthcare Center LLC..D.......626 798-0558
1570 N Fair Oaks Ave Pasadena (91103) *(P-21449)*
Legacy Prtners Residential Inc..B.......949 930-6600
5141 California Ave # 100 Irvine (92617) *(P-23050)*
Legacy Tile and Stone Inc..E.......951 296-1096
26825 Jefferson Ave Ste D Murrieta (92562) *(P-1419)*
Legal Enterprise, Calabasas *Also called Litigtion Rsrces of America-CA (P-18579)*
Legal Solutions Holdings Inc..C.......800 244-3495
955 Overland Ct Ste 200 San Dimas (91773) *(P-21608)*
Legal Support Network LLC..D.......213 975-9850
1533 Wilshire Blvd Los Angeles (90017) *(P-18575)*
Legal Vision Group LLC..E.......310 945-5550
2030 Paddock Ln Norco (92860) *(P-4356)*
Legalzoomcom Inc (PA)..B.......323 962-8600
101 N Brand Blvd Fl 11 Glendale (91203) *(P-18098)*
Legend Pump & Well Service Inc..E.......909 384-1000
1324 W Rialto Ave San Bernardino (92410) *(P-433)*
Legend3d Inc..D.......858 793-4420
1500 Cotner Ave Ste 1 Los Angeles (90025) *(P-19140)*
Legendary Entertainment LLC..D.......818 688-7006
2900 W Alameda Ave Burbank (91505) *(P-19141)*
Leggett & Platt Incorporated..D.......909 937-1010
1050 S Dupont Ave Ontario (91761) *(P-3552)*
Leggett & Platt 0302, Valencia *Also called Leggett & Platt Incorporated (P-3657)*
Leggett & Platt Incorporated..E.......661 775-8500
29120 Commerce Center Dr # 1 Valencia (91355) *(P-3657)*
Legion Creative Group..E.......323 498-1100
500 N Brand Blvd Ste 1800 Glendale (91203) *(P-4537)*
Lehigh Cement West Inc..C.......661 822-4445
13573 E Tehachapi Blvd Tehachapi (93561) *(P-5978)*
Lehman Foods Inc..E.......818 837-7600
1145 Arroyo St Ste B San Fernando (91340) *(P-2474)*
Lehrer Brllnprfktion Werks Inc (PA)..D.......818 407-1890
20801 Nordhoff St Chatsworth (91311) *(P-5697)*
Lei AG Seattle, Los Angeles *Also called Lowe Enterprises Inc (P-16546)*
Leibovic & Tysch, Sherman Oaks *Also called Health Advocates (P-21578)*
Leidos Inc..D.......714 257-6400
590 W Central Ave Ste I Brea (92821) *(P-22847)*
Leidos Government Services Inc..C.......323 721-6979
500 N Via Val Verde Montebello (90640) *(P-18198)*
Leigh Jerry California Inc (PA)..B.......818 909-6200
7860 Nelson Rd Panorama City (91402) *(P-14391)*
Leight Sales Co Inc..D.......310 223-1000
1611 S Catalina Ave L45 Redondo Beach (90277) *(P-13809)*
Leighton & Associates, Irvine *Also called Gradient Engineers Inc (P-22562)*
Leighton and Associates Inc (PA)..D.......949 250-1421
17781 Cowan Irvine (92614) *(P-23466)*
Leiner Health Products Inc (HQ)..A.......631 200-2000
901 E 233rd St Carson (90745) *(P-4843)*
Leiner Health Products Inc..C.......714 898-9936
7366 Orangewood Ave Garden Grove (92841) *(P-4844)*
Leiner Health Products Inc..D.......661 775-1422
27655b Avenue Hopkins Valencia (91355) *(P-4845)*
Leisure Care LLC..B.......818 713-0900
8138 Woodlake Ave West Hills (91304) *(P-20535)*
Leisure Care LLC..C.......714 974-1616
380 S Anaheim Hills Rd Anaheim (92807) *(P-22124)*
Leisure Components, Cerritos *Also called Sedenquist-Fraser Entps Inc (P-10132)*
Leisure Court Nursing Center, Anaheim *Also called 1135 N Leisure Ct Inc (P-20236)*
Leisure Glen Convalescent Ctr, Glendale *Also called Buena Ventura Care Center Inc (P-20566)*
Leisure World Pharmacy, Seal Beach *Also called Tenet Healthsystem Medical Inc (P-20107)*
Leisure World Resales, Laguna Hills *Also called Professional Cmnty MGT Cal Inc (P-15959)*
Lejon of California Inc..E.......951 736-1229
1229 Railroad St Corona (92882) *(P-3061)*
Lejon Tulliani, Corona *Also called Lejon of California Inc (P-3061)*
LEK Consulting LLC..E.......310 209-9800
1100 Glendon Ave Ste 2100 Los Angeles (90024) *(P-23260)*
Lekos Dye & Finishing Inc..D.......310 763-0900
3131 E Harcourt St Compton (90221) *(P-2613)*
Lemonlight Media Inc..D.......310 402-0275
226 S Glasgow Ave Inglewood (90301) *(P-19142)*
Lemyn LLC..F.......714 617-2410
511 S Harbor Blvd La Habra (90631) *(P-5043)*
Lemyn Organics, La Habra *Also called Lemyn LLC (P-5043)*
Lenders Investment Corp..D.......714 540-4747
18101 Von Karman Ave # 400 Irvine (92612) *(P-15207)*
Lenlyn Ltd Which Will Do Bus I (HQ)..D.......310 417-3432
6151 W Century Blvd # 11 Los Angeles (90045) *(P-15129)*
Lennar Builders, Irvine *Also called Lennar Homes California Inc (P-621)*
Lennar Corporation..D.......949 349-8000
15131 Alton Pkwy Ste 190 Irvine (92618) *(P-680)*
Lennar Homes California Inc (HQ)..C.......949 349-8000
15131 Alton Pkwy Ste 190 Irvine (92618) *(P-621)*
Lennar Multi Family Community, Aliso Viejo *Also called LMC Hollywood Highland (P-784)*
Lennar Partners of Los Angeles (PA)..D.......949 885-8500
4350 Von Karman Ave # 200 Newport Beach (92660) *(P-18576)*
Lenntek Corporation..E.......310 534-2738
1610 Lockness Pl Torrance (90501) *(P-9286)*
Lenovati Inc (PA)..E.......323 307-9878
3251 E 26th St Vernon (90058) *(P-14392)*
Lenox Financial Mortgage Corp..B.......949 428-5100
200 Sandpointe Ave # 800 Santa Ana (92707) *(P-15208)*
Lens Technology I LLC..F.......714 940-6602
45 Parker Ste 100 Irvine (92618) *(P-10844)*
Leo Hoffman Chevrolet Inc (PA)..C.......626 968-8411
17300 Gale Ave City of Industry (91748) *(P-18750)*
Leoben Company..F.......951 284-9653
16692 Burke Ln Huntington Beach (92647) *(P-11707)*
Leoch Battery Corporation (HQ)..D.......949 588-5853
19751 Descartes Unit A Foothill Ranch (92610) *(P-8921)*
Leon Krous Drilling Inc..E.......818 833-4654
9300 Borden Ave Sun Valley (91352) *(P-434)*
Leonard Chaidez Inc..D.......714 279-8173
2298 N Batavia St Orange (92865) *(P-358)*
Leonard Chaidez Tree Service, Orange *Also called Leonard Chaidez Inc (P-358)*
Leonard Craft Co LLC..D.......714 549-0678
3501 W Segerstrom Ave Santa Ana (92704) *(P-11322)*
Leonard Roofing Inc..C.......951 506-3811
43280 Bus Pk Dr Ste 107 Temecula (92590) *(P-1495)*
Leonards Carpet Service Inc (PA)..D.......714 630-1930
1121 N Red Gum St Anaheim (92806) *(P-3658)*
Leonards Molded Products Inc..E.......661 253-2227
25031 Anza Dr Valencia (91355) *(P-5388)*
Leonesse Cellars, Temecula *Also called Temecula Valley Winery MGT LLC (P-2228)*
Leonesse Cellars LLC..E.......951 302-7601
38311 De Portola Rd Temecula (92592) *(P-2202)*
Leonetti Company, Tujunga *Also called F J & J Corporation (P-19232)*
Leonid M Glsman DDS A Dntl Cor..C.......323 560-4514
5021 Florence Ave Bell (90201) *(P-20186)*
Leport Educational Inst Inc..B.......914 374-8860
1 Technology Dr Bldg A Irvine (92618) *(P-22027)*
Leport Schools, Irvine *Also called Leport Educational Inst Inc (P-22027)*
Leprino Foods Company..B.......559 924-7722
490 F St Lemoore (93245) *(P-1777)*
Leprino Foods Company..C.......559 924-7939
351 Belle Haven Dr Lemoore (93245) *(P-1778)*
Lereta LLC (PA)..B.......626 543-1765
901 Corporate Center Dr Pomona (91768) *(P-15274)*
LEROY HAYNES CENTER, La Verne *Also called Haynes Family Programs Inc (P-22111)*
Lesco, Torrance *Also called American Ultraviolet West Inc (P-7684)*
Lester Lithograph Inc..E.......714 491-3981
1128 N Gilbert St Anaheim (92801) *(P-4357)*
Lets Do Lunch..D.......310 523-3664
310 W Alondra Blvd Gardena (90248) *(P-2475)*
Lets Go Apparel Inc (PA)..E.......213 863-1767
1729 E Washington Blvd Los Angeles (90021) *(P-3076)*
Letterhead Factory Inc..F.......310 538-3321
1007 E Dominguez St Ste H Carson (90746) *(P-4358)*
Levco Fab Inc..E.......909 465-0840
10757 Fremont Ave Ontario (91762) *(P-7540)*
Levecke LLC..E.......951 681-8600
10810 Inland Ave Jurupa Valley (91752) *(P-2203)*
Level 23 Fab..E.......714 979-2323
2117 S Anne St Santa Ana (92704) *(P-6628)*
Level 99, Gardena *Also called Phoenix Textile Inc (P-14313)*
Level Four Business MGT LLC..E.......310 914-1600
11812 San Vicente Blvd # 400 Los Angeles (90049) *(P-23467)*
Level Furnished Living, Los Angeles *Also called Onni Properties LLC (P-23078)*
Levi Strauss & Co..F.......310 246-9044
316 N Beverly Dr Beverly Hills (90210) *(P-2772)*
Levine Leichtman Capital..D.......310 275-5335
345 N Maple Dr Ste 300 Beverly Hills (90210) *(P-16211)*
Levity Entertainment Group LLC..E.......310 417-4861
6701 Center Dr W Fl 11 Los Angeles (90045) *(P-23261)*
Levity Live, Oxnard *Also called Comedy Club Oxnard LLC (P-19556)*
Levity of Brea LLC..D.......714 482-0700
180 S Brea Blvd Brea (92821) *(P-19579)*
Lewis Barricade Inc..D.......661 363-0912
4000 Westerly Pl Ste 100 Newport Beach (92660) *(P-5274)*

ALPHABETIC

Employee Codes: A=Over 500 employees, B=251-500
C=101-250, D=51-100, E=20-50 F=10-19
2022 Southern California Business
Directory and Buyers Guide
© Mergent Inc. 1-800-342-5647
1187

Lewis Brsbois Bsgard Smith LLP......D......951 252-6150
28765 Single Oak Dr # 14 Temecula (92590) *(P-21609)*
Lewis Brsbois Bsgard Smith LLP (PA)......A......**213 250-1800**
633 W 5th St Ste 4000 Los Angeles (90071) *(P-21610)*
Lewis Brsbois Bsgard Smith LLP......D......909 387-1130
650 E Hospitality Ln # 600 San Bernardino (92408) *(P-21611)*
Lewis Companies (PA)......C......**909 985-0971**
1156 N Mountain Ave Upland (91786) *(P-681)*
Lewis Development Co (PA)......C......**909 946-7506**
1156 N Mountain Ave Upland (91786) *(P-783)*
Lewis Homes, Upland *Also called Lewis Development Co (P-783)*
Lewis Marenstein Wicke Sherwin......E......818 703-6000
20750 Ventura Blvd # 400 Woodland Hills (91364) *(P-21612)*
Lexani Wheel Corporation......D......951 368-7526
34420 Gateway Dr Palm Desert (92211) *(P-10091)*
Lexicon Marketing (usa) Inc (PA)......B......**323 782-8282**
640 S San Vicente Blvd Los Angeles (90048) *(P-13534)*
Lexington Scenery & Props Inc......C......818 768-5768
12800 Rangoon St Arleta (91331) *(P-1446)*
Lexisnexis Risk Assets Inc......C......949 222-0028
2112 Bus Ctr Dr Ste 150 Irvine (92614) *(P-15588)*
Lexmar Distribution Inc......E......909 620-7001
200 Erie St Pomona (91768) *(P-12061)*
Lexmark International Inc......E......714 641-1007
575 Anton Blvd Fl 3 Costa Mesa (92626) *(P-8274)*
Lexor Inc......D......714 444-4144
7400 Hazard Ave Westminster (92683) *(P-11708)*
Lexus of Cerritos, Cerritos *Also called Bargain Rent-A-Car (P-13021)*
Lexus Santa Monica, Santa Monica *Also called Volkswagen Santa Monica Inc (P-18808)*
Lexxiom Inc......B......909 581-7313
99 N San Antonio Ave # 3 Upland (91786) *(P-23051)*
Ley Grand Foods Corporation......E......626 336-2244
287 S 6th Ave La Puente (91746) *(P-2015)*
Leyen Food LLC (PA)......D......**626 333-8812**
14328 Lomitas Ave City of Industry (91746) *(P-14596)*
Lf Illumination LLC......D......818 885-1335
9200 Deering Ave Chatsworth (91311) *(P-9094)*
Lf Sportswear Inc (PA)......E......**310 437-4100**
5333 Mcconnell Ave Los Angeles (90066) *(P-2855)*
Lf Visuals Inc......F......760 345-5571
39620 Entrepreneur Ln Palm Desert (92211) *(P-2729)*
Lfk Law......D......310 300-8464
9595 Wilshire Blvd # 900 Beverly Hills (90212) *(P-21613)*
Lfp Ecommerce LLC......D......314 428-5069
210 N Sunset Ave West Covina (91790) *(P-18577)*
Lg Battery......F......323 569-3116
8973 Lotta Ave South Gate (90280) *(P-9825)*
Lg Nanoh2o Inc......E......424 218-4000
21250 Hawthorne Blvd # 33 Torrance (90503) *(P-5227)*
Lg-Led Solutions Limited......E......626 587-8506
15902 Halliburton Rd A Hacienda Heights (91745) *(P-9138)*
LGarde Inc......E......714 259-0771
15181 Woodlawn Ave Tustin (92780) *(P-8206)*
Lh Indian Wells Operating LLC......C......760 341-2200
4500 Indian Wells Ln Indian Wells (92210) *(P-16540)*
Lh Universal Operating LLC......B......818 980-1212
333 Unversal Hollywood Dr Universal City (91608) *(P-16541)*
Liberman Broadcasting Inc (PA)......D......**818 729-5300**
1845 W Empire Ave Burbank (91504) *(P-12700)*
Liberty Container Company......C......323 564-4211
4224 Santa Ana St South Gate (90280) *(P-3817)*
Liberty Debt Relief LLC......D......800 756-8447
333 City Blvd W Fl 17 Orange (92868) *(P-16963)*
Liberty Dental Plan Cal Inc......B......949 223-0007
340 Commerce Ste 100 Irvine (92602) *(P-15440)*
Liberty Dental Plan Corp (PA)......C......**888 703-6999**
340 Commerce Ste 100 Irvine (92602) *(P-15441)*
Liberty Dental Plan Nevada Inc......D......888 703-6999
340 Commerce Irvine (92602) *(P-15442)*
Liberty Entertainment Inc (HQ)......B......**310 964-5000**
2230 E Imperial Hwy El Segundo (90245) *(P-12773)*
Liberty Hardware Mfg Corp......D......909 605-2300
5555 Jurupa St Ontario (91761) *(P-13810)*
Liberty Industries......F......626 575-3206
10754 Lower Azusa Rd El Monte (91731) *(P-8663)*
Liberty Landscaping Inc (PA)......C......**951 683-2999**
5212 El Rivino Rd Riverside (92509) *(P-323)*
Liberty Love, Commerce *Also called Cure Apparel Llc (P-2841)*
Liberty Packg & Extruding Inc......E......323 722-5124
3015 Supply Ave Commerce (90040) *(P-3885)*
Liberty Paper, Vernon *Also called D D Office Products Inc (P-3750)*
Liberty School, Paso Robles *Also called Treana Winery LLC (P-2232)*
Liberty Utilities Pk Wtr Corp (HQ)......D......**562 923-0711**
9750 Washburn Rd Downey (90241) *(P-12899)*
Liberty Vegetable Oil Company......E......562 921-3567
15306 Carmenita Rd Santa Fe Springs (90670) *(P-2131)*
Libra Cable Technologies Inc......F......310 618-8182
Monterey Business Park 27 Torrance (90503) *(P-9740)*
Library Reproduction Service, Los Angeles *Also called The Microfilm Company of Cal (P-4139)*
License Frame Inc......F......714 903-7550
15462 Electronic Ln Huntington Beach (92649) *(P-7381)*
Licher Direct Mail Inc......E......626 795-3333
980 Seco St Pasadena (91103) *(P-4359)*
Lida Childrens Wear Inc......E......626 967-8868
3113 E California Blvd Pasadena (91107) *(P-3034)*
Lidlaw Educational Services, Rancho Cucamonga *Also called Durham School Services L P (P-11922)*
Lieberman RES Worldwide LLC (PA)......C......**310 553-0550**
1900 Avenue Of The Stars Los Angeles (90067) *(P-22892)*
Lief Labs, Valencia *Also called Lief Organics LLC (P-4846)*
Lief Organics LLC (PA)......E......**661 775-2500**
28903 Avenue Paine Valencia (91355) *(P-4846)*
Life Alert Emrgncy Rsponse Inc (PA)......C......**800 247-0000**
16027 Ventura Blvd # 400 Encino (91436) *(P-18393)*
Life Care Center of Bellflower, Bellflower *Also called Life Care Centers America Inc (P-20397)*
Life Care Center of La Habra, La Habra *Also called Life Care Centers America Inc (P-20391)*
Life Care Center of Norwalk, Norwalk *Also called Life Care Centers America Inc (P-20398)*
Life Care Center San Gabriel, San Gabriel *Also called Life Care Centers America Inc (P-20393)*
Life Care Centers America Inc......C......562 690-0852
1233 W La Habra Blvd La Habra (90631) *(P-20391)*
Life Care Centers America Inc......C......562 947-8691
12200 La Mirada Blvd La Mirada (90638) *(P-20392)*
Life Care Centers America Inc......C......626 289-5365
909 W Santa Anita Ave San Gabriel (91776) *(P-20393)*
Life Care Centers America Inc......C......626 289-8889
901 W Santa Anita Ave San Gabriel (91776) *(P-20394)*
Life Care Centers America Inc......C......949 380-9380
25652 Old Trabuco Rd Lake Forest (92630) *(P-20395)*
Life Care Centers America Inc......C......562 943-7156
11926 La Mirada Blvd La Mirada (90638) *(P-20396)*
Life Care Centers America Inc......C......562 867-1761
16910 Woodruff Ave Bellflower (90706) *(P-20397)*
Life Care Centers America Inc......C......562 921-6624
12350 Rosecrans Ave Norwalk (90650) *(P-20398)*
Life Care Centers America Inc......C......760 252-2515
27555 Rimrock Rd Barstow (92311) *(P-20399)*
Life Enchancing Therapies, Upland *Also called Inland Empire Therapy Provider (P-20216)*
Life Is Life LLC......F......310 584-7541
7888 Cherry Ave Ste C Fontana (92336) *(P-1779)*
Life Media Inc......E......800 201-9440
7657 Winnetka Ave Ste 504 Winnetka (91306) *(P-4080)*
Life Paint Company (PA)......E......**562 944-6391**
12927 Sunshine Ave Santa Fe Springs (90670) *(P-5101)*
Life Science Outsourcing Inc......D......714 672-1090
830 Challenger St Brea (92821) *(P-11007)*
Life Steps Foundation Inc......D......805 349-9810
2255 S Depot St Santa Maria (93455) *(P-21838)*
Life Steps Foundation Inc......D......805 474-8431
218 Carmen Ln Ste 108 Santa Maria (93458) *(P-21839)*
Life Steps Foundation Inc......D......562 436-0751
500 E 4th St Long Beach (90802) *(P-21840)*
Life Steps Foundation Inc......D......805 549-0150
1107 Johnson Ave San Luis Obispo (93401) *(P-21841)*
Life Tech Clnical Svcs Lab Inc (HQ)......E......**866 522-1585**
405 N Wilmington Ave Compton (90220) *(P-22848)*
Life Time Inc......C......949 492-1515
111 Avenida Vista Montana San Clemente (92672) *(P-19456)*
Life Time Fitness, San Clemente *Also called Life Time Inc (P-19456)*
Life Time Fitness Inc......C......949 238-2700
28221 Crown Valley Pkwy Laguna Niguel (92677) *(P-21450)*
Lifebloom Corporation......E......562 944-6800
925 W Lambert Rd Ste B Brea (92821) *(P-4847)*
Lifecare Assurance Company, Woodland Hills *Also called 21st Century Lf & Hlth Co Inc (P-15373)*
Lifecare Assurance Company......C......818 887-4436
21600 Oxnard St Fl 16 Woodland Hills (91367) *(P-15381)*
Lifegas, Burbank *Also called Linde Gas North America LLC (P-4641)*
Lifeline Ambulance, Montebello *Also called Eastwestproto Inc (P-11861)*
Lifeline Medical Transport, Ventura *Also called Ojai Ambulance Inc (P-11863)*
Lifemed of California......E......800 543-3633
13948 Mountain Ave Chino (91710) *(P-11008)*
Liferay Inc (PA)......C......**877 543-3729**
1400 Montefino Ave # 100 Diamond Bar (91765) *(P-18043)*
Lifesource Water Systems Inc (PA)......E......**626 792-9996**
523 S Fair Oaks Ave Pasadena (91105) *(P-8392)*
Lifestream, San Bernardino *Also called Blood Bnk San Brnrdino Rvrside (P-21391)*
Lifetech Resources LLC......D......805 944-1199
700 Science Dr Moorpark (93021) *(P-14256)*
Lifetime Entrmt Svcs LLC......B......310 556-7500
2049 Century Park E # 840 Los Angeles (90067) *(P-12733)*
Lifetime TV Network, Los Angeles *Also called Lifetime Entrmt Svcs LLC (P-12733)*
Lifeworks (us) Ltd......D......888 577-3784
27715 Jefferson Ave # 103 Temecula (92590) *(P-23262)*
Lifoam Industries LLC......D......323 587-1934
2340 E 52nd St Vernon (90058) *(P-5432)*
Lifoam Industries LLC......D......714 891-5035
15671 Industry Ln Huntington Beach (92649) *(P-3818)*
Lifoam Mfg, Vernon *Also called Lifoam Industries LLC (P-5432)*
Lift Aviation, Rancho Dominguez *Also called Fairway Import-Export Inc (P-11415)*
Lift By Encore, Huntington Beach *Also called Irish Interiors Inc (P-10356)*
Lift By Encore, Huntington Beach *Also called Encore Seats Inc (P-10322)*
Lifted Research Group, Irvine *Also called Hwmm (P-14337)*
Light Composite Corporation......E......949 858-8820
22322 Gilberto Rcho STA Marg (92688) *(P-6524)*
Light House, Torrance *Also called Takuyo Corporation (P-4034)*
Light House Group, The, Pacific Palisades *Also called Lighthouse Capital Funding (P-16274)*
Lightbox, Irvine *Also called Digital Map Products Inc (P-12783)*
Lightclub USA, Chatsworth *Also called Lightcraft Otdoor Environments (P-9065)*
Lightcraft Otdoor Environments......F......818 349-2663
9811 Owensmouth Ave Ste 1 Chatsworth (91311) *(P-9065)*

Lightcrest LLC......E......888 320-8495
1112 Montana Ave 705 Santa Monica (90403) ***(P-18044)***
Lightcross Inc......F......626 236-4500
2630 Corporate Pl Monterey Park (91754) ***(P-9741)***
Lightform, Carpinteria *Also called Forms and Surfaces Company LLC* ***(P-6034)***
Lighthouse Capital Funding......E......310 230-8335
15332 Antioch St Ste 540 Pacific Palisades (90272) ***(P-16274)***
Lighthouse Healthcare Ctr LLC......D......323 564-4461
2222 Santa Ana S Los Angeles (90059) ***(P-20400)***
Lighthouse Property MGT Inc (PA)......**D......210 340-7072**
15332 Antioch St 540 Pacific Palisades (90272) ***(P-23052)***
Lighthouse Trucking, Montebello *Also called Beacon Concrete Inc* ***(P-6073)***
Lighting Resources LLC......D......909 923-7252
805 E Francis St Ontario (91761) ***(P-12955)***
Lighting Technologies Intl LLC......C......626 480-0755
13700 Live Oak Ave Baldwin Park (91706) ***(P-13640)***
Lightning Dversion Systems LLC......F......714 841-1080
16572 Burke Ln Huntington Beach (92647) ***(P-9040)***
Lightningfasttrafficschool.com, San Bernardino *Also called Web Educational Services Inc* ***(P-18007)***
Lights of America Inc......A......909 444-2000
749 S Lemon Ave Walnut (91789) ***(P-9066)***
Lights of America Inc (PA)......**B......909 594-7883**
13602 12th St Ste B Chino (91710) ***(P-9067)***
Lightspeed Software Inc......E......661 716-7600
1800 19th St Bakersfield (93301) ***(P-17905)***
Lightthipe Substation, Long Beach *Also called Southern California Edison Co* ***(P-12849)***
Lightway Industries......E......661 257-0286
28435 Industry Dr Valencia (91355) ***(P-9095)***
Likom Caseworks USA Inc (HQ)......**E......210 587-7824**
17800 Castleton St # 220 City of Industry (91748) ***(P-8227)***
Lil O Blossom Inc......F......949 675-3885
2025 W Balboa Blvd Ste A Newport Beach (92663) ***(P-3905)***
Lily Bleu Inc......E......310 225-2522
1406 W 178th St Gardena (90248) ***(P-14393)***
Lima Trading LLC......E......323 588-7434
3251 E Slauson Ave Vernon (90058) ***(P-13140)***
Limbach Company LP......C......714 653-7000
1709 Apollo Ct Seal Beach (90740) ***(P-1094)***
Liminex Inc......C......888 310-0410
2030 E Maple Ave El Segundo (90245) ***(P-17653)***
Limnexus LLP (PA)......**D......213 955-9500**
707 Wilshire Blvd # 4600 Los Angeles (90017) ***(P-21614)***
Limoneira Company (PA)......**B......805 525-5541**
1141 Cummings Rd Ofc Santa Paula (93060) ***(P-180)***
Limpus Prints Inc......F......714 545-5078
1820 S Santa Fe St Santa Ana (92705) ***(P-4538)***
Lin Consulting LLC......E......714 650-8595
15086 Beach Blvd Midway City (92655) ***(P-10543)***
Lina Gale (usa) Inc......D......909 595-8898
22067 Ferrero Walnut (91789) ***(P-14257)***
Linabond Inc......E......805 484-7373
1161 Avenida Acaso Camarillo (93012) ***(P-7382)***
Linc Western Air LP......D......949 330-1535
152 Technology Dr Irvine (92618) ***(P-1095)***
Lincare Inc......D......870 972-8839
17777 Center Court Dr N # 55 Cerritos (90703) ***(P-21184)***
Lincare Inc......D......661 833-3333
4300 Stine Rd Ste 603 Bakersfield (93313) ***(P-21185)***
Lincoln Composite Mtls Inc......F......714 898-8350
15422 Electronic Ln Huntington Beach (92649) ***(P-4700)***
Lincoln Iron Works......E......310 684-2543
507 7th St Santa Monica (90402) ***(P-6204)***
Lincoln Plaza Hotel Inc......D......626 571-8818
123 S Lincoln Ave Monterey Park (91755) ***(P-16542)***
Lincoln Trning Ctr Rhblttion W......D......626 442-0621
2643 Loma Ave South El Monte (91733) ***(P-21959)***
Linda Loma Univ Hlth Care (HQ)......**A......909 558-2806**
11370 Anderson St # 3900 Loma Linda (92354) ***(P-20833)***
Linda Loma Univ Hlth Care (PA)......**A......909 558-4729**
11175 Campus St Loma Linda (92350) ***(P-19961)***
Linda Valley Care Center, Loma Linda *Also called Chancellor Hlth Care Cal I Inc* ***(P-20570)***
Linda Yorba Water District (PA)......**D......714 701-3000**
1717 E Miraloma Ave Placentia (92870) ***(P-12900)***
Lindbergh Child Care Center, Lynwood *Also called Lynwood Unified School Dst* ***(P-22032)***
Lindblade Metal Works, La Mirada *Also called Lindblade Metalworks Inc* ***(P-6629)***
Lindblade Metalworks Inc......E......714 670-7172
14355 Macaw St La Mirada (90638) ***(P-6629)***
Linde Gas & Equipment Inc......E......310 816-9397
2006 E 223rd St Bldg 1 Long Beach (90810) ***(P-4640)***
Linde Gas North America LLC......F......626 855-8344
614 S Glenwood Pl Burbank (91506) ***(P-4641)***
Linder Equipment Co......E......559 685-5000
311 E Kern Ave Tulare (93274) ***(P-19048)***
Lindsay Windows California LLC......F......760 247-1082
13510 Central Rd Apple Valley (92308) ***(P-6707)***
Lindsey & Sons......D......657 306-5369
1226 E 76th St Los Angeles (90001) ***(P-18578)***
Lindsey Doors Inc......E......760 775-1959
81101 Indio Blvd Ste D16 Indio (92201) ***(P-5452)***
Lindsey Manufacturing Co......C......626 969-3471
760 N Georgia Ave Azusa (91702) ***(P-7103)***
Lindsey Mfg, Indio *Also called Lindsey Doors Inc* ***(P-5452)***
Lindsey Systems, Azusa *Also called Lindsey Manufacturing Co* ***(P-7103)***
Line Hotel, The, Los Angeles *Also called Sydell Hotels LLC* ***(P-16748)***
Line One Laboratories Inc USA (PA)......**C......818 886-2288**
9600 Lurline Ave Chatsworth (91311) ***(P-5389)***
Line Publications Inc......F......310 234-9501
9800 S La Cienega Blvd # 10 Inglewood (90301) ***(P-4081)***
Linea Pelle Inc (PA)......**F......310 231-9950**
7107 Valjean Ave Van Nuys (91406) ***(P-5871)***
Linea Solutions Inc......D......310 443-4191
10940 Wilshire Blvd Los Angeles (90024) ***(P-23263)***
Lineage Logistics Holdings LLC......C......951 369-0230
2344 Fleetwood Dr Riverside (92509) ***(P-12578)***
Lineage Logistics Holdings LLC......C......909 874-1200
2551 S Lilac Ave Bloomington (92316) ***(P-12114)***
Linear Industries Ltd (PA)......**D......626 303-1130**
1850 Enterprise Way Monrovia (91016) ***(P-13995)***
Linen Salvage Et Cie LLC......E......323 904-3100
1073 Stearns Dr Los Angeles (90035) ***(P-2674)***
Liner Law, Los Angeles *Also called Liner LLP* ***(P-21615)***
Liner LLP......C......310 500-3500
1100 Glendon Ave 14th Los Angeles (90024) ***(P-21615)***
Liner Technologies Inc......E......909 594-6610
4821 Chino Ave Chino (91710) ***(P-5698)***
Linfinity Microelectronics, Garden Grove *Also called Microsemi Corp - Anlog Mxed Sg* ***(P-9542)***
Ling's, South El Monte *Also called Out of Shell LLC* ***(P-2503)***
Link Logistics Solutions Inc......D......800 932-3383
220 W Victoria St Compton (90220) ***(P-12479)***
Links Medical Products Inc (PA)......**E......949 753-0001**
9249 Research Dr Irvine (92618) ***(P-11009)***
Links Sign Lngage Intrprting S, Long Beach *Also called Goodwill Srving The Pple Sther* ***(P-18532)***
Linksys LLC......C......408 526-4000
120 Theory Irvine (92617) ***(P-13742)***
Linksys LLC......C......310 751-5100
12045 Waterfront Dr Playa Vista (90094) ***(P-13743)***
Linksys LLC (HQ)......**B......949 270-8500**
121 Theory Irvine (92617) ***(P-13744)***
Linksys Usa Inc......D......310 751-5100
12045 Waterfront Dr Playa Vista (90094) ***(P-13745)***
Linn's Main Bin, Cambria *Also called Linns Fruit Bin Inc* ***(P-2078)***
Linnco LLC......C......661 616-3900
5201 Truxtun Ave Bakersfield (93309) ***(P-455)***
Linns Fruit Bin Inc (PA)......**E......805 927-1499**
2535 Village Ln Ste A Cambria (93428) ***(P-2078)***
Linpac USA Holdings Inc......D......714 845-2845
10540 Talbert Ave Fountain Valley (92708) ***(P-5699)***
Linquest Corporation (PA)......**C......323 924-1600**
5140 W Goldleaf Cir # 40 Los Angeles (90056) ***(P-22601)***
Linwood Grdns Convalescent Ctr, Visalia *Also called Far West Inc* ***(P-20341)***
Linzer Products, San Fernando *Also called Ahi Investment Inc* ***(P-14908)***
Lion Tank Line Inc......E......323 726-1966
5801 Randolph St Commerce (90040) ***(P-5252)***
Lions Gate Entertainment Inc (HQ)......**D......310 449-9200**
2700 Colorado Ave Ste 200 Santa Monica (90404) ***(P-19143)***
Lions Gate Films Inc......C......310 449-9200
2700 Colorado Ave Santa Monica (90404) ***(P-19144)***
Lionsgate Productions Inc......A......310 255-3937
2700 Colorado Ave Ste 200 Santa Monica (90404) ***(P-19260)***
Lip Ink International......F......310 414-9246
225 Arena St El Segundo (90245) ***(P-14258)***
Lippert Components Mfg Inc......E......909 628-5557
1021 Walnut Ave Pomona (91766) ***(P-5962)***
Liquid Advertising Inc......D......310 450-2653
138 Eucalyptus Dr El Segundo (90245) ***(P-17029)***
Liquid Graphics Inc......C......949 486-3588
2701 S Harbor Blvd Unit A Santa Ana (92704) ***(P-2820)***
Liquid Packaging, Paramount *Also called Vast Enterprises* ***(P-5299)***
Liquid Technologies Inc......E......909 393-9475
14425 Yorba Ave Chino (91710) ***(P-5044)***
Liquidate Direct LLC......E......800 750-7617
2929 Washington Blvd Fl 2 Marina Del Rey (90292) ***(P-18045)***
Lisi Aerospace, City of Industry *Also called Monadnock Company* ***(P-6528)***
Lisi Aerospace......E......310 326-8110
2600 Skypark Dr Torrance (90505) ***(P-11010)***
Lisi Aerospace North Amer Inc......A......310 326-8110
2600 Skypark Dr Torrance (90505) ***(P-6268)***
Lite Extrusions Mfg Inc......E......323 770-4298
15025 S Main St Gardena (90248) ***(P-5453)***
Litepanels Inc......E......818 752-7009
20600 Plummer St Chatsworth (91311) ***(P-9022)***
Lith-O-Roll Corporation......E......626 579-0340
9521 Telstar Ave El Monte (91731) ***(P-7920)***
Lithia, Temecula *Also called DCH Acura of Temecula* ***(P-18896)***
Lithographix Inc (PA)......**B......323 770-1000**
12250 Crenshaw Blvd Hawthorne (90250) ***(P-4360)***
Lithotech International LLC......F......626 443-4210
9950 Baldwin Pl El Monte (91731) ***(P-4539)***
Litigtion Rsrces of America-CA (PA)......**D......818 878-9227**
4232-1 Las Virgenes Rd Calabasas (91302) ***(P-18579)***
Lito Childrens Wear Inc......F......323 260-4692
3730 Union Pacific Ave Los Angeles (90023) ***(P-2745)***
Liton Lighting, Los Angeles *Also called Eema Industries Inc* ***(P-9127)***
Little Brothers Bakery LLC......D......310 225-3790
320 W Alondra Blvd Gardena (90248) ***(P-2016)***
Little Castle Furniture Co Inc......E......805 278-4646
301 Todd Ct Oxnard (93030) ***(P-3507)***
Little Company Mary Hospital......A......310 540-7676
4101 Torrance Blvd Torrance (90503) ***(P-20834)***
Little Einsteins LLC......D......818 560-1000
500 S Buena Vista St Burbank (91521) ***(P-4133)***
Little Firefighter Corporation......F......714 834-0410
204 S Center St Santa Ana (92703) ***(P-7449)***
Little Folk Visuals, Palm Desert *Also called Lf Visuals Inc* ***(P-2729)***

ALPHABETIC

Little People Pre-School ....D....909 989-2804
9974 19th St Rancho Cucamonga (91737) ***(P-22028)***
Little Peoples ....D....951 849-1959
39514 Brookside Ave Cherry Valley (92223) ***(P-22125)***
Little Scholars Montessori ....E....818 343-1794
18706 Hatteras St Tarzana (91356) ***(P-22029)***
Little Ssters of The Poor Los ....D....310 548-0625
2100 S Western Ave San Pedro (90732) ***(P-20401)***
Littlejohn-Reuland Corporation ....E....323 587-5255
4575 Pacific Blvd Vernon (90058) ***(P-1276)***
Live Nation Concerts Inc ....E....310 867-7132
9348 Civic Center Dr Lbby Beverly Hills (90210) ***(P-19362)***
Live Nation Entertainment Inc (PA) ....**C....310 867-7000**
9348 Civic Center Dr Lbby Beverly Hills (90210) ***(P-18580)***
Live Nation Mtours (usa) Inc (HQ) ....**D....310 867-7000**
9348 Civic Center Dr Beverly Hills (90210) ***(P-19322)***
Live Nation Worldwide Inc ....A....310 867-7000
9348 Civic Center Dr Lbby Beverly Hills (90210) ***(P-19363)***
Live Oak Rehab, San Gabriel *Also called Longwood Management Corp* ***(P-20606)***
Liveoffice LLC ....D....877 253-2793
900 Corporate Pointe Culver City (90230) ***(P-17906)***
Liveuniverse Inc ....D....310 492-2200
9255 W Sunset Blvd # 1010 West Hollywood (90069) ***(P-17088)***
Livhome Inc (PA) ....**A....800 807-5854**
5670 Wilshire Blvd # 500 Los Angeles (90036) ***(P-21186)***
Living Colors Inc ....D....818 893-5068
16026 Rayen St North Hills (91343) ***(P-1188)***
Living Desert ....C....760 346-5694
47900 Portola Ave Palm Desert (92260) ***(P-22238)***
Living Spaces Furniture LLC (PA) ....**C....714 523-2000**
14501 Artesia Blvd La Mirada (90638) ***(P-13141)***
Living Way Industries Inc ....F....661 298-3200
20734 Centre Pointe Pkwy Santa Clarita (91350) ***(P-4361)***
Livingston Mem Vna Hlth Corp ....B....805 642-0239
1996 Eastman Ave Ste 101 Ventura (93003) ***(P-23053)***
Livingston Mem Vsting Nrse Ass, Ventura *Also called Livingston Mem Vna Hlth Corp* ***(P-23053)***
Ljg, Irvine *Also called La Jolla Group Inc* ***(P-18569)***
Ljr Blanchard Grinding, Gardena *Also called L J R Grinding Corp* ***(P-8658)***
Llamas Plastics Inc ....C....818 362-0371
12970 Bradley Ave Sylmar (91342) ***(P-10368)***
LLC Marsh Perkins ....F....760 880-4558
80080 Via Pessaro La Quinta (92253) ***(P-3077)***
LLC Woodward West ....C....661 822-7900
28400 Stallion Springs Dr Tehachapi (93561) ***(P-16824)***
Llc, Hula Media Services, Burbank *Also called Hula Post Productions Inc* ***(P-19132)***
Lloyd Design Corporation ....D....818 768-6001
19731 Nordhoff St Northridge (91324) ***(P-10092)***
Lloyd Mats, Northridge *Also called Lloyd Design Corporation* ***(P-10092)***
Lloyd Staffing Inc ....B....631 777-7600
18000 Studebaker Rd # 700 Cerritos (90703) ***(P-17497)***
LLP Moss Adams ....D....818 577-1822
21700 Oxnard St Ste 300 Woodland Hills (91367) ***(P-22802)***
LLP Moss Adams ....C....310 477-0450
10960 Wilshire Blvd # 1100 Los Angeles (90024) ***(P-22803)***
LLP Moss Adams ....D....949 221-4000
2040 Main St Ste 900 Irvine (92614) ***(P-22804)***
LLUMC, Loma Linda *Also called Loma Linda University Med Ctr* ***(P-20837)***
Lmb Heeger, South El Monte *Also called Heeger Inc* ***(P-8915)***
Lmb Mortgage Services Inc (HQ) ....**C....310 348-6800**
4859 W Slauson Ave # 405 Los Angeles (90056) ***(P-15209)***
Lmb Opco LLC ....B....310 348-6800
12181 Bluff Creek Dr Playa Vista (90094) ***(P-15245)***
LMC Enterprises (PA) ....**D....562 602-2116**
6401 Alondra Blvd Paramount (90723) ***(P-4968)***
LMC Enterprises ....E....310 632-7124
19402 S Susana Rd Compton (90221) ***(P-4969)***
LMC Hollywood Highland ....B....949 448-1600
95 Enterprise Ste 200 Aliso Viejo (92656) ***(P-784)***
LMD Intgrted Lgistics Svcs Inc (PA) ....**D....310 605-5100**
3136 E Victoria St Compton (90221) ***(P-12219)***
Lmno Cable Group, Encino *Also called Lmno Productions Inc* ***(P-19145)***
Lmno Productions Inc ....D....818 995-5555
15821 Ventura Blvd # 320 Encino (91436) ***(P-19145)***
LMS Corporation ....E....310 641-4222
300 Crprate Pinte Ste 301 Culver City (90230) ***(P-18581)***
LMS Reinforcing Steel Group, Corona *Also called LMS Reinforcing Steel Usa LP* ***(P-7024)***
LMS Reinforcing Steel Usa LP (PA) ....**E....604 598-9930**
26365 Earthmover Cir Corona (92883) ***(P-7024)***
Lmw Enterprises LLC ....F....562 944-1969
10558 Norwalk Blvd Santa Fe Springs (90670) ***(P-8344)***
Lni Custom Manufacturing Inc ....E....310 978-2000
15542 Broadway Center St Gardena (90248) ***(P-6973)***
Lo Bue Bros Inc ....C....559 562-6367
713 E Hermosa St Lindsay (93247) ***(P-181)***
Lo Bue Bros East, Lindsay *Also called Lo Bue Bros Inc* ***(P-181)***
Loaded Boards Inc ....F....310 839-1800
10575 Virginia Ave Culver City (90232) ***(P-10497)***
Loan Administration Netwrk Inc ....D....949 752-5246
2082 Bus Ctr Dr Ste 250 Irvine (92612) ***(P-17437)***
Loandepot Inc (PA) ....**A....888 337-6888**
26642 Towne Centre Dr Foothill Ranch (92610) ***(P-15210)***
Loandepotcom LLC ....A....661 202-1700
42455 10th St W Ste 109 Lancaster (93534) ***(P-15211)***
Loandepotcom LLC ....A....760 797-6000
901 N Palm Canyon Dr # 107 Palm Springs (92262) ***(P-15212)***
Loandepotcom LLC (HQ) ....**A....888 337-6888**
26642 Towne Centre Dr Foothill Ranch (92610) ***(P-15213)***

Lobby Traffic Systems Inc ....F....800 486-8606
8583 Irvine Center Dr # 10 Irvine (92618) ***(P-10896)***
Lobel Financial Corporation (PA) ....**D....714 995-3333**
1150 N Magnolia Ave Anaheim (92801) ***(P-15145)***
Lobue Laser & Eye Medical Ctrs (PA) ....**D....951 696-1135**
40700 California Oaks Rd Murrieta (92562) ***(P-19962)***
Local 12, Redlands *Also called Interntional Un Oper Engineers* ***(P-22292)***
Local Corporation (PA) ....**D....949 784-0800**
7555 Irvine Center Dr Irvine (92618) ***(P-17030)***
Local Hero Bookstore and Cafe, Ojai *Also called Dmz Studio Inc* ***(P-4127)***
Local Inttive Hlth Auth For Lo (PA) ....**A....213 694-1250**
1055 W 7th St Fl 10 Los Angeles (90017) ***(P-15443)***
Local Neon Co Inc ....E....310 978-2000
12536 Chadron Ave Hawthorne (90250) ***(P-11567)***
Local.com, Irvine *Also called Local Corporation* ***(P-17030)***
Locale Lifestyle Magazine LLC ....E....949 436-8910
2755 Bristol St Ste 295 Costa Mesa (92626) ***(P-4082)***
Locale Magazine, Costa Mesa *Also called Locale Lifestyle Magazine LLC* ***(P-4082)***
Lochaber Cornwall Inc ....F....714 935-0302
675 N Eckhoff St Ste D Orange (92868) ***(P-8095)***
Lock America Inc ....F....951 277-5180
9168 Stellar Ct Corona (92883) ***(P-6525)***
Lock-Ridge Tool Company Inc ....D....909 865-8309
2000 Pomona Blvd Pomona (91768) ***(P-7161)***
Lockheed Martin Aeronautics Co, Palmdale *Also called Lockheed Martin Corporation* ***(P-10598)***
Lockheed Martin Corporation ....C....760 386-2572
South Loop Bldg 821 Fort Irwin (92310) ***(P-12220)***
Lockheed Martin Corporation ....A....661 572-7428
1011 Lockheed Way Palmdale (93599) ***(P-10598)***
Lockheed Martin Unmanned ....D....805 503-4340
125 Venture Dr Ste 110 San Luis Obispo (93401) ***(P-18046)***
Lockton Companies LLC- Pacifi (HQ) ....**B....213 689-0500**
777 S Figueroa St # 5200 Los Angeles (90017) ***(P-15589)***
Lockton Insurance Brokers, Los Angeles *Also called Lockton Companies LLC-Pacifi* ***(P-15589)***
Lockwood Industries LLC (PA) ....**C....661 702-6999**
28525 Industry Dr Valencia (91355) ***(P-9532)***
Lodestone LLC ....F....714 970-0900
4769 E Wesley Dr Anaheim (92807) ***(P-7891)***
Lodestone Pacific, Anaheim *Also called R H Barden Inc* ***(P-9640)***
Loeb & Loeb LLP (PA) ....**C....310 282-2000**
10100 Santa Monica Blvd # 2200 Los Angeles (90067) ***(P-21616)***
Loews Hollywood Hotel LLC ....B....323 450-2235
1755 N Highland Ave Hollywood (90028) ***(P-16543)***
Loews Santa Monica Beach Hotel, Santa Monica *Also called Dtrs Santa Monica LLC* ***(P-16421)***
Logans Candies ....F....909 984-5410
125 W B St Ontario (91762) ***(P-2093)***
Logi Graphics Incorporated ....F....714 841-3686
17592 Metzler Ln Huntington Beach (92647) ***(P-9423)***
Logic Mate Inc ....F....213 623-4422
412 W Broadway Fl 3 Glendale (91204) ***(P-17654)***
Logicmonitor Inc (PA) ....**A....805 394-8632**
820 State St Fl 5 Santa Barbara (93101) ***(P-18128)***
Logicube Inc (PA) ....**E....888 494-8832**
19755 Nordhoff Pl Chatsworth (91311) ***(P-8275)***
Login Consulting Services Inc ....D....310 607-9091
300 Continental Blvd # 405 El Segundo (90245) ***(P-18199)***
Logistar LLC ....D....323 274-9651
3030 S Atl Blvd Unit B Vernon (90058) ***(P-13142)***
Logistical Support LLC ....C....818 341-3344
20409 Prairie St Chatsworth (91311) ***(P-10220)***
Logistical Support LLC ....C....818 341-3344
20409 Prairie St Chatsworth (91311) ***(P-14062)***
Logistics, Bell *Also called De Well Container Shipping Inc* ***(P-12443)***
Logitech Inc ....C....510 795-8500
3 Jenner Ste 180 Irvine (92618) ***(P-8276)***
Logix Federal Credit Union (PA) ....**C....888 718-5328**
2340 N Hollywood Way Burbank (91505) ***(P-15072)***
Logo Expressions, Ontario *Also called Dennis Foland Inc* ***(P-14152)***
Logomark Inc ....C....714 675-6100
1201 Bell Ave Tustin (92780) ***(P-14948)***
Logomart Corporation ....F....714 458-3181
600 W 15th St Long Beach (90813) ***(P-4540)***
Lois Lauer Realty (PA) ....**C....909 748-7000**
1998 Orange Tree Ln Redlands (92374) ***(P-15912)***
Lola Belle Brands LLC ....F....855 226-3526
631 S Palm Ave Alhambra (91803) ***(P-11709)***
Lollicup Tea Zone, Chino *Also called Lollicup USA Inc* ***(P-3842)***
Lollicup USA Inc (HQ) ....**B....626 965-8882**
6185 Kimball Ave Chino (91708) ***(P-3842)***
Loma Linda Catering Center, Loma Linda *Also called Loma Linda University Med Ctr* ***(P-20838)***
Loma Linda Community Hospital, Loma Linda *Also called Loma Linda University Med Ctr* ***(P-20842)***
Loma Linda Healthcare Sys 605, Loma Linda *Also called Veterans Health Administration* ***(P-20149)***
Loma Linda Hospice, San Bernardino *Also called Loma Linda University Med Ctr* ***(P-20402)***
Loma Linda Pharmacy, Loma Linda *Also called Loma Linda University Med Ctr* ***(P-20841)***
Loma Linda University Med Ctr ....D....909 558-4000
26780 Barton Rd Redlands (92373) ***(P-20835)***
Loma Linda University Med Ctr ....D....909 558-2100
11370 Anderson St 2100 Loma Linda (92354) ***(P-20836)***
Loma Linda University Med Ctr (HQ) ....**A....909 558-4000**
11234 Anderson St Loma Linda (92354) ***(P-20837)***

Loma Linda University Med Ctr......D......909 558-8244
11175 Campus St Loma Linda (92350) ***(P-20838)***
Loma Linda University Med Ctr......D......909 558-9275
1710 Barton Rd Redlands (92373) ***(P-20839)***
Loma Linda University Med Ctr......D......909 824-6904
268 W Hospitality Ln # 300 San Bernardino (92408) ***(P-20402)***
Loma Linda University Med Ctr......D......909 558-4385
11370 Anderson St Loma Linda (92354) ***(P-20840)***
Loma Linda University Med Ctr......D......909 558-4216
11223 Campus St Loma Linda (92354) ***(P-20841)***
Loma Linda University Med Ctr......D......909 796-0167
25333 Barton Rd Loma Linda (92350) ***(P-20842)***
Loma Lnda Univ Fmly Med Group......D......909 558-6600
25455 Barton Rd Ste 204b Loma Linda (92354) ***(P-19963)***
Loma Scientific International......F......310 539-8655
3115 Kashiwa St Torrance (90505) ***(P-9287)***
Lombard Enterprises Inc......E......562 692-7070
3619 San Gbriel Rver Pkwy Pico Rivera (90660) ***(P-4362)***
Lombard Graphics, Pico Rivera *Also called Lombard Enterprises Inc* ***(P-4362)***
Lombardy Holdings Inc (PA)......C......951 808-4550
151 Kalmus Dr Ste F6 Costa Mesa (92626) ***(P-961)***
Lomita Care Center, Lomita *Also called Lomita Verde Inc* ***(P-20600)***
Lomita Medical Offices, Lomita *Also called Kaiser Foundation Hospitals* ***(P-19906)***
Lomita Verde Inc......D......310 325-1970
1955 Lomita Blvd Lomita (90717) ***(P-20600)***
Lompoc Convlsnt Care Ctr, Lompoc *Also called Lompoc Valley Medical Center* ***(P-20845)***
Lompoc Family YMCA, Lompoc *Also called Channel Islnds Yung MNS Chrstn* ***(P-22326)***
LOMPOC SKILLED CARE CENTER, Lompoc *Also called Lompoc Valley Medical Center* ***(P-20844)***
Lompoc Sklled Nrsing Rhbltion, Lompoc *Also called Ghc of Lompoc LLC* ***(P-21306)***
Lompoc Valley Medical Center......C......805 735-9229
1111 E Ocean Ave Ste 2 Lompoc (93436) ***(P-20843)***
Lompoc Valley Medical Center (PA)......B......805 737-3300
1515 E Ocean Ave Lompoc (93436) ***(P-20844)***
Lompoc Valley Medical Center......C......805 736-3466
216 N 3rd St Lompoc (93436) ***(P-20845)***
Lompoc-Vandenberg Afb, Lompoc *Also called Serco Services Inc* ***(P-17710)***
Lonestar Sierra LLC......C......866 575-5680
1820 W Orangewood Ave Orange (92868) ***(P-13996)***
Long Bch - Lkwood Orthpd Med G......D......562 633-3787
5750 Downey Ave Ste 308 Lakewood (90712) ***(P-19964)***
Long Bch Hose Coupling Co Inc......F......562 901-2970
1265 W 16th St Long Beach (90813) ***(P-13997)***
Long Bch Museum Art Foundation......D......562 439-2119
2300 E Ocean Blvd Long Beach (90803) ***(P-22224)***
Long Bch Rscue Mssion Fndation......D......562 423-2500
1430 Pacific Ave Long Beach (90813) ***(P-21842)***
Long Beach Airport, Long Beach *Also called City of Long Beach* ***(P-12347)***
Long Beach Cap, Long Beach *Also called Long Beach Cmnty Action Partnr* ***(P-22196)***
Long Beach Care Center Inc......C......562 426-6141
2615 Grand Ave Long Beach (90815) ***(P-20403)***
Long Beach City of, Long Beach *Also called Stearns Park* ***(P-3632)***
Long Beach Cmnty Action Partnr......D......562 216-4600
117 W Victoria St Long Beach (90805) ***(P-22196)***
Long Beach Convention Center, Long Beach *Also called Smg Holdings LLC* ***(P-15698)***
Long Beach Day Nursery......D......562 421-1488
3965 N Bellflower Blvd Long Beach (90808) ***(P-22030)***
Long Beach Golden Sails Inc......D......562 596-1631
23545 Crenshaw Blvd # 100 Torrance (90505) ***(P-16544)***
Long Beach Hilton, The, Long Beach *Also called World Trade Ctr Ht Assoc Ltd* ***(P-16804)***
Long Beach Marriott, Long Beach *Also called Ruffin Hotel Corp of Cal* ***(P-16677)***
Long Beach Medical Center......B......562 933-7701
450 E Spring St Ste 11 Long Beach (90806) ***(P-20846)***
Long Beach Medical Center (HQ)......A......562 933-2000
2801 Atlantic Ave Fl 2 Long Beach (90806) ***(P-20847)***
Long Beach Medical Center......B......562 933-0085
1720 Termino Ave Long Beach (90804) ***(P-20848)***
Long Beach Memorial Med Ctr......B......562 933-0432
1057 Pine Ave Long Beach (90813) ***(P-20849)***
Long Beach Pain Center, Long Beach *Also called Healthsmart Pacific Inc* ***(P-20783)***
Long Beach Public Trnsp Co (PA)......A......562 599-8571
1963 E Anaheim St Long Beach (90813) ***(P-11815)***
Long Beach Seafoods Co......E......562 432-7300
4643 Hackett Ave Lakewood (90713) ***(P-2346)***
Long Beach Transit, Long Beach *Also called Long Beach Public Trnsp Co* ***(P-11815)***
Long Beach Unified School Dst......D......562 426-6176
2700 Pine Ave Long Beach (90806) ***(P-11935)***
Long Beach Unified School Dst......C......562 426-5571
3038 Delta Ave Long Beach (90810) ***(P-15913)***
Long Beach Woodworks LLC......F......562 437-2293
1261 Highland Ave Glendale (91202) ***(P-3397)***
Long Beach Yacht Club......D......562 598-9401
6201 E Appian Way Long Beach (90803) ***(P-19580)***
Long Machine Inc......E......951 296-0194
27450 Colt Ct Temecula (92590) ***(P-8664)***
Long Pine Leathers, Vernon *Also called Jejomi Designs Inc* ***(P-3058)***
Long Point Development LLC......A......310 265-2800
100 Terranea Way Rancho Palos Verdes (90275) ***(P-16545)***
Long-Lok LLC......E......424 209-8726
20531 Belshaw Ave Carson (90746) ***(P-10369)***
Long-Lok Fasteners Corporation......E......310 667-4200
20501 Belshaw Ave Carson (90746) ***(P-13998)***
Longbar Grinding Inc......F......562 921-1983
13121 Arctic Cir Santa Fe Springs (90670) ***(P-8665)***
Longo Lexus, El Monte *Also called El Monte Automotive Group Inc* ***(P-18788)***
Longo Scion, El Monte *Also called D Longo Inc* ***(P-18821)***
Longs Drug Stores Cal Inc......D......805 530-0283
155 W Los Angeles Ave Moorpark (93021) ***(P-18410)***
Longs Drug Stores Cal Inc......E......805 499-4006
451 S Reino Rd Newbury Park (91320) ***(P-18411)***
Longs Drug Stores Cal Inc......D......909 886-4984
1540 E Highland Ave San Bernardino (92404) ***(P-18412)***
Longs Drug Stores Cal Inc......D......805 588-0290
4400 Coffee Rd Bakersfield (93308) ***(P-18413)***
Longs Drug Stores Cal Inc......D......661 254-3766
25880 Mcbean Pkwy Santa Clarita (91355) ***(P-18414)***
Longs Drug Stores Cal Inc......E......805 581-1504
3935 Cochran St Simi Valley (93063) ***(P-18415)***
Longs Drug Stores Cal LLC......C......805 493-1502
1822 E Avnida De Los Arbl Thousand Oaks (91362) ***(P-18416)***
Longs Drug Stores Cal LLC......C......310 377-6728
901 Silver Spur Rd Rllng HLS Est (90274) ***(P-18417)***
Longs Drug Stores Cal LLC......C......760 327-1374
1785 E Palm Canyon Dr Palm Springs (92264) ***(P-18418)***
Longs Drug Stores Cal LLC......C......909 884-5364
404 E Base Line St San Bernardino (92410) ***(P-18419)***
Longstar Healthpro Inc......F......909 468-9215
4010 Valley Blvd Ste 101 Walnut (91789) ***(P-14705)***
Longwood Management, San Dimas *Also called San Dimas Retirement Center* ***(P-15748)***
Longwood Management Corp......C......310 679-1461
11834 Inglewood Ave Hawthorne (90250) ***(P-20404)***
Longwood Management Corp......D......323 735-5146
2000 W Washington Blvd Los Angeles (90018) ***(P-20601)***
Longwood Management Corp......C......562 693-5240
7716 Pickering Ave Whittier (90602) ***(P-20850)***
Longwood Management Corp......D......818 246-7174
605 W Broadway Glendale (91204) ***(P-20602)***
Longwood Management Corp......C......818 881-7414
7836 Reseda Blvd Reseda (91335) ***(P-20851)***
Longwood Management Corp......C......818 360-1864
17922 San Frnando Msn Granada Hills (91344) ***(P-20405)***
Longwood Management Corp......C......626 280-2293
8101 Hill Dr Rosemead (91770) ***(P-20406)***
Longwood Management Corp......C......626 280-4820
8035 Hill Dr Rosemead (91770) ***(P-20407)***
Longwood Management Corp......D......323 737-7778
2190 W Adams Blvd Los Angeles (90018) ***(P-20603)***
Longwood Management Corp......D......213 382-8461
1240 S Hoover St Los Angeles (90006) ***(P-20604)***
Longwood Management Corp......D......818 980-8200
11429 Ventura Blvd Studio City (91604) ***(P-20605)***
Longwood Management Corp......C......323 933-1560
1900 S Longwood Ave Los Angeles (90016) ***(P-20408)***
Longwood Management Corp......D......626 289-3763
537 W Live Oak St San Gabriel (91776) ***(P-20606)***
Longwood Management Corp......D......562 432-5751
1913 E 5th St Long Beach (90802) ***(P-20607)***
Lonix Pharmaceutical Inc......F......626 287-4700
5001 Earle Ave Rosemead (91770) ***(P-1799)***
Loomworks Apparel, Irvine *Also called Delta Galil USA Inc* ***(P-14370)***
Looney Bins Inc (HQ)......D......818 485-8200
12153 Montague St Pacoima (91331) ***(P-12956)***
Lopez & Associates Engineers, El Monte *Also called R and L Lopez Associates Inc* ***(P-22642)***
Lopez Pallets Inc......F......909 823-0865
11080 Redwood Ave Fontana (92337) ***(P-3398)***
Loran Inc......E......405 340-0660
1705 E Colton Ave Redlands (92374) ***(P-8877)***
Lorber Industries California......E......310 275-1568
823 N Roxbury Dr Beverly Hills (90210) ***(P-2659)***
Lorber Industries of Claif, Beverly Hills *Also called Lorber Industries California* ***(P-2659)***
Loren Electric Sign & Lighting, Whittier *Also called Loren Industries* ***(P-11568)***
Loren Industries......E......562 699-1122
12226 Coast Dr Whittier (90601) ***(P-11568)***
Lorenz Inc......E......760 427-1815
1749 Stergios Rd Calexico (92231) ***(P-9889)***
Loritz & Associates Inc......E......714 694-0200
24895 La Palma Ave Yorba Linda (92887) ***(P-5700)***
Lorser Industries Inc......E......619 917-4298
9636 Arby Dr Beverly Hills (90210) ***(P-9424)***
Lortz & Son Mfg Co......C......281 241-9418
4042 Patton Way Bakersfield (93308) ***(P-7277)***
Lortz Manufacturing, Bakersfield *Also called Lortz & Son Mfg Co* ***(P-7277)***
Los Adobes De Maria, Santa Maria *Also called Peoples Self-Help Housing Corp* ***(P-23494)***
Los Alamitos Medical Ctr Inc (HQ)......A......714 826-6400
3751 Katella Ave Los Alamitos (90720) ***(P-20852)***
Los Alamitos Race Course......C......714 820-2800
4961 Katella Ave Cypress (90720) ***(P-19430)***
Los Altos Food Products LLC......C......626 330-6555
450 Baldwin Park Blvd City of Industry (91746) ***(P-14543)***
Los Angeles Angels of Anaheim, Anaheim *Also called Angels Baseball LP* ***(P-19407)***
Los Angeles Apparel Inc......B......323 745-4986
647 E 59th St Los Angeles (90001) ***(P-3078)***
Los Angeles At Home, Burbank *Also called Silverado Senior Living Inc* ***(P-20467)***
Los Angeles Athletic Club Inc......C......213 625-2211
431 W 7th St Los Angeles (90014) ***(P-19457)***
Los Angeles Board Mills Inc......D......323 685-8900
1600 Barranca Pkwy Irvine (92606) ***(P-3773)***
Los Angeles Board of Education, Los Angeles *Also called Los Angeles Unified School Dst* ***(P-23469)***
Los Angeles Branch, Los Angeles *Also called Federal Rsrve Bnk San Frncisco* ***(P-14988)***
Los Angeles Branch, Commerce *Also called Jfc International Inc* ***(P-14699)***
Los Angeles Brass Products, Huntington Park *Also called Los Angles Pump Valve Pdts Inc* ***(P-8016)***

ALPHABETIC

Employee Codes: A=Over 500 employees, B=251-500
C=101-250, D=51-100, E=20-50 F=10-19
2022 Southern California Business
Directory and Buyers Guide
© Mergent Inc. 1-800-342-5647
1191

Los Angeles Bus Jurnl Assoc ....E......323 549-5225
11150 Santa Monica Blvd # 350 Los Angeles (90025) (P-4083)
Los Angeles Business Journal, Los Angeles Also called Cbj LP (P-4055)
Los Angeles Capital MGT LLC (PA) ....D......310 479-9998
11150 Santa Monica Blvd # 200 Los Angeles (90025) (P-16132)
Los Angeles Cardiology Assoc (HQ) ....D......213 977-0419
1245 Wilshire Blvd # 703 Los Angeles (90017) (P-19965)
Los Angeles Chargers, Costa Mesa Also called Chargers Football Company LLC (P-19413)
Los Angeles Church of Christ, Santa Monica Also called Los Angeles Intl Ch
Chrst (P-17655)
Los Angeles City Hauling, Sun Valley Also called USA Waste of California Inc (P-12987)
Los Angeles Clippers, Los Angeles Also called LA Sports Properties Inc (P-19420)
Los Angeles Cnty Mseum of Art ....D......323 857-6000
5905 Wilshire Blvd Los Angeles (90036) (P-22225)
Los Angeles Cold Storage, Los Angeles Also called Standard-Southern
Corporation (P-12179)
Los Angeles Cold Storage Co, Los Angeles Also called Standard-Southern
Corporation (P-12177)
Los Angeles Conven and Exh ....B......213 741-1151
1201 S Figueroa St Los Angeles (90015) (P-15676)
Los Angeles Convention Center, Los Angeles Also called AEG Management Lacc
LLC (P-22968)
Los Angeles Country Club ....C......310 276-6104
10101 Wilshire Blvd Los Angeles (90024) (P-19581)
Los Angeles County, Pacoima Also called County of Los Angeles (P-19772)
Los Angeles County Bar Assn (PA) ....D......213 627-2727
200 S Spring St Los Angeles (90012) (P-22272)
Los Angeles County Fair Assn (PA) ....D......909 623-3111
1101 W Mckinley Ave Pomona (91768) (P-19654)
Los Angeles County Pub Works, South Gate Also called County of Los Angeles (P-21408)
Los Angeles Cty Rnch Los Amgos ....A......562 385-7111
7601 Imperial Hwy Downey (90242) (P-20536)
Los Angeles Daily News Pubg Co ....E......818 713-3883
21860 Burbank Blvd # 200 Woodland Hills (91367) (P-4003)
Los Angeles Dependency Lawyers ....D......323 859-5546
901 Corporate Center Dr # 52 Monterey Park (91754) (P-21617)
Los Angeles Dept Convetion Tou, Los Angeles Also called Los Angeles Conven and
Exh (P-15676)
Los Angeles Dept Wtr & Pwr ....B......323 256-8079
4030 Crenshaw Blvd Los Angeles (90008) (P-12901)
Los Angeles Dept Wtr & Pwr ....B......213 367-1342
11801 Sheldon St Sun Valley (91352) (P-12902)
Los Angeles Dept Wtr & Pwr ....B......760 878-2156
201 S Webster St Independence (93526) (P-12903)
Los Angeles Dept Wtr & Pwr (HQ) ....A......213 367-1320
111 N Hope St Los Angeles (90012) (P-12904)
Los Angeles Dept Wtr & Pwr ....D......213 367-4211
111 N Hope St Los Angeles (90012) (P-12808)
Los Angeles Dept Wtr & Pwr ....B......213 367-5706
1141 W 2nd St Bldg D Los Angeles (90012) (P-12905)
Los Angeles Dept Wtr & Pwr ....B......310 524-8500
12700 Vista Del Mar Playa Del Rey (90293) (P-12878)
Los Angeles District Office, Glendale Also called State Compensation Insur Fund (P-15483)
Los Angeles Dodgers LLC ....A......323 224-1507
1000 Vin Scully Ave Los Angeles (90090) (P-19421)
Los Angeles Downtown News, Los Angeles Also called Civic Center News Inc (P-3963)
Los Angeles Education Partnr ....D......213 622-5237
1541 Wilshire Blvd # 200 Los Angeles (90017) (P-22197)
Los Angeles Engineering Inc ....C......626 869-1400
633 N Barranca Ave Covina (91723) (P-22602)
Los Angeles Equestrian Center ....D......818 840-9063
480 W Riverside Dr Burbank (91506) (P-213)
Los Angeles Federal Credit Un (PA) ....D......818 242-8640
300 S Glendale Ave # 100 Glendale (91205) (P-15073)
Los Angeles Fiber Co, Vernon Also called Marspring Corporation (P-3554)
Los Angeles Free Clinic ....C......323 653-1990
5205 Melrose Ave Los Angeles (90038) (P-19966)
Los Angeles Free Clinic (PA) ....D......323 653-8622
8405 Beverly Blvd Los Angeles (90048) (P-19967)
Los Angeles Freightliner, Fontana Also called Los Angeles Truck Centers LLC (P-13032)
Los Angeles Galvanizing Co ....D......323 583-2263
2518 E 53rd St Huntington Park (90255) (P-7383)
Los Angeles Homeless Svcs Auth ....A......213 683-3333
707 Wilshire Blvd # 1000 Los Angeles (90017) (P-21843)
Los Angeles Intl Ch Chrst ....C......213 351-2300
2716 Ocean Park Blvd # 20 Santa Monica (90405) (P-17655)
Los Angeles Junction Rlwy Co ....D......323 277-2004
4433 Exchange Ave Vernon (90058) (P-11796)
Los Angeles Lawyer Magazine, Los Angeles Also called Los Angeles County Bar
Assn (P-22272)
Los Angeles Lgbt Center (PA) ....C......323 993-7618
1625 Schrader Blvd Los Angeles (90028) (P-22198)
Los Angeles Ltg Mfg Co Inc ....D......626 454-8300
10141 Olney St El Monte (91731) (P-13641)
Los Angeles Magazine, Los Angeles Also called Emmis Publishing Corporation (P-14872)
Los Angeles Mem Coliseum Comm ....B......213 747-7111
3911 S Figueroa St Los Angeles (90037) (P-22455)
Los Angeles Mills Inc ....F......213 622-8031
2331 E 8th St Los Angeles (90021) (P-2580)
Los Angeles Mission Inc (PA) ....D......213 629-1227
6732 Brynhurst Ave Apt 3 Los Angeles (90043) (P-22126)
Los Angeles Organizing ....E......310 407-0539
10900 Wilshire Blvd # 710 Los Angeles (90024) (P-19582)
Los Angeles Orphans Home Soc (HQ) ....C......323 463-2119
815 N El Centro Ave Los Angeles (90038) (P-22127)
Los Angeles Philharmonic Assn (PA) ....C......213 972-7300
151 S Grand Ave Los Angeles (90012) (P-19364)

Los Angeles Philharmonic Assn ....A......323 850-2060
2301 N Highland Ave Los Angeles (90068) (P-19365)
Los Angeles Plant, Cypress Also called Hitachi Automotive Systems (P-8917)
Los Angeles Police Credit Un (PA) ....D......818 787-6520
16150 Sherman Way Van Nuys (91406) (P-15114)
Los Angeles Poultry Co Inc ....D......323 232-1619
4816 Long Beach Ave Los Angeles (90058) (P-1762)
Los Angeles Ppr Box & Bd Mills, Irvine Also called Los Angeles Board Mills Inc (P-3773)
Los Angeles Produce Distrs LLC (HQ) ....E......562 448-5555
1601 E Olympic Blvd Los Angeles (90021) (P-14643)
Los Angeles Rams LLC (PA) ....D......314 982-7267
29899 Agoura Rd Agoura Hills (91301) (P-19422)
Los Angeles Rams LLC ....D......310 277-4700
10271 W Pico Blvd Los Angeles (90064) (P-23054)
Los Angeles Refining Co ....F......310 522-6000
2101 E Pacific Coast Hwy Wilmington (90744) (P-5253)
Los Angeles Regional Food Bank ....C......323 234-3030
1734 E 41st St Vernon (90058) (P-21844)
Los Angeles Regional Office, Pasadena Also called Employee Benefits Security
ADM (P-15515)
Los Angeles Residential Comm F ....D......661 296-8636
29890 Bouquet Canyon Rd Santa Clarita (91390) (P-22128)
Los Angeles Rubber Company (PA) ....D......323 263-4131
2915 E Washington Blvd Los Angeles (90023) (P-13999)
Los Angeles Salad Intl Inc ....E......626 322-9000
623 W La Habra Blvd La Habra (90631) (P-1890)
Los Angeles Sentinel Inc ....D......323 299-3800
3800 Crenshaw Blvd Los Angeles (90008) (P-4004)
Los Angeles Sleeve Co Inc ....E......562 945-7578
12051 Rivera Rd Santa Fe Springs (90670) (P-10093)
Los Angeles Truck Centers LLC ....C......909 510-4000
13800 Valley Blvd Fontana (92335) (P-13032)
Los Angeles Turf Club Inc (HQ) ....B......626 574-6330
285 W Huntington Dr Arcadia (91007) (P-19431)
Los Angeles Unified School Dst ....D......310 354-3417
1208 Magnolia Ave Gardena (90247) (P-23468)
Los Angeles Unified School Dst ....D......818 346-3540
6200 Winnetka Ave Woodland Hills (91367) (P-21960)
Los Angeles Unified School Dst ....D......323 549-2018
1406 S Highland Ave Los Angeles (90019) (P-23055)
Los Angeles Unified School Dst ....D......323 265-1898
333 S Beaudry Ave Fl 29 Los Angeles (90017) (P-23469)
Los Angeles Unified School Dst ....D......818 360-2361
10535 Zelzah Ave Granada Hills (91344) (P-23470)
Los Angeles Unified School Dst ....D......818 763-6497
12215 Albers St North Hollywood (91607) (P-22346)
Los Angeles Waves Netball Club ....E......310 346-7211
2059 Artesia Blvd Apt 81 Torrance (90504) (P-22456)
Los Angeles World Airports, Los Angeles Also called Lawa Inc (P-12360)
Los Angeles World Airports (PA) ....B......310 646-7911
6320 W 96th St Los Angeles (90045) (P-12361)
Los Angeles Wraps, Torrance Also called Sirena Incorporated (P-4574)
Los Angels Unified School Dst, Gardena Also called Los Angeles Unified School
Dst (P-23468)
Los Angels Ambulatory Care Ctr, Los Angeles Also called Veterans Health
Administration (P-20153)
Los Angles Arbrtum Fndtion Inc ....D......626 821-3222
301 N Baldwin Ave Arcadia (91007) (P-22239)
Los Angles Area Chmber Cmmerce ....D......213 580-7500
350 S Bixel St Los Angeles (90017) (P-22251)
Los Angles Chmber Orchstra Soc ....D......213 622-7001
510 W 6th St Ste 1001 Los Angeles (90014) (P-19366)
Los Angles Cllege Chiropractic, Whittier Also called Southern Cal Univ Hlth
Scences (P-20234)
Los Angles Cnty Cntl Jail Hosp, Los Angeles Also called County of Los Angeles (P-20740)
Los Angles Cnty Dvlpmntal Svcs ....C......213 383-1300
3303 Wilshire Blvd # 700 Los Angeles (90010) (P-21451)
Los Angles Cnty Employees Assn ....D......213 368-8660
1545 Wilshire Blvd Los Angeles (90017) (P-22293)
Los Angles Cnty Emplyees Rtrme (PA) ....C......626 564-6000
300 N Lake Ave Ste 720 Pasadena (91101) (P-15516)
Los Angles Cnty Mseum Ntral Hs (PA) ....C......213 763-3466
900 Exposition Blvd Los Angeles (90007) (P-22199)
Los Angles Cnty Mtro Trnsp Aut, Los Angeles Also called Los Angles Cnty Mtro Trnsp
Aut (P-11821)
Los Angles Cnty Mtro Trnsp Aut ....A......310 643-3804
14724 Aviation Blvd Lawndale (90260) (P-11816)
Los Angles Cnty Mtro Trnsp Aut ....A......213 922-6308
9201 Canoga Ave Chatsworth (91311) (P-11817)
Los Angles Cnty Mtro Trnsp Aut ....F......213 922-5887
900 Lyon St Los Angeles (90012) (P-11818)
Los Angles Cnty Mtro Trnsp Aut ....A......213 922-6301
1130 E 6th St Los Angeles (90021) (P-11819)
Los Angles Cnty Mtro Trnsp Aut ....A......213 922-6203
630 W Avenue 28 Los Angeles (90065) (P-11820)
Los Angles Cnty Mtro Trnsp Aut ....A......213 922-6202
1 Gateway Plz Los Angeles (90012) (P-11821)
Los Angles Cnty Mtro Trnsp Aut (PA) ....A......323 466-3876
1 Gateway Plz Fl 25 Los Angeles (90012) (P-11822)
Los Angles Cnty Mtro Trnsp Aut ....A......213 922-6207
8800 Santa Monica Blvd Los Angeles (90069) (P-11823)
Los Angles Cnty Mtro Trnsp Aut ....A......213 922-6215
11900 Branford St Sun Valley (91352) (P-11824)
Los Angles Cnty Mtro Trnsp Aut ....A......213 533-1506
720 E 15th St Los Angeles (90021) (P-11825)
Los Angles Cnty Mtro Trnsp Aut ....A......213 922-5012
470 Bauchet St Los Angeles (90012) (P-11826)

Mergent e-mail: customerrelations@mergent.com
1192

2022 Southern California Business
Directory and Buyers Guide

(P-0000) Products & Services Section entry number
(PA)=Parent Co (HQ)=Headquarters (DH)=Div Headquarters

ALPHABETIC SECTION | Lowes Home Centers LLC

Los Angles Cnty Mtro Trnsp Aut ....A.......310 392-8636
100 Sunset Ave Venice (90291) *(P-11827)*

Los Angles Cnty Mtro Trnsp Aut ....A.......213 244-6783
818 W 7th St Ste 500 Los Angeles (90017) *(P-11828)*

Los Angles Cnty Mtro Trnsp Aut ....A.......213 626-4455
320 S Santa Fe Ave Los Angeles (90013) *(P-11829)*

Los Angles Dst Off Policy Svcs, Monterey Park *Also called State Compensation Insur Fund (P-15485)*

Los Angles Free Clnic Hllywood ....D.......323 653-8622
8405 Beverly Blvd Los Angeles (90048) *(P-19968)*

Los Angles Fund For Pub Edcatn (PA) ....**D.......310 912-3444**
10250 Constellation Blvd Los Angeles (90067) *(P-22200)*

Los Angles Jewish HM For Aging (PA) ....**B.......818 774-3000**
7150 Tampa Ave Reseda (91335) *(P-20409)*

Los Angles Jewish HM For Aging ....B.......818 774-3000
18855 Victory Blvd Reseda (91335) *(P-20410)*

Los Angles Pump Valve Pdts Inc ....E.......323 277-7788
2528 E 57th St Huntington Park (90255) *(P-8016)*

Los Angles Ryal Vsta Golf Crse, Walnut *Also called Los Angles Ryal Vsta Golf Crse (P-19583)*

Los Angles Ryal Vsta Golf Crse ....D.......909 595-7441
20055 Colima Rd Walnut (91789) *(P-19583)*

Los Angles Sction Nat Cncil JW (PA) ....**E.......323 651-2930**
543 N Fairfax Ave Los Angeles (90036) *(P-21845)*

Los Angles Tmes Cmmnctions LLC (PA) ....**A.......213 237-5000**
2300 E Imperial Hwy El Segundo (90245) *(P-4005)*

Los Angles Tmes Cmmnctions LLC ....E.......213 237-7987
145 S Spring St Los Angeles (90012) *(P-4006)*

Los Angles Trism Convention Bd (PA) ....**E.......213 624-7300**
633 W 5th St Ste 1800 Los Angeles (90071) *(P-18582)*

Los Angles Universal Preschool ....C.......213 416-1200
515 S Figueroa St Ste 900 Los Angeles (90071) *(P-22031)*

Los Cabos Mexican Foods, Santa Fe Springs *Also called MCI Foods Inc (P-2483)*

Los Dos Valles Harvstg & Pkg ....C.......805 739-1688
2365 Westgate Rd Santa Maria (93455) *(P-156)*

Los Feliz Ford Inc (PA) ....**D.......818 502-1901**
1101 S Brand Blvd Glendale (91204) *(P-18751)*

Los Olivos Packaging Inc (PA) ....**C.......323 261-2218**
929 Ridgecrest St Monterey Park (91754) *(P-1866)*

Los Osos Community Svcs Dst ....E.......805 528-9370
2122 9th St Ste 110 Los Osos (93402) *(P-22201)*

LOS OSOS CSD, Los Osos *Also called Los Osos Community Svcs Dst (P-22201)*

Los Palos Convalescent Hosp, San Pedro *Also called San Pedro Convalescent HM Inc (P-20457)*

Los Pericos Food Products LLC ....E.......909 623-5625
2301 Valley Blvd Pomona (91768) *(P-2476)*

Los Robles Bank ....D.......805 373-6763
33 W Thousand Oaks Blvd Thousand Oaks (91360) *(P-15030)*

Los Robles Regional Med Ctr ....C.......805 370-4531
150 Via Merida Westlake Village (91362) *(P-19969)*

Los Robles Regional Med Ctr ....B.......805 494-0880
2200 Lynn Rd Thousand Oaks (91360) *(P-20853)*

Los Robles Regional Med Ctr (HQ) ....**A.......805 497-2727**
215 W Janss Rd Thousand Oaks (91360) *(P-20854)*

Los Serranos Golf & Cntry CLB, Chino Hills *Also called Los Serranos Golf Club (P-19497)*

Los Serranos Golf Club ....C.......909 597-1769
15656 Yorba Ave Chino Hills (91709) *(P-19497)*

Lost & Wander, Vernon *Also called Vxb & Orfwid Inc (P-3008)*

Lost Dutchmans Minings Assn (HQ) ....**E.......951 699-4749**
43445 Bus Pk Dr Ste 113 Temecula (92590) *(P-375)*

Lost International LLC ....F.......949 600-6950
170 Technology Dr Irvine (92618) *(P-2821)*

Lotus Clinical Research LLC ....D.......626 381-9830
100 W California Blvd Pasadena (91105) *(P-21075)*

Lotus Communications Corp (PA) ....**D.......323 512-2225**
3301 Barham Blvd Ste 200 Los Angeles (90068) *(P-12701)*

Lotus Hygiene Systems Inc ....E.......714 259-8805
1621 E Saint Andrew Pl Santa Ana (92705) *(P-5992)*

Lotus Labels, Brea *Also called President Enterprise Inc (P-4558)*

Lotus Orient Corp (PA) ....**E.......626 285-5796**
411 S California St San Gabriel (91776) *(P-2892)*

Lou Ana Foods, Brea *Also called Ventura Foods LLC (P-2133)*

Louden Madelon, Vernon *Also called National Corset Supply House (P-3018)*

Louidar LLC ....E.......951 676-5047
33820 Rancho Cal Rd Temecula (92591) *(P-2204)*

Louie Almeida & Settler (PA) ....**D.......818 461-9559**
303 N Glenoaks Blvd # 400 Burbank (91502) *(P-21618)*

Louis Levin & Son Inc ....E.......562 802-8066
13550 Larwin Cir Santa Fe Springs (90670) *(P-8666)*

Louis Sardo Upholstery Inc (PA) ....**D.......310 327-0532**
512 W Rosecrans Ave Gardena (90248) *(P-3625)*

Louis W Osborn Co., La Mirada *Also called Headwaters Construction Inc (P-5976)*

Lounge Fly, Walnut *Also called Loungefly LLC (P-11487)*

Lounge Spa Inc ....D.......310 745-1646
4016 East Blvd Los Angeles (90066) *(P-19458)*

Loungefly LLC ....E.......818 718-5600
108 S Mayo Ave Walnut (91789) *(P-11487)*

Louroe Electronics Inc ....E.......818 994-6498
6955 Valjean Ave Van Nuys (91406) *(P-18394)*

Lovco Construction Inc ....C.......562 595-1601
1300 E Burnett St Signal Hill (90755) *(P-1600)*

Love At First Bite Catering ....D.......714 369-0561
18281 Gothard St Ste 108 Huntington Beach (92648) *(P-16964)*

Love Stitch, Los Angeles *Also called Clothing Illustrated Inc (P-2934)*

Love Style, Vernon *Also called Love Tree Fashion Inc (P-14394)*

Love Tree Fashion Inc ....E.......213 747-3755
2154 E 51st St Vernon (90058) *(P-14394)*

Loveis Corp ....F.......818 408-9504
9588 Topanga Canyon Blvd Chatsworth (91311) *(P-11011)*

Lovemarks Inc ....E.......213 514-5888
1100 S San Pedro St C01 Los Angeles (90015) *(P-2856)*

Low Voltage Architecture Inc ....F.......310 573-7588
11715 San Vicente Blvd Los Angeles (90049) *(P-9890)*

Lowe Enterprises Inc (PA) ....**C.......310 820-6661**
11777 San Vicente Blvd # 900 Los Angeles (90049) *(P-16546)*

Lowe Enterprises Inc ....D.......310 820-6661
11777 San Vicente Blvd # 900 Los Angeles (90049) *(P-16057)*

Lowe Enterprises Inv MGT (HQ) ....**D.......310 820-6661**
11777 San Vicente Blvd Los Angeles (90049) *(P-16158)*

Lowe Enterprises RE Group ....B.......310 820-6661
11777 San Vicente Blvd Los Angeles (90049) *(P-16058)*

Lowe Enterprises Rlty Svcs Inc (HQ) ....**B.......310 820-6661**
11777 San Vicente Blvd Los Angeles (90049) *(P-23056)*

Lowe Enterprises Rlty Svcs Inc ....A.......818 990-9555
16133 Ventura Blvd # 535 Encino (91436) *(P-15914)*

Lowermybills, Los Angeles *Also called Lmb Mortgage Services Inc (P-15209)*

Lowermybills.com, Playa Vista *Also called Lmb Opco LLC (P-15245)*

Lowers Industrial Supply, Santa Fe Springs *Also called Lowers Wldg & Fabrication Inc (P-8667)*

Lowers Wldg & Fabrication Inc ....F.......562 946-4521
10847 Painter Ave Santa Fe Springs (90670) *(P-8667)*

Lowes Home Centers LLC ....C.......562 496-8120
2840 N Bellflower Blvd Long Beach (90815) *(P-13219)*

Lowes Home Centers LLC ....C.......909 476-9697
11399 Foothill Blvd Rancho Cucamonga (91730) *(P-13220)*

Lowes Home Centers LLC ....C.......949 589-5005
30481 Avnida De Las Flres Rancho Santa Margari (92688) *(P-13221)*

Lowes Home Centers LLC ....C.......760 949-9565
14333 Bear Valley Rd Victorville (92392) *(P-13222)*

Lowes Home Centers LLC ....C.......818 686-4300
13500 Paxton St Pacoima (91331) *(P-13223)*

Lowes Home Centers LLC ....C.......951 723-1930
30472 Haun Rd Menifee (92584) *(P-13224)*

Lowes Home Centers LLC ....C.......805 602-9051
2445 Golden Hill Rd Paso Robles (93446) *(P-13225)*

Lowes Home Centers LLC ....C.......949 369-4644
907 Avenida Pico San Clemente (92673) *(P-13226)*

Lowes Home Centers LLC ....C.......951 509-5500
9851 Magnolia Ave Riverside (92503) *(P-13227)*

Lowes Home Centers LLC ....C.......760 771-5566
78865 Highway 111 La Quinta (92253) *(P-13228)*

Lowes Home Centers LLC ....C.......562 926-0826
14873 Carmenita Rd Norwalk (90650) *(P-13229)*

Lowes Home Centers LLC ....C.......909 627-6039
13251 Peyton Dr Chino Hills (91709) *(P-13230)*

Lowes Home Centers LLC ....C.......818 610-1960
8383 Topanga Canyon Blvd West Hills (91304) *(P-13231)*

Lowes Home Centers LLC ....C.......909 982-4795
1659 W Foothill Blvd Upland (91786) *(P-13232)*

Lowes Home Centers LLC ....C.......661 297-1400
26415 Bouquet Canyon Rd Santa Clarita (91350) *(P-13233)*

Lowes Home Centers LLC ....C.......760 866-1901
5201 E Ramon Rd Palm Springs (92264) *(P-13234)*

Lowes Home Centers LLC ....C.......818 557-2300
2000 W Empire Ave Burbank (91504) *(P-13235)*

Lowes Home Centers LLC ....C.......714 447-6140
1500 N Lemon St Anaheim (92801) *(P-13236)*

Lowes Home Centers LLC ....C.......951 461-8916
24701 Madison Ave Murrieta (92562) *(P-13237)*

Lowes Home Centers LLC ....C.......323 327-4000
2800 W 120th St Hawthorne (90250) *(P-13238)*

Lowes Home Centers LLC ....C.......562 942-9909
8600 Washington Blvd Pico Rivera (90660) *(P-13239)*

Lowes Home Centers LLC ....C.......951 656-1859
12400 Day St Moreno Valley (92553) *(P-13240)*

Lowes Home Centers LLC ....C.......909 305-2960
633 W Bonita Ave San Dimas (91773) *(P-13241)*

Lowes Home Centers LLC ....C.......562 690-5122
1380 S Beach Blvd La Habra (90631) *(P-13242)*

Lowes Home Centers LLC ....C.......661 588-6420
7825 Rosedale Hwy Bakersfield (93308) *(P-13243)*

Lowes Home Centers LLC ....C.......562 421-9996
7300 E Carson St Long Beach (90808) *(P-13244)*

Lowes Home Centers LLC ....C.......661 267-9888
39500 Lowes Dr Palmdale (93551) *(P-13245)*

Lowes Home Centers LLC ....C.......951 296-1618
40390 Winchester Rd Temecula (92591) *(P-13246)*

Lowes Home Centers LLC ....C.......310 787-1469
22255 S Western Ave Torrance (90501) *(P-13247)*

Lowes Home Centers LLC ....C.......559 624-4300
4144 S Mooney Blvd Visalia (93277) *(P-13248)*

Lowes Home Centers LLC ....C.......805 675-8800
500 S Mills Rd Ventura (93003) *(P-13249)*

Lowes Home Centers LLC ....C.......909 350-7900
16851 Sierra Lakes Pkwy Fontana (92336) *(P-13250)*

Lowes Home Centers LLC ....C.......951 256-9004
1285 Magnolia Ave Corona (92879) *(P-13251)*

Lowes Home Centers LLC ....C.......951 492-7000
350 S Sanderson Ave Hemet (92545) *(P-13252)*

Lowes Home Centers LLC ....C.......661 699-1000
6200 Colony St Bakersfield (93307) *(P-13253)*

Lowes Home Centers LLC ....C.......909 307-8883
1725 W Redlands Blvd Redlands (92373) *(P-13254)*

Lowes Home Centers LLC ....C.......661 341-9000
730 W Avenue K Lancaster (93534) *(P-13255)*

Lowes Home Centers LLC ....C.......760 337-6700
2053 N Imperial Ave El Centro (92243) *(P-13256)*

ALPHABETIC

Lowes Home Centers LLC ....C 714 907-9006
8175 Warner Ave Huntington Beach (92647) *(P-13257)*

Lowes Home Centers LLC ....C 661 533-9900
37080 47th St E Palmdale (93552) *(P-13258)*

Lowes Home Centers LLC ....C 760 961-3000
12189 Apple Valley Rd Apple Valley (92308) *(P-13259)*

Lowes Home Centers LLC ....C 951 253-6000
29335 Central Ave Lake Elsinore (92532) *(P-13260)*

Lowes Home Centers LLC ....C 805 426-2780
1275 Simi Town Center Way Simi Valley (93065) *(P-13261)*

Lowes Home Centers LLC ....C 818 477-9022
19601 Nordhoff St Northridge (91324) *(P-13262)*

Lowes Home Centers LLC ....C 909 969-9053
2390 S Grove Ave Ontario (91761) *(P-13263)*

Lowes Home Centers LLC ....C 559 366-5000
1145 E Prosperity Ave Tulare (93274) *(P-13264)*

Lowes Home Centers LLC ....C 310 602-2090
2700 Skypark Dr Torrance (90505) *(P-13265)*

Lowes Home Centers LLC ....C 661 889-9000
1601 Columbus St Bakersfield (93305) *(P-13266)*

Lowes Home Centers LLC ....C 626 217-1133
17789 Castleton St City of Industry (91748) *(P-13267)*

Lowes Home Centers LLC ....C 951 256-9034
6413 Pats Ranch Rd Jurupa Valley (91752) *(P-13268)*

Lowes Home Centers LLC ....C 714 913-2663
2500 Park Ave Tustin (92782) *(P-13269)*

Lowes Home Centers LLC ....C 559 802-9055
3020 N Demaree St Visalia (93291) *(P-13270)*

Lowes Home Centers LLC ....C 559 306-5000
500 W Vandalia Ave Porterville (93257) *(P-13271)*

Lowes Home Centers LLC ....C 909 438-9000
4777 Chino Hills Pkwy Chino Hills (91709) *(P-13272)*

Lowes Home Centers LLC ....C 661 678-4430
19001 Golden Valley Rd Santa Clarita (91387) *(P-13273)*

Lowes Home Centers LLC ....C 559 410-9000
1955 W Lacey Blvd Hanford (93230) *(P-13274)*

Lowes Home Centers LLC ....C 909 557-9010
27847 Greenspot Rd Highland (92346) *(P-13275)*

Lowratscom 1st Lbrty Cal State, Buena Park *Also called Sun West Mortgage Company Inc (P-15232)*

Lozano Enterprises, Los Angeles *Also called La Opinion LP (P-4000)*

Lozano Plumbing Services Inc ....C 951 683-4840
3615 Presley Ave Riverside (92507) *(P-1096)*

LPA Inc (PA) ....C **949 261-1001**
5301 California Ave # 100 Irvine (92617) *(P-22729)*

LPC Commercial Services Inc ....C 213 362-9080
915 Wilshire Blvd Ste 250 Los Angeles (90017) *(P-16059)*

Lpcc, Camarillo *Also called Las Posas Country Club (P-19578)*

Lpcc 6008, Ontario *Also called Leggett & Platt Incorporated (P-3552)*

Lps Agency Sales & Posting Inc (PA) ....D **714 247-7503**
3210 El Cmino Real Ste 20 Irvine (92602) *(P-18583)*

Lpsh Holdings Inc (PA) ....B **855 647-5061**
7100 W Florida Ave Hemet (92545) *(P-1097)*

Lpsh Holdings Inc ....D 951 926-1176
3570 W Florida Ave # 168 Hemet (92545) *(P-1098)*

Lqr Property LLC ....B 760 564-4111
49499 Eisenhower Dr La Quinta (92253) *(P-16547)*

LR Baggs Corporation ....E 805 929-3545
483 N Frontage Rd Nipomo (93444) *(P-11346)*

Lrb Millwork & Casework Inc ....F 951 328-0105
2760 S Iowa Ave Colton (92324) *(P-3263)*

Lrc Coil Company, Santa Fe Springs *Also called Lmw Enterprises LLC (P-8344)*

Lres Corporation (PA) ....D **714 520-5737**
765 The City Dr S Ste 300 Orange (92868) *(P-15915)*

Lrw Group, Los Angeles *Also called Lieberman RES Worldwide LLC (P-22892)*

Lrw Investments LLC ....D 310 337-1944
9700 Bellanca Ave Los Angeles (90045) *(P-18768)*

Lsa Associates Inc (PA) ....C **949 553-0666**
20 Executive Park Ste 200 Irvine (92614) *(P-23471)*

Lsf Central Cal Adult Svcs, Santa Maria *Also called Life Steps Foundation Inc (P-21839)*

Lsf9 Cypress LP (PA) ....A **714 380-3127**
2741 Walnut Ave Ste 200 Tustin (92780) *(P-13333)*

Lsf9 Cypress Parent LLC (HQ) ....A **714 380-3127**
2741 Walnut Ave Ste 200 Tustin (92780) *(P-13334)*

Lsf9 Cypress Parent 2 LLC ....A 714 380-3127
2741 Walnut Ave Ste 200 Tustin (92780) *(P-13335)*

LSI Products Inc ....F 951 343-9270
12885 Wildflower Ln Riverside (92503) *(P-10094)*

Lspace America LLC ....E 949 596-8726
3500 Hyland Ave Ste 100 Costa Mesa (92626) *(P-2857)*

Lt Foods Americas Inc (HQ) ....D **562 340-4040**
11130 Warland Dr Cypress (90630) *(P-1946)*

Lt Security Inc (PA) ....C **626 435-2838**
17333 Freedom Way City of Industry (91748) *(P-13746)*

Ltd Tech Inc ....F 805 480-1886
2630 Lavery Ct Ste B Newbury Park (91320) *(P-7905)*

LTI, Irvine *Also called Lens Technology I LLC (P-10844)*

Ltp Modern Machine Inc ....F 562 795-1701
10900 Walker St Cypress (90630) *(P-19049)*

Ltr, South Gate *Also called Lunday-Thagard Company (P-5300)*

LTS Associate Inc (PA) ....E **626 435-2838**
17333 Freedom Way City of Industry (91748) *(P-13747)*

Lu & Weber Corporation ....D 714 590-3620
10521 Garden Grove Blvd Garden Grove (92843) *(P-21187)*

Lubeco Inc ....E 562 602-1791
6859 Downey Ave Long Beach (90805) *(P-5297)*

Lubrication Scientifics Inc ....F 714 557-0664
17651 Armstrong Ave Irvine (92614) *(P-7450)*

Lubrication Scientifics LLC ....E 714 557-0664
17651 Armstrong Ave Irvine (92614) *(P-8128)*

Lubrigreen, Irvine *Also called Biosynthetic Technologies LLC (P-7928)*

Lubrizol Corporation ....F 949 212-1863
30211 Ave D Las Bandras Rancho Santa Margari (92688) *(P-5228)*

Lucare Corporation ....F 818 583-7731
1292 Journeys End Dr La Canada Flintridge (91011) *(P-11282)*

Lucas & Lewellen Vineyards Inc (PA) ....E **805 686-9336**
1645 Copenhagen Dr Solvang (93463) *(P-14844)*

Lucas Design International Inc (PA) ....D **213 387-4444**
606 S Hill St Ste 1001 Los Angeles (90014) *(P-14132)*

Lucas Lwllen Vnyrds Tasting Rm, Solvang *Also called Lucas & Lewellen Vineyards Inc (P-14844)*

Lucas Oil Products Inc (PA) ....C **951 270-0154**
302 N Sheridan St Corona (92878) *(P-14786)*

Luce Communications LLC ....D 657 600-6812
22895 Eastpark Dr Yorba Linda (92887) *(P-5229)*

Lucent Diamonds Inc ....E 424 777-2390
22809 Pacific Coast Hwy Malibu (90265) *(P-11337)*

Lucix Corporation (HQ) ....D **805 987-6645**
800 Avenida Acaso Ste E Camarillo (93012) *(P-9742)*

Lucix Corporation ....D 805 987-3677
3883 Via Pescador Camarillo (93012) *(P-9743)*

Lucky Dog AG Services, Santa Maria *Also called Red Dog Management Inc (P-23097)*

Lucky Farms Inc ....D 909 799-6688
1194 E Brier Dr San Bernardino (92408) *(P-17)*

Lucky Strike Entertainment Inc ....C 213 542-4880
800 W Olympic Blvd # 250 Los Angeles (90015) *(P-19399)*

Lucky Strike Entertainment Inc (PA) ....E **818 933-3752**
15260 Ventura Blvd # 1110 Sherman Oaks (91403) *(P-11434)*

Lucky Strike Entertainment LLC ....C 818 933-3752
6801 Hollywood Blvd # 143 Los Angeles (90028) *(P-19400)*

Lucky Strike Entertainment LLC ....C 248 374-3420
15260 Ventura Blvd # 1110 Sherman Oaks (91403) *(P-19401)*

Lucky Strike Entertainment LLC ....C 818 933-0872
15260 Ventura Blvd # 1110 Sherman Oaks (91403) *(P-19402)*

Lucky Strike Entertainment LLC ....C 248 374-3420
20 City Blvd W Ste G2 Orange (92868) *(P-19403)*

Lucky Strike Novi, Sherman Oaks *Also called Lucky Strike Entertainment LLC (P-19401)*

Lucky-13 Apparel, Los Alamitos *Also called Blue Sphere Inc (P-2743)*

Lucy Ann, Torrance *Also called Obatake Inc (P-11327)*

Luma Comfort LLC ....E 855 963-9247
6600 Katella Ave Cypress (90630) *(P-9008)*

Luma Pictures Inc ....C 310 888-8738
1453 3rd Street Promenade # 400 Santa Monica (90401) *(P-19146)*

Lumaforge Llc An Owc Company ....F 818 741-2858
1311 S Flower St Burbank (91502) *(P-8207)*

Lumar Metals, Rancho Cucamonga *Also called Lur Inc (P-6974)*

Lumber City Corp ....D 805 522-0533
2695 Cochran St Simi Valley (93065) *(P-83)*

Lumber City Corp ....D 805 497-2753
3775 E Thousand Oaks Blvd Westlake Village (91362) *(P-13276)*

Lumenton Inc ....F 323 904-0202
5461 W Jefferson Blvd Los Angeles (90016) *(P-9139)*

Lumenton Lighting, Los Angeles *Also called Lumenton Inc (P-9139)*

Lumina Alliance ....D 805 781-6400
51 Zaca Ln Ste 150 San Luis Obispo (93401) *(P-21846)*

Lumina At Home, Los Angeles *Also called Lumina Healthcare LLC (P-21188)*

Lumina Healthcare LLC (PA) ....D **888 958-6462**
5220 Pcf Cncrse Dr Ste 12 Los Angeles (90045) *(P-21188)*

Lumination Lighting & Tech Inc ....C 855 283-1100
1515 240th St Harbor City (90710) *(P-9096)*

Luminit LLC ....E 310 320-1066
1850 W 205th St Torrance (90501) *(P-10845)*

Lumio Inc ....F 586 861-2408
6355 Topanga Canyon Blvd # 335 Woodland Hills (91367) *(P-9533)*

Luna Imaging Inc ....E 323 908-1400
2702 Media Center Dr Los Angeles (90065) *(P-17907)*

Lund Motion Products Inc ....E 949 221-0023
15651 Mosher Ave Tustin (92780) *(P-10095)*

Lunday-Thagard Company (HQ) ....C **562 928-7000**
9302 Garfield Ave South Gate (90280) *(P-5300)*

Lunday-Thagard Company ....E 562 928-6990
9301 Garfield Ave South Gate (90280) *(P-5284)*

Lundberg Survey Inc ....E 805 383-2400
911 Via Alondra Camarillo (93012) *(P-4084)*

Lungsal International Inc ....F 714 671-9788
360 Thor Pl Brea (92821) *(P-14949)*

Lungsal USA, Brea *Also called Lungsal International Inc (P-14949)*

Lunwood Developmental Care ....D 310 223-5920
14925 S Atlantic Ave Compton (90221) *(P-20608)*

Lupitas Bakery Inc (PA) ....F **323 752-2391**
1848 W Florence Ave Los Angeles (90047) *(P-2017)*

Luppen Holdings Inc (PA) ....E **323 581-8121**
3050 Leonis Blvd Vernon (90058) *(P-7162)*

Lur Inc ....F 909 623-4999
9936 Albany Ave Rancho Cucamonga (91701) *(P-6974)*

Luran Inc ....E 661 257-6303
24927 Avenue Tibbitts K Valencia (91355) *(P-8668)*

Lusive Decor ....D 323 227-9207
3400 Medford St Los Angeles (90063) *(P-23472)*

Lusk Quality Machine Products ....E 661 272-0630
39457 15th St E Palmdale (93550) *(P-8669)*

Luster Cote Inc ....F 909 355-9995
10841 Business Dr Fontana (92337) *(P-7384)*

Lutheran Health Facility, Burbank *Also called Front Prch Cmmnties Svcs - Cas (P-20588)*

Lux Solutions LLC (PA) ....D **770 591-0463**
12123 Barringer St South El Monte (91733) *(P-19367)*

ALPHABETIC SECTION M-7 Consolidation Inc

Luxe City Center, Los Angeles *Also called Emerik Hotel Corp* ***(P-16432)***
Luxe Homecare Inc (PA)..............D.......**310 454-5500**
881 Alma Real Dr Pacific Palisades (90272) ***(P-21189)***
Luxe Light and Home, Los Angeles *Also called Lusive Decor* ***(P-23472)***
Luxe Sunset Boulevard Hotel, Los Angeles *Also called E H Summit Inc* ***(P-16423)***
Luxe Travel Group, Irvine *Also called Luxe Travel Management Inc* ***(P-12392)***
Luxe Travel Management Inc (HQ)..............D.......**949 336-1000**
18650 Macarthur Blvd # 100 Irvine (92612) ***(P-12392)***
Luxfer Gas Cylinder, Riverside *Also called Luxfer Inc* ***(P-10370)***
Luxfer Inc (HQ)..............D.......**951 684-5110**
3016 Kansas Ave Bldg 1 Riverside (92507) ***(P-10370)***
Luxfer Inc..............E.......951 684-5110
1995 3rd St Riverside (92507) ***(P-6311)***
Luxfer Inc..............E.......951 351-4100
6825 Jurupa Ave Riverside (92504) ***(P-7104)***
Luxor Industries International..............E.......909 469-4757
1250 E Franklin Ave Pomona (91766) ***(P-3264)***
Luxre Realty Inc..............D.......949 498-3702
222 Avenida Del Mar San Clemente (92672) ***(P-15916)***
Lvl 10 Entertainment LLC..............E.......424 298-5119
6444 San Fernando Rd # 55 Glendale (91201) ***(P-19368)***
Lvp Cy Paso Robles LLC..............E.......805 239-9700
120 S Vine St Paso Robles (93446) ***(P-16548)***
Lymi Inc (PA)..............D.......**855 756-0560**
2263 E Vernon Ave Vernon (90058) ***(P-14395)***
Lynam Industries Inc..............D.......951 360-1919
13050 Santa Ana Ave Fontana (92337) ***(P-6864)***
Lynberg & Watkins A Prof Corp (PA)..............E.......**213 624-8700**
1150 S Olive St Fl 18 Los Angeles (90015) ***(P-21619)***
Lynberg & Watkins Attys At Law, Los Angeles *Also called Lynberg & Watkins A Prof Corp* ***(P-21619)***
Lynch Ambulance Service, Anaheim *Also called Filyn Corporation* ***(P-11867)***
Lynch Ready Mix Concrete Co..............F.......805 647-2817
11011 Azahar St Ste 4 Ventura (93004) ***(P-6099)***
Lyncole Grunding Solutions LLC..............E.......310 214-4000
3547 Voyager St Ste 204 Torrance (90503) ***(P-9041)***
Lyncole Xit Grounding, Torrance *Also called Lyncole Grunding Solutions LLC* ***(P-9041)***
Lynde-Ordway Company Inc..............F.......714 957-1311
5402 Commercial Dr Huntington Beach (92649) ***(P-8318)***
Lynn Products Inc..............A.......310 530-5966
2645 W 237th St Torrance (90505) ***(P-8277)***
Lynwood Adult Day Care, Compton *Also called Lunwood Developmental Care* ***(P-20608)***
Lynwood Medical Offices, Lynwood *Also called Kaiser Foundation Hospitals* ***(P-19907)***
Lynwood Pattern Service Inc..............E.......310 631-2225
603 S Hope Ave Ontario (91761) ***(P-6398)***
Lynwood Unified School Dst..............D.......310 631-7308
12120 Lindbergh Ave Lynwood (90262) ***(P-22032)***
Lynx Innovation Inc (PA)..............C.......**949 345-1847**
500 Wald Irvine (92618) ***(P-13748)***
Lynx Phtnic Ntworks A Del Corp..............E.......818 802-0244
6303 Owensmouth Ave Fl 10 Woodland Hills (91367) ***(P-9237)***
Lyons Security Service Inc (PA)..............C.......**714 401-4850**
505 S Villa Real Ste 203a Anaheim (92807) ***(P-18295)***
Lyonsgate Realty Inc..............E.......561 961-4934
6317 Simpson Ave North Hollywood (91606) ***(P-15917)***
Lytle Screen Printing Inc..............F.......714 969-2424
21572 Surveyor Cir Huntington Beach (92646) ***(P-7909)***
Lz Management Group LLC (PA)..............D.......**213 383-4800**
3680 Wilshire Blvd # 206 Los Angeles (90010) ***(P-23057)***
M & A Custom Doors, Harbor City *Also called Joanka Inc* ***(P-6703)***
M & A Plastics Inc..............F.......818 768-0479
11735 Sheldon St Sun Valley (91352) ***(P-5701)***
M & B Window Fashions, Los Angeles *Also called Hd Window Fashions Inc* ***(P-3710)***
M & C, Los Angeles *Also called Murchison & Cumming LLP* ***(P-21638)***
M & G Jewelers Inc..............D.......909 989-2929
10823 Edison Ct Rancho Cucamonga (91730) ***(P-11323)***
M & J Seafood Company Inc..............D.......562 529-2786
6859 Walthall Way Paramount (90723) ***(P-14572)***
M & L Pharmaceuticals Inc..............E.......909 890-0078
629 S Allen St San Bernardino (92408) ***(P-4848)***
M & M Distributors, Los Angeles *Also called Wiemar Distributors Inc* ***(P-14667)***
M & M Florists Inc..............D.......661 298-7088
27592 Sierra Hwy Canyon Country (91351) ***(P-14040)***
M & M Plumbing Inc..............D.......951 354-5388
6782 Columbus St Riverside (92504) ***(P-1099)***
M & M Service..............F.......909 802-2050
972 E 1st St Pomona (91766) ***(P-6865)***
M & N Consulting Inc..............D.......818 349-9400
21358 Nordhoff St Chatsworth (91311) ***(P-12141)***
M & O Perry Industries Inc..............E.......951 734-9838
412 N Smith Ave Corona (92878) ***(P-8073)***
M & R Engineering Co..............F.......714 991-8480
227 E Meats Ave Orange (92865) ***(P-7038)***
M & R Joint Venture Electrical..............D.......909 598-7700
231 Benton Ct Walnut (91789) ***(P-1277)***
M & R Plating Corporation..............F.......818 896-2700
12375 Montague St Pacoima (91331) ***(P-7278)***
M & S Acquisition Corporation (PA)..............C.......**213 385-1515**
707 Wilshire Blvd # 5200 Los Angeles (90017) ***(P-15918)***
M & S Security Services Inc..............D.......661 397-9616
2900 L St Bakersfield (93301) ***(P-18296)***
M & S Trading Inc..............D.......714 241-7190
15778 Gateway Cir Tustin (92780) ***(P-14341)***
M & T Aerospace Inc..............F.......714 591-5154
10492 Trask Ave Garden Grove (92843) ***(P-10194)***
M & W Machine Corporation..............E.......714 541-2652
1642 E Edinger Ave Ste A Santa Ana (92705) ***(P-8670)***
M 86 Security, Irvine *Also called M86 Americas Inc* ***(P-13412)***
M A C, Northridge *Also called Mikuni American Corporation* ***(P-13073)***
M A G, Santa Maria *Also called Microwave Applications Group* ***(P-22614)***
M and M Stamping Corp..............F.......909 590-2704
13821 Oaks Ave Chino (91710) ***(P-6630)***
M Argeso & Co Inc..............F.......626 573-3000
2628 River Ave Rosemead (91770) ***(P-5254)***
M Arthur Gensler Jr Assoc Inc..............C.......213 927-3600
500 S Figueroa St Los Angeles (90071) ***(P-22730)***
M Block & Sons Inc..............C.......909 335-6684
26875 Pioneer Ave Redlands (92374) ***(P-12221)***
M C, Los Angeles *Also called Muir-Chase Plumbing Co Inc* ***(P-1104)***
M C C, Torrance *Also called Medical Chemical Corporation* ***(P-5233)***
M C C, Brea *Also called Mercury Casualty Company* ***(P-15469)***
M C C Equipment Rentals Inc..............D.......909 795-9300
32389 Dunlap Blvd Yucaipa (92399) ***(P-962)***
M C E, Torrance *Also called Magnetic Component Engrg Inc* ***(P-7563)***
M Caratan Disc Inc..............C.......661 725-2566
33787 Cecil Ave Delano (93215) ***(P-49)***
M D D, Burbank *Also called US Steel Rule Dies Inc* ***(P-7841)***
M D H, Monrovia *Also called Radcal Corporation* ***(P-10906)***
M D H Burner & Boiler Co Inc..............F.......562 630-2875
12106 Center St South Gate (90280) ***(P-8049)***
M D Manufacturing Inc..............F.......661 283-7550
34970 Mcmurtrey Ave Bakersfield (93308) ***(P-8393)***
M E D Inc..............D.......562 921-0464
14001 Marquardt Ave Santa Fe Springs (90670) ***(P-10096)***
M E I, Santa Barbara *Also called Motion Engineering Inc* ***(P-8282)***
M E Nollkamper Inc (PA)..............E.......**951 737-9300**
940 Manor Way Corona (92882) ***(P-23264)***
M E T, Murrieta *Also called Medical Extrusion Tech Inc* ***(P-5706)***
M F G Eurotec Inc..............F.......760 863-0033
84464 Cabazon Center Dr Indio (92201) ***(P-3477)***
M F G West, Adelanto *Also called Molded Fiber GL Companies - W* ***(P-5716)***
M F Salta Co Inc (PA)..............D.......**562 421-2512**
20 Executive Park Ste 150 Irvine (92614) ***(P-23265)***
M G A Investment Co Inc..............F.......805 543-9050
3211 Broad St Ste 201 San Luis Obispo (93401) ***(P-4188)***
M Gaw Inc..............D.......818 503-7997
6910 Farmdale Ave North Hollywood (91605) ***(P-1672)***
M I E, Temecula *Also called Molding Intl & Engrg Inc* ***(P-5718)***
M I I, Bakersfield *Also called Mechanical Industries Inc* ***(P-1577)***
M I M, Long Beach *Also called GTM Management Company Inc* ***(P-998)***
M I P, Covina *Also called Moores Ideal Products LLC* ***(P-11385)***
M I T Inc..............E.......714 899-6066
15202 Pipeline Ln Huntington Beach (92649) ***(P-7813)***
M K Products Inc..............D.......949 798-1425
16882 Armstrong Ave Irvine (92606) ***(P-7892)***
M K Smith Chevrolet..............C.......909 628-8961
12845 Central Ave Chino (91710) ***(P-18937)***
M L Services Inc..............D.......800 272-2179
5 Peters Canyon Rd # 140 Irvine (92606) ***(P-1278)***
M L Stern & Co LLC (HQ)..............C.......**323 658-4400**
8350 Wilshire Blvd # 300 Beverly Hills (90211) ***(P-15275)***
M M C, Covina *Also called Davita Magan Management Inc* ***(P-19781)***
M M Direct Marketing Inc..............C.......714 265-4100
14271 Corporate Dr Garden Grove (92843) ***(P-17133)***
M M Fab Inc..............D.......310 763-3800
2300 E Gladwick St Compton (90220) ***(P-14306)***
M M P, Long Beach *Also called Maruhide Marine Products Inc* ***(P-14573)***
M M S, Claremont *Also called Micro Matrix Systems* ***(P-7166)***
M M S Trading Inc..............F.......323 587-1082
5390 Rickenbacker Rd Bell (90201) ***(P-14950)***
M N M Manufacturing Inc..............D.......310 898-1099
3019 E Harcourt St Compton (90221) ***(P-6708)***
M Nexon Inc..............D.......213 858-5930
222 N Pacific Coast Hwy # 300 El Segundo (90245) ***(P-17908)***
M O Dion & Sons Inc (PA)..............D.......**562 432-3946**
1543 W 16th St Long Beach (90813) ***(P-14805)***
M O M G Orthopedics, Pico Rivera *Also called Montebello Orthpd Med Group* ***(P-19989)***
M P C Industrial Products Inc..............E.......949 863-0106
2150 Mcgaw Ave Irvine (92614) ***(P-7279)***
M P C Industries, Irvine *Also called M P C Industrial Products Inc* ***(P-7279)***
M P M Building Services Inc..............E.......818 708-9676
7011 Hayvenhurst Ave F Van Nuys (91406) ***(P-4970)***
M P Vacuum Truck Service, Bakersfield *Also called MP Environmental Svcs Inc* ***(P-12961)***
M S E, Sylmar *Also called Matthews Studio Equipment Inc* ***(P-11283)***
M S E Media Solutions, Commerce *Also called MSE Media Solutions Inc* ***(P-9837)***
M S I, South El Monte *Also called Manufacturers Service Inc* ***(P-13913)***
M S International Inc (PA)..............B.......**714 685-7500**
2095 N Batavia St Orange (92865) ***(P-13307)***
M T C, El Monte *Also called Mutual Trading Co Inc* ***(P-14712)***
M T C, City of Industry *Also called Micro-Technology Concepts Inc* ***(P-13415)***
M T D, Santa Barbara *Also called Santa Barbara Metro Trnst Dst* ***(P-11839)***
M T S, Bakersfield *Also called MTS Stimulation Services Inc* ***(P-521)***
M W Sausse & Co Inc (PA)..............D.......**661 257-3311**
28744 Witherspoon Pkwy Valencia (91355) ***(P-8959)***
M Wave Design Corporation..............F.......805 499-8825
82 W Cochran St Ste B Simi Valley (93065) ***(P-13749)***
M Z T, Santa Ana *Also called Macro-Z-Technology Company* ***(P-898)***
M&C Hotel Interests Inc..............C.......310 399-9344
530 Pico Blvd Santa Monica (90405) ***(P-16549)***
M-5 Steel Mfg Inc (PA)..............E.......**323 263-9383**
11778 San Marino St Ste A Rancho Cucamonga (91730) ***(P-6866)***
M-7 Consolidation Inc..............C.......310 898-3456
475 W Apra St Compton (90220) ***(P-12480)***

ALPHABETIC

Employee Codes: A=Over 500 employees, B=251-500
C=101-250, D=51-100, E=20-50 F=10-19
2022 Southern California Business
Directory and Buyers Guide
© Mergent Inc. 1-800-342-5647
1195

M-I LLC....E....661 321-5400
4400 Fanucchi Way Shafter (93263) *(P-515)*
M-Industrial Enterprises....E....949 413-7513
11 Via Onagro Rcho STA Marg (92688) *(P-8671)*
M-N-Z Janitorial Services Inc....C....323 851-4115
2109 W Burbank Blvd Burbank (91506) *(P-17258)*
M29 Technology and Design....F....805 489-9402
133 Bridge St Ste B Arroyo Grande (93420) *(P-17909)*
M6 Dev LLC....E....714 533-2101
1801 S Harbor Blvd Anaheim (92802) *(P-16550)*
M8 Dev LLC....D....714 782-7500
640 W Katella Ave Anaheim (92802) *(P-16551)*
M86 Americas Inc (HQ)....D....714 282-6111
8845 Irvine Center Dr # 101 Irvine (92618) *(P-13412)*
Maas-Hansen Steel, Westminster *Also called Neighborhood Steel LLC (P-13579)*
Mabel Baas Inc....E....805 520-8075
3960 Royal Ave Simi Valley (93063) *(P-7385)*
Mac M McCully Co, Moorpark *Also called Mc Cully Mac M Corporation (P-8923)*
Mac Performance Exhaust, Temecula *Also called MAC Products Inc (P-6205)*
MAC Products Inc....E....951 296-3077
43214 Black Deer Loop # 113 Temecula (92590) *(P-6205)*
Macdonald Carbide Co....E....626 960-4034
525 S Prospero Dr West Covina (91791) *(P-7814)*
Macerich Company (PA)....D....310 394-6000
401 Wilshire Blvd Ste 700 Santa Monica (90401) *(P-16239)*
Macgregor Yacht Corporation....E....310 621-2206
1631 Placentia Ave Costa Mesa (92627) *(P-10467)*
Machine Building Spc Inc....E....323 666-8289
1977 Blake Ave Los Angeles (90039) *(P-7943)*
Machine Precision Components....F....562 404-0500
14014 Dinard Ave Santa Fe Springs (90670) *(P-8672)*
Machine Tools Supply, Tustin *Also called Mt Supply Inc (P-14006)*
Machinehome Inc....E....858 336-9471
8960 Toronto Ave Rancho Cucamonga (91730) *(P-13143)*
Machining Time Savers Inc....D....714 635-7373
1338 S State College Pkwy Anaheim (92806) *(P-13912)*
Mackenzie Laboratories Inc....E....909 394-9007
1163 Nicole Ct Glendora (91740) *(P-9534)*
Mackie International Inc (PA)....E....951 346-0530
4193 Flat Rock Dr Ste 200 Riverside (92505) *(P-1820)*
Macom Technology Solutions Inc....F....310 320-6160
4000 Macarthur Blvd # 101 Newport Beach (92660) *(P-9288)*
Macpherson Oil Company LLC....E....661 556-6096
24118 Round Mountain Rd Bakersfield (93308) *(P-456)*
Macro Air Technologies, San Bernardino *Also called Macroair Technologies Inc (P-8050)*
Macro-Pro Inc (PA)....C....562 595-0900
2400 Grand Ave Long Beach (90815) *(P-18584)*
Macro-Z-Technology Company (PA)....D....714 564-1130
841 E Washington Ave Santa Ana (92701) *(P-898)*
Macroair Technologies Inc (PA)....E....909 890-2270
794 S Allen St San Bernardino (92408) *(P-8050)*
Macs Lift Gate Inc (PA)....E....562 529-3465
2801 E South St Long Beach (90805) *(P-11710)*
Mactech Magazine, Westlake Village *Also called Xplain Corporation (P-4115)*
Mad Dogg Athletics Inc (PA)....D....310 823-7008
2111 Narcissus Ct Venice (90291) *(P-14396)*
Madaco Safety Products Inc....F....909 614-1756
1313 N Grand Ave 249 Walnut (91789) *(P-14168)*
Madaluxe Eyewear, Seal Beach *Also called Madaluxe Group LLC (P-14397)*
Madaluxe Group LLC (PA)....E....562 296-1055
1760 Apollo Ct Seal Beach (90740) *(P-14397)*
Madden Corporation....D....714 922-1670
733 W Taft Ave Orange (92865) *(P-11980)*
Mader News Inc....D....818 551-5000
913 Ruberta Ave Glendale (91201) *(P-14875)*
Madisn/Grham Clor Graphics Inc....B....323 261-7171
150 N Myers St Los Angeles (90033) *(P-4363)*
Madison Inc of Oklahoma....D....918 224-6990
18000 Studebaker Rd Cerritos (90703) *(P-6631)*
Madison Club Owners Assn....C....760 777-9320
53035 Meriwether Way La Quinta (92253) *(P-19498)*
Madison Club, The, La Quinta *Also called Madison Club Owners Assn (P-19498)*
Madison Creek Partners LLC (PA)....D....949 449-2500
26522 La Alameda Ste 300 Mission Viejo (92691) *(P-20411)*
Madison Industries (HQ)....E....323 583-4061
18000 Studebaker Rd # 305 Cerritos (90703) *(P-7001)*
Madison Radiology Med Group....D....626 793-8189
65 N Madison Ave Ste M250 Pasadena (91101) *(P-19970)*
Madn Aircraft Hinge....E....661 257-3430
26911 Ruether Ave Ste Q Santa Clarita (91351) *(P-10195)*
Madonna Inn Inc....C....805 543-3000
100 Madonna Rd San Luis Obispo (93405) *(P-19459)*
Madrid Pro Designs Inc....F....714 897-5656
5271 Business Dr Huntington Beach (92649) *(P-14084)*
Madrona Carwash Inc (PA)....E....310 373-9736
3405 Sepulveda Blvd Torrance (90505) *(P-18915)*
Madsen Products Incorporated....F....714 894-1816
15321 Connector Ln Huntington Beach (92649) *(P-8673)*
Maesa Home, Los Angeles *Also called Latitudes Intl Fragrance Inc (P-14946)*
Maf Industries Inc (HQ)....D....559 897-2905
36470 Highway 99 Traver (93673) *(P-8074)*
Mafab Inc (PA)....D....714 893-0551
1925 Century Park E # 650 Los Angeles (90067) *(P-16104)*
Mag Aerospace Industries LLC....B....801 400-7944
1500 Glenn Curtiss St Carson (90746) *(P-6548)*
Mag Aerospace Industries, Inc., Carson *Also called Mag Aerospace Industries LLC (P-6548)*
Mag Instrument Inc (PA)....A....909 947-1006
2001 S Hellman Ave Ontario (91761) *(P-9140)*

Magco Drilling Inc....C....626 969-1000
1391 Manchester Rd San Dimas (91773) *(P-1562)*
Magensa LLC....F....562 546-6689
1710 Apollo Ct Seal Beach (90740) *(P-8315)*
Maggz Adult Buddy Care LLC....E....818 396-3338
5850 Canoga Ave Woodland Hills (91367) *(P-23058)*
Magic Acquisition Corp....B....661 382-4700
23920 Creekside Rd Valencia (91355) *(P-18852)*
Magic Castles Inc....D....323 851-3313
7001 Franklin Ave Los Angeles (90028) *(P-19584)*
Magic Gumball International....F....818 716-1888
9310 Mason Ave Chatsworth (91311) *(P-2094)*
Magic International, Santa Monica *Also called Mens Apparel Guild In Cal Inc (P-22252)*
Magic Jump Inc....E....818 847-1313
9165 Glenoaks Blvd Sun Valley (91352) *(P-17361)*
Magic Plastics Inc (PA)....D....800 369-0303
25215 Avenue Stanford Santa Clarita (91355) *(P-5702)*
Magic Ram Inc....F....213 380-5555
3540 Wilshire Blvd # 716 Los Angeles (90010) *(P-8278)*
Magic Software Enterprises Inc....E....949 250-1718
24422 Avnida De La Crlota Carlota Laguna Hills (92653) *(P-17910)*
Magic Workforce Solutions LLC....A....310 246-6153
9100 Wilsh Blvd Ste 700e Beverly Hills (90212) *(P-23381)*
Magicall Inc....F....805 484-4300
4550 Calle Alto Camarillo (93012) *(P-8922)*
Magma Consulting Group LLC....D....415 315-9364
830 Traction Ave 3a Los Angeles (90013) *(P-18200)*
Magma Products LLC....D....562 627-0500
3940 Pixie Ave Lakewood (90712) *(P-8992)*
Magmalabs, Los Angeles *Also called Magma Consulting Group LLC (P-18200)*
Magna Tool Inc....E....714 826-2500
5594 Market Pl Cypress (90630) *(P-8674)*
Magna-Pole Products Inc (PA)....F....310 453-3806
1904 14th St Ste 107 Santa Monica (90404) *(P-3688)*
Magnasync-Moviola, Burbank *Also called Magnasync/Moviola Corporation (P-9182)*
Magnasync/Moviola Corporation....E....818 845-8066
1400 W Burbank Blvd Burbank (91506) *(P-9182)*
Magnell Associate Inc....E....626 271-1320
17708 Rowland St City of Industry (91748) *(P-8164)*
Magnell Associate Inc (HQ)....C....626 271-9700
17560 Rowland St City of Industry (91748) *(P-13413)*
Magnesium Alloy Pdts Co Inc....E....310 605-1440
2420 N Alameda St Compton (90222) *(P-6366)*
Magnesium Alloy Products Co LP....E....323 636-2276
2420 N Alameda St Compton (90222) *(P-6367)*
Magnesium International Inc (PA)....F....808 741-9712
2798 Redwing Cir Costa Mesa (92626) *(P-6334)*
Magnet Sales & Mfg Co Inc (HQ)....D....310 391-7213
11250 Playa Ct Culver City (90230) *(P-5999)*
Magnetech Industrial Svcs Inc....E....559 651-0606
7515 W Sunnyview Ave Visalia (93291) *(P-19014)*
Magnetic Component Engrg Inc (PA)....D....310 784-3100
2830 Lomita Blvd Torrance (90505) *(P-7563)*
Magnetic Design Labs Inc....F....714 558-3355
1636 E Edinger Ave Ste H Santa Ana (92705) *(P-9744)*
Magnetic Metals Corporation....C....714 828-4625
2475 W La Palma Ave Anaheim (92801) *(P-7759)*
Magnetic Sensors Corporation....E....714 630-8380
1365 N Mccan St Anaheim (92806) *(P-9745)*
Magnetics Test Lab Inc....F....951 270-0215
23167 Temescal Canyon Rd Corona (92883) *(P-13642)*
Magnetika Inc (PA)....D....310 527-8100
2041 W 139th St Gardena (90249) *(P-13643)*
Magnetron Power Inventions Inc....E....310 462-6970
2226 W 232nd St Torrance (90501) *(P-457)*
Magnite Inc (PA)....C....310 207-0272
6080 Center Dr Ste 400 Los Angeles (90045) *(P-17031)*
Magnolia Convalescent Hospital, Riverside *Also called Magnolia Rhblttion Nursing Ctr (P-20609)*
Magnolia Eductl RES Foundation (PA)....C....714 892-5066
250 E 1st St Ste 1500 Los Angeles (90012) *(P-22202)*
Magnolia Grdns Convalescent HM, Granada Hills *Also called Longwood Management Corp (P-20405)*
Magnolia Rhblttion Nursing Ctr....C....951 688-4321
8133 Magnolia Ave Riverside (92504) *(P-20609)*
Magnolia Science Academy, Los Angeles *Also called Magnolia Eductl RES Foundation (P-22202)*
Magnotek Manufacturing Inc....E....951 653-8461
6510 Box Springs Blvd Riverside (92507) *(P-9632)*
Magnum Abrasives Inc....E....909 890-1100
758 S Allen St San Bernardino (92408) *(P-6154)*
Magnus Caster-Pro, Irvine *Also called Monroe Magnus LLC (P-13812)*
Magnuson Products LLC....E....805 642-8833
1990 Knoll Dr Ste A Ventura (93003) *(P-10097)*
Magnuson Superchargers, Ventura *Also called Magnuson Products LLC (P-10097)*
Magor Mold LLC....D....909 592-3663
420 S Lone Hill Ave San Dimas (91773) *(P-7815)*
Magparts (HQ)....C....626 334-7897
1545 W Roosevelt St Azusa (91702) *(P-6399)*
Magtech & Power Conversion Inc....E....714 451-0106
1146 E Ash Ave Fullerton (92831) *(P-9633)*
Magtek Inc (PA)....C....562 546-6400
1710 Apollo Ct Seal Beach (90740) *(P-8279)*
Mahar Manufacturing Corp (PA)....E....323 581-9988
2834 E 46th St Vernon (90058) *(P-11361)*
Mahavaipulya Buddhist Assn....E....714 220-0028
8781 Knott Ave Buena Park (90620) *(P-18585)*
Mahavir Hospitality LLC....D....760 352-5152
1455 Ocotillo Dr El Centro (92243) *(P-16552)*

Mergent e-mail: customerrelations@mergent.com
1196
2022 Southern California Business Directory and Buyers Guide
(P-0000) Products & Services Section entry number
(PA)=Parent Co (HQ)=Headquarters (DH)=Div Headquarters

ALPHABETIC SECTION
Maple Dairy LP

Mahmood Izadi Inc F 310 325-0463
3115 Lomita Blvd Torrance (90505) *(P-8129)*
Maidenform LLC C 323 724-9558
100 Citadel Dr Ste 323 Commerce (90040) *(P-3017)*
Mail Handling Group Inc C 952 975-5000
2840 Madonna Dr Fullerton (92835) *(P-4364)*
Mail Handling Services, Fullerton *Also called Mail Handling Group Inc (P-4364)*
Mailing Pros Inc F 714 892-7251
5261 Business Dr Huntington Beach (92649) *(P-3761)*
Maimone Liquidating Corp (PA) **D 626 286-5691**
1390 E Palm St Altadena (91001) *(P-18795)*
Main Electric Supply Co LLC (PA) **D 949 833-3052**
3600 W Segerstrom Ave Santa Ana (92704) *(P-13644)*
Main Electric Supply Co LLC E 323 753-5131
8146 Byron Rd Whittier (90606) *(P-13645)*
Main Electric Supply Co LLC E 805 654-8600
1700 Morse Ave Ventura (93003) *(P-13646)*
Main Street Banner, Carpinteria *Also called Dsy Educational Corporation (P-3194)*
Main Street Fibers Inc D 909 986-6310
608 E Main St Ontario (91761) *(P-12957)*
Main Street Management LLC (PA) **D 310 640-3100**
2015 Manhattan Beach Blvd # 1 Redondo Beach (90278) *(P-15919)*
Main Street Specialty Surgery D 714 704-1900
280 S Mn St Ste 100 Orange (92868) *(P-20855)*
Mainfreight Inc (HQ) **D 310 900-1974**
1400 Glenn Curtiss St Carson (90746) *(P-12481)*
Mainline Sales Inc (PA) **D 714 300-0641**
659 E Ball Rd Anaheim (92805) *(P-23266)*
Mainstreet Communications Inc (PA) **F 951 682-2005**
4093 Market St Riverside (92501) *(P-17152)*
Maintainance Department, Artesia *Also called A B C Unified School District (P-17208)*
Maintech Incorporated C 714 921-8000
2401 N Glassell St Orange (92865) *(P-17656)*
Maintech Resources Inc E 562 804-0664
9112 Rose St Bellflower (90706) *(P-1624)*
Maintenance Department, Garden Grove *Also called Garden Grove Unified Schl Dst (P-17245)*
Maintenance Dept., La Canada *Also called La Canada Unified School Dst (P-11944)*
Maintnc/Pration/Transportation, Rialto *Also called Rialto Unified School District (P-23101)*
Majestic Garlic Inc F 951 677-0555
2222 Foothill Blvd Ste E La Canada (91011) *(P-1891)*
Majestic Industry Hills LLC A 626 810-4455
1 Industry Hills Pkwy City of Industry (91744) *(P-16553)*
Majestic Print Inc F 951 509-2539
4017 Trail Creek Rd Riverside (92505) *(P-4365)*
Majestic Printing Systems, Riverside *Also called Majestic Print Inc (P-4365)*
Major Fulfillment LLC F 310 204-1874
13707 S Figueroa St Los Angeles (90061) *(P-4366)*
Makabi 26 Inc F 323 588-7666
2850 E 44th St Vernon (90058) *(P-5703)*
Makallon La Jolla Properties, Newport Beach *Also called Makar Properties LLC (P-16060)*
Makar Anaheim LLC A 714 740-4431
777 W Convention Way Anaheim (92802) *(P-16554)*
Makar Properties LLC (PA) **A 949 255-1100**
4100 Macarthur Blvd # 150 Newport Beach (92660) *(P-16060)*
Maker Studios Inc (HQ) **C 310 606-2182**
3515 Eastham Dr Culver City (90232) *(P-19369)*
Makita USA Inc (HQ) **C 714 522-8088**
14930 Northam St La Mirada (90638) *(P-13811)*
Mako Inc F 323 262-2168
736 Monterey Pass Rd Monterey Park (91754) *(P-2617)*
Mako Industries SC Inc E 714 632-1400
1280 N Red Gum St Anaheim (92806) *(P-10800)*
Malaga Financial Corporation (PA) **D 310 375-9000**
2514 Via Tejon Palos Verdes Estates (90274) *(P-15055)*
Malakan Inc (PA) **E 310 910-9270**
412 1/2 S Central Ave Glendale (91204) *(P-3352)*
Malanis Inc F 562 924-7274
18307 Pioneer Blvd Artesia (90701) *(P-14133)*
Malbon Golf LLC E 323 433-4028
13101 W Wash Blvd Ste 426 Los Angeles (90066) *(P-11435)*
Malcolm & Cisneros A Law Corp C 949 252-1039
2112 Business Center Dr # 100 Irvine (92612) *(P-21620)*
Malcolm Cisneros, Irvine *Also called Malcolm & Cisneros A Law Corp (P-21620)*
Malcolm Demille Inc F 805 929-4353
650 S Frontage Rd Nipomo (93444) *(P-11324)*
Malcolm Smith Motorcycles Inc D 951 687-1300
7599 Indiana Ave Riverside (92504) *(P-16854)*
Malibu Castle, Aliso Viejo *Also called Apex Parks Group LLC (P-19633)*
Malibu Castle E 210 341-6663
27061 Aliso Creek Rd # 100 Aliso Viejo (92656) *(P-19519)*
Malibu Ceramic Works F 310 455-2485
903 Fairbanks Ave Long Beach (90813) *(P-5989)*
Malibu Conference Center Inc B 818 889-6440
327 Latigo Canyon Rd Malibu (90265) *(P-15677)*
Malibu Design Group E 323 271-1700
1748 Camino Lindo South Pasadena (91030) *(P-14398)*
Malibu Kitchen, Malibu *Also called Marys Country Kitchen (P-2079)*
Malibu Leather Inc C 310 985-0707
510 W 6th St Ste 1002 Los Angeles (90014) *(P-5910)*
Malibu Limousine Service, Marina Del Rey *Also called Executive Network Entps Inc (P-11864)*
Malibu Times Inc E 310 456-5507
3864 Las Flores Canyon Rd Malibu (90265) *(P-4007)*
Mallcraft Inc D 626 765-9100
2225 Windsor Ave Altadena (91001) *(P-785)*
Maloof Naman Builders Inc D 818 775-0040
9614 Cozycroft Ave Chatsworth (91311) *(P-13864)*
Mamba Logistics Inc D 661 234-8050
23749 Fitzgerald St West Hills (91304) *(P-11981)*
Mamco Inc (PA) **C 951 776-9300**
764 Ramona Expy Ste C Perris (92571) *(P-899)*
Mammography Center, Lompoc *Also called Lompoc Valley Medical Center (P-20843)*
Mammoth Media Inc D 832 315-0833
1447 2nd St Santa Monica (90401) *(P-4008)*
Mammoth Water, Montebello *Also called Unix Packaging LLC (P-2302)*
Mamolos Cntntl Bailey Bakeries C 805 496-0045
2734 Townsgate Rd Westlake Village (91361) *(P-14706)*
Managed Dental Care C 818 598-6599
6200 Canoga Ave Ste 100 Woodland Hills (91367) *(P-15444)*
Managed Dental Care California, Woodland Hills *Also called Managed Dental Care (P-15444)*
Managed Health Network C 714 934-5519
7755 Center Ave Ste 700 Huntington Beach (92647) *(P-15445)*
Management 360 D 310 272-7000
9111 Wilshire Blvd Beverly Hills (90210) *(P-19323)*
Management Applied Prgrm Inc (PA) **C 562 463-5000**
13191 Crossroads Pkwy N # 205 City of Industry (91746) *(P-18099)*
Management Success, Monrovia *Also called Leekilpatrick Management Inc (P-23259)*
Management Trust Assn Inc D 805 496-5514
100 E Thousand Oaks Blvd Thousand Oaks (91360) *(P-16187)*
Management Trust Assn Inc D 951 694-1758
4160 Temescal Canyon Rd # 202 Corona (92883) *(P-16188)*
Management Trust Assn Inc (PA) **D 714 285-2626**
15661 Red Hill Ave # 201 Tustin (92780) *(P-16189)*
Management Trust Assn Inc C 562 926-3372
12607 Hiddencreek Way R Cerritos (90703) *(P-23267)*
Management Trust, The, Tustin *Also called Management Trust Assn Inc (P-16189)*
Manatt Phelps & Phillips LLP E 714 371-2500
695 Town Center Dr # 1400 Costa Mesa (92626) *(P-21621)*
Manchster Mnor Cnvlescent Hosp D 323 753-1789
837 W Manchester Ave Los Angeles (90044) *(P-20412)*
Mandalay Baseball Properties, Los Angeles *Also called Mandalay Spt Action Entrmt LLC (P-19423)*
Mandalay Generating Station, Oxnard *Also called NRG California South LP (P-12809)*
Mandalay Spt Action Entrmt LLC (PA) **D 323 549-4300**
4751 Wilshire Blvd Fl 3 Los Angeles (90010) *(P-19423)*
Maneri Sign Co Inc E 310 327-6261
1928 W 135th St Gardena (90249) *(P-11569)*
Maneri Sign Co Inc F 310 327-6261
1100 Main St Irvine (92614) *(P-11570)*
Maney Aircraft Inc E 909 390-2500
1305 S Wanamaker Ave Ontario (91761) *(P-10371)*
Mangan Inc (PA) **D 310 835-8080**
3901 Via Oro Ave Long Beach (90810) *(P-22603)*
Manhattan Beachwear Inc D 714 892-7354
10700 Valley View St Cypress (90630) *(P-2969)*
Manhattan Beachwear LLC (PA) **D 657 384-2110**
10855 Bus Ctr Dr Ste C Cypress (90630) *(P-3043)*
Manhattan Confectioners Inc F 310 257-0260
2530 W 237th St Torrance (90505) *(P-2095)*
Manhattan Country Club, Manhattan Beach *Also called 1334 Partners LP (P-19526)*
Manhattan Stitching Co Inc E 714 521-9479
8362 Artesia Blvd Ste E Buena Park (90621) *(P-3158)*
Manhole Adjusting Inc E 323 725-1387
9500 Beverly Rd Pico Rivera (90660) *(P-900)*
Maniaci Group Inc D 310 541-4824
500 Silver Spur Rd # 121 Rllng HLS Est (90275) *(P-15590)*
Manley Laboratories Inc E 909 627-4256
13880 Magnolia Ave Chino (91710) *(P-6206)*
Mann+hmmel Wtr Fluid Sltons In (HQ) **D 805 964-8003**
93 S La Patera Ln Goleta (93117) *(P-8394)*
Manning Kass Ellrod Rmrez Trst (PA) **C 213 624-6900**
801 S Figueroa St Fl 15 Los Angeles (90017) *(P-21622)*
Mannkind Corporation (PA) **C 818 661-5000**
30930 Russell Ranch Rd Westlake Village (91362) *(P-4849)*
Manor At Santa Teresita Hosp, Duarte *Also called Santa Teresita Inc (P-20936)*
Manske Dental Corporation (PA) **D 424 354-9336**
1355 N Sierra Bonita Ave West Hollywood (90046) *(P-20187)*
Manson Construction Co D 562 983-2340
340 Golden Shore Ste 310 Long Beach (90802) *(P-1001)*
Mantels & More Corp F 323 869-9764
2909 Tanager Ave Commerce (90040) *(P-6140)*
Manti - Machine Co Inc F 714 902-1465
11782 Western Ave Ste 15 Stanton (90680) *(P-8675)*
Manufacture, Vernon *Also called D I F Group Inc (P-23012)*
Manufacturer, Paramount *Also called Z-Tronix Inc (P-9806)*
Manufacturer and Distributor, Corona *Also called Approved Aeronautics LLC (P-10274)*
Manufacturers Bank (HQ) **C 213 489-6200**
515 S Figueroa St Fl 4 Los Angeles (90071) *(P-15031)*
Manufacturers of Wood Products, Santa Barbara *Also called Architctral Mllwk Snta Barbara (P-3231)*
Manufacturers Service Inc E 323 283-1013
9715 Klingerman St South El Monte (91733) *(P-13913)*
Manufacturing, Chino *Also called Manley Laboratories Inc (P-6206)*
Manufacturing, Valencia *Also called King Henrys Inc (P-2362)*
Manufacturing/Distributrion, Long Beach *Also called Jf Fixtures & Design LLC (P-18559)*
Many LLC D 310 399-1515
17575 Pacific Coast Hwy Pacific Palisades (90272) *(P-17032)*
MAOF, Montebello *Also called Mexican Amrcn Oprtnty Fndation (P-21850)*
Mapcargo Global Logistics (PA) **D 310 297-8300**
2501 Santa Fe Ave Redondo Beach (90278) *(P-12482)*
Maple Dairy LP D 661 396-9600
15857 Bear Mountain Blvd Bakersfield (93311) *(P-134)*

ALPHABETIC

Employee Codes: A=Over 500 employees, B=251-500
C=101-250, D=51-100, E=20-50 F=10-19
2022 Southern California Business
Directory and Buyers Guide
© Mergent Inc. 1-800-342-5647
1197

Maplegrove Gluten Free Foods..........F.......909 334-7828
5010 Eucalyptus Ave Chino (91710) ***(P-2477)***
Mar Cor Purification Inc..........E.......800 633-3080
6351 Orangethorpe Ave Buena Park (90620) ***(P-8395)***
Mar Engineering Company..........E.......818 765-4805
7350 Greenbush Ave North Hollywood (91605) ***(P-8676)***
Mar Vista Resources LLC..........F.......559 992-4535
745 North Ave Corcoran (93212) ***(P-5157)***
Mar-Kell Seal, Irvine *Also called Quadion LLC* ***(P-15341)***
Maranatha Sheet Metal Inc..........D.......714 602-7764
411 N Sullivan St Santa Ana (92703) ***(P-1496)***
Marathon Industries Inc..........C.......661 286-1520
25597 Springbrook Ave Santa Clarita (91350) ***(P-13033)***
Marathon Land Inc..........C.......805 488-3585
2599 E Hueneme Rd Oxnard (93033) ***(P-84)***
Marathon Productions Inc..........F.......818 748-1100
2900 W Alameda Ave # 800 Burbank (91505) ***(P-9289)***
Marathon Truck Bodies, Santa Clarita *Also called Marathon Industries Inc* ***(P-13033)***
Maravilla Foundation (PA)..........**C.......323 721-4162**
5729 Union Pacific Ave Commerce (90022) ***(P-22457)***
Marbella Country Club..........C.......949 248-3700
30800 Golf Club Dr San Juan Capistrano (92675) ***(P-19585)***
Marbil Industries Inc..........E.......714 974-4032
2201 N Glassell St Orange (92865) ***(P-10801)***
Marbleworks, Huntington Beach *Also called Tile & Marble Design Co Inc* ***(P-1423)***
Marborg Industries (PA)..........**C.......805 963-1852**
728 E Yanonali St Santa Barbara (93103) ***(P-12958)***
Marborg Recovery LP..........C.......805 963-1852
14470 Calle Real Goleta (93117) ***(P-12959)***
Marcea Inc..........F.......213 746-5191
1742 Crenshaw Blvd Torrance (90501) ***(P-2970)***
March Products Inc..........D.......909 622-4800
4645 Troy Ct Jurupa Valley (92509) ***(P-11711)***
Marchem Solvay Group, Long Beach *Also called Solvay USA Inc* ***(P-4670)***
Marco Fine Arts Galleries Inc..........E.......310 615-1818
4860 W 147th St Hawthorne (90250) ***(P-4541)***
Marco's Auto Body, Altadena *Also called Maimone Liquidating Corp* ***(P-18795)***
Marcus & Millchap Real Estate (HQ)..........**D.......818 212-2250**
23975 Park Sorrento # 400 Calabasas (91302) ***(P-15920)***
Marcus & Millichap Inc (PA)..........**B.......818 212-2250**
23975 Park Sorrento # 400 Calabasas (91302) ***(P-15921)***
Marcus Buckingham Company LLC..........D.......323 302-9810
8350 Wilshire Blvd # 200 Beverly Hills (90211) ***(P-23268)***
Marcus Hotels Inc..........C.......818 980-8000
4222 Vineland Ave North Hollywood (91602) ***(P-16555)***
Marcus Mllchap RE Inv Svcs ATL (HQ)..........**D.......818 212-2250**
23975 Park Sorrento # 400 Calabasas (91302) ***(P-15922)***
MAREBLU NATURALS, Anaheim *Also called 180 Snacks Inc* ***(P-2109)***
Marflex, Vernon *Also called Marspring Corporation* ***(P-2692)***
Margarita Vineyards LLC..........F.......805 226-8600
679 Calf Canyon Hwy Creston (93432) ***(P-2205)***
Marge Carson Inc (PA)..........**D.......626 571-1111**
13300 Crssrads Pkwy N Ste City of Industry (91746) ***(P-3508)***
Margus Automotive Elc Exch..........F.......323 232-5281
165 E Jefferson Blvd Los Angeles (90011) ***(P-10098)***
Mariak Industries Inc..........B.......310 661-4400
575 W Manville St Rancho Dominguez (90220) ***(P-13177)***
Mariak Window Fashion, Rancho Dominguez *Also called Mariak Industries Inc* ***(P-13177)***
Marian Community Clinic..........C.......805 739-3867
117 W Bunny Ave Santa Maria (93458) ***(P-20856)***
Marian Regional Medical Center, Santa Maria *Also called Dignity Health* ***(P-20749)***
Maricopa Packers, Bakersfield *Also called Sun Pacific Maricopa* ***(P-186)***
Marie Callender Pie Shops Inc..........D.......714 963-6791
18889 Brookhurst St Fountain Valley (92708) ***(P-2018)***
Marie Callender's Pie Shops, Rancho Palos Verdes *Also called Pie Rise Ltd* ***(P-2029)***
Marie Callender's Pie Shops, Fountain Valley *Also called Marie Callender Pie Shops Inc* ***(P-2018)***
Marie Callender's Pie Shops, Azusa *Also called Pie Place* ***(P-14717)***
Marie Cllender Wholesalers Inc..........A.......951 737-6760
170 E Rincon St Corona (92879) ***(P-14528)***
Marie Edward Vineyards Inc..........E.......661 363-5038
6901 E Brundage Ln Bakersfield (93307) ***(P-7613)***
Marika LLC..........D.......323 888-7755
5553-B Bandini Blvd Bell (90201) ***(P-2971)***
Marina Care Center, Culver City *Also called D K Fortune & Associates Inc* ***(P-20577)***
Marina City Club LP A Cali..........C.......310 822-0611
4333 Admiralty Way Marina Del Rey (90292) ***(P-15739)***
MARINA DEL REY HOSPITAL, Marina Del Rey *Also called Cfhs Holdings Inc* ***(P-20712)***
Marina International Hotel, Venice *Also called Outrigger Hotels Hawaii* ***(P-16601)***
Marina Landscape Maint Inc..........B.......714 939-6600
1900 S Lewis St Anaheim (92805) ***(P-266)***
Marina Shipyard, Long Beach *Also called Indel Engineering Inc* ***(P-10466)***
Marine Holding US Corp..........A.......805 529-2000
6000 Condor Dr Moorpark (93021) ***(P-16275)***
Marine Technical Services Inc..........D.......310 549-8030
211 N Marine Ave Wilmington (90744) ***(P-18586)***
Mariner's Village, Marina Del Rey *Also called E & S Ring Management Corp* ***(P-15841)***
Marino Enterprises Inc..........E.......909 476-0343
10671 Civic Center Dr Rancho Cucamonga (91730) ***(P-10372)***
Mariposa Horticultural Entps, Irwindale *Also called Mariposa Landscapes Inc* ***(P-324)***
Mariposa Landscapes Inc (PA)..........**C.......626 960-0196**
6232 Santos Diaz St Irwindale (91702) ***(P-324)***
Maripro, Goleta *Also called L3 Technologies Inc* ***(P-22599)***
Marisa Foods LLC..........F.......562 437-7775
1401 Santa Fe Ave Long Beach (90813) ***(P-1740)***
Maritz, Torrance *Also called Inmoment Research LLC* ***(P-12406)***
Mark & Fred Enterprises..........C.......714 821-1993
645 S Beach Blvd Anaheim (92804) ***(P-20413)***
Mark 1 Mortgage Corporation (PA)..........**E.......714 752-5700**
1342 E Chapman Ave Orange (92866) ***(P-15246)***
Mark 1 Restoration Service LLC..........D.......714 283-9990
3360 E La Palma Ave Anaheim (92806) ***(P-21847)***
Mark Christopher Chevrolet Inc (PA)..........**C.......909 321-5860**
2131 E Convention Ctr Way Ontario (91764) ***(P-10099)***
Mark Christopher Hummer, Ontario *Also called Mark Christopher Chevrolet Inc* ***(P-10099)***
Mark Clemons..........C.......760 361-1531
4584 Adobe Rd Twentynine Palms (92277) ***(P-12062)***
Mark Kislinger MD Inc..........D.......626 335-2020
210 S Grand Ave Ste 106 Glendora (91741) ***(P-19971)***
Mark Land Electric Inc..........B.......818 883-5110
7876 Deering Ave Canoga Park (91304) ***(P-1279)***
Mark Optics Inc..........E.......714 545-6684
1424 E Saint Gertrude Pl Santa Ana (92705) ***(P-10846)***
Mark Roberts, Santa Ana *Also called Celmol Inc* ***(P-14919)***
Mark Sheffield Construction..........E.......661 589-8520
9105 Langley Rd Bakersfield (93312) ***(P-516)***
Mark V Products, Corona *Also called 2nd Gen Productions Inc* ***(P-4950)***
Markel Corp..........B.......818 595-0600
21600 Oxnard St Ste 900 Woodland Hills (91367) ***(P-15591)***
Market Fixtures Unlimited Inc (PA)..........**F.......562 803-5553**
13235 Woodruff Ave Downey (90242) ***(P-13853)***
Market Scan Info Systems Inc..........D.......800 658-7226
815 Camarillo Springs Rd Camarillo (93012) ***(P-17657)***
Marketwire Inc (HQ)..........**D.......310 765-3200**
100 N Pacific Coast Hwy # 32 El Segundo (90245) ***(P-18407)***
Markland Industries Inc (PA)..........**C.......714 245-2850**
1111 E Mcfadden Ave Santa Ana (92705) ***(P-10498)***
Marko Foam Products Inc (PA)..........**E.......949 417-3307**
7441 Vincent Cir Huntington Beach (92648) ***(P-5513)***
Markwins Beauty Brands, Walnut *Also called Lina Gale (usa) Inc* ***(P-14257)***
Markwins Beauty Brands Inc (PA)..........**C.......909 595-8898**
22067 Ferrero Walnut (91789) ***(P-14259)***
Markwins Beauty Products Inc..........D.......909 595-8898
22067 Ferrero City of Industry (91789) ***(P-14260)***
Markzware..........E.......949 756-5100
1805 E Dyer Rd Ste 101 Santa Ana (92705) ***(P-17911)***
Markzware Software, Santa Ana *Also called Markzware* ***(P-17911)***
Marlee Manufacturing Inc..........E.......909 390-3222
4711 E Guasti Rd Ontario (91761) ***(P-11012)***
Marleon Inc..........E.......310 679-1242
3202 W Rosecrans Ave Hawthorne (90250) ***(P-18989)***
Marlin Designs LLC..........C.......949 637-7257
1900 E Warner Ave Ste J Santa Ana (92705) ***(P-3509)***
Marlin Equity Partners LLC (PA)..........**D.......310 364-0100**
338 Pier Ave Hermosa Beach (90254) ***(P-15331)***
Marlin Operations Group Inc (PA)..........**D.......310 364-0100**
338 Pier Ave Hermosa Beach (90254) ***(P-16276)***
Marlinda Imperial Hospital, Pasadena *Also called Two Palms Nursing Center Inc* ***(P-20633)***
Marlinda Management Inc (PA)..........**C.......310 631-6122**
3351 E Imperial Hwy Lynwood (90262) ***(P-20610)***
Marlora Investments LLC..........D.......562 494-3311
3801 E Anaheim St Long Beach (90804) ***(P-20414)***
Marlora Post Accute Rhblttion, Long Beach *Also called Marlora Investments LLC* ***(P-20414)***
Marmol Rdzner An Archtctral Co..........D.......310 826-6222
12210 Nebraska Ave Los Angeles (90025) ***(P-22731)***
Marna Health Services Inc..........D.......909 882-2965
4280 Cypress Dr San Bernardino (92407) ***(P-20611)***
Marne Construction Inc..........D.......714 935-0995
749 N Poplar St Orange (92868) ***(P-1538)***
Maroney Company..........F.......818 882-2722
9016 Winnetka Ave Northridge (91324) ***(P-8677)***
Marples Gears Inc..........E.......626 570-1744
808 W Santa Anita Ave San Gabriel (91776) ***(P-8082)***
Marquez & Marquez Food PR, South Gate *Also called Marquez Marquez Inc* ***(P-2363)***
Marquez Brothers Entps Inc..........C.......626 330-3310
15480 Valley Blvd City of Industry (91746) ***(P-14475)***
Marquez Marquez Inc..........E.......562 408-0960
11821 Industrial Ave South Gate (90280) ***(P-2363)***
Marriott, Los Angeles *Also called Renaissance Hotel Operating Co* ***(P-16660)***
Marriott, Visalia *Also called Welcome Group Management LLC* ***(P-16782)***
Marriott, Newport Beach *Also called Wj Newport LLC* ***(P-16802)***
Marriott, Burbank *Also called Shc Burbank II LLC* ***(P-16703)***
Marriott, Lake Arrowhead *Also called Lake Arrwhead Rsort Oprtor Inc* ***(P-16533)***
Marriott, Santa Monica *Also called Windsor Capital Group Inc* ***(P-16794)***
Marriott, Fullerton *Also called Merritt Hospitality LLC* ***(P-16565)***
Marriott, Woodland Hills *Also called HEI Hospitality LLC* ***(P-16469)***
Marriott, Baldwin Park *Also called Ols Hotels & Resorts LLC* ***(P-16594)***
Marriott, Bakersfield *Also called Bakersfield Inn Inc* ***(P-16336)***
Marriott, Riverside *Also called Windsor Capital Group Inc* ***(P-16801)***
Marriott Burbank, Burbank *Also called AWH Burbank Hotel LLC* ***(P-16331)***
Marriott International Inc..........A.......310 641-5700
5855 W Century Blvd Los Angeles (90045) ***(P-16556)***
Marriott International Inc..........B.......949 724-3606
18000 Von Karman Ave Irvine (92612) ***(P-16557)***
Marriott International Inc..........D.......949 503-5700
31692 El Camino Real San Juan Capistrano (92675) ***(P-16558)***
Marriott International Inc..........C.......213 284-3862
900 W Olympic Blvd Los Angeles (90015) ***(P-16559)***
Marriott Rsrts Hspitality Corp..........B.......760 779-1200
1091 Pinehurst Ln Palm Desert (92260) ***(P-16560)***
Marriott Ventura Beach, Ventura *Also called Oly-Remington Ventura LLC* ***(P-16595)***
Marriotts Shadow Ridge..........C.......760 674-2600
9003 Shadow Ridge Rd Palm Desert (92211) ***(P-16561)***

Marrow Meadows, Walnut *Also called M & R Joint Venture Electrical (P-1277)*
Marrs Printing Inc.....D.....909 594-9459
860 Tucker Ln City of Industry (91789) *(P-4367)*
Mars Air Systems LLC.....D.....310 532-1555
14716 S Broadway Gardena (90248) *(P-8051)*
Mars Food Us LLC (HQ).....**B.....310 933-0670**
2001 E Cashdan St Ste 201 Rancho Dominguez (90220) *(P-2478)*
Mars Petcare Us Inc.....E.....909 887-8131
2765 Lexington Way San Bernardino (92407) *(P-1959)*
Mars Petcare Us Inc.....E.....760 261-7900
13243 Nutro Way Victorville (92395) *(P-1960)*
Mars Printing and Packaging, City of Industry *Also called Marrs Printing Inc (P-4367)*
Marsh Consulting Group.....D.....239 433-5500
2626 Summer Ranch Rd Paso Robles (93446) *(P-18587)*
Marsh Risk & Insurance Svcs.....A.....213 624-5555
633 W 5th St Ste 1200 Los Angeles (90071) *(P-15592)*
Marshall S Ezralow & Assoc, Calabasas *Also called MSE Enterprises Inc (P-15929)*
Marshall, Spector MD, San Gabriel *Also called Facey Medical Foundation (P-21426)*
Marspring Corporation (PA).....**E.....323 589-5637**
4920 S Boyle Ave Vernon (90058) *(P-2692)*
Marspring Corporation.....E.....800 522-5252
4920 S Boyle Ave Vernon (90058) *(P-3553)*
Marspring Corporation.....E.....310 484-6849
5190 S Santa Fe Ave Vernon (90058) *(P-3554)*
Martek Power, Torrance *Also called Sure Power Inc (P-9789)*
Marthas Village & Kitchen.....D.....760 347-4741
83791 Date Ave Indio (92201) *(P-21848)*
Martin AC Partners Inc.....C.....213 683-1900
444 S Flower St Ste 1200 Los Angeles (90071) *(P-22732)*
Martin Archery, Los Angeles *Also called Martin Sports Inc (P-11436)*
Martin Associates Group Inc (PA).....**D.....213 483-6490**
950 S Grand Ave Fl 4 Los Angeles (90015) *(P-22604)*
Martin Automotive Inc.....D.....909 394-9899
1959 Auto Centre Dr Glendora (91740) *(P-18853)*
Martin Bauer Inc.....F.....310 669-2100
20710 S Alameda St Long Beach (90810) *(P-2332)*
Martin Bros/Marcowall Inc (PA).....**C.....310 532-5335**
17104 S Figueroa St Gardena (90248) *(P-1385)*
Martin Chevrolet.....D.....323 772-6494
23505 Hawthorne Blvd Torrance (90505) *(P-18854)*
Martin E-Z Stick Labels.....F.....562 906-1577
12921 Sunnyside Pl Santa Fe Springs (90670) *(P-4542)*
Martin Enterprises, Highland *Also called Tj Composites Inc (P-6931)*
Martin Erattrud Co, Gardena *Also called Baxstra Inc (P-3214)*
Martin Inst For Chrstnity Cltu, Santa Barbara *Also called Westmont College (P-17760)*
Martin Integrated Systems.....D.....714 998-9100
1525 W Orange Grove Ave D Orange (92868) *(P-1386)*
Martin Lther King Jr-Los Angle.....C.....424 338-8000
1680 E 120th St Los Angeles (90059) *(P-21452)*
MARTIN LUTHER KING, JR. COMMUN, Los Angeles *Also called Martin Lther King Jr-Los Angle (P-21452)*
Martin Sports Inc (PA).....**F.....509 529-2554**
1100 Glendon Ave Ste 920 Los Angeles (90024) *(P-11436)*
Martin, John A & Associates, Los Angeles *Also called Martin Associates Group Inc (P-22604)*
Martin-Chandler Inc.....F.....323 321-5119
122 E Alondra Blvd Gardena (90248) *(P-8678)*
Martin/Brattrud Inc.....D.....323 770-4171
1224 W 132nd St Gardena (90247) *(P-3510)*
Martinez & Turek, Rialto *Also called Martinez and Turek Inc (P-8679)*
Martinez and Turek Inc.....C.....909 820-6800
300 S Cedar Ave Rialto (92376) *(P-8679)*
Martinez Steel Corporation.....C.....909 946-0686
1500 S Haven Ave Ste 150 Ontario (91761) *(P-1574)*
Martinez Steel Inc.....D.....909 946-0686
8920 Vernon Ave Ste 128 Montclair (91763) *(P-1575)*
Martins Quality Truck Body Inc.....F.....310 632-5978
1831 W El Segundo Blvd Compton (90222) *(P-9957)*
Martinsound Inc.....F.....626 281-3555
1151 W Valley Blvd Alhambra (91803) *(P-22849)*
Martinsound Recording Studios, Alhambra *Also called Martinsound Inc (P-22849)*
Marton Precision Mfg LLC.....E.....714 808-6523
1365 S Acacia Ave Fullerton (92831) *(P-10221)*
Marty's Cutting Service, Vernon *Also called Martys Cutting Inc (P-18588)*
Martys Cutting Inc.....D.....323 582-5758
2615 Fruitland Ave Vernon (90058) *(P-18588)*
Maruchan Inc (HQ).....**B.....949 789-2300**
15800 Laguna Canyon Rd Irvine (92618) *(P-2479)*
Maruhachi Ceramics America Inc.....E.....800 736-6221
1985 Sampson Ave Corona (92879) *(P-5990)*
Maruhide Marine Products Inc.....D.....562 435-6509
2145 W 17th St Long Beach (90813) *(P-14573)*
Maruichi American Corporation.....D.....562 903-8600
11529 Greenstone Ave Santa Fe Springs (90670) *(P-6250)*
Marukan Vinegar U S A Inc (HQ).....**E.....562 630-6060**
16203 Vermont Ave Paramount (90723) *(P-2480)*
Marukome USA Inc.....F.....949 863-0110
17132 Pullman St Irvine (92614) *(P-2481)*
Marvel Studios LLC (HQ).....**C.....310 727-2700**
500 S Buena Vista St Burbank (91521) *(P-16894)*
Marvell Semiconductor Inc.....C.....949 614-7700
15485 Sand Canyon Ave Irvine (92618) *(P-9535)*
Marvic Inc.....F.....818 992-0078
7945 Deering Ave Canoga Park (91304) *(P-6867)*
Marvin Engineering Co Inc (PA).....**A.....310 674-5030**
261 W Beach Ave Inglewood (90302) *(P-22605)*
Marvin Group The, Inglewood *Also called Marvin Land Systems Inc (P-9958)*
Marvin Group, The, Inglewood *Also called Marvin Engineering Co Inc (P-22605)*
Marvin Land Systems Inc.....E.....310 674-5030
261 W Beach Ave Inglewood (90302) *(P-9958)*
Marvin Test Solutions Inc.....D.....949 263-2222
1770 Kettering Irvine (92614) *(P-10764)*
Marway Power Solutions, Santa Ana *Also called Marway Power Systems Inc (P-8280)*
Marway Power Systems Inc (PA).....**E.....714 917-6200**
1721 S Grand Ave Santa Ana (92705) *(P-8280)*
Marwell Corporation.....F.....909 794-4192
1094 Wabash Ave Mentone (92359) *(P-8899)*
Mary Hlth SCK Cnvlscnt &NRsng.....D.....805 498-3644
2929 Theresa Dr Newbury Park (91320) *(P-20415)*
Marycrest Manor.....C.....310 838-2778
10664 Saint James Dr Culver City (90230) *(P-20612)*
Marys Country Kitchen.....F.....310 456-7845
3900 Cross Creek Rd Ste 3 Malibu (90265) *(P-2079)*
Maryvale.....D.....626 280-6510
7600 Graves Ave Rosemead (91770) *(P-22129)*
Maryvale Day Care Center.....C.....626 357-1514
2502 Huntington Dr Duarte (91010) *(P-22033)*
Maryvale Edcatn Fmly Rsrce Ctr, Duarte *Also called Maryvale Day Care Center (P-22033)*
MASADA HOMES, Gardena *Also called Counseling and Research Assoc (P-22096)*
Mascorro Leather Inc.....E.....323 724-6759
1303 S Gerhart Ave Commerce (90022) *(P-5913)*
Mashburn Trnsp Svcs Inc.....C.....661 763-5724
1423 Kern St Taft (93268) *(P-12063)*
Mashindustries Inc.....E.....714 736-9600
7150 Village Dr Buena Park (90621) *(P-3735)*
Masimo Americas Inc.....D.....949 297-7000
52 Discovery Irvine (92618) *(P-11013)*
Masimo Corporation.....E.....949 297-7000
9600 Jeronimo Rd Irvine (92618) *(P-11226)*
Masimo Corporation.....E.....949 297-7000
40 Parker Irvine (92618) *(P-11227)*
Masimo Corporation (PA).....**B.....949 297-7000**
52 Discovery Irvine (92618) *(P-11228)*
Masimo Semiconductor Inc.....F.....603 595-8900
52 Discovery Irvine (92618) *(P-9536)*
Mask Technology Inc.....E.....714 557-3383
2601 Oak St Santa Ana (92707) *(P-9746)*
Mason Electric Co.....B.....818 361-3366
13955 Balboa Blvd Sylmar (91342) *(P-10373)*
Masonite Entry Door Corp.....F.....951 243-2261
25100 Globe St Moreno Valley (92551) *(P-3265)*
Masonry Concepts Inc.....D.....562 802-3700
15408 Cornet St Santa Fe Springs (90670) *(P-1349)*
Mass Systems, Baldwin Park *Also called Ametek Ameron LLC (P-10675)*
Massachusetts Electric Company.....D.....909 962-6001
1925 Wright Ave Ste C La Verne (91750) *(P-23059)*
Massachusetts Mutl Lf Insur Co.....D.....323 965-6339
8383 Wilshire Blvd # 600 Beverly Hills (90211) *(P-15364)*
Massmutual, Beverly Hills *Also called Massachusetts Mutl Lf Insur Co (P-15364)*
Masten Space Systems Inc.....E.....661 824-3423
1570 Sabovich St 25 Mojave (93501) *(P-10515)*
Master & Sons Inc.....D.....661 299-9090
24922 Anza Dr Ste B Valencia (91355) *(P-17259)*
Master Arts Engraving, Anaheim *Also called Master Arts Inc (P-4633)*
Master Arts Inc.....F.....714 240-4550
3737 E Miraloma Ave Anaheim (92806) *(P-4633)*
Master Builders LLC.....A.....909 987-1758
9060 Haven Ave Rancho Cucamonga (91730) *(P-5230)*
Master Enterprises Inc.....E.....626 442-1821
2025 Lee Ave South El Monte (91733) *(P-6868)*
Master Fab Inc.....F.....951 277-4772
9210 Stellar Ct Corona (92883) *(P-6869)*
Master Machine Products, Riverside *Also called Metric Machining (P-8693)*
Master Powder Coating Inc.....E.....562 863-4135
13721 Bora Dr Santa Fe Springs (90670) *(P-5102)*
Master Research & Mfg Inc.....D.....562 483-8789
13528 Pumice St Norwalk (90650) *(P-10374)*
Master-Chef's Linen Rental, Los Angeles *Also called American Textile Maint Co (P-16844)*
Masterite Division, Los Angeles *Also called Dcx-Chol Enterprises Inc (P-9362)*
Masters In Metal Inc.....E.....805 988-1992
131 Lombard St Oxnard (93030) *(P-5996)*
Mastey De Paris Inc.....E.....661 257-4814
25413 Rye Canyon Rd Valencia (91355) *(P-5045)*
Mastroianni Family Entps Ltd.....B.....310 952-1700
10581 Garden Grove Blvd Garden Grove (92843) *(P-16965)*
Mat Cactus Mfg Co.....E.....626 969-0444
930 W 10th St Azusa (91702) *(P-2693)*
Matches Inc.....B.....760 899-1919
1700 E Araby St Ste 64 Palm Springs (92264) *(P-4734)*
Matchmaster Dyg & Finshg Inc.....F.....323 233-4281
3700 S Broadway Los Angeles (90007) *(P-2675)*
Matchmaster Dyg & Finshg Inc (PA).....**C.....323 232-2061**
3750 S Broadway Los Angeles (90007) *(P-2676)*
Matchmaster Dyg & Finshg Inc.....D.....323 232-2061
3750 Broadway Pl Los Angeles (90007) *(P-2646)*
Materals MGT At St Mary Med Ct, Apple Valley *Also called St Mary Medical Center LLC (P-20968)*
Materia Inc (PA).....**C.....626 584-8400**
60 N San Gabriel Blvd Pasadena (91107) *(P-4661)*
Material Control Inc.....D.....661 617-6033
6901 District Blvd Ste A Bakersfield (93313) *(P-7564)*
Material Handling Supply Inc (HQ).....**D.....562 921-7715**
12900 Firestone Blvd Santa Fe Springs (90670) *(P-13914)*
Material Sciences Corporation.....E.....562 699-4550
3730 Capitol Ave City of Industry (90601) *(P-6301)*
Material Supply Inc (PA).....**C.....951 801-5004**
11700 Industry Ave Fontana (92337) *(P-6870)*

ALPHABETIC

Employee Codes: A=Over 500 employees, B=251-500
C=101-250, D=51-100, E=20-50 F=10-19
2022 Southern California Business Directory and Buyers Guide
© Mergent Inc. 1-800-342-5647
1199

Matesta Corporation C 949 874-6052
5620 Knott Ave Buena Park (90621) ***(P-14399)***

Matich Corporation (PA) **D 909 382-7400**
1596 E Harry Shepard Blvd San Bernardino (92408) ***(P-901)***

Matko, San Bernardino *Also called Mkkr Inc* ***(P-7858)***

Matrix Aviation Services Inc C 310 337-3037
6171 W Century Blvd # 10 Los Angeles (90045) ***(P-12416)***

Matrix Document Imaging Inc E 626 966-9959
527 E Rowland St Ste 214 Covina (91723) ***(P-4543)***

Matrix Environmental Inc D 562 236-2704
2330 Cherry Indus Cir Long Beach (90805) ***(P-1673)***

Matrix Group International Inc D 626 960-6205
1520 W Cameron Ave West Covina (91790) ***(P-622)***

Matrix Industries Inc B 562 236-2700
2330 E Cherry Indus Cir Long Beach (90805) ***(P-1674)***

Matrix International Tex Inc E 323 582-9100
1363 S Bonnie Beach Pl Commerce (90023) ***(P-14307)***

Matrix Surfaces Inc D 714 696-5449
5449 E La Palma Ave Anaheim (92807) ***(P-1420)***

Matrix USA Inc E 714 825-0404
2730 S Main St Santa Ana (92707) ***(P-9425)***

Matsmatsmats.com, Woodland Hills *Also called Tinyinklingcom LLC* ***(P-5416)***

Matson Company F 805 643-7166
213 N Olive St Ventura (93001) ***(P-7386)***

Matson Industrial Finishing, Ventura *Also called Nyd Livet Technologies Inc* ***(P-7392)***

Matsuda House Printing Inc E 310 532-1533
1825 W 169th St Ste A Gardena (90247) ***(P-4368)***

Matsui International Co Inc (HQ) **C 310 767-7812**
1501 W 178th St Gardena (90248) ***(P-5231)***

Matsushita International Corp (PA) **D 949 498-1000**
1141 Via Callejon San Clemente (92673) ***(P-16277)***

Matt Construction Corporation (PA) **C 562 903-2277**
9814 Norwalk Blvd Ste 100 Santa Fe Springs (90670) ***(P-23269)***

Matt Gyl Decauwer, Ontario *Also called Gyl Decauwer LLP* ***(P-22788)***

Mattco Forge Inc (HQ) **E 562 634-8635**
16443 Minnesota Ave Paramount (90723) ***(P-7091)***

Mattel Inc (PA) **A 310 252-2000**
333 Continental Blvd El Segundo (90245) ***(P-11362)***

Mattel Direct Import Inc (HQ) **E 310 252-2000**
333 Continental Blvd El Segundo (90245) ***(P-11382)***

Mattel Operations Inc F 310 252-2000
333 Continental Blvd El Segundo (90245) ***(P-11383)***

Matteo LLC E 213 617-2813
1000 E Cesar E Chavez Ave Los Angeles (90033) ***(P-3107)***

Mattern Sausages Inc F 714 628-9630
1003 N Parker St Orange (92867) ***(P-1715)***

Matthew Warren Inc E 805 928-3851
901 W Mccoy Ln Santa Maria (93455) ***(P-7465)***

Matthew Warren Inc D 800 237-5225
5959 Triumph St Commerce (90040) ***(P-7466)***

Matthews Manufacturing Inc F 323 980-4373
3301 E 14th St Los Angeles (90023) ***(P-6871)***

Matthews RE Inv Svcs Inc (PA) **D 866 889-0550**
841 Apollo St Ste 150 El Segundo (90245) ***(P-15923)***

Matthews Studio Equipment Inc E 818 843-6715
15148 Bledsoe St Sylmar (91342) ***(P-11283)***

Matz Rubber Co Inc F 323 849-5170
1209 Chestnut St Burbank (91506) ***(P-5390)***

Maud Booth Family Center, North Hollywood *Also called Volunteers of Amer Los Angeles* ***(P-21919)***

Maui Toys F 330 747-4333
2951 28th St Ste 1000 Santa Monica (90405) ***(P-11437)***

Maul Mfg Inc (PA) **E 714 641-0727**
3041 S Shannon St Santa Ana (92704) ***(P-8680)***

Maurer Marine Inc F 949 645-7673
873 W 17th St Costa Mesa (92627) ***(P-10468)***

Maurice & Maurice Engrg Inc E 760 949-5151
17579 Mesa St Ste B4 Hesperia (92345) ***(P-6284)***

Maurice Carrie Winery F 951 676-1711
34225 Rancho Cal Rd Temecula (92591) ***(P-2206)***

Maurice Kraiem & Company E 213 629-0038
228 S Beverly Dr Beverly Hills (90212) ***(P-14134)***

Maury Microwave Inc C 909 987-4715
2900 Inland Empire Blvd Ontario (91764) ***(P-13750)***

Mave Enterprises Inc E 818 767-4533
11555 Cantara St Ste B-E North Hollywood (91605) ***(P-2096)***

Mavenlink Inc (PA) **C 949 336-7610**
6501 Irvine Center Dr # 25 Irvine (92618) ***(P-17658)***

Maverick Abrasives Corporation D 714 854-9531
4340 E Miraloma Ave Anaheim (92807) ***(P-6155)***

Maverick Aerospace Inc F 714 578-1700
3718 Capitol Ave City of Industry (90601) ***(P-10375)***

Maverick Aerospace LLC D 714 578-1700
3718 Capitol Ave City of Industry (90601) ***(P-10376)***

Maverick Hospitality Inc D 714 730-7717
17662 Irvine Blvd Ste 4 Tustin (92780) ***(P-16562)***

Max Group Corporation (PA) **D 626 935-0050**
17011 Green Dr City of Industry (91745) ***(P-13414)***

Max Leon Inc (PA) **D 626 797-6886**
3100 New York Dr Pasadena (91107) ***(P-2972)***

Max Q, Ontario *Also called Maximum Quality Metal Pdts Inc* ***(P-6632)***

Max Studio.com, Pasadena *Also called Max Leon Inc* ***(P-2972)***

Max/Mr Imaging Inc D 818 382-2220
17530 Ventura Blvd # 105 Encino (91316) ***(P-21076)***

Maxair Systems, Irvine *Also called Bio-Medical Devices Inc* ***(P-10946)***

Maxar Space Robotics LLC (HQ) **E 626 296-1373**
1250 Lincoln Ave Ste 100 Pasadena (91103) ***(P-22606)***

Maxar Space Robotics LLC D 626 296-1373
1250 Lincoln Ave Ste 100 Pasadena (91103) ***(P-22607)***

Maxco Supply Inc D 559 646-6700
8419 Di Giorgio Rd Lamont (93241) ***(P-14212)***

Maxgen Energy Services LLC (HQ) **D 714 908-5266**
1222 Vine St Ste 301 Paso Robles (93446) ***(P-12875)***

Maxim Healthcare Services Inc D 661 964-6350
28470 Ave Stnford Ste 250 Valencia (91355) ***(P-17498)***

Maxim Healthcare Services Inc D 805 489-2685
104 Traffic Way Ste A Arroyo Grande (93420) ***(P-17499)***

Maxim Healthcare Services Inc D 805 278-4593
500 E Esplanade Dr Oxnard (93036) ***(P-17500)***

Maxim Healthcare Services Inc C 866 465-5678
3580 Wilshire Blvd # 100 Los Angeles (90010) ***(P-21190)***

Maxim Healthcare Services Inc D 951 694-0100
1 Ridgegate Dr Ste 130 Temecula (92590) ***(P-17501)***

Maxim Healthcare Services Inc D 951 684-4148
1845 Bus Ctr Dr Ste 112 San Bernardino (92408) ***(P-17502)***

Maxim Healthcare Services Inc C 760 243-3377
560 E Hospitality Ln # 400 San Bernardino (92408) ***(P-21191)***

Maxim Healthcare Services Inc D 661 322-3039
5201 California Ave # 200 Bakersfield (93309) ***(P-17503)***

Maxim Healthcare Services Inc D 626 962-6453
801 Corporate Center Dr # 21 Pomona (91768) ***(P-17504)***

Maxim Lighting Intl Inc (PA) **C 626 956-4200**
253 Vineland Ave City of Industry (91746) ***(P-13647)***

Maxim Lighting Intl Inc E 626 956-4200
247 Vineland Ave City of Industry (91746) ***(P-9068)***

Maximum Quality Metal Pdts Inc E 909 902-5018
1017 E Acacia St Ontario (91761) ***(P-6632)***

Maxon Auto Corporation F 626 400-6464
8599 Enterprise Way Chino (91710) ***(P-3774)***

Maxon Crs LLC E 424 236-4660
5400 W Rosecrans Ave # 105 Hawthorne (90250) ***(P-10453)***

Maxon Industries Inc D 562 464-0099
11921 Slauson Ave Santa Fe Springs (90670) ***(P-10100)***

Maxon Lift Corporation C 562 464-0099
11921 Slauson Ave Santa Fe Springs (90670) ***(P-13915)***

Maxtrol Corporation E 714 245-0506
1701 E Edinger Ave Ste B6 Santa Ana (92705) ***(P-9426)***

Maxus USA, Los Angeles *Also called Essense* ***(P-23533)***

Maxwell Alarm Screen Mfg Inc E 818 773-5533
20327 Nordhoff St Chatsworth (91311) ***(P-11571)***

Maxwell Petersen Associates E 714 230-3150
412 Olive Ave Ste 208 Huntington Beach (92648) ***(P-4085)***

Maxwell Sign and Decal Div, Chatsworth *Also called Maxwell Alarm Screen Mfg Inc* ***(P-11571)***

Maxxess Systems Inc (PA) **F 714 772-1000**
22661 Old Canal Rd Yorba Linda (92887) ***(P-17912)***

Maxxon Company, City of Industry *Also called Dennison Inc* ***(P-6960)***

Maxzone Vehicle Lighting Corp (HQ) **E 909 822-3288**
15889 Slover Ave Unit A Fontana (92337) ***(P-13072)***

Maya Bkrsfeld Cinemas Oper LLC E 213 805-5333
1000 California Ave Bakersfield (93304) ***(P-19283)***

Maya Cinemas Bakersfield, Bakersfield *Also called Maya Bkrsfeld Cinemas Oper LLC* ***(P-19283)***

Maya Cinemas Delano, Delano *Also called Maya Delano Cinemas Oper LLC* ***(P-19284)***

Maya Delano Cinemas Oper LLC E 213 805-5333
401 Woollomes Ave Delano (93215) ***(P-19284)***

Maya Steels Fabrication Inc D 310 532-8830
301 E Compton Blvd Gardena (90248) ***(P-6633)***

Mayer Baking Co, Torrance *Also called Kopykake Enterprises Inc* ***(P-7159)***

Mayesh Wholesale Florist Inc (PA) **E 310 342-0980**
5401 W 104th St Los Angeles (90045) ***(P-14887)***

Mayoni Enterprises D 818 896-0026
10320 Glenoaks Blvd Pacoima (91331) ***(P-6872)***

MAYWOOD ACRES HEALTHCARE, Oxnard *Also called Milwood Healthcare Inc* ***(P-15679)***

Mazzei Injector Company LLC E 661 363-6500
500 Rooster Dr Bakersfield (93307) ***(P-8396)***

MB Coatings Inc E 714 625-2118
571 N Poplar St Ste G Orange (92868) ***(P-18589)***

MB Herzog Electric Inc C 562 531-2002
15709 Illinois Ave Paramount (90723) ***(P-1280)***

Mb2 Raceway Inc (PA) **D 818 364-8000**
13943 Balboa Blvd Sylmar (91342) ***(P-19432)***

MBC Systems, Santa Ana *Also called Medical Network Inc* ***(P-23060)***

Mbit Wireless Inc (PA) **C 949 205-4559**
4340 Von Karman Ave # 140 Newport Beach (92660) ***(P-12609)***

MBK Enterprises Inc E 818 998-1477
9959 Canoga Ave Chatsworth (91311) ***(P-11122)***

MBK Laguna, Irvine *Also called MBK Real Estate Companies* ***(P-16061)***

MBK Real Estate Companies E 949 789-8300
4 Park Plz Ste 1700 Irvine (92614) ***(P-16061)***

MBK Real Estate Ltd A Cal Ltd (HQ) **D 949 789-8300**
4 Park Plz Ste 1700 Irvine (92614) ***(P-16062)***

MBK Senior Living LLC (PA) **A 949 242-1400**
4 Park Plz Ste 1700 Irvine (92614) ***(P-15740)***

MBK Tape Solutions, Chatsworth *Also called MBK Enterprises Inc* ***(P-11122)***

Mbm, Ontario *Also called McLane Foodservice Dist Inc* ***(P-12270)***

Mbm, Irvine *Also called McLane Foodservice Dist Inc* ***(P-14529)***

Mbm Distribution, Ontario *Also called McLane Foodservice Dist Inc* ***(P-14597)***

Mc Cully Mac M Corporation E 805 529-0661
12012 Hertz Ave Moorpark (93021) ***(P-8923)***

Mc Graw Commercial Insur Svc D 714 939-9875
8185 E Kaiser Blvd Anaheim (92808) ***(P-15593)***

Mc Laughlin Engrg & Min Inc (PA) **D 951 699-7957**
27636 Ynez Rd Ste L7 Temecula (92591) ***(P-902)***

Mc Products Inc E 949 888-7100
23331 Antonio Pkwy Rcho STA Marg (92688) ***(P-5232)***

Mc Welco Products, Hesperia *Also called Mc-Kinley Welding Corp* ***(P-7164)***

ALPHABETIC SECTION | Medennium Inc

Mc William & Son Inc ....F....626 969-1821
421 S Irwindale Ave Azusa (91702) *(P-7163)*
Mc-Kinley Welding Corp ....E....760 244-8876
6730 Santa Fe Ave E Hesperia (92345) *(P-7164)*
Mc2 Sabtech Holdings Inc ....E....714 221-5000
22705 Savi Ranch Pkwy Yorba Linda (92887) *(P-8165)*
McBain Systems A Cal Ltd Prtnr ....E....805 581-6800
756 Lakefield Rd Ste G Westlake Village (91361) *(P-13535)*
McC Pipeline, Yucaipa *Also called M C C Equipment Rentals Inc (P-962)*
McCain & Mccain Inc ....F....661 322-7764
3801 Gilmore Ave Bakersfield (93308) *(P-8681)*
MCCALLUM THEATRE, Palm Desert *Also called Friends of Cultural Center Inc (P-19310)*
McCarthy Bldg Companies Inc ....B....949 851-8383
20401 Sw Birch St Ste 200 Newport Beach (92660) *(P-786)*
McCarthy Bldg Companies Inc ....D....949 851-8383
20401 Sw Birch St Ste 300 Newport Beach (92660) *(P-787)*
McCarthy Bldg Companies Inc ....D....949 851-8383
1113 S Bush St Orange (92868) *(P-788)*
McCarthy Bldg Companies Inc ....D....949 851-8383
6363 Regent St Huntington Park (90255) *(P-789)*
McCarthy Bldg Companies Inc ....D....949 851-8383
18943 Airport Way Santa Ana (92707) *(P-790)*
McCarthy Construction, Lawndale *Also called McCarthy Framing Cnstr Inc (P-791)*
McCarthy Framing Cnstr Inc ....D....310 219-3038
15133 Grevillea Ave Lawndale (90260) *(P-791)*
McConnells Fine Ice Creams LLC ....E....805 963-8813
800 Del Norte Blvd Oxnard (93030) *(P-14544)*
McCoppin Enterprises ....E....818 240-4840
6641 San Fernando Rd Glendale (91201) *(P-8682)*
McCormick Fresh Herbs LLC ....D....323 278-9750
1575 W Walnut Pkwy Compton (90220) *(P-2482)*
McCrometer Inc (HQ) ....**C....951 652-6811**
3255 W Stetson Ave Hemet (92545) *(P-10706)*
McDaniel Inc ....F....909 591-8353
10807 Monte Vista Ave Montclair (91763) *(P-6269)*
McDonald's, Reseda *Also called Valley Management Associates (P-15522)*
McDowell Craig Off Systems Inc ....D....562 921-4441
13146 Firestone Blvd Norwalk (90650) *(P-3614)*
McDowell-Craig Office Furn, Norwalk *Also called McDowell Craig Off Systems Inc (P-3614)*
McElroy Metal Mill Inc ....D....760 246-5545
17031 Koala Rd Adelanto (92301) *(P-7002)*
McGarry Mechanical Inc ....F....714 630-4600
1370 N Mccan St Anaheim (92806) *(P-1497)*
McGraw Insurance Services, Anaheim *Also called Mc Graw Commercial Insur Svc (P-15593)*
McGrever Dnlee Very Spcial Chc, Azusa *Also called Morris National Inc (P-14711)*
McGuff Pharmaceuticals Inc ....E....714 918-7277
2921 W Macarthur Blvd # 1 Santa Ana (92704) *(P-4850)*
McGuire Contracting Inc ....D....909 357-1200
16579 Slover Ave Fontana (92337) *(P-1539)*
McGuire Grinding Inc ....F....805 238-9000
2754 Concrete Ct Paso Robles (93446) *(P-8683)*
McGuire Talent Inc ....D....909 527-7006
8608 Utica Ave Ste 220 Rancho Cucamonga (91730) *(P-19324)*
McGuirewoods LLP ....E....310 315-8200
1800 Century Park E Fl 8 Los Angeles (90067) *(P-21623)*
McGuirewoods LLP ....E....213 627-2268
355 S Grand Ave Ste 4200 Los Angeles (90071) *(P-21624)*
McHael G Fortansce Physcl Thra ....C....626 446-7027
24630 Washington Ave # 200 Murrieta (92562) *(P-20226)*
McHem Inc (PA) ....**D....541 913-7892**
2425 Golden Hill Rd Paso Robles (93446) *(P-14787)*
MCI Foods Inc ....C....562 977-4000
13013 Molette St Santa Fe Springs (90670) *(P-2483)*
McIntyre Company (PA) ....**D....909 962-6322**
2817 E Cedar St Ste 200 Ontario (91761) *(P-1576)*
McK Enterprises Inc ....D....805 483-5292
910 Commercial Ave Oxnard (93030) *(P-2484)*
McKee Electric, Bakersfield *Also called Surgener Electric Inc (P-1323)*
McKeever Danlee Confectionary ....C....626 334-8964
760 N Mckeever Ave Azusa (91702) *(P-2097)*
McKenna Boiler Works Inc ....E....323 221-1171
1510 N Spring St Los Angeles (90012) *(P-19050)*
McKenna Labs Inc (PA) ....**E....714 687-6888**
1601 E Orangethorpe Ave Fullerton (92831) *(P-4851)*
McKesson Mdcl-Srgcal Mdmart In ....D....800 755-2090
2800 E Philadelphia St Ontario (91761) *(P-14261)*
McKesson Medical-Surgical Inc ....D....805 375-8800
1525 Rnch Conejo Blvd # 104 Newbury Park (91320) *(P-14262)*
McKinley Childrens Center Inc (PA) ....**C....909 599-1227**
180 Via Verde Ste 200 San Dimas (91773) *(P-22130)*
McKinley Equipment Corporation (PA) ....**E....800 770-6094**
17611 Armstrong Ave Irvine (92614) *(P-13916)*
McKool Smith Hennigan ....D....213 694-1200
300 S Grand Ave Ste 2900 Los Angeles (90071) *(P-21625)*
McL Fresh, Commerce *Also called 4 Earth Farms LLC (P-14610)*
McLane Foodservice Inc ....C....951 867-3555
14813 Meridian Pkwy Riverside (92518) *(P-14476)*
McLane Foodservice Dist Inc ....D....909 912-3700
1051 Wineville Ave # 100 Ontario (91764) *(P-14597)*
McLane Foodservice Dist Inc ....D....252 955-9547
1051 Wineville Ave # 100 Ontario (91764) *(P-12270)*
McLane Foodservice Dist Inc ....D....714 562-6893
6800 Artesia Blvd Buena Park (90620) *(P-14598)*
McLane Foodservice Dist Inc ....D....909 484-6100
3051 N Church St Rancho Cucamonga (91730) *(P-14599)*
McLane Foodservice Dist Inc ....D....714 863-0163
17872 Cartwright Rd Irvine (92614) *(P-14529)*
McLane Manufacturing Inc ....D....562 633-8158
6814 Foster Bridge Blvd Bell Gardens (90201) *(P-7628)*
McLaren Industries Inc (PA) ....**F....310 212-1333**
1515 W 190th St Ste 528 Gardena (90248) *(P-5304)*
McLellan Equipment Inc ....E....559 582-8100
13221 Crown Ave Hanford (93230) *(P-9990)*
McLellan Industries Inc ....D....650 873-8100
13221 Crown Ave Hanford (93230) *(P-9991)*
MCM Construction Inc ....C....909 875-0533
19010 Slover Ave Bloomington (92316) *(P-929)*
McMaster-Carr Supply Company ....B....562 692-5911
9630 Norwalk Blvd Santa Fe Springs (90670) *(P-14000)*
McMillin Communities Inc ....C....951 506-3303
41687 Temeku Dr Temecula (92591) *(P-19499)*
McMillin Mfg Corp ....E....323 981-8585
40 E Verdugo Ave Burbank (91502) *(P-6873)*
McMillin Wire Products, Burbank *Also called McMillin Mfg Corp (P-6873)*
McMurray Stern, Santa Fe Springs *Also called Gatehouse Msi LLC (P-1437)*
McMurtrie & Mcmurtrie Inc ....E....626 815-0177
915 W 5th St Azusa (91702) *(P-3221)*
McNeilus Truck and Mfg Inc ....E....909 370-2100
401 N Pepper Ave Colton (92324) *(P-9992)*
McNichols Company ....E....562 921-3344
14108 Arbor Pl Cerritos (90703) *(P-13577)*
McO Inc ....E....909 627-3574
13925 Benson Ave Chino (91710) *(P-10101)*
MCP Industries Inc (PA) ....**F....951 736-1881**
708 S Temescal St Ste 101 Corona (92879) *(P-5391)*
McPrint Corp ....F....714 632-9966
327 E Commercial St Pomona (91767) *(P-4369)*
McPrint Direct, Pomona *Also called McPrint Corp (P-4369)*
McStarlite, Harbor City *Also called Basmat Inc (P-6793)*
McWhirter Steel Inc ....D....661 951-8998
42211 7th St E Lancaster (93535) *(P-6634)*
MD Engineering Inc ....E....951 736-5390
1550 Consumer Cir Corona (92878) *(P-8684)*
MD Stainless Services ....E....562 904-7022
8241 Phlox St Downey (90241) *(P-7541)*
Md-Staff, Temecula *Also called Applied Statistics & MGT Inc (P-17788)*
Mdc Interior Solutions LLC ....E....800 621-4006
6900 E Washington Blvd Los Angeles (90040) *(P-3079)*
Mddr Inc ....C....714 792-1993
555 Vanguard Way Brea (92821) *(P-1100)*
Mdi East Inc (HQ) ....**D....951 509-6918**
6918 Ed Perkic St Riverside (92504) *(P-5704)*
Mds, Tarzana *Also called Universal Merchandise Inc (P-2752)*
Mds Consulting (PA) ....**D....949 251-8821**
17320 Red Hill Ave # 350 Irvine (92614) *(P-22608)*
ME & My Big Ideas LLC ....D....877 462-6241
17777 Newhope St Fountain Valley (92708) *(P-14097)*
Meade Instruments Corp ....D....949 451-1450
27 Hubble Irvine (92618) *(P-10847)*
Meadow Decor Inc ....F....909 923-2558
1477 E Cedar St Ste F Ontario (91761) *(P-3567)*
Meadows Mechanical, Gardena *Also called Meadows Sheet Metal and AC Inc (P-6874)*
Meadows Sheet Metal and AC Inc ....E....310 615-1125
333 Crown Vista Dr Gardena (90248) *(P-6874)*
Meadows, The, Culver City *Also called E & S Ring Management Corp (P-15843)*
Mearsk, San Pedro *Also called APM Terminals Pacific LLC (P-12424)*
Meat Packers Butchers Sup Inc ....F....323 268-8514
2820 E Washington Blvd Los Angeles (90023) *(P-7944)*
Meathead Movers Inc (PA) ....**D....805 544-6328**
3600 S Higuera St San Luis Obispo (93401) *(P-12064)*
Mec-CCC S All N One ....E....909 529-0013
13800 Prkcnter Ln Apt 304 Tustin (92782) *(P-517)*
Mechanical Drives and Belting, Los Angeles *Also called Los Angeles Rubber Company (P-13999)*
Mechanical Industries Inc ....E....661 634-9477
314 Yampa St Bakersfield (93307) *(P-1577)*
Mechanix Wear LLC (PA) ....**C....800 222-4296**
28525 Witherspoon Pkwy Valencia (91355) *(P-3049)*
Mechanized Enterprises Inc ....F....714 630-5512
1140 N Kraemer Blvd Ste M Anaheim (92806) *(P-8685)*
Mechanized Science Seals Inc ....E....714 898-5602
5322 Mcfadden Ave Huntington Beach (92649) *(P-10897)*
Meco-Nag Corporation ....F....818 764-2020
7306 Laurel Canyon Blvd North Hollywood (91605) *(P-5881)*
Med Focus/California Radiology, Santa Monica *Also called Stephen B Meisel MD A Med Corp (P-20098)*
Med-Legal LLC (PA) ....**C....626 653-5160**
955 Overland Ct Ste 200 San Dimas (91773) *(P-21626)*
Med-Life Ambulance Services ....D....818 242-1785
4304 Alger St Los Angeles (90039) *(P-11878)*
Med-Pharmex Inc ....C....909 593-7875
2727 Thompson Creek Rd Pomona (91767) *(P-4852)*
Medasend Biomedical Inc (PA) ....**C....800 200-3581**
1402 Daisy Ave Long Beach (90813) *(P-21453)*
Medata Inc (PA) ....**D....714 918-1310**
5 Peters Canyon Rd # 250 Irvine (92606) *(P-17913)*
Medcor Group Inc ....D....714 221-8511
725 W Twn Cntry Rd # 300 Orange (92868) *(P-22805)*
Medcor Revenue Services, Orange *Also called Medcor Group Inc (P-22805)*
Mededge Inc ....F....310 745-2290
11965 Venice Blvd Ste 407 Los Angeles (90066) *(P-11014)*
Medegen LLC (HQ) ....**E....909 390-9080**
4501 E Wall St Ontario (91761) *(P-5705)*
Medeia Inc ....F....800 433-4609
7 W Figueroa St Ste 215 Santa Barbara (93101) *(P-11015)*
Medennium Inc (PA) ....**E....949 789-9000**
9 Parker Ste 150 Irvine (92618) *(P-11255)*

ALPHABETIC

Employee Codes: A=Over 500 employees, B=251-500
C=101-250, D=51-100, E=20-50 F=10-19
2022 Southern California Business
Directory and Buyers Guide
© Mergent Inc. 1-800-342-5647
1201

Medgear, Cerritos *Also called LA Triumph Inc* (P-2784)
Media Arts Lab, Santa Monica *Also called Tbwa Worldwide Inc* (P-17060)
Media Blast & Abrasive Inc ....F......714 257-0484
 591 Apollo St Brea (92821) (P-8397)
Media Gobbler Inc ....E......323 203-3222
 6427 W Sunset Blvd Los Angeles (90028) (P-17914)
Media King Inc ....E......626 288-4558
 140 W Valley Blvd 201a San Gabriel (91776) (P-9891)
Media Services, Los Angeles *Also called Oberman Tivoli & Pickert Inc* (P-18056)
Media Temple Inc ....C......877 578-4000
 12655 W Jefferson Blvd # 40 Los Angeles (90066) (P-12653)
Mediabrands Worldwide Inc ....B......323 370-8000
 5700 Wilshire Blvd # 400 Los Angeles (90036) (P-17033)
Mediacentric Integration Inc ....D......310 325-7900
 20610 Manhattan Pl # 128 Torrance (90501) (P-18201)
Mediachase Ltd ....D......323 988-1071
 8447 Wilshire Blvd # 102 Beverly Hills (90211) (P-17659)
Medianews Group Inc ....C......661 257-5200
 24800 Ave Rockefeller Valencia (91355) (P-4009)
Mediaplex Inc (HQ) ....D......818 575-4500
 30699 Russell Ranch Rd # 2 Westlake Village (91362) (P-17034)
Mediapointe Inc ....F......805 480-3700
 3952 Camino Ranchero Camarillo (93012) (P-9183)
Mediatek USA Inc ....E......408 526-1899
 1 Ada Ste 200 Irvine (92618) (P-8166)
Medic-1 Ambulance Service Inc ....D......909 592-8840
 1305 W Arrow Hwy Ste 206 San Dimas (91773) (P-11879)
Medical Billing Services, Monrovia *Also called California Business Bureau Inc* (P-22765)
Medical Brkthrugh Mssage Chirs ....E......408 677-7702
 28577 Industry Dr Valencia (91355) (P-11712)
Medical Center, San Bernardino *Also called Far West Inc* (P-20343)
Medical Center Gift Shop ....D......714 537-7100
 12601 Garden Grove Blvd Garden Grove (92843) (P-20857)
Medical Center of Garden Grove, Garden Grove *Also called Medical Center Gift Shop* (P-20857)
Medical Chemical Corporation ....E......310 787-6800
 19250 Van Ness Ave Torrance (90501) (P-5233)
Medical Device Manufacturing, Brea *Also called Life Science Outsourcing Inc* (P-11007)
Medical Extrusion Tech Inc (PA) ....E......951 698-4346
 26608 Pierce Cir Ste A Murrieta (92562) (P-5706)
Medical Eye Services Inc ....D......714 619-4660
 345 Baker St Costa Mesa (92626) (P-15594)
Medical Genetics, Los Angeles *Also called Cedars-Sinai Medical Center* (P-20705)
Medical Group, Temple City *Also called Davita Medical Management LLC* (P-19782)
Medical Group Bverly Hills Inc ....E......310 247-4646
 250 N Robertson Blvd # 60 Beverly Hills (90211) (P-19972)
Medical Imaging Partners LLC ....D......626 446-0080
 638 W Duarte Rd Ste 2 Arcadia (91007) (P-19973)
Medical Lab Svcs Med Group Inc ....D......951 834-9020
 25470 Med Ctr Dr Ste 105 Murrieta (92562) (P-21077)
Medical Management Cons Inc (PA) ....E......310 659-3835
 8150 Beverly Blvd Los Angeles (90048) (P-17505)
Medical Network Inc ....D......949 863-0022
 1809 E Dyer Rd Ste 311 Santa Ana (92705) (P-23060)
Medical Packaging Corporation ....D......805 388-2383
 941 Avenida Acaso Camarillo (93012) (P-11123)
Medical Spc Managers Inc ....C......714 571-5000
 1 City Blvd W Ste 1100 Orange (92868) (P-23270)
Medical Specialty Billing, Orange *Also called Medical Spc Managers Inc* (P-23270)
Medical Tactile Inc ....F......310 641-8228
 5500 W Rosecrans Ave A Hawthorne (90250) (P-11016)
Medicl Imgng Ctr of Southrn CA ....D......310 829-9788
 2811 Wilshire Blvd # 100 Santa Monica (90403) (P-19974)
Medico Professional Linen Svc, Los Angeles *Also called American Textile Maint Co* (P-16840)
Medicool Inc ....F......310 782-2200
 20460 Gramercy Pl Torrance (90501) (P-11017)
Medicrest of California 1 ....D......909 626-1294
 5119 Bandera St Montclair (91763) (P-20416)
Mediland Corporation ....D......562 630-9696
 7027 Motz St Paramount (90723) (P-5920)
Medina Concrete Construction ....E......909 474-9640
 2368 W 1st Ave San Bernardino (92407) (P-1540)
Medina Construction, Riverside *Also called Bens Asphalt & Maint Co Inc* (P-863)
Mediscan Diagnostic Svcs LLC ....D......818 758-4224
 21050 Califa St Ste 100 Woodland Hills (91367) (P-17438)
Mediscan Staffing Services, Woodland Hills *Also called Mediscan Diagnostic Svcs LLC* (P-17438)
Meditech Health Services Inc (PA) ....B......800 538-0900
 1650 Palma Dr Ste 101 Ventura (93003) (P-21454)
Mediterraneotaste Inc (PA) ....E......714 395-6755
 3400 Irvine Ave Newport Beach (92660) (P-1854)
Medium Large LLC ....F......424 271-9411
 13217 Jamboree Rd Tustin (92782) (P-19147)
Medivision Inc ....F......714 563-2772
 4883 E La Palma Ave # 503 Anaheim (92807) (P-11229)
Medivision Optics, Anaheim *Also called Medivision Inc* (P-11229)
Medley Communications Inc (PA) ....C......951 245-5200
 43015 Black Deer Loop Temecula (92590) (P-1281)
Medlin & Sons, Whittier *Also called Medlin and Son Engrg Svc Inc* (P-8686)
Medlin and Son Engrg Svc Inc ....E......562 464-5889
 12484 Whittier Blvd Whittier (90602) (P-8686)
Medlin Development ....E......909 825-5296
 320 Tropicana Ranch Rd Colton (92324) (P-325)
Medlin Ramps ....E......877 463-3546
 14903 Marquardt Ave Santa Fe Springs (90670) (P-7760)
Medline Industries Inc ....E......909 799-8983
 1455 Research Dr Redlands (92374) (P-13499)

Medmen, Culver City *Also called Mme Florida LLC* (P-18599)
Medpoint Management ....E......818 702-0100
 6400 Canoga Ave Ste 163 Woodland Hills (91367) (P-19975)
Medrano Raymundo ....F......909 947-5507
 1752 S Bon View Ave Ontario (91761) (P-2703)
Medresponse (PA) ....C......818 442-9222
 7040 Hayvenhurst Ave Van Nuys (91406) (P-11880)
Medsco Fabrication & Dist Inc ....D......323 263-0511
 958 N Eastern Ave Los Angeles (90063) (P-6635)
Medstop Medical, North Hollywood *Also called Morigon Technologies LLC* (P-13502)
Medterra Cbd LLC ....D......800 971-1288
 9805 Research Dr Irvine (92618) (P-9)
Medtronic 3f Therapeutics Inc ....C......949 399-1675
 1851 E Deere Ave Santa Ana (92705) (P-11230)
Medtronic Ats Medical Inc ....D......949 380-9333
 1851 E Deere Ave Santa Ana (92705) (P-11018)
Medtronic Minimed Inc (HQ) ....A......800 646-4633
 18000 Devonshire St Northridge (91325) (P-11019)
Medtronic PS Medical Inc (HQ) ....C......805 571-3769
 5290 California Ave # 100 Irvine (92617) (P-11020)
Medusind Solutions Inc (PA) ....A......949 240-8895
 31103 Rancho Viejo Rd San Juan Capistrano (92675) (P-18590)
Medway Plastics Corporation ....C......562 630-1175
 2250 E Cherry Indus Cir Long Beach (90805) (P-5707)
Mee Audio, City of Industry *Also called S2e Inc* (P-9192)
Meerkat Inc ....F......909 877-0093
 434 S Yucca Ave Rialto (92376) (P-8687)
Mega Appraisers Inc ....A......818 246-7370
 14724 Ventura Blvd # 800 Sherman Oaks (91403) (P-18591)
Mega Brands America Inc (HQ) ....D......949 727-9009
 333 Continental Blvd El Segundo (90245) (P-11384)
Mega Led Technology, Commerce *Also called Mega Sign Inc* (P-11572)
Mega Machinery Inc ....E......951 300-9300
 6688 Doolittle Ave Riverside (92503) (P-7988)
Mega Plus Pcb Incorporated ....F......714 550-0265
 1479 E Warner Ave Santa Ana (92705) (P-9427)
Mega Sign Inc ....E......888 315-7446
 5900 S Eastrn Ave Ste 141 Commerce (90040) (P-11572)
Megabrand Kitchen & Bath Inc ....E......562 229-0088
 15600 Blackburn Ave Norwalk (90650) (P-13277)
Megamex Foods LLC (PA) ....D......714 385-4500
 333 S Anita Dr Ste 1000 Orange (92868) (P-14477)
Meganutra Inc ....F......949 835-2591
 17332 Irvine Blvd Ste 101 Tustin (92780) (P-1800)
Meggitt Arcft Braking Systems, Gardena *Also called Nasco Aircraft Brake Inc* (P-10386)
Meggitt Control Systems, North Hollywood *Also called Meggitt North Hollywood Inc* (P-10379)
Meggitt Ctrl Systms-Vntura Cnt, Simi Valley *Also called Meggitt Safety Systems Inc* (P-9892)
Meggitt Defense Systems Inc ....B......949 465-7700
 9801 Muirlands Blvd Irvine (92618) (P-10377)
Meggitt North Hollywood Inc ....E......818 691-6258
 10092 Foxrun Rd Santa Ana (92705) (P-10378)
Meggitt North Hollywood Inc (HQ) ....C......818 765-8160
 12838 Saticoy St North Hollywood (91605) (P-10379)
Meggitt Polymers & Composites, Simi Valley *Also called Meggitt-Usa Inc* (P-10382)
Meggitt Safety Systems Inc ....D......805 584-4100
 1785 Voyager Ave Simi Valley (93063) (P-10380)
Meggitt Safety Systems Inc (HQ) ....C......805 584-4100
 1785 Voyager Ave Simi Valley (93063) (P-9892)
Meggitt Safety Systems Inc ....C......805 584-4100
 1785 Voyager Ave Simi Valley (93063) (P-10381)
Meggitt-Usa Inc (HQ) ....B......805 526-5700
 1955 Surveyor Ave Simi Valley (93063) (P-10382)
Meggitt-Usa Services Inc ....F......805 526-5700
 1955 Surveyor Ave Simi Valley (93063) (P-10383)
Megiddo Global LLC ....E......844 477-7007
 17101 Central Ave Ste 1c Carson (90746) (P-11124)
Meguiars Inc (HQ) ....E......949 752-8000
 17991 Mitchell S Irvine (92614) (P-4971)
Meguiars Inc ....F......651 733-1110
 18001 Mitchell S Irvine (92614) (P-8398)
MEI Rigging & Crating LLC ....D......714 712-5888
 14555 Alondra Blvd La Mirada (90638) (P-7989)
Meisei Tools LLC ....F......805 497-2626
 948 Tourmaline Dr Thousand Oaks (91320) (P-6486)
Mejico Express Inc (PA) ....C......714 690-8300
 14849 Firestone Blvd Fl 1 La Mirada (90638) (P-12330)
Mekong Printing Inc ....E......714 558-9595
 2421 W 1st St Santa Ana (92703) (P-4370)
Mel Bernie and Company Inc (PA) ....C......818 841-1928
 3000 W Empire Ave Burbank (91504) (P-14135)
Melcast, Cerritos *Also called Molino Company* (P-4376)
Melco Steel Inc ....E......626 334-7875
 1100 W Foothill Blvd Azusa (91702) (P-6743)
Melfred Borzall Inc ....E......805 614-4344
 2712 Airpark Dr Santa Maria (93455) (P-7736)
Melissa Trinidad ....E......805 536-0954
 3589 Vine St Paso Robles (93446) (P-5046)
Melissas World Variety Produce, Vernon *Also called World Variety Produce Inc* (P-14668)
Melkes Machine Inc ....E......626 448-5062
 9928 Hayward Way South El Monte (91733) (P-8688)
Melko Logistic Group Corp (PA) ....D......626 363-6300
 15000 Nelson Ave City of Industry (91744) (P-12115)
Mellano & Co (PA) ....D......213 622-0796
 766 Wall St Los Angeles (90014) (P-14888)
Mellano Enterprises, Los Angeles *Also called Mellano & Co* (P-14888)
Melling Sintered Metals, Gardena *Also called Melling Tool Rush Metals LLC* (P-6459)

Mergent e-mail: customerrelations@mergent.com
1202

2022 Southern California Business
Directory and Buyers Guide

(P-0000) Products & Services Section entry number
(PA)=Parent Co (HQ)=Headquarters (DH)=Div Headquarters

ALPHABETIC SECTION Merqbiz LLC

Melling Tool Rush Metals LLC ....E....580 725-3295
16100 S Figueroa St Gardena (90248) ***(P-6459)***

Melmarc Products Inc ....C....714 549-2170
752 S Campus Ave Ontario (91761) ***(P-3159)***

Melmet Steven J Law Ofc ....D....949 263-1000
2912 Daimler St Santa Ana (92705) ***(P-21627)***

Melton Intl Tackle Inc ....E....714 978-9192
1375 S State College Blvd Anaheim (92806) ***(P-14951)***

Melville Winery LLC ....F....805 735-7030
5185 E Highway 246 Lompoc (93436) ***(P-2207)***

Membrane Switch and Panel Inc ....E....714 957-6905
3198 Arprt Loop Dr Ste K Costa Mesa (92626) ***(P-9747)***

Memco Holdings Inc ....C....310 277-0057
10390 Santa Monica Blvd # 210 Los Angeles (90025) ***(P-15924)***

Memeged Tevuot Shemesh (PA) ....**C....866 575-1211**
5550 Topanga Canyon Blvd # 280 Woodland Hills (91367) ***(P-1101)***

Memor Ortho Surgic Group A M ....D....562 424-6666
2760 Atlantic Ave Long Beach (90806) ***(P-19976)***

Memorex Products Inc ....C....562 653-2800
17777 Center Court Dr N # 80 Cerritos (90703) ***(P-13689)***

MEMORIAL CARE MEDICAL CENTERS, Fountain Valley *Also called Memorial Health Services* ***(P-20858)***

MEMORIAL CENTER, Bakersfield *Also called Bakersfield Memorial Hospital* ***(P-20685)***

Memorial Health Services (PA) ....**A....714 377-2900**
17360 Brookhurst St # 160 Fountain Valley (92708) ***(P-20858)***

Memorial Healthtec Labratories ....A....714 962-4677
9920 Talbert Ave Fountain Valley (92708) ***(P-22850)***

Memorial Healthtec Labratories (HQ) ....**E....562 933-0777**
2865 Atlantic Ave Ste 203 Long Beach (90806) ***(P-20859)***

Memorial Hlth Svcs - Univ Cal (PA) ....**A....562 933-2000**
2801 Atlantic Ave Long Beach (90806) ***(P-20860)***

Memorial Hospital of Gardena, Gardena *Also called Gardena Hospital LP* ***(P-20774)***

Memorialcare Med Foundation (PA) ....**C....714 389-5353**
17360 Brookhurst St Fountain Valley (92708) ***(P-22347)***

Memorlcare Srgcal Ctr At Ornge ....D....714 369-1100
18111 Brookhurst St # 3200 Fountain Valley (92708) ***(P-20861)***

Memory Experts Intl USA Inc (HQ) ....**E....714 258-3000**
1651 E Saint Andrew Pl Santa Ana (92705) ***(P-8208)***

Men Tking Over Rfrming Soc Inc ....D....323 338-6633
6630 Crenshaw Blvd Los Angeles (90043) ***(P-21849)***

Menasha Packaging Company LLC ....D....562 698-3705
8110 Sorensen Ave Santa Fe Springs (90670) ***(P-3819)***

Menasha Packaging Company LLC ....F....909 442-0668
1686 W Base Line Rd # 200 Rialto (92376) ***(P-3820)***

Menifee Union School District (PA) ....**D....951 672-1851**
29775 Haun Rd Sun City (92586) ***(P-23061)***

Menifee Valley Hospital Center, Sun City *Also called Physicians For Healthy Hospita* ***(P-20888)***

Menke Marketing Devices, Santa Fe Springs *Also called Menke Marking Devices Inc* ***(P-13917)***

Menke Marking Devices Inc ....E....562 921-1380
10440 Pioneer Blvd Ste 4 Santa Fe Springs (90670) ***(P-13917)***

Menlo Microsystems Inc ....E....949 771-0277
49 Discovery Ste 150 Irvine (92618) ***(P-9537)***

Mens Apparel Guild In Cal Inc ....C....310 857-7500
2901 28th St Ste 100 Santa Monica (90405) ***(P-22252)***

Mental Health Dept of, Artesia *Also called County of Los Angeles* ***(P-21293)***

Mental Health Dept of, Long Beach *Also called County of Los Angeles* ***(P-19775)***

Mentor California, Bakersfield *Also called Alliance Childrens Services* ***(P-22079)***

Mentor Mdia USA Sup Chain MGT ....D....909 930-0800
865 S Washington Ave San Bernardino (92408) ***(P-23062)***

Mentor Worldwide LLC ....B....805 681-6000
5425 Hollister Ave Santa Barbara (93111) ***(P-13500)***

Mentor Worldwide LLC (HQ) ....**C....800 636-8678**
31 Technology Dr Ste 200 Irvine (92618) ***(P-11125)***

Menzies Aviation (texas) Inc ....D....909 937-3998
1049 S Vineyard Ave Ontario (91761) ***(P-12362)***

MEOW LOGISTICS, Walnut *Also called Straight Forwarding Inc* ***(P-12533)***

Mer-Mar Electronics, Hesperia *Also called Geeriraj Inc* ***(P-9410)***

Mercado Latino Inc ....E....310 537-1062
1420 W Walnut St Compton (90220) ***(P-11713)***

Mercado Latino Inc (PA) ....**D....626 333-6862**
245 Baldwin Park Blvd City of Industry (91746) ***(P-14478)***

Mercedes Benz of Bakersfield, Bakersfield *Also called Sangera Buick Inc* ***(P-18871)***

Mercedes Diaz Homes Inc ....D....562 945-4576
7239 Washington Ave # 100 Whittier (90602) ***(P-22131)***

Mercedes-Benz RE ....E....310 547-6086
4031 Via Oro Ave Long Beach (90810) ***(P-22851)***

Mercer Global Securities LLC ....D....805 565-1681
1801 E Cabrillo Blvd A Santa Barbara (93108) ***(P-15332)***

Merchant of Tennis Inc ....A....310 855-1946
1118 S La Cienega Blvd Los Angeles (90035) ***(P-18592)***

Merchant of Tennis Inc ....A....909 923-3388
1625 Proforma Ave Ontario (91761) ***(P-18593)***

Merchant Services, Irvine *Also called Universal Card Inc* ***(P-18708)***

Merchants Bank California N A ....D....310 549-4350
1 Civic Plaza Dr Ste 100 Carson (90745) ***(P-15032)***

Merchants Building Maint Co ....D....714 973-9272
1639 E Edinger Ave Ste C Santa Ana (92705) ***(P-17260)***

Merchants Building Maint Co (PA) ....**A....323 881-6701**
1190 Monterey Pass Rd Monterey Park (91754) ***(P-17261)***

Merchants Building Maint Co ....D....909 622-8260
1995 W Holt Ave Pomona (91768) ***(P-17262)***

Merchants Building Maint Co ....C....323 881-8902
606 Monterey Paca Rd 20 Monterey Park (91754) ***(P-17263)***

Merchants Landscape Services ....C....909 981-1022
8748 Industrial Ln 1 Rancho Cucamonga (91730) ***(P-267)***

Merchants Metals LLC ....E....951 686-1888
6466 Mission Blvd Riverside (92509) ***(P-6229)***

Merci Life LLC ....F....317 341-4109
321 N Pass Ave Ste 144 Burbank (91505) ***(P-4752)***

Merco Manufacturing Co, Walnut *Also called Aero Pacific Corporation* ***(P-10244)***

Mercury Air Cargo Inc (HQ) ....**C....310 258-6100**
2780 Skypark Dr Ste 300 Torrance (90505) ***(P-12363)***

Mercury Broach Company Inc ....F....626 443-5904
2546 Seaman Ave El Monte (91733) ***(P-7856)***

Mercury Casualty Company (HQ) ....**A....323 937-1060**
555 W Imperial Hwy Brea (92821) ***(P-15469)***

Mercury Engineering Corp ....E....562 861-7816
5630 Imperial Hwy South Gate (90280) ***(P-8689)***

Mercury General Corporation (PA) ....**A....323 937-1060**
4484 Wilshire Blvd Los Angeles (90010) ***(P-15470)***

Mercury Insurance Broker, Santa Monica *Also called Mercury Insurance Company* ***(P-15472)***

Mercury Insurance Company ....D....714 671-6700
555 W Imperial Hwy Brea (92821) ***(P-15471)***

Mercury Insurance Company ....B....310 451-4943
1433 Santa Monica Blvd Santa Monica (90404) ***(P-15472)***

Mercury Insurance Company ....B....714 255-5000
1700 Greenbriar Ln Brea (92821) ***(P-15473)***

Mercury Insurance Company (HQ) ....**C....323 937-1060**
4484 Wilshire Blvd Los Angeles (90010) ***(P-15474)***

Mercury Insurance Company ....B....661 291-6470
27200 Tourney Rd Ste 400 Valencia (91355) ***(P-15475)***

Mercury Insurance Services LLC ....A....323 937-1060
4484 Wilshire Blvd Los Angeles (90010) ***(P-15476)***

Mercury Magnetics Inc ....E....818 998-7791
10050 Remmet Ave Chatsworth (91311) ***(P-9634)***

Mercury Media, Los Angeles *Also called Diversfied Mrcury Cmmnctons LL* ***(P-17095)***

Mercury Metal Die & Ltr Co Inc (PA) ....**F....951 674-8717**
600 3rd St Ste A Lake Elsinore (92530) ***(P-7387)***

Mercury Plastics Inc ....D....323 264-2400
2939 E Washington Blvd Los Angeles (90023) ***(P-5433)***

Mercury Plastics Inc (HQ) ....**B....626 961-0165**
14825 Salt Lake Ave City of Industry (91746) ***(P-3886)***

Mercury Security Products LLC ....F....562 986-9105
4811 Arprt Plz Dr Ste 300 Long Beach (90815) ***(P-9893)***

Mercury Systems Inc ....C....805 388-1345
400 Del Norte Blvd Oxnard (93030) ***(P-9428)***

Mercury Systems Inc ....D....714 898-8200
10855 Bus Ctr Dr Ste A Cypress (90630) ***(P-18100)***

Mercury United Electronics Inc ....F....909 466-0427
9804 Cres Ctr Dr Ste 603 Rancho Cucamonga (91730) ***(P-9748)***

Mercury World Cargo, Torrance *Also called Mercury Air Cargo Inc* ***(P-12363)***

Mercy Hospital, Bakersfield *Also called Dean L Davis MD* ***(P-21766)***

Mercy House Living Centers ....C....714 836-7188
807 N Garfield St Santa Ana (92701) ***(P-22253)***

Mercy Hse Trnstnal Living Ctrs, Santa Ana *Also called Mercy House Living Centers* ***(P-22253)***

Meredith Baer & Associates, South Gate *Also called Meribear Productions Inc* ***(P-18594)***

Merelex Corporation ....E....310 208-0551
10884 Weyburn Ave Los Angeles (90024) ***(P-4662)***

Merex Inc ....E....805 446-2700
1283 Flynn Rd Camarillo (93012) ***(P-10765)***

Merex Group, El Segundo *Also called Kellstrom Holding Corporation* ***(P-14060)***

Merge Mobile Inc ....E....949 234-6248
1311 Calle Batido Ste 240 San Clemente (92673) ***(P-17660)***

Mergis Group, The, Irvine *Also called Randstad Professionals Us LLC* ***(P-17452)***

Meribear Productions Inc ....D....310 204-5353
4100 Ardmore Ave South Gate (90280) ***(P-18594)***

Merical LLC (PA) ....**C....714 238-7225**
2995 E Miraloma Ave Anaheim (92806) ***(P-18595)***

Meridan Sport Club LLC (PA) ....**D....818 698-2900**
12100 W Olympic Blvd Los Angeles (90064) ***(P-19460)***

Meridian Graphics Inc ....D....949 833-3500
2652 Dow Ave Tustin (92780) ***(P-4371)***

Meridian Medical Offices, Riverside *Also called Kaiser Foundation Hospitals* ***(P-19916)***

Meridian Moulding Inc ....F....951 279-5220
330 Cessna Cir Corona (92878) ***(P-14169)***

Meridian Rail Acquisition ....C....909 478-0541
1475 Cooley Ct San Bernardino (92408) ***(P-12579)***

Meridian Textiles Inc (PA) ....**D....323 869-5700**
6415 Canning St Commerce (90040) ***(P-14308)***

Meristar San Pedro Hilton LLC ....C....310 514-3344
2800 Via Cabrillo Marina San Pedro (90731) ***(P-16563)***

Merit Aluminum Inc (PA) ....**C....951 735-1770**
2480 Railroad St Corona (92878) ***(P-6312)***

Merit Companies The, Irvine *Also called Firstservice Residential* ***(P-15867)***

Merit Logistics LLC ....A....949 481-0685
33332 Valle Rd Ste 100 San Juan Capistrano (92675) ***(P-12580)***

Merit Medical Systems Inc ....E....801 208-4793
6 Journey Ste 125 Aliso Viejo (92656) ***(P-11021)***

Meritek Electronics Corp (PA) ....**D....626 373-1728**
5160 Rivergrade Rd Baldwin Park (91706) ***(P-7990)***

Merito.com, Van Nuys *Also called Chef Merito Inc* ***(P-2407)***

Merle Norman Cosmetics Inc (PA) ....**B....310 641-3000**
9130 Bellanca Ave Los Angeles (90045) ***(P-5047)***

Merlex Stucco Inc ....F....877 547-8822
2911 N Orange Olive Rd Orange (92865) ***(P-6182)***

Merlex Stucco Mfg, Orange *Also called Merlex Stucco Inc* ***(P-6182)***

Merli Concrete Pumping, Gardena *Also called Stefan Merli Plastering Co Inc* ***(P-1551)***

Merlot Film Productions Inc ....C....323 575-2906
7800 Beverly Blvd Los Angeles (90036) ***(P-19148)***

Merqbiz LLC ....E....855 637-7249
300 N Cntntl Blvd Ste 640 El Segundo (90245) ***(P-7915)***

ALPHABETIC

Merrick Engineering Inc (PA) ....C......951 737-6040
 1275 Quarry St Corona (92879) *(P-5708)*
Merrill Corporation Inc ....E......310 552-5288
 10635 Santa Monica Blvd # 350 Los Angeles (90025) *(P-4544)*
Merrill Lynch Pierce Fenner ....E......310 858-1500
 9560 Wilshire Blvd Fl 3 Beverly Hills (90212) *(P-15276)*
Merrill Lynch Prce Fnner Smith ....D......818 340-9500
 21215 Burbank Blvd # 600 Woodland Hills (91367) *(P-15277)*
Merrill Lynch Prce Fnner Smith ....D......714 429-2800
 650 Town Center Dr # 500 Costa Mesa (92626) *(P-15278)*
Merrill Lynch Prce Fnner Smith ....D......661 802-0764
 730 W Lancaster Blvd Lancaster (93534) *(P-15279)*
Merrill Lynch Prce Fnner Smith ....D......760 862-1400
 74800 Us Highway 111 Indian Wells (92210) *(P-15280)*
Merrill Lynch Prce Fnner Smith ....D......949 467-3760
 520 Nwport Ctr Dr Ste 190 Newport Beach (92660) *(P-15281)*
Merrill Lynch Prce Fnner Smith ....D......800 964-5182
 300 E Esplanade Dr # 215 Oxnard (93036) *(P-15282)*
Merrill Lynch Prce Fnner Smith ....D......949 456-8082
 28202 Cabot Rd Laguna Niguel (92677) *(P-15283)*
Merrill Lynch Prce Fnner Smith ....D......310 477-3400
 100 Wilshire Blvd Ste 300 Santa Monica (90401) *(P-15284)*
Merrill Lynch Prce Fnner Smith ....D......949 235-5050
 100 Spectrum Center Dr Irvine (92618) *(P-15285)*
Merrill Lynch Prce Fnner Smith ....D......909 476-5100
 901 Via Piemonte Ste 503 Ontario (91764) *(P-15286)*
Merrill Lynch Prce Fnner Smith ....C......805 695-7028
 1096 Coast Village Rd Santa Barbara (93108) *(P-18596)*
Merrill Lynch Prce Fnner Smith ....D......805 963-0333
 1424 State St Santa Barbara (93101) *(P-15287)*
Merrill Lynch Prce Fnner Smith ....D......661 326-7700
 5080 California Ave # 102 Bakersfield (93309) *(P-15288)*
Merrill Lynch Prce Fnner Smith ....D......714 257-4400
 145 S State College Blvd Brea (92821) *(P-15289)*
Merrill Lynch Prce Fnner Smith ....D......310 407-3900
 2049 Century Park E # 1100 Los Angeles (90067) *(P-15290)*
Merrill Lynch Prce Fnner Smith ....D......310 536-1600
 2301 Rosecrans Ave # 3150 El Segundo (90245) *(P-15291)*
Merrill Lynch Prce Fnner Smith ....D......800 637-7455
 800 E Colo Blvd Ste 400 Pasadena (91101) *(P-15292)*
Merrill Lynch Prce Fnner Smith ....D......562 493-1300
 3010 Old Ranch Pkwy # 15 Seal Beach (90740) *(P-15293)*
Merrill Lynch Prce Fnner Smith ....D......805 381-2600
 2815 Townsgate Rd Ste 300 Westlake Village (91361) *(P-15294)*
Merrill Lynch Prce Fnner Smith ....D......805 596-2222
 1020 Marsh St San Luis Obispo (93401) *(P-15295)*
Merrimans Incorporated ....E......909 795-5301
 32195 Dunlap Blvd Yucaipa (92399) *(P-6636)*
Merritt Hospitality LLC ....C......562 983-3400
 701 W Ocean Blvd Long Beach (90831) *(P-16564)*
Merritt Hospitality LLC ....C......714 738-7800
 2701 Nutwood Ave Fullerton (92831) *(P-16565)*
Merry An Cejka 323 560-3949
 4601 Cecilia St Cudahy (90201) *(P-8690)*
Meruelo Enterprises Inc (PA) ....A......562 745-2300
 9550 Firestone Blvd # 105 Downey (90241) *(P-792)*
Mesa Associates Inc ....C......909 979-6609
 3670 W Temple Ave Ste 152 Pomona (91768) *(P-22609)*
Mesa Cnsld Wtr Dst Imprv Corp (PA) ....D......949 631-1200
 1965 Placentia Ave Costa Mesa (92627) *(P-12906)*
Mesa Energy Systems Inc (HQ) ....C......949 460-0460
 2 Cromwell Irvine (92618) *(P-1102)*
Mesa Management Inc ....D......949 851-0995
 1451 Quail St Ste 201 Newport Beach (92660) *(P-15925)*
Mesa Pointe Stadium 12, Costa Mesa Also called Edwards Theatres Circuit Inc *(P-19273)*
Mesa Safe Company Inc ....E......714 202-8000
 337 W Freedom Ave Orange (92865) *(P-7565)*
Mesa Verde Country Club ....C......714 549-0377
 3000 Club House Rd Costa Mesa (92626) *(P-19586)*
Mesa Verde Partners ....C......714 540-7500
 1701 Golf Course Dr Costa Mesa (92626) *(P-19500)*
Mesa Verde Prosecute Care, Costa Mesa Also called Mesa Vrde Cnvalescent Hosp
Inc *(P-20417)*
Mesa Vineyard Management Inc (PA) ....D......805 434-4100
 110 Gibson Rd Templeton (93465) *(P-225)*
Mesa Vrde Cnvalescent Hosp Inc ....C......949 548-5584
 661 Center St Costa Mesa (92627) *(P-20417)*
MESA WATER DISTRICT, Costa Mesa Also called Mesa Cnsld Wtr Dst Imprv Corp *(P-12906)*
Mesmerize, Los Angeles Also called Kamiran Inc *(P-2851)*
Mesquite Cattle Feeders Inc ....E......760 344-2944
 1504 Us Highway 78 Brawley (92227) *(P-124)*
Message Broadcast LLC ....E......949 428-3111
 4685 Macarthur Ct Ste 250 Newport Beach (92660) *(P-18597)*
Messenger Express (PA) ....C......213 614-0475
 5435 Cahuenga Blvd Ste C North Hollywood (91601) *(P-12142)*
Messer LLC ....F......562 903-1290
 13117 Meyer Rd Whittier (90605) *(P-4642)*
Messer LLC ....F......310 533-8394
 2535 Del Amo Blvd Torrance (90503) *(P-4643)*
Messer LLC ....F......626 855-8366
 660 Baldwin Park Blvd City of Industry (91746) *(P-4644)*
Mestek Inc 310 835-7500
 1220 E Watson Center Rd Carson (90745) *(P-8345)*
Metagenics Inc (HQ) ....C......949 366-0818
 25 Enterprise Ste 200 Aliso Viejo (92656) *(P-14263)*
Metal Analysis, Santa Fe Springs Also called Bodycote W Cast Anlytcal Svc I *(P-6433)*
Metal Art of California Inc (PA) ....D......714 532-7100
 640 N Cypress St Orange (92867) *(P-11573)*
Metal Cast Inc ....E......714 285-9792
 2002 W Chestnut Ave Santa Ana (92703) *(P-6277)*

Metal Chem Inc ....E......818 727-9951
 21514 Nordhoff St Chatsworth (91311) *(P-7280)*
Metal Coaters California Inc ....D......909 987-4681
 9123 Center Ave Rancho Cucamonga (91730) *(P-7388)*
Metal Coaters System, Rancho Cucamonga Also called Metal Coaters California
Inc *(P-7388)*
Metal Container Corporation ....C......951 354-0444
 7155 Central Ave Riverside (92504) *(P-6465)*
Metal Container Corporation ....C......951 360-4500
 10980 Inland Ave Jurupa Valley (91752) *(P-6466)*
Metal Cutting Service Inc ....F......626 968-4764
 16233 Gale Ave City of Industry (91745) *(P-8691)*
Metal Engineering Inc ....E......626 334-1819
 1642 S Sacramento Ave Ontario (91761) *(P-6875)*
Metal Finishing Division, South Gate Also called Anadite Cal Restoration Tr *(P-7210)*
Metal Improvement Company LLC ....D......818 983-1952
 6940 Farmdale Ave North Hollywood (91605) *(P-6445)*
Metal Improvement Company LLC ....E......949 855-8010
 35 Argonaut Ste A1 Laguna Hills (92656) *(P-6446)*
Metal Improvement Company LLC ....D......818 407-6280
 20751 Superior St Chatsworth (91311) *(P-6447)*
Metal Preparations 213 628-5176
 1000 E Ocean Blvd Unit 41 Long Beach (90802) *(P-7281)*
METAL PRODUCTS ENGINEERING, Vernon Also called Luppen Holdings Inc *(P-7162)*
Metal Supply LLC ....D......562 634-9940
 11810 Center St South Gate (90280) *(P-6637)*
Metal Surfaces Intl LLC ....C......562 927-1331
 6060 Shull St Bell Gardens (90201) *(P-7282)*
Metal Tek Engineering Inc ....F......909 821-4158
 7426 Cherry Ave Ste 210 Fontana (92336) *(P-3266)*
Metal Tite Products (PA) ....D......562 695-0645
 4880 Gregg Rd Pico Rivera (90660) *(P-6709)*
Metal X Direct Inc ....F......949 336-0055
 1555 Mesa Verde Dr E 11g Costa Mesa (92626) *(P-6975)*
Metal-Fab Services Indust Inc ....E......714 630-7771
 2500 E Miraloma Way Anaheim (92806) *(P-6876)*
Metalcast, Santa Ana Also called Metal Cast Inc *(P-6277)*
Metalite Manufacturing, Pacoima Also called Hanmar LLC *(P-7149)*
Metalore Inc ....E......310 643-0360
 750 S Douglas St El Segundo (90245) *(P-8692)*
Metalpro Industries Inc ....E......661 294-0764
 28064 Avenue Stanford H Santa Clarita (91355) *(P-6877)*
Metals USA Building Pdts LP ....D......714 522-7852
 6450 Caballero Blvd Ste A Buena Park (90620) *(P-6638)*
Metals USA Building Pdts LP (HQ) ....A......713 946-9000
 955 Columbia St Brea (92821) *(P-6328)*
Metals USA Building Pdts LP ....C......800 325-1305
 1951 S Parco Ave Ste C Ontario (91761) *(P-6329)*
Metcalfe Security Inc ....D......213 605-2785
 3161 Bostonian Dr Los Alamitos (90720) *(P-1282)*
Metco Fourslide Manufacturing, Gardena Also called Metco Manufacturing Inc *(P-7165)*
Metco Manufacturing Inc ....E......310 516-6547
 17540 S Denver Ave Gardena (90248) *(P-7165)*
Metcoe Skylight Specialites, Gardena Also called Weiss Sheet Metal Company *(P-1509)*
Method Studios LLC ....D......310 434-6500
 3401 Exposition Blvd Santa Monica (90404) *(P-19149)*
Methodist Hosp Southern Cal (PA) ....A......626 898-8000
 300 W Huntington Dr Arcadia (91007) *(P-20862)*
Metra Electronics Corporation ....E......562 470-6601
 3201 E 59th St Long Beach (90805) *(P-10102)*
Metric Machining (PA) ....E......909 947-9222
 3263 Trade Center Dr Riverside (92507) *(P-8693)*
Metric Precision, Huntington Beach Also called AMG Torrance LLC *(P-10268)*
Metric Products Inc (PA) ....E......310 815-9000
 4630 Leahy St Culver City (90232) *(P-3021)*
Metro Bldrs & Engineers Group, Newport Beach Also called Houalla Enterprises Ltd *(P-773)*
Metro Building Maintenance, Brea Also called US Metro Group Inc *(P-17299)*
Metro Digital Printing Inc ....E......714 545-8400
 3311 W Macarthur Blvd Santa Ana (92704) *(P-4372)*
Metro Truck Body Incorporated ....E......310 532-5570
 1201 W Jon St Torrance (90502) *(P-9993)*
Metro-Goldwyn-Mayer Inc (HQ) ....B......310 449-3000
 245 N Beverly Dr Beverly Hills (90210) *(P-19150)*
Metrolink, Los Angeles Also called Southern Cal Rgional Rail Auth *(P-11843)*
Metrolink Doc, Pomona Also called Southern Cal Rgional Rail Auth *(P-11842)*
Metromedia Technologies Inc ....E......818 552-6500
 311 Parkside Dr San Fernando (91340) *(P-8281)*
Metronome Software LLC ....E......949 273-5190
 2 S Pointe Dr Ste 140 Lake Forest (92630) *(P-17915)*
Metropole Hotel ....D......310 510-1884
 205 Crescent Ave Avalon (90704) *(P-16566)*
Metropolis Hotel MGT LLC ....C......213 683-4855
 899 Francisco St Los Angeles (90017) *(P-16567)*
Metropolitan Home Mortgage Inc ....D......949 428-0161
 3090 Bristol St Ste 600 Costa Mesa (92626) *(P-15214)*
Metropolitan News Company, Los Angeles Also called Grace Communications Inc *(P-3983)*
Metropolitan News Company ....E......951 369-5890
 3540 12th St Riverside (92501) *(P-4010)*
Metropolitan W Asset MGT LLC (HQ) ....D......213 244-0000
 865 S Figueroa St Los Angeles (90017) *(P-15296)*
Metropolitan Waste Disposal, Paramount Also called Calmet Inc *(P-12935)*
Metropolitan Water District ....B......909 593-7474
 700 Moreno Ave La Verne (91750) *(P-12907)*
Metropolitan Water Lavern, La Verne Also called Metropolitan Water Disrict *(P-12907)*
Metropro Road Services Inc (PA) ....D......714 556-7600
 957 W 17th St Costa Mesa (92627) *(P-18938)*
Metrostudy, Costa Mesa Also called Hanley Wood Mkt Intelligence *(P-22882)*

Metrostudy Inc ....C.......714 619-7800
4000 Macarthur Blvd # 400 Newport Beach (92660) ***(P-23271)***
Mettler Electronics Corp ....E.......714 533-2221
1333 S Claudina St Anaheim (92805) ***(P-11022)***
Meundies Inc ....E.......888 552-6775
3650 Holdrege Ave Los Angeles (90016) ***(P-2645)***
Meus, Cypress *Also called Mitsubishi Electric Us Inc* ***(P-1625)***
Mevsa, Cypress *Also called Mitsubshi Elc Vsual Sltons AME* ***(P-9752)***
Mexapparel Inc (PA)........E.......323 364-8600
2344 E 38th St Vernon (90058) ***(P-2785)***
Mexicali Inc ....C.......661 327-3861
631 18th St Bakersfield (93301) ***(P-16966)***
Mexicali Restaurant, Bakersfield *Also called Mexicali Inc* ***(P-16966)***
Mexican Amrcn Oprtnty Fndation (PA)........D.......323 890-9600
401 N Garfield Ave Montebello (90640) ***(P-21850)***
Mexican Amrcn Oprtnty Fndation ....D.......323 264-4333
330 S Ford Blvd Los Angeles (90022) ***(P-22034)***
Meyco Machine and Tool Inc ....E.......714 435-1546
11579 Martens River Cir Fountain Valley (92708) ***(P-7857)***
Meyer Coatings Inc ....E.......714 467-4600
1927 N Glassell St Orange (92865) ***(P-1189)***
Meyer Construction Services, Orange *Also called Meyer Coatings Inc* ***(P-1189)***
Meyers Research LLC (PA)........C.......714 619-7800
4000 Macarthur Blvd # 400 Newport Beach (92660) ***(P-22893)***
Meza Pallet Inc ....F.......909 829-0223
14619 Merrill Ave Fontana (92335) ***(P-3399)***
Mf Inc ....C.......213 627-2498
2010 E 15th St Los Angeles (90021) ***(P-2858)***
Mf Services Company LLC (HQ)........D.......949 474-5800
4350 Von Karman Ave # 400 Newport Beach (92660) ***(P-23272)***
Mfb Worldwide Inc (PA)........F.......323 562-2339
4901 Patata St 201-204 Cudahy (90201) ***(P-2730)***
Mfi Inc ....F.......949 887-8691
363 San Miguel Dr Ste 200 Newport Beach (92660) ***(P-11714)***
Mfi Recovery Center (PA)........D.......951 683-6596
5870 Arlington Ave # 103 Riverside (92504) ***(P-21319)***
Mflex, Irvine *Also called Multi-Fineline Electronix Inc* ***(P-9430)***
Mflex Delaware Inc ....A.......949 453-6800
101 Academy Ste 250 Irvine (92617) ***(P-9429)***
MGA Entertainment Inc (PA)........B.......818 894-2525
9220 Winnetka Ave Chatsworth (91311) ***(P-14098)***
MGB Construction Inc ....C.......951 342-0303
91 Commercial Ave Riverside (92507) ***(P-623)***
Mge Underground Inc ....D.......805 238-3510
2501 Golden Hill Rd Paso Robles (93446) ***(P-1601)***
Mgid Inc (PA)........D.......424 322-8059
1149 3rd St Ste 210 Santa Monica (90403) ***(P-23273)***
Mgl, Santa Ana *Also called Gerald Michael Ltd* ***(P-14334)***
MGM, Beverly Hills *Also called Metro-Goldwyn-Mayer Inc* ***(P-19150)***
MGM and Ua Services Company ....A.......310 449-3000
245 N Beverly Dr Beverly Hills (90210) ***(P-23536)***
MGM Holdings II Inc (HQ)........D.......310 449-3000
245 N Beverly Dr Beverly Hills (90210) ***(P-19151)***
MGM Studios, Beverly Hills *Also called MGM Holdings II Inc* ***(P-19151)***
MGM Transformer Co ....D.......323 726-0888
5701 Smithway St Commerce (90040) ***(P-8878)***
Mgr Design International Inc ....C.......805 981-6400
1950 Williams Dr Oxnard (93036) ***(P-11715)***
MGT Industries Inc ....D.......310 324-3152
19034 S Vermont Ave Gardena (90248) ***(P-23063)***
MGT Industries Inc (PA)........C.......310 516-5900
13889 S Figueroa St Los Angeles (90061) ***(P-2973)***
Mh Sub I LLC (PA)........A.......310 280-4000
909 N Pacific Coast Hwy # 11 El Segundo (90245) ***(P-17035)***
Mhh Holdings Inc ....C.......949 651-9903
5653 Alton Pkwy Irvine (92618) ***(P-14707)***
Mhh Holdings Inc ....C.......626 744-9370
415 S Lake Ave Ste 108 Pasadena (91101) ***(P-14708)***
Mhm Services Inc ....C.......805 904-6678
230 Station Way Arroyo Grande (93420) ***(P-21320)***
MHRP Resort Inc ....D.......760 249-5808
24510 Highway 2 Wrightwood (92397) ***(P-16568)***
Mhx LLC ....D.......800 234-2098
22707 Wilmington Ave Carson (90745) ***(P-12483)***
Mias Fashion Mfg Co Inc ....B.......562 906-1060
12623 Cisneros Ln Santa Fe Springs (90670) ***(P-14400)***
Mic ....E.......661 401-0070
2960 Pacini St Bakersfield (93314) ***(P-13918)***
Micha-Rettenmaier Partnership ....D.......714 280-1645
351 Hospital Rd Ste 507 Newport Beach (92663) ***(P-19977)***
Michael Baker Intl Inc ....D.......909 974-4900
3536 Concours Ste 110 Ontario (91764) ***(P-22610)***
Michael Baker Intl Inc ....D.......760 346-7481
75410 Gerald Ford Dr # 100 Palm Desert (92211) ***(P-22611)***
Michael Baker Intl Inc ....D.......951 676-8042
40810 County Center Dr # 100 Temecula (92591) ***(P-22612)***
Michael Baker Intl Inc ....D.......805 383-3373
5051 Verdugo Way Ste 300 Camarillo (93012) ***(P-22613)***
Michael D Molinari MD Facg Inc ....F.......951 734-9930
341 Magnolia Ave Ste 207 Corona (92879) ***(P-19978)***
Michael D Wilson Inc ....E.......559 568-1115
19774 Orange Belt Dr Strathmore (93267) ***(P-7566)***
Michael Levine Inc (PA)........D.......213 622-6259
920 Maple Ave Los Angeles (90015) ***(P-14309)***
Michael Madden Co Inc ....D.......800 834-6248
2825 Warner Ave Irvine (92606) ***(P-14213)***
Michael P Byko DDS A Prof Corp (PA)........D.......909 888-7817
164 W Hospitality Ln # 14 San Bernardino (92408) ***(P-20188)***
Michael Sullivan & Assoc LLP ....C.......310 337-4480
400 Continental Blvd # 250 El Segundo (90245) ***(P-21628)***
Michael-Antonio Studio, Montclair *Also called E M S Trading Inc* ***(P-14435)***
Michaelson Connor & Boul (PA)........D.......714 230-3600
5312 Bolsa Ave Huntington Beach (92649) ***(P-23274)***
Michelle Barrionuevo-Mazzini (PA)........F.......415 706-1677
1224 Pendio Irvine (92620) ***(P-11716)***
Michelle Pasternak, Los Angeles *Also called SM 10000 Property LLC* ***(P-16074)***
Michelson Laboratories Inc (PA)........D.......562 928-0553
6280 Chalet Dr Commerce (90040) ***(P-22952)***
Michigan Metal Partitions, Anaheim *Also called Weis/Robart Partitions Inc* ***(P-6984)***
Micop, Oxnard *Also called Mixtec/Ndgena Cmnty Orgnzing P* ***(P-21851)***
Micro Analog Inc ....C.......909 392-8277
1861 Puddingstone Dr La Verne (91750) ***(P-9538)***
Micro Express, Irvine *Also called A S A Engineering Inc* ***(P-8144)***
Micro Gage ....E.......626 443-1741
9537 Telstar Ave Ste 131 El Monte (91731) ***(P-9539)***
Micro Matrix Systems (PA)........E.......909 626-8544
1899 Salem Ct Claremont (91711) ***(P-7166)***
Micro Plastics Inc ....E.......818 882-0244
20821 Dearborn St Chatsworth (91311) ***(P-9042)***
Micro Steel Inc ....E.......818 348-8701
7850 Alabama Ave Canoga Park (91304) ***(P-10535)***
Micro Surface Engr Inc (PA)........E.......323 582-7348
1550 E Slauson Ave Los Angeles (90011) ***(P-6460)***
Micro Therapeutics Inc (HQ)........D.......949 837-3700
9775 Toledo Way Irvine (92618) ***(P-11023)***
Micro-OHM Corporation ....F.......626 357-5377
1075 Hamilton Rd Duarte (91010) ***(P-9616)***
Micro-Pro Microfilming Svcs, Long Beach *Also called Macro-Pro Inc* ***(P-18584)***
Micro-TEC, Chatsworth *Also called Wallace E Miller Inc* ***(P-8844)***
Micro-Technology Concepts Inc ....D.......626 839-6800
17837 Rowland St City of Industry (91748) ***(P-13415)***
Micro/Sys Inc ....E.......818 244-4600
158 W Pomona Ave Monrovia (91016) ***(P-8167)***
Microcool ....F.......760 322-1111
72216 Northshore St # 103 Thousand Palms (92276) ***(P-10707)***
Microcosm Inc ....E.......310 219-2700
3111 Lomita Blvd Torrance (90505) ***(P-10527)***
Microdyn-Nadir Us, Inc., Goleta *Also called Mann+hmmel Wtr Fluid Sltons In* ***(P-8394)***
Microdyne Plastics Inc ....D.......909 503-4010
1901 E Cooley Dr Colton (92324) ***(P-5709)***
Microfabrica Inc ....E.......888 964-2763
7911 Haskell Ave Van Nuys (91406) ***(P-9749)***
Microfinancial Incorporated ....C.......805 367-8900
2801 Townsgate Rd Westlake Village (91361) ***(P-17362)***
Microlease Inc (HQ)........D.......866 520-0200
6060 Sepulveda Blvd Van Nuys (91411) ***(P-17363)***
Micrometals Inc (PA)........C.......714 970-9400
5615 E La Palma Ave Anaheim (92807) ***(P-9750)***
Micromold Inc ....F.......951 684-7130
2100 Iowa Ave Riverside (92507) ***(P-5710)***
Micron Instruments, Simi Valley *Also called Piezo-Metrics Inc* ***(P-9559)***
Micronova Manufacturing Inc ....E.......310 784-6990
3431 Lomita Blvd Torrance (90505) ***(P-3108)***
Microplate, Inglewood *Also called Multichrome Company Inc* ***(P-7284)***
Microplex Inc ....F.......714 630-8220
1070 Ortega Way Placentia (92870) ***(P-9540)***
Microprint Inc ....E.......626 369-1950
133 Puente Ave City of Industry (91746) ***(P-4373)***
Microscale Industries Inc ....E.......714 593-1422
18435 Bandilier Cir Fountain Valley (92708) ***(P-4374)***
Microsemi Communications Inc (HQ)........C.......805 388-3700
4721 Calle Carga Camarillo (93012) ***(P-9541)***
Microsemi Corp - Anlog Mxed Sg (HQ)........A.......714 898-8121
11861 Western Ave Garden Grove (92841) ***(P-9542)***
Microsemi Corp - High Prfmce T (HQ)........D.......949 380-6100
11861 Western Ave Garden Grove (92841) ***(P-9543)***
Microsemi Corp-Power MGT Group ....C.......714 994-6500
11861 Western Ave Garden Grove (92841) ***(P-8960)***
Microsemi Corporation (HQ)........E.......949 380-6100
11861 Western Ave Garden Grove (92841) ***(P-9544)***
Micross Holdings Inc ....D.......215 997-3200
11150 Santa Monica Blvd Los Angeles (90025) ***(P-9545)***
Microtek Lab Inc (HQ)........C.......310 687-5823
13337 South St Cerritos (90703) ***(P-13362)***
Microtronix Systems Co, Huntington Beach *Also called Kwl Industrial Company* ***(P-13911)***
Microvention Inc (HQ)........A.......714 258-8000
35 Enterprise Aliso Viejo (92656) ***(P-11024)***
Microvention Terumo, Aliso Viejo *Also called Microvention Inc* ***(P-11024)***
Microvoice Corporation ....E.......805 389-2922
345 Willis Ave Camarillo (93010) ***(P-9290)***
Microvoice Systems, Camarillo *Also called Microvoice Corporation* ***(P-9290)***
Microwave Applications Group ....E.......805 928-5711
3030 Industrial Pkwy Santa Maria (93455) ***(P-22614)***
Microwave Dynamics ....F.......949 679-7788
16541 Scientific Irvine (92618) ***(P-9291)***
Mid Coast Suppliers Inc ....F.......805 543-0871
60 Prado Rd San Luis Obispo (93401) ***(P-13336)***
Mid Rckland Imging Prtners Inc (HQ)........E.......310 445-2800
1510 Cotner Ave Los Angeles (90025) ***(P-21078)***
Mid-Century Insurance Company (HQ)........C.......323 932-7116
6303 Owensmouth Ave Woodland Hills (91367) ***(P-15477)***
Mid-Cities Association Inc (PA)........D.......310 537-4510
14208 Towne Ave Los Angeles (90061) ***(P-21961)***
Mid-State Concrete Pdts Inc ....E.......805 928-2855
1625 E Donovan Rd Ste C Santa Maria (93454) ***(P-6039)***

ALPHABETIC

Employee Codes: A=Over 500 employees, B=251-500
C=101-250, D=51-100, E=20-50 F=10-19
2022 Southern California Business
Directory and Buyers Guide
© Mergent Inc. 1-800-342-5647
1205

Mid-West Fabricating Co ... E ... 562 698-9615
8623 Dice Rd Santa Fe Springs (90670) *(P-10103)*

Mid-West Wholesale Hardware Co ... E ... 714 630-4751
1641 S Sunkist St Anaheim (92806) *(P-6526)*

Mida Industries Inc ... C ... 562 616-1020
6101 Obispo Ave Long Beach (90805) *(P-17264)*

Midas Express Los Angeles Inc ... C ... 310 609-0366
11854 Alameda St Lynwood (90262) *(P-12222)*

Midland Industries ... D ... 800 821-5725
659 E Ball Rd Anaheim (92805) *(P-14001)*

Midmark Diagnostics Group, Gardena *Also called Brentwood Medical Tech Corp (P-13481)*

Midnight Cellars Inc ... F ... 805 239-8904
2925 Anderson Rd Paso Robles (93446) *(P-2208)*

Midnight Cellars Winery, Paso Robles *Also called Midnight Cellars Inc (P-2208)*

Midnight Manufacturing LLC ... E ... 714 833-6130
2535 Conejo Spectrum St Thousand Oaks (91320) *(P-4753)*

Midnight Mission (PA) ... **D ... 213 624-9258**
601 S San Pedro St Los Angeles (90014) *(P-22348)*

Midnight Sun Enterprises Inc ... D ... 310 532-2427
19900 Normandie Ave Torrance (90502) *(P-23473)*

Midrange Software Inc ... F ... 818 762-8539
12223 Otsego St Valley Village (91607) *(P-17916)*

Midstream Energy Partners USA ... E ... 661 765-4087
9224 Tupman Rd Tupman (93276) *(P-381)*

Midthrust Imports Inc ... E ... 213 749-6651
830 E 14th Pl Los Angeles (90021) *(P-2653)*

Midway Car Rental, North Hollywood *Also called Midway Rent A Car Inc (P-18752)*

Midway Clinic Cars, Los Angeles *Also called Midway Rent A Car Inc (P-18746)*

Midway International Inc ... E ... 562 921-2255
13131 166th St Cerritos (90703) *(P-14952)*

Midway Rent A Car Inc ... D ... 818 985-9770
4201 Lankershim Blvd North Hollywood (91602) *(P-18752)*

Midway Rent A Car Inc ... D ... 310 330-4600
6225 W Century Blvd Los Angeles (90045) *(P-18744)*

Midway Rent A Car Inc ... D ... 424 293-4855
11231 S La Cienega Blvd Los Angeles (90045) *(P-18745)*

Midway Rent A Car Inc ... D ... 310 445-4355
1800 S Sepulveda Blvd Los Angeles (90025) *(P-18746)*

Midwest Rubber, Ontario *Also called Ace Calendering Entps Inc (P-5364)*

Mieron Inc ... F ... 626 466-9040
9160 Rose St Bellflower (90706) *(P-11025)*

Mig Capital LLC (PA) ... **C ... 949 474-5800**
660 Newport Center Dr # 450 Newport Beach (92660) *(P-15333)*

Mig Management Services LLC ... D ... 949 474-5800
660 Newport Center Dr Newport Beach (92660) *(P-23064)*

Mighty Enterprises Inc ... D ... 310 516-7478
19706 Normandie Ave Torrance (90502) *(P-13919)*

Mighty Green, Costa Mesa *Also called Inveco Inc (P-7271)*

Mighty Soy Inc ... F ... 323 266-6969
1227 S Eastern Ave Los Angeles (90022) *(P-7945)*

Mighty USA, Torrance *Also called Mighty Enterprises Inc (P-13919)*

Mikado Hotels Inc ... E ... 818 763-9141
12600 Riverside Dr North Hollywood (91607) *(P-16569)*

Mikawaya, Vernon *Also called Mochi Ice Cream Company LLC (P-2020)*

Mike Campbell & Associates Ltd ... A ... 626 369-3981
10907 Downey Ave Ste 203 Downey (90241) *(P-12175)*

Mike Campbell Assoc Logictics, Downey *Also called Mike Campbell & Associates Ltd (P-12175)*

Mike Cims Inc ... E ... 562 428-8390
2300 E Curry St Long Beach (90805) *(P-3511)*

Mike Dyell Machine Shop Inc (PA) ... **F ... 909 350-4101**
160 S Linden Ave Rialto (92376) *(P-8694)*

Mike Kenney Tool Inc ... E ... 714 577-9262
2900 Saturn St Ste A Brea (92821) *(P-8695)*

Mike Parker Landscape, Santa Ana *Also called Mpl Enterprises Inc (P-327)*

Mike Rovner Construction Inc ... C ... 949 458-1562
22600 Lambert St Lake Forest (92630) *(P-23065)*

Mike's Business Card, Orange *Also called Bishop Inc (P-1474)*

Mikelson Machine Shop Inc ... E ... 626 448-3920
2546 Merced Ave South El Monte (91733) *(P-8696)*

Miken Clothing, Commerce *Also called Miken Sales Inc (P-14401)*

Miken Sales Inc (PA) ... **D ... 323 266-2560**
7230 Oxford Way Commerce (90040) *(P-14401)*

Mikes Precision Welding Inc ... F ... 951 676-4744
28073 Diaz Rd Ste D Temecula (92590) *(P-18990)*

Mikhail Darafeev Inc (PA) ... **E ... 909 613-1818**
5075 Edison Ave Chino (91710) *(P-3478)*

Mikron Products Inc ... E ... 909 545-8600
3701 E Conant St Long Beach (90808) *(P-5359)*

Mikuni American Corporation (HQ) ... **D ... 310 676-0522**
8910 Mikuni Ave Northridge (91324) *(P-13073)*

Mil-Spec Magnetics Inc ... E ... 909 598-8116
169 Pacific St Pomona (91768) *(P-9635)*

Milani Cosmetics, Culver City *Also called New Milani Group LLC (P-14269)*

Milbank Global Securities, Los Angeles *Also called Milbank Tweed Hdley McCloy LLP (P-21629)*

Milbank Tweed Hdley McCloy LLP ... C ... 424 386-4000
2029 Century Park E # 3300 Los Angeles (90067) *(P-21629)*

Milco Waterjet, Huntington Beach *Also called Milco Wire Edm Inc (P-8697)*

Milco Wire Edm Inc ... F ... 714 373-0098
15221 Connector Ln Huntington Beach (92649) *(P-8697)*

Mile High Valet, Dana Point *Also called Ciri - Stroup Inc (P-16948)*

Mile Square Golf Course ... C ... 714 962-5541
10401 Warner Ave Fountain Valley (92708) *(P-19501)*

Miles Construction Group Inc ... E ... 951 260-2504
41725 Elm St Ste 303 Murrieta (92562) *(P-624)*

Milestone Health Care Center, Costa Mesa *Also called Newport Sbacute Healthcare Ctr (P-20424)*

Milgard Manufacturing LLC ... C ... 805 581-6325
355 E Easy St Simi Valley (93065) *(P-5963)*

Milgard Manufacturing LLC ... C ... 480 763-6000
26879 Diaz Rd Temecula (92590) *(P-5711)*

Milgard Windows, Temecula *Also called Milgard Manufacturing LLC (P-5711)*

Milgard-Simi Valley, Simi Valley *Also called Milgard Manufacturing LLC (P-5963)*

Milgro, Oxnard *Also called Victoria Nursery Inc (P-14897)*

Military California Department ... B ... 562 795-2065
11300 Lexington Dr # 100 Los Alamitos (90720) *(P-23395)*

Milken Family Foundation ... C ... 310 570-4800
1250 4th St Fl 1 Santa Monica (90401) *(P-22349)*

Milken Institute ... E ... 310 570-4600
1250 4th St Santa Monica (90401) *(P-22914)*

Milky Mama LLC ... F ... 877 886-4559
10722 Arrow Rte Ste 104 Rancho Cucamonga (91730) *(P-2019)*

Millbrook Kitchens Inc ... F ... 310 684-3366
15960 Downey Ave Paramount (90723) *(P-3326)*

Millcraft Inc ... D ... 714 632-9621
2850 E White Star Ave Anaheim (92806) *(P-3267)*

Millennia Stainless Inc ... D ... 562 946-3545
10016 Romandel Ave Santa Fe Springs (90670) *(P-14002)*

Millennial Home Lending Inc ... D ... 818 812-5150
9200 Oakdale Ave Ste 501 Chatsworth (91311) *(P-15215)*

Millennium Biltmore Hotel, Los Angeles *Also called Whb Corporation (P-16787)*

Millennium Space Systems Inc (HQ) ... **E ... 310 683-5840**
2265 E El Segundo Blvd El Segundo (90245) *(P-10599)*

Miller and Associates, Los Angeles *Also called Imhoff & Associates PC (P-21584)*

Miller Automotive Group Inc (HQ) ... **B ... 818 787-8400**
5425 Van Nuys Blvd Sherman Oaks (91401) *(P-18855)*

Miller Brewing Co ... F ... 626 353-1604
15801 1st St Irwindale (91706) *(P-2150)*

Miller Castings Inc (PA) ... **B ... 562 695-0461**
2503 Pacific Park Dr Whittier (90601) *(P-6270)*

Miller Children's Hospital, Long Beach *Also called Long Beach Medical Center (P-20847)*

Miller Environmental Inc ... C ... 714 385-0099
1130 W Trenton Ave Orange (92867) *(P-1617)*

Miller Gasket Co, San Fernando *Also called J Miller Co Inc (P-5344)*

Miller Nissan, Sherman Oaks *Also called Miller Automotive Group Inc (P-18855)*

Miller Woodworking Inc ... E ... 310 257-6806
1429 259th St Harbor City (90710) *(P-3268)*

Millers American Honey Inc ... E ... 909 825-1722
1455 Riverview Dr San Bernardino (92408) *(P-2485)*

Millers Fab & Weld Corp ... E ... 951 359-3100
6100 Industrial Ave Riverside (92504) *(P-6639)*

Millers Woodworking, Tustin *Also called GL Woodworking Inc (P-3445)*

Millie and Severson Inc ... D ... 562 493-3611
3601 Serpentine Dr Los Alamitos (90720) *(P-708)*

Million Corporation ... D ... 626 969-1888
1300 W Optical Dr Ste 600 Irwindale (91702) *(P-4545)*

Millipart Inc (PA) ... **F ... 626 963-4101**
412 W Carter Dr Glendora (91740) *(P-8698)*

Mills ASAP Reprographics (PA) ... **F ... 805 772-2019**
495 Morro Bay Blvd Morro Bay (93442) *(P-3915)*

Mills Corporation ... D ... 909 484-8300
1 Mills Cir Ste 1 # 1 Ontario (91764) *(P-15678)*

Mills Iron Works ... D ... 323 321-6520
14834 S Maple Ave Gardena (90248) *(P-14003)*

Millwood Cabinet Co Inc ... F ... 661 327-0371
2321 Virginia Ave Bakersfield (93307) *(P-3327)*

Millwork Holdings, Irvine *Also called Alton Irvine Inc (P-13125)*

Millworks Etc Inc ... E ... 805 499-3400
1250 Commercial Ave Oxnard (93030) *(P-6710)*

Millworks By Design Inc ... E ... 818 597-1326
4525 Runway St Simi Valley (93063) *(P-3269)*

Millworx Prcsion Machining Inc ... E ... 951 371-2683
506 Malloy Ct Corona (92878) *(P-8699)*

Milodon Incorporated ... E ... 805 577-5950
2250 Agate Ct Simi Valley (93065) *(P-10104)*

Milwaukee Electric Tool Corp ... D ... 714 827-1301
1130 N Magnolia Ave Anaheim (92801) *(P-14004)*

Milwood Healthcare Inc ... C ... 626 274-4345
2641 S C St Oxnard (93033) *(P-15679)*

Mimg Medical Management LLC ... D ... 949 282-1600
26522 La Alameda Ste 120 Mission Viejo (92691) *(P-23066)*

Mimi Chica (PA) ... **F ... 323 264-9278**
161 W 33rd St Los Angeles (90007) *(P-2974)*

Mimi Chica Design, Los Angeles *Also called Mimi Chica (P-2974)*

Min-E-Con LLC ... D ... 949 250-0087
17312 Eastman Irvine (92614) *(P-9661)*

Minal Inc (PA) ... **D ... 323 957-8787**
1080 N Western Ave Los Angeles (90029) *(P-19979)*

Minatronic Inc ... F ... 805 239-8864
1139 13th St Paso Robles (93446) *(P-9751)*

Mind Research Institute ... C ... 949 345-8700
5281 California Ave # 300 Irvine (92617) *(P-22915)*

Mindbody Inc (PA) ... **C ... 877 755-4279**
4051 Broad St Ste 220 San Luis Obispo (93401) *(P-18101)*

Mindless Entertainment, North Hollywood *Also called 51 Minds Entertainment LLC (P-19341)*

Mindrum Precision Inc ... E ... 909 989-1728
10000 4th St Rancho Cucamonga (91730) *(P-10739)*

Mindrum Precision Products, Rancho Cucamonga *Also called Mindrum Precision Inc (P-10739)*

Mindshow ... E ... 213 531-0277
333 S Grand Ave Ste 4325 Los Angeles (90071) *(P-17917)*

Mergent e-mail: customerrelations@mergent.com
1206
2022 Southern California Business Directory and Buyers Guide
(P-0000) Products & Services Section entry number
(PA)=Parent Co (HQ)=Headquarters (DH)=Div Headquarters

Mindspark Inc..........E.......310 396-9292
21021 Ventura Blvd # 220 Woodland Hills (91364) *(P-17661)*

Mindspeed Technologies LLC (HQ)..........A.......949 579-3000
4000 Macarthur Blvd Newport Beach (92660) *(P-9546)*

Mindspeed Technologies, Inc., Newport Beach *Also called Mindspeed Technologies LLC (P-9546)*

Mine Fashion, Los Angeles *Also called Edgemine Inc (P-14372)*

Mineral King Rdlgcal Med Group..........D.......559 734-9244
1700 S Court St Ste F Visalia (93277) *(P-19980)*

Ming Medical Offices, Bakersfield *Also called Kaiser Foundation Hospitals (P-19894)*

Mini-Flex Corporation..........F.......805 644-1474
2472 Eastman Ave Ste 29 Ventura (93003) *(P-8700)*

Minilec Service Inc..........E.......818 341-1125
9207 Deering Ave Ste A Chatsworth (91311) *(P-18944)*

Minilec Service-Los Angeles BR, Chatsworth *Also called Minilec Service Inc (P-18944)*

Miniluxe Inc..........D.......424 442-1630
11965 San Vicente Blvd Los Angeles (90049) *(P-16908)*

Minka Group, Corona *Also called Minka Lighting Inc (P-13648)*

Minka Lighting Inc (PA)..........D.......951 735-9220
1151 Bradford Cir Corona (92882) *(P-13648)*

Minsley Inc..........E.......909 458-1100
989 S Monterey Ave Ontario (91761) *(P-2486)*

Mintie Corporation (PA)..........C.......323 225-4111
777 N Georgia Ave Azusa (91702) *(P-17265)*

Mintie Technologies, Azusa *Also called Mintie Corporation (P-17265)*

Minton-Spidell Inc (PA)..........F.......310 836-0403
8467 Steller Dr Culver City (90232) *(P-3479)*

Minus K Technology Inc..........C.......310 348-9656
460 Hindry Ave Ste C Inglewood (90301) *(P-10898)*

Minuteman Press, Van Nuys *Also called Printcom Inc (P-4395)*

Minuteman Press, Rancho Cucamonga *Also called Lee Maxton Inc (P-4355)*

Miracle Bedding Corporation..........E.......562 908-2370
3700 Capitol Ave City of Industry (90601) *(P-3555)*

Mirada, Long Beach *Also called Motion Theory Inc (P-17180)*

Mirada Hills Rehabilitation..........D.......562 947-8691
12200 La Mirada Blvd La Mirada (90638) *(P-20613)*

Mirada Hlls Rehb Cnvlscent Hos, La Mirada *Also called Life Care Centers America Inc (P-20392)*

Miramax LLC..........C.......310 409-4321
1901 Avenue Of The Stars # 2000 Los Angeles (90067) *(P-19152)*

Miramax Film Ny LLC (HQ)..........D.......310 409-4321
1901 Avenue Of The Stars # 2000 Los Angeles (90067) *(P-19153)*

Miramed Global Services Inc..........C.......805 277-1017
199 E Thsand Oaks Blvd Thousand Oaks (91360) *(P-23474)*

Miramonte Enterprises LLC..........C.......951 658-9441
275 N San Jacinto St Hemet (92543) *(P-20418)*

Mirion Technologies Gds Inc (HQ)..........C.......949 419-1000
2652 Mcgaw Ave Irvine (92614) *(P-22953)*

Mirth Corporation..........D.......714 389-1200
611 Anton Blvd Ste 500 Costa Mesa (92626) *(P-17918)*

Mis Sciences Corp..........C.......818 847-0213
2550 N Hollywood Way # 4 Burbank (91505) *(P-12654)*

Mishima Foods USA Inc (PA)..........D.......310 787-1533
3812 Sepulveda Blvd # 505 Torrance (90505) *(P-14479)*

Miss Cristina, Los Angeles *Also called Miss Kim Inc (P-2893)*

Miss Kim Inc..........F.......213 741-0888
911 New Depot St Apt 9 Los Angeles (90012) *(P-2893)*

Mission Ambltory Srgcenter Ltd..........D.......949 364-2201
26730 Crown Valley Pkwy Mission Viejo (92691) *(P-20863)*

Mission Ambulance Inc..........D.......951 272-2300
1055 E 3rd St Corona (92879) *(P-11881)*

MISSION BARGAIN CENTER, Oxnard *Also called Rescue Mission Alliance (P-22460)*

Mission Beverage Co (HQ)..........C.......323 266-6238
550 S Mission Rd Los Angeles (90033) *(P-14831)*

Mission Care Center, Riverside *Also called Riverside Equities LLC (P-20449)*

Mission Care Center, Rosemead *Also called Ensign Group Inc (P-20331)*

Mission Community Hospital, Panorama City *Also called Deanco Healthcare LLC (P-20743)*

Mission Country Disposal..........D.......805 543-0875
4388 Old Santa Fe Rd San Luis Obispo (93401) *(P-12960)*

Mission Crtical Composites LLC..........E.......714 831-2100
15400 Graham St Ste 102 Huntington Beach (92649) *(P-10384)*

Mission Custom Extrusion Inc..........E.......909 822-1581
10904 Beech Ave Fontana (92337) *(P-5712)*

Mission Flavors Fragrances Inc..........F.......949 461-3344
25882 Wright El Toro (92610) *(P-2333)*

Mission Hills Country Club Inc..........C.......760 324-9400
34600 Mission Hills Dr Rancho Mirage (92270) *(P-19587)*

Mission Hills Mortgage Bankers, Irvine *Also called Mission Hills Mortgage Corp (P-15216)*

Mission Hills Mortgage Corp (HQ)..........C.......714 972-3832
18500 Von Karman Ave # 1100 Irvine (92612) *(P-15216)*

Mission Hills Senior Living..........D.......760 770-7737
34560 Bob Hope Dr Rancho Mirage (92270) *(P-22132)*

Mission Hosp Regional Med Ctr (PA)..........A.......949 364-1400
27700 Medical Center Rd Mission Viejo (92691) *(P-20864)*

Mission Inn Hotel and Spa, The, Riverside *Also called Historic Mission Inn Corp (P-16481)*

Mission Internal Med Group Inc..........D.......949 364-3570
26800 Crown Valley Pkwy # 103 Mission Viejo (92691) *(P-19981)*

Mission Internal Med Group Inc..........D.......949 364-3605
27882 Forbes Rd Ste 110 Laguna Niguel (92677) *(P-19982)*

Mission Kleensweep Prod Inc..........D.......323 223-1405
13644 Live Oak Ln Baldwin Park (91706) *(P-4944)*

Mission Laboratories, Baldwin Park *Also called Mission Kleensweep Prod Inc (P-4944)*

Mission Ldscp Companies Inc..........C.......714 545-9962
536 E Dyer Rd Santa Ana (92707) *(P-268)*

Mission Ldscp Companies Inc..........C.......800 545-9963
16672 Millikan Ave Irvine (92606) *(P-269)*

Mission Linen & Unf Svc 178, Anaheim *Also called Mission Linen Supply (P-16857)*

Mission Linen & Uniform Svc, Lancaster *Also called Mission Linen Supply (P-16855)*

Mission Linen & Uniform Svc, Oxnard *Also called Mission Linen Supply (P-16858)*

Mission Linen & Uniform Svc, Chino *Also called Mission Linen Supply (P-16859)*

Mission Linen & Uniform Svc, Santa Barbara *Also called Mission Linen Supply (P-16862)*

Mission Linen & Uniform Svc, Montebello *Also called Mission Linen Supply (P-16863)*

Mission Linen & Uniform Svc, Palm Springs *Also called Mission Linen Supply (P-16864)*

Mission Linen & Uniform Svc, Santa Maria *Also called Mission Linen Supply (P-16865)*

Mission Linen & Uniform Svc, Visalia *Also called Mission Linen Supply (P-16866)*

Mission Linen & Uniform Svc 4, Santa Barbara *Also called Mission Linen Supply (P-16860)*

Mission Linen Supply..........D.......661 948-5052
619 W Avenue I Lancaster (93534) *(P-16855)*

Mission Linen Supply..........D.......805 772-4451
399 Errol St Morro Bay (93442) *(P-16856)*

Mission Linen Supply..........D.......909 364-8752
1260 N Jefferson St Anaheim (92807) *(P-16857)*

Mission Linen Supply..........D.......805 485-6794
505 Maulhardt Ave Oxnard (93030) *(P-16858)*

Mission Linen Supply..........D.......909 393-6857
5400 Alton Way Chino (91710) *(P-16859)*

Mission Linen Supply..........D.......805 963-0414
725 E Montecito St Santa Barbara (93103) *(P-16860)*

Mission Linen Supply..........D.......818 764-0720
12629 Saticoy St S North Hollywood (91605) *(P-16861)*

Mission Linen Supply..........D.......805 962-7687
712 E Montecito St Santa Barbara (93103) *(P-16862)*

Mission Linen Supply..........D.......323 888-8971
721 Washington Blvd Montebello (90640) *(P-16863)*

Mission Linen Supply..........D.......760 778-5288
1275 Montalvo Way Palm Springs (92262) *(P-16864)*

Mission Linen Supply..........D.......805 922-3579
602 S Western Ave Santa Maria (93458) *(P-16865)*

Mission Linen Supply..........D.......559 625-5423
520 E Mineral King Ave Visalia (93292) *(P-16837)*

Mission Linen Supply..........D.......559 291-7181
520 E Mineral King Ave Visalia (93292) *(P-16866)*

Mission Medical Clinic, Pomona *Also called Western Univ Hlth Sciences (P-20162)*

Mission Microwave Tech LLC..........D.......951 893-4925
6060 Phyllis Dr Cypress (90630) *(P-9292)*

Mission Plastics Inc..........C.......909 947-7287
1930 S Parco Ave Ontario (91761) *(P-5713)*

Mission Pools of Escondido..........C.......949 588-0100
22600 Lambert St Ste 1104 Lake Forest (92630) *(P-1675)*

Mission Pools of Lake Forest, Lake Forest *Also called Mission Pools of Escondido (P-1675)*

Mission Ready Mix, Ventura *Also called Lynch Ready Mix Concrete Co (P-6099)*

Mission Rubber Co, Corona *Also called MCP Industries Inc (P-5391)*

Mission Rubber Company LLC (HQ)..........C.......951 736-1313
1660 Leeson Ln Corona (92879) *(P-14005)*

Mission Series Inc..........E.......714 736-1000
1585 W Mission Blvd Pomona (91766) *(P-14264)*

Mission Service Inc..........A.......323 266-2593
1800 Avenue Of The Stars # 1400 Los Angeles (90067) *(P-18856)*

Mission Terrace, Santa Barbara *Also called Cliff View Terrace Inc (P-22093)*

Mission Viejo Country Club..........C.......949 582-1550
26200 Country Club Dr Mission Viejo (92691) *(P-19588)*

Mission Viejo Pateadores Inc..........E.......949 350-5590
7 El Corzo Rcho STA Marg (92688) *(P-19424)*

Mission Viejo Surgicenter, Mission Viejo *Also called Saddlback Vly Srgcal Med Group (P-20046)*

Mission View Health Center, San Luis Obispo *Also called Compass Health Inc (P-20286)*

Mission Volkswagen Inc..........D.......949 493-4511
32922 Valle Rd San Juan Capistrano (92675) *(P-18857)*

Misyd Corp (PA)..........D.......213 742-1800
30 Fremont Pl Los Angeles (90005) *(P-3035)*

Mitchell Buckman Inc (PA)..........D.......559 733-1181
500 N Santa Fe St Visalia (93292) *(P-15595)*

Mitchell Fabrication..........E.......909 590-0393
4564 Mission Blvd Montclair (91763) *(P-6640)*

Mitchell Processing LLC..........E.......909 519-5759
2778 Pomona Blvd Pomona (91768) *(P-5392)*

Mitchell Rubber Products LLC (PA)..........C.......951 681-5655
1880 Iowa Ave Ste 400 Riverside (92507) *(P-5393)*

Mitchell Silberberg Knupp LLP (PA)..........B.......310 312-2000
2049 Century Park E Fl 18 Los Angeles (90067) *(P-21630)*

Mitchell Slbrberg Knupp Fndtio, Los Angeles *Also called Mitchell Silberberg Knupp LLP (P-21630)*

Mitchellamazing, Montclair *Also called Amazing Steel Company (P-6585)*

Mitco Industries Inc (PA)..........E.......909 877-0800
2235 S Vista Ave Bloomington (92316) *(P-8701)*

Mitratech Holdings Inc..........C.......323 964-0000
5900 Wilshire Blvd # 1500 Los Angeles (90036) *(P-17919)*

Mitsubishi Cement Corporation..........C.......760 248-7373
5808 State Highway 18 Lucerne Valley (92356) *(P-5979)*

Mitsubishi Cement Corporation..........B.......562 495-0600
1150 Pier F Ave Long Beach (90802) *(P-5980)*

Mitsubishi Chemical Crbn Fbr..........C.......800 929-5471
1822 Reynolds Ave Irvine (92614) *(P-5187)*

Mitsubishi Elc Pwr Pdts Inc..........E.......909 447-8410
1065 Bonita Ave La Verne (91750) *(P-8900)*

Mitsubishi Electric Us Inc (HQ)..........C.......714 220-2500
5900 Katella Ave Ste C Cypress (90630) *(P-1625)*

Mitsubishi Electric Us Inc..........D.......714 934-5300
7345 Orangewood Ave Garden Grove (92841) *(P-13751)*

Mitsubishi Materials USA Corp (HQ)..........E.......714 352-6100
3535 Hyland Ave Ste 200 Costa Mesa (92626) *(P-13920)*

Mitsubishi Motors Cr Amer Inc (HQ)..........B.......714 799-4730
6400 Katella Ave Cypress (90630) *(P-15146)*

Employee Codes: A=Over 500 employees, B=251-500
C=101-250, D=51-100, E=20-50 F=10-19
2022 Southern California Business
Directory and Buyers Guide
© Mergent Inc. 1-800-342-5647
1207

Mitsubishi Warehouse Cal Corp D 310 886-5500
3040 E Victoria St Compton (90221) ***(P-12223)***

Mitsubshi Elc Vsual Sltons AME C 800 553-7278
10833 Valley View St # 300 Cypress (90630) ***(P-9752)***

Mitsuwa Corporation D 714 557-6699
665 Paularino Ave Costa Mesa (92626) ***(P-14441)***

Mittal Ram D 310 769-6669
100 E Hillcrest Blvd Inglewood (90301) ***(P-13834)***

Mixed Nuts Inc E 323 587-6887
7909 Crossway Dr Pico Rivera (90660) ***(P-2113)***

Mixmor Inc F 323 664-1941
3131 Casitas Ave Los Angeles (90039) ***(P-7646)***

Mixtec/Ndgena Cmnty Orgnzing P D 805 483-1166
135 Magnolia Ave Oxnard (93030) ***(P-21851)***

Miyako Oriental Foods Inc F 626 962-9633
4287 Puente Ave Baldwin Park (91706) ***(P-2119)***

Mizell Senior Center Inc D 760 323-5689
480 S Sunrise Way Palm Springs (92262) ***(P-21852)***

Mizkan America Inc D 909 484-8743
10037 8th St Rancho Cucamonga (91730) ***(P-2487)***

Mj Best Videographer LLC C 209 208-8432
14005 S Berendo Ave Apt 3 Gardena (90247) ***(P-9184)***

Mj Diaz Backhoe Service Inc F 951 496-4949
968 White Ranch Cir Corona (92881) ***(P-7647)***

Mj-Pak, Costa Mesa *Also called Plastoker Inc* ***(P-5761)***

Mjc America Ltd (PA) **E 888 876-5387**
20035 E Walnut Dr N Walnut (91789) ***(P-9009)***

Mjc Engineering and Tech Inc F 714 890-0618
15401 Assembly Ln Huntington Beach (92649) ***(P-7761)***

Mjck Corporation F 888 992-8437
3222 E Washington Blvd Vernon (90058) ***(P-2639)***

MJM Expert Pipe Fbrcation Wldg E 661 330-8698
3404 Wrenwood St Bakersfield (93309) ***(P-6641)***

Mjp Empire Inc (PA) **C 714 564-7900**
1682 Langley Ave Fl 2 Irvine (92614) ***(P-1190)***

Mjw Inc D 323 778-8900
1328 W Slauson Ave Los Angeles (90044) ***(P-8017)***

MJW Investments (PA) **D 310 395-3430**
1640 5th St Ste 112 Santa Monica (90401) ***(P-15680)***

Mk Diamond Products Inc (PA) **C 310 539-5221**
1315 Storm Pkwy Torrance (90501) ***(P-7882)***

Mk Diamonds & Jewelry, Beverly Hills *Also called Maurice Kraiem & Company* ***(P-14134)***

Mk Magnetics Inc D 760 246-6373
17030 Muskrat Ave Adelanto (92301) ***(P-6230)***

Mk Manufacturing, Irvine *Also called M K Products Inc* ***(P-7892)***

Mk Printing, Santa Ana *Also called Mekong Printing Inc* ***(P-4370)***

Mk Tool and Abrasive Inc F 562 776-8818
4710 S Eastern Ave Los Angeles (90040) ***(P-6156)***

Mkkr Inc E 909 890-5994
430 E Parkcenter Cir N San Bernardino (92408) ***(P-7858)***

Mkni, Visalia *Also called Morgan Kleppe and Nash LLC* ***(P-15598)***

Mkr Medical Supply Inc C 310 830-3980
1950 E 220th St Ste 203 Long Beach (90810) ***(P-13501)***

Mks Color Composite, Compton *Also called Permalite Plastics Corp* ***(P-5122)***

Mkt Innovations, Brea *Also called Mike Kenney Tool Inc* ***(P-8695)***

Mkt Innovations D 714 524-7668
2900 Saturn St Ste A Brea (92821) ***(P-8702)***

Mktg Inc A 310 972-7900
5800 Bristol Pkwy Ste 500 Culver City (90230) ***(P-18598)***

ML Kishigo Mfg Co LLC D 949 852-1963
11250 Slater Ave Fountain Valley (92708) ***(P-3080)***

Mladen Buntich Cnstr Co Inc D 909 920-9977
1500 W 9th St Upland (91786) ***(P-963)***

Mlife Hospice Inc (PA) **D 909 996-2508**
7786 Lemon Pepper Ave Fontana (92336) ***(P-20537)***

MMC, Los Angeles *Also called Marsh Risk & Insurance Svcs* ***(P-15592)***

MMC, Los Angeles *Also called Medical Management Cons Inc* ***(P-17505)***

Mmd Equipment, Simi Valley *Also called Rajysan Incorporated* ***(P-13934)***

Mme Florida LLC (PA) **D 678 826-8622**
10115 Jefferson Blvd Culver City (90232) ***(P-18599)***

Mmi Services Inc C 661 589-9366
4042 Patton Way Bakersfield (93308) ***(P-518)***

Mmiw Welding & Fabrication, Springville *Also called Theodore B Martin* ***(P-19000)***

Mmp Sheet Metal Inc E 562 691-1055
501 Commercial Way La Habra (90631) ***(P-6878)***

Mmxviii Holdings Inc E 800 672-3974
20251 Sw Acacia St # 120 Newport Beach (92660) ***(P-11574)***

Mnm Corporation (PA) **E 213 627-3737**
110 E 9th St Ste A777 Los Angeles (90079) ***(P-4086)***

MNS Engineers Inc (PA) **D 805 692-6921**
201 N Calle Cesar Chavez Santa Barbara (93103) ***(P-22615)***

MNX Global Logistics Corp (HQ) **D 310 981-0918**
5000 Arprt Plz Dr Ste 100 Long Beach (90815) ***(P-12484)***

Moaddel Law Firm APC E 323 999-5099
3435 Wilshire Blvd # 243 Los Angeles (90010) ***(P-21631)***

Mob Scene LLC (PA) **C 323 648-7200**
8447 Wilshire Blvd # 100 Beverly Hills (90211) ***(P-17036)***

Mob Scene Creative Productions, Beverly Hills *Also called Mob Scene LLC* ***(P-17036)***

Mobile Equipment Appraisers, Bakersfield *Also called Mobile Equipment Company* ***(P-7698)***

Mobile Equipment Company E 661 327-8476
3610 Gilmore Ave Bakersfield (93308) ***(P-7698)***

Mobile Messenger Americas Inc (PA) **C 310 957-3300**
6601 Center Dr W Ste 700 Los Angeles (90045) ***(P-18600)***

Mobile Money Inc (HQ) **D 562 948-3916**
7633 Industry Ave Pico Rivera (90660) ***(P-15130)***

Mobile Net Posa Inc F 213 863-0351
835 Wilshire Blvd Ste 200 Los Angeles (90017) ***(P-17920)***

Mobile Video Systems Inc (PA) **F 888 721-5777**
23905 Clinton Kth Rd Wildomar (92595) ***(P-9293)***

Mobilenet Services Inc (PA) **C 949 951-4444**
18 Morgan Ste 200 Irvine (92618) ***(P-22616)***

Mobilitie Services LLC B 877 399-7070
660 Nwport Ctr Dr Ste 200 Newport Beach (92660) ***(P-12655)***

Mobilityware, Irvine *Also called Upstanding LLC* ***(P-18004)***

Mobilityware LLC (PA) **D 949 788-9900**
440 Exchange Ste 100 Irvine (92602) ***(P-17662)***

Mobis Parts America LLC (HQ) **D 786 515-1101**
10550 Talbert Ave Fl 4 Fountain Valley (92708) ***(P-13074)***

Mobis Parts America LLC E 949 450-0014
10550 Talbert Ave 4 Fountain Valley (92708) ***(P-10105)***

Mobis Wholesale, Carpinteria *Also called Ocean Breeze International* ***(P-88)***

Moc Products Company Inc (PA) **D 818 794-3500**
12306 Montague St Pacoima (91331) ***(P-5234)***

Mocean LLC C 310 481-0808
2440 S Sepulveda Blvd # 150 Los Angeles (90064) ***(P-18102)***

Mochi Ice Cream Company LLC (PA) **E 323 587-5504**
5563 Alcoa Ave Vernon (90058) ***(P-2020)***

Mod 2, Los Angeles *Also called Mod2 Inc* ***(P-17921)***

Mod Vid Film, Glendale *Also called Modern Videofilm Inc* ***(P-19154)***

Mod-Electronics Inc E 310 322-2136
142 Sierra St El Segundo (90245) ***(P-11302)***

Mod2 Inc E 213 747-8424
3317 S Broadway Los Angeles (90007) ***(P-17921)***

Modaan Inc (PA) **F 949 786-0223**
4250 Barranca Pkwy Ste I Irvine (92604) ***(P-2021)***

Model Lyfe F 224 325-5933
5405 Wilshire Blvd Los Angeles (90036) ***(P-4087)***

Model Lyfe Magazine, Los Angeles *Also called Model Lyfe* ***(P-4087)***

Model Match Inc F 949 525-9405
209 Avnida Fbrcnte Ste 15 San Clemente (92672) ***(P-17922)***

Modern Aire Ventilating, North Hollywood *Also called Modern-Aire Ventilating Inc* ***(P-6879)***

Modern Building Inc E 951 297-3311
29991 Cyn Hls Rd Ste 1709 Lake Elsinore (92532) ***(P-709)***

Modern Campus USA Inc D 805 484-9400
1320 Flynn Rd Ste 100 Camarillo (93012) ***(P-17663)***

Modern Candle Co Inc E 323 441-0104
12884 Bradley Ave Sylmar (91342) ***(P-14953)***

Modern Candles, Sylmar *Also called Modern Candle Co Inc* ***(P-14953)***

Modern Concepts Inc D 310 637-0013
3121 E Ana St E Rncho Dmngz (90221) ***(P-5714)***

Modern Dev Co A Ltd Partnr D 949 646-6400
7900 All America City Way Paramount (90723) ***(P-18601)***

Modern Engine Inc E 818 409-9494
701 Sonora Ave Glendale (91201) ***(P-8703)***

Modern Gourmet Foods, Irvine *Also called Coastal Cocktails Inc* ***(P-2262)***

Modern Imaging Solutions Inc E 800 511-7585
22122 Sherman Way Ste 209 Canoga Park (91303) ***(P-13144)***

Modern Manufacturing Inc E 714 254-0156
4110 E La Palma Ave Anaheim (92807) ***(P-8704)***

Modern Outdoor Designs LLC F 818 785-0171
16787 Schoenborn St North Hills (91343) ***(P-18602)***

Modern Parking Inc B 310 821-1081
14110 Palawan Way Marina Del Rey (90292) ***(P-18769)***

Modern Plating, Los Angeles *Also called Alco Plating Corp* ***(P-7202)***

Modern Studio Equipment Inc F 818 764-8574
16200 Stagg St Van Nuys (91406) ***(P-11284)***

Modern Videofilm Inc C 818 637-6800
1733 Flower St Glendale (91201) ***(P-19154)***

Modern Woodworks Inc E 800 575-3475
7949 Deering Ave Canoga Park (91304) ***(P-3446)***

Modern-Aire Ventilating Inc E 818 765-9870
7319 Lankershim Blvd North Hollywood (91605) ***(P-6879)***

Modified Plastics Inc (PA) **E 714 546-4667**
1240 E Glenwood Pl Santa Ana (92707) ***(P-5715)***

Modivcare Inc E 661 765-7025
1021 4th St Taft (93268) ***(P-21321)***

Modivcare Solutions LLC C 714 503-6871
7441 Lincoln Way 225 Garden Grove (92841) ***(P-12485)***

Modrine Limited D 213 269-5466
750 N Diamond Bar Blvd Diamond Bar (91765) ***(P-17664)***

Moducom, La Crescenta *Also called Modular Communications Systems* ***(P-9294)***

Modulant, Long Beach *Also called Product Data Intgrtion Tech In* ***(P-18059)***

Modular Communications Systems E 818 764-1333
2629 Foothill Blvd La Crescenta (91214) ***(P-9294)***

Modular Metal Fabricators Inc C 951 242-3154
24600 Nandina Ave Moreno Valley (92551) ***(P-6880)***

Modular Office Solutions Inc E 909 476-4200
11701 6th St Rancho Cucamonga (91730) ***(P-3615)***

Modvans, Ventura *Also called Webtez Inc* ***(P-10557)***

Modway Furniture, Fontana *Also called Modway Inc* ***(P-13145)***

Modway Inc D 323 729-3299
15816 Santa Ana Ave Fontana (92337) ***(P-13145)***

Moehair Usa Inc F 888 663-7032
1061 S Melrose St Ste A Placentia (92870) ***(P-5048)***

Moelis & Company LLC D 310 443-2300
1999 Avenue Of The Stars Los Angeles (90067) ***(P-16190)***

Moeller Mfg & Sup LLC E 714 999-5551
630 E Lambert Rd Brea (92821) ***(P-6527)***

Moffatt & Nichol D 657 261-2699
555 Anton Blvd Ste 400 Costa Mesa (92626) ***(P-22617)***

Mohawk Medical Group Inc D 661 324-4747
9500 Stockdale Hwy # 200 Bakersfield (93311) ***(P-19983)***

Mohawk Western Plastics Inc E 909 593-7547
1496 Arrow Hwy La Verne (91750) ***(P-3887)***

Moiola Bros Cattle Feeders, Brawley *Also called Moiola Bros Cttle Fders Ltd A* ***(P-125)***

Moiola Bros Cttle Fders Ltd A......D......760 344-1919
1594 Gonder Rd Brawley (92227) *(P-125)*
Mojave Copy & Printing Inc......F......760 241-7898
12402 Industrial Blvd E10 Victorville (92395) *(P-4375)*
Mojave Foods Corporation......C......323 890-8900
6200 E Slauson Ave Commerce (90040) *(P-2488)*
Mojave Gold LLC......F......760 397-0408
74100 Fillmore St Thermal (92274) *(P-14709)*
Mola Inc......C......323 582-0088
2957 E 46th St Vernon (90058) *(P-14402)*
Mold Vision Inc......F......951 245-8020
18351 Pasadena St Lake Elsinore (92530) *(P-7816)*
Molded Devices, Riverside *Also called Mdi East Inc (P-5704)*
Molded Fiber GL Companies - W......D......760 246-4042
9400 Holly Rd Adelanto (92301) *(P-5716)*
Molded Interconnect Industries, Foothill Ranch *Also called Lantic Inc (P-5696)*
Moldex-Metric Inc......B......310 837-6500
10111 Jefferson Blvd Culver City (90232) *(P-11126)*
Molding Corporation America......E......818 890-7877
10349 Norris Ave Pacoima (91331) *(P-5717)*
Molding Intl & Engrg Inc......E......951 296-5010
42136 Avenida Alvarado Temecula (92590) *(P-5718)*
Moldings Plus Inc......E......909 947-3310
1856 S Grove Ave Ontario (91761) *(P-3270)*
Moleculum......F......714 619-5139
3128 Red Hill Ave Costa Mesa (92626) *(P-5255)*
Molina Healthcare Inc......D......909 546-7116
790 E Foothill Blvd Rialto (92376) *(P-21455)*
Molina Healthcare Inc......D......888 562-5442
604 Pine Ave Long Beach (90802) *(P-21456)*
Molina Healthcare Inc (PA)......A......562 435-3666**
200 Oceangate Ste 100 Long Beach (90802) *(P-19984)*
Molina Healthcare Inc......D......562 435-3666
1 Golden Shore Long Beach (90802) *(P-21457)*
Molina Healthcare California......C......800 526-8196
200 Oceangate Ste 100 Long Beach (90802) *(P-19985)*
Molina Healthcare New York Inc......C......888 562-5442
200 Oceangate Ste 100 Long Beach (90802) *(P-19986)*
Molina Hlthcare Cal Prtner Pla......A......562 435-3666
200 Oceangate Ste 100 Long Beach (90802) *(P-15382)*
Molina Information Systems LLC (HQ)......A......916 561-8540
200 Oceangate Ste 100 Long Beach (90802) *(P-18129)*
Molina Medicaid Solutions, Long Beach *Also called Molina Information Systems LLC (P-18129)*
Molina Pathways LLC......B......562 491-5773
200 Oceangate Ste 100 Long Beach (90802) *(P-19987)*
Molinari, Michael D MD, Corona *Also called Michael D Molinari MD Facg Inc (P-19978)*
Molino Company......D......323 726-1000
13712 Alondra Blvd Cerritos (90703) *(P-4376)*
Moller Retail Inc......F......805 299-8200
6591 Collins Dr Ste E11 Moorpark (93021) *(P-519)*
Molly Max, Los Angeles *Also called Assoluto Inc (P-2919)*
Molnar Engineering Inc......E......818 993-3495
20731 Marilla St Chatsworth (91311) *(P-8705)*
Momeni Engineering LLC......E......714 897-9301
15662 Commerce Ln Huntington Beach (92649) *(P-8706)*
Momentfeed Inc......D......310 853-3336
3415 S Sepulveda Blvd # 1100 Los Angeles (90034) *(P-23275)*
Momentous Insurance Brkg Inc......D......818 933-2700
5990 Sepulvda Blvd # 550 Van Nuys (91411) *(P-15596)*
Momentum Management LLC......F......310 329-2599
1206 W Jon St Torrance (90502) *(P-5394)*
Momentum Textiles LLC (PA)......E......949 833-8886
17811 Fitch Irvine (92614) *(P-14310)*
Momentum Work Inc (PA)......D......805 566-9000
5320 Carpinteria Ave G Carpinteria (93013) *(P-21962)*
Moms Orange County......E......714 972-2610
1128 W Santa Ana Blvd Santa Ana (92703) *(P-21192)*
Monadnock Company......C......626 964-6581
16728 Gale Ave City of Industry (91745) *(P-6528)*
Monarch Art & Frame Inc......E......818 373-6180
7700 Gloria Ave Van Nuys (91406) *(P-19051)*
Monarch Beach Golf Links (HQ)......D......949 240-8247
50 Monarch Beach Resort N Dana Point (92629) *(P-19502)*
Monarch Healthcare A Medical (HQ)......B......949 923-3200
11 Technology Dr Irvine (92618) *(P-19988)*
Monarch Landscape Holdings LLC (PA)......D......213 816-1750
550 S Hope St Ste 1675 Los Angeles (90071) *(P-326)*
Monarch Litho Inc (PA)......E......323 727-0300
1501 Date St Montebello (90640) *(P-4377)*
Monarch Nut Company LLC......C......661 725-6458
786 Road 188 Delano (93215) *(P-182)*
Monarch Prcision Deburring Inc......F......714 258-0342
1514 E Edinger Ave Ste C Santa Ana (92705) *(P-7737)*
Monark LP......D......310 769-6669
2804 W El Segundo Blvd Gardena (90249) *(P-15741)*
Monco Products Inc......E......714 891-2788
7562 Acacia Ave Garden Grove (92841) *(P-5719)*
Mondrian Holdings LLC......B......323 848-6004
8440 W Sunset Blvd West Hollywood (90069) *(P-16570)*
Mondrian Hotel, Los Angeles *Also called Morgans Hotel Group MGT LLC (P-16573)*
Monex Deposit A Cal Ltd Partnr......D......949 752-1400
4910 Birch St Newport Beach (92660) *(P-16133)*
Moneyline Lending Services, Irvine *Also called Genpact Mortgage Services Inc (P-15195)*
Monica Ros School......D......805 646-8184
783 Mcnell Rd Ojai (93023) *(P-22035)*
Monique Suraci......D......951 677-8111
41885 Ivy St Murrieta (92562) *(P-19461)*
Monkee Inc......E......626 848-1555
16104 E Cypress St Covina (91722) *(P-18603)*
Mono Engineering Corp......E......818 772-4998
20977 Knapp St Chatsworth (91311) *(P-8707)*
Monobind Sales Inc (PA)......E......949 951-2665
100 N Pointe Dr Lake Forest (92630) *(P-11026)*
Monocent Inc......F......424 310-0777
9237 Eton Ave Chatsworth (91311) *(P-4924)*
Monogram Aerospace Fas Inc......C......323 722-4760
3423 Garfield Ave Commerce (90040) *(P-6529)*
Monogram Systems, Carson *Also called Zodiac Wtr Waste Aero Systems (P-10449)*
Monopole Inc......F......818 500-8585
4661 Alger St Los Angeles (90039) *(P-5103)*
Monoprice Inc (HQ)......C......909 989-6887
1 Pointe Dr Ste 400 Brea (92821) *(P-14170)*
Monoprice.com, Brea *Also called Monoprice Inc (P-14170)*
Monroe Magnus LLC (PA)......F......714 771-2630
2805 Barranca Pkwy Irvine (92606) *(P-13812)*
Monrovia Growes, Azusa *Also called Monrovia Nursery Company (P-85)*
Monrovia Memorial Hospital, Monrovia *Also called Alakor Healthcare LLC (P-20668)*
Monrovia Nursery Company (PA)......A......626 334-9321
817 E Monrovia Pl Azusa (91702) *(P-85)*
Monrovia Ranch Market, Victorville *Also called E & T Foods Inc (P-141)*
Monrovia Service Center, Monrovia *Also called Southern California Edison Co (P-12829)*
Monrow Inc......E......213 741-6007
1404 S Main St Ste C Los Angeles (90015) *(P-2859)*
MONSIEUR MARCEL, Los Angeles *Also called Strouk Group LLC (P-14607)*
Monster Beverage Company......E......866 322-4466
1990 Pomona Rd Corona (92878) *(P-2271)*
Monster Beverage Corporation (PA)......A......951 739-6200
1 Monster Way Corona (92879) *(P-2272)*
Monster Energy Company (HQ)......A......951 739-6200
1 Monster Way Corona (92879) *(P-14710)*
Monster Vending......E......909 223-5522
8545 Devon Ln Garden Grove (92844) *(P-5720)*
Montage Beverly Hills, Beverly Hills *Also called Montage Hotels & Resorts LLC (P-16571)*
Montage Hotels & Resorts LLC......D......310 499-4199
225 N Canon Dr Beverly Hills (90210) *(P-16571)*
Montage Hotels & Resorts LLC......A......949 715-6000
30801 Coast Hwy Laguna Beach (92651) *(P-23067)*
Montage Hotels & Resorts LLC (PA)......A......949 715-5002
3 Ada Ste 100 Irvine (92618) *(P-16572)*
Montage Laguna Beach, Laguna Beach *Also called Montage Hotels & Resorts LLC (P-23067)*
Montage Laguna Beach, Irvine *Also called Montage Hotels & Resorts LLC (P-16572)*
Montclair Bronze Inc (PA)......E......909 986-2664
5621 State St Montclair (91763) *(P-6409)*
Montclair Community Health Ctr, Chino *Also called Health Service Alliance (P-21434)*
Montclair Mental Health Offs, Montclair *Also called Kaiser Foundation Hospitals (P-21314)*
Montclair Mnor Cnvlescent Hosp, Montclair *Also called Medicrest of California 1 (P-20416)*
Montclair Wood Corporation......F......909 985-0302
545 N Mountain Ave Upland (91786) *(P-3222)*
Monte De Oro Winery......F......951 491-6551
35820 Rancho Cal Rd Temecula (92591) *(P-2209)*
Monte Nido Holdings LLC......D......310 472-3728
520 S Sepulveda Blvd # 208 Los Angeles (90049) *(P-20227)*
Monte Vista Child Care Ctr Inc (PA)......D......909 544-0040
13342 Victoria St Rancho Cucamonga (91739) *(P-22036)*
Monte Vista Grove Homes......D......626 796-6135
2889 San Pasqual St Pasadena (91107) *(P-22133)*
Montebello Container Co LLC (HQ)......D......562 404-6221
16069 Shoemaker Ave Cerritos (90703) *(P-3821)*
Montebello Orthpd Med Group......D......562 654-6899
6758 Passons Blvd Pico Rivera (90660) *(P-19989)*
Montebello Plastics LLC......E......323 728-6814
601 W Olympic Blvd Montebello (90640) *(P-5434)*
Montecito Country Club Inc......D......805 969-0800
920 Summit Rd Santa Barbara (93108) *(P-19589)*
Montecito Family YMCA, Santa Barbara *Also called Channel Islnds Yung MNS Chrstn (P-22329)*
Montecito Heights, Los Angeles *Also called Rockport ADM Svcs LLC (P-20451)*
Montecito Retirement Assn......B......805 969-8011
300 Hot Springs Rd Santa Barbara (93108) *(P-20419)*
Monterey Bay Beverage Co Inc......E......818 784-4885
14535 Benefit St Unit 4 Sherman Oaks (91403) *(P-1867)*
Monterey Canyon LLC (PA)......D......213 741-0209
1515 E 15th St Los Angeles (90021) *(P-2975)*
Monterey Machine Products......F......626 967-2242
1504 W Industrial Park St Covina (91722) *(P-8708)*
Monterey Park Hospital, Monterey Park *Also called Monterey Park Hospital (P-20865)*
Monterey Park Hospital......C......626 570-9000
900 S Atlantic Blvd Monterey Park (91754) *(P-20865)*
Monterey Pk Convalescent Hosp......D......626 280-0280
416 N Garfield Ave Monterey Park (91754) *(P-20614)*
Montessori On The Lake, Lake Forest *Also called Environments For Learning Inc (P-22012)*
Montrose Envmtl Group Inc (PA)......B......949 988-3500
1 Park Plz Ste 1000 Irvine (92614) *(P-23475)*
Montrose Msrmnts Analytics LLC (HQ)......E......949 988-3500
1 Park Plz Ste 1000 Irvine (92614) *(P-23476)*
Montrose Water and Sustainabil......D......949 988-3500
1 Park Plz Ste 1000 Irvine (92614) *(P-23477)*
Monty Ventsam Inc......F......818 768-6424
9495 San Fernando Rd Sun Valley (91352) *(P-3271)*
Mony Life Insurance Company......D......714 939-6669
333 S Anita Dr Ste 750 Orange (92868) *(P-15597)*
Moog Aircraft Group, Torrance *Also called Moog Inc (P-10602)*

ALPHABETIC

Employee Codes: A=Over 500 employees, B=251-500
C=101-250, D=51-100, E=20-50 F=10-19
2022 Southern California Business
Directory and Buyers Guide
© Mergent Inc. 1-800-342-5647
1209

Moog Inc ....C.......818 341-5156
21339 Nordhoff St Chatsworth (91311) ***(P-10600)***
Moog Inc ....B.......805 618-3900
7406 Hollister Ave Goleta (93117) ***(P-10601)***
Moog Inc ....B.......310 533-1178
1218 W Jon St Torrance (90502) ***(P-8961)***
Moog Inc ....B.......310 533-1178
20263 S Western Ave Torrance (90501) ***(P-10602)***
Moog Jon Street Warehouse, Torrance *Also called Moog Inc* ***(P-8961)***
Mooney Inds Prcsion McHning In.......F.......818 998-0199
8744 Remmet Ave Canoga Park (91304) ***(P-8709)***
Mooney International, Chino *Also called Soaring America Corporation* ***(P-10203)***
Moonstar Mfg Inc ....F.......323 581-1656
5101 Pacific Blvd Vernon (90058) ***(P-2860)***
Moonstone Hotel Properties, Cambria *Also called Moonstone Management Corp* ***(P-15926)***
Moonstone Management Corp (PA).......C.......805 927-4200**
2905 Burton Dr Cambria (93428) ***(P-15926)***
Moore Farms Inc.......E.......661 854-5588
916 S Derby St Arvin (93203) ***(P-2489)***
Moore Foundations Inc ....E.......818 698-4737
7046 Darby Ave Reseda (91335) ***(P-22350)***
Moore Industries - Europe Inc (HQ).......F.......818 894-7111**
16650 Schoenborn St Sepulveda (91343) ***(P-10708)***
Moore Law Group A Prof Corp ....D.......714 431-2000
3710 S Susan St Ste 210 Santa Ana (92704) ***(P-21632)***
Moorefield Construction Inc (PA).......D.......714 972-0700**
600 N Tustin Ave Ste 210 Santa Ana (92705) ***(P-793)***
Moores Ideal Products LLC ....E.......626 339-9007
830 W Golden Grove Way Covina (91722) ***(P-11385)***
Moose Toys LLC ....D.......310 341-4642
737 Campus Sq W El Segundo (90245) ***(P-11363)***
Mophie Inc (HQ).......C.......888 866-7443**
15495 Sand Canyon Ave # 400 Irvine (92618) ***(P-9295)***
Moravek Biochemicals Inc (PA).......E.......714 990-2018**
577 Mercury Ln Brea (92821) ***(P-4663)***
Morehouse Foods Inc.......E.......626 854-1655
760 Epperson Dr City of Industry (91748) ***(P-1892)***
Morehouse-Cowles LLC.......E.......909 627-7222
13930 Magnolia Ave Chino (91710) ***(P-7991)***
Moreno Valley Family Hlth Ctr, Moreno Valley *Also called Community Health Systems Inc* ***(P-19757)***
Moreno Valley Heacock Med Offs, Moreno Valley *Also called Kaiser Foundation Hospitals* ***(P-16182)***
Morettis Design Collection.......E.......310 638-5555
16926 Keegan Ave Ste C Carson (90746) ***(P-3480)***
Morgan Kleppe and Nash LLC.......D.......559 732-3436
501 N Church St Visalia (93291) ***(P-15598)***
Morgan & Slates Mfg & Sup Inc (PA).......F.......559 582-4417**
12918 Hanford Armona Rd Hanford (93230) ***(P-18991)***
Morgan Fabrics Corporation (PA) ....D.......323 583-9981**
4265 Exchange Ave Vernon (90058) ***(P-14311)***
Morgan Gallacher Inc.......E.......562 695-1232
8707 Millergrove Dr Santa Fe Springs (90670) ***(P-4972)***
Morgan Linen Service, Los Angeles *Also called Morgan Services Inc* ***(P-16867)***
Morgan Marine, Simi Valley *Also called Catalina Yachts Inc* ***(P-10460)***
Morgan Products Inc.......E.......661 257-3022
28103 Avenue Stanford Santa Clarita (91355) ***(P-8710)***
Morgan Services Inc.......D.......213 485-9666
905 Yale St Los Angeles (90012) ***(P-16867)***
Morgan Stnley Smith Barney LLC.......D.......818 715-1800
21650 Oxnard St Ste 1800 Woodland Hills (91367) ***(P-15297)***
Morgan Stnley Smith Barney LLC.......C.......310 285-4800
9665 Wilshire Blvd # 600 Beverly Hills (90212) ***(P-15155)***
Morgan Stnley Smith Barney LLC.......D.......714 674-4100
10 Pointe Dr Ste 400 Brea (92821) ***(P-15298)***
Morgan Stnley Smith Barney LLC.......D.......805 565-4447
1111 Coast Village Rd Santa Barbara (93108) ***(P-15299)***
Morgan Stnley Smith Barney LLC.......D.......951 682-1181
3750 University Ave # 600 Riverside (92501) ***(P-15300)***
Morgan Stnley Smith Barney LLC.......C.......760 568-3500
74199 El Paseo Ste 201 Palm Desert (92260) ***(P-15033)***
Morgan Stnley Smith Barney LLC.......C.......800 490-5412
28202 Cabot Rd Ste 150 Laguna Niguel (92677) ***(P-15034)***
Morgan Stnley Smith Barney LLC.......D.......805 963-3381
1014 Santa Barbara St Santa Barbara (93101) ***(P-15301)***
Morgan Trner Frman Invstgators, Beverly Hills *Also called Morgan Turner Freeman* ***(P-18297)***
Morgan Turner Freeman (PA) ....D.......310 800-3502**
433 N Camden Dr Beverly Hills (90210) ***(P-18297)***
Morgans Hotel Group MGT LLC.......C.......323 650-8999
8440 W Sunset Blvd Los Angeles (90069) ***(P-16573)***
Morgner Construction MGT, Los Angeles *Also called Morgner Technology Management* ***(P-23068)***
Morgner Technology Management ....D.......323 900-0030
1880 Century Park E # 1402 Los Angeles (90067) ***(P-23068)***
Morigon Technologies LLC.......E.......818 764-8880
7615 Fulton Ave North Hollywood (91605) ***(P-13502)***
Morin Corporation.......E.......909 428-3747
10707 Commerce Way Fontana (92337) ***(P-7003)***
Morin Industrial Technology, Huntington Beach *Also called M I T Inc* ***(P-7813)***
Morin West, Fontana *Also called Morin Corporation* ***(P-7003)***
Morinaga America Inc (HQ).......E.......949 732-1155**
4 Park Plz Ste 750 Irvine (92614) ***(P-2098)***
Morinaga Nutritional Foods Inc ....F.......310 787-0200
3838 Del Amo Blvd Ste 201 Torrance (90503) ***(P-2490)***
Morley Construction Company (HQ).......D.......310 399-1600**
3330 Ocean Park Blvd # 101 Santa Monica (90405) ***(P-1541)***

Morningside Community Assn.......D.......760 328-3323
82 Mayfair Dr Rancho Mirage (92270) ***(P-22351)***
Morningside of Fullerton, Fullerton *Also called Corecare I I I* ***(P-22095)***
Moroccanoil Inc (PA) ....D.......888 700-1817**
16311 Ventura Blvd # 120 Encino (91436) ***(P-14265)***
Morongo Bsin Amblance Assn Inc.......D.......760 366-8474
61828 Chollita Rd Joshua Tree (92252) ***(P-11882)***
Morphosis Architects ....D.......310 453-2247
3440 Wesley St Culver City (90232) ***(P-22733)***
Morphotrak LLC (HQ) ....C.......714 238-2000**
5515 E La Palma Ave # 100 Anaheim (92807) ***(P-18047)***
Morrell's Metal Finishing, Compton *Also called Morrells Electro Plating Inc* ***(P-7283)***
Morrells Electro Plating Inc.......E.......310 639-1024
432 E Euclid Ave Compton (90222) ***(P-7283)***
Morris & Willner Partners.......D.......949 705-0682
2151 Michelson Dr Ste 185 Irvine (92612) ***(P-23276)***
Morris Automotive Supply, Fontana *Also called CH Morris Co Inc* ***(P-13050)***
Morris Enterprises Inc ....F.......818 894-9103
16799 Schoenborn St North Hills (91343) ***(P-5721)***
Morris Group International, City of Industry *Also called Acorn Engineering Company* ***(P-6985)***
Morris Group International (PA) ....C.......626 336-4561**
15125 Proctor Ave City of Industry (91746) ***(P-7004)***
Morris Grritano Insur Agcy Inc.......D.......805 543-6887
1122 Laurel Ln San Luis Obispo (93401) ***(P-15599)***
Morris Levin and Son ....C.......559 686-8665
1816 S K St Tulare (93274) ***(P-1103)***
Morris Levin Rentl & Parts Ctr, Tulare *Also called Morris Levin and Son* ***(P-1103)***
Morris National Inc (HQ).......D.......626 385-2000**
760 N Mckeever Ave Azusa (91702) ***(P-14711)***
Morris Polich & Purdy LLP (PA) ....D.......213 891-9100**
1055 W 7th St Ste 2400 Los Angeles (90017) ***(P-21633)***
Morris, Phyllis, West Hollywood *Also called Phyllis Morris Originals* ***(P-13147)***
Morrison & Foerster LLP.......C.......213 892-5200
707 Wilshire Blvd # 6000 Los Angeles (90017) ***(P-21634)***
Morrison Concrete Inc.......E.......562 802-1450
14114 Rosecrans Ave Ste C Santa Fe Springs (90670) ***(P-1542)***
Morrison Landscape.......E.......714 571-0455
1225 E Wakeham Ave Santa Ana (92705) ***(P-270)***
Morrow-Meadows Corporation (PA).......A.......858 974-3650**
231 Benton Ct City of Industry (91789) ***(P-1283)***
Morse Industrial, Ontario *Also called Regal Beloit America Inc* ***(P-13664)***
Morse Micro Inc ....D.......949 501-7080
40 Waterworks Way Irvine (92618) ***(P-9547)***
Mortan Industries Inc.......F.......951 682-2215
880 Columbia Ave Ste 2 Riverside (92507) ***(P-5395)***
Mortech Manufacturing.......D.......626 334-1471
411 N Aerojet Dr Azusa (91702) ***(P-3626)***
Mortgage Capital Partners Inc (PA).......D.......310 295-2900**
12400 Wilshire Blvd # 900 Los Angeles (90025) ***(P-15217)***
Mortgage Guy Inc (PA) ....D.......310 625-8809**
8721 W Sunset Blvd Ph 10 West Hollywood (90069) ***(P-15218)***
Mortgage Works Financial, Redlands *Also called Mountain West Financial Inc* ***(P-15219)***
Morton Grinding Inc ....C.......661 298-0895
201 E Avenue K15 Lancaster (93535) ***(P-11499)***
Morton Manufacturing, Lancaster *Also called Morton Grinding Inc* ***(P-11499)***
Moseley Associates Inc (HQ).......C.......805 968-9621**
82 Coromar Dr Goleta (93117) ***(P-9296)***
Moss & Company Inc (PA) ....D.......310 453-0911**
15300 Ventura Blvd # 418 Sherman Oaks (91403) ***(P-15927)***
Motec USA, Huntington Beach *Also called JGM Automotive Tooling Inc* ***(P-7985)***
Motek Industries.......F.......626 960-6005
14434 Joanbridge St Baldwin Park (91706) ***(P-8711)***
Mother Plucker Feather Co Inc ....F.......213 637-0411
2511 W 3rd St Ste 102 Los Angeles (90057) ***(P-11717)***
Mothers Club Family Lrng Ctr.......D.......626 792-2687
980 N Fair Oaks Ave Pasadena (91103) ***(P-21853)***
Mothership Technologies Inc ....D.......310 905-8677
3213 S La Cienega Blvd Los Angeles (90016) ***(P-17665)***
Motion Engineering Inc (HQ) ....D.......805 696-1200**
33 S La Patera Ln Santa Barbara (93117) ***(P-8282)***
Motion Pcture Indust Pnsion Hl ....C.......818 769-0007
11365 Ventura Blvd # 300 Studio City (91604) ***(P-15517)***
Motion Picture and TV Fund (PA).......A.......818 876-1777**
23388 Mulholland Dr # 200 Woodland Hills (91364) ***(P-20866)***
Motion Picture Licensing Corp (PA) ....D.......800 462-8855**
5455 S Centinela Ave Los Angeles (90066) ***(P-18604)***
Motion Solutions, Aliso Viejo *Also called Bearing Engineers Inc* ***(P-13973)***
Motion Theory Inc.......D.......310 396-9433
444 W Ocean Blvd Ste 1400 Long Beach (90802) ***(P-17180)***
Motionloft Inc ....E.......415 580-7671
13681 Newport Ave Ste 8 Tustin (92780) ***(P-10802)***
Motivational Fulfillmen, Chino *Also called Motivational Marketing Inc* ***(P-12224)***
Motivational Fulfillment, Chino *Also called Motivational Marketing Inc* ***(P-12486)***
Motivational Marketing Inc.......D.......909 517-2200
15785 Mountain Ave Chino (91708) ***(P-12224)***
Motivational Marketing Inc.......D.......909 517-2200
16133 Fern Ave Chino (91708) ***(P-12486)***
Motivational Marketing Inc (PA) ....C.......909 517-2200**
15820 Euclid Ave Chino (91708) ***(P-18605)***
Motive Energy Inc (PA).......D.......714 888-2525**
125 E Coml St Bldg B Anaheim (92801) ***(P-13649)***
Motive Nation, Downey *Also called Rockview Dairies Inc* ***(P-14733)***
Motivtnal Flfllment Lgstics Sv, Chino *Also called Motivational Marketing Inc* ***(P-18605)***
Motobell USA Inc.......F.......909 608-2830
260 Corporate Way Upland (91786) ***(P-9297)***
Motolease Funding LLC.......D.......310 601-4779
5200 W Century Blvd # 75 Los Angeles (90045) ***(P-15165)***

Motor Technology Inc......D......951 270-6200
2301 Wardlow Cir Corona (92878) ***(P-8924)***
Motor Vehicle Software Corp (PA)......**C......818 706-1949**
29901 Agoura Rd Agoura Hills (91301) ***(P-13416)***
Motorcar Parts of America Inc (PA)......**A......310 212-7910**
2929 California St Torrance (90503) ***(P-10106)***
Motorola Solutions Inc......C......954 723-4730
6101 W Century Blvd Los Angeles (90045) ***(P-9298)***
Motors & Controls Whse Inc......E......714 956-0480
1440 N Burton Pl Anaheim (92806) ***(P-13752)***
Motorshield LLC......F......323 396-9200
3364 Garfield Ave Commerce (90040) ***(P-5104)***
Motorsport Aftrmrket Group Inc (PA)......**F......917 838-4002**
13861 Rosecrans Ave Santa Fe Springs (90670) ***(P-10107)***
Motoshieldpro, Commerce *Also called Motorshield LLC* ***(P-5104)***
Moulton Nguel Wtr Dst Pub Fclt (PA)......**D......949 831-2500**
27500 La Paz Rd Laguna Niguel (92677) ***(P-12908)***
Mount Palomar Winery, Temecula *Also called Louidar LLC* ***(P-2204)***
Mount San Jcnto Winter Pk Auth......D......760 325-1449
1 Tramway Rd Palm Springs (92262) ***(P-19655)***
Mountain Gear Corporation......C......626 851-2488
4889 4th St Irwindale (91706) ***(P-14342)***
Mountain High Resort Assoc LLC......D......760 249-5808
24512 Highway 2 Wrightwood (92397) ***(P-15928)***
Mountain High Ski Resort, Wrightwood *Also called MHRP Resort Inc* ***(P-16568)***
Mountain News & Shopper, Lake Arrowhead *Also called Hi-Desert Publishing Company* ***(P-3987)***
Mountain Top Comm Svcs LLC......E......909 798-4400
1902 Orange Tree Ln # 14 Redlands (92374) ***(P-23478)***
Mountain View Chevrolet Inc......D......909 985-2866
1079 W Foothill Blvd Upland (91786) ***(P-18796)***
Mountain View Child Care Inc......C......818 252-5863
10716 La Tuna Canyon Rd Sun Valley (91352) ***(P-22037)***
Mountain View Child Care Inc (PA)......**B......909 796-6915**
1720 Mountain View Ave Loma Linda (92354) ***(P-20867)***
Mountain View Children'c Ctr, El Monte *Also called Mountain View Elmntary Schl Ds* ***(P-22038)***
Mountain View Country Club Inc......D......760 771-4311
80375 Pomelo La Quinta (92253) ***(P-19590)***
Mountain View Elmntary Schl Ds......D......626 652-4250
2109 Burkett Rd El Monte (91733) ***(P-22038)***
Mountain View Montessori Schl (PA)......**D......805 453-3197**
4640 Granada Pl Santa Barbara (93110) ***(P-22039)***
Mountain Vista Golf Course At......D......760 200-2200
38180 Del Webb Blvd Palm Desert (92211) ***(P-19656)***
Mountain W Dialysis Svcs LLC (HQ)......**E......310 536-2400**
601 Hawaii St El Segundo (90245) ***(P-21254)***
Mountain West Financial Inc (PA)......**B......909 793-1500**
1209 Nevada St Ste 200 Redlands (92374) ***(P-15219)***
Mountains Community Hosp Fndtn......C......909 336-3651
29101 Hospital Rd Lake Arrowhead (92352) ***(P-20868)***
Mountasia Family Fun Center, Santa Clarita *Also called Mountasia of Santa Clarita* ***(P-16967)***
Mountasia Family Fun Center......D......661 253-4386
21516 Golden Triangle Rd Santa Clarita (91350) ***(P-19520)***
Mountasia of Santa Clarita......D......661 253-4386
21516 Golden Triangle Rd Santa Clarita (91350) ***(P-16967)***
Mouse Graphics, Costa Mesa *Also called Orange Coast Reprographics Inc* ***(P-4383)***
Mousepad Designs, Cerritos *Also called Mpd Holdings Inc* ***(P-8284)***
Mover Services Inc......E......310 868-5143
721 E Compton Blvd Rancho Dominguez (90220) ***(P-1676)***
Movieclips.com, Los Angeles *Also called Zefr Inc* ***(P-17766)***
Movieline Magazine, Inglewood *Also called Line Publications Inc* ***(P-4081)***
Moving Image Technologies LLC......E......714 751-7998
17760 Newhope St Ste B Fountain Valley (92708) ***(P-11285)***
Moviola Digital, Burbank *Also called Filmtools Inc* ***(P-13344)***
Movits, Carson *Also called O W I Inc* ***(P-9185)***
Mowery Thomason Inc......C......714 666-1717
1225 N Red Gum St Anaheim (92806) ***(P-1387)***
Moxa Americas Inc......E......714 528-6777
601 Valencia Ave Ste 100 Brea (92823) ***(P-8283)***
Moxie Pest Ctrl Orange Cnty LP......E......951 272-4000
18 Technology Dr Ste 154 Irvine (92618) ***(P-17203)***
Moyes Custom Furniture Inc......E......714 729-0234
3431 E La Palma Ave Ste 3 Anaheim (92806) ***(P-18964)***
Moyles Centl Vly Hlth Care Inc (PA)......**C......559 688-0288**
999 N M St Tulare (93274) ***(P-20420)***
Moyles Centl Vly Hlth Care Inc......D......559 782-1509
1100 W Morton Ave Porterville (93257) ***(P-20421)***
Moyles Health Care Inc......A......559 686-1601
604 E Merritt Ave Tulare (93274) ***(P-20615)***
Mp Aero LLC......D......818 901-9828
7701 Woodley Ave Van Nuys (91406) ***(P-1677)***
Mp Biomedicals LLC (HQ)......**E......949 833-2500**
9 Goddard Irvine (92618) ***(P-10803)***
MP Environmental Svcs Inc (PA)......**C......800 458-3036**
3400 Manor St Bakersfield (93308) ***(P-12961)***
Mp Mine Operations LLC......C......702 277-0848
67750 Bailey Rd Mountain Pass (92366) ***(P-583)***
MPA, Torrance *Also called Motorcar Parts of America Inc* ***(P-10106)***
Mpb Furniture Corporation......E......760 375-4800
414 W Ridgecrest Blvd Ridgecrest (93555) ***(P-3512)***
Mpbs Industries, Los Angeles *Also called Meat Packers Butchers Sup Inc* ***(P-7944)***
Mpc Productions LLC......D......310 418-8115
12035 Killion St Sherman Oaks (91401) ***(P-19370)***
Mpd Holdings Inc......E......562 777-1051
16200 Commerce Way Cerritos (90703) ***(P-8284)***
Mpi, Newbury Park *Also called Multilayer Prototypes Inc* ***(P-9431)***
Mpl Enterprises Inc......D......714 545-1717
2302 S Susan St Santa Ana (92704) ***(P-327)***
Mpm & Associates, Van Nuys *Also called M P M Building Services Inc* ***(P-4970)***
Mpo Videotronics Inc (PA)......**D......805 499-8513**
5069 Maureen Ln Moorpark (93021) ***(P-11286)***
Mpower Holding Corporation (HQ)......**A......866 699-8242**
515 S Flower St Fl 36 Los Angeles (90071) ***(P-12656)***
MPS Anzon LLC......C......626 471-3553
11911 Clark St Arcadia (91006) ***(P-11127)***
MPS Industries Incorporated (PA)......**E......310 325-1043**
19210 S Vermont Ave # 405 Gardena (90248) ***(P-8879)***
MPS Medical Inc......E......714 672-1090
830 Challenger St Ste 200 Brea (92821) ***(P-11027)***
MPS Security, Murrieta *Also called National Bus Invstigations Inc* ***(P-18608)***
Mpulse Mobile Inc (PA)......**B......888 678-5735**
16530 Ventura Blvd # 500 Encino (91436) ***(P-12657)***
Mq Power, Cypress *Also called Multiquip Inc* ***(P-13650)***
Mr Clean Maintenance Systems, Bloomington *Also called Chiro Inc* ***(P-14034)***
Mr Lock, Corona *Also called Lock America Inc* ***(P-6525)***
MR Mold & Engineering Corp......E......714 996-5511
1150 Beacon St Brea (92821) ***(P-7817)***
Mr T Transport......F......562 602-5536
15535 Garfield Ave Paramount (90723) ***(P-520)***
Mr Tortilla Inc......E......818 307-7414
1112 Arroyo St San Fernando (91340) ***(P-2491)***
Mr. Nature, Cerritos *Also called G & P Group Inc* ***(P-2112)***
Mrca Fire Division......E......818 880-4752
1670 Las Virgenes Cyn Rd Calabasas (91302) ***(P-22352)***
Mrs Appletree's Bakery, Baldwin Park *Also called Distinct Indulgence Inc* ***(P-1996)***
MRS Foods Incorporated (PA)......**E......714 554-2791**
4406 W 5th St Santa Ana (92703) ***(P-2492)***
Mrs Redds Pie Co Inc......E......909 825-4800
150 S La Cadena Dr Colton (92324) ***(P-2022)***
Mrt Inc......D......949 348-2292
19781 Pauling Foothill Ranch (92610) ***(P-17134)***
Mrv Crane, Delano *Also called Mrv Service Air Inc* ***(P-18948)***
Mrv Service Air Inc......F......661 725-3400
937 High St Delano (93215) ***(P-18948)***
MS Aerospace Inc......B......818 833-9095
13928 Balboa Blvd Sylmar (91342) ***(P-7070)***
Ms Bellows, Huntington Beach *Also called Mechanized Science Seals Inc* ***(P-10897)***
Ms Bubbles Inc (PA)......**D......323 544-0300**
2731 S Alameda St Los Angeles (90058) ***(P-14403)***
MS Industrial Shtmtl Inc......C......951 272-6610
1731 Pomona Rd Corona (92878) ***(P-1498)***
Msblous LLC......D......909 929-9689
11671 Dayton Dr Rancho Cucamonga (91730) ***(P-12225)***
MSC Metalworking, City of Industry *Also called Rutland Tool & Supply Co* ***(P-14016)***
MSC-La, City of Industry *Also called Material Sciences Corporation* ***(P-6301)***
Mscp V CC Parent LLC (HQ)......**D......323 634-0156**
5900 Wilshire Blvd # 110 Los Angeles (90036) ***(P-17439)***
Mscsoftware Corporation (HQ)......**C......714 540-8900**
5161 California Ave # 200 Irvine (92617) ***(P-17923)***
Mscsoftware Corporation (PA)......**C......323 258-9111**
815 Colorado Blvd Los Angeles (90041) ***(P-17924)***
MSE Enterprises Inc (PA)......**D......818 223-3500**
23622 Calabasas Rd # 200 Calabasas (91302) ***(P-15929)***
MSE Media Solutions Inc......F......323 721-1656
5711 Sheila St Commerce (90040) ***(P-9837)***
Msg Forum LLC......D......310 330-7339
3900 W Manchester Blvd Inglewood (90305) ***(P-15681)***
MSI Computer Corp (HQ)......**D......626 913-0828**
901 Canada Ct City of Industry (91748) ***(P-13417)***
MSI Hvac, Fontana *Also called Material Supply Inc* ***(P-6870)***
MSI Orange Showroom & Dist Ctr, Orange *Also called M S International Inc* ***(P-13307)***
MSI Structural Steel LLC......E......562 473-0066
11810 Center St South Gate (90280) ***(P-6642)***
Msl Electric Inc......D......714 693-4837
2918 E La Jolla St Anaheim (92806) ***(P-1284)***
MSM Industries Inc......E......951 735-0834
12660 Magnolia Ave Riverside (92503) ***(P-22618)***
MSP Group Inc......E......310 660-0022
206 W 140th St Los Angeles (90061) ***(P-2581)***
Msr Desert Resort LP......A......760 564-5730
49499 Eisenhower Dr La Quinta (92253) ***(P-16574)***
Msr Hotels & Resorts Inc......D......661 325-9700
5101 California Ave # 204 Bakersfield (93309) ***(P-16278)***
Msr Hotels & Resorts Inc......B......310 543-4566
3701 Torrance Blvd Torrance (90503) ***(P-16575)***
MSRS INC......C......310 952-9000
945 E Church St Riverside (92507) ***(P-4701)***
Mt Calvary Lthran Chrch-Mssuri......D......909 861-2740
23300 Golden Springs Dr Diamond Bar (91765) ***(P-22040)***
Mt Rubidoux Convalescent Hosp, San Bernardino *Also called Waterman Convalescent Hosp Inc* ***(P-20502)***
Mt Rubidouxidence Opco LLC......C......951 681-2200
6401 33rd St Riverside (92509) ***(P-20422)***
Mt Sinai Mem Pk & Mortuary, Los Angeles *Also called Sinai Temple* ***(P-16930)***
Mt Sinai Mem Pk & Mortuary, Los Angeles *Also called Sinai Temple* ***(P-16931)***
Mt Supply Inc (HQ)......**C......800 938-6658**
2752 Walnut Ave Tustin (92780) ***(P-14006)***
Mt View Farming Inc......D......559 688-2906
23595 Road 140 Tulare (93274) ***(P-50)***
Mtc Financial Inc......E......949 252-8300
17100 Gillette Ave Irvine (92614) ***(P-16191)***
Mtc Financial Inc......D......949 252-8300
17100 Gillette Ave Irvine (92614) ***(P-23069)***
Mtc Transportation, Twentynine Palms *Also called Mark Clemons* ***(P-12062)***

A
L
P
H
A
B
E
T
I
C

Employee Codes: A=Over 500 employees, B=251-500
C=101-250, D=51-100, E=20-50 F=10-19
2022 Southern California Business
Directory and Buyers Guide
© Mergent Inc. 1-800-342-5647
1211

Mtc Worldwide Corp ...D ...626 839-6800
17837 Rowland St City of Industry (91748) ***(P-13418)***

Mtd Kitchen Inc ...D ...818 764-2254
13213 Sherman Way North Hollywood (91605) ***(P-3272)***

MTI De Baja Inc ...E ...951 654-2333
915 Industrial Way San Jacinto (92582) ***(P-10603)***

MTI Film LLC ...F ...323 465-6487
1016 N Sycamore Ave Los Angeles (90038) ***(P-17666)***

MTI Laboratory Inc ...E ...310 955-3700
201 Continental Blvd # 300 El Segundo (90245) ***(P-9299)***

MTI Technology Corporation (PA) ...C ...**949 251-1101**
15461 Red Hill Ave # 200 Tustin (92780) ***(P-8209)***

Mtil, El Segundo *Also called MTI Laboratory Inc* ***(P-9299)***

Mtl Distribution, Corona *Also called Magnetics Test Lab Inc* ***(P-13642)***

Mtm Pharmacy Fairview, Santa Ana *Also called Fairview Mtm Pharma Inc* ***(P-4820)***

Mtn Government Services Inc (HQ) ...F ...**954 538-4000**
1821 E Dyer Rd Ste 125 Santa Ana (92705) ***(P-7005)***

Mtroiz International ...E ...661 998-8013
150 S Kenmore Ave Los Angeles (90004) ***(P-13753)***

MTS Stimulation Services Inc (PA) ...F ...**661 589-5804**
7131 Charity Ave Bakersfield (93308) ***(P-521)***

Mtv Networks, Los Angeles *Also called Viacom Networks* ***(P-19196)***

Mueller Gages Company ...E ...626 287-2911
318 Agostino Rd San Gabriel (91776) ***(P-7859)***

Mufg Americas Leasing Corp (HQ) ...D ...**213 488-3700**
445 S Figueroa St # 2700 Los Angeles (90071) ***(P-17364)***

Mufg Union Bank Foundation ...A ...213 236-5000
445 S Figueroa St Ste 710 Los Angeles (90071) ***(P-15003)***

Muhlhauser Enterprises Inc (PA) ...E ...**909 877-2792**
25825 Adams Ave Murrieta (92562) ***(P-6643)***

Muhlhauser Steel, Murrieta *Also called Muhlhauser Enterprises Inc* ***(P-6643)***

Muhlhauser Steel Inc ...E ...909 877-2792
25825 Adams Ave Murrieta (92562) ***(P-6644)***

Muir Elementary School, Long Beach *Also called Long Beach Unified School Dst* ***(P-15913)***

Muir-Chase Plumbing Co Inc ...D ...818 500-1940
4530 Brazil St Ste 1 Los Angeles (90039) ***(P-1104)***

Mulechain Inc ...D ...888 456-8881
2901 W Coast Hwy Ste 200 Newport Beach (92663) ***(P-11982)***

Mulgrew Arcft Components Inc ...D ...626 256-1375
1810 S Shamrock Ave Monrovia (91016) ***(P-10385)***

Mulholland SEC & Patrol Inc ...B ...818 755-0202
11454 San Vicente Blvd Los Angeles (90049) ***(P-18298)***

Mullen & Henzell LLP ...E ...805 966-1501
112 E Victoria St Santa Barbara (93101) ***(P-21635)***

Mullen Technologies Inc (PA) ...E ...**714 613-1900**
1405 Pioneer St Brea (92821) ***(P-9959)***

Mulligan Family Fun Center, Redondo Beach *Also called Mulligan Limited* ***(P-19521)***

Mulligan Limited (PA) ...D ...**714 484-6799**
1801 S Catalina Ave # 306 Redondo Beach (90277) ***(P-19521)***

Mulroses Usa Inc ...D ...213 489-1761
741 S San Pedro St Los Angeles (90014) ***(P-86)***

Multi Mechanical Inc ...D ...714 632-7404
469 Blaine St Corona (92879) ***(P-1105)***

Multi Specialty Medical Svc, Visalia *Also called Visalia Medical Clinic Inc* ***(P-20156)***

Multi-Fineline Electronix Inc (HQ) ...A ...**949 453-6800**
101 Academy Ste 250 Irvine (92617) ***(P-9430)***

Multi-Link International Corp ...E ...562 941-5380
12235 Los Nietos Rd Santa Fe Springs (90670) ***(P-5514)***

Multi-Pak Corporation ...D ...818 709-0508
20131 Bahama St Chatsworth (91311) ***(P-18606)***

Multichrome Company Inc (PA) ...E ...**310 216-1086**
1013 W Hillcrest Blvd Inglewood (90301) ***(P-7284)***

Multicoat Products Inc ...F ...949 888-7100
23331 Antonio Pkwy Rcho STA Marg (92688) ***(P-5105)***

Multicultural Rdo Brdcstg Inc ...D ...626 844-8882
747 E Green St Pasadena (91101) ***(P-12702)***

Multilayer Prototypes Inc ...F ...805 498-9390
2513 Teller Rd Newbury Park (91320) ***(P-9431)***

Multimedia Led Inc (PA) ...F ...**951 280-7500**
4225 Prado Rd Ste 108 Corona (92878) ***(P-9753)***

Multipak, Chatsworth *Also called Multi-Pak Corporation* ***(P-18606)***

Multiquip Inc (HQ) ...B ...**310 537-3700**
6141 Katella Ave Ste 200 Cypress (90630) ***(P-13650)***

Munchkin Inc (PA) ...C ...**800 344-2229**
7835 Gloria Ave Van Nuys (91406) ***(P-5476)***

Munger Tolles & Olson LLP ...C ...213 683-9100
350 S Grand Ave Fl 50 Los Angeles (90071) ***(P-21636)***

Munger Bros LLC ...A ...661 721-0390
786 Road 188 Delano (93215) ***(P-71)***

Munger Farm, Delano *Also called Munger Bros LLC* ***(P-71)***

Munger Farms, Delano *Also called Monarch Nut Company LLC* ***(P-182)***

Munger Tolles Olson Foundation (PA) ...B ...**213 683-9100**
350 S Grand Ave Fl 50 Los Angeles (90071) ***(P-21637)***

Municpal Wtr Dst Ornge Cnty Wt ...D ...714 963-3058
18700 Ward St Fountain Valley (92708) ***(P-12909)***

Mur-Sol Builders Inc ...E ...626 447-0558
119 E Saint Joseph St Arcadia (91006) ***(P-662)***

Murad LLC (HQ) ...C ...**310 726-0600**
2121 Park Pl Fl 1 El Segundo (90245) ***(P-4853)***

Muranaka Farm ...C ...805 529-0201
11018 W Los Angeles Ave Moorpark (93021) ***(P-115)***

Murano Group ...D ...949 409-1079
30211 Avnida De Las Bndra Ste Rancho Santa Margari (92688) ***(P-18299)***

Murcal Inc ...E ...661 272-4700
41343 12th St W Palmdale (93551) ***(P-13651)***

Murchison & Cumming LLP (PA) ...D ...**213 623-7400**
801 S Grand Ave Ste 900 Los Angeles (90017) ***(P-21638)***

Murcor Inc ...C ...909 623-4001
740 Corp Ctr Dr Pomona (91768) ***(P-15930)***

Murphy & Beane Inc ...D ...310 649-4470
5901 Green Valley Cir # 145 Culver City (90230) ***(P-21639)***

Murphy OBrien Inc ...D ...310 453-2539
407 N Maple Dr Ste 1 Beverly Hills (90210) ***(P-23382)***

Murphy-Rodgers Incorporated ...F ...714 525-2952
1340 Valwood St La Habra (90631) ***(P-13921)***

Murray Company, E Rncho Dmngz *Also called Murray Plumbing and Htg Corp* ***(P-1106)***

Murray Plumbing and Htg Corp (PA) ...A ...**310 637-1500**
18414 S Santa Fe Ave E Rncho Dmngz (90221) ***(P-1106)***

Murrays Hardware ...F ...714 543-4023
210 S Main St Santa Ana (92701) ***(P-6711)***

Murrey International Inc ...F ...310 532-6091
25701 Weston Dr Laguna Niguel (92677) ***(P-11438)***

Murrieta Day Spa, Murrieta *Also called Monique Suraci* ***(P-19461)***

Murrietta Circuits ...C ...714 970-2430
5000 E Landon Dr Anaheim (92807) ***(P-9432)***

Murtaugh Myer Nlson Trglia LLP ...D ...949 794-4000
2603 Main St Ste 900 Irvine (92614) ***(P-21640)***

Musclepharm Corporation (PA) ...D ...**800 292-3909**
4500 Park Granada Ste 2 Calabasas (91302) ***(P-1801)***

Muse Presentation Technologies, Irvine *Also called Producers Inc* ***(P-17368)***

Museum Associates ...B ...323 857-6172
5905 Wilshire Blvd Los Angeles (90036) ***(P-22226)***

Museum of Contemporary Art (PA) ...C ...**213 626-6222**
250 S Grand Ave Los Angeles (90012) ***(P-22227)***

Museum of Latin American Art ...E ...562 437-1689
628 Alamitos Ave Long Beach (90802) ***(P-22228)***

Music Academy of West ...D ...805 969-4726
1070 Fairway Rd Santa Barbara (93108) ***(P-19371)***

Music Center, Los Angeles *Also called Performing Arts Ctr Los Angles* ***(P-19327)***

Music Intllgnce Neuro Dev Inst, Irvine *Also called Mind Research Institute* ***(P-22915)***

Music Market Update, Los Angeles *Also called Hits Magazine Inc* ***(P-14874)***

Musick Peeler & Garrett LLP (PA) ...C ...**213 629-7600**
624 S Grand Ave Ste 2000 Los Angeles (90017) ***(P-21641)***

Mutesix Group Inc ...C ...310 215-3467
5800 Bristol Pkwy Ste 500 Culver City (90230) ***(P-17037)***

Mutesix, An Iprospect Company, Culver City *Also called Mutesix Group Inc* ***(P-17037)***

Muth Development Co Inc ...F ...714 527-2239
11100 Beach Blvd Stanton (90680) ***(P-6010)***

Muth Machine Works ...D ...951 685-1521
4510 Rutile St Riverside (92509) ***(P-23277)***

Muth Machine Works (HQ) ...E ...**714 527-2239**
8042 Katella Ave Stanton (90680) ***(P-8712)***

Mutt Couture Inc (PA) ...E ...**805 469-6888**
973 E Fthill Blvd Ste 105 San Luis Obispo (93405) ***(P-2765)***

Mutual Liquid Gas & Eqp Co Inc (PA) ...E ...**310 515-0553**
17117 S Broadway Gardena (90248) ***(P-13922)***

Mutual Propane, Gardena *Also called Mutual Liquid Gas & Eqp Co Inc* ***(P-13922)***

Mutual Trading Co Inc (HQ) ...C ...**213 626-9458**
4200 Shirley Ave El Monte (91731) ***(P-14712)***

Mutual Trading Co Inc ...D ...213 229-9393
843 E 4th St Los Angeles (90013) ***(P-14954)***

Muzik Inc (PA) ...E ...**646 345-6500**
9220 W Sunset Blvd # 112 West Hollywood (90069) ***(P-9754)***

Mv Medical Management ...D ...323 257-7637
1860 Colo Blvd Ste 200 Los Angeles (90041) ***(P-23278)***

Mv Transportation Inc ...D ...562 259-9911
7231 Rosecrans Ave Paramount (90723) ***(P-11830)***

Mve + Partners Inc (PA) ...D ...**949 809-3388**
1900 Main St Ste 800 Irvine (92614) ***(P-22734)***

Mventix Inc (PA) ...B ...**818 337-3747**
21600 Oxnard St Ste 1700 Woodland Hills (91367) ***(P-18607)***

Mvm Products LLC ...F ...949 366-1470
946 Calle Amanecer Ste E San Clemente (92673) ***(P-11287)***

Mvp Rv Inc ...E ...951 848-4288
40 E Verdugo Ave Burbank (91502) ***(P-10544)***

Mw Components - Corona, Corona *Also called Ameriflex Inc* ***(P-7527)***

Mw Partners, Irvine *Also called Morris & Willner Partners* ***(P-23276)***

Mwb Copy Products Inc (HQ) ...E ...**800 736-7979**
5700 Warland Dr Cypress (90630) ***(P-13363)***

MWH Americas Inc ...C ...805 683-2409
437 2nd St Solvang (93463) ***(P-22619)***

Mwla Inc ...D ...310 841-2505
8780 National Blvd Culver City (90232) ***(P-22041)***

Mws Precision Wire Inds Inc ...D ...818 991-8553
31200 Cedar Valley Dr Westlake Village (91362) ***(P-13578)***

Mws Wire Industries, Westlake Village *Also called Mws Precision Wire Inds Inc* ***(P-13578)***

Mwss, Irvine *Also called Montrose Water and Sustainabil* ***(P-23477)***

Mx Electronics Mfg Inc (HQ) ...D ...**714 258-0200**
1651 E Saint Andrew Pl Santa Ana (92705) ***(P-6353)***

MXF Designs Inc ...D ...323 266-1451
5327 Valley Blvd Los Angeles (90032) ***(P-2861)***

My Day Counts, Anaheim *Also called Orange Cnty Adult Achvment Ctr* ***(P-21860)***

My Eye Media LLC ...D ...818 559-7200
2211 N Hollywood Way Burbank (91505) ***(P-17925)***

My Favorite Company Inc (PA) ...F ...**310 659-3611**
8322 Beverly Blvd Ste 302 Los Angeles (90048) ***(P-2099)***

My Gym Enterprises, Sherman Oaks *Also called Gym Consulting Inc* ***(P-23231)***

My Kids Dentist ...B ...951 600-1062
24635 Madison Ave Ste E Murrieta (92562) ***(P-20189)***

My Kids Dentist (PA) ...D ...**909 854-1437**
17000 Red Hill Ave Irvine (92614) ***(P-20190)***

My Machine Inc ...F ...626 214-9223
5140 Commerce Dr Baldwin Park (91706) ***(P-8713)***

My Michelle, La Puente *Also called Mymichelle Company LLC* ***(P-2862)***

My Tech USA, Corona *Also called Hardy Frames Inc* ***(P-6203)***

My Wireless, Santa Ana *Also called BP Communications Inc* ***(P-12628)***

Mergent e-mail: customerrelations@mergent.com
1212
2022 Southern California Business Directory and Buyers Guide
(P-0000) Products & Services Section entry number
(PA)=Parent Co (HQ)=Headquarters DH)=Div Headquarters

Mycom North America Inc (PA)...E...**310 328-1362**
19475 Gramercy Pl Torrance (90501) ***(P-13854)***
Mydyer.com, Irvine *Also called Providence Industries LLC* ***(P-2787)***
Mye Technologies Inc...E...661 964-0217
28460 Westinghouse Pl Valencia (91355) ***(P-9894)***
Myers & Sons Hi-Way Safety Inc (PA)...D...**909 591-1781**
13310 5th St Chino (91710) ***(P-11575)***
Myers FSI, Ontario *Also called Myers Power Products Inc* ***(P-8901)***
Myers Mixers LLC...E...323 560-4723
8376 Salt Lake Ave Cudahy (90201) ***(P-8130)***
Myers Power Products Inc (PA)...C...**909 923-1800**
2950 E Philadelphia St Ontario (91761) ***(P-8901)***
Myevaluationscom Inc...E...646 422-0554
11111 W Olympic Blvd Los Angeles (90064) ***(P-17667)***
Mygnar Inc (PA)...F...**626 676-5415**
2525 Main St Ste 300 Santa Monica (90405) ***(P-8285)***
Mymichelle Company LLC (HQ)...B...**626 934-4166**
13077 Temple Ave La Puente (91746) ***(P-2862)***
Mynela LLC...E...323 522-9080
1025 W 190th St Ste 220 Gardena (90248) ***(P-20228)***
Mynela Staffing, Gardena *Also called Mynela LLC* ***(P-20228)***
Myogenix Incorporated...E...800 950-0348
4725 Allene Way San Luis Obispo (93401) ***(P-4854)***
Myojo USA Inc...F...909 464-1411
6220 Prescott Ct Chino (91710) ***(P-2377)***
Myotek Industries Incorporated (PA)...D...**949 502-3776**
1278 Glenneyre St Ste 431 Laguna Beach (92651) ***(P-9826)***
Myricom Inc...E...626 821-5555
3871 E Colo Blvd Ste 101 Pasadena (91107) ***(P-8168)***
Myron & Davis, Jurupa Valley *Also called Johnson Safety Inc* ***(P-14165)***
Myst Therapeutics Inc...D...415 516-8450
570 Westwood Plz Bldg 114 Los Angeles (90095) ***(P-22852)***
Mywi Fabricators Inc...F...626 279-6994
2115-2119 Edwards Ave South El Monte (91733) ***(P-6645)***
Myyogaworks, Culver City *Also called Yogaworks Inc* ***(P-19682)***
N A T C O, Glendale *Also called North American Textile Co LLC* ***(P-3178)***
N A Tomatobank...D...626 759-9200
901 S Baldwin Ave Arcadia (91007) ***(P-15048)***
N D Industries, Santa Fe Springs *Also called ND Industries Inc* ***(P-14007)***
N G I, Brea *Also called Nevell Group Inc* ***(P-796)***
N H Research Incorporated...D...949 474-3900
16601 Hale Ave Irvine (92606) ***(P-10766)***
N P A, Los Angeles *Also called National Promotions & Advg Inc* ***(P-17038)***
N Qiagen Amercn Holdings Inc (HQ)...C...**800 426-8157**
27220 Turnberry Ln # 200 Valencia (91355) ***(P-14266)***
N S C Channel Islands Inc...B...805 485-1908
2300 Wankel Way Oxnard (93030) ***(P-19990)***
N S Haas Inc...F...805 874-1155
649 Beachport Dr Port Hueneme (93041) ***(P-3590)***
N Stitches Prints Inc...F...310 366-7537
16009 S Broadway Gardena (90248) ***(P-3160)***
N T S, Woodland Hills *Also called Network Telephone Services Inc* ***(P-18612)***
N Trans/Sub Regional Office, Valencia *Also called Southern California Edison Co* ***(P-23114)***
N-U Enterprise, Irvine *Also called Ancca Corporation* ***(P-1363)***
N/S Corporation (PA)...D...**310 412-7074**
235 W Florence Ave Inglewood (90301) ***(P-8399)***
N2 Acquisition Company Inc...D...714 942-3563
14440 Myford Rd Irvine (92606) ***(P-16105)***
N2 Imaging Systems, Irvine *Also called N2 Acquisition Company Inc* ***(P-16105)***
N2w Engineering Inc...D...714 716-1711
3240 El Cmino Real Ste 15 Irvine (92602) ***(P-23479)***
Nabors Well Services Co...D...805 648-2731
2567 N Ventura Ave C Ventura (93001) ***(P-522)***
Nabors Well Services Co...D...661 588-6140
1025 Earthmover Ct Bakersfield (93314) ***(P-523)***
Nabors Well Services Co...D...310 639-7074
19431 S Santa Fe Ave Compton (90221) ***(P-524)***
Nabors Well Services Co...D...661 589-3970
7515 Rosedale Hwy Bakersfield (93308) ***(P-525)***
Nabors Well Services Co...D...310 639-7074
19431 S Santa Fe Ave Compton (90221) ***(P-526)***
Nabors Well Services Co...D...661 392-7668
1954 James Rd Bakersfield (93308) ***(P-527)***
Nac Mfg Inc...F...909 472-3033
601 Kettering Dr Ontario (91761) ***(P-5158)***
Nada Appraisal Guide, Costa Mesa *Also called National Appraisal Guides Inc* ***(P-4189)***
Nadin Company...E...818 500-8908
1815 Flower St Glendale (91201) ***(P-4855)***
Nafees Memon...D...818 997-1666
6819 Sepulveda Blvd # 312 Van Nuys (91405) ***(P-18300)***
Nafees Mmon Cmmand Intl SEC Sv, Van Nuys *Also called Nafees Memon* ***(P-18300)***
Nafhc, Santa Maria *Also called North American Fire Hose Corp* ***(P-5321)***
NAFTA Distributors...D...800 956-2382
5120 Santa Ana St Ontario (91761) ***(P-14480)***
Naftex Westside Partners Limit...D...310 277-9004
1900 Avenue Of The Stars Los Angeles (90067) ***(P-407)***
Nagles Veal Inc...E...909 383-7075
1411 E Base Line St San Bernardino (92410) ***(P-1716)***
Nail Alliance - North Amer Inc (PA)...B...**714 773-9758**
1545 Moonstone Brea (92821) ***(P-16909)***
Nailpro, Encino *Also called Creative Age Publications Inc* ***(P-4060)***
Nakamura-Beeman Inc...E...562 696-1400
8520 Wellsford Pl Santa Fe Springs (90670) ***(P-3591)***
Nakase Brothers Wholesale Nurs (PA)...D...**949 855-4388**
9441 Krepp Dr Huntington Beach (92646) ***(P-14889)***
Nakase Brothers Wholesale Nurs...C...949 855-4388
20621 Lake Forest Dr Lake Forest (92630) ***(P-14890)***
Naked Juice Co Glendora Inc...B...626 873-2600
1333 S Mayflower Ave # 100 Monrovia (91016) ***(P-1868)***
Naked Princess Worldwide LLC (PA)...F...**310 271-1199**
11766 Wilshire Blvd Fl 9 Los Angeles (90025) ***(P-5049)***
Nalco Company LLC...D...310 900-5400
2111 E Dominguez St Long Beach (90810) ***(P-5235)***
Nalco Wtr Prtrtment Sltons LLC...E...714 792-0708
704 Richfield Rd Placentia (92870) ***(P-8400)***
Nallatech Inc...D...805 383-8997
741 Flynn Rd Camarillo (93012) ***(P-13754)***
Nally & Millie, Los Angeles *Also called MXF Designs Inc* ***(P-2861)***
Namm California (PA)...D...**909 605-8058**
3990 Concours Ste 500 Ontario (91764) ***(P-23279)***
Nanka Seimen Co...F...323 585-9967
3030 Leonis Blvd Vernon (90058) ***(P-2378)***
Nannette Keller, Tehachapi *Also called Keller Classics Inc* ***(P-2904)***
Nannocare Inc...F...818 823-7594
2570 Corp Pl Ste E103 Monterey Park (91754) ***(P-11718)***
Nano Filter Inc...D...949 316-8866
22310 Bonita St Carson (90745) ***(P-11719)***
Nanofilm, Westlake Village *Also called Interntional Photo Plates Corp* ***(P-7270)***
Nanoflowx LLC...E...323 396-9200
3364 Garfield Ave Commerce (90040) ***(P-7389)***
Nanoknee, Arroyo Grande *Also called Applied Orthopedic Design* ***(P-11088)***
Nanoprecision Products Inc...E...310 597-4991
802 Calle Plano Camarillo (93012) ***(P-7167)***
Nanoskin Car Care Products, Santa Fe Springs *Also called Total Import Solutions Inc* ***(P-13099)***
Nantbioscience Inc...D...310 883-1300
9920 Jefferson Blvd Culver City (90232) ***(P-13503)***
Nantcell Inc...C...310 883-1300
2040 E Mariposa Ave El Segundo (90245) ***(P-22916)***
Nantcell Inc...D...562 397-3639
9920 Jefferson Blvd Culver City (90232) ***(P-22853)***
Nantenergy LLC...D...310 905-4866
2040 E Mariposa Ave El Segundo (90245) ***(P-8925)***
Nanthealth Inc (HQ)...B...**310 883-1300**
2040 E Mariposa Ave El Segundo (90245) ***(P-18048)***
Nantomics LLC (PA)...D...**310 883-1300**
9920 Jefferson Blvd Culver City (90232) ***(P-22954)***
Nantworks LLC (PA)...C...**310 883-1300**
9920 Jefferson Blvd Culver City (90232) ***(P-18049)***
Napd, Bakersfield *Also called New Advnces For Pple With Dsbl* ***(P-22203)***
Napoleon Perdis Cosmetics Inc...D...323 817-3611
16825 Saticoy St Van Nuys (91406) ***(P-14267)***
Nappcote, Canoga Park *Also called American Metal & Paint Inc* ***(P-6586)***
Naranjo Pallets...F...323 637-8019
6653 Loveland St Bell Gardens (90201) ***(P-3400)***
Narayan Corporation...E...310 719-7330
13432 Estrella Ave Gardena (90248) ***(P-5477)***
Narcotics Annymous Wrld Svcs I...E...818 773-9999
19737 Nordhoff Pl Chatsworth (91311) ***(P-4134)***
Nasco Aircraft Brake Inc...D...310 532-4430
13300 Estrella Ave Gardena (90248) ***(P-10386)***
Nasco Gourmet Foods Inc...D...714 279-2100
22720 Savi Ranch Pkwy Yorba Linda (92887) ***(P-1869)***
Nashua Corporation...D...323 583-8828
13341 Cambridge St Santa Fe Springs (90670) ***(P-3762)***
Nashville Wire Pdts Mfg Co LLC...E...714 736-0081
10727 Commerce Way Ste C Fontana (92337) ***(P-7504)***
Nasif Hicks Harris & Co LLP...D...805 966-1521
104 W Anapamu St Ste B Santa Barbara (93101) ***(P-22806)***
Nasmyth Tmf Inc...D...818 954-9504
29102 Hancock Pkwy Valencia (91355) ***(P-7285)***
Naso Industries Corporation...E...805 650-1231
3007 Bunsen Ave Ste Q Ventura (93003) ***(P-9433)***
Naso Technologies, Ventura *Also called Naso Industries Corporation* ***(P-9433)***
Nasser Company Inc (PA)...D...**714 279-2100**
22720 Savi Ranch Pkwy Yorba Linda (92887) ***(P-14481)***
Nasser Company of Arizona, Yorba Linda *Also called Nasser Company Inc* ***(P-14481)***
Nasty Gal Inc (HQ)...E...**213 542-3436**
2049 Century Park E # 3400 Los Angeles (90067) ***(P-14442)***
NAT'L ASSN FOR HISPANIC ELDERL, Pasadena *Also called La Asccion Ncnal Pro Prsnas My* ***(P-21835)***
Natals Inc...E...310 866-8145
5681 W Jefferson Blvd Los Angeles (90016) ***(P-4856)***
Natel Engineering, Chatsworth *Also called Epic Technologies LLC* ***(P-9232)***
Natel Engineering Company LLC (PA)...C...**818 495-8617**
9340 Owensmouth Ave Chatsworth (91311) ***(P-9755)***
Natel Engineering Holdings Inc...E...818 734-6500
9340 Owensmouth Ave Chatsworth (91311) ***(P-9434)***
Nathan Anthony Furniture, Vernon *Also called Yen-Nhai Inc* ***(P-3522)***
Nation Surfboard Mfg Inc...F...949 370-6607
216 Avnida Fbrcnte Ste 10 San Clemente (92672) ***(P-11439)***
National Advanced Endoscopy De...E...818 227-2720
22134 Sherman Way Canoga Park (91303) ***(P-11028)***
National Appraisal Guides Inc...E...714 556-8511
3186 Airway Ave Ste K Costa Mesa (92626) ***(P-4189)***
National Assn For Hispanic, Los Angeles *Also called La Asccion Ncnal Pro Prsnas My* ***(P-21834)***
National Attny Collection Svcs...B...818 547-9760
700 N Brand Blvd Fl 2 Glendale (91203) ***(P-21642)***
National Band Saw Company...F...661 294-9552
1055 W Avenue L12 Lancaster (93534) ***(P-7946)***
National Bus Invstigations Inc...D...951 677-3500
25020 Las Brisas Rd Ste A Murrieta (92562) ***(P-18608)***
National Business Group Inc (PA)...D...**818 221-6000**
15319 Chatsworth St Mission Hills (91345) ***(P-17312)***

ALPHABETIC

Employee Codes: A=Over 500 employees, B=251-500 C=101-250, D=51-100, E=20-50 F=10-19
2022 Southern California Business Directory and Buyers Guide
© Mergent Inc. 1-800-342-5647
1213

National Cement Co Cal Inc (HQ) ....D....**818 728-5200**
15821 Ventura Blvd # 475 Encino (91436) ***(P-6100)***

National Cement Company Inc (HQ) ....E....**818 728-5200**
15821 Ventura Blvd # 475 Encino (91436) ***(P-5981)***

National Cmnty Renaissance Cal (PA) ....D....**909 483-2444**
9421 Haven Ave Rancho Cucamonga (91730) ***(P-16063)***

National Cmnty Rnssnce Dev Cor (PA) ....D....**909 483-2444**
9421 Haven Ave Rancho Cucamonga (91730) ***(P-16834)***

National Cnstr Rentals Inc (HQ) ....D....**818 221-6000**
15319 Chatsworth St Mission Hills (91345) ***(P-17365)***

National Commercial Services ....D....818 701-4400
6644 Valjean Ave Ste 100 Van Nuys (91406) ***(P-17115)***

National Community Renaissance (PA) ....D....**909 483-2444**
9421 Haven Ave Rancho Cucamonga (91730) ***(P-16064)***

National Construction & Maint ....E....909 888-7042
23846 Sunnymead Blvd # 10 Moreno Valley (92553) ***(P-794)***

National Copy Cartridge, Tustin *Also called US Print & Toner Inc* ***(P-11483)***

National Corset Supply House (PA) ....D....**323 261-0265**
3240 E 26th St Vernon (90058) ***(P-3018)***

National Diversified Sales Inc (HQ) ....C....**559 562-9888**
21300 Victory Blvd # 215 Woodland Hills (91367) ***(P-5722)***

National Dyeing, Vernon *Also called AS Match Dyeing Co Inc* ***(P-2655)***

National Emblem Inc (PA) ....C....**310 515-5055**
3925 E Vernon St Long Beach (90815) ***(P-3161)***

National Ewp Inc ....F....909 931-4014
5566 Arrow Hwy Montclair (91763) ***(P-377)***

National Explrtion Wells Pumps, Montclair *Also called National Ewp Inc* ***(P-377)***

National Fail Safe Inc ....E....562 493-5447
6442 Industry Way Westminster (92683) ***(P-1285)***

National Fail-Safe SEC Systems, Westminster *Also called National Fail Safe Inc* ***(P-1285)***

National Film Laboratories ....D....323 466-0281
900 Glenneyre St Laguna Beach (92651) ***(P-19241)***

National Filter Media Corp ....D....760 246-4551
17130 Muskrat Ave Ste B Adelanto (92301) ***(P-8131)***

National Financial Svcs LLC ....A....949 476-0157
19200 Von Karman Ave Irvine (92612) ***(P-15302)***

National Fuel Cell RES Ctr ....F....949 824-1509
1002 Health Sciences Rd Irvine (92617) ***(P-7699)***

National Genetics Institute ....C....310 996-6610
2440 S Sepulveda Blvd # 235 Los Angeles (90064) ***(P-22955)***

National Graphics LLC ....E....805 644-9212
200 N Elevar St Oxnard (93030) ***(P-4378)***

National Gypsum Mfg Office ....F....562 435-4465
1850 Pier B St Long Beach (90813) ***(P-6129)***

National Hot Rod Association (PA) ....C....**626 914-4761**
2035 E Financial Way Glendora (91741) ***(P-19433)***

National Hrdwood Flrg Moulding, Van Nuys *Also called Katzirs Floor & HM Design Inc* ***(P-13175)***

National Insurance Crime Bur ....D....818 895-2867
15545 Devonshire St # 309 Mission Hills (91345) ***(P-15600)***

National Link Incorporated ....D....909 670-1900
2235 Auto Centre Dr Glendora (91740) ***(P-13364)***

National Logistics Team LLC ....E....951 369-5841
21496 Main St Grand Terrace (92313) ***(P-12143)***

National Media Inc (HQ) ....E....**310 377-6877**
609 Deep Valley Dr # 200 Rllng HLS Est (90274) ***(P-4011)***

National Media Inc ....F....310 372-0388
2615 Pcf Cast Hwy Ste 329 Hermosa Beach (90254) ***(P-4012)***

National Medical Products Inc ....F....949 768-1147
57 Parker Irvine (92618) ***(P-5723)***

National Mentor Inc ....E....661 387-1000
2131 Mars Ct Bakersfield (93308) ***(P-22134)***

National Mentor Holdings Inc ....C....951 677-1453
30033 Technology Dr Murrieta (92563) ***(P-22135)***

National Metal Stampings Inc ....D....661 945-1157
42110 8th St E Lancaster (93535) ***(P-7168)***

National Millworks Llc ....F....619 823-0395
32020 Allen Ave Hemet (92545) ***(P-3447)***

National Monitoring Center, Lake Forest *Also called Advanced Protection Inds LLC* ***(P-18364)***

National Mustang Racers Assn, Santa Ana *Also called Promedia Companies* ***(P-4100)***

National O Rings, Downey *Also called Hutchinson Seal Corporation* ***(P-5341)***

National Orange Show (PA) ....C....**909 888-6788**
689 S E St San Bernardino (92408) ***(P-18609)***

National Packaging Products, Commerce *Also called Yavar Manufacturing Co Inc* ***(P-3847)***

National Paving Company Inc ....D....951 369-1332
4361 Fort Dr Riverside (92509) ***(P-903)***

National Promotions & Advg Inc ....E....310 558-8555
3434 Overland Ave Los Angeles (90034) ***(P-17038)***

National Ready Mix ....F....818 728-5200
15821 Ventura Blvd # 475 Encino (91436) ***(P-6101)***

National Ready Mixed Con Co (HQ) ....E....**818 728-5200**
15821 Ventura Blvd # 475 Encino (91436) ***(P-6102)***

National Research Group Inc ....B....323 817-2000
6255 W Sunset Blvd Fl 19 Los Angeles (90028) ***(P-22894)***

National Retail Trnsp Inc ....D....310 631-8951
500 W Victoria St Compton (90220) ***(P-12065)***

National Retail Trnsp Inc ....D....951 243-6110
400 Harley Knox Blvd Perris (92571) ***(P-12066)***

National Retail Trnsp Inc ....D....310 605-3777
355 W Carob St Compton (90220) ***(P-12067)***

National Safety Services ....E....714 679-9118
3400 Avenue Of The Arts F214 Costa Mesa (92626) ***(P-23480)***

National Sales Corp ....D....323 586-0200
7250 Oxford Way Commerce (90040) ***(P-14955)***

National Security Tech LLC ....A....805 681-2432
5520 Ekwill St Ste B Goleta (93111) ***(P-22620)***

National Sign & Marketing Corp ....D....909 591-4742
13580 5th St Chino (91710) ***(P-11576)***

National Signal Inc ....E....714 441-7707
2440 Artesia Ave Fullerton (92833) ***(P-10553)***

National Teleconsultants Inc ....C....818 265-4400
550 N Brand Blvd Fl 17 Glendale (91203) ***(P-22621)***

National Therapeutic Svcs Inc (PA) ....D....**866 311-0003**
3822 Campus Dr Ste 100 Newport Beach (92660) ***(P-21322)***

National Tour Intgrted Rsrces ....E....949 215-6330
23141 Arroyo Vis Ste 100 Rcho STA Marg (92688) ***(P-23280)***

National Trench Safety LLC ....C....562 602-1642
13217 Laureldale Ave Downey (90242) ***(P-17313)***

National Tube & Steel, Mission Hills *Also called National Business Group Inc* ***(P-17312)***

National Veterinary Assoc Inc (HQ) ....A....**805 777-7722**
29229 Canwood St Ste 100 Agoura Hills (91301) ***(P-201)***

National Wholesale Lumber, Pixley *Also called Correa Pallet Inc* ***(P-3384)***

Nationbuilder, Los Angeles *Also called 3dna Corp* ***(P-17534)***

Nations Capital Group LLC ....E....818 793-2050
5353 Balboa Blvd Ste 300 Encino (91316) ***(P-15156)***

Nations Petroleum Cal LLC ....D....661 387-6402
9600 Ming Ave Ste 300 Bakersfield (93311) ***(P-458)***

Nations Surgery Center, Encino *Also called Nations Capital Group LLC* ***(P-15156)***

Nationwide, Tustin *Also called Wood Gutmann Bogart Insur Brkg* ***(P-15651)***

Nationwide, Cerritos *Also called Poliseek Ais Insur Sltions Inc* ***(P-15614)***

Nationwide, Cerritos *Also called Petra Risk Solutions* ***(P-15613)***

Nationwide, Cerritos *Also called Auto Insurance Specialists LLC* ***(P-15539)***

Nationwide, Riverside *Also called Insurance Inc Southern Cal* ***(P-15584)***

Nationwide, Newport Beach *Also called Alliant Insurance Services Inc* ***(P-23409)***

Nationwide, Glendale *Also called Arthur J Gallagher Risk Mgmt* ***(P-15538)***

Nationwide, Woodland Hills *Also called Grosslight Insurance Inc* ***(P-15574)***

Nationwide, San Luis Obispo *Also called Morris Grritano Insur Agcy Inc* ***(P-15599)***

Nationwide, Pasadena *Also called United Agencies Inc* ***(P-15639)***

Nationwide, Los Angeles *Also called Koram Insurance Center Inc* ***(P-15587)***

Nationwide, Visalia *Also called Arthur J Gallagher & Co* ***(P-15536)***

Nationwide, Irvine *Also called Sullivncrtsmnroe Insur Svcs LL* ***(P-23336)***

Nationwide, Cypress *Also called Pacific Pioneer Insur Group* ***(P-15608)***

Nationwide Environmental Svcs, Norwalk *Also called Joes Sweeping Inc* ***(P-12954)***

Nationwide Guard Services Inc ....B....909 608-1112
9327 Frway View Pl Ste 20 Rancho Cucamonga (91730) ***(P-18301)***

Nationwide Jewelry Mfrs Inc ....F....213 489-1215
631 S Olive St Ste 790 Los Angeles (90014) ***(P-11325)***

Nationwide Legal LLC (PA) ....C....**213 249-9999**
1609 James M Wood Blvd Los Angeles (90015) ***(P-21643)***

Nationwide Litho Inc ....F....626 542-0371
11728 Goldring Rd Arcadia (91006) ***(P-4546)***

Nationwide Medical Group Inc ....D....661 328-0245
501 W Columbus St Ste A Bakersfield (93301) ***(P-21048)***

Nationwide Plastic Products ....F....310 366-7585
16809 Gramercy Pl Gardena (90247) ***(P-5435)***

Nationwide Theatres Corp (HQ) ....D....**310 657-8420**
120 N Robertson Blvd Fl 3 Los Angeles (90048) ***(P-19296)***

Nationwide Theatres Corp ....A....562 421-8448
2500 Carson St Lakewood (90712) ***(P-19404)***

Nationwide Trans Inc (PA) ....D....**909 355-3211**
1633 S Campus Ave Ontario (91761) ***(P-12487)***

Natren Inc ....D....805 371-4737
3105 Willow Ln Thousand Oaks (91361) ***(P-2493)***

Natrol LLC (PA) ....C....**818 739-6000**
21411 Prairie St Chatsworth (91311) ***(P-4857)***

Natural and Healthy Products, South Gate *Also called Ibitta Enterprises Inc* ***(P-14472)***

Natural Balance Pet Foods Inc (HQ) ....E....**800 829-4493**
100 N First St Ste 200 Burbank (91502) ***(P-1972)***

Natural Elements, Vernon *Also called L A S A M Inc* ***(P-3033)***

Natural Envmtl Protection Co ....E....909 620-8028
750 S Reservoir St Pomona (91766) ***(P-4702)***

Natural Food Mill, Corona *Also called Food For Life Baking Co Inc* ***(P-2001***

Natural History Museum of Los ....B....213 763-3442
900 Exposition Blvd Los Angeles (90007) ***(P-22229)***

Naturalife Eco Vite Labs ....D....310 370-1563
20433 Earl St Torrance (90503) ***(P-1802)***

Nature's Bounty, Anaheim *Also called Nbty Manufacturing LLC* ***(P-4858)***

Nature's Flavors, Orange *Also called Newport Flavors & Fragrances* ***(P-2334)***

Nature's Glory, North Hollywood *Also called Cosmo - Pharm Inc* ***(P-4741)***

Nature-Cide, Canoga Park *Also called Pacific Shore Holdings Inc* ***(P-4868)***

Natures Image Inc ....E....949 680-4400
20361 Hermana Cir Lake Forest (92630) ***(P-271)***

Natures Produce ....C....323 235-4343
3305 Bandini Blvd Vernon (90058) ***(P-14644)***

Natureware Inc ....D....714 251-4510
6590 Darin Way Cypress (90630) ***(P-14268)***

Naturvet, Temecula *Also called Garmon Corporation* ***(P-11674)***

Natutac, Cerritos *Also called Winning Laboratories Inc* ***(P-4770)***

Navair WD ....D....760 939-1970
1 Admin Cir Ridgecrest (93555) ***(P-22622)***

Navajo Concrete Inc ....F....805 238-0955
2484 Ramada Dr Paso Robles (93446) ***(P-6103)***

Navajo Investments Inc (PA) ....D....**949 863-9200**
17962 Cowan Irvine (92614) ***(P-12337)***

Navajo Rock & Block, Paso Robles *Also called Navajo Concrete Inc* ***(P-6103)***

Naval Hosp Twntynine Plms Gfeb, Twentynine Palms *Also called Navy United States Department* ***(P-21458)***

Navco Security Systems, Fullerton *Also called North American Video Corp* ***(P-13756)***

Navcom Defense Electronics Inc (PA) ....E....**951 268-9205**
9129 Stellar Ct Corona (92883) ***(P-10604)***

Navcom Technology Inc (HQ) ....D....**310 381-2000**
20780 Madrona Ave Torrance (90503) ***(P-9300)***

Mergent e-mail: customerrelations@mergent.com
1214
2022 Southern California Business Directory and Buyers Guide
(P-0000) Products & Services Section entry number
(PA)=Parent Co (HQ)=Headquarters (DH)=Div Headquarters

ALPHABETIC SECTION | **Network Automation Inc**

Naver Band Inc......F......323 847-1750
5750 Wilshire Blvd # 640 Los Angeles (90036) ***(P-17926)***
Navigage Foundation (PA)......**D......818 790-2522**
849 Foothill Blvd Ste 8 La Canada (91011) ***(P-20423)***
Navigant Cymetrix Corporation......D......424 201-6300
1515 W 190th St Ste 350 Gardena (90248) ***(P-23070)***
Navigator Yachts and Pdts Inc......E......951 657-2117
364 Malbert St Perris (92570) ***(P-10469)***
Navigators Management Co Inc......D......949 255-4860
19100 Von Karman Ave Irvine (92612) ***(P-23071)***
Navy United States Department......D......760 830-2124
1145 Sturgis Rd Twentynine Palms (92278) ***(P-21458)***
Nazca Solutions Inc......E......612 279-6100
4 First American Way Santa Ana (92707) ***(P-17927)***
Naztech, Valencia *Also called Hypercel Corporation* ***(P-13727)***
Nazzareno Electric Co Inc......D......714 712-4744
1250 E Gene Autry Way Anaheim (92805) ***(P-1286)***
NBC Consulting Inc......D......310 798-5000
2110 Artesia Blvd Ste 323 Redondo Beach (90278) ***(P-23281)***
NBC Subsidiary (knbc-Tv) LLC......C......818 684-5746
100 Unvrsal Cy Plz Bldg 2 Universal City (91608) ***(P-12734)***
NBC Suite Hotel......D......310 640-3600
1440 E Imperial Ave El Segundo (90245) ***(P-16576)***
NBC Universal Studios Inc (HQ)......**D......818 777-5000**
3900 Lnkrshim Blvd Ste 42 Universal City (91608) ***(P-19155)***
Nbcuniversal Television Dist, Universal City *Also called Universal Cy Stdios Prdctons L* ***(P-19193)***
Nbp, Claremont *Also called New Bedford Panoramex Corp* ***(P-9141)***
Nbty Manufacturing LLC......C......714 765-8323
5115 E La Palma Ave Anaheim (92807) ***(P-4858)***
NC Dynamics Incorporated......C......562 634-7392
6925 Downey Ave Long Beach (90805) ***(P-8714)***
NC Dynamics LLC......C......562 634-7392
3401 E 69th St Long Beach (90805) ***(P-8715)***
NC Interactive LLC......D......512 623-8700
1 Polaris Way Ste 110 Aliso Viejo (92656) ***(P-18202)***
Nc4 Soltra LLC......D......408 489-5579
21515 Hawthorne Blvd # 52 Torrance (90503) ***(P-17928)***
Nccs, Irvine *Also called Numerical Ctrl Cmpt Sciences* ***(P-17681)***
Ncdi, Long Beach *Also called NC Dynamics Incorporated* ***(P-8714)***
NCJW LA, Los Angeles *Also called Los Angles Sction Nat Cncil JW* ***(P-21845)***
Ncla Inc......F......562 926-6252
1388 W Foothill Blvd Azusa (91702) ***(P-3931)***
NCM, Moreno Valley *Also called National Construction & Maint* ***(P-794)***
Ncompass International LLC......C......323 785-1700
12101 Crenshaw Blvd # 800 Hawthorne (90250) ***(P-23282)***
Ncsoft, Aliso Viejo *Also called NC Interactive LLC* ***(P-18202)***
Ncstar Inc......F......866 627-8278
18031 Cortney Ct City of Industry (91748) ***(P-10848)***
ND Industries Inc......D......562 926-3321
13929 Dinard Ave Santa Fe Springs (90670) ***(P-14007)***
Ndi (PA)......**D......818 368-5650**
17106 Devonshire St Northridge (91325) ***(P-15601)***
Nds, Woodland Hills *Also called National Diversified Sales Inc* ***(P-5722)***
Nds Americas Inc (HQ)......**D......714 434-2100**
3500 Hyland Ave Costa Mesa (92626) ***(P-12774)***
NDT Metal Finishing Inc......F......818 807-1381
11370 Luddington St Sun Valley (91352) ***(P-7286)***
NDT Systems Inc......E......714 893-2438
5542 Buckingham Dr Ste A Huntington Beach (92649) ***(P-10899)***
Ndti, Ridgecrest *Also called New Directions Tech Inc* ***(P-18052)***
Nea Electronics Inc......E......805 292-4010
14370 White Sage Rd Moorpark (93021) ***(P-9662)***
Neal Feay Company......D......805 967-4521
133 S La Patera Ln Goleta (93117) ***(P-6313)***
Neal Trucking Inc......D......951 685-5048
9749 Bellegrave Ave Riverside (92509) ***(P-11983)***
Near-Cal Corp......E......951 245-5400
512 Chaney St Lake Elsinore (92530) ***(P-795)***
Neardata Inc......D......818 249-2469
4502 Dyer St Ste 103 La Crescenta (91214) ***(P-23283)***
Neardata Systems, La Crescenta *Also called Neardata Inc* ***(P-23283)***
Nearfield Systems Inc......D......310 525-7000
19730 Magellan Dr Torrance (90502) ***(P-10767)***
Neasi-Weber International LLC (PA)......**E......818 895-6900**
25115 Ave Stnford Ste 220 Valencia (91355) ***(P-17668)***
Nectar Sleep, Walnut *Also called Resident Home LLC* ***(P-13151)***
Nectave Inc......F......714 736-9811
6700 Caballero Blvd Buena Park (90620) ***(P-2494)***
Ned L Webster Concrete Cnstr......D......805 529-4900
8800 Grimes Canyon Rd Moorpark (93021) ***(P-1543)***
Neftaly Imports LLC......B......909 329-1276
1700 S Milliken Ave Ontario (91761) ***(P-18610)***
Neg282 LLC......B......760 786-2387
51880 Highway 190 Death Valley (92328) ***(P-16577)***
Negranti Construciton, Cayucos *Also called Negranti Construction* ***(P-1602)***
Negranti Construction......E......805 995-3357
1424 Old Creek Rd Cayucos (93430) ***(P-1602)***
Neighborhood Church, Visalia *Also called Neighborhood Mennonite* ***(P-17929)***
Neighborhood Healthcare......D......951 225-6400
41840 Enterprise Cir N Temecula (92590) ***(P-21459)***
Neighborhood Mennonite......E......559 732-9107
5505 W Riggin Ave Visalia (93291) ***(P-17929)***
Neighborhood Steel LLC (HQ)......**E......714 236-8700**
5555 Garden Grove Blvd Westminster (92683) ***(P-13579)***
Neill Aircraft Co......B......562 432-7981
1260 W 15th St Long Beach (90813) ***(P-10387)***
Neilson Marketing Services, Laguna Hills *Also called Nms Data Inc* ***(P-23482)***
Neiman & Company, Van Nuys *Also called Neiman/Hoeller Inc* ***(P-11577)***
Neiman/Hoeller Inc......D......818 781-8600
6842 Valjean Ave Van Nuys (91406) ***(P-11577)***
Nekter Juice Bar Inc (PA)......**D......949 660-0071**
1844 Carnegie Ave Santa Ana (92705) ***(P-16212)***
Nellix Inc......E......650 213-8700
2 Musick Irvine (92618) ***(P-11029)***
Nellson Nutraceutical Inc......B......844 635-5766
5115 E La Palma Ave Anaheim (92807) ***(P-2100)***
Nellxo LLC......E......909 320-8501
5990 Bald Eagle Dr Fontana (92336) ***(P-7169)***
Nelson & Associates Inc......D......562 921-4423
12816 Leffingwell Ave Santa Fe Springs (90670) ***(P-13652)***
Nelson Adams Inc......F......909 256-8938
160 N Cactus Ave Rialto (92376) ***(P-3627)***
Nelson Bros Property MGT Inc......C......949 916-7300
16b Journey Ste 200 Aliso Viejo (92656) ***(P-23072)***
Nelson Brothers Property MGT, Aliso Viejo *Also called Nelson Bros Property MGT Inc* ***(P-23072)***
Nelson Case Corporation......F......714 528-2215
650 S Jefferson St Ste A Placentia (92870) ***(P-3378)***
Nelson Dunn, Cerritos *Also called Amphenol Nelson-Dunn Tech Inc* ***(P-13886)***
Nelson Engineering Llc......E......714 893-7999
11600 Monarch St Garden Grove (92841) ***(P-8716)***
Nelson Moving & Storage Inc......E......949 582-0380
25742 Atlantic Ocean Dr Lake Forest (92630) ***(P-12116)***
Nelson Name Plate Company (HQ)......**C......323 663-3971**
2800 Casitas Ave Los Angeles (90039) ***(P-7390)***
Nelson North American, Lake Forest *Also called Nelson Moving & Storage Inc* ***(P-12116)***
Nelson Sports Inc......E......562 944-8081
12810 Florence Ave Santa Fe Springs (90670) ***(P-5884)***
Nelson-Miller, Los Angeles *Also called Nelson Name Plate Company* ***(P-7390)***
Neo Tech, Chatsworth *Also called Natel Engineering Company LLC* ***(P-9755)***
Neo Tech, Chatsworth *Also called Oncore Manufacturing LLC* ***(P-22623)***
Neo Tech Natel Epic Oncore, Chatsworth *Also called Oncore Manufacturing Svcs Inc* ***(P-9435)***
Neocomp Systems Inc......D......818 700-8722
21541 Nordhoff St Ste F Chatsworth (91311) ***(P-18149)***
Neogov, El Segundo *Also called Governmentjobscom Inc* ***(P-17869)***
Neomend Inc......D......949 783-3300
60 Technology Dr Irvine (92618) ***(P-11030)***
Neon Energy Corporation......E......661 829-2505
1401 Coml Way Ste 200 Bakersfield (93309) ***(P-459)***
Neonroots LLC......C......310 907-9210
8560 W Sunset Blvd # 500 West Hollywood (90069) ***(P-17669)***
Neopacific Holdings Inc......E......818 786-2900
14940 Calvert St Van Nuys (91411) ***(P-5724)***
Neotech Products LLC......D......661 775-7466
28430 Witherspoon Pkwy Valencia (91355) ***(P-13504)***
Neoteryx LLC......E......310 787-8747
421 Amapola Ave Torrance (90501) ***(P-22854)***
Neovia Logistics Dist LP......D......909 657-4900
5750 E Francis St Ontario (91761) ***(P-12226)***
Neovia Logistics Dist LP......C......626 359-4500
600 Live Oak Ave Irwindale (91706) ***(P-12488)***
Nepco, Pomona *Also called Natural Envmtl Protection Co* ***(P-4702)***
Nephrology, Los Angeles *Also called Cedars-Sinai Medical Center* ***(P-20694)***
Neptune Foods, Vernon *Also called Fishermans Pride Prcessors Inc* ***(P-2345)***
Ner Precious Metals Inc......D......310 367-3179
640 St Hill St Ste 450 Los Angeles (90014) ***(P-14136)***
Nerdist Channel LLC......E......818 333-2705
2900 W Alameda Ave # 15 Burbank (91505) ***(P-9301)***
Nerdist Industries, Burbank *Also called Nerdist Channel LLC* ***(P-9301)***
Nero, Garden Grove *Also called Vorsteiner Inc* ***(P-5423)***
Nesbitt Prtners San Luis Obspo......D......805 549-0800
333 Madonna Rd San Luis Obispo (93405) ***(P-16578)***
Nestle Dist Ctr & Logistics, Jurupa Valley *Also called Nestle Usa Inc* ***(P-1933)***
Nestle Ice Cream Company LLC......A......661 398-3500
7301 District Blvd Bakersfield (93313) ***(P-14545)***
Nestle Refrigerated Food Co......B......818 549-6000
800 N Brand Blvd Fl 5 Glendale (91203) ***(P-2379)***
Nestle Usa Inc......C......661 398-3536
7301 District Blvd Bakersfield (93313) ***(P-1803)***
Nestle Usa Inc......D......951 360-7200
3450 Dulles Dr Jurupa Valley (91752) ***(P-1933)***
Net Shapes Inc......C......909 947-3231
1336 E Francis St Ste B Ontario (91761) ***(P-6271)***
Netapp Inc......C......818 227-5025
6320 Canoga Ave Ste 1500 Woodland Hills (91367) ***(P-18050)***
Netball America Inc......E......888 221-3650
5101 Audrey Dr Huntington Beach (92649) ***(P-19591)***
Netflix Wrldwide Prdctions LLC (HQ)......**A......310 734-2900**
5808 W Sunset Blvd Fl 11 Los Angeles (90028) ***(P-19242)***
Netlist Inc (PA)......**D......949 435-0025**
175 Technology Dr Ste 150 Irvine (92618) ***(P-9548)***
Netmarble Us Inc......D......213 222-7712
600 Wilshire Blvd # 1100 Los Angeles (90017) ***(P-4190)***
Neto Express LLC......D......818 625-5615
7536 Goodland Ave North Hollywood (91605) ***(P-12068)***
Netsol Technologies Inc (PA)......**A......818 222-9197**
23975 Park Sorrento # 250 Calabasas (91302) ***(P-17930)***
Netsource Technology Inc......F......949 713-0800
951 Calle Negocio Ste B San Clemente (92673) ***(P-13755)***
Nettwerk Music Group LLC (HQ)......**E......323 301-4200**
1545 Wilcox Ave Ste 103 Los Angeles (90028) ***(P-18611)***
Network Automation Inc......E......213 738-1700
3530 Wilshire Blvd # 1800 Los Angeles (90010) ***(P-17931)***

ALPHABETIC

Employee Codes: A=Over 500 employees, B=251-500
C=101-250, D=51-100, E=20-50 F=10-19
2022 Southern California Business
Directory and Buyers Guide
© Mergent Inc. 1-800-342-5647
1215

Network Capital Funding Corp (PA)....B....**949 442-0060**
7700 Irvine Center Dr # 3 Irvine (92618) ***(P-15220)***
Network Intgrtion Partners Inc....D....909 919-2800
11981 Jack Benny Dr # 10 Rancho Cucamonga (91739) ***(P-18051)***
Network Management Group Inc (PA)....C....**323 263-2632**
1100 S Flower St Ste 3110 Los Angeles (90015) ***(P-23073)***
Network Medical Management Inc....C....626 282-0288
1668 S Grfeld Ave Ste 100 Alhambra (91801) ***(P-23074)***
Network Telephone Services Inc (PA)....D....**800 742-5687**
21135 Erwin St Woodland Hills (91367) ***(P-18612)***
Network Television Time Inc (PA)....E....**877 468-8899**
3929 Clearford Ct Westlake Village (91361) ***(P-4191)***
Networks Electronic Co LLC....E....818 341-0440
9750 De Soto Ave Chatsworth (91311) ***(P-7433)***
Netwrix Corporation (HQ)....D....**888 638-9749**
300 Spectrum Center Dr # 200 Irvine (92618) ***(P-17932)***
Neudesic LLC (PA)....C....**949 754-4500**
200 Spectrum Center Dr # 2000 Irvine (92618) ***(P-17670)***
Neuintel LLC (PA)....D....**949 625-6117**
20 Pacifica Ste 1000 Irvine (92618) ***(P-17671)***
Neuro Drinks, Sherman Oaks *Also called Neurobrands LLC* ***(P-14713)***
Neurobrands LLC....C....310 393-6444
15303 Ventura Blvd # 675 Sherman Oaks (91403) ***(P-14713)***
Neurolenses, Costa Mesa *Also called Eyebrain Medical Inc* ***(P-11252)***
Neuron Esb, Irvine *Also called Neudesic LLC* ***(P-17670)***
Neuroptics Inc....E....949 250-9792
9223 Research Dr Irvine (92618) ***(P-11031)***
Neuroscience Gamma Knife Ctr, Thousand Oaks *Also called Los Robles Regional Med Ctr* ***(P-20853)***
Neurosmith LLC....E....562 296-1100
1000 N Studebaker Rd # 3 Long Beach (90815) ***(P-11386)***
Neurostructures Inc....F....800 352-6103
199 Technology Dr Ste 110 Irvine (92618) ***(P-11128)***
Neurosurgical Associates (PA)....D....**661 799-2542**
25751 Mcbean Pkwy Ste 305 Valencia (91355) ***(P-19991)***
Neurovasc Technologies Inc....F....949 258-9946
3 Jenner Ste 100 Irvine (92618) ***(P-11032)***
Neutraderm Inc....E....818 534-3190
20660 Nordhoff St Chatsworth (91311) ***(P-5050)***
Neutron Plating Inc....F....714 632-9241
2993 E Blue Star St Anaheim (92806) ***(P-7287)***
Neutronic Stamping & Plating, Corona *Also called Ravlich Enterprises LLC* ***(P-7304)***
Nevada Window Supply Inc....E....951 300-0100
1455 Columbia Ave Riverside (92507) ***(P-3273)***
Nevell Group Inc (PA)....C....**714 579-7501**
3001 Enterprise St # 200 Brea (92821) ***(P-796)***
Neversoft Entertainment Inc....E....818 610-4100
21255 Burbank Blvd # 600 Woodland Hills (91367) ***(P-17672)***
Nevins Adams Properties, Santa Barbara *Also called Nevins/Adams Properties Inc* ***(P-15682)***
Nevins/Adams Properties Inc (PA)....C....**805 963-2884**
920 Garden St Ste A Santa Barbara (93101) ***(P-15682)***
Nevion Usa Inc....D....805 247-8575
400 W Ventura Blvd # 155 Camarillo (93010) ***(P-9302)***
New Advnces For Pple With Dsbl....D....661 322-9735
4032 Jewett Ave Bakersfield (93301) ***(P-22203)***
New Advnces For Pple With Dsbl....D....661 327-0188
1120 21st St Bakersfield (93301) ***(P-22204)***
New Age Enclosures, Santa Maria *Also called Alltec Integrated Mfg Inc* ***(P-5554)***
New Age Lamirada Inn, La Mirada *Also called Kam Sang Company Inc* ***(P-16519)***
New Air LLC....E....657 257-4349
6600 Katella Ave Cypress (90630) ***(P-13690)***
New Albertsons Inc....C....310 540-6824
21035 Hawthorne Blvd Torrance (90503) ***(P-18420)***
New Alliance Insurance Brokers....E....424 205-6700
3700 Santa Fe Ave Ste 300 Long Beach (90810) ***(P-15602)***
New American Funding, Porter Ranch *Also called Broker Solutions Inc* ***(P-15151)***
New American Funding, Tustin *Also called Broker Solutions Inc* ***(P-23179)***
New Bay Dialysis LLC (HQ)....E....**310 536-2400**
601 Hawaii St El Segundo (90245) ***(P-21255)***
New Bedford Panoramex Corp....E....909 982-9806
1480 N Claremont Blvd Claremont (91711) ***(P-9141)***
New CAM Commerce Solutions LLC....D....714 338-0200
5555 Garden Grove Blvd # 100 Westminster (92683) ***(P-17673)***
New Century Industries Inc....E....562 634-9551
7231 Rosecrans Ave Paramount (90723) ***(P-10108)***
New Century Media Corp....E....562 695-1000
2727 Pellissier Pl City of Industry (90601) ***(P-14171)***
New Century Mortgage Corp....A....949 440-7030
18400 Von Karman Ave # 1000 Irvine (92612) ***(P-15221)***
New Century Snacks, Commerce *Also called Snak Club LLC* ***(P-2116)***
New Chef Fashion Inc....D....323 581-0300
3223 E 46th St Vernon (90058) ***(P-2746)***
New Classic Furniture, Fontana *Also called New Classic HM Furnishing Inc* ***(P-13178)***
New Classic HM Furnishing Inc (PA)....D....**909 484-7676**
7351 Mcguire Ave Fontana (92336) ***(P-13178)***
New Cntury Mtals Southeast Inc....A....562 356-6804
15723 Shoemaker Ave Norwalk (90650) ***(P-6335)***
New Crew Production Corp....C....323 234-8880
1100 W 135th St Gardena (90247) ***(P-18613)***
New Directions Inc (PA)....D....**310 914-4045**
11303 Wilshire Blvd Los Angeles (90025) ***(P-21854)***
New Directions For Veterans, Los Angeles *Also called New Directions Inc* ***(P-21854)***
New Directions Tech Inc (PA)....D....**760 384-2444**
137 W Drummond Ave Ste A Ridgecrest (93555) ***(P-18052)***
New Dream Network LLC....D....323 375-3842
707 Wilshire Blvd # 5050 Los Angeles (90017) ***(P-12658)***

New Economics For Women (PA)....D....**213 483-2060**
303 Loma Dr Los Angeles (90017) ***(P-21855)***
New Figueroa Hotel Inc....D....213 627-8971
1000 S Hope St Apt 201 Los Angeles (90015) ***(P-16579)***
New First Fincl Resources LLC....C....949 223-2160
100 Spectrum Center Dr # 400 Irvine (92618) ***(P-15365)***
New Flyer of America Inc....E....909 456-3566
2880 Jurupa St Ontario (91761) ***(P-9960)***
New Frnters Ntral Mrktplace 10, San Luis Obispo *Also called Northern Holdings* ***(P-1618)***
New Generation Engrg Cnstr Inc....E....424 329-3950
22815 Frampton Ave Torrance (90501) ***(P-13308)***
New Generation Wellness Inc (PA)....C....**949 863-0340**
46 Corporate Park Ste 200 Irvine (92606) ***(P-4859)***
New Glaspro Inc....E....800 776-2368
9401 Ann St Santa Fe Springs (90670) ***(P-5964)***
New Gold Manufacturing Inc....F....818 847-1020
2150 N Lincoln St Burbank (91504) ***(P-11326)***
New Green Day LLC....E....323 566-7603
1710 E 111th St Los Angeles (90059) ***(P-3744)***
New Greenscreen Incorporated....D....951 685-9660
11445 Pacific Ave Fontana (92337) ***(P-6881)***
New Greenscreen Incorporated....E....800 767-9378
5500 Jurupa St Ontario (91761) ***(P-3689)***
New Hope Harvesting LLC....D....805 478-4469
918 Nita Ct Santa Maria (93454) ***(P-157)***
New Horizon Vending, Garden Grove *Also called Monster Vending* ***(P-5720)***
New Horizons Center & Workshop, North Hills *Also called New Hrzns Srving Indvdals With* ***(P-2069)***
New Horizons Picture, Los Angeles *Also called Concorde-New Horizons Corp* ***(P-19110)***
New Hrzns Srving Indvdals With (PA)....D....**818 894-9301**
15725 Parthenia St North Hills (91343) ***(P-2069)***
New Icon Inc (PA)....F....**626 620-4387**
15136 Valley Blvd City of Industry (91746) ***(P-2731)***
New Image Commercial Flrg Inc....F....909 796-3400
10444 Corporate Dr Ste B Redlands (92374) ***(P-11620)***
New Image Flooring, Redlands *Also called New Image Commercial Flrg Inc* ***(P-11620)***
New Inspiration Brdcstg Co Inc (HQ)....A....**805 987-0400**
4880 Santa Rosa Rd Camarillo (93012) ***(P-12703)***
New Legend Inc....B....855 210-2300
8613 Etiwanda Ave Rancho Cucamonga (91739) ***(P-12069)***
New Maverick Desk Inc....C....310 217-1554
15100 S Figueroa St Gardena (90248) ***(P-3592)***
New Milani Group LLC....D....323 582-9404
10000 Wash Blvd Ste 210 Culver City (90232) ***(P-14269)***
New Mode Sportswear....F....714 899-7800
12762 Monarch St Garden Grove (92841) ***(P-14343)***
New Origins Accessories Inc (PA)....F....**909 869-7559**
3980 Valley Blvd Ste D Walnut (91789) ***(P-11488)***
New Power Inc....D....800 980-9825
887 Marlborough Ave Riverside (92507) ***(P-1107)***
New Pride Corporation....D....323 584-6608
5101 Pacific Blvd Vernon (90058) ***(P-14404)***
New Printing, Van Nuys *Also called Digital Room Holdings Inc* ***(P-4507)***
New Regency Productions Inc (PA)....D....**310 369-8300**
10201 W Pico Blvd Bldg 12 Los Angeles (90064) ***(P-19156)***
New Spirit Naturals Inc (PA)....E....**909 592-4445**
615 W Allen Ave San Dimas (91773) ***(P-19992)***
New Technology Plastics Inc....E....562 941-6034
7110 Fenwick Ln Westminster (92683) ***(P-4703)***
New Times Media Group, San Luis Obispo *Also called Slo New Times Inc* ***(P-4030)***
New Vista Behavioral Hlth LLC....D....949 284-0095
3 Park Plz Ste 550 Irvine (92614) ***(P-20538)***
New Vista Health Services....C....310 477-5501
1516 Sawtelle Blvd Los Angeles (90025) ***(P-20616)***
New Vista Health Services....C....818 352-1421
8647 Fenwick St Sunland (91040) ***(P-20617)***
New Vista Health Services Inc....D....909 626-0117
501 S College Ave Claremont (91711) ***(P-22136)***
New Vsta Nrsing Rhbltation Ctr, Sunland *Also called New Vista Health Services* ***(P-20617)***
New Vsta Post Acute Care Ctr W, Los Angeles *Also called New Vista Health Services* ***(P-20616)***
New Wave Entertainment, Burbank *Also called NW Entertainment Inc* ***(P-19157)***
New World Medical Incorporated....F....909 466-4304
10763 Edison Ct Rancho Cucamonga (91730) ***(P-11033)***
New York Frozen Foods Inc....E....626 338-3000
5100 Rivergrade Rd Baldwin Park (91706) ***(P-2023)***
New-Indy Containerboard, Ontario *Also called New-Indy Ontario LLC* ***(P-3764)***
New-Indy Containerboard, Oxnard *Also called New-Indy Oxnard LLC* ***(P-3765)***
New-Indy Containerboard LLC (HQ)....D....**909 296-3400**
3500 Porsche Way Ste 150 Ontario (91764) ***(P-3763)***
New-Indy Ontario LLC....C....909 390-1055
5100 Jurupa St Ontario (91761) ***(P-3764)***
New-Indy Oxnard LLC....C....805 986-3881
5936 Perkins Rd Oxnard (93033) ***(P-3765)***
New-Indy Tripaq LLC (PA)....D....**562 404-6965**
16069 Shoemaker Ave Cerritos (90703) ***(P-17181)***
Newair, Cypress *Also called New Air LLC* ***(P-13690)***
Neway Packaging Corp (PA)....D....**602 454-9000**
1973 E Via Arado Rancho Dominguez (90220) ***(P-14214)***
Neways Inc....E....949 264-1542
28202 Cabot Rd Ste 100 Laguna Niguel (92677) ***(P-9756)***
Newbasis LLC....C....951 787-0600
2626 Kansas Ave Riverside (92507) ***(P-6040)***
Newbasis West LLC....C....951 787-0600
2626 Kansas Ave Riverside (92507) ***(P-6041)***
Newbook International Inc....D....310 855-3773
3680 Wilshire Blvd P04 Los Angeles (90010) ***(P-23481)***

Mergent e-mail: customerrelations@mergent.com
1216
2022 Southern California Business Directory and Buyers Guide
(P-0000) Products & Services Section entry number
(PA)=Parent Co (HQ)=Headquarters (DH)=Div Headquarters

Newby Rubber Inc E 661 327-5137
320 Industrial St Bakersfield (93307) *(P-5396)*
Newco Distributors Inc D 909 291-2240
9060 Rochester Ave Rancho Cucamonga (91730) *(P-14865)*
Newco International Inc F 818 834-7100
13600 Vaughn St San Fernando (91340) *(P-3481)*
Newegg.com, City of Industry *Also called Magnell Associate Inc (P-8164)*
Newhall Signal, Santa Clarita *Also called Signal (P-4028)*
Newhere Inc (PA) E **888 991-7471**
19851 Nordhoff Pl Ste 105 Chatsworth (91311) *(P-4860)*
Newhouse Upholstery E 626 444-1370
2309 Edwards Ave El Monte (91733) *(P-3628)*
Newhouse Upholstery Mfg, El Monte *Also called Newhouse Upholstery (P-3628)*
Newlight Technologies Inc E 714 556-4500
14382 Astronautics Ln Huntington Beach (92647) *(P-5725)*
Newlon Rouge LLC F 310 458-7737
1640 5th St Ste 218 Santa Monica (90401) *(P-4013)*
Newman and Sons Inc (PA) E **805 522-1646**
2655 1st St Ste 210 Simi Valley (93065) *(P-6042)*
Newman Bros California Inc (PA) F **951 782-0102**
1901 Massachusetts Ave Riverside (92507) *(P-3274)*
Newman Garrison + Partners Inc D 949 756-0818
3100 Bristol St Ste 400 Costa Mesa (92626) *(P-22735)*
Newmar, Huntington Beach *Also called Roi Development Corp (P-8981)*
Newmar Power LLC C 800 854-3906
15272 Newsboy Cir Huntington Beach (92649) *(P-9613)*
Newmeyer & Dillion LLP (PA) C **949 854-7000**
895 Dove St Fl 5 Newport Beach (92660) *(P-21644)*
Newport Apparel Corporation (PA) D **310 605-1900**
1215 W Walnut St Compton (90220) *(P-14405)*
Newport Bay Hospital, Newport Beach *Also called Beacon Healthcare Services (P-21276)*
Newport Beach Country Club Inc D 949 644-9550
1 Clubhouse Dr Newport Beach (92660) *(P-19592)*
Newport Beach Spaghetti, Newport Beach *Also called Osf International Inc (P-16599)*
Newport Beach Surgery Ctr LLC C 949 631-0988
361 Hospital Rd Ste 124 Newport Beach (92663) *(P-19993)*
Newport Brass, Santa Ana *Also called Brasstech Inc (P-6553)*
Newport Center Medical Group D 949 644-3555
400 Nwport Ctr Dr Ste 502 Newport Beach (92660) *(P-19994)*
Newport Corporation (HQ) A **949 863-3144**
1791 Deere Ave Irvine (92606) *(P-10660)*
Newport Diagnostic Center Inc (PA) D **949 760-3025**
1605 Avocado Ave Newport Beach (92660) *(P-19995)*
Newport Energy E 408 230-7545
19200 Von Karman Ave # 4 Irvine (92612) *(P-460)*
Newport Fab LLC D 949 435-8000
4321 Jamboree Rd Newport Beach (92660) *(P-9549)*
Newport Flavors & Fragrances E 714 771-2200
833 N Elm St Orange (92867) *(P-2334)*
Newport Glassworks, Stanton *Also called Newport Optical Industries (P-10849)*
Newport Hospitality Group Inc C 661 323-1900
801 Truxtun Ave Bakersfield (93301) *(P-16580)*
Newport Hotel Capital LLC C 714 758-0900
1221 S Harbor Blvd Anaheim (92805) *(P-16581)*
Newport Industrial Glass Inc E 714 484-7500
8610 Central Ave Stanton (90680) *(P-5965)*
Newport Laminates Inc E 714 545-8335
3121 W Central Ave Santa Ana (92704) *(P-5726)*
Newport Meat Company, Irvine *Also called Newport Meat Southern Cal Inc (P-14600)*
Newport Meat Southern Cal Inc C 949 399-4200
16691 Hale Ave Irvine (92606) *(P-14600)*
Newport Medical Instrs Inc B 949 642-3910
1620 Sunflower Ave Costa Mesa (92626) *(P-11034)*
Newport Mesa Inn LLC D 949 650-3020
2642 Newport Blvd Costa Mesa (92627) *(P-16582)*
Newport Mesa Memory Care Cmnty, Costa Mesa *Also called Silverado Senior Living Inc (P-20471)*
Newport Mesa Unified Schl Dst D 714 424-5090
2985 Barrish St Bldg E Costa Mesa (92626) *(P-21460)*
Newport Mesa Unified Schl Dst D 949 515-6940
900 Goldenrod Ave Corona Del Mar (92625) *(P-22042)*
Newport Mesa Usd Campus C F 714 424-8939
2985 Bear St Costa Mesa (92626) *(P-4379)*
Newport Optical Industries (PA) E **714 484-8100**
10564 Fern Ave Stanton (90680) *(P-10849)*
Newport Plastic Inc E 714 549-1955
1525 E Edinger Ave Santa Ana (92705) *(P-5727)*
Newport Plastics LLC (PA) E **800 854-8402**
1525 E Edinger Ave Santa Ana (92705) *(P-5728)*
Newport Sbacute Healthcare Ctr D 949 631-4282
2570 Newport Blvd Costa Mesa (92627) *(P-20424)*
Newport Television LLC B 661 283-1700
2120 L St Bakersfield (93301) *(P-12735)*
News Corp - Fox, Los Angeles *Also called Twentieth Cntury Fox Japan Inc (P-17192)*
News Group, The, Orange *Also called Great Atlantic News LLC (P-14873)*
News Media Inc F 805 237-6060
502 First St Paso Robles (93446) *(P-4014)*
News Publishers' Press, Glendale *Also called P E N Inc (P-4020)*
News Review, The, Ridgecrest *Also called Sierra View Inc (P-4027)*
Newshire Investment, Los Angeles *Also called Otts Asia Moorer Devon (P-16282)*
Newtex Industries Inc D 323 277-0900
9654 Hermosa Ave Rancho Cucamonga (91730) *(P-11720)*
Newton Heat Treating Co Inc D 626 964-6528
19235 E Walnut Dr N City of Industry (91748) *(P-6448)*
Newvac LLC (HQ) D **310 525-1205**
9330 De Soto Ave Chatsworth (91311) *(P-9043)*
Newvac LLC C 310 990-0401
9330 Desoto Ave Chatsworth (91311) *(P-9364)*
Newvac LLC D 747 202-7333
9330 De Soto Ave Chatsworth (91311) *(P-9365)*
Newvac LLC E 747 202-7333
9330 De Soto Ave Chatsworth (91311) *(P-9757)*
Newvac Division, Chatsworth *Also called Newvac LLC (P-9364)*
Newval Chemical, Orange *Also called Marne Construction Inc (P-1538)*
Nexa 3d, Ventura *Also called Nexa3d Inc (P-8286)*
Nexa3d Inc E 805 465-9001
1923 Eastman Ave Ste 200 Ventura (93003) *(P-8286)*
Nexcare Collaborative (PA) E **818 907-0322**
15477 Ventura Blvd Sherman Oaks (91403) *(P-21856)*
Nexgen Air Heating and Plbg, Anaheim *Also called Nexgen Air Los Angeles (P-1108)*
Nexgen Air Los Angeles (PA) D **714 331-9633**
700 N Valley St Ste Jk Anaheim (92801) *(P-1108)*
Nexgen Pharma, Irvine *Also called New Generation Wellness Inc (P-4859)*
Nexgenix Inc (PA) B **714 665-6240**
2 Peters Canyon Rd # 200 Irvine (92606) *(P-17674)*
Nexgrill Industries Inc (PA) D **909 598-8799**
14050 Laurelwood Pl Chino (91710) *(P-13179)*
Nexinfo Solutions Inc E 714 368-1452
8502 E Chapman Ave # 364 Orange (92869) *(P-13419)*
Nexjet Corporation F 562 395-3030
180 E Ocean Blvd Ste 1010 Long Beach (90802) *(P-10196)*
Nexon America, El Segundo *Also called M Nexon Inc (P-17908)*
Nexrange Industries, City of Industry *Also called Duro Corporation (P-8990)*
Nexsan Corporation (HQ) D **408 724-9809**
325 E Hillcrest Dr # 150 Thousand Oaks (91360) *(P-12787)*
Nexstar Digital LLC D 310 971-9300
12777 W Jefferson Blvd Los Angeles (90066) *(P-17039)*
Next Auto Tech Center E 323 483-6767
6821 Crenshaw Blvd Los Angeles (90043) *(P-2601)*
Next Day Flyers, Van Nuys *Also called Postcard Press Inc (P-4557)*
Next Day Frame Inc D 310 886-0851
11560 Wright Rd Lynwood (90262) *(P-3568)*
Next ERA, Vernon *Also called Peter K Inc (P-2982)*
Next Generation, Commerce *Also called J & F Design Inc (P-2953)*
Next Intent Inc E 805 781-6755
865 Via Esteban San Luis Obispo (93401) *(P-8717)*
Next Point Bearing Group LLC E 818 988-1880
28364 Avenue Crocker Valencia (91355) *(P-8029)*
Next Trucking Inc C 855 688-6398
2383 Utah Ave Ste 108 El Segundo (90245) *(P-12489)*
Next Venture Inc D 818 637-2888
560 Rverdale Drv Glendale Glendale (91204) *(P-797)*
Nextclientcom Inc F 661 222-7755
25000 Avenue Stanford # 125 Valencia (91355) *(P-4192)*
Nextex International, South Gate *Also called Nextrade Inc (P-2732)*
Nextgen Healthcare Info System (HQ) D **949 255-2600**
18111 Von Karman Ave # 800 Irvine (92612) *(P-17675)*
Nexthealth West Hollywood Inc F 310 295-2075
24955 Pacific Coast Hwy Malibu (90265) *(P-19996)*
Nextpoint Inc (PA) D **310 360-5904**
8750 Wilshire Blvd 300e Beverly Hills (90211) *(P-12659)*
Nextrade Inc (PA) E **562 944-9950**
12411 Industrial Ave South Gate (90280) *(P-2732)*
Nexus California Inc E 909 937-1000
4551 Brickell Privado St Ontario (91761) *(P-5436)*
Nexus Healthcare Solutions Inc E 310 448-2693
648 N St Andrews Pl Los Angeles (90004) *(P-21461)*
Nexxen Apparel Inc (PA) F **323 267-9900**
1555 Los Palos St Los Angeles (90023) *(P-2976)*
Nexxrad Teleradiology Partners, Signal Hill *Also called RAD-Image Med Group Inc A Cal (P-20034)*
Nfl Network, Culver City *Also called Nfl Properties LLC (P-19425)*
Nfl Properties LLC D 310 840-4635
10950 Wash Blvd Ste 100 Culver City (90232) *(P-19425)*
Nga 911 LLC D 877 899-8337
8383 Wilshire Blvd # 800 Beverly Hills (90211) *(P-17676)*
Ngd Systems Inc E 949 870-9148
355 Goddard Ste 200 Irvine (92618) *(P-8210)*
Ngork Dental Corporation (PA) D **714 200-4095**
275 S Arroyo Pkwy # 511 Pasadena (91105) *(P-20191)*
Ngp Motors Inc C 818 980-9800
5500 Lankershim Blvd North Hollywood (91601) *(P-18900)*
Nguoi Viet Newspaper, Westminster *Also called Nguoi Viet Vtnamese People Inc (P-4015)*
Nguoi Viet Vtnamese People Inc (PA) E **714 892-9414**
14771 Moran St Westminster (92683) *(P-4015)*
Nguyen Minh F 949 646-2584
300 Old Newport Blvd Newport Beach (92663) *(P-13420)*
Nhk Laboratories Inc (PA) D **562 903-5835**
12230 Florence Ave Santa Fe Springs (90670) *(P-4861)*
Nhn Global Inc (PA) D **424 672-1177**
3530 Wilshire Blvd # 160 Los Angeles (90010) *(P-14406)*
Nhr Newco Holdings LLC (HQ) C **805 964-9975**
6500 Hollister Ave # 210 Santa Barbara (93117) *(P-13421)*
Nhra, Glendora *Also called National Hot Rod Association (P-19433)*
Nhs Western Division Inc D 909 947-9931
175 N Indian Hill Blvd # 203 Claremont (91711) *(P-625)*
Nht Global Inc D 972 241-6525
609 Deep Valley Dr # 395 Rllng HLS Est (90274) *(P-14270)*
Ni Industries Inc D 309 283-3355
7300 E Slauson Ave Commerce (90040) *(P-7025)*
Niagara Bottling Intl LLC F 909 230-5000
2560 E Philadelphia St Ontario (91761) *(P-2273)*
Nibbelink Masonry Cnstr Corp D 661 948-7859
2010 W Avenue K Lancaster (93536) *(P-1350)*
Nic Partners, Rancho Cucamonga *Also called Network Intgrtion Partners Inc (P-18051)*

Employee Codes: A=Over 500 employees, B=251-500
C=101-250, D=51-100, E=20-50 F=10-19
2022 Southern California Business Directory and Buyers Guide
© Mergent Inc. 1-800-342-5647
1217

Nicholas Michael Designs Inc....C....714 562-8101
2330 Raymer Ave Fullerton (92833) ***(P-3569)***
Nichols Farms, Hanford *Also called Nichols Pistachio* ***(P-2114)***
Nichols Inst Reference Labs (HQ)....A....**949 728-4000**
33608 Ortega Hwy San Juan Capistrano (92675) ***(P-21079)***
Nichols Lumber, Baldwin Park *Also called Survey Stake and Marker Inc* ***(P-3455)***
Nichols Lumber & Hardware Co....D....626 960-4802
13470 Dalewood St Baldwin Park (91706) ***(P-13278)***
Nichols Pistachio....C....559 584-6811
13762 1st Ave Hanford (93230) ***(P-2114)***
Nick Alexander Imports....C....800 800-6425
6333 S Alameda St Los Angeles (90001) ***(P-18939)***
Nick's Cabinet Doors, Azusa *Also called Nicks Doors Inc* ***(P-3275)***
Nicks Doors Inc....F....626 812-6491
1052 W Kirkwall Rd Azusa (91702) ***(P-3275)***
Nicksons Machine Shop Inc....E....805 925-2525
914 W Betteravia Rd Santa Maria (93455) ***(P-8718)***
Nico Nat Mfg Corp....E....323 721-1900
2624 Yates Ave Commerce (90040) ***(P-3659)***
Nicola, Los Angeles *Also called Taad Group Inc* ***(P-2868)***
Niconat Manufacturing, Commerce *Also called Nico Nat Mfg Corp* ***(P-3659)***
Niedwick Corporation....E....714 771-9999
967 N Eckhoff St Orange (92867) ***(P-8719)***
Niedwick Machine Co, Orange *Also called Niedwick Corporation* ***(P-8719)***
Nielsen Audio Inc....D....310 824-5906
6080 Center Dr Fl 6 Los Angeles (90045) ***(P-22895)***
Nielsens Creamery (PA)....E....**559 686-4744**
21346 Road 140 Tulare (93274) ***(P-135)***
Nieves Landscape Inc....C....714 835-7332
1629 E Edinger Ave Santa Ana (92705) ***(P-272)***
Nightscaping Outdoor Lighting, Redlands *Also called Loran Inc* ***(P-8877)***
Nihon Kohden America Inc (HQ)....C....**949 580-1555**
15353 Barranca Pkwy Irvine (92618) ***(P-13505)***
Niitakaya Usa Inc (PA)....E....**323 720-5050**
1801 Aeros Way Montebello (90640) ***(P-14714)***
Nijjar Realty Inc (PA)....D....**626 575-0062**
4900 Santa Anita Ave 2b El Monte (91731) ***(P-15931)***
Nike Usa Inc....B....310 670-6770
222 E Redondo Beach Blvd C Gardena (90248) ***(P-19426)***
Nikkel Iron Works Corporation....F....661 746-4904
17045 S Central Vly Hwy Shafter (93263) ***(P-7614)***
Nikken Global Inc (HQ)....C....**949 789-2000**
18301 Von Karman Ave # 1 Irvine (92612) ***(P-14041)***
Nikken International Inc (PA)....C....**949 789-2000**
18301 Von Karman Ave Irvine (92612) ***(P-14956)***
Nikkiso Cosmodyne, Seal Beach *Also called Cosmodyne LLC* ***(P-7968)***
Nikko Enterprise Corporation....E....562 941-6080
13168 Sandoval St Santa Fe Springs (90670) ***(P-2347)***
Niknejad Inc....E....310 477-0407
6855 Hayvenhurst Ave Van Nuys (91406) ***(P-4380)***
Nile Ai Inc....E....818 689-9107
15260 Ventura Blvd # 141 Sherman Oaks (91403) ***(P-17933)***
Nils Inc (PA)....F....**714 755-1600**
3151 Airway Ave Ste V Costa Mesa (92626) ***(P-2977)***
Nils Skiwear, Costa Mesa *Also called Nils Inc* ***(P-2977)***
Nimbus Data Inc....E....650 276-4500
5151 California Ave # 100 Irvine (92617) ***(P-18203)***
Nimbus Water Systems....F....951 984-2800
42445 Avenida Alvarado Temecula (92590) ***(P-8401)***
Nina Mia Inc....D....714 773-5588
826 Enterprise Way Fullerton (92831) ***(P-2495)***
Nina Religion, Huntington Park *Also called Saydel Inc* ***(P-5066)***
Ninas Mexican Foods Inc....E....909 468-5888
20631 Valley Blvd Ste A Walnut (91789) ***(P-2496)***
Nine Network Australia, Los Angeles *Also called Channel 9 Australia Inc* ***(P-12711)***
Niner Wine Estates LLC....E....805 239-2233
2400 W Highway 46 Paso Robles (93446) ***(P-2210)***
Ninja Jump Inc....D....323 255-5418
3221 N San Fernando Rd Los Angeles (90065) ***(P-11387)***
Ninos Latino Unidos FSA....D....562 801-5454
10016 Pioneer Blvd # 123 Santa Fe Springs (90670) ***(P-22137)***
Ninth Avenue Foods, City of Industry *Also called Heritage Distributing Company* ***(P-1795)***
Nippon Ex Nec Lgstics Amer Inc....D....310 604-6100
18615 S Ferris Pl Rancho Dominguez (90220) ***(P-11984)***
Nippon Express USA Inc....E....310 532-6300
970 Francisco St Torrance (90502) ***(P-12490)***
Nippon Express USA Inc....D....310 535-7200
2233 E Grand Ave El Segundo (90245) ***(P-12491)***
Nippon Express USA Inc....D....310 527-4237
19500 S Vermont Ave Torrance (90502) ***(P-12492)***
Nippon Travel Agency Amer Inc....D....310 768-1817
1411 W 190th St Ste 650 Gardena (90248) ***(P-12393)***
Nippon Travel Agency PCF Inc (HQ)....D....**310 768-0017**
1025 W 190th St Ste 300 Gardena (90248) ***(P-12394)***
Niron Inc....E....909 598-1526
20541 Earlgate St Walnut (91789) ***(P-7818)***
Nis America Inc....E....714 540-1199
4 Hutton Cntre Dr Ste 650 Santa Ana (92707) ***(P-17934)***
Nissan of Tustin....C....714 669-8282
30 Auto Center Dr Tustin (92782) ***(P-15166)***
Nissi Trim, Los Angeles *Also called Ckcc Inc* ***(P-3170)***
Nissin Foods USA Company Inc (HQ)....C....**310 327-8478**
2001 W Rosecrans Ave Gardena (90249) ***(P-2380)***
Nissin Intl Trnspt USA Inc (HQ)....E....**310 222-8500**
1540 W 190th St Torrance (90501) ***(P-12493)***
Nite-Lite Signs Inc....E....818 341-0987
25583 Avenue Stanford Valencia (91355) ***(P-1678)***
Nitro 2 Go Inc....F....909 864-4886
1420 Richardson St San Bernardino (92408) ***(P-4754)***
Nitro Circus Live Usa Inc....D....760 231-1840
946 W 17th St Costa Mesa (92627) ***(P-19593)***
Nitto Avecia Pharma Svcs Inc (HQ)....C....**949 951-4425**
10 Vanderbilt Irvine (92618) ***(P-4862)***
Nittobo America Inc....C....951 677-5629
25549 Adams Ave Murrieta (92562) ***(P-4937)***
Niusource Inc....F....909 631-2895
14266 Euclid Ave Chino (91710) ***(P-23284)***
Nix Healthcare System, Los Angeles *Also called Nix Hospitals System LLC* ***(P-20869)***
Nix Hospitals System LLC (HQ)....C....**210 271-1800**
3415 S Sepulveda Blvd # 900 Los Angeles (90034) ***(P-20869)***
Nk Sign Industry Inc....F....661 348-9580
2546 S Union Ave Bakersfield (93307) ***(P-11578)***
Nkmax America Inc....D....949 396-6830
3001 Daimler St Santa Ana (92705) ***(P-21080)***
Nksfb LLC....E....310 277-4657
10960 Wilshire Blvd Fl 5 Los Angeles (90024) ***(P-17677)***
NL&a Collections Inc....E....323 277-6266
6323 Maywood Ave Huntington Park (90255) ***(P-9069)***
Nlms Elite Construction Co....F....626 205-8417
1254 S Waterman Ave San Bernardino (92408) ***(P-626)***
Nmc Group Inc....E....714 223-3525
300 E Cypress St Brea (92821) ***(P-14008)***
Nms Data Inc....E....949 472-2700
23172 Plaza Pointe Dr # 205 Laguna Hills (92653) ***(P-23482)***
Nms Properties Inc....D....310 656-2700
10960 Wilshire Blvd Los Angeles (90024) ***(P-15932)***
Nmsp Inc (HQ)....D....**310 484-2322**
2205 W 126th St Ste A Hawthorne (90250) ***(P-10109)***
Nmsp Inc....E....951 734-2453
1451 E 6th St Corona (92879) ***(P-10110)***
Nna Insurance Services LLC....C....818 739-4071
9350 De Soto Ave Chatsworth (91311) ***(P-15603)***
Nnn Realty Advisors Inc....B....714 667-8252
1551 N Tustin Ave Ste 300 Santa Ana (92705) ***(P-15933)***
Nnn Realty Investors LLC....B....714 667-8252
19700 Fairchild Ste 300 Irvine (92612) ***(P-16279)***
No Holidays Corporation....E....310 848-7351
1137 El Centro St Apt E South Pasadena (91030) ***(P-663)***
No Nuts LLC....F....805 309-2420
750 Calle Plano Camarillo (93012) ***(P-2101)***
No Prssure Prssure Wshg Svcs L....E....951 477-1988
41880 Kalmia St Ste 165 Murrieta (92562) ***(P-4973)***
No World Borders (PA)....D....**949 718-4427**
620 Newport Center Dr Newport Beach (92660) ***(P-23483)***
Noah's New York Bagels, Westminster *Also called Einstein Noah Rest Group Inc* ***(P-1770)***
Noarus Investments Inc....D....310 649-2440
5850 W Centinela Ave Los Angeles (90045) ***(P-18858)***
Noarus Tgg....D....714 895-5595
9444 Trask Ave Garden Grove (92844) ***(P-18859)***
Nobbe Orthopedics Inc....C....805 687-7508
3010 State St Santa Barbara (93105) ***(P-11129)***
Nobel Biocare Usa LLC....B....714 282-4800
22715 Savi Ranch Pkwy Yorba Linda (92887) ***(P-21111)***
Nobel Biocare USA LLC....F....714 282-4800
22715 Savi Ranch Pkwy Yorba Linda (92887) ***(P-11182)***
Noble Energy, Seal Beach *Also called Samedan Oil Corporation* ***(P-463)***
Noble Investment Group LLC....C....562 436-3000
333 E Ocean Blvd Long Beach (90802) ***(P-16583)***
Noble Rents Inc....D....855 767-4424
8314 Slauson Ave Pico Rivera (90660) ***(P-17314)***
Noble/Utah Long Beach LLC....C....562 436-3000
333 E Ocean Blvd Long Beach (90802) ***(P-16584)***
Nobles Medical Tech Inc....E....714 427-0398
17080 Newhope St Fountain Valley (92708) ***(P-11035)***
Noblesse Oblige Inc....C....760 353-3336
2015 Silsbee Rd El Centro (92243) ***(P-158)***
Noevir Holding America Inc (HQ)....E....**949 660-1111**
1095 Main St Irvine (92614) ***(P-14271)***
Nogales Investors LLC....D....310 276-7439
9229 W Sunset Blvd # 900 Los Angeles (90069) ***(P-16280)***
Nogales Investors MGT LLC (PA)....C....**310 276-7439**
9229 W Sunset Blvd # 900 Los Angeles (90069) ***(P-16134)***
Nohl Ranch Inn, Anaheim *Also called Leisure Care LLC* ***(P-22124)***
Noka LLC....F....214 455-3888
15332 Antioch St Ste 199 Pacific Palisades (90272) ***(P-6467)***
Nongshim America Inc (HQ)....C....**909 481-3698**
12155 6th St Rancho Cucamonga (91730) ***(P-14482)***
Nopomo Garbage, San Luis Obispo *Also called South County Sanitary Svc Inc* ***(P-12982)***
Nor-Cal Beverage Co Inc....E....714 526-8600
1226 N Olive St Anaheim (92801) ***(P-18614)***
Nora Lighting Inc....C....800 686-6672
6505 Gayhart St Commerce (90040) ***(P-13653)***
Norac Additives LLC....D....909 321-5952
100 W Fthill Blvd Ste 101 San Dimas (91773) ***(P-14788)***
Norac Inc (PA)....D....**626 334-2907**
405 S Motor Ave Azusa (91702) ***(P-5142)***
Norac Pharma, Azusa *Also called S&B Pharma Inc* ***(P-4763)***
Norberts Athletic Products Inc....F....310 830-6672
354 W Gardena Blvd Gardena (90248) ***(P-11440)***
Norcal Inc....C....714 224-3949
1400 Moonstone Brea (92821) ***(P-1447)***
Norcal Beverage Co, Anaheim *Also called Nor-Cal Beverage Co Inc* ***(P-18614)***
Norcal Inc....C....714 224-3949
1400 Moonstone Brea (92821) ***(P-1448)***
Norcal Pottery Products Inc....C....909 390-3745
5700 E Airport Dr Ontario (91761) ***(P-13180)***

Mergent e-mail: customerrelations@mergent.com
1218
2022 Southern California Business Directory and Buyers Guide
(P-0000) Products & Services Section entry number
(PA)=Parent Co (HQ)=Headquarters (DH)=Div Headquarters

Norchem Corporation (PA) ....D....323 221-0221
5649 Alhambra Ave Los Angeles (90032) ***(P-7992)***

Norco Injection Molding Inc ....D....909 393-4000
14325 Monte Vista Ave Chino (91710) ***(P-5729)***

Norco Plastics, Chino *Also called Norco Injection Molding Inc* ***(P-5729)***

Norco Plastics Inc ....D....909 393-4000
14325 Monte Vista Ave Chino (91710) ***(P-5730)***

Norco Ranch Inc (HQ) ....B....951 737-6735
12005 Cabernet Dr Fontana (92337) ***(P-144)***

Nordhavn Yachts, Dana Point *Also called Pacific Asian Enterprises Inc* ***(P-18625)***

Nordson Medical (ca) LLC ....D....657 215-4200
7612 Woodwind Dr Huntington Beach (92647) ***(P-11036)***

Norfox, City of Industry *Also called Norman Fox & Co* ***(P-14790)***

Noritsu-America Corporation (HQ) ....C....714 521-9040
6900 Noritsu Ave Buena Park (90620) ***(P-13347)***

Noritz America Corporation (HQ) ....D....714 433-2905
11160 Grace Ave Fountain Valley (92708) ***(P-13848)***

Norm Harboldt ....F....714 596-4242
17592 Gothard St Huntington Beach (92647) ***(P-7391)***

Norm Tessier Cabinets Inc ....F....909 987-8955
11989 6th St Rancho Cucamonga (91730) ***(P-3328)***

Norman Fox & Co ....E....323 973-4900
5511 S Boyle Ave Vernon (90058) ***(P-14789)***

Norman Fox & Co (PA) ....E....800 632-1777
14970 Don Julian Rd City of Industry (91746) ***(P-14790)***

Norman Charter, La Palma *Also called Norman International Inc* ***(P-13181)***

Norman Industrial Mtls Inc (PA) ....C....818 729-3333
8300 San Fernando Rd Sun Valley (91352) ***(P-13580)***

Norman Industrial Mtls Inc ....E....949 250-3343
2481 Alton Pkwy Irvine (92606) ***(P-13581)***

Norman International, Vernon *Also called Norman Paper and Foam Co Inc* ***(P-3888)***

Norman International Inc ....D....562 946-0420
28 Centerpointe Dr # 120 La Palma (90623) ***(P-13181)***

Norman Paper and Foam Co Inc ....E....323 582-7132
4501 S Santa Fe Ave Vernon (90058) ***(P-3888)***

Norman Wireline Service Inc ....F....661 399-5697
1301 James Rd Bakersfield (93308) ***(P-528)***

Normandie Casino & Showroom, Rancho Palos Verdes *Also called Normandie Club LP* ***(P-19657)***

Normandie Club LP ....D....310 352-3486
57 Via Malona Rancho Palos Verdes (90275) ***(P-19657)***

Normandie Country Bakery Inc (PA) ....F....323 939-5528
3022 S Cochran Ave Los Angeles (90016) ***(P-2024)***

Normandy Refinishers Inc ....E....626 792-9202
355 S Rosemead Blvd Pasadena (91107) ***(P-7288)***

Normans Nursery Inc (PA) ....E....626 285-9795
8665 Duarte Rd San Gabriel (91775) ***(P-14891)***

Normans Nursery Inc ....C....805 684-1411
5770 Casitas Pass Rd Carpinteria (93013) ***(P-87)***

Normans Nursery Inc ....C....805 684-5442
5800 Via Real Carpinteria (93013) ***(P-14892)***

Normans Nursery Inc ....C....626 285-9795
20500 Ramona Blvd Baldwin Park (91706) ***(P-14893)***

Normont Hydraulic Sls Svc Inc ....F....951 676-2155
43123 Business Park Dr Temecula (92590) ***(P-13923)***

Norotos Inc ....C....714 662-3113
201 E Alton Ave Santa Ana (92707) ***(P-8720)***

Norstar Office Products Inc (PA) ....E....323 262-1919
5353 Jillson St Commerce (90040) ***(P-3593)***

North Amercn Science Assoc Inc ....D....949 951-3110
9 Morgan Irvine (92618) ***(P-22956)***

North American Acceptance Corp ....C....714 868-3195
3191 Red Hill Ave Ste 100 Costa Mesa (92626) ***(P-15147)***

North American Client Svcs Inc (PA) ....C....949 240-2423
25910 Acero Ste 350 Mission Viejo (92691) ***(P-23075)***

North American Composites Co ....E....909 605-8977
4990 Vanderbilt St Ontario (91761) ***(P-4704)***

North American Fire Hose Corp ....D....805 922-7076
910 Noble Way Santa Maria (93454) ***(P-5321)***

North American Foam & Packg, Fullerton *Also called Gold Venture Inc* ***(P-5509)***

North American Med MGT Cal Inc (HQ) ....D....909 605-8000
3281 E Guasti Rd Fl 7 Ontario (91761) ***(P-23076)***

North American Pet Products, Corona *Also called Pet Partners Inc* ***(P-11734)***

North American Textile Co LLC (PA) ....E....818 409-0019
346 W Cerritos Ave Glendale (91204) ***(P-3178)***

North American Title Co Inc ....C....714 550-6400
505 S Main St Ste 101 Orange (92868) ***(P-15510)***

North American Video Corp (PA) ....E....714 779-7499
1335 S Acacia Ave Fullerton (92831) ***(P-13756)***

North Amrcn SEC Investigations ....D....323 634-1911
550 E Carson Plaza Dr # 22 Carson (90746) ***(P-18302)***

North Anaheim Surgery Center, Anaheim *Also called Vanguard Health Systems Inc* ***(P-20132)***

North Bay Pool and Spa, Monrovia *Also called Vivopools LLC* ***(P-18718)***

North County Sand and Grav Inc ....F....951 928-2881
26227 Sherman Rd Sun City (92585) ***(P-572)***

North County Times ....E....951 676-4315
28441 Rancho California R Temecula (92590) ***(P-4016)***

North Highland Company LLC ....C....818 509-5100
4640 Lankershim Blvd # 30 North Hollywood (91602) ***(P-23285)***

North Hollywood Medical Offs, North Hollywood *Also called Kaiser Foundation Hospitals* ***(P-19908)***

North Kern S Tulare Hosp Dst ....C....661 720-2126
1509 Tokay St Delano (93215) ***(P-20870)***

North La County Regional Ctr (PA) ....B....818 778-1900
9200 Oakdale Ave Ste 100 Chatsworth (91311) ***(P-23484)***

North Orange Coast Pntg Inc ....D....951 279-2694
3969 Sierra Ave Norco (92860) ***(P-1191)***

North Orange County Svc Ctr, Fullerton *Also called Southern California Edison Co* ***(P-12835)***

North Ornge Cnty Cmnty Cllege ....C....714 992-7008
330 E Chapman Ave Fullerton (92832) ***(P-13422)***

North Pk Apartments Hsing Corp (PA) ....E....661 399-3084
601 Douglas St Bakersfield (93308) ***(P-15742)***

North Ranch Country Club ....C....818 889-3531
4761 Valley Spring Dr Westlake Village (91362) ***(P-19594)***

North Ranch Management Corp ....D....800 410-2153
9754 Deering Ave Chatsworth (91311) ***(P-5902)***

North Shore Greenhouses Inc ....C....760 397-0400
82900 Johnson St Thermal (92274) ***(P-100)***

North Shore Living Herbs, Thermal *Also called North Shore Greenhouses Inc* ***(P-100)***

North West Pharmanaturals, Brea *Also called Beacon Manufacturing Inc* ***(P-4738)***

Northbound Treatment Services, Newport Beach *Also called National Therapeutic Svcs Inc* ***(P-21322)***

Northcross Paper Co Inc ....E....818 998-3774
9667 Canoga Ave Chatsworth (91311) ***(P-14215)***

Northeast Newspapers Inc ....E....213 727-1117
621 W Beverly Blvd Montebello (90640) ***(P-4017)***

Northeast Valley Health Corp ....D....818 361-8464
531 5th St Unit A San Fernando (91340) ***(P-19997)***

Northeast Valley Health Corp ....D....661 287-1551
23763 Valencia Blvd Valencia (91355) ***(P-19998)***

Northeast Valley Health Corp ....D....818 340-3570
7107 Remmet Ave Canoga Park (91303) ***(P-21462)***

Northeast Valley Health Corp ....D....661 673-8888
26974 Rainbow Glen Dr Canyon Country (91351) ***(P-21463)***

Northeast Valley Health Corp ....D....818 432-4400
7223 Fair Ave Sun Valley (91352) ***(P-21464)***

Northeast Valley Health Corp (PA) ....D....818 898-1388
1172 N Maclay Ave San Fernando (91340) ***(P-21857)***

Northeast Valley Health Corp ....D....818 365-8086
1600 San Fernando Rd San Fernando (91340) ***(P-19999)***

Northeast Valley Health Corp ....D....818 778-6240
7138 Van Nuys Blvd Van Nuys (91405) ***(P-20000)***

Northeast Valley Health Corp ....D....818 765-8656
7843 Lankershim Blvd North Hollywood (91605) ***(P-20001)***

Northeast Valley Health Corp ....D....818 896-0531
12756 Van Nuys Blvd Pacoima (91331) ***(P-20002)***

Northeast Valley Health Corp ....D....818 988-6335
8215 Van Nuys Blvd Ste 21 Panorama City (91402) ***(P-20003)***

Northern Holdings ....D....805 785-0194
1531 Froom Ranch Way San Luis Obispo (93405) ***(P-1618)***

Northern Inyo Healthcare Dst ....B....760 873-5811
150 Pioneer Ln Bishop (93514) ***(P-20871)***

NORTHERN INYO HOSPITAL, Bishop *Also called Northern Inyo Healthcare Dst* ***(P-20871)***

Northern Ornge Cnty Ent Mdcl (PA) ....D....714 441-0133
1955 Sunny Crest Dr # 108 Fullerton (92835) ***(P-20004)***

Northern Pionr Healthcare Inc (HQ) ....E....949 487-9500
27101 Puerta Real Mission Viejo (92691) ***(P-21465)***

Northern Trust Company ....E....310 282-3800
2049 Century Park E # 3600 Los Angeles (90067) ***(P-15004)***

NORTHPOINT DAY TREATMENT SCH, Northridge *Also called Child and Family Guidance Ctr* ***(P-21287)***

Northrdge Tr-Mdlity Imging Inc ....F....818 709-2468
9449 De Soto Ave Chatsworth (91311) ***(P-10661)***

Northridge Diagnostic Center ....C....818 773-6500
8227 Reseda Blvd Reseda (91335) ***(P-20005)***

Northridge Emergency Med Group ....D....818 700-5603
18300 Roscoe Blvd Northridge (91325) ***(P-20872)***

Northridge Hosp Foundation Aux ....D....818 885-5341
18300 Roscoe Blvd Northridge (91325) ***(P-20873)***

Northridge Hospital Med Ctr, Northridge *Also called Dignity Health* ***(P-20752)***

Northridge Nursing Center, Reseda *Also called Longwood Management Corp* ***(P-20851)***

Northrop Grmman Elctrnic Syste, Azusa *Also called Northrop Grumman Systems Corp* ***(P-10622)***

Northrop Grmman Innvtion Syste ....D....818 887-8100
9401 Corbin Ave Northridge (91324) ***(P-10605)***

Northrop Grumman Aerospace, Redondo Beach *Also called Northrop Grumman Intl Inc* ***(P-10607)***

Northrop Grumman CMS, Woodland Hills *Also called Northrop Grumman Systems Corp* ***(P-18053)***

Northrop Grumman Corporation ....C....310 332-1000
1 Hornet Way El Segundo (90245) ***(P-10606)***

Northrop Grumman Federal Cr Un (PA) ....D....310 808-4000
879 W 190th St Ste 800 Gardena (90248) ***(P-15074)***

Northrop Grumman Intl Inc ....E....310 812-4321
2420 Santa Fe Ave Redondo Beach (90278) ***(P-10607)***

Northrop Grumman Intl Trdg Inc ....B....818 715-3607
21240 Burbank Blvd Woodland Hills (91367) ***(P-10608)***

Northrop Grumman Systems Corp ....C....310 812-5149
1 Space Park Blvd Redondo Beach (90278) ***(P-9303)***

Northrop Grumman Systems Corp ....B....310 556-4911
6411 W Imperial Hwy Los Angeles (90045) ***(P-10609)***

Northrop Grumman Systems Corp ....A....818 715-4040
21240 Burbank Blvd Ms29 Woodland Hills (91367) ***(P-10610)***

Northrop Grumman Systems Corp ....C....818 676-1321
5500 Canoga Ave 31 Woodland Hills (91367) ***(P-22855)***

Northrop Grumman Systems Corp ....C....310 632-1846
1 Hornet Way Dept Mt00w5 El Segundo (90245) ***(P-10611)***

Northrop Grumman Systems Corp ....C....805 684-6641
2601 Camino Del Sol Oxnard (93030) ***(P-10612)***

Northrop Grumman Systems Corp ....C....818 715-4854
21240 Burbank Blvd Woodland Hills (91367) ***(P-18053)***

Northrop Grumman Systems Corp ....B....661 272-7000
3520 E Avenue M Palmdale (93550) ***(P-10197)***

Northrop Grumman Systems Corp ....C....805 278-2074
2700 Camino Del Sol Oxnard (93030) ***(P-10613)***

Employee Codes: A=Over 500 employees, B=251-500
C=101-250, D=51-100, E=20-50 F=10-19

2022 Southern California Business
Directory and Buyers Guide

© Mergent Inc. 1-800-342-5647

1219

Northrop Grumman Systems Corp C 818 715-2597
21200 Burbank Blvd Woodland Hills (91367) ***(P-10614)***

Northrop Grumman Systems Corp C 760 380-4268
Bldg 806 Fort Irwin (92310) ***(P-10615)***

Northrop Grumman Systems Corp C 818 887-8110
9401 Corbin Ave Northridge (91324) ***(P-10616)***

Northrop Grumman Systems Corp C 714 240-6521
6033 Bandini Blvd Commerce (90040) ***(P-10617)***

Northrop Grumman Systems Corp C 714 240-6521
600 Pine Ave Goleta (93117) ***(P-10618)***

Northrop Grumman Systems Corp C 480 355-7716
2401 E El Segundo Blvd El Segundo (90245) ***(P-10619)***

Northrop Grumman Systems Corp C 805 315-5728
1467 Fairway Dr Santa Maria (93455) ***(P-10620)***

Northrop Grumman Systems Corp C 805 987-9739
5161 Verdugo Way Camarillo (93012) ***(P-18054)***

Northrop Grumman Systems Corp C 310 764-3000
1762 Glenn Curtiss St Carson (90746) ***(P-17678)***

Northrop Grumman Systems Corp C 818 249-5252
2550 Honolulu Ave Montrose (91020) ***(P-10621)***

Northrop Grumman Systems Corp C 626 812-1000
1100 W Hollyvale St Azusa (91702) ***(P-10622)***

Northrop Grumman Systems Corp C 661 540-0446
3520 E Avenue M Palmdale (93550) ***(P-10623)***

Northrop Grumman Systems Corp C 855 737-8364
1 Space Park Blvd Redondo Beach (90278) ***(P-23485)***

Northrop Grumman Systems Corp C 310 812-4321
2477 Manhattan Beach Blvd Redondo Beach (90278) ***(P-10624)***

Northrop Grumman Systems Corp C 626 812-1464
1111 W 3rd St Azusa (91702) ***(P-10625)***

Northrop Grumman Systems Corp C 310 332-1000
1 Hornet Way El Segundo (90245) ***(P-10626)***

Northrop Grumman Systems Corp B 310 812-1089
1 Space Park Blvd Redondo Beach (90278) ***(P-10198)***

Northrop Grumman Systems Corp B 310 812-4321
1 Space Park Blvd D Redondo Beach (90278) ***(P-10199)***

Northrop Grumman Systems Corp C 703 713-4096
862 E Hospitality Ln San Bernardino (92408) ***(P-10627)***

Northstar, Irvine *Also called Custom Business Solutions Inc* ***(P-13355)***

Northstar Contg Group Inc D 714 639-7600
13320 Cambridge St Santa Fe Springs (90670) ***(P-1619)***

Northstar Dem & Remediation LP (HQ) **C 714 672-3500**
404 N Berry St Brea (92821) ***(P-1620)***

Northstar Engineering, Rancho Cucamonga *Also called James Magna Ltd* ***(P-18899)***

Northwest Excavating Inc D 818 349-5861
18201 Napa St Northridge (91325) ***(P-17315)***

Northwest Group Llc E 310 327-4670
1535 W 139th St Gardena (90249) ***(P-14312)***

Northwest Hotel Corporation (PA) **C 714 776-6120**
1380 S Harbor Blvd Anaheim (92802) ***(P-16585)***

Northwest Landscape Services, Los Angeles *Also called Vaughn Weedman Inc* ***(P-348)***

Northwest Recycler Core, Riverside *Also called Recycler Core Company Inc* ***(P-12970)***

Northwestern Converting Co D 800 959-3402
2395 Railroad St Corona (92878) ***(P-3109)***

Norton Packaging Inc E 323 588-6167
5800 S Boyle Ave Vernon (90058) ***(P-5731)***

NORTON SCIENCE AND LANGUAGE AC, Apple Valley *Also called High Dsert Prtnr In Acdmic Exc* ***(P-22884)***

Norton Smon Mseum Art At Psden D 626 449-6840
411 W Colorado Blvd Pasadena (91105) ***(P-22230)***

Norwalk Meadows Nursing Ctr LP C 562 864-2541
10625 Leffingwell Rd Norwalk (90650) ***(P-20425)***

Norwalk Medical Offices, Norwalk *Also called Kaiser Foundation Hospitals* ***(P-19909)***

Norwich Aero Products Inc (HQ) **E 607 336-7636**
6900 Orangethorpe Ave B Buena Park (90620) ***(P-10628)***

Nossaman LLP (PA) **D 213 612-7800**
777 S Figueroa St # 3400 Los Angeles (90017) ***(P-21645)***

Nossaman LLP D 760 918-0500
777 S Figueroa St # 3400 Los Angeles (90017) ***(P-21646)***

Nossaman LLP D 949 833-7800
18101 Von Karman Ave # 1800 Irvine (92612) ***(P-21647)***

Not Only Jeans Inc E 213 765-9725
3004 S Main St Los Angeles (90007) ***(P-2582)***

Not Your Daughters Jeans, Vernon *Also called Nydj Apparel LLC* ***(P-14407)***

Notellage Corporation D 323 257-8151
4681 Eagle Rock Blvd Los Angeles (90041) ***(P-20618)***

Nothing To Wear Inc (PA) **E 310 328-0408**
630 Maple Ave Torrance (90503) ***(P-2863)***

Noticiero Semanal Advertising F 559 784-5000
115 E Oak Ave Porterville (93257) ***(P-4018)***

Notron Manufacturing Inc F 818 247-7739
801 Milford St Glendale (91203) ***(P-8721)***

Notthoff Engineering, Huntington Beach *Also called AMG Huntington Beach LLC* ***(P-22486)***

Notthoff Engineering LA Inc D 714 894-9802
5416 Argosy Ave Huntington Beach (92649) ***(P-10388)***

Nourmand & Associates E 310 274-4000
421 N Beverly Dr Ste 200 Beverly Hills (90210) ***(P-15934)***

Noushig Inc E 805 983-2903
451 Lombard St Oxnard (93030) ***(P-2025)***

Nova, Huntington Park *Also called NL&a Collections Inc* ***(P-9069)***

Nova Container Freight Station, Carson *Also called H Rauvel Inc* ***(P-12212)***

Nova Development, Calabasas *Also called Avanquest North America LLC* ***(P-17558)***

Nova Lifestyle Inc (PA) **E 323 888-9999**
6565 E Washington Blvd Commerce (90040) ***(P-3482)***

Nova Medical Products, Carson *Also called Nova Ortho-Med Inc* ***(P-13506)***

Nova Ortho-Med Inc (PA) **D 310 352-3600**
1470 Beachey Pl Carson (90746) ***(P-13506)***

Nova Skilled Home Health Inc C 323 658-6232
3300 N San Fernando Blvd Burbank (91504) ***(P-21466)***

Nova Steel Company, Corona *Also called Ckkm Inc* ***(P-13557)***

Nova Transportation Services, Compton *Also called H Rauvel Inc* ***(P-12050)***

Novacap LLC B 661 295-5920
25111 Anza Dr Valencia (91355) ***(P-13757)***

Novalogic Inc (PA) **D 818 380-1997**
27489 Agoura Rd Ste 300 Agoura Hills (91301) ***(P-17679)***

Novare Nat Settlement Svc LLC E 714 352-4088
320 Commerce Ste 150 Irvine (92602) ***(P-15005)***

Novasignal Corp F 818 317-4999
2440 S Sepulveda Blvd # 1 Los Angeles (90064) ***(P-11037)***

Novastor Corporation (PA) **E 805 579-6700**
29209 Canwood St Ste 200 Agoura Hills (91301) ***(P-17935)***

Novatime Technology Inc (HQ) **D 909 895-8100**
9680 Haven Ave Ste 200 Rancho Cucamonga (91730) ***(P-17440)***

Novipax Inc D 909 392-1750
1941 N White Ave La Verne (91750) ***(P-14216)***

Novo Distribution LLC C 951 742-5273
31 Heron Ln Riverside (92507) ***(P-13279)***

Nowcom LLC C 323 746-6888
4751 Wilshire Blvd # 205 Los Angeles (90010) ***(P-18204)***

NP Mechanical Inc B 951 667-4220
9129 Stellar Ct Corona (92883) ***(P-1109)***

Npg Inc (PA) **D 951 940-0200**
1354 Jet Way Perris (92571) ***(P-5275)***

Npms Natural Products Mil Svcs, Gardena *Also called BDS Natural Products Inc* ***(P-2396)***

Nrea-TRC 711 LLC C 213 488-3500
711 S Hope St Los Angeles (90017) ***(P-16586)***

NRG California South LP D 805 984-5241
393 Harbor Blvd Oxnard (93035) ***(P-12809)***

NRG California South LP D 909 899-7241
8996 Etiwanda Ave Rancho Cucamonga (91739) ***(P-12810)***

NRG California South LP D 760 254-5241
37000 E Santa Fe St Daggett (92327) ***(P-12811)***

NRG Clean Power Inc E 818 444-2020
7012 Owensmouth Ave Canoga Park (91303) ***(P-12812)***

NRG El Segundo Operations Inc D 310 615-6344
301 Vista Del Mar El Segundo (90245) ***(P-12813)***

NRG Power Inc D 714 424-6484
3011 S Shannon St Santa Ana (92704) ***(P-1287)***

Nri Distribution, Los Angeles *Also called Nri Usa LLC* ***(P-12494)***

Nri Usa LLC (PA) **D 323 345-6456**
13200 S Broadway Los Angeles (90061) ***(P-12494)***

NRLL LLC B 949 768-7777
1 Mauchly Irvine (92618) ***(P-16281)***

Nrp Holding Co Inc (PA) **C 949 583-1000**
1 Mauchly Irvine (92618) ***(P-16106)***

NS Wash Systems, Inglewood *Also called N/S Corporation* ***(P-8399)***

Nsa Holdings Inc F 951 686-1400
888 Marlborough Ave Riverside (92507) ***(P-5732)***

Nsbn, Los Angeles *Also called Cliftonlarsonallen LLP* ***(P-22773)***

Nsi - Natural Sourcing Intl, Encino *Also called Nsi Group LLC* ***(P-18615)***

Nsi Architectural, Anaheim *Also called Onesolution Light and Control* ***(P-13654)***

Nsi Group LLC (PA) **E 818 639-8335**
17031 Ventura Blvd Encino (91316) ***(P-18615)***

NSK Prcsion Amer Snta Fe Sprng, Cerritos *Also called NSK Precision America Inc* ***(P-14009)***

NSK Precision America Inc C 562 968-1000
13921 Bettencourt St Cerritos (90703) ***(P-14009)***

Nsv International Corp D 562 438-3836
1250 E 29th St Signal Hill (90755) ***(P-13075)***

Nta America, Gardena *Also called Nippon Travel Agency Amer Inc* ***(P-12393)***

Nta Pacific, Gardena *Also called Nippon Travel Agency PCF Inc* ***(P-12394)***

Ntrust Infotech Inc D 562 207-1600
230 Commerce Ste 180 Irvine (92602) ***(P-17936)***

Ntt Data Inc D 213 228-2500
1000 Corporate Center Dr # 140 Monterey Park (91754) ***(P-18055)***

Nu Health Products, Walnut *Also called Nu-Health Products Co* ***(P-4755)***

Nu Venture Diving Co E 805 815-4044
1600 Beacon Pl Oxnard (93033) ***(P-8036)***

Nu-Health California LLC F 800 806-0519
16910 Cherie Pl Carson (90746) ***(P-1870)***

Nu-Health Products Co E 909 869-0666
20875 Currier Rd Walnut (91789) ***(P-4755)***

Nu-Hope Laboratories Inc E 818 899-7711
12640 Branford St Pacoima (91331) ***(P-11038)***

Nu-Steel Trade LLC E 310 329-2263
15005 S Avalon Blvd Gardena (90248) ***(P-13582)***

Nu-Way SEC Invstgtive Svcs Inc D 760 243-7577
14368 St Andrews Dr Ste D Victorville (92395) ***(P-18303)***

Nubile, Los Angeles *Also called Semore Inc* ***(P-2774)***

Nubity Inc (PA) **E 213 408-4675**
2767 Tumbleweed Ave Simi Valley (93065) ***(P-17680)***

Nucast Industries Inc D 951 277-8888
23220 Park Canyon Dr Corona (92883) ***(P-6043)***

Nuconic Packaging LLC E 323 588-9033
4889 Loma Vista Ave Vernon (90058) ***(P-5733)***

Nucourse Distribution Inc D 866 655-4366
22342 Avenida Empresa # 200 Rcho STA Marg (92688) ***(P-13758)***

Nuevo Amnecer Latino Chld Svcs (PA) **D 323 720-9951**
5400 Pomona Blvd Los Angeles (90022) ***(P-21858)***

Nugier Hydraulics, Gardena *Also called Nugier Press Company Inc* ***(P-7762)***

Nugier Press Company Inc E 310 515-6025
18031 La Salle Ave Gardena (90248) ***(P-7762)***

Numatech West (kmp) LLC D 909 706-3627
1201 E Lexington Ave Pomona (91766) ***(P-3822)***

ALPHABETIC SECTION Obatake Inc

Number Holdings Inc (PA) .... C **323 980-8145**
4000 Union Pacific Ave Commerce (90023) ***(P-14957)***

Numecent Inc .... E 949 833-2800
530 Technology Dr Ste 375 Irvine (92618) ***(P-17937)***

Numerical Ctrl Cmpt Sciences (PA) .... F **949 852-3664**
2600 Michelson Dr # 1700 Irvine (92612) ***(P-17681)***

Numotion, Cypress *Also called Atg - Designing Mobility Inc **(P-13477)***

Nuorder Inc (PA) .... F **310 954-1313**
1901 Avenue Of The Stars # 175 Los Angeles (90067) ***(P-17938)***

Nuphoton Technologies Inc .... F 951 696-8366
41610 Corning Pl Murrieta (92562) ***(P-9895)***

Nupla LLC .... C 818 768-6800
11912 Sheldon St Sun Valley (91352) ***(P-6487)***

Nurse Next Door, Anaheim *Also called St Joseph Health Per Care Svcs **(P-21214)***

Nursecore Management Svcs LLC .... B 805 938-7660
1010 S Broadway Ste A Santa Maria (93454) ***(P-22138)***

Nurses Tuch HM Hlth Prvder Inc .... E 818 500-4877
135 S Jackson St Ste 100 Glendale (91205) ***(P-21193)***

Nurturing Tots Inc .... D 818 996-1602
535 Avenue B A Redondo Beach (90277) ***(P-22043)***

Nuset Inc .... E 626 246-1668
2432 Peck Rd City of Industry (90601) ***(P-6530)***

Nuspace Inc (HQ) .... E **562 497-3200**
4401 E Donald Douglas Dr Long Beach (90808) ***(P-8722)***

Nutrade Inc .... F 949 477-2300
2808 Willis St Santa Ana (92705) ***(P-2583)***

Nutrawise Health & Beauty Corp (PA) .... D **949 900-2400**
9600 Toledo Way Irvine (92618) ***(P-4863)***

Nutri Granulations, La Mirada *Also called JM Huber Micropowders Inc **(P-4660)***

Nutrilite, Buena Park *Also called Access Business Group LLC **(P-14769)***

Nutripharm USA Inc .... F 626 962-9871
15046 Nelson Ave Ste 1 City of Industry (91744) ***(P-4756)***

Nutrition Services, Hemet *Also called Hemet Unified School District **(P-22948)***

Nutrition Services Department, Costa Mesa *Also called Newport Mesa Unified Schl Dst **(P-21460)***

Nutrition Without Borders LLC .... F 310 845-7745
4641 Leahy St Culver City (90232) ***(P-8322)***

Nuvair, Oxnard *Also called Nu Venture Diving Co **(P-8036)***

Nuvasive Spclzed Orthpdics Inc .... D 949 837-3600
101 Enterprise Ste 100 Aliso Viejo (92656) ***(P-11039)***

Nuvet Labs, Westlake Village *Also called Vitavet Labs Inc **(P-11790)***

Nuvia Water Technologies Inc .... D 951 734-7400
108 Business Center Dr Corona (92878) ***(P-18616)***

Nuvision Fincl Federal Cr Un (PA) .... C **714 375-8000**
7812 Edinger Ave Ste 100 Huntington Beach (92647) ***(P-15075)***

Nux Group Inc .... F 323 780-4700
5164 Alcoa Ave Vernon (90058) ***(P-2584)***

Nuzuna Corporation .... D 949 432-4824
1451 Quail St Ste 104 Newport Beach (92660) ***(P-19462)***

Nuzuna Fitness, Newport Beach *Also called Nuzuna Corporation **(P-19462)***

NVE Inc (PA) .... D **323 512-8400**
700 N San Vicnte Blvd West Hollywood (90069) ***(P-23286)***

Nvision Laser Eye Centers Inc .... D 949 951-1457
24022 Calle De La Plata Laguna Hills (92653) ***(P-20006)***

NW Entertainment Inc (PA) .... C **818 295-5000**
2660 W Olive Ave Burbank (91505) ***(P-19157)***

NW Packaging LLC (PA) .... D **909 706-3627**
1201 E Lexington Ave Pomona (91766) ***(P-14958)***

Nwi, Valencia *Also called Neasi-Weber International LLC **(P-17668)***

Nwp Services Corporation (HQ) .... C **949 253-2500**
535 Anton Blvd Ste 1100 Costa Mesa (92626) ***(P-17939)***

Nxt Biomedical LLC .... F 201 658-6455
5270 California Ave # 300 Irvine (92617) ***(P-11231)***

Nxt Factory Inc (PA) .... F **805 340-2340**
1923 Eastman Ave Ste 200 Ventura (93003) ***(P-5311)***

NY Transport Inc .... D 909 355-9832
10191 Redwood Ave Fontana (92335) ***(P-12070)***

Nyd Livet Technologies Inc .... F 805 643-7166
213 N Olive St Ventura (93001) ***(P-7392)***

Nydj Apparel LLC .... C 323 581-9040
5401 S Soto St Vernon (90058) ***(P-14407)***

Nylok LLC .... E 714 635-3993
313 N Euclid Way Anaheim (92801) ***(P-7071)***

Nylok Western Fastener, Anaheim *Also called Nylok LLC **(P-7071)***

Nylon Molding, Brea *Also called Nmc Group Inc **(P-14008)***

Nyx Industries Inc .... F 909 937-3923
9452 Resenda Ave Fontana (92335) ***(P-7615)***

Nzg Specialties Inc (PA) .... D **310 216-7575**
2580 Santa Fe Ave Redondo Beach (90278) ***(P-14483)***

O & K Inc (PA) .... C **323 846-5700**
2121 E 37th St Vernon (90058) ***(P-14408)***

O & S Precision Inc .... E 818 718-8876
20630 Nordhoff St Chatsworth (91311) ***(P-8723)***

O C M, Los Angeles *Also called Old Country Millwork Inc **(P-7886)***

O D I, Riverside *Also called Edge Plastics Inc **(P-5635)***

O E C, Santa Maria *Also called Oilfield Envmtl Compliance Inc **(P-22957)***

O E C Shipg Los Angeles Inc .... E 562 926-7186
13100 Alondra Blvd # 100 Cerritos (90703) ***(P-12495)***

O H I, Irvine *Also called European Ht Invstors I I A Cal **(P-16438)***

O Industries Corporation .... F 310 719-2289
1930 W 139th St Gardena (90249) ***(P-3223)***

O P F, Oxnard *Also called Oxnard Prcsion Fabrication Inc **(P-6885)***

O P I Products Inc (HQ) .... B **818 759-8688**
13034 Saticoy St North Hollywood (91605) ***(P-14042)***

O W I Inc .... F 310 515-1900
17141 Kingsview Ave Carson (90746) ***(P-9185)***

O'Neal U S A, Camarillo *Also called Jim ONeal Distributing Inc **(P-10494)***

O'Neill Sportswear, Irvine *Also called La Jolla Sport USA Inc **(P-14340)***

O.C. Metro Magazine, Newport Beach *Also called Churm Publishing Inc **(P-3961)***

O.H. Kruse Grain and Milling, Goshen *Also called Western Milling LLC **(P-16302)***

Oak Creek LP .... D 909 860-5440
21725 Gateway Center Dr Diamond Bar (91765) ***(P-16587)***

Oak Design Corporation .... F 909 628-9597
13272 6th St Chino (91710) ***(P-3594)***

Oak Grove Center, Murrieta *Also called Oak Grove Inst Foundation Inc **(P-20007)***

Oak Grove Inst Foundation Inc (PA) .... B **951 677-5599**
24275 Jefferson Ave Murrieta (92562) ***(P-20007)***

Oak Manufacturing Company Inc .... E 323 581-8087
2850 E Vernon Ave Vernon (90058) ***(P-8323)***

Oak Paper Products Co Inc (PA) .... C **323 268-0507**
3686 E Olympic Blvd Los Angeles (90023) ***(P-14217)***

Oak Park Manor, Claremont *Also called New Vista Health Services Inc **(P-22136)***

Oak Parks Inns Inc .... D 805 481-4448
775 N Oak Park Blvd Grover Beach (93433) ***(P-16588)***

Oak Ridge Landworks .... D 805 630-8377
3106 Tanglewood Ct Thousand Oaks (91360) ***(P-328)***

Oak Springs Nursery Inc .... D 818 367-5832
13761 Eldridge Ave Sylmar (91342) ***(P-13013)***

Oak Street Physical Therapy, Lomita *Also called Kaiser Foundation Hospitals **(P-21316)***

Oak Tree Furniture Inc .... F 562 944-0754
13681 Newport Ave Ste 8 Tustin (92780) ***(P-3483)***

Oak View Group LLC (PA) .... C **310 209-3164**
11755 Wilshire Blvd Fl 9 Los Angeles (90025) ***(P-19658)***

Oak-It Inc .... D 310 719-3999
845 Sandhill Ave Carson (90746) ***(P-3660)***

Oak-It Inc .... F 951 735-5973
143 Business Center Dr Corona (92878) ***(P-3276)***

Oakcroft Associates Inc (PA) .... E **323 261-5122**
750 Monterey Pass Rd Monterey Park (91754) ***(P-13865)***

Oakdale Memorial Park (PA) .... D **626 335-0281**
1401 S Grand Ave Glendora (91740) ***(P-16087)***

Oakhurst Industries Inc (PA) .... C **323 724-3000**
2050 S Tubeway Ave Commerce (90040) ***(P-2026)***

Oakley Inc (HQ) .... A **949 951-0991**
1 Icon Foothill Ranch (92610) ***(P-11256)***

Oakley Sales Corp .... C 949 672-6925
1 Icon Foothill Ranch (92610) ***(P-11257)***

Oakmont Country Club .... C 818 542-4260
3100 Country Club Dr Glendale (91208) ***(P-19595)***

Oakmont of Orange LLC .... E 714 880-8624
630 The City Dr S Orange (92868) ***(P-22139)***

Oakridge Landscape Inc (PA) .... C **661 295-7228**
28064 Avenue Stanford K Valencia (91355) ***(P-148)***

Oaks Diagnostics Inc (PA) .... D **310 855-0035**
6310 San Vicente Blvd Los Angeles (90048) ***(P-20008)***

Oaktree Capital Group LLC (HQ) .... D **213 830-6300**
333 S Grand Ave Fl 28 Los Angeles (90071) ***(P-16135)***

Oaktree Capital Management LP (PA) .... C **213 830-6300**
333 S Grand Ave Fl 28 Los Angeles (90071) ***(P-15334)***

Oaktree Cpitl Group Hldings LP (PA) .... A **213 830-6300**
333 S Grand Ave Fl 28 Los Angeles (90071) ***(P-16136)***

Oaktree Holdings Inc .... A 213 830-6300
333 Suth Grnd Ave Fl 28 Flr 28 Los Angeles (90071) ***(P-16137)***

Oaktree Intl Holdings LLC (HQ) .... D **213 830-6300**
333 S Grand Ave Fl 28 Los Angeles (90071) ***(P-15335)***

Oaktree Real Estate Opprtnties (HQ) .... D **213 830-6300**
333 S Grand Ave Fl 28 Los Angeles (90071) ***(P-16138)***

Oaktree Real Estate Opprtnties .... B 213 830-6300
333 S Grand Ave Fl 28 Los Angeles (90071) ***(P-16139)***

Oaktree Strategic Income LLC .... A 213 830-6300
333 S Grand Ave Fl 28 Los Angeles (90071) ***(P-16140)***

Oakwood Corporate Housing Inc (PA) .... B **877 902-0832**
1 World Trade Ctr # 2400 Long Beach (90831) ***(P-16812)***

Oakwood Interiors, Ontario *Also called Lanpar Inc **(P-3475)***

Oakwood Temporary Housing, Long Beach *Also called Worldwide Corporate Housing LP **(P-16814)***

Oakwood Worldwide, Long Beach *Also called Worldwide Corporate Housing LP **(P-16815)***

Oakwood Worldwide, Long Beach *Also called R & B Realty Group LP **(P-15962)***

Oakwood Worldwide LLC (HQ) .... C **877 902-0832**
1 World Trade Ctr # 2400 Long Beach (90831) ***(P-23077)***

Oasis Alloy Wheels Inc .... F 714 533-3286
400 S Lemon St Anaheim (92805) ***(P-6400)***

Oasis Brands Inc .... D 540 658-2830
100 S Anaheim Blvd # 280 Anaheim (92805) ***(P-14218)***

Oasis Date Garden Inc .... E 760 399-5665
59111 Grapefruit Blvd Thermal (92274) ***(P-2497)***

Oasis Hcp 2 LLC (PA) .... C **323 987-5954**
4601 Wilshire Blvd # 220 Los Angeles (90010) ***(P-20426)***

Oasis Medical Inc (PA) .... D **909 305-5400**
510-528 S Vermont Ave Glendora (91741) ***(P-11258)***

Oasis Mental Health Treatment, Palm Springs *Also called Oasis Rehabilitation Center **(P-21467)***

Oasis Metal Works, Anaheim *Also called Oasis Alloy Wheels Inc **(P-6400)***

Oasis Rehabilitation Center (HQ) .... E **760 863-8638**
2283 N Viminal Rd Palm Springs (92262) ***(P-21467)***

Oasis West Realty LLC .... D 310 860-6666
9850 Wilshire Blvd Beverly Hills (90210) ***(P-16589)***

Oasis West Realty LLC (PA) .... B **310 274-8066**
1800 Century Park E # 500 Los Angeles (90067) ***(P-16159)***

Obagi Cosmeceuticals LLC (PA) .... C **800 636-7546**
3760 Kilroy Arprt Way Long Beach (90806) ***(P-4864)***

Obagi Medical, Long Beach *Also called Obagi Cosmeceuticals LLC **(P-4864)***

Obatake Inc .... F 310 782-2730
20309 Gramercy Pl Ste A Torrance (90501) ***(P-11327)***

ALPHABETIC

Oberman Tivoli & Pickert Inc....C....310 440-9600
500 S Sepulveda Blvd # 500 Los Angeles (90049) *(P-18056)*

Oblong Industries Inc (HQ)....C....**213 683-8863**
923 E 3rd St Ste 111 Los Angeles (90013) *(P-17682)*

OBryant Electric Inc....C....818 407-1986
9314 Eton Ave Chatsworth (91311) *(P-1288)*

Observatories of The Carnegie, Pasadena *Also called Carnegie Institution Wash (P-22902)*

Observer Group Newspaper....E....661 324-9466
1219 20th St Bakersfield (93301) *(P-4019)*

Oc 405 Partners Joint Venture....D....858 251-2200
3100 W Lake Center Dr # 200 Santa Ana (92704) *(P-930)*

Oc Fleet Service Inc....F....714 460-8069
8270 Monroe Ave Stanton (90680) *(P-10454)*

OC FOOD BANK, Garden Grove *Also called Community Action Prtnr Ornge C (P-21753)*

Oc Metals Inc....E....714 668-0783
2720 S Main St Ste B Santa Ana (92707) *(P-6882)*

Occam Networks Inc (HQ)....C....**805 692-2900**
6868 Cortona Dr Santa Barbara (93117) *(P-9238)*

Occupational Therapy Training, Torrance *Also called Special Service For Groups Inc (P-22212)*

Ocdm, Tustin *Also called Orange County Direct Mail Inc (P-17135)*

Ocean Avenue LLC....B....310 576-7777
101 Wilshire Blvd Santa Monica (90401) *(P-16590)*

Ocean Blue Envmtl Svcs Inc (PA)....D....**562 624-4120**
925 W Esther St Long Beach (90813) *(P-11985)*

Ocean Blue Express Inc (PA)....D....**310 719-2500**
255 W Victoria St Compton (90220) *(P-12496)*

Ocean Breeze International....D....805 684-1747
3910 Via Real Carpinteria (93013) *(P-88)*

Ocean Direct LLC (HQ)....C....**424 266-9300**
13771 Gramercy Pl Gardena (90249) *(P-2348)*

Ocean Dream, South Pasadena *Also called Malibu Design Group (P-14398)*

Ocean Duke Corporation....E....310 326-3198
21250 Hawthorne Blvd # 500 Torrance (90503) *(P-14574)*

Ocean Fresh Fish Seafood Mktg, Los Angeles *Also called Ocean Group Inc (P-14575)*

Ocean Group Inc (PA)....D....**213 622-3677**
1100 S Santa Fe Ave Los Angeles (90021) *(P-14575)*

Ocean Park Community Center....D....310 828-6717
1447 16th St Santa Monica (90404) *(P-23486)*

Ocean Pavers Inc....F....949 340-6363
12 Endless Vis Aliso Viejo (92656) *(P-7648)*

Ocean Protecta Incorporated....E....714 891-2628
1240 Pioneer St Ste B Brea (92821) *(P-10470)*

Ocean Queen 87 Inc....E....323 585-1200
4511 Everett Ave Vernon (90058) *(P-14576)*

Ocean Technology Systems, Santa Ana *Also called Undersea Systems Intl Inc (P-9925)*

Oceania Inc....E....562 926-8886
14209 Gannet St La Mirada (90638) *(P-5437)*

Oceania International LLC....E....949 407-8904
23661 Birtcher Dr Lake Forest (92630) *(P-6336)*

Oceanwide Repairs, Long Beach *Also called APR Engineering Inc (P-10451)*

Oceanx LLC (HQ)....D....**310 774-4088**
100 N Pcf Cast Hwy Ste 15 El Segundo (90245) *(P-18617)*

Ocelot Engineering Inc....C....800 841-2960
555 S H St San Bernardino (92410) *(P-13076)*

Ocfit Lb LLC (PA)....D....**949 701-7702**
151 Kalmus Dr Ste F3a Costa Mesa (92626) *(P-19463)*

Oci, Santa Fe Springs *Also called Office Chairs Inc (P-3595)*

Ocip, Anaheim *Also called Orange County Indus Plas Inc (P-14759)*

Ocm Pe Holdings LP....A....213 830-6213
333 S Grand Ave Fl 28 Los Angeles (90071) *(P-9758)*

Ocm Real Estate Opprtnties Fun....B....213 830-6300
333 S Grand Ave Fl 28 Los Angeles (90071) *(P-16141)*

Ocmban, Irvine *Also called Ocmbc Inc (P-15222)*

Ocmbc Inc....C....714 479-0999
19000 Macarthur Blvd # 200 Irvine (92612) *(P-15222)*

Oconca Shipping (lax) Inc....E....909 625-5555
10628 Central Ave Montclair (91763) *(P-12497)*

Oconca Shipping New York, Montclair *Also called Oconca Shipping (lax) Inc (P-12497)*

OConnell Landscape Maint Inc....B....800 339-1106
860 E Watson Center Rd Carson (90745) *(P-329)*

Ocpc Inc....D....949 475-1900
2485 Da Vinci Irvine (92614) *(P-4381)*

Ocs America Inc (HQ)....E....**310 417-0650**
11100 Hindry Ave Los Angeles (90045) *(P-18618)*

Ocs Bookstore, Los Angeles *Also called Ocs America Inc (P-18618)*

Octa, Orange *Also called Orange County Trnsp Auth (P-11834)*

Odcombe Press (nashville)....E....615 793-5414
859 Lawrence Dr Newbury Park (91320) *(P-4382)*

Oddworld Inhabitants Inc....F....805 503-3000
869 Monterey St San Luis Obispo (93401) *(P-17940)*

ODonnell Manufacturing Inc....E....562 944-9671
14811 Via Defrancesco Ave Riverside (92508) *(P-8724)*

Ods Technologies LP (HQ)....C....**310 242-9400**
6701 Center Dr W Ste 160 Los Angeles (90045) *(P-12736)*

Odu-Usa Inc (HQ)....D....**805 484-0540**
300 Camarillo Ranch Rd A Camarillo (93012) *(P-13759)*

Odwalla Inc....D....310 342-3920
700 Isis Ave Inglewood (90301) *(P-1871)*

Odyssey Healthcare Inc....D....714 245-7420
525 Cabrillo Park Dr # 150 Santa Ana (92701) *(P-20427)*

Odyssey Healthcare Bakersfield, Bakersfield *Also called Kindred Healthcare LLC (P-21180)*

Odyssey Innovative Designs, San Gabriel *Also called Hsiao & Montano Inc (P-5893)*

Oec Group, Cerritos *Also called O E C Shipg Los Angeles Inc (P-12495)*

Oel/Hhh Inc....D....818 246-6050
1833 Victory Blvd Glendale (91201) *(P-22736)*

Oem LLC....E....714 449-7500
311 S Highland Ave Fullerton (92832) *(P-8725)*

OEM Materials & Supplies Inc....E....714 564-9600
1500 Ritchey St Santa Ana (92705) *(P-3766)*

OEM Parts Network Inc....F....909 944-8030
10763 Bell Ct Rancho Cucamonga (91730) *(P-7588)*

Off Broadway, La Verne *Also called Fortress Inc (P-3584)*

Offenhauser Sales Corp....F....323 225-1307
5300 Alhambra Ave Los Angeles (90032) *(P-10111)*

Office Chairs Inc....D....562 302-0464
14815 Radburn Ave Santa Fe Springs (90670) *(P-3595)*

Office of Inspector General, Los Angeles *Also called Los Angles Cnty Mtro Trnsp Aut (P-11828)*

Office Pride, Visalia *Also called Cleaning For King Inc (P-17227)*

Office Star Products, Ontario *Also called Blumenthal Distributing Inc (P-13129)*

Office Xpress Inc....E....818 884-5737
7705 Alabama Ave Canoga Park (91304) *(P-14195)*

Officeworks Inc....D....951 784-2534
11801 Pierce St Fl 2 Riverside (92505) *(P-17441)*

Offiserve Inc....D....714 547-9500
14370 Myford Rd Ste 100 Irvine (92606) *(P-13365)*

Offline Inc (PA)....E....**213 742-9001**
2250 Maple Ave Los Angeles (90011) *(P-3022)*

Offshore Crane & Service Co (PA)....D....**805 648-3348**
1375 N Olive St Ste A Ventura (93001) *(P-17316)*

Ofs Brands Holdings Inc....A....714 903-2257
5559 Mcfadden Ave Huntington Beach (92649) *(P-3596)*

Oggi Corp, Anaheim *Also called Asdak International (P-6000)*

Oheck LLC....E....323 923-2700
5830 Bickett St Huntington Park (90255) *(P-3059)*

Ohi Resort Hotels LLC....D....714 867-5555
12021 Harbor Blvd Garden Grove (92840) *(P-16591)*

Ohio River Dialysis LLC (HQ)....E....**310 536-2400**
601 Hawaii St El Segundo (90245) *(P-21256)*

Ohl International, Carson *Also called Geodis Usa Inc (P-12461)*

Ohno America Inc....E....770 773-3820
18781 Winnwood Ln Santa Ana (92705) *(P-2694)*

Ohsung Display USA Inc (HQ)....E....**760 482-5788**
203 S Waterman Ave El Centro (92243) *(P-8979)*

Oil Country Manufacturing Inc....C....305 643-1200
300 W Stanley Ave Ventura (93001) *(P-7674)*

Oil Well Service Company (PA)....C....**562 612-0600**
10840 Norwalk Blvd Santa Fe Springs (90670) *(P-529)*

Oil Well Service Company....D....661 746-4809
10255 Enos Ln Shafter (93263) *(P-530)*

Oil Well Service Company....D....805 525-2103
1015 Mission Rock Rd Santa Paula (93060) *(P-531)*

Oilfield Electric & Motor, Ventura *Also called Oilfield Electric Company (P-1289)*

Oilfield Electric Company....D....805 648-3131
1801 N Ventura Ave Ventura (93001) *(P-1289)*

Oilfield Envmtl Compliance Inc (PA)....D....**805 922-4772**
307 Roemer Way Ste 300 Santa Maria (93454) *(P-22957)*

Oj Insulation LP (PA)....C....**800 707-9278**
600 S Vincent Ave Azusa (91702) *(P-1388)*

Ojai Ambulance Inc....C....805 653-9111
632 E Thompson Blvd Ventura (93001) *(P-11883)*

Ojai Valley Athletic Club....D....805 646-7213
409 Fox St Ojai (93023) *(P-19596)*

Ojai Valley Community Hospital, Ojai *Also called Community Memorial Health Sys (P-20731)*

Ojai Valley Inn & Spa, Ojai *Also called Ovis LLC (P-16603)*

Ojai Valley Inn Golf Course....D....805 646-2420
905 Country Club Rd Ojai (93023) *(P-16592)*

Ojai Valley Spa, Ojai *Also called Ojai Valley Inn Golf Course (P-16592)*

Ojai Vly Fmly Medicine Group....D....805 646-7246
117 Pirie Rd Ste D Ojai (93023) *(P-20009)*

Okonite Company Inc....D....805 922-6682
2900 Skyway Dr Santa Maria (93455) *(P-6354)*

Ola Nation LLC....E....310 256-0638
915 W Barbara Ave West Covina (91790) *(P-2894)*

Ola805 LLC (PA)....F....**805 258-7680**
1482 E Valley Rd Ste 701 Santa Barbara (93108) *(P-5051)*

Olam Tomato Processors Inc....E....559 447-1390
1175 S 19th Ave Lemoore (93245) *(P-1872)*

Olaplex Holdings Inc (PA)....F....**310 691-0776**
1187 Coast Village Rd 1-52 Santa Barbara (93108) *(P-5052)*

Olaplex Intermediate Inc (HQ)....E....**805 452-8110**
1187 Coast Village Rd 1-52 Santa Barbara (93108) *(P-14272)*

Olaplex Intermediate II Inc (HQ)....E....**805 452-8110**
1187 Coast Village Rd 1-52 Santa Barbara (93108) *(P-14273)*

Old An Inc....F....949 263-1400
17651 Armstrong Ave Irvine (92614) *(P-11721)*

Old Candle LLC (PA)....E....**818 436-2776**
7630 Balasiano Ave West Hills (91304) *(P-11722)*

Old Country Millwork Inc....E....323 234-2940
5855 Hooper Ave Los Angeles (90001) *(P-7886)*

Old English Mil & Woodworks, Santa Clarita *Also called Old English Mil Woodworks Inc (P-3277)*

Old English Mil Woodworks Inc (PA)....E....**661 294-9171**
27772 Avenue Scott Santa Clarita (91355) *(P-3277)*

Old Fashion Lavash, Los Angeles *Also called Lavash Corporation of America (P-2014)*

Old Guys Rule, Ventura *Also called Streamline Dsign Slkscreen Inc (P-2827)*

Old New York Bagel Deli Co Inc (PA)....E....**805 484-3354**
4972 Verdugo Way Camarillo (93012) *(P-2027)*

Old New York Deli & Bagel Co, Camarillo *Also called Old New York Bagel Deli Co Inc (P-2027)*

Old Prospectors Assn Amer LLC....E....951 699-4749
25819 Jefferson Ave # 110 Murrieta (92562) *(P-4088)*

Old Pueblo Ranch Inc....E....800 367-7522
316 N Ford Blvd Los Angeles (90022) *(P-2498)*

Mergent e-mail: customerrelations@mergent.com
1222
2022 Southern California Business Directory and Buyers Guide
(P-0000) Products & Services Section entry number
(PA)=Parent Co (HQ)=Headquarters (DH)=Div Headquarters

Old Republic Title Company C 818 240-1936
101 N Brand Blvd Ste 1400 Glendale (91203) *(P-15511)*
Old Spaghetti Factory-Duarte, Duarte *Also called Osf International Inc (P-16970)*
Old Spc Inc E 310 533-0748
202 W 140th St Los Angeles (90061) *(P-7289)*
Old Time Farming Inc (PA) C **805 349-3886**
1141 Tama Ln Santa Maria (93455) *(P-116)*
Oldcast Precast (HQ) E **951 788-9720**
2434 Rubidoux Blvd Riverside (92509) *(P-6044)*
Oldcastle Buildingenvelope Inc D 323 722-2007
5631 Ferguson Dr Commerce (90022) *(P-5966)*
Oldcastle Infrastructure Inc E 951 928-8713
19940 Hansen Ave Nuevo (92567) *(P-6883)*
Oldcastle Infrastructure Inc E 951 788-9720
2434 Rubidoux Blvd Riverside (92509) *(P-6045)*
Olde Thompson LLC C 805 983-0388
3250 Camino Del Sol Oxnard (93030) *(P-5236)*
Oldenkamp Trucking Inc (PA) D **661 833-3400**
10303 S Enos Ln Bakersfield (93311) *(P-11986)*
Olea Kiosks Inc D 562 924-2644
13845 Artesia Blvd Cerritos (90703) *(P-8287)*
Olen Commercial Realty Corp B 949 644-6536
7 Corporate Plaza Dr Newport Beach (92660) *(P-15683)*
Olen Companies, The, Newport Beach *Also called Olen Residential Realty Corp (P-664)*
Olen Residential Realty, Newport Beach *Also called Olen Commercial Realty Corp (P-15683)*
Olen Residential Realty Corp (HQ) D **949 644-6536**
7 Corporate Plaza Dr Newport Beach (92660) *(P-664)*
Oleumtech Corporation E 949 305-9009
19762 Pauling Foothill Ranch (92610) *(P-10709)*
Oliphant Tool Company F 714 903-6336
15652 Chemical Ln Huntington Beach (92649) *(P-7819)*
Olive Crest (PA) B **714 543-5437**
2130 E 4th St Ste 200 Santa Ana (92705) *(P-22140)*
Olive View-Ucla Medical Center (PA) A **818 364-1555**
14445 Olive View Dr Sylmar (91342) *(P-20010)*
Oliver Healthcare Packaging Co D 714 864-3500
1145 N Ocean Cir Anaheim (92806) *(P-13924)*
Olivet International Inc (PA) D **951 681-8888**
11015 Hopkins St Jurupa Valley (91752) *(P-14172)*
Olloclip, Huntington Beach *Also called Premier Systems Usa Inc (P-13428)*
Ols Hotels & Resorts LLC A 310 855-1115
733 W Knoll Dr West Hollywood (90069) *(P-16593)*
Ols Hotels & Resorts LLC A 626 962-6000
14635 Bldwin Pk Towne Ctr Baldwin Park (91706) *(P-16594)*
Olson Company LLC (PA) D **562 596-4770**
3010 Old Ranch Pkwy # 100 Seal Beach (90740) *(P-16065)*
Olson Company, The, Seal Beach *Also called Olson Urban Housing LLC (P-16066)*
Olson Homes, Seal Beach *Also called Olson Company LLC (P-16065)*
Olson Urban Housing LLC D 562 596-4770
3010 Old Ranch Pkwy # 100 Seal Beach (90740) *(P-16066)*
Oltmans Construction Co (PA) D **562 948-4242**
10005 Mission Mill Rd Whittier (90601) *(P-710)*
Oltmans Construction Co B 805 495-9553
270 Conejo Ridge Ave # 210 Thousand Oaks (91361) *(P-711)*
Oltmans Investment Company LLC D 562 948-4242
10005 Mission Mill Rd Whittier (90601) *(P-15684)*
Oltmans Property Management, Whittier *Also called Oltmans Investment Company LLC (P-15684)*
Oly-Remington Ventura LLC D 805 643-6000
2055 Harbor Blvd Ventura (93001) *(P-16595)*
Olympia Convalescent Hospital C 213 487-3000
1100 S Alvarado St Los Angeles (90006) *(P-20619)*
Olympia Health Care LLC A 323 938-3161
5900 W Olympic Blvd Los Angeles (90036) *(P-20874)*
Olympia Medical Center, Los Angeles *Also called Olympia Health Care LLC (P-20874)*
Olympic Security, Bellflower *Also called Advent Securities Investments (P-15261)*
Olympix Fitness LLC D 562 366-4600
4101 E Olympic Plz Long Beach (90803) *(P-19464)*
Olympus Property D 661 393-1700
3411 State Rd Bakersfield (93308) *(P-15761)*
Om Food Sejal Enterprises Inc D 626 712-3138
449 W Allen Ave Ste 111 San Dimas (91773) *(P-23287)*
Omar Leather Co F 323 227-5220
4557 Valley Blvd Los Angeles (90032) *(P-5914)*
Omega Case Company Inc F 818 238-9263
2231 N Hollywood Way Burbank (91505) *(P-3416)*
Omega Insurance Services E 714 973-0311
721 S Parker St Ste 300 Orange (92868) *(P-15604)*
Omega Leads Inc E 310 394-6786
1509 Colorado Ave Santa Monica (90404) *(P-9759)*
Omega Moulding West LLC C 323 261-3510
5500 Lindbergh Ln Bell (90201) *(P-13182)*
Omega Precision E 562 946-2491
13040 Telegraph Rd Santa Fe Springs (90670) *(P-8726)*
Omega Products Corp E 714 935-0900
282 S Anita Dr Fl 3 Orange (92868) *(P-6183)*
Omega/Cinema Props Inc D 323 466-8201
1515 E 15th St Los Angeles (90021) *(P-19243)*
Omelet LLC (PA) D **213 427-6400**
3540 Hayden Ave Culver City (90232) *(P-17040)*
OMelveny & Myers LLP (PA) A **213 430-6000**
400 S Hope St Fl 19 Los Angeles (90071) *(P-21648)*
Omics Group Inc B 650 268-9744
5716 Corsa Ave Ste 110 Westlake Village (91362) *(P-4089)*
Omni Connection Intl Inc B 951 898-6232
126 Via Trevizio Corona (92879) *(P-9760)*
Omni Family Health (PA) D **661 459-1900**
4900 California Ave 400b Bakersfield (93309) *(P-20011)*
Omni Foods Manufacturing, Paramount *Also called Pioneer Trading Inc (P-14718)*
Omni Hotels Corporation D 760 568-2727
41000 Bob Hope Dr Rancho Mirage (92270) *(P-16596)*
Omni Metal Finishing Inc (PA) D **714 979-9414**
11665 Coley River Cir Fountain Valley (92708) *(P-7290)*
Omni Optical Products Inc E 714 692-1400
22605 La Palma Ave # 502 Yorba Linda (92887) *(P-19052)*
Omni Optical Products Inc (PA) E **714 634-5700**
17282 Eastman Irvine (92614) *(P-10900)*
Omni Seals, Inc., Rancho Cucamonga *Also called Smith International Inc (P-546)*
Omnia Italian Design LLC C 909 393-4400
4900 Edison Ave Chino (91710) *(P-13146)*
Omnia Leather Motion Inc C 909 393-4400
4950 Edison Ave Chino (91710) *(P-3110)*
Omnical Inc F 818 837-7531
557 Jessie St San Fernando (91340) *(P-11130)*
Omniduct, Buena Park *Also called ECB Corp (P-1058)*
Omnikron Systems Inc D 818 591-7890
20920 Warner Center Ln A Woodland Hills (91367) *(P-18205)*
Omniprint Inc E 949 833-0080
1923 E Deere Ave Santa Ana (92705) *(P-8288)*
Omnisil E 805 644-2514
5401 Everglades St Ventura (93003) *(P-9550)*
Omniteam Inc C 562 923-9660
9300 Hall Rd Downey (90241) *(P-13855)*
Omnitrans Inc D 909 379-7100
4748 Arrow Hwy Montclair (91763) *(P-11831)*
Omnitron Systems Tech Inc D 949 250-6510
38 Tesla Irvine (92618) *(P-13760)*
Omp Inc (HQ) C **562 628-1007**
3760 Kilroy Arprt Way Long Beach (90806) *(P-14274)*
Omron Delta Tau, Chatsworth *Also called Delta Tau Data Systems Inc Cal (P-8119)*
Omstar Environmental Products, Wilmington *Also called D-1280-X Inc (P-5250)*
Omtek Inc E 805 687-9629
3722 Calle Cita Santa Barbara (93105) *(P-9551)*
Omya Inc D 760 248-5200
7299 Crystal Creek Rd Lucerne Valley (92356) *(P-4664)*
On Call Consulting, Thousand Oaks *Also called Miramed Global Services Inc (P-23474)*
On Central Realty Inc (PA) B **818 476-3000**
1625 W Glenoaks Blvd Glendale (91201) *(P-15935)*
On Target Solutions LLC (PA) D **949 543-3200**
17691 Mitchell N Ste A Irvine (92614) *(P-12788)*
On The Rise Inc D 760 964-7473
305 E Buena Vista St Barstow (92311) *(P-22205)*
On-Gard Metals Inc F 562 622-9057
8638 Cleta St Downey (90241) *(P-6295)*
On-Line Power Incorporated (PA) E **323 721-5017**
14000 S Broadway Los Angeles (90061) *(P-8880)*
Oncehub Inc F 650 206-5585
340 S Lemon Ave Ste 5585 Walnut (91789) *(P-17941)*
Oncocyte Corporation (PA) E **949 409-7600**
15 Cushing Irvine (92618) *(P-4925)*
Oncore Manufacturing LLC (HQ) A **818 734-6500**
9340 Owensmouth Ave Chatsworth (91311) *(P-22623)*
Oncore Manufacturing Svcs Inc C 510 360-2222
9340 Owensmouth Ave Chatsworth (91311) *(P-9435)*
Ondax Inc F 626 357-9600
850 E Duarte Rd Monrovia (91016) *(P-10850)*
One California Plaza, Los Angeles *Also called Hill Farrer & Burrill (P-21580)*
One Call Plumber Goleta D 805 284-0441
140 Nectarine Ave Apt 4 Goleta (93117) *(P-16968)*
One Call Plumber Santa Barbara D 805 364-6337
1016 Cliff Dr Apt 309 Santa Barbara (93109) *(P-1110)*
One Clothing, Vernon *Also called O & K Inc (P-14408)*
One Events Inc D 310 498-5471
8581 Santa Monica Blvd West Hollywood (90069) *(P-16969)*
One Identity LLC (HQ) E **949 754-8000**
4 Polaris Way Aliso Viejo (92656) *(P-17683)*
One Lambda Inc (HQ) B **747 494-1000**
22801 Roscoe Blvd West Hills (91304) *(P-22856)*
One LLP (PA) D **949 502-2870**
4000 Macarthur Blvd # 500 Newport Beach (92660) *(P-21649)*
One Seventeen Global, San Juan Capistrano *Also called 117 Global LLC (P-18423)*
One Silver Serve Inc E 818 995-6444
17835 Ventura Blvd # 108 Encino (91316) *(P-17266)*
One Source Supply Solutions, Buena Park *Also called Onesource Distributors LLC (P-13655)*
One Step Gps LLC E 818 659-2031
675 Glenoaks Blvd Unit C San Fernando (91340) *(P-10629)*
One Stop Label Corporation E 909 230-9380
1641 S Baker Ave Ontario (91761) *(P-4547)*
One Stop Parts Source LLC (HQ) D **949 955-2600**
2610 S Birch St Santa Ana (92707) *(P-13077)*
One Touch Office Technology, Torrance *Also called One Touch Solutions Inc (P-7921)*
One Touch Solutions Inc F 310 320-6868
370 Amapola Ave Ste 106 Torrance (90501) *(P-7921)*
One Town Center Associates LLC E 714 435-2100
3315 Fairview Rd Costa Mesa (92626) *(P-15685)*
One Up Manufacturing LLC E 310 749-8347
550 E Airline Way Gardena (90248) *(P-3775)*
One World Meat Company LLC F 800 782-1670
6363 Knott Ave Buena Park (90620) *(P-1741)*
One-Way Manufacturing Inc E 714 630-8833
1195 N Osprey Cir Anaheim (92807) *(P-7542)*
Onecharge Biz, Garden Grove *Also called Onecharge Inc (P-9812)*
Onecharge Inc E 833 895-8624
12472 Industry St Garden Grove (92841) *(P-9812)*
Onegeneration (PA) D **818 708-6625**
17400 Victory Blvd Van Nuys (91406) *(P-22044)*

A L P H A B E T I C

Employee Codes: A=Over 500 employees, B=251-500
C=101-250, D=51-100, E=20-50 F=10-19
2022 Southern California Business Directory and Buyers Guide
© Mergent Inc. 1-800-342-5647
1223

Onegenrtion Adult Dycare Chldc, Van Nuys *Also called Onegeneration* ***(P-22044)***
ONeil Capital Management Inc ... C ... 310 448-6400
12655 Beatrice St Los Angeles (90066) ***(P-4466)***
ONeil Digital Solutions LLC ... C ... 310 448-6407
12655 Beatrice St Los Angeles (90066) ***(P-18619)***
Onelegacy (PA) ... **D ... 213 625-0665**
221 S Figueroa St Ste 500 Los Angeles (90012) ***(P-21468)***
Onesolution Light and Control ... D ... 714 490-5540
225 S Loara St Anaheim (92802) ***(P-13654)***
Onesource Distributors LLC ... D ... 562 401-1264
6530 Altura Blvd Buena Park (90620) ***(P-13655)***
Onewest Bank NA ... D ... 562 433-0971
3500 E 7th St Long Beach (90804) ***(P-15051)***
Onex Automation, Duarte *Also called Onex Enterprises Corporation* ***(P-8132)***
Onex Enterprises Corporation ... F ... 626 358-6639
1824 Flower Ave Duarte (91010) ***(P-8132)***
Onex Rf Inc ... F ... 626 358-6639
1824 Flower Ave Duarte (91010) ***(P-7893)***
Online Capital, Newport Beach *Also called RMR Financial LLC* ***(P-15250)***
Online Land Planning LLC ... E ... 310 594-7782
856 Avenue B Redondo Beach (90277) ***(P-23487)***
Online Media Technologies Ltd ... F ... 209 279-5320
1633 Amador Ln Newbury Park (91320) ***(P-17942)***
Only You Rx Skin Care, Valencia *Also called Professional Skin Care Inc* ***(P-5063)***
Onni Properties LLC ... C ... 213 568-0278
888 S Olive St Los Angeles (90014) ***(P-23078)***
Onnik Shoe Company Inc ... F ... 818 506-5353
11443 Chandler Blvd North Hollywood (91601) ***(P-5882)***
Onquest Heaters Inc (HQ) ... **C ... 909 451-0499**
180 E Arrow Hwy San Dimas (91773) ***(P-22624)***
Onrad Inc ... D ... 800 848-5876
1770 Iowa Ave Ste 280 Riverside (92507) ***(P-20012)***
Onrad Medical Group, Riverside *Also called Onrad Inc* ***(P-20012)***
Onshore Technologies Inc ... E ... 310 533-4888
2771 Plaza Del Amo # 802 Torrance (90503) ***(P-9761)***
Onsight Ways Technology, Newport Beach *Also called Bluestone Medical Inc* ***(P-10951)***
Ontario Automotive LLC ... C ... 909 974-3800
1401 Auto Center Dr Ontario (91761) ***(P-13034)***
Ontario Convention Center, Ontario *Also called Smg Food and Beverage LLC* ***(P-18669)***
Ontario Convention Center Corp ... C ... 909 937-3000
2000 E Convention Ctr Way Ontario (91764) ***(P-18620)***
Ontario Foam Products, Ontario *Also called Androp Packaging Inc* ***(P-3783)***
Ontario Healthcare Center, Ontario *Also called Kf Ontario Healthcare LLC* ***(P-20599)***
Ontario Hospitality Properties ... D ... 909 946-9600
3400 Shelby St Ontario (91764) ***(P-16597)***
Ontario International Airport, Ontario *Also called Virgin Atlantic Airways Ltd* ***(P-12373)***
Ontario Mills Shopping Center, Ontario *Also called Mills Corporation* ***(P-15678)***
Ontario Refrigeration Svc Inc (PA) ... **D ... 909 984-2771**
635 S Mountain Ave Ontario (91762) ***(P-1111)***
Ontario Vineyard Medical Offs, Ontario *Also called Kaiser Foundation Hospitals* ***(P-19910)***
Ontario/Montclair YMCA, Ontario *Also called West End Yung MNS Christn Assn* ***(P-22375)***
Ontic Engineering and Mfg Inc (PA) ... **C ... 818 678-6555**
20400 Plummer St Chatsworth (91311) ***(P-14063)***
Ontrac, Santa Maria *Also called Express Messenger Systems Inc* ***(P-12130)***
Ontrac, Compton *Also called Express Messenger Systems Inc* ***(P-12132)***
Ontrak Inc (PA) ... **A ... 310 444-4300**
2120 Colorado Ave Ste 230 Santa Monica (90404) ***(P-21025)***
Ontraport Inc ... C ... 805 568-1424
2040 Alameda Padre Serra Santa Barbara (93103) ***(P-23079)***
Onyx Global Hr LLC (PA) ... **D ... 866 715-4806**
110 Pine Ave Ste 920 Long Beach (90802) ***(P-23288)***
Onyx Industries Inc (PA) ... **D ... 310 539-8830**
1227 254th St Harbor City (90710) ***(P-7039)***
Onyx Industries Inc ... D ... 310 851-6161
521 W Rosecrans Ave Gardena (90248) ***(P-7040)***
Onyx Pharmaceuticals Inc ... A ... 650 266-0000
1 Amgen Center Dr Newbury Park (91320) ***(P-4865)***
Onyx Shutters, City of Industry *Also called Tje Company* ***(P-6721)***
Opal Service Inc (PA) ... **E ... 714 935-0900**
282 S Anita Dr Orange (92868) ***(P-6184)***
Oparc (PA) ... **E ... 909 982-4090**
9029 Vernon Ave Montclair (91763) ***(P-21963)***
OPEN America Inc ... C ... 562 428-9210
4300 Long Beach Blvd # 45 Long Beach (90807) ***(P-17267)***
Openpopcom Inc (PA) ... **D ... 714 249-7044**
12539 Carson St Hawaiian Gardens (90716) ***(P-23488)***
Openworks, Long Beach *Also called OPEN America Inc* ***(P-17267)***
Openx Technologies Inc (HQ) ... **B ... 855 673-6948**
888 E Walnut St Fl 2 Pasadena (91101) ***(P-17041)***
Operam Inc ... D ... 855 673-7261
1041 N Formosa Ave 500 West Hollywood (90046) ***(P-23289)***
Operating Engineers Funds Inc (PA) ... **C ... 866 400-5200**
100 Corson St Ste 222 Pasadena (91103) ***(P-16192)***
Operation Safe House Inc (PA) ... **D ... 951 358-4418**
9685 Hayes St Riverside (92503) ***(P-21859)***
Operation Technology Inc (PA) ... **D ... 949 462-0100**
17 Goodyear Ste 100 Irvine (92618) ***(P-17684)***
Opex Communications Inc ... E ... 562 968-5420
1677 E 28th St Signal Hill (90755) ***(P-12660)***
Ophir Rf Inc ... E ... 310 306-5556
5300 Beethoven St Fl 3 Los Angeles (90066) ***(P-9304)***
Ophthalmic Facial Plastic (PA) ... **D ... 310 276-0044**
9735 Wilshire Blvd # 300 Beverly Hills (90212) ***(P-20013)***
Ophthalmology Assoc of Vly, Encino *Also called Opthamology Associates of Vly* ***(P-20014)***
Ophthonix Inc ... E ... 760 842-5600
900 Glenneyre St Laguna Beach (92651) ***(P-11259)***
Opiant Pharmaceuticals Inc ... F ... 310 598-5410
233 Wilshire Blvd Ste 280 Santa Monica (90401) ***(P-4866)***
Opolo Vineyards Inc ... D ... 805 238-9593
2801 Townsgate Rd Ste 123 Westlake Village (91361) ***(P-2211)***
Oppenheimer Group, Chino Hills *Also called David Oppenheimer and Co I LLC* ***(P-14462)***
Oppenheimer Group, Carson *Also called David Oppenheimer and Co I LLC* ***(P-14464)***
Oprah Winfrey Network, West Hollywood *Also called Own LLC* ***(P-12775)***
Opsec Specialized Protection ... D ... 661 942-3999
44262 Division St Ste A Lancaster (93535) ***(P-18304)***
Optec Displays Inc ... D ... 626 369-7188
1700 S De Soto Pl Ste A Ontario (91761) ***(P-11579)***
Optek Group Inc ... F ... 949 629-2558
23 Corporate Plaza Dr # 150 Newport Beach (92660) ***(P-11232)***
Optex Incorporated ... D ... 800 966-7839
18730 S Wilmington Ave # 100 Compton (90220) ***(P-9346)***
Opthamology Associates of Vly ... D ... 818 990-3623
16311 Ventura Blvd # 750 Encino (91436) ***(P-20014)***
Opti-Forms Inc ... D ... 951 296-1300
42310 Winchester Rd Temecula (92590) ***(P-7291)***
Optic Arts Holdings Inc ... E ... 213 250-6069
716 Monterey Pass Rd Monterey Park (91754) ***(P-9097)***
Optical Corporation (HQ) ... **E ... 818 725-9750**
9731 Topanga Canyon Pl Chatsworth (91311) ***(P-10851)***
Optical Zonu Corporation ... F ... 818 780-9701
7510 Hazeltine Ave Van Nuys (91405) ***(P-9239)***
Optim Microwave Inc ... F ... 805 482-7093
4020 Adolfo Rd Camarillo (93012) ***(P-9305)***
Optima Network Services Inc (HQ) ... **D ... 305 599-1800**
15345 Frfeld Rnch Rd Ste Chino Hills (91709) ***(P-23537)***
Optima Tax Relief LLC ... C ... 714 361-4636
3100 S Harbor Blvd # 250 Santa Ana (92704) ***(P-16939)***
Optima Technology Corporation ... B ... 949 253-5768
17062 Murphy Ave Irvine (92614) ***(P-8289)***
Optimal Home Health Care Inc ... D ... 661 410-4000
1227 Chester Ave Bakersfield (93301) ***(P-21194)***
Optimal Hospice Care, Bakersfield *Also called Bristol Hospice Foundation Cal* ***(P-22447)***
Optimal Hospice Care, Bakersfield *Also called Bristol Hospice Foundation Cal* ***(P-20526)***
Optimis Services Inc ... F ... 310 230-2780
225 Mantua Rd Pacific Palisades (90272) ***(P-17943)***
Optimiscorp ... E ... 310 230-2780
200 Mantua Rd Pacific Palisades (90272) ***(P-17944)***
Optimum Inc (PA) ... **C ... 909 990-0767**
17890 Valley Blvd Bloomington (92316) ***(P-22625)***
Optimum Bioenergy Intl Corp ... F ... 714 903-8872
2463 Pomona Rd Corona (92878) ***(P-4757)***
Optimum Con Fundations USA Inc ... D ... 877 212-7994
6258 Rustic Ln Jurupa Valley (92509) ***(P-1544)***
Option One Home Med Eqp Inc ... D ... 909 478-5413
1220 Research Dr Ste A Redlands (92374) ***(P-17303)***
Options Family of Services ... E ... 805 462-8544
5755 Valentina Ave Atascadero (93422) ***(P-21323)***
Optivus Proton Therapy Inc ... D ... 909 799-8300
1475 Victoria Ct San Bernardino (92408) ***(P-10901)***
Opto 22 ... C ... 951 695-3000
43044 Business Park Dr Temecula (92590) ***(P-9762)***
Opto Diode Corporation ... E ... 805 465-8700
1260 Calle Suerte Camarillo (93012) ***(P-9552)***
Opto-Knowledge Systems Inc ... E ... 310 756-0520
19805 Hamilton Ave Torrance (90502) ***(P-22857)***
Optodyne Incorporation ... E ... 310 635-7481
21345 Hawthorne Blvd # 2 Torrance (90503) ***(P-9306)***
Optoknowledge, Torrance *Also called Opto-Knowledge Systems Inc* ***(P-22857)***
Optosigma Corporation ... E ... 949 851-5881
3210 S Croddy Way Santa Ana (92704) ***(P-10852)***
Optronics, Goleta *Also called Karl Storz Imaging Inc* ***(P-10895)***
Optumrx Inc (HQ) ... **B ... 714 825-3600**
2300 Main St Irvine (92614) ***(P-15446)***
Oracle Corp ... A ... 650 506-7000
17901 Von Karman Ave # 800 Irvine (92614) ***(P-23538)***
Oracle Corporation ... B ... 626 315-7513
1 Bolero Mission Viejo (92692) ***(P-17945)***
Oral Essentials Inc ... F ... 888 773-5273
436 N Roxbury Dr Beverly Hills (90210) ***(P-5053)***
Orange Bakery Inc ... D ... 949 454-1247
75 Parker Irvine (92618) ***(P-15686)***
Orange Bakery Inc (HQ) ... **C ... 949 863-1377**
17751 Cowan Irvine (92614) ***(P-2028)***
Orange Bang Inc ... E ... 818 833-1000
13115 Telfair Ave Sylmar (91342) ***(P-2274)***
Orange Belt Adventures, Visalia *Also called Orange Belt Stages* ***(P-11913)***
Orange Belt Stages (PA) ... **D ... 559 733-4408**
2134 E Mineral King Ave Visalia (93292) ***(P-11913)***
Orange Circle Studio Corp ... D ... 949 727-0800
8687 Research Dr Ste 150 Irvine (92618) ***(P-4548)***
Orange City Mills Ltd Partnr ... D ... 317 636-1600
20 City Blvd W Ste C5 Orange (92868) ***(P-15687)***
Orange Cnty Adult Achvment Ctr ... C ... 714 744-5301
225 W Carl Karcher Way Anaheim (92801) ***(P-21860)***
Orange Cnty Cncil Boy Scuts AM (PA) ... **D ... 714 546-4990**
2 Irvine Park Rd Orange (92869) ***(P-22353)***
Orange Cnty Emplyees Rtrment S ... D ... 714 558-6200
2223 S Wellington Ave Santa Ana (92701) ***(P-16142)***
Orange Cnty George M Raymond N, Orange *Also called Raymond Group* ***(P-23096)***
Orange Cnty Hlth Auth A Pub AG ... B ... 714 246-8500
505 City Pkwy W Orange (92868) ***(P-22273)***
Orange Cnty Name Plate Co Inc ... D ... 714 522-7693
13201 Arctic Cir Santa Fe Springs (90670) ***(P-11580)***
Orange Cnty Rescue Mission Inc (PA) ... **D ... 714 247-4300**
1 Hope Dr Tustin (92782) ***(P-21861)***
Orange Coast Building Svcs Inc ... C ... 714 453-6300
2191 S Dupont Dr Anaheim (92806) ***(P-712)***

Mergent e-mail: customerrelations@mergent.com
1224
2022 Southern California Business
Directory and Buyers Guide
(P-0000) Products & Services Section entry number
(PA)=Parent Co (HQ)=Headquarters (DH)=Div Headquarters

Orange Coast Ctr For Surgl Cr, Fountain Valley *Also called Memorlcare Srgcal Ctr At Ornge* ***(P-20861)***
Orange Coast Kommunications ....B....949 862-1133
5900 Wilshire Blvd # 1000 Los Angeles (90036) ***(P-4090)***
Orange Coast Magazine, Los Angeles *Also called Orange Coast Kommunications* ***(P-4090)***
Orange Coast Memorial Med Ctr (HQ) ....**A....714 378-7000**
9920 Talbert Ave Fountain Valley (92708) ***(P-20875)***
Orange Coast Reprographics Inc ....E....949 548-5571
659 W 19th St Costa Mesa (92627) ***(P-4383)***
Orange Coast Service Center, Westminster *Also called Southern California Edison Co* ***(P-12850)***
Orange Coast Title Company (PA) ....**D....714 558-2836**
1551 N Tustin Ave Ste 300 Santa Ana (92705) ***(P-18621)***
Orange Coast Wns Med Group Inc ....D....949 829-5500
24411 Health Center Dr # 200 Laguna Hills (92653) ***(P-23290)***
Orange County At Home, Irvine *Also called Silverado Senior Living Inc* ***(P-20468)***
Orange County Business Journal, Irvine *Also called Cbj LP* ***(P-4056)***
Orange County Direct Mail Inc ....E....714 444-4412
2672 Dow Ave Tustin (92780) ***(P-17135)***
Orange County Erectors Inc ....E....714 502-8455
517 E La Palma Ave Anaheim (92801) ***(P-7006)***
Orange County Head Start Inc (PA) ....**D....714 241-8920**
2501 Pullman St Santa Ana (92705) ***(P-22045)***
Orange County Health Care Agcy ....D....714 568-5683
405 W 5th St Ste 700 Santa Ana (92701) ***(P-22274)***
Orange County Homecare LLC (PA) ....**D....949 390-7308**
630 Roosevelt Irvine (92620) ***(P-21195)***
Orange County Hospice, Irvine *Also called Silverado Senior Living Inc* ***(P-20469)***
Orange County Indus Plas Inc (PA) ....**E....714 632-9450**
4811 E La Palma Ave Anaheim (92807) ***(P-14759)***
Orange County Internet Xchange ....D....714 450-7109
2001 E Dyer Rd Ste 102 Santa Ana (92705) ***(P-12661)***
Orange County Label Co Inc ....F....714 437-1010
301 W Dyer Rd Ste D Santa Ana (92707) ***(P-4549)***
Orange County Pike Alumni Assn ....B....702 832-6211
6653 Iron Horse Ln Eastvale (92880) ***(P-17685)***
Orange County Plating Coinc ....F....714 532-4610
940 N Parker St 960 Orange (92867) ***(P-7292)***
Orange County Plst Co Inc ....C....714 957-1971
3191 Arprt Loop Dr Ste B1 Costa Mesa (92626) ***(P-1389)***
Orange County Printing, Irvine *Also called Kelmscott Communications LLC* ***(P-4348)***
Orange County Produce LLC ....D....949 451-0880
11405 Jeffrey Rd Irvine (92602) ***(P-32)***
Orange County Register, El Toro *Also called Freedom Communications Inc* ***(P-3977)***
Orange County Royale Convlscnt (PA) ....**B....714 546-6450**
1030 W Warner Ave Santa Ana (92707) ***(P-20620)***
Orange County Sanitation (PA) ....**B....714 962-2411**
10844 Ellis Ave Fountain Valley (92708) ***(P-12962)***
Orange County Screw Pdts Inc ....E....714 630-7433
2993 E La Palma Ave Anaheim (92806) ***(P-8727)***
Orange County Service Center, San Clemente *Also called San Diego Gas & Electric Co* ***(P-12873)***
Orange County Services Inc (PA) ....**D....310 515-1001**
3801 Lenawee Ave Culver City (90232) ***(P-1112)***
Orange County Thermal Inds Inc ....D....714 279-9416
1350 N Hundley St Anaheim (92806) ***(P-1390)***
ORANGE COUNTY TRANSIT DISTRICT, Orange *Also called Orange County Trnsp Auth* ***(P-11833)***
Orange County Trnsp Auth ....D....714 560-6282
11790 Cardinal Cir Garden Grove (92843) ***(P-11832)***
Orange County Trnsp Auth (PA) ....**B....714 636-7433**
550 S Main St Orange (92868) ***(P-11833)***
Orange County Trnsp Auth ....A....714 999-1726
600 S Main St Ste 910 Orange (92868) ***(P-11834)***
Orange County Water District ....D....714 378-3200
14980 River Rd Eastvale (92880) ***(P-12910)***
Orange County Water District ....D....714 378-3200
18700 Ward St Fountain Valley (92708) ***(P-12911)***
Orange County Water District ....D....714 378-3320
4060 E La Palma Ave Anaheim (92807) ***(P-12912)***
Orange County-Irvine Med Ctr, Irvine *Also called Kaiser Foundation Hospitals* ***(P-16186)***
Orange Countys Credit Union (PA) ....**C....714 755-5900**
1721 E Saint Andrew Pl Santa Ana (92705) ***(P-15076)***
Orange Courier Inc ....B....714 384-3600
15300 Desman Rd La Mirada (90638) ***(P-18622)***
Orange Health Solutions Inc ....D....661 310-9333
28480 Ave Stnford Ste 300 Valencia (91355) ***(P-17686)***
Orange Hlthcare Wllness Cntre ....C....714 633-3568
920 W La Veta Ave Orange (92868) ***(P-20428)***
Orange Logic LLC (PA) ....**D....949 396-2233**
19100 Von Karman Ave # 900 Irvine (92612) ***(P-8169)***
Orange Mtal Spnning Stmping In ....E....714 754-0770
2601 Orange Ave Santa Ana (92707) ***(P-7170)***
Orange Show Fairgrounds The, San Bernardino *Also called National Orange Show* ***(P-18609)***
Orange Vise Company LLC ....F....714 482-3952
940 S Via Rodeo Placentia (92870) ***(P-7860)***
Orange Woodworks Inc ....E....714 997-2600
1215 N Parker St Orange (92867) ***(P-3278)***
Orangegrid LLC ....E....657 220-1519
145 S State College Blvd Brea (92821) ***(P-17946)***
Orangepeople LLC ....D....949 535-1308
300 Spectrum Center Dr # 40 Irvine (92618) ***(P-23539)***
Orangetree Convalescent Hosp ....C....951 785-6060
4000 Harrison St Riverside (92503) ***(P-20876)***
Orangewood Foundation ....D....714 619-0200
1575 E 17th St Santa Ana (92705) ***(P-21862)***

Orbit Intl Inc ....E....909 468-5160
4965 Firenza Dr Cypress (90630) ***(P-9763)***
Orbit Systems, Laguna Niguel *Also called Aot Electronics Inc* ***(P-8235)***
Orbita Corp (PA) ....**F....213 746-4783**
1136 Crocker St Los Angeles (90021) ***(P-3050)***
Orbital Sciences LLC ....B....703 406-5000
2401 E El Segundo Blvd El Segundo (90245) ***(P-10630)***
Orbital Sciences LLC ....B....818 887-8345
1151 W Reeves Ave Ridgecrest (93555) ***(P-10631)***
Orbital Sciences LLC ....B....805 734-5400
Talo Rd Bldg 1555 Lompoc (93437) ***(P-10632)***
Orbits Lightwave Inc ....E....626 513-7400
41 S Chester Ave Pasadena (91106) ***(P-5938)***
Orbo Corporation ....E....562 806-6171
1000 S Euclid St La Habra (90631) ***(P-3629)***
Orbo Manufacturing Inc ....E....562 222-4535
12740 Lakeland Rd Santa Fe Springs (90670) ***(P-3179)***
Orchard - Post Acute Care Ctr ....C....562 693-7701
12385 Washington Blvd Whittier (90606) ***(P-20429)***
Orchard Holdings Group Inc ....D....949 502-8300
1 Venture Ste 300 Irvine (92618) ***(P-15936)***
Orchard Horror Film LLC ....E....212 203-6147
15715 Woodvale Rd Encino (91436) ***(P-19372)***
Orchard Medical Offices, Downey *Also called Kaiser Foundation Hospitals* ***(P-19896)***
Orchid MPS ....D....714 549-9203
3233 W Harvard St Santa Ana (92704) ***(P-11040)***
Orchid Orthopedis, Arcadia *Also called MPS Anzon LLC* ***(P-11127)***
Orco Block, Stanton *Also called Muth Development Co Inc* ***(P-6010)***
Orco Block & Hardscape (PA) ....**D....714 527-2239**
11100 Beach Blvd Stanton (90680) ***(P-6011)***
Orco Block & Hardscape ....E....951 928-3619
26380 Palomar Rd Romoland (92585) ***(P-6012)***
Ordermark Inc ....D....833 673-3762
12045 Waterfront Dr # 400 Playa Vista (90094) ***(P-18103)***
Oregon PCF Bldg Pdts Maple Inc ....C....909 627-4043
2401 E Philadelphia St Ontario (91761) ***(P-13280)***
Orepac Millwork Products, Ontario *Also called Oregon PCF Bldg Pdts Maple Inc* ***(P-13280)***
Oreq Corporation ....D....951 296-5076
42306 Remington Ave Temecula (92590) ***(P-23080)***
Organic Inc ....D....310 543-4600
390 Amapola Ave Ste 8 Torrance (90501) ***(P-18206)***
Organic By Nature Inc (PA) ....**E....562 901-0177**
2610 Homestead Pl Compton (90220) ***(P-4758)***
Organic Milling Inc ....D....800 638-8686
505 W Allen Ave San Dimas (91773) ***(P-1949)***
Organic Milling Corporation (PA) ....**C....909 599-0961**
505 W Allen Ave San Dimas (91773) ***(P-2499)***
Organic Milling Corporation ....E....909 305-0185
305 S Acacia St Ste A San Dimas (91773) ***(P-2500)***
Organztion Amrcn Kdaly Edctors ....E....310 441-3555
10801 National Blvd # 590 Los Angeles (90064) ***(P-22458)***
Orgatech Omegalux, Orange *Also called Western Lighting Inds Inc* ***(P-13678)***
Oriental Motor USA Corporation (HQ) ....**D....310 715-3300**
570 Alaska Ave Torrance (90503) ***(P-13656)***
Origen Food Inc (PA) ....**E....800 420-4927**
230 W Avenue 26 Ste 239 Los Angeles (90031) ***(P-2501)***
Original Mowbrays Tree Svc Inc (PA) ....**C....909 383-7009**
686 E Mill St San Bernardino (92408) ***(P-359)***
Original Parts Group Inc (PA) ....**D....562 594-1000**
1770 Saturn Way Seal Beach (90740) ***(P-7112)***
Original Seatbeltbag , The, Santa Ana *Also called Harveys Industries Inc* ***(P-14379)***
Original Sid Blackman Plbg Inc ....D....760 352-3632
1160 S 2nd St El Centro (92243) ***(P-1113)***
Original Whistle Stop Inc ....E....626 796-7791
2490 E Colorado Blvd Pasadena (91107) ***(P-11388)***
Orion Ornamental Iron Inc ....E....818 752-0688
6918 Tujunga Ave North Hollywood (91605) ***(P-6531)***
Orion Pictures Corporation ....A....310 449-3000
245 N Beverly Dr Beverly Hills (90210) ***(P-19158)***
Orion Plastics Corporation ....D....310 223-0370
700 W Carob St Compton (90220) ***(P-4705)***
Orion Tech, City of Industry *Also called Compucase Corporation* ***(P-8195)***
Orlandini Entps Pcf Die Cast ....C....323 725-1332
6155 S Eastern Ave Commerce (90040) ***(P-6418)***
Orlando Spring Corp ....E....562 594-8411
5341 Argosy Ave Huntington Beach (92649) ***(P-7488)***
Orlando Wilshire Investments ....C....323 658-6600
8384 W 3rd St Los Angeles (90048) ***(P-16598)***
Orlando, The, Los Angeles *Also called Orlando Wilshire Investments* ***(P-16598)***
Orly International Inc (PA) ....**D....818 994-1001**
7710 Haskell Ave Van Nuys (91406) ***(P-5054)***
Ormco Corporation ....B....714 516-7400
1889 W Mission Blvd Pomona (91766) ***(P-11183)***
Ormco Corporation ....E....909 962-5705
200 S Kraemer Blvd Brea (92821) ***(P-11184)***
Ormco Corporation (HQ) ....**D....714 516-7400**
1717 W Collins Ave Orange (92867) ***(P-11185)***
Ormond Beach LP ....D....805 496-4948
1259 E Thousand Oaks Blvd Thousand Oaks (91362) ***(P-15688)***
Orora North America ....E....818 896-3449
12708 Branford St Pacoima (91331) ***(P-14219)***
Orora North America ....C....714 562-6002
6200 Caballero Blvd Buena Park (90620) ***(P-14220)***
Orora Packaging Solutions (HQ) ....**D....714 562-6000**
6600 Valley View St Buena Park (90620) ***(P-14221)***
Orora Packaging Solutions ....C....323 832-2000
1640 S Greenwood Ave Montebello (90640) ***(P-14222)***
Orora Visual LLC ....D....714 879-2400
1600 E Valencia Dr Fullerton (92831) ***(P-4550)***

ALPHABETIC

Employee Codes: A=Over 500 employees, B=251-500
C=101-250, D=51-100, E=20-50 F=10-19
2022 Southern California Business Directory and Buyers Guide
© Mergent Inc. 1-800-342-5647
1225

Ortega Manufacturing Inc.....F.....951 766-9363
3960 Industrial Ave Hemet (92545) *(P-11723)*

Ortel A Division Emcore Co (HQ).....C.....**626 293-3400**
2015 Chestnut St Alhambra (91803) *(P-9553)*

Orthalliance Inc.....A.....310 792-1300
21535 Hawthorne Blvd # 20 Torrance (90503) *(P-22206)*

Orthalliances, Torrance *Also called Orthalliance Inc (P-22206)*

Ortho Engineering Inc (PA).....E.....**310 559-5996**
17402 Chtswrth St Ste 200 Granada Hills (91344) *(P-11131)*

Orthodental International Inc.....D.....760 357-8070
280 Campillo St Ste J Calexico (92231) *(P-11186)*

Orthopaedic Hospital (PA).....C.....**213 742-1000**
403 W Adams Blvd Los Angeles (90007) *(P-20877)*

ORTHOPAEDIC INSTITUTE FOR CHIL, Los Angeles *Also called Orthopaedic Hospital (P-20877)*

Orthopedic Consultants (PA).....E.....**818 788-7343**
16311 Ventura Blvd # 800 Encino (91436) *(P-20015)*

Orthopedics Department, Los Angeles *Also called Southern Cal Prmnnte Med Group (P-20081)*

Orthowest, Laguna Hills *Also called South Cnty Orthpd Spclsts A ME (P-20068)*

Ortiz Enterprises Incorporated (PA).....D.....**949 753-1414**
6 Cushing Ste 200 Irvine (92618) *(P-904)*

Ortronics Inc.....C.....714 776-5420
1443 S Sunkist St Anaheim (92806) *(P-6884)*

Osata Enterprises Inc.....D.....888 445-6237
225 S Aviation Blvd El Segundo (90245) *(P-14443)*

Osf International Inc.....D.....949 675-8654
2110 Newport Blvd Newport Beach (92663) *(P-16599)*

Osf International Inc.....D.....626 358-2115
1431 Buena Vista St Duarte (91010) *(P-16970)*

Oshyn Inc.....D.....213 483-1770
100 W Broadway Ste 330 Long Beach (90802) *(P-17687)*

OSI Digital Inc (PA).....E.....**818 992-2700**
5950 Canoga Ave Ste 300 Woodland Hills (91367) *(P-18207)*

OSI Electronics Inc (HQ).....C.....**310 978-0516**
12533 Chadron Ave Hawthorne (90250) *(P-9436)*

OSI Industries LLC.....D.....951 684-4500
1155 Mt Vernon Ave Riverside (92507) *(P-11724)*

OSI Laserscan Inc.....E.....310 978-0516
12525 Chadron Ave Hawthorne (90250) *(P-9896)*

OSI Optoelectronics Inc.....E.....805 987-0146
1240 Avenida Acaso Camarillo (93012) *(P-9554)*

OSI Staffing Inc.....D.....562 261-5753
10913 La Reina Ave Ste B Downey (90241) *(P-17442)*

OSI Subsidiary Inc.....C.....310 978-0516
12525 Chadron Ave Hawthorne (90250) *(P-9897)*

OSI Systems Inc (PA).....B.....**310 978-0516**
12525 Chadron Ave Hawthorne (90250) *(P-9555)*

Osmosis Technology Inc.....E.....714 670-9303
6900 Hermosa Cir Buena Park (90620) *(P-8402)*

Osmotik, Buena Park *Also called Osmosis Technology Inc (P-8402)*

Ospreydata Inc.....F.....619 971-4662
32242 Paseo Adelanto C San Juan Capistrano (92675) *(P-10804)*

Osr Enterprises Inc.....E.....805 925-1831
1910 E Stowell Rd Santa Maria (93454) *(P-17947)*

Osram Sylvania Inc.....C.....909 923-3003
1651 S Archibald Ave Ontario (91761) *(P-12227)*

Ossur Americas Inc (HQ).....B.....**800 233-6263**
27051 Towne Centre Dr # 100 Foothill Ranch (92610) *(P-11132)*

Ost Crane Service, Ventura *Also called Ost Trucks and Cranes Inc (P-18623)*

Ost Trucks and Cranes Inc.....D.....805 643-9963
2951 N Ventura Ave Ventura (93001) *(P-18623)*

Otafuku Foods Inc.....E.....562 404-4700
13117 Molette St Santa Fe Springs (90670) *(P-2502)*

OTasty Foods Inc.....D.....626 330-1229
160 S Hacienda Blvd City of Industry (91745) *(P-14484)*

Otb Acquisition LLC.....D.....520 458-0540
770 S Brea Blvd Ste 227 Brea (92821) *(P-16600)*

Otimo Inc.....E.....323 233-8894
2937 S Alameda St Vernon (90058) *(P-2759)*

Otis Elevator Company.....E.....323 342-4500
2701 Media Center Dr # 2 Los Angeles (90065) *(P-13925)*

Otis Elevator Company.....C.....818 241-2828
512 Paula Ave Ste A Glendale (91201) *(P-13926)*

Otis Elevator Company.....E.....805 683-3979
5733 Hollister Ave Ste B Goleta (93117) *(P-7680)*

Otis Textile, Los Angeles *Also called Textiles & Son LLC (P-2739)*

Ots, Irvine *Also called On Target Solutions LLC (P-12788)*

Ott Textile Inc (PA).....E.....**626 566-5858**
10507 Valley Blvd Ste 858 El Monte (91731) *(P-2733)*

Ottano Inc.....E.....805 547-2088
11555 Los Osos Valley Rd San Luis Obispo (93405) *(P-2151)*

Otto Cap, Ontario *Also called Otto International Inc (P-14344)*

Otto Instrument Service Inc (PA).....E.....**909 930-5800**
1441 Valencia Pl Ontario (91761) *(P-10389)*

Otto International Inc (PA).....E.....**909 937-1998**
3550 Jurupa St Ste A Ontario (91761) *(P-14344)*

Otts Asia Moorer Devon.....C.....323 603-6959
10015 Baring Cross St Los Angeles (90044) *(P-16282)*

OUR HOUSE, Victorville *Also called Family Assistance Program (P-21781)*

Our Watch.....D.....714 622-5852
12832 Valley View St # 211 Garden Grove (92845) *(P-21196)*

Out of Shell LLC.....C.....626 401-1923
9658 Remer St South El Monte (91733) *(P-2503)*

Outdoor Dimensions LLC.....C.....714 578-9555
5325 E Hunter Ave Anaheim (92807) *(P-3448)*

Outdoor Galore Inc (PA).....F.....**661 831-8662**
6801 White Ln Ste A1 Bakersfield (93309) *(P-7505)*

Outdoor Products, View Park *Also called Outdoor Recreation Group (P-3129)*

Outdoor Recreation Group (PA).....E.....**323 226-0830**
3450 Mount Vernon Dr View Park (90008) *(P-3129)*

Outex, La Canada Flintridge *Also called Lucare Corporation (P-11282)*

Outfront Media LLC.....E.....323 222-7171
1731 Workman St Los Angeles (90031) *(P-17076)*

Outlook Amusements Inc.....C.....818 433-3800
3746 Foothill Blvd La Crescenta (91214) *(P-18208)*

Outlook Resources Inc.....D.....714 522-2452
14930 Alondra Blvd La Mirada (90638) *(P-3162)*

Output Inc.....F.....310 795-6099
1418 N Spring St Ste 102 Los Angeles (90012) *(P-17948)*

Outrigger Hotels Hawaii.....D.....310 301-2000
4200 Admiralty Way Venice (90292) *(P-16601)*

Outrigger Hotels Hawaii.....D.....323 491-9015
8462 W Sunset Blvd West Hollywood (90069) *(P-16602)*

Outside Lines Inc.....E.....714 637-4747
2150 S Twne Cntre Pl Ste Anaheim (92806) *(P-273)*

Outsource Utility Contr Corp.....C.....714 238-9263
8015 E Crystal Dr Anaheim (92807) *(P-12814)*

Ovation Fertility (PA).....D.....**818 858-1074**
15821 Ventura Blvd # 625 Encino (91436) *(P-20016)*

Ovation Home Loans, Irvine *Also called Carnegie Mortgage LLC (P-15237)*

Ovation LLC.....D.....310 430-7575
12910 Culver Blvd Ste J Los Angeles (90066) *(P-12737)*

Ovation R&G LLC (PA).....D.....**310 430-7575**
2850 Ocean Park Blvd # 225 Santa Monica (90405) *(P-9307)*

Over & Over Ready Mix Inc.....D.....818 983-1588
8216 Tujunga Ave Sun Valley (91352) *(P-6046)*

Overair Inc.....E.....949 503-7503
3001 S Susan St Santa Ana (92704) *(P-10200)*

Overhill Farms Inc (HQ).....C.....**323 582-9977**
2727 E Vernon Ave Vernon (90058) *(P-2504)*

Overland Pacific & Cutler LLC (PA).....D.....**800 400-7356**
5000 Arprt Plz Dr Ste 250 Long Beach (90815) *(P-18624)*

Overseenet (PA).....C.....**213 408-0080**
550 S Hope St Ste 200 Los Angeles (90071) *(P-17042)*

Ovis LLC.....A.....805 646-5511
905 Country Club Rd Ojai (93023) *(P-16603)*

Owb Packers LLC.....E.....760 351-2700
57 Shank Rd Brawley (92227) *(P-1717)*

Owen Design Group, Pasadena *Also called Owen Group Limited Partnership (P-23081)*

Owen Group Limited Partnership (HQ).....D.....**800 600-6936**
600 N Rosemead Blvd # 205 Pasadena (91107) *(P-23081)*

Owen Trailers Inc.....E.....951 361-4557
9020 Jurupa Rd Riverside (92509) *(P-10167)*

Owens & Minor Distribution Inc.....A.....805 524-0243
452 Sespe Ave Fillmore (93015) *(P-14173)*

Owl Education and Training Inc.....B.....949 797-2000
2465 Campus Dr Irvine (92612) *(P-21964)*

Own LLC.....C.....323 602-5500
1041 N Formosa Ave West Hollywood (90046) *(P-12775)*

Owning Corporation.....B.....949 269-3300
1 City Blvd W Ste 1000 Orange (92868) *(P-15937)*

Oxford Instrs Asylum RES Inc (HQ).....D.....**805 696-6466**
7416 Hollister Ave Santa Barbara (93117) *(P-10805)*

Oxford Palace Hotel.....D.....213 382-7756
745 S Oxford Ave Los Angeles (90005) *(P-16604)*

Oxigen Beverages (usa) Inc.....F.....424 284-2177
12130 Millennium Los Angeles (90094) *(P-2275)*

Oxigenesis Inc.....F.....805 549-0275
2917 Union Rd Ste B Paso Robles (93446) *(P-2276)*

Oxnard 2 Warehouse, Oxnard *Also called Sunrise Growers Inc (P-2530)*

Oxnard 2103 E Gnzles Rd Med Of, Oxnard *Also called Kaiser Foundation Hospitals (P-19913)*

Oxnard 2200 E Gnzles Rd Med Of, Oxnard *Also called Kaiser Foundation Hospitals (P-19911)*

Oxnard City Hall, Oxnard *Also called City of Oxnard (P-23191)*

Oxnard Family Circle Adhc, Oxnard *Also called Family Circle Inc (P-21783)*

Oxnard Lemon Company.....E.....805 483-1173
2001 Sunkist Cir Oxnard (93033) *(P-1906)*

Oxnard Pallet Company, Oxnard *Also called E Vasquez Distributors Inc (P-3388)*

Oxnard Prcsion Fabrication Inc.....E.....805 985-0447
2200 Teal Club Rd Oxnard (93030) *(P-6885)*

Oxnard Veterans Center, Oxnard *Also called Veterans Health Administration (P-20145)*

Oxpros, Canoga Park *Also called Office Xpress Inc (P-14195)*

P & D Consultants Inc (HQ).....E.....**714 835-4447**
999 W Town And Country Rd Orange (92868) *(P-22626)*

P & L Development LLC.....E.....323 567-2482
11865 Alameda St Lynwood (90262) *(P-4867)*

P & R Paper Supply Co Inc (HQ).....C.....**909 389-1807**
1898 E Colton Ave Redlands (92374) *(P-14223)*

P A C E, Los Angeles *Also called Pacific Asian Cnsrtium In Empl (P-21965)*

P A P, Anaheim *Also called Precision Anodizing & Pltg Inc (P-7297)*

P A T H, Los Angeles *Also called People Assisting Homeless (P-21866)*

P A X Industries, Costa Mesa *Also called Tk Pax Inc (P-5324)*

P B I, Long Beach *Also called Pbi-Birkenwald Market Eqp Inc (P-13465)*

P C A Electronics Inc.....E.....818 892-0761
16799 Schoenborn St North Hills (91343) *(P-13761)*

P C M, Foothill Ranch *Also called Professional Cmnty MGT Cal Inc (P-15956)*

P C P Inc.....F.....626 813-6166
13462 Brooks Dr Baldwin Park (91706) *(P-14959)*

P C S C, Torrance *Also called Proprietary Controls Systems (P-10904)*

P C Services, Indio *Also called Alliance Protection Service (P-732)*

P E N Inc.....F.....818 954-0775
215 Allen Ave Glendale (91201) *(P-4020)*

P F Plastics Inc.....F.....909 392-4488
2044 Wright Ave La Verne (91750) *(P-3570)*

P H S Management Group (PA)..........E.......**714 547-7551**
721 N Eckhoff St Orange (92868) ***(P-23291)***
P J Milligan & Associates, Santa Barbara *Also called P J Milligan Company LLC* ***(P-3484)***
P J Milligan Company LLC (PA)..........F.......**805 963-4038**
436 E Gutierrez St Santa Barbara (93101) ***(P-3484)***
P K Engineering & Mfg Co Inc..........F.......805 628-9556
200 E Shell Rd 2b Ventura (93001) ***(P-11041)***
P K Metal, Los Angeles *Also called P Kay Metal Inc* ***(P-6337)***
P Kay Metal Inc (PA)..........E.......**323 585-5058**
2448 E 25th St Los Angeles (90058) ***(P-6337)***
P L C Lighting, Chatsworth *Also called PLC Imports Inc* ***(P-13660)***
P L M, Los Angeles *Also called Prudential Lighting Corp* ***(P-9100)***
P M Rehrig Inc (HQ)..........C.......**323 262-5145**
4010 E 26th St Vernon (90058) ***(P-5734)***
P Murphy & Associates Inc..........C.......818 841-2002
359 E Magnolia Blvd Ste G Burbank (91502) ***(P-17688)***
P P I, Corona *Also called Preproduction Plastics Inc* ***(P-5775)***
P P I, Buena Park *Also called Premiere Packaging Inds Inc* ***(P-14968)***
P P Mfg Co Inc..........E.......562 921-3640
13130 Arctic Cir Santa Fe Springs (90670) ***(P-7171)***
P R N Convalescent Hospital..........D.......818 352-3158
7912 Topley Ln Sunland (91040) ***(P-20430)***
P R P, Costa Mesa *Also called Profit Recovery Partners LLC* ***(P-23496)***
P R P Multisource Inc..........E.......951 681-6100
3836 Wacker Dr Jurupa Valley (91752) ***(P-8075)***
P S E Boilers, Santa Fe Springs *Also called Pacific Steam Equipment Inc* ***(P-6745)***
P S I, Beaumont *Also called Precision Stampings Inc* ***(P-9045)***
P T I, Torrance *Also called Plasma Technology Incorporated* ***(P-7400)***
P T I, Bloomington *Also called Products/Techniques Inc* ***(P-5109)***
P T I, Santa Ana *Also called Parpro Technologies Inc* ***(P-9437)***
P T Industries Inc..........F.......562 961-3431
3220 Industry Dr Signal Hill (90755) ***(P-6886)***
P T P, Carson *Also called Pacific Toll Processing Inc* ***(P-6207)***
P V T Supply, Paramount *Also called Wagner Plate Works West Inc* ***(P-6765)***
P W C, San Dimas *Also called Pacific W Space Cmmnctions Inc* ***(P-964)***
P W Pipe, Perris *Also called Pw Eagle Inc* ***(P-5471)***
P W S, San Luis Obispo *Also called Protective Wther Strctures Inc* ***(P-715)***
P&Y T-Shrts Silk Screening Inc..........E.......323 585-4604
2126 E 52nd St Vernon (90058) ***(P-7910)***
P-Cove Enterprises Inc..........D.......818 341-1101
8745 Remmet Ave Canoga Park (91304) ***(P-18057)***
P-W Western Inc..........D.......562 463-9055
9415 Kruse Rd Pico Rivera (90660) ***(P-6744)***
P-W Wiring Systems LLC..........F.......562 463-9055
9415 Kruse Rd Pico Rivera (90660) ***(P-9663)***
P.E.P., Pomona *Also called Performnce Engineered Pdts Inc* ***(P-5743)***
P.S. Services, Anaheim *Also called 3s Sign Services Inc* ***(P-11517)***
P5 Graphics and Displays Inc..........E.......714 808-1645
625 Fee Ana St Placentia (92870) ***(P-17182)***
P8ge Consulting Inc..........E.......310 666-2301
8406 Beverly Blvd Los Angeles (90048) ***(P-23489)***
Paamco, Newport Beach *Also called Pacific Altrntive Asset MGT LL* ***(P-15336)***
Paat & Kimmel Development Inc..........D.......909 315-8074
600 N Mountain Ave Upland (91786) ***(P-798)***
Pabco Building Products LLC..........D.......323 581-6113
4460 Pacific Blvd Vernon (90058) ***(P-6130)***
Pabco Clay Products LLC..........D.......323 568-1860
4301 Firestone Blvd South Gate (90280) ***(P-13309)***
Pabco Paper, Vernon *Also called Pabco Building Products LLC* ***(P-6130)***
Pabst Brewing Company LLC (PA)..........C.......**310 470-0962**
10635 Santa Monica Blvd Los Angeles (90025) ***(P-2152)***
Pac Fill Inc..........E.......818 409-0117
5471 W San Fernando Rd Los Angeles (90039) ***(P-1838)***
Pac Foundries Inc..........C.......805 488-6451
705 Industrial Way Port Hueneme (93041) ***(P-6419)***
Pac Foundries Inc..........C.......805 986-1308
705 Industrial Way Port Hueneme (93041) ***(P-6410)***
Pac Foundry Inc..........F.......323 773-2363
8333 Wilcox Ave Cudahy (90201) ***(P-6272)***
Pac-Dent Inc..........E.......909 839-0888
670 Endeavor Cir Brea (92821) ***(P-11187)***
Pac-Rancho Inc (HQ)..........C.......**909 987-4721**
11000 Jersey Blvd Rancho Cucamonga (91730) ***(P-6273)***
Pacc, Canyon Country *Also called Pure Autism Counseling Ctr Inc* ***(P-21331)***
Pace Development Cabinetry Inc..........E.......714 842-5336
7642 Windfield Dr Huntington Beach (92647) ***(P-799)***
Pace International LLC..........F.......559 651-4877
1104 N Nevada St Visalia (93291) ***(P-4974)***
Pace Lithographers Inc..........E.......626 913-2108
18030 Cortney Ct City of Industry (91748) ***(P-23540)***
Pace Marketing Communications, City of Industry *Also called Pace Lithographers Inc* ***(P-23540)***
Pace Punches Inc..........D.......949 428-2750
297 Goddard Irvine (92618) ***(P-7820)***
Pace Sportswear Inc..........F.......714 891-8716
12781 Monarch St Garden Grove (92841) ***(P-2978)***
Pace Transducer Co, Canoga Park *Also called C J Instruments Inc* ***(P-10874)***
Pacer Print..........F.......888 305-3144
9655 De Soto Ave Chatsworth (91311) ***(P-4384)***
Pacer Technology (HQ)..........C.......**909 987-0550**
3281 E Guasti Rd Ste 260 Ontario (91761) ***(P-5188)***
Pacesetter Inc..........C.......818 493-2715
13150 Telfair Ave Sylmar (91342) ***(P-11233)***
Pacesetter Inc (HQ)..........A.......**818 362-6822**
15900 Valley View Ct Sylmar (91342) ***(P-11234)***
Pacesetter Inc..........C.......323 773-0591
4946 Florence Ave Bell (90201) ***(P-11235)***
Pacesetter Fabrics LLC (HQ)..........F.......**213 741-9999**
11450 Sheldon St Sun Valley (91352) ***(P-2734)***
Pachulski Stang Zehl Jones LLP (PA)..........D.......**310 277-6910**
10100 Santa Monica Blvd # 1300 Los Angeles (90067) ***(P-21650)***
Pacifcare Hlth Plan Admnstrtor (HQ)..........B.......**714 825-5200**
3120 W Lake Center Dr Santa Ana (92704) ***(P-15447)***
Pacific Accent Incorporated..........F.......909 563-1600
623 S Doubleday Ave Ontario (91761) ***(P-9010)***
Pacific Advnced Cvil Engrg Inc (PA)..........D.......**714 481-7300**
17520 Newhope St Ste 200 Fountain Valley (92708) ***(P-22627)***
Pacific Aerospace Machine Inc..........E.......714 534-1444
3002 S Rosewood Ave Santa Ana (92707) ***(P-8728)***
Pacific Aggregates Inc..........D.......951 245-2460
28251 Lake St Lake Elsinore (92530) ***(P-6104)***
Pacific Air Cargo LLC..........D.......310 645-2178
6041 W Imperial Hwy Los Angeles (90045) ***(P-12498)***
Pacific Altrntive Asset MGT LL (HQ)..........C.......**949 261-4900**
660 Nwport Ctr Dr Ste 930 Newport Beach (92660) ***(P-15336)***
Pacific American Fish Co Inc (PA)..........C.......**323 319-1551**
5525 S Santa Fe Ave Vernon (90058) ***(P-14577)***
Pacific Aquascape Inc..........D.......714 843-5734
17520 Newhope St Ste 120 Fountain Valley (92708) ***(P-1679)***
Pacific Archtectural Mllwk Inc (PA)..........D.......**562 905-3200**
1031 S Leslie St La Habra (90631) ***(P-3279)***
Pacific Asian Cnsrtium In Empl (PA)..........C.......**213 353-3982**
1055 Wilshire Blvd # 147 Los Angeles (90017) ***(P-21965)***
Pacific Asian Enterprises Inc (PA)..........E.......**949 496-4848**
25001 Dana Dr Dana Point (92629) ***(P-18625)***
Pacific Asset Holding LLC..........C.......949 219-3011
700 Newport Center Dr Newport Beach (92660) ***(P-15366)***
Pacific Athletic Wear Inc..........D.......714 751-8006
7340 Lampson Ave Garden Grove (92841) ***(P-2979)***
Pacific Ave Cpitl Partners LLC..........A.......424 254-9774
2321 Rosecrans Ave # 3255 El Segundo (90245) ***(P-16160)***
Pacific Aviation Corporation (PA)..........C.......**310 646-4015**
201 Continental Blvd # 220 El Segundo (90245) ***(P-12364)***
Pacific Award Metals Inc (HQ)..........D.......**626 814-4410**
1450 Virginia Ave Baldwin Park (91706) ***(P-6887)***
Pacific Award Metals Inc..........D.......909 390-9880
10302 Birtcher Dr Jurupa Valley (91752) ***(P-13326)***
Pacific Award Metals Inc..........E.......360 694-9530
10302 Birtcher Dr Jurupa Valley (91752) ***(P-6888)***
Pacific Barcode Inc..........E.......951 587-8717
27531 Enterprise Cir W 201c Temecula (92590) ***(P-7922)***
Pacific Bay Lending Group..........D.......714 367-5125
7390 Lincoln Way Garden Grove (92841) ***(P-15247)***
Pacific Bay Properties (PA)..........E.......**949 440-7200**
4041 Macarthur Blvd # 500 Newport Beach (92660) ***(P-627)***
Pacific Bell Telephone Company..........A.......310 515-2898
3847 Cardiff Ave Culver City (90232) ***(P-12610)***
Pacific Beverage Co..........D.......805 922-7901
900 Fairway Dr Santa Maria (93455) ***(P-14832)***
Pacific Beverage Co..........D.......805 278-5600
401 Del Norte Blvd Oxnard (93030) ***(P-14833)***
Pacific Beverage Co..........D.......805 438-5766
22255 El Camino Real Santa Margarita (93453) ***(P-14834)***
Pacific Beverage Company, Oxnard *Also called Pacific Beverage Co* ***(P-14833)***
Pacific Broach & Engrg Assoc..........F.......714 632-5678
1513 N Kraemer Blvd Anaheim (92806) ***(P-8729)***
Pacific Building Care Inc (PA)..........B.......**949 261-1234**
3001 Red Hill Ave 6-210 Costa Mesa (92626) ***(P-17268)***
Pacific Building Maint Inc..........D.......805 969-5221
130 Garden St Ste B Santa Barbara (93101) ***(P-17269)***
Pacific Building Maint Inc (PA)..........D.......**805 642-0214**
1601 Ives Ave Ste E Oxnard (93033) ***(P-17270)***
Pacific Cambria Inc..........D.......805 927-6114
2905 Burton Dr Cambria (93428) ***(P-16605)***
Pacific Cast Fther Cushion LLC (HQ)..........C.......**562 801-9995**
7600 Industry Ave Pico Rivera (90660) ***(P-3111)***
Pacific Cast Products, Ontario *Also called Alumistar Inc* ***(P-6385)***
Pacific Casual LLC..........E.......805 445-8310
1060 Avenida Acaso Camarillo (93012) ***(P-3531)***
Pacific Catalina Hotel Inc..........B.......310 510-9255
888 Country Club Dr Avalon (90704) ***(P-16606)***
Pacific Cchways Chrtr Svcs Inc..........D.......714 892-5000
11771 Markon Dr Garden Grove (92841) ***(P-11914)***
Pacific Chemical Dist Corp (HQ)..........D.......**714 521-7161**
6250 Caballero Blvd Buena Park (90620) ***(P-12271)***
Pacific Child and Family Assoc, Glendale *Also called Verdugo Hills Psychtherapy Ctr* ***(P-20138)***
Pacific City Bank..........D.......714 263-1800
13140 Yale Ave Irvine (92620) ***(P-15049)***
Pacific City Hotel LLC..........B.......714 698-6100
21080 Pacific Coast Hwy Huntington Beach (92648) ***(P-16607)***
Pacific Clay Products Inc..........C.......661 857-1401
14741 Lake St Lake Elsinore (92530) ***(P-13310)***
Pacific Club (PA)..........D.......**949 955-1123**
4110 Macarthur Blvd Newport Beach (92660) ***(P-19597)***
Pacific Coachworks Inc..........C.......951 686-7294
3411 N Perris Blvd Bldg 1 Perris (92571) ***(P-10545)***
Pacific Coast Bach Label Inc..........E.......213 612-0314
3015 S Grand Ave Los Angeles (90007) ***(P-2677)***
Pacific Coast Bolt Corporation..........E.......562 944-9549
12748 Florence Ave Santa Fe Springs (90670) ***(P-14010)***
Pacific Coast Bus Times Inc..........F.......805 560-6950
14 E Carrillo St Ste A Santa Barbara (93101) ***(P-4021)***
Pacific Coast Cheer Inc (PA)..........D.......**951 894-7438**
25815 Jefferson Ave Murrieta (92562) ***(P-19659)***

ALPHABETIC

Employee Codes: A=Over 500 employees, B=251-500
C=101-250, D=51-100, E=20-50 F=10-19
2022 Southern California Business
Directory and Buyers Guide
© Mergent Inc. 1-800-342-5647
1227

Pacific Coast Elevator Corp.......C.......323 345-2550
3041 Roswell St Los Angeles (90065) ***(P-19053)***

Pacific Coast Fabrication Inc.......F.......714 536-8385
1390 N Hundley St Anaheim (92806) ***(P-11725)***

Pacific Coast Home Furn Inc (PA).......**F.......323 838-7808**
2424 Saybrook Ave Commerce (90040) ***(P-3112)***

Pacific Coast Ironworks Inc.......F.......323 585-1320
8831 Miner St Los Angeles (90002) ***(P-6646)***

Pacific Coast Lacquer, Los Angeles *Also called Berg Lacquer Co* ***(P-14905)***

Pacific Coast Lighting, Ventura *Also called Lamps Plus Inc* ***(P-9092)***

Pacific Coast Lighting Inc (HQ).......**C.......800 709-9004**
20238 Plummer St Chatsworth (91311) ***(P-9142)***

Pacific Coast Lighting Group, Chatsworth *Also called Pacific Coast Lighting Inc* ***(P-9142)***

Pacific Coast Mfg Inc.......D.......909 627-7040
5270 Edison Ave Chino (91710) ***(P-8993)***

Pacific Coast Pallets Inc.......F.......626 937-6565
15151 Salt Lake Ave La Puente (91746) ***(P-3401)***

Pacific Coast Produce Inc.......E.......805 240-3385
950 Mountain View Ave # 1 Oxnard (93030) ***(P-14645)***

Pacific Coast Sightseeing Tour.......C.......714 507-1157
2001 S Manchester Ave Anaheim (92802) ***(P-12407)***

Pacific Coast Sportswear, Fountain Valley *Also called Watt Enterprise Inc* ***(P-2832)***

Pacific Coast Tree Experts.......C.......805 506-1211
21525 Strathern St Canoga Park (91304) ***(P-360)***

Pacific Communications, Irvine *Also called Allergan Usa Inc* ***(P-4780)***

Pacific Communities Bldr Inc (PA).......**D.......949 660-8988**
1000 Dove St Ste 300 Newport Beach (92660) ***(P-628)***

Pacific Compensation Corp (HQ).......**D.......602 631-2300**
3011 Townsgate Rd Ste 120 Westlake Village (91361) ***(P-15605)***

Pacific Compensation Insur Co.......C.......818 575-8500
3011 Townsgate Rd Ste 120 Westlake Village (91361) ***(P-15606)***

Pacific Computer Products Inc.......E.......714 549-7535
2210 S Huron Dr Santa Ana (92704) ***(P-11480)***

Pacific Concept Laundry, Los Angeles *Also called E & C Fashion Inc* ***(P-18508)***

Pacific Consolidated Inds LLC.......D.......951 479-0860
12201 Magnolia Ave Riverside (92503) ***(P-8133)***

Pacific Containerprint Inc.......E.......909 465-0365
5951 Riverside Dr Apt 4 Chino (91710) ***(P-4551)***

Pacific Contntl Textiles Inc (HQ).......**C.......310 604-1100**
2880 E Ana St Compton (90221) ***(P-2678)***

Pacific Contours Corporation.......D.......714 693-1260
5340 E Hunter Ave Anaheim (92807) ***(P-10390)***

Pacific Couriers, El Monte *Also called Integrated Parcel Network* ***(P-12138)***

Pacific Couriers Inc.......E.......714 278-6100
4373 Santa Anita Ave A El Monte (91731) ***(P-12144)***

Pacific Culinary Group Inc.......E.......626 284-1328
566 Monterey Pass Rd Monterey Park (91754) ***(P-2505)***

Pacific Dental Services LLC (PA).......**B.......714 845-8500**
17000 Red Hill Ave Irvine (92614) ***(P-20192)***

Pacific Design Directions Inc.......E.......714 685-7766
8171 E Kaiser Blvd Anaheim (92808) ***(P-629)***

Pacific Diagnostic Labs LLC (PA).......**C.......805 879-8100**
454 S Patterson Ave Santa Barbara (93111) ***(P-21081)***

Pacific Die Casting Corp.......C.......323 725-1308
6155 S Eastern Ave Commerce (90040) ***(P-6368)***

Pacific Die Services Inc.......E.......562 907-4463
7626 Baldwin Pl Whittier (90602) ***(P-7821)***

Pacific Drayage Services LLC.......C.......901 746-3794
550 W Artesia Blvd Compton (90220) ***(P-11987)***

Pacific Duct Inc.......E.......909 635-1335
5499 Brooks St Montclair (91763) ***(P-6889)***

Pacific Eagle International (PA).......**B.......562 972-3813**
12674 Hoover St Garden Grove (92841) ***(P-18305)***

Pacific Earth Resources (PA).......**D.......805 986-8277**
305 Hueneme Rd Camarillo (93012) ***(P-89)***

Pacific Echo Inc.......D.......310 539-1822
23540 Telo Ave Torrance (90505) ***(P-14011)***

Pacific Edge Mktg Group Inc (PA).......**D.......818 879-0946**
5155 Clareton Dr Ste 100 Agoura Hills (91301) ***(P-14845)***

Pacific Edge Wine and Spirits, Agoura Hills *Also called Pacific Edge Mktg Group Inc* ***(P-14845)***

Pacific Embroidery LLC.......F.......714 630-4757
1189 N Kraemer Blvd Anaheim (92806) ***(P-18626)***

Pacific Energy Resources Ltd (PA).......**F.......562 628-1526**
111 W Ocean Blvd Ste 1240 Long Beach (90802) ***(P-408)***

Pacific Erth Rsrces Ltd A Cal.......D.......209 892-3000
315 Hueneme Rd Camarillo (93012) ***(P-90)***

Pacific Fibre & Rope Co Inc.......F.......310 834-4567
903 Flint Ave 927 Wilmington (90744) ***(P-2716)***

Pacific Fire Safety, Pomona *Also called Ferguson Fire Fabrication Inc* ***(P-13827)***

Pacific Foam, Ontario *Also called Induspac California Inc* ***(P-4697)***

Pacific Forge Inc.......D.......909 390-0701
10641 Etiwanda Ave Fontana (92337) ***(P-7092)***

Pacific Gardens Med Ctr LLC.......C.......562 860-0401
21530 Pioneer Blvd Hawaiian Gardens (90716) ***(P-23082)***

Pacific Gas and Electric Co.......C.......559 386-2052
34453 Pleymouth Avenal (93204) ***(P-12815)***

Pacific Gas and Electric Co.......C.......805 545-4562
4340 Old Santa Fe Rd San Luis Obispo (93401) ***(P-12816)***

Pacific Gas and Electric Co.......A.......805 506-5280
9 Mi Nw Of Avila Bch Avila Beach (93424) ***(P-12817)***

Pacific Gas and Electric Co.......C.......760 253-2925
35863 Fairview Rd Hinkley (92347) ***(P-12818)***

Pacific Gas and Electric Co.......C.......805 546-5267
800 Price Canyon Rd Pismo Beach (93449) ***(P-12819)***

Pacific Gas and Electric Co.......C.......760 326-2615
145453 Nat Trails Hwy Needles (92363) ***(P-12820)***

Pacific Gas and Electric Co.......C.......661 398-5918
4201 Arrow St Bakersfield (93308) ***(P-12821)***

Pacific Gas and Electric Co.......C.......805 434-4418
160 Cow Meadow Pl Templeton (93465) ***(P-12822)***

Pacific Green Trucking Inc.......F.......310 830-4528
512 E C St Wilmington (90744) ***(P-10478)***

Pacific Handy Cutter Inc (HQ).......**E.......714 562-1033**
17819 Gillette Ave Irvine (92614) ***(P-6488)***

Pacific Hardware Sales, Anaheim *Also called A J Fasteners Inc* ***(P-7054)***

Pacific Haven Convalescent HM, Garden Grove *Also called Pacific Haven Convalescent HM* ***(P-20621)***

Pacific Haven Convalescent HM.......D.......714 534-1942
12072 Trask Ave Garden Grove (92843) ***(P-20621)***

Pacific Health and Welness, Redondo Beach *Also called NBC Consulting Inc* ***(P-23281)***

Pacific Health Corporation.......B.......714 619-7797
3699 Wilshire Blvd # 540 Los Angeles (90010) ***(P-20878)***

Pacific Heritg HM Fashion Inc.......E.......909 598-5200
901 Lawson St City of Industry (91748) ***(P-13183)***

Pacific Hospitality Design Inc.......E.......323 278-7998
2620 S Malt Ave Commerce (90040) ***(P-3630)***

Pacific Hotel Management Inc.......C.......949 608-1091
4545 Macarthur Blvd Newport Beach (92660) ***(P-16608)***

Pacific Housing Management (PA).......**D.......714 508-1777**
945 Katella St Laguna Beach (92651) ***(P-15938)***

Pacific Hsptlist Assoc A Med C.......D.......949 610-7245
361 Hospital Rd Ste 521 Newport Beach (92663) ***(P-22254)***

Pacific Huntington Hotel Corp.......A.......626 568-3900
1401 S Oak Knoll Ave Pasadena (91106) ***(P-16609)***

Pacific Hydrotech Corporation.......C.......951 943-8803
314 E 3rd St Perris (92570) ***(P-22628)***

Pacific Income Advisers Inc (PA).......**E.......310 393-1424**
1299 Ocean Ave Ste 210 Santa Monica (90401) ***(P-15337)***

Pacific Indemnity Company.......B.......213 622-2334
555 S Flower St Ste 300 Los Angeles (90071) ***(P-15607)***

Pacific Industrial Electric, Brea *Also called Pacific Intl Elc Co Inc* ***(P-1290)***

Pacific Interior Design, Anaheim *Also called Pacific Design Directions Inc* ***(P-629)***

Pacific Intl Elc Co Inc.......D.......714 990-9280
230 N Orange Ave Brea (92821) ***(P-1290)***

Pacific Investment MGT Co LLC (HQ).......**C.......949 720-6000**
650 Newport Center Dr Newport Beach (92660) ***(P-16143)***

Pacific Kiln Insulations Inc.......E.......951 697-4422
14370 Veterans Way Moreno Valley (92553) ***(P-8096)***

Pacific Label Inc.......E.......714 237-1276
1511 E Edinger Ave Santa Ana (92705) ***(P-4552)***

Pacific Labor Services Inc.......E.......805 488-4625
5690 Cypress Rd Oxnard (93033) ***(P-16813)***

Pacific Life & Annuity Company.......A.......949 219-3011
700 Newport Center Dr Newport Beach (92660) ***(P-15367)***

Pacific Life Fund Advisors LLC.......A.......949 260-9000
700 Newport Center Dr Newport Beach (92660) ***(P-23083)***

Pacific Life Fund Advisors LLC (HQ).......**D.......800 800-7646**
700 Newport Center Dr Newport Beach (92660) ***(P-15338)***

Pacific Life Global Funding.......D.......949 219-3011
700 Newport Center Dr Newport Beach (92660) ***(P-15157)***

Pacific Life Insurance Company.......D.......949 219-5200
45 Enterprise 4 Aliso Viejo (92656) ***(P-15368)***

Pacific Lighting Mfr Inc.......D.......310 327-7711
2329 E Pacifica Pl Compton (90220) ***(P-13657)***

Pacific Lighting Mfr Inc.......D.......310 327-7711
2661 E Del Amo Blvd Compton (90221) ***(P-13658)***

Pacific Lock Company (PA).......**E.......661 294-3707**
25605 Hercules St Valencia (91355) ***(P-6532)***

PACIFIC LODGE BOY'S HOME, Woodland Hills *Also called Pacific Lodge Youth Svcs Inc* ***(P-22141)***

Pacific Lodge Youth Svcs Inc.......C.......818 347-1577
4900 Serrania Ave Woodland Hills (91364) ***(P-22141)***

Pacific Logistics Corp (PA).......**C.......562 478-4700**
7255 Rosemead Blvd Pico Rivera (90660) ***(P-12499)***

Pacific Ltg & Standards Co.......E.......310 603-9344
2815 Los Flores Blvd Lynwood (90262) ***(P-9098)***

Pacific Manufacturing MGT Inc.......D.......323 263-9000
3110 E 12th St Los Angeles (90023) ***(P-3690)***

Pacific Maritime Freight Inc.......D.......562 590-8188
1512 Pier C St Long Beach (90813) ***(P-12296)***

Pacific Medical Group Inc.......D.......949 493-1030
212 Avenida Fabricante San Clemente (92672) ***(P-13507)***

Pacific Mercantile Bank (HQ).......**E.......714 438-2500**
949 S Coast Dr Ste 300 Costa Mesa (92626) ***(P-15035)***

Pacific Metal Products, Los Angeles *Also called Basic Industries Intl Inc* ***(P-6729)***

Pacific Metal Stampings Inc.......E.......661 257-7656
28415 Witherspoon Pkwy Valencia (91355) ***(P-7172)***

Pacific Metals Group LLC.......E.......909 218-8889
787 S Wanamaker Ave Ontario (91761) ***(P-13583)***

Pacific Miniatures, Fullerton *Also called Pacmin Incorporated* ***(P-11728)***

Pacific Monarch Resorts Inc.......D.......949 228-1396
7 Grenada St Laguna Niguel (92677) ***(P-16610)***

Pacific Monarch Resorts Inc.......D.......951 342-7970
981 Iowa Ave Ste C Riverside (92507) ***(P-16611)***

Pacific Monarch Resorts Inc (PA).......**D.......949 609-2400**
4000 Macarthur Blvd # 600 Newport Beach (92660) ***(P-15939)***

Pacific Monarch Resorts Inc.......D.......949 248-2944
34630 Pacific Coast Hwy Capistrano Beach (92624) ***(P-16612)***

Pacific Mutual Distributors, Newport Beach *Also called Pacific Select Distributors* ***(P-15303)***

Pacific Natural Spices, Commerce *Also called Pacific Spice Company Inc* ***(P-2506)***

Pacific Naturals, Pacoima *Also called Gscm Ventures Inc* ***(P-5028)***

Pacific Occptnal Medicine Svcs.......E.......562 997-2290
2776 Pacific Ave Long Beach (90806) ***(P-20879)***

Pacific Oil Cooler Service In.......E.......909 593-8400
1677 Curtiss Ct La Verne (91750) ***(P-12365)***

Pacific Operators Inc ....E....805 899-3144
205 E Carrillo St Ste 200 Santa Barbara (93101) *(P-435)*
Pacific Outdoor Living, Sun Valley *Also called Pacific Pavingstone Inc (P-1545)*
Pacific Packaging Components, Baldwin Park *Also called P C P Inc (P-14959)*
Pacific Packaging McHy LLC ....E....951 393-2200
200 River Rd Corona (92878) *(P-7947)*
Pacific Pallet Co, Glendale *Also called Long Beach Woodworks LLC (P-3397)*
Pacific Palms Healthcare LLC (PA) ....C....**562 433-6791**
1020 Termino Ave Long Beach (90804) *(P-20431)*
Pacific Panel Products Corp ....E....626 851-0444
15601 Arrow Hwy Irwindale (91706) *(P-3449)*
Pacific Paper Box Company (PA) ....E....**323 771-7733**
3928 Encino Hills Pl Encino (91436) *(P-3779)*
Pacific Paper Converting Inc (PA) ....D....**323 888-1330**
6023 Bandini Blvd Los Angeles (90040) *(P-14960)*
Pacific Park, Santa Monica *Also called Santa Monica Amusements LLC (P-19524)*
Pacific Parts International, Canoga Park *Also called Richard Huetter Inc (P-13085)*
Pacific Pavingstone Inc ....C....818 244-4000
8309 Tujunga Ave Unit 201 Sun Valley (91352) *(P-1545)*
Pacific Perforating Inc ....E....661 768-9224
25090 Highway 33 Fellows (93224) *(P-532)*
Pacific Pharma Inc ....A....714 246-4600
18600 Von Karman Ave Irvine (92612) *(P-14275)*
Pacific Pioneer Insur Group (PA) ....D....**714 228-7888**
6363 Katella Ave Cypress (90630) *(P-15608)*
Pacific Piston Ring Co Inc ....D....310 836-3322
3620 Eastham Dr Culver City (90232) *(P-8433)*
Pacific Plastics Inc ....D....714 990-9050
111 S Berry St Brea (92821) *(P-5469)*
Pacific Plating, Sun Valley *Also called Kvr Investment Group Inc (P-7987)*
Pacific Play Tents Inc ....E....323 269-0431
2801 E 12th St Los Angeles (90023) *(P-3142)*
Pacific Plms Conference Resort, City of Industry *Also called Majestic Industry Hills LLC (P-16553)*
Pacific Pprbd Converting LLC (PA) ....E....**909 476-6466**
8865 Utica Ave Ste A Rancho Cucamonga (91730) *(P-3932)*
Pacific Precision Labs Inc ....F....818 700-8977
9430 Lurline Ave Chatsworth (91311) *(P-10902)*
Pacific Precision Metals Inc ....C....951 226-1500
1100 E Orangethorpe Ave # 253 Anaheim (92801) *(P-7173)*
Pacific Premier Bancorp Inc (PA) ....D....**949 864-8000**
17901 Von Karman Ave # 1 Irvine (92614) *(P-15036)*
Pacific Premier Bank (HQ) ....D....**714 431-4000**
17901 Von Karman Ave # 1 Irvine (92614) *(P-15037)*
Pacific Premier Bank ....D....213 626-0085
333 S Grand Ave Ste 3560 Los Angeles (90071) *(P-15038)*
Pacific Press, Anaheim *Also called Wasser Filtration Inc (P-8142)*
Pacific Process Systems Inc (PA) ....D....**661 321-9681**
7401 Rosedale Hwy Bakersfield (93308) *(P-533)*
Pacific Protection Svcs Inc (PA) ....C....**818 313-9369**
22144 Clarendon St # 110 Woodland Hills (91367) *(P-18306)*
Pacific Quality Packaging Corp ....D....714 257-1234
660 Neptune Ave Brea (92821) *(P-3823)*
Pacific Quartz Inc ....E....714 546-8133
900 Glenneyre St Laguna Beach (92651) *(P-10853)*
Pacific Rebar Inc ....D....909 984-7199
501 S Oaks Ave Ontario (91762) *(P-13584)*
Pacific Relocation Consultants, Long Beach *Also called Overland Pacific & Cutler LLC (P-18624)*
Pacific Restoration Group Inc ....E....951 940-6069
325 E Ellis Ave Perris (92570) *(P-274)*
Pacific Rim Contractors Inc ....D....714 641-7380
1315 E Saint Andrew Pl B Santa Ana (92705) *(P-1391)*
Pacific Rim Mech Contrs Inc ....C....714 285-2600
1701 E Edinger Ave Ste F2 Santa Ana (92705) *(P-1114)*
Pacific Rim Printers & Mailers, Culver City *Also called Econ-O-Plate Inc (P-4288)*
Pacific Rim Realty Group ....E....805 553-9562
740 Lucille Ct Moorpark (93021) *(P-15940)*
Pacific Scientific Company (HQ) ....E....**805 526-5700**
1785 Voyager Ave Simi Valley (93063) *(P-10633)*
Pacific Sd/Pcfic Arbor Nrsries, Camarillo *Also called Pacific Earth Resources (P-89)*
Pacific Seismic Products Inc ....E....661 942-4499
233 E Avenue H8 Lancaster (93535) *(P-7451)*
Pacific Select Distributors ....D....949 219-3011
700 Newport Center Dr # 4 Newport Beach (92660) *(P-15303)*
Pacific Shore Holdings Inc ....E....818 998-0996
8236 Remmet Ave Canoga Park (91304) *(P-4868)*
Pacific Shores Med Group Inc (HQ) ....D....**562 590-0345**
1043 Elm Ave Ste 104 Long Beach (90813) *(P-20017)*
Pacific Sky Supply Inc ....D....818 768-3700
8230 San Fernando Rd Sun Valley (91352) *(P-10391)*
Pacific Snow Valley Resort LLC ....D....909 866-3121
40650 Village Dr Big Bear Lake (92315) *(P-16613)*
Pacific Sod, Camarillo *Also called Pacific Erth Rsrces Ltd A Cal (P-90)*
Pacific South Bay Dialysis LLC (HQ) ....E....**310 371-4244**
20911 Earl St Ste 160 Torrance (90503) *(P-21257)*
Pacific Southwest Cont LLC ....E....559 651-5500
9525 W Nicholas Ct Visalia (93291) *(P-3824)*
Pacific Southwest Instruments, Corona *Also called Pacwest Instrument Labs Inc (P-19054)*
Pacific Specialty Insurance Co ....E....800 303-5000
5515 E La Palma Ave # 150 Anaheim (92807) *(P-15609)*
Pacific Spice Company Inc ....D....323 726-9190
6430 E Slauson Ave Commerce (90040) *(P-2506)*
Pacific Stainless, Colton *Also called S & S Installations Inc (P-8409)*
Pacific Steam Equipment Inc ....E....562 906-9292
11748 Slauson Ave Santa Fe Springs (90670) *(P-6745)*
Pacific Stone Design Inc ....E....714 836-5757
1201 E Wakeham Ave Santa Ana (92705) *(P-6047)*
Pacific Strucframe LLC ....D....951 405-8536
1600 Chicago Ave Ste R11 Riverside (92507) *(P-1499)*
Pacific Suites Hotel, Santa Monica *Also called Windsor Capital Group Inc (P-16791)*
Pacific Sun Labor ....D....760 556-5085
350 G St Brawley (92227) *(P-218)*
Pacific Surveys LLC ....F....909 949-0850
1785 W Arrow Rte Upland (91786) *(P-534)*
Pacific Surveys LLC (PA) ....F....**909 625-6262**
4456 Via Saint Ambrose Claremont (91711) *(P-535)*
Pacific Symphony ....D....714 755-5788
17620 Fitch Ste 100 Irvine (92614) *(P-19373)*
Pacific Systems Interiors Inc ....C....310 436-6820
190 E Arrow Hwy Ste D San Dimas (91773) *(P-1392)*
Pacific Tank & Cnstr Inc ....E....805 237-2929
17995 E Highway 46 Shandon (93461) *(P-6746)*
Pacific Theaters Inc (PA) ....C....**310 657-8420**
120 N Robertson Blvd Fl 3 Los Angeles (90048) *(P-19285)*
Pacific Theatres Entrmt Corp (HQ) ....D....**310 659-9432**
120 N Robertson Blvd Fl 3 Los Angeles (90048) *(P-19286)*
Pacific Toll Processing Inc ....E....310 952-4992
24724 Wilmington Ave Carson (90745) *(P-6207)*
Pacific Toxicology Labs ....D....818 598-3110
9348 De Soto Ave Chatsworth (91311) *(P-21082)*
Pacific Transformer Corp ....C....714 779-0450
5399 E Hunter Ave Anaheim (92807) *(P-8881)*
Pacific Trellis Fruit LLC (PA) ....C....**323 859-9600**
2301 E 7th St Ste C200 Los Angeles (90023) *(P-14646)*
Pacific Urethanes LLC ....C....909 390-8400
1671 Champagne Ave Ste A Ontario (91761) *(P-3113)*
Pacific Utlity Instllation Inc ....D....714 970-6430
510 Malloy Ct Corona (92878) *(P-1291)*
Pacific Valuation ....E....949 271-6377
15615 Alton Pkwy Ste 450 Irvine (92618) *(P-15941)*
Pacific Ventures Ltd ....C....626 576-0737
2200 W Valley Blvd Alhambra (91803) *(P-23084)*
Pacific Vial Mfg Inc ....F....323 721-7004
2800 Supply Ave Commerce (90040) *(P-11726)*
Pacific Vial Mfg Inc ....E....323 721-7004
2738 Supply Ave Commerce (90040) *(P-5929)*
Pacific W Space Cmmnctions Inc ....D....909 592-4321
900 W Gladstone St San Dimas (91773) *(P-964)*
Pacific Wave Systems Inc ....D....714 893-0152
2525 W 190th St Torrance (90504) *(P-9308)*
Pacific West Construction ....E....310 997-2340
1601 Pcf Cast Hwy Ste 160 Hermosa Beach (90254) *(P-630)*
Pacific West Litho Inc ....D....714 579-0868
3291 E Miraloma Ave Anaheim (92806) *(P-4385)*
Pacific Western Container, Santa Ana *Also called Blower-Dempsay Corporation (P-3787)*
Pacific Western Sales (PA) ....D....**714 572-6730**
2980 Enterprise St Ste A Brea (92821) *(P-14961)*
Pacific Westline Inc ....D....714 956-2442
1536 W Embassy St Anaheim (92802) *(P-3661)*
Pacific Wire Products Inc ....E....818 755-6400
10725 Vanowen St North Hollywood (91605) *(P-7506)*
Pacific World Corporation (PA) ....D....**949 598-2400**
100 Technology Dr Ste 200 Irvine (92618) *(P-5055)*
Pacific Wtrprfing Rstrtion Inc ....E....909 444-3052
2845 Pomona Blvd Pomona (91768) *(P-5237)*
Pacifica Beauty LLC ....D....844 332-8440
1090 Eugenia Pl Ste 200 Carpinteria (93013) *(P-11727)*
Pacifica Hospital of Valley, Sun Valley *Also called Pacifica of Valley Corporation (P-20880)*
Pacifica Hotel Company (HQ) ....E....**805 957-0095**
39 Argonaut Aliso Viejo (92656) *(P-15942)*
Pacifica Ht Cnfrnce Ctr A Cal ....D....310 649-1776
6161 W Centinela Ave Culver City (90230) *(P-16614)*
Pacifica International, Carpinteria *Also called Pacifica Beauty LLC (P-11727)*
Pacifica of Valley Corporation ....A....818 767-3310
9449 San Fernando Rd Sun Valley (91352) *(P-20880)*
Pacifica Services Inc ....D....626 405-0131
106 S Mentor Ave Ste 200 Pasadena (91106) *(P-22629)*
Pacifica Trucks LLC ....D....310 549-1351
1450 Dominguez St Carson (90810) *(P-12500)*
Pacificare Health Systems, Cypress *Also called Uhc of California (P-15462)*
Pacificare Health Systems LLC (HQ) ....A....**714 952-1121**
5995 Plaza Dr Cypress (90630) *(P-21197)*
Pacifico Bindery Inc ....F....714 744-1510
544 W Angus Ave Orange (92868) *(P-4619)*
Pacifictech Molded Pdts Inc ....E....714 279-9928
22805 Savi Ranch Pkwy Yorba Linda (92887) *(P-5397)*
Paciolan LLC (HQ) ....C....**866 722-4652**
5291 California Ave # 100 Irvine (92617) *(P-17949)*
Pack West Machinery, Corona *Also called Pacific Packaging McHy LLC (P-7947)*
Pack West Machinery Co, Corona *Also called W J Ellison Co Inc (P-8081)*
Packaging Dist Assembly Group ....F....661 607-0600
24730 Avenue Rockefeller Valencia (91355) *(P-3776)*
Packaging Holdings Inc ....E....831 634-0940
1030 N Anderson Rd Exeter (93221) *(P-8076)*
Packaging Spectrum, Los Angeles *Also called Advance Paper Box Company (P-3782)*
Packaging Systems Inc ....E....661 253-5700
26435 Summit Cir Santa Clarita (91350) *(P-5189)*
Packard Realty Inc ....C....310 649-5151
9901 S La Cienega Blvd Los Angeles (90045) *(P-16615)*
Packers Bar M, Los Angeles *Also called Serv-Rite Meat Company Inc (P-1719)*
Packers Food Products Inc ....E....913 262-6200
701 W Kimberly Ave # 210 Placentia (92870) *(P-1907)*
Packers Manufacturing Inc ....F....559 732-4886
4212 W Hemlock Ave Visalia (93277) *(P-7948)*
Packetfabric Inc ....D....844 475-8322
9920 Jefferson Blvd Culver City (90232) *(P-12662)*

ALPHABETIC

Employee Codes: A=Over 500 employees, B=251-500
C=101-250, D=51-100, E=20-50 F=10-19
2022 Southern California Business Directory and Buyers Guide
© Mergent Inc. 1-800-342-5647
1229

Packline Technologies Inc....E....559 591-3150
5929 Avenue 408 Dinuba (93618) ***(P-8077)***
Packline USA LLC....F....909 392-8000
9555 Hyssop Dr Rancho Cucamonga (91730) ***(P-5735)***
Paclights LLC (PA)....**F....800 980-6386**
15318 El Prado Rd Chino (91710) ***(P-9099)***
Paclo, Pico Rivera *Also called Pacific Logistics Corp* ***(P-12499)***
Pacmet Aerospace, Ontario *Also called Pacific Metals Group LLC* ***(P-13583)***
Pacmin Incorporated (PA)....**D....714 447-4478**
2021 Raymer Ave Fullerton (92833) ***(P-11728)***
Pacobond Inc....E....818 768-5002
9344 Glenoaks Blvd Sun Valley (91352) ***(P-3897)***
Pacon Inc....C....626 814-4654
4249 Puente Ave Baldwin Park (91706) ***(P-3767)***
Pactiv Packaging Inc (HQ)....**A....323 513-9000**
3751 Seville Ave Vernon (90058) ***(P-14962)***
Pactrack Inc....D....213 201-5856
4373 Santa Anita Ave A El Monte (91731) ***(P-12501)***
Pacwest Bancorp (PA)....**C....310 887-8500**
9701 Wilshire Blvd # 700 Beverly Hills (90212) ***(P-15006)***
Pacwest Instrument Labs Inc....D....951 737-0790
1721 Railroad St Corona (92878) ***(P-19054)***
Pacwest Security Services....C....909 948-0279
2990 Inland Empire Blvd Ontario (91764) ***(P-18307)***
Pacwest Security Services....C....213 413-3500
1545 Wilshire Blvd # 302 Los Angeles (90017) ***(P-18308)***
Paderia LLC....F....949 478-5273
18279 Brookhurst St Ste 1 Fountain Valley (92708) ***(P-2070)***
Padi Americas Inc....C....949 858-7234
30151 Tomas Rcho STA Marg (92688) ***(P-22275)***
Padilla Construction Company....C....714 685-8500
1620 N Brian St Orange (92867) ***(P-1393)***
Padywell Corp....E....626 359-9149
835 Meridian St Duarte (91010) ***(P-4553)***
Pafco, Vernon *Also called Pacific American Fish Co Inc* ***(P-14577)***
Page Private School....D....323 272-3429
419 S Robertson Blvd Beverly Hills (90211) ***(P-22046)***
Pagliei Collection Inc....F....805 693-9101
2363 Alamo Pintado Rd Los Olivos (93441) ***(P-11489)***
Pai Enterprises, Los Angeles *Also called Pai Gp Inc* ***(P-5967)***
Pai Gp Inc....D....323 549-5355
5914 Crenshaw Blvd Los Angeles (90043) ***(P-5967)***
Paige LLC (HQ)....**C....310 733-2100**
10119 Jefferson Blvd Culver City (90232) ***(P-2786)***
Paige Premium Denim, Culver City *Also called Paige LLC* ***(P-2786)***
Paiho North America Corp....E....661 257-6611
16051 El Prado Rd Chino (91708) ***(P-11500)***
Paint Specialists Inc....F....818 771-0552
8629 Bradley Ave Sun Valley (91352) ***(P-7393)***
Paint-Chem Inc....F....213 747-7725
1680 Miller Ave Los Angeles (90063) ***(P-5106)***
Painted Rhino Inc....E....951 656-5524
14310 Veterans Way Moreno Valley (92553) ***(P-5535)***
Pair of Thieves, Culver City *Also called Stateside Merchants LLC* ***(P-2764)***
Paisano Publications LLC (PA)....**D....818 889-8740**
28210 Dorothy Dr Agoura Hills (91301) ***(P-4091)***
Paisano Publications Inc....D....818 889-8740
28210 Dorothy Dr Agoura Hills (91301) ***(P-4092)***
Paisleyriversoapco, Paso Robles *Also called Melissa Trinidad* ***(P-5046)***
Paiute Palace Casino, Bishop *Also called Bishop Paiute Gaming Corp* ***(P-16353)***
Pak Group LLC....E....626 316-6555
236 N Chester Ave Ste 200 Pasadena (91106) ***(P-2071)***
Pak West Paper & Packaging, Santa Ana *Also called Blower-Dempsay Corporation* ***(P-14914)***
Pakedge Device & Software Inc....E....714 880-4511
17011 Beach Blvd Ste 600 Huntington Beach (92647) ***(P-17950)***
Paklab, Chino *Also called Universal Packg Systems Inc* ***(P-5077)***
Paklab, Chino *Also called Universal Packg Systems Inc* ***(P-12257)***
Palace Entertainment Inc (HQ)....**E....949 261-0404**
5160 Campus Dr Newport Beach (92660) ***(P-19660)***
Palace Sports & Entrmt LLC, Beverly Hills *Also called Pse Holding LLC* ***(P-19428)***
Palace Textile Inc....D....323 587-7756
8453 Terradell St Pico Rivera (90660) ***(P-7911)***
Palace Textiles, Pico Rivera *Also called Palace Textile Inc* ***(P-7911)***
Paladar Mfg Inc....D....760 775-4222
53973 Polk St Coachella (92236) ***(P-11347)***
Palermo Family LP....E....213 542-3300
140 W Providencia Ave Burbank (91502) ***(P-2507)***
Palette Life Sciences Inc....E....805 869-7020
27 E Cota St Ste 401 Santa Barbara (93101) ***(P-4759)***
Palisades Group LLC....D....424 280-7560
11755 Wilshire Blvd # 1700 Los Angeles (90025) ***(P-15304)***
Palisades Interactive, Santa Monica *Also called Palisades Media Group Inc* ***(P-17043)***
Palisades Media Group Inc (PA)....**D....310 564-5400**
1601 Clver Feld Bvld Ste Santa Monica (90404) ***(P-17043)***
Palisades Ranch Inc....B....323 581-6161
5925 Alcoa Ave Vernon (90058) ***(P-14485)***
Pallet Depot Inc....D....916 645-0490
19049 Avenue 242 Lindsay (93247) ***(P-3402)***
Pallet Masters Inc....D....323 758-1713
655 E Florence Ave Los Angeles (90001) ***(P-3403)***
Palm Canyon Resort & Spa, Palm Springs *Also called Diamond Resorts LLC* ***(P-16406)***
Palm Desert Community Assn, Palm Desert *Also called Sun City Palm Dsert Cmnty Assn* ***(P-22370)***
Palm Desert Greens Association....D....760 346-8005
73750 Country Club Dr Palm Desert (92260) ***(P-22354)***
Palm Desert Hospitality LLC....C....760 568-1600
36999 Cook St Palm Desert (92211) ***(P-16616)***
Palm Desert Medical Offices, Palm Desert *Also called Kaiser Foundation Hospitals* ***(P-19914)***
Palm Desert Resorter Assn....D....760 345-1954
77333 Country Club Dr B Palm Desert (92211) ***(P-22355)***
Palm Desert Veterans Center, Palm Desert *Also called Veterans Health Administration* ***(P-20146)***
Palm Garden Hotel, Thousand Oaks *Also called Ventu Park LLC* ***(P-16770)***
Palm Grove Health Care, Torrance *Also called Unified Inv Programs Inc* ***(P-21492)***
Palm Grove Healthcare, Beaumont *Also called David-Kleis II LLC* ***(P-21410)***
Palm Mountain Resort & Spa....D....760 325-1301
155 S Belardo Rd Palm Springs (92262) ***(P-16617)***
Palm Springs Art Museum Inc....D....760 322-4800
101 N Museum Dr Palm Springs (92262) ***(P-22231)***
Palm Springs Disposal Services....D....760 327-1351
4690 E Mesquite Ave Palm Springs (92264) ***(P-12963)***
Palm Springs Life....F....760 325-2333
303 N Indian Canyon Dr Palm Springs (92262) ***(P-4093)***
Palm Springs Motors Inc....C....760 699-6695
69-200a Highway 111 Cathedral City (92234) ***(P-18860)***
Palm Springs Plating, Palm Springs *Also called Ken Hoffmann Inc* ***(P-7275)***
Palm Springs Renaissance, Palm Springs *Also called Remington Hotel Corporation* ***(P-16658)***
Palm Springs Rental Agency Inc....E....760 320-7451
225 S Civic Dr Ste 1-7 Palm Springs (92262) ***(P-16618)***
PALM SPRINGS SENIOR CENTER, Palm Springs *Also called Mizell Senior Center Inc* ***(P-21852)***
Palm Sprng Ford Lncoln Mercury, Cathedral City *Also called Palm Springs Motors Inc* ***(P-18860)***
Palm Sprng Pwr Basbal CLB Inc....D....760 778-4487
1901 E Baristo Rd Palm Springs (92262) ***(P-19427)***
Palm Sprng Riviera Resorts Spa, Palm Springs *Also called Riviera Reincarnate LLC* ***(P-16667)***
Palm Ter Hlth Care Rhblitation, Laguna Hills *Also called Gate Three Healthcare LLC* ***(P-20354)***
Palm Valley School....D....760 328-0861
35525 Da Vall Dr Rancho Mirage (92270) ***(P-23490)***
Palmcrest Grand Care Ctr Inc....D....562 595-4551
3501 Cedar Ave Long Beach (90807) ***(P-20432)***
Palmdale Heat Treating Inc....F....661 274-8604
38834 17th St E Palmdale (93550) ***(P-6449)***
Palmdale Med Mental Hlth Svcs, Santa Clarita *Also called American Health Services LLC* ***(P-19708)***
Palmdale Medical Offices, Palmdale *Also called Kaiser Foundation Hospitals* ***(P-16184)***
Palmdale Resort Inc....D....661 947-8055
38630 5th St W Palmdale (93551) ***(P-16619)***
Palmdale Water District....D....661 947-4111
2029 E Avenue Q Palmdale (93550) ***(P-12913)***
Palmer Tank & Construction Inc....E....661 834-1110
2464 S Union Ave Bakersfield (93307) ***(P-536)***
Palmieri Tyler Wner Wlhelm Wld....D....949 851-9400
1900 Main St Ste 700 Irvine (92614) ***(P-21651)***
Palms Golf Club Inc....D....760 771-2606
57000 Palms Dr La Quinta (92253) ***(P-19503)***
Palo Verde Health Care Dst....C....760 922-4115
250 N 1st St Blythe (92225) ***(P-20881)***
Palo Verde Hospital, Blythe *Also called Palo Verde Health Care Dst* ***(P-20881)***
Palo Verde Hospital Assn....C....760 922-4115
250 N 1st St Blythe (92225) ***(P-20882)***
Palo Verde Irrigation District....D....760 922-3144
180 W 14th Ave Blythe (92225) ***(P-13014)***
Palomar Products Inc....D....949 858-8836
23042 Arroyo Vis Rcho STA Marg (92688) ***(P-9347)***
Palos Verdes Golf & Cntry CLB, Palos Verdes Estates *Also called Palos Verdes Golf Club* ***(P-19598)***
Palos Verdes Golf Club....D....310 375-2759
3301 Via Campesina Palos Verdes Estates (90274) ***(P-19598)***
Palos Vrdes Fmly Immdate Med C....E....310 541-7911
26516 Crenshaw Blvd Pls Vrds Pnsl (90274) ***(P-20883)***
Palp Inc....C....562 599-5841
2230 Lemon Ave Long Beach (90806) ***(P-905)***
Palumbo Lawyers LLP (PA)....**D....949 442-0300**
20 Journey Aliso Viejo (92656) ***(P-21652)***
Pam's Delivery Svc & Nat Msgnr, Orange *Also called Madden Corporation* ***(P-11980)***
Pama Management Co....E....951 929-0340
123 N Inez St Ste 16 Hemet (92543) ***(P-23085)***
Pamc Ltd (PA)....**A....213 624-8411**
531 W College St Los Angeles (90012) ***(P-20884)***
Pamc Health Foundation, Los Angeles *Also called Pamc Ltd* ***(P-20884)***
Pamco, Sun Valley *Also called Precision Arcft Machining Inc* ***(P-8741)***
Pamco Machine Works Inc....E....909 941-7260
9359 Feron Blvd Rancho Cucamonga (91730) ***(P-8730)***
Pamona Valley Medical Group (PA)....**D....909 932-1045**
600 City Pkwy W Ste 800 Orange (92868) ***(P-20018)***
Pampa Regional Medical Center, Ontario *Also called Prime Hlthcare Svcs - Pmpa LLC* ***(P-20908)***
Pampanga Foods Company Inc....D....714 773-0537
1835 N Orngthrp Park A Anaheim (92801) ***(P-1742)***
Pan American Bank Fsb....B....949 224-1917
18191 Von Karman Ave # 300 Irvine (92612) ***(P-15052)***
Pan American Properties Inc....E....714 505-5544
17491 Irvine Blvd Ste 100 Tustin (92780) ***(P-15689)***
Pan Pacific Petroleum Co Inc (PA)....**D....562 928-0100**
9302 Garfield Ave South Gate (90280) ***(P-12071)***
Pan Pacific Petroleum Co Inc....C....661 589-3200
1850 Coffee Rd Bakersfield (93308) ***(P-12072)***
Pan-Pacific Mechanical LLC (PA)....**C....949 474-9170**
18250 Euclid St Fountain Valley (92708) ***(P-1115)***

Panacea Inc .... D 562 860-2869
14905 Parmnt Blvd Ste H Paramount (90723) ***(P-22858)***

Panadent Corporation .... E 909 783-1841
580 S Rancho Ave Colton (92324) ***(P-11188)***

Panalpina Inc .... D 310 819-4060
19900 S Vermont Ave Ste A Torrance (90502) ***(P-12502)***

Panaroma Gardens, Panorama City *Also called Ensign Group Inc* ***(P-20329)***

Panasonic Avionics Corporation (HQ) .... **B 949 672-2000**
26200 Enterprise Way Lake Forest (92630) ***(P-22630)***

Panattoni Development Co Inc (PA) .... **D 916 381-1561**
2442 Dupont Dr Irvine (92612) ***(P-16067)***

Panavision Group, Woodland Hills *Also called Panavision Inc* ***(P-17366)***

Panavision Inc (PA) .... **A 818 316-1000**
6101 Variel Ave Woodland Hills (91367) ***(P-17366)***

Panavision International LP (HQ) .... **B 818 316-1080**
6101 Variel Ave Woodland Hills (91367) ***(P-11288)***

PANCAN, Manhattan Beach *Also called Pancrtic Cncer Action Ntwrk In* ***(P-21469)***

Panco Mens Products Inc .... E 760 342-4368
45605 Citrus Ave Indio (92201) ***(P-5056)***

Pancrtic Cncer Action Ntwrk In (PA) .... **C 310 725-0025**
1500 Rosecrans Ave # 200 Manhattan Beach (90266) ***(P-21469)***

Panda Express, Rosemead *Also called Panda Systems Inc* ***(P-16213)***

Panda Systems Inc .... C 626 799-9898
1683 Walnut Grove Ave Rosemead (91770) ***(P-16213)***

Pandol & Sons .... D 661 725-3755
401 Road 192 Delano (93215) ***(P-51)***

Pandora Marketing LLC .... D 800 705-6856
26970 Aliso Viejo Pkwy # 150 Aliso Viejo (92656) ***(P-23292)***

Panel Products Inc .... E 310 830-3331
21818 S Wilmington Ave # 411 Long Beach (90810) ***(P-10634)***

Panel Shop Inc .... E 951 739-7000
2800 Palisades Dr Corona (92878) ***(P-8902)***

Panel Works, Santa Fe Springs *Also called JC Hanscom Inc* ***(P-3351)***

Pango Group Inc .... D 818 502-0400
6100 San Fernando Rd Glendale (91201) ***(P-15943)***

Panini Kabob Grill, Irvine *Also called Sanan Inc* ***(P-23506)***

Pankl Aerospace Systems .... D 562 207-6300
16615 Edwards Rd Cerritos (90703) ***(P-6420)***

Pankl Holdings Inc (HQ) .... **D 949 567-9000**
1902 Mcgaw Ave Irvine (92614) ***(P-10112)***

Panob Corp .... E 909 947-8008
1531 E Cedar St Ontario (91761) ***(P-5736)***

Panoramic Software Corporation .... F 877 558-8526
9650 Research Dr Irvine (92618) ***(P-17951)***

Panosoft, Irvine *Also called Panoramic Software Corporation* ***(P-17951)***

Panrosa Enterprises Inc .... D 951 339-5888
550 Monica Cir Corona (92878) ***(P-4945)***

Papa Cantella's Sausage Plant, Vernon *Also called Papa Cantellas Incorporated* ***(P-1743)***

Papa Cantellas Incorporated .... D 323 584-7272
3341 E 50th St Vernon (90058) ***(P-1743)***

Papco Parts, Chatsworth *Also called Papco Screw Products Inc* ***(P-7738)***

Papco Screw Products Inc .... F 818 341-2266
9410 De Soto Ave Ste A Chatsworth (91311) ***(P-7738)***

Pape Material Handling Inc .... D 562 692-9311
2600 Peck Rd City of Industry (90601) ***(P-7715)***

Pape Material Handling Inc .... C 562 463-8000
2615 Pellissier Pl City of Industry (90601) ***(P-13927)***

Paper Company, The, Irvine *Also called Michael Madden Co Inc* ***(P-14213)***

Paper Company, The, Irvine *Also called Imperial Bag & Paper Co LLC* ***(P-14211)***

Paper Crane, Los Angeles *Also called Lovemarks Inc* ***(P-2856)***

Paper Cutters, Los Angeles *Also called Pacific Paper Converting Inc* ***(P-14960)***

Paper Mart Indus & Ret Packg, Orange *Also called Frick Paper Company* ***(P-14209)***

Paper Surce Converting Mfg Inc .... E 323 583-3800
2015 E 48th St Vernon (90058) ***(P-3768)***

Paper-Pak Industries, La Verne *Also called Novipax Inc* ***(P-14216)***

Papercon Packaging Division, City of Industry *Also called Bagcraftpapercon I LLC* ***(P-3894)***

Papercutters Inc .... E 323 888-1330
6023 Bandini Blvd Los Angeles (90040) ***(P-3856)***

Papich Construction Co Inc (PA) .... **C 805 473-3016**
398 Sunrise Ter Arroyo Grande (93420) ***(P-631)***

Par Engineering Inc .... E 626 964-8700
17855 Arenth Ave City of Industry (91748) ***(P-1116)***

PAR SERVICES, Culver City *Also called Exceptional Chld Foundation* ***(P-21950)***

Par Services, Los Angeles *Also called Exceptional Chld Foundation* ***(P-21951)***

Para Plate, Cerritos *Also called Para-Plate & Plastics Co Inc* ***(P-7923)***

Para Sempre Inc .... D 310 444-0555
11322 Idaho Ave Ste 202 Los Angeles (90025) ***(P-23293)***

Para Tech Coating, Laguna Hills *Also called Metal Improvement Company LLC* ***(P-6446)***

Para-Plate & Plastics Co Inc .... E 562 404-3434
15910 Shoemaker Ave Cerritos (90703) ***(P-7923)***

Parable Christian Store, San Luis Obispo *Also called Parable Group Inc* ***(P-16214)***

Parable Group Inc (PA) .... **D 805 543-2644**
102 Cross St Ste 210 San Luis Obispo (93401) ***(P-16214)***

Paracelsus Los Angeles Comm .... C 323 267-0477
4081 E Olympic Blvd Los Angeles (90023) ***(P-20885)***

Parachute Home Inc .... C 310 903-0353
3525 Eastham Dr Culver City (90232) ***(P-3114)***

Parade Designs Inc .... F 213 627-4019
1327 S Myrtle Ave Monrovia (91016) ***(P-14137)***

Paradigm 360 Inc .... E 951 638-9917
41593 Winchester Rd # 200 Temecula (92590) ***(P-15610)***

Paradigm 360 Insur Fincl Svcs, Temecula *Also called Paradigm 360 Inc* ***(P-15610)***

Paradigm Communications Corp .... E 310 395-5757
401 Wilshire Blvd Ste 900 Santa Monica (90401) ***(P-12663)***

Paradigm Contract Mfg LLC .... F 714 889-7074
5531 Belle Ave Cypress (90630) ***(P-11729)***

Paradigm Industries Inc .... D 310 965-1900
2522 E 37th St Vernon (90058) ***(P-18627)***

Paradigm Label Inc .... F 951 372-9212
10258 Birtcher Dr Jurupa Valley (91752) ***(P-4554)***

Paradigm Music LLC (PA) .... **D 310 288-8000**
360 N Crescent Dr Beverly Hills (90210) ***(P-19325)***

Paradigm Packaging East LLC .... E 909 985-2750
9177 Center Ave Rancho Cucamonga (91730) ***(P-5737)***

Paradigm Packaging West, Rancho Cucamonga *Also called Paradigm Packaging East LLC* ***(P-5737)***

Paradigm Talent Agency LLC .... D 310 288-8000
6725 W Sunset Blvd Los Angeles (90028) ***(P-19326)***

Paradis .... F 818 248-1004
2323 Honolulu Ave Montrose (91020) ***(P-1821)***

Paradise Garden Center Inc .... F 951 789-0386
7109 Dufferin Ave Riverside (92504) ***(P-13877)***

Paradise Kitchen Doors, Pomona *Also called Gonzalez Feliciano* ***(P-3252)***

Paradise Manufacturing Co Inc .... E 909 477-3460
13364 Aerospace Dr 100 Victorville (92394) ***(P-3143)***

Paradise Printing Inc .... E 714 228-9628
13474 Pumice St Norwalk (90650) ***(P-4386)***

Paragon Building Products Inc (PA) .... **E 951 549-1155**
2191 5th St Ste 111 Norco (92860) ***(P-6048)***

Paragon Industries Inc .... D 661 396-0555
4301 Ashe Rd Bakersfield (93313) ***(P-13311)***

Paragon Industries Inc .... D 714 778-1800
1515 E Winston Rd Anaheim (92805) ***(P-13312)***

Paragon Laboratories, Torrance *Also called Naturalife Eco Vite Labs* ***(P-1802)***

Paragon Language Services Inc (PA) .... **F 323 966-4655**
5055 Wilshire Blvd # 835 Los Angeles (90036) ***(P-18628)***

Paragon Partners Ltd (PA) .... **D 714 379-3376**
5660 Katella Ave Ste 100 Cypress (90630) ***(P-23491)***

Paragon Plastics Co Div, Chino *Also called Consolidated Plastics Corp* ***(P-14757)***

Paragon Precision, Valencia *Also called Princeton Tool Inc* ***(P-10223)***

Paragon Textiles Inc .... D 310 323-7500
13003 S Figueroa St Los Angeles (90061) ***(P-14409)***

Paramont Metal & Supply Co, Paramount *Also called George Jue Mfg Co Inc* ***(P-7881)***

Paramount Asphalt, Paramount *Also called Paramount Petroleum Corp* ***(P-5256)***

Paramount Citrus, Delano *Also called Wonderful Company LLC* ***(P-67)***

Paramount Citrus Packing Co, Delano *Also called Wonderful Citrus Packing LLC* ***(P-193)***

Paramount Dairy Inc .... C 562 361-1800
15255 Texaco Ave Paramount (90723) ***(P-1839)***

Paramount Extrusions Company (PA) .... **E 562 634-3291**
6833 Rosecrans Ave Paramount (90723) ***(P-6314)***

Paramount Fabricators, Rancho Cucamonga *Also called Paramunt Plstic Fbricators Inc* ***(P-5739)***

Paramount Farms, Los Angeles *Also called Wonderful Pstchios Almonds LLC* ***(P-2118)***

Paramount Forge Inc .... E 323 775-6803
1721 E Colon St Wilmington (90744) ***(P-7093)***

Paramount Grinding Service .... E 562 630-6940
7311 Madison St Ste C Paramount (90723) ***(P-8731)***

Paramount Home Care Inc .... D 714 994-1250
12235 Beach Blvd Ste 102 Stanton (90680) ***(P-21198)***

Paramount Laminates Inc (PA) .... **D 562 531-7580**
15527 Vermont Ave Paramount (90723) ***(P-5454)***

Paramount Laminates & Cabinets, Paramount *Also called Paramount Laminates Inc* ***(P-5454)***

Paramount Licensing Inc .... E 323 956-5634
5555 Melrose Ave Los Angeles (90038) ***(P-16215)***

Paramount Machine Co Inc .... E 909 484-3600
10824 Edison Ct Rancho Cucamonga (91730) ***(P-8732)***

Paramount Panels Inc (PA) .... **E 909 947-8008**
1531 E Cedar St Ontario (91761) ***(P-5738)***

Paramount Petroleum Corp (HQ) .... **C 562 531-2060**
14700 Downey Ave Paramount (90723) ***(P-5256)***

Paramount Pictures Corporation (HQ) .... **A 323 956-5000**
5555 Melrose Ave Los Angeles (90038) ***(P-19159)***

Paramount Properties, Westlake Village *Also called Rodeo Realty Inc* ***(P-15983)***

Paramount Properties, Beverly Hills *Also called Rodeo Realty Inc* ***(P-15984)***

Paramount Properties, Woodland Hills *Also called Rodeo Realty Inc* ***(P-15988)***

Paramount Properties Encino BR, Encino *Also called Rodeo Realty Inc* ***(P-15981)***

Paramount Studios, Los Angeles *Also called Paramount Pictures Corporation* ***(P-19159)***

Paramount Swap Meet, Paramount *Also called Modern Dev Co A Ltd Partnr* ***(P-18601)***

Paramount Window & Doors, San Bernardino *Also called Paramount Windows & Doors* ***(P-3280)***

Paramount Windows & Doors .... F 909 888-4688
723 W Mill St San Bernardino (92410) ***(P-3280)***

Paramout Farms, Lost Hills *Also called Roll Properties Intl Inc* ***(P-16289)***

Paramunt Contrs Developers Inc .... E 323 464-7050
6464 W Sunset Blvd # 700 Los Angeles (90028) ***(P-15944)***

Paramunt Plstic Fbricators Inc .... E 909 987-4757
11251 Jersey Blvd Rancho Cucamonga (91730) ***(P-5739)***

Parasoft Corporation (PA) .... **E 626 256-3680**
101 E Huntington Dr Fl 2 Monrovia (91016) ***(P-13423)***

Parco LLC (HQ) .... **C 909 947-2200**
1801 S Archibald Ave Ontario (91761) ***(P-5347)***

Parentsquare Inc .... D 888 496-3168
6144 Calle Real Ste 200a Goleta (93117) ***(P-17952)***

Parex Usa Inc (HQ) .... **E 714 778-2266**
2150 Eastridge Ave Riverside (92507) ***(P-6185)***

Parex Usa Inc .... E 951 653-3549
2150 Eastridge Ave Riverside (92507) ***(P-6186)***

Parisa Lingerie & Swim Wear, Northridge *Also called Afr Apparel International Inc* ***(P-3012)***

Park Cleaners Inc (PA) .... **D 626 281-5942**
419 Mcgroarty St San Gabriel (91776) ***(P-16868)***

ALPHABETIC

Employee Codes: A=Over 500 employees, B=251-500
C=101-250, D=51-100, E=20-50 F=10-19

2022 Southern California Business
Directory and Buyers Guide

© Mergent Inc. 1-800-342-5647
1231

Park Engineering and Mfg Co ....E....714 521-4660
6430 Roland St Buena Park (90621) *(P-8733)*
Park Hotels & Resorts Inc ....D....714 990-6000
900 E Birch St Brea (92821) *(P-16620)*
Park Hotels & Resorts Inc ....C....310 415-3340
9876 Wilshire Blvd Beverly Hills (90210) *(P-16621)*
Park Inn, Anaheim *Also called Badalian Enterprises Inc (P-16335)*
Park Landscape Maint 1-2-3-4, Rcho STA Marg *Also called Park Landscape Maintenance (P-330)*
Park Landscape Maintenance (PA) ....B....**949 546-8300**
22421 Gilberto Ste A Rcho STA Marg (92688) *(P-330)*
Park Landscape Maintenance ....E....909 605-8878
5140 E Airport Dr Ste B Ontario (91761) *(P-331)*
Park Marino Convalescent Ctr ....C....626 463-4105
2585 E Washington Blvd Pasadena (91107) *(P-20622)*
Park Newport Apartments, Newport Beach *Also called Park Newport Ltd (P-15743)*
Park Newport Ltd (PA) ....D....**949 644-1900**
1 Park Newport Newport Beach (92660) *(P-15743)*
Park Paseo, Glendale *Also called Cal Southern Presbt Homes (P-15721)*
Park Place Ford LLC ....D....909 946-5555
555 W Foothill Blvd Upland (91786) *(P-18797)*
Park Place Inn, Anaheim *Also called Stovall Stovall & OConnell (P-16734)*
Park Regency Inc ....D....818 363-6116
10146 Balboa Blvd Granada Hills (91344) *(P-15945)*
Park Regency Club Apts, Downey *Also called PRC Multi-Family LLC (P-15745)*
Park Steel Co Inc ....F....310 638-6101
515 E Pine St Compton (90222) *(P-6647)*
Park Uniform Rentals, San Gabriel *Also called Park Cleaners Inc (P-16868)*
Park Vista At Morningside, Fullerton *Also called Corecare V A Cal Ltd Partnr (P-20291)*
Park Vue Inn, Anaheim *Also called Scalzo Hospitality Inc (P-16698)*
Park West Companies Inc (PA) ....B....**949 546-8300**
22421 Gilberto Ste A Rcho STA Marg (92688) *(P-332)*
Park West Enterprises Inc ....E....909 383-8341
2586 Shenandoah Way San Bernardino (92407) *(P-2127)*
Park West Landscape Inc ....D....310 363-4100
13105 Crenshaw Blvd Hawthorne (90250) *(P-333)*
Park West Rescom Inc ....D....949 546-8300
22421 Gilberto Rcho STA Marg (92688) *(P-334)*
Parkco Building Company ....D....714 444-1441
24795 State Highway 74 Perris (92570) *(P-800)*
Parker Boiler Co, Commerce *Also called Sid E Parker Boiler Mfg Co Inc (P-6752)*
Parker Milliken Clark OHar ....D....818 784-8087
555 S Flower St Ste 3000 Los Angeles (90071) *(P-21653)*
Parker Palm Springs LLC ....D....760 770-5000
4200 E Palm Canyon Dr Palm Springs (92264) *(P-16622)*
Parker Pumper Helmet Co, Jurupa Valley *Also called Racing Plus Inc (P-11137)*
Parker Stanbury LLP (PA) ....D....**619 528-1259**
444 S Flower St Ste 1900 Los Angeles (90071) *(P-21654)*
Parker Station, Woodland Hills *Also called Guarachi Wine Partners Inc (P-14843)*
Parker-Hannifin Corporation ....C....949 833-3000
16666 Von Karman Ave Irvine (92606) *(P-10222)*
Parker-Hannifin Corporation ....C....949 833-3000
16666 Von Karman Ave Irvine (92606) *(P-8445)*
Parker-Hannifin Corporation ....C....310 608-5600
19610 S Rancho Way Rancho Dominguez (90220) *(P-9636)*
Parking Company of America ....D....562 862-2118
3165 Garfield Ave Commerce (90040) *(P-18770)*
Parking Concepts Inc ....C....714 543-5725
1020 W Civic Center Dr Santa Ana (92703) *(P-18771)*
Parking Concepts Inc ....C....310 208-1611
1036 Broxton Ave Los Angeles (90024) *(P-18772)*
Parking Concepts Inc ....C....213 746-5764
1801 Georgia St Los Angeles (90015) *(P-18773)*
Parking Concepts Inc ....C....310 821-1081
14110 Palawan Way Lab Venice (90292) *(P-18774)*
Parking Concepts Inc ....C....213 623-2661
800 Wilshire Blvd Los Angeles (90017) *(P-18775)*
Parking Concepts Inc ....C....310 322-5008
12001 Vista Del Mar Playa Del Rey (90293) *(P-18776)*
Parking Network Inc ....C....213 613-1500
1625 W Olympic Blvd # 1010 Los Angeles (90015) *(P-1680)*
Parking Veterans LLC ....E....714 699-3541
18282 Gramercy Dr North Tustin (92705) *(P-16971)*
Parkinson Enterprises Inc ....D....714 626-0275
135 S State College Blvd # 625 Brea (92821) *(P-3597)*
Parks and Recreation Dept, Lakewood *Also called County of Los Angeles (P-19480)*
Parks and Recreation Dept, Pomona *Also called County of Los Angeles (P-19481)*
Parks and Recreation, Dept of, Wilmington *Also called County of Los Angeles (P-19482)*
Parks Optical ....F....805 522-6722
80 W Easy St Ste 3 Simi Valley (93065) *(P-10854)*
Parktree Community Health Ctr, Pomona *Also called Pomona Community Health Center (P-22276)*
Parkview Cmnty Hosp Med Ctr ....A....951 354-7404
3865 Jackson St Riverside (92503) *(P-20886)*
Parkview Jlian Cnvlescent Hosp ....C....661 831-9150
1801 Julian Ave Bakersfield (93304) *(P-20433)*
Parkview Julian LLC ....C....661 831-9150
1801 Julian Ave Bakersfield (93304) *(P-20434)*
Parkview Julian Healthcare Ctr, Bakersfield *Also called Parkview Julian LLC (P-20434)*
Parkwood Landscape Maint Inc ....D....818 988-9677
16443 Hart St Van Nuys (91406) *(P-335)*
Parmela Creamery, Fontana *Also called Life Is Life LLC (P-1779)*
Parpro Technologies Inc ....C....714 545-8886
2700 S Fairview St Santa Ana (92704) *(P-9437)*
Parquet By Dian Inc ....D....310 527-3779
16601 S Main St Gardena (90248) *(P-3224)*

Parrot Communications Intl Inc ....E....818 567-4700
26321 Ferry Ct Santa Clarita (91350) *(P-4193)*
Parrot Media Network, Santa Clarita *Also called Parrot Communications Intl Inc (P-4193)*
Pars Publishing Corp ....F....818 280-0540
4485 Runway St Simi Valley (93063) *(P-4387)*
Parsons Constructors Inc ....A....626 440-2000
100 W Walnut St Pasadena (91124) *(P-23086)*
Parsons Engrg Science Inc (HQ) ....B....**626 440-2000**
100 W Walnut St Pasadena (91124) *(P-22631)*
Parsons Government Svcs Inc (HQ) ....D....**949 768-8161**
25531 Cmmrcntre Dr Ste 12 Lake Forest (92630) *(P-22632)*
Parsons Group Inc (PA) ....D....**805 564-3341**
1921 State St Ste A Santa Barbara (93101) *(P-15744)*
Parsons Gvrnment Svcs Intl Inc ....C....626 440-6000
100 W Walnut St Pasadena (91124) *(P-801)*
Parsons Project Services Inc ....D....626 440-4000
100 W Walnut St Pasadena (91124) *(P-713)*
Parsons Services Company ....A....626 440-2000
100 W Walnut St Pasadena (91124) *(P-22633)*
Parsons Wtr Infrastructure Inc ....D....626 440-7000
100 W Walnut St Pasadena (91124) *(P-22634)*
Parter Medical Products Inc ....C....310 327-4417
17015 Kingsview Ave Carson (90746) *(P-13508)*
Participant Media LLC (PA) ....D....**310 550-5100**
331 Foothill Rd Fl 3 Beverly Hills (90210) *(P-19160)*
Partner Assessment Corporation (PA) ....C....**800 419-4923**
2154 Torrance Blvd # 200 Torrance (90501) *(P-22635)*
Partner Concepts Inc ....D....805 745-7199
811 Camino Viejo Santa Barbara (93108) *(P-4094)*
Partner Engineering & Science, Torrance *Also called Partner Assessment Corporation (P-22635)*
Partners Capital Group Inc (PA) ....D....**949 916-3900**
201 Sandpointe Ave # 220 Santa Ana (92707) *(P-18629)*
Partners Federal Credit Union (PA) ....D....**800 948-6677**
100 N First St Ste 400 Burbank (91502) *(P-15077)*
Partners In Leadership LLC (HQ) ....D....**951 694-5596**
27555 Ynez Rd Ste 200 Temecula (92591) *(P-23294)*
Partners Information Tech (HQ) ....D....**714 736-4487**
888 S Disneyland Dr # 500 Anaheim (92802) *(P-18209)*
Parts Authority LLC ....C....305 676-3410
4277 Transport St Ventura (93003) *(P-13078)*
Parts Expediting and Dist Co ....E....562 944-3199
10805 Artesia Blvd # 112 Cerritos (90703) *(P-10113)*
Parts Out Inc (PA) ....F....**626 560-1540**
1875 Century Park E # 2200 Los Angeles (90067) *(P-9827)*
Party Time Ice ....F....310 833-0187
983 N Pacific Ave San Pedro (90731) *(P-2373)*
Pasadena Center Operating Co ....C....626 795-9311
300 E Green St Pasadena (91101) *(P-18630)*
Pasadena Chld Training Soc ....C....626 798-0853
2933 El Nido Dr Altadena (91001) *(P-22142)*
PASADENA CONVENTION CENTER, Pasadena *Also called Pasadena Center Operating Co (P-18630)*
Pasadena Hospital Assn Ltd (PA) ....A....**626 397-5000**
100 W California Blvd Pasadena (91105) *(P-20435)*
Pasadena Hospital Assn Ltd ....B....626 397-3322
716 S Fair Oaks Ave Pasadena (91105) *(P-20436)*
Pasadena Hotel Dev Ventr LP ....D....626 449-4000
303 Cordova St Pasadena (91101) *(P-16623)*
Pasadena Humane Society ....D....626 792-7151
361 S Raymond Ave Pasadena (91105) *(P-22459)*
Pasadena Madows Nursing Ctr LP ....D....626 796-1103
150 Bellefontaine St Pasadena (91105) *(P-20437)*
Pasadena Manor Retirement Ht, Los Angeles *Also called Ruchel Enterprises (P-15747)*
Pasadena Newspapers Inc (PA) ....C....**626 578-6300**
2 N Lake Ave Ste 150 Pasadena (91101) *(P-4022)*
Pasadena Rehabilitation Inst, Pasadena *Also called Algos Inc A Medical Corp (P-21272)*
Pasadena Senior Center ....D....626 795-4331
85 E Holly St Pasadena (91103) *(P-21863)*
Pasadena Service Federal Cr Un ....D....626 351-9651
670 N Rosemead Blvd Pasadena (91107) *(P-15078)*
Pasadena Star-News, Pasadena *Also called Pasadena Newspapers Inc (P-4022)*
Pasadena Unified School Dst ....D....626 798-9171
740 W Woodbury Rd Pasadena (91104) *(P-17271)*
Pasco, Buena Park *Also called Yeager Enterprises Corp (P-6162)*
Pasco Corporation of America ....E....503 289-6500
19191 S Vt Ave Ste 420 Torrance (90502) *(P-1934)*
Pasco Industries Inc ....F....714 992-2051
2040 Redondo Pl Fullerton (92835) *(P-11514)*
Pasea Hotel & Spa, Huntington Beach *Also called Pacific City Hotel LLC (P-16607)*
Pasha Stevedoring Terminals LP ....E....310 233-2006
802 S Fries Ave Wilmington (90744) *(P-12289)*
Pasha Stevedoring Terminals LP ....D....415 927-6353
802 Suth Fries Ave La Hbr Wilmington (90744) *(P-12276)*
Paso Robles Hotel, Paso Robles *Also called Paso Robles Inn LLC (P-16624)*
Paso Robles Inn LLC ....D....805 238-2660
1103 Spring St Paso Robles (93446) *(P-16624)*
Paso Robles Press, Paso Robles *Also called News Media Inc (P-4014)*
Paso Robles Tank Inc (HQ) ....D....**805 227-1641**
825 26th St Paso Robles (93446) *(P-6208)*
Pass, Orange *Also called Prototype & Short-Run Svcs Inc (P-7178)*
Pass Resources Center, Beaumont *Also called ARC Riverside (P-21715)*
Passages, Malibu *Also called Grasshopper House Partners LLC (P-21307)*
Passco Companies LLC (PA) ....D....**949 442-1000**
2050 Main St Ste 650 Irvine (92614) *(P-15946)*
Passport Foods (svc) LLC ....C....909 627-7312
2539 E Philadelphia St Ontario (91761) *(P-2508)*

Passport Technology Usa Inc............E.......818 957-5471
101 N Brand Blvd Ste 1230 Glendale (91203) ***(P-19055)***
Password Enterprise Inc............E.......562 988-8889
3200 E 29th St Long Beach (90806) ***(P-6421)***
Passy-Muir Inc (PA)............**E.......949 833-8255**
17992 Mitchell S Ste 200 Irvine (92614) ***(P-11133)***
Pasta Mia, Fullerton *Also called Nina Mia Inc* ***(P-2495)***
Pasta Piccinini Inc............D.......626 798-0841
950 N Fair Oaks Ave Pasadena (91103) ***(P-14715)***
Patagonia Inc............F.......626 795-0319
47 N Fair Oaks Ave Pasadena (91103) ***(P-3081)***
Pathfinder Health Inc............E.......714 636-5649
10051 Lampson Ave Garden Grove (92840) ***(P-21199)***
Pathnostics, Irvine *Also called Cap Diagnostics LLC* ***(P-21061)***
Pathway Capital Management LP (PA)............**D.......949 622-1000**
18575 Jamboree Rd Ste 700 Irvine (92612) ***(P-23087)***
Pathways I Sober Living Inc (PA)............**D.......626 373-6006**
13312 Ranchero Rd Oak Hills (92344) ***(P-21864)***
Pathways La (PA)............**E.......213 427-2700**
3325 Wilshire Blvd # 110 Los Angeles (90010) ***(P-21865)***
Patientpop Inc............D.......844 487-8399
214 Wilshire Blvd Santa Monica (90401) ***(P-17953)***
Patina Freight Inc............D.......909 444-1025
525 S Lemon Ave Walnut (91789) ***(P-12228)***
Patina Freight Inc............D.......310 764-4395
1650 S Central Ave Compton (90220) ***(P-12503)***
Patina Products, Arroyo Grande *Also called Layne Laboratories Inc* ***(P-2728)***
Patio & Door Outlet Inc (PA)............**E.......714 974-9900**
410 W Fletcher Ave Orange (92865) ***(P-3571)***
Patio Guys, Santa Ana *Also called Guys Patio Inc* ***(P-18963)***
Patio Outlet, Orange *Also called Patio & Door Outlet Inc* ***(P-3571)***
Patric Communications Inc (PA)............**D.......619 579-2898**
15215 Alton Pkwy Ste 200 Irvine (92618) ***(P-1292)***
Patricia Edwards, Commerce *Also called Superb Chair Corporation* ***(P-3520)***
Patricks Cabinets............F.......909 823-2524
10160 Redwood Ave Fontana (92335) ***(P-3329)***
Patriot Brokerage Inc............D.......910 227-4142
7840 Foothill Blvd Ste H Sunland (91040) ***(P-12504)***
Patriot Communications LLC (PA)............**D.......888 833-4711**
3415 S Sepulveda Blvd # 8 Los Angeles (90034) ***(P-23492)***
Patriot Polishing Company............F.......310 903-7409
47260 Wrangler Rd Aguanga (92536) ***(P-4975)***
Patriot Products, Irwindale *Also called Pertronix Inc* ***(P-9828)***
Patrol Black Knight Inc............D.......213 985-6499
505 S Pcf Ave Unit 201 San Pedro (90731) ***(P-18309)***
Patron Solutions LLC............C.......949 823-1700
5171 California Ave # 200 Irvine (92617) ***(P-17954)***
Pattern Knitting Mills Inc............E.......310 801-1126
7963 Paramount Blvd Pico Rivera (90660) ***(P-2640)***
Patterson Kincaid LLC............D.......323 584-3559
5175 S Soto St Vernon (90058) ***(P-2980)***
Patterson Ritner Lockwood (PA)............**E.......818 241-8001**
620 N Brand Blvd Fl 3 Glendale (91203) ***(P-21655)***
Patton Door and Gate, Palm Springs *Also called Door Service Company* ***(P-6223)***
Patton State Hospital, Patton *Also called State Hospitals Cal Dept* ***(P-21028)***
Pauba Valley Elem. School, Temecula *Also called Temecula Vly Unified Schl Dst* ***(P-22371)***
Paul Calvo and Company............E.......626 814-8000
1619 W Garvey Ave N # 201 West Covina (91790) ***(P-15947)***
Paul Ferrante Inc............E.......310 854-4412
8464 Melrose Pl West Hollywood (90069) ***(P-11730)***
Paul Hastings LLP (PA)............**A.......213 683-6000**
515 S Flower St Fl 25 Los Angeles (90071) ***(P-21656)***
Paul Hubbs Construction Inc (PA)............**F.......951 360-3990**
542 W C St Colton (92324) ***(P-565)***
Paul Mitchell John Systems (PA)............**D.......800 793-8790**
20705 Centre Pointe Pkwy Santa Clarita (91350) ***(P-14276)***
Paulco Precision Inc............F.......310 679-4900
13916 Cordary Ave Hawthorne (90250) ***(P-8734)***
Pauley Plastic LLC............F.......760 240-3737
17177 Navajo Rd Apple Valley (92307) ***(P-5740)***
Paulson Manufacturing Corp............D.......951 676-2451
46752 Rainbow Canyon Rd Temecula (92592) ***(P-11134)***
Paulus Engineering Inc............D.......714 632-3322
2871 E Coronado St Anaheim (92806) ***(P-965)***
Pavement Coatings Co (PA)............**C.......714 826-3011**
10240 San Sevaine Way Jurupa Valley (91752) ***(P-906)***
Pavement Recycling Systems Inc............D.......661 948-5599
46205 Division St Lancaster (93535) ***(P-5276)***
Pavement Recycling Systems Inc (PA)............**C.......951 682-1091**
10240 San Sevaine Way Jurupa Valley (91752) ***(P-14119)***
Pavilion Surgery Center LLC............D.......714 744-8850
1140 W La Veta Ave Orange (92868) ***(P-20019)***
Pavletich Elc Cmmnications Inc (PA)............**D.......661 589-9473**
6308 Seven Seas Ave Bakersfield (93308) ***(P-1293)***
Paw, Chatsworth *Also called Performance Automotive Whl Inc* ***(P-13079)***
Pax Tag & Label Inc............E.......626 579-2000
9528 Rush St Ste C El Monte (91733) ***(P-4555)***
Paydarfar Industries Inc............D.......949 481-3267
26054 Acero Mission Viejo (92691) ***(P-13424)***
Payden & Rygel (PA)............**C.......213 625-1900**
333 S Grand Ave Ste 4000 Los Angeles (90071) ***(P-15339)***
Payless Kitchen Cabinets, Glendale *Also called Carpet Wagon-Glendale Inc* ***(P-3314)***
Paymentmax Processing Inc............F.......805 557-1692
600 Hampshire Rd Ste 120 Westlake Village (91361) ***(P-8316)***
Payne & Fears LLP (PA)............**D.......949 851-1101**
4 Park Plz Ste 1100 Irvine (92614) ***(P-21657)***
Payne Magnetics Inc............D.......626 332-6207
854 W Front St Covina (91722) ***(P-9637)***
Payoff Inc............D.......949 430-0630
3200 Park Center Dr # 800 Costa Mesa (92626) ***(P-15148)***
Payrollcentric Inc............E.......310 258-9703
2100 W Century Blvd Los Angeles (90047) ***(P-17955)***
Payton Technology Corporation............D.......714 885-8000
17665 Newhope St Ste B Fountain Valley (92708) ***(P-9556)***
Pb Fasteners, Gardena *Also called SPS Technologies LLC* ***(P-14020)***
Pbb Inc............E.......909 923-6250
1311 E Philadelphia St Ontario (91761) ***(P-13813)***
Pbc Companies, Brea *Also called Peterson Bros Contruction Inc* ***(P-1547)***
Pbc Pavers Inc............D.......714 278-0488
1560 W Lambert Rd Brea (92821) ***(P-1192)***
Pbf & E LLC............E.......213 427-0340
3014 W Olympic Blvd Los Angeles (90006) ***(P-2335)***
Pbf Energy Western Region LLC (HQ)............**C.......973 455-7500**
111 W Ocean Blvd Ste 1500 Long Beach (90802) ***(P-5257)***
Pbfy Flexible Packaging, Brea *Also called Pacific Western Sales* ***(P-14961)***
Pbi-Birkenwald Market Eqp Inc (PA)............**E.......562 595-4785**
2667 Gundry Ave Long Beach (90755) ***(P-13465)***
PC Club Inc (HQ)............**D.......626 839-8080**
18537 Gale Ave City of Industry (91748) ***(P-13425)***
PC Mechanical Inc............E.......805 925-2888
2803 Industrial Pkwy Santa Maria (93455) ***(P-537)***
PC Recycle, Newbury Park *Also called Fc Management Services* ***(P-7975)***
PC Vaughan Mfg Corp............C.......805 278-2555
1278 Mercantile St Oxnard (93030) ***(P-8134)***
PCA Aerospace Inc (PA)............**D.......714 841-1750**
17800 Gothard St Huntington Beach (92647) ***(P-10392)***
Pcamp, Commerce *Also called Parking Company of America* ***(P-18770)***
PCC Aerostructures, North Hollywood *Also called Klune Industries Inc* ***(P-10363)***
PCC Rollmet Inc............D.......949 221-5333
1822 Deere Ave Irvine (92606) ***(P-6286)***
PCI, Riverside *Also called Pacific Consolidated Inds LLC* ***(P-8133)***
PCI Care Venture I............D.......661 949-2177
43454 30th St W Ofc Lancaster (93536) ***(P-20438)***
PCI Care Venture I............D.......559 735-0828
3120 W Caldwell Ave Visalia (93277) ***(P-20439)***
PCI Holding Company Inc (PA)............**F.......951 479-0860**
12201 Magnolia Ave Riverside (92503) ***(P-8135)***
PCI Industries Inc............E.......323 889-6770
700 S Vail Ave Montebello (90640) ***(P-11731)***
PCI Industries Inc............E.......323 728-0004
6490 Fleet St Commerce (90040) ***(P-11732)***
PCI Industries Inc............E.......323 728-0004
6501 Potello St Commerce (90040) ***(P-6890)***
PCL Construction Services Inc............C.......818 246-3481
655 N Central Ave # 1600 Glendale (91203) ***(P-802)***
PCL Construction Services Inc............C.......818 509-7816
100 Universal City Plz North Hollywood (91608) ***(P-803)***
PCL Industrial Services Inc............B.......661 832-3995
1500 S Union Ave Bakersfield (93307) ***(P-804)***
Pcm, Aliso Viejo *Also called Professional Community MGT Cal* ***(P-23091)***
Pcm, Laguna Woods *Also called Professional Cmnty MGT Cal Inc* ***(P-15958)***
Pcm, Foothill Ranch *Also called Professional Cmnty MGT Cal Inc* ***(P-15755)***
Pcm Inc (HQ)............**A.......310 354-5600**
200 N Pacific Coast Hwy El Segundo (90245) ***(P-13426)***
Pcn3 Inc............E.......562 493-4124
11082 Winners Cir Ste B Los Alamitos (90720) ***(P-805)***
Pcs Mobile Solutions LLC............D.......323 567-2490
3534 Tweedy Blvd South Gate (90280) ***(P-12664)***
Pcs Property Managment LLC............C.......310 231-1000
11859 Wilshire Blvd # 60 Los Angeles (90025) ***(P-15948)***
Pct, Compton *Also called Pacific Contntl Textiles Inc* ***(P-2678)***
Pct-Gw Carbide Tools Usa Inc............F.......562 921-7898
13701 Excelsior Dr Santa Fe Springs (90670) ***(P-4665)***
Pcv Murcor Real Estate Svcs, Pomona *Also called Murcor Inc* ***(P-15930)***
Pcwc, Ontario *Also called Chino-Pacific Warehouse Corp* ***(P-12189)***
Pcx Aerosystems - Santa Ana, Santa Ana *Also called Integral Aerospace LLC* ***(P-10354)***
Pd Group............E.......760 674-3028
41945 Boardwalk Ste L Palm Desert (92211) ***(P-11581)***
Pd Liquidation Inc............C.......818 772-0100
21350 Lassen St Chatsworth (91311) ***(P-14963)***
Pd Products LLC............E.......818 772-0100
21350 Lassen St Chatsworth (91311) ***(P-2735)***
Pda Group, Valencia *Also called Packaging Dist Assembly Group* ***(P-3776)***
Pdc LLC............E.......626 334-5000
4675 Vinita Ct Chino (91710) ***(P-7822)***
PDC Capital Group LLC............D.......866 500-8550
250 Fischer Ave Costa Mesa (92626) ***(P-16068)***
Pdc-Identicard, Valencia *Also called Precision Dynamics Corporation* ***(P-3873)***
Pdf Print Communications Inc (PA)............**D.......562 426-6978**
2630 E 28th St Long Beach (90755) ***(P-4388)***
Pdma Ventures Inc............E.......714 777-8770
22951 La Palma Ave Yorba Linda (92887) ***(P-11189)***
PDQ Engineering Inc............E.......805 482-1334
1199 Avenida Acaso Ste F Camarillo (93012) ***(P-8735)***
Pds, Irvine *Also called Pacific Dental Services LLC* ***(P-20192)***
Pds Tech Inc............C.......214 647-9600
3100 S Harbor Blvd # 135 Santa Ana (92704) ***(P-17443)***
Pdu Lad Corporation (PA)............**D.......626 442-7711**
11165 Valley Spring Ln North Hollywood (91602) ***(P-7394)***
Pea Soup Andersen's Restaurant, Buellton *Also called Carpenters Southwest ADM Corp* ***(P-16945)***
Peabody Engineering & Sup Inc............E.......951 734-7711
13435 Estelle St Corona (92879) ***(P-7993)***
Peace Kim Dentistry Inc (PA)............**D.......949 679-8762**
4 Longbourn Aisle Irvine (92603) ***(P-20193)***

ALPHABETIC

Employee Codes: A=Over 500 employees, B=251-500
C=101-250, D=51-100, E=20-50 F=10-19
2022 Southern California Business
Directory and Buyers Guide
© Mergent Inc. 1-800-342-5647
1233

Peach Inc..C.......323 654-2333
1311 N Highland Ave Los Angeles (90028) ***(P-12145)***
Peacock Stes Resort Ltd Partnr...D.......714 535-8255
1745 S Anaheim Blvd Anaheim (92805) ***(P-16625)***
Peak Operator II LLC..F.......805 436-2555
300 E Esplanade Dr # 181 Oxnard (93036) ***(P-461)***
Peak Seasons, Riverside *Also called Tom Leonard Investment Co Inc* ***(P-11780)***
Pearce Services LLC (HQ)...**E.......805 467-2528**
1222 Vine St Ste 301 Paso Robles (93446) ***(P-23493)***
Pearlman Brown & Wax LLP (PA)...**D.......818 501-4343**
15910 Ventura Blvd Fl 18 Encino (91436) ***(P-21658)***
Pearlman Enterprises Inc (HQ)..**D.......800 969-5561**
6210 Garfield Ave Commerce (90040) ***(P-6157)***
Pearpoint Inc...E.......760 343-7350
39740 Garand Ln Ste B Palm Desert (92211) ***(P-9309)***
Pearson Dental Supplies Inc (PA)...**C.......818 362-2600**
13161 Telfair Ave Sylmar (91342) ***(P-13509)***
Pearson Engineering Corp..F.......626 442-7436
2505 Loma Ave South El Monte (91733) ***(P-7395)***
Pearson Ford Co (PA)..**C.......877 743-0421**
5900 Sycamore Canyon Blvd Riverside (92507) ***(P-18901)***
Pearson Surgical Supply Co, Sylmar *Also called Pearson Dental Supplies Inc* ***(P-13509)***
PEC HI FI, Irvine *Also called Solvere Inc* ***(P-12669)***
PEC Tool, Torrance *Also called Fun Properties Inc* ***(P-6480)***
Pechanga Development Corp...A.......951 695-4655
45000 Pechanga Pkwy Temecula (92592) ***(P-16626)***
Pechanga Resort & Casino, Temecula *Also called Pechanga Development Corp* ***(P-16626)***
Pechanga Resorts Incorporated...D.......888 732-4264
45000 Pechanga Pkwy Temecula (92592) ***(P-16627)***
Pecific Grinding, Fullerton *Also called Kryler Corp* ***(P-7276)***
Peck Jones Construction, Santa Monica *Also called Jones Brothers Cnstr Corp* ***(P-777)***
Peck Road Gravel Pit..F.......626 574-7570
128 Live Oak Ave Monrovia (91016) ***(P-573)***
Pecs, Rancho Cucamonga *Also called Professnal Elec Cnstr Svcs Inc* ***(P-1302)***
Pedavena Mould and Die Co Inc...E.......310 327-2814
12464 Mccann Dr Santa Fe Springs (90670) ***(P-8736)***
Pedco, Cerritos *Also called Parts Expediting and Dist Co* ***(P-10113)***
Pedestal Capital II LLC...D.......562 863-5555
13111 Sycamore Dr Norwalk (90650) ***(P-16283)***
Pediatric & Family Medical Ctr..C.......213 342-3325
1530 S Olive St Los Angeles (90015) ***(P-20020)***
Pediatric Cancer Research, Orange *Also called Childrens Healthcare Cal* ***(P-19748)***
Pediatric Therapy Network...C.......310 328-0276
1815 W 213th St Ste 100 Torrance (90501) ***(P-21324)***
Peed Equipment Company..E.......951 657-0900
43466 Business Park Dr Temecula (92590) ***(P-17317)***
Peei, Los Angeles *Also called Playboy Enterprises Intl* ***(P-4195)***
Peen-Rite Inc...E.......818 767-3676
11662 Sheldon St Sun Valley (91352) ***(P-6450)***
Peep Inc..F.......213 748-5500
720 Towne Ave Los Angeles (90021) ***(P-2981)***
Peep Studio, Los Angeles *Also called Peep Inc* ***(P-2981)***
Peerless Building Maint Co, Chatsworth *Also called Tuttle Family Enterprises Inc* ***(P-17294)***
Peerless Injection Molding LLC..E.......714 689-1920
14321 Corp Dr Garden Grove (92843) ***(P-5741)***
Peerless Maintenance Svc Inc..B.......714 871-3380
1100 S Euclid St La Habra (90631) ***(P-17272)***
Peerless Materials Company..E.......323 266-0313
4442 E 26th St Vernon (90058) ***(P-4976)***
Peets Coffee & Tea LLC..D.......818 546-1030
1151 Glendale Galleria Glendale (91210) ***(P-14716)***
Pegasus Communications Inc (PA)...**E.......818 907-1900**
16633 Ventura Blvd # 1010 Encino (91436) ***(P-19161)***
Pegasus Foods, Los Angeles *Also called Astrochef LLC* ***(P-1916)***
Pegasus HM Hlth Care A Cal Cor..D.......818 551-1932
132 N Artsakh Ave Glendale (91206) ***(P-21200)***
Pegasus Home Health Services, Glendale *Also called Pegasus HM Hlth Care A Cal Cor* ***(P-21200)***
Pegasus Maritime Inc..D.......714 728-8565
535 N Brand Blvd Ste 400 Glendale (91203) ***(P-12505)***
Pegasus Squire Inc..D.......866 208-6837
12021 Wilshire Blvd # 77 Los Angeles (90025) ***(P-18210)***
Pegasus Transit Inc...D.......805 988-1540
210 Beedy St Oxnard (93036) ***(P-11907)***
Peggs Company Inc (PA)..**D.......253 584-9548**
4851 Felspar St Riverside (92509) ***(P-19056)***
Pehl Futz Futz Tgrden Accntnts..D.......951 658-3277
1045 E Morton Pl Hemet (92543) ***(P-22807)***
Peking Noodle Co Inc..E.......323 223-0897
1514 N San Fernando Rd Los Angeles (90065) ***(P-2381)***
Pelco By Schneider Electric, Chino *Also called Schneider Electric Usa Inc* ***(P-12242)***
Pelican Biopharma LLC...E.......310 326-4700
23215 Early Ave Torrance (90505) ***(P-4869)***
Pelican Products Inc (PA)...**B.......310 326-4700**
23215 Early Ave Torrance (90505) ***(P-9143)***
Pelican Rope Works..F.......714 545-0116
1600 E Mcfadden Ave Santa Ana (92705) ***(P-2717)***
Peltek Holdings Inc...E.......949 855-8010
35 Argonaut Ste A1 Laguna Hills (92656) ***(P-7396)***
Pem, Buena Park *Also called Park Engineering and Mfg Co* ***(P-8733)***
Pena Grading & Demolition Inc...E.......818 768-5202
11253 Vinedale St Sun Valley (91352) ***(P-907)***
Pena Trucking, Sun Valley *Also called Pena Grading & Demolition Inc* ***(P-907)***
Pena's Recycling Center, Cutler *Also called Penas Disposal Inc* ***(P-12964)***
Penas Disposal Inc..D.......559 528-3909
12094 Avenue 408 Cutler (93615) ***(P-12964)***
Pencil Grip Inc (PA)..**F.......310 315-3545**
21200 Superior St Ste A Chatsworth (91311) ***(P-3916)***
Pendarvis Manufacturing Inc...E.......714 992-0950
1808 N American St Anaheim (92801) ***(P-8737)***
Pendragon North Amer Auto Inc...D.......949 365-8750
26400 La Alameda Ste 112 Mission Viejo (92691) ***(P-18902)***
Penelope Holdings Corp (HQ)...**E.......805 452-8110**
1187 Coast Village Rd 1-52 Santa Barbara (93108) ***(P-14277)***
Penelope Intermediate Corp (HQ)...**E.......805 452-8110**
1187 Coast Village Rd 1-52 Santa Barbara (93108) ***(P-14278)***
Penguin Pumps Incorporated..E.......818 504-2391
7932 Ajay Dr Sun Valley (91352) ***(P-8018)***
Penhall Holding Company...D.......714 772-6450
1801 W Penhall Way Anaheim (92801) ***(P-1546)***
Peninsula Beverly Hill's, Beverly Hills *Also called Belvedere Hotel Partnership* ***(P-16342)***
Peninsula Beverly Hills, The, Beverly Hills *Also called Belvedere Partnership* ***(P-16343)***
Peninsula Laboratories LLC..F.......310 539-4171
3132 Kashiwa St Torrance (90505) ***(P-4870)***
Peninsula Packaging LLC (HQ)..**D.......559 594-6813**
1030 N Anderson Rd Exeter (93221) ***(P-11733)***
Peninsula Packaging Company, Exeter *Also called Peninsula Packaging LLC* ***(P-11733)***
Peninsula Publishing Inc..E.......949 631-1307
1602 Monrovia Ave Newport Beach (92663) ***(P-4095)***
Penn Elcom Inc (HQ)...**E.......714 230-6200**
7465 Lampson Ave Garden Grove (92841) ***(P-13814)***
Penn Elcom Hardware, Garden Grove *Also called Penn Elcom Inc* ***(P-13814)***
Penn Engineering Components..E.......818 503-1511
29045 Avenue Penn Valencia (91355) ***(P-13815)***
Pennant Healthcare Inc (HQ)...**C.......949 487-9500**
27101 Puerta Real Ste 450 Mission Viejo (92691) ***(P-20440)***
Penney Lawn Service Inc...D.......661 587-4788
4000 Allen Rd Bakersfield (93314) ***(P-336)***
Penney Opco LLC...D.......559 732-4171
2115 S Mooney Blvd Visalia (93277) ***(P-16910)***
Penney Opco LLC...D.......626 445-6454
400 S Baldwin Ave Lowr Arcadia (91007) ***(P-16911)***
Penney Opco LLC...D.......805 497-6811
280 W Hillcrest Dr Thousand Oaks (91360) ***(P-16912)***
Penney Opco LLC...D.......626 960-3711
1203 Plaza Dr West Covina (91790) ***(P-16913)***
Pennoyer-Dodge Co...E.......818 547-2100
6650 San Fernando Rd Glendale (91201) ***(P-7861)***
Penny Lane Centers (PA)...**B.......818 892-3423**
15305 Rayen St North Hills (91343) ***(P-22207)***
Penny Lawn Service, Bakersfield *Also called Penney Lawn Service Inc* ***(P-336)***
Pennymac, Agoura Hills *Also called Private Nat Mrtg Accptance LLC* ***(P-1522[illegible])***
Pennymac Corp...D.......818 878-8416
27001 Agoura Rd Agoura Hills (91301) ***(P-15248)***
Pennymac Financial Svcs Inc (PA)..**B.......818 224-7442**
3043 Townsgate Rd Westlake Village (91361) ***(P-15223)***
Pennymac Mortgage Inv Tr (PA)...**A.......818 224-7442**
6101 Condor Dr Moorpark (93021) ***(P-15224)***
Penrose Coping Company, Sun Valley *Also called Precision Tile Co* ***(P-6051)***
Pensinmark Rtirement Group LLC..D.......805 456-6260
24 E Cota St Ste 200 Santa Barbara (93101) ***(P-23295)***
Pension Group Inc...D.......949 768-4015
23046 Avnida De La Crltlo Carlotalota Laguna Hills (92653) ***(P-15611)***
Penske Business Media LLC (HQ)..**D.......310 321-5000**
11175 Santa Monica Blvd # 9 Los Angeles (90025) ***(P-4096)***
Penske Honda Ontario, Ontario *Also called Ontario Automotive LLC* ***(P-13034)***
Penske Motor Group LLC..B.......626 859-1200
2010 E Garvey Ave S West Covina (91791) ***(P-18735)***
Penske Motorcars Mercedes Benz, West Covina *Also called Pmb Motorcars LLC* ***(P-18861)***
Penta Financial Inc...E.......818 882-3872
14399 Princeton Ave Moorpark (93021) ***(P-9366)***
Penta Laboratories, Moorpark *Also called Penta Financial Inc* ***(P-9366)***
Penta Laboratories LLC..F.......818 882-3872
2359 Knoll Dr Ste A Ventura (93003) ***(P-9367)***
Pentair Pool Products, Moorpark *Also called Pentair Water Pool and Spa Inc* ***(P-8403)***
Pentair Water Pool and Spa Inc..E.......805 553-5003
10951 W Los Angeles Ave Moorpark (93021) ***(P-8403)***
Pentel of America Ltd (HQ)..**C.......310 320-3831**
2715 Columbia St Torrance (90503) ***(P-14196)***
Pentland USA Inc (HQ)...**E.......516 365-1333**
35 W Haley St Santa Barbara (93101) ***(P-14444)***
Pentrate Metal Processing...E.......323 269-2121
3517 E Olympic Blvd Los Angeles (90023) ***(P-7293)***
Pentron Clinical Tech LLC...D.......203 265-7397
1717 W Collins Ave Orange (92867) ***(P-21083)***
Penwal Industries Inc...D.......909 466-1555
10611 Acacia St Rancho Cucamonga (91730) ***(P-806)***
People Assisting Homeless...C.......323 644-2216
340 N Madison Ave Los Angeles (90004) ***(P-21866)***
People Concern..C.......310 883-1222
1751 Cloverfield Blvd Santa Monica (90404) ***(P-21867)***
People Concern..C.......310 450-0650
1751 Cloverfield Blvd Santa Monica (90404) ***(P-21868)***
People Creating Success Inc...D.......661 225-9700
1607 E Palmdale Blvd H Palmdale (93550) ***(P-21869)***
People Creating Success Inc...C.......805 644-9480
380 Arneill Rd Camarillo (93010) ***(P-20021)***
People Creating Success Inc...D.......805 692-5290
5350 Hollister Ave Ste I Santa Barbara (93111) ***(P-21870)***
People Media Inc..F.......800 600-7111
8800 W Sunset Blvd 3 West Hollywood (90069) ***(P-4023)***
People's Place, Torrance *Also called Topwin Corporation* ***(P-14356)***
Peoples Care Inc..C.......760 962-1900
13901 Amargosa Rd Ste 101 Victorville (92392) ***(P-21201)***

Peoples Care Inc.......C.......562 320-0174
12215 Telg Rd Ste 208 Santa Fe Springs (90670) ***(P-22047)***
Peoples Chice HM Ln Scrties Co (PA).......**D.......949 494-6167**
7515 Irvine Center Dr Irvine (92618) ***(P-15225)***
Peoples Choice Staffing Inc.......D.......951 735-0550
4218 Green River Rd # 101 Corona (92878) ***(P-17444)***
Peoples Sausage Company.......F.......213 627-8633
1132 E Pico Blvd Los Angeles (90021) ***(P-1744)***
Peoples Self-Help Housing Corp.......D.......805 349-9341
1026 W Boone St Santa Maria (93458) ***(P-23494)***
Peppermint Ridge (PA).......**D.......951 273-7320**
825 Magnolia Ave Corona (92879) ***(P-22143)***
Pepsi Bottling Group.......F.......714 522-9742
6230 Descanso Ave Buena Park (90620) ***(P-2277)***
Pepsi Cola Btlg of Bkersfield.......E.......661 327-9992
215 E 21st St Bakersfield (93305) ***(P-2278)***
Pepsico, Buena Park *Also called Pepsi Bottling Group* ***(P-2277)***
Pepsico, Riverside *Also called Bottling Group LLC* ***(P-2260)***
Pepsico.......F.......562 818-9429
1650 E Central Ave San Bernardino (92408) ***(P-2279)***
Pepsico Inc.......F.......323 785-2820
8530 Wilshire Blvd # 300 Beverly Hills (90211) ***(P-2280)***
Perera Cnstr & Design Inc.......E.......909 484-6350
2890 Inland Empire Blvd Ontario (91764) ***(P-378)***
Perez Contracting LLC.......C.......661 399-2700
12620 Snow Rd Bakersfield (93314) ***(P-226)***
Perfect 10 Satellite, Fontana *Also called Perfectvision Mfg Inc* ***(P-16914)***
Perfect Banner, The, Aliso Viejo *Also called Perfect Impression Inc* ***(P-18631)***
Perfect Impression Inc.......E.......949 305-0797
27111 Aliso Creek Rd # 145 Aliso Viejo (92656) ***(P-18631)***
Perfection Glass Inc.......E.......951 674-0240
554 3rd St Lake Elsinore (92530) ***(P-1587)***
Perfection Machine & Tl Works, Los Angeles *Also called Perfection Machine and Tl Work* ***(P-8738)***
Perfection Machine and Tl Work.......E.......213 749-5095
1568 E 22nd St Los Angeles (90011) ***(P-8738)***
Perfection Pet Brands, Visalia *Also called Perfection Pet Foods LLC* ***(P-1961)***
Perfection Pet Foods LLC (HQ).......**E.......559 302-4880**
1111 N Miller Park Ct Visalia (93291) ***(P-1961)***
Perfectvision Mfg Inc.......C.......909 355-0478
10837 Commerce Way Ste A Fontana (92337) ***(P-16914)***
Performance Aluminum Products.......E.......909 391-4131
520 S Palmetto Ave Ontario (91762) ***(P-6369)***
Performance Automotive Whl Inc (PA).......**D.......805 499-8973**
20235 Nordhoff St Chatsworth (91311) ***(P-13079)***
Performance Building Services.......C.......949 364-4364
22642 Lambert St Ste 409 Lake Forest (92630) ***(P-17273)***
Performance Cleanroom Services, Lake Forest *Also called Performance Building Services* ***(P-17273)***
Performance Composites Inc.......C.......310 328-6661
1418 S Alameda St Compton (90221) ***(P-5939)***
Performance Contracting Inc.......D.......913 310-7120
4955 E Landon Dr Anaheim (92807) ***(P-1626)***
Performance Designed Pdts LLC (PA).......**D.......323 248-9236**
2300 W Empire Ave Ste 600 Burbank (91504) ***(P-14099)***
Performance Engineered Pdts.......E.......909 594-7487
3270 Pomona Blvd Pomona (91768) ***(P-5742)***
Performance Forge Inc.......E.......323 722-3460
7401 Telegraph Rd Montebello (90640) ***(P-7094)***
Performance Health Med Group (PA).......**E.......310 540-9699**
21707 Hawthorne Blvd # 20 Torrance (90503) ***(P-21470)***
Performance Machine Tech Inc.......E.......661 294-8617
25141 Avenue Stanford Valencia (91355) ***(P-8739)***
Performance Materials Corp (HQ).......**D.......805 482-1722**
1150 Calle Suerte Camarillo (93012) ***(P-4706)***
Performance Nissan, Duarte *Also called Gpi Ca-Niii Inc* ***(P-18835)***
Performance Powder Inc.......E.......714 632-0600
2940 E La Jolla St Ste A Anaheim (92806) ***(P-7397)***
Performance Sheets LLC.......C.......626 333-0195
440 Baldwin Park Blvd City of Industry (91746) ***(P-1500)***
PERFORMANCE TEAM FREIGHT SYSTEM, INC., Santa Fe Springs *Also called Performance Team Frt Sys Inc* ***(P-12229)***
Performance Team Frt Sys Inc.......D.......562 741-1300
12816 Shoemaker Ave Santa Fe Springs (90670) ***(P-12229)***
Performance Team Frt Sys Inc.......C.......562 345-2200
1331 Torrance Blvd Torrance (90501) ***(P-12506)***
Performance Team Frt Sys Inc.......C.......424 358-6943
1651 California St Redlands (92374) ***(P-12507)***
Performance Team LLC.......C.......801 301-1732
1651 California St Ste A Redlands (92374) ***(P-12508)***
Performance Team LLC.......D.......310 241-4100
401 Westmont Dr San Pedro (90731) ***(P-12230)***
Performance Team LLC (HQ).......**C.......562 345-2200**
2240 E Maple Ave El Segundo (90245) ***(P-12509)***
Performance Water Products Inc.......F.......714 736-0137
6902 Aragon Cir Buena Park (90620) ***(P-8404)***
Performing Arts Ctr Los Angles.......C.......213 972-7512
135 N Grand Ave Ste 314 Los Angeles (90012) ***(P-19327)***
Performio Usa Inc (PA).......**D.......833 817-7084**
18191 Von Karman Ave # 1 Irvine (92612) ***(P-17689)***
Performnce Engineered Pdts Inc.......D.......909 594-7487
3270 Pomona Blvd Pomona (91768) ***(P-5743)***
Peric Oil Tool, Bakersfield *Also called Weatherford Completion Systems* ***(P-558)***
Perillo Industries Inc.......E.......805 498-9838
2150 Anchor Ct Ste A Newbury Park (91320) ***(P-13762)***
Perimeter Solutions LP.......E.......909 983-0772
10667 Jersey Blvd Rancho Cucamonga (91730) ***(P-4666)***
Perimetrics LLC.......F.......310 826-4905
11661 San Vicente Blvd # 800 Los Angeles (90049) ***(P-6005)***
Perkins.......E.......818 764-9293
7312 Varna Ave Ste A North Hollywood (91605) ***(P-7894)***
Perkins Development Group Inc (PA).......**D.......213 447-4464**
8306 Wilshire Blvd Beverly Hills (90211) ***(P-714)***
Perkins Family Restaurant, North Hollywood *Also called Perkins* ***(P-7894)***
Perkowitz & Ruth Architects, Long Beach *Also called Rdc-S111 Inc* ***(P-22739)***
Permalite Plastics Corp.......E.......310 669-9492
3121 E Ana St Compton (90221) ***(P-5122)***
Permanente Medical Group Inc.......A.......310 325-5111
25825 Vermont Ave Harbor City (90710) ***(P-20022)***
Permaswage USA, Gardena *Also called Designed Metal Connections Inc* ***(P-10309)***
Perona Langer Beck A Prof Corp.......D.......562 426-6155
300 E San Antonio Dr Long Beach (90807) ***(P-21659)***
Perpetual Motion Group Inc.......F.......818 982-4300
11939 Sherman Rd North Hollywood (91605) ***(P-6648)***
Perr & Knight Inc (PA).......**D.......310 230-9339**
401 Wilshire Blvd Ste 300 Santa Monica (90401) ***(P-15612)***
Perricone Juices, Beaumont *Also called Beaumont Juice Inc* ***(P-1859)***
Perrin Bernard Supowitz LLC (HQ).......**D.......323 981-2800**
5496 Lindbergh Ln Bell (90201) ***(P-14224)***
Perris Valley AVI Svcs Inc.......D.......951 657-3904
2091 Goetz Rd Perris (92570) ***(P-17506)***
Perris Valley Cmnty Hosp LLC (PA).......**C.......951 436-5000**
2224 Medical Center Dr Perris (92571) ***(P-20887)***
Perris Valley Government Svcs, Perris *Also called Perris Valley AVI Svcs Inc* ***(P-17506)***
Perry Coast Construction Inc.......C.......951 774-0677
14130 Meridian Pkwy Riverside (92518) ***(P-807)***
Perseption, Vernon *Also called W & W Concept Inc* ***(P-3009)***
Persian Bks Englsh-Prsian Bks, Pacoima *Also called Ketab Corporation* ***(P-4186)***
Person & Covey Inc.......E.......818 937-5000
616 Allen Ave Glendale (91201) ***(P-5057)***
Personal Touch Clg & Maint Inc (PA).......**D.......949 727-4135**
340 Goddard Irvine (92618) ***(P-17274)***
Pertronix Inc (PA).......**E.......909 599-5955**
440 E Arrow Hwy San Dimas (91773) ***(P-10667)***
Pertronix Inc.......E.......909 599-5955
15601 Cypress Ave Unit B Irwindale (91706) ***(P-9828)***
Pest Options Inc.......D.......714 224-7378
135 N Manchester Ave Anaheim (92802) ***(P-17204)***
Pet Partners Inc (PA).......**C.......951 279-9888**
450 N Sheridan St Corona (92878) ***(P-11734)***
Petco Animal Sups Stores Inc.......F.......323 852-1370
8161 Beverly Blvd Los Angeles (90048) ***(P-14964)***
Peter Brasseler Holdings LLC.......D.......805 658-2643
4837 Mcgrath St Ventura (93003) ***(P-11042)***
Peter Brasseler Holdings LLC.......D.......805 650-5209
4837 Mcgrath St Ste J Ventura (93003) ***(P-13510)***
Peter Cohen Companies, Los Angeles *Also called Piet Retief Inc* ***(P-2984)***
Peter K Inc (PA).......**C.......323 585-5343**
5175 S Soto St Vernon (90058) ***(P-2982)***
Peter Wylan DDS.......D.......562 925-3765
10318 Rosecrans Ave Bellflower (90706) ***(P-20194)***
Petersen-Dean Inc.......D.......661 254-3322
21616 Golden Triangle Rd # 101 Santa Clarita (91350) ***(P-1501)***
Petersendean, Santa Clarita *Also called Petersen-Dean Inc* ***(P-1501)***
Peterson Bros Construction, Brea *Also called Pbc Pavers Inc* ***(P-1192)***
Peterson Bros Contruction Inc.......A.......714 278-0488
1560 W Lambert Rd Brea (92821) ***(P-1547)***
Peterson's Spices, Pico Rivera *Also called GPde Slva Spces Incrporation* ***(P-2447)***
Petit Ermitage, West Hollywood *Also called Valadon Hotel LLC* ***(P-16768)***
Petra Geotechnical Inc (PA).......**D.......714 549-8921**
3198 Arprt Loop Dr Ste A2 Costa Mesa (92626) ***(P-22636)***
Petra Risk Solutions (PA).......**D.......800 466-8951**
13950 Cerritos Corprt Dr A Cerritos (90703) ***(P-15613)***
Petra-1 LP.......F.......866 334-3702
12386 Osborne Pl Pacoima (91331) ***(P-5058)***
Petrelli Electric Inc.......D.......661 268-7312
11615 Davenport Rd Agua Dulce (91390) ***(P-1294)***
Petro-Lud Inc.......F.......661 747-4779
12625 Jomani Dr Ste 104 Bakersfield (93312) ***(P-436)***
Petrochem Insulation Inc.......D.......310 638-6663
19010 S Alameda St Compton (90221) ***(P-1394)***
Petrol Advertising Inc.......E.......323 644-3720
443 N Varney St Burbank (91502) ***(P-17044)***
Petroquip, Santa Ana *Also called G W Maintenance Inc* ***(P-13984)***
Pevelers Custom Interiors Inc.......F.......310 214-5049
4203 Spencer St Torrance (90503) ***(P-632)***
Pexco Aerospace Inc.......E.......714 894-9922
5451 Argosy Ave Huntington Beach (92649) ***(P-4707)***
Pexs International Inc.......C.......626 365-6706
1400 Midvale Ave Apt 408 Los Angeles (90024) ***(P-18211)***
Pezeme, Los Angeles *Also called Choon Inc* ***(P-2882)***
Pf Candle Co, Commerce *Also called Pommes Frites Candle Co* ***(P-11737)***
Pff Bancorp Inc (PA).......**A.......213 683-6393**
2058 N Mills Ave Ste 139 Claremont (91711) ***(P-15053)***
Pfister Faucets, Foothill Ranch *Also called Price Pfister Inc* ***(P-6564)***
Pfitech, Huntington Beach *Also called Precise Fit Limited One LLC* ***(P-17445)***
Pfs, Sylmar *Also called Professional Finishing Systems* ***(P-7176)***
PG&e, Avenal *Also called Pacific Gas and Electric Co* ***(P-12815)***
PG&e, San Luis Obispo *Also called Pacific Gas and Electric Co* ***(P-12816)***
PG&e, Avila Beach *Also called Pacific Gas and Electric Co* ***(P-12817)***
PG&e, Hinkley *Also called Pacific Gas and Electric Co* ***(P-12818)***
PG&e, Pismo Beach *Also called Pacific Gas and Electric Co* ***(P-12819)***
PG&e, Needles *Also called Pacific Gas and Electric Co* ***(P-12820)***

ALPHABETIC

PG&e, Bakersfield *Also called Pacific Gas and Electric Co* ***(P-12821)***

PG&e, Templeton *Also called Pacific Gas and Electric Co* ***(P-12822)***

Pgc Construction Inc ....E....760 549-4121
42309 Winchester Rd Ste C Temecula (92590) ***(P-633)***

Pgi Pacific Graphics Intl ....E....626 336-7707
14938 Nelson Ave City of Industry (91744) ***(P-4389)***

Pgs 360, City of Industry *Also called Prime Global Solutions Inc* ***(P-12510)***

PH Corporation ....F....949 646-7775
1718 Placentia Ave Costa Mesa (92627) ***(P-13659)***

PH Design, Commerce *Also called Pacific Hospitality Design Inc* ***(P-3630)***

Phantom Access Systems LLC ....F....949 753-1280
631 Wald Irvine (92618) ***(P-9898)***

Phaostron Instr Electronic Co, Azusa *Also called Phaostron Instr Electronic Co* ***(P-8903)***

Phaostron Instr Electronic Co ....D....626 969-6801
717 N Coney Ave Azusa (91702) ***(P-8903)***

Pharma Alliance Group Inc ....F....661 294-7955
28452 Constellation Rd Valencia (91355) ***(P-4871)***

Pharma Pac, Grover Beach *Also called H J Harkins Company Inc* ***(P-4828)***

Pharmaceutic Litho Label Inc ....D....805 285-5162
3990 Royal Ave Simi Valley (93063) ***(P-4872)***

Pharmaco Inc ....D....310 328-3897
19500 Normandie Ave Torrance (90502) ***(P-21202)***

Pharmaco-Kinesis Corporation ....E....310 641-2700
10604 S La Cienega Blvd Inglewood (90304) ***(P-11043)***

Pharmaskincare, Sun Valley *Also called Spa De Soleil Inc* ***(P-14291)***

Pharmatech Manufacturing Inc ....E....805 404-7169
4480 Shopping Ln Simi Valley (93063) ***(P-1804)***

Pharmavite LLC (HQ) ....**B....818 221-6200**
8531 Fallbrook Ave West Hills (91304) ***(P-4760)***

Pharr-Palomar Inc ....A....714 522-4811
6781 8th St Buena Park (90620) ***(P-2701)***

Phase 2 Cellars LLC ....E....805 782-0300
4910 Edna Rd San Luis Obispo (93401) ***(P-2212)***

Phase Four Inc ....F....310 648-8454
129 Sierra St El Segundo (90245) ***(P-10528)***

Phase Research, Costa Mesa *Also called Fire and Safety Elec Inc* ***(P-8952)***

PHC, Irvine *Also called Pacific Handy Cutter Inc* ***(P-6488)***

PHD Marketing Inc ....D....909 620-1000
1373 Ridgeway St Pomona (91768) ***(P-14965)***

Phelps Group ....E....310 752-4400
12121 W Bluff Dr Ste 200 Playa Vista (90094) ***(P-17045)***

Phelps United LLC ....D....657 212-8050
3183 Red Hill Ave Costa Mesa (92626) ***(P-13427)***

Phenix Enterprises Inc (PA) ....**E....909 469-0411**
1785 Mount Vernon Ave Pomona (91768) ***(P-9994)***

Phenix Technology Corporation ....E....951 272-4938
3453 Durahart St Riverside (92507) ***(P-8136)***

Phenix Truck Bodies and Eqp, Pomona *Also called Phenix Enterprises Inc* ***(P-9994)***

Phenomenex Inc (HQ) ....**C....310 212-0555**
411 Madrid Ave Torrance (90501) ***(P-10806)***

Phenomenon Mktg & Entrmt LLC (PA) ....**D....323 648-4000**
5900 Wilshire Blvd Fl 28 Los Angeles (90036) ***(P-23296)***

PHF II Burbank LLC ....C....818 843-6000
2500 N Hollywood Way Burbank (91505) ***(P-16628)***

Phg Engineering Services LLC ....D....714 283-8288
900 E Katella Ave Ste F Orange (92867) ***(P-22637)***

PHI (PA) ....**F....626 968-9680**
14955 Salt Lake Ave City of Industry (91746) ***(P-7763)***

PHI Hydraulics, City of Industry *Also called PHI* ***(P-7763)***

Phiaro Incorporated ....E....949 727-1261
9016 Research Dr Irvine (92618) ***(P-11735)***

Phibro-Tech Inc ....E....562 698-8036
8851 Dice Rd Santa Fe Springs (90670) ***(P-4667)***

Phifer Incorporated ....C....626 968-0438
14408 Nelson Ave City of Industry (91744) ***(P-7507)***

Phifer Western, City of Industry *Also called Phifer Incorporated* ***(P-7507)***

Phil Inter Pharma Usa Inc (PA) ....**F....909 982-3670**
8767 Lanyard Ct Rancho Cucamonga (91730) ***(P-4873)***

Philadelphia Gear, Santa Fe Springs *Also called Timken Gears & Services Inc* ***(P-7099)***

Philatron International (PA) ....**C....562 802-0452**
15315 Cornet St Santa Fe Springs (90670) ***(P-9899)***

Philip Morris USA Inc ....D....949 453-3500
185 Technology Dr Irvine (92618) ***(P-2550)***

Philips Elec N Amer Corp ....C....626 480-0755
13700 Live Oak Ave Baldwin Park (91706) ***(P-10855)***

Philips Med Systems Clvland In ....D....949 699-2300
1 Marconi Irvine (92618) ***(P-13511)***

Philips North America LLC ....C....909 574-1800
11201 Iberia St Ste A Jurupa Valley (91752) ***(P-9070)***

Philips Rs North America LLC ....F....562 483-6805
14101 Rosecrans Ave Ste F La Mirada (90638) ***(P-11135)***

Philips Tool & Die Inc ....E....909 947-8712
1620 S Marigold Ave Ontario (91761) ***(P-7823)***

Phillips 66 Co Carbon Group ....E....805 489-4050
2555 Willow Rd Arroyo Grande (93420) ***(P-7994)***

Phillips Bros Plastics Inc ....F....310 532-8020
17831 S Western Ave Gardena (90248) ***(P-5455)***

Phillips Machine & Wldg Co Inc ....E....626 855-4600
16125 Gale Ave City of Industry (91745) ***(P-18992)***

Phillips Plywood Co Inc ....D....818 897-7736
13599 Desmond St Pacoima (91331) ***(P-13281)***

Phillps-Mdisize Costa Mesa LLC ....C....949 477-9495
3545 Harbor Blvd Costa Mesa (92626) ***(P-11044)***

Philmont Management Inc ....D....213 380-0159
3450 Wilshire Blvd # 850 Los Angeles (90010) ***(P-808)***

Phiten Usa Inc (HQ) ....**E....310 225-4300**
22301 S Wstn Ave Ste 103 Torrance (90501) ***(P-16915)***

Phoenix Aerial Systems Inc ....F....323 577-3366
10131 National Blvd Los Angeles (90034) ***(P-10903)***

Phoenix Arms ....E....909 937-6900
4231 E Brickell St Ontario (91761) ***(P-7429)***

Phoenix Cars LLC ....E....909 987-0815
1500 Lakeview Loop Anaheim (92807) ***(P-9961)***

Phoenix Club Inc ....D....714 224-0194
1340 S Sanderson Ave Anaheim (92806) ***(P-22356)***

Phoenix Custom Packaging, Santa Fe Springs *Also called Camper Packaging LLC* ***(P-1788)***

Phoenix Engineering, Orange *Also called His Industries Inc* ***(P-8071)***

Phoenix Engineering Co Inc ....D....310 532-1134
2480 Armacost Ave Los Angeles (90064) ***(P-17507)***

Phoenix Engineering Tech LLC ....D....714 918-0630
17117 Leal Ave Cerritos (90703) ***(P-22638)***

Phoenix House Orange County ....C....714 953-9373
1207 E Fruit St Santa Ana (92701) ***(P-22144)***

Phoenix Houses Los Angeles Inc ....D....818 686-3000
11600 Eldridge Ave Lake View Terrace (91342) ***(P-22145)***

Phoenix Immigration & Educatn, Lompoc *Also called Citiznship Immigration Svcs US* ***(P-21531)***

Phoenix Motorcars, Anaheim *Also called Phoenix Cars LLC* ***(P-9961)***

Phoenix Personnel, Los Angeles *Also called Phoenix Engineering Co Inc* ***(P-17507)***

Phoenix Pumps California Inc ....E....858 278-2223
5143 Azusa Canyon Rd Baldwin Park (91706) ***(P-8019)***

Phoenix Satellite TV US Inc ....E....626 388-1188
3810 Durbin St Baldwin Park (91706) ***(P-12776)***

Phoenix Technologies Ltd (HQ) ....**E....408 570-1000**
150 S Los Robles Ave # 5 Pasadena (91101) ***(P-17956)***

Phoenix Textile Inc ....D....213 239-9640
910 S Los Angeles St Los Angeles (90015) ***(P-18632)***

Phoenix Textile Inc (PA) ....**D....310 715-7090**
14600 S Broadway Gardena (90248) ***(P-14313)***

Phone Check Solutions LLC ....B....310 365-1855
16027 Ventura Bllvd 605 Encino (91436) ***(P-17690)***

Phonepower, Northridge *Also called Quality Speaks LLC* ***(P-12666)***

Phonesuit, Santa Monica *Also called Gc Technology LLC* ***(P-9275)***

Phonesuit Inc ....E....310 774-0282
1431 7th St Ste 201 Santa Monica (90401) ***(P-9310)***

Photo Fabricators Inc ....D....818 781-1010
7648 Burnet Ave Van Nuys (91405) ***(P-9438)***

Photo Sciences Incorporated (PA) ....**E....310 634-1500**
2542 W 237th St Torrance (90505) ***(P-8290)***

Photonic Corp ....F....310 642-7975
5800 Uplander Way Ste 100 Culver City (90230) ***(P-4390)***

Photothermal Spectroscopy Corp ....F....805 730-3310
325 Chapala St Santa Barbara (93101) ***(P-10807)***

Photronics California, Burbank *Also called Photronics Inc* ***(P-11289)***

Photronics Inc (HQ) ....**B....203 740-5653**
2428 N Ontario St Burbank (91504) ***(P-11289)***

Phs Staffing, Seal Beach *Also called Premier Healthcare Svcs LLC* ***(P-17446***

Phx Investment Properties LLC ....E....949 474-7368
2532 Dupont Dr Irvine (92612) ***(P-18633)***

Phyllis Morris Originals (PA) ....**F....310 289-6868**
8772 Beverly Blvd West Hollywood (90048) ***(P-13147)***

Phyllis Morris Originals ....E....310 289-4800
655 N Robertson Blvd Los Angeles (90069) ***(P-13148)***

Physical Distribution Svc Inc (PA) ....**D....323 881-0886**
16000 Heron Ave La Mirada (90638) ***(P-12231)***

Physicans Dalysis Acquisitions (HQ) ....**E....310 536-2400**
601 Hawaii St El Segundo (90245) ***(P-21258)***

Physicans Formula Holdings Inc (HQ) ....**D....626 334-3395**
22067 Ferrero Walnut (91789) ***(P-5059)***

PHYSICIAN OFFICE SUPPORT SERVI, Torrance *Also called Torrance Health Assn Inc* ***(P-20978)***

Physician Support Systems Inc (HQ) ....**E....717 653-5340**
1131 W 6th St Ste 300 Ontario (91762) ***(P-22808)***

Physician Weblink MGT Svcs, Irvine *Also called Syntiro Healthcare Services* ***(P-23120)***

Physicians Automated Lab Inc (HQ) ....**D....661 325-0744**
820 34th St Ste 102 Bakersfield (93301) ***(P-21084)***

Physicians Automated Lab Inc ....D....661 325-0744
2920 F St Ste A2 Bakersfield (93301) ***(P-21085)***

Physicians Automated Lab Inc ....D....661 431-1176
9830 Brimhall Rd Unit 100 Bakersfield (93312) ***(P-20023)***

Physicians Automated Labs, Bakersfield *Also called Physicians Automated Lab Inc* ***(P-20023)***

Physicians Choice LLC ....D....818 340-9988
21860 Burbank Blvd # 120 Woodland Hills (91367) ***(P-22809)***

Physicians Choice HM Hlth Inc ....E....310 793-1616
3220 Sepulveda Blvd # 100 Torrance (90505) ***(P-21203)***

Physicians For Healthy Hospita ....B....951 679-8888
28400 Mccall Blvd Sun City (92585) ***(P-20888)***

Physicians Formula Inc (HQ) ....**D....626 334-3395**
22067 Ferrero City of Industry (91789) ***(P-5060)***

Physicians Formula Cosmt Inc ....D....626 334-3395
22067 Ferrero City of Industry (91789) ***(P-5061)***

Physicians Referral Service, Lancaster *Also called Lancaster Crdlgy Med Group Inc* ***(P-19956)***

Physpeed Corporation ....F....805 259-3101
4055 Mission Oaks Blvd Camarillo (93012) ***(P-9557)***

Phyto Tech Corp (PA) ....**E....949 635-1990**
30111 Tomas Rcho STA Marg (92688) ***(P-4874)***

PI Variables Inc ....F....949 415-9411
3002 Dow Ave Ste 138 Tustin (92780) ***(P-9348)***

Piazza Trucking, South Gate *Also called Samuel J Piazza & Son Inc* ***(P-12117)***

Pic Manufacturing Inc ....F....805 238-5451
410 Sherwood Rd Paso Robles (93446) ***(P-7924)***

Pickleback Nola LLC ....E....504 605-0911
1102 7th Pl Hermosa Beach (90254) ***(P-19162)***

Picnic At Ascot Inc ....E....310 674-3098
3237 W 131st St Hawthorne (90250) ***(P-3417)***

Mergent e-mail: customerrelations@mergent.com
1236
2022 Southern California Business Directory and Buyers Guide
(P-0000) Products & Services Section entry number
(PA)=Parent Co (HQ)=Headquarters (DH)=Div Headquarters

Picnic Time Inc ....E....805 529-7400
5131 Maureen Ln Moorpark (93021) ***(P-14966)***
Pico Cleaner Inc (PA) ....**D....310 274-2431**
9150 W Pico Blvd Los Angeles (90035) ***(P-16876)***
Pico Instruments LLC ....F....949 910-6448
23232 Peralta Dr Ste 121 Laguna Hills (92653) ***(P-9558)***
Pico Party Rents, Simi Valley *Also called Pico Rents Inc* ***(P-17367)***
Pico Pica Foods, Wilmington *Also called Juanitas Foods* ***(P-1852)***
Pico Rents Inc ....D....310 275-9431
4646 E Los Angeles Ave Simi Valley (93063) ***(P-17367)***
Pictsweet Company ....B....805 928-4414
732 Hanson Way Santa Maria (93458) ***(P-1935)***
Picture This Framing Inc ....F....714 447-8749
631 S State College Blvd Fullerton (92831) ***(P-3450)***
Pie Place ....D....626 963-9475
1175 E Alosta Ave Azusa (91702) ***(P-14717)***
Pie Rise Ltd ....E....310 832-4559
29051 S Western Ave Rancho Palos Verdes (90275) ***(P-2029)***
Pie Town Productions Inc ....D....818 255-9300
5433 Laurel Canyon Blvd North Hollywood (91607) ***(P-19163)***
Piecemaker's Country Store, Costa Mesa *Also called Piecemakers LLC* ***(P-14314)***
Piecemakers LLC ....E....714 641-3112
1720 Adams Ave Costa Mesa (92626) ***(P-14314)***
Piedmont Airlines Inc ....C....562 421-1806
4100 E Donald Douglas Dr Long Beach (90808) ***(P-12312)***
Piedras Machine Corporation ....F....562 602-1500
15154 Downey Ave Ste B Paramount (90723) ***(P-8740)***
Piege Co (PA) ....**D....818 727-9100**
20120 Plummer St Chatsworth (91311) ***(P-14345)***
Piehl, Joel J DDS, Hawthorne *Also called Schnierow Dental Care* ***(P-20198)***
Pieology Franchise LLC ....D....949 774-2380
2642 Michelle Dr Ste 100 Tustin (92780) ***(P-16216)***
Pieology Pizzeria, Tustin *Also called Pieology Franchise LLC* ***(P-16216)***
Pieper and Associates Inc ....D....310 515-5600
19823 Hamilton Ave Torrance (90502) ***(P-23383)***
Pier Pont Hotel LP ....E....805 643-6144
550 San Jon Rd Ventura (93001) ***(P-16629)***
Pierce Brothers (HQ) ....**D....818 763-9121**
10621 Victory Blvd North Hollywood (91606) ***(P-16925)***
Pierce-Spafford Metals Co Inc ....C....714 895-7756
7373 Hunt Ave Garden Grove (92841) ***(P-13585)***
Pierco, Eastvale *Also called Cal-Mold Incorporated* ***(P-5592)***
Pierco Incorporated ....F....909 251-7100
680 Main St Riverside (92501) ***(P-11736)***
Pierpont Inn Inc ....D....805 643-0245
550 San Jon Rd Ventura (93001) ***(P-16630)***
Pierre Landscape Inc ....C....626 587-2121
5455 2nd St Irwindale (91706) ***(P-275)***
Pierre Mitri (PA) ....**F....213 747-1838**
1138 Wall St Los Angeles (90015) ***(P-2983)***
Piet Retief Inc ....E....323 732-8312
1914 6th Ave Los Angeles (90018) ***(P-2984)***
Piezo-Metrics Inc (PA) ....**E....805 522-4676**
4584 Runway St Simi Valley (93063) ***(P-9559)***
Piggy Toes Press, Inglewood *Also called Intervisual Books Inc* ***(P-4131)***
Pih Health Inc (PA) ....**A....562 698-0811**
12401 Washington Blvd Whittier (90602) ***(P-20889)***
Pih Health Good Samaritan Hosp (HQ) ....**A....213 977-2121**
1225 Wilshire Blvd Los Angeles (90017) ***(P-20890)***
Pih Health Hospital - Downey (HQ) ....**A....562 698-0811**
11500 Brookshire Ave Downey (90241) ***(P-20891)***
Pih Health Hospital - Whitti ....A....562 904-5482
11500 Brookshire Ave Downey (90241) ***(P-20892)***
Pih Health Whittier Hospital (PA) ....**A....562 698-0811**
12401 Washington Blvd Whittier (90602) ***(P-20893)***
Pilgrim Operations LLC ....B....818 478-4500
12020 Chanl Blvd Ste 200 North Hollywood (91607) ***(P-13348)***
Pilgrim Place In Claremont (PA) ....**C....909 399-5500**
625 Mayflower Rd Claremont (91711) ***(P-20623)***
Pilot Automotive, City of Industry *Also called Pilot Inc* ***(P-12232)***
Pilot Inc (PA) ....**D....626 937-6988**
13000 Temple Ave City of Industry (91746) ***(P-12232)***
Pilot Painting & Construction, Cypress *Also called Power Maintenance Services Inc* ***(P-1193)***
Pimco, Newport Beach *Also called Pacific Investment MGT Co LLC* ***(P-16143)***
Pimco Global Advisors LLC (HQ) ....**D....949 219-2200**
840 Nwport Ctr Dr Ste 100 Newport Beach (92660) ***(P-16144)***
Pimco Mortgage Income Tr Inc ....B....949 720-6000
650 Newport Center Dr Newport Beach (92660) ***(P-16193)***
Pin Concepts, Sun Valley *Also called Pincraft Inc* ***(P-11490)***
Pincraft Inc ....E....818 248-0077
7933 Ajay Dr Sun Valley (91352) ***(P-11490)***
Pindler & Pindler Inc (PA) ....**D....805 531-9090**
11910 Poindexter Ave Moorpark (93021) ***(P-14315)***
Pine Grove Hospital Corp ....C....818 348-0500
9449 San Fernando Rd Sun Valley (91352) ***(P-21026)***
Pinecraft Custom Shutters Inc ....F....949 642-9317
946 W 17th St Costa Mesa (92627) ***(P-3281)***
Pinegrove Industries Inc ....E....805 485-3700
2001 Cabot Pl Oxnard (93030) ***(P-4391)***
Pinky Los Angeles, Burbank *Also called Vesture Group Incorporated* ***(P-3047)***
Pinnacle Communication Svcs, Glendale *Also called Pinnacle Networking Svcs Inc* ***(P-1295)***
Pinnacle Contracting Corp ....E....818 888-6548
21800 Burbank Blvd # 210 Woodland Hills (91367) ***(P-809)***
Pinnacle Escrow Company, Northridge *Also called Pinnacle Estate Properties* ***(P-15949)***
Pinnacle Estate Properties (PA) ....**C....818 993-4707**
9137 Reseda Blvd Northridge (91324) ***(P-15949)***
Pinnacle Housing, Fort Irwin *Also called Pinnacle Irwin LLC* ***(P-15950)***
Pinnacle Irwin LLC (PA) ....**D....760 386-4663**
4553 Tippecanoe St Fort Irwin (92310) ***(P-15950)***
Pinnacle Networking Svcs Inc ....D....818 241-6009
730 Fairmont Ave Glendale (91203) ***(P-1295)***
Pinnacle Precision Shtmtl Corp (PA) ....**C....714 777-3129**
5410 E La Palma Ave Anaheim (92807) ***(P-6891)***
Pinnacle Rvrside Hspitality LP ....C....951 784-8000
3400 Market St Riverside (92501) ***(P-16631)***
Pinnacle Travel Services LLC ....C....310 414-1787
390 N Pacific Coast Hwy El Segundo (90245) ***(P-12395)***
Pinnacle Veterinary Center, Santa Clarita *Also called Delphic Enterprises Inc* ***(P-198)***
Pinner Construction Co Inc (PA) ....**D....714 490-4000**
1255 S Lewis St Anaheim (92805) ***(P-810)***
Pinnpack Packaging LLC (HQ) ....**D....805 385-4100**
875 Michigan Ave Riverside (92507) ***(P-5744)***
Pioneer Broach Company (PA) ....**E....323 728-1263**
6434 Telegraph Rd Commerce (90040) ***(P-7862)***
Pioneer Circuits Inc ....B....714 641-3132
3000 S Shannon St Santa Ana (92704) ***(P-9439)***
Pioneer Custom Elec Pdts Corp ....D....562 944-0626
10640 Springdale Ave Santa Fe Springs (90670) ***(P-8882)***
Pioneer Diecasters Inc ....F....323 245-6561
4209 Chevy Chase Dr Los Angeles (90039) ***(P-6370)***
Pioneer Medical Group Inc ....D....562 867-8681
10230 Artesia Blvd # 300 Bellflower (90706) ***(P-20894)***
Pioneer Medical Group Inc ....D....562 597-4181
2220 Clark Ave Long Beach (90815) ***(P-20895)***
Pioneer North America Inc (HQ) ....**F....310 952-2000**
2050 W 190th St Ste 100 Torrance (90504) ***(P-13691)***
Pioneer Packing Inc (PA) ....**E....714 540-9751**
2430 S Grand Ave Santa Ana (92705) ***(P-14225)***
Pioneer Photo Albums Inc (PA) ....**C....818 882-2161**
9801 Deering Ave Chatsworth (91311) ***(P-4611)***
Pioneer Sands LLC ....E....661 746-5789
9952 Enos Ln Bakersfield (93314) ***(P-577)***
Pioneer Sands LLC ....E....949 728-0171
31302 Ortega Hwy San Juan Capistrano (92675) ***(P-578)***
Pioneer Theatres Inc ....C....310 532-8183
2500 Redondo Beach Blvd Torrance (90504) ***(P-18634)***
Pioneer Trading Inc ....E....562 531-3842
6305 Alondra Blvd Paramount (90723) ***(P-14718)***
Pioneers Mem Healthcare Dst (PA) ....**A....760 351-3333**
207 W Legion Rd Brawley (92227) ***(P-20896)***
PIONEERS MEMORIAL HOSPITAL, Brawley *Also called Pioneers Mem Healthcare Dst* ***(P-20896)***
PIP PRINTING, Mission Viejo *Also called Postal Instant Press Inc* ***(P-4392)***
PIP Printing, Downey *Also called Jeb-Phi Inc* ***(P-4343)***
PIP Printing, Riverside *Also called Mainstreet Communications Inc* ***(P-17152)***
PIP Printing, Hemet *Also called Jsm Productions Inc* ***(P-4344)***
Pipe Dream Products, Chatsworth *Also called Pd Liquidation Inc* ***(P-14963)***
Pipe Dream Products, Chatsworth *Also called Pd Products LLC* ***(P-2735)***
Pipe Restoration Inc ....E....714 564-7600
3122 W Alpine St Santa Ana (92704) ***(P-1117)***
Pipeline, Rllng HLS Est *Also called Graphic Prints Inc* ***(P-3174)***
Pipeline Group LLC ....C....949 296-8375
2850 Redhill Ave Ste 110 Santa Ana (92705) ***(P-23088)***
Pipeline Health LLC (PA) ....**B....310 379-2134**
111 N Sepulveda Blvd # 21 Manhattan Beach (90266) ***(P-20897)***
Pipeline Restoration Plbg Inc ....E....949 510-2281
2700 S Main St Santa Ana (92707) ***(P-1118)***
Pipeliner Crm ....F....424 280-6445
15243 La Cruz Dr Unit 492 Pacific Palisades (90272) ***(P-17957)***
Pipelinersales Corporation (PA) ....**E....888 843-6699**
15243 La Cruz Dr Unit 492 Pacific Palisades (90272) ***(P-17958)***
PIPLINE, Oxnard *Also called West Coast Wldg & Piping Inc* ***(P-19004)***
Pipsticks Inc ....E....805 439-1692
1304 Garden St Ste 1 San Luis Obispo (93401) ***(P-3917)***
Pircher Nichols & Meeks (PA) ....**D....310 201-0132**
1925 Century Park E # 1700 Los Angeles (90067) ***(P-21660)***
Pirtek Sfo, Indian Wells *Also called Hart Sales LLC* ***(P-7903)***
Pismo Beach Ht Investments LLC ....E....805 773-1011
147 Stimson Ave Pismo Beach (93449) ***(P-16632)***
Pismo Coast Village Inc ....D....805 773-1811
165 S Dolliver St Pismo Beach (93449) ***(P-16633)***
Pitbull Gym Incorporated ....F....909 980-7960
10782 Edison Ct Rancho Cucamonga (91730) ***(P-5745)***
Pitman Family Farms ....D....559 585-3330
10365 Iona Ave Hanford (93230) ***(P-1973)***
Pittman Outdoors, Placentia *Also called Pittman Products Intl Inc* ***(P-5746)***
Pittman Products Intl Inc ....F....562 926-6660
650 S Jefferson St Ste D Placentia (92870) ***(P-5746)***
Pitts & Bachmann Realtors Inc ....D....805 969-5005
1482 E Valley Rd Ste 44 Santa Barbara (93108) ***(P-15951)***
Pitts & Bachmann Realtors Inc ....D....805 963-1391
1436 State St Santa Barbara (93101) ***(P-15952)***
Pivot Interiors Inc ....D....949 988-5400
3200 Park Center Dr # 100 Costa Mesa (92626) ***(P-1296)***
Pivot Technology Solutions ....C....714 845-4547
15461 Springdale St Huntington Beach (92649) ***(P-18212)***
Pixelogic Media Partners LLC (HQ) ....**C....818 861-2001**
4000 W Alameda Ave # 110 Burbank (91505) ***(P-19244)***
Pixi Inc ....D....310 670-7767
10351 Santa Monica Blvd # 410 Los Angeles (90025) ***(P-14279)***
Pixi Beauty, Los Angeles *Also called Pixi Inc* ***(P-14279)***
Pixior LLC (PA) ....**C....323 721-2221**
5901 S Eastern Ave Commerce (90040) ***(P-18635)***
Pjbs Holdings Inc (PA) ....**D....661 822-5273**
1401 Goodrick Dr Tehachapi (93561) ***(P-12965)***

ALPHABETIC

Employee Codes: A=Over 500 employees, B=251-500 C=101-250, D=51-100, E=20-50 F=10-19
2022 Southern California Business Directory and Buyers Guide
© Mergent Inc. 1-800-342-5647
1237

Pjy Inc ....E 323 583-7737
3251 Leonis Blvd Vernon (90058) ***(P-2585)***

Pl Development, Lynwood *Also called P & L Development LLC* ***(P-4867)***

Placentia Linda Hospital, Placentia *Also called Tenet Healthsystem Medical Inc* ***(P-21055)***

Plan Member Financial Corp ....D 800 874-6910
6187 Carpinteria Ave Carpinteria (93013) ***(P-15340)***

Planet Green Cartridges Inc ....D 818 725-2596
20724 Lassen St Chatsworth (91311) ***(P-11481)***

Planetizen Inc ....E 877 260-7526
3530 Wilshire Blvd # 1285 Los Angeles (90010) ***(P-4194)***

Planmember Services, Carpinteria *Also called Plan Member Financial Corp* ***(P-15340)***

Planned Parenthood Los Angeles (PA) ....**D 213 284-3200**
400 W 30th St Los Angeles (90007) ***(P-21325)***

Planned Prnthood Cal Cntl Cast (PA) ....**D 805 963-2445**
518 Garden St Santa Barbara (93101) ***(P-21326)***

Plannet Consulting LLC ....D 714 982-5800
180 N Rverview Dr Ste 240 Anaheim (92808) ***(P-18213)***

Plant 16, Van Nuys *Also called Weststar Cinemas Inc* ***(P-19290)***

Plant 2, Harbor City *Also called Hansen Engineering Co* ***(P-10343)***

Plant Ranch LLC ....F 818 384-9727
242 N Avenue 25 Ste 114 Los Angeles (90031) ***(P-2509)***

Plantation Golf Club Inc ....D 760 775-3688
50994 Monroe St Indio (92201) ***(P-19599)***

Plantel Nurseries Inc ....D 805 349-8952
2775 E Clark Ave Santa Maria (93455) ***(P-14894)***

Plantel Nurseries Inc (PA) ....**E 805 349-8952**
2775 E Clark Ave Santa Maria (93455) ***(P-91)***

Plantel Nurseries Inc ....C 805 934-4300
3990 Foxen Canyon Rd Santa Maria (93454) ***(P-92)***

Plantel Tranplanting Services, Santa Maria *Also called Plantel Nurseries Inc* ***(P-91)***

Planters Hay Inc ....D 760 344-0620
1295 E St 78 Brawley (92227) ***(P-14866)***

Plas-Tal Manufacturing Co, Santa Fe Springs *Also called Brunton Enterprises Inc* ***(P-6593)***

Plas-Tech Sealing Tech LLC ....F 951 737-2228
252 Mariah Cir Fl 2 Corona (92879) ***(P-5190)***

Plascor Inc ....C 951 328-1010
972 Columbia Ave Riverside (92507) ***(P-5478)***

Plasidyne Engineering & Mfg ....E 562 531-0510
3230 E 59th St Long Beach (90805) ***(P-5747)***

Plaskolite West LLC ....E 310 637-2103
2225 E Del Amo Blvd Compton (90220) ***(P-4708)***

Plasma Biolife Services L P ....E 951 497-4407
23727 Sunnymead Blvd Moreno Valley (92553) ***(P-14280)***

Plasma Biolife Services L P ....E 909 863-3025
2065 E Highland Ave San Bernardino (92404) ***(P-21471)***

Plasma Coating Corporation ....E 310 532-1951
1900 W Walnut St Compton (90220) ***(P-7398)***

Plasma Coating Tech Inc ....F 661 670-8810
24971 Avenue Stanford Valencia (91355) ***(P-7399)***

Plasma Division, Corona *Also called PVA Tepla America Inc* ***(P-8750)***

Plasma Rggedized Solutions Inc ....E 714 893-6063
5452 Business Dr Huntington Beach (92649) ***(P-7294)***

Plasma Technology Incorporated (PA) ....**D 310 320-3373**
1754 Crenshaw Blvd Torrance (90501) ***(P-7400)***

Plasthec Molding Inc ....E 909 947-4267
1945 S Grove Ave Ontario (91761) ***(P-5748)***

Plastic and Metal Center Inc ....E 949 770-0610
23162 La Cadena Dr Laguna Hills (92653) ***(P-5749)***

Plastic Dress-Up, North Hollywood *Also called Pdu Lad Corporation* ***(P-7394)***

Plastic Dress-Up Company ....D 626 442-7711
11077 Rush St South El Monte (91733) ***(P-5750)***

Plastic Engineering Tech LLC ....E 909 390-1323
4502 Brickell Privado St Ontario (91761) ***(P-5751)***

Plastic Fabrication Tech LLC ....F 773 509-1700
2320 E Cherry Indus Cir Long Beach (90805) ***(P-5752)***

Plastic Innovations Inc ....F 951 361-0251
10513 San Sevaine Way Jurupa Valley (91752) ***(P-5456)***

Plastic Mart Inc ....F 310 268-1404
43535 Gadsden Ave Ste F Lancaster (93534) ***(P-4709)***

Plastic Processing Co, Gardena *Also called Narayan Corporation* ***(P-5477)***

Plastic Processing Corp ....F 310 719-7330
13432 Estrella Ave Gardena (90248) ***(P-5753)***

Plastic Sales Southern Inc ....E 714 375-7900
425 Havana Ave Long Beach (90814) ***(P-14760)***

Plastic Specialties & Tech Inc ....C 909 869-8069
19555 Arenth Ave City of Industry (91748) ***(P-5754)***

Plastic Technologies Inc ....E 951 360-6055
4720 Felspar St Riverside (92509) ***(P-5755)***

Plastic Tops Inc ....F 714 738-8128
521 E Jamie Ave La Habra (90631) ***(P-3691)***

Plasticbagsonsalecom Inc ....F 951 710-1340
4023 Trail Creek Rd Riverside (92505) ***(P-14226)***

Plasticolor Molded Pdts Inc (PA) ....**C 714 525-3880**
801 S Acacia Ave Fullerton (92831) ***(P-5457)***

Plastics Development Corp ....E 949 492-0217
960 Calle Negocio San Clemente (92673) ***(P-5756)***

Plastics Plus Technology Inc ....E 909 747-0555
1495 Research Dr Redlands (92374) ***(P-5757)***

Plastics Research Corporation ....D 909 391-9050
1400 S Campus Ave Ontario (91761) ***(P-5458)***

Plastifab Inc ....E 909 596-1927
1425 Palomares St La Verne (91750) ***(P-5459)***

Plastifab/Leed Plastics, La Verne *Also called Plastifab Inc* ***(P-5459)***

Plastiject LLC ....F 562 926-6705
14811 Spring Ave Santa Fe Springs (90670) ***(P-5758)***

Plastique Unique Inc ....E 310 839-3968
3383 Livonia Ave Los Angeles (90034) ***(P-5759)***

Plasto Tech International Inc ....E 949 458-1880
4 Autry Irvine (92618) ***(P-5760)***

Plastoker Inc ....F 714 598-5920
1690 Scenic Ave Costa Mesa (92626) ***(P-5761)***

Plastopan Industries Inc (PA) ....**E 323 231-2225**
812 E 59th St Los Angeles (90001) ***(P-3838)***

Plastpro 2000 Inc (PA) ....**C 310 693-8600**
5200 W Century Blvd Fl 9 Los Angeles (90045) ***(P-5762)***

Plastpro Doors, Los Angeles *Also called Plastpro 2000 Inc* ***(P-5762)***

Plasvacc USA Inc ....F 805 434-0321
1535 Templeton Rd Templeton (93465) ***(P-11045)***

Plateronics Processing Inc ....E 818 341-2191
9164 Independence Ave Chatsworth (91311) ***(P-7295)***

Platescan Inc ....F 949 851-1600
20101 Sw Birch St Ste 250 Newport Beach (92660) ***(P-7174)***

Plating, Chatsworth *Also called Electro Adapter Inc* ***(P-9034)***

Platinum, Fullerton *Also called Ultra Wheel Company* ***(P-10148)***

Platinum Boss Intl Intllgnce L ....D 818 416-5216
18735 Gilmore St Reseda (91335) ***(P-18310)***

Platinum Boss Intl Prtction Sv ....E 818 416-5216
18735 Gilmore St Reseda (91335) ***(P-18311)***

Platinum Clg Indianapolis LLC ....B 310 584-8000
1522 2nd St Santa Monica (90401) ***(P-17275)***

Platinum Disc LLC ....D 608 784-6620
10203 Santa Monica Blvd # 5 Los Angeles (90067) ***(P-14174)***

Platinum Distribution, Yorba Linda *Also called Nasco Gourmet Foods Inc* ***(P-1869)***

Platinum Empire Group Inc ....C 310 821-5888
2430 Amsler St Ste B Torrance (90505) ***(P-17508)***

Platinum Equity Partners LLC ....D 310 712-1850
360 N Crescent Dr South Beverly Hills (90210) ***(P-16161)***

Platinum Group Companies Inc (PA) ....**C 818 721-3800**
22560 La Quilla Dr Chatsworth (91311) ***(P-16107)***

Platinum Healthcare Staffing, Torrance *Also called Platinum Empire Group Inc* ***(P-17508)***

Platinum Landscape Inc ....C 760 200-3673
42575 Melanie Pl Ste C Palm Desert (92211) ***(P-276)***

Platinum Performance Inc ....D 800 553-2400
760 Mcmurray Rd Buellton (93427) ***(P-18798)***

Platinum Performance Inc (HQ) ....**E 800 553-2400**
90 Thomas Rd Buellton (93427) ***(P-14281)***

Platinum Roofing Inc ....D 408 280-5028
11500 W Olympic Blvd # 530 Los Angeles (90064) ***(P-1502)***

Platinum Visual Systems, Corona *Also called ABC School Equipment Inc* ***(P-13532)***

Plaxicon Co, Rancho Cucamonga *Also called Plaxicon Holding Corporation* ***(P-5479)***

Plaxicon Holding Corporation ....A 909 944-6868
10660 Acacia St Rancho Cucamonga (91730) ***(P-5479)***

Playa Proper Jv LLC ....D 310 645-0400
8639 Lincoln Blvd Los Angeles (90045) ***(P-16634)***

Playboy Enterprises Inc ....D 310 424-1800
10960 Wilshire Blvd Fl 22 Los Angeles (90024) ***(P-4097)***

Playboy Enterprises Inc (HQ) ....**B 310 424-1800**
10960 Wilshire Blvd Fl 22 Los Angeles (90024) ***(P-4098)***

Playboy Enterprises Intl ....D 310 424-1800
10960 Wilshire Blvd Fl 22 Los Angeles (90024) ***(P-4195)***

Playboy Entrmt Group Inc (HQ) ....**C 323 276-4000**
2300 W Empire Ave Burbank (91504) ***(P-19164)***

Playboy Jewelry, Los Angeles *Also called Lucas Design International Inc* ***(P-4132)***

Players West Amusements Inc (PA) ....**C 805 983-1400**
2360 Sturgis Rd Ste A Oxnard (93030) ***(P-19513)***

Playhouse Dental (PA) ....**D 323 269-5437**
3000 Whittier Blvd Los Angeles (90023) ***(P-20195)***

Playhut Inc ....E 909 869-8083
18560 San Jose Ave City of Industry (91748) ***(P-11389)***

Playmax Surfacing Inc ....F 951 250-6039
1950 Compton Ave Ste 111 Corona (92881) ***(P-5398)***

Plaza De La Raza Child Dev Svc (PA) ....**D 562 776-1301**
13300 Crssrds Pkwy N 44 440 N La Puente (91746) ***(P-22048)***

Plaza De La Raza Child Develop ....D 323 224-1788
225 N Avenue 25 Los Angeles (90031) ***(P-22049)***

Plaza De La Raza Child Develop ....D 562 695-1070
6411 Norwalk Blvd Whittier (90606) ***(P-22050)***

PLC Imports Inc ....E 818 349-1600
9667 Owensmouth Ave # 201 Chatsworth (91311) ***(P-13660)***

PLD Enterprises Inc ....D 213 626-4444
440 Stanford Ave Los Angeles (90013) ***(P-14578)***

Pleasant Hawaiian Holiday, Westlake Village *Also called Pleasant Holidays LLC* ***(P-12396)***

Pleasant Holidays LLC (HQ) ....**B 818 991-3390**
2404 Townsgate Rd Westlake Village (91361) ***(P-12396)***

Plexi Fab Inc ....F 714 447-8494
1142 E Elm Ave Fullerton (92831) ***(P-5763)***

Plexicor Inc (PA) ....**E 714 918-8700**
3598 Cadillac Ave Costa Mesa (92626) ***(P-18395)***

Plh Products Inc ....B 714 739-6622
10541 Calle Lee Ste 119 Los Alamitos (90720) ***(P-3429)***

Plott Family Care Centers, Riverside *Also called Orangetree Convalescent Hosp* ***(P-20876)***

Plott Family Home Care, San Bernardino *Also called Plott Management Co* ***(P-20441)***

Plott Management Co ....D 909 883-0288
264 E 18th St San Bernardino (92404) ***(P-20441)***

Plowboy Landscapes Inc ....D 805 643-4966
2190 N Ventura Ave Ventura (93001) ***(P-337)***

Pls Diabetic Shoe Company Inc ....E 818 734-7080
21500 Osborne St Canoga Park (91304) ***(P-5312)***

Plt Enterprises Inc ....D 805 389-5335
809 Calle Plano Camarillo (93012) ***(P-9044)***

Pluckys Dump Rental LLC ....E 323 540-3510
10136 Bowman Ave South Gate (90280) ***(P-6747)***

Plugg ME LNc ....E 949 705-4472
18100 Von Karman Ave # 850 Irvine (92612) ***(P-17959)***

Plum Creek Timberlands LP ....C 909 949-2255
615 N Benson Ave Upland (91786) ***(P-3212)***

Plum Healthcare Group LLC ....D 909 793-2609
1620 W Fern Ave Redlands (92373) ***(P-18636)***

Plumbing Master, Riverside *Also called Lozano Plumbing Services Inc* ***(P-1096)***
Plumbing Piping & Cnstr Inc ....D....714 821-0490
5950 Lakeshore Dr Cypress (90630) ***(P-1119)***
Plumbing Products Company Inc ....F....760 343-3306
77551 El Duna Ct Ste I Palm Desert (92211) ***(P-6563)***
Plumbing Systems West Inc ....D....909 794-3823
31491 Outer Highway 10 Redlands (92373) ***(P-1120)***
Plumbingandfire Inc ....E....818 764-9800
11120 Sherman Way Sun Valley (91352) ***(P-13835)***
Plus Products, Adelanto *Also called Carberry LLC* ***(P-11649)***
Plush Home Inc ....F....323 852-1912
6507 Lindenhurst Ave Los Angeles (90048) ***(P-3485)***
Plustek Technology Inc ....F....714 670-7713
9830 Norwalk Blvd Ste 155 Santa Fe Springs (90670) ***(P-8291)***
Pluto Inc (HQ) ....**D....323 746-0500**
6100 Wilshire Blvd # 1550 Los Angeles (90048) ***(P-19165)***
Pluto TV, Los Angeles *Also called Pluto Inc* ***(P-19165)***
Plycraft Industries Inc ....C....323 587-8101
2100 E Slauson Ave Huntington Park (90255) ***(P-3353)***
Plymouth Christian School, Whittier *Also called Plymouth Congregational Church* ***(P-22051)***
Plymouth Congregational Church ....D....562 692-1228
12058 Beverly Blvd Whittier (90601) ***(P-22051)***
Plymouth Village, Redlands *Also called Humangood Norcal* ***(P-20597)***
PM Realty Group LP ....D....949 390-5500
3 Park Plz Ste 450 Irvine (92614) ***(P-15690)***
PM Realty Group LP ....D....949 553-8246
4680 Macarthur Ct Newport Beach (92660) ***(P-15953)***
Pmac Lending Services Inc (PA) ....**D....909 614-2000**
6 Pointe Dr Ste 150 Brea (92821) ***(P-15226)***
Pmb Motorcars LLC (HQ) ....**D....626 859-1200**
2010 E Garvey Ave S West Covina (91791) ***(P-18861)***
PMBC, Costa Mesa *Also called Pacific Mercantile Bank* ***(P-15035)***
Pmc Inc (HQ) ....**A....818 896-1101**
12243 Branford St Sun Valley (91352) ***(P-10393)***
PMC Capital Partners LLC ....A....818 896-1101
12243 Branford St Sun Valley (91352) ***(P-16284)***
PMC Global Inc (PA) ....**B....818 896-1101**
12243 Branford St Sun Valley (91352) ***(P-5515)***
PMC Leaders In Chemicals Inc (HQ) ....**C....818 896-1101**
12243 Branford St Sun Valley (91352) ***(P-5516)***
Pmd Industries Inc ....E....949 222-0999
703 Randolph Ave Costa Mesa (92626) ***(P-1297)***
Pmic, Los Angeles *Also called Practice Management Info Corp* ***(P-4135)***
Pmk-Bnc Inc (PA) ....**D....310 854-0455**
1840 Century Park E # 1400 Los Angeles (90067) ***(P-23384)***
Pmk-Bnc Inc ....E....310 854-4800
8687 Melrose Ave Fl 8th Los Angeles (90069) ***(P-23385)***
Pml Inc ....D....310 671-4345
201 W Beach Ave Inglewood (90302) ***(P-18637)***
Pmp Products Inc ....F....310 549-5122
19827 Hamilton Ave Torrance (90502) ***(P-5895)***
Pmr Precision Mfg & Rbr Co Inc ....E....909 605-7525
1330 Etiwanda Ave Ontario (91761) ***(P-5399)***
Pmt Crdit Risk Trnsf Tr 2015-2 ....D....818 224-7442
3043 Townsgate Rd Westlake Village (91361) ***(P-16194)***
PNa Construction Tech Inc ....E....661 326-1700
301 Espee St Ste E Bakersfield (93301) ***(P-6892)***
PNC Proactive Nthrn Cont LLC ....E....909 390-5624
602 S Rockefeller Ave A Ontario (91761) ***(P-3825)***
Pneudraulics Inc ....B....909 980-5366
8575 Helms Ave Rancho Cucamonga (91730) ***(P-10635)***
Pneumatic Tube Carrier, Duarte *Also called Lee Machine Products* ***(P-7812)***
Png Builders ....D....626 256-9539
2392 Bateman Ave Duarte (91010) ***(P-665)***
Pnk Enterprises Inc ....E....818 765-3770
12901 Saticoy St North Hollywood (91605) ***(P-7567)***
Pnmac Gmsr Issuer Trust ....A....818 746-2271
3043 Townsgate Rd Westlake Village (91361) ***(P-16195)***
Pnmac Holdings Inc (HQ) ....**B....818 224-7442**
3043 Townsgate Rd Westlake Village (91361) ***(P-15227)***
Pocino Foods Company ....D....626 968-8000
14250 Lomitas Ave City of Industry (91746) ***(P-1745)***
Poetry Corporation (PA) ....**E....213 765-8957**
2111 Long Beach Ave Los Angeles (90058) ***(P-2906)***
Point Conception Inc ....E....949 589-6890
23121 Arroyo Vis Ste A Rcho STA Marg (92688) ***(P-2985)***
Point360 (PA) ....**C....818 565-1400**
2701 Media Center Dr Los Angeles (90065) ***(P-19245)***
Pointdirect Transport Inc ....D....909 371-0837
10858 Almond Ave Fontana (92337) ***(P-12073)***
Polagram, Los Angeles *Also called Wellmade Inc* ***(P-23364)***
Polar Tankers Inc ....C....310 519-8260
60 Berth San Pedro (90731) ***(P-12277)***
Polar Tankers Inc (HQ) ....**D....562 388-1400**
300 Oceangate Long Beach (90802) ***(P-12278)***
Polaris E-Commerce Inc ....E....714 907-0582
1941 E Occidental St Santa Ana (92705) ***(P-8020)***
Polaris Music, Los Angeles *Also called Eti Systems* ***(P-10692)***
Polaris Sales Inc ....F....951 343-9270
12885 Wildflower Ln Riverside (92503) ***(P-6649)***
Pole Position Raceway Inc (PA) ....**D....951 817-5032**
1594 E Bentley Dr Corona (92879) ***(P-19434)***
Poliseek Ais Insur Sltions Inc ....D....866 480-7335
17785 Center Court Dr N # 25 Cerritos (90703) ***(P-15614)***
Polishing The Professional, Culver City *Also called Davina Douthard Inc* ***(P-23431)***
Polk Street Offices, Riverside *Also called Kaiser Foundation Hospitals* ***(P-20225)***
Polley Inc (PA) ....**F....562 868-9861**
11936 Front St Norwalk (90650) ***(P-8137)***
Pollo Campero, Los Angeles *Also called Adir Restaurants Corp* ***(P-16200)***
Pollstar LLC ....D....559 271-7900
1100 Glendon Ave Ste 2100 Los Angeles (90024) ***(P-4099)***
Pollstar.com, Los Angeles *Also called Pollstar LLC* ***(P-4099)***
Pollution Ctrl Specialists Inc ....F....949 474-0137
1354 Ritchey St Santa Ana (92705) ***(P-8052)***
Pollys 208, Huntington Beach *Also called Pollys Pies Inc* ***(P-14719)***
Pollys Pies Inc ....D....714 964-4424
9791 Adams Ave Huntington Beach (92646) ***(P-14719)***
Polsinelli LLP, Los Angeles *Also called Polsinelli PC* ***(P-21661)***
Polsinelli PC ....D....310 556-1801
2049 Century Park E Los Angeles (90067) ***(P-21661)***
Poly-Fiber Inc (PA) ....**F....951 684-4280**
4343 Fort Dr Riverside (92509) ***(P-5107)***
Poly-Tainer Inc (PA) ....**C....805 526-3424**
450 W Los Angeles Ave Simi Valley (93065) ***(P-5480)***
Polyalloys Injected Metals Inc ....D....310 715-9800
14000 Avalon Blvd Los Angeles (90061) ***(P-7661)***
Polycarbin Inc (PA) ....**D....203 615-3797**
2640 N San Fernando Rd Los Angeles (90065) ***(P-4710)***
Polycell Packaging Corporation ....E....562 483-6000
12851 Midway Pl Cerritos (90703) ***(P-14967)***
Polycraft Inc ....E....951 296-0860
42075 Avenida Alvarado Temecula (92590) ***(P-4556)***
Polyfet Rf Devices Inc ....E....805 484-9582
1110 Avenida Acaso Camarillo (93012) ***(P-9560)***
Polymasters Industries Inc ....F....213 564-7824
2821 Century Blvd South Gate (90280) ***(P-5764)***
Polymer Concepts Tech Inc ....F....760 240-4999
13522 Manhasset Rd Apple Valley (92308) ***(P-5348)***
Polymer Logistics Inc ....D....951 567-2900
1725 Sierra Ridge Dr Riverside (92507) ***(P-5765)***
Polymerpak LLC ....C....559 651-1965
6941 W Goshen Ave Visalia (93291) ***(P-5766)***
Polypeptide Laboratories Inc (HQ) ....**D....310 782-3569**
365 Maple Ave Torrance (90503) ***(P-21086)***
Polytech Color & Compounding ....F....909 923-7008
847 S Wanamaker Ave Ontario (91761) ***(P-5767)***
Polytechnic School ....B....626 792-2147
1030 E California Blvd Pasadena (91106) ***(P-22052)***
Polytex Manufacturing Inc (PA) ....**F....323 726-0140**
1140 S Hope St Los Angeles (90015) ***(P-2704)***
Pom Medical LLC ....D....805 306-2105
5456 Endeavour Ct Moorpark (93021) ***(P-13512)***
Pommes Frites Candle Co ....E....213 488-2016
7300 E Slauson Ave Commerce (90040) ***(P-11737)***
Pomona College ....D....909 621-8000
333 N College Way Claremont (91711) ***(P-17136)***
Pomona Community Health Center ....D....909 630-7927
1450 E Holt Ave Pomona (91767) ***(P-22276)***
Pomona Quality Foam LLC ....D....909 628-7844
1279 Philadelphia St Pomona (91766) ***(P-5517)***
Pomona Valley Hospital Med Ctr (PA) ....**A....909 865-9500**
1798 N Garey Ave Pomona (91767) ***(P-20898)***
Pomwonderful LLC (HQ) ....**C....310 966-5800**
11444 W Olympic Blvd Los Angeles (90064) ***(P-14720)***
Pond Heifer Ranch, Wasco *Also called Rockview Farms Inc* ***(P-137)***
Ponder Environmental Svcs Inc ....E....661 589-7771
19484 Broken Ct Shafter (93263) ***(P-23396)***
Ponderosa Electric Inc ....D....949 253-3100
3911 E La Palma Ave Ste D Anaheim (92807) ***(P-1298)***
Ponderosa Yorba Linda LLC ....E....714 974-8880
125 S Festival Dr Anaheim (92808) ***(P-16635)***
Ponte Winery ....F....951 694-8855
35053 Rancho Cal Rd Temecula (92591) ***(P-2213)***
Pontrelli & Larricchia Ltd ....E....323 583-6690
6080 Malburg Way Vernon (90058) ***(P-14601)***
Pontrlli-Laricchia Sausage Mfg, Vernon *Also called Pontrelli & Larricchia Ltd* ***(P-14601)***
Pool Pals Division, Temecula *Also called Oreq Corporation* ***(P-23080)***
Pool Water Products (PA) ....**F....949 756-1666**
17872 Mitchell N Ste 250 Irvine (92614) ***(P-14085)***
Poor Richard's Press, San Luis Obispo *Also called Prpco* ***(P-4410)***
Poor Richards Press, San Luis Obispo *Also called Ws Packaging-Blake Printery* ***(P-4461)***
Pop 82 Inc ....F....714 523-8500
8211 Orangethorpe Ave Buena Park (90621) ***(P-2602)***
Pop Chips, E Rncho Dmngz *Also called Sonora Mills Foods Inc* ***(P-2526)***
Pop Media Networks LLC (HQ) ....**C....323 856-4000**
5510 Lincoln Blvd Ste 400 Playa Vista (90094) ***(P-19374)***
Pop Plastics Acrylic Disp Inc ....F....714 523-8500
8211 Orangethorpe Ave Buena Park (90621) ***(P-5768)***
Pope Mortgage & Associates Inc ....D....909 466-5380
2980 Inland Empire Blvd Ontario (91764) ***(P-15249)***
Pope Plastics Inc ....E....818 701-1850
9134 Independence Ave Chatsworth (91311) ***(P-7824)***
Popla International Inc ....E....909 923-6899
1740 S Sacramento Ave Ontario (91761) ***(P-1953)***
Popsalot Gourmet Popcorn, Paramount *Also called Popsalot LLC* ***(P-2364)***
Popsalot LLC ....E....213 761-0156
7723 Somerset Blvd Paramount (90723) ***(P-2364)***
Populus Financial Group Inc ....C....951 509-3506
6302 Van Buren Blvd Riverside (92503) ***(P-15131)***
Port of Long Beach ....C....562 283-7000
415 W Ocean Blvd Long Beach (90802) ***(P-12290)***
Port of Los Angeles ....D....310 732-3508
425 S Palos Verdes St San Pedro (90731) ***(P-12291)***
Porta - Kan Sanitation Inc (PA) ....**C....562 463-8282**
4320 San Gbriel Rver Pkwy Pico Rivera (90660) ***(P-12966)***
Porter Boiler Service Inc ....E....562 426-2528
1166 E 23rd St Signal Hill (90755) ***(P-19057)***
Porter Valley Catering, Northridge *Also called Porter Valley Country Club* ***(P-19600)***

ALPHABETIC

Employee Codes: A=Over 500 employees, B=251-500
C=101-250, D=51-100, E=20-50 F=10-19
2022 Southern California Business
Directory and Buyers Guide
© Mergent Inc. 1-800-342-5647
1239

Porter Valley Country Club ....C....818 360-1071
19216 Singing Hills Dr Northridge (91326) ***(P-19600)***

Portermatt Electric Inc ....D....714 596-8788
5431 Production Dr Huntington Beach (92649) ***(P-1299)***

Porterville Annex, Porterville *Also called Family Healthcare Network* ***(P-19815)***

Porterville Concrete Pipe Inc ....E....559 784-6187
474 S Main St Porterville (93257) ***(P-6049)***

Porterville Convalescent Hosp, Porterville *Also called Moyles Centl Vly Hlth Care Inc* ***(P-20421)***

Porterville Developmental Ctr, Porterville *Also called Developmental Svcs Cal Dept* ***(P-20313)***

Porterville Dialysis Center ....B....559 781-5551
385 Pearson Dr Porterville (93257) ***(P-21259)***

Porterville Hemodialysis, Porterville *Also called Porterville Dialysis Center* ***(P-21259)***

Porterville Recorder, Porterville *Also called Noticiero Semanal Advertising* ***(P-4018)***

Porterville Sheltered Workshop ....D....559 684-9168
1853 E Cross Ave Tulare (93274) ***(P-13513)***

Porto Inc ....D....760 709-3737
12 S San Gorgonio Ave # 2 Banning (92220) ***(P-21871)***

Portofino Hotel Partners LP ....C....310 379-8481
260 Portofino Way Redondo Beach (90277) ***(P-16636)***

Portofino Inn & Suites Anaheim ....A....714 782-7600
1831 S Harbor Blvd Anaheim (92802) ***(P-16637)***

Portos Bakery West Covina Inc ....B....626 214-3490
584 S Sunset Ave West Covina (91790) ***(P-14721)***

Portos Food Product Inc ....D....323 480-8400
2085 Garfield Ave Commerce (90040) ***(P-2030)***

Posada Royale Hotel & Suites ....D....805 584-6300
1775 Madera Rd Simi Valley (93065) ***(P-16638)***

Posadas Usa Inc ....C....714 522-2122
7828 Orangethorpe Ave Buena Park (90621) ***(P-16639)***

Posca Brothers Dental Lab Inc ....D....562 427-1811
641 W Willow St Long Beach (90806) ***(P-21112)***

Posey Co, Ontario *Also called Posey Products LLC* ***(P-13514)***

Posey Products LLC (HQ) ....**C....626 443-3143**
2530 Lndsay Prvado Dr Uni Ontario (91761) ***(P-13514)***

Posh Peanut Inc (PA) ....**D....805 335-1960**
2279 Ward Ave Simi Valley (93065) ***(P-14410)***

Poshpeanut, Simi Valley *Also called Posh Peanut Inc* ***(P-14410)***

Positive Behavior Steps Corp ....D....626 940-5180
1050 Lakes Dr Ste 225 West Covina (91790) ***(P-21327)***

Positive Concepts Inc (PA) ....**E....714 685-5800**
2021 N Glassell St Orange (92865) ***(P-3933)***

Post Alarm Systems (PA) ....**D....626 446-7159**
47 E Saint Joseph St Arcadia (91006) ***(P-18396)***

Post Alarm Systems Patrol Svcs, Arcadia *Also called Post Alarm Systems* ***(P-18396)***

Post Group Inc (PA) ....**C....323 462-2300**
1415 N Cahuenga Blvd Los Angeles (90028) ***(P-19246)***

Post Modern Edit LLC (PA) ....**D....949 608-8700**
1821 E Dyer Rd Ste 125 Santa Ana (92705) ***(P-19166)***

Post Publishing LLC ....F....818 291-1100
620 W Elk Ave Glendale (91204) ***(P-4196)***

Post Surgical Recovery Center, Huntington Beach *Also called Friedman Professional Mgt Co* ***(P-19825)***

Postaer Rubin and Associates (PA) ....**B....310 394-4000**
2525 Colorado Ave Ste 100 Santa Monica (90404) ***(P-17046)***

Postal Instant Press Inc (HQ) ....**E....949 348-5000**
26722 Plaza Mission Viejo (92691) ***(P-4392)***

Postalio Inc ....F....408 616-9284
75 Higuera St Ste 240 San Luis Obispo (93401) ***(P-23297)***

Postcard Press Inc (PA) ....**E....855 898-9870**
8000 Haskell Ave Van Nuys (91406) ***(P-4557)***

Postvision Inc ....F....818 840-0777
2605 E Fthill Blvd Ste 10 Glendora (91740) ***(P-8211)***

Potential Industries Inc (PA) ....**C....310 807-4466**
922 E E St Wilmington (90744) ***(P-12967)***

Potter Roemer LLC (HQ) ....**D....626 855-4890**
17451 Hurley St City of Industry (91744) ***(P-13282)***

Poundex Associates Corporation ....D....909 444-5878
21490 Baker Pkwy City of Industry (91789) ***(P-13149)***

Pouring With Heart LLC ....F....213 817-5321
515 W 7th St Los Angeles (90014) ***(P-2214)***

Povac Investments Inc ....E....626 405-0400
388 Cordova St Ste 280 Pasadena (91101) ***(P-811)***

Powder Painting By Sundial, Sun Valley *Also called Sundial Industries Inc* ***(P-7417)***

Powdercoat Services LLC ....E....714 533-2251
1747 W Lincoln Ave Ste K Anaheim (92801) ***(P-7401)***

Powell Works Inc ....B....909 861-6699
17807 Maclaren St Ste B La Puente (91744) ***(P-13928)***

Power - Trim Co ....F....714 523-8560
6060 Phyllis Dr Cypress (90630) ***(P-7629)***

Power Acoustik Electronics, Montebello *Also called Epsilon Electronics Inc* ***(P-13685)***

Power Aire Inc ....F....800 526-7661
8055 E Crystal Dr Anaheim (92807) ***(P-8904)***

Power Brands Consulting LLC ....E....818 989-9646
5805 Sepulveda Blvd # 501 Van Nuys (91411) ***(P-2153)***

Power Circuits Inc ....C....714 327-3000
2630 S Harbor Blvd Santa Ana (92704) ***(P-9440)***

Power Fasteners Inc ....E....323 232-4362
650 E 60th St Los Angeles (90001) ***(P-7072)***

Power Generation Entps Inc ....C....818 484-8550
11411 Cumpston St Ste 104 North Hollywood (91601) ***(P-13929)***

Power Maintenance Services Inc ....D....714 229-5900
5555 Corporate Ave Cypress (90630) ***(P-1193)***

Power Plus, Anaheim *Also called SRbray LLC* ***(P-1319)***

Power Plus International Inc (PA) ....**D....714 507-1881**
5500 E La Palma Ave Anaheim (92807) ***(P-13661)***

Power Pros Exhaust Systems, Placentia *Also called Power Pros Racg Exhust Systems* ***(P-10114)***

Power Pros Racg Exhust Systems ....F....714 777-3278
817 S Lakeview Ave Ste J Placentia (92870) ***(P-10114)***

Power Pt Inc (PA) ....**F....951 490-4149**
1500 Crafton Ave Bldg 100 Mentone (92359) ***(P-7716)***

Power Services, Los Angeles *Also called On-Line Power Incorporated* ***(P-8880)***

Powerfull Systems Inc ....E....310 836-9333
5222 Venice Blvd Los Angeles (90019) ***(P-1300)***

Powers Holdings Inc ....F....559 651-2222
1601 Clancy Ct Visalia (93291) ***(P-9764)***

Powersource Talent LLC ....C....424 835-0878
12655 W Jefferson Blvd Los Angeles (90066) ***(P-23298)***

Powerstorm Ess, Rancho Palos Verdes *Also called Powerstorm Holdings Inc* ***(P-9813)***

Powerstorm Holdings Inc ....F....424 327-2991
31244 Palos Verdes Dr W # 245 Rancho Palos Verdes (90275) ***(P-9813)***

Powertec Company Inc ....D....951 332-1198
5150 E La Palma Ave # 209 Anaheim (92807) ***(P-908)***

Ppc Enterprises Inc ....C....951 354-5402
5920 Rickenbacker Ave Riverside (92504) ***(P-1121)***

PPG Aerospace, Valencia *Also called PRC - Desoto International Inc* ***(P-5191)***

PPG Aerospace, Sylmar *Also called Sierracin/Sylmar Corporation* ***(P-5819)***

PPG Aerospace, Mojave *Also called PRC - Desoto International Inc* ***(P-5192)***

PPG Industries Inc ....E....661 824-4532
11601 United St Mojave (93501) ***(P-5108)***

Ppmc, Corona *Also called Primary Provider MGT Co Inc* ***(P-23089)***

Pponext West Inc ....B....838 446-6098
1501 Hughes Way Ste 400 Long Beach (90810) ***(P-21472)***

Ppp LLC ....F....323 832-9627
601 W Olympic Blvd Montebello (90640) ***(P-5769)***

Pps Parking Inc ....A....949 223-8707
1800 E Garry Ave Ste 107 Santa Ana (92705) ***(P-16972)***

Ppst Inc (PA) ....**E....800 421-1921**
17692 Fitch Irvine (92614) ***(P-9765)***

Practice Management Info Corp (PA) ....**F....323 954-0224**
4727 Wilshire Blvd # 302 Los Angeles (90010) ***(P-4135)***

Prajin 1 Stop Distributors Inc (PA) ....**E....323 395-5302**
5701 Pacific Blvd 5711 Huntington Park (90255) ***(P-14175)***

Prajin Discount Distributors, Huntington Park *Also called Prajin 1 Stop Distributors Inc* ***(P-14175)***

Pramira Inc ....C....800 678-1169
2552 Walnut Ave Ste 200 Tustin (92780) ***(P-18214)***

Pranalytica Inc ....F....310 458-3345
1101 Colorado Ave Santa Monica (90401) ***(P-11046)***

Prata Inc ....E....512 823-1002
202 Bicknell Ave Santa Monica (90405) ***(P-17960)***

Prats/Coffee Inc ....D....323 780-4022
4652 E 3rd St Los Angeles (90022) ***(P-812)***

Praxis Musical Instruments Inc ....F....714 532-6655
19122 S Vermont Ave Gardena (90248) ***(P-7489)***

PRC, Ontario *Also called Plastics Research Corporation* ***(P-5458)***

PRC - Desoto International Inc (HQ) ....**B....661 678-4209**
24811 Ave Rockefeller Valencia (91355) ***(P-5191)***

PRC - Desoto International Inc ....C....661 824-4532
11601 United St Mojave (93501) ***(P-5192)***

PRC Composites LLC (PA) ....**D....909 391-2006**
1400 S Campus Ave Ontario (91761) ***(P-5770)***

PRC Composites LLC ....E....909 464-1520
13477 12th St Chino (91710) ***(P-5771)***

PRC Multi-Family LLC ....D....562 803-5000
10000 Imperial Hwy Downey (90242) ***(P-15745)***

Prdctions N Fremantle Amer Inc (HQ) ....**D....818 748-1100**
2900 W Alameda Ave # 800 Burbank (91505) ***(P-19328)***

Pre Con Industries Inc ....E....805 481-7305
950 Riata Ln Nipomo (93444) ***(P-1449)***

Pre Con Industries Inc (PA) ....**D....805 345-3147**
725 Oak St Santa Maria (93454) ***(P-1450)***

Precast Innovations Inc ....E....714 921-4060
1670 N Main St Orange (92867) ***(P-6050)***

Precept Inc (HQ) ....**D....949 955-1430**
130 Theory Ste 200 Irvine (92617) ***(P-15615)***

Precept Group The, Irvine *Also called Precept Inc* ***(P-15615)***

Precious Metals Plating Co Inc ....F....714 546-6271
2635 Orange Ave Santa Ana (92707) ***(P-7296)***

Precise Aerospace Mfg Inc ....E....951 898-0500
224 Glider Cir Corona (92878) ***(P-5772)***

Precise Air Systems Inc ....D....818 646-9757
5467 W San Fernando Rd Los Angeles (90039) ***(P-1122)***

Precise Die and Finishing ....E....818 773-9337
9400 Oso Ave Chatsworth (91311) ***(P-7825)***

Precise Distribution Inc ....E....951 367-1037
12215 Holly St Riverside (92509) ***(P-12233)***

Precise Fit Limited One LLC ....B....310 824-1800
17011 Beach Blvd Ste 900 Huntington Beach (92647) ***(P-17445)***

Precise Industries Inc ....C....714 482-2333
610 Neptune Ave Brea (92821) ***(P-6893)***

Precise Iron Doors Inc ....E....818 338-6269
12331 Foothill Blvd Sylmar (91342) ***(P-6712)***

Precise Media Services Inc ....E....909 481-3305
888 Vintage Ave Ontario (91764) ***(P-9223)***

Precise Plastic Products, Corona *Also called Precise Aerospace Mfg Inc* ***(P-5772)***

Precise-Full Service Media, Ontario *Also called Precise Media Services Inc* ***(P-9223)***

Preciseq Inc ....D....310 709-6094
11601 Wilshire Blvd Fl 5 Los Angeles (90025) ***(P-18215)***

Precision Aerial Services Inc ....F....909 484-8259
2020 Lowell St Rialto (92377) ***(P-18940)***

Precision Aerospace Corp ....D....909 945-9604
11155 Jersey Blvd Ste A Rancho Cucamonga (91730) ***(P-10394)***

Mergent e-mail: customerrelations@mergent.com
1240
2022 Southern California Business Directory and Buyers Guide
(P-0000) Products & Services Section entry number
(PA)=Parent Co (HQ)=Headquarters (DH)=Div Headquarters

Precision Anodizing & Pltg Inc..........D.......714 996-1601
1601 N Miller St Anaheim (92806) ***(P-7297)***
Precision Arcft Machining Inc..........E.......818 768-5900
10640 Elkwood St Sun Valley (91352) ***(P-8741)***
Precision Babbitt Co Inc..........F.......562 531-9173
1007 S Whitemarsh Ave Compton (90220) ***(P-8106)***
Precision Circuits West Inc..........F.......714 435-9670
3310 W Harvard St Santa Ana (92704) ***(P-9441)***
Precision Coil Spring Company..........D.......626 444-0561
10107 Rose Ave El Monte (91731) ***(P-7490)***
Precision Companies Inc..........F.......909 548-2700
15088 La Palma Dr Chino (91710) ***(P-3282)***
Precision Copy (PA)..........**F.......949 833-1213**
1413 E Edinger Ave Santa Ana (92705) ***(P-17153)***
Precision Cutting Tools Inc..........E.......562 921-7898
5572 Fresca Dr La Palma (90623) ***(P-7863)***
Precision Deburring Services..........E.......562 944-4497
4440 Manning Rd Pico Rivera (90660) ***(P-7739)***
Precision Diecut, Chino *Also called Pdc LLC* ***(P-7822)***
Precision Doors & Millwork, Chino *Also called Precision Companies Inc* ***(P-3282)***
Precision Dynamics Corporation (HQ)..........**C.......818 897-1111**
25124 Sprngfeld Ct Ste 20 Valencia (91355) ***(P-3873)***
Precision Energy Efficient Ltg, Yorba Linda *Also called Precision Fluorescent West Inc* ***(P-13662)***
Precision Engineered Products, Sunland *Also called Engineered Products By Lee Ltd* ***(P-8582)***
Precision Engineering Inds Inc..........F.......818 767-8590
11627 Cantara St North Hollywood (91605) ***(P-9766)***
Precision Engineering Industry, North Hollywood *Also called Precision Engineering Inds Inc* ***(P-9766)***
Precision Enterprises, Stanton *Also called CJ Enterprises* ***(P-7788)***
Precision Fastener Tooling Inc..........E.......714 898-8558
11530 Western Ave Stanton (90680) ***(P-7764)***
Precision Fiberglass Products..........F.......310 539-7470
3105 Kashiwa St Torrance (90505) ***(P-9052)***
Precision Fluorescent West Inc (HQ)..........**D.......352 692-5900**
23281 La Palma Ave Yorba Linda (92887) ***(P-13662)***
Precision Forging Dies Inc..........E.......562 861-1878
10710 Sessler St South Gate (90280) ***(P-7826)***
Precision Frrites Ceramics Inc..........D.......714 901-7622
5432 Production Dr Huntington Beach (92649) ***(P-8742)***
Precision Glass & Optics, Santa Ana *Also called Buk Optics Inc* ***(P-10827)***
Precision Glass Bevelling Inc..........F.......818 989-2727
15201 Keswick St Ste A Van Nuys (91405) ***(P-5940)***
Precision Granite Company, Azusa *Also called Precision Granite Usa Inc* ***(P-6141)***
Precision Granite Usa Inc..........F.......562 696-8328
174 N Aspan Ave Azusa (91702) ***(P-6141)***
Precision Hermetic Tech Inc..........D.......909 381-6011
1940 W Park Ave Redlands (92373) ***(P-9767)***
Precision Iron Works..........F.......562 220-2303
4815 Slauson Ave Maywood (90270) ***(P-6650)***
Precision Landscape & Turf..........E.......714 525-2318
940 S Leslie St La Habra (90631) ***(P-277)***
Precision Machining, Glendale *Also called Premac Inc* ***(P-8744)***
Precision Measurement Labs, Inglewood *Also called Pml Inc* ***(P-18637)***
Precision Metal Crafts..........E.......562 468-7080
16920 Gridley Pl Cerritos (90703) ***(P-6651)***
Precision Millwork LLC..........F.......661 402-5021
14300 Davenport Rd Ste 4a Agua Dulce (91390) ***(P-3283)***
Precision Molded Products Inc..........E.......951 354-0779
12660 Magnolia Ave Riverside (92503) ***(P-5773)***
Precision Netwrk Solutions LLC..........D.......562 318-4242
4259 Deeboyar Ave Lakewood (90712) ***(P-18638)***
Precision Offset Inc..........D.......949 752-1714
15201 Woodlawn Ave Tustin (92780) ***(P-4393)***
Precision Optical, Costa Mesa *Also called Sellers Optical Inc* ***(P-10860)***
Precision Performance Products (PA)..........**F.......909 356-4868**
7747 Edison Ave Fontana (92336) ***(P-1681)***
Precision Pipeline LLC..........B.......909 229-6858
10400 Trademark St Rancho Cucamonga (91730) ***(P-966)***
Precision Plastics Packaging, Anaheim *Also called Interlink Inc* ***(P-4339)***
Precision Pwdred Met Parts Inc..........E.......909 595-5656
145 Atlantic St Pomona (91768) ***(P-6461)***
Precision Resources, Hawthorne *Also called Paulco Precision Inc* ***(P-8734)***
Precision Services Group, Tustin *Also called Precision Offset Inc* ***(P-4393)***
Precision Sheet Metal, Gardena *Also called Artistic Welding* ***(P-6788)***
Precision Stampg Solutions Inc..........E.......951 845-1174
500 Egan Ave Beaumont (92223) ***(P-7175)***
Precision Stampings Inc (PA)..........**E.......951 845-1174**
500 Egan Ave Beaumont (92223) ***(P-9045)***
Precision Steel Products Inc..........E.......310 523-2002
13124 Avalon Blvd Los Angeles (90061) ***(P-6894)***
Precision Technology and Mfg..........E.......951 788-0252
3147 Durahart St Riverside (92507) ***(P-7041)***
Precision Tile Co..........F.......818 767-7673
11140 Penrose St Sun Valley (91352) ***(P-6051)***
Precision Tube Bending..........D.......562 921-6723
13626 Talc St Santa Fe Springs (90670) ***(P-10395)***
Precision Waterjet, Anaheim *Also called Jbb Inc* ***(P-9879)***
Precision Waterjet Inc..........E.......888 538-9287
4900 E Hunter Ave Anaheim (92807) ***(P-8743)***
Precision Welding Inc..........E.......661 729-3436
241 Enterprise Pkwy Lancaster (93534) ***(P-6652)***
Precision Wire Products Inc (PA)..........**C.......323 890-9100**
6150 Sheila St Commerce (90040) ***(P-7508)***
Preco Aircraft Motors Inc..........F.......626 799-3549
1133 Mission St South Pasadena (91030) ***(P-9829)***
Precon Inc..........E.......714 630-7632
3131 E La Palma Ave Anaheim (92806) ***(P-7740)***
Precon Gage, Anaheim *Also called Precon Inc* ***(P-7740)***
Preferred Brokers Inc (PA)..........**D.......661 836-2345**
9100 Ming Ave Ste 100 Bakersfield (93311) ***(P-15954)***
Preferred Excellent Care Phrm, Garden Grove *Also called Lu & Weber Corporation* ***(P-21187)***
Preferred Frzr Svcs - Lbf LLC..........D.......323 263-8811
4901 Bandini Blvd Vernon (90058) ***(P-12176)***
Preferred Pump Inc..........F.......805 922-8510
1740 Carlotti Dr Santa Maria (93454) ***(P-8021)***
Premac Inc..........F.......818 241-8370
625 Thompson Ave Glendale (91201) ***(P-8744)***
Premere Event Services, Huntington Beach *Also called Love At First Bite Catering* ***(P-16964)***
Premier America Credit Union (PA)..........**C.......818 772-4000**
19867 Prairie St Lbby Chatsworth (91311) ***(P-15115)***
Premier Aquatic Services Llc..........D.......949 716-3333
6 Journey Ste 160 Aliso Viejo (92656) ***(P-19601)***
Premier Business Centers, Irvine *Also called Premier Office Centers LLC* ***(P-18639)***
Premier Care Ctr For Palm Sprn, Palm Springs *Also called Ensign Palm I LLC* ***(P-20332)***
Premier Commercial Bancorp..........D.......714 978-2400
2400 E Katella Ave # 125 Anaheim (92806) ***(P-15039)***
Premier Disability Svcs LLC..........D.......310 280-4000
909 N Pacific Coast Hwy # 11 El Segundo (90245) ***(P-22208)***
Premier Drywall, Santa Maria *Also called Pre Con Industries Inc* ***(P-1450)***
Premier Food Services Inc..........B.......760 843-8000
14359 Amargosa Rd Ste F Victorville (92392) ***(P-14486)***
Premier Fuel Distributors Inc..........C.......760 423-3610
156 E La Cadena Dr Riverside (92507) ***(P-5143)***
Premier Gear & Machining Inc..........E.......951 278-5505
2360 Pomona Rd Corona (92878) ***(P-7095)***
Premier Healthcare Svcs LLC (HQ)..........**C.......626 204-7930**
3030 Old Ranch Pkwy # 100 Seal Beach (90740) ***(P-17446)***
Premier Infusion Care, Torrance *Also called Pharmaco Inc* ***(P-21202)***
Premier Magnetics Inc..........E.......949 452-0511
20381 Barents Sea Cir Lake Forest (92630) ***(P-9638)***
Premier Mailing Inc..........E.......562 408-2134
14522 Garfield Ave Paramount (90723) ***(P-17137)***
Premier Mailing Services, Paramount *Also called Premier Mailing Inc* ***(P-17137)***
Premier Meat Company, Vernon *Also called Wayne Provision Co Inc* ***(P-14609)***
Premier Medical Transport Inc..........D.......888 353-9556
260 N Palm St 200 Brea (92821) ***(P-11884)***
Premier Medical Trnsp Inc..........D.......909 433-3939
575 Maple Ct Ste A Colton (92324) ***(P-11885)***
Premier Mop & Broom, Corona *Also called Northwestern Converting Co* ***(P-3109)***
Premier Office Centers LLC (PA)..........**E.......949 253-4616**
2102 Business Center Dr Irvine (92612) ***(P-18639)***
Premier Otptent Srgery Ctr Inc..........C.......909 370-2190
900 E Washington St # 155 Colton (92324) ***(P-20024)***
Premier Packaging/Assembly, Santa Fe Springs *Also called Haringa Inc* ***(P-18537)***
Premier Plumbing Company, Riverside *Also called Ppc Enterprises Inc* ***(P-1121)***
Premier Residential Svcs LLC..........D.......760 773-4081
43100 Cook St Ste 101 Palm Desert (92211) ***(P-16973)***
Premier Signs Service Inc..........F.......951 204-7693
2985 Durahart St Riverside (92507) ***(P-1301)***
Premier Steel Structures Inc..........E.......951 356-6655
13345 Estelle St Corona (92879) ***(P-6653)***
Premier Systems Usa Inc (PA)..........**F.......657 204-9861**
16291 Gothard St Huntington Beach (92647) ***(P-13428)***
Premier Tile & Marble..........D.......310 516-1712
15000 S Main St Gardena (90248) ***(P-1421)***
Premier Trailer Mfg Inc..........E.......559 651-2212
30517 Ivy Rd Visalia (93291) ***(P-10554)***
Premiere Medical Group..........D.......909 469-9498
1770 N Orng Grv Ave Pomona (91767) ***(P-20025)***
Premiere Packaging Inds Inc..........D.......562 799-9200
6530 Altura Blvd Buena Park (90620) ***(P-14968)***
Premiere Packing, Shafter *Also called Grimmway Enterprises Inc* ***(P-108)***
Premiere Radio Network Inc (HQ)..........**C.......818 377-5300**
15260 Ventura Blvd # 400 Sherman Oaks (91403) ***(P-19329)***
Premio, Irvine *Also called Prestige International USA Inc* ***(P-15616)***
Premio Inc (PA)..........**C.......626 839-3100**
918 Radecki Ct City of Industry (91748) ***(P-8170)***
Premium Outlet Partners LP..........D.......805 445-8520
740 Ventura Blvd Camarillo (93010) ***(P-15691)***
Premium Outlet Partners LP..........D.......951 849-6641
48400 Seminole Dr Cabazon (92230) ***(P-15692)***
Premium Pet Foods, Irwindale *Also called J&R Taylor Brothers Assoc Inc* ***(P-1958)***
Premium Plastics Machine Inc..........E.......562 633-7723
15956 Downey Ave Paramount (90723) ***(P-5774)***
Premium Trnsp Svcs Inc (PA)..........**C.......310 816-0260**
18735 S Ferris Pl Rancho Dominguez (90220) ***(P-12234)***
Premium Windows, Paramount *Also called Mediland Corporation* ***(P-5920)***
Preproduction Plastics Inc..........E.......951 340-9680
210 Teller St Corona (92879) ***(P-5775)***
Pres-Tek Plastics Inc (PA)..........**D.......909 360-1600**
10700 7th St Rancho Cucamonga (91730) ***(P-5776)***
Presbia, Aliso Viejo *Also called Presbibio LLC* ***(P-11260)***
Presbibio LLC..........E.......949 502-7010
36 Plateau Aliso Viejo (92656) ***(P-11260)***
Presbyterian Church USA, Los Angeles *Also called Bel Air Presbyterian Church* ***(P-21986)***
Presbyterian Health Physicians..........B.......562 464-4717
6557 Greenleaf Ave Whittier (90601) ***(P-20899)***
Presbyterian Inter Cmnty Hosp, Whittier *Also called Interhealth Services Inc* ***(P-21176)***
Preschool Services Department (PA)..........**D.......909 383-2000**
662 S Tippecanoe Ave San Bernardino (92415) ***(P-22053)***

ALPHABETIC

Employee Codes: A=Over 500 employees, B=251-500
C=101-250, D=51-100, E=20-50 F=10-19
2022 Southern California Business
Directory and Buyers Guide
© Mergent Inc. 1-800-342-5647
1241

Prescience Corporation ....D 949 600-8631
125 Columbia Ste A Aliso Viejo (92656) ***(P-22639)***
Presentation Folder Inc ....E 714 289-7000
1130 N Main St Orange (92867) ***(P-3900)***
Presentation Products Inc (PA) ....**D 714 367-2900**
16751 Knott Ave La Mirada (90638) ***(P-18058)***
President Enterprise Inc ....E 714 671-9577
655 Tamarack Ave Brea (92821) ***(P-4558)***
Presidental Services Inc (PA) ....**C 661 259-8987**
23404 Lyons Ave Ste 223 Santa Clarita (91321) ***(P-17126)***
Presort Center of Fresno LLC ....E 559 498-6151
496 S Uruapan Way Dinuba (93618) ***(P-17138)***
Press Colorcom, Santa Fe Springs *Also called Ace Commercial Inc* ***(P-4222)***
Press Forge Company ....D 562 531-4962
7700 Jackson St Paramount (90723) ***(P-7096)***
Press-Enterprise Company (PA) ....**A 951 684-1200**
3450 14th St Riverside (92501) ***(P-4024)***
Pressed Juicery Inc ....F 310 214-2144
21540 Hawthorne Blvd Torrance (90503) ***(P-14722)***
Pressed Juicery Inc ....F 818 225-8985
23500 Park Sorrento Calabasas (91302) ***(P-14723)***
Pressed Juicery Inc ....F 805 966-0099
651 Paseo Nuevo Santa Barbara (93101) ***(P-14724)***
Pressed Juicery Inc ....F 949 650-0661
1116 Irvine Ave Newport Beach (92660) ***(P-14725)***
Pressed Juicery Inc ....F 714 258-7266
2348 Park Ave Tustin (92782) ***(P-1873)***
Pressed Juicery Inc ....F 949 715-7006
7922 E Coast Hwy Newport Beach (92657) ***(P-14726)***
Pressure Profile Systems Inc ....F 310 641-8100
5757 W Century Blvd # 600 Los Angeles (90045) ***(P-10710)***
Prestige Asssted Lving At Lncs, Lancaster *Also called PCI Care Venture I* ***(P-20438)***
Prestige Asssted Lving At Vsli, Visalia *Also called PCI Care Venture I* ***(P-20439)***
Prestige Auto Collision Inc ....D 949 470-6031
23726 Via Fabricante Mission Viejo (92691) ***(P-18799)***
Prestige Beauty Care, Pomona *Also called Mission Series Inc* ***(P-14264)***
Prestige Cosmetics Inc ....F 714 375-0395
17780 Gothard St Huntington Beach (92647) ***(P-5062)***
Prestige Fuels, Fontana *Also called Bdeebz Investment Inc* ***(P-16248)***
Prestige International USA Inc (HQ) ....**D 949 870-1640**
19800 Macarthur Blvd # 400 Irvine (92612) ***(P-15616)***
Prestige Mold Incorporated ....D 909 980-6600
11040 Tacoma Dr Rancho Cucamonga (91730) ***(P-7827)***
Prestige Preschools Inc (PA) ....**D 818 957-1170**
3795 La Crescenta Ave # 2 Glendale (91208) ***(P-22054)***
Prestige Stations Inc (HQ) ....**C 714 670-5145**
4 Centerpointe Dr La Palma (90623) ***(P-18941)***
Prestone Products Corporation ....E 424 271-4836
19500 Mariner Ave Torrance (90503) ***(P-5238)***
Pretium Packaging LLC ....C 714 777-9580
5235 E Hunter Ave Anaheim (92807) ***(P-5777)***
Pretzelmaker, Santa Paula *Also called Fowlie Enterprises Inc* ***(P-2064)***
Prevost Car (us) Inc ....E 951 360-2550
3384 Deforest Cir Mira Loma (91752) ***(P-13080)***
Prevounce Health LLC ....F 800 618-7738
1426 Hidden Valley Rd Thousand Oaks (91361) ***(P-11738)***
Price Law Group A Prof Corp (PA) ....**C 818 995-4540**
15760 Ventura Blvd # 1100 Encino (91436) ***(P-21662)***
Price Manufacturing Co Inc ....E 951 371-5660
372 N Smith Ave Corona (92878) ***(P-7042)***
Price Pfister Inc ....C 949 672-4003
19701 Da Vinci Foothill Ranch (92610) ***(P-6564)***
Price Pfister Inc (HQ) ....**A 949 672-4000**
19701 Da Vinci Lake Forest (92610) ***(P-6565)***
Price Pfister Brass Mfg, Lake Forest *Also called Price Pfister Inc* ***(P-6565)***
Price Postel and Parma LLP ....D 805 962-0011
200 E Carrillo St Ste 400 Santa Barbara (93101) ***(P-21663)***
Pricespider, Irvine *Also called Neuintel LLC* ***(P-17671)***
Pride Auto Body, Van Nuys *Also called Pride Collision Centers Inc* ***(P-18800)***
Pride Cleaning Co Inc ....E 818 295-2510
1900 W Burbank Blvd Burbank (91506) ***(P-18640)***
Pride Collision Centers Inc (HQ) ....**D 818 909-0660**
7950 Haskell Ave Van Nuys (91406) ***(P-18800)***
Pride Companies, Burbank *Also called Pride Cleaning Co Inc* ***(P-18640)***
Pride Metal Polishing Inc ....F 626 350-1326
10822 Saint Louis Dr El Monte (91731) ***(P-7298)***
Prima Royale, Pasadena *Also called Prima Royale Enterprises Ltd* ***(P-14445)***
Prima Royale Enterprises Ltd ....E 626 960-8388
150 S Los Robles Ave # 100 Pasadena (91101) ***(P-14445)***
Primal Blueprint, Oxnard *Also called Primal Nutrition LLC* ***(P-14283)***
Primal Elements Inc ....D 714 899-0757
18062 Redondo Cir Huntington Beach (92648) ***(P-14282)***
Primal Nutrition LLC ....E 310 317-4414
1101 Maulhardt Ave Oxnard (93030) ***(P-14283)***
Primary Color Inc ....D 714 824-8930
11130 Holder St Cypress (90630) ***(P-17183)***
Primary Color Systems Corp (PA) ....**B 949 660-7080**
11130 Holder St Cypress (90630) ***(P-4394)***
Primary Color Systems Corp ....E 310 841-0250
401 Coral Cir El Segundo (90245) ***(P-4559)***
Primary Critical Care Medical ....C 818 847-9950
620 N Brand Blvd Ste 500 Glendale (91203) ***(P-20026)***
Primary Provider MGT Co Inc (PA) ....**D 951 280-7700**
2115 Compton Ave Ste 301 Corona (92881) ***(P-23089)***
Prime Administration LLC ....A 323 549-7155
357 S Curson Ave Los Angeles (90036) ***(P-16240)***
Prime Alliance LLC ....E 310 764-1000
360 W Victoria St Compton (90220) ***(P-2650)***

Prime Alloy Steel Casting, Port Hueneme *Also called Pac Foundries Inc* ***(P-6410)***
Prime Converting Corporation ....E 909 476-9500
9121 Pttsbrgh Ave Ste 100 Rancho Cucamonga (91730) ***(P-3934)***
Prime Focus Technologies Inc ....D 310 895-9550
2255 N Ontario St Ste 230 Burbank (91504) ***(P-23495)***
Prime Focus World, Culver City *Also called Dneg North America Inc* ***(P-19229)***
Prime Forming & Cnstr Sups Inc ....E 714 547-6710
1500a E Chestnut Ave Santa Ana (92701) ***(P-6052)***
Prime Global Solutions Inc (PA) ....**D 800 424-7746**
15805 E Valley Blvd City of Industry (91744) ***(P-12510)***
Prime Group, Los Angeles *Also called Prime Administration LLC* ***(P-16240)***
Prime Halthcare Foundation Inc (PA) ....**D 909 235-4400**
3480 E Guasti Rd Ontario (91761) ***(P-20900)***
Prime Health Care ....B 909 394-2727
1350 W Covina Blvd San Dimas (91773) ***(P-22055)***
Prime Healthcare Anaheim LLC ....A 714 827-3000
3033 W Orange Ave Anaheim (92804) ***(P-20901)***
Prime Healthcare Centinela LLC ....A 310 673-4660
555 E Hardy St Inglewood (90301) ***(P-20902)***
Prime Healthcare Services, Ontario *Also called Bio-Med Services Inc* ***(P-20689)***
Prime Healthcare Services-Mont ....A 909 625-5411
5000 San Bernardino St Montclair (91763) ***(P-20903)***
Prime Healthcare Svcs III LLC, Montclair *Also called Prime Hlthcare Srvcs-Mntclair* ***(P-20906)***
Prime Hlthcare Hntngton Bch LL ....B 714 843-5000
17772 Beach Blvd Huntington Beach (92647) ***(P-20904)***
Prime Hlthcare Srvcs-Mntclair ....D 909 625-5411
5000 San Bernardino St Montclair (91763) ***(P-20905)***
Prime Hlthcare Srvcs-Mntclair (HQ) ....**B 909 625-5411**
5000 San Bernardino St Montclair (91763) ***(P-20906)***
Prime Hlthcare Svcs - Encino H ....B 818 995-5000
16237 Ventura Blvd Encino (91436) ***(P-20907)***
Prime Hlthcare Svcs - Pmpa LLC (HQ) ....**B 909 235-4400**
3300 E Guasti Rd Ste 300 Ontario (91761) ***(P-20908)***
Prime Hlthcare Svcs - San Dmas ....B 909 599-6811
1350 W Covina Blvd San Dimas (91773) ***(P-20909)***
Prime Hlthcare Svcs - Shrman O ....B 818 981-7111
4929 Van Nuys Blvd Sherman Oaks (91403) ***(P-20910)***
Prime Hlthcare Svcs - St John (HQ) ....**E 913 680-6000**
3500 S 4th St Ontario (91761) ***(P-20911)***
Prime Hospitality LLC (PA) ....**C 909 212-8000**
2155 E Convention Ctr Way Ontario (91764) ***(P-16640)***
Prime Hospitality Services LLC (PA) ....**D 661 321-9424**
8300 Granite Falls Dr Bakersfield (93312) ***(P-16641)***
Prime Mso LLC ....D 818 937-9969
550 N Brand Blvd Ste 900 Glendale (91203) ***(P-21328)***
Prime One Inc ....C 310 378-1944
22410 Hawthorne Blvd # 4 Torrance (90505) ***(P-17447)***
Prime Plating, Sun Valley *Also called Schmidt Industries Inc* ***(P-7311)***
Prime Plating Aerospace Inc ....E 818 768-9100
11321 Goss St Sun Valley (91352) ***(P-7299)***
Prime Tech Cabinets Inc ....C 949 757-4900
2215 S Standard Ave Santa Ana (92707) ***(P-1451)***
Prime Time International, Coachella *Also called Sun and Sands Enterprises LLC* ***(P-14655)***
Prime Transport Inc (PA) ....**D 909 972-1300**
14726 Ramona Ave Ste 104 Chino (91710) ***(P-12581)***
Prime Value Logistic Inc ....E 213 218-3917
16700 Valley View Ave # 30 La Mirada (90638) ***(P-12511)***
Prime Value Logistics, La Mirada *Also called Prime Value Logistic Inc* ***(P-12511)***
Prime Wheel Corporation ....B 310 326-5080
23920 Vermont Ave Harbor City (90710) ***(P-10115)***
Prime Wheel Corporation ....E 310 819-4123
17680 S Figueroa St Gardena (90248) ***(P-10116)***
Prime Wheel Corporation (PA) ....**A 310 516-9126**
17705 S Main St Gardena (90248) ***(P-10117)***
Prime Wheel of Figueroa, Gardena *Also called Prime Wheel Corporation* ***(P-10116)***
Prime Wire & Cable Inc (HQ) ....**C 888 445-9955**
1330 Valley Vista Dr Diamond Bar (91765) ***(P-6355)***
Prime-Line Products LLC (HQ) ....**E 909 887-8118**
26950 San Bernardino Ave Redlands (92374) ***(P-13816)***
Primebore Drctonal Boring Corp ....F 909 821-4643
10822 Vernon Ave Ontario (91762) ***(P-437)***
Primecare Moreno Valley Inc ....D 951 371-8440
2275 Sampson Ave Ste 111 Corona (92879) ***(P-20027)***
Primecare Quality HM Care Inc ....D 949 681-3515
2372 Morse Ave Irvine (92614) ***(P-634)***
Primetime International Inc ....D 760 399-4166
86705 Avenue 54 Ste A Coachella (92236) ***(P-14647)***
Primex Clinical Labs Inc (PA) ....**D 818 779-0496**
16742 Stagg St Ste 120 Van Nuys (91406) ***(P-21087)***
Primex Farms LLC (PA) ....**E 661 758-7790**
16070 Wildwood Rd Wasco (93280) ***(P-2115)***
Primo Sandblasting, Huntington Beach *Also called Norm Harboldt* ***(P-7391)***
Primor Huntington Park Inc ....F 323 365-3200
6334 Pacific Blvd Huntington Park (90255) ***(P-11190)***
Primordial Diagnostics Inc ....E 800 462-1926
3233 Mission Oaks Blvd P Camarillo (93012) ***(P-10711)***
Primus Inc ....D 714 527-2261
17901 Jamestown Ln Huntington Beach (92647) ***(P-11582)***
Primus Group Inc (PA) ....**E 805 922-0055**
2810 Industrial Pkwy Santa Maria (93455) ***(P-23299)***
Primus Labs, Santa Maria *Also called Primus Group Inc* ***(P-23299)***
Primus Lighting Inc ....F 626 442-4600
3570 Lexington Ave El Monte (91731) ***(P-9144)***
Primus Pipe and Tube Inc (HQ) ....**E 562 808-8000**
5855 Obispo Ave Long Beach (90805) ***(P-6251)***
Prince Lionheart Inc (PA) ....**E 805 922-2250**
2421 Westgate Rd Santa Maria (93455) ***(P-5778)***

Princess Cruise Lines Ltd...A...213 745-0314
1242 E 25th St Los Angeles (90011) ***(P-14411)***
Princess Cruise Lines Ltd...A...661 753-2197
24833 Anza Dr Santa Clarita (91355) ***(P-12397)***
Princess Cruise Lines Ltd (HQ)...A...661 753-0000
24305 Town Center Dr Santa Clarita (91355) ***(P-12279)***
Princess Cruise Lines Ltd...A...661 753-0000
24200 Magic Mountain Pkwy Santa Clarita (91355) ***(P-12408)***
Princess Cruises, Santa Clarita *Also called Princess Cruise Lines Ltd* ***(P-12397)***
Princess Cruises, Santa Clarita *Also called Princess Cruise Lines Ltd* ***(P-12279)***
Princess Cruises and Tours Inc (HQ)...D...206 336-6000
24305 Town Center Dr # 200 Valencia (91355) ***(P-12398)***
Princess Paper Inc...E...323 588-4777
4455 Fruitland Ave Vernon (90058) ***(P-3906)***
Princess Paradise, Walnut *Also called Diana Did-It Designs Inc* ***(P-3075)***
Princeton Case-West Inc...E...805 928-8840
1444 W Mccoy Ln Santa Maria (93455) ***(P-5779)***
Princeton Technology Inc...E...949 851-7776
1691 Browning Irvine (92606) ***(P-8292)***
Princeton Tool Inc...F...661 257-1380
25620 Rye Canyon Rd Ste A Valencia (91355) ***(P-10223)***
Principle Plastics...E...310 532-3411
1136 W 135th St Gardena (90247) ***(P-5313)***
Principles Inc (PA)...D...323 681-2575
1680 N Fair Oaks Ave Pasadena (91103) ***(P-21329)***
Prindle Decker & Amaro LLP (PA)...D...562 436-3946
310 Golden Shore Fl 4 Long Beach (90802) ***(P-21664)***
Pringle's Draperies, Garden Grove *Also called L C Pringle Sales Inc* ***(P-3713)***
Print Printing, Anaheim *Also called Crescent Inc* ***(P-4268)***
Print Shop, San Bernardino *Also called San Brnrdino Cmnty College Dst* ***(P-4570)***
Printcom Inc...F...818 891-8282
14675 Titus St Van Nuys (91402) ***(P-4395)***
Printec Ht Electronics LLC...E...714 484-7597
501 Sally Pl Fullerton (92831) ***(P-9561)***
Printech, Placentia *Also called High Five Inc* ***(P-4316)***
Printery Inc...F...949 757-1930
1762 Kaiser Ave Irvine (92614) ***(P-4396)***
Printfirm Inc...F...818 992-1005
21352 Nordhoff St Ste 104 Chatsworth (91311) ***(P-4397)***
Printing 4him, Ontario *Also called Ultimate Print Source Inc* ***(P-4443)***
Printing Connection , The, Newbury Park *Also called H J S Graphics* ***(P-4308)***
Printing Division Inc...F...714 685-0111
1933 N Main St Orange (92865) ***(P-4398)***
Printing Impressions, Goleta *Also called JD Business Solutions Inc* ***(P-4342)***
Printing Island Corporation...F...714 668-1000
11535 Martens River Cir Fountain Valley (92708) ***(P-4399)***
Printing Management Associates...F...562 407-9977
17128 Edwards Rd Cerritos (90703) ***(P-4400)***
Printing Palace Inc (PA)...F...310 451-5151
2300 Lincoln Blvd Santa Monica (90405) ***(P-4401)***
Printing Place, The, Palm Desert *Also called Wanda Matranga* ***(P-4452)***
Printing Rsources Southern Cal, Upland *Also called Helens Place Inc* ***(P-4314)***
Printograph Inc...F...818 252-3000
7625 N San Fernando Rd Burbank (91505) ***(P-4402)***
Printronix LLC (PA)...D...714 368-2300
7700 Irvine Center Dr # 700 Irvine (92618) ***(P-8293)***
Printronix Holding Corp...E...714 368-2300
7700 Irvine Center Dr # 70 Irvine (92618) ***(P-8294)***
Printrunner LLC...E...888 296-5760
8000 Haskell Ave Van Nuys (91406) ***(P-4403)***
Prints 4 Life...E...661 942-2233
43145 Business Ctr Pkwy Lancaster (93535) ***(P-4404)***
Printxcel - Visalia...F...559 636-6290
1424 E Tulare Ave Visalia (93292) ***(P-4405)***
Priority Building Services LLC (PA)...B...714 255-2940
521 Mercury Ln Brea (92821) ***(P-17276)***
Priority Ctr Ending The Gnrtna...D...714 543-4333
1940 E Deere Ave Ste 100 Santa Ana (92705) ***(P-21872)***
Priority Landscape Services, Brea *Also called Priority Building Services LLC* ***(P-17276)***
Priority Lighting Inc...F...800 709-1119
77551 El Duna Ct Ste H Palm Desert (92211) ***(P-9145)***
Priority One Med Trnspt Inc (PA)...D...909 948-4400
9327 Fairway View Pl # 300 Rancho Cucamonga (91730) ***(P-11886)***
Priority Pallet Inc...E...951 769-9399
1060 E Third St Beaumont (92223) ***(P-3404)***
Priority Posting and Pubg Inc...F...714 338-2568
17501 Irvine Blvd Ste 1 Tustin (92780) ***(P-4197)***
Prism Aerospace...E...951 582-2850
3087 12th St Riverside (92507) ***(P-6895)***
PRISM AEROSPACE DBA JET MANUFACTURING, Corona *Also called Jet Manufacturing Inc* ***(P-6858)***
Prism Software Corporation...E...949 855-3100
184 Technology Dr Ste 201 Irvine (92618) ***(P-17961)***
Prison Ride Share Network...E...314 703-5245
1541 S California Ave Compton (90221) ***(P-4198)***
Prison Rideshare Network, Compton *Also called Prison Ride Share Network* ***(P-4198)***
Private Brand Mdsg Corp...E...213 749-0191
214 W Olympic Blvd Los Angeles (90015) ***(P-2895)***
Private Label Pc LLC...C...626 965-8686
748 Epperson Dr City of Industry (91748) ***(P-13429)***
Private Medical-Care Inc...A...562 924-8311
12898 Towne Center Dr Cerritos (90703) ***(P-15448)***
Private Nat Mrtg Accptance LLC (HQ)...A...818 224-7401
6101 Condor Dr Agoura Hills (91301) ***(P-15228)***
Private Suite Lax LLC...D...310 907-9950
6871 W Imperial Hwy Los Angeles (90045) ***(P-11835)***
Privilege International Inc...D...323 585-0777
2323 Firestone Blvd South Gate (90280) ***(P-13150)***

Prl Aluminum Inc...D...626 968-7507
14760 Don Julian Rd City of Industry (91746) ***(P-6315)***
Prl Glass Systems Inc...D...877 775-2586
14760 Don Julian Rd City of Industry (91746) ***(P-5968)***
Prn Ambulance LLC...B...818 810-3600
8928 Sepulveda Blvd North Hills (91343) ***(P-11887)***
Prn Radio Networks, Sherman Oaks *Also called Premiere Radio Network Inc* ***(P-19329)***
Pro America Premium Tools, Baldwin Park *Also called American Kal Enterprises Inc* ***(P-13794)***
Pro American Premium Tools, Baldwin Park *Also called Kal-Cameron Manufacturing Corp* ***(P-6483)***
Pro Armor, Riverside *Also called Polaris Sales Inc* ***(P-6649)***
Pro Building Maintenance Inc...C...951 279-3386
149 N Maple St Ste H Corona (92878) ***(P-17277)***
Pro Cal, South Gate *Also called Productivity California Inc* ***(P-5782)***
Pro Circuit Products Inc (PA)...E...951 738-8050
2771 Wardlow Rd Corona (92882) ***(P-10499)***
Pro Circuit Products & Racing, Corona *Also called Pro Circuit Products Inc* ***(P-10499)***
Pro Corporation...C...949 660-9544
17682 Mitchell N Ste 100 Irvine (92614) ***(P-17448)***
Pro Design Group Inc...E...310 767-1032
438 E Alondra Blvd Gardena (90248) ***(P-5780)***
Pro Detention Inc...D...714 881-3680
2238 N Glassell St Ste E Orange (92865) ***(P-6231)***
Pro Document Solutions Inc (PA)...E...805 238-6680
1760 Commerce Way Paso Robles (93446) ***(P-4406)***
Pro Group, Irvine *Also called Professnal Rprgraphic Svcs Inc* ***(P-4560)***
Pro Group Inc...C...951 271-3000
4160 Temescal Canyon Rd # 500 Corona (92883) ***(P-15955)***
Pro Loaders Inc...C...909 355-5531
14032 Santa Ana Ave Fontana (92337) ***(P-12512)***
Pro Med Hlth Netwrk Pomona Vly, Orange *Also called Pamona Valley Medical Group* ***(P-20018)***
Pro Media Merchants...F...818 957-7114
3746 Foothill Blvd La Crescenta (91214) ***(P-4407)***
Pro Safety & Rescue Inc...D...888 269-5095
3701 Pegasus Dr Ste 124 Bakersfield (93308) ***(P-23300)***
Pro Safety Inc...C...562 364-7450
20503 Belshaw Ave Carson (90746) ***(P-13930)***
Pro Spray Equipment, San Bernardino *Also called Wcs Distributing Inc* ***(P-13962)***
Pro Structural Inc...D...951 526-2010
29190 Riverside Dr Lake Elsinore (92530) ***(P-1351)***
Pro Systems, Fontana *Also called Pro-Systems Fabricators Inc* ***(P-9900)***
Pro Tech Thermal Services...E...951 272-5808
1954 Tandem Norco (92860) ***(P-6451)***
Pro Tool Services Inc...E...661 393-9222
1704 Sunnyside Ct Bakersfield (93308) ***(P-7864)***
Pro Tour Memorabilia LLC...E...424 303-7200
700 N San Vicente Blvd G696 West Hollywood (90069) ***(P-3451)***
Pro Vote Solutions, Paso Robles *Also called Pro Document Solutions Inc* ***(P-4406)***
Pro Wax, Tustin *Also called Baf Industries* ***(P-4957)***
Pro-Action Products, Van Nuys *Also called Neopacific Holdings Inc* ***(P-5724)***
Pro-Craft Construction Inc...C...909 790-5222
500 Iowa St Ste 100 Redlands (92373) ***(P-1123)***
Pro-Dex Inc (PA)...C...949 769-3200
2361 Mcgaw Ave Irvine (92614) ***(P-11047)***
Pro-Lite Inc...F...714 668-9988
3505 Cadillac Ave Ste D Costa Mesa (92626) ***(P-11583)***
Pro-Mart Industries Inc (PA)...E...949 428-7700
17421 Von Karman Ave Irvine (92614) ***(P-3115)***
Pro-Systems Fabricators Inc (PA)...F...909 350-9147
14643 Hawthorne Ave Fontana (92335) ***(P-9900)***
Pro-Tech Design & Mfg Inc...D...562 207-1680
14561 Marquardt Ave Santa Fe Springs (90670) ***(P-18641)***
Pro-Tech Mats Industries Inc...F...760 343-3667
72370 Quarry Trl Ste A Thousand Palms (92276) ***(P-5400)***
Pro-Tek Consulting (PA)...C...805 807-5571
21300 Victory Blvd # 240 Woodland Hills (91367) ***(P-18216)***
Pro-Vac Inc...E...661 765-7298
26857 Henry Rd Fellows (93224) ***(P-538)***
Pro-Wash Inc...D...323 756-6000
9117 S Main St Los Angeles (90003) ***(P-16873)***
Pro-Youth...B...559 374-2030
505 N Court St Visalia (93291) ***(P-22357)***
Pro-Youth Heart, Visalia *Also called Pro-Youth* ***(P-22357)***
Proactiv, El Segundo *Also called Guthy-Renker LLC* ***(P-23230)***
Proactive Packg & Display LLC (HQ)...D...909 390-5624
602 S Rockefeller Ave Ontario (91761) ***(P-14969)***
Proactive Risk Management Inc...D...213 840-8856
22617 Hawthorne Blvd Torrance (90505) ***(P-23090)***
Probe Racing Components Inc...E...310 784-2977
5022 Onyx St Torrance (90503) ***(P-8434)***
Prober & Raphael A Law Corp...D...818 227-0100
20750 Ventura Blvd # 100 Woodland Hills (91364) ***(P-21665)***
Prober & Raphael, ALC, Woodland Hills *Also called Prober & Raphael A Law Corp* ***(P-21665)***
Procases Inc...F...323 585-4447
8205 Industry Ave Pico Rivera (90660) ***(P-3379)***
Procel Temporary Services Inc...D...310 372-0560
108 W Walnut St Fl 1 Gardena (90248) ***(P-17509)***
Procelebrity, Arcadia *Also called Tee Top of California Inc* ***(P-14354)***
Processes By Martin Inc...E...310 637-1855
12150 Alameda St Lynwood (90262) ***(P-7402)***
Processing Office, Corcoran *Also called J G Boswell Company* ***(P-177)***
Processors Mailing Inc...E...626 358-5600
761 N Dodsworth Ave Covina (91724) ***(P-4408)***
Processors The, Covina *Also called Processors Mailing Inc* ***(P-4408)***

ALPHABETIC

Employee Codes: A=Over 500 employees, B=251-500
C=101-250, D=51-100, E=20-50 F=10-19
2022 Southern California Business
Directory and Buyers Guide
© Mergent Inc. 1-800-342-5647
1243

Procore Technologies Inc (PA) A 866 477-6267
6309 Carpinteria Ave Carpinteria (93013) *(P-17691)*
Procter & Gamble Mfg Co C 513 627-4678
18125 Rowland St City of Industry (91748) *(P-4946)*
Procter & Gamble Paper Pdts Co A 805 485-8871
800 N Rice Ave Oxnard (93030) *(P-3907)*
Procurementiq, Los Angeles *Also called Ibisworld Inc (P-4181)*
Prodege LLC (PA) B 310 294-9599
2030 E Maple Ave Ste 200 El Segundo (90245) *(P-17692)*
Prodigy Investigations, Irvine *Also called Fraud Fighters Inc (P-18277)*
Produce Available Inc (PA) D 805 483-5292
910 Commercial Ave Oxnard (93030) *(P-14648)*
Producer -Writers Guild D 818 846-1015
2900 W Alameda Ave # 1100 Burbank (91505) *(P-15518)*
Producers Inc D 714 850-1008
1751 Langley Ave Irvine (92614) *(P-17368)*
Product Data Intgrtion Tech In (PA) D 562 495-6500
111 W Ocean Blvd Fl 4 Long Beach (90802) *(P-18059)*
Product Dsign Developments Inc F 714 898-6895
15611 Container Ln Huntington Beach (92649) *(P-5781)*
Product Solutions Inc E 714 545-9757
1182 N Knollwood Cir Anaheim (92801) *(P-8405)*
Product Transportation, Long Beach *Also called Sfpp LP (P-12376)*
Production Associates Inc (PA) D 310 598-7200
77899 Wolf Rd Ste 107 Palm Desert (92211) *(P-19167)*
Production Data Inc E 661 327-4776
1210 33rd St Bakersfield (93301) *(P-539)*
Production Delivery Svcs Inc D 562 777-0060
806 W Valencia Mesa Dr Fullerton (92835) *(P-12074)*
Production Engineering & Mch, Fontana *Also called Cavallo & Cavallo Inc (P-8543)*
Production Engineering & Mch E 909 721-2455
14955 Hilton Dr Fontana (92336) *(P-21088)*
PRODUCTION FACILITIES UNLIMITE, La Puente *Also called San Gabriel Vly Training Ctr (P-21966)*
Production Industries, Brea *Also called Production Systems Group Inc (P-3736)*
Production Lapping Company E 626 359-0611
124 E Chestnut Ave Monrovia (91016) *(P-8745)*
Production Lapping Company F 626 359-0611
120 E Chestnut Ave Monrovia (91016) *(P-8746)*
Production Systems Group Inc E 714 990-8997
895 Beacon St Brea (92821) *(P-3736)*
Production Transport, Fullerton *Also called Production Delivery Svcs Inc (P-12074)*
Productive Playhouse Inc B 323 250-3445
25231 Paseo De Alicia # 2 Laguna Hills (92653) *(P-18642)*
Productivity California Inc C 562 923-3100
10533 Sessler St South Gate (90280) *(P-5782)*
Productplan LLC E 805 618-2975
10 E Yanonali St Ste 2a Santa Barbara (93101) *(P-17962)*
Products/Techniques Inc F 909 877-3951
3271 S Riverside Ave Bloomington (92316) *(P-5109)*
Productsgo LLC E 714 242-4299
14515 Alondra Blvd La Mirada (90638) *(P-12513)*
Professional Cabinet Solutions A 909 614-2900
2111 Eastridge Ave Riverside (92507) *(P-3330)*
Professional Cabinet Solutions C 909 614-2900
2111 Eastridge Ave Riverside (92507) *(P-3331)*
Professional Cmnty MGT Cal Inc (PA) E 800 369-7260
27051 Twne Cntre Dr Ste 2 Foothill Ranch (92610) *(P-15956)*
Professional Cmnty MGT Cal Inc C 951 845-2191
850 Country Club Dr Banning (92220) *(P-15957)*
Professional Cmnty MGT Cal Inc C 949 206-0580
24351 El Toro Rd Laguna Woods (92637) *(P-15958)*
Professional Cmnty MGT Cal Inc D 949 768-7261
27051 Towne Centre Dr Foothill Ranch (92610) *(P-15755)*
Professional Cmnty MGT Cal Inc C 949 597-4200
23522 Paseo De Valencia Laguna Hills (92653) *(P-15959)*
Professional Community MGT Cal C 949 380-0725
23081 Via Campo Verde Aliso Viejo (92656) *(P-23091)*
Professional Construction Svcs, Rancho Cucamonga *Also called Rwc Enterprises Inc (P-22648)*
Professional Finishing Systems F 818 365-8888
12341 Gladstone Ave Sylmar (91342) *(P-7176)*
Professional Parking (HQ) C 714 722-0242
2799 E 21st St Signal Hill (90755) *(P-18777)*
Professional Produce D 323 277-1550
2570 E 25th St Los Angeles (90058) *(P-14649)*
Professional Security Cons (PA) A 310 207-7729
11454 San Vicente Blvd # 2 Los Angeles (90049) *(P-18312)*
Professional Skin Care Inc (PA) E 661 257-7771
25028 Avenue Kearny Valencia (91355) *(P-5063)*
Professional Svcs Med Group, Huntington Park *Also called All Care Medical Group Inc (P-19689)*
Professnal Cmmnctons Netwrk LP (PA) E 951 275-9149
6774 Magnolia Ave Riverside (92506) *(P-18643)*
Professnal Elec Cnstr Svcs Inc C 909 373-4100
9112 Santa Anita Ave Rancho Cucamonga (91730) *(P-1302)*
Professnal Rprgraphic Svcs Inc E 949 748-5400
17731 Cowan Irvine (92614) *(P-4560)*
Professnal Svcs - Archtectural, Redondo Beach *Also called Online Land Planning LLC (P-23487)*
Professonal Tele Answering Svc, Chatsworth *Also called Seven One Inc (P-18664)*
Profile Planing Mill, Santa Ana *Also called Strata Forest Products Inc (P-3213)*
Profit Recovery Partners LLC D 949 851-2777
1600 Sunflower Ave # 100 Costa Mesa (92626) *(P-23496)*
Proform Inc D 707 752-9010
1140 S Rockefeller Ave Ontario (91761) *(P-21089)*
Proform Labs, Ontario *Also called Proform Inc (P-21089)*
Proformance Manufacturing Inc E 951 279-1230
1922 Elise Cir Corona (92879) *(P-7177)*
Programmed Composites Inc C 951 520-7300
250 Klug Cir Corona (92880) *(P-10396)*
Prographics Inc E 626 287-0417
9200 Lower Azusa Rd Rosemead (91770) *(P-4409)*
Progression Drywall Corp, Lancaster *Also called Excel Contractors Inc (P-604)*
Progressive Converting Inc F 909 392-2201
280 W Bonita Ave Pomona (91767) *(P-3935)*
Progressive Label Inc E 323 415-9770
2545 Yates Ave Commerce (90040) *(P-3936)*
Progressive Management Systems, West Covina *Also called RM Galicia Inc (P-17116)*
Progressive Manufacturing, Fullerton *Also called Progrssive Intgrated Solutions (P-4561)*
Progressive Marketing Group, Commerce *Also called Progressive Produce LLC (P-14650)*
Progressive Marketing Pdts Inc D 714 888-1700
4571 Avenida Del Este Yorba Linda (92886) *(P-7007)*
Progressive Power Group Inc E 714 899-2300
12552 Western Ave Garden Grove (92841) *(P-1124)*
Progressive Produce LLC (HQ) D 323 890-8100
5790 Peachtree St Commerce (90040) *(P-14650)*
Progressive Products Inc F 951 784-9930
8804 Windmill Pl Riverside (92508) *(P-2736)*
Progrssive Intgrated Solutions D 714 237-0980
377 S Acacia Ave Fullerton (92831) *(P-4561)*
Project Access Inc (PA) D 949 253-6200
2100 W Orangewood Ave # 2 Orange (92868) *(P-21873)*
Project Independence (PA) D 714 549-3464
3505 Cadillac Ave O103 Costa Mesa (92626) *(P-22146)*
Project Management, Rcho STA Marg *Also called M-Industrial Enterprises (P-8671)*
Project Skyline Intermediate H A 310 712-1850
360 N Crescent Dr Bldg S Beverly Hills (90210) *(P-16108)*
Project Social T LLC E 323 266-4500
615 S Clarence St Los Angeles (90023) *(P-2864)*
Prolabs Factory Inc E 818 646-3677
15001 Oxnard St Van Nuys (91411) *(P-5064)*
Prolacta Bioscience Inc B 626 599-9260
1800 Highland Ave Duarte (91010) *(P-1805)*
Prolacta Bioscience Inc (PA) C 626 599-9260
757 Baldwin Park Blvd City of Industry (91746) *(P-4938)*
Proland Property Managment LLC (PA) D 213 738-8175
2510 W 7th St Fl 2 Los Angeles (90057) *(P-15960)*
Prolifics Testing Inc E 925 485-9535
24025 Park Sorrento # 405 Calabasas (91302) *(P-17693)*
Proline Manufacturing, Banning *Also called DT Mattson Enterprises Inc (P-11372)*
Prologic Rdmption Slutions Inc (PA) A 310 322-7774
2121 Rosecrans Ave El Segundo (90245) *(P-18644)*
Proma Inc E 310 327-0035
730 Kingshill Pl Carson (90746) *(P-11191)*
Promach Filling Systems LLC E 951 393-2200
200 River Rd Corona (92878) *(P-10712)*
Promag, South Gate *Also called C&C Metal Form & Tooling Inc (P-7132)*
Promart Dazz, Irvine *Also called Pro-Mart Industries Inc (P-3115)*
Promedia Companies E 714 444-2426
3518 W Lake Center Dr D Santa Ana (92704) *(P-4100)*
Promega Biosciences LLC D 805 544-8524
277 Granada Dr San Luis Obispo (93401) *(P-4761)*
Promises Promises Inc E 213 749-7725
3121 S Grand Ave Los Angeles (90007) *(P-2896)*
Promo Shop Inc (PA) D 310 821-1780
5420 Mcconnell Ave Los Angeles (90066) *(P-23301)*
Promote Media LP D 323 433-7950
8484 Wilshire Blvd # 630 Beverly Hills (90211) *(P-23302)*
Promotonal Design Concepts Inc D 626 579-4454
9872 Rush St South El Monte (91733) *(P-5401)*
Prompt Delivery Inc D 858 549-8000
5757 Wilshire Blvd Ph 3 Los Angeles (90036) *(P-18645)*
Pronto Drilling Inc (PA) E 562 777-0900
9501 Santa Fe Springs Rd Santa Fe Springs (90670) *(P-8747)*
Pronto Janitorial Services Inc D 562 273-5997
12561 Persing Dr Whittier (90606) *(P-17278)*
Pronto Laser Cutting Inc F 310 327-7820
13323 S Normandie Ave Gardena (90249) *(P-9901)*
Propak Logistics Inc D 951 934-7160
11555 Iberia St Jurupa Valley (91752) *(P-12582)*
Property Care Building Svc LLC E 626 623-6420
126 La Porte St Ste F Arcadia (91006) *(P-17279)*
Property I D, Los Angeles *Also called I D Property Corporation (P-15887)*
Property Insight LLC A 877 747-2537
2510 Redhill Ave Santa Ana (92705) *(P-16041)*
Property Management Assoc Inc (PA) C 323 295-2000
6011 Bristol Pkwy Culver City (90230) *(P-15961)*
Propertyplus Insur Agcy Inc B 818 432-2640
21820 Burbank Blvd # 130 Woodland Hills (91367) *(P-15617)*
Proplas Technologies, Garden Grove *Also called Peerless Injection Molding LLC (P-5741)*
Proponent Main Whse, Brea *Also called Kirkhill Aircraft Parts Co (P-14061)*
Proportion Foods LLC E 515 735-9800
3501 E Vernon Ave Vernon (90058) *(P-2510)*
Proprietary Controls Systems E 310 303-3600
3830 Del Amo Blvd 102 Torrance (90503) *(P-10904)*
Pros Incorporated D 661 589-5400
3400 Patton Way Bakersfield (93308) *(P-540)*
Proscape Landscape, Signal Hill *Also called Fenderscape Inc (P-256)*
Prosearch Strategies LLC C 877 447-7291
3250 Wilshire Blvd # 301 Los Angeles (90010) *(P-22896)*
Prosight Specty Insur Grp Inc D 818 230-8200
101 N Brand Blvd Ste 1900 Glendale (91203) *(P-15618)*
Prosoft Technology Inc (HQ) C 661 716-5100
9201 Camino Media Ste 200 Bakersfield (93311) *(P-12789)*

Prospect Enterprises Inc (PA) ....C........213 599-5700
625 Kohler St Los Angeles (90021) *(P-14579)*
Prospect Medical Group Inc (HQ) ....B........714 796-5900
1920 E 17th St Ste 200 Santa Ana (92705) *(P-23092)*
Prospect Medical Holdings Inc (PA) ....B........310 943-4500
3415 S Sepulveda Blvd # 9 Los Angeles (90034) *(P-20028)*
Prospect Medical Systems Inc (HQ) ....C........714 667-8156
600 City Pkwy W Ste 800 Orange (92868) *(P-23093)*
Prosthtic Orthtic Group Ornge ....F........949 242-2237
26300 La Alameda Ste 120 Mission Viejo (92691) *(P-11136)*
Prosum Inc (PA) ....D........310 426-0600
2201 Park Pl Ste 102 El Segundo (90245) *(P-18104)*
Prosum Inc ....D........949 732-1122
3990 Westerly Pl Ste 100 Newport Beach (92660) *(P-18105)*
Prosum Technology Services, El Segundo *Also called Prosum Inc (P-18104)*
Protab Laboratories ....C........949 635-1930
25902 Towne Centre Dr Foothill Ranch (92610) *(P-4875)*
Protech Systems, Riverside *Also called Alectro Inc (P-8862)*
Protect-US ....C........714 721-8127
12391 Lewis St Ste 201 Garden Grove (92840) *(P-18313)*
Protected Outcomes Corporation ....D........203 545-9565
9663 Santa Monica Blvd Beverly Hills (90210) *(P-18314)*
Protective Industries Inc ....D........310 537-2300
18704 S Ferris Pl Rancho Dominguez (90220) *(P-5783)*
Protective Wther Strctures Inc ....F........805 547-8797
5290 Orcutt Rd San Luis Obispo (93401) *(P-715)*
Proterra Inc ....B........864 438-0000
393 Cheryl Ln City of Industry (91789) *(P-9962)*
Proto Homes LLC ....E........310 271-7544
917 W 17th St Los Angeles (90015) *(P-10546)*
Proto Space Engineering Inc ....E........626 442-8273
2214 Loma Ave South El Monte (91733) *(P-8748)*
Protocast, Chatsworth *Also called John List Corporation (P-7885)*
Protool Co, Tustin *Also called Bernhardt and Bernhardt Inc (P-7722)*
Prototype & Short-Run Svcs Inc ....E........714 449-9661
1310 W Collins Ave Orange (92867) *(P-7178)*
Prototype Express LLC ....F........714 751-3533
3506 W Lake Center Dr D Santa Ana (92704) *(P-9902)*
Prototype Industries Inc (PA) ....E........949 680-4890
26035 Acero Ste 100 Mission Viejo (92691) *(P-4199)*
Prototypes Centers For Innov ....C........213 542-3838
1000 N Alameda St Ste 390 Los Angeles (90012) *(P-21874)*
Protravel International LLC ....D........310 271-9566
9171 Wilshire Blvd # 428 Beverly Hills (90210) *(P-12399)*
Protype, Orange *Also called G P Manufacturing Inc (P-8598)*
Proulx Manufacturing Inc ....E........909 980-0662
11433 6th St Rancho Cucamonga (91730) *(P-5784)*
Provena Foods Inc (HQ) ....D........909 627-1082
5010 Eucalyptus Ave Chino (91710) *(P-1746)*
Providence Health & Services F ....A........818 843-5111
501 S Buena Vista St Burbank (91505) *(P-20912)*
Providence Health & Services S ....D........310 832-3311
1300 W 7th St San Pedro (90732) *(P-20913)*
Providence Health & Svcs - Ore ....C........818 365-8051
15031 Rinaldi St Mission Hills (91345) *(P-20914)*
Providence Health System ....A........818 843-5111
501 S Buena Vista St Burbank (91505) *(P-20915)*
Providence Health System ....C........310 370-5895
3551 Voyager St Ste 201 Torrance (90503) *(P-16196)*
Providence Health System ....C........310 370-5895
4101 Torrance Blvd Torrance (90503) *(P-21204)*
Providence Holy Cross Med Ctr, Mission Hills *Also called Providence Health & Svcs - Ore (P-20914)*
Providence Holy Cross Medical (PA) ....A........818 365-8051
15031 Rinaldi St Mission Hills (91345) *(P-20916)*
Providence Industries LLC ....D........562 420-9091
18191 Von Karman Ave # 100 Irvine (92612) *(P-2787)*
Providence Little Company of M, San Pedro *Also called Providence Health & Services S (P-20913)*
Providence Rest Partners LLC ....D........323 460-4170
5955 Melrose Ave Los Angeles (90038) *(P-16285)*
Providence Speech Hearing Ctr ....E........714 639-4990
1301 W Providence Ave Orange (92868) *(P-21330)*
Providence St Johns Hlth Ctr ....B........310 829-6562
2121 Santa Monica Blvd Santa Monica (90404) *(P-20917)*
Providence St Joseph Health ....A........949 430-3963
4 Park Plz Ste 150 Irvine (92614) *(P-20029)*
Providence St Joseph Health ....A........949 430-3960
57 Prism Irvine (92618) *(P-21205)*
Providence St Joseph Health ....A........818 843-5111
501 S Buena Vista St Burbank (91505) *(P-20030)*
Providence Tarzana Medical Ctr ....A........818 881-0800
18321 Clark St Tarzana (91356) *(P-20918)*
Provident Bank, Riverside *Also called Provident Savings Bank (P-15041)*
Provident Financial Management ....D........310 282-0477
3130 Wilshire Blvd # 600 Santa Monica (90403) *(P-23094)*
Provident Fincl Holdings Inc (PA) ....D........951 686-6060
3756 Central Ave Riverside (92506) *(P-15040)*
Provident Savings Bank (HQ) ....C........951 782-6177
6570 Magnolia Ave Riverside (92506) *(P-15041)*
Providnce Holy Cross Fundation, Burbank *Also called Providence Health & Services F (P-20912)*
Provivi Inc (PA) ....E........310 828-2307
1701 Colorado Ave Santa Monica (90404) *(P-5144)*
Proximity Technologies, Irvine *Also called Secure Channels Inc (P-17707)*
Prp Seats, Temecula *Also called Kamm Industries Inc (P-3177)*
Prpco ....E........805 543-6844
2226 Beebee St San Luis Obispo (93401) *(P-4410)*
Prs Industries, Ontario *Also called Inland Powder Coating Corp (P-7375)*
Prsi, Jurupa Valley *Also called Pavement Recycling Systems Inc (P-14119)*
Prudential, Thousand Oaks *Also called Gemmm Corp (P-15873)*
Prudential, Irvine *Also called Brer Affiliates LLC (P-16203)*
Prudential, Glendale *Also called On Central Realty Inc (P-15935)*
Prudential Insur Co of Amer ....D........818 901-0028
5990 Sepulvda Blvd # 300 Van Nuys (91411) *(P-15619)*
Prudential Lighting Corp (PA) ....C........213 477-1694
1774 E 21st St Los Angeles (90058) *(P-9100)*
Prudential Overall Supply (PA) ....D........949 250-4855
1661 Alton Pkwy Irvine (92606) *(P-16885)*
Prutel Joint Venture ....A........949 240-2000
1 Ritz Carlton Dr Dana Point (92629) *(P-16642)*
Prx International Corp (PA) ....D........714 624-0789
23332 Madero Ste H Mission Viejo (92691) *(P-9768)*
PS, Los Angeles *Also called Private Suite Lax LLC (P-11835)*
PS Arts ....E........310 586-1017
2947 S Sepulveda Blvd Los Angeles (90064) *(P-23497)*
PS Business Parks Inc (PA) ....D........818 244-8080
701 Western Ave Glendale (91201) *(P-16241)*
PS LPT Properties Investors (HQ) ....D........818 244-8080
701 Western Ave Glendale (91201) *(P-12235)*
Ps2 (PA) ....D........310 243-2980
17903 S Hobart Blvd Gardena (90248) *(P-1194)*
Psav, Cerritos *Also called Audio Visual Headquarters (P-17333)*
Psav Holdings LLC (PA) ....B........562 366-0138
111 W Ocean Blvd Ste 1110 Long Beach (90802) *(P-17369)*
PSC, Visalia *Also called Pacific Southwest Cont LLC (P-3824)*
PSC Circuits Inc ....F........626 373-1728
5160 Rivergrade Rd Baldwin Park (91706) *(P-9442)*
PSC Industrial Outsourcing LP ....C........310 325-1600
19340 Van Ness Ave Torrance (90501) *(P-19058)*
PSC Industrial Outsourcing LP ....D........661 833-9991
200 Old Yard Dr Bakersfield (93307) *(P-541)*
Pscmb Repairs Inc ....E........626 448-7778
12145 Slauson Ave Santa Fe Springs (90670) *(P-8749)*
Pse Holding LLC (HQ) ....B........248 377-0165
360 N Crescent Dr Beverly Hills (90210) *(P-19428)*
Psg California LLC (PA) ....B........909 422-1700
22069 Van Buren St Grand Terrace (92313) *(P-8022)*
PSI Management Team Inc ....D........562 236-3860
12342 Mccann Dr Santa Fe Springs (90670) *(P-1002)*
Psitech Inc ....F........714 964-7818
18368 Bandilier Cir Fountain Valley (92708) *(P-8171)*
PSM Industries Inc (PA) ....D........888 663-8256
14000 Avalon Blvd Los Angeles (90061) *(P-7568)*
Psomas (PA) ....C........213 223-1400
555 S Flower St Ste 4300 Los Angeles (90071) *(P-22755)*
Pssc Labs ....F........949 380-7288
20432 N Sea Cir Lake Forest (92630) *(P-8212)*
PSW Inc ....F........951 371-7100
281 Corporate Terrace St Corona (92879) *(P-2511)*
Psychic Eye Book Shops Inc (PA) ....D........818 906-8263
13435 Ventura Blvd Sherman Oaks (91423) *(P-19661)*
Pszyjw, Los Angeles *Also called Pachulski Stang Zehl Jones LLP (P-21650)*
Pt Gaming LLC ....A........323 260-5060
235 Oregon St El Segundo (90245) *(P-16643)*
Pta CA Cngress of Parnts Palm ....D........818 952-8360
5025 Palm Dr La Canada (91011) *(P-22358)*
Pta California Congress of Par ....E........559 622-3195
2121 E Laura Ave Visalia (93292) *(P-22359)*
Ptac Rail Ranch Elem School ....D........951 696-1404
25030 Via Santee Murrieta (92563) *(P-22360)*
Ptb Sales Inc (PA) ....E........626 334-0500
1361 Mountain View Cir Azusa (91702) *(P-8037)*
Pti Technologies Inc (HQ) ....C........805 604-3700
501 Del Norte Blvd Oxnard (93030) *(P-10397)*
Ptm & W Industries Inc ....E........562 946-4511
10640 Painter Ave Santa Fe Springs (90670) *(P-5460)*
Ptm Images, West Hollywood *Also called Pro Tour Memorabilia LLC (P-3451)*
Ptm Images LLC ....F........310 881-8053
10990 Wilshire Blvd # 140 Los Angeles (90024) *(P-3737)*
Pts Advance ....C........949 268-4000
1775 Flight Way Ste 100 Tustin (92782) *(P-17449)*
Ptsi Managed Services Inc ....D........626 440-3118
100 W Walnut St Pasadena (91124) *(P-22640)*
Public Agency Resources ....D........714 940-6300
2125 E Katella Ave # 200 Anaheim (92806) *(P-23303)*
Public Communications Svcs Inc ....C........310 231-1000
11859 Wilshire Blvd # 60 Los Angeles (90025) *(P-12665)*
Public Counsel ....D........213 385-2977
610 S Ardmore Ave Los Angeles (90005) *(P-21666)*
Public Defender- Main Office, Riverside *Also called County of Riverside (P-21540)*
Public Fclities Resources Dept, Santa Ana *Also called County of Orange (P-4505)*
Public Hlth Fndation Entps Inc (PA) ....A........800 201-7320
13300 Crssrds Pkwy N City of Industry (91746) *(P-22361)*
Public Investment Corporation ....C........310 451-5227
4340 Eucalyptus Ave Chino (91710) *(P-16069)*
Public Mdia Group Southern Cal (PA) ....C........714 241-4100
2900 W Alameda Ave # 600 Burbank (91505) *(P-12738)*
Public Storage (PA) ....C........818 244-8080
701 Western Ave Glendale (91201) *(P-16242)*
Public Works, Dept of, La Puente *Also called County of Los Angeles (P-7640)*
Public Works, Dept of, Malibu *Also called County of Los Angeles (P-7641)*
Publish Brand Inc ....F........714 890-1908
15731 Graham St Huntington Beach (92649) *(P-4200)*
Puente Hills Chevrolet, City of Industry *Also called Leo Hoffman Chevrolet Inc (P-18750)*

ALPHABETIC

Employee Codes: A=Over 500 employees, B=251-500
C=101-250, D=51-100, E=20-50 F=10-19
2022 Southern California Business
Directory and Buyers Guide
© Mergent Inc. 1-800-342-5647
1245

Puente Ready Mix Services Inc (PA) ....E......626 968-0711
 209 N California Ave City of Industry (91744) (P-6105)
Pulitzer Community Newspapers, Hanford Also called Hanford Sentinel Inc (P-3984)
Pull-N-Pac, Huntington Park Also called Crown Poly Inc (P-3882)
Pulp Story, Los Angeles Also called Quality Produced LLC (P-1908)
Pulp Studio Incorporated ....D......310 815-4999
 2100 W 139th St Gardena (90249) (P-17184)
Pulse Instruments, Camarillo Also called Primordial Diagnostics Inc (P-10711)
Pulse Instruments ....E......310 515-5330
 1234 Francisco St Torrance (90502) (P-10768)
Pulse One Care LLC ....E......310 657-9300
 1260 S La Cienega Blvd Los Angeles (90035) (P-21875)
Puma Biotechnology Inc (PA) ....B......424 248-6500
 10880 Wilshire Blvd # 2150 Los Angeles (90024) (P-4876)
Pumpkin Patch, Anaheim Also called Branvid Ltd Inc (P-17334)
Punch Press Products Inc ....D......323 581-7151
 2035 E 51st St Vernon (90058) (P-7828)
Punch Studio LLC (PA) ....C......310 390-9900
 6025 W Slauson Ave Culver City (90230) (P-14197)
Pupil Transportation, Whittier Also called County of Los Angeles (P-11918)
Pura Naturals Inc (HQ) ....F......949 273-8100
 23615 El Toro Rd Ste X300 Lake Forest (92630) (P-5065)
Pura Naturals Inc ....E......949 273-8100
 3401 Space Center Ct # 811 Jurupa Valley (91752) (P-3556)
Purchasing Department, El Centro Also called Imperial Irrigation District (P-12871)
Purchasing Department, Ventura Also called Community Mem Hosp San Bnvntur (P-20729)
Pure Autism Counseling Ctr Inc ....D......661 360-7730
 17728 Sierra Hwy Canyon Country (91351) (P-21331)
Pure-Chem Products Company Inc ....E......714 995-4141
 8371 Monroe Ave Stanton (90680) (P-5239)
Pureform Global Inc ....F......310 666-4869
 5700 Melrose Ave Apt 208 Los Angeles (90038) (P-5145)
Pureformance Cables, Torrance Also called Lynn Products Inc (P-8277)
Puregear, Irwindale Also called Superior Communications Inc (P-13777)
Puretec Industrial Water, Oxnard Also called J Harris Indus Wtr Trtmnt Inc (P-13831)
Puretek Corporation ....C......818 361-3949
 7900 Nelson Rd Unit A Panorama City (91402) (P-4877)
Puretek Corporation (PA) ....E......818 361-3316
 1145 Arroyo St Ste D San Fernando (91340) (P-4878)
Puri Tech Inc ....E......951 360-8380
 3167 Progress Cir Jurupa Valley (91752) (P-8406)
Puroflux Corporation ....F......805 579-0216
 2121 Union Pl Simi Valley (93065) (P-9639)
Purosil LLC (HQ) ....C......951 271-3900
 708 S Temescal St Ste 101 Corona (92879) (P-4732)
Purus International Inc ....F......760 775-4500
 82860 Avenue 45 Indio (92201) (P-5402)
Putnam Accessory Group Inc ....E......323 306-1330
 4455 Fruitland Ave Vernon (90058) (P-2986)
PVA Tepla America Inc (HQ) ....E......951 371-2500
 251 Corporate Terrace St Corona (92879) (P-8750)
Pvd Coatings LLC ....F......714 899-4892
 5271 Argosy Ave Huntington Beach (92649) (P-7403)
Pvhmc, Pomona Also called Pomona Valley Hospital Med Ctr (P-20898)
Pvp Advanced Eo Systems Inc ....E......714 508-2740
 14312 Franklin Ave # 100 Tustin (92780) (P-10856)
Pw Eagle Inc ....B......800 621-4404
 5200 W Century Blvd Fl 10 Los Angeles (90045) (P-5470)
Pw Eagle Inc ....B......951 657-7400
 23711 Rider St Perris (92570) (P-5471)
PW Gillibrand Co Inc (PA) ....D......805 526-2195
 4537 Ish Dr Simi Valley (93063) (P-579)
PW Stephens Envmtl Inc (PA) ....C......714 892-2028
 15201 Pipeline Ln Ste B Huntington Beach (92649) (P-1682)
Pw Wiring Systems, Pico Rivera Also called P-W Wiring Systems LLC (P-9663)
Pwp, Vernon Also called Pactiv Packaging Inc (P-14962)
Pws Inc (PA) ....D......323 721-8832
 12020 Garfield Ave South Gate (90280) (P-14043)
Pylo Health, Thousand Oaks Also called Prevounce Health LLC (P-11738)
Pyramid Enterprises Inc (PA) ....D......661 702-1420
 28368 Constellation Rd # 380 Valencia (91355) (P-19662)
Pyramid Flowers Inc ....C......805 382-8070
 3813 Doris Ave Oxnard (93030) (P-93)
Pyramid Mold & Tool ....E......909 476-2555
 10155 Sharon Cir Rancho Cucamonga (91730) (P-7829)
Pyramid Peak Corporation ....D......949 769-8600
 450 Nwport Ctr Dr Ste 650 Newport Beach (92660) (P-16286)
Pyramid Powder Coating Inc ....F......818 768-5898
 12251 Montague St Pacoima (91331) (P-7404)
Pyramid Systems Inc ....E......559 582-9345
 10105 8 3/4 Ave Hanford (93230) (P-3662)
Pyrenees French Bakery Inc ....E......661 322-7159
 717 E 21st St Bakersfield (93305) (P-2031)
Pyro-Comm Systems Inc (PA) ....C......714 902-8000
 15531 Container Ln Huntington Beach (92649) (P-1303)
Q & B Foods Inc (HQ) ....D......626 334-8090
 15547 1st St Irwindale (91706) (P-1893)
Q C M Inc ....E......714 414-1173
 285 Gemini Ave Brea (92821) (P-8980)
Q C Poultry, Commerce Also called Ingenue Inc (P-1760)
Q Railing USA Inc ....F......714 259-1372
 14321 Franklin Ave Ste A Tustin (92780) (P-3284)
Q S H Properties Inc ....F......714 957-9200
 2701 Hotel Ter Santa Ana (92705) (P-16644)
Q S San Luis Obispo LP ....D......805 541-5001
 1631 Monterey St San Luis Obispo (93401) (P-16645)
Q Team ....F......714 228-4465
 6400 Dale St Buena Park (90621) (P-4411)

Q&A Clothing, Los Angeles Also called Q&A7 LLC (P-2987)
Q&A7 LLC ....F......323 364-4250
 2155 E 7th St Ste 150 Los Angeles (90023) (P-2987)
Q-Flex Inc ....E......714 364-0101
 1301 E Hunter Ave Santa Ana (92705) (P-9443)
Q-Mark Manufacturing Inc ....F......949 457-1913
 30051 Comercio Rcho STA Marg (92688) (P-10713)
Q-See, Anaheim Also called Digital Periph Solutions Inc (P-9171)
Q-Tech Corporation ....C......310 836-7900
 6161 Chip Ave Cypress (90630) (P-13763)
Q1 Test Inc ....E......909 390-9718
 1100 S Grove Ave Ste B2 Ontario (91761) (P-10398)
Q4 Services LLC ....F......949 421-7856
 1108 W Barkley Ave Orange (92868) (P-9349)
Qad Inc (PA) ....A......805 566-6000
 100 Innovation Pl Santa Barbara (93108) (P-17963)
Qad Inc ....F......805 684-6614
 6450 Via Real Carpinteria (93013) (P-17964)
Qantas Vctons Nwmans Vacations, Long Beach Also called Helloworld Travel Svcs USA Inc (P-12385)
Qbi LLC (PA) ....D......818 594-4900
 21031 Ventura Blvd # 1200 Woodland Hills (91364) (P-22810)
Qc Manufacturing Inc ....D......951 325-6340
 26040 Ynez Rd Temecula (92591) (P-8053)
QED Inc ....E......714 546-6010
 2920 Halladay St Santa Ana (92705) (P-10714)
QED Software LLC ....E......310 214-3118
 304 Tejon Pl Palos Verdes Estates (90274) (P-17965)
Qf Liquidation Inc (PA) ....C......949 930-3400
 25242 Arctic Ocean Dr Lake Forest (92630) (P-10118)
Qfi Prv Aerospace, Torrance Also called Quality Forming LLC (P-10400)
Qg Printing Corp ....F......951 571-2500
 6688 Box Springs Blvd Riverside (92507) (P-4101)
Qg Printing IL LLC ....C......951 571-2500
 6688 Box Springs Blvd Riverside (92507) (P-4412)
Qic US Management Inc ....C......310 955-1670
 222 N Pacific Coast Hwy El Segundo (90245) (P-23095)
Qlogic LLC (HQ) ....C......949 389-6000
 15485 Sand Canyon Ave Irvine (92618) (P-9562)
Qma Inc ....F......805 529-5395
 1645 E Lemonwood Dr Santa Paula (93060) (P-8751)
Qmadix Inc ....D......818 988-4300
 9321 Eton Ave Chatsworth (91311) (P-13764)
Qmerit Electrification LLC (PA) ....C......888 272-0090
 2 Venture Ste 550 Irvine (92618) (P-23498)
Qmp Inc ....E......661 294-6860
 25070 Avenue Tibbitts Valencia (91355) (P-8407)
Qnap Inc ....D......909 598-6933
 168 University Pkwy Pomona (91768) (P-22859)
Qology Direct LLC ....C......310 341-4420
 12130 Millennium Ste 600 Los Angeles (90094) (P-18646)
Qorvo California Inc ....E......805 480-5050
 950 Lawrence Dr Newbury Park (91320) (P-9769)
Qorvo US, Newbury Park Also called Qorvo California Inc (P-9769)
Qpc Fiber Optic LLC ....E......949 361-8855
 27612 El Lazo Laguna Niguel (92677) (P-6356)
Qpc Laser, Sylmar Also called Laser Operations LLC (P-9530)
Qpc Lasers Inc ....F......818 986-0000
 15632 Roxford St Sylmar (91342) (P-9563)
Qpe Inc ....F......949 263-0381
 1372 Mcgaw Ave Irvine (92614) (P-4467)
Qpi Holdings Inc (HQ) ....D......310 539-2855
 22906 Frampton Ave Torrance (90501) (P-10399)
Qre Operating LLC ....D......213 225-5900
 707 Wilshire Blvd # 4600 Los Angeles (90017) (P-462)
Qsc Inc (PA) ....B......800 854-4079
 1675 Macarthur Blvd Costa Mesa (92626) (P-9186)
Qsc Audio, Costa Mesa Also called Qsc LLC (P-9186)
Qsi 2011 Inc (PA) ....F......949 855-6885
 2302 Martin Ste 475 Irvine (92612) (P-17966)
Qspac Industries Inc (PA) ....D......562 407-3868
 15020 Marquardt Ave Santa Fe Springs (90670) (P-5193)
Qst Ingredients and Packg Inc ....F......909 989-4343
 9734-40 6th St Rch Rancho Cucamonga (91730) (P-2512)
Qtc Management Inc (HQ) ....D......800 260-1515
 924 Overland Ct San Dimas (91773) (P-21473)
Qtc Mdcal Group Inc A Med Corp ....A......800 260-1515
 924 Overland Ct San Dimas (91773) (P-21474)
Quad Graphics, Riverside Also called Qg Printing IL LLC (P-4412)
Quad Knopf Inc (PA) ....E......559 733-0440
 901 E Main St Visalia (93292) (P-22641)
Quad R Tech, Harbor City Also called Onyx Industries Inc (P-7039)
Quadion LLC ....A......714 546-0994
 17651 Armstrong Ave Irvine (92614) (P-15341)
Quadra Productions Inc ....D......310 244-1234
 10202 Washington Blvd Culver City (90232) (P-19168)
Quadriga USA Enterprises Inc ....F......888 669-9994
 28410 Witherspoon Pkwy Valencia (91355) (P-3937)
Quadrotech Solutions Inc (PA) ....F......302 660-0166
 4 Polaris Way Aliso Viejo (92656) (P-17967)
Quadrtech Corporation ....F......310 523-1697
 521 W Rosecrans Ave Gardena (90248) (P-11338)
Quaglino Roofing, San Luis Obispo Also called James A Quaglino Inc (P-1490)
Quail Park Retirement Vlg LLC ....D......559 624-3500
 4520 W Cypress Ave Visalia (93277) (P-20539)
Quake City Caps, Los Angeles Also called Quake City Casuals Inc (P-14346)
Quake City Casuals Inc ....C......213 746-0540
 1800 S Flower St Los Angeles (90015) (P-14346)
Quaker, Whittier Also called AC Products Inc (P-5176)

Quaker City Plating.....C.....562 945-3721
11729 Washington Blvd Whittier (90606) ***(P-7300)***
Quaker City Plating & Silvrsm, Whittier *Also called Quaker City Plating* ***(P-7300)***
QUAKER GARDENS, Stanton *Also called California Friends Homes* ***(P-22088)***
Quaker Oats Company.....E.....714 526-8800
2501 E Orangethorpe Ave Fullerton (92831) ***(P-12236)***
Qual-Pro Corporation (HQ).....C.....310 329-7535
18510 S Figueroa St Gardena (90248) ***(P-9444)***
Quali-Tech Manufacturing, Calexico *Also called Lakim Industries Incorporated* ***(P-11513)***
Qualified Benefits, Woodland Hills *Also called Qbi LLC* ***(P-22810)***
Qualis Automotive LLC.....D.....859 689-7772
21046 Figueroa St Carson (90745) ***(P-18862)***
Qualitask Inc.....E.....714 237-0900
2840 E Gretta Ln Anaheim (92806) ***(P-8752)***
Quality Aluminum Forge LLC.....C.....714 639-8191
793 N Cypress St Orange (92867) ***(P-7105)***
Quality Behavior Solutions Inc.....D.....818 991-7722
1212 W Avenue J Ste 200 Lancaster (93534) ***(P-21332)***
Quality Car Care Products Inc.....E.....626 359-9174
2734 Huntington Dr Duarte (91010) ***(P-4668)***
Quality Components Co, Rcho STA Marg *Also called Q-Mark Manufacturing Inc* ***(P-10713)***
Quality Container Corp.....F.....909 482-1850
866 Towne Center Dr Pomona (91767) ***(P-3857)***
Quality Control Plating Inc.....E.....909 605-0206
4425 E Airport Dr Ste 113 Ontario (91761) ***(P-7301)***
Quality Control Solutions Inc.....E.....951 676-1616
43339 Bus Pk Dr Ste 101 Temecula (92590) ***(P-10905)***
Quality Fabrication Inc (PA).....D.....818 407-5015
9631 Irondale Ave Chatsworth (91311) ***(P-6896)***
Quality First Woodworks Inc.....C.....714 632-0480
1264 N Lakeview Ave Anaheim (92807) ***(P-3452)***
QUALITY FOAM PACKAGING, Lake Elsinore *Also called Aerofoam Industries Inc* ***(P-3618)***
Quality Foam Packaging Inc.....E.....951 245-4429
31855 Corydon St Lake Elsinore (92530) ***(P-5518)***
Quality Forming LLC.....D.....310 539-2855
22906 Frampton Ave Torrance (90501) ***(P-10400)***
Quality Grinding Co Inc.....F.....714 228-2100
6800 Caballero Blvd Buena Park (90620) ***(P-7865)***
Quality Heat Treating Inc.....E.....818 840-8212
3305 Burton Ave Burbank (91504) ***(P-6452)***
Quality Industry Repair, Santa Fe Springs *Also called Pscmb Repairs Inc* ***(P-8749)***
Quality Inn, San Luis Obispo *Also called Q S San Luis Obispo LP* ***(P-16645)***
Quality Inn, Blythe *Also called Anup Inc* ***(P-16326)***
Quality Inn, Santa Ana *Also called Q S H Properties Inc* ***(P-16644)***
Quality Instant Printing, San Dimas *Also called Am-PM Printing Inc* ***(P-4226)***
Quality Laminating, Pacoima *Also called Phillips Plywood Co Inc* ***(P-13281)***
Quality Magnetics Corporation.....E.....310 632-1941
18025 Adria Maru Ln Carson (90746) ***(P-7569)***
Quality Marble & Granite, Ontario *Also called Regards Enterprises Inc* ***(P-3434)***
Quality Marine, Los Angeles *Also called Allaquaria LLC* ***(P-14909)***
Quality Packaging and Engrg, Irvine *Also called Qpe Inc* ***(P-4467)***
Quality Painting Co.....F.....626 964-2529
19136 San Jose Ave Rowland Heights (91748) ***(P-7405)***
Quality Produced LLC (PA).....E.....310 592-8834
11693 San Vicente Blvd Los Angeles (90049) ***(P-1908)***
Quality Production Svcs Inc.....D.....310 406-3350
18711 S Broadwick St Compton (90220) ***(P-1395)***
Quality Reimbursement Services.....D.....626 445-5092
150 N Santa Anita Ave Arcadia (91006) ***(P-22811)***
Quality Resources Dist LLC.....E.....510 378-6861
16254 Beaver Rd Adelanto (92301) ***(P-11739)***
Quality Rubber Sourcing Inc.....F.....805 544-7770
3988 Short St Ste 110 San Luis Obispo (93401) ***(P-4733)***
Quality Service Pac Industry, Santa Fe Springs *Also called Qspac Industries Inc* ***(P-5193)***
Quality Shutters Inc.....E.....951 683-4939
3359 Chicago Ave Ste A Riverside (92507) ***(P-3285)***
Quality Speaks LLC (PA).....C.....818 264-4400
9221 Corbin Ave Ste 260 Northridge (91324) ***(P-12666)***
Quality Sprayers Inc.....D.....562 376-5177
3020 E La Palma Ave Anaheim (92806) ***(P-147)***
Quality Tech Mfg Inc.....E.....909 465-9565
170 W Mindanao St Bloomington (92316) ***(P-10201)***
Quality Temp Staffing, Granada Hills *Also called Siracusa Enterprises Inc* ***(P-17465)***
Quality Vessel Engineering Inc.....F.....562 696-2100
8515 Chetle Ave Santa Fe Springs (90670) ***(P-6748)***
Quallion LLC.....C.....818 833-2000
12744 San Fernando Rd # 100 Sylmar (91342) ***(P-9817)***
Qualls Stud Welding Pdts Inc.....F.....562 923-7883
9459 Washburn Rd Downey (90242) ***(P-13931)***
Qualontime Corporation.....F.....714 523-4751
19 Senisa Irvine (92612) ***(P-8753)***
Qualstar Corporation (PA).....F.....805 583-7744
1267 Flynn Rd Camarillo (93012) ***(P-8213)***
Quanex Screens LLC.....F.....909 349-0600
13611 Santa Ana Ave Fontana (92337) ***(P-6713)***
Quanmax Usa Inc.....D.....949 272-2930
25 Delamesa E Irvine (92620) ***(P-13430)***
Quantimetrix Corporation.....D.....310 536-0006
2005 Manhattan Beach Blvd Redondo Beach (90278) ***(P-4926)***
Quantos Payroll, Los Angeles *Also called Film Payroll Services Inc* ***(P-22784)***
Quantum Alliance Inc.....F.....818 415-2085
511 E Mountain St Glendale (91207) ***(P-8214)***
Quantum Automation.....E.....714 854-0800
4400 E La Palma Ave Anaheim (92807) ***(P-13663)***
Quantum Bhvioral Solutions Inc (PA).....D.....626 531-6999
445 S Figueroa St # 3100 Los Angeles (90071) ***(P-20229)***
Quantum Bhvioral Solutions Inc.....D.....626 531-6999
2400 E Katella Ave # 800 Anaheim (92806) ***(P-20230)***
Quantum Concept Inc.....F.....323 888-8601
5701 S Eastrn Ave Ste 220 Commerce (90040) ***(P-2822)***
Quantum Corporation, Irvine *Also called Certance LLC* ***(P-8193)***
Quantum Four Labs LLC.....F.....213 217-9777
3310 Fruitland Ave Vernon (90058) ***(P-4879)***
Quantum Solutions Inc.....E.....818 577-4555
5146 Douglas Fir Rd # 205 Calabasas (91302) ***(P-18217)***
Quantum Technologies, Lake Forest *Also called Qf Liquidation Inc* ***(P-10118)***
Quantum Technologies Inc.....F.....949 399-4500
25242 Arctic Ocean Dr Lake Forest (92630) ***(P-409)***
Quantum World Technologies Inc.....B.....805 834-0532
199 W Hillcrest Dr Ste 11 Thousand Oaks (91360) ***(P-17450)***
Quantum-Dynamics Co.....F.....818 719-0142
6414 Independence Ave Woodland Hills (91367) ***(P-10715)***
Quarry At La Quinta Inc (PA).....D.....760 777-1100
41865 Boardwalk Ste 214 Palm Desert (92211) ***(P-19504)***
Quarton Usa Inc.....F.....888 532-2221
3230 Fallow Field Dr Diamond Bar (91765) ***(P-9903)***
Quartz Logistics Inc.....D.....626 606-2001
780 Nogales St Ste D City of Industry (91748) ***(P-12514)***
Quechan Gaming Commission, Winterhaven *Also called Quechan Indian Tribe* ***(P-19663)***
Quechan Indian Tribe.....D.....760 572-2413
450 Quechan Rd Winterhaven (92283) ***(P-19663)***
Queen Beach Printers Inc.....E.....562 436-8201
937 Pine Ave Long Beach (90813) ***(P-4413)***
Queen Mary Hotel, Long Beach *Also called RMS Foundation Inc* ***(P-16668)***
Queen Mary, The, Long Beach *Also called Urban Commons Queensway LLC* ***(P-16763)***
Queen of The Valley Campus, West Covina *Also called Citrus Vly Hlth Partners Inc* ***(P-20723)***
Queen of The Valley Hospital, West Covina *Also called Emanate Health Medical Center* ***(P-20766)***
Queen of Valley Hospital.....D.....626 962-4011
1115 S Sunset Ave West Covina (91790) ***(P-20919)***
Queensbay Hotel LLC.....D.....562 481-3910
700 Queensway Dr Long Beach (90802) ***(P-16646)***
Queenscare Fmly Clinics-Eastsd, Los Angeles *Also called Queenscare Health Centers* ***(P-20031)***
Queenscare Health Centers.....D.....323 780-4510
4816 E 3rd St Los Angeles (90022) ***(P-20031)***
Queenscare Health Centers.....D.....323 644-6180
4618 Fountain Ave Los Angeles (90029) ***(P-20032)***
Quest Components Inc.....E.....626 333-5858
14711 Clark Ave City of Industry (91745) ***(P-13765)***
Quest Dgnstics Clncal Labs Inc.....D.....661 964-6582
26081 Avenue Hall 150 Valencia (91355) ***(P-21090)***
Quest Dgnstics Clncal Labs Inc.....D.....562 424-3039
701 E 28th St Ste 113 Long Beach (90806) ***(P-21091)***
Quest Dgnstics Clncal Labs Inc.....D.....562 945-7771
15141 Whittier Blvd # 12 Whittier (90603) ***(P-21092)***
Quest Dgnstics Nchols Inst Vln, Valencia *Also called Specialty Laboratories Inc* ***(P-21096)***
Quest Diagnostics, West Hills *Also called Unilab Corporation* ***(P-21100)***
Quest Diagnostics Nichols Inst (HQ).....A.....949 728-4000
33608 Ortega Hwy San Juan Capistrano (92675) ***(P-10808)***
Quest Group (PA).....D.....949 585-0111
2621 White Rd Irvine (92614) ***(P-14176)***
Quest Intl Monitor Svc Inc (PA).....D.....949 581-9900
60-65 Parker Irvine (92618) ***(P-18150)***
Quest Nutrition LLC.....D.....562 272-0180
777 S Avi Blvd Ste 100 El Segundo (90245) ***(P-14727)***
Quest Nutrition LLC.....E.....562 446-3321
2221 Park Pl El Segundo (90245) ***(P-2513)***
Quest Software Inc (HQ).....A.....949 754-8000
4 Polaris Way Aliso Viejo (92656) ***(P-18060)***
Quest Software Inc.....D.....949 754-8000
4 Polaris Way Aliso Viejo (92656) ***(P-17968)***
Questsoft Corporation.....E.....949 837-9506
24411 Ridge Route Dr # 220 Laguna Hills (92653) ***(P-17694)***
Questus Inc (PA).....E.....415 677-5719
3350 E Birch St Ste 110 Brea (92821) ***(P-18106)***
Questys Solutions, Irvine *Also called Qsi 2011 Inc* ***(P-17966)***
Quetico LLC (PA).....C.....909 628-6200
5610 Daniels St Chino (91710) ***(P-14970)***
Quick Lane, Fontana *Also called Sunrise Ford* ***(P-13035)***
Quick Lane, Hawthorne *Also called South Bay Ford Inc* ***(P-18872)***
Quick Lane, Riverside *Also called Raceway Ford Inc* ***(P-18863)***
Quick Systems Inc.....E.....702 335-3574
5042 Wilshire Blvd # 28533 Los Angeles (90036) ***(P-1125)***
Quickrete, Corona *Also called Quikrete California LLC* ***(P-6053)***
Quiel Bros Elc Sign Svc Co Inc.....E.....909 885-4476
272 S I St San Bernardino (92410) ***(P-11584)***
Quiet Cannon Montebello Inc.....D.....323 724-4500
901 Via San Clemente Montebello (90640) ***(P-16974)***
Quigley-Simpson La, Los Angeles *Also called Quigly-Simpson Heppelwhite Inc* ***(P-17047)***
Quigly-Simpson Heppelwhite Inc.....C.....310 996-5800
11601 Wilshire Blvd Fl 7 Los Angeles (90025) ***(P-17047)***
Quik Pick Express LLC.....C.....310 763-3000
23610 Banning Blvd Carson (90745) ***(P-12515)***
Quik Pick Express LLC (PA).....C.....310 763-3000
1021 E 233rd St Carson (90745) ***(P-12516)***
Quik-Shor, Downey *Also called Westar Manufacturing Inc* ***(P-1703)***
Quikrete California LLC.....C.....951 277-3155
3940 Temescal Canyon Rd Corona (92883) ***(P-6053)***
Quikstor, Encino *Also called Calstar Systems Group Inc* ***(P-9857)***
Quikturn Prof Scrnprinting Inc.....F.....800 784-5419
567 S Melrose St Placentia (92870) ***(P-4562)***
Quill Distribution Center, Ontario *Also called Quill LLC* ***(P-12237)***
Quill LLC.....D.....909 390-0600
1500 S Dupont Ave Ontario (91761) ***(P-12237)***

Employee Codes: A=Over 500 employees, B=251-500
C=101-250, D=51-100, E=20-50 F=10-19
2022 Southern California Business
Directory and Buyers Guide
© Mergent Inc. 1-800-342-5647
1247

Quilter Laboratories LLC...F.......714 519-6114
1700 Sunflower Ave Costa Mesa (92626) ***(P-11348)***
Quilting House...F.......949 476-7090
16872 Millikan Ave Irvine (92606) ***(P-3116)***
Quinn Company...D.......559 992-2193
510 Pickerell Ave Corcoran (93212) ***(P-13866)***
Quinn Company...D.......818 767-7171
13275 Golden State Rd Sylmar (91342) ***(P-13867)***
Quinn Company...D.......661 393-5800
2200 Pegasus Dr Bakersfield (93308) ***(P-13868)***
Quinn Company...D.......805 485-2171
801 Del Norte Blvd Oxnard (93030) ***(P-13869)***
Quinn Company...D.......805 925-8611
1655 Carlotti Dr Santa Maria (93454) ***(P-13870)***
Quinn Company...F.......888 987-8466
3359 Pomona Blvd Pomona (91768) ***(P-7616)***
Quinn Emnuel Urqhart Sllvan LL (PA)...B.......213 443-3000
865 S Figueroa St Fl 10 Los Angeles (90017) ***(P-21667)***
Quinn Shepherd Machinery...B.......562 463-6000
10006 Rose Hills Rd City of Industry (90601) ***(P-13871)***
Quinstar Technology Inc...D.......310 320-1111
24085 Garnier St Torrance (90505) ***(P-13766)***
Quintile Wealth Management LLC...E.......310 806-4000
11150 Santa Monica Blvd # 400 Los Angeles (90025) ***(P-23304)***
Quintron Systems Inc (PA)...E.......805 928-4343
2105 S Blosser Rd Santa Maria (93458) ***(P-9240)***
Quoc Viet Foods...E.......714 283-3131
1967 N Glassell St Orange (92865) ***(P-14728)***
Quotit Corporation...C.......714 564-5000
721 S Parker St Ste 330 Orange (92868) ***(P-18061)***
Qupid Shoe, Walnut *Also called East Lion Corporation* ***(P-14436)***
Qy Research Inc...D.......626 295-2442
17890 Castleton St City of Industry (91748) ***(P-22897)***
Qycell Corporation...E.......909 390-6644
600 Etiwanda Ave Ontario (91761) ***(P-5519)***
Qyk Brands LLC...C.......949 312-7119
12101 Western Ave Garden Grove (92841) ***(P-14284)***
R & A Technical Inc...F.......951 549-6945
232 N Sherman Ave Ste D Corona (92882) ***(P-7949)***
R & B Plastics Inc...F.......714 229-8419
227 E Meats Ave Orange (92865) ***(P-5785)***
R & B Realty Group LP...A.......310 478-1021
1 World Trade Ctr # 2400 Long Beach (90831) ***(P-15962)***
R & B Reinforcing Steel Corp...D.......909 591-1726
13581 5th St Chino (91710) ***(P-1578)***
R & B Wholesale Distrs Inc (PA)...D.......909 230-5400
2350 S Milliken Ave Ontario (91761) ***(P-13692)***
R & B Wire Products Inc...E.......714 549-3355
2902 W Garry Ave Santa Ana (92704) ***(P-7509)***
R & D Fasteners, Rancho Cucamonga *Also called Doubleco Incorporated* ***(P-7062)***
R & D Nova Inc...F.......951 781-7332
833 Marlborough Ave 200 Riverside (92507) ***(P-11236)***
R & D Steel Inc...E.......310 631-6183
1136 S Santa Fe Ave Compton (90221) ***(P-6654)***
R & I Industries Inc...E.......909 923-7747
2910 S Archibald Ave A Ontario (91761) ***(P-6655)***
R & J Fabricators Inc...E.......951 817-0300
1121 Railroad St Ste 102 Corona (92882) ***(P-3738)***
R & J Material Handling Inc...F.......951 735-0000
345 Adams Cir Corona (92882) ***(P-13932)***
R & L Brosamer Inc...B.......559 739-8215
2916 W Main St Visalia (93291) ***(P-813)***
R & R Ductwork LLC...F.......562 944-9660
12820 Lakeland Rd Santa Fe Springs (90670) ***(P-6897)***
R & R Electric...E.......310 785-0288
2029 Century Park E A4 Los Angeles (90067) ***(P-1304)***
R & R Fabrications Inc...E.......562 693-0500
13438 Lambert Rd Whittier (90605) ***(P-6656)***
R & R Industries, San Clemente *Also called Rosen & Rosen Industries Inc* ***(P-11443)***
R & R Industries Inc...E.......800 234-5611
204 Avenida Fabricante San Clemente (92672) ***(P-3082)***
R & R Metal Fabricators...F.......626 960-6400
14846 Ramona Blvd Baldwin Park (91706) ***(P-6657)***
R & R Pumping Unit Repr & Svc, Ventura *Also called Richard Yarbrough* ***(P-543)***
R & R Rubber Molding Inc...E.......626 575-8105
2444 Loma Ave South El Monte (91733) ***(P-5403)***
R & R Services Corporation...E.......818 889-2562
31119 Via Colinas Ste 502 Westlake Village (91362) ***(P-5404)***
R & S Automation Inc...E.......800 962-3111
283 W Bonita Ave Pomona (91767) ***(P-6714)***
R & S Manufacturing & Sup Inc...F.......909 622-5881
16616 Garfield Ave Paramount (90723) ***(P-5110)***
R & S Mfg, Pomona *Also called R & S Mfg Southern Cal Inc* ***(P-6715)***
R & S Mfg Southern Cal Inc...F.......909 596-2090
283 W Bonita Ave Pomona (91767) ***(P-6715)***
R & S Overhead Door of So Cal...E.......714 680-0600
1617 N Orangethorpe Way Anaheim (92801) ***(P-6716)***
R & S Processing Co Inc...D.......562 531-0738
15712 Illinois Ave Paramount (90723) ***(P-5405)***
R A F LP (PA)...D.......714 633-1442
1702 Fairhaven Ave Santa Ana (92705) ***(P-16926)***
R A Reed Electric Company (PA)...E.......323 587-2284
5503 S Boyle Ave Vernon (90058) ***(P-19015)***
R and I Holdings Inc...E.......562 483-0577
2145 Dashwood St Lakewood Lakewood (90712) ***(P-16109)***
R and L Lopez Associates Inc (PA)...D.......626 330-5296
3649 Tyler Ave El Monte (91731) ***(P-22642)***
R B R Meat Company Inc...D.......323 973-4868
5151 Alcoa Ave Vernon (90058) ***(P-1718)***
R B Welding Inc...E.......310 324-8680
155 E Redondo Beach Blvd Gardena (90248) ***(P-18993)***
R C Hotels Inc...D.......714 891-0123
7667 Center Ave Huntington Beach (92647) ***(P-16647)***
R C I P Inc...F.......714 530-1239
1476 N Hundley St Anaheim (92806) ***(P-8754)***
R C Industries, Anaheim *Also called R C I P Inc* ***(P-8754)***
R C L Lodging Systems Inc...D.......661 833-3000
1045 E Valley Blvd A205 San Gabriel (91776) ***(P-16648)***
R C Products Corp...E.......949 858-8820
22322 Gilberto Rcho STA Marg (92688) ***(P-6533)***
R D D USA Division, Commerce *Also called RDD Enterprises Inc* ***(P-3144)***
R D Mathis Company...E.......562 426-7049
2840 Gundry Ave Signal Hill (90755) ***(P-6219)***
R D Rubber Technology Corp...E.......562 941-4800
12870 Florence Ave Santa Fe Springs (90670) ***(P-5360)***
R G Canning Enterprises Inc...C.......323 560-7469
4515 E 59th Pl Maywood (90270) ***(P-18647)***
R G Hansen & Associates (PA)...F.......805 564-3388
5951 Encina Rd Ste 106 Goleta (93117) ***(P-10716)***
R Gas LLC...F.......559 592-2456
30045 Road 196 Exeter (93221) ***(P-5258)***
R H Barden Inc...F.......714 970-0900
4769 E Wesley Dr Anaheim (92807) ***(P-9640)***
R H D, Corona *Also called Ranch House Doors Inc* ***(P-1452)***
R H Strasbaugh (PA)...D.......805 541-6424
825 Buckley Rd San Luis Obispo (93401) ***(P-7741)***
R K Fabrication Inc...F.......714 630-9654
1283 N Grove St Anaheim (92806) ***(P-4711)***
R K Properties, Long Beach *Also called Rance King Properties Inc* ***(P-15746)***
R Kern Engineering & Mfg Corp...D.......909 664-2440
13912 Mountain Ave Chino (91710) ***(P-9664)***
R L Anodizing...F.......818 252-3804
11331 Penrose St Sun Valley (91352) ***(P-7302)***
R L Anodizing & Plating, Sun Valley *Also called R L Anodizing* ***(P-7302)***
R L Jones-San Diego Inc (PA)...D.......760 357-3177
1778 Zinetta Rd Ste A Calexico (92231) ***(P-12517)***
R Lang Company...D.......559 651-0701
8240 W Doe Ave Visalia (93291) ***(P-6717)***
R M A Group (PA)...D.......909 980-6096
12130 Santa Margarita Ct Rancho Cucamonga (91730) ***(P-22643)***
R M Baker Machine and Tl Inc...F.......562 697-4007
815 W Front St Covina (91722) ***(P-8755)***
R M I, Van Nuys *Also called Rothlisberger Mfg A Cal Corp* ***(P-8777)***
R M I, Gardena *Also called Rotational Molding Inc* ***(P-5800)***
R Mc Closkey Insurance Agency...C.......949 223-8100
4001 Macarthur Blvd # 300 Newport Beach (92660) ***(P-15620)***
R N D Enterprises, Lancaster *Also called BDR Industries Inc* ***(P-12751)***
R P Direct, Santa Monica *Also called Postaer Rubin and Associates* ***(P-17046)***
R P M Centerless Grinding, Norco *Also called RPM Grinding Co Inc* ***(P-8780)***
R P S Resort Corp...C.......760 327-8311
1600 N Indian Canyon Dr Palm Springs (92262) ***(P-16649)***
R Planet Earth LLC...C.......213 320-0601
3200 Fruitland Ave Vernon (90058) ***(P-12968)***
R R Donnelley & Sons Company...E.......310 784-8485
18915 S Laurel Park Rd Rancho Dominguez (90220) ***(P-17139)***
R Ranch Market...D.......714 573-1182
1112 Walnut Ave Tustin (92780) ***(P-145)***
R S R Steel Fabrication Inc...E.......760 244-2210
11040 I Ave Hesperia (92345) ***(P-6209)***
R T A, Riverside *Also called Riverside Transit Agency* ***(P-11836)***
R T C Group...E.......949 226-2000
905 Calle Amanecer # 150 San Clemente (92673) ***(P-4102)***
R W Swarens Associates Inc...E.......626 579-0943
10768 Lower Azusa Rd El Monte (91731) ***(P-9101)***
R W Zant Co (PA)...D.......323 980-5457
1470 E 4th St Los Angeles (90033) ***(P-14602)***
R&M Deese Inc...E.......951 734-7342
1875 Sampson Ave Corona (92879) ***(P-11585)***
R&R Electric, Redondo Beach *Also called Ricardo Ramos* ***(P-1309)***
R&R Machine Products Inc...F.......909 885-7500
760 W Mill St San Bernardino (92410) ***(P-7043)***
R-Cold Inc...D.......951 436-5476
1221 S G St Perris (92570) ***(P-8346)***
R-Con General Building Inc (PA)...D.......818 235-6465
18017 Chtswrth St Ste 665 Granada Hills (91344) ***(P-1683)***
R-F Circuits and Assembly Inc...F.......805 499-7788
3533 Old Conejo Rd # 107 Newbury Park (91320) ***(P-9445)***
R1 Concepts Inc...D.......714 777-2323
13140 Midway Pl Cerritos (90703) ***(P-13081)***
R3 Performance Products Inc...F.......760 909-0846
531 Old Woman Springs Rd Yucca Valley (92284) ***(P-10119)***
RA Industries LLC...E.......714 557-2322
900 Glenneyre St Laguna Beach (92651) ***(P-8756)***
RABBIT RIDGE VINEYARDS, Paso Robles *Also called Rabbit Ridge Wine Sales Inc* ***(P-2215)***
Rabbit Ridge Wine Sales Inc (PA)...F.......661 877-7525
1172 San Marcos Rd Paso Robles (93446) ***(P-2215)***
RAC, Corcoran *Also called Recreational Assn Corcoran* ***(P-22362)***
Racaar Circuit Industries Inc...F.......818 998-7566
9225 Alabama Ave Ste F Chatsworth (91311) ***(P-9446)***
Race Pak, Rcho STA Marg *Also called Racepak LLC* ***(P-9963)***
Race Pro Products, Bloomington *Also called Rpp Products Inc* ***(P-14806)***
Race Technologies LLC...F.......714 438-1118
17422 Murphy Ave Irvine (92614) ***(P-10120)***
Raceline Wheels, Garden Grove *Also called Allied Wheel Components Inc* ***(P-10015)***
Racepak LLC...E.......949 709-5555
30402 Esperanza Rcho STA Marg (92688) ***(P-10121)***

Racepak LLC...E...888 429-4709
30402 Esperanza Rcho STA Marg (92688) ***(P-9963)***
Racer Media & Marketing Inc...F...949 417-6700
17030 Red Hill Ave Irvine (92614) ***(P-4103)***
Raceway Ford Inc...C...951 571-9300
5800 Sycamore Canyon Blvd Riverside (92507) ***(P-18863)***
Rachas Inc...E...626 671-2440
9080 Foothill Blvd Rancho Cucamonga (91730) ***(P-19465)***
Rachas Inc...E...714 290-0636
135 N Beach Blvd Anaheim (92801) ***(P-19466)***
Rachlin Architects Inc...D...310 204-3400
8640 National Blvd Culver City (90232) ***(P-22737)***
Racing Beat Inc...E...714 779-8677
4789 E Wesley Dr Anaheim (92807) ***(P-7597)***
Racing Plus Inc...E...951 360-5906
3834 Wacker Dr Jurupa Valley (91752) ***(P-11137)***
Racing Power Company...E...909 468-3690
815 Tucker Ln Walnut (91789) ***(P-10122)***
Rack Depot Inc...E...562 777-9809
10226 Greenleaf Ave Santa Fe Springs (90670) ***(P-13933)***
Rack Installations Svcs Inc...E...909 261-2243
1256 Brooks St Ste E Ontario (91762) ***(P-3692)***
Rackmountpro.com, La Puente *Also called Yang-Ming International Corp* ***(P-18077)***
RAD Onc Inc...D...562 492-6695
2650 Elm Ave Ste 201 Long Beach (90806) ***(P-20033)***
RAD-Image Med Group Inc A Cal...D...562 912-2500
2651 Walnut Ave Signal Hill (90755) ***(P-20034)***
Radarsonics Inc...F...714 630-7288
1190 N Grove St Anaheim (92806) ***(P-9770)***
Radcal Corporation...E...626 357-7921
426 W Duarte Rd Monrovia (91016) ***(P-10906)***
Radford Alexander Corporation...D...310 523-2555
14700 S Avalon Blvd Gardena (90248) ***(P-11988)***
Radford Cabinets Inc...D...661 729-8931
216 E Avenue K8 Lancaster (93535) ***(P-3486)***
Radford Studio Center Inc...B...818 655-5000
4024 Radford Ave Studio City (91604) ***(P-19330)***
Radiabeam Technologies LLC (PA)...**F...310 822-5845**
1717 Stewart St Santa Monica (90404) ***(P-13536)***
Radial South LP...B...610 491-7000
2225 Alder Ave Rialto (92377) ***(P-12238)***
Radian Audio Engineering Inc...E...714 288-8900
2720 Kimball Ave Pomona (91767) ***(P-9311)***
Radian Memory Systems Inc...E...818 222-4080
5010 N Pkwy Ste 205 Calabasas (91302) ***(P-8215)***
Radiance Lightworks Inc...F...818 879-1516
4607 Lkview Cyn Rd Ste 50 Westlake Village (91361) ***(P-9023)***
Radiant Services Corp (PA)...**C...310 327-6300**
651 W Knox St Gardena (90248) ***(P-16838)***
Radiation Oncology, Long Beach *Also called RAD Onc Inc* ***(P-20033)***
Radiation Protection & Spc Inc...F...714 771-7702
1531 W Orangewood Ave Orange (92868) ***(P-6898)***
Radica Enterprises Ltd (HQ)...**D...310 252-2000**
333 Continental Blvd El Segundo (90245) ***(P-14100)***
Radica USA, El Segundo *Also called Radica Enterprises Ltd* ***(P-14100)***
Radio Disney Group LLC...D...818 569-5000
3800 W Alameda Ave # 115 Burbank (91505) ***(P-12704)***
Radio Korea USA, Los Angeles *Also called Infokorea Inc* ***(P-4074)***
Radio Station Kfbs, La Mirada *Also called Far East Broadcasting Co Inc* ***(P-12691)***
Radiology Partners Inc (HQ)...**B...424 290-8004**
2101 E El Segundo Blvd # 40 El Segundo (90245) ***(P-20035)***
Radiology Support Devices Inc...E...310 518-0527
1904 E Dominguez St Long Beach (90810) ***(P-11048)***
Radiometer America Inc (HQ)...**E...800 736-0600**
250 S Kraemer Blvd Msb1sw Brea (92821) ***(P-13515)***
Radison Hotel Newport Beach, Newport Beach *Also called Pacific Hotel Management Inc* ***(P-16608)***
Radisson Hotel At Usc...C...213 748-4141
3540 S Figueroa St Los Angeles (90007) ***(P-16650)***
Radisson Hotel La Westside, Culver City *Also called Pacifica Ht Cnfrnce Ctr A Cal* ***(P-16614)***
Radisson Hotel Santa Maria...D...805 928-8000
3455 Skyway Dr Santa Maria (93455) ***(P-16651)***
Radisson Inn, Los Angeles *Also called Radisson Hotel At Usc* ***(P-16650)***
Radisson Inn, Santa Maria *Also called Radisson Hotel Santa Maria* ***(P-16651)***
Radisson Inn, Los Angeles *Also called Radlax Gateway Hotel LLC* ***(P-16652)***
Radisson Inn, San Bernardino *Also called First Hotels International Inc* ***(P-16443)***
Radix Textile Inc...D...323 234-1667
600 E Wash Blvd Ste C2 Los Angeles (90015) ***(P-14316)***
Radlax Gateway Hotel LLC...A...310 670-9000
6225 W Century Blvd Los Angeles (90045) ***(P-16652)***
Radleys...E...310 765-2223
3780 Wilshire Blvd # 110 Los Angeles (90010) ***(P-19169)***
Radnet Inc (PA)...**B...310 445-2800**
1510 Cotner Ave Los Angeles (90025) ***(P-21093)***
Radnet Management I Inc...C...661 945-5855
44725 10th St W Ste 150 Lancaster (93534) ***(P-20036)***
Radnet Mnaged Imaging Svcs Inc (HQ)...**C...310 445-2800**
1510 Cotner Ave Los Angeles (90025) ***(P-20037)***
Radnoti Glass Technology Inc...F...626 357-8827
541 E Edna Pl Covina (91723) ***(P-22860)***
Radon Boats, Goleta *Also called DR Radon Boatbuilding Inc* ***(P-10463)***
Rael Inc...E...800 573-1516
6940 Beach Blvd Unit D301 Buena Park (90621) ***(P-3908)***
Raemica Inc...E...909 864-1990
7759 Victoria Ave Highland (92346) ***(P-1747)***
Rafco Products Brickform, Rancho Cucamonga *Also called Rafco-Brickform LLC* ***(P-7866)***
Rafco-Brickform LLC (PA)...**D...909 484-3399**
11061 Jersey Blvd Rancho Cucamonga (91730) ***(P-7866)***
Raffles Lrmitage Beverly Hills...C...310 278-3344
9291 Burton Way Beverly Hills (90210) ***(P-16653)***
Rafu Shimpo...E...213 629-2231
701 E 3rd St Ste 130 Los Angeles (90013) ***(P-4025)***
Raging Waters Group Inc...A...909 802-2200
111 Raging Waters Dr San Dimas (91773) ***(P-19522)***
Rahn Industries Incorporated (PA)...**D...562 908-0680**
2630 Pacific Park Dr Whittier (90601) ***(P-8347)***
Rai Care Ctrs Sthern Cal II LL...D...760 347-3986
46767 Monroe St Ste 101 Indio (92201) ***(P-21260)***
Rai Care Ctrs Sthern Cal II LL...D...310 673-6865
1416 Centinela Ave Inglewood (90302) ***(P-21261)***
Rai Care Ctrs Sthern Cal II LL...D...760 346-7588
41501 Corporate Way Palm Desert (92260) ***(P-21262)***
Rai Centinela Inglewood, Inglewood *Also called Rai Care Ctrs Sthern Cal II LL* ***(P-21261)***
Rai Corporate Way Palm Desert, Palm Desert *Also called Rai Care Ctrs Sthern Cal II LL* ***(P-21262)***
Railmakers Inc...F...949 642-6506
864 W 18th St Costa Mesa (92627) ***(P-6658)***
Railpros Inc (PA)...**C...714 734-8765**
15265 Alton Pkwy Ste 140 Irvine (92618) ***(P-22644)***
Railstech Inc...E...267 315-2998
730 Arizona Ave Santa Monica (90401) ***(P-17969)***
Rain Bird Corporation (PA)...**C...626 812-3400**
970 W Sierra Madre Ave Azusa (91702) ***(P-7475)***
Rain Bird Distribution Corp...E...626 963-9311
1000 W Sierra Madre Ave Azusa (91702) ***(P-1003)***
Rain For Rent, Bakersfield *Also called Western Oilfields Supply Co* ***(P-17384)***
Rain Mstr Irrgtion Systems Inc...E...805 527-4498
5825 Jasmine St Riverside (92504) ***(P-10717)***
Rainbo Record Mfg Corp (PA)...**E...818 280-1100**
8960 Eton Ave Canoga Park (91304) ***(P-9224)***
Rainbo Records & Cassettes, Canoga Park *Also called Rainbo Record Mfg Corp* ***(P-9224)***
Rainbow Camp Inc...E...310 456-3066
26619 Marigold Ct Calabasas (91302) ***(P-19664)***
Rainbow Disposal Co Inc (HQ)...**C...714 847-3581**
17121 Nichols Ln Huntington Beach (92647) ***(P-12969)***
Rainbow Magnetics Incorporated...F...714 540-4777
1 Whatney Irvine (92618) ***(P-4414)***
Rainbow Refuse Recycling, Huntington Beach *Also called Rainbow Disposal Co Inc* ***(P-12969)***
Rainbow Sublymation Inc...E...213 489-5001
2438 E 11th St Los Angeles (90021) ***(P-4563)***
Raintree Business Products Inc...E...949 859-0801
23101 Terra Dr Laguna Hills (92653) ***(P-4415)***
Raintree Systems Inc...C...951 252-9400
30650 Rancho California R Temecula (92591) ***(P-17695)***
Raise 3d Inc...F...888 963-9028
43 Tesla Irvine (92618) ***(P-13431)***
Raise 3d Technologies Inc...E...949 482-2040
43 Tesla Irvine (92618) ***(P-8295)***
Raise Praise Inc...F...805 498-1747
845 Rnch Conejo Blvd Newbury Park (91320) ***(P-11349)***
Raj Manufacturing LLC...E...714 838-3110
2692 Dow Ave Tustin (92780) ***(P-2988)***
Raj Manufacturing Inc (PA)...**F...714 838-3110**
2692 Dow Ave Tustin (92780) ***(P-15963)***
Rajysan Incorporated (PA)...**E...661 775-4920**
4175 Guardian St Simi Valley (93063) ***(P-13934)***
Rakar Incorporated...E...805 487-2721
1700 Emerson Ave Oxnard (93033) ***(P-5786)***
Rakworx Inc...C...949 215-1362
23122 Alcalde Dr Ste C Laguna Hills (92653) ***(P-18151)***
Ralco Holdings Inc (HQ)...**A...949 440-5500**
13861 Rosecrans Ave Santa Fe Springs (90670) ***(P-13082)***
Raleigh Enterprises Inc (PA)...**C...310 899-8900**
5300 Melrose Ave Fl 4 Los Angeles (90038) ***(P-16654)***
Raleigh Holdings, Los Angeles *Also called Raleigh Enterprises Inc* ***(P-16654)***
Raleigh Sunset Marquis Ho...D...310 358-3759
1200 Alta Loma Rd Los Angeles (90069) ***(P-16655)***
Ralis Services Corp...C...844 347-2547
1 City Blvd W Ste 600 Orange (92868) ***(P-23305)***
Ralison International Inc...E...909 393-0008
15328 Central Ave Chino (91710) ***(P-14120)***
Rally Holdings LLC...A...817 919-6833
17771 Mitchell N Irvine (92614) ***(P-13083)***
Ralph Brennan Rest Group LLC...D...714 776-5200
1590 S Disneyland Dr Anaheim (92802) ***(P-23306)***
Ralph E Ames Machine Works...E...310 328-8523
2301 Dominguez Way Torrance (90501) ***(P-8757)***
Ralphs Logistics - Compton DC, Compton *Also called Kroger Co* ***(P-12217)***
Ram Off Road Accessories Inc...E...323 266-3850
3901 Medford St Los Angeles (90063) ***(P-10123)***
Ram Technologies, Walnut *Also called KS Electronics Inc* ***(P-9527)***
Rama Corporation...E...951 654-7351
600 W Esplanade Ave San Jacinto (92583) ***(P-8097)***
Rama Food Manufacture Corp (PA)...**E...909 923-5305**
1486 E Cedar St Ontario (91761) ***(P-2514)***
Ramada By Wyndham, Irvine *Also called Western National Securities* ***(P-16033)***
Ramada Inn, Costa Mesa *Also called Trigild International Inc* ***(P-16757)***
Ramcar Batteries Inc...E...323 726-1212
2700 Carrier Ave Commerce (90040) ***(P-13084)***
Ramcast Ornamental Sup Co Inc...E...909 469-4767
1450 E Mission Blvd Pomona (91766) ***(P-13586)***
Ramcast Steel, Pomona *Also called Ramcast Ornamental Sup Co Inc* ***(P-13586)***
Ramco, Simi Valley *Also called Recycled Aggregate Mtls Co Inc* ***(P-5277)***
Ramco Employment Services, Oxnard *Also called Ramco Enterprises LP* ***(P-183)***

ALPHABETIC

Employee Codes: A=Over 500 employees, B=251-500
C=101-250, D=51-100, E=20-50 F=10-19
2022 Southern California Business
Directory and Buyers Guide
© Mergent Inc. 1-800-342-5647
1249

Ramco Enterprises LP...A...805 922-9888
325 Plaza Dr Ste 1 Santa Maria (93454) ***(P-17451)***
Ramco Enterprises LP...A...805 486-9328
520 E 3rd St Ste B Oxnard (93030) ***(P-183)***
Ramda Metal Specialties Inc...E...310 538-2136
13012 Crenshaw Blvd Gardena (90249) ***(P-6899)***
Rami Designs Inc...F...949 588-8288
24 Hammond Ste E Irvine (92618) ***(P-6976)***
Ramirez Pallets Inc...E...909 822-2066
8431 Sultana Ave Fontana (92335) ***(P-3405)***
Ramisons Inc...F...714 323-7134
1534 S Harbor Blvd Anaheim (92802) ***(P-2102)***
Ramkade Insurance Services...A...818 444-1340
21550 Oxnard St Ste 500 Woodland Hills (91367) ***(P-15621)***
Ramko Injection Inc...D...951 929-0360
3551 Tanya Ave Hemet (92545) ***(P-5787)***
Ramona Auto Services Inc...D...909 986-1785
2451 S Euclid Ave Ontario (91762) ***(P-18864)***
Ramona Care Inc...C...626 442-5721
11900 Ramona Blvd El Monte (91732) ***(P-20442)***
Ramona Community Services Corp (HQ)...C...951 658-9288
890 W Stetson Ave Ste A Hemet (92543) ***(P-21206)***
Ramona Nrsing Rhbilitation Ctr, El Monte *Also called Ramona Care Inc* ***(P-20442)***
Ramona Rhblttion Post Acute Ca, Hemet *Also called Ramona Rhblttion Post Acute CA* ***(P-20920)***
Ramona Rhblttion Post Acute CA...C...951 652-0011
485 W Johnston Ave Hemet (92543) ***(P-20920)***
Ramona Vna & Hospice, Hemet *Also called Ramona Community Services Corp* ***(P-21206)***
Ramp Engineering Inc...E...562 531-8030
6850 Walthall Way Paramount (90723) ***(P-8758)***
Rampone Industries LLC...E...949 581-8701
2761 Dow Ave Tustin (92780) ***(P-7510)***
Ramtec Associates Inc...E...714 996-7477
3200 E Birch St Ste B Brea (92821) ***(P-5788)***
Ranar Manufacturing Corp...F...310 414-4122
149 Lomita St El Segundo (90245) ***(P-4564)***
Rance King Properties Inc (PA)...C...562 240-1000
3737 E Broadway Long Beach (90803) ***(P-15746)***
Ranch At Laguna Beach, The, Laguna Beach *Also called Laguna Bch Golf Bnglow Vlg LLC* ***(P-143)***
Ranch House Doors Inc...D...951 278-2884
1527 Pomona Rd Corona (92878) ***(P-1452)***
Ranching Shop, Corcoran *Also called J G Boswell Company* ***(P-3)***
Rancho California Ldscpg Inc...E...310 768-1680
13801 S Western Ave Gardena (90249) ***(P-338)***
Rancho California Water Dst (PA)...C...951 296-6900
42135 Winchester Rd Temecula (92590) ***(P-12914)***
Rancho Ccamonga Cmnty Hosp LLC...D...909 581-6400
10841 White Oak Ave Rancho Cucamonga (91730) ***(P-20921)***
Rancho Cucamonga Medical Offs, Rancho Cucamonga *Also called Kaiser Foundation Hospitals* ***(P-19885)***
Rancho Foods Inc...D...323 585-0503
2528 E 37th St Vernon (90058) ***(P-14603)***
Rancho Ford Inc...C...951 699-1302
26895 Ynez Rd Temecula (92591) ***(P-18801)***
Rancho Laguna Farms LLC...D...805 925-7805
2410 W Main St Santa Maria (93458) ***(P-117)***
Rancho Los Amigos Nationa (PA)...A...562 401-7111
7601 Imperial Hwy Downey (90242) ***(P-21876)***
Rancho Mission Viejo LLC...D...949 240-3363
28811 Ortega Hwy San Juan Capistrano (92675) ***(P-15964)***
Rancho Monterey Apartments, Tustin *Also called Irvine APT Communities LP* ***(P-15735)***
Rancho Pacific Electric Inc...E...909 476-1022
9063 Santa Anita Ave Rancho Cucamonga (91730) ***(P-1305)***
Rancho Physical Therapy Inc (PA)...C...951 696-9353
24630 Washington Ave # 200 Murrieta (92562) ***(P-20231)***
Rancho Pino Verdi, Lucerne Valley *Also called Casa Clina Hosp Ctrs For Hlthc* ***(P-21730)***
Rancho Ready Mix...D...951 674-0488
28251 Lake St Lake Elsinore (92530) ***(P-6106)***
Rancho Research Institute...C...562 401-8111
7601 Imperial Hwy Downey (90242) ***(P-22917)***
Rancho San Antonio Boys HM Inc (PA)...D...818 882-6400
21000 Plummer St Chatsworth (91311) ***(P-22147)***
Rancho Santa Ana Botanic Grdn...D...909 625-8767
1500 N College Ave Claremont (91711) ***(P-22240)***
Rancho Sisquoc Winery, Santa Maria *Also called Flood Ranch Company* ***(P-2185)***
Rancho Speciality Hospital, Rancho Cucamonga *Also called Rancho Ccamonga Cmnty Hosp LLC* ***(P-20921)***
Rancho Springs Medical Center, Murrieta *Also called Southwest Healthcare Sys Aux* ***(P-20953)***
Rancho Technology Inc...F...909 987-3966
10783 Bell Ct Rancho Cucamonga (91730) ***(P-8296)***
Rancho Vista Development Co...D...661 272-9082
3905 Club Rancho Dr Palmdale (93551) ***(P-19505)***
Rancho Vista Golf Course, Palmdale *Also called Rancho Vista Development Co* ***(P-19505)***
Rancon Real Estate Corporation...D...951 677-1800
41391 Kalmia St Ste 100 Murrieta (92562) ***(P-15965)***
Rand Technology LLC (PA)...D...949 255-5700
15225 Alton Pkwy Unit 100 Irvine (92618) ***(P-13767)***
Randall - McAnany Company...D...310 822-3344
1528 W 178th St Gardena (90248) ***(P-1195)***
Randall Hv Foods LLC...C...323 261-6565
2905 E 50th St Vernon (90058) ***(P-14604)***
Randell Equipment & Mfg, Delano *Also called Randell Equiptment & Mfg* ***(P-7617)***
Randell Equiptment & Mfg...F...661 725-6380
1408 S Lexington St Delano (93215) ***(P-7617)***
Randstad Engineering, El Segundo *Also called Randstad Professionals Us LLC* ***(P-17510)***
Randstad Finance & Accounting, Cerritos *Also called Randstad Professionals Us LLC* ***(P-17453)***
Randstad Professionals Us LLC...D...781 213-1500
3333 Michelson Dr Ste 210 Irvine (92612) ***(P-17452)***
Randstad Professionals Us LLC...D...424 246-4400
2321 Rosecrans Ave # 2215 El Segundo (90245) ***(P-17510)***
Randstad Professionals Us LLC...D...562 468-0111
17777 Center Court Dr N # 225 Cerritos (90703) ***(P-17453)***
Randy Nix Cstm Wldg & Mfg Inc...E...559 562-1958
22700 Road 196 Lindsay (93247) ***(P-18994)***
Ranir LLC...E...866 373-7374
6 Centerpointe Dr Ste 640 La Palma (90623) ***(P-11192)***
Rankin-Delux Inc (PA)...F...951 685-0081
3245 Corridor Dr Eastvale (91752) ***(P-8408)***
Ranscapes Inc...E...866 883-9297
30 Hughes Ste 209 Irvine (92618) ***(P-17280)***
Rantec Microwave Systems Inc (PA)...D...818 223-5000
31186 La Baya Dr Westlake Village (91362) ***(P-10636)***
Rantec Power Systems Inc (HQ)...D...805 596-6000
1173 Los Olivos Ave Los Osos (93402) ***(P-13768)***
Raoul Textiles Inc...F...805 965-1694
110 Los Aguajes Ave Santa Barbara (93101) ***(P-4565)***
Raouls Hnd-Scrned Yrdage Prntw, Santa Barbara *Also called Raoul Textiles Inc* ***(P-4565)***
RAP Security Inc...D...323 560-3493
4630 Cecilia St Cudahy (90201) ***(P-3693)***
Rapid Conn Inc...E...949 951-3722
25172 Arctic Ocean Dr # 106 Lake Forest (92630) ***(P-13587)***
Rapid Manufacturing A (PA)...C...714 974-2432
8080 E Crystal Dr Anaheim (92807) ***(P-7511)***
Rapid Manufacturing Inc...F...818 899-4377
9724 Eton Ave Chatsworth (91311) ***(P-11740)***
Rapid Product Solutions Inc...E...805 485-7234
2240 Celsius Ave Ste D Oxnard (93030) ***(P-8759)***
Rapiscan Holdings Inc (HQ)...D...310 978-0516
12525 Chadron Ave Hawthorne (90250) ***(P-16287)***
Rapiscan Systems Inc (HQ)...A...310 978-1457
2805 Columbia St Torrance (90503) ***(P-11209)***
Rapiscan Systems Inc...E...310 978-1457
3232 W El Segundo Blvd Hawthorne (90250) ***(P-9904)***
Rapp Worldwide California Inc (PA)...C...310 563-7200
12777 W Jefferson Blvd Los Angeles (90066) ***(P-17048)***
Rapp Worldwide Inc...D...310 563-7200
12777 W Jefferson Blvd Los Angeles (90066) ***(P-17049)***
Rare Beauty LLC...D...424 502-1900
222 N Pacific Coast Hwy El Segundo (90245) ***(P-14285)***
Rashman Corporation...D...818 993-3030
8600 Wilbur Ave Northridge (91324) ***(P-13516)***
Rasmussen Iron Works Inc...D...562 696-8718
12028 Philadelphia St Whittier (90601) ***(P-6573)***
Raspadoxpress...D...818 367-9838
13796 Foothill Blvd Sylmar (91342) ***(P-19665)***
Raspadoxpress...E...818 892-6969
8610 Van Nuys Blvd Panorama City (91402) ***(P-4201)***
Rastaclat LLC...E...424 287-0902
100 W Broadway Ste 3000 Long Beach (90802) ***(P-11328)***
Ratespecial Interactive LLC (PA)...D...626 376-4702
46 Smith Aly Ste 230 Pasadena (91103) ***(P-17050)***
Ratpac Dimmers, Van Nuys *Also called Data Lights Rigging LLC* ***(P-8894)***
Raudmans Craig Victory Circle...E...661 833-4600
700 S Mount Vernon Ave # 10 Bakersfield (93307) ***(P-10555)***
Ravine Waterpark LLC...C...805 237-8500
2301 Airport Rd Paso Robles (93446) ***(P-19523)***
Ravine Waterpark, The, Paso Robles *Also called Ravine Waterpark LLC* ***(P-19523)***
Ravlich Enterprises LLC...E...310 533-0748
202 W 140th St Los Angeles (90061) ***(P-7303)***
Ravlich Enterprises LLC (PA)...E...714 964-8900
100 Business Center Dr Corona (92878) ***(P-7304)***
Raw Juicery Inc...F...213 221-6081
915 Mateo St Ste 207 Los Angeles (90021) ***(P-1909)***
Rawlings Mechanical Corp (PA)...D...323 875-2040
11615 Pendleton St Sun Valley (91352) ***(P-1126)***
Ray Chinn Construction Inc...E...661 327-2731
424 24th St Bakersfield (93301) ***(P-7765)***
Ray Foster Dental Equipment...E...714 897-7795
5421 Commercial Dr Huntington Beach (92649) ***(P-11193)***
Ray Gaskin Service...E...909 574-7000
14312 Arrow Hwy Baldwin Park (91706) ***(P-19059)***
Rayco B Products, Monrovia *Also called Rayco Burial Products Inc* ***(P-6900)***
Rayco Burial Products Inc...E...626 357-1996
1601 Raymond Ave Monrovia (91016) ***(P-6900)***
Rayco Electronic Mfg Inc...E...310 329-2660
1220 W 130th St Gardena (90247) ***(P-9641)***
Raykorvay Inc...F...714 632-8680
1070 N Kraemer Pl Anaheim (92806) ***(P-11364)***
Raymak Automotive Inc...E...310 329-8910
15600 S Main St Gardena (90248) ***(P-18865)***
Raymond Group (PA)...D...714 771-7670
520 W Walnut Ave Orange (92868) ***(P-23096)***
Raymond Handling Solutions Inc (HQ)...C...562 944-8067
9939 Norwalk Blvd Santa Fe Springs (90670) ***(P-13935)***
Raypak Inc (HQ)...B...805 278-5300
2151 Eastman Ave Oxnard (93030) ***(P-6574)***
Raytheon Applied Signal...D...714 917-0255
160 N Rverview Dr Ste 300 Anaheim (92808) ***(P-9350)***
Raytheon Cmmand Ctrl Sltons LL...E...714 446-3232
2000 E El Segundo Blvd El Segundo (90245) ***(P-13769)***
Raytheon Cmmand Ctrl Sltons LL (HQ)...A...714 446-3118
1801 Hughes Dr Fullerton (92833) ***(P-13770)***
Raytheon Company...C...805 967-5511
6380 Hollister Ave Goleta (93117) ***(P-9905)***

Mergent e-mail: customerrelations@mergent.com
1250
2022 Southern California Business Directory and Buyers Guide
(P-0000) Products & Services Section entry number
(PA)=Parent Co (HQ)=Headquarters (DH)=Div Headquarters

Raytheon Company D 310 647-1000
1921 Mariposa St El Segundo (90245) ***(P-10637)***
Raytheon Company F 714 446-2584
1801 Hughes Dr Fullerton (92833) ***(P-10638)***
Raytheon Company B 310 647-1000
2000 E El Segundo Blvd El Segundo (90245) ***(P-10639)***
Raytheon Company D 805 562-2941
75 Coromar Dr Goleta (93117) ***(P-18648)***
Raytheon Company A 310 647-9438
2000 E El Segundo Blvd El Segundo (90245) ***(P-10640)***
Raytheon Technologies Corp F 714 984-1467
2727 E Imperial Hwy Brea (92821) ***(P-10401)***
Razor USA LLC (PA) **D 562 345-6000**
12723 166th St Cerritos (90703) ***(P-14086)***
Razzor Technologies Inc F 949 202-5846
1 Park Plz Fl 6 Irvine (92614) ***(P-17970)***
Rba Builders Inc D 714 895-9000
17601 Sampson Ln Huntington Beach (92647) ***(P-814)***
Rbabs Investments 1 LLC E 818 577-7171
5967 W 3rd St Ste 102 Los Angeles (90036) ***(P-15966)***
Rbb Architects Inc (PA) **D 310 479-1473**
10980 Wilshire Blvd Los Angeles (90024) ***(P-22738)***
Rbc Lubron Bearing Systems Inc (HQ) **F 714 841-3007**
13141 Molette St Santa Fe Springs (90670) ***(P-6287)***
Rbc Southwest Products Inc D 626 358-0181
5001b Commerce Dr Baldwin Park (91706) ***(P-14012)***
Rbc Transport Dynamics Corp C 203 267-7001
3131 W Segerstrom Ave Santa Ana (92704) ***(P-14013)***
Rbd Hotel Palm Springs LLC D 760 322-9000
285 N Palm Canyon Dr Palm Springs (92262) ***(P-16656)***
Rbf Associates, Camarillo *Also called Michael Baker Intl Inc* ***(P-22613)***
Rbf Group International F 626 333-5700
1441 W 2nd St Pomona (91766) ***(P-3598)***
Rbf Lifestyle Holdings, Pomona *Also called Rbf Group International* ***(P-3598)***
Rbg Holdings Corp (PA) **A 818 782-6445**
7855 Haskell Ave Ste 350 Van Nuys (91406) ***(P-11441)***
Rbm Conveyor Systems Inc E 909 620-1333
1432 Royal Blvd Glendale (91207) ***(P-7950)***
Rbs Glass Designs, Van Nuys *Also called Precision Glass Bevelling Inc* ***(P-5940)***
Rbw Industries Inc D 909 591-5359
5788 Schaefer Ave Chino (91710) ***(P-10124)***
Rbz Vineyards LLC E 805 542-0133
2324 W Highway 46 Paso Robles (93446) ***(P-2216)***
RC Construction Services, Rialto *Also called Robert Clapper Cnstr Svcs Inc* ***(P-817)***
RC Furniture Inc D 626 964-4100
1111 Jellick Ave City of Industry (91748) ***(P-3513)***
RC Wendt Painting Inc C 714 960-2700
21612 Surveyor Cir Huntington Beach (92646) ***(P-1196)***
Rcan Inc D 559 585-8010
600 E 11th St Hanford (93230) ***(P-22148)***
Rci Rack Cnvyor Instltion Inc E 909 381-4818
39700 Grand Ave Cherry Valley (92223) ***(P-7692)***
RCP Block & Brick Inc D 951 677-1489
25725 Jefferson Ave Murrieta (92562) ***(P-13313)***
Rcrv Inc (PA) **E 323 235-7300**
4715 S Alameda St Vernon (90058) ***(P-14412)***
Rcs World Travel, Ventura *Also called Registration Ctrl Systems Inc* ***(P-18650)***
RCWD, Temecula *Also called Rancho California Water Dst* ***(P-12914)***
RD Metal Polishing Inc F 909 594-8393
244 Pioneer Pl Pomona (91768) ***(P-7305)***
Rdc-S111 Inc (PA) **C 562 628-8000**
245 E 3rd St Long Beach (90802) ***(P-22739)***
RDD Enterprises Inc F 213 746-0020
4638 E Washinton Blvd Commerce (90040) ***(P-2747)***
RDD Enterprises Inc E 213 742-0666
4638 E Washington Blvd Commerce (90040) ***(P-3144)***
RDfabricators Inc F 714 634-2078
11880 Western Ave Stanton (90680) ***(P-6901)***
Rdl Reference Laboratory, Beverly Hills *Also called Rheumatology Diagnostics Lab* ***(P-21094)***
RDM Electric Co Inc (PA) **D 909 591-0990**
4260 E Brickell St Ontario (91761) ***(P-1306)***
RDM Industries F 714 690-0380
14310 Gannet St La Mirada (90638) ***(P-14761)***
Rdr Precision Tech Inc F 661 322-8450
11000 Kern Canyon Rd A Bakersfield (93306) ***(P-7675)***
RDS Logistics Group (PA) **D 909 355-4100**
8600 Banana Ave Fontana (92335) ***(P-11989)***
RE Bilt Metalizing Co F 323 277-8200
2229 E 38th St Vernon (90058) ***(P-8760)***
Re/Max, Los Alamitos *Also called College Park Realty Inc* ***(P-15823)***
Re/Max, Upland *Also called Diamond Ridge Corporation* ***(P-15837)***
Re/Max, Northridge *Also called Remax Olson & Associates Inc* ***(P-15974)***
Re/Max, Ventura *Also called Rgc Services Inc* ***(P-15976)***
Re/Max, Cypress *Also called Riphagen & Bullerdick Inc* ***(P-15978)***
Re/Max, Camarillo *Also called Rgc Services Inc* ***(P-15977)***
Re/Max E 661 616-4040
201 New Stine Rd Ste 300 Bakersfield (93309) ***(P-15967)***
Re/Max Bch Cties Rlty Mrquee P D 310 376-2225
400 S Sepulveda Blvd # 100 Manhattan Beach (90266) ***(P-15968)***
RE/Max of Valencia Inc (PA) **C 661 255-2650**
25101 The Old Rd Santa Clarita (91381) ***(P-15969)***
Reach Out West End D 909 982-8641
1126 W Foothill Blvd # 150 Upland (91786) ***(P-22209)***
Reachlocal Inc (HQ) **A 818 274-0260**
21700 Oxnard St Ste 1600 Woodland Hills (91367) ***(P-17051)***
Reading Entertainment Inc (HQ) **D 213 235-2226**
500 Citadel Dr Ste 300 Commerce (90040) ***(P-19287)***
Reading International Inc (PA) **A 213 235-2240**
5995 Sepulveda Blvd # 300 Culver City (90230) ***(P-19288)***
Ready Industries Inc F 213 749-2041
1520 E 15th St Los Angeles (90021) ***(P-4416)***
Ready Pac Foods Inc (HQ) **A 626 856-8686**
4401 Foxdale St Irwindale (91706) ***(P-2515)***
Ready Reproductions, Los Angeles *Also called Ready Industries Inc* ***(P-4416)***
Readylink Inc D 760 343-7000
72030 Metroplex Dr Thousand Palms (92276) ***(P-17454)***
Readylink Healthcare D 760 343-7000
72030 Metroplex Dr Thousand Palms (92276) ***(P-17455)***
Readymix -Fontana Rm, Fontana *Also called Cemex Cnstr Mtls PCF LLC* ***(P-6080)***
Readymix -Redlands Rm Dual, Highland *Also called Cemex Cnstr Mtls PCF LLC* ***(P-6079)***
Reagent World Inc F 909 947-7779
2100 Main St Ste 106 Irvine (92614) ***(P-13537)***
Real Estate Digital LLC C 800 234-2139
20411 Sw Birch St Ste 250 Newport Beach (92660) ***(P-17696)***
Real Estate Image Inc (PA) **C 714 502-3900**
1415 S Acacia Ave Fullerton (92831) ***(P-17140)***
Real Estate Trainers Inc E 800 282-2352
212 Twne Cntre Pl Ste 100 Anaheim (92806) ***(P-4104)***
Real Good Food Company LLC C 818 299-4179
444 E Santa Clara St Ventura (93001) ***(P-14729)***
Real Plating Inc E 909 623-2304
1245 W 2nd St Pomona (91766) ***(P-7306)***
Real Software Systems LLC (PA) **E 818 313-8000**
21255 Burbank Blvd # 220 Woodland Hills (91367) ***(P-17971)***
Real Vision Foods LLC E 253 228-5050
8707 Utica Ave Rancho Cucamonga (91730) ***(P-1936)***
Realselect Inc C 661 803-5188
3063 W Chapman Ave # 620 Orange (92868) ***(P-15970)***
Realty One Group Inc D 951 565-8105
19322 Jesse Ln Riverside (92508) ***(P-15971)***
Reason Foundation E 310 391-2245
5737 Mesmer Ave Los Angeles (90230) ***(P-18649)***
Rebar Engineering Inc C 562 946-2461
10706 Painter Ave Santa Fe Springs (90670) ***(P-1579)***
Rebas Inc C 562 941-4155
12907 Imperial Hwy Santa Fe Springs (90670) ***(P-13936)***
Rebecca International Inc E 323 973-2602
4587 E 48th St Vernon (90058) ***(P-3163)***
Rebel Jeans, Los Angeles *Also called Be Bop Clothing* ***(P-2923)***
Rebound Therapeutics Corp E 949 305-8111
13900 Alton Pkwy Ste 120 Irvine (92618) ***(P-11049)***
Rebuilt Metalizing Chrome Pltg, Vernon *Also called RE Bilt Metalizing Co* ***(P-8760)***
Rec Solar Commercial Corp C 844 732-7652
3450 Broad St Ste 105 San Luis Obispo (93401) ***(P-1127)***
Recell Usa Inc F 951 353-1600
10321 Magnolia Ave Riverside (92505) ***(P-2551)***
Reche Cyn Regional Rehab Ctr, Colton *Also called Cambridge Sierra Holdings LLC* ***(P-20273)***
Recom Group E 909 599-1370
449 Borrego Ct San Dimas (91773) ***(P-13771)***
Recon Refractory & Cnstr Inc E 562 988-7981
3914 Cherry Ave Ste B Long Beach (90807) ***(P-22645)***
Reconserve Inc (HQ) **E 310 458-1574**
2811 Wilshire Blvd # 410 Santa Monica (90403) ***(P-1974)***
Reconserve of Maryland, Santa Monica *Also called Dext Company of Maryland* ***(P-1964)***
Record Technology Inc E 805 484-2747
486 Dawson Dr Ste 4s Camarillo (93012) ***(P-9225)***
Recovery Solutions Santa Ana, Santa Ana *Also called CRC Health Corporate* ***(P-21295)***
Recp/Wndsor Port Hueneme Ventr, Port Hueneme *Also called Windsor Capital Group Inc* ***(P-16799)***
Recreational Assn Corcoran D 559 992-5171
900 Dairy Ave Corcoran (93212) ***(P-22362)***
Recruit 360 C 949 250-4420
457 Ogle St Costa Mesa (92627) ***(P-17456)***
Recycled Aggregate Mtls Co Inc (PA) **F 805 522-1646**
2655 1st St Ste 210 Simi Valley (93065) ***(P-5277)***
Recycled Paper Products, Santa Fe Springs *Also called Gabriel Container* ***(P-3805)***
Recycled Wood Products, Pomona *Also called Rwp Transfer Inc* ***(P-14181)***
Recycler Classified, Sherman Oaks *Also called E Z Buy E Z Sell Recycler Corp* ***(P-3973)***
Recycler Core Company Inc D 951 276-1687
2727 Kansas Ave Riverside (92507) ***(P-12970)***
Red Blossom Sales Inc A 805 349-9404
865 Black Rd Santa Maria (93458) ***(P-33)***
Red Brick Corporation F 323 549-9444
5364 Venice Blvd Los Angeles (90019) ***(P-4417)***
Red Bull Distribution Co Inc (HQ) **C 916 515-3501**
1740 Stewart St Santa Monica (90404) ***(P-14730)***
Red Bull Media Hse N Amer Inc (HQ) **C 310 393-4647**
1740 Stewart St Santa Monica (90404) ***(P-14731)***
Red Bull Media Hse N Amer Inc D 310 393-4647
1630 Stewart St Ste A Santa Monica (90404) ***(P-2281)***
Red Carpet Car Wash, Visalia *Also called Bowie Enterprises* ***(P-18907)***
Red Chamber Co (PA) **B 323 234-9000**
1912 E Vernon Ave Vernon (90058) ***(P-14580)***
Red Digital Cinema Camera Co, Foothill Ranch *Also called Redcom LLC* ***(P-11290)***
Red Dog Management Inc (PA) **C 805 925-1414**
2240 A St Santa Maria (93455) ***(P-23097)***
Red Earth Casino, Thermal *Also called Torres-Mrtnez Dsert Chlla Inda* ***(P-16755)***
Red Earth Casino C 760 395-1200
3089 Norm Niver Rd Thermal (92274) ***(P-16657)***
Red Fish Grill, Anaheim *Also called Ralph Brennan Rest Group LLC* ***(P-23306)***
Red Gate Software Inc E 626 993-3949
144 W Colo Blvd Ste 200 Pasadena (91105) ***(P-17972)***
Red Hawk Fire & SEC CA Inc (HQ) **D 818 683-1500**
7605 N San Fernando Rd Los Angeles (90065) ***(P-1307)***

Employee Codes: A=Over 500 employees, B=251-500
C=101-250, D=51-100, E=20-50 F=10-19
2022 Southern California Business
Directory and Buyers Guide
© Mergent Inc. 1-800-342-5647
1251

Red Hill Country Club.....D.....909 982-1358
8358 Red Hl Cntry Clb Dr Rancho Cucamonga (91730) ***(P-19602)***

Red Interactive Agency LLC (PA).....**D.....310 399-4242**
3420 Ocean Park Blvd # 3080 Santa Monica (90405) ***(P-17052)***

Red Peak Group LLC.....D.....818 222-7762
23975 Park Sorrento # 410 Calabasas (91302) ***(P-23307)***

Red Pocket Inc.....D.....888 993-3888
2060d E Avnida De Los Arb Thousand Oaks (91362) ***(P-12667)***

Red Pocket Mobile, Thousand Oaks *Also called Red Pocket Inc* ***(P-12667)***

Red Pointe Roofing LP (PA).....**D.....714 685-0010**
1814 N Neville St Orange (92865) ***(P-1503)***

Red Rock Pallet Company.....E.....530 852-7744
81153 Red Rock Rd La Quinta (92253) ***(P-12518)***

Red Star Coffee, Goleta *Also called Santa Barbara Coffee LLC* ***(P-2357)***

Red Star Fertilizer Co.....F.....909 597-4801
17132 Hellman Ave Eastvale (92880) ***(P-5159)***

Redart Corporation.....F.....714 774-9444
2549 Eastbluff Dr Newport Beach (92660) ***(P-3631)***

Redbarn Pet Products Inc (PA).....**C.....562 495-7315**
3229 E Spring St Ste 310 Long Beach (90806) ***(P-14971)***

Redbarn Premium Pet Products, Long Beach *Also called Redbarn Pet Products Inc* ***(P-14971)***

Redbull Distribution Co Colo, Santa Monica *Also called Red Bull Distribution Co Inc* ***(P-14730)***

Redcom LLC (HQ).....**B.....949 404-4084**
94 Icon Foothill Ranch (92610) ***(P-11290)***

Redding Tree Growers Corp.....D.....559 594-9299
18985 Avenue 256 Apt A Exeter (93221) ***(P-372)***

Redlands Cmnty Hosp Foundation.....C.....909 793-1382
1875 Barton Rd Redlands (92373) ***(P-20624)***

Redlands Community Hospital, Redlands *Also called RHS Corp* ***(P-23100)***

Redlands Community Hospital (PA).....**D.....909 335-5500**
350 Terracina Blvd Redlands (92373) ***(P-20922)***

Redlands Country Club.....D.....909 793-2661
1749 Garden St Redlands (92373) ***(P-19603)***

Redlands Daily Facts, Redlands *Also called Califrnia Nwspapers Ltd Partnr* ***(P-3958)***

Redlands Employment Services.....C.....951 688-0083
4295 Jurupa St Ste 110 Ontario (91761) ***(P-17457)***

Redlands Employment Services (PA).....**B.....909 792-3413**
499 W State St Redlands (92373) ***(P-17458)***

Redlands Fmly Prctice Med Grou.....D.....909 793-3208
1520 Barton Rd Redlands (92373) ***(P-20038)***

Redlands Foothill Groves.....E.....909 793-2164
304 9th St Redlands (92374) ***(P-184)***

Redlands Ford Inc.....D.....909 793-3211
1121 W Colton Ave Redlands (92374) ***(P-18802)***

Redlands Health Care Group, Redlands *Also called Plum Healthcare Group LLC* ***(P-18636)***

Redlands Healthcare Center, Redlands *Also called Ash Holdings LLC* ***(P-20247)***

Redlands Recycling, Riverside *Also called Riverside Scrap Ir & Met Corp* ***(P-14121)***

Redlands Staffing Services, Ontario *Also called Redlands Employment Services* ***(P-17457)***

Redline Detection LLC (PA).....**E.....714 579-6961**
828 W Taft Ave Orange (92865) ***(P-10907)***

Redline Prcision Machining Inc.....F.....909 483-1273
907 E Francis St Ontario (91761) ***(P-8761)***

Redman Container, Carson *Also called Calko Transport Company Inc* ***(P-12109)***

Redman Equipment & Mfg Co.....E.....310 329-1134
19800 Normandie Ave Torrance (90502) ***(P-19060)***

Redondo Beach Brewing Co Inc.....E.....310 316-8477
1814 S Catalina Ave Redondo Beach (90277) ***(P-2154)***

Redtrac, Bakersfield *Also called Water Associates LLC* ***(P-9327)***

Redwood, Culver City *Also called Wovexx Holdings Inc* ***(P-12794)***

Redwood Scientific Tech Inc.....E.....310 693-5401
11450 Sheldon St Sun Valley (91352) ***(P-4880)***

Redwood Wellness LLC.....E.....323 843-2676
11814 Jefferson Blvd Culver City (90230) ***(P-2737)***

Redworks Industries LLC.....E.....949 334-7081
23986 Aliso Creek Rd Laguna Niguel (92677) ***(P-3453)***

Reed LLC.....E.....909 287-2100
13822 Oaks Ave Chino (91710) ***(P-8023)***

Reed Electric & Field Service, Vernon *Also called R A Reed Electric Company* ***(P-19015)***

Reed Manufacturing, Chino *Also called Reed LLC* ***(P-8023)***

Reed Smith LLP.....C.....213 457-8000
355 S Grand Ave Ste 2900 Los Angeles (90071) ***(P-21668)***

Reed Thomas Company Inc.....D.....714 558-7691
1025 N Santiago St Santa Ana (92701) ***(P-1603)***

Reedex Inc.....E.....714 894-0311
15526 Commerce Ln Huntington Beach (92649) ***(P-9771)***

Reel Efx Inc.....E.....818 762-1710
5539 Riverton Ave North Hollywood (91601) ***(P-11741)***

Reel Security California Inc.....D.....818 928-4737
15303 Ventura Blvd # 1080 Sherman Oaks (91403) ***(P-18315)***

Reeve Store Equipment Company (PA).....**D.....562 949-2535**
9131 Bermudez St Pico Rivera (90660) ***(P-3694)***

Reeves Extruded Products Inc.....D.....661 854-5970
1032 Stockton Ave Arvin (93203) ***(P-5789)***

Refinery Av LLC.....E.....818 843-0004
15301 Ventura Blvd # 300 Sherman Oaks (91403) ***(P-17185)***

Refinery, The, Sherman Oaks *Also called Waldberg Inc* ***(P-17092)***

Reflections and Enclave Hoa, Irvine *Also called Keystone PCF Property MGT Inc* ***(P-15901)***

Reformation, The, Vernon *Also called Lymi Inc* ***(P-14395)***

Refresco Beverages US Inc.....E.....909 915-1400
631 S Waterman Ave San Bernardino (92408) ***(P-2282)***

Refresco Beverages US Inc.....E.....909 915-1430
499 E Mill St San Bernardino (92408) ***(P-2283)***

Refresco Beverages US Inc.....C.....951 685-0481
11751 Pacific Ave Fontana (92337) ***(P-1874)***

Refridgerator Manufacters LLC.....E.....562 229-0500
17018 Edwards Rd Cerritos (90703) ***(P-8998)***

Refrigeration Hdwr Sup Corp.....E.....818 768-3636
9021 Norris Ave Sun Valley (91352) ***(P-13856)***

Refrigerator Manufacters Inc (PA).....**E.....562 926-2006**
17018 Edwards Rd Cerritos (90703) ***(P-8999)***

Refrigerator Manufacturers LLC.....E.....562 926-2006
17018 Edwards Rd Cerritos (90703) ***(P-8348)***

Refrigrated Trck Solutions LLC.....E.....323 594-4500
1115 E Dominguez St Carson (90746) ***(P-10168)***

Refuse Department, Lemoore *Also called City of Lemoore* ***(P-12939)***

Regal Beloit America Inc.....F.....909 591-9561
3505 E Francis St Ontario (91761) ***(P-13664)***

Regal Cultured Marble Inc.....F.....909 802-2388
1239 E Franklin Ave Pomona (91766) ***(P-6142)***

Regal Kitchens LLC.....F.....786 953-6578
3480 Sunset Ln Oxnard (93035) ***(P-3332)***

Regal Machine & Engrg Inc.....E.....323 773-7462
5200 E 60th St Maywood (90270) ***(P-8762)***

Regal Medical Group Inc (PA).....**C.....818 654-3400**
8510 Balboa Blvd Ste 275 Northridge (91325) ***(P-22277)***

Regal Technology Partners Inc.....D.....714 835-1162
2921 Daimler St Santa Ana (92705) ***(P-13432)***

Regal-Piedmont Plastics LLC.....E.....562 404-4014
17000 Valley View Ave La Mirada (90638) ***(P-14762)***

Regan Paving, Corona *Also called Charles C Regan Inc* ***(P-871)***

Regards Enterprises Inc.....F.....909 983-0655
731 S Taylor Ave Ontario (91761) ***(P-3434)***

Regency Enterprises, Los Angeles *Also called New Regency Productions Inc* ***(P-19156)***

Regency Enterprises Inc (PA).....**B.....818 901-0255**
9261 Jordan Ave Chatsworth (91311) ***(P-13665)***

Regency Health Services, Covina *Also called Covina Rehabilitation Center* ***(P-20306)***

Regency Inn, Costa Mesa *Also called US Hotel and Resort MGT Inc* ***(P-16765)***

Regency Lighting, Chatsworth *Also called Regency Enterprises Inc* ***(P-13665)***

Regency Park El Molino, Pasadena *Also called Regency Park Senior Living Inc* ***(P-15972)***

Regency Park Oak Knoll, Pasadena *Also called Regency Park Senior Living Inc* ***(P-22149)***

Regency Park Senior Living Inc.....D.....626 396-4911
255 S Oak Knoll Ave Pasadena (91101) ***(P-22149)***

Regency Park Senior Living Inc.....C.....626 578-0460
245 S El Molino Ave Pasadena (91101) ***(P-15972)***

Regent LP (PA).....**D.....310 299-4100**
9720 Wilshire Blvd Beverly Hills (90212) ***(P-16288)***

Regent Aerospace Corporation (PA).....**C.....661 257-3000**
28110 Harrison Pkwy Valencia (91355) ***(P-1684)***

Regents of The University Cal.....D.....310 267-9308
1250 16th St Santa Monica (90404) ***(P-21475)***

Regents of Uc.....D.....310 827-3700
4560 Admiralty Way # 100 Marina Del Rey (90292) ***(P-20039)***

Regional Connector Constrs.....E.....951 368-6400
1995 Agua Mansa Rd Riverside (92509) ***(P-635)***

Regional Ctr Orange Cnty Inc (PA).....**B.....714 796-5100**
1525 N Tustin Ave Santa Ana (92705) ***(P-21877)***

Regis Contractors LP.....B.....949 253-0455
18825 Bardeen Ave Irvine (92612) ***(P-666)***

Regis Corporation.....E.....310 274-8791
9403 Santa Monica Blvd Beverly Hills (90210) ***(P-16916)***

Registrar of Voters, Santa Ana *Also called County of Orange* ***(P-22393)***

Registration Ctrl Systems Inc (PA).....**D.....805 654-0171**
1833 Portola Rd Unit B Ventura (93003) ***(P-18650)***

Registry Mntring Insur Svcs In.....D.....800 400-4924
5388 Sterling Center Dr Westlake Village (91361) ***(P-15973)***

Rehababilities Inc.....C.....310 473-4448
11835 W Olympic Blvd Los Angeles (90064) ***(P-17459)***

Rehabfocus Home Health Inc (HQ).....**E.....209 524-8700**
27071 Aliso Creek Rd Aliso Viejo (92656) ***(P-21207)***

Rehabilitation Assoc Med Group.....D.....562 424-8111
2840 Long Beach Blvd # 13 Long Beach (90806) ***(P-20040)***

Rehabilitation Ctr Bakersfield, Bakersfield *Also called Bakersfeld Hlthcare Wllness CN* ***(P-20558)***

Rehabilitation Inst of Sthrn C, Orange *Also called Rio* ***(P-21334)***

Rehabilitation Inst Orange Cnty, Santa Ana *Also called Reimagine Network* ***(P-21333)***

Rehabltion Cntre of Bvrly Hlls.....C.....323 782-1500
580 S San Vicente Blvd Los Angeles (90048) ***(P-20443)***

Rehablttion Cntre of Bkrsfield, Bakersfield *Also called Bakersfield Healthcare* ***(P-20251)***

Rehablttion Ctr of Ornge Cnty.....C.....714 826-2330
9021 Knott Ave Buena Park (90620) ***(P-20444)***

Rehabworks At Freedom Village, Lake Forest *Also called Freedom Village Healthcare Ctr* ***(P-20346)***

Rehrig Pacific Holdings Inc (PA).....**B.....323 262-5145**
4010 E 26th St Vernon (90058) ***(P-5790)***

Reichhold Chemicals, Azusa *Also called Reichhold LLC 2* ***(P-4712)***

Reichhold LLC 2.....F.....626 334-4974
237 S Motor Ave Azusa (91702) ***(P-4712)***

Reid Metal Finishing, Santa Ana *Also called Electrode Technologies Inc* ***(P-7250)***

Reid Plastics Customer Svcs, City of Industry *Also called Altium Packaging LLC* ***(P-5557)***

Reid Products Inc.....E.....760 240-1355
21430 Waalew Rd Apple Valley (92307) ***(P-8763)***

Reimagine Network (PA).....**C.....714 633-7400**
1601 E Saint Andrew Pl Santa Ana (92705) ***(P-21333)***

Reinhardt Brothers MBL & Tile.....F.....310 325-0174
1450 W 228th St Ste 17 Torrance (90501) ***(P-1422)***

Reinhold Industries Inc (HQ).....**C.....562 944-3281**
12827 Imperial Hwy Santa Fe Springs (90670) ***(P-5791)***

Reisner Enterprises Inc.....F.....951 786-9478
1403 W Linden St Riverside (92507) ***(P-8764)***

Reiter Affl Companies LLC (PA).....**C.....805 483-1000**
730 S A St Oxnard (93030) ***(P-34)***

Reiter Berry Farms Inc (PA) ..... **C** **805 483-1000**
730 S A St Oxnard (93030) ***(P-35)***

Related/Normont Dev Co LLC ..... D 949 660-7272
18201 Von Karman Ave # 900 Irvine (92612) ***(P-16070)***

Relational Center ..... F 323 935-1807
2717 S Robertson Blvd # 1 Los Angeles (90034) ***(P-17973)***

Relativity Space Inc ..... B 424 393-4309
3500 E Burnett St Long Beach (90815) ***(P-10529)***

Relax Medical Systems Inc ..... F 800 405-7677
3260 E Willow St Signal Hill (90755) ***(P-11742)***

Relaxis, San Clemente *Also called Sensory Neurostimulation Inc* ***(P-4892)***

Reldom Corporation ..... E 562 498-3346
3241 Industry Dr Signal Hill (90755) ***(P-9906)***

Releasepoint, Claremont *Also called Western Feld Invstigations Inc* ***(P-18135)***

Reliable Building Products Inc ..... E 323 566-5000
9301 Rayo Ave South Gate (90280) ***(P-6659)***

Reliable Circuits Mfg Inc ..... F 310 373-2174
3080 Lomita Blvd Torrance (90505) ***(P-9447)***

Reliable Co, Glendale *Also called Coinmach Corporation* ***(P-16872)***

Reliable Energy Management Inc ..... D 562 984-5511
6829 Walthall Way Paramount (90723) ***(P-1128)***

Reliable Packaging Systems Inc ..... F 714 572-1094
1300 N Jefferson St Anaheim (92807) ***(P-5194)***

Reliable Sheet Metal Works, Fullerton *Also called Gard Inc* ***(P-6842)***

Reliable Tape Products, Vernon *Also called Chua & Sons Co Inc* ***(P-2616)***

Reliable Wholesale Lumber Inc (PA) ..... **D** **714 848-8222**
7600 Redondo Cir Huntington Beach (92648) ***(P-13283)***

Reliance Carpet Cushion, Huntington Park *Also called Reliance Upholstery Sup Co Inc* ***(P-3117)***

Reliance Company, Los Angeles *Also called Zastrow Construction Inc* ***(P-675)***

Reliance Steel & Aluminum Co (PA) ..... **D** **213 687-7700**
350 S Grand Ave Ste 5100 Los Angeles (90071) ***(P-13588)***

Reliance Steel & Aluminum Co ..... D 562 695-0467
9351 Norwalk Blvd Santa Fe Springs (90670) ***(P-13589)***

Reliance Steel & Aluminum Co ..... C 714 736-4800
15090 Northam St La Mirada (90638) ***(P-13590)***

Reliance Steel & Aluminum Co ..... C 323 583-6111
2537 E 27th St Vernon (90058) ***(P-13591)***

Reliance Steel & Aluminum Co ..... D 562 944-3322
12034 Greenstone Ave Santa Fe Springs (90670) ***(P-13592)***

Reliance Steel Company, Vernon *Also called Reliance Steel & Aluminum Co* ***(P-13591)***

Reliance Upholstery Sup Co Inc ..... D 323 321-2300
4920 S Boyle Ave Huntington Park (90255) ***(P-3117)***

Reliant Foodservice, Temecula *Also called Canadas Finest Foods Inc* ***(P-1896)***

Relief-Mart Inc ..... E 805 379-4300
28505 Canwood St Ste C Agoura Hills (91301) ***(P-3557)***

Relocity Inc ..... C 323 207-9160
10250 Constellation Blvd Los Angeles (90067) ***(P-23098)***

Relton Corporation ..... D 800 423-1505
317 Rolyn Pl Arcadia (91007) ***(P-5240)***

REM Eye Wear, Sun Valley *Also called REM Optical Company Inc* ***(P-13538)***

REM Optical Company Inc ..... D 818 504-3950
10941 La Tuna Canyon Rd Sun Valley (91352) ***(P-13538)***

Remanfctured Converter MBL LLC ..... F 714 744-8988
582 N Batavia St Orange (92868) ***(P-8107)***

Remanufactured Converter MBL, Orange *Also called Remanfctured Converter MBL LLC* ***(P-8107)***

Remarkable Industries Inc (PA) ..... **E** **800 579-4380**
6355 Topanga Canyon Blvd # 321 Woodland Hills (91367) ***(P-11743)***

Remax Legends, Alta Loma *Also called Inland Empire RE Solutions* ***(P-15890)***

Remax Olson & Associates Inc ..... D 818 366-3300
11141 Tampa Ave Northridge (91326) ***(P-15974)***

Remco Mch & Fabrication Inc ..... F 909 877-3530
1966 S Date Ave Bloomington (92316) ***(P-8765)***

Remedy Intelligent Staffing, Aliso Viejo *Also called Remedytemp Inc* ***(P-17512)***

Remedy Intlligent Staffing LLC (HQ) ..... **D** **805 882-2200**
3820 State St Ste A Santa Barbara (93105) ***(P-17511)***

Remedytemp Inc (HQ) ..... **C** **949 425-7600**
101 Enterprise Ste 100 Aliso Viejo (92656) ***(P-17512)***

Remington Hotel Corporation ..... D 760 322-6000
888 E Tahquitz Canyon Way Palm Springs (92262) ***(P-16658)***

Remington Hotel Corporation ..... D 310 553-6561
1150 S Beverly Dr Los Angeles (90035) ***(P-16659)***

Remington Roll Forming Inc ..... E 626 350-5196
2445 Chico Ave El Monte (91733) ***(P-6244)***

Remo Inc (PA) ..... **B** **661 294-5600**
28101 Industry Dr Valencia (91355) ***(P-11350)***

Remstek Corp, Temecula *Also called Inners Tasks LLC* ***(P-8161)***

Renaissance Doors & Windows, Rcho STA Marg *Also called Renaissnce Frnch Dors Sash Inc* ***(P-3286)***

Renaissance Hotel Clubsport, Aliso Viejo *Also called L & O Aliso Viejo LLC* ***(P-16530)***

Renaissance Hotel Operating Co ..... B 310 337-2800
9620 Airport Blvd Los Angeles (90045) ***(P-16660)***

Renaissance Hotel Operating Co ..... A 760 773-4444
44400 Indian Wells Ln Indian Wells (92210) ***(P-16661)***

Renaissance Indian Wells, Indian Wells *Also called Renaissance Hotel Operating Co* ***(P-16661)***

Renaissance Palm Springs, Palm Springs *Also called HHC Trs Portsmouth LLC* ***(P-16473)***

Renaissnce Frnch Dors Sash Inc (PA) ..... **C** **714 578-0090**
38 Segada Rcho STA Marg (92688) ***(P-3286)***

Renal Center, Orange *Also called St Joseph Hospital of Orange* ***(P-20964)***

Renau Corporation ..... E 818 341-1994
9309 Deering Ave Chatsworth (91311) ***(P-10718)***

Renau Electronic Laboratories, Chatsworth *Also called Renau Corporation* ***(P-10718)***

Renaud's Patisserie & Bistro, Santa Barbara *Also called Renauds Bakery and Bistro Inc* ***(P-2032)***

Renauds Bakery and Bistro Inc (PA) ..... **D** **805 569-2400**
3315 State St Santa Barbara (93105) ***(P-2032)***

Renco Encoders Inc ..... B 805 968-1525
26 Coromar Dr Goleta (93117) ***(P-8926)***

Renee Claire Inc, Los Angeles *Also called Camp Smidgemore Inc* ***(P-2929)***

Renew Health Group LLC ..... E 310 625-2838
107 W Lemon Ave Monrovia (91016) ***(P-23308)***

Renkus-Heinz Inc (PA) ..... **D** **949 588-9997**
19201 Cook St Foothill Ranch (92610) ***(P-9187)***

Reno Tenco, Boron *Also called Rio Tinto Minerals Inc* ***(P-383)***

Renova Energy Corp ..... E 760 568-3413
75181 Mediterranean Palm Desert (92211) ***(P-1129)***

Renovo Solutions LLC ..... B 714 599-7969
4 Executive Cir Ste 185 Irvine (92614) ***(P-23099)***

Rent What, Compton *Also called Sew What Inc* ***(P-3094)***

Rentech Inc (PA) ..... **B** **310 571-9800**
10880 Wilshire Blvd # 1101 Los Angeles (90024) ***(P-5301)***

Rentech Ntrgn Pasadena Spa LLC ..... E 310 571-9805
10877 Wilshire Blvd # 71 Los Angeles (90024) ***(P-5160)***

Rentokil North America Inc ..... D 562 802-2238
15415 Marquardt Ave Santa Fe Springs (90670) ***(P-14867)***

Rentspree Inc ..... E 323 515-7757
15303 Ventura Blvd # 1150 Sherman Oaks (91403) ***(P-17697)***

Reny & Co Inc ..... F 626 962-3078
4505 Littlejohn St Baldwin Park (91706) ***(P-5792)***

Renymed, Baldwin Park *Also called Reny & Co Inc* ***(P-5792)***

Renzoni Vineyards Inc ..... E 951 302-8466
37350 De Portola Rd Temecula (92592) ***(P-52)***

Rep-Kote Products Inc ..... F 909 355-1288
10938 Beech Ave Fontana (92337) ***(P-5285)***

Repair Tech International, Van Nuys *Also called Repairtech International Inc* ***(P-12366)***

Repairtech International Inc ..... E 818 989-2681
7850 Gloria Ave Van Nuys (91406) ***(P-12366)***

Repet Inc ..... C 909 594-5333
14207 Monte Vista Ave Chino (91710) ***(P-5461)***

Repipe1 Restoration Inc ..... E 626 252-0778
19326 Ventura Blvd # 200 Tarzana (91356) ***(P-542)***

Replacement Parts Inds Inc ..... E 818 882-8611
625 Cochran St Simi Valley (93065) ***(P-11194)***

Reprints Desk Inc ..... D 310 477-0354
15821 Ventura Blvd # 165 Encino (91436) ***(P-18130)***

Republic Bag Inc (PA) ..... **D** **951 734-9740**
580 E Harrison St Corona (92879) ***(P-3889)***

Republic Fence Co Inc (PA) ..... **E** **818 341-5323**
11309 Danube Ave Granada Hills (91344) ***(P-1685)***

Republic Furniture Mfg Inc ..... E 323 235-2144
2241 E 49th St Vernon (90058) ***(P-3514)***

Republic Indemnity Co Amer (HQ) ..... **C** **818 990-9860**
4500 Park Granada Ste 300 Calabasas (91302) ***(P-15478)***

Republic Machinery Co Inc (PA) ..... **E** **310 518-1100**
800 Sprucelake Dr Harbor City (90710) ***(P-7742)***

Republic Master Chefs Textile, Long Beach *Also called American Textile Maint Co* ***(P-16842)***

Republic Uniform, Long Beach *Also called American Textile Maint Co* ***(P-16841)***

Rerubber LLC ..... F 909 786-2811
115 N Del Rosa Dr Ste C San Bernardino (92408) ***(P-12971)***

RES-Care Inc ..... D 760 775-2887
45691 Monroe St Ste 6 Indio (92201) ***(P-20540)***

RES-Care Inc ..... D 951 653-1311
22635 Alessandro Blvd Moreno Valley (92553) ***(P-20541)***

RES-Care Inc ..... D 909 596-5360
2120 Foothill Blvd # 205 La Verne (91750) ***(P-20542)***

Res.net, Lake Forest *Also called US Real Estate Services Inc* ***(P-16026)***

Reschedge, Walnut *Also called Oncehub Inc* ***(P-17941)***

Rescom Overhead Doors Inc ..... F 909 799-8555
1430 Richardson St San Bernardino (92408) ***(P-1453)***

Rescue Mission Alliance (PA) ..... **D** **805 487-1234**
315 N A St Oxnard (93030) ***(P-22460)***

Research Affiliates Capital LP ..... D 949 325-8700
620 Nwport Ctr Dr Ste 900 Newport Beach (92660) ***(P-15342)***

Research Affiliates MGT LLC ..... D 949 325-8700
620 Nwport Ctr Dr Ste 900 Newport Beach (92660) ***(P-15343)***

Research Metal Industries Inc ..... E 310 352-3200
1970 W 139th St Gardena (90249) ***(P-8766)***

Research Way Ll LLC ..... F 608 830-6300
1900 Main St Ste 375 Irvine (92614) ***(P-4881)***

Research Way Partners, Irvine *Also called Research Way Ll LLC* ***(P-4881)***

Resecurity Inc ..... E 888 273-8276
445 S Figueroa St # 3100 Los Angeles (90071) ***(P-13433)***

Reseda Dodge Sales Inc ..... D 805 581-9090
4470 Winnetka Ave Woodland Hills (91364) ***(P-18866)***

Reserve Club ..... D 760 674-2222
49400 Desert Butte Trl Indian Wells (92210) ***(P-19604)***

Reshape Weightloss Inc (HQ) ..... **E** **949 429-6680**
1001 Calle Amanecer San Clemente (92673) ***(P-11237)***

Residence Inn Anaheim, Anaheim *Also called M8 Dev LLC* ***(P-16551)***

Residence Inn By Marriott, Oxnard *Also called Windsor Capital Group Inc* ***(P-16789)***

Residence Inn By Marriott, Torrance *Also called Msr Hotels & Resorts Inc* ***(P-16575)***

Residence Inn By Marriott, Los Angeles *Also called Sunstone Hotel Properties Inc* ***(P-16741)***

Residence Inn By Marriott, Manhattan Beach *Also called Sunstone Hotel Properties Inc* ***(P-16742)***

Residence Inn By Marriott, Los Angeles *Also called Beverly Sunstone Hills LLC* ***(P-16350)***

Residence Inn By Marriott, La Mirada *Also called B S A Partners* ***(P-16334)***

Residence Inn By Marriott, Aliso Viejo *Also called Sunstone Hotel Properties Inc* ***(P-16743)***

Residences At Stevens Pond, Los Angeles *Also called Stevens Pond APT Propty Ownr* ***(P-15750)***

Resident Group Services Inc (PA) ..... **C** **714 630-5300**
1156 N Grove St Anaheim (92806) ***(P-339)***

ALPHABETIC

Employee Codes: A=Over 500 employees, B=251-500
C=101-250, D=51-100, E=20-50 F=10-19
2022 Southern California Business
Directory and Buyers Guide
© Mergent Inc. 1-800-342-5647
1253

Resident Home LLC (PA) .... **C.......888 863-2827**
340 S Lemon Ave 9599 Walnut (91789) ***(P-13151)***

Residential Bancorp (PA) .... **D.......330 499-8333**
22632 Goln Spgs Dr Ste 20 Diamond Bar (91765) ***(P-15229)***

Residential Design Service, Irvine *Also called LARK Industries Inc* ***(P-18572)***

Residential Fire Systems Inc .... D.......714 666-8450
8085 E Crystal Dr Anaheim (92807) ***(P-1130)***

Residnce Inn Anheim Hlls Yrba, Anaheim *Also called Ponderosa Yorba Linda LLC* ***(P-16635)***

Residnce Inn Anheim Rsort Ar/G, Garden Grove *Also called Chatham Rigg LLC* ***(P-16049)***

Residnce Inn By Mrriot Lx/Cntu, Los Angeles *Also called Svi Lax LLC* ***(P-16745)***

Residual Income Opprtnties Inc .... F.......818 991-1999
4580 E Thsand Oaks Blvd S Westlake Village (91362) ***(P-5259)***

Resinart Corporation .... E.......949 642-3665
1621 Placentia Ave Costa Mesa (92627) ***(P-5793)***

Resinart Plastics, Costa Mesa *Also called Resinart Corporation* ***(P-5793)***

Resmed Motor Technologies Inc .... C.......818 428-6400
9540 De Soto Ave Chatsworth (91311) ***(P-8927)***

Resort At Pelican Hill LLC .... C.......949 467-6800
22701 Pelican Hill Rd S Newport Coast (92657) ***(P-16662)***

Resort Campground Intl, Lytle Creek *Also called Burlingame Industries Inc* ***(P-16830)***

Resort Parking Services Inc .... C.......760 328-4041
39755 Berkey Dr B Palm Desert (92211) ***(P-18778)***

RESOURCE CENTER, Long Beach *Also called Womenshelter of Long Beach* ***(P-22377)***

Resource Collection Inc .... D.......310 219-3272
3771 W 242nd St Ste 205 Torrance (90505) ***(P-17281)***

Resource Environmental Inc .... D.......562 468-7000
13100 Alondra Blvd # 108 Cerritos (90703) ***(P-815)***

Resource Label Group LLC .... E.......310 603-8910
1360 W Walnut Pkwy Compton (90220) ***(P-4468)***

Resource Management Group Inc (PA) .... **D.......858 677-0884**
2301 E 7th St Ste A337 Los Angeles (90023) ***(P-12519)***

Resources Connection Inc (PA) .... **A.......714 430-6400**
17101 Armstrong Ave # 100 Irvine (92614) ***(P-23309)***

Resources Connection LLC (HQ) .... **D.......714 430-6400**
17101 Armstrong Ave # 100 Irvine (92614) ***(P-17460)***

Resources Global Professionals, Irvine *Also called Resources Connection LLC* ***(P-17460)***

Response Envelope Inc (PA) .... **C.......909 923-5855**
1340 S Baker Ave Ontario (91761) ***(P-4566)***

Responsible Med Solutions Corp .... E.......951 308-0024
41715 Winchester Rd # 101 Temecula (92590) ***(P-20041)***

Restaurant Investment, Los Angeles *Also called Providence Rest Partners LLC* ***(P-16285)***

Restaurants Bars & Food Svcs, Los Angeles *Also called Fish House Partners One LLC* ***(P-16262)***

Restor-Tech Cnstr Cnslting Inc (PA) .... **D.......323 249-2277**
9125 Long Beach Blvd South Gate (90280) ***(P-23499)***

RESTORATION SOBER LIVING HOMES, Inglewood *Also called Christ-Centered Ministries* ***(P-22449)***

Restore Motion, Foothill Ranch *Also called Team Makena LLC* ***(P-13523)***

Result Group Inc .... F.......480 777-7130
2603 Main St Ste 710 Irvine (92614) ***(P-18062)***

Retail, South El Monte *Also called Kureiji Inc* ***(P-2853)***

Retail Print Media Inc .... E.......424 488-6950
2355 Crenshaw Blvd # 135 Torrance (90501) ***(P-4567)***

Rethink Label Systems, Anaheim *Also called Labeltronix LLC* ***(P-4534)***

Retina Associates Orange Cnty (PA) .... **D.......949 707-5125**
23521 Paseo De Valencia Laguna Hills (92653) ***(P-20042)***

Retirement Housing Foundation (PA) .... **D.......562 257-5100**
911 N Studebaker Rd # 100 Long Beach (90815) ***(P-15975)***

Rettig Machine Inc .... E.......909 793-7811
301 Kansas St Redlands (92373) ***(P-18995)***

Reuland Electric Co (PA) .... **C.......626 964-6411**
17969 Railroad St City of Industry (91748) ***(P-8928)***

Reunify LLC .... D.......310 893-1736
12121 Wilshire Blvd # 505 Los Angeles (90025) ***(P-16975)***

Rev Co Spring Mfanufacturing .... F.......562 949-1958
9915 Alburtis Ave Santa Fe Springs (90670) ***(P-7491)***

Revasum Inc .... C.......805 541-6424
825 Buckley Rd Ste 200 San Luis Obispo (93401) ***(P-9564)***

Revchem Composites Inc (PA) .... **D.......909 877-8477**
2720 S Willow Ave B Bloomington (92316) ***(P-13327)***

Revchem Plastics, Bloomington *Also called Revchem Composites Inc* ***(P-13327)***

Revco Industries Inc (PA) .... **E.......562 777-1588**
10747 Norwalk Blvd Santa Fe Springs (90670) ***(P-14014)***

Reveal Windows & Doors, La Habra *Also called Pacific Archtectural Mllwk Inc* ***(P-3279)***

Reverse Medical Corporation .... D.......949 215-0660
13700 Alton Pkwy Ste 167 Irvine (92618) ***(P-11050)***

REVIVALS THRIFT STORES, Palm Springs *Also called Desert Aids Project* ***(P-21767)***

Revolt Media and Tv LLC .... C.......323 645-3000
1800 N Highland Ave Fl 7 Los Angeles (90028) ***(P-12739)***

Rew, Riverside *Also called Roy E Whitehead Inc* ***(P-1454)***

Rex Creamery, Commerce *Also called Heritage Distributing Company* ***(P-1837)***

Rexford Industrial Realty Inc (PA) .... **C.......310 966-1680**
11620 Wilshire Blvd Fl 10 Los Angeles (90025) ***(P-16243)***

Rexhall Industries Inc .... E.......661 726-5470
26857 Tannahill Ave Canyon Country (91387) ***(P-10174)***

Rexnord Industries LLC .... F.......814 969-3665
14650 Miller Ave Fontana (92336) ***(P-8108)***

Rey-Crest Roofg Waterproofing, Los Angeles *Also called Rey-Crest Roofg Waterproofing* ***(P-1686)***

Rey-Crest Roofg Waterproofing .... D.......323 257-9329
3065 Verdugo Rd Los Angeles (90065) ***(P-1686)***

Reyes Coca-Cola Bottling LLC (PA) .... **B.......213 744-8616**
3 Park Plz Ste 600 Irvine (92614) ***(P-2284)***

Reyes Coca-Cola Bottling LLC .... D.......661 324-6531
4320 Ride St Bakersfield (93313) ***(P-2285)***

Reyes Coca-Cola Bottling LLC .... D.......562 803-8100
8729 Cleta St Downey (90241) ***(P-2286)***

Reyes Coca-Cola Bottling LLC .... D.......805 644-2211
5335 Walker St Ventura (93003) ***(P-2287)***

Reyes Coca-Cola Bottling LLC .... D.......760 396-4500
86375 Industrial Way Coachella (92236) ***(P-2288)***

Reyes Coca-Cola Bottling LLC .... D.......805 925-2629
120 E Jones St Santa Maria (93454) ***(P-2289)***

Reyes Coca-Cola Bottling LLC .... D.......909 980-3121
10670 6th St Rancho Cucamonga (91730) ***(P-2290)***

Reyes Coca-Cola Bottling LLC .... D.......805 614-3702
1000 Fairway Dr Santa Maria (93455) ***(P-2291)***

Reyes Coca-Cola Bottling LLC .... D.......562 536-8847
11634 Patton Rd Downey (90241) ***(P-2292)***

Reyes Coca-Cola Bottling LLC .... D.......323 278-2600
666 Union St Montebello (90640) ***(P-2293)***

Reyes Coca-Cola Bottling LLC .... D.......714 974-1901
700 W Grove Ave Orange (92865) ***(P-2294)***

Reyes Coca-Cola Bottling LLC .... E.......818 362-4307
12925 Bradley Ave Sylmar (91342) ***(P-14732)***

Reyes Coca-Cola Bottling LLC .... D.......213 744-8659
1338 E 14th St Los Angeles (90021) ***(P-2295)***

Reyes Coca-Cola Bottling LLC .... D.......760 241-2653
15346 Anacapa Rd Victorville (92392) ***(P-2296)***

Reyes Coca-Cola Bottling LLC .... D.......760 352-1561
126 S 3rd St El Centro (92243) ***(P-2297)***

Reynaldos Mexican Food Co Inc .... F.......562 803-3188
11929 Woodruff Ave Downey (90241) ***(P-2516)***

Reynaldos Mexican Food Co LLC (PA) .... **C.......562 803-3188**
3301 E Vernon Ave Vernon (90058) ***(P-2517)***

Reynard Corporation .... E.......949 366-8866
1020 Calle Sombra San Clemente (92673) ***(P-10857)***

Reyrich Plastics Inc .... E.......909 484-8444
1704 S Vineyard Ave Ontario (91761) ***(P-5794)***

Rezek Equipment .... E.......909 885-6221
970 Reece St San Bernardino (92411) ***(P-22646)***

Rezex Corporation .... E.......213 622-2015
1930 E 51st St Vernon (90058) ***(P-2679)***

Rf Digital Corporation .... C.......949 610-0008
1601 Pcf Cast Hwy Ste 290 Hermosa Beach (90254) ***(P-9565)***

Rfc Wire Forms Inc .... D.......909 467-0559
525 Brooks St Ontario (91762) ***(P-7512)***

Rfl Global Inc .... F.......323 235-2580
732 E Jefferson Blvd Los Angeles (90011) ***(P-17974)***

RG Costumes & Accessories Inc .... E.......626 858-9559
726 Arrow Grand Cir Covina (91722) ***(P-3083)***

RGA Electric Inc .... D.......562 941-6380
10207 Freeman Ave Santa Fe Springs (90670) ***(P-1308)***

Rgb Systems Inc (PA) .... **C.......714 491-1500**
1025 E Ball Rd Ste 100 Anaheim (92805) ***(P-8297)***

Rgbx Inc .... D.......714 524-1350
16971 Imperial Hwy Yorba Linda (92886) ***(P-22056)***

Rgc Services Inc (PA) .... **C.......805 644-1242**
5720 Ralston St Ste 100 Ventura (93003) ***(P-15976)***

Rgc Services Inc .... D.......805 484-1600
601 E Daily Dr Ste 102 Camarillo (93010) ***(P-15977)***

RGF Enterprises Inc .... E.......951 734-6922
220 Citation Cir Corona (92878) ***(P-7406)***

Rggd Inc (PA) .... **D.......323 581-6617**
4950 S Santa Fe Ave Vernon (90058) ***(P-14177)***

Rgis LLC .... C.......248 651-2511
500 E Olive Ave Ste 240 Burbank (91501) ***(P-18651)***

Rgis LLC .... C.......714 938-0663
1937 W Chapman Ave Orange (92868) ***(P-18652)***

Rgis LLC .... D.......951 369-7131
6529 Rverside Ave Ste 215 Riverside (92506) ***(P-18653)***

Rgs Services, Anaheim *Also called Resident Group Services Inc* ***(P-339)***

Rhapsody Clothing Inc .... D.......213 614-8887
810 E Pico Blvd Ste 24 Los Angeles (90021) ***(P-2989)***

Rheumatology Diagnostics Lab .... D.......310 253-5455
324 S Beverly Dr Beverly Hills (90212) ***(P-21094)***

Rhf Plymouth Tower .... D.......951 248-0456
3401 Lemon St Ofc Riverside (92501) ***(P-20445)***

Rhi Inc (PA) .... **C.......818 508-3800**
5841 Lankershim Blvd North Hollywood (91601) ***(P-18867)***

Rhino Ready Mix Trucking Inc (PA) .... **E.......661 679-3643**
3701 Pegasus Dr Ste 126 Bakersfield (93308) ***(P-11990)***

RHO Chem LLC (HQ) .... **E.......323 776-6234**
425 Isis Ave Inglewood (90301) ***(P-13008)***

RHS Corp .... F.......909 335-5500
350 Terracina Blvd Redlands (92373) ***(P-23100)***

Rhythm & Hues Studios, El Segundo *Also called Rhythm and Hues Inc* ***(P-19170)***

Rhythm and Hues Inc (PA) .... **C.......310 448-7500**
2100 E Grand Ave Ste A El Segundo (90245) ***(P-19170)***

Ria Envia Inc (HQ) .... **A.......714 543-8448**
6565 Knott Ave Buena Park (90620) ***(P-18654)***

Ria Financial Service, Buena Park *Also called Continental Exch Solutions Inc* ***(P-15126)***

Ria Financial Services, Buena Park *Also called Continental Exch Solutions Inc* ***(P-18490)***

Rialto Concrete Products, Rialto *Also called Kti Incorporated* ***(P-6038)***

Rialto Record, San Bernardino *Also called Inland Empire Cmnty Newspapers* ***(P-3994)***

Rialto Unified School District .... D.......909 820-7864
625 W Rialto Ave Rialto (92376) ***(P-23101)***

Ricardo Defense Inc (HQ) .... **D.......805 882-1884**
175 Cremona Dr Ste 140 Goleta (93117) ***(P-10125)***

Ricardo Ramos .... E.......310 785-0288
2803 Carlsbad St Redondo Beach (90278) ***(P-1309)***

Ricaurte Precision Inc .... E.......714 667-0632
1550 E Mcfadden Ave Santa Ana (92705) ***(P-8767)***

Rice Drywall Inc .... D.......714 543-5400
919 E 6th St Santa Ana (92701) ***(P-1396)***

Rice Field Corporation .... C.......626 968-6917
14500 Valley Blvd City of Industry (91746) ***(P-1748)***

Rich Chicks LLC ....E....209 879-4104
13771 Gramercy Pl Gardena (90249) ***(P-1763)***

Richard Bagdasarian Inc ....D....760 396-2168
65500 Lincoln St Mecca (92254) ***(P-53)***

Richard Cantrell (PA) ....**D....310 399-5511**
1661 9th St Santa Monica (90404) ***(P-14413)***

Richard Huetter Inc ....D....818 700-8001
21050 Osborne St Canoga Park (91304) ***(P-13085)***

Richard K Newman and Assoc Inc (PA) ....**E....661 634-1130**
121 Monterey St Bakersfield (93305) ***(P-16869)***

Richard K Newman and Assoc Inc ....D....661 634-1218
5600 Auburn St Ste V Bakersfield (93306) ***(P-16877)***

Richard Nixon Foundation ....D....714 701-6832
18001 Yorba Linda Blvd Yorba Linda (92886) ***(P-22232)***

Richard Tyler, Alhambra *Also called Tyler Trafficante Inc* ***(P-2751)***

Richard Wilson Wellington ....D....626 812-7881
1025 N Todd Ave Azusa (91702) ***(P-94)***

Richard Yarbrough ....E....805 643-1021
2493 N Ventura Ave Ventura (93001) ***(P-543)***

Richards Watson & Gershon PC (PA) ....**C....213 626-8484**
355 S Grand Ave Fl 40 Los Angeles (90071) ***(P-21669)***

Richards Neon Shop Inc ....E....951 279-6767
4375 Prado Rd Ste 102 Corona (92878) ***(P-11586)***

Richardson Group ....D....714 997-3970
413 S Glassell St Orange (92866) ***(P-816)***

Richfield Engineering Inc ....E....714 524-3741
1135 Fee Ana St Placentia (92870) ***(P-6749)***

Richland Chevrolet Co Corp ....D....661 746-4981
511 Central Ave Shafter (93263) ***(P-18903)***

Richman Management Corporation ....B....760 832-8520
35400 Bob Hope Dr Ste 107 Rancho Mirage (92270) ***(P-18316)***

Richman Management Corporation ....B....909 296-6189
41743 Entp Cir N Ste 209 Temecula (92590) ***(P-18317)***

Richmond Plastering Inc ....E....562 924-4202
12102 Centralia Rd Ste B Hawaiian Gardens (90716) ***(P-1397)***

Richwell Steel Co Inc ....D....310 324-4455
134 W 168th St Gardena (90248) ***(P-1580)***

Rick Hamm Construction Inc ....D....714 532-0815
201 W Carleton Ave Orange (92867) ***(P-909)***

Rick Solomon Enterprises Inc (PA) ....**D....310 280-3700**
8460 Higuera St Culver City (90232) ***(P-14347)***

Rico Corporation (HQ) ....**C....818 394-2700**
8484 San Fernando Rd Sun Valley (91352) ***(P-11351)***

Rico Farm Labor Inc ....E....805 525-4523
735 E Pleasant St Santa Paula (93060) ***(P-227)***

Rico Holdings Inc ....F....818 394-2700
8484 San Fernando Rd Sun Valley (91352) ***(P-11352)***

Rico Products, Sun Valley *Also called Rico Corporation* ***(P-11351)***

Ricoh Electronics Inc ....C....714 566-6079
2310 Redhill Ave Santa Ana (92705) ***(P-11291)***

Ricoh Electronics Inc ....E....714 259-1220
17482 Pullman St Irvine (92614) ***(P-8319)***

Ricoh Prtg Systems Amer Inc (HQ) ....**B....805 578-4000**
2390 Ward Ave Ste A Simi Valley (93065) ***(P-8298)***

Ricon Corp (HQ) ....**C....818 267-3000**
1135 Aviation Pl San Fernando (91340) ***(P-11744)***

Ride At Home Care, Corona *Also called Bmb 1 LLC* ***(P-20562)***

RIDE ON TRANSPORTATION, San Luis Obispo *Also called United Crbral Plsy Assn San Lu* ***(P-11895)***

Rider Best Inc (PA) ....**E....626 336-8388**
428 S 9th Ave City of Industry (91746) ***(P-9188)***

Ridge Wallet LLC ....F....818 636-2832
2448 Main St Santa Monica (90405) ***(P-5911)***

Ridgecrest Healthcare Inc (PA) ....**C....323 344-0601**
1131 N China Lake Blvd Ridgecrest (93555) ***(P-20446)***

Ridgecrest Regional Hospital (PA) ....**B....760 446-3551**
1081 N China Lake Blvd Ridgecrest (93555) ***(P-20923)***

Ridgecrest Service Center, Ridgecrest *Also called Southern California Edison Co* ***(P-12857)***

Ridgetop Energy LLC ....E....661 822-2400
7021 Oak Creek Rd Mojave (93501) ***(P-12823)***

Riedon Inc (PA) ....**C....626 284-9901**
300 Cypress Ave Alhambra (91801) ***(P-9617)***

Riggins Engineering Inc ....E....818 782-7010
13932 Saticoy St Van Nuys (91402) ***(P-8768)***

Right Angle Solutions Inc ....E....951 934-3081
6315 Pedley Rd Jurupa Valley (92509) ***(P-23500)***

Right At Home, Fountain Valley *Also called In Home Comfort and Care Inc* ***(P-21174)***

Rightime Enterprise (PA) ....**E....323 574-0310**
2716 E Florence Ave Huntington Park (90255) ***(P-1937)***

Rightscale Inc ....C....805 500-4164
402 E Gutierrez St Santa Barbara (93101) ***(P-17698)***

Rightsourcing Inc (HQ) ....**D....800 660-9544**
9 Executive Cir Ste 290 Irvine (92614) ***(P-17513)***

Rightway, Vernon *Also called R B R Meat Company Inc* ***(P-1718)***

Rigiflex Technology Inc ....F....714 688-1500
1166 N Grove St Anaheim (92806) ***(P-9448)***

Rignoli Pacific, Monterey Park *Also called Rigoli Enterprises Inc* ***(P-9907)***

Rigoli Enterprises Inc ....F....626 573-0242
1983 Potrero Grande Dr Monterey Park (91755) ***(P-9907)***

Rigos Equipment Mfg LLC ....E....626 813-6621
14501 Joanbridge St Baldwin Park (91706) ***(P-6902)***

Rigos Sheet Metal, Baldwin Park *Also called Rigos Equipment Mfg LLC* ***(P-6902)***

Rika Corporation ....D....949 830-9050
332 W Brenna Ln Orange (92867) ***(P-1581)***

Rim of World Unified Schl Dst ....D....909 336-0330
27614 Hwy 18 Across Bldg Lake Arrowhead (92352) ***(P-11936)***

Rima Enterprises Inc ....D....714 893-4534
16417 Ladona Cir Huntington Beach (92649) ***(P-7925)***

Rima-System, Huntington Beach *Also called Rima Enterprises Inc* ***(P-7925)***

Rincon Consultants Inc ....C....805 547-0900
1530 Monterey St Ste D San Luis Obispo (93401) ***(P-23501)***

Rincon Engineering Corporation ....E....805 684-0935
6325 Carpinteria Ave Carpinteria (93013) ***(P-8769)***

Rincon Iron Inc ....F....805 455-2904
531 Montgomery Ave Oxnard (93036) ***(P-6977)***

Rincon Ironworks, Oxnard *Also called Rincon Iron Inc* ***(P-6977)***

Rincon Pacific LLC ....D....805 986-8806
1312 Del Norte Rd Camarillo (93010) ***(P-36)***

Rincon Technology Inc (PA) ....**E....805 684-8100**
810 E Montecito St Santa Barbara (93103) ***(P-13539)***

Ring LLC (HQ) ....**B....800 656-1918**
1523 26th St Santa Monica (90404) ***(P-8883)***

Ring of Fire, Van Nuys *Also called Rof LLC* ***(P-2788)***

Rio ....C....714 633-7400
1800 E La Veta Ave Orange (92866) ***(P-21334)***

Rio Hondo Education Consortium ....D....562 945-0150
7200 Greenleaf Ave # 300 Whittier (90602) ***(P-21878)***

Rio Tinto Minerals Inc ....C....760 762-7121
14486 Borax Rd Boron (93516) ***(P-383)***

Rio Vista Development Co Inc (PA) ....**C....818 980-8000**
4222 Vineland Ave North Hollywood (91602) ***(P-16663)***

Riot Games Inc (HQ) ....**A....310 207-1444**
12333 W Olympic Blvd Los Angeles (90064) ***(P-17699)***

Riot Glass Inc ....E....800 580-2303
17941 Brookshire Ln Huntington Beach (92647) ***(P-9908)***

Rip Curl Inc (HQ) ....**D....714 422-3600**
193 Avenida La Pata San Clemente (92673) ***(P-11442)***

Rip Curl USA, San Clemente *Also called Rip Curl Inc* ***(P-11442)***

Riphagen & Bullerdick Inc ....E....714 763-2100
5925 Ball Rd Cypress (90630) ***(P-15978)***

Risa Tech Inc ....E....949 951-5815
26632 Towne Cntre Dr 210 Foothill Ranch (92610) ***(P-17700)***

Risco Inc ....E....951 769-2899
390 Risco Cir Beaumont (92223) ***(P-7073)***

Rise Bar, Irvine *Also called Divine Foods Inc* ***(P-2084)***

Rising Sun Chinese Food, Foothill Ranch *Also called Kds Donut Chinese Foods* ***(P-2011)***

Risvolds Inc ....D....323 770-2674
1234 W El Segundo Blvd Gardena (90247) ***(P-2518)***

Rite Screen, Rancho Cucamonga *Also called J T Walker Industries Inc* ***(P-6702)***

Rite-Way Meat Packers Inc ....D....323 826-2144
5151 Alcoa Ave Vernon (90058) ***(P-14605)***

Ritec, Simi Valley *Also called Rugged Info Tech Eqp Corp* ***(P-8299)***

Ritual, Los Angeles *Also called Natals Inc* ***(P-4856)***

Ritz Carlton Rancho Mirage, Rancho Mirage *Also called Ritz-Carlton Hotel Company LLC* ***(P-16666)***

Ritz-Carlton Hotel Company LLC ....B....949 240-5020
1 Ritz Carlton Dr Dana Point (92629) ***(P-16664)***

Ritz-Carlton Hotel Company LLC ....A....805 968-0100
8301 Hollister Ave Santa Barbara (93117) ***(P-16665)***

Ritz-Carlton Hotel Company LLC ....B....760 321-8282
68900 Frank Sinatra Dr Rancho Mirage (92270) ***(P-16666)***

Ritz-Carlton Laguna Niguel, Dana Point *Also called Prutel Joint Venture* ***(P-16642)***

Rive Gauche Cafe, Sherman Oaks *Also called Watt Construction Company* ***(P-15758)***

River Ridge Farms Inc ....D....805 647-6880
3135 Los Angeles Ave Oxnard (93036) ***(P-95)***

River Ridge Golf Club, Oxnard *Also called High Tide and Green Grass Inc* ***(P-19495)***

River Valley Dialysis LLC (HQ) ....**E....310 536-2400**
601 Hawaii St El Segundo (90245) ***(P-21263)***

River Valley Precast Inc ....F....928 764-3839
14796 Washington Dr Fontana (92335) ***(P-6054)***

Rivera Sanitarium Inc ....D....562 949-2591
7246 Rosemead Blvd Pico Rivera (90660) ***(P-20447)***

Riverbench LLC (PA) ....**E....805 937-8340**
6020 Foxen Canyon Rd Santa Maria (93454) ***(P-54)***

Riverbench Vineyard & Winery, Santa Maria *Also called Riverbench LLC* ***(P-54)***

Riversd-San Brnrdino Cnty Indi (PA) ....**B....909 864-1097**
11980 Mount Vernon Ave Grand Terrace (92313) ***(P-20043)***

Riverside Auto Auction, Anaheim *Also called Califrnia Auto Dalers Exch LLC* ***(P-13022)***

Riverside Blltin Jrupa This We, Riverside *Also called Metropolitan News Company* ***(P-4010)***

Riverside Care Inc ....C....951 683-7111
4301 Caroline Ct Riverside (92506) ***(P-20448)***

Riverside Cmnty Hlth Systems (HQ) ....**A....951 788-3000**
4445 Magnolia Ave Fl 6 Riverside (92501) ***(P-20924)***

Riverside Cnty Flood Ctrl Wtr ....C....951 955-1200
1995 Market St Riverside (92501) ***(P-23541)***

Riverside Community Hospital, Riverside *Also called Riverside Cmnty Hlth Systems* ***(P-20924)***

Riverside Companion Services, San Bernardino *Also called Maxim Healthcare Services Inc* ***(P-17502)***

Riverside County Off Educatn ....C....760 320-8266
1055 E Vista Chino Palm Springs (92262) ***(P-23502)***

RIVERSIDE COUNTY REGIONAL MEDI, Riverside *Also called Riverside Univ Hlth Sys Fndtio* ***(P-20925)***

Riverside District Office, Riverside *Also called State Compensation Insur Fund* ***(P-15484)***

Riverside Equities LLC ....C....951 688-2222
8487 Magnolia Ave Riverside (92504) ***(P-20449)***

Riverside Foundary, Riverside *Also called Oldcast Precast* ***(P-6044)***

Riverside Lamination Corp ....F....951 682-0100
3016 Kansas Ave Bldg 6 Riverside (92507) ***(P-5195)***

Riverside Machine Works Inc ....F....951 685-7416
6301 Baldwin Ave Riverside (92509) ***(P-8770)***

Riverside Marriott, Riverside *Also called Pinnacle Rvrside Hspitality LP* ***(P-16631)***

Riverside Med Clnic Ptient Ctr, Riverside *Also called Riverside Medical Clinic Inc* ***(P-20044)***

Riverside Medical Center, Riverside *Also called Kaiser Foundation Hospitals* ***(P-19944)***

Employee Codes: A=Over 500 employees, B=251-500
C=101-250, D=51-100, E=20-50 F=10-19
2022 Southern California Business Directory and Buyers Guide
© Mergent Inc. 1-800-342-5647
1255

Riverside Medical Clinic Inc (PA) ...B ...**951 683-6370**
3660 Arlington Ave Riverside (92506) ***(P-20044)***
Riverside Research Institute ...D ...949 631-0107
3333 W Coast Hwy Ste 101 Newport Beach (92663) ***(P-22918)***
Riverside Scrap Ir & Met Corp (PA) ...E ...**951 686-2120**
2993 6th St Riverside (92507) ***(P-14121)***
Riverside Sheriffs Association ...D ...951 653-5152
21810 Cactus Ave March ARB (92518) ***(P-22294)***
Riverside Tent and Awng Co Inc ...F ...951 683-1925
231 E Alcandro Blvd Ste A Riverside (92508) ***(P-3130)***
Riverside Transit Agency (PA) ...B ...**951 565-5000**
1825 3rd St Riverside (92507) ***(P-11836)***
Riverside Univ Hlth Sys Fndtio (PA) ...A ...**951 358-5000**
4065 County Circle Dr Riverside (92503) ***(P-20925)***
Riverton Steel Construction ...F ...323 564-1881
10130 Adella Ave South Gate (90280) ***(P-1582)***
Riverwalk PST-Cute Rhblitation, Mission Viejo *Also called Rock Canyon Healthcare Inc* ***(P-21209)***
Riviera Finance of Texas Inc ...D ...562 777-1300
10430 Pioneer Blvd Ste 1 Santa Fe Springs (90670) ***(P-15158)***
Riviera Health Care Center, Pico Rivera *Also called Riviera Nursing & Conva* ***(P-20450)***
Riviera Nursing & Conva ...C ...562 806-2576
8203 Telegraph Rd Pico Rivera (90660) ***(P-20450)***
Riviera Palm Sprng A Trbute Pr, Palm Springs *Also called Agre Dcp Palm Sprng Tenant LLC* ***(P-16315)***
Riviera Reincarnate LLC ...D ...760 327-8311
1600 N Indian Canyon Dr Palm Springs (92262) ***(P-16667)***
Riviera Shores, Capistrano Beach *Also called Pacific Monarch Resorts Inc* ***(P-16612)***
RJ Acquisition Corp (PA) ...C ...**323 318-1107**
3260 E 26th St Vernon (90058) ***(P-4568)***
Rj Airwash LLC (PA) ...E ...**818 342-8800**
6860 Canby Ave Ste 109 Reseda (91335) ***(P-10471)***
RJ Allen Inc ...D ...714 539-1022
10392 Stanford Ave Garden Grove (92840) ***(P-17318)***
RJ Noble Company (PA) ...C ...**714 637-1550**
15505 E Lincoln Ave Orange (92865) ***(P-910)***
RJ Singer International Inc ...E ...323 735-1717
3737 Ross St Vernon (90058) ***(P-5896)***
RJA Industries Inc ...E ...818 998-5124
9640 Topanga Canyon Pl J Chatsworth (91311) ***(P-9772)***
Rjb Enterprises Inc ...E ...714 484-3101
2579 W Woodland Dr Anaheim (92801) ***(P-1310)***
Rjn Investigations Inc ...D ...951 686-7638
360 E 1st St Ste 696 Tustin (92780) ***(P-18318)***
Rk Sports LLC (PA) ...F ...**714 794-4400**
16761 Viewpoint Ln # 268 Huntington Beach (92647) ***(P-10126)***
Rlh Fire Protection Inc (PA) ...D ...**661 322-9344**
4300 Stine Rd Ste 800 Bakersfield (93313) ***(P-1131)***
Rlh Industries Inc ...E ...714 532-1672
936 N Main St Orange (92867) ***(P-9241)***
Rlv Tuned Exhaust Products Inc ...E ...805 925-5461
2351 Thompson Way Bldg A Santa Maria (93455) ***(P-10127)***
RM Galicia Inc ...C ...626 813-6200
1521 W Cameron Ave # 100 West Covina (91790) ***(P-17116)***
Rm Partners Inc ...E ...714 765-5725
1439 S State College Blvd Anaheim (92806) ***(P-1469)***
RMA Group, Rancho Cucamonga *Also called R M A Group* ***(P-22643)***
Rmbb Properties LLC (PA) ...D ...**310 473-5562**
9190 W Olympic Blvd Beverly Hills (90212) ***(P-15693)***
Rmd Group Inc ...B ...562 866-9288
2311 E South St Long Beach (90805) ***(P-23310)***
Rmg Recycling, Los Angeles *Also called Resource Management Group Inc* ***(P-12519)***
Rmi Utility Services Inc ...D ...323 589-9498
2323 E Vernon Ave Vernon (90058) ***(P-23311)***
Rmis, Westlake Village *Also called Registry Mntring Insur Svcs In* ***(P-15973)***
Rmla Inc ...F ...213 749-4333
1972 E 20th St Vernon (90058) ***(P-3044)***
RMR Financial LLC (HQ) ...D ...**408 355-2000**
610 Newport Center Dr Newport Beach (92660) ***(P-15250)***
RMR Products Inc (PA) ...E ...**818 890-0896**
11011 Glenoaks Blvd Ste 1 Pacoima (91331) ***(P-6055)***
RMS, Signal Hill *Also called Relax Medical Systems Inc* ***(P-11742)***
RMS Foundation Inc ...A ...562 435-3511
1126 Queens Hwy Long Beach (90802) ***(P-16668)***
Rms/Endlgix Sdways Merger Corp ...E ...949 595-7200
2 Musick Irvine (92618) ***(P-11051)***
Rnbs Corporation ...E ...714 998-1828
725 S Paseo Prado Anaheim (92807) ***(P-8172)***
Rnc, Los Angeles *Also called Rnovate Inc* ***(P-8109)***
Rnc Capital Management LLC ...D ...310 477-6543
11601 Wilshire Blvd Ph 25 Los Angeles (90025) ***(P-15344)***
Rnc Genter Capital Management, Los Angeles *Also called Rnc Capital Management LLC* ***(P-15344)***
Rnd Contractors Inc ...E ...909 429-8500
14796 Jurupa Ave Ste A Fontana (92337) ***(P-6660)***
Rnd Enterprises, Chatsworth *Also called BDR Industries Inc* ***(P-8237)***
Rnj Printing Corporation ...F ...310 638-7768
116 23rd Pl Manhattan Beach (90266) ***(P-4418)***
Rnl Design, Los Angeles *Also called Stantec Architecture Inc* ***(P-18677)***
Rnovate Inc ...F ...213 489-1617
834 S Broadway Los Angeles (90014) ***(P-8109)***
RNS Channel Letters, Corona *Also called Richards Neon Shop Inc* ***(P-11586)***
Ro Gar Mfg, El Centro *Also called Rogar Manufacturing Inc* ***(P-9774)***
Ro Rocket Design Inc (PA) ...D ...**213 784-0014**
1031 W Mnchstr Blvd Inglewood (90301) ***(P-22740)***
Roadex America Inc ...D ...310 878-9800
2132 E Dominguez St Ste B Long Beach (90810) ***(P-12239)***
Roadium Open Air Market, Torrance *Also called Pioneer Theatres Inc* ***(P-18634)***
Roadrunner Shuttle, Camarillo *Also called Airport Connection Inc* ***(P-11802)***
Roadwire Distinctive Inds, Santa Fe Springs *Also called Distinctive Inds Texas Inc* ***(P-3056)***
Rob Inc ...D ...562 806-5589
6760 Foster Bridge Blvd Bell Gardens (90201) ***(P-2773)***
Robar Enterprises Inc (PA) ...C ...**760 244-5456**
17671 Bear Valley Rd Hesperia (92345) ***(P-6107)***
Robb Curtco Media LLC ...E ...310 589-7700
22741 Pcf Cast Hwy Ste 40 Malibu (90265) ***(P-4105)***
Robb Report Collection ...E ...310 589-7700
29160 Heathercliff Rd # 200 Malibu (90265) ***(P-4106)***
Robbins Precast, Corona *Also called Nucast Industries Inc* ***(P-6043)***
Robert Ballard Rehab Hospital (HQ) ...C ...**909 473-1200**
1760 W 16th St San Bernardino (92411) ***(P-20232)***
Robert Clapper Cnstr Svcs Inc ...D ...909 829-3688
2223 N Locust Ave Rialto (92377) ***(P-817)***
Robert Consl Englekirk Strctrl (PA) ...D ...**323 733-6673**
2116 Arlington Ave Lbby Los Angeles (90018) ***(P-22647)***
Robert D Vandereyk ...D ...559 909-3195
9441 Avenue 104 Pixley (93256) ***(P-136)***
Robert F Chapman Inc ...D ...661 940-9482
43100 Exchange Pl Lancaster (93535) ***(P-6903)***
Robert H Oliva Inc ...E ...818 700-1035
19863 Nordhoff St Northridge (91324) ***(P-8771)***
Robert Half International Inc ...D ...951 779-9081
2280 Market St Ste 220 Riverside (92501) ***(P-17461)***
Robert Heely Construction, Bakersfield *Also called Robert Heely Construction LP* ***(P-544)***
Robert Heely Construction LP (PA) ...E ...**661 617-1400**
5401 Woodmere Dr Bakersfield (93313) ***(P-544)***
Robert Kinsella Inc ...D ...949 453-9533
15375 Barranca Pkwy G107 Irvine (92618) ***(P-14487)***
Robert M Hadley Company Inc ...D ...805 658-7286
4054 Transport St Ventura (93003) ***(P-9642)***
Robert Moreno Insurance Svcs ...C ...714 578-3318
3110 E Guasti Rd Ste 500 Ontario (91761) ***(P-15622)***
Robert P Martin Company ...F ...323 686-2220
2209 Seaman Ave South El Monte (91733) ***(P-6232)***
Robert P Von Zabern ...F ...951 734-7215
4121 Tigris Way Riverside (92503) ***(P-11052)***
Robert Quintero Labor Contg ...E ...559 732-6954
1827 S Bardo St Visalia (93277) ***(P-17462)***
Robert Rnzoni Vineyards Winery, Temecula *Also called Renzoni Vineyards Inc* ***(P-52)***
Robert Vander Eyk & Sons Dairy, Pixley *Also called Robert D Vandereyk* ***(P-136)***
Robert W Wiesmantel ...F ...562 634-0442
15345 Allen St Paramount (90723) ***(P-8772)***
Robert's Engineering, Anaheim *Also called Roberts Precision Engrg Inc* ***(P-8773)***
Robert's Lumber, Bloomington *Also called Roberts Lumber Sales Inc* ***(P-13284)***
Roberto Martinez Inc ...F ...800 257-6462
1050 Calle Cordillera # 103 San Clemente (92673) ***(P-11329)***
Roberts & Associates Inc ...D ...951 727-4357
8175 Limonite Ave Ste A Riverside (92509) ***(P-21208)***
Roberts Lumber Sales Inc ...D ...909 350-9164
2661 S Lilac Ave Bloomington (92316) ***(P-13284)***
Roberts Precision Engrg Inc ...E ...714 635-4485
1345 S Allec St Anaheim (92805) ***(P-8773)***
Roberts Research Laboratory ...F ...310 320-7310
23150 Kashiwa Ct Torrance (90505) ***(P-7434)***
Robertson Honda, North Hollywood *Also called Rhi Inc* ***(P-18867)***
Robertsons Rdymx Ltd A Cal Ltd (HQ) ...D ...**951 493-6500**
200 S Main St Ste 200 # 200 Corona (92882) ***(P-6108)***
Robertsons Rdymx Ltd A Cal Ltd ...D ...800 834-7557
200 S Main St Ste 200 # 200 Corona (92882) ***(P-6109)***
Robertsons Rdymx Ltd A Cal Ltd ...D ...909 425-2930
27401 3rd St Highland (92346) ***(P-6110)***
Robertsons Ready Mix Ltd ...C ...702 798-0568
16952 S D St Victorville (92395) ***(P-13314)***
Robertsons Ready Mix Ltd ...D ...760 244-7239
9635 C Ave Hesperia (92345) ***(P-6111)***
Robertsons Ready Mix Ltd ...D ...760 373-4815
7900 Moss Ave California City (93505) ***(P-6112)***
Robin Singh Eductl Svcs Inc ...D ...310 460-7199
8383 Wilshire Blvd # 810 Beverly Hills (90211) ***(P-23503)***
Robin's Jeans, Bell Gardens *Also called Rob Inc* ***(P-2773)***
Robinson Engineering Corp ...F ...951 361-8000
3575 Grapevine St Jurupa Valley (91752) ***(P-7887)***
Robinson Helicopter Co Inc ...A ...310 539-0508
2901 Airport Dr Torrance (90505) ***(P-10402)***
Robinson Pharma Inc ...E ...714 241-0235
3701 W Warner Ave Santa Ana (92704) ***(P-4882)***
Robinson Pharma Inc ...E ...714 241-0235
2811 S Harbor Blvd Santa Ana (92704) ***(P-4883)***
Robinson Pharma Inc ...E ...714 241-0235
2811 S Harbor Blvd Santa Ana (92704) ***(P-4884)***
Robinson Pharma Inc (PA) ...B ...**714 241-0235**
3330 S Harbor Blvd Santa Ana (92704) ***(P-4885)***
Robinson Pharma Inc ...E ...714 241-0235
2811 S Harbor Blvd Santa Ana (92704) ***(P-4886)***
Robinson Printing Inc ...E ...951 296-0300
42685 Rio Nedo Temecula (92590) ***(P-4569)***
Robinson Textiles Inc ...F ...310 527-8110
24532 Woodward Ave Lomita (90717) ***(P-2748)***
Robot-Gxg Inc ...E ...660 324-0030
8960 Toronto Ave Rancho Cucamonga (91730) ***(P-9189)***
Robray Hotel Partnership LLP ...D ...760 325-4372
222 S Indian Canyon Dr Palm Springs (92262) ***(P-16669)***
ROC-Aire Corp ...E ...909 784-3385
2198 Pomona Blvd Pomona (91768) ***(P-8774)***
Rock Blue ...D ...703 314-0208
601 Foothill Rd Ojai (93023) ***(P-22278)***

Rock Canyon Healthcare Inc ....C....719 404-1000
27101 Puerta Real Ste 450 Mission Viejo (92691) ***(P-21209)***
Rock Paper Scissors LLC ....E....310 586-0600
2308 Broadway Santa Monica (90404) ***(P-19171)***
ROCK REVIVAL, Vernon *Also called Rcrv Inc* ***(P-14412)***
Rock Structures-Rip Rap ....E....951 371-1112
11126 Silverton Ct Corona (92881) ***(P-6172)***
Rock-It Cargo USA LLC ....D....310 410-0935
5343 W Imperial Hwy # 900 Los Angeles (90045) ***(P-12520)***
Rock-Ola Manufacturing Corp ....D....310 328-1306
1445 Sepulveda Blvd Torrance (90501) ***(P-9190)***
Rockefeller Group Dev Corp ....C....949 468-1800
4 Park Plz Ste 840 Irvine (92614) ***(P-16071)***
Rocker Industries, Huntington Beach *Also called Rocker Solenoid Company* ***(P-9773)***
Rocker Solenoid Company ....D....310 534-5660
5492 Bolsa Ave Huntington Beach (92649) ***(P-9773)***
Rocket Lab Usa Inc ....A....714 465-5737
3881 Mcgowen St Long Beach (90808) ***(P-10516)***
Rockjock, Corona *Also called John Currie Performance Group* ***(P-7986)***
Rockley Photonics Inc (HQ) ....**C....626 304-9960**
234 E Colo Blvd Ste 600 Pasadena (91101) ***(P-9566)***
Rockport ADM Svcs LLC ....D....323 223-3441
4585 N Figueroa St Los Angeles (90065) ***(P-20451)***
Rockport ADM Svcs LLC (PA) ....**D....323 330-6500**
5900 Wilshire Blvd # 1600 Los Angeles (90036) ***(P-23102)***
Rockport Healthcare Services, Los Angeles *Also called Rockport ADM Svcs LLC* ***(P-23102)***
Rockview Dairies Inc (PA) ....**C....562 927-5511**
7011 Stewart And Gray Rd Downey (90241) ***(P-14733)***
Rockview Farms Inc ....D....661 792-3583
11695 Jumper Ave Wasco (93280) ***(P-137)***
Rockwell Collins Inc ....E....760 768-4732
1757 Carr Rd Ste 100e Calexico (92231) ***(P-10403)***
Rockwell Enterprises Inc ....E....626 796-1511
15194 Prairie Ave Lawndale (90260) ***(P-14972)***
Rockwest Technology Group Inc ....F....323 256-8700
3370 N San Fernando Rd Los Angeles (90065) ***(P-5795)***
Rocky Mtn Dialysis Svcs LLC (HQ) ....**E....310 536-2400**
601 Hawaii St El Segundo (90245) ***(P-21264)***
Rodax Distributors ....D....818 765-6400
7230 Coldwater Canyon Ave North Hollywood (91605) ***(P-19172)***
Rode Microphones LLC ....C....310 328-7456
2745 Raymond Ave Signal Hill (90755) ***(P-9191)***
Rodeo Realty Inc ....D....818 986-7300
15300 Ventura Blvd # 500 Sherman Oaks (91403) ***(P-15979)***
Rodeo Realty Inc ....D....310 873-0100
11940 San Vicente Blvd Los Angeles (90049) ***(P-15980)***
Rodeo Realty Inc ....D....818 285-3700
17501 Ventura Blvd Encino (91316) ***(P-15981)***
Rodeo Realty Inc ....D....818 308-8273
12345 Ventura Blvd Ste A Studio City (91604) ***(P-15982)***
Rodeo Realty Inc ....D....805 494-0449
100 N Wstlke Blvd 100 # 100 Westlake Village (91362) ***(P-15983)***
Rodeo Realty Inc (PA) ....**D....818 349-9997**
9171 Wilshire Blvd # 321 Beverly Hills (90210) ***(P-15984)***
Rodeo Realty Inc ....D....818 349-9997
9338 Reseda Blvd Ste 102 Northridge (91324) ***(P-15985)***
Rodeo Realty Inc ....D....805 582-8700
2424 Erringer Rd Northridge (91324) ***(P-15986)***
Rodeo Realty Inc ....D....818 657-4609
23901 Calabasas Rd # 1050 Calabasas (91302) ***(P-15987)***
Rodeo Realty Inc ....D....818 999-2030
21031 Ventura Blvd # 100 Woodland Hills (91364) ***(P-15988)***
Rodon Products Inc ....F....714 898-3528
15481 Electronic Ln Ste A Huntington Beach (92649) ***(P-9643)***
Rodriguez Brothers Auto Parts (PA) ....**F....714 772-7278**
812 N Anaheim Blvd Anaheim (92805) ***(P-8775)***
Roettele Industries ....F....909 606-8252
15485 Dupont Ave Chino (91710) ***(P-5349)***
Rof LLC ....E....818 933-4000
7800 Arprt Bus Pkwy Stdio Van Nuys (91406) ***(P-2788)***
Rogar Manufacturing Inc ....C....760 335-3700
866 E Ross Ave El Centro (92243) ***(P-9774)***
Roger Industry ....F....714 896-0765
11552 Knott St Ste 5 Garden Grove (92841) ***(P-9449)***
Roger R Caruso Enterprises Inc ....E....714 778-6006
2911 Norton Ave Lynwood (90262) ***(P-3406)***
Rogers & Cowan Inc (HQ) ....**D....310 854-8100**
8687 Melrose Ave Ste 7 Los Angeles (90069) ***(P-23386)***
Rogers Corporation ....D....562 404-8942
13937 Rosecrans Ave Santa Fe Springs (90670) ***(P-5406)***
Rogers Holding Company Inc ....D....714 257-4850
1130 Columbia St Brea (92821) ***(P-10404)***
Rogers Poultry Co (PA) ....**D....323 585-0802**
5050 S Santa Fe Ave Vernon (90058) ***(P-14549)***
Rogers Poultry Co ....D....800 585-0802
2020 E 67th St Los Angeles (90001) ***(P-14550)***
Rogerson Aircraft Corporation (PA) ....**D....949 660-0666**
16940 Von Karman Ave Irvine (92606) ***(P-10641)***
Rogerson Kratos ....C....626 449-3090
403 S Raymond Ave Pasadena (91105) ***(P-10642)***
Rogue Games Inc ....E....650 483-8008
4056 Ventura Canyon Ave Sherman Oaks (91423) ***(P-17701)***
Rohde & Schwarz Usa Inc ....F....818 846-3600
2255 N Ontario St Ste 150 Burbank (91504) ***(P-10769)***
Rohrback Cosasco Systems Inc (HQ) ....**D....562 949-0123**
11841 Smith Ave Santa Fe Springs (90670) ***(P-10719)***
Roi Development Corp ....E....714 751-0488
15272 Newsboy Cir Huntington Beach (92649) ***(P-8981)***
Rojo's, Cypress *Also called Simply Fresh LLC* ***(P-2350)***

Rok Drinks LLC ....E....323 654-2740
17383 W Sunset Blvd # 300 Pacific Palisades (90272) ***(P-2244)***
Roland Corporation US (HQ) ....**C....323 890-3700**
5100 S Eastern Ave Los Angeles (90040) ***(P-14178)***
Roland Dga Corporation (HQ) ....**C....949 727-2100**
15363 Barranca Pkwy Irvine (92618) ***(P-13434)***
Rolenn Manufacturing Inc (PA) ....**E....951 682-1185**
2065 Roberta St Riverside (92507) ***(P-5796)***
Rolex Watch Service Center Cal, Beverly Hills *Also called Rolex Watch USA Inc* ***(P-18962)***
Rolex Watch USA Inc ....D....310 271-6200
9420 Wilshire Blvd # 400 Beverly Hills (90212) ***(P-18962)***
Roll Along Vans Inc ....E....714 528-9600
1350 E Yorba Linda Blvd Placentia (92870) ***(P-10128)***
Roll Properties Intl Inc ....C....661 797-6500
13646 Highway 33 Lost Hills (93249) ***(P-16289)***
Roll-A-Shade Inc (PA) ....**E....951 245-5077**
12101 Madera Way Riverside (92503) ***(P-3714)***
Roller Bones, Goleta *Also called Skate One Corp* ***(P-11447)***
Rolling Hills Vineyard Inc ....E....310 541-5098
4213 Pascal Pl Pls Vrds Pnsl (90274) ***(P-2217)***
Rolling Oaks Radiology Inc ....C....805 778-1513
415 Rolling Oaks Dr # 16 Thousand Oaks (91361) ***(P-20045)***
Rollins Inc ....C....323 722-2279
2585 Commerce Way Commerce (90040) ***(P-17205)***
Rollins Leasing LLC ....D....626 913-7186
18305 Arenth Ave City of Industry (91748) ***(P-18736)***
Rollins Truck Rental-Leasing, City of Industry *Also called Rollins Leasing LLC* ***(P-18736)***
Romac Supply Co Inc ....D....323 721-5810
7400 Bandini Blvd Commerce (90040) ***(P-8905)***
Romakk Engineering, Northridge *Also called Robert H Oliva Inc* ***(P-8771)***
Roman Catholic Bishp of Fresno ....D....559 561-4499
43816 Sierra Dr Three Rivers (93271) ***(P-16825)***
Roman Cthlic Diocese of Orange ....C....949 766-6000
22062 Antonio Pkwy Rcho STA Marg (92688) ***(P-4107)***
Roman Cthlic Diocese of Orange ....C....714 528-1794
801 N Bradford Ave Placentia (92870) ***(P-18655)***
Roman Cthlic Diocese of Orange ....C....714 544-1533
1311 Sycamore Ave Tustin (92780) ***(P-22057)***
Roman Upholstery Mfg Inc ....F....310 479-3252
2008 Cotner Ave Los Angeles (90025) ***(P-3515)***
Romar Group Inc (PA) ....**D....213 621-4403**
837 Traction Ave Unit 406 Los Angeles (90013) ***(P-2760)***
Romeo Power Inc (PA) ....**E....833 467-2237**
4380 Ayers Ave Vernon (90058) ***(P-10129)***
Romeo Power Technology, Vernon *Also called Romeo Systems Inc* ***(P-9909)***
Romeo Systems Inc ....C....323 675-2180
4380 Ayers Ave Vernon (90058) ***(P-9909)***
Romeros Food Products Inc (PA) ....**D....562 802-1858**
15155 Valley View Ave Santa Fe Springs (90670) ***(P-2519)***
Romex Textiles Inc (PA) ....**E....213 749-9090**
1430 Griffith Ave Los Angeles (90021) ***(P-14317)***
Ron Teeguarden Enterprises Inc (PA) ....**E....323 556-8188**
5670 Wilshire Blvd # 1500 Los Angeles (90036) ***(P-4762)***
Ronald L Wolfe & Assoc Inc ....E....805 964-6770
173 Chapel St Santa Barbara (93111) ***(P-15989)***
Ronald Reagan Building, Los Angeles *Also called Ucla Health* ***(P-20985)***
Ronald Reagan Ucla Medical Ctr, Los Angeles *Also called University Cal Los Angeles* ***(P-20988)***
Ronald Rgan Prsdntial Fndtion ....D....805 522-2977
40 Presidential Dr # 200 Simi Valley (93065) ***(P-22233)***
Ronald Rgan Prsdntial Lib Fndt, Simi Valley *Also called Ronald Rgan Prsdntial Fndtion* ***(P-22233)***
Ronan Engineering Company (PA) ....**D....661 702-1344**
28209 Avenue Stanford Valencia (91355) ***(P-10720)***
Ronan Engnrng/Rnan Msrment Div, Valencia *Also called Ronan Engineering Company* ***(P-10720)***
Roncelli Plastics Inc ....D....800 250-6516
330 W Duarte Rd Monrovia (91016) ***(P-4713)***
Ronco Plastics Inc ....E....714 259-1385
15022 Parkway Loop Ste B Tustin (92780) ***(P-5797)***
Ronford Products Inc ....E....909 622-7446
1116 E 2nd St Pomona (91766) ***(P-5798)***
Rongcheng Trading LLC ....E....626 338-1090
19319 Arenth Ave City of Industry (91748) ***(P-14606)***
Ronlo Engineering Ltd ....E....805 388-3227
955 Flynn Rd Camarillo (93012) ***(P-8776)***
Ronman Products Inc ....F....714 735-3146
8440 Kass Dr Buena Park (90621) ***(P-6462)***
Ronsin Photocopy Inc (PA) ....**D....909 594-5995**
215 Lemon Creek Dr Walnut (91789) ***(P-18656)***
Roofline Supply SRS Dist ....D....909 623-8191
2016 S Reservoir St Pomona (91766) ***(P-13328)***
Roosevelt Hotel LLC ....C....323 466-7000
7000 Hollywood Blvd Los Angeles (90028) ***(P-16670)***
Rootstrap Inc ....C....310 907-9210
8306 Wilshire Blvd # 249 Beverly Hills (90211) ***(P-17702)***
Ropak Corporation (HQ) ....**B....714 845-2845**
10540 Talbert Ave 200w Fountain Valley (92708) ***(P-5799)***
Ropak Packaging, Fountain Valley *Also called Ropak Corporation* ***(P-5799)***
Ropers Majeski A Prof Corp ....C....213 312-2000
445 S Figueroa St # 3000 Los Angeles (90071) ***(P-21670)***
Ros Electrical Sup Eqp Co LLC ....E....562 695-9000
9529 Slauson Ave Pico Rivera (90660) ***(P-13666)***
Rosa Brothers Milk Co Inc (PA) ....**E....559 582-8825**
10090 2nd Ave Hanford (93230) ***(P-1822)***
Rosanna Inc ....C....714 751-5100
3350 Avenue Of The Arts Costa Mesa (92626) ***(P-16671)***

Employee Codes: A=Over 500 employees, B=251-500
C=101-250, D=51-100, E=20-50 F=10-19
2022 Southern California Business
Directory and Buyers Guide
© Mergent Inc. 1-800-342-5647
1257

Rosano Partners .... E 213 802-0300
3530 Wilshire Blvd # 1700 Los Angeles (90010) ***(P-15990)***
Rosary Academy Parent Council .... D 714 879-6302
1340 N Acacia Ave Fullerton (92831) ***(P-22363)***
Roscoe Moss Company, Los Angeles *Also called Roscoe Moss Manufacturing Co* ***(P-6252)***
Roscoe Moss Manufacturing Co (PA) .... **D 323 261-4185**
4360 Worth St Los Angeles (90063) ***(P-6252)***
Roscoe Real Estate Ltd Partnr .... C 310 260-7500
1819 Ocean Ave Santa Monica (90401) ***(P-16672)***
Rose & Shore Inc .... B 323 826-2144
5151 Alcoa Ave Vernon (90058) ***(P-18657)***
Rose Art Industries, El Segundo *Also called Mega Brands America Inc* ***(P-11384)***
Rose Bowl Aquatics Center .... D 626 564-0330
360 N Arroyo Blvd Pasadena (91103) ***(P-19605)***
Rose Brand Wipers Inc .... D 818 505-6290
11440 Sheldon St Sun Valley (91352) ***(P-19331)***
Rose Chem Intl - USA Corp .... E 678 510-8864
25 Rainbow Fls Irvine (92603) ***(P-4887)***
Rose Genuine Inc .... F 213 747-4120
834 S Broadway Ste 1100 Los Angeles (90014) ***(P-3036)***
Rose Hills Co, Whittier *Also called Rose Hills Mortuary Inc* ***(P-16927)***
Rose Hills Company (HQ) .... **A 562 699-0921**
3888 Workman Mill Rd Whittier (90601) ***(P-16088)***
Rose Hills Holdings Corp (HQ) .... **B 562 699-0921**
3888 Workman Mill Rd Whittier (90601) ***(P-16089)***
Rose Hills Mem Pk & Mortuary, Whittier *Also called Rose Hills Company* ***(P-16088)***
Rose Hills Mem Pk & Mortuary, Whittier *Also called Rose Hills Holdings Corp* ***(P-16089)***
Rose Hills Mortuary Inc .... D 562 699-0921
3888 Workman Mill Rd Whittier (90601) ***(P-16927)***
Rose International Inc .... C 636 812-4000
450 N Brand Blvd Fl 6 Glendale (91203) ***(P-17703)***
Rose International Inc .... C 636 812-4000
17701 Cowan Ste 230 Irvine (92614) ***(P-23504)***
Rose K Tarlow Antiques Ltd (PA) .... **D 323 651-2202**
425 N Robertson Blvd West Hollywood (90048) ***(P-14179)***
Rose Villa Healthcare Center, Bellflower *Also called Bell Villa Care Associates LLC* ***(P-20253)***
Rosecrans Care Center, Gardena *Also called Health Care Investments Inc* ***(P-20372)***
Roselm Industries Inc .... E 626 442-6840
2510 Seaman Ave South El Monte (91733) ***(P-9312)***
Rosemary Childrens Services (PA) .... **C 626 844-3033**
36 S Kinneloa Ave 200 Pasadena (91107) ***(P-22150)***
Rosemont Realty LLC (PA) .... **C 505 992-5100**
2000 Avenue Of The Stars # 550 Los Angeles (90067) ***(P-15991)***
Rosen & Rosen Industries Inc .... D 949 361-9238
204 Avenida Fabricante San Clemente (92672) ***(P-11443)***
Rosen Electronics LLC .... D 951 898-9808
2500 E Francis St Ontario (91761) ***(P-14180)***
Rosendin Electric Inc .... A 714 739-1334
1730 S Anaheim Way Anaheim (92805) ***(P-1311)***
Rosendin Holdings Inc (PA) .... **A 213 891-9619**
400 S Hope St Los Angeles (90071) ***(P-1312)***
Rosenthal Group, The, Venice *Also called Trg Inc* ***(P-16018)***
Rosewill Inc .... A 800 575-9885
17560 Rowland St City of Industry (91748) ***(P-8173)***
Rosewood Retirement Community, Bakersfield *Also called Humangood Norcal* ***(P-20596)***
Roshan Trading Inc .... E 213 622-9904
2734 E 46th St Vernon (90058) ***(P-14318)***
Ross Baker Towing Inc .... C 818 886-7411
8750 Vanalden Ave Northridge (91324) ***(P-18942)***
Ross Baker Towing Service, Northridge *Also called Ross Baker Towing Inc* ***(P-18942)***
Ross Bindery Inc .... C 562 623-4565
15310 Spring Ave Santa Fe Springs (90670) ***(P-4620)***
Ross Fabrication & Welding Inc .... F 661 393-1242
1154 Basta Ave Bakersfield (93308) ***(P-3454)***
Ross Name Plate Company .... E 323 725-6812
2 Red Plum Cir Monterey Park (91755) ***(P-11587)***
Ross Racing Pistons .... D 310 536-0100
625 S Douglas St El Segundo (90245) ***(P-8435)***
Rossier Park School, Buena Park *Also called Rossier Park School* ***(P-23312)***
Rossier Park School .... D 714 562-0441
7100 Knott Ave Buena Park (90620) ***(P-23312)***
Rostar Filters, Oxnard *Also called PC Vaughan Mfg Corp* ***(P-8134)***
Rotary and Miission Systems, Fort Irwin *Also called Lockheed Martin Corporation* ***(P-12220)***
Rotating Prcsion McHanisms Inc .... E 818 349-9774
8750 Shirley Ave Northridge (91324) ***(P-9313)***
Rotational Molding Inc .... D 310 327-5401
17038 S Figueroa St Gardena (90248) ***(P-5800)***
Rotax Incorporated .... E 323 589-5999
2940 Leonis Blvd Vernon (90058) ***(P-2990)***
Rotech Engineering Inc .... E 714 632-0532
1020 S Melrose St Ste A Placentia (92870) ***(P-9775)***
Roth Capital Partners LLC (PA) .... **D 800 678-9147**
888 San Clemente Dr # 400 Newport Beach (92660) ***(P-15305)***
Roth Staffing Companies LP (PA) .... **D 714 939-8600**
450 N State College Blvd Orange (92868) ***(P-17514)***
Rothenberger USA LLC .... F 323 268-1381
955 Monterey Pass Rd Monterey Park (91754) ***(P-7743)***
Rothlisberger Mfg A Cal Corp .... F 818 786-9462
14718 Arminta St Van Nuys (91402) ***(P-8777)***
Roto Dynamics Inc .... E 714 685-0183
1925 N Lime St Orange (92865) ***(P-5801)***
Roto Lite Inc .... E 909 923-4353
84701 Avenue 48 Coachella (92236) ***(P-5802)***
Roto Power Inc .... F 951 751-9850
191 Granite St Ste A Corona (92879) ***(P-5803)***
Roto West Enterprises Inc .... F 714 899-2030
15651 Container Ln Huntington Beach (92649) ***(P-5804)***

Rotolo Chevrolet Inc .... C 866 756-9776
16666 S Highland Ave Fontana (92336) ***(P-18868)***
Rotorcraft Support Inc .... D 818 997-7667
67 D St Fillmore (93015) ***(P-12367)***
Roughan Associates At Linc .... E 626 351-0991
465 N Halstead St Ste 120 Pasadena (91107) ***(P-23505)***
Roundabout Entertainment Inc .... D 818 842-9300
217 S Lake St Burbank (91502) ***(P-19173)***
Rovi Guides Inc (HQ) .... **D 323 817-4600**
2233 N Ontario St Ste 100 Burbank (91504) ***(P-19375)***
Row Management Ltd Inc .... B 310 887-3671
499 N Canon Dr Beverly Hills (90210) ***(P-15992)***
Rowland Convalescent Hosp Inc .... D 626 967-2741
330 W Rowland St Covina (91723) ***(P-20452)***
Rowland, The, Covina *Also called Rowland Convalescent Hosp Inc* ***(P-20452)***
Rox Medical Inc (PA) .... **F 949 276-8968**
150 Calle Iglesia Ste A San Clemente (92672) ***(P-11053)***
Roy & Val Tool Grinding Inc .... E 818 341-2434
10131 Canoga Ave Chatsworth (91311) ***(P-8778)***
Roy E Hanson Jr Mfg (PA) .... **D 213 747-7514**
1600 E Washington Blvd Los Angeles (90021) ***(P-6750)***
Roy E Whitehead Inc .... D 951 682-1490
2245 Via Cerro Riverside (92509) ***(P-1454)***
Roy Miller Freight Lines LLC (PA) .... **D 714 632-5511**
3165 E Coronado St Anaheim (92806) ***(P-11991)***
Royal Adhesives & Sealants LLC .... E 310 830-9904
800 E Anaheim St Wilmington (90744) ***(P-5241)***
Royal Airline Linen Inc .... D 310 677-9885
125 N Ash Ave Inglewood (90301) ***(P-16839)***
Royal Apparel Inc .... E 626 579-5168
4331 Baldwin Ave El Monte (91731) ***(P-2991)***
Royal Blue Inc .... E 310 888-0156
9025 Wilshire Blvd # 301 Beverly Hills (90211) ***(P-3118)***
Royal Cabinets, Pomona *Also called Royal Industries Inc* ***(P-3334)***
Royal Cabinets Inc .... A 909 629-8565
1299 E Phillips Blvd Pomona (91766) ***(P-3333)***
Royal Care Skilled Nursing Ctr, Long Beach *Also called Covenant Care California LLC* ***(P-20297)***
Royal Coatings, Simi Valley *Also called Mabel Baas Inc* ***(P-7385)***
Royal Custom Designs LLC .... C 909 591-8990
13951 Monte Vista Ave Chino (91710) ***(P-3516)***
Royal Equestrian Apartments, Burbank *Also called Alliance Residential LLC* ***(P-15657)***
Royal Family Kids Camps Inc .... C 714 438-2494
3000 W Macarthur Blvd # 412 Santa Ana (92704) ***(P-16826)***
Royal Flex Circuits Inc .... E 562 404-0626
15505 Cornet St Santa Fe Springs (90670) ***(P-9450)***
Royal Industries, Eastvale *Also called Royal Range California Inc* ***(P-8994)***
Royal Industries Inc .... C 909 629-8565
1299 E Phillips Blvd Pomona (91766) ***(P-3334)***
Royal Interpack North Amer Inc .... E 951 787-6925
475 Palmyrita Ave Riverside (92507) ***(P-5805)***
Royal Manufacturing Inds Inc .... F 714 668-9199
600 W Warner Ave Santa Ana (92707) ***(P-6904)***
Royal Metal, Santa Ana *Also called Ted Rieck Enterprises Inc* ***(P-6928)***
Royal Oak Motor Hotel .... D 805 544-4410
214 Madonna Rd San Luis Obispo (93405) ***(P-16673)***
Royal Paper Box Co California (PA) .... **C 323 728-7041**
1105 S Maple Ave Montebello (90640) ***(P-14973)***
Royal Paper Corp (PA) .... **D 562 903-9030**
10232 Palm Dr Santa Fe Springs (90670) ***(P-14227)***
Royal Plasticware, Gardena *Also called La Palm Furnitures & ACC Inc* ***(P-3156)***
Royal Plywood Company LLC (PA) .... **D 562 404-2989**
14171 Park Pl Cerritos (90703) ***(P-13285)***
Royal Poultry, Vernon *Also called Golden West Trading Inc* ***(P-14594)***
Royal Range California Inc .... D 951 360-1600
3245 Corridor Dr Eastvale (91752) ***(P-8994)***
Royal Specialty Undwrt Inc .... C 818 922-6700
15303 Ventura Blvd # 500 Sherman Oaks (91403) ***(P-15479)***
Royal Supply Midwest, Santa Fe Springs *Also called Royal Paper Corp* ***(P-14227)***
Royal Terrace Healthcare .... D 626 256-4654
1340 Highland Ave Duarte (91010) ***(P-20453)***
Royal Trim .... F 323 583-2121
2529 Chambers St Vernon (90058) ***(P-3180)***
Royal Truck Body, Carson *Also called Fortress Resources LLC* ***(P-18830)***
Royal Welding & Fabricating, Fullerton *Also called Cook and Cook Incorporated* ***(P-6739)***
Royal West Drywall Inc .... D 951 271-4600
2008 2nd St Norco (92860) ***(P-1398)***
Royal Wine Corporation .... E 805 983-1560
3201 Camino Del Sol Oxnard (93030) ***(P-2218)***
Royal-Pedic Mattress Mfg LLC (PA) .... **E 310 278-9594**
341 N Robertson Blvd Beverly Hills (90211) ***(P-3558)***
Rozak Engineering Inc .... F 714 446-8855
556 S State College Blvd Fullerton (92831) ***(P-8779)***
Roze Room Hospice, Culver City *Also called L & A Care Corporation* ***(P-20534)***
Rozge Cosmoceutical, Van Nuys *Also called CDM Corp* ***(P-4999)***
Rp Realty Partners LLC .... E 310 207-6990
990 W 8th St Ste 600 Los Angeles (90017) ***(P-15694)***
RPC Legacy Inc .... F 818 787-9000
14600 Arminta St Van Nuys (91402) ***(P-6534)***
Rpd Hotels 18 LLC (PA) .... **A 213 746-1531**
1801 S La Cnega Blvd # 301 Los Angeles (90035) ***(P-16674)***
RPI, Simi Valley *Also called Replacement Parts Inds Inc* ***(P-11194)***
Rplanet Erth Los Angles Hldngs .... D 833 775-2638
5300 S Boyle Ave Vernon (90058) ***(P-5806)***
RPM, Northridge *Also called Rotating Prcsion McHanisms Inc* ***(P-9313)***
RPM Consolidated Services Inc (HQ) .... **D 714 388-3500**
1901 Raymer Ave Fullerton (92833) ***(P-12240)***

Mergent e-mail: customerrelations@mergent.com
1258
2022 Southern California Business Directory and Buyers Guide
(P-0000) Products & Services Section entry number
(PA)=Parent Co (HQ)=Headquarters (DH)=Div Headquarters

RPM Grinding Co Inc ....F....951 273-0602
1755 Commerce St Norco (92860) ***(P-8780)***
RPM Plastic Molding Inc ....E....714 630-9300
2821 E Miraloma Ave Anaheim (92806) ***(P-5807)***
RPM Products Inc (PA) ....**E....949 888-8543**
30065 Comercio Rcho STA Marg (92688) ***(P-5350)***
RPM Transportation Inc (HQ) ....**C....714 388-3500**
11660 Arroyo Ave Santa Ana (92705) ***(P-12075)***
Rpp Products Inc (PA) ....**F....800 657-4811**
2756 S Riverside Ave Bloomington (92316) ***(P-14806)***
RPS, Orange *Also called Radiation Protection & Spc Inc* ***(P-6898)***
RPS Inc ....E....818 350-8088
20331 Corisco St Chatsworth (91311) ***(P-7513)***
Rpsz Construction LLC ....E....314 677-5831
1201 W 5th St Ste T340 Los Angeles (90017) ***(P-11444)***
RR Donnelley, Rancho Dominguez *Also called R R Donnelley & Sons Company* ***(P-17139)***
Rrds Inc (PA) ....**F....949 482-6200**
12 Goodyear Ste 100 Irvine (92618) ***(P-10858)***
Rri, Downey *Also called Rancho Research Institute* ***(P-22917)***
Rri Energy Coolwater Inc ....A....760 254-5290
37000 E Santa Fe St Daggett (92327) ***(P-12824)***
Rrm Construction Inc ....E....562 440-3539
9135 Cord Ave Downey (90240) ***(P-667)***
Rrm Design Group (PA) ....**D....805 439-0442**
3765 S Higuera St Ste 102 San Luis Obispo (93401) ***(P-22741)***
Rrt Enterprises LP (PA) ....**B....310 397-2372**
3966 Marcasel Ave Los Angeles (90066) ***(P-20454)***
Rrt Enterprises LP ....B....323 653-1521
855 N Fairfax Ave Los Angeles (90046) ***(P-20455)***
Rrz Enterprises Inc ....F....714 683-2820
5521 Schaefer Ave Chino (91710) ***(P-14348)***
Rsa Engineered Products LLC ....D....805 584-4150
110 W Cochran St Ste A Simi Valley (93065) ***(P-10405)***
Rsdg International Inc ....F....626 256-4190
2127 Aralia St Newport Beach (92660) ***(P-3037)***
Rsg Group USA Inc ....A....214 574-4653
7000 Romaine St Ste 201 West Hollywood (90038) ***(P-16110)***
Rsg/Aames Security Inc ....E....562 529-5100
3300 E 59th St Long Beach (90805) ***(P-9351)***
RSI Construction Inc ....D....949 720-1116
620 Newport Center Dr # 12 Newport Beach (92660) ***(P-668)***
RSI Home Products Inc (HQ) ....**A....714 449-2200**
400 E Orangethorpe Ave Anaheim (92801) ***(P-3532)***
RSI Home Products Mfg Inc ....D....714 449-2200
400 E Orangethorpe Ave Anaheim (92801) ***(P-3533)***
RSI Home Products Sales Inc ....D....714 449-2200
400 E Orangethorpe Ave Anaheim (92801) ***(P-13184)***
RSI Insurance Brokers Inc (HQ) ....**E....714 546-6616**
4000 Westerly Pl Ste 110 Newport Beach (92660) ***(P-15623)***
RSI Leasing LLC ....D....626 966-6129
1314 E Puente Ave West Covina (91790) ***(P-17370)***
Rsk Tool Incorporated ....E....310 537-3302
410 W Carob St Compton (90220) ***(P-5808)***
RSR Metal Spinning Inc ....F....626 814-2339
850 E Edna Pl Covina (91723) ***(P-7179)***
Rss Inc (PA) ....**D....909 321-5958**
3939 E Guasti Rd Ste A Ontario (91761) ***(P-1504)***
Rsui Group, Sherman Oaks *Also called Royal Specialty Undwrt Inc* ***(P-15479)***
Rt Pasad Hotel Partners LP ....D....626 403-7600
180 N Fair Oaks Ave Pasadena (91103) ***(P-16675)***
Rt Rogers Brewing Co LLC ....F....818 371-0838
38 E Montecito Ave Ste 1 Sierra Madre (91024) ***(P-2155)***
RTC Aerospace, Chatsworth *Also called Cliffdale Manufacturing LLC* ***(P-10531)***
RTC Aerospace, Chatsworth *Also called Logistical Support LLC* ***(P-10220)***
RTC Arspace - Chtswrth Div Inc (PA) ....**C....818 341-3344**
20409 Prairie St Chatsworth (91311) ***(P-8440)***
Rte Enterprises Inc ....D....818 999-5300
21530 Roscoe Blvd Canoga Park (91304) ***(P-1197)***
Rte Welding, Fontana *Also called Tikos Tanks Inc* ***(P-19001)***
Rti Los Angeles, Norwalk *Also called New Cntury Mtals Southeast Inc* ***(P-6335)***
Rti Pierce-Spafford, Garden Grove *Also called Pierce-Spafford Metals Co Inc* ***(P-13585)***
Rti Services Inc ....D....323 725-6370
2836 Vail Ave Commerce (90040) ***(P-18658)***
Rtie Holdings LLC ....F....714 765-8200
1800 E Via Burton Anaheim (92806) ***(P-9776)***
Rtm Products Inc ....E....562 926-2400
13120 Arctic Cir Santa Fe Springs (90670) ***(P-6210)***
Rtr Bakery Inc ....E....714 415-2233
2640 Walnut Ave Ste C Tustin (92780) ***(P-14734)***
Rtr Industries LLC ....E....714 996-0050
3943 E La Palma Ave Anaheim (92807) ***(P-8436)***
RTS Powder Coating Inc (PA) ....**E....909 393-5404**
15121 Sierra Bonita Ln Chino (91710) ***(P-7407)***
Rubber Plastic & Metal Pdts, Rcho STA Marg *Also called RPM Products Inc* ***(P-5350)***
Rubber Teck Division, Long Beach *Also called Rubbercraft Corp Cal Ltd* ***(P-5361)***
Rubbercraft Corp Cal Ltd (HQ) ....**C....562 354-2800**
3701 E Conant St Long Beach (90808) ***(P-5361)***
Rubberite Corp (PA) ....**F....714 546-6464**
301 Goetz Ave Santa Ana (92707) ***(P-5407)***
Rubberite Cypress Spnge Rbr Pd, Santa Ana *Also called Rubberite Corp* ***(P-5407)***
Ruben & Leon Inc ....F....310 486-6648
5002 Venice Blvd Los Angeles (90019) ***(P-11588)***
Ruben & Leon Inc ....E....323 937-4445
5002 Venice Blvd Los Angeles (90019) ***(P-18955)***
Ruben and Sharam, Vernon *Also called RJ Singer International Inc* ***(P-5896)***
Rubicon B Hacienda LLC ....D....424 290-5000
525 N Pacific Coast Hwy El Segundo (90245) ***(P-16676)***
Rubicon Gear Inc ....D....951 356-3800
225 Citation Cir Corona (92878) ***(P-7097)***
Rubidoux Community Svcs Dst ....D....951 684-7580
3590 Rubidoux Blvd Riverside (92509) ***(P-22255)***
Rubio Arts Corporation ....C....407 849-1643
1313 S Harbor Blvd Anaheim (92802) ***(P-23542)***
Ruby Creek Resources Inc ....E....212 671-0404
11835 W Olympic Blvd Los Angeles (90064) ***(P-23313)***
Ruby Industrial Tech LLC ....E....909 390-7919
910 S Wanamaker Ave Ontario (91761) ***(P-14015)***
Ruby Rox, Los Angeles *Also called Misyd Corp* ***(P-3035)***
Rucci Inc ....E....323 778-9000
6700 11th Ave Los Angeles (90043) ***(P-11745)***
Ruchel Enterprises ....C....213 389-6900
4032 Wilshire Blvd Los Angeles (90010) ***(P-15747)***
Ruffin Hotel Corp of Cal ....B....562 425-5210
4700 Airport Plaza Dr Long Beach (90815) ***(P-16677)***
Rugby Laboratories Inc (HQ) ....**D....951 270-1400**
311 Bonnie Cir Corona (92878) ***(P-14286)***
Ruggable LLC (PA) ....**E....310 295-0098**
18005 Savarona Way Carson (90746) ***(P-2695)***
Rugged Info Tech Eqp Corp (PA) ....**E....805 577-9710**
25 E Easy St Simi Valley (93065) ***(P-8299)***
Rugged Notebooks, Anaheim *Also called Rnbs Corporation* ***(P-8172)***
Ruggeri Marble and Granite Inc ....D....310 513-2155
16001 S San Pedro St C Gardena (90248) ***(P-6143)***
Ruiteng Internet Technology Co ....C....302 597-7438
1344 W Foothill Blvd D Azusa (91702) ***(P-18107)***
Ruiz Flour Tortillas, Riverside *Also called Ruiz Mexican Foods Inc* ***(P-2520)***
Ruiz Food Products Inc (PA) ....**A....559 591-5510**
501 S Alta Ave Dinuba (93618) ***(P-1938)***
Ruiz Mexican Foods Inc (PA) ....**C....909 947-7811**
1200 Marlborough Ave A Riverside (92507) ***(P-2520)***
Run The Play Entertainment LLC ....F....800 978-9638
9350 Wilshire Blvd Beverly Hills (90212) ***(P-19376)***
Runa Hr Holdings Inc ....D....562 883-3546
3067 E 1st St Long Beach (90803) ***(P-17704)***
Runway Inc ....D....310 636-2000
1330 Vine St Los Angeles (90028) ***(P-19247)***
Runway Liquidation LLC (HQ) ....**A....323 589-2224**
2761 Fruitland Ave Vernon (90058) ***(P-14414)***
Rush Business Forms Inc ....E....714 630-5661
3860 E Eagle Dr Ste A Anaheim (92807) ***(P-11589)***
Rush Computer Rentals, West Hills *Also called Electro Rent Corporation* ***(P-17347)***
Rushmore Loan MGT Svcs LLC (PA) ....**A....949 727-4798**
15480 Laguna Canyon Rd Irvine (92618) ***(P-15230)***
Russ Bassett Corp ....C....562 945-2445
8189 Byron Rd Whittier (90606) ***(P-3487)***
Russ International Inc ....E....310 329-7121
1658 W 132nd St Gardena (90249) ***(P-6905)***
Russell Fabrication Corp ....E....661 861-8495
4940 Gilmore Ave Bakersfield (93308) ***(P-7543)***
Russell Fisher Partnership ....E....714 842-4453
16061 Beach Blvd Huntington Beach (92647) ***(P-18916)***
Russell Kc & Son ....F....559 686-3236
375 E Paige Ave Tulare (93274) ***(P-7618)***
Russell Sigler Inc ....C....951 656-3737
14751 Meridian Pkwy March ARB (92518) ***(P-12146)***
Russell Sigler Inc ....D....909 390-7838
2641 E Lindsey Privado Dr Ontario (91761) ***(P-1132)***
Rustic Canyon Group LLC ....D....310 998-8000
1025 Westwood Blvd Los Angeles (90024) ***(P-16290)***
Rustic Canyon Partners, Los Angeles *Also called Rustic Canyon Group LLC* ***(P-16290)***
Rutan & Tucker LLP (PA) ....**C....714 641-5100**
18575 Jamboree Rd Ste 900 Irvine (92612) ***(P-21671)***
Rutherford Co Inc (PA) ....**D....323 666-5284**
2107 Crystal St Los Angeles (90039) ***(P-1399)***
Rutland Tool & Supply Co (HQ) ....**C....562 566-5000**
2225 Workman Mill Rd City of Industry (90601) ***(P-14016)***
Ruuhwa Dann and Associates Inc (PA) ....**D....909 467-4800**
1541 Brooks St Ontario (91762) ***(P-12972)***
Ruzannas Decor ....E....323 472-0505
608 S Hill St Ste Gl118 Los Angeles (90014) ***(P-18659)***
Rvshilfy LLC ....E....313 329-0146
1515 E 15th St Los Angeles (90021) ***(P-13124)***
Rvtlzation Anaheim II Partners ....D....714 520-4041
1515 S Calle Del Mar Anaheim (92802) ***(P-15993)***
RW&g, Los Angeles *Also called Richards Watson & Gershon PC* ***(P-21669)***
Rwc Enterprises Inc ....E....909 373-4100
9130 Santa Anita Ave Rancho Cucamonga (91730) ***(P-22648)***
Rwp Transfer Inc ....E....909 868-6882
1313 E Phillips Blvd Pomona (91766) ***(P-14181)***
RWS Research & Development Inc ....F....818 364-6766
15853 Olden St Sylmar (91342) ***(P-7476)***
Rxsight Inc (PA) ....**C....949 521-7830**
100 Columbia Ste 120 Aliso Viejo (92656) ***(P-11261)***
Ryan Herco Flow Solutions, Burbank *Also called Ryan Herco Products Corp* ***(P-13836)***
Ryan Herco Products Corp (HQ) ....**D....818 841-1141**
3010 N San Fernando Blvd Burbank (91504) ***(P-13836)***
Ryan Press, Buena Park *Also called Q Team* ***(P-4411)***
Ryan Shroads ....E....310 936-5966
5110 E Washington Blvd Commerce (90040) ***(P-18660)***
Ryans Express Trnsp Svcs Inc (PA) ....**D....310 219-2960**
19500 Mariner Ave Torrance (90503) ***(P-11915)***
Rydell Chevrolet-Northridge, Northridge *Also called San Fernando Valley Auto LLC* ***(P-18870)***
Ryder Intgrted Lgstics Cal LLC ....D....909 356-8555
10641 Almond Ave Fontana (92337) ***(P-18737)***

ALPHABETIC

Employee Codes: A=Over 500 employees, B=251-500
C=101-250, D=51-100, E=20-50 F=10-19
2022 Southern California Business
Directory and Buyers Guide
© Mergent Inc. 1-800-342-5647
1259

Rynoclad Technologies Inc ....C.......951 264-3441
780 E Francis St Ste M Ontario (91761) ***(P-1588)***

Ryo Rio Tinto Minerals ....F.......310 522-5322
300 Falcon St Wilmington (90744) ***(P-379)***

Ryot Corp ....D.......323 356-1787
11995 Bluff Creek Dr Playa Vista (90094) ***(P-17186)***

Rytan Inc ....F.......310 328-6553
1648 W 134th St Gardena (90249) ***(P-7744)***

Ryvec Inc ....E.......714 520-5592
251 E Palais Rd Anaheim (92805) ***(P-4645)***

S & H Cabinets and Mfg Inc ....E.......909 357-0551
10860 Mulberry Ave Fontana (92337) ***(P-3599)***

S & H Machine Inc (PA) ....**F.......818 846-9847**
900 N Lake St Burbank (91502) ***(P-8781)***

S & H Machine Inc ....E.......626 448-5062
9928 Hayward Way South El Monte (91733) ***(P-7459)***

S & K Plating Inc ....F.......310 632-7141
2727 N Compton Ave Compton (90222) ***(P-7307)***

S & K Theatrical Drap Inc ....F.......818 503-0596
7313 Varna Ave North Hollywood (91605) ***(P-3093)***

S & R Cnc Machining, Valencia *Also called Salvador Ramirez* ***(P-10224)***

S & S Bindery Inc ....E.......909 596-2213
2366 1st St La Verne (91750) ***(P-4621)***

S & S Construction Co, Beverly Hills *Also called Shapell Industries LLC* ***(P-16072)***

S & S Foods LLC ....C.......626 633-1609
1120 W Foothill Blvd Azusa (91702) ***(P-1749)***

S & S Installations Inc ....E.......909 370-1730
294 W Olive St Colton (92324) ***(P-8409)***

S & S Numerical Control Inc ....E.......818 341-4141
19841 Nordhoff St Northridge (91324) ***(P-8782)***

S & S Paving Inc ....D.......818 591-0668
23875 Ventura Blvd # 202 Calabasas (91302) ***(P-911)***

S & S Precision Mfg Inc ....E.......714 754-6664
2101 S Yale St Santa Ana (92704) ***(P-8783)***

S & S Precision Sheetmetal, Canoga Park *Also called B S K T Inc* ***(P-8514)***

S & W Plastic Stores Inc (PA) ....**E.......909 390-0090**
14270 Albers Way Chino (91710) ***(P-14763)***

S & W Plastics Supply, Chino *Also called S & W Plastic Stores Inc* ***(P-14763)***

S 2 K, Chatsworth *Also called S2k Graphics Inc* ***(P-11590)***

S A Camp Companies (PA) ....**E.......661 399-4451**
17876 Zerker Rd Bakersfield (93308) ***(P-13878)***

S A I, Van Nuys *Also called Search Associates Inc* ***(P-17463)***

S and C Precision Inc ....E.......626 338-7149
5045 Calmview Ave Baldwin Park (91706) ***(P-9777)***

S and H Rubber Company Inc ....E.......714 525-0277
1141 E Elm Ave Fullerton (92831) ***(P-5408)***

S B H Hotel Corporation ....A.......909 889-0133
285 E Hospitality Ln San Bernardino (92408) ***(P-16678)***

S B Hotel Partners ....D.......805 963-9757
17 W Haley St Santa Barbara (93101) ***(P-16679)***

S Bravo Systems Inc ....E.......323 888-4133
2929 Vail Ave Commerce (90040) ***(P-6751)***

S C A, Victorville *Also called Comav Technical Services LLC* ***(P-12350)***

S C A G, Los Angeles *Also called Cal Southern Assn Governments* ***(P-23422)***

S C Hydraulic Engineering, Brea *Also called Southern Cal Hydrlic Engrg Cor* ***(P-13939)***

S C I R E, Long Beach *Also called Southern Cal Inst For RES Edca* ***(P-22921)***

S C L, Gardena *Also called Schumacher Cargo Logistics Inc* ***(P-12523)***

S C P M G, Fontana *Also called Southern Cal Prmnnte Med Group* ***(P-20946)***

S C P M G, Colton *Also called Southern Cal Prmnnte Med Group* ***(P-20082)***

S C P M G, Culver City *Also called Southern Cal Prmnnte Med Group* ***(P-20083)***

S C P M G, Inglewood *Also called Southern Cal Prmnnte Med Group* ***(P-20084)***

S C P M G, Anaheim *Also called Southern Cal Prmnnte Med Group* ***(P-20086)***

S C P M G, San Juan Capistrano *Also called Southern Cal Prmnnte Med Group* ***(P-20087)***

S C P M G, Santa Ana *Also called Southern Cal Prmnnte Med Group* ***(P-20088)***

S C P M G, San Dimas *Also called Southern Cal Prmnnte Med Group* ***(P-15460)***

S C P M G, Cudahy *Also called Southern Cal Prmnnte Med Group* ***(P-20089)***

S C P M G, Woodland Hills *Also called Southern Cal Prmnnte Med Group* ***(P-20090)***

S C P M G, Santa Clarita *Also called Southern Cal Prmnnte Med Group* ***(P-20091)***

S C P M G, Harbor City *Also called Permanente Medical Group Inc* ***(P-20022)***

S C R, Costa Mesa *Also called South Coast Repertory Inc* ***(P-19332)***

S C Village, Bellflower *Also called S J S Enterprise Inc* ***(P-19666)***

S C Yamamoto, La Habra *Also called Shinsuke Clifford Yamamoto Inc* ***(P-342)***

S Callan Company Inc ....D.......818 841-3284
1126 N Hollywood Way Burbank (91505) ***(P-17053)***

S D I, Visalia *Also called Spraying Devices Inc* ***(P-7621)***

S D I, Upland *Also called Sign Development Inc* ***(P-11595)***

S D I, Camarillo *Also called Structural Diagnostics Inc* ***(P-10913)***

S D S, Ontario *Also called Specialized Dairy Service Inc* ***(P-7620)***

S E C C Corporation ....D.......760 246-6218
16224 Koala Rd Adelanto (92301) ***(P-967)***

S E O P Inc ....C.......949 682-7906
1621 Alton Pkwy Ste 150 Irvine (92606) ***(P-23314)***

S E P E Inc ....E.......714 241-7373
245 Fischer Ave Ste C4 Costa Mesa (92626) ***(P-8174)***

S E Pipe Line Construction Co ....D.......562 868-9771
11832 Bloomfield Ave Santa Fe Springs (90670) ***(P-968)***

S F Broadcasting of Wisconsin ....C.......310 586-2410
2425 Olympic Blvd Santa Monica (90404) ***(P-12740)***

S F Technology, Cerritos *Also called UFO Designs* ***(P-10147)***

S G D Enterprises ....E.......323 658-1047
14937 Delano St Van Nuys (91411) ***(P-340)***

S G S Produce, Los Angeles *Also called Shapiro-Gilman-Shandler Co* ***(P-14654)***

S J Amoroso Cnstr Co LLC ....D.......650 654-1900
275 Baker St Ste B Costa Mesa (92626) ***(P-818)***

S J S Enterprise Inc ....C.......949 489-9000
9030 Somerset Blvd Bellflower (90706) ***(P-19666)***

S J S Link International Inc (PA) ....**E.......310 860-7666**
468 N Camden Dr Ste 311 Beverly Hills (90210) ***(P-14530)***

S K Laboratories Inc ....D.......714 595-9800
5420 E La Palma Ave Anaheim (92807) ***(P-4888)***

S K Labs, Anaheim *Also called S K Laboratories Inc* ***(P-4888)***

S K Pharmaceuticals Inc ....F.......949 235-5265
31473 Rancho Viejo Rd San Juan Capistrano (92675) ***(P-4889)***

S L Fusco Inc (PA) ....**E.......310 868-1010**
1966 E Via Arado Rancho Dominguez (90220) ***(P-7745)***

S R J, San Clemente *Also called Julius Steve Construction Inc* ***(P-704)***

S R Machining Inc ....E.......951 520-9486
640 Parkridge Ave Norco (92860) ***(P-8784)***

S R Machining-Properties LLC ....C.......951 520-9486
640 Parkridge Ave Norco (92860) ***(P-8785)***

S R Mutual Funds, City of Industry *Also called California Country Club* ***(P-19551)***

S S I, Oxnard *Also called Synectic Solutions Inc* ***(P-18223)***

S S I, Irvine *Also called Seal Science Inc* ***(P-5351)***

S S Schaffer Co Inc ....F.......323 560-1430
5637 District Blvd Vernon (90058) ***(P-7746)***

S S W Mechanical Cnstr Inc ....C.......760 327-1481
670 S Oleander Rd Palm Springs (92264) ***(P-1133)***

S Studio Inc ....F.......213 388-7400
3030 W 6th St Los Angeles (90020) ***(P-2907)***

S T Moll Inc (PA) ....**D.......951 658-3145**
3223 W Florida Ave Hemet (92545) ***(P-18869)***

S W K Properties LLC ....C.......714 481-6300
2726 S Grand Ave Lbby Santa Ana (92705) ***(P-16680)***

S W K Properties LLC (PA) ....**D.......213 383-9204**
3807 Wilshire Blvd # 122 Los Angeles (90010) ***(P-16681)***

S&B Development Group LLC ....E.......213 446-2818
1901 Avenue Of The Stars # 200 Los Angeles (90067) ***(P-2603)***

S&B Filters Inc ....D.......909 947-0015
15461 Slover Ave Ste A Fontana (92337) ***(P-10130)***

S&B Industry Inc ....E.......909 569-4155
105 S Puente St Brea (92821) ***(P-5809)***

S&B Pharma Inc ....D.......626 334-2908
405 S Motor Ave Azusa (91702) ***(P-4763)***

S&E Gourmet Cuts Inc ....C.......909 370-0155
1055 E Cooley Ave San Bernardino (92408) ***(P-14565)***

S&F Management Company LLC (PA) ....**A.......310 385-1090**
9200 W Sunset Blvd # 700 West Hollywood (90069) ***(P-20456)***

S&S Flavours, Brea *Also called Scisorek & Son Flavors Inc* ***(P-2336)***

S-Energy America Inc (HQ) ....**F.......949 281-7897**
1170 N Gilbert St Anaheim (92801) ***(P-9567)***

S2e Inc ....F.......626 965-1008
817 Lawson St City of Industry (91748) ***(P-9192)***

S2k Graphics Inc ....E.......818 885-3900
9255 Deering Ave Chatsworth (91311) ***(P-11590)***

SA Camp Pump and Drilling Co, Bakersfield *Also called SA Camp Pump Company* ***(P-19061)***

SA Camp Pump Company ....D.......661 399-2976
17876 Zerker Rd Bakersfield (93308) ***(P-19061)***

SA Kitsinian Inc ....F.......818 988-9961
27101 Mcbean Pkwy Valencia (91355) ***(P-14138)***

SA Recycling LLC ....D.......909 622-3337
11614 Eastend Ave Chino (91710) ***(P-12973)***

SA Recycling LLC (PA) ....**C.......714 632-2000**
2411 N Glassell St Orange (92865) ***(P-12974)***

SA Recycling LLC ....D.......661 723-1383
42353 8th St E Lancaster (93535) ***(P-12975)***

SA Serving Lines Inc ....E.......714 848-7529
226 W Carleton Ave Orange (92867) ***(P-6906)***

Sa-Tech, Oxnard *Also called Systems Application & Tech Inc* ***(P-22664)***

Saa, Culver City *Also called Shlemmer Algaze Associates* ***(P-22742)***

Saab Enterprises Inc ....F.......909 823-2228
1433 Miller Dr Colton (92324) ***(P-1750)***

Saalex Corp (PA) ....**C.......805 482-1070**
811 Camarillo Springs Rd A Camarillo (93012) ***(P-22649)***

Saalex Solutions, Camarillo *Also called Saalex Corp* ***(P-22649)***

Saatchi & Saatchi N Amer LLC ....C.......310 437-2500
13031 W Jefferson Blvd Los Angeles (90094) ***(P-17054)***

Sabal Capital Partners LLC ....D.......949 255-1007
465 N Halstead St Ste 105 Pasadena (91107) ***(P-16291)***

Saban Brands LLC (HQ) ....**D.......310 557-5230**
10100 Santa Monica Blvd # 500 Los Angeles (90067) ***(P-23315)***

Saban Capital Group Inc (PA) ....**D.......310 557-5100**
10100 Santa Monica Blvd Los Angeles (90067) ***(P-16292)***

SABAN COMMUNITY CLINIC, Los Angeles *Also called Los Angeles Free Clinic* ***(P-19967)***

Saban Research Institute, The, Los Angeles *Also called Childrens Hospital Los Angeles* ***(P-20719)***

Saber, Temecula *Also called South Coast Piering Inc* ***(P-832)***

Sabina Motors & Controls, Anaheim *Also called Motors & Controls Whse Inc* ***(P-13752)***

Sabio Mobile Inc ....E.......818 805-3678
16350 Ventura Blvd D82 Encino (91436) ***(P-17089)***

Sabra Health Care Ltd Partnr (HQ) ....**D.......949 255-7100**
18500 Von Karman Ave # 5 Irvine (92612) ***(P-16162)***

Sabred International Packg Inc ....E.......714 996-2800
3740 Prospect Ave Yorba Linda (92886) ***(P-5520)***

Sabrin Corporation ....F.......626 792-3813
2836 E Walnut St Pasadena (91107) ***(P-10406)***

Sac Health System (PA) ....**D.......909 382-7100**
1455 3rd Ave San Bernardino (92408) ***(P-20196)***

Sac International Steel Inc (PA) ....**D.......323 232-2467**
6130 Avalon Blvd Los Angeles (90003) ***(P-13593)***

Sac-TEC Labs Inc (PA) ....**E.......310 375-5295**
24301 Wilmington Ave Carson (90745) ***(P-9568)***

Mergent e-mail: customerrelations@mergent.com
1260
2022 Southern California Business Directory and Buyers Guide
(P-0000) Products & Services Section entry number
(PA)=Parent Co (HQ)=Headquarters (DH)=Div Headquarters

Saca Technologies Inc ....D.......888 603-9030
5101 E La Palma Ave # 200 Anaheim (92807) ***(P-18218)***
Sada Systems Inc ....C.......818 766-2400
5250 Lankershim Blvd # 620 North Hollywood (91601) ***(P-18219)***
Sadaf Foods, Vernon *Also called Soofer Co Inc* ***(P-14737)***
Saddlback Vly Srgcal Med Group ....C.......949 364-1007
26732 Crown Valley Pkwy Mission Viejo (92691) ***(P-20046)***
Saddleback Educational Inc ....F.......714 640-5200
151 Kalmus Dr Ste J1 Costa Mesa (92626) ***(P-4136)***
Saddleback Eye Center, Laguna Hills *Also called Charles C Manger III MD Inc* ***(P-19744)***
Saddleback Memorial Med Ctr (HQ) ....**A.......949 837-4500**
24451 Health Center Dr # 1 Laguna Hills (92653) ***(P-20926)***
Saddleback Stair & Millwork ....F.......949 460-0384
23291 Peralta Dr Ste B4 Laguna Hills (92653) ***(P-3287)***
Saddleback Valley Service Ctr, Irvine *Also called Southern California Edison Co* ***(P-12847)***
Saddlemen Corporation ....D.......310 638-1222
17801 S Susana Rd Compton (90221) ***(P-13086)***
Sadie & Sage LLC (PA) ....**F.......213 234-2188**
673 Monterey Pass Rd Monterey Park (91754) ***(P-2865)***
Saehan Bank (PA) ....**E.......213 368-7700**
3200 Wilshire Blvd # 700 Los Angeles (90010) ***(P-15042)***
Saeilo Manufacturing Inds, Santa Fe Springs *Also called SMI Ca Inc* ***(P-8796)***
Saf-T-Co Supply ....E.......714 547-9975
1300 E Normandy Pl Santa Ana (92705) ***(P-9053)***
Safariland LLC ....B.......909 923-7300
4700 E Airport Dr Ontario (91761) ***(P-11138)***
SAFE HOUSE SHELTER, Riverside *Also called Operation Safe House Inc* ***(P-21859)***
Safe Place For Youth Inc ....D.......310 902-2283
1821 E 68th St Apt 108 Long Beach (90805) ***(P-21879)***
Safe Plating Inc ....D.......626 810-1872
18001 Railroad St City of Industry (91748) ***(P-7308)***
Safe Refuge ....D.......562 987-5722
1041 Redondo Ave Long Beach (90804) ***(P-21335)***
Safeco Insurance Company Amer ....C.......818 956-4250
330 N Brand Blvd Ste 680 Glendale (91203) ***(P-15624)***
Safeguard Dental Plan, Aliso Viejo *Also called Safeguard Health Plans Inc* ***(P-15450)***
Safeguard Envirogroup Inc ....E.......626 512-7585
153 Lowell Ave Glendora (91741) ***(P-10809)***
Safeguard Health Entps Inc (HQ) ....**B.......800 880-1800**
95 Enterprise Ste 100 Aliso Viejo (92656) ***(P-15449)***
Safeguard Health Plans Inc (HQ) ....**D.......800 880-1800**
95 Enterprise Ste 100 Aliso Viejo (92656) ***(P-15450)***
Safeguard On Demand Inc ....C.......800 640-2327
11037 Warner Ave 297 Fountain Valley (92708) ***(P-18319)***
Safeland Industrial Supply Inc (PA) ....**E.......909 786-1967**
8949 9th St Ste 130 Rancho Cucamonga (91730) ***(P-6233)***
Safety Security Patrol LLC ....D.......909 888-7778
560 N Arrowhead Ave 3b San Bernardino (92401) ***(P-18320)***
Safety Systems Hawaii ....E.......808 847-4017
P.O. Box 5299 Irvine (92616) ***(P-11591)***
Safetypark Corporation (PA) ....**C.......310 899-0490**
13420 Beach Ave Marina Del Rey (90292) ***(P-18779)***
Safeway Sign Company ....E.......760 246-7070
9875 Yucca Rd Adelanto (92301) ***(P-11592)***
Saffola Quality Foods, Ontario *Also called Ventura Foods LLC* ***(P-1766)***
Safran, Anaheim *Also called Morphotrak LLC* ***(P-18047)***
Safran Cabin Galleys Us Inc (HQ) ....**A.......714 861-7300**
17311 Nichols Ln Huntington Beach (92647) ***(P-10407)***
Safran Cabin Inc (HQ) ....**B.......714 934-0000**
5701 Bolsa Ave Huntington Beach (92647) ***(P-10408)***
Safran Cabin Inc ....C.......562 344-4780
11240 Warland Dr Cypress (90630) ***(P-10409)***
Safran Cabin Materials LLC ....E.......909 947-4115
1945 S Grove Ave Ontario (91761) ***(P-10410)***
Safran Pass Innovations LLC (HQ) ....**D.......714 854-8600**
3151 E Imperial Hwy Brea (92821) ***(P-17705)***
Safran Seats Santa Maria LLC ....A.......805 922-5995
2641 Airpark Dr Santa Maria (93455) ***(P-10411)***
Sag- Aftra Federal Credit Un ....D.......818 562-3400
134 N Kenwood St Burbank (91505) ***(P-15079)***
Sag-Aftra Foundation ....E.......323 549-6708
5757 Wilshire Blvd Ph 1 Los Angeles (90036) ***(P-22295)***
Sag-Aftra Plaza, Los Angeles *Also called Chrome River Technology* ***(P-17816)***
Saga Kapital Group Inc ....D.......714 294-4132
108 Saybrook Irvine (92620) ***(P-23103)***
Sage Associates Inc (PA) ....**D.......949 724-9600**
2361 Campus Dr Ste 111 Irvine (92612) ***(P-22650)***
Sage Goddess Inc ....E.......650 733-6639
21010 Figueroa St Carson (90745) ***(P-11330)***
Sage Hospitality Resources LLC ....C.......626 357-5211
700 W Huntington Dr Monrovia (91016) ***(P-16682)***
Sage Software Holdings Inc (HQ) ....**B.......866 530-7243**
6561 Irvine Center Dr Irvine (92618) ***(P-17975)***
Sage Staffing Consultants Inc (PA) ....**C.......661 254-4026**
27441 Tourney Rd Ste 150 Valencia (91355) ***(P-17515)***
Sage The Label, Monterey Park *Also called Sadie & Sage LLC* ***(P-2865)***
Sagepoint Financial Inc ....B.......949 756-1462
3723 Birch St Ste 9 Newport Beach (92660) ***(P-15345)***
Sagepoint Financial Inc ....D.......310 792-0801
3655 Torrance Blvd # 480 Torrance (90503) ***(P-15346)***
Sageview Advisory Group LLC (PA) ....**D.......949 955-1395**
4000 Macarthur Blvd # 1050 Newport Beach (92660) ***(P-15347)***
Saharan Motor Hotel Inc ....D.......323 874-6700
7212 W Sunset Blvd Los Angeles (90046) ***(P-16683)***
SAI Industries ....E.......818 842-6144
631 Allen Ave Glendale (91201) ***(P-7430)***
SAI Management Co Inc ....D.......714 772-5050
1600 S Harbor Blvd Anaheim (92802) ***(P-16684)***
Saia Motor Freight Line LLC ....D.......909 356-2808
14731 Santa Ana Ave Fontana (92337) ***(P-12076)***
Saia Motor Freight Line LLC ....D.......310 217-1499
14719 S San Pedro St Gardena (90248) ***(P-12077)***
Saia Motor Freight Line LLC ....D.......323 277-2880
2550 E 28th St Vernon (90058) ***(P-12078)***
Saiful/Bquet Cnslting Strl Eng (PA) ....**D.......626 304-2616**
155 N Lake Ave Fl 6 Pasadena (91101) ***(P-22651)***
Sailing Innovation (us) Inc ....A.......626 965-6665
17870 Castleton St # 220 City of Industry (91748) ***(P-9193)***
Saint Anthony Retreat, Three Rivers *Also called Roman Catholic Bishp of Fresno* ***(P-16825)***
Saint Barnabas Senior Services, Los Angeles *Also called St Brnbas Snior Ctr Los Angle* ***(P-21894)***
Saint Cecilia School, Tustin *Also called Roman Cthlic Diocese of Orange* ***(P-22057)***
Saint Frncis Winery Tasting Rm (PA) ....**E.......707 833-4668**
100 Pythian Rd Camarillo (93012) ***(P-2219)***
Saint Jhns Hlth Ctr Foundation ....C.......310 315-6111
2200 Santa Monica Blvd Santa Monica (90404) ***(P-20047)***
Saint Jhns Hlth Ctr Foundation ....D.......310 829-8970
2020 Santa Monica Blvd Santa Monica (90404) ***(P-20927)***
Saint John's Hospital X Ray, Long Beach *Also called Dignity Health* ***(P-20750)***
Saint John's Well Child Center, Los Angeles *Also called St Jhns Well Child Fmly Ctr I* ***(P-20200)***
Saint Johns Cancer Institute ....D.......310 449-5253
2200 Santa Monica Blvd Santa Monica (90404) ***(P-22919)***
SAINT JOSEPH CENTER VOLUNTEER, Venice *Also called St Joseph Center* ***(P-21895)***
Saint Joseph Hlth Sys Hospice, Anaheim *Also called St Joseph Hospice* ***(P-21896)***
Saint Jseph Communications Inc (PA) ....**E.......626 331-3549**
1243 E Shamwood St West Covina (91790) ***(P-19174)***
Saint Nine America Inc ....E.......562 921-5300
10700 Norwalk Blvd Santa Fe Springs (90670) ***(P-11445)***
SAINT VINCENT'S INSTITUTION, Santa Barbara *Also called St Vincents Institution* ***(P-21897)***
Saint-Gobain Ceramics Plas Inc ....C.......714 701-3900
4905 E Hunter Ave Anaheim (92807) ***(P-5146)***
Saint-Gobain Prfmce Plas Corp ....C.......714 893-0470
7301 Orangewood Ave Garden Grove (92841) ***(P-4714)***
Saitex (usa) LLC ....F.......323 391-6116
6074 Malburg Way Vernon (90058) ***(P-2586)***
Sajahtera Inc ....A.......310 276-2251
9641 Sunset Blvd Beverly Hills (90210) ***(P-16685)***
Saje Natural Wellness USA Inc (HQ) ....**D.......310 317-0421**
1421 Abbot Kinney Blvd Venice (90291) ***(P-21476)***
Sakura Finetek USA Inc (HQ) ....**C.......310 972-7800**
1750 W 214th St Torrance (90501) ***(P-13517)***
Sakura Noodle Inc ....F.......213 623-2396
620 E 7th St Los Angeles (90021) ***(P-2382)***
Salad Time Farms, Baldwin Park *Also called Tanimura Antle Fresh Foods Inc* ***(P-191)***
Saladish Inc ....F.......626 304-3100
12 W Colorado Blvd Pasadena (91105) ***(P-2521)***
Salameh & Mahmood DDS Inc (PA) ....**D.......949 830-6510**
24102 El Toro Rd Ste A Laguna Woods (92637) ***(P-20197)***
Salco Dynamic Solutions Inc (PA) ....**E.......714 374-7500**
6248 Surfpoint Cir Huntington Beach (92648) ***(P-5298)***
Salco Oil, Huntington Beach *Also called Salco Dynamic Solutions Inc* ***(P-5298)***
Salco Products, Fontana *Also called Nyx Industries Inc* ***(P-7615)***
Saleen Automotive Inc (PA) ....**E.......800 888-8945**
2735 Wardlow Rd Corona (92882) ***(P-7113)***
Saleen Incorporated (PA) ....**C.......714 400-2121**
2735 Wardlow Rd Corona (92882) ***(P-9964)***
Salem Music Network Inc ....F.......805 987-0400
4880 Santa Rosa Rd # 300 Camarillo (93012) ***(P-9314)***
Salem Polymer Industries ....F.......818 331-9475
5500 Owensmouth Ave # 133 Woodland Hills (91367) ***(P-11746)***
Sales Advantage Group, Corona *Also called Temps Plus Inc* ***(P-17473)***
Salesforcecom Inc ....E.......310 752-7000
1442 2nd St Santa Monica (90401) ***(P-17976)***
Salimar Inc ....D.......661 327-9651
2842 Summit Cir Bakersfield (93306) ***(P-16686)***
Salman, Brea *Also called Parkinson Enterprises Inc* ***(P-3597)***
Salon Brandy, Compton *Also called California Decor* ***(P-3235)***
Salsbury Industries Inc (PA) ....**B.......323 846-6700**
18300 Central Ave Carson (90746) ***(P-3695)***
Salson Logistics Inc ....D.......973 986-0200
1331 Torrance Blvd Torrance (90501) ***(P-12521)***
Salus Homecare, Irvine *Also called Orange County Homecare LLC* ***(P-21195)***
Salvador Ramirez ....F.......661 702-1813
25334 Avenue Stanford B Valencia (91355) ***(P-10224)***
Salvation Army (HQ) ....**C.......562 264-3600**
16941 Keegan Ave Carson (90746) ***(P-21880)***
Salvation Army ....D.......714 832-7100
10200 Pioneer Rd Tustin (92782) ***(P-21881)***
Salvation Army Western Ttry, Carson *Also called Salvation Army* ***(P-21880)***
Sam & Lavi, Los Angeles *Also called Valmas Inc* ***(P-2899)***
Sam Hill & Sons Inc ....E.......805 620-0828
2627 Beene Rd Ventura (93003) ***(P-969)***
Sam Israel Viner, Marina Del Rey *Also called Samvco* ***(P-9011)***
Sam Schaffer Inc ....E.......323 263-7524
4477 Sheila St Commerce (90023) ***(P-19062)***
Samaritan Imaging Center ....A.......213 977-2140
1245 Wilshire Blvd # 205 Los Angeles (90017) ***(P-21095)***
SAMARITIN HOUSE, Long Beach *Also called Long Bch Rscue Mssion Fndation* ***(P-21842)***
Sambazon Inc (PA) ....**D.......877 726-2296**
209 Avnida Fbrcnte Ste 20 San Clemente (92672) ***(P-14651)***
Same Swim LLC ....D.......323 582-2588
2333 E 49th St Vernon (90058) ***(P-14415)***
Samedan Oil Corporation ....D.......661 319-5038
1360 Landing Ave Seal Beach (90740) ***(P-463)***

A L P H A B E T I C

Employee Codes: A=Over 500 employees, B=251-500
C=101-250, D=51-100, E=20-50 F=10-19
2022 Southern California Business
Directory and Buyers Guide
© Mergent Inc. 1-800-342-5647
1261

Samiyatex, Los Angeles *Also called Paragon Textiles Inc* ***(P-14409)***

Sampav Inc ....F........909 984-8646
15802 Ellington Way Chino Hills (91709) ***(P-2749)***

Sample Tile and Stone Inc ....E........951 776-8562
1410 Richardson St San Bernardino (92408) ***(P-6144)***

Samson Pharmaceuticals Inc ....E........323 722-3066
5635 Smithway St Commerce (90040) ***(P-4890)***

Samson Products Inc ....E........323 726-9070
6285 Randolph St Commerce (90040) ***(P-3696)***

Samsung Electronics Amer Inc ....B........323 374-6300
5601 E Slauson Ave # 200 Commerce (90040) ***(P-13693)***

Samsung Electronics Amer Inc ....D........310 537-7000
18600 S Broadwick St Rancho Dominguez (90220) ***(P-13694)***

Samtech Automotive Usa Inc ....E........310 638-9955
1130 E Dominguez St Carson (90746) ***(P-7766)***

Samtech International, Carson *Also called Samtech Automotive Usa Inc* ***(P-7766)***

Samtex Fabrics Inc ....E........213 742-0200
2424 E 28th St Vernon (90058) ***(P-12522)***

Samuel Son & Co (usa) Inc ....E........323 722-0300
12389 Lower Azusa Rd Arcadia (91006) ***(P-13594)***

Samuel Son & Co (usa) Inc ....E........951 781-7800
2345 Fleetwood Dr Riverside (92509) ***(P-6316)***

Samuel J Piazza & Son Inc (PA) ....**D........323 357-1999**
9001 Rayo Ave South Gate (90280) ***(P-12117)***

Samvco ....F........310 980-5680
14016 Bora Bora Way Marina Del Rey (90292) ***(P-9011)***

Samy Co, Cypress *Also called Hoyu America Co* ***(P-14250)***

San Antnio Ambltory Srgcal Ctr ....D........909 579-1500
901 San Bernardino Rd 2n Upland (91786) ***(P-20048)***

San Antnio Behavioral Hlth LLC (PA) ....**D........310 566-0640**
1333 2nd St Ste 650 Santa Monica (90401) ***(P-21477)***

San Antonio Gift Shop, Los Angeles *Also called San Antonio Winery Inc* ***(P-2220)***

San Antonio Regional Hospital (PA) ....**A........909 985-2811**
999 San Bernardino Rd Upland (91786) ***(P-20928)***

San Antonio Winery Inc (PA) ....**C........323 223-1401**
737 Lamar St Los Angeles (90031) ***(P-2220)***

San Bernardino California City (PA) ....**B........909 384-7272**
290 N D St San Bernardino (92401) ***(P-21672)***

San Bernardino Canning Co., San Bernardino *Also called Refresco Beverages US Inc* ***(P-2283)***

San Bernardino Care Company ....C........909 884-4781
467 E Gilbert St San Bernardino (92404) ***(P-20625)***

San Bernardino County Sun, The, San Bernardino *Also called Sun Company San Bernardino Cal* ***(P-4032)***

San Bernardino Family YMCA, San Bernardino *Also called YMCA of East Valley* ***(P-22382)***

San Bernardino Fics, San Bernardino *Also called Victor Cmnty Support Svcs Inc* ***(P-21365)***

San Bernardino Hilton (HQ) ....**C........909 889-0133**
285 E Hospitality Ln San Bernardino (92408) ***(P-16687)***

San Brnrdino Cmnty College Dst ....C........909 384-4444
701 S Mount Vernon Ave San Bernardino (92410) ***(P-12705)***

San Brnrdino Cmnty College Dst ....E........909 888-6511
701 S Mount Vernon Ave San Bernardino (92410) ***(P-4570)***

San Brnrdino Cnty Prbtion Offc ....B........909 887-2544
4370 Hallmark Pkwy # 105 San Bernardino (92407) ***(P-21882)***

San Brnrdno Cnty Ret Med Tr ....D........909 387-6053
157 W 5th St San Bernardino (92415) ***(P-22256)***

San Clemente Sportfishing Inc ....D........949 496-5794
34675 Golden Lantern St Dana Point (92629) ***(P-19667)***

San Clemente Villas By Sea Inc ....D........949 489-3400
660 Camino De Los Mares San Clemente (92673) ***(P-22151)***

San Dego Nghborhood Newspapers, Cypress *Also called Community Media Corporation* ***(P-3966)***

San Diego Daily Transcript ....D........619 232-4381
34 Emerald Gln Laguna Niguel (92677) ***(P-3769)***

San Diego Gas & Electric Co ....D........949 361-8090
662 Camino De Los Mares San Clemente (92673) ***(P-12873)***

San Dimas Community Hospital, San Dimas *Also called Prime Health Care* ***(P-22055)***

San Dimas Community Hospital, San Dimas *Also called Prime Hlthcare Svcs - San Dmas* ***(P-20909)***

San Dimas Golf Inc ....C........909 599-8486
1400 Avenida Entrada San Dimas (91773) ***(P-19606)***

San Dimas Medical Group Inc ....D........661 663-4800
100 Old River Rd Bakersfield (93311) ***(P-20049)***

San Dimas Retirement Center (PA) ....**D........909 599-8441**
834 W Arrow Hwy San Dimas (91773) ***(P-15748)***

San Fernando City of Inc ....D........818 832-2400
10605 Balboa Blvd Ste 100 Granada Hills (91344) ***(P-21336)***

San Fernando City of Inc ....D........818 898-7340
505 S Huntington St San Fernando (91340) ***(P-21883)***

San Fernando Health Center, San Fernando *Also called Northeast Valley Health Corp* ***(P-19999)***

San Fernando Valley Auto LLC ....C........818 832-1600
18600 Devonshire St Northridge (91324) ***(P-18870)***

San Fernando Valley Bus Jurnl, Woodland Hills *Also called Cbj LP* ***(P-4054)***

San Fernando Vly Pallet Co Inc (PA) ....**F........818 341-1200**
21540 Nordhoff St Chatsworth (91311) ***(P-3407)***

San Frnndo Vly Cmnty Mntal HLT (PA) ....**D........818 901-4830**
16360 Roscoe Blvd Fl 2 Van Nuys (91406) ***(P-21337)***

San Frnndo Vly Intrfith Cncil ....D........818 885-5220
8956 Vanalden Ave Northridge (91324) ***(P-21884)***

San Frnndo Vly Urlgcal Med Gro ....D........818 996-4242
18370 Burbank Blvd # 407 Tarzana (91356) ***(P-20050)***

San Gabriel Convalescent Ctr, Rosemead *Also called Longwood Management Corp* ***(P-20407)***

San Gabriel Country Club ....D........626 287-9671
350 E Hermosa Dr San Gabriel (91775) ***(P-19607)***

San Gabriel Transit Inc ....D........626 430-3650
14913 Ramona Blvd Baldwin Park (91706) ***(P-11901)***

San Gabriel Transit Inc (PA) ....**C........626 258-1310**
3650 Rockwell Ave El Monte (91731) ***(P-11837)***

San Gabriel Valley Cab Co, El Monte *Also called San Gabriel Transit Inc* ***(P-11837)***

San Gabriel Valley Medical Ctr ....A........626 289-5454
438 W Las Tunas Dr San Gabriel (91776) ***(P-20929)***

San Gabriel Valley Water Co (PA) ....**C........626 448-6183**
11142 Garvey Ave El Monte (91733) ***(P-12915)***

San Gabriel Valley Water Co ....C........909 822-2201
8440 Nuevo Ave Fontana (92335) ***(P-12916)***

San Gabriel Vly Surgical Ctr, West Covina *Also called Surgical Center of West Covina* ***(P-20100)***

San Gabriel Vly Training Ctr (PA) ....**D........626 330-3185**
400 S Covina Blvd La Puente (91746) ***(P-21966)***

SAN GABRIEL/POMONA REGIONAL CE, Pomona *Also called San Gbrl/Pmona Vlleys Dvlpmnta* ***(P-21885)***

San Gbriel Ambltory Srgery Ctr ....B........626 300-5300
207 S Santa Anita St San Gabriel (91776) ***(P-20051)***

San Gbrl/Pmona Vlleys Dvlpmnta ....B........909 620-7722
75 Rancho Camino Dr Pomona (91766) ***(P-21885)***

San Gorgonio Memorial Hospital ....A........951 845-1121
600 N Highland Sprng Ave Banning (92220) ***(P-20930)***

San Grgnio Mem Hosp Foundation (PA) ....**C........951 845-1121**
600 N Highland Sprng Ave Banning (92220) ***(P-20931)***

San Jacinto Healthcare, Hemet *Also called Miramonte Enterprises LLC* ***(P-20413)***

San Joaquin Bit Service Inc ....C........661 834-3233
2543 S Union Ave Bakersfield (93307) ***(P-13937)***

San Joaquin Community Hospital, Bakersfield *Also called Kaiser Foundation Hospitals* ***(P-20809)***

San Joaquin Community Hospital (PA) ....**A........661 395-3000**
2615 Chester Ave Bakersfield (93301) ***(P-20932)***

San Joaquin Refining Co Inc ....C........661 327-4257
3500 Shell St Bakersfield (93308) ***(P-5260)***

San Joaquin Valley Railroad Co ....D........559 592-1857
221 N F St Exeter (93221) ***(P-11797)***

San Joaquin Window Inc ....C........909 946-3697
1455 Columbia Ave Riverside (92507) ***(P-6718)***

San Jose Medical Group / MGT, Woodland Hills *Also called Verity Medical Foundation* ***(P-20139)***

San Jquin Hlls Trnsp Crrdor AG (PA) ....**D........949 754-3400**
125 Pacifica Ste 100 Irvine (92618) ***(P-912)***

San Juan Cpstrano Mmory Care C, San Juan Capistrano *Also called Silverado Senior Living Inc* ***(P-20472)***

San Juan Golf Inc ....D........949 493-1167
32120 San Juan Creek Rd San Juan Capistrano (92675) ***(P-19506)***

San Juan Hill Country Club, San Juan Capistrano *Also called San Juan Golf Inc* ***(P-19506)***

San Luis Ambulance Service Inc ....C........805 543-2626
3546 S Higuera St San Luis Obispo (93401) ***(P-11888)***

San Luis Dgnstc Ctr A Cal Ltd ....D........805 542-9700
1100 Monterey St San Luis Obispo (93401) ***(P-20052)***

San Luis Diagnostic Med Assoc, San Luis Obispo *Also called San Luis Dgnstc Ctr A Cal Ltd* ***(P-20052)***

San Luis Obispo County YMCA ....D........805 544-7225
5785 Los Ranchos Rd San Luis Obispo (93401) ***(P-22364)***

San Luis Obispo Golf Cntry CLB ....C........805 543-3400
255 Country Club Dr San Luis Obispo (93401) ***(P-19608)***

San Luis Obispo VA Cboc, San Luis Obispo *Also called Veterans Health Administration* ***(P-20143)***

San Luis Obspo Rgnal Trnst Aut ....D........805 781-4465
179 Cross St Ste A San Luis Obispo (93401) ***(P-11838)***

San Manuel Indian Bingo Casino (PA) ....**A........909 864-5050**
777 San Manuel Blvd Highland (92346) ***(P-19668)***

San Marco's Tortilla & Market, Los Angeles *Also called Tortilleria San Marcos* ***(P-2542)***

San Marino Plastering Inc ....D........714 693-7840
4501 E La Palma Ave # 200 Anaheim (92807) ***(P-1400)***

San Miguel Produce Inc ....B........805 488-0981
600 E Hueneme Rd Oxnard (93033) ***(P-18)***

San Pedro Convalescent HM Inc ....D........310 832-6431
1430 W 6th St San Pedro (90732) ***(P-20457)***

San Pedro Fish Market LLC ....D........323 775-2921
1190 Nagoya Way 78 San Pedro (90731) ***(P-14581)***

San Pedro Ownership Inc ....D........310 514-3344
2800 Via Cabrillo Marina San Pedro (90731) ***(P-16688)***

San Pedro Sign Company ....E........310 549-4661
701 Lakme Ave Wilmington (90744) ***(P-11593)***

San Val Alarm System, Thousand Palms *Also called San Val Corp* ***(P-278)***

San Val Corp (PA) ....**B........760 346-3999**
72203 Adelaid St Thousand Palms (92276) ***(P-278)***

San Yi US Investment Co Inc ....E........626 607-2006
303 E Valley Blvd San Gabriel (91776) ***(P-16689)***

San-Mar Construction Co Inc ....C........714 693-5400
4875 E La Palma Ave # 601 Anaheim (92807) ***(P-819)***

Sanan Inc ....E........949 679-9200
8505 Irvine Center Dr Irvine (92618) ***(P-23506)***

Sanctus LLC ....C........248 594-2396
250 Broadway St Laguna Beach (92651) ***(P-23104)***

Sand Canyon Corporation (HQ) ....**D........949 727-9425**
7595 Irvine Center Dr # 12 Irvine (92618) ***(P-15251)***

Sandberg Furniture Mfg Co Inc (PA) ....**C........323 582-0711**
5705 Alcoa Ave Vernon (90058) ***(P-3488)***

Sandee Plastic Extrusions ....E........323 979-4020
14932 Gwenchris Ct Paramount (90723) ***(P-5810)***

Sander Langston LP ....C........949 863-9200
17962 Cowan Irvine (92614) ***(P-820)***

Sanders & Wohrman Corporation ....C........714 919-0446
709 N Poplar St Orange (92868) ***(P-1198)***

Mergent e-mail: customerrelations@mergent.com
1262
2022 Southern California Business
Directory and Buyers Guide
(P-0000) Products & Services Section entry number
(PA)=Parent Co (HQ)=Headquarters (DH)=Div Headquarters

Sanders Candy Factory Inc........E......626 814-2038
5051 Calmview Ave Baldwin Park (91706) ***(P-2103)***

Sanders Composites Inc (HQ)........**E......562 354-2800**
3701 E Conant St Long Beach (90808) ***(P-10412)***

Sanders Composites Industries, Long Beach *Also called Sanders Composites Inc* ***(P-10412)***

Sanders Inds Holdings Inc (HQ)........**F......562 354-2920**
3701 E Conant St Long Beach (90808) ***(P-4715)***

Sandhrst Cnvlscent Group Ltd A........D......310 675-3304
13922 Cerise Ave Hawthorne (90250) ***(P-20458)***

Sandia Plastics Inc........E......714 901-8400
15571 Container Ln Huntington Beach (92649) ***(P-5811)***

Sandpiper Golf Course, Goleta *Also called Sandpiper Golf Trust LLC* ***(P-19507)***

Sandpiper Golf Trust LLC........D......805 968-1541
7925 Hollister Ave Goleta (93117) ***(P-19507)***

Sandridge Partners LP........D......408 738-4444
19087 Milan Rd Buttonwillow (93206) ***(P-10)***

Sandy Lake Animal Hospital, Los Angeles *Also called Veternary Ctrs of Amrica-Texas* ***(P-208)***

Sangera Buick Inc........D......661 833-5200
5600 Gasoline Alley Dr Bakersfield (93313) ***(P-18871)***

Sani-Tech West Inc (HQ)........**D......805 389-0400**
1020 Flynn Rd Camarillo (93012) ***(P-5322)***

Sanie Manufacturing Company........F......714 751-7700
2600 S Yale St Santa Ana (92704) ***(P-6978)***

Sanitec Industries Inc........D......818 523-1942
10700 Sherman Way Burbank (91505) ***(P-12976)***

Sanitek Products Inc........F......323 245-6781
3959 Goodwin Ave Los Angeles (90039) ***(P-4977)***

Sanittion Dstrcts Los Angles C........A......562 908-4288
1955 Workman Mill Rd Whittier (90601) ***(P-12977)***

Sanko Electronics America Inc (HQ)........**F......310 618-1677**
20700 Denker Ave Ste A Torrance (90501) ***(P-10131)***

Sanluisina, Chino Hills *Also called Andrew LLC* ***(P-1941)***

Sanmina Corporation........C......714 913-2200
2950 Red Hill Ave Costa Mesa (92626) ***(P-9451)***

Sanrio Inc (HQ)........**D......650 952-2880**
2050 W 190th St Ste 205 Torrance (90504) ***(P-14101)***

Sans Wine & Spirits Co........F......714 423-3883
17885 Sky Park Cir Ste J Irvine (92614) ***(P-2221)***

Sansani Cleaning Solutions LLC........F......310 630-9033
551 E 64th St Apt 3 Long Beach (90805) ***(P-8410)***

Sansum Clinic (PA)........**D......805 681-7700**
470 S Patterson Ave Santa Barbara (93111) ***(P-20053)***

Santa Ana Clnica Mdica Gen Med........E......323 221-1111
2208 W 7th St Los Angeles (90057) ***(P-20054)***

Santa Ana Country Club........D......714 556-3000
20382 Newport Blvd Santa Ana (92707) ***(P-19609)***

Santa Ana District Office, Santa Ana *Also called State Compensation Insur Fund* ***(P-15480)***

Santa Ana Plating (PA)........**D......310 923-8305**
1726 E Rosslynn Ave Fullerton (92831) ***(P-7309)***

Santa Ana Radiology Center........D......714 835-6055
1100 N Tustin Ave Ste A Santa Ana (92705) ***(P-20055)***

Santa Ana Watershed Prj Auth........D......951 354-4220
11615 Sterling Ave Riverside (92503) ***(P-12917)***

Santa Anita Associates (PA)........**D......626 447-2764**
405 S Santa Anita Ave Arcadia (91006) ***(P-19508)***

Santa Anita Cnvlscent Hosp Rtr........C......626 579-0310
5522 Gracewood Ave Temple City (91780) ***(P-20459)***

Santa Anita Golf Course, Arcadia *Also called Santa Anita Associates* ***(P-19508)***

Santa Anita Park, Arcadia *Also called Los Angeles Turf Club Inc* ***(P-19431)***

Santa Barbara City of........D......805 962-6464
1100 Anacapa St Dept 3 Santa Barbara (93101) ***(P-12409)***

Santa Barbara Coffee LLC........F......805 683-2555
6489 Calle Real Ste G Goleta (93117) ***(P-2357)***

Santa Barbara Coffee & Tea Inc........D......805 898-3700
321 Motor Way Santa Barbara (93101) ***(P-2358)***

Santa Barbara Control Systems........F......805 683-8833
5375 Overpass Rd Santa Barbara (93111) ***(P-10721)***

Santa Barbara Convalescent Ctr, Santa Barbara *Also called California Convalescent Hosp* ***(P-20269)***

Santa Barbara Cottage........D......805 879-8900
5333 Hollister Ave # 250 Santa Barbara (93111) ***(P-20933)***

Santa Barbara Design Studio (PA)........**D......805 966-3883**
1600 Pacific Ave Oxnard (93033) ***(P-6006)***

Santa Barbara Family YMCA, Santa Barbara *Also called Channel Islnds Yung MNS Chrstn* ***(P-22328)***

Santa Barbara Farms LLC (PA)........**C......805 736-9776**
1200 Union Sugar Ave Lompoc (93436) ***(P-19)***

Santa Barbara Group, Santa Barbara *Also called Tecolote Research Inc* ***(P-23341)***

Santa Barbara Independent Inc........E......805 965-5205
12 E Figueroa St Santa Barbara (93101) ***(P-4026)***

Santa Barbara Indus Finshg, Goleta *Also called Sbif Inc* ***(P-7408)***

Santa Barbara Inn, Santa Barbara *Also called Interstate Hotels Resorts Inc* ***(P-16506)***

Santa Barbara Metro Trnst Dst (PA)........**C......805 963-3364**
550 Olive St Santa Barbara (93101) ***(P-11839)***

Santa Barbara Museum of Art (PA)........**D......805 963-4364**
1130 State St Santa Barbara (93101) ***(P-22234)***

Santa Barbara News-Press Info, Santa Barbara *Also called Ampersand Publishing LLC* ***(P-3944)***

Santa Barbara San Luis Obispo........C......800 421-2560
4050 Calle Real Santa Barbara (93110) ***(P-15383)***

Santa Barbara Service Center, Goleta *Also called Southern California Edison Co* ***(P-12845)***

Santa Barbara Surgical Ctr Inc........D......805 569-3226
3045 De La Vina St Santa Barbara (93105) ***(P-20056)***

Santa Barbara Trnsp Corp........C......661 510-0566
42138 7th St W Lancaster (93534) ***(P-11937)***

Santa Barbara Trnsp Corp........C......559 738-5780
1131 E Houston Ave Visalia (93292) ***(P-11938)***

Santa Barbara Trnsp Corp (HQ)........**D......805 681-8355**
6414 Hollister Ave Goleta (93117) ***(P-11939)***

Santa Barbara Trnsp Corp........C......805 928-0402
1331 Jason Way Santa Maria (93455) ***(P-11940)***

Santa Barbarba Roasting, Santa Barbara *Also called Santa Barbara Coffee & Tea Inc* ***(P-2358)***

Santa Brbara Cmnty College Dst........B......805 683-4191
525 Anacapa St Santa Barbara (93101) ***(P-16917)***

Santa Brbara Cttage Hosp Fndti (HQ)........**A......805 682-7111**
400 W Pueblo St Santa Barbara (93105) ***(P-20934)***

Santa Brbara Mseum Ntral Hstor........D......805 682-4711
2559 Puesta Del Sol Santa Barbara (93105) ***(P-22235)***

Santa Brbara V A Otptent Clnic, Santa Barbara *Also called Veterans Health Administration* ***(P-20148)***

Santa Brbara Zlgcal Foundation........C......805 962-1673
500 Ninos Dr Santa Barbara (93103) ***(P-22241)***

Santa Catalina Island Company (PA)........**C......310 510-2000**
4 Park Plz Ste 420 Irvine (92614) ***(P-12410)***

Santa Clarita Concrete........E......661 252-2012
16164 Sierra Hwy Santa Clarita (91390) ***(P-1548)***

Santa Clarita Plastic Molding........E......661 294-2257
24735 Avenue Rockefeller Valencia (91355) ***(P-5812)***

Santa Clarita Swim Club, Valencia *Also called Academy Swim Club* ***(P-19527)***

SANTA CLARITA VALLEY SENIOR CE, Santa Clarita *Also called Santa Clrita Vly Cmmttee On AG* ***(P-21886)***

Santa Clarita Valley Wtr Agcy........C......661 259-2737
26521 Summit Cir Santa Clarita (91350) ***(P-12918)***

Santa Clarita Water Division, Santa Clarita *Also called Santa Clarita Valley Wtr Agcy* ***(P-12918)***

Santa Clrita Hlth Care Assn In (PA)........**D......661 253-8000**
23845 Mcbean Pkwy Santa Clarita (91355) ***(P-23105)***

Santa Clrita Vly Cmmttee On AG........D......661 259-9444
22900 Market St Santa Clarita (91321) ***(P-21886)***

Santa Clrita Vly Wtr Agcy Fing........C......661 259-2737
27234 Bouquet Canyon Rd Santa Clarita (91350) ***(P-12919)***

Santa Fe Enterprises Inc........E......562 692-7596
11654 Pike St Santa Fe Springs (90670) ***(P-7830)***

Santa Fe Extruders Inc........F......562 921-8991
15315 Marquardt Ave Santa Fe Springs (90670) ***(P-5813)***

Santa Fe Footwear Corporation........F......562 941-9689
9988 Santa Fe Springs Rd Santa Fe Springs (90670) ***(P-5885)***

Santa Fe Machine Works Inc........E......909 350-6877
14578 Rancho Vista Dr Fontana (92335) ***(P-8786)***

Santa Fe Middle School, Hemet *Also called Hemet Unified School District* ***(P-22452)***

Santa Fe Rubber Products Inc........E......562 693-2776
12306 Washington Blvd Whittier (90606) ***(P-5409)***

Santa Fe Supply Company, Santa Fe Springs *Also called Philatron International* ***(P-9899)***

Santa Fe Textiles Inc........F......949 251-1960
17370 Mount Herrmann St Fountain Valley (92708) ***(P-2618)***

Santa Margarita Water District (PA)........**D......949 459-6400**
26111 Antonio Pkwy Rcho STA Marg (92688) ***(P-12920)***

Santa Maria Cinema 10, Santa Maria *Also called Edwards Theatres Circuit Inc* ***(P-19279)***

Santa Maria Enrgy Holdings LLC........E......805 938-3320
2811 Airpark Dr Santa Maria (93455) ***(P-464)***

Santa Maria Hotel Corp........D......805 928-6000
2100 N Broadway Santa Maria (93454) ***(P-16690)***

Santa Maria Public Airport Dst........D......805 922-1726
3217 Terminal Dr Santa Maria (93455) ***(P-12368)***

Santa Maria Tire Inc (PA)........**D......805 347-4793**
2170 Hutton Rd Bldg A Nipomo (93444) ***(P-18810)***

Santa Maria Wisdom Center, Santa Maria *Also called Life Steps Foundation Inc* ***(P-21838)***

Santa Mnica Wlshire Imging LLC........E......323 549-3055
5455 Wilshire Blvd # 112 Los Angeles (90036) ***(P-20057)***

Santa Monica City of........D......310 451-5444
1334 5th St Santa Monica (90401) ***(P-11904)***

Santa Monica Amusements LLC........B......310 451-9641
380 Santa Monica Pier Santa Monica (90401) ***(P-19524)***

Santa Monica Bay Physcians........D......310 459-2363
881 Alma Real Dr Ste 214 Pacific Palisades (90272) ***(P-20058)***

Santa Monica Bay Physicians He (PA)........**D......310 417-5900**
5767 W Century Blvd Los Angeles (90045) ***(P-20059)***

Santa Monica City of........E......310 826-6712
1228 S Bundy Dr Los Angeles (90025) ***(P-8411)***

Santa Monica Daily Press, Santa Monica *Also called Newlon Rouge LLC* ***(P-4013)***

Santa Monica Days Inn........D......310 829-6333
3007 Santa Monica Blvd Santa Monica (90404) ***(P-16691)***

Santa Monica Family YMCA........D......310 451-7387
1332 6th St Santa Monica (90401) ***(P-22365)***

Santa Monica Hotel Owner LLC........C......310 395-3332
1707 4th St Santa Monica (90401) ***(P-16692)***

Santa Monica Millworks........E......805 643-0010
2568 Channel Dr Ste C Ventura (93003) ***(P-3335)***

Santa Monica Orthopedic (PA)........**D......310 315-2018**
2020 Santa Monica Blvd # 230 Santa Monica (90404) ***(P-20060)***

Santa Monica Pet Med Ctr Inc........D......310 393-8218
1534 14th St Santa Monica (90404) ***(P-202)***

Santa Monica Plastics Llc........F......310 403-2849
1602 Stanford St Santa Monica (90404) ***(P-5814)***

Santa Monica Propeller Svc Inc........F......310 390-6233
3135 Dnald Douglas Loop S Santa Monica (90405) ***(P-10413)***

Santa Monica Proper Hotel, Santa Monica *Also called Santa Monica Proper Jv LLC* ***(P-16693)***

Santa Monica Proper Jv LLC........C......310 620-9990
700 Wilshire Blvd Santa Monica (90401) ***(P-16693)***

Santa Monica Seafood Company (PA)........**D......310 886-7900**
18531 S Broadwick St Rancho Dominguez (90220) ***(P-2349)***

ALPHABETIC

Employee Codes: A=Over 500 employees, B=251-500
C=101-250, D=51-100, E=20-50 F=10-19

2022 Southern California Business
Directory and Buyers Guide

© Mergent Inc. 1-800-342-5647
1263

Santa Monica Ucla Medical Ctr, Santa Monica *Also called Regents of The University Cal* ***(P-21475)***
Santa Mrgrita Cthlic High Schl, Rcho STA Marg *Also called Roman Cthlic Diocese of Orange* ***(P-4107)***
Santa Mria Vly Yung MNS Chrstn.......C.......805 937-8521
3400 Skyway Dr Santa Maria (93455) ***(P-22366)***
Santa Paula Hospital, Santa Paula *Also called Ventura County Medical Center* ***(P-20135)***
Santa Paula Memorial Hospital.......D.......805 933-9131
845 N 10th St Ste 3 Santa Paula (93060) ***(P-20935)***
Santa Rosa Berry Farms LLC.......B.......805 981-3060
3500 Camino Ave Ste 250 Oxnard (93030) ***(P-37)***
Santa Teresita Inc (PA).......**B.......626 359-3243**
819 Buena Vista St Duarte (91010) ***(P-20936)***
Santa Ynez Valley Marriott, Buellton *Also called Kang Family Partners LLC* ***(P-16520)***
Santa Ynez Vineyards, Santa Barbara *Also called Lafond Vineyard Inc* ***(P-2201)***
Santa Ynez Vly Cttage Hosp Inc.......D.......805 688-6431
2050 Viborg Rd Solvang (93463) ***(P-20937)***
Santana Formal Accessories Inc.......F.......818 898-3677
707 Arroyo St Ste B San Fernando (91340) ***(P-2750)***
Santec Inc.......E.......310 542-0063
3501 Challenger St Fl 2 Torrance (90503) ***(P-6566)***
Santee Systems Services II LL.......E.......323 445-0044
229 E Gage Ave Los Angeles (90003) ***(P-19467)***
Santos Precision Inc.......E.......714 957-0299
2220 S Anne St Santa Ana (92704) ***(P-8787)***
Santoshi Corporation.......E.......626 444-7118
2439 Seaman Ave El Monte (91733) ***(P-7310)***
Sanwa Jutaku Co Ltd.......D.......562 861-1900
8425 Firestone Blvd Downey (90241) ***(P-16694)***
Sanyo Denki America Inc (HQ).......**D.......310 783-5400**
468 Amapola Ave Torrance (90501) ***(P-13435)***
Sanyo Foods Corp America (HQ).......**E.......714 891-3671**
11955 Monarch St Garden Grove (92841) ***(P-2383)***
Sapa Extrusions Inc.......C.......909 947-7682
2821 E Philadelphia St A Ontario (91761) ***(P-6317)***
Sapphire Chandelier LLC.......D.......714 879-3660
505 Porter Way Placentia (92870) ***(P-9102)***
Sapphire Clean Rooms LLC (PA).......**C.......714 316-5036**
505 Porter Way Placentia (92870) ***(P-13540)***
Sapphire Manufacturing Inc.......E.......714 401-3117
505 Porter Way Placentia (92870) ***(P-6979)***
Sapphire Softech Solutions LLC.......D.......888 357-5222
123 E 9th St Ste 323 Upland (91786) ***(P-18220)***
Saputo Cheese USA Inc.......B.......559 687-8411
800 E Paige Ave Tulare (93274) ***(P-1780)***
SARA, Cypress *Also called Scientfic Applctons RES Assoc* ***(P-22862)***
Sarah Elizabeth Treusdell.......E.......661 949-0131
921 W Avenue J Ste C Lancaster (93534) ***(P-21338)***
Saratech, Mission Viejo *Also called Paydarfar Industries Inc* ***(P-13424)***
Sarco Inc.......E.......949 888-5548
30412 Esperanza Rcho STA Marg (92688) ***(P-13772)***
Sardo Bus & Coach Upholstery, Gardena *Also called Louis Sardo Upholstery Inc* ***(P-3625)***
Saritasa LLC (PA).......**D.......949 200-6839**
20411 Sw Birch St Ste 330 Newport Beach (92660) ***(P-18108)***
Saroyan Lumber and Moulding Co, Huntington Park *Also called Saroyan Lumber Company Inc* ***(P-13286)***
Saroyan Lumber Company Inc (PA).......**D.......800 624-9309**
6230 S Alameda St Huntington Park (90255) ***(P-13286)***
SARR Industries Inc.......E.......818 998-7735
8975 Fullbright Ave Chatsworth (91311) ***(P-8788)***
Sarris Interiors, Paramount *Also called Sibyl Shepard Inc* ***(P-3119)***
Sas Entertainment Partners Inc.......E.......213 400-1901
6224 Greenleaf Ave Whittier (90601) ***(P-19377)***
Sas Manufacturing Inc.......E.......951 734-1808
405 N Smith Ave Corona (92878) ***(P-9778)***
Sas Safety Corporation.......D.......562 427-2775
3031 Gardenia Ave Long Beach (90807) ***(P-11139)***
Sas Textiles Inc.......D.......323 277-5555
3100 E 44th St Vernon (90058) ***(P-2654)***
Satco Inc (PA).......**C.......310 322-4719**
1601 E El Segundo Blvd El Segundo (90245) ***(P-3408)***
Satellite Management Co (PA).......**C.......714 558-2411**
1010 E Chestnut Ave Santa Ana (92701) ***(P-15994)***
Satellite Pros, Ontario *Also called Jeeva Corp* ***(P-1269)***
Sather Installation, Murrieta *Also called Sl Inc* ***(P-1455)***
Saticoy Country Club.......D.......805 647-1153
4450 Clubhouse Dr Somis (93066) ***(P-19610)***
Saticoy Fruit Exchange, Santa Paula *Also called Saticoy Lemon Association* ***(P-185)***
Saticoy Fruit Exchange, Ventura *Also called Saticoy Lemon Association* ***(P-65)***
Saticoy Lemon Association (PA).......**D.......805 654-6500**
103 N Peck Rd Santa Paula (93060) ***(P-185)***
Saticoy Lemon Association.......D.......805 654-6500
7560 Bristol Rd Ventura (93003) ***(P-65)***
Saticoy Lemon Association.......C.......805 654-6543
600 E 3rd St Oxnard (93030) ***(P-22257)***
Satterfield Aerospace, Northridge *Also called S & S Numerical Control Inc* ***(P-8782)***
Saturn Fasteners Inc.......C.......818 973-1807
425 S Varney St Burbank (91502) ***(P-6535)***
Sauer Brands Inc.......D.......805 597-8900
184 Suburban Rd San Luis Obispo (93401) ***(P-2522)***
Savage Services Corporation.......D.......562 400-2044
8636 Sorensen Ave Santa Fe Springs (90670) ***(P-11992)***
Savala Equipment Company Inc (PA).......**D.......949 552-1859**
16402 Construction Cir E Irvine (92606) ***(P-17319)***
Savala Equipment Rentals, Irvine *Also called Savala Equipment Company Inc* ***(P-17319)***
Savant Construction Inc.......D.......909 614-4300
13830 Mountain Ave Chino (91710) ***(P-821)***
Save Queen LLC.......D.......562 435-3511
429 Shoreline Village Dr I Long Beach (90802) ***(P-16695)***
Savedailycom Inc (HQ).......**D.......562 795-7500**
1503 S Coast Dr Ste 330 Costa Mesa (92626) ***(P-18063)***
Savice Inc.......D.......949 888-2444
30052 Tomas Rcho STA Marg (92688) ***(P-22367)***
Savin & Bursk Law Offices of.......D.......818 368-8646
10663 Yarmouth Ave Granada Hills (91344) ***(P-21673)***
Saviynt Inc (PA).......**C.......310 641-1664**
1301 E El Segundo Blvd El Segundo (90245) ***(P-23316)***
Sawpa, Riverside *Also called Santa Ana Watershed Prj Auth* ***(P-12917)***
Sawtelle & Rosprim Machine Sp, Corcoran *Also called Corcoran Sawtelle Rosprim Inc* ***(P-6607)***
Say It With A Sock LLC.......F.......800 208-0879
11111 Santa Monica Blvd Los Angeles (90025) ***(P-2622)***
Say It With A Sock LLC (PA).......**E.......424 284-8416**
10200 Venice Blvd Ste 108 Culver City (90232) ***(P-2623)***
Sayari Shahrzad.......E.......310 903-6368
4822 Aqueduct Ave Encino (91436) ***(P-14349)***
Saydel Inc (PA).......**F.......323 585-2800**
2475 E Slauson Ave Huntington Park (90255) ***(P-5066)***
Sazerac Company Inc.......F.......310 604-8717
2202 E Del Amo Blvd Carson (90749) ***(P-2245)***
Sb Waterman Holdings Inc (PA).......**C.......909 883-8611**
1700 N Waterman Ave San Bernardino (92404) ***(P-20061)***
Sbb Roofing Inc (PA).......**C.......323 254-2888**
3310 Verdugo Rd Los Angeles (90065) ***(P-1505)***
SBE Contracting.......E.......714 544-5066
17256 Red Hill Ave Irvine (92614) ***(P-1313)***
SBE Electrical Contracting Inc.......C.......714 544-5066
2817 Mcgaw Ave Irvine (92614) ***(P-1314)***
SBE Entertainment Group LLC (HQ).......**D.......323 655-8000**
2535 Las Vegas Blvd S Los Angeles (90036) ***(P-16696)***
SBE Hotel Group LLC.......D.......323 655-8000
8000 Beverly Blvd Los Angeles (90048) ***(P-16697)***
Sbif Inc.......E.......805 683-1711
873 S Kellogg Ave Goleta (93117) ***(P-7408)***
Sbnw LLC (PA).......**C.......213 234-5122**
320 W 31st St Los Angeles (90007) ***(P-5903)***
SC Beverage Inc.......F.......562 463-8918
2300 Peck Rd City of Industry (90601) ***(P-7951)***
SC Fuels, Orange *Also called Southern Counties Oil Co* ***(P-14797)***
Sca Enterprises Inc (PA).......**D.......818 845-7621**
3817 W Magnolia Blvd Burbank (91505) ***(P-18661)***
Scaled Composites LLC.......B.......661 824-4541
1624 Flight Line Mojave (93501) ***(P-10202)***
Scales, Covina *Also called American Scale Co Inc* ***(P-13375)***
Scalzo Hospitality Inc.......D.......714 772-3691
1570 S Harbor Blvd Anaheim (92802) ***(P-16698)***
Scan Group (PA).......**B.......562 308-2733**
3800 Kilroy Arprt Way Long Beach (90806) ***(P-15451)***
Scan Health Plan, Long Beach *Also called Senior Care* ***(P-15452)***
Scarborough Farms Inc.......C.......805 483-9113
731 Pacific Ave Oxnard (93030) ***(P-118)***
Scarrott Metallurgical Co, Los Angeles *Also called Interntonal Metallurgical Svcs* ***(P-6441)***
Scat Enterprises Inc.......D.......310 370-5501
1400 Kingsdale Ave Redondo Beach (90278) ***(P-13087)***
Scattergood Generation Plant, Playa Del Rey *Also called Los Angeles Dept Wtr & Pwr* ***(P-12878)***
Scb Distributors, Gardena *Also called A B P Inc* ***(P-14907)***
Scb Division, Bell Gardens *Also called Cal Southern Braiding Inc* ***(P-9687)***
Scb Division of Dcx-Chol, Bell *Also called Dcx-Chol Enterprises Inc* ***(P-9700)***
Scci, Orcutt *Also called Spiess Construction Co Inc* ***(P-973)***
Scdrg Inc.......D.......818 874-0830
473 S Carnegie Dr San Bernardino (92408) ***(P-17055)***
SCE, Rosemead *Also called Southern California Edison Co* ***(P-12827)***
SCE FCU, Baldwin Park *Also called SCE Federal Credit Union* ***(P-15080)***
SCE Federal Credit Union (PA).......**D.......626 960-6888**
12701 Schabarum Ave Baldwin Park (91706) ***(P-15080)***
Scenario Cockram USA Inc (HQ).......**C.......818 650-0999**
605 8th St San Fernando (91340) ***(P-1687)***
Scenewise Inc.......F.......310 466-7692
2201 Park Pl Ste 100 El Segundo (90245) ***(P-9838)***
Scenic Express Inc.......E.......323 254-4351
9380 San Fernando Rd Sun Valley (91352) ***(P-1688)***
Scenic Route Inc.......E.......818 896-6006
13516 Desmond St Pacoima (91331) ***(P-1689)***
Sceptre Inc.......E.......626 369-3698
16800 Gale Ave City of Industry (91745) ***(P-9779)***
Schachtel Corporation (PA).......**F.......818 597-1222**
5236 Colodny Dr Ste 200 Agoura Hills (91301) ***(P-4419)***
Schaeffler Group USA Inc.......C.......949 234-9799
34700 Pcf Cast Hwy Ste 20 Capistrano Beach (92624) ***(P-8030)***
Schafer Bros Trnsf Pano Mvers (PA).......**D.......310 835-7231**
1981 E 213th St Carson (90810) ***(P-12241)***
Schafer Logistics, Carson *Also called Schafer Bros Trnsf Pano Mvers* ***(P-12241)***
Schaffer Laboratories Inc.......F.......714 202-1594
8441 Monroe Ave Stanton (90680) ***(P-5462)***
Schamas Mfg Coinc.......F.......626 334-6870
6356 N Irwindale Ave Irwindale (91702) ***(P-7649)***
Schaumbond Group Inc (PA).......**B.......626 215-4998**
225 S Lake Ave Ste 300 Pasadena (91101) ***(P-16163)***
Schecter Guitar Research Inc.......E.......818 767-1029
10953 Pendleton St Sun Valley (91352) ***(P-11353)***
Schellinger Spring Inc.......E.......909 373-0799
8477 Utica Ave Rancho Cucamonga (91730) ***(P-7467)***
Scherzer International Corp (PA).......**D.......818 227-2770**
21650 Oxnard St Ste 300 Woodland Hills (91367) ***(P-18662)***

Mergent e-mail: customerrelations@mergent.com
1264
2022 Southern California Business Directory and Buyers Guide
(P-0000) Products & Services Section entry number
(PA)=Parent Co (HQ)=Headquarters (DH)=Div Headquarters

Scheu Manufacturing Co (PA).......F.......909 982-8933
297 Stowell St Upland (91786) *(P-6575)*
Schick Moving & Storage Co (PA).......D.......**714 731-5500**
2721 Michelle Dr Tustin (92780) *(P-12118)*
Schindler Elevator Corporation.......C.......818 336-3000
16450 Fthill Blvd Ste 200 Sylmar (91342) *(P-19063)*
Schlumberger Technology Corp.......D.......661 864-4750
2841 Pegasus Dr Bakersfield (93308) *(P-545)*
Schlumberger Well Services, Bakersfield *Also called Schlumberger Technology Corp (P-545)*
Schmidt Industries Inc.......F.......323 344-6400
91 Sequoia Dr Pasadena (91105) *(P-11747)*
Schmidt Industries Inc.......D.......818 768-9100
11321 Goss St Sun Valley (91352) *(P-7311)*
Schmitt House, El Monte *Also called Hope Hse For Mltple Hndcpped I (P-22115)*
Schn, Glendale *Also called Adventist Hlth Systm/West Corp (P-20661)*
Schneider Elc Buildings LLC.......C.......310 900-2385
100 W Victoria St Long Beach (90805) *(P-9910)*
Schneider Electric.......F.......949 713-9200
1660 Scenic Ave Costa Mesa (92626) *(P-9911)*
Schneider Electric Usa Inc.......D.......909 438-2295
14725 Monte Vista Ave Chino (91710) *(P-12242)*
Schneiders Manufacturing Inc.......E.......818 771-0082
11122 Penrose St Sun Valley (91352) *(P-8789)*
Schnierow Dental Care.......D.......310 377-6453
13450 Hawthorne Blvd Hawthorne (90250) *(P-20198)*
Scholls, Ontario *Also called Distribution Alternatives Inc (P-12199)*
Schoolsfirst Federal Credit Un.......D.......800 462-8328
5305 Alton Pkwy Irvine (92604) *(P-15081)*
Schoolsfirst Federal Credit Un.......D.......800 462-8328
161 E 40th St San Bernardino (92404) *(P-15082)*
Schoolsfirst Federal Credit Un.......D.......800 462-8328
12831 Moreno Beach Dr Moreno Valley (92555) *(P-15083)*
Schoolsfirst Federal Credit Un.......D.......800 462-8328
26892 La Paz Rd Aliso Viejo (92656) *(P-15084)*
Schoolsfirst Federal Credit Un (PA).......B.......**714 258-4000**
2115 N Broadway Santa Ana (92706) *(P-15085)*
Schoolsfirst Federal Credit Un.......D.......714 258-4000
9125 Imperial Hwy Ste A Downey (90242) *(P-15086)*
Schoolsfirst Federal Credit Un.......D.......480 777-5995
15442 Del Amo Ave Tustin (92780) *(P-15087)*
Schrader-Bridgeport Intl Inc.......C.......909 930-2475
2018 E Cedar St Ontario (91761) *(P-19064)*
Schreiber Foods Inc.......E.......714 490-7360
1901 Via Burton Fullerton (92831) *(P-1781)*
Schrey & Sons Mold Co Inc.......E.......661 294-2260
24735 Avenue Rockefeller Valencia (91355) *(P-7831)*
Schrillo Company LLC.......E.......818 894-8241
16750 Schoenborn St North Hills (91343) *(P-7074)*
Schroeder Iron Corporation.......E.......909 428-6471
8417 Beech Ave Fontana (92335) *(P-6661)*
Schulz Engineering, Sylmar *Also called Dg Engineering Corp (P-10583)*
Schulz Industries, Paramount *Also called Schulz Leather Company Inc (P-3145)*
Schulz Leather Company Inc.......F.......562 633-1081
16247 Minnesota Ave Paramount (90723) *(P-3145)*
Schumacher Cargo Logistics Inc (PA).......E.......**562 408-6677**
550 W 135th St Gardena (90248) *(P-12523)*
Schurman Fine Papers.......C.......951 653-1934
22500 Town Cir Moreno Valley (92553) *(P-4605)*
Schwarzkopf Inc (HQ).......E.......**310 641-0990**
600 Corporate Pointe # 1100 Culver City (90230) *(P-11748)*
SCI, North Hollywood *Also called Pierce Brothers (P-16925)*
SCI, Santa Ana *Also called Semiconductor Components Inc (P-9570)*
SCI, Pomona *Also called Structural Composites Inds LLC (P-6756)*
Sci Inc.......D.......951 245-7511
18501 Collier Ave B106 Lake Elsinore (92530) *(P-1549)*
SCI Western Region Inc.......D.......818 286-0640
10621 Victory Blvd North Hollywood (91606) *(P-16928)*
SCI-Tech Glassblowing Inc.......F.......805 523-9790
5555 Tech Cir Moorpark (93021) *(P-5941)*
Scico, Irvine *Also called Santa Catalina Island Company (P-12410)*
Scicon Technologies Corp (PA).......E.......**661 295-8630**
27525 Nwhll Rnch Rd Ste 2 Valencia (91355) *(P-22652)*
Science 37 Holdings Inc (PA).......A.......**984 377-3737**
600 Crprate Pinte Ste 320 Culver City (90230) *(P-22861)*
Science of Skincare LLC.......D.......818 254-7961
3333 N San Fernando Blvd Burbank (91504) *(P-14287)*
Scientfic Applctons RES Assoc (PA).......D.......**714 224-4410**
6300 Gateway Dr Cypress (90630) *(P-22862)*
Scientific Cutting Tools Inc.......E.......805 584-9495
220 W Los Angeles Ave Simi Valley (93065) *(P-7867)*
Scientific Spray Finishes Inc.......E.......714 871-5541
315 S Richman Ave Fullerton (92832) *(P-7409)*
Scientific Surface Inds Inc.......F.......805 499-5100
855 Rancho Conejo Blvd Newbury Park (91320) *(P-3663)*
Scisorek & Son Flavors Inc.......E.......714 524-0550
2951 Enterprise St Brea (92821) *(P-2336)*
SCLARC, Los Angeles *Also called South Cntl Los Angles Rgnal CT (P-22210)*
Scodan Systems Inc.......F.......626 444-1020
12373 Barringer St South El Monte (91733) *(P-7098)*
Scope City (PA).......E.......**805 522-6646**
2978 Topaz Ave Simi Valley (93063) *(P-10859)*
Scope Packaging Inc.......D.......714 998-4411
13400 Nelson Ave City of Industry (91746) *(P-3826)*
Scopely Inc (PA).......C.......**323 400-6618**
3530 Hayden Ave Ste A Culver City (90232) *(P-17977)*
Score Sports, Wilmington *Also called American Soccer Company Inc (P-2797)*
Scoreusa Institute.......D.......714 909-0688
528 19th St Huntington Beach (92648) *(P-22920)*

Scorpio Enterprises.......D.......562 946-9464
12556 Mccann Dr Santa Fe Springs (90670) *(P-1134)*
Scorpion Design LLC.......A.......661 702-0100
27750 Entertainment Dr Valencia (91355) *(P-23317)*
Scosche Industries Inc.......C.......805 486-4450
1550 Pacific Ave Oxnard (93033) *(P-9194)*
Scott Craft Co, Cudahy *Also called Merry An Cejka (P-8690)*
Scott Engineering Inc.......E.......909 594-9637
5051 Edison Ave Chino (91710) *(P-8982)*
Scott's Pavillon, Pasadena *Also called Pasadena Senior Center (P-21863)*
Scottel Voice & Data Inc.......C.......310 737-7300
6100 Center Dr Ste 720 Los Angeles (90045) *(P-18956)*
Scottex Inc.......E.......310 516-1411
12828 S Broadway Los Angeles (90061) *(P-3200)*
Scottish American Insurance (PA).......D.......**714 550-5050**
2002 E Mcfadden Ave # 100 Santa Ana (92705) *(P-15625)*
Scotts Temecula Operations LLC (HQ).......C.......**951 719-1700**
42375 Remington Ave Temecula (92590) *(P-7630)*
Scotts- Hyponex, Jurupa Valley *Also called Hyponex Corporation (P-5156)*
Scpe, Walnut *Also called Cal Southern Packg Eqp Inc (P-13894)*
SCR Molding Inc.......E.......951 736-5490
2340 Pomona Rd Corona (92878) *(P-5815)*
Scratch Financial Inc.......D.......855 727-2395
225 S Lake Ave Ste 250 Pasadena (91101) *(P-18663)*
Scratchpay, Pasadena *Also called Scratch Financial Inc (P-18663)*
Screamline Investment Corp.......C.......323 201-0114
2130 S Tubeway Ave Commerce (90040) *(P-12411)*
Screen Actors Guild - American.......C.......818 954-9400
3601 W Olive Ave Fl 2 Burbank (91505) *(P-15519)*
Screen Actors Guild-Producers, Burbank *Also called Screen Actors Guild - American (P-15519)*
Screen Art Inc.......F.......714 891-4185
15162 Triton Ln Huntington Beach (92649) *(P-4571)*
Screen Gems Inc.......D.......310 244-4000
10202 Washington Blvd Culver City (90232) *(P-19175)*
Screen Printers Resource Inc.......F.......714 441-1155
1251 Burton St Fullerton (92831) *(P-4572)*
Screening Systems Inc (PA).......E.......**949 855-1751**
36 Blackbird Ln Aliso Viejo (92656) *(P-10810)*
Screw Conveyor Pacific Corp.......C.......559 651-2131
7807 W Doe Ave Visalia (93291) *(P-7693)*
Screwmatic Inc.......D.......626 334-7831
925 W 1st St Azusa (91702) *(P-8790)*
Scribble Press Inc.......E.......212 288-2928
1109 Montana Ave Santa Monica (90403) *(P-4202)*
Scribeamerica LLC.......C.......877 819-5900
840 Apollo St Ste 231 El Segundo (90245) *(P-21478)*
Scribemd LLC.......D.......714 543-8911
1310 W Stewart Dr Ste 212 Orange (92868) *(P-20062)*
Scripla LLC.......F.......818 925-1460
11134 Sepulveda Blvd Mission Hills (91345) *(P-17978)*
Scripto, Ontario *Also called Calico Brands Inc (P-14918)*
Scripto-Tokai Corporation (HQ).......D.......**909 930-5000**
2055 S Haven Ave Ontario (91761) *(P-11749)*
Scully Leather Wear, Oxnard *Also called Scully Sportswear Inc (P-3060)*
Scully Sportswear Inc.......D.......805 483-6339
1701 Pacific Ave Oxnard (93033) *(P-3060)*
Sculptor Body Molding (PA).......E.......**818 761-3767**
10817 W Stallion Ranch Rd Sunland (91040) *(P-5816)*
Scv Facilities Services Inc.......D.......310 803-4588
1907 W 75th St Los Angeles (90047) *(P-17282)*
SDC Technologies Inc (HQ).......E.......**714 939-8300**
45 Parker Ste 100 Irvine (92618) *(P-5111)*
Sdg Enterprises.......D.......805 777-7978
822 Hampshire Rd Ste H Westlake Village (91361) *(P-1135)*
Sdi, Simi Valley *Also called Special Devices Incorporated (P-10135)*
Sdi LLC.......F.......949 583-1001
21 Morgan Ste 150 Irvine (92618) *(P-13773)*
Sdi LLC.......E.......949 351-1866
21 Morgan Ste 150 Irvine (92618) *(P-8791)*
Sdi Industries Inc (PA).......C.......**818 890-6002**
13000 Pierce St Pacoima (91331) *(P-7694)*
SDI Media USA Inc (HQ).......A.......**310 388-8800**
6060 Center Dr Ste 100 Los Angeles (90045) *(P-19176)*
Sdl, Los Angeles *Also called Language Weaver Inc (P-17652)*
Sdmv Hotel Partners LP.......D.......949 516-0088
520 Newport Center Dr # 2 Newport Beach (92660) *(P-15695)*
SE Acqstion Lncaster Cal Inc (HQ).......D.......**661 942-1139**
44831 Cedar Ave Lancaster (93534) *(P-16929)*
SE Industries Inc.......F.......714 744-3200
300 W Collins Ave Orange (92867) *(P-3336)*
SE Software Inc.......F.......888 504-9876
3340 Ocean Park Blvd # 1005 Santa Monica (90405) *(P-17979)*
Se-Gl Products Inc.......E.......951 737-8320
20521 Teresita Way Lake Forest (92630) *(P-6907)*
Sea Breeze Collision, Tustin *Also called Sterling Collision LLC (P-18805)*
Sea Breeze Financial Svcs Inc.......C.......949 223-9700
18191 Von Karman Ave # 1 Irvine (92612) *(P-15231)*
Sea Breeze Health Care Inc.......C.......714 847-9671
7781 Garfield Ave Huntington Beach (92648) *(P-20460)*
Sea Breeze Mortgage Services, Irvine *Also called Sea Breeze Financial Svcs Inc (P-15231)*
Sea Cliffs Restaurant & Lounge, Pismo Beach *Also called Cliffs Resort LLC (P-16949)*
Sea Critters, Culver City *Also called Ecoly International Inc (P-5017)*
Sea Dwelling Creatures Inc.......D.......310 676-9697
5515 W 104th St Los Angeles (90045) *(P-14974)*
Sea Electric LLC.......E.......424 376-3660
436 Alaska Ave Torrance (90503) *(P-8929)*
Sea Magazine, Fountain Valley *Also called Duncan McIntosh Company Inc (P-4067)*

Employee Codes: A=Over 500 employees, B=251-500
C=101-250, D=51-100, E=20-50 F=10-19
2022 Southern California Business
Directory and Buyers Guide
© Mergent Inc. 1-800-342-5647
1265

ALPHABETIC

Sea Pac Engineering Inc ... D ... 213 487-6130
625 S Nh Ave Fl 2 Flr 2 Los Angeles (90005) *(P-822)*

Sea Shield Marine Products ... E ... 909 594-2507
20832 Currier Rd Walnut (91789) *(P-6371)*

Sea Snack Foods Inc (PA) ... E ... 213 622-2204
914 E 11th St Los Angeles (90021) *(P-14582)*

Sea Win Inc ... E ... 213 688-2899
526 Stanford Ave Los Angeles (90013) *(P-14583)*

Sea/Sue Inc (HQ) ... C ... 805 526-1919
195 W Los Angeles Ave Simi Valley (93065) *(P-12978)*

Seabiscuit Motorsports Inc ... E ... 714 898-9763
10800 Valley View St Cypress (90630) *(P-8437)*

Seaboard Envelope Co Inc ... E ... 626 960-4559
15601 Cypress Ave Irwindale (91706) *(P-3911)*

Seaborn Canvas ... E ... 310 519-1208
435 N Harbor Blvd Ste B1 San Pedro (90731) *(P-3201)*

Seabreeze Management Co Inc (PA) ... D ... 949 855-1800
26840 Aliso Viejo Pkwy Aliso Viejo (92656) *(P-23106)*

Seachrome Corporation ... C ... 310 427-8010
1906 E Dominguez St Long Beach (90810) *(P-6549)*

Seacrest Beach Resort, Pismo Beach *Also called Seacrest Oceanfront Hotel (P-16699)*

Seacrest Convalescent Hosp Inc ... D ... 310 833-3526
1416 W 6th St San Pedro (90732) *(P-20461)*

Seacrest Oceanfront Hotel ... D ... 805 773-4608
2241 Price St Pismo Beach (93449) *(P-16699)*

Seafood Ranch Grill Inc ... D ... 909 590-7232
2120 Grand Ave Ste A Chino Hills (91709) *(P-146)*

Seagra Technology Inc (PA) ... E ... 949 419-6796
14252 Culver Dr Irvine (92604) *(P-8300)*

Seal & Packing Supply, Bakersfield *Also called Shar-Craft Inc (P-14017)*

Seal Beach Family Med Group, Seal Beach *Also called Turner John McDonald MD (P-20114)*

Seal Methods Inc (PA) ... D ... 562 944-0291
11915 Shoemaker Ave Santa Fe Springs (90670) *(P-3874)*

Seal Science Inc (HQ) ... D ... 949 253-3130
17131 Daimler St Irvine (92614) *(P-5351)*

Sealing Corporation ... F ... 818 765-7327
7353 Greenbush Ave B North Hollywood (91605) *(P-5352)*

Sealtight Technology, Santa Barbara *Also called B&B Hardware Inc (P-7056)*

Seaman Products of California ... F ... 818 768-4881
12329 Gladstone Ave Sylmar (91342) *(P-10414)*

Search Agency Inc (HQ) ... D ... 310 873-5700
801 N Brand Blvd Ste 1020 Glendale (91203) *(P-23318)*

Search Associates Inc ... D ... 818 988-5600
5900 Sepulveda Blvd # 104 Van Nuys (91411) *(P-17463)*

Search123 ... D ... 818 575-4600
30699 Russell Ranch Rd # 2 Westlake Village (91362) *(P-12668)*

Searing Industries Inc ... C ... 909 948-3030
8901 Arrow Rte Rancho Cucamonga (91730) *(P-6211)*

Searles Valley Minerals Inc ... E ... 760 372-2259
80201 Trona Rd Trona (93562) *(P-580)*

Searles Valley Minerals Inc ... E ... 760 672-2053
13068 Main St Trona (93562) *(P-581)*

Sears, Ontario *Also called Innovel Solutions Inc (P-12472)*

Sears Roebuck and Co ... C ... 714 256-7328
100 Brea Mall Brea (92821) *(P-19065)*

Sears Roebuck and Co ... C ... 909 390-4210
5691 E Philadelphia St Ontario (91761) *(P-19066)*

Sears Roebuck and Co ... C ... 805 569-6700
3845 State St Santa Barbara (93105) *(P-19067)*

Sears Home Imprv Pdts Inc ... C ... 626 671-1892
730 S Orange Ave West Covina (91790) *(P-636)*

Sears Home Imprv Pdts Inc ... C ... 562 485-4904
2900 N Bellflower Blvd Long Beach (90815) *(P-637)*

Sears Home Imprv Pdts Inc ... C ... 626 988-9134
5665 Rosemead Blvd Temple City (91780) *(P-638)*

Season Produce Co Inc ... B ... 213 689-0008
1601 E Olympic Blvd # 315 Los Angeles (90021) *(P-14652)*

Seasonic Electronics Inc ... F ... 626 969-9966
301 Aerojet Ave Azusa (91702) *(P-9780)*

Seatech Consulting Group Inc ... E ... 310 356-6828
609 Deep Valley Dr # 200 Rllng HLS Est (90274) *(P-18221)*

Seating Component Mfg Inc ... F ... 714 693-3376
3951 E Miraloma Ave Anaheim (92806) *(P-3572)*

Seattle Arprt Hospitality LLC ... D ... 310 476-6411
170 N Church Ln Los Angeles (90049) *(P-16700)*

Seattle Tnnel Prtners A Jint V ... B ... 206 971-8701
555 Anton Blvd Ste 1000 Costa Mesa (92626) *(P-639)*

Seaworld Global Logistics ... B ... 310 579-9164
9350 Wilshire Blvd # 203 Beverly Hills (90212) *(P-12524)*

Seb, Chino *Also called Specilty Enzymes Btechnologies (P-5148)*

SEC, Moorpark *Also called Semiconductor Equipment Corp (P-9571)*

Sechrist Industries Inc ... D ... 714 579-8400
4225 E La Palma Ave Anaheim (92807) *(P-11054)*

Seco Industries, Commerce *Also called Specialty Enterprises Co (P-5522)*

Secom International (PA) ... D ... 310 641-1290
15905 S Broadway Gardena (90248) *(P-18064)*

Second Generation Inc ... D ... 213 743-8700
1950 Naomi Ave Los Angeles (90011) *(P-2992)*

Second Hrvest Fd Bnk Ornge CNT ... D ... 949 653-2900
8014 Marine Way Irvine (92618) *(P-21887)*

Second Image National LLC (PA) ... C ... 800 229-7477
170 E Arrow Hwy San Dimas (91773) *(P-17154)*

Second Sight Medical Pdts Inc ... C ... 818 833-5000
13170 Telfair Ave Sylmar (91342) *(P-11055)*

Second Spectrum Inc ... D ... 213 995-6860
312 E 1st St Los Angeles (90012) *(P-17706)*

Second Street Corporation ... C ... 310 394-5454
1111 2nd St Santa Monica (90403) *(P-16701)*

Secrom Inc ... D ... 310 830-4010
345 E Carson St Carson (90745) *(P-20626)*

Sectran Armored Truck Service, Pico Rivera *Also called Sectran Security Incorporated (P-18321)*

Sectran Security Incorporated (PA) ... C ... 562 948-1446
7633 Industry Ave Pico Rivera (90660) *(P-18321)*

Secura Key, Chatsworth *Also called Soundcraft Inc (P-9916)*

Secure Channels Inc (PA) ... F ... 949 208-7525
2102 Bus Ctr Dr Ste 130 Irvine (92612) *(P-17707)*

Secure Comm Systems Inc (HQ) ... C ... 714 547-1174
1740 E Wilshire Ave Santa Ana (92705) *(P-9315)*

Secure Data Recovery Services, Los Angeles *Also called World Acceptance Group Corp (P-18136)*

Secure One Data Solutions LLC ... D ... 562 924-7056
11090 Artesia Blvd Ste D Cerritos (90703) *(P-18109)*

Secure Technology Company ... D ... 714 991-6500
2000 W Corporate Way Anaheim (92801) *(P-9452)*

Secure Transportation Company ... D ... 951 737-7300
12785 Magnolia Ave # 102 Riverside (92503) *(P-11889)*

Secureauth Corporation (PA) ... D ... 949 777-6959
38 Discovery Ste 100 Irvine (92618) *(P-17708)*

Secured Funding Corporation ... A ... 714 689-6749
2955 Red Hill Ave Costa Mesa (92626) *(P-15252)*

Securitas SEC Svcs USA Inc ... B ... 818 706-6800
4330 Park Terrace Dr Westlake Village (91361) *(P-18322)*

Securitas SEC Svcs USA Inc ... C ... 310 787-0747
400 Crenshaw Blvd Ste 200 Torrance (90503) *(P-18323)*

Securitas SEC Svcs USA Inc ... C ... 818 706-6800
4330 Park Terrace Dr Westlake Village (91361) *(P-18324)*

Securitech Security Svcs Inc ... C ... 213 387-5050
2733 N San Fernando Rd Los Angeles (90065) *(P-18325)*

Security 20/20 Inc ... F ... 310 475-7780
8543 Venice Blvd Los Angeles (90034) *(P-23507)*

Security and Patrol Services, Fountain Valley *Also called Safeguard On Demand Inc (P-18319)*

Security Base Group Inc ... E ... 213 444-1555
2447 Pacific Coast Hwy # 2 Hermosa Beach (90254) *(P-18326)*

Security Front Desk, Mc Kittrick *Also called Aera Energy Services Company (P-422)*

Security Guard Services, Highland *Also called Synolo Security (P-18344)*

Security Indust Spcialists Inc ... C ... 323 924-9147
477 N Oak St Inglewood (90302) *(P-18327)*

Security Indust Spcialists Inc (PA) ... A ... 310 215-5100
6071 Bristol Pkwy Culver City (90230) *(P-18328)*

Security Metal Products Corp (HQ) ... F ... 310 641-6690
5678 Concours Ontario (91764) *(P-6719)*

Security Paving Company Inc (PA) ... D ... 818 362-9200
3075 Townsgate Rd Ste 210 Westlake Village (91361) *(P-913)*

Security Pro USA, Los Angeles *Also called Security 20/20 Inc (P-23507)*

Security Signal Devices Inc (PA) ... E ... 800 888-0444
1740 N Lemon St Anaheim (92801) *(P-18397)*

Security Specialists, San Fernando *Also called Tyan Inc (P-18347)*

Security Textile Corporation ... E ... 213 747-2673
1457 E Washington Blvd Los Angeles (90021) *(P-3181)*

Securityman, Ontario *Also called Teklink Security Inc (P-9922)*

Securtas Crtcal Infrstrcture S ... B ... 310 817-2177
1835 W Orangewood Ave # 2 Orange (92868) *(P-18329)*

Securtas Crtcal Infrstrcture S ... B ... 805 685-1100
Rm 117 Bldg 7525 Vandenberg Afb (93437) *(P-18330)*

Securtas Crtcal Infrstrcture S ... B ... 310 426-3300
360 N Pacific Coast Hwy # 30 El Segundo (90245) *(P-18331)*

Secuto Music, Burbank *Also called Roundabout Entertainment Inc (P-19173)*

Sedas Printing Inc ... F ... 323 469-1034
5335 Santa Monica Blvd Los Angeles (90029) *(P-4420)*

Sedenquist-Fraser Entps Inc ... E ... 562 924-5763
16730 Gridley Rd Cerritos (90703) *(P-10132)*

Sedgwick Claims MGT Svcs Inc ... D ... 714 572-1207
3230 E Imperial Hwy Brea (92821) *(P-15626)*

Sedgwick Claims MGT Svcs Inc ... D ... 818 591-9444
24025 Park Sorrento # 200 Calabasas (91302) *(P-15627)*

Sedway Group, Los Angeles *Also called Cbre Consulting Inc (P-23183)*

Seedorff Acme, Anaheim *Also called A P Seedorff & Company Inc (P-8940)*

Seeds of Change Inc ... C ... 310 764-7700
2555 S Dominguez Hills Dr Rancho Dominguez (90220) *(P-14868)*

Seek Capital LLC ... D ... 855 978-6106
6420 Wilshire Blvd # 500 Los Angeles (90048) *(P-23319)*

Seeley Brothers, Brea *Also called Norcal Inc (P-1448)*

Seeley Brothers, Brea *Also called Norcal Inc (P-1447)*

Seems Plumbing Co Inc ... E ... 310 297-4969
5400 W Rosecrans Ave Lowr Hawthorne (90250) *(P-1136)*

Sees Candies Inc (HQ) ... B ... 800 347-7337
20600 S Alameda St Carson (90810) *(P-2104)*

Sega of America Inc ... D ... 415 806-0169
6430 Oak Cyn Ste 150 Irvine (92618) *(P-11750)*

Sega of America Inc (HQ) ... E ... 949 788-0455
6400 Oak Cyn Ste 100 Irvine (92618) *(P-11751)*

Segway Inc ... C ... 603 222-6000
2350 W Valley Blvd Alhambra (91803) *(P-10500)*

Sehanson Inc ... D ... 714 778-1900
2121 E Via Burton Anaheim (92806) *(P-10415)*

Seidner-Miller Inc ... C ... 909 305-2000
1949 Auto Centre Dr Glendora (91740) *(P-18803)*

Seiko Epson, Los Alamitos *Also called Epson America Inc (P-8255)*

Seismic Reservoir 2020 Inc ... E ... 562 697-9711
3 Pointe Dr Ste 212 Brea (92821) *(P-465)*

Seiu Local 2015 ... C ... 213 985-0384
2910 Beverly Blvd Los Angeles (90057) *(P-22296)*

Seiu Local 721 ... C ... 213 368-8660
1545 Wilshire Blvd # 100 Los Angeles (90017) *(P-22297)*

Mergent e-mail: customerrelations@mergent.com
1266
2022 Southern California Business Directory and Buyers Guide
(P-0000) Products & Services Section entry number
(PA)=Parent Co (HQ)=Headquarters (DH)=Div Headquarters

Seiu United Service Workers W (PA)....D....213 284-7705
828 W Washington Blvd Los Angeles (90015) ***(P-22298)***
Seiu-Usww, Los Angeles *Also called Seiu United Service Workers W* ***(P-22298)***
Sekai Electronics Inc (PA)....E....**949 783-5740**
38 Waterworks Way Irvine (92618) ***(P-9316)***
Sela Healthcare Inc (PA)....C....**909 985-1981**
867 E 11th St Upland (91786) ***(P-20462)***
Sela Healthcare Inc....B....818 341-9800
20554 Roscoe Blvd Canoga Park (91306) ***(P-20463)***
Selane Products Inc (PA)....D....**818 998-7460**
9129 Lurline Ave Chatsworth (91311) ***(P-11195)***
Selarom....F....626 614-6744
3234 Concord Ave Alhambra (91803) ***(P-17980)***
Select Data Inc....C....714 577-1000
4175 E La Palma Ave # 205 Anaheim (92807) ***(P-17709)***
Select Graphics....F....714 537-5250
11931 Euclid St Garden Grove (92840) ***(P-4421)***
Select Home Care....D....805 777-3855
2393 Townsgate Rd Ste 100 Westlake Village (91361) ***(P-21210)***
Select Office Systems Inc....F....818 861-8320
1811 W Magnolia Blvd Burbank (91506) ***(P-5209)***
Select Personnel Services, Santa Barbara *Also called Select Temporaries LLC* ***(P-17464)***
Select Staffing, Santa Barbara *Also called Employbridge LLC* ***(P-17418)***
Select Temporaries LLC (HQ)....D....**805 882-2200**
3820 State St Santa Barbara (93105) ***(P-17464)***
Selecta Products Inc (PA)....D....**661 823-7050**
1200 E Tehachapi Blvd Tehachapi (93561) ***(P-13667)***
Selecta Switch, Tehachapi *Also called Selecta Products Inc* ***(P-13667)***
Selectabed, Agoura Hills *Also called Relief-Mart Inc* ***(P-3557)***
Selectforce, Irvine *Also called Accurate Background LLC* ***(P-18117)***
Selectra Industries Corp....D....323 581-8500
5166 Alcoa Ave Vernon (90058) ***(P-3019)***
Self Esteem, Montebello *Also called All Access Apparel Inc* ***(P-3027)***
Self Help Enterprises (PA)....D....**559 651-1000**
8445 W Elowin Ct Visalia (93291) ***(P-15995)***
Self Realization Fellowship, Los Angeles *Also called Self-Realization Fellowship Ch* ***(P-4203)***
Self Serve Auto Dismantlers (PA)....C....**714 630-8901**
3200 E Frontera St Anaheim (92806) ***(P-12979)***
Self-Insured Schools Cal (PA)....C....**661 636-4000**
1300 17th St 5 Bakersfield (93301) ***(P-15520)***
Self-Realization Fellowship Ch (PA)....E....**323 225-2471**
3880 San Rafael Ave Los Angeles (90065) ***(P-4203)***
Sellers Optical Inc....D....949 631-6800
320 Kalmus Dr Costa Mesa (92626) ***(P-10860)***
Selman Chevrolet Company....C....714 633-3521
1800 E Chapman Ave Orange (92867) ***(P-18753)***
Seloah Gourmet Food, Tustin *Also called Country House* ***(P-2083)***
Seltzer-Doren Company, Canoga Park *Also called Seltzer-Doren Management Co* ***(P-15749)***
Seltzer-Doren Management Co....D....818 709-5210
20201 Sherman Way Ste 209 Canoga Park (91306) ***(P-15749)***
Selu College, Inglewood *Also called Beckett Enterprise* ***(P-23171)***
Sema, Diamond Bar *Also called Specialty Equipment Mkt Assn* ***(P-22261)***
Sema Inc (PA)....C....**949 830-1400**
4 Mason Ste A Irvine (92618) ***(P-22812)***
Semco....E....909 799-9666
1495 S Gage St San Bernardino (92408) ***(P-10908)***
Semi-Kinetics Inc....D....949 830-7364
20191 Windrow Dr Ste A Lake Forest (92630) ***(P-9453)***
Semicoa, Costa Mesa *Also called Falkor Partners LLC* ***(P-9508)***
Semicoa Corporation....D....714 979-1900
333 Mccormick Ave Costa Mesa (92626) ***(P-9569)***
Semiconductor Components Inc....F....714 547-6059
1353 E Edinger Ave Santa Ana (92705) ***(P-9570)***
Semiconductor Equipment Corp....F....805 529-2293
5154 Goldman Ave Moorpark (93021) ***(P-9571)***
Semiconductor Process Eqp Corp....E....661 257-0934
27963 Franklin Pkwy Valencia (91355) ***(P-9572)***
Semiconductorstore.com, El Segundo *Also called Symmetry Electronics LLC* ***(P-9587)***
Seminis Inc (HQ)....B....**805 485-7317**
2700 Camino Del Sol Oxnard (93030) ***(P-22863)***
Seminis Vegetable Seeds Inc (HQ)....A....**855 733-3834**
2700 Camino Del Sol Oxnard (93030) ***(P-14869)***
Semiq Incorporated....F....949 273-4373
20692 Prism Pl Lake Forest (92630) ***(P-9573)***
Semore Inc....F....213 746-4122
1437 Santee St Ste 201 Los Angeles (90015) ***(P-2774)***
Semtech Corporation (PA)....C....**805 498-2111**
200 Flynn Rd Camarillo (93012) ***(P-9574)***
Sencha Naturals Inc....F....213 353-9908
1101 Monterey Pass Rd A Monterey Park (91754) ***(P-2105)***
Seneca Resources Company LLC....F....661 391-3540
4800 Corporate Ct Bakersfield (93311) ***(P-466)***
Senegence International, Foothill Ranch *Also called Sgii Inc* ***(P-14288)***
Senfeng Laser Usa Inc....F....562 319-8053
5989 Rickenbacker Rd Commerce (90040) ***(P-9912)***
Senga Engineering Inc....E....714 549-8011
1525 E Warner Ave Santa Ana (92705) ***(P-8792)***
Senior Care (PA)....A....**562 989-5100**
3800 Kilroy Airport Way Long Beach (90806) ***(P-15452)***
Senior Care Action Ntwrk Fndti....D....562 492-9878
2501 Cherry Ave Ste 380 Long Beach (90755) ***(P-15453)***
Senior Health and Activity Ctr, Los Angeles *Also called Altamed Health Services Corp* ***(P-19703)***
Senior Keiro Health Care....D....323 263-9651
325 S Boyle Ave Los Angeles (90033) ***(P-22152)***
Senior Nutrition Program, Los Angeles *Also called Jewish Family Svc Los Angeles* ***(P-21822)***
Senior Operations LLC....B....818 260-2900
2980 N San Fernando Blvd Burbank (91504) ***(P-10416)***
Senior Wellness Innovation Grp (PA)....D....**562 746-2182**
7403 Adwen St Downey (90241) ***(P-341)***
Senju Fire Protection Corp....F....949 333-1281
30 Muller Ste 112 Irvine (92618) ***(P-8138)***
Senju Sprinkler, Irvine *Also called Senju Fire Protection Corp* ***(P-8138)***
Senju Usa Inc....F....818 719-7190
21700 Oxnard St Ste 1070 Woodland Hills (91367) ***(P-4891)***
Senna Tree Company LLC....D....818 957-5755
9255 Sunland Blvd Sun Valley (91352) ***(P-361)***
Senor Snacks Holdings, Fullerton *Also called Senor Snacks Inc* ***(P-2365)***
Senor Snacks Inc....F....714 739-1073
2325 Raymer Ave Fullerton (92833) ***(P-2365)***
Senor Snacks Manufacturing Ltd....F....714 739-1073
2325 Raymer Ave Fullerton (92833) ***(P-2106)***
Sensata Technologies Inc....D....805 716-0322
1461 Lawrence Dr Thousand Oaks (91320) ***(P-8301)***
Sense Fashion Corporation....F....626 454-3381
2415 Merced Ave South El Monte (91733) ***(P-2866)***
Sense Fashions, South El Monte *Also called Sense Fashion Corporation* ***(P-2866)***
Senso-Metrics Inc....F....805 527-3640
4584 Runway St Simi Valley (93063) ***(P-10909)***
Sensonetics Inc....F....714 799-1616
11164 Young River Ave Fountain Valley (92708) ***(P-9575)***
Sensor Systems Inc....B....818 341-5366
8929 Fullbright Ave Chatsworth (91311) ***(P-10643)***
Sensors and Integrated Systems, Brea *Also called Raytheon Technologies Corp* ***(P-10401)***
Sensory Neurostimulation Inc....F....949 492-0550
1235 Puerta Del Sol # 600 San Clemente (92673) ***(P-4892)***
Sensoscientific Inc....F....800 279-3101
685 Cochran St Ste 200 Simi Valley (93065) ***(P-10722)***
Sentiments Inc (PA)....F....**323 843-2080**
5353 E Slauson Ave Commerce (90040) ***(P-11752)***
Sentinel Monitoring Corp (HQ)....D....**949 453-1550**
220 Technology Dr Ste 200 Irvine (92618) ***(P-18398)***
Sentinel Offender Services LLC (PA)....D....**949 453-1550**
1290 N Hancock St Ste 103 Anaheim (92807) ***(P-18399)***
Sentinel Peak Rsources Cal LLC....D....661 395-5214
1200 Discovery Dr Ste 100 Bakersfield (93309) ***(P-467)***
Sentinel Peak Rsources Cal LLC....D....323 298-2200
5640 S Fairfax Ave Los Angeles (90056) ***(P-468)***
Sentran L L C (PA)....F....**888 545-8988**
4355 E Lowell St Ste F Ontario (91761) ***(P-10910)***
Seollem Corporation....F....323 265-3266
2856 E Pico Blvd Los Angeles (90023) ***(P-2789)***
Sephora Co LLC (PA)....F....**760 798-7654**
6103 Obispo Ave Long Beach (90805) ***(P-5067)***
Sepulveda Ambltory Care Ctr Cl, North Hills *Also called Veterans Health Administration* ***(P-20147)***
Sepulveda Golf Course, Encino *Also called County of Los Angeles* ***(P-19483)***
Sequel Contractors Inc....E....562 802-7227
13546 Imperial Hwy Santa Fe Springs (90670) ***(P-914)***
Sequent Medical Inc....D....949 830-9600
35 Enterprise Aliso Viejo (92656) ***(P-11056)***
Sequoia Beverage Company LP....C....559 651-2444
2122 N Plaza Dr Visalia (93291) ***(P-14835)***
Sequoia Concepts Inc....D....818 409-6000
28632 Roadside Dr Ste 110 Agoura Hills (91301) ***(P-17117)***
Sequoia Consultants Inc (PA)....D....**714 974-6316**
361 W Grove Ave Orange (92865) ***(P-22653)***
Sequoia Environmental Svcs Inc....D....949 480-4742
1 University Dr Aliso Viejo (92656) ***(P-279)***
Sequoia Exploration Inc....E....661 303-0564
5913 Sundale Ave Bakersfield (93309) ***(P-410)***
Sequoia Financial Services, Agoura Hills *Also called Sequoia Concepts Inc* ***(P-17117)***
Sequoia National Park, Seq Natl Pk *Also called DNC Prks Rsorts At Sequoia Inc* ***(P-16414)***
Sequoia Natural History Assn, Three Rivers *Also called Sequoia Parks Conservancy* ***(P-4137)***
Sequoia Parks Conservancy....E....559 565-3759
47050 Generals Hwy # 10 Three Rivers (93271) ***(P-4137)***
Sequoia Pure Water Inc....F....310 637-8500
1640 W 134th St Compton (90222) ***(P-2298)***
Serco Mold Inc (PA)....E....**626 331-0517**
2009 Wright Ave La Verne (91750) ***(P-5817)***
Serco Services Inc....D....805 736-3584
701 N St Ste A Lompoc (93437) ***(P-17710)***
Sercomp LLC (PA)....D....**805 299-0020**
5401 Tech Cir Ste 200 Moorpark (93021) ***(P-11482)***
Serendipity Hearing Inc (PA)....D....**562 922-1718**
5555 Garden Grove Blvd # 200 Westminster (92683) ***(P-20233)***
Serfin Funds Transfer (PA)....D....**626 457-3070**
1000 S Fremont Ave A-O Alhambra (91803) ***(P-15132)***
Sergio Shoes, North Hollywood *Also called Onnik Shoe Company Inc* ***(P-5882)***
Serpa Packaging Solutions, Visalia *Also called Food Machinery Sales Inc* ***(P-8068)***
Serpac Electronic Enclosures, La Verne *Also called Serco Mold Inc* ***(P-5817)***
Serra Community Med Clinic Inc....C....818 768-3000
9375 San Fernando Rd Sun Valley (91352) ***(P-20063)***
Serra Laser and Waterjet Inc....E....714 680-6211
1740 N Orangethorpe Park Anaheim (92801) ***(P-9913)***
Serra Manufacturing Corp (PA)....D....**310 537-4560**
3039 E Las Hermanas St Compton (90221) ***(P-7180)***
Serrano Industries Inc....E....562 777-8180
9922 Tabor Pl Santa Fe Springs (90670) ***(P-8793)***
Serv-Rite Meat Company Inc....D....323 227-1911
2515 N San Fernando Rd Los Angeles (90065) ***(P-1719)***
Serve People Inc....D....714 352-2911
1206 E 17th St Ste 101 Santa Ana (92701) ***(P-22461)***

ALPHABETIC

Employee Codes: A=Over 500 employees, B=251-500
C=101-250, D=51-100, E=20-50 F=10-19
2022 Southern California Business
Directory and Buyers Guide
© Mergent Inc. 1-800-342-5647
1267

Servers Direct LLC ....D....800 576-7931
20480 Business Pkwy Walnut (91789) ***(P-13436)***
Servexo ....B....323 527-9994
1515 W 190th St Ste 170 Gardena (90248) ***(P-18332)***
Servexo Protective Service, Gardena *Also called Servexo* ***(P-18332)***
Service 1st Electrical Svcs ....E....714 630-9699
1092 N Armando St Anaheim (92806) ***(P-1315)***
Service Benefits LLC ....D....312 576-2247
8201 Beverly Blvd Ste 302 West Hollywood (90048) ***(P-23320)***
Service Chemicals, Carson *Also called East West Enterprises* ***(P-6224)***
Service Employee Intl Un, Los Angeles *Also called Los Angles Cnty Employees Assn* ***(P-22293)***
Service Employee Union, Commerce *Also called Hospital Svc Emplyees Un Lcal* ***(P-22290)***
Service First Contractors ....E....714 573-2200
2510 N Grand Ave Ste 110 Santa Ana (92705) ***(P-823)***
Service Genius Los Angeles Inc ....D....818 200-3379
9761 Variel Ave Chatsworth (91311) ***(P-1137)***
Service Master By ARS, Gardena *Also called Disaster Rstrtion Prfssnals In* ***(P-601)***
Service Quick Inc (PA) ....C....**213 700-4332**
18724 S Broadwick St Compton (90220) ***(P-18957)***
ServiceMaster, Valencia *Also called Master & Sons Inc* ***(P-17259)***
ServiceMaster, Santa Maria *Also called Skylstad-Schoelen Co Inc* ***(P-17285)***
ServiceMaster By Best Pros Inc ....D....951 515-9051
6474 Western Ave Riverside (92505) ***(P-17283)***
Servicetitan Inc (PA) ....D....**855 899-0970**
801 N Brand Blvd Ste 700 Glendale (91203) ***(P-17711)***
Servicmster Clean By Integrity, Santa Barbara *Also called Pacific Building Maint Inc* ***(P-17269)***
Servicmster Clean By Integrity, Oxnard *Also called Pacific Building Maint Inc* ***(P-17270)***
Servicon Systems Inc ....A....310 970-0700
3329 Jack Northrop Ave Hawthorne (90250) ***(P-1550)***
Servis One Inc ....D....888 738-5873
7505 Irvine Center Dr Irvine (92618) ***(P-15253)***
Serviz Inc ....D....818 381-4826
15303 Ventura Blvd # 1600 Sherman Oaks (91403) ***(P-16976)***
SERVPRO Encino/Sherman Oaks, Encino *Also called One Silver Serve Inc* ***(P-17266)***
SERVPRO Jeffries Global, Beverly Hills *Also called Jeffries Global Inc* ***(P-1667)***
SERVPRO of Beverly Hills, Beverly Hills *Also called D&A Endeavors Inc* ***(P-1653)***
Sesa Inc (PA) ....E....**714 779-9700**
20391 Via Guadalupe Yorba Linda (92887) ***(P-17187)***
Sesloc Federal Credit Union (PA) ....D....**805 543-1816**
3855 Broad St San Luis Obispo (93401) ***(P-15088)***
Sessa Manufacturing & Welding ....E....805 644-2284
2932 Golf Course Dr Ventura (93003) ***(P-7181)***
Setarehshenas Dental Corp ....C....805 583-5700
1197 E Los Angeles Ave Simi Valley (93065) ***(P-20199)***
Setco LLC ....C....812 424-2904
4875 E Hunter Ave Anaheim (92807) ***(P-5818)***
Settlers Jerky Inc ....E....909 444-3999
307 Paseo Sonrisa Walnut (91789) ***(P-1751)***
Setton Pstchio Terra Bella Inc (HQ) ....D....**559 535-6050**
9370 Road 234 Terra Bella (93270) ***(P-14735)***
Sev-Cal Tool Inc ....F....714 549-3347
3231 Halladay St Santa Ana (92705) ***(P-7868)***
Seven Licensing Company LLC ....D....323 881-0308
5401 S Soto St Vernon (90058) ***(P-14416)***
Seven Oaks Country Club ....C....661 664-6404
2000 Grand Lakes Ave Bakersfield (93311) ***(P-19611)***
Seven One Inc (PA) ....D....**818 904-3435**
21540 Prairie St Ste E Chatsworth (91311) ***(P-18664)***
Seven Resorts Inc (PA) ....D....**949 588-7100**
9771 Irvine Center Dr Irvine (92618) ***(P-16702)***
Seven7 Brands, Vernon *Also called Seven Licensing Company LLC* ***(P-14416)***
Severson Group Incorporated (PA) ....D....**562 493-3611**
3601 Serpentine Dr Los Alamitos (90720) ***(P-824)***
Sew What Inc ....E....310 639-6000
1978 E Gladwick St Compton (90220) ***(P-3094)***
Sewer Rodding Equipment Co (PA) ....E....**310 301-9009**
3217 Carter Ave Marina Del Rey (90292) ***(P-8412)***
Sewing Collection Inc ....D....323 264-2223
3113 E 26th St Vernon (90058) ***(P-5353)***
Sextant Wines, Paso Robles *Also called Rbz Vineyards LLC* ***(P-2216)***
Sexual Recovery Institute Inc ....B....310 360-0130
1964 Westwood Blvd # 400 Los Angeles (90025) ***(P-21888)***
Sexy Hair Concepts LLC ....E....818 435-0800
21551 Prairie St Chatsworth (91311) ***(P-21967)***
Seychelle Envmtl Tech Inc ....F....949 234-1999
32963 Calle Perfecto San Juan Capistrano (92675) ***(P-8413)***
Seyfarth Shaw LLP ....C....213 270-9600
601 S Figueroa St # 3300 Los Angeles (90017) ***(P-21674)***
Seyfarth Shaw LLP ....C....310 277-7200
2029 Century Park E # 3400 Los Angeles (90067) ***(P-21675)***
Seymour Duncan, Santa Barbara *Also called Duncan Carter Corporation* ***(P-11341)***
SF Technology Inc ....F....562 924-5763
16730 Gridley Rd Cerritos (90703) ***(P-11753)***
Sfadia Inc ....D....323 622-1930
8485 Artesia Blvd Ste A Buena Park (90621) ***(P-1316)***
Sfc, Perris *Also called Stretch Forming Corporation* ***(P-6921)***
SFE, Santa Fe Springs *Also called Santa Fe Enterprises Inc* ***(P-7830)***
Sfmc, Lynwood *Also called St Francis Medical Center* ***(P-20958)***
Sfn Group Inc ....A....949 727-8500
114 Pacifica Ste 210 Irvine (92618) ***(P-17516)***
Sfpp LP ....D....909 877-2373
2319 S Riverside Ave Bloomington (92316) ***(P-12375)***
Sfpp LP ....D....323 636-4447
20410 S Wilmington Ave Long Beach (90810) ***(P-12376)***
Sfpp LP (HQ) ....C....**714 560-4400**
1100 W Town And Country R Orange (92868) ***(P-12377)***
Sfs, Brea *Also called Kirkhill Inc* ***(P-10362)***
Sft Realty Galway Downs LLC ....D....951 232-1880
38801 Los Porralitos Temecula (92592) ***(P-15996)***
Sfv LLC ....E....818 339-8881
8949 Reseda Blvd 227-2 Northridge (91324) ***(P-21211)***
SGB Better Baking Co LLC ....D....818 787-9992
14528 Blythe St Van Nuys (91402) ***(P-2033)***
SGB Bubbles Baking Co LLC ....D....818 786-1700
15215 Keswick St Van Nuys (91405) ***(P-2034)***
SGB Enterprises Inc ....E....661 294-8306
24844 Anza Dr Ste A Valencia (91355) ***(P-8228)***
SGC International Inc ....F....323 318-2998
6489 Corvette St Commerce (90040) ***(P-5921)***
SGF Produce Holding Corp ....F....714 630-6292
701 W Kimberly Ave # 210 Placentia (92870) ***(P-14653)***
Sgi Logistics ....E....310 513-5339
2500 Broadway Ste F125 Santa Monica (90404) ***(P-11993)***
Sgii Inc (PA) ....C....**949 521-6161**
19651 Alter Foothill Ranch (92610) ***(P-14288)***
Sgl Composites Inc (HQ) ....E....**424 329-5250**
1551 W 139th St Gardena (90249) ***(P-3839)***
Sgl Technic LLC (HQ) ....D....**661 257-0500**
28176 Avenue Stanford Valencia (91355) ***(P-6168)***
Sgp.id11, Huntington Beach *Also called Scoreusa Institute* ***(P-22920)***
Sgps Inc ....D....310 538-4175
15823 S Main St Gardena (90248) ***(P-11754)***
Sgt Boardriders Inc ....F....714 274-8000
7403 Slater Ave Huntington Beach (92647) ***(P-5410)***
Sgvmi, West Covina *Also called Specilty Hosp San Gbriel Vly M* ***(P-20955)***
Shadecraft Inc ....E....818 502-0700
116 W Del Mar Blvd Pasadena (91105) ***(P-7695)***
Shading Solutions, Los Angeles *Also called Powerfull Systems Inc* ***(P-1300)***
Shadow Animation LLC ....E....323 466-7771
940 N Mansfield Ave Los Angeles (90038) ***(P-19177)***
Shadow Hills Convalescent Home, Sunland *Also called Arcadia Convalescent Hosp Inc* ***(P-20246)***
Shadow Hlls Cnvlscent Hosp Inc ....D....818 352-4438
10158 Sunland Blvd Sunland (91040) ***(P-20464)***
Shadow Holdings LLC (HQ) ....B....**661 252-3807**
26455 Ruether Ave Santa Clarita (91350) ***(P-5068)***
Shadow Industries Inc ....F....714 995-4353
8941 Electric St Cypress (90630) ***(P-10547)***
Shadow Mtn Rsort Rcquet CLB Tn, Palm Desert *Also called Destination Residences LLC* ***(P-16405)***
Shadow Trailers, Cypress *Also called Shadow Industries Inc* ***(P-10547)***
Shadowmachine LLC (PA) ....D....**323 466-7388**
940 N Mansfield Ave Los Angeles (90038) ***(P-19178)***
Shady Canyon Golf Club Inc ....C....949 856-7000
100 Shady Canyon Dr Irvine (92603) ***(P-19612)***
Shafton Inc ....F....818 985-5025
4427 Sancola Ave Toluca Lake (91602) ***(P-3084)***
Shaka Wear, Los Angeles *Also called Gino Corporation* ***(P-2756)***
Shamrock Companies, The, Anaheim *Also called Shamrock Supply Company Inc* ***(P-13817)***
Shamrock Foods Company ....B....951 685-6314
12400 Riverside Dr Eastvale (91752) ***(P-14736)***
Shamrock Holdings Inc (PA) ....D....**818 845-4444**
4444 W Lkeside Dr Ste 150 Burbank (91505) ***(P-15348)***
Shamrock Holdings Cal Inc (HQ) ....D....**818 845-4444**
4444 W Lakeside Dr Lbby Burbank (91505) ***(P-15997)***
Shamrock Holdings California, Burbank *Also called Shamrock Holdings Inc* ***(P-15348)***
Shamrock Manufacturing, Chino *Also called Shamrock Marketing Co Inc* ***(P-11140)***
Shamrock Marketing Co Inc (HQ) ....F....**909 591-8855**
5445 Daniels St Chino (91710) ***(P-11140)***
Shamrock Supply Company Inc (PA) ....D....**714 575-1800**
3366 E La Palma Ave Anaheim (92806) ***(P-13817)***
Shandin Hlls Bhvior Thrapy Ctr, San Bernardino *Also called Sunbrdge Shndin Hlls Rhblttion* ***(P-20484)***
Shandon Properties, Beverly Hills *Also called Gang Tyre Ramer & Brown Inc* ***(P-21562)***
Shane Hunter LLC ....E....415 627-7730
1013 S Los Angeles St # 1000 Los Angeles (90015) ***(P-3085)***
Shani Darden Skincare Inc ....E....310 745-3150
1800 Century Park E # 400 Los Angeles (90067) ***(P-5069)***
Shank Kretz Mch Auto Parts Inc ....F....760 344-4541
375 N 8th St Brawley (92227) ***(P-13088)***
Shapco Inc (PA) ....F....**310 264-1666**
1666 20th St Ste 100 Santa Monica (90404) ***(P-13595)***
Shapell Industries LLC (HQ) ....D....**323 655-7330**
8383 Wilshire Blvd # 700 Beverly Hills (90211) ***(P-16072)***
Shapiro-Gilman-Shandler Co (HQ) ....D....**213 593-1200**
739 Decatur St Los Angeles (90021) ***(P-14654)***
Shapp International Trdg Inc ....C....818 348-3000
6000 Reseda Blvd Ste J Tarzana (91356) ***(P-13287)***
Shapp Internatioonal, Tarzana *Also called Shapp International Trdg Inc* ***(P-13287)***
Shar-Craft Inc (PA) ....E....**661 324-4985**
1103 33rd St Bakersfield (93301) ***(P-14017)***
Shara-Tex Inc ....E....323 587-7200
3338 E Slauson Ave Vernon (90058) ***(P-2647)***
Share Our Selves Corporation ....D....949 609-8199
1 Purpose Dr Lake Forest (92630) ***(P-21479)***
Shared Services, Torrance *Also called Securitas SEC Svcs USA Inc* ***(P-18323)***
Sharon Havriluk ....E....714 630-1313
1164 N Kraemer Pl Anaheim (92806) ***(P-4612)***
Sharp Dots.com, Pico Rivera *Also called Sharpdots LLC* ***(P-8302)***
Sharp Fabric, Los Angeles *Also called Elijah Textiles Inc* ***(P-13168)***

Mergent e-mail: customerrelations@mergent.com
1268
2022 Southern California Business Directory and Buyers Guide
(P-0000) Products & Services Section entry number
(PA)=Parent Co (HQ)=Headquarters (DH)=Div Headquarters

Sharp Industries LLC.....F.....951 323-3677
1525 3rd St Ste K Riverside (92507) *(P-11755)*
Sharp Profiles LLC.....F.....760 246-9446
828 W Cienega Ave San Dimas (91773) *(P-6489)*
Sharpcast, Los Angeles *Also called Sugarsync Inc (P-17990)*
Sharpdots LLC.....F.....626 599-9696
3733 San Gabriel River Pk Pico Rivera (90660) *(P-8302)*
Shason Inc (PA).....D.....323 269-6666
5525 S Soto St Vernon (90058) *(P-14319)*
Shasta Beverages Inc.....D.....714 523-2280
14405 Artesia Blvd La Mirada (90638) *(P-2299)*
Shaver Specialty Co Inc.....E.....310 370-6941
20608 Earl St Torrance (90503) *(P-7952)*
Shawmut Design and Cnstr, Los Angeles *Also called Shawmut Woodworking & Sup Inc (P-825)*
Shawmut Woodworking & Sup Inc.....C.....323 602-1000
11390 W Olympic Blvd Fl 2 Los Angeles (90064) *(P-825)*
Shawnan, Downey *Also called Sialic Contractors Corporation (P-915)*
Shaxon Industries Inc.....D.....714 779-1140
4852 E La Palma Ave Anaheim (92807) *(P-8216)*
Shc Burbank II LLC.....C.....818 843-6000
2500 N Hollywood Way Burbank (91505) *(P-16703)*
Shea Convalescent Hospital, Whittier *Also called Longwood Management Corp (P-20850)*
Shea Hmes Ltd Prtnr A Cal Ltd (HQ).....E.....909 594-9500
655 Brea Canyon Rd Walnut (91789) *(P-640)*
Shea Homes, Walnut *Also called Shea La Quinta LLC (P-15696)*
Shea Homes Vantis LLC.....D.....909 594-9500
655 Brea Canyon Rd Walnut (91789) *(P-669)*
Shea La Quinta LLC.....D.....909 594-9500
655 Brea Canyon Rd Walnut (91789) *(P-15696)*
Shea Properties MGT Co Inc.....B.....949 389-7000
130 Vantis Dr Ste 200 Aliso Viejo (92656) *(P-15697)*
Sheer Design Inc (PA).....E.....310 306-2121
6309 Esplanade Playa Del Rey (90293) *(P-5070)*
Sheervision Inc (PA).....F.....310 265-8918
4030 Palos Verdes Dr N # 104 Rllng HLS Est (90274) *(P-11057)*
Sheet Metal Prototype Inc.....E.....818 772-2715
19420 Londelius St Northridge (91324) *(P-6908)*
Sheet Metal Service.....F.....714 446-0196
2310 E Orangethorpe Ave Anaheim (92806) *(P-6909)*
Sheet Metal Specialists LLC.....E.....951 351-6828
11698 Warm Springs Rd Riverside (92505) *(P-6910)*
Sheetmetal Engineering.....E.....805 306-0390
1780 Voyager Ave Simi Valley (93063) *(P-6911)*
Sheffield Manufacturing Inc.....F.....818 767-4948
13849 Magnolia Ave Chino (91710) *(P-8794)*
Shelby Carroll Intl Inc (PA).....D.....310 538-2914
19021 S Figueroa St Gardena (90248) *(P-9965)*
Shelcore Inc (PA).....E.....818 883-2400
7811 Lemona Ave Van Nuys (91405) *(P-11390)*
Shelcore Toys, Van Nuys *Also called Shelcore Inc (P-11390)*
Sheldon Mechanical Corporation.....D.....661 286-1361
26015 Avenue Hall Santa Clarita (91355) *(P-1138)*
Shell New Energies US LLC (HQ).....E.....888 751-8560
767 S Alameda St Ste 200 Los Angeles (90021) *(P-17712)*
Shell Oil Company.....C.....714 991-9200
511 N Brookhurst St Anaheim (92801) *(P-23321)*
Shen Zhen New World II LLC.....D.....818 980-1212
333 Unversal Hollywood Dr Universal City (91608) *(P-16704)*
Shepard Bros Inc (PA).....C.....562 697-1366
503 S Cypress St La Habra (90631) *(P-8414)*
Shepard-Thomason Company.....D.....714 773-5539
901 S Leslie St La Habra (90631) *(P-10133)*
Sheppard Mllin Rchter Hmpton L (PA).....B.....213 620-1780
333 S Hope St Fl 43 Los Angeles (90071) *(P-21676)*
SHEPPARD MULLIN, Los Angeles *Also called Sheppard Mllin Rchter Hmpton L (P-21676)*
Sheraton, Universal City *Also called Shen Zhen New World II LLC (P-16704)*
Sheraton, Los Angeles *Also called Nrea-TRC 711 LLC (P-16586)*
Sheraton, Los Angeles *Also called Hazens Investment LLC (P-16468)*
Sheraton, Los Angeles *Also called S W K Properties LLC (P-16681)*
Sheraton, Universal City *Also called Lh Universal Operating LLC (P-16541)*
Sheraton Inn Bakersfield, Bakersfield *Also called Msr Hotels & Resorts Inc (P-16278)*
Sheraton LLC.....D.....310 642-1111
6101 W Century Blvd Los Angeles (90045) *(P-16705)*
Sheraton LLC.....D.....909 204-6100
11960 Foothill Blvd Rancho Cucamonga (91739) *(P-16706)*
Sheraton Los Angles San Gbriel, San Gabriel *Also called San Yi US Investment Co Inc (P-16689)*
Sheraton Pasadena, Pasadena *Also called Pasadena Hotel Dev Ventr LP (P-16623)*
Sheraton Pk Ht At Anheim Rsort, Anaheim *Also called 1855 S Hbr Blvd Drv Hldngs LLC (P-16306)*
Sheraton Pk Ht At Anheim Rsort, Anaheim *Also called Anaheim - 1855 S Hbr Blvd Owne (P-16319)*
Sheraton Pk Ht At Anheim Rsort, Anaheim *Also called Anaheim Hotel LLC (P-16321)*
SHERATON SUITES FAIRPLEX, Pomona *Also called Fairplex Child Development Ctr (P-22013)*
Shercon Inc.....D.....800 228-3218
18704 S Ferris Pl Rancho Dominguez (90220) *(P-5411)*
Sherman Corporation.....E.....310 671-2117
10803 Los Jardines E Fountain Valley (92708) *(P-8795)*
Sherman Oaks Health System.....D.....818 981-7111
4929 Van Nuys Blvd Sherman Oaks (91403) *(P-20938)*
Sherman Oaks Hospital, Sherman Oaks *Also called Prime Hlthcare Svcs - Shrman O (P-20910)*
Sherman Oaks Hspice Care Group.....E.....714 733-1333
1855 W Katella Ave # 255 Orange (92867) *(P-20543)*
Sherman Village Hlth Care Ctr, North Hollywood *Also called Hillsdale Group LP (P-20595)*
Sherry Kline, Commerce *Also called Pacific Coast Home Furn Inc (P-3112)*
Sherton Grdn Grove Anheim S Ht.....E.....714 703-8400
12221 Harbor Blvd Garden Grove (92840) *(P-16707)*
Sherwood Country Club.....C.....805 496-3036
320 W Stafford Rd Thousand Oaks (91361) *(P-19613)*
Sherwood Guest Home, Lynwood *Also called Marlinda Management Inc (P-20610)*
Sheryl Lowe Designs LLC.....E.....805 969-1742
1187 Coast Village Rd # 156 Santa Barbara (93108) *(P-18665)*
Shg Holdings Corp (PA).....E.....310 410-4907
201 Hindry Ave Inglewood (90301) *(P-7883)*
Shibui Apartments, Torrance *Also called Hunt Enterprises Inc (P-15886)*
Shield E A Sewer Construction, Bakersfield *Also called E A Shields Inc (P-947)*
Shield Healthcare, Valencia *Also called Shield-Denver Health Care Ctr (P-13518)*
Shield Security Inc (HQ).....B.....714 210-1501
1551 N Tustin Ave Ste 650 Santa Ana (92705) *(P-18333)*
Shield Security Inc.....B.....818 239-5800
21110 Vanowen St Canoga Park (91303) *(P-18334)*
Shield Security Inc.....B.....562 283-1100
150 E Wardlow Rd Long Beach (90807) *(P-18335)*
Shield Security Inc.....B.....909 920-1173
265 N Euclid Ave Upland (91786) *(P-18336)*
Shield-Denver Health Care Ctr (HQ).....C.....661 294-4200
27911 Franklin Pkwy Valencia (91355) *(P-13518)*
Shields For Families (PA).....D.....323 242-5000
11601 S Western Ave Los Angeles (90047) *(P-21049)*
Shields For Families.....D.....310 603-1050
11705 Deputy Yamamoto Pl A Lynwood (90262) *(P-21050)*
Shields For Families.....D.....310 604-4446
3209 N Alameda St Compton (90222) *(P-21051)*
Shift Calendars Inc.....F.....626 967-5862
809 N Glendora Ave Covina (91724) *(P-4422)*
Shift Digital, Laguna Beach *Also called Sanctus LLC (P-23104)*
Shift Packaging LLC.....F.....206 412-4253
14261 Proctor Ave Ste A La Puente (91746) *(P-4947)*
Shii LLC.....E.....909 354-8000
2151 E Cnvntn Ctr Way # 222 Ontario (91764) *(P-15998)*
Shilpark Paint Corporation (PA).....E.....323 732-7093
1640 S Vermont Ave Los Angeles (90006) *(P-14906)*
Shim-It Corporation.....F.....951 734-8300
1691 California Ave Corona (92881) *(P-10417)*
Shimada Enterprises Inc.....E.....562 802-8811
14009 Dinard Ave Santa Fe Springs (90670) *(P-9146)*
Shimadzu Medical Systems USA, Long Beach *Also called Shimadzu Precision Instrs Inc (P-14064)*
Shimadzu Precision Instrs Inc (HQ).....D.....562 420-6226
3645 N Lakewood Blvd Long Beach (90808) *(P-14064)*
Shimadzu Precision Instrs Inc.....D.....310 217-8855
20101 S Vermont Ave Torrance (90502) *(P-13519)*
Shimano North Amer Holdg Inc (HQ).....C.....949 951-5003
1 Holland Irvine (92618) *(P-14087)*
Shims Bargain Inc (PA).....D.....323 881-0099
2600 S Soto St Vernon (90058) *(P-14975)*
Shims Bargain Inc.....D.....323 726-8800
7030 E Slauson Ave Commerce (90040) *(P-716)*
Shimtech US, Santa Clarita *Also called Lamsco West Inc (P-5695)*
Shine Food Inc (PA).....E.....310 329-3829
19216 Normandie Ave Torrance (90502) *(P-1855)*
Shine Food Inc.....D.....310 533-6010
21100 S Western Ave Torrance (90501) *(P-1939)*
Shining Star Dialysis Inc (HQ).....E.....310 536-2400
601 Hawaii St El Segundo (90245) *(P-21265)*
Shinsuke Clifford Yamamoto Inc.....D.....714 992-5783
2031 Emery Ave La Habra (90631) *(P-342)*
Ship & Shore Environmental Inc.....E.....562 997-0233
2474 N Palm Dr Signal Hill (90755) *(P-13938)*
Shipping Department, Anaheim *Also called Disneyland Resort (P-12556)*
Shire-NPS Pharmaceuticals Inc.....A.....818 241-3700
4501 Colorado Blvd Los Angeles (90039) *(P-4893)*
Shivay Hospitality Inc.....D.....323 702-7103
1738 N Las Palmas Ave Los Angeles (90028) *(P-16708)*
Shlemmer Algaze Associates (PA).....D.....310 215-3991
6083 Bristol Pkwy Culver City (90230) *(P-22742)*
Shmaze Custom Coatings, Lake Forest *Also called Shmaze Industries Inc (P-7410)*
Shmaze Industries Inc.....E.....949 583-1448
20792 Canada Rd Lake Forest (92630) *(P-7410)*
Sho-Air International Inc (PA).....E.....949 476-9111
5401 Argosy Ave Ste 102 Huntington Beach (92649) *(P-12525)*
Shock Doctor Inc (PA).....D.....800 233-6956
11488 Slater Ave Fountain Valley (92708) *(P-11446)*
Shock Doctor Sports, Fountain Valley *Also called Shock Doctor Inc (P-11446)*
Shockhound, City of Industry *Also called Hot Topic Inc (P-2779)*
Shoes For Crews Intl Inc.....E.....561 683-5090
760 Baldwin Park Blvd City of Industry (91746) *(P-5877)*
Shoffeitt Pipeline Inc.....D.....949 581-1600
15801 Rockfield Blvd L Irvine (92618) *(P-970)*
Shogun Labs Inc (PA).....D.....206 679-1302
340 S Lemon Ave 1085 Walnut (91789) *(P-22958)*
Shook Hardy & Bacon LLP.....C.....949 475-1500
5 Park Plz Ste 1600 Irvine (92614) *(P-21677)*
Shop Buru, Los Angeles *Also called Bu Ru LLC (P-2926)*
Shop Services Inc.....F.....661 768-1775
27622 Highway 33 Fellows (93224) *(P-19068)*
Shop4techcom.....E.....909 248-2725
13745 Seminole Dr Chino (91710) *(P-8217)*
Shopper Inc.....B.....805 527-6700
3987 Heritage Oak Ct Simi Valley (93063) *(P-13466)*
Shopzilla.com, Santa Monica *Also called Connexity Inc (P-12632)*

ALPHABETIC

Employee Codes: A=Over 500 employees, B=251-500 C=101-250, D=51-100, E=20-50 F=10-19
2022 Southern California Business Directory and Buyers Guide
© Mergent Inc. 1-800-342-5647
1269

Shore Front LLC E 714 612-3751
3973 Trolley Ct Brea (92823) ***(P-2523)***
Shore Western Manufacturing E 626 357-3251
225 W Duarte Rd Monrovia (91016) ***(P-10811)***
Shorecliff Properties, Pismo Beach *Also called Tic Hotels Inc* ***(P-16754)***
Shoreline Ambulance Corp D 714 847-9107
15105 S Broadway Gardena (90248) ***(P-11890)***
Shoreline Care Center, Oxnard *Also called Covenant Care California LLC* ***(P-20298)***
Shorett Printing Inc (PA) E **714 545-4689**
250 W Rialto Ave San Bernardino (92408) ***(P-4573)***
Shoring & Excavating, Santa Fe Springs *Also called Shoring Engineers* ***(P-1690)***
Shoring Engineers D 562 944-9331
12645 Clark St Santa Fe Springs (90670) ***(P-1690)***
Short Load Concrete Inc E 714 524-7013
605 E Commercial St Anaheim (92801) ***(P-6113)***
Shortcuts Software Inc E 714 622-6600
7711 Center Ave Ste 550 Huntington Beach (92647) ***(P-17981)***
Show Group Production Services, Gardena *Also called Sgps Inc* ***(P-11754)***
Show Off Time, Ventura *Also called Fnc Medical Corporation* ***(P-5021)***
Show Offs F 909 885-5223
1696 W Mill St Unit 10 Colton (92324) ***(P-3664)***
Showbiz Drapery, Van Nuys *Also called Showbiz Enterprises Inc* ***(P-17371)***
Showbiz Enterprises Inc (PA) E **818 989-5005**
15541 Lanark St Van Nuys (91406) ***(P-17371)***
Showerdoordirect LLC E 310 327-8060
20100 Normandie Ave Torrance (90502) ***(P-6912)***
Showershapes, Ventura *Also called G W Surfaces* ***(P-1660)***
Showroom Interiors LLC C 323 348-1551
8905 Rex Rd Pico Rivera (90660) ***(P-17372)***
Showtime Custom Coach Inc E 909 867-7025
2461 Deep Creek Dr Running Springs (92382) ***(P-18804)***
Shred-Tech Usa LLC F 909 923-2783
1100 S Grove Ave Ontario (91761) ***(P-7717)***
Shrin LLC D 714 850-0303
900 E Arlee Pl Anaheim (92805) ***(P-13089)***
Shriner's Hospital, Pasadena *Also called Shriners Hspitals For Children* ***(P-21052)***
Shriners Hspitals For Children C 213 388-3151
909 S Fair Oaks Ave Pasadena (91105) ***(P-21052)***
Shuttercraft of California, Santa Fe Springs *Also called Steiner & Mateer Inc* ***(P-3292)***
Shutters On The Beach, Santa Monica *Also called By The Blue Sea LLC* ***(P-16362)***
Shutters On The Beach, Santa Monica *Also called Edward Thomas Hospitality Corp* ***(P-16427)***
Shuttle Smart Inc C 310 338-9466
6150 W 96th St Los Angeles (90045) ***(P-11840)***
Shyam Bhaskar MD Inc (PA) D **559 635-7100**
231 W Noble Ave Visalia (93277) ***(P-20064)***
Shye West Inc (PA) E **949 486-4598**
43 Corporate Park Ste 102 Irvine (92606) ***(P-11594)***
Shyft Group Inc E 323 276-1933
1130 S Vail Ave Montebello (90640) ***(P-9966)***
Si, Fontana *Also called California Steel Inds Inc* ***(P-6192)***
SI Inc E 951 304-9444
26035 Jefferson Ave Murrieta (92562) ***(P-1455)***
Si Manufacturing Inc E 714 956-7110
1440 S Allec St Anaheim (92805) ***(P-9644)***
Sia Engineering (usa) Inc D 310 693-7108
7001 W Imperial Hwy Los Angeles (90045) ***(P-22654)***
Sialic Contractors Corporation D 562 803-9977
12240 Woodruff Ave Downey (90241) ***(P-915)***
Sibyl Shepard Inc E 562 531-8612
8225 Alondra Blvd Paramount (90723) ***(P-3119)***
Sid E Parker Boiler Mfg Co Inc D 323 727-9800
5930 Bandini Blvd Commerce (90040) ***(P-6752)***
Sid-Mar Inc E 213 626-8121
23303 La Palma Ave Yorba Linda (92887) ***(P-4423)***
Siegfried Irvine, Irvine *Also called Alliance Medical Products Inc* ***(P-10931)***
Siemens Energy Inc D 949 448-0600
6 Journey Ste 200 Aliso Viejo (92656) ***(P-4204)***
Siemens Hlthcare Dgnostics Inc D 310 645-8200
5210 Pacific Concourse Dr Los Angeles (90045) ***(P-11058)***
Siemens Industry Inc F 714 891-3964
7485 Anaconda Ave Garden Grove (92841) ***(P-9242)***
Siemens Medical Solutions, Los Angeles *Also called Siemens Hlthcare Dgnostics Inc* ***(P-11058)***
Siemens Mobility Inc A 714 284-0206
1026 E Lacy Ave Anaheim (92805) ***(P-9243)***
Siemens Rail Automation Corp D 909 532-5405
9568 Archibald Ave Rancho Cucamonga (91730) ***(P-9352)***
Sientra Inc (PA) C **805 562-3500**
420 S Fairview Ave # 200 Santa Barbara (93117) ***(P-11141)***
Sierra Aerospace LLC F 805 526-8669
2263 Ward Ave Simi Valley (93065) ***(P-10225)***
Sierra Alloys Company D 626 969-6711
5467 Ayon Ave Irwindale (91706) ***(P-7106)***
Sierra Aluminum, Riverside *Also called Samuel Son & Co (usa) Inc* ***(P-6316)***
Sierra Automated Sys/Eng Corp E 818 840-6749
2821 Burton Ave Burbank (91504) ***(P-9317)***
Sierra Canyon Inc D 818 882-8121
11052 Independence Ave Chatsworth (91311) ***(P-19669)***
Sierra Canyon Day Camp, Chatsworth *Also called Sierra Canyon Inc* ***(P-19669)***
Sierra Corporate MGT Inc (PA) D **714 575-5130**
320 N Park Vista St Anaheim (92806) ***(P-23107)***
Sierra Forest Products C 559 535-4893
9000 Road 234 Terra Bella (93270) ***(P-13288)***
Sierra Group, Glendale *Also called Next Venture Inc* ***(P-797)***
Sierra Group Inc F 760 377-1000
1129 N Calvert Blvd Ridgecrest (93555) ***(P-12369)***

Sierra Hotel Group LLC D 909 822-7300
10543 Sierra Ave Fontana (92337) ***(P-16709)***
Sierra International McHy LLC D 661 327-7073
1620 E Brundage Ln Frnt Bakersfield (93307) ***(P-14122)***
Sierra Landscape Development E 626 447-5260
2209 1/2 Chico Ave South El Monte (91733) ***(P-280)***
Sierra Lathing Company Inc C 909 421-0211
1189 Leiske Dr Rialto (92376) ***(P-1401)***
Sierra Medical Group, Lancaster *Also called Sierra Primary Care Medical* ***(P-20065)***
Sierra Monolithics Inc (HQ) D **310 698-1000**
103 W Torrance Blvd Redondo Beach (90277) ***(P-23508)***
Sierra Pacific Constrs Inc D 747 888-5000
22212 Ventura Blvd # 300 Woodland Hills (91364) ***(P-826)***
Sierra Pacific Engrg & Pdts, Long Beach *Also called SPEP Acquisition Corp* ***(P-6538)***
Sierra Pacific Farms Inc (PA) D **951 699-9980**
43406 Business Park Dr Temecula (92590) ***(P-228)***
Sierra Primary Care Medical (PA) D **661 945-9411**
44469 10th St W Lancaster (93534) ***(P-20065)***
Sierra Springs Apartments, San Bernardino *Also called Woodman Realty Inc* ***(P-16034)***
Sierra Systems Inc (PA) C **310 536-6288**
222 N Pacific Coast Hwy # 1310 El Segundo (90245) ***(P-23322)***
Sierra Technical Services Inc F 661 823-1092
101 Commercial Way Unit D Tehachapi (93561) ***(P-6274)***
Sierra Traffic Service Inc F 805 388-2474
225 W Loop Dr Camarillo (93010) ***(P-9353)***
Sierra View Dst Hosp Leag Inc (PA) A **559 784-1110**
465 W Putnam Ave Porterville (93257) ***(P-20066)***
Sierra View Inc E 760 371-4301
109 N Sanders St Ridgecrest (93555) ***(P-4027)***
Sierra View Medical Center, Porterville *Also called Sierra View Dst Hosp Leag Inc* ***(P-20066)***
Sierra Vista Extended Stay, Brea *Also called Otb Acquisition LLC* ***(P-16600)***
Sierra Vista Family Medical D 805 582-4000
1227 E Los Angeles Ave Simi Valley (93065) ***(P-21480)***
Sierra Vista Hospital Inc (HQ) A **805 546-7600**
1010 Murray Ave San Luis Obispo (93405) ***(P-20939)***
Sierra Vista Regional Med Ctr, San Luis Obispo *Also called Sierra Vista Hospital Inc* ***(P-20939)***
Sierra Woodworking Inc F 949 493-4528
960 6th St Ste 101a Norco (92860) ***(P-3288)***
Sierracin Corporation (HQ) A **818 741-1656**
12780 San Fernando Rd Sylmar (91342) ***(P-5112)***
Sierracin/Sylmar Corporation A 818 362-6711
12780 San Fernando Rd Sylmar (91342) ***(P-5819)***
Sigma Faction Inc E 951 416-0961
31681 Riverside Dr Lake Elsinore (92530) ***(P-23108)***
Sigma Services Inc (PA) D **805 642-8377**
2140 Eastman Ave Ste 110 Ventura (93003) ***(P-827)***
Sigma Supply & Dist Inc F 818 246-4624
701 W Harvard St Glendale (91204) ***(P-13520)***
Sigmanet Inc (HQ) C **909 230-7500**
4290 E Brickell St Ontario (91761) ***(P-13437)***
Sigmatronix Inc F 714 436-1618
2109 S Susan St Santa Ana (92704) ***(P-9195)***
Sign Development Inc F 909 920-5535
1366 W 9th St Upland (91786) ***(P-11595)***
Sign Factory Printing & Offic F 760 357-0098
120 N 4th St El Centro (92243) ***(P-11596)***
Sign Industries Inc E 909 930-0303
2101 Carrillo Privado Ontario (91761) ***(P-11597)***
Sign Mart, Orange *Also called Metal Art of California Inc* ***(P-11573)***
Sign Pipers Inc F 657 215-3957
17451 Nichols Ln Ste C Huntington Beach (92647) ***(P-11598)***
Sign Specialists Corporation E 714 641-0064
111 W Dyer Rd Ste F Santa Ana (92707) ***(P-11599)***
Sign-A-Rama, Palm Desert *Also called Pd Group* ***(P-11581)***
Signage Solutions Corporation E 714 491-0299
2231 S Dupont Dr Anaheim (92806) ***(P-11600)***
Signal D 661 259-1234
26330 Diamond Pl Ste 100 Santa Clarita (91350) ***(P-4028)***
Signal Health Police Dept E 562 989-7200
2745 Walnut Ave Signal Hill (90755) ***(P-22368)***
Signal Hill Petroleum Inc E 562 595-6440
2633 Cherry Ave Signal Hill (90755) ***(P-469)***
Signal Sciences Corp F 424 289-0342
600 Corporate Pointe # 1200 Culver City (90230) ***(P-17982)***
Signature Control Systems D 949 580-3640
16485 Laguna Canyon Rd # 130 Irvine (92618) ***(P-7619)***
Signature Flexible Packg LLC D 323 887-1997
19310 San Jose Ave City of Industry (91748) ***(P-5196)***
Signature Fresh, City of Industry *Also called Ssre Holdings LLC* ***(P-1720)***
Signature Propellers, Santa Ana *Also called Hill Marine Products LLC* ***(P-8618)***
Signature Rsrces Insur Fncl Sv D 949 930-2400
19900 Macarthur Blvd Irvine (92612) ***(P-15628)***
Signature Tech Group Inc F 818 890-7611
11960 Borden Ave San Fernando (91340) ***(P-9781)***
Signco, Yorba Linda *Also called Sesa Inc* ***(P-17187)***
Signs and Services Company E 714 761-8200
10980 Boatman Ave Stanton (90680) ***(P-11601)***
Signs of Success Inc E 805 925-7545
2350 Skyway Dr Ste 10 Santa Maria (93455) ***(P-11602)***
Signum Systems Corporation F 805 383-3682
1211 Flynn Rd Unit 104 Camarillo (93012) ***(P-10770)***
Signworld America Inc (PA) D **844 900-7446**
12023 Arrow Rte Rancho Cucamonga (91739) ***(P-11603)***
Sigtronics Corporation E 909 305-9399
178 E Arrow Hwy San Dimas (91773) ***(P-9354)***
Sigue Corporation (PA) D **818 837-5939**
13190 Telfair Ave Sylmar (91342) ***(P-18666)***

Sika Corporation.....F.....562 941-0231
12767 Imperial Hwy Santa Fe Springs (90670) *(P-5242)*
Sikama International Inc.....F.....805 962-1000
118 E Gutierrez St Santa Barbara (93101) *(P-7895)*
Silao Tortilleria Inc.....E.....626 961-0761
250 N California Ave City of Industry (91744) *(P-2524)*
Silent Valley Club Inc.....D.....951 849-4501
46305 Poppet Flats Rd Banning (92220) *(P-16710)*
Silenx Corporation.....F.....562 941-4200
10606 Shoemaker Ave Ste A Santa Fe Springs (90670) *(P-10723)*
Silgan Containers Corporation (HQ).....**D.....818 710-3700**
21600 Oxnard St Ste 1600 Woodland Hills (91367) *(P-6468)*
Silgan Containers LLC (HQ).....**D.....818 710-3700**
21600 Oxnard St Ste 1600 Woodland Hills (91367) *(P-6469)*
Silgan Containers Mfg Corp (HQ).....**B.....818 710-3700**
21600 Oxnard St Ste 1600 Woodland Hills (91367) *(P-6470)*
Silicon Tech Inc.....B.....949 476-1130
3009 Daimler St Santa Ana (92705) *(P-8218)*
Silicontech, Santa Ana *Also called Silicon Tech Inc (P-8218)*
Silla Automotive LLC.....D.....661 392-8880
1901 Mineral Ct Ste C Bakersfield (93308) *(P-13090)*
Sillcrest Nursing Home, San Bernardino *Also called Marna Health Services Inc (P-20611)*
Silmar Division, Hawthorne *Also called Ip Corporation (P-4698)*
Silo City Inc.....E.....661 387-0179
1401 S Union Ave Bakersfield (93307) *(P-7650)*
Silpak Inc (PA).....**F.....909 625-0056**
470 E Bonita Ave Pomona (91767) *(P-4716)*
Silq Technologies Corporation.....F.....310 806-9202
607 Charles E Young Dr E Los Angeles (90095) *(P-8098)*
Siltanen Inc.....D.....310 321-5200
353 Coral Cir El Segundo (90245) *(P-17077)*
Siltanen & Partners Advg, El Segundo *Also called Siltanen Inc (P-17077)*
Silver Cinemas Acquisition Co (HQ).....**D.....310 473-6701**
700 N San Vicnte Blvd G460 West Hollywood (90069) *(P-19289)*
Silver Creek Industries LLC.....C.....951 943-5393
2830 Barrett Ave Perris (92571) *(P-828)*
Silver Lake Medical Center, Los Angeles *Also called Success Healthcare 1 LLC (P-21219)*
Silver Lakes Association.....D.....760 245-1606
15273 Orchard Hill Ln Helendale (92342) *(P-22369)*
Silver Rock Resort Golf Club.....D.....760 777-8884
79179 Ahmanson Ln La Quinta (92253) *(P-19509)*
Silver Saddle Ranch & Club Inc.....D.....760 373-8617
20751 Aristotle Dr California City (93505) *(P-16073)*
Silver Star Distribution, Irvine *Also called Str Worldwide Inc (P-14352)*
Silver Strand.....E.....818 701-9707
8945 Fullbright Ave Chatsworth (91311) *(P-1456)*
Silverado Energy Company.....D.....949 752-5588
18101 Von Karman Ave # 9 Irvine (92612) *(P-12825)*
Silverado Framing & Cnstr.....D.....951 352-1100
3091 E La Cadena Dr Riverside (92507) *(P-641)*
Silverado Senior Living Inc.....D.....424 257-6418
514 N Prospect Ave # 120 Redondo Beach (90277) *(P-20465)*
Silverado Senior Living Inc (PA).....**D.....949 240-7200**
6400 Oak Cyn Ste 200 Irvine (92618) *(P-20466)*
Silverado Senior Living Inc.....D.....747 477-2618
601 S Glenoaks Blvd Burbank (91502) *(P-20467)*
Silverado Senior Living Inc.....D.....858 869-0538
6400 Oak Cyn Ste 150 Irvine (92618) *(P-20468)*
Silverado Senior Living Inc.....D.....949 240-7744
6400 Oak Cyn Ste 150 Irvine (92618) *(P-20469)*
Silverado Senior Living Inc.....D.....805 230-2626
4520 E Thousand Oaks Blvd Westlake Village (91362) *(P-20470)*
Silverado Senior Living Inc.....D.....949 945-0189
350 W Bay St Costa Mesa (92627) *(P-20471)*
Silverado Senior Living Inc.....D.....949 988-0921
30311 Camino Capistrano San Juan Capistrano (92675) *(P-20472)*
Silverado Senior Living Inc.....D.....626 872-3941
1118 N Stoneman Ave Alhambra (91801) *(P-20473)*
Silverado Senior Living Inc.....D.....818 746-2583
25100 Calabasas Rd Calabasas (91302) *(P-20474)*
Silverado Senior Living Inc.....D.....323 984-7313
330 N Hayworth Ave Los Angeles (90048) *(P-20475)*
Silverado Snior Lving Hldngs.....A.....949 240-7200
6400 Oak Cyn Ste 200 Irvine (92618) *(P-22153)*
Silverline Construction Inc (PA).....**C.....310 327-4970**
1421 W 132nd St Gardena (90249) *(P-829)*
Silveron Industries Inc.....F.....909 598-4533
182 S Brent Cir City of Industry (91789) *(P-8962)*
Silverrest, Fullerton *Also called Brentwood Home LLC (P-3544)*
Silverscreen Healthcare Inc.....C.....909 793-1382
1875 Barton Rd Redlands (92373) *(P-20627)*
Silverstein, Sylvain S MD, Van Nuys *Also called Vanowen Medical Associates (P-20133)*
Silverwood Landscape Cnstr Inc.....E.....714 427-6134
2209 S Lyon St Santa Ana (92705) *(P-343)*
Silvester California, Los Angeles *Also called Silvestri Studio Inc (P-11756)*
Silvestri Studio Inc (PA).....**D.....323 277-4420**
8125 Beach St Los Angeles (90001) *(P-11756)*
Silvus Technologies Inc (PA).....**D.....310 479-3333**
10990 Wilshire Blvd # 1500 Los Angeles (90024) *(P-9318)*
Sim Ideation, Irvine *Also called Specialty Interior Mfg Inc (P-13095)*
Simex-Iwerks, Santa Clarita *Also called Iwerks Entertainment Inc (P-9876)*
Simi Valley Chrysler, Woodland Hills *Also called Reseda Dodge Sales Inc (P-18866)*
Simi Valley Family YMCA, Simi Valley *Also called Young MNS Chrstn Assn Sthast V (P-19683)*
Simi Vly Care & Rehabilitation, Simi Valley *Also called Chase Group Llc (P-22876)*
Simi Vly Hosp & Hlth Care Svcs, Simi Valley *Also called Simi Vly Hosp & Hlth Care Svcs (P-20941)*
Simi Vly Hosp & Hlth Care Svcs.....C.....805 955-6000
2750 Sycamore Dr Simi Valley (93065) *(P-20940)*
Simi Vly Hosp & Hlth Care Svcs (HQ).....**A.....805 955-6000**
2975 Sycamore Dr Simi Valley (93065) *(P-20941)*
Simi West Inc.....C.....760 346-5502
999 Enchanted Way Simi Valley (93065) *(P-16711)*
Simi YMCA Elementary Site, Simi Valley *Also called Young MNS Chrstn Assn Sthast V (P-22388)*
Simmons Construction Inc.....E.....661 636-1321
19252 Flightpath Way Bakersfield (93308) *(P-830)*
Simon and Gladstone A Prof, Irvine *Also called Berger Kahn A Law Corporation (P-21513)*
Simon G Jewelry Inc.....E.....818 500-8595
528 State St Glendale (91203) *(P-14139)*
Simoniz Janss Mall Car Wash, Thousand Oaks *Also called Wash Depot Auto Centers LP (P-18918)*
Simons Brick Corporation.....E.....951 279-1000
4301 Firestone Blvd South Gate (90280) *(P-6174)*
Simple Green, Huntington Beach *Also called Sunshine Makers Inc (P-4979)*
Simple Science Inc.....E.....949 335-1099
1626 Ohms Way Costa Mesa (92627) *(P-18667)*
Simplehuman LLC (PA).....**D.....310 436-2250**
19850 Magellan Dr Torrance (90502) *(P-13185)*
Simplex Isolation Systems, Fontana *Also called Simplex Strip Doors LLC (P-5438)*
Simplex Strip Doors LLC (PA).....**E.....800 854-7951**
14500 Miller Ave Fontana (92336) *(P-5438)*
Simplex Supplies Inc.....E.....618 594-6450
1370 Valley Vista Dr # 200 Diamond Bar (91765) *(P-6662)*
Simply Display.....F.....888 767-0676
12200 Los Nietos Rd Santa Fe Springs (90670) *(P-11604)*
Simply Fresh LLC.....C.....714 562-5000
11215 Knott Ave Ste A Cypress (90630) *(P-2350)*
Simply Straws LLC.....F.....855 787-2974
1725 Monrovia Ave Ste C3 Costa Mesa (92627) *(P-5942)*
Simpson Automotive Inc.....D.....714 690-6200
6600 Auto Center Dr Buena Park (90621) *(P-18904)*
Simpson Buick Pontiac GMC, Buena Park *Also called Simpson Automotive Inc (P-18904)*
Simpson House Inn Inc.....D.....805 963-7067
121 E Arrellaga St Santa Barbara (93101) *(P-16712)*
Simpson Industries Inc.....E.....310 605-1224
1093 E Bedmar St Carson (90746) *(P-4894)*
Simpson Strong-Tie Company Inc.....C.....714 871-8373
12246 Holly St Riverside (92509) *(P-3367)*
Simpsonsimpson Industries, Carson *Also called Simpson Industries Inc (P-4894)*
Simso Tex Sublimation (PA).....**D.....310 885-9717**
3028 E Las Hermanas St Compton (90221) *(P-3182)*
Simulations Plus Inc (PA).....**D.....661 723-7723**
42505 10th St W Ste 103 Lancaster (93534) *(P-18065)*
Sinai Temple.....C.....323 469-6000
5950 Forest Lawn Dr Los Angeles (90068) *(P-16930)*
Sinai Temple (PA).....**B.....310 474-1518**
10400 Wilshire Blvd Los Angeles (90024) *(P-16931)*
Sinanian Development Inc.....D.....818 996-9666
18980 Ventura Blvd # 200 Tarzana (91356) *(P-831)*
Sincere Orient Commercial Corp.....D.....626 333-8882
15222 Valley Blvd City of Industry (91746) *(P-2525)*
Sincere Orient Food Company, City of Industry *Also called Sincere Orient Commercial Corp (P-2525)*
Sinecera Inc.....D.....626 962-1087
5397 3rd St Irwindale (91706) *(P-18668)*
Sing Tao Newspapers Ltd.....D.....626 839-8200
17059 Green Dr City of Industry (91745) *(P-4029)*
Sing Tao Nwspapers Los Angeles, City of Industry *Also called Sing Tao Newspapers Ltd (P-4029)*
Singapore Airlines Limited.....C.....310 647-1922
222 N Pcf Cast Hwy Ste 16 El Segundo (90245) *(P-12313)*
Singerlewak LLP (PA).....**C.....310 477-3924**
10960 Wilshire Blvd Fl 7 Los Angeles (90024) *(P-22813)*
Singod Investors Vi LLC.....D.....714 326-7800
1600 S Clementine St Anaheim (92802) *(P-4669)*
Singularity 6 Corporation (PA).....**F.....310 963-1655**
12203 W Pico Blvd Los Angeles (90064) *(P-17983)*
Sion & Shamoneil Fmly Partner, Vernon *Also called Bobco Metals LLC (P-13550)*
Sipa Medical Group, Bakersfield *Also called Truxtun Psychtric Med Group LP (P-20112)*
Sir Speedy, Whittier *Also called George Coriaty (P-4302)*
Sir Speedy Inc (HQ).....**E.....949 348-5000**
26722 Plaza Mission Viejo (92691) *(P-4424)*
Siracusa Enterprises Inc.....D.....818 831-1130
17737 Chtswrth St Ste 200 Granada Hills (91344) *(P-17465)*
Sirena Incorporated.....F.....866 548-5353
22717 S Western Ave Torrance (90501) *(P-4574)*
SIS, Culver City *Also called Security Indust Specialists Inc (P-18328)*
Sisc, Bakersfield *Also called Self-Insured Schools Cal (P-15520)*
Sisneros Inc.....E.....562 777-9797
12717 Los Nietos Rd Santa Fe Springs (90670) *(P-3616)*
Sisneros Office Furntiure, Santa Fe Springs *Also called Sisneros Inc (P-3616)*
Sissell Bros.....E.....323 261-0106
4322 E 3rd St Los Angeles (90022) *(P-6056)*
Sisters of Nzareth Los Angeles.....D.....310 839-2361
3333 Manning Ave Los Angeles (90064) *(P-22154)*
Sisters of Saint Joseph, Fullerton *Also called St Jude Heritage Med Group (P-20965)*
Sisters of Soul SOS Yuth Fmly.....D.....909 533-4889
937 Via Lata Ste 400 Colton (92324) *(P-22258)*
Sisters of St Joseph Orange.....A.....562 430-4638
240 Ocean Ave Seal Beach (90740) *(P-20942)*
Sistone Inc.....F.....818 988-9918
15530 Lanark St Van Nuys (91406) *(P-3665)*
Sit On It, Buena Park *Also called Exemplis LLC (P-3609)*

ALPHABETIC

Employee Codes: A=Over 500 employees, B=251-500
C=101-250, D=51-100, E=20-50 F=10-19
2022 Southern California Business Directory and Buyers Guide
© Mergent Inc. 1-800-342-5647
1271

Site Crew Inc ....B....714 668-0100
3185 Airway Ave Ste G Costa Mesa (92626) ***(P-17284)***
Siteserver Inc ....E....805 579-7831
4514 Ish Dr Simi Valley (93063) ***(P-23509)***
Sitestuff Yardi Systems I (PA)....**C....805 966-3666**
430 S Fairview Ave Goleta (93117) ***(P-23323)***
Sitonit, Cypress *Also called Exemplis LLC* ***(P-3611)***
Sitonit Seating Inc....A....714 995-4800
6415 Katella Ave Cypress (90630) ***(P-13152)***
Sitrick Brincko Group LLC....D....310 788-2850
1840 Century Park E # 800 Los Angeles (90067) ***(P-23324)***
Six Continents Hotels Inc....C....661 343-3316
612 Wainwight Ct Lebec (93243) ***(P-16713)***
Six Eleven Limited Inc....F....818 764-5810
11921 Sherman Way North Hollywood (91605) ***(P-6145)***
Sizzix, Lake Forest *Also called Ellison Educational Eqp Inc* ***(P-7914)***
Sizzler USA Restaurants Inc (HQ)....**C....949 273-4497**
25910 Acero Ste 350 Mission Viejo (92691) ***(P-16217)***
Sj Controls Inc....E....562 494-1400
2248 Obispo Ave Ste 203 Long Beach (90755) ***(P-10724)***
SJ Distributors Inc....D....888 988-2328
6116 Walker Ave Maywood (90270) ***(P-14531)***
SJ&I Bias Binding & Tex Co Inc....E....213 747-5271
1950 E 20th St Vernon (90058) ***(P-3183)***
Sk Chemicals America Inc....F....949 336-8088
3 Park Plz Ste 430 Irvine (92614) ***(P-4717)***
Sk Drapes, North Hollywood *Also called S & K Theatrical Drap Inc* ***(P-3093)***
SK&a, Irvine *Also called Iqvia Inc* ***(P-22890)***
Skadden Arps Slate Meagher & F....C....213 687-5000
300 S Grand Ave Ste 3400 Los Angeles (90071) ***(P-21678)***
SKANSKA ROCKY MOUNTAIN DISTRICT, Riverside *Also called Skanska USA Cvil W Rcky Mtn Ds* ***(P-1004)***
Skanska USA Cvil W Cal Dst Inc (HQ)....**A....951 684-5360**
1995 Agua Mansa Rd Riverside (92509) ***(P-916)***
Skanska USA Cvil W Rcky Mtn Ds (HQ)....**D....970 565-8000**
1995 Agua Mansa Rd Riverside (92509) ***(P-1004)***
Skat-Trak....E....909 795-2505
654 Avenue K Calimesa (92320) ***(P-5305)***
Skate One Corp....D....805 964-1330
6860 Cortona Dr Ste B Goleta (93117) ***(P-11447)***
Skaug Truck Body Works....F....818 365-9123
1404 1st St San Fernando (91340) ***(P-9995)***
SKB Corporation (PA)....**B....714 637-1252**
434 W Levers Pl Orange (92867) ***(P-5820)***
Skechers Collection LLC....E....310 318-3100
228 Manhattan Beach Blvd Manhattan Beach (90266) ***(P-5314)***
Skechers USA Inc....E....310 318-3100
330 S Sepulveda Blvd Manhattan Beach (90266) ***(P-5315)***
Skechers USA Inc (PA)....**D....310 318-3100**
228 Manhattan Beach Blvd # 200 Manhattan Beach (90266) ***(P-5886)***
Skechers USA Inc II (HQ)....**D....800 746-3411**
228 Manhattan Beach Blvd # 200 Manhattan Beach (90266) ***(P-5316)***
Skeffington Enterprises Inc....D....714 540-1700
2200 S Yale St Santa Ana (92704) ***(P-16111)***
Sketchers, Manhattan Beach *Also called Skechers Collection LLC* ***(P-5314)***
Skid Row Housing Trust, Los Angeles *Also called Srht Property Holding LLC* ***(P-16009)***
Skilled Nursing Facility, Taft *Also called West Side Dst Hosp Foundation* ***(P-21007)***
Skillz Inc (PA)....**B....415 762-0511**
2121 Avenue Of The Stars Los Angeles (90067) ***(P-17713)***
Skin Health Experts LLC....D....323 655-7546
8428 Melrose Pl Los Angeles (90069) ***(P-19468)***
Skinfood Usa Inc....D....818 998-1142
9301 Tampa Ave Unit 59 Northridge (91324) ***(P-14289)***
Skirball Cultural Center....C....310 440-4500
2701 N Sepulveda Blvd Los Angeles (90049) ***(P-22236)***
Sklar Bov Solutions Inc....E....323 266-7111
3137 E 26th St Vernon (90058) ***(P-7570)***
Skm Industries Inc....F....661 294-8373
28966 Hancock Pkwy Valencia (91355) ***(P-7182)***
Skog Furniture, Pomona *Also called Aw Industries Inc* ***(P-3463)***
Skullduggery Inc....F....714 777-6425
5433 E La Palma Ave Anaheim (92807) ***(P-11391)***
Skurka Aerospace Inc (HQ)....**C....805 484-8884**
4600 Calle Bolero Camarillo (93012) ***(P-8930)***
Sky Court USA Inc....B....805 497-9991
880 S Westlake Blvd Westlake Village (91361) ***(P-16714)***
Sky Jeans Inc....E....323 778-2065
6600 Avalon Blvd Ste 102 Los Angeles (90003) ***(P-2587)***
Sky One Inc....F....909 622-3333
1793 W 2nd St Pomona (91766) ***(P-5994)***
Sky Rider Equipment Co Inc....E....714 632-6890
1180 N Blue Gum St Anaheim (92806) ***(P-3559)***
Sky Zone LLC (HQ)....**C....310 734-0300**
1201 W 5th St Ste T340 Los Angeles (90017) ***(P-19378)***
Skyco Shading Systems Inc....E....714 708-3038
3411 W Fordham Ave Santa Ana (92704) ***(P-3289)***
Skyco Skylights Inc....E....949 629-4090
401 Goetz Ave Santa Ana (92707) ***(P-5922)***
Skyguard LLC....E....703 262-0500
2945 Townsgate Rd Ste 200 Westlake Village (91361) ***(P-9914)***
Skyhill Financial Inc....D....714 657-3938
5762 Bolsa Ave Ste 110 Huntington Beach (92649) ***(P-15999)***
Skyline Cabinet & Millworks, Bakersfield *Also called Spalinger Enterprises Inc* ***(P-3666)***
Skyline Flwr Growers Shippers, Nipomo *Also called L J T Flowers Inc* ***(P-14863)***
Skyline Healthcare Center, Los Angeles *Also called Skyline Hlthcare Wllness Ctr L* ***(P-20476)***
Skyline Hlthcare Wllness Ctr L....D....323 665-1185
3032 Rowena Ave Los Angeles (90039) ***(P-20476)***
Skyline International Inc....F....714 290-8866
6663 Leanne St Eastvale (91752) ***(P-9782)***
Skyline Seating, Westminster *Also called Dang Tha* ***(P-3621)***
Skyline Security MGT Inc (PA)....**D....562 622-7114**
10642 Downey Ave Ste 205 Downey (90241) ***(P-18400)***
Skylock Industries....E....201 637-9505
1290 W Optical Dr Azusa (91702) ***(P-10418)***
Skylock Industries LLC....D....626 334-2391
1290 W Optical Dr Azusa (91702) ***(P-10419)***
Skylstad-Schoelen Co Inc....D....805 349-0503
3130 Skyway Dr Ste 701 Santa Maria (93455) ***(P-17285)***
Skynet USA Asset MGT Inc....E....702 969-5599
17011 Beach Blvd Fl 9th Huntington Beach (92647) ***(P-23325)***
Skyone Federal Credit Union (PA)....**D....310 491-7500**
14600 Aviation Blvd Hawthorne (90250) ***(P-15089)***
Skypark At Santa's Village, Skyforest *Also called Spsv Entertainment LLC* ***(P-19380)***
Skypower Holdings LLC....C....323 860-4900
4700 Wilshire Blvd Los Angeles (90010) ***(P-1139)***
Skyview Capital LLC....D....310 273-6000
2000 Avenue Of The Stars # 810 Los Angeles (90067) ***(P-15159)***
Skywest Airlines Inc....D....951 926-9511
32128 Chagall Ct Winchester (92596) ***(P-12314)***
Skywest Airlines Inc....D....951 600-9181
26818 Bahama Way Murrieta (92563) ***(P-12315)***
Skyworks Solutions Inc (PA)....**A....949 231-3000**
5260 California Ave Irvine (92617) ***(P-9576)***
Skyworks Solutions Inc....F....301 874-6408
1767 Carr Rd Ste 105 Calexico (92231) ***(P-8983)***
SL Power Electronics Corp (HQ)....**D....800 235-5929**
6050 King Dr Ste A Ventura (93003) ***(P-13774)***
Slade Gorton & Co Inc....D....714 676-4200
1 Centerpointe Dr Ste 311 La Palma (90623) ***(P-14584)***
Slade Industrial Landscape Inc....D....818 885-1916
8838 Zelzah Ave Sherwood Forest (91325) ***(P-281)***
Slalom LLC....C....949 450-1100
300 Spectrum Center Dr # 1500 Irvine (92618) ***(P-23510)***
Slapfish Huntington Beach LLC....E....714 963-3900
10661 Ellis Ave Ste F Fountain Valley (92708) ***(P-1894)***
Slater Inc....D....909 822-6800
11045 Rose Ave Fontana (92337) ***(P-1005)***
Slaters 50/50 Inc (PA)....**C....714 685-1103**
5801 E Camino Pinzon Anaheim (92807) ***(P-16218)***
Slauson Plaza Med Group, Pico Rivera *Also called Altamed Health Services Corp* ***(P-21380)***
Slch Inc (PA)....**E....626 798-0558**
1920 N Fair Oaks Ave Pasadena (91103) ***(P-20477)***
Sleepcomp West LLC....E....562 946-3222
10006 Santa Fe Springs Rd Santa Fe Springs (90670) ***(P-5521)***
Sleepow Ltd....E....646 688-0808
11706 Darlington Ave Los Angeles (90049) ***(P-2588)***
Sleepy Giant Entertainment Inc....C....949 464-7986
4 San Joaquin Plz Ste 200 Newport Beach (92660) ***(P-17714)***
Sleepy Giant Entertainment Inc....D....714 460-4113
3501 Jamboree Rd Ste 5000 Newport Beach (92660) ***(P-19379)***
Slide Go, Redlands *Also called Prime-Line Products LLC* ***(P-13816)***
Slimsuit, Bell *Also called Carol Wior Inc* ***(P-2930)***
Sll Inc....F....323 581-9040
5401 S Soto St Vernon (90058) ***(P-2993)***
SLM Services, Simi Valley *Also called Specialized Ldscp MGT Svcs Inc* ***(P-233)***
Slo New Times Inc....E....805 546-8208
1010 Marsh St San Luis Obispo (93401) ***(P-4030)***
SLO TRANSITIONS, San Luis Obispo *Also called Transitions - Mental Hlth Assn* ***(P-21355)***
Sloanled, Ventura *Also called The Sloan Company Inc* ***(P-13670)***
Slogcc, San Luis Obispo *Also called San Luis Obispo Golf Cntry CLB* ***(P-19508)***
Slorta, San Luis Obispo *Also called San Luis Obspo Rgnal Trnst Aut* ***(P-11838)***
Sls Hotel At Beverly Hills....D....310 247-0400
465 S La Cienega Blvd Los Angeles (90048) ***(P-16715)***
SM 10000 Property LLC....D....305 374-5700
10000 Santa Monica Blvd Los Angeles (90067) ***(P-16074)***
SM Tire, Nipomo *Also called Santa Maria Tire Inc* ***(P-18810)***
SMA Builders Inc....E....818 994-8306
16134 Leadwell St Van Nuys (91406) ***(P-642)***
Small Business Advertising Inc....E....818 262-8923
5304 Derry Ave Ste L Agoura Hills (91301) ***(P-17101)***
Small Wnders Hndcrfted Mntres....F....818 703-7450
7033 Canoga Ave Ste 5 Canoga Park (91303) ***(P-11757)***
Smart LLC....E....310 674-8135
14108 S Western Ave Gardena (90249) ***(P-5821)***
Smart & Final Stores Inc....C....949 675-2396
3049 E Coast Hwy Corona Del Mar (92625) ***(P-14488)***
Smart & Final Stores Inc....C....323 549-9586
4550 W Pico Blvd Los Angeles (90019) ***(P-14489)***
Smart & Final Stores Inc....C....909 592-2190
1005 W Arrow Hwy San Dimas (91773) ***(P-14490)***
Smart & Final Stores Inc....C....909 773-1813
13346 Limonite Ave Eastvale (92880) ***(P-14491)***
Smart & Final Stores Inc....C....805 566-2174
850 Linden Ave Carpinteria (93013) ***(P-14492)***
Smart & Final Stores Inc....C....714 549-2362
1308 W Edinger Ave Santa Ana (92704) ***(P-14493)***
Smart & Final Stores Inc....C....626 330-2495
15427 Amar Rd La Puente (91744) ***(P-14494)***
Smart & Final Stores Inc....C....818 368-6409
18555 Devonshire St Northridge (91324) ***(P-14495)***
Smart & Final Stores Inc....C....562 438-0450
644 Redondo Ave Long Beach (90814) ***(P-14496)***
Smart & Final Stores Inc....C....805 237-0323
2121 Spring St Paso Robles (93446) ***(P-14497)***
Smart & Final Stores Inc....C....949 581-1212
26911 Trabuco Rd Mission Viejo (92691) ***(P-14498)***

Mergent e-mail: customerrelations@mergent.com
1272
2022 Southern California Business Directory and Buyers Guide
(P-0000) Products & Services Section entry number
(PA)=Parent Co (HQ)=Headquarters (DH)=Div Headquarters

Smart & Final Stores Inc ....C....323 497-8528
615 N Pacific Coast Hwy Redondo Beach (90277) ***(P-14499)***

Smart & Final Stores Inc ....C....323 855-8434
240 S Diamond Bar Blvd Diamond Bar (91765) ***(P-14500)***

Smart & Final Stores Inc ....C....818 954-8631
3830 W Verdugo Ave Burbank (91505) ***(P-14501)***

Smart & Final Stores Inc ....C....661 722-6210
5038 W Avenue N Palmdale (93551) ***(P-14502)***

Smart & Final Stores Inc ....C....818 889-8253
5770 Lindero Canyon Rd Westlake Village (91362) ***(P-14503)***

Smart & Final Stores Inc ....C....805 647-4276
7800 Telegraph Rd Ventura (93004) ***(P-14504)***

Smart & Final Stores Inc ....C....562 907-7037
13003 Whittier Blvd Whittier (90602) ***(P-14505)***

Smart & Final Stores Inc ....C....626 334-5189
303 E Foothill Blvd Azusa (91702) ***(P-14506)***

Smart & Final Stores Inc ....C....805 520-6035
5135 E Los Angeles Ave Simi Valley (93063) ***(P-14507)***

Smart & Final Stores LLC (HQ) ....**B....323 869-7500**
600 Citadel Dr Commerce (90040) ***(P-14508)***

Smart & Final Stores LLC (HQ) ....**B....323 869-7500**
600 Citadel Dr Commerce (90040) ***(P-14509)***

Smart Action Company LLC ....E....310 776-9200
300 Continental Blvd # 350 El Segundo (90245) ***(P-17984)***

Smart Choice Investments Inc (PA) ....**D....310 944-6985**
7121 Magnolia Ave Riverside (92504) ***(P-17466)***

Smart Circle International LLC (PA) ....**D....949 587-9207**
4490 Von Karman Ave Newport Beach (92660) ***(P-23326)***

Smart Circle, The, Newport Beach *Also called Smart Circle International LLC* ***(P-23326)***

Smart Elec & Assembly Inc ....C....714 772-2651
2000 W Corporate Way Anaheim (92801) ***(P-9454)***

Smart Energy Solar Inc ....C....800 405-1978
1641 Comm St Corona (92880) ***(P-1140)***

Smart Energy Systems Inc (PA) ....**C....909 703-9609**
15495 Sand Canyon Ave # 100 Irvine (92618) ***(P-17715)***

Smart Energy USA, Corona *Also called Smart Energy Solar Inc* ***(P-1140)***

Smart Foam Pads, Lake Forest *Also called Advanced Innvtive Rcvery Tech* ***(P-3539)***

Smart Foods LLC ....E....818 660-2238
3398 Leonis Blvd Vernon Vernon (90058) ***(P-1954)***

Smart Living Company, Simi Valley *Also called Specialty Merchandise Corp* ***(P-14976)***

Smart Systems Technologies (PA) ....**D....949 367-9375**
9 Goodyear Irvine (92618) ***(P-18401)***

Smart Wax, Gardena *Also called Smart LLC* ***(P-5821)***

Smartest Edu Inc ....F....833 463-6761
10880 Wilshire Blvd # 11 Los Angeles (90024) ***(P-17985)***

Smarthomepro, Irvine *Also called Smartlabs Inc* ***(P-10668)***

Smartlabs Inc ....D....800 762-7846
1621 Alton Pkwy Ste 100 Irvine (92606) ***(P-10668)***

Smartstop Op, Ladera Ranch *Also called Smartstop Self Storage* ***(P-12243)***

Smartstop Self Storage (HQ) ....**D....949 429-6600**
111 Corporate Dr Ste 120 Ladera Ranch (92694) ***(P-12243)***

Smartstop Self Storage Inc (HQ) ....**D....949 429-6600**
111 Corporate Dr Ste 120 Ladera Ranch (92694) ***(P-12244)***

SMC Grease Specialist Inc ....E....951 788-6042
1600 W Pellisier Rd Colton (92324) ***(P-12980)***

SMC Networks Inc (HQ) ....**D....949 679-8029**
20 Mason Irvine (92618) ***(P-13438)***

Smci, Costa Mesa *Also called Software Management Cons Inc* ***(P-17719)***

Smci, Glendale *Also called Software Management Cons LLC* ***(P-18222)***

SMD Holdings 2019 Inc ....F....310 953-4800
121 W Lexington Dr # 412 Glendale (91203) ***(P-17986)***

SMD Logistics Inc (PA) ....**C....760 352-3194**
101 E Main St Heber (92249) ***(P-12526)***

Smg Food and Beverage LLC (PA) ....**D....909 937-3000**
2000 E Convention Ctr Way Ontario (91764) ***(P-18669)***

Smg Holdings LLC ....D....562 499-7611
300 E Ocean Blvd Long Beach (90802) ***(P-15698)***

Smg Management Facility, Ontario *Also called Ontario Convention Center Corp* ***(P-18620)***

Smg Stone Company Inc ....D....818 767-0000
8460 San Fernando Rd Sun Valley (91352) ***(P-1352)***

SMI Architectural Millwork Inc ....E....714 567-0112
2116 W Chestnut Ave Santa Ana (92703) ***(P-3290)***

SMI Ca Inc ....E....562 926-9407
14340 Iseli Rd Santa Fe Springs (90670) ***(P-8796)***

SMI Millwork, Santa Ana *Also called SMI Architectural Millwork Inc* ***(P-3290)***

Smi, Scb, Los Angeles *Also called Dcx-Chol Enterprises Inc* ***(P-9360)***

Smile Brands Group Inc (PA) ....**D....714 668-1300**
100 Spectrum Center Dr # 100 Irvine (92618) ***(P-23109)***

Smile Housing Corporation ....D....805 772-6066
800 Quintana Rd Ste 2c Morro Bay (93442) ***(P-21339)***

Smile Keepers, Inglewood *Also called Interdent Inc* ***(P-20181)***

Smile Wide Dental, Irvine *Also called Universal Care Inc* ***(P-21361)***

Smith & Company, Los Angeles *Also called A S G Corporation* ***(P-11622)***

Smith Broadcasting Group Inc (PA) ....**C....805 965-0400**
2315 Red Rose Way Santa Barbara (93109) ***(P-23110)***

Smith Broadcasting Group Inc ....B....805 882-3933
730 Miramonte Dr Santa Barbara (93109) ***(P-12741)***

Smith Bros Inc (PA) ....**D....805 449-2841**
2301 Townsgate Rd Ste A Westlake Village (91361) ***(P-1457)***

Smith Bros Cstm Met Fbrication, South El Monte *Also called Smith Bros Strl Stl Pdts Inc* ***(P-6212)***

Smith Bros Finished Carpentry, Westlake Village *Also called Smith Bros Inc* ***(P-1457)***

Smith Bros Strl Stl Pdts Inc ....F....626 350-1872
1535 Potrero Ave South El Monte (91733) ***(P-6212)***

Smith Brothers Restaurant Inc ....D....626 577-2400
100 Corson St Lbby Pasadena (91103) ***(P-23111)***

Smith Electric Service, Santa Maria *Also called Smith McHncl-Lctrical-Plumbing* ***(P-717)***

Smith International Inc ....C....909 906-7900
11031 Jersey Blvd Ste A Rancho Cucamonga (91730) ***(P-546)***

Smith Ironworks, Hesperia *Also called Endura Steel Inc* ***(P-13565)***

Smith McHncl-Lctrical-Plumbing ....C....805 621-5000
1340 W Betteravia Rd Santa Maria (93455) ***(P-717)***

Smith Micro Software Inc ....F....949 362-5800
120 Vantis Dr Ste 350 Aliso Viejo (92656) ***(P-17987)***

Smith Packing Inc (PA) ....**C....805 348-1818**
111 W Chapel St Santa Maria (93458) ***(P-159)***

Smith Residential Care Fcilty (PA) ....**D....559 584-8451**
318 E 4th St Hanford (93230) ***(P-21212)***

Smith, Malcolm Motorsports, Riverside *Also called Malcolm Smith Motorcycles Inc* ***(P-16854)***

Smith-Emery Company (PA) ....**C....213 745-5312**
781 E Washington Blvd Los Angeles (90021) ***(P-23327)***

Smithco Plastics Inc (PA) ....**F....714 545-9107**
3330 W Harvard St Santa Ana (92704) ***(P-5822)***

Smithfield Foods, Vernon *Also called Clougherty Packing LLC* ***(P-1710)***

Smiths Action Plastic Inc (PA) ....**F....714 836-4141**
645 S Santa Fe St Santa Ana (92705) ***(P-5536)***

Smiths Interconnect Inc ....D....805 267-0100
375 Conejo Ridge Ave Thousand Oaks (91361) ***(P-9783)***

Smiths Intrcnnect Americas Inc ....B....714 371-1100
1231 E Dyer Rd Ste 235 Santa Ana (92705) ***(P-9784)***

Sml Space Maintainers Labs, Chatsworth *Also called Selane Products Inc* ***(P-11195)***

Smoke Tree Inc ....D....760 327-1221
1850 Smoke Tree Ln Palm Springs (92264) ***(P-16716)***

Smoke Tree Ranch, Palm Springs *Also called Smoke Tree Inc* ***(P-16716)***

Smokeless Selects LLC (PA) ....**F....619 564-8250**
27576 Commerce Center Dr # 114 Temecula (92590) ***(P-2552)***

Smoothie Inc ....F....310 598-7113
3600 Wilshire Blvd # 172 Los Angeles (90010) ***(P-1910)***

SMS Fabrications Inc ....E....951 351-6828
11698 Warm Springs Rd Riverside (92505) ***(P-6913)***

SMS Transportation Inc ....D....310 527-9200
18516 S Broadway Gardena (90248) ***(P-21679)***

SMS Transportation Svcs Inc ....C....213 489-5367
865 S Figueroa St # 2750 Los Angeles (90017) ***(P-11841)***

Smt Electronics Mfg Inc ....E....714 751-8894
2630 S Shannon St Santa Ana (92704) ***(P-9577)***

Smurfit Kappa North Amer LLC ....B....626 322-2123
440 Baldwin Park Blvd City of Industry (91746) ***(P-3827)***

Smwd Inc (PA) ....**D....323 904-4680**
3800 Barham Blvd Ste 410 Los Angeles (90068) ***(P-12742)***

Snack It Forward LLC ....E....310 242-5517
6080 Center Dr Ste 600 Los Angeles (90045) ***(P-2366)***

Snacknation, Los Angeles *Also called Awesome Office Inc* ***(P-14557)***

Snak Club LLC ....D....323 278-9578
5560 E Slauson Ave Commerce (90040) ***(P-2116)***

Snap Inc (PA) ....**A....310 399-3339**
2772 Dnald Douglas Loop N Santa Monica (90405) ***(P-17716)***

SNAPCHAT, Santa Monica *Also called Snap Inc* ***(P-17716)***

Snapcomms Inc ....D....805 715-0300
155 N Lake Ave Fl 9 Pasadena (91101) ***(P-17717)***

Snapnrack Inc ....F....877 732-2860
775 Fiero Ln Ste 200 San Luis Obispo (93401) ***(P-6536)***

Snappays Mobile Inc ....E....310 869-6942
14140 Ventura Blvd Sherman Oaks (91423) ***(P-17718)***

Snapshot Hair & Extensions LLC ....F....877 783-5658
2892 N Bellflower Blvd Long Beach (90815) ***(P-11758)***

Snapware Corporation ....C....951 361-3100
2325 Cottonwood Ave Riverside (92508) ***(P-5823)***

Snell & Wilmer LLP ....D....714 427-7000
600 Anton Blvd Ste 1400 Costa Mesa (92626) ***(P-21680)***

Snf Management ....D....310 385-1090
9200 W Sunset Blvd # 700 West Hollywood (90069) ***(P-23112)***

Snk Lodging Inc ....D....760 872-2423
636 N Main St Bishop (93514) ***(P-16717)***

Snow Ball Trading Company (PA) ....**D....626 893-9415**
1352 S Diamond Bar Blvd B Diamond Bar (91765) ***(P-13849)***

Snow Summit Mountain Resort, Big Bear City *Also called Snow Summit Ski Corporation* ***(P-19670)***

Snow Summit Ski Corporation (PA) ....**C....909 866-5766**
880 Summit Blvd Big Bear Lake (92315) ***(P-16718)***

Snow Summit Ski Corporation ....D....909 585-2517
43101 Goldmine Dr Big Bear City (92314) ***(P-19670)***

Snow Valley Mountain Sports Pk, Running Springs *Also called Snow Valley Mtn Resort LLC* ***(P-16827)***

Snow Valley Mtn Resort LLC ....D....909 867-2751
Hwy 18 Running Springs (92382) ***(P-16827)***

Snowball Trading, Diamond Bar *Also called Snow Ball Trading Company* ***(P-13849)***

Snowbounders Ski Club ....D....714 892-4897
5402 Tattershall Ave Westminster (92683) ***(P-19614)***

Snowkap Enterprises Inc (PA) ....**E....909 370-4444**
1405 E Washington St Colton (92324) ***(P-18670)***

Snowmass Apparel Inc (PA) ....**E....949 788-0617**
15225 Alton Pkwy Irvine (92618) ***(P-14417)***

Snowpure LLC ....E....949 240-2188
130 Calle Iglesia Ste A San Clemente (92672) ***(P-8415)***

Snowpure Water Technologies, San Clemente *Also called Snowpure LLC* ***(P-8415)***

Snowsound USA, Santa Fe Springs *Also called Atlantic Representations Inc* ***(P-3525)***

Snyder Langston, Irvine *Also called Sander Langston LP* ***(P-820)***

So Cal Land Maintenance Inc ....D....714 231-1454
3121 E La Palma Ave Ste K Anaheim (92806) ***(P-17286)***

So Cal Sandbags Inc ....D....951 277-3404
12620 Bosley Ln Corona (92883) ***(P-14018)***

So Cal Ship Services ....D....310 519-8411
971 S Seaside Ave San Pedro (90731) ***(P-12284)***

ALPHABETIC

Employee Codes: A=Over 500 employees, B=251-500
C=101-250, D=51-100, E=20-50 F=10-19
2022 Southern California Business
Directory and Buyers Guide
© Mergent Inc. 1-800-342-5647
1273

So Cal Tractor Sales Co Inc .... F 818 252-1900
30517 The Old Rd Castaic (91384) *(P-18996)*

SO Tech/Spcl Op Tech Inc (PA) .... E **310 202-9007**
206 Star Of India Ln Carson (90746) *(P-14320)*

So-Cal Strl Stl Fbrication Inc .... E 909 877-1299
130 S Spruce Ave Rialto (92376) *(P-1583)*

So-Cal Value Added, Camarillo *Also called Plt Enterprises Inc (P-9044)*

So-Cal Value Added LLC .... E 805 389-5335
809 Calle Plano Camarillo (93012) *(P-9785)*

Soaptronic LLC .... E 949 465-8955
20562 Crescent Bay Dr Lake Forest (92630) *(P-4978)*

Soaring America Corporation .... E 909 270-2628
8354 Kimball Ave F360 Chino (91708) *(P-10203)*

Sobaliving Llc .... E 800 595-3803
22669 Pacific Coast Hwy Malibu (90265) *(P-21481)*

Sober Living By Sea Inc (HQ) .... D **949 673-6696**
2800 Lafayette Rd Ste D Newport Beach (92663) *(P-21340)*

Soberlink Healthcare LLC .... F 714 975-7200
16787 Beach Blvd 211 Huntington Beach (92647) *(P-10911)*

Soboba Band Luiseno Indians .... A 951 665-1000
22777 Soboba Rd San Jacinto (92583) *(P-18671)*

Soboba Casino, San Jacinto *Also called Soboba Band Luiseno Indians (P-18671)*

Sobriety House, Long Beach *Also called Safe Refuge (P-21335)*

Socal Cleaning & Insulation, Santa Ana *Also called TMC Fluid Systems Inc (P-8057)*

Socal Office Technologies, Cypress *Also called Mwb Copy Products Inc (P-13363)*

Socal Uniform Rental, San Gabriel *Also called Cal Southern Services (P-16850)*

Socco Plastic Coating Company .... E 909 987-4753
11251 Jersey Blvd Rancho Cucamonga (91730) *(P-7411)*

Social Gaming Network, Culver City *Also called Jam City Inc (P-17897)*

Social Junky Inc .... E 323 347-9847
7874 Palmetto Ave Fontana (92336) *(P-4939)*

Social Science Service Center .... D 909 421-7120
18612 Santa Ana Ave Bloomington (92316) *(P-21053)*

Social Sciences, Irvine *Also called University California Irvine (P-20992)*

Social Service Professionals, Los Angeles *Also called Rehababilities Inc (P-17459)*

Social Services Cal Dept .... D 951 782-4200
3737 Main St Ste 700 Riverside (92501) *(P-21889)*

Social Studies School Service .... D 310 839-2436
10200 Jefferson Blvd Culver City (90232) *(P-13541)*

Socialcom Inc .... D 310 289-4477
13468 Beach Ave Marina Del Rey (90292) *(P-23328)*

Society of St Vncent De Paul C (PA) .... D **323 226-9645**
210 N Avenue 21 Los Angeles (90031) *(P-22462)*

Society6 LLC .... D 310 394-6400
1655 26th St Santa Monica (90404) *(P-18110)*

Soco Group Inc .... D 951 657-2350
240 E 1st St Perris (92570) *(P-14807)*

Soco Group Inc .... D 760 352-4683
350 E Main St El Centro (92243) *(P-14808)*

Soco Petroleum, El Centro *Also called Soco Group Inc (P-14808)*

Soco Petroleum Group, Perris *Also called Soco Group Inc (P-14807)*

Soderberg Manufacturing Co Inc .... D 909 595-1291
20821 Currier Rd Walnut (91789) *(P-9118)*

Sodexo Management Inc .... B 310 646-3738
450 World Way Los Angeles (90045) *(P-23329)*

Soex Group, Vernon *Also called Soex West Usa LLC (P-14350)*

Soex West Usa LLC (PA) .... B **323 264-8300**
3294 E 26th St Vernon (90058) *(P-14350)*

Sofa U Love LLC (PA) .... E **323 464-3397**
1207 N Western Ave Los Angeles (90029) *(P-3517)*

Soffa Electric Inc .... E 323 728-0230
5901 Corvette St Commerce (90040) *(P-10725)*

Soffietti Co .... D 909 907-2277
236 W Orange Show San Bernardino (92408) *(P-13818)*

Sofie Biosciences Inc (PA) .... C **310 215-3159**
160 Briston Pkwy Ste 200 Culver City (90230) *(P-22864)*

Sofitel Los Angeles, Los Angeles *Also called Accor Corp (P-16313)*

Soft Gel Technologies Inc (HQ) .... D **323 726-0700**
6982 Bandini Blvd Commerce (90040) *(P-4895)*

Soft-Touch Tissue, Vernon *Also called Paper Surce Converting Mfg Inc (P-3768)*

Softline Home Fashions Inc .... E 310 630-4848
13130 S Normandie Ave Gardena (90249) *(P-14321)*

Softscript Inc .... A 310 451-2110
2215 Campus Dr El Segundo (90245) *(P-17194)*

Softub Inc (PA) .... D **858 602-1920**
24700 Avenue Rockefeller Valencia (91355) *(P-11759)*

Software, Encino *Also called Phone Check Solutions LLC (P-17690)*

Software Dynamics Incorporated .... C 818 992-3299
8501 Fllbrook Ave Ste 200 Canoga Park (91304) *(P-18066)*

Software Management Cons Inc .... C 714 662-1841
959 S Coast Dr Ste 415 Costa Mesa (92626) *(P-17719)*

Software Management Cons LLC (HQ) .... B **818 240-3177**
500 N Brand Blvd Ste 1100 Glendale (91203) *(P-18222)*

Software Products & Svcs Group, Santa Barbara *Also called Tecolote Research Inc (P-23342)*

Soho Carpet & Rugs, Santa Ana *Also called Ohno America Inc (P-2694)*

Soilmoisture Equipment Corp .... E 805 964-3525
801 S Kellogg Ave Goleta (93117) *(P-10912)*

Sol-Pak Thermoforming Inc .... E 323 582-3333
3388 Fruitland Ave Vernon (90058) *(P-14764)*

Sola Impact Fund II LP .... E 323 306-4648
9221 Kalmia St Los Angeles (90002) *(P-16000)*

Sola Impact Fund II LP .... E 323 306-4648
1401 E 52nd St Los Angeles (90011) *(P-16001)*

Sola Impact Fund II LP .... E 323 306-4648
1639 E 92nd St Los Angeles (90002) *(P-16002)*

Sola Impact Fund II LP .... E 323 306-4648
629 E 48th St Los Angeles (90011) *(P-16003)*

Sola Impact Fund II LP .... E 323 306-4648
11809 Robin St Los Angeles (90059) *(P-16004)*

Sola Impact Fund II LP .... E 323 306-4648
6415 Makee Ave Los Angeles (90001) *(P-16005)*

Sola Rentals Inc .... E 323 306-4648
8629 S Vermont Ave Los Angeles (90044) *(P-17373)*

Solace Cst LLC (HQ) .... D **310 919-5401**
11111 Santa Monica Blvd Los Angeles (90025) *(P-6753)*

Solag Disposal Co, San Juan Capistrano *Also called Solag Incorporated (P-12981)*

Solag Incorporated .... B 949 728-1206
31641 Ortege Hwy San Juan Capistrano (92675) *(P-12981)*

Solar Electronics Company, North Hollywood *Also called A T Parker Inc (P-9845)*

Solar Energy LLC .... D 818 449-5816
21600 Oxnard St Ste 1200 Woodland Hills (91367) *(P-1141)*

Solar Link International Inc .... C 909 605-7789
4652 E Brickell St Ste A Ontario (91761) *(P-14019)*

Solar Spectrum LLC .... B 844 777-6527
27368 Via Industria # 101 Temecula (92590) *(P-1142)*

Solara Engineering, Sun Valley *Also called Excelity (P-6415)*

Solarflare Communications Inc (PA) .... D **949 581-6830**
7505 Irvine Center Dr Irvine (92618) *(P-8175)*

Solari Enterprises Inc .... C 714 282-2520
1507 W Yale Ave Orange (92867) *(P-15699)*

Solariant Capital LLC .... C 626 544-0279
301 N Lake Ave Ste 950 Pasadena (91101) *(P-16112)*

Solaris Paper Inc (HQ) .... C **562 653-1680**
100 S Anaheim Blvd # 280 Anaheim (92805) *(P-14228)*

Solarreserve Inc .... D 310 315-2200
520 Broadway Fl 6 Santa Monica (90401) *(P-12826)*

Solarreserve LLC (PA) .... F **310 315-2200**
520 Broadway Fl 6 Santa Monica (90401) *(P-6576)*

Solartis LLC .... E 310 251-4861
1601 N Sepulveda Blvd # 6 Manhattan Beach (90266) *(P-17720)*

Solatron Enterprises, Torrance *Also called Mahmood Izadi Inc (P-8129)*

Solcius LLC .... D 951 772-0030
12155 Magnolia Ave 12b Riverside (92503) *(P-1143)*

Soldermask Inc .... F 714 842-1987
17905 Metzler Ln Huntington Beach (92647) *(P-9455)*

SOLE Designs Inc .... F 626 452-8642
11685 Mcbean Dr El Monte (91732) *(P-3518)*

Sole Society Group Inc .... C 310 220-0808
11248 Playa Ct B Culver City (90230) *(P-5874)*

Sole Source Technology LLC .... F 949 500-3371
1968 S Coast Hwy 680 Laguna Beach (92651) *(P-8303)*

Sole Survivor Corporation .... F 818 338-3760
28632 Roadside Dr Ste 200 Agoura Hills (91301) *(P-2994)*

Sole Technology Inc (PA) .... C **949 460-2020**
26921 Fuerte Lake Forest (92630) *(P-5887)*

Soleffect .... F 323 275-9945
13009 Los Nietos Rd Santa Fe Springs (90670) *(P-3715)*

Solemnity Personnel .... E 323 718-3979
5670 E Washington Blvd Commerce (90040) *(P-17467)*

Solestage Inc .... E 909 576-1309
17651 Railroad St City of Industry (91748) *(P-18067)*

Soleus International, Walnut *Also called Mjc America Ltd (P-9009)*

Solex Contracting Inc .... C 951 308-1706
42146 Remington Ave Temecula (92590) *(P-971)*

Solheim Lutheran Home .... C 323 257-7518
2236 Merton Ave Los Angeles (90041) *(P-22155)*

Solid Commerce, Marina Del Rey *Also called Liquidate Direct LLC (P-18045)*

Solid Oak Software Inc (PA) .... E **805 568-5415**
319 W Mission St Santa Barbara (93101) *(P-13439)*

Solid State Devices Inc .... C 562 404-4474
14701 Firestone Blvd La Mirada (90638) *(P-9578)*

Solid-Scope Machining Co Inc .... F 310 523-2366
17925 Adria Maru Ln Carson (90746) *(P-6537)*

Soligen 2006, Northridge *Also called DC Partners Inc (P-6391)*

Solo Enterprise Corp .... E 626 961-3591
220 N California Ave City of Industry (91744) *(P-8797)*

Solo Golf, City of Industry *Also called Solo Enterprise Corp (P-8797)*

Solugenix Corporation (PA) .... C **866 749-7658**
601 Valencia Ave Ste 260 Brea (92823) *(P-18068)*

Solutions Unlimited, Fullerton *Also called Wilsons Art Studio Inc (P-4596)*

Solvay Composite Materials, Anaheim *Also called Cytec Engineered Materials Inc (P-6390)*

Solvay USA Inc .... F 310 669-5300
20851 S Santa Fe Ave Long Beach (90810) *(P-4670)*

Solver Inc .... E 310 691-5300
10780 Santa Monica Blvd # 370 Los Angeles (90025) *(P-13440)*

Solvere Inc .... E 949 707-0035
15560 Rckfeld Blvd Ste B1 Irvine (92618) *(P-12669)*

Soma Magnetics Corporation .... F 714 447-0782
585 S State College Blvd Fullerton (92831) *(P-8884)*

Somar Corporation .... E 310 329-1446
13006 Halldale Ave Gardena (90249) *(P-6914)*

Some Crust Bakery, Claremont *Also called Feemster Co Inc (P-1999)*

Someone's In The Kitchen, Tarzana *Also called JMJ Enterprises Inc (P-16961)*

Somis Pacific AG Management, Temecula *Also called Sierra Pacific Farms Inc (P-228)*

Sona Chaandi Jewelry, Artesia *Also called Malanis Inc (P-14133)*

Sonance, San Clemente *Also called Dana Innovations (P-9169)*

Sonance .... D 949 492-7777
212 Avenida Fabricante San Clemente (92672) *(P-13695)*

Sonar Entertainment Inc (PA) .... B **424 230-7140**
2834 Colorado Ave Ste 300 Santa Monica (90404) *(P-19261)*

Sonatech Division, Santa Barbara *Also called Alta Properties Inc (P-9853)*

Sonendo Inc (PA) .... C **949 766-3636**
26061 Merit Cir Ste 102 Laguna Hills (92653) *(P-11196)*

Sonesta Los Angles Arprt Lax L .... C 310 642-7500
5985 W Century Blvd Los Angeles (90045) *(P-16719)*

Sonfarrel ... E ... 714 630-7280
3000 E La Jolla St Anaheim (92806) ***(P-5824)***
Sonfarrel Aerospace LLC ... D ... 714 630-7280
3010 E La Jolla St Anaheim (92806) ***(P-6401)***
Songs Dcmmssning Solutions LLC ... F ... 801 649-2223
5000 Pacific Coast Hwy San Clemente (92674) ***(P-4671)***
Songs Music Publishing LLC ... F ... 323 939-3511
7656 W Sunset Blvd Los Angeles (90046) ***(P-4205)***
Sonic Industries Inc ... C ... 310 532-8382
20030 Normandie Ave Torrance (90502) ***(P-22655)***
Sonic Plating Company, Gardena *Also called Granath & Granath Inc* ***(P-7264)***
Sonicsensory Inc (PA) ... **F ... 213 336-3747**
1163 Logan St Los Angeles (90026) ***(P-5317)***
Sonix, Torrance *Also called Lenntek Corporation* ***(P-9286)***
Sonnet Technologies Inc ... E ... 949 587-3500
8 Autry Irvine (92618) ***(P-9915)***
Sonora Bakery Inc ... E ... 323 269-2253
4484 Whittier Blvd Los Angeles (90022) ***(P-2035)***
Sonora Face Co ... E ... 323 560-8188
5233 Randolph St Maywood (90270) ***(P-3354)***
Sonora Mills Foods Inc (PA) ... **C ... 310 639-5333**
3064 E Maria St E Rncho Dmngz (90221) ***(P-2526)***
Sonos Inc (PA) ... **D ... 805 965-3001**
614 Chapala St Santa Barbara (93101) ***(P-9196)***
Sonus Group LLC ... F ... 888 316-5351
43537 Ridge Park Dr # 100 Temecula (92590) ***(P-10134)***
Sonus Hring Care Professionals, Westminster *Also called Serendipity Hearing Inc* ***(P-20233)***
Sony Dadc US Inc ... F ... 310 760-8500
4499 Glencoe Ave Marina Del Rey (90292) ***(P-9839)***
Sony Media Cloud Services LLC ... E ... 877 683-9124
10202 Washington Blvd Culver City (90232) ***(P-19179)***
Sony Pctres HM Entrmt Online I (HQ) ... **C ... 310 244-4000**
10202 Washington Blvd Culver City (90232) ***(P-19180)***
Sony Pctres Wrldwide Acqstons ... D ... 310 244-4000
10202 Washington Blvd Culver City (90232) ***(P-19181)***
Sony Pictures Entrmt Inc (HQ) ... **A ... 310 244-4000**
10202 Washington Blvd Culver City (90232) ***(P-19182)***
Sony Pictures Imageworks Inc ... A ... 310 840-8000
9050 Washington Blvd Culver City (90232) ***(P-18111)***
Sony Pictures Studios, Culver City *Also called Sony Pictures Entrmt Inc* ***(P-19182)***
Sony Pictures Television Inc (HQ) ... **B ... 310 244-7625**
10202 Washington Blvd Culver City (90232) ***(P-19183)***
Soofer Co Inc ... D ... 323 234-6666
2828 S Alameda St Vernon (90058) ***(P-14737)***
Sophia Lyn Convalescent Hosp, Pasadena *Also called Slch Inc* ***(P-20477)***
Soprano, Los Angeles *Also called SSC Apparel Inc* ***(P-2996)***
Soren McAdam Christianson LLP ... D ... 909 798-2222
2068 Orange Tree Ln # 100 Redlands (92374) ***(P-22814)***
Sorenson Engineering Inc (PA) ... **C ... 909 795-2434**
32032 Dunlap Blvd Yucaipa (92399) ***(P-7044)***
Sorma USA LLC ... B ... 559 651-1269
9810 W Ferguson Ave Visalia (93291) ***(P-3890)***
Soroptmist Intl Huntington Bch ... E ... 714 271-9305
212 Utica Ave Huntington Beach (92648) ***(P-22463)***
SOS Beauty Inc ... F ... 424 285-1405
700 N San Vicnte Blvd G460 West Hollywood (90069) ***(P-14290)***
SOS Metals Inc (HQ) ... **C ... 310 217-8848**
201 E Gardena Blvd Gardena (90248) ***(P-14123)***
SOS Security Incorporated ... D ... 310 392-9600
3000 S Robertson Blvd # 100 Los Angeles (90034) ***(P-18337)***
SOS Security LLC ... D ... 310 859-8248
331 N Beverly Dr Ste 3 Beverly Hills (90210) ***(P-18338)***
Sotec USA LLC ... E ... 909 525-5861
3076 S Edenglen Ave Ontario (91761) ***(P-7662)***
Soto Company Inc ... D ... 949 493-9403
34275 Camino Capistrano A Capistrano Beach (92624) ***(P-344)***
Soto Food Service, City of Industry *Also called Soto Provision Inc* ***(P-13186)***
Soto Provision Inc ... D ... 626 458-4600
488 Parriott Pl W City of Industry (91745) ***(P-13186)***
Sound Investment Group ... F ... 714 515-4001
16402 Gothard St Ste E Huntington Beach (92647) ***(P-13091)***
Sound Services, West Hollywood *Also called Ssi/Advanced Post Services LLC* ***(P-19184)***
Sound Storm Laboratories LLC ... F ... 805 983-8008
3451 Lunar Ct Oxnard (93030) ***(P-9197)***
Soundboks Inc ... F ... 310 774-0480
800 Wilshire Blvd Los Angeles (90017) ***(P-17374)***
Soundcraft Inc ... E ... 818 882-0020
20301 Nordhoff St Chatsworth (91311) ***(P-9916)***
Soup Bases Loaded Inc ... E ... 909 230-6890
2355 E Francis St Ontario (91761) ***(P-2527)***
Source Code LLC ... E ... 562 903-1500
9808 Alburtis Ave Santa Fe Springs (90670) ***(P-8176)***
Source Freight System LLC (PA) ... **D ... 323 887-3884**
812 Union St Montebello (90640) ***(P-12527)***
Source It USA Inc ... E ... 714 318-4428
1150 S Olive St Los Angeles (90015) ***(P-18069)***
Source Logistic, Montebello *Also called Source Freight System LLC* ***(P-12527)***
Source Logistics Center Corp ... D ... 323 887-3884
812 Union St Montebello (90640) ***(P-12528)***
Source Photonics Usa Inc (PA) ... **C ... 818 773-9044**
8521 Fllbrook Ave Ste 200 West Hills (91304) ***(P-9579)***
Source Photonics Usa Inc ... F ... 818 407-5007
8917 Fullbright Ave Chatsworth (91311) ***(P-9580)***
Sourcery LLC ... F ... 949 380-0466
27051 Burbank Foothill Ranch (92610) ***(P-13668)***
Sourcery Wire, Foothill Ranch *Also called Sourcery LLC* ***(P-13668)***
Sourcing Solutions, Costa Mesa *Also called Phelps United LLC* ***(P-13427)***
Souriau Usa Inc (HQ) ... **E ... 805 238-2840**
1750 Commerce Way Paso Robles (93446) ***(P-9046)***

South American Imaging Inc ... F ... 805 824-4036
2360 Eastman Ave Ste 110 Oxnard (93030) ***(P-8931)***
South Bay Center For Cmnty Dev, Wilmington *Also called South Bay Ctr For Counseling* ***(P-21890)***
South Bay Corporation ... F ... 310 532-5353
1335 W 134th St Gardena (90247) ***(P-5412)***
South Bay Ctr For Counseling ... D ... 310 414-2090
540 N Marine Ave Wilmington (90744) ***(P-21890)***
South Bay Fabrication Inc ... E ... 714 894-1314
15421 Electronic Ln Huntington Beach (92649) ***(P-18672)***
South Bay Ford Inc (PA) ... **C ... 310 644-0211**
5100 W Rosecrans Ave Hawthorne (90250) ***(P-18872)***
South Bay Freight System LLC (PA) ... **D ... 626 271-9800**
900 Turnbull Canyon Rd City of Industry (91745) ***(P-12529)***
South Bay Group, City of Industry *Also called South Bay Freight System LLC* ***(P-12529)***
South Bay International Inc ... E ... 909 718-5000
8570 Hickory Ave Rancho Cucamonga (91739) ***(P-3560)***
South Bay Public Warehouse ... D ... 310 637-1133
490 W Manville St Compton (90220) ***(P-12245)***
South Bay Senior Services Inc ... D ... 310 338-8558
8929 S Sepulveda Blvd # 314 Los Angeles (90045) ***(P-21213)***
South Bay Toyota ... C ... 310 323-7800
18416 S Western Ave Gardena (90248) ***(P-18873)***
South Bay Wire & Cable Co LLC ... D ... 951 659-2183
54125 Maranatha Dr Idyllwild (92549) ***(P-6234)***
South Baylo Acupuncture Clinic, Los Angeles *Also called South Baylo University* ***(P-21341)***
South Baylo University ... C ... 213 999-0297
2727 W 6th St Los Angeles (90057) ***(P-21341)***
South Central Family Hlth Ctr ... D ... 323 908-4200
4425 S Central Ave Los Angeles (90011) ***(P-20067)***
South China Sheet Metal Inc ... E ... 323 225-1522
1740 Albion St Los Angeles (90031) ***(P-1144)***
South Cntl Hlth Rhblttion Prgr ... D ... 310 667-4070
2620 Industry Way Lynwood (90262) ***(P-21342)***
South Cntl Los Angles Rgnal CT (PA) ... **C ... 213 744-7000**
2500 S Western Ave Los Angeles (90018) ***(P-22210)***
South Cnty Lxus At Mssion Vejo ... C ... 949 347-3400
28242 Marguerite Pkwy Mission Viejo (92692) ***(P-18943)***
South Cnty Orthpd Spclsts A ME ... D ... 949 586-3200
24331 El Toro Rd Ste 200 Laguna Hills (92637) ***(P-20068)***
South Coast Air Qulty MGT Dst (PA) ... **A ... 909 396-2000**
21865 Copley Dr Diamond Bar (91765) ***(P-23511)***
South Coast Auto Insurance, Huntington Beach *Also called Freeway Insurance* ***(P-15572)***
South Coast Baking LLC (PA) ... **D ... 949 851-9654**
1722 Kettering Irvine (92614) ***(P-2072)***
South Coast Baking Co., Irvine *Also called South Coast Baking LLC* ***(P-2072)***
South Coast Childrens Soc Inc ... C ... 909 478-3377
24950 Redlands Blvd Loma Linda (92354) ***(P-21891)***
South Coast Childrens Soc Inc ... C ... 909 364-9788
11780 Central Ave Chino (91710) ***(P-21892)***
South Coast Circuits Inc ... D ... 714 966-2108
3506 W Lake Center Dr A Santa Ana (92704) ***(P-9456)***
South Coast Eye Care Centers ... D ... 949 588-2020
24022 Calle De La Plata Laguna Hills (92653) ***(P-20069)***
South Coast Global Med Ctr Inc ... D ... 714 953-3582
1301 N Tustin Ave Santa Ana (92705) ***(P-20070)***
South Coast Health Wellness ... E ... 951 686-9001
4768 Palm Ave Riverside (92501) ***(P-20478)***
SOUTH COAST IRON, La Habra *Also called Ironwood Fabrication Inc* ***(P-7088)***
South Coast Mechanical Inc ... D ... 714 738-6644
800 E Orangethorpe Ave Anaheim (92801) ***(P-1145)***
South Coast Piering Inc ... D ... 800 922-2488
43300 Bus Pk Dr Ste 204 Temecula (92590) ***(P-832)***
South Coast Plaza LLC (PA) ... **D ... 714 546-0110**
3333 Bristol St Ofc Costa Mesa (92626) ***(P-15700)***
South Coast Plaza LLC ... D ... 714 435-2000
3333 Bristol St Ofc Costa Mesa (92626) ***(P-15701)***
South Coast Plaza Mall, Costa Mesa *Also called South Coast Plaza LLC* ***(P-15701)***
South Coast Plaza Security ... C ... 714 435-2180
695 Town Center Dr Ste 50 Costa Mesa (92626) ***(P-23113)***
South Coast Plaza Village, Costa Mesa *Also called South Coast Plaza LLC* ***(P-15700)***
South Coast Repertory Inc ... D ... 714 708-5500
655 Town Center Dr Costa Mesa (92626) ***(P-19332)***
South Coast Screen and Casing ... F ... 310 632-3200
19112 S Santa Fe Ave Compton (90221) ***(P-7676)***
South Coast Stairs Inc ... E ... 949 858-1685
30251 Tomas Rcho STA Marg (92688) ***(P-3291)***
South Coast Trnsp & Dist Inc ... D ... 310 816-0280
1424 S Raymond Ave Fullerton (92831) ***(P-11994)***
South Coast Water, Santa Ana *Also called Hannah Industries Inc* ***(P-8385)***
South Coast Water District ... D ... 949 499-4555
34152 Del Obispo St Dana Point (92629) ***(P-23330)***
South Coast Westin Hotel Co ... D ... 714 540-2500
686 Anton Blvd Costa Mesa (92626) ***(P-16720)***
South Coast Winery Inc ... E ... 951 587-9463
34843 Rancho Cal Rd Temecula (92591) ***(P-2222)***
South Coast Winery Resort Spa, Temecula *Also called South Coast Winery Inc* ***(P-2222)***
South County Sanitary Svc Inc ... D ... 805 489-4246
4388 Old Santa Fe Rd San Luis Obispo (93401) ***(P-12982)***
South Gate Care Centers, South Gate *Also called Far West Inc* ***(P-20342)***
South Gate Engineering LLC ... C ... 909 628-2779
13477 Yorba Ave Chino (91710) ***(P-6754)***
South Hills Country Club ... D ... 626 339-1231
2655 S Citrus St West Covina (91791) ***(P-19615)***
South Orange County Ww Auth ... F ... 949 234-5400
34156 Del Obispo St Dana Point (92629) ***(P-5243)***
South Ornge Cnty Srgcal Med Gr ... D ... 949 457-7900
24411 Health Center Dr # 350 Laguna Hills (92653) ***(P-20071)***

Employee Codes: A=Over 500 employees, B=251-500
C=101-250, D=51-100, E=20-50 F=10-19
2022 Southern California Business Directory and Buyers Guide
© Mergent Inc. 1-800-342-5647
1275

South Seas Imports, Compton *Also called M M Fab Inc (P-14306)*

South Valley Almond Co LLC....................C.......661 391-9000
15443 Beech Ave Wasco (93280) *(P-14752)*

South Valley Farms, Wasco *Also called South Valley Almond Co LLC (P-14752)*

South Valley Materials Inc....................F.......559 594-4142
1132 N Belmont Rd Exeter (93221) *(P-6114)*

South Valley Materials Inc....................F.......559 582-0532
7761 Hanford Armona Rd Hanford (93230) *(P-6115)*

South West Sun Solar Inc....................E.......714 582-3909
13752 Harbor Blvd Garden Grove (92843) *(P-1146)*

Southbay BMW, Torrance *Also called Southbay European Inc (P-18905)*

Southbay European Inc....................D.......310 939-7300
18800 Hawthorne Blvd Torrance (90504) *(P-18905)*

Southcoast Cabinet Inc (PA)....................E.......909 594-3089
755 Pinefalls Ave Walnut (91789) *(P-3337)*

Southcoast Dyeing & Finishing, Santa Ana *Also called Chroma Systems (P-16879)*

Southeast Industries, Downey *Also called ARC Los Angles Orange Counties (P-21939)*

Southeast Kern Weekender, Tehachapi *Also called Tehachapi News Inc (P-4036)*

Southeastern Westminster, Westminster *Also called Southern California Edison Co (P-12846)*

Southern Asthma Assoc Southern, Mission Viejo *Also called Allergy & Asthma Assoc Cal (P-19691)*

Southern CA Hlth & Rhbltn Prg....................C.......310 631-8004
2610 Industry Way Ste A Lynwood (90262) *(P-20072)*

Southern Cal Alchol DRG Prgram (PA)....................D.......562 923-4545
11500 Paramount Blvd Downey (90241) *(P-21343)*

Southern Cal Appraisal Co, Burbank *Also called Sca Enterprises Inc (P-18661)*

Southern Cal Bndery Miling Inc....................F.......909 829-1949
10661 Business Dr Fontana (92337) *(P-4622)*

Southern Cal Dgnstc Imging Inc (PA)....................D.......714 995-5471
408 S Beach Blvd Ste 106 Anaheim (92804) *(P-20073)*

Southern Cal Disc Tire Co Inc....................C.......951 929-2130
600 W Florida Ave Hemet (92543) *(P-13092)*

Southern Cal Disc Tire Co Inc....................C.......714 901-8226
15672 Springdale St Huntington Beach (92649) *(P-13093)*

Southern Cal Disc Tire Co Inc....................C.......626 335-2883
705 S Grand Ave Glendora (91740) *(P-13094)*

Southern Cal Disc Tire Co Inc....................C.......805 639-0166
4640 Telephone Rd Ventura (93003) *(P-18874)*

Southern Cal Disc Tire Co Inc....................C.......310 324-2569
20741 Avalon Blvd Carson (90746) *(P-13119)*

Southern Cal Edson - Prvate Ch, Rosemead *Also called Southern California Edison Co (P-12837)*

Southern Cal Fd Allergy Inst, Long Beach *Also called Transltnal Plmnary Immnlogy RE (P-20111)*

Southern Cal Halthcare Sys Inc....................D.......310 836-7000
3828 Delmas Ter Culver City (90232) *(P-20943)*

Southern Cal Halthcare Sys Inc (HQ)....................C.......310 943-4500
3415 S Sepulveda Blvd # 9 Los Angeles (90034) *(P-20944)*

Southern Cal Hosp At Culver Cy, Culver City *Also called Brotman Medical Center Inc (P-20690)*

Southern Cal Hosp At Culver Cy, Culver City *Also called Southern Cal Halthcare Sys Inc (P-20943)*

Southern Cal Hsing Rights Ctr....................D.......213 387-8400
3255 Wilshire Blvd Los Angeles (90010) *(P-21893)*

Southern Cal Hydrlic Engrg Cor....................E.......714 257-4800
1130 Columbia St Brea (92821) *(P-13939)*

Southern Cal Ibw-Neca ADM Corp (PA)....................D.......323 221-5861
100 Corson St Ste 200 Pasadena (91103) *(P-15521)*

Southern Cal Inst For RES Edca....................D.......562 826-8139
5901 E 7th St 151 Long Beach (90822) *(P-22921)*

Southern Cal Orthopedics, La Mirada *Also called Healthpointe Medical Group Inc (P-19837)*

Southern Cal Orthpd Inst LP (PA)....................C.......818 901-6600
6815 Noble Ave Ste 400 Van Nuys (91405) *(P-20074)*

Southern Cal Pipe Trades, Los Angeles *Also called Defined Cntrbtion Tr Fund For (P-16176)*

Southern Cal Pipe Trades ADM, Los Angeles *Also called Southern Cal Pipe Trades ADM (P-16197)*

Southern Cal Pipe Trades ADM (PA)....................D.......213 385-6161
501 Shatto Pl Ste 500 Los Angeles (90020) *(P-16197)*

Southern Cal Presbt Homes, Glendale *Also called Humangood Socal (P-15726)*

Southern Cal Prmnnte Med Group....................C.......949 262-5780
6 Willard Irvine (92604) *(P-20075)*

Southern Cal Prmnnte Med Group....................C.......800 272-3500
13652 Cantara St Panorama City (91402) *(P-15454)*

Southern Cal Prmnnte Med Group....................C.......661 398-5085
3501 Stockdale Hwy Bakersfield (93309) *(P-20076)*

Southern Cal Prmnnte Med Group....................C.......866 984-7483
10800 Magnolia Ave Riverside (92505) *(P-15455)*

Southern Cal Prmnnte Med Group....................C.......310 604-5700
3830 Mrtin Lther King Jr Lynwood (90262) *(P-20077)*

Southern Cal Prmnnte Med Group....................A.......661 290-3100
26415 Carl Boyer Dr Santa Clarita (91350) *(P-20945)*

Southern Cal Prmnnte Med Group....................C.......323 857-2000
6041 Cadillac Ave Los Angeles (90034) *(P-20078)*

Southern Cal Prmnnte Med Group....................C.......800 780-1230
25825 Vermont Ave Harbor City (90710) *(P-20079)*

Southern Cal Prmnnte Med Group....................A.......909 427-5000
9961 Sierra Ave Fontana (92335) *(P-20946)*

Southern Cal Prmnnte Med Group....................C.......323 783-5455
4841 Hollywood Blvd Los Angeles (90027) *(P-20080)*

Southern Cal Prmnnte Med Group....................C.......626 960-4844
1511 W Garvey Ave N West Covina (91790) *(P-15456)*

Southern Cal Prmnnte Med Group....................C.......714 734-4500
17542 17th St Ste 300 Tustin (92780) *(P-15457)*

Southern Cal Prmnnte Med Group....................C.......323 783-4893
4760 W Sunset Blvd Los Angeles (90027) *(P-20081)*

Southern Cal Prmnnte Med Group (HQ)....................D.......626 405-5704
393 Walnut Dr Pasadena (91107) *(P-15458)*

Southern Cal Prmnnte Med Group....................C.......323 564-7911
1465 E 103rd St Los Angeles (90002) *(P-15459)*

Southern Cal Prmnnte Med Group....................C.......909 370-2501
789 E Cooley Dr Colton (92324) *(P-20082)*

Southern Cal Prmnnte Med Group....................C.......310 737-4900
5620 Mesmer Ave Culver City (90230) *(P-20083)*

Southern Cal Prmnnte Med Group....................C.......310 419-3306
110 N La Brea Ave Inglewood (90301) *(P-20084)*

Southern Cal Prmnnte Med Group....................C.......714 841-7293
18081 Beach Blvd Huntington Beach (92648) *(P-20085)*

Southern Cal Prmnnte Med Group....................C.......714 279-4675
411 N Lakeview Ave Anaheim (92807) *(P-20086)*

Southern Cal Prmnnte Med Group....................C.......949 234-2139
30400 Camino Capistrano San Juan Capistrano (92675) *(P-20087)*

Southern Cal Prmnnte Med Group....................C.......714 967-4760
1900 E 4th St Santa Ana (92705) *(P-20088)*

Southern Cal Prmnnte Med Group....................C.......909 394-2505
1255 W Arrow Hwy San Dimas (91773) *(P-15460)*

Southern Cal Prmnnte Med Group....................C.......323 562-6459
7825 Atlantic Ave Cudahy (90201) *(P-20089)*

Southern Cal Prmnnte Med Group....................C.......818 592-3038
21263 Erwin St Woodland Hills (91367) *(P-20090)*

Southern Cal Prmnnte Med Group....................C.......661 222-2150
27107 Tourney Rd Santa Clarita (91355) *(P-20091)*

Southern Cal Prmnnte Med Group....................C.......562 657-2200
9353 Imprl Hwy Grdn Med Downey (90242) *(P-15461)*

Southern Cal Prmnnte Med Group....................C.......949 376-8619
23781 Maquina Mission Viejo (92691) *(P-21482)*

Southern Cal Prmnnte Med Group....................C.......661 334-2020
5055 California Ave Bakersfield (93309) *(P-20092)*

Southern Cal Rgional Rail Auth....................C.......213 808-7043
2704 N Garey Ave Pomona (91767) *(P-11842)*

Southern Cal Rgional Rail Auth (PA)....................C.......213 452-0200
900 Wilshire Blvd # 1500 Los Angeles (90017) *(P-11843)*

Southern Cal Spcialty Care Inc....................C.......714 564-7800
1901 College Ave Santa Ana (92706) *(P-20947)*

Southern Cal Spcialty Care Inc....................C.......626 339-5451
845 N Lark Ellen Ave West Covina (91791) *(P-20948)*

Southern Cal Spcialty Care Inc (HQ)....................D.......562 944-1900
14900 Imperial Hwy La Mirada (90638) *(P-20949)*

Southern Cal Tchnical Arts Inc....................E.......714 524-2626
370 E Crowther Ave Placentia (92870) *(P-8798)*

Southern Cal Tele & Enrgy, Temecula *Also called Southern California Tele Co (P-12670)*

Southern Cal Trck Bdies Sls In....................F.......909 469-1132
1131 E 2nd St Pomona (91766) *(P-9996)*

Southern Cal Univ Hlth Scences....................E.......562 947-8755
16200 Amber Valley Dr Whittier (90604) *(P-20234)*

Southern California Bancorp....................D.......949 766-3015
22342 Avnida Empresa Ste Rancho Santa Margari (92688) *(P-15043)*

Southern California Carriers, Heber *Also called C S Transport Inc (P-11960)*

Southern California Cen, Long Beach *Also called Memor Ortho Surgic Group A M (P-19976)*

Southern California Edison Co (HQ)....................A.......626 302-1212
2244 Walnut Grove Ave Rosemead (91770) *(P-12827)*

Southern California Edison Co....................C.......626 543-8081
4900 Rivergrade Rd 2b1 Irwindale (91706) *(P-12828)*

Southern California Edison Co....................C.......626 303-8480
1440 S California Ave Monrovia (91016) *(P-12829)*

Southern California Edison Co....................C.......760 873-0715
4000 Bishop Creek Rd Bishop (93514) *(P-12830)*

Southern California Edison Co....................C.......714 934-0838
14799 Chestnut St Westminster (92683) *(P-12831)*

Southern California Edison Co....................C.......626 302-5101
8380 Klingerman St Rosemead (91770) *(P-12832)*

Southern California Edison Co....................C.......626 543-6093
4900 Rivergrade Rd Baldwin Park (91706) *(P-12833)*

Southern California Edison Co....................C.......800 336-2822
26125 Menifee Rd Romoland (92585) *(P-12834)*

Southern California Edison Co....................C.......714 870-3225
1851 W Valencia Dr Fullerton (92833) *(P-12835)*

Southern California Edison Co....................C.......805 496-3406
3589 Foothill Dr Westlake Village (91361) *(P-12836)*

Southern California Edison Co....................C.......626 302-1212
2131 Walnut Grove Ave Rosemead (91770) *(P-12837)*

Southern California Edison Co....................C.......909 274-1925
2 Innovation Way Fl 1 Pomona (91768) *(P-12838)*

Southern California Edison Co....................C.......714 973-5481
1241 S Grand Ave Santa Ana (92705) *(P-12839)*

Southern California Edison Co....................C.......559 625-7126
4175 S Laspina St Tulare (93274) *(P-12840)*

Southern California Edison Co....................C.......818 999-1880
3589 Foothill Dr Thousand Oaks (91361) *(P-12841)*

Southern California Edison Co....................C.......626 815-7296
6000 N Irwindale Ave A Irwindale (91702) *(P-12842)*

Southern California Edison Co....................C.......909 469-0251
265 N East End Ave Pomona (91767) *(P-12843)*

Southern California Edison Co....................C.......310 608-5029
1924 E Cashdan St Compton (90220) *(P-12844)*

Southern California Edison Co....................C.......805 683-5291
103 Love Pl Goleta (93117) *(P-12845)*

Southern California Edison Co....................C.......661 607-0207
28250 Gateway Village Dr Valencia (91355) *(P-23114)*

Southern California Edison Co....................C.......714 895-0420
7300 Fenwick Ln Westminster (92683) *(P-12846)*

Southern California Edison Co....................C.......949 587-5416
14155 Bake Pkwy Irvine (92618) *(P-12847)*

Southern California Edison Co....................C.......626 633-3070
6042 N Irwindale Ave A Irwindale (91702) *(P-12848)*

ALPHABETIC SECTION Spacex, San Pedro

Southern California Edison Co..........C.......562 529-7301
6900 Orange Ave Long Beach (90805) ***(P-12849)***
Southern California Edison Co..........C.......714 895-0163
7333 Bolsa Ave Westminster (92683) ***(P-12850)***
Southern California Edison Co..........C.......626 814-4212
13025 Los Angeles St Irwindale (91706) ***(P-12851)***
Southern California Edison Co..........C.......909 592-3757
800 W Cienega Ave San Dimas (91773) ***(P-12852)***
Southern California Edison Co..........C.......562 903-3191
9901 Geary Ave Santa Fe Springs (90670) ***(P-12853)***
Southern California Edison Co..........C.......562 491-3803
125 Elm Ave Long Beach (90802) ***(P-12854)***
Southern California Edison Co..........C.......760 951-3172
12353 Hesperia Rd Victorville (92395) ***(P-12855)***
Southern California Edison Co..........C.......626 812-7380
6090 N Irwindale Ave Irwindale (91702) ***(P-12856)***
Southern California Edison Co..........C.......760 375-1821
510 S China Lake Blvd Ridgecrest (93555) ***(P-12857)***
Southern California Edison Co..........C.......714 895-0119
7400 Fenwick Ln Westminster (92683) ***(P-12858)***
Southern California Edison Co..........C.......714 283-8568
1900 E Taft Ave Orange (92865) ***(P-12859)***
Southern California Edison Co..........C.......626 308-6193
501 S Marengo Ave Alhambra (91803) ***(P-12860)***
Southern California Gas Co (HQ)..........A.......213 244-1200
555 W 5th St Los Angeles (90013) ***(P-12866)***
Southern California Gas Co..........C.......213 244-1200
1600 Corporate Center Dr Monterey Park (91754) ***(P-12867)***
Southern California Gas Tower..........A.......213 244-1200
555 W 5th St Los Angeles (90013) ***(P-12868)***
Southern California Golf Assn (PA)..........D.......818 980-3630
3740 Cahuenga Blvd North Hollywood (91604) ***(P-22259)***
Southern California Ice Co..........F.......310 325-1040
22921 Lockness Ave Torrance (90501) ***(P-2374)***
Southern California Lrng Corp..........E.......818 639-9692
2970 Huntington Dr San Marino (91108) ***(P-22058)***
Southern California Mar Assn..........D.......714 850-4004
3333 Fairview Rd Costa Mesa (92626) ***(P-18875)***
Southern California Messenger, Los Angeles *Also called Prompt Delivery Inc* ***(P-18645)***
Southern California Mtl Hdlg, Whittier *Also called Equipment Depot Inc* ***(P-13900)***
Southern California Plas Inc..........D.......714 751-7084
3122 Maple St Santa Ana (92707) ***(P-4718)***
Southern California Regional, Indio *Also called Granite Construction Company* ***(P-881)***
Southern California Tele Co (PA)..........D.......951 693-1880
27515 Enterprise Cir W Temecula (92590) ***(P-12670)***
Southern California Trane, Brea *Also called Trane US Inc* ***(P-8351)***
Southern Counties Bldg Maint (PA)..........C.......805 928-9900
1035 N Armando St Ste F Anaheim (92806) ***(P-17287)***
Southern Counties Oil Co (PA)..........D.......714 744-7140
1800 W Katella Ave # 400 Orange (92867) ***(P-14797)***
Southern Electronics, Pomona *Also called Electrocube Inc* ***(P-9707)***
Southern Glazer's of CA, Cerritos *Also called Southern Glzers Wine Sprits WA* ***(P-14846)***
Southern Glzers Wine Sprits WA..........B.......562 926-2000
17101 Valley View Ave Cerritos (90703) ***(P-14846)***
Southern Implants Inc..........C.......949 273-8505
5 Holland Ste 209 Irvine (92618) ***(P-23115)***
Southern International Packg, Rancho Palos Verdes *Also called Western Summit Mfg Corp* ***(P-5442)***
Southern Inyo Healthcare Dst..........C.......760 876-5501
501 E Locust St Lone Pine (93545) ***(P-20950)***
Southern Management Corp..........C.......213 312-2268
808 S Olive St Los Angeles (90014) ***(P-17288)***
Southern Neng Eggs Acqstion LL (HQ)..........E.......951 332-3300
12005 Capperney Dr Fontana (92337) ***(P-14551)***
Southern Sierra Energy Company..........C.......949 752-5588
18101 Von Karman Ave # 9 Irvine (92612) ***(P-12861)***
Southern Sierra Medical Center..........D.......760 446-6404
105 E Sydnor Ave 100 Ridgecrest (93555) ***(P-20951)***
Southern Sierra Medical Clinic, Ridgecrest *Also called Ridgecrest Regional Hospital* ***(P-20923)***
Southern States Realty..........A.......626 302-1212
2244 Walnut Grove Ave Rosemead (91770) ***(P-16006)***
Southern Valley Chemical Co..........F.......661 366-3308
101 Sycamore Rd Arvin (93203) ***(P-5172)***
Southland Arthritis Osteo..........E.......951 672-1866
949 Calhoun Pl Ste F Hemet (92543) ***(P-20093)***
Southland Care, San Juan Capistrano *Also called Ensign Southland LLC* ***(P-20334)***
Southland Container Corp..........B.......909 937-9781
1600 Champagne Ave Ontario (91761) ***(P-3828)***
Southland Credit Union (PA)..........D.......562 862-6831
10701 Los Alamitos Blvd Los Alamitos (90720) ***(P-15090)***
Southland Home Fabrics Inc..........F.......310 475-1637
10629 W Pico Blvd Los Angeles (90064) ***(P-3164)***
Southland Industries (PA)..........E.......800 613-6240
12131 Western Ave Garden Grove (92841) ***(P-1147)***
Southland Integrated Svcs Inc (PA)..........D.......714 558-6009
1618 W 1st St Santa Ana (92703) ***(P-22211)***
Southland Lutheran Home, Norwalk *Also called Front Prch Cmmnties Svcs - Cas* ***(P-20589)***
Southland Polymers Inc..........E.......562 921-0444
14030 Gannet St Santa Fe Springs (90670) ***(P-4719)***
Southland Publishing Inc (PA)..........F.......626 584-1500
50 S Delacey Ave Ste 200 Pasadena (91105) ***(P-4031)***
Southland Rgonal Assn Realtors (PA)..........D.......818 786-2110
7232 Balboa Blvd Van Nuys (91406) ***(P-22260)***
Southland Tool Mfg Inc..........F.......714 632-8198
1430 N Hundley St Anaheim (92806) ***(P-7869)***
Southland Transit Inc (PA)..........C.......626 258-1310
3650 Rockwell Ave El Monte (91731) ***(P-11844)***
Southland Transit Co, Baldwin Park *Also called San Gabriel Transit Inc* ***(P-11901)***
Southwest Airlines Co..........D.......949 252-5200
18601 Airport Way Ste 237 Santa Ana (92707) ***(P-12316)***
Southwest Airlines Co..........D.......310 665-5700
100 World Way Ste 328 Los Angeles (90045) ***(P-12317)***
Southwest Atlanta Dia (HQ)..........E.......310 536-2400
601 Hawaii St El Segundo (90245) ***(P-21266)***
Southwest Con Structures Inc..........D.......951 278-0377
124 River Rd Corona (92878) ***(P-917)***
Southwest Concrete Products..........D.......909 983-9789
519 S Benson Ave Ontario (91762) ***(P-6057)***
Southwest Contractors (PA)..........E.......661 588-0484
136 Allen Rd 100 Bakersfield (93314) ***(P-972)***
Southwest Convalesant, Hawthorne *Also called Windsor Anaheim Healthcare* ***(P-20511)***
Southwest Crpnters Trning Fund..........D.......213 386-8590
533 S Fremont Ave Los Angeles (90071) ***(P-22299)***
Southwest Data Products, San Bernardino *Also called Innovative Metal Inds Inc* ***(P-7023)***
Southwest Dealer Services Inc (PA)..........C.......949 707-4200
8659 Research Dr Ste 100 Irvine (92618) ***(P-18673)***
Southwest Healthcare Sys Aux..........A.......800 404-6627
38977 Sky Canyon Dr # 200 Murrieta (92563) ***(P-20952)***
Southwest Healthcare Sys Aux (HQ)..........B.......951 696-6000
25500 Medical Center Dr Murrieta (92562) ***(P-20953)***
Southwest Inspection and Tstg..........D.......562 941-2990
441 Commercial Way La Habra (90631) ***(P-18674)***
Southwest Inspection Testing, La Habra *Also called Southwest Inspection and Tstg* ***(P-18674)***
Southwest Landscape Inc..........D.......714 545-1084
2205 S Standard Ave Santa Ana (92707) ***(P-282)***
Southwest Machine & Plastic Co..........E.......626 963-6919
620 W Foothill Blvd Glendora (91741) ***(P-10420)***
Southwest Material Hdlg Inc (PA)..........C.......951 727-0477
3725 Nobel Ct Jurupa Valley (91752) ***(P-18675)***
Southwest Offset Prtg Co Inc (PA)..........B.......310 965-9154
13650 Gramercy Pl Gardena (90249) ***(P-4425)***
Southwest Patrol Inc..........D.......909 861-1884
556 N Dmnd Bar Blvd # 207 Diamond Bar (91765) ***(P-18339)***
Southwest Plastics Co, Glendora *Also called Southwest Machine & Plastic Co* ***(P-10420)***
Southwest Plating Co Inc..........F.......323 753-3781
1344 W Slauson Ave Los Angeles (90044) ***(P-7312)***
Southwest Ppline Trnchless Cor (PA)..........D.......310 329-8717
22118 S Vermont Ave Torrance (90502) ***(P-19069)***
Southwest Products Corporation..........F.......360 887-7400
2875 Cherry Ave Signal Hill (90755) ***(P-7598)***
Southwest Protective Svcs Inc..........C.......760 996-1285
404 W Heil Ave El Centro (92243) ***(P-18340)***
Southwest Rgnal Cncil Crpnters (PA)..........E.......213 385-1457
533 S Fremont Ave Fl 10 Los Angeles (90071) ***(P-22300)***
Southwest Rgnal Cncil Crpnters..........D.......818 364-9303
15881 Valley View Ct Sylmar (91342) ***(P-22301)***
Southwest Security, El Centro *Also called Southwest Protective Svcs Inc* ***(P-18340)***
Southwest Sign Company, Corona *Also called Fovell Enterprises Inc* ***(P-11556)***
Southwest Site Services Inc..........D.......866 892-8451
963 Main St Riverside (92501) ***(P-17375)***
Southwest Toyota Lift, Jurupa Valley *Also called Southwest Material Hdlg Inc* ***(P-18675)***
Southwest Traders Incorporated (PA)..........C.......951 699-7800
27565 Diaz Rd Temecula (92590) ***(P-14510)***
Southwestern Industries Inc (PA)..........D.......310 608-4422
2615 Homestead Pl Rancho Dominguez (90220) ***(P-7747)***
Southwestern Orthpd Med Corp..........E.......562 803-0600
3416 The Strand Manhattan Beach (90266) ***(P-20094)***
Southwind Foods LLC (PA)..........C.......323 262-8222
20644 S Fordyce Ave Carson (90810) ***(P-14585)***
Southwire Inc..........B.......310 886-8300
20250 S Alameda St Compton (90221) ***(P-6302)***
Southwire Inc (HQ)..........F.......310 884-8500
11695 Pacific Ave Fontana (92337) ***(P-6303)***
Southwood Garden Apartments, Long Beach *Also called Intervest Property MGT Inc* ***(P-15728)***
Sovereign Arts Met Finshg LLC..........F.......714 742-9944
1336 N Mccadden Pl Los Angeles (90028) ***(P-7313)***
Sovereign Health of California, San Clemente *Also called Dual Diagnosis Trtmnt Ctr Inc* ***(P-21300)***
Sovereign Healthcare Oc LLC (PA)..........D.......949 706-9900
27401 Los Altos Ste 200 Mission Viejo (92691) ***(P-20954)***
Soyfoods of America..........E.......626 358-3836
1091 Hamilton Rd Duarte (91010) ***(P-2120)***
Sp, City of Industry *Also called Scope Packaging Inc* ***(P-3826)***
Spa De Soleil Inc..........E.......818 504-3200
10443 Arminta St Sun Valley (91352) ***(P-14291)***
Spa Resort Casino (PA)..........A.......888 999-1995
401 E Amado Rd Palm Springs (92262) ***(P-16721)***
Spa Resort Casino..........C.......760 883-1034
100 N Indian Canyon Dr Palm Springs (92262) ***(P-16722)***
Space Components, Commerce *Also called Atk Space Systems LLC* ***(P-10571)***
Space Exploration Tech Corp..........E.......714 330-8668
2700 Miner St San Pedro (90731) ***(P-10517)***
Space Exploration Tech Corp (PA)..........A.......310 363-6000
1 Rocket Rd Hawthorne (90250) ***(P-10518)***
Space Systems Division, El Segundo *Also called Orbital Sciences LLC* ***(P-10630)***
Space-Lok Inc..........C.......310 527-6150
13306 Halldale Ave Gardena (90249) ***(P-10421)***
Spaceship Company, The, Mojave *Also called Galactic Co LLC* ***(P-10514)***
Spacestor Inc..........F.......310 410-0220
5450 W 83rd St Los Angeles (90045) ***(P-3600)***
Spacesystems Holdings LLC..........F.......714 226-1400
4398 Corporate Center Dr Los Alamitos (90720) ***(P-8939)***
Spacex, San Pedro *Also called Space Exploration Tech Corp* ***(P-10517)***

ALPHABETIC

Employee Codes: A=Over 500 employees, B=251-500
C=101-250, D=51-100, E=20-50 F=10-19
2022 Southern California Business
Directory and Buyers Guide
© Mergent Inc. 1-800-342-5647
1277

Spacex, Hawthorne *Also called Space Exploration Tech Corp* ***(P-10518)***

Spacex LLC ....B....310 970-5845
12533 Crenshaw Blvd Hawthorne (90250) ***(P-10519)***

Spalinger Enterprises Inc. ....E....661 834-4550
800 S Mount Vernon Ave Bakersfield (93307) ***(P-3666)***

Span-O-Matic Inc ....E....714 256-4700
825 Columbia St Brea (92821) ***(P-6915)***

Spangler Industries Inc ....C....951 735-5000
1711 N Delilah St Corona (92879) ***(P-5413)***

Spanish Brdcstg Sys of Cal ....D....310 203-0900
7007 Nw 77th Ave Los Angeles (90064) ***(P-12706)***

Spanish Hills Club LLC ....D....805 388-5000
999 Crestview Ave Camarillo (93010) ***(P-19616)***

Spanish Hills Country Club (PA) ....**C....805 389-1644**
999 Crestview Ave Camarillo (93010) ***(P-19617)***

Sparitual, Van Nuys *Also called Orly International Inc* ***(P-5054)***

Spark Compass, Los Angeles *Also called Total Cmmnicator Solutions Inc* ***(P-17999)***

Sparkle Uniform & Linen Svc, Bakersfield *Also called Richard K Newman and Assoc Inc* ***(P-16869)***

Sparling Instruments LLC ....E....626 444-0571
4097 Temple City Blvd El Monte (91731) ***(P-13940)***

Spartak Enterprises Inc ....F....951 360-0610
11186 Venture Dr Jurupa Valley (91752) ***(P-3562)***

Spartan, Los Alamitos *Also called Dc-001 Inc* ***(P-10581)***

Spartan Inc ....D....661 327-1205
3030 M St Bakersfield (93301) ***(P-6663)***

Spartan Manufacturing Co ....E....714 894-1955
7081 Patterson Dr Garden Grove (92841) ***(P-8799)***

Spartan Motors Gtb LLC ....F....323 276-1933
1130 S Vail Ave Montebello (90640) ***(P-9997)***

Spartan Truck Company Inc ....E....818 899-1111
12266 Branford St Sun Valley (91352) ***(P-9998)***

Spates Fabricators Inc ....D....760 397-4122
85435 Middleton St Thermal (92274) ***(P-3368)***

Spatz Corporation ....C....805 487-2122
1600 Westar Dr Oxnard (93033) ***(P-5071)***

Spatz Laboratories, Oxnard *Also called Spatz Corporation* ***(P-5071)***

Spaulding Crusher Parts, Perris *Also called Spaulding Equipment Company* ***(P-7663)***

Spaulding Equipment Company (PA) ....**E....951 943-4531**
75 Paseo Adelanto Perris (92570) ***(P-7663)***

Spc Building Services, Riverside *Also called J M V B Inc* ***(P-1184)***

SPD Department, Los Angeles *Also called Steriltek Inc* ***(P-18680)***

SPD Manufacturing Inc ....F....985 302-1902
1101 E Truslow Ave Fullerton (92831) ***(P-2604)***

Spearman Aerospace Inc ....E....714 523-4751
9215 Greenleaf Ave Santa Fe Springs (90670) ***(P-22656)***

Spearman Clubs Inc (PA) ....**E....949 496-2070**
23500 Clubhouse Dr Laguna Niguel (92677) ***(P-19671)***

Spearmint Rhino Cmpnies Wrldwi ....D....951 371-3788
1875 Tandem Norco (92860) ***(P-23116)***

Spearmint Rhino Gentlemens CLB, Torrance *Also called Midnight Sun Enterprises Inc* ***(P-23473)***

Spears Manufacturing, Sylmar *Also called RWS Research & Development Inc* ***(P-7476)***

Spears Manufacturing Co (PA) ....**C....818 364-1611**
15853 Olden St Sylmar (91342) ***(P-13879)***

Spec, Valencia *Also called Semiconductor Process Eqp Corp* ***(P-9572)***

Spec Engineering Co Inc ....E....818 780-3045
13754 Saticoy St Van Nuys (91402) ***(P-8800)***

Spec Formliners Inc ....E....714 429-9500
1038 E 4th St Santa Ana (92701) ***(P-6058)***

Spec Services Inc ....B....714 963-8077
10540 Talbert Ave 100e Fountain Valley (92708) ***(P-22657)***

Spec Tool Company ....E....323 723-9533
11805 Wakeman St Santa Fe Springs (90670) ***(P-10422)***

Special Devices Incorporated ....A....805 387-1000
2655 1st St Ste 300 Simi Valley (93065) ***(P-10135)***

Special Dispatch Cal Inc (PA) ....**D....714 521-8200**
234 Loma Ave Long Beach (90803) ***(P-12119)***

Special Needs Network ....E....323 291-7100
4401 Crenshaw Blvd # 215 Los Angeles (90043) ***(P-21054)***

Special Service For Groups Inc ....C....310 323-6887
19401 S Vt Ave Ste A200 Torrance (90502) ***(P-22212)***

Special Service For Groups Inc (PA) ....**D....213 368-1888**
905 E 8th St Los Angeles (90021) ***(P-21968)***

Special Service For Groups Inc ....C....213 553-1800
520 S La Fyte Pk Pl 30 Los Angeles (90057) ***(P-22213)***

Special-T, North Hollywood *Also called Specialty Coatings & Chem Inc* ***(P-5114)***

Speciality Labs, Fullerton *Also called Magtech & Power Conversion Inc* ***(P-9633)***

Specialized Coating, Huntington Beach *Also called Specilzed Crmic Pwdr Cting Inc* ***(P-7413)***

Specialized Dairy Service Inc ....E....909 923-3420
1710 E Philadelphia St Ontario (91761) ***(P-7620)***

Specialized Elevator Svcs LLC (PA) ....**D....562 407-1200**
14320 Iseli Rd Santa Fe Springs (90670) ***(P-13941)***

Specialized Ldscp MGT Svcs Inc ....D....805 520-7590
4212 Past Los Angles Ave Simi Valley (93063) ***(P-283)***

Specialized Milling Corp ....E....909 357-7890
10330 Elm Ave Fontana (92337) ***(P-5113)***

Specialized Pdts & Design Inc ....F....714 289-1428
1428 N Manzanita St Orange (92867) ***(P-5147)***

Specialized Screen Prtg Inc ....F....714 964-1230
18435 Bandilier Cir Fountain Valley (92708) ***(P-4575)***

Specialteam Medical Svc Inc ....F....714 694-0348
22445 La Palma Ave Ste F Yorba Linda (92887) ***(P-11059)***

Specialty Car Wash System ....F....909 869-6300
146 Mercury Cir Pomona (91768) ***(P-8416)***

Specialty Coating Systems Inc ....D....909 390-8818
4435 E Airport Dr Ste 100 Ontario (91761) ***(P-7412)***

Specialty Coatings & Chem Inc ....E....818 983-0055
7360 Varna Ave North Hollywood (91605) ***(P-5114)***

Specialty Concepts Inc ....F....818 998-5238
2393 Teller Rd Ste 106 Newbury Park (91320) ***(P-8963)***

Specialty Construction Inc ....D....805 543-1706
645 Clarion Ct San Luis Obispo (93401) ***(P-1317)***

Specialty Division, Santa Fe Springs *Also called Distinctive Industries* ***(P-3172)***

Specialty Enterprises Co ....D....323 726-9721
6858 E Acco St Commerce (90040) ***(P-5522)***

Specialty Equipment Co ....F....714 258-1622
1921 E Pomona St Santa Ana (92705) ***(P-9999)***

Specialty Equipment Mkt Assn (PA) ....**D....909 396-0289**
1575 Valley Vista Dr Diamond Bar (91765) ***(P-22261)***

Specialty Fabrications Inc ....E....805 579-9730
2674 Westhills Ct Simi Valley (93065) ***(P-6916)***

Specialty Finishes, Fontana *Also called Specialized Milling Corp* ***(P-5113)***

Specialty Interior Mfg Inc ....E....714 296-8618
16751 Millikan Ave Irvine (92606) ***(P-13095)***

Specialty International Inc ....E....813 768-8810
11144 Penrose St Ste 11 Sun Valley (91352) ***(P-7183)***

Specialty Laboratories Inc (HQ) ....**A....661 799-6543**
27027 Tourney Rd Valencia (91355) ***(P-21096)***

Specialty Merchandise Corp (PA) ....**E....805 578-5500**
4100 Guardian St Ste 112 Simi Valley (93063) ***(P-14976)***

Specialty Metal Fabrication, Goleta *Also called Tan Set Corporation* ***(P-6667)***

Specialty Minerals Inc ....C....760 248-5300
6565 Meridian Rd Lucerne Valley (92356) ***(P-4672)***

Specialty Motions Inc ....E....951 735-8722
5480 Smokey Mountain Way Yorba Linda (92887) ***(P-8031)***

Specialty Motors Inc ....F....800 232-2612
28420 Witherspoon Pkwy Valencia (91355) ***(P-8932)***

Specialty Paper Mills Inc ....C....562 692-8737
8844 Millergrove Dr Santa Fe Springs (90670) ***(P-3770)***

Specialty Restaurants Corp ....C....818 843-5013
1250 E Harvard Rd Burbank (91501) ***(P-16977)***

Specialty Risk Services Inc ....D....714 674-1000
1 Pointe Dr Ste 220 Brea (92821) ***(P-15629)***

Specialty Rock Inc ....F....909 334-2265
5405 Alton Pkwy Irvine Irvine (92604) ***(P-574)***

Specialty Surface Grinding Inc ....E....310 538-4352
345 W 131st St Los Angeles (90061) ***(P-8801)***

Specialty Surgical Centers ....E....949 341-3499
15825 Laguna Canyon Rd # 200 Irvine (92618) ***(P-20095)***

Specialty Team Plastering Inc ....C....805 966-3858
4652 Vintage Ranch Ln Santa Barbara (93110) ***(P-1402)***

Specific Media LLC (HQ) ....**D....949 861-8888**
2722 Michelson Dr Ste 100 Irvine (92612) ***(P-17056)***

Specilty Enzymes Btechnologies, Chino *Also called Cal-India Foods International* ***(P-5129)***

Specilty Enzymes Btechnologies ....F....909 613-1660
13591 Yorba Ave Chino (91710) ***(P-5148)***

Specilty Hosp San Gbriel Vly M ....D....626 339-5451
845 N Lark Ellen Ave West Covina (91791) ***(P-20955)***

Specilzed Crmic Pwdr Cting Inc ....F....714 901-2628
5862 Research Dr Huntington Beach (92649) ***(P-7413)***

Specilzed Foster Care Pasadena, Pasadena *Also called County of Los Angeles* ***(P-21406)***

Specilzed Fster Care Chtsworth, Chatsworth *Also called County of Los Angeles* ***(P-21404)***

Specimen Contracting, Sunland *Also called Brightview Tree Company* ***(P-365)***

Spectra Apparel, Chino *Also called Rrz Enterprises Inc* ***(P-14348)***

Spectra Clinical Labs Inc ....D....562 776-8440
14601 S Broadway Gardena (90248) ***(P-21097)***

Spectra Color Inc ....E....951 277-0200
9116 Stellar Ct Corona (92883) ***(P-4646)***

Spectra Company ....C....909 599-0760
2510 Supply St Pomona (91767) ***(P-1353)***

Spectra I California ....D....310 835-0808
21818 S Wilmington Ave # 402 Carson (90810) ***(P-1318)***

Spectra Industrial Electric, Carson *Also called Spectra I California* ***(P-1318)***

Spectra Premium (usa) Corp ....D....951 653-0640
2220 Almond Ave Redlands (92374) ***(P-13096)***

Spectra USA, Chino *Also called Isiqalo LLC* ***(P-2637)***

Spectrasensors Inc ....E....909 980-4238
11027 Arrow Rte Rancho Cucamonga (91730) ***(P-10812)***

Spectrasensors Inc (HQ) ....**E....909 948-4102**
11027 Arrow Rte Rancho Cucamonga (91730) ***(P-10813)***

Spectrolab Inc ....E....818 365-4611
12500 Gladstone Ave Sylmar (91342) ***(P-9581)***

Spectrum Bags, Cerritos *Also called Ips Industries Inc* ***(P-5676)***

Spectrum Brands Inc ....A....949 672-4003
19701 Da Vinci Lake Forest (92610) ***(P-9818)***

Spectrum Brands Hardware and H, Foothill Ranch *Also called Spectrum Hhi* ***(P-16978)***

Spectrum Brands Hhi, Lake Forest *Also called Spectrum Brands Inc* ***(P-9818)***

Spectrum Cnstr Group Inc ....D....949 299-1400
16 Goodyear Ste 140 Irvine (92618) ***(P-718)***

Spectrum Hhi ....D....949 672-4000
19701 Da Vinci Foothill Ranch (92610) ***(P-16978)***

Spectrum Hotel Group LLC ....D....949 471-8888
90 Pacifica Irvine (92618) ***(P-16723)***

Spectrum Information Svcs LLC (PA) ....**D....949 752-7070**
16 Technology Dr Ste 107 Irvine (92618) ***(P-17141)***

Spectrum Instruments Inc ....F....909 971-9710
570 E Arrow Hwy Ste D San Dimas (91773) ***(P-10771)***

Spectrum Lab & Phrm Pdts, Gardena *Also called Spectrum Laboratory Pdts Inc* ***(P-14791)***

Spectrum Laboratory Pdts Inc ....E....520 292-3103
14422 S San Pedro St Gardena (90248) ***(P-14791)***

Spectrum Lifesciences LLC (HQ) ....**F....310 885-4600**
18617 S Broadwick St Rancho Dominguez (90220) ***(P-4764)***

Spectrum MGT Holdg Co LLC ....D....323 657-0899
3550 Wilshire Blvd Los Angeles (90010) ***(P-12777)***

Mergent e-mail: customerrelations@mergent.com
1278
2022 Southern California Business Directory and Buyers Guide
(P-0000) Products & Services Section entry number
(PA)=Parent Co (HQ)=Headquarters (DH)=Div Headquarters

Spectrum MGT Holdg Co LLC ....C....714 657-1060
6021 Katella Ave Ste 100 Cypress (90630) ***(P-12778)***
Spectrum Plating Company, Los Angeles *Also called Ravlich Enterprises LLC* ***(P-7303)***
Spectrum Scientific Inc ....E....949 260-9900
16692 Hale Ave Ste A Irvine (92606) ***(P-10861)***
Speed-O-Pin International ....F....562 433-4911
1401 Freeman Ave Long Beach (90804) ***(P-3716)***
Speedo USA Inc ....B....657 465-3800
6251 Katella Ave Cypress (90630) ***(P-2823)***
Speeds Oil Tool Service Inc ....D....805 925-1369
1573 E Betteravia Rd Santa Maria (93454) ***(P-11995)***
Speedway Usa Inc ....E....760 245-6211
14800 Seventh St Victorville (92395) ***(P-19435)***
Speedwear.com, Huntington Beach *Also called Gachupin Enterprises LLC* ***(P-4518)***
Speedy Circuits, Huntington Beach *Also called Coast To Coast Circuits Inc* ***(P-9393)***
Spektrum Manufacturing Inc ....F....949 702-2807
1939 S Susan St Santa Ana (92704) ***(P-2790)***
Spencer Aerospace Mfg LLC ....D....805 452-3536
28510 Industry Dr Valencia (91355) ***(P-7460)***
Spencer Home Decor, City of Industry *Also called Spencer N Enterprises LLC* ***(P-3120)***
Spencer N Enterprises LLC ....D....626 448-0374
425 S Lemon Ave City of Industry (91789) ***(P-3120)***
Spencer Recovery Centers Inc (PA) ....**D....949 376-3705**
1316 S Coast Hwy Laguna Beach (92651) ***(P-21344)***
Spenco Machine & Manufacturing ....F....951 699-5566
27556 Commerce Center Dr Temecula (92590) ***(P-8802)***
Spenuzza Inc (HQ) ....**C....951 281-1830**
1128 Sherborn St Corona (92879) ***(P-8417)***
SPEP Acquisition Corp (PA) ....**D....310 608-0693**
4041 Via Oro Ave Long Beach (90810) ***(P-6538)***
Spf Capital Real Estate LLC ....D....310 519-8200
601 S Palos Verdes St San Pedro (90731) ***(P-16724)***
Sph Holdings Inc (HQ) ....**C....714 441-3900**
4120 N Palm St Fullerton (92835) ***(P-719)***
Sphere Alliance Inc ....E....951 352-2400
3087 12th St Riverside (92507) ***(P-4720)***
Spidell Publishing Inc ....E....714 776-7850
1134 N Gilbert St Anaheim (92801) ***(P-4206)***
Spiess Construction Co Inc ....D....805 937-5859
201 S Broadway St Ste 140 Orcutt (93455) ***(P-973)***
Spigen Inc ....D....949 502-5121
9975 Toledo Way Ste 100 Irvine (92618) ***(P-14765)***
Spigen Sgp, Irvine *Also called Spigen Inc* ***(P-14765)***
Spill Magic Inc ....E....714 557-2001
630 Young St Santa Ana (92705) ***(P-3771)***
Spilo Worldwide Inc ....D....213 687-8600
100 Wilshire Blvd Ste 700 Santa Monica (90401) ***(P-14044)***
Spin Products Inc ....E....909 590-7000
13878 Yorba Ave Chino (91710) ***(P-5825)***
Spinelli Graphic Inc ....F....562 431-3232
10621 Bloomfield St Ste 2 Los Alamitos (90720) ***(P-4576)***
Spiniello Companies ....C....909 629-1000
2650 Pomona Blvd Pomona (91768) ***(P-974)***
Spinitar, La Mirada *Also called Presentation Products Inc* ***(P-18058)***
Spinlaunch Inc ....D....650 516-7746
4350 E Conant St Long Beach (90808) ***(P-23331)***
Spinnaker Coating LLC ....C....714 482-1006
566 Vanguard Way Brea (92821) ***(P-3875)***
Spinning, Venice *Also called Mad Dogg Athletics Inc* ***(P-14396)***
Spintek Filtration Inc ....F....714 236-9190
10863 Portal Dr Los Alamitos (90720) ***(P-8139)***
Spira Manufacturing Corp ....E....818 764-8222
650 Jessie St San Fernando (91340) ***(P-5354)***
Spiral Ppr Tube & Core Co Inc ....E....562 801-9705
5200 Industry Ave Pico Rivera (90660) ***(P-3840)***
Spiral Technology Inc ....D....661 723-3148
229 E Avenue K8 Ste 105 Lancaster (93535) ***(P-22658)***
Spirent Calabasas, Calabasas *Also called Spirent Communications Inc* ***(P-13441)***
Spirent Communications Inc (HQ) ....**B....818 676-2300**
27349 Agoura Rd Calabasas (91301) ***(P-13441)***
Spireon Inc (PA) ....**C....800 557-1449**
16802 Aston Ste 150 Irvine (92606) ***(P-17721)***
Spirit Active Wear, Vernon *Also called Spirit Clothing Company* ***(P-2995)***
Spirit Clothing Company ....E....213 784-0251
2211 E 37th St Vernon (90058) ***(P-2995)***
Splash Events Inc (PA) ....**D....408 287-8600**
80 Icon Foothill Ranch (92610) ***(P-17188)***
Spm, Anaheim *Also called Bace Manufacturing Inc* ***(P-5573)***
Spn Investments Inc ....F....562 777-1140
6481 Orangethorpe Ave # 12 Buena Park (90620) ***(P-11448)***
Sport Chalet LLC ....D....714 848-0988
16242 Beach Blvd Huntington Beach (92647) ***(P-19672)***
Sport Chalet LLC ....D....661 253-3883
25560 The Old Rd Stevenson Ranch (91381) ***(P-14088)***
Sport Chalet LLC ....D....949 476-9555
2983 Michelson Dr Irvine (92612) ***(P-19673)***
Sport Kites Inc ....F....714 998-6359
500 W Blueridge Ave Orange (92865) ***(P-10204)***
Sport Pins International Inc ....F....909 985-4549
888 Berry Ct Ste A Upland (91786) ***(P-11491)***
Sport Tek, Commerce *Also called Sportek International Inc* ***(P-14351)***
Sportek International Inc ....F....213 239-6700
2425 S Eastern Ave Commerce (90040) ***(P-14351)***
Sportifeye Optics Inc ....E....626 521-5600
1854 Business Center Dr Duarte (91010) ***(P-11262)***
Sportsman Steel Gun Safe, Long Beach *Also called Sportsmen Steel Safe Fabg Co* ***(P-7571)***
Sportsmen Steel Safe Fabg Co (PA) ....**E....562 984-0244**
6311 N Paramount Blvd Long Beach (90805) ***(P-7571)***
Sportsmens Ldge Rest Spcial Ev, Studio City *Also called Sportsmens Lodge Restaurant* ***(P-16979)***
Sportsmens Lodge Hotel LLC ....D....818 769-4700
12825 Ventura Blvd Studio City (91604) ***(P-16725)***
Sportsmens Lodge Restaurant ....D....818 755-5000
12833 Ventura Blvd Studio City (91604) ***(P-16979)***
Sportsrobe Inc ....E....310 559-3999
8654 Hayden Pl Culver City (90232) ***(P-2824)***
Spotlight 29 Casino, Coachella *Also called 29 Palms Enterprises Corp* ***(P-19629)***
Spotlite America Corporation (PA) ....**E....310 829-0200**
9937 Jefferson Blvd # 110 Culver City (90232) ***(P-5943)***
Spragues Ready Mix, Irwindale *Also called Spragues Rock and Sand Company* ***(P-6116)***
Spragues Ready Mix Concrete, Simi Valley *Also called Spragues Rock and Sand Company* ***(P-6117)***
Spragues Rock and Sand Company (PA) ....**E....626 445-2125**
230 Longden Ave Irwindale (91706) ***(P-6116)***
Spragues Rock and Sand Company ....F....805 522-7010
5400 Bennett Rd Simi Valley (93063) ***(P-6117)***
Spray Enclosure Tech Inc ....E....909 419-7011
1427 N Linden Ave Rialto (92376) ***(P-6917)***
Spray Tech, Rialto *Also called Spray Enclosure Tech Inc* ***(P-6917)***
Spraying Devices Inc ....F....559 734-5555
447 E Caldwell Ave Visalia (93277) ***(P-7621)***
Sprayline Enterprises Inc ....F....909 627-8411
10774 Grand Ave Ontario (91762) ***(P-7414)***
Spreadco Inc ....E....760 351-0747
803 Us Highway 78 Brawley (92227) ***(P-2665)***
Spreckels Sugar Company Inc ....B....760 344-3110
395 W Keystone Rd Brawley (92227) ***(P-2080)***
Spring Industries, Ventura *Also called Juengermann Inc* ***(P-7464)***
Spring Senior Assisted Living, Torrance *Also called Genesis Healthcare LLC* ***(P-20356)***
Spring Valley Post Acute LLC ....C....760 245-6477
14973 Hesperia Rd Victorville (92395) ***(P-20479)***
Springboard, Los Angeles *Also called Evolve Media Holdings LLC* ***(P-17012)***
Springcoin Inc ....D....847 322-6349
4551 Glencoe Ave Ste 100 Marina Del Rey (90292) ***(P-17988)***
Springhill SMC LLC ....D....310 727-9595
14620 Aviation Blvd Hawthorne (90250) ***(P-16726)***
Springhill Suites, Hawthorne *Also called Springhill SMC LLC* ***(P-16726)***
Springhill Suites, Anaheim *Also called M6 Dev LLC* ***(P-16550)***
Springhill Suites, Temecula *Also called Starwood Hospitality LLC* ***(P-16729)***
Springhill Suites LLC ....D....626 821-5400
99 N 2nd Ave Arcadia (91006) ***(P-16727)***
Springpudic, Los Angeles *Also called Cuevas Mattress Inc* ***(P-3545)***
Springs Club Inc ....D....760 328-0254
1 Duke Dr Rancho Mirage (92270) ***(P-19618)***
SPRINGS COUNTRY CLUB, THE, Rancho Mirage *Also called Springs Club Inc* ***(P-19618)***
Sprint, Anaheim *Also called Arch Telecom Inc* ***(P-12590)***
Sprint Communications Co LP ....C....562 943-8907
15582 Whittwood Ln Whittier (90603) ***(P-12611)***
Sprint Communications Co LP ....C....951 303-8501
31754 Temecula Pkwy Ste A Temecula (92592) ***(P-18131)***
Sprint Communications Co LP ....C....310 216-9093
5381 W Centinela Ave Los Angeles (90045) ***(P-13775)***
Sprint Communications Co LP ....C....714 534-2107
12913 Harbor Blvd Ste Q4 Garden Grove (92840) ***(P-18132)***
Sprint Communications Co LP ....C....626 339-0430
1316 N Azusa Ave Covina (91722) ***(P-18133)***
Sprint Communications Co LP ....C....951 461-9786
23865 Clinton Keith Rd Wildomar (92595) ***(P-12612)***
Sprint Communications Co LP ....C....951 340-1924
3580 Grand Oaks Corona (92881) ***(P-13776)***
Sprint Communications Co LP ....C....661 951-8927
44416 Valley Central Way Lancaster (93536) ***(P-12613)***
Sprint Communications Co LP ....C....818 755-7100
111 Unversal Hollywood Dr Universal City (91608) ***(P-12671)***
Sprint Communications Co LP ....C....909 382-6030
1505 E Enterprise Dr San Bernardino (92408) ***(P-12672)***
Sprint Intl Cmmunications Corp ....C....562 408-6978
9 Lakewood Center Mall Lakewood (90712) ***(P-12614)***
Sprintray Inc ....C....800 914-8004
2705 Media Center Dr 2 Los Angeles (90065) ***(P-23332)***
Sprite Industries Incorporated ....E....951 735-1015
1791 Railroad St Corona (92878) ***(P-10814)***
Sprite Showers, Corona *Also called Sprite Industries Incorporated* ***(P-10814)***
Sproutime, Sun Valley *Also called Foodology LLC* ***(P-2435)***
Sprouts Farmers Market Inc ....C....888 577-7688
280 De Berry St Colton (92324) ***(P-12246)***
SPS Inc ....F....714 632-8333
3000 E Miraloma Ave Anaheim (92806) ***(P-3369)***
SPS Technologies LLC ....B....714 545-9311
1224 E Warner Ave Santa Ana (92705) ***(P-11501)***
SPS Technologies LLC ....B....310 323-6222
1700 W 132nd St Gardena (90249) ***(P-14020)***
SPS Technologies LLC ....E....714 892-5571
12570 Knott St Garden Grove (92841) ***(P-7075)***
SPS Technologies LLC ....B....714 371-1925
1224 E Warner Ave Santa Ana (92705) ***(P-11502)***
SPS Technologies LLC ....D....562 426-9411
14800 S Figueroa St Gardena (90248) ***(P-14021)***
Spsv Entertainment LLC ....D....909 744-9373
28950 State Highway 18 Skyforest (92385) ***(P-19380)***
Spus7 125 Cambridgepark LP ....D....213 683-4200
515 S Flower St Ste 3100 Los Angeles (90071) ***(P-16007)***
Spus7 150 Cambridgepark LP ....C....213 683-4200
515 S Flower St Ste 3100 Los Angeles (90071) ***(P-16008)***
SPX Corporation ....D....714 434-2576
17815 Newhope St Ste M Fountain Valley (92708) ***(P-6755)***

Employee Codes: A=Over 500 employees, B=251-500
C=101-250, D=51-100, E=20-50 F=10-19
2022 Southern California Business
Directory and Buyers Guide
© Mergent Inc. 1-800-342-5647
1279

Spyder Manufacturing Inc ....F 714 528-8010
545 Porter Way Placentia (92870) (P-7631)
Spyke Inc ....E 562 803-1700
12155 Pangborn Ave Downey (90241) (P-10501)
Sqa Services Inc ....B 800 333-6180
425 Via Corta Ste 203 Palos Verdes Estates (90274) (P-23333)
Squar Milner, Irvine Also called Squar Mlner Ptrson Mrnda Wllms (P-22815)
Squar Mlner Ptrson Mrnda Wllms (PA) ....C 949 222-2999
18500 Von Karman Ave # 10 Irvine (92612) (P-22815)
Square Enix Inc ....C 310 846-0400
999 N Pcf Cast Hwy Fl 3 Flr 3 El Segundo (90245) (P-13442)
Square Enix Amer Holdings Inc (HQ) ....E 310 321-6979
999 N Pacific Coast Hwy # 3 El Segundo (90245) (P-13443)
Square H Brands Inc ....C 323 267-4600
2731 S Soto St Vernon (90058) (P-1752)
Sr Plastics Company LLC (PA) ....D 951 520-9486
640 Parkridge Ave Norco (92860) (P-5826)
SRbray LLC (PA) ....E 714 765-7551
5500 E La Palma Ave Anaheim (92807) (P-1319)
Srd Engineering Inc ....D 714 630-2480
5300 Highland Ct Yorba Linda (92886) (P-975)
Sream Inc ....E 951 245-6999
12869 Temescal Canyon Rd A Corona (92883) (P-5969)
Srht Property Holding LLC ....C 213 683-0522
1317 E 7th St Los Angeles (90021) (P-16009)
SRI International ....C 805 542-9330
4111 Broad St Ste 220 San Luis Obispo (93401) (P-22922)
SRS Protection Inc ....C 805 744-7122
2064 Eastman Ave Ste 110 Ventura (93003) (P-18341)
Ss Brewtech, Tustin Also called CM Brewing Technologies LLC (P-8375)
SS Heritage Inn Ontario LLC ....D 909 937-5000
3595 E Guasti Rd Ontario (91761) (P-16728)
SS Metal Fabricators ....F 949 631-4272
2501 S Birch St Santa Ana (92707) (P-6664)
SSC Apparel Inc ....F 213 748-5511
2025 Long Beach Ave Los Angeles (90058) (P-2996)
SSC Construction Inc ....D 951 278-1177
4195 Chino Hills Pkwy Chino Hills (91709) (P-22659)
SSC Racing, Palm Desert Also called Karbz Inc (P-10084)
Sscor Inc ....F 818 504-4054
11064 Randall St Sun Valley (91352) (P-11060)
Ssd Systems, Anaheim Also called Security Signal Devices Inc (P-18397)
Ssdi, La Mirada Also called Solid State Devices Inc (P-9578)
SSG ADMINISTRATIVE OFFICES, Los Angeles Also called Special Service For Groups Inc (P-21968)
Ssi Surfaces, Newbury Park Also called Scientific Surface Inds Inc (P-3663)
Ssi/Advanced Post Services LLC ....D 323 969-9333
7165 W Sunset Blvd West Hollywood (90046) (P-19184)
Ssl Robotics LLC, Pasadena Also called Maxar Space Robotics LLC (P-22606)
Ssre Holdings LLC ....D 800 314-2098
18901 Railroad St City of Industry (91748) (P-1720)
Sst IV 8020 Las Vgas Blvd S LL ....D 949 429-6600
10 Terrace Rd Ladera Ranch (92694) (P-12247)
Sst Technologies ....E 562 803-3361
9801 Everest St Downey (90242) (P-9582)
Sst Vacuum Reflow Systems, Downey Also called Sst Technologies (P-9582)
Sstmas Y Aranda Eqpos Hdrlicos ....E 619 245-4502
280 Campillo St Ste L Calexico (92231) (P-13942)
Ssw, Palm Springs Also called S S W Mechanical Cnstr Inc (P-1133)
St Annes Maternity Home ....C 213 381-2931
155 N Occidental Blvd Los Angeles (90026) (P-22156)
St Baldricks Foundation Inc (PA) ....D 626 792-8247
1333 S Mayflower Ave # 40 Monrovia (91016) (P-22279)
St Bernardine Med Ctr Aux Inc ....C 909 881-4320
2101 N Waterman Ave San Bernardino (92404) (P-20956)
St Bernardine Medical Center ....B 909 883-8711
2101 N Waterman Ave San Bernardino (92404) (P-20957)
St Brnbas Snior Ctr Los Angle ....D 213 388-4444
675 S Carondelet St Los Angeles (90057) (P-21894)
St Francis Medical Center (HQ) ....D 310 900-8900
3630 E Imperial Hwy Lynwood (90262) (P-20958)
St George Auto Center Inc (PA) ....D 909 341-1189
10325 Central Ave Montclair (91763) (P-18906)
St George Logistics, Compton Also called Patina Freight Inc (P-12503)
St Jhns Lthran Ch Bakersfield ....C 661 665-7815
4500 Buena Vista Rd Bakersfield (93311) (P-17722)
St Jhns Well Child Fmly Ctr I (PA) ....D 323 541-1600
808 W 58th St Los Angeles (90037) (P-20200)
St John Knits, Irvine Also called St John Knits Intl Inc (P-2998)
St John Knits Inc (HQ) ....A 949 225-8857
17522 Armstrong Ave Irvine (92614) (P-2997)
St John Knits Intl Inc (HQ) ....C 949 863-1171
17522 Armstrong Ave Irvine (92614) (P-2998)
St John's Health Centre, Santa Monica Also called Saint Jhns Hlth Ctr Foundation (P-20927)
St Johns Lthran Schl Chldren C, Bakersfield Also called St Jhns Lthran Ch Bakersfield (P-17722)
St Johns Regional Medical Ctr, Oxnard Also called Dignity Health (P-20754)
St Joseph Center ....D 310 396-6468
204 Hampton Dr Venice (90291) (P-21895)
St Joseph Health Per Care Svcs (PA) ......D 714 712-7100
200 W Center St Promenade Anaheim (92805) (P-21214)
St Joseph Health Per Care Svcs ....D 800 365-1110
1315 Corona Pointe Ct Corona (92879) (P-21215)
St Joseph Hospice ....C 714 712-7100
200 W Center St Promenade Anaheim (92805) (P-21896)
St Joseph Hospital ....E 714 744-8601
1000 W La Veta Ave Orange (92868) (P-20959)

St Joseph Hospital of Orange ....C 714 771-8222
1310 W Stewart Dr Ste 203 Orange (92868) (P-20960)
St Joseph Hospital of Orange ....C 714 771-8006
363 S Main St Ste 211 Orange (92868) (P-20961)
St Joseph Hospital of Orange (HQ) ....A 714 633-9111
1100 W Stewart Dr Orange (92868) (P-20962)
St Joseph Hospital of Orange ....C 714 568-5500
3345 Michelson Dr Ste 100 Irvine (92612) (P-20963)
St Joseph Hospital of Orange ....C 714 771-8037
1100 W Stewart Dr Orange (92868) (P-20964)
St Josephs Physical Rehab Svcs, Orange Also called St Joseph Hospital of Orange (P-20960)
St Josephs School, Placentia Also called Roman Cthlic Diocese of Orange (P-18655)
St Jseph Heritg Med Group LLC (PA) ......C 714 633-1011
2212 E 4th St Ste 201 Santa Ana (92705) (P-20096)
St Jseph Hlth Sys HM Care Svc ....A 714 712-9500
200 W Center St Promenade Anaheim (92805) (P-21216)
St Jude Heritage Med Group ....D 714 449-6200
1835 Sunny Crest Dr Fullerton (92835) (P-20965)
St Jude Heritage Medical Group ....D 714 528-4211
4300 Rose Dr Yorba Linda (92886) (P-20097)
St Jude Hospital (HQ) ....A 714 871-3280
101 E Valencia Mesa Dr Fullerton (92835) (P-20966)
St Jude Medical Center, Fullerton Also called St Jude Hospital (P-20966)
St Louis Rams, Agoura Hills Also called Los Angeles Rams LLC (P-19422)
St Marks Episcopal Church ....D 909 920-5565
330 E 16th St Upland (91784) (P-22059)
St Mary Medical Center (HQ) ....A 562 491-9000
1050 Linden Ave Long Beach (90813) (P-20967)
St Mary Medical Center LLC ....D 760 946-8767
16000 Kasota Rd Apple Valley (92307) (P-20968)
St Mary Medical Center LLC (PA) ....A 760 242-2311
18300 Us Highway 18 Apple Valley (92307) (P-20969)
St Mary's School of Nursing, Long Beach Also called St Mary Medical Center (P-20967)
St Marys Medical Center ....A 562 491-9230
1050 Linden Ave Long Beach (90813) (P-23334)
St Paul Brands Inc ....E 714 903-1000
11555 Monarch St Ste B Garden Grove (92841) (P-4735)
St Pierre Gonzalez Enterprises ....F 714 491-2191
419 E La Palma Ave Anaheim (92801) (P-7415)
St Supertec, Paramount Also called Supertec Machinery Inc (P-7748)
St Timothy School ....D 310 474-1811
10479 W Pico Blvd Los Angeles (90064) (P-22060)
ST VINCENT DE PAUL SOCIETY OF, Los Angeles Also called Society of St Vncent De Paul C (P-22462)
St Vincent De Paul Vlg Inc ....D 619 233-8500
28225 Driza Mission Viejo (92692) (P-22464)
St Vincent Health Care, Pasadena Also called Vincent Hayley Enterprises (P-21004)
St Vincents Institution ....D 805 683-6381
4200 Calle Real Santa Barbara (93110) (P-21897)
St Vncent Snior Ctzen Ntrtn P (PA) ....D 213 484-7775
2303 Miramar St Los Angeles (90057) (P-22280)
St. Edna Sb-Cute Rhblttion Ctr, Santa Ana Also called Covenant Care California LLC (P-20302)
St. Johns Pleasant Valley Hosp, Camarillo Also called Dignity Health (P-20753)
ST. VINCENT MEALS ON WHEELS, Los Angeles Also called St Vncent Snior Ctzen Ntrtn P (P-22280)
STA, Thousand Palms Also called Sunline Transit Agency (P-11845)
Staar Surgical Company (PA) ....B 626 303-7902
25651 Atlantic Ocean Dr A1 Lake Forest (92630) (P-11263)
Staar Surgical Company ....F 626 303-7902
15102 Redhiill Ave Tustin (92780) (P-11264)
Stabile Plating Company Inc ....E 626 339-9091
1150 E Edna Pl Covina (91724) (P-7314)
Staco Switch, Irvine Also called Staco Systems Inc (P-8906)
Staco Systems Inc (HQ) ....D 949 297-8700
7 Morgan Irvine (92618) (P-8906)
Stadco (PA) ....C 323 227-8888
107 S Avenue 20 Los Angeles (90031) (P-7870)
Staff Assistance Inc (PA) ....B 818 894-7879
72 Moody Ct Ste 100 Thousand Oaks (91360) (P-21217)
Staff Assistance Inc ....B 805 371-9980
72 Moody Ct Ste 100 Thousand Oaks (91360) (P-17468)
Staff Pro Inc (PA) ....A 714 230-7200
1400 N Harbor Blvd # 700 Fullerton (92835) (P-18402)
Staffchex Inc ....A 818 709-6100
20537 Devonshire St Chatsworth (91311) (P-17469)
Staffing Solutions, Santa Ana Also called L&T Staffing Inc (P-17436)
Staffrehab ....A 888 835-0894
5000 Birch St Newport Beach (92660) (P-21345)
Stainless Fixtures Inc ....F 909 622-1615
3323 Russell St Riverside (92501) (P-3739)
Stainless Fixtures Inc ....E 909 622-1615
1250 E Franklin Ave Pomona (91766) (P-3740)
Stainless Industrial Companies ....D 310 575-9400
11111 Santa Monica Blvd Los Angeles (90025) (P-7832)
Stainless Micro-Polish Inc ....E 714 632-8903
1286 N Grove St Anaheim (92806) (P-7315)
Stainless Process Systems Inc ....F 805 483-7100
1650 Beacon Pl Oxnard (93033) (P-6665)
Stainless Stl Fabricators Inc ....D 714 739-9904
15120 Desman Rd La Mirada (90638) (P-13943)
Stainless Technologies LLC ....F 559 651-0460
19425 W Grove Ave Visalia (93291) (P-18997)
Stainless Works Inc ....F 559 688-4310
201 E Owens Ave Tulare (93274) (P-18998)
Stake Fastener, Chino Also called Dupree Inc (P-7064)

Mergent e-mail: customerrelations@mergent.com
1280

2022 Southern California Business
Directory and Buyers Guide

(P-0000) Products & Services Section entry number
(PA)=Parent Co (HQ)=Headquarters (DH)=Div Headquarters

Stampscom Inc (PA) ....B....**310 482-5800**
1990 E Grand Ave El Segundo (90245) ***(P-17142)***
Stan Tashman & Associates Inc....D....310 460-7600
8675 Wash Blvd Ste 203 Culver City (90232) ***(P-23117)***
Stance Inc (PA)....C....**949 391-9030**
197 Avenida La Pata San Clemente (92673) ***(P-14418)***
Stand 8, Long Beach *Also called Talent & Acquisition LLC* ***(P-17729)***
Stand Strong, San Luis Obispo *Also called Lumina Alliance* ***(P-21846)***
Standard Armament, Glendale *Also called SAI Industries* ***(P-7430)***
Standard Cable Usa Inc....F....949 888-0842
23126 Arroyo Vis Rcho STA Marg (92688) ***(P-7514)***
Standard Concrete Products Inc (HQ)....E....**310 829-4537**
13550 Live Oak Ln Baldwin Park (91706) ***(P-6118)***
Standard Homeopathic Company (PA)....D....**310 768-0700**
13301 S Main St Los Angeles (90061) ***(P-4896)***
Standard Hotel, The, Los Angeles *Also called 550 Flower St Operations LLC* ***(P-16310)***
Standard Industries Inc....D....661 387-1110
6505 Zerker Rd Shafter (93263) ***(P-13329)***
Standard Insurance Company....D....714 634-8200
500 N State College Blvd # 1000 Orange (92868) ***(P-15369)***
Standard Lumber Company Inc (HQ)....E....**559 651-2037**
27770 Entertainment Dr Valencia (91355) ***(P-3409)***
Standard Metal Products Inc....E....310 532-9861
1541 W 132nd St Gardena (90249) ***(P-7316)***
Standard Textile Co Inc....D....800 999-0400
6980 Sycamore Canyon Blvd Riverside (92507) ***(P-18676)***
Standard Tool & Die Co, Los Angeles *Also called Stadco* ***(P-7870)***
Standard Wire & Cable Co (PA)....E....**310 609-1811**
2050 E Vista Bella Way Rancho Dominguez (90220) ***(P-6357)***
Standard-Southern Corporation....D....213 624-1831
400 S Central Ave Los Angeles (90013) ***(P-12177)***
Standard-Southern Corporation....C....213 624-1831
440 S Central Ave Los Angeles (90013) ***(P-12178)***
Standard-Southern Corporation....C....213 624-1831
715 E 4th St Los Angeles (90013) ***(P-12179)***
Standardvision LLC....E....323 222-3630
3370 N San Fernando Rd Los Angeles (90065) ***(P-11605)***
Standridge Granite Corporation....E....562 946-6334
9437 Santa Fe Springs Rd Santa Fe Springs (90670) ***(P-6146)***
Staness Jonekos Entps Inc....E....818 606-2710
4000 W Magnolia Blvd D Burbank (91505) ***(P-2528)***
Stanford Advanced Materials, Lake Forest *Also called Oceania International LLC* ***(P-6336)***
Stanford Materials Corporation....F....949 380-7362
23661 Birtcher Dr Lake Forest (92630) ***(P-4647)***
Stanford Mu Corporation....E....310 605-2888
20725 Annalee Ave Carson (90746) ***(P-10536)***
Stanford Transportation Inc....D....661 302-3288
10201 Alondra Dr Bakersfield (93311) ***(P-11996)***
Stang Industrial Products, Corona *Also called Stang Industries Inc* ***(P-11760)***
Stang Industries Inc....F....714 556-0222
2616 Research Dr Ste B Corona (92882) ***(P-11760)***
Stanley Access Tech LLC....E....909 628-9272
15750 Jurupa Ave Fontana (92337) ***(P-6490)***
Stanley Healthcare Center....D....714 893-0026
14102 Springdale St Westminster (92683) ***(P-20628)***
Stanley M Scher Inc (PA)....D....**213 746-1922**
2716 S Main St Los Angeles (90007) ***(P-13097)***
Stanley Steemer of Los Angles (PA)....C....**626 791-9400**
841 W Foothill Blvd Azusa (91702) ***(P-16881)***
Stantec Architecture Inc....C....213 955-9775
801 S Figueroa St Ste 300 Los Angeles (90017) ***(P-18677)***
Stantec Architecture Inc....C....949 923-6000
38 Technology Dr Ste 100 Irvine (92618) ***(P-22743)***
Stantec Architecture Inc....D....626 796-9141
300 N Lake Ave Ste 400 Pasadena (91101) ***(P-22744)***
Stantec Consulting Svcs Inc....D....626 796-9141
300 N Lake Ave Ste 400 Pasadena (91101) ***(P-22660)***
Stantec Consulting Svcs Inc....C....949 923-6000
38 Technology Dr Ste 100 Irvine (92618) ***(P-22745)***
Stantec Energy & Resources Inc (HQ)....C....**661 396-3770**
5500 Ming Ave Ste 410 Bakersfield (93309) ***(P-22756)***
Stantec Holdings Del III Inc....B....661 396-3770
5500 Ming Ave Ste 300 Bakersfield (93309) ***(P-16113)***
Stantec Oil and Gas, Bakersfield *Also called Stantec Holdings Del III Inc* ***(P-16113)***
Stanton Carpet Corp....E....562 945-8711
2209 Pine Ave Manhattan Beach (90266) ***(P-2696)***
Stantru Reinforcing Steel, Fontana *Also called Stantru Resources Inc* ***(P-720)***
Stantru Resources Inc....D....909 587-1441
11175 Redwood Ave Fontana (92337) ***(P-720)***
Stanzino Inc....D....818 602-5171
17937 Santa Rita St Encino (91316) ***(P-2589)***
Stanzino Inc (PA)....D....**213 746-8822**
16325 S Avalon Blvd Gardena (90248) ***(P-2590)***
Star Die Casting Inc....D....562 698-0627
12209 Slauson Ave Santa Fe Springs (90670) ***(P-6539)***
Star Die Casting Inc....F....714 536-2999
19215 Woodlands Dr Huntington Beach (92648) ***(P-7833)***
Star Ford Lincoln Mercury, Glendale *Also called Los Feliz Ford Inc* ***(P-18751)***
Star Link Company Inc....F....310 787-8299
3300 Fujita St Torrance (90505) ***(P-17189)***
Star Lion, Los Angeles *Also called Starlion Inc* ***(P-2761)***
Star Milling Co....C....951 657-3143
24067 Water Ave Perris (92570) ***(P-1975)***
Star Nail International, Valencia *Also called Star Nail Products Inc* ***(P-14292)***
Star Nail Products Inc....D....661 257-3376
29120 Avenue Paine Valencia (91355) ***(P-14292)***
Star of Ca LLC....D....805 379-1401
299 W Hillcrest Dr Thousand Oaks (91360) ***(P-21483)***
Star of Ca LLC....D....818 986-7827
15260 Ventura Blvd Sherman Oaks (91403) ***(P-21484)***
Star of Ca LLC (HQ)....C....**805 644-7827**
4880 Market St Ventura (93003) ***(P-21485)***
Star of California....D....805 466-1638
8834 Morro Rd Atascadero (93422) ***(P-21486)***
Star Plastic Design....D....310 530-7119
25914 President Ave Harbor City (90710) ***(P-5827)***
Star Pro Security Patrol Inc....C....714 617-5056
3303 Harbor Blvd Ste B3 Costa Mesa (92626) ***(P-18342)***
Star Scrap Metal Company Inc....D....562 921-5045
1509 S Bluff Rd Montebello (90640) ***(P-12983)***
Star Shield Solutions LLC....D....866 662-4477
4315 Santa Ana St Ontario (91761) ***(P-5828)***
Star View Chldren Fmly Svcs In....D....310 868-5379
1085 W Victoria St Compton (90220) ***(P-21898)***
Star-Kist, Carson *Also called Big Heart Pet Brands* ***(P-1860)***
Star-Luck Enterprise Inc....F....661 665-9999
11807 Harrington St Bakersfield (93311) ***(P-10726)***
Starco Enterprises Inc (PA)....D....**323 266-7111**
3137 E 26th St Vernon (90058) ***(P-7995)***
Starco Group Inc (PA)....D....**909 989-9898**
9160 Hyssop Dr Rancho Cucamonga (91730) ***(P-18678)***
Starcom Worldwide Inc....C....818 753-7200
5200 Lankershim Blvd # 60 North Hollywood (91601) ***(P-17057)***
Stardust Diamond Corp....E....213 239-9999
550 S Hill St Ste 1420 Los Angeles (90013) ***(P-11339)***
Stargate Digital, South Pasadena *Also called Stargate Films Inc* ***(P-19185)***
Stargate Films Inc (PA)....D....**626 403-8403**
1001 El Centro St South Pasadena (91030) ***(P-19185)***
Stark Services....D....818 985-2003
12444 Victory Blvd # 300 North Hollywood (91606) ***(P-18112)***
Starlight Educational Center, Westminster *Also called Westview Services Inc* ***(P-21979)***
Starlion Inc....E....323 233-8823
706 E 32nd St Los Angeles (90011) ***(P-2761)***
Starpint 1031 Property MGT LLC....C....310 247-0550
450 N Roxbury Dr Ste 1050 Beverly Hills (90210) ***(P-16010)***
Starrett Kinemetric Engrg Inc....E....949 348-1213
26052 Merit Cir Ste 103 Laguna Hills (92653) ***(P-7871)***
Starscroll, Los Angeles *Also called Twelve Signs Inc* ***(P-4109)***
Start Pace Head....D....213 989-3222
1541 Wilshire Blvd # 200 Los Angeles (90017) ***(P-22061)***
Startel Corporation (PA)....D....**949 863-8700**
16 Goodyear B-125 Irvine (92618) ***(P-17723)***
Starwood Hospitality LLC....D....951 699-4477
28220 Jefferson Ave Temecula (92590) ***(P-16729)***
Starwood Hotel....C....310 641-7740
5990 Green Valley Cir Culver City (90230) ***(P-16730)***
Starwood Hotels & Resorts, Costa Mesa *Also called South Coast Westin Hotel Co* ***(P-16720)***
Starwood Hotels & Resorts, Culver City *Also called Starwood Hotel* ***(P-16730)***
Starwood Htls & Rsrts Wrldwde....C....909 622-2220
601 W Mckinley Ave Pomona (91768) ***(P-16731)***
Starz Inc....F....877 595-6789
23016 Lk Frest Dr Ste D30 Laguna Hills (92653) ***(P-13521)***
Starz Tipz, Laguna Hills *Also called Starz Inc* ***(P-13521)***
Stason Pharmaceuticals Inc (PA)....E....**949 380-0752**
11 Morgan Irvine (92618) ***(P-4897)***
Statco Engrg & Fabricators Inc (PA)....E....**714 375-6300**
7595 Reynolds Cir Huntington Beach (92647) ***(P-13944)***
State Bar of California....D....213 765-1520
845 S Figueroa St Los Angeles (90017) ***(P-22281)***
State Bar of California....D....805 544-7551
755 Santa Rosa St Ste 310 San Luis Obispo (93401) ***(P-22282)***
State Compensation Insur Fund....D....714 565-5000
1750 E 4th St Fl 3 Santa Ana (92705) ***(P-15480)***
State Compensation Insur Fund....D....661 664-4000
9801 Camino Media Ste 101 Bakersfield (93311) ***(P-15481)***
State Compensation Insur Fund....D....714 565-7000
1750 E 4th St Ste 260 Santa Ana (92705) ***(P-15482)***
State Compensation Insur Fund....D....888 782-8338
655 N Central Ave Ste 200 Glendale (91203) ***(P-15483)***
State Compensation Insur Fund....D....888 782-8338
6301 Day St Riverside (92507) ***(P-15484)***
State Compensation Insur Fund....D....888 782-8338
2901 N Ventura Rd Ste 100 Oxnard (93036) ***(P-15384)***
State Compensation Insur Fund....D....323 266-5000
900 Corporate Center Dr Monterey Park (91754) ***(P-15485)***
State Farm Insurance, Bakersfield *Also called State Farm Mutl Auto Insur Co* ***(P-15630)***
State Farm Mutl Auto Insur Co....D....309 766-2311
900 Old River Rd 400 Bakersfield (93311) ***(P-15630)***
State Hospitals Cal Dept....B....714 957-5000
2501 Harbor Blvd Costa Mesa (92626) ***(P-21027)***
State Hospitals Cal Dept....B....909 425-7000
3102 E Highland Ave Patton (92369) ***(P-21028)***
State Hospitals Cal Dept....B....805 468-2000
10333 El Camino Real Atascadero (93422) ***(P-21029)***
State Pipe & Supply Inc....E....909 356-5670
2180 N Locust Ave Rialto (92377) ***(P-6213)***
State Pipe & Supply Inc (HQ)....D....**909 877-9999**
183 S Cedar Ave Rialto (92376) ***(P-13596)***
State Ready Mix Inc (PA)....E....**805 647-2817**
1011 Azahar St Ste 1 Ventura (93004) ***(P-6119)***
Statek Corporation (HQ)....C....**714 639-7810**
512 N Main St Orange (92868) ***(P-9786)***
Stater Bros Markets....E....714 963-0949
10114 Adams Ave Huntington Beach (92646) ***(P-2073)***
Stater Bros Markets....E....714 991-5310
1131 N State College Blvd Anaheim (92806) ***(P-2036)***

A L P H A B E T I C

Employee Codes: A=Over 500 employees, B=251-500
C=101-250, D=51-100, E=20-50 F=10-19

2022 Southern California Business
Directory and Buyers Guide

© Mergent Inc. 1-800-342-5647
1281

States Drawer Box Spc LLC ....D 714 744-4247
1482 N Batavia St Orange (92867) ***(P-13289)***
States Logistics Services Inc ....D 714 523-1276
7221 Cate Dr Buena Park (90621) ***(P-12530)***
States Logistics Services Inc ....D 714 523-1276
7151 Cate Dr Buena Park (90621) ***(P-12248)***
States Logistics Services Inc (PA) ....**C 714 521-6520**
5650 Dolly Ave Buena Park (90621) ***(P-12531)***
Stateside Merchants LLC ....E 424 251-5190
5813 Washington Blvd Culver City (90232) ***(P-2764)***
Statewide Distributors, Ontario *Also called USA Sales Inc* ***(P-2553)***
Statewide Safety & Signs Inc (HQ) ....**E 805 929-5070**
522 Lindon Ln Nipomo (93444) ***(P-17376)***
Statewide Safety and Signs I ....B 714 468-1919
522 Lindon Ln Nipomo (93444) ***(P-9355)***
Stationery Exchange, Yorba Linda *Also called Sid-Mar Inc* ***(P-4423)***
Stauber Prfmce Ingredients Inc (HQ) ....**D 714 441-3900**
4120 N Palm St Fullerton (92835) ***(P-4765)***
Stavatti Industries Ltd ....E 651 238-5369
3670 El Camino Dr San Bernardino (92404) ***(P-376)***
Stavros Enterprises Inc ....E 888 463-2293
681 Arrow Grand Cir Covina (91722) ***(P-19070)***
STC Netcom Inc (PA) ....**D 951 685-8181**
11611 Industry Ave Fontana (92337) ***(P-1320)***
Stci, Rancho Cucamonga *Also called Superior Tank Co Inc* ***(P-6758)***
Steadfast Coml MGT Co Inc (HQ) ....**D 949 852-0700**
4343 Von Karman Ave # 30 Newport Beach (92660) ***(P-16011)***
Steadfast Companies, Irvine *Also called Steadfast Management Co Inc* ***(P-16012)***
Steadfast Income Reit Inc (HQ) ....**C 949 852-0700**
18100 Von Karman Ave # 500 Irvine (92612) ***(P-16244)***
Steadfast Management Co Inc (PA) ....**B 949 748-3000**
18100 Von Karman Ave # 500 Irvine (92612) ***(P-16012)***
Steady Clothing Inc ....F 714 444-2058
2851 E White Star Ave A Anaheim (92806) ***(P-2825)***
Stearns Corporation ....E 805 582-2710
2280 Ward Ave Ste 100 Simi Valley (93065) ***(P-5072)***
Stearns Park ....F 562 570-1685
4520 E 23rd St Long Beach (90815) ***(P-3632)***
Stearns Product Dev Corp (PA) ....**D 951 657-0379**
20281 Harvill Ave Perris (92570) ***(P-8140)***
Stec Inc (HQ) ....**B 415 222-9996**
3355 Michelson Dr Ste 100 Irvine (92612) ***(P-8219)***
Stec International Holding Inc ....C 949 476-1180
3001 Daimler St Santa Ana (92705) ***(P-8220)***
Stecher Enterprises Inc ....F 714 484-6900
8536 Central Ave Stanton (90680) ***(P-7492)***
Steel Products International, Los Angeles *Also called Precision Steel Products Inc* ***(P-6894)***
Steel Services Co, Vernon *Also called S S Schaffer Co Inc* ***(P-7746)***
Steel Unlimited Inc ....D 909 873-1222
3200 Myers St Riverside (92503) ***(P-13597)***
Steel Works Etc, Oxnard *Also called Millworks Etc Inc* ***(P-6710)***
Steel-Tech Industrial Corp ....E 951 270-0144
1268 Sherborn St Corona (92879) ***(P-6666)***
Steelclad Inc ....F 714 529-0277
2664 Saturn St Ste A Brea (92821) ***(P-547)***
Steelco USA, Chino *Also called West Coast Steel & Proc LLC* ***(P-6279)***
Steeldeck Inc ....E 323 290-2100
13147 S Western Ave Gardena (90249) ***(P-11761)***
Steeldyne Industries ....E 714 630-6200
2871 E La Cresta Ave Anaheim (92806) ***(P-6918)***
Steelhouse Inc ....C 310 773-3331
3644 Eastham Dr Culver City (90232) ***(P-17058)***
Steelscape LLC ....E 909 987-4711
11200 Arrow Rte Rancho Cucamonga (91730) ***(P-7416)***
Steelworks Etc Inc ....F 805 487-3000
1250 Commercial Ave Oxnard (93030) ***(P-6720)***
Stefan Merli Plastering Co Inc (PA) ....**D 310 323-0404**
1230 W 130th St Gardena (90247) ***(P-1551)***
Stein Industries Inc (PA) ....**E 714 522-4560**
4005 Artesia Ave Fullerton (92833) ***(P-6919)***
Steinberg Architects, Los Angeles *Also called Steinberg Hart* ***(P-22746)***
Steinberg Hart (PA) ....**D 408 295-5446**
818 W 7th St Ste 1100 Los Angeles (90017) ***(P-22746)***
Steiner & Mateer Inc ....F 562 464-9082
8333 Secura Way Santa Fe Springs (90670) ***(P-3292)***
Steiny & Company, Corona *Also called Computer Service Company* ***(P-9336)***
Stell Industries Inc ....E 951 369-8777
1951 S Parco Ave Ste B Ontario (91761) ***(P-7008)***
Stellant Systems Inc (HQ) ....**D 310 517-6000**
3100 Lomita Blvd Torrance (90505) ***(P-9368)***
Stellar Engineering, Anaheim *Also called APT Manufacturing LLC* ***(P-7721)***
Stellar Exploration Inc ....E 805 459-1425
835 Airport Dr San Luis Obispo (93401) ***(P-10520)***
Stellar Industries ....E 818 472-5432
1524 Patricia Ave Simi Valley (93065) ***(P-11762)***
Stellar Microelectronics Inc ....C 661 775-3500
9340 Owensmouth Ave Chatsworth (91311) ***(P-9583)***
Step Up On Second Street Inc (PA) ....**D 310 394-6889**
1328 2nd St Ofc Santa Monica (90401) ***(P-21218)***
Stephen B Meisel MD A Med Corp (HQ) ....**D 310 828-8843**
2811 Wilshire Blvd # 900 Santa Monica (90403) ***(P-20098)***
Stepstone Inc (PA) ....**E 310 327-7474**
17025 S Main St Gardena (90248) ***(P-6059)***
Stepstone Inc ....E 310 327-7474
13238 S Figueroa St Los Angeles (90061) ***(P-6060)***
Steril-Aire Inc ....E 818 565-1128
2840 N Lima St Burbank (91504) ***(P-9147)***
Sterile Proc Svcs Amer LLC (PA) ....**D 562 428-5858**
2240 E Artesia Blvd Long Beach (90805) ***(P-18679)***
Steriltek Inc ....D 213 977-2298
637 S Lucas St Los Angeles (90046) ***(P-18680)***
Sterisyn Inc ....E 805 991-9694
11969 Challenger Ct Moorpark (93021) ***(P-4898)***
Sterling BMW, Newport Beach *Also called Sterling Motors Ltd* ***(P-18754)***
Sterling Carpets & Flooring, Anaheim *Also called Rm Partners Inc* ***(P-1469)***
Sterling Collision LLC (PA) ....**D 714 259-1111**
1111 Bell Ave Ste A Tustin (92780) ***(P-18805)***
Sterling Dry Cleaners, Los Angeles *Also called Sterling Westwood Inc* ***(P-16878)***
Sterling Motors Ltd ....D 949 645-5900
3000 W Coast Hwy Newport Beach (92663) ***(P-18754)***
Sterling Pacific Meat Co., Commerce *Also called Interstate Meat Co Inc* ***(P-7939)***
Sterling Plumbing Inc ....D 714 641-5480
3111 W Central Ave Santa Ana (92704) ***(P-1148)***
Sterling Shutters, Costa Mesa *Also called Pinecraft Custom Shutters Inc* ***(P-3281)***
Sterling Westwood Inc ....D 310 287-2431
3405 Overland Ave Los Angeles (90034) ***(P-16878)***
Sterndahl Enterprises Inc ....E 818 834-8199
11861 Branford St Sun Valley (91352) ***(P-1199)***
Sterno LLC (HQ) ....**E 800 669-6699**
1880 Compton Ave Ste 101 Corona (92881) ***(P-8418)***
Sterno Candle Lamp, Corona *Also called Sterno Group Companies LLC* ***(P-8419)***
Sterno Group Companies LLC (HQ) ....**E 951 682-9600**
1880 Compton Ave Ste 101 Corona (92881) ***(P-8419)***
Sternocandlelamp Holdings Inc ....A 951 682-9600
1880 Compton Ave Ste 101 Corona (92881) ***(P-15306)***
Steve Leshner Clear Systems ....F 818 764-9223
13438 Wyandotte St North Hollywood (91605) ***(P-5829)***
Steve Thomas BMW, Camarillo *Also called Thomas Bavarian Mtr Works Inc* ***(P-18879)***
Steven Engineering Inc ....E 650 588-9200
2398 Railroad St Corona (92878) ***(P-22661)***
Steven Global Freight Services, Redondo Beach *Also called Stevens Global Logistics Inc* ***(P-12532)***
Steven Handelman Studios (PA) ....**E 305 884-9070**
716 N Milpas St Santa Barbara (93103) ***(P-6262)***
Stevens Global Logistics Inc (PA) ....**D 310 216-5645**
3700 Redondo Beach Ave Redondo Beach (90278) ***(P-12532)***
Stevens Pond APT Propty Ownr (PA) ....**D 310 268-8344**
11766 Wilshire Blvd # 1500 Los Angeles (90025) ***(P-15750)***
Steves Plating Corporation ....C 818 842-2184
3111 N San Fernando Blvd Burbank (91504) ***(P-3697)***
Stewart Filmscreen Corp (PA) ....**C 310 326-1422**
1161 Sepulveda Blvd Torrance (90502) ***(P-11292)***
Stewart Title California Inc ....C 818 502-2700
525 N Brand Blvd Ste 200 Glendale (91203) ***(P-16042)***
Stg Auto Group, Montclair *Also called St George Auto Center Inc* ***(P-18906)***
Stic-Adhesive Products Co Inc ....C 323 268-2956
3950 Medford St Los Angeles (90063) ***(P-5197)***
Stillhouse LLC ....E 323 498-1111
8201 Beverly Blvd Ste 300 Los Angeles (90048) ***(P-2246)***
Stinson Commercial Trnsp ....D 626 807-6265
1443 E Washngtn Blvd Pasadena (91104) ***(P-11997)***
Stitch Industries Inc ....E 888 282-0842
6055 E Wash Blvd Ste 900 Commerce (90040) ***(P-3519)***
Stjohn God Rtirement Care Ctr ....C 323 731-0641
2468 S St Andrews Pl Los Angeles (90018) ***(P-20480)***
Stk ....F 310 659-3535
930 Hilgard Ave Los Angeles (90024) ***(P-11763)***
Stm Networks Inc ....D 949 273-6800
2 Faraday Irvine (92618) ***(P-9319)***
Stm Wireless, Irvine *Also called Stm Networks Inc* ***(P-9319)***
Stmicroelectronics Inc ....E 949 347-0717
85 Enterprise Ste 300 Aliso Viejo (92656) ***(P-9584)***
Stockbridge/Sbe Holdings LLC ....A 323 655-8000
5900 Wilshire Blvd # 3100 Los Angeles (90036) ***(P-16732)***
Stockcross Financial Svcs Inc (HQ) ....**E 800 993-2015**
9464 Wilshire Blvd Beverly Hills (90212) ***(P-15307)***
Stockdale Christian School, Bakersfield *Also called First Assmbly of God Bkrsfield* ***(P-22015)***
Stockdale Country Club ....D 661 832-0310
7001 Stockdale Hwy Bakersfield (93309) ***(P-19619)***
Stockdale Medical Offices, Bakersfield *Also called Kaiser Foundation Hospitals* ***(P-19933)***
Stockmar Industrial, Long Beach *Also called Elite Craftsman* ***(P-17240)***
Stoll Metalcraft Inc ....C 661 295-0401
24808 Anza Dr Valencia (91355) ***(P-6920)***
Stolo Cabinets Inc (PA) ....**E 714 529-7303**
860 Challenger St Brea (92821) ***(P-3601)***
Stolo Custom Cabinets, Brea *Also called Stolo Cabinets Inc* ***(P-3601)***
Stolpman Vineyards LLC ....E 805 736-5000
1700 Industrial Way B Lompoc (93436) ***(P-2223)***
Stone Age Equipment Inc (PA) ....**E 909 798-4222**
1411 W State St Redlands (92373) ***(P-14446)***
Stone Canyon Inds Holdings LLC (PA) ....**E 424 316-2061**
1875 Century Park E # 320 Los Angeles (90067) ***(P-23335)***
Stone Canyon Industries LLC (PA) ....**E 310 570-4869**
1875 Century Park E # 320 Los Angeles (90067) ***(P-5830)***
Stone Entertainment, Costa Mesa *Also called Volcom LLC* ***(P-18719)***
Stone Harbor Inc ....F 323 277-2777
5015 District Blvd Vernon (90058) ***(P-2738)***
Stone Image Inc ....F 561 547-1177
7311 Fulton Ave North Hollywood (91605) ***(P-6147)***
Stone Land Company (PA) ....**D 559 947-3185**
28521 Nevada Ave Stratford (93266) ***(P-4)***
Stone Manufacturing Company, Gardena *Also called Tomorrows Heirlooms Inc* ***(P-6540)***
Stone Ranch, Stratford *Also called Stone Land Company* ***(P-4)***
Stonebridge Rlty Advisors Inc ....B 949 597-8700
27102 Towne Centre Dr Foothill Ranch (92610) ***(P-16733)***
Stonecalibre LLC (PA) ....**D 310 774-0014**
2049 Century Park E # 2550 Los Angeles (90067) ***(P-16293)***

Stonefire Grill Inc (PA)..........B.......**805 413-0300**
30401 Agoura Rd Ste 130 Agoura Hills (91301) ***(P-17724)***
Stoneland, North Hollywood *Also called Arriaga Usa Inc* ***(P-561)***
Stoneland, North Hollywood *Also called Arriaga Usa Inc* ***(P-1411)***
Stoneriver Inc..........D.......714 705-8227
770 The Cy Dr S Ste 5000 Orange (92868) ***(P-17725)***
Stony Apparel Corp (PA)..........D.......**323 981-9080**
1500 S Evergreen Ave Los Angeles (90023) ***(P-2999)***
Stop Hop Center, Carson *Also called Anschutz Sthern Cal Spt Cmplex* ***(P-19408)***
Stop Look Plastics Inc, La Habra *Also called Stop-Look Sign Co Intl Inc* ***(P-11606)***
Stop-Look Sign Co Intl Inc..........F.......562 690-7576
401 Commercial Way La Habra (90631) ***(P-11606)***
Storage West, Los Angeles *Also called Laaco Ltd* ***(P-15760)***
Store & Online, City of Industry *Also called Solestage Inc* ***(P-18067)***
Storefront Door Repair, Huntington Beach *Also called Storefront Repair Inc* ***(P-1458)***
Storefront Repair Inc..........F.......714 842-1337
17032 Palmdale Ln Ste B Huntington Beach (92647) ***(P-1458)***
Stories International Inc..........F.......310 242-8409
400 Corporate Pointe Culver City (90230) ***(P-4207)***
Storm Industries Inc (PA)..........D.......**310 534-5232**
23223 Normandie Ave Torrance (90501) ***(P-7622)***
Storm Manufacturing, Torrance *Also called FCkingston Co* ***(P-7444)***
Storm Manufacturing Group Inc..........D.......310 326-8287
23201 Normandie Ave Torrance (90501) ***(P-7452)***
Storquest Self Storage (HQ)..........D.......**310 451-2130**
201 Wilshire Blvd Ste 102 Santa Monica (90401) ***(P-12249)***
Stoughton Printing Co..........E.......626 961-3678
130 N Sunset Ave City of Industry (91744) ***(P-4426)***
Stovall Stovall & OConnell..........D.......714 776-4800
1544 S Harbor Blvd Anaheim (92802) ***(P-16734)***
Str Worldwide Inc..........A.......949 276-5990
17462 Von Karman Ave Irvine (92614) ***(P-14352)***
Stracon Inc..........F.......949 851-2288
1672 Kaiser Ave Ste 1 Irvine (92614) ***(P-9917)***
Strada Wheels Inc..........F.......626 336-1634
560 S Magnolia Ave Ontario (91762) ***(P-6214)***
Stradling Ycca Crlson Ruth A P (PA)..........C.......**949 725-4000**
660 Nwport Ctr Dr Ste 160 Newport Beach (92660) ***(P-21681)***
Straight Down Clothing Company, San Luis Obispo *Also called Straight Down Enterprises* ***(P-2826)***
Straight Down Enterprises (PA)..........E.......**805 543-3086**
625 Clarion Ct San Luis Obispo (93401) ***(P-2826)***
Straight Forwarding Inc..........D.......909 594-3400
20275 Business Pkwy Walnut (91789) ***(P-12533)***
Straight Talk Counseling Ctr, La Mirada *Also called Straight Talk Inc* ***(P-21899)***
Straight Talk Inc..........D.......562 943-0195
13710 La Mirada Blvd La Mirada (90638) ***(P-21899)***
Strand Art Company Inc..........E.......714 777-0444
4700 E Hunter Ave Anaheim (92807) ***(P-5831)***
Strand Products Inc (PA)..........E.......**800 343-7985**
2233 Knoll Dr Ventura (93003) ***(P-11238)***
Strata Forest Products Inc (PA)..........E.......**714 751-0800**
2600 S Susan St Santa Ana (92704) ***(P-3213)***
Stratacare Llc..........C.......949 743-1200
17838 Gillette Ave Ste D Irvine (92614) ***(P-17726)***
Stratasys Direct Inc (HQ)..........C.......**661 295-4400**
28309 Avenue Crocker Valencia (91355) ***(P-5832)***
Stratasys Direct Manufacturing, Valencia *Also called Stratasys Direct Inc* ***(P-5832)***
Strategic Distribution L P..........C.......818 671-2100
9800 De Soto Ave Chatsworth (91311) ***(P-2791)***
Strategic Materials Inc..........D.......323 887-6831
7000 Bandini Blvd Commerce (90040) ***(P-12984)***
Strategic Medical Ventures LLC (PA)..........F.......**949 355-5212**
280 Newport Center Dr Newport Beach (92660) ***(P-11210)***
Strategy Companion Corp..........D.......714 460-8398
3240 El Camino Real # 120 Irvine (92602) ***(P-17989)***
Strathmore Ladder, Strathmore *Also called Michael D Wilson Inc* ***(P-7566)***
Stratoflight (HQ)..........D.......**949 622-0700**
25540 Rye Canyon Rd Valencia (91355) ***(P-10423)***
Stratos Renewables Corporation..........E.......310 402-5901
9440 Santa Monica Blvd Beverly Hills (90210) ***(P-5149)***
Stratus Group Duo LLC..........E.......323 581-3663
4401 S Downey Rd Vernon (90058) ***(P-2300)***
Stratus Real Estate Inc..........D.......626 441-5549
435 Garfield Ave South Pasadena (91030) ***(P-15254)***
Stratus Real Estate Inc..........D.......310 549-7028
1100 N Banning Blvd # 11 Wilmington (90744) ***(P-15255)***
Stratus Realestate, South Pasadena *Also called Stratus Real Estate Inc* ***(P-15254)***
Straub Distributing Co Ltd (PA)..........C.......**714 779-4000**
4633 E La Palma Ave Anaheim (92807) ***(P-14836)***
Strawberry Farms Golf Club LLC..........C.......949 551-2560
11 Strawberry Farm Rd Irvine (92612) ***(P-19510)***
Streamline Avionics Inc..........E.......949 861-8151
17672 Armstrong Ave Irvine (92614) ***(P-8885)***
Streamline Dsign Slkscreen Inc (PA)..........D.......**805 884-1025**
1299 S Wells Rd Ventura (93004) ***(P-2827)***
Streamline Finishes Inc..........D.......949 600-8964
26429 Rancho Pkwy S # 140 Lake Forest (92630) ***(P-833)***
Strech Plastics Incorporated..........E.......951 922-2224
900 John St Ste J Banning (92220) ***(P-14065)***
Street Glow Inc..........D.......310 631-1881
2710 E El Presidio St Carson (90810) ***(P-9119)***
Streets Ahead Inc..........E.......323 277-0860
5510 S Soto St Unit B Vernon (90058) ***(P-3062)***
Stremicks Heritage Foods LLC (HQ)..........B.......**714 775-5000**
4002 Westminster Ave Santa Ana (92703) ***(P-1840)***
Stretch Art, Gardena *Also called Ar-Ce Inc* ***(P-11467)***
Stretch Forming Corporation..........D.......951 443-0911
804 S Redlands Ave Perris (92570) ***(P-6921)***
Stretto Inc (PA)..........D.......**949 222-1212**
410 Exchange Ste 100 Irvine (92602) ***(P-21682)***
Streuter Fastel Timtel, San Clemente *Also called Streuter Technologies* ***(P-13598)***
Streuter Technologies..........E.......949 369-7676
208 Avnida Fbrcnte Ste 20 San Clemente (92672) ***(P-13598)***
Stria, Bakersfield *Also called Technosocialworkcom LLC* ***(P-18113)***
Strike Technology Inc..........E.......562 437-3428
24311 Wilmington Ave Carson (90745) ***(P-9787)***
Stringking Inc (PA)..........C.......**310 503-8901**
19100 S Vermont Ave Gardena (90248) ***(P-3086)***
Strong Hand Tools, Santa Fe Springs *Also called Valtra Inc* ***(P-13958)***
Stronghold Engineering Inc (PA)..........D.......**951 684-9303**
150 W Walnut Ave Perris (92571) ***(P-834)***
Stroock & Stroock & Lavan LLP..........C.......310 556-5800
2029 Century Park E # 1800 Los Angeles (90067) ***(P-21683)***
Strouk Group LLC..........D.......323 939-7792
6333 W 3rd St Ste 150 Los Angeles (90036) ***(P-14607)***
Structural Composites Inds LLC (HQ)..........C.......**909 594-7777**
336 Enterprise Pl Pomona (91768) ***(P-6756)***
Structural Concrete Group Inc..........E.......818 923-0984
11038 Washington Blvd Whittier (90606) ***(P-1552)***
Structural Diagnostics Inc..........E.......805 987-7755
650 Via Alondra Camarillo (93012) ***(P-10913)***
Structure Cast, Bakersfield *Also called Golden Empire Con Pdts Inc* ***(P-1524)***
Structurecast..........D.......661 833-4490
8261 Mccutchen Rd Bakersfield (93311) ***(P-6061)***
Struers Inc..........E.......310 320-6288
1724 Gramercy Ave Torrance (90501) ***(P-13522)***
STS, Tehachapi *Also called Sierra Technical Services Inc* ***(P-6274)***
STS Instruments Inc..........E.......580 223-4773
17711 Mitchell N Irvine (92614) ***(P-10772)***
STS Metals, Irwindale *Also called Sierra Alloys Company* ***(P-7106)***
Stuart C. Gildred Family YMCA, Santa Ynez *Also called Channel Islnds Yung MNS Chrstn* ***(P-22331)***
Stuart Cellars LLC..........F.......951 676-6414
41006 Simi Ct Temecula (92591) ***(P-2224)***
Stuart-Dean Co Inc..........F.......714 544-4460
14731 Franklin Ave Ste L Tustin (92780) ***(P-7317)***
Stud Welding Systems Inc..........F.......626 330-7434
15306 Proctor Ave City of Industry (91745) ***(P-7076)***
Student Sports LLC..........F.......310 791-1142
23954 Madison St Torrance (90505) ***(P-2697)***
Student Transportation America, Santa Maria *Also called Santa Barbara Trnsp Corp* ***(P-11940)***
Studex, Gardena *Also called Quadrtech Corporation* ***(P-11338)***
Studio 71 LP..........C.......323 370-1500
8383 Wilshire Blvd # 1050 Beverly Hills (90211) ***(P-17090)***
Studio Distribution Svcs LLC..........C.......818 954-6000
4000 Warner Blvd Burbank (91522) ***(P-19186)***
Studio OH, Irvine *Also called Orange Circle Studio Corp* ***(P-4548)***
Studio Systems Inc (PA)..........E.......**323 634-3400**
5700 Wilshire Blvd # 600 Los Angeles (90036) ***(P-4208)***
Studio9d8 Inc..........E.......626 350-0832
9743 Alesia St South El Monte (91733) ***(P-2641)***
Stull Industries Inc..........E.......951 248-9789
1315 W Flint St Lake Elsinore (92530) ***(P-10136)***
Sturgeon & Son, Bakersfield *Also called Sturgeon Services Intl Inc* ***(P-1604)***
Sturgeon Services Intl, Santa Maria *Also called Sturgeon Son Grading & Pav Inc* ***(P-22662)***
Sturgeon Services Intl Inc (PA)..........E.......**661 322-4408**
3511 Gilmore Ave Bakersfield (93308) ***(P-1604)***
Sturgeon Services Intl Inc..........B.......661 322-4408
3511 Gilmore Ave Bakersfield (93308) ***(P-7651)***
Sturgeon Son Grading & Pav Inc (PA)..........C.......**661 322-4408**
3511 Gilmore Ave Bakersfield (93308) ***(P-1605)***
Sturgeon Son Grading & Pav Inc..........C.......805 938-0618
6516 Cat Canyon Rd Santa Maria (93454) ***(P-22662)***
Stussy Inc..........D.......949 474-9255
17426 Daimler St Irvine (92614) ***(P-14353)***
Stutman Treister Glatt Prof Co, Los Angeles *Also called Stutman Trster Glatt Prof Corp* ***(P-21684)***
Stutman Trster Glatt Prof Corp..........D.......310 228-5600
1901 Avenue Of The Los Angeles (90067) ***(P-21684)***
Stutz Packing Company..........F.......760 342-1666
82689 Avenue 45 Indio (92201) ***(P-1884)***
Stutzman Plating, Los Angeles *Also called Virgil M Stutzman Inc* ***(P-7330)***
Stv Architects Inc..........C.......213 482-9444
1055 W 7th St Ste 3150 Los Angeles (90017) ***(P-22747)***
Stx Productions LLC (PA)..........D.......**310 742-2300**
3900 W Alameda Ave Fl 32 Burbank (91505) ***(P-19262)***
Style Cft Grphic Cmmunications, Rcho STA Marg *Also called Style Craft Marketing Inc* ***(P-17190)***
Style Craft Marketing Inc..........E.......949 709-2000
22922 Avenida Empresa Rcho STA Marg (92688) ***(P-17190)***
Style Knits Inc..........F.......323 890-9080
1745 Chapin Rd Montebello (90640) ***(P-2642)***
Styrotek Inc..........C.......661 725-4957
345 Road 176 Delano (93215) ***(P-5523)***
Su Casa Ending Dom Violence..........D.......562 421-6537
3750 E Anaheim St Ste 100 Long Beach (90804) ***(P-21900)***
Su Mano Inc..........E.......562 529-8835
16394 Downey Ave Paramount (90723) ***(P-5872)***
Sub-Zero Excavating Inc..........D.......805 522-5043
1916 Duncan St Simi Valley (93065) ***(P-1606)***
Subchondral Solutions Inc..........F.......888 410-5622
1127 Wilshire Blvd Los Angeles (90017) ***(P-11142)***

Employee Codes: A=Over 500 employees, B=251-500
C=101-250, D=51-100, E=20-50 F=10-19
2022 Southern California Business
Directory and Buyers Guide
© Mergent Inc. 1-800-342-5647
1283

Submersible Systems LLC .... F 714 842-6566
7413 Slater Ave Huntington Beach (92647) ***(P-11449)***

Subsidy of Be Aerospace, Fullerton *Also called ADB Industries* ***(P-6426)***

Substance Abuse Program .... E 951 791-3350
1370 S State St Ste A Hemet (92543) ***(P-9585)***

Subtractive Inc (PA) .... **D 310 664-0540**
Santa Monica Airport N 28 Santa Monica (90405) ***(P-12743)***

Subway, Brea *Also called Shore Front LLC* ***(P-2523)***

Success Healthcare 1 LLC (PA) .... **A 213 989-6100**
1711 W Temple St Los Angeles (90026) ***(P-21219)***

Success Strategies Inst Inc .... D 949 721-6808
6 Hutton Cntre Dr Ste 700 Santa Ana (92707) ***(P-21969)***

Successor Agency To The Norco, Norco *Also called City of Norco* ***(P-23429)***

Succetti Group Inc .... E 949 335-2292
5020 Campus Dr Newport Beach (92660) ***(P-23512)***

Sue Wong, Los Angeles *Also called S Studio Inc* ***(P-2907)***

Suez Water Indiana LLC .... E 310 414-0183
1935 S Hughes Way El Segundo (90245) ***(P-10727)***

Suez Wts Services Usa Inc .... D 562 942-2200
7777 Industry Ave Pico Rivera (90660) ***(P-8420)***

Sugar Foods Corporation .... C 818 768-7900
9500 El Dorado Ave Sun Valley (91352) ***(P-18681)***

Sugar Foods Corporation .... D 323 727-8290
6190 E Slauson Ave Commerce (90040) ***(P-2037)***

Sugar Lips Inc .... F 213 742-9001
2250 Maple Ave Los Angeles (90011) ***(P-2591)***

Sugar Spice Evrything Nice Inc (PA) .... **D 949 307-8674**
27000 Alicia Pkwy Ste E Laguna Niguel (92677) ***(P-22062)***

Sugared + Bronzed LLC (PA) .... **D 410 493-3467**
34241 E Pcf Cast Hwy Ste Dana Point (92629) ***(P-16980)***

Sugarfina USA LLC .... C 855 784-2734
1700 E Walnut Ave Ste 500 El Segundo (90245) ***(P-2107)***

Sugarlips Clothing, Los Angeles *Also called Sugar Lips Inc* ***(P-2591)***

Sugarsync Inc .... E 650 571-5105
6922 Hollywood Blvd # 500 Los Angeles (90028) ***(P-17990)***

Suheung-America Corporation (HQ) .... **E 714 854-9882**
428 Saturn St Brea (92821) ***(P-4899)***

Sui Companies, Riverside *Also called Steel Unlimited Inc* ***(P-13597)***

Suissa Miller Advertising LLC .... D 310 392-9666
8687 Melrose Ave West Hollywood (90069) ***(P-17059)***

Sukarne, City of Industry *Also called Viz Cattle Corporation* ***(P-1724)***

Sukut Construction LLC .... D 714 540-5351
4010 W Chandler Ave Santa Ana (92704) ***(P-976)***

Sukut Construction Inc .... C 714 540-5351
4010 W Chandler Ave Santa Ana (92704) ***(P-1607)***

Sullivans Stone Factory Inc .... E 760 347-5535
83778 Avenue 45 Indio (92201) ***(P-6148)***

Sullivncrtsmnroe Insur Svcs LL (PA) .... **C 800 427-3253**
1920 Main St Ste 600 Irvine (92614) ***(P-23336)***

Sully-Miller Contracting Co (HQ) .... **B 714 578-9600**
135 S State College Blvd # 400 Brea (92821) ***(P-918)***

Sully-Miller Holding Corp .... D 714 578-9600
135 S State College Blvd # 400 Brea (92821) ***(P-919)***

Sulmeyerkupetz A Prof Corp (PA) .... **D 213 617-5221**
333 S Hope St Ste 3500 Los Angeles (90071) ***(P-21685)***

Sulzer Bingham Pumps, Santa Fe Springs *Also called Sulzer Pump Services (us) Inc* ***(P-8024)***

Sulzer Electro-Mechanical Serv .... E 909 825-7971
620 S Rancho Ave Colton (92324) ***(P-19016)***

Sulzer Pump Services (us) Inc .... E 562 903-1000
9856 Jordan Cir Santa Fe Springs (90670) ***(P-8024)***

Sumaria Systems Inc .... D 805 606-4973
105 13th St Vandenberg Afb (93437) ***(P-22663)***

Sumi Office Services, Carson *Also called Sumi Printing & Binding Inc* ***(P-4427)***

Sumi Printing & Binding Inc .... F 310 769-1600
1139 E Janis St Carson (90746) ***(P-4427)***

Sumitomo Rubber North Amer Inc (HQ) .... **C 909 466-1116**
8656 Haven Ave Rancho Cucamonga (91730) ***(P-13120)***

Summer Rio Corp (PA) .... **F 626 854-1498**
17501 Rowland St City of Industry (91748) ***(P-5318)***

Summer Systems Inc .... D 661 257-4419
28942 Hancock Pkwy Valencia (91355) ***(P-835)***

Summerwood Winery & Inn Inc .... E 805 227-1365
2175 Arbor Rd Paso Robles (93446) ***(P-16735)***

Summit Commercial Prpts Inc (HQ) .... **C 310 648-7500**
400 Continental Blvd # 160 El Segundo (90245) ***(P-16294)***

Summit Electric & Data Inc .... F 661 775-9901
27913 Smyth Dr Valencia (91355) ***(P-9918)***

Summit Equipment Rentals LLC .... D 951 246-3313
26105 Sherman Rd A Menifee (92585) ***(P-17377)***

Summit Fire Protection .... D 909 793-0676
520 Texas St Redlands (92374) ***(P-1149)***

Summit Hotel Trs 111 LLC (PA) .... **D 805 389-9898**
50 W Daily Dr Camarillo (93010) ***(P-16736)***

Summit Hotel Trs 129 LLC (PA) .... **D 949 425-9500**
110 Vantis Dr Aliso Viejo (92656) ***(P-16737)***

Summit Interconnect Inc (HQ) .... **C 714 239-2433**
223 N Crescent Way Anaheim (92801) ***(P-9457)***

Summit Interconnect - Anaheim, Anaheim *Also called Kca Electronics Inc* ***(P-9419)***

Summit Interconnect Orange, Orange *Also called Fabricated Components Corp* ***(P-9404)***

Summit Machine LLC .... C 909 923-2744
2880 E Philadelphia St Ontario (91761) ***(P-8803)***

Summit Rentals, Menifee *Also called Summit Equipment Rentals LLC* ***(P-17377)***

Summit Surgery Center, Santa Barbara *Also called Summit Vntres Santa Barbara LP* ***(P-20099)***

Summit Trail Hlth Holdings LLC .... D 949 487-9500
29222 Rncho Vejo Rd Ste 1 San Juan Capistrano (92675) ***(P-20481)***

Summit Vntres Santa Barbara LP .... D 805 898-2797
231 W Pueblo St Santa Barbara (93105) ***(P-20099)***

Sun & Sail Club, Lake Forest *Also called Lake Frest No II Mstr Hmwners* ***(P-22344)***

Sun & Sun Industries Inc .... D 714 210-5141
2101 S Yale St Santa Ana (92704) ***(P-9103)***

Sun and Sands Enterprises LLC (PA) .... **D 760 399-4278**
86705 Avenue 54 Ste A Coachella (92236) ***(P-14655)***

Sun Badge Co .... E 909 930-1444
2248 S Baker Ave Ontario (91761) ***(P-11764)***

Sun Chlorella USA Corp .... D 310 891-0600
3305 Kashiwa St Torrance (90505) ***(P-14738)***

Sun City Palm Dsert Cmnty Assn (PA) .... **D 760 200-2100**
38180 Del Webb Blvd Palm Desert (92211) ***(P-22370)***

Sun Coast Merchandise Corp .... C 323 720-9700
6600 Bandini Blvd Commerce (90040) ***(P-14182)***

Sun Community Federal Cr Un .... D 760 337-4200
1001 E Us Highway 98 Calexico (92231) ***(P-15091)***

Sun Company San Bernardino Cal (PA) .... **B 909 889-9666**
4030 Georgia Blvd San Bernardino (92407) ***(P-4032)***

Sun Country Marine Inc .... D 909 390-6600
17092 Pullman St Irvine (92614) ***(P-19071)***

Sun Dairy Co, Los Angeles *Also called Pac Fill Inc* ***(P-1838)***

Sun Delivery LLC .... E 336 472-5000
51 Zaca Ln Ste 120 San Luis Obispo (93401) ***(P-11998)***

Sun Express, Fontana *Also called Hanks Inc* ***(P-11970)***

Sun Glo Foods, Fullerton *Also called Khyber Foods Incorporated* ***(P-2460)***

Sun Haven Care Inc .... D 714 870-0060
201 E Bastanchury Rd Fullerton (92835) ***(P-20482)***

Sun Hill Properties Inc (HQ) .... **C 818 506-2500**
555 Unversal Hollywood Dr Universal City (91608) ***(P-16738)***

Sun Ice USA, Riverside *Also called Mackie International Inc* ***(P-1820)***

Sun Lakes Country Club, Banning *Also called Professional Cmnty MGT Cal Inc* ***(P-15957)***

Sun Life Cnada US Holdings Inc .... C 949 930-1570
4675 Macarthur Ct Ste 770 Newport Beach (92660) ***(P-15349)***

Sun Mar Healthcare, Orange *Also called Sun Mar Management Services* ***(P-20629)***

Sun Mar Management Service, Monterey Park *Also called Monterey Pk Convalescent Hosp* ***(P-20614)***

Sun Mar Management Services, Anaheim *Also called Sun Mar Nursing Center Inc* ***(P-20630)***

Sun Mar Management Services .... D 714 385-1006
500 N State College Blvd Orange (92868) ***(P-20629)***

Sun Mar Management Services .... C 951 687-3842
8171 Magnolia Ave Riverside (92504) ***(P-20483)***

Sun Mar Nursing Center Inc .... D 714 776-1720
1720 W Orange Ave Anaheim (92804) ***(P-20630)***

Sun Pac Storage Containers Inc .... F 949 458-2347
23222 Olive Ave Ste A Lake Forest (92630) ***(P-3410)***

Sun Pacific Cold Storage, Bakersfield *Also called Exeter Packers Inc* ***(P-12173)***

Sun Pacific Farming, Bakersfield *Also called 7th Standard Ranch Company* ***(P-39)***

Sun Pacific Farming, Bakersfield *Also called Sun Pacific Marketing Coop Inc* ***(P-14657)***

Sun Pacific Farming Coop Inc (PA) .... **B 559 592-7121**
1250 E Myer Ave Exeter (93221) ***(P-229)***

Sun Pacific Farming Coop Inc .... D 661 399-0376
33374 Lerdo Hwy Bakersfield (93308) ***(P-230)***

Sun Pacific Farms, Bakersfield *Also called Sun Pacific Farming Coop Inc* ***(P-230)***

Sun Pacific Maricopa .... D 661 847-1015
31452 Old River Rd Bakersfield (93311) ***(P-186)***

Sun Pacific Marketing Coop Inc .... B 213 612-9957
33502 Lerdo Hwy Bakersfield (93308) ***(P-23337)***

Sun Pacific Marketing Coop Inc .... B 559 784-6845
20715 Ave 8 Richgrove (93261) ***(P-14656)***

Sun Pacific Marketing Coop Inc .... B 661 847-1015
31452 Old River Rd Bakersfield (93311) ***(P-14657)***

Sun Pacific Packers, Exeter *Also called Exeter Packers Inc* ***(P-167)***

Sun Pacific Shippers, Pasadena *Also called Exeter Packers Inc* ***(P-62)***

Sun Plastics Inc .... E 323 888-6999
7140 E Slauson Ave Commerce (90040) ***(P-3891)***

Sun Power Source (PA) .... **F 805 644-2520**
1650 Palma Dr Ventura (93003) ***(P-9148)***

Sun Precision Machining Inc .... F 951 817-0056
1651 Market St Ste A Corona (92880) ***(P-8804)***

Sun Rich Foods .... F 714 632-7577
1240 N Barsten Way Anaheim (92806) ***(P-13945)***

Sun Rich Foods Intl Corp .... E 714 632-7577
1240 N Barsten Way Anaheim (92806) ***(P-2529)***

Sun Rich Fresh Foods USA Inc (PA) .... **C 951 735-3800**
515 E Rincon St Corona (92879) ***(P-187)***

Sun Stone Sales, Temecula *Also called Sunstone Components Group Inc* ***(P-7184)***

Sun Ten Laboratories Inc .... E 949 587-1238
9250 Jeronimo Rd Irvine (92618) ***(P-4900)***

Sun Ten Labs Liquidation Co .... E 949 587-0509
9250 Jeronimo Rd Irvine (92618) ***(P-14739)***

Sun Valley Dairy, Sun Valley *Also called Svd Inc* ***(P-14546)***

Sun Valley Extrusion, Los Angeles *Also called Sun Valley Products Inc* ***(P-6318)***

Sun Valley Ltg Standards Inc .... D 661 233-2000
660 W Avenue O Palmdale (93551) ***(P-9104)***

Sun Valley Products Inc .... E 818 247-8350
4640 Sperry St Los Angeles (90039) ***(P-6318)***

Sun Valley Products Inc (HQ) .... **E 818 247-8350**
4626 Sperry St Los Angeles (90039) ***(P-6319)***

Sun West Mortgage Company Inc (PA) .... **D 800 453-7884**
6131 Orangethorpe Ave # 500 Buena Park (90620) ***(P-15232)***

Sun World Inc .... A 805 833-6460
5544 California Ave # 280 Bakersfield (93309) ***(P-188)***

Sun World International Inc (PA) .... **A 661 392-5000**
16351 Driver Rd Bakersfield (93308) ***(P-189)***

Sun World International LLC (HQ) .... **B 661 392-5000**
5701 Truxtun Ave Ste 200 Bakersfield (93309) ***(P-119)***

Mergent e-mail: customerrelations@mergent.com
1284
2022 Southern California Business Directory and Buyers Guide
(P-0000) Products & Services Section entry number
(PA)=Parent Co (HQ)=Headquarters (DH)=Div Headquarters

Sun-Gro Commodities Inc (PA)....E....661 393-2612
34575 Famoso Rd Bakersfield (93308) ***(P-1976)***
Sun-Mate Corp....F....818 700-0572
19730 Ventura Blvd Ste 18 Woodland Hills (91364) ***(P-11392)***
SunAmerica Inc (HQ)....A....310 772-6000
1 Sun America Ctr Fl 38 Los Angeles (90067) ***(P-15120)***
SunAmerica Investments Inc (HQ)....D....310 772-6000
1 Sun America Ctr Fl 37 Los Angeles (90067) ***(P-23118)***
SunAmerica Investments Inc....C....310 772-6000
1 Sun America Ctr Fl 38 Los Angeles (90067) ***(P-16145)***
Sunbeam Trailer Products Inc....E....714 373-5000
5312 Production Dr Huntington Beach (92649) ***(P-9120)***
Sunbelt of California, La Verne *Also called Sunbelt USA Inc* ***(P-14183)***
Sunbelt USA Inc (PA)....F....909 593-0500
1941 Yeager Ave La Verne (91750) ***(P-14183)***
Sunbrdge Shndin Hlls Rhblttion....D....909 881-3896
4164 N 4th Ave San Bernardino (92407) ***(P-20484)***
Sunbritetv LLC (HQ)....E....805 214-7250
2630 Townsgate Rd Ste F Westlake Village (91361) ***(P-9320)***
Sunburst Products Inc....E....949 722-0158
1570 Corporate Dr Ste F Costa Mesa (92626) ***(P-11303)***
Suncal, Santa Ana *Also called Argent Management LLC* ***(P-15772)***
Sunco Lighting Inc....E....844 334-9938
27811 Hancock Pkwy Ste A Valencia (91355) ***(P-13669)***
Suncore Inc....E....949 450-0054
15 Hubble Ste 200 Irvine (92618) ***(P-9586)***
Sundale Fndtion For Stdnts Cmn....C....559 688-3419
13990 Avenue 240 Tulare (93274) ***(P-22063)***
Sundale School, Tulare *Also called Sundale Fndtion For Stdnts Cmn* ***(P-22063)***
Sundance Spas Inc (HQ)....E....909 606-7733
13925 City Center Dr # 200 Chino Hills (91709) ***(P-11765)***
Sunderstorm LLC....F....818 605-6682
1146 N Central Ave Glendale (91202) ***(P-11766)***
Sundial Industries Inc....E....818 767-4477
8421 Telfair Ave Sun Valley (91352) ***(P-7417)***
Sundial Powder Coatings Inc....E....818 767-4477
8421 Telfair Ave Sun Valley (91352) ***(P-7418)***
Sundown Foods USA Inc....E....909 606-6797
10891 Business Dr Fontana (92337) ***(P-1875)***
Sundown Liquidating Corp (PA)....C....714 540-8950
401 Goetz Ave Santa Ana (92707) ***(P-5923)***
Sunflower Gardens Inc....D....714 641-0959
3730 S Greenville St Santa Ana (92704) ***(P-20485)***
Sungevity, Temecula *Also called Solar Spectrum LLC* ***(P-1142)***
Sunkist Growers Inc (PA)....C....661 290-8900
27770 Entertainment Dr Valencia (91355) ***(P-14658)***
Sunland Aerospace Fasteners....E....818 485-8929
12920 Pierce St Pacoima (91331) ***(P-7077)***
Sunland Ford Inc....D....760 241-7751
15330 Palmdale Rd Victorville (92392) ***(P-18876)***
Sunland Ford-Lincoln-Mercury, Victorville *Also called Sunland Ford Inc* ***(P-18876)***
Sunland Scaffold....D....951 595-9402
24885 Whitewood Rd # 106 Murrieta (92563) ***(P-1691)***
Sunland Shutters, Long Beach *Also called Ta Chen International Inc* ***(P-13599)***
Sunland Woodworks....F....818 982-3110
7253 Lankershim Blvd North Hollywood (91605) ***(P-3225)***
Sunline Transit Agency....C....760 972-4059
790 Vine Ave Coachella (92236) ***(P-11891)***
Sunline Transit Agency (PA)....C....760 343-3456
32505 Harry Oliver Trl Thousand Palms (92276) ***(P-11845)***
Sunn America Inc....E....909 944-5756
10280 Indiana Ct Rancho Cucamonga (91730) ***(P-17378)***
Sunny America & Global Autotec....E....714 544-0400
2681 Dow Ave Ste A Tustin (92780) ***(P-10137)***
Sunny Rose Glen LLC....D....951 679-3355
29620 Bradley Rd Sun City (92586) ***(P-22157)***
Sunny View Care Center, Los Angeles *Also called Longwood Management Corp* ***(P-20601)***
Sunnygem LLC....B....661 758-0491
500 N F St Wasco (93280) ***(P-1876)***
Sunnyside Nursing Center, Torrance *Also called Fh & Hf-Torrance I LLC* ***(P-20344)***
Sunon Inc (PA)....E....714 255-0208
1075 W Lambert Rd Ste A Brea (92821) ***(P-8054)***
Sunpower By Green Convergence, Valencia *Also called Green Convergence* ***(P-13829)***
Sunpro Solar Inc....D....951 678-7733
34859 Frederick St # 101 Wildomar (92595) ***(P-1150)***
Sunrider Eastern Europe Inc (PA)....C....310 781-3808
1625 Abalone Ave Torrance (90501) ***(P-14293)***
Sunridge Nurseries Inc....D....661 363-8463
441 Vineland Rd Bakersfield (93307) ***(P-149)***
Sunrise Brands LLC (PA)....E....323 780-8250
5401 S Soto St Vernon (90058) ***(P-14419)***
Sunrise Cntry CLB Rncho Mrage....D....760 328-6549
71601 Country Club Dr Rancho Mirage (92270) ***(P-19620)***
Sunrise Dairy, Vernon *Also called Sunrise Food Service Inc* ***(P-138)***
Sunrise Food Service Inc....D....323 264-8364
2307 E 49th St Vernon (90058) ***(P-138)***
Sunrise Ford, North Hollywood *Also called Ngp Motors Inc* ***(P-18900)***
Sunrise Ford....C....909 822-4401
16005 Valley Blvd Fontana (92335) ***(P-13035)***
Sunrise Growers Inc....C....612 619-9545
2640 Sturgis Rd Oxnard (93030) ***(P-2530)***
Sunrise Pillow Co Inc....F....626 401-9283
2215 Merced Ave El Monte (91733) ***(P-3121)***
Sunrise Senior Living LLC....D....949 248-8855
31741 Rancho Viejo Rd San Juan Capistrano (92675) ***(P-20486)***
Sunrise Senior Living MGT Inc....C....909 447-5259
120 W San Jose Ave Claremont (91711) ***(P-22158)***
Sunrun Installation Svcs Inc....C....818 255-5462
13012 Saticoy St Ste 1 North Hollywood (91605) ***(P-23513)***
Sunrun Installation Svcs Inc (HQ)....D....415 580-6900
775 Fiero Ln Ste 200 San Luis Obispo (93401) ***(P-1151)***
Sunrun Installation Svcs Inc....B....805 658-1236
5777 Olivas Park Dr O Ventura (93003) ***(P-1152)***
Sunsation Inc....E....909 542-0280
100 S Cambridge Ave Claremont (91711) ***(P-1911)***
Sunscape Eyewear Inc....D....949 553-0590
17526 Von Karman Ave A Irvine (92614) ***(P-14184)***
Sunset Landscape Maintenance....D....949 455-4636
27201 Burbank El Toro (92610) ***(P-284)***
Sunset Lighting Services, Irvine *Also called M L Services Inc* ***(P-1278)***
Sunset Manor Convalescent Hosp, El Monte *Also called Gibralter Convalescent Hosp* ***(P-20593)***
Sunset Plaza Hotel....D....323 656-8090
8400 W Sunset Blvd Ste 3a West Hollywood (90069) ***(P-16739)***
Sunset Property Services, Irvine *Also called Jonset Corporation* ***(P-13007)***
Sunset Signs and Printing Inc....E....714 255-9104
2906 E Coronado St Anaheim (92806) ***(P-11607)***
Sunset Tower Hotel LLC....D....323 654-7100
8358 W Sunset Blvd Los Angeles (90069) ***(P-16740)***
Sunshine Behavioral Health LLC (PA)....D....949 835-4375
30950 Rncho Vejo Rd Ste 2 San Juan Capistrano (92675) ***(P-21346)***
Sunshine Enterprises, Monterey Park *Also called DHm International Corp* ***(P-2940)***
Sunshine Floral Inc....D....805 684-1177
4595 Foothill Rd Carpinteria (93013) ***(P-14895)***
Sunshine Floral LLC....D....805 982-8822
1070 S Rice Ave Ste 1 Oxnard (93033) ***(P-14896)***
Sunshine Makers Inc (PA)....D....562 795-6000
15922 Pacific Coast Hwy Huntington Beach (92649) ***(P-4979)***
Sunshine Metal Clad Inc....D....661 366-0575
7201 Edison Hwy Bakersfield (93307) ***(P-1403)***
Sunsports LP....E....949 273-6202
7 Holland Irvine (92618) ***(P-5875)***
Sunstar Spa Covers Inc (HQ)....E....858 602-1950
26074 Avenue Hall Ste 13 Valencia (91355) ***(P-11767)***
Sunstone Components Group Inc (HQ)....D....951 296-5010
42136 Avenida Alvarado Temecula (92590) ***(P-7184)***
Sunstone Hotel Properties Inc....C....310 228-4100
1177 S Beverly Dr Los Angeles (90035) ***(P-16741)***
Sunstone Hotel Properties Inc....C....310 546-7627
1700 N Sepulveda Blvd Manhattan Beach (90266) ***(P-16742)***
Sunstone Hotel Properties Inc (HQ)....C....949 330-4000
120 Vantis Dr Ste 350 Aliso Viejo (92656) ***(P-16743)***
Suntreat Pkg Shipg A Ltd Prtnr....C....559 562-4991
391 Oxford Ave Lindsay (93247) ***(P-12558)***
Suntsu Electronics Inc....E....949 783-7300
142 Technology Dr Ste 150 Irvine (92618) ***(P-9788)***
Sunvair Inc (HQ)....D....661 294-3777
29145 The Old Rd Valencia (91355) ***(P-8805)***
Sunvair Aerospace Group Inc (PA)....D....661 294-3777
29145 The Old Rd Valencia (91355) ***(P-19072)***
Sunvair Overhaul Inc....E....661 257-6123
29145 The Old Rd Valencia (91355) ***(P-10424)***
Sunwest Bank (HQ)....E....714 730-4441
2050 Main St Ste 300 Irvine (92614) ***(P-15044)***
Sunwest Electric Inc....C....714 630-8700
3064 E Miraloma Ave Anaheim (92806) ***(P-1321)***
Super 8 Motel, Bakersfield *Also called Tiburon Hospitality LLC* ***(P-16753)***
Super 8 Motel Goleta....C....805 967-5591
6021 Hollister Ave Goleta (93117) ***(P-16744)***
Super Center Concepts Inc....C....323 241-6789
10211 Avalon Blvd Los Angeles (90003) ***(P-2038)***
Super Center Concepts Inc....C....323 562-8980
7300 Atlantic Ave Cudahy (90201) ***(P-2074)***
Super Color Digital LLC (PA)....E....949 622-0010
16761 Hale Ave Irvine (92606) ***(P-4577)***
Super Glue, Ontario *Also called Pacer Technology* ***(P-5188)***
Super73 Inc (PA)....E....949 313-6340
16591 Noyes Ave Irvine (92606) ***(P-10502)***
Superb Chair Corporation....E....562 776-1771
6861 Watcher St Commerce (90040) ***(P-3520)***
Supercuts, Downey *Also called Jlm & Mag Associates Inc* ***(P-16906)***
Superform USA Incorporated....E....951 351-4100
6825 Jurupa Ave Riverside (92504) ***(P-7107)***
Superior Awning Inc....E....818 780-7200
14555 Titus St Panorama City (91402) ***(P-3146)***
Superior Bias Trims, Vernon *Also called SJ&I Bias Binding & Tex Co Inc* ***(P-3183)***
Superior Cattle Feeders LLC (PA)....D....760 348-2218
551 S Industrial Ave Calipatria (92233) ***(P-126)***
Superior Communications Inc (PA)....C....877 522-4727
5027 Irwindale Ave # 900 Irwindale (91706) ***(P-13777)***
Superior Connector Plating Inc....E....714 774-1174
1901 E Cerritos Ave Anaheim (92805) ***(P-7318)***
Superior Construction Inc....D....951 808-8780
265 N Joy St Corona (92879) ***(P-643)***
Superior Dairy Products Co....F....559 582-0481
325 N Douty St Hanford (93230) ***(P-1823)***
Superior Duct Fabrication Inc....C....909 620-8565
1683 Mount Vernon Ave Pomona (91768) ***(P-6922)***
Superior Elec Mech & Plbg Inc....B....909 357-9400
8613 Helms Ave Rancho Cucamonga (91730) ***(P-1322)***
Superior Electric Mtr Svc Inc....F....323 583-1040
4622 Alcoa Ave Vernon (90058) ***(P-19017)***
Superior Electrical Advg Inc (PA)....D....562 495-3808
1700 W Anaheim St Long Beach (90813) ***(P-11608)***
Superior Equipment Solutions....D....323 722-7900
1085 Bixby Dr Hacienda Heights (91745) ***(P-8995)***
Superior Filtration Pdts LLC....F....951 681-1700
3401 Space Center Ct 811b Jurupa Valley (91752) ***(P-8055)***

ALPHABETIC

Employee Codes: A=Over 500 employees, B=251-500
C=101-250, D=51-100, E=20-50 F=10-19
2022 Southern California Business Directory and Buyers Guide
© Mergent Inc. 1-800-342-5647
1285

Superior Food Machinery Inc ... E ... 562 949-0396
8311 Sorensen Ave Santa Fe Springs (90670) ***(P-7953)***

Superior Fruit LLC ... C ... 805 485-2519
4324 E Vineyard Ave Oxnard (93036) ***(P-38)***

Superior Galleries Inc (HQ) ... **E ... 818 444-8699**
20011 Ventura Blvd Woodland Hills (91364) ***(P-14140)***

Superior Gunite (HQ) ... **C ... 818 896-9199**
12306 Van Nuys Blvd Sylmar (91342) ***(P-1553)***

Superior Honey Company, San Bernardino *Also called Millers American Honey Inc* ***(P-2485)***

Superior Inds Intl Hldings LLC (HQ) ... **C ... 818 781-4973**
7800 Woodley Ave Van Nuys (91406) ***(P-10138)***

Superior Interlocking Pavers ... F ... 818 838-0833
27305 Live Oak Rd Ste A Castaic (91384) ***(P-7652)***

Superior Jig Inc ... E ... 714 525-4777
1540 N Orangethorpe Way Anaheim (92801) ***(P-7834)***

Superior Lithographics Inc ... D ... 323 263-8400
3055 Bandini Blvd Vernon (90058) ***(P-4428)***

Superior Masonry Walls Ltd ... D ... 909 370-1800
300 W Olive St Ste A Colton (92324) ***(P-1354)***

Superior Metal Fabricators Inc ... E ... 951 360-2474
4768 Felspar St Riverside (92509) ***(P-6923)***

Superior Metal Finishing Inc ... F ... 310 464-8010
1733 W 134th St Gardena (90249) ***(P-7319)***

Superior Metal Shapes Inc ... E ... 909 947-3455
4730 Eucalyptus Ave Chino (91710) ***(P-6320)***

Superior Millwork of Sb Inc ... F ... 805 685-1744
7330 Hollister Ave Ste B Goleta (93117) ***(P-3338)***

Superior Mold Co ... E ... 909 947-7028
1927 E Francis St Ontario (91761) ***(P-5833)***

Superior Nut Co Inc ... F ... 323 223-2431
5200 Valley Blvd Los Angeles (90032) ***(P-14566)***

Superior Paving Company Inc ... D ... 951 739-9200
1880 N Delilah St Corona (92879) ***(P-920)***

Superior Plating, Anaheim *Also called Superior Connector Plating Inc* ***(P-7318)***

Superior Plating Inc ... E ... 818 252-1088
9001 Glenoaks Blvd Sun Valley (91352) ***(P-7320)***

Superior Press, Santa Fe Springs *Also called Superior Printing Inc* ***(P-4578)***

Superior Printing Inc ... D ... 888 590-7998
9440 Norwalk Blvd Santa Fe Springs (90670) ***(P-4578)***

Superior Ready Mix Concrete LP ... D ... 760 352-4341
802 E Main St El Centro (92243) ***(P-6120)***

Superior Ready Mix Concrete LP ... D ... 951 277-3553
24635 Temescal Canyon Rd Corona (92883) ***(P-6121)***

Superior Ready Mix Concrete LP ... D ... 951 658-9225
1130 N State St Hemet (92543) ***(P-6122)***

Superior Ready Mix Concrete LP ... D ... 760 343-3418
72270 Varner Rd Thousand Palms (92276) ***(P-6123)***

Superior Seafood Co, Los Angeles *Also called PLD Enterprises Inc* ***(P-14578)***

Superior Sod I LP ... C ... 909 923-5068
17821 17th St Ste 165 Tustin (92780) ***(P-96)***

Superior Spring Company ... E ... 714 490-0881
1260 S Talt Ave Anaheim (92806) ***(P-7493)***

Superior Stone Products Inc ... F ... 714 635-7775
923 E Arlee Pl Anaheim (92805) ***(P-6149)***

Superior Storage Tank Inc ... F ... 714 226-1914
14700 Industry Cir La Mirada (90638) ***(P-6757)***

Superior Super Warehouse, Cudahy *Also called Super Center Concepts Inc* ***(P-2074)***

Superior Tank Co Inc (PA) ... **E ... 909 912-0580**
9500 Lucas Ranch Rd Rancho Cucamonga (91730) ***(P-6758)***

Superior Tech Inc ... F ... 909 364-2300
13850 Benson Ave Chino (91710) ***(P-6253)***

Superior Technologies, Chino *Also called Superior Tech Inc* ***(P-6253)***

Superior Trailer Works ... E ... 909 350-0185
13700 Slover Ave Fontana (92337) ***(P-7718)***

Superior Wall Systems, South Gate *Also called Sws Panel and Truss Inc* ***(P-11769)***

Superior Wall Systems Inc ... B ... 714 278-0000
1232 E Orangethorpe Ave Fullerton (92831) ***(P-1404)***

Superior Warehouse, Los Angeles *Also called Super Center Concepts Inc* ***(P-2038)***

Superior Window Coverings Inc ... E ... 818 762-6685
7683 N San Fernando Rd Burbank (91505) ***(P-3095)***

Superior-Studio Spc Inc ... E ... 323 278-0100
2239 Yates Ave Commerce (90040) ***(P-11768)***

Supermedia LLC ... B ... 626 331-9440
1270 E Garvey St Covina (91724) ***(P-4209)***

Superprint Lithographics Inc ... F ... 562 698-8001
8332 Secura Way Santa Fe Springs (90670) ***(P-4429)***

Supershuttle Orange County Inc ... B ... 310 222-5500
531 Van Ness Ave Torrance (90501) ***(P-11846)***

Supersprings International Inc ... E ... 805 745-5553
505 Maple St Carpinteria (93013) ***(P-7468)***

Supertec Machinery Inc ... F ... 562 220-1675
6435 Alondra Blvd Paramount (90723) ***(P-7748)***

Support Technologies Inc ... F ... 949 442-2957
1939 Deere Ave Irvine (92606) ***(P-17991)***

Supra National Express Inc ... C ... 310 549-7105
1411 E Watson Center Rd Carson (90745) ***(P-12534)***

Supreme Abrasives ... E ... 949 250-8644
1021 Fuller St Santa Ana (92701) ***(P-6158)***

Supreme Almonds California Inc ... D ... 661 746-6475
16897 Highway 43 Wasco (93280) ***(P-57)***

Supreme Enterprise, Santa Fe Springs *Also called Kingsolver Inc* ***(P-11512)***

Supreme Graphics Inc ... F ... 310 531-8300
1201 N Miller St Anaheim (92806) ***(P-4430)***

Supreme Machine Products Inc ... F ... 909 974-0349
302 Sequoia Ave Ontario (91761) ***(P-8806)***

Supreme Steel Treating Inc ... E ... 626 350-5865
2466 Seaman Ave El Monte (91733) ***(P-6453)***

Surco Products Inc ... F ... 310 323-2520
14001 S Main St Los Angeles (90061) ***(P-6980)***

Sure Forming Systems Inc ... E ... 562 598-6348
10602 Humbolt St Los Alamitos (90720) ***(P-1554)***

Sure Power Inc ... F ... 310 542-8561
1111 Knox St Torrance (90502) ***(P-9789)***

Sureco Hlth Lf Insur Agcy Inc ... D ... 949 333-0263
201 Sandpointe Ave # 600 Santa Ana (92707) ***(P-15631)***

Surefire LLC (PA) ... **B ... 714 545-9444**
18300 Mount Baldy Cir Fountain Valley (92708) ***(P-11143)***

Suregrip International Co ... D ... 562 923-0724
5519 Rawlings Ave South Gate (90280) ***(P-11450)***

Surestay, Los Angeles *Also called Saharan Motor Hotel Inc* ***(P-16683)***

Surf City Garage ... F ... 714 894-1707
5872 Engineer Dr Huntington Beach (92649) ***(P-4980)***

Surf City Still Works LLC ... F ... 714 253-7606
16561 Gemini Ln Huntington Beach (92647) ***(P-2247)***

Surf Sand Hotel, Laguna Beach *Also called JC Resorts LLC* ***(P-23041)***

Surf To Summit Inc ... F ... 805 964-1896
7234 Hollister Ave Goleta (93117) ***(P-11451)***

Surface Pumps Inc (PA) ... **D ... 661 393-1545**
3301 Unicorn Rd Bakersfield (93308) ***(P-13946)***

Surge Globl Bkries Hldings LLC (PA) ... **C ... 818 896-0525**
13336 Paxton St Pacoima (91331) ***(P-14740)***

Surgener Electric Inc ... D ... 661 399-3321
732 Angus Ln Bakersfield (93308) ***(P-1323)***

Surgeon Worldwide Inc ... E ... 707 501-7962
3855 S Hill St Los Angeles (90037) ***(P-5883)***

Surgery Center of South Bay, Torrance *Also called Bay Citis Surgery Centre L P* ***(P-19719)***

Surgical Center of West Covina ... D ... 626 960-6623
1250 S Sunset Ave Ste 100 West Covina (91790) ***(P-20100)***

Surgicare La Veta Ltd A Cal Lt ... D ... 714 744-0900
681 S Parker St Ste 150 Orange (92868) ***(P-20101)***

Surrounding Elements LLC ... E ... 949 582-9000
33051 Calle Aviador Ste A San Juan Capistrano (92675) ***(P-3534)***

Surterre Properties Inc (PA) ... **C ... 949 717-7100**
1400 Nwport Ctr Dr Ste 10 Newport Beach (92660) ***(P-16013)***

Surveillance Systems Group Inc ... F ... 877 687-3939
3175 Sedona Ct Ontario (91764) ***(P-18343)***

Survey Junkie, Glendale *Also called Disqo Inc* ***(P-22879)***

Survey Stake and Marker Inc ... E ... 626 960-4802
13470 Dalewood St Baldwin Park (91706) ***(P-3455)***

Survios Inc ... E ... 310 736-1503
4501 Glencoe Ave Marina Del Rey (90292) ***(P-18070)***

Susanna Beverly Hills, Beverly Hills *Also called Susannas Inc* ***(P-2897)***

Susannas Inc ... F ... 310 276-7510
9647 Santa Monica Blvd Beverly Hills (90210) ***(P-2897)***

Suss McRtec Phtnic Systems Inc ... D ... 951 817-3700
2520 Palisades Dr Corona (92882) ***(P-9919)***

Suss Microtec Inc (HQ) ... **C ... 408 940-0300**
2520 Palisades Dr Corona (92882) ***(P-7996)***

Sustainable Agriculture, Rancho Dominguez *Also called Seeds of Change Inc* ***(P-14868)***

Sutter Health ... C ... 805 966-1600
25 W Micheltorena St Santa Barbara (93101) ***(P-20970)***

Sutter Securities Incorporated ... D ... 415 352-6300
6 Venture Ste 395 Irvine (92618) ***(P-15308)***

Suttles Plumbing & Mech Corp ... D ... 818 718-9779
2267 Agate Ct Simi Valley (93065) ***(P-1153)***

Sutura Inc ... E ... 714 427-0398
17080 Newhope St Fountain Valley (92708) ***(P-11144)***

Suzhou South ... B ... 626 322-0101
18351 Colima Rd Ste 82 Rowland Heights (91748) ***(P-8317)***

Suzuki Motor of America Inc (HQ) ... **C ... 714 996-7040**
3251 E Imperial Hwy Brea (92821) ***(P-7599)***

Suzuki USA, Brea *Also called Suzuki Motor of America Inc* ***(P-7599)***

Svd Inc ... D ... 818 504-1775
8088 San Fernando Rd Sun Valley (91352) ***(P-14546)***

Svevia Usa Inc ... F ... 909 559-4134
14567 Rancho Vista Dr Fontana (92335) ***(P-11473)***

Svf Flow Controls Inc ... E ... 562 802-2255
5595 Fresca Dr La Palma (90623) ***(P-13947)***

Svi Lax LLC ... D ... 310 281-0300
5933 W Century Blvd Los Angeles (90045) ***(P-16745)***

Svo Enterprise ... E ... 626 406-4770
9854 Baldwin Pl El Monte (91731) ***(P-3051)***

SW Fixtures Inc ... F ... 909 595-2506
3940 Valley Blvd Ste C Walnut (91789) ***(P-3667)***

Swagbucks, El Segundo *Also called Prodege LLC* ***(P-17692)***

Swan Fence Incorporated ... E ... 310 669-8000
600 W Manville St Compton (90220) ***(P-6235)***

Swaner Hardwood Co Inc (PA) ... **D ... 818 953-5350**
5 W Magnolia Blvd Burbank (91502) ***(P-3355)***

Swann Communications USA Inc ... D ... 562 777-2551
12636 Clark St Santa Fe Springs (90670) ***(P-13778)***

Swartz Glass Company Inc (PA) ... **F ... 310 392-0001**
821 Lincoln Blvd Venice (90291) ***(P-1589)***

Swatfame Inc (PA) ... **B ... 626 961-7928**
16425 Gale Ave City of Industry (91745) ***(P-14420)***

Swc Group Inc ... F ... 888 982-1628
20529 E Walnut Dr N Walnut (91789) ***(P-3843)***

Sweatheory LLC ... D ... 310 956-2307
1503 N Cahuenga Blvd Los Angeles (90028) ***(P-19469)***

Sweatheory Wellness LLC ... D ... 310 844-3662
6427 W Sunset Blvd 106 Los Angeles (90028) ***(P-21487)***

Sweda Company LLC ... C ... 626 357-9999
17411 E Valley Blvd City of Industry (91744) ***(P-14141)***

Sweden & Martina Inc ... E ... 844 862-7846
600 Anton Blvd Ste 1134 Costa Mesa (92626) ***(P-11061)***

Sweegen Inc ... F ... 949 635-1984
30452 Esperanza Rcho STA Marg (92688) ***(P-5150)***

Sweetener Products Inc..........D.......323 234-2200
2050 E 38th St Vernon (90058) ***(P-14741)***
Sweetener Products Company, Vernon *Also called Sweetener Products Inc* ***(P-14741)***
Sweetgrace Home Hlth Svcs LLC..........D.......909 463-7400
6101 Cherry Ave Fontana (92336) ***(P-21488)***
Sweety Novelty Inc..........F.......310 533-6010
633 Monterey Pass Rd Monterey Park (91754) ***(P-1824)***
Sweis Inc (PA)..........D.......310 375-0558**
23760 Hawthorne Blvd Torrance (90505) ***(P-14045)***
Swift Beef Company..........C.......951 571-2237
15555 Meridian Pkwy Riverside (92518) ***(P-1753)***
Swift Fab..........F.......310 366-7295
515 E Alondra Blvd Gardena (90248) ***(P-6924)***
Swift Leasing Co LLC..........D.......909 347-0500
14392 Valley Blvd Fontana (92335) ***(P-12079)***
Swift Media Entertainment Inc..........D.......310 308-3694
5340 Alla Rd Ste 101 Los Angeles (90066) ***(P-18682)***
Swift-Cor Precision Inc..........E.......310 354-1207
344 W 157th St Gardena (90248) ***(P-6925)***
Swinford Electric Inc..........E.......714 578-8888
1150 E Elm Ave Fullerton (92831) ***(P-1324)***
Swinks Creations Inc (PA)..........D.......805 522-0412
2769 Wanda Ave Simi Valley (93065) ***(P-285)***
Swiss Cabinet..........F.......818 571-9917
12430 Montague St Ste 212 Pacoima (91331) ***(P-3339)***
Swiss House, Glendora *Also called Grico Precision Inc* ***(P-8610)***
Swiss Machine Products, Anaheim *Also called Farrell Brothers Holding Corp* ***(P-8586)***
Swiss Park Banquet Center..........F.......562 699-1525
1905 Workman Mill Rd Whittier (90601) ***(P-9012)***
Swiss Productions Inc..........E.......805 654-8525
2801 Golf Course Dr Ventura (93003) ***(P-5463)***
Swiss RE Underwriters Agency (HQ)..........C.......818 226-0028
26050 Mureau Rd Calabasas (91302) ***(P-15385)***
Swiss Wire EDM..........F.......714 540-2903
3505 Cadillac Ave Ste J1 Costa Mesa (92626) ***(P-8807)***
Swiss-Micron Inc..........D.......949 589-0430
22361 Gilberto Ste A Rcho STA Marg (92688) ***(P-7045)***
Swissmann Engineering Inc..........F.......760 223-0663
14019 Park Palisades Dr Bakersfield (93306) ***(P-7872)***
Swissport Cargo Services LP..........C.......310 910-9541
11001 Aviation Blvd Los Angeles (90045) ***(P-12370)***
Swissport Usa Inc..........D.......310 345-1986
7025 W Imperial Hwy Los Angeles (90045) ***(P-12371)***
Swissport Usa Inc..........D.......310 910-9560
11001 Aviation Blvd Los Angeles (90045) ***(P-12372)***
Swisstex California Inc (PA)..........D.......310 516-6800
13660 S Figueroa St Los Angeles (90061) ***(P-18683)***
Switching Systems, Anaheim *Also called Xp Power Inc* ***(P-9805)***
Sws, Fullerton *Also called Superior Wall Systems Inc* ***(P-1404)***
Sws Panel and Truss Inc..........F.......323 923-4900
4231 Liberty Blvd South Gate (90280) ***(P-11769)***
Swt Stockton, Temecula *Also called Southwest Traders Incorporated* ***(P-14510)***
Swvl LLC..........F.......424 248-3677
2118 Wilshire Blvd # 400 Santa Monica (90403) ***(P-4210)***
Swvp Westlake LLC..........C.......805 557-1234
880 S Westlake Blvd Westlake Village (91361) ***(P-16746)***
Syagen Technology LLC..........D.......714 258-4400
1251 E Dyer Rd Ste 140 Santa Ana (92705) ***(P-10815)***
Sybron Dental Specialties Inc (HQ)..........C.......714 516-7400
1717 W Collins Ave Orange (92867) ***(P-11197)***
Sybron Endo, Orange *Also called Ormco Corporation* ***(P-11185)***
Syc International Inc..........E.......888 300-9168
16027 Brookhurst St I305 Fountain Valley (92708) ***(P-3741)***
Sycamore Cogeneration Co (PA)..........D.......661 615-4630
1546 China Grade Loop Bakersfield (93308) ***(P-12862)***
SYCAMORE COURT APT, Newport Beach *Also called 10632 Bolsa Avenue LP* ***(P-15715)***
Sycamore Mineral Spring Resort..........D.......805 595-7302
1215 Avila Beach Dr San Luis Obispo (93405) ***(P-16747)***
Sycamores School, Altadena *Also called Pasadena Chld Training Soc* ***(P-22142)***
Sydell Hotels LLC..........C.......213 381-7411
3515 Wilshire Blvd Los Angeles (90010) ***(P-16748)***
Sygma Inc..........E.......562 906-8880
13168 Flores St Santa Fe Springs (90670) ***(P-7873)***
Sygma Network Inc..........C.......661 723-0405
46905 47th St W Lancaster (93536) ***(P-14511)***
Sygma Network, The, Sun Valley *Also called Sugar Foods Corporation* ***(P-18681)***
Sylmark Group, Van Nuys *Also called Sylmark Inc* ***(P-23119)***
Sylmark Inc (PA)..........D.......818 217-2000
7821 Orion Ave Ste 200 Van Nuys (91406) ***(P-23119)***
Sylvan Learning Center, San Marino *Also called Southern California Lrng Corp* ***(P-22058)***
Sylvester Winery Inc..........F.......805 227-4000
5115 Buena Vista Dr Paso Robles (93446) ***(P-2225)***
Symbolic Displays Inc..........D.......714 258-2811
1917 E Saint Andrew Pl Santa Ana (92705) ***(P-10425)***
Symes Cadillac Inc..........D.......626 689-4386
3475 E Colorado Blvd Pasadena (91107) ***(P-18877)***
Symes Cadillac of Pasadena, Pasadena *Also called Symes Cadillac Inc* ***(P-18877)***
Symmetry Electronics LLC (HQ)..........E.......310 536-6190
222 N Pacific Coast Hwy # 10 El Segundo (90245) ***(P-9587)***
Symrise Inc..........E.......949 276-4600
332 Forest Ave Laguna Beach (92651) ***(P-2337)***
Synchronized Technologies Inc..........F.......213 368-3760
7536 Tyrone Ave Van Nuys (91405) ***(P-8304)***
Synchrotech, Van Nuys *Also called Synchronized Technologies Inc* ***(P-8304)***
Syncis Insurance Solutions Inc (PA)..........C.......424 233-1764
301 E Ocean Blvd Ste 1170 Long Beach (90802) ***(P-15632)***
Syncreon America Inc..........D.......909 610-4511
14780 Bar Harbor Rd Ste B Fontana (92336) ***(P-12535)***
Synear Foods Usa LLC..........E.......818 341-3588
9601 Canoga Ave Chatsworth (91311) ***(P-721)***
Synectic Solutions Inc (PA)..........D.......805 483-4800
1701 Pacific Ave Ste 260 Oxnard (93033) ***(P-18223)***
Synergetic Tech Group Inc..........E.......909 305-4711
1712 Earhart La Verne (91750) ***(P-10426)***
Synergistic Research Inc..........F.......949 476-0000
11208 Young River Ave Fountain Valley (92708) ***(P-7515)***
Synergy Beverages, Vernon *Also called Gts Living Foods LLC* ***(P-2267)***
Synergy Direct Response, Santa Ana *Also called Cowboy Direct Response* ***(P-11538)***
Synergy Microsystems Inc (HQ)..........D.......858 452-0020
28965 Avenue Penn Valencia (91355) ***(P-8177)***
Syneron Inc (HQ)..........C.......866 259-6661
3 Goodyear Ste A Irvine (92618) ***(P-11239)***
Syneron Candela, Irvine *Also called Syneron Inc* ***(P-11239)***
Synertech PM Inc..........F.......714 898-9151
11711 Monarch St Garden Grove (92841) ***(P-6422)***
Syng Inc..........D.......770 354-0915
120 Mildred Ave Venice (90291) ***(P-9198)***
Synolo Security..........E.......909 907-4605
7231 Boulder Ave Pmb 650 Highland (92346) ***(P-18344)***
Synoptek Inc (PA)..........D.......949 241-8600
19520 Jamboree Rd Ste 110 Irvine (92612) ***(P-18224)***
Syntiant Corp..........D.......949 774-4887
7555 Irvine Center Dr # 200 Irvine (92618) ***(P-9588)***
Syntiro Healthcare Services (PA)..........D.......949 923-3438
7 Technology Dr Irvine (92618) ***(P-23120)***
Sypris Data Systems Inc (HQ)..........E.......909 962-9400
160 Via Verde San Dimas (91773) ***(P-8221)***
Sysco Los Angeles Inc..........A.......909 595-9595
20701 Currier Rd Walnut (91789) ***(P-14512)***
Sysco Riverside Inc..........B.......951 601-5300
15750 Meridian Pkwy Riverside (92518) ***(P-14513)***
Sysco Ventura Inc..........B.......805 205-7000
3100 Sturgis Rd Oxnard (93030) ***(P-14514)***
Sysparc, Van Nuys *Also called Bijan Rad Inc* ***(P-7966)***
Syspro Impact Software Inc..........C.......714 437-1000
1775 Flight Way Ste 150 Tustin (92782) ***(P-13444)***
Systech Solutions Inc (PA)..........D.......818 550-9690
500 N Brand Blvd Ste 1900 Glendale (91203) ***(P-17727)***
Systechs, Orange *Also called Cruz Modular Inc* ***(P-12111)***
System Supply Stationery Corp..........F.......310 223-0880
1251 E Walnut St Carson (90746) ***(P-14198)***
System Technical Support Corp..........E.......310 845-9400
960 Knox St Bldg B Torrance (90502) ***(P-8964)***
System1 LLC (PA)..........C.......310 256-4882
4235 Redwood Ave Los Angeles (90066) ***(P-23338)***
Systems Application & Tech Inc..........D.......805 487-7373
1000 Town Center Dr # 110 Oxnard (93036) ***(P-22664)***
Systems Division, Irvine *Also called Sdi LLC* ***(P-13773)***
Systems Experience Inc..........D.......310 215-9000
6033 W Century Blvd # 820 Los Angeles (90045) ***(P-23514)***
Systems Integrated LLC..........E.......714 998-0900
2200 N Glassell St Orange (92865) ***(P-10914)***
Systems Paving Inc (PA)..........D.......949 263-8301
1570 Brookhollow Dr Santa Ana (92705) ***(P-921)***
Systems Printing Inc..........F.......714 832-4677
14311 Chambers Rd Tustin (92780) ***(P-4626)***
Systems Technology Inc..........D.......909 799-9950
1350 Riverview Dr San Bernardino (92408) ***(P-8078)***
Systems Wire & Cable Limited..........F.......310 532-7870
1165 N Stanford Ave Los Angeles (90059) ***(P-7516)***
Syston Cable Technology Corp..........E.......888 679-7866
15278 El Prado Rd Chino (91710) ***(P-9920)***
Syxsense Inc..........D.......949 270-1903
65 Enterprise Ste 375 Aliso Viejo (92656) ***(P-17728)***
T & D Services Inc..........F.......951 304-1190
42363 Guava St Murrieta (92562) ***(P-438)***
T & F Sheet Mtls Fab McHning I..........E.......310 516-8548
15607 New Century Dr Gardena (90248) ***(P-6926)***
T & H Store Fixtures, Commerce *Also called Teichman Enterprises Inc* ***(P-3698)***
T & J Sausage Kitchen, Anaheim *Also called T&J Sausage Kitchen Inc* ***(P-1754)***
T & L Air Conditioning Inc..........E.......626 294-9888
164 W Live Oak Ave Arcadia (91007) ***(P-10669)***
T & M Machining..........E.......805 983-6716
331 Irving Dr Oxnard (93030) ***(P-8808)***
T & S Die Cutting..........F.......562 802-1731
13301 Alondra Blvd Ste A Santa Fe Springs (90670) ***(P-7835)***
T & T Box Company Inc..........E.......909 465-0848
1353 Philadelphia St Pomona (91766) ***(P-3846)***
T & T Enterprises, Corona *Also called Thalasinos Enterprises Inc* ***(P-14024)***
T & T Foods Inc..........E.......323 588-2158
3080 E 50th St Vernon (90058) ***(P-1856)***
T & T Solutions Inc..........D.......818 676-1786
7018 Owensmouth Ave # 201 Canoga Park (91303) ***(P-18225)***
T & T Truck & Crane Service, Ventura *Also called Offshore Crane & Service Co* ***(P-17316)***
T & W Converters Inc..........F.......818 241-1707
15020 Marquardt Ave Santa Fe Springs (90670) ***(P-14229)***
T A Rivard Inc..........D.......951 360-8596
8884 Jurupa Rd Riverside (92509) ***(P-977)***
T Allance One - Palm Sprng LLC..........D.......760 322-7000
67967 Vista Chino Cathedral City (92234) ***(P-19674)***
T and T Industries Inc (PA)..........F.......714 284-6555
1835 Dawns Way Ste A Fullerton (92831) ***(P-7517)***
T Boyer Company..........E.......949 642-2431
1656 Babcock St Costa Mesa (92627) ***(P-1325)***
T C P, Santa Monica *Also called Tennenbaum Capitl Partners LLC* ***(P-16296)***
T D Whitton Construction Inc..........E.......661 834-5894
4801 Wible Rd Bakersfield (93313) ***(P-286)***

ALPHABETIC

Employee Codes: A=Over 500 employees, B=251-500
C=101-250, D=51-100, E=20-50 F=10-19
2022 Southern California Business Directory and Buyers Guide
© Mergent Inc. 1-800-342-5647
1287

T E B Inc..........F.......909 941-8100
8754 Lion St Rancho Cucamonga (91730) ***(P-8809)***
T E M P, Gardena *Also called Thermlly Engnred Mnfctred Pdts* ***(P-6761)***
T F S, Camarillo *Also called Technical Film Systems Inc* ***(P-11293)***
T F X, Oxnard *Also called Trans Fx Inc* ***(P-11782)***
T Hasegawa USA Inc (HQ)..........**E.......714 522-1900**
14017 183rd St Cerritos (90703) ***(P-2338)***
T Hasegawa USA Inc..........D.......951 264-1121
2026 Cecilia Cir Corona (92881) ***(P-2531)***
T Joseph Raoof MD Inc..........F.......818 788-5060
16133 Ventura Blvd # 340 Encino (91436) ***(P-20102)***
T L C Transportation Staffing (HQ)..........**D.......714 541-5415**
1600 E 4th St Ste 340 Santa Ana (92701) ***(P-17470)***
T L Fabrications LP..........D.......562 802-3980
2921 E Coronado St Anaheim (92806) ***(P-18999)***
T L Timmerman Construction..........E.......760 244-2532
9845 Santa Fe Ave E Hesperia (92345) ***(P-3370)***
T M B, San Fernando *Also called Jme Inc* ***(P-13638)***
T M Cobb Company (PA)..........**E.......951 248-2400**
500 Palmyrita Ave Riverside (92507) ***(P-3293)***
T M I, Gardena *Also called Timbucktoo Manufacturing Inc* ***(P-8421)***
T M Mian & Associates Inc..........D.......818 591-2300
24150 Park Sorrento Calabasas (91302) ***(P-16749)***
T M Mian & Associates Inc..........D.......805 983-8600
2000 Solar Dr Oxnard (93036) ***(P-16750)***
T M P Services Inc (PA)..........**E.......951 213-3900**
2929 Kansas Ave Riverside (92507) ***(P-7009)***
t McGee Electric Inc..........D.......909 591-6461
2390 S Reservoir St Pomona (91766) ***(P-1326)***
T McGee Electric Inc..........E.......909 591-6461
12375 Mills Ave Ste 2 Chino (91710) ***(P-9047)***
T P R Traffic Solutions (PA)..........**F.......800 821-2913**
13217 Laureldale Ave Downey (90242) ***(P-18684)***
T Points Inc..........E.......323 846-9176
350 W Mrtn Lthr King Jr Los Angeles (90037) ***(P-16892)***
T Q M Apparel Group, Los Angeles *Also called High-End Knitwear Inc* ***(P-2636)***
T R I, Yucaipa *Also called Technical Resource Industries* ***(P-9048)***
T R L, Rancho Cucamonga *Also called TRL Systems Incorporated* ***(P-1331)***
T S I, Valencia *Also called Tape Specialty Inc* ***(P-13780)***
T S M, Los Angeles *Also called Tubular Specialties Mfg Inc* ***(P-5993)***
T Y R, Seal Beach *Also called Tyr Sport Inc* ***(P-14424)***
T&D Trenchless, Murrieta *Also called T & D Services Inc* ***(P-438)***
T&J Sausage Kitchen Inc..........E.......714 632-8350
2831 E Miraloma Ave Anaheim (92806) ***(P-1754)***
T-1 Lighting Inc..........F.......626 234-2328
9929 Pioneer Blvd Santa Fe Springs (90670) ***(P-9105)***
T-Force Inc (PA)..........**D.......949 208-1527**
4695 Macarthur Ct Newport Beach (92660) ***(P-23515)***
T-Rex Grilles, Corona *Also called T-Rex Truck Products Inc* ***(P-7114)***
T-Rex Truck Products Inc..........D.......800 287-5900
2365 Railroad St Corona (92878) ***(P-7114)***
T.com Ontario Fc T-9479, Ontario *Also called Target Corporation* ***(P-12251)***
T.S.c, Altadena *Also called Tom Sawyer Camps Inc* ***(P-16828)***
T/O Printing, Westlake Village *Also called Thousand Oaks Prtg & Spc Inc* ***(P-18689)***
T/Q Systems Inc..........E.......949 455-0478
25131 Arctic Ocean Dr Lake Forest (92630) ***(P-8810)***
T2c Inc..........F.......213 741-5232
1348 S Flower St Los Angeles (90015) ***(P-2867)***
T3 Micro Inc (PA)..........**F.......310 452-2888**
228 Main St Ste 3 Venice (90291) ***(P-11770)***
T3 Motion Inc..........E.......951 737-7300
425 Klug Cir Corona (92878) ***(P-10503)***
T3 Motion Inc..........E.......909 737-7300
425 Klug Cir Corona (92878) ***(P-10504)***
Ta Aerospace Co (HQ)..........**C.......661 775-1100**
28065 Franklin Pkwy Valencia (91355) ***(P-5414)***
Ta Aerospace Co..........C.......661 702-0448
28065 Franklin Pkwy Valencia (91355) ***(P-4721)***
Ta Chen International Inc (HQ)..........**C.......562 808-8000**
5855 Obispo Ave Long Beach (90805) ***(P-13599)***
Ta Division, Valencia *Also called Ta Aerospace Co* ***(P-4721)***
TA Industries Inc (HQ)..........**D.......562 466-1000**
11130 Bloomfield Ave Santa Fe Springs (90670) ***(P-13837)***
Taad Group Inc (HQ)..........**F.......213 545-0009**
1601 Perrino Pl Ste B Los Angeles (90023) ***(P-2868)***
Tabc Inc (HQ)..........**A.......562 984-3305**
6375 N Paramount Blvd Long Beach (90805) ***(P-10139)***
Taber Company Inc..........D.......714 543-7100
1442 Ritchey St Santa Ana (92705) ***(P-3294)***
Tablas Creek Vineyard LLC..........F.......805 237-1231
9339 Adelaida Rd Paso Robles (93446) ***(P-2226)***
Tabletops Unlimited Inc (PA)..........**D.......310 549-6000**
23000 Avalon Blvd Carson (90745) ***(P-13187)***
Tacer, Van Nuys *Also called Town & Cntry Event Rentals Inc* ***(P-17379)***
Tachi Palace Casino Resort..........A.......559 924-7751
17225 Jersey Ave Lemoore (93245) ***(P-16751)***
Tackle Specialties Inc..........F.......310 538-0535
1245 W 132nd St Gardena (90247) ***(P-11452)***
Taco Bell Corp (HQ)..........**A.......949 863-4500**
1 Glen Bell Way Irvine (92618) ***(P-16219)***
Taco Works Inc..........E.......805 541-1556
3424 Sacramento Dr San Luis Obispo (93401) ***(P-2367)***
Tacori By B & T Jewelers, Glendale *Also called Tacori Enterprises* ***(P-14142)***
Tacori Enterprises..........D.......818 863-1536
1736 Gardena Ave Glendale (91204) ***(P-14142)***
Tactical Command Inds Inc (HQ)..........**E.......925 219-1097**
4700 E Airport Dr Ontario (91761) ***(P-9356)***
Tactical Communications Corp..........E.......805 987-4100
473 Post St Camarillo (93010) ***(P-9357)***
Tactical Micro Inc (HQ)..........**E.......714 547-1174**
1740 E Wilshire Ave Santa Ana (92705) ***(P-9921)***
Tactsquad, Corona *Also called Amwear USA Inc* ***(P-2740)***
Tad Group LLC..........C.......949 476-3601
5000 Birch St Ste 3000 Newport Beach (92660) ***(P-18403)***
Tad Pgs Inc..........A.......800 261-3779
12062 Valley View St # 108 Garden Grove (92845) ***(P-17517)***
Tad Pgs Inc..........A.......571 451-2428
10805 Holder St Ste 250 Cypress (90630) ***(P-17518)***
Tae Gwang Inc..........F.......323 233-2882
4922 S Figueroa St Los Angeles (90037) ***(P-11609)***
Tae Life Sciences Us LLC (HQ)..........**E.......949 830-2117**
19641 Da Vinci Foothill Ranch (92610) ***(P-11240)***
Tae Life Sciences Us LLC..........D.......949 344-6112
19571 Pauling Foothill Ranch (92610) ***(P-22865)***
Tae Technologies Inc (PA)..........**C.......949 830-2117**
19631 Pauling Foothill Ranch (92610) ***(P-22866)***
Taft Electric Company (PA)..........**B.......805 642-0121**
1694 Eastman Ave Ventura (93003) ***(P-1327)***
Taft Production Company..........D.......661 765-7194
950 Petroleum Club Rd Taft (93268) ***(P-384)***
Tag Rag, Los Angeles *Also called Fetish Group Inc* ***(P-2808)***
Tag Toys Inc..........D.......310 639-4566
1810 S Acacia Ave Compton (90220) ***(P-11771)***
Tag-It Pacific Inc..........D.......818 444-4100
21900 Burbank Blvd # 270 Woodland Hills (91367) ***(P-2680)***
Tagtime Usa Inc..........B.......323 587-1555
4601 District Blvd Vernon (90058) ***(P-3938)***
Tahiti Cabinets Inc..........D.......714 693-0618
5419 E La Palma Ave Anaheim (92807) ***(P-3742)***
Tahiti Trading Company, Riverside *Also called Tropical Functional Labs LLC* ***(P-1806)***
Tailbroom Media Grop, North Hollywood *Also called Pilgrim Operations LLC* ***(P-13348)***
Tailgate Printing Inc..........D.......714 966-3035
2930 S Fairview St Santa Ana (92704) ***(P-4431)***
Tait & Associates Inc..........E.......714 560-8222
2131 S Dupont Dr Anaheim (92806) ***(P-6759)***
Tait Environmental Svcs Inc (PA)..........**D.......714 560-8200**
701 Parkcenter Dr Santa Ana (92705) ***(P-1692)***
Tajen Graphics Inc..........E.......714 527-3122
2100 W Lincoln Ave Ste B Anaheim (92801) ***(P-4432)***
Tajima /Crl, Vernon *Also called Tajima USA Dissolving Corp* ***(P-6981)***
Tajima USA Dissolving Corp..........D.......323 588-1281
2503 E Vernon Ave Vernon (90058) ***(P-6981)***
Tajima USA Inc..........E.......310 604-8200
19925 S Susana Rd Compton (90221) ***(P-7912)***
Takagi-Ao Smith T W H Co LLC..........F.......949 770-7171
5 Whatney Irvine (92618) ***(P-9016)***
Takane USA Inc (HQ)..........**C.......310 212-1411**
369 Van Ness Way Ste 715 Torrance (90501) ***(P-11304)***
Take A Break Paper..........E.......323 333-7773
263 W Olive Ave 307 Burbank (91502) ***(P-4033)***
Takeda Pharmaceuticals..........F.......805 375-6700
1700 Rancho Conejo Blvd Thousand Oaks (91320) ***(P-4901)***
Takeda Thousand Oaks, Thousand Oaks *Also called Takeda Pharmaceuticals* ***(P-4901)***
Tako Tyko Sign & Lighting, Los Angeles *Also called Ruben & Leon Inc* ***(P-11588)***
Takuyo Corporation..........F.......310 782-6927
2958 Columbia St Torrance (90503) ***(P-4034)***
Takyo Tyco, Los Angeles *Also called Ruben & Leon Inc* ***(P-18955)***
Talbert Medical Center, Downey *Also called Davita Medical Management LLC* ***(P-21411)***
Talbert Medical Center, Santa Ana *Also called Davita Medical Management LLC* ***(P-21415)***
Talbert Medical Group, Long Beach *Also called Davita Medical Management LLC* ***(P-21412)***
Talbot Insurance & Fincl Svcs, Santa Barbara *Also called Caesar and Seider Insur Svcs* ***(P-15545)***
Talco Plastics Inc (PA)..........**D.......951 531-2000**
1000 W Rincon St Corona (92878) ***(P-12985)***
Talco Plastics Inc..........D.......562 630-1224
3270 E 70th St Long Beach (90805) ***(P-5834)***
Talega Golf Club, San Clemente *Also called Heritage Golf Group LLC* ***(P-19492)***
Talega Golf Club, San Clemente *Also called Won & Jay Inc* ***(P-19512)***
Talent & Acquisition LLC..........C.......213 742-1972
100 W Broadway Ste 650 Long Beach (90802) ***(P-17729)***
Talentscale Inc..........D.......760 458-7633
28693 Old Town Front St Temecula (92590) ***(P-10205)***
Talespin Reality Labs Inc (PA)..........**D.......323 452-6998**
600 Corporate Pointe # 1130 Culver City (90230) ***(P-17730)***
Talimar Systems Inc..........E.......714 557-4884
3105 W Alpine St Santa Ana (92704) ***(P-3633)***
Talins Inc..........F.......310 378-3715
17800 S Main St Ste 121 Gardena (90248) ***(P-6927)***
Tall Mouse Arts & Crafts Inc..........D.......714 693-4900
13233 South St Cerritos (90703) ***(P-14102)***
Talladium Inc (PA)..........**E.......661 295-0900**
27360 Muirfield Ln Valencia (91355) ***(P-11198)***
Talley & Associates, Santa Fe Springs *Also called Talley Inc* ***(P-13779)***
Talley Farms..........C.......805 489-2508
2900 Lopez Dr Arroyo Grande (93420) ***(P-190)***
Talley Inc (PA)..........**C.......562 906-8000**
12976 Sandoval St Santa Fe Springs (90670) ***(P-13779)***
Talley Metal Fabrication, San Jacinto *Also called J Talley Corporation* ***(P-6964)***
Talley Vineyards..........F.......805 489-0446
3031 Lopez Dr Arroyo Grande (93420) ***(P-2227)***
Talon International Inc (PA)..........**C.......818 444-4100**
21900 Burbank Blvd # 101 Woodland Hills (91367) ***(P-14322)***
Talon Therapeutics Inc..........D.......949 788-6700
157 Technology Dr Irvine (92618) ***(P-4902)***
Talsco, Garden Grove *Also called Jvr Sheetmetal Fabrication Inc* ***(P-10132)***

Talyarps Corporation ....E....310 559-2335
3465 S La Cienega Blvd Los Angeles (90016) ***(P-5115)***
Tam O'Shanter Inn, Los Angeles *Also called Lawrys Restaurants II Inc* ***(P-16962)***
Tam Printing Inc ....F....714 224-4488
2961 E White Star Ave Anaheim (92806) ***(P-4433)***
Tama Trading Company ....D....213 748-8262
1920 E 20th St Vernon (90058) ***(P-14742)***
Tamco (HQ) ....**B....909 899-0660**
12459 Arrow Rte Rancho Cucamonga (91739) ***(P-6215)***
Tammy Taylor Nails Inc ....E....949 250-9287
2001 E Deere Ave Santa Ana (92705) ***(P-4722)***
Tampico Spice Co Incorporated ....E....323 235-3154
5901 S Central Ave 5941 Los Angeles (90001) ***(P-2532)***
Tampico Spice Company, Los Angeles *Also called Tampico Spice Co Incorporated* ***(P-2532)***
Tamshell Corp ....D....951 272-9395
237 Glider Cir Corona (92878) ***(P-5835)***
Tan Set Corporation ....F....805 967-4567
1 S Fairview Ave Goleta (93117) ***(P-6667)***
Tanaka Farms ....D....949 653-2100
5380 University Dr Irvine (92612) ***(P-14743)***
Tandem Care Plg A Pub Bneft Co ....D....310 281-0028
1925 Century Park E # 1700 Los Angeles (90067) ***(P-21220)***
Tandem Design Inc ....E....714 978-7272
1846 W Sequoia Ave Orange (92868) ***(P-11772)***
Tandem Exhibit, Orange *Also called Tandem Design Inc* ***(P-11772)***
Tandex Test Labs Inc ....E....626 962-7166
15849 Business Center Dr Irwindale (91706) ***(P-22959)***
Tanimura Antle Fresh Foods Inc ....B....831 424-6100
4401 Foxdale St Baldwin Park (91706) ***(P-191)***
Tanimura Antle Fresh Foods Inc ....C....805 483-2358
761 Commercial Ave Oxnard (93030) ***(P-12250)***
Tanz Publishing Inc (PA) ....**E....949 231-2290**
94 Seton Rd Irvine (92612) ***(P-4211)***
Taotao Manufacturer Inc (PA) ....**E....626 688-9880**
9833 Garibaldi Ave Temple City (91780) ***(P-11773)***
Taotao Manufacturer Inc ....F....626 688-9880
9073 Arcadia Ave San Gabriel (91775) ***(P-11774)***
Tap Worldwide LLC (HQ) ....**A....310 900-5500**
400 W Artesia Blvd Compton (90220) ***(P-13098)***
Tapatio Foods LLC ....F....323 587-8933
4685 District Blvd Vernon (90058) ***(P-1877)***
Tapatio Hot Sauce, Vernon *Also called Tapatio Foods LLC* ***(P-1877)***
Tape and Label Converters Inc ....E....562 945-3486
8231 Allport Ave Santa Fe Springs (90670) ***(P-3876)***
Tape Specialty Inc ....E....661 702-9030
24831 Avenue Tibbitts Valencia (91355) ***(P-13780)***
Tapia Brothers Co, Maywood *Also called Tapia Enterprises Inc* ***(P-14515)***
Tapia Enterprises Inc (PA) ....**D....323 560-7415**
6067 District Blvd Maywood (90270) ***(P-14515)***
Tara, Lomita *Also called Torrance Amateur Rdo Assn Inc* ***(P-22465)***
Tara Enterprises Inc ....F....661 510-2206
27023 Mack Bean Pkwy Valencia (91355) ***(P-3340)***
Tarazi Specialty Foods LLC ....F....909 628-3601
13727 Seminole Dr Chino (91710) ***(P-2533)***
Tarbell Financial Corporation (PA) ....**D....714 972-0988**
1403 N Tustin Ave Ste 380 Santa Ana (92705) ***(P-15256)***
Tarbell Realtors, Anaheim *Also called F M Tarbell Co* ***(P-15850)***
Tarbell Realtors, Santa Ana *Also called F M Tarbell Co* ***(P-15851)***
Tarbell Realtors, Palm Desert *Also called F M Tarbell Co* ***(P-15852)***
Target Corporation ....C....909 937-5500
1505 S Haven Ave Ontario (91761) ***(P-12251)***
Target Mdia Prtners Intractive, North Hollywood *Also called Target Mdia Prtners Intrctive* ***(P-4579)***
Target Mdia Prtners Intrctive (HQ) ....**F....323 930-3123**
5200 Lankershim Blvd # 35 North Hollywood (91601) ***(P-4579)***
Target Media Partners Oper LLC ....F....323 930-3123
5900 Wilshire Blvd # 550 Los Angeles (90036) ***(P-4035)***
Target Specialty Products, Santa Fe Springs *Also called Rentokil North America Inc* ***(P-14867)***
Target Specialty Products, Santa Fe Springs *Also called Western Exterminator Company* ***(P-17206)***
Target Technology Company LLC ....E....949 788-0909
564 Wald Irvine (92618) ***(P-9840)***
Targeted Medical Pharma Inc (PA) ....**E....310 474-9809**
2980 N Beverly Glen Cir # 301 Los Angeles (90077) ***(P-4903)***
Targus International LLC (PA) ....**C....714 765-5555**
1211 N Miller St Anaheim (92806) ***(P-14977)***
Targus US LLC ....E....714 765-5555
1211 N Miller St Anaheim (92806) ***(P-5897)***
Tarlow R Antiques, West Hollywood *Also called Rose K Tarlow Antiques Ltd* ***(P-14179)***
Tarpin Corporation ....E....714 891-6944
5361 Business Dr Huntington Beach (92649) ***(P-7836)***
Tarrant Apparel Group, Los Angeles *Also called C M G Inc* ***(P-2928)***
Tarsadia Hotels, Newport Beach *Also called Uka LLC* ***(P-16761)***
Tarsco Holdings LLC ....C....562 869-0200
11905 Regentview Ave Downey (90241) ***(P-19073)***
Tartan Fashion Inc ....E....626 575-2828
4357 Rowland Ave El Monte (91731) ***(P-2828)***
Tarzana Treatment Centers Inc ....D....818 654-3815
320 E Palmdale Blvd Palmdale (93550) ***(P-21347)***
Tarzana Treatment Centers Inc (PA) ....**C....818 996-1051**
18646 Oxnard St Tarzana (91356) ***(P-21348)***
Tarzana Treatment Centers Inc ....D....562 428-4111
5190 Atlantic Ave Lakewood (90805) ***(P-21349)***
Tarzana Treatment Centers Inc ....D....562 218-1868
2101 Magnolia Ave Long Beach (90806) ***(P-21350)***
Tarzana Treatment Centers Inc ....D....661 726-2630
44447 10th St W Lancaster (93534) ***(P-21351)***
Tarzana Treatment Ctr, Lancaster *Also called Tarzana Treatment Centers Inc* ***(P-21351)***
Tarzana Trtmnt Ctrs LNG Bch O, Lakewood *Also called Tarzana Treatment Centers Inc* ***(P-21349)***
Taschen America LLC (PA) ....**F....323 463-4441**
6121 W Sunset Blvd Los Angeles (90028) ***(P-4138)***
Taseon Inc ....F....408 240-7800
515 S Flower St Fl 25 Los Angeles (90071) ***(P-10773)***
Task Force For Reg Autostaff, Monrovia *Also called Trap* ***(P-18695)***
Tasker Metal Products ....F....213 765-5400
1823 S Hope St Los Angeles (90015) ***(P-10140)***
Taslimi Construction Co Inc ....D....310 447-3000
1805 Colorado Ave Santa Monica (90404) ***(P-836)***
Taste Nirvana International, Corona *Also called PSW Inc* ***(P-2511)***
Tasteful Selections LLC ....C....661 588-1053
13003 Di Giorgio Rd Arvin (93203) ***(P-14744)***
Tattooed Chef Inc (PA) ....**D....562 602-0822**
6305 Alondra Blvd Paramount (90723) ***(P-2534)***
Tatung Company America Inc (HQ) ....**D....310 637-2105**
2850 E El Presidio St Long Beach (90810) ***(P-9321)***
Tavistock Restaurants LLC ....C....714 939-8686
20 City Blvd W Ste R1 Orange (92868) ***(P-2156)***
Tawa Services Inc (PA) ....**C....714 521-8899**
6338 Regio Ave Buena Park (90620) ***(P-14745)***
Tawa Supermarket Inc (PA) ....**D....714 521-8899**
6281 Regio Ave Buena Park (90620) ***(P-1940)***
Tax and Financial Group, Newport Beach *Also called R Mc Closkey Insurance Agency* ***(P-15620)***
Tax Credit Co LLC (PA) ....**D....323 927-0752**
6121 W Sunset Blvd Fl 2 Los Angeles (90028) ***(P-16940)***
Tax Problem Center, Los Angeles *Also called Authority Tax Services LLC* ***(P-18452)***
Tay Ho, Santa Ana *Also called West Lake Food Corporation* ***(P-1725)***
Tay Ho Food Corporation ....F....714 973-2286
2430 Cape Cod Way Santa Ana (92703) ***(P-1857)***
Tayco Engineering Inc ....C....714 952-2240
10874 Hope St Cypress (90630) ***(P-10521)***
Taylor & Assoc Architects Inc (PA) ....**D....949 574-1325**
17850 Fitch Irvine (92614) ***(P-22748)***
Taylor Communications Inc ....F....951 203-9011
8972 Cuyamaca St Corona (92883) ***(P-4600)***
Taylor Communications Inc ....F....714 708-2005
535 Anton Blvd Ste 530 Costa Mesa (92626) ***(P-4601)***
Taylor Communications Inc ....F....714 664-8865
400 N Tustin Ave Ste 275 Santa Ana (92705) ***(P-4602)***
Taylor Design, Irvine *Also called Taylor & Assoc Architects Inc* ***(P-22748)***
Taylor Graphics Inc ....E....949 752-5200
1582 Browning Irvine (92606) ***(P-4580)***
Taylor Morrison California LLC ....D....949 341-1200
100 Spectrum Center Dr # 1450 Irvine (92618) ***(P-16075)***
Taylor Morse Ltd ....E....949 707-5031
23422 Mill Creek Dr # 135 Laguna Hills (92653) ***(P-17155)***
Taylor Print Vsual Imprssons I ....E....909 357-0661
4100 E Jurupa Ave Ste 106 Ontario (91761) ***(P-14199)***
Taylor Technology Services Inc ....C....714 986-1559
3230 E Imperial Hwy # 302 Brea (92821) ***(P-4581)***
Taylor-Dunn Manufacturing Co (HQ) ....**D....714 956-4040**
2114 W Ball Rd Anaheim (92804) ***(P-7719)***
Taylored Services LLC (HQ) ....**D....909 510-4800**
1495 E Locust St Ontario (91761) ***(P-12252)***
Taylored Services Holdings LLC (HQ) ....**D....909 510-4800**
1495 E Locust St Ontario (91761) ***(P-12253)***
Taylored Svcs Parent Co Inc (PA) ....**D....909 510-4800**
1495 E Locust St Ontario (91761) ***(P-12536)***
Taylors Appliance ....E....951 683-6365
6140 Magnolia Ave Riverside (92506) ***(P-19074)***
TBG Insurance Services Corp ....C....310 203-8770
100 N Pacific Coast Hwy # 500 El Segundo (90245) ***(P-15633)***
Tbs, Huntington Beach *Also called Transprttion Brkg Spclists Inc* ***(P-12001)***
TBS Contracting Inc ....D....714 894-2206
13602 Milton Ave Westminster (92683) ***(P-922)***
Tbwa Chiat/Day Inc ....B....310 305-5000
5353 Grosvenor Blvd Los Angeles (90066) ***(P-18685)***
Tbwa Worldwide Inc ....C....310 305-4400
1017 16th St Apt C Santa Monica (90403) ***(P-17060)***
Tbyci LLC ....F....805 985-6800
3615 Victoria Ave Oxnard (93035) ***(P-10472)***
Tc Cosmotronic Inc ....D....949 660-0740
4663 E Guasti Rd Ste A Ontario (91761) ***(P-9458)***
Tca Architects Inc (PA) ....**D....949 862-0270**
18821 Bardeen Ave Irvine (92612) ***(P-22749)***
Tca Precision Products LLC ....F....714 257-4850
1130 Columbia St Brea (92821) ***(P-10427)***
Tccsc, Los Angeles *Also called Tessie Clvland Cmnty Svcs Corp* ***(P-21901)***
Tcg Capital Management LP ....C....310 633-2900
12180 Millennium Ste 500 Playa Vista (90094) ***(P-16295)***
Tcg Software Services Inc ....B....714 665-6200
320 Commerce Ste 200 Irvine (92602) ***(P-17731)***
TCI Engineering Inc ....D....909 984-1773
1416 Brooks St Ontario (91762) ***(P-9967)***
TCI Supply Inc ....E....213 745-7756
121 E 18th St Los Angeles (90015) ***(P-17289)***
TCI Transportation Services (PA) ....**B....323 269-3033**
4950 Triggs St Commerce (90022) ***(P-12080)***
Tcj Manufacturing LLC ....E....213 488-8400
2744 E 11th St Los Angeles (90023) ***(P-3000)***
Tck USA Corporation ....F....323 269-2969
2580 Corp Pl Ste F101 Monterey Park (91754) ***(P-5198)***
TCS, Chatsworth *Also called Telemtry Cmmnctons Systems Inc* ***(P-9322)***
Tcsc, Irvine *Also called Traffic Control & Safety Corp* ***(P-13954)***

ALPHABETIC

Tct Advanced Machining Inc ....F....714 871-9371
2454 Fender Ave Ste C Fullerton (92831) ***(P-8811)***
Tct Circuit Supply Inc ....D....714 644-9700
560 S Melrose St Placentia (92870) ***(P-14022)***
Tct Mobile Inc ....D....949 892-2990
25 Edelman Ste 200 Irvine (92618) ***(P-23121)***
Tcw Absolute Return Credit LLC ....D....213 244-0000
865 S Figueroa St # 2100 Los Angeles (90017) ***(P-16146)***
Tcw Group Inc (PA) ....**B....213 244-0000**
865 S Figueroa St # 1800 Los Angeles (90017) ***(P-15350)***
Tcw Trends Inc ....E....310 533-5177
2886 Columbia St Torrance (90503) ***(P-3001)***
Td Industries ....E....949 939-3685
3 Ironwood Cir Trabuco Canyon (92679) ***(P-11775)***
Tda Magnetics LLC ....F....424 213-1585
1175 W Victoria St Rancho Dominguez (90220) ***(P-7572)***
Tdg Operations LLC ....D....559 781-4116
600 S E St Porterville (93257) ***(P-2702)***
Tdg Operations LLC ....E....323 724-9000
340 S Avenue 17 Los Angeles (90031) ***(P-2698)***
Tdg Operations LLC ....E....323 724-9000
6433 Gayhart St Commerce (90040) ***(P-2699)***
Tdi Signs ....E....562 436-5188
13158 Arctic Cir Santa Fe Springs (90670) ***(P-11610)***
Tdi2 Custom Packaging Inc ....F....714 751-6782
17391 Mount Cliffwood Cir Fountain Valley (92708) ***(P-3892)***
Teac America Inc (HQ) ....**E....323 726-0303**
10410 Pioneer Blvd Ste 1 Santa Fe Springs (90670) ***(P-13445)***
Teacher Created Materials Inc ....C....714 891-2273
5301 Oceanus Dr Huntington Beach (92649) ***(P-4212)***
Teacher Created Resources Inc ....D....714 230-7060
12621 Western Ave Garden Grove (92841) ***(P-4213)***
Teacherzone Inc ....F....855 970-9663
31899 Del Obispo St San Juan Capistrano (92675) ***(P-17992)***
Teague Custom Marine Inc ....E....661 295-7000
28115 Avenue Stanford Valencia (91355) ***(P-19075)***
Tealove Inc ....E....714 408-8245
9810 Sierra Ave Ste A Fontana (92335) ***(P-2535)***
Team Inc ....E....310 514-2312
1515 240th St Harbor City (90710) ***(P-6454)***
Team Air Inc (PA) ....**E....909 823-1957**
12771 Brown Ave Riverside (92509) ***(P-8349)***
Team Air Conditioning Eqp, Riverside *Also called Team Air Inc* ***(P-8349)***
Team Companies LLC (PA) ....**D....818 558-3261**
901 W Alameda Ave Ste 100 Burbank (91506) ***(P-22816)***
Team Dykspra (PA) ....**D....951 898-6482**
2315 California Ave Corona (92881) ***(P-18917)***
Team Fashion ....F....323 589-3388
2303 E 55th St Vernon (90058) ***(P-2869)***
Team Finish Inc ....D....714 671-9190
155 Arovista Cir Ste A Brea (92821) ***(P-1555)***
Team Garage LLC ....D....714 913-9900
3200 Bristol St Ste 300 Costa Mesa (92626) ***(P-17061)***
Team Group LLC ....D....951 688-8593
4076 Flat Rock Dr Riverside (92505) ***(P-23122)***
Team Industrial Services, Harbor City *Also called Team Inc* ***(P-6454)***
Team Makena LLC (PA) ....**D....949 474-1753**
27051 Towne Centre Dr # 180 Foothill Ranch (92610) ***(P-13523)***
Team Manufacturing Inc ....E....310 639-0251
2625 Homestead Pl Rancho Dominguez (90220) ***(P-7185)***
Team One, Encino *Also called Team-One Emplyment Spclsts LLC* ***(P-17471)***
Team Post-Op Inc ....C....949 253-5500
17256 Red Hill Ave Irvine (92614) ***(P-13524)***
Team Services, Burbank *Also called Team Companies LLC* ***(P-22816)***
Team USA (PA) ....**F....323 826-9888**
2154 E 51st St Vernon (90058) ***(P-9968)***
Team West Contracting Corp ....D....951 340-3426
2733 S Vista Ave Bloomington (92316) ***(P-1693)***
Team-One Emplyment Spclsts LLC ....D....310 481-4480
15720 Ventura Blvd # 607 Encino (91436) ***(P-17471)***
Team-One Staffing Services Inc ....A....951 616-3515
15720 Ventura Blvd # 607 Encino (91436) ***(P-17472)***
Teaman Ramirez & Smith Inc ....D....951 274-9500
4201 Brockton Ave Ste 100 Riverside (92501) ***(P-22817)***
Teamone Employment, Encino *Also called Team-One Staffing Services Inc* ***(P-17472)***
Teaonic, Van Nuys *Also called Happy Cells Inc* ***(P-2268)***
TEC, Compton *Also called Thermal Equipment Corporation* ***(P-6760)***
TEC Color Craft (PA) ....**E....909 392-9000**
1860 Wright Ave La Verne (91750) ***(P-4434)***
TEC Color Craft Products, La Verne *Also called TEC Color Craft* ***(P-4434)***
TEC Lighting Inc ....F....714 529-5068
115 Arovista Cir Brea (92821) ***(P-9149)***
Tecan Sp Inc ....D....626 962-0010
14180 Live Oak Ave Baldwin Park (91706) ***(P-13542)***
Tecfar Manufacturing Inc ....F....818 767-0677
8525 Telfair Ave Sun Valley (91352) ***(P-8812)***
Tech Electronic Systems Inc ....E....909 986-4395
404 S Euclid Ave Ontario (91762) ***(P-9790)***
Tech Knowledge Associates LLC ....D....714 735-3810
1 Centerpointe Dr Ste 200 La Palma (90623) ***(P-19076)***
Tech Powers, Santa Fe Springs *Also called Turbine Eng Cmpnents Tech Corp* ***(P-7108)***
Tech Systems Inc ....B....714 523-5404
7372 Walnut Ave Ste J Buena Park (90620) ***(P-13781)***
Tech Town Inc ....E....818 621-2744
1157 N Brand Blvd Glendale (91202) ***(P-17732)***
Techflex Packaging LLC ....D....424 266-9400
13771 Gramercy Pl Gardena (90249) ***(P-14978)***
Techmer Pm Inc ....B....310 632-9211
18420 S Laurel Park Rd Compton (90220) ***(P-4723)***
Techncolor Crative Svcs USA Inc (HQ) ....**B....818 260-3800**
6040 W Sunset Blvd Los Angeles (90028) ***(P-19248)***
Techncolor Crative Svcs USA Inc ....E....323 467-1244
8921 Lindblade St Culver City (90232) ***(P-19249)***
Techncolor Vdocassette Mich Inc (HQ) ....**B....805 445-1122**
3233 Mission Oaks Blvd Camarillo (93012) ***(P-19250)***
Techni-Cast Corp ....D....562 923-4585
11220 Garfield Ave South Gate (90280) ***(P-6423)***
Technic Inc ....E....714 632-0200
1170 N Hawk Cir Anaheim (92807) ***(P-7321)***
Technical America Inc ....D....951 272-9540
301 N Smith Ave Corona (92878) ***(P-22665)***
Technical Devices, Torrance *Also called Winther Technologies Inc* ***(P-7897)***
Technical Devices Company ....E....310 618-8437
560 Alaska Ave Torrance (90503) ***(P-7896)***
Technical Film Systems Inc ....F....805 384-9470
4725 Calle Quetzal Ste A Camarillo (93012) ***(P-11293)***
Technical Heaters Inc ....F....818 361-7185
10959 Tuxford St Sun Valley (91352) ***(P-5323)***
Technical Manufacturing W LLC ....E....661 295-7226
24820 Avenue Tibbitts Valencia (91355) ***(P-11776)***
Technical Micro Cons Inc (PA) ....**E....310 559-3982**
807 N Park View Dr # 150 El Segundo (90245) ***(P-23339)***
Technical Resource Industries (PA) ....**E....909 446-1109**
12854 Daisy Ct Yucaipa (92399) ***(P-9048)***
Technical Screen Printing Inc ....F....714 541-8590
677 N Hariton St Orange (92868) ***(P-4582)***
Technical Services, San Bernardino *Also called Northrop Grumman Systems Corp* ***(P-10627)***
Technical Trouble Shooting Inc ....F....661 257-1202
27822 Fremont Ct B Valencia (91355) ***(P-8813)***
Technicolor Inc ....B....818 260-4577
2255 N Ontario St Ste 180 Burbank (91504) ***(P-18421)***
Technicolor Connected USA, Lebec *Also called Technicolor Usa Inc* ***(P-9199)***
Technicolor Content Services, Glendale *Also called Technicolor Usa Inc* ***(P-9201)***
Technicolor Disc Services Corp (HQ) ....**C....805 445-1122**
3233 Mission Oaks Blvd Camarillo (93012) ***(P-9841)***
Technicolor HM Entrmt Svcs Inc (HQ) ....**B....805 445-1122**
3233 Mission Oaks Blvd Camarillo (93012) ***(P-19251)***
Technicolor Lab, Burbank *Also called Technicolor Inc* ***(P-18421)***
Technicolor Usa Inc ....A....661 496-1309
4049 Industrial Pkwy Dr Lebec (93243) ***(P-9199)***
Technicolor Usa Inc ....C....818 500-9090
1507 Railroad St Glendale (91204) ***(P-9200)***
Technicolor Usa Inc ....C....818 260-3651
440 W Los Feliz Rd Glendale (91204) ***(P-9201)***
Technicolor Video Service, Camarillo *Also called Techncolor Vdocassette Mich Inc* ***(P-19250)***
Technicolor Video Services, Camarillo *Also called Technicolor HM Entrmt Svcs Inc* ***(P-19251)***
Technicon Design Corporation ....D....949 218-1300
26522 La Alameda Ste 150 Mission Viejo (92691) ***(P-18686)***
Technicote Inc ....E....951 372-0627
1141 California Ave Corona (92881) ***(P-5199)***
Technifex Products LLC ....E....661 294-3800
25261 Rye Canyon Rd Valencia (91355) ***(P-6159)***
Techniform International Corp ....C....909 877-6886
375 S Cactus Ave Rialto (92376) ***(P-8814)***
Technip Stone Wbster Prcess Te ....D....909 447-3600
555 W Arrow Hwy Claremont (91711) ***(P-22666)***
Technique Designs Inc ....F....760 904-6223
63665 19th Ave North Palm Springs (92258) ***(P-3668)***
Techno Coatings Inc ....D....714 774-4671
785 E Debra Ln Anaheim (92805) ***(P-837)***
Techno Coatings Inc ....D....714 774-4671
795 Debra St Anaheim (92805) ***(P-838)***
Technologent, Irvine *Also called Thomas Gallaway Corporation* ***(P-17734)***
Technology Management Concepts, El Segundo *Also called Technical Micro Cons Inc* ***(P-23339)***
Technology Resource Center Inc (PA) ....**D....714 542-1004**
2101 E 4th St Ste 130a Santa Ana (92705) ***(P-18226)***
Technology Training Corp (PA) ....**F....310 320-8110**
369 Van Ness Way Ste 735 Torrance (90501) ***(P-18687)***
Technology Training Corp ....D....310 644-7777
3238 W 131st St Hawthorne (90250) ***(P-4435)***
Technosocialworkcom LLC ....D....661 617-6601
4300 Resnik Ct Unit 103 Bakersfield (93313) ***(P-18113)***
Technotronix Inc ....E....714 630-9200
1381 N Hundley St Anaheim (92806) ***(P-9459)***
Techture Inc ....E....323 347-6209
1010 Wilshire Blvd # 120 Los Angeles (90017) ***(P-4214)***
Techvalve Industries LLC ....F....714 264-7950
21061 Morningside Dr Trabuco Canyon (92679) ***(P-11777)***
Tecno Industrial Engrg Inc ....E....562 623-4517
13528 Pumice St Norwalk (90650) ***(P-8815)***
Teco Diagnostics ....D....714 693-7788
1268 N Lakeview Ave Anaheim (92807) ***(P-4927)***
Tecolote Research Inc ....D....310 640-4700
2120 E Grand Ave Ste 200 El Segundo (90245) ***(P-23340)***
Tecolote Research Inc ....D....805 964-6963
5266 Hollister Ave # 301 Santa Barbara (93111) ***(P-23341)***
Tecolote Research Inc ....D....805 964-6963
5383 Hollister Ave # 100 Santa Barbara (93111) ***(P-23342)***
Tecomet Inc ....B....626 334-1519
503 S Vincent Ave Azusa (91702) ***(P-11062)***
Tecon Pacific, Fontana *Also called Clark - Pacific Corporation* ***(P-6024)***
Tecta America Southern Cal Inc ....D....714 973-6233
1217 E Wakeham Ave Santa Ana (92705) ***(P-1506)***
Ted Ford Jones Inc (PA) ....**C....714 521-3110**
6211 Beach Blvd Buena Park (90621) ***(P-18878)***
Ted Levine Drum Co (PA) ....**D....626 579-1084**
1817 Chico Ave South El Monte (91733) ***(P-19077)***

Ted Rieck Enterprises Inc ....F....714 542-4763
1228 S Wright St Santa Ana (92705) ***(P-6928)***
Tee -N -Jay Manufacturing Inc ....E....818 504-2961
9145 Glenoaks Blvd Sun Valley (91352) ***(P-6929)***
Tee Top of California Inc (PA) ....**E....626 303-1868**
11801 Goldring Rd Arcadia (91006) ***(P-14354)***
Teen Bell, Los Angeles *Also called Touch ME Fashion Inc* ***(P-3005)***
Tehachapi News Inc (PA) ....**F....661 822-6828**
411 N Mill St Tehachapi (93561) ***(P-4036)***
Tei Struthers Wells, Santa Fe Springs *Also called Wells Struthers Corporation* ***(P-6767)***
Teichman Enterprises Inc ....E....323 278-9000
6100 Bandini Blvd Commerce (90040) ***(P-3698)***
Teixeira Farms Desert Inc ....D....805 928-3801
2600 Bonita Lateral Rd Santa Maria (93458) ***(P-20)***
Tejon Ranch Co (PA) ....**C....661 248-3000**
4436 Lebec Rd Lebec (93243) ***(P-58)***
Tek Enterprises Inc ....F....818 785-5971
7730 Airport Bus Pkwy Van Nuys (91406) ***(P-9791)***
Tekia Inc ....E....949 699-1300
17 Hammond Ste 414 Irvine (92618) ***(P-11265)***
Teklam Corporation, Corona *Also called B/E Aerospace Inc* ***(P-10286)***
Teklink Security Inc ....F....909 230-6668
4601 E Airport Dr Ontario (91761) ***(P-9922)***
Teknor Apex, City of Industry *Also called Teknor Color Company* ***(P-4724)***
Teknor Color Company ....F....626 336-7709
420 S 6th Ave City of Industry (91746) ***(P-4724)***
Teksun Inc ....F....310 479-0794
1549 N Poinsettia Pl # 1 Los Angeles (90046) ***(P-5836)***
Tektest Inc ....E....626 446-6175
225 N 2nd Ave Arcadia (91006) ***(P-9665)***
Tekworks Inc ....D....877 835-9675
12742 Knott St Garden Grove (92841) ***(P-12673)***
Telacu, Commerce *Also called East Los Angeles Community Un* ***(P-15152)***
Telacu Construction MGT Inc ....E....714 541-2390
604 N Eckhoff St Orange (92868) ***(P-23123)***
Telacu Industries Inc (HQ) ....**E....323 721-1655**
5400 E Olympic Blvd # 300 Commerce (90022) ***(P-16076)***
Telatemp Corporation ....E....714 414-0343
2910 E La Palma Ave Ste C Anaheim (92806) ***(P-10915)***
Telco Food, Colton *Also called HC Brill* ***(P-2077)***
Telecare Act 7 ....D....562 929-6688
12440 Firestone Blvd # 30 Norwalk (90650) ***(P-21352)***
Telecare Corporation ....C....562 630-8672
6060 N Paramount Blvd Long Beach (90805) ***(P-21353)***
Telecom Lease Advisors LLC (HQ) ....**E....877 418-5238**
4640 Admiralty Way # 1030 Marina Del Rey (90292) ***(P-23343)***
Telecommunication, Beverly Hills *Also called Nga 911 LLC* ***(P-17676)***
Teledyne Analytical Instrs, City of Industry *Also called Teledyne Instruments Inc* ***(P-10728)***
Teledyne Battery Products, Redlands *Also called Teledyne Technologies Inc* ***(P-9814)***
Teledyne Controls, El Segundo *Also called Teledyne Technologies Inc* ***(P-9793)***
Teledyne Controls LLC ....A....310 765-3600
501 Continental Blvd El Segundo (90245) ***(P-10644)***
Teledyne Defense Elec LLC ....C....310 823-5491
1001 Knox St Torrance (90502) ***(P-9792)***
Teledyne Instruments Inc ....C....626 934-1500
16830 Chestnut St City of Industry (91748) ***(P-10728)***
Teledyne Instruments Inc ....E....818 882-7266
9810 Variel Ave Chatsworth (91311) ***(P-10816)***
Teledyne Redlake Masd LLC (HQ) ....**E....805 373-4545**
1049 Camino Dos Rios Thousand Oaks (91360) ***(P-10817)***
Teledyne Reson Inc ....E....805 964-6260
5212 Verdugo Way Camarillo (93012) ***(P-14066)***
Teledyne Reynolds, Torrance *Also called Teledyne Defense Elec LLC* ***(P-9792)***
Teledyne Scientific Imaging LLC ....D....805 373-4979
5212 Verdugo Way Camarillo (93012) ***(P-22867)***
Teledyne Scientific Imaging LLC (HQ) ....**C....805 373-4545**
1049 Camino Dos Rios Thousand Oaks (91360) ***(P-22868)***
Teledyne Scientific Company, Thousand Oaks *Also called Teledyne Scientific Imaging LLC* ***(P-22868)***
Teledyne Technologies Inc ....B....310 765-3600
501 Continental Blvd El Segundo (90245) ***(P-9793)***
Teledyne Technologies Inc (PA) ....**C....805 373-4545**
1049 Camino Dos Rios Thousand Oaks (91360) ***(P-9794)***
Teledyne Technologies Inc ....B....310 822-8229
12964 Panama St Los Angeles (90066) ***(P-9795)***
Teledyne Technologies Inc ....D....909 793-3131
840 W Brockton Ave Redlands (92374) ***(P-9814)***
Telemedicine Corp ....E....888 472-2853
8920 Wilshire Blvd # 310 Beverly Hills (90211) ***(P-21489)***
Telemetry Systems, Goleta *Also called Acroamatics Inc* ***(P-9248)***
Telemtry Cmmnctons Systems Inc ....E....818 718-6248
10020 Remmet Ave Chatsworth (91311) ***(P-9322)***
Telenet Voip Inc ....D....310 253-9000
850 N Park View Dr El Segundo (90245) ***(P-18958)***
Teleperformance, Pasadena *Also called Tpusa - Fhcs Inc* ***(P-18139)***
Teles Properties Inc (PA) ....**D....424 202-3200**
9470 Wilshire Blvd # 120 Beverly Hills (90212) ***(P-16014)***
Telescape, Los Angeles *Also called Truconnect Communications Inc* ***(P-12675)***
Telesector Resources Group Inc ....B....626 813-4538
5010 Azusa Canyon Rd Baldwin Park (91706) ***(P-23344)***
Telesign Holdings Inc (HQ) ....**E....310 740-9700**
13274 Fiji Way Ste 600 Marina Del Rey (90292) ***(P-17993)***
Telesis Community Credit Union (PA) ....**D....818 885-1226**
9301 Winnetka Ave Chatsworth (91311) ***(P-15092)***
Telestar International Corp ....E....909 598-3636
5536 Balboa Blvd Encino (91316) ***(P-23345)***
Telestar Material, Encino *Also called Telestar International Corp* ***(P-23345)***
Teletrac Inc (HQ) ....**B....714 897-0877**
310 Commerce Ste 100 Irvine (92602) ***(P-12790)***
Teletrac Navman US Ltd (HQ) ....**E....866 527-9896**
310 Commerce Ste 100 Irvine (92602) ***(P-10645)***
Teletronics Technology Corp ....E....661 273-7033
190 Sierra Ct Ste A3 Palmdale (93550) ***(P-10646)***
Television Games Network, Los Angeles *Also called Ods Technologies LP* ***(P-12736)***
Tell Steel Inc ....D....562 435-4826
2345 W 17th St Long Beach (90813) ***(P-13600)***
Temalpakh Inc ....D....760 770-5778
73750 Spyder Cir Palm Desert (92211) ***(P-839)***
Temblor Brewing LLC ....E....661 489-4855
3200 Buck Owens Blvd Bakersfield (93308) ***(P-2157)***
Temco, Laguna Beach *Also called C & B Delivery Services* ***(P-12186)***
Temco Logistics, Laguna Beach *Also called Home Express Delivery Svc LLC* ***(P-12470)***
Temecula 24 Hour Care, Temecula *Also called Responsible Med Solutions Corp* ***(P-20041)***
Temecula Hhg Hotel Dev LP ....C....951 331-3622
28400 Rancho Cal Rd Temecula (92590) ***(P-16752)***
Temecula Homecare, Temecula *Also called Maxim Healthcare Services Inc* ***(P-17501)***
Temecula Precision Mfg, Temecula *Also called Temecula Precison Fabrication* ***(P-8816)***
Temecula Precison Fabrication ....F....951 699-4066
42201 Sarah Way Temecula (92590) ***(P-8816)***
Temecula Quality Plating Inc ....E....951 296-9875
42147 Roick Dr Temecula (92590) ***(P-7322)***
Temecula Stadium Cinemas 15, Temecula *Also called Edwards Theatres Circuit Inc* ***(P-19277)***
Temecula T-Shirt Printers Inc ....F....951 296-0184
41607 Enterprise Cir N A Temecula (92590) ***(P-4583)***
Temecula Valley Drywall Inc ....D....951 600-1742
41228 Raintree Ct Murrieta (92562) ***(P-1405)***
Temecula Valley Unified School ....D....951 695-7110
40516 Roripaugh Rd Temecula (92591) ***(P-11941)***
Temecula Valley Winery MGT LLC ....D....951 699-8896
27495 Diaz Rd Temecula (92590) ***(P-2228)***
Temecula Vly Unified Schl Dst ....D....951 302-5140
33125 Regina Dr Temecula (92592) ***(P-22371)***
Temeka Advertising Inc ....D....951 277-2525
9073 Pulsar Ct Corona (92883) ***(P-3669)***
Temeka Group, Corona *Also called Temeka Advertising Inc* ***(P-3669)***
Temeku Hills, Temecula *Also called McMillin Communities Inc* ***(P-19499)***
Tempest Telecom Solutions LLC (PA) ....**D....805 879-4800**
136 W Canon Perdido St # 100 Santa Barbara (93101) ***(P-23516)***
Temple Israel of Hollywood (PA) ....**D....323 876-8330**
7300 Hollywood Blvd Los Angeles (90046) ***(P-16932)***
Temple Jdea of W San Frnndo Vl ....D....818 758-3800
5429 Lindley Ave Tarzana (91356) ***(P-22064)***
Temple Judea Nursery School, Tarzana *Also called Temple Jdea of W San Frnndo Vl* ***(P-22064)***
Temple Pk Cnvalescent Hosp Inc ....D....213 380-2035
2411 W Temple St Los Angeles (90026) ***(P-20631)***
Templeton Community Svc Dst ....D....805 434-4900
420 Crocker St Templeton (93465) ***(P-12921)***
Templeton Surgery Center LLC ....B....805 434-3550
1310 Las Tablas Rd # 104 Templeton (93465) ***(P-20103)***
Tempo Industries, Irvine *Also called Tempo Lighting Inc* ***(P-9106)***
Tempo Lighting Inc ....E....949 442-1601
1961 Mcgaw Ave Irvine (92614) ***(P-9106)***
Tempo Plastic Co ....F....559 651-7711
1227 N Miller Park Ct Visalia (93291) ***(P-5524)***
Temporary Staffing Union ....A....714 728-5186
19800 Macarthur Blvd Irvine (92612) ***(P-22302)***
Temps Plus Inc ....D....951 549-8309
268 N Lincoln Ave Ste 12 Corona (92882) ***(P-17473)***
Tempted Apparel Corp ....E....323 859-2480
4516 Loma Vista Ave Vernon (90058) ***(P-3002)***
Temptron Engineering Inc ....E....818 346-4900
7823 Deering Ave Canoga Park (91304) ***(P-10916)***
Tempus LLC ....D....800 917-5055
2041 Rosecrans Ave # 245 El Segundo (90245) ***(P-17474)***
Ten Days Manufacturing ....C....888 222-1575
458 Commercial Rd San Bernardino (92408) ***(P-14023)***
Ten Publishing Media LLC (PA) ....**C....310 531-9900**
831 S Douglas St Ste 100 El Segundo (90245) ***(P-19252)***
Ten-X Finance Inc ....C....949 465-8523
15295 Alton Pkwy Irvine (92618) ***(P-16015)***
Tencate Advanced Armor USA Inc (HQ) ....**D....805 845-4085**
120 Cremona Dr Ste 130 Goleta (93117) ***(P-7431)***
Tencate Performance Composite, Camarillo *Also called Performance Materials Corp* ***(P-4706)***
Tender Home Healthcare Inc ....D....323 466-2345
3550 Wilshire Blvd # 700 Los Angeles (90010) ***(P-21221)***
Tenenblatt Corporation ....D....323 232-2061
3750 Broadway Pl Los Angeles (90007) ***(P-2648)***
Tenet, La Quinta *Also called Desert Regional Med Ctr Inc* ***(P-20745)***
Tenet, Palm Springs *Also called Desert Regional Med Ctr Inc* ***(P-20746)***
Tenet, Palm Springs *Also called Desert Regional Med Ctr Inc* ***(P-20747)***
Tenet Health Systems Norris ....B....323 865-3000
1441 Eastlake Ave Los Angeles (90089) ***(P-20971)***
Tenet Healthsystem Medical Inc ....D....760 347-6191
47111 Monroe St Indio (92201) ***(P-21490)***
Tenet Healthsystem Medical Inc ....C....714 966-8191
13032 Earlham St Santa Ana (92705) ***(P-20972)***
Tenet Healthsystem Medical Inc ....D....562 531-2550
3700 South St Lakewood (90712) ***(P-20104)***
Tenet Healthsystem Medical Inc ....C....562 531-2550
16331 Arthur St Cerritos (90703) ***(P-20973)***
Tenet Healthsystem Medical Inc ....D....714 524-4820
1301 N Tustin Ave Santa Ana (92705) ***(P-20105)***

ALPHABETIC

Tenet Healthsystem Medical Inc ....C....714 428-6800
1400 S Duglaca Rd Ste 250 Anaheim (92806) ***(P-20974)***

Tenet Healthsystem Medical Inc ....D....805 546-7698
3751 Katella Ave Los Alamitos (90720) ***(P-20106)***

Tenet Healthsystem Medical Inc ....D....714 993-2000
1301 N Rose Dr Placentia (92870) ***(P-21055)***

Tenet Healthsystem Medical Inc ....D....562 493-9581
1661 Golden Rain Rd Seal Beach (90740) ***(P-20107)***

Tenex Health Inc ....D....949 454-7500
26902 Vista Ter Lake Forest (92630) ***(P-11063)***

Tennenbaum Capitl Partners LLC (HQ) ....**D....310 566-1000**
2951 28th St Ste 1000 Santa Monica (90405) ***(P-16296)***

Tennessee Hospitalists Inc ....D....888 447-2362
4605 Lankershim Blvd North Hollywood (91602) ***(P-20975)***

Tennis Channel Inc (HQ) ....**D....310 392-1920**
3003 Exposition Blvd Santa Monica (90404) ***(P-19333)***

Tentek Inc (PA) ....**C....818 551-7100**
101 N Brand Blvd Ste 1660 Glendale (91203) ***(P-18227)***

Teridian Semiconductor Corp (HQ) ....**D....714 508-8800**
6440 Oak Cyn Ste 100 Irvine (92618) ***(P-9589)***

Teridian Smicdtr Holdings Corp (HQ) ....**D....714 508-8800**
6440 Oak Cyn Ste 100 Irvine (92618) ***(P-9590)***

Terminal Freezers, Oxnard *Also called Fresh Innovations LLC* ***(P-2370)***

Termo Company ....E....562 595-7401
3275 Cherry Ave Long Beach (90807) ***(P-470)***

Terra Pacific Landscape (HQ) ....**D....714 567-0177**
12891 Nelson St Garden Grove (92840) ***(P-287)***

Terra Universal Inc ....C....714 526-0100
800 S Raymond Ave Fullerton (92831) ***(P-8056)***

Terrace View Care Center, Fullerton *Also called Sun Haven Care Inc* ***(P-20482)***

Terrace, The, Grand Terrace *Also called Emeritus Corporation* ***(P-20325)***

Terran Orbital Corporation (PA) ....**E....212 496-2300**
15330 Barranca Pkwy Irvine (92618) ***(P-10522)***

Terranea Resort, Rancho Palos Verdes *Also called Long Point Development LLC* ***(P-16545)***

Terravant Wine Company LLC (PA) ....**C....805 688-4245**
70 Industrial Way Buellton (93427) ***(P-2229)***

Terry Hines & Assoc, Burbank *Also called GL Nemirow Inc* ***(P-17015)***

Terry Hinge & Hardware, Van Nuys *Also called RPC Legacy Inc* ***(P-6534)***

Tesco Products ....E....661 257-0153
25601 Avenue Stanford Santa Clarita (91355) ***(P-7749)***

Teserra (PA) ....**B....760 340-9000**
86100 Avenue 54 Coachella (92236) ***(P-1694)***

Tesoro Refining & Mktg Co LLC ....D....951 461-3063
39224 Winchester Rd Murrieta (92563) ***(P-14809)***

Tesoro Refining & Mktg Co LLC ....D....562 728-2215
5905 N Paramount Blvd Long Beach (90805) ***(P-5261)***

Tesoro Refining & Mktg Co LLC ....D....877 837-6762
2101 E Pacific Coast Hwy Wilmington (90744) ***(P-14810)***

Tesoro Refining & Mktg Co LLC ....D....805 521-0615
3907 E Telegraph Rd Piru (93040) ***(P-14811)***

Tessa Mia Corp ....E....877 740-5757
9565 Vassar Ave Chatsworth (91311) ***(P-3341)***

Tessie Clvland Cmnty Svcs Corp ....D....323 586-7333
8019 Compton Ave Ste 219 Los Angeles (90001) ***(P-21901)***

Test-Rite Products Corp (HQ) ....**D....909 605-9899**
1900 Burgundy Pl Ontario (91761) ***(P-13188)***

Testan Law A Professional Corp (PA) ....**E....805 604-1816**
31330 Oak Crest Dr Westlake Village (91361) ***(P-21686)***

Testequity LLC (PA) ....**C....805 498-9933**
6100 Condor Dr Moorpark (93021) ***(P-18959)***

Testing Company LLC (PA) ....**C....714 379-0280**
12802 Valley View St Garden Grove (92845) ***(P-21098)***

Testmasters, Beverly Hills *Also called Robin Singh Eductl Svcs Inc* ***(P-23503)***

Testronic Inc ....C....818 845-3223
111 N First St Ste 204 Burbank (91502) ***(P-19253)***

Testronic Labs, Burbank *Also called Testronic Inc* ***(P-19253)***

Tetra Tech Inc (PA) ....**C....626 351-4664**
3475 E Foothill Blvd Pasadena (91107) ***(P-22667)***

Tetra Tech Inc ....D....949 263-0846
17885 Von Karman Ave # 500 Irvine (92614) ***(P-22668)***

Tetra Tech Bas Inc (HQ) ....**D....909 860-7777**
21700 Copley Dr Ste 200 Diamond Bar (91765) ***(P-22669)***

Tetra Tech Ec Inc ....D....949 809-5000
17885 Von Karman Ave # 500 Irvine (92614) ***(P-10818)***

Tetra Tech Executive Svcs Inc ....C....626 470-2400
3475 E Foothill Blvd Pasadena (91107) ***(P-17475)***

Tetra Tech Holding LLC (HQ) ....**B....626 351-4664**
3475 E Foothill Blvd Pasadena (91107) ***(P-22670)***

Tetra Tech International Inc (HQ) ....**D....626 351-4664**
3475 E Foothill Blvd Pasadena (91107) ***(P-22671)***

Tetra Tech Nus Inc ....C....412 921-7090
3475 E Foothill Blvd Pasadena (91107) ***(P-22672)***

Tetracam Inc ....F....818 718-2119
21601 Devonshire St # 310 Chatsworth (91311) ***(P-11294)***

Teutonic Holdings LLC (PA) ....**D....818 264-4400**
9221 Corbin Ave Ste 260 Northridge (91324) ***(P-12674)***

Teva Foods Inc ....E....323 267-8110
4401 S Downey Rd Vernon (90058) ***(P-2536)***

Teva Parenteral Medicines Inc ....A....949 455-4700
19 Hughes Irvine (92618) ***(P-4904)***

Tex Rhino Inc ....F....909 548-3910
15080 Hilton Dr Fontana (92336) ***(P-3829)***

Tex-Coat LLC ....E....323 233-3111
417 E Weber Ave Compton (90222) ***(P-5116)***

Texas Home Health America LP (PA) ....**D....972 201-3800**
1455 Auto Center Dr # 200 Ontario (91761) ***(P-21222)***

Texas Instruments Incorporated ....C....714 731-7110
14351 Myford Rd Tustin (92780) ***(P-9591)***

Texollini Inc ....C....310 537-3400
2575 E El Presidio St Long Beach (90810) ***(P-2710)***

Textile Products Inc ....E....714 761-0401
2512-2520 W Woodland Dr Anaheim (92801) ***(P-2605)***

Textile Unlimited Corporation (PA) ....**B....310 263-7400**
20917 Higgins Ct Torrance (90501) ***(P-2762)***

Textiles & Son LLC (PA) ....**E....323 965-9888**
1750 W Adams Blvd Los Angeles (90018) ***(P-2739)***

Texture Design, Anaheim *Also called Textured Design Furniture Inc* ***(P-3489)***

Textured Design Furniture Inc ....E....714 502-9121
1303 S Claudina St Anaheim (92805) ***(P-3489)***

TFC Manufacturing Inc ....D....562 426-9559
4001 Watson Plaza Dr Lakewood (90712) ***(P-6930)***

Tfcf Inc ....F....562 469-3444
11718 Burke St Santa Fe Springs (90670) ***(P-2660)***

Tfd Incorporated ....E....714 630-7127
1180 N Tustin Ave Anaheim (92807) ***(P-10862)***

Tfn Architectural Signage Inc (PA) ....**E....714 556-0990**
3411 W Lake Center Dr Santa Ana (92704) ***(P-11611)***

Thai Print USA LLC (PA) ....**F....626 872-6600**
8666 Garvey Ave Ste C Rosemead (91770) ***(P-4436)***

Thai Union North America Inc (HQ) ....**E....424 397-8556**
2150 E Grand Ave El Segundo (90245) ***(P-2342)***

Thaihot Investment Co US Ltd ....A....949 242-5300
18201 Von Karman Ave # 60 Irvine (92612) ***(P-21099)***

Thalasinos Enterprises Inc ....E....951 340-0911
1220 Railroad St Corona (92882) ***(P-14024)***

Thales Avionics Inc ....E....949 381-3033
48 Discovery Irvine (92618) ***(P-10428)***

Thales Avionics Inc ....E....949 790-2500
58 Discovery Irvine (92618) ***(P-10429)***

Tharp Truck Rental Inc (PA) ....**C....559 782-5800**
15243 Road 192 Porterville (93257) ***(P-19078)***

Tharpe & Howell (PA) ....**D....818 205-9955**
15250 Ventura Blvd Fl 9 Sherman Oaks (91403) ***(P-21687)***

Thatgamecompany Inc ....E....310 453-4906
1520 Cloverfield Blvd D Santa Monica (90404) ***(P-19514)***

Thc - Orange County Inc ....C....310 642-0325
5525 W Slauson Ave Los Angeles (90056) ***(P-20976)***

The China Press, San Gabriel *Also called Asia-Pacific California Inc* ***(P-3948)***

The Community Medical Group of (PA) ....**D....818 707-9603**
8510 Balboa Blvd Ste 150 Northridge (91325) ***(P-20108)***

The Eberly Company, Beverly Hills *Also called Charles & Cynthia Eberly Inc* ***(P-15722)***

The Fifty Five Foundry Inc ....E....612 760-5900
1100 Highland Ave Manhattan Beach (90266) ***(P-17733)***

The Goodwin Company, Garden Grove *Also called Goodwin Ammonia Company* ***(P-4942)***

The Ligature Inc (HQ) ....**E....323 585-6000**
4909 Alcoa Ave Vernon (90058) ***(P-4437)***

The Microfilm Company of Cal ....F....310 354-2610
14214 S Figueroa St Los Angeles (90061) ***(P-4139)***

The Orange County Printing Co, Irvine *Also called Ocpc Inc* ***(P-4381)***

The Orthopedic Institute of ....A....213 977-2010
616 Witmer St Los Angeles (90017) ***(P-20109)***

The Quiet Cannon, Montebello *Also called Quiet Cannon Montebello Inc* ***(P-16974)***

The Rule Group, Newport Beach *Also called Trg Insurance Services* ***(P-1563[illegible])***

The Rutter Group, Culver City *Also called West Publishing Corporation* ***(P-4143)***

The Sloan Company Inc (PA) ....**C....805 676-3200**
5725 Olivas Park Dr Ventura (93003) ***(P-13670)***

The Teecor Group Inc ....D....213 632-2350
1450 S Burlington Ave Los Angeles (90006) ***(P-1695)***

The Timing Inc (PA) ....**E....323 589-5577**
2809 S Santa Fe Ave Vernon (90058) ***(P-14421)***

The Valley Club of Montecito ....E....805 969-2215
1901 E Valley Rd Santa Barbara (93108) ***(P-19621)***

The Wave, Los Angeles *Also called Wave Community Newspapers Inc* ***(P-4043)***

The White Sheet, Palm Desert *Also called Associated Desert Shoppers Inc* ***(P-4152)***

The/Studio ....F....877 647-6447
800 Wilshire Blvd Ste 200 Los Angeles (90017) ***(P-18688)***

Theatredreams La/Chi L P ....E....323 308-6363
6801 Hollywood Blvd # 18 Los Angeles (90028) ***(P-19334)***

Thebouqs.com, Marina Del Rey *Also called Bouqs Company* ***(P-14877)***

Thebrain Technologies LP ....F....310 751-5000
11522 W Washington Blvd Los Angeles (90066) ***(P-17994)***

Theodore B Martin ....E....559 360-2559
17530 Doran Dr Springville (93265) ***(P-19000)***

Theodore Robins Inc ....D....949 642-0010
2060 Harbor Blvd Costa Mesa (92627) ***(P-13036)***

Theodore Robins Ford, Costa Mesa *Also called Theodore Robins Inc* ***(P-13036)***

Theorem LLC, Woodland Hills *Also called Citrusbyte LLC* ***(P-17578)***

Therabreath, Los Angeles *Also called Dr Harold Katz LLC* ***(P-5014)***

Therapak LLC (HQ) ....**C....909 267-2000**
651 Wharton Dr Claremont (91711) ***(P-13525)***

Therapeutic Industries Inc ....F....760 343-2502
72096 Dunham Way Ste E Thousand Palms (92276) ***(P-11064)***

Therapy For Kids Inc ....D....714 870-6116
233 Orangefair Mall Fullerton (92832) ***(P-21354)***

Therm Core Products, San Bernardino *Also called Caldesso LLC* ***(P-8085)***

Therm Pacific, Commerce *Also called Hkf Inc* ***(P-13846)***

Therm-O-Namel Inc ....E....310 631-7866
2780 Mrtin Lther King Jr Lynwood (90262) ***(P-7419)***

Therma Holdings LLC ....E....626 446-1854
2390 Bateman Ave Duarte (91010) ***(P-1154)***

Therma-Tek Range Corp ....E....570 455-9491
9121 Atlanta Ave Ste 331 Huntington Beach (92646) ***(P-9017)***

Thermal Air, Anaheim *Also called General Engineering Wstn Inc* ***(P-1074)***

Thermal Energy Solutions Inc ....F....661 489-4100
100 Quantico Ave Bakersfield (93307) ***(P-978)***

Thermal Engrg Intl USA Inc (HQ)......D......**323 726-0641**
18000 Studebaker Rd # 400 Cerritos (90703) ***(P-22673)***
Thermal Equipment Corporation......E......310 328-6600
2030 E University Dr Compton (90220) ***(P-6760)***
Thermal ID Technologies Inc......F......408 656-6809
2707 Saturn St Brea (92821) ***(P-10819)***
Thermal Rite, Commerce *Also called Crowntonka California Inc* ***(P-8335)***
Thermal Structures Inc (HQ)......B......**951 736-9911**
2362 Railroad St Corona (92878) ***(P-10226)***
Thermal Structures Inc......E......951 256-8051
2380 Railroad St Corona (92878) ***(P-10227)***
Thermal-Vac Technology Inc......E......714 997-2601
1221 W Struck Ave Orange (92867) ***(P-6455)***
Thermalair Inc (HQ)......D......**714 630-3200**
1140 N Red Gum St Anaheim (92806) ***(P-1155)***
Thermalrite, Rancho Cucamonga *Also called Everidge Inc* ***(P-8339)***
Thermaprint Corp......E......949 583-0800
11 Autry Ste B Irvine (92618) ***(P-11295)***
Thermech Corporation......E......714 533-3183
1773 W Lincoln Ave Ste I Anaheim (92801) ***(P-3858)***
Thermech Engineering, Anaheim *Also called Thermech Corporation* ***(P-3858)***
Thermeon Corporation (PA)......F......**714 731-9191**
1175 Warner Ave Tustin (92780) ***(P-17995)***
Thermlly Engnred Mnfctred Pdts......E......310 523-9934
543 W 135th St Gardena (90248) ***(P-6761)***
Thermo Power Industries......E......562 799-0087
10570 Humbolt St Los Alamitos (90720) ***(P-1406)***
Thermo Trilogy, Wasco *Also called Certis USA LLC* ***(P-5168)***
Thermobile, Santa Ana *Also called Hood Manufacturing Inc* ***(P-5664)***
Thermodyne International Ltd......C......909 923-9945
1841 S Business Pkwy Ontario (91761) ***(P-5837)***
Thermolab, Sun Valley *Also called Technical Heaters Inc* ***(P-5323)***
Thermometrics Corporation (PA)......E......**818 886-3755**
18714 Parthenia St Northridge (91324) ***(P-10729)***
Thermomix, Thousand Oaks *Also called Vorwerk LLC* ***(P-7190)***
Thermostatic Industries, Rancho Cucamonga *Also called Newtex Industries Inc* ***(P-11720)***
Thermtronix Corporation (PA)......E......**760 246-4500**
17129 Muskrat Ave Adelanto (92301) ***(P-8099)***
Theta Digital Corporation......E......818 572-4300
1749 Chapin Rd Montebello (90640) ***(P-9202)***
Theta Oilfield Services Inc......E......661 633-2792
5201 California Ave # 370 Bakersfield (93309) ***(P-548)***
Thetradedesk, Ventura *Also called Trade Desk Inc* ***(P-17741)***
Thewrap......F......424 273-4787
2260 S Centinela Ave # 150 Los Angeles (90064) ***(P-4037)***
Thg Brands Inc......E......844 694-8327
1810 Abalone Ave Torrance (90501) ***(P-2537)***
Thi Inc......D......714 444-4643
1525 E Edinger Ave Santa Ana (92705) ***(P-11065)***
Thi Holdings (delaware) Inc......B......661 266-7423
2140 E Palmdale Blvd O Palmdale (93550) ***(P-15634)***
Thibiant International Inc......B......818 709-1345
20320 Prairie St Chatsworth (91311) ***(P-5073)***
Thiel Capital LLC (PA)......E......**323 990-2030**
9200 W Sunset Blvd # 1110 West Hollywood (90069) ***(P-23346)***
Thienes Apparel Inc......E......626 575-2818
1811 Floradale Ave South El Monte (91733) ***(P-2643)***
Thiessen Products Inc......C......805 482-6913
555 Dawson Dr Ste A Camarillo (93012) ***(P-8817)***
Thin Film Devices, Anaheim *Also called Tfd Incorporated* ***(P-10862)***
Thin Metal Sales Inc......F......909 393-2273
5721 Schaefer Ave Chino (91710) ***(P-6668)***
Thin-Lite Corporation......E......805 987-5021
530 Constitution Ave Camarillo (93012) ***(P-9150)***
Thingap Inc......E......805 477-9741
4035 Via Pescador Camarillo (93012) ***(P-8933)***
Think Together......B......562 236-3835
12016 Telegraph Rd Santa Fe Springs (90670) ***(P-19470)***
Think Together......A......909 723-1400
202 E Airport Dr Ste 200 San Bernardino (92408) ***(P-22065)***
Think Together......A......626 373-2311
800 S Barranca Ave # 120 Covina (91723) ***(P-22066)***
Think Together......A......951 571-9944
22620 Goldencrest Dr # 104 Moreno Valley (92553) ***(P-22067)***
Thinkcp Technologies, Irvine *Also called H Co Computer Products* ***(P-8202)***
Thinkom Solutions Inc......C......310 371-5486
4881 W 145th St Hawthorne (90250) ***(P-12791)***
Thinkwell Group Inc (PA)......D......**818 333-3444**
2710 Media Center Dr Los Angeles (90065) ***(P-19335)***
Third Floor North Company, Santa Ana *Also called Tfn Architectural Signage Inc* ***(P-11611)***
Thirkettle Corporation (PA)......D......**951 637-1400**
4050 Flat Rock Dr Riverside (92505) ***(P-13948)***
Thistle Roller Co Inc......E......323 685-5322
209 Van Norman Rd Montebello (90640) ***(P-7926)***
Thoma Electric Inc......D......805 543-3850
3562 Empleo St Ste C San Luis Obispo (93401) ***(P-1328)***
Thoma Electric Co, San Luis Obispo *Also called Thoma Electric Inc* ***(P-1328)***
Thomas Bavarian Mtr Works Inc......D......805 482-8878
411 E Daily Dr Camarillo (93010) ***(P-18879)***
Thomas Burt......F......626 301-9065
5095 Brooks St Montclair (91763) ***(P-4438)***
Thomas Container & Packaging, Pomona *Also called T & T Box Company Inc* ***(P-3846)***
Thomas Gallaway Corporation (PA)......D......**949 716-9500**
100 Spectrum Center Dr # 700 Irvine (92618) ***(P-17734)***
Thomas James Capital Inc......C......949 481-7026
26940 Aliso Viejo Pkwy # 100 Aliso Viejo (92656) ***(P-15351)***
Thompco Inc......E......805 933-8048
899 Mission Rock Rd Santa Paula (93060) ***(P-13872)***
Thompson & Colegate LLP......E......951 682-5550
3610 14th St Lowr Riverside (92501) ***(P-21688)***
Thompson ADB Industries, Westminster *Also called Thompson Industries Ltd* ***(P-10430)***
Thompson Building Materials, Fontana *Also called Edessa Inc* ***(P-6028)***
Thompson Building Materials, Fontana *Also called Valori Sand & Gravel Company* ***(P-13317)***
Thompson Cnstr Sup Door Frame, Corona *Also called Fennel Inc* ***(P-1436)***
Thompson Family Farms LLC......E......714 848-7536
16478 Beach Blvd Ste 391 Westminster (92683) ***(P-120)***
Thompson Gundrilling Inc......E......323 873-4045
13840 Saticoy St Van Nuys (91402) ***(P-6260)***
Thompson Indus Sup A Ltd Lblty......F......714 632-8895
3945 E La Palma Ave Anaheim (92807) ***(P-14025)***
Thompson Industries Ltd......D......310 679-9193
7155 Fenwick Ln Westminster (92683) ***(P-10430)***
Thompson Magnetics Inc......E......951 676-0243
42255 Baldaray Cir Ste C Temecula (92590) ***(P-9796)***
Thompson Pipe Group Inc......E......909 822-0200
3011 N Laurel Ave Rialto (92377) ***(P-3939)***
Thompson Tank Inc......F......562 869-7711
8029 Phlox St Downey (90241) ***(P-6762)***
Thomson International Inc......F......661 845-1111
11220 S Vineland Rd Bakersfield (93307) ***(P-121)***
Thornton Steel & Ir Works Inc......F......714 491-8800
1323 S State College Pkwy Anaheim (92806) ***(P-6982)***
Thornton Winery......D......951 699-0099
32575 Rancho Cal Rd Temecula (92591) ***(P-2230)***
Thoro—Packaging (HQ)......C......**951 278-2100**
1467 Davril Cir Corona (92878) ***(P-14979)***
Thorock Metals Inc......E......310 537-1597
1213 S Pacific Coast Hwy Redondo Beach (90277) ***(P-6296)***
Thorpe Technologies Inc (HQ)......E......**562 903-8230**
449 W Allen Ave Ste 119 San Dimas (91773) ***(P-22674)***
Thosand Oaks 145 Hdncamp Rd Me, Thousand Oaks *Also called Kaiser Foundation Hospitals* ***(P-19919)***
Thousand Oaks 322 E Thsand Oak, Thousand Oaks *Also called Kaiser Foundation Hospitals* ***(P-19920)***
Thousand Oaks Prtg & Spc Inc......C......818 706-8330
5334 Sterling Center Dr Westlake Village (91361) ***(P-18689)***
Thousand Oaks Service Center, Thousand Oaks *Also called Southern California Edison Co* ***(P-12841)***
Thousand Oaks Surgical Hosp LP......D......805 777-7750
401 Rolling Oaks Dr Thousand Oaks (91361) ***(P-20977)***
Three Dots LLC......D......714 799-6333
7340 Lampson Ave Garden Grove (92841) ***(P-2870)***
Three Plus One Inc......F......213 623-3070
3007 Fruitland Ave Vernon (90058) ***(P-2871)***
Three Sons Inc......D......562 801-4100
5201 Industry Ave Pico Rivera (90660) ***(P-14608)***
Three Star Rfrgn Engrg Inc......E......310 327-9090
21720 S Wilmington Ave Long Beach (90810) ***(P-8350)***
Three-D Plastics Inc (PA)......E......**323 849-1316**
430 N Varney St Burbank (91502) ***(P-5838)***
Three-D Traffics Works, Burbank *Also called Three-D Plastics Inc* ***(P-5838)***
Thrifty Oil Co (PA)......E......**562 921-3581**
13116 Imperial Hwy Santa Fe Springs (90670) ***(P-15702)***
Thrifty Payless Inc......A......626 571-0122
9200 Telstar Ave El Monte (91731) ***(P-1825)***
Thrio Inc......E......858 299-7191
5230 Las Virgenes Rd # 21 Calabasas (91302) ***(P-18690)***
Thunderbird Country Club......D......760 328-2161
70737 Country Club Dr Rancho Mirage (92270) ***(P-19622)***
Thunderbird Industries Inc......F......909 394-1633
695 W Terrace Dr San Dimas (91773) ***(P-7837)***
Thunderbolt Manufacturing Inc......E......714 632-0397
641 S State College Blvd Fullerton (92831) ***(P-8818)***
Thyde Inc (PA)......C......**951 817-2300**
300 El Sobrante Rd Corona (92879) ***(P-18691)***
Ti Inc......F......559 972-1475
13802 Avenue 352 Visalia (93292) ***(P-5161)***
Tl Limited LLC (PA)......D......**323 877-5991**
20335 Ventura Blvd Woodland Hills (91364) ***(P-17996)***
Tl Wire, Walnut *Also called Tree Island Wire (usa) Inc* ***(P-6236)***
Tiancheng Intl Inc USA......F......909 947-5577
2851 E Philadelphia St Ontario (91761) ***(P-4905)***
Tianello Inc......C......323 231-0599
138 W 38th St Los Angeles (90037) ***(P-2872)***
Tianello By Steve Barraza, Los Angeles *Also called Tianello Inc* ***(P-2872)***
Tibban Manufacturing Inc......E......760 961-1160
12593 Highline Dr Apple Valley (92308) ***(P-11778)***
Tiburon Hospitality LLC......C......661 322-1012
901 Real Rd Bakersfield (93309) ***(P-16753)***
Tic, Panorama City *Also called Import Collection* ***(P-14939)***
Tic Hotels Inc......D......805 773-4671
2555 Price St Pismo Beach (93449) ***(P-16754)***
Ticketmaster Entertainment LLC......A......800 653-8000
8800 W Sunset Blvd West Hollywood (90069) ***(P-19675)***
Ticketmster New Vntres Hldngs (HQ)......A......**800 653-8000**
7060 Hollywood Blvd Fl 2 Los Angeles (90028) ***(P-19676)***
Tickets.com, Inc., Costa Mesa *Also called Ticketscom LLC* ***(P-19336)***
Ticketscom LLC (HQ)......C......**714 327-5400**
535 Anton Blvd Ste 250 Costa Mesa (92626) ***(P-19336)***
Ticketsocket Inc......E......917 283-0436
2901 W Coast Hwy Ste 200 Newport Beach (92663) ***(P-17735)***
Ticketswest, Irvine *Also called Paciolan LLC* ***(P-17949)***
Ticonium Division, City of Industry *Also called Cmp Industries LLC* ***(P-11164)***
Ticor Title Insurance Company (HQ)......D......**616 302-3121**
131 N El Molino Ave # 13 Pasadena (91101) ***(P-15512)***

ALPHABETIC

Tidavater Inc.....C.....818 848-4151
2107 W Alameda Ave Burbank (91506) ***(P-18692)***

Tidings.....E.....213 637-7360
3424 Wilshire Blvd Los Angeles (90010) ***(P-4038)***

Tidwell Excav Acquisition Inc.....D.....805 647-4707
1691 Los Angeles Ave Ventura (93004) ***(P-1608)***

Tierra Del Sol Foundation (PA).....D.....**818 352-1419**
9919 Sunland Blvd Sunland (91040) ***(P-22159)***

Tierra Del Sol Foundation.....D.....909 626-8301
250 W 1st St Ste 120 Claremont (91711) ***(P-19677)***

Tierra Del Soul, Claremont *Also called Tierra Del Sol Foundation* ***(P-19677)***

Tiffany Coachworks Inc.....F.....951 657-2680
420 N Mckinley St 111-465 Corona (92879) ***(P-9969)***

Tiffany Dale Inc (PA).....D.....**714 739-2700**
14765 Industry Cir La Mirada (90638) ***(P-13189)***

Tiffany Homecare Inc (PA).....B.....**818 886-1602**
9700 Reseda Blvd Ste 105 Northridge (91324) ***(P-21223)***

Tiffanys Liu.....D.....415 644-0846
9465 Wilshire Blvd Beverly Hills (90212) ***(P-21902)***

Tig/M LLC.....E.....818 709-8500
9160 Jordan Ave Chatsworth (91311) ***(P-7696)***

Tiger Case Hole Services, Signal Hill *Also called Tiger Cased Hole Services Inc* ***(P-549)***

Tiger Cased Hole Services Inc.....E.....562 426-4044
2828 Junipero Ave Signal Hill (90755) ***(P-549)***

Tiger Tanks Inc.....E.....661 363-8335
3397 Edison Hwy Bakersfield (93307) ***(P-10548)***

Tikos Tanks Inc.....E.....951 757-8014
14561 Hawthorne Ave Fontana (92335) ***(P-19001)***

Tiktok Inc (HQ).....C.....**844 523-3993**
5800 Bristol Pkwy Culver City (90230) ***(P-17736)***

Tikun Olam Adelanto LLC.....F.....833 468-4586
541 S Spring St Unit 213 Los Angeles (90013) ***(P-4766)***

Tikun Olam Adelanto LLC (PA).....F.....**833 468-4586**
16605 Koala Rd Adelanto (92301) ***(P-4767)***

Tile & Marble Design Co Inc.....E.....714 847-6472
7421 Vincent Cir Huntington Beach (92648) ***(P-1423)***

Tile King.....F.....909 599-7300
949 N Cataract Ave Ste C San Dimas (91773) ***(P-13315)***

Tiller Constructors Partnr Inc.....D.....714 771-5600
306 W Katella Ave Ste A Orange (92867) ***(P-840)***

Tilton Engineering Inc.....E.....805 688-2353
25 Easy St Buellton (93427) ***(P-10141)***

Tim Guzzy Services Inc.....E.....626 813-0626
5136 Calmview Ave Baldwin Park (91706) ***(P-8819)***

Tim Hofer Inc.....C.....559 732-6676
148 N Akers St Visalia (93291) ***(P-17290)***

Timberlake Painting, Murrieta *Also called Temecula Valley Drywall Inc* ***(P-1405)***

Timbucktoo Manufacturing Inc.....E.....310 323-1134
1633 W 134th St Gardena (90249) ***(P-8421)***

Timco, Hesperia *Also called T L Timmerman Construction* ***(P-3370)***

Time and Alarm Systems (PA).....D.....**951 685-1761**
3828 Wacker Dr Jurupa Valley (91752) ***(P-1329)***

Time Financial Services, Woodland Hills *Also called Ramkade Insurance Services* ***(P-15621)***

Time Masters, Los Angeles *Also called AMG Employee Management Inc* ***(P-11300)***

Time Warner, Los Angeles *Also called Spectrum MGT Holdg Co LLC* ***(P-12777)***

Time Warner, Cypress *Also called Spectrum MGT Holdg Co LLC* ***(P-12778)***

Time Warner Cable Inc.....D.....760 335-4800
313 N 8th St El Centro (92243) ***(P-12779)***

Timec Companies Inc.....C.....310 885-4710
2997 E Maria St E Rncho Dmngz (90221) ***(P-1006)***

Timemed Labeling Systems Inc (HQ).....D.....**818 897-1111**
27770 N Entrmt Dr Ste 200 Valencia (91355) ***(P-5415)***

Timeshare Compliance, Aliso Viejo *Also called Pandora Marketing LLC* ***(P-23292)***

Timevalue Software.....E.....949 727-1800
22 Mauchly Irvine (92618) ***(P-17997)***

Timing Fashion, Vernon *Also called The Timing Inc* ***(P-14421)***

Timken Gears & Services Inc.....F.....310 605-2600
12935 Imperial Hwy Santa Fe Springs (90670) ***(P-7099)***

Timmons Volkswagen, Long Beach *Also called Walter Timmons Enterprises Inc* ***(P-18887)***

Timmons Wood Products Inc.....E.....951 940-4700
4675 Wade Ave Perris (92571) ***(P-3456)***

Tinco Sheet Metal Inc.....C.....323 263-0511
958 N Eastern Ave Los Angeles (90063) ***(P-1507)***

Tinnovate LLC.....E.....909 860-6900
6255 Providence Way Eastvale (92880) ***(P-13782)***

Tinson LLC.....E.....901 494-6405
450 N Brand Blvd Glendale (91203) ***(P-23347)***

Tinyinklingcom LLC.....E.....877 777-6287
6303 Owensmouth Ave Fl 10 Woodland Hills (91367) ***(P-5416)***

Tiodize Co Inc (PA).....F.....**714 898-4377**
5858 Engineer Dr Huntington Beach (92649) ***(P-7420)***

Tiodize Co Inc.....E.....714 898-4377
15701 Industry Ln Huntington Beach (92649) ***(P-14812)***

Tireco Inc (PA).....C.....**310 767-7990**
500 W 190th St Ste 600 Gardena (90248) ***(P-13121)***

Tires Warehouse LLC.....C.....714 432-8851
18203 Mount Baldy Cir Fountain Valley (92708) ***(P-13122)***

Tis Industries LLC (PA).....E.....**626 336-3821**
16815 E Johnson Dr City of Industry (91745) ***(P-11779)***

Titan Medical Enterprises Inc.....F.....562 903-7236
11100 Greenstone Ave Santa Fe Springs (90670) ***(P-4906)***

Titan Metal Fabricators Inc (PA).....D.....**805 487-5050**
352 Balboa Cir Camarillo (93012) ***(P-6669)***

Titan Oilfield Services Inc.....E.....661 861-1630
21535 Kratzmeyer Rd Bakersfield (93314) ***(P-550)***

Titan Solar, Woodland Hills *Also called Memeged Tevuot Shemesh* ***(P-1101)***

Titanium Coating Services Inc.....F.....714 860-4229
720 N Valley St Ste G-H Anaheim (92801) ***(P-7421)***

Title365 Company (HQ).....B.....**877 365-9365**
5000 Birch St Ste 300 Newport Beach (92660) ***(P-16043)***

Tivoli LLC.....E.....714 957-6101
17110 Armstrong Ave Irvine (92614) ***(P-9024)***

Tivoli Industries Inc.....E.....714 957-6101
1550 E Saint Gertrude Pl Santa Ana (92705) ***(P-9151)***

Tj Aerospace Inc.....E.....714 891-3564
12601 Monarch St Garden Grove (92841) ***(P-10431)***

Tj Composites Inc.....E.....951 928-8713
7231 Boulder Ave Highland (92346) ***(P-6931)***

Tj Cross Engineers Inc.....D.....661 831-8782
200 New Stine Rd Ste 270 Bakersfield (93309) ***(P-22675)***

Tj Giant Llc.....F.....562 906-1060
12623 Cisneros Ln Santa Fe Springs (90670) ***(P-4584)***

Tjc CA, San Pedro *Also called Jankovich Company* ***(P-14796)***

Tje Company.....E.....909 869-7777
18343 Gale Ave City of Industry (91748) ***(P-6721)***

Tjs Metal Manufacturing Inc.....E.....310 604-1545
10847 Drury Ln Lynwood (90262) ***(P-6983)***

Tk and Company Watches.....F.....213 545-1971
5827 W Pico Blvd Los Angeles (90019) ***(P-11331)***

Tk Carsites Inc.....D.....714 937-1239
2975 Red Hill Ave Costa Mesa (92626) ***(P-17737)***

Tk Elevator Corporation.....D.....714 423-6340
10955 Matthews Dr Tustin (92782) ***(P-13949)***

Tk Elevator Corporation.....D.....323 278-2801
6048 Triangle Dr Commerce (90040) ***(P-13950)***

Tk Elevator Corporation.....D.....818 847-2568
2850 N California St Burbank (91504) ***(P-13951)***

Tk Elevator Corporation.....D.....714 939-0888
1601 S Sunkist St Ste A Anaheim (92806) ***(P-13952)***

Tk Pax Inc.....E.....714 850-1330
1561 Macarthur Blvd Costa Mesa (92626) ***(P-5324)***

Tka, La Palma *Also called Tech Knowledge Associates LLC* ***(P-19076)***

Tl Fab LP.....C.....562 802-3980
2921 E Coronado St Anaheim (92806) ***(P-6670)***

Tl Machine Inc.....D.....714 554-4154
14272 Commerce Dr Garden Grove (92843) ***(P-7046)***

TL Shield & Associates Inc.....E.....818 509-8228
1030 Arroyo St San Fernando (91340) ***(P-7681)***

TLC Sportswear Inc.....F.....805 375-2494
5049 Jacobs Ct Oak Park (91377) ***(P-14422)***

Tln Inc.....D.....208 880-9935
6801 Ave 304 Goshen (93227) ***(P-12081)***

Tm Claims Service Inc.....D.....626 568-7800
800 E Colorado Blvd Pasadena (91101) ***(P-15635)***

TMC Aero, Los Angeles *Also called TMC Ice Protection Systems LLC* ***(P-10647)***

TMC Aero, Murrieta *Also called TMC Ice Protection Systems LLC* ***(P-10648)***

TMC Fluid Systems Inc.....F.....714 553-0944
1228 Village Way Ste H Santa Ana (92705) ***(P-8057)***

TMC Ice Protection Systems LLC (PA).....E.....**951 677-6934**
10850 Wilshire Blvd # 12 Los Angeles (90024) ***(P-10647)***

TMC Ice Protection Systems LLC.....E.....951 677-6934
25775 Jefferson Ave Murrieta (92562) ***(P-10648)***

Tmd Worldwide Incorporated.....F.....949 306-8877
12 Alisal Ct Aliso Viejo (92656) ***(P-17998)***

TMJ Concepts, Ventura *Also called TMJ Solutions Inc* ***(P-11066)***

TMJ Products Inc.....F.....626 576-4063
515 S Palm Ave Ste 6 Alhambra (91803) ***(P-10228)***

TMJ Solutions Inc.....D.....805 650-3391
6059 King Dr Ventura (93003) ***(P-11066)***

Tmp, Los Angeles *Also called Targeted Medical Pharma Inc* ***(P-4903)***

Tms America, Torrance *Also called Total Management Svcs Amer Inc* ***(P-17476)***

Tms International.....F.....818 894-1414
1521 Railroad St Glendale (91204) ***(P-6216)***

TMT Industries Inc.....D.....909 493-3441
14774 Jurupa Ave Fontana (92337) ***(P-12082)***

TMW Corporation (PA).....C.....**818 362-5665**
15148 Bledsoe St Sylmar (91342) ***(P-10432)***

Tmx Aerospace.....C.....562 215-4410
12821 Carmenita Rd Unit F Santa Fe Springs (90670) ***(P-13601)***

Tmx Engineering LLC.....D.....714 641-5884
2141 S Standard Ave Santa Ana (92707) ***(P-22676)***

Tmx Engineering and Mfg Corp.....D.....714 641-5884
2141 S Standard Ave Santa Ana (92707) ***(P-8820)***

TN Sheet Metal Inc.....F.....714 593-0100
18385 Bandilier Cir Fountain Valley (92708) ***(P-6932)***

Tnhc Realty and Cnstr Inc (PA).....C.....**949 382-7800**
15231 Laguna Canyon Rd # 25 Irvine (92618) ***(P-644)***

Tnp Instruments Inc.....F.....310 532-2222
119 Star Of India Ln Carson (90746) ***(P-9797)***

TNT Electric Signs Co, Long Beach *Also called Dynamite Sign Group Inc* ***(P-11544)***

TNT Packaging Corporation.....F.....714 671-9012
300 Thor Pl Brea (92821) ***(P-3859)***

TNT Plastic Molding Inc (PA).....C.....**951 808-9700**
725 E Harrison St Corona (92879) ***(P-5839)***

TNT Welding, Fontana *Also called Precision Performance Products* ***(P-1581)***

TO HELP EVERYONE HEALTH AND WE, Los Angeles *Also called Clinic Inc* ***(P-19751)***

Toad & Co International Inc (PA).....E.....**805 957-1474**
2020 Alameda Padre Serra Santa Barbara (93103) ***(P-3003)***

Toan D Nguyen DDS Inc (PA).....D.....**562 926-3354**
511 E 1st St Ste C Tustin (92780) ***(P-20201)***

Tobacco Crush, Riverside *Also called Recell Usa Inc* ***(P-2551)***

Tobin Lucks, Woodland Hills *Also called Joseph C Sansone Company* ***(P-21593)***

Tobin Steel Company Inc.....D.....714 541-2268
817 E Santa Ana Blvd Santa Ana (92701) ***(P-6671)***

Todai Ssb Inc.....D.....909 869-7727
19481 San Jose Ave City of Industry (91748) ***(P-16220)***

Today Cleaners, Bakersfield *Also called Richard K Newman and Assoc Inc* ***(P-16877)***
Today Pvc Bending Inc...F...714 953-5707
501 N Garfield St Santa Ana (92701) ***(P-9054)***
Tofasco of America Inc (PA)...D...909 392-8282
1661 Fairplex Dr La Verne (91750) ***(P-23124)***
Tognazzini Beverage Service...E...805 928-1144
241 Roemer Way Santa Maria (93454) ***(P-2301)***
Toiyabe Indian Health Prj Inc (PA)...D...760 873-8461
250 N See Vee Ln Bishop (93514) ***(P-20202)***
Tokai Intl Holdings Inc (PA)...E...909 930-5000
2055 S Haven Ave Ontario (91761) ***(P-16114)***
Tokio Marine Michido, Pasadena *Also called Tm Claims Service Inc* ***(P-15635)***
Tokyopop Inc...D...323 920-5967
5200 W Century Blvd Fl 7 Los Angeles (90045) ***(P-4140)***
Tolar Manufacturing Co Inc...E...951 808-0081
258 Mariah Cir Corona (92879) ***(P-6672)***
Tolco Incorporated...F...951 656-3111
6480 Box Springs Blvd Riverside (92507) ***(P-7010)***
Tolemar Inc...F...714 362-8166
5221 Oceanus Dr Huntington Beach (92649) ***(P-10505)***
Tolemar Manufacturing, Huntington Beach *Also called Tolemar Inc* ***(P-10505)***
Toll Global Forwarding USA Inc (HQ)...E...626 363-2400
2000 E Carson St Carson (90810) ***(P-12537)***
Toll Global Fwdg Scs USA Inc...D...951 360-8310
3355 Dulles Dr Jurupa Valley (91752) ***(P-12538)***
Toll Global Fwdg Scs USA Inc...D...732 750-9000
400-450 Westmont Dr San Pedro (90731) ***(P-12539)***
Toller Enterprises Inc (PA)...E...805 374-9455
2251 Townsgate Rd Westlake Village (91361) ***(P-10473)***
Tollfreeforwarding.com, Cerritos *Also called Ifncom Inc* ***(P-12648)***
Tolosa Winery, San Luis Obispo *Also called Courtside Cellars LLC* ***(P-2180)***
Tom Anderson Guitar Works, Newbury Park *Also called Raise Praise Inc* ***(P-11349)***
Tom Anderson Guitarworks...F...805 498-1747
845 Rancho Conejo Blvd Newbury Park (91320) ***(P-11354)***
Tom Bell Chevrolet, Redlands *Also called Dick Dewese Chevrolet Inc* ***(P-18824)***
Tom Byer Roofing Service Inc...E...714 847-9332
17712 Metzler Ln Huntington Beach (92647) ***(P-1508)***
Tom Ferry Your Coach, Santa Ana *Also called Success Strategies Inst Inc* ***(P-21969)***
Tom Harris Inc...F...951 352-5700
5821 Wilderness Ave Riverside (92504) ***(P-2538)***
Tom Leonard Investment Co Inc...E...951 351-7778
7240 Sycamore Canyon Blvd Riverside (92508) ***(P-11780)***
Tom Malloy Corporation (PA)...E...310 327-5554
206 N Central Ave Compton (90220) ***(P-13873)***
Tom Ponton Industries Inc...F...714 998-9073
22901 Savi Ranch Pkwy Yorba Linda (92887) ***(P-23348)***
Tom Sawyer Camps Inc...D...626 794-1156
707 W Woodbury Rd Ste F Altadena (91001) ***(P-16828)***
Tom York Enterprises Inc...D...323 581-6194
2050 E 48th St Vernon (90058) ***(P-5840)***
Tomarco Contractor Spc Inc (PA)...D...714 523-1771
14848 Northam St La Mirada (90638) ***(P-13819)***
Tomarco Fastening Systems, La Mirada *Also called Tomarco Contractor Spc Inc* ***(P-13819)***
Tomasini Inc...F...323 231-2349
1001 E 60th St Los Angeles (90001) ***(P-2606)***
Tomi Engineering Inc...D...714 556-1474
414 E Alton Ave Santa Ana (92707) ***(P-8821)***
Tomitribe Corporation...E...310 526-7676
1519 6th St Apt 503 Santa Monica (90401) ***(P-17738)***
Tomlin Scientific Inc...F...714 523-7971
6780 8th St Buena Park (90620) ***(P-14813)***
Tommy Gun Plastering Inc...D...909 795-9966
944 4th St Calimesa (92320) ***(P-1407)***
Tomorrows Heirlooms Inc...E...310 323-6720
1636 W 135th St Gardena (90249) ***(P-6540)***
Tomorrows Look Inc...D...949 596-8400
17462 Von Karman Ave Irvine (92614) ***(P-2661)***
Toms Backhoe Services Inc...F...951 634-4075
2026 Roanoke St San Jacinto (92582) ***(P-7653)***
Toms Truck Center Inc...C...714 835-1978
1008 E 4th St Santa Ana (92701) ***(P-13037)***
Tone It Up Inc...E...310 376-7645
1110 Manhattan Ave Manhattan Beach (90266) ***(P-2539)***
Toner Supply USA Inc...E...818 504-6540
8055 Lankershim Blvd # 11 North Hollywood (91605) ***(P-13446)***
Toni & Guy Hairdressing (PA)...E...949 721-1666
1177 Newport Center Dr Newport Beach (92660) ***(P-16918)***
Tonnage Industrial LLC...E...800 893-9681
2130 W Cowles St Long Beach (90813) ***(P-14026)***
Tonopah Solar Energy LLC...D...310 315-2200
520 Broadway Fl 6 Santa Monica (90401) ***(P-1156)***
Tonusa LLC...F...626 961-8700
16770 E Johnson Dr City of Industry (91745) ***(P-3342)***
Tonys Express Inc (PA)...C...909 427-8700
10613 Jasmine St Fontana (92337) ***(P-12254)***
Tool & Jig Plating Co, Whittier *Also called Aguilar Williams Inc* ***(P-7201)***
Toor Farming LLC...D...559 500-1331
27725 Road 92 Visalia (93277) ***(P-122)***
Tooth and Nail Winery...F...805 369-6100
3090 Anderson Rd Paso Robles (93446) ***(P-2231)***
Top Deck Investments Inc...E...714 956-7712
731 E Ball Rd Ste 102 Anaheim (92805) ***(P-16016)***
Top Finance Company, Chatsworth *Also called Platinum Group Companies Inc* ***(P-16107)***
Top Heavy Clothing Company Inc (PA)...D...951 442-8839
28381 Vincent Moraga Dr Temecula (92590) ***(P-2763)***
Top Line Mfg Inc...E...562 633-0605
7032 Alondra Blvd Paramount (90723) ***(P-6541)***
Top Priority Couriers Inc (PA)...D...951 781-1000
1257 Columbia Ave Ste D1 Riverside (92507) ***(P-12147)***
Top-Shelf Fixtures LLC...D...909 627-7423
5263 Schaefer Ave Chino (91710) ***(P-7518)***
Topa Insurance Company (HQ)...D...310 201-0451
1800 Avenue Of The Stars # 1200 Los Angeles (90067) ***(P-15636)***
Topa Property Group Inc (HQ)...C...310 203-9199
1800 Avenue Of The Stars # 1200 Los Angeles (90067) ***(P-15703)***
Topa Topa Brewing...F...805 324-4150
120 Santa Barbara St Santa Barbara (93101) ***(P-2158)***
Topac USA Inc (HQ)...A...949 462-6000
25530 Commercentre Dr Lake Forest (92630) ***(P-13366)***
Topaz Systems Inc (PA)...E...805 520-8282
875 Patriot Dr Ste A Moorpark (93021) ***(P-8305)***
Topco Sales, Simi Valley *Also called Wsm Investments LLC* ***(P-16224)***
Topland Logistics Inc (PA)...D...562 908-6988
2727 Workman Mill Rd City of Industry (90601) ***(P-12540)***
Topland Trucking Inc (HQ)...D...562 908-6988
2727 Workman Mill Rd City of Industry (90601) ***(P-11999)***
Topocean Consolidation Service (PA)...C...562 908-1688
2727 Workman Mill Rd City of Industry (90601) ***(P-12541)***
Topper Manufacturing Corp...F...310 375-5000
23880 Madison St Torrance (90505) ***(P-8422)***
Topper Plastics Inc...F...626 331-0561
461 E Front St Covina (91723) ***(P-5525)***
Tops Auto Parks, Los Angeles *Also called Paramunt Contrs Developers Inc* ***(P-15944)***
Tops Slt Inc...C...562 968-2000
8550 Chetle Ave Ste B Whittier (90606) ***(P-3901)***
Topson Downs California Inc (PA)...C...310 558-0300
3840 Watseka Ave Culver City (90232) ***(P-14355)***
Topson Downs California Inc...C...310 558-0300
3545 Motor Ave Los Angeles (90034) ***(P-2908)***
Topwin Corporation (PA)...D...310 325-2255
1808 Abalone Ave Torrance (90501) ***(P-14356)***
Torah-Aura Productions Inc...F...323 585-1847
2710 Supply Ave Commerce (90040) ***(P-4141)***
Tornante-MDP Joe Holding LLC (PA)...F...310 228-6800
233 S Beverly Dr Beverly Hills (90212) ***(P-14103)***
Toro Enterprises Inc...D...805 483-4515
2101 Ventura Blvd Oxnard (93036) ***(P-923)***
Torrance Amateur Rdo Assn Inc...E...310 245-0989
2162 248th St Lomita (90717) ***(P-22465)***
Torrance Care Center West Inc...C...310 370-4561
4333 Torrance Blvd Torrance (90503) ***(P-20487)***
Torrance Family Medicine Ctr, Manhattan Beach *Also called Torrance Mem Physicians Netwrk* ***(P-20979)***
Torrance Health Assn Inc (PA)...A...310 325-9110
3330 Lomita Blvd Torrance (90505) ***(P-20978)***
Torrance Manufacturing, Chatsworth *Also called Torrance Prcsion Machining Inc* ***(P-8822)***
Torrance Marriott Hotel, Torrance *Also called Xld Group LLC* ***(P-16808)***
Torrance Mem Physicians Netwrk (HQ)...E...310 939-7847
855 Manhattan Beach Blvd Manhattan Beach (90266) ***(P-20979)***
Torrance Memorial Breast Diagn, Manhattan Beach *Also called Torrance Memorial Medical Ctr* ***(P-20983)***
Torrance Memorial Medical Ctr...A...310 784-6316
3333 Skypark Dr Ste 200 Torrance (90505) ***(P-20980)***
Torrance Memorial Medical Ctr...A...310 784-3740
22411 Hawthorne Blvd Torrance (90505) ***(P-20981)***
Torrance Memorial Medical Ctr (HQ)...A...310 325-9110
3330 Lomita Blvd Torrance (90505) ***(P-20982)***
Torrance Memorial Medical Ctr...A...310 939-7847
855 Manhattan Beach Blvd # 208 Manhattan Beach (90266) ***(P-20983)***
Torrance Orthpdic Spt Medicine, Torrance *Also called John J Ohara MD A Medical Corp* ***(P-19857)***
Torrance Prcsion Machining Inc...F...818 709-7838
9530 Owensmouth Ave Ste 8 Chatsworth (91311) ***(P-8822)***
Torrance Refining Company LLC...A...310 212-2800
3700 W 190th St Torrance (90504) ***(P-5262)***
Torrance Steel Window Co Inc...E...310 328-9181
1819 Abalone Ave Torrance (90501) ***(P-6722)***
Torrence Municipal Airport, Torrance *Also called City of Torrance* ***(P-12348)***
Torrence Trading Inc...E...310 649-1188
21041 S Wstn Ave Ste 200 Torrance (90501) ***(P-11393)***
Torres Construction Corp (PA)...D...323 257-7460
1370 N El Molino Ave Pasadena (91104) ***(P-722)***
Torres-Mrtnez Dsert Chlla Inda...D...760 395-1200
3089 Norm Niver Rd Thermal (92274) ***(P-16755)***
Tortilleria La California Inc...F...323 221-8940
2241 Cypress Ave Los Angeles (90065) ***(P-2540)***
Tortilleria La Mejor...D...559 747-0739
684 S Farmersville Blvd Farmersville (93223) ***(P-2541)***
Tortilleria San Marcos...F...323 263-0208
1927 E 1st St Los Angeles (90033) ***(P-2542)***
Toscana Country Club Inc...C...760 404-1444
76009 Via Club Villa Indian Wells (92210) ***(P-19623)***
Tosco - Tool Specialty Company...E...323 232-3561
1011 E Slauson Ave Los Angeles (90011) ***(P-7874)***
Toshiba Amer Bus Solutions Inc (HQ)...B...949 462-6000
25530 Commercentre Dr Lake Forest (92630) ***(P-13367)***
Toshiba Amer Elctrnic Cmpnnts (HQ)...B...949 462-7700
5231 California Ave Irvine (92617) ***(P-9203)***
Toshiba Amer Info Systems Inc...D...949 300-9435
225 Sonoma Aisle Irvine (92618) ***(P-8178)***
Toshiba Amer Info Systems Inc...C...949 583-3000
9740 Irvine Blvd Fl 1 Irvine (92618) ***(P-8179)***
Toshiba Business Solutions, Lake Forest *Also called Topac USA Inc* ***(P-13366)***
Toshiba Education Center...C...949 583-3000
9740 Irvine Blvd Irvine (92618) ***(P-22898)***
Toska Inc...F...213 746-0088
1100 S San Pedro St I06 Los Angeles (90015) ***(P-3004)***

ALPHABETIC

Employee Codes: A=Over 500 employees, B=251-500
C=101-250, D=51-100, E=20-50 F=10-19
2022 Southern California Business
Directory and Buyers Guide
© Mergent Inc. 1-800-342-5647
1295

Tot Squad Services LLC ... F ... 310 895-9983
13412 Ventura Blvd # 300 Sherman Oaks (91423) ***(P-21903)***

Total Beauty Media Inc (HQ) ... **F ... 310 295-9593**
1158 26th St Ste 535 Santa Monica (90403) ***(P-4108)***

Total Brand Delivery, Camarillo *Also called Corprint Incorporated* ***(P-4503)***

Total Clean, La Verne *Also called Haaker Equipment Company* ***(P-13027)***

Total Cmmnicator Solutions Inc ... D ... 619 277-1488
11150 Santa Monica Blvd # 600 Los Angeles (90025) ***(P-17999)***

Total Cost Involved, Ontario *Also called TCI Engineering Inc* ***(P-9967)***

Total Education Solutions Inc (PA) ... **E ... 323 341-5580**
625 Fair Oaks Ave Ste 300 South Pasadena (91030) ***(P-23517)***

Total Fincl & Insur Svcs Inc ... D ... 310 477-7500
300 Crprate Pinte Ste 250 Culver City (90230) ***(P-15637)***

Total Garments, Westlake Village *Also called Hec Inc* ***(P-13725)***

Total Health Environment LLC ... E ... 714 637-1010
743 W Taft Ave Orange (92865) ***(P-13526)***

Total Immersion, Los Angeles *Also called Dfusion Software Inc* ***(P-17596)***

Total Import Solutions Inc ... F ... 562 691-6818
14700 Radburn Ave Santa Fe Springs (90670) ***(P-13099)***

Total Intermodal Services Inc ... D ... 562 427-6300
2757 E Del Amo Blvd Compton (90221) ***(P-12292)***

Total Logistics Online LLC ... D ... 714 526-3559
628 N Gilbert St Fullerton (92833) ***(P-12542)***

Total Management Svcs Amer Inc ... E ... 310 328-0867
21151 S Wstn Ave Ste 139 Torrance (90501) ***(P-17476)***

Total Paper Services Inc ... F ... 714 780-0131
100 S Anaheim Blvd # 250 Anaheim (92805) ***(P-11781)***

Total Petroleum Services Inc ... D ... 714 907-0117
7071 Warner Ave Ste F-397 Huntington Beach (92647) ***(P-14814)***

Total Process Solutions LLC ... E ... 661 829-7910
1400 Norris Rd Bakersfield (93308) ***(P-8025)***

Total Recon Solutions Inc ... D ... 949 584-8417
27 Oakbrook Trabuco Canyon (92679) ***(P-23349)***

Total Renal Care Inc ... D ... 760 947-7405
14135 Main St Ste 501 Hesperia (92345) ***(P-21267)***

Total Resources Intl Inc (PA) ... **D ... 909 594-1220**
420 S Lemon Ave Walnut (91789) ***(P-11145)***

Total Structures Inc ... E ... 805 676-3322
1696 Walter St Ventura (93003) ***(P-9152)***

Total Telco Specialists Inc ... D ... 805 541-2232
602 W Southern Ave Orange (92865) ***(P-18960)***

Total Trnsp Logistics Inc ... D ... 951 360-9521
4325 Etiwanda Ave Ste A Jurupa Valley (91752) ***(P-12083)***

Total Vision LLC ... C ... 949 652-7242
27271 Las Ramblas 200a Mission Viejo (92691) ***(P-20207)***

Total-Western Inc (HQ) ... **C ... 562 220-1450**
8049 Somerset Blvd Paramount (90723) ***(P-551)***

Totally Kids Rhbilitation Hosp, Loma Linda *Also called Mountain View Child Care Inc* ***(P-20867)***

Totally Kids Spcalty Hlth Care, Sun Valley *Also called Mountain View Child Care Inc* ***(P-22037)***

Totex Manufacturing Inc ... D ... 310 326-2028
3050 Lomita Blvd Torrance (90505) ***(P-5841)***

Totten Tubes Inc (PA) ... **D ... 626 812-0220**
500 W Danlee St Azusa (91702) ***(P-13602)***

Touch Litho Company ... F ... 562 927-8899
7215 E Gage Ave Commerce (90040) ***(P-4439)***

Touch ME Fashion Inc (PA) ... **E ... 323 234-9200**
906 E 60th St Los Angeles (90001) ***(P-3005)***

Touchdown Technologies Inc ... E ... 626 472-6732
5188 Commerce Dr Baldwin Park (91706) ***(P-9592)***

Touchtone Corporation ... E ... 714 755-2810
3151 Airway Ave Ste I3 Costa Mesa (92626) ***(P-17739)***

Toughbuilt Industries Inc (PA) ... **F ... 949 528-3100**
25371 Cmmrcntre Dr Dte 20 20 Dte Lake Forest (92630) ***(P-6491)***

Tour Master, Calabasas Hills *Also called Helmet House LLC* ***(P-14336)***

Tourcoach Transportation, Commerce *Also called Screamline Investment Corp* ***(P-12411)***

Tow Industries, West Covina *Also called Baatz Enterprises Inc* ***(P-9936)***

Towbes Group Inc (PA) ... **D ... 805 962-2121**
33 E Carrillo St Ste 200 Santa Barbara (93101) ***(P-16077)***

Tower Energy Group (PA) ... **C ... 310 538-8000**
1983 W 190th St Ste 100 Torrance (90504) ***(P-14815)***

Tower Hmtlogy Onclogy Med Grou ... D ... 310 888-8680
9090 Wilshire Blvd # 200 Beverly Hills (90211) ***(P-20110)***

Tower Industries Inc ... C ... 909 947-2723
1720 S Bon View Ave Ontario (91761) ***(P-8823)***

Tower Mechanical Products Inc ... C ... 714 947-2723
1720 S Bon View Ave Ontario (91761) ***(P-10649)***

Tower Semicdtr Newport Bch Inc (HQ) ... **A ... 949 435-8000**
4321 Jamboree Rd Newport Beach (92660) ***(P-9593)***

Tower St John Imaging, Los Angeles *Also called Santa Mnica Wlshire Imging LLC* ***(P-20057)***

Towerjazz, Newport Beach *Also called Tower Semicdtr Newport Bch Inc* ***(P-9593)***

Towmaster Tire & Wheel, Anaheim *Also called Greenball Corp* ***(P-13117)***

Town & Cntry Event Rentals Inc (PA) ... **B ... 818 908-4211**
7725 Airport Bus Pkwy Van Nuys (91406) ***(P-17379)***

Town & Cntry Event Rentals Inc ... B ... 805 770-5729
1 N Calle Cesar Chavez Santa Barbara (93103) ***(P-17380)***

Town Cntry Mnor of Chrstn Mssn ... C ... 714 547-7581
555 E Memory Ln Ofc Ofc Santa Ana (92706) ***(P-20488)***

Towne Park Brew Inc ... E ... 714 844-2492
1566 W Lincoln Ave Anaheim (92801) ***(P-2159)***

TownePlace Stes Irvine Lk Fres, Lake Forest *Also called TP Heritg Inn Lk Forest LLC* ***(P-16756)***

TownePlace Suites El Centro, El Centro *Also called El Centro Hospitality 2 LLC* ***(P-16429)***

Townsend Industries Inc ... D ... 661 837-1795
4401 Stine Rd Bakersfield (93313) ***(P-11146)***

Townsend Industries Inc ... D ... 661 837-1795
4833 N Hills Dr Bakersfield (93308) ***(P-11147)***

Townsteel Inc ... D ... 626 965-8917
17901 Railroad St City of Industry (91748) ***(P-13290)***

Toy Barn, Oxnard *Also called Players West Amusements Inc* ***(P-19513)***

Toye Corporation ... E ... 818 882-4000
9230 Deering Ave Chatsworth (91311) ***(P-8306)***

Toymax International Inc (HQ) ... **D ... 310 456-7799**
22619 Pacific Coast Hwy Malibu (90265) ***(P-11394)***

Toyo Tire Hldings Americas Inc (HQ) ... **E ... 562 431-6502**
5665 Plaza Dr Ste 200 Cypress (90630) ***(P-5306)***

Toyon Research Corporation (PA) ... **C ... 805 968-6787**
6800 Cortona Dr Goleta (93117) ***(P-22677)***

Toyota Industries N Amer Inc ... E ... 562 941-4155
12907 Imperial Hwy Santa Fe Springs (90670) ***(P-13953)***

Toyota Logistics Services Inc (HQ) ... **C ... 310 468-4000**
19001 S Western Ave Torrance (90501) ***(P-9970)***

Toyota Material Hdlg Solutions, Santa Fe Springs *Also called Rebas Inc* ***(P-13936)***

Toyota of Glendora, Glendora *Also called Seidner-Miller Inc* ***(P-18803)***

Toyota of Orange Inc ... C ... 714 639-6750
1400 N Tustin St Orange (92867) ***(P-13038)***

Toyota of Oxnard, Oxnard *Also called D C H California Motors Inc* ***(P-18820)***

Toyota of Riverside Inc ... C ... 951 687-1622
7870 Indiana Ave Riverside (92504) ***(P-18880)***

Toyota Scion Place, Garden Grove *Also called Noarus Tgg* ***(P-18859)***

Toyota-Lift of Los Angeles, Santa Fe Springs *Also called Toyota Industries N Amer Inc* ***(P-13953)***

TP Heritg Inn Lk Forest LLC ... E ... 949 461-0470
23150 Lake Center Dr Lake Forest (92630) ***(P-16756)***

TP Products, San Fernando *Also called Triumph Precision Products* ***(P-7047)***

TP Solar Inc ... F ... 562 808-2171
16310 Downey Ave Paramount (90723) ***(P-8100)***

Tp-Link USA Corporation (HQ) ... **C ... 626 333-0234**
10 Mauchly Irvine (92618) ***(P-13447)***

Tpi, Covina *Also called Topper Plastics Inc* ***(P-5525)***

Tpl Communications, Panorama City *Also called D X Communications Inc* ***(P-9266)***

Tpsi, Paramount *Also called TP Solar Inc* ***(P-8100)***

Tpusa - Fhcs Inc (HQ) ... **B ... 213 873-5100**
215 N Marengo Ave Ste 160 Pasadena (91101) ***(P-18139)***

Tpx Communications, Los Angeles *Also called US Telepacific Corp* ***(P-12676)***

Tpx Communications, Los Angeles *Also called Mpower Holding Corporation* ***(P-12656)***

Trace3 LLC (HQ) ... **D ... 949 333-2300**
7565 Irvine Center Dr # 20 Irvine (92618) ***(P-23350)***

Trackr Inc ... D ... 855 981-1690
7410 Hollister Ave Santa Barbara (93117) ***(P-17740)***

Tracy & Ryder, Rcho STA Marg *Also called Park West Companies Inc* ***(P-332)***

Tracy & Ryder Landscape Inc ... D ... 949 858-7017
22421 Gilberto Ste A Rcho STA Marg (92688) ***(P-345)***

Tracy Industries Inc ... C ... 562 692-9034
3200 E Guasti Rd Ste 100 Ontario (91761) ***(P-7600)***

Trade Desk Inc (PA) ... **A ... 805 585-3434**
42 N Chestnut St Ventura (93001) ***(P-17741)***

Trade News International Inc ... E ... 818 848-6397
4444 W Riverside Dr # 202 Burbank (91505) ***(P-17091)***

Trademark Cosmetics Inc ... E ... 951 683-2631
545 Columbia Ave Riverside (92507) ***(P-5074)***

Trademark Plastics Inc ... C ... 909 941-8810
807 Palmyrita Ave Riverside (92507) ***(P-7997)***

Tradenet Enterprise Inc ... D ... 888 595-3956
1580 Magnolia Ave Corona (92879) ***(P-11612)***

Trader Joe Fontana Warehouse, Fontana *Also called World Class Distribution Inc* ***(P-12263)***

Tradesmen International LLC ... D ... 949 588-3280
16880 Valley View Ave La Mirada (90638) ***(P-23125)***

Tradestyle, Los Angeles *Also called Tutoring Expert Services LLC* ***(P-18002)***

Tradewind Seafood Inc ... E ... 805 483-8555
1505 Mountain View Ave Oxnard (93030) ***(P-14586)***

Tradewinds, Monrovia *Also called Headwinds* ***(P-10491)***

Tradition Golf Club, La Quinta *Also called Chapman Golf Development LLC* ***(P-19554)***

Tradition Golf Club Associates ... D ... 760 564-3355
78505 Avenue 52 La Quinta (92253) ***(P-19624)***

Traffic Control & Safety Corp (PA) ... **D ... 949 553-8272**
1100 Main St Irvine (92614) ***(P-13954)***

Traffic Management Inc (PA) ... **C ... 562 595-4278**
4900 Arprt Plz Dr Ste 300 Long Beach (90815) ***(P-18693)***

Traffic Works Inc ... E ... 323 582-0616
5720 Soto St Huntington Park (90255) ***(P-5439)***

Trail Lines Inc ... D ... 562 758-6980
9415 Sorensen Ave Santa Fe Springs (90670) ***(P-12000)***

Trailer Park Inc ... D ... 310 845-8400
6922 Hollywood Blvd Fl 12 Los Angeles (90028) ***(P-17062)***

Trailer Park Inc ... D ... 310 845-3000
9000 W Sunset Blvd # 915 Los Angeles (90069) ***(P-17063)***

Trailer Park Inc (PA) ... **D ... 310 845-3000**
6922 Hollywood Blvd # 1200 Los Angeles (90028) ***(P-17064)***

Train Reaction, Huntington Beach *Also called West Coast Trends Inc* ***(P-11458)***

Trak Machine Tools, Rancho Dominguez *Also called Southwestern Industries Inc* ***(P-7747)***

Trammell Crow Centl Texas Ltd ... D ... 310 765-2600
2221 Rosecrans Ave El Segundo (90245) ***(P-16017)***

Trams Inc (HQ) ... **D ... 310 641-8726**
7 Lower Blackwater Cyn Rd Rolling Hills (90274) ***(P-18071)***

Trams International, Bell Gardens *Also called Bus Services Corporation* ***(P-10025)***

Trane US Inc ... D ... 626 913-7123
3253 E Imperial Hwy Brea (92821) ***(P-8351)***

Trans Fx Inc ... F ... 805 485-6110
2361 Eastman Ave Oxnard (93030) ***(P-11782)***

Trans-Dapt California Inc ... E ... 562 921-0404
12438 Putnam St Whittier (90602) ***(P-10142)***

Trans-Pak Incorporated ... C ... 310 618-6937
2601 S Garnsey St Santa Ana (92707) ***(P-18694)***

Mergent e-mail: customerrelations@mergent.com
1296
2022 Southern California Business Directory and Buyers Guide
(P-0000) Products & Services Section entry number
(PA)=Parent Co (HQ)=Headquarters DH)=Div Headquarters

Trans-West Ford Truck Sls Inc (PA) ....D....909 770-5127
10150 Cherry Ave Fontana (92335) *(P-13100)*
Trans-West Services Inc ....B....661 381-2900
8503 Crippen St Bakersfield (93311) *(P-18345)*
Transamerican Dissolution LLC (PA) ....C....310 900-5500
400 W Artesia Blvd Compton (90220) *(P-13101)*
Transcendent Security Services ....E....562 850-3313
3553 Atl Ave Ste 1197 Long Beach (90807) *(P-18346)*
Transcentra Inc ....A....310 603-0105
20500 Belshaw Ave Carson (90746) *(P-18072)*
Transchem Coatings, Los Angeles *Also called Paint-Chem Inc (P-5106)*
Transco, El Monte *Also called Transgo (P-10143)*
Transcontinental Ontario Inc ....E....909 390-8866
5601 Santa Ana St Ontario (91761) *(P-3860)*
Transcosmos Onmiconnect LLC ....D....310 630-0072
879 W 190th St Ste 1050 Gardena (90248) *(P-23126)*
Transdev North America Inc ....D....909 394-2307
1224 N San Dimas Cyn Rd San Dimas (91773) *(P-11800)*
Transdev Services Inc ....B....626 357-7912
5640 Peck Rd Arcadia (91006) *(P-11892)*
Transducer Techniques LLC ....E....951 719-3965
42480 Rio Nedo Temecula (92590) *(P-10917)*
Transgo ....E....626 443-7456
2621 Merced Ave El Monte (91733) *(P-10143)*
Transit Air Cargo Inc ....C....714 571-0393
2204 E 4th St Santa Ana (92705) *(P-12543)*
Transit Care Inc ....F....818 267-3002
7900 Nelson Rd Panorama City (91402) *(P-5924)*
Transit Control Systems, Santa Ana *Also called Anello Corporation (P-10933)*
Transition Team, The, Beverly Hills *Also called Beverly Hills Escrow A Cal (P-15789)*
Transitions - Mental Hlth Assn (PA) ....D....805 540-6500
784 High St San Luis Obispo (93401) *(P-21355)*
Transline Technology Inc ....E....714 533-8300
1106 S Technology Cir Anaheim (92805) *(P-9460)*
Translogic Incorporated ....E....714 890-0058
5641 Engineer Dr Huntington Beach (92649) *(P-10730)*
Transltnal Plmnary Immnlogy RE ....D....562 490-9900
701 E 28th St Ste 419 Long Beach (90806) *(P-20111)*
Transmrica Rtirement Svcs Corp (PA) ....C....866 498-4557
1150 S Olive St Ste T-91 Los Angeles (90015) *(P-15370)*
Transom Capital Group LLC (PA) ....D....424 293-2818
10990 Wilshire Blvd # 44 Los Angeles (90024) *(P-16297)*
Transonic Combustion Inc ....E....805 465-5145
461 Calle San Pablo Camarillo (93012) *(P-7601)*
Transpacific Financial Inc (PA) ....D....626 447-7888
185 W Chestnut Ave Monrovia (91016) *(P-23351)*
Transpak Los Angeles, Santa Ana *Also called Trans-Pak Incorporated (P-18694)*
Transparent Devices Inc ....E....805 499-5000
853 Lawrence Dr Newbury Park (91320) *(P-8307)*
Transparent Products Inc ....E....661 294-9787
28064 Avenue Stanford E Valencia (91355) *(P-8229)*
Transphorm Inc (PA) ....D....805 456-1300
75 Castilian Dr Ste 200 Goleta (93117) *(P-9594)*
Transplant Connect Inc ....E....310 392-1400
12121 Wilshire Blvd # 205 Los Angeles (90025) *(P-18000)*
Transportation, Lake Arrowhead *Also called Rim of World Unified Schl Dst (P-11936)*
Transportation Bureau, Los Angeles *Also called County of Los Angeles (P-12568)*
Transportation Chrtr Svcs Inc ....E....714 396-0346
1931 N Batavia St Orange (92865) *(P-11916)*
Transportation Department, Culver City *Also called City of Culver City (P-22246)*
Transportation Department, Long Beach *Also called Long Beach Unified School Dst (P-11935)*
Transprttion Brkg Spclists Inc ....B....714 754-4230
15170 Transistor Ln Huntington Beach (92649) *(P-12001)*
Transtech Engineers Inc (PA) ....D....909 595-8599
13367 Benson Ave Chino (91710) *(P-22678)*
Transwest Truck Center LLC ....D....909 770-5170
10150 Cherry Ave Fontana (92335) *(P-13102)*
Trantronics Inc ....E....949 553-1234
1822 Langley Ave Irvine (92614) *(P-9461)*
Trap ....D....626 572-5610
1833 S Mountain Ave Monrovia (91016) *(P-18695)*
Trapac LLC (HQ) ....E....380 830-2000
630 W Hrry Brdges Blvd Br 136 Berths Wilmington (90744) *(P-12293)*
Trapdoor Ensemble ....E....310 951-4836
11236 Valley Spring Ln North Hollywood (91602) *(P-19337)*
Travel America Inc (HQ) ....E....949 474-0404
17672 Cowan Bldg B Irvine (92614) *(P-15757)*
Travel Store ....D....714 529-1947
633 S Brea Blvd Brea (92821) *(P-12400)*
Travel Store (PA) ....D....310 575-5540
11601 Wilshire Blvd # 30 Los Angeles (90025) *(P-12401)*
Travelers Choice Travelware ....D....909 529-7688
2805 S Reservoir St Pomona (91766) *(P-5898)*
Travelers Club Luggage Inc ....D....714 523-8808
5911 Fresca Dr La Palma (90623) *(P-14185)*
Travelodge, Santa Ana *Also called Chen & Huang Partners LP (P-16380)*
Travelstore, Los Angeles *Also called Travel Store (P-12401)*
Travis Industries, Sun Valley *Also called Travis-American Group LLC (P-3295)*
Travis Snyder ....E....909 338-6302
27248 Hwy 189 Ste Ab-06 Blue Jay (92317) *(P-7654)*
Travis-American Group LLC ....F....714 258-1200
11450 Sheldon St Sun Valley (91352) *(P-3295)*
Travismathew LLC (HQ) ....F....562 799-6900
15202 Graham St Huntington Beach (92649) *(P-2829)*
Traxx Corporation ....D....909 623-8032
1201 E Lexington Ave Pomona (91766) *(P-11783)*
TRC Companies Inc ....E....661 837-0022
2820 Pegasus Dr Bakersfield (93308) *(P-23518)*
TRC Operating Company Inc ....F....661 763-0081
805 Blackgold Ct Taft (93268) *(P-411)*
TRC Solutions Inc (HQ) ....C....949 753-0101
9685 Research Dr Ste 100 Irvine (92618) *(P-23519)*
Trc-Indiana Llc (HQ) ....E....310 536-2400
601 Hawaii St El Segundo (90245) *(P-21268)*
Tre Milano LLC ....F....310 260-8888
2730 Monterey St Ste 101 Torrance (90503) *(P-11784)*
Tre Venezie Inc ....D....818 985-4669
4100 Cahuenga Blvd Toluca Lake (91602) *(P-16981)*
Treana Winery LLC ....E....805 237-2932
4280 Second Wind Way Paso Robles (93446) *(P-2232)*
Treasure Garden Inc (PA) ....E....626 814-0168
13401 Brooks Dr Baldwin Park (91706) *(P-3535)*
Treasure Hlls Hlth Hldings LLC ....D....949 487-9500
29222 Rncho Vejo Rd Ste 1 San Juan Capistrano (92675) *(P-20489)*
Tredc, Porterville *Also called Tule River Economic Dev (P-23520)*
Tree House Pad & Paper Inc ....D....800 213-4184
2341 Pomona Rd Ste 108 Corona (92878) *(P-3918)*
Tree Island Wire (usa) Inc ....D....909 899-1673
5080 Hallmark Pkwy San Bernardino (92407) *(P-7519)*
Tree Island Wire (usa) Inc (HQ) ....C....909 594-7511
3880 Valley Blvd Walnut (91789) *(P-6236)*
Tree Island Wire (usa) Inc ....C....909 594-7511
13470 Philadelphia Ave Fontana (92337) *(P-6237)*
Tree Island Wire (usa) Inc ....C....909 595-6617
3880 W Valley Blvd Pomona (91769) *(P-6238)*
Tree Island Wire USA, San Bernardino *Also called Tree Island Wire (usa) Inc (P-7519)*
Treeland Farms, Woodland Hills *Also called Boething Treeland Nursery Co (P-12016)*
Treepeople Inc ....E....818 753-4600
12601 Mulholland Dr Beverly Hills (90210) *(P-362)*
Treivush Industries ....D....213 745-7774
940 W Washington Blvd Los Angeles (90015) *(P-3006)*
Trellborg Sling Sltions US Inc (HQ) ....C....714 415-0280
2761 Walnut Ave Tustin (92780) *(P-11067)*
Trelleborg Sealing Solutions ....D....805 239-4284
3034 Propeller Dr Paso Robles (93446) *(P-11068)*
Trench Plate Rental, Downey *Also called National Trench Safety LLC (P-17313)*
Trench Shoring Company, Compton *Also called Tom Malloy Corporation (P-13873)*
Trend Design Inc ....F....805 498-0457
1200 Lawrence Dr Ste 465 Newbury Park (91320) *(P-17191)*
Trend Graphics Screenprinting, Newbury Park *Also called Trend Design Inc (P-17191)*
Trend Manor Furn Mfg Co Inc ....E....626 964-6493
17047 Gale Ave City of Industry (91745) *(P-3490)*
TREND OFFSET PRINTING SERVICES INCORPORATED, Los Alamitos *Also called Trend Offset Printing Svcs Inc (P-4440)*
Trend Offset Printing Svcs Inc ....B....562 598-2446
3791 Catalina St Los Alamitos (90720) *(P-4440)*
Trend Technologies LLC (HQ) ....C....909 597-7861
4626 Eucalyptus Ave Chino (91710) *(P-6933)*
Trendnet Inc (PA) ....D....310 961-5500
20675 Manhattan Pl Torrance (90501) *(P-13448)*
Trendshift LLC ....D....866 644-8877
13274 Fiji Way Ste 250 Marina Del Rey (90292) *(P-17742)*
Trepanning Specialities Inc ....E....562 633-8110
16201 Illinois Ave Paramount (90723) *(P-8824)*
Trepanning Specialties, Paramount *Also called Trepanning Specialities Inc (P-8824)*
Trey Arch LLC ....D....310 581-4700
3420 Ocean Park Blvd # 2000 Santa Monica (90405) *(P-13449)*
Trg Inc ....D....310 396-6750
1350 Abbot Kinney Blvd # 101 Venice (90291) *(P-16018)*
Trg Insurance Services ....D....949 474-1550
3620 Birch St Ste 100 Newport Beach (92660) *(P-15638)*
Tri - Star Win Coverings Inc ....E....818 718-3188
19555 Prairie St Northridge (91324) *(P-13190)*
Tri City Mental Health Center, Pomona *Also called Tri-City Mental Health Auth (P-21356)*
Tri Models Inc ....D....714 896-0823
5191 Oceanus Dr Huntington Beach (92649) *(P-10206)*
Tri Pointe Contractors LP (HQ) ....D....949 478-8600
5 Peters Canyon Rd # 100 Irvine (92606) *(P-682)*
Tri Pointe Homes Inc ....C....714 389-5933
57 Furlong Irvine (92602) *(P-670)*
Tri Pointe Homes Inc (HQ) ....C....949 438-1400
19540 Jamboree Rd Ste 300 Irvine (92612) *(P-671)*
Tri Precision Sheetmetal Inc ....E....714 632-8838
845 N Elm St Orange (92867) *(P-6934)*
Tri Service Co Inc ....E....626 442-3270
2465 Loma Ave South El Monte (91733) *(P-5244)*
Tri State Truss Corporation ....E....760 326-3868
600 River Rd Needles (92363) *(P-3371)*
Tri Tek Electronics Inc ....E....661 295-0020
25358 Avenue Stanford Valencia (91355) *(P-9798)*
Tri-City Mental Health Auth (PA) ....D....909 623-6131
2008 N Garey Ave Pomona (91767) *(P-21356)*
Tri-Cnties Assn For Dvlpmntlly (PA) ....D....805 962-7881
520 E Montecito St Santa Barbara (93103) *(P-21904)*
Tri-Cnties Assn For Dvlpmntlly ....C....805 543-2833
1146 Farmhouse Ln San Luis Obispo (93401) *(P-21905)*
Tri-Co Building Supply Inc ....E....805 343-2555
695 Obispo St Guadalupe (93434) *(P-3372)*
Tri-Counties Association F ....D....805 922-4640
1234 Fairway Dr A Santa Maria (93455) *(P-22283)*
TRI-COUNTIES REGIONAL CENTER, Santa Barbara *Also called Tri-Cnties Assn For Dvlpmntlly (P-21904)*
Tri-Counties Regional Center, San Luis Obispo *Also called Tri-Cnties Assn For Dvlpmntlly (P-21905)*

ALPHABETIC

Employee Codes: A=Over 500 employees, B=251-500 C=101-250, D=51-100, E=20-50 F=10-19
2022 Southern California Business Directory and Buyers Guide
© Mergent Inc. 1-800-342-5647
1297

Tri-Dim Filter Corporation ... E ... 626 826-5893
15271 Fairfield Ranch Rd # 150 Chino Hills (91709) ***(P-8058)***

Tri-Fanucchi Farms Inc ... D ... 661 858-2264
3728 David Rd Arvin (93203) ***(P-21)***

Tri-Fitting Mfg Company ... F ... 626 442-2000
10414 Rush St South El Monte (91733) ***(P-10433)***

Tri-J Metal Heat Treating Co (PA) ... **F ... 909 622-9999**
327 E Commercial St Pomona (91767) ***(P-6456)***

Tri-Marine Fish Company LLC ... D ... 310 547-1144
220 Cannery St San Pedro (90731) ***(P-14587)***

Tri-Mountain, Irwindale *Also called Mountain Gear Corporation* ***(P-14342)***

Tri-Net Inc ... F ... 909 483-3555
14721 Hilton Dr Fontana (92336) ***(P-10774)***

Tri-Net Technology Inc ... D ... 909 598-8818
21709 Ferrero Walnut (91789) ***(P-8308)***

Tri-Signal Integration Inc (PA) ... **D ... 818 566-8558**
28110 Avenue Stanford D Santa Clarita (91355) ***(P-1330)***

Tri-Star Dyeing & Finshg Inc ... D ... 562 483-0123
15125 Marquardt Ave Santa Fe Springs (90670) ***(P-2614)***

Tri-Star Electronics Intl Inc (HQ) ... **B ... 310 536-0444**
2201 Rosecrans Ave El Segundo (90245) ***(P-13783)***

Tri-Star Laminates Inc ... E ... 949 587-3200
20322 Windrow Dr Ste 100 Lake Forest (92630) ***(P-9462)***

Tri-Star Technologies Inc ... F ... 310 567-9243
1111 E El Segundo Blvd El Segundo (90245) ***(P-11241)***

Tri-Tech Logistics LLC ... C ... 855 373-7049
3230 E Imperial Hwy # 140 Brea (92821) ***(P-12544)***

Tri-Tech Metals Inc ... F ... 909 948-1401
9039 Charles Smith Ave Rancho Cucamonga (91730) ***(P-13603)***

Tri-Tech Precision Inc ... F ... 714 970-1363
1863 N Case St Orange (92865) ***(P-10434)***

Tri-Tech Restoration Cnstr Inc ... F ... 800 900-8448
3301 N San Fernando Blvd Burbank (91504) ***(P-552)***

Tri-Tech Restoration Co Inc ... D ... 818 565-3900
3301 N San Fernando Blvd Burbank (91504) ***(P-723)***

Tri-Tech Systems Inc (PA) ... **B ... 818 222-6811**
23801 Calabasas Rd # 2022 Calabasas (91302) ***(P-17743)***

Tri-Union Seafoods LLC (HQ) ... **D ... 858 558-9662**
2150 E Grand Ave El Segundo (90245) ***(P-14588)***

Tri-West Ltd (PA) ... **C ... 562 692-9166**
12005 Pike St Santa Fe Springs (90670) ***(P-13191)***

Triad Bellows Design & Mfg Inc ... E ... 714 204-4444
2897 E La Cresta Ave Anaheim (92806) ***(P-6673)***

Triad Properties ... D ... 805 648-5008
995 Riverside St Ventura (93001) ***(P-15704)***

Triad Systems International, Calabasas *Also called Tri-Tech Systems Inc* ***(P-17743)***

Triage Entertainment LLC ... D ... 310 417-4800
6701 Center Dr W Ste 300 Los Angeles (90045) ***(P-19187)***

Triage Partners LLC ... D ... 562 634-0058
15717 Texaco Ave Paramount (90723) ***(P-18228)***

Triangle Rock Products LLC ... B ... 818 553-8820
500 N Brand Blvd Ste 500 # 500 Glendale (91203) ***(P-566)***

Triangle Services Inc ... D ... 562 696-0712
7032 Comstock Ave Ste 207 Whittier (90602) ***(P-17291)***

Triangle Tool & Die Corp ... F ... 562 944-2117
13189 Flores St Santa Fe Springs (90670) ***(P-8825)***

Triangle West, Santa Fe Springs *Also called Gale/Triangle Inc* ***(P-11967)***

Tribe Media Corp ... E ... 213 368-1661
3250 Wilshire Blvd Los Angeles (90010) ***(P-4039)***

Tribeworx LLC ... D ... 800 949-3432
4 San Joaquin Plz Ste 150 Newport Beach (92660) ***(P-18001)***

Tribridge Holdings LLC ... B ... 813 287-8887
523 W 6th St Ste 830 Los Angeles (90014) ***(P-17744)***

Tribune Studios, Los Angeles *Also called 5800 Sunset Productions Inc* ***(P-3942)***

Trical Inc ... E ... 559 651-0736
28679 Rd 68 Visalia (93277) ***(P-5173)***

Trical Inc ... E ... 951 737-6960
1029 Railroad St Corona (92882) ***(P-5174)***

Trical Inc ... E ... 661 824-2494
1667 Purdy Rd Mojave (93501) ***(P-5175)***

Tricap International LLC ... D ... 509 703-8780
19067 S Reyes Ave Compton (90221) ***(P-12545)***

Tricir Technologies, City of Industry *Also called Lanstreetcom* ***(P-8226)***

Trico Leasing Company LLC ... E ... 877 259-9997
30154 Rhone Dr Rancho Palos Verdes (90275) ***(P-14027)***

Trico Sports Inc ... E ... 818 899-7705
13541 Desmond St Pacoima (91331) ***(P-10506)***

Tricom Management Inc ... C ... 714 630-2029
4025 E La Palma Ave # 10 Anaheim (92807) ***(P-23127)***

Tricom Research Inc ... D ... 949 250-6024
17791 Sky Park Cir Ste J Irvine (92614) ***(P-9323)***

Tricom Service Corp (PA) ... **E ... 888 415-6911**
2384 -1801 W Olympic Blvd Pasadena (91199) ***(P-17292)***

Tricon American Homes LLC ... C ... 844 874-2661
15771 Red Hill Ave Tustin (92780) ***(P-645)***

Tricor America Inc ... D ... 310 676-0800
12441 Eucalyptus Ave 7 Hawthorne (90250) ***(P-12546)***

Tricor Refining LLC ... E ... 661 393-7110
1134 Manor St Bakersfield (93308) ***(P-5263)***

Tridant Solutions Inc ... D ... 310 292-7382
453 N Lake Ave Pasadena (91101) ***(P-23352)***

Trident Dental Labratories, Hawthorne *Also called Trident Labs LLC* ***(P-21113)***

Trident Labs LLC ... C ... 310 915-9121
12000 Aviation Blvd Hawthorne (90250) ***(P-21113)***

Trident Plating Inc ... E ... 562 906-2556
10046 Romandel Ave Santa Fe Springs (90670) ***(P-7323)***

Trifoil Imaging, Chatsworth *Also called Northrdge Tr-Mdlity Imging Inc* ***(P-10661)***

Trigild International Inc ... D ... 949 645-2221
1680 Superior Ave Costa Mesa (92627) ***(P-16757)***

Trigon Components Inc (PA) ... **D ... 714 990-1367**
935 Mariner St Brea (92821) ***(P-9614)***

Trigon Electronics Inc ... E ... 714 633-7442
22865 Savi Ranch Pkwy A Yorba Linda (92887) ***(P-9923)***

Trilar Management Group ... C ... 951 925-2021
1025 S Gilbert St Hemet (92543) ***(P-23128)***

Trilogy Day Spa, Manhattan Beach *Also called Trilogy Squaw Spa LLC* ***(P-16919)***

Trilogy Golf At La Quinta ... C ... 760 771-0707
60151 Trilogy Pkwy La Quinta (92253) ***(P-19511)***

Trilogy Plumbing Inc ... C ... 714 441-2952
1525 S Sinclair St Anaheim (92806) ***(P-1157)***

Trilogy Squaw Spa LLC ... E ... 310 760-0044
451 Manhattan Beach Blvd Manhattan Beach (90266) ***(P-16919)***

Trim Quick, Corona *Also called Vinylvisions Company LLC* ***(P-5118)***

Trim To Trade, Palm Desert *Also called Plumbing Products Company Inc* ***(P-6563)***

Trim-Lok Inc (PA) ... **C ... 714 562-0500**
6855 Hermosa Cir Buena Park (90620) ***(P-5842)***

Trimana, Los Angeles *Also called High Rise Gdies Rest Group Inc* ***(P-16208)***

Trimark Orange County, Irvine *Also called Trimark Raygal LLC* ***(P-13467)***

Trimark Raygal LLC ... C ... 949 474-1000
210 Commerce Irvine (92602) ***(P-13467)***

Trimas Aerospace, Simi Valley *Also called Rsa Engineered Products LLC* ***(P-10405)***

Trimatic, Pasadena *Also called C & D Precision Components Inc* ***(P-8536)***

Trimedyne Inc (PA) ... **F ... 949 951-3800**
519 N Smith Ave Ste 105 Corona (92878) ***(P-11242)***

Trinamix Inc (PA) ... **B ... 408 507-3583**
35 Amoret Dr Irvine (92602) ***(P-23353)***

Trinity Brdcstg Netwrk Inc ... C ... 714 665-3619
2442 Michelle Dr Tustin (92780) ***(P-12744)***

Trinity Broadcasting Network, Tustin *Also called Trinity Christian Center of SA* ***(P-12745)***

Trinity Care & Nutria, Cerritos *Also called Trinitycare LLC* ***(P-21224)***

Trinity Christian Center of SA (PA) ... **C ... 714 665-3619**
2442 Michelle Dr Tustin (92780) ***(P-12745)***

Trinity Christn Ctr Santa Ana, Tustin *Also called Trinity Brdcstg Netwrk Inc* ***(P-12744)***

Trinity Equipment Inc ... D ... 951 790-1905
2650 S La Cadena Dr Colton (92324) ***(P-13468)***

Trinity Health Systems (PA) ... **D ... 626 960-1971**
14318 Ohio St Baldwin Park (91706) ***(P-20490)***

Trinity Home Care, Torrance *Also called Providence Health System* ***(P-21204)***

Trinity International Inds LLC ... E ... 800 985-5506
930 E 233rd St Carson (90745) ***(P-5843)***

Trinity Lighweight, Frazier Park *Also called Trnlwb LLC* ***(P-11785)***

Trinity Office Furniture Inc ... F ... 909 888-5551
1050 W Rialto Ave San Bernardino (92410) ***(P-3602)***

Trinity Process Solutions Inc ... E ... 714 701-1112
4740 E Bryson St Anaheim (92807) ***(P-7544)***

Trinity Youth Services (PA) ... **D ... 909 825-5588**
201 N Indian Hill Blvd # 201 Claremont (91711) ***(P-22160)***

Trinitycare LLC (PA) ... **E ... 818 709-4221**
13030 Alondra Blvd Cerritos (90703) ***(P-21224)***

Trinium Technologies, Palos Verdes Estates *Also called QED Software LLC* ***(P-17965)***

Trinus Corporation ... E ... 818 246-1143
1030 Fallen Leaf Rd Arcadia (91006) ***(P-17745)***

Trio Engineered Products Inc (HQ) ... **E ... 626 851-3966**
505 W Foothill Blvd Azusa (91702) ***(P-7655)***

Trio Manufacturing Inc ... C ... 310 640-6123
601 Lairport St El Segundo (90245) ***(P-10435)***

Trio Metal Stamping Inc ... D ... 626 336-1228
15318 Proctor Ave City of Industry (91745) ***(P-6935)***

Trio Tool & Die Co (PA) ... **F ... 310 644-4431**
3340 W El Segundo Blvd Hawthorne (90250) ***(P-7838)***

Tripadvisor LLC ... D ... 323 464-5181
6141 Franklin Ave Los Angeles (90028) ***(P-16758)***

Triple B Forwarders, Carson *Also called Triple B Forwarders Inc* ***(P-12547)***

Triple B Forwarders Inc (PA) ... **C ... 310 604-5840**
1511 Glenn Curtiss St Carson (90746) ***(P-12547)***

Triple DOT Corp ... E ... 714 241-0888
3302 S Susan St Santa Ana (92704) ***(P-5481)***

Triple E Manufacturing ... E ... 661 831-7553
2121 S Union Ave Bakersfield (93307) ***(P-7954)***

Triple H Food Processors LLC ... D ... 951 352-5700
5821 Wilderness Ave Riverside (92504) ***(P-2543)***

Triple R Transportation Inc ... D ... 661 725-6494
978 Rd 192 Delano (93215) ***(P-11893)***

Triple-E Machinery Moving Inc ... D ... 626 444-1137
3301 Gilman Rd El Monte (91732) ***(P-12084)***

Trisar Inc ... F ... 714 972-2626
2200 W Orangewood Ave # 235 Orange (92868) ***(P-4585)***

Tristar Industrial LLC ... D ... 562 634-6425
5875 Obispo Ave Long Beach (90805) ***(P-14028)***

Tristar Insurance Group Inc (PA) ... **A ... 562 495-6600**
100 Oceangate Ste 700 Long Beach (90802) ***(P-15486)***

Tristar Television Music Inc ... E ... 310 244-4000
10202 Washington Blvd Culver City (90232) ***(P-19338)***

Tristart Risk Management, Long Beach *Also called Tristar Insurance Group Inc* ***(P-15486)***

Triton Chandelier Inc ... F ... 714 957-9600
1301 Dove St Ste 900 Newport Beach (92660) ***(P-9107)***

Triton Media Group LLC ... C ... 661 294-9000
8935 Lindblade St Culver City (90232) ***(P-12707)***

Triumph Acttion Systems - Vlnc ... C ... 661 702-7537
28150 Harrison Pkwy Valencia (91355) ***(P-10436)***

Triumph Equipment Inc ... F ... 909 947-5983
13434 S Ontario Ave Ontario (91761) ***(P-10437)***

Triumph Group, Valencia *Also called Triumph Acttion Systems - Vlnc* ***(P-10436)***

Triumph Group, Calexico *Also called Triumph Insulation Systems LLC* ***(P-10439)***

Triumph Group Inc ... F ... 760 768-1700
2401 Portico Blvd Calexico (92231) ***(P-10438)***

Triumph Insulation Systems LLC A 760 618-7543
1754 Carr Rd Ste 103 Calexico (92231) ***(P-10439)***
Triumph Precision Products E 818 897-4700
13636 Vaughn St Ste A San Fernando (91340) ***(P-7047)***
Triumph Processing Inc C 323 563-1338
2605 Industry Way Lynwood (90262) ***(P-7324)***
Triumph Structures - Brea, Brea *Also called Alatus Aerosystems* ***(P-10263)***
Triune Enterprises Inc E 310 719-1600
13711 S Normandie Ave Gardena (90249) ***(P-3861)***
Triune Enterprises Mfg, Gardena *Also called Triune Enterprises Inc* ***(P-3861)***
Trivascular Inc (HQ) C **707 543-8800**
2 Musick Irvine (92618) ***(P-11069)***
Trivascular Technologies Inc (HQ) D **707 543-8800**
2 Musick Irvine (92618) ***(P-11070)***
Triview Glass Industries LLC D 626 363-7980
279 Shawnan Ln La Habra (90631) ***(P-5970)***
Trivista Business Group Inc (PA) C **949 218-4830**
18565 Jamboree Rd Ste 350 Irvine (92612) ***(P-23354)***
Triways Inc D 951 361-4840
11201 Iberia St Ste B Jurupa Valley (91752) ***(P-12085)***
Trixxi Clothing Company Inc (PA) C **323 585-4200**
6817 E Acco St Commerce (90040) ***(P-2898)***
Triyar Sv LLC (PA) B **310 234-2888**
10850 Wilshire Blvd Los Angeles (90024) ***(P-16019)***
TRL Systems Incorporated D 909 390-8392
9531 Milliken Ave Rancho Cucamonga (91730) ***(P-1331)***
Trlg Intermediate Holdings LLC (PA) D **323 266-3072**
1888 Rosecrans Ave Manhattan Beach (90266) ***(P-3045)***
TRM Manufacturing Inc C 951 256-8550
375 Trm Cir Corona (92879) ***(P-5440)***
Trnlwb LLC A 661 245-3736
17410 Lockwood Valley Rd Frazier Park (93225) ***(P-11785)***
Troesh Readymix Inc E 805 928-3764
2280 Hutton Rd Nipomo (93444) ***(P-6124)***
Trojan Battery Company (HQ) B **562 236-3000**
12380 Clark St Santa Fe Springs (90670) ***(P-9819)***
Trojan Battery Holdings LLC (HQ) D **800 423-6569**
12380 Clark St Santa Fe Springs (90670) ***(P-9815)***
Trojan Professional Svcs Inc D 714 816-7169
4410 Cerritos Ave Los Alamitos (90720) ***(P-18134)***
Trojan Rivet F 818 245-1065
1835 Dana St Glendale (91201) ***(P-7078)***
Trona Railway Company A 760 372-2312
13068 Main St Trona (93562) ***(P-11798)***
Troon Golf LLC C 760 346-4653
44500 Indian Wells Ln Indian Wells (92210) ***(P-23129)***
Troop Real Estate Inc D 805 487-2892
2365 E Vineyard Ave Oxnard (93036) ***(P-16020)***
Troop Real Estate Inc D 805 402-3028
4165 E Thsand Oaks Ste 10 Westlake Village (91362) ***(P-16021)***
Troop Real Estate Inc (PA) D **805 581-3200**
1308 Madera Rd Ste 8 Simi Valley (93065) ***(P-16022)***
Troop Real Estate Inc D 805 921-0030
586 W Main St Santa Paula (93060) ***(P-16023)***
Troop Real Estate Inc D 805 640-1440
236 W Ojai Ave Ste 100 Ojai (93023) ***(P-16024)***
Trophies Etc F 805 484-4121
2255 Pleasant Valley Rd K Camarillo (93012) ***(P-18696)***
Tropi-Con Foods Inc F 949 472-2200
3691 Noakes St Los Angeles (90023) ***(P-7573)***
Tropical Asphalt LLC (PA) F **714 739-1408**
14435 Macaw St La Mirada (90638) ***(P-5286)***
Tropical Functional Labs LLC F 951 688-2619
7111 Arlington Ave Ste F Riverside (92503) ***(P-1806)***
Tropical Plaza Nursery Inc D 714 998-4100
9642 Santiago Blvd Villa Park (92867) ***(P-346)***
Tropical Preserving Co Inc E 213 748-5108
1711 E 15th St Los Angeles (90021) ***(P-1878)***
Tropical Roofing Products CA, La Mirada *Also called Tropical Asphalt LLC* ***(P-5286)***
Tropicale Foods Inc E 909 635-0390
1237 W State St Ontario (91762) ***(P-1826)***
Tropitone Furniture Co Inc (HQ) B **949 595-2010**
5 Marconi Irvine (92618) ***(P-3536)***
Trouble At The Mill, Huntington Park *Also called Cotton Generation Inc* ***(P-3030)***
Troutman Ppper Hmlton Snders L D 949 622-2700
5 Park Plz Ste 1400 Irvine (92614) ***(P-21689)***
Troutman Sanders, Irvine *Also called Troutman Ppper Hmlton Snders L* ***(P-21689)***
Troy Lee Designs LLC (PA) D **951 371-5219**
155 E Rincon St Corona (92879) ***(P-14089)***
Troy Metal Products, Goleta *Also called Neal Feay Company* ***(P-6313)***
Troy Products, Montebello *Also called Troy Sheet Metal Works Inc* ***(P-7115)***
Troy Sheet Metal Works Inc (PA) D **323 720-4100**
1024 S Vail Ave Montebello (90640) ***(P-7115)***
Troy-Csl Lighting Inc D 626 336-4511
14508 Nelson Ave City of Industry (91744) ***(P-9071)***
Troyer Contracting Company Inc D 562 944-6452
10122 Freeman Ave Santa Fe Springs (90670) ***(P-1696)***
Troygould PC D 310 553-4441
1801 Century Park E # 1600 Los Angeles (90067) ***(P-21690)***
Trs Staffing Solutions, Aliso Viejo *Also called Fluor Corporation* ***(P-22550)***
Tru Form Industries, Santa Fe Springs *Also called Tru-Form Industries Inc* ***(P-7186)***
Tru-Cut Inc E 310 630-0422
141 E 157th St Gardena (90248) ***(P-7632)***
Tru-Form Industries Inc (PA) D **562 802-2041**
14511 Anson Ave Santa Fe Springs (90670) ***(P-7186)***
Tru-Form Plastics Inc E 310 327-9444
14600 Hoover St Westminster (92683) ***(P-5844)***
Tru-Wood Products, Azusa *Also called McMurtrie & Mcmurtrie Inc* ***(P-3221)***
Truabutment Inc D 714 956-1488
17742 Cowan Irvine (92614) ***(P-11199)***
Truaire, Santa Fe Springs *Also called TA Industries Inc* ***(P-13837)***
Truck Club Publishing Inc F 323 726-8620
7807 Telegraph Rd Ste H Montebello (90640) ***(P-4142)***
Truck Terminal, Bakersfield *Also called Pan Pacific Petroleum Co Inc* ***(P-12072)***
Truck Underwriters Association (HQ) A **323 932-3200**
4680 Wilshire Blvd Los Angeles (90010) ***(P-22284)***
Truck Underwriters Association A 323 932-3200
6303 Owensmouth Ave Fl 1 Woodland Hills (91367) ***(P-15371)***
Truconnect Communications Inc (PA) C **512 919-2641**
1149 S Hill St Ste 400 Los Angeles (90015) ***(P-12675)***
True Air Mechanical Inc C 888 316-0642
4 Faraday Irvine (92618) ***(P-1158)***
True Cast Concrete Products, Sun Valley *Also called Gibbel Bros Inc* ***(P-6092)***
True Design Inc F 562 699-2001
9427 Norwalk Blvd Santa Fe Springs (90670) ***(P-3343)***
True Digital Surgery, Goleta *Also called Digital Surgery Systems Inc* ***(P-10970)***
True Family Enterprises (PA) D **888 665-8638**
27156 Burbank Foothill Ranch (92610) ***(P-16164)***
True Fresh Hpp LLC F 949 922-8801
6535 Caballero Blvd B Buena Park (90620) ***(P-10670)***
True Grit, Newport Beach *Also called Calor Apparel Group Intl Corp* ***(P-3013)***
True Home Heating and AC, Irvine *Also called True Air Mechanical Inc* ***(P-1158)***
True Investments LLC (PA) E **949 258-9720**
2260 University Dr Newport Beach (92660) ***(P-16298)***
True Position Technologies LLC D 661 294-0030
24900 Avenue Stanford Valencia (91355) ***(P-8826)***
True Precision Machining Inc E 805 964-4545
175 Indstrial Way Bellton Buellton Buellton (93427) ***(P-8827)***
True Religion Apparel, Gardena *Also called Guru Denim LLC* ***(P-14378)***
True Religion Apparel Inc (HQ) B **323 266-3072**
500 W 190th St Ste 300 Gardena (90248) ***(P-2775)***
True Religion Brand Jeans, Gardena *Also called True Religion Apparel Inc* ***(P-2775)***
True Religion Jeans, Manhattan Beach *Also called True Religion Sales LLC* ***(P-14423)***
True Religion Sales LLC (HQ) B **323 266-3072**
1888 Rosecrans Ave # 1000 Manhattan Beach (90266) ***(P-14423)***
True Vision Displays Inc F 562 407-0630
16402 Berwyn Rd Cerritos (90703) ***(P-9799)***
True Warrior LLC E 661 237-6588
21226 Lone Star Way Santa Clarita (91390) ***(P-3087)***
True Wrld Fods Los Angeles LLC D 323 846-3300
4200 S Alameda St Vernon (90058) ***(P-14589)***
Truecar Inc (PA) E **800 200-2000**
120 Broadway Ste 200 Santa Monica (90401) ***(P-17746)***
Truesdail Laboratories Inc E 714 730-6239
3337 Michelson Dr Irvine (92612) ***(P-22869)***
Truevision 3d Surgical, Goleta *Also called Truevision Systems Inc* ***(P-11071)***
Truevision Systems Inc E 805 963-9700
315 Bollay Dr Ste 101 Goleta (93117) ***(P-11071)***
Truex Inc E 310 657-9900
11925 Wilshire Blvd Fl 2 Los Angeles (90025) ***(P-12792)***
Truform Construction Corp E 714 630-7447
1041 N Shepard St Anaheim (92806) ***(P-1459)***
Truframe, Visalia *Also called R Lang Company* ***(P-6717)***
Trugreen, Santa Ana *Also called Landcare USA LLC* ***(P-265)***
Trugreen, Simi Valley *Also called Landcare USA LLC* ***(P-315)***
Trugreen, Riverside *Also called Landcare USA LLC* ***(P-316)***
Trugreen, Canoga Park *Also called Landcare USA LLC* ***(P-319)***
Trugreen Lndcare Michael Bogan, Santa Fe Springs *Also called Landcare USA LLC* ***(P-317)***
Truitt Oilfield Maint Corp B 661 871-4099
1051 James Rd Bakersfield (93308) ***(P-553)***
Truly Green Solutions LLC E 818 206-4404
9601 Variel Ave Chatsworth (91311) ***(P-9153)***
Trump Card LLC (HQ) D **949 360-7340**
23807 Aliso Creek Rd Laguna Niguel (92677) ***(P-12002)***
Trumpia, Anaheim *Also called Docircle Inc* ***(P-12634)***
Truog-Ryding Company Inc D 805 371-9222
2659 Townsgate Rd Ste 101 Westlake Village (91361) ***(P-23355)***
Truspro, Guadalupe *Also called Tri-Co Building Supply Inc* ***(P-3372)***
Trussworks International Inc D 714 630-2772
1275 E Franklin Ave Pomona (91766) ***(P-6674)***
Trust Automation Inc D 805 544-0761
125 Venture Dr Ste 110 San Luis Obispo (93401) ***(P-22679)***
Trustee Corps, Irvine *Also called Mtc Financial Inc* ***(P-16191)***
Trustee Corps, Irvine *Also called Mtc Financial Inc* ***(P-23069)***
Truteam of California Inc D 805 345-3239
2389 A St Santa Maria (93455) ***(P-1408)***
Truthmd LLC D 949 637-4296
32932 Pcf Cast Hwy Ste 14 Dana Point (92629) ***(P-18229)***
Trutouch Technologies Inc F 909 703-5963
2020 Iowa Ave Ste 102 Riverside (92507) ***(P-10918)***
Truvida Recovery D 949 283-4679
45 Timberland Aliso Viejo (92656) ***(P-21357)***
Truwest Inc E 714 895-2444
5592 Engineer Dr Huntington Beach (92649) ***(P-2830)***
Truxtun Psychtric Med Group LP D 661 323-6410
6313 Schirra Ct Bakersfield (93313) ***(P-20112)***
Truxtun Radiology Med Group LP (HQ) B **661 325-6800**
1817 Truxtun Ave Bakersfield (93301) ***(P-20113)***
Trv Investments LLC (HQ) D **661 378-3846**
3001 Calloway Dr Bakersfield (93312) ***(P-16299)***
Tryad Service Corporation D 661 391-1524
5900 E Lerdo Hwy Shafter (93263) ***(P-554)***
Trymax F 661 391-1572
5900 E Lerdo Hwy Shafter (93263) ***(P-7545)***

ALPHABETIC

Employee Codes: A=Over 500 employees, B=251-500
C=101-250, D=51-100, E=20-50 F=10-19
2022 Southern California Business Directory and Buyers Guide
© Mergent Inc. 1-800-342-5647
1299

Tryvision ....E......760 780-0408
  15056 Dakota St Victorville (92394) *(P-21906)*
TS Enterprises Inc ....E......760 360-5991
  78250 Highway 111 La Quinta (92253) *(P-4627)*
TSC Auto ID Technology America (HQ) ....C......909 468-0100
  3040 Saturn St Ste 200 Brea (92821) *(P-14029)*
TSC Precision Machining Inc ....F......714 542-3182
  1311 E Saint Gertrude Pl A Santa Ana (92705) *(P-8828)*
TSCM Corporation ....D......714 841-1988
  17791 Jamestown Ln Huntington Beach (92647) *(P-17293)*
Tst Inc (PA) ....B......951 685-2155
  13428 Benson Ave Chino (91710) *(P-6297)*
TST Molding LLC ....E......951 296-6200
  42322 Avenida Alvarado Temecula (92590) *(P-5845)*
Tst/Impreso California Inc ....E......909 357-7190
  10589 Business Dr Fontana (92337) *(P-4603)*
Tsu Corporate Services, North Hollywood Also called Toner Supply USA Inc *(P-13446)*
TT Elctrnics Pwr Sltons US Inc ....C......626 967-6021
  1330 E Cypress St Covina (91724) *(P-9800)*
TT Machine Corp ....F......714 534-5288
  11651 Anabel Ave Garden Grove (92843) *(P-8829)*
TT Trucking Services LLC ....D......323 790-3408
  12745 Jade Rd Victorville (92392) *(P-12003)*
TTI Floor Care North Amer Inc ....D......440 996-2802
  13055 Valley Blvd Fontana (92335) *(P-5325)*
TTI Performance Exhaust, Corona Also called Tube Technologies Inc *(P-10144)*
TTI Technologies, Exeter Also called Exeter Engineering Inc *(P-166)*
Ttl Holdings LLC (HQ) ....B......909 597-7861
  4626 Eucalyptus Ave Chino (91710) *(P-5846)*
Ttm Printed Circuit Group Inc (HQ) ....A......714 327-3000
  2630 S Harbor Blvd Santa Ana (92704) *(P-9463)*
Ttm Technologies Inc (PA) ....B......714 327-3000
  200 Sandpointe Ave # 400 Santa Ana (92707) *(P-9464)*
Ttm Technologies Inc ....B......714 688-7200
  3140 E Coronado St Anaheim (92806) *(P-9465)*
Tts, Orange Also called Total Telco Specialists Inc *(P-18960)*
Ttsi, Rancho Dominguez Also called Premium Trnsp Svcs Inc *(P-12234)*
TTT Innovations LLC ....E......818 201-8828
  20850 Plummer St Chatsworth (91311) *(P-11786)*
TTT West Coast Inc ....D......818 972-0500
  3000 W Alameda Ave # 125 Burbank (91505) *(P-19188)*
Tu Vets Printing ....F......323 723-4569
  5635 E Beverly Blvd Los Angeles (90022) *(P-4441)*
Tu-K Industries Inc ....E......562 927-3365
  5702 Firestone Pl South Gate (90280) *(P-5075)*
Tua Fashion Inc (PA) ....F......213 422-2384
  8936 Appian Way Los Angeles (90046) *(P-2592)*
Tua USA, Los Angeles Also called Tua Fashion Inc *(P-2592)*
Tube Bending LLC ....F......562 692-5829
  4747 Citrus Dr Pico Rivera (90660) *(P-7546)*
Tube One Industries Inc ....F......951 300-2998
  4055 Garner Rd Riverside (92501) *(P-6254)*
Tube Technologies Inc ....E......951 371-4878
  1555 Consumer Cir Corona (92878) *(P-10144)*
Tube-Tainer Inc ....E......562 945-3711
  8174 Byron Rd Whittier (90606) *(P-3841)*
Tubing Seal Cap Co, Anaheim Also called Pacific Precision Metals Inc *(P-7173)*
Tubular Specialties Mfg Inc ....D......310 515-4801
  13011 S Spring St Los Angeles (90061) *(P-5993)*
Tucker Rocky Distribution, Visalia Also called Ed Tucker Distributor Inc *(P-13056)*
Tuff Kote Systems Inc ....F......714 522-7341
  7033 Orangethorpe Ave B Buena Park (90621) *(P-5117)*
Tuff Stuff Products ....B......559 535-5778
  9600 Road 256 Terra Bella (93270) *(P-4725)*
Tuffer Manufacturing Co Inc ....E......714 526-3077
  163 E Liberty Ave Anaheim (92801) *(P-10650)*
Tuffstuff Fitness Intl Inc ....C......909 629-1600
  13971 Norton Ave Chino (91710) *(P-11453)*
Tul Inc ....F......909 444-0577
  663 Brea Canyon Rd Ste 6 Walnut (91789) *(P-6542)*
TULARE DISTRICT HOSPITAL, Tulare Also called Tulare Local Health Care Dst *(P-20984)*
Tulare Local Health Care Dst ....A......559 685-3462
  869 N Cherry St Tulare (93274) *(P-20984)*
Tulare Nrsing Rhbilitation Ctr, Tulare Also called Tulare Nrsing Rhblttion Hosp I *(P-20491)*
Tulare Nrsing Rhblttion Hosp I ....D......559 686-8581
  680 E Merritt Ave Tulare (93274) *(P-20491)*
Tule River Economic Dev ....D......559 781-4271
  31071 Highway 190 Porterville (93257) *(P-23520)*
Tule River Indian Hlth Ctr Inc ....D......559 784-2316
  380 N Reservation Rd Porterville (93257) *(P-21358)*
Tumbleweed Day Camp, Los Angeles Also called Tumbleweed Eductl Entps Inc *(P-19678)*
Tumbleweed Eductl Entps Inc ....C......310 444-3232
  1024 Hanley Ave Los Angeles (90049) *(P-19678)*
Tunnelworks Services Inc (PA) ....D......562 201-4036
  13502 Whittier Blvd Ste H Whittier (90605) *(P-23356)*
Tur-Bo Jet Products Co Inc ....D......626 285-1294
  5025 Earle Ave Rosemead (91770) *(P-9645)*
Turbine Eng Cmpnents Tech Corp ....C......562 908-0200
  8839 Pioneer Blvd Santa Fe Springs (90670) *(P-7108)*
Turbine Repair Services LLC (PA) ....C......909 947-2256
  1838 E Cedar St Ontario (91761) *(P-7589)*
Turbo Coil Inc ....E......626 644-6254
  1532 Sinaloa Ave Pasadena (91104) *(P-8352)*
Turbo Refrigeration Systems ....E......626 599-9777
  1740 Evergreen St Duarte (91010) *(P-8353)*
Turbonetics Holdings Inc ....E......805 581-0333
  651 Via Alondra Ste 715 Camarillo (93012) *(P-10145)*
Turley Wine Cellars ....F......805 434-1030
  2900 Vineyard Dr Templeton (93465) *(P-2233)*

Turman Construction Co Inc ....D......661 831-0905
  4301 Park Circle Dr Bakersfield (93309) *(P-924)*
Turn Around Communications Inc ....C......626 443-2400
  100 N Barranca St Ste 260 West Covina (91791) *(P-979)*
Turn Key Logistics Inc ....C......714 931-1625
  14939 Summit Dr Eastvale (92880) *(P-12583)*
Turner John McDonald MD ....D......562 799-7071
  1198 Pacific Coast Hwy I Seal Beach (90740) *(P-20114)*
Turner Construction Company ....B......714 940-9000
  1900 S State College Blvd # 200 Anaheim (92806) *(P-841)*
Turner Fiberfill Inc ....E......323 724-7957
  1600 Date St Montebello (90640) *(P-4736)*
Turner Precision, Gardena Also called Aldo Fragale *(P-8485)*
Turner Techtronics Inc ....C......949 724-1339
  17845 Sky Park Cir Irvine (92614) *(P-18152)*
TURNINGPOINT SCHOOL, Culver City Also called Mwla Inc *(P-22041)*
Turnupseed Electric Service ....D......559 686-1541
  1580 S K St Tulare (93274) *(P-1332)*
Turret Lathe Specialists Inc ....F......714 520-0058
  875 S Rose Pl Anaheim (92805) *(P-8830)*
Turtle Entertainment America,, Burbank Also called Esl Gaming America Inc *(P-19351)*
Turtle Rock Cdc, Irvine Also called Child Development Incorporated *(P-21998)*
Turtle Rock Preschool Inc ....D......949 754-1685
  1 Concordia Irvine (92612) *(P-22068)*
Turtle Storage Ltd ....E......805 933-3688
  401 S Beckwith Rd Santa Paula (93060) *(P-3699)*
Turtleback Case, Sylmar Also called Leather Pro Inc *(P-5909)*
Tustin Executive Center, Tustin Also called Southern Cal Prmnnte Med Group *(P-15457)*
Tustin Executive Center, Tustin Also called Kaiser Foundation Hospitals *(P-21177)*
Tustin Memorial Academy ....D......714 730-7546
  12712 Browning Ave Santa Ana (92705) *(P-22372)*
Tustin Memorial Academy Pto, Santa Ana Also called Tustin Memorial Academy *(P-22372)*
Tustin Ranch Golf Club, Tustin Also called Crown Golf Properties LP *(P-23200)*
Tustin Ranch Medical Offices, Tustin Also called Kaiser Foundation Hospitals *(P-19921)*
Tustin Saab, Tustin Also called Nissan of Tustin *(P-15166)*
Tutor Perini Corporation (PA) ....C......318 362-8391
  15901 Olden St Sylmar (91342) *(P-842)*
Tutor Time Learning Ctrs LLC ....C......866 930-7975
  17150 Soledad Canyon Rd Canyon Country (91387) *(P-22069)*
Tutor Time Learning Ctrs LLC ....C......866 930-7975
  10420 Alta Loma Dr Rancho Cucamonga (91737) *(P-22070)*
Tutor Time Learning Ctrs LLC ....C......714 484-1000
  5805 Corporate Ave Cypress (90630) *(P-22071)*
Tutor-Saliba Corporation (HQ) ....D......818 362-8391
  15901 Olden St Sylmar (91342) *(P-843)*
Tutoring Expert Services LLC ....F......424 297-8318
  3751 Motor Ave Unit 34394 Los Angeles (90034) *(P-18002)*
Tuttle Click Ford, Irvine Also called Tuttle-Click Ford Inc *(P-18881)*
Tuttle Family Enterprises Inc ....B......818 534-2566
  9510 Topanga Canyon Blvd Chatsworth (91311) *(P-17294)*
Tuttle-Click Ford Inc ....C......949 855-1704
  43 Auto Center Dr Irvine (92618) *(P-18881)*
TV Guide Entrmt Group LLC ....B......310 360-1441
  2700 Colorado Ave Ste 200 Santa Monica (90404) *(P-13696)*
Tvb (usa) Inc (HQ) ....E......562 345-9871
  15411 Blackburn Ave Norwalk (90650) *(P-12746)*
Tvguide.com, Playa Vista Also called Pop Media Networks LLC *(P-19374)*
TW Security Corp (HQ) ....C......949 932-1000
  5 Park Plz Ste 400 Irvine (92614) *(P-13450)*
TW Services Inc ....B......714 441-2400
  2751 E Chapman Ave # 204 Fullerton (92831) *(P-12584)*
Twdc Enterprises 18 Corp (HQ) ....B......818 560-1000
  500 S Buena Vista St Burbank (91521) *(P-12747)*
Twed-Dells Inc ....E......714 754-6900
  1900 S Susan St Santa Ana (92704) *(P-5971)*
Twelve Signs Inc ....F......310 553-8000
  3369 S Robertson Blvd Los Angeles (90034) *(P-4109)*
Twentieth Cntury Fox HM Entrmt (HQ) .....A......310 369-1000
  10201 W Pico Blvd Los Angeles (90064) *(P-19189)*
Twentieth Cntury Fox Intl TV In (HQ) ....D......310 369-1000
  10201 W Pico Blvd Los Angeles (90064) *(P-12748)*
Twentieth Cntury Fox Film Corp (HQ) ....D......310 369-1000
  10201 W Pico Blvd Los Angeles (90064) *(P-19190)*
Twentieth Cntury Fox Film Corp ....C......310 369-2582
  2121 Avenue Of The Stars Los Angeles (90067) *(P-19191)*
Twentieth Cntury Fox Intl Corp (HQ) ....A......310 969-5300
  10201 W Pico Blvd Bldg 1 Los Angeles (90064) *(P-19263)*
Twentieth Cntury Fox Japan Inc ....A......310 369-4636
  10201 W Pico Blvd Los Angeles (90064) *(P-17192)*
Twentieth Television Inc ....D......310 584-2000
  1999 S Bundy Dr Los Angeles (90025) *(P-12749)*
Twenty Four 7 Globl Sltons Inc ....E......323 319-2724
  1460 Beachey Pl Carson (90746) *(P-3052)*
Twenty Mile Productions LLC ....C......412 251-0767
  11833 Miss Ave Ste 101 Los Angeles (90025) *(P-19381)*
Twenty4seven Hotels Corp ....B......949 734-6400
  520 Newport Center Dr # 520 Newport Beach (92660) *(P-23130)*
Twila True Collaborations LLC ....E......949 258-9720
  27156 Burbank Foothill Ranch (92610) *(P-5076)*
Twilight Technology Inc (PA) ....F......714 257-2257
  325 N Shepard St Anaheim (92806) *(P-9595)*
Twin Cities Community Hosp Inc ....B......805 434-3500
  1100 Las Tablas Rd Templeton (93465) *(P-20115)*
Twin Coast Metrology Inc (PA) ....F......310 709-2308
  333 Wshngton Blvd Ste 362 Marina Del Rey (90292) *(P-10863)*
Twin Eagles Inc ....C......562 802-3488
  13259 166th St Cerritos (90703) *(P-8996)*

Twin Peak Industries Inc ... E ... 800 259-5906
12420 Montague St Ste E Pacoima (91331) *(P-11454)*
Twin Power Indus Solutions, Murrieta *Also called Twin Power Usa LLC (P-1333)*
Twin Power Usa LLC ... E ... 714 609-6014
40424 Jacob Way Murrieta (92563) *(P-1333)*
Twining Inc (PA) ... **C ... 562 426-3355**
2883 E Spring St Ste 300 Long Beach (90806) *(P-22960)*
Twining Laboratories, Long Beach *Also called Twining Inc (P-22960)*
Twist Tite Mfg Inc ... E ... 562 229-0990
13344 Cambridge St Santa Fe Springs (90670) *(P-7079)*
Two Brothers Racing Inc ... F ... 714 550-6070
167 Via Trevizio Corona (92879) *(P-10507)*
Two Bunch Palms LLC (PA) ... **C ... 760 329-8791**
67425 Two Bunch Palms Trl Desert Hot Springs (92240) *(P-16759)*
Two Lads Inc (PA) ... **E ... 323 584-0064**
5001 Hampton St Vernon (90058) *(P-11503)*
Two Palms Nursing Center Inc (PA) ... **E ... 626 798-8991**
2637 E Washington Blvd Pasadena (91107) *(P-20632)*
Two Palms Nursing Center Inc ... C ... 626 796-1103
150 Bellefontaine St Pasadena (91105) *(P-20633)*
Two Roads Prof Resources Inc ... D ... 714 901-3804
5122 Bolsa Ave Ste 112 Huntington Beach (92649) *(P-17519)*
TWR Enterprises Inc ... C ... 951 279-2000
1661 Railroad St Corona (92878) *(P-1460)*
Txd International Usa Inc ... F ... 909 947-6568
2336 S Vineyard Ave A Ontario (91761) *(P-4040)*
Tyan Inc ... D ... 818 785-5831
1500 Glenoaks Blvd San Fernando (91340) *(P-18347)*
Tyler Trafficante Inc (PA) ... **D ... 323 869-9299**
700 S Palm Ave Alhambra (91803) *(P-2751)*
Typecraft Inc ... E ... 626 795-8093
2040 E Walnut St Pasadena (91107) *(P-4442)*
Typecraft Wood & Jones, Pasadena *Also called Typecraft Inc (P-4442)*
Tyr Sport Inc ... D ... 562 430-1380
1790 Apollo Ct Seal Beach (90740) *(P-14424)*
Tyte Jeans, Commerce *Also called 4 What Its Worth Inc (P-2794)*
Tyvak Nn-Satellite Systems Inc ... D ... 949 753-1020
15330 Barranca Pkwy Irvine (92618) *(P-10523)*
Tz, Los Angeles *Also called Toska Inc (P-3004)*
U A L, Irvine *Also called United Agribusiness League (P-22262)*
U C I Distribution Plus, Pasadena *Also called United Couriers Inc (P-12318)*
U C L Incorporated (PA) ... **D ... 323 235-0099**
620 S Hacienda Blvd City of Industry (91745) *(P-12086)*
U C L A Conference & Catering ... D ... 310 825-5305
330 De Neve Dr Ste L16 Los Angeles (90024) *(P-16982)*
U F C Pension Trust Fund, Cypress *Also called Cal Southern United Food (P-15514)*
U F I, Los Angeles *Also called United Fabrics Intl Inc (P-14323)*
U Gym LLC (PA) ... **D ... 714 668-0911**
1501 Quail St Ste 100 Newport Beach (92660) *(P-19471)*
U I G, Lake Forest *Also called United Industries Group Inc (P-22682)*
U M S Inc ... E ... 661 324-5454
317 Mount Vernon Ave Bakersfield (93307) *(P-7325)*
U S Architectural Lighting, Palmdale *Also called US Pole Company Inc (P-9108)*
U S Bearings, Baldwin Park *Also called Rbc Southwest Products Inc (P-14012)*
U S Bowling Corporation ... F ... 909 548-0644
5480 Schaefer Ave Chino (91710) *(P-11455)*
U S C, Glendale *Also called Usc Vrdugo Hlls Hosp Fundation (P-20997)*
U S L, San Luis Obispo *Also called Ultra-Stereo Labs Inc (P-9924)*
U S Managers Realty Inc ... D ... 310 607-0003
2101 Rosecrans Ave # 5252 El Segundo (90245) *(P-23131)*
U S Precision Manufacturing, Riverside *Also called US Precision Sheet Metal Inc (P-6937)*
U S Saw & Blades, Santa Ana *Also called US Saws Inc (P-7656)*
U S Technical Institute, Placentia *Also called US Computers Inc (P-8309)*
U S Trust Company NA ... B ... 213 861-5000
515 S Flower St Ste 2700 Los Angeles (90071) *(P-15352)*
U S Weatherford L P ... C ... 661 589-9483
2815 Fruitvale Ave Bakersfield (93308) *(P-555)*
U S Weatherford L P ... E ... 661 746-3415
19608 Broken Ct Shafter (93263) *(P-471)*
U S Wheel Corporation ... E ... 714 892-0021
15702 Producer Ln Huntington Beach (92649) *(P-10146)*
U S Xpress Inc ... A ... 760 768-6707
363 Nina Lee Rd Calexico (92231) *(P-12087)*
U T L A, Los Angeles *Also called United Teachers-Los Angeles (P-22306)*
U-Nav Microelectronics Corp ... D ... 949 453-2727
8 Hughes Irvine (92618) *(P-18230)*
U-Nited Printing and Copy Ctr, Van Nuys *Also called Printrunner LLC (P-4403)*
U-Sun Textiles Inc ... F ... 310 609-1155
3104 E Ana St Compton (90221) *(P-2607)*
U.S. Healthworks Medical Group, Valencia *Also called US Healthworks Inc (P-20127)*
U.S. Horizon Mfg, Valencia *Also called US Horizon Manufacturing Inc (P-5925)*
U.S. Rnal Care Earl St Dalysis, Torrance *Also called Pacific South Bay Dialysis LLC (P-21257)*
U.S. Specialty Vehicles, Yorba Linda *Also called American HX Auto Trade Inc (P-9934)*
UAS, Los Angeles *Also called Cal State La Univ Aux Svcs Inc (P-22996)*
Ubi Energy Corporation ... C ... 310 283-6978
9465 Wilshire Blvd # 300 Beverly Hills (90212) *(P-5264)*
Ubiquity Broadcasting Corp (HQ) ... **E ... 949 489-7600**
9801 Research Dr Irvine (92618) *(P-18697)*
Ubm Canon LLC (HQ) ... **C ... 310 445-4200**
2901 28th St Ste 100 Santa Monica (90405) *(P-4110)*
Ubtech Robotics Corp ... E ... 213 261-7153
767 S Alameda St Ste 330 Los Angeles (90021) *(P-7906)*
Uc Advantage Inc ... E ... 949 540-3403
92 Argonaut Ste 200 Aliso Viejo (92656) *(P-23357)*
Uc Irvine Hlth Rgonal Burn Ctr, Orange *Also called University California Irvine (P-20122)*
Uc Irvine Medical Center, Orange *Also called University California Irvine (P-20989)*
Uca General Insurance, Cypress *Also called United Chinese American Genera (P-15640)*
Ucan Zippers, Los Angeles *Also called Catame Inc (P-11495)*
UCI Construction Inc ... D ... 661 587-0192
3900 Fruitvale Ave Bakersfield (93308) *(P-22680)*
UCI Division Plastic Surgery, Orange *Also called University California Irvine (P-22818)*
UCI Family Health Center, Santa Ana *Also called University California Irvine (P-20123)*
UCI Health Blood Donor Center, Irvine *Also called University California Irvine (P-21494)*
UCI Westminster Medical Center, Westminster *Also called University California Irvine (P-20991)*
Ucla Copy Services ... E ... 310 794-6371
555 Westwood Plz Ste B Los Angeles (90095) *(P-17156)*
Ucla Dept of Design Media, Los Angeles *Also called Associated Students UCLA (P-17160)*
Ucla Foundation ... B ... 310 794-3193
10889 Wilshire Blvd # 11 Los Angeles (90024) *(P-16170)*
Ucla Hbr Dlysis Ctr Med Fndtio, Torrance *Also called Harbor-Ucla Med Foundation Inc (P-21245)*
Ucla Health ... D ... 310 825-9111
757 Westwood Plz Los Angeles (90095) *(P-20985)*
Ucla Health System Auxiliary ... B ... 310 267-4327
10920 Wilshire Blvd Los Angeles (90024) *(P-21225)*
Ucla Healthcare ... D ... 310 319-4560
1821 Wilshire Blvd Fl 6 Santa Monica (90403) *(P-20986)*
Ucla Mdcn SC Phrmclgy, Los Angeles *Also called Associated Students UCLA (P-19717)*
Ucp Dronfield North, Sylmar *Also called United Crbral Plsy/Spstic Chld (P-20635)*
Ucview, Northridge *Also called ATI Solutions Inc (P-9332)*
Udash Corporation (PA) ... **F ... 805 526-5222**
4511 Ish Dr Simi Valley (93063) *(P-10651)*
UDC, Anaheim *Also called Universal Dust Cllctr Mfg Sup (P-724)*
Uec, Cypress *Also called United Exchange Corp (P-18698)*
Ueis, Long Beach *Also called Undercurrent Educational (P-2766)*
Ufc Gym, Newport Beach *Also called U Gym LLC (P-19471)*
Ufcw Local 770, Los Angeles *Also called United Food and Commercial (P-22305)*
UFO Designs (PA) ... **F ... 714 892-4420**
5812 Machine Dr Huntington Beach (92649) *(P-5847)*
UFO Designs ... E ... 562 924-5763
16730 Gridley Rd Cerritos (90703) *(P-10147)*
UFO Inc ... E ... 323 588-5450
2110 Belgrave Ave Huntington Park (90255) *(P-5848)*
Ufp Riverside LLC ... E ... 951 826-3000
2100 Avalon St Riverside (92509) *(P-14030)*
Ufp Technologies Inc ... E ... 714 662-0277
20211 S Susana Rd Compton (90221) *(P-5526)*
Ugm Citatah Inc (PA) ... **C ... 562 921-9549**
13220 Cambridge St Santa Fe Springs (90670) *(P-13316)*
Ugmc, Santa Fe Springs *Also called Ugm Citatah Inc (P-13316)*
Uhc of California (HQ) ... **A ... 714 952-1121**
5995 Plaza Dr Cypress (90630) *(P-15462)*
Uhg Lax Prop Llc ... C ... 310 322-0999
1985 E Grand Ave El Segundo (90245) *(P-16760)*
Uhp Healthcare, Inglewood *Also called Watts Health Foundation Inc (P-20548)*
UHS, Chino *Also called Canyon Ridge Hospital Inc (P-21016)*
Uhs-Corona Inc (HQ) ... **A ... 951 737-4343**
800 S Main St Corona (92882) *(P-20987)*
Uhs-Corona Inc ... C ... 951 736-7200
730 Magnolia Ave Corona (92879) *(P-21359)*
UIC, Orange *Also called University California Irvine (P-20121)*
Uka LLC ... D ... 949 610-8000
620 Nwport Ctr Dr Ste 140 Newport Beach (92660) *(P-16761)*
Uline Inc ... D ... 909 605-7090
2950 Jurupa St Ontario (91761) *(P-14980)*
Ullman Sails Inc (PA) ... **F ... 714 432-1860**
2710 S Croddy Way Santa Ana (92704) *(P-3147)*
Uls Express Inc ... C ... 310 631-0800
2850 E Del Amo Blvd Compton (90221) *(P-12004)*
Ulti-Mate Connector Inc ... C ... 714 637-7099
1872 N Case St Orange (92865) *(P-9666)*
Ultimaster, Montebello *Also called Spartan Motors Gtb LLC (P-9997)*
Ultimate, Downey *Also called Altamed Health Services Corp (P-19695)*
Ultimate Communication Systems, Anaheim *Also called Rjb Enterprises Inc (P-1310)*
Ultimate Demo, Pomona *Also called Ultimate Removal Inc (P-646)*
Ultimate Ears Consumer LLC ... A ... 949 502-8340
3 Jenner Ste 180 Irvine (92618) *(P-11148)*
Ultimate Landscaping MGT ... D ... 714 502-9711
700 E Sycamore St Anaheim (92805) *(P-347)*
Ultimate Maintenance Svcs Inc ... E ... 310 542-1474
4237 Redondo Beach Blvd Lawndale (90260) *(P-17295)*
Ultimate Metal Finishing Corp ... E ... 323 890-9100
6150 Sheila St Commerce (90040) *(P-7422)*
Ultimate Paper Box Company, City of Industry *Also called Boxes R Us Inc (P-3789)*
Ultimate Print Source Inc ... E ... 909 947-5292
2070 S Hellman Ave Ontario (91761) *(P-4443)*
Ultimate Removal Inc ... C ... 909 524-0800
2168 Pomona Blvd Pomona (91768) *(P-646)*
Ultimate Solutions, Huntington Beach *Also called Sandia Plastics Inc (P-5811)*
Ultimate Sound Inc ... B ... 909 861-6200
1200 S Diamond Bar Blvd # 200 Diamond Bar (91765) *(P-9204)*
Ultimate Staffing Services, Orange *Also called Roth Staffing Companies LP (P-17514)*
Ultimatte Corporation ... E ... 818 993-8007
5828 Calvin Ave Tarzana (91356) *(P-9324)*
Ultra Built Kitchens Inc ... E ... 323 232-3362
1814 E 43rd St Los Angeles (90058) *(P-3344)*
Ultra Chem Labs Corp ... F ... 909 605-1640
4581 Brickell Privado St Ontario (91761) *(P-4981)*
Ultra Mobile, Costa Mesa *Also called Uvnv Inc (P-12677)*

ALPHABETIC

Employee Codes: A=Over 500 employees, B=251-500
C=101-250, D=51-100, E=20-50 F=10-19
2022 Southern California Business
Directory and Buyers Guide
© Mergent Inc. 1-800-342-5647
1301

Ultra Pro Acquisition LLC ....E....323 725-1975
6049 E Slauson Ave Commerce (90040) ***(P-4613)***

Ultra Pro International LLC (PA) ....D....**323 890-2100**
6049 E Slauson Ave Commerce (90040) ***(P-4614)***

Ultra Solutions LLC ....E....909 628-1778
1137 E Philadelphia St Ontario (91761) ***(P-13527)***

Ultra TEC Manufacturing Inc ....F....714 542-0608
1025 E Chestnut Ave Santa Ana (92701) ***(P-7998)***

Ultra Wheel Company ....E....714 449-7100
586 N Gilbert St Fullerton (92833) ***(P-10148)***

Ultra-Stereo Labs Inc ....E....805 549-0161
181 Bonetti Dr San Luis Obispo (93401) ***(P-9924)***

Ultraglas Inc ....E....818 772-7744
9200 Gazette Ave Chatsworth (91311) ***(P-13337)***

Ultragraphics Inc ....E....818 295-3994
2800 N Naomi St Burbank (91504) ***(P-17159)***

Ultramar Inc ....E....661 944-2496
9508 E Palmdale Blvd Palmdale (93591) ***(P-5265)***

Ultramar Inc ....E....310 834-7254
961 S La Paloma Ave Wilmington (90744) ***(P-556)***

Ultramet ....D....818 899-0236
12173 Montague St Pacoima (91331) ***(P-7326)***

Ultrastar Cinemas, Redlands *Also called American Cinemas Group Inc* ***(P-19268)***

Ultraviolet Devices Inc ....D....661 295-8140
26145 Technology Dr Valencia (91355) ***(P-13850)***

Ultron Systems Inc ....F....805 529-1485
5105 Maureen Ln Moorpark (93021) ***(P-9596)***

Uma Enterprises Inc (PA) ....D....**310 631-1166**
350 W Apra St Compton (90220) ***(P-13192)***

Uma Home Decor, Compton *Also called Uma Enterprises Inc* ***(P-13192)***

Umbrla Inc ....D....888 909-5564
3242 Halladay St Ste 202 Santa Ana (92705) ***(P-7623)***

Umc Acquisition Corp (PA) ....E....**562 940-0300**
9151 Imperial Hwy Downey (90242) ***(P-6338)***

Umeken USA Inc (PA) ....D....**888 941-3311**
13012 Moore St Cerritos (90703) ***(P-14746)***

Umex, Downey *Also called Universal Mlding Extrusion Inc* ***(P-6321)***

Umeya Inc ....E....213 626-8341
414 Crocker St Los Angeles (90013) ***(P-2075)***

Umeya Rice Cake Co, Los Angeles *Also called Umeya Inc* ***(P-2075)***

Umg Commercial Services Inc (HQ) ....D....**310 235-4700**
2220 Colorado Ave Santa Monica (90404) ***(P-4215)***

Umgd, Santa Monica *Also called Umg Commercial Services Inc* ***(P-4215)***

Umgee USA Inc ....F....323 526-9138
1565 E 23rd St Los Angeles (90011) ***(P-2873)***

Umina Brothers Inc (PA) ....D....**213 622-9206**
1601 E Olympic Blvd # 403 Los Angeles (90021) ***(P-14659)***

Ump, Corona *Also called United Metal Products Inc* ***(P-6463)***

Umpco Inc ....D....714 897-3531
7100 Lampson Ave Garden Grove (92841) ***(P-6543)***

Ums Banking, Glendale *Also called United Merchant Svcs Cal Inc* ***(P-13368)***

Umx, Walnut *Also called Universal Mercantile Exch Inc* ***(P-11613)***

Un Deux Trois Inc (PA) ....E....**323 588-1067**
2301 E 7th St Los Angeles (90023) ***(P-3046)***

UNAC/UHCP, San Dimas *Also called Associations of United Nurses* ***(P-22287)***

Unalisys, Glendale *Also called Universal Asset Lnding Info Sy* ***(P-17747)***

Unbrako LLC ....F....310 817-2400
11939 Woodruff Ave Downey (90241) ***(P-13820)***

Unbroken Studios LLC ....D....310 741-2670
2121 Park Pl Ste 100 El Segundo (90245) ***(P-18003)***

Uncks Unique Plastics Inc ....F....909 983-5181
1215 Brooks St Ontario (91762) ***(P-5849)***

Uncle Bum's Gourmet Sauces, Riverside *Also called Tom Harris Inc* ***(P-2538)***

Unconditional Love Inc ....D....888 860-6888
17383 W Sunset Blvd 200b Pacific Palisades (90272) ***(P-14425)***

Undercurrent Educational ....D....800 430-1183
3350 E 7th St Ste 343 Long Beach (90804) ***(P-2766)***

Undersea Systems Intl Inc ....D....714 754-7848
3133 W Harvard St Santa Ana (92704) ***(P-9925)***

Underwater Systems Inc ....F....714 229-9268
10603 Progress Way Cypress (90630) ***(P-22681)***

Underwraps Costume Corporation ....F....818 349-5300
9600 Irondale Ave Chatsworth (91311) ***(P-3088)***

Underwraps Costumes, Chatsworth *Also called Underwraps Costume Corporation* ***(P-3088)***

Unfold Agency Inc (PA) ....D....**323 963-3108**
11801 Teale St Culver City (90230) ***(P-17065)***

Unger Fabrik LLC (PA) ....C....**626 469-8080**
18525 Railroad St City of Industry (91748) ***(P-2874)***

UNI Filter Inc ....E....714 535-6933
1468 Manhattan Ave Fullerton (92831) ***(P-10149)***

UNI Healthcare Inc ....E....661 222-9984
25129 The Old Rd Ste 204 Stevenson Ranch (91381) ***(P-21491)***

UNI Hosiery Co Inc (PA) ....C....**213 228-0100**
1911 E Olympic Blvd Los Angeles (90021) ***(P-14357)***

UNI-Caps LLC ....E....714 529-8400
540 Lambert Rd Brea (92821) ***(P-4768)***

UNI-Sport Inc ....E....310 217-4587
16933 Gramercy Pl Gardena (90247) ***(P-4444)***

Unical Aviation Inc (PA) ....C....**909 348-1700**
680 S Lemon Ave City of Industry (91789) ***(P-14067)***

Unical Defense Inc ....E....909 348-1500
680 S Lemon Ave Ste A City of Industry (91789) ***(P-14068)***

Unicare Medical Transportation, Riverside *Also called Empire Med Transportations LLC* ***(P-12453)***

Unichem Enterprises, Ontario *Also called Imp International Inc* ***(P-4749)***

Unico American Corporation (PA) ....D....**818 591-9800**
26050 Mureau Rd Calabasas (91302) ***(P-15487)***

Unico Logistics Usa Inc ....E....310 835-5656
357 Van Ness Way Ste 100 Torrance (90501) ***(P-11894)***

Unicom Electric Inc ....F....626 964-7873
565 Brea Canyon Rd Ste A Walnut (91789) ***(P-9358)***

Unified Aircraft Services Inc (PA) ....D....**909 877-0535**
1571 S Lilac Ave Bloomington (92316) ***(P-12559)***

Unified Field Services Corp ....E....661 325-8962
6906 Downing Ave Bakersfield (93308) ***(P-412)***

Unified Inv Programs Inc (PA) ....E....**310 782-1878**
2368 Torrance Blvd # 200 Torrance (90501) ***(P-21492)***

Unified Nutrimeals ....D....323 923-9335
5469 Ferguson Dr Commerce (90022) ***(P-2544)***

Unified Valet Parking Inc ....D....818 822-5807
99 S Chester Ave Fl 2 Pasadena (91106) ***(P-18780)***

Unifirst Corporation ....C....909 390-8670
700 Etiwanda Ave Ste C Ontario (91761) ***(P-16886)***

Uniform Accessories, Northridge *Also called Rashman Corporation* ***(P-13516)***

Unify Financial Federal Cr Un (PA) ....D....**310 536-5000**
1899 Western Way Ste 100 Torrance (90501) ***(P-15093)***

Unigro, San Bernardino *Also called L & L Nursery Supply Inc* ***(P-14862)***

Unilab Corporation (HQ) ....B....**818 737-6000**
8401 Fallbrook Ave West Hills (91304) ***(P-21100)***

Unilabel, Santa Fe Springs *Also called Universal Label Printers* ***(P-4587)***

Unimark, Gardena *Also called Matsui International Co Inc* ***(P-5231)***

Uninet Imaging Inc (PA) ....E....**424 675-3300**
3232 W El Segundo Blvd Hawthorne (90250) ***(P-13349)***

Union 76, Los Angeles *Also called Kim Chong* ***(P-18563)***

Union Bank of California (PA) ....D....**909 350-7176**
11551 Foothill Blvd Rancho Cucamonga (91730) ***(P-15007)***

Union Building Maintenance, Commerce *Also called Uniserve Facilities Svcs Corp* ***(P-17296)***

Union Pacific Lines, Long Beach *Also called Union Pacific Railroad Company* ***(P-11799)***

Union Pacific Railroad Company ....B....562 490-7000
2401 E Sepulveda Blvd Long Beach (90810) ***(P-11799)***

Union Sup Comsy Solutions Inc ....C....785 357-5005
2301 E Pacifica Pl Rancho Dominguez (90220) ***(P-14516)***

Union Technology Corp ....E....323 266-6871
718 Monterey Pass Rd Monterey Park (91754) ***(P-13784)***

Unique Carpets Ltd ....D....951 352-8125
7360 Jurupa Ave Riverside (92504) ***(P-13193)***

Unique Image Inc ....F....818 727-7785
19365 Bus Center Dr Ste 4 Northridge (91324) ***(P-4445)***

Unique Protective Services, Santa Clarita *Also called Cottrell Paul Enterprises LLC* ***(P-18266)***

Unique Sales, Vernon *Also called Zk Enterprises Inc* ***(P-2833)***

Unirex Corp ....E....323 589-4000
2288 E 27th St Vernon (90058) ***(P-9597)***

Unirex Technologies, Vernon *Also called Unirex Corp* ***(P-9597)***

Unis LLC (PA) ....C....**909 839-2600**
218 Machlin Ct Ste A Walnut (91789) ***(P-12548)***

Unis LLC ....D....310 747-7388
19914 S Via Baron Rancho Dominguez (90220) ***(P-12255)***

Uniserve Facilities Svcs Corp (PA) ....B....**213 533-1000**
2363 S Atlantic Blvd Commerce (90040) ***(P-17296)***

Uniserve Facilities Svcs Corp ....B....310 440-6747
1200 Getty Center Dr Los Angeles (90049) ***(P-17297)***

Unison Electric ....E....714 375-5915
16652 Gemini Ln Huntington Beach (92647) ***(P-1334)***

Unisource Solutions Inc (PA) ....C....**562 654-3500**
8350 Rex Rd Pico Rivera (90660) ***(P-13153)***

Unisun Multinational, Chino *Also called Ht Multinational Inc* ***(P-10076)***

Unit Industries Inc (PA) ....F....**714 871-4161**
3122 Maple St Santa Ana (92707) ***(P-9667)***

Unitech Deco Inc ....F....818 700-1373
19731 Bahama St Northridge (91324) ***(P-4586)***

Unitech Industries, Northridge *Also called Unitech Deco Inc* ***(P-4586)***

United Aeronautical Corp ....E....818 764-2102
7360 Laurel Canyon Blvd North Hollywood (91605) ***(P-14069)***

United Agencies Inc (PA) ....D....**818 952-8818**
301 E Colo Blvd Ste 200 Pasadena (91101) ***(P-15639)***

United Agribusiness League (PA) ....E....**800 223-4590**
54 Corporate Park Irvine (92606) ***(P-22262)***

United Amrcn Indian Invlvment (PA) ....C....**213 202-3970**
1125 W 6th St Ste 103 Los Angeles (90017) ***(P-21360)***

United Artists Entrmt LLC (PA) ....D....**310 449-3000**
245 N Beverly Dr Beverly Hills (90210) ***(P-19382)***

United Artists Pictures Inc (HQ) ....C....**310 449-3000**
10250 Constellation Blvd Los Angeles (90067) ***(P-19192)***

United Artists Productions Inc ....C....310 449-3000
10250 Constellation Blvd Los Angeles (90067) ***(P-19264)***

United Artists Television Corp ....C....310 449-3000
10250 Constellation Blvd Los Angeles (90067) ***(P-19265)***

United Audio Video Group Inc ....E....818 980-6700
7651 Densmore Ave Van Nuys (91406) ***(P-9842)***

United Bakery Equipment Co Inc (PA) ....D....**310 635-8121**
19216 S Laurel Park Rd Rancho Dominguez (90220) ***(P-8079)***

United Blood Svcs Centl Coast, Ventura *Also called Vitalant* ***(P-21496)***

United Brothers Concrete Inc ....C....760 346-1013
41905 Boardwalk Ste K Palm Desert (92211) ***(P-1556)***

United Bys Grls Clubs Snta BRB ....D....805 967-1612
5701 Hollister Ave Goleta (93117) ***(P-22373)***

United Cabinet Company Inc ....E....909 796-3015
1510 S Mountain View Ave San Bernardino (92408) ***(P-3345)***

United California, Downey *Also called United Drill Bushing Corp* ***(P-7875)***

United California Corporation ....D....562 803-1521
12200 Woodruff Ave Downey (90241) ***(P-7839)***

United Cargo Logistics, City of Industry *Also called U C L Incorporated* ***(P-12086)***

United Carports LLC ....F....800 757-6742
7280 Sycamore Canyon Blvd # 1 Riverside (92508) ***(P-7011)***

United Chinese American Genera (PA) ... E ... **714 228-7800**
6363 Katella Ave Cypress (90630) *(P-15640)*
United Contractors Inc ... D ... 714 828-6275
8032 Chester Ave Stanton (90680) *(P-1335)*
United Convalescent Facilities ... D ... 626 629-6950
230 E Adams Blvd Los Angeles (90011) *(P-20634)*
United Couriers Inc (HQ) ... C ... **213 383-3611**
3280 E Foothill Blvd Pasadena (91107) *(P-12318)*
United Cpitl Fncl Advisers LLC ... D ... 949 999-8500
620 Nwport Ctr Dr Ste 500 Newport Beach (92660) *(P-15353)*
United Crbral Plsy Assn Ornge ... B ... 949 333-6400
1251 E Dyer Rd Ste 150 Santa Ana (92705) *(P-21907)*
United Crbral Plsy Assn San Lu ... D ... 805 543-2039
3620 Sacramento Dr # 201 San Luis Obispo (93401) *(P-11895)*
United Crbral Plsy/Spstic Chld ... D ... 818 364-5911
13272 Dronfield Ave Sylmar (91342) *(P-20635)*
United Crbral Plsy/Spstic Chld ... D ... 818 727-1067
9205 White Oak Ave Northridge (91325) *(P-20544)*
United Drill Bushing Corp ... C ... 562 803-1521
12200 Woodruff Ave Downey (90241) *(P-7875)*
United Duralume Products Inc ... F ... 714 773-4011
350 S Raymond Ave Fullerton (92831) *(P-6936)*
United El Segundo Inc (PA) ... D ... **310 323-3992**
4130 Cover St Long Beach (90808) *(P-16025)*
United Exchange Corp (PA) ... D ... **562 977-4500**
5836 Corp Ave Ste 200 Cypress (90630) *(P-18698)*
United Fabricare Supply Inc (PA) ... D ... **310 886-3790**
1237 W Walnut St Compton (90220) *(P-14046)*
United Fabrics Intl Inc ... D ... 213 749-8200
1723 S Central Ave Los Angeles (90021) *(P-14323)*
United Facility Solutions Inc ... B ... 310 743-3000
19208 S Vermont Ave # 200 Gardena (90248) *(P-18348)*
United Farm Workers America (PA) ... C ... **661 822-5571**
29700 Wdford Tehachapi Rd Keene (93531) *(P-22303)*
United Fmly Care Inc A Med Cor ... C ... 909 874-1679
8110 Mango Ave Ste 104 Fontana (92335) *(P-20116)*
United Food & Commercl Workers (PA) ... D ... **714 995-4601**
8530 Stanton Ave Buena Park (90620) *(P-22304)*
United Food and Commercial (PA) ... D ... **213 487-7070**
630 Shatto Pl Ste 300 Los Angeles (90005) *(P-22305)*
United Food Group LLC ... F ... 323 588-5286
3425 E Vernon Ave Vernon (90058) *(P-1721)*
United Gastroenterologists, Murrieta *Also called United Medical Doctors (P-20117)*
United Guard Security Inc (PA) ... B ... **800 228-2505**
879 W 190th St Ste 280 Gardena (90248) *(P-18349)*
United Imaging, Woodland Hills *Also called United Ribbon Company Inc (P-13369)*
United Ind Taxi Drivers (PA) ... D ... **323 462-1088**
900 N Alvarado St Los Angeles (90026) *(P-11902)*
United Industries Group Inc ... E ... 949 759-3200
11 Rancho Cir Lake Forest (92630) *(P-22682)*
United Irrigation Inc ... D ... 760 347-6161
44907 Golf Center Pkwy # 3 Indio (92201) *(P-13015)*
United Launch Alliance LLC ... C ... 303 269-5876
1579 Utah Ave Bldg 7525 Vandenberg Afb (93437) *(P-10524)*
United Material Handling Inc ... D ... 951 657-4900
23900 Brodiaea Ave Moreno Valley (92553) *(P-13955)*
United Media Services Inc ... C ... 714 693-8168
4955 E Hunter Ave Anaheim (92807) *(P-9843)*
United Medical Doctors ... D ... 951 566-5229
28078 Baxter Rd Ste 530 Murrieta (92563) *(P-20117)*
United Medical Imaging Inc (PA) ... D ... **310 943-8400**
1762 Westwood Blvd # 230 Los Angeles (90024) *(P-20118)*
United Medical Management Inc ... C ... 909 886-5291
1680 N Waterman Ave San Bernardino (92404) *(P-20636)*
United Medical-IV Pharmacy, Cerritos *Also called Lincare Inc (P-21184)*
United Memorial Products Inc ... E ... 562 699-3578
4845 Pioneer Blvd Whittier (90601) *(P-6062)*
United Memorial/Matthews Intl, Whittier *Also called United Memorial Products Inc (P-6062)*
United Merchant Svcs Cal Inc ... D ... 818 246-6767
750 Fairmont Ave Ste 201 Glendale (91203) *(P-13368)*
United Metal Products Inc ... F ... 951 739-9535
234 N Sherman Ave Corona (92882) *(P-6463)*
United Methodist Federal Cr Un (PA) ... C ... **909 946-4096**
9040 Benson Ave Montclair (91763) *(P-15094)*
United Network Info Svcs, Walnut *Also called Unis LLC (P-12548)*
United Oil, Long Beach *Also called United El Segundo Inc (P-16025)*
United Online Inc (HQ) ... D ... **818 287-3000**
30870 Russell Ranch Rd # 250 Westlake Village (91362) *(P-16983)*
United Online Advg Netwrk Inc ... D ... 818 287-3000
21301 Burbank Blvd Woodland Hills (91367) *(P-17066)*
United Owners Services, Anaheim *Also called Tricom Management Inc (P-23127)*
United Pacific Designs, Vernon *Also called UPD INC (P-11365)*
United Pacific Waste ... D ... 562 699-7600
4334 San Gbriel Rver Pkwy Pico Rivera (90660) *(P-12986)*
United Panam Financial Corp (PA) ... B ... **949 224-1226**
1071 Camelback St Ste 100 Newport Beach (92660) *(P-18882)*
United Paradyne Corporation ... D ... 805 734-2359
P.O. Box 5368 Santa Barbara (93150) *(P-23132)*
United Paradyne Corporation ... D ... 805 734-4734
Utah & 10th St Bldg 7525 Lompoc (93437) *(P-23133)*
United Parcel Service Inc ... C ... 858 541-2336
160 W Main St El Centro (92243) *(P-12148)*
United Parcel Service Inc ... C ... 760 325-1762
650 N Commercial Rd Palm Springs (92262) *(P-12149)*
United Parcel Service Inc ... C ... 800 742-5877
2800 W 227th St Torrance (90505) *(P-12150)*
United Parcel Service Inc ... D ... 323 837-1220
2747 Vail Ave Commerce (90040) *(P-18699)*
United Parcel Service Inc ... D ... 805 474-9134
1820 Railroad St Oceano (93445) *(P-18700)*
United Parcel Service Inc ... C ... 760 375-7861
711 W Ridgecrest Blvd Ridgecrest (93555) *(P-12151)*
United Parcel Service Inc ... C ... 760 872-7661
2915 N Sierra Hwy Bishop (93514) *(P-12152)*
United Parcel Service Inc ... C ... 760 252-5766
2790 E Main St Barstow (92311) *(P-12153)*
United Parcel Service Inc ... D ... 949 643-6634
22 Brookline Aliso Viejo (92656) *(P-18701)*
United Parcel Service Inc ... D ... 323 260-8957
3333 S Downey Rd Vernon (90058) *(P-12331)*
United Parcel Service Inc ... C ... 310 217-2646
17115 S Western Ave Gardena (90247) *(P-12154)*
United Parcel Service Inc ... C ... 909 974-7212
3140 E Jurupa Ave Ontario (91761) *(P-12155)*
United Parcel Service Inc ... D ... 951 928-5221
25283 Sherman Rd Sun City (92585) *(P-12332)*
United Parcel Service Inc ... C ... 661 824-9391
1522 Sabovich St Mojave (93501) *(P-12156)*
United Parcel Service Inc ... C ... 310 474-0019
10690 Santa Monica Blvd Los Angeles (90025) *(P-12157)*
United Parcel Service Inc ... D ... 909 974-7250
3221 E Jurupa Ontario (91764) *(P-18702)*
United Parcel Service Inc ... D ... 909 974-7190
Ontario Airport Ontario (91758) *(P-12333)*
United Parcel Service Inc ... D ... 310 670-5849
5720 Avion Dr Bay 8 Los Angeles (90045) *(P-12319)*
United Parcel Service Inc ... D ... 909 906-5700
2925 Jurupa St Ontario (91761) *(P-12320)*
United Parcel Service Inc ... D ... 800 742-5877
1457 E Victoria Ave San Bernardino (92408) *(P-12321)*
United Parcel Service Inc ... D ... 951 757-8176
19440 Arenth Ave City of Industry (91748) *(P-12322)*
United Parcel Service Inc ... D ... 909 349-4343
10760 Tamarind Ave Bloomington (92316) *(P-12323)*
United Parcel Service Inc ... C ... 800 828-8264
290 W Avenue L Lancaster (93534) *(P-12158)*
United Parcel Service Inc ... C ... 404 828-6000
16000 Arminta St Van Nuys (91406) *(P-12159)*
United Parcel Service Inc ... D ... 909 605-7740
3110 Jurupa St Ontario (91761) *(P-12324)*
United Parcel Service Inc ... C ... 562 404-3236
13233 Moore St Cerritos (90703) *(P-12160)*
United Parcel Service Inc ... D ... 626 280-8012
201 W Garvey Ave Ste 102 Monterey Park (91754) *(P-18703)*
United Parcel Service Inc ... D ... 818 735-0945
4607 Lakeview Canyon Rd Westlake Village (91361) *(P-18704)*
United Parcel Service Inc ... C ... 801 973-3400
3601 Sacramento Dr San Luis Obispo (93401) *(P-12161)*
United Parcel Service Inc ... C ... 805 964-7848
505 Pine Ave Goleta (93117) *(P-12162)*
United Parcel Service Inc ... C ... 805 922-7851
309 Cooley Ln Santa Maria (93455) *(P-12163)*
United Parcel Service Inc ... C ... 760 365-3158
56174 29th Palms Hwy Yucca Valley (92284) *(P-12164)*
United Parcel Service Inc ... C ... 805 375-1832
1501 Rancho Conejo Blvd Newbury Park (91320) *(P-12165)*
United Parcel Service Inc ... C ... 323 729-6762
3000 E Washington Blvd Los Angeles (90023) *(P-12166)*
United Parcel Service Inc ... C ... 909 974-7000
3140 Jurupa St Ontario (91761) *(P-12167)*
United Parcel Service Inc ... D ... 951 749-3400
11811 Landon Dr Eastvale (91752) *(P-18705)*
United Parcel Service Inc ... C ... 805 642-6784
2559 Palma Dr Ventura (93003) *(P-12168)*
United Parcel Service Inc ... C ... 626 814-6216
1100 Baldwin Park Blvd Baldwin Park (91706) *(P-12169)*
United Parcel Service Inc ... D ... 866 553-1069
91 W Easy St Simi Valley (93065) *(P-18706)*
United Paving Company, Corona *Also called Superior Paving Company Inc (P-920)*
United Pharma LLC ... C ... 714 738-8999
2317 Moore Ave Fullerton (92833) *(P-5245)*
United Precision Corp ... E ... 818 576-9540
20810 Plummer St Chatsworth (91311) *(P-8831)*
United Pumping Service Inc ... D ... 626 961-9326
14000 Valley Blvd City of Industry (91746) *(P-12005)*
United Ribbon Company Inc ... D ... 818 716-1515
21201 Oxnard St Woodland Hills (91367) *(P-13369)*
United Riggers & Erectors Inc (PA) ... D ... **909 978-0400**
4188 Valley Blvd Walnut (91789) *(P-1627)*
United Scope LLC (HQ) ... E ... **949 333-0001**
14370 Myford Rd Ste 150 Irvine (92606) *(P-10864)*
United Seal Coating Slurryseal ... F ... 805 563-4922
3463 State St Ste 522 Santa Barbara (93105) *(P-844)*
United Service Tech Inc ... D ... 714 224-1406
181 W Orangethorpe Ave D Placentia (92870) *(P-19079)*
United Site Services Cal Inc (PA) ... E ... **626 462-9110**
242 Live Oak Ave Irwindale (91706) *(P-17381)*
United Srgcal Prtners Intl Inc ... D ... 310 325-4555
3445 Pcf Cast Hwy Ste 110 Torrance (90505) *(P-20119)*
United States Bakery ... E ... 323 232-6124
457 E Martin Luthr Kng Jr Los Angeles (90011) *(P-2039)*
United States Fire Insur Co ... D ... 213 797-3100
777 S Figueroa St # 1500 Los Angeles (90017) *(P-15641)*
United States Gypsum Company ... D ... 908 232-8900
401 Van Ness Ave Torrance (90501) *(P-6131)*
United States Gypsum Company ... D ... 760 358-3200
3810 Evan Hewes Hwy Imperial (92251) *(P-6132)*
United States Logistics Group ... E ... 562 989-9555
2700 Rose Ave Ste A Signal Hill (90755) *(P-10169)*

Employee Codes: A=Over 500 employees, B=251-500 C=101-250, D=51-100, E=20-50 F=10-19
2022 Southern California Business Directory and Buyers Guide
© Mergent Inc. 1-800-342-5647
1303

United States Technical Svcs .... C 714 374-6300
16541 Gothard St Ste 214 Huntington Beach (92647) ***(P-18231)***

United Stationers, City of Industry *Also called Essendant Co* ***(P-14194)***

United Surface Solutions LLC .... E 562 693-0202
11901 Burke St Santa Fe Springs (90670) ***(P-7999)***

United Syatt America Corp (PA) .... **C 714 568-1938**
920 E 1st St Santa Ana (92701) ***(P-13103)***

United Taxi San Fernando Vly, Los Angeles *Also called United Ind Taxi Drivers* ***(P-11902)***

United Teachers-Los Angeles .... D 213 487-5560
3303 Wilshire Blvd Fl 10 Los Angeles (90010) ***(P-22306)***

United Technologies Corp .... D 562 944-6244
11120 Norwalk Blvd Santa Fe Springs (90670) ***(P-10440)***

United Technology, City of Industry *Also called Faircom Inc* ***(P-9507)***

United Testing Systems Inc .... E 714 638-2322
1375 S Acacia Ave Fullerton (92831) ***(P-10919)***

United Transport Service Inc .... E 844 258-2262
6750 Black Forest Dr Eastvale (92880) ***(P-18707)***

United Vision Financial Inc .... C 818 285-0211
16027 Ventura Blvd # 200 Encino (91436) ***(P-15257)***

United Vlve Div of Fderal Inds .... F 310 297-4000
645 Hawaii St El Segundo (90245) ***(P-14070)***

United Way Inc (PA) .... **D 213 808-6220**
1150 S Olive St Ste T-500 Los Angeles (90015) ***(P-22214)***

United Way Greater Los Angeles, Los Angeles *Also called United Way Inc* ***(P-22214)***

United Wealth Control, Bakersfield *Also called B & L Casing Service LLC* ***(P-478)***

United Western Enterprises Inc .... E 805 389-1077
850 Flynn Rd Ste 200 Camarillo (93012) ***(P-7423)***

United Wholesale Lumber Co, Valencia *Also called Standard Lumber Company Inc* ***(P-3409)***

United Wireless Inc (HQ) .... **D 951 471-5999**
31915 Mission Trl Lake Elsinore (92530) ***(P-12615)***

Unitek It Education, Newport Beach *Also called Unitek Learning Inc* ***(P-18232)***

Unitek Learning Inc (PA) .... **D 510 249-1060**
1401 Dove St Ste 340 Newport Beach (92660) ***(P-18232)***

Unitek Technology Inc .... F 909 930-5700
10211 Bellegrave Ave Jurupa Valley (91752) ***(P-8180)***

Unity Courier Service Inc (PA) .... **C 323 255-9800**
3231 Fletcher Dr Los Angeles (90065) ***(P-12170)***

Unity Digital, Costa Mesa *Also called Unity Sales International Inc* ***(P-11296)***

Unity Sales International Inc .... E 714 800-1700
2950 Airway Ave Ste A12 Costa Mesa (92626) ***(P-11296)***

Univar Solutions USA Inc .... C 323 727-7005
2600 Garfield Ave Commerce (90040) ***(P-14792)***

Universal Asphalt Co Inc .... E 562 941-0201
10610 Painter Ave Santa Fe Springs (90670) ***(P-925)***

Universal Asset Lnding Info Sy (HQ) .... **D 678 854-9451**
505 N Brand Blvd Ste 830 Glendale (91203) ***(P-17747)***

Universal Bank (PA) .... **D 626 854-2818**
3455 S Nogales St Fl 2 West Covina (91792) ***(P-15054)***

Universal Card Inc .... B 949 861-4000
9012 Research Dr Ste 200 Irvine (92618) ***(P-18708)***

Universal Care Inc (PA) .... **B 562 424-6200**
19762 Macarthur Blvd # 100 Irvine (92612) ***(P-21361)***

Universal Cble Productions LLC .... D 818 777-0351
100 Universal City Plz Universal City (91608) ***(P-19383)***

Universal Ctrl Solutions Corp .... F 818 898-3380
19770 Bahama St Northridge (91324) ***(P-8965)***

Universal Cushion Company Inc (PA) .... **E 323 887-8000**
1610 Mandeville Canyon Rd Los Angeles (90049) ***(P-3122)***

Universal Custom Courier, San Fernando *Also called Universal Mail Delivery Svc* ***(P-12006)***

Universal Cy Stdios Prdctons L (HQ) .... **A 818 777-1000**
100 Universal City Plz Universal City (91608) ***(P-19193)***

Universal Defense .... E 909 626-4178
412 Cucamonga Ave Claremont (91711) ***(P-6763)***

Universal Dust Cllctr Mfg Sup (PA) .... **D 714 630-8588**
1041 N Kraemer Pl Anaheim (92806) ***(P-724)***

Universal Dyeing and Prtg Inc .... E 213 746-0818
2303 E 11th St Los Angeles (90021) ***(P-2666)***

Universal Dynamics Inc .... E 626 480-0035
5313 3rd St Irwindale (91706) ***(P-472)***

Universal Forest Products, Riverside *Also called Ufp Riverside LLC* ***(P-14030)***

Universal Framing Products, Santa Clarita *Also called Universal Wood Moulding Inc* ***(P-13194)***

Universal Home Care Inc .... C 323 653-9222
151 N San Vicente Blvd Beverly Hills (90211) ***(P-21226)***

Universal Hosiery Inc .... D 661 702-8444
28337 Constellation Rd Valencia (91355) ***(P-2624)***

Universal Label Printers .... E 562 944-0234
13003 Los Nietos Rd Santa Fe Springs (90670) ***(P-4587)***

Universal Logistics System Inc (HQ) .... **D 310 631-0800**
2850 Del Amo Blvd Carson (90810) ***(P-12256)***

Universal Mail Delivery Svc (PA) .... **D 818 365-3144**
501 S Brand Blvd 104 San Fernando (91340) ***(P-12006)***

Universal Meat Company, Rancho Cucamonga *Also called Formosa Meat Company Inc* ***(P-1732)***

Universal Mercantile Exch Inc .... F 909 839-0556
21128 Commerce Point Dr Walnut (91789) ***(P-11613)***

Universal Merchandise Inc .... F 818 344-2044
5422 Aura Ave Tarzana (91356) ***(P-2752)***

Universal Metal Plating .... F 626 969-7932
704 S Taylor Ave Montebello (90640) ***(P-7327)***

Universal Metal Plating (PA) .... **F 626 969-7931**
1526 W 1st St Irwindale (91702) ***(P-18806)***

Universal Mlding Extrusion Inc (HQ) .... **C 562 401-1015**
9151 Imperial Hwy Downey (90242) ***(P-6321)***

Universal Molding Company, Downey *Also called Umc Acquisition Corp* ***(P-6338)***

Universal Molding Company (HQ) .... **C 310 886-1750**
9151 Imperial Hwy Downey (90242) ***(P-6339)***

Universal Mus Group Dist Corp .... D 818 508-9550
111 Unvrsal Hllywood Dr S Universal City (91608) ***(P-18709)***

Universal Mus Investments Inc (HQ) .... **D 888 583-7176**
2220 Colorado Ave Santa Monica (90404) ***(P-18710)***

Universal Music Group Inc (PA) .... **D 310 865-4000**
2220 Colorado Ave Santa Monica (90404) ***(P-18711)***

Universal Music Publishing Inc .... D 310 235-4700
2100 Colorado Ave Santa Monica (90404) ***(P-4216)***

Universal Packg Systems Inc (PA) .... **A 909 517-2442**
14570 Monte Vista Ave Chino (91710) ***(P-5077)***

Universal Packg Systems Inc .... C 909 517-2442
14570 Monte Vista Ave Chino (91710) ***(P-12257)***

Universal Pain MGT Med Corp (PA) .... **D 661 267-6876**
819 Auto Center Dr Ste A Palmdale (93551) ***(P-20120)***

Universal Pctres HM Entrmt LLC (HQ) .... **A 818 777-1000**
100 Unvrsal Cy Plz Bldg 1 Universal City (91608) ***(P-19194)***

Universal Plant Svcs Cal Inc .... D 310 618-1600
20545 Belshaw Ave A Carson (90746) ***(P-8832)***

Universal Plastic Mold, Baldwin Park *Also called Upm Inc* ***(P-7840)***

Universal Printing Svcs Inc .... F 951 788-1500
26012 Atlantic Ocean Dr Lake Forest (92630) ***(P-4446)***

Universal Products, Rancho Cucamonga *Also called Proulx Manufacturing Inc* ***(P-5784)***

Universal Protection Gp LLC (PA) .... **C 714 619-9700**
1551 N Tustin Ave Ste 650 Santa Ana (92705) ***(P-18350)***

Universal Protection Svc LP (HQ) .... **A 714 619-9700**
1551 N Tustin Ave Ste 650 Santa Ana (92705) ***(P-18351)***

Universal Prtction SEC Systems (HQ) .... **E 714 288-2227**
1815 E Wilshire Ave # 91 Santa Ana (92705) ***(P-18352)***

Universal Punch Corp .... D 714 556-4488
4001 W Macarthur Blvd Santa Ana (92704) ***(P-7767)***

Universal Saw Company Inc .... F 562 921-8832
13316 Arctic Cir Santa Fe Springs (90670) ***(P-19080)***

Universal Screw Products .... F 310 371-1170
20421 Earl St Torrance (90503) ***(P-7048)***

Universal Services America LP .... A 760 200-2865
77725 Enfield Ln Palm Desert (92211) ***(P-18353)***

Universal Services America LP .... A 714 923-3700
1815 E Wilshire Ave # 91 Santa Ana (92705) ***(P-17298)***

Universal Services America LP (HQ) .... **D 866 877-1965**
1551 N Tustin Ave Fl 6 Santa Ana (92705) ***(P-18354)***

Universal Shopping Plaza A CA .... C 714 521-8899
6281 Regio Ave Buena Park (90620) ***(P-15705)***

Universal Stdios Licensing LLC .... C 818 695-1273
100 Universal City Plz Universal City (91608) ***(P-16221)***

Universal Steel Services Inc .... D 626 960-1455
5034 Heintz St Baldwin Park (91706) ***(P-6675)***

Universal Studios, Universal City *Also called Creative Park Productions LLC* ***(P-19112)***

Universal Studios Company LLC (HQ) .... **B 818 777-1000**
100 Universal City Plz North Hollywood (91608) ***(P-19195)***

Universal Surface Techlgy Inc .... E 310 352-6969
13023 S Main St Los Angeles (90061) ***(P-4948)***

Universal Technical Inst Inc .... D 909 484-1929
9494 Haven Ave Rancho Cucamonga (91730) ***(P-18712)***

Universal Trailers Inc .... E 951 784-0543
2750 Mulberry St Riverside (92501) ***(P-10556)***

Universal Wire Inc .... F 626 285-2288
1705 S Campus Ave Ontario (91761) ***(P-7520)***

Universal Wood Moulding Inc (PA) .... **E 661 362-6262**
21139 Centre Pointe Pkwy Santa Clarita (91350) ***(P-13194)***

UNIVERSITY BOOKSTORE, Long Beach *Also called Forty-Niner Shops Inc* ***(P-16811)***

University Business Ctr Assoc .... D 601 354-3555
5425 Hollister Ave # 160 Santa Barbara (93111) ***(P-15706)***

University Cal Los Angeles .... C 310 825-7852
Ucla Boelter Hall 420 Wes Los Angeles (90095) ***(P-22923)***

University Cal Los Angeles .... A 310 825-9111
757 Westwood Plz Los Angeles (90095) ***(P-20988)***

University California Irvine .... C 714 456-6966
101 The City Dr S Ste 313 Orange (92868) ***(P-20121)***

University California Irvine .... A 714 456-6170
101 The City Dr S Bldg 1a Orange (92868) ***(P-20122)***

University California Irvine .... C 949 939-7106
31865 Circle Dr Laguna Beach (92651) ***(P-21493)***

University California Irvine .... C 714 480-2443
800 N Main St Santa Ana (92701) ***(P-20123)***

University California Irvine .... C 949 644-5245
43 Cambria Dr Corona Del Mar (92625) ***(P-20124)***

University California Irvine .... C 949 646-2267
1640 Newport Blvd Ste 340 Costa Mesa (92627) ***(P-20125)***

University California Irvine .... A 714 456-6011
101 The City Dr S Orange (92868) ***(P-20989)***

University California Irvine .... D 949 824-2819
2220 Engineering Gateway Irvine (92697) ***(P-22870)***

University California Irvine .... C 949 824-2662
106 B Student Ctr Irvine (92697) ***(P-21494)***

University California Irvine .... B 714 456-5558
200 S Manchester Ave # 400 Orange (92868) ***(P-20990)***

University California Irvine .... C 714 456-7890
101 The City Dr S Orange (92868) ***(P-20126)***

University California Irvine .... B 714 775-3066
15355 Brookhurst St # 102 Westminster (92683) ***(P-20991)***

University California Irvine .... C 949 824-7725
3151 Social Science Plz Irvine (92697) ***(P-20992)***

University California Irvine .... D 714 456-6655
200 S Manchester Ave # 400 Orange (92868) ***(P-22818)***

University Credit Union .... C 310 477-6628
1500 S Sepulveda Blvd Los Angeles (90025) ***(P-15095)***

University Frames Inc .... E 714 575-5100
3060 E Miraloma Ave Anaheim (92806) ***(P-3457)***

University Marelich Mech Inc .... D 714 632-2600
1000 N Kraemer Pl Anaheim (92806) ***(P-1159)***

Mergent e-mail: customerrelations@mergent.com
1304
2022 Southern California Business Directory and Buyers Guide
(P-0000) Products & Services Section entry number
(PA)=Parent Co (HQ)=Headquarters (DH)=Div Headquarters

University Park Healthcare Ctr, Los Angeles *Also called United Convalescent Facilities* ***(P-20634)***
University Southern California ....A.......323 442-8500
1500 San Pablo St Los Angeles (90033) ***(P-20993)***
Uniweb Inc (PA) ....**D.......951 279-7999**
222 S Promenade Ave Corona (92879) ***(P-3700)***
Uniwell Corporation ....C.......714 522-7000
7000 Beach Blvd Buena Park (90620) ***(P-16762)***
Uniworld Boutique River Cruise, Encino *Also called Uniworld River Cruises Inc* ***(P-12402)***
Uniworld River Cruises Inc (HQ) ....**C.......818 382-2322**
17323 Ventura Blvd # 300 Encino (91316) ***(P-12402)***
Unix Packaging LLC ....C.......213 627-5050
9 Minson Way Montebello (90640) ***(P-2302)***
Unrivaled Brands Inc (PA) ....**E.......888 909-5564**
3242 Halladay St Ste 202 Santa Ana (92705) ***(P-7624)***
Uns Electric Inc ....E.......714 690-3660
6565 Valley View St La Palma (90623) ***(P-13671)***
Uoc USA Inc ....F.......949 328-3366
15251 Alton Pkwy Ste 100 Irvine (92618) ***(P-11072)***
Up Packaging Enterprise ....F.......626 715-2838
3228 Gabriella St West Covina (91792) ***(P-3777)***
UPD INC ....D.......323 588-8811
4507 S Maywood Ave Vernon (90058) ***(P-11365)***
UPF Corporation ....E.......661 323-8227
3747 Standard St Bakersfield (93308) ***(P-6173)***
Upholstery Workroom, Los Angeles *Also called Custom Upholstered Furn Inc* ***(P-3500)***
Upland Community Care Inc ....C.......909 985-1903
1221 E Arrow Hwy Upland (91786) ***(P-20492)***
Upland Fab Inc ....E.......909 933-9185
1445 Brooks St Ste L Ontario (91762) ***(P-5850)***
Upland Rehabilitation Care Ctr, Upland *Also called Upland Community Care Inc* ***(P-20492)***
Upm Inc ....B.......626 962-4001
13245 Los Angeles St Baldwin Park (91706) ***(P-7840)***
Upm Raflatac Inc ....E.......909 390-4657
1105 Auto Center Dr Ontario (91761) ***(P-3877)***
Upper Crust Enterprises Inc ....D.......213 625-0038
411 Center St Los Angeles (90012) ***(P-2545)***
Uprite Construction Corp ....D.......949 877-8877
2211 Michelson Dr Ste 500 Irvine (92612) ***(P-725)***
UPS, El Centro *Also called United Parcel Service Inc* ***(P-12148)***
UPS, Palm Springs *Also called United Parcel Service Inc* ***(P-12149)***
UPS, Torrance *Also called United Parcel Service Inc* ***(P-12150)***
UPS, Commerce *Also called United Parcel Service Inc* ***(P-18699)***
UPS, Oceano *Also called United Parcel Service Inc* ***(P-18700)***
UPS, Ridgecrest *Also called United Parcel Service Inc* ***(P-12151)***
UPS, Bishop *Also called United Parcel Service Inc* ***(P-12152)***
UPS, Barstow *Also called United Parcel Service Inc* ***(P-12153)***
UPS, Aliso Viejo *Also called United Parcel Service Inc* ***(P-18701)***
UPS, Vernon *Also called United Parcel Service Inc* ***(P-12331)***
UPS, Gardena *Also called United Parcel Service Inc* ***(P-12154)***
UPS, Ontario *Also called United Parcel Service Inc* ***(P-12155)***
UPS, Sun City *Also called United Parcel Service Inc* ***(P-12332)***
UPS, Mojave *Also called United Parcel Service Inc* ***(P-12156)***
UPS, Los Angeles *Also called United Parcel Service Inc* ***(P-12157)***
UPS, Ontario *Also called United Parcel Service Inc* ***(P-18702)***
UPS, Ontario *Also called United Parcel Service Inc* ***(P-12333)***
UPS, Los Angeles *Also called United Parcel Service Inc* ***(P-12319)***
UPS, Ontario *Also called United Parcel Service Inc* ***(P-12320)***
UPS, San Bernardino *Also called United Parcel Service Inc* ***(P-12321)***
UPS, City of Industry *Also called United Parcel Service Inc* ***(P-12322)***
UPS, Bloomington *Also called United Parcel Service Inc* ***(P-12323)***
UPS, Lancaster *Also called United Parcel Service Inc* ***(P-12158)***
UPS, Van Nuys *Also called United Parcel Service Inc* ***(P-12159)***
UPS, Ontario *Also called United Parcel Service Inc* ***(P-12324)***
UPS, Cerritos *Also called United Parcel Service Inc* ***(P-12160)***
UPS, Monterey Park *Also called United Parcel Service Inc* ***(P-18703)***
UPS, Westlake Village *Also called United Parcel Service Inc* ***(P-18704)***
UPS, San Luis Obispo *Also called United Parcel Service Inc* ***(P-12161)***
UPS, Goleta *Also called United Parcel Service Inc* ***(P-12162)***
UPS, Santa Maria *Also called United Parcel Service Inc* ***(P-12163)***
UPS, Yucca Valley *Also called United Parcel Service Inc* ***(P-12164)***
UPS, Newbury Park *Also called United Parcel Service Inc* ***(P-12165)***
UPS, Los Angeles *Also called United Parcel Service Inc* ***(P-12166)***
UPS, Ontario *Also called United Parcel Service Inc* ***(P-12167)***
UPS, Eastvale *Also called United Parcel Service Inc* ***(P-18705)***
UPS, Ventura *Also called United Parcel Service Inc* ***(P-12168)***
UPS, Baldwin Park *Also called United Parcel Service Inc* ***(P-12169)***
UPS, Simi Valley *Also called United Parcel Service Inc* ***(P-18706)***
Upstanding LLC ....C.......949 788-9900
440 Exchange Ste 100 Irvine (92602) ***(P-18004)***
Upton Engineering & Mfg Co, South El Monte *Also called Bci Inc* ***(P-8519)***
Uptown, Los Angeles *Also called Lets Go Apparel Inc* ***(P-3076)***
Urban Armor Gear LLC (HQ) ....**E.......949 329-0500**
28202 Cabot Rd Ste 300 Laguna Niguel (92677) ***(P-5851)***
Urban Commons Queensway LLC ....A.......562 499-1611
1126 Queens Hwy Long Beach (90802) ***(P-16763)***
Urban Commons Queensway LLC (PA) ....**D.......562 499-1750**
1126 Qeens Hwy Queen Mary Long Beach (90802) ***(P-16764)***
Urban Concepts, Vernon *Also called Anns Trading Company Inc* ***(P-14911)***
Urban Decal LLC (HQ) ....**E.......949 574-9712**
833 W 16th St Newport Beach (92663) ***(P-5078)***
Urban Decay Cosmetics, Newport Beach *Also called Urban Decal LLC* ***(P-5078)***
Urban Expressions Inc ....E.......310 593-4574
5500 Union Pacific Ave Commerce (90022) ***(P-5904)***
Urban Futures Inc ....D.......714 283-9334
17821 17th St Ste 245 Tustin (92780) ***(P-23521)***
Urban Group, The, Santa Barbara *Also called Parsons Group Inc* ***(P-15744)***
Urban Insight Inc ....F.......213 792-2000
3530 Wilshire Blvd # 128 Los Angeles (90010) ***(P-18073)***
Uremet Corporation ....E.......657 257-4027
7012 Belgrave Ave Garden Grove (92841) ***(P-4726)***
Urethane Polymer International ....F.......909 357-7200
10880 Poplar Ave Fontana (92337) ***(P-5246)***
Urgent Care Center, Montclair *Also called Prime Hlthcare Srvcs-Mntclair* ***(P-20905)***
Uriman Inc (HQ) ....**E.......714 257-2080**
650 N Puente St Brea (92821) ***(P-9830)***
Urm Technologies Inc ....E.......661 705-0500
28486 Wstnghuse Pl Ste 13 Valencia (91355) ***(P-23134)***
Urocare Products Inc ....F.......909 621-6013
2735 Melbourne Ave Pomona (91767) ***(P-5417)***
Urological Associates, Tarzana *Also called San Frnndo Vly Urlgcal Med Gro* ***(P-20050)***
Urovant Sciences Inc (HQ) ....**E.......949 226-6029**
5281 California Ave # 100 Irvine (92617) ***(P-4907)***
URS Group Inc ....D.......951 571-2220
6721 Sycamore Canyon Blvd Riverside (92507) ***(P-22683)***
URS Group Inc ....D.......213 996-2200
300 S Grand Ave Ste 1100 Los Angeles (90071) ***(P-22684)***
URS Group Inc ....D.......213 996-2200
915 Wilshire Blvd Ste 700 Los Angeles (90017) ***(P-22685)***
URS Group Inc ....D.......562 420-2933
3995 Via Oro Ave Long Beach (90810) ***(P-22686)***
URS Resources LLC (HQ) ....**E.......626 331-0359**
999 W Town And Country Rd Orange (92868) ***(P-22687)***
US 3, Santa Ana *Also called Utility Systems Scnce Sftwr In* ***(P-17749)***
US Alliance Group Inc ....E.......949 888-8580
29883 Snta Mrgrita Pkwy S Rcho STA Marg (92688) ***(P-18713)***
US Apothecary Crown Labs, Santa Fe Springs *Also called Titan Medical Enterprises Inc* ***(P-4906)***
US Arcades LLC (PA) ....**D.......818 888-8738**
11684 Ventura Blvd Studio City (91604) ***(P-19515)***
US Architectural Lighting, Palmdale *Also called Sun Valley Ltg Standards Inc* ***(P-9104)***
US Armor Corporation ....E.......562 207-4240
10715 Bloomfield Ave Santa Fe Springs (90670) ***(P-11149)***
US Bankcard Services Inc ....D.......888 888-8872
17171 Gale Ave Ste 110 City of Industry (91745) ***(P-18714)***
US Best Repair Service Inc ....C.......888 750-2378
1652 Edinger Ave Ste E Tustin (92780) ***(P-647)***
US Best Repairs, Tustin *Also called US Best Repair Service Inc* ***(P-647)***
US Blanks, Vernon *Also called LA Brands LLC* ***(P-14339)***
US Blanks LLC (PA) ....**E.......310 225-6774**
14700 S San Pedro St Gardena (90248) ***(P-4727)***
US Borax Inc ....A.......760 762-7000
14486 Borax Rd Boron (93516) ***(P-4673)***
US Carenet Services LLC ....C.......661 945-7350
42225 10th St W Ste 2b Lancaster (93534) ***(P-21227)***
US Computers Inc ....F.......714 528-0514
181 W Orangethorpe Ave C Placentia (92870) ***(P-8309)***
US Continental Marketing Inc (PA) ....**D.......951 808-8888**
310 Reed Cir Corona (92879) ***(P-4982)***
US Core Pins Inc ....F.......714 540-2846
2115 S Hathaway St Santa Ana (92705) ***(P-8833)***
US Critical LLC (PA) ....**D.......949 916-9326**
6 Orchard Ste 150 Lake Forest (92630) ***(P-8222)***
US Data Management LLC (PA) ....**D.......888 231-0816**
535 Chapala St Santa Barbara (93101) ***(P-18233)***
US Dental Inc ....E.......562 404-3500
13043 166th St Cerritos (90703) ***(P-11200)***
US Display Group Inc ....E.......951 444-4567
235 Radio Rd Corona (92879) ***(P-3830)***
US Donuts & Yogurt ....E.......562 695-8867
11719 Whittier Blvd Whittier (90601) ***(P-2040)***
US Door and Fence LLC ....E.......951 300-0010
3880 Garner Rd Riverside (92501) ***(P-3203)***
US Duty Gear Inc ....F.......909 391-8800
1946 S Grove Ave Ontario (91761) ***(P-5915)***
US Facility Solutions LLC (PA) ....**D.......888 904-7900**
17541 17th St Ste 200 Tustin (92780) ***(P-23397)***
US Family Care, San Bernardino *Also called Caremark Rx Inc* ***(P-19734)***
US Family Care, Rialto *Also called Caremark Rx Inc* ***(P-19735)***
US Family Care, Hesperia *Also called Caremark Rx Inc* ***(P-19736)***
US Foods Inc ....C.......714 670-3500
15155 Northam St La Mirada (90638) ***(P-14517)***
US Gold Trading Inc (PA) ....**F.......818 558-7766**
117 E Providencia Ave Burbank (91502) ***(P-11332)***
US Hanger Company LLC ....E.......310 323-8030
17501 S Denver Ave Gardena (90248) ***(P-6239)***
US Hardship Group LLC ....E.......877 777-0174
260 Newport Center Dr # 100 Newport Beach (92660) ***(P-16984)***
US Healthworks Inc (HQ) ....**D.......661 678-2300**
28035 Avenue Stanford Valencia (91355) ***(P-20127)***
US Horizon Manufacturing Inc ....E.......661 775-1675
28539 Industry Dr Valencia (91355) ***(P-5925)***
US Hosiery Inc ....F.......213 742-0101
1415 S Main St Los Angeles (90015) ***(P-2625)***
US Hotel and Resort MGT Inc ....C.......949 650-2988
2544 Newport Blvd Costa Mesa (92627) ***(P-16765)***
US Hybrid Corporation (HQ) ....**E.......310 212-1200**
2660 Columbia St Torrance (90503) ***(P-10150)***
US Industrial Tool & Sup Co ....E.......310 464-8400
14083 S Normandie Ave Gardena (90249) ***(P-7768)***

ALPHABETIC

Employee Codes: A=Over 500 employees, B=251-500
C=101-250, D=51-100, E=20-50 F=10-19
2022 Southern California Business
Directory and Buyers Guide
© Mergent Inc. 1-800-342-5647
1305

US International Media LLC (PA)......C......**310 482-6700**
3415 S Sepulveda Blvd # 8 Los Angeles (90034) ***(P-17067)***

US Lines LLC (HQ)......D......**714 751-3333**
3501 Jamboree Rd Ste 300 Newport Beach (92660) ***(P-12549)***

US Logistics, Signal Hill *Also called United States Logistics Group* ***(P-10169)***

US Metro Group Inc......A......213 382-6435
135 S State College Blvd Brea (92821) ***(P-17299)***

US Motor Works LLC (PA)......C......**562 404-0488**
14722 Anson Ave Santa Fe Springs (90670) ***(P-10151)***

US Outdoor, Los Angeles *Also called US International Media LLC* ***(P-17067)***

US Pharmatech Inc......F......310 219-6003
2927 Lomita Blvd Ste A Torrance (90505) ***(P-4908)***

US Pole Company Inc (PA)......D......**800 877-6537**
660 W Avenue O Palmdale (93551) ***(P-9108)***

US Polymers Inc......D......323 727-6888
5910 Bandini Blvd Commerce (90040) ***(P-6322)***

US Polymers Inc (PA)......D......**323 728-3023**
1057 S Vail Ave Montebello (90640) ***(P-5852)***

US Precision Sheet Metal Inc......D......951 276-2611
4020 Garner Rd Riverside (92501) ***(P-6937)***

US Print & Toner Inc......E......619 562-6995
14751 Franklin Ave Ste B Tustin (92780) ***(P-11483)***

US Radiator Corporation (PA)......E......**323 826-0965**
4423 District Blvd Vernon (90058) ***(P-10152)***

US Real Estate Services Inc......D......949 598-9920
25520 Commercentre Dr # 1 Lake Forest (92630) ***(P-16026)***

US Rigging Supply Corp......E......714 545-7444
1600 E Mcfadden Ave Santa Ana (92705) ***(P-7521)***

US Rubber Recycling Inc......E......909 825-1200
1231 Lincoln St Colton (92324) ***(P-5418)***

US Rubber Roller Company Inc......F......951 682-2221
1516 7th St Riverside (92507) ***(P-5419)***

US Saws Inc (PA)......F......**860 668-2402**
3702 W Central Ave Santa Ana (92704) ***(P-7656)***

US Security Associates, Burbank *Also called US Security Associates Inc* ***(P-18355)***

US Security Associates Inc......B......818 697-1809
455 N Moss St Burbank (91502) ***(P-18355)***

US Security Associates Inc......B......714 352-0773
2275 W 190th St Ste 100 Torrance (90504) ***(P-18356)***

US Sensor Corp......D......714 639-1000
1832 W Collins Ave Orange (92867) ***(P-9598)***

US Skillserve Inc......A......909 621-4751
9620 Fremont Ave Montclair (91763) ***(P-20493)***

US Steel Rule Dies Inc......F......562 921-0690
40 E Verdugo Ave Burbank (91502) ***(P-7841)***

US Telepacific Corp (HQ)......E......**877 487-8722**
515 S Flower St Ste 4500 Los Angeles (90071) ***(P-12676)***

US Tower Corp......D......559 564-6000
1099 W Ropes Ave Woodlake (93286) ***(P-6676)***

US Tower Corp (PA)......E......**785 524-9966**
1099 W Ropes Ave Woodlake (93286) ***(P-6677)***

US Toyo Fan Corporation (HQ)......D......**626 338-1111**
16025 Arrow Hwy Ste F Irwindale (91706) ***(P-8059)***

US Trust, Los Angeles *Also called U S Trust Company NA* ***(P-15352)***

US Union Tool Inc (HQ)......E......**714 521-6242**
1260 N Fee Ana St Anaheim (92807) ***(P-7750)***

US Wheel, Huntington Beach *Also called U S Wheel Corporation* ***(P-10146)***

USA, Long Beach *Also called Su Casa Ending Dom Violence* ***(P-21900)***

USA Express Tire and Service......D......949 494-7111
350 Broadway St Ste A Laguna Beach (92651) ***(P-18883)***

USA Extruded Plastics Inc......F......714 991-6061
965 E Discovery Ln Anaheim (92801) ***(P-5853)***

USA Sales Inc......E......909 390-9606
1560 S Archibald Ave Ontario (91761) ***(P-2553)***

USA Staffing Inc......D......805 269-2677
505 Higuera St San Luis Obispo (93401) ***(P-17520)***

USA Travel Services LLC......A......207 899-8803
714 Washington Blvd Marina Del Rey (90292) ***(P-22466)***

USA Vision Systems Inc (HQ)......E......**949 583-1519**
9301 Irvine Blvd Irvine (92618) ***(P-9926)***

USA Waste of California Inc......D......818 252-3112
9081 Tujunga Ave Sun Valley (91352) ***(P-12987)***

USA-Srdc Corporation (HQ)......E......**310 418-7064**
500 W 140th St Gardena (90248) ***(P-14124)***

Usag, Rcho STA Marg *Also called US Alliance Group Inc* ***(P-18713)***

Usc Care Medical Group Inc (PA)......C......**323 442-5100**
1510 San Pablo St Ste 649 Los Angeles (90033) ***(P-20994)***

Usc Crdiothoracic Surgeons Inc......D......323 442-5849
1520 San Pablo St # 4300 Los Angeles (90033) ***(P-20128)***

Usc Credit Union......D......213 821-7100
3720 S Flower St Los Angeles (90089) ***(P-15096)***

Usc Emergency Medicine Assoc......D......323 226-6667
1200 N State St Ste 1011 Los Angeles (90033) ***(P-20129)***

Usc Keck School of Medicine (HQ)......C......**323 442-2830**
1975 Zonal Ave Ste Kam500 Los Angeles (90089) ***(P-20995)***

Usc Srgcal Edcatn RES Fndation, Los Angeles *Also called Usc Surgeons Incorporated* ***(P-20130)***

Usc Surgeons Incorporated......D......323 442-5910
1510 San Pablo St Ste 514 Los Angeles (90033) ***(P-20130)***

Usc University Hospital, Los Angeles *Also called University Southern California* ***(P-20993)***

Usc Verdugo Hills Hospital LLC......A......818 790-7100
1812 Verdugo Blvd Glendale (91208) ***(P-20996)***

Usc Vrdugo Hlls Hosp Fundation (HQ)......B......**800 872-2273**
1812 Verdugo Blvd Glendale (91208) ***(P-20997)***

Uscb Inc (PA)......C......**213 985-2111**
355 S Grand Ave Ste 3200 Los Angeles (90071) ***(P-17118)***

Uscb America, Los Angeles *Also called Uscb Inc* ***(P-17118)***

Usdm Life Science, Santa Barbara *Also called US Data Management LLC* ***(P-18233)***

Used Cardboard Boxes Inc......D......323 724-2500
4032 Wilshire Blvd # 402 Los Angeles (90010) ***(P-14230)***

Usedmac Inc......F......866 769-4777
665 E Los Angeles Ave Simi Valley (93065) ***(P-8230)***

Usfi Inc......D......310 768-1937
110 W Walnut St 221 Gardena (90248) ***(P-14518)***

USG Ceilings Plus LLC......E......323 724-8166
6711 E Washington Blvd Commerce (90040) ***(P-7187)***

Ushio America Inc (HQ)......D......**714 236-8600**
5440 Cerritos Ave Cypress (90630) ***(P-13672)***

Usit Co, Gardena *Also called US Industrial Tool & Sup Co* ***(P-7768)***

Usl Parallel Products Cal......E......909 980-1200
12281 Arrow Rte Rancho Cucamonga (91739) ***(P-5151)***

Usmilk Nutrition Inc......F......951 888-2228
28381 Vincent Moraga Dr Temecula (92590) ***(P-2160)***

Usoc Bio-Medical Services, Irvine *Also called Usoc Medical* ***(P-19081)***

Usoc Medical......D......949 243-9109
20 Morgan Irvine (92618) ***(P-19081)***

Uspar Enterprises Inc......F......909 591-7506
2037 S Vineyard Ave Ontario (91761) ***(P-9072)***

USS Cal Builders Inc......C......714 828-4882
8031 Main St Stanton (90680) ***(P-845)***

UST, Los Angeles *Also called Universal Surface Techlgy Inc* ***(P-4948)***

UST Global Inc (HQ)......D......**949 716-8757**
5 Polaris Way Aliso Viejo (92656) ***(P-17748)***

Usts, Huntington Beach *Also called United States Technical Svcs* ***(P-18231)***

Utah Pacific Construction Co......D......951 677-9876
40940 Eleanora Way Murrieta (92562) ***(P-980)***

Utak Laboratories Inc......E......661 294-3935
25020 Avenue Tibbitts Valencia (91355) ***(P-5152)***

Utbbb Inc......D......562 594-4411
10711 Bloomfield St Los Alamitos (90720) ***(P-2076)***

UTC Aerospace Systems, Santa Fe Springs *Also called United Technologies Corp* ***(P-10440)***

Uti, Rancho Cucamonga *Also called Universal Technical Inst Inc* ***(P-18712)***

Utility Refrigerator......E......818 764-6200
12160 Sherman Way North Hollywood (91605) ***(P-8354)***

Utility Systems Scnce Sftwr In (PA)......D......**714 542-1004**
601 Parkcenter Dr Ste 209 Santa Ana (92705) ***(P-17749)***

Utility Trailer Mfg Co (PA)......B......**626 964-7319**
17295 Railroad St Ste A City of Industry (91748) ***(P-10170)***

Utility Trailer Mfg Co......C......909 594-6026
17295 Railroad St Ste A City of Industry (91748) ***(P-10171)***

Utility Trailer Mfg Co......C......909 428-8300
15567 Valley Blvd Fontana (92335) ***(P-10172)***

Utility Trlr Sls Southern Cal, Fontana *Also called Utility Trailer Mfg Co* ***(P-10172)***

Utility Trlr Sls Sthern Cal LL (PA)......D......**877 275-4887**
15567 Valley Blvd Fontana (92335) ***(P-13039)***

Utility Vault Co......E......559 688-6686
4491 S K St Tulare (93274) ***(P-6063)***

Utiliuse, Riverside *Also called Thirkettle Corporation* ***(P-13948)***

Utopia Lighting, Compton *Also called Pacific Lighting Mfr Inc* ***(P-13657)***

Utopia Lighting, Compton *Also called Pacific Lighting Mfr Inc* ***(P-13658)***

Utopia Lighting......F......310 327-7711
2329 E Pacifica Pl Compton (90220) ***(P-8886)***

Uttam Composites LLC......F......714 894-5300
11700 Monarch St Garden Grove (92841) ***(P-6764)***

Uvnv Inc (PA)......C......**888 777-0446**
1550 Scenic Ave Ste 100 Costa Mesa (92626) ***(P-12677)***

Uvw Inc......F......714 482-2914
511 S Harbor Blvd Ste G La Habra (90631) ***(P-5854)***

Uwe, Camarillo *Also called United Western Enterprises Inc* ***(P-7423)***

V & F Fabrication Company Inc......E......714 265-0630
13902 Seaboard Cir Garden Grove (92843) ***(P-6678)***

V & L Produce Inc......C......323 589-3125
2550 E 25th St Vernon (90058) ***(P-14660)***

V & M Plating Co......F......310 532-5633
14024 Avalon Blvd Los Angeles (90061) ***(P-7328)***

V & M Precision Grinding Co., Brea *Also called Rogers Holding Company Inc* ***(P-10404)***

V & S Engineering Company Ltd......E......714 898-7869
5766 Research Dr Huntington Beach (92649) ***(P-8834)***

V & V Manufacturing Inc......F......626 330-0641
15320 Proctor Ave City of Industry (91745) ***(P-11492)***

V 3, Oxnard *Also called V3 Printing Corporation* ***(P-4447)***

V A Anderson Enterprises Inc (PA)......D......**714 990-6100**
400 Atlas St Brea (92821) ***(P-18715)***

V A Desert PCF Federal Cr Un......C......562 498-1250
5901 E 7th St Long Beach (90822) ***(P-15097)***

V and C Manufacturing and......F......615 374-2076
655 E Ball Rd Anaheim (92805) ***(P-11787)***

V and L Back Hoe Service Inc......F......818 898-1997
447 N Hagar St San Fernando (91340) ***(P-7657)***

V B Z, Richgrove *Also called Vincent B Zaninovich Sons Inc* ***(P-55)***

V C A Central Animal Hospital......D......909 981-2855
281 N Central Ave Upland (91786) ***(P-203)***

V I P Tots Inc......D......951 652-7611
41915 Acacia Ave Hemet (92544) ***(P-22072)***

V J Provision Inc......F......818 843-3945
410 S Varney St Burbank (91502) ***(P-1722)***

V M I, Visalia *Also called Voltage Multipliers Inc* ***(P-9603)***

V M P Inc......F......661 294-9934
24830 Avenue Tibbitts Valencia (91355) ***(P-7049)***

V M S, Glendora *Also called Venue Management Systems Inc* ***(P-18357)***

V Manufacturing Logistics Inc......E......909 869-6200
20501 Earlgate St Walnut (91789) ***(P-5079)***

V O I C E, Banning *Also called J & L Daycare* ***(P-22119)***

V P H, Van Nuys *Also called Valley Presbyterian Hospital* ***(P-21000)***

V Q Orthocare, Irvine *Also called Vision Quest Industries Inc* ***(P-11151)***

V R Gifts, Brea *Also called Vesuki Inc (P-7575)*
V Todays Inc ....C....310 781-9100
19800 S Vermont Ave Torrance (90502) *(P-16766)*
V Troth Inc ....D....661 948-4646
1801 W Avenue K Ste 101 Lancaster (93534) *(P-16027)*
V Twest Inc ....F....714 521-2167
16222 Phoebe Ave La Mirada (90638) *(P-3670)*
V Twin Magazine, Agoura Hills *Also called Paisano Publications LLC (P-4091)*
V&H Performance LLC ....D....562 921-7461
13861 Rosecrans Ave Santa Fe Springs (90670) *(P-10508)*
V&M Prcsion Machining Grinding, Brea *Also called Tca Precision Products LLC (P-10427)*
V.O.I.C.E., Loma Linda *Also called J & L Daycare (P-22118)*
V/ Twins, Agoura Hills *Also called Paisano Publications Inc (P-4092)*
V3, Oxnard *Also called Ventura Printing Inc (P-4588)*
V3 Printing Corporation ....D....805 981-2600
200 N Elevar St Oxnard (93030) *(P-4447)*
VA HSR&d Center of Excellence, North Hills *Also called Veterans Health Administration (P-20150)*
VA Santa Maria Cboc, Santa Maria *Also called Veterans Health Administration (P-20144)*
Vacation Bay Hotel Prpts Inc ....C....949 494-8566
647 S Coast Hwy Laguna Beach (92651) *(P-16767)*
Vacation Interval Realty, Newport Beach *Also called Pacific Monarch Resorts Inc (P-15939)*
Vacation Marketing Group, Riverside *Also called Pacific Monarch Resorts Inc (P-16611)*
Vacation Palm Springs RE Inc ....C....760 778-7832
901 E Tahquitz Canyon Way B200 Palm Springs (92262) *(P-16028)*
Vacation Village Hotel, Laguna Beach *Also called Vacation Bay Hotel Prpts Inc (P-16767)*
Vacco Industries (HQ) ....**C....626 443-7121**
10350 Vacco St South El Monte (91733) *(P-7477)*
Vadnais Trenchless Svcs Inc ....C....858 550-1460
26000 Commercentre Dr Lake Forest (92630) *(P-981)*
Vae Industries Corporation ....E....714 842-7500
5402 Research Dr Huntington Beach (92649) *(P-3148)*
Vaga Industries, South El Monte *Also called Pearson Engineering Corp (P-7395)*
Vagabond Inns, Los Angeles *Also called Rpd Hotels 18 LLC (P-16674)*
Vagrant Records Inc ....F....323 302-0100
6351 Wilshire Blvd # 101 Los Angeles (90048) *(P-4615)*
Vagthols Rsdntial Care Ctr Inc ....C....323 464-6067
6537 Fountain Ave Los Angeles (90028) *(P-22161)*
Vahe Enterprises Inc ....D....323 235-6657
750 E Slauson Ave Los Angeles (90011) *(P-10000)*
Vahi Toyota Inc (PA) ....**C....760 241-6484**
14612 Valley Center Dr Victorville (92395) *(P-18884)*
Val Pak Products ....F....661 252-0115
20731 Centre Pointe Pkwy Santa Clarita (91350) *(P-5420)*
Val Plastic USA L L C ....F....909 390-9600
4570 Eucalyptus Ave Ste C Chino (91710) *(P-7625)*
Val USA Manufacturer Inc ....E....626 839-8069
1050 W Central Ave Ste A Brea (92821) *(P-11788)*
Val-Pro Inc ....D....213 689-0844
1661 Mcgarry St Los Angeles (90021) *(P-14661)*
Valadon Hotel LLC ....D....310 854-1114
8822 Cynthia St West Hollywood (90069) *(P-16768)*
Valco Construction, Bakersfield *Also called Gilliam & Sons Inc (P-1595)*
Valco Planer Works Inc ....E....323 582-6355
6131 Maywood Ave Huntington Park (90255) *(P-7842)*
Valco Precision Works, Huntington Park *Also called Valco Planer Works Inc (P-7842)*
Valeant Biomedicals Inc (HQ) ....**D....949 461-6000**
1 Enterprise Aliso Viejo (92656) *(P-14793)*
Valence Lynwood, Lynwood *Also called Triumph Processing Inc (P-7324)*
Valence Surface Tech LLC ....F....562 531-7666
7718 Adams St Paramount (90723) *(P-6679)*
Valencia Bros Inc ....D....760 353-2168
257 Maple Ave El Centro (92243) *(P-1557)*
Valencia Brothers Concrete, El Centro *Also called Valencia Bros Inc (P-1557)*
Valencia Country Club, Valencia *Also called CF Valencia Arcis LLC (P-19553)*
Valencia Country Club, Valencia *Also called Heritage Golf Group LLC (P-19493)*
VALENCIA GARDENS HEALTH CARE CENTER, Riverside *Also called Riverside Care Inc (P-20448)*
Valencia Hotel Ltd Partnership ....D....661 253-2400
25259 The Old Rd Santa Clarita (91381) *(P-16769)*
Valencia Mold, Valencia *Also called Valencia Plastics Inc (P-5855)*
Valencia Pipe Company ....D....661 257-3923
28305 Livingston Ave Valencia (91355) *(P-5472)*
Valencia Plastics Inc ....F....661 257-0066
25611 Hercules St Valencia (91355) *(P-5855)*
Valero, Wilmington *Also called Ultramar Inc (P-556)*
Valero Ref Company-California ....A....562 491-6754
2401 E Anaheim St Wilmington (90744) *(P-5266)*
Valet Parking Svc A Cal Partnr (PA) ....**A....323 465-5873**
6933 Hollywood Blvd Los Angeles (90028) *(P-18781)*
Valet Services, Bell Gardens *Also called Anitsa Inc (P-16835)*
Valew Welding & Fabrication, Adelanto *Also called Hayes Welding Inc (P-18981)*
Valiant Technical Services Inc ....D....757 628-9500
1785 Utah Ave Lompoc (93437) *(P-10455)*
Valley Animal Medical Center ....A....760 342-4711
46920 Jefferson St Indio (92201) *(P-204)*
Valley Base Materials, Westlake Village *Also called Security Paving Company Inc (P-913)*
Valley Bulk Inc ....D....760 843-0574
17649 Turner Rd Victorville (92394) *(P-12088)*
Valley Business Printers Inc ....D....818 362-7771
6355 Topanga Canyon Blvd # 225 Woodland Hills (91367) *(P-4448)*
Valley Care Center, Porterville *Also called Wescordon Incorporated (P-20504)*
Valley Care Olive View Med Ctr, Sylmar *Also called Olive View-Ucla Medical Center (P-20010)*
Valley Careidence Opco LLC ....D....559 784-8371
661 W Poplar Ave Porterville (93257) *(P-20494)*
Valley Clark Plbg & Htg Co Inc (PA) ....**E....818 782-1047**
7640 Gloria Ave Ste L Van Nuys (91406) *(P-1160)*
Valley Community Healthcare ....B....818 763-8836
6801 Coldwater Canyon Ave 1b North Hollywood (91605) *(P-20131)*
Valley Couriers Inc ....D....909 605-2999
181 S Wineville Ave Ste O Ontario (91761) *(P-12007)*
Valley Cutting System Inc ....F....559 684-1229
1455 N Belmont Rd Exeter (93221) *(P-7751)*
Valley Department Store, Chino Hills *Also called Sampav Inc (P-2749)*
Valley Engravers, Santa Clarita *Also called Valley Precision Metal Product (P-6938)*
Valley Eye Center Group, Van Nuys *Also called George M Rajacich MD PC (P-19830)*
Valley Forge Acquisition Corp ....F....626 969-8701
444 S Motor Ave Azusa (91702) *(P-7100)*
Valley Friction Materials ....F....323 875-1783
12036 Carson St Hawaiian Gardens (90716) *(P-13104)*
Valley Garbage Rubbish Co Inc ....C....805 614-1131
1850 W Betteravia Rd Santa Maria (93455) *(P-12988)*
Valley Health System Svc Corp ....D....951 765-4702
301 N San Jacinto St Hemet (92543) *(P-20998)*
Valley Healthcare, San Bernardino *Also called United Medical Management Inc (P-20636)*
Valley Hunt Club ....D....626 793-7134
520 S Orange Grove Blvd Pasadena (91105) *(P-22374)*
Valley Indus X-Ray Insptn Svcs ....D....661 399-8497
3700 Pegasus Dr Ste 100 Bakersfield (93308) *(P-18716)*
Valley Instrument Service Inc (PA) ....**C....661 327-8681**
3536 Brian Way Bakersfield (93308) *(P-13956)*
Valley Insurance Service Inc (HQ) ....**D....626 966-3664**
4695 Macarthur Ct Ste 600 Newport Beach (92660) *(P-15642)*
Valley Insurance Service Inc ....B....949 707-4080
23181 Verdugo Dr Ste 100b Laguna Hills (92653) *(P-15643)*
Valley Lght Ctr For Scial Advn ....C....626 337-6200
5360 Irwindale Ave Irwindale (91706) *(P-21970)*
Valley Light Industries, Irwindale *Also called Valley Lght Ctr For Scial Advn (P-21970)*
Valley Management Associates (PA) ....**D....818 881-6801**
18747 Sherman Way Frnt Reseda (91335) *(P-15522)*
Valley Med Group Lompoc Inc ....D....805 736-1253
136 N 3rd St Lompoc (93436) *(P-20999)*
Valley Metal Supply Inc ....F....818 837-6566
12950 Bradley Ave Sylmar (91342) *(P-13330)*
Valley Metal Treating Inc ....E....909 623-6316
355 S East End Ave Pomona (91766) *(P-6457)*
Valley Molding & Frame, North Hollywood *Also called Valley Wholesale Supply Corp (P-13195)*
Valley News Gardens, Gardena *Also called Gardena Valley News Inc (P-3980)*
Valley Oak Cabinets, Santa Ynez *Also called Valley Oaks Industries (P-3603)*
Valley Oaks Industries ....F....805 688-2754
3550 E Highway 246 Ste Ae Santa Ynez (93460) *(P-3603)*
VALLEY OASIS, Lancaster *Also called Antelope Vly Dom Vlnce Council (P-21713)*
Valley of Sun Cosmetics LLC ....C....310 327-9062
535 Patrice Pl Gardena (90248) *(P-14294)*
Valley of The Sun Labs, Gardena *Also called Valley of Sun Cosmetics LLC (P-14294)*
Valley Perforating LLC ....D....661 324-4964
3201 Gulf St Bakersfield (93308) *(P-8835)*
Valley Plating Works Inc ....F....323 838-9211
5900 Sheila St Commerce (90040) *(P-7329)*
Valley Power Services Inc ....E....909 969-9345
425 S Hacienda Blvd City of Industry (91745) *(P-8934)*
Valley Power Systems Inc (PA) ....**D....626 333-1243**
425 S Hacienda Blvd City of Industry (91745) *(P-13957)*
Valley Precision Metal Product ....E....661 607-0100
27771 Avenue Hopkins Santa Clarita (91355) *(P-6938)*
Valley Presbyterian Hospital ....A....818 782-6600
15107 Vanowen St Van Nuys (91405) *(P-21000)*
Valley Printers, Woodland Hills *Also called Valley Business Printers Inc (P-4448)*
Valley Processing, City of Industry *Also called Hexpol Compounding CA Inc (P-5380)*
Valley Republic Bank ....D....661 371-2000
5000 California Ave # 110 Bakersfield (93309) *(P-15045)*
Valley Rsrce Ctr For Rtrded In (PA) ....**E....951 766-8659**
1285 N Santa Fe St Hemet (92543) *(P-21971)*
Valley Spuds, Oxnard *Also called McK Enterprises Inc (P-2484)*
Valley Spuds of Oxnard, Oxnard *Also called Produce Available Inc (P-14648)*
Valley Store Front Jwish Fmly, North Hollywood *Also called Jewish Family Svc Los Angeles (P-21823)*
Valley Strong Credit Union ....D....661 725-1014
1828 Cecil Ave Delano (93215) *(P-15098)*
Valley Strong Credit Union (PA) ....**D....661 833-7900**
11500 Bolthouse Dr Bakersfield (93311) *(P-15099)*
Valley Strong Credit Union ....D....661 833-7920
3901 Mount Vernon Ave Bakersfield (93306) *(P-15100)*
Valley Strong Credit Union ....D....661 833-7940
8200 Stockdale Hwy Ste P Bakersfield (93311) *(P-15101)*
Valley Strong Credit Union ....D....661 833-7900
6101 Coffee Rd Bakersfield (93308) *(P-15102)*
Valley Substation, Romoland *Also called Southern California Edison Co (P-12834)*
Valley Sun Mech Cnstr Inc ....D....661 321-9070
4205 Atlas Ct Bakersfield (93308) *(P-1697)*
Valley Tool and Machine Co Inc ....E....909 595-2205
111 Explorer St Pomona (91768) *(P-8836)*
Valley Village ....C....818 446-0366
8727 Fenwick St Sunland (91040) *(P-20545)*
Valley Village (PA) ....**D....818 587-9450**
20830 Sherman Way Winnetka (91306) *(P-21908)*
Valley Vsta Nrsing Trnstnal Ca, North Hollywood *Also called Valley Vsta Nrsing Trnstnal CA (P-20495)*

ALPHABETIC

Employee Codes: A=Over 500 employees, B=251-500
C=101-250, D=51-100, E=20-50 F=10-19
2022 Southern California Business
Directory and Buyers Guide
© Mergent Inc. 1-800-342-5647
1307

Valley Vsta Nrsing Trnstnal CA ....C....818 763-6275
6120 Vineland Ave North Hollywood (91606) *(P-20495)*
Valley Wholesale Supply Corp (PA) ....D....818 769-5656
10708 Vanowen St North Hollywood (91605) *(P-13195)*
Valley Wide Recreation Pk Dst (PA) ....D....951 654-1505
901 W Esplanade Ave San Jacinto (92582) *(P-19679)*
Valley-HI Toyota Honda, Victorville *Also called Vahi Toyota Inc (P-18884)*
Valley-Todeco Inc (HQ) ....C....800 992-4444
12975 Bradley Ave Sylmar (91342) *(P-7080)*
Valleycrest Productions Ltd ....D....818 560-5391
500 S Buena Vista St Burbank (91521) *(P-12750)*
Valmas Inc ....F....323 677-2211
1233 S Boyle Ave Los Angeles (90023) *(P-2899)*
Valmont Coatings Inc ....F....310 549-2200
2226 E Dominguez St Long Beach (90810) *(P-7424)*
Valmont Ctngs Clwest Glvnizing, Long Beach *Also called Valmont Coatings Inc (P-7424)*
Valori Sand & Gravel Company ....C....909 350-3000
11027 Cherry Ave Fontana (92337) *(P-13317)*
Valterra Products LLC (PA) ....E....818 898-1671
15230 San Fernando Missio Mission Hills (91345) *(P-7478)*
Valtra Inc (PA) ....E....562 949-8625
8750 Pioneer Blvd Santa Fe Springs (90670) *(P-13958)*
Valtron Technologies Inc ....D....805 257-0333
28309 Avenue Crocker Santa Clarita (91355) *(P-18153)*
Value Options-V B H, Cypress *Also called Valueoptions of California (P-15644)*
Valueoptions of California ....C....800 228-1286
5665 Plaza Dr Ste 400 Cypress (90630) *(P-15644)*
Valverde Construction Inc ....D....562 906-1826
10936 Shoemaker Ave Santa Fe Springs (90670) *(P-982)*
Valvoline Instant Oil Change, Costa Mesa *Also called EZ Lube LLC (P-18932)*
Van Brunt Foundry Inc ....F....323 569-2832
5136 Chakemco St South Gate (90280) *(P-6402)*
Van Daele Development Corp ....C....951 354-6800
2900 Adams St Ste C25 Riverside (92504) *(P-683)*
Van Daele Homes, Riverside *Also called Van Daele Development Corp (P-683)*
Van Dorpe Chou Associates Inc ....E....714 978-9780
1845 W Orangewood Ave # 210 Orange (92868) *(P-22688)*
Van Grace Quality Injection ....F....323 931-5255
9164 Appleby St Downey (90240) *(P-5856)*
Van King & Storage Inc ....D....562 921-0555
13535 Larwin Cir Santa Fe Springs (90670) *(P-12089)*
Van Mart Inc (PA) ....F....949 698-2447
15192 Goldenwest Cir Westminster (92683) *(P-10001)*
Van Mart, The, Westminster *Also called Van Mart Inc (P-10001)*
Van Nuys Care Center Inc ....D....818 343-0700
16955 Vanowen St Van Nuys (91406) *(P-20637)*
Van's Gifts, Long Beach *Also called Farm Street Designs Inc (P-14841)*
Vance & Hines, Santa Fe Springs *Also called V&H Performance LLC (P-10508)*
Vance Corporation ....E....909 355-4333
17761 Slover Ave Bloomington (92316) *(P-926)*
Vance Executive Protection, Los Angeles *Also called Andrews International Inc (P-18250)*
Vancrest Construction Corp ....E....323 256-0011
7171 N Figueroa St Los Angeles (90042) *(P-846)*
Vandersteen Audio ....E....559 582-0324
116 W 4th St Hanford (93230) *(P-9205)*
Vanderveer Industrial Plas LLC ....E....714 579-7700
515 S Melrose St Placentia (92870) *(P-5857)*
Vanguard Health Systems Inc ....B....714 635-6272
1154 N Euclid St Anaheim (92801) *(P-20132)*
Vanguard Hospice Care Inc (PA) ....D....951 371-5681
1450 W 6th St Ste 215 Corona (92882) *(P-16147)*
Vanguard Lgistics Svcs USA Inc (HQ) ....C....310 637-3700
2665 E Del Amo Blvd E Rncho Dmngz (90221) *(P-12258)*
Vanguard Lgistics Svcs USA Inc (HQ) ....D....310 847-3000
5000 Arprt Plz Dr Ste 200 Long Beach (90815) *(P-12550)*
Vanguard Printing, Oxnard *Also called DBC Printing Incorporated (P-4273)*
Vanguard Space Tech Inc ....C....858 587-4210
4398 Corporate Center Dr Los Alamitos (90720) *(P-22689)*
Vanguard Tool & Manufacturing, Rancho Cucamonga *Also called Vanguard Tool & Mfg Co Inc (P-7188)*
Vanguard Tool & Mfg Co Inc ....E....909 980-9392
8388 Utica Ave Rancho Cucamonga (91730) *(P-7188)*
Vanguard Univ Southern Cal ....C....714 556-3610
55 Fair Dr Costa Mesa (92626) *(P-22467)*
Vaniman Manufacturing, Murrieta *Also called Vmc International LLC (P-11202)*
Vanomation Inc ....E....877 228-2992
9241 Research Dr Irvine (92618) *(P-8080)*
Vanowen Medical Associates ....D....818 778-1920
15211 Vanowen St Ste 100 Van Nuys (91405) *(P-20133)*
Vans Inc (HQ) ....B....714 755-4000
1588 S Coast Dr Costa Mesa (92626) *(P-5319)*
Vans Manufacturing Inc ....F....805 522-6267
330 E Easy St Ste C Simi Valley (93065) *(P-8837)*
Vans Shoes, Costa Mesa *Also called Vans Inc (P-5319)*
Vantage Apparel, Santa Ana *Also called Vantage Custom Classics Inc (P-14358)*
Vantage Associates Inc ....E....562 968-1400
12333 Los Nietos Rd Santa Fe Springs (90670) *(P-10441)*
Vantage Associates Inc ....E....800 995-8322
12333 Los Nietos Rd Santa Fe Springs (90670) *(P-5537)*
Vantage Associates Inc (PA) ....E....619 477-6940
12333 Los Nietos Rd Santa Fe Springs (90670) *(P-10537)*
Vantage Associates Inc ....D....562 968-1400
12333 Los Nietos Rd Santa Fe Springs (90670) *(P-5858)*
Vantage Company, Orange *Also called W Corporation (P-23525)*
Vantage Custom Classics Inc ....E....714 755-1133
3321 S Susan St Santa Ana (92704) *(P-14358)*
Vantage Led, Corona *Also called Tradenet Enterprise Inc (P-11612)*
Vantage Master Machine Company, Santa Fe Springs *Also called Vantage Associates Inc (P-10441)*
Vantage Point Products Corp (PA) ....D....562 946-1718
9115 Dice Rd Ste 18 Santa Fe Springs (90670) *(P-9206)*
Vantage Vehicle Group, Corona *Also called Vantage Vehicle Intl Inc (P-9831)*
Vantage Vehicle Intl Inc ....E....951 735-1200
1740 N Delilah St Corona (92879) *(P-9831)*
Vantari Medical LLC ....F....949 783-5300
15440 Laguna Canyon Rd # 26 Irvine (92618) *(P-10920)*
Vapex-Genex-Precision, Los Angeles *Also called Electrical Rebuilders Sls Inc (P-9823)*
Vaquero Energy Inc ....E....661 616-0600
4700 Stockdale Hwy # 120 Bakersfield (93309) *(P-557)*
Vaquero Energy Incorporated ....E....661 363-7240
15545 Hermosa Rd Bakersfield (93307) *(P-413)*
Varco De Mexico Holdings Inc ....D....714 978-1900
743 N Eckhoff St Orange (92868) *(P-17382)*
Varco Heat Treating, Garden Grove *Also called Diversfied Mtllrgical Svcs Inc (P-6439)*
Varco Systems, Orange *Also called Varco De Mexico Holdings Inc (P-17382)*
Variable Image Printing ....F....949 296-1444
16540 Aston Ste A Irvine (92606) *(P-4449)*
Variable Speed Solutions Inc ....F....714 847-5957
16182 Gothard St Ste I Huntington Beach (92647) *(P-18949)*
Variations In Stone Inc ....D....949 438-8337
360 La Perle Pl Costa Mesa (92627) *(P-1355)*
Varner Bros Inc ....D....661 399-2944
1808 Roberts Ln Bakersfield (93308) *(P-12989)*
Varner Family Ltd Partnership (PA) ....D....661 399-1163
5900 E Lerdo Hwy Shafter (93263) *(P-16198)*
Varsity Contractors Inc ....C....949 586-8283
24155 Laguna Hills Mall Laguna Hills (92653) *(P-17300)*
Vasinda Investments Inc ....D....661 324-4277
5353 Truckston Ave Bakersfield (93309) *(P-17521)*
Vasindas Around Clock Care Inc ....E....661 395-5820
5251 Office Park Dr # 403 Bakersfield (93309) *(P-22162)*
Vast Enterprises ....F....562 633-3224
7739 Monroe St Paramount (90723) *(P-5299)*
Vaughans Industrial Repair Inc ....E....562 633-2660
16224 Garfield Ave Paramount (90723) *(P-13959)*
Vaughn Weedman Inc (PA) ....C....425 481-0919
550 S Hope St Ste 1675 Los Angeles (90071) *(P-348)*
Vault Prep Inc ....E....310 971-9091
2500 Broadway Ste F125 Santa Monica (90404) *(P-6064)*
Vault Pro ....F....800 299-6929
13607 Pumice St Santa Fe Springs (90670) *(P-7574)*
Vayan Marketing Group LLC ....E....310 943-4990
10877 Wilshire Blvd Fl 12 Los Angeles (90024) *(P-23358)*
VCA Animal Hospitals Inc (HQ) ....C....310 571-6500
12401 W Olympic Blvd Los Angeles (90064) *(P-205)*
VCA Code Group ....E....714 363-4700
1845 W Orangewood Ave # 210 Orange (92868) *(P-22690)*
VCA Engineering, Orange *Also called Van Dorpe Chou Associates Inc (P-22688)*
VCA Inc (HQ) ....A....310 571-6500
12401 W Olympic Blvd Los Angeles (90064) *(P-13528)*
VCA Prfessional Animal Lab Inc ....D....310 571-6500
12401 W Olympic Blvd Los Angeles (90064) *(P-206)*
VCA TLC Animal Hospital, Los Angeles *Also called VCA Animal Hospitals Inc (P-205)*
Vci Construction LLC (HQ) ....D....909 946-0905
1921 W 11th St Ste A Upland (91786) *(P-983)*
Vci Event Technology Inc ....C....714 772-2002
1261 S Simpson Cir Anaheim (92806) *(P-17383)*
Vclad Laminates Inc ....E....626 442-2100
2103 Seaman Ave South El Monte (91733) *(P-5464)*
Vdi Motor Sports, Lake Elsinore *Also called Vertical Doors Inc (P-3717)*
Veatch Carlson Grogan & Nelson ....E....213 381-2861
1055 Wilshire Blvd Fl 11 Los Angeles (90017) *(P-21691)*
Vector Electronics & Tech Inc ....E....818 985-8208
11115 Vanowen St North Hollywood (91605) *(P-9466)*
Vector Launch LLC (PA) ....C....202 888-3063
15261 Connector Ln Huntington Beach (92649) *(P-7435)*
Vector Resources Inc (PA) ....B....310 436-1000
20917 Higgins Ct Torrance (90501) *(P-1336)*
Vectorusa, Torrance *Also called Vector Resources Inc (P-1336)*
Veeco Electro Fab Inc ....E....714 630-8020
1176 N Osprey Cir Anaheim (92807) *(P-9467)*
Vefo Inc ....E....909 598-3856
3202 Factory Dr Pomona (91768) *(P-5527)*
Veg-Fresh Farms LLC ....C....800 422-5535
1400 W Rincon St Corona (92878) *(P-14662)*
Veg-Land Inc ....E....714 871-6712
1518 E Valencia Dr Fullerton (92831) *(P-12172)*
Vegatek Corporation ....D....949 502-0090
470 Wald Irvine (92618) *(P-17750)*
Vege - Kurl Inc ....D....818 956-5582
412 W Cypress St Glendale (91204) *(P-5080)*
Vege-Mist Inc ....D....310 353-2300
407 E Redondo Beach Blvd Gardena (90248) *(P-8355)*
Vege-Tech Company, Glendale *Also called Vege - Kurl Inc (P-5080)*
Vehicle Accessory Center LLC ....D....909 987-8237
10863 Jersey Blvd Ste 101 Rancho Cucamonga (91730) *(P-13105)*
Veinviewer, Cypress *Also called Christie Medical Holdings Inc (P-11218)*
Vellios Automotive Machine Sp, Lawndale *Also called Vellios Machine Shop Inc (P-8838)*
Vellios Machine Shop Inc ....E....310 643-8540
4625 29th Mnhttan Bch Blv Lawndale (90260) *(P-8838)*
Velocitel Rf Inc ....C....949 809-4999
2415 Campus Dr Ste 200 Irvine (92612) *(P-22691)*
Velocity Arospc - Burbank Inc (HQ) ....D....818 246-8431
2840 N Ontario St Burbank (91504) *(P-19082)*
Velocity Arospc - Edn AVI Inc ....F....818 988-8826
6720 Valjean Ave Van Nuys (91406) *(P-22692)*

Velocity Commercial Capitl LLC ....E......818 532-3700
30699 Russell Ranch Rd Westlake Village (91362) *(P-15258)*

Velocity Financial LLC (PA) ....**D......818 532-3700**
30699 Russell Ranch Rd Westlake Village (91362) *(P-15259)*

Velocity Tech Solutions Inc 949 417-0260
111 Pacifica Ste 320 Irvine (92618) *(P-18114)*

Velvet Heart, Los Angeles *Also called Tcj Manufacturing LLC (P-3000)*

Venator Americas LLC 323 269-7311
3700 E Olympic Blvd Los Angeles (90023) *(P-4648)*

Venco Western Inc (PA) ....**C......805 981-2400**
2400 Eastman Ave Oxnard (93030) *(P-349)*

Vendor Direct Solutions LLC (PA) ....**C......213 362-5622**
515 S Figueroa St # 1900 Los Angeles (90071) *(P-17751)*

Vendor Surveillance Corp ....C......949 833-2111
2525 Main St Ste 100 Irvine (92614) *(P-23359)*

Venegas Farming LLC ....E......805 529-5038
8002 Balcom Canyon Rd Somis (93066) *(P-219)*

Venice Baking Co ....E......310 322-7357
134 Main St El Segundo (90245) *(P-2041)*

Venice Fmly Clinic Foundation (PA) ....**C......310 664-7703**
604 Rose Ave Venice (90291) *(P-20134)*

Venida Packing Company ....C......559 592-2816
19823 Avenue 300 Exeter (93221) *(P-14981)*

Venoco Inc ....E......805 644-1400
4483 Mcgrath St Ste 101 Ventura (93003) *(P-414)*

Venoco Inc ....E......805 961-2305
7979 Hollister Ave Goleta (93117) *(P-5267)*

Venstar Inc ....F......818 341-8760
9250 Owensmouth Ave Chatsworth (91311) *(P-8356)*

Ventegra Inc A Cal Beneft Corp ....D......858 551-8111
450 N Brand Blvd Ste 600 Glendale (91203) *(P-23522)*

Ventritex, Sylmar *Also called Pacesetter Inc (P-11234)*

Ventsam Sash & Door Mfg Co, Sun Valley *Also called Monty Ventsam Inc (P-3271)*

Ventu Park LLC ....D......805 716-4200
495 N Ventu Park Rd Thousand Oaks (91320) *(P-16770)*

Ventura Aerospace Inc ....F......818 540-3130
31355 Agoura Rd Westlake Village (91361) *(P-10442)*

Ventura Coastal LLC (PA) ....**D......805 653-7000**
2325 Vista Del Mar Dr Ventura (93001) *(P-1912)*

Ventura County Credit Union (PA) ....**D......805 477-4000**
2575 Vista Del Mar Dr Ventura (93001) *(P-15103)*

Ventura County Lemon Coops ....D......805 385-3345
245 E Colonia Rd Oxnard (93030) *(P-14663)*

Ventura County Medi-Cal Manage 888 301-1228
711 E Daily Dr Ste 106 Camarillo (93010) *(P-21495)*

Ventura County Medical Center ....D......805 652-6729
300 Hillmont Ave Ventura (93003) *(P-20235)*

Ventura County Medical Center ....C......805 933-8600
845 N 10th St Ste 3 Santa Paula (93060) *(P-20135)*

Ventura County Medical Center (PA) ....**C......805 652-6000**
3291 Loma Vista Rd Ventura (93003) *(P-20136)*

Ventura County Medical Center ....C......805 652-6201
3291 Loma Vista Rd # 343 Ventura (93003) *(P-20137)*

Ventura County Reporter, Pasadena *Also called Southland Publishing Inc (P-4031)*

Ventura County Star ....E......805 437-0138
771 E Daily Dr Ste 300 Camarillo (93010) *(P-4041)*

Ventura Family YMCA, Ventura *Also called Channel Islnds Yung MNS Chrstn (P-22330)*

Ventura Feed and Pet Sups Inc ....E......805 648-5035
980 E Front St Ventura (93001) *(P-11789)*

Ventura Foods LLC ....D......714 257-3700
2900 Jurupa St Ontario (91761) *(P-2132)*

Ventura Foods LLC ....E......323 262-9157
2900 Jurupa St Ontario (91761) *(P-1766)*

Ventura Foods LLC (PA) ....**C......714 257-3700**
40 Pointe Dr Brea (92821) *(P-2133)*

Ventura Harbor Boatyard Inc ....E......805 654-1433
1415 Spinnaker Dr Ventura (93001) *(P-10474)*

Ventura Hospice, Westlake Village *Also called Silverado Senior Living Inc (P-20470)*

Ventura Hsptality Partners LLC ....C......805 648-2100
450 Harbor Blvd Ventura (93001) *(P-16771)*

Ventura Hydrulic Mch Works Inc ....E......805 656-1760
1555 Callens Rd Ventura (93003) *(P-8839)*

Ventura Medical Management LLC ....B......805 477-6220
2601 E Main St Ventura (93003) *(P-23135)*

Ventura Pacific Co, Oxnard *Also called Ventura County Lemon Coops (P-14663)*

Ventura Printing Inc (PA) ....**D......805 981-2600**
200 N Elevar St Oxnard (93030) *(P-4588)*

Ventura Rgional Sanitation Dst 805 525-8217
3500 Toland Rd Santa Paula (93060) *(P-12990)*

Ventura Technology Group ....E......805 581-0800
855 E Easy St Ste 104 Simi Valley (93065) *(P-9599)*

Ventura Transfer Company (PA) ....**D......310 549-1660**
2418 E 223rd St Long Beach (90810) *(P-12090)*

Ventura Yuth Conservation Camp, Camarillo *Also called County of Ventura (P-21763)*

Ventura Yuth Crrctional Fcilty, Camarillo *Also called Juvenile Justice Division Cal (P-23044)*

Venture Aviator ....E......212 913-9746
4136 Del Rey Ave Ste 662 Marina Del Rey (90292) *(P-17752)*

Venture Design Services Inc (PA) ....**C......714 765-3740**
1051 S East St Anaheim (92805) *(P-22871)*

Venturedyne Ltd ....D......909 793-2788
1320 W Colton Ave Redlands (92374) *(P-8060)*

Venturi Astrolab Inc ....F......310 989-1264
12536 Chadron Ave Hawthorne (90250) *(P-10525)*

Venue Management Systems Inc ....A......626 445-6000
2041 E Gladstone St Ste A Glendora (91740) *(P-18357)*

Venus Alloys Inc (PA) ....**E......714 635-8800**
1415 S Allec St Anaheim (92805) *(P-6372)*

Venus Bridal Gowns, San Gabriel *Also called Lotus Orient Corp (P-2892)*

Venus Foods Inc ....E......626 369-5188
770 S Stimson Ave City of Industry (91745) *(P-1723)*

Venus Group Inc ....C......949 609-1299
25861 Wright Foothill Ranch (92610) *(P-13196)*

Venus Laboratories Inc ....D......714 891-3100
11150 Hope St Cypress (90630) *(P-4674)*

Venus Textiles, Foothill Ranch *Also called Venus Group Inc (P-13196)*

Ver Sales Inc (PA) ....**D......818 567-3000**
2509 N Naomi St Burbank (91504) *(P-13604)*

Verde Cosmetic Labs LLC ....F......818 284-4080
19845 Nordhokk St Northridge (91324) *(P-5081)*

Verdugo Hills Hospital Inc ....D......818 790-7100
1812 Verdugo Blvd Glendale (91208) *(P-21001)*

Verdugo Hills Psychtherapy Ctr (PA) ....**D......818 241-6780**
410 Arden Ave Ste 201 Glendale (91203) *(P-20138)*

Verdugo Hospice Care Center, Los Angeles *Also called Alta Verdugo Consulting Inc (P-20521)*

Verdugo Mental Health ....D......818 244-7257
1540 E Colorado St Glendale (91205) *(P-21362)*

Verdugo Tool & Engrg Co Inc 818 998-1101
20600 Superior St Chatsworth (91311) *(P-7189)*

Verengo Inc (HQ) ....**A......310 803-9053**
20285 S Wstn Ave Ste 200 Torrance (90501) *(P-1628)*

Verengo Solar, Torrance *Also called Verengo Inc (P-1628)*

Verifi Inc ....D......323 655-5789
8391 Beverly Blvd Ste 310 Los Angeles (90048) *(P-23360)*

Veris Manufacturing, Brea *Also called Q C M Inc (P-8980)*

Veritas Health Services Inc ....A......909 464-8600
5451 Walnut Ave Chino (91710) *(P-21002)*

Veritas Technologies LLC ....C......310 202-0757
16501 Ventura Blvd # 400 Encino (91436) *(P-17753)*

Veritone Inc (PA) ....**D......888 507-1737**
575 Anton Blvd Ste 100 Costa Mesa (92626) *(P-18115)*

Veritxt/Clfornia Reporting LLC ....E......714 432-1711
20 Corporate Park Irvine (92606) *(P-17195)*

Verity Health System Cal Inc ....D......310 900-2000
3680 E Imperial Hwy # 306 Lynwood (90262) *(P-21003)*

Verity Medical Foundation (PA) ....**D......408 278-3000**
6300 Canoga Ave Ste 1500 Woodland Hills (91367) *(P-20139)*

Verizon, Indio *Also called Frontier California Inc (P-12637)*

Verizon, Santa Maria *Also called Frontier California Inc (P-12638)*

Verizon, San Fernando *Also called Frontier California Inc (P-12639)*

Verizon, Bishop *Also called Frontier California Inc (P-12640)*

Verizon, Huntington Beach *Also called Frontier California Inc (P-12641)*

Verizon, Baldwin Park *Also called Telesector Resources Group Inc (P-23344)*

Verizon, Westlake Village *Also called Frontier California Inc (P-12642)*

Verizon Communications Inc ....D......626 858-1739
176 E Badillo St Covina (91723) *(P-12616)*

Verizon Connect Telo Inc (HQ) ....**C......949 389-5500**
15505 Sand Canyon Ave Irvine (92618) *(P-18116)*

Verizon Digital Media Svcs Inc (HQ) ....**B......310 396-7400**
13031 W Jefferson Blvd Los Angeles (90094) *(P-18234)*

Verizon Media Inc (HQ) ....**A......310 907-3016**
11995 Bluff Creek Dr Los Angeles (90094) *(P-12617)*

Verizon Services Corp ....B......310 315-1100
2530 Wilshire Blvd Fl 1 Santa Monica (90403) *(P-12618)*

Verizon South Inc ....B......805 681-8527
424 S Patterson Ave Goleta (93111) *(P-12619)*

Verizon Wireless, Tarzana *Also called Cellco Partnership (P-12597)*

Verizon Wireless, Compton *Also called Cellco Partnership (P-12598)*

Verizon Wireless, Taft *Also called Cellco Partnership (P-12600)*

Verizon Wireless, Orange *Also called Cellco Partnership (P-12601)*

Verizon Wireless, Norwalk *Also called Cellco Partnership (P-12603)*

Verizon Wireless, Irvine *Also called 4g Wireless Inc (P-12589)*

Verizon Wireless, San Clemente *Also called Cellco Partnership (P-12604)*

Verizon Wireless (PA) ....**C......949 286-7000**
15505 Sand Canyon Ave Irvine (92618) *(P-12620)*

Verlo Industries Inc ....F......714 236-2191
5032 Apollo Cir Los Alamitos (90720) *(P-3701)*

Vermont Care Center, Torrance *Also called Geri-Care II Inc (P-20591)*

Vermont Fuel Inc ....F......818 339-6623
2202 S Vermont Ave Los Angeles (90007) *(P-4949)*

Vern Fonk Insurance Svcs Inc (HQ) ....**D......714 252-2500**
7711 Center Ave Ste 200 Huntington Beach (92647) *(P-15645)*

Vernon Central Warehouse Inc ....C......323 234-2200
2050 E 38th St Vernon (90058) *(P-12120)*

Vernon Warehouse Co, Vernon *Also called Vernon Central Warehouse Inc (P-12120)*

Verona Quartz Inc ....F......818 962-3668
9415 Telfair Ave Sun Valley (91352) *(P-13318)*

Veronicas Auto Insur Svcs Inc (PA) ....**D......909 723-1910**
290 W Orange Show Rd # 1 San Bernardino (92408) *(P-15646)*

Verrix LLC ....F......949 668-1234
1330 Calle Avanzado # 200 San Clemente (92673) *(P-11073)*

Versa Products Inc (PA) ....**C......310 353-7100**
14105 Avalon Blvd Los Angeles (90061) *(P-3617)*

Versa Stage, Torrance *Also called Forrester Eastland Corporation (P-11670)*

Versaclimber, Santa Ana *Also called Heart Rate Inc (P-11424)*

Versafab Corp (PA) ....**E......800 421-1822**
15919 S Broadway Gardena (90248) *(P-6939)*

Versailles On The Lake, Santa Ana *Also called Domino Realty Management Co (P-15723)*

Versante, Monterey Park *Also called Direct Wheel Inc (P-10046)*

Versatables.com, Los Angeles *Also called Versa Products Inc (P-3617)*

Versatile Building Pdts LLC ....F......714 829-2600
245 W Carl Karcher Way Anaheim (92801) *(P-1461)*

Versity Investments LLC ....D......877 827-6272
20 Enterprise Ste 400 Aliso Viejo (92656) *(P-15309)*

Employee Codes: A=Over 500 employees, B=251-500
C=101-250, D=51-100, E=20-50 F=10-19

2022 Southern California Business
Directory and Buyers Guide

© Mergent Inc. 1-800-342-5647

1309

Vertex China, Pomona *Also called Sky One Inc* ***(P-5994)***

Vertex Coatings Inc ....D....909 923-5795
1291 W State St Ontario (91762) ***(P-1200)***

Vertex Diamond Tool Co Inc ....E....909 599-1129
940 W Cienega Ave San Dimas (91773) ***(P-7876)***

Vertical Doors Inc ....E....951 273-1069
542 3rd St Lake Elsinore (92530) ***(P-3717)***

Vertical Fiber Technologies, Montebello *Also called Vft Inc* ***(P-3123)***

Vertical Tank Inc ....F....415 686-8796
4807 Matterhorn Way Bakersfield (93312) ***(P-3718)***

Vertiflex Inc ....E....442 325-5900
25155 Rye Canyon Loop Valencia (91355) ***(P-11074)***

Vertos Medical Inc ....D....949 349-0008
95 Enterprise Ste 325 Aliso Viejo (92656) ***(P-11075)***

Very Special Chocolats Inc ....C....626 334-7838
760 N Mckeever Ave Azusa (91702) ***(P-2108)***

Vescio Enterprises Inc (PA) ....**D....323 263-7225**
4915 E Olympic Blvd Los Angeles (90022) ***(P-13960)***

Vescio Manufacturing Intl, Santa Fe Springs *Also called Vescio Threading Co* ***(P-8840)***

Vescio Threading Co ....D....562 802-1868
14002 Anson Ave Santa Fe Springs (90670) ***(P-8840)***

Vescom Corporation (PA) ....**A....207 945-5051**
1125 W 190th St Gardena (90248) ***(P-18358)***

Vessels Club Restaurant, Cypress *Also called Los Alamitos Race Course* ***(P-19430)***

Vest Inc ....D....800 421-6370
6023 Alcoa Ave Vernon (90058) ***(P-6255)***

Vesta, Corona *Also called Extrumed Inc* ***(P-5643)***

Vesta Foodservice, Santa Fe Springs *Also called LA Specialty Produce Co* ***(P-14641)***

Vesta Luxury Home Staging, Pico Rivera *Also called Showroom Interiors LLC* ***(P-17372)***

Vesta Solutions Inc (HQ) ....**B....951 719-2100**
42555 Rio Nedo Temecula (92590) ***(P-9244)***

Vesture Group Incorporated ....E....818 842-0200
3405 W Pacific Ave Burbank (91505) ***(P-3047)***

Vesuki Inc ....F....562 245-4000
1350 W Lambert Rd Ste A Brea (92821) ***(P-7575)***

Vet National Inc ....E....805 692-8487
3621 State St Santa Barbara (93105) ***(P-13673)***

Vet National Mail, Santa Barbara *Also called Vet National Inc* ***(P-13673)***

Vetco Hospitals Inc (HQ) ....**D....858 483-4145**
4790 Irvine Blvd Ste 105 Irvine (92620) ***(P-207)***

Veteran Company, Los Angeles *Also called Veteran Enterprise Inc* ***(P-2593)***

Veteran Enterprise Inc ....F....323 937-2233
620 Gladys Ave Los Angeles (90021) ***(P-2593)***

Veterans Affairs US Dept ....D....714 568-9802
888 W Santa Ana Blvd Santa Ana (92701) ***(P-20140)***

Veterans Health Administration ....C....818 895-9344
16111 Plummer St North Hills (91343) ***(P-20141)***

Veterans Health Administration ....C....310 478-3711
11301 Wilshire Blvd Los Angeles (90073) ***(P-20142)***

Veterans Health Administration ....C....805 543-1233
1288 Morro St Ste 200 San Luis Obispo (93401) ***(P-20143)***

Veterans Health Administration ....C....805 354-6000
1550 E Main St Santa Maria (93454) ***(P-20144)***

Veterans Health Administration ....B....805 983-6384
250 Citrus Grove Ln # 250 Oxnard (93036) ***(P-20145)***

Veterans Health Administration ....C....760 341-5570
41865 Boardwalk Ste 103 Palm Desert (92211) ***(P-20146)***

Veterans Health Administration ....C....818 891-7711
16111 Plummer St North Hills (91343) ***(P-20147)***

Veterans Health Administration ....C....805 683-1491
4440 Calle Real Santa Barbara (93110) ***(P-20148)***

Veterans Health Administration ....C....909 825-7084
11201 Benton St Loma Linda (92357) ***(P-20149)***

Veterans Health Administration ....C....818 895-9449
16111 Plummer St North Hills (91343) ***(P-20150)***

Veterans Health Administration ....C....714 780-5400
1801 W Romneya Dr Ste 303 Anaheim (92801) ***(P-20151)***

Veterans Health Administration ....C....661 632-1871
1801 Westwind Dr Bakersfield (93301) ***(P-20152)***

Veterans Health Administration ....C....213 253-2677
351 E Temple St Los Angeles (90012) ***(P-20153)***

Veterans Health Administration ....C....661 323-8387
1110 Golden Valley Fwy Bakersfield (93301) ***(P-20154)***

Veterinary Centers America VCA, Los Angeles *Also called Vicar Operating Inc* ***(P-209)***

Veterinary Pharmaceuticals Inc ....D....559 582-6800
13159 Hanford Armona Rd Hanford (93230) ***(P-14295)***

Veterinary Service Inc ....E....951 328-4900
935 Palmyrita Ave Riverside (92507) ***(P-13529)***

Veterinary Service Inc ....E....559 651-1633
1607 N Plaza Dr Visalia (93291) ***(P-13530)***

Veternary Ctrs of Amrica-Texas (HQ) ....**D....310 571-6500**
12401 W Olympic Blvd Los Angeles (90064) ***(P-208)***

Vfs Fire Protection Services, Orange *Also called Bernel Inc* ***(P-1033)***

Vft Inc ....E....323 728-2280
1040 S Vail Ave Montebello (90640) ***(P-3123)***

Vi-Star Gear Co Inc ....E....323 774-3750
7312 Jefferson St Paramount (90723) ***(P-7101)***

Via Care Cmnty Hlth Ctr Inc ....D....323 268-9191
507 S Atlantic Blvd Los Angeles (90022) ***(P-20155)***

Via Trading Corporation ....D....877 202-3616
2520 Industry Way Lynwood (90262) ***(P-14982)***

Via Verde Country Club, San Dimas *Also called San Dimas Golf Inc* ***(P-19606)***

Viacare Inc (PA) ....**D....562 591-1411**
1206 Walnut Ave Long Beach (90813) ***(P-20638)***

Viacom Consumer Products Inc, Los Angeles *Also called Paramount Licensing Inc* ***(P-16215)***

Viacom Networks ....D....310 752-8000
1575 N Gower St Ste 100 Los Angeles (90028) ***(P-19196)***

Viade Products Inc ....E....805 484-2114
354 Dawson Dr Camarillo (93012) ***(P-11201)***

Vianh Company Inc ....E....714 590-9808
13841 A Better Way 10c Garden Grove (92843) ***(P-8841)***

Viant, Irvine *Also called Interactive Media Holdings Inc* ***(P-17023)***

Viant Technology LLC (HQ) ....**E....949 861-8888**
2722 Michelson Dr Ste 100 Irvine (92612) ***(P-17068)***

Viant US, Irvine *Also called Viant Technology LLC* ***(P-17068)***

Viasys Respiratory Care Inc ....F....714 283-2228
1100 Bird Center Dr Palm Springs (92262) ***(P-11076)***

Viasys Respiratory Care Inc ....D....714 283-2228
22745 Savi Ranch Pkwy Yorba Linda (92887) ***(P-11077)***

Viavi Solutions Inc ....D....805 465-1875
3601 Calle Tecate Camarillo (93012) ***(P-9245)***

Vibiana Events LLC ....D....213 626-1507
214 S Main St Los Angeles (90012) ***(P-16985)***

Vibra Finish Co (PA) ....**E....805 578-0033**
2220 Shasta Way Simi Valley (93065) ***(P-6160)***

Vibrahone, Simi Valley *Also called Vibra Finish Co* ***(P-6160)***

Vibrex, Valencia *Also called M W Sausse & Co Inc* ***(P-8959)***

Vicar Operating Inc (HQ) ....**B....310 571-6500**
12401 W Olympic Blvd Los Angeles (90064) ***(P-209)***

Victor Cmnty Support Svcs Inc ....C....760 987-8225
15095 Amargosa Rd Ste 201 Victorville (92394) ***(P-21363)***

Victor Cmnty Support Svcs Inc ....C....760 245-4695
14360 St Andrews Dr Ste 1 Victorville (92395) ***(P-21364)***

Victor Cmnty Support Svcs Inc ....C....909 890-5930
1908 Bsneca Ctr Dr Ste 10 San Bernardino (92408) ***(P-21365)***

Victor Martin Inc ....E....323 587-3101
1640 W 132nd St Gardena (90249) ***(P-3537)***

Victor Wire & Cable Corp ....F....310 842-9933
12915 S Spring St Los Angeles (90061) ***(P-6358)***

Victor Wire and Cable LLC ....F....310 842-9933
12915 S Spring St Los Angeles (90061) ***(P-6359)***

Victoria Care Center ....D....805 642-1736
5445 Everglades St Ventura (93003) ***(P-20496)***

Victoria Nursery Inc (PA) ....**D....805 985-0855**
1085 Victoria Ave Oxnard (93030) ***(P-14897)***

Victoria Place Community Assn ....D....909 981-4131
195 N Euclid Ave Upland (91786) ***(P-22468)***

Victoria Skimboards ....F....949 494-0059
2955 Laguna Canyon Rd # 1 Laguna Beach (92651) ***(P-11456)***

Victorious RED ....E....657 529-8911
4260 Artesia Ave Unit B Fullerton (92833) ***(P-1621)***

Victorville Daily Press, Victorville *Also called Gatehouse Media LLC* ***(P-3981)***

Victorville Disposal Inc ....D....909 429-4200
9890 Cherry Ave Fontana (92335) ***(P-12991)***

Victorville Homecare, San Bernardino *Also called Maxim Healthcare Services Inc* ***(P-21191)***

Victorvlle Trsure Holdings LLC ....D....760 245-6565
15494 Palmdale Rd Victorville (92392) ***(P-16772)***

Victory Circle Chassis & Parts, Bakersfield *Also called Raudmans Craig Victory Circle* ***(P-10555)***

Victory Display & Store Fixs, Compton *Also called Gemco Display and Str Fixs LLC* ***(P-13456)***

Victory Foam Inc (PA) ....**D....949 474-0690**
3 Holland Irvine (92618) ***(P-14983)***

Victory Intl Group LLC ....C....949 407-5888
14748 Pipeline Ave Ste B Chino Hills (91709) ***(P-14104)***

Victory Koredrry, Huntington Beach *Also called Victory Professional Pdts Inc* ***(P-3007)***

Victory Oil Company ....D....310 519-9500
461 W 6th St Ste 300 San Pedro (90731) ***(P-415)***

Victory Professional Pdts Inc ....E....714 887-0621
5601 Engineer Dr Huntington Beach (92649) ***(P-3007)***

Victory Shell, Westlake Village *Also called Conico Roro Inc* ***(P-18911)***

Victory Sportswear Inc ....E....626 359-5400
2381 Buena Vista St Duarte (91010) ***(P-14984)***

Victory Studio, Burbank *Also called Warner Bros Entertainment Inc* ***(P-19205)***

Vida Corporation ....F....626 839-4912
17807 Maclaren St Ste A City of Industry (91744) ***(P-9844)***

VIDA NUEVA, Los Angeles *Also called Tidings* ***(P-4038)***

Vidal Sassoon Salon, Beverly Hills *Also called Regis Corporation* ***(P-16915)***

Vident ....D....714 221-6700
22705 Savi Ranch Pkwy Yorba Linda (92887) ***(P-13531)***

VIDEO GAME, Santa Monica *Also called Thatgamecompany Inc* ***(P-19514)***

Video Sensing Division, Tustin *Also called Canon Medical Systems USA Inc* ***(P-13482)***

Video Vice Data Communications ....B....714 897-6300
12681 Pala Dr Garden Grove (92841) ***(P-12793)***

Videoamp Inc (PA) ....**D....949 294-0351**
2229 S Carmelina Ave Los Angeles (90064) ***(P-18005)***

Videocam, Anaheim *Also called Vci Event Technology Inc* ***(P-17383)***

Videssence LLC (PA) ....**E....626 579-0943**
10768 Lower Azusa Rd El Monte (91731) ***(P-9073)***

Vie De France 108, Vernon *Also called Vie De France Yamazaki Inc* ***(P-2042)***

Vie De France Yamazaki Inc ....A....323 582-1241
3046 E 50th St Vernon (90058) ***(P-2042)***

Viele & Sons Inc ....D....714 447-3663
1820 E Valencia Dr Fullerton (92831) ***(P-14519)***

Viele & Sons Instnl Groc, Fullerton *Also called Viele & Sons Inc* ***(P-14519)***

Viento Funding II LLC ....F....609 524-4500
18101 Von Karman Ave 1700a Irvine (92612) ***(P-8935)***

VIETNAMESE COMMUNITY OF ORANGE, Santa Ana *Also called Southland Integrated Svcs Inc* ***(P-22211)***

Vietnumber, Huntington Beach *Also called Filanity Corporation* ***(P-12635)***

View Heights Convalescent Hosp, Los Angeles *Also called Amada Enterprises Inc* ***(P-20242)***

Mergent e-mail: customerrelations@mergent.com
1310
2022 Southern California Business Directory and Buyers Guide
(P-0000) Products & Services Section entry number
(PA)=Parent Co (HQ)=Headquarters (DH)=Div Headquarters

View Park Convalescent Center, Los Angeles *Also called Burlington Convalescent Hosp* ***(P-20267)***
View Park Convalescent Center, Los Angeles *Also called Burlington Convalescent Hosp* ***(P-20268)***
Viewsonic Corporation (PA) ... **C ... 909 444-8888**
10 Pointe Dr Ste 200 Brea (92821) ***(P-8310)***
Vifah, Mentone *Also called Dropship Vendor Group LLC* ***(P-3469)***
Vig Furniture, Vernon *Also called Lima Trading LLC* ***(P-13140)***
Vigilant Drone Defense Inc ... E ... 424 275-8282
1055 W 7th St Fl 33 Los Angeles (90017) ***(P-7576)***
Vignolo Farms Inc ... C ... 661 746-2148
33342 Dresser Ave Bakersfield (93308) ***(P-5)***
Vijall Inc ... E ... 818 700-0071
21900 Marilla St Chatsworth (91311) ***(P-14794)***
Viking Fabrication, Riverside *Also called Tolco Incorporated* ***(P-7010)***
Viking Ocean Cruises, Woodland Hills *Also called Viking River Cruises Inc* ***(P-12403)***
Viking Office Products Inc (HQ) ... **B ... 562 490-1000**
3366 E Willow St Signal Hill (90755) ***(P-14200)***
Viking Products, Orange *Also called Pro Detention Inc* ***(P-6231)***
Viking Products Inc ... E ... 949 379-5100
20 Doppler Irvine (92618) ***(P-7877)***
Viking River Cruises Inc (HQ) ... **A ... 818 227-1234**
5700 Canoga Ave Ste 200 Woodland Hills (91367) ***(P-12403)***
Viking Rubber Products Inc ... F ... 310 868-5200
2600 Homestead Pl Compton (90220) ***(P-5421)***
Viktor Benes Bakeries, Westlake Village *Also called Mamolos Cntntl Bailey Bakeries* ***(P-14706)***
Villa Alamar, Santa Barbara *Also called Bankers Mrtg Rlty Advsors Snta* ***(P-22084)***
Villa Convalescent Hosp Inc ... D ... 951 689-5788
8965 Magnolia Ave Riverside (92503) ***(P-20497)***
Villa Dolce Gelato, Van Nuys *Also called Dolce Dolci LLC* ***(P-1814)***
Villa Ford Inc ... C ... 714 637-8222
2550 N Tustin St Orange (92865) ***(P-18807)***
Villa Furniture Mfg Co ... C ... 714 535-7272
13760 Midway St Cerritos (90703) ***(P-3634)***
Villa International, Cerritos *Also called Villa Furniture Mfg Co* ***(P-3634)***
Villa Maria Care Center, Baldwin Park *Also called Trinity Health Systems* ***(P-20490)***
Villa Park Landscape (PA) ... **D ... 714 538-3788**
739 W Katella Ave Ste B Orange (92867) ***(P-288)***
Villa Park Substation, Orange *Also called Southern California Edison Co* ***(P-12859)***
Villa Serena Healthcare Center ... D ... 562 437-2797
723 E 9th St Long Beach (90813) ***(P-20498)***
Villa Toscana Properties LLC ... D ... 213 223-2261
633 W 5th St Ste 2600 Los Angeles (90071) ***(P-16029)***
Villa Venetia ... B ... 714 540-1800
2775 Mesa Verde Dr E Costa Mesa (92626) ***(P-15260)***
Village 8, Westlake Village *Also called Weststar Cinemas Inc* ***(P-19291)***
Village At Northridge ... C ... 818 514-4497
9222 Corbin Ave Northridge (91324) ***(P-22163)***
Village At Sherman Oaks LLC ... C ... 818 994-7900
5450 Vesper Ave Sherman Oaks (91411) ***(P-22164)***
Village At Sydney Creek, San Luis Obispo *Also called Village Pacific MGT Group Inc* ***(P-20499)***
Village At Sydney Creek, San Luis Obispo *Also called Village Pacific MGT Group Inc* ***(P-20500)***
Village Center Ultramar, Palmdale *Also called Ultramar Inc* ***(P-5265)***
Village Family Services (PA) ... **D ... 818 755-8786**
6736 Laurel Canyon Blvd # 200 North Hollywood (91606) ***(P-21366)***
Village Nurseries Whl LLC (PA) ... **E ... 714 279-3100**
1589 N Main St Orange (92867) ***(P-14898)***
Village Nurseries Whl LLC ... B ... 951 657-3940
20099 Santa Rosa Mine Rd Perris (92570) ***(P-14899)***
Village Pacific MGT Group Inc ... D ... 805 543-2350
1234 Laurel Ln San Luis Obispo (93401) ***(P-20499)***
Village Pacific MGT Group Inc (PA) ... **D ... 805 543-2300**
55 Broad St San Luis Obispo (93405) ***(P-20500)***
Village Rdshow Entrmt Group US (PA) ... **E ... 310 385-4300**
10100 Santa Monica Blvd Los Angeles (90067) ***(P-19197)***
Village Rdshow Entrmt Group US ... E ... 310 867-8000
9268 W 3rd St Beverly Hills (90210) ***(P-19198)***
Village Road Show Pictures USA ... D ... 310 385-4300
10100 Santa Monica Blvd Los Angeles (90067) ***(P-19199)***
Village The, San Juan Capistrano *Also called Freedom Properties-Hemet LLC* ***(P-15668)***
Village West Health Center, Riverside *Also called Air Force Village West Inc* ***(P-20240)***
Villlage News Inc ... E ... 760 451-3488
41740 Enterprise Cir S Temecula (92590) ***(P-4042)***
Vim Tools, La Verne *Also called Durston Manufacturing Company* ***(P-6477)***
Vin Dibona Productions, Los Angeles *Also called Cara Communications Corp* ***(P-19107)***
Vinatronic Inc ... F ... 714 845-3480
15571 Industry Ln Huntington Beach (92649) ***(P-9468)***
Vincent B Zaninovich Sons Inc ... A ... 661 720-9031
20715 Ave 8 Richgrove (93261) ***(P-55)***
Vincent Contractors Inc ... B ... 714 693-1726
4501 E La Palma Ave # 200 Anaheim (92807) ***(P-1356)***
Vincent Hayley Enterprises ... D ... 626 398-8182
1810 N Fair Oaks Ave Pasadena (91103) ***(P-21004)***
Vincent Huang & Associates LLC (PA) ... **D ... 909 861-9600**
1550 Valley Vista Dr Diamond Bar (91765) ***(P-12678)***
Vinci Brands LLC ... C ... 949 838-5111
1775 Flight Ste 300 Irvine (92606) ***(P-8181)***
Vinculums Services LLC ... C ... 949 783-3552
10 Pasteur Ste 100 Irvine (92618) ***(P-23523)***
Vinotemp International Corp ... E ... 310 886-3332
700 W 16th St Long Beach (90813) ***(P-3573)***
Vintage Associates Inc ... C ... 760 772-3673
78755 Darby Rd Bermuda Dunes (92203) ***(P-350)***
Vintage Club ... D ... 760 340-0500
75001 Vintage Dr W Indian Wells (92210) ***(P-19625)***
Vintage Design LLC (HQ) ... **D ... 949 900-5400**
25200 Commercentre Dr Lake Forest (92630) ***(P-1470)***
Vintage Nursery, Bermuda Dunes *Also called Vintage Associates Inc* ***(P-350)***
Vintage Production California, Santa Clarita *Also called California Resources Prod Corp* ***(P-398)***
Vintage Senior Housing LLC ... B ... 805 583-3500
5300 E Los Angeles Ave Simi Valley (93063) ***(P-15751)***
Vintage Senior Living, Newport Beach *Also called Vintage Senior Management Inc* ***(P-15752)***
Vintage Senior Management Inc ... C ... 818 954-9500
2721 W Willow St Burbank (91505) ***(P-21909)***
Vintage Senior Management Inc (PA) ... **A ... 949 719-4080**
23 Corporate Plaza Dr # 190 Newport Beach (92660) ***(P-15752)***
Vintage Simi Hills, Simi Valley *Also called Vintage Senior Housing LLC* ***(P-15751)***
Vintique Inc ... E ... 714 634-1932
1828 W Sequoia Ave Orange (92868) ***(P-10153)***
Vinyl Technology Inc ... C ... 626 443-5257
200 Railroad Ave Monrovia (91016) ***(P-3862)***
Vinylvisions Company LLC ... E ... 800 321-8746
1233 Enterprise Ct Corona (92882) ***(P-5118)***
Vioski Inc ... F ... 626 359-4571
1625 S Magnolia Ave Monrovia (91016) ***(P-3521)***
VIP Rubber Company Inc (PA) ... **C ... 562 905-3456**
540 S Cypress St La Habra (90631) ***(P-5422)***
VIP TOTS, Hemet *Also called V I P Tots Inc* ***(P-22072)***
VIP Tours of California Inc ... D ... 310 216-7507
1419 E Maple Ave El Segundo (90245) ***(P-12412)***
VIP Transport Inc ... E ... 951 272-3700
2703 Wardlow Rd Corona (92882) ***(P-12091)***
Vipstore USA Co ... B ... 626 934-7880
13674 Star Ruby Ave Eastvale (92880) ***(P-14985)***
Virco Inc (HQ) ... **C ... 310 533-0474**
2027 Harpers Way Torrance (90501) ***(P-13154)***
Virco Mfg Corporation (PA) ... **A ... 310 533-0474**
2027 Harpers Way Torrance (90501) ***(P-3635)***
Virgil M Stutzman Inc ... F ... 323 732-9146
5045 Exposition Blvd Los Angeles (90016) ***(P-7330)***
Virgil Walker Inc ... F ... 661 797-4101
24856 Avenue Rockefeller Valencia (91355) ***(P-6680)***
Virgil Walker Inc ... E ... 661 294-9142
29102 Hancock Pkwy Valencia (91355) ***(P-9615)***
Virgin Atlantic Airways Ltd ... D ... 888 747-7474
2900 E Arprt Dr Ste 1243 Ontario (91761) ***(P-12373)***
Virgin Fish Inc (PA) ... **C ... 310 391-6161**
1000 Corporate Pointe # 150 Culver City (90230) ***(P-11896)***
Virgin Orbit LLC (PA) ... **A ... 562 384-4400**
4022 E Conant St Long Beach (90808) ***(P-10526)***
Virginia Cntry CLB of Long Bch ... C ... 562 427-0924
4602 N Virginia Rd Long Beach (90807) ***(P-19626)***
Virginia Park LLC ... F ... 816 592-0776
2225 Via Cerro Ste A Riverside (92509) ***(P-2546)***
Virginia Park Foods, Riverside *Also called Virginia Park LLC* ***(P-2546)***
Virtis-Us LLC (PA) ... **F ... 855 796-1457**
11601 Wilshire Blvd 5thf Los Angeles (90025) ***(P-18404)***
Virtium LLC ... D ... 949 888-2444
30052 Tomas Rcho STA Marg (92688) ***(P-13451)***
Visalia Cams, Visalia *Also called Visalia Ctr 4 Ambltry Med Srgr* ***(P-11150)***
Visalia Country Club ... D ... 559 734-3733
625 N Ranch St Visalia (93291) ***(P-19627)***
Visalia Ctr 4 Ambltry Med Srgr ... F ... 559 740-4094
842 S Akers St Visalia (93277) ***(P-11150)***
Visalia Electric Motor Service, Visalia *Also called Visalia Electric Motor Sp Inc* ***(P-19018)***
Visalia Electric Motor Sp Inc ... E ... 559 651-0606
7515 W Sunnyview Ave Visalia (93291) ***(P-19018)***
Visalia Medical Clinic Inc (PA) ... **B ... 559 733-5222**
5400 W Hillsdale Ave Visalia (93291) ***(P-20156)***
Visalia Pallet LLC ... E ... 559 627-4829
5932 W Elowin Dr Visalia (93291) ***(P-3411)***
Vishay Spectoral Electronics, Ontario *Also called Vishay Thin Film LLC* ***(P-9600)***
Vishay Spectro, Ontario *Also called Vishay Techno Components LLC* ***(P-8966)***
Vishay Techno Components LLC ... C ... 909 923-3313
4051 Greystone Dr Ontario (91761) ***(P-8966)***
Vishay Thin Film LLC ... F ... 909 923-3313
4051 Greystone Dr Ontario (91761) ***(P-9600)***
Vishay Transducers Ltd ... E ... 626 363-7500
2930 Inland Empire Blvd # 100 Ontario (91764) ***(P-9601)***
Visible Graphics Inc ... F ... 818 787-0477
9736 Eton Ave Chatsworth (91311) ***(P-11614)***
Vision 33 Inc (PA) ... **C ... 949 420-3300**
6 Hughes Ste 220 Irvine (92618) ***(P-18235)***
Vision Engrg Met Stamping Inc ... D ... 661 575-0933
114 Grand Cypress Ave Palmdale (93551) ***(P-9109)***
Vision Envelope & Prtg Co Inc (PA) ... **E ... 310 324-7062**
13707 S Figueroa St Los Angeles (90061) ***(P-3912)***
Vision Essntals By Kser Prmnnt, Bakersfield *Also called Kaiser Foundation Hospitals* ***(P-19930)***
Vision Imaging Supplies Inc ... E ... 818 710-7200
9540 Cozycroft Ave Chatsworth (91311) ***(P-11484)***
Vision Produce Acquisition LLC ... E ... 213 622-4435
1651 Bay St Los Angeles (90021) ***(P-14664)***
Vision Quest Industries Inc (PA) ... **D ... 949 261-6382**
18011 Mitchell S Ste A Irvine (92614) ***(P-11151)***
Vision Realty Managements, Beverly Hills *Also called Starpint 1031 Property MGT LLC* ***(P-16010)***
Vision Solutions Inc (PA) ... **D ... 949 253-6500**
15300 Barranca Pkwy Irvine (92618) ***(P-17754)***

Employee Codes: A=Over 500 employees, B=251-500
C=101-250, D=51-100, E=20-50 F=10-19
2022 Southern California Business
Directory and Buyers Guide
© Mergent Inc. 1-800-342-5647
1311

Vision To Learn ...... E 800 485-9196
12100 Wilshire Blvd # 1275 Los Angeles (90025) *(P-22469)*
Visionaire, Long Beach Also called E4site Inc *(P-17605)*
Visionaire Lighting LLC ...... D 310 512-6480
19645 S Rancho Way Rancho Dominguez (90220) *(P-9110)*
Visionary Sleep LLC ...... D 909 605-2010
2060 S Wineville Ave A Ontario (91761) *(P-3561)*
Visionary Vr Inc ...... F 323 868-7443
409 N Plymouth Blvd Los Angeles (90004) *(P-18006)*
Visit Anaheim, Anaheim Also called Anaheim/Orange Cnty Visitor Bu *(P-18444)*
Visiting Angels, Chino Also called Angels In Motion LLC *(P-21134)*
Visiting Angels Riverside Cnty, Riverside Also called Roberts & Associates Inc *(P-21208)*
Visiting Nrse Assn of Inland C (PA) ...... A 951 413-1200
600 W Santa Ana Blvd # 1 Santa Ana (92701) *(P-21228)*
Visiting Nrse Assn Orange Cnty (PA) ...... D 949 263-4700
2520 Redhill Ave Santa Ana (92705) *(P-21229)*
Visiting Nurse & Hospice Care, Santa Barbara Also called Visiting Nurse & Hospice Care *(P-21230)*
Visiting Nurse & Hospice Care (PA) ...... C 805 965-5555
509 E Montecito St # 200 Santa Barbara (93103) *(P-21230)*
Vislink LLC ...... E 714 998-2121
1158 N Gilbert St Anaheim (92801) *(P-9325)*
Vista Community Clinic ...... D 951 245-2735
30195 Fraser Dr Lake Elsinore (92530) *(P-20157)*
Vista Del Campo, Irvine Also called American Cmpus Communities Inc *(P-16810)*
Vista Del Mar Child Fmly Svcs (PA) ...... B 310 836-1223
3200 Motor Ave Los Angeles (90034) *(P-22165)*
Vista Ford Inc ...... D 805 983-6511
1501 Auto Center Dr Oxnard (93036) *(P-18885)*
Vista Ford of Oxnard, Oxnard Also called Vista Ford Inc *(P-18885)*
Vista Hospital San Gabriel Vly, Baldwin Park Also called Vista Spclty Hosp Sthern Cal L *(P-21005)*
Vista Investments LLC (PA) ...... C 310 725-8200
2225 Campus Dr El Segundo (90245) *(P-16773)*
Vista Metals Corp (PA) ...... C 909 823-4278
13425 Whittram Ave Fontana (92335) *(P-6323)*
Vista Pacifica Center, Jurupa Valley Also called Vista Pacifica Enterprises Inc *(P-20501)*
Vista Pacifica Enterprises Inc (PA) ...... C 951 682-4833
3674 Pacific Ave Jurupa Valley (92509) *(P-20501)*
Vista Paint Corporation (PA) ...... C 714 680-3800
2020 E Orangethorpe Ave Fullerton (92831) *(P-5119)*
Vista Spclty Hosp Sthern Cal L ...... C 626 388-2700
14148 Francisquito Ave Baldwin Park (91706) *(P-21005)*
Vista Specialty Hosp Riverside, Perris Also called Perris Valley Cmnty Hosp LLC *(P-20887)*
Vista Steel Co Inc (PA) ...... E 805 964-4732
6100 Francis Botello Rd Goleta (93117) *(P-7026)*
Vista Steel Co Inc ...... E 805 653-1189
331 W Lewis St Ventura (93001) *(P-1007)*
Vit Best, Santa Ana Also called Vitabest Nutrition Inc *(P-4910)*
Vita North America, Yorba Linda Also called Vident *(P-13531)*
Vita Science Health Products, Long Beach Also called Get *(P-8383)*
Vita-Herb Nutriceuticals Inc ...... E 714 632-3726
172 E La Jolla St Placentia (92870) *(P-4909)*
Vita-Pakt Citrus Products Co (PA) ...... E 626 332-1101
4825 Calloway Dr Ste 102 Bakersfield (93312) *(P-1879)*
Vita-Ray Productions LLC ...... F 310 220-8963
1600 Rosecrans Ave Manhattan Beach (90266) *(P-11297)*
Vitabest Nutrition Inc ...... B 714 368-1181
2906 S Tech Center Dr Santa Ana (92705) *(P-4910)*
Vitabri Canopies, Huntington Beach Also called Vae Industries Corporation *(P-3148)*
Vitachrome Graphics Group Inc ...... E 818 957-0900
3710 Park Pl Montrose (91020) *(P-4589)*
Vitacig Inc ...... E 310 402-6937
433 N Camden Dr Fl 6 Beverly Hills (90210) *(P-2554)*
Vital Research LLC ...... D 323 951-1670
6380 Wilshire Blvd # 170 Los Angeles (90048) *(P-22924)*
Vitalant ...... D 805 654-1603
2223 Eastman Ave Ste A Ventura (93003) *(P-21496)*
Vitamer Laboratories, Irvine Also called Anabolic Incorporated *(P-4784)*
Vitamin Records, Los Angeles Also called CMH Records Inc *(P-9212)*
Vitas Healthcare Corp Cal (HQ) ...... E 305 374-4143
7888 Mission Grove Pkwy S Riverside (92508) *(P-21231)*
Vitas Healthcare Corporation ...... D 858 805-6254
9106 Pulsar Ct Ste D Corona (92883) *(P-20546)*
Vitas Healthcare Corporation ...... D 805 437-2100
333 N Lantana St Ste 124 Camarillo (93010) *(P-20547)*
Vitavet Labs Inc ...... E 818 865-2600
5717 Corsa Ave Westlake Village (91362) *(P-11790)*
Vitawest Nutraceuticals Inc ...... F 888 557-8012
10880 Mulberry Ave Fontana (92337) *(P-1807)*
Vitco Distributors Inc ...... D 909 355-1300
715 E California St Ontario (91761) *(P-14520)*
Vitco Food Service, Ontario Also called Vitco Distributors Inc *(P-14520)*
Vitek Indus Video Pdts Inc ...... E 661 294-8043
28492 Constellation Rd Valencia (91355) *(P-11298)*
Vitesse Manufacturing & Dev ...... C 805 388-3700
11861 Western Ave Garden Grove (92841) *(P-9602)*
Vitesse Semiconductor, Garden Grove Also called Vitesse Manufacturing & Dev *(P-9602)*
Vitu, Agoura Hills Also called Motor Vehicle Software Corp *(P-13416)*
Viva America Marketing (PA) ...... D 949 645-6100
1239 Victoria St Costa Mesa (92627) *(P-23361)*
Viva Concepts, Vernon Also called Viva Holdings LLC *(P-3919)*
Viva Holdings LLC (PA) ...... F 818 243-1363
4210 Charter St Vernon (90058) *(P-3919)*
Viva Life Science Inc ...... C 949 645-6100
350 Paularino Ave Costa Mesa (92626) *(P-14296)*

Viva Print LLC (HQ) ...... F 818 243-1363
1025 N Brand Blvd Ste 300 Glendale (91202) *(P-3920)*
Vivid Digital ...... D 818 908-0481
1933 N Bronson Ave # 209 Los Angeles (90068) *(P-17755)*
Vivid Entertainment LLC ...... D 323 845-4557
3599 Cahuenga Blvd W Los Angeles (90068) *(P-19200)*
Vivid Interactive, Los Angeles Also called Vivid Digital *(P-17755)*
Vivometrics Inc ...... D 805 667-2225
16030 Ventura Blvd # 470 Encino (91436) *(P-11243)*
Vivopools Inc ...... D 818 952-2121
825 S Primrose Ave Ste H Monrovia (91016) *(P-18717)*
Vivopools LLC ...... D 888 702-8486
245 W Foothill Blvd Monrovia (91016) *(P-18718)*
Vivotein LLC ...... F 918 344-8742
231 S Pleasant Ave Ontario (91761) *(P-1977)*
Viz Cattle Corporation ...... E 310 884-5260
17890 Castleton St # 350 City of Industry (91748) *(P-1724)*
Vizio Inc (PA) ...... C 855 833-3221
39 Tesla Irvine (92618) *(P-9207)*
Vizio Holding Corp ...... A 949 428-2525
39 Tesla Irvine (92618) *(P-9208)*
Vizualogic LLC ...... C 407 509-3421
1493 E Bentley Dr Ste 102 Corona (92879) *(P-8000)*
Vline Industries, Simi Valley Also called Computer Metal Products Corp *(P-6811)*
Vm International, Riverside Also called MSRS INC *(P-4701)*
Vmc Holdings Group Corp ...... E 818 993-1466
9667 Owensmouth Ave # 202 Chatsworth (91311) *(P-8182)*
Vmc International LLC ...... F 760 723-1498
25799 Jefferson Ave Murrieta (92562) *(P-11202)*
VME Acquisition Corp (PA) ...... F 805 384-2748
820 Flynn Rd Camarillo (93012) *(P-11152)*
Vmg Partners LLC ...... D 310 775-8603
2000 Avenue Of The Stars Los Angeles (90067) *(P-15354)*
Vna Home Health Systems, Santa Ana Also called Visiting Nrse Assn Orange Cnty *(P-21229)*
Vna Hspice Plltive Care Sthern (PA) ...... C 909 624-3574
412 E Vanderbilt Way # 10 San Bernardino (92408) *(P-21232)*
Vna Private Duty Care, San Bernardino Also called Vna Hspice Plltive Care Sthern *(P-21232)*
Vnaic, Santa Ana Also called Visiting Nrse Assn of Inland C *(P-21228)*
Voa, Los Angeles Also called Volunteers of Amer Los Angeles *(P-21920)*
Voa Plainview Head Start, Tujunga Also called Volunteers of Amer Los Angeles *(P-21916)*
Vocational Imprv Program Inc (PA) ...... D 909 483-5924
9210 Rochester Ave Rancho Cucamonga (91730) *(P-21972)*
Vocational Visions ...... C 949 837-7280
26041 Pala Mission Viejo (92691) *(P-21973)*
Voestalpine High Prfmce Mtls, Walnut Also called Edro Engineering Inc *(P-7799)*
Vogue Developement, Irvine Also called Vogue Enterprise Inc *(P-13197)*
Vogue Enterprise Inc ...... C 949 833-9787
1801 Kettering Irvine (92614) *(P-13197)*
Vogue Sign Inc ...... E 805 487-7222
715 Commercial Ave Oxnard (93030) *(P-11615)*
Voice Assist Inc ...... F 949 655-6400
100 Spectrum Center Dr # 90 Irvine (92618) *(P-9801)*
Voiceboard Corporation ...... E 805 389-3100
473 Post St Camarillo (93010) *(P-8183)*
Voit Commercial Brokerage, Irvine Also called Voit Development Manager Inc *(P-16078)*
Voit Development Manager Inc ...... D 949 851-5110
2020 Main St Ste 100 Irvine (92614) *(P-16078)*
Voit Real Estate Services LLC ...... D 949 851-5100
2020 Main St Irvine (92614) *(P-16079)*
Volant Cool Air Intakes Inc ...... C 909 476-7225
10285 Indiana Ct Rancho Cucamonga (91730) *(P-5859)*
Volcom LLC (HQ) ...... C 949 646-2175
1740 Monrovia Ave Costa Mesa (92627) *(P-18719)*
Voler Softgoods (PA) ...... D 805 473-7808
21 Saratoga Ave Grover Beach (93433) *(P-3089)*
Volkswagen of Van Nuys Inc ...... D 323 873-3311
300 Hitchcock Way Santa Barbara (93105) *(P-18886)*
Volkswagen Santa Monica Inc ...... C 310 829-1888
2440 Santa Monica Blvd Santa Monica (90404) *(P-18808)*
Vollmer-Gray Engrg Labs Inc ...... D 562 427-8435
2421 N Palm Dr Signal Hill (90755) *(P-22693)*
Volt Consulting Group Ltd ...... C 800 654-2624
2401 N Glassell St Orange (92865) *(P-17477)*
Volt Industries ...... F 323 982-0815
1831 Phillips Way Los Angeles (90042) *(P-11791)*
Volt Information Sciences Inc (PA) ...... E 714 921-8800
2401 N Glassell St Orange (92865) *(P-17522)*
Volt Management Corp ...... D 805 237-0882
715 6th St Paso Robles (93446) *(P-17523)*
Volt Management Corp ...... D 310 316-8523
19191 S Vt Ave Ste 950 Torrance (90502) *(P-17524)*
Volt Management Corp ...... B 800 654-2624
2411 N Glassell St Orange (92865) *(P-17525)*
Volt Management Corp ...... D 626 931-1437
100 N Citrus St Ste 150 West Covina (91791) *(P-17526)*
Volt Management Corp ...... D 714 879-9330
1400 N Harbor Blvd # 103 Fullerton (92835) *(P-17527)*
Volt Management Corp ...... D 805 560-8658
1300 Santa Barbara St A Santa Barbara (93101) *(P-17528)*
Volt Management Corp (HQ) ...... E 800 654-2624
2401 N Glassell St Orange (92865) *(P-17529)*
Volt Management Corp ...... D 951 789-8133
1650 Iowa Ave Ste 140 Riverside (92507) *(P-17530)*
Volt Management Corp ...... D 805 485-0506
1701 Solar Dr Ste 145 Oxnard (93030) *(P-17531)*
Volt Telecom Group, Corona Also called Volt Telecom Group Inc *(P-23524)*
Volt Telecom Group Inc ...... B 951 493-8900
218 Helicopter Cir Corona (92878) *(P-23524)*

ALPHABETIC SECTION Wadco Industries Inc

Volt Temporary Services, Orange *Also called Volt Management Corp* ***(P-17525)***
Volt Workforce Solutions, Torrance *Also called Volt Management Corp* ***(P-17524)***
Volt Workforce Solutions, West Covina *Also called Volt Management Corp* ***(P-17526)***
Volt Workforce Solutions, Fullerton *Also called Volt Management Corp* ***(P-17527)***
Volt Workforce Solutions, Santa Barbara *Also called Volt Management Corp* ***(P-17528)***
Volt Workforce Solutions, Orange *Also called Volt Management Corp* ***(P-17529)***
Volt Workforce Solutions, Riverside *Also called Volt Management Corp* ***(P-17530)***
Volt Workforce Solutions, Oxnard *Also called Volt Management Corp* ***(P-17531)***
Voltage Multipliers Inc (PA)........C.......**559 651-1402**
8711 W Roosevelt Ave Visalia (93291) ***(P-9603)***
Voltedge LLC........F.......949 877-8900
500 Nwport Ctr Dr Ste 910 Newport Beach (92660) ***(P-8184)***
Voltege Inc (PA)........E.......**949 273-3822**
11 Pastora Foothill Ranch (92610) ***(P-7027)***
Volume Services Inc........C.......323 644-6038
5333 Zoo Dr Los Angeles (90027) ***(P-19680)***
Volunteers America Head Start, San Fernando *Also called Child Care Resource Center Inc* ***(P-21997)***
Volunteers of Amer Los Angeles........D.......213 749-0362
1032 W 18th St Los Angeles (90015) ***(P-21910)***
Volunteers of Amer Los Angeles........D.......818 834-9097
10896 Lehigh Ave Pacoima (91331) ***(P-21911)***
Volunteers of Amer Los Angeles........D.......818 367-8841
13550 Herron St Sylmar (91342) ***(P-21912)***
Volunteers of Amer Los Angeles........D.......323 780-3770
522 N Dangler Ave Los Angeles (90022) ***(P-21913)***
Volunteers of Amer Los Angeles........D.......626 337-9878
1760 W Cameron Ave # 104 West Covina (91790) ***(P-21914)***
Volunteers of Amer Los Angeles........D.......661 290-2829
25141 Avenida Rondel Valencia (91355) ***(P-21915)***
Volunteers of Amer Los Angeles........D.......818 352-5974
10819 Plainview Ave Tujunga (91042) ***(P-21916)***
Volunteers of Amer Los Angeles........D.......714 426-9834
2100 N Broadway Ste 300 Santa Ana (92706) ***(P-21917)***
Volunteers of Amer Los Angeles........D.......818 769-3617
6724 Tujunga Ave North Hollywood (91606) ***(P-21918)***
Volunteers of Amer Los Angeles........D.......818 506-0597
11243 Kittridge St North Hollywood (91606) ***(P-21919)***
Volunteers of Amer Los Angeles........D.......213 627-8002
515 E 6th St Fl 9 Los Angeles (90021) ***(P-21920)***
Volunteers of Amer Los Angeles........D.......818 834-8957
12550 Van Nuys Blvd Pacoima (91331) ***(P-21921)***
Volunteers of Amer Los Angeles........D.......310 830-3404
334 Figueroa St Wilmington (90744) ***(P-21922)***
Voluspa, Irvine *Also called Flame and Wax Inc* ***(P-11668)***
Volvo Construction Eqp & Svcs........E.......951 277-7620
22099 Knabe Rd Corona (92883) ***(P-7658)***
Vomar Products Inc........E.......818 610-5115
7800 Deering Ave Canoga Park (91304) ***(P-4590)***
Vomela Specialty Company........E.......562 944-3853
9810 Bell Ranch Dr Santa Fe Springs (90670) ***(P-4450)***
Vonnic Inc........E.......626 964-2345
16610 Gale Ave City of Industry (91745) ***(P-11299)***
Vons 2030, Stevenson Ranch *Also called Vons Companies Inc* ***(P-2043)***
Vons 2111, Newhall *Also called Vons Companies Inc* ***(P-2048)***
Vons 2124, Tujunga *Also called Vons Companies Inc* ***(P-2046)***
Vons 2139, Pasadena *Also called Vons Companies Inc* ***(P-2044)***
Vons 2381, Corona *Also called Vons Companies Inc* ***(P-2047)***
Vons 2407, Brawley *Also called Vons Companies Inc* ***(P-2045)***
Vons 2560, Grover Beach *Also called Vons Companies Inc* ***(P-7955)***
Vons Companies Inc........D.......661 254-3570
25850 The Old Rd Stevenson Ranch (91381) ***(P-2043)***
Vons Companies Inc........D.......805 481-2492
1758 W Grand Ave Grover Beach (93433) ***(P-7955)***
Vons Companies Inc........D.......626 798-7603
1390 N Allen Ave Pasadena (91104) ***(P-2044)***
Vons Companies Inc........D.......760 351-3002
475 W Main St Brawley (92227) ***(P-2045)***
Vons Companies Inc........D.......818 353-4917
7789 Foothill Blvd Tujunga (91042) ***(P-2046)***
Vons Companies Inc........D.......951 278-8284
535 N Mckinley St Corona (92879) ***(P-2047)***
Vons Companies Inc........D.......661 259-9214
24160 Lyons Ave Newhall (91321) ***(P-2048)***
Vopak Terminal Long Beach Inc........D.......310 521-7969
3601 Dock St San Pedro (90731) ***(P-13338)***
Vorsteiner Inc........F.......714 379-4600
11621 Markon Dr Garden Grove (92841) ***(P-5423)***
Vortech Engineering Inc........E.......805 247-0226
1650 Pacific Ave Oxnard (93033) ***(P-8061)***
Vortex Doors, Irvine *Also called Vortex Industries Inc* ***(P-1462)***
Vortex Electronics, San Fernando *Also called Arturo Gonzalez* ***(P-9381)***
Vortex Industries Inc (PA)........E.......**714 434-8000**
20 Odyssey Irvine (92618) ***(P-1462)***
Vortex Whirlpool Systems Inc........F.......951 940-4556
26035 Jefferson Ave Murrieta (92562) ***(P-5538)***
Vorwaller & Brooks Inc........D.......760 262-6300
72182 Corporate Way Thousand Palms (92276) ***(P-648)***
Vorwerk LLC........D.......805 413-0800
3255 E Thousand Oaks Blvd B Thousand Oaks (91362) ***(P-7190)***
Votaw Precision Technologies........C.......562 944-0661
13153 Lakeland Rd Santa Fe Springs (90670) ***(P-10652)***
Vox DJS, Torrance *Also called Kace Entertainment Inc* ***(P-19360)***
Voyager Learning Company........F.......909 923-3120
2060 Lynx Pl Unit G Ontario (91761) ***(P-4217)***
Voyant Beauty, Chatsworth *Also called Aware Products LLC* ***(P-4991)***

Vpet Usa LLC........D.......909 605-1668
12925 Marlay Ave Fontana (92337) ***(P-18720)***
Vpls Inc........E.......213 406-9000
1744 W Katella Ave # 200 Orange (92867) ***(P-12679)***
Vpm Management Inc........C.......949 863-1500
2400 Main St Ste 201 Irvine (92614) ***(P-23136)***
Vpt Direct, Santa Fe Springs *Also called Vantage Point Products Corp* ***(P-9206)***
Vsa and Associates Inc........D.......562 698-2468
6571 Altura Blvd Ste 100 Buena Park (90620) ***(P-22694)***
Vsmpo Tirus US........E.......909 230-9020
2850 E Cedar St Ontario (91761) ***(P-6340)***
Vsmpo-Tirus US Inc........E.......909 230-9020
2850 E Cedar St Ontario (91761) ***(P-6341)***
Vtc Enterprises (PA)........B.......**805 928-5000**
2445 A St Santa Maria (93455) ***(P-21974)***
Vti Instruments Corporation (HQ)........E.......**949 955-1894**
2031 Main St Irvine (92614) ***(P-9927)***
Vtl Amplifiers Inc........E.......909 627-5944
4774 Murrieta St Ste 10 Chino (91710) ***(P-9209)***
Vts Sheetmetal Specialist Co........E.......714 237-1420
1041 N Grove St Anaheim (92806) ***(P-6940)***
Vu Holdings LLC........D.......661 808-4004
55 Fair Dr Costa Mesa (92626) ***(P-21497)***
Vubiquity Holdings Inc (HQ)........C.......**818 526-5000**
15301 Ventura Blvd # 3000 Sherman Oaks (91403) ***(P-12780)***
Vulcan Construction Mtls LLC........F.......661 810-2285
35800 146th St E Pearblossom (93553) ***(P-6125)***
Vulcan Materials, Glendale *Also called Calmat Co* ***(P-5269)***
Vvd Comuunications, Garden Grove *Also called Video Vice Data Communications* ***(P-12793)***
Vwise Inc........D.......949 716-1276
85 Enterprise Ste 320 Aliso Viejo (92656) ***(P-17756)***
Vxb & Orfwid Inc........E.......213 222-0030
5041 S Santa Fe Ave B Vernon (90058) ***(P-3008)***
Vxi Global Solutions LLC (PA)........A.......**213 739-4720**
220 W 1st St Fl 3 Los Angeles (90012) ***(P-18721)***
W & M Textile, Vernon *Also called Jml Textile Inc* ***(P-2577)***
W & W Concept Inc........D.......323 233-9202
4890 S Alameda St Vernon (90058) ***(P-3009)***
W A Benjamin Electric Co........E.......213 749-7731
1615 Staunton Ave Los Angeles (90021) ***(P-8907)***
W A Rasic Cnstr Co Inc (PA)........B.......**562 928-6111**
4150 Long Beach Blvd Long Beach (90807) ***(P-984)***
W A Thompson Inc (PA)........D.......**661 832-5101**
5101 District Blvd Bakersfield (93313) ***(P-14837)***
W B Mason Co Inc........E.......888 926-2766
5911 E Washington Blvd Commerce (90040) ***(P-4451)***
W B Powell Inc........D.......951 270-0095
630 Parkridge Ave Norco (92860) ***(P-3296)***
W B Starr Inc........D.......949 770-8835
20602 Canada Rd Lake Forest (92630) ***(P-351)***
W B Walton Enterprises Inc........E.......951 683-0930
4185 Hallmark Pkwy San Bernardino (92407) ***(P-9326)***
W Cellars Inc........F.......714 655-2025
927 N La Cienega Blvd Los Angeles (90069) ***(P-2161)***
W Corporation........D.......714 532-8800
1643 W Orange Grove Ave Orange (92868) ***(P-23525)***
W Diamond Supply Co (HQ)........D.......**909 859-8939**
19321 E Walnut Dr N City of Industry (91748) ***(P-13198)***
W E O'Neil Construction, Rancho Cucamonga *Also called WE Oneil Construction Co Cal* ***(P-847)***
W G A, Irvine *Also called Western Growers Association* ***(P-22263)***
W G Holt Inc........D.......949 859-8800
23351 Madero Mission Viejo (92691) ***(P-9604)***
W J Ellison Co Inc........E.......626 814-4766
200 River Rd Corona (92878) ***(P-8081)***
W L Rubottom Co........D.......805 648-6943
320 W Lewis St Ventura (93001) ***(P-3346)***
W Los Angeles........B.......310 208-8765
930 Hilgard Ave Los Angeles (90024) ***(P-16774)***
W Machine Works Inc........E.......818 890-8049
13814 Del Sur St San Fernando (91340) ***(P-8842)***
W N G Construction Jv Inc (PA)........D.......**714 524-7100**
4175 E La Palma Ave # 125 Anaheim (92807) ***(P-726)***
W O R K, Carpinteria *Also called Momentum Work Inc* ***(P-21962)***
W P Keith Co Inc........E.......562 948-3636
8323 Loch Lomond Dr Pico Rivera (90660) ***(P-8101)***
W Plastics Inc........E.......800 442-9727
41573 Dendy Pkwy Ste 2543 Temecula (92590) ***(P-5441)***
W T E, Ontario *Also called Wallner Expac Inc* ***(P-7907)***
W Why W Enterprises Inc........D.......626 969-4292
2671 Pomona Blvd Pomona (91768) ***(P-12121)***
W&J Business Ventures LLC........C.......310 645-7700
8620 Airport Blvd Los Angeles (90045) ***(P-16775)***
W.J. Byrnes & Co. Los Angeles, El Segundo *Also called Byrnes W J & Co of Los Angeles* ***(P-12425)***
W2005 Wyn Hotels LP........D.......323 887-8100
5757 Telegraph Rd Commerce (90040) ***(P-16776)***
W5 Concepts Inc........E.......323 231-2415
2049 E 38th St Vernon (90058) ***(P-2875)***
Waag, Van Nuys *Also called Wsw Corp* ***(P-10160)***
Wabash National Trlr Ctrs Inc........E.......765 771-5300
16025 Slover Ave Fontana (92337) ***(P-13106)***
Wac Lighting, Ontario *Also called Wangs Alliance Corporation* ***(P-9074)***
Waco Products, Santa Ana *Also called Ackley Metal Products Inc* ***(P-8465)***
Wad Productions Inc........D.......818 260-5673
3500 W Olive Ave Ste 1000 Burbank (91505) ***(P-19201)***
Wadco Industries Inc........E.......909 874-7800
2625 S Willow Ave Bloomington (92316) ***(P-6681)***

ALPHABETIC

Employee Codes: A=Over 500 employees, B=251-500
C=101-250, D=51-100, E=20-50 F=10-19
2022 Southern California Business
Directory and Buyers Guide
© Mergent Inc. 1-800-342-5647
1313

Wadco Steel Sales, Bloomington *Also called Wadco Industries Inc* **(P-6681)**

Waddington North America Inc ....C.......626 913-4022
1135 Samuelson St City of Industry (91748) **(P-5860)**

Wade & Lowe A Prof Corp....D.......949 753-1000
7700 Irvine Center Dr # 700 Irvine (92618) **(P-21692)**

Wade Melvin Banner DMD (PA) ....D.......626 594-0374
2060 E Route 66 Ste 105 Glendora (91740) **(P-20203)**

Wagner Die Supply Inc (PA)....E.......909 947-3044
2041 Elm Ct Ontario (91761) **(P-7843)**

Wagner Financials, Manhattan Beach *Also called GBS Financial Corp* **(P-18524)**

Wagner Plate Works West Inc (PA) ....E.......562 531-6050
14015 Garfield Ave Paramount (90723) **(P-6765)**

Wagner, Kendall S MD, Fullerton *Also called Fullerton Orthpd Srgery Med Gr* **(P-19826)**

Wah Hung Group Inc (PA) ....E.......626 571-8700
1000 E Garvey Ave Monterey Park (91755) **(P-10154)**

Wah Hung Group Inc ....E.......626 571-8700
283 E Garvey Ave Monterey Park (91755) **(P-10155)**

Wahlco Inc....C.......714 979-7300
15 Marconi Ste B Irvine (92618) **(P-8843)**

Wakunaga of America Co Ltd (HQ)....D.......949 855-2776
23501 Madero Mission Viejo (92691) **(P-4911)**

Walco Inc....F.......909 483-3333
9017 Arrow Rte Rancho Cucamonga (91730) **(P-8001)**

Waldberg Inc ....D.......818 843-0004
15301 Ventura Blvd # 300 Sherman Oaks (91403) **(P-17092)**

Walden Environment....D.......818 365-3665
6345 Balboa Blvd Ste 130 Encino (91316) **(P-20639)**

Walden Family Services, Encino *Also called Walden Environment* **(P-20639)**

Walden House Inc....C.......626 258-0300
12423 Dahlia Ave El Monte (91732) **(P-22166)**

Walden Structures Inc ....B.......909 389-9100
1000 Bristol St N 126 Newport Beach (92660) **(P-3430)**

Waldorf Astoria Beverly Hills, Beverly Hills *Also called Oasis West Realty LLC* **(P-16589)**

Waldorf Astria Mnrc Bch Rsort, Dana Point *Also called Cph Monarch Hotel LLC* **(P-16397)**

Walin Group Inc....F.......714 444-5980
2950 Grace Ln Ste C Costa Mesa (92626) **(P-8141)**

Walker & Dunlop Inc....D.......301 215-5500
12100 Wilshire Blvd # 1500 Los Angeles (90025) **(P-15233)**

Walker & Zanger LLC (HQ)....D.......818 280-8300
16719 Schoenborn St A North Hills (91343) **(P-13319)**

Walker Advertising LLC....E.......310 519-4050
20101 Hamilton Ave # 300 Torrance (90502) **(P-17069)**

Walker Corporation....E.......909 390-4300
1555 S Vintage Ave Ontario (91761) **(P-7191)**

Walker Design Inc....E.......818 252-7788
9255 San Fernando Rd Sun Valley (91352) **(P-10456)**

Walker Engineering Enterprises, Sun Valley *Also called Walker Design Inc* **(P-10456)**

Walker Foods Inc....D.......323 268-5191
237 N Mission Rd Los Angeles (90033) **(P-1880)**

Walker Products....E.......714 554-5151
14291 Commerce Dr Garden Grove (92843) **(P-10156)**

Walker Spring & Stamping Corp ....C.......909 390-4300
1555 S Vintage Ave Ontario (91761) **(P-7192)**

Walking Company Holdings Inc (PA)....C.......805 963-8727
1800 Avenue Of The Stars # 300 Los Angeles (90067) **(P-14359)**

Wall Street Alley T-Shirt Co....E.......661 324-6207
4125 E Brundage Ln Bakersfield (93307) **(P-14426)**

Wall To Wall Builders Inc....E.......909 246-7003
35350 Twin Willow Rd Murrieta (92563) **(P-672)**

Wallace E Miller Inc....E.......818 998-0444
9155 Alabama Ave Ste B Chatsworth (91311) **(P-8844)**

Wallace Wood Products ....F.......951 654-9311
1247 S Buena Vista St C San Jacinto (92583) **(P-3671)**

Wallner Expac Inc (PA)....D.......909 481-8800
1274 S Slater Cir Ontario (91761) **(P-7907)**

Wally & Pat Enterprises....E.......310 532-2031
13530 S Budlong Ave Gardena (90247) **(P-11792)**

Wally Park, Los Angeles *Also called Lrw Investments LLC* **(P-18768)**

Walnut Manor Care Center, Anaheim *Also called Front Prch Cmmnties Svcs - Cas* **(P-20584)**

Walnut Valley Water District ....D.......909 595-7554
271 Brea Canyon Rd Walnut (91789) **(P-12922)**

Walong Marketing Inc (PA)....D.......714 670-8899
6281 Regio Ave Buena Park (90620) **(P-14747)**

Walsworth Franklin & Bevins, Orange *Also called Walswrth Frnklin Bevins McCall* **(P-21693)**

Walswrth Frnklin Bevins McCall (PA) ....D.......714 634-2522
1 City Blvd W Ste 500 Orange (92868) **(P-21693)**

Walt Disney Company (PA)....A.......818 560-1000
500 S Buena Vista St Burbank (91521) **(P-19525)**

Walt Disney Imagineering (HQ) ....A.......818 544-6500
1401 Flower St Glendale (91201) **(P-19254)**

Walt Disney Music Company (HQ) ....A.......818 560-1000
500 S Buena Vista St Burbank (91521) **(P-19202)**

Walt Disney Pictures ....B.......818 409-2200
811 Sonora Ave Glendale (91201) **(P-19255)**

Walt Disney Pictures and TV ....D.......818 560-1000
500 S Buena Vista St Burbank (91521) **(P-19267)**

Walt Disney Records Direct (HQ)....A.......818 560-1000
500 S Buena Vista St Burbank (91521) **(P-19203)**

Walt Dsney Imgnring RES Dev In....D.......714 781-3152
1200 N Miller St Unit D Anaheim (92806) **(P-3090)**

Walter Timmons Enterprises Inc....D.......562 595-4601
3940 Cherry Ave Long Beach (90807) **(P-18887)**

Walters Family Partnership ....C.......760 320-6868
400 E Tahquitz Canyon Way Palm Springs (92262) **(P-16777)**

Walters Wholesale Electric Co (HQ)....E.......562 988-3100
18626 S Susana Rd Compton (90221) **(P-13674)**

Walters Wholesale Electric Co....F.......951 943-7708
425 W Rider St Ste C1 Perris (92571) **(P-13675)**

Walton Associated Companies ....D.......626 963-8505
2001 E Fincl Way Ste 200 Glendora (91741) **(P-649)**

Walton Company Inc ....E.......714 847-8800
17900 Sampson Ln Huntington Beach (92647) **(P-3458)**

Walton Company, The, Glendora *Also called Walton Associated Companies* **(P-649)**

Walton Construction Inc ....D.......909 267-7777
358 E Foothill Blvd # 100 San Dimas (91773) **(P-673)**

Walton Construction Services, San Dimas *Also called Walton Construction Inc* **(P-673)**

Walton Electric Corporation ....C.......909 981-5051
755 N Central Ave Ste A Upland (91786) **(P-9359)**

Walton Motors & Controls Inc....F.......626 442-4610
1843 Floradale Ave South El Monte (91733) **(P-13676)**

Wamco Inc (PA) ....F.......714 545-5560
17752 Fitch Irvine (92614) **(P-13677)**

Wanda Matranga ....F.......760 773-4701
41651 Corporate Way Ste 5 Palm Desert (92260) **(P-4452)**

Wangs Alliance Corporation....E.......909 230-9401
1750 S Archibald Ave Ontario (91761) **(P-9074)**

Wanu Water Inc ....F.......310 401-1733
12424 Wilshire Blvd # 1115 Los Angeles (90025) **(P-2303)**

Warco, Orange *Also called West American Rubber Co LLC* **(P-5424)**

Warco, Orange *Also called West American Rubber Co LLC* **(P-5425)**

Ward Enterprises ....F.......661 251-4890
10332 Trumbull St California City (93505) **(P-8845)**

Wardlow 2 LP (PA) ....D.......562 432-8066
333 S Grand Ave Ste 4070 Los Angeles (90071) **(P-19083)**

Ware Disposal Inc....C.......714 834-0234
1451 Manhattan Ave Fullerton (92831) **(P-12992)**

Ware Malcomb (PA) ....C.......949 660-9128
10 Edelman Irvine (92618) **(P-22750)**

Warehouse and Distribution, Jurupa Valley *Also called Triways Inc* **(P-12085)**

Warmington Homes (PA)....C.......714 434-4435
3090 Pullman St Costa Mesa (92626) **(P-684)**

Warmington Homes....C.......949 679-3100
15615 Alton Pkwy Ste 150 Irvine (92618) **(P-685)**

Warmington Residential Cal Inc....C.......714 557-5511
3090 Pullman St Costa Mesa (92626) **(P-650)**

Warner Bros Consumer Pdts Inc (HQ)....C.......818 954-7980
4001 W Olive Ave Burbank (91505) **(P-23526)**

Warner Bros Distributing Inc (HQ) ....B.......818 954-6000
4000 Warner Blvd Burbank (91522) **(P-23137)**

Warner Bros Enterprises LLC (HQ)....D.......818 954-6000
4000 Warner Blvd Burbank (91522) **(P-19204)**

Warner Bros Entertainment Inc (HQ) ....A.......818 954-6000
4000 Warner Blvd Burbank (91522) **(P-19205)**

Warner Bros Entertainment Inc....C.......818 954-2209
3500 W Olive Ave Ste 200 Burbank (91505) **(P-19206)**

Warner Bros FE Inc (HQ)....C.......212 484-8000
4000 Warner Blvd Bldg 178 Burbank (91522) **(P-19207)**

Warner Bros Home Entrmt Group (HQ) ....D.......818 954-6000
4000 Warner Blvd Burbank (91522) **(P-19384)**

Warner Bros Home Entrmt Inc....A.......818 954-6000
4000 Warner Blvd Bldg 160 Burbank (91522) **(P-19208)**

Warner Bros Intl TV Dist Inc ....D.......818 954-6000
4000 Warner Blvd Burbank (91522) **(P-19209)**

Warner Bros Pictures Inc ....E.......818 954-6000
4000 Warner Blvd Burbank (91522) **(P-19210)**

Warner Bros Records Inc (HQ)....B.......818 846-9090
777 S Santa Fe Ave Los Angeles (90021) **(P-18722)**

Warner Bros Studio Facilities, Burbank *Also called Warner Bros Entertainment Inc* **(P-19206)**

Warner Bros Transatlantic Inc (HQ) ....A.......818 977-0018
4000 Warner Blvd Burbank (91522) **(P-19266)**

Warner Chemical Mfg ....E.......310 715-3000
14803 S Spring St Gardena (90248) **(P-9971)**

Warner Food Management Co Inc....C.......818 285-2160
4917 Genesta Ave Encino (91316) **(P-23362)**

Warner Pacific Insur Svcs Inc (PA) ....C.......408 298-4049
32110 Agoura Rd Westlake Village (91361) **(P-15647)**

Warner/Chappell Music Inc (HQ) ....C.......310 441-8600
777 S Santa Fe Ave Los Angeles (90021) **(P-4218)**

Warren & Baerg Mfg Inc ....E.......559 591-6790
39950 Road 108 Dinuba (93618) **(P-7626)**

Warren Collins and Assoc Inc (PA) ....E.......909 548-6708
5470 Daniels St Chino (91710) **(P-1008)**

Warren Distributing Inc (PA)....D.......562 789-3360
3435 Wilshire Blvd # 990 Los Angeles (90010) **(P-13107)**

Warren Drye Kelley....E.......310 712-6100
10100 Santa Monica Blvd # 2300 Los Angeles (90067) **(P-21694)**

Warren E & P, Long Beach *Also called Warren E&P Inc* **(P-473)**

Warren E&P Inc....D.......214 393-9688
400 Oceangate Ste 200 Long Beach (90802) **(P-473)**

Warrens Department Store Inc ....F.......888 577-2735
9800 De Soto Ave Chatsworth (91311) **(P-2753)**

Wasco Sales and Marketing Inc ....E.......805 739-2747
2245 A St Santa Maria (93455) **(P-9049)**

Wash Depot Auto Centers LP ....D.......805 379-4900
467 N Moorpark Rd Thousand Oaks (91360) **(P-18918)**

Wash Mltfmily Ldry Systems LLC (PA) ....C.......310 643-8491
100 N Pacific Coast Hwy El Segundo (90245) **(P-16874)**

Washburn Grove Management Inc....E.......909 322-4690
27781 Fairview Ave Hemet (92544) **(P-3204)**

Washington Garment Dyeing (PA)....E.......213 747-1111
1341 E Washington Blvd Los Angeles (90021) **(P-2667)**

Washington Grment Dyg Fnshg In....E.......213 747-1111
1332 E 18th St Los Angeles (90021) **(P-2662)**

Washington Iron Works, Gardena *Also called Washington Orna Ir Works Inc* **(P-1698)**

Washington Orna Ir Works Inc (PA) ....C.......310 327-8660
17926 S Broadway Gardena (90248) **(P-1698)**

Wassef, E W MD Facs, Lakewood *Also called Long Bch - Lkwood Orthpd Med G* **(P-19964)**

Wasser Filtration Inc (PA) ....D....714 696-6450
1215 N Fee Ana St Anaheim (92807) *(P-8142)*
Wasserman Comden & Casselman (PA) ....D....323 872-0995
5567 Reseda Blvd Ste 330 Tarzana (91356) *(P-21695)*
Wasserman Media Group LLC (PA) ....C....310 407-0200
10900 Wilshire Blvd Fl 12 Los Angeles (90024) *(P-23363)*
Waste Management Cal Inc (HQ) ....C....877 836-6526
9081 Tujunga Ave Sun Valley (91352) *(P-12993)*
Waste Management Cal Inc ....C....661 947-7197
1200 W City Ranch Rd Palmdale (93551) *(P-12994)*
Waste Management Cal Inc ....C....805 522-7023
2801 N Madera Rd Simi Valley (93065) *(P-12995)*
Waste Management Cal Inc ....C....951 277-1740
10910 Dawson Canyon Rd Corona (92883) *(P-12996)*
Waste Management Recycling ....C....818 767-6180
9227 Tujunga Ave Sun Valley (91352) *(P-12008)*
Waste MGT Collectn Recycl Inc ....D....951 242-0421
17700 Indian St Moreno Valley (92551) *(P-12997)*
Waste MGT Collectn Recycl Inc ....D....714 637-3010
1800 S Grand Ave Santa Ana (92705) *(P-17320)*
Waste MGT Collectn Recycl Inc ....D....626 960-7551
13940 Live Oak Ave Baldwin Park (91706) *(P-12998)*
Waste MGT Collectn Recycl Inc ....D....310 532-6511
1449 W Rosecrans Ave Gardena (90249) *(P-12999)*
Waste MGT Collectn Recycl Inc ....D....949 451-2600
16122 Construction Cir E Irvine (92606) *(P-13000)*
Waste MGT Collectn Recycl Inc ....D....909 242-0421
17700 Indian St Moreno Valley (92551) *(P-13001)*
Wastech Controls & Engrg Inc ....E....818 998-3500
20600 Nordhoff St Chatsworth (91311) *(P-13961)*
Watch L.A., Los Angeles *Also called Pierre Mitri (P-2983)*
Water Associates LLC ....E....661 281-6077
34929 Flyover Ct Bakersfield (93308) *(P-9327)*
Water Filter Exchange Inc ....F....818 808-2541
875 N Todd Ave Azusa (91702) *(P-8143)*
Water Purification, Rancho Dominguez *Also called Parker-Hannifin Corporation (P-9636)*
Water Treatment Plant, Riverside *Also called City of Riverside (P-8372)*
Water Well Solutions, Exeter *Also called Willitts Equipment Company Inc (P-19086)*
Watercraft Mix Inc ....E....310 884-9755
2018 N Bahama Ave Los Angeles (90059) *(P-6126)*
Watercrest Inc ....E....909 390-3944
4850 E Airport Dr Ontario (91761) *(P-6766)*
Waterdance Corporation (PA) ....E....818 656-0005
7340 Melrose St Buena Park (90621) *(P-8446)*
Waterdance West, Buena Park *Also called Waterdance Corporation (P-8446)*
Waterfront Design Group LLC ....E....213 746-5800
122 E Washington Blvd Los Angeles (90015) *(P-2831)*
Waterfront Hotel LLC ....B....714 845-8000
21100 Pacific Coast Hwy Huntington Beach (92648) *(P-16778)*
Waterhealth International Inc ....D....949 716-5790
9601 Irvine Center Dr Irvine (92618) *(P-8423)*
Waterman Convalescent Hosp Inc ....D....951 681-2200
6401 33rd St Riverside (92509) *(P-21056)*
Waterman Convalescent Hosp Inc (PA) ....C....909 882-1215
1850 N Waterman Ave San Bernardino (92404) *(P-20502)*
Waterman Valve LLC (HQ) ....C....559 562-4000
25500 Road 204 Exeter (93221) *(P-8424)*
Watermark, Riverside *Also called Irrometer Company Inc (P-10892)*
Watermark Rtrment Cmmnties Inc ....C....760 346-5420
41505 Carlotta Dr Palm Desert (92211) *(P-20503)*
Waterprfing Rofg Solutions Inc ....D....310 571-0892
11041 Santa Monica Blvd Los Angeles (90025) *(P-1699)*
Waters Edge Wineries Inc ....F....909 468-9463
8560 Vineyard Ave Ste 408 Rancho Cucamonga (91730) *(P-2234)*
Waters Edge Winery, Rancho Cucamonga *Also called Waters Edge Wineries Inc (P-2234)*
Watersentinel, Temecula *Also called Aquamor LLC (P-8364)*
Waterstone Faucets, Murrieta *Also called Waterstone LLC (P-13838)*
Waterstone LLC ....C....951 304-0520
41180 Raintree Ct Murrieta (92562) *(P-13838)*
Watertalent LLC ....E....424 832-7217
10877 Wilshire Blvd # 708 Los Angeles (90024) *(P-23527)*
Waterway Plastics, Oxnard *Also called B & S Plastics Inc (P-5572)*
Watkins Construction Co Inc ....D....661 763-5395
112 E Cedar St Taft (93268) *(P-985)*
Watson Cogeneration Co Inc ....D....310 816-8100
22850 Wilmington Ave Carson (90745) *(P-12863)*
Watsons Profiling Corp ....F....909 923-5500
1460 S Balboa Ave Ontario (91761) *(P-8846)*
Watt Commercial Properties, Santa Monica *Also called Watt Properties Inc (P-16080)*
Watt Communities ....D....310 314-2430
2716 Ocean Park Blvd # 2025 Santa Monica (90405) *(P-18723)*
Watt Companies Inc (PA) ....C....310 314-2430
2716 Ocean Park Blvd # 20 Santa Monica (90405) *(P-16030)*
Watt Construction Company (PA) ....D....818 905-6601
14106 Ventura Blvd # 200 Sherman Oaks (91423) *(P-15758)*
Watt Enterprise Inc ....F....714 963-0781
10575 Bechler River Ave Fountain Valley (92708) *(P-2832)*
Watt Properties Inc (PA) ....D....310 314-2430
2716 Ocean Park Blvd # 2025 Santa Monica (90405) *(P-16080)*
Watts Health Foundation Inc (HQ) ....B....310 424-2220
3405 W Imperial Hwy # 304 Inglewood (90303) *(P-20548)*
Watts Health Foundation Inc ....D....323 750-5284
8005 S Figueroa St Los Angeles (90003) *(P-21057)*
Watts Healthcare Corporation ....C....323 241-1780
700 W Imperial Hwy Los Angeles (90044) *(P-20158)*
Watts Healthcare Corporation (PA) ....C....323 564-4331
10300 Compton Ave Los Angeles (90002) *(P-20159)*
Watts Labor Community Action ....C....323 563-5639
4142 Palmwood Dr Apt 11 Los Angeles (90008) *(P-21923)*

Wave Community Newspapers Inc (PA) ....E....323 290-3000
3731 Wilshire Blvd # 840 Los Angeles (90010) *(P-4043)*
Wave Plastic Surgery Ctr Inc (PA) ....D....213 383-4800
3680 Wilshire Blvd Fl 2 Los Angeles (90010) *(P-21006)*
Wave Plstic Srgery Asthtic Lse, Los Angeles *Also called Wave Plastic Surgery Ctr Inc (P-21006)*
Wave Precision Inc ....F....805 529-3324
5390 Kazuko Ct Moorpark (93021) *(P-10865)*
Wavefunction Inc ....F....949 955-2120
18401 Von Karman Ave # 370 Irvine (92612) *(P-17757)*
Waveline Creative LLC ....E....805 469-1549
1299 S Wells Rd Ventura (93004) *(P-4591)*
Wavenet Inc (PA) ....F....310 885-4200
707 E Sepulveda Blvd Carson (90745) *(P-6240)*
Wavestream Corporation (HQ) ....C....909 599-9080
545 W Terrace Dr San Dimas (91773) *(P-9802)*
Wawona Packing Co LLC (PA) ....A....559 528-4000
12133 Avenue 408 Cutler (93615) *(P-14665)*
Wax Jean By Ambiance, Los Angeles *Also called Ambiance USA Inc (P-2915)*
Way Out West Inc ....E....310 769-6937
21800 Oxnard St Ste 770 Woodland Hills (91367) *(P-2792)*
Wayfinder Family Services ....E....909 305-1948
1045 Bonita Ave La Verne (91750) *(P-22167)*
Wayfinder Family Services ....E....909 305-1948
1045 Bonita Ave La Verne (91750) *(P-22168)*
Wayforward Technologies Inc ....E....661 286-2769
28738 The Old Rd Valencia (91355) *(P-17758)*
Waymakers (PA) ....D....714 492-1010
1221 E Dyer Rd Ste 120 Santa Ana (92705) *(P-21924)*
Wayne J Sand & Gravel Inc ....E....805 529-1323
9455 Buena Vista St Moorpark (93021) *(P-575)*
Wayne Perry Inc (PA) ....C....714 826-0352
8281 Commonwealth Ave Buena Park (90621) *(P-1700)*
Wayne Provision Co Inc (PA) ....D....323 277-5888
5030 Gifford Ave Vernon (90058) *(P-14609)*
Wayne Tool & Die Co ....F....818 364-1611
15853 Olden St Sylmar (91342) *(P-6217)*
Wb Music Corp (HQ) ....C....310 441-8600
10585 Santa Monica Blvd # 200 Los Angeles (90025) *(P-4219)*
Wbp Associates Inc ....F....626 575-0747
2017 Seaman Ave South El Monte (91733) *(P-3702)*
Wbt Group LLC ....E....323 735-1201
1401 S Shamrock Ave Monrovia (91016) *(P-11793)*
Wbt Industries, Monrovia *Also called Wbt Group LLC (P-11793)*
Wca, Los Angeles *Also called West Coast Ambulance Corp (P-11897)*
Wcbm Company (PA) ....E....323 262-3274
1812 W 135th St Gardena (90249) *(P-11504)*
Wcc Inc ....F....661 251-3865
20717 Centre Pointe Pkwy Santa Clarita (91350) *(P-1701)*
Wcct Global Inc (PA) ....C....714 668-1500
5630 Cerritos Ave Cypress (90630) *(P-22925)*
Wco Hotels Inc (HQ) ....D....323 636-3251
1150 W Magic Way Anaheim (92802) *(P-16779)*
Wco Hotels Inc ....A....714 635-2300
1600 S Disneyland Dr Anaheim (92802) *(P-16780)*
WCP Inc ....D....562 653-9797
17730 Crusader Ave Cerritos (90703) *(P-5861)*
Wcs Distributing Inc ....E....909 888-2015
268 W Orange Show Ln San Bernardino (92408) *(P-13962)*
Wdi, Los Angeles *Also called Warren Distributing Inc (P-13107)*
We Do Graphics Inc ....E....714 997-7390
1150 N Main St Orange (92867) *(P-4453)*
We Five-R Corporation ....E....323 263-6757
1507 S Sunol Dr Los Angeles (90023) *(P-7331)*
WE Oneil Construction Co Cal ....D....909 466-5300
9485 Haven Ave Ste 101 Rancho Cucamonga (91730) *(P-847)*
We Pack It All, Duarte *Also called Bershtel Enterprises LLC (P-18459)*
We The Pie People LLC ....E....818 349-1880
9909 Topanga Canyon Blvd # 159 Chatsworth (91311) *(P-1827)*
Weapons System Division, Northridge *Also called Northrop Grumman Systems Corp (P-10616)*
Weatherford Completion Systems ....F....661 746-1391
19468 Creek Rd Bakersfield (93314) *(P-558)*
Weatherford International LLC ....F....805 643-1279
250 W Stanley Ave Ventura (93001) *(P-559)*
Weaver and Tidwell LLP ....D....310 382-5380
1230 Rosecrans Ave # 510 Manhattan Beach (90266) *(P-22751)*
Web CAM, Riverside *Also called Webcam Inc (P-10157)*
Web Design, Laguna Beach *Also called Exploremypc (P-17174)*
Web Educational Services Inc ....F....866 719-2159
524 N Mtn View Ave Ste 3 San Bernardino (92401) *(P-18007)*
Web4 Inc ....D....714 974-2670
8175 E Kaiser Blvd 100 Anaheim (92808) *(P-17759)*
Webasto Charging Systems Inc (HQ) ....D....626 415-4000
1333 S Mayflower Ave # 100 Monrovia (91016) *(P-13108)*
Webb Del California Corp (HQ) ....B....760 772-5300
39755 Berkey Dr Palm Desert (92211) *(P-16081)*
Webb Massey Co Inc ....E....714 639-6012
201 W Carleton Ave Orange (92867) *(P-3563)*
Webber EMI, Ontario *Also called Emission Methods Inc (P-10881)*
Webcam Inc ....F....951 369-5144
1815 Massachusetts Ave Riverside (92507) *(P-10157)*
Webcor Builders, Los Angeles *Also called Webcor Construction LP (P-848)*
Webcor Construction LP ....A....213 239-2800
550 S Hope St Ste 2100 Los Angeles (90071) *(P-848)*
Webedoctor Inc ....F....714 990-3999
335 N Puente St Ste B Brea (92821) *(P-18008)*

ALPHABETIC

Employee Codes: A=Over 500 employees, B=251-500
C=101-250, D=51-100, E=20-50 F=10-19
2022 Southern California Business Directory and Buyers Guide
© Mergent Inc. 1-800-342-5647
1315

Weber Distribution LLC (PA) ....B....**855 469-3237**
13530 Rosecrans Ave Santa Fe Springs (90670) ***(P-12180)***

Weber Drilling Co Inc....E....310 670-7708
401 Hindry Ave Inglewood (90301) ***(P-7664)***

Weber Logistics, Santa Fe Springs *Also called Weber Distribution LLC* ***(P-12180)***

Weber Metals Inc....B....562 602-0260
16706 Garfield Ave Paramount (90723) ***(P-7109)***

Weber Orthopedic LP (PA)....D....**800 221-5465**
1185 E Main St Santa Paula (93060) ***(P-11153)***

Weber Precision Graphics, Santa Ana *Also called Artisan Nameplate Awards Corp* ***(P-4481)***

Weber Printing Company Inc....E....310 639-5064
1124 E Del Amo Blvd Carson (90746) ***(P-4454)***

Webtez Inc....F....805 856-6585
1679 Donlon St Ste 202 Ventura (93003) ***(P-10557)***

Webtoon Entertainment Inc (PA)....D....**323 297-3410**
5700 Wilshire Blvd # 220 Los Angeles (90036) ***(P-19385)***

Weckerle Cosmetics Usa Inc....E....310 328-7000
525 Maple Ave Torrance (90503) ***(P-14297)***

Weckerle Sales Corporation, Torrance *Also called Weckerle Cosmetics Usa Inc* ***(P-14297)***

Wedbush Securities Inc (HQ)....B....**213 688-8000**
1000 Wilshire Blvd # 800 Los Angeles (90017) ***(P-15310)***

Wedgewood Hspitality Group Inc....E....951 491-8110
43385 Business Park Dr Temecula (92590) ***(P-16986)***

Wedgewood Inc (PA)....B....**310 640-3070**
2015 Manhattan Beach Blvd Redondo Beach (90278) ***(P-16300)***

Weed Army Community Hospital, Fort Irwin *Also called Department of Army* ***(P-20744)***

Weekend Balita, La Crescenta *Also called Balita Media Inc* ***(P-3952)***

Weekendz Off, The, Commerce *Also called Weekendz-Off Inc* ***(P-14360)***

Weekendz-Off Inc....E....323 888-9966
6838 E Acco St Commerce (90040) ***(P-14360)***

WEI-Chuan USA Inc....E....323 838-0088
13031 Temple Ave La Puente (91746) ***(P-14532)***

WEI-Chuan USA Inc (PA)....C....**626 225-7168**
13031 Temple Ave City of Industry (91746) ***(P-14533)***

Weider Health and Fitness....B....818 884-6800
21100 Erwin St Woodland Hills (91367) ***(P-2339)***

Weider Leasing Inc....D....818 884-6800
21100 Erwin St Woodland Hills (91367) ***(P-4111)***

Weingart Center Association....C....213 622-6359
566 S San Pedro St Los Angeles (90013) ***(P-21925)***

WEINGART CENTER FOR THE HOMELE, Los Angeles *Also called Weingart Center Association* ***(P-21925)***

Weis/Robart Partitions Inc....F....714 666-0822
3501 E La Palma Ave Anaheim (92806) ***(P-6984)***

Weiser Iron Inc....E....909 429-4600
64 Sundance Dr Pomona (91766) ***(P-6682)***

Weiss Sheet Metal Company....E....310 354-2700
1715 W 135th St Gardena (90249) ***(P-1509)***

Weitz & Luxenberg PC....D....310 247-0921
1880 Century Park E # 700 Los Angeles (90067) ***(P-21696)***

Welaco, Bakersfield *Also called Well Analysis Corporation Inc* ***(P-3205)***

Welch Management Corporation....D....909 981-4302
1233 W Foothill Blvd Upland (91786) ***(P-16920)***

Welcome Baby, Santa Ana *Also called Priority Ctr Ending The Gnrtna* ***(P-21872)***

Welcome Group Inc (PA)....B....**860 741-2211**
222 N Pacific Coast Hwy # 2222 El Segundo (90245) ***(P-16781)***

Welcome Group Management LLC....D....310 378-6666
300 S Court St Visalia (93291) ***(P-16782)***

Welcome Skateboards Inc....F....949 305-9200
26792 Vista Ter Lake Forest (92630) ***(P-11457)***

Weld-It Co, Commerce *Also called Sam Schaffer Inc* ***(P-19062)***

Weld-On Adhesives, Compton *Also called Ips Corporation* ***(P-5186)***

Weldcraft Industries Inc....F....559 784-4322
18794 Avenue 96 Terra Bella (93270) ***(P-7627)***

Weldex Corporation (PA)....B....**714 761-2100**
6751 Katella Ave Cypress (90630) ***(P-9605)***

Weldlogic Inc....D....805 375-1670
2651 Lavery Ct Newbury Park (91320) ***(P-19002)***

Weldstone Portable Welders, Anaheim *Also called Lodestone LLC* ***(P-7891)***

Welk Resort Group Inc....C....760 770-9755
34567 Cathedral Canyon Dr Cathedral City (92234) ***(P-16783)***

Welkin Welkin Capitl Group LLC (PA)....D....**323 312-3200**
7190 W Sunset Blvd Los Angeles (90046) ***(P-16301)***

Well Analysis Corporation Inc (PA)....E....**661 283-9510**
5500 Woodmere Dr Bakersfield (93313) ***(P-3205)***

Wella Operations US LLC....B....818 999-5112
4500 Park Granada Ste 100 Calabasas (91302) ***(P-14298)***

Wellbore Navigation Inc (PA)....F....**714 259-7760**
1240 N Jefferson St Ste M Anaheim (92807) ***(P-10921)***

Wellington Foods Inc....E....562 989-0111
1930 California Ave Corona (92881) ***(P-2547)***

Wellmade Inc....D....213 221-1123
800 E 12th St Los Angeles (90021) ***(P-23364)***

Wellman & Company....F....310 980-4918
12931 Venice Blvd Los Angeles (90066) ***(P-4728)***

Wellnest Emtonal Hlth Wellness (PA)....C....**323 373-2400**
3031 S Vermont Ave Los Angeles (90007) ***(P-21926)***

Wellpoint Inc....C....805 375-1605
319 N San Dimas Ave Ste F San Dimas (91773) ***(P-15372)***

Wells Fargo Advisors, Seal Beach *Also called Wells Fargo Clearing Svcs LLC* ***(P-15311)***

Wells Fargo Bank Ltd....D....213 253-6227
333 S Grand Ave Ste 500 Los Angeles (90071) ***(P-15008)***

Wells Fargo Capital Fin LLC (HQ)....D....**310 453-7300**
2450 Colo Ave Ste 3000w Santa Monica (90404) ***(P-15167)***

Wells Fargo Clearing Svcs LLC....E....562 594-1220
3020 Old Ranch Pkwy # 190 Seal Beach (90740) ***(P-15311)***

Wells Struthers Corporation....E....814 726-1000
10375 Slusher Dr Santa Fe Springs (90670) ***(P-6767)***

Welnav, Anaheim *Also called Wellbore Navigation Inc* ***(P-10921)***

Welovefine, Los Angeles *Also called Mf Inc* ***(P-2858)***

Wems Inc (PA)....D....**310 644-0251**
4650 W Rosecrans Ave Hawthorne (90250) ***(P-8062)***

Wems Electronics, Hawthorne *Also called Wems Inc* ***(P-8062)***

Wendy's, Cypress *Also called WKS Frosty Corporation* ***(P-16222)***

Wenzlau Engineering Inc....D....310 604-3400
2950 E Harcourt St Compton (90221) ***(P-13785)***

Wepower LLC....E....866 385-9463
32 Journey Ste 250 Aliso Viejo (92656) ***(P-7590)***

Werner Corporation....E....951 277-4586
25050 Maitri Rd Corona (92883) ***(P-6127)***

Werner Systems Inc....E....714 838-4444
14321 Myford Rd Tustin (92780) ***(P-6330)***

Wes Go Inc....E....818 504-1200
8211 Lankershim Blvd North Hollywood (91605) ***(P-4592)***

Wesanco Inc....E....714 739-4989
14870 Desman Rd La Mirada (90638) ***(P-10443)***

Wesco Aircraft, Valencia *Also called Falcon Aerospace Holdings LLC* ***(P-14056)***

Wesco Aircraft Hardware Corp....B....661 775-7200
27727 Avenue Scott Valencia (91355) ***(P-14071)***

Wescom Central Credit Union (PA)....B....**888 493-7266**
123 S Marengo Ave Pasadena (91101) ***(P-15116)***

Wescordon Incorporated (PA)....D....**559 784-8371**
661 W Poplar Ave Porterville (93257) ***(P-20504)***

Wesfac Inc (HQ)....D....**562 861-2160**
9300 Hall Rd Downey (90241) ***(P-8425)***

Weslar Inc....D....661 702-1362
28310 Constellation Rd Valencia (91355) ***(P-1463)***

Weslend Financial, Santa Ana *Also called Lenox Financial Mortgage Corp* ***(P-15208)***

Wesley Allen Inc (PA)....C....**323 231-4275**
1001 E 60th St Los Angeles (90001) ***(P-3538)***

Wespac, Downey *Also called Wesfac Inc* ***(P-8425)***

Wessco Intl Ltd A Cal Ltd Prtn (PA)....E....**310 477-4272**
11400 W Olympic Blvd Los Angeles (90064) ***(P-3131)***

Wessex Industries Inc....E....562 944-5760
8619 Red Oak St Rancho Cucamonga (91730) ***(P-7547)***

West American Energy Corp....F....661 747-7732
4949 Buckley Way Ste 207 Bakersfield (93309) ***(P-439)***

West American Rubber Co LLC (PA)....C....**714 532-3355**
1337 W Braden Ct Orange (92868) ***(P-5424)***

West American Rubber Co LLC....C....714 532-3355
750 N Main St Orange (92868) ***(P-5425)***

West Anaheim Care Center, Anaheim *Also called Mark & Fred Enterprises* ***(P-20413)***

WEST ANAHEIM MEDICAL CENTER, Anaheim *Also called Prime Healthcare Anaheim LLC* ***(P-20901)***

West Angeles Ch God In Chrst....C....323 731-2567
3010 Crenshaw Blvd Los Angeles (90016) ***(P-15707)***

West Angeles Christian Academy, Los Angeles *Also called West Angeles Ch God In Chrst* ***(P-15707)***

West Area Opportunity Center, Santa Monica *Also called Casa De Hermandad* ***(P-11408)***

West Bay Company LLC....E....805 969-5803
132 E Carrillo St Santa Barbara (93101) ***(P-2235)***

West Bay Imports Inc....E....323 720-5777
7245 Oxford Way Commerce (90040) ***(P-14986)***

West Bent Bolt Division, Santa Fe Springs *Also called Mid-West Fabricating Co* ***(P-10103)***

West Bond Inc (PA)....E....**714 978-1551**
1551 S Harris Ct Anaheim (92806) ***(P-8847)***

West Bsin Wtr Rclamation Plant, El Segundo *Also called Suez Water Indiana LLC* ***(P-10727)***

West Cast Fire Integration Inc....D....909 824-7980
891 Iowa Ave Riverside (92507) ***(P-18405)***

West Cast Hndcrfted Albums Inc....E....626 253-0335
1717 S Hoover St Ste 101 Los Angeles (90006) ***(P-4616)***

West Central Food Service, Norwalk *Also called West Central Produce Inc* ***(P-14666)***

West Central Produce Inc....B....213 629-3600
12840 Leyva St Norwalk (90650) ***(P-14666)***

West Cntinela Vly Care Ctr Inc....D....310 674-3216
950 S Flower St Inglewood (90301) ***(P-20505)***

West Coast Aerospace Inc....F....310 518-0633
24224 Broad St Carson (90745) ***(P-14031)***

West Coast Aerospace Inc (PA)....D....**310 518-3167**
220 W E St Wilmington (90744) ***(P-11505)***

West Coast Aggregate Supply....F....760 342-7598
92500 Airport Blvd Thermal (92274) ***(P-576)***

West Coast Air Conditioning, Oxnard *Also called Gmh Inc* ***(P-18947)***

West Coast Airlines, Riverside *Also called West Coast Unlimited* ***(P-9972)***

West Coast Albums, Los Angeles *Also called West Cast Hndcrfted Albums Inc* ***(P-4616)***

West Coast Ambulance Corp....D....310 435-1862
6739 S Victoria Ave Los Angeles (90043) ***(P-11897)***

West Coast Arborists Inc....C....805 671-5092
11405 Nardo St Ventura (93004) ***(P-363)***

West Coast Arborists Inc....C....909 783-6544
21718 Walnut Ave Grand Terrace (92313) ***(P-364)***

West Coast Aviation Svcs LLC (PA)....E....**949 852-8340**
19711 Campus Dr Ste 200 Santa Ana (92707) ***(P-23365)***

West Coast Business Prtrs Inc....F....818 709-4980
9822 Independence Ave Chatsworth (91311) ***(P-4455)***

West Coast Button Mfg Co, Gardena *Also called Wcbm Company* ***(P-11504)***

West Coast Catrg Trcks Mfg Inc....F....323 278-1279
1217 Goodrich Blvd Commerce (90022) ***(P-3491)***

West Coast Chain Mfg Co....E....909 923-7800
4245 Pacific Privado Ontario (91761) ***(P-9928)***

West Coast Charters, Santa Ana *Also called West Coast Aviation Svcs LLC* ***(P-23365)***

West Coast Construction, Riverside *Also called Perry Coast Construction Inc* ***(P-807)***

West Coast Consulting LLC....C....949 250-4102
9233 Research Dr Ste 200 Irvine (92618) ***(P-18009)***

ALPHABETIC SECTION Western Costume Co

West Coast Corporation ....E....909 923-7800
4245 Pacific Privado Ontario (91761) ***(P-9929)***

West Coast Coupon Inc ....E....818 341-2400
9400 Oso Ave Chatsworth (91311) ***(P-17102)***

West Coast Custom Sheet Metal ....E....818 252-7500
8125 Lankershim Blvd North Hollywood (91605) ***(P-6941)***

West Coast Digital, Chatsworth *Also called West Coast Business Prtrs Inc* ***(P-4455)***

West Coast Distribution Inc (PA) ....**D....323 588-6508**
2602 E 37th St Vernon (90058) ***(P-12259)***

West Coast Drywall & Co Inc ....B....951 778-3592
1610 W Linden St Riverside (92507) ***(P-1409)***

West Coast Electric & Pwr Inc ....D....562 447-3254
741 E Ball Rd Ste 206 Anaheim (92805) ***(P-12864)***

West Coast Firestopping Inc ....D....714 935-1104
1130 W Trenton Ave Orange (92867) ***(P-1702)***

West Coast Foundry LLC (HQ) ....**E....323 583-1421**
2450 E 53rd St Huntington Park (90255) ***(P-6278)***

West Coast Furn Framers Inc ....E....760 669-5275
17402 Eucalyptus St Hesperia (92345) ***(P-3226)***

West Coast Gasket Co ....D....714 869-0123
300 Ranger Ave Brea (92821) ***(P-5355)***

West Coast Interiors Inc ....A....951 778-3592
1610 W Linden St Riverside (92507) ***(P-1201)***

West Coast Labels, Placentia *Also called Cinton Inc* ***(P-3868)***

West Coast Laboratories Inc ....E....310 527-6163
156 E 162nd St Gardena (90248) ***(P-4912)***

West Coast Laboratories Inc (PA) ....**F....323 321-4774**
116 E Alondra Blvd Gardena (90248) ***(P-4913)***

West Coast Ltg & Enrgy Inc ....D....951 296-0680
18550 Minthorn St Lake Elsinore (92530) ***(P-1337)***

West Coast Machining Inc ....F....562 229-1087
14560 Marquardt Ave Santa Fe Springs (90670) ***(P-8848)***

West Coast Manufacturing Inc ....E....714 897-4221
1822 Western Ave Stanton (90680) ***(P-7193)***

West Coast Materials, Buena Park *Also called West Coast Sand and Gravel Inc* ***(P-13320)***

West Coast Metal Stamping Inc ....E....714 792-0322
550 W Crowther Ave Placentia (92870) ***(P-7194)***

West Coast Mfg & Whsng, Ontario *Also called Idx Los Angeles LLC* ***(P-3686)***

West Coast Milling, Lancaster *Also called Pavement Recycling Systems Inc* ***(P-5276)***

West Coast Motor Sports, Perris *Also called West Coast Yamaha Inc* ***(P-8110)***

West Coast Painting, Riverside *Also called West Coast Interiors Inc* ***(P-1201)***

West Coast Physical Therapy, Laguna Niguel *Also called Mission Internal Med Group Inc* ***(P-19982)***

West Coast Radiology Center, Santa Ana *Also called Santa Ana Radiology Center* ***(P-20055)***

West Coast Rags, Long Beach *Also called Coastal Closeouts Inc* ***(P-18482)***

West Coast Sand and Gravel Inc (PA) ....**D....714 522-0282**
7282 Orangethorpe Ave Buena Park (90621) ***(P-13320)***

West Coast Service Center, Ontario *Also called Vsmpo-Tirus US Inc* ***(P-6341)***

West Coast Steel & Proc LLC (PA) ....**C....909 393-8405**
3534 Philadelphia St Chino (91710) ***(P-6279)***

West Coast Storm Inc (PA) ....**E....909 890-5700**
9701 Wilshire Blvd # 1000 Beverly Hills (90212) ***(P-23398)***

West Coast Surfaces Inc ....E....951 699-0600
27620 Commerce Center Dr # 107 Temecula (92590) ***(P-1471)***

West Coast Switchgear (HQ) ....**D....562 802-3441**
13837 Bettencourt St Cerritos (90703) ***(P-8908)***

West Coast Timber Corp ....F....714 893-4374
6221 Apache Rd Westminster (92683) ***(P-3206)***

West Coast Trends Inc ....E....714 843-9288
17811 Jamestown Ln Huntington Beach (92647) ***(P-11458)***

West Coast Trimmings Corp (PA) ....**F....323 587-0701**
7100 Wilson Ave Los Angeles (90001) ***(P-2619)***

West Coast Turf (PA) ....**E....760 340-7300**
42540 Melanie Pl Palm Desert (92211) ***(P-97)***

West Coast Unlimited ....E....951 352-1234
11161 Pierce St Riverside (92505) ***(P-9972)***

West Coast Vinyl Windows, Cerritos *Also called WCP Inc* ***(P-5861)***

West Coast Welding & Cnstr ....F....805 604-1222
390 S Del Norte Blvd Oxnard (93030) ***(P-19003)***

West Coast Wldg & Piping Inc ....D....805 246-5841
640 W Hueneme Rd Oxnard (93033) ***(P-19004)***

West Coast Yamaha Inc ....E....951 943-2061
1622 Illinois Ave Perris (92571) ***(P-8110)***

West Coast-Accudyne Inc ....E....562 927-2546
7180 Scout Ave Bell (90201) ***(P-7769)***

West Covina Foster Family Agcy ....D....626 814-9085
1107 S Glendora Ave West Covina (91790) ***(P-15648)***

West Covina Lanes, West Covina *Also called Bowlero Corp* ***(P-19388)***

West Covina Medical Clinic Inc (PA) ....**C....626 960-8614**
1500 W West Covina Pkwy West Covina (91790) ***(P-20160)***

WEST COVINA PHYSICAL THERAPY, West Covina *Also called Doctors Hospital W Covina Inc* ***(P-20758)***

West Dermatology Med MGT Inc ....C....909 793-3000
680 Nwport Ctr Dr Ste 150 Newport Beach (92660) ***(P-20161)***

West End Yung MNS Christn Assn ....C....909 477-2780
1257 E D St Ontario (91764) ***(P-22375)***

West End Yung MNS Christn Assn ....C....909 597-7445
5665 Edison Ave Chino (91710) ***(P-22376)***

West Fargo Capital Finance, Los Angeles *Also called Foothill Group Inc* ***(P-15001)***

West Hills Construction Inc ....E....800 515-5270
423 Jenks Cir Ste 101 Corona (92878) ***(P-727)***

West Lake Food Corporation ....D....714 973-2286
301 N Sullivan St Santa Ana (92703) ***(P-1725)***

West Los Angeles V A Med Ctr, Los Angeles *Also called Veterans Health Administration* ***(P-20142)***

West Newport Oil Company ....E....949 631-1100
1080 W 17th St Costa Mesa (92627) ***(P-416)***

West Pacific Medical Lab, Santa Fe Springs *Also called California Lab Sciences LLC* ***(P-22934)***

West Pico Distributors LLC ....D....323 586-9050
5201 S Downey Rd Vernon (90058) ***(P-14521)***

West Pico Foods Inc ....C....323 586-9050
5201 S Downey Rd Vernon (90058) ***(P-14534)***

West Publishing Corporation ....C....800 747-3161
800 Crprate Pinte Ste 150 Culver City (90230) ***(P-4143)***

West Publishing Corporation ....C....424 243-2100
800 Crprate Pinte Ste 150 Culver City (90230) ***(P-18074)***

West Side Dst Hosp Foundation ....D....805 763-4211
110 E North St Taft (93268) ***(P-21007)***

West Side Recreation & Pk Dst ....E....661 763-4246
500 Cascade Pl Taft (93268) ***(P-19472)***

West Side Rehab Corporation ....C....323 231-4174
1755 Kings Way Los Angeles (90069) ***(P-15708)***

West States Skanska Inc ....C....970 565-4903
1995 Agua Mansa Rd Riverside (92509) ***(P-986)***

West Valley Christian Church ....D....818 884-4710
22450 Sherman Way West Hills (91307) ***(P-22073)***

West Valley Christian School, West Hills *Also called West Valley Christian Church* ***(P-22073)***

West Valley Occupational Ctr, Woodland Hills *Also called Los Angeles Unified School Dst* ***(P-21960)***

West Valley Plating Inc ....F....818 709-1684
21061 Superior St Ste A Chatsworth (91311) ***(P-7332)***

West Wood Products Inc ....E....310 631-8978
2943 E Las Hermanas St Compton (90221) ***(P-13291)***

West World Productions Inc ....E....310 276-9500
420 N Camden Dr Beverly Hills (90210) ***(P-4112)***

West-Bag Inc ....E....323 264-0750
1161 Monterey Pass Rd Monterey Park (91754) ***(P-5862)***

West-Tech Mechanical Inc ....F....909 635-1170
5589 Brooks St Ste A Montclair (91763) ***(P-1161)***

Westair Gases & Equipment Inc ....C....661 387-6800
3901 Buck Owens Blvd Bakersfield (93308) ***(P-13963)***

Westaire Engineering Inc ....F....323 587-3347
5820 S Alameda St Vernon (90058) ***(P-8357)***

Westamerica Communications Inc ....D....949 340-8942
26012 Atlantic Ocean Dr Lake Forest (92630) ***(P-23543)***

Westar Manufacturing Inc ....E....562 633-0581
13217 Laureldale Ave Downey (90242) ***(P-1703)***

Westar Nutrition Corp (PA) ....**E....949 645-6100**
350 Paularino Ave Costa Mesa (92626) ***(P-4769)***

Westates Inc ....E....714 523-7600
6800 Orangethorpe Ave H Buena Park (90620) ***(P-4456)***

Westates Automotive Promotions, Buena Park *Also called Westates Inc* ***(P-4456)***

Westbrook Ops LLC ....D....818 832-2300
24151 Ventura Blvd # 200 Calabasas (91302) ***(P-19211)***

Westco Industries Inc ....E....909 874-8700
2625 S Willow Ave Bloomington (92316) ***(P-6683)***

Westcoast Brush Mfg Inc ....E....909 627-7170
1330 Philadelphia St Pomona (91766) ***(P-11515)***

Westcoast Grinding Corporation ....F....818 890-1841
10517 San Fernando Rd Pacoima (91331) ***(P-8849)***

Westcoast Rotor Inc ....E....310 327-5050
119 W 154th St Gardena (90248) ***(P-13964)***

Westcoast Tool Products, Sun Valley *Also called Accu-Grinding Inc* ***(P-7844)***

Westcoast Warehousing LLC ....E....310 537-9958
100 W Manville St Rancho Dominguez (90220) ***(P-12260)***

Westcoe Escrow Division, Riverside *Also called Westcoe Realtors Inc* ***(P-16031)***

Westcoe Realtors Inc ....D....951 784-2500
7191 Magnolia Ave Riverside (92504) ***(P-16031)***

Westcorp Engineering, Riverside *Also called Reisner Enterprises Inc* ***(P-8764)***

Westech Products Inc ....E....951 279-4496
1242 Enterprise Ct Corona (92882) ***(P-11470)***

Westech Wax Products, Corona *Also called Westech Products Inc* ***(P-11470)***

Westerlay Orchids LP ....C....805 684-5411
3504 Via Real Carpinteria (93013) ***(P-98)***

Western Abrasives Inc ....F....323 588-1245
4383 Fruitland Ave Vernon (90058) ***(P-6161)***

Western Air & Refrigeration, Seal Beach *Also called Limbach Company LP* ***(P-1094)***

Western Allied Corporation ....E....562 944-6341
12046 Florence Ave Santa Fe Springs (90670) ***(P-1162)***

Western Asset Core Plus Bond P ....C....626 844-9400
385 E Colorado Blvd Pasadena (91101) ***(P-16148)***

Western Asset Management Co (HQ) ....**E....626 844-9265**
385 E Colorado Blvd # 250 Pasadena (91101) ***(P-16149)***

Western Asset Management Co ....E....626 844-9400
385 E Colorado Blvd # 250 Pasadena (91101) ***(P-16150)***

Western Asset Mrtg Capitl Corp ....A....626 844-9400
385 E Colorado Blvd Pasadena (91101) ***(P-16245)***

Western Bagel Baking Corp (PA) ....**C....818 786-5847**
7814 Sepulveda Blvd Van Nuys (91405) ***(P-2049)***

Western Bagel Baking Corp ....F....818 887-5451
21749 Ventura Blvd Woodland Hills (91364) ***(P-2050)***

Western Bagel Baking Corp ....E....310 479-4823
11628 Santa Monica Blvd # 12 Los Angeles (90025) ***(P-2051)***

Western Bagel Too, Los Angeles *Also called Western Bagel Baking Corp* ***(P-2051)***

Western Case Incorporated ....D....951 214-6380
231 E Alessandro Blvd Riverside (92508) ***(P-5863)***

Western Connection, Carol Rose, Vernon *Also called B Boston & Associates Inc* ***(P-14362)***

Western Convelescence, Los Angeles *Also called Longwood Management Corp* ***(P-20603)***

Western Converting Spc Inc ....E....909 392-4578
2886 Metropolitan Pl Pomona (91767) ***(P-4593)***

Western Corrugated Design Inc ....E....562 695-9295
8741 Pioneer Blvd Santa Fe Springs (90670) ***(P-3831)***

Western Costume Co (HQ) ....**E....818 760-0900**
11041 Vanowen St North Hollywood (91605) ***(P-16987)***

ALPHABETIC

Employee Codes: A=Over 500 employees, B=251-500
C=101-250, D=51-100, E=20-50 F=10-19
2022 Southern California Business
Directory and Buyers Guide
© Mergent Inc. 1-800-342-5647
1317

Western Dental & Orthodontics, Orange *Also called Western Dental Services Inc* ***(P-20204)***
Western Dental Services Inc (HQ).....**B**.......**714 480-3000**
530 S Main St Ste 600 Orange (92868) ***(P-20204)***
Western Dermato Pathology Svcs, San Luis Obispo *Also called Central Cast Pthlogy Cons Inc* ***(P-21062)***
Western Die & Printing Corp.....F.......323 665-0474
3109 Casitas Ave Los Angeles (90039) ***(P-4594)***
Western Distribution Center, Riverside *Also called Standard Textile Co Inc* ***(P-18676)***
Western Division Regional Off, Long Beach *Also called Southern California Edison Co* ***(P-12854)***
Western Drug, Glendale *Also called H and H Drug Stores Inc* ***(P-13492)***
Western Drug Medical Supply, San Bernardino *Also called H and H Drug Stores Inc* ***(P-13493)***
Western Edge Inc.....F.......661 947-3900
37957 Sierra Hwy Palmdale (93550) ***(P-7425)***
Western Energy Services Corp.....C.......403 984-5916
3430 Getty St Bakersfield (93308) ***(P-17321)***
Western Environmental Inc.....E.......760 396-0222
62150 Gene Welmas Way Mecca (92254) ***(P-10671)***
Western Equipment Mfg, Corona *Also called Western Equipment Mfg Inc* ***(P-7659)***
Western Equipment Mfg Inc.....E.......951 284-2000
1160 Olympic Dr Corona (92881) ***(P-7659)***
Western Exterminator Company.....D.......562 802-2238
15415 Marquardt Ave Santa Fe Springs (90670) ***(P-17206)***
Western Fab Inc.....F.......760 949-1441
9823 E Ave Hesperia (92345) ***(P-7577)***
Western Fabricators, Hesperia *Also called Western Fab Inc* ***(P-7577)***
Western Feld Invstigations Inc (PA).....**D**.......**800 999-9589**
405 W Foothill Blvd # 204 Claremont (91711) ***(P-18135)***
Western Fiber Co Inc.....E.......661 854-5556
4234a Sandrini Rd Arvin (93203) ***(P-7752)***
Western Forge Die, Huntington Beach *Also called Tarpin Corporation* ***(P-7836)***
Western Freight Carrier Inc (PA).....**D**.......**310 767-1042**
321 E Gardena Blvd Gardena (90248) ***(P-12092)***
Western Gage Corporation.....E.......805 445-1410
3316 Maya Linda Ste A Camarillo (93012) ***(P-7878)***
Western General Holding Co (PA).....**C**.......**818 880-9070**
5230 Las Virgenes Rd # 100 Calabasas (91302) ***(P-15488)***
Western General Insurance Co.....C.......818 880-9070
5230 Las Virgenes Rd # 10 Calabasas (91302) ***(P-15489)***
Western Glass Co, Pomona *Also called Da-Ly Glass Corp* ***(P-5951)***
Western Golf Inc.....F.......800 448-4409
1340 N Jefferson St Anaheim (92807) ***(P-11459)***
Western Golf Car Mfg Inc.....D.......760 671-6691
69391 Dillon Rd Desert Hot Springs (92241) ***(P-11460)***
Western Golf Car Sales Co, Desert Hot Springs *Also called Western Golf Car Mfg Inc* ***(P-11460)***
Western Growers Association (PA).....**C**.......**949 863-1000**
15525 Sand Canyon Ave Irvine (92618) ***(P-22263)***
Western Hardware Company, Walnut *Also called Hardware Imports Inc* ***(P-9989)***
Western Hardware Company.....E.......909 595-6201
161 Commerce Way Walnut (91789) ***(P-6544)***
Western Health Resources.....E.......559 537-2860
440 Greenfield Ave Ste B Hanford (93230) ***(P-23366)***
Western Highway Products, Huntington Beach *Also called Primus Inc* ***(P-11582)***
Western Hydrostatics Inc (PA).....**E**.......**951 784-2133**
1956 Keats Dr Riverside (92501) ***(P-8447)***
Western Illuminated Plas Inc.....E.......714 895-3067
14451 Edwards St Westminster (92683) ***(P-9111)***
Western Inn Upland Co Inc.....D.......909 949-4800
1191 E Foothill Blvd Upland (91786) ***(P-16784)***
Western Integrated Mtls Inc (PA).....**E**.......**562 634-2823**
3310 E 59th St Long Beach (90805) ***(P-3297)***
Western Lighting Inds Inc.....E.......626 969-6820
205 W Blueridge Ave Orange (92865) ***(P-13678)***
Western Med Center-Santa Ana, Santa Ana *Also called Western Medical Center Aux* ***(P-21008)***
Western Medical Center Aux (HQ).....**C**.......**714 835-3555**
1301 N Tustin Ave Santa Ana (92705) ***(P-21008)***
Western Medical Management LLC.....E.......949 260-6575
3333 Michelson Dr Ste 735 Irvine (92612) ***(P-23138)***
Western Mesquite Mines Inc.....E.......928 341-4653
6502 E Us Highway 78 Brawley (92227) ***(P-6288)***
Western Methods, Valencia *Also called Stratoflight* ***(P-10423)***
Western Mfg & Distrg LLC.....E.......805 988-1010
835 Flynn Rd Camarillo (93012) ***(P-10509)***
Western Milling LLC (HQ).....**C**.......**559 302-1000**
31120 W St Goshen (93227) ***(P-16302)***
Western Motor Works Inc.....F.......310 382-6896
8332 Osage Ave Los Angeles (90045) ***(P-7913)***
Western Mutual Insurance Co.....D.......818 879-2142
27489 Agoura Rd Agoura Hills (91301) ***(P-15490)***
Western National Contractors.....D.......949 862-6200
8 Executive Cir Irvine (92614) ***(P-23139)***
Western National Group LP.....D.......949 862-6200
8 Executive Cir Irvine (92614) ***(P-16032)***
Western National Prpts LLC (PA).....**C**.......**949 862-6200**
8 Executive Cir Irvine (92614) ***(P-674)***
Western National Securities (PA).....**C**.......**949 862-6200**
8 Executive Cir Irvine (92614) ***(P-16033)***
Western Oilfields Supply Co (PA).....**C**.......**661 399-9124**
3404 State Rd Bakersfield (93308) ***(P-17384)***
Western Operations, Rancho Cucamonga *Also called Gentex Corporation* ***(P-22841)***
Western Operations Center, Westlake Village *Also called Securitas SEC Svcs USA Inc* ***(P-18322)***
Western Outdoor News, San Clemente *Also called Western Outdoors Publications* ***(P-4044)***
Western Outdoors Publications (PA).....**E**.......**949 366-0030**
1211 Puerta Del Sol # 270 San Clemente (92673) ***(P-4044)***
Western Overseas Corporation (PA).....**E**.......**562 985-0616**
10731 Walker St Ste B Cypress (90630) ***(P-12551)***
Western Pacific Distrg LLC.....C.......714 974-6837
341 W Meats Ave Orange (92865) ***(P-13321)***
Western Pacific Pulp and Paper (HQ).....**D**.......**562 803-4401**
9400 Hall Rd Downey (90241) ***(P-3745)***
Western Pacific Roofing Corp.....C.......661 273-1336
3462 E La Campana Way Palm Springs (92262) ***(P-1510)***
Western PCF Crane & Eqp LLC (HQ).....**E**.......**562 286-6618**
8600 Calabash Ave Fontana (92335) ***(P-17322)***
Western PCF Stor Solutions Inc (PA).....**D**.......**909 451-0303**
300 E Arrow Hwy San Dimas (91773) ***(P-3703)***
Western Plastic Products, Stanton *Also called Schaffer Laboratories Inc* ***(P-5462)***
Western Plastics Temecula, Temecula *Also called W Plastics Inc* ***(P-5441)***
Western Precision Aero LLC.....E.......714 893-7999
11600 Monarch St Garden Grove (92841) ***(P-8850)***
Western Printing and Label, Orange *Also called Western Prtg & Graphics LLC* ***(P-4457)***
Western Prtg & Graphics LLC (PA).....**E**.......**714 532-3946**
675 N Main St Orange (92868) ***(P-4457)***
Western Regional Cancer Center, Santa Ana *Also called Tenet Healthsystem Medical Inc* ***(P-20105)***
Western Saw Manufacturers Inc.....E.......805 981-0999
3200 Camino Del Sol Oxnard (93030) ***(P-6493)***
Western Screw Products Inc.....E.......562 698-5793
11770 Slauson Ave Santa Fe Springs (90670) ***(P-7050)***
Western Sheet Metals Inc.....E.......951 272-3600
280 E Harrison St Corona (92879) ***(P-6942)***
Western Sheld Acquisitions LLC (PA).....**F**.......**310 527-6212**
2146 E Gladwick St Rancho Dominguez (90220) ***(P-4469)***
Western Shield Label, Rancho Dominguez *Also called Western Sheld Acquisitions LLC* ***(P-4469)***
Western Sierra Landscapes Inc.....E.......805 983-0070
2400 Eastman Ave Oxnard (93030) ***(P-289)***
Western Single Ply Inc.....E.......909 574-9735
8535 Sultana Ave Ste B Fontana (92335) ***(P-1511)***
Western Staffing Solutions LLC.....C.......951 545-4449
1235 Carbide Dr Corona (92881) ***(P-17478)***
Western States Envelope Corp.....D.......714 449-0909
2301 Raymer Ave Fullerton (92833) ***(P-4595)***
Western States Packaging Inc.....E.......818 686-6045
13276 Paxton St Pacoima (91331) ***(P-3893)***
Western States Wholesale Inc (PA).....**D**.......**909 947-0028**
1420 S Bon View Ave Ontario (91761) ***(P-6013)***
Western Summit Mfg Corp.....E.......626 333-3333
30200 Cartier Dr Rancho Palos Verdes (90275) ***(P-5442)***
Western Supreme Inc.....C.......213 627-3861
846 Produce Ct Los Angeles (90021) ***(P-1764)***
Western Telematic Inc.....E.......949 586-9950
5 Sterling Irvine (92618) ***(P-8311)***
Western Tube & Conduit Corp (HQ).....**C**.......**310 537-6300**
2001 E Dominguez St Long Beach (90810) ***(P-9055)***
Western Univ Hlth Sciences.....D.......909 865-2565
360 E Mission Blvd Pomona (91766) ***(P-20162)***
Westfall Technik, Corona *Also called 10 Day Parts Inc* ***(P-5539)***
Westfield LLC (HQ).....**B**.......**813 926-4600**
2049 Century Park E # 4100 Los Angeles (90067) ***(P-15709)***
Westfield America Inc (HQ).....**C**.......**310 478-4456**
2049 Century Park E Fl 41 Los Angeles (90067) ***(P-15710)***
Westfield America Ltd Partnr.....B.......310 277-3898
2049 Century Park E # 4100 Los Angeles (90067) ***(P-15711)***
Westgage Grdn Convalescent Ctr, Visalia *Also called Far West Inc* ***(P-20530)***
Westgate Gardens Care Ctr Inc.....D.......559 733-0901
4525 W Tulare Ave Visalia (93277) ***(P-20506)***
Westgate Manufacturing, Vernon *Also called Westgate Mfg Inc* ***(P-9930)***
Westgate Mfg Inc.....D.......877 805-2252
2462 E 28th St Vernon (90058) ***(P-9930)***
Westin Automotive Products Inc (PA).....**E**.......**626 960-6762**
320 W Covina Blvd San Dimas (91773) ***(P-3184)***
Westin Long Beach Hotel, The, Long Beach *Also called Noble/Utah Long Beach LLC* ***(P-16584)***
Westin Long Beach Hotel, The, Long Beach *Also called Noble Investment Group LLC* ***(P-16583)***
Westlake Diagnostic Center, Thousand Oaks *Also called Rolling Oaks Radiology Inc* ***(P-20045)***
Westlake Engrg Roto Form.....E.......805 525-8800
1041 E Santa Barbara St Santa Paula (93060) ***(P-5864)***
Westlake Financial Services, Los Angeles *Also called Westlake Services LLC* ***(P-15168)***
Westlake Health Care Center.....B.......805 494-1233
1101 Crenshaw Blvd Los Angeles (90019) ***(P-20507)***
Westlake Properties Inc.....C.......818 889-0230
31943 Agoura Rd Westlake Village (91361) ***(P-16785)***
Westlake Services LLC (HQ).....**C**.......**323 692-8800**
4751 Wilshire Blvd # 100 Los Angeles (90010) ***(P-15168)***
Westlake Village Inn, Westlake Village *Also called Westlake Properties Inc* ***(P-16785)***
Westland Floral, Carpinteria *Also called Westland Orchids Inc* ***(P-14901)***
Westland Flral Carpinteria Inc.....E.......805 684-4011
1400 Cravens Ln Carpinteria (93013) ***(P-14900)***
Westland Orchids Inc.....E.......805 684-1436
1400 Cravens Ln Carpinteria (93013) ***(P-14901)***
Westmed Ambulance Inc.....D.......310 456-3830
3872 Las Flores Canyon Rd Malibu (90265) ***(P-11898)***
Westmed Ambulance Inc (PA).....**C**.......**510 614-1420**
13933 Crenshaw Blvd Hawthorne (90250) ***(P-11899)***
Westminster Gardens.....D.......626 359-2571
1420 Santo Domingo Ave Duarte (91010) ***(P-20640)***

Westminster Press Inc ....E....714 210-2881
4906 W 1st St Santa Ana (92703) ***(P-4458)***
Westmont College ....B....805 565-6000
955 La Paz Rd Santa Barbara (93108) ***(P-17760)***
Westmont Industries LLC (PA) ....**E....562 944-6137**
10805 Painter Ave Uppr Santa Fe Springs (90670) ***(P-7700)***
Westpac Labs Inc (PA) ....**B....562 906-5227**
10200 Pioneer Blvd # 500 Santa Fe Springs (90670) ***(P-21101)***
Westpac Labs Inc ....B....562 906-5227
10200 Pioneer Blvd # 500 Santa Fe Springs (90670) ***(P-22961)***
Westpac Materials, Orange *Also called Western Pacific Distrg LLC* ***(P-13321)***
Westpoint Marketing Intl Inc ....D....323 233-0233
5901 Avalon Blvd Los Angeles (90003) ***(P-18724)***
Westrec Properties Inc ....B....818 907-0400
16633 Ventura Blvd Fl 6 Encino (91436) ***(P-23140)***
Westridge Laboratories Inc ....E....714 259-9400
1671 E Saint Andrew Pl Santa Ana (92705) ***(P-5082)***
Westrock Cp LLC ....D....951 273-7900
2577 Research Dr Corona (92882) ***(P-4459)***
Westrock Rkt Company ....C....626 859-7633
536 S 2nd Ave Covina (91723) ***(P-3832)***
Westrux International Inc (PA) ....**D....562 404-1020**
15555 Valley View Ave Santa Fe Springs (90670) ***(P-18738)***
Westside Accessories Inc (PA) ....**E....626 858-5452**
8920 Vernon Ave Ste 128 Montclair (91763) ***(P-3063)***
Westside Crdvsclar Med Group I (PA) ....**D....310 623-1150**
99 N La Cienega Blvd # 10 Beverly Hills (90211) ***(P-20163)***
Westside Jewish Cmnty Ctr Inc (PA) ....**C....323 938-2531**
5870 W Olympic Blvd Los Angeles (90036) ***(P-22215)***
Westside Medical ASC Los Ang, Beverly Hills *Also called Westside Crdvsclar Med Group I* ***(P-20163)***
Westside Resources Inc ....E....800 944-3939
8850 Research Dr Irvine (92618) ***(P-11203)***
Westside Security Patrol, Bakersfield *Also called M & S Security Services Inc* ***(P-18296)***
Weststar Cinemas Inc ....C....818 779-0323
7876 Van Nuys Blvd Van Nuys (91402) ***(P-19290)***
Weststar Cinemas Inc ....C....805 379-8966
180 Promenade Way Ste R Westlake Village (91362) ***(P-19291)***
Weststar Cinemas Inc ....C....805 658-6544
1440 Eastman Ave Ventura (93003) ***(P-19292)***
Weststar Cinemas Inc ....C....818 707-9987
29045 Agoura Rd Agoura Hills (91301) ***(P-19293)***
Westveiw Vo Ser, Anaheim *Also called Westview Services Inc* ***(P-21977)***
Westview Cmnty Arts Program, Anaheim *Also called Westview Services Inc* ***(P-20508)***
Westview Services Inc ....D....626 962-0956
1515 W Cameron Ave # 310 West Covina (91790) ***(P-21975)***
Westview Services Inc ....D....818 242-0068
301 E Glenoaks Blvd Ste 2 Glendale (91207) ***(P-21927)***
Westview Services Inc ....D....951 699-0047
27576 Commerce Center Dr # 1 Temecula (92590) ***(P-21976)***
Westview Services Inc ....C....714 956-4199
1701 S Euclid St Ste E Anaheim (92802) ***(P-20508)***
Westview Services Inc ....D....714 530-2703
9776 Katella Ave Anaheim (92804) ***(P-21977)***
Westview Services Inc ....D....714 879-3980
626 W Commonwealth Ave Fullerton (92832) ***(P-21928)***
Westview Services Inc ....D....714 635-2444
1655 S Euclid St Ste A Anaheim (92802) ***(P-21978)***
Westview Services Inc ....D....714 418-2090
9421 Edinger Ave Westminster (92683) ***(P-21979)***
Westview Vocational Services, Temecula *Also called Westview Services Inc* ***(P-21976)***
Westview Vocational Services, Anaheim *Also called Westview Services Inc* ***(P-21978)***
Westway Magazine, Costa Mesa *Also called Auto Club Enterprises* ***(P-4053)***
Westwind Engineering Inc ....C....310 831-3454
625 Esplanade Unit 70 Redondo Beach (90277) ***(P-22695)***
Westwind Engineering Inc ....D....310 831-3454
553 N Pcf Coastte B179 B Redondo Beach (90277) ***(P-22696)***
Westwind Equity Investors, Newport Beach *Also called Windjmmer Cpitl Invstors III L* ***(P-16304)***
Westwood Building Materials Co ....E....310 643-9158
15708 Inglewood Ave Lawndale (90260) ***(P-6128)***
Westwood Express Messenger Svc, Los Angeles *Also called Express Group Inc* ***(P-12128)***
Westwood Healthcare Center LP ....D....310 826-0821
12121 Santa Monica Blvd Los Angeles (90025) ***(P-20509)***
Westwood Insurance Agency (HQ) ....**D....818 990-9715**
8407 Fllbrook Ave Ste 200 Canoga Park (91304) ***(P-15649)***
Westwood Laboratories Inc (PA) ....**E....626 969-3305**
710 S Ayon Ave Azusa (91702) ***(P-5083)***
Westwood Marquis Hotel & Grdns, Los Angeles *Also called W Los Angeles* ***(P-16774)***
Wet (PA) ....**C....818 769-6200**
10847 Sherman Way Sun Valley (91352) ***(P-18725)***
Wet Design, Sun Valley *Also called Wet* ***(P-18725)***
Wet N Wild Los Angeles, City of Industry *Also called Markwins Beauty Products Inc* ***(P-14260)***
Wetransfer Corporation ....D....626 626-5565
2116 Zeno Pl Venice (90291) ***(P-17761)***
Wetzel & Sons Mvg & Stor Inc ....D....818 890-0992
12400 Osborne St Pacoima (91331) ***(P-12122)***
Wetzel Trucking, Pacoima *Also called Wetzel & Sons Mvg & Stor Inc* ***(P-12122)***
Wfg Lenders Services LLC (HQ) ....**D....503 387-3636**
2625 Townsgate Rd Ste 101 Westlake Village (91361) ***(P-16044)***
Wfg National Title Insur Co (PA) ....**D....818 476-4000**
700 N Brand Blvd Ste 1100 Glendale (91203) ***(P-15513)***
Whale Logistics (usa) Inc (PA) ....**D....714 891-8265**
6320 Caballero Blvd Buena Park (90620) ***(P-12585)***
Whaling Packaging Co ....E....310 518-6021
21020 S Wilmington Ave Carson (90810) ***(P-12560)***
Wham-O Inc ....D....818 963-4200
6301 Owensmouth Ave # 700 Woodland Hills (91367) ***(P-14105)***
Wharf, The, Ventura *Also called Ventura Feed and Pet Sups Inc* ***(P-11789)***
What Kids Want Inc ....F....818 775-0375
19428 Londelius St Northridge (91324) ***(P-11395)***
Whatever It Takes Inc ....D....760 329-6000
10805 Palm Dr Desert Hot Springs (92240) ***(P-16786)***
Whb Corporation ....A....213 624-1011
506 S Grand Ave Los Angeles (90071) ***(P-16787)***
Wheel and Tire Club Inc ....E....714 422-3505
1301 Burton St Fullerton (92831) ***(P-6218)***
Wheel of Fortune, Culver City *Also called Quadra Productions Inc* ***(P-19168)***
Whelan Security Co ....B....310 343-8628
400 Continental Blvd El Segundo (90245) ***(P-18359)***
Where 2 Get It Inc (HQ) ....**D....714 660-4870**
222 S Harbor Blvd Ste 600 Anaheim (92805) ***(P-18236)***
Whi Solutions Inc ....C....661 257-2120
28470 Ave Stnford Ste 200 Valencia (91355) ***(P-13452)***
White Bottle Inc ....E....949 788-1998
10579 Dale Ave Stanton (90680) ***(P-5865)***
White Cap 301, Santa Clarita *Also called White Cap Supply Group Inc* ***(P-13339)***
White Cap Construction Supply ....A....949 794-5300
1815 Ritchey St Santa Ana (92705) ***(P-13874)***
White Cap Supply Group Inc ....A....661 294-7737
28255 Kelly Johnson Pkwy Santa Clarita (91355) ***(P-13339)***
White Crane, Indio *Also called Whites Crane Service Inc* ***(P-17323)***
White Horse Logistics Inc ....E....909 947-7822
12400 Philadelphia Ave Eastvale (91752) ***(P-12586)***
White House Sanitation Inc ....D....951 943-1550
18916 Seaton Ave Perris (92570) ***(P-19084)***
White Mem Cmnty Hlth Ctr A Cal ....D....323 987-1222
1828 E Cesar E Chavez Ave # 5000 Los Angeles (90033) ***(P-20164)***
White Mem Pediatrics Med Group ....D....323 987-1200
1701 E Cesar E Chavez Ave # 456 Los Angeles (90033) ***(P-21009)***
White Memorial Med Group Inc (PA) ....**D....323 987-1300**
1701 E Cesar E Chavez Ave Los Angeles (90033) ***(P-20165)***
White Memorial Medical Center ....A....323 260-5739
1720 E Cesar E Chavez Ave Los Angeles (90033) ***(P-20166)***
White Memorial Medical Center (HQ) ....**A....323 268-5000**
1720 E Cesar E Chavez Ave Los Angeles (90033) ***(P-21010)***
White Oak Housing Foundation, Northridge *Also called United Crbral Plsy/Spstic Chld* ***(P-20544)***
White Rabbit Partners Inc ....C....310 975-1450
9000 W Sunset Blvd West Hollywood (90069) ***(P-22169)***
White Wave Foods, City of Industry *Also called Wwf Operating Company LLC* ***(P-1842)***
White Zuckerman Warsavsky Luna (PA) ....**D....818 981-4226**
15490 Ventura Blvd # 300 Sherman Oaks (91403) ***(P-22819)***
Whitefield Medical Lab & Rdlgy, Pomona *Also called Whitefield Medical Lab Inc* ***(P-21102)***
Whitefield Medical Lab Inc (PA) ....**E....909 625-2114**
764 Indigo Ct Ste A Pomona (91767) ***(P-21102)***
Whitefox Defense Tech Inc ....E....805 225-4506
833 Buckley Rd San Luis Obispo (93401) ***(P-6381)***
Whitehall Manufacturing Inc ....D....626 336-4561
15125 Proctor Ave City of Industry (91746) ***(P-11154)***
Whites Crane Service Inc ....D....760 347-3401
45524 Towne St Indio (92201) ***(P-17323)***
Whites Hvac Services Inc ....F....805 801-0167
131 E Knotts St Nipomo (93444) ***(P-8358)***
Whites Steel Inc (PA) ....**F....760 347-3401**
45524 Towne St Indio (92201) ***(P-1584)***
Whitewater Rock & Sup Co Inc ....E....760 325-2747
58645 Old Highway 60 Whitewater (92282) ***(P-13322)***
Whiting Door Mfg Corp ....D....909 877-0120
301 S Milliken Ave Ontario (91761) ***(P-19085)***
Whiting-Turner Contracting Co ....C....818 879-8100
29209 Canwood St Ste 100 Agoura Hills (91301) ***(P-849)***
Whiting-Turner Contracting Co ....C....949 863-0800
250 Commerce Ste 150 Irvine (92602) ***(P-850)***
Whitman Ptrson Capitl Partners (PA) ....**D....818 483-1060**
3075 Townsgate Rd Ste 210 Westlake Village (91361) ***(P-16788)***
Whitmor Plstic Wire Cable Corp (PA) ....**E....661 257-2400**
27737 Avenue Hopkins Santa Clarita (91355) ***(P-7522)***
Whitmor Plstic Wire Cable Corp ....E....661 257-2400
28420 Stanford Ave Valencia (91355) ***(P-7523)***
Whitmor Wire and Cable, Santa Clarita *Also called Whitmor Plstic Wire Cable Corp* ***(P-7522)***
Whitmor Wirenetics, Valencia *Also called Whitmor Plstic Wire Cable Corp* ***(P-7523)***
Whittaker Corporation ....E....805 526-5700
1955 Surveyor Ave Fl 2 Simi Valley (93063) ***(P-10444)***
Whitten Machine ....F....559 686-3428
4770 S K St Tulare (93274) ***(P-8851)***
Whittier Fertilizer Company ....D....562 699-3461
9441 Kruse Rd Pico Rivera (90660) ***(P-5162)***
Whittier Filtration Inc (HQ) ....**E....714 986-5300**
120 S State College Blvd Brea (92821) ***(P-8426)***
Whittier Hills Health Care Ctr, Whittier *Also called Ensign Whittier East LLC* ***(P-20335)***
Whittier Hills Health Care Ctr, Whittier *Also called Ensign Group Inc* ***(P-20330)***
Whittier Hospital Med Ctr Inc ....C....562 945-3561
9080 Colima Rd Whittier (90605) ***(P-21011)***
Whittier Mailing Products Inc (PA) ....**E....562 464-3000**
13019 Park St Santa Fe Springs (90670) ***(P-8320)***
Whittier Millwork Co, Whittier *Also called Avca Fixture System Inc* ***(P-3676)***
Whittier Narrow Golf Course ....C....626 288-1044
8640 Rush St Rosemead (91770) ***(P-19681)***
Whittier Service Center, Santa Fe Springs *Also called Southern California Edison Co* ***(P-12853)***
Whittier Union High Schl Dist ....C....562 693-8826
7200 Greenleaf Ave # 170 Whittier (90602) ***(P-21929)***

ALPHABETIC

Who Dat Nation Trnsp LLC....D....760 403-7237
13186 Rincon Rd Apple Valley (92308) ***(P-12587)***

Who What Wear, West Hollywood *Also called Clique Brands Inc* ***(P-4059)***

Whole Health Pharmacy....E....949 305-0788
1415 N Broadway Santa Ana (92706) ***(P-14299)***

Wholesale Fuels Inc....D....661 327-4900
2200 E Brundage Ln Bakersfield (93307) ***(P-14816)***

Wholesale Shutter Company Inc....F....951 845-8786
411 Olive Ave Beaumont (92223) ***(P-3298)***

Wick Communications Co....E....760 379-3667
6404 Lake Isabella Blvd Lake Isabella (93240) ***(P-4045)***

Wicoro Inc (HQ)....E....626 962-4489
919 N Sunset Ave West Covina (91790) ***(P-20641)***

Wide Open Industries LLC....E....949 635-2292
21088 Bake Pkwy Ste 100 Lake Forest (92630) ***(P-9973)***

Wide USA Corporation....F....714 300-0540
2210 E Winston Rd Anaheim (92806) ***(P-8231)***

Widescreen Review, Temecula *Also called Wsr Publishing Inc* ***(P-4113)***

Wieland Brookes, Santa Fe Springs *Also called Wieland Metal Services LLC* ***(P-13605)***

Wieland Metal Services LLC....D....562 968-2100
10634 Shoemaker Ave Santa Fe Springs (90670) ***(P-13605)***

Wieland Metal Services W LLC (HQ)....D....714 692-1000
5100 S Archibald Ave Ontario (91762) ***(P-13606)***

Wiemar Distributors Inc....D....213 747-7036
1953 S Alameda St Los Angeles (90058) ***(P-14667)***

Wiens Cellars LLC....E....951 694-9892
35055 Via Del Ponte Temecula (92592) ***(P-2236)***

Wiggins Lift Co Inc....E....805 485-7821
2571 Cortez St Oxnard (93036) ***(P-13965)***

Wilbur Curtis Co Inc....B....800 421-6150
6913 W Acco St Montebello (90640) ***(P-16115)***

Wilbur Curtis Co Inc....C....323 837-2300
6913 W Acco St Montebello (90640) ***(P-8427)***

Wilbur Curtis Co Inc....B....323 837-2300
6913 W Acco St Montebello (90640) ***(P-8428)***

Wilco Building Corporation....F....805 765-4188
2005 Palma Dr Ste A Ventura (93003) ***(P-3299)***

Wilcompute....F....818 674-0506
38713 Tierra Subida Ave Palmdale (93551) ***(P-10775)***

Wilcox Machine Co....D....562 927-5353
7180 Scout Ave Bell Gardens (90201) ***(P-8852)***

Wild Creek Healthcare Inc (HQ)....E....775 359-3161
27101 Puerta Real Ste 450 Mission Viejo (92691) ***(P-21498)***

Wild Lizard, Los Angeles *Also called Bb Co Inc* ***(P-2922)***

Wilden Pump, Grand Terrace *Also called Psg California LLC* ***(P-8022)***

Wildflour Bakery & Cafe LLC....D....818 575-7280
21160 Califa St Woodland Hills (91367) ***(P-14748)***

Wildlife Waystation....E....818 899-5201
14831 Lttle Tjunga Cyn Rd Sylmar (91342) ***(P-22470)***

Wildomar Medical Offices, Wildomar *Also called Kaiser Foundation Hospitals* ***(P-20811)***

Wilkins Design and Mfg Inc....E....714 564-3351
2619 Oak St Santa Ana (92707) ***(P-6684)***

Will-Mann Inc....E....714 870-0350
225 E Santa Fe Ave Fullerton (92832) ***(P-6943)***

Willard Marine Inc....D....714 666-2150
1250 N Grove St Anaheim (92806) ***(P-10475)***

Willdan Engineering....D....909 386-0200
650 E Hospitality Ln # 250 San Bernardino (92408) ***(P-22697)***

Willdan Engineering....D....562 908-6200
13191 Crssrads Pkwy N Ste City of Industry (91746) ***(P-22698)***

Willdan Engineering....D....805 653-6597
374 Poli St Ste 101 Ventura (93001) ***(P-22699)***

Willdan Group Inc (PA)....C....800 424-9144
2401 E Katella Ave # 300 Anaheim (92806) ***(P-22700)***

William Bounds Ltd....E....310 375-0505
23625 Madison St Torrance (90505) ***(P-7956)***

William Getz Corp....F....714 516-2050
539 W Walnut Ave Orange (92868) ***(P-11461)***

William Hzmlhlch Archtects Inc....D....949 250-0607
680 Nwport Ctr Dr Ste 300 Newport Beach (92660) ***(P-22752)***

William James Cellars (PA)....E....805 478-9412
613 Woodgreen Way Nipomo (93444) ***(P-2237)***

William Lyon Homes (HQ)....B....949 833-3600
4695 Macarthur Ct Ste 800 Newport Beach (92660) ***(P-651)***

William Lyon Homes Inc (HQ)....D....949 833-3600
4695 Macarthur Ct Ste 800 Newport Beach (92660) ***(P-652)***

William Morris Consulting, Beverly Hills *Also called William Mrris Endvor Entrmt LL* ***(P-19340)***

William Morris Endeavor Entrmt, Beverly Hills *Also called William Mrris Endvor Entrmt FN* ***(P-19339)***

William Morris Rodeo Inc (HQ)....D....310 859-4000
151 El Camino Dr Beverly Hills (90212) ***(P-15712)***

William Mrris Endvor Entrmt FN (HQ)....C....310 285-9000
9601 Wilshire Blvd Fl 3 Beverly Hills (90210) ***(P-19339)***

William Mrris Endvor Entrmt LL....B....310 285-9000
9601 Wilshire Blvd Fl 3 Beverly Hills (90210) ***(P-19340)***

William Oneil & Co Inc (PA)....C....310 448-6800
12655 Beatrice St Los Angeles (90066) ***(P-15312)***

William Warren Properties Inc....D....310 454-1500
201 Wilshire Blvd Ste 102 Santa Monica (90401) ***(P-15753)***

Williams Aerospace & Mfg Inc (HQ)....E....805 446-2700
999 Avenida Acaso Camarillo (93012) ***(P-14072)***

Williams Comfort Products, Colton *Also called Williams Furnace Co* ***(P-8359)***

Williams Furnace Co (HQ)....C....562 450-3602
250 W Laurel St Colton (92324) ***(P-8359)***

Williams Mfg Aero Machining....F....818 898-2272
12727 Foothill Blvd Sylmar (91342) ***(P-7479)***

Williamson Granados....F....424 296-5494
15004 Paramount Blvd Paramount (90723) ***(P-2900)***

Willick Engineering Co Inc....F....562 946-4242
12516 Lakeland Rd Santa Fe Springs (90670) ***(P-11211)***

Willis Electric Inc....E....661 324-2781
4465 Buck Owens Blvd Bakersfield (93308) ***(P-18961)***

Willis Electric Company, Bakersfield *Also called Willis Electric Inc* ***(P-18961)***

Willis Machine Inc....E....805 604-4500
11000 Alto Dr Oak View (93022) ***(P-8853)***

Willis, Burton F MD, Huntington Beach *Also called Edinger Medical Group Inc* ***(P-19802)***

Willits Perpetual LLC....D....818 668-6800
21600 Oxnard St Woodland Hills (91367) ***(P-18726)***

Willitts Equipment Company Inc....E....559 594-5020
30548 Road 196 Exeter (93221) ***(P-19086)***

Willow, Vernon *Also called Complete Clothing Company* ***(P-2883)***

Willow Springs LLC....D....951 789-4405
17241 Van Buren Blvd Riverside (92504) ***(P-20167)***

Wills Wing, Orange *Also called Sport Kites Inc* ***(P-10204)***

Wilmay Inc....D....805 524-2603
893 Oak Ave Fillmore (93015) ***(P-18727)***

Wilmington Ironworks, Wilmington *Also called Wilmington Machine Inc* ***(P-8854)***

Wilmington Machine Inc....E....310 518-3213
432 W C St Wilmington (90744) ***(P-8854)***

Wilmington Woodworks Inc....E....310 834-1015
318 E C St Wilmington (90744) ***(P-3412)***

Wilorco, Carson *Also called Strike Technology Inc* ***(P-9787)***

Wilschur Design and Mfg, Santa Ana *Also called Wilkins Design and Mfg Inc* ***(P-6684)***

Wilsey Foods Inc....A....714 257-3700
40 Pointe Dr Brea (92821) ***(P-2134)***

Wilshire Advisors LLC (PA)....C....310 451-3051
1299 Ocean Ave Ste 700 Santa Monica (90401) ***(P-23367)***

Wilshire Boulevard Temple....C....323 261-6135
4334 Whittier Blvd Los Angeles (90023) ***(P-16090)***

Wilshire Country Club....D....323 934-6050
301 N Rossmore Ave Los Angeles (90004) ***(P-19628)***

Wilshire Kingsley Inc....D....213 382-6677
3575 Wilshire Blvd Los Angeles (90010) ***(P-15713)***

Wilshire Precision Pdts Inc....E....818 765-4571
7353 Hinds Ave North Hollywood (91605) ***(P-8855)***

Wilson & Hampton Pntg Contrs....D....714 772-5091
1524 W Mable St Anaheim (92802) ***(P-1202)***

Wilson Creek Wnery Vnyards Inc....C....951 699-9463
35960 Rancho Cal Rd Temecula (92591) ***(P-2238)***

Wilson Cycles Sports Corp....E....951 894-5545
26145 Jefferson Ave # 205 Murrieta (92562) ***(P-10510)***

Wilsons Art Studio Inc....D....714 870-7030
501 S Acacia Ave Fullerton (92831) ***(P-4596)***

Wilwood Engineering....C....805 388-1188
4700 Calle Bolero Camarillo (93012) ***(P-10158)***

Win Fat Food LLC....F....323 261-1869
700 Monterey Pass Rd A Monterey Park (91754) ***(P-1765)***

Win Soon Inc....E....323 564-5070
4569 Firestone Blvd South Gate (90280) ***(P-1841)***

Win-Dor Inc (PA)....C....714 576-2030
450 Delta Ave Brea (92821) ***(P-1464)***

Winbo Usa Inc....E....951 738-9978
2120 California Ave Ste 2 Corona (92881) ***(P-6944)***

Winc Inc....C....855 282-5829
5340 Alla Rd Ste 105 Los Angeles (90066) ***(P-2239)***

Winchell's Donut House, Long Beach *Also called Winchells Franchising LLC* ***(P-2052)***

Winchell's Donut House, San Fernando *Also called Winchells Franchising LLC* ***(P-2053)***

Winchells Franchising LLC....E....562 437-8463
1695 W Pacific Coast Hwy Long Beach (90810) ***(P-2052)***

Winchells Franchising LLC....E....818 361-9017
14530 Brand Blvd San Fernando (91340) ***(P-2053)***

Windermere RE Coachella Vly, Indian Wells *Also called Bennion Deville Fine Homes Inc* ***(P-15786)***

Windes Inc (PA)....D....562 435-1191
3780 Kilroy Arprt Way Long Beach (90806) ***(P-22820)***

Windjmmer Capitl Investors III, Santa Ana *Also called Jwc Environmental Inc* ***(P-13908)***

Windjmmer Capitl Investors LLC....D....949 706-9989
610 Newport Center Dr Newport Beach (92660) ***(P-16303)***

Windjmmer Cpitl Invstors III L....A....949 706-9989
610 Nwport Ctr Dr Ste 110 Newport Beach (92660) ***(P-16304)***

Window Products Management Inc....F....805 677-6800
5917 Olivas Park Dr Ste F Ventura (93003) ***(P-3300)***

Windsor Anaheim Healthcare....E....562 422-9219
3232 E Artesia Blvd Long Beach (90805) ***(P-20510)***

Windsor Anaheim Healthcare....E....310 675-3304
13922 Cerise Ave Hawthorne (90250) ***(P-20511)***

Windsor Anaheim Healthcare (PA)....C....714 826-8950
3415 W Ball Rd Anaheim (92804) ***(P-20512)***

Windsor Capital Group Inc....D....805 988-0627
2101 W Vineyard Ave Oxnard (93036) ***(P-16789)***

Windsor Capital Group Inc....D....805 735-8311
1117 N H St Lompoc (93436) ***(P-16790)***

Windsor Capital Group Inc....D....310 566-1100
3250 Ocean Park Blvd # 35 Santa Monica (90405) ***(P-16791)***

Windsor Capital Group Inc....D....310 566-1100
3250 Ocean Park Blvd # 35 Santa Monica (90405) ***(P-16792)***

Windsor Capital Group Inc....D....209 577-3825
3250 Ocean Park Blvd # 35 Santa Monica (90405) ***(P-16793)***

Windsor Capital Group Inc....D....209 577-3825
3250 Ocean Park Blvd # 35 Santa Monica (90405) ***(P-16794)***

Windsor Capital Group Inc....D....714 990-6000
900 E Birch St Brea (92821) ***(P-16795)***

Windsor Capital Group Inc....D....951 676-5656
29345 Rancho California Temecula (92591) ***(P-16796)***

Windsor Capital Group Inc....D....310 566-1100
3250 Ocean Park Blvd # 35 Santa Monica (90405) ***(P-16797)***

Mergent e-mail: customerrelations@mergent.com
1320
2022 Southern California Business Directory and Buyers Guide
(P-0000) Products & Services Section entry number
(PA)=Parent Co (HQ)=Headquarters (DH)=Div Headquarters

Windsor Capital Group Inc ....D......310 566-1100
3250 Ocean Park Blvd # 35 Santa Monica (90405) ***(P-16798)***
Windsor Capital Group Inc ....D......805 986-5353
350 E Hueneme Rd Port Hueneme (93041) ***(P-16799)***
Windsor Capital Group Inc ....D......714 241-3800
1325 E Dyer Rd Santa Ana (92705) ***(P-16800)***
Windsor Capital Group Inc ....D......951 276-1200
1510 University Ave Riverside (92507) ***(P-16801)***
Windsor Crt Asssted Living LLC ....E......760 327-8351
201 S Sunrise Way Palm Springs (92262) ***(P-20513)***
Windsor Cypress Grdns Hlthcare ....A......951 688-3643
9025 Colorado Ave Riverside (92503) ***(P-20642)***
Windsor Foods, Ontario *Also called Ajinomoto Foods North Amer Inc* ***(P-1914)***
Windsor Gardens of Fullerton, Fullerton *Also called Windsor Grdns Hlthcare Ctr Fll* ***(P-20516)***
Windsor Gardens of Long Beach, Long Beach *Also called Windsor Anaheim Healthcare* ***(P-20510)***
Windsor Grdns Cnvlescent Ctr A, Anaheim *Also called Windsor Anaheim Healthcare* ***(P-20512)***
Windsor Grdns Cnvlscent Ctr Hw, Hawthorne *Also called Sandhrst Cnvlscent Group Ltd A* ***(P-20458)***
Windsor Grdns Cnvlscent Hosp I ....D......888 234-4442
9200 W Sunset Blvd West Hollywood (90069) ***(P-20514)***
Windsor Grdns Cnvlscent Hosp I ....D......323 937-5466
915 Crenshaw Blvd Los Angeles (90019) ***(P-20515)***
Windsor Grdns Hlthcare Ctr Fll ....D......714 871-6020
245 E Wilshire Ave Fullerton (92832) ***(P-20516)***
Windsor Insurance Assoc Inc ....E......818 710-9890
21820 Burbank Blvd # 100 Woodland Hills (91367) ***(P-15650)***
Windsor Palms Care Ctr Artesia, Artesia *Also called Windsor Twin Plms Hlthcare Ctr* ***(P-20517)***
Windsor Twin Plms Hlthcare Ctr ....C......562 865-0271
11900 Artesia Blvd Artesia (90701) ***(P-20517)***
Windward Yacht & Repair Inc ....F......310 823-4581
13645 Fiji Way Venice (90292) ***(P-10476)***
Windward Yacht Center, Venice *Also called Windward Yacht & Repair Inc* ***(P-10476)***
Windy Balloon Company, Gardena *Also called South Bay Corporation* ***(P-5412)***
Wine Country Gift Baskets, Fullerton *Also called Houdini Inc* ***(P-14938)***
Wine Country Party & Events, Torrance *Also called Bright Event Rentals LLC* ***(P-17335)***
Wine Dept, Los Angeles *Also called Youngs Market Company LLC* ***(P-14849)***
Wine Warehouse, Commerce *Also called Ben Myerson Candy Co Inc* ***(P-14838)***
Wine Wrangler Inc ....F......805 238-5700
2985 Theatre Dr Ste 7 Paso Robles (93446) ***(P-2240)***
Winegardner Masonry Inc ....E......909 795-9711
32147 Dunlap Blvd Ste A Yucaipa (92399) ***(P-1357)***
Wingate By Wyndham, Inglewood *Also called Lax Hotel Investment Co Inc* ***(P-16536)***
Winit America Inc ....F......626 606-0308
381 Brea Canyon Rd Walnut (91789) ***(P-8312)***
Winning Laboratories Inc ....F......562 921-6880
16218 Arthur St Cerritos (90703) ***(P-4770)***
Winning Performance Pdts Inc ....E......818 367-1041
13010 Bradley Ave Sylmar (91342) ***(P-18728)***
Winning Team Inc ....F......661 295-1428
24922 Anza Dr Ste E Valencia (91355) ***(P-3165)***
Winonics Inc ....C......714 626-3755
1257 S State College Blvd Fullerton (92831) ***(P-9469)***
Winstar Textile Inc ....E......626 357-1133
16815 E Johnson Dr City of Industry (91745) ***(P-3038)***
Winter & Bain Mfg Inc (PA) ....**F......213 749-3568**
1417 Elwood St Los Angeles (90021) ***(P-7682)***
Winter Park Utility Svcs LLC (PA) ....**D......714 283-6080**
8141 E Kaiser Blvd # 212 Anaheim (92808) ***(P-987)***
Winther Technologies Inc (PA) ....**E......310 618-8437**
560 Alaska Ave Torrance (90503) ***(P-7897)***
Wipex Corp (PA) ....**D......909 714-4623**
10808 Foothill Blvd Rancho Cucamonga (91730) ***(P-10159)***
Wira Co, El Monte *Also called Jans Enterprises Corporation* ***(P-14696)***
Wire Cut Company Inc ....E......714 994-1170
6750 Caballero Blvd Buena Park (90620) ***(P-8856)***
Wire Harness & Cable Assembly, Santa Monica *Also called Omega Leads Inc* ***(P-9759)***
Wire Technology Corporation ....E......310 635-6935
9527 Laurel St Los Angeles (90002) ***(P-6360)***
Wireless Technology Inc ....E......805 339-9696
2064 Eastman Ave Ste 113 Ventura (93003) ***(P-9210)***
Wirenetics Co, Valencia *Also called Circle W Enterprises Inc* ***(P-7497)***
Wiretech Inc (PA) ....**D......323 722-4933**
6440 Canning St Commerce (90040) ***(P-6241)***
Wirz & Co ....F......909 825-6970
444 Colton Ave Colton (92324) ***(P-4460)***
Wise & Healthy Aging ....D......818 876-1402
23388 Mulholland Dr # 60 Woodland Hills (91364) ***(P-21930)***
Wise Living Inc ....E......323 541-0410
2001 W 60th St Los Angeles (90047) ***(P-3574)***
Wismettac Asian Foods Inc (HQ) ....**C......562 802-1900**
13409 Orden Dr Santa Fe Springs (90670) ***(P-14522)***
Wismettac Fresh Fish, Santa Fe Springs *Also called Wismettac Asian Foods Inc* ***(P-14522)***
Within Unlimited Inc ....E......310 664-1400
3760 Motor Ave Los Angeles (90034) ***(P-18422)***
Wixen Music Publishing Inc ....F......818 591-7355
24025 Park Sorrento # 130 Calabasas (91302) ***(P-4144)***
Wj Newport LLC ....C......949 476-2001
4500 Macarthur Blvd Newport Beach (92660) ***(P-16802)***
Wjb Bearings Inc ....E......909 598-6238
535 Brea Canyon Rd City of Industry (91789) ***(P-7110)***
Wjbradley Mortgage Capital, Newport Beach *Also called Emery Financial Inc* ***(P-15241)***
WKS Frosty Corporation (HQ) ....**D......562 425-1402**
5856 Corp Ave Ste 200 Cypress (90630) ***(P-16222)***
WKS Restaurant Corporation (PA) ....**A......562 425-1402**
5856 Corp Ave Ste 200 Cypress (90630) ***(P-16223)***
Wlcac, Los Angeles *Also called Watts Labor Community Action* ***(P-21923)***
Wm Bolthouse Farms Inc (HQ) ....**A......661 366-7209**
7200 E Brundage Ln Bakersfield (93307) ***(P-22)***
Wm J Matson Company ....F......805 684-9410
213 N Olive St Ventura (93001) ***(P-7426)***
WM Klorman Construction Corp ....D......818 591-5969
23047 Ventura Blvd Fl 2 Woodland Hills (91364) ***(P-851)***
Wm Technology Inc ....B......844 933-3627
41 Discovery Irvine (92618) ***(P-18010)***
Wm Vandergeest Ldscp Care Inc ....D......714 545-8432
3342 W Castor St Santa Ana (92704) ***(P-352)***
WMc Prcsion McHning Grnding ....E......714 773-0059
1234 E Ash Ave Ste A Fullerton (92831) ***(P-8857)***
WMS Transportation, Ventura *Also called Sam Hill & Sons Inc* ***(P-969)***
Wna City of Industry, City of Industry *Also called Wna Comet West Inc* ***(P-5866)***
Wna City of Industry, City of Industry *Also called Waddington North America Inc* ***(P-5860)***
Wna Comet West Inc ....C......626 913-0724
927 S Azusa Ave City of Industry (91748) ***(P-5866)***
Wng, Irvine *Also called Western National Group LP* ***(P-16032)***
Wolf Rfkin Shpiro Schlman Rbk (PA) ....**D......310 445-8817**
11400 W Olympic Blvd Los Angeles (90064) ***(P-21697)***
Wolf Firm A Law Corporation ....D......949 720-9200
1851 E 1st St Ste 100 Santa Ana (92705) ***(P-21698)***
Wolfe & Associates, Santa Barbara *Also called Ronald L Wolfe & Assoc Inc* ***(P-15989)***
Wolfgang Enterprise Inc ....F......951 848-7680
13977 The Merge St Unit B Eastvale (92880) ***(P-18729)***
Wolverine Intrmdate Hldg II Co (PA) ....**B......310 712-1850**
360 N Crescent Dr Bldg S Beverly Hills (90210) ***(P-23141)***
Wolverine Top Holding Corp ....D......661 772-7500
360 N Crescent Dr Bldg S Beverly Hills (90210) ***(P-16116)***
Womble Bond Dickinson (us) LLP ....C......310 207-3800
12400 Wilshire Blvd # 600 Los Angeles (90025) ***(P-21699)***
Womenshelter of Long Beach ....E......562 437-7233
4201 Long Beach Blvd # 102 Long Beach (90807) ***(P-22377)***
Won & Jay Inc ....E......949 369-6226
990 Avenida Talega San Clemente (92673) ***(P-19512)***
Wonderful Agency ....A......310 966-8600
11444 W Olympic Blvd # 210 Los Angeles (90064) ***(P-17070)***
Wonderful Almond Cooperative ....E......310 966-5800
11444 W Olympic Blvd 10th Los Angeles (90064) ***(P-2117)***
Wonderful Citrus Cooperative (PA) ....**A......661 720-2400**
1901 S Lexington St Delano (93215) ***(P-192)***
Wonderful Citrus LLC (HQ) ....**C......661 720-2400**
1701 S Lexington St Delano (93215) ***(P-66)***
Wonderful Citrus Packing LLC ....F......661 720-2400
1701 S Lexington St Delano (93215) ***(P-1881)***
Wonderful Citrus Packing LLC (HQ) ....**B......661 720-2400**
1901 S Lexington St Delano (93215) ***(P-193)***
Wonderful Company LLC ....B......661 720-2400
1901 S Lexington St Delano (93215) ***(P-67)***
Wonderful Company LLC ....B......559 781-7438
5001 California Ave Bakersfield (93309) ***(P-194)***
Wonderful Company LLC ....B......661 720-2609
11444 W Olympic Blvd # 210 Los Angeles (90064) ***(P-195)***
Wonderful Company LLC ....B......661 399-4456
6801 E Lerdo Hwy Shafter (93263) ***(P-196)***
Wonderful Orchards LLC (HQ) ....**C......661 399-4456**
6801 E Lerdo Hwy Shafter (93263) ***(P-59)***
Wonderful Orchards LLC ....C......661 797-6400
13646 Highway 33 Lost Hills (93249) ***(P-60)***
Wonderful Orchards LLC ....C......661 797-2509
21707 Lerdo Hwy Mc Kittrick (93251) ***(P-61)***
Wonderful Pstchios Almonds LLC (HQ) ....**E......310 966-4650**
11444 W Olympic Blvd Los Angeles (90064) ***(P-2118)***
Wonderfulpistachiosandalmonds, Lost Hills *Also called Wonderful Orchards LLC* ***(P-60)***
Wonderware, Lake Forest *Also called Aveva Software LLC* ***(P-18019)***
Wonderware Corporation (HQ) ....**B......949 727-3200**
26561 Rancho Pkwy S Lake Forest (92630) ***(P-18011)***
Wondros, Los Angeles *Also called Hungry Heart Media Inc* ***(P-19133)***
Wongdoody Inc ....E......310 280-7800
8500 Steller Dr Ste 5 Culver City (90232) ***(P-17071)***
Woobo Distribution ....F......714 522-5505
16261 Phoebe Ave La Mirada (90638) ***(P-2162)***
Wood Bros Inc ....D......559 924-7715
14147 18th Ave Lemoore (93245) ***(P-1009)***
Wood Castle Construction Inc ....E......626 966-8600
770 W Golden Grove Way Covina (91722) ***(P-653)***
Wood Gutmann Bogart Insur Brkg ....D......714 505-7000
15901 Red Hill Ave # 100 Tustin (92780) ***(P-15651)***
Wood Smith Henning Berman LLP (PA) ....**E......310 481-7600**
10960 Wilshire Blvd Fl 18 Los Angeles (90024) ***(P-21700)***
Wood Space Industries Inc ....F......714 996-4552
429 W Levers Pl Orange (92867) ***(P-12272)***
Woodbine Lgacy/Playa Owner LLC ....D......678 292-4962
6161 W Centinela Ave Culver City (90230) ***(P-16803)***
Woodbridge Glass, Tustin *Also called Werner Systems Inc* ***(P-6330)***
Woodbridge Glass Inc ....C......714 838-4444
14321 Myford Rd Tustin (92780) ***(P-1590)***
Woodbridge Village Association ....D......949 786-1800
31 Creek Rd Irvine (92604) ***(P-22378)***
Woodie Woodpeckers Woodworks ....F......818 999-2090
21268 Deering Ct Canoga Park (91304) ***(P-3347)***
Woodland Bedrooms Inc ....F......562 408-1558
3423 Merced St Los Angeles (90065) ***(P-3492)***
Woodman Realty Inc ....C......909 425-5324
26030 Base Line St Apt 97 San Bernardino (92410) ***(P-16034)***

ALPHABETIC

Woodmill Seating Inc F 909 622-1615
1250 E Franklin Ave Pomona (91766) *(P-3301)*
Woodpecker Cabinet Inc E 310 404-4805
21512 Nordhoff St Chatsworth (91311) *(P-3348)*
Woodruff Spradlin & Smart D 714 558-7000
555 Anton Blvd Ste 1200 Costa Mesa (92626) *(P-21701)*
Woodruff Convalescent Center, Duarte *Also called Estrella Inc (P-20337)*
Woods Electric Company, Santa Fe Springs *Also called Harris L Woods Elec Contr (P-1262)*
Woods Maintenance Services Inc C 818 764-2515
7250 Coldwater Canyon Ave North Hollywood (91605) *(P-1704)*
Woodville Inc F 323 636-0223
11680 Wright Rd Lynwood (90262) *(P-3493)*
Woodward Duarte, Duarte *Also called Woodward Hrt Inc (P-10445)*
Woodward Hrt Inc (HQ) A **661 294-6000**
25200 Rye Canyon Rd Santa Clarita (91355) *(P-8967)*
Woodward Hrt Inc C 626 359-9211
1700 Business Center Dr Duarte (91010) *(P-10445)*
Woodwork Pioneers Corp E 714 991-1017
1757 S Claudina Way Anaheim (92805) *(P-3302)*
Woojin Is America Inc F 626 386-0101
12521 Mccann Dr Santa Fe Springs (90670) *(P-10479)*
Woongjin Coway USA Inc., Los Angeles *Also called Coway Usa Inc (P-8045)*
Word and Brown, Orange *Also called Omega Insurance Services (P-15604)*
Word and Brown Hearing Ctr, Orange *Also called Providence Speech Hearing Ctr (P-21330)*
Word For Today D 714 825-9673
3232 W Macarthur Blvd A Santa Ana (92704) *(P-4145)*
Work Force Services Inc C 661 327-5019
1811 Oak St Bakersfield (93301) *(P-17532)*
Work Force Staffing, Bakersfield *Also called Work Force Services Inc (P-17532)*
Work Inc C 805 739-0451
3070 Skyway Dr Ste 104 Santa Maria (93455) *(P-21931)*
Workbook Inc F 323 856-0008
110 N Doheny Dr Beverly Hills (90211) *(P-4146)*
Workcare Inc C 714 978-7488
300 S Harbor Blvd Ste 600 Anaheim (92805) *(P-23399)*
Workforce Enterprises Wfe Inc E 909 718-8915
800 N Haven Ave Ste 330 Ontario (91764) *(P-17479)*
Working With Autism Inc D 818 501-4240
14724 Ventura Blvd # 1110 Sherman Oaks (91403) *(P-21367)*
Workmens Auto Insurance Co D 213 742-8700
714 W Olympic Blvd # 800 Los Angeles (90015) *(P-15491)*
Workrite Uniform Company Inc (HQ) B **805 483-0175**
1701 Lombard St Ste 200 Oxnard (93030) *(P-16887)*
Works Entertainment LLC E 310 623-7436
11333 Iowa Ave Los Angeles (90025) *(P-19386)*
Works Floor & Wall, The, Palm Desert *Also called Temalpakh Inc (P-839)*
Worksite Labs Inc D 657 444-9146
1890 E Miraloma Ave Ste D Placentia (92870) *(P-22962)*
Workway Inc C 949 553-8700
19742 Macarthur Blvd # 235 Irvine (92612) *(P-17480)*
World Acceptance Group Corp (PA) D **800 388-1266**
3255 Chnga Blvd W Ste 301 Los Angeles (90068) *(P-18136)*
World Class Cheerleading Inc E 877 923-2645
20212 Hart St Winnetka (91306) *(P-11462)*
World Class Distribution Inc D 909 574-4140
800 S Shamrock Ave Monrovia (91016) *(P-12261)*
World Class Distribution Inc D 909 574-4140
343 S Lena Rd San Bernardino (92408) *(P-12262)*
World Class Distribution Inc (HQ) C **909 574-4140**
10288 Calabash Ave Fontana (92335) *(P-12263)*
World Journal La LLC (HQ) C **323 268-4982**
1588 Corporate Center Dr Monterey Park (91754) *(P-4046)*
World Mvie Awrds Orgnztion Wma D 833 375-5857
9171 Wilshire Blvd 500a Beverly Hills (90210) *(P-22379)*
World Oil Corp B 562 928-0100
9302 Garfield Ave South Gate (90280) *(P-417)*
World Oil Marketing Company (PA) E **562 928-0100**
9302 Garfield Ave South Gate (90280) *(P-5278)*
World Peas Brand, Los Angeles *Also called Snack It Forward LLC (P-2366)*
World Private Security Inc C 818 894-1800
16921 Parthenia St # 201 Northridge (91343) *(P-18360)*
WORLD SERVICE OFFICE, Chatsworth *Also called Narcotics Annymous Wrld Svcs I (P-4134)*
World Svc Wst/La Inflght Svc L C 310 538-7000
1812 W 135th St Gardena (90249) *(P-12374)*
World Trade Ctr Ht Assoc Ltd D 562 983-3400
701 W Ocean Blvd Long Beach (90831) *(P-16804)*
World Trade Printing Company, Garden Grove *Also called Wtpc Inc (P-4462)*
World Trend Inc (PA) F **909 620-9945**
1920 W Holt Ave Pomona (91768) *(P-11516)*
World Upholstery & Trim Inc F 805 921-0100
1320 E Main St Santa Paula (93060) *(P-3185)*
World Variety Produce Inc B 800 588-0151
5325 S Soto St Vernon (90058) *(P-14668)*
World Vision International (HQ) C **626 303-8811**
800 W Chestnut Ave Monrovia (91016) *(P-22471)*
World Water Inc E 562 940-1964
9848 Everest St Downey (90242) *(P-10731)*
World Wind & Solar, Tehachapi *Also called World Wind Electrical Svcs Inc (P-1338)*
World Wind & Solar, Paso Robles *Also called Worldwind Services LLC (P-1339)*
World Wind Electrical Svcs Inc A 661 822-4877
228 W Tehachapi Blvd Tehachapi (93561) *(P-1338)*
Worldlink East, Los Angeles *Also called Worldlink LLC (P-18730)*
Worldlink LLC (PA) D **323 866-5900**
6100 Wilshire Blvd # 1400 Los Angeles (90048) *(P-18730)*
Worldmark At Palm Springs, Palm Springs *Also called Worldmark Club (P-16805)*
Worldmark Club D 760 416-4428
1177 N Palm Canyon Dr Palm Springs (92262) *(P-16805)*
Worldstage Inc (PA) D **714 508-1858**
1111 Bell Ave Ste A Tustin (92780) *(P-23142)*
Worldwide Inc D 310 276-7171
9601 Wilshire Blvd Beverly Hills (90210) *(P-16035)*
Worldwide Aeros Corp D 818 344-3999
1734 Aeros Way Montebello (90640) *(P-10207)*
Worldwide Corporate Housing LP C 972 392-4747
1 World Trade Ctr # 2400 Long Beach (90831) *(P-16814)*
Worldwide Corporate Housing LP (HQ) A **562 473-7371**
1 World Trade Ctr # 2400 Long Beach (90831) *(P-16815)*
Worldwide Envmtl Pdts Inc (PA) D **714 990-2700**
1100 Beacon St Brea (92821) *(P-10732)*
Worldwide Holdings Inc (PA) D **213 236-4500**
725 S Figueroa St # 1900 Los Angeles (90017) *(P-15652)*
Worldwide Intgrted Rsurces Inc D 323 838-8938
7171 Telegraph Rd Montebello (90640) *(P-14047)*
Worldwide Produce, Los Angeles *Also called Green Farms California LLC (P-14635)*
Worldwide Security Assoc Inc (HQ) B **310 743-3000**
10311 S La Cienega Blvd Los Angeles (90045) *(P-18361)*
Worldwide Specialties Inc C 323 587-2200
2420 Modoc St Los Angeles (90021) *(P-2548)*
Worldwind Services LLC A 661 822-4877
1222 Vine St Ste 301 Paso Robles (93446) *(P-1339)*
Worley Field Services Inc D 310 816-8939
2422 E 223rd St Carson (90810) *(P-23544)*
Worley Field Services Inc D 949 224-7585
2600 Michelson Dr Ste 500 Irvine (92612) *(P-1010)*
Worxsitehr Insur Solutions Inc D 877 479-3591
5000 Parkway Calabasas # 302 Calabasas (91302) *(P-15653)*
Wovexx Holdings Inc (HQ) D **310 424-2080**
10381 Jefferson Blvd Culver City (90232) *(P-12794)*
Wp Electric Communications Inc E 909 606-3510
14198 Albers Way Chino (91710) *(P-1340)*
Wpa Worldwide Production Agcy (PA) D **310 659-9965**
144 N Robertson Blvd West Hollywood (90048) *(P-19212)*
Wpromote LLC (PA) C **310 421-4844**
2100 E Grand Ave Fl 1 El Segundo (90245) *(P-23368)*
Wrap News Inc E 424 248-0612
2260 S Centinela Ave # 15 Los Angeles (90064) *(P-18408)*
Wrap, The, Los Angeles *Also called Wrap News Inc (P-18408)*
Wright Finlay & Zak LLP D 949 477-5050
4665 Macarthur Ct Ste 200 Newport Beach (92660) *(P-21702)*
Wright Bus Graphics Cal Inc F 800 310-3676
13602 12th St Ste A Chino (91710) *(P-14201)*
Wright Business Graphics Calif, Chino *Also called Wright Business Graphics LLC (P-4604)*
Wright Business Graphics LLC E 909 614-6700
13602 12th St Ste A Chino (91710) *(P-4604)*
Writers Guild America West Inc C 323 951-4000
7000 W 3rd St Los Angeles (90048) *(P-22307)*
Writing Company, Culver City *Also called Social Studies School Service (P-13541)*
Ws Packaging-Blake Printery E 805 543-6844
2224 Beebee St San Luis Obispo (93401) *(P-4461)*
Wsa Group Inc (PA) E **310 743-3000**
19208 S Vermont Ave 200 Gardena (90248) *(P-18362)*
WSH&b, Los Angeles *Also called Wood Smith Henning Berman LLP (P-21700)*
Wsm Investments LLC C 818 332-4600
3990b Heritage Oak Ct Simi Valley (93063) *(P-16224)*
Wsp USA Inc D 714 973-4880
1100 W Town And Cntry 2 Orange (92868) *(P-22701)*
Wsr Publishing Inc (PA) F **951 676-4914**
27645 Commerce Center Dr Temecula (92590) *(P-4113)*
Wsw Corp (PA) E **818 989-5008**
16000 Strathern St Van Nuys (91406) *(P-10160)*
Wt Partnership, Santa Monica *Also called Wtp America LLC (P-23528)*
Wtb Technology F 661 327-9604
245 Industrial St Bakersfield (93307) *(P-5163)*
Wti, Ventura *Also called Wireless Technology Inc (P-9210)*
Wti Distribution Inc D 909 597-8410
5491 E Francis St Ontario (91761) *(P-12264)*
Wtp America LLC (HQ) D **310 356-4636**
520 Broadway Ste 200 Santa Monica (90401) *(P-23528)*
Wtpc Inc E 714 903-2500
12082 Western Ave Garden Grove (92841) *(P-4462)*
Wun, Goleta *Also called Yardi Kube Inc (P-18013)*
Wurms Janitorial Service Inc D 951 582-0003
544 Bateman Cir Corona (92878) *(P-17301)*
Wurth Louis and Company (HQ) D **714 529-1771**
895 Columbia St Brea (92821) *(P-13821)*
WV Communications Inc E 805 376-1820
1125 Bus Ctr Cir Ste A Newbury Park (91320) *(P-9328)*
Wwcot Architects, Riverside *Also called Dlr Group Inc (P-22714)*
Wwf Operating Company LLC E 626 810-1775
18275 Arenth Ave Bldg 1 City of Industry (91748) *(P-1842)*
Www.b-Dazzle.com, Redondo Beach *Also called B Dazzle Inc (P-11367)*
Wyatt Precision Machine Inc E 562 634-0524
3301 E 59th St Long Beach (90805) *(P-7051)*
Wyatt Technology Corporation (PA) C **805 681-9009**
6330 Hollister Ave Goleta (93117) *(P-10820)*
Wyland Galleries, Rcho STA Marg *Also called Wyland International LLC (P-14987)*
Wyland International LLC (PA) E **949 643-7070**
30265 Tomas Rcho STA Marg (92688) *(P-14987)*
Wyle Services Corporation (HQ) A **310 563-6800**
1960 E Grand Ave Ste 900 El Segundo (90245) *(P-22702)*
Wymore Inc E 760 352-2045
697 S Dogwood Rd El Centro (92243) *(P-19005)*
Wynden Stark LLC (HQ) C **424 271-4156**
1038 Princeton Dr Ste B Marina Del Rey (90292) *(P-17481)*

Wyndham - Santa Monica, Santa Monica *Also called Djont/Jpm Hsptlity Lsg Spe LLC* ***(P-16412)***
Wyndham Anaheim Garden Grove, Garden Grove *Also called Ohi Resort Hotels LLC* ***(P-16591)***
Wyndham Collection LLC ....E....888 522-8476
1175 Aviation Pl San Fernando (91340) ***(P-3349)***
Wyndham Garden Pierpont Inn, Ventura *Also called Fpl LLC* ***(P-16449)***
Wyndham Hotels & Resorts, Fullerton *Also called Anaheim Park Hotel* ***(P-16323)***
Wyndham International Inc ....C....714 992-1700
222 W Houston Ave Fullerton (92832) ***(P-16806)***
Wynne Systems Inc (HQ) ....D....949 224-6300
2601 Main St Ste 270 Irvine (92614) ***(P-17762)***
Wyrefab Inc ....E....310 523-2147
15711 S Broadway Gardena (90248) ***(P-7524)***
Wytcote Inc ....F....877 472-5587
3 Park Plz Ste 480 Irvine (92614) ***(P-18075)***
Wyvern Technologies ....E....714 966-0710
1205 E Warner Ave Santa Ana (92705) ***(P-9803)***
X Prize Foundation Inc ....E....310 741-4880
800 Crprate Pinte Ste 350 Culver City (90230) ***(P-22926)***
X Weapon Security ....D....818 818-9950
297 Country Club Dr Simi Valley (93065) ***(P-23545)***
X-Act Finish & Trim Inc ....D....951 582-9229
248 Glider Cir Corona (92878) ***(P-1465)***
X-Igent Printing Inc ....F....323 837-9779
1001 Goodrich Blvd Commerce (90022) ***(P-4463)***
X1 Discovery Inc ....E....877 999-1347
617 W 7th St Ste 604 Los Angeles (90017) ***(P-17763)***
Xanterra Parks & Resorts Inc ....C....760 786-2345
Hwy 190 Death Valley (92328) ***(P-16807)***
Xantrex LLC (HQ) ....D....800 241-3897
15272 Newsboy Cir Huntington Beach (92649) ***(P-8984)***
Xbiz ....F....310 820-0228
4929 Wilshire Blvd # 960 Los Angeles (90010) ***(P-4114)***
Xcast Labs Inc (PA) ....C....310 861-4700
1880 Century Park E # 1415 Los Angeles (90067) ***(P-17764)***
Xceed Financial Credit Union (PA) ....D....800 932-8222
888 N Nash St El Segundo (90245) ***(P-15104)***
XCEL Mechanical Systems Inc ....C....310 660-0090
1710 W 130th St Gardena (90249) ***(P-1163)***
Xcelerium Inc ....F....949 244-3668
530 Technology Dr Ste 100 Irvine (92618) ***(P-9606)***
Xcom Wireless Inc ....F....562 981-0077
2700 Rose Ave Ste E Signal Hill (90755) ***(P-9329)***
Xcvi LLC (PA) ....C....213 749-2661
2311 S Santa Fe Ave Los Angeles (90058) ***(P-2594)***
Xdbs Corporation ....D....844 932-7356
3501 Jack Northrop Ave Hawthorne (90250) ***(P-22899)***
Xdbsb2b, Hawthorne *Also called Xdbs Corporation* ***(P-22899)***
Xdr Radiology, Los Angeles *Also called Cyber Medical Imaging Inc* ***(P-11165)***
XEL Group, Aliso Viejo *Also called XEL USA Inc* ***(P-9607)***
XEL USA Inc ....E....949 425-8686
21 Argonaut Ste B Aliso Viejo (92656) ***(P-9607)***
Xencor Inc ....C....626 305-5900
111 W Lemon Ave Monrovia (91016) ***(P-4914)***
Xenel International USA (HQ) ....F....805 496-2227
2637 Townsgate Rd Ste 300 Westlake Village (91361) ***(P-16117)***
Xerox Education Services LLC (HQ) ....D....310 830-9847
2277 E 220th St Long Beach (90810) ***(P-13370)***
Xerxes Corporation ....E....714 630-0012
1210 N Tustin Ave Anaheim (92807) ***(P-4729)***
Xgrass Turf Direct, Anaheim *Also called Leonards Carpet Service Inc* ***(P-3658)***
Xi Enterprise Inc ....D....661 266-3200
2140 E Palmdale Blvd Palmdale (93550) ***(P-19473)***
Xidas Inc ....F....949 930-0147
46 Waterworks Way Irvine (92618) ***(P-9804)***
Xirgo Technologies LLC ....D....805 319-4079
188 Camino Ruiz Fl 2 Camarillo (93012) ***(P-9931)***
Xirrus Inc ....D....805 262-1600
2545 W Hillcrest Dr # 220 Newbury Park (91320) ***(P-10733)***
Xld Group LLC ....D....310 316-3636
3635 Fashion Way Torrance (90503) ***(P-16808)***
Xlr8 Services Inc ....E....949 498-9578
1020 Calle Negocio Ste A San Clemente (92673) ***(P-22703)***
Xlsoft Corporation ....F....949 453-2781
12 Mauchly Ste K Irvine (92618) ***(P-18012)***
Xmultiple Technologies (PA) ....E....805 579-1100
543 Country Club Dr B-128 Simi Valley (93065) ***(P-8185)***
Xmultiple/Xrjax, Simi Valley *Also called Xmultiple Technologies* ***(P-8185)***
Xorail Inc ....C....904 443-0083
430 N Vineyard Ave # 220 Ontario (91764) ***(P-22704)***
Xos Inc ....C....818 316-1890
3550 Tyburn St Unit 100 Los Angeles (90065) ***(P-9832)***
Xos Fleet Inc ....E....818 316-1890
3550 Tyburn St Los Angeles (90065) ***(P-9974)***
Xos Trucks, Los Angeles *Also called Xos Fleet Inc* ***(P-9974)***
Xp Power Inc ....D....714 712-2642
1590 S Sinclair St Anaheim (92806) ***(P-9805)***
Xp Power LLC ....D....714 597-7100
15641 Red Hill Ave # 100 Tustin (92780) ***(P-13786)***
Xp Systems Corporation (HQ) ....C....805 532-9100
405 Science Dr Moorpark (93021) ***(P-18076)***
Xperience Restaurant Group (PA) ....D....562 346-1200
11065 Knott Ave Ste A Cypress (90630) ***(P-23143)***
Xplain Corporation ....E....805 494-9797
705 Lakefield Rd Ste I Westlake Village (91361) ***(P-4115)***
Xpo Logistics Freight Inc ....D....760 768-0280
298 Rood Rd Calexico (92231) ***(P-12093)***
Xpo Logistics Freight Inc ....D....805 541-4581
219a Tank Farm Rd San Luis Obispo (93401) ***(P-12094)***
Xpo Logistics Freight Inc ....D....661 324-2947
226 Washington St Bakersfield (93307) ***(P-12095)***
Xpo Logistics Freight Inc ....D....818 890-2095
12466 Montague St Pacoima (91331) ***(P-12096)***
Xpo Logistics Freight Inc ....D....714 282-7717
2102 N Batavia St Orange (92865) ***(P-12097)***
Xpo Logistics Freight Inc ....D....805 485-6466
2900 Camino Del Sol Oxnard (93030) ***(P-12098)***
Xpo Logistics Freight Inc ....D....949 581-9030
20697 Prism Pl Lake Forest (92630) ***(P-12099)***
Xpo Logistics Freight Inc ....D....213 744-0664
1955 E Washington Blvd Los Angeles (90021) ***(P-12100)***
Xpo Logistics Freight Inc ....D....760 922-8538
12555 Mesa Dr Blythe (92225) ***(P-12101)***
Xpo Logistics Freight Inc ....D....951 685-1244
13364 Marlay Ave Fontana (92337) ***(P-12102)***
Xpo Logistics Freight Inc ....D....562 946-8331
12903 Lakeland Rd Santa Fe Springs (90670) ***(P-12103)***
Xpo Stacktrain LLC ....C....310 661-4000
2700 E Imperial Hwy Lynwood (90262) ***(P-12552)***
Xponential Fitness Inc (HQ) ....B....949 346-3000
17877 Von Karman Ave # 100 Irvine (92614) ***(P-19474)***
Xpower Manufacture Inc ....E....626 285-3301
668 S 6th Ave City of Industry (91746) ***(P-10672)***
Xr LLC ....E....714 847-9292
15251 Pipeline Ln Huntington Beach (92649) ***(P-11155)***
Xrp Inc (PA) ....F....562 861-4765
5630 Imperial Hwy South Gate (90280) ***(P-10161)***
Xs Scuba Inc (PA) ....E....714 424-0434
4040 W Chandler Ave Santa Ana (92704) ***(P-11463)***
Xse Group Inc ....C....888 272-8340
92 Argonaut Ste 235 Aliso Viejo (92656) ***(P-14202)***
Xsential, Gardena *Also called Techflex Packaging LLC* ***(P-14978)***
Xy Corp Inc ....F....760 323-0333
1258 Montalvo Way Ste A Palm Springs (92262) ***(P-7770)***
Xzavier, Vernon *Also called Mjck Corporation* ***(P-2639)***
Y B S Enterprises Inc ....F....818 848-7790
3116 W Vanowen St Burbank (91505) ***(P-9246)***
Y I C, Carson *Also called Yun Industrial Co Ltd* ***(P-9470)***
Y&R-Wcj Spectrum, Irvine *Also called Young & Rubicam LLC* ***(P-17072)***
Yaesu Usa Inc ....E....714 827-7600
6125 Phyllis Dr Cypress (90630) ***(P-9330)***
Yamaha Corporation of America (HQ) ....B....714 522-9011
6600 Orangethorpe Ave Buena Park (90620) ***(P-14186)***
Yamaha Guitar Group Inc (HQ) ....C....818 575-3600
26580 Agoura Rd Calabasas (91302) ***(P-11355)***
Yamaha Guitar Group Inc ....E....818 575-3900
26664 Agoura Rd Calabasas (91302) ***(P-11356)***
Yamaha Motor Corporation USA (HQ) ....B....714 761-7300
6555 Katella Ave Cypress (90630) ***(P-13109)***
Yamaha Music Corporation U S A, Buena Park *Also called Yamaha Corporation of America* ***(P-14186)***
Yamajirushi Miso, Baldwin Park *Also called Miyako Oriental Foods Inc* ***(P-2119)***
Yamamoto of Orient Inc (HQ) ....C....909 594-7356
122 Voyager St Pomona (91768) ***(P-15714)***
YAMAMOTOYAMA OF AMERICA, Pomona *Also called Yamamoto of Orient Inc* ***(P-15714)***
Yamasa Enterprises ....E....213 626-2211
515 Stanford Ave Los Angeles (90013) ***(P-2343)***
Yamasa Fish Cake, Los Angeles *Also called Yamasa Enterprises* ***(P-2343)***
Yamazaki California Inc ....F....213 624-2773
123 Japanese Vlg Plz Mall Los Angeles (90012) ***(P-2054)***
Yang-Ming International Corp ....E....626 956-0100
595 Yorbita Rd La Puente (91744) ***(P-18077)***
Yankee Doodles, Marina Del Rey *Also called 3rd Street Billiard Club Inc* ***(P-19630)***
Yankon Industries Inc (PA) ....E....909 591-2345
13445 12th St Chino (91710) ***(P-9112)***
Yardi Kube Inc ....E....805 699-2040
430 S Fairview Ave Goleta (93117) ***(P-18013)***
Yardi Systems Inc (PA) ....B....951 203-6951
430 S Fairview Ave Santa Barbara (93117) ***(P-17765)***
Yardney Water MGT Systems, Riverside *Also called Yardney Water MGT Systems Inc* ***(P-8429)***
Yardney Water MGT Systems Inc (PA) ....E....951 656-6716
6666 Box Springs Blvd Riverside (92507) ***(P-8429)***
Yates & Associates, Santa Ana *Also called Scottish American Insurance* ***(P-15625)***
Yavar Manufacturing Co Inc ....E....323 722-2040
1900 S Tubeway Ave Commerce (90040) ***(P-3847)***
Yawitz Inc ....E....909 865-5599
1379 Ridgeway St Pomona (91768) ***(P-9075)***
Ybcc Inc ....E....626 213-3945
17800 Castleton St # 386 City of Industry (91748) ***(P-1808)***
Yeager Enterprises Corp ....D....714 994-2040
7100 Village Dr Buena Park (90621) ***(P-6162)***
Yeager Manufacturing Corp (PA) ....E....714 879-2800
2320 E Orangethorpe Ave Anaheim (92806) ***(P-10446)***
Yebo Group Inc ....E....949 502-3317
2652 Dow Ave Tustin (92780) ***(P-3780)***
Yebo Printing, Tustin *Also called Yebo Group Inc* ***(P-3780)***
Yee Yuen Laundry and Clrs Inc ....D....323 734-7205
2575 S Normandie Ave Los Angeles (90007) ***(P-16870)***
Yee Yuen Linen Service, Los Angeles *Also called Yee Yuen Laundry and Clrs Inc* ***(P-16870)***
Yellow Magic Incorporated ....F....951 506-4005
41571 Date St Murrieta (92562) ***(P-18014)***
Yellowpagescom LLC (HQ) ....B....818 937-5500
611 N Brand Blvd Ste 500 Glendale (91203) ***(P-18731)***

Employee Codes: A=Over 500 employees, B=251-500 C=101-250, D=51-100, E=20-50 F=10-19
2022 Southern California Business Directory and Buyers Guide
© Mergent Inc. 1-800-342-5647
1323

Yen-Nhai Inc ....E....323 584-1315
4940 District Blvd Vernon (90058) ***(P-3522)***
Yes To Carrots, Pasadena *Also called Yes To Inc* ***(P-5084)***
Yes To Inc ....E....626 365-1976
177 E Colo Blvd Ste 110 Pasadena (91105) ***(P-5084)***
Yesco, Jurupa Valley *Also called Young Electric Sign Company* ***(P-11616)***
Yeshiva Rav Isacsohn Academy, Los Angeles *Also called Yeshivath Torath Emeth Academy* ***(P-22074)***
Yeshivath Torath Emeth Academy (PA) ....**C....323 549-3170**
540 N La Brea Ave Los Angeles (90036) ***(P-22074)***
Yesterdays Sportswear, Paso Robles *Also called Lakeshirts LLC* ***(P-3157)***
Yew Bio-Pharm Group Inc (PA) ....**D....626 401-9588**
9460 Telstar Ave Ste 6 El Monte (91731) ***(P-369)***
Yf Art Holdings Gp LLC ....A....678 441-1400
9130 W Sunset Blvd Los Angeles (90069) ***(P-16118)***
Yf Manufacture Inc ....F....626 768-0029
2455 Maple Ave Pomona (91767) ***(P-6007)***
Yhb Long Beach LLC ....D....562 597-4401
2640 N Lakewood Blvd Long Beach (90815) ***(P-16809)***
Yinlun Tdi LLC (HQ) ....**C....909 390-3944**
4850 E Airport Dr Ontario (91761) ***(P-10162)***
Ymarketing LLC ....D....714 545-2550
4000 Macarthur Blvd # 350 Newport Beach (92660) ***(P-23369)***
YMCA, Burbank *Also called Young MNS Chrstn Assn Brbank C* ***(P-22385)***
YMCA, Alhambra *Also called Young Men Chrstn Assoc W San G* ***(P-21932)***
YMCA, Los Angeles *Also called Young MNS Chrstn Assn Mtro Los* ***(P-22386)***
YMCA, Santa Maria *Also called Santa Mria Vly Yung MNS Chrstn* ***(P-22366)***
YMCA Camp Edwards, Angelus Oaks *Also called YMCA of East Valley* ***(P-22381)***
YMCA CRESCENTA-CANADA, La Canada *Also called Crescenta-Canada YMCA* ***(P-22334)***
YMCA of East Valley (PA) ....**C....909 798-9622**
500 E Citrus Ave Redlands (92373) ***(P-22380)***
YMCA of East Valley ....D....909 794-1702
42842 Jenks Lake Rd E Angelus Oaks (92305) ***(P-22381)***
YMCA of East Valley ....D....909 881-9622
808 E 21st St San Bernardino (92404) ***(P-22382)***
YMCA of East Valley ....D....909 425-9622
7793 Central Ave Highland (92346) ***(P-22383)***
YMCA Simi Valley Family, Simi Valley *Also called Young MNS Chrstn Assn Sthast V* ***(P-22389)***
Ymi Jeanswear, Los Angeles *Also called YMi Jeanswear Inc* ***(P-2901)***
YMi Jeanswear Inc (PA) ....**F....323 581-7700**
1155 S Boyle Ave Los Angeles (90023) ***(P-2901)***
YMi Jeanswear Inc ....D....213 746-6681
1015 Wall St Ste 115 Los Angeles (90015) ***(P-3010)***
Yobs Technologies Inc ....E....213 713-3825
615 Childs Way 370 Los Angeles (90089) ***(P-19213)***
Yocup Company ....F....310 884-9888
13711 S Main St Los Angeles (90061) ***(P-3844)***
Yoga Works Inc (HQ) ....**E....310 664-6470**
2215 Main St Santa Monica (90405) ***(P-19475)***
Yogaworks, Santa Monica *Also called Yoga Works Inc* ***(P-19475)***
Yogaworks Inc (HQ) ....**D....310 664-6470**
5780 Uplander Way Culver City (90230) ***(P-19682)***
Yogurtland Franchising Inc (PA) ....**D....949 265-8000**
17801 Cartwright Rd Irvine (92614) ***(P-16225)***
Yokohama Corp North America (HQ) ....**C....540 389-5426**
1 Macarthur Pl Ste 800 Santa Ana (92707) ***(P-5307)***
Yokohama Tire, Santa Ana *Also called Yokohama Corp North America* ***(P-5307)***
Yonekyu USA Inc ....D....323 581-4194
611 N 20th St Montebello (90640) ***(P-1755)***
Yoplait U S A Inc ....F....310 632-9502
1055 Sandhill Ave Carson (90746) ***(P-1843)***
Yorba Linda Country Club, Garden Grove *Also called Sanyo Foods Corp America* ***(P-2383)***
Yorba Park Medical Group, Santa Ana *Also called St Jseph Heritg Med Group LLC* ***(P-20096)***
York Employment Services Inc ....D....909 581-0181
980 Ontario Mills Dr C Ontario (91764) ***(P-17482)***
York Enterprises South Inc ....D....714 842-6611
18255 Beach Blvd Huntington Beach (92648) ***(P-18888)***
Yosemite Capital Mangagement, Newport Beach *Also called Hmwc Cpas & Business Advisors* ***(P-22789)***
Yoshimasa Display Case Inc ....E....213 637-9999
108 Pico St Pomona (91766) ***(P-3672)***
Yoshimura RES & Dev Amer Inc ....D....909 628-4722
5420 Daniels St Ste A Chino (91710) ***(P-13110)***
Youbar Inc ....D....626 537-1851
445 Wilson Way City of Industry (91744) ***(P-14567)***
Youbetcom Inc (HQ) ....**D....818 668-2100**
2600 W Olive Ave Fl 5 Burbank (91505) ***(P-19436)***
Youcare Pharma (usa) Inc ....D....951 258-3114
132 Business Center Dr Corona (92878) ***(P-4915)***
Young & Rubicam LLC ....B....949 754-2000
7535 Irvine Center Dr Irvine (92618) ***(P-17072)***
Young & Rubicam LLC ....C....949 754-2100
7535 Irvine Center Dr Irvine (92618) ***(P-17073)***
Young & Rubicam LLC ....C....213 930-5000
4751 Wilshire Blvd # 201 Los Angeles (90010) ***(P-17074)***
Young & Rubicam LLC ....B....949 224-6300
1735 Irvine Center Dr Irvine (92618) ***(P-23370)***
Young Dental, Cerritos *Also called US Dental Inc* ***(P-11200)***
Young Electric Sign Company ....E....909 923-7668
10235 Bellegrave Ave Jurupa Valley (91752) ***(P-11616)***
Young Engineering & Mfg Inc (PA) ....**E....909 394-3225**
560 W Terrace Dr San Dimas (91773) ***(P-10734)***
Young Engineers Inc ....D....949 581-9411
25841 Commercentre Dr Lake Forest (92630) ***(P-6545)***
Young Knitting Mills ....E....323 980-8677
3499 E 15th St Los Angeles (90023) ***(P-2644)***
Young Machine Inc ....F....909 464-0405
12282 Colony Ave Chino (91710) ***(P-8858)***
Young Men Chrstn Assoc W San G (PA) ....**D....626 576-0226**
401 Corto St Alhambra (91801) ***(P-21932)***
Young Mens Christian Associat ....D....562 524-2376
525 E 7th St Long Beach (90813) ***(P-22384)***
Young Mens Christn Assocation, Highland *Also called YMCA of East Valley* ***(P-22383)***
Young MNS Chrstn Assn Brbank C (PA) ....**D....818 845-8551**
321 E Magnolia Blvd Burbank (91502) ***(P-22385)***
Young MNS Chrstn Assn Mtro Los (PA) ....**D....213 380-6448**
625 S New Hampshire Ave Los Angeles (90005) ***(P-22386)***
Young MNS Chrstn Assn Mtro Los ....E....818 763-5126
5142 Tujunga Ave North Hollywood (91601) ***(P-22075)***
Young MNS Chrstn Assn of Glnda ....D....818 484-8256
140 N Louise St Glendale (91206) ***(P-22387)***
Young MNS Chrstn Assn Sthast V ....E....805 520-6775
2925 Fletcher St Simi Valley (93065) ***(P-22388)***
Young MNS Chrstn Assn Sthast V ....E....805 527-5730
828 Gibson Ave Simi Valley (93065) ***(P-22389)***
Young MNS Chrstn Assn Sthast V ....D....805 583-5338
3200 Cochran St Simi Valley (93065) ***(P-19683)***
Young MNS Chrstn Assn Sthast V ....E....805 523-7613
4031 N Moorpark Rd Thousand Oaks (91360) ***(P-22390)***
Young Realtors ....D....805 497-0947
971 S Westlake Blvd # 100 Westlake Village (91361) ***(P-16036)***
Young Sung (usa) Inc ....F....213 427-2580
1122 S Alvarado St Los Angeles (90006) ***(P-3202)***
Young Wns Chrstn Assn Grter Lo ....D....323 295-4280
2501 W Vernon Ave Los Angeles (90008) ***(P-22391)***
Young Wns Chrstn Assn Grter Lo ....D....323 295-4288
2519 W Vernon Ave Los Angeles (90008) ***(P-22392)***
Younger Mfg Co (PA) ....**B....310 783-1533**
2925 California St Torrance (90503) ***(P-11266)***
Younger Optics, Torrance *Also called Younger Mfg Co* ***(P-11266)***
Youngs Holdings Inc (PA) ....**D....714 368-4615**
15 Enterprise Ste 100 Aliso Viejo (92656) ***(P-14847)***
Youngs Iron Works Inc ....F....818 768-3877
9133 De Garmo Ave Sun Valley (91352) ***(P-1585)***
Youngs Market Company LLC (HQ) ....**B....800 317-6150**
14402 Franklin Ave Tustin (92780) ***(P-14848)***
Youngs Market Company LLC ....D....213 629-3929
500 S Central Ave Los Angeles (90013) ***(P-14849)***
Youngs Market Company LLC ....D....909 393-4540
6711 Bickmore Ave Chino (91708) ***(P-14850)***
Your Practice Online LLC (PA) ....**D....877 388-8569**
4590 Macarthur Blvd # 500 Newport Beach (92660) ***(P-23371)***
Your Way Fumigation Inc ....D....951 699-9116
1660 Chicago Ave Ste N9 Riverside (92507) ***(P-17207)***
Yourtex Fashions Inc ....C....323 581-6600
2060 E Via Arado Compton (90220) ***(P-18732)***
Youth Enterprise Inc ....E....310 902-9266
231 E Alessndro Blvd Riverside (92508) ***(P-21368)***
Youth Services, Long Beach *Also called Altamed Health Services Corp* ***(P-21381)***
Youth To People Inc ....E....309 648-5500
708 Traction Ave Los Angeles (90013) ***(P-5085)***
Yti, San Pedro *Also called Yusen Terminals LLC* ***(P-12294)***
Yti Enterprises Inc ....F....714 632-8696
1260 S State College Pkwy Anaheim (92806) ***(P-3459)***
Yucaipa Companies LLC (PA) ....**C....310 789-7200**
9130 W Sunset Blvd Los Angeles (90069) ***(P-23529)***
Yucaipa Disposal Inc ....C....909 429-4200
9890 Cherry Ave Fontana (92335) ***(P-13002)***
Yucaipa Valley Water District (PA) ....**D....909 797-5117**
12770 2nd St Yucaipa (92399) ***(P-12923)***
Yuciapa & Calimesa News Mirror, Yucaipa *Also called Hi-Desert Publishing Company* ***(P-3986)***
Yue Feng Inc ....D....310 253-9795
145 S Fairfax Ave Los Angeles (90036) ***(P-21933)***
Yukevich / Cvanaugh A Law Corp (PA) ....**D....213 362-7777**
355 S Grand Ave Fl 15 Los Angeles (90071) ***(P-21703)***
Yuko Systems, Torrance *Also called Phiten Usa Inc* ***(P-16915)***
Yuma Lakes Resort, Earp *Also called Colorado River Adventures Inc* ***(P-16831)***
Yumi, Los Angeles *Also called Caer Inc* ***(P-1846)***
Yummy Foods LLC ....D....323 965-0600
5520 San Vicente Blvd Los Angeles (90019) ***(P-12009)***
Yun Industrial Co Ltd ....E....310 715-1898
161 Selandia Ln Carson (90746) ***(P-9470)***
Yuneec USA Inc ....D....855 284-8888
9227 Haven Ave Ste 210 Rancho Cucamonga (91730) ***(P-13787)***
Yusen Logistics Americas Inc ....C....310 518-3008
2417 E Carson St Ste 100 Carson (90810) ***(P-12553)***
Yusen Terminals LLC (HQ) ....**D....310 548-8000**
701 New Dock St San Pedro (90731) ***(P-12294)***
Yutaka Electric Intl Inc ....F....626 962-7770
5116 Azusa Canyon Rd Baldwin Park (91706) ***(P-8985)***
Yvonne J Bryson MD, Los Angeles *Also called Childrens Health Center* ***(P-19747)***
YWCA, Los Angeles *Also called Young Wns Chrstn Assn Grter Lo* ***(P-22391)***
YWCA of La-Burbank Blvd, North Hollywood *Also called Los Angeles Unified School Dst* ***(P-22346)***
Z B P Inc ....F....323 266-3363
2871 E Pico Blvd Los Angeles (90023) ***(P-3940)***
Z C & R Coating For Optics Inc ....E....310 381-3060
1401 Abalone Ave Torrance (90501) ***(P-10866)***
Z Industries, Los Angeles *Also called Active Window Products* ***(P-6687)***
Z Manufacturing Inc ....E....909 593-2191
2679 Sierra Way La Verne (91750) ***(P-7578)***
Z P M Inc ....E....805 681-3511
5770 Thornwood Dr Ste C Goleta (93117) ***(P-8430)***

Z-Barten Productions, Los Angeles *Also called Z B P Inc* ***(P-3940)***
Z-Best Concrete Inc.....D.....951 774-1870
2575 Main St Riverside (92501) ***(P-1558)***
Z-Tronix Inc.....E.....562 808-0800
6327 Alondra Blvd Paramount (90723) ***(P-9806)***
Za Management.....D.....310 271-2200
250 N Robertson Blvd # 10 Beverly Hills (90211) ***(P-23144)***
Zabin Industries Inc (PA).....**D.....213 749-1215**
3957 S Hill St Ste A Los Angeles (90037) ***(P-14324)***
Zaca Mesa Winery, Los Olivos *Also called Cushman Winery Corporation* ***(P-14839)***
Zada International Printing, Chatsworth *Also called Havana Graphic Center Inc* ***(P-4313)***
Zadara Storage Inc.....D.....949 251-0360
9245 Research Drv Irvine Irvine (92618) ***(P-8223)***
Zadro Inc.....E.....714 892-9200
14462 Astronautics Ln # 101 Huntington Beach (92647) ***(P-5972)***
Zadro Products Inc.....E.....714 892-9200
14462 Astronautics Ln # 101 Huntington Beach (92647) ***(P-5973)***
Zalemark Holding Company Inc.....F.....888 682-6885
15260 Ventura Blvd # 120 Sherman Oaks (91403) ***(P-11333)***
Zambezi LLC.....D.....310 450-6800
10441 Jefferson Blvd Culver City (90232) ***(P-17103)***
Zapp Packaging Inc.....D.....909 930-1500
1921 S Business Pkwy Ontario (91761) ***(P-3778)***
Zastrow Construction Inc.....D.....323 478-1956
3267 Verdugo Rd Los Angeles (90065) ***(P-675)***
Zbe Inc.....E.....805 576-1600
1035 Cindy Ln Carpinteria (93013) ***(P-8968)***
Zbs Law LLP.....D.....714 848-7920
30 Corporate Park Ste 450 Irvine (92606) ***(P-21704)***
Zebrasci Inc (PA).....**F.....800 217-3032**
27973 Diaz Rd Temecula (92590) ***(P-8002)***
Zeco Systems Inc.....D.....888 751-8560
767 S Alameda St Ste 200 Los Angeles (90021) ***(P-14798)***
Zee Consulting, Bakersfield *Also called Contrband Ctrl Specialists Inc* ***(P-5215)***
Zefr Inc.....C.....310 392-3555
4101 Redwood Ave Los Angeles (90066) ***(P-17766)***
Zeghani, Glendale *Also called Simon G Jewelry Inc* ***(P-14139)***
Zelouf West Ltd (PA).....**E.....213 417-1346**
110 E 9th St Ste B743 Los Angeles (90079) ***(P-2608)***
Zelzah Pharmacy Inc (PA).....**E.....818 609-0692**
17911 Ventura Blvd Encino (91316) ***(P-4916)***
Zemarc Corporation (PA).....**E.....323 721-5598**
6431 Flotilla St Commerce (90040) ***(P-13966)***
Zenana, Los Angeles *Also called Kc Exclusive Inc* ***(P-14389)***
Zenith A Fairfax Company, The, Woodland Hills *Also called Zenith Insurance Company* ***(P-15492)***
Zenith American Solutions Inc.....C.....626 732-2100
1325 N Grand Ave Ste 100 Covina (91724) ***(P-18733)***
Zenith Insurance Company, Woodland Hills *Also called Zenith National Insurance Corp* ***(P-15493)***
Zenith Insurance Company (HQ).....**B.....818 713-1000**
21255 Califa St Woodland Hills (91367) ***(P-15492)***
Zenith Manufacturing Inc.....E.....818 767-2106
3087 12th St Riverside (92507) ***(P-10447)***
Zenith National Insurance Corp (HQ).....**D.....818 713-1000**
21255 Califa St Woodland Hills (91367) ***(P-15493)***
Zenith Screw Products Inc.....E.....562 941-0281
10910 Painter Ave Santa Fe Springs (90670) ***(P-7052)***
Zenlayer Inc.....B.....909 718-3558
21680 Gateway Center Dr # 350 Diamond Bar (91765) ***(P-12680)***
Zenner Performance Meters Inc.....E.....951 849-8822
1910 E Westward Ave Banning (92220) ***(P-10740)***
Zensho USA Corporation.....A.....760 585-8455
27261 Las Ramblas Ste 240 Mission Viejo (92691) ***(P-23372)***
Zeons Inc.....B.....323 302-8299
291 S Cienega Blvd 102 Beverly Hills (90211) ***(P-5944)***
Zephyr Manufacturing Co Inc.....D.....310 410-4907
201 Hindry Ave Inglewood (90301) ***(P-7884)***
Zephyr Tool Group, Inglewood *Also called Zephyr Manufacturing Co Inc* ***(P-7884)***
Zephyr Tool Group, Inglewood *Also called Shg Holdings Corp* ***(P-7883)***
Zerep Management Corporation (PA).....**D.....626 968-1796**
17445 Railroad St City of Industry (91748) ***(P-13003)***
Zero Energy Contracting LLC.....D.....626 701-3180
13850 Cerritos Corprt Dr Cerritos (90703) ***(P-1164)***
Zero Gravity Corporation.....E.....805 388-8803
912 Pancho Rd Ste A Camarillo (93012) ***(P-10511)***
Zero Gravity Group, Camarillo *Also called Zero Gravity Corporation* ***(P-10511)***
Zerotruck.....F.....714 675-7117
3687 W Mcfadden Ave Santa Ana (92704) ***(P-9975)***
Zest.ai, Burbank *Also called Zestfinance Inc* ***(P-17767)***
Zestfinance Inc.....D.....323 450-3000
3900 W Alameda Ave Fl 30 Burbank (91505) ***(P-17767)***
Zet-Tek Machining, Yorba Linda *Also called Zet-Tek Precision Machining* ***(P-8859)***
Zet-Tek Precision Machining, Yorba Linda *Also called Pdma Ventures Inc* ***(P-11189)***
Zet-Tek Precision Machining (PA).....**F.....714 777-8770**
22951 La Palma Ave Yorba Linda (92887) ***(P-8859)***
Zettler Components Inc (PA).....**C.....949 831-5000**
75 Columbia Orange (92868) ***(P-13788)***
Zettler Magnetics Inc.....C.....949 831-5000
75 Columbia Aliso Viejo (92656) ***(P-8887)***
Zevia LLC.....D.....310 202-7000
15821 Ventura Blvd # 145 Encino (91436) ***(P-2304)***
Zia Aamir.....E.....714 337-7861
2043 Imperial St Los Angeles (90021) ***(P-6685)***
Zico Beverages LLC (HQ).....**D.....866 729-9426**
2101 E El Segundo Blvd # 40 El Segundo (90245) ***(P-2305)***
Ziegenfelder Company.....E.....909 590-0493
12290 Colony Ave Chino (91710) ***(P-1828)***
Ziehm Instrumentarium.....E.....407 615-8560
4181 Latham St Riverside (92501) ***(P-11212)***
Ziffren B B F G-L S&C Fnd.....C.....310 552-3388
1801 Century Park W Los Angeles (90067) ***(P-21705)***
Zillionaire Empress Danielle B.....A.....310 461-9923
8549 Wilshire Blvd # 817 Beverly Hills (90211) ***(P-16151)***
Zim Industries Inc.....C.....661 393-9661
7212 Fruitvale Ave Bakersfield (93308) ***(P-1563)***
Zimmer Gnsul Frsca Archtcts LL.....C.....213 617-1901
515 S Flower St Ste 3700 Los Angeles (90071) ***(P-22753)***
Zimmer Gnsul Frsca Partnr Amer, Los Angeles *Also called Zimmer Gnsul Frsca Archtcts LL* ***(P-22753)***
Zimmer Intermed Inc.....F.....909 392-0882
1647 Yeager Ave La Verne (91750) ***(P-11156)***
Zimmer Melia & Associates Inc (PA).....**D.....615 377-0118**
6832 Presidio Dr Huntington Beach (92648) ***(P-11157)***
Zina Sterling Silver Inc.....F.....310 286-2206
3268 Motor Ave Los Angeles (90034) ***(P-14143)***
Zina Sterling Silver & Gifts, Los Angeles *Also called Zina Sterling Silver Inc* ***(P-14143)***
Zion Automotive Group, Cerritos *Also called R1 Concepts Inc* ***(P-13081)***
Zipco, Riverside *Also called Zenith Manufacturing Inc* ***(P-10447)***
Zippy Usa Inc.....D.....949 366-9525
1 Morgan Irvine (92618) ***(P-13679)***
Ziprecruiter Inc.....A.....877 252-1062
604 Arizona Ave Santa Monica (90401) ***(P-23373)***
Zk Enterprises Inc.....E.....213 622-7012
4368 District Blvd Vernon (90058) ***(P-2833)***
Zmp Aquisition Corporation.....F.....714 278-6500
4141 N Palm St Fullerton (92835) ***(P-8969)***
Znat Insurance Company.....C.....818 713-1000
21255 Califa St Woodland Hills (91367) ***(P-15654)***
Zo Skin Health Inc (HQ).....**D.....949 988-7524**
9685 Research Dr Irvine (92618) ***(P-5086)***
Zoasis Corporation.....E.....800 745-4725
1960 E Grand Ave Ste 555 El Segundo (90245) ***(P-4116)***
Zodiac Aerospace.....F.....909 652-9700
11340 Jersey Blvd Rancho Cucamonga (91730) ***(P-10448)***
Zodiac Inflight Innovations US, Brea *Also called Safran Pass Innovations LLC* ***(P-17705)***
Zodiac Wtr Waste Aero Systems.....C.....310 884-7000
1500 Glenn Curtiss St Carson (90746) ***(P-10449)***
Zodiak Services America.....E.....310 884-7200
6734 Valjean Ave Van Nuys (91406) ***(P-10450)***
Zoic Inc.....C.....310 838-0770
3582 Eastham Dr Culver City (90232) ***(P-19214)***
Zoic Studios, Culver City *Also called Zoic Inc* ***(P-19214)***
Zonda Intelligence, Newport Beach *Also called Metrostudy Inc* ***(P-23271)***
Zonex Systems, Huntington Beach *Also called California Economizer* ***(P-8945)***
Zoo Digital Production LLC.....D.....310 220-3939
2201 Park Pl Ste 100 El Segundo (90245) ***(P-19215)***
Zoo Printing Inc (PA).....**D.....310 253-7751**
1225 Los Angeles St Glendale (91204) ***(P-4464)***
Zoo Printing Trade Printer, Glendale *Also called Zoo Printing Inc* ***(P-4464)***
Zooey Apparel Inc.....E.....310 315-2880
1526 Cloverfield Blvd C Santa Monica (90404) ***(P-3011)***
Zoominfo Technologies LLC.....C.....360 783-6924
Dept La 24789 Pasadena (91185) ***(P-18137)***
Zpower LLC.....C.....805 445-7789
4765 Calle Quetzal Camarillo (93012) ***(P-8986)***
Zt Plus.....F.....626 208-3440
1321 Mountain View Cir Azusa (91702) ***(P-9608)***
Zumar Industries Inc.....D.....562 941-4633
9719 Santa Fe Springs Rd Santa Fe Springs (90670) ***(P-11617)***
Zuru LLC.....F.....424 277-1274
228 Nevada St El Segundo (90245) ***(P-11396)***
Zwift Inc (PA).....**B.....855 469-9438**
111 W Ocean Blvd Ste 1800 Long Beach (90802) ***(P-18015)***
Zymo Research Corporation (PA).....**D.....949 679-1190**
17062 Murphy Ave Irvine (92614) ***(P-22872)***
Zynx Health Incorporated (HQ).....**E.....310 954-1950**
6420 Wilshire Blvd # 1250 Los Angeles (90048) ***(P-17768)***
Zyris Inc.....E.....805 560-9888
6868 Cortona Dr Ste A Santa Barbara (93117) ***(P-11204)***
Zyxel Communications Inc.....D.....714 632-0882
1130 N Miller St Anaheim (92806) ***(P-12681)***

Employee Codes: A=Over 500 employees, B=251-500
C=101-250, D=51-100, E=20-50 F=10-19
2022 Southern California Business
Directory and Buyers Guide
© Mergent Inc. 1-800-342-5647
1325

COUNTY/CITY CROSS-REFERENCE INDEX

ENTRY#	ENTRY#	ENTRY#	ENTRY#	ENTRY#
Running Springs	Harmony	Guadalupe	Ivanhoe	Camarillo
San Bernardino	Los Osos	Lompoc	Lindsay	Fillmore
Skyforest	Morro Bay	Los Olivos	Orosi	Moorpark
Trona	Nipomo	New Cuyama	Pixley	Newbury Park
Twentynine Palms	Oceano	Orcutt	Porterville	Oak Park
Upland	Paso Robles	Santa Barbara	Richgrove	Oak View
Victorville	Pismo Beach	Santa Maria	Seq Natl Pk	Ojai
Wrightwood	San Luis Obispo	Santa Ynez	Springville	Oxnard
Yucaipa	San Miguel	Solvang	Strathmore	Piru
Yucca Valley	San Simeon	Vandenberg Afb	Terra Bella	Port Hueneme
San Luis Obispo	Santa Margarita		Three Rivers	Santa Paula
	Shandon	**Tulare**	Tipton	Simi Valley
Arroyo Grande	Shell Beach	Badger	Traver	Somis
Atascadero	Templeton	Cutler	Tulare	Thousand Oaks
Avila Beach		Dinuba	Visalia	Ventura
Cambria	**Santa Barbara**	Earlimart	Woodlake	Westlake Village
Cayucos	Buellton	Exeter	**Ventura**	
Creston	Carpinteria	Farmersville	Agoura Hills	
Grover Beach	Goleta	Goshen		

GEOGRAPHIC SECTION

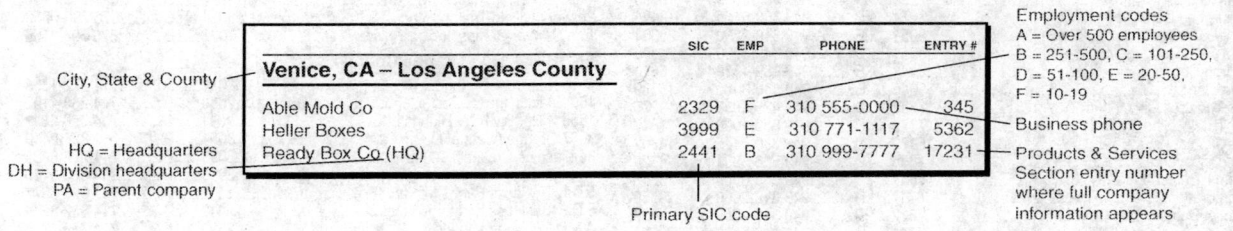

	SIC	EMP	PHONE	ENTRY #
Venice, CA – Los Angeles County				
Able Mold Co	2329	F	310 555-0000	345
Heller Boxes	3999	E	310 771-1117	5362
Ready Box Co (HQ)	2441	B	310 999-7777	17231

City, State & County

HQ = Headquarters
DH = Division headquarters
PA = Parent company

Primary SIC code

Employment codes
A = Over 500 employees
B = 251-500, C = 101-250,
D = 51-100, E = 20-50,
F = 10-19

Business phone

Products & Services
Section entry number
where full company
information appears

- Listings in this section are sorted alphabetically by city.
- Listings within each city are sorted alphabetically by company name.

ACTON, CA - Los Angeles County
County of Los Angeles	8069	D	661 223-8700	21041
Ferreira Service Inc (PA)	1711	D	925 831-9330	1066

ADELANTO, CA - San Bernardino County
Adelanto Elementary School Dst	2099	E	760 530-7680	2385
Amko Service Company	7699	D	760 246-3600	19024
Andersen Industries Inc	3715	E	760 246-8766	10163
Cageco Inc	3523	E	800 605-4859	7608
California Silica Products LLC	2819	E	909 947-0028	4654
Carberry LLC (HQ)	3999	E	800 564-0842	11649
Centerline Wood Products	5099	D	760 246-4530	14148
Clark - Pacific Corporation	3272	E	626 962-8755	6023
Cwp Cabinets Inc	1751	C	760 246-4530	1433
Dar-Ken Inc	3053	E	760 246-4010	5335
Ducommun Aerostructures Inc	3728	C	760 246-4191	10315
Fiber Care Baths Inc	3088	D	760 246-0019	5531
Flavor House Inc	2087	E	760 246-9131	2325
Furniture Technologies Inc	2426	C	760 246-9180	3219
General Atomic Aeron	3721	C	760 388-8208	10185
Hayes Welding Inc (PA)	7692	D	760 246-4878	18981
Inca Plastics Molding Co Inc	3089	F	760 246-8087	5673
McElroy Metal Mill Inc	3448	D	760 246-5545	7002
Mk Magnetics Inc	3315	D	760 246-6373	6230
Molded Fiber GL Companies - W	3089	D	760 246-4042	5716
National Filter Media Corp	3569	D	760 246-4551	8131
Quality Resources Dist LLC	3999	E	510 378-6861	11739
S E C C Corporation	1623	C	760 246-6218	967
Safeway Sign Company	3993	E	760 246-7070	11592
Thermtronix Corporation (PA)	3567	C	760 246-4500	8099
Tikun Olam Adelanto LLC (PA)	2833	F	833 468-4586	4767

AGOURA, CA - Los Angeles County
Joni and Friends Foundation (PA)	8322	D	818 707-5664	21828

AGOURA HILLS, CA - Los Angeles County
1st Century Builders Inc	1521	F	818 254-7183	588
Acorn Newspaper Inc	2711	E	818 706-0266	3943
Albert & Mackenzie LLP (PA)	8111	C	818 575-9876	21501
Allstate Technologies Inc (PA)	4813	D	818 889-7600	12625
American Travel Solutions LLC	4724	D	818 359-6514	12382
Athas Capital Group Inc	6162	D	877 877-1477	15174
Bergelectric Corp	1731	D	818 991-8600	1220
Brightview Golf Maint Inc (DH)	0781	D	818 223-8500	237
Cydcor LLC (PA)	8742	D	805 277-5500	23204
Davidson Hotel Partners Lp	7011	A	818 707-1220	16404
Edge Solutions Consulting Inc (PA)	3571	D	818 591-3500	8154
Ess LLC	1711	D	888 303-6424	1065
Evergreen Licensing LLC	2833	F	844 270-2700	4744
Farmers Fincl Solutions LLC (PA)	6411	D	818 584-0200	15563
First Student Inc	4151	D	818 707-2082	11930
Internet Machines Corporation (PA)	3577	D	818 575-2100	8269
J Bee NP Publishing Ltd	2741	F	818 706-0266	4185
James H Cowan & Associates Inc	0782	D	310 457-2574	312
Los Angeles Rams LLC (PA)	7941	D	314 982-7267	19422
Motor Vehicle Software Corp (PA)	5045	C	818 706-1949	13416
National Veterinary Assoc Inc (HQ)	0742	A	805 777-7222	201
Novalogic Inc (PA)	7371	D	818 880-1997	17679
Novastor Corporation (PA)	7372	E	805 579-6700	17935
Pacific Mktg Group Inc (PA)	5182	D	818 879-0946	14845
Paisano Publications LLC (PA)	2721	E	818 889-8740	4091
Paisano Publications Inc	2721	E	818 889-8740	4092
Pennymac Corp	6163	A	818 878-8416	15248
Private Nat Mrtg Accptance LLC (DH)	6162	A	818 224-7401	15228
Relief-Mart Inc	2515	E	805 379-4300	3557
Schachtel Corporation (PA)	2752	F	818 597-1222	4419
Sequoia Concepts Inc	7322	E	818 409-6000	17117
Small Business Advertising Inc	7319	E	818 262-8923	17101
Sole Survivor Corporation	2339	F	818 338-3760	2994
Stonefire Grill Inc (PA)	7371	E	805 413-0300	17724
Western Mutual Insurance Co	6331	D	818 879-2142	15490

Weststar Cinemas Inc	7832	C	818 707-9987	19293
Whiting-Turner Contracting Co	1542	C	818 879-8100	849
Coldwell Bankers Residential (PA)	6531	D	818 575-2660	15820

AGUA DULCE, CA - Los Angeles County
Agua Dulce Vineyards LLC	2084	E	661 268-7402	2164
Door & Hardware Installers Inc	2431	E	661 298-9383	3245
Petrelli Electric Inc	1731	D	661 268-7312	1294
Precision Millwork LLC	2431	F	661 402-5021	3283

AGUANGA, CA - Riverside County
Patriot Polishing Company	2842	F	310 903-7409	4975

ALHAMBRA, CA - Los Angeles County
Ahmc Inc	8011	D	626 570-1606	19687
Air Blast Inc	3564	E	626 576-0144	8039
Alhambra Foundry Company Ltd	3321	E	626 289-4294	6256
Alhambra Hospital Med Ctr LP	8062	C	626 570-1606	20669
APC-Lsma Dsmc (HQ)	8099	C	626 282-0288	21384
Apollo Medical Holdings Inc (PA)	8741	D	626 282-0288	22977
Ariston Hospitality Inc	2599	E	626 458-8668	3722
Asia-Pacific California Inc (PA)	2711	D	323 318-2254	3947
Atherton Baptist Homes	8051	C	626 863-1710	20249
Automobile Club Southern Cal	8699	D	626 289-4491	22408
Binoptics LLC	8711	E	607 257-3200	22500
Coast To Coast Met Finshg Corp	3471	E	626 282-2122	7240
Comprhnsive Crdvsclar Spcalist (PA)	2834	F	626 281-8663	4809
Copy Solutions Inc	2752	E	323 307-0900	4263
County of Los Angeles	4941	B	626 458-4000	12885
Crown Pavers Inc	3531	F	323 636-3365	7642
Drew Chain Security Corp	7381	D	626 457-8626	18271
Dsp Winner Inc	3631	F	858 336-9471	8989
Eastern Los Angeles RE (PA)	8322	C	626 299-4700	21776
Emcore Corporation (PA)	3674	C	626 293-3400	9502
Emcore Corporation	3674	C	626 293-3400	9503
Ethos Management Inc	8741	E	626 456-3669	23022
Gala Deluxe Corporation (PA)	2752	E	626 283-4804	4301
Gracing Brand Management Inc	2369	B	626 297-2472	3042
Holmes Body Shop-Alhambra	7532	D	626 282-6173	18792
Inveserve Corporation	6531	E	626 458-3435	15892
Lola Belle Brands LLC	3999	F	855 226-3526	11709
Martinsound Inc	8731	F	626 281-3555	22849
Network Medical Management Inc	8741	C	626 282-0288	23074
Ortel A Division Emcore Co (HQ)	3674	C	626 293-3400	9553
Pacific Ventures Ltd	8741	C	626 576-0737	23084
Riedon Inc (PA)	3676	C	626 284-9901	9617
Segway Inc	3751	C	603 222-6000	10500
Selarom	7372	F	626 614-6744	17980
Serfin Funds Transfer (PA)	6099	D	626 457-3070	15132
Silverado Senior Living Inc	8051	D	626 872-3941	20473
Southern California Edison Co	4911	D	626 308-6193	12860
TMJ Products Inc	3724	F	626 576-4063	10228
Tyler Trafficante (PA)	2311	D	323 869-9299	2751
Young Men Chrstn Assoc W San G (PA)	8322	D	626 576-0226	21932

ALISO VIEJO, CA - Orange County
Agile Technologies Inc	3674	E	949 454-8030	9479
Ambry Genetics Corporation (DH)	8071	D	949 900-5500	21059
American Assn Crtcal Care Nrse	8331	E	949 362-2000	21937
American Zettler Inc (HQ)	5065	E	949 831-5000	13700
Americas Moneyline Inc	6163	E	800 247-6663	15236
Apex Parks Group LLC	7999	D	210 341-6663	19633
Astronic	3672	C	949 454-1180	9383
Avanir Pharmaceuticals Inc (DH)	2834	B	949 389-6700	4790
AZ Displays Inc	3679	E	949 831-5000	9679
Basketball Marketing Co Inc	8742	D	610 249-2255	23168
Bearing Engineers Inc (PA)	5085	C	949 586-7442	13973
Biovail Technologies Ltd	2834	D	703 995-2400	4800
Brainchip Inc (HQ)	7372	F	949 330-6750	17806
Bridgeport Products Inc	3161	E	949 348-8800	5889
Brightview Landscape Svcs Inc	0781	E	310 829-4707	242
Brightview Landscape Svcs Inc	0781	C	949 480-4187	247

Employment Codes: A=Over 500 employees, B=251-500,
C=101-250, D=51-100, E=20-50 F=10-19

2022 Southern California Business
Directory and Buyers Guide

© Mergent Inc. 1-800-342-5647

1329

GEOGRAPHIC

	SIC	EMP	PHONE	ENTRY #
Centon Electronics Inc **(PA)**	3572	D	949 855-9111	8192
Clarient Inc **(DH)**	3841	B	949 445-7300	10963
Cloudstaff LLC	7299	C	888 551-5339	16950
CNT Acquisition Corp **(DH)**	3674	B	949 380-6100	9491
Covenant Care California LLC **(HQ)**	8051	E	949 349-1200	20301
Covenant Care Dubuque LLC	8051	D	949 349-1200	20303
Custom Iron Corporation	3441	E	949 939-4379	6610
Datallegro Inc	5045	D	949 680-3000	13389
Edwards Theatres Circuit Inc	7832	D	949 425-3838	19275
Eeye Inc **(HQ)**	7372	D	949 333-1900	17842
Efuel LLC	5172	D	949 330-7145	14802
Epicuren Discovery	2835	D	949 588-5807	4920
First Team RE - Orange Cnty	6531	C	949 389-0004	15866
Fluor Corporation	8711	D	949 349-2000	22550
Fluor Daniel Construction Co **(DH)**	1622	B	949 349-2000	928
Fluor Daniel Eurasia Inc **(DH)**	8711	A	949 349-2000	22551
Fluor Industrial Services Inc	7349	C	949 439-2000	17243
Fluor Plant Services Intl Inc	8711	D	949 349-2000	22552
Fluoramec LLC **(HQ)**	8711	E	949 349-2000	22553
Focus Healthcare Holdings Inc **(HQ)**	8099	E	949 349-1200	21427
Fuel Injection Engineering Co	3714	F	949 360-0909	10064
Global Wave Group	7372	F	949 916-9800	17867
Indie Semiconductor Inc	3674	C	949 608-0854	9515
Information MGT Resources Inc **(PA)**	7373	C	949 215-8889	18038
Interntnal Litigation Svcs Inc	5044	E	888 313-4457	13360
Ixys Intgrted Crcits Div AV In	3674	C	949 831-4622	9525
JMJ Financial Group **(PA)**	6162	E	949 340-6336	15206
Ju-Ju-Be Intl LLC	2393	E	877 258-5823	3128
Kaiser Foundation Hospitals	8011	C	949 425-3150	19860
L & O Aliso Viejo LLC	7011	D	949 643-6700	16530
Lauras House	8322	D	949 361-3775	21837
LMC Hollywood Highland	1542	B	949 448-1600	784
Malibu Castle	7996	E	210 341-6663	19519
Merit Medical Systems Inc	3841	E	801 208-4793	11021
Metagenics Inc **(DH)**	5122	C	949 366-0818	14263
Microvention Inc **(DH)**	3841	A	714 258-8000	11024
NC Interactive LLC	7379	D	512 623-8700	18202
Nelson Bros Property MGT Inc	8741	C	949 916-7300	23072
Nuvasive Spclzed Orthpdics Inc	3841	D	949 837-3600	11039
Ocean Pavers Inc	3531	F	949 340-6363	7648
One Identity LLC **(DH)**	7371	E	949 754-8000	17683
Pacific Life Insurance Company	6311	D	949 219-5200	15368
Pacifica Hotel Company **(HQ)**	6531	E	805 957-0095	15942
Palumbo Lawyers LLP **(PA)**	8111	D	949 442-0300	21652
Pandora Marketing LLC	8742	D	800 705-6856	23292
Perfect Impression Inc	7389	E	949 305-0797	18631
Premier Aquatic Services Llc	7997	D	949 716-3333	19601
Presbibio LLC	3851	E	949 502-7010	11260
Prescience Corporation	8711	D	949 600-8631	22639
Professional Community MGT Cal	8741	C	949 380-0725	23091
Quadrotech Solutions Inc **(PA)**	7372	F	302 660-0166	17967
Quest Software Inc **(HQ)**	7373	A	949 754-8000	18060
Quest Software Inc	7372	D	949 754-8000	17968
Rehabfocus Home Health Inc **(DH)**	8082	E	209 524-8700	21207
Remedytemp Inc **(DH)**	7363	C	949 425-7600	17512
Rxsight Inc **(PA)**	3851	C	949 521-7830	11261
Safeguard Health Entps Inc **(HQ)**	6324	B	800 880-1800	15449
Safeguard Health Plans Inc **(DH)**	6324	D	800 880-1800	15450
Schoolsfirst Federal Credit Un	6061	D	800 462-8328	15084
Screening Systems Inc **(PA)**	3826	E	949 855-1751	10810
Seabreeze Management Co Inc **(PA)**	8741	D	949 855-1800	23106
Sequent Medical Inc	3841	D	949 830-9600	11056
Sequoia Environmental Svcs Inc	0781	D	949 480-4742	279
Shea Properties MGT Co Inc	6512	B	949 389-7000	15697
Siemens Energy Inc	2741	D	949 448-0600	4204
Smith Micro Software Inc	7372	F	949 362-5800	17987
Stmicroelectronics Inc	3674	E	949 347-0717	9584
Summit Hotel Trs 129 LLC **(PA)**	7011	D	949 425-9500	16737
Sunstone Hotel Properties Inc **(DH)**	7011	C	949 330-4000	16743
Syxsense Inc	7371	D	949 270-1903	17728
Thomas James Capital Inc	6282	C	949 481-7026	15351
Tmd Worldwide Incorporated	7372	F	949 306-8877	17998
Truvida Recovery	8093	D	949 283-4679	21357
Uc Advantage Inc	8742	E	949 540-3403	23357
United Parcel Service Inc	7389	D	949 643-6634	18701
UST Global Inc **(HQ)**	7371	D	949 716-8757	17748
Valeant Biomedicals Inc **(DH)**	5169	D	949 461-6000	14793
Versity Investments LLC	6211	D	877 827-6272	15309
Vertos Medical Inc	3841	D	949 349-0008	11075
Vwise Inc	7371	D	949 716-1276	17756
Wepower LLC	3511	E	866 385-9463	7590
XEL USA Inc	3674	E	949 425-8686	9607
Xse Group Inc	5112	C	888 272-8340	14202
Youngs Holdings Inc **(PA)**	5182	D	714 368-4615	14847
Zettler Magnetics Inc	3612	C	949 831-5000	8887

ALTA LOMA, CA - San Bernardino County

	SIC	EMP	PHONE	ENTRY #
Ascension Constructors Inc **(PA)**	1521	D	909 242-3106	594
EDM Intrnational Logistics Inc	3086	F	626 588-2299	5498
Inland Empire RE Solutions	6531	D	909 476-1000	15890

ALTADENA, CA - Los Angeles County

	SIC	EMP	PHONE	ENTRY #
3becom Inc **(PA)**	7372	F	818 726-0007	17770
Altadena Town and Country Club	7997	D	626 345-9088	19530
Anre Technologies Inc	7371	C	818 627-5433	17549
Blue Marble Rehab Inc	7372	F	626 296-6400	17802
Dockum Research Laboratory Inc	3843	F	626 794-1821	11170
Five Acres-The Boys & Girls &	8361	B	626 798-6793	22102
Honeybee Robotics Ltd	3569	E	303 774-7613	8124
Maimone Liquidating Corp **(PA)**	7532	D	626 286-5691	18795
Mallcraft Inc	1542	D	626 765-9100	785
Pasadena Chld Training Soc	8361	C	626 798-0853	22142
Tom Sawyer Camps Inc	7032	D	626 794-1156	16828

ANAHEIM, CA - Orange County

	SIC	EMP	PHONE	ENTRY #
1135 N Leisure Ct Inc	8051	D	714 772-1353	20236
180 Snacks Inc	2068	E	714 238-1192	2109
1855 S Hbr Blvd Drv Hldngs LLC	7011	C	714 750-1811	16306
3067 Orange Avenue LLC	8051	D	714 827-2440	20237
3d Machine Co Inc	3599	E	714 777-8985	8449
3s Sign Services Inc	3993	E	714 683-1120	11517
5 Day Business Forms Mfg Inc **(PA)**	5112	D	213 623-3577	14189
5 Day Business Forms Mfg Inc	5112	D	714 632-8674	14190
A & D Precision Mfg Inc	3599	E	714 779-2714	8452
A & G Instr Svc Clibration Inc	3491	F	714 630-7400	7436
A & R Powder Coating Inc	3479	F	714 630-0709	7333
A & R Wholesale Distrs Inc	5145	D	714 777-7742	14553
A D S Gold Inc	3341	F	714 632-1888	6289
A J Fasteners Inc	3452	E	714 630-1556	7054
A P Seedorff & Company Inc	3625	F	714 252-5330	8940
A-1 Enterprises Inc	1799	E	714 630-3390	1631
ABB Inc	3612	D	714 630-4111	8860
Absolute Packaging Inc	2657	E	714 630-3020	3845
Action Enterprises Inc	3089	F	714 978-0333	5544
Action Innovations Inc	3089	F	714 978-0333	5545
Adcraft Products Co Inc	2759	E	714 776-1230	4477
Advanced Global Tech Group	3678	E	714 281-8020	9646
Advanced Manufacturing Tech	3699	A	714 238-1438	9848
Advanced Tech Plating	3471	F	714 630-7093	7198
Advanced Thermal Sciences Corp	3674	E	714 688-4200	9476
Advantage Mailing LLC **(PA)**	7331	C	714 538-3881	17130
Advantage-Crown Sls & Mktg LLC **(DH)**	5141	A	714 780-3000	14449
Adventure City Inc	7999	D	714 821-3311	19631
Adwest Technologies Inc **(HQ)**	3564	E	714 632-8595	8038
Aerofab Corporation	3441	F	714 635-0902	6582
Aerospace Parts Holdings Inc	3728	A	949 877-3630	10253
Affluent Target Marketing Inc	2721	F	714 446-6280	4051
Aggressive Engineering Corp	5084	F	714 995-8313	13881
Aircraft Repair & Overhaul Svc **(PA)**	4581	E	714 630-9494	12338
Albd Electric and Cable	1731	D	949 440-1216	1211
Aldoc Inc	1711	D	714 836-3477	1022
Alexanders Grand Salon	7231	D	714 282-6438	16895
Aliantel Inc	8748	D	714 829-1650	23407
Alstyle AP & Activewear MGT Co **(HQ)**	5137	A	714 765-0400	14361
Alstyle Apparel LLC	2211	A	714 765-0400	2556
Altamed Health Services Corp	8011	C	714 635-0593	19698
Altura Comm Solutions LLC **(DH)**	5065	D	714 948-8400	13699
American Circuit Tech Inc **(PA)**	3672	E	714 777-2480	9378
American Fabrication Corp **(PA)**	3714	D	714 632-1709	10017
American Sanitary Supply Inc	5087	D	714 632-3010	14032
Ampco Contracting Inc	4959	C	949 955-2255	13004
Anacom General Corporation	3651	E	714 774-8484	9158
Anaheim - 1855 S Hbr Blvd Owne	7011	D	714 750-1811	16319
Anaheim Arena Management LLC	7941	A	714 704-2400	19405
Anaheim Automation Inc	3625	E	714 992-6990	8943
Anaheim Custom Extruders Inc	3089	E	714 693-8508	5563
Anaheim Ducks Hockey Club LLC **(PA)**	7941	C	714 940-2900	19406
Anaheim Global Medical Center	8062	A	714 533-6220	20675
Anaheim Harbor Medical Group **(PA)**	8011	E	714 533-4511	19709
Anaheim Healthcare Center LLC	8051	D	714 816-0540	20244
Anaheim Hills Auto Body Inc	7532	D	714 632-8266	18783
Anaheim Hotel LLC	7011	C	714 750-1811	16321
Anaheim Plaza Hotel Inc	7011	C	714 772-5900	16324
Anaheim Regional Medical Ctr	8062	C	714 774-1450	20676
Anaheim Regional Medical Ctr	8062	C	714 999-3847	20677
Anaheim Regional Medical Ctr **(PA)**	8069	A	714 774-1450	21031
Anaheim Wire Products Inc	3496	E	714 563-8300	7495
Anaheim/Orange Cnty Visitor Bu **(PA)**	7389	D	714 765-8888	18444
Anamex Corporation **(PA)**	7371	E	714 779-7055	17546
Angels Baseball LP **(PA)**	7941	A	714 940-2000	19407
Apex Technology Holdings Inc	3812	A	321 270-3630	10567
Apple Paper Converting Inc	2679	E	714 632-3195	3922
Applied General Agency Inc **(PA)**	6411	D	800 498-6880	15534
APT Electronics Inc	3672	C	714 687-6760	9380
APT Manufacturing LLC	3541	F	714 632-0040	7721
Aquatic Co	3088	C	714 993-1220	5529
Aquatic Industries Inc	3088	E	800 877-2005	5530
Arch Telecom Inc **(PA)**	4812	B	714 312-2724	12590
Arch-Rite Inc	2431	E	714 630-9305	3230
Arden Engineering Inc **(DH)**	3728	E	949 877-3642	10276
Arizona Tile LLC	5032	D	714 978-6403	13292
Artisan Glass and Design Inc	1799	D	714 542-0507	1636
Artistic Pltg & Met Finshg Inc	3471	E	619 661-1691	7215
Ascent Manufacturing LLC	3469	E	714 540-6414	7125
Asco Power Services Inc	3699	F	714 283-4000	9856
Asdak International	3269	E	714 449-0733	6000
Aseptic Innovations Inc	3221	E	714 584-2110	5927
Astro-Tek Industries LLC	3728	D	714 238-0022	10280
AT&T Corp	4812	B	714 284-2878	12591
ATI Restoration LLC **(PA)**	1799	C	714 283-9990	1638
Atlas Magnetics Inc	3679	E	714 632-9718	9677
Atrium Door & Win Co Ariz Inc	5031	C	714 693-0601	13203
Automobile Club Southern Cal	8699	D	714 774-2392	22406
Automobile Club Southern Cal	8699	D	714 921-2850	22412
Avalon Building Maint Inc **(PA)**	7349	C	714 693-2407	17216
B & B Specialties Inc **(PA)**	3429	D	714 985-3000	6504

Mergent email: customerrelations@mergent.com
1330
2022 Southern California Business Directory and Buyers Guide
(P-0000) Products & Services Section entry number
(PA)=Parent Co (HQ)=Headquarters (DH)=Div Headquarters

GEOGRAPHIC SECTION ANAHEIM, CA

	SIC	EMP	PHONE	ENTRY #
B & B Specialties Inc	5072	D	714 985-3075	13797
B & Cawnings Inc	3444	E	714 632-3303	6791
B & E Enterprises	3751	F	714 630-3731	10481
Bace Manufacturing Inc **(HQ)**	3089	A	714 630-6002	5573
Badalian Enterprises Inc	7011	D	714 635-4082	16335
Bananafish Productions Inc	3231	F	714 956-2129	5946
Bassani Manufacturing	3498	E	714 630-1821	7530
Bcp Systems Inc	7378	D	714 202-3900	18144
Bechler Cams Inc	3599	F	714 774-5150	8520
Behavioral Health Works Inc	8093	D	800 249-1266	21278
Bell Pipe & Supply Co	5085	E	714 772-3200	13975
Best Cheer Stone Inc **(PA)**	5032	E	714 399-1588	13294
Best Interiors Inc **(PA)**	1742	C	714 490-7999	1367
Best Western Stovalls Inn **(PA)**	7011	D	714 956-4430	16345
Bielski Services Inc	7349	D	714 630-2316	17219
Birchwood Lighting Inc	3648	E	714 550-7118	9125
Black Oxide Industries Inc	3471	E	714 870-9610	7223
Block Tops Inc **(PA)**	2541	E	714 978-5080	3639
Borbon Incorporated	1721	C	714 994-0170	1171
Botanx LLC	2844	E	714 854-1601	4995
Bowers & Kelly Products Inc	3086	E	714 630-1285	5493
Bpo Management Services Inc **(HQ)**	7372	C	714 974-2670	17804
Bpo Management Services Inc **(PA)**	7371	D	714 972-2670	17572
Bradfield Manufacturing Inc	3446	F	714 543-8348	6953
Branded Group Inc	8742	C	323 940-1444	23175
Branvid Ltd Inc	7359	E	714 630-0661	17334
Bravo Sign & Design Inc	1799	F	714 284-0500	1642
Brice Tool & Stamping	3469	F	714 630-6400	7131
Bridgford Foods Corporation **(HQ)**	2045	B	714 526-5533	1951
Bridgford Marketing Company **(DH)**	5147	D	714 526-5533	14592
Bridport Erie Aviation Inc	7699	D	714 634-8801	19025
Brightview Landscape Svcs Inc	0781	C	714 215-7423	240
Brook & Whittle Limited	2759	E	714 634-3466	4489
Brownco Construction Co Inc	1521	D	714 935-9600	596
Bud Wil Inc	3086	E	714 630-1242	5494
Buds Cotton Inc	2844	E	714 223-7800	4996
Bunzl Distribution Cal LLC **(DH)**	5113	D	714 688-1900	14204
Burt L Howe & Associates	8111	D	714 701-9180	21525
Butler Inc	3452	F	310 323-3114	7059
C & S Assembly Inc	3679	D	866 779-8939	9685
C T L Printing Inds Inc	2759	E	714 635-2980	4490
C-G Systems Inc	1731	E	714 632-8882	1228
Caballero & Sons Inc	6221	E	562 368-1644	15313
Cabinets R US	2434	E	562 483-6886	3311
Cadence Aerospace LLC **(PA)**	3728	E	949 877-3630	10291
Cadence Aerospace LLC	3728	E	425 353-0405	10292
Cal Tech Precision Inc	3728	D	714 992-4130	10293
Cal-State Auto Parts Inc **(PA)**	5013	C	714 630-5950	13049
California Safety Agency	7381	E	866 996-6990	18260
Califrnia Auto Dalers Exch LLC	5012	B	714 996-2400	13022
Canyon Composites Incorporated	3728	E	714 991-8181	10295
Capsule Manufacturing Inc	1389	D	949 245-4151	487
Carrington Mrtg Holdings LLC	6162	C	888 267-0584	15181
Castle Inn Inc	7011	D	855 214-3079	16370
Castle Press	2791	F	800 794-0858	4624
CAT Exteriors Inc	1761	E	714 985-6906	1477
CBS Fasteners Inc	3452	E	714 779-6368	7060
Ced Anaheim 018	3699	F	714 956-5156	9859
Cemtrol Inc	3571	F	714 666-6606	8150
Certifix Inc	3999	F	714 496-3850	11652
Chad Industries Incorporated	3569	E	714 938-0080	8114
Champions Choice Inc	2992	F	714 635-4491	5289
Cheek Machine Corp	3599	E	714 279-9486	8552
Chuaolson Enterprises Inc	5072	E	714 630-4751	13799
Cinderella Motel	7011	D	559 432-0118	16382
Cintas Corporation	7389	D	714 646-2550	18479
Ciscos Shop Inc	3432	F	657 230-9158	6557
CM School Supply Inc	3944	F	714 680-6681	11369
Coast 2 Coast Cables LLC	3357	E	714 666-1062	6348
Coast Sign Incorporated	3993	C	714 520-9144	11535
Coast2coast Public Safety LLC	7382	E	833 262-7877	18368
Coastal Building Services Inc	7349	B	714 775-2855	17228
Colortech Label Inc	2759	F	714 999-5545	4501
Comfort California Inc	7011	C	714 750-3131	16387
Community Close-Up Westminster	2711	D	714 704-5811	3965
Computed Tool & Engrg Inc	3544	E	714 630-3911	7791
Concourse Recreation Center **(PA)**	7933	D	714 666-2695	19397
Concrete West Construction Inc	8742	F	949 448-9940	23196
Conestoga Hotel	7011	D	714 535-0300	16388
Consolidated Design West Inc	7336	E	714 999-1476	17166
Control AC Svc Corp	1711	D	714 777-8600	1047
Cost Saver Tours	4725	E	714 935-2569	12405
Countertop Factory **(PA)**	2491	F	562 903-4080	3431
Country Villa Service Corp **(PA)**	8741	D	310 574-3733	23007
Coventry Court Health Center	8051	C	714 636-2800	20305
Cppg Inc	7389	E	714 572-3662	18494
Craftech EDM Corporation	3089	C	714 630-8117	5617
Crafters Companion	3944	E	714 630-2444	11370
Craftsman Cutting Dies Inc **(PA)**	3423	E	714 776-8995	6475
Craftsman Unity LLC	3423	C	714 776-8995	6476
Creative Press LLC **(PA)**	2752	D	714 774-5060	4267
Crescent Inc	2752	E	714 992-6030	4268
Cresco Manufacturing Inc	3599	E	714 525-2326	8564
Crest Coating Inc	3479	D	714 635-7090	7355
Cristek Interconnects Inc **(HQ)**	3678	C	714 696-5200	9651
Crystal Cal Lab Inc	3679	E	714 991-1580	9698
Custom Industries Inc	3231	E	714 779-9101	5949

	SIC	EMP	PHONE	ENTRY #
Custom Laminators Inc	3083	F	714 778-0895	5448
Cytec Engineered Materials Inc	2821	E	714 632-8444	4686
Cytec Engineered Materials Inc	3365	C	714 632-1174	6390
D & D Gear Incorporated	3728	C	714 692-6570	10306
D & S Industries Inc	3728	F	714 779-8074	10307
D-Mac Inc	2451	E	714 808-3918	3419
D/K Mechanical Contractors Inc	1711	D	714 970-0180	1051
Daisy Scout Publishing	2741	F	714 630-6611	4165
Danny Ryan Precision Contg Inc	1795	D	949 642-6664	1612
Danville Materials LLC	3843	E	714 399-0334	11166
Davita Medical Management LLC	8099	D	714 995-1000	21413
Demoldco Plastics Inc	3089	E	714 577-9391	5623
Development Resource Cons Inc **(PA)**	8711	D	714 685-6860	22530
Dg Holdings Inc	3714	F	714 891-9300	10045
DG Performance Spc Inc	3799	D	714 961-8850	10549
Di Overnite LLC	4215	D	877 997-7447	12127
Diamodent Inc	3843	E	888 281-8850	11169
Digital Periph Solutions Inc	3651	E	714 998-3440	9171
Direct Edge Media Inc **(PA)**	2759	F	714 221-8686	4508
Direct Edge Screenworks Inc	2752	E	714 579-3686	4277
Disney Enterprises Inc	7011	A	714 778-6600	16407
Disney Enterprises Inc	7812	D	407 397-6000	19117
Disneyland International	7011	A	714 956-6746	16408
Disneyland International **(DH)**	7996	C	714 781-4565	19517
Disneyland Resort **(DH)**	7011	C	714 781-4000	16409
Disneyland Resort	4783	B	714 781-7560	12556
Display Fabrication Group Inc	2399	E	714 373-2100	3193
Dma Greencare Contracting Inc	0782	E	714 630-9470	302
DMS Facility Services Inc	7349	A	949 975-1366	17239
DMS Facility Services LLC	8711	A	949 975-1366	22534
Docircle Inc	4813	E	415 484-4221	12634
Donco & Sons Inc	1731	E	714 779-0099	1244
Doubltree Suites By Hilton LLC	7011	C	714 750-3000	16419
Dretloh Aircraft Supply Inc **(PA)**	3728	F	714 632-6982	10313
DSV Solutions LLC	4731	C	714 630-0110	12450
Dynaflex International	3949	E	714 630-0909	11413
Eaco Corporation **(PA)**	5065	D	714 876-2490	13715
Eagle Ridge Paper Ltd **(HQ)**	2621	C	714 780-1799	3751
Eagle Trs 1 LLC	7011	D	657 439-0060	16425
Earthscapes Landscape Inc	0781	E	714 936-7810	254
Econolite Control Products Inc **(PA)**	3669	C	714 630-3700	9339
Ecotech Rfrgn & Hvac Inc	1711	D	888 833-8100	1059
Edco Plastics Inc	3089	E	714 772-1986	5634
Edge Mortgage Advisory Co LLC	8748	D	714 564-5800	23434
Edward Thomas Companies	7011	C	714 782-7500	16426
Electron Beam Engineering Inc	7692	F	714 491-5990	18977
Eleganza Tiles Inc **(PA)**	1743	D	714 224-1700	1415
Elite Enfrcment SEC Sltons Inc **(PA)**	7381	C	866 354-8308	18273
Ellsworth Trck Auto Machining	5013	F	714 761-2500	13058
Elysium Tiles Inc	3253	F	714 991-7885	5986
Emazing Lights LLC	3648	E	626 628-6482	9131
Emergency Vehicle Group Inc	5012	E	714 238-0110	13025
Emitcon Inc	3824	F	714 632-8595	10737
Empi Inc	5013	D	714 446-9606	13059
Endress & Hauser Conducta Inc	3826	E	800 835-5474	10792
Endress + Hauser Inc	3823	F	714 577-5600	10691
Eps Corporate Holdings Inc	5074	D	714 635-3131	13825
Etherwan Systems Inc	7379	D	714 779-3800	18177
Exactax Inc **(PA)**	7291	D	714 284-4802	16936
Excelsior Nutrition Inc	2833	E	657 999-5188	4746
Expo Dyeing & Finishing Inc	2269	C	714 220-9583	2670
Express Messenger Systems Inc	4215	D	949 235-1400	12129
F M Tarbell Co	6531	D	714 772-8990	15850
Fabrication Network Inc	3444	F	714 393-5282	6836
Fairfeld Inn By Mrrott Ltd Prt	7011	D	714 772-6777	16440
Falck Mobile Health Corp	4119	D	714 828-7750	11866
Family Tree Produce Inc	5148	C	714 693-5688	14627
Fantasia Distribution Inc	2131	F	714 817-8300	2555
Farrell Brothers Holding Corp	3599	F	714 630-3417	8586
Fci Lender Services Inc	7322	C	800 931-2424	17111
Ferra Aerospace Inc	3728	E	918 787-2220	10326
Filyn Corporation	4119	C	714 632-0225	11867
Fire & Gas Detection Tech Inc	3669	F	714 671-8500	9342
Firmenich	2869	D	714 535-2871	5136
First Choice Physcn Partners **(HQ)**	8011	E	714 428-2311	19823
First Team RE - Orange Cnty	6531	C	714 974-9191	15865
Fjs Inc	7011	C	714 905-1050	16445
Flawless Vape Whl & Dist Inc	5194	D	714 406-2933	14902
Foam Concepts Inc	3086	E	714 693-1037	5501
Foam Plastics & Rbr Pdts Corp	3086	F	714 779-0990	5505
Foreseeson Custom Displays Inc **(PA)**	3577	E	714 300-0540	8257
Formula Consultants Inc	7371	F	714 778-0123	17618
Fortel Traffic Inc	8711	F	714 701-9800	22555
Fortress Holding Group LLC	6719	D	714 202-8710	16100
Freeman Expositions LLC	7389	C	714 254-3400	18521
Freight Management Inc	8742	D	714 632-1440	23222
Friedl Corporation	3714	E	714 443-0122	10062
Front Prch Cmmnties Svcs - Cas	8059	C	714 776-7150	20584
Furniture Solutions Inc	2521	E	714 666-0424	3585
G C Landscape Inc	0782	E	714 535-5640	306
G4s Justice Services LLC	7382	D	800 589-6003	18380
GBS Linens Inc **(PA)**	7213	D	714 778-6448	16853
Gear Manufacturing Inc	3728	E	714 792-2895	10334
Gemini Mfg & Engrg Inc	3544	E	714 999-0010	7803
General Engineering Wstn Inc **(PA)**	1711	D	714 630-3200	1074
General Power Systems Inc	3679	E	714 956-9321	9716
General Procurement Inc **(PA)**	5045	C	949 679-7960	13402

GEOGRAPHIC

	SIC	EMP	PHONE	ENTRY #
Genesis Computer Systems Inc	5045	E	714 632-3648	13403
Gentry Golf Maintenance	3949	E	714 630-3541	11419
George Drumheller Properties	7011	D	714 779-0252	16453
George T Hall Co Inc **(PA)**	5075	E	909 825-9751	13844
Ges US (new England) Inc	3679	C	978 459-4434	9717
Giddens Industries Inc **(DH)**	3728	C	425 353-0405	10336
Gledhill/Lyons Inc	3728	E	714 502-0274	10337
Global Paper Solutions Inc	2621	E	714 687-6102	3753
Gmp Laboratories America Inc	2834	D	714 630-2467	4825
Go-Staff Inc	7361	C	657 242-9350	17425
Graffiti Shield Inc	3081	F	714 575-1100	5431
Greenball Corp **(PA)**	5014	E	714 782-3060	13117
Greenfields Outdoor Fitnes Inc	3949	F	888 315-9037	11422
Greengro Technologies Inc **(PA)**	7372	E	714 367-6538	17873
GT Styling Corp	3089	E	714 644-9214	5658
Haddads Fine Arts Inc	2893	E	714 996-2100	5204
Harris Freeman & Co Inc **(PA)**	5149	B	714 765-7525	14694
Harris Spice Company Inc	2099	E	714 507-1919	2448
Harrys Dye and Wash Inc	2261	E	714 446-0300	2658
Hba Incorporated	1741	D	714 635-8602	1346
Hestan Commercial Corporation	3639	C	714 869-2380	9015
HHC Ha Trs Inc	7011	E	714 750-4321	16472
HI Anaheim LLC	7011	D	714 533-1500	16474
Highland Lumber Sales Inc	5031	D	714 778-2293	13215
Hippo Corporation	5199	F	714 229-9152	14936
Hitech Metal Fabrication Corp	3441	D	714 635-3505	6621
Hob Entertainment LLC	7929	D	714 778-2583	19352
Holiday Garden SF Corp	7011	D	714 533-3555	16483
Holiday Inn	7011	E	714 748-7777	16484
Holiday Inn Ex Anheim Main Gat	7011	D	714 772-7755	16485
House Seven Gables RE Inc	6531	D	714 974-7000	15883
House Seven Gables RE Inc	6531	D	714 282-0306	15885
Hoyt Roofs Inc	1761	E	714 773-1820	1489
Hunter Easterday Corporation	7349	C	714 238-3400	17250
Hydro-Dig Inc	0781	D	714 772-9947	262
IAC Industries	2599	E	714 990-8997	3731
Ideal Fasteners Inc	5085	E	714 630-7840	13990
In Oakwood Cnstr Rstrtion Svcs **(DH)**	1521	E	714 529-8300	614
Infinity Drywall Contg Inc	1742	D	714 634-2255	1380
Infosend Inc **(PA)**	8721	D	714 993-2690	22794
Inland Litho LLC	2752	D	714 993-6000	4334
Innovative Organics Inc	2869	E	714 701-3900	5138
Intense Lighting LLC	3646	D	714 630-9877	9090
Interlink Inc	2752	D	714 905-7700	4339
Interlog Corporation	3679	E	714 529-7808	9730
Internal Revenue Service	7291	D	714 512-2818	16938
International West Inc	3444	D	714 632-9190	6855
Interstate Electronics Corp **(DH)**	3825	B	714 758-0500	10760
Interstate Electronics Corp	8742	D	714 758-0500	23245
Interstate Electronics Corp	3825	D	714 758-0500	10761
Interstate Electronics Corp	3663	D	714 758-3395	9279
Interstate Electronics Corp	5065	D	714 758-0500	13733
Ironwood Electric Inc	3699	E	714 630-2350	9874
Isuzu North America Corp **(HQ)**	5084	C	714 935-9300	13907
J&S Goodwin Inc **(HQ)**	3537	C	714 956-4040	7711
Jabil Inc	3672	E	714 938-0080	9417
Jaco Engineering	3599	E	714 991-1680	8638
Jan Pro Clg Systems Sthern Cal	7349	C	714 220-0500	17253
Jasper Electronics	3679	E	714 917-0749	9734
JB Bostick Company Inc **(PA)**	1611	D	714 238-2121	892
Jbb Inc	3699	E	888 538-9287	9879
JDC Development Group Inc	2449	F	714 575-1108	3415
Jellco Container Inc	2653	D	714 666-2728	3813
Jorge Ulloa	3999	F	714 630-0499	11697
K & J Wire Products Corp	3446	E	714 816-0360	6969
Kaiser Foundation Hospitals	8011	C	714 279-4675	19858
Kaiser Foundation Hospitals	8062	A	714 644-2000	20806
Kaiser Foundation Hospitals	8011	C	888 988-2800	19886
Kaiser Foundation Hospitals	8011	C	888 988-2800	19888
Kaiser Foundation Hospitals	6324	C	714 284-6634	15415
Karcher Environmental Inc **(PA)**	1799	E	714 385-1490	1670
Kca Electronics Inc	3672	C	714 239-2433	9419
Keenan Hpkins Sder Stwell Cntr **(PA)**	1742	D	714 695-3670	1384
Kempton Machine Works Inc	3545	E	714 990-0596	7855
Ken Real Estate Lease Ltd	7011	D	714 778-1700	16522
Ken Starr Inc	1711	D	714 632-8789	1089
Kendon Industries LLC	3792	E	714 630-7144	10542
Kesa Incorporated	7382	E	714 956-2827	18391
Kinsbursky Bros Supply Inc **(PA)**	5093	D	714 738-8516	14118
Kisco Senior Living LLC	6513	D	714 872-9785	15736
Korean Community Services Inc	8069	C	714 527-6561	21047
Kretus Group Inc **(PA)**	5032	E	714 738-6640	13306
L3 Technologies Inc	3663	C	714 758-4222	9284
Labeltronix LLC	2759	D	800 429-4321	4534
Legacy Farms LLC	5148	C	714 736-1800	14642
Leisure Care LLC	8361	C	714 974-1616	22124
Leonards Carpet Service Inc **(PA)**	2541	D	714 630-1930	3658
Lester Lithograph Inc	2752	E	714 491-3981	4357
Lobel Financial Corporation **(PA)**	6141	D	714 995-3333	15145
Lodestone LLC	3548	F	714 970-0900	7891
Lowes Home Centers LLC	5031	C	714 447-6140	13236
Lyons Security Service Inc **(PA)**	7381	C	714 401-4850	18295
M6 Dev LLC	7011	E	714 533-2101	16550
M8 Dev LLC	7011	E	714 782-7500	16551
Machining Time Savers Inc	5084	D	714 635-7373	13912
Magnetic Metals Corporation	3542	C	714 828-4625	7759
Magnetic Sensors Corporation	3679	E	714 630-8380	9745
Mainline Sales Inc **(PA)**	8742	D	714 300-0641	23266
Makar Anaheim LLC	7011	A	714 740-4431	16554
Mako Industries SC Inc	3826	E	714 632-1400	10800
Marina Landscape Maint Inc	0781	B	714 939-6600	266
Mark & Fred Enterprises	8051	C	714 821-1993	20413
Mark 1 Restoration Service LLC	8322	D	714 283-9990	21847
Master Arts Inc	2796	F	714 240-4550	4633
Matrix Surfaces Inc	1743	D	714 696-5449	1420
Maverick Abrasives Corporation	3291	D	714 854-9531	6155
Mc Graw Commercial Insur Svc	6411	D	714 939-9875	15593
McGarry Mechanical Inc	1761	F	714 630-4600	1497
Mechanized Enterprises Inc	3599	F	714 630-5512	8685
Medivision Inc	3845	F	714 563-2772	11229
Melton Intl Tackle Inc	5199	E	714 978-9192	14951
Merical LLC **(PA)**	7389	C	714 238-7225	18595
Metal-Fab Services Indust Inc	3444	E	714 630-7771	6876
Mettler Electronics Corp	3841	E	714 533-2221	11022
Micrometals Inc **(PA)**	3679	C	714 970-9400	9750
Mid-West Wholesale Hardware Co	3429	E	714 630-4751	6526
Midland Industries	5085	D	800 821-5725	14001
Millcraft Inc	2431	D	714 632-9621	3267
Milwaukee Electric Tool Corp	5085	D	714 827-1301	14004
Mission Linen Supply	7213	D	909 364-8752	16857
Modern Manufacturing Inc	3599	E	714 254-0156	8704
Morphotrak LLC **(DH)**	7373	C	714 238-2000	18047
Motive Energy Inc **(PA)**	5063	D	714 888-2525	13649
Motors & Controls Whse Inc	5065	E	714 956-0480	13752
Mowery Thomason Inc	1742	C	714 666-1717	1387
Moyes Custom Furniture Inc	7641	E	714 729-0234	18964
Msl Electric Inc	1731	D	714 693-4837	1284
Murrietta Circuits	3672	C	714 970-2430	9432
Nazzareno Electric Co Inc	1731	D	714 712-4744	1286
Nbty Manufacturing LLC	2834	C	714 765-8323	4858
Nellson Nutraceutical Inc	2064	B	844 635-5766	2100
Neutron Plating Inc	3471	F	714 632-9241	7287
Newport Hotel Capital LLC	7011	C	714 758-0900	16581
Nexgen Air Los Angeles **(PA)**	1711	D	714 331-9633	1108
Nor-Cal Beverage Co Inc	7389	E	714 526-8600	18614
Northwest Hotel Corporation **(PA)**	7011	C	714 776-6120	16585
Nylok LLC	3452	E	714 635-3993	7071
Oasis Alloy Wheels Inc	3365	F	714 533-3286	6400
Oasis Brands Inc	5113	D	540 658-2830	14218
Oliver Healthcare Packaging Co	5084	D	714 864-3500	13924
One-Way Manufacturing Inc	3498	E	714 630-8833	7542
Onesolution Light and Control	5063	D	714 490-5540	13654
Orange Cnty Adult Achvment Ctr	8322	C	714 744-5301	21860
Orange Coast Building Svcs Inc	1541	C	714 453-6300	712
Orange County Erectors Inc	3448	E	714 502-8455	7006
Orange County Indus Plas Inc **(PA)**	5162	E	714 632-9450	14759
Orange County Screw Pdts Inc	3599	E	714 630-7433	8727
Orange County Thermal Inds Inc	1742	D	714 279-9416	1390
Orange County Water District	4941	D	714 378-3320	12912
Ortronics Inc	3444	C	714 776-5420	6884
Outdoor Dimensions LLC	2499	C	714 578-9555	3448
Outside Lines Inc	0781	E	714 637-4747	273
Outsource Utility Contr Corp	4911	C	714 238-9263	12814
Pacific Broach & Engrg Assoc	3599	F	714 632-5678	8729
Pacific Coast Fabrication Inc	3999	F	714 536-8385	11725
Pacific Coast Sightseeing Tour	4725	C	714 507-1157	12407
Pacific Contours Corporation	3728	D	714 693-1260	10390
Pacific Design Directions Inc	1521	E	714 685-7766	629
Pacific Embroidery LLC	7389	F	714 630-4757	18626
Pacific Precision Metals Inc	3469	C	951 226-1500	7173
Pacific Specialty Insurance Co	6411	E	800 303-5000	15609
Pacific Transformer Corp	3612	C	714 779-0450	8881
Pacific West Litho Inc	2752	D	714 579-0868	4385
Pacific Westline Inc	2541	D	714 956-2442	3661
Pampanga Foods Company Inc	2013	D	714 773-0537	1742
Paragon Industries Inc	5032	D	714 778-1800	13312
Partners Information Tech **(HQ)**	7379	D	714 736-4487	18209
Paulus Engineering Inc	1623	D	714 632-3322	965
Peacock Stes Resort Ltd Partnr	7011	D	714 535-8255	16625
Pendarvis Manufacturing Inc	3599	E	714 992-0950	8737
Penhall Holding Company	1771	D	714 772-6450	1546
Performance Contracting Inc	1796	D	913 310-7120	1626
Performance Powder Inc	3479	E	714 632-0600	7397
Pest Options Inc	7342	D	714 224-7378	17204
Phoenix Cars LLC	3711	E	909 987-0815	9961
Phoenix Club Inc	8641	D	714 224-0194	22356
Pinnacle Precision Shtmtl Corp **(PA)**	3444	C	714 777-3129	6891
Pinner Construction Co Inc **(PA)**	1542	D	714 490-4000	810
Plannet Consulting LLC	7379	D	714 982-5800	18213
Ponderosa Electric Inc	1731	D	949 253-3100	1298
Ponderosa Yorba Linda LLC	7011	E	714 974-8880	16635
Portofino Inn & Suites Anaheim	7011	A	714 782-7600	16637
Powdercoat Services LLC	3479	E	714 533-2251	7401
Power Aire Inc	3613	F	800 526-7661	8904
Power Plus International Inc **(PA)**	5063	D	714 507-1881	13661
Powertec Company Inc	1611	D	951 332-1198	908
Precision Anodizing & Pltg Inc	3471	D	714 996-1601	7297
Precision Waterjet Inc	3599	E	888 538-9287	8743
Precon Inc	3541	E	714 630-7632	7740
Premier Commercial Bancorp	6022	D	714 978-2400	15039
Pretium Packaging LLC	3089	C	714 777-9580	5777
Prime Healthcare Anaheim LLC	8062	A	714 827-3000	20901
Product Solutions Inc	3589	E	714 545-9757	8405
Public Agency Resources	8742	D	714 940-6300	23303

Mergent email: customerrelations@mergent.com
1332
2022 Southern California Business Directory and Buyers Guide
(P-0000) Products & Services Section entry number
(PA)=Parent Co (HQ)=Headquarters (DH)=Div Headquarters

	SIC	EMP	PHONE	ENTRY #
Qualitask Inc	3599	E	714 237-0900	8752
Quality First Woodworks Inc	2499	C	714 632-0480	3452
Quality Sprayers Inc	0711	D	562 376-5177	147
Quantum Automation	5063	E	714 854-0800	13663
Quantum Bhvioral Solutions Inc	8049	D	626 531-6999	20230
R & S Overhead Door of So Cal	3442	E	714 680-0600	6716
R C I P Inc	3599	F	714 630-1239	8754
R H Barden Inc	3677	F	714 970-0900	9640
R K Fabrication Inc	2821	F	714 630-9654	4711
Rachas Inc	7991	E	714 290-0636	19466
Racing Beat Inc	3519	E	714 779-8677	7597
Radarsonics Inc	3679	F	714 630-7288	9770
Ralph Brennan Rest Group LLC	8742	D	714 776-5200	23306
Ramisons Inc	2064	F	714 323-7134	2102
Rapid Manufacturing A **(PA)**	3496	C	714 974-2432	7511
Raykorvay Inc	3942	F	714 632-8680	11364
Raytheon Applied Signal	3669	D	714 917-0255	9350
Real Estate Trainers Inc	2721	E	800 282-2352	4104
Reliable Packaging Systems Inc	2891	F	714 572-1094	5194
Resident Group Services Inc **(PA)**	0782	C	714 630-5300	339
Residential Fire Systems Inc	1711	D	714 666-8450	1130
Rgb Systems Inc **(PA)**	3577	C	714 491-1500	8297
Rigiflex Technology Inc	3672	F	714 688-1500	9448
Rjb Enterprises Inc	1731	E	714 484-3101	1310
Rm Partners Inc	1752	E	714 765-5725	1469
Rnbs Corporation	3571	E	714 998-1828	8172
Roberts Precision Engrg Inc	3599	E	714 635-4485	8773
Rodriguez Brothers Auto Parts **(PA)**	3599	F	714 772-7278	8775
Rosendin Electric Inc	1731	A	714 739-1334	1311
Roy Miller Freight Lines LLC **(PA)**	4212	D	714 632-5511	11991
RPM Plastic Molding Inc	3089	E	714 630-9300	5807
RSI Home Products Inc **(HQ)**	2514	A	714 449-2200	3532
RSI Home Products Mfg Inc	2514	D	714 449-2200	3533
RSI Home Products Sales Inc	5023	D	714 449-2200	13184
Rtie Holdings LLC	3679	F	714 765-8200	9776
Rtr Industries LLC	3592	E	714 996-0050	8436
Rubio Arts Corporation	8999	C	407 849-1643	23542
Rush Business Forms Inc	3993	E	714 630-5661	11589
Rvtlzation Anaheim II Partners	6531	D	714 520-4041	15993
Ryvec Inc	2816	E	714 520-5592	4645
S K Laboratories Inc	2834	D	714 695-9800	4888
S-Energy America Inc **(HQ)**	3674	F	949 281-7897	9567
Saca Technologies Inc	7379	D	888 603-9030	18218
SAI Management Co Inc	7011	D	714 772-5050	16684
Saint-Gobain Ceramics Plas Inc	2869	C	714 701-3900	5146
San Marino Plastering Inc	1742	D	714 693-7840	1400
San-Mar Construction Co Inc	1542	C	714 693-5400	819
Scalzo Hospitality Inc	7011	D	714 772-3691	16698
Seating Component Mfg Inc	2519	F	714 693-3376	3572
Sechrist Industries Inc	3841	D	714 579-8400	11054
Secure Technology Company	3672	D	714 991-6500	9452
Security Signal Devices Inc **(PA)**	7382	E	800 888-0444	18397
Sehanson Inc	3728	D	714 778-1900	10415
Select Data Inc	7371	C	714 577-1000	17709
Self Serve Auto Dismantlers **(PA)**	4953	C	714 630-8901	12979
Sentinel Offender Services LLC **(PA)**	7382	D	949 453-1550	18399
Serra Laser and Waterjet Inc	3699	E	714 680-6211	9913
Service 1st Electrical Svcs	1731	E	714 630-9699	1315
Setco LLC	3089	C	812 424-2904	5818
Shamrock Supply Company Inc **(PA)**	5072	D	714 575-1800	13817
Sharon Havriluk	2782	E	714 630-1313	4612
Shaxon Industries Inc	3572	D	714 779-1140	8216
Sheet Metal Service	3444	F	714 446-0196	6909
Shell Oil Company	8742	C	714 991-9200	23321
Short Load Concrete Inc	3273	E	714 524-7013	6113
Shrin LLC	5013	D	714 850-0303	13089
Si Manufacturing Inc	3677	E	714 956-7110	9644
Siemens Mobility Inc	3661	A	714 284-0206	9243
Sierra Corporate MGT Inc **(PA)**	8741	D	714 575-5130	23107
Signage Solutions Corporation	3993	E	714 491-0299	11600
Singod Investors Vi LLC	2819	D	714 326-7800	4669
Skullduggery Inc	3944	F	714 777-6425	11391
Sky Rider Equipment Co Inc	2515	E	714 632-6890	3559
Slaters 50/50 Inc **(PA)**	6794	C	714 685-1103	16218
Smart Elec & Assembly Inc	3672	C	714 772-2651	9454
So Cal Land Maintenance Inc	7349	D	714 231-1454	17286
Solaris Paper Inc **(DH)**	5113	C	562 653-1680	14228
Sonfarrel	3089	E	714 630-7280	5824
Sonfarrel Aerospace LLC	3365	D	714 630-7280	6401
South Coast Mechanical Inc	1711	D	714 738-6644	1145
Southern Cal Dgnstc Imging Inc **(PA)**	8011	D	714 995-5471	20073
Southern Cal Prmnnte Med Group	8011	C	714 279-4675	20086
Southern Counties Bldg Maint **(PA)**	7349	C	805 928-9900	17287
Southland Tool Mfg Inc	3545	F	714 632-8198	7869
Spidell Publishing Inc	2741	E	714 776-7850	4206
SPS Inc	2439	F	714 632-8333	3369
SRbray LLC **(PA)**	1731	E	714 765-7551	1319
St Joseph Health Per Care Svcs **(PA)**	8082	D	714 712-7100	21214
St Joseph Hospice	8322	C	714 712-7100	21896
St Jseph Hlth Sys HM Care Svc	8082	A	714 712-9500	21216
St Pierre Gonzalez Enterprises	3479	F	714 491-2191	7415
Stainless Micro-Polish Inc	3471	E	714 632-8903	7315
Stater Bros Markets	2051	E	714 991-5310	2036
Steady Clothing Inc	2329	F	714 444-2058	2825
Steeldyne Industries	3444	E	714 630-6200	6918
Stovall Stovall & OConnell	7011	D	714 776-4800	16734
Strand Art Company Inc	3089	E	714 777-0444	5831

	SIC	EMP	PHONE	ENTRY #
Straub Distributing Co Ltd **(PA)**	5181	C	714 779-4000	14836
Summit Interconnect Inc **(HQ)**	3672	C	714 239-2433	9457
Sun Mar Nursing Center Inc	8059	D	714 776-1720	20630
Sun Rich Foods	5084	F	714 632-7577	13945
Sun Rich Foods Intl Corp	2099	E	714 632-7577	2529
Sunset Signs and Printing Inc	3993	E	714 255-9104	11607
Sunwest Electric Inc	1731	C	714 630-8700	1321
Superior Connector Plating Inc	3471	E	714 774-1174	7318
Superior Jig Inc	3544	E	714 525-4777	7834
Superior Spring Company	3495	E	714 490-0881	7493
Superior Stone Products Inc	3281	F	714 635-7775	6149
Supreme Graphics Inc	2752	F	310 531-8300	4430
T L Fabrications LP	7692	D	562 802-3980	18999
T&J Sausage Kitchen Inc	2013	E	714 632-8350	1754
Tahiti Cabinets Inc	2599	D	714 693-0618	3742
Tait & Associates Inc	3443	E	714 560-8222	6759
Tajen Graphics Inc	2752	E	714 527-3122	4432
Tam Printing Inc	2752	F	714 224-4488	4433
Targus International LLC **(PA)**	5199	C	714 765-5555	14977
Targus US LLC	3161	E	714 765-5555	5897
Taylor-Dunn Manufacturing Co **(DH)**	3537	D	714 956-4040	7719
Technic Inc	3471	E	714 632-0200	7321
Techno Coatings Inc	1542	D	714 774-4671	837
Techno Coatings Inc	1542	D	714 774-4671	838
Technotronix Inc	3672	E	714 630-9200	9459
Teco Diagnostics	2835	D	714 693-7788	4927
Telatemp Corporation	3829	E	714 414-0343	10915
Tenet Healthsystem Medical Inc	8062	C	714 428-6800	20974
Textile Products Inc	2221	E	714 761-0401	2605
Textured Design Furniture Inc	2511	E	714 502-9121	3489
Tfd Incorporated	3827	E	714 630-7127	10862
Thermalair Inc **(HQ)**	1711	D	714 630-3200	1155
Thermech Corporation	2671	E	714 533-3183	3858
Thompson Indus Sup A Ltd Lblty	5085	F	714 632-8895	14025
Thornton Steel & Ir Works Inc	3446	F	714 491-8800	6982
Titanium Coating Services Inc	3479	F	714 860-4229	7421
Tk Elevator Corporation	5084	D	714 939-0888	13952
Tl Fab LP	3441	C	562 802-3980	6670
Top Deck Investments Inc	6531	E	714 956-7712	16016
Total Paper Services Inc	3999	F	714 780-0131	11781
Towne Park Brew Inc	2082	E	714 844-2492	2159
Transline Technology Inc	3672	E	714 533-8300	9460
Triad Bellows Design & Mfg Inc	3441	E	714 204-4444	6673
Tricom Management Inc	8741	C	714 630-2029	23127
Trilogy Plumbing Inc	1711	C	714 441-2952	1157
Trinity Process Solutions Inc	3498	E	714 701-1112	7544
Truform Construction Corp	1751	E	714 630-7447	1459
Ttm Technologies Inc	3672	B	714 688-7200	9465
Tuffer Manufacturing Co Inc	3812	E	714 526-3077	10650
Turner Construction Company	1542	B	714 940-9000	841
Turret Lathe Specialists Inc	3599	F	714 520-0058	8830
Twilight Technology Inc **(PA)**	3674	F	714 257-2257	9595
Ultimate Landscaping MGT	0782	D	714 502-9711	347
United Media Services Inc	3695	C	714 693-8168	9843
Universal Dust Cllctr Mfg Sup **(PA)**	1541	D	714 630-8588	724
University Frames Inc	2499	E	714 575-5100	3457
University Marelich Mech Inc	1711	D	714 632-2600	1159
US Union Tool Inc **(HQ)**	3541	E	714 521-6242	7750
USA Extruded Plastics Inc	3089	F	714 991-6061	5853
V and C Manufacturing and	3999	F	615 374-2076	11787
Vanguard Health Systems Inc	8011	B	714 635-6272	20132
Vci Event Technology Inc	7359	C	714 772-2002	17383
Veeco Electro Fab Inc	3672	E	714 630-8020	9467
Venture Design Services Inc **(PA)**	8731	C	714 765-3740	22871
Venus Alloys Inc **(PA)**	3363	E	714 635-8800	6372
Versatile Building Pdts LLC	1751	F	714 829-2600	1461
Veterans Health Administration	8011	C	714 780-5400	20151
Vincent Contractors Inc	1741	B	714 693-1726	1356
Vislink LLC	3663	E	714 998-2121	9325
Vts Sheetmetal Specialist Co	3444	E	714 237-1420	6940
W N G Construction Jv Inc **(PA)**	1541	D	714 524-7100	726
Walt Dsney Imgnring RES Dev In	2389	D	714 781-3152	3090
Wasser Filtration Inc **(PA)**	3569	D	714 696-6450	8142
Wco Hotels Inc **(DH)**	7011	D	323 636-3251	16779
Wco Hotels Inc	7011	A	714 635-2300	16780
Web4 Inc	7371	D	714 974-2670	17759
Weis/Robart Partitions Inc	3446	F	714 666-0822	6984
Wellbore Navigation Inc **(PA)**	3829	F	714 259-7760	10921
West Bond Inc **(PA)**	3599	E	714 978-1551	8847
West Coast Electric & Pwr Inc	4911	D	562 447-3254	12864
Western Golf Inc	3949	F	800 448-4409	11459
Westview Services Inc	8051	C	714 956-4199	20508
Westview Services Inc	8331	D	714 530-2703	21977
Westview Services Inc	8331	D	714 635-2444	21978
Where 2 Get It Inc **(HQ)**	7379	D	714 660-4870	18236
Wide USA Corporation	3575	F	714 300-0540	8231
Willard Marine Inc	3732	D	714 666-2150	10475
Willdan Group Inc **(PA)**	8711	C	800 424-9144	22700
Wilson & Hampton Pntg Contrs	1721	D	714 772-5091	1202
Windsor Anaheim Healthcare **(PA)**	8051	C	714 826-8950	20512
Winter Park Utility Svcs LLC **(PA)**	1623	D	714 283-6080	987
Woodwork Pioneers Corp	2431	E	714 991-1017	3302
Workcare Inc	8744	C	714 978-7488	23399
Xerxes Corporation	2821	E	714 630-0012	4729
Xp Power Inc	3679	D	714 712-2642	9805
Yeager Manufacturing Corp **(PA)**	3728	E	714 879-2800	10446
Yti Enterprises Inc	2499	F	714 632-8696	3459

Employment Codes: A=Over 500 employees, B=251-500, C=101-250, D=51-100, E=20-50 F=10-19

2022 Southern California Business Directory and Buyers Guide

© Mergent Inc. 1-800-342-5647

1333

	SIC	EMP	PHONE	ENTRY #
Zyxel Communications Inc	4813	D	714 632-0882	12681

ANGELUS OAKS, CA - San Bernardino County

	SIC	EMP	PHONE	ENTRY #
YMCA of East Valley	8641	D	909 794-1702	22381

ANZA, CA - Riverside County

	SIC	EMP	PHONE	ENTRY #
Cahuilla Creek Rest & Casino	7999	C	951 763-1200	19638
County of Riverside	8099	C	951 763-5611	21409

APPLE VALLEY, CA - San Bernardino County

	SIC	EMP	PHONE	ENTRY #
Automobile Club Southern Cal	8699	D	760 247-4110	22437
BEST Opportunities Inc	8331	C	760 628-0111	21944
Brightview Tree Company	0781	D	760 955-2560	249
Cemex Cement Inc	3273	C	760 381-7616	6078
EE Pauley Plastic Extrusion	3089	F	760 240-3737	5637
Front Prch Cmmnties Svcs - Cas	8051	C	760 240-5051	20347
High Dsert Prtnr In Acdmic Exc	8732	B	760 946-5414	22884
Induction Technology Corp	3567	E	760 246-7333	8090
Lindsay Windows California LLC	3442	F	760 247-1082	6707
Lowes Home Centers LLC	5031	C	760 961-3000	13259
Pauley Plastic LLC	3089	F	760 240-3737	5740
Polymer Concepts Tech Inc	3053	F	760 240-4999	5348
Reid Products Inc	3599	E	760 240-1355	8763
St Mary Medical Center LLC	8062	D	760 946-8767	20968
St Mary Medical Center LLC **(PA)**	8062	A	760 242-2311	20969
Tibban Manufacturing Inc	3999	E	760 961-1160	11778
Who Dat Nation Trnsp LLC	4789	D	760 403-7237	12587

ARCADIA, CA - Los Angeles County

	SIC	EMP	PHONE	ENTRY #
365 Delivery Inc	4212	D	818 815-5005	11945
Arcadia Convalescent Hosp Inc **(PA)**	8059	C	626 445-2170	20555
Arcadia Gardens MGT Corp	8052	D	626 574-8571	20523
Arcadia Hotel Venture LP	7011	D	626 445-8525	16328
Arroyo Insurance Services Inc **(PA)**	6411	D	626 799-9532	15535
Automobile Club Southern Cal	8699	D	626 445-6687	22411
Avantra Real Estate Services	6531	E	626 357-7028	15780
Bendick Precision Inc	3599	E	626 445-0217	8524
Cardenas Enterprises Inc	2542	F	323 588-0137	3679
Century 21 Ludecke Inc **(PA)**	6531	D	626 445-0123	15808
Christian Arcadia School	8351	D	626 574-8229	22003
Coach Usa Inc	4142	D	626 357-7912	11910
Commercial Roofing Systems Inc	1761	D	626 359-5354	1480
Country Villa Service Corp	8051	C	626 445-2421	20295
Danco Anodizing Inc **(PA)**	3471	E	626 445-3303	7245
Dardanella Electric Corp	5063	D	818 445-5009	13622
David S Tsai DDS Inc **(PA)**	2834	F	626 358-9136	4812
Dear John Denim Inc	2211	F	626 350-5100	2567
Dynapro	3537	F	626 898-4411	7708
Enas Media Inc	3652	E	626 962-1115	9215
Evergreen Chemicals USA LLC	2869	F	626 821-9236	5135
Galileo Technologies Corp	1311	D	626 447-3100	403
Gar Enterprises **(PA)**	5045	D	626 574-1175	13398
Heprand Hospitality Inc	7011	D	626 574-5600	16471
Human Designs Prosthetic **(HQ)**	3842	F	562 988-2414	11113
Los Angeles Turf Club Inc **(DH)**	7948	B	626 574-6330	19431
Los Angles Arbrtum Fndtion Inc	8422	D	626 821-3222	22239
Medical Imaging Partners LLC	8011	D	626 446-0080	19973
Methodist Hosp Southern Cal **(PA)**	8062	A	626 898-8000	20862
MPS Anzon LLC	3842	C	626 471-3553	11127
Mur-Sol Builders Inc	1522	E	626 447-0558	662
N A Tomatobank	6029	D	626 759-9200	15048
Nationwide Litho Inc	2759	F	626 542-0371	4546
Penney Opco LLC	7231	D	626 445-6454	16911
Post Alarm Systems **(PA)**	7382	D	626 446-7159	18396
Property Care Building Svc LLC	7349	E	626 623-6420	17279
Quality Reimbursement Services	8721	D	626 445-5092	22811
Relton Corporation	2899	D	800 423-1505	5240
Samuel Son & Co (usa) Inc	5051	E	323 722-0300	13594
Santa Anita Associates **(PA)**	7992	D	626 447-2764	19508
Springhill Suites LLC	7011	D	626 821-5400	16727
T & L Air Conditioning Inc	3822	E	626 294-9888	10669
Tee Top of California Inc **(PA)**	5136	E	626 303-1868	14354
Tektest Inc	3678	E	626 446-6175	9665
Transdev Services Inc	4119	B	626 357-7912	11892
Trinus Corporation	7371	E	818 246-1143	17745

ARLETA, CA - Los Angeles County

	SIC	EMP	PHONE	ENTRY #
International Envmtl Corp	0782	D	818 892-9341	310
Lexington Scenery & Props Inc	1751	C	818 768-5768	1446

ARROYO GRANDE, CA - San Luis Obispo County

	SIC	EMP	PHONE	ENTRY #
Alliance Ready Mix Inc **(PA)**	3273	D	805 343-0360	6066
Ameri-Kleen	7349	C	805 546-0706	17214
Anderson Burton Cnstr Inc **(PA)**	1542	D	805 481-5096	735
Applied Orthopedic Design	3842	F	805 481-3685	11088
Community Action Partnership	8111	D	805 489-4026	21534
Compass Health Inc	8051	C	805 489-8137	20288
Corbett Canyon Vineyards	2084	F	805 782-9463	2178
Crosno Construction Inc	3441	E	805 343-7437	6609
Gould Welding Inc	7692	F	805 489-9353	18979
Greenheart Farms Inc	0191	B	805 481-2234	107
Laetitia Vineyard & Winery Inc	2084	D	805 481-1772	2200
Layne Laboratories Inc	2299	E	805 242-7918	2728
M29 Technology and Design	7372	F	805 489-9402	17909
Maxim Healthcare Services Inc	7363	D	805 489-2685	17499
Mhm Services Inc	8093	C	805 904-6678	21320
Papich Construction Co Inc **(PA)**	1521	E	805 473-3016	631
Phillips 66 Co Carbon Group	3559	E	805 489-4050	7994
Talley Farms	0723	C	805 489-2508	190
Talley Vineyards	2084	F	805 489-0446	2227

ARTESIA, CA - Los Angeles County

	SIC	EMP	PHONE	ENTRY #
A B C Unified School District	7349	D	562 865-1676	17208
Artesia Christian Home Inc	8059	C	562 865-5218	20556
Automobile Club Southern Cal	8699	D	562 924-6636	22444
Cal Plate **(PA)**	3555	D	562 403-3000	7917
County of Los Angeles	8093	D	562 402-0688	21293
E R G Home Health Provider	8082	D	562 403-1070	21162
Kukdong Apparel America Inc	7389	E	562 403-0044	18568
Malanis Inc	5094	F	562 924-7274	14133
Windsor Twin Plms Hlthcare Ctr	8051	C	562 865-0271	20517

ARVIN, CA - Kern County

	SIC	EMP	PHONE	ENTRY #
Arvin-Edison Water Storage Dst **(PA)**	4941	E	661 854-5573	12880
Evergreen Health Care LLC	8051	A	661 854-4475	20339
Grimmway Enterprises Inc	1541	B	661 854-6240	700
Grimmway Enterprises Inc	8741	C	661 854-6200	23033
Grimmway Enterprises Inc	0723	C	661 854-6250	173
Grimmway Enterprises Inc	0723	C	661 854-6200	174
Kern Ridge Growers LLC	0723	B	661 854-3141	178
Moore Farms Inc	2099	E	661 854-5588	2489
Reeves Extruded Products Inc	3089	D	661 854-5970	5789
Southern Valley Chemical Co	2879	F	661 366-3308	5172
Tasteful Selections LLC	5149	C	661 588-1053	14744
Tri-Fanucchi Farms Inc	0161	D	661 858-2264	21
Western Fiber Co Inc	3541	E	661 854-5556	7752

ATASCADERO, CA - San Luis Obispo County

	SIC	EMP	PHONE	ENTRY #
Central Coast Seafoods	5146	C	805 462-3474	14568
Compass Health Inc	8051	C	805 466-9254	20289
Datazeo Inc	7372	F	805 461-3458	17835
Experts Exchange LLC	7379	D	805 787-0603	18178
Options Family of Services	8093	E	805 462-8544	21323
Star of California	8099	D	805 466-1638	21486
State Hospitals Cal Dept	8063	B	805 468-2000	21029

AVALON, CA - Los Angeles County

	SIC	EMP	PHONE	ENTRY #
Guided Discoveries Inc	7032	D	310 510-1622	16822
Intervrsity Chrstn Fllwshp/Usa	7032	B	310 510-0015	16823
Metropole Hotel	7011	D	310 510-1884	16566
Pacific Catalina Hotel Inc	7011	B	310 510-9255	16606

AVENAL, CA - Kings County

	SIC	EMP	PHONE	ENTRY #
Adventist Hlth Systm/West Corp	8062	D	559 386-5200	20651
Adventist Hlth Systm/West Corp	8062	D	559 386-5364	20658
Pacific Gas and Electric Co	4911	C	559 386-2052	12815

AVILA BEACH, CA - San Luis Obispo County

	SIC	EMP	PHONE	ENTRY #
Gander Publishing Inc	2731	E	805 541-5523	4129
Pacific Gas and Electric Co	4911	A	805 506-5280	12817

AZUSA, CA - Los Angeles County

	SIC	EMP	PHONE	ENTRY #
3ality Digital LLC **(PA)**	7812	D	818 970-7756	19087
A & B Aerospace Inc	3599	E	626 334-2976	8451
Acme Portable Machines Inc	3571	E	626 610-1888	8145
Advanced Vehicle Mfg Inc **(PA)**	3429	F	866 622-8628	6496
Ancra International LLC	3537	E	626 765-4818	7702
Ancra International LLC **(HQ)**	3537	C	626 765-4800	7703
Arrietta Incorporated	2099	E	626 334-0302	2392
Artisan Screen Printing Inc	2759	C	626 815-2700	4482
Artistic Entrmt Svcs LLC	7929	D	626 334-9388	19344
BK Signs Inc	3993	F	626 334-5600	11526
Bojer Inc	2392	E	626 334-1711	3096
Buena Vista Food Products Inc **(DH)**	5149	C	626 815-8859	14677
California Amforge Corporation	3312	C	626 334-4931	6191
California Pediatric Fmly Svcs	8322	D	626 812-0055	21727
Casa Colina Hospital and Cente	8049	C	626 334-8735	20210
Cee Jay Research & Sales LLC	2759	F	626 815-1530	4493
Cemex Cement Inc	5032	B	626 969-1747	13296
Chipmasters Manufacturing Inc **(PA)**	3599	F	626 804-8178	8553
County of Los Angeles	8011	D	626 969-7885	19773
D W Mack Co Inc	3053	E	626 969-1817	5334
Dependble Incontinence Sup Inc	2676	E	626 812-0044	3903
Dhb Delivery LLC	4215	D	626 588-7562	12126
Dolphin Spas Inc	3999	F	626 334-0099	11661
Ducommun Incorporated	3677	E	626 812-9666	9629
Gale Banks Engineering	3519	C	626 969-9600	7595
Hallett Boats LLC	3732	F	626 969-8844	10465
Hannemann Fiberglass Inc	3714	F	626 969-7317	10071
Hanson Distributing Company **(PA)**	5013	C	626 224-9800	13062
Heidi Corporation	1771	D	626 333-6317	1529
Heppner Hardwoods Inc	5031	D	626 969-7983	13214
I/O Controls Corporation **(PA)**	3625	D	626 812-5353	8956
I2k LLC	7911	E	626 969-7780	19299
Inovativ Inc	3334	E	626 969-5300	6282
Inwesco Incorporated **(PA)**	3315	D	626 334-7115	6228
Jans Towing Inc **(PA)**	7549	C	626 334-1383	18936
Jar Machine Fabrication Inc	3599	F	626 939-1111	8640
Le Petit Sheet Metal Inc	3444	F	626 334-4415	6863
Lindsey Manufacturing Co	3463	C	626 969-3471	7103
Magparts **(DH)**	3365	C	626 334-7897	6399
Mat Cactus Mfg Co	2273	E	626 969-0444	2693
Mc William & Son Inc	3469	F	626 969-1821	7163
McKeever Danlee Confectionary	2064	C	626 334-8964	2097
McMurtrie & Mcmurtrie Inc	2426	E	626 815-0177	3221
Melco Steel Inc	3443	E	626 334-7875	6743
Mintie Corporation **(PA)**	7349	C	323 225-4111	17265
Monrovia Nursery Company **(PA)**	0181	A	626 334-9321	85

Mergent email: customerrelations@mergent.com
1334

2022 Southern California Business
Directory and Buyers Guide

(P-0000) Products & Services Section entry number
(PA)=Parent Co (HQ)=Headquarters (DH)=Div Headquarters

	SIC	EMP	PHONE	ENTRY #
Morris National Inc **(HQ)**	5149	D	626 385-2000	14711
Mortech Manufacturing	2531	D	626 334-1471	3626
Ncla Inc	2679	F	562 926-6252	3931
Nicks Doors Inc	2431	F	626 812-6491	3275
Norac Inc **(PA)**	2869	D	626 334-2907	5142
Northrop Grumman Systems Corp	3812	C	626 812-1000	10622
Northrop Grumman Systems Corp	3812	C	626 812-1464	10625
Oj Insulation LP **(PA)**	1742	C	800 707-9278	1388
Phaostron Instr Electronic Co	3613	D	626 969-6801	8903
Pie Place	5149	D	626 963-9475	14717
Precision Granite Usa Inc	3281	F	562 696-8328	6141
Ptb Sales Inc **(PA)**	3563	E	626 334-0500	8037
Rain Bird Corporation **(PA)**	3494	C	626 812-3400	7475
Rain Bird Distribution Corp	1629	E	626 963-9311	1003
Reichhold LLC 2	2821	F	626 334-4974	4712
Richard Wilson Wellington	0181	D	626 812-7881	94
Ruiteng Internet Technology Co	7374	C	302 597-7438	18107
S & S Foods LLC	2013	C	626 633-1609	1749
S&B Pharma Inc	2833	D	626 334-2908	4763
Screwmatic Inc	3599	D	626 334-7831	8790
Seasonic Electronics Inc	3679	F	626 969-9966	9780
Skylock Industries	3728	E	201 637-9505	10418
Skylock Industries LLC	3728	D	626 334-2391	10419
Smart & Final Stores Inc	5141	C	626 334-5189	14506
Stanley Steemer of Los Angles **(PA)**	7217	C	626 791-9400	16881
Tecomet Inc	3841	B	626 334-1519	11062
Totten Tubes Inc **(PA)**	5051	D	626 812-0220	13602
Trio Engineered Products Inc **(HQ)**	3531	E	626 851-3966	7655
Valley Forge Acquisition Corp	3462	F	626 969-8701	7100
Very Special Chocolats Inc	2066	C	626 334-7838	2108
Water Filter Exchange Inc	3569	F	818 808-2541	8143
Westwood Laboratories Inc **(PA)**	2844	E	626 969-3305	5083
Zt Plus	3674	F	626 208-3440	9608

BADGER, CA - Tulare County

	SIC	EMP	PHONE	ENTRY #
Christian Hartland Association	7032	D	559 337-2349	16819

BAKERSFIELD, CA - Kern County

	SIC	EMP	PHONE	ENTRY #
3g Rebar Inc	3449	F	661 588-0294	7012
7th Standard Ranch Company	0172	B	661 399-0416	39
A-C Electric Company **(PA)**	1731	E	661 410-0000	1205
Accelerated Envmtl Svcs Inc	7349	D	661 765-4003	17211
Acco Engineered Systems Inc	3585	F	661 631-1975	8325
Ace Hydraulic Sales & Svc Inc	5084	F	661 327-0571	13880
Advance Beverage Co Inc	5181	D	661 833-3783	14818
Advanced Cmbstn Prcess Cntrls	7699	F	661 615-1193	19019
Aera Energy Services Company **(HQ)**	1381	A	661 665-5000	421
AG Spray Equipment Inc	3523	F	661 391-9081	7602
Ag-Wise Enterprises Inc **(PA)**	0762	C	661 325-1567	220
Agstar Services Inc **(PA)**	3089	F	661 303-5556	5550
Alder & Co LLC	2511	F	661 326-0320	3460
Alfred Louie Incorporated	2099	F	661 831-2520	2388
Alliance Childrens Services	8361	C	661 863-0350	22079
Ally Enterprises	1389	E	661 412-9933	475
American Bottling Company	2086	F	661 323-7921	2250
Ameripride Services Inc	7213	C	661 324-7941	16845
Anatesco Inc	1389	F	661 399-6990	476
Anthony Vineyards Inc **(PA)**	0172	E	661 858-6211	41
Ardent Companies Inc	1731	D	661 633-1465	1215
Arrival Communications Inc **(DH)**	7389	D	661 716-2100	18449
Asbury Transportation Co	4213	D	661 327-2271	12012
Athletic Schlarship Connection	6733	E	909 705-5875	16173
Automobile Club Southern Cal	8699	D	661 327-4661	22410
B & B Pipe and Tool Co	3599	E	661 323-8208	8512
B & B Surplus Inc **(PA)**	5051	D	661 589-0381	13547
B & L Casing Service LLC	1389	F	661 589-9080	478
B C Laboratories Inc	8734	D	661 327-4911	22931
Bakersfeld Assn For Rtrded Ctz	8331	C	661 834-2272	21942
Bakersfeld Bhvral Hlthcare Hos	8063	C	661 398-1800	21015
Bakersfeld Hlthcare Wllness CN	8059	D	661 872-2121	20558
Bakersfield Country Club	7997	D	661 871-4000	19535
Bakersfield Elc Mtr Repr Inc	7694	D	661 327-3583	19006
Bakersfield Healthcare	8051	D	661 872-2121	20251
Bakersfield Inn Inc	7011	C	661 323-1900	16336
Bakersfield Machine Co Inc	3599	D	661 709-1992	8516
Bakersfield Memorial Hospital	8062	A	661 327-1792	20685
Bakersfield Westwind Corp	6531	C	661 327-2121	15782
Banks Pest Control	7342	C	661 323-7858	17198
Basic Energy Services Inc	1389	E	661 588-3800	480
Baymarr Constructors Inc	1771	C	661 395-1676	1515
Beautologie MGT Group Inc	8011	E	661 327-3800	19720
Berry Petroleum Company LLC **(HQ)**	1311	C	661 616-3900	390
Bidart Bros **(PA)**	0212	C	661 832-2447	127
Bolthouse Farms	0161	A	661 366-7205	11
Bolthouse Investment Company	0161	F	661 366-7209	12
Boyd & Boyd Industries **(PA)**	3565	F	661 631-8400	8064
Boys Girls Clubs of Kern Cnty	8641	D	661 325-3730	22314
Braun Electric Company Inc **(HQ)**	1731	E	661 633-1451	1223
Bristol Hospice Foundation Cal **(PA)**	8699	D	661 410-3000	22447
Bristol Hospice Foundation Cal	8052	D	661 716-4000	20526
Brown Armstrong Accntancy Corp	8721	D	661 324-4971	22763
Bryant Fuel Systems LLC	3443	E	661 334-5462	6731
Burkshine Enterprises Inc **(PA)**	7231	D	661 399-4321	16900
Burtch Trucking Inc	1611	D	661 399-1736	864
Buttonwillow Warehouse Co Inc **(HQ)**	5191	D	661 695-6500	14857
Bwf Banducci Inc	2873	F	661 302-6625	5153
C & H Testing Service Inc **(PA)**	1389	E	661 589-4030	482
C MBA Rn Inc	8082	D	661 395-1700	21145
C&J Well Services LLC	1389	A	661 589-5220	483
California Physicians Service	6324	D	661 631-2277	15389
Califrnia Grnhse Frm II Ltd PR	7389	D	949 715-3987	18466
Calpi Inc	1389	E	661 589-5648	486
Cameron West Coast Inc	5082	D	661 837-4980	13857
Canyon Hills Assembly God Ch	8351	D	661 871-1150	21995
Car Wash Partners Inc	7542	B	661 377-1020	18908
Car Wash Partners Inc	7542	D	661 231-3689	18909
Carlos Shower Doors Inc	3231	E	661 204-6689	5948
Carneros Energy Inc	1311	F	661 616-5600	400
Casing Specialties Inc	1389	E	661 399-5522	488
Cencal Machine Company	3599	F	661 392-7831	8545
Central California Cnstr Inc	1389	E	661 978-8230	489
Central Cardiology Med Clinic	8011	C	661 395-0000	19742
Centre For Neuro Skills **(PA)**	8093	B	661 872-3408	21286
Century Hlth Staffing Svcs Inc	7361	C	661 322-0606	17405
Century Rubber Company Inc	3069	F	661 366-7009	5370
Cfp Designs Inc	1711	D	661 903-8940	1043
Chartec LLC	7379	D	661 281-4000	18167
CJ Berry Well Services MGT LLC	1389	A	661 589-5220	490
Cjm Automotive Group Inc	7538	D	661 832-3000	18819
CL Knox Inc	1389	D	661 837-0477	492
Clinica Sierra Vista **(PA)**	8011	D	661 635-3050	19753
Cni Thl Propco Fe LLC	7011	D	661 325-9700	16385
Coastal Products Company Inc	3561	E	661 323-0487	8006
Cognito Company Inc	3714	E	661 588-8085	10034
Community Action Partnr Kern	8322	D	661 871-6055	21751
Community Action Partnr Kern **(PA)**	8322	E	661 336-5236	21752
Community Action Partnr Kern	8361	D	661 336-5300	22094
Computational Systems Inc	3823	C	661 832-5306	10686
Consolidated Fibrgls Pdts Co	3296	D	661 323-6026	6170
Construction Specialty Svc Inc	1623	D	661 864-7573	945
Contra Costa Electric Inc	1731	C	661 322-4036	1236
Contrband Ctrl Specialists Inc	2899	E	661 322-3363	5215
Coretex Products Inc **(PA)**	2844	F	661 834-6805	5002
County of Kern	8062	A	661 326-2054	20736
Crestwood Behavioral Hlth Inc	8322	D	661 363-8127	21764
Crestwood Behavioral Hlth Inc	8011	A	661 363-0124	19777
Crown Drilling Services Inc	1381	F	661 479-0710	425
Crystal Geyser Water Company	2086	E	661 323-6296	2263
Crystal Geyser Water Company	2086	E	661 321-0896	2264
Crystal Organic Farms LLC	0191	A	661 845-5200	103
Cummins Pacific LLC	3714	E	661 325-9404	10037
Cw Industries Inc	5094	D	661 399-5422	14129
D M Camp & Sons **(PA)**	0191	D	661 399-5511	104
Davidson Enterprises Inc	1799	E	661 325-2145	1654
Dean L Davis MD	8322	E	661 632-5000	21766
Delaney Manufacturing Inc **(PA)**	3999	E	661 587-6681	11656
Delta Trading LP	2951	E	661 834-5560	5270
Dhv Industries Inc	5085	D	661 392-8948	13981
Diaz Plastering Inc	1742	D	661 244-8228	1372
Diversified Prj Svcs Intl Inc **(PA)**	8711	D	661 371-2800	22533
Diversified Utility Svcs Inc	1623	B	661 325-3212	946
DMS-Bkl Drywall & Intr Systems	1742	E	415 508-4968	1373
Domino Plastics Mfg Inc	3089	E	661 396-3744	5628
Douglass Truck Bodies Inc	3713	E	661 327-0258	9983
Downhole Stabilization Inc	3533	E	661 631-1044	7668
Downs Equipment Rentals Inc **(PA)**	7353	D	661 615-6119	17307
Drill Cool Systems Inc **(PA)**	5084	F	661 633-2665	13898
Dunbar Electric Sign Company	3993	E	661 323-2600	11543
Dv Custom Farming LLC	0191	D	661 858-2888	105
E & B Ntral Resources Mgt Corp **(PA)**	1382	D	661 679-1714	449
E A Shields Inc	1623	F	661 325-5969	947
E and B Natural Resources	1382	D	661 679-1700	450
Electric Motor Works Inc	7694	E	661 327-4271	19010
Elmer F Karpe Inc	6531	E	661 847-4800	15845
Elysium Jennings LLC	1381	C	661 679-1700	427
Elysium West LLC	1389	E	661 679-1700	496
Energy Link Indus Svcs Inc	3599	E	661 765-4444	8581
Engineered Well Svc Intl Inc	1389	F	866 913-6283	498
Enova Solutions Inc	2899	F	661 327-2405	5218
Ensign US Drlg Cal Inc **(HQ)**	3541	C	661 589-0111	7731
Esparza Enterprises Inc **(PA)**	7363	A	661 831-0002	17492
Esparza Enterprises Inc	7361	B	661 831-0002	17421
Esparza Enterprises Inc	7361	B	661 631-0347	17423
Esparza Enterprises Inc	4213	A	661 631-0347	12036
Esys Energy Control Company	1731	D	661 833-1902	1249
Evergreen At Lakeport LLC	8051	D	661 871-3133	20338
Excalibur Well Services Corp	1381	C	661 589-5338	428
Exeter Packers Inc	4222	C	661 399-0416	12173
Farley Machine Inc	3533	E	661 397-4987	7669
Farm Credit West	6159	D	661 399-7360	15164
First Assmbly of God Bkrsfield	8351	D	661 327-2227	22015
First Energy Services Inc	1389	E	661 387-1972	502
Frontier Mechanical Inc	1711	D	661 589-6203	1072
Garcia Roofing Inc	1761	E	661 325-5736	1486
Gene Wtson Cnstr A Cal Ltd Prt	1389	E	661 763-5254	503
Generis Holdings LP **(PA)**	0161	E	661 366-7209	15
Gentiva Hospice	8082	C	661 324-1232	21166
Geo Drilling Fluids Inc **(PA)**	5169	E	661 325-5919	14782
Geo Guidance Drilling Svcs Inc **(PA)**	1381	E	661 833-9999	429
Georg Fischer Harvel LLC	3084	E	661 396-0653	5466
Gilliam & Sons Inc	1794	E	661 589-0913	1595
Giumarra Vineyards Corporation	0172	C	661 395-7071	46
Glam and Glits Nail Design Inc	2844	D	661 393-4800	5024
Global Elastomeric Pdts Inc	3533	D	661 831-5380	7670
Golden Empire Con Pdts Inc	1771	D	661 833-4490	1524

GEOGRAPHIC

Employment Codes: A=Over 500 employees, B=251-500, C=101-250, D=51-100, E=20-50 F=10-19

2022 Southern California Business Directory and Buyers Guide

© Mergent Inc. 1-800-342-5647

1335

	SIC	EMP	PHONE	ENTRY #
Golden Empire Mortgage Inc **(PA)**	6162	D	661 328-1600	15196
Golden Empire Mortgage Inc **(PA)**	6162	D	661 328-1600	15197
Golden Empire Transit District **(PA)**	4111	C	661 869-2438	11811
Golden State Drilling Inc	1381	D	661 589-0730	430
Good Smrtan Hosp A Cal Ltd Prt	8062	B	661 903-9555	20780
Gottstein Contracting Corp	5082	D	661 322-8934	13860
Grant Construction Inc	1751	C	661 588-4586	1438
Grayson Service Inc	1389	E	661 589-5444	504
Greers Bnner A Bakersfield Inc	1711	D	661 322-5858	1077
Gregory A Stainer MD Facs	8011	D	661 393-2331	19834
Griffith Company	1611	B	661 392-6640	884
Grimmway Enterprises Inc	0723	C	661 845-5200	175
Gsf Properties Inc	6531	D	661 834-1498	15878
Guardsmark LLC	7381	C	661 325-5906	18285
Guinn Corporation	1794	D	661 325-6109	1596
Gundlach Plbg & Shtmtl Co Ltd	1711	D	661 327-3052	1079
Haberfelde Ford **(PA)**	7538	C	661 328-3600	18839
Haberfelde Ford	7538	D	661 837-6400	18840
Hall Ambulance Service Inc	4119	D	661 322-8741	11873
Hall Ambulance Service Inc **(PA)**	4119	D	661 322-8741	11874
Hall Letter Shop Inc	2752	F	661 327-3228	4309
Hancor Inc	3084	E	661 366-1520	5467
Harrell Holdings **(PA)**	2711	C	661 322-5627	3985
Hathaway LLC	1311	E	661 393-2004	405
Health Net LLC	6324	C	661 321-3904	15398
Healthcare Finance Direct LLC	8742	D	661 616-4400	23234
Heart Center A Medical Corp	8011	D	661 324-4100	19839
Heart Hospital of Bk LLC	8062	B	661 316-6000	20784
Heritage Medical Group Inc **(PA)**	8011	C	661 327-4411	19843
HF Cox Inc **(PA)**	4213	D	661 366-3236	12053
Hills Wldg & Engrg Contr Inc	1389	D	661 746-5400	507
Hoffman Hospice of The Valley	8052	D	661 410-1010	20532
Hoover Treated Wood Pdts Inc	2491	F	661 833-0429	3433
Houchin Blood Services **(PA)**	8099	D	661 323-4222	21439
Houchin Blood Services	8099	D	661 327-8541	21440
Houchin Community Blood Bank	8099	D	661 323-4222	21441
Hps Mechanical Inc **(PA)**	1711	C	661 397-2121	1082
Hudson Valve Co Inc	3491	E	661 831-6208	7445
Humangood Norcal	8059	D	661 834-0620	20596
Hydril Company	3533	D	661 588-9332	7671
Impax Automation LLC	5084	E	661 391-8210	13904
Indepndent Lving Ctr Kern Cnty	8322	D	661 325-1063	21813
Industrial Data Communications	5084	E	661 589-4477	13905
Industrial Medical Group	8011	D	661 327-2225	19851
Innovative Engrg Systems Inc **(PA)**	8711	D	661 381-7800	22576
Irish Farms Co Inc **(PA)**	0761	E	661 746-4392	215
J Flying Manufacturing	3061	F	805 839-9229	5358
J G Boswell Company	0131	C	661 327-7721	2
Jaguars Wroght Iron	3446	F	661 323-5015	6965
Jims Steel Supply LLC	8742	E	661 324-6514	23250
Jims Supply Co Inc **(PA)**	5051	D	661 616-6977	13573
John M Phillips LLC	1389	E	661 327-3118	513
Jts Modular Inc	3448	E	661 835-9270	7000
K S Fabrication & Machine Inc	1623	C	661 617-1700	958
Kaiser Foundation Hospitals	8062	A	661 412-6777	20803
Kaiser Foundation Hospitals	8011	C	877 524-7373	19887
Kaiser Foundation Hospitals	8062	A	661 395-3000	20809
Kaiser Foundation Hospitals	8011	C	877 524-7373	19889
Kaiser Foundation Hospitals	8011	C	661 337-7160	19890
Kaiser Foundation Hospitals	8011	C	877 524-7373	19891
Kaiser Foundation Hospitals	8011	C	877 524-7373	19894
Kaiser Foundation Hospitals	8011	C	877 524-7373	19930
Kaiser Foundation Hospitals	8011	C	661 398-5011	19933
Kaiser Foundation Hospitals	6324	C	661 334-2020	15416
Kba Engineering LLC	3533	D	661 323-0487	7672
Kearn Alternative Care Inc **(PA)**	8082	B	661 631-2036	21178
Kenai Drilling Limited	1781	C	661 587-0117	1561
Kern Cmnty Cllege Dst Fndation	8331	D	661 336-5117	21958
Kern County Hospital Authority **(PA)**	8062	A	661 326-2102	20825
Kern Federal Credit Union	6061	D	661 327-9461	15070
Kern Health Systems Inc	8011	D	661 664-5000	19950
Kern Rdlgy Imaging Systems Inc **(PA)**	8011	D	661 326-9600	19951
Kern Rdlgy Imaging Systems Inc	8011	D	661 322-9958	19952
Kern Regional Center **(PA)**	8399	C	661 327-8531	22192
Kern Security Corporation	7382	D	661 363-6874	18390
Kern Steel Fabrication Inc **(PA)**	3441	D	661 327-9588	6626
Kindred Healthcare LLC	8082	D	661 324-1232	21180
Kirschenman Enterprises Inc	0191	D	661 366-5736	114
Klassen Corporation **(PA)**	1542	D	661 327-0875	779
Klein Denatale Goldner Et Al **(PA)**	8111	C	661 401-7755	21599
KS Industries LP **(PA)**	1623	A	661 617-1700	960
Ksi Engineering Inc	8711	D	661 617-1700	22598
Le Beau Thelen LLP	8111	D	661 325-8962	21607
Lightspeed Software Inc	7372	E	661 716-7600	17905
Lincare Inc	8082	D	661 833-3333	21185
Linnco LLC	1382	C	661 616-3900	455
Longs Drug Stores Cal Inc	7384	D	805 588-0290	18413
Lortz & Son Mfg Co	3471	C	281 241-9418	7277
Lowes Home Centers LLC	5031	C	661 588-6420	13243
Lowes Home Centers LLC	5031	C	661 699-1000	13253
Lowes Home Centers LLC	5031	C	661 889-9000	13266
M & S Security Services Inc	7381	D	661 397-9616	18296
M D Manufacturing Inc	3589	F	661 283-7550	8393
Macpherson Oil Company LLC	1382	E	661 556-6096	456
Maple Dairy LP	0241	D	661 396-9600	134
Marie Edward Vineyards Inc	3523	E	661 363-5038	7613
Mark Sheffield Construction	1389	E	661 589-8520	516
Material Control Inc	3499	D	661 617-6033	7564
Maxim Healthcare Services Inc	7363	D	661 322-3039	17503
Maya Bkrsfeld Cinemas Oper LLC	7832	E	213 805-5333	19283
Mazzei Injector Company LLC	3589	E	661 363-6500	8396
McCain & Mccain Inc	3599	F	661 322-7764	8681
Mechanical Industries Inc	1791	E	661 634-9477	1577
Merrill Lynch Prce Fnner Smith	6211	D	661 326-7700	15288
Mexicali Inc	7299	C	661 327-3861	16966
Mic	5084	E	661 401-0070	13918
Millwood Cabinet Co Inc	2434	F	661 327-0371	3327
MJM Expert Pipe Fbrcation Wldg	3441	E	661 330-8698	6641
Mmi Services Inc	1389	C	661 589-9366	518
Mobile Equipment Company	3536	E	661 327-8476	7698
Mohawk Medical Group Inc	8011	D	661 324-4747	19983
MP Environmental Svcs Inc **(PA)**	4953	C	800 458-3036	12961
Msr Hotels & Resorts Inc	6799	D	661 325-9700	16278
MTS Stimulation Services Inc **(PA)**	1389	F	661 589-5804	521
Nabors Well Services Co	1389	D	661 588-6140	523
Nabors Well Services Co	1389	D	661 589-3970	525
Nabors Well Services Co	1389	D	661 392-7668	527
National Mentor Inc	8361	E	661 387-1000	22134
Nations Petroleum Cal LLC	1382	D	661 387-6402	458
Nationwide Medical Group Inc	8069	D	661 328-0245	21048
Neon Energy Corporation	1382	E	661 829-2505	459
Nestle Ice Cream Company LLC	5143	A	661 398-3500	14545
Nestle Usa Inc	2023	C	661 398-3536	1803
New Advnces For Pple With Dsbl	8399	D	661 322-9735	22203
New Advnces For Pple With Dsbl	8399	D	661 327-0183	22204
Newby Rubber Inc	3069	E	661 327-5137	5396
Newport Hospitality Group Inc	7011	C	661 323-1900	16580
Newport Television LLC	4833	B	661 283-1700	12735
Nk Sign Industry Inc	3993	F	661 348-9580	11578
Norman Wireline Service Inc	1389	F	661 399-5697	528
North Pk Apartments Hsing Corp **(PA)**	6513	E	661 399-3084	15742
Observer Group Newspaper	2711	E	661 324-9466	4019
Oldenkamp Trucking Inc **(PA)**	4212	D	661 833-3400	11986
Olympus Property	6519	D	661 393-1700	15761
Omni Family Health **(PA)**	8011	D	661 459-1900	20011
Optimal Home Health Care Inc	8082	D	661 410-4000	21194
Outdoor Galore Inc **(PA)**	3496	F	661 831-8662	7505
Pacific Gas and Electric Co	4911	C	661 398-5918	12821
Pacific Process Systems Inc **(PA)**	1389	D	661 321-9681	533
Palmer Tank & Construction Inc	1389	E	661 834-1110	536
Pan Pacific Petroleum Co Inc	4213	C	661 589-3200	12072
Paragon Industries Inc	5032	D	661 396-0555	13311
Parkview Jlian Cnvlescent Hosp	8051	C	661 831-9150	20433
Parkview Julian LLC	8051	C	661 831-9150	20434
Pavletich Elc Cmmnications Inc **(PA)**	1731	D	661 589-9473	1293
PCL Industrial Services Inc	1542	B	661 832-3995	804
Penney Lawn Service Inc	0782	D	661 587-4788	336
Pepsi Cola Btlg of Bkersfield	2086	E	661 327-9992	2278
Perez Contracting LLC	0762	C	661 399-2700	226
Petro-Lud Inc	1381	F	661 747-4779	436
Physicians Automated Lab Inc **(DH)**	8071	D	661 325-0744	21084
Physicians Automated Lab Inc	8071	D	661 325-0744	21085
Physicians Automated Lab Inc	8011	D	661 431-1176	20023
Pioneer Sands LLC	1446	E	661 746-5789	577
PNa Construction Tech Inc	3444	E	661 326-1700	6892
Preferred Brokers Inc **(PA)**	6531	D	661 836-2345	15954
Prime Hospitality Services LLC **(PA)**	7011	D	661 321-9424	16641
Pro Safety & Rescue Inc	8742	D	888 269-5095	23300
Pro Tool Services Inc	3545	E	661 393-9222	7864
Production Data Inc	1389	E	661 327-4776	539
Pros Incorporated	1389	D	661 589-5400	540
Prosoft Technology Inc **(HQ)**	4899	C	661 716-5100	12789
PSC Industrial Outsourcing LP	1389	D	661 833-9991	541
Pyrenees French Bakery Inc	2051	E	661 322-7159	2031
Quinn Company	5082	D	661 393-5800	13868
Raudmans Craig Victory Circle	3799	E	661 833-4600	10555
Ray Chinn Construction Inc	3542	E	661 327-2731	7765
Rdr Precision Tech Inc	3533	F	661 322-8450	7675
Re/Max	6531	E	661 616-4040	15967
Reyes Coca-Cola Bottling LLC	2086	D	661 324-6531	2285
Rhino Ready Mix Trucking Inc **(PA)**	4212	E	661 679-3643	11990
Richard K Newman and Assoc Inc **(PA)**	7213	E	661 634-1130	16869
Richard K Newman and Assoc Inc	7216	D	661 634-1218	16877
Rlh Fire Protection Inc **(PA)**	1711	D	661 322-9344	1131
Robert Heely Construction LP **(PA)**	1389	E	661 617-1400	544
Ross Fabrication & Welding Inc	2499	F	661 393-1242	3454
Russell Fabrication Corp	3498	E	661 861-8495	7543
S A Camp Companies **(PA)**	5083	E	661 399-4451	13878
SA Camp Pump Company	7699	D	661 399-2976	19061
Salimar Inc	7011	D	661 327-9651	16686
San Dimas Medical Group Inc	8011	D	661 663-4800	20049
San Joaquin Bit Service Inc	5084	C	661 834-3233	13937
San Joaquin Community Hospital **(PA)**	8062	A	661 395-3000	20932
San Joaquin Refining Co Inc	2911	C	661 327-4257	5260
Sangera Buick Inc	7538	D	661 833-5200	18871
Schlumberger Technology Corp	1389	D	661 864-4750	545
Self-Insured Schools Cal **(PA)**	6371	C	661 636-4000	15520
Seneca Resources Company LLC	1382	F	661 391-3540	466
Sentinel Peak Rsources Cal LLC	1382	D	661 395-5214	467
Sequoia Exploration Inc	1311	E	661 303-0564	410
Seven Oaks Country Club	7997	C	661 664-6404	19611
Shar-Craft Inc **(PA)**	5085	E	661 324-4985	14017
Sierra International McHy LLC	5093	D	661 327-7073	14122
Silla Automotive LLC	5013	D	661 392-8880	13090

Mergent email: customerrelations@mergent.com
1336
2022 Southern California Business Directory and Buyers Guide
(P-0000) Products & Services Section entry number
(PA)=Parent Co (HQ)=Headquarters (DH)=Div Headquarters

GEOGRAPHIC SECTION BANNING, CA

	SIC	EMP	PHONE	ENTRY #
Silo City Inc	3531	E	661 387-0179	7650
Simmons Construction Inc	1542	E	661 636-1321	830
Southern Cal Prmnnte Med Group	8011	C	661 398-5085	20076
Southern Cal Prmnnte Med Group	8011	C	661 334-2020	20092
Southwest Contractors **(PA)**	1623	E	661 588-0484	972
Spalinger Enterprises Inc	2541	E	661 834-4550	3666
Spartan Inc	3441	D	661 327-1205	6663
St Jhns Lthran Ch Bakersfield	7371	C	661 665-7815	17722
Stanford Transportation Inc	4212	D	661 302-3288	11996
Stantec Energy & Resources Inc **(HQ)**	8713	C	661 396-3770	22756
Stantec Holdings Del III Inc	6719	B	661 396-3770	16113
Star-Luck Enterprise Inc	3823	F	661 665-9999	10726
State Compensation Insur Fund	6331	D	661 664-4000	15481
State Farm Mutl Auto Insur Co	6411	D	309 766-2311	15630
Stockdale Country Club	7997	D	661 832-0310	19619
Structurecast	3272	D	661 833-4490	6061
Sturgeon Services Intl Inc **(PA)**	1794	E	661 322-4408	1604
Sturgeon Services Intl Inc	3531	B	661 322-4408	7651
Sturgeon Son Grading & Pav Inc **(PA)**	1794	C	661 322-4408	1605
Sun Pacific Farming Coop Inc	0762	D	661 399-0376	230
Sun Pacific Maricopa	0723	D	661 847-1015	186
Sun Pacific Marketing Coop Inc	8742	B	213 612-9957	23337
Sun Pacific Marketing Coop Inc	5148	B	661 847-1015	14657
Sun World Inc	0723	A	805 833-6460	188
Sun World International Inc **(PA)**	0723	A	661 392-5000	189
Sun World International LLC **(HQ)**	0191	B	661 392-5000	119
Sun-Gro Commodities Inc **(PA)**	2048	E	661 393-2612	1976
Sunridge Nurseries Inc	0721	D	661 363-8463	149
Sunshine Metal Clad Inc	1742	D	661 366-0575	1403
Surface Pumps Inc **(PA)**	5084	D	661 393-1545	13946
Surgener Electric Inc	1731	D	661 399-3321	1323
Swissmann Engineering Inc	3545	F	760 223-0663	7872
Sycamore Cogeneration Co **(PA)**	4911	D	661 615-4630	12862
T D Whitton Construction Inc	0781	E	661 834-5894	286
Technosocialworkcom LLC	7374	D	661 617-6601	18113
Temblor Brewing LLC	2082	E	661 489-4855	2157
Thermal Energy Solutions Inc	1623	F	661 489-4100	978
Theta Oilfield Services Inc	1389	E	661 633-2792	548
Thomson International Inc	0191	F	661 845-1111	121
Tiburon Hospitality LLC	7011	C	661 322-1012	16753
Tiger Tanks Inc	3795	E	661 363-8335	10548
Titan Oilfield Services Inc	1389	E	661 861-1630	550
Tj Cross Engineers Inc	8711	D	661 831-8782	22675
Total Process Solutions LLC	3561	E	661 829-7910	8025
Townsend Industries Inc	3842	D	661 837-1795	11146
Townsend Industries Inc	3842	D	661 837-1795	11147
Trans-West Services Inc	7381	B	661 381-2900	18345
TRC Companies Inc	8748	E	661 837-0022	23518
Tricor Refining LLC	2911	E	661 393-7110	5263
Triple E Manufacturing	3556	E	661 831-7553	7954
Truitt Oilfield Maint Corp	1389	B	661 871-4099	553
Truxtun Psychtric Med Group LP	8011	D	661 323-6410	20112
Truxtun Radiology Med Group LP **(HQ)**	8011	B	661 325-6800	20113
Trv Investments LLC **(HQ)**	6799	D	661 378-3846	16299
Turman Construction Co Inc	1611	D	661 831-0905	924
U M S Inc	3471	E	661 324-5454	7325
U S Weatherford L P	1389	C	661 589-9483	555
UCI Construction Inc	8711	D	661 587-0192	22680
Unified Field Services Corp	1311	E	661 325-8962	412
UPF Corporation	3296	E	661 323-8227	6173
Valley Indus X-Ray Insptn Svcs	7389	D	661 399-8497	18716
Valley Instrument Service Inc **(PA)**	5084	C	661 327-8681	13956
Valley Perforating LLC	3599	D	661 324-4964	8835
Valley Republic Bank	6022	D	661 371-2000	15045
Valley Strong Credit Union **(PA)**	6061	D	661 833-7900	15099
Valley Strong Credit Union	6061	D	661 833-7920	15100
Valley Strong Credit Union	6061	D	661 833-7940	15101
Valley Strong Credit Union	6061	D	661 833-7900	15102
Valley Sun Mech Cnstr Inc	1799	D	661 321-9070	1697
Vaquero Energy Inc	1389	E	661 616-0600	557
Vaquero Energy Incorporated	1311	E	661 363-7240	413
Varner Bros Inc	4953	D	661 399-2944	12989
Vasinda Investments Inc	7363	D	661 324-4277	17521
Vasindas Around Clock Care Inc	8361	E	661 395-5820	22162
Vertical Tank Inc	2591	F	415 686-8796	3718
Veterans Health Administration	8011	C	661 632-1871	20152
Veterans Health Administration	8011	C	661 323-8387	20154
Vignolo Farms Inc	0131	C	661 746-2148	5
Vita-Pakt Citrus Products Co **(PA)**	2033	E	626 332-1101	1879
W A Thompson Inc **(PA)**	5181	D	661 832-5101	14837
Wall Street Alley T-Shirt Co	5137	E	661 324-6207	14426
Water Associates LLC	3663	E	661 281-6077	9327
Weatherford Completion Systems	1389	F	661 746-1391	558
Well Analysis Corporation Inc **(PA)**	2411	E	661 283-9510	3205
West American Energy Corp	1381	F	661 747-7732	439
Westair Gases & Equipment Inc	5084	C	661 387-6800	13963
Western Energy Services Corp	7353	C	403 984-5916	17321
Western Oilfields Supply Co **(PA)**	7359	C	661 399-9124	17384
Wholesale Fuels Inc	5172	D	661 327-4900	14816
Willis Electric Inc	7629	E	661 324-2781	18961
Wm Bolthouse Farms Inc **(HQ)**	0161	A	661 366-7209	22
Wonderful Company LLC	0723	B	559 781-7438	194
Work Force Services Inc	7363	C	661 327-5019	17532
Wtb Technology	2873	F	661 327-9604	5163
Xpo Logistics Freight Inc	4213	D	661 324-2947	12095
Zim Industries Inc	1781	C	661 393-9661	1563

BALDWIN PARK, CA - Los Angeles County

	SIC	EMP	PHONE	ENTRY #
American Kal Enterprises Inc **(PA)**	5072	D	626 338-7308	13794
American Mzhou Dngpo Group Inc	8741	D	626 820-9239	22975
Ametek Ameron LLC	3812	E	626 337-4640	10565
Ametek Ameron LLC **(HQ)**	3823	D	626 856-0101	10675
Anura Plastic Engineerign	3089	E	626 814-9684	5564
Assa Abloy Rsdential Group Inc **(HQ)**	5072	C	626 961-0413	13795
B & B Red-I-Mix Concrete Inc	3273	F	626 359-8371	6072
Baldwin Hospitality LLC	7011	D	626 446-2988	16337
Baldwin Hospitality LLC	7011	D	626 962-6000	16338
Baldwin Park Unified Schl Dst	8351	D	626 337-2711	21984
C&M Industries	3999	F	626 391-5102	11643
Cedarwood-Young Company **(PA)**	4953	C	626 962-4047	12937
Cedarwood-Young Company	5093	D	626 962-4047	14112
Cera Inc	3821	E	626 814-2688	10654
Checkworks Inc	2782	D	626 333-1444	4607
Condor Outdoor Products Inc **(PA)**	3949	E	626 358-3270	11410
Crosstown Elec & Data Inc	1731	D	626 813-6693	1238
Crowner Sheet Metal Pdts Inc	1761	E	626 960-4971	1481
Denovo Dental Inc	3843	E	626 480-0182	11167
Distinct Indulgence Inc	2051	E	818 546-1700	1996
Exquisite Corporation	2844	F	626 856-0200	5020
Fabtronic Inc	3444	E	626 962-3293	6837
Falcon Electric Inc	3612	F	626 962-7770	8870
First Avenue Inc	1761	D	626 856-2076	1485
First Student Inc	4151	C	855 870-8747	11926
Freudenberg Medical LLC	3841	C	626 814-9684	10983
Front Edge Technology Inc	3691	E	626 856-8979	9810
G & I Islas Industries Inc **(PA)**	3556	E	626 960-5020	7936
G K Tool Corp	5072	D	626 338-7300	13807
Gammill Electric Inc	1731	F	626 812-4515	1258
Garden View Care Center Inc	8051	E	626 962-7095	20351
Georg Fischer Signet LLC	3823	D	626 571-2770	10697
George Fischer Inc **(HQ)**	3599	B	626 571-2770	8605
Golden State Habilitation Conv **(PA)**	8051	C	626 962-3274	20362
Gr8 Care Inc	8051	D	626 337-7229	20365
Haynes Building Service LLC	7349	C	626 359-6100	17249
Health Care Provider Labs Inc	8071	D	626 813-3800	21070
Hemosure Inc	2899	E	888 436-6787	5222
Ideal Transit Inc	4111	E	626 448-2690	11812
Jax and Bones Inc	3999	E	626 363-9350	11694
Kaiser Foundation Hospitals	8011	C	310 922-8916	19859
Kaiser Foundation Hospitals	6324	A	626 851-1011	15404
Kal-Cameron Manufacturing Corp **(HQ)**	3423	D	626 338-7308	6483
Kci Newport Inc	2599	F	877 302-5302	3734
Knd Development 52 LLC	8062	D	626 388-2700	20830
Lawrence Roll Up Doors Inc **(PA)**	3442	E	626 962-4163	6706
Lighting Technologies Intl LLC	5063	C	626 480-0755	13640
Meritek Electronics Corp **(PA)**	3559	D	626 373-1728	7990
Mission Kleensweep Prod Inc	2841	D	323 223-1405	4944
Miyako Oriental Foods Inc	2075	F	626 962-9633	2119
Motek Industries	3599	F	626 960-6005	8711
My Machine Inc	3599	F	626 214-9223	8713
New York Frozen Foods Inc	2051	E	626 338-3000	2023
Nichols Lumber & Hardware Co	5031	D	626 960-4802	13278
Normans Nursery Inc	5193	C	626 285-9795	14893
Ols Hotels & Resorts LLC	7011	A	626 962-6000	16594
P C P Inc	5199	F	626 813-6166	14959
Pacific Award Metals Inc **(HQ)**	3444	D	626 814-4410	6887
Pacon Inc	2621	C	626 814-4654	3767
Philips Elec N Amer Corp	3827	C	626 480-0755	10855
Phoenix Pumps California Inc	3561	E	858 278-2223	8019
Phoenix Satellite TV US Inc	4841	E	626 388-1188	12776
PSC Circuits Inc	3672	F	626 373-1728	9442
R & R Metal Fabricators	3441	F	626 960-6400	6657
Ray Gaskin Service	7699	E	909 574-7000	19059
Rbc Southwest Products Inc	5085	D	626 358-0181	14012
Reny & Co Inc	3089	F	626 962-3078	5792
Rigos Equipment Mfg LLC	3444	E	626 813-6621	6902
S and C Precision Inc	3679	E	626 338-7149	9777
San Gabriel Transit Inc	4121	D	626 430-3650	11901
Sanders Candy Factory Inc	2064	E	626 814-2038	2103
SCE Federal Credit Union **(PA)**	6061	D	626 960-6888	15080
Southern California Edison Co	4911	C	626 543-6093	12833
Standard Concrete Products Inc **(HQ)**	3273	E	310 829-4537	6118
Survey Stake and Marker Inc	2499	E	626 960-4802	3455
Tanimura Antle Fresh Foods Inc	0723	B	831 424-6100	191
Tecan Sp Inc	5049	D	626 962-0010	13542
Telesector Resources Group Inc	8742	B	626 813-4538	23344
Tim Guzzy Services Inc	3599	E	626 813-0626	8819
Touchdown Technologies Inc	3674	E	626 472-6732	9592
Treasure Garden Inc **(PA)**	2514	E	626 814-0168	3535
Trinity Health Systems **(PA)**	8051	D	626 960-1971	20490
United Parcel Service Inc	4215	C	626 814-6216	12169
Universal Steel Services Inc	3441	D	626 960-1455	6675
Upm Inc	3544	B	626 962-4001	7840
Vista Spclty Hosp Sthern Cal L	8062	C	626 388-2700	21005
Waste MGT Collectn Recycl Inc	4953	D	626 960-7551	12998
Yutaka Electric Intl Inc	3629	F	626 962-7770	8985

BANNING, CA - Riverside County

	SIC	EMP	PHONE	ENTRY #
C Brent Peeke DDS Inc **(PA)**	8021	D	951 845-4685	20171
Century Publishing	2759	F	951 849-4586	4494
DT Mattson Enterprises Inc	3944	E	951 849-9781	11372
Green Thumb Produce Inc	5148	C	951 849-4711	14636
J & L Daycare	8361	D	951 849-1429	22119
Porto Inc	8322	D	760 709-3737	21871

GEOGRAPHIC

Employment Codes: A=Over 500 employees, B=251-500, C=101-250, D=51-100, E=20-50 F=10-19

2022 Southern California Business Directory and Buyers Guide

© Mergent Inc. 1-800-342-5647

1337

	SIC	EMP	PHONE	ENTRY #
Professional Cmnty MGT Cal Inc	6531	C	951 845-2191	15957
San Gorgonio Memorial Hospital	8062	A	951 845-1121	20930
San Grgnio Mem Hosp Foundation **(PA)**	8062	C	951 845-1121	20931
Silent Valley Club Inc	7011	D	951 849-4501	16710
Strech Plastics Incorporated	5088	E	951 922-2224	14065
Zenner Performance Meters Inc	3824	E	951 849-8822	10740

BARSTOW, CA - San Bernardino County

	SIC	EMP	PHONE	ENTRY #
Barstow Healthcare MGT Inc **(DH)**	8742	E	831 319-4194	23167
Country Side Inn Ontario LP	7011	D	909 390-7778	16390
First Student Inc	4151	C	760 256-2333	11932
Five Star Food Containers Inc	3086	C	626 437-6219	5500
Green Valley Foods Product	2022	F	760 964-1105	1773
Hentrel Greathouse Foundation	8641	D	302 513-4056	22341
Holiday Inn Ex Ht & Suites LLC	7011	D	760 253-9200	16486
Hospital of Barstow Inc **(DH)**	8062	C	760 256-1761	20794
Kar Ice Service Inc **(PA)**	2097	F	760 256-2648	2372
Life Care Centers America Inc	8051	C	760 252-2515	20399
On The Rise Inc	8399	D	760 964-7473	22205
United Parcel Service Inc	4215	C	760 252-5766	12153

BEAUMONT, CA - Riverside County

	SIC	EMP	PHONE	ENTRY #
Anderson Chrnesky Strl Stl Inc	3441	D	951 769-5700	6587
ARC Riverside	8322	D	951 845-3385	21715
Beaumont Juice Inc	2033	D	951 769-7171	1859
Beaumont Unfied Schl Dst Pub F	8351	B	951 845-6580	21985
Bogh Engineering Inc	1771	D	951 845-5130	1518
CJ Foods Mfg Beaumont Corp	3999	E	951 916-9300	11653
David-Kleis II LLC	8099	D	951 845-3125	21410
Dura Plastic Products Inc **(HQ)**	3089	D	951 845-3161	5631
Focus Vsion Clnic Optmetry Inc **(PA)**	8042	D	951 845-4749	20206
Kpu Roofing	1761	E	909 586-2531	1493
Precision Stampg Solutions Inc	3469	E	951 845-1174	7175
Precision Stampings Inc **(PA)**	3643	E	951 845-1174	9045
Priority Pallet Inc	2448	E	951 769-9399	3404
Risco Inc	3452	E	951 769-2899	7073
Wholesale Shutter Company Inc	2431	F	951 845-8786	3298

BELL, CA - Los Angeles County

	SIC	EMP	PHONE	ENTRY #
Briarcrest Nursing Center Inc	8051	D	562 927-2641	20263
Carol Wior Inc	2339	E	562 927-0052	2930
Dcx-Chol Enterprises Inc	3679	E	562 927-5531	9700
De Well Container Shipping Inc	4731	D	310 735-8600	12443
El Aviso Magazine	5192	E	323 586-9199	14871
Fam LLC **(PA)**	2231	C	323 888-7755	2612
Fam Ppe LLC	5099	C	323 888-7755	14155
Flores Brothers Inc	2099	F	562 806-9128	2433
Hain Celestial Group Inc	2844	C	323 859-0553	5029
Hg Graphic & Printing	2752	F	323 412-3866	4315
Human Services Association **(PA)**	8322	D	562 806-5400	21807
J P Turgeon & Sons Inc	3471	E	323 773-3105	7272
Jwch Institute Inc	8733	C	323 562-5813	22911
Leonid M Glsman DDS A Dntl Cor	8021	C	323 560-4514	20186
M M S Trading Inc	5199	F	323 587-1082	14950
Marika LLC	2339	D	323 888-7755	2971
Omega Moulding West LLC	5023	C	323 261-3510	13182
Pacesetter Inc	3845	C	323 773-0591	11235
Perrin Bernard Supowitz LLC **(HQ)**	5113	D	323 981-2800	14224
West Coast-Accudyne Inc	3542	E	562 927-2546	7769

BELL GARDENS, CA - Los Angeles County

	SIC	EMP	PHONE	ENTRY #
Anitsa Inc	7211	C	213 237-0533	16835
Bell Gardens Bicycle Club Inc	7999	A	562 806-4646	19637
Bicycle Casino LP	7011	A	562 806-4646	16351
Bus Services Corporation	3714	E	562 231-1770	10025
Cal Southern Braiding Inc	3679	D	562 927-5531	9687
Carnevale & Lohr Inc	3281	E	562 927-8311	6136
Del Rio Sanitarium Inc	8051	C	562 927-6586	20309
Eurocraft Archtectural Met Inc	3446	E	323 771-1323	6961
Flexco Inc	3728	E	562 927-2525	10328
Infinity Kitchen Products Inc	3444	F	562 806-5771	6852
McLane Manufacturing Inc	3524	D	562 633-8158	7628
Metal Surfaces Intl LLC	3471	C	562 927-1331	7282
Naranjo Pallets	2448	F	323 637-8019	3400
Rob Inc	2325	D	562 806-5589	2773
Wilcox Machine Co	3599	D	562 927-5353	8852

BELLFLOWER, CA - Los Angeles County

	SIC	EMP	PHONE	ENTRY #
Advent Securities Investments **(PA)**	6211	E	562 920-5467	15261
Bell Villa Care Associates LLC	8051	D	562 925-4252	20253
Black & Decker (us) Inc	3546	F	562 925-7551	7879
Bryant Rubber Corp	3053	C	310 530-2530	5329
County of Los Angeles	8011	D	562 804-8111	19769
Cutting Edge Creative LLC	2542	D	562 907-7007	3681
Danco Valve Company	3491	E	562 925-2588	7443
Empire Transportation	4141	B	562 529-2676	11906
Express Sheet Metal Product	3444	E	562 925-9340	6834
George Chevrolet	7515	D	562 925-2500	18749
Habitat For Hmnity Grter Los A	8399	E	310 323-4663	22185
Harbor Health Care Inc	8361	C	562 866-7054	22108
Hollywood Sports Park LLC	7389	D	562 867-9600	18545
Ice Man Inc	2097	E	562 633-4423	2371
Jwch Institute Inc	8099	B	562 867-7999	21445
Kaiser Foundation Hospitals	6324	C	562 461-3084	15426
Kevin White	2711	F	562 231-6642	3999
Life Care Centers America Inc	8051	C	562 867-1761	20397
Maintech Resources Inc	1796	E	562 804-0664	1624
Mieron Inc	3841	F	626 466-9040	11025
Peter Wylan DDS	8021	D	562 925-3765	20194

	SIC	EMP	PHONE	ENTRY #
Pioneer Medical Group Inc	8062	D	562 867-8681	20894
S J S Enterprise Inc	7999	C	949 489-9000	19666

BERMUDA DUNES, CA - Riverside County

	SIC	EMP	PHONE	ENTRY #
Bermuda Dunes Country Club	7997	E	760 360-2481	19544
Earth Systems Southwest **(HQ)**	8711	D	760 345-1588	22537
KDI Elements	1743	D	760 345-9933	1417
Vintage Associates Inc	0782	C	760 772-3673	350

BEVERLY HILLS, CA - Los Angeles County

	SIC	EMP	PHONE	ENTRY #
Academy Foundation **(HQ)**	7819	E	310 247-3000	19217
Academy Mpic Arts & Sciences **(PA)**	8621	D	310 247-3000	22264
Agency For Performing Arts Inc	7922	D	310 888-4200	19302
Agency For Performing Arts Inc **(PA)**	7922	D	310 557-9049	19303
Agoura Health Products LLC **(PA)**	5122	D	800 852-0477	14232
American Health Connection	7389	A	424 226-0420	18443
American Solar LLC	3433	E	323 250-1307	6568
Anderson Assoc Staffing Corp **(PA)**	7363	C	323 930-3170	17485
APA Incorporated	8742	D	310 888-4200	23160
Artica & Arbox LLC	2389	F	213 446-6272	3067
Beautiful Group LLC **(PA)**	7231	C	310 299-4100	16896
Bedford Surgical Center Inc	8071	D	310 271-6996	21060
Belvedere Hotel Partnership	7011	B	310 551-2888	16342
Belvedere Partnership	7011	B	310 551-2888	16343
Bernardi Financial Inc	2311	E	323 581-1900	2742
Beverly Hills Courier Inc	2711	E	310 278-1322	3953
Beverly Hills Escrow A Cal	6531	D	310 273-9850	15789
Beverly Hlls Onclogy Med Group	8069	D	310 432-8900	21035
Beverly Holdings Inc	7011	C	310 274-7777	16349
Bloom Hergott Diemer Cook LLC	8111	D	310 859-6800	21518
Blue Lagoon Textile Inc	7389	E	213 590-4545	18461
Brillstein Entrmt Partners LLC **(PA)**	7812	D	310 205-5100	19103
BW Hotel LLC	7011	A	310 275-5200	16361
Bwr Public Relations	8743	D	310 248-6100	23378
Capricor Therapeutics Inc **(PA)**	2834	F	310 358-3200	4804
Casewise Systems Inc **(DH)**	5045	D	424 284-4101	13381
Cedars-Sinai Medical Center	8062	B	310 967-1884	20702
Cedars-Sinai Medical Center	8062	B	310 385-3326	20703
Cedars-Sinai Medical Center	8062	B	310 385-3400	20707
Century Pacific Realty Corp	6552	C	310 729-9922	16048
Charles & Cynthia Eberly Inc	6513	D	323 937-6468	15722
City National Asset MGT Inc	8742	D	310 888-6441	23190
City National Securities Inc	6021	C	310 888-6393	14999
Collective MGT Group LLC	8741	C	323 655-8585	23006
Condor Productions LLC	7819	D	310 449-3000	19223
Credit Monkey LLC	7323	D	877 701-7307	17121
Crescent Hotel	7011	D	310 247-0505	16398
Cznd Inc	7929	D	323 378-6505	19346
D&A Endeavors Inc	1799	D	310 390-7540	1653
Decorators Rug Warehouse Inc **(PA)**	2273	D	310 638-8300	2688
Drywired Defense LLC	3479	F	310 684-3891	7358
El Camino Management Company	8741	D	310 276-3154	23020
Endeavor Group Holdings Inc **(PA)**	7941	D	310 285-9000	19415
ERA Products Inc	2531	F	310 324-4908	3623
Fashion World Incorporated	5136	C	310 273-6544	14332
Gang Tyre Ramer & Brown Inc	8111	E	310 777-7158	21562
Gersh Agency Inc **(PA)**	7922	D	310 274-6611	19311
Ggwh LLC	7011	E	310 786-1700	16455
Ghp Management Corporation	8741	B	310 432-1441	23030
Gores Group LLC **(PA)**	6211	D	310 209-3010	15268
GPh Medical & Legal Services **(PA)**	8051	C	213 207-2700	20364
Harris Construction Inc	2752	F	310 246-0188	4312
Heritage Auctions Inc	7389	D	310 300-8390	18541
Hillquest SEC Patrol Svcs Inc	7382	E	213 213-9763	18384
Hilton Inns Inc **(HQ)**	7011	A	310 278-4321	16476
Hollywood Reporter	2711	E	323 525-2150	3991
Hollywood Reporter LLC	2711	E	323 525-2000	3992
Honeymoon Real Estate LP	7011	D	310 277-5221	16490
House Blues Houston Rest Corp	7929	C	310 867-7000	19355
House Blues Orlando Rest Corp	7929	C	310 867-7000	19356
IMG Worldwide LLC **(PA)**	5137	C	424 653-1900	14381
Insomniac Inc	7929	C	323 874-7020	19358
Insomniac Holdings LLC **(HQ)**	7929	C	323 874-7020	19359
Instant Tuck Inc	2392	E	310 955-8824	3103
Jeffries Global Inc	1799	D	888 255-3488	1667
Kate Somerville Skincare LLC **(PA)**	2834	D	323 655-7546	4838
Keller Wllams Rlty Bvrly Hills	6531	D	310 432-6400	15899
Kennedy-Wilson Inc **(PA)**	6531	C	310 887-6400	15900
Kevidko Inc	2621	F	310 601-0060	3758
Klooma Holdings Inc	7372	E	305 747-3315	17902
L F P Inc **(PA)**	2721	D	323 651-3525	4077
La Peer Surgery Center LLC	8011	D	310 360-9119	19954
Lane & Kuschner Medical Group	8011	D	310 858-0104	19958
Laseraway Medical Group Inc **(PA)**	8011	C	888 252-7497	19960
Levi Strauss & Co	2325	F	310 246-9044	2772
Levine Leichtman Capital	6794	D	310 275-5335	16211
Lfk Law	8111	D	310 300-8464	21613
Live Nation Concerts Inc	7929	E	310 867-7132	19362
Live Nation Entertainment Inc **(PA)**	7389	C	310 867-7000	18580
Live Nation Mtours (usa) Inc **(HQ)**	7922	D	310 867-7000	19322
Live Nation Worldwide Inc	7929	A	310 867-7000	19363
Lorber Industries California	2261	E	310 275-1568	2659
Lorser Industries Inc	3672	E	619 917-4298	9424
M L Stern & Co LLC **(DH)**	6211	C	323 658-4400	15275
Magic Workforce Solutions LLC	8743	A	310 246-6153	23381
Management 360	7922	D	310 272-7000	19323
Marcus Buckingham Company LLC	8742	D	323 302-9810	23268
Massachusetts Mutl Lf Insur Co	6311	D	323 965-6339	15364

Mergent email: customerrelations@mergent.com
1338

2022 Southern California Business
Directory and Buyers Guide

(P-0000) Products & Services Section entry number
(PA)=Parent Co (HQ)=Headquarters (DH)=Div Headquarters

	SIC	EMP	PHONE	ENTRY #
Maurice Kraiem & Company	5094	E	213 629-0038	14134
Mediachase Ltd	7371	D	323 988-1071	17659
Medical Group Bverly Hills Inc	8011	E	310 247-4646	19972
Merrill Lynch Pierce Fenner	6211	E	310 858-1500	15276
Metro-Goldwyn-Mayer Inc **(DH)**	7812	B	310 449-3000	19150
MGM and Ua Services Company	8999	A	310 449-3000	23536
MGM Holdings II Inc **(HQ)**	7812	D	310 449-3000	19151
Mob Scene LLC **(PA)**	7311	C	323 648-7200	17036
Montage Hotels & Resorts LLC	7011	D	310 499-4199	16571
Morgan Stnley Smith Barney LLC	6153	C	310 285-4800	15155
Morgan Turner Freeman **(PA)**	7381	D	310 800-3502	18297
Murphy OBrien Inc	8743	D	310 453-2539	23382
Nextpoint Inc **(PA)**	4813	D	310 360-5904	12659
Nga 911 LLC	7371	D	877 899-8337	17676
Nourmand & Associates	6531	E	310 274-4000	15934
Oasis West Realty LLC	7011	D	310 860-6666	16589
Ophthalmic Facial Plastic **(PA)**	8011	D	310 276-0044	20013
Oral Essentials Inc	2844	F	888 773-5273	5053
Orion Pictures Corporation	7812	A	310 449-3000	19158
Pacwest Bancorp **(PA)**	6021	C	310 887-8500	15006
Page Private School	8351	D	323 272-3429	22046
Paradigm Music LLC **(PA)**	7922	D	310 288-8000	19325
Park Hotels & Resorts Inc	7011	C	310 415-3340	16621
Participant Media LLC **(PA)**	7812	D	310 550-5100	19160
Pepsico Inc	2086	F	323 785-2820	2280
Perkins Development Group Inc **(PA)**	1541	D	213 447-4464	714
Platinum Equity Partners LLC	6726	D	310 712-1850	16161
Project Skyline Intermediate H	6719	A	310 712-1850	16108
Promote Media LP	8742	D	323 433-7950	23302
Protected Outcomes Corporation	7381	D	203 545-9565	18314
Protravel International LLC	4724	D	310 271-9566	12399
Pse Holding LLC **(DH)**	7941	B	248 377-0165	19428
Raffles Lrmitage Beverly Hills	7011	C	310 278-3344	16653
Regent LP **(PA)**	6799	D	310 299-4100	16288
Regis Corporation	7231	E	310 274-8791	16916
Rheumatology Diagnostics Lab	8071	D	310 253-5455	21094
Rmbb Properties LLC **(PA)**	6512	D	310 473-5562	15693
Robin Singh Eductl Svcs Inc	8748	D	310 460-7199	23503
Rodeo Realty Inc **(PA)**	6531	D	818 349-9997	15984
Rolex Watch USA Inc	7631	D	310 271-6200	18962
Rootstrap Inc	7371	C	310 907-9210	17702
Row Management Ltd Inc	6531	B	310 887-3671	15992
Royal Blue Inc	2392	E	310 888-0156	3118
Royal-Pedic Mattress Mfg LLC **(PA)**	2515	E	310 278-9594	3558
Run The Play Entertainment LLC	7929	F	800 978-9638	19376
S J S Link International Inc **(PA)**	5142	E	310 860-7666	14530
Sajahtera Inc	7011	A	310 276-2251	16685
Seaworld Global Logistics	4731	B	310 579-9164	12524
Shapell Industries LLC **(HQ)**	6552	D	323 655-7330	16072
SOS Security LLC	7381	D	310 859-8248	18338
Starpint 1031 Property MGT LLC	6531	C	310 247-0550	16010
Stockcross Financial Svcs Inc **(DH)**	6211	E	800 993-2015	15307
Stratos Renewables Corporation	2869	E	310 402-5901	5149
Studio 71 LP	7313	C	323 370-1500	17090
Susannas Inc	2335	F	310 276-7510	2897
Telemedicine Corp	8099	E	888 472-2853	21489
Teles Properties Inc **(PA)**	6531	D	424 202-3200	16014
Tiffanys Liu	8322	D	415 644-0846	21902
Tornante-MDP Joe Holding LLC **(PA)**	5092	F	310 228-6800	14103
Tower Hmtlogy Onclogy Med Grou	8011	D	310 888-8680	20110
Treepeople Inc	0783	E	818 753-4600	362
Ubi Energy Corporation	2911	C	310 283-6978	5264
United Artists Entrmt LLC **(PA)**	7929	D	310 449-3000	19382
Universal Home Care Inc	8082	C	323 653-9222	21226
Village Rdshow Entrmt Group US	7812	E	310 867-8000	19198
Vitacig Inc	2111	E	310 402-6937	2554
West Coast Storm Inc **(PA)**	8744	E	909 890-5700	23398
West World Productions Inc	2721	E	310 276-9500	4112
Westside Crdvsclar Med Group I **(PA)**	8011	D	310 623-1150	20163
William Morris Rodeo Inc **(HQ)**	6512	D	310 859-4000	15712
William Mrris Endvor Entrmt FN **(DH)**	7922	C	310 285-9000	19339
William Mrris Endvor Entrmt LL	7922	B	310 285-9000	19340
Wolverine Intrmdate Hldg II Co **(PA)**	8741	B	310 712-1850	23141
Wolverine Top Holding Corp	6719	D	661 772-7500	16116
Workbook Inc	2731	F	323 856-0008	4146
World Mvie Awrds Orgnztion Wma	8641	D	833 375-5857	22379
Worldwide Inc	6531	D	310 276-7171	16035
Za Management	8741	D	310 271-2200	23144
Zeons Inc	3229	B	323 302-8299	5944
Zillionaire Empress Danielle B	6722	A	310 461-9923	16151

BIG BEAR CITY, CA - San Bernardino County

	SIC	EMP	PHONE	ENTRY #
Snow Summit Ski Corporation	7999	D	909 585-2517	19670

BIG BEAR LAKE, CA - San Bernardino County

	SIC	EMP	PHONE	ENTRY #
Action Response Team Inc	3826	F	909 585-9019	10776
Alderwood Group LLC **(PA)**	8741	D	909 866-6445	22970
Bear Vly Cmnty Healthcare Dst **(PA)**	8062	C	909 866-6501	20686
Big Bear Bowling Barn Inc	1799	E	909 878-2695	1639
Big Bear Lake Resort Assn Inc	7011	E	909 866-6190	16352
Hi-Desert Publishing Company	2711	E	909 866-3456	3989
Pacific Snow Valley Resort LLC	7011	D	909 866-3121	16613
Snow Summit Ski Corporation **(PA)**	7011	C	909 866-5766	16718

BISHOP, CA - Inyo County

	SIC	EMP	PHONE	ENTRY #
Best Wstn Bshp Hlday Spa Lodge	7011	D	760 873-3543	16346
Bishop Care Center	8051	D	760 872-1000	20256
Bishop Paiute Gaming Corp	7011	C	760 872-6005	16353
Cal-Tron Corporation	3089	E	760 873-8491	5593
Eastern Sierra Transit Auth	4111	E	760 872-1901	11805
Frontier California Inc	4813	B	760 872-0812	12640
High Sierra Plastics	3089	F	760 873-5600	5662
Northern Inyo Healthcare Dst	8062	B	760 873-5811	20871
Snk Lodging Inc	7011	D	760 872-2423	16717
Southern California Edison Co	4911	C	760 873-0715	12830
Toiyabe Indian Health Prj Inc **(PA)**	8021	D	760 873-8461	20202
United Parcel Service Inc	4215	C	760 872-7661	12152

BLOOMINGTON, CA - San Bernardino County

	SIC	EMP	PHONE	ENTRY #
Accurate Delivery Systems Inc	4212	D	951 823-8870	11953
Acts For Children **(PA)**	8361	D	909 877-5590	22077
Advance Powder Coatings LLC	3479	F	909 543-0014	7337
Atlas Pacific Corporation **(PA)**	5093	E	909 421-1200	14110
Calmex Engineering Inc	1771	D	909 546-1311	1519
Chiro Inc **(PA)**	5087	B	909 879-1160	14034
Cummins Pacific LLC	3519	F	909 877-0433	7592
Dura Technologies Inc	2851	C	909 877-8477	5096
Empire Oil Co	5172	A	909 877-0226	14803
Englewood Marketing Group LLC	4731	D	909 875-3649	12454
Ftdi West Inc	4225	D	909 473-1111	12207
Gxo Logistics Supply Chain Inc	4225	A	336 309-6201	12210
Heater Designs Inc	3567	E	909 421-0971	8089
Hogan Co Inc	3315	E	909 421-0245	6227
Hydraulic Shop Inc	3537	E	909 875-9336	7709
Lineage Logistics Holdings LLC	4214	C	909 874-1200	12114
MCM Construction Inc	1622	C	909 875-0533	929
Mitco Industries Inc **(PA)**	3599	E	909 877-0800	8701
Optimum Inc **(PA)**	8711	C	909 990-0767	22625
Products/Techniques Inc	2851	F	909 877-3951	5109
Quality Tech Mfg Inc	3721	E	909 465-9565	10201
Remco Mch & Fabrication Inc	3599	F	909 877-3530	8765
Revchem Composites Inc **(PA)**	5033	D	909 877-8477	13327
Roberts Lumber Sales Inc	5031	D	909 350-9164	13284
Rpp Products Inc **(PA)**	5172	F	800 657-4811	14806
Sfpp LP	4612	D	909 877-2373	12375
Social Science Service Center	8069	D	909 421-7120	21053
Team West Contracting Corp	1799	D	951 340-3426	1693
Unified Aircraft Services Inc **(PA)**	4783	D	909 877-0535	12559
United Parcel Service Inc	4512	D	909 349-4343	12323
Vance Corporation	1611	E	909 355-4333	926
Wadco Industries Inc	3441	E	909 874-7800	6681
Westco Industries Inc	3441	E	909 874-8700	6683

BLUE JAY, CA - San Bernardino County

	SIC	EMP	PHONE	ENTRY #
Alpine Camp Conference Ctr Inc	7999	D	909 337-6287	19632
Travis Snyder	3531	E	909 338-6302	7654

BLYTHE, CA - Riverside County

	SIC	EMP	PHONE	ENTRY #
Anup Inc	7011	D	760 921-2300	16326
Blythe Energy Inc	1321	F	760 922-9950	419
Crawford Associates	1771	E	760 922-6804	1520
Fisher Ranch LLC	0723	D	760 922-4151	170
Hayday Farms Inc	0139	D	760 922-4713	7
Inland Builders Supply Inc	5031	E	760 922-0361	13217
Palo Verde Health Care Dst	8062	C	760 922-4115	20881
Palo Verde Hospital Assn	8062	C	760 922-4115	20882
Palo Verde Irrigation District	4971	D	760 922-3144	13014
Xpo Logistics Freight Inc	4213	D	760 922-8538	12101

BORON, CA - Kern County

	SIC	EMP	PHONE	ENTRY #
Hall Ambulance Service Inc	4119	E	760 762-6402	11872
Rio Tinto Minerals Inc	1241	C	760 762-7121	383
US Borax Inc	2819	A	760 762-7000	4673

BRAWLEY, CA - Imperial County

	SIC	EMP	PHONE	ENTRY #
Border Valley Trading Ltd	5191	D	760 344-6700	14854
Border Valley Trading Ltd	5191	D	760 344-6700	14855
Brawley Union High School Dist **(PA)**	8351	C	760 312-6068	21991
Broma Applicators LLC	5191	E	760 351-0101	14856
City of Brawley **(PA)**	8611	D	760 344-8941	22245
Crown Citrus Company Inc	2037	F	760 344-1930	1897
Esparza Enterprises Inc	0762	C	760 344-2031	221
Fiesta Mexican Foods Inc	2051	E	760 344-3580	2000
Grimmway Enterprises Inc	7538	C	760 344-0204	18837
Mesquite Cattle Feeders Inc	0211	E	760 344-2944	124
Moiola Bros Cttle Fders Ltd A	0211	D	760 344-1919	125
Owb Packers LLC	2011	E	760 351-2700	1717
Pacific Sun Labor	0761	D	760 556-5085	218
Pioneers Mem Healthcare Dst **(PA)**	8062	A	760 351-3333	20896
Planters Hay Inc	5191	D	760 344-0620	14866
Shank Kretz Mch Auto Parts Inc	5013	F	760 344-4541	13088
Spreadco Inc	2262	E	760 351-0747	2665
Spreckels Sugar Company Inc	2063	B	760 344-3110	2080
Vons Companies Inc	2051	D	760 351-3002	2045
Western Mesquite Mines Inc	3339	E	928 341-4653	6288

BREA, CA - Orange County

	SIC	EMP	PHONE	ENTRY #
3-V Fastener Co Inc	3452	D	949 888-7700	7053
Able Wire Edm Inc	3599	F	714 255-1967	8460
Absolute Screenprint Inc	2396	C	714 529-2120	3166
Acepex Management Corporation	8744	C	909 625-6900	23387
Acosta Inc	5141	C	714 988-1500	14448
Aer Technologies Inc	7699	B	714 871-7357	19020
Aerospace Engineering LLC	3728	C	714 996-8178	10251
Aerospace Systems Strctres LLC	3728	F	626 965-1630	10255
Air Treatment Corporation **(PA)**	5075	D	909 869-7975	13839
Alatus Aerosystems **(PA)**	3728	A	610 965-1630	10262

GEOGRAPHIC

	SIC	EMP	PHONE	ENTRY #
Alatus Aerosystems	3728	D	714 732-0559	10263
Alatus Aerosystems	3728	D	626 498-7376	10264
Albertsons LLC	4225	A	714 990-8200	12184
American Financial Network Inc **(PA)**	6162	C	909 606-3905	15170
American First Credit Union **(PA)**	6061	D	562 691-1112	15057
Amwest Funding Corp	6153	D	714 831-3333	15149
Antaira Technologies LLC **(PA)**	3669	E	714 386-7036	9331
Apollo Electric	1731	D	714 256-8414	1214
Applied Cmpsite Structures Inc **(HQ)**	3728	C	714 990-6300	10273
AST Sportswear Inc **(PA)**	2361	B	714 223-2030	3028
Avery Dennison Corporation	2672	B	714 674-8500	3864
Avery Products Corporation **(DH)**	2678	A	714 675-8500	3913
B & W Precision Inc	3599	F	714 447-0971	8513
B O A Inc	2329	E	714 256-8960	2802
Beacon Manufacturing Inc	2833	E	714 529-0980	4738
Beckman Coulter Inc	3841	C	818 970-2161	10945
Bedard Machine Inc	3599	F	714 990-4846	8521
Belt Drives Ltd	3751	E	714 693-1313	10483
Benevolence Food Products LLC	2099	E	888 832-3738	2397
Bergman Kprs LLC **(PA)**	1542	C	714 924-7000	743
Brookdale Brea	8051	E	714 706-9968	20265
Burns & McDonnell Inc	8711	D	714 256-1595	22505
California Automobile Insur Co **(HQ)**	6331	D	714 232-8669	15465
Capco Unlimited	3399	F	714 257-0154	6458
Carolina Lquid Chmistries Corp	3841	F	336 722-8910	10959
Clean America Inc	3699	F	562 694-5990	9860
Cmre Financial Services Inc	7322	B	714 528-3200	17106
Consolidated Aerospace Mfg LLC	3429	E	714 989-2802	6512
Contract Services Group Inc	7349	C	714 582-1800	17232
Coolsys Inc **(HQ)**	7623	B	714 510-9577	18946
Coolsys Coml Indus Sltions Inc **(DH)**	1711	A	714 510-9609	1048
Coyle Reproductions Inc **(PA)**	2752	C	866 269-5373	4265
Crossroads Software Inc	7372	F	714 990-6433	17829
Curtiss-Wrght Flow Ctrl Svc LL **(HQ)**	8711	D	949 498-3350	22525
D G Industries	3541	F	714 990-3787	7726
Darbo Manufacturing Company	2339	E	714 529-7693	2936
Database Works Inc	7372	F	714 203-8800	17834
Diversfied Cmmnctions Svcs Inc	4813	D	714 888-2284	12633
DSI Logistics LLC **(PA)**	4789	D	800 335-6557	12569
Educational Ideas Incorporated	2731	D	714 990-4332	4128
Electronic Precision Spc Inc	3471	E	714 256-8950	7256
Emergency Ambulance Service	4119	D	714 990-1331	11862
Emet Lending Group Inc	6162	D	714 933-9800	15189
Energy Berkeley Office US Dept	8733	C	510 486-7089	22908
Energy Cnvrsion Applctions Inc	3612	F	714 256-2166	8869
Envista Holdings Corporation **(PA)**	3843	A	714 817-7000	11173
Esmart Massage Inc	3634	F	657 341-0360	9004
Evangelical Christian Cr Un	6062	C	714 671-5700	15112
Evangelical Christian Cr Un **(PA)**	6062	C	714 671-5700	15113
Evga Corporation **(PA)**	5045	E	714 528-4500	13396
Fineline Circuits & Technology	3672	E	714 529-2942	9406
Foxlink International Inc **(HQ)**	3643	E	714 256-1777	9037
Foxlink World Circuit Tech	3672	E	714 256-0877	9407
Garmin International Inc	3812	D	909 444-5000	10589
Gentekk Industries LLC **(PA)**	3999	E	714 985-9280	11677
Glen Ivy Hot Springs	7299	C	714 990-2090	16957
Goodrich Corporation	3728	C	714 984-1461	10340
Griffith Company **(PA)**	1611	D	714 984-5500	883
Harbor Truck Bodies Inc	3713	D	714 996-0411	9988
Hemocue Inc	5047	D	800 881-1611	13495
Hill Brothers Chemical Company **(PA)**	5169	C	714 998-8800	14783
Hot Dogger Tours Inc	4142	C	714 988-4088	11912
Iddea California LLC	3714	F	714 257-7389	10078
Imperial Cal Products Inc	3469	E	714 990-9100	7152
IMS Flightdeck LLC	5045	C	714 854-8600	13406
Insight Envmtl Engrg Cnstr Inc **(PA)**	8711	D	714 678-6700	22577
Isys Solutions Inc	8742	D	714 521-7656	23246
Jade Range LLC	3631	C	714 961-2400	8991
Jewelers Touch	3915	E	714 579-1616	11336
Jilk Heavy Construction Inc	1629	D	310 830-6323	1000
Kaiser Foundation Hospitals	8011	C	714 672-5100	19877
Kanex	3699	E	714 332-1681	9880
Kanex Pro Inc	2298	F	714 332-1681	2715
Kelly-Wright Hardwoods Inc	5031	F	714 632-9930	13218
Kingson Mold & Machine Inc	3544	E	714 871-0221	7810
Kirkhill Aircraft Parts Co **(PA)**	5088	C	714 223-5400	14061
Kirkhill Inc **(HQ)**	3728	A	714 529-4901	10362
Kirkhill Inc	3053	A	714 529-4901	5345
Kirkhill Inc	3053	A	714 529-4901	5346
Kprs Construction Services Inc **(PA)**	1542	D	714 672-0800	780
Kworld (usa) Computer Inc	3663	E	626 581-0867	9282
La Paz Products Inc	2087	E	714 990-0982	2331
Lance Soll & Lunghard LLP	8721	D	714 672-0022	22801
Ledconn Corp	3648	E	714 256-2111	9137
Leidos Inc	8731	D	714 257-6400	22847
Levity of Brea LLC	7997	D	714 482-0700	19579
Life Science Outsourcing Inc	3841	D	714 672-1090	11007
Lifebloom Corporation	2834	E	562 944-6800	4847
Lungsal International Inc	5199	F	714 671-9788	14949
Mddr Inc	1711	C	714 792-1993	1100
Media Blast & Abrasive Inc	3589	F	714 257-0484	8397
Mercury Casualty Company **(HQ)**	6331	A	323 937-1060	15469
Mercury Insurance Company	6331	D	714 671-6700	15471
Mercury Insurance Company	6331	B	714 255-5000	15473
Merrill Lynch Prce Fnner Smith	6211	D	714 257-4400	15289
Metals USA Building Pdts LP **(DH)**	3355	A	713 946-9000	6328
Mike Kenney Tool Inc	3599	E	714 577-9262	8695
Mkt Innovations	3599	D	714 524-7668	8702
Moeller Mfg & Sup LLC	3429	E	714 999-5551	6527
Monoprice Inc **(HQ)**	5099	C	909 989-6887	14170
Moravek Biochemicals Inc **(PA)**	2819	E	714 990-2018	4663
Morgan Stnley Smith Barney LLC	6211	D	714 674-4100	15298
Moxa Americas Inc	3577	E	714 528-6777	8283
MPS Medical Inc	3841	E	714 672-1090	11027
MR Mold & Engineering Corp	3544	E	714 996-5511	7817
Mullen Technologies Inc **(PA)**	3711	E	714 613-1900	9959
Nail Alliance - North Amer Inc **(PA)**	7231	B	714 773-9758	16909
Nevell Group Inc **(PA)**	1542	C	714 579-7501	796
Nmc Group Inc	5085	E	714 223-3525	14008
Norcal Inc	1751	C	714 224-3949	1447
Norcal Inc	1751	C	714 224-3949	1448
Northstar Dem & Remediation LP **(DH)**	1795	C	714 672-3500	1620
Ocean Protecta Incorporated	3732	E	714 891-2628	10470
Orangegrid LLC	7372	E	657 220-1519	17946
Ormco Corporation	3843	E	909 962-5705	11184
Otb Acquisition LLC	7011	D	520 458-0540	16600
Pac-Dent Inc	3843	E	909 839-0888	11187
Pacific Intl Elc Co Inc	1731	D	714 990-9280	1290
Pacific Plastics Inc	3084	D	714 990-9050	5469
Pacific Quality Packaging Corp	2653	D	714 257-1234	3823
Pacific Western Sales **(PA)**	5199	D	714 572-6730	14961
Park Hotels & Resorts Inc	7011	D	714 990-6000	16620
Parkinson Enterprises Inc	2521	D	714 626-0275	3597
Pbc Pavers Inc	1721	D	714 278-0488	1192
Peterson Bros Contruction Inc	1771	A	714 278-0488	1547
Pmac Lending Services Inc **(PA)**	6162	D	909 614-2000	15226
Precise Industries Inc	3444	C	714 482-2333	6893
Premier Medical Transport Inc	4119	D	888 353-9556	11884
President Enterprise Inc	2759	E	714 671-9577	4558
Priority Building Services LLC **(PA)**	7349	B	714 255-2940	17276
Production Systems Group Inc	2599	E	714 990-8997	3736
Q C M Inc	3629	E	714 414-1173	8980
Questus Inc **(PA)**	7374	E	415 677-5719	18106
Radiometer America Inc **(HQ)**	5047	E	800 736-0600	13515
Ramtec Associates Inc	3089	E	714 996-7477	5788
Raytheon Technologies Corp	3728	F	714 984-1467	10401
Rogers Holding Company Inc	3728	D	714 257-4850	10404
S&B Industry Inc	3089	E	909 569-4155	5809
Safran Pass Innovations LLC **(HQ)**	7371	D	714 854-8600	17705
Scisorek & Son Flavors Inc	2087	E	714 524-0550	2336
Sears Roebuck and Co	7699	C	714 256-7328	19065
Sedgwick Claims MGT Svcs Inc	6411	D	714 572-1207	15626
Seismic Reservoir 2020 Inc	1382	E	562 697-9711	465
Shore Front LLC	2099	E	714 612-3751	2523
Solugenix Corporation **(PA)**	7373	C	866 749-7658	18068
Southern Cal Hydrlic Engrg Cor	5084	E	714 257-4800	13939
Span-O-Matic Inc	3444	E	714 256-4700	6915
Specialty Risk Services Inc	6411	D	714 674-1000	15629
Spinnaker Coating LLC	2672	C	714 482-1006	3875
Steelclad Inc	1389	F	714 529-0277	547
Stolo Cabinets Inc **(PA)**	2521	E	714 529-7303	3601
Suheung-America Corporation **(HQ)**	2834	E	714 854-9882	4899
Sully-Miller Contracting Co **(DH)**	1611	B	714 578-9600	918
Sully-Miller Holding Corp	1611	D	714 578-9600	919
Sunon Inc **(PA)**	3564	E	714 255-0208	8054
Suzuki Motor of America Inc **(HQ)**	3519	C	714 996-7040	7599
Taylor Technology Services Inc	2759	C	714 986-1559	4581
Tca Precision Products LLC	3728	F	714 257-4850	10427
Team Finish Inc	1771	D	714 671-9190	1555
TEC Lighting Inc	3648	F	714 529-5068	9149
Thermal ID Technologies Inc	3826	F	408 656-6809	10819
TNT Packaging Corporation	2671	F	714 671-9012	3859
Trane US Inc	3585	D	626 913-7123	8351
Travel Store	4724	D	714 529-1947	12400
Tri-Tech Logistics LLC	4731	C	855 373-7049	12544
Trigon Components Inc **(PA)**	3675	D	714 990-1367	9614
TSC Auto ID Technology America **(HQ)**	5085	C	909 468-0100	14029
UNI-Caps LLC	2833	E	714 529-8400	4768
Uriman Inc **(HQ)**	3694	E	714 257-2080	9830
US Metro Group Inc	7349	A	213 382-6435	17299
V A Anderson Enterprises Inc **(PA)**	7389	D	714 990-6100	18715
Val USA Manufacturer Inc	3999	E	626 839-8069	11788
Ventura Foods LLC **(PA)**	2079	C	714 257-3700	2133
Vesuki Inc	3499	F	562 245-4000	7575
Viewsonic Corporation **(PA)**	3577	C	909 444-8888	8310
Webedoctor Inc	7372	F	714 990-3999	18008
West Coast Gasket Co	3053	D	714 869-0123	5355
Whittier Filtration Inc **(DH)**	3589	E	714 986-5300	8426
Wilsey Foods Inc	2079	A	714 257-3700	2134
Win-Dor Inc **(PA)**	1751	C	714 576-2030	1464
Windsor Capital Group Inc	7011	D	714 990-6000	16795
Worldwide Envmtl Pdts Inc **(PA)**	3823	D	714 990-2700	10732
Wurth Louis and Company **(DH)**	5072	D	714 529-1771	13821

BUELLTON, CA - Santa Barbara County

	SIC	EMP	PHONE	ENTRY #
Aero Industries LLC	3599	B	805 688-6734	8473
Carpenters Southwest ADM Corp	7299	C	805 688-5581	16945
Central Coast Agriculture Inc **(PA)**	0191	D	805 694-8594	102
GP Machining Inc	3599	E	805 686-0852	8608
Infraredvision Technology Corp	3674	C	805 686-8848	9517
Kang Family Partners LLC	7011	C	805 688-1000	16520
Platinum Performance Inc	7532	D	800 553-2400	18798
Platinum Performance Inc **(HQ)**	5122	E	800 553-2400	14281
Terravant Wine Company LLC **(PA)**	2084	C	805 688-4245	2229
Tilton Engineering Inc	3714	E	805 688-2353	10141

Mergent email: customerrelations@mergent.com
1340

2022 Southern California Business
Directory and Buyers Guide

(P-0000) Products & Services Section entry number
(PA)=Parent Co (HQ)=Headquarters (DH)=Div Headquarters

	SIC	EMP	PHONE	ENTRY #
True Precision Machining Inc	3599	E	805 964-4545	8827

BUENA PARK, CA - Orange County

	SIC	EMP	PHONE	ENTRY #
A J Parent Company Inc **(PA)**	7389	D	714 521-1100	18426
AAA Network Solutions Inc	1731	D	714 484-2711	1208
Abad Foam Inc	3086	E	714 994-2223	5482
Access Business Group LLC	5169	C	714 562-6200	14768
Access Business Group LLC	5169	C	714 562-7914	14769
Advanced Prof Imging Med Group **(PA)**	8011	C	714 995-5400	19685
Alloy Die Casting Co	3363	C	714 521-9800	6362
AM Machining Inc	5088	E	714 367-0830	14051
Amada America Inc **(HQ)**	5084	D	714 739-2111	13884
Amada North America Inc **(HQ)**	5084	B	714 739-2111	13885
Ameripec Inc	2086	C	714 690-9191	2254
Aqua Products Inc	3581	F	714 670-0691	8321
Atlas Construction Supply Inc	5032	E	714 441-9500	13293
AW Die Engraving Inc	3544	E	714 521-7910	7780
Awesome Products Inc **(PA)**	2842	C	714 562-8873	4955
Buena Park Medical Group Inc **(PA)**	8011	E	714 994-5290	19726
Cambium Business Group Inc **(PA)**	5021	C	714 670-1171	13130
Communications Supply Corp	4899	D	714 670-7711	12781
Continental Exch Solutions Inc	7389	D	562 345-2100	18490
Continental Exch Solutions Inc **(HQ)**	6099	A	714 522-7044	15126
Creative Impressions Inc	3081	E	714 521-4441	5429
Cyu Lithographics Inc	2752	E	888 878-9898	4271
Derm Cosmetic Labs Inc **(PA)**	5122	E	714 562-8873	14240
ECB Corp **(PA)**	1711	D	714 385-8900	1058
Eidim Group Inc	3648	F	562 777-1009	9128
Elwin Inc	2591	E	714 752-6962	3709
Erika Records Inc	3652	E	714 228-5420	9216
Esquivel Designs LLC **(PA)**	5139	D	714 670-2200	14437
Exemplis LLC	2522	E	714 995-4800	3609
Exemplis LLC	2522	E	714 898-5500	3610
Four Seasons Building Products	3448	F	714 522-7852	6995
Fueling and Service Tech Inc	5084	D	714 523-0194	13902
G & G Door Products Inc	3442	E	714 228-2008	6701
Ganahl Lumber Company	5031	D	714 522-2864	13209
Haley Bros Inc **(HQ)**	2431	C	714 670-2112	3253
Hi-Tech Labels Incorporated **(PA)**	3599	E	714 670-2150	8617
Hochiki America Corporation	5063	C	714 522-2246	13633
Houdini Inc	4225	C	714 228-4406	12214
Innovative Bedg Solutions Inc	5023	F	714 994-2223	13174
Interntional Color Posters Inc	2759	E	949 768-1005	4529
Island Snacks Inc	2064	E	714 994-1228	2089
Jaz Distribution Inc	3462	F	714 521-3888	7089
JP Crown House Dental Lab Inc **(PA)**	8072	D	714 323-8555	21109
Jxp Tech Inc	5065	F	714 723-0696	13739
King Supply Company LLC	1799	D	714 670-8980	1671
Knotts Berry Farm LLC **(HQ)**	7996	B	714 827-1776	19518
Knotts Berry Farm LLC	7011	D	714 995-1111	16527
Krikorian Premiere Theatre LLC	7832	D	714 826-7469	19281
Leach International Corp **(DH)**	3728	B	714 736-7537	10367
Mahavaipulya Buddhist Assn	7389	E	714 220-0028	18585
Manhattan Stitching Co Inc	2395	E	714 521-9479	3158
Mar Cor Purification Inc	3589	E	800 633-3080	8395
Mashindustries Inc	2599	E	714 736-9600	3735
Matesta Corporation	5137	C	949 874-6052	14399
McLane Foodservice Dist Inc	5147	D	714 562-6893	14598
Metals USA Building Pdts LP	3441	D	714 522-7852	6638
Nectave Inc	2099	F	714 736-9811	2494
Noritsu-America Corporation **(HQ)**	5043	C	714 521-9040	13347
Norwich Aero Products Inc **(DH)**	3812	E	607 336-7636	10628
One World Meat Company LLC	2013	F	800 782-1670	1741
Onesource Distributors LLC	5063	D	562 401-1264	13655
Orora North America	5113	C	714 562-6002	14220
Orora Packaging Solutions **(HQ)**	5113	D	714 562-6000	14221
Osmosis Technology Inc	3589	E	714 670-9303	8402
Pacific Chemical Dist Corp **(HQ)**	4226	D	714 521-7161	12271
Park Engineering and Mfg Co	3599	E	714 521-4660	8733
Pepsi Bottling Group	2086	F	714 522-9742	2277
Performance Water Products Inc	3589	F	714 736-0137	8404
Pharr-Palomar Inc	2281	A	714 522-4811	2701
Pop 82 Inc	2221	F	714 523-8500	2602
Pop Plastics Acrylic Disp Inc	3089	F	714 523-8500	5768
Posadas Usa Inc	7011	C	714 522-2122	16639
Premiere Packaging Inds Inc	5199	D	562 799-9200	14968
Q Team	2752	F	714 228-4465	4411
Quality Grinding Co Inc	3545	F	714 228-2100	7865
Rael Inc	2676	E	800 573-1516	3908
Rehabltion Ctr of Ornge Cnty	8051	C	714 826-2330	20444
Ria Envia Inc **(HQ)**	7389	A	714 543-8448	18654
Ronman Products Inc	3399	F	714 735-3146	6462
Rossier Park School	8742	D	714 562-0441	23312
Sfadia Inc	1731	D	323 622-1930	1316
Simpson Automotive Inc	7539	D	714 690-6200	18904
Spn Investments Inc	3949	F	562 777-1140	11448
States Logistics Services Inc	4731	D	714 523-1276	12530
States Logistics Services Inc	4225	D	714 523-1276	12248
States Logistics Services Inc **(PA)**	4731	C	714 521-6520	12531
Sun West Mortgage Company Inc **(PA)**	6162	D	800 453-7884	15232
Tawa Services Inc **(PA)**	5149	C	714 521-8899	14745
Tawa Supermarket Inc **(PA)**	2038	D	714 521-8899	1940
Tech Systems Inc	5065	B	714 523-5404	13781
Ted Ford Jones Inc **(PA)**	7538	C	714 521-3110	18878
Tomlin Scientific Inc	5172	F	714 523-7971	14813
Trim-Lok Inc **(PA)**	3089	C	714 562-0500	5842
True Fresh Hpp LLC	3822	F	949 922-8801	10670
Tuff Kote Systems Inc	2851	F	714 522-7341	5117
United Food & Commercl Workers **(PA)**	8631	D	714 995-4601	22304
Universal Shopping Plaza A CA	6512	C	714 521-8899	15705
Uniwell Corporation	7011	C	714 522-7000	16762
Vsa and Associates Inc	8711	D	562 698-2468	22694
Walong Marketing Inc **(PA)**	5149	D	714 670-8899	14747
Waterdance Corporation **(PA)**	3594	E	818 656-0005	8446
Wayne Perry Inc **(PA)**	1799	C	714 826-0352	1700
West Coast Sand and Gravel Inc **(PA)**	5032	D	714 522-0282	13320
Westates Inc	2752	E	714 523-7600	4456
Whale Logistics (usa) Inc **(PA)**	4789	D	714 891-8265	12585
Wire Cut Company Inc	3599	E	714 994-1170	8856
Yamaha Corporation of America **(HQ)**	5099	B	714 522-9011	14186
Yeager Enterprises Corp	3291	D	714 994-2040	6162

BURBANK, CA - Los Angeles County

	SIC	EMP	PHONE	ENTRY #
24/7 Studio Equipment Inc	3663	E	818 840-8247	9247
716 Management Inc	1522	D	818 471-4956	654
939 Holdings Inc	4832	D	818 525-5000	12683
939 Investment LLC **(PA)**	4832	C	818 525-5000	12684
A Its Laugh Productions Inc	7812	D	818 848-8787	19089
A-1 Hospice Care Inc	8052	D	818 237-2700	20518
ABC Cable Networks Group **(HQ)**	4832	C	818 460-7477	12685
ABC Family Worldwide Inc **(HQ)**	7812	B	818 560-1000	19090
ABC Signature Studios Inc	4833	D	818 569-7500	12708
Accratronics Seals Corporation	3679	D	818 843-1500	9670
Ace Industrial Supply Inc **(PA)**	1521	C	818 252-1981	590
Acsco Products Inc	3714	E	818 953-2240	10004
Advanced Publishing Tech Inc	2741	F	818 557-3035	4148
Alliance Residential LLC	6512	C	818 841-2441	15657
Allianz Globl Risks US Insur **(DH)**	6331	C	818 260-7500	15463
Allianz Underwriters Insur Co	6331	D	818 260-7500	15464
American Fdrtion Mscans Lcal 4	8631	C	323 462-2161	22285
American Fine Arts Foundry LLC	3366	F	818 848-7593	6404
Anabelle Hotel Inc	7011	D	818 845-7800	16318
and Syndicated Productions Inc	7812	D	818 308-5200	19094
Andrews International Inc	7381	C	818 260-9586	18249
Andrews International Inc **(PA)**	7381	A	818 487-4060	18251
Angels Hand Hospice Care Inc **(PA)**	8052	D	818 782-2516	20522
Annex Pro Inc	7372	E	800 682-6639	17782
Aramark Unf & Career AP LLC	7213	D	818 973-3700	16846
Aramark Unf & Career AP LLC **(DH)**	7218	C	818 973-3700	16883
Aramark Uniform Mfg Co	3999	F	800 999-8989	11632
Ardwin Inc	4213	C	818 767-7777	12011
Arte De Mexico Inc **(PA)**	2522	D	818 753-4559	3606
Astra Communications Inc	3663	E	818 859-7305	9255
Atlas Digital LLC **(PA)**	7812	D	323 762-2626	19098
Automobile Club Southern Cal	8699	D	818 843-2833	22441
AWH Burbank Hotel LLC	7011	D	813 843-6000	16331
Bandy Manufacturing LLC	3728	D	818 846-9020	10288
Blu Digital Group Inc	7371	D	818 294-7695	17568
Bonanza Productions Inc	7929	A	818 954-4212	19345
Borrmann Metal Center **(DH)**	5051	D	818 846-7171	13551
BRC Imagination Arts Inc **(PA)**	7812	D	818 841-8084	19102
Bryant Ranch Prepack	5122	E	818 764-7225	14235
Bucy Die Casting	3544	F	818 843-5044	7783
Buena Vista International Inc **(DH)**	7822	E	818 560-1000	19257
Buena Vista International Inc	7812	C	818 295-5200	19104
Buena Vista Television **(DH)**	7383	C	818 560-1878	18406
Buildit Engineering Co Inc	3354	F	818 244-6666	6304
Burbank Dental Laboratory Inc	8072	C	818 841-2256	21103
Burbank Emrgncy Med Group Inc	8011	D	818 506-5778	19729
Burbank Steel Treating Inc	3398	E	818 842-0975	6434
Bvs Entertainment Inc **(DH)**	7812	E	818 460-6917	19106
California Insulated Wire &	3357	D	818 569-4930	6345
Cardona Manufacturing Corp	3728	E	818 841-8358	10297
Career Strategies Tmpry Inc	7361	D	213 385-0440	17404
Carter Plating Inc	3471	E	818 842-1325	7236
Cast & Crew Payroll LLC **(PA)**	8721	C	818 848-6022	22767
Centerpoint Mfg Co Inc	3599	E	818 842-2147	8546
Cheque Guard Inc	7371	D	818 563-9335	17576
Chevys Restaurants LLC	7299	D	818 846-6999	16946
Christys Edtorial Film Sup Inc	5043	D	818 845-1755	13343
Chulada Inc	2833	F	818 841-6536	4740
City of Burbank	4931	B	818 238-3550	12869
Color Service Inc	2752	F	323 283-4793	4256
Comco Inc	3589	E	818 333-8500	8376
Come Land Inc **(PA)**	7349	B	818 567-2455	17229
Come Land Maint Svc Co Inc	7349	A	818 567-2455	17230
Connell Processing Inc	3471	E	818 845-7661	7242
Corday Productions Inc **(PA)**	7812	D	818 295-2821	19111
Crane Aerospace Inc	3812	E	818 526-2600	10580
Cw Network LLC **(PA)**	4833	C	818 977-2500	12713
Cydwoq Inc	3131	E	818 848-8307	5873
Deluxe Entertainment Svcs Inc	7819	D	323 960-7303	19225
Deluxe Entrmt Svcs Group Inc **(PA)**	7929	D	818 565-3600	19347
Deluxe Laboratories Inc **(HQ)**	7819	A	323 462-6171	19226
Deluxe Media Inc **(PA)**	7819	A	818 565-3697	19227
Disney Book Group LLC **(DH)**	2731	D	818 560-1000	4126
Disney Enterprises Inc **(DH)**	4832	A	818 560-1000	12687
Disney Incorporated **(DH)**	7812	C	818 560-1000	19118
Disney Interactive Studios Inc	7371	B	818 553-5000	17598
Disney Online	4833	D	818 553-7200	12714
Disney Publishing Worldwide **(DH)**	2721	D	212 633-4400	4066
Disney Regional Entrmt Inc **(DH)**	7999	C	818 560-1000	19643
Doremi Cinema LLC	3861	F	818 562-1101	11274
Draco Broadcast Inc	3663	E	818 736-5788	9268
Dvs Media Services **(PA)**	7334	F	818 841-6750	17149
Earthwise Bag Company Inc	3812	F	818 847-2174	10584

Employment Codes: A=Over 500 employees, B=251-500, C=101-250, D=51-100, E=20-50 F=10-19
2022 Southern California Business Directory and Buyers Guide
© Mergent Inc. 1-800-342-5647
1341

	SIC	EMP	PHONE	ENTRY #
Eastwest Clothing Inc **(PA)**	2331	E	323 980-1177	2842
Eaton Aerospace LLC	3812	C	818 550-4200	10585
Eckert Zegler Isotope Pdts Inc	3829	E	661 309-1010	10878
Eckert Zegler Isotope Pdts Inc	3829	E	661 309-1010	10880
Effective Graphics NC Inc	2796	E	310 323-2223	4629
Electrosonic Inc **(DH)**	8711	D	818 333-3600	22540
Enbio Corp	8742	C	818 953-9976	23212
Entertainment Partners Inc **(PA)**	8721	B	818 955-6000	22780
Eon Innovative Technology Inc	7382	D	213 381-0061	18377
Eros Stx Global Corporation	7841	A	818 524-7000	19297
Esl Gaming America Inc	7929	E	818 861-7315	19351
ESM Aerospace Inc	3444	E	818 841-3653	6828
Estrella Communications Inc	4833	D	818 260-5700	12719
Estrella Media Inc	4832	D	818 729-5316	12690
Evolution Film & Tape Inc	7812	D	818 260-0300	19122
Excelline Food Products LLC	2038	E	818 701-7710	1926
Fact Foundation	7389	B	818 729-8105	18516
Farmers Insur Group Fdral Cr U **(PA)**	6061	D	323 209-6000	15063
Filmtools Inc **(PA)**	5043	E	323 467-1116	13344
Final Film	7336	D	323 467-0700	17175
Foto-Kem Industries Inc **(PA)**	7819	B	818 846-3102	19235
Frasco Inc **(PA)**	7381	D	818 848-3888	18276
Front Prch Cmmnties Svcs - Cas	8059	D	626 570-5293	20588
Ftp Productions LLC **(PA)**	7812	C	818 560-2977	19127
G Printing Inc	2759	E	818 246-1156	4516
Gat - Arln Ground Support Inc	4729	D	818 847-9127	12415
Gentle Giant Studios Inc	7389	D	818 504-3555	18526
Gerhardt Gear Co Inc	3714	E	818 842-6700	10066
GL Nemirow Inc	7311	D	818 562-9433	17015
Global Entertainment Inds Inc	1799	D	818 567-0000	1661
Global Service Resources Inc	7371	D	800 679-7658	17626
Golden Fleece Designs	2394	F	323 849-1901	3140
Gotprint	2752	F	877 922-7374	4304
Granite Software Inc	7372	F	818 252-1950	17870
Hanger Inc	3842	E	818 563-9590	11109
Haskel International LLC **(HQ)**	3561	C	818 843-4000	8014
HK Aerspace Krkhill Arcft Prts	5085	D	818 559-9783	13986
Hollywood Records Inc	3652	E	818 560-5670	9220
Honey Isabells Inc	0279	E	800 708-8485	140
Hood Container Corporation	3999	F	818 848-1648	11687
Hula Post Productions Inc	7812	D	818 954-0200	19132
Hutchinson Arospc & Indust Inc	3728	C	818 843-1000	10345
Hutchinson Arospc & Indust Inc	3069	C	818 843-1000	5382
Hydra-Electric Company **(PA)**	3613	C	818 843-6211	8898
Hydro-Aire Inc **(DH)**	3728	B	818 526-2600	10348
Ies Commercial Inc	1731	D	713 860-1500	1267
IKEA Purchasing Svcs US Inc	8741	C	818 841-3500	23039
Image IV Systems Inc **(PA)**	5044	D	323 849-3049	13357
Information Tech Partners Inc	7379	D	800 789-7487	18187
Insomniac Games Inc **(PA)**	3944	B	818 729-2400	11377
International Fmly Entrmt Inc **(DH)**	4841	C	818 560-1000	12772
J L Fisher Inc	7359	D	818 846-8366	17357
Jake Hey Incorporated	7384	C	323 856-5280	18409
JP Allen Inc	7011	B	818 841-4770	16514
JP Allen Extended Stay	7011	E	818 841-4770	16515
Kan-Di-Ki LLC **(HQ)**	8071	A	818 549-1880	21073
Kh9100 LLC	3851	F	818 972-2580	11254
Krca Television LLC **(DH)**	4833	D	818 563-5722	12731
Lakeside Golf Club	7992	D	818 984-0601	19496
Lawyers Title Company **(HQ)**	6361	E	818 767-0425	15506
Lbi Media Holdings Inc **(HQ)**	4832	D	818 563-5722	12698
Le Bleu Chateau Inc	8361	E	818 843-3141	22123
Legendary Entertainment LLC	7812	D	818 688-7006	19141
Liberman Broadcasting Inc **(PA)**	4832	D	818 729-5300	12700
Linde Gas North America LLC	2813	F	626 855-8344	4641
Little Einsteins LLC	2731	D	818 560-1000	4133
Logix Federal Credit Union **(PA)**	6061	C	888 718-5328	15072
Los Angeles Equestrian Center	0752	D	818 840-9063	213
Louie Almeida & Settler **(PA)**	8111	D	818 461-9559	21618
Lowes Home Centers LLC	5031	C	818 557-2300	13235
Lumaforge Llc An Owc Company	3572	F	818 741-2858	8207
M-N-Z Janitorial Services Inc	7349	C	323 851-4115	17258
Magnasync/Moviola Corporation	3651	E	818 845-8066	9182
Marathon Productions Inc	3663	F	818 748-1100	9289
Marvel Studios LLC **(HQ)**	7221	C	310 727-2700	16894
Matz Rubber Co Inc	3069	F	323 849-5170	5390
McMillin Mfg Corp	3444	E	323 981-8585	6873
Mel Bernie and Company Inc **(PA)**	5094	C	818 841-1928	14135
Merci Life LLC	2833	F	317 341-4109	4752
Mis Sciences Corp	4813	C	818 847-0213	12654
Mvp Rv Inc	3792	E	951 848-4288	10544
My Eye Media LLC	7372	D	818 559-7200	17925
Natural Balance Pet Foods Inc **(DH)**	2048	E	800 829-4493	1972
Nerdist Channel LLC	3663	E	818 333-2705	9301
New Gold Manufacturing Inc	3911	F	818 847-1020	11326
Nova Skilled Home Health Inc	8099	C	323 658-6232	21466
NW Entertainment Inc **(PA)**	7812	C	818 295-5000	19157
Omega Case Company Inc	2449	F	818 238-9263	3416
P Murphy & Associates Inc	7371	C	818 841-2002	17688
Palermo Family LP	2099	E	213 542-3300	2507
Partners Federal Credit Union **(PA)**	6061	D	800 948-6677	15077
Performance Designed Pdts LLC **(PA)**	5092	D	323 248-9236	14099
Petrol Advertising Inc	7311	E	323 644-3720	17044
PHF II Burbank LLC	7011	C	818 843-6000	16628
Photronics Inc **(DH)**	3861	B	203 740-5653	11289
Pixelogic Media Partners LLC **(DH)**	7819	C	818 861-2001	19244
Playboy Entrmt Group Inc **(DH)**	7812	C	323 276-4000	19164
Prdctions N Fremantle Amer Inc **(DH)**	7922	D	818 748-1100	19328
Pride Cleaning Co Inc	7389	E	818 295-2510	18640
Prime Focus Technologies Inc	8748	D	310 895-9550	23495
Printograph Inc	2752	F	818 252-3000	4402
Producer -Writers Guild	6371	D	818 846-1015	15518
Providence Health & Services F	8062	A	818 843-5111	20912
Providence Health System	8062	A	818 843-5111	20915
Providence St Joseph Health	8011	A	818 843-5111	20030
Public Mdia Group Southern Cal **(PA)**	4833	C	714 241-4100	12738
Quality Heat Treating Inc	3398	E	818 840-8212	6452
Radio Disney Group LLC	4832	D	818 569-5000	12704
Rgis LLC	7389	C	248 651-2511	18651
Rohde & Schwarz Usa Inc	3825	F	818 846-3600	10769
Roundabout Entertainment Inc	7812	D	818 842-9300	19173
Rovi Guides Inc **(DH)**	7929	D	323 817-4600	19375
Ryan Herco Products Corp **(HQ)**	5074	D	818 841-1141	13836
S & H Machine Inc **(PA)**	3599	F	818 846-9847	8781
S Callan Company Inc	7311	D	818 841-3284	17053
Sag- Aftra Federal Credit Un	6061	D	818 562-3400	15079
Sanitec Industries Inc	4953	D	818 523-1942	12976
Saturn Fasteners Inc	3429	C	818 973-1807	6535
Sca Enterprises Inc **(PA)**	7389	D	818 845-7621	18661
Science of Skincare LLC	5122	D	818 254-7961	14287
Screen Actors Guild - American	6371	C	818 954-9400	15519
Select Office Systems Inc	2893	F	818 861-8320	5209
Senior Operations LLC	3728	B	818 260-2900	10416
Shamrock Holdings Inc **(PA)**	6282	D	818 845-4444	15348
Shamrock Holdings Cal Inc **(HQ)**	6531	D	818 845-4444	15997
Shc Burbank II LLC	7011	C	818 843-6000	16703
Sierra Automated Sys/Eng Corp	3663	E	818 840-6749	9317
Silverado Senior Living Inc	8051	D	747 477-26[illegible]8	20467
Smart & Final Stores Inc	5141	C	818 954-8631	14501
Specialty Restaurants Corp	7299	C	818 843-5013	16977
Staness Jonekos Entps Inc	2099	E	818 606-2710	2528
Steril-Aire Inc	3648	E	818 565-1128	9147
Steves Plating Corporation	2542	C	818 842-2184	3697
Studio Distribution Svcs LLC	7812	C	818 954-6000	19186
Stx Productions LLC **(PA)**	7822	D	310 742-2300	19262
Superior Window Coverings Inc	2391	E	818 762-6685	3095
Swaner Hardwood Co Inc **(PA)**	2435	D	818 953-5350	3355
Take A Break Paper	2711	E	323 333-7773	4033
Team Companies LLC **(PA)**	8721	D	818 558-3261	22816
Technicolor Inc	7384	B	818 260-4577	18421
Testronic Inc	7819	C	818 845-3223	19253
Three-D Plastics Inc **(PA)**	3089	E	323 849-1316	5838
Tidavater Inc	7389	C	818 848-4151	18692
Tk Elevator Corporation	5084	D	818 847-2568	13951
Trade News International Inc	7313	E	818 848-6397	17091
Tri-Tech Restoration Cnstr Inc	1389	F	800 900-8448	552
Tri-Tech Restoration Co Inc	1541	D	818 565-3900	723
TTT West Coast Inc	7812	D	818 972-0500	19188
Twdc Enterprises 18 Corp **(HQ)**	4833	B	818 560-1000	12747
Ultragraphics Inc	7335	E	818 295-3994	17159
US Gold Trading Inc **(PA)**	3911	F	818 558-7766	11332
US Security Associates Inc	7381	B	818 697-1809	18355
US Steel Rule Dies Inc	3544	F	562 921-0690	7841
V J Provision Inc	2011	F	818 843-3945	1722
Valleycrest Productions Ltd	4833	D	818 560-5391	12750
Velocity Arospc - Burbank Inc **(HQ)**	7699	D	818 246-8431	19082
Ver Sales Inc **(PA)**	5051	D	818 567-3000	13604
Vesture Group Incorporated	2369	E	818 842-0200	3047
Vintage Senior Management Inc	8322	C	818 954-9500	21909
Wad Productions Inc	7812	D	818 260-5673	19201
Walt Disney Company **(PA)**	7996	A	818 560-1000	19525
Walt Disney Music Company **(DH)**	7812	A	818 560-1000	19202
Walt Disney Pictures and TV	7829	D	818 560-1000	19267
Walt Disney Records Direct **(DH)**	7812	A	818 560-1000	19203
Warner Bros Consumer Pdts Inc **(DH)**	8748	C	818 954-7980	23526
Warner Bros Distributing Inc **(DH)**	8741	B	818 954-6000	23137
Warner Bros Enterprises LLC **(DH)**	7812	D	818 954-6000	19204
Warner Bros Entertainment Inc **(DH)**	7812	A	818 954-6000	19205
Warner Bros Entertainment Inc	7812	C	818 954-2209	19206
Warner Bros FE Inc **(DH)**	7812	C	212 484-8000	19207
Warner Bros Home Entrmt Group **(DH)**	7929	D	818 954-6000	19384
Warner Bros Home Entrmt Inc	7812	A	818 954-6000	19208
Warner Bros Intl TV Dist Inc	7812	D	818 954-6000	19209
Warner Bros Pictures Inc	7812	E	818 954-6000	19210
Warner Bros Transatlantic Inc **(DH)**	7822	A	818 977-0018	19266
Y B S Enterprises Inc	3661	F	818 848-7790	9246
Youbetcom Inc **(HQ)**	7948	D	818 668-2100	19436
Young MNS Chrstn Assn Brbank C **(PA)**	8641	D	818 845-8551	22385
Zestfinance Inc	7371	D	323 450-3000	17767

BUTTONWILLOW, CA - Kern County

	SIC	EMP	PHONE	ENTRY #
B W Implement Co	3523	E	661 764-5254	7605
Clean Harbors Buttonwillow LLC	4953	D	661 762-6200	12940
JG Boswell Tomato - Kern LLC	2033	E	661 764-9000	1865
Sandridge Partners LP	0139	D	408 738-4444	10

CABAZON, CA - Riverside County

	SIC	EMP	PHONE	ENTRY #
Casino Morongo	7996	D	951 849-3080	19516
Centric Brands Inc	2211	E	951 797-5077	2562
Hadley Fruit Orchards Inc **(PA)**	2034	E	951 849-5255	1882
Premium Outlet Partners LP	6512	D	951 849-6641	15692

CALABASAS, CA - Los Angeles County

	SIC	EMP	PHONE	ENTRY #
23627 Calabasas Road LLC	7011	D	818 222-5300	16307
Able Cable Inc **(PA)**	7629	C	818 223-3600	18950

Mergent email: customerrelations@mergent.com
1342

2022 Southern California Business
Directory and Buyers Guide

(P-0000) Products & Services Section entry number
(PA)=Parent Co (HQ)=Headquarters (DH)=Div Headquarters

	SIC	EMP	PHONE	ENTRY #
AIA Holdings Inc **(PA)**	7389	D	818 222-4999	18438
Ale USA Inc	3663	A	818 878-4816	9250
Amawaterways LLC **(PA)**	4724	C	800 626-0126	12381
American Hmes 4 Rent MGT Hldng	6798	D	805 413-5300	16228
American Homes 4 Rent **(PA)**	6798	C	805 413-5300	16229
Apex Holding Co	5172	D	818 876-0161	14800
Arcoro Holdings Corp	7372	F	877 252-2168	17789
Arcs Commercial Mortgage Co LP **(DH)**	6162	C	818 676-3274	15173
Atlas Database Software Corp **(PA)**	7371	C	818 340-7080	17555
Avanquest North America LLC **(HQ)**	7371	D	818 591-9600	17558
Blk International LLC	2086	E	424 282-3443	2258
Boys and Girls Club	7997	E	818 225-8406	19548
Brightview Companies LLC **(DH)**	1629	C	818 223-8500	989
Brightview Landscape Dev Inc **(DH)**	0781	E	818 223-8500	238
Cartel Marketing Inc	6411	C	818 483-1130	15549
Catapult Communications Corp **(DH)**	7372	D	818 871-1800	17811
Ccf International LLC	2051	F	818 871-3000	1990
Center For Civic Education **(PA)**	8733	D	818 591-9321	22905
Crusader Insurance Company	6331	D	818 591-9800	15466
David Shield Security Inc	7381	D	310 849-4950	18269
Davis Research LLC	8732	C	818 591-2408	22878
Dts Inc **(DH)**	7819	C	818 436-1000	19230
Dts LLC	3651	E	818 436-1000	9172
Durham School Services L P	4151	C	818 880-4257	11921
Electric Solidus LLC	2741	E	917 692-7764	4170
Ellie Mae Inc	7371	C	818 223-2000	17607
Fulcrum Microsystems Inc	3674	D	818 871-8100	9509
Global Edge LLC	7372	E	888 315-2692	17866
Grant & Weber **(PA)**	7322	C	818 878-7700	17113
Help Children World Foundation	8322	B	818 706-9848	21800
Idrive Inc	7379	D	818 594-5972	18185
Indegene Inc **(DH)**	8733	E	732 750-2901	22910
Informa Research Services Inc **(HQ)**	8732	C	818 880-8877	22887
Ixia **(HQ)**	3825	A	818 871-1800	10762
Knight-Calabasas LLC **(PA)**	7997	D	818 222-3200	19573
Lab Support LLC **(HQ)**	7363	C	818 878-7900	17496
Lantz Security Systems Inc	7382	C	818 871-0193	18392
Las Virgenes Municipal Wtr Dst	4941	C	818 251-2100	12898
Litigtion Rsrces of Amrca-CA **(PA)**	7389	D	818 878-9227	18579
Marcus & Millchap Real Estate **(DH)**	6531	D	818 212-2250	15920
Marcus & Millichap Inc **(PA)**	6531	B	818 212-2250	15921
Marcus Mllchap RE Inv Svcs ATL **(DH)**	6531	D	818 212-2250	15922
Mrca Fire Division	8641	E	818 880-4752	22352
MSE Enterprises Inc **(PA)**	6531	D	818 223-3500	15929
Musclepharm Corporation **(PA)**	2023	D	800 292-3909	1801
Netsol Technologies Inc **(PA)**	7372	A	818 222-9197	17930
Pressed Juicery Inc	5149	F	818 225-8985	14723
Prolifics Testing Inc	7371	E	925 485-9535	17693
Quantum Solutions Inc	7379	E	818 577-4555	18217
Radian Memory Systems Inc	3572	E	818 222-4080	8215
Rainbow Camp Inc	7999	E	310 456-3066	19664
Red Peak Group LLC	8742	D	818 222-7762	23307
Republic Indemnity Co Amer **(DH)**	6331	C	818 990-9860	15478
Rodeo Realty Inc	6531	D	818 657-4609	15987
S & S Paving Inc	1611	D	818 591-0668	911
Sedgwick Claims MGT Svcs Inc	6411	D	818 591-9444	15627
Silverado Senior Living Inc	8051	D	818 746-2583	20474
Spirent Communications Inc **(HQ)**	5045	B	818 676-2300	13441
Swiss RE Underwriters Agency **(DH)**	6321	C	818 226-0028	15385
T M Mian & Associates Inc	7011	D	818 591-2300	16749
Thrio Inc	7389	E	858 299-7191	18690
Tri-Tech Systems Inc **(PA)**	7371	B	818 222-6811	17743
Unico American Corporation **(PA)**	6331	D	818 591-9800	15487
Wella Operations US LLC	5122	B	818 999-5112	14298
Westbrook Ops LLC	7812	D	818 832-2300	19211
Western General Holding Co **(PA)**	6331	C	818 880-9070	15488
Western General Insurance Co	6331	C	818 880-9070	15489
Wixen Music Publishing Inc	2731	F	818 591-7355	4144
Worxsitehr Insur Solutions Inc	6411	D	877 479-3591	15653
Yamaha Guitar Group Inc **(HQ)**	3931	C	818 575-3600	11355
Yamaha Guitar Group Inc	3931	E	818 575-3900	11356

CALABASAS HILLS, CA - Los Angeles County

	SIC	EMP	PHONE	ENTRY #
Ccf China Operating Corp	2051	E	818 871-3000	1989
Cheesecake Factory Inc **(PA)**	2051	A	818 871-3000	1992
Helmet House LLC **(PA)**	5136	C	800 421-7247	14336
Houston Cheesecake Fctry Corp	2051	E	818 871-3000	2007

CALEXICO, CA - Imperial County

	SIC	EMP	PHONE	ENTRY #
ARC - Imperial Valley	8093	E	760 768-1944	21274
Asco LP	3443	C	877 208-4316	6726
Bradford Soap Mexico Inc	2841	B	760 768-4539	4940
Circle Produce Co Inc	5148	E	760 357-5454	14617
Clover Imaging Group LLC	3861	E	760 357-9277	11271
Coppel Corporation	5021	D	760 357-3707	13132
Creation Tech Calexico Inc **(HQ)**	3672	E	760 336-8543	9396
Cs Manfacturing Indus Svcs Inc **(PA)**	3678	F	760 890-7746	9652
Hirsh Industries-Mexicali Div	3999	F	515 299-3200	11685
Imperial Valley Foods Inc	2037	B	760 203-1896	1900
Lakim Industries Incorporated **(PA)**	3991	E	310 637-8900	11513
Lorenz Inc	3699	E	760 427-1815	9889
Orthodental International Inc	3843	D	760 357-8070	11186
R L Jones-San Diego Inc **(PA)**	4731	D	760 357-3177	12517
Rockwell Collins Inc	3728	E	760 768-4732	10403
Skyworks Solutions Inc	3629	F	301 874-6408	8983
Sstmas Y Aranda Eqpos Hdrlicos	5084	E	619 245-4502	13942
Sun Community Federal Cr Un	6061	D	760 337-4200	15091
Triumph Group Inc	3728	F	760 768-1700	10438
Triumph Insulation Systems LLC	3728	A	760 618-7543	10439
U S Xpress Inc	4213	A	760 768-6707	12087
Xpo Logistics Freight Inc	4213	D	760 768-0280	12093

CALIFORNIA CITY, CA - Kern County

	SIC	EMP	PHONE	ENTRY #
Creative Accents	2273	E	760 373-1222	2685
Robertsons Ready Mix Ltd	3273	D	760 373-4815	6112
Silver Saddle Ranch & Club Inc	6552	D	760 373-8617	16073
Ward Enterprises	3599	F	661 251-4890	8845

CALIMESA, CA - Riverside County

	SIC	EMP	PHONE	ENTRY #
Skat-Trak	3011	E	909 795-2505	5305
Tommy Gun Plastering Inc	1742	D	909 795-9966	1407

CALIPATRIA, CA - Imperial County

	SIC	EMP	PHONE	ENTRY #
Ancon Marine	1799	D	760 348-9606	1634
Brandt Co Inc	0211	D	760 348-2295	123
Calenergy LLC	1731	B	402 231-1527	1229
Earthrise Nutritionals LLC	2099	E	760 348-5027	2427
Superior Cattle Feeders LLC **(PA)**	0211	D	760 348-2218	126

CAMARILLO, CA - Ventura County

	SIC	EMP	PHONE	ENTRY #
Abel Automatics LLC	3451	E	805 388-3721	7028
Aecom C&E Inc	8711	D	805 388-3775	22479
Affiliated Communications Inc	7389	C	805 447-2101	18436
Airborne Technologies Inc	3728	D	805 389-3700	10259
Airport Connection Inc	4111	C	805 389-8196	11802
Americon	2521	F	805 987-0412	3576
Amt Datasouth Corp **(PA)**	8731	E	805 388-5799	22824
Applied Engineering MGT Corp	7371	C	805 484-1909	17551
Artisan Vehicle Systems Inc	3711	D	805 402-6856	9935
Askgene Pharma Inc	2834	E	805 807-9868	4788
Astrofoam Molding Company Inc	3089	F	805 482-7276	5571
Barrett Business Services Inc	7361	A	805 987-0331	17396
Barta-Schoenewald Inc **(PA)**	3621	C	805 389-1935	8909
Basso Distributing Coinc	5181	D	805 656-1946	14821
Battery-Biz Inc	3694	D	800 848-6782	9820
Belport Company Inc **(PA)**	3843	F	805 484-1051	11161
Bestforms Inc	2761	E	805 388-0503	4598
BKM Office Environments Inc **(PA)**	1799	F	805 339-6388	1641
Cal Simba Inc **(PA)**	3914	E	805 240-1177	11334
Cal-Sensors Inc **(PA)**	3812	E	707 303-3837	10575
California Internet LP **(PA)**	4813	D	805 225-4638	12630
Califrnia Dsgners Chice Cstm C	2434	E	805 987-5820	3313
Califrnia State Univ Chnnel Is	3612	D	805 437-2670	8864
Camarillo Healthcare Center	8741	D	805 482-9805	22997
Camland Inc	7692	F	805 485-9242	18972
Casa Pcfica Ctrs For Chldren F **(PA)**	8322	C	805 482-3260	21732
Central Purchasing LLC **(HQ)**	5085	B	800 444-3353	13978
Channel Islnds Yung MNS Chrstn	8641	D	805 484-0423	22327
Chargetek Inc	3629	F	805 444-7792	8973
Chauhan Industries Inc	3728	F	805 484-1616	10299
Ciao Wireless Inc	3679	D	805 389-3224	9691
CK Technologies Inc **(PA)**	3823	E	805 987-4801	10685
Coastal Grading and Excavating	1794	E	805 445-6433	1593
Cooper Interconnect Inc **(DH)**	3643	D	805 484-0543	9029
Corprint Incorporated	2759	F	818 839-5316	4503
County of Ventura	4581	D	805 388-4274	12355
County of Ventura	8322	C	805 983-1332	21763
Crockett Graphics Inc **(PA)**	2653	D	805 987-8577	3797
Cudoform Inc	3469	F	805 617-0818	7137
Cushman & Wakefield Cal Inc	6531	A	805 322-7244	15829
Data Exchange Corporation **(PA)**	5045	B	805 388-1711	13388
Delicate Productions Inc **(PA)**	7922	D	415 484-1174	19309
Devorss & Co	5192	F	805 322-9010	14870
Dex Corporation	8711	C	805 388-1711	22531
Dial Security Inc **(PA)**	7382	C	805 389-6700	18371
Dignity Health	8062	C	805 389-5800	20753
Directv Group Holdings LLC	4841	C	805 207-6675	12758
DP Technology LLC **(HQ)**	7371	D	805 388-6000	17602
Earthcore Industries Inc	3999	F	805 484-7350	11663
Elder Care Alliance Camarillo	8361	D	510 769-2700	22101
Electronic Clearing House Inc **(HQ)**	7372	D	805 419-8700	17844
Engense Inc	3312	F	805 484-8317	6200
Eurasia Power LLC	5065	E	805 383-1234	13719
Futureflite Inc	2531	E	818 653-2145	3624
Galtech Computer Corporation	2521	E	805 376-1060	3586
Gbl Systems Corporation	7373	E	805 987-4345	18032
Gc International Inc **(PA)**	3365	E	805 389-4631	6396
Gc International Inc	3652	F	805 389-4631	9218
Gms Landscapes Inc	3432	D	805 402-3925	6562
Golden State Medical Sup Inc	5047	C	805 477-9866	13489
Golden State Medical Supply	5099	D	805 477-8966	14159
Gsms Inc **(PA)**	2834	D	805 477-9866	4827
Gtran Inc **(PA)**	3679	E	805 445-4500	9719
Hanson Lab Solutions Inc	3821	E	805 498-3121	10659
Hi-Temp Insulation Inc	1742	B	805 484-2774	1377
Houweling Nurseries Oxnard Inc	5141	B	805 271-5105	14471
Hte Acquisition LLC	3599	E	805 987-5449	8623
Hygiena LLC **(PA)**	2835	B	805 388-2383	4922
Infab LLC	3842	D	805 987-5255	11115
Innovative Integration Inc	3823	E	805 520-3300	10703
Institute For Applied Bhvior A	8049	D	805 987-5886	20221
Insulfab Inc	3296	E	805 482-2751	6171
Interconnect Systems Intl LLC **(DH)**	3674	D	805 482-2870	9520
Interface Community **(PA)**	8322	D	805 485-6114	21816
J C Industries Inc	3999	F	805 389-4040	11692
Jim ONeal Distributing Inc	3751	E	805 426-3300	10494

GEOGRAPHIC

Employment Codes: A=Over 500 employees, B=251-500, C=101-250, D=51-100, E=20-50 F=10-19

2022 Southern California Business Directory and Buyers Guide

© Mergent Inc. 1-800-342-5647

1343

	SIC	EMP	PHONE	ENTRY #
Johanson Dielectrics Inc **(HQ)**	3675	C	805 389-1166	9611
Johanson Technology Inc	3675	C	805 389-1166	9612
Juvenile Justice Division Cal	8741	C	805 485-7951	23044
K9 Ballistics Inc	3999	F	844 772-3125	11699
Kaiser Foundation Hospitals	8011	C	888 515-3500	19893
Kinamed Inc	3842	E	805 384-2748	11120
Koltov Inc **(PA)**	3172	E	805 764-0280	5908
La Workout Inc	7991	C	805 482-8884	19455
Las Posas Country Club	7997	D	805 482-4518	19578
Ledingedge Lighting Inc **(PA)**	3646	F	805 383-8493	9093
Linabond Inc	3479	E	805 484-7373	7382
Lucix Corporation **(HQ)**	3679	D	805 987-6645	9742
Lucix Corporation	3679	D	805 987-3677	9743
Lundberg Survey Inc	2721	E	805 383-2400	4084
Magicall Inc	3621	F	805 484-4300	8922
Market Scan Info Systems Inc	7371	D	800 658-7226	17657
Mediapointe Inc	3651	F	805 480-3700	9183
Medical Packaging Corporation	3842	D	805 388-2383	11123
Merex Inc	3825	E	805 446-2700	10765
Michael Baker Intl Inc	8711	D	805 383-3373	22613
Microsemi Communications Inc **(DH)**	3674	C	805 388-3700	9541
Microvoice Corporation	3663	E	805 389-2922	9290
Modern Campus USA Inc	7371	D	805 484-9400	17663
Nallatech Inc	5065	D	805 383-8997	13754
Nanoprecision Products Inc	3469	E	310 597-4991	7167
Nevion Usa Inc	3663	D	805 247-8575	9302
New Inspiration Brdcstg Co Inc **(HQ)**	4832	A	805 987-0400	12703
No Nuts LLC	2064	F	805 309-2420	2101
Northrop Grumman Systems Corp	7373	C	805 987-9739	18054
Odu-Usa Inc **(HQ)**	5065	D	805 484-0540	13759
Old New York Bagel Deli Co Inc **(PA)**	2051	E	805 484-3354	2027
Optim Microwave Inc	3663	F	805 482-7093	9305
Opto Diode Corporation	3674	E	805 465-8700	9552
OSI Optoelectronics Inc	3674	E	805 987-0146	9554
Pacific Casual LLC	2514	E	805 445-8310	3531
Pacific Earth Resources **(PA)**	0181	D	805 986-8277	89
Pacific Erth Rsrces Ltd A Cal	0181	D	209 892-3000	90
PDQ Engineering Inc	3599	E	805 482-1334	8735
People Creating Success Inc	8011	C	805 644-9480	20021
Performance Materials Corp **(HQ)**	2821	D	805 482-1722	4706
Physpeed Corporation	3674	F	805 259-3101	9557
Plt Enterprises Inc	3643	D	805 389-5335	9044
Polyfet Rf Devices Inc	3674	E	805 484-9582	9560
Premium Outlet Partners LP	6512	D	805 445-8520	15691
Primordial Diagnostics Inc	3823	E	800 462-1926	10711
Qualstar Corporation **(PA)**	3572	F	805 583-7744	8213
Record Technology Inc	3652	E	805 484-2747	9225
Rgc Services Inc	6531	D	805 484-1600	15977
Rincon Pacific LLC	0171	D	805 986-8806	36
Ronlo Engineering Ltd	3599	E	805 388-3227	8776
Saalex Corp **(PA)**	8711	C	805 482-1070	22649
Saint Frncis Winery Tasting Rm **(PA)**	2084	E	707 833-4668	2219
Salem Music Network Inc	3663	F	805 987-0400	9314
Sani-Tech West Inc **(HQ)**	3052	D	805 389-0400	5322
Semtech Corporation **(PA)**	3674	C	805 498-2111	9574
Sierra Traffic Service Inc	3669	F	805 388-2474	9353
Signum Systems Corporation	3825	F	805 383-3682	10770
Skurka Aerospace Inc **(DH)**	3621	E	805 484-8884	8930
So-Cal Value Added LLC	3679	E	805 389-5335	9785
Spanish Hills Club LLC	7997	D	805 388-5000	19616
Spanish Hills Country Club **(PA)**	7997	E	805 389-1644	19617
Structural Diagnostics Inc	3829	E	805 987-7755	10913
Summit Hotel Trs 111 LLC **(PA)**	7011	D	805 389-9898	16736
Tactical Communications Corp	3669	E	805 987-4100	9357
Technclor Vdocassette Mich Inc **(DH)**	7819	B	805 445-1122	19250
Technical Film Systems Inc	3861	F	805 384-9470	11293
Technicolor Disc Services Corp **(HQ)**	3695	C	805 445-1122	9841
Technicolor HM Entrmt Svcs Inc **(HQ)**	7819	B	805 445-1122	19251
Teledyne Reson Inc	5088	E	805 964-6260	14066
Teledyne Scentific Imaging LLC	8731	D	805 373-4979	22867
Thiessen Products Inc	3599	C	805 482-6913	8817
Thin-Lite Corporation	3648	E	805 987-5021	9150
Thingap Inc	3621	E	805 477-9741	8933
Thomas Bavarian Mtr Works Inc	7538	D	805 482-8878	18879
Titan Metal Fabricators Inc **(PA)**	3441	D	805 487-5050	6669
Transonic Combustion Inc	3519	E	805 465-5145	7601
Trophies Etc	7389	F	805 484-4121	18696
Turbonetics Holdings Inc	3714	E	805 581-0333	10145
United Western Enterprises Inc	3479	E	805 389-1077	7423
Ventura County Medi-Cal Manage	8099	D	888 301-1228	21495
Ventura County Star	2711	E	805 437-0138	4041
Viade Products Inc	3843	E	805 484-2114	11201
Viavi Solutions Inc	3661	D	805 465-1875	9245
Vitas Healthcare Corporation	8052	D	805 437-2100	20547
VME Acquisition Corp **(PA)**	3842	F	805 384-2748	11152
Voiceboard Corporation	3571	E	805 389-3100	8183
Western Gage Corporation	3545	E	805 445-1410	7878
Western Mfg & Distrg LLC	3751	E	805 988-1010	10509
Williams Aerospace & Mfg Inc **(HQ)**	5088	E	805 446-2700	14072
Wilwood Engineering	3714	C	805 388-1188	10158
Xirgo Technologies LLC	3699	D	805 319-4079	9931
Zero Gravity Corporation	3751	E	805 388-8803	10511
Zpower LLC	3629	C	805 445-7789	8986

CAMBRIA, CA - San Luis Obispo County

	SIC	EMP	PHONE	ENTRY #
Linns Fruit Bin Inc **(PA)**	2053	E	805 927-1499	2078
Moonstone Management Corp **(PA)**	6531	C	805 927-4200	15926
Pacific Cambria Inc	7011	D	805 927-6114	16605

CANOGA PARK, CA - Los Angeles County

	SIC	EMP	PHONE	ENTRY #
24-7 Caregivers Registry Inc	8082	C	800 687-8066	21114
A Yafa Pen Company	5112	E	818 704-8888	14191
Aerojet Rocketdyne De Inc **(HQ)**	2869	A	818 586-1000	5123
Allman Products Inc	3086	E	818 715-0093	5486
American Landscape Inc	0781	C	818 999-2041	232
American Landscape MGT Inc **(PA)**	0781	C	818 999-2041	233
American Metal & Paint Inc	3441	F	818 882-6333	6586
American Mfg Netwrk Inc	3599	F	818 786-1113	8496
APn Business Resources Inc	8742	D	818 717-9980	23161
Atlantis Enterprises Inc	5199	E	818 712-0572	14913
Azimc Investments Inc	5013	C	818 678-1200	13047
B S K T Inc	3599	F	818 349-1566	8514
Barrys Printing Inc	2752	E	818 998-8600	4236
Best Data Products Inc	3577	D	818 534-1414	8239
Buyers Consultation Svc Inc **(PA)**	5065	D	818 341-4820	13706
C J Instruments Inc	3829	E	818 996-4131	10874
Canyon Oaks Nursing and Rehab	8059	D	818 887-7050	20569
Catholic Charities of La Inc	8322	E	818 883-6015	21733
Computrition Inc **(HQ)**	7371	D	818 961-3999	17583
Den-Mat Corporation	2844	C	800 445-0345	5011
Dependable Dodge Inc	7532	E	818 883-9060	18787
Emac Assembly Corp	3679	F	818 882-2999	9708
Glastar Corporation	3559	E	818 341-0301	7980
Green Thumb International Inc	5193	D	818 340-6400	14885
Haven Hills Inc	8322	D	818 887-7481	21798
Hmi Associates Inc	7381	C	818 887-6800	18287
Home Depot USA Inc	7359	C	818 887-7083	17354
Interamerican Motor LLC **(HQ)**	5013	C	800 874-8925	13067
Landcare USA LLC	0782	D	818 346-7552	319
Mark Land Electric Inc	1731	B	818 883-5110	1279
Marvic Inc	3444	F	818 992-0078	6867
Micro Steel Inc	3769	E	818 348-8701	10535
Modern Imaging Solutions Inc	5021	E	800 511-7585	13144
Modern Woodworks Inc	2499	E	800 575-3475	3446
Mooney Inds Prcsion McHning In	3599	F	818 998-0199	8709
National Advanced Endoscopy De	3841	E	818 227-2720	11028
Northeast Valley Health Corp	8099	D	818 340-3570	21462
NRG Clean Power Inc	4911	E	818 444-2020	12812
Office Xpress Inc	5112	E	818 884-5737	14195
P-Cove Enterprises Inc	7373	D	818 341-1101	18057
Pacific Coast Tree Experts	0783	C	805 506-1211	360
Pacific Shore Holdings Inc	2834	E	818 998-0996	4868
Pls Diabetic Shoe Company Inc	3021	E	818 734-7080	5312
Rainbo Record Mfg Corp **(PA)**	3652	E	818 280-1100	9224
Richard Huetter Inc	5013	D	818 700-8001	13085
Rte Enterprises Inc	1721	D	818 999-5300	1197
Sela Healthcare Inc	8051	B	818 341-9800	20463
Seltzer-Doren Management Co	6513	D	818 709-5210	15749
Shield Security Inc	7381	B	818 239-5800	18334
Small Wnders Hndcrfted Mntres	3999	F	818 703-7450	11757
Software Dynamics Incorporated	7373	C	818 992-3299	18066
T & T Solutions Inc	7379	D	818 676-1786	18225
Temptron Engineering Inc	3829	E	818 346-4900	10916
Vomar Products Inc	2759	E	818 610-5115	4590
Westwood Insurance Agency **(DH)**	6411	D	818 990-9715	15649
Woodie Woodpeckers Woodworks	2434	F	818 999-2090	3347

CANYON COUNTRY, CA - Los Angeles County

	SIC	EMP	PHONE	ENTRY #
Commercial Display Systems LLC	3585	E	818 361-8160	8332
Design Masonry Inc	1741	D	661 252-2784	1342
M & M Florists Inc	5087	D	661 298-7088	14040
Northeast Valley Health Corp	8099	D	661 673-8888	21463
Pure Autism Counseling Ctr Inc	8093	D	661 360-7730	21331
Rexhall Industries Inc	3716	E	661 726-5470	10174
Tutor Time Learning Ctrs LLC	8351	C	866 930-7975	22069

CANYON LAKE, CA - Riverside County

	SIC	EMP	PHONE	ENTRY #
A Caregiver LLC	8082	E	951 676-4190	21123
Canyon Lk Property Owners Assn	8641	D	951 244-6841	22323
Cbabr Inc **(PA)**	6531	D	951 640-7056	15799
Golding Publications	2791	F	951 244-1966	4625

CAPISTRANO BEACH, CA - Orange County

	SIC	EMP	PHONE	ENTRY #
Capistrano Dispatch	2711	F	949 388-7700	3959
Pacific Monarch Resorts Inc	7011	D	949 248-2944	16612
Schaeffler Group USA Inc	3562	C	949 234-9799	8030
Soto Company Inc	0782	D	949 493-9403	344

CARPINTERIA, CA - Santa Barbara County

	SIC	EMP	PHONE	ENTRY #
After-Party2 Inc	7359	D	805 563-3800	17328
AGIA Inc **(PA)**	6411	C	805 566-9191	15529
Beacon West Energy Group LLC	8711	D	805 816-2790	22499
Bega North America Inc	3648	D	805 684-0533	9124
Brand Flower Farms Inc **(PA)**	5193	C	805 684-5531	14878
Carpinteria Motor Inn Inc	7011	E	805 684-0473	16368
Clipper Windpower PLC	3511	A	805 690-3275	7581
CP Opco LLC	7359	D	805 566-3566	17341
Dac International Inc	3541	E	805 684-8307	7727
Dako North America Inc	7389	D	805 566-3037	18500
Ditec Co	3841	F	805 566-7800	10971
Dsy Educational Corporation	2399	F	805 684-8111	3194
Essex Electronics Inc	3674	E	805 684-7601	9506
Forms and Surfaces Inc	3446	D	805 684-8626	6962
Forms and Surfaces Company LLC	3272	C	805 684-8626	6034
Freudenberg Medical LLC **(DH)**	3842	C	805 684-3304	11108
Gallup & Stribling Orchids LLC	5193	E	805 684-1998	14883
Gigavac LLC **(HQ)**	3625	F	805 684-8401	8953

Mergent email: customerrelations@mergent.com
1344
2022 Southern California Business Directory and Buyers Guide
(P-0000) Products & Services Section entry number
(PA)=Parent Co (HQ)=Headquarters (DH)=Div Headquarters

GEOGRAPHIC SECTION CATHEDRAL CITY, CA

	SIC	EMP	PHONE	ENTRY #
Helix Medical	3842	F	805 576-5458	11111
Inhealth Technologies	3842	E	800 477-5969	11116
Island Brewing Co	2082	F	805 745-8272	2148
Jimenez Nursery Inc	0181	D	805 684-7955	80
Momentum Work Inc **(PA)**	8331	D	805 566-9000	21962
Normans Nursery Inc	0181	C	805 684-1411	87
Normans Nursery Inc	5193	C	805 684-5442	14892
Ocean Breeze International	0181	D	805 684-1747	88
Pacifica Beauty LLC	3999	D	844 332-8440	11727
Plan Member Financial Corp	6282	D	800 874-6910	15340
Procore Technologies Inc **(PA)**	7371	A	866 477-6267	17691
Qad Inc	7372	F	805 684-6614	17964
Rincon Engineering Corporation	3599	E	805 684-0935	8769
Smart & Final Stores Inc	5141	C	805 566-2174	14492
Sunshine Floral Inc	5193	D	805 684-1177	14895
Supersprings International Inc	3493	E	805 745-5553	7468
Westerlay Orchids LP	0181	C	805 684-5411	98
Westland Flral Carpinteria Inc	5193	E	805 684-4011	14900
Westland Orchids Inc	5193	E	805 684-1436	14901
Zbe Inc	3625	E	805 576-1600	8968

CARSON, CA - Los Angeles County

	SIC	EMP	PHONE	ENTRY #
4as Trucking	4212	E	424 308-9563	11946
A & R Engineering Co Inc	3599	D	310 603-9060	8455
Allianz Globl Invstors Amer LP **(HQ)**	6799	D	310 549-0729	16246
Altium Packaging LLC	3085	F	310 952-8736	5473
Ampam Parks Mechanical Inc	1711	A	310 835-1532	1027
Anemostat Inc	5031	E	310 835-7500	13200
Anemostat Door Products Inc	3442	F	310 835-7500	6690
Anschutz Sthern Cal Spt Cmplex	7941	C	310 630-2000	19408
Apw Knox-Seeman Warehouse Inc **(HQ)**	5013	D	310 604-4373	13043
Arctic Glacier USA Inc	2097	C	310 638-0321	2368
Auto Parts Warehouse Inc **(PA)**	5013	E	800 913-6119	13044
Bakkavor Foods Usa Inc **(DH)**	5149	B	704 522-1977	14674
Belden Inc	3357	A	310 639-9473	6343
Big Heart Pet Brands	2033	C	310 519-3791	1860
Braun Linen Service Inc	7213	E	310 719-8661	16848
Brentwood Originals Inc **(PA)**	2392	C	925 202-9290	3097
Bristol Farms **(HQ)**	2099	D	310 233-4700	2400
Buswest LLC **(HQ)**	4141	D	310 984-3900	11905
C Preme Limited LLC	3949	F	310 355-0498	11407
Cal-Coast Pkg & Crating Inc	2441	E	310 518-7215	3377
Cali-Fame Los Angeles Inc	2353	D	310 747-5263	3025
Calko Transport Company Inc	4214	D	310 816-0602	12109
Calwest Galvanizing Corp	3479	E	310 549-2200	7351
Capital Cooking Equipment Inc	3433	E	562 903-1168	6569
Cardic Machine Products Inc	3599	F	310 884-3400	8541
Carson Operating Company LLC	7011	D	310 830-9200	16369
Carson Senior Assisted Living	8361	D	310 830-4010	22089
CCL Tube Inc **(HQ)**	3089	C	310 635-4444	5603
Cedarlane Natural Foods Inc **(PA)**	2099	D	310 886-7720	2406
Cedarlane Natural Foods Inc	2038	A	310 527-7833	1922
Cirrus Enterprises LLC	5162	D	310 204-6159	14753
City Fashion Express Inc	4731	D	310 223-1010	12435
Clay Dunn Enterprises Inc	1711	C	310 549-1698	1046
Cmp Display Systems Inc	3089	D	805 499-3642	5608
Coastal Doors	3442	F	562 665-5585	6694
Color Spot Nurseries Inc	5193	D	310 549-7470	14879
Cosway Company Inc **(PA)**	2844	E	310 900-4100	5009
County of Los Angeles	8631	C	310 847-4018	22289
Crate Modular Inc	3448	D	310 405-0829	6991
Custom Goods LLC	4225	D	310 241-6700	12192
Custom Goods LLC	4225	D	310 241-6700	12193
Custom Goods LLC **(PA)**	4225	E	310 241-6700	12194
Cwd LLC **(DH)**	3714	E	310 218-1082	10039
David Oppenheimer and Co I LLC	5141	D	310 900-7140	14464
Dependable Highway Express Inc	4213	D	310 522-4111	12031
Dermalogica LLC **(HQ)**	2844	C	310 900-4000	5012
Dianas Mexican Food Pdts Inc	2099	D	310 834-4886	2423
DMC Power Inc **(PA)**	3643	D	310 323-1616	9032
Dmf Inc	3645	D	323 934-7779	9062
DSA Signage	3993	F	877 305-4911	11542
Ducommun Aerostructures Inc	3728	C	310 513-7200	10316
Ducommun Labarge Tech Inc **(HQ)**	3728	C	310 513-7200	10318
Duro-Sense Corp	3823	F	310 533-6877	10690
Dynamex Corporation	2298	D	310 329-0399	2714
East West Enterprises	3315	E	310 632-9933	6224
Elite 4 Print Inc	2752	E	310 366-1344	4290
Elite Color Technologies Inc	2759	F	310 324-3040	4513
Empire Container Corporation	2653	D	310 537-8190	3800
Evo Manufacturing Inc	3999	F	714 879-8913	11665
Forensic Analytical Spc Inc	8734	D	310 763-2374	22945
Fortress Resources LLC **(HQ)**	7538	C	562 633-9951	18830
General Mills Inc	2026	E	310 605-6108	1835
Geodis Usa Inc	4731	D	310 518-6467	12461
Giuliano-Pagano Corporation	2051	D	310 537-7700	2004
Global Billiard Mfg Co Inc	3949	F	310 764-5000	11420
Gms Molds **(PA)**	3544	E	310 684-1168	7804
Gordon Laboratories Inc	2844	C	310 327-5240	5026
Grand View Geranium Grdns Inc	0181	D	310 217-0490	78
Gs Brothers Inc **(PA)**	0782	C	310 833-1369	308
H & C Headwear Inc **(PA)**	5136	D	310 324-5263	14335
H Rauvel Inc **(PA)**	4225	D	310 604-0060	12212
Hanjin Transportation Co Ltd	4731	D	310 522-5030	12467
Hankyu Hanshin Express USA Inc **(DH)**	4731	E	630 285-7100	12468
Harvard Grand Inv Inc A Cal	6799	D	310 513-7560	16267
Howmet Corporation	3324	C	310 847-8152	6266
Huck International Inc	3452	C	310 830-8200	7067
Hydroform USA Incorporated	3728	C	310 632-6353	10349
I & I Sports Supply Company **(PA)**	3949	E	310 715-6800	11427
Interface Welding	7699	E	310 323-4944	19045
JB Dental Supply Co Inc **(PA)**	5047	C	310 202-8855	13496
Jnj Operations LLC	3999	E	855 525-6545	11695
Jobar International Inc	5199	D	310 222-8682	14942
Johnson Laminating Coating Inc	3083	D	310 635-4929	5451
Js Apparel Inc	2329	D	310 631-6333	2815
Kaiser Foundation Hospitals	6324	C	310 816-5440	15423
Kaiser Foundation Hospitals	8093	C	310 513-6707	21318
Klx LLC	4213	D	559 684-1037	12057
Kole Imports	5199	D	310 834-0004	14944
Kts Kitchens Inc	2099	C	310 764-0850	2461
Kw International Inc	4731	D	310 354-6944	12475
Leiner Health Products Inc **(HQ)**	2834	A	631 200-2000	4843
Letterhead Factory Inc	2752	F	310 538-3321	4358
Long-Lok LLC	3728	E	424 209-8726	10369
Long-Lok Fasteners Corporation	5085	E	310 667-4200	13998
Mag Aerospace Industries LLC	3431	B	801 400-7944	6548
Mainfreight Inc **(HQ)**	4731	D	310 900-1974	12481
Megiddo Global LLC	3842	E	844 477-7007	11124
Merchants Bank California N A	6022	D	310 549-4350	15032
Mestek Inc	3585	C	310 835-7500	8345
Mhx LLC	4731	D	800 234-2098	12483
Morettis Design Collection	2511	E	310 638-5555	3480
Nano Filter Inc	3999	D	949 316-8866	11719
North Amrcn SEC Investigations	7381	D	323 634-1911	18302
Northrop Grumman Systems Corp	7371	C	310 764-3000	17678
Nova Ortho-Med Inc **(PA)**	5047	D	310 352-3600	13506
Nu-Health California LLC	2033	F	800 806-0519	1870
O W I Inc	3651	F	310 515-1900	9185
Oak-It Inc	2541	D	310 719-3999	3660
OConnell Landscape Maint Inc	0782	B	800 339-1106	329
Pacific Toll Processing Inc	3312	E	310 952-4992	6207
Pacifica Trucks LLC	4731	D	310 549-1351	12500
Parter Medical Products Inc	5047	C	310 327-4417	13508
Pro Safety Inc	5084	C	562 364-7450	13930
Proma Inc	3843	E	310 327-0035	11191
Qualis Automotive LLC	7538	D	859 689-7772	18862
Quality Magnetics Corporation	3499	E	310 632-1941	7569
Quik Pick Express LLC	4731	C	310 763-3000	12515
Quik Pick Express LLC **(PA)**	4731	C	310 763-3000	12516
Refrigrated Trck Solutions LLC	3715	E	323 594-4500	10168
Ruggable LLC **(PA)**	2273	E	310 295-0098	2695
Sac-TEC Labs Inc **(PA)**	3674	E	310 375-5295	9568
Sage Goddess Inc	3911	E	650 733-6639	11330
Salsbury Industries Inc **(PA)**	2542	B	323 846-6700	3695
Salvation Army **(HQ)**	8322	C	562 264-3600	21880
Samtech Automotive Usa Inc	3542	E	310 638-9955	7766
Sazerac Company Inc	2085	F	310 604-8717	2245
Schafer Bros Trnsf Pano Mvers **(PA)**	4225	D	310 835-7231	12241
Secrom Inc	8059	D	310 830-4010	20626
Sees Candies Inc **(DH)**	2064	B	800 347-7337	2104
Simpson Industries Inc	2834	E	310 605-1224	4894
SO Tech/Spcl Op Tech Inc **(PA)**	5131	E	310 202-9007	14320
Solid-Scope Machining Co Inc	3429	F	310 523-2366	6537
Southern Cal Disc Tire Co Inc	5014	C	310 324-2569	13119
Southwind Foods LLC **(PA)**	5146	C	323 262-8222	14585
Spectra I California	1731	D	310 835-0808	1318
Stanford Mu Corporation	3769	E	310 605-2888	10536
Street Glow Inc	3647	D	310 631-1881	9119
Strike Technology Inc	3679	E	562 437-3428	9787
Sumi Printing & Binding Inc	2752	F	310 769-1600	4427
Supra National Express Inc	4731	C	310 549-7105	12534
System Supply Stationery Corp	5112	F	310 223-0880	14198
Tabletops Unlimited Inc **(PA)**	5023	D	310 549-6000	13187
Tnp Instruments Inc	3679	F	310 532-2222	9797
Toll Global Forwarding USA Inc **(HQ)**	4731	E	626 363-2400	12537
Transcentra Inc	7373	A	310 603-0105	18072
Trinity International Inds LLC	3089	E	800 985-5506	5843
Triple B Forwarders Inc **(PA)**	4731	C	310 604-5840	12547
Twenty Four 7 Globl Sltons Inc	2385	E	323 319-2724	3052
Universal Logistics System Inc **(DH)**	4225	D	310 631-0800	12256
Universal Plant Svcs Cal Inc	3599	D	310 618-1600	8832
Watson Cogeneration Co Inc	4911	D	310 816-8100	12863
Wavenet Inc **(PA)**	3315	F	310 885-4200	6240
Weber Printing Company Inc	2752	E	310 639-5064	4454
West Coast Aerospace Inc	5085	F	310 518-0633	14031
Whaling Packaging Co	4783	E	310 518-6021	12560
Worley Field Services Inc	8999	D	310 816-8939	23544
Yoplait U S A Inc	2026	F	310 632-9502	1843
Yun Industrial Co Ltd	3672	E	310 715-1898	9470
Yusen Logistics Americas Inc	4731	C	310 518-3008	12553
Zodiac Wtr Waste Aero Systems	3728	C	310 884-7000	10449

CASTAIC, CA - Los Angeles County

	SIC	EMP	PHONE	ENTRY #
Castaic Lake RV Park Inc	2451	F	661 257-3340	3418
Castaic Truck Stop Inc	2911	E	661 295-1374	5249
Clay Castaic Manufacturing Co	3251	F	661 259-3066	5983
County of Los Angeles	8069	D	661 223-8700	21044
So Cal Tractor Sales Co Inc	7692	F	818 252-1900	18996
Superior Interlocking Pavers	3531	F	818 838-0833	7652

CATHEDRAL CITY, CA - Riverside County

	SIC	EMP	PHONE	ENTRY #
American Golf Corporation	7997	D	702 431-2191	19531
Big Lgue Dreams Consulting LLC	7032	D	760 324-5600	16817
Desert Prncess HM Owners CLB I	7997	E	760 322-1655	19559
Developmental Svcs Cal Dept	8099	A	760 770-6248	21420

GEOGRAPHIC

Employment Codes: A=Over 500 employees, B=251-500, C=101-250, D=51-100, E=20-50 F=10-19
2022 Southern California Business Directory and Buyers Guide
© Mergent Inc. 1-800-342-5647
1345

	SIC	EMP	PHONE	ENTRY #
Enterprise Portable Welding	3842	F	760 328-6316	11102
Heartland Payment Systems Inc	7389	D	760 324-0133	18540
Palm Springs Motors Inc	7538	C	760 699-6695	18860
T Allance One - Palm Sprng LLC	7999	D	760 322-7000	19674
Welk Resort Group Inc	7011	C	760 770-9755	16783

CAYUCOS, CA - San Luis Obispo County

	SIC	EMP	PHONE	ENTRY #
Negranti Construction	1794	E	805 995-3357	1602

CERRITOS, CA - Los Angeles County

	SIC	EMP	PHONE	ENTRY #
A & H Engineering & Mfg Inc	3599	E	562 623-9717	8453
AB Mauri Food Inc	2099	E	562 483-4619	2384
Advanced Uv Inc **(PA)**	3589	E	562 407-0299	8361
Allstate Floral Inc	6411	C	562 926-2989	15530
Alpha Dental of Utah Inc	3843	E	562 467-7759	11159
Amphenol Nelson-Dunn Tech Inc **(HQ)**	5084	E	714 249-7700	13886
Apex Computer Systems Inc	7378	D	562 926-6820	18143
Apperson Inc **(PA)**	2761	D	562 356-3333	4597
ARI Industries Inc	3585	D	714 993-3700	8329
Arjo Inc	5047	C	714 412-1170	13476
Artistic Coverings Inc	3086	E	562 404-9343	5489
Atkinson Andlson Loya Ruud Rom **(PA)**	8111	C	562 653-3200	21506
Audio Visual Headquarters **(DH)**	7359	E	310 603-0652	17333
Auditboard Inc **(PA)**	7371	E	877 769-5444	17556
Auto Insurance Specialists LLC **(DH)**	6411	C	562 345-6247	15539
Award Packaging Spc Corp	2653	E	323 727-1200	3784
Axelacare Holdings Inc	8082	A	714 522-8802	21137
Bargain Rent-A-Car	5012	C	562 865-7447	13021
Berkshire Hthway HM Svcs CA Rp **(PA)**	6531	D	562 860-2625	15787
Bermingham Cntrls Inc A Cal Co **(PA)**	3491	E	562 860-0463	7438
Better Beverages Inc **(PA)**	2087	D	562 924-8321	2310
Big 5 Electronics Inc	3651	E	562 941-4669	9164
Biospace Inc	8731	D	323 932-6503	22832
Blairs Metal Polsg Pltg Co Inc	3471	E	562 860-7106	7224
Blc Wc Inc **(PA)**	2759	C	562 926-1452	4487
Calnetix Inc **(PA)**	8711	D	562 293-1660	22510
Calnetix Technologies LLC **(HQ)**	3621	E	562 293-1660	8910
Captek Holdings LLC	2023	E	562 921-9511	1789
Captek Midco Inc **(HQ)**	2077	C	562 921-9511	2125
Captek Softgel Intl Inc **(DH)**	2834	B	562 921-9511	4806
Caravan Canopy Intl Inc	2394	E	714 367-3000	3135
Caremore Health Plan **(HQ)**	8011	C	562 622-2950	19737
City of Cerritos	7922	C	562 916-8500	19307
Clio Inc	3495	E	562 926-3724	7485
College Hospital Inc **(PA)**	8063	B	562 924-9581	21018
Community Family Guidance Ctr **(PA)**	8093	D	562 865-6444	21289
Complete Office California Inc	5021	D	714 880-1222	13131
Corelis Inc	3679	E	562 926-6727	9696
Crest Financial Corporation **(DH)**	6411	D	562 733-6500	15558
Ctcoa LLC	3728	E	562 407-5375	10305
David Levy Co Inc	5065	E	562 404-9998	13714
Dec Fabricators Inc	3499	F	562 403-3626	7552
Dji Service LLC	3728	F	818 235-0788	10311
Dji Technology Inc	3861	E	818 235-0789	11273
Docupak Inc	2782	E	714 670-7944	4610
Dool Fna Inc	2221	C	562 483-4100	2596
Eco-Air Products Inc	5075	F	562 801-0133	13841
Edco Health Info Solution	7389	D	909 793-0613	18511
Eide Industries Inc	2394	D	562 402-8335	3138
Enterprise Bank & Trust	6022	C	562 345-9092	15021
Eplica Inc	7361	C	562 977-4300	17420
Evergreen Hospice Care Inc **(PA)**	8082	C	562 865-9006	21163
Faith Com Inc **(PA)**	8748	D	562 719-9300	23440
Foam Molders and Specialties **(PA)**	3086	D	562 924-7757	5503
Foam Molders and Specialties	3086	E	562 924-7757	5504
Ftg Inc **(PA)**	3714	F	562 865-9200	10063
Funtastic Factory Inc	3599	F	562 777-1140	8595
G & P Group Inc	2068	F	323 268-2686	2112
Geek Squad Inc	7379	D	562 402-1555	18183
Golden Star Technology Inc **(PA)**	7378	D	562 345-8700	18147
Hansai Inc	1389	F	714 539-3311	506
Helix Electric Inc	1731	C	562 941-7200	1263
Ifncom Inc **(PA)**	4813	D	213 452-1505	12648
Inbody Co Ltd	3845	E	323 932-6503	11224
International Coatings Co Inc **(PA)**	2891	E	562 926-1010	5185
IPC Cal Flex Inc	3672	E	714 952-0373	9414
Ips Industries Inc	3089	D	562 623-2555	5676
Kaiser Foundation Hospitals	8011	C	800 823-4040	19892
Kaltec Electronics Inc **(PA)**	3861	F	813 888-9555	11281
LA Triumph Inc	2326	E	562 404-7657	2784
Lincare Inc	8082	D	870 972-8839	21184
Lloyd Staffing Inc	7363	B	631 777-7600	17497
Madison Inc of Oklahoma	3441	D	918 224-6990	6631
Madison Industries **(HQ)**	3448	E	323 583-4061	7001
Management Trust Assn Inc	8742	C	562 926-3372	23267
McNichols Company	5051	E	562 921-3344	13577
Memorex Products Inc	5064	C	562 653-2800	13689
Microtek Lab Inc **(HQ)**	5044	C	310 687-5823	13362
Midway International Inc	5199	E	562 921-2255	14952
Molino Company	2752	D	323 726-1000	4376
Montebello Container Co LLC **(HQ)**	2653	D	562 404-6221	3821
Mpd Holdings Inc	3577	E	562 777-1051	8284
New-Indy Tripaq LLC **(PA)**	7336	D	562 404-6965	17181
NSK Precision America Inc	5085	C	562 968-1000	14009
O E C Shipg Los Angeles Inc	4731	E	562 926-7186	12495
Olea Kiosks Inc	3577	D	562 924-2644	8287
Pankl Aerospace Systems	3369	D	562 207-6300	6420
Para-Plate & Plastics Co Inc	3555	E	562 404-3434	7923
Parts Expediting and Dist Co	3714	E	562 944-3199	10113
Petra Risk Solutions **(PA)**	6411	D	800 466-8951	15613
Phoenix Engineering Tech LLC	8711	D	714 918-0630	22638
Poliseek Ais Insur Sltions Inc	6411	D	866 480-7335	15614
Polycell Packaging Corporation	5199	E	562 483-6000	14967
Precision Metal Crafts	3441	E	562 468-7080	6651
Printing Management Associates	2752	F	562 407-9977	4400
Private Medical-Care Inc	6324	A	562 924-8311	15448
R1 Concepts Inc	5013	D	714 777-2323	13081
Randstad Professionals Us LLC	7361	D	562 468-0111	17453
Razor USA LLC **(PA)**	5091	D	562 345-6000	14086
Refriderator Manufacters LLC	3632	E	562 229-0500	8998
Refrigerator Manufacters Inc **(PA)**	3632	E	562 926-2006	8999
Refrigerator Manufacturers LLC	3585	E	562 926-2006	8348
Resource Environmental Inc	1542	D	562 468-7000	815
Royal Plywood Company LLC **(PA)**	5031	D	562 404-2989	13285
Secure One Data Solutions LLC	7374	D	562 924-7056	18109
Sedenquist-Fraser Entps Inc	3714	E	562 924-5763	10132
SF Technology Inc	3999	F	562 924-5763	11753
Southern Glzers Wine Sprits WA	5182	B	562 926-2000	14846
T Hasegawa USA Inc **(HQ)**	2087	E	714 522-1900	2338
Tall Mouse Arts & Crafts Inc	5092	D	714 693-4900	14102
Tenet Healthsystem Medical Inc	8062	C	562 531-2550	20973
Thermal Engrg Intl USA Inc **(HQ)**	8711	D	323 726-0641	22673
Trinitycare LLC **(PA)**	8082	E	818 709-4221	21224
True Vision Displays Inc	3679	F	562 407-0630	9799
Twin Eagles Inc	3631	C	562 802-3488	8996
UFO Designs	3714	E	562 924-5763	10147
Umeken USA Inc **(PA)**	5149	D	888 941-3311	14746
United Parcel Service Inc	4215	C	562 404-3236	12160
US Dental Inc	3843	E	562 404-3500	11200
Villa Furniture Mfg Co	2531	C	714 535-7272	3634
WCP Inc	3089	D	562 653-9797	5861
West Coast Switchgear **(HQ)**	3613	D	562 802-3441	8908
Winning Laboratories Inc	2833	F	562 921-6380	4770
Zero Energy Contracting LLC	1711	D	626 701-3180	1164

CHATSWORTH, CA - Los Angeles County

	SIC	EMP	PHONE	ENTRY #
A & S Mold and Die Corp	3089	D	818 341-5393	5540
A B C Plastics Inc	3083	F	818 775-0065	5446
Aaron Thomas & Associates Inc	7331	E	818 727-9040	17127
Aben Machine Products Inc	3599	F	818 960-4502	8459
Absolute Machining Inc	3441	F	818 709-7367	6579
Academic Ch Choir Gwns Mfg Inc	2389	E	818 886-3697	3064
Access Control Security Inc **(PA)**	7381	D	714 835-3800	18238
Accunex Inc	8711	E	818 882-5858	22473
Adco Container Company	5085	E	818 998-2565	13969
Aderans Hair Goods Inc **(HQ)**	5131	E	818 428-1626	14301
Advanced Cosmetic RES Labs Inc	3999	E	818 709-9945	11626
Aero Mechanism Precision Inc	3599	E	818 886-1855	8474
Aeroantenna Technology Inc	3812	C	818 993-3842	10560
Aerojet Rocketdyne De Inc	2869	C	818 586-1000	5124
Aitech Defense Systems Inc	3699	E	818 700-2000	9850
Aitech Rugged Group Inc **(PA)**	3699	E	818 700-2000	9851
Align Aerospace LLC **(PA)**	3728	B	818 727-7800	10265
All Tmperatures Controlled Inc	1711	D	818 882-1478	1023
Alliance Metal Products Inc	3444	C	818 709-1204	6779
Allied Trading Group Inc	8742	E	818 576-9277	23151
Allsale Electric Inc	5063	D	818 715-0181	13611
Allstate Imaging Inc **(PA)**	5044	D	818 678-4550	13351
Almack Liners Inc	2335	E	818 718-5878	2876
American Copak Corporation	7389	C	818 576-1000	18442
Andrews Powder Coating Inc	3479	E	818 700-1030	7342
Ansell Sndel Med Solutions LLC	3842	E	818 534-2500	11087
Apparel Prod Svcs Globl LLC	2339	E	818 700-3700	2918
Aram Precision Tool & Die Inc	3599	F	818 998-1000	8499
Armada Engineering LLC	8711	F	818 280-5138	22493
Audionics System Inc	3651	F	818 345-9599	9160
Automoco LLC	3714	E	707 544-4761	10020
Avenue Lighting	3229	F	800 798-0409	5931
Avet Industries Inc	3949	F	818 576-9895	11404
Avn Media Network Inc	2731	E	818 718-5788	4120
Aware Products Inc	2844	E	818 206-6700	4990
Aware Products LLC	2844	C	818 206-6700	4991
BDR Industries Inc	3577	E	818 341-2112	8237
Bellami Hair LLC	7231	C	844 235-5264	16899
Bey-Berk International **(PA)**	3499	E	818 773-7534	7550
Breakaway Press Inc	2752	E	818 727-7388	4240
Cac Fabrication Inc	3441	F	818 882-2626	6595
Cali Framing Supplies LLC	7699	E	818 899-7777	19026
California Psychcare Inc **(PA)**	8049	D	813 401-0661	20209
Califrnia Dluxe Wndows Inds In **(PA)**	2431	E	813 349-5566	3237
Califrnia Trade Converters Inc	2631	E	818 899-1455	3772
Canoga Perkins Corporation **(HQ)**	3669	D	818 718-6300	9335
Careismatic Brands Inc **(PA)**	3143	C	818 671-2100	5876
Cbol Corporation	5065	C	818 704-8200	13708
Celesco Transducer Products	3679	F	818 701-2701	9690
Challenge Publications Inc	2721	F	818 700-6868	4057
Chatsworth Products Inc **(PA)**	3499	E	818 735-6100	7551
Chemsil Silicones Inc	5169	E	818 700-0302	14776
Child Care Resource Center Inc **(PA)**	8322	C	818 717-1000	21737
Ciphertex LLC	3577	F	818 773-8989	8245
Circuit Services Llc	3672	E	818 701-5391	9391
Classic Cosmetics Inc **(PA)**	2844	C	818 773-9042	5000
Cliffdale Manufacturing LLC	3769	C	318 341-3344	10531
Clm Group Inc	2844	E	318 349-2549	5001
Clover Imaging Group LLC	5085	B	815 431-8100	13979
Colbrit Manufacturing Co Inc	3544	E	818 709-3608	7790

Mergent email: customerrelations@mergent.com
1346
2022 Southern California Business
Directory and Buyers Guide
(P-0000) Products & Services Section entry number
(PA)=Parent Co (HQ)=Headquarters (DH)=Div Headquarters

	SIC	EMP	PHONE	ENTRY #
Color Design Laboratory Inc	7389	E	818 341-8200	18484
Comet Electric Inc	1731	C	818 340-0965	1234
Cooner Sales Company LLC **(PA)**	5051	F	818 882-8311	13560
County of Los Angeles	8099	D	818 717-4644	21404
Cpcc Inc	8059	D	818 882-3200	20575
Crunch LLC	7991	D	951 327-0202	19441
Crunch LLC	7991	D	719 301-1760	19442
Crunch Fitness	7991	D	805 522-5454	19443
CU Vehicles LLC	7515	D	818 885-1226	18748
Custom Control Sensors Inc	3625	E	818 341-4610	8947
Custom Control Sensors LLC **(PA)**	3613	B	818 341-4610	8892
Custom Control Sensors Intl	3613	E	818 341-4610	8893
Custom Design Iron Works Inc	3364	F	818 700-9182	6376
Datadirect Networks Inc **(PA)**	3572	C	818 700-7600	8196
Delta Fabrication Inc	3444	D	818 407-4000	6819
Delta Hi-Tech	3599	C	818 407-4000	8570
Delta Tau Data Systems Inc Cal **(HQ)**	3569	C	818 998-2095	8119
Dolphin Imaging Systems LLC	7371	C	818 435-1368	17601
DOT Copy Inc	2752	D	818 341-6666	4280
Double K Industries Inc	3523	F	818 772-2887	7609
Duclos Lenses Inc	7699	F	818 773-0600	19034
Dwa Alminum Composites USA Inc	3365	E	818 998-1504	6393
Dynamic Sciences Intl Inc	3663	E	818 226-6262	9270
Dynamo Aviation Inc	4581	D	818 785-9561	12357
Dytran Instruments Inc	3679	C	818 700-7818	9702
Egremont Schools Inc	8351	D	818 363-7803	22011
Eisenberg International Corp **(PA)**	5136	D	818 365-8161	14331
Electro Adapter Inc	3643	D	818 998-1198	9034
Electronic Health Plans Inc	8099	D	818 734-4700	21422
Epic Technologies LLC **(HQ)**	3661	C	818 495-8617	9232
Erbaviva Inc	2833	E	818 998-7112	4743
Exhart Envmtl Systems Inc **(PA)**	3999	F	818 576-9628	11666
Featherock Inc **(PA)**	1499	F	818 882-3888	586
Federal Manufacturing Corp	3452	E	818 341-9825	7065
Firan Tech Group USA Corp **(HQ)**	3812	C	818 407-4024	10588
Flowmetrics Inc	3823	F	818 407-3420	10693
Fluid Line Technology Corp	3841	E	818 998-8848	10982
Formology Lab Inc	2844	F	424 452-0377	5022
Ftg Aerospace Inc **(DH)**	3364	E	818 407-4024	6380
Ftg Circuits Inc **(DH)**	3672	D	818 407-4024	9408
General Ribbon Corp	3955	B	818 709-1234	11478
Genesis Tech Partners LLC	7699	C	800 950-2647	19039
Globalvision Systems Inc	3572	F	888 227-7967	8200
GPA Printing CA LLC	2752	F	818 618-1500	4305
Graphic Research Inc	3672	E	818 886-7340	9412
H2w	5099	F	800 578-3088	14162
Happy Jump Inc	7999	F	818 886-3991	19652
Havana Graphic Center Inc	2752	E	818 841-3774	4313
Health Advocates LLC	8399	B	818 995-9500	22188
Heritage Cabinet Co Inc	2541	F	818 786-4900	3650
Houston Ontic Inc	3599	E	818 678-6555	8622
Hydraulics International Inc **(PA)**	3728	B	818 998-1231	10346
Hydraulics International Inc	3728	E	818 998-1231	10347
Hydromach Inc	3769	E	818 341-0915	10533
Imperial Enterprises Inc	3229	E	818 886-5028	5937
Impress Communications Inc	2752	D	818 701-8800	4327
Innovative Cosmetic Labs Inc	2844	F	818 349-1121	5032
Intelligent Cmpt Solutions Inc **(PA)**	3825	E	818 998-5805	10757
International Precision Inc	3599	E	818 882-3933	8627
Invelop Inc	3523	E	818 772-2887	7612
Iog Products LLC	3674	F	818 350-5070	9523
Ironman Inc	7692	E	818 341-0980	18982
J & J Products Inc	3499	F	818 998-4250	7561
J & P Precision Deburring Inc	3599	F	818 998-6079	8632
J B Whl Roofg Bldg Sups Inc **(DH)**	5033	D	818 998-0440	13325
Jackson Engineering Co Inc	3612	E	818 886-9567	8875
Joerns LLC **(HQ)**	5047	C	800 966-6662	13497
John List Corporation	3547	E	818 882-7848	7885
Jt Windows Inc	1751	E	818 709-7950	1444
Kdc/One Cosmetic Labs Amer Inc	2844	C	818 998-3511	5038
Keith E Archambeau Sr Inc	3444	E	818 718-6110	6861
Kerning Data Systems Inc	3555	F	818 882-8712	7919
Kingdom Enterprise Films LLC	7812	E	818 963-2513	19139
Labeling Hurst Systems LLC	2759	F	818 701-0710	4532
Lasalle Intl Hldings Group Inc	3533	F	818 233-8000	7673
Lehrer Brllnprfktion Werks Inc **(PA)**	3089	D	818 407-1890	5697
Lf Illumination LLC	3646	D	818 885-1335	9094
Lightcraft Otdoor Environments	3645	F	818 349-2663	9065
Line One Laboratories Inc USA **(PA)**	3069	C	818 886-2288	5389
Litepanels Inc	3641	E	818 752-7009	9022
Logicube Inc **(PA)**	3577	E	888 494-8832	8275
Logistical Support LLC	3724	C	818 341-3344	10220
Logistical Support LLC	5088	C	818 341-3344	14062
Los Angles Cnty Mtro Trnsp Aut	4111	A	213 922-6308	11817
Loveis Corp	3841	F	818 408-9504	11011
M & N Consulting Inc	4215	D	818 349-9400	12141
Magic Gumball International	2064	F	818 716-1888	2094
Maloof Naman Builders Inc	5082	D	818 775-0040	13864
Maxwell Alarm Screen Mfg Inc	3993	E	818 773-5533	11571
MBK Enterprises Inc	3842	E	818 998-1477	11122
Mercury Magnetics Inc	3677	E	818 998-7791	9634
Metal Chem Inc	3471	E	818 727-9951	7280
Metal Improvement Company LLC	3398	D	818 407-6280	6447
MGA Entertainment Inc **(PA)**	5092	B	818 894-2525	14098
Micro Plastics Inc	3643	E	818 882-0244	9042
Millennial Home Lending Inc	6162	D	818 812-5150	15215
Minilec Service Inc	7622	E	818 341-1125	18944
Molnar Engineering Inc	3599	E	818 993-3495	8705
Mono Engineering Corp	3599	E	818 772-4998	8707
Monocent Inc	2835	F	424 310-0777	4924
Moog Inc	3812	C	818 341-5156	10600
Multi-Pak Corporation	7389	D	818 709-0508	18606
Narcotics Annymous Wrld Svcs I	2731	E	818 773-9999	4134
Natel Engineering Company LLC **(PA)**	3679	C	818 495-8617	9755
Natel Engineering Holdings Inc	3672	E	818 734-6500	9434
Natrol LLC **(PA)**	2834	C	818 739-6000	4857
Neocomp Systems Inc	7378	D	818 700-8722	18149
Networks Electronic Co LLC	3489	E	818 341-0440	7433
Neutraderm Inc	2844	E	818 534-3190	5050
Newhere Inc **(PA)**	2834	E	888 991-7471	4860
Newvac LLC **(HQ)**	3643	D	310 525-1205	9043
Newvac LLC	3671	C	310 990-0401	9364
Newvac LLC	3671	D	747 202-7333	9365
Newvac LLC	3679	E	747 202-7333	9757
Nna Insurance Services LLC	6411	C	818 739-4071	15603
North La County Regional Ctr **(PA)**	8748	B	818 778-1900	23484
North Ranch Management Corp	3171	D	800 410-2153	5902
Northcross Paper Co Inc	5113	E	818 998-3774	14215
Northrdge Tr-Mdlity Imging Inc	3821	F	818 709-2468	10661
O & S Precision Inc	3599	E	818 718-8876	8723
OBryant Electric Inc	1731	C	818 407-1986	1288
Oncore Manufacturing LLC **(HQ)**	8711	A	818 734-6500	22623
Oncore Manufacturing Svcs Inc	3672	C	510 360-2222	9435
Ontic Engineering and Mfg Inc **(PA)**	5088	C	818 678-6555	14063
Optical Corporation **(DH)**	3827	E	818 725-9750	10851
Pacer Print	2752	F	888 305-3144	4384
Pacific Coast Lighting Inc **(HQ)**	3648	C	800 709-9004	9142
Pacific Precision Labs Inc	3829	F	818 700-8977	10902
Pacific Toxicclogy Labs	8071	D	818 598-3110	21082
Papco Screw Products Inc	3541	F	818 341-2266	7738
Pd Liquidation Inc	5199	C	818 772-0100	14963
Pd Products LLC	2299	E	818 772-0100	2735
Pencil Grip Inc **(PA)**	2678	F	310 315-3545	3916
Performance Automotive Whl Inc **(PA)**	5013	D	805 499-8973	13079
Piege Co **(PA)**	5136	D	818 727-9100	14345
Pioneer Photo Albums Inc **(PA)**	2782	C	818 882-2161	4611
Planet Green Cartridges Inc	3955	D	818 725-2596	11481
Plateronics Processing Inc	3471	E	818 341-2191	7295
Platinum Group Companies Inc **(PA)**	6719	C	818 721-3800	16107
PLC Imports Inc	5063	E	818 349-1600	13660
Pope Plastics Inc	3544	E	818 701-1850	7824
Precise Die and Finishing	3544	E	818 773-9337	7825
Premier America Credit Union **(PA)**	6062	C	818 772-4000	15115
Printfirm Inc	2752	F	818 992-1005	4397
Qmadix Inc	5065	D	818 988-4300	13764
Quality Fabrication Inc **(PA)**	3444	D	818 407-5015	6896
Racaar Circuit Industries Inc	3672	F	818 998-7566	9446
Rancho San Antonio Boys HM Inc **(PA)**	8361	D	818 882-6400	22147
Rapid Manufacturing Inc	3999	F	818 899-4377	11740
Regency Enterprises Inc **(PA)**	5063	B	818 901-0255	13665
Renau Corporation	3823	E	818 341-1994	10718
Resmed Motor Technologies Inc	3621	C	818 428-6400	8927
RJA Industries Inc	3679	E	818 998-5124	9772
Roy & Val Tool Grinding Inc	3599	E	818 341-2434	8778
RPS Inc	3496	E	818 350-8088	7513
RTC Arspace - Chtswrth Div Inc **(PA)**	3593	C	818 341-3344	8440
S2k Graphics Inc	3993	E	818 885-3900	11590
San Fernando Vly Pallet Co Inc **(PA)**	2448	F	818 341-1200	3407
SARR Industries Inc	3599	E	818 998-7735	8788
Selane Products Inc **(PA)**	3843	D	818 998-7460	11195
Sensor Systems Inc	3812	B	818 341-5366	10643
Service Genius Los Angeles Inc	1711	D	818 200-3379	1137
Seven One Inc **(PA)**	7389	D	818 904-3435	18664
Sexy Hair Concepts LLC	8331	E	818 435-0800	21967
Sierra Canyon Inc	7999	D	818 882-8121	19669
Silver Strand	1751	E	818 701-9707	1456
Soundcraft Inc	3699	E	818 882-0020	9916
Source Photonics Usa Inc	3674	F	818 407-5007	9580
Staffchex Inc	7361	A	818 709-6100	17469
Stellar Microelectronics Inc	3674	C	661 775-3500	9583
Strategic Distribution L P	2326	C	818 671-2100	2791
Synear Foods Usa LLC	1541	E	818 341-3588	721
Teledyne Instruments Inc	3826	E	818 882-7266	10816
Telemtry Cmmnctons Systems Inc	3663	E	818 718-6248	9322
Telesis Community Credit Union **(PA)**	6061	D	818 885-1226	15092
Tessa Mia Corp	2434	E	877 740-5757	3341
Tetracam Inc	3861	F	818 718-2119	11294
Thibiant International Inc	2844	B	818 709-1345	5073
Tig/M LLC	3535	E	818 709-8500	7696
Torrance Prcsion Machining Inc	3599	F	818 709-7838	8822
Toye Corporation	3577	E	818 882-4000	8306
Truly Green Solutions LLC	3648	E	818 206-4404	9153
TTT Innovations LLC	3999	E	818 201-8828	11786
Tuttle Family Enterprises Inc	7349	B	818 534-2566	17294
Ultraglas Inc	5039	E	818 772-7744	13337
Underwraps Costume Corporation	2389	F	818 349-5300	3088
United Precision Corp	3599	E	818 576-9540	8831
Venstar Inc	3585	F	818 341-8760	8356
Verdugo Tool & Engrg Co Inc	3469	F	818 998-1101	7189
Vijall Inc	5169	E	818 700-0071	14794
Visible Graphics Inc	3993	F	818 787-0477	11614
Vision Imaging Supplies Inc	3955	E	818 710-7200	11484
Vmc Holdings Group Corp	3571	E	818 993-1466	8182
Wallace E Miller Inc	3599	E	818 998-0444	8844

GEOGRAPHIC

Employment Codes: A=Over 500 employees, B=251-500, C=101-250, D=51-100, E=20-50 F=10-19

2022 Southern California Business Directory and Buyers Guide

© Mergent Inc. 1-800-342-5647

1347

	SIC	EMP	PHONE	ENTRY #
Warrens Department Store Inc	2311	F	888 577-2735	2753
Wastech Controls & Engrg Inc	5084	E	818 998-3500	13961
We The Pie People LLC	2024	E	818 349-1880	1827
West Coast Business Prtrs Inc	2752	F	818 709-4980	4455
West Coast Coupon Inc	7319	E	818 341-2400	17102
West Valley Plating Inc	3471	F	818 709-1684	7332
Woodpecker Cabinet Inc	2434	E	310 404-4805	3348

CHERRY VALLEY, CA - Riverside County

	SIC	EMP	PHONE	ENTRY #
Little Peoples	8361	D	951 849-1959	22125
Rci Rack Cnvyor Instltion Inc	3535	E	909 381-4818	7692

CHINO, CA - San Bernardino County

	SIC	EMP	PHONE	ENTRY #
A Plus International Inc **(PA)**	5047	D	909 591-5168	13469
ABC Precision Sheet Metal Inc	3444	F	951 741-6667	6772
Accent Plastics Inc **(HQ)**	3089	D	951 273-7777	5542
Acepex Management Corporation	8741	B	909 591-1999	22965
Acorn-Gencon Plastics LLC	3089	D	909 591-8461	5543
Acornvac Inc	3432	E	909 902-1141	6550
Action Gypsum Supply West LP **(PA)**	5099	D	909 993-5655	14144
Advanced Precision Inc	3441	F	909 591-4244	6581
Advantage Pntg Solutions Inc	1721	D	951 739-9204	1166
Air Craftors Engineering Inc	3599	F	909 900-0635	8483
Alaco Ladder Company	2499	E	909 591-7561	3436
Albers Mfg Co Inc **(PA)**	3523	E	909 597-5537	7603
Alston Tascom Inc	3661	F	909 517-3660	9226
Altium Packaging LP	3089	C	909 590-7334	5559
Alvarado Manufacturing Co Inc	3829	D	909 591-8431	10868
Am-TEC Total Security Inc **(PA)**	7382	D	909 573-4678	18366
American Beef Packers Inc	0751	C	909 628-4888	210
American Solar Advantage Inc	3674	E	877 765-2388	9481
Angels In Motion LLC	8082	D	909 590-9102	21134
Anthony California Inc **(PA)**	3645	E	909 627-0351	9058
Aranda Tooling Inc	3599	D	714 379-6565	8500
Arnold-Gonsalves Engrg Inc	3599	E	909 465-1579	8502
Artiva USA Inc **(PA)**	3645	E	909 628-1388	9060
Asrock America Inc	3672	E	909 590-8308	9382
AST Enzymes	2869	F	800 608-1688	5127
Aut Inc	2711	F	909 393-9961	3951
Automobile Club Southern Cal	8699	D	909 591-9451	22427
Aviation Maintenance Group Inc	4581	D	714 469-0515	12342
Avient Colorants USA LLC	2869	C	909 606-1325	5128
B E & P Enterprises LLC **(PA)**	2499	E	909 591-7561	3439
Balaji Trading Inc	3661	D	909 444-7999	9227
Baronhr LLC	7361	D	909 517-3800	17394
Base Lite Corporation	3645	E	909 444-2776	9061
Beckman Coulter Inc	3826	D	909 597-3967	10783
Bellzi Inc	3942	F	888 317-1502	11357
Berry Global Inc	3089	C	909 465-9055	5580
Bright Shark Powder Coating	3479	F	909 591-1385	7350
Bti Aerospace & Electronics	3599	E	909 465-1569	8532
C & M Spring Engrg Co Inc	3495	E	909 597-2030	7484
C G Motor Sports Inc	3089	F	909 628-1440	5590
Cal-India Foods International	2869	E	909 613-1660	5129
Campbell Painting Inc	1721	D	919 591-4300	1173
Canyon Ridge Hospital Inc	8063	A	909 590-3700	21016
Champion Pblications Chino Inc	2711	F	909 628-5501	3960
Chino Ice Service	2097	F	909 628-2105	2369
Chino Medical Group Inc	8011	D	909 591-6446	19749
Chino Mfg & Repair Inc	7539	F	909 628-0519	18895
Closetmaid LLC	3496	E	909 590-4444	7498
Consolidated Plastics Corp **(PA)**	5162	E	909 393-8222	14757
Contract Labeling Service Inc	7389	E	909 937-0344	18491
Corona Millworks Company **(PA)**	2434	C	909 606-3288	3316
CPI Advanced Inc	3612	F	909 597-5533	8866
Craneveyor Midwest Corp	3446	E	909 627-6801	6957
Darly Filtration Inc **(PA)**	5085	E	909 591-7999	13980
Diamond Wipes Intl Inc **(PA)**	2844	D	909 230-9888	5013
Dick Farrell Industries Inc	3567	F	909 613-9424	8088
Diversified Coatings Linings	1771	E	909 591-6366	1522
DL Long Landscaping Inc	0781	D	909 628-5531	253
Duke Pacific Inc	1761	D	909 591-0191	1483
Dupree Inc	3452	E	909 597-4889	7064
Eep Holdings LLC **(PA)**	3089	B	909 597-7861	5638
El & El Wood Products Corp **(PA)**	2431	C	909 591-0339	3248
El Prado Golf Course LP	7992	D	909 597-1751	19486
Elecnor Inc **(DH)**	1711	C	909 993-5470	1060
Esm Plastics Inc	3599	F	909 591-7658	8583
Esslinger Engineering Inc	3714	E	909 539-0544	10054
Exhaust Gas Technologies Inc	3714	F	909 548-8100	10056
Fenchem Inc **(HQ)**	2023	E	909 597-8880	1792
Ferco Color Inc	2821	E	909 930-0773	4692
Flatiron West Inc	1622	C	909 597-8413	927
Fonegear LLC	3661	F	909 627-7999	9233
Gano Excel (usa) Inc	5149	D	626 338-8081	14689
General Photonics Corp	3661	D	909 590-5473	9234
Generation Construction Inc	1521	C	909 923-2077	606
Gluten Free Foods Mfg LLC **(PA)**	2099	D	909 823-8230	2442
Gmp Nutrition Enterprises Inc	2834	F	909 628-8889	4826
Golden Gate Hosiery Inc	2252	F	909 464-0805	2621
Great Pacific Elbow Company	3444	E	909 606-5551	6847
Gro-Power Inc	2873	E	909 393-3744	5155
H2 Environmental	3292	F	909 628-0369	6164
Hanson Truss Inc	2439	B	909 591-9256	3362
Harrington Industrial Plas LLC **(PA)**	5074	D	909 597-8641	13830
Hazelrigg Claims MGT Svcs Inc **(HQ)**	6411	D	909 606-6373	15578
Health Service Alliance	8099	D	909 464-9675	21434
Hi-Lite Manufacturing Co Inc	3646	D	909 465-1999	9089

	SIC	EMP	PHONE	ENTRY #
Ht Multinational Inc	3714	E	626 964-2686	10076
Hussmann Corporation	3585	B	909 590-4910	8342
Hyundai Amer Technical Ctr Inc	8734	D	909 627-3525	22949
Impact Printing & Graphics	2752	E	909 614-1678	4325
Imperial Rubber Products Inc	3555	E	909 393-0528	7918
Inland Empire Utlties Agcy A M **(PA)**	4941	D	909 993-1600	12893
Inter-Packing Inc	3086	F	909 465-5555	5512
Interior Experts Gen Bldrs Inc	1742	D	909 203-4922	1381
Isiqalo LLC	2253	B	714 683-2820	2637
Jacuzzi Inc **(DH)**	3589	C	909 606-7733	8389
Jacuzzi Products Co	3088	B	909 548-7732	5533
Jpm Industries Inc	1521	E	909 592-2292	615
June A Grothe Construction Inc	1542	D	909 993-9393	778
Kaiser Foundation Hospitals	6324	C	888 750-0036	15403
Kaiser Foundation Hospitals	6324	C	888 750-0036	15424
Karat Packaging Inc **(PA)**	3089	D	626 965-8882	5687
Kemper Enterprises Inc	3423	E	909 627-6191	6484
Larin Corp	3423	E	909 464-0605	6485
Lifemed of California	3841	E	800 543-3633	11008
Lights of America Inc **(PA)**	3645	B	909 594-7883	9067
Liner Technologies Inc	3089	E	909 594-6610	5698
Liquid Technologies Inc	2844	E	909 393-9475	5044
Lollicup USA Inc **(HQ)**	2656	B	626 965-8882	3842
M and M Stamping Corp	3441	F	909 590-2704	6630
M K Smith Chevrolet	7549	C	909 628-8961	18937
Manley Laboratories Inc	3312	E	909 627-4256	6206
Maplegrove Gluten Free Foods	2099	F	909 334-7828	2477
Maxon Auto Corporation	2631	F	626 400-6464	3774
McO Inc	3714	E	909 627-3571	10101
Mikhail Darafeev Inc **(PA)**	2511	E	909 613-1813	3478
Mission Linen Supply	7213	D	909 393-6857	16859
Morehouse-Cowles LLC	3559	E	909 627-7222	7991
Motivational Marketing Inc	4225	D	909 517-2200	12224
Motivational Marketing Inc	4731	D	909 517-2200	12486
Motivational Marketing Inc **(PA)**	7389	C	909 517-2200	18605
Myers & Sons Hi-Way Safety Inc **(PA)**	3993	D	909 591-1781	11575
Myojo USA Inc	2098	F	909 464-1411	2377
National Sign & Marketing Corp	3993	D	909 591-4742	11576
Nexgrill Industries Inc **(PA)**	5023	D	909 598-8799	13179
Niusource Inc	8742	F	909 631-2895	23284
Norco Injection Molding Inc	3089	D	909 393-4000	5729
Norco Plastics Inc	3089	D	909 393-4000	5730
Oak Design Corporation	2521	F	909 628-9597	3594
Omnia Italian Design LLC	5021	C	909 393-4400	13146
Omnia Leather Motion Inc	2392	C	909 393-4400	3110
Pacific Coast Mfg Inc	3631	D	909 627-7040	8993
Pacific Containerprint Inc	2759	E	909 465-0365	4551
Paclights LLC **(PA)**	3646	F	800 980-6386	9099
Paiho North America Corp	3965	E	661 257-6611	11500
Pdc LLC	3544	E	626 334-5000	7822
PRC Composites LLC	3089	E	909 464-1520	5771
Precision Companies Inc	2431	F	909 548-2700	3282
Prime Transport Inc **(PA)**	4789	D	909 972-1300	12581
Provena Foods Inc **(HQ)**	2013	D	909 627-1082	1746
Public Investment Corporation	6552	C	310 451-5227	16069
Quetico LLC **(PA)**	5199	C	909 628-6200	14970
R & B Reinforcing Steel Corp	1791	D	909 591-1726	1578
R Kern Engineering & Mfg Corp	3678	D	909 664-2440	9664
Ralison International Inc	5093	E	909 393-0008	14120
Rbw Industries Inc	3714	D	909 591-5359	10124
Reed LLC	3561	E	909 287-2100	8023
Repet Inc	3083	C	909 594-5333	5461
Roettele Industries	3053	F	909 606-8252	5349
Royal Custom Designs LLC	2512	C	909 591-8990	3516
Rrz Enterprises Inc	5136	F	714 683-2820	14348
RTS Powder Coating Inc **(PA)**	3479	E	909 393-5404	7407
S & W Plastic Stores Inc **(PA)**	5162	E	909 390-0090	14763
SA Recycling LLC	4953	D	909 622-3337	12973
Savant Construction Inc	1542	D	909 614-4300	821
Schneider Electric Usa Inc	4225	D	909 438-2295	12242
Scott Engineering Inc	3629	E	909 594-9637	8982
Shamrock Marketing Co Inc **(HQ)**	3842	F	909 591-8855	11140
Sheffield Manufacturing Inc	3599	F	818 767-4948	8794
Shop4techcom	3572	E	909 243-2725	8217
Soaring America Corporation	3721	E	909 270-2628	10203
South Coast Childrens Soc Inc	8322	C	909 364-9788	21892
South Gate Engineering LLC	3443	C	909 628-2779	6754
Specilty Enzymes Btechnologies	2869	F	909 613-1660	5148
Spin Products Inc	3089	E	909 590-7000	5825
Superior Metal Shapes Inc	3354	E	909 947-3455	6320
Superior Tech Inc	3317	F	909 364-2300	6253
Syston Cable Technology Corp	3699	E	888 679-7866	9920
T McGee Electric Inc	3643	E	909 591-6461	9047
Tarazi Specialty Foods LLC	2099	F	909 628-3601	2533
Thin Metal Sales Inc	3441	F	909 393-2273	6668
Top-Shelf Fixtures LLC	3496	D	909 627-7423	7518
Transtech Engineers Inc **(PA)**	8711	D	909 595-8599	22678
Trend Technologies LLC **(DH)**	3444	C	909 597-7861	6933
Tst Inc **(PA)**	3341	B	951 685-2155	6297
Ttl Holdings LLC **(HQ)**	3089	B	909 597-7861	5846
Tuffstuff Fitness Intl Inc	3949	C	909 629-1600	11453
U S Bowling Corporation	3949	F	909 548-0644	11455
Universal Packg Systems Inc **(PA)**	2844	A	909 517-2442	5077
Universal Packg Systems Inc	4225	C	909 517-2442	12257
Val Plastic USA L L C	3523	F	909 390-9600	7625
Veritas Health Services Inc	8062	A	909 464-8600	21002
Vtl Amplifiers Inc	3651	E	909 627-5944	9209

Mergent email: customerrelations@mergent.com
1348

2022 Southern California Business
Directory and Buyers Guide

(P-0000) Products & Services Section entry number
(PA)=Parent Co (HQ)=Headquarters (DH)=Div Headquarters

	SIC	EMP	PHONE	ENTRY #
Warren Collins and Assoc Inc **(PA)**	1629	E	909 548-6708	1008
West Coast Steel & Proc LLC **(PA)**	3325	C	909 393-8405	6279
West End Yung MNS Christn Assn	8641	C	909 597-7445	22376
Wp Electric Communications Inc	1731	E	909 606-3510	1340
Wright Bus Graphics Cal Inc	5112	F	800 310-3676	14201
Wright Business Graphics LLC	2761	E	909 614-6700	4604
Yankon Industries Inc **(PA)**	3646	E	909 591-2345	9112
Yoshimura RES & Dev Amer Inc	5013	D	909 628-4722	13110
Young Machine Inc	3599	F	909 464-0405	8858
Youngs Market Company LLC	5182	D	909 393-4540	14850
Ziegenfelder Company	2024	E	909 590-0493	1828

CHINO HILLS, CA - San Bernardino County

	SIC	EMP	PHONE	ENTRY #
Andrew LLC	2041	F	909 270-9356	1941
Boys Republic **(PA)**	8361	C	909 902-6690	22085
Camp Franchise Systems LLC **(PA)**	7032	D	909 325-6011	16818
Crmls Inc	6512	C	909 859-2040	15663
David Oppenheimer and Co I LLC	5141	D	909 631-2600	14462
Dynamic Enterprises Inc	3599	E	562 944-0271	8576
Flatiron Electric Group Inc	1731	E	714 228-9631	1256
Hoya Surgical Optics Inc	3841	E	909 680-3900	10988
Jacuzzi Brands LLC **(DH)**	3999	E	909 606-1416	11693
Jacuzzi Products Co **(DH)**	3088	C	909 606-1416	5532
Jupiter Holding I Corp **(HQ)**	5091	E	909 606-1416	14082
Los Serranos Golf Club	7992	C	909 597-1769	19497
Lowes Home Centers LLC	5031	C	909 627-6039	13230
Lowes Home Centers LLC	5031	C	909 438-9000	13272
Optima Network Services Inc **(DH)**	8999	D	305 599-1800	23537
Sampav Inc	2311	F	909 984-8646	2749
Seafood Ranch Grill Inc	0291	D	909 590-7232	146
SSC Construction Inc	8711	D	951 278-1177	22659
Sundance Spas Inc **(DH)**	3999	E	909 606-7733	11765
Tri-Dim Filter Corporation	3564	E	626 826-5893	8058
Victory Intl Group LLC	5092	C	949 407-5888	14104

CITY OF INDUSTRY, CA - Los Angeles County

	SIC	EMP	PHONE	ENTRY #
17400 Inc	4214	D	626 913-1800	12104
Abacus Business Capital Inc	5141	E	909 594-8080	14447
Accolade Pharma USA	2834	E	626 279-9699	4775
Acorn Engineering Company **(PA)**	3448	A	800 488-8999	6985
Acromil LLC **(HQ)**	3728	C	626 964-2522	10235
Acromil Corporation **(PA)**	3728	C	626 964-2522	10237
Addice Inc **(PA)**	3577	D	626 617-7779	8233
Adtech Photonics Inc	3674	E	626 956-1000	9474
Advanced Industrial Cmpt Inc **(PA)**	5045	D	909 895-8989	13372
Airgas Safety Inc	5084	F	562 699-5239	13882
Alaska Diesel Electric	7539	C	626 934-6211	18892
Allfast Fastening Systems LLC	5072	D	626 968-9388	13790
Allied Entertainment Group Inc **(PA)**	7812	B	626 330-0600	19093
Alpha Imaging Technology	5047	F	626 330-0808	13470
Alta-Dena Certified Dairy LLC **(DH)**	0241	B	626 964-6401	130
Altium Packaging LLC	3089	F	888 425-7343	5557
America Chung Nam LLC **(HQ)**	5093	C	909 839-8383	14108
American Foam Fiber & Sups Inc **(PA)**	2299	D	626 969-7268	2719
American Future Tech Corp	5045	C	888 462-3899	13374
American Paper & Plastics LLC	5199	C	626 444-0000	14910
Anning-Johnson Company	1742	E	626 369-7131	1364
Arakelian Enterprises Inc **(PA)**	4953	A	626 336-3636	12927
Aremac Heat Treating Inc	3398	E	626 333-3898	6429
Articouture Inc	5136	E	626 336-7299	14326
Asi Networks Inc	7379	F	800 251-1336	18159
Assa Abloy Rsdential Group Inc	5072	A	626 369-4718	13796
Astrophysics Inc **(PA)**	3844	C	909 598-5488	11206
Austin Pang Glv Mfg USA Corp **(HQ)**	5099	E	562 777-0088	14146
Avatar Technology Inc	5045	E	909 598-7696	13377
Bagcraftpapercon I LLC	2674	D	626 961-6766	3894
Battery Technology Inc **(PA)**	3691	D	626 336-6878	9807
Bentley Mills Inc **(PA)**	2273	C	626 333-4585	2683
Best Formulations	2899	F	626 912-9998	5213
Best Formulations Inc	2099	C	626 912-9998	2398
Blackseries Campers Inc	3715	E	833 822-6737	10164
Blue Pacific Flavors Inc	2087	E	626 934-0099	2311
Boiling Point Rest S CA Inc	7361	B	626 551-5181	17397
Boss Litho Inc	2752	E	626 912-7088	4239
Boxes R Us Inc	2653	D	626 820-5410	3789
Bridgestone Hosepower LLC	5085	F	562 699-9500	13977
Brilliant Imaging Group Inc	5084	F	626 333-1868	13892
Bryan Press Inc	2752	F	626 961-9257	4241
Burton James Inc	2512	D	626 961-7221	3496
California Access Scaffold LLC	1799	D	310 324-3388	1645
California Country Club	7997	D	626 333-4571	19551
California Expanded Met Pdts **(PA)**	3444	D	626 369-3564	6802
California Hydroforming Co Inc	3444	F	626 912-0036	6803
California Steel and Tube	5051	C	626 968-5511	13553
Cameron Energy Services Corp	8741	D	562 321-9183	22998
Cardinal Paint and Powder Inc	2851	D	626 937-6767	5091
Carrara Marble Co Amer Inc **(PA)**	5032	D	626 961-6010	13295
Carryout Bags LLC **(PA)**	2671	D	626 279-7000	3852
Cast Parts Inc	3324	C	626 937-3444	6264
Central Blower Co	3564	E	626 330-3182	8043
Cenveo Worldwide Limited	5112	B	626 369-4921	14193
CH Image Inc	2752	F	626 336-6063	4249
Chefs Warehouse West Coast LLC **(HQ)**	5141	D	626 465-4200	14460
China Master USA Entrmt Co	3299	E	626 810-9372	6179
Chronomite Laboratories Inc	3822	E	310 534-2300	10664
Circle Racing Wheels Inc **(PA)**	3714	F	800 959-2100	10030
Citifinancial Credit Company	6141	C	626 712-8780	15142
Classic Distrg & Bev Group Inc	5181	B	626 934-3700	14824
Clay Laguna Co **(HQ)**	3295	D	626 330-0631	6165
Clayton Manufacturing Company **(PA)**	3569	C	626 443-9381	8115
Clayton Manufacturing Inc **(HQ)**	3569	D	626 443-9381	8116
Clemson Distribution Inc **(PA)**	5143	E	909 595-2770	14540
Closet World Inc	1751	D	626 855-0846	1430
Closet World Inc	1799	C	800 576-7717	1649
Closets By Design Inc	2541	E	562 699-9945	3642
Cmp Industries LLC **(PA)**	3843	E	518 434-3147	11164
Coi Rubber Products Inc	2822	B	626 965-9966	4730
Commercial Lbr & Pallet Co Inc **(PA)**	2448	C	626 968-0631	3383
Compucase Corporation	3572	A	626 336-6588	8195
Consolidated Devices Inc **(HQ)**	3679	E	626 965-0668	9695
Continental Marketing Svc Inc	2393	F	626 626-8888	3125
Cosmos Food Co Inc	2099	E	323 221-9142	2412
Cpp Ind	3812	E	909 595-2252	10579
Cryomax USA Inc **(HQ)**	4225	F	626 330-3388	12191
Custom Alloy Sales Inc **(PA)**	3341	F	626 369-3641	6290
Cwd LLC	3711	D	626 961-5775	9941
D & D Wholesale Distrs Inc	5148	D	626 333-2111	14619
D-Tech Optoelectronics Inc	3669	E	626 956-1100	9337
Dacor **(DH)**	3631	D	626 799-1000	8988
Databyte Technology Inc **(PA)**	5064	E	626 305-0500	13683
Delori-Nutifood Products Inc	2099	E	626 965-3006	2420
Delta Creative Inc	5092	C	800 423-4135	14096
Dennison Inc	3446	E	626 965-8917	6960
Derek and Constance Lee Corp **(PA)**	2013	D	909 595-8831	1731
Dfa Dairy Brands Fluid LLC	5143	B	800 395-7004	14541
Dreyers Grand Ice Cream Inc	2024	C	909 444-2253	1816
Duro Corporation	3631	F	626 839-6541	8990
E-Sceptre Inc	8731	D	888 350-8989	22836
EAC Intrnational Logistics Inc	4789	E	877 668-7837	12570
Edwards Vacuum LLC	5085	D	626 532-5585	13982
El Encanto Healthcare & Rehab	8051	D	626 336-1274	20318
Elmco Sales Inc **(PA)**	5074	D	626 855-4831	13823
Elmco/Duddy Inc **(HQ)**	5074	E	626 333-9942	13824
Engineering Model Assoc Inc **(PA)**	3089	E	626 912-7011	5641
Eonstar Ledlight Corp	7389	C	626 693-8084	18514
Essendant Co	5112	D	626 961-0011	14194
Estes Express Lines	4213	D	626 333-9090	12039
Evans Industries Inc	3499	E	626 912-1688	7556
Ever Win International Corp	5065	E	626 810-8218	13720
Expert Pharmaceutical LLC	2834	F	626 581-4008	4819
Exxel Outdoors Inc	2399	C	626 369-7278	3195
Ezviz Inc	7382	C	855 693-9849	18378
Faircom Inc	3674	D	626 820-9900	9507
Finance America Mortgage LLC	6162	D	562 478-4664	15192
Forever Link International Inc	5139	E	877 839-9899	14438
Fortune Dynamic Inc	5139	D	909 979-8318	14439
Fox Luggage Inc	5099	D	323 588-1688	14156
Fremarc Industries Inc **(PA)**	2511	D	626 965-0802	3471
Freshpoint Southern Cal Inc	5148	C	626 855-1400	14630
Frize Corporation	1541	D	800 834-2127	698
Furniture America Cal Inc **(PA)**	5021	D	909 718-7276	13137
GBT Inc	5045	C	626 854-9338	13399
Gels Logistics Inc	4731	D	909 610-2277	12460
General Sealants	2891	C	626 961-0211	5183
Gff Inc	2035	D	323 232-6255	1888
Golden State Foods Corp	2038	B	626 465-7500	1928
Golden West Packg Group LLC **(PA)**	2653	B	888 501-5893	3808
Goldencorr Sheets LLC	2653	C	626 369-6446	3809
Gordon Brush Mfg Co Inc **(PA)**	3991	E	323 724-7777	11511
Goulds Pumps	3561	F	562 949-2113	8011
Gracing Inc	2325	E	626 269-6818	2769
Graycon Inc	1711	E	626 961-9640	1076
Grifols Usa LLC	5047	B	626 435-2600	13491
Grifols Wrldwide Oprtons USA I	8099	D	626 435-2600	21431
H & H Specialties Inc	3999	E	626 575-0776	11682
Harbor Green Grain LP	2048	E	310 991-8089	1966
Harvard Label LLC	2621	C	626 333-8881	3755
Hd Supply Facilities Maint Ltd	7359	D	909 594-3843	17352
Herald Christian Health Center	8011	D	626 286-8700	19841
Heritage Distributing Company	2023	E	626 333-9526	1795
Hexpol Compounding CA Inc	3069	D	626 961-0311	5380
Hikvision USA Inc **(HQ)**	7382	C	909 895-0400	18383
Hill Brothers Chemical Company	2812	F	626 333-2251	4635
Hitchcock Automotive Resources	8742	D	626 839-8400	23235
Hitex Dyeing & Finishing Inc	2399	E	626 363-0160	3199
Home Organizers Inc	1751	A	562 699-9945	1440
Hot Topic Inc **(DH)**	2326	A	626 839-4681	2779
Hps Performance Products	3052	F	626 747-9200	5320
Hydro Extrusion Usa LLC	3354	B	626 964-3411	6310
Ideal Printing Co Inc	2752	E	626 964-2019	4319
Importla LLC	2599	F	626 336-8118	3732
Integral Engrg Fabrication Inc	3441	E	626 369-0958	6623
Invenlux Corporation	3674	F	626 277-4163	9522
Iridium Technology Group **(PA)**	5099	D	626 839-7488	14164
ITT LLC	3625	D	562 908-4144	8958
J P Original Corp **(PA)**	5139	D	626 839-4300	14440
Jada Group Inc	3944	D	626 810-8382	11378
Jon Brooks Inc **(PA)**	3295	D	626 330-0631	6167
K-1 Packaging Group **(PA)**	2752	C	626 964-9384	4346
K-Tops Plastic Mfg Inc	3999	E	626 575-9679	11698
Kaiser Foundation Hospitals	8011	C	562 463-4377	19895
Klm Management Company	5143	D	626 330-3479	14542
Labels-R-Us Inc	2759	E	626 333-4001	4533
Langers Juice Company Inc	2037	B	626 336-3100	1905
Lanstreetcom	3575	F	626 964-2000	8226

Employment Codes: A=Over 500 employees, B=251-500, C=101-250, D=51-100, E=20-50 F=10-19

2022 Southern California Business Directory and Buyers Guide

© Mergent Inc. 1-800-342-5647

1349

	SIC	EMP	PHONE	ENTRY #
Lee & Ro Inc **(PA)**	8711	E	626 912-3391	22600
Lee Kum Kee (usa) Foods Inc	2099	D	626 709-1888	2473
Lee Kum Kee (usa) Inc **(DH)**	5149	E	626 709-1888	14704
Leo Hoffman Chevrolet Inc **(PA)**	7515	C	626 968-8411	18750
Leyen Food LLC **(PA)**	5147	D	626 333-8812	14596
Likom Caseworks USA Inc **(HQ)**	3575	E	210 587-7824	8227
Los Altos Food Products LLC	5143	C	626 330-6555	14543
Lowes Home Centers LLC	5031	C	626 217-1133	13267
Lt Security Inc **(PA)**	5065	C	626 435-2838	13746
LTS Associate Inc **(PA)**	5065	E	626 435-2838	13747
Magnell Associate Inc	3571	E	626 271-1320	8164
Magnell Associate Inc **(DH)**	5045	C	626 271-9700	13413
Majestic Industry Hills LLC	7011	A	626 810-4455	16553
Management Applied Prgrm Inc **(PA)**	7374	C	562 463-5000	18099
Marge Carson Inc **(PA)**	2512	D	626 571-1111	3508
Markwins Beauty Products Inc	5122	D	909 595-8898	14260
Marquez Brothers Entps Inc	5141	C	626 330-3310	14475
Marrs Printing Inc	2752	D	909 594-9459	4367
Material Sciences Corporation	3353	E	562 699-4550	6301
Maverick Aerospace Inc	3728	F	714 578-1700	10375
Maverick Aerospace LLC	3728	D	714 578-1700	10376
Max Group Corporation **(PA)**	5045	D	626 935-0050	13414
Maxim Lighting Intl Inc **(PA)**	5063	C	626 956-4200	13647
Maxim Lighting Intl Inc	3645	E	626 956-4200	9068
Melko Logistic Group Corp **(PA)**	4214	D	626 363-6300	12115
Mercado Latino Inc **(PA)**	5141	D	626 333-6862	14478
Mercury Plastics Inc **(HQ)**	2673	B	626 961-0165	3886
Messer LLC	2813	F	626 855-8366	4644
Metal Cutting Service Inc	3599	F	626 968-4764	8691
Micro-Technology Concepts Inc	5045	D	626 839-6800	13415
Microprint Inc	2752	E	626 369-1950	4373
Miracle Bedding Corporation	2515	E	562 908-2370	3555
Monadnock Company	3429	C	626 964-6581	6528
Morehouse Foods Inc	2035	E	626 854-1655	1892
Morris Group International **(PA)**	3448	C	626 336-4561	7004
Morrow-Meadows Corporation **(PA)**	1731	A	858 974-3650	1283
MSI Computer Corp **(HQ)**	5045	D	626 913-0828	13417
Mtc Worldwide Corp	5045	D	626 839-6800	13418
Ncstar Inc	3827	F	866 627-8278	10848
New Century Media Corp	5099	E	562 695-1000	14171
New Icon Inc **(PA)**	2299	F	626 620-4387	2731
Newton Heat Treating Co Inc	3398	D	626 964-6528	6448
Norman Fox & Co **(PA)**	5169	E	800 632-1777	14790
Nuset Inc	3429	E	626 246-1668	6530
Nutripharm USA Inc	2833	F	626 962-9871	4756
OTasty Foods Inc	5141	D	626 330-1229	14484
Pace Lithographers Inc	8999	E	626 913-2108	23540
Pacific Heritg HM Fashion Inc	5023	E	909 598-5200	13183
Pape Material Handling Inc	3537	D	562 692-9311	7715
Pape Material Handling Inc	5084	C	562 463-8000	13927
Par Engineering Inc	1711	E	626 964-8700	1116
PC Club Inc **(HQ)**	5045	D	626 839-8080	13425
Performance Sheets LLC	1761	C	626 333-0195	1500
Pgi Pacific Graphics Intl	2752	E	626 336-7707	4389
PHI **(PA)**	3542	F	626 968-9680	7763
Phifer Incorporated	3496	C	626 968-0438	7507
Phillips Machine & Wldg Co Inc	7692	E	626 855-4600	18992
Physicians Formula Inc **(DH)**	2844	D	626 334-3395	5060
Physicians Formula Cosmt Inc	2844	D	626 334-3395	5061
Pilot Inc **(PA)**	4225	D	626 937-6988	12232
Plastic Specialties & Tech Inc	3089	C	909 869-8069	5754
Playhut Inc	3944	E	909 869-8083	11389
Pocino Foods Company	2013	D	626 968-8000	1745
Potter Roemer LLC **(HQ)**	5031	D	626 855-4890	13282
Poundex Associates Corporation	5021	D	909 444-5878	13149
Premio Inc **(PA)**	3571	C	626 839-3100	8170
Prime Global Solutions Inc **(PA)**	4731	D	800 424-7746	12510
Private Label Pc LLC	5045	C	626 965-8686	13429
Prl Aluminum Inc	3354	D	626 968-7507	6315
Prl Glass Systems Inc	3231	D	877 775-2586	5968
Procter & Gamble Mfg Co	2841	C	513 627-4678	4946
Prolacta Bioscience Inc **(PA)**	2836	C	626 599-9260	4938
Proterra Inc	3711	B	864 438-0000	9962
Public Hlth Fndation Entps Inc **(PA)**	8641	A	800 201-7320	22361
Puente Ready Mix Services Inc **(PA)**	3273	E	626 968-0711	6105
Quartz Logistics Inc	4731	D	626 606-2001	12514
Quest Components Inc	5065	E	626 333-5858	13765
Quinn Shepherd Machinery	5082	B	562 463-6000	13871
Qy Research Inc	8732	D	626 295-2442	22897
RC Furniture Inc	2512	D	626 964-4100	3513
Reuland Electric Co **(PA)**	3621	C	626 964-6411	8928
Rice Field Corporation	2013	C	626 968-6917	1748
Rider Best Inc **(PA)**	3651	E	626 336-8388	9188
Rollins Leasing LLC	7513	D	626 913-7186	18736
Rongcheng Trading LLC	5147	E	626 338-1090	14606
Rosewill Inc	3571	A	800 575-9885	8173
Rutland Tool & Supply Co **(HQ)**	5085	C	562 566-5000	14016
S2e Inc	3651	F	626 965-1008	9192
Safe Plating Inc	3471	D	626 810-1872	7308
Sailing Innovation (us) Inc	3651	A	626 965-6665	9193
SC Beverage Inc	3556	F	562 463-8918	7951
Sceptre Inc	3679	E	626 369-3698	9779
Scope Packaging Inc	2653	D	714 998-4411	3826
Shoes For Crews Intl Inc	3143	E	561 683-5090	5877
Signature Flexible Packg LLC	2891	D	323 887-1997	5196
Silao Tortilleria Inc	2099	E	626 961-0761	2524
Silveron Industries Inc	3625	F	909 598-4533	8962
Sincere Orient Commercial Corp	2099	D	626 333-8882	2525
Sing Tao Newspapers Ltd	2711	D	626 839-8200	4029
Smurfit Kappa North Amer LLC	2653	B	626 322-2123	3827
Solestage Inc	7373	E	909 576-1309	18067
Solo Enterprise Corp	3599	E	626 961-3591	8797
Soto Provision Inc	5023	D	626 458-4600	13186
South Bay Freight System LLC **(PA)**	4731	D	626 271-9800	12529
Spencer N Enterprises LLC	2392	D	626 448-0374	3120
Ssre Holdings LLC	2011	D	800 314-2098	1720
Stoughton Printing Co	2752	E	626 961-3678	4426
Stud Welding Systems Inc	3452	F	626 330-7434	7076
Summer Rio Corp **(PA)**	3021	F	626 854-1498	5318
Swatfame Inc **(PA)**	5137	B	626 961-7928	14420
Sweda Company LLC	5094	C	626 357-9999	14141
Teknor Color Company	2821	F	626 336-7709	4724
Teledyne Instruments Inc	3823	C	626 934-1500	10728
Tis Industries LLC **(PA)**	3999	E	626 336-3821	11779
Tje Company	3442	E	909 869-7777	6721
Todai Ssb Inc	6794	D	909 869-7727	16220
Tonusa LLC	2434	F	626 961-8700	3342
Topland Logistics Inc **(PA)**	4731	D	562 908-6988	12540
Topland Trucking Inc **(HQ)**	4212	D	562 908-6988	11999
Topocean Consolidation Service **(PA)**	4731	C	562 908-1688	12541
Townsteel Inc	5031	D	626 965-8917	13290
Trend Manor Furn Mfg Co Inc	2511	E	626 964-6493	3490
Trio Metal Stamping Inc	3444	D	626 336-1228	6935
Troy-Csl Lighting Inc	3645	D	626 336-4511	9071
U C L Incorporated **(PA)**	4213	D	323 235-0099	12086
Unger Fabrik LLC **(PA)**	2331	C	626 469-8080	2874
Unical Aviation Inc **(PA)**	5088	C	909 348-1700	14067
Unical Defense Inc	5088	E	909 348-1500	14068
United Parcel Service Inc	4512	D	951 757-8176	12322
United Pumping Service Inc	4212	D	626 961-9326	12005
US Bankcard Services Inc	7389	D	888 888-8872	18714
Utility Trailer Mfg Co **(PA)**	3715	B	626 964-73[illegible]9	10170
Utility Trailer Mfg Co	3715	C	909 594-6026	10171
V & V Manufacturing Inc	3961	F	626 330-0641	11492
Valley Power Services Inc	3621	E	909 969-9345	8934
Valley Power Systems Inc **(PA)**	5084	D	626 333-1243	13957
Venus Foods Inc	2011	E	626 369-5188	1723
Vida Corporation	3695	F	626 839-4912	9844
Viz Cattle Corporation	2011	E	310 884-5260	1724
Vonnic Inc	3861	E	626 964-2345	11299
W Diamond Supply Co **(DH)**	5023	D	909 859-8939	13198
Waddington North America Inc	3089	C	626 913-4022	5860
WEI-Chuan USA Inc **(PA)**	5142	C	626 225-7168	14533
Whitehall Manufacturing Inc	3842	D	626 336-4561	11154
Willdan Engineering	8711	D	562 908-6200	22698
Winstar Textile Inc	2361	E	626 357-1133	3038
Wjb Bearings Inc	3463	E	909 598-6238	7110
Wna Comet West Inc	3089	C	626 913-0724	5866
Wwf Operating Company LLC	2026	E	626 810-1775	1842
Xpower Manufacture Inc	3822	E	626 285-3301	10672
Ybcc Inc	2023	E	626 213-3945	1808
Youbar Inc	5145	D	626 537-[illegible]851	14567
Zerep Management Corporation **(PA)**	4953	D	626 968-[illegible]796	13003

CLAREMONT, CA - Los Angeles County

	SIC	EMP	PHONE	ENTRY #
Atmc Incorporated **(PA)**	1731	D	909 390-0470	1218
Baumann Engineering	3599	D	909 621-4181	8517
Ben Bollinger Productions Inc	7922	D	909 626-3296	19304
Bluebridge Prof Svcs Inc	8082	D	909 625-6151	21139
Bon Appetit Management Co	8741	C	909 607-2788	22990
Claremont Courier Inc	2711	F	909 621-4761	3964
Claremont Tennis Club	7997	C	909 625 9515	19555
Conveyor Mfg & Svc Inc	3535	F	909 621-0406	7688
Corey Nursery Co Inc **(PA)**	5193	D	909 621-6886	14880
Epitome Enterprises LLC	7371	D	909 625-4728	17608
Feemster Co Inc	2051	F	909 621-9772	1999
Front Porch Communities	8099	D	909 626-3490	21428
Front Prch Cmmnties Svcs - Cas	8059	C	909 626-1227	20586
Green Spot Packaging Inc	2086	E	909 625-8771	2266
Hl Rel Connectors Inc	3643	B	909 626-1820	9038
Isn Global Enterprises Inc	7375	F	909 670-0601	18126
Kaiser Foundation Hospitals	8062	A	888 750-0036	20816
Micro Matrix Systems **(PA)**	3469	E	909 626-8544	7166
New Bedford Panoramex Corp	3648	E	909 982-9806	9141
New Vista Health Services Inc	8361	D	909 625-0117	22136
Nhs Western Division Inc	1521	D	909 947-9931	625
Pacific Surveys LLC **(PA)**	1389	F	909 625-6262	535
Pff Bancorp Inc **(PA)**	6035	A	213 683-6393	15053
Pilgrim Place In Claremont **(PA)**	8059	C	909 399-5500	20623
Pomona College	7331	D	909 621-8000	17136
Rancho Santa Ana Botanic Grdn	8422	D	909 625-8767	22240
Sunrise Senior Living MGT Inc	8361	C	909 447-5259	22158
Sunsation Inc	2037	E	909 542-0280	1911
Technip Stone Wbster Prcess Te	8711	D	909 447-3600	22666
Therapak LLC **(DH)**	5047	D	909 267-2000	13525
Tierra Del Sol Foundation	7999	D	909 626-8301	19677
Trinity Youth Services **(PA)**	8361	D	909 825-5588	22160
Universal Defense	3443	E	909 626-4178	6763
Western Feld Invstigations Inc **(PA)**	7375	D	800 999-9589	18135

COACHELLA, CA - Riverside County

	SIC	EMP	PHONE	ENTRY #
29 Palms Enterprises Corp	7999	A	760 775-5566	19629
Anthony Vineyards Inc	0172	D	760 391-5488	40
Armtec Countermeasures Co **(DH)**	3812	C	760 398-0143	10569
Armtec Defense Products Co **(DH)**	3489	B	760 398-0143	7432

Mergent email: customerrelations@mergent.com
1350

2022 Southern California Business
Directory and Buyers Guide

(P-0000) Products & Services Section entry number
(PA)=Parent Co (HQ)=Headquarters (DH)=Div Headquarters

	SIC	EMP	PHONE	ENTRY #
Augustine Gaming MGT Corp	7371	D	760 391-9500	17557
Desert Valley Date Inc	0723	E	760 398-0999	165
Desert Valley Date LLC	5149	D	760 398-0999	14686
Esparza Enterprises Inc	7361	B	760 398-0349	17422
L&D Farm Labor	0761	E	760 408-6311	217
Paladar Mfg Inc	3931	D	760 775-4222	11347
Primetime International Inc	5148	D	760 399-4166	14647
Reyes Coca-Cola Bottling LLC	2086	D	760 396-4500	2288
Roto Lite Inc	3089	E	909 923-4353	5802
Sun and Sands Enterprises LLC **(PA)**	5148	D	760 399-4278	14655
Sunline Transit Agency	4119	C	760 972-4059	11891
Teserra **(PA)**	1799	B	760 340-9000	1694

COLTON, CA - San Bernardino County

	SIC	EMP	PHONE	ENTRY #
A-Avis HM Svcs Plbg Htg AC Inc	1711	D	909 825-3600	1012
A-Z Bus Sales Inc **(PA)**	5012	D	951 781-7188	13016
A-Z Emissions Solutions Inc	3699	E	951 781-1856	9846
Als Garden Art Inc **(PA)**	3299	B	909 424-0221	6176
Ardent Mills LLC	2041	F	951 201-1170	1942
Arrowhead Regional Medical Ctr	8062	A	909 580-1000	20683
Black Diamond Blade Company **(PA)**	3531	E	800 949-9014	7636
Bob Hubbard Horse Trnsp Inc **(PA)**	4212	E	951 369-3770	11958
Boyd Specialties LLC	2013	D	909 219-5120	1728
Brithinee Electric	5063	D	909 825-7971	13617
Cal Portland Cement Co	3273	E	909 423-0436	6074
California Churros Corporation	2051	C	909 370-4777	1987
Cambridge Sierra Holdings LLC	8051	B	909 370-4411	20273
Cemex Materials LLC	3273	D	909 825-1500	6082
Charter Hospice Colton LLC	8052	C	909 825-2969	20527
Clariant Corporation	2672	E	909 825-1793	3869
Cummings Resources LLC	3993	E	951 248-1130	11539
Dairy Queen	2024	E	909 422-1501	1812
E-Z Up Directcom	2394	E	909 426-0060	3137
Ecology Recycling Services LLC	4953	D	909 370-1318	12948
Elizabeth Shutters Inc	3442	E	909 825-1531	6697
Entercom Media Corp	4832	D	909 825-9525	12689
Erf Enterprises Inc	3713	F	909 825-4080	9986
Frank Kams & Associates Inc	2449	F	909 382-0047	3414
Greenpath Recovery West Inc	5093	D	909 954-0686	14116
Gxo Logistics Supply Chain Inc	4225	D	951 512-1201	12211
Hawa Corporation **(PA)**	2013	F	909 825-8882	1734
HC Brill	2053	E	909 825-7343	2077
High-Light Electric Inc	1731	D	951 352-9646	1265
Inland Eye Inst Med Group Inc **(PA)**	8011	D	909 825-3425	19852
Jon-Lin Frozen Foods **(PA)**	5142	C	909 825-8542	14524
Kaiser Foundation Hospitals	6733	D	909 427-5521	16183
King Equipment LLC	7353	D	909 986-5300	17311
Lrb Millwork & Casework Inc	2431	F	951 328-0105	3263
McNeilus Truck and Mfg Inc	3713	E	909 370-2100	9992
Medlin Development	0782	E	909 825-5296	325
Microdyne Plastics Inc	3089	D	909 503-4010	5709
Mrs Redds Pie Co Inc	2051	E	909 825-4800	2022
Panadent Corporation	3843	E	909 783-1841	11188
Paul Hubbs Construction Inc **(PA)**	1429	F	951 360-3990	565
Premier Medical Trnsp Inc	4119	D	909 433-3939	11885
Premier Otptent Srgery Ctr Inc	8011	C	909 370-2190	20024
S & S Installations Inc	3589	E	909 370-1730	8409
Saab Enterprises Inc	2013	F	909 823-2228	1750
Show Offs	2541	F	909 885-5223	3664
Sisters of Soul SOS Yuth Fmly	8611	D	909 533-4889	22258
SMC Grease Specialist Inc	4953	E	951 788-6042	12980
Snowkap Enterprises Inc **(PA)**	7389	E	909 370-4444	18670
Southern Cal Prmnnte Med Group	8011	C	909 370-2501	20082
Sprouts Farmers Market Inc	4225	C	888 577-7688	12246
Sulzer Electro-Mechanical Serv	7694	E	909 825-7971	19016
Superior Masonry Walls Ltd	1741	D	909 370-1800	1354
Trinity Equipment Inc	5046	D	951 790-1905	13468
US Rubber Recycling Inc	3069	E	909 825-1200	5418
Williams Furnace Co **(DH)**	3585	C	562 450-3602	8359
Wirz & Co	2752	F	909 825-6970	4460

COMMERCE, CA - Los Angeles County

	SIC	EMP	PHONE	ENTRY #
4 Earth Farms LLC **(PA)**	5148	B	323 201-5800	14610
4 What Its Worth Inc **(PA)**	2329	D	323 728-4503	2794
99 Cents Only Stores LLC **(HQ)**	4225	B	323 980-8145	12181
A-1 Metal Products Inc	3444	E	323 721-3334	6771
Aahs Enterprises Inc	3993	F	323 838-9130	11519
AB&r Inc	2339	E	323 727-0007	2911
Abisco Products Co	2782	E	562 906-9330	4606
Acclaim Lighting LLC	3646	F	323 213-4626	9077
Acco Engineered Systems Inc	7389	E	323 201-0931	18432
Adj Products LLC **(PA)**	5063	C	323 582-2650	13608
Advanced Process Services Inc	3491	E	323 278-6530	7437
Ajg Inc	2386	E	323 346-0171	3053
Alarin Aircraft Hinge Inc	3429	E	323 725-1666	6497
Alcast Mfg Inc **(PA)**	3365	E	310 542-3581	6384
Allegro Pacific Corporation	3172	F	323 724-0101	5905
Alliance Apparel Inc	2331	E	323 888-8900	2834
Alloy Machining and Honing Inc	3599	E	323 726-8248	8490
Alloy Machining Services Inc	3599	F	323 725-2545	8491
Altamed Health Services Corp **(PA)**	8011	C	323 725-8751	19701
Amcor Flexibles LLC	2671	A	323 721-6777	3848
American Brass & Alum Fndry Co	3432	E	800 545-9988	6552
American Graphic Board Inc	2621	E	323 721-0585	3748
American Intl Inds Inc	2844	A	323 728-2999	4988
American Security Force Inc	7381	D	323 722-8585	18248
Amerifoods Trading Company LLC **(DH)**	5141	A	323 869-7500	14453
Apex Drum Company Inc	2449	F	323 721-8994	3413
Arbo Box Inc	2441	F	562 404-2726	3374
Architectural Enterprises Inc	3446	E	323 268-4000	6950
Arevalo Tortilleria Inc	2099	E	323 888-1711	2390
Arthurmade Plastics Inc	3089	D	323 721-7325	5568
Asco Sintering Co	3429	E	323 725-3550	6498
Atk Space Systems LLC **(DH)**	3812	E	323 722-0222	10571
B & B Battery (usa) Inc **(PA)**	3692	F	323 278-1900	9816
Balance Foods Inc	5145	E	323 838-5555	14559
Ball of Cotton Inc	2253	F	323 888-9448	2626
Ben Myerson Candy Co Inc **(PA)**	5182	B	800 331-2829	14838
Biorx Pharmaceuticals Inc	2834	E	323 725-3100	4799
Bluprint Clothing Corp	2331	D	323 780-4347	2838
Bonded Fiberloft Inc	2211	B	323 726-7820	2560
Bottlemate Inc **(PA)**	3089	E	323 887-9009	5584
Bridge Publications Inc **(PA)**	2731	E	323 888-6200	4122
Brk Group LLC	2299	E	562 949-4394	2722
Buy Fresh Produce Inc	5148	D	323 796-0127	14616
California Commerce Club Inc	7011	A	323 721-2100	16365
Califrnia Intermodal Assoc Inc **(PA)**	4213	E	323 562-7788	12019
Capitol Steel Fabricators Inc	3441	E	323 721-5460	6599
Caraustar Cstm Packg Group Inc	2655	D	323 724-5989	3834
Carmi Flvr & Fragrance Co Inc **(PA)**	2087	E	323 888-9240	2314
Cee Sportswear	2339	F	323 726-8158	2931
Central Bsin Mncpl Wtr Dst Fin	4941	D	323 201-5500	12882
Centric Brands LLC	1541	D	323 837-3700	691
Century Snacks LLC	5145	B	323 278-9578	14560
Century Wire & Cable Inc	3357	D	800 999-5566	6347
Ceramic Decorating Company Inc	7389	E	323 268-5135	18476
Chameleon Beverage Company Inc **(PA)**	2086	D	323 724-8223	2261
Cisco Bros Corp **(PA)**	2512	C	323 778-8612	3498
Color Image Apparel Inc **(PA)**	2361	E	855 793-3100	3029
Colorcom Inc	2752	D	323 246-4640	4257
Commercial Intr Resources Inc	2512	D	562 926-5885	3499
Community Manufacturing Inc	3531	F	323 720-8811	7639
Crown Plz Ht At Cmmerce Casino	7011	D	323 728-3600	16400
Crowntonka California Inc	3585	E	909 230-6720	8335
Ctd Machines Inc	3541	F	213 689-4455	7725
Cure Apparel Llc	2331	F	562 927-7460	2841
D J American Supply Inc	5099	C	323 582-2650	14150
Dart International A Corp **(HQ)**	4225	C	323 264-8746	12197
Dart Transportation Svc A Corp **(PA)**	7513	C	323 981-8205	18734
Dart Warehouse Corporation **(HQ)**	4225	B	323 264-1011	12198
Deamco Corporation	3535	E	323 890-1190	7690
Deco Enterprises Inc	3646	D	323 726-2575	9082
Deskmakers Inc	2521	E	323 264-2260	3583
DNam Apparel Industries LLC	2339	E	323 859-0114	2941
Dynaflex Products **(PA)**	3713	D	323 724-1555	9984
East Los Angeles Community Un **(PA)**	6153	E	323 721-1655	15152
El Clasificado	2741	D	323 278-5310	4169
El Guapo Spices Inc **(PA)**	5149	D	213 312-1300	14687
Elation Lighting Inc	3648	D	323 582-3322	9129
Elite Lighting	3648	C	323 888-1973	9130
Elkay Plastics Co Inc **(PA)**	5162	D	323 722-7073	14758
Ernest Packaging **(PA)**	5199	C	800 233-7788	14927
Eti Sound Systems Inc	3651	E	323 835-6660	9175
Fast Sportswear Inc	2339	F	323 720-1078	2944
Fedex Smartpost Inc	4215	D	323 888-8879	12135
Fleming Metal Fabricators	3713	E	323 723-8203	9987
Floride Products LLC **(PA)**	2819	E	323 201-4363	4658
Fungs Village Inc	2098	E	323 881-1600	2376
Furniture Technics Inc	2511	E	562 802-0261	3473
Galaxy Enterprises Inc	3999	E	323 728-3980	11673
Gehr Group Inc **(PA)**	7011	C	323 728-5558	16452
Gehr Hospitality New York LLC **(DH)**	6512	D	323 728-5558	15669
Gehr Industries Inc **(HQ)**	3357	C	323 728-5558	6350
General Industrial Repair	3599	E	323 278-0873	8603
Gibson Overseas Inc	5023	A	323 832-8900	13171
Ginger Golden Products Inc	2035	F	323 838-1070	1889
Glamour Industries Co **(PA)**	5122	B	323 728-2999	14244
Globe Iron Foundry Inc	3321	D	323 723-8983	6258
Gold Coast Ingredients Inc	2099	D	323 724-8935	2443
Grocers Specialty Company **(DH)**	5141	E	323 264-5200	14470
H-D Specialty Groups Inc	3479	F	323 516-6186	7370
Haldeman Inc	1711	E	323 726-7011	1081
Haley Indus Ctings Linings Inc	3479	E	323 588-8086	7372
Hallmark Lighting LLC	3646	D	818 885-5010	9087
Heritage Distributing Company **(PA)**	2026	E	323 838-1225	1837
Hidden Jeans Inc	2211	E	213 746-4223	2574
Hkf Inc **(PA)**	5075	D	323 225-1318	13846
Hollywood Bed Spring Mfg Inc **(PA)**	3429	D	323 887-9500	6521
Hospital Svc Emplyees Un Lcal	8631	D	323 734-8399	22290
Hospitality Wood Products Inc	2431	F	562 806-5564	3255
Huhtamaki Inc	3086	D	323 269-0151	5511
Image Micro Spare Parts Inc	3621	E	562 776-9808	8918
Indio Products Inc	2899	E	323 720-9117	5223
Ineos Composites Us LLC	5169	D	323 767-1300	14785
Ingenue Inc	2015	D	323 726-8084	1760
Ink Makers Inc	2893	F	323 728-7500	5206
Interntional Tea Importers Inc **(PA)**	2099	D	562 801-9600	2453
Interstate Electric Co Inc **(PA)**	5046	D	323 724-0420	13460
Interstate Meat Co Inc	3556	E	323 838-9400	7939
Ivy Enterprises Inc	8748	B	323 887-8661	23456
Iworks Us Inc	3641	D	323 278-8363	9021
J & F Design Inc	2339	D	323 526-4444	2953
J & S Building Maintenance Inc	7349	E	562 714-4033	17252
J Michelle of California	2269	F	323 585-8500	2673
Jfc International Inc **(HQ)**	5149	C	323 721-6100	14698

GEOGRAPHIC

	SIC	EMP	PHONE	ENTRY #
Jfc International Inc	5149	C	323 721-6900	14699
JP Products LLC	2511	E	310 237-6237	3474
Justman Packaging & Display	5046	D	323 728-8888	13463
Kate Somerville Skincare LLC	5122	D	310 623-6822	14255
Kerry Ingredients	2099	F	323 430-9718	2459
Kingdom Mattress Co Inc	2515	E	562 630-5531	3551
Kirk API Containers	3089	E	323 278-5400	5692
L Tech Network Services Inc	1731	D	562 222-1121	1273
La Xpress Air & Heating Svcs	2741	D	310 856-9678	4187
LCI Laundry Inc	2335	C	323 767-1900	2891
Liberty Packg & Extruding Inc	2673	E	323 722-5124	3885
Lion Tank Line Inc	2911	E	323 726-1966	5252
Maidenform LLC	2341	C	323 724-9558	3017
Mantels & More Corp	3281	F	323 869-9764	6140
Maravilla Foundation **(PA)**	8699	C	323 721-4162	22457
Mascorro Leather Inc	3199	E	323 724-6759	5913
Matrix International Tex Inc	5131	E	323 582-9100	14307
Matthew Warren Inc	3493	D	800 237-5225	7466
Mega Sign Inc	3993	E	888 315-7446	11572
Meridian Textiles Inc **(PA)**	5131	D	323 869-5700	14308
MGM Transformer Co	3612	D	323 726-0888	8878
Michelson Laboratories Inc **(PA)**	8734	D	562 928-0553	22952
Miken Sales Inc **(PA)**	5137	D	323 266-2560	14401
Mojave Foods Corporation	2099	C	323 890-8900	2488
Monogram Aerospace Fas Inc	3429	C	323 722-4760	6529
Motorshield LLC	2851	F	323 396-9200	5104
MSE Media Solutions Inc	3695	F	323 721-1656	9837
Nanoflowx LLC	3479	E	323 396-9200	7389
National Sales Corp	5199	D	323 586-0200	14955
Ni Industries Inc	3449	D	309 283-3355	7025
Nico Nat Mfg Corp	2541	E	323 721-1900	3659
Nora Lighting Inc	5063	C	800 686-6672	13653
Norstar Office Products Inc **(PA)**	2521	E	323 262-1919	3593
Northrop Grumman Systems Corp	3812	C	714 240-6521	10617
Nova Lifestyle Inc **(PA)**	2511	E	323 888-9999	3482
Number Holdings Inc **(PA)**	5199	C	323 980-8145	14957
Oakhurst Industries Inc **(PA)**	2051	C	323 724-3000	2026
Oldcastle Buildingenvelope Inc	3231	D	323 722-2007	5966
Orlandini Entps Pcf Die Cast	3369	C	323 725-1332	6418
Pacific Coast Home Furn Inc **(PA)**	2392	F	323 838-7808	3112
Pacific Die Casting Corp	3363	C	323 725-1308	6368
Pacific Hospitality Design Inc	2531	E	323 278-7998	3630
Pacific Spice Company Inc	2099	D	323 726-9190	2506
Pacific Vial Mfg Inc	3999	F	323 721-7004	11726
Pacific Vial Mfg Inc	3221	E	323 721-7004	5929
Parking Company of America	7521	D	562 862-2118	18770
PCI Industries Inc	3999	E	323 728-0004	11732
PCI Industries Inc	3444	E	323 728-0004	6890
Pearlman Enterprises Inc **(DH)**	3291	D	800 969-5561	6157
Pioneer Broach Company **(PA)**	3545	E	323 728-1263	7862
Pixior LLC **(PA)**	7389	C	323 721-2221	18635
Pommes Frites Candle Co	3999	E	213 488-2016	11737
Portos Food Product Inc	2051	D	323 480-8400	2030
Precision Wire Products Inc **(PA)**	3496	C	323 890-9100	7508
Progressive Label Inc	2679	E	323 415-9770	3936
Progressive Produce LLC **(HQ)**	5148	D	323 890-8100	14650
Quantum Concept Inc	2329	F	323 888-8601	2822
Ramcar Batteries Inc	5013	E	323 726-1212	13084
RDD Enterprises Inc	2311	F	213 746-0020	2747
RDD Enterprises Inc	2394	E	213 742-0666	3144
Reading Entertainment Inc **(HQ)**	7832	D	213 235-2226	19287
Rollins Inc	7342	C	323 722-2279	17205
Romac Supply Co Inc	3613	D	323 721-5810	8905
Rti Services Inc	7389	D	323 725-6370	18658
Ryan Shroads	7389	E	310 936-5966	18660
S Bravo Systems Inc	3443	E	323 888-4133	6751
Sam Schaffer Inc	7699	E	323 263-7524	19062
Samson Pharmaceuticals Inc	2834	E	323 722-3066	4890
Samson Products Inc	2542	E	323 726-9070	3696
Samsung Electronics Amer Inc	5064	B	323 374-6300	13693
Screamline Investment Corp	4725	C	323 201-0114	12411
Senfeng Laser Usa Inc	3699	F	562 319-8053	9912
Sentiments Inc **(PA)**	3999	F	323 843-2080	11752
SGC International Inc	3211	F	323 318-2998	5921
Shims Bargain Inc	1541	D	323 726-8800	716
Sid E Parker Boiler Mfg Co Inc	3443	D	323 727-9800	6752
Smart & Final Stores LLC **(HQ)**	5141	B	323 869-7500	14508
Smart & Final Stores LLC **(DH)**	5141	B	323 869-7500	14509
Snak Club LLC	2068	D	323 278-9578	2116
Soffa Electric Inc	3823	E	323 728-0230	10725
Soft Gel Technologies Inc **(HQ)**	2834	D	323 726-0700	4895
Solemnity Personnel	7361	E	323 718-3979	17467
Specialty Enterprises Co	3086	D	323 726-9721	5522
Sportek International Inc	5136	F	213 239-6700	14351
Stitch Industries Inc	2512	E	888 282-0842	3519
Strategic Materials Inc	4953	D	323 887-6831	12984
Sugar Foods Corporation	2051	D	323 727-8290	2037
Sun Coast Merchandise Corp	5099	C	323 720-9700	14182
Sun Plastics Inc	2673	E	323 888-6999	3891
Superb Chair Corporation	2512	E	562 776-1771	3520
Superior-Studio Spc Inc	3999	E	323 278-0100	11768
TCI Transportation Services **(PA)**	4213	B	323 269-3033	12080
Tdg Operations LLC	2273	E	323 724-9000	2699
Teichman Enterprises Inc	2542	E	323 278-9000	3698
Telacu Industries Inc **(HQ)**	6552	E	323 721-1655	16076
Tk Elevator Corporation	5084	D	323 278-2801	13950
Torah-Aura Productions Inc	2731	F	323 585-1847	4141
Touch Litho Company	2752	F	562 927-8899	4439
Trixxi Clothing Company Inc **(PA)**	2335	E	323 585-4200	2898
Ultimate Metal Finishing Corp	3479	E	323 890-9100	7422
Ultra Pro Acquisition LLC	2782	E	323 725-1975	4613
Ultra Pro International LLC **(PA)**	2782	D	323 890-2100	4614
Unified Nutrimeals	2099	D	323 923-9335	2544
Uniserve Facilities Svcs Corp **(PA)**	7349	B	213 533-1000	17296
United Parcel Service Inc	7389	D	323 837-1220	18699
Univar Solutions USA Inc	5169	C	323 727-7005	14792
Urban Expressions Inc	3171	E	310 593-4574	5904
US Polymers Inc	3354	D	323 727-6888	6322
USG Ceilings Plus LLC	3469	E	323 724-8166	7187
Valley Plating Works Inc	3471	F	323 838-9211	7329
W B Mason Co Inc	2752	E	888 926-2766	4451
W2005 Wyn Hotels LP	7011	D	323 887-8100	16776
Weekendz-Off Inc	5136	E	323 888-9966	14360
West Bay Imports Inc	5199	E	323 720-5777	14986
West Coast Catrg Trcks Mfg Inc	2511	F	323 278-1279	3491
Wiretech Inc **(PA)**	3315	D	323 722-4933	6241
X-Igent Printing Inc	2752	F	323 837-9779	4463
Yavar Manufacturing Co Inc	2657	E	323 722-2040	3847
Zemarc Corporation **(PA)**	5084	E	323 721-5598	13966

COMPTON, CA - Los Angeles County

	SIC	EMP	PHONE	ENTRY #
A J R Trucking Inc	4212	D	562 989-9555	11950
AAA Plating & Inspection Inc	3471	D	323 979-8930	7195
Ace Clearwater Enterprises Inc	3544	E	310 538-5380	7773
Advanced Materials Inc **(HQ)**	3086	F	310 537-5444	5484
AITA Clutch Inc	3714	E	323 585-4140	10014
Ajr Trucking Inc	4212	C	562 989-9555	11954
Alameda Construction Svcs Inc	1442	E	310 635-3277	567
Allan Kidd	3643	E	310 762-1600	9026
American Dawn Inc **(PA)**	2299	D	800 821-2221	2718
Andrew Alexander Inc	3111	D	323 752-0066	5867
Anoroc Precision Shtmtl Inc	3444	E	310 515-6015	6786
Apex Logistics Intl Inc **(PA)**	4731	D	310 665-0288	12423
Asbury Environmental Services **(PA)**	4212	D	310 886-3400	11956
Barkens Hardchrome Inc	3559	E	310 632-2000	7964
Bay Cities Italian Bakery Inc	2051	F	310 608-1881	1983
Beauchamp Distributing Company	5181	D	310 639-5320	14822
Benettis Italia Inc	5021	E	310 537-8036	13127
Beyondsoft Consulting Inc	8748	C	310 532-2822	23418
BHC Industries Inc	3471	E	310 632-2000	7222
Blake H Brown Inc **(DH)**	5084	D	310 764-0110	13891
Bowman Plating Co Inc	3471	C	310 639-4343	7226
Brinderson LP **(DH)**	8711	C	714 466-7100	22503
Brybradan Inc	3999	F	323 230-8604	11642
California Cartage Company Inc	4225	D	888 537-1432	12187
California Decor	2431	F	310 603-9944	3235
California Pak Intl Inc	3612	E	310 223-2500	8863
CCC Property Holdings LLC	6719	C	310 609-1957	16096
Celebrity Casinos Inc	7011	B	310 631-3838	16373
Cellco Partnership	4812	D	310 603-0101	12598
Circle Industrial Mfg Corp **(PA)**	3567	E	310 638-5101	8086
Circle Industrial Mfg Corp	3542	F	310 638-5101	7758
CK Steel Inc	3441	F	310 638-0855	6600
Color Ad Inc	7311	E	310 632-5500	17000
Colosseum Athletics Corp	5136	D	310 667-8341	14330
Compton Unified School Dst	8322	D	310 898-6470	21756
Compton Unified School Dst	8351	D	310 898-6008	22008
Compton Unified School Dst	7389	D	310 639-4321	18486
Concrete Mold Corporation	3544	D	310 537-5171	7792
Concrete Tie Industries Inc **(PA)**	5032	D	310 628-2328	13300
Continental Forge Company **(PA)**	3462	D	310 603-1014	7083
Contractors Cargo Company **(PA)**	4213	D	310 609-1957	12025
Cordelia Lighting Inc	5063	C	310 886-3490	13620
Cotton Knits Trading	2259	E	310 884-9600	2652
County of Los Angeles	8099	D	310 885-2100	21403
County of Los Angeles	8099	D	310 668-6845	21405
Crew Inc	1794	D	310 608-6860	1594
Cri Sub 1 **(DH)**	2521	E	310 537-1657	3581
Crossfield Products Corp **(PA)**	2821	E	310 886-9100	4685
Custom Iron Design **(PA)**	3446	F	310 537-5936	6959
De Menno-Kerdoon Trading Co **(HQ)**	2911	C	310 537-7100	5251
Demenno Kerdoon	1382	E	310 537-7100	446
Dhx-Dependable Hawaiian Ex Inc **(PA)**	4731	C	310 537-2000	12446
Diamond Mattress Company Inc **(PA)**	2515	D	310 638-0363	3547
Dna Specialty Inc	5013	D	310 767-4070	13055
Durham School Services L P	4151	C	310 767-5820	11919
Dxterity Diagnostics Inc **(PA)**	8733	E	310 537-7857	22907
E M E Inc	3471	C	310 639-1621	7249
Edmund Kim International Inc **(PA)**	2329	E	310 604-1100	2806
Electronic Stamping Corp	3613	F	310 639-2120	8897
Element Mtrls Tech HB Inc	8734	D	310 632-8500	22940
Epsilon Plastics Inc	5199	D	310 609-1320	14926
Evans Hydro Inc	7699	E	310 608-5801	19036
Evox Productions LLC **(PA)**	7371	D	310 605-1400	17612
Excellon Acquisition LLC **(HQ)**	3559	E	310 668-7700	7973
Express Messenger Systems Inc	4215	D	800 359-2959	12132
F R T International Inc **(PA)**	4225	D	310 604-8208	12205
Fastener Innovation Tech Inc	3451	D	310 538-1111	7035
Fleetwood Continental Inc	3366	D	310 609-1477	6407
Florence Filter Corporation	5075	D	310 637-1137	13843
Fmf Racing	3751	C	310 631-4363	10490
Foam Factory Inc	3086	E	310 603-9808	5502
Foamex LP	4225	C	323 774-5600	12206
Forming Specialties Inc	3728	E	310 639-1122	10330
Foster Poultry Farms	2015	B	310 223-1499	1758

Mergent email: customerrelations@mergent.com
1352

2022 Southern California Business
Directory and Buyers Guide

(P-0000) Products & Services Section entry number
(PA)=Parent Co (HQ)=Headquarters (DH)=Div Headquarters

	SIC	EMP	PHONE	ENTRY #
Fs - Precision Tech Co LLC	3369	D	310 638-0595	6417
Fusion Finish LLC (PA)	3479	E	562 773-5303	7366
Gemco Display and Str Fixs LLC (PA)	5046	D	800 262-1126	13456
General Petroleum Corporation (HQ)	5172	C	562 983-7300	14804
Global Mail Inc	4731	C	310 735-0800	12463
Golden Gate Steel Inc	3441	F	310 638-0855	6619
Gourmet Foods Inc (PA)	5141	C	310 632-3300	14469
Great Eastern Entertainment Co	2741	E	310 638-5058	4178
H Rauvel Inc	4213	C	562 989-3333	12050
Hammond Power Solutions Inc	5063	D	310 537-4690	13632
Henkel US Operations Corp	2843	C	310 764-4600	4984
Hf Group Inc (PA)	3861	C	310 605-0755	11277
Idemia America Corp	3089	C	310 884-7900	5670
Ilco Industries Inc	3498	E	310 631-8655	7539
Industrial Valco Inc (PA)	5085	E	310 635-0711	13993
Innovative Stamping Inc	3469	E	310 537-6996	7153
Interstate Foods Inc	5144	C	310 635-0426	14548
Ipme	3499	C	866 237-6302	7560
Ips Corporation (PA)	2891	C	310 898-3300	5186
Jack Rubin & Sons Inc (PA)	5051	E	310 635-5407	13570
Jbi LLC	2514	E	310 537-2910	3529
Jimway Inc	3648	D	310 886-3718	9136
Kawai America Corporation (HQ)	5099	E	310 631-1771	14166
Kens Spray Equipment Inc (DH)	3479	D	310 635-9995	7380
Kizure Product Co Inc	3634	E	310 604-0058	9007
Kroger Co	4225	B	859 630-6959	12217
Lekos Dye & Finishing Inc	2231	E	310 763-0900	2613
Life Tech Clnical Svcs Lab Inc (DH)	8731	E	866 522-1585	22848
Link Logistics Solutions Inc	4731	E	800 932-3383	12479
LMC Enterprises	2842	D	310 632-7124	4969
LMD Intgrted Lgistics Svcs Inc (PA)	4731	D	310 605-5100	12219
Lunwood Developmental Care	8059	D	310 223-5920	20608
M M Fab Inc	5131	D	310 763-3800	14306
M N M Manufacturing Inc	3442	D	310 898-1099	6708
M-7 Consolidation Inc	4731	C	310 898-3456	12480
Magnesium Alloy Pdts Co Inc	3363	E	310 605-1440	6366
Magnesium Alloy Products Co LP	3363	E	323 636-2276	6367
Martins Quality Truck Body Inc	3711	F	310 632-5978	9957
McCormick Fresh Herbs LLC	2099	D	323 278-9750	2482
Mercado Latino Inc	3999	E	310 537-1062	11713
Mitsubishi Warehouse Cal Corp	4225	D	310 886-5500	12223
Morrells Electro Plating Inc	3471	E	310 639-1024	7283
Nabors Well Services Co	1389	D	310 639-7074	524
Nabors Well Services Co	1389	D	310 639-7074	526
National Retail Trnsp Inc	4213	D	310 631-8951	12065
National Retail Trnsp Inc	4213	D	310 605-3777	12067
Newport Apparel Corporation (PA)	5137	D	310 605-1900	14405
Ocean Blue Express Inc (PA)	4731	D	310 719-2500	12496
Optex Incorporated	3669	C	800 966-7839	9346
Organic By Nature Inc (PA)	2833	E	562 901-0177	4758
Orion Plastics Corporation	2821	D	310 223-0700	4705
Pacific Contntl Textiles Inc (HQ)	2269	C	310 604-1100	2678
Pacific Drayage Services LLC	4212	C	901 746-3794	11987
Pacific Lighting Mfr Inc	5063	D	310 327-7711	13657
Pacific Lighting Mfr Inc	5063	D	310 327-7711	13658
Park Steel Co Inc	3441	F	310 638-6101	6647
Patina Freight Inc	4731	D	310 764-4395	12503
Performance Composites Inc	3229	C	310 328-6661	5939
Permalite Plastics Corp	2865	E	310 669-9492	5122
Petrochem Insulation Inc	1742	D	310 638-6663	1394
Plaskolite West LLC	2821	D	310 637-2103	4708
Plasma Coating Corporation	3479	E	310 532-1951	7398
Precision Babbitt Co Inc	3568	F	562 531-9173	8106
Prime Alliance LLC	2258	E	310 764-1000	2650
Prison Ride Share Network	2741	E	314 703-5245	4198
Quality Production Svcs Inc	1742	D	310 406-3350	1395
R & D Steel Inc	3441	E	310 631-6183	6654
Resource Label Group LLC	2754	E	310 603-8910	4468
Rsk Tool Incorporated	3089	D	310 537-3302	5808
S & K Plating Inc	3471	F	310 632-7141	7307
Saddlemen Corporation	5013	D	310 638-1222	13086
Sequoia Pure Water Inc	2086	E	310 637-8500	2298
Serra Manufacturing Corp (PA)	3469	D	310 537-4560	7180
Service Quick Inc (PA)	7629	C	213 700-4332	18957
Sew What Inc	2391	E	310 639-6000	3094
Shields For Families	8069	D	310 604-4446	21051
Simso Tex Sublimation (PA)	2396	D	310 885-9717	3182
South Bay Public Warehouse	4225	D	310 637-1133	12245
South Coast Screen and Casing	3533	F	310 632-3200	7676
Southern California Edison Co	4911	C	310 608-5029	12844
Southwire Inc	3353	B	310 886-8300	6302
Star View Chldren Fmly Svcs In	8322	D	310 868-5379	21898
Swan Fence Incorporated	3315	E	310 669-8000	6235
Tag Toys Inc	3999	D	310 639-4566	11771
Tajima USA Inc	3552	E	310 604-8200	7912
Tap Worldwide LLC (DH)	5013	A	310 900-5500	13098
Techmer Pm Inc	2821	D	310 632-9211	4723
Tex-Coat LLC	2851	E	323 233-3111	5116
Thermal Equipment Corporation	3443	E	310 328-6600	6760
Tom Malloy Corporation (PA)	5082	D	310 327-5554	13873
Total Intermodal Services Inc	4491	D	562 427-6300	12292
Transamerican Dissolution LLC (PA)	5013	C	310 900-5500	13101
Tricap International LLC	4731	D	509 703-8780	12545
U-Sun Textiles Inc	2221	F	310 609-1155	2607
Ufp Technologies Inc	3086	D	714 662-0277	5526
Uls Express Inc	4212	D	310 631-0800	12004
Uma Enterprises Inc (PA)	5023	D	310 631-1166	13192
United Fabricare Supply Inc (PA)	5087	D	310 886-3790	14046
Utopia Lighting	3612	F	310 327-7711	8886
Viking Rubber Products Inc	3069	F	310 868-5200	5421
Walters Wholesale Electric Co (HQ)	5063	E	562 988-3100	13674
Wenzlau Engineering Inc	5065	D	310 604-3400	13785
West Wood Products Inc	5031	D	310 631-8978	13291
Yourtex Fashions Inc	7389	C	323 581-6600	18732

CORCORAN, CA - Kings County

	SIC	EMP	PHONE	ENTRY #
Adventist Hlth Systm/West Corp	8062	D	559 992-2800	20659
Corcoran Irrigation District	4971	C	559 992-5165	13010
Corcoran Sawtelle Rosprim Inc	3441	E	559 992-2117	6607
Crookshanks Sales Co	3273	C	559 992-5077	6088
Hansen Equipment Company LLC	0762	E	559 992-3111	223
Hansen Ranches	0191	D	559 992-3111	109
J G Boswell Company	0723	D	559 992-2141	177
J G Boswell Company	0212	D	559 992-5011	128
J G Boswell Company	0131	C	559 992-5141	3
Karl M Smith Inc	3444	E	559 992-4109	6859
Mar Vista Resources LLC	2873	F	559 992-4535	5157
Quinn Company	5082	D	559 992-2193	13866
Recreational Assn Corcoran	8641	D	559 992-5171	22362

CORONA, CA - Riverside County

	SIC	EMP	PHONE	ENTRY #
10 Day Parts Inc	3089	E	951 279-4810	5539
2nd Gen Productions Inc	2842	E	800 877-6282	4950
A and M Ornamental Iron & Wldg	3446	F	951 734-6730	6945
A M Ortega Construction Inc	1731	C	951 360-1352	1203
ABC School Equipment Inc	5049	D	951 817-2200	13532
Ability Counts Inc (PA)	8331	D	951 734-6595	21934
Absolute Graphic Tech USA Inc	3625	C	909 597-1133	8941
Accurate Grinding and Mfg Corp	3724	E	951 479-0909	10210
Ace Heaters LLC	3585	E	951 738-2230	8326
Acker Stone Industries Inc (DH)	3272	C	951 674-0047	6014
Acm Technologies Inc (PA)	5044	D	951 738-9898	13350
Acromil LLC	3728	D	951 808-9929	10236
Actavis LLC	2834	C	909 270-1400	4776
Actron Manufacturing Inc	3429	C	951 371-0885	6495
Adonis Inc	2844	C	951 432-3960	4987
Advanced Flow Engineering Inc (PA)	3714	C	951 493-7155	10008
Aero Automatic Sprinkler Co	1711	D	951 273-1889	1018
Aero-Craft Hydraulics Inc	3728	C	951 736-4690	10246
Agile Sourcing Partners Inc	4939	C	951 279-4154	12876
AK Constructors Inc	1542	C	951 280-0269	731
All American Asphalt (PA)	1611	A	951 736-7600	853
All American Asphalt	1611	A	951 736-7617	854
All American Asphalt	1611	A	951 736-7617	856
All Integrated Solutions LLC	3949	F	951 817-3328	11399
All Manufacturers Inc	3841	C	951 280-4200	10930
Allied Construction Services	1521	C	951 405-3193	591
Alpha Laser	3699	F	951 582-0285	9852
American Electric Supply Inc (PA)	5063	C	951 734-7910	13612
American National Mfg Inc	2515	C	951 273-7888	3541
American Power SEC Svc Inc	7381	D	866 974-9994	18245
Ameriflex Inc	3498	D	951 737-5557	7527
Amerisourcebergen Drug Corp	5122	C	951 371-2000	14233
Ames Construction Inc	1751	C	951 356-1275	1427
AMF Support Surfaces Inc (DH)	2515	C	951 549-6800	3542
Amrapur Overseas Incorporated (PA)	2299	E	714 893-8808	2721
Amwear USA Inc	2311	E	800 858-6755	2740
Anaco Inc	3568	C	951 372-2732	8102
Approved Aeronautics LLC	3728	C	951 200-3730	10274
Aqua Mix Inc	2842	C	951 256-3040	4953
Aqua Performance Inc	5091	C	951 340-2056	14073
Aquatic Co	3088	C	714 993-1220	5528
Aqueous Technologies Corp	3589	E	909 944-7771	8365
Architectural Design Signs Inc (PA)	3993	C	951 278-0680	11523
Arizona Pipeline Company	1623	C	951 270-3100	935
Artistic Plastics Inc	3089	F	951 808-9700	5569
Arvinyl Laminates LP	3081	C	951 371-7800	5427
Aseptic Sltons USA Vntures LLC	2086	C	951 736-9230	2256
Asturies Manufacturing Co Inc	3728	C	951 270-1766	10281
Aurora Bhvioral Healthcare LLC (HQ)	8063	C	951 549-8032	21013
Auto Buyline Systems Inc (PA)	5012	C	951 271-8999	13020
Automobile Club Southern Cal	8699	D	951 808-9624	22438
Avalon Mfg Co Incoirporated	3556	F	951 340-0280	7927
Azteca Landscape (PA)	0782	C	909 673-0889	292
Aztecs Telecom Inc	7389	D	714 373-1560	18454
B/E Aerospace Inc	3728	C	951 278-4563	10286
Bbva USA	6022	C	951 279-7071	15012
Beador Construction Co Inc	1611	D	951 674-7352	861
Bergelectric Corp	1731	C	951 520-0851	1219
Best- In- West	2395	E	909 947-6507	3151
Bills Pipes Inc	3751	E	951 371-1329	10484
Biolase Inc	3843	D	949 361-1200	11162
Blue Desert International Inc	3589	D	951 273-7575	8369
Blue Sky Natural Beverage Co	2086	F	800 426-3777	2259
Bmb 1 LLC	8059	D	951 741-0663	20562
Boudreau Pipeline Corporation	1623	B	951 493-6780	938
Brasscraft Manufacturing Co	3494	D	951 735-4375	7471
Bu LLC	2082	F	951 277-7470	2141
C&R Systems Inc (PA)	1731	C	951 270-0255	1227
Cadence Gourmet LLC	2099	E	951 444-9269	2402
Caliber Sealing Solutions Inc (PA)	3053	F	949 461-0555	5330
California Wire Products Corp	3496	C	951 371-7730	7496
Cannon Fabrication Inc	1761	D	951 278-1830	1476
Canyon Tire Sales Inc (PA)	5014	E	951 603-0615	13113
Carr Management Inc	3089	D	951 277-4800	5601

GEOGRAPHIC

	SIC	EMP	PHONE	ENTRY #
Carter Holt Harvey Holdings	3312	F	951 272-8180	6195
Case Automation Corporation	3535	E	951 493-6666	7687
Cemex Materials LLC	3273	D	951 277-2420	6081
Century Blinds Inc	2591	D	951 734-3762	3708
Certainteed Corona Inc	3089	C	951 272-1300	5604
Cgpc America Corporation	2821	E	951 332-4100	4682
Chandler Aggregates Inc **(PA)**	1411	E	951 277-1341	562
Charles C Regan Inc	1611	D	951 735-8100	871
Circor Aerospace Inc **(HQ)**	3491	C	951 270-6200	7440
Circor Instrmentation Tech Inc	3492	F	951 270-6200	7454
Ckkm Inc **(PA)**	5051	E	951 371-8484	13557
Clay Corona Company **(PA)**	1542	E	951 277-2667	756
Columbia Aluminum Products LLC	3441	D	323 728-7361	6601
Combustion Associates Inc	4911	E	951 272-6999	12797
Community Access Ntwrk Non Prf **(PA)**	8322	D	951 279-1333	21749
Computer Service Company	3669	E	951 738-1444	9336
Computrus Inc	3443	E	951 245-9103	6737
Cooper Engineering Inc	8711	E	951 736-6135	22518
Core-Mark Intrrlted Cmpnies In **(DH)**	5199	E	951 272-4790	14923
Corona Clipper Inc	5072	D	951 737-6515	13801
Corona Magnetics Inc	3677	C	951 735-7558	9626
Cremach Tech Inc **(PA)**	3541	C	951 735-3194	7724
Crossrads Chrstn Schols Corona	8351	C	951 278-3199	22009
CTA Manufacturing Inc	2393	E	951 280-2400	3126
Currie Enterprises	3714	E	714 528-6957	10038
Custom Quality Door & Trim Inc	2431	E	951 278-0066	3239
Dal Chem Inc	5171	D	951 279-9830	14795
Dart Container Corp California **(PA)**	3086	B	951 735-8115	5496
David Engineering & Mfg Inc	3469	E	951 735-5200	7140
De La Torre Ldscp & Maint Corp	0782	D	951 549-3525	299
Decra Roofing Systems Inc **(DH)**	3444	D	951 272-8180	6817
Della Robbia Inc	2515	E	951 372-9199	3546
Developlus Inc	3999	C	951 738-8595	11658
Dietzgen Corporation	2679	E	951 278-3259	3926
Dita Inc **(PA)**	3851	E	949 599-2700	11248
Diversified Mfg Tech Inc	3544	F	714 577-7000	7797
Do It American Mfg Company LLC	3499	F	951 254-9204	7553
Eagle Glen Country Club LLC	7992	D	951 272-4653	19485
Ebs General Engineering Inc	1611	D	951 279-6869	876
Eclypse International Corp **(PA)**	3825	F	951 371-8008	10749
Eibach Inc	3493	D	951 256-8300	7463
Electrasem Corp	3822	D	951 371-6140	10665
Empire Demolition Inc	1795	D	909 393-8300	1613
Engineered Food Systems	3589	E	714 921-9913	8380
Ergononmic Comfort Design Inc	2522	F	951 277-1558	3608
Esl Power Systems Inc	3643	D	800 922-4188	9036
Excel Cabinets Inc	2434	E	951 279-4545	3319
Excel Landscape Inc	0782	C	951 735-9650	304
Extrumed Inc **(DH)**	3089	D	951 547-7400	5643
F & L Tools Corporation	3728	F	951 279-1555	10324
Fender Musical Instrs Corp	3931	A	480 596-9690	11342
Fennel Inc	1751	D	951 284-2020	1436
Fire Sprinkler Systems Inc **(PA)**	1711	D	800 915-3473	1068
Fireblast Global Inc	3569	E	951 277-8319	8122
First Student Inc	4173	C	951 736-3234	11943
First Team RE - Orange Cnty	6531	C	951 270-2800	15861
Fischer Mold Incorporated	3089	D	951 279-1140	5645
Fleetwood Enterprises Inc **(DH)**	3799	A	951 354-3000	10550
Fleetwood Homes of Kentucky **(DH)**	2451	D	800 688-1745	3424
Fleetwood Homes of PA **(DH)**	2451	D	717 367-8222	3425
Fletcher Bldg Holdings USA Inc **(DH)**	3444	D	951 272-8180	6839
Food For Life Baking Co Inc **(PA)**	2051	D	951 273-3031	2001
Four Seasons Rest Eqp Inc	3444	E	951 278-9100	6841
Fovell Enterprises Inc	3993	E	951 734-6275	11556
Fst Sand & Gravel Inc	5032	E	951 277-8440	13305
Gail Materials Inc	1442	E	951 667-6106	571
Ganahl Lumber Company	2431	D	951 278-4000	3250
General Container	2653	D	714 562-8700	3807
Gibson Performance Corporation	3714	D	951 372-1220	10067
Green River Golf Corporation	7992	D	714 970-8411	19490
H & H Transportation LLC	4213	D	951 817-2300	12049
Halo Unlimted Inc	8099	D	714 692-2270	21432
Handbill Printers LP	2752	E	951 547-5910	4310
Hannan Products Corp **(PA)**	3565	F	951 735-1587	8070
Hardy Frames Inc	3312	D	951 245-9525	6203
Hillcrest Contracting Inc	1611	D	951 273-9600	887
Hitachi Astemo Ohio Mfg Inc	3714	D	951 340-0702	10074
Hoosier Inc	3089	D	951 272-3070	5665
HP Communications Inc **(PA)**	1623	C	951 572-1200	955
Hub Distributing Inc **(HQ)**	5137	B	951 340-3149	14380
Index Fresh Inc **(PA)**	5148	D	909 877-0999	14639
Infinity Plumbing Designs Inc	1711	B	951 737-4436	1083
Inland Mailing Services Inc	2752	F	951 371-6245	4335
International Wind Inc **(PA)**	3724	E	562 240-3963	10217
Interstate Cabinet Inc	3999	E	951 736-0777	11691
Irwin Aviation Inc	3728	E	951 372-9555	10359
Irwin International Inc **(PA)**	5088	D	951 372-9555	14057
Jayco Interface Technology Inc	3679	E	951 738-2000	9736
Jayco/Mmi Inc	3679	E	951 738-2000	9737
Jet Manufacturing Inc	3444	D	951 736-9316	6858
Jhawar Industries LLC	3567	E	951 340-4646	8092
JJ Mac Intyre Co Inc **(PA)**	7322	C	951 898-4300	17114
Johasee Rebar Inc	3441	E	661 589-0972	6625
John Currie Performance Group	3559	E	714 367-1580	7986
Johnson Caldraul Inc	3728	E	951 340-1067	10361
Joor Bros Welding Inc	5051	F	951 737-3950	13574
K & W Manufacturing Co Inc	3429	E	951 277-3300	6523
K S Printing Inc	2752	F	951 268-5180	4345
K&B Electric LLC	8711	C	951 808-9501	22593
K&B Engineering	8711	C	951 808-9501	22594
Kaiser Fndtion Hlth Plan GA In	6324	C	951 270-1200	15401
Kaiser Foundation Hospitals	8011	C	951 898-7370	19872
Kaiser Foundation Hospitals	8099	C	866 984-7483	21447
Kaiser Foundation Hospitals	6733	D	866 984-7483	16185
Kap Medical	3829	E	951 340-4360	10894
Kec Engineering	1611	C	951 734-3010	894
Kobelco Compressors Amer Inc	3563	D	951 739-3030	8034
Kobelco Compressors Amer Inc **(DH)**	3563	B	951 739-3030	8035
Kpc Group Inc **(PA)**	8742	D	951 782-8812	23253
Kurz Transfer Products LP	3999	E	951 738-9521	11703
La Steel Services Inc	1791	E	951 393-2013	1573
Landscape Development Inc	0782	C	951 371-9370	320
Laneaire	3444	F	951 808-3658	6862
Laurence-Hovenier Inc	1751	C	951 736-2990	1445
LDI Mechanical Inc **(PA)**	1711	B	951 340-9685	1093
Le Elegant Bath Inc	3088	C	951 734-0238	5534
Leepers Wood Turning Co Inc **(PA)**	2431	E	562 422-6525	3262
Lejon of California Inc	2387	E	951 736-1229	3061
LMS Reinforcing Steel Usa LP **(PA)**	3449	E	604 598-9930	7024
Lock America Inc	3429	F	951 277-5180	6525
Lowes Home Centers LLC	5031	C	951 256-9004	13251
Lucas Oil Products Inc **(PA)**	5169	C	951 270-0154	14786
M & O Perry Industries Inc	3565	E	951 734-9838	8073
M E Nollkamper Inc **(PA)**	8742	E	951 737-9300	23264
Magnetics Test Lab Inc	5063	F	951 270-0215	13642
Management Trust Assn Inc	6733	D	951 694-1758	16188
Marie Cllender Wholesalers Inc	5142	A	951 737-6760	14528
Maruhachi Ceramics America Inc	3259	E	800 736-6221	5990
Master Fab Inc	3444	F	951 277-4772	6869
MCP Industries Inc **(PA)**	3069	E	951 736-1881	5391
MD Engineering Inc	3599	E	951 736-5390	8684
Meridian Moulding Inc	5099	F	951 279-5220	14169
Merit Aluminum Inc **(PA)**	3354	C	951 735-1770	6312
Merrick Engineering Inc **(PA)**	3089	C	951 737-6040	5708
Michael D Molinari MD Facg Inc	8011	F	951 734-9930	19978
Millworx Prcsion Machining Inc	3599	E	951 371-2683	8699
Minka Lighting Inc **(PA)**	5063	D	951 735-9220	13648
Mission Ambulance Inc	4119	D	951 272-2300	11881
Mission Rubber Company LLC **(HQ)**	5085	C	951 736-1313	14005
Mj Diaz Backhoe Service Inc	3531	F	951 496-4949	7647
Monster Beverage Company	2086	E	866 322-4466	2271
Monster Beverage Corporation **(PA)**	2086	A	951 739-6200	2272
Monster Energy Company **(HQ)**	5149	A	951 739-6200	14710
Motor Technology Inc	3621	D	951 270-6200	8924
MS Industrial Shtmtl Inc	1761	C	951 272-6610	1498
Multi Mechanical Inc	1711	D	714 632-7404	1105
Multimedia Led Inc **(PA)**	3679	F	951 280-7500	9753
Navcom Defense Electronics Inc **(PA)**	3812	E	951 268-9205	10604
Nmsp Inc	3714	E	951 734-2453	10110
Northwestern Converting Co	2392	D	800 959-3402	3109
NP Mechanical Inc	1711	B	951 667-4220	1109
Nucast Industries Inc	3272	D	951 277-8888	6043
Nuvia Water Technologies Inc	7389	D	951 734-7400	18616
Oak-It Inc	2431	F	951 735-5973	3276
Omni Connection Intl Inc	3679	B	951 898-6232	9760
Optimum Bioenergy Intl Corp	2833	F	714 903-8872	4757
Pacific Packaging McHy LLC	3556	E	951 393-2200	7947
Pacific Utlity Instllation Inc	1731	D	714 970-6430	1291
Pacwest Instrument Labs Inc	7699	D	951 737-0790	19054
Panel Shop Inc	3613	E	951 739-7000	8902
Panrosa Enterprises Inc	2841	D	951 339-5888	4945
Peabody Engineering & Sup Inc	3559	E	951 734-7711	7993
Peoples Choice Staffing Inc	7361	D	951 735-0550	17444
Peppermint Ridge **(PA)**	8361	D	951 273-7320	22143
Pet Partners Inc **(PA)**	3999	C	951 279-9888	11734
Plas-Tech Sealing Tech LLC	2891	F	951 737-2228	5190
Playmax Surfacing Inc	3069	F	951 250-6039	5398
Pole Position Raceway Inc **(PA)**	7948	D	951 817-5032	19434
Precise Aerospace Mfg Inc	3089	E	951 898-0500	5772
Premier Gear & Machining Inc	3462	E	951 278-5505	7095
Premier Steel Structures Inc	3441	E	951 356-6655	6653
Preproduction Plastics Inc	3089	E	951 340-9680	5775
Price Manufacturing Co Inc	3451	E	951 371-5660	7042
Primary Provider MGT Co Inc **(PA)**	8741	D	951 280-7700	23089
Primecare Moreno Valley Inc	8011	D	951 371-8440	20027
Pro Building Maintenance Inc	7349	C	951 279-3386	17277
Pro Circuit Products Inc **(PA)**	3751	E	951 738-8050	10499
Pro Group Inc	6531	C	951 271-3000	15955
Proformance Manufacturing Inc	3469	E	951 279-1230	7177
Programmed Composites Inc	3728	C	951 520-7300	10396
Promach Filling Systems LLC	3823	E	951 393-2200	10712
PSW Inc	2099	F	951 371-7100	2511
Purosil LLC **(HQ)**	2822	C	951 271-3900	4732
PVA Tepla America Inc **(HQ)**	3599	E	951 371-2500	8750
Quikrete California LLC	3272	C	951 277-3155	6053
R & A Technical Inc	3556	F	951 549-6945	7949
R & J Fabricators Inc	2599	E	951 817-0300	3738
R & J Material Handling Inc	5084	F	951 735-0000	13932
R&M Deese Inc	3993	E	951 734-7342	11585
Ranch House Doors Inc	1751	D	951 278-2884	1452
Ravlich Enterprises LLC **(PA)**	3471	E	714 964-8900	7304
Republic Bag Inc **(PA)**	2673	D	951 734-9740	3889
RGF Enterprises Inc	3479	E	951 734-6922	7406
Richards Neon Shop Inc	3993	E	951 279-6767	11586

Mergent email: customerrelations@mergent.com
1354

2022 Southern California Business
Directory and Buyers Guide

(P-0000) Products & Services Section entry number
(PA)=Parent Co (HQ)=Headquarters (DH)=Div Headquarters

GEOGRAPHIC SECTION

COSTA MESA, CA

	SIC	EMP	PHONE	ENTRY #
Robertsons Rdymx Ltd A Cal Ltd **(HQ)**	3273	D	951 493-6500	6108
Robertsons Rdymx Ltd A Cal Ltd	3273	D	800 834-7557	6109
Rock Structures-Rip Rap	3296	E	951 371-1112	6172
Roto Power Inc	3089	F	951 751-9850	5803
Rubicon Gear Inc	3462	D	951 356-3800	7097
Rugby Laboratories Inc **(DH)**	5122	D	951 270-1400	14286
Saleen Automotive Inc **(PA)**	3465	E	800 888-8945	7113
Saleen Incorporated **(PA)**	3711	C	714 400-2121	9964
Sas Manufacturing Inc	3679	E	951 734-1808	9778
SCR Molding Inc	3089	E	951 736-5490	5815
Shim-It Corporation	3728	F	951 734-8300	10417
Smart Energy Solar Inc	1711	C	800 405-1978	1140
So Cal Sandbags Inc	5085	D	951 277-3404	14018
Southwest Con Structures Inc	1611	D	951 278-0377	917
Spangler Industries Inc	3069	C	951 735-5000	5413
Spectra Color Inc	2816	E	951 277-0200	4646
Spenuzza Inc **(HQ)**	3589	C	951 281-1830	8417
Sprint Communications Co LP	5065	C	951 340-1924	13776
Sprite Industries Incorporated	3826	E	951 735-1015	10814
Sream Inc	3231	E	951 245-6999	5969
St Joseph Health Per Care Svcs	8082	D	800 365-1110	21215
Stang Industries Inc	3999	F	714 556-0222	11760
Steel-Tech Industrial Corp	3441	E	951 270-0144	6666
Sterno LLC **(DH)**	3589	E	800 669-6699	8418
Sterno Group Companies LLC **(HQ)**	3589	E	951 682-9600	8419
Sternocandlelamp Holdings Inc	6211	A	951 682-9600	15306
Steven Engineering Inc	8711	E	650 588-9200	22661
Sun Precision Machining Inc	3599	F	951 817-0056	8804
Sun Rich Fresh Foods USA Inc **(PA)**	0723	C	951 735-3800	187
Superior Construction Inc	1521	D	951 808-8780	643
Superior Paving Company Inc	1611	D	951 739-9200	920
Superior Ready Mix Concrete LP	3273	D	951 277-3553	6121
Suss McRtec Phtnic Systems Inc	3699	D	951 817-3700	9919
Suss Microtec Inc **(HQ)**	3559	C	408 940-0300	7996
T Hasegawa USA Inc	2099	D	951 264-1121	2531
T-Rex Truck Products Inc	3465	D	800 287-5900	7114
T3 Motion Inc	3751	E	951 737-7300	10503
T3 Motion Inc	3751	E	909 737-7300	10504
Talco Plastics Inc **(PA)**	4953	D	951 531-2000	12985
Tamshell Corp	3089	D	951 272-9395	5835
Taylor Communications Inc	2761	F	951 203-9011	4600
Team Dykspra **(PA)**	7542	D	951 898-6482	18917
Technical America Inc	8711	D	951 272-9540	22665
Technicote Inc	2891	E	951 372-0627	5199
Temeka Advertising Inc	2541	D	951 277-2525	3669
Temps Plus Inc	7361	D	951 549-8309	17473
Thalasinos Enterprises Inc	5085	E	951 340-0911	14024
Thermal Structures Inc **(DH)**	3724	B	951 736-9911	10226
Thermal Structures Inc	3724	E	951 256-8051	10227
Thoro—Packaging **(DH)**	5199	C	951 278-2100	14979
Thyde Inc **(PA)**	7389	C	951 817-2300	18691
Tiffany Coachworks Inc	3711	F	951 657-2680	9969
TNT Plastic Molding Inc **(PA)**	3089	C	951 808-9700	5839
Tolar Manufacturing Co Inc	3441	E	951 808-0081	6672
Tradenet Enterprise Inc	3993	D	888 595-3956	11612
Tree House Pad & Paper Inc	2678	D	800 213-4184	3918
Trical Inc	2879	E	951 737-6960	5174
Trimedyne Inc **(PA)**	3845	F	949 951-3800	11242
TRM Manufacturing Inc	3081	C	951 256-8550	5440
Troy Lee Designs LLC **(PA)**	5091	D	951 371-5219	14089
Tube Technologies Inc	3714	E	951 371-4878	10144
Two Brothers Racing Inc	3751	F	714 550-6070	10507
TWR Enterprises Inc	1751	C	951 279-2000	1460
Uhs-Corona Inc **(HQ)**	8062	A	951 737-4343	20987
Uhs-Corona Inc	8093	C	951 736-7200	21359
United Metal Products Inc	3399	F	951 739-9535	6463
Uniweb Inc **(PA)**	2542	D	951 279-7999	3700
US Continental Marketing Inc **(PA)**	2842	D	951 808-8888	4982
US Display Group Inc	2653	E	951 444-4567	3830
Vanguard Hospice Care Inc **(PA)**	6722	D	951 371-5681	16147
Vantage Vehicle Intl Inc	3694	E	951 735-1200	9831
Veg-Fresh Farms LLC	5148	C	800 422-5535	14662
Vinylvisions Company LLC	2851	E	800 321-8746	5118
VIP Transport Inc	4213	E	951 272-3700	12091
Vitas Healthcare Corporation	8052	D	858 805-6254	20546
Vizualogic LLC	3559	C	407 509-3421	8000
Volt Telecom Group Inc	8748	B	951 493-8900	23524
Volvo Construction Eqp & Svcs	3531	E	951 277-7620	7658
Vons Companies Inc	2051	D	951 278-8284	2047
W J Ellison Co Inc	3565	E	626 814-4766	8081
Waste Management Cal Inc	4953	C	951 277-1740	12996
Wellington Foods Inc	2099	E	562 989-0111	2547
Werner Corporation	3273	E	951 277-4586	6127
West Hills Construction Inc	1541	E	800 515-5270	727
Westech Products Inc	3952	E	951 279-4496	11470
Western Equipment Mfg Inc	3531	E	951 284-2000	7659
Western Sheet Metals Inc	3444	E	951 272-3600	6942
Western Staffing Solutions LLC	7361	C	951 545-4449	17478
Westrock Cp LLC	2752	D	951 273-7900	4459
Winbo Usa Inc	3444	E	951 738-9978	6944
Wurms Janitorial Service Inc	7349	D	951 582-0003	17301
X-Act Finish & Trim Inc	1751	D	951 582-9229	1465
Youcare Pharma (usa) Inc	2834	D	951 258-3114	4915

CORONA DEL MAR, CA - Orange County

	SIC	EMP	PHONE	ENTRY #
Balboa Yacht Club	7997	E	949 673-3515	19537
Broker Solutions Inc	6162	D	800 450-2010	15177
Ecc Capital Corporation **(PA)**	6162	A	949 954-7060	15188
Newport Mesa Unified Schl Dst	8351	D	949 515-6940	22042
Smart & Final Stores Inc	5141	C	949 675-2396	14488
University California Irvine	8011	C	949 644-5245	20124

COSTA MESA, CA - Orange County

	SIC	EMP	PHONE	ENTRY #
4 Gen Digital	2752	F	714 486-1150	4221
ABC Bus Inc	5012	D	714 444-5888	13017
Accredited Nursing Services	8082	C	714 973-1234	21126
Accumedical USA Inc	3841	F	714 929-1020	10924
Adaptive Shelters LLC	2452	E	949 923-5444	3426
Adopt-A-Highway Maintenance	1611	C	800 200-0003	852
Advanced Conservation Technolo	3433	F	714 668-1200	6567
Advanced Micro Instruments Inc	3826	E	714 848-5533	10777
Agility Powertrain Systems LLC **(DH)**	5013	B	949 236-5520	13040
All-Rite Leasing Company Inc	7349	B	714 957-1822	17213
Altametrics Hosting LLC	5045	C	800 676-1281	13373
Amen Clinics Inc A Med Corp **(PA)**	8011	D	888 564-2700	19706
Andersen Tax LLC	7291	D	949 885-4550	16934
Andrew L Youngquist Cnstr Inc	1542	D	949 862-5611	736
ARC **(PA)**	7334	E	714 424-8500	17145
Arnel Commercial Properties **(PA)**	6513	C	714 481-5023	15719
Arnel Development Company **(PA)**	1542	D	714 481-5000	738
Asana Recovery	8093	E	702 786-2396	21275
Aspen Brands Corporation	2511	F	702 946-9430	3462
Associated Microbreweries Inc	2082	D	714 546-2739	2137
Astro Haven Enterprises Inc	3829	F	949 215-3777	10870
Auto Club Enterprises **(PA)**	6321	A	714 850-5111	15377
Auto Club Enterprises	2721	C	714 885-2376	4053
Automobile Club Southern Cal	6411	D	213 741-3686	15541
Automobile Club Southern Cal	6411	C	714 885-1343	15543
Ayres Group **(PA)**	7011	B	714 540-6060	16333
Baier Marine Company Inc	3429	E	800 455-3917	6505
Baker & Hostetler LLP	8111	D	714 754-6600	21508
Balboa Capital Corporation **(PA)**	6153	C	949 756-0800	15150
Balboa Water Group LLC **(HQ)**	3625	B	714 384-0384	8944
Barto Signal Petroleum Inc	1389	F	949 631-8066	479
Bay Ornamental Iron Inc	3446	E	949 548-1015	6952
Bdfco Inc	3669	D	714 228-2900	9333
Benq America Corp **(HQ)**	5045	D	714 559-4900	13380
Bio Creative Enterprises	2844	F	714 352-3600	4992
Boyd & Associates	7381	C	714 835-5423	18256
Brand Amp LLC	8743	D	949 438-1060	23376
Brookfeld Sthland Holdings LLC	1521	C	714 427-6868	595
California Ticketscom Inc **(DH)**	7922	C	714 327-5400	19305
Captive-Aire Systems Inc	3444	E	714 957-1500	6804
Cardflex Inc	7389	D	714 361-1900	18468
Casanova Pndrill Pblicidad Inc **(PA)**	7311	D	949 474-5001	16998
CCI Industries Inc **(PA)**	3089	E	714 662-3879	5602
Center Club	8641	D	714 662-3414	22324
Cevians LLC	3211	D	714 619-5135	5917
Cfbtel	3661	F	949 381-2525	9229
Champions Bowling & Embroidery	7933	F	714 968-5033	19396
Chargers Football Company LLC **(PA)**	7941	D	619 280-2121	19413
Chet Cooper	2721	F	949 854-8700	4058
Chup Corporation	2752	F	949 455-0676	4252
Coach Inc	3171	F	949 365-0771	5899
Coast Sheet Metal Inc	3444	E	949 645-2224	6809
Competent Care Inc	8082	D	714 545-4818	21153
Concept Studio Inc	3253	F	949 759-0606	5985
Contech Engnered Solutions Inc	3317	D	714 281-7883	6246
Cooksey Tlen Gage Dffy Woog A **(PA)**	8111	D	714 431-1100	21537
Cornell Ptrson Arospc Tech LLC	3672	F	714 656-5376	9395
County of Orange	4581	C	949 252-5006	12353
Creative Design Consultants **(PA)**	7389	D	714 641-4868	18496
Crescent Healthcare Inc	8082	D	949 646-2267	21156
Crisp Enterprises Inc **(PA)**	7334	D	714 668-5955	17147
Crystaliner Corp	3732	F	949 548-0292	10462
Cytec Aerospace Mtls CA Inc	2295	C	714 899-0400	2707
Darcy AK Corporation	3599	F	949 650-5566	8568
Delphi Display Systems Inc	3577	D	714 825-3400	8250
Developmental Svcs Cal Dept	8331	B	714 957-5151	21949
Donahue Schrber Rlty Group Inc **(PA)**	6531	D	714 545-1400	15840
Donahue Schriber Rlty Group LP **(PA)**	6512	D	714 545-1400	15665
Ds Lakeshore LP	8641	D	916 286-5231	22336
Durrani Investments Corp	5169	E	424 292-3424	14778
Dynamic Cooking Systems Inc	3589	A	714 372-7000	8379
EBA & M Corporation **(PA)**	6324	D	714 668-8920	15396
Edwards Theatres Circuit Inc	7832	C	714 428-0962	19273
El Metate Inc	2051	C	949 646-9362	1997
El Pollo Loco Holdings Inc **(PA)**	6794	C	714 599-5000	16206
Elesco	5063	E	714 673-6600	13626
Empire Leasing Inc	1751	D	949 646-7400	1434
Ensign Group Inc	8051	D	949 642-0387	20327
Ev Infrastructure LLC	1731	E	714 908-5266	1251
Eventure Interactive Inc	7372	F	855 986-5669	17850
Experian Holdings Inc **(DH)**	7323	C	714 830-7000	17123
Experian Info Solutions Inc **(DH)**	7323	A	714 830-7000	17124
Experian Mktg Solutions LLC	7323	A	714 830-7000	17125
Eyebrain Medical Inc **(PA)**	3851	F	949 339-5157	11252
EZ Lube LLC	7549	D	714 966-1647	18932
Falkor Partners LLC	3674	E	714 721-8772	9508
Fgr 1 LLC	7372	E	800 653-3517	17855
Fineline Woodworking Inc	2431	D	714 540-5468	3249
Fire and Safety Elec Inc	3625	F	714 850-1320	8952
Fisher & Paykel Appliances Inc **(DH)**	3639	C	949 790-8900	9014
Fisker Auto & Tech Group LLC	3711	C	714 723-3247	9946
Flare Group	3728	E	714 850-2080	10327
Flat White Economy Inv USA LLC	4953	C	949 344-5013	12951

GEOGRAPHIC

Employment Codes: A=Over 500 employees, B=251-500, C=101-250, D=51-100, E=20-50 F=10-19

2022 Southern California Business Directory and Buyers Guide

© Mergent Inc. 1-800-342-5647

1355

Company	SIC	EMP	PHONE	ENTRY #
Flora Gold LLC	3999	F	949 252-1122	11669
Food Sales West Inc (PA)	5141	D	714 966-2900	14466
Fox Rent A Car Inc	7514	D	310 342-5155	18740
Fxc Corporation	2399	D	714 557-8032	3197
Fxc Corporation (PA)	3429	E	714 556-7400	6518
Grand Prix Road Trends Inc (PA)	3312	E	949 645-7022	6202
GSP Precision Inc	3599	E	818 845-2212	8611
Hanford Hotels Inc	7011	C	714 557-3000	16462
Hanley Wood Mkt Intelligence (HQ)	8732	C	714 540-8500	22882
Hartley Company	3951	E	949 646-9643	11464
Hexagon Agility Inc	1321	F	949 236-5520	420
Hospice Touch Inc (PA)	8082	C	714 327-1936	21171
Hst Lessee South Coast LP	7011	D	714 540-2500	16494
Human Options Inc	8322	E	949 757-3635	21806
Hurley International LLC (PA)	2329	C	949 548-9375	2813
Husky Injction Mlding Systems	3089	D	714 545-8200	5669
Hykso Inc	8742	D	213 785-3372	23238
I D Brand LLC	2396	F	949 422-7057	3175
I O Interconnect Ltd (PA)	3678	E	714 564-1111	9656
ID Supply	2759	E	714 728-6478	4526
Impac Technologies Inc	3663	E	714 427-2000	9278
Innovative Cnstr Solutions	8744	C	714 893-6366	23394
Insight Investments LLC (DH)	7377	D	714 939-2300	18140
Inveco Inc	3471	E	949 378-3850	7271
Irvine Sensors Corporation	3674	E	714 444-8700	9524
Jds Hospitality Group	7011	E	949 631-6000	16512
JG Plastics Group LLC	3089	E	714 751-4266	5684
L & L Custom Shutters Inc	2431	F	714 996-9539	3260
Lambda Research Optics Inc	3826	E	714 327-0600	10799
Laurus Construction Corp	1542	E	714 641-0318	781
Lava Products Inc	2752	E	949 951-7191	4353
Lexmark International Inc	3577	E	714 641-1007	8274
Locale Lifestyle Magazine LLC	2721	E	949 436-8910	4082
Lombardy Holdings Inc (PA)	1623	C	951 808-4550	961
Lspace America LLC	2331	E	949 596-8726	2857
Macgregor Yacht Corporation	3732	E	310 621-2206	10467
Magnesium International Inc (PA)	3356	F	808 741-9712	6334
Manatt Phelps & Phillips LLP	8111	D	714 371-2500	21621
Maurer Marine Inc	3732	F	949 645-7673	10468
Medical Eye Services Inc	6411	D	714 619-4660	15594
Membrane Switch and Panel Inc	3679	E	714 957-6905	9747
Merrill Lynch Prce Fnner Smith	6211	D	714 429-2800	15278
Mesa Cnsld Wtr Dst Imprv Corp (PA)	4941	C	949 631-1200	12906
Mesa Verde Country Club	7997	C	714 549-0377	19586
Mesa Verde Partners	7992	C	714 540-7500	19500
Mesa Vrde Cnvalescent Hosp Inc	8051	C	949 548-5584	20417
Metal X Direct Inc	3446	F	949 336-0055	6975
Metropolitan Home Mortgage Inc	6162	D	949 428-0161	15214
Metropro Road Services Inc (PA)	7549	D	714 556-7600	18938
Mirth Corporation	7372	D	714 389-1200	17918
Mitsubishi Materials USA Corp (HQ)	5084	E	714 352-6100	13920
Mitsuwa Corporation	5139	C	714 557-6699	14441
Moffatt & Nichol	8711	D	657 261-2699	22617
Moleculum	2911	F	714 619-5139	5255
National Appraisal Guides Inc	2741	C	714 556-8511	4189
National Safety Services	8748	E	714 679-9118	23480
Nds Americas Inc (DH)	4841	D	714 434-2100	12774
Newman Garrison + Partners Inc	8712	E	949 756-0818	22735
Newport Medical Instrs Inc	3841	B	949 642-3910	11034
Newport Mesa Inn LLC	7011	D	949 650-3020	16582
Newport Mesa Unified Schl Dst	8099	D	714 424-5090	21460
Newport Mesa Usd Campus C	2752	F	714 424-8939	4379
Newport Sbacute Healthcare Ctr	8051	D	949 631-4282	20424
Nils Inc (PA)	2339	F	714 755-1600	2977
Nitro Circus Live Usa Inc	7997	D	760 231-1840	19593
North American Acceptance Corp	6141	C	714 868-3195	15147
Nwp Services Corporation (DH)	7372	C	949 253-2500	17939
Ocfit Lb LLC (DH)	7991	D	949 701-7702	19463
One Town Center Associates LLC	6512	E	714 435-2100	15685
Orange Coast Reprographics Inc	2752	E	949 548-5571	4383
Orange County Plst Co Inc	1742	C	714 957-1971	1389
Pacific Building Care Inc (PA)	7349	B	949 261-1234	17268
Pacific Mercantile Bank (HQ)	6022	E	714 438-2500	15035
Payoff Inc	6141	D	949 430-0630	15148
PDC Capital Group LLC	6552	D	866 500-8550	16068
Petra Geotechnical Inc (PA)	8711	D	714 549-8921	22636
PH Corporation	5063	F	949 646-7775	13659
Phelps United LLC	5045	D	657 212-8050	13427
Phillps-Mdisize Costa Mesa LLC	3841	C	949 477-9495	11044
Piecemakers Inc	5131	E	714 641-3112	14314
Pinecraft Custom Shutters Inc	2431	F	949 642-9317	3281
Pivot Interiors Inc	1731	D	949 988-5400	1296
Plastoker Inc	3089	F	949 598-5920	5761
Plexicor Inc (PA)	7382	E	714 918-8700	18395
Pmd Industries Inc	1731	E	949 222-0999	1297
Pro-Lite Inc	3993	F	714 668-9988	11583
Profit Recovery Partners LLC	8748	D	949 851-2777	23496
Project Independence (PA)	8361	D	714 549-3464	22146
Qsc LLC (PA)	3651	B	800 854-4079	9186
Quilter Laboratories LLC	3931	F	714 519-6114	11348
Railmakers Inc	3441	F	949 642-6506	6658
Recruit 360	7361	C	949 250-4420	17456
Resinart Corporation	3089	E	949 642-3665	5793
Rosanna Inc	7011	E	714 751-5000	16671
S E P E Inc	3571	E	714 241-7373	8174
S J Amoroso Cnstr Co LLC	1542	D	650 654-1900	818
Saddleback Educational Inc	2731	F	714 640-5200	4136
Sanmina Corporation	3672	C	714 913-2200	9451
Savedailycom Inc (HQ)	7373	D	562 795-7500	18063
Schneider Electric	3699	F	949 713-9200	9911
Seattle Tnnel Prtners A Jint V	1521	B	206 971-8701	639
Secured Funding Corporation	6163	A	714 689-6749	15252
Sellers Optical Inc	3827	D	949 631-6800	10860
Semicoa Corporation	3674	D	714 979-1900	9569
Silverado Senior Living Inc	8051	D	949 945-0189	20471
Simple Science Inc	7389	E	949 335-1099	18667
Simply Straws LLC	3229	F	855 787-2974	5942
Site Crew Inc	7349	B	714 668-0100	17284
Snell & Wilmer LLP	8111	D	714 427-7000	21680
Software Management Cons Inc	7371	C	714 662-1841	17719
South Coast Plaza LLC (PA)	6512	D	714 546-0110	15700
South Coast Plaza LLC	6512	D	714 435-2000	15701
South Coast Plaza Security	8741	C	714 435-2180	23113
South Coast Repertory Inc	7922	D	714 708-5500	19332
South Coast Westin Hotel Co	7011	D	714 540-2500	16720
Southern California Mar Assn	7538	D	714 850-4004	18875
Star Pro Security Patrol Inc	7381	C	714 617-5056	18342
State Hospitals Cal Dept	8063	B	714 957-5000	21027
Sunburst Products Inc	3873	E	949 722-0150	11303
Sweden & Martina Inc	3841	C	844 862-7846	11061
Swiss Wire EDM	3599	F	714 540-2903	8807
T Boyer Company	1731	E	949 642-2431	1325
Taylor Communications Inc	2761	F	714 708-2005	4601
Team Garage LLC	7311	D	714 913-9900	17061
Theodore Robins Inc	5012	D	949 642-0015	13036
Ticketscom LLC (DH)	7922	C	714 327-5400	19336
Tk Carsites Inc	7371	D	714 937-1229	17737
Tk Pax Inc	3052	E	714 850-1330	5324
Touchtone Corporation	7371	E	714 755-2810	17739
Trigild International Inc	7011	D	949 645-2221	16757
Unity Sales International Inc	3861	E	714 800-1700	11296
University California Irvine	8011	C	949 646-2267	20125
US Hotel and Resort MGT Inc	7011	C	949 650-2938	16765
Uvnv Inc (PA)	4813	C	888 777-0446	12677
Vanguard Univ Southern Cal	8699	C	714 556-3610	22467
Vans Inc (DH)	3021	B	714 755-4000	5319
Variations In Stone Inc	1741	D	949 438-8537	1355
Veritone Inc (PA)	7374	D	888 507-1737	18115
Villa Venetia	6163	B	714 540-1800	15260
Viva America Marketing Inc (PA)	8742	C	949 645-6100	23361
Viva Life Science Inc	5122	C	949 645-6100	14296
Volcom LLC (HQ)	7389	C	949 646-2175	18719
Vu Holdings LLC	8099	C	661 808-4004	21497
Walin Group Inc	3569	F	714 444-5980	8141
Warmington Homes (PA)	1531	C	714 434-4435	684
Warmington Residential Cal Inc	1521	C	714 557-5511	650
West Newport Oil Company	1311	E	949 631-1100	416
Westar Nutrition Corp (PA)	2833	C	949 645-6100	4469
Woodruff Spradlin & Smart	8111	D	714 558-7000	21701

COVINA, CA - Los Angeles County

Company	SIC	EMP	PHONE	ENTRY #
A-1 Event & Party Rentals	7299	D	626 967-0500	16941
Altamed Health Services Corp	6321	C	626 214-1480	15375
American Scale Co Inc	5045	E	800 773-7225	13375
Anvil Cases Inc	3161	C	626 968-4100	5888
Apricot Designs Inc	3841	D	626 966-3299	10940
AR Industries	3999	F	626 332-8918	11631
Aubrey Industries	3646	F	626 261-4242	9079
Azusa Engineering Inc	3714	C	626 966-4071	10021
Baltazar Construction Inc	1771	C	626 339-8620	1514
Bowlero Corp	7933	D	626 339-1286	19387
Briteworks Inc	7349	C	626 337-0099	17220
Caco-Pacific Corporation (PA)	3544	C	626 331-3361	7784
Cal Empire Engineering Inc	1795	D	626 915-8030	1610
Charter Bhvral Hlth Sys S C/Ch	8063	C	626 966-1632	21017
Chemeor Inc	2843	E	626 966-3808	4983
Citrus Vly Hlth Partners Inc	8099	B	626 732-3100	21398
Cobel Technologies Inc	3613	F	626 332-2100	8890
Composites Horizons LLC (DH)	3728	C	626 331-0861	10302
Covina Rehabilitation Center	8051	C	626 967-3874	20306
Cozzia USA LLC (HQ)	3699	F	626 667-2272	9863
Cwf Inc	7359	D	626 967-0500	17344
Dauntless Industries Inc	3544	E	626 966-4494	7794
Davita Magan Management Inc (DH)	8011	C	626 331-6411	19781
Emanate Health Medical Center	8062	A	626 858-8515	20765
Emanate Health Medical Center	8062	A	626 331-7331	20767
Emanate Health Medical Group (PA)	8062	A	626 331-7331	20768
Haemonetics Manufacturing Inc (HQ)	3841	C	626 339-7388	10986
Jf Ready Mix Inc	3273	C	626 818-1204	6097
LAg and Associates LLC	7389	D	909 242-4394	18570
Los Angeles Engineering Inc	8711	C	626 869-1400	22602
Matrix Document Imaging Inc	2759	C	626 966-9959	4543
Monkee Inc	7389	E	626 848-1555	18603
Monterey Machine Products	3599	F	626 967-2242	8708
Moores Ideal Products LLC	3944	E	626 339-9007	11385
Payne Magnetics Inc	3677	D	626 332-6207	9637
Processors Mailing Inc	2752	E	626 358-5600	4408
R M Baker Machine and TI Inc	3599	F	562 697-4007	8755
Radnoti Glass Technology Inc	8731	F	626 357-8827	22860
RG Costumes & Accessories Inc	2389	E	626 858-9559	3083
Rowland Convalescent Hosp Inc	8051	D	626 967-2741	20452
RSR Metal Spinning Inc	3469	F	626 814-2339	7179
Shift Calendars Inc	2752	F	626 967-5862	4422
Sprint Communications Co LP	7375	C	626 339-0430	18133
Stabile Plating Company Inc	3471	E	626 339-9091	7314

	SIC	EMP	PHONE	ENTRY #
Stavros Enterprises Inc	7699	E	888 463-2293	19070
Supermedia LLC	2741	B	626 331-9440	4209
Think Together	8351	A	626 373-2311	22066
Topper Plastics Inc	3086	F	626 331-0561	5525
TT Elctrnics Pwr Sltons US Inc	3679	C	626 967-6021	9800
Verizon Communications Inc	4812	D	626 858-1739	12616
Westrock Rkt Company	2653	C	626 859-7633	3832
Wood Castle Construction Inc	1521	E	626 966-8600	653
Zenith American Solutions Inc	7389	C	626 732-2100	18733

CRESTON, CA - San Luis Obispo County

	SIC	EMP	PHONE	ENTRY #
Margarita Vineyards LLC	2084	F	805 226-8600	2205

CUDAHY, CA - Los Angeles County

	SIC	EMP	PHONE	ENTRY #
All American Frame & Bedg Corp	2514	F	323 773-7415	3524
Consolidated Foundries Inc	3365	C	323 773-2363	6389
Dur-Red Products	3444	E	323 771-9000	6822
G E Shell Core Co	3544	E	323 773-4242	7802
Grace Machine Co Inc	3599	F	323 771-6215	8609
HF Cox Inc	4212	B	323 587-2359	11974
Kaiser Foundation Hospitals	8011	C	323 562-6400	19879
Kaiser Foundation Hospitals	8062	A	323 562-6400	20812
Merry An Cejka	3599	E	323 560-3949	8690
Mfb Worldwide Inc **(PA)**	2299	F	323 562-2339	2730
Myers Mixers LLC	3569	E	323 560-4723	8130
Pac Foundry Inc	3324	F	323 773-2363	6272
RAP Security Inc	2542	D	323 560-3493	3693
Southern Cal Prmnnte Med Group	8011	C	323 562-6459	20089
Super Center Concepts Inc	2052	C	323 562-8980	2074

CULVER CITY, CA - Los Angeles County

	SIC	EMP	PHONE	ENTRY #
24hr Homecare LLC	8082	D	310 258-9525	21117
A-1 Electric Service Co Inc	1731	E	310 204-1077	1204
Advanced Medical Reviews LLC	7363	D	310 575-0900	17484
Aegis SEC & Investigations Inc	7381	C	310 838-2787	18239
Allies For Every Child Inc	8351	D	310 846-4100	21982
Alpine Interiors Corporation **(PA)**	5023	E	310 390-7639	13156
Altor Bioscience LLC	8731	D	954 443-8600	22823
Anonymous Content LLC **(PA)**	7812	D	310 558-6000	19095
Apic Corporation	3674	D	310 642-7975	9482
Beats Electronics LLC **(PA)**	3679	F	424 268-3055	9681
Beats Electronics LLC	3651	B	424 326-4679	9162
Blind Decker Productions Inc **(PA)**	7812	D	310 264-4247	19101
Blur Studio Inc	7371	D	424 258-3145	17570
Borin Manufacturing Inc	3443	E	310 822-1000	6730
Brotman Medical Center Inc	8062	B	310 836-7000	20690
Cal Southern Graphics Corp **(PA)**	2752	D	310 559-3600	4245
Cambridge Equities LP	2836	E	858 350-2300	4933
Carbon 38 Inc	7389	D	888 723-5838	18467
Century Wilshire Inc	7011	D	310 558-9400	16375
Charles David of California **(PA)**	5139	D	310 348-5050	14432
City of Culver City	8611	D	310 253-6525	22246
City of Culver City	4131	E	310 253-6510	11903
Clay Designs Inc	3269	F	562 432-3991	6002
Clutter Inc **(PA)**	7299	C	800 805-4023	16951
Columbia Pictures Inds Inc **(DH)**	7812	C	310 244-4000	19109
Crp Centinela LP	7011	D	901 821-4117	16401
D K Fortune & Associates Inc	8059	C	310 391-7266	20577
Daring Foods Inc **(PA)**	5142	C	855 862-5825	14523
Davina Douthard Inc	8748	F	310 540-5120	23431
Didi Hirsch Psychiatric Svc **(PA)**	8322	C	310 390-6612	21769
Dneg North America Inc **(PA)**	7819	D	323 461-7887	19229
E & S Ring Management Corp	6531	C	310 670-5983	15843
Ecoly International Inc	2844	F	818 718-6982	5017
Econ-O-Plate Inc	2752	E	310 342-5900	4288
Exceptional Chld Foundation	8641	C	310 915-6606	22337
Exceptional Chld Foundation **(PA)**	8331	C	310 204-3300	21950
Exodus Recovery Inc **(PA)**	8093	C	310 945-3350	21305
Exodus Recovery Ctr At Brotman **(PA)**	8069	D	310 253-9494	21045
Farchitecture Bb LLC	2024	E	917 701-2777	1817
Fortune Casuals LLC **(PA)**	2331	D	310 733-2100	2843
Fulltone Musical Products Inc	3931	F	310 204-0155	11343
Funimation Global Group LLC **(DH)**	7812	C	972 355-7300	19128
Gebbs Healthcare Solutions **(HQ)**	8748	C	201 227-0088	23444
Genex **(HQ)**	7371	C	424 672-9500	17625
Given Imaging Los Angeles LLC	3845	C	310 641-8492	11223
GK Management Co Inc **(PA)**	6531	C	310 204-2050	15874
Globecast America Incorporated **(DH)**	4841	B	310 845-3900	12770
Goldrich & Kest Industries LLC **(PA)**	6552	A	310 204-2050	16051
Goldrichkest **(PA)**	6552	C	310 204-2050	16052
Grand Casino On Main Inc	2051	F	310 253-9066	2006
Harel General Contractors Inc	1542	E	310 558-8304	768
Hawkins Brown USA Inc	8712	B	310 600-2695	22719
Health and Happiness H&H Inc	2023	F	619 330-6030	1794
HI LLC	8732	D	757 655-4113	22883
Honeybee Health Inc **(PA)**	8099	C	310 559-5903	21438
I AM Beyond LLC	2339	F	310 882-6476	2952
Integrated Magnetics Inc	3621	E	310 391-7213	8919
Integrated Tech Group Inc **(PA)**	3499	C	310 391-7213	7559
Investment Tech Group Inc	6211	C	310 216-6777	15272
Ipsos Otx Corporation **(HQ)**	8732	C	310 736-3400	22889
Jam City Inc **(PA)**	7372	C	310 205-4800	17897
JC Promotions Inc	8742	F	310 870-1183	23249
Jeopardy Productions Inc	7812	C	310 244-8855	19136
Joico Laboratories Inc	2844	D	626 321-4100	5035
Kfa LLP	8712	D	310 399-7975	22726
Kovel/Fuller LLC	7311	D	310 841-4444	17028
Kpmg LLP	8721	D	703 286-8175	22798
L & A Care Corporation	8052	D	310 202-7693	20534
Liveoffice LLC	7372	D	877 253-2793	17906
LMS Corporation	7389	E	310 641-4222	18581
Loaded Boards Inc	3751	F	310 839-1800	10497
Magnet Sales & Mfg Co Inc **(HQ)**	3264	D	310 391-7213	5999
Maker Studios Inc **(DH)**	7929	C	310 606-2182	19369
Marycrest Manor	8059	C	310 838-2778	20612
Metric Products Inc **(PA)**	2342	E	310 815-9000	3021
Minton-Spidell Inc **(PA)**	2511	F	310 836-0403	3479
Mktg Inc	7389	A	310 972-7900	18598
Mme Florida LLC **(PA)**	7389	D	678 826-8622	18599
Moldex-Metric Inc	3842	B	310 837-6500	11126
Morphosis Architects	8712	D	310 453-2247	22733
Murphy & Beane Inc	8111	D	310 649-4470	21639
Mutesix Group Inc	7311	C	310 215-3467	17037
Mwla Inc	8351	D	310 841-2505	22041
Nantbioscience Inc	5047	D	310 883-1300	13503
Nantcell Inc	8731	D	562 397-3639	22853
Nantomics LLC **(PA)**	8734	D	310 883-1300	22954
Nantworks LLC **(PA)**	7373	C	310 883-1300	18049
New Milani Group LLC	5122	D	323 582-9404	14269
Nfl Properties LLC	7941	D	310 840-4635	19425
Nutrition Without Borders LLC	3581	F	310 845-7745	8322
Omelet LLC **(PA)**	7311	D	213 427-6400	17040
Orange County Services Inc **(PA)**	1711	D	310 515-1001	1112
Pacific Bell Telephone Company	4812	A	310 515-2898	12610
Pacific Piston Ring Co Inc	3592	D	310 836-3322	8433
Pacifica Ht Cnfrnce Ctr A Cal	7011	D	310 649-1776	16614
Packetfabric Inc	4813	D	844 475-8322	12662
Paige LLC **(HQ)**	2326	C	310 733-2100	2786
Parachute Home Inc	2392	C	310 903-0353	3114
Photonic Corp	2752	F	310 642-7975	4390
Property Management Assoc Inc **(PA)**	6531	C	323 295-2000	15961
Punch Studio LLC **(PA)**	5112	C	310 390-9900	14197
Quadra Productions Inc	7812	D	310 244-1234	19168
Rachlin Architects Inc	8712	D	310 204-3400	22737
Reading International Inc **(PA)**	7832	A	213 235-2240	19288
Redwood Wellness LLC	2299	E	323 843-2676	2737
Rick Solomon Enterprises Inc **(PA)**	5136	D	310 280-3700	14347
Say It With A Sock LLC **(PA)**	2252	E	424 284-8416	2623
Schwarzkopf Inc **(DH)**	3999	E	310 641-0990	11748
Science 37 Holdings Inc **(PA)**	8731	A	984 377-3737	22861
Scopely Inc **(PA)**	7372	C	323 400-6618	17977
Screen Gems Inc	7812	D	310 244-4000	19175
Security Indust Spcialists Inc **(PA)**	7381	A	310 215-5100	18328
Shlemmer Algaze Associates **(PA)**	8712	D	310 215-3991	22742
Signal Sciences Corp	7372	F	424 289-0342	17982
Social Studies School Service	5049	D	310 839-2436	13541
Sofie Biosciences Inc **(PA)**	8731	C	310 215-3159	22864
Sole Society Group Inc	3131	C	310 220-0808	5874
Sony Media Cloud Services LLC	7812	E	877 683-9124	19179
Sony Pctres HM Entrmt Online I **(DH)**	7812	C	310 244-4000	19180
Sony Pctres Wrldwide Acqstons	7812	D	310 244-4000	19181
Sony Pictures Entrmt Inc **(DH)**	7812	A	310 244-4000	19182
Sony Pictures Imageworks Inc	7374	A	310 840-8000	18111
Sony Pictures Television Inc **(DH)**	7812	B	310 244-7625	19183
Southern Cal Hlthcare Sys Inc	8062	D	310 836-7000	20943
Southern Cal Prmnnte Med Group	8011	C	310 737-4900	20083
Sportsrobe Inc	2329	E	310 559-3999	2824
Spotlite America Corporation **(PA)**	3229	E	310 829-0200	5943
Stan Tashman & Associates Inc	8741	D	310 460-7600	23117
Starwood Hotel	7011	C	310 641-7740	16730
Stateside Merchants LLC	2322	E	424 251-5190	2764
Steelhouse Inc	7311	C	310 773-3331	17058
Stories International Inc	2741	F	310 242-8409	4207
Talespin Reality Labs Inc **(PA)**	7371	D	323 452-6998	17730
Technclor Crative Svcs USA Inc	7819	E	323 467-1244	19249
Tiktok Inc **(DH)**	7371	C	844 523-3993	17736
Topson Downs California Inc **(PA)**	5136	C	310 558-0300	14355
Total Fincl & Insur Svcs Inc	6411	D	310 477-7500	15637
Tristar Television Music Inc	7922	E	310 244-4000	19338
Triton Media Group LLC	4832	C	661 294-9000	12707
Unfold Agency Inc **(PA)**	7311	D	323 963-3108	17065
Virgin Fish Inc **(PA)**	4119	C	310 391-6161	11896
West Publishing Corporation	2731	C	800 747-3161	4143
West Publishing Corporation	7373	C	424 243-2100	18074
Wongdoody Inc	7311	E	310 280-7800	17071
Woodbine Lgacy/Playa Owner LLC	7011	D	678 292-4962	16803
Wovexx Holdings Inc **(DH)**	4899	D	310 424-2080	12794
X Prize Foundation Inc	8733	E	310 741-4880	22926
Yogaworks Inc **(HQ)**	7999	D	310 664-6470	19682
Zambezi LLC	7319	D	310 450-6800	17103
Zoic Inc	7812	C	310 838-0770	19214

CUTLER, CA - Tulare County

	SIC	EMP	PHONE	ENTRY #
Penas Disposal Inc	4953	D	559 528-3909	12964
Wawona Packing Co LLC **(PA)**	5148	A	559 528-4000	14665

CYPRESS, CA - Orange County

	SIC	EMP	PHONE	ENTRY #
Advanex Americas Inc **(HQ)**	3495	C	714 995-4519	7481
Alltrade Tools LLC	5072	E	310 522-9008	13792
Applied Research Assoc Inc	8731	D	505 881-8074	22825
Atg - Designing Mobility Inc **(DH)**	5047	E	562 921-0258	13477
Awake Inc	2335	E	818 365-9361	2879
B2b Staffing Services Inc	7363	B	714 243-4104	17486
Cal Southern United Food	6371	C	714 220-2297	15514
Cavotec Dabico US Inc	3728	E	714 947-0005	10298
Cavotec Inet US Inc	3531	D	714 947-0005	7638

GEOGRAPHIC

Employment Codes: A=Over 500 employees, B=251-500, C=101-250, D=51-100, E=20-50 F=10-19
2022 Southern California Business Directory and Buyers Guide
© Mergent Inc. 1-800-342-5647
1357

	SIC	EMP	PHONE	ENTRY #
Cavotec US Holdings Inc **(HQ)**	3532	E	714 545-7900	7660
Christie Dgtal Systems USA Inc **(DH)**	5043	C	714 236-8610	13342
Christie Digital Systems Inc **(HQ)**	3861	C	714 236-8610	11270
Christie Medical Holdings Inc	3845	E	714 236-8610	11218
Community Media Corporation **(PA)**	2711	D	714 220-0292	3966
Consoldted Med Bo-Analysis Inc **(PA)**	8071	D	714 657-7369	21064
Contiki US Holdings Inc	4725	D	714 935-0808	12404
Creative Teaching Press Inc **(PA)**	2731	D	714 799-2100	4125
Daiwa Corporation	5091	D	562 375-6800	14075
Dameron Alloy Foundries **(PA)**	3325	D	310 631-5165	6275
DAndrea Graphic Corportion	7336	D	310 642-0260	17170
Dean Goodman Inc	6531	D	714 229-8999	15834
Diasorin Molecular LLC	2835	C	562 240-6500	4919
Drs Ntwork Imaging Systems LLC	3674	D	714 220-3800	9499
Easy Choice Health Plan Inc **(DH)**	6321	D	866 999-3945	15379
Exemplis LLC **(PA)**	2522	E	714 995-4800	3611
Focus Diagnostics Inc	8071	B	714 220-1900	21067
Focus Technologies Holding Co	8071	E	800 838-4548	21068
Glory Global Solutions Inc	7371	D	714 897-7545	17627
Healthcare Synergy Inc	7371	D	714 229-8700	17630
Healthsmart Management Service	6411	D	714 947-8600	15580
Hitachi Automotive Systems	3621	D	310 212-0200	8917
Hoyu America Co	5122	D	714 230-3000	14250
Hybrid Promotions LLC **(PA)**	5136	B	714 952-3866	14338
Interntional Tech Systems Corp	5065	E	714 761-8886	13732
J & F Machine Inc	3599	E	714 527-3499	8631
J Perez Associates Inc **(PA)**	1799	D	562 801-5397	1666
Kone Inc	7699	E	714 890-7080	19046
Kushco Holdings Inc **(PA)**	3089	D	714 462-4603	5693
Los Alamitos Race Course	7948	C	714 820-2800	19430
Lt Foods Americas Inc **(HQ)**	2041	D	562 340-4040	1946
Ltp Modern Machine Inc	7699	F	562 795-1701	19049
Luma Comfort LLC	3634	E	855 963-9247	9008
Magna Tool Inc	3599	E	714 826-2500	8674
Manhattan Beachwear Inc	2339	D	714 892-7354	2969
Manhattan Beachwear LLC **(PA)**	2369	D	657 384-2110	3043
Mercury Systems Inc	7374	D	714 898-8200	18100
Mission Microwave Tech LLC	3663	D	951 893-4925	9292
Mitsubishi Electric Us Inc **(DH)**	1796	C	714 220-2500	1625
Mitsubishi Motors Cr Amer Inc **(DH)**	6141	B	714 799-4730	15146
Mitsubshi Elc Vsual Sltons AME	3679	C	800 553-7278	9752
Multiquip Inc **(DH)**	5063	B	310 537-3700	13650
Mwb Copy Products Inc **(DH)**	5044	E	800 736-7979	13363
Natureware Inc	5122	D	714 251-4510	14268
New Air LLC	5064	E	657 257-4349	13690
Orbit Intl Inc	3679	E	909 468-5160	9763
Pacific Pioneer Insur Group **(PA)**	6411	D	714 228-7888	15608
Pacificare Health Systems LLC **(HQ)**	8082	A	714 952-1121	21197
Paradigm Contract Mfg LLC	3999	F	714 889-7074	11729
Paragon Partners Ltd **(PA)**	8748	D	714 379-3376	23491
Plumbing Piping & Cnstr Inc	1711	D	714 821-0490	1119
Power - Trim Co	3524	F	714 523-8560	7629
Power Maintenance Services Inc	1721	D	714 229-5900	1193
Primary Color Inc	7336	D	714 824-8930	17183
Primary Color Systems Corp **(PA)**	2752	B	949 660-7080	4394
Q-Tech Corporation	5065	C	310 836-7900	13763
Riphagen & Bullerdick Inc	6531	E	714 763-2100	15978
Safran Cabin Inc	3728	C	562 344-4780	10409
Scientfic Applctons RES Assoc **(PA)**	8731	D	714 224-4410	22862
Seabiscuit Motorsports Inc	3592	E	714 898-9763	8437
Shadow Industries Inc	3792	F	714 995-4353	10547
Simply Fresh LLC	2092	C	714 562-5000	2350
Sitonit Seating Inc	5021	A	714 995-4800	13152
Spectrum MGT Holdg Co LLC	4841	C	714 657-1060	12778
Speedo USA Inc	2329	B	657 465-3800	2823
Tad Pgs Inc	7363	A	571 451-2428	17518
Tayco Engineering Inc	3761	C	714 952-2240	10521
Toyo Tire Hldings Americas Inc **(HQ)**	3011	E	562 431-6502	5306
Tutor Time Learning Ctrs LLC	8351	C	714 484-1000	22071
Uhc of California **(DH)**	6324	A	714 952-1121	15462
Underwater Systems Inc	8711	F	714 229-9268	22681
United Chinese American Genera **(PA)**	6411	E	714 228-7800	15640
United Exchange Corp **(PA)**	7389	D	562 977-4500	18698
Ushio America Inc **(HQ)**	5063	D	714 236-8600	13672
Valueoptions of California	6411	C	800 228-1286	15644
Venus Laboratories Inc	2819	D	714 891-3100	4674
Wcct Global Inc **(PA)**	8733	C	714 668-1500	22925
Weldex Corporation **(PA)**	3674	B	714 761-2100	9605
Western Overseas Corporation **(PA)**	4731	E	562 985-0616	12551
WKS Frosty Corporation **(HQ)**	6794	D	562 425-1402	16222
WKS Restaurant Corporation **(PA)**	6794	A	562 425-1402	16223
Xperience Restaurant Group **(PA)**	8741	D	562 346-1200	23143
Yaesu Usa Inc	3663	E	714 827-7600	9330
Yamaha Motor Corporation USA **(HQ)**	5013	B	714 761-7300	13109

DAGGETT, CA - San Bernardino County

	SIC	EMP	PHONE	ENTRY #
NRG California South LP	4911	D	760 254-5241	12811
Rri Energy Coolwater Inc	4911	A	760 254-5290	12824

DANA POINT, CA - Orange County

	SIC	EMP	PHONE	ENTRY #
Circuit Automation Inc	3672	F	714 763-4180	9389
Ciri - Stroup Inc	7299	B	949 488-3104	16948
Cph Monarch Hotel LLC	7011	A	949 234-3200	16397
Ergs Aim Hotel Realty LLC	7011	D	949 661-1100	16436
Its All About Cake Inc	2051	F	949 240-7100	2008
Kanstul Musical Instrs Inc	3931	E	714 563-1000	11345
Monarch Beach Golf Links **(HQ)**	7992	D	949 240-8247	19502
Pacific Asian Enterprises Inc **(PA)**	7389	E	949 496-4848	18625
Prutel Joint Venture	7011	A	949 240-2000	16642
Ritz-Carlton Hotel Company LLC	7011	B	949 240-5020	16664
San Clemente Sportfishing Inc	7999	D	949 496-5794	19667
South Coast Water District	8742	D	949 499-4555	23330
South Orange County Ww Auth	2899	F	949 234-5400	5243
Sugared + Bronzed LLC **(PA)**	7299	D	410 493-3467	16980
Truthmd LLC	7379	D	949 637-4296	18229

DEATH VALLEY, CA - Inyo County

	SIC	EMP	PHONE	ENTRY #
Neg282 LLC	7011	B	760 786-2387	16577
Xanterra Parks & Resorts Inc	7011	C	760 786-2345	16807

DELANO, CA - Kern County

	SIC	EMP	PHONE	ENTRY #
Agri-Cel Inc	3086	E	661 792-2107	5485
Anthony Welded Products Inc **(PA)**	3537	E	661 721-7211	7705
Asv Wines Inc **(PA)**	2084	F	661 792-3159	2166
Ayo Foods LLC	2026	E	661 345-5457	1831
Castlerock Farms LLC	2084	E	661 721-1933	2173
City of Delano	3589	E	661 721-3352	8371
Crowne Cold Storage LLC	8742	E	661 725-6458	23201
Dan Tudor & Sons **(PA)**	0172	D	661 792-2933	44
Delano Dst Sklled Nrsing Fclty	8051	D	661 720-2100	20311
Delano Growers Grape Products	2087	D	661 725-3255	2319
Hronis Inc A California Corp **(PA)**	0174	C	661 725-2503	63
M Caratan Disc Inc	0172	C	661 725-2566	49
Maya Delano Cinemas Oper LLC	7832	E	213 805-5333	19284
Monarch Nut Company LLC	0723	C	661 725-6458	182
Mrv Service Air Inc	7623	F	661 725-3400	18948
Munger Bros LLC	0179	A	661 721-0390	71
North Kern S Tulare Hosp Dst	8062	C	661 720-2126	20870
Pandol & Sons	0172	D	661 725-3755	51
Randell Equipment & Mfg	3523	F	661 725-6380	7617
Styrotek Inc	3086	C	661 725-4957	5523
Triple R Transportation Inc	4119	D	661 725-6494	11893
Valley Strong Credit Union	6061	D	661 725-1014	15098
Wonderful Citrus Cooperative **(PA)**	0723	A	661 720-2400	192
Wonderful Citrus LLC **(HQ)**	0174	C	661 720-2400	66
Wonderful Citrus Packing LLC	2033	F	661 720-2400	1881
Wonderful Citrus Packing LLC **(HQ)**	0723	B	661 720-2400	193
Wonderful Company LLC	0174	B	661 720-2400	67

DESERT HOT SPRINGS, CA - Riverside County

	SIC	EMP	PHONE	ENTRY #
Back Support Systems Inc	3086	F	760 329-1472	5492
Desert Hot Sprng Real Prpts In	6512	D	760 329-6000	15664
Two Bunch Palms LLC **(PA)**	7011	C	760 329-8791	16759
Western Golf Car Mfg Inc	3949	D	760 671-6391	11460
Whatever It Takes Inc	7011	D	760 329-6000	16786

DIAMOND BAR, CA - Los Angeles County

	SIC	EMP	PHONE	ENTRY #
24-Hour Med Staffing Svcs LLC	7361	C	909 895-8960	17385
Bait Inc **(PA)**	5065	E	909 595-1712	13702
Burnaby Intl Tech Corp	5063	D	888 930-2090	13618
Cdnetworks Inc **(DH)**	4813	D	408 228-3379	12631
Central Health Plan Cal Inc	8082	C	626 938-7120	21147
Dynamic Woodworks Inc	2431	F	562 483-3400	3247
Ecmm Services Inc	3955	C	714 988-3388	11477
Fkc International Inc **(PA)**	8732	D	909 869-3000	22880
Garden Pals Inc	3423	E	909 605-0200	6481
Genius Products Nt Inc	2086	C	510 671-0219	2265
Gohz Inc	3621	E	800 603-1219	8914
Golden State Holdg Group Corp **(PA)**	4412	A	909 860-7668	12275
Graybar Electric Company Inc	5063	C	909 451-4300	13631
K2 Label & Printing Inc	2752	E	626 922-8108	4347
Kaiser Foundation Hospitals	8011	C	800 780-1277	19897
Liferay Inc **(PA)**	7373	C	877 543-3729	18043
Modrine Limited	7371	D	213 269-5466	17664
Mt Calvary Lthran Chrch-Mssuri	8351	D	909 861-2740	22040
Oak Creek LP	7011	D	909 860-5440	16587
Prime Wire & Cable Inc **(HQ)**	3357	C	888 445-9955	6355
Quarton Usa Inc	3699	F	888 532-2221	9903
Residential Bancorp **(PA)**	6162	D	330 493-8333	15229
Simplex Supplies Inc	3441	E	618 594-6450	6662
Smart & Final Stores Inc	5141	C	323 855-8434	14500
Snow Ball Trading Company **(PA)**	5075	D	626 893-9415	13849
South Coast Air Qulty MGT Dst **(PA)**	8748	A	909 396-2000	23511
Southwest Patrol Inc	7381	D	909 861-1884	18339
Specialty Equipment Mkt Assn **(PA)**	8611	D	909 396-0289	22261
Tetra Tech Bas Inc **(HQ)**	8711	D	909 860-7777	22669
Ultimate Sound Inc	3651	B	909 861-6200	9204
Vincent Huang & Associates LLC **(PA)**	4813	D	909 861-9600	12678
Zenlayer Inc	4813	B	909 718-3558	12680

DINUBA, CA - Tulare County

	SIC	EMP	PHONE	ENTRY #
Adventist Health System	8011	A	559 595-9890	19686
Adventist Hlth Systm/West Corp	8062	D	559 591-1906	20653
Adventist Hlth Systm/West Corp	8062	D	559 591-3342	20657
City of Dinuba	4119	D	559 595-9999	11858
Gillette Citrus Company	0723	D	559 626-4236	171
Integrated Voting Systems Inc	7389	E	559 498-0281	18550
Kaweah Delta Health Care Dst	8062	C	559 591-5513	20817
Packline Technologies Inc	3565	E	559 591-3150	8077
Presort Center of Fresno LLC	7331	E	559 498-6151	17138
Ruiz Food Products Inc **(PA)**	2038	A	559 591-5510	1938
Warren & Baerg Mfg Inc	3523	E	559 591-6790	7626

DOWNEY, CA - Los Angeles County

	SIC	EMP	PHONE	ENTRY #
A-1 Engraving Co Inc	3479	E	562 861-2216	7334
Abianca Khanna LLC	5169	F	833 225-7527	14766
Advanced Building Systems Inc	3999	E	818 652-4252	11625

Mergent email: customerrelations@mergent.com
1358
2022 Southern California Business Directory and Buyers Guide
(P-0000) Products & Services Section entry number
(PA)=Parent Co (HQ)=Headquarters (DH)=Div Headquarters

	SIC	EMP	PHONE	ENTRY #
Alpha Grinding Inc	3599	F	562 803-1509	8493
Altamed Health Services Corp	8011	C	562 923-9414	19695
ARC Los Angles Orange Counties **(PA)**	8331	D	562 803-1556	21939
Arrow Abrasive Company Inc	3291	E	562 869-2282	6150
Automobile Club Southern Cal	8699	D	562 904-5970	22414
Blastco Texas Inc	1721	D	562 869-0200	1170
Bradley Manufacturing Co Inc	3089	E	562 923-5556	5585
Cal Pipe Manufacturing Inc **(PA)**	3498	E	562 803-4388	7531
Calpipe Industries LLC **(HQ)**	5051	D	562 803-4388	13555
Can Lines Engineering Inc **(PA)**	3565	D	562 861-2996	8065
Commercial Truck Eqp Co LLC	3713	D	562 803-4466	9979
County of Los Angeles	8093	D	562 401-7088	21290
Cummins Pacific LLC	3519	F	866 934-4373	7591
Davita Medical Management LLC	8099	D	562 923-4911	21411
Downey Community Health Center	8051	C	562 862-6506	20316
Downey Grinding Co	3541	E	562 803-5556	7730
E J Lauren LLC	2512	E	562 803-1113	3502
Ebus Inc	3713	E	562 904-3474	9985
Ensign Group Inc	8051	D	562 923-9301	20328
Farwest Corrosion Control Co **(PA)**	1799	D	310 532-9524	1655
Financial Partners Credit Un **(PA)**	6061	D	562 904-3000	15064
Healthcare Ctr of Downey LLC	8051	C	562 869-0978	20373
Huntington Radiology	8011	D	562 904-1111	19849
Hutchinson Seal Corporation **(DH)**	3053	A	248 375-4190	5341
Instant Web LLC	2752	E	562 658-2020	4336
J F Duncan Industries Inc **(PA)**	3589	D	562 862-4269	8387
Jeb-Phi Inc	2752	E	562 861-0863	4343
Jlm & Mag Associates Inc	7231	D	562 869-3343	16906
Jobsite Stud Welding	7692	F	855 885-7883	18985
Kaiser Foundation Hospitals	6324	B	562 657-9000	15405
Kaiser Foundation Hospitals	8011	C	800 823-4040	19896
Kaiser Foundation Hospitals	8011	C	800 823-4040	19898
Kaiser Foundation Hospitals	8011	C	817 372-8201	19922
Kaiser Foundation Hospitals	6324	C	562 622-4190	15433
Keyline Sales Inc	5074	E	562 904-3910	13832
Kf Fiberglass Inc **(PA)**	3714	F	562 869-1536	10086
Kirkhill Inc	3069	D	562 803-1117	5386
Lakewood Park Health Ctr Inc **(PA)**	7389	B	562 869-0978	18571
Leach Grain & Milling Co Inc	5191	E	562 869-4451	14864
Liberty Utilities Pk Wtr Corp **(DH)**	4941	D	562 923-0711	12899
Los Angeles Cty Rnch Los Amgos	8052	A	562 385-7111	20536
Market Fixtures Unlimited Inc **(PA)**	5078	F	562 803-5553	13853
MD Stainless Services	3498	E	562 904-7022	7541
Meruelo Enterprises Inc **(PA)**	1542	A	562 745-2300	792
Mike Campbell & Associates Ltd	4222	A	626 369-3981	12175
National Trench Safety LLC	7353	C	562 602-1642	17313
Omniteam Inc	5078	C	562 923-9660	13855
On-Gard Metals Inc	3341	F	562 622-9057	6295
OSI Staffing Inc	7361	D	562 261-5753	17442
Pih Health Hospital - Downey **(HQ)**	8062	A	562 698-0811	20891
Pih Health Hospital - Whitti	8062	A	562 904-5482	20892
PRC Multi-Family LLC	6513	D	562 803-5000	15745
Qualls Stud Welding Pdts Inc	5084	F	562 923-7883	13931
Rancho Los Amigos Nationa **(PA)**	8322	A	562 401-7111	21876
Rancho Research Institute	8733	C	562 401-8111	22917
Reyes Coca-Cola Bottling LLC	2086	D	562 803-8100	2286
Reyes Coca-Cola Bottling LLC	2086	D	562 536-8847	2292
Reynaldos Mexican Food Co Inc	2099	F	562 803-3188	2516
Rockview Dairies Inc **(PA)**	5149	C	562 927-5511	14733
Rrm Construction Inc	1522	E	562 440-3539	667
Sanwa Jutaku Co Ltd	7011	D	562 861-1900	16694
Schoolsfirst Federal Credit Un	6061	D	714 258-4000	15086
Senior Wellness Innovation Grp **(PA)**	0782	D	562 746-2182	341
Sialic Contractors Corporation	1611	D	562 803-9977	915
Skyline Security MGT Inc **(PA)**	7382	D	562 622-7114	18400
Southern Cal Alchol DRG Prgram **(PA)**	8093	D	562 923-4545	21343
Southern Cal Prmnnte Med Group	6324	C	562 657-2200	15461
Spyke Inc	3751	E	562 803-1700	10501
Sst Technologies	3674	E	562 803-3361	9582
T P R Traffic Solutions **(PA)**	7389	F	800 821-2913	18684
Tarsco Holdings LLC	7699	C	562 869-0200	19073
Thompson Tank Inc	3443	F	562 869-7711	6762
Umc Acquisition Corp **(PA)**	3356	E	562 940-0300	6338
Unbrako LLC	5072	F	310 817-2400	13820
United California Corporation	3544	D	562 803-1521	7839
United Drill Bushing Corp	3545	C	562 803-1521	7875
Universal Mlding Extrusion Inc **(DH)**	3354	C	562 401-1015	6321
Universal Molding Company **(HQ)**	3356	C	310 886-1750	6339
Van Grace Quality Injection	3089	F	323 931-5255	5856
Wesfac Inc **(HQ)**	3589	D	562 861-2160	8425
Westar Manufacturing Inc	1799	E	562 633-0581	1703
Western Pacific Pulp and Paper **(HQ)**	2611	D	562 803-4401	3745
World Water Inc	3823	E	562 940-1964	10731

DUARTE, CA - Los Angeles County

	SIC	EMP	PHONE	ENTRY #
A & B Brush Mfg Corp	3991	E	626 303-8856	11506
Accu-Sembly Inc	3672	D	626 357-3447	9370
Advantage Ford Lincoln Mercury	7532	D	626 305-9188	18782
Assembly Automation Industries	3549	E	626 303-2777	7899
Baxco Pharmaceutical Inc	2834	F	626 610-7088	4794
Beckman RES Inst of The Cy Hop	8011	C	626 359-8111	19723
Bershtel Enterprises LLC **(PA)**	7389	C	626 301-9214	18459
City Hope National Medical Ctr	8062	A	626 256-4673	20724
Cosmo Fiber Corporation **(PA)**	2759	E	626 256-6098	4504
Davita Medical Management LLC	8011	D	626 358-0269	19792
Delafield Corporation **(PA)**	3599	C	626 303-0740	8569
Endodent Inc	3843	E	626 359-5715	11172
ESP Group Ltd	5137	D	626 301-0280	14374
Estrella Inc	8051	C	562 925-6418	20337
Gpi Ca-Niii Inc	7538	D	626 305-3000	18835
Humangood Socal	8361	C	626 359-8141	22116
Justice Bros Dist Co Inc	2843	E	626 359-9174	4985
Lee Machine Products	3544	F	626 301-4105	7812
Maryvale Day Care Center	8351	C	626 357-1514	22033
Micro-OHM Corporation	3676	F	626 357-5377	9616
Onex Enterprises Corporation	3569	F	626 358-6639	8132
Onex Rf Inc	3548	F	626 358-6639	7893
Osf International Inc	7299	D	626 358-2115	16970
Padywell Corp	2759	E	626 359-9149	4553
Png Builders	1522	E	626 256-9539	665
Prolacta Bioscience Inc	2023	B	626 599-9260	1805
Quality Car Care Products Inc	2819	E	626 359-9174	4668
Royal Terrace Healthcare	8051	D	626 256-4654	20453
Santa Teresita Inc **(PA)**	8062	B	626 359-3243	20936
Soyfoods of America	2075	E	626 358-3836	2120
Sportifeye Optics Inc	3851	E	626 521-5600	11262
Therma Holdings LLC	1711	E	626 446-1854	1154
Turbo Refrigeration Systems	3585	F	626 599-9777	8353
Victory Sportswear Inc	5199	E	626 359-5400	14984
Westminster Gardens	8059	D	626 359-2571	20640
Woodward Hrt Inc	3728	C	626 359-9211	10445

E RNCHO DMNGZ, CA - Los Angeles County

	SIC	EMP	PHONE	ENTRY #
Audio Video Color Corporation **(PA)**	2671	B	424 213-7500	3850
Beu Industries Inc	2671	F	310 885-9626	3851
Coy Industries Inc	3444	D	310 603-2970	6813
Dependable Global Express Inc **(PA)**	4731	C	310 537-2000	12444
Industrial Tctnics Brings Corp **(DH)**	3562	C	310 537-3750	8028
Modern Concepts Inc	3089	D	310 637-0013	5714
Murray Plumbing and Htg Corp **(PA)**	1711	A	310 637-1500	1106
Sonora Mills Foods Inc **(PA)**	2099	C	310 639-5333	2526
Timec Companies Inc	1629	C	310 885-4710	1006
Vanguard Lgistics Svcs USA Inc **(DH)**	4225	C	310 637-3700	12258

EARLIMART, CA - Tulare County

	SIC	EMP	PHONE	ENTRY #
Cal Treehouse Almonds LLC **(PA)**	2068	C	559 757-5020	2111

EARP, CA - San Bernardino County

	SIC	EMP	PHONE	ENTRY #
Colorado River Adventures Inc **(PA)**	7033	C	760 663-3737	16831

EASTVALE, CA - Riverside County

	SIC	EMP	PHONE	ENTRY #
Axis Unlimited Inc	8742	D	714 476-1341	23165
Cal-Mold Incorporated	3089	E	951 361-6400	5592
Califrnia Indus Rfrgn Mchs Inc	3585	F	951 361-0040	8331
CJ Logistics America LLC	4212	C	909 605-7233	11962
Dz Trading Ltd	5099	D	951 479-5700	14153
K-Cal Group Inc **(PA)**	2024	F	626 922-1103	1819
Keystone Automotive Warehouse	5013	D	951 277-5237	13071
Orange County Pike Alumni Assn	7371	B	702 832-6211	17685
Orange County Water District	4941	D	714 378-3200	12910
Rankin-Delux Inc **(PA)**	3589	F	951 685-0081	8408
Red Star Fertilizer Co	2873	F	909 597-4801	5159
Royal Range California Inc	3631	D	951 360-1600	8994
Shamrock Foods Company	5149	B	951 685-6314	14736
Skyline International Inc	3679	F	714 290-8866	9782
Smart & Final Stores Inc	5141	C	909 773-1813	14491
Tinnovate LLC	5065	E	909 860-6900	13782
Turn Key Logistics Inc	4789	C	714 931-1625	12583
United Parcel Service Inc	7389	D	951 749-3400	18705
United Transport Service Inc	7389	E	844 258-2262	18707
Vipstore USA Co	5199	B	626 934-7880	14985
White Horse Logistics Inc	4789	E	909 947-7822	12586
Wolfgang Enterprise Inc	7389	F	951 848-7680	18729

EDISON, CA - Kern County

	SIC	EMP	PHONE	ENTRY #
Giumarra Vineyards Corporation **(PA)**	0172	B	661 395-7000	47
Johnston Farms Fmly Ltd Partnr	0174	D	661 366-3201	64
Kirschenman Enterprises Sls LP	7389	C	661 366-5736	18565

EDWARDS, CA - Kern County

	SIC	EMP	PHONE	ENTRY #
Centech Group Inc	7389	E	661 275-5688	18474
Jt3 LLC	8711	C	661 277-4900	22592

EL CENTRO, CA - Imperial County

	SIC	EMP	PHONE	ENTRY #
Accentcare HM Hlth El Cntro In	8082	C	760 352-4022	21124
ARC - Imperial Valley **(PA)**	8322	D	760 352-0180	21714
Associated Desert Newspaper **(DH)**	2711	E	760 337-3400	3949
California Department Trnsp	1611	D	760 352-1129	868
Centene Chwp	6324	C	760 482-5593	15393
Clinicas De Slud Del Peblo Inc **(PA)**	8011	D	760 344-9951	19754
Complete Metal Fabrication Inc	3441	F	760 353-0260	6604
Coyne Companies LLC	2741	F	760 353-1016	4164
El Centro Hospitality LLC	7011	C	760 353-2600	16428
El Centro Hospitality 2 LLC	7011	C	760 370-3800	16429
El Centro Rgnal Med Ctr Fndtio **(PA)**	8062	A	760 339-7100	20761
Ew Corprtion Indus Fabricators **(PA)**	3441	D	760 337-0020	6616
Hay Kuhn Inc	5199	E	760 353-0124	14935
I N C Builders Inc	7363	B	760 352-4200	17495
Imperial Irrigation District	4931	E	760 339-9253	12871
Imperial Irrigation District	4931	E	760 339-9800	12872
Imperial Printers **(PA)**	2752	F	760 352-4374	4326
Joe Heger Farms LLC	0191	C	760 353-5111	113
K C Welding Inc	7692	F	760 352-3832	18987
Labrucherie Produce LLC	2099	E	760 352-2170	2469
Lowes Home Centers LLC	5031	C	760 337-6700	13256
Mahavir Hospitality LLC	7011	D	760 352-5152	16552
Noblesse Oblige Inc	0722	C	760 353-3336	158

GEOGRAPHIC

Employment Codes: A=Over 500 employees, B=251-500, C=101-250, D=51-100, E=20-50 F=10-19
2022 Southern California Business Directory and Buyers Guide
© Mergent Inc. 1-800-342-5647
1359

	SIC	EMP	PHONE	ENTRY #
Ohsung Display USA Inc **(HQ)**	3629	E	760 482-5788	8979
Original Sid Blackman Plbg Inc	1711	D	760 352-3632	1113
Reyes Coca-Cola Bottling LLC	2086	D	760 352-1561	2297
Rogar Manufacturing Inc	3679	C	760 335-3700	9774
Sign Factory Printing & Offic	3993	F	760 357-0098	11596
Soco Group Inc	5172	D	760 352-4683	14808
Southwest Protective Svcs Inc	7381	C	760 996-1285	18340
Superior Ready Mix Concrete LP	3273	D	760 352-4341	6120
Time Warner Cable Inc	4841	D	760 335-4800	12779
United Parcel Service Inc	4215	C	858 541-2336	12148
Valencia Bros Inc	1771	D	760 353-2168	1557
Wymore Inc	7692	E	760 352-2045	19005

EL MONTE, CA - Los Angeles County

	SIC	EMP	PHONE	ENTRY #
Able Rise Limited Corp	7389	E	626 416-5680	18430
Access Services	4111	D	213 270-6000	11801
Aero-k	3599	E	626 350-5125	8475
Ahm Gemch Inc	8062	C	626 579-7777	20664
All New Stamping Co	3469	C	626 443-8813	7122
Altamed Health Services Corp	8099	D	323 889-7847	21376
Altamed Health Services Corp	8099	D	626 453-8466	21382
American Apparel ACC Inc **(PA)**	3089	E	626 350-3828	5561
Andari Fashion Inc	2329	C	626 575-2759	2798
Applied Coatings & Linings	3479	E	626 280-6354	7344
Architectural Window Shades	5023	D	626 578-1936	13158
Automobile Club Southern Cal	6411	D	626 442-0944	15542
Bangkit (usa) Inc	5112	D	626 672-0888	14192
Citiznship Immigration Svcs US	8111	C	626 448-0135	21530
Craneveyor Corp **(PA)**	3536	D	626 442-1524	7697
D Longo Inc	7538	B	626 580-6000	18821
Davita Medical Management LLC	8011	D	626 444-0333	19789
Dianas Mexican Food Pdts Inc	2099	E	626 444-0555	2424
Driftwood Dairy Holding Corp	2099	F	626 444-9591	2426
Eighty One Enterprise Inc	5137	E	626 371-1980	14373
El Gallito Market Inc	2099	E	626 442-1190	2428
El Monte Automotive Group Inc	7532	C	626 580-6200	18788
El Monte Convalescent Hospital	8051	D	626 442-1500	20319
Envirogenics Systems Company	1629	D	818 573-9220	995
ERs SEC Alarm Systems Inc	5063	D	626 579-2525	13627
Eurmax Canopy Inc	3444	F	626 279-1622	6831
Exterran Inc	7353	D	626 455-0739	17308
Fanboys Window Factory Inc **(PA)**	3442	E	626 280-8787	6699
Firefighter Cancer Support Ntw	8322	E	866 994-3276	21788
First Student Inc	4111	B	626 448-9446	11806
Flexfirm Holdings LLC	2295	F	323 283-1173	2708
GAI Manufacturing Co LLC	3534	F	626 443-8616	7678
Georgia Atkison Snf LLC	8051	D	626 444-2535	20358
Gibralter Convalescent Hosp	8059	D	626 443-9425	20593
Gill Corporation **(PA)**	3089	C	626 443-6094	5653
Gsl Tech Inc	2023	F	877 572-9617	1793
Herald Christian Health Center **(PA)**	8011	D	626 286-8700	19842
Home Paradise LLC	3469	F	626 284-9999	7150
Hope Hse For Mltple Hndcpped I **(PA)**	8361	D	626 443-1313	22115
Industrial Machine & Mfg Co	3441	E	626 444-0181	6622
Inovit Inc	3714	F	626 444-4775	10082
Integrated Parcel Network	4215	B	714 278-6100	12138
Jans Enterprises Corporation	5149	E	626 575-2000	14696
Jansen Ornamental Supply Co	3446	E	626 442-0271	6966
Justin Inc	3612	E	626 444-4516	8876
K T Lucky Co Inc	5149	D	626 579-7272	14700
L & N Fixtures Inc	2541	E	626 442-4778	3655
La Chapalita Inc **(PA)**	2099	E	626 443-8556	2463
LA Web Inc	1721	E	626 453-8800	1187
Lanty Inc	2099	C	626 582-8001	2470
LAweb Offset Printing Inc	2759	E	626 454-2469	4535
Lawrence Equipment Leasing Inc **(PA)**	3556	C	626 442-2894	7942
Liberty Industries	3599	F	626 575-3206	8663
Lith-O-Roll Corporation	3555	E	626 579-0340	7920
Lithotech International LLC	2759	E	626 443-4210	4539
Los Angeles Ltg Mfg Co Inc	5063	D	626 454-8300	13641
Mercury Broach Company Inc	3545	F	626 443-5904	7856
Micro Gage	3674	E	626 443-1741	9539
Mountain View Elmntary Schl Ds	8351	D	626 652-4250	22038
Mutual Trading Co Inc **(DH)**	5149	C	213 626-9458	14712
Newhouse Upholstery	2531	E	626 444-1370	3628
Nijjar Realty Inc **(PA)**	6531	D	626 575-0062	15931
Ott Textile Inc **(PA)**	2299	E	626 566-5858	2733
Pacific Couriers Inc	4215	E	714 278-6100	12144
Pactrack Inc	4731	D	213 201-5856	12501
Pax Tag & Label Inc	2759	E	626 579-2000	4555
Precision Coil Spring Company	3495	D	626 444-0561	7490
Pride Metal Polishing Inc	3471	F	626 350-1326	7298
Primus Lighting Inc	3648	F	626 442-4600	9144
R and L Lopez Associates Inc **(PA)**	8711	D	626 330-5296	22642
R W Swarens Associates Inc	3646	E	626 579-0943	9101
Ramona Care Inc	8051	C	626 442-5721	20442
Remington Roll Forming Inc	3316	E	626 350-5196	6244
Royal Apparel Inc	2339	E	626 579-5168	2991
San Gabriel Transit Inc **(PA)**	4111	C	626 258-1310	11837
San Gabriel Valley Water Co **(PA)**	4941	C	626 448-6183	12915
Santoshi Corporation	3471	E	626 444-7118	7310
SOLE Designs Inc	2512	F	626 452-8642	3518
Southland Transit Inc **(PA)**	4111	C	626 258-1310	11844
Sparling Instruments LLC	5084	E	626 444-0571	13940
Sunrise Pillow Co Inc	2392	F	626 401-9283	3121
Supreme Steel Treating Inc	3398	E	626 350-5865	6453
Svo Enterprise	2381	E	626 406-4770	3051
Tartan Fashion Inc	2329	E	626 575-2828	2828
Thrifty Payless Inc	2024	A	626 571-0122	1825
Transgo	3714	E	626 443-7456	10143
Triple-E Machinery Moving Inc	4213	D	626 444-1137	12084
Videssence LLC **(PA)**	3645	E	626 579-0943	9073
Walden House Inc	8361	C	626 258-0300	22166
Yew Bio-Pharm Group Inc **(PA)**	0811	D	626 401-9588	369

EL SEGUNDO, CA - Los Angeles County

	SIC	EMP	PHONE	ENTRY #
18 Media Inc **(PA)**	2721	F	650 324-1818	4047
24hr Homecare LLC **(PA)**	8082	A	310 906-3683	21115
24hr Homecare LLC	8082	C	310 375-5353	21116
A-Mark Precious Metals Inc **(PA)**	5094	C	310 587-1477	14125
Abl Space Systems Company	3761	D	424 321-5049	10512
Aerojet Rcketdyne Holdings Inc **(PA)**	3812	D	310 252-8100	10561
Aerospace Engrg Support Corp	3728	E	310 297-4050	10252
Air New Zealand Limited	4512	D	310 648-7000	12301
Anthos Group Inc	8742	E	888 778-2986	23159
Asp Henry Holdings Inc	6719	A	310 955-9200	16095
Asset Athene Management L P **(HQ)**	8741	D	310 698-4444	22980
AT&T Corp	4813	C	303 596-8431	12626
Atk Space Systems LLC	3812	D	310 343-3799	10573
Austin Dialysis Centers LP **(HQ)**	8092	E	310 536-2400	21233
Avasant LLC **(PA)**	8742	D	310 643-3030	23162
Bandai America Incorporated **(DH)**	3944	D	714 816-9751	11368
Bear Nash Productions	7819	D	310 428-5167	19221
Bellwether Asset MGT Inc	8741	D	310 525-3022	22985
Beyond Meat Inc **(PA)**	2038	E	866 756-4112	1917
Beyond Meat Inc	2038	E	310 567-3323	1918
BMC	7372	E	310 321-5555	17803
BMC Group Inc	8111	D	310 321-5555	21519
Boeing Coml Satellite Svcs Inc **(HQ)**	3663	E	310 335-6682	9257
Boeing Comsatcom Services Inc **(HQ)**	3721	D	310 335-6682	10179
Boeing Satellite Systems	3812	D	310 364-5088	10574
Boeing Satellite Systems Inc	3721	A	310 568-2735	10181
Boeing Satellite Systems Inc **(HQ)**	3663	E	310 791-7450	9258
Boeing Stllite Systems Intl In **(HQ)**	5088	E	310 364-4000	14053
Browntrout Publishers Inc **(PA)**	2741	E	424 290-6122	4158
BT Americas Inc	5065	D	646 487-7400	13705
Byrnes W J & Co of Los Angeles	4731	D	310 615-2325	12425
California Physicians Service	6324	D	310 744-2668	15390
Carson Kurtzman Consultants **(DH)**	8111	C	310 823-9000	21528
Central KY Dialysis Ctrs LLC **(HQ)**	8092	E	310 536-2400	21234
Century Pk Capitl Partners LLC **(PA)**	6726	C	310 867-2210	16153
Cetera Financial Group Inc **(PA)**	7389	D	866 489-3100	18477
Chevron Corporation	1311	A	310 615-5000	401
Cls Trnsprttion Los Angles LLC **(HQ)**	4119	C	310 414-8189	11859
Computershare Inc	6289	A	800 522-6645	15355
Continental Dialysis Ctr Inc **(HQ)**	8092	E	310 536-2400	21235
Continental Graphics Corp	2752	D	310 662-2307	4262
Cookingcom Inc	5046	C	310 664-1283	13454
Core Nutrition LLC	5149	E	310 640-0500	14685
Craig Tools Inc	3545	E	310 322-0614	7851
Dallas-Fort Wrth Nephrology LP **(HQ)**	8092	E	310 536-2400	21236
David & Goliath LLC	7311	C	310 445-5200	17003
Davinci Schools	7389	E	310 725-5800	18501
Davita - Riverside LLC **(HQ)**	8092	E	310 536-2400	21237
Davita Medical Management LLC **(HQ)**	8011	A	310 354-4200	19791
Design People	7374	C	800 969-5799	18083
Dfds International Corporation	4731	D	310 414-1516	12445
Dialysis North Atlanta LLC **(HQ)**	8092	E	310 536-2400	21240
Directv Inc	4841	B	888 388-4249	12755
Directv Enterprises LLC	4841	A	310 535-5000	12756
Directv Group Holdings LLC **(HQ)**	4812	C	310 964-5000	12606
Directv Group Inc **(DH)**	4841	C	310 964-5000	12760
Directv Holdings LLC **(DH)**	4841	A	310 964-5000	12761
Directv International Inc **(DH)**	4841	C	310 964-6460	12762
Directv Sports Network LLC **(DH)**	4841	D	310 964-5000	12763
Diverse Journeys Inc **(PA)**	8322	D	310 643-7403	21771
Djont Operations LLC	7011	C	310 640-3600	16410
Dkp Designs Inc	3999	F	310 322-6000	11659
Dtv Network Systems Inc **(PA)**	4841	C	800 531-5000	12767
Dva Healthcare Tuscaloosa LLC **(HQ)**	8092	E	310 536-2400	21241
Edwards Technologies Inc	1731	C	310 536-7070	1245
Efficient Pwr Conversion Corp **(PA)**	3674	D	310 615-0279	9501
El Segundo Bread Bar LLC	2051	E	310 615-9898	1998
El Segundo Eductl Foundation	8399	B	310 615-2650	22182
En Pointe Technologies Sls LLC	5045	C	310 337-6151	13391
Esaloncom LLC	7231	C	866 550-2424	16902
Etonien LLC **(PA)**	8748	D	310 321-5800	23439
Ev Connect Inc	1731	D	310 751-7997	1250
F & E Arcft Mint Los Angles LL	4581	B	310 338-0063	12358
Far Out Toys Inc	3942	E	310 480-7554	11360
Federal Industries Inc	3494	F	310 297-4040	7473
Felcor Lax Lessee LLC	7011	E	310 640-3600	16441
Flight Microwave Corporation	3559	E	310 607-9819	7977
Fujitsu Glovia Inc **(HQ)**	7371	C	310 563-7000	17622
Glentek Inc	3621	D	310 322-3026	8913
Governmentjobscom Inc	7372	C	310 426-6304	17869
Greater Las Vegas Dialysis LLC **(HQ)**	8092	E	310 536-2400	21243
Griffin Capital Holdings Corp	6799	D	310 469-6100	16265
Gurucul Solutions LLC	7372	E	213 291-6888	17877
Guthy-Renker LLC **(PA)**	8742	D	760 773-9022	23230
Hco Holding I Corporation **(HQ)**	6719	D	323 583-5000	16102
Hco Holding II Corporation	2952	A	310 955-9200	5280
Hemilane Inc	2085	F	424 277-1134	2242
Henry Company LLC **(HQ)**	2952	D	310 955-9200	5281
Hlb90067 Inc **(PA)**	2844	F	626 689-8614	5030
Hnc Parent Inc **(PA)**	2952	D	310 955-9200	5282

Mergent email: customerrelations@mergent.com
1360
2022 Southern California Business Directory and Buyers Guide
(P-0000) Products & Services Section entry number
(PA)=Parent Co (HQ)=Headquarters (DH)=Div Headquarters

	SIC	EMP	PHONE	ENTRY #
Houston Kidney Center/Total R **(HQ)**	8092	E	310 536-2400	21248
Hr Cloud Inc **(PA)**	7372	D	510 909-1993	17880
Ibftech Inc	7361	D	424 217-8010	17430
Ignited LLC **(PA)**	7311	C	310 773-3100	17020
Infineon Tech Americas Corp **(HQ)**	3674	A	310 726-8200	9516
Infineon Tech Americas Corp	8721	A	310 726-8000	22793
Infonet Services Corporation **(DH)**	4813	A	310 335-2600	12651
Integra Technologies Inc	3674	E	310 606-0855	9519
Integrated Data Services Inc **(PA)**	7371	D	310 647-3439	17640
Irise **(PA)**	7371	D	800 556-0399	17644
Ispace Inc	7379	C	310 563-3800	18193
Itochu Aviation Inc **(DH)**	5088	E	310 640-2770	14058
J L Cooper Electronics Inc	3679	E	310 322-9990	9732
Jal Avionet USA **(HQ)**	5045	E	310 606-1000	13410
Jumpstart Games Inc	7371	D	424 645-4311	17647
Karl Storz Endscpy-America Inc	3841	D	508 248-9011	10999
Karl Storz Endscpy-America Inc **(HQ)**	3841	B	424 218-8100	11000
Kellstrom Holding Corporation **(PA)**	5088	D	561 222-7455	14060
Kidney Centers Michigan LLC **(HQ)**	8092	E	310 536-2400	21253
Kinkisharyo International LLC **(HQ)**	3743	F	424 276-1803	10477
Kubic Marketing Inc **(HQ)**	5091	C	310 297-1600	14083
L E Coppersmith Inc **(PA)**	4731	D	310 607-8000	12477
Lambs & Ivy Inc	2392	D	310 322-3800	3106
Landmark Dividend LLC **(PA)**	6531	C	323 306-2683	15907
Ld Acquisition Company 16 LLC	6799	D	310 294-8160	16273
Liberty Entertainment Inc **(DH)**	4841	B	310 964-5000	12773
Liminex Inc	7371	C	888 310-0410	17653
Lip Ink International	5122	F	310 414-9246	14258
Liquid Advertising Inc	7311	D	310 450-2653	17029
Login Consulting Services Inc	7379	D	310 607-9091	18199
Los Angles Tmes Cmmnctions LLC **(PA)**	2711	A	213 237-5000	4005
M Nexon Inc	7372	D	213 858-5930	17908
Marketwire Inc **(HQ)**	7383	D	310 765-3200	18407
Mattel Inc **(PA)**	3942	A	310 252-2000	11362
Mattel Direct Import Inc **(HQ)**	3944	E	310 252-2000	11382
Mattel Operations Inc	3944	F	310 252-2000	11383
Matthews RE Inv Svcs Inc **(PA)**	6531	D	866 889-0550	15923
Mega Brands America Inc **(DH)**	3944	D	949 727-9009	11384
Merqbiz LLC	3554	E	855 637-7249	7915
Merrill Lynch Prce Fnner Smith	6211	D	310 536-1600	15291
Metalore Inc	3599	E	310 643-0360	8692
Mh Sub I LLC **(PA)**	7311	A	310 280-4000	17035
Michael Sullivan & Assoc LLP	8111	C	310 337-4480	21628
Millennium Space Systems Inc **(HQ)**	3812	E	310 683-5840	10599
Mod-Electronics Inc	3873	E	310 322-2136	11302
Moose Toys LLC	3942	D	310 341-4642	11363
Mountain W Dialysis Svcs LLC **(HQ)**	8092	E	310 536-2400	21254
MTI Laboratory Inc	3663	E	310 955-3700	9299
Murad LLC **(HQ)**	2834	C	310 726-0600	4853
Nantcell Inc	8733	C	310 883-1300	22916
Nantenergy LLC	3621	D	310 905-4866	8925
Nanthealth Inc **(HQ)**	7373	B	310 883-1300	18048
NBC Suite Hotel	7011	D	310 640-3600	16576
New Bay Dialysis LLC **(HQ)**	8092	E	310 536-2400	21255
Next Trucking Inc	4731	C	855 688-6398	12489
Nippon Express USA Inc	4731	D	310 535-7200	12491
Northrop Grumman Corporation	3812	C	310 332-1000	10606
Northrop Grumman Systems Corp	3812	C	310 632-1846	10611
Northrop Grumman Systems Corp	3812	C	480 355-7716	10619
Northrop Grumman Systems Corp	3812	C	310 332-1000	10626
NRG El Segundo Operations Inc	4911	D	310 615-6344	12813
Oceanx LLC **(HQ)**	7389	D	310 774-4088	18617
Ohio River Dialysis LLC **(HQ)**	8092	E	310 536-2400	21256
Orbital Sciences LLC	3812	B	703 406-5000	10630
Osata Enterprises Inc	5139	D	888 445-6237	14443
Pacific Ave Cpitl Partners LLC	6726	A	424 254-9774	16160
Pacific Aviation Corporation **(PA)**	4581	C	310 646-4015	12364
Pcm Inc **(HQ)**	5045	A	310 354-5600	13426
Performance Team LLC **(DH)**	4731	C	562 345-2200	12509
Phase Four Inc	3764	F	310 648-8454	10528
Physicans Dalysis Acquisitions **(HQ)**	8092	E	310 536-2400	21258
Pinnacle Travel Services LLC	4724	C	310 414-1787	12395
Premier Disability Svcs LLC	8399	D	310 280-4000	22208
Primary Color Systems Corp	2759	E	310 841-0250	4559
Prodege LLC **(PA)**	7371	B	310 294-9599	17692
Prologic Rdmption Slutions Inc **(PA)**	7389	A	310 322-7774	18644
Prosum Inc **(PA)**	7374	D	310 426-0600	18104
Pt Gaming LLC	7011	A	323 260-5060	16643
Qic US Management Inc **(HQ)**	8741	C	310 955-1670	23095
Quest Nutrition LLC	5149	D	562 272-0180	14727
Quest Nutrition LLC	2099	E	562 446-3321	2513
Radica Enterprises Ltd **(DH)**	5092	D	310 252-2000	14100
Radiology Partners Inc **(HQ)**	8011	B	424 290-8004	20035
Ranar Manufacturing Corp	2759	F	310 414-4122	4564
Randstad Professionals Us LLC	7363	D	424 246-4400	17510
Rare Beauty LLC	5122	D	424 502-1900	14285
Raytheon Cmmand Ctrl Sltons LL	5065	E	714 446-3232	13769
Raytheon Company	3812	D	310 647-1000	10637
Raytheon Company	3812	B	310 647-1000	10639
Raytheon Company	3812	A	310 647-9438	10640
Rhythm and Hues Inc **(PA)**	7812	C	310 448-7500	19170
River Valley Dialysis LLC **(HQ)**	8092	E	310 536-2400	21263
Rocky Mtn Dialysis Svcs LLC **(HQ)**	8092	E	310 536-2400	21264
Ross Racing Pistons	3592	D	310 536-0100	8435
Rubicon B Hacienda LLC	7011	D	424 290-5000	16676
Satco Inc **(PA)**	2448	C	310 322-4719	3408
Saviynt Inc **(PA)**	8742	C	310 641-1664	23316
Scenewise Inc	3695	F	310 466-7692	9838
Scribeamerica LLC	8099	C	877 819-5900	21478
Securtas Crtcal Infrstrcture S	7381	B	310 426-3300	18331
Shining Star Dialysis Inc **(HQ)**	8092	E	310 536-2400	21265
Sierra Systems Inc **(PA)**	8742	E	310 536-6288	23322
Siltanen Inc	7312	D	310 321-5200	17077
Singapore Airlines Limited	4512	C	310 647-1922	12313
Smart Action Company LLC	7372	E	310 776-9200	17984
Softscript Inc	7338	A	310 451-2110	17194
Southwest Atlanta Dia **(HQ)**	8092	E	310 536-2400	21266
Square Enix Inc	5045	C	310 846-0400	13442
Square Enix Amer Holdings Inc **(HQ)**	5045	E	310 321-6979	13443
Stampscom Inc **(PA)**	7331	B	310 482-5800	17142
Suez Water Indiana LLC	3823	E	310 414-0183	10727
Sugarfina USA LLC	2064	C	855 784-2734	2107
Summit Commercial Prpts Inc **(HQ)**	6799	C	310 648-7500	16294
Symmetry Electronics LLC **(DH)**	3674	E	310 536-6190	9587
TBG Insurance Services Corp	6411	C	310 203-8770	15633
Technical Micro Cons Inc **(PA)**	8742	E	310 559-3982	23339
Tecolote Research Inc	8742	D	310 640-4700	23340
Teledyne Controls LLC	3812	A	310 765-3600	10644
Teledyne Technologies Inc	3679	B	310 765-3600	9793
Telenet Voip Inc	7629	D	310 253-9000	18958
Tempus LLC	7361	D	800 917-5055	17474
Ten Publishing Media LLC **(PA)**	7819	C	310 531-9900	19252
Thai Union North America Inc **(HQ)**	2091	E	424 397-8556	2342
Trammell Crow Centl Texas Ltd	6531	D	310 765-2600	16017
Trc-Indiana Llc **(HQ)**	8092	E	310 536-2400	21268
Tri-Star Electronics Intl Inc **(HQ)**	5065	B	310 536-0444	13783
Tri-Star Technologies Inc	3845	F	310 567-9243	11241
Tri-Union Seafoods LLC **(DH)**	5146	D	858 558-9662	14588
Trio Manufacturing Inc	3728	C	310 640-6123	10435
U S Managers Realty Inc	8741	D	310 607-0003	23131
Uhg Lax Prop Llc	7011	C	310 322-0999	16760
Unbroken Studios LLC	7372	D	310 741-2670	18003
United Vlve Div of Fderal Inds	5088	F	310 297-4000	14070
Venice Baking Co	2051	E	310 322-7357	2041
VIP Tours of California Inc	4725	D	310 216-7507	12412
Vista Investments LLC **(PA)**	7011	C	310 725-8200	16773
Wash Mltfmily Ldry Systems LLC **(PA)**	7215	C	310 643-8491	16874
Welcome Group Inc **(PA)**	7011	B	860 741-2211	16781
Whelan Security Co	7381	B	310 343-8628	18359
Wpromote LLC **(PA)**	8742	C	310 421-4844	23368
Wyle Services Corporation **(DH)**	8711	A	310 563-6800	22702
Xceed Financial Credit Union **(PA)**	6061	D	800 932-8222	15104
Zico Beverages LLC **(HQ)**	2086	D	866 729-9426	2305
Zoasis Corporation	2721	E	800 745-4725	4116
Zoo Digital Production LLC	7812	D	310 220-3939	19215
Zuru LLC	3944	F	424 277-1274	11396

EL TORO, CA - Orange County

	SIC	EMP	PHONE	ENTRY #
Beverly Hillcrest Oil Corp	1311	F	949 598-7300	392
Freedom Communications Inc	2711	E	949 454-7300	3977
Kott Koatings Inc **(PA)**	6794	F	949 770-5055	16210
Mission Flavors Fragrances Inc	2087	F	949 461-3344	2333
Sunset Landscape Maintenance	0781	D	949 455-4636	284

ENCINO, CA - Los Angeles County

	SIC	EMP	PHONE	ENTRY #
24hr Homecare LLC	8082	D	818 385-0227	21118
A-Able Inc **(PA)**	7342	D	323 658-5779	17196
ABS By Allen Schwartz LLC **(HQ)**	2339	C	213 895-4400	2912
ABs Clothing Collection Inc	2339	F	213 895-4400	2913
Alex A Khadavi MD Inc	8011	E	818 528-2500	19688
Answer Financial Inc **(HQ)**	7389	C	818 644-4000	18447
Aquarius Rags LLC **(PA)**	2335	E	213 895-4400	2877
Automobile Club Southern Cal	8699	D	818 997-6230	22399
Bovitz Inc	8732	D	818 806-0800	22875
California Respiratory Care	2899	D	818 379-9999	5214
Calstar Systems Group Inc	3699	E	818 922-2000	9857
Capna Fabrication	3556	E	888 416-6777	7929
Caulipower LLC	2038	E	844 422-8544	1921
Columbia Fabricating Co Inc	3446	E	818 247-4220	6956
Concrete Holding Co Cal Inc	3273	A	818 788-4228	6085
County of Los Angeles	7992	D	818 995-1170	19483
Creative Age Publications Inc	2721	E	818 782-7328	4060
Culture AMP Inc **(HQ)**	7372	E	415 326-8453	17830
D3publisher of America Inc	7372	D	310 268-0820	17832
Degenerate Sound Inc **(PA)**	1731	D	818 385-1933	1242
Ect News Network Inc	2741	F	818 461-9700	4168
Elizabeth Glaser Pedia	8099	D	310 231-0400	21423
EMI-Jay Inc	7299	F	888 779-9733	16955
Encino Center Car Wash Inc	7542	E	818 788-6300	18913
Encino Trzana Regional Med Ctr	8062	B	818 995-5000	20769
Exer Holding Company LLC	8011	E	818 287-0894	19808
F6s Network Limited	8731	D	619 818-4363	22839
First Republic Bank	6022	D	818 263-8798	15026
Garage Equipment Supply Inc	3559	F	805 530-0027	7979
Graypay LLC	7372	F	818 387-6735	17871
Hemar Rousso & Heald L L P	8111	E	818 501-3800	21579
Ipressroom Inc	7372	E	310 499-0544	17893
Ksl Media Inc	7319	C	212 468-3395	17100
Life Alert Emrgncy Rsponse Inc **(PA)**	7382	C	800 247-0000	18393
Lmno Productions Inc	7812	D	818 995-5555	19145
Lowe Enterprises Rlty Svcs Inc	6531	A	818 990-9555	15914
Max/Mr Imaging Inc	8071	D	818 382-2220	21076
Moroccanoil Inc **(PA)**	5122	D	888 700-1817	14265
Mpulse Mobile Inc **(PA)**	4813	B	888 678-5735	12657
National Cement Co Cal Inc **(DH)**	3273	D	818 728-5200	6100

GEOGRAPHIC

Employment Codes: A=Over 500 employees, B=251-500, C=101-250, D=51-100, E=20-50 F=10-19

2022 Southern California Business Directory and Buyers Guide

© Mergent Inc. 1-800-342-5647

1361

	SIC	EMP	PHONE	ENTRY #
National Cement Company Inc **(HQ)**	3241	E	818 728-5200	5981
National Ready Mix	3273	F	818 728-5200	6101
National Ready Mixed Con Co **(DH)**	3273	E	818 728-5200	6102
Nations Capital Group LLC	6153	E	818 793-2050	15156
Nsi Group LLC **(PA)**	7389	E	818 639-8335	18615
One Silver Serve Inc	7349	E	818 995-6444	17266
Opthamology Associates of Vly	8011	D	818 990-3623	20014
Orchard Horror Film LLC	7929	E	212 203-6147	19372
Orthopedic Consultants **(PA)**	8011	E	818 788-7343	20015
Ovation Fertility **(PA)**	8011	D	818 858-1074	20016
Pacific Paper Box Company **(PA)**	2652	E	323 771-7733	3779
Pearlman Brown & Wax LLP **(PA)**	8111	D	818 501-4343	21658
Pegasus Communications Inc **(PA)**	7812	E	818 907-1900	19161
Phone Check Solutions LLC	7371	B	310 365-1855	17690
Price Law Group A Prof Corp **(PA)**	8111	C	818 995-4540	21662
Prime Hlthcare Svcs - Encino H	8062	B	818 995-5000	20907
Reprints Desk Inc	7375	D	310 477-0354	18130
Rodeo Realty Inc	6531	D	818 285-3700	15981
Sabio Mobile Inc	7313	E	818 805-3678	17089
Sayari Shahrzad	5136	E	310 903-6368	14349
Stanzino Inc	2211	D	818 602-5171	2589
T Joseph Raoof MD Inc	8011	F	818 788-5060	20102
Team-One Emplyment Spclsts LLC	7361	D	310 481-4480	17471
Team-One Staffing Services Inc	7361	A	951 616-3515	17472
Telestar International Corp	8742	E	909 598-3636	23345
United Vision Financial Inc	6163	C	818 285-0211	15257
Uniworld River Cruises Inc **(HQ)**	4724	C	818 382-2322	12402
Veritas Technologies LLC	7371	C	310 202-0757	17753
Vivometrics Inc	3845	F	805 667-2225	11243
Walden Environment	8059	D	818 365-3665	20639
Warner Food Management Co Inc	8742	C	818 285-2160	23362
Westrec Properties Inc	8741	B	818 907-0400	23140
Zelzah Pharmacy Inc **(PA)**	2834	E	818 609-0692	4916
Zevia LLC	2086	D	310 202-7000	2304

EXETER, CA - Tulare County

	SIC	EMP	PHONE	ENTRY #
Amarillo Wind Machine LLC	3523	F	559 592-4256	7604
Bowsmith Inc **(PA)**	7218	D	559 592-9485	16884
Central California Baking Co	2051	C	559 592-2270	1991
Exeter Engineering Inc	0723	D	559 592-3161	166
Exeter Mercantile Company	3523	F	559 592-2121	7611
Exeter Packers Inc **(PA)**	0723	C	559 592-5168	167
Exeter Specialties	2037	F	559 592-5999	1899
Exeter-Ivanhoe Citrus Assn	0723	D	559 592-3141	169
Farmers Insurance Exchange	6411	B	559 594-4149	15567
Foothills Sun-Gazette	2711	F	559 592-3171	3976
Fruit Growers Supply Company	2653	E	559 592-6550	3804
Kaweah Delta Health Care Dst	8062	C	559 592-7128	20818
Packaging Holdings Inc	3565	E	831 634-0940	8076
Peninsula Packaging LLC **(DH)**	3999	D	559 594-6813	11733
R Gas LLC	2911	F	559 592-2456	5258
Redding Tree Growers Corp	0851	D	559 594-9299	372
San Joaquin Valley Railroad Co	4011	D	559 592-1857	11797
South Valley Materials Inc	3273	F	559 594-4142	6114
Sun Pacific Farming Coop Inc **(PA)**	0762	B	559 592-7121	229
Valley Cutting System Inc	3541	F	559 684-1229	7751
Venida Packing Company	5199	C	559 592-2816	14981
Waterman Valve LLC **(HQ)**	3589	C	559 562-4000	8424
Willitts Equipment Company Inc	7699	E	559 594-5020	19086

FARMERSVILLE, CA - Tulare County

	SIC	EMP	PHONE	ENTRY #
Claudes Buggies Inc	5013	E	559 733-8222	13052
Tortilleria La Mejor	2099	D	559 747-0739	2541

FELLOWS, CA - Kern County

	SIC	EMP	PHONE	ENTRY #
Dwaynes Engineering & Cnstr	1389	F	661 762-7261	495
Pacific Perforating Inc	1389	E	661 768-9224	532
Pro-Vac Inc	1389	E	661 765-7298	538
Shop Services Inc	7699	F	661 768-1775	19068

FILLMORE, CA - Ventura County

	SIC	EMP	PHONE	ENTRY #
Allied Avocados & Citrus Inc	0723	D	805 625-7155	160
Ameron International Corp	3272	C	425 258-2616	6016
Ameron International Corp	3272	D	805 524-0223	6017
Brightview Tree Company	0811	D	714 546-7975	367
California Watercress Inc **(PA)**	0161	D	805 524-4808	13
Fillmore Convalescent Ctr LLC	8059	D	805 524-0083	20581
Growit LLC	8711	E	949 305-4004	22564
Honey Bennetts Farm Inc **(PA)**	2099	E	805 521-1375	2450
Owens & Minor Distribution Inc	5099	A	805 524-0243	14173
Rotorcraft Support Inc	4581	D	818 997-7667	12367
Wilmay Inc	7389	D	805 524-2603	18727

FONTANA, CA - San Bernardino County

	SIC	EMP	PHONE	ENTRY #
101 Vertical Fabrication Inc	5051	D	909 428-6000	13543
A&R Tarpaulins Inc	2394	E	909 829-4444	3132
Advanti Racing Usa LLC **(DH)**	3714	F	951 272-5930	10009
Alabama Metal Industries Corp	3446	D	909 350-9280	6949
Allied West Paper Corp	2621	D	909 349-0710	3747
American Die Casting Inc	3364	E	909 356-7768	6374
American Security Products Co	3499	C	951 685-9680	7548
Amerit Fleet Solutions Inc	7549	A	909 357-0100	18921
Anfinson Lumber Sales Inc **(PA)**	5031	D	951 681-4707	13201
Apple Tree International Corp	3571	E	626 679-7025	8149
Aqua-Serv Engineers Inc **(HQ)**	5169	C	951 681-9696	14772
Assisvis Inc	3084	F	909 628-2031	5465
Avilas Garden Art **(PA)**	3272	D	909 350-4546	6019
B&B Industrial Services Inc **(PA)**	1741	B	909 428-3167	1341
Bab Steering Hydraulics **(PA)**	3714	E	208 573-4502	10022
Bdeebz Investment Inc **(PA)**	6799	D	909 646-9498	16248
Becker Specialty Corporation	3677	E	909 356-1095	9621
Bluefield Associates Inc	2844	E	909 476-6027	4994
Bowlero Corp	7933	D	909 822-9900	19395
Boyd Flotation Inc	2515	E	314 997-5222	3543
Bridgestone Americas	7534	D	909 770-8523	18809
Brightview Landscape Svcs Inc	0781	C	909 946-3196	243
Budway Enterprises Inc **(PA)**	4213	D	909 463-0500	12017
Burrtec Waste Industries Inc **(HQ)**	4953	C	909 429-4200	12933
California Speedway Corp	7948	E	909 429-5000	19429
California Steel Inds Inc **(PA)**	3312	A	909 350-6300	6192
California Steel Inds Inc	3312	E	909 350-6300	6193
Cannon Gasket Inc	3053	E	909 355-1547	5331
Canyon Steel Fabricators Inc	3441	E	951 683-2352	6598
Cargo Solution Brokerage Inc	4212	C	909 350-1644	11961
Cargo Solution Express Inc **(PA)**	4213	C	909 350-1644	12020
Castle Importing Inc	2022	F	909 428-9200	1769
Cattrac Construction Inc	1629	D	909 355-1146	992
Cavallo & Cavallo Inc	3599	F	909 428-6994	8543
Cemex Cnstr Mtls PCF LLC	3273	F	909 355-8754	6080
CH Morris Co Inc	5013	E	909 829-4481	13050
Clark - Pacific Corporation	3272	E	909 823-1433	6024
Complete Logistics Company	4213	C	909 427-9800	12024
Continental Coatings Inc	2851	F	909 355-1200	5093
Corbell Products Inc **(PA)**	3441	E	909 574-9139	6606
Costco Wholesale Corporation	5199	C	909 823-8270	14924
Creative Stone Mfg Inc **(PA)**	3272	C	909 357-8295	6026
Crown Technical Systems **(PA)**	3613	C	951 332-4170	8891
CRST International Inc	4213	C	909 829-1313	12027
Cvc Technologies Inc	3565	E	909 355-0311	8067
Cyi Pins Ltd	3452	F	626 600-9017	7061
Dalton Trucking Inc **(PA)**	4225	C	909 823-0663	12196
Daniel Gerard Worldwide Inc	5051	D	951 361-1111	13562
Dennie Manning Concrete Inc	3273	F	909 823-7521	6089
Desert Coastal Transport Inc **(PA)**	4213	D	909 357-3395	12033
Dispatch Transportation LLC	7359	E	909 355-5531	17346
Dispatch Trucking LLC **(PA)**	4731	D	909 355-5531	12447
Door Components Inc	3442	C	909 770-5700	6695
Dorel Juvenile Group Inc	3089	E	909 428-0295	5629
DSM&t Co Inc	3694	C	909 357-7960	9822
DSV Solutions LLC	4731	C	909 349-6100	12448
Eaton Electrical Inc	3625	E	951 685-5788	8950
Ecoplast Corporation Inc	3089	E	909 346-0450	5633
Edessa Inc	3272	E	909 823-1377	6028
Eight Point Trailer Corp	7539	E	909 357-9227	18897
Estes Express Lines	4213	D	909 427-9850	12038
Exel Inc	4225	E	909 350-6976	12203
Express Contractors Inc	7217	D	951 360-6500	16880
Express Messenger Systems Inc	4215	D	804 334-5000	12133
Fab Services West Inc	3449	D	909 350-7500	7020
Fabco Steel Fabrication Inc	3441	E	909 350-1535	6617
Fedex Freight West Inc	4213	B	909 357-3555	12045
Finnco Services Incorporated	7359	D	909 355-0707	17349
Fontana Foundry Corporation	3365	E	909 822-6128	6395
Fontana Paper Mills Inc	2952	D	909 823-4100	5279
Fontana Resources At Work	8331	C	909 428-3833	21952
Fontana Wood Treating Inc	2491	F	909 357-2136	3432
Forged Metals Inc	3462	C	909 350-9260	7086
Foundation Pile Inc	1629	D	909 350-1584	997
Friends Group Express Inc	4213	D	909 346-6814	12046
G O Pallets Inc	2448	F	909 823-4663	3390
General Motors LLC	4225	D	951 361-6302	12208
Golden State Grating Inc	3446	F	909 854-2489	6963
Gonsalves & Santucci Inc	1771	B	909 350-0474	1526
Great Northern Corporation	2671	E	951 361-4770	3855
Hanks Inc	4212	D	909 350-8365	11970
Hartman Industries	5051	D	909 423-0114	13569
Hawk Transportation Inc	4213	D	800 709-4295	12051
Heartland Express Inc Iowa	4213	A	319 625-3600	12052
High Tech Machine Shop S-Corp	3519	F	909 356-5437	7596
Hub Group Trucking Inc	4212	B	909 770-8950	11976
Ifco Systems North America Inc	2448	E	909 356-0697	3393
Indorama Vntres Sstnble Sltion	2821	E	951 727-8318	4696
Industrial Insulations Inc **(PA)**	3644	F	909 574-7433	9051
Inland Cc Inc	1771	C	909 355-1318	1531
Inland Kenworth Inc **(HQ)**	5012	C	909 823-9955	13031
Integrated Intermodal Svcs Inc	7379	D	909 355-4100	18189
JE Thomson & Company LLC	3537	F	626 334-7190	7712
Jensen Enterprises Inc	3272	B	909 357-7264	6037
Jeti Inc **(PA)**	7692	F	909 357-2966	18984
Jocer Enterprises Inc	1542	E	909 822-0500	775
Kaden Cash LLC	7929	E	818 714-4665	19361
Kaiser Foundation Hospitals	8011	C	909 609-3800	19884
Kaiser Foundation Hospitals	8011	C	866 205-3595	19900
Kaiser Foundation Hospitals	8011	C	909 427-5000	19932
Kaiser Foundation Hospitals	6324	C	909 427-3910	15432
Life Is Life LLC	2022	F	310 584-7541	1779
Lopez Pallets Inc	2448	F	909 823-0865	3398
Los Angeles Truck Centers LLC	5012	C	909 510-4000	13032
Lowes Home Centers LLC	5031	C	909 350-7900	13250
Luster Cote Inc	3479	F	909 355-9995	7384
Lynam Industries Inc	3444	D	951 360-1919	6864
Material Supply Inc **(PA)**	3444	C	951 801-5004	6870
Maxzone Vehicle Lighting Corp **(HQ)**	5013	E	909 822-3288	13072
McGuire Contracting Inc	1771	D	909 357-1200	1539
Metal Tek Engineering Inc	2431	F	909 821-4158	3266
Meza Pallet Inc	2448	F	909 829-0223	3399

Mergent email: customerrelations@mergent.com
1362

2022 Southern California Business
Directory and Buyers Guide

(P-0000) Products & Services Section entry number
(PA)=Parent Co (HQ)=Headquarters (DH)=Div Headquarters

	SIC	EMP	PHONE	ENTRY #
Mission Custom Extrusion Inc	3089	E	909 822-1581	5712
Mlife Hospice Inc **(PA)**	8052	D	909 996-2508	20537
Modway Inc	5021	D	323 729-3299	13145
Morin Corporation	3448	E	909 428-3747	7003
Nashville Wire Pdts Mfg Co LLC	3496	E	714 736-0081	7504
Nellxo LLC	3469	E	909 320-8501	7169
New Classic HM Furnishing Inc **(PA)**	5023	D	909 484-7676	13178
New Greenscreen Incorporated	3444	D	951 685-9660	6881
Norco Ranch Inc **(DH)**	0291	B	951 737-6735	144
NY Transport Inc	4213	D	909 355-9832	12070
Nyx Industries Inc	3523	F	909 937-3923	7615
Pacific Forge Inc	3462	D	909 390-0701	7092
Patricks Cabinets	2434	F	909 823-2524	3329
Perfectvision Mfg Inc	7231	C	909 355-0478	16914
Pointdirect Transport Inc	4213	D	909 371-0837	12073
Precision Performance Products **(PA)**	1799	F	909 356-4868	1681
Pro Loaders Inc	4731	C	909 355-5531	12512
Pro-Systems Fabricators Inc **(PA)**	3699	F	909 350-9147	9900
Production Engineering & Mch	8071	E	909 721-2455	21088
Quanex Screens LLC	3442	F	909 349-0600	6713
Ramirez Pallets Inc	2448	E	909 822-2066	3405
RDS Logistics Group **(PA)**	4212	D	909 355-4100	11989
Refresco Beverages US Inc	2033	C	951 685-0481	1874
Rep-Kote Products Inc	2952	F	909 355-1288	5285
Rexnord Industries LLC	3568	F	814 969-3665	8108
River Valley Precast Inc	3272	F	928 764-3839	6054
Rnd Contractors Inc	3441	E	909 429-8500	6660
Rotolo Chevrolet Inc	7538	C	866 756-9776	18868
Ryder Intgrted Lgstics Cal LLC	7513	D	909 356-8555	18737
S & H Cabinets and Mfg Inc	2521	E	909 357-0551	3599
S&B Filters Inc	3714	D	909 947-0015	10130
Saia Motor Freight Line LLC	4213	D	909 356-2808	12076
San Gabriel Valley Water Co	4941	C	909 822-2201	12916
Santa Fe Machine Works Inc	3599	E	909 350-6877	8786
Schroeder Iron Corporation	3441	E	909 428-6471	6661
Sierra Hotel Group LLC	7011	D	909 822-7300	16709
Simplex Strip Doors LLC **(PA)**	3081	E	800 854-7951	5438
Slater Inc	1629	D	909 822-6800	1005
Social Junky Inc	2836	E	323 347-9847	4939
Southern Cal Bndery Miling Inc	2789	F	909 829-1949	4622
Southern Cal Prmnnte Med Group	8062	A	909 427-5000	20946
Southern Neng Eggs Acqstion LL **(DH)**	5144	E	951 332-3300	14551
Southwire Inc **(HQ)**	3353	F	310 884-8500	6303
Specialized Milling Corp	2851	E	909 357-7890	5113
Stanley Access Tech LLC	3423	E	909 628-9272	6490
Stantru Resources Inc	1541	D	909 587-1441	720
STC Netcom Inc **(PA)**	1731	D	951 685-8181	1320
Sundown Foods USA Inc	2033	E	909 606-6797	1875
Sunrise Ford	5012	C	909 822-4401	13035
Superior Trailer Works	3537	E	909 350-0185	7718
Svevia Usa Inc	3953	F	909 559-4134	11473
Sweetgrace Home Hlth Svcs LLC	8099	D	909 463-7400	21488
Swift Leasing Co LLC	4213	D	909 347-0500	12079
Syncreon America Inc	4731	D	909 610-4511	12535
Tealove Inc	2099	E	714 408-8245	2535
Tex Rhino Inc	2653	F	909 548-3910	3829
Tikos Tanks Inc	7692	E	951 757-8014	19001
TMT Industries Inc	4213	D	909 493-3441	12082
Tonys Express Inc **(PA)**	4225	C	909 427-8700	12254
Trans-West Ford Truck Sls Inc **(PA)**	5013	D	909 770-5127	13100
Transwest Truck Center LLC	5013	D	909 770-5170	13102
Tree Island Wire (usa) Inc	3315	C	909 594-7511	6237
Tri-Net Inc	3825	F	909 483-3555	10774
Tst/Impreso California Inc	2761	E	909 357-7190	4603
TTI Floor Care North Amer Inc	3052	D	440 996-2802	5325
United Fmly Care Inc A Med Cor	8011	C	909 874-1679	20116
Urethane Polymer International	2899	F	909 357-7200	5246
Utility Trailer Mfg Co	3715	C	909 428-8300	10172
Utility Trlr Sls Sthern Cal LL **(PA)**	5012	D	877 275-4887	13039
Valori Sand & Gravel Company	5032	C	909 350-3000	13317
Victorville Disposal Inc	4953	D	909 429-4200	12991
Vista Metals Corp **(PA)**	3354	C	909 823-4278	6323
Vitawest Nutraceuticals Inc	2023	F	888 557-8012	1807
Vpet Usa LLC	7389	D	909 605-1668	18720
Wabash National Trlr Ctrs Inc	5013	E	765 771-5300	13106
Western PCF Crane & Eqp LLC **(DH)**	7353	E	562 286-6618	17322
Western Single Ply Inc	1761	E	909 574-9735	1511
World Class Distribution Inc **(DH)**	4225	C	909 574-4140	12263
Xpo Logistics Freight Inc	4213	D	951 685-1244	12102
Yucaipa Disposal Inc	4953	C	909 429-4200	13002

FOOTHILL RANCH, CA - Orange County

	SIC	EMP	PHONE	ENTRY #
A & J Manufacturing Company	3469	E	714 544-9570	7116
Allied Components Intl	3677	E	949 356-1780	9619
Avion Graphics Inc	2752	E	949 472-0438	4232
Azure Microdynamics Inc	3599	D	949 699-3344	8511
Bal Seal Engineering LLC **(DH)**	3495	B	949 460-2100	7483
Baldwin Hardware Corporation **(DH)**	3429	A	949 672-4000	6506
Carttronics LLC **(HQ)**	3699	E	888 696-2278	9858
Chroma Systems Solutions Inc **(HQ)**	3825	D	949 297-4848	10747
Debisys Inc **(PA)**	6099	D	949 699-1401	15127
E2 Managetech Inc **(HQ)**	8711	D	281 407-0820	22536
Elite Global Solutions Inc	2821	F	949 709-4872	4691
Frontech N Fujitsu Amer Inc **(DH)**	3578	C	949 855-5500	8314
Gatekeeper Systems Inc **(PA)**	3699	E	949 268-1414	9870
Global Solutions Integration	8711	D	949 307-1849	22561
Hampton Products Intl Corp **(PA)**	5072	D	949 472-4256	13808
Hubbell Power Systems Inc	5063	D	949 305-3311	13634
Ibaset Inc **(PA)**	8748	D	949 598-5200	23452
Ibaset Federal Services LLC **(PA)**	7371	D	949 598-5200	17635
Image Distribution Services **(PA)**	2752	E	949 754-9000	4322
Image Options	7319	C	949 586-7665	17099
Kaiser Aluminum Corporation **(PA)**	3334	D	949 614-1740	6283
Kaiser Aluminum Fab Pdts LLC **(HQ)**	3353	A	949 614-1740	6300
Kaiser Foundation Hospitals	8011	C	800 922-2000	19899
Kawasaki Motors Corp USA **(HQ)**	5013	B	949 837-4683	13069
Kds Donut Chinese Foods	2051	F	949 588-1688	2011
Lantic Inc	3089	E	949 830-9951	5696
Ld Holdings Group LLC **(HQ)**	8742	E	888 337-6888	23257
Leoch Battery Corporation **(HQ)**	3621	D	949 588-5853	8921
Loandepot Inc **(PA)**	6162	A	888 337-6888	15210
Loandepotcom LLC **(DH)**	6162	A	888 337-6888	15213
Mrt Inc	7331	D	949 348-2292	17134
Oakley Inc **(DH)**	3851	A	949 951-0991	11256
Oakley Sales Corp	3851	C	949 672-6925	11257
Oleumtech Corporation	3823	E	949 305-9009	10709
Ossur Americas Inc **(HQ)**	3842	B	800 233-6263	11132
Price Pfister Inc	3432	C	949 672-4003	6564
Professional Cmnty MGT Cal Inc **(PA)**	6531	E	800 369-7260	15956
Professional Cmnty MGT Cal Inc	6514	D	949 768-7261	15755
Protab Laboratories	2834	C	949 635-1930	4875
Redcom LLC **(HQ)**	3861	B	949 404-4084	11290
Renkus-Heinz Inc **(PA)**	3651	D	949 588-9997	9187
Risa Tech Inc	7371	E	949 951-5815	17700
Sgii Inc **(PA)**	5122	C	949 521-6161	14288
Sourcery LLC	5063	F	949 380-0466	13668
Spectrum Hhi	7299	D	949 672-4000	16978
Splash Events Inc **(PA)**	7336	D	408 287-8600	17188
Stonebridge Rlty Advisors Inc	7011	B	949 597-8700	16733
Tae Life Sciences Us LLC **(HQ)**	3845	E	949 830-2117	11240
Tae Life Sciences Us LLC	8731	D	949 344-6112	22865
Tae Technologies Inc **(PA)**	8731	C	949 830-2117	22866
Team Makena LLC **(PA)**	5047	D	949 474-1753	13523
True Family Enterprises **(PA)**	6726	D	888 665-8638	16164
Twila True Collaborations LLC	2844	E	949 258-9720	5076
Venus Group Inc	5023	C	949 609-1299	13196
Voltege Inc **(PA)**	3449	E	949 273-3822	7027

FORT IRWIN, CA - San Bernardino County

	SIC	EMP	PHONE	ENTRY #
Department of Army	8062	D	760 380-3114	20744
Lockheed Martin Corporation	4225	C	760 386-2572	12220
Northrop Grumman Systems Corp	3812	C	760 380-4268	10615
Pinnacle Irwin LLC **(PA)**	6531	D	760 386-4663	15950

FOUNTAIN VALLEY, CA - Orange County

	SIC	EMP	PHONE	ENTRY #
Action Bag & Cover Inc	2393	D	714 965-7777	3124
Adrienne Designs LLC	3911	F	714 558-1209	11306
Advanced Architectural Frames	3442	E	424 209-6018	6689
Advanced Charging Tech Inc	3629	E	877 228-5922	8970
Architectural Doors Inc **(PA)**	5031	D	714 898-3667	13202
Atlantc-Pcfic Proc Systems Inc **(PA)**	7389	C	714 241-1402	18451
Avatar Machine LLC	3599	E	714 434-2737	8508
Banzai Foods LLC	2099	F	714 200-9933	2394
Boys Girls CLB Huntington Vly **(PA)**	8641	D	714 531-2582	22313
California Heart Associates	8011	D	714 546-2238	19732
CCS Los Angeles Janitorial LLC	7349	A	714 966-5600	17224
Ceridian Tax Service Inc	8721	B	714 963-1311	22768
Chefs Toys LLC **(HQ)**	5046	C	508 399-2400	13453
City of Fountain Valley	1623	E	714 593-4441	942
Compuvac Industries Inc	3563	F	949 574-5085	8033
Custom Enamelers Inc	3479	E	714 540-7884	7356
Design Catapult Manufacturing	3841	F	949 522-6789	10968
Duncan McIntosh Company Inc **(PA)**	2721	E	949 660-6150	4067
Elwyn Pennsylvania and Del	8093	D	714 557-6313	21304
Epe Industries Usa Inc **(HQ)**	3086	F	800 315-0336	5499
Express Lens Lab Inc	3851	F	714 545-1024	11251
Fountain Vly Rgnal Hosp Med CT	8062	A	714 966-7200	20772
Freightgate Inc	7372	E	714 799-2833	17862
Gaffoglio Fmly Mtlcrafters Inc **(PA)**	3231	C	714 444-2000	5953
Genesis Group Sftwr Developers	7372	E	714 630-4297	17865
Gfmi Aerospace & Defense Inc	3728	E	714 361-4444	10335
Hyundai Motor America **(HQ)**	5012	B	714 965-3000	13029
In Home Comfort and Care Inc	8082	D	714 485-4120	21174
Interconnect Solutions Co LLC **(PA)**	3629	D	909 545-6140	8978
Interconnect Solutions Co LLC	3679	C	714 556-7007	9727
Jmg Security Systems Inc	1731	D	714 545-8882	1270
Joy Products California Inc	3953	E	714 437-7250	11472
KB Sheetmetal Fabrication Inc	3444	E	714 979-1780	6860
Kingston Digital Inc **(HQ)**	3577	C	714 435-2600	8270
Kingston Technology Corp **(PA)**	3577	E	714 435-2600	8271
Ktc-Tu Corporation	3674	F	714 435-2600	9528
Linpac USA Holdings Inc	3089	D	714 845-2845	5699
Marie Callender Pie Shops Inc	2051	D	714 963-6791	2018
ME & My Big Ideas LLC	5092	D	877 462-6241	14097
Memorial Health Services **(PA)**	8062	A	714 377-2900	20858
Memorial Healthtec Labratories	8731	A	714 962-4677	22850
Memorialcare Med Foundation **(PA)**	8641	C	714 389-5353	22347
Memorlcare Srgcal Ctr At Ornge	8062	D	714 369-1100	20861
Meyco Machine and Tool Inc	3545	E	714 435-1546	7857
Microscale Industries Inc	2752	E	714 593-1422	4374
Mile Square Golf Course	7992	C	714 962-5541	19501
ML Kishigo Mfg Co LLC	2389	D	949 852-1963	3080
Mobis Parts America LLC **(HQ)**	5013	D	786 515-1101	13074
Mobis Parts America LLC	3714	E	949 450-0014	10105
Moving Image Technologies LLC	3861	E	714 751-7998	11285
Municpal Wtr Dst Ornge Cnty Wt	4941	D	714 963-3058	12909

GEOGRAPHIC

Employment Codes: A=Over 500 employees, B=251-500, C=101-250, D=51-100, E=20-50 F=10-19

2022 Southern California Business Directory and Buyers Guide

© Mergent Inc. 1-800-342-5647

1363

Company	SIC	EMP	PHONE	ENTRY #
Nobles Medical Tech Inc	3841	E	714 427-0398	11035
Noritz America Corporation (HQ)	5075	D	714 433-2905	13848
Omni Metal Finishing Inc (PA)	3471	C	714 979-9414	7290
Orange Coast Memorial Med Ctr (HQ)	8062	A	714 378-7000	20875
Orange County Sanitation (PA)	4953	B	714 962-2411	12962
Orange County Water District	4941	D	714 378-3200	12911
Pacific Advnced Cvil Engrg Inc (PA)	8711	D	714 481-7300	22627
Pacific Aquascape Inc	1799	D	714 843-5734	1679
Paderia LLC	2052	F	949 478-5273	2070
Pan-Pacific Mechanical LLC (PA)	1711	C	949 474-9170	1115
Payton Technology Corporation	3674	D	714 885-8000	9556
Printing Island Corporation	2752	F	714 668-1000	4399
Psitech Inc	3571	F	714 964-7818	8171
Ropak Corporation (DH)	3089	B	714 845-2845	5799
Safeguard On Demand Inc	7381	C	800 640-2327	18319
Santa Fe Textiles Inc	2241	F	949 251-1960	2618
Sensonetics Inc	3674	E	714 799-1616	9575
Sherman Corporation	3599	E	310 671-2117	8795
Shock Doctor Inc (PA)	3949	D	800 233-6956	11446
Slapfish Huntington Beach LLC	2035	E	714 963-3900	1894
Spec Services Inc	8711	B	714 963-8077	22657
Specialized Screen Prtg Inc	2759	F	714 964-1230	4575
SPX Corporation	3443	D	714 434-2576	6755
Surefire LLC (PA)	3842	B	714 545-9444	11143
Sutura Inc	3842	E	714 427-0398	11144
Syc International Inc	2599	E	888 300-9168	3741
Synergistic Research Inc	3496	F	949 476-0000	7515
Tdi2 Custom Packaging Inc	2673	E	714 751-6782	3892
Tires Warehouse LLC	5014	C	714 432-8851	13122
TN Sheet Metal Inc	3444	F	714 593-0100	6932
Watt Enterprise Inc	2329	F	714 963-0781	2832

FRAZIER PARK, CA - Kern County

Company	SIC	EMP	PHONE	ENTRY #
Trnlwb LLC	3999	A	661 245-3736	11785

FULLERTON, CA - Orange County

Company	SIC	EMP	PHONE	ENTRY #
24hr Homecare LLC	8082	D	714 881-4245	21119
Accurate Laminated Pdts Inc	2542	E	714 632-2773	3674
Achem Industry America Inc (PA)	5085	E	562 802-0998	13968
Adams Rite Aerospace Inc (DH)	3728	C	714 278-6500	10239
ADB Industries	3398	B	310 679-9193	6426
Adept Builder LLC	6513	E	949 933-2785	15717
Advanced Equipment Corporation (PA)	2542	E	714 635-5350	3675
Advanced Image Direct LLC	7331	E	714 502-3900	17129
Aero Engineering Inc	3599	F	714 879-6200	8472
Aerofit LLC	3498	C	714 521-5060	7526
AJ Kirkwood & Associates Inc	1731	B	714 505-1977	1210
Altura Holdings LLC (HQ)	6722	E	714 948-8400	16121
American Window Covering Inc	7216	F	714 879-3880	16875
Americo Builders LLC	1521	C	714 430-7730	592
AMS American Mech Svcs MD Inc	1711	C	714 888-6820	1028
Amtrend Corporation	2541	D	714 630-2070	3637
Anaheim Park Hotel	7011	A	714 992-1700	16323
Anderco Inc	2431	E	714 446-9508	3229
Anderson Air Conditioning LP	1711	D	714 998-6850	1029
Arborland Enterprises Inc	8351	D	714 871-2311	21983
Aurident Inc	3843	E	714 870-1851	11160
Automobile Club Southern Cal	8699	D	714 871-2333	22428
Bakery Ex Southern Cal LLC	5149	C	714 446-9470	14673
Bbe Sound Inc (PA)	3931	E	714 897-6766	11340
Beckman Instruments Inc	3826	D	714 871-4848	10784
Biomed Instruments Inc	3845	F	714 459-5716	11215
Bon Suisse Inc	8748	F	714 578-0001	23421
Brentwood Home LLC (PA)	2515	C	562 949-3759	3544
Bushnell Ribbon Corporation	3955	E	562 948-1410	11474
Byrnes & Kiefer Co	2087	D	714 554-4000	2312
C & L Refrigeration Corp	1711	C	800 901-4822	1041
Cardservice International Inc	7389	D	714 773-1778	18469
Cargill Incorporated	2079	E	323 588-2274	2128
Chefmaster	2099	E	714 554-4000	2408
Chubby Gorilla Inc (PA)	3089	D	844 365-5218	5606
CJ Foods Manufacturing Corp	2099	E	714 888-3500	2410
Common Collabs LLC	2087	E	714 519-3245	2316
Consolidated Aerospace Mfg LLC (HQ)	3812	C	714 989-2797	10578
Cook and Cook Incorporated	3443	C	714 680-6669	6739
Corecare I I I	8361	C	714 256-8000	22095
Corecare V A Cal Ltd Partnr	8051	C	714 256-1000	20291
Corru-Kraft IV	2653	F	714 773-0124	3796
Cove Four-Slide Stamping Corp (PA)	3496	D	516 379-4232	7499
Custom Autosound Mfg Inc	3651	E	714 535-1091	9168
Dae Shin Usa Inc	2221	D	714 578-8900	2595
Delta Pacific Activewear Inc	2253	D	714 871-9281	2629
Delta Stag Manufacturing	3713	E	562 904-6444	9982
Direct Drive Systems Inc	3621	D	714 872-5500	8912
Dr Smoothie Brands Inc	2087	F	714 449-9787	2321
Dr Smoothie Enterprises	2087	E	714 449-9787	2322
Ejays Machine Co Inc	3599	E	714 879-0558	8578
Ellingson Inc	3599	E	714 773-1923	8579
Excel Construction Svcs Inc (PA)	1541	D	714 680-9200	697
EZ Lube LLC	7549	D	714 871-9980	18931
Faac	3699	E	800 221-8278	9868
Florence Crttnton Svcs Ornge C	8361	B	714 680-9000	22103
Fluid Power Ctrl Systems Inc	3823	E	714 525-3727	10694
Foam-Craft Inc	3086	C	714 459-9971	5506
Fullerton Hlthcare Wllness CNT	8051	C	714 992-5701	20548
Fullerton Orthpd Srgery Med Gr	8011	D	714 879-0050	19826
Fullerton Printing Inc	2752	F	714 870-7500	4300
Future Foam Inc	3086	E	714 871-2344	5507
Future Foam Inc	3086	C	714 459-9971	5508
Gard Inc	3444	E	714 738-5891	6842
Gaylords HRI Meats	2011	F	714 526-2278	1712
General Linear Systems Inc	3677	F	714 994-4822	9631
Gigatera Communications	3679	D	714 515-1100	9718
Global Mfg Solutions LLC	3357	C	562 356-3222	6351
Gold Venture Inc	3086	C	909 623-1810	5509
Golden Pacific Seafoods Inc	3556	E	714 589-8888	7937
Golden West Technology	3672	C	714 738-3775	9411
Goodman North America LLC	2621	D	714 680-7460	3754
Hidden Villa Ranch Produce Inc	5144	B	714 680-3447	14547
Houdini Inc (PA)	5199	D	714 525-0325	14938
Howmet Globl Fstning Systems I	3324	F	714 871-1550	6267
HP It Services Incorporated	3577	E	714 844-7737	8262
Huoyen International Inc	7011	F	714 635-9000	16496
Ideal Graphics Inc	2752	F	714 632-3398	4318
Independent Options Inc	8361	D	714 738-1400	22117
Interntnal Cnnctors Cable Corp	3661	C	888 275-4422	9235
Jonel Engineering	3596	E	714 879-2360	8448
Kaylas Cake Corporation	5149	E	714 869-1522	14701
Khyber Foods Incorporated	2099	F	714 879-0900	2460
Kims Welding and Iron Works	3462	F	714 680-7700	7090
Kip Steel Inc	3316	E	714 461-1051	6243
Kryler Corp	3471	E	714 871-9611	7276
Lange Precision Inc	3599	F	714 870-5421	8660
Laser Industries Inc	3599	D	714 532-3271	8662
Magtech & Power Conversion Inc	3677	E	714 451-0105	9633
Mail Handling Group Inc	2752	C	952 975-5000	4364
Marton Precision Mfg LLC	3724	E	714 808-6523	10221
McKenna Labs Inc (PA)	2834	E	714 687-6888	4851
Merritt Hospitality LLC	7011	C	714 738-7800	16565
National Signal Inc	3799	E	714 441-7707	10553
Nicholas Michael Designs Inc	2519	C	714 562-8101	3569
Nina Mia Inc	2099	E	714 773-5538	2495
North American Video Corp (PA)	5065	E	714 779-7499	13756
North Ornge Cnty Cmmty Cllege	5045	C	714 992-7008	13422
Northern Ornge Cnty Ent Mdcl (PA)	8011	D	714 441-0133	20004
Oem LLC	3599	E	714 449-7500	8725
Orora Visual LLC	2759	D	714 879-2400	4550
Pacmin Incorporated (PA)	3999	D	714 447-4278	11728
Pasco Industries Inc	3991	E	714 992-2051	11514
Picture This Framing Inc	2499	F	714 447-8749	3450
Plasticolor Molded Pdts Inc (PA)	3083	C	714 525-3880	5457
Plexi Fab Inc	3089	F	714 447-8494	5763
Printec Ht Electronics LLC	3674	E	714 484-7597	9561
Production Delivery Svcs Inc	4213	D	562 777-0060	12074
Progrssive Intgrated Solutions	2759	D	714 237-0980	4561
Quaker Oats Company	4225	E	714 526-8800	12236
Raytheon Cmmand Ctrl Sltons LL (DH)	5065	A	714 446-3118	13770
Raytheon Company	3812	F	714 446-2584	10638
Real Estate Image Inc (PA)	7331	C	714 502-3900	17140
Rosary Academy Parent Council	8641	B	714 879-6302	22363
Rozak Engineering Inc	3599	F	714 446-3855	8779
RPM Consolidated Services Inc (HQ)	4225	D	714 388-3500	12240
S and H Rubber Company Inc	3069	E	714 525-0277	5408
Santa Ana Plating (PA)	3471	D	310 923-8305	7309
Schreiber Foods Inc	2022	E	714 490-7360	1781
Scientific Spray Finishes Inc	3479	E	714 871-5541	7409
Screen Printers Resource Inc	2759	F	714 441-1155	4572
Senor Snacks Inc	2096	F	714 739-1073	2365
Senor Snacks Manufacturing Ltd	2064	E	714 739-1073	2106
Soma Magnetics Corporation	3612	F	714 447-0782	8884
South Coast Trnsp & Dist Inc	4212	D	310 816-0280	11994
Southern California Edison Co	4911	C	714 870-3225	12835
SPD Manufacturing Inc	2221	F	985 302-1902	2604
Sph Holdings Inc (HQ)	1541	C	714 441-3900	719
St Jude Heritage Med Group	8062	D	714 449-6200	20965
St Jude Hospital (DH)	8062	A	714 871-3280	20966
Staff Pro Inc (PA)	7382	A	714 230-7200	18402
Stauber Prfmce Ingredients Inc (HQ)	2833	D	714 441-3900	4765
Stein Industries Inc (PA)	3444	D	714 522-4560	6919
Sun Haven Care Inc	8051	D	714 870-0060	20482
Superior Wall Systems Inc	1742	B	714 278-0000	1404
Swinford Electric Inc	1731	E	714 578-8888	1324
T and T Industries Inc (PA)	3496	F	714 264-6555	7517
Tct Advanced Machining Inc	3599	F	714 871-9371	8811
Terra Universal Inc	3564	C	714 526-0100	8056
Therapy For Kids Inc	8093	D	714 870-6116	21354
Thunderbolt Manufacturing Inc	3599	E	714 632-0397	8818
Total Logistics Online LLC	4731	D	714 526-3559	12542
TW Services Inc	4789	B	714 441-2400	12584
Ultra Wheel Company	3714	E	714 449-7100	10148
UNI Filter Inc	3714	E	714 535-6933	10149
United Duralume Products Inc	3444	E	714 773-4011	6936
United Pharma LLC	2899	C	714 738-8999	5245
United Testing Systems Inc	3829	E	714 638-2322	10919
Veg-Land Inc	4221	E	714 871-6712	12172
Victorious RED	1795	E	657 529-8911	1621
Viele & Sons Inc	5141	E	714 147-3663	14519
Vista Paint Corporation (PA)	2851	C	714 380-3800	5119
Volt Management Corp	7363	D	714 879-9330	17527
Ware Disposal Inc	4953	C	714 834-0234	12992
Western States Envelope Corp	2759	D	714 449-0909	4595
Westview Services Inc	8322	D	714 879-3980	21928
Wheel and Tire Club Inc	3312	E	714 422-3505	6218
Will-Mann Inc	3444	E	714 870-0350	6943
Wilsons Art Studio Inc	2759	D	714 870-7030	4596

	SIC	EMP	PHONE	ENTRY #
Windsor Grdns Hlthcare Ctr Fll	8051	D	714 871-6020	20516
Winonics Inc	3672	C	714 626-3755	9469
WMc Prcsion McHning Grnding	3599	E	714 773-0059	8857
Wyndham International Inc	7011	C	714 992-1700	16806
Zmp Aquisition Corporation	3625	F	714 278-6500	8969

GARDEN GROVE, CA - Orange County

	SIC	EMP	PHONE	ENTRY #
A Q Pharmaceuticals Inc	2834	E	714 903-1000	4771
Aaron Thomas Company Inc **(PA)**	7389	C	714 894-4468	18428
Abbey-Properties LLC **(PA)**	6512	D	562 435-2100	15656
Accutherm Refrigeraton Inc	1711	D	714 766-7800	1013
Advanced Aerospace	3585	F	714 265-6200	8327
Advanced Phrm Svcs Inc	5122	F	714 903-1006	14231
Aero Dynamic Machining Inc	3599	D	714 379-1073	8471
AGR Group Inc	8742	A	714 245-7151	23148
Allied Wheel Components Inc	3714	E	714 893-4160	10015
American Metal Bearing Company	3562	E	714 892-5527	8026
Anaheim Marriott Suites	7011	D	714 750-1000	16322
Arch Precision Components	3728	E	714 961-9200	10275
B & E Manufacturing Co Inc	3728	E	714 898-2269	10285
Bankers Investment Group Inc	6162	C	714 618-1736	15175
Basic Electronics Inc	3679	E	714 530-2400	9680
Baton Lock & Hardware Co Inc	3429	E	714 265-3636	6507
Beauty & Health International	2834	E	714 903-9730	4796
Boys Grls Clubs Grdn Grove Inc **(PA)**	8699	C	714 530-0430	22446
Brinks Incorporated	7381	C	714 903-9272	18259
Buffalo Spot MGT Group LLC	8741	C	949 354-0884	22993
C & A Transducers Inc	3679	F	714 554-9188	9684
Cali Chem Inc	2844	E	714 265-3740	4997
Cali Food Company Inc	2032	E	714 821-8630	1847
California Shirt Printer Inc	5136	D	714 898-9946	14329
Caster Technology Corp **(PA)**	5051	F	714 893-6886	13556
Catalina Cylinders Inc **(PA)**	3443	D	714 890-0999	6733
Chapman Hbr Sklled Nrsing Care	8051	D	714 971-5517	20280
Chatham Rigg LLC	6552	E	714 591-4000	16049
Chemical Methods Assoc LLC **(DH)**	3589	E	714 898-8781	8370
Closet World Inc	1799	C	714 890-5860	1650
Coastline High Prfmce Ctngs Lt	3663	F	714 372-3263	9262
Coastline Metal Finishing Corp	3471	D	714 895-9099	7241
Commercial Cstm Sting Uphl Inc	2599	D	714 850-0520	3723
Community Action Prtnr Ornge C	8322	C	714 897-6670	21753
Compass Group Usa Inc	7359	C	714 899-2520	17338
Crystal Cathedral Ministries **(PA)**	7812	C	714 622-2900	19114
CTS Cement Manufacturing Corp **(PA)**	2891	E	714 379-8260	5179
Cushman & Wakefield Cal Inc	6531	A	714 591-0451	15828
Custom Pack Inc	3221	F	714 534-2201	5928
Customfab Inc	3111	C	714 891-9119	5868
D & S Custom Plating Inc	3714	F	714 537-5411	10040
Diversfied Mtllrgical Svcs Inc	3398	E	714 895-7777	6439
Elasco Inc	2821	D	714 373-4767	4689
Elasco Urethane Inc	2821	E	714 895-7031	4690
Electron Plating III Inc	3471	E	714 554-2210	7254
Elite Screens Inc	3861	E	877 511-1211	11275
Elrob Inc	5065	D	714 230-6122	13717
Envise **(HQ)**	1711	D	800 613-6240	1063
Envise	1711	D	714 901-5800	1064
Evans Manufacturing Inc **(PA)**	3993	C	714 379-6100	11552
Exigent Sensors LLC	3669	E	949 439-1321	9341
Expo-3 International Inc	3993	E	714 379-8383	11553
F T B & Son Inc	3444	E	714 891-8003	6835
Fei-Zyfer Inc **(HQ)**	3663	B	714 933-4000	9273
Fourbro Inc	2329	F	714 277-3858	2809
G Brothers Construction Inc	1742	E	714 590-3070	1376
Garden Grove Medical Investors **(HQ)**	8051	D	714 534-1041	20350
Garden Grove Unified Schl Dst	2731	D	714 663-6101	4130
Garden Grove Unified Schl Dst	7349	D	714 663-6185	17245
GKN Aerospace	3721	E	714 653-7531	10187
GKN Arspace Trnsprncy Systems **(DH)**	3089	B	714 893-7531	5654
Goodwin Ammonia Company **(PA)**	2841	F	714 894-0531	4941
Goodwin Ammonia Company	2841	D	714 894-0531	4942
Griton Industries Inc **(PA)**	3291	F	714 554-8875	6153
Harbor Suites LLC	7011	E	714 703-8800	16463
House Foods America Corp **(HQ)**	2099	B	714 901-4350	2451
Houston Bazz Co	3469	D	714 898-2666	7151
Hyatt Die Cast Engrg Corp - S	3363	E	714 622-2131	6364
Hycor Biomedical LLC	3841	C	714 933-3000	10989
I Copy Inc	3599	E	562 921-0202	8625
In Garden Grove Cnvlscent Hosp	8059	D	714 638-9470	20598
Infinite Engineering Inc	3599	F	714 534-4688	8626
Innovated Solutions Inc	3559	F	949 222-1088	7984
Innovative Casework Mfg Inc	3999	E	714 890-9100	11690
Innovative Metal Designs Inc	5013	E	714 799-6700	13066
Iron Grip Barbell Company Inc	3949	D	714 850-6900	11430
Irvine APT Communities LP	6513	C	714 537-8500	15733
J L Wingert Company	3589	D	714 379-5519	8388
Janitorial Equipment Svcs Inc	7349	D	951 205-8937	17254
Jason Tool and Engineering Inc	3089	E	714 895-5067	5679
Jvr Sheetmetal Fabrication Inc	3721	E	714 841-2464	10192
Kaiser Foundation Hospitals	8011	C	714 741-3448	19863
Kenneth Corp	8062	A	714 537-5160	20824
Kimberly Machine Inc	3599	E	714 539-0151	8655
King Instrument Company Inc	3823	E	714 891-0008	10704
King Shock Technology Inc	3714	D	719 394-3754	10087
Kittyhawk Inc	3398	E	714 895-5024	6442
Kittyhawk Products CA LLC	3398	E	714 895-5024	6443
Kpi Services Inc	3398	E	714 895-5024	6444
L C Pringle Sales Inc **(PA)**	2591	E	714 892-1524	3713
Leiner Health Products Inc	2834	C	714 898-9936	4844
Lu & Weber Corporation	8082	D	714 590-3620	21187
M & T Aerospace Inc	3721	F	714 591-5154	10194
M M Direct Marketing Inc	7331	C	714 265-4100	17133
Mastroianni Family Entps Ltd	7299	B	310 952-1700	16965
Medical Center Gift Shop	8062	D	714 537-7100	20857
Microsemi Corp - Anlog Mxed Sg **(DH)**	3674	A	714 898-8121	9542
Microsemi Corp - High Prfmce T **(DH)**	3674	D	949 380-6100	9543
Microsemi Corp-Power MGT Group	3625	C	714 994-6500	8960
Microsemi Corporation **(HQ)**	3674	E	949 380-6100	9544
Mitsubishi Electric Us Inc	5065	D	714 934-5300	13751
Modivcare Solutions LLC	4731	C	714 503-6871	12485
Monco Products Inc	3089	E	714 891-2788	5719
Monster Vending	3089	E	909 223-5522	5720
Nelson Engineering Llc	3599	E	714 893-7999	8716
New Mode Sportswear	5136	F	714 899-7800	14343
Noarus Tgg	7538	D	714 895-5595	18859
Ohi Resort Hotels LLC	7011	D	714 867-5555	16591
Onecharge Inc	3691	E	833 895-8624	9812
Orange County Trnsp Auth	4111	D	714 560-6282	11832
Our Watch	8082	D	714 622-5852	21196
Pace Sportswear Inc	2339	F	714 891-8716	2978
Pacific Athletic Wear Inc	2339	D	714 751-8006	2979
Pacific Bay Lending Group	6163	D	714 367-5125	15247
Pacific Cchways Chrtr Svcs Inc	4142	D	714 892-5000	11914
Pacific Eagle International **(PA)**	7381	B	562 972-3813	18305
Pacific Haven Convalescent HM	8059	D	714 534-1942	20621
Pathfinder Health Inc	8082	E	714 636-5649	21199
Peerless Injection Molding LLC	3089	E	714 689-1920	5741
Penn Elcom Inc **(HQ)**	5072	E	714 230-6200	13814
Pierce-Spafford Metals Co Inc	5051	C	714 895-7756	13585
Progressive Power Group Inc	1711	E	714 899-2300	1124
Protect-US	7381	C	714 721-8127	18313
Qyk Brands LLC	5122	C	949 312-7119	14284
RJ Allen Inc	7353	D	714 539-1022	17318
Roger Industry	3672	F	714 896-0765	9449
Saint-Gobain Prfmce Plas Corp	2821	C	714 893-0470	4714
Sanyo Foods Corp America **(DH)**	2098	E	714 891-3671	2383
Select Graphics	2752	F	714 537-5250	4421
Sherton Grdn Grove Anheim S Ht	7011	E	714 703-8400	16707
Siemens Industry Inc	3661	F	714 891-3964	9242
South West Sun Solar Inc	1711	E	714 582-3909	1146
Southland Industries **(PA)**	1711	E	800 613-6240	1147
Spartan Manufacturing Co	3599	E	714 894-1955	8799
Sprint Communications Co LP	7375	C	714 534-2107	18132
SPS Technologies LLC	3452	E	714 892-5571	7075
St Paul Brands Inc	2824	E	714 903-1000	4735
Synertech PM Inc	3369	F	714 898-9151	6422
Tad Pgs Inc	7363	A	800 261-3779	17517
Teacher Created Resources Inc	2741	D	714 230-7060	4213
Tekworks Inc	4813	D	877 835-9675	12673
Terra Pacific Landscape **(HQ)**	0781	D	714 567-0177	287
Testing Company LLC **(PA)**	8071	C	714 379-0280	21098
Three Dots LLC	2331	D	714 799-6333	2870
Tj Aerospace Inc	3728	E	714 891-3564	10431
Tl Machine Inc	3451	D	714 554-4154	7046
TT Machine Corp	3599	F	714 534-5288	8829
Umpco Inc	3429	D	714 897-3531	6543
Uremet Corporation	2821	E	657 257-4027	4726
Uttam Composites LLC	3443	F	714 894-5300	6764
V & F Fabrication Company Inc	3441	E	714 265-0630	6678
Vianh Company Inc	3599	E	714 590-9808	8841
Video Vice Data Communications	4899	B	714 897-6300	12793
Vitesse Manufacturing & Dev	3674	C	805 388-3700	9602
Vorsteiner Inc	3069	F	714 379-4600	5423
Walker Products	3714	E	714 554-5151	10156
Western Precision Aero LLC	3599	E	714 893-7999	8850
Wtpc Inc	2752	E	714 903-2500	4462

GARDENA, CA - Los Angeles County

	SIC	EMP	PHONE	ENTRY #
3 - D Polymers	3069	F	310 324-7694	5362
A & A Machine & Dev Co Inc	3599	F	310 532-7706	8450
A and M Welding Inc	7692	E	310 329-2700	18965
A B P Inc	5199	F	310 532-9400	14907
A M Cabinets Inc **(PA)**	2521	D	310 532-1919	3575
A Royal Wolf Portable Stor Inc	5085	E	310 719-1048	13967
A&W Precision Machining Inc	3599	F	310 527-7242	8457
Abrasive Finishing Co	3398	F	310 323-7175	6424
Ace Air Manufacturing	3728	F	310 323-7246	10233
Acrylicore Inc	3083	F	310 515-4846	5447
Administrative Svcs Coop Inc	4121	C	310 715-1968	11900
Advanced Foam Inc	3086	E	310 515-0728	5483
Advantage Products Group LLC	2399	E	310 371-2060	3189
Aerodynamic Plating Co	3471	E	310 329-7959	7200
Ahf-Ducommun Incorporated **(HQ)**	3728	C	310 380-5390	10257
Air Fayre USA Inc	2099	C	310 808-1061	2387
Alan Pre-Fab Building Corp	2452	F	310 538-0333	3427
Aldo Fragale	3599	E	310 324-0050	8485
Aleksandar Inc	1751	F	310 516-7700	1424
All Year Roofing Inc	1761	D	310 851-9440	1473
All-Ways Metal Inc	3444	E	310 217-1177	6778
Ambuserve Inc	4119	D	310 644-0500	11848
American Aircraft Products Inc	3444	D	310 532-7434	6782
American Cabinet Works	2431	E	310 715-6815	3228
American Guard Services Inc **(PA)**	7381	B	310 645-6200	18244
American Maple Inc	3949	F	310 515-8881	11400
American Stream Solar Inc	7299	E	888 919-6636	16943
Americhip Inc **(PA)**	2752	E	310 323-3697	4229
Amfoam Inc **(PA)**	3086	D	310 327-4003	5488

GEOGRAPHIC

Employment Codes: A=Over 500 employees, B=251-500, C=101-250, D=51-100, E=20-50 F=10-19
2022 Southern California Business Directory and Buyers Guide
© Mergent Inc. 1-800-342-5647
1365

	SIC	EMP	PHONE	ENTRY #
AMG Construction Group	1611	D	800 310-2609	858
Anvil Steel Corporation	1791	D	310 329-5811	1566
Ar-Ce Inc	3952	F	310 771-1960	11467
Arandas Woodcraft Inc	2434	E	310 538-9945	3304
Arena Painting Contractors Inc	1721	D	310 316-2446	1169
Arktura LLC **(HQ)**	2519	E	310 532-1050	3565
Artistic Welding	3444	D	310 515-4922	6788
Artists Guild of America	8999	F	310 532-3331	23530
Arto Brick / California Pavers	3251	E	310 768-8500	5982
Autoflow Products Co	3823	F	310 515-2866	10678
Autozone Inc	5013	D	310 525-2333	13046
Avcorp Cmpsite Fabrication Inc	3728	B	310 970-5658	10283
B & W Tile Co Inc **(PA)**	3253	E	310 538-9579	5984
Bake R Us Inc	2051	E	310 630-5873	1980
Barco Uniforms Inc	2311	C	310 323-7315	2741
Barnes Plastics Inc	3089	E	310 329-6301	5576
Baxstra Inc	2426	E	323 770-4171	3214
Bay Cities Tin Shop Inc	3444	E	310 660-0351	6794
Bcd Food Inc	2099	F	310 323-1200	2395
BDS Natural Products Inc **(PA)**	2099	E	310 518-2227	2396
Behavior Frontiers LLC	8049	D	310 856-0800	20208
Behavioral Health Services Inc **(PA)**	8322	E	310 679-9031	21720
Better Nutritionals LLC	2023	E	310 356-9019	1784
Binder Metal Products Inc	3469	D	800 233-0896	7128
Bixolon America Inc	3577	E	858 764-4580	8240
Bremik International Inc	2741	D	310 715-6622	4157
Brentwood Medical Tech Corp	5047	D	800 624-8950	13481
Brightview Landscape Svcs Inc	0781	C	310 327-8700	248
Briles Aerospace Inc	3452	D	310 701-2087	7058
Budget Industrial Unf Sup Inc	7213	D	310 532-7550	16849
Caitac Garment Processing Inc	2261	B	310 217-9888	2657
Cal Pacific Dyeing & Finishing	2269	F	310 327-3792	2669
California Supply Inc **(PA)**	5113	D	310 532-2500	14206
California Waste Services LLC	4953	C	310 538-5998	12934
Carson Trailer Inc **(PA)**	3792	D	310 835-0876	10538
Cast-Rite Corporation	3544	D	310 532-2080	7785
Cast-Rite International Inc **(PA)**	3369	D	310 532-2080	6413
Cbm Consulting Inc	8711	D	310 329-0102	22512
Centron Industries Inc	3663	E	310 324-6443	9261
Century Precision Engrg Inc	3599	E	310 538-0015	8548
CH Laboratories Inc **(PA)**	2834	E	310 516-8273	4808
Charles E Thomas Company Inc **(PA)**	1542	D	310 323-6730	751
Chief Neon Sign Co Inc	3993	F	310 327-1317	11533
Cilajet LLC	2842	E	310 320-8000	4960
City of Gardena	4111	D	310 324-1475	11803
Classic Tile & Mosaic Inc **(PA)**	5032	D	310 538-9605	13298
Claud Townsley Inc	1761	D	310 527-6770	1478
Clean Water Technology Inc **(HQ)**	3589	E	310 380-4648	8373
Cleanstreet LLC	4959	C	800 225-7316	13005
Clegg Industries Inc	3993	C	310 225-3800	11534
Cloud B Inc	3942	E	310 781-3833	11358
CM Laundry LLC	7219	D	310 436-6170	16888
Colich Sons	1623	D	323 770-2920	944
Comprehensive Dist Svcs Inc	4789	C	310 523-1546	12567
Continental Bdr Specialty Corp **(PA)**	2782	C	310 324-8227	4608
Cosway Company Inc	2844	E	310 527-9135	5008
Counseling and Research Assoc **(PA)**	8361	C	310 715-2020	22096
Custom Displays Inc	2541	F	323 770-8074	3645
Custom Metal Finishing Corp	3559	E	310 532-5075	7971
Cytydel Plastics Inc	3089	F	310 523-2884	5620
D and J Marketing Inc	2396	E	310 538-1583	3171
Dasol Inc	3641	C	310 327-6700	9019
DCH Gardena Honda	7538	C	310 515-5700	18823
Del Mar Industries **(PA)**	3364	D	323 321-0600	6377
Del Mar Industries	3364	E	310 327-2634	6378
Designed Metal Connections Inc **(DH)**	3728	B	310 323-6200	10309
Disaster Rstrtion Prfssnals In	1521	D	310 301-8030	601
Doringer Manufacturing Co Inc	3541	F	310 366-7766	7729
Ducommun Aerostructures Inc **(HQ)**	3724	B	310 380-5390	10213
Duggan & Associates Inc	1721	D	323 965-1502	1177
Eagle Security Services Inc	7381	C	310 642-0656	18272
El Dorado Enterprises Inc	7011	A	310 719-9800	16430
Elite Engineering Contrs Inc	8711	E	310 465-8333	22541
Elro Manufacturing Company **(PA)**	3993	E	310 380-7444	11548
Eptronics Inc	3646	F	310 536-0700	9083
Eternal Star Corporation	2678	E	310 768-1945	3914
Evergreen Oil Inc **(HQ)**	2992	C	949 757-7770	5295
F R T International Inc	4225	D	310 329-5700	12204
Faber Enterprises Inc	3492	C	310 323-6200	7457
Faraday Fture Intllgent Elc In **(PA)**	3711	D	424 276-7616	9945
FAraday&future Inc	8711	A	424 276-7616	22547
Finntech Inc	3599	F	310 323-0790	8589
First Student Inc	4151	A	310 769-2400	11934
Gamma Aerospace LLC	3599	E	310 532-4480	8599
Gardena Flores	8051	D	310 323-4570	20352
Gardena Hospital LP	8062	A	310 532-4200	20774
Gardena Retirement Center Inc	8051	D	310 327-4091	20353
Gardena Valley News Inc	2711	E	310 329-6351	3980
Geiger Plastics Inc	3089	E	310 327-9926	5649
Gina B Ltd	5023	F	310 366-7926	13172
Global Casuals Inc	2329	D	310 817-2828	2811
Global Paratransit Inc	4119	B	310 715-7550	11871
Gloria Lance Inc **(PA)**	2331	D	310 767-4400	2844
Granath & Granath Inc	3471	E	310 327-5740	7264
Grow More Inc	2879	D	310 515-1700	5170
Gsp Metal Finishing Inc	3471	E	818 744-1328	7265
GT Precision Inc	3451	C	310 323-4374	7037

	SIC	EMP	PHONE	ENTRY #
Guardsmark LLC	7381	D	310 522-9603	18283
Guru Denim LLC **(DH)**	5137	C	323 266-3072	14378
Hamilton Technology Corp	3646	F	310 217-1191	9088
Hammer Collection Inc	2512	E	310 515-0276	3505
Hansens Welding Inc	7692	E	310 329-6888	18980
Harbor Distributing LLC	5181	D	310 538-5483	14828
Health Care Investments Inc	8051	C	310 323-3194	20372
HI Tech Heat Treating Inc	3398	F	310 532-3705	6440
Hi-Craft Metal Products	3444	E	310 323-6949	6851
His Life Woodworks	2431	E	310 756-0170	3254
Hotel Pacific Garden	7011	D	310 532-5200	16493
HUD Industries	3556	F	310 327-7110	7938
Impresa Aerospace LLC	3728	C	310 354-1200	10351
Inca One Corporation	3675	E	310 808-0001	9610
J & S Inc	3599	E	310 719-7144	8634
J&L Press Inc **(PA)**	2752	F	818 549-8344	4341
Jabi Enterprises Inc	7549	D	310 323-8436	18935
Jayem Enterprises Inc	5051	D	310 329-2263	13571
JH Bryant Jr Inc **(PA)**	1541	E	310 532-1840	703
Jk Imaging Ltd	5043	D	310 755-6848	13346
Jomar Industries Inc	7389	E	323 770-0505	18561
K C Hilites Inc	3647	E	928 635-2607	9117
K C Restoration Co Inc	1389	E	310 280-0597	514
Kaiser Foundation Hospitals	8011	C	310 325-5111	19861
Kaiser Foundation Hospitals	8011	C	800 780-1230	19901
Kaiser Foundation Hospitals	8011	C	310 325-5111	19927
Kaiser Foundation Hospitals	8062	A	310 517-2956	20813
Karrior Electric Vehicles Inc	3537	F	310 515-7600	7713
Kings Hawaiian Bakery W Inc **(HQ)**	5142	E	310 533-3250	14525
Knk Apparel Inc	2326	F	310 768-3333	2783
Kubra America West Inc	8721	D	310 756-17[illegible]7	22800
L J R Grinding Corp	3599	F	310 532-7232	8658
L&F Wood LLC	2431	F	310 400-5559	3261
La Dye & Print Inc	5137	E	310 327-3200	14390
La Mousse Desserts Inc	2038	E	310 478-6051	1932
La Palm Furnitures & ACC Inc **(PA)**	2395	D	310 217-2700	3156
Landcare USA LLC	0782	D	310 719-1008	318
Learning Resources Inc	3999	E	800 995-4436	11706
Lets Do Lunch	2099	D	310 523-3664	2475
Lily Bleu Inc	5137	E	310 225-2522	14393
Lite Extrusions Mfg Inc	3083	E	323 770-4298	5453
Little Brothers Bakery LLC	2051	D	310 225-3790	2016
Lni Custom Manufacturing Inc	3446	E	310 978-2000	6973
Los Angeles Unified School Dst	8748	D	310 354-3417	23468
Louis Sardo Upholstery Inc **(PA)**	2531	D	310 327-0532	3625
Magnetika Inc **(PA)**	5063	D	310 527-8100	13643
Maneri Sign Co Inc	3993	E	310 327-6261	11569
Mars Air Systems LLC	3564	D	310 532-1555	8051
Martin Bros/Marcowall Inc **(PA)**	1742	C	310 532-5335	1385
Martin-Chandler Inc	3599	F	323 321-5119	8678
Martin/Brattrud Inc	2512	D	323 770-4171	3510
Matsuda House Printing Inc	2752	E	310 532-1533	4368
Matsui International Co Inc **(HQ)**	2899	C	310 767-7812	5231
Maya Steels Fabrication Inc	3441	D	310 532-8830	6633
McLaren Industries Inc **(PA)**	3011	F	310 212-1333	5304
Meadows Sheet Metal and AC Inc	3444	E	310 615 1125	6874
Melling Tool Rush Metals LLC	3399	E	580 725 3295	6459
Metco Manufacturing Inc	3469	E	310 516-6547	7165
MGT Industries Inc	8741	D	310 324-3152	23063
Mills Iron Works	5085	D	323 321-6520	14003
Mj Best Videographer LLC	3651	C	209 208-8432	9184
Monark LP	6513	D	310 769-6669	15741
MPS Industries Incorporated **(PA)**	3612	E	310 325-1043	8879
Mutual Liquid Gas & Eqp Co Inc **(PA)**	5084	E	310 515-0553	13922
Mynela LLC	8049	E	323 522-9080	20228
N Stitches Prints Inc	2395	F	310 366-7537	3160
Narayan Corporation	3085	E	310 719-7330	5477
Nasco Aircraft Brake Inc	3728	D	310 532-4430	10386
Nationwide Plastic Products	3081	F	310 366-7585	5435
Navigant Cymetrix Corporation	8741	D	424 201-6300	23070
New Crew Production Corp	7389	C	323 234-8880	18613
New Maverick Desk Inc	2521	C	310 217-1554	3592
Nike Usa Inc	7941	B	310 670-6770	19426
Nippon Travel Agency Amer Inc	4724	D	310 768-1817	12393
Nippon Travel Agency PCF Inc **(DH)**	4724	D	310 768-0017	12394
Nissin Foods USA Company Inc **(HQ)**	2098	C	310 327-8478	2380
Norberts Athletic Products Inc	3949	F	310 830-6672	11440
Northrop Grumman Federal Cr Un **(PA)**	6061	D	310 808-4000	15074
Northwest Group Llc	5131	E	310 327-4670	14312
Nu-Steel Trade LLC	5051	E	310 329-2263	13582
Nugier Press Company Inc	3542	E	310 515-6025	7762
O Industries Corporation	2426	F	310 719-2289	3223
Ocean Direct LLC **(HQ)**	2092	C	424 266-9300	2348
One Up Manufacturing LLC	2631	E	310 749-8347	3775
Onyx Industries Inc	3451	D	310 851-6161	7040
Parquet By Dian Inc	2426	D	310 527-3779	3224
Phillips Bros Plastics Inc	3083	F	310 532-8020	5455
Phoenix Textile Inc **(PA)**	5131	D	310 715-7090	14313
Plastic Processing Corp	3089	F	310 719-7330	5753
Praxis Musical Instruments Inc	3495	F	714 532-6655	7489
Premier Tile & Marble	1743	D	310 516-1712	1421
Prime Wheel Corporation	3714	E	310 819-4123	10116
Prime Wheel Corporation **(PA)**	3714	A	310 516-9126	10117
Principle Plastics	3021	E	310 532-3411	5313
Pro Design Group Inc	3089	E	310 767-1032	5780
Procel Temporary Services Inc	7363	D	310 372-0560	17509
Pronto Laser Cutting Inc	3699	F	310 327-7820	9901

Mergent email: customerrelations@mergent.com
1366

2022 Southern California Business
Directory and Buyers Guide

(P-0000) Products & Services Section entry number
(PA)=Parent Co (HQ)=Headquarters (DH)=Div Headquarters

	SIC	EMP	PHONE	ENTRY #
Ps2 **(PA)**	1721	D	310 243-2980	1194
Pulp Studio Incorporated	7336	D	310 815-4999	17184
Quadrtech Corporation	3915	F	310 523-1697	11338
Qual-Pro Corporation **(HQ)**	3672	C	310 329-7535	9444
R B Welding Inc	7692	E	310 324-8680	18993
Radford Alexander Corporation	4212	D	310 523-2555	11988
Radiant Services Corp **(PA)**	7211	C	310 327-6300	16838
Ramda Metal Specialties Inc	3444	E	310 538-2136	6899
Rancho California Ldscpg Inc	0782	E	310 768-1680	338
Randall - McAnany Company	1721	D	310 822-3344	1195
Rayco Electronic Mfg Inc	3677	E	310 329-2660	9641
Raymak Automotive Inc	7538	E	310 329-8910	18865
Research Metal Industries Inc	3599	E	310 352-3200	8766
Rich Chicks LLC	2015	E	209 879-4104	1763
Richwell Steel Co Inc	1791	D	310 324-4455	1580
Risvolds Inc	2099	D	323 770-2674	2518
Rotational Molding Inc	3089	D	310 327-5401	5800
Ruggeri Marble and Granite Inc	3281	D	310 513-2155	6143
Russ International Inc	3444	E	310 329-7121	6905
Rytan Inc	3541	F	310 328-6553	7744
Saia Motor Freight Line LLC	4213	D	310 217-1499	12077
Schumacher Cargo Logistics Inc **(PA)**	4731	E	562 408-6677	12523
Secom International **(PA)**	7373	D	310 641-1290	18064
Servexo	7381	B	323 527-9994	18332
Sgl Composites Inc **(DH)**	2655	E	424 329-5250	3839
Sgps Inc	3999	D	310 538-4175	11754
Shelby Carroll Intl Inc **(PA)**	3711	D	310 538-2914	9965
Shoreline Ambulance Corp	4119	D	714 847-9107	11890
Silverline Construction Inc **(PA)**	1542	C	310 327-4970	829
Smart LLC	3089	E	310 674-8135	5821
SMS Transportation Inc	8111	D	310 527-9200	21679
Softline Home Fashions Inc	5131	E	310 630-4848	14321
Somar Corporation	3444	E	310 329-1446	6914
SOS Metals Inc **(DH)**	5093	C	310 217-8848	14123
South Bay Corporation	3069	F	310 532-5353	5412
South Bay Toyota	7538	C	310 323-7800	18873
Southwest Offset Prtg Co Inc **(PA)**	2752	B	310 965-9154	4425
Space-Lok Inc	3728	C	310 527-6150	10421
Spectra Clinical Labs Inc	8071	D	562 776-8440	21097
Spectrum Laboratory Pdts Inc	5169	E	520 292-3103	14791
SPS Technologies LLC	5085	B	310 323-6222	14020
SPS Technologies LLC	5085	D	562 426-9411	14021
Standard Metal Products Inc	3471	E	310 532-9861	7316
Stanzino Inc **(PA)**	2211	D	213 746-8822	2590
Steeldeck Inc	3999	E	323 290-2100	11761
Stefan Merli Plastering Co Inc **(PA)**	1771	D	310 323-0404	1551
Stepstone Inc **(PA)**	3272	E	310 327-7474	6059
Stringking Inc **(PA)**	2389	C	310 503-8901	3086
Superior Metal Finishing Inc	3471	F	310 464-8010	7319
Swift Fab	3444	F	310 366-7295	6924
Swift-Cor Precision Inc	3444	E	310 354-1207	6925
T & F Sheet Mtls Fab McHning I	3444	E	310 516-8548	6926
Tackle Specialties Inc	3949	F	310 538-0535	11452
Talins Inc	3444	F	310 378-3715	6927
Techflex Packaging LLC	5199	D	424 266-9400	14978
Thermlly Engnred Mnfctred Pdts	3443	E	310 523-9934	6761
Timbucktoo Manufacturing Inc	3589	E	310 323-1134	8421
Tireco Inc **(PA)**	5014	C	310 767-7990	13121
Tomorrows Heirlooms Inc	3429	E	310 323-6720	6540
Transcosmos Onmiconnect LLC	8741	D	310 630-0072	23126
Triune Enterprises Inc	2671	E	310 719-1600	3861
Tru-Cut Inc	3524	E	310 630-0422	7632
True Religion Apparel Inc **(HQ)**	2325	B	323 266-3072	2775
UNI-Sport Inc	2752	E	310 217-4587	4444
United Facility Solutions Inc	7381	B	310 743-3000	18348
United Guard Security Inc **(PA)**	7381	B	800 228-2505	18349
United Parcel Service Inc	4215	C	310 217-2646	12154
US Blanks LLC **(PA)**	2821	E	310 225-6774	4727
US Hanger Company LLC	3315	E	310 323-8030	6239
US Industrial Tool & Sup Co	3542	E	310 464-8400	7768
USA-Srdc Corporation **(DH)**	5093	E	310 418-7064	14124
Usfi Inc	5141	D	310 768-1937	14518
Valley of Sun Cosmetics LLC	5122	C	310 327-9062	14294
Vege-Mist Inc	3585	D	310 353-2300	8355
Versafab Corp **(PA)**	3444	E	800 421-1822	6939
Vescom Corporation **(PA)**	7381	A	207 945-5051	18358
Victor Martin Inc	2514	E	323 587-3101	3537
Wally & Pat Enterprises	3999	E	310 532-2031	11792
Warner Chemical Mfg	3711	E	310 715-3000	9971
Washington Orna Ir Works Inc **(PA)**	1799	C	310 327-8660	1698
Waste MGT Collectn Recycl Inc	4953	D	310 532-6511	12999
Wcbm Company **(PA)**	3965	E	323 262-3274	11504
Weiss Sheet Metal Company	1761	E	310 354-2700	1509
West Coast Laboratories Inc	2834	E	310 527-6163	4912
West Coast Laboratories Inc **(PA)**	2834	F	323 321-4774	4913
Westcoast Rotor Inc	5084	E	310 327-5050	13964
Western Freight Carrier Inc **(PA)**	4213	D	310 767-1042	12092
World Svc Wst/La Inflght Svc L	4581	C	310 538-7000	12374
Wsa Group Inc **(PA)**	7381	E	310 743-3000	18362
Wyrefab Inc	3496	E	310 523-2147	7524
XCEL Mechanical Systems Inc	1711	C	310 660-0090	1163

GLENDALE, CA - Los Angeles County

	SIC	EMP	PHONE	ENTRY #
2310 Catalina LLC	7389	D	818 696-2040	18424
4 Over LLC **(HQ)**	2759	C	818 246-1170	4470
4 Over LLC	2759	F	818 246-1170	4471
Adventist Hlth Systm/West Corp	8062	D	818 409-8540	20656
Adventist Hlth Systm/West Corp	8062	D	818 409-8050	20661
Aero Mfg & Pltg Co LLC	3471	E	818 241-2844	7199
Alexander Henry Fabrics Inc	5131	E	818 562-8200	14302
All Care Home Health Provider	8082	D	818 241-2473	21130
All For Hlth Hlth For All Inc **(PA)**	8011	C	818 409-3020	19690
All4-Pcb (north America) Inc	3599	F	866 734-9403	8488
Allen Gwynn Chevrolet Inc	7515	D	818 240-0000	18747
Allesandro Automatic Inc	3599	F	323 663-8253	8489
Alls Well Inc **(PA)**	7361	D	818 240-8688	17390
Ambiance Transportation LLC	4789	D	818 955-5757	12563
Ambrit Industries Inc	3542	E	818 243-1224	7753
Amco Foods Inc	8742	B	818 247-4716	23154
American Imaging MGT Inc	6321	A	847 310-0366	15376
American Transportation Co LLC	4789	D	818 660-2343	12564
Amgen Distribution Inc	4213	D	760 989-4424	12010
Arthur J Gallagher Risk Mgmt	6411	D	818 539-2300	15538
Asab Inc **(DH)**	7338	C	818 551-7300	17193
Assign Corporation	7379	C	818 247-7100	18160
Associates First Capital Corp	6141	C	818 248-7055	15138
At-Tech Staffing Services Inc **(PA)**	7361	D	818 240-8688	17392
Automation Plating Corporation	3471	E	323 245-4951	7219
Automobile Club Southern Cal	8699	D	818 240-2200	22443
Avery Corp	8731	C	626 304-2000	22827
Avery Dennison Corporation **(PA)**	2672	A	626 304-2000	3863
Avery Dennison Foundation	2672	E	626 304-2000	3866
Axiomprint Inc	2752	F	747 888-7777	4233
Axis Construction Inc	1542	D	818 545-9292	741
Bartholomew Barry & Associates	8111	D	818 543-4000	21512
Baxter International Inc	2834	F	818 550-4500	4795
Begroup **(PA)**	8059	D	818 638-4563	20559
Beyond Limits Inc **(PA)**	7379	C	818 643-2344	18164
Btrade LLC	7372	E	818 334-4433	17808
Buena Ventura Care Center Inc	8059	D	818 247-4476	20566
Bunim-Murray Productions	7812	C	818 756-5100	19105
Cal Southern Presbt Homes	6513	D	818 247-0420	15721
California Community News LLC	2711	D	818 843-8700	3954
California Credit Union **(PA)**	6062	C	818 291-6700	15107
Califrnia Elctrmechanical Repr	7699	F	818 840-9211	19027
Califrnia Insur Guarantee Assn	6411	C	818 844-4300	15547
Calmat Co **(DH)**	2951	C	818 553-8821	5269
Campbell Center	8699	E	818 242-2434	22448
Carpet Wagon-Glendale Inc **(PA)**	2434	F	818 937-9545	3314
Caspian Commercial Plbg Inc	1711	D	818 649-2500	1042
Caviar Express Inc	2741	F	818 956-1566	4161
Cellco Partnership	4812	D	818 500-7779	12599
Challenger Ornamental Ir Works	3446	F	818 507-7030	6955
Chromatic Inc Lithographers	2752	E	818 242-5785	4251
Ciba Insurance Svcs Cal Inc **(PA)**	6411	D	818 638-8525	15551
Cigna Behavioral Health of Cal	6324	B	800 753-0540	15394
Cigna Healthcare Cal Inc **(DH)**	6324	B	818 500-6262	15395
Coda Energy Holdings LLC	3699	E	626 775-3900	9861
Coinmach Corporation **(PA)**	7215	D	818 637-4300	16872
Color Inc	2752	E	818 240-1350	4255
Color Depot Inc	2759	F	818 500-9033	4499
Compspec Inc	8742	D	818 551-4200	23195
Country Villa Service Corp	8051	C	818 246-5516	20294
Countrywide Home Loans Inc	6162	A	818 550-8700	15185
Cryst Mark Inc A Swan Techno C	3559	E	818 240-7520	7970
Custom Characters Inc	2389	F	818 507-5940	3072
Cygnet Stampng & Fabrictng Inc	3469	E	818 240-7574	7138
Cygnet Stampng & Fabrictng Inc **(PA)**	3469	E	818 240-7574	7139
Denttio Inc	3843	F	323 254-1000	11168
Dignity Hlth MGT Svcs Orgnztio	8741	E	661 716-7100	23018
Dine Brands Global Inc **(PA)**	6794	B	818 240-6055	16205
Dish Network Corporation	4841	D	818 334-8740	12765
Disney Interactive Studios Inc	7371	B	818 560-1000	17597
Disney Research Pittsburgh	8731	C	412 623-1800	22834
Disney Worldwide Services Inc	7379	D	818 560-1250	18173
Disqo Inc	8732	D	818 237-2186	22879
Dma Claims Management Inc **(PA)**	6411	C	323 342-6800	15561
Dreamworks Animation Pubg LLC	7812	A	818 695-5000	19119
Dwa Holdings LLC **(DH)**	7812	D	818 695-5000	19120
E Z Staffing Inc **(PA)**	7361	B	818 845-2500	17415
Emeritus Corporation	8051	C	818 246-7457	20323
Employers Compensation Insur **(DH)**	6411	C	818 549-4600	15562
Equity Title Company **(DH)**	6541	D	818 291-4400	16038
First Group Holdings Inc	6799	D	855 910-5626	16261
First Interstate Services Inc	7382	B	818 638-3435	18379
Forest Lawn Co	6553	C	818 241-4151	16082
Forest Lawn Memorial-Park Assn **(PA)**	6553	B	323 254-3131	16083
Forest Lawn Mortuary **(HQ)**	7261	B	323 254-3131	16922
Fortner Eng & Mfg Inc	3599	E	818 240-7740	8592
Front Prch Cmmnties Oprting Gr	8059	C	800 233-3709	20583
Front Prch Cmmnties Svcs - Cas **(PA)**	8059	D	818 729-8100	20585
Fuse LLC **(DH)**	7389	C	323 256-8900	18523
Gavin De Becker & Assoc GP LLC	8742	C	818 505-0177	23224
Gcg Corporation	3471	E	818 247-8508	7261
General Networks Corporation	7379	D	818 249-1962	18184
Ggis Insurance Services Inc	6411	C	818 553-2110	15573
Glendale Adventist Medical Ctr	8082	E	818 409-8379	21167
Glendale Adventist Medical Ctr **(HQ)**	8062	A	818 409-8000	20776
Glendale Associates Ltd	6512	D	818 246-6737	15670
Glendale Eye Medical Group **(PA)**	8011	D	818 956-1010	19831
Glendale Mem Hosp & Hlth Ctr	8062	D	818 502-1900	20777
Glenoaks Convalescent Hospital	8062	D	818 240-4300	20778
Global Asylum Incorporated	7812	E	323 850-1214	19129
Grandall Distributing Co Inc	7389	E	818 242-6640	18533
Griffith Pk Rhbltation Ctr LLC	8051	D	818 845-8507	20368

Employment Codes: A=Over 500 employees, B=251-500, C=101-250, D=51-100, E=20-50 F=10-19

2022 Southern California Business Directory and Buyers Guide

© Mergent Inc. 1-800-342-5647

1367

	SIC	EMP	PHONE	ENTRY #
Gsa Design Inc	7389	E	818 241-2558	18535
H and H Drug Stores Inc **(PA)**	5047	D	818 956-6691	13492
H L Moe Co Inc **(PA)**	1711	C	818 572-2100	1080
Health Data Vision Inc **(PA)**	7374	D	866 969-3222	18093
Hemodialysis Inc **(PA)**	8092	E	818 500-8736	21246
Hl Temp Forming Co	3599	F	714 529-6556	8616
Howroyd-Wright Emplymnt Agcy **(HQ)**	7361	C	818 240-8688	17428
Howroyd-Wright Emplymnt Agcy	7361	C	818 240-8688	17429
Humangood Socal **(HQ)**	6513	D	818 247-0420	15726
Huntmix Inc	2951	C	818 548-5200	5273
Hutchinson & Bloodgood LLP **(PA)**	8721	D	818 637-5000	22791
Informtion Intgrtion Group Inc	7372	E	818 956-3744	17887
Ink Mill LLC	2893	F	626 304-2000	5207
Insite Digestive Health Care	8011	D	626 817-2900	19855
International Bus Mchs Corp	3571	A	818 553-8100	8162
Interpreting Services Intl LLC	7389	D	818 753-9181	18552
Interstate Rhbltation Svcs LLC	8093	C	818 244-5656	21313
Isovac Engineering Inc	7389	E	818 552-6200	18557
JP Allen Extended Stay **(PA)**	7011	D	818 956-0202	16516
JP Weaver & Company	3299	E	818 500-1740	6181
Kabc-TV	4833	D	818 863-7171	12729
Kaiser Foundation Hospitals	8011	C	800 954-8000	19903
Kaiser Foundation Hospitals	8011	C	818 552-3000	19936
Kennard Development Group	1522	D	818 241-0800	660
Kradjian Importing Company Inc **(PA)**	5149	D	818 502-1313	14703
Ksm Healthcare Inc	8051	D	818 242-1183	20390
La Follette Johnson De Haas **(PA)**	8111	C	213 426-3600	21602
Latino Film Inst Yuth Cnema PR	7819	D	626 222-9252	19240
LDI Operations LLC	3999	C	818 240-7500	11705
Legalzoomcom Inc **(PA)**	7374	B	323 962-8600	18098
Legion Creative Group	2759	E	323 498-1100	4537
Logic Mate Inc	7371	F	213 623-4422	17654
Long Beach Woodworks LLC	2448	F	562 437-2293	3397
Longwood Management Corp	8059	D	818 246-7174	20602
Los Angeles Federal Credit Un **(PA)**	6061	D	818 242-8640	15073
Los Feliz Ford Inc **(PA)**	7515	D	818 502-1901	18751
Lvl 10 Entertainment LLC	7929	E	424 298-5119	19368
Mader News Inc	5192	D	818 551-5000	14875
Malakan Inc **(PA)**	2435	E	310 910-9270	3352
McCoppin Enterprises	3599	E	818 240-4840	8682
Modern Engine Inc	3599	E	818 409-9494	8703
Modern Videofilm Inc	7812	C	818 637-6800	19154
Nadin Company	2834	E	818 500-8908	4855
National Attny Collection Svcs	8111	B	818 547-9760	21642
National Teleconsultants Inc	8711	C	818 265-4400	22621
Nestle Refrigerated Food Co	2098	B	818 549-6000	2379
Next Venture Inc	1542	D	818 637-2888	797
North American Textile Co LLC **(PA)**	2396	E	818 409-0019	3178
Notron Manufacturing Inc	3599	F	818 247-7739	8721
Nurses Tuch HM Hlth Prvder Inc	8082	E	818 500-4877	21193
Oakmont Country Club	7997	C	818 542-4260	19595
Oel/Hhh Inc	8712	D	818 246-6050	22736
Old Republic Title Company	6361	C	818 240-1936	15511
On Central Realty Inc **(PA)**	6531	B	818 476-3000	15935
Otis Elevator Company	5084	C	818 241-2828	13926
P E N Inc	2711	F	818 954-0775	4020
Pango Group Inc	6531	D	818 502-0400	15943
Passport Technology Usa Inc	7699	E	818 957-5471	19055
Patterson Ritner Lockwood **(PA)**	8111	E	818 241-8001	21655
PCL Construction Services Inc	1542	C	818 246-3481	802
Peets Coffee & Tea LLC	5149	D	818 546-1030	14716
Pegasus HM Hlth Care A Cal Cor	8082	D	818 551-1932	21200
Pegasus Maritime Inc	4731	D	714 728-8565	12505
Pennoyer-Dodge Co	3545	E	818 547-2100	7861
Person & Covey Inc	2844	E	818 937-5000	5057
Pinnacle Networking Svcs Inc	1731	D	818 241-6009	1295
Post Publishing LLC	2741	F	818 291-1100	4196
Premac Inc	3599	F	818 241-8370	8744
Prestige Preschools Inc **(PA)**	8351	D	818 957-1170	22054
Primary Critical Care Medical	8011	C	818 847-9950	20026
Prime Mso LLC	8093	D	818 937-9969	21328
Prosight Specty Insur Grp Inc	6411	D	818 230-8200	15618
PS Business Parks Inc **(PA)**	6798	D	818 244-8080	16241
PS LPT Properties Investors **(HQ)**	4225	D	818 244-8080	12235
Public Storage **(PA)**	6798	C	818 244-8080	16242
Quantum Alliance Inc	3572	F	818 415-2085	8214
Rbm Conveyor Systems Inc	3556	E	909 620-1333	7950
Rose International Inc	7371	C	636 812-4000	17703
Safeco Insurance Company Amer	6411	C	818 956-4250	15624
SAI Industries	3484	E	818 842-6144	7430
Search Agency Inc **(DH)**	8742	D	310 873-5700	23318
Servicetitan Inc **(PA)**	7371	D	855 899-0970	17711
Sigma Supply & Dist Inc	5047	F	818 246-4624	13520
Simon G Jewelry Inc	5094	E	818 500-8595	14139
SMD Holdings 2019 Inc	7372	F	310 953-4800	17986
Software Management Cons LLC **(HQ)**	7379	B	818 240-3177	18222
State Compensation Insur Fund	6331	D	888 782-8338	15483
Stewart Title California Inc	6541	C	818 502-2700	16042
Sunderstorm LLC	3999	F	818 605-6682	11766
Systech Solutions Inc **(PA)**	7371	D	818 550-9690	17727
Tacori Enterprises	5094	D	818 863-1536	14142
Tech Town Inc	7371	E	818 621-2744	17732
Technicolor Usa Inc	3651	C	818 500-9090	9200
Technicolor Usa Inc	3651	C	818 260-3651	9201
Tentek Inc **(PA)**	7379	C	818 551-7100	18227
Tinson LLC	8742	E	901 494-6405	23347
Tms International	3312	F	818 894-1414	6216
Triangle Rock Products LLC	1429	B	818 553-8820	566
Trojan Rivet	3452	F	818 245-1065	7078
United Merchant Svcs Cal Inc	5044	D	818 246-6767	13368
Universal Asset Lnding Info Sy **(DH)**	7371	D	678 854-9451	17747
Usc Verdugo Hills Hospital LLC	8062	A	818 790-7100	20996
Usc Vrdugo Hlls Hosp Fundation **(HQ)**	8062	B	800 872-2273	20997
Vege - Kurl Inc	2844	D	818 956-5582	5080
Ventegra Inc A Cal Beneft Corp	8748	D	858 551-8111	23522
Verdugo Hills Hospital Inc	8062	C	818 790-7100	21001
Verdugo Hills Psychtherapy Ctr **(PA)**	8011	D	818 241-6780	20138
Verdugo Mental Health	8093	D	818 244-7257	21362
Viva Print LLC **(HQ)**	2678	F	818 243-1363	3920
Walt Disney Imagineering **(DH)**	7819	A	818 544-6500	19254
Walt Disney Pictures	7819	B	818 409-2200	19255
Westview Services Inc	8322	D	818 242-0068	21927
Wfg National Title Insur Co **(PA)**	6361	D	818 476-4000	15513
Yellowpagescom LLC **(DH)**	7389	B	818 937-5500	18731
Young MNS Chrstn Assn of Glnda	8641	D	818 484-8256	22387
Zoo Printing Inc **(PA)**	2752	D	310 253-7751	4464

GLENDORA, CA - Los Angeles County

	SIC	EMP	PHONE	ENTRY #
Action Stamping Inc	3469	E	626 914-7466	7120
Americas Christian Credit Un **(PA)**	6061	D	626 208-5400	15058
Automobile Club Southern Cal	8699	D	626 963-853[illegible]	22407
BR Building Resources Co	1542	C	626 963-4880	747
Building Elctronic Contrls Inc **(PA)**	1731	E	909 305-1600	1226
Calportland	1442	D	760 343-3403	568
Calportland Company **(DH)**	3241	D	626 852-6200	5975
CJd Construction Svcs Inc	1389	E	626 335-1116	491
Cliftonlarsonallen LLP	8721	D	626 857-7300	22772
CPC Services Inc	3273	E	626 852-6200	6087
Deccofelt Corporation	2299	E	626 963-8511	2723
East Valley Glendora Hosp LLC	8062	B	626 852-5000	20759
Electro-Tech Products Inc	3679	E	909 592-1434	9706
Emanate Health	8062	A	626 857-3477	20763
Ensign San Dimas LLC	8059	C	626 963-7531	20579
Foothill Hsptl-Mrris L Jhnston **(PA)**	8062	D	626 857-3145	20771
Glendora Country Club	7997	D	626 335-4051	19564
Grico Precision Inc	3599	F	626 963-0368	8610
Hallmark Metals Inc	3444	E	626 335-1263	6849
Harbor Glen Care Center	8051	B	626 963-7531	20371
HP Core Co Inc	3543	E	323 582-1688	7771
Mackenzie Laboratories Inc	3674	E	909 394-9007	9534
Mark Kislinger MD Inc	8011	D	626 335-2020	19971
Martin Automotive Inc	7538	D	909 394-9399	18853
Millipart Inc **(PA)**	3599	F	626 963-4101	8698
National Hot Rod Association **(PA)**	7948	C	626 914-4761	19433
National Link Incorporated	5044	D	909 670-[illegible]900	13364
Oakdale Memorial Park **(PA)**	6553	D	626 335-0281	16087
Oasis Medical Inc **(PA)**	3851	D	909 305-5400	11258
Postvision Inc	3572	F	818 840-0777	8211
Safeguard Envirogroup Inc	3826	E	626 512-7585	10809
Seidner-Miller Inc	7532	C	909 305-2000	18803
Southern Cal Disc Tire Co Inc	5013	C	626 335-2883	13094
Southwest Machine & Plastic Co	3728	E	626 963-6919	10420
Venue Management Systems Inc	7381	A	626 445-6000	18357
Wade Melvin Banner DMD **(PA)**	8021	D	626 594 0374	20203
Walton Associated Companies	1521	D	626 963-8505	649

GOLETA, CA - Santa Barbara County

	SIC	EMP	PHONE	ENTRY #
6500 Hllister Ave Partners LLC	6512	D	805 722-1362	15655
ABC - Clio Inc **(PA)**	2731	C	805 968-1911	4118
Acroamatics Inc	3663	F	805 967-9909	9248
Advanced Vision Science Inc	3851	E	805 683-3851	11244
Alta-Dena Certified Dairy LLC	2026	C	805 685-8328	1830
Appfolio Inc **(PA)**	7372	A	805 364-6093	17786
Arguello Inc	1382	E	805 567-1632	440
Atk Space Systems LLC	3812	D	805 685-2262	10572
Atomica Corp	3674	C	805 681-2807	9485
Bardex Corporation **(PA)**	5084	D	805 964-7747	13888
Biopac Systems Inc	3826	E	805 685-0066	10786
Boone Printing & Graphics Inc	2752	D	805 683-2349	4237
C N C Machining Inc	3599	E	805 681-8855	8537
Calient Technologies Inc **(PA)**	3661	E	805 695-4800	9228
Caribbean Coffee Company Inc	2043	E	805 692-2200	1947
Cbrite Inc	3823	E	805 722-1121	10684
CMC Rescue Inc	5099	D	805 562-9120	14149
Community Action Comm Snta BRB **(PA)**	8399	E	805 964-8857	22176
Connectpoint Inc	7372	E	805 682-8900	17825
Cottage Health System	8062	D	805 967-3411	20734
Deckers Outdoor Corporation **(PA)**	2389	A	805 967-7611	3073
Deployable Space Systems Inc	8711	E	805 722-8090	22528
Devereux Foundation	8093	D	805 968-2525	21298
Devereux Foundation	8093	D	805 968-2525	21299
Digital Surgery Systems Inc	3841	E	805 978-5400	10970
DR Radon Boatbuilding Inc	3732	F	805 692-2170	10463
Electro Optical Industries	3827	E	805 964-6701	10833
Enerpro Inc	5065	E	805 683-2114	13718
Ergomotion Inc	5021	D	805 979-9400	13136
Far West Technology Inc	3829	F	805 964-3615	10883
Flir Commercial Systems Inc **(DH)**	3826	B	805 964-9797	10794
Flir Motion Ctrl Systems Inc	3559	D	650 692-3900	7978
Glen Annie Golf Club	7992	D	805 968-6400	19489
Hanson Aggrgtes Md-Pacific Inc	4212	E	805 967-2371	11971
Image-X Enterprises Inc	7371	E	805 964-3535	17637
Impulse Internet Services LLC	4813	D	805 456-5800	12649
Inogen Inc **(PA)**	3841	C	805 562-0500	10995
Intouch Technologies Inc **(HQ)**	7372	B	805 562-8686	17890

Mergent email: customerrelations@mergent.com
1368
2022 Southern California Business Directory and Buyers Guide

(P-0000) Products & Services Section entry number
(PA)=Parent Co (HQ)=Headquarters (DH)=Div Headquarters

	SIC	EMP	PHONE	ENTRY #
Intri-Plex Technologies Inc **(HQ)**	3599	C	805 683-3414	8629
Ipt Holding Inc **(PA)**	3469	D	805 683-3414	7154
JD Business Solutions Inc	2752	E	805 962-8193	4342
Juniper Networks Inc	7373	D	805 880-2000	18041
Karl Storz Endscpy-America Inc	3841	D	800 964-5563	11001
Karl Storz Imaging Inc	3841	E	805 968-5563	11002
Karl Storz Imaging Inc **(HQ)**	3829	B	805 968-5563	10895
Kitson Landscape MGT Inc	0782	D	805 681-9460	313
Kyocera Sld Laser Inc **(HQ)**	3699	D	805 696-6999	9883
L3 Technologies Inc	8711	D	805 683-3881	22599
Las Cmbres Obsrvtory Globl Tls	8733	E	805 880-1600	22913
Launchpint Elc Prplsion Sltons	3728	E	805 683-9659	10366
Mann+hmmel Wtr Fluid Sltons In **(DH)**	3589	D	805 964-8003	8394
Marborg Recovery LP	4953	C	805 963-1852	12959
Moog Inc	3812	B	805 618-3900	10601
Moseley Associates Inc **(HQ)**	3663	C	805 968-9621	9296
National Security Tech LLC	8711	A	805 681-2432	22620
Neal Feay Company	3354	D	805 967-4521	6313
Northrop Grumman Systems Corp	3812	C	714 240-6521	10618
One Call Plumber Goleta	7299	D	805 284-0441	16968
Otis Elevator Company	3534	E	805 683-3979	7680
Parentsquare Inc	7372	D	888 496-3168	17952
R G Hansen & Associates **(PA)**	3823	F	805 564-3388	10716
Raytheon Company	3699	C	805 967-5511	9905
Raytheon Company	7389	D	805 562-2941	18648
Renco Encoders Inc	3621	B	805 968-1525	8926
Ricardo Defense Inc **(DH)**	3714	D	805 882-1884	10125
Sandpiper Golf Trust LLC	7992	D	805 968-1541	19507
Santa Barbara Coffee LLC	2095	F	805 683-2555	2357
Santa Barbara Trnsp Corp **(HQ)**	4151	D	805 681-8355	11939
Sbif Inc	3479	E	805 683-1711	7408
Sitestuff Yardi Systems I **(PA)**	8742	C	805 966-3666	23323
Skate One Corp	3949	D	805 964-1330	11447
Soilmoisture Equipment Corp	3829	E	805 964-3525	10912
Southern California Edison Co	4911	C	805 683-5291	12845
Super 8 Motel Goleta	7011	C	805 967-5591	16744
Superior Millwork of Sb Inc	2434	F	805 685-1744	3338
Surf To Summit Inc	3949	F	805 964-1896	11451
Tan Set Corporation	3441	F	805 967-4567	6667
Tencate Advanced Armor USA Inc **(DH)**	3484	D	805 845-4085	7431
Toyon Research Corporation **(PA)**	8711	C	805 968-6787	22677
Transphorm Inc **(PA)**	3674	D	805 456-1300	9594
Truevision Systems Inc	3841	E	805 963-9700	11071
United Bys Grls Clubs Snta BRB	8641	D	805 967-1612	22373
United Parcel Service Inc	4215	C	805 964-7848	12162
Venoco Inc	2911	E	805 961-2305	5267
Verizon South Inc	4812	B	805 681-8527	12619
Vista Steel Co Inc **(PA)**	3449	E	805 964-4732	7026
Wyatt Technology Corporation **(PA)**	3826	C	805 681-9009	10820
Yardi Kube Inc	7372	E	805 699-2040	18013
Z P M Inc	3589	E	805 681-3511	8430

GOSHEN, CA - Tulare County

	SIC	EMP	PHONE	ENTRY #
Tln Inc	4213	D	208 880-9935	12081
Western Milling LLC **(HQ)**	6799	C	559 302-1000	16302

GRANADA HILLS, CA - Los Angeles County

	SIC	EMP	PHONE	ENTRY #
A Cori Partnership	8059	E	818 368-2802	20549
Aegis Senior Communities LLC	8082	C	818 363-3373	21129
Bethlhem Evang Lthran Ch Grnad	8351	D	818 360-4777	21989
Brite-Lite Neon Corp	3993	F	818 763-4798	11530
Financial Info Netwrk Inc	7371	E	818 782-0331	17615
Fox Printing Company Inc **(PA)**	2752	E	818 768-6110	4297
Garys Leather Inc	3172	F	818 831-9977	5907
In Granada Hlls Cnvlscent Hosp	8051	D	818 891-1745	20378
Kaiser Foundation Hospitals	8011	C	818 832-7200	19902
Longwood Management Corp	8051	C	818 360-1864	20405
Los Angeles Unified School Dst	8748	D	818 360-2361	23470
Ortho Engineering Inc **(PA)**	3842	E	310 559-5996	11131
Park Regency Inc	6531	D	818 363-6116	15945
R-Con General Building Inc **(PA)**	1799	D	818 235-6465	1683
Republic Fence Co Inc **(PA)**	1799	E	818 341-5323	1685
San Fernando City of Inc	8093	D	818 832-2400	21336
Savin & Bursk Law Offices of	8111	D	818 368-8646	21673
Siracusa Enterprises Inc	7361	D	818 831-1130	17465

GRAND TERRACE, CA - San Bernardino County

	SIC	EMP	PHONE	ENTRY #
City News Group Inc	2711	F	909 370-1200	3962
Emeritus Corporation	8051	C	909 420-0153	20325
Grand Terrace Care Center **(PA)**	8051	D	909 825-5221	20367
Griswold Pump Company	3561	E	909 422-1700	8012
Keystone NPS LLC **(DH)**	8399	D	909 633-6354	22194
National Logistics Team LLC	4215	E	951 369-5841	12143
Psg California LLC **(PA)**	3561	B	909 422-1700	8022
Riversd-San Brnrdino Cnty Indi **(PA)**	8011	B	909 864-1097	20043
West Coast Arborists Inc	0783	C	909 783-6544	364

GROVER BEACH, CA - San Luis Obispo County

	SIC	EMP	PHONE	ENTRY #
C F W Research & Dev Co	3351	F	805 489-8750	6298
H J Harkins Company Inc	2834	E	805 929-1333	4828
Hotlix **(PA)**	2064	E	805 473-0596	2088
Oak Parks Inns Inc	7011	D	805 481-4448	16588
Voler Softgoods **(PA)**	2389	D	805 473-7808	3089
Vons Companies Inc	3556	D	805 481-2492	7955

GUADALUPE, CA - Santa Barbara County

	SIC	EMP	PHONE	ENTRY #
Byrd Harvest Inc	0722	D	805 343-1608	151
Guadalupe Cooling Company Inc	0723	D	805 343-2331	176
Guadalupe Union School Dst **(PA)**	8741	C	805 343-2114	23034
Tri-Co Building Supply Inc	2439	E	805 343-2555	3372

HACIENDA HEIGHTS, CA - Los Angeles County

	SIC	EMP	PHONE	ENTRY #
Able Microsystems Corporation	7373	E	626 723-7777	18016
Barhena Inc	3589	E	888 383-8800	8368
Brio Water Technology Inc	5078	E	800 781-1680	13851
Cotton Tale Designs Inc	2392	F	714 435-9558	3100
Courtyard Management Corp	7011	D	626 965-1700	16395
CSX Corporation	4011	C	626 336-1377	11795
Easterncctv (usa) LLC	3699	C	626 961-8810	9866
Heights Insurance Group Inc **(PA)**	6411	D	626 333-1111	15581
Joy International Trading Inc	3944	F	626 736-5987	11381
Lg-Led Solutions Limited	3648	E	626 587-8506	9138
Superior Equipment Solutions	3631	D	323 722-7900	8995

HANFORD, CA - Kings County

	SIC	EMP	PHONE	ENTRY #
Adventist Health System/West	8062	D	559 537-0305	20646
Adventist Health System/West	8062	D	559 537-2510	20649
Adventist Hlth Systm/West Corp	8062	D	888 443-2273	20654
Adventist Med Center-Hanford **(HQ)**	8062	E	559 582-9000	20662
Adventist Med Center-Hanford	8062	B	559 537-1377	20663
All Health Services Corp **(PA)**	7361	D	559 583-9101	17389
Baker Commodities Inc	2077	E	559 686-4797	2123
Beco Dairy Automation Inc	5083	F	559 582-2566	13875
Britz Fertilizers Inc	3523	D	559 582-0942	7607
California Bio-Productex Inc	2869	E	559 582-5308	5130
Central Valley Meat Co Inc **(PA)**	2011	C	559 583-9624	1709
City Hanford Public Imprv Corp	1623	D	559 585-2550	941
Danell Bros Inc	0722	D	559 582-1251	153
Danell Custom Harvesting LLC	0722	C	559 582-1251	154
Educational Employees Cr Un	6062	D	559 587-4460	15111
Family Healthcare Network	8011	C	559 582-2013	19818
Hacienda Rhbltion Hlth Care C	8051	C	559 582-9221	20370
Hanford Community Hospital **(HQ)**	8062	A	559 582-9000	20781
Hanford Sentinel Inc	2711	B	559 582-0471	3984
High Plains Ranch LLC **(PA)**	0241	C	559 583-1277	133
Hood Packaging Corporation	5199	C	559 585-2040	14937
Jvac Inc	7538	D	559 584-5531	18846
Kings Cabinet Systems	2521	F	559 584-9662	3588
Kings Cmnty Action Orgnztion I **(PA)**	8322	D	559 582-4386	21831
Kings Nrsing Rhbltion Hosp In	8051	E	559 582-4414	20387
Kings Rehabilitation Ctr Inc **(PA)**	8322	D	559 582-9234	21832
Lacey Milling Company	2041	F	559 584-6634	1945
Lowes Home Centers LLC	5031	C	559 410-9000	13274
McLellan Equipment Inc	3713	E	559 582-8100	9990
McLellan Industries Inc	3713	D	650 873-8100	9991
Morgan & Slates Mfg & Sup Inc **(PA)**	7692	F	559 582-4417	18991
Nichols Pistachio	2068	C	559 584-6811	2114
Pitman Family Farms	2048	D	559 585-3330	1973
Pyramid Systems Inc	2541	E	559 582-9345	3662
Rcan Inc	8361	D	559 585-8010	22148
Rosa Brothers Milk Co Inc **(PA)**	2024	E	559 582-8825	1822
Smith Residential Care Fcilty **(PA)**	8082	D	559 584-8451	21212
South Valley Materials Inc	3273	F	559 582-0532	6115
Superior Dairy Products Co	2024	F	559 582-0481	1823
Vandersteen Audio	3651	E	559 582-0324	9205
Veterinary Pharmaceuticals Inc	5122	D	559 582-6800	14295
Western Health Resources	8742	E	559 537-2860	23366

HARBOR CITY, CA - Los Angeles County

	SIC	EMP	PHONE	ENTRY #
A & J Industries Inc	2441	F	310 216-2170	3373
Basmat Inc **(PA)**	3444	D	310 325-2063	6793
Bennett Entps A Cal Ldscp Cntg	0781	D	310 534-3543	234
Brea Canon Oil Co Inc	1311	F	310 326-4002	393
Cal Partitions Inc	2542	E	310 539-1911	3678
Corn Maiden Foods Inc	2032	D	310 784-0400	1848
County of Los Angeles	8011	D	310 257-4989	19768
Decco Graphics Inc	3469	E	310 534-2861	7141
Hansen Engineering Co	3728	F	310 534-3870	10343
Joanka Inc	3442	F	310 326-8940	6703
Kaiser Foundation Hospitals	8011	C	310 325-5111	19929
Kaiser Foundation Hospitals	8011	C	310 517-3400	19947
La Espanola Meats Inc	2013	E	310 539-0455	1739
Lumination Lighting & Tech Inc	3646	C	855 283-1100	9096
Miller Woodworking Inc	2431	E	310 257-6806	3268
Onyx Industries Inc **(PA)**	3451	D	310 539-8830	7039
Permanente Medical Group Inc	8011	A	310 325-5111	20022
Prime Wheel Corporation	3714	B	310 326-5080	10115
Republic Machinery Co Inc **(PA)**	3541	E	310 518-1100	7742
Southern Cal Prmnnte Med Group	8011	C	800 780-1230	20079
Star Plastic Design	3089	D	310 530-7119	5827
Team Inc	3398	E	310 514-2312	6454

HARMONY, CA - San Luis Obispo County

	SIC	EMP	PHONE	ENTRY #
Harmony Cellars	2084	F	805 927-1625	2191

HAWAIIAN GARDENS, CA - Los Angeles County

	SIC	EMP	PHONE	ENTRY #
Consolidated Color Corporation	2851	E	562 420-7714	5092
Hawaiian Gardens Casino	7011	A	562 860-5887	16466
Howard Contracting Inc	1794	E	562 596-2969	1597
Openpopcom Inc **(PA)**	8748	D	714 249-7044	23488
Pacific Gardens Med Ctr LLC	8741	C	562 860-0401	23082
Richmond Plastering Inc	1742	E	562 924-4202	1397
Valley Friction Materials	5013	F	323 875-1783	13104

HAWTHORNE, CA - Los Angeles County

	SIC	EMP	PHONE	ENTRY #
Acuna Dionisio Able	3599	F	310 978-4741	8468
All Cartage Transportation Inc **(PA)**	4214	D	310 970-0600	12105
Amag Technology Inc **(DH)**	3577	E	310 518-2380	8234

GEOGRAPHIC

Employment Codes: A=Over 500 employees, B=251-500, C=101-250, D=51-100, E=20-50 F=10-19
2022 Southern California Business Directory and Buyers Guide
© Mergent Inc. 1-800-342-5647
1369

	SIC	EMP	PHONE	ENTRY #
Astro Machine Co Inc	3599	F	310 679-8291	8505
Averitt Express Inc	4213	D	310 970-9520	12013
Blue Chip Moving and Stor Inc	4213	D	323 463-6888	12015
Calpak Usa Inc	3672	D	310 937-7335	9386
Crown Transportation Inc	4119	D	310 737-0888	11860
Dolphin Medical Inc (HQ)	3845	D	800 448-6506	11220
Eaglerider Finance LLC	7389	D	310 321-3191	18510
Epirus Inc	7372	E	310 620-8678	17847
Equinox-76th Street Inc	7991	D	310 727-9543	19444
Eureka Restaurant Group LLC (PA)	8741	B	310 331-8233	23023
Firstclass Foods - Trojan Inc	2011	C	310 676-2500	1711
Fulham Co Inc	3612	E	323 779-2980	8872
Glen-Mac Swiss Co	3678	E	310 978-4555	9655
Honda Stephan T MD Inc	8011	D	323 757-2118	19845
Inspectorate America Corp	7389	C	800 424-0099	18549
Intelligent SCM LLC (PA)	4731	D	310 775-9195	12473
Interntonal Strl Engineers Inc	8711	D	310 643-7310	22580
Ip Corporation	2821	E	323 757-1801	4698
Lithographix Inc (PA)	2752	B	323 770-1000	4360
Local Neon Co Inc	3993	E	310 978-2000	11567
Longwood Management Corp	8051	C	310 679-1461	20404
Lowes Home Centers LLC	5031	C	323 327-4000	13238
Marco Fine Arts Galleries Inc	2759	E	310 615-1818	4541
Marleon Inc	7692	E	310 679-1242	18989
Maxon Crs LLC	3731	E	424 236-4660	10453
Medical Tactile Inc	3841	F	310 641-8228	11016
Ncompass International LLC	8742	E	323 785-1700	23282
Nmsp Inc (HQ)	3714	D	310 484-2322	10109
OSI Electronics Inc (HQ)	3672	E	310 978-0516	9436
OSI Laserscan Inc	3699	E	310 978-0516	9896
OSI Subsidiary Inc	3699	C	310 978-0516	9897
OSI Systems Inc (PA)	3674	B	310 978-0516	9555
Park West Landscape Inc	0782	D	310 363-4100	333
Paulco Precision Inc	3599	F	310 679-4900	8734
Picnic At Ascot Inc	2449	D	310 674-3098	3417
Rapiscan Holdings Inc (HQ)	6799	D	310 978-0516	16287
Rapiscan Systems Inc	3699	E	310 978-1457	9904
Sandhrst Cnvlscent Group Ltd A	8051	E	310 675-3304	20458
Schnierow Dental Care	8021	D	310 377-6453	20198
Seems Plumbing Co Inc	1711	E	310 297-4969	1136
Servicon Systems Inc	1771	A	310 970-0700	1550
Skyone Federal Credit Union (PA)	6061	D	310 491-7500	15089
South Bay Ford Inc (PA)	7538	C	310 644-0211	18872
Space Exploration Tech Corp (PA)	3761	A	310 363-6000	10518
Spacex Inc	3761	B	310 970-5845	10519
Springhill SMC LLC	7011	D	310 727-9595	16726
Technology Training Corp	2752	C	310 644-7777	4435
Thinkom Solutions Inc	4899	C	310 371-5486	12791
Tricor America Inc	4731	D	310 676-0800	12546
Trident Labs LLC	8072	C	310 915-9121	21113
Trio Tool & Die Co (PA)	3544	F	310 644-4431	7838
Uninet Imaging Inc (PA)	5043	C	424 675-3300	13349
Venturi Astrolab Inc	3761	F	310 989-1264	10525
Wems Inc (PA)	3564	D	310 644-0251	8062
Westmed Ambulance Inc (PA)	4119	C	510 614-1420	11899
Windsor Anaheim Healthcare	8051	E	310 675-3304	20511
Xdbs Corporation	8732	D	844 932-7356	22899

HEBER, CA - Imperial County

	SIC	EMP	PHONE	ENTRY #
C S Transport Inc	4212	D	760 666-5661	11960
Gibson and Schaefer Inc (PA)	3273	E	619 352-3535	6093
SMD Logistics Inc (PA)	4731	C	760 352-3194	12526

HELENDALE, CA - San Bernardino County

	SIC	EMP	PHONE	ENTRY #
Silver Lakes Association	8641	D	760 245-1606	22369

HEMET, CA - Riverside County

	SIC	EMP	PHONE	ENTRY #
Advanced Erosion Services	2951	F	951 929-8780	5268
Automobile Club Southern Cal	8699	D	951 652-6202	22434
Brazeau Thoroughbred Farms LP	3523	E	951 201-2278	7606
Califrnia Prcast Stone Mfg Inc	3272	F	951 657-7913	6020
Casa-Pacifica Inc	8361	B	951 658-3369	22090
Casa-Pacifica Inc	8361	B	951 766-5116	22091
Emeritus Corporation	8051	C	951 744-9861	20321
EZ Lube LLC	2992	D	951 766-1996	5296
Hemet Unified School District	8734	D	951 765-5100	22948
Hemet Unified School District	8699	D	951 765-6287	22452
Jack Gosch Ford Inc	7538	D	951 658-3181	18842
Johnre Care LLC	8051	E	951 658-6374	20383
Jsm Productions Inc	2752	F	951 929-5771	4344
Lake Hemet Municipal Water Dst (PA)	4941	D	951 658-3241	12897
Lowes Home Centers LLC	5031	C	951 492-7000	13252
Lpsh Holdings Inc (PA)	1711	B	855 647-5061	1097
Lpsh Holdings Inc	1711	C	951 926-1176	1098
McCrometer Inc (HQ)	3823	C	951 652-6811	10706
Miramonte Enterprises LLC	8051	C	951 658-9441	20418
National Millworks Llc	2499	F	619 823-0395	3447
Ortega Manufacturing Inc	3999	F	951 766-9363	11723
Pama Management Co	8741	E	951 929-0340	23085
Pehl Futz Futz Tgrden Accntnts	8721	D	951 658-3277	22807
Ramko Injection Inc	3089	D	951 929-0360	5787
Ramona Community Services Corp (HQ)	8082	C	951 658-9288	21206
Ramona Rhblttion Post Acute CA	8062	C	951 652-0011	20920
S T Moll Inc (PA)	7538	D	951 658-3145	18869
Southern Cal Disc Tire Co Inc	5013	C	951 929-2100	13092
Southland Arthritis Osteo	8011	E	951 672-1866	20093
Substance Abuse Program	3674	E	951 791-3350	9585
Superior Ready Mix Concrete LP	3273	D	951 658-9225	6122

	SIC	EMP	PHONE	ENTRY #
Trilar Management Group	8741	C	951 925-2021	23128
V I P Tots Inc	8351	D	951 652-7611	22072
Valley Health System Svc Corp	8062	D	951 765-4702	20998
Valley Rsrce Ctr For Rtrded In (PA)	8331	E	951 766-8659	21971
Washburn Grove Management Inc	2411	E	909 322-4690	3204

HERMOSA BEACH, CA - Los Angeles County

	SIC	EMP	PHONE	ENTRY #
Dedicated Media Inc (PA)	7311	D	310 524-9400	17005
Easy Reader Inc	2711	E	310 372-4611	3974
Gps Flyers	8742	D	951 588-7777	23227
Hammitt Inc	3161	D	310 292-5200	5892
Jealous Devil LLC	5199	E	800 446-0135	14940
Marlin Equity Partners LLC (PA)	6282	C	310 364-0100	15331
Marlin Operations Group Inc (PA)	6799	D	310 364-0100	16276
National Media Inc	2711	F	310 372-0388	4012
Pacific West Construction	1521	E	310 997-2340	630
Pickleback Nola LLC	7812	E	504 605-0911	19162
Rf Digital Corporation	3674	C	949 610-0008	9565
Security Base Group Inc	7381	E	213 444-1555	18326

HESPERIA, CA - San Bernardino County

	SIC	EMP	PHONE	ENTRY #
A Terrycable California Corp	3714	E	760 244-935*	10002
Aj Special Coatings Inc	3479	F	760 646-2813	7340
Arizona Pipeline Company (PA)	1623	B	760 244-8212	934
Best Way Disposal Co Inc	4953	D	760 244-9773	12930
Brown Hnycutt Truss Systems In	2439	E	760 244-8887	3356
C & M Wood Industries	2591	E	760 949-3292	3707
Cal Southern Components Inc	2439	F	760 949-5144	3357
Caremark Rx Inc	8011	E	760 948-6606	19736
Davita Inc	8092	C	310 536-2406	21238
Daytec Center LLC	3751	F	760 995-35'5	10489
Dial Precision Inc	3599	E	760 947-3557	8572
Dynasty Staffing Solutionsinc	7361	E	909 727-3801	17414
Endura Steel Inc (HQ)	5051	F	760 244-9325	13565
Geeriraj Inc	3672	E	760 244-6149	9410
Hannaknapp Realty Inc	6531	E	760 244-8557	15879
Hesperia Holding Inc	2439	D	760 244-8737	3363
Hesperia Unified School Dst	2099	E	760 948-1051	2449
Jesse Alexander Transport	4789	D	760 669-0379	12574
Maurice & Maurice Engrg Inc	3334	E	760 949-5151	6284
Mc-Kinley Welding Corp	3469	E	760 244-8876	7164
R S R Steel Fabrication Inc	3312	E	760 244-2210	6209
Robar Enterprises Inc (PA)	3273	C	760 244-5456	6107
Robertsons Ready Mix Ltd	3273	D	760 244-7239	6111
T L Timmerman Construction	2439	E	760 244-2532	3370
Total Renal Care Inc	8092	D	760 947-7405	21267
West Coast Furn Framers Inc	2426	E	760 669-5275	3226
Western Fab Inc	3499	F	760 949-1441	7577

HIGHLAND, CA - San Bernardino County

	SIC	EMP	PHONE	ENTRY #
Automobile Club Southern Cal	8699	D	909 381-2211	22401
Beaver Medical Group LP (HQ)	8011	C	909 425-3321	19722
Cedar Holdings LLC	8051	D	909 862-9611	20277
Cemex Cnstr Mtls PCF LLC	3273	F	909 335-3105	6079
East Valley Water District	4941	D	909 889-9501	12888
Immanuel Bptst Ch of San Brnrd	8351	D	909 862-3641	22022
In-Roads Creative Programs (PA)	8322	A	909 864-1551	21811
Innovative Product Brands Inc	3841	E	909 864-7477	10994
Kcb Towers Inc	1791	D	909 862-0322	1572
Lowes Home Centers LLC	5031	C	909 557-9010	13275
Raemica Inc	2013	D	909 864-1990	1747
Robertsons Rdymx Ltd A Cal Ltd	3273	D	909 425-2930	6110
San Manuel Indian Bingo Casino (PA)	7999	A	909 864-5050	19668
Synolo Security	7381	E	909 907-4605	18344
Tj Composites Inc	3444	E	951 928-8713	6931
YMCA of East Valley	8641	E	909 425-9622	22383

HINKLEY, CA - San Bernardino County

	SIC	EMP	PHONE	ENTRY #
Pacific Gas and Electric Co	4911	C	760 253-2925	12818

HOLLYWOOD, CA - Los Angeles County

	SIC	EMP	PHONE	ENTRY #
Battery Marketing Inc	7311	D	323 467-7267	16995
Body Glove International LLC	2329	F	310 374-3441	2804
Equinox-76th Street Inc	7991	D	323 471-0130	19445
Loews Hollywood Hotel LLC	7011	C	323 450-2235	16543

HOLTVILLE, CA - Imperial County

	SIC	EMP	PHONE	ENTRY #
Heritage Farms LLC (PA)	0191	D	442 283-5145	110

HUNTINGTON BEACH, CA - Orange County

	SIC	EMP	PHONE	ENTRY #
A Growing Concern Landscapes	0781	D	714 843-5137	231
Acceliot Inc	8731	F	657 845-4250	22821
Ace Parking Management Inc	7521	C	714 845-8000	18760
ADS LLC	3823	F	714 379-9778	10673
Advanced Cmpsite Pdts Tech Inc	3089	C	714 895-5544	5546
Advanced Cutting Tools Inc	3423	E	714 842-9376	6473
Aerodynamic Engineering Inc	3599	E	714 891-2651	8477
Aerodyne Prcsion Machining Inc	3599	E	714 891-1311	8478
AES Huntington Beach LLC	4911	E	714 374-1476	12796
Aire-Rite AC & Rfrgn Inc	1711	D	714 895-2338	1021
Airtech International Inc (PA)	3728	C	714 899-8100	10261
All West Plastics Inc	3082	E	714 394-9922	5443
Alltek Company U S A Inc	5084	C	714 375-9785	13883
Alpha Omega Cmpt Ntwrk Svcs In	7378	F	714 962-3129	18141
Alphalogix Inc	3695	F	714 901-1456	9833
American Automated Engrg Inc	3769	D	714 898-9951	10530
American Precision Hydraulics	3542	E	714 903-8610	7755
Americare Medservices Inc	4119	D	310 632-1141	11853
AMG Huntington Beach LLC	8711	E	714 894-9802	22486

	SIC	EMP	PHONE	ENTRY #
AMG Torrance LLC **(DH)**	3728	D	310 515-2584	10268
Applied Computer Solutions **(DH)**	7371	D	714 861-2200	17550
Automobile Club Southern Cal	8699	D	714 848-2227	22422
Bare Nothings Inc **(PA)**	2339	E	714 848-8532	2921
Bartco Lighting Inc	5063	D	714 230-3200	13616
Bent Manufacturing Co Bdaa Inc	3089	F	714 842-0600	5578
BJs Restaurant Operations Co	8741	C	714 500-2440	22988
Blue-White Industries Ltd **(PA)**	3824	D	714 893-8529	10735
Boardriders Inc **(HQ)**	2329	A	714 889-5404	2803
Boeing Company	3761	B	714 896-3311	10513
Boeing Encore Interiors LLC	3728	E	949 559-0930	10289
Boeing Intllctual Prprty Lcnsi	3721	B	562 797-2020	10180
Brymax Construction Svcs Inc	1711	D	949 200-9619	1040
Buena Park Tool & Engrg Inc	3599	F	714 843-6215	8533
C & C Boats Inc	4499	E	714 969-0900	12298
C-Guy Industries Inc **(PA)**	3999	F	714 587-9575	11644
Cal-Aurum Industries	3471	E	714 898-0996	7233
California Closet Co O **(PA)**	1799	C	714 899-4905	1646
California Economizer	3625	E	714 898-9963	8945
California Faucets Inc	3432	E	657 400-1639	6554
California Faucets Inc **(PA)**	3432	E	714 890-0450	6555
Cambro Manufacturing Company **(PA)**	3089	B	714 848-1555	5597
Careworks Health Services	8322	D	949 859-4700	21728
Child Development Incorporated	6531	C	714 842-4064	15813
Clarendon Specialty Fas Inc	5072	D	714 842-2603	13800
Classic Camaro Inc	5013	C	714 847-6887	13051
Coast To Coast Circuits Inc **(PA)**	3672	E	714 891-9441	9393
Coastline Cnstr & Awng Co Inc	1521	D	714 891-9798	598
Cobham Exeter Inc	3663	E	714 841-4976	9263
Colepro Inc	2426	F	714 488-0996	3216
Confie Seguros Inc **(DH)**	6411	C	714 252-2500	15554
Confie Seguros Holdings II Co **(PA)**	6411	C	714 252-2500	15555
Confie Seguros Texas Inc **(HQ)**	6411	D	714 252-2649	15556
Conversion Devices Inc	3845	F	714 898-6551	11219
Covid Clinic Inc	8011	D	877 219-8378	19776
Creative Costuming Designs Inc	2211	E	714 895-0982	2566
Crenshaw Die and Mfg Corp	3544	D	949 475-5505	7793
Critchfeld Mech Inc Sthern Cal	1711	D	949 390-2900	1050
Curlin Medical Inc **(HQ)**	3561	D	714 897-9301	8009
Custom Building Products LLC **(DH)**	2891	D	800 272-8786	5181
D & D Technologies USA Inc	3315	E	949 852-5140	6221
Davita Medical Management LLC	8099	D	714 968-0068	21414
DC Shoes Inc **(DH)**	2329	C	714 889-4206	2805
Delfin Design & Mfg Inc	3089	E	949 888-4644	5622
Direct Chassislink Inc	7359	C	657 216-5846	17345
Dix Metals Inc	5051	D	714 677-0777	13563
Donoco Industries Inc	3229	E	714 893-7889	5934
Douglas Fir Holdings LLC	8051	C	714 842-5551	20315
Dynamet Incorporated	3356	E	714 375-3150	6331
Dynatrac Products Co Inc	3714	F	714 596-4461	10049
Edinger Medical Group Inc	8011	D	714 965-2500	19802
Electronic Waveform Lab Inc	3841	E	714 843-0463	10977
Element Materials **(DH)**	8734	D	714 892-1961	22939
Encore Seats Inc	3728	E	949 559-0930	10322
Enhanced Vision Systems Inc **(HQ)**	3827	D	800 440-9476	10834
Fedex Office & Print Svcs Inc	7334	E	714 892-1452	17150
Fibreform Electronics Inc	3599	E	714 898-9641	8587
Filanity Corporation	4813	D	714 475-3521	12635
Flw Inc	5064	D	714 751-7512	13686
Fotis and Son Imports Inc	3556	E	714 894-9022	7933
Fox Hills Industries	3321	E	714 893-1940	6257
Freeway Insurance **(PA)**	6411	C	714 252-2500	15572
Friedman Professional Mgt Co	8011	D	714 842-1426	19825
Frontier California Inc	4813	B	714 375-6713	12641
Gac Brokerage Inc **(PA)**	7011	D	714 846-2732	16451
Gachupin Enterprises LLC	2759	F	714 375-4111	4518
Galkos Construction Inc **(PA)**	7299	C	714 373-8545	16956
Gearment Inc	2269	D	323 822-9999	2672
Glacier Design Systems Inc **(PA)**	2082	F	714 897-2337	2145
Glen Beverly Laboratories Inc **(PA)**	8621	D	714 848-5777	22270
Global Exprnce Specialists Inc	7389	C	619 498-6300	18529
Goodwill Inds Orange Cnty Cal	8331	D	714 881-3986	21955
Grani Installation Inc **(PA)**	1542	D	714 898-0441	767
Graphic Ink Corp	7336	E	714 901-2805	17177
Great Western Grinding Inc	7389	F	714 890-6592	18534
Guardian Health Care Svcs Inc	8322	E	714 377-7767	21795
Guhring Inc	3545	E	714 841-3582	7854
H & M Nursery Supply Corp	5191	F	714 898-1311	14860
H2 Home Collection Inc	2392	E	714 916-9513	3102
Harbor Distributing LLC **(HQ)**	5181	C	714 933-2400	14827
Harris Industries Inc **(PA)**	2672	E	714 898-8048	3872
HB Products LLC	2759	E	714 799-6967	4524
Home & Body Company **(PA)**	2842	E	714 842-8000	4964
Horsemen Inc	7381	D	714 847-4243	18288
House Seven Gables RE Inc	6531	D	714 500-3300	15882
House Seven Gables RE Inc	6531	D	714 754-6262	15884
Huntington Bch Senior Hsing LP	6513	C	714 842-4006	15727
Huntington Valley Inds Inc	5085	F	714 892-0256	13989
Hytron Mfg Co Inc	3599	E	714 903-6701	8624
I Hot Leads	7374	D	714 960-8028	18095
Iconn Engineering LLC	3495	E	714 696-8826	7487
Ideal Pallet System Inc	2448	F	714 847-9657	3392
IEPC Corp	7371	F	714 892-4443	17636
Ink Direct	2893	F	714 418-1999	5205
Inkwright LLC	2752	E	714 892-3300	4333
Innocean Wrldwide Americas LLC **(HQ)**	7311	B	714 861-5200	17021
Innovative Plastics Inc	3083	E	714 891-8800	5450

	SIC	EMP	PHONE	ENTRY #
Intertrade Aviation Corp	3728	F	714 895-3335	10355
Irish Interiors Inc **(HQ)**	3728	C	949 559-0930	10356
Irish Interiors Holdings Inc	3728	C	562 344-1700	10357
Irish International	3724	C	949 559-0930	10218
Italias Pizza Kitchen Ltd **(PA)**	2038	F	714 861-8178	1930
JCM Industries Inc **(PA)**	2542	E	714 902-9000	3687
Jet Performance Products Inc	3694	E	714 848-5500	9824
JGM Automotive Tooling Inc	3559	E	714 895-7001	7985
Johnson Manufacturing Inc	3599	E	714 903-0393	8645
Jolyn Clothing Company LLC	2339	E	714 794-2149	2959
Kadan Consultants Incorporated	3599	F	562 988-1165	8649
Kaiser Foundation Hospitals	6733	D	714 841-7293	16180
Karls Custom Sash & Doors LLC	2431	F	714 842-7877	3257
Kastle Stair Inc **(PA)**	2431	E	714 596-2600	3258
Kettenbach LP	3843	E	877 532-2123	11180
Kwl Industrial Company	5084	E	714 847-3268	13911
Laird Coatings Corporation	2851	D	714 894-5252	5100
Landmark Health LLC **(PA)**	8082	B	657 237-2450	21183
Leda Corporation	3769	E	714 841-7821	10534
Leoben Company	3999	F	951 284-9653	11707
License Frame Inc	3479	F	714 903-7550	7381
Lifoam Industries LLC	2653	D	714 891-5035	3818
Lightning Dversion Systems LLC	3643	F	714 841-1080	9040
Lincoln Composite Mtls Inc	2821	F	714 898-8350	4700
Logi Graphics Incorporated	3672	D	714 841-3686	9423
Love At First Bite Catering	7299	D	714 369-0561	16964
Lowes Home Centers LLC	5031	C	714 907-9006	13257
Lynde-Ordway Company Inc	3579	F	714 957-1311	8318
Lytle Screen Printing Inc	3552	E	714 969-2424	7909
M I T Inc	3544	E	714 899-6066	7813
Madrid Pro Designs Inc	5091	F	714 897-5656	14084
Madsen Products Incorporated	3599	F	714 894-1816	8673
Mailing Pros Inc	2621	F	714 892-7251	3761
Managed Health Network	6324	C	714 934-5519	15445
Marko Foam Products Inc **(PA)**	3086	E	949 417-3307	5513
Maxwell Petersen Associates	2721	E	714 230-3150	4085
Mechanized Science Seals Inc	3829	E	714 898-5602	10897
Michaelson Connor & Boul **(PA)**	8742	D	714 230-3600	23274
Milco Wire Edm Inc	3599	F	714 373-0098	8697
Mission Crtical Composites LLC	3728	E	714 831-2100	10384
Mjc Engineering and Tech Inc	3542	F	714 890-0618	7761
Momeni Engineering LLC	3599	E	714 897-9301	8706
Nakase Brothers Wholesale Nurs **(PA)**	5193	D	949 855-4388	14889
NDT Systems Inc	3829	E	714 893-2438	10899
Netball America Inc	7997	E	888 221-3650	19591
Newlight Technologies Inc	3089	E	714 556-4500	5725
Newmar Power LLC	3675	C	800 854-3906	9613
Nordson Medical (ca) LLC	3841	D	657 215-4200	11036
Norm Harboldt	3479	F	714 596-4242	7391
Notthoff Engineering LA Inc	3728	D	714 894-9802	10388
Nuvision Fincl Federal Cr Un **(PA)**	6061	C	714 375-8000	15075
Ofs Brands Holdings Inc	2521	A	714 903-2257	3596
Oliphant Tool Company	3544	F	714 903-6336	7819
Orlando Spring Corp	3495	E	562 594-8411	7488
Pace Development Cabinetry Inc	1542	E	714 842-5336	799
Pacific City Hotel LLC	7011	B	714 698-6100	16607
Pakedge Device & Software Inc	7372	E	714 880-4511	17950
PCA Aerospace Inc **(PA)**	3728	D	714 841-1750	10392
Pexco Aerospace Inc	2821	E	714 894-9922	4707
Pivot Technology Solutions	7379	C	714 845-4547	18212
Plasma Rggedized Solutions Inc	3471	E	714 893-6063	7294
Pollys Pies Inc	5149	D	714 964-4424	14719
Portermatt Electric Inc	1731	D	714 596-8788	1299
Precise Fit Limited One LLC	7361	B	310 824-1800	17445
Precision Frrites Ceramics Inc	3599	D	714 901-7622	8742
Premier Systems Usa Inc **(PA)**	5045	F	657 204-9861	13428
Prestige Cosmetics Inc	2844	F	714 375-0395	5062
Primal Elements Inc	5122	D	714 899-0757	14282
Prime Hlthcare Hntngton Bch LL	8062	B	714 843-5000	20904
Primus Inc	3993	D	714 527-2261	11582
Product Dsign Developments Inc	3089	F	714 898-6895	5781
Publish Brand Inc	2741	F	714 890-1908	4200
Pvd Coatings LLC	3479	F	714 899-4892	7403
PW Stephens Envmtl Inc **(PA)**	1799	C	714 892-2028	1682
Pyro-Comm Systems Inc **(PA)**	1731	C	714 902-8000	1303
R C Hotels Inc	7011	D	714 891-0123	16647
Rainbow Disposal Co Inc **(HQ)**	4953	C	714 847-3581	12969
Ray Foster Dental Equipment	3843	E	714 897-7795	11193
Rba Builders Inc	1542	D	714 895-9000	814
RC Wendt Painting Inc	1721	C	714 960-2700	1196
Reedex Inc	3679	E	714 894-0311	9771
Reliable Wholesale Lumber Inc **(PA)**	5031	C	714 848-8222	13283
Rima Enterprises Inc	3555	D	714 893-4534	7925
Riot Glass Inc	3699	E	800 580-2303	9908
Rk Sports LLC **(PA)**	3714	F	714 794-4400	10126
Rocker Solenoid Company	3679	D	310 534-5660	9773
Rodon Products Inc	3677	F	714 898-3528	9643
Roi Development Corp	3629	E	714 751-0488	8981
Roto West Enterprises Inc	3089	F	714 899-2030	5804
Russell Fisher Partnership	7542	E	714 842-4453	18916
Safran Cabin Galleys Us Inc **(HQ)**	3728	A	714 861-7300	10407
Safran Cabin Inc **(HQ)**	3728	B	714 934-0000	10408
Salco Dynamic Solutions Inc **(PA)**	2992	E	714 374-7500	5298
Sandia Plastics Inc	3089	E	714 901-8400	5811
Scoreusa Institute	8733	D	714 909-0688	22920
Screen Art Inc	2759	F	714 891-4185	4571
Sea Breeze Health Care Inc	8051	C	714 847-9671	20460

	SIC	EMP	PHONE	ENTRY #
Sgt Boardriders Inc	3069	F	714 274-8000	5410
Sho-Air International Inc **(PA)**	4731	F	949 476-9111	12525
Shortcuts Software Inc	7372	E	714 622-6600	17981
Sign Pipers Inc	3993	F	657 215-3957	11598
Skyhill Financial Inc	6531	D	714 657-3938	15999
Skynet USA Asset MGT Inc	8742	E	702 969-5599	23325
Soberlink Healthcare LLC	3829	F	714 975-7200	10911
Soldermask Inc	3672	F	714 842-1987	9455
Soroptmist Intl Huntington Bch	8699	E	714 271-9305	22463
Sound Investment Group	5013	F	714 515-4001	13091
South Bay Fabrication Inc	7389	E	714 894-1314	18672
Southern Cal Disc Tire Co Inc	5013	C	714 901-8226	13093
Southern Cal Prmnnte Med Group	8011	C	714 841-7293	20085
Specilzed Crmic Pwdr Cting Inc	3479	F	714 901-2628	7413
Sport Chalet LLC	7999	D	714 848-0988	19672
Star Die Casting Inc	3544	F	714 536-2999	7833
Statco Engrg & Fabricators Inc **(PA)**	5084	E	714 375-6300	13944
Stater Bros Markets	2052	E	714 963-0949	2073
Storefront Repair Inc	1751	F	714 842-1337	1458
Submersible Systems LLC	3949	F	714 842-6566	11449
Sunbeam Trailer Products Inc	3647	E	714 373-5000	9120
Sunshine Makers Inc **(PA)**	2842	D	562 795-6000	4979
Surf City Garage	2842	F	714 894-1707	4980
Surf City Still Works LLC	2085	F	714 253-7606	2247
Tarpin Corporation	3544	E	714 891-6944	7836
Teacher Created Materials Inc	2741	C	714 891-2273	4212
Therma-Tek Range Corp	3639	E	570 455-9491	9017
Tile & Marble Design Co Inc	1743	E	714 847-6472	1423
Tiodize Co Inc **(PA)**	3479	F	714 898-4377	7420
Tiodize Co Inc	5172	E	714 898-4377	14812
Tolemar Inc	3751	F	714 362-8166	10505
Tom Byer Roofing Service Inc	1761	E	714 847-9332	1508
Total Petroleum Services Inc	5172	D	714 907-0117	14814
Translogic Incorporated	3823	E	714 890-0058	10730
Transprttion Brkg Spclists Inc	4212	B	714 754-4230	12001
Travismathew LLC **(HQ)**	2329	F	562 799-6900	2829
Tri Models Inc	3721	D	714 896-0823	10206
Truwest Inc	2329	E	714 895-2444	2830
TSCM Corporation	7349	D	714 841-1988	17293
Two Roads Prof Resources Inc	7363	D	714 901-3804	17519
U S Wheel Corporation	3714	E	714 892-0021	10146
UFO Designs **(PA)**	3089	F	714 892-4420	5847
Unison Electric	1731	E	714 375-5915	1334
United States Technical Svcs	7379	C	714 374-6300	18231
V & S Engineering Company Ltd	3599	E	714 898-7869	8834
Vae Industries Corporation	2394	E	714 842-7500	3148
Variable Speed Solutions Inc	7623	F	714 847-5957	18949
Vector Launch LLC **(PA)**	3489	C	202 888-3063	7435
Vern Fonk Insurance Svcs Inc **(DH)**	6411	D	714 252-2500	15645
Victory Professional Pdts Inc	2339	E	714 887-0621	3007
Vinatronic Inc	3672	F	714 845-3480	9468
Walton Company Inc	2499	E	714 847-8800	3458
Waterfront Hotel LLC	7011	B	714 845-8000	16778
West Coast Trends Inc	3949	E	714 843-9288	11458
Xantrex LLC **(HQ)**	3629	D	800 241-3897	8984
Xr LLC	3842	E	714 847-9292	11155
York Enterprises South Inc	7538	D	714 842-6611	18888
Zadro Inc	3231	E	714 892-9200	5972
Zadro Products Inc	3231	E	714 892-9200	5973
Zimmer Melia & Associates Inc **(PA)**	3842	D	615 377-0118	11157

HUNTINGTON PARK, CA - Los Angeles County

	SIC	EMP	PHONE	ENTRY #
Acme Castings Inc	3366	E	323 583-3129	6403
Acme Screw Products	3449	E	323 581-8611	7013
Aircraft Foundry Co Inc	3365	E	323 587-3171	6383
Aircraft Xray Laboratories Inc	8734	D	323 587-4141	22927
All Care Medical Group Inc	8011	D	408 278-3550	19689
Altamed Health Services Corp	8011	C	323 277-7678	19699
B F McGilla Inc	3498	E	323 581-8288	7528
Bodycote Thermal Proc Inc	3471	D	323 583-1231	7225
Cal-Pac Chemical Co Inc	2819	F	323 585-2178	4651
Canterbury Designs Inc	3446	E	323 936-7111	6954
Chhp Holdings II LLC **(HQ)**	8062	B	323 583-1931	20716
Chhp Management LLC	8062	D	323 583-1931	20717
Citizens of Humanity LLC **(PA)**	2339	C	323 923-1240	2932
Cotton Generation Inc	2361	F	323 581-8555	3030
Covenant Care California LLC	8051	D	323 589-5941	20299
Covert Iron Works	3322	F	323 560-2792	6261
Crown Poly Inc	2673	C	323 268-1298	3882
GM Windows & Doors Inc	2431	F	323 771-0348	3251
Huntington Park Dialysis LLC	8092	D	323 585-7605	21249
J Heyri Inc	2331	E	323 588-1234	2848
Kuk Rim USA Inc	2281	C	323 277-9256	2700
Los Angeles Galvanizing Co	3479	D	323 583-2263	7383
Los Angles Pump Valve Pdts Inc	3561	E	323 277-7788	8016
McCarthy Bldg Companies Inc	1542	D	949 851-8383	789
NL&a Collections Inc	3645	E	323 277-6266	9069
Oheck LLC	2386	E	323 923-2700	3059
Plycraft Industries Inc	2435	C	323 587-8101	3353
Prajin 1 Stop Distributors Inc **(PA)**	5099	E	323 395-5302	14175
Primor Huntington Park Inc	3843	F	323 365-3200	11190
Reliance Upholstery Sup Co Inc	2392	D	323 321-2300	3117
Rightime Enterprise **(PA)**	2038	E	323 574-0310	1937
Saroyan Lumber Company Inc **(PA)**	5031	D	800 624-9309	13286
Saydel Inc **(PA)**	2844	F	323 585-2800	5066
Traffic Works Inc	3081	E	323 582-0616	5439
UFO Inc	3089	E	323 588-5450	5848
Valco Planer Works Inc	3544	E	323 582-6355	7842

	SIC	EMP	PHONE	ENTRY #
West Coast Foundry LLC **(HQ)**	3325	E	323 583-1421	6278

IDYLLWILD, CA - Riverside County

	SIC	EMP	PHONE	ENTRY #
Guided Discoveries Inc	7032	D	951 659-6062	16821
Jeb Holdings Corp **(PA)**	5065	D	951 659-2183	13735
South Bay Wire & Cable Co LLC	3315	D	951 659-2183	6234

IMPERIAL, CA - Imperial County

	SIC	EMP	PHONE	ENTRY #
Imperial Irrigation District **(PA)**	4911	A	800 303-7756	12806
Imperial Irrigation District	4971	E	760 339-9220	13011
Imperial Premix LLC **(PA)**	2048	F	760 355-7997	1969
Imperial Roof Truss Inc	2439	E	760 355-1809	3365
Imperial Valley Family Care **(PA)**	8351	D	760 355-7730	22023
United States Gypsum Company	3275	D	760 358-3200	6132

INDEPENDENCE, CA - Inyo County

	SIC	EMP	PHONE	ENTRY #
Eastern California Museum **(PA)**	8412	B	760 878-0292	22221
Los Angeles Dept Wtr & Pwr	4941	B	760 878-2156	12903

INDIAN WELLS, CA - Riverside County

	SIC	EMP	PHONE	ENTRY #
Bennion Deville Fine Homes Inc	6531	B	760 674-3452	15786
Bjz LLC	8082	C	760 851-0740	21138
Dhccnp	7997	D	760 340-4646	19560
Eldorado Country Club	7997	C	760 346-808[illegible]	19562
Hart Sales LLC	3549	F	650 532-9200	7903
Indian Wells Country Club Inc	7997	D	760 345-256[illegible]	19569
Indian Wells Property LLC	7011	D	442 305-4500	16502
Indian Wells Resort Hotel	7011	D	760 345-6466	16503
Lh Indian Wells Operating LLC	7011	C	760 341-2200	16540
Merrill Lynch Prce Fnner Smith	6211	D	760 862-1400	15280
Renaissance Hotel Operating Co	7011	A	760 773-4444	16661
Reserve Club	7997	D	760 674-2222	19604
Toscana Country Club Inc	7997	C	760 404-1444	19623
Troon Golf LLC	8741	C	760 346-4653	23129
Vintage Club	7997	D	760 340-0500	19625

INDIO, CA - Riverside County

	SIC	EMP	PHONE	ENTRY #
A Plus Cabinets Inc	2434	F	760 322-5252	3303
All Wall Inc	1742	D	760 600-5108	1362
Alliance Protection Service	1542	E	760 347-3747	732
Brodie Holdings Inc	1751	E	760 775-3744	1428
Cabazon Band Mission Indians	7011	A	760 342-5000	16364
Coachella Vly Rescue Mission	8322	D	760 347-3512	21747
Commercial Lighting Inds Inc	5063	D	800 755-0[illegible]55	13619
Coronet Concrete Products Inc **(PA)**	3273	E	760 398-2441	6086
Desert Recreation District **(PA)**	7999	D	760 347-3484	19642
East Valley Tourist Dev Auth	7999	A	760 342-5000	19645
Elite Anywhere Corp **(PA)**	4731	D	917 860-9247	12452
Fiesta Ford Inc	7538	C	760 775-7777	18828
Frontier California Inc	4813	B	760 342-0500	12637
Granite Construction Company	1611	B	760 775-7500	881
Heritage Palms Hoa	7992	D	760 772-7334	19494
John F Kennedy Mem Hosp Aux	8062	A	760 347-6191	20799
Kaiser Foundation Hospitals	8011	C	866 984-7483	19904
Kash Organization	6732	D	702 330-9215	16168
Lindsey Doors Inc	3083	E	760 775-1959	5452
M F G Eurotec Inc	2511	F	760 863-0033	3477
Marthas Village & Kitchen	8322	D	760 347-4741	21848
Panco Mens Products Inc	2844	E	760 342-4368	5056
Plantation Golf Club Inc	7997	D	760 775-3688	19599
Purus International Inc	3069	F	760 775-4500	5402
Rai Care Ctrs Sthern Cal II LL	8092	D	760 347-3986	21260
RES-Care Inc	8052	D	760 775-2887	20540
Stutz Packing Company	2034	F	760 342-1666	1884
Sullivans Stone Factory Inc	3281	E	760 347-5535	6148
Tenet Healthsystem Medical Inc	8099	D	760 347-6191	21490
United Irrigation Inc	4971	D	760 347-6161	13015
Valley Animal Medical Center	0742	A	760 342-4711	204
Whites Crane Service Inc	7353	D	760 347-3401	17323
Whites Steel Inc **(PA)**	1791	F	760 347-3401	1584

INGLEWOOD, CA - Los Angeles County

	SIC	EMP	PHONE	ENTRY #
A H Machine Inc	3599	E	310 672-0016	8456
Aero Port Services Inc **(PA)**	7382	A	310 623-8230	18365
After-Party2 Inc **(HQ)**	7359	C	310 202-0011	17329
Air-Sea Forwarders Inc **(PA)**	4731	D	310 216-1616	12418
Allied Guard Services Inc **(PA)**	7381	D	424 227-9912	18240
American Egle Prtctive Svcs In	7381	D	310 412-0019	18243
Antique Designs Ltd Inc	2521	E	310 671-5400	3577
Apollo Couriers Inc **(PA)**	4215	D	310 337-0377	12124
Automobile Club Southern Cal	8699	D	310 673-5170	22424
Autonomous Medical Devices Inc **(PA)**	3826	E	424 331-0900	10782
Beckett Enterprise	8742	E	310 686-3817	23171
C C M D Inc	3471	E	310 673-5532	7231
Carpet USA Ltd **(PA)**	5023	D	310 390-8570	13164
Centinela Consulting Group Inc	3272	F	310 674-2115	6021
Centinela Valley Care Center	8361	D	310 674-3216	22092
Centra Freight Services Inc	4731	D	310 568-8810	12431
Century Skill Care	8051	D	310 672-1012	20279
Cfhs Holdings Inc	8062	B	310 673-4660	20713
Christ-Centered Ministries	8699	E	310 528-4538	22449
CP Opco LLC **(HQ)**	7299	A	310 966-4900	16952
Creamer Printing Co	2752	F	310 671-9491	4266
Dedicated Dental Systems Inc	8021	D	661 397-5513	20173
Dolphin Hkg Ltd **(PA)**	5199	D	310 215-3356	14925
Doorking Inc **(PA)**	3699	C	310 645-0023	9865
Empower Rf Systems Inc **(PA)**	3663	D	310 412-8100	9271
Engineered Magnetics Inc	3629	E	310 649-9000	8975
Everbrands Inc	2844	E	855 595-2999	5019

Mergent email: customerrelations@mergent.com
1372
2022 Southern California Business Directory and Buyers Guide
(P-0000) Products & Services Section entry number
(PA)=Parent Co (HQ)=Headquarters (DH)=Div Headquarters

GEOGRAPHIC SECTION IRVINE, CA

	SIC	EMP	PHONE	ENTRY #
Farrar Grinding Company	3728	E	323 678-4879	10325
Gentle Dental Service Corp **(DH)**	8021	D	800 277-1112	20179
Glp Designs Inc	2599	F	310 652-6800	3730
Goodman Food Products Inc **(PA)**	2099	C	310 674-3180	2446
Hayes Protective Services Inc	7381	C	323 755-2282	18286
Industrious Software Solution	7372	F	310 672-8700	17884
Inglewood Cmtry Mortuary Inc	7261	D	310 412-6811	16924
Inglewood Park Cemetery **(PA)**	6553	C	310 412-6500	16085
Interdent Inc **(HQ)**	8021	D	310 765-2400	20181
Interdent Service Corporation **(DH)**	8021	E	310 765-2400	20183
Intervisual Books Inc	2731	F	302 636-5400	4131
Iron Mountain Info MGT LLC	4731	D	818 848-9766	12474
Kaiser Foundation Hospitals	6324	C	800 954-8000	15434
Kaiser Foundation Hospitals	8011	C	310 419-3303	19946
L and W Developers LLC	6552	E	310 654-8428	16055
Lax Hotel Investment Co Inc	7011	D	310 846-3200	16536
Lax In-Flite Services LLC	3699	F	310 677-9885	9888
Lemonlight Media Inc	7812	D	310 402-0275	19142
Line Publications Inc	2721	F	310 234-9501	4081
Marvin Engineering Co Inc **(PA)**	8711	A	310 674-5030	22605
Marvin Land Systems Inc	3711	E	310 674-5030	9958
Minus K Technology Inc	3829	C	310 348-9656	10898
Mittal Ram	5074	D	310 769-6669	13834
Msg Forum LLC	6512	D	310 330-7339	15681
Multichrome Company Inc **(PA)**	3471	E	310 216-1086	7284
N/S Corporation **(PA)**	3589	D	310 412-7074	8399
Odwalla Inc	2033	D	310 342-3920	1871
Pharmaco-Kinesis Corporation	3841	E	310 641-2700	11043
Pml Inc	7389	D	310 671-4345	18637
Prime Healthcare Centinela LLC	8062	A	310 673-4660	20902
Rai Care Ctrs Sthern Cal II LL	8092	D	310 673-6865	21261
RHO Chem LLC **(DH)**	4959	E	323 776-6234	13008
Ro Rocket Design Inc **(PA)**	8712	D	213 784-0014	22740
Royal Airline Linen Inc	7211	D	310 677-9885	16839
Security Indust Spcialists Inc	7381	C	323 924-9147	18327
Shg Holdings Corp **(PA)**	3546	E	310 410-4907	7883
Southern Cal Prmnnte Med Group	8011	C	310 419-3306	20084
Watts Health Foundation Inc **(HQ)**	8052	B	310 424-2220	20548
Weber Drilling Co Inc	3532	E	310 670-7708	7664
West Cntinela Vly Care Ctr Inc	8051	D	310 674-3216	20505
Zephyr Manufacturing Co Inc	3546	D	310 410-4907	7884

INYOKERN, CA - Kern County

	SIC	EMP	PHONE	ENTRY #
Firequick Products Inc	3569	E	760 371-4279	8123
Firequick Products Inc	2899	F	760 377-5766	5220
Herbert Rizzardini	2048	F	760 377-4571	1967
Indian Wells Companies	2082	F	760 377-4290	2147

IRVINE, CA - Orange County

	SIC	EMP	PHONE	ENTRY #
24hr Homecare LLC	8082	D	949 607-8115	21120
3 Point Distribution LLC	2329	E	949 266-2700	2793
3h Communication Systems Inc	4813	E	949 529-1583	12621
3M Technical Ceramics Inc **(HQ)**	3299	A	949 862-9600	6175
3y Power Technology Inc	3679	F	949 450-0152	9668
4g Wireless Inc **(PA)**	4812	C	949 748-6100	12589
5 Arches LLC	6163	D	949 387-8092	15234
511 Inc **(DH)**	2231	B	949 800-1511	2609
A & H Communications Inc	1623	C	949 250-4555	931
A S A Engineering Inc	3571	F	949 460-9911	8144
A-Info Inc	3728	E	949 346-7326	10232
Abbott	2834	F	949 769-5018	4772
ABC Imaging of Washington	2759	F	949 419-3728	4474
ABM Onsite Services Inc	7381	A	949 863-9100	18237
Above & Beyond Balloons Inc	3999	E	949 586-8470	11623
ABS Consulting Inc	8711	D	714 734-4242	22472
Acclarent Inc	3841	B	650 687-5888	10923
Accretive Solutions Inc **(HQ)**	8721	A	312 994-4600	22757
Accurate Background LLC **(PA)**	7375	B	800 784-3911	18117
Ace Parking Management Inc	7521	D	949 769-3696	18757
Acme Communications Inc **(PA)**	4833	D	714 245-9499	12709
Acti Corporation Inc	3651	E	949 753-0352	9155
Action Property Management Inc **(PA)**	6514	D	949 450-0202	15754
Activision Blizzard Inc	7372	D	949 955-1380	17774
Adams/Strter Cvil Engneers Inc	8711	D	949 474-2330	22475
Adenna LLC	3842	F	909 510-6999	11078
Adex Electronics Inc	3674	F	949 597-1772	9473
Advanced Sterlization **(HQ)**	3841	C	800 595-0200	10925
Advanced Vsual Image Dsign LLC	2752	E	951 279-2138	4224
Advancedware Corporation	7371	F	949 609-1240	17540
Advantage Sales & Mktg Inc **(DH)**	8742	C	949 797-2900	23147
Advantage Solutions Inc **(HQ)**	7311	A	949 797-2900	16991
Advantage Systems Inc	7371	F	949 250-0260	17541
Advantest Test Solutions Inc **(DH)**	3674	D	949 523-6900	9477
Aeroflex Incorporated	3674	D	800 843-1553	9478
Agendia Inc	8093	C	949 540-6300	21270
Agents West Inc	3699	E	949 614-0293	9849
Agility Holdings Inc **(DH)**	4731	D	714 617-6300	12417
Ahtna-CDM JV	1541	E	714 824-3470	686
Aids Svcs Fndation Orange Cnty	8322	D	949 809-5700	21709
Alcon Lensx Inc **(DH)**	3841	C	949 753-1393	10926
Alcon Manufacturing Ltd **(PA)**	2834	C	949 753-1393	4777
Alcon Vision LLC	3841	A	949 753-6488	10928
Alcone Marketing Group Inc **(HQ)**	7311	D	949 595-5322	16992
All Counties Courier Inc	4215	C	714 599-9300	12123
Allergan Sales LLC **(DH)**	2834	A	862 261-7000	4778
Allergan Spclty Thrpeutics Inc	2834	A	714 246-4500	4779
Allergan Usa Inc	2834	A	714 427-1900	4780
Alliance Healthcare Svcs Inc **(DH)**	8071	C	949 242-5300	21058
Alliance Medical Products Inc **(DH)**	3841	C	949 768-4690	10931
Alorica Inc **(PA)**	7389	D	949 527-4600	18440
Alpha Star Corporation	7372	E	562 961-7827	17781
Alphaeon Corporation **(HQ)**	5047	D	949 284-4555	13471
Alteryx Inc **(PA)**	7373	E	888 836-4274	18017
Alton Irvine Inc	5021	D	949 428-4141	13125
Aluratek Inc	3651	E	949 468-2046	9157
American Arium	3674	E	949 623-7090	9480
American Audio Component Inc	3679	E	909 596-3788	9673
American Cmpus Communities Inc	7021	D	949 854-0900	16810
American Healthcare Reit Inc **(PA)**	6798	D	949 270-9200	16227
American Liberty Capital Corp	6163	C	949 623-0288	15235
American Medical Tech Inc	5047	D	949 553-0359	13473
American Relays Inc	3625	E	562 926-2837	8942
American Scence Tech As T Corp	3721	D	310 773-1978	10176
Americor Funding Inc	7299	C	866 333-8686	16944
Ameripark LLC	7521	B	949 279-7525	18763
Ametek Aerospace	3823	F	949 473-6754	10674
Ampronix Inc	5047	D	949 273-8000	13475
Anabolic Incorporated	2834	E	949 863-0340	4784
Ancca Corporation	1742	D	949 553-0084	1363
Anderson & Howard Electric Inc	1731	C	949 250-4555	1213
Andrew Lauren Company Inc	7389	C	949 861-4222	18445
Anduril Industries Inc **(PA)**	3812	C	949 891-1607	10566
Anheuser-Busch LLC	5181	C	949 263-9270	14820
Antis Roofg Waterproofing LLC	1799	D	949 461-9222	1635
Aperto Property Management Inc **(PA)**	6519	C	949 873-4200	15759
Apollo Instruments Inc	3827	F	949 756-3111	10826
Apollotek International Inc	2899	E	800 787-1244	5212
Applied Cardiac Systems Inc	3841	D	949 855-9366	10934
Aquatec International Inc	3561	D	949 225-2200	8004
Arbitech LLC	5045	D	949 376-6650	13376
Arbonne International LLC **(DH)**	2834	E	949 770-2610	4786
Arcules Inc	7371	E	949 439-0053	17553
Aria Group Incorporated	8711	D	949 475-2915	22491
Arkham Technology Limited **(PA)**	8711	F	949 585-0404	22492
Artistic Maintenance Inc	0782	D	949 733-8690	291
Asics America Corporation **(HQ)**	5139	C	949 453-8888	14429
Aspen Medical Products LLC	3841	D	949 681-0200	10941
Assi Security **(PA)**	1731	D	949 955-0244	1216
Astron Corporation	3677	E	949 458-7277	9620
Astronics Test Systems Inc **(DH)**	3825	C	800 722-2528	10743
AT&T Corp	4812	D	949 622-8240	12592
Aten Technology Inc	3577	D	949 428-1111	8236
Atkinson Construction Inc	1611	B	303 410-2540	860
Atlas Franchise Management Inc	8741	D	949 239-1760	22981
Atlas Hospitality Group	6531	D	949 622-3400	15774
Atlas Sheet Metal Inc	3444	F	949 600-8787	6789
Attom Data Solutions LLC **(PA)**	6531	D	949 502-8300	15775
Auctioncom Inc	6531	C	800 499-6199	15776
Auctioncom LLC **(PA)**	6531	A	949 859-2777	15777
Autogravity Corporation	6141	D	949 392-8777	15140
Automatic Data Processing Inc	7374	C	949 751-0360	18079
Automobile Club Southern Cal	8699	D	714 973-1211	22398
Avalonbay Communities Inc	6531	E	949 955-6200	15779
Avente Inc	7379	E	844 385-1556	18161
Axent Corporation Limited	2676	F	949 900-4349	3902
Axiom Memory Solutions Inc	5045	D	949 581-1450	13378
Axon Networks Inc	7371	D	949 310-4429	17559
Axonics Inc	8731	D	949 396-6322	22829
Aztek Incorporated	7373	E	949 770-8406	18020
B Braun Medical Inc	3841	A	610 691-5400	10942
Balt Usa LLC	5047	D	949 788-1443	13479
Barrot Corporation	3544	E	949 852-1640	7782
Barton Perreira LLC	3851	E	949 305-5360	11245
Bausch & Lomb Incorporated	2834	D	949 788-6000	4792
Bausch & Lomb Incorporated	3851	C	949 788-6000	11246
Baxalta US Inc	7389	B	949 474-6301	18458
Baxter Healthcare Corporation	3841	C	949 474-6301	10944
Baywa RE Solar Projects LLC **(DH)**	3674	F	949 398-3915	9487
BDS Marketing LLC **(DH)**	7311	B	949 472-6700	16996
BDS Solutions Group LLC **(DH)**	7311	E	949 472-6700	16997
Beacon Resources LLC	8742	C	949 955-1773	23169
Berger Kahn A Law Corporation **(PA)**	8111	D	949 474-1880	21513
Best Best & Krieger LLP	8111	E	949 263-2600	21515
Best Life and Health Insur Co	6311	D	949 253-4080	15357
Beta Bionics Inc	3845	E	949 297-6635	11214
Bi-Search International Inc	3679	D	714 258-4500	9682
Bigrentz Inc **(PA)**	7353	D	855 999-5438	17305
Bio-Medical Devices Inc	3841	E	949 752-9642	10946
Bio-Medical Devices Intl Inc	3841	E	800 443-3842	10947
Bio-Nutritional RES Group Inc **(PA)**	2023	C	714 427-6990	1785
Biodot Inc **(HQ)**	3823	D	949 440-3685	10681
Biomerica Inc **(PA)**	2835	D	949 645-2111	4918
Biorad Inc	3826	E	949 598-1200	10787
Bioray Inc	2023	F	949 305-7454	1786
Bioriginal Food & Science	2023	E	949 622-9030	1787
Biosense Webster Inc **(HQ)**	3845	C	909 839-8500	11217
Biosynthetic Technologies LLC **(HQ)**	3556	F	949 390-5910	7928
Bit Group Usa Inc **(PA)**	3841	D	949 238-1200	10950
Bitvore Corp	7372	E	866 869-5151	17797
Bivar Inc	3679	E	949 951-8808	9683
Bk Sems Usa Inc	2499	F	949 390-7120	3440
Black Knght RE Data Sltons LLC **(DH)**	6531	A	626 808-9000	15792
Blind Squirrel Games Inc	7372	E	714 460-0860	17800
Blitzz Technology Inc	3663	E	949 380-7709	9256
Blizzard Entertainment Inc **(HQ)**	7372	D	949 955-1380	17801

GEOGRAPHIC

Employment Codes: A=Over 500 employees, B=251-500, C=101-250, D=51-100, E=20-50 F=10-19
2022 Southern California Business Directory and Buyers Guide
© Mergent Inc. 1-800-342-5647
1373

	SIC	EMP	PHONE	ENTRY #
Bogart Construction Inc	1542	D	949 453-1400	744
Bomel Construction Co Inc **(PA)**	1542	D	714 921-1660	745
Boral Roofing LLC **(DH)**	1761	E	949 756-1605	1475
Boys Grls Clubs Cntl Ornge Cas **(PA)**	8641	D	714 543-5540	22317
Brady Vorwerck Rydr & Cspno **(PA)**	8111	D	480 456-9888	21522
Breathe Technologies Inc	3842	E	949 988-7700	11093
Brer Affiliates LLC **(DH)**	6794	C	949 794-7900	16203
Bridgwter Consulting Group Inc	8742	D	949 535-1755	23177
Brightview Landscape Dev Inc	1711	D	714 546-7975	1038
Brinderson LP	8711	D	714 466-7100	22504
Broadley-James Corporation	3826	D	949 829-5555	10788
Brooker Associates	0783	D	949 559-4877	354
Brooksamerica Mortgage Corp	6162	E	714 429-4500	15178
Brown and Streza LLP	8742	D	949 453-2900	23180
Bsh Home Appliances Corp **(DH)**	7629	C	949 440-7100	18953
Budget Blinds LLC **(HQ)**	7389	D	949 404-1100	18463
Buy Insta Slim Inc	2326	F	949 263-2301	2777
Cadence Design Systems Inc	7372	E	949 788-6080	17809
Caerus Marketing Group LLC	8742	D	877 627-2509	23181
Calamp Corp **(PA)**	3663	B	949 600-5600	9260
Calico Building Services Inc	7349	C	949 380-8707	17222
Camden Solar LLC	3674	E	940 398-3915	9488
Cannon Cochran MGT Svcs Inc	6411	D	949 474-6500	15548
Canon USA Inc	5043	B	949 753-4000	13341
Cap Diagnostics LLC	8071	D	714 966-1221	21061
Capital Prvate Clent Svcs Fnds	6722	D	949 975-5000	16126
Cardlogix	3577	F	949 380-1312	8243
Carnegie Mortgage LLC	6163	B	949 379-7000	15237
Cartel Industries LLC	3444	E	949 474-3200	6807
Cas Medical Systems Inc **(HQ)**	3841	F	203 488-6056	10960
Cbj LP	2721	E	949 833-8373	4056
Center For Autism &	8093	E	949 203-8872	21284
Centerline Mortgage Capitl Inc	6799	D	949 221-6685	16253
Centralize Leasing Corp	6159	D	949 252-2000	15162
Certance LLC **(HQ)**	3572	B	949 856-7800	8193
Certified Wtr Dmage Rstrtion E	7349	E	800 417-1776	17225
Cfp Fire Protection Inc	1711	D	949 727-3277	1044
Cg Oncology Inc	2834	E	949 409-3700	4807
Cgtech **(HQ)**	7373	E	949 753-1050	18022
Change Lending LLC **(PA)**	6162	D	949 423-6814	15182
Chen-Tech Industries Inc **(DH)**	3841	E	949 855-6716	10961
Child Development Incorporated	8351	B	949 854-5060	21998
Childrens Hospital Orange Cnty	8062	C	949 387-2586	20722
China Manufacturing Netwrk LLC	8742	F	949 756-0015	23189
Choose Manufacturing Co LLC	3672	E	714 327-1698	9388
Chromadex Corporation **(PA)**	2833	E	949 419-0288	4739
Chronicle Technology Inc	3674	F	949 651-8968	9489
Cie Digital Labs LLC	7319	D	949 381-6200	17094
Citigroup Inc	6021	D	949 726-5124	14997
City Ventures LLC **(PA)**	6531	B	949 258-7555	15816
CK Franchising Inc **(DH)**	8082	B	800 498-8144	21148
Clariphy Communications Inc **(DH)**	3674	C	949 861-3074	9490
Clark Cnstr Group - Cal Inc	1541	B	714 754-0764	693
Clark Cnstr Group - Cal LP	1542	B	714 429-9779	755
Clearflow Inc **(PA)**	3841	E	714 916-5010	10964
Clearpath Lending	6163	C	949 502-3577	15238
Clearview Orthopedic Dev LLC	3841	F	949 752-7885	10965
Clindatrix	8731	D	949 428-6600	22833
Cloudcover Iot Inc	7372	E	888 511-2022	17819
Cloudvirga Inc	7372	D	949 799-2643	17820
Club Speed LLC	7372	E	951 817-7073	17821
Cnm Marketing Inc	2759	F	866 792-5265	4496
Coast Composites LLC **(PA)**	3599	B	949 455-0665	8559
Coast To Coast Bus Eqp Inc **(PA)**	5044	D	949 457-7300	13353
Coastal Cocktails Inc	2086	E	949 250-3129	2262
Coda Automotive Inc	3714	E	949 830-7000	10033
Codazen Inc	7371	D	949 916-6266	17580
Cofiroute Usa LLC	4785	C	949 754-0198	12561
Colimatic Usa Inc	3565	F	949 600-6440	8066
Columbia Sanitary Products Inc	3432	E	949 474-0777	6559
Combimatrix Corporation **(HQ)**	3826	D	949 753-0624	10789
Commerce Home Mortgage LLC	6162	D	949 769-3526	15184
Commerce Velocity LLC	7372	E	949 756-8950	17822
Commonwealth Equity Svcs LLC	8742	D	949 336-6440	23194
Commonwealth Land Title Insur	6361	C	949 460-4500	15500
Compugroup Medical Inc	7372	E	949 789-0500	17823
Computer Assisted Mfg Tech LLC	3599	E	949 263-8911	8561
Computer EMB Specialists	7389	E	949 852-8888	18487
Concept Development Llc	3672	E	949 623-8000	9394
Conduent Wkrs Cmpnstion Hldngs **(HQ)**	8099	E	860 678-7877	21400
Conexant Systems Inc	3674	F	949 483-5714	9492
Conexant Systems LLC **(HQ)**	3674	B	949 483-4600	9493
Connectec Company Inc **(PA)**	3643	D	949 252-1077	9028
Consoldted Fire Protection LLC **(HQ)**	7389	A	949 727-3277	18489
Contec Microelectronics USA	5045	D	949 250-4025	13383
Cooper Microelectronics Inc	3674	E	949 553-8352	9495
Cor Medica Technology **(PA)**	8011	E	949 353-4554	19762
Corelogic Inc	6531	E	714 250-6400	15826
Corelogic Credco LLC **(DH)**	7323	C	800 255-0792	17120
Corsair Elec Connectors Inc	3678	C	949 833-0273	9650
Cosemi Technologies Inc **(HQ)**	3674	F	949 623-9816	9496
Council On Aging - Sthern Cal	8322	D	714 479-0107	21757
Courtney Inc **(PA)**	1799	D	949 222-2050	1651
Courtyard Management Corp	7011	D	949 453-1033	16393
Cp-Carrillo Inc	3592	E	949 567-9000	8431
Cp-Carrillo Inc **(DH)**	3592	C	949 567-9000	8432
CPS Receivables Five LLC	7322	D	949 753-6800	17108

	SIC	EMP	PHONE	ENTRY #
Creative Maintenance Systems	7349	D	949 852-2871	17233
Critical Io LLC	3577	F	949 553-2200	8247
Cryoport Systems LLC **(HQ)**	3559	F	949 540-7204	7969
Crystal Tips Holdings	3061	E	800 944-3939	5357
Cs Systems Inc	3577	E	949 475-9100	8248
Ctc Global Corporation **(PA)**	3643	C	949 428-8500	9030
Cummins Pacific LLC **(HQ)**	3519	D	949 253-6000	7593
Cushman & Wakefield Cal Inc	6531	A	949 474-4004	15833
Custom Business Solutions Inc **(PA)**	5044	D	949 380-7674	13355
Cwpnc Inc	1721	D	714 564-7904	1175
Cybercoders Inc	7361	C	949 885-5151	17409
Cybernet Manufacturing Inc	3571	A	949 600-8000	8152
Cycle News Inc **(PA)**	2711	E	949 863-7082	3967
D & S Media Group Inc	2721	F	714 881-4700	4063
D P S Inc	1721	C	714 564-7900	1176
D-Link Systems Incorporated	5045	C	714 885-6000	13386
D7 LLC	8741	D	808 630-9169	23013
DAd Investments	2099	E	310 627-6316	2417
Dana Capital Group Inc **(PA)**	6163	D	949 789-0200	15239
Dane Elec Corp USA **(HQ)**	5045	E	949 450-2900	13387
Danone Us LLC	2024	C	949 474-9670	1813
Darius E Lin MD Inc	8011	D	215 601-6899	19779
Data Circle Inc	3674	F	949 260-6569	9497
Database Marketing Group Inc	7331	D	714 727-0800	17131
Davita Inc	8092	B	949 930-4400	21239
Daz Inc	3613	F	949 724-8800	8895
Db Studios Inc	3999	E	949 833-0100	11655
De Vries International Inc **(PA)**	1389	D	949 252-1212	494
Decision Ready Solutions Inc	6162	E	949 400-1126	15186
Decisionpoint Systems Intl Inc **(HQ)**	7373	E	949 465-0065	18028
Decton Inc **(PA)**	7361	C	949 851-0111	17411
Decwood Inc	5031	E	949 588-9663	13207
Delafoil Holdings Inc **(PA)**	3444	B	949 752-4580	6818
Delcan Corporation	8711	C	714 562-5725	22527
Dellarobbia Inc **(PA)**	2512	E	949 251-9532	3501
Delta Galil USA Inc	5137	D	949 296-0380	14370
Denken Solutions Inc	7371	C	949 630-5263	17593
Developers Surety Indemnity Co **(DH)**	6351	D	949 263-3300	15496
Diality Inc	3841	F	949 916-5851	10969
Diamon Fusion Intl Inc	2899	F	949 388-8000	5217
Digital Map Products Inc	4899	D	949 333-5111	12783
Dinsmore & Associates Inc	3081	F	714 641-7111	5430
Disco Print Whl 46 Sup Cmpnies	7373	F	949 261-8457	18029
Divine Foods Inc	2064	E	800 440-6476	2084
Dkn Hotel LLC **(PA)**	7011	B	714 427-4320	16413
Documedia Group **(PA)**	2752	F	949 567-9930	4278
Doing Good Works	2759	F	949 354-0400	4509
Dongsuk Park DDS Inc	8021	D	714 734-0900	20175
DOT Printer Inc **(PA)**	2752	D	949 474-1100	4283
Drybar Holdings LLC **(PA)**	7231	B	310 776-6330	16901
Duke Energy Corporation	4911	C	949 727-7434	12801
Dynabook Americas Inc **(HQ)**	3571	B	949 583-3000	8153
Dynalloy Inc	3679	E	714 436-1206	9701
Dynamic Auto Images Inc	7542	B	714 771-3400	18912
Dyntek Inc **(PA)**	7379	C	949 271-6700	18175
Dzyne Technologies Inc	8711	E	703 454-0704	22535
Earthrise Nutritionals LLC **(HQ)**	0191	E	949 623-0980	106
Eaton Aerospace LLC	3812	E	949 452-9500	10586
Edison Capital	4911	C	909 594-3789	12802
Edwards Lfesciences Foundation	3842	F	949 250-2806	11096
Edwards Lfsciences Cardiaq LLC	3841	D	949 387-2615	10976
Edwards Lfscnces Wrld Trade Co **(HQ)**	3842	D	949 250-2500	11097
Edwards Lifesciences Corp **(PA)**	3842	A	949 250-2500	11098
Edwards Lifesciences Corp PR	3842	D	949 250-2500	11099
Edwards Lifesciences Fing LLC	3999	D	949 250-3480	11664
Edwards Lifesciences LLC **(HQ)**	8011	A	949 250-2500	19803
Edwards Lifesciences US Inc	3845	C	949 250-2500	11221
Edwards Theatres Circuit Inc	7832	C	949 854-8811	19278
Egs Financial Care Inc **(DH)**	7322	B	877 217-4423	17110
Ekedal Concrete Inc	1771	D	949 729-8082	1523
Electric On Target Inc	1711	D	949 247-3842	1061
Electrolurgy Inc	3471	D	949 250-4494	7252
Emcor Group Inc	3824	E	949 475-6020	10736
EMI Solutions Inc	3679	F	949 206-9960	9709
Empcc Inc	1721	C	714 564-7900	1178
Enclarity Inc	7374	A	949 797-7160	18085
Encrypted Access Corporation	3577	E	714 371-4125	8254
Endologix Inc **(PA)**	3841	B	949 595-7200	10978
Endologix Canada LLC	3841	D	949 595-7200	10979
Enevate Corporation	3691	D	949 243-0399	9809
Entrepreneur Media Inc **(PA)**	2721	D	949 261-2325	4069
Envveno Medical Corporation	3841	F	949 261-2900	10980
Eon Reality Inc **(PA)**	5045	C	949 460-2000	13392
Ephesoft Inc **(PA)**	5045	D	949 335-5335	13393
Equinox-76th Street Inc	7991	D	949 296-1700	19448
Equinox-76th Street Inc	8049	D	949 975-8400	20214
Equus Products Inc	3825	E	714 424-6779	10750
Ernst & Young LLP	8721	B	949 794-2300	22782
Es Engineering Services LLC	8711	D	949 988-3500	22546
Essex Properties LLC	6531	D	949 798-8100	15846
Ethicon Inc	3842	B	949 581-5799	11103
Eturns Inc	7372	E	949 265-2626	17849
Eurofins Eag Engrg Science LLC	8734	E	949 521-6200	22943
European Ht Invstors I I A Cal **(PA)**	7011	E	949 474-7368	16438
Eveg Inc	7371	E	844 221-3359	17611
Evergreen Holdings Inc **(PA)**	2992	E	949 757-7770	5294
Evolve Dental Technologies Inc	3843	E	949 713-0909	11174

Mergent email: customerrelations@mergent.com
1374

2022 Southern California Business
Directory and Buyers Guide

(P-0000) Products & Services Section entry number
(PA)=Parent Co (HQ)=Headquarters (DH)=Div Headquarters

	SIC	EMP	PHONE	ENTRY #
Evr Lending Inc **(PA)**	6531	D	949 753-7888	15848
Eworkplace Manufacturing Inc	5045	C	949 583-1646	13397
Exult Inc	8742	A	949 856-8800	23213
Eyeonics Inc	3851	E	949 788-6000	11253
Ezaki Glico USA Corporation	2064	F	949 251-0144	2085
Farstone Technology Inc	3695	C	949 336-4321	9835
FCA US LLC	3714	F	949 450-5111	10058
FEC Fture Contrs Engineers Inc	1611	D	949 328-9758	878
Federal Custom Cable LLC	5065	E	949 851-3114	13722
Federal Express Corporation	7389	B	800 463-3339	18518
Federal Express Corporation	4512	E	949 862-4500	12306
Fema Electronics Corporation	3679	E	714 825-0140	9712
Fieldstone Communities Inc **(PA)**	1531	C	949 790-5400	676
Filtronics Inc	3589	F	714 630-5040	8381
Finance America LLC **(HQ)**	6162	C	949 440-1000	15191
Finis LLC	3577	D	949 250-4929	8256
First Amercn Prof RE Svcs Inc **(HQ)**	6531	C	714 250-1400	15855
First Foundation Advisors **(HQ)**	6282	D	949 202-4100	15327
First Foundation Inc **(PA)**	6022	C	949 202-4160	15024
First Student Inc	4151	C	855 870-8747	11927
First Team RE - Orange Cnty **(PA)**	6531	C	888 236-1943	15860
First Transit Inc	4111	C	949 857-7211	11809
Firstservice Residential **(HQ)**	6531	C	949 448-6000	15867
Fisher & Paykel Healthcare Inc	5047	C	949 453-4000	13487
Fit Electronics Inc **(HQ)**	8731	D	949 270-8500	22840
Five Point Holdings LLC **(PA)**	6531	C	949 349-1000	15869
Flame and Wax Inc	3999	E	949 752-4000	11668
Fleet Management Solutions Inc	3663	E	800 500-6009	9274
Flexicare Incorporated	5047	D	949 450-9999	13488
Flexpoint Funding Corporation **(PA)**	6163	C	949 250-4466	15243
Fluxergy Inc **(PA)**	8711	D	949 305-4201	22554
Fmh Aerospace Corp	3728	D	714 751-1000	10329
Foampro Mfg Inc	3991	D	949 252-0112	11510
Foothill / Estrn Trnsp Crrdor	1611	D	949 754-3400	879
Ford Motor Land Dev Corp	6512	B	949 242-6606	15667
Foundation Lead Group LLC	8742	D	877 477-2311	23220
Fox Head Inc **(PA)**	5136	C	408 776-8800	14333
Fragomen Del Rey Bernse	8111	D	949 660-3504	21558
Fraud Fighters Inc	7381	E	800 576-6116	18277
FSI Coating Technologies Inc	2851	E	949 540-1140	5098
Fugro Roadware Inc	7549	D	949 536-5175	18933
Fuscoe Engineering Inc **(PA)**	8711	D	949 474-1960	22559
Futek Advanced Sensor Tech Inc	3823	C	949 465-0900	10696
GA Services LLC	7379	E	949 752-6515	18180
Gabe Inc	8748	D	949 679-2727	23443
Gan Limited	7371	B	702 964-5777	17623
Gary Bale Redi-Mix Con Inc	3273	D	949 786-9441	6091
Gateway Inc **(DH)**	3571	C	949 471-7000	8156
Gateway Manufacturing LLC	3575	E	949 471-7000	8224
Gateway US Retail Inc	3571	D	949 471-7000	8157
Gdr Group Inc	7379	D	949 453-8818	18181
Genea Energy Partners Inc	7373	D	714 694-0536	18034
General Tool Inc	5085	D	949 261-2322	13985
Genpact Mortgage Services Inc **(HQ)**	6162	D	949 417-5131	15195
Gensia Sicor Inc **(HQ)**	2834	A	949 455-4700	4822
Georg Fischer LLC **(DH)**	5051	D	714 731-8800	13566
Getac Inc	5045	D	949 681-2900	13404
Gfk Etilize Inc **(DH)**	8732	D	888 608-1212	22881
Ghost Management Group LLC	7313	C	949 870-1400	17085
Gkk Corporation **(PA)**	8712	D	949 250-1500	22716
Gkk Works **(HQ)**	8712	D	949 250-1500	22717
Global Debt Management Llc **(PA)**	7389	D	949 825-7800	18528
Global Language Solutions LLC	7389	D	949 798-1400	18530
Global Locate Inc	3674	D	949 926-5000	9511
Global Metal Solutions Inc	3471	E	949 872-2995	7263
Global Pcci (gpc) **(PA)**	3469	C	757 637-9000	7147
Global Risk MGT Solutions LLC	8742	D	949 759-8500	23225
Global Vision Holdings Inc	2099	F	949 281-6438	2441
Glovis America Inc **(HQ)**	4731	C	714 435-2960	12464
Golden Hotels Ltd Partnership	7011	C	949 833-2770	16456
Golden State Foods Corp **(PA)**	2087	E	949 247-8000	2328
Golden West Partners Inc **(PA)**	8748	B	949 477-3090	23446
Good Culture LLC	2026	E	949 545-9945	1836
Goodix Technology Inc	3577	F	858 554-0352	8259
Goodman North America LLC **(PA)**	6531	D	949 407-0100	15875
Gordian Medical Inc	5047	B	714 556-0200	13490
Gradient Engineers Inc	8711	C	949 477-0555	22562
Grand Fusion Housewares LLC **(PA)**	3089	E	888 614-7263	5656
Graphtec America Inc **(DH)**	3823	E	949 770-6010	10698
Greenhouse Agency Inc	8742	D	949 752-7542	23228
Greens Group Inc	7011	C	949 829-4902	16457
Greenwave Reality Inc	7373	E	714 805-9283	18035
Griswold Controls LLC **(PA)**	3494	D	949 559-6000	7474
Guaranteed Rate Inc	6162	C	424 354-5344	15199
H Co Computer Products **(PA)**	3572	E	949 833-3222	8202
Hammes Company	8741	D	949 705-0900	23035
Hanwha Q Cells America Inc	3674	C	949 748-5996	9513
Hardesty LLC **(PA)**	7361	E	949 407-6625	17426
Haymarket Worldwide Inc	2721	D	949 417-6700	4072
Healthquest Laboratories Inc **(PA)**	8071	D	714 418-5867	21071
Helix Semiconductors **(PA)**	3674	D	949 748-6057	9514
Henkel Chemical Management LLC	2891	C	888 943-6535	5184
HIC Corporation **(PA)**	2721	F	949 261-1636	4073
Hitachi Solutions America Ltd **(DH)**	5045	E	949 242-1300	13405
Hoag Orthopedic Institute LLC	8062	D	949 764-8690	20791
Home Franchise Concepts LLC **(PA)**	1771	D	949 404-1100	1530
Home Junction Inc	7371	D	858 777-9533	17631
Homefacts Management LLC	2741	F	949 502-8300	4180
Horiba Americas Holding Inc **(HQ)**	3826	A	949 250-4811	10797
Horiba Instruments Inc **(DH)**	3826	C	949 250-4811	10798
Horizon Communication Tech Inc **(PA)**	4899	D	714 982-3900	12786
Hormel Foods Corp Svcs LLC	2013	E	949 753-5350	1735
House of Lashes	3999	F	714 515-4162	11688
Hunsaker & Assoc Irvine Inc **(PA)**	8711	D	949 583-1010	22572
Hwmm **(HQ)**	5136	D	949 581-1144	14337
Hyper Ice Inc **(PA)**	3949	E	714 524-3742	11426
Hyundai Amer Technical Ctr Inc	8711	D	734 337-2500	22573
Hyundai Capital America **(DH)**	6141	B	714 965-3000	15144
I-Flow LLC	3841	A	800 448-3569	10990
I/O Magic Corporation	3571	F	949 707-4800	8158
Icf Jones & Stokes Inc	8742	D	949 333-6600	23240
Icl Systems Inc **(PA)**	7373	D	877 425-8725	18036
Iconn Inc	5063	E	800 286-6742	13635
Ignite Health LLC **(PA)**	7311	D	949 861-3200	17019
Illumnate Educatn Holdings Inc **(PA)**	7372	D	949 656-3133	17882
Immport Therapeutics Inc	3844	E	949 679-4068	11208
Impac Funding Corporation **(HQ)**	6162	C	949 475-3600	15202
Impac Mortgage Corp	6162	B	949 475-3600	15203
Impac Mortgage Holdings Inc **(PA)**	6162	C	949 475-3600	15204
Imperial Bag & Paper Co LLC	5113	D	800 834-6248	14211
Imperial Hotel Group LLC	7389	E	949 474-7368	18547
Inari Medical Inc	3841	C	877 927-4747	10993
Incipio Technologies Inc **(PA)**	3577	E	949 250-4929	8263
Incomnet Communications Corp	4813	D	949 251-8000	12650
Indemnity Company California **(DH)**	6411	D	949 263-3300	15582
Infinite Electronics Inc **(HQ)**	3679	D	949 261-1920	9726
Infinite Electronics Intl Inc **(DH)**	3678	B	949 261-1920	9657
Informa Business Media Inc	2741	E	949 252-1146	4183
Ingram Micro Inc **(HQ)**	5045	A	714 566-1000	13407
Ingram Micro Management Co **(DH)**	5045	C	714 566-1000	13408
Inhouseit Inc	7378	D	949 660-5655	18148
Innova Electronics Corporation	3714	E	714 241-6800	10081
Innovative Tech & Engrg Inc	3577	E	949 955-2501	8266
Insco Insurance Services Inc **(DH)**	6411	D	949 263-3415	15583
Inspiria Inc **(PA)**	8711	D	949 206-0606	22578
Integrated Polymer Inds Inc	3479	E	949 788-1050	7376
Integrus LLC	5044	D	714 547-9500	13359
Interactive Media Holdings Inc **(DH)**	7311	E	949 861-8888	17023
Interctive Dsplay Slutions Inc	3679	E	949 727-1959	9728
Interior Logic Group Inc **(HQ)**	7389	A	800 959-8333	18551
Interlink Electronics Inc **(PA)**	3679	D	805 484-8855	9729
Intermed Video Tech Inc	3651	E	203 270-9100	9181
International Rectifier Corp **(PA)**	3674	E	949 453-1008	9521
International Sensor Tech	3829	E	949 452-9000	10890
International Silicon Company	2869	E	929 291-0056	5140
International Vitamin Corp **(PA)**	2834	D	949 664-5500	4832
Interntnal Plymr Solutions Inc	3491	E	949 458-3731	7446
Interpore Cross Intl Inc **(DH)**	3842	D	949 453-3200	11117
Intratek Computer Inc	7379	C	949 334-4200	18191
Invasix Inc	8731	D	855 418-5306	22844
INX Prints Inc	2262	D	949 660-9190	2664
Iqvia Inc **(DH)**	8732	D	949 476-2167	22890
Irvine APT Communities LP	6513	C	949 854-4942	15732
Irvine APT Communities LP **(HQ)**	6513	C	949 720-5600	15734
Irvine Electronics Inc	3672	D	949 250-0315	9415
Irvine Pharmaceutical Svcs Inc	8734	D	949 439-6677	22951
Irvine Ranch Water District **(PA)**	4941	C	949 453-5300	12894
Irvine Ranch Water District	4941	C	949 453-5300	12895
Iscope Corp	3827	F	949 333-0001	10843
Isotis Orthobiologics Inc	8731	C	949 595-8710	22845
It Division Inc	7371	C	678 648-2709	17645
ITT Cannon LLC	3625	C	714 557-4700	8957
Ivantis Inc **(PA)**	3841	C	949 600-9650	10996
Ixos Software Inc **(PA)**	5045	D	949 784-8000	13409
J & M Realty Company **(PA)**	6531	D	949 261-2727	15893
J F Fong Inc	3841	F	949 553-8885	10997
J5 Infrastructure Partners LLC	4812	D	949 299-5258	12608
Jackson Tidus A Law Corp **(PA)**	8111	D	949 752-8585	21590
Jacobs Project Management Co	8711	D	949 224-7695	22588
Jacobus Consulting Inc	8742	E	949 727-0720	23248
Jae Electronics Inc **(HQ)**	5065	E	949 753-2600	13734
Janteq Corp **(PA)**	3663	E	949 215-2603	9280
Jaybee Huntington LLC	7011	D	562 756-3124	16511
JBa Consulting Engineers Inc	8711	D	949 419-3030	22589
Jelight Company Inc **(PA)**	5063	D	949 380-8774	13637
Jeremywell International Inc	3569	F	949 588-6888	8126
Jetsuite Inc **(PA)**	4522	C	949 892-4300	12336
Jnr Inc	8742	D	949 476-2788	23251
Jonathan Engnred Slutions Corp **(HQ)**	3429	E	714 665-4400	6522
Jones Day Limited Partnership	8111	D	949 851-3939	21592
Jonset Corporation	4959	D	949 551-5151	13007
Joseph Company Intl Inc	3411	E	949 474-2200	6464
Jsn Industries Inc	3089	D	949 458-0050	5686
Jsn Packaging Products Inc	3082	D	949 458-0050	5445
Jump Start Juice Bar	2037	F	949 754-3120	1902
Justenough Software Corp Inc **(HQ)**	7372	E	949 706-5400	17899
Jynormus LLC	4813	F	949 436-2112	12652
K Hovnanian Companies Cal Inc **(HQ)**	1521	D	714 368-4500	616
Kaiser Foundation Hospitals	8062	A	949 262-5780	20800
Kaiser Foundation Hospitals	6324	C	949 932-5000	15402
Kaiser Foundation Hospitals	8011	C	949 262-5760	19864
Kaiser Foundation Hospitals	8011	C	949 932-2604	19868
Kaiser Foundation Hospitals	6733	D	949 932-5000	16186
Kajabi LLC	7375	E	855 452-5224	18127

Employment Codes: A=Over 500 employees, B=251-500, C=101-250, D=51-100, E=20-50 F=10-19

2022 Southern California Business Directory and Buyers Guide

© Mergent Inc. 1-800-342-5647

1375

	SIC	EMP	PHONE	ENTRY #
Karma Automotive LLC	3711	A	714 723-3247	9955
Karman Topco LP **(PA)**	8748	A	949 797-2900	23460
Kasdan Smnds Riley Vaughan LLP **(PA)**	8111	D	949 851-9000	21594
Keating Dental Arts	8072	C	949 955-2100	21110
Kelley Blue Book Co Inc **(DH)**	2721	D	949 770-7704	4076
Kelmscott Communications LLC	2752	B	949 475-1900	4348
Keystone PCF Property MGT Inc **(PA)**	6531	D	949 833-2600	15901
Kids Healthy Foods LLC	5149	E	949 260-4950	14702
Kitara Media Corp **(HQ)**	7311	E	201 539-2200	17027
Kite Electric Inc	1731	C	949 380-7471	1272
Kme Cnc Inc	3549	F	714 345-5816	7904
Knight LLC **(HQ)**	3569	D	949 595-4800	8127
Knobbe Martens Olson Bear LLP **(PA)**	8111	B	949 760-0404	21600
Kodella LLC	7379	C	786 408-7995	18195
Koder Inc	7371	E	415 906-4157	17648
Koeller Nbker Crlson Hluck LLP **(PA)**	8111	D	949 864-3400	21601
Kofax Inc **(PA)**	7371	B	949 783-1000	17649
Kofax Limited **(DH)**	7372	A	949 783-1000	17903
Kool Blast Gas	3841	F	949 420-9675	11005
Kore1 Inc	7379	D	949 706-6990	18196
Kratos Instruments LLC	3812	F	949 660-0666	10595
Ksl II Mngement Operations LLC	7011	D	760 564-8000	16529
Ktgy Group Inc **(PA)**	8712	D	949 851-2133	22727
Kyocera Dcment Solutions W LLC	5044	C	800 996-9591	13361
L T Litho & Printing Co	2752	F	949 466-8584	4351
La Jolla Group Inc **(PA)**	7389	C	949 428-2800	18569
La Jolla Sport USA Inc **(PA)**	5136	D	949 428-2800	14340
Lance Rygg Dental Corp **(PA)**	8021	C	714 508-3600	20185
Landmark Event Staffing	7381	A	714 293-4248	18292
Lantronix Inc **(PA)**	3577	B	949 453-3990	8272
LARK Industries Inc **(DH)**	7389	C	714 701-4200	18572
Laser Spectrum Inc **(PA)**	3699	F	949 551-8225	9886
Lasergraphics Inc	3577	E	949 753-8282	8273
Law Offces Les Zeve A Prof Cor	8111	C	714 848-7920	21605
Lawyers Title Insurance Corp	6361	C	949 223-5575	15507
Lawyers Title Insurance Corp	6361	C	949 223-5575	15509
Lba Inc	8742	D	949 833-0400	23256
Lba Realty LLC **(PA)**	6531	E	949 833-0400	15908
Leadingway Corporation **(PA)**	7373	F	949 509-6589	18042
Learfield Communications LLC	4832	D	949 823-1729	12699
Ledra Brands Inc	5023	C	714 259-9959	13176
Lee & Assoc Coml RE Svcs Inc - **(PA)**	6531	E	949 727-1200	15909
Legacy Prtners Residential Inc	8741	B	949 930-6600	23050
Leighton and Associates Inc **(PA)**	8748	D	949 250-1421	23466
Lenders Investment Corp	6162	D	714 540-4747	15207
Lennar Corporation	1531	D	949 349-8000	680
Lennar Homes California Inc **(DH)**	1521	C	949 349-8000	621
Lens Technology I LLC	3827	F	714 940-6602	10844
Leport Educational Inst Inc	8351	B	914 374-8860	22027
Lexisnexis Risk Assets Inc	6411	C	949 222-0028	15588
Liberty Dental Plan Cal Inc	6324	B	949 223-0007	15440
Liberty Dental Plan Corp **(PA)**	6324	C	888 703-6999	15441
Liberty Dental Plan Nevada Inc	6324	D	888 703-6999	15442
Linc Western Air LP	1711	D	949 330-1535	1095
Links Medical Products Inc **(PA)**	3841	E	949 753-0001	11009
Linksys LLC	5065	C	408 526-4000	13742
Linksys LLC **(DH)**	5065	B	949 270-8500	13744
LLP Moss Adams	8721	D	949 221-4000	22804
Loan Administration Netwrk Inc	7361	D	949 752-5246	17437
Lobby Traffic Systems Inc	3829	F	800 486-8606	10896
Local Corporation **(PA)**	7311	D	949 784-0800	17030
Logitech Inc	3577	C	510 795-8500	8276
Los Angeles Board Mills Inc	2631	D	323 685-8900	3773
Lost International LLC	2329	F	949 600-6950	2821
LPA Inc **(PA)**	8712	C	949 261-1001	22729
Lps Agency Sales & Posting Inc **(PA)**	7389	D	714 247-7503	18583
Lsa Associates Inc **(PA)**	8748	C	949 553-0666	23471
Lubrication Scientifics Inc	3491	F	714 557-0664	7450
Lubrication Scientifics LLC	3569	E	714 557-0664	8128
Luxe Travel Management Inc **(HQ)**	4724	D	949 336-1000	12392
Lynx Innovation Inc **(PA)**	5065	C	949 345-1847	13748
M F Salta Co Inc **(PA)**	8742	D	562 421-2512	23265
M K Products Inc	3548	D	949 798-1425	7892
M L Services Inc	1731	D	800 272-2179	1278
M P C Industrial Products Inc	3471	E	949 863-0106	7279
M86 Americas Inc **(DH)**	5045	D	714 282-6111	13412
Malcolm & Cisneros A Law Corp	8111	C	949 252-1039	21620
Maneri Sign Co Inc	3993	F	310 327-6261	11570
Marriott International Inc	7011	B	949 724-3606	16557
Maruchan Inc **(HQ)**	2099	B	949 789-2300	2479
Marukome USA Inc	2099	F	949 863-0110	2481
Marvell Semiconductor Inc	3674	C	949 614-7700	9535
Marvin Test Solutions Inc	3825	D	949 263-2222	10764
Masimo Americas Inc	3841	D	949 297-7000	11013
Masimo Corporation	3845	E	949 297-7000	11226
Masimo Corporation	3845	E	949 297-7000	11227
Masimo Corporation **(PA)**	3845	B	949 297-7000	11228
Masimo Semiconductor Inc	3674	F	603 595-8900	9536
Mavenlink Inc **(PA)**	7371	C	949 336-7610	17658
MBK Real Estate Companies	6552	E	949 789-8300	16061
MBK Real Estate Ltd A Cal Ltd **(HQ)**	6552	D	949 789-8300	16062
MBK Senior Living LLC **(PA)**	6513	A	949 242-1400	15740
McKinley Equipment Corporation **(PA)**	5084	E	800 770-6094	13916
McLane Foodservice Dist Inc	5142	D	714 863-0163	14529
Mds Consulting **(PA)**	8711	D	949 251-8821	22608
Meade Instruments Corp	3827	D	949 451-1450	10847
Medata Inc **(PA)**	7372	D	714 918-1310	17913
Medennium Inc **(PA)**	3851	E	949 789-9000	11255
Mediatek USA Inc	3571	E	408 526-1899	8166
Medterra Cbd LLC	0139	D	800 971-1288	9
Medtronic PS Medical Inc **(DH)**	3841	C	805 571-3769	11020
Meggitt Defense Systems Inc	3728	B	949 465-7700	10377
Meguiars Inc **(HQ)**	2842	E	949 752-8000	4971
Meguiars Inc	3589	F	651 733-1110	8398
Menlo Microsystems Inc	3674	E	949 771-0277	9537
Mentor Worldwide LLC **(DH)**	3842	C	800 636-8678	11125
Merrill Lynch Prce Fnner Smith	6211	D	949 235-5050	15285
Mesa Energy Systems Inc **(HQ)**	1711	C	949 460-0460	1102
Mflex Delaware Inc	3672	A	949 453-6800	9429
Mhh Holdings Inc	5149	C	949 651-9903	14707
Michael Madden Co Inc	5113	D	800 834-6248	14213
Michelle Barrionuevo-Mazzini **(PA)**	3999	F	415 706-1677	11716
Micro Therapeutics Inc **(HQ)**	3841	D	949 837-3700	11023
Microwave Dynamics	3663	F	949 679-7788	9291
Min-E-Con LLC	3678	D	949 250-0087	9661
Mind Research Institute	8733	C	949 345-8700	22915
Mirion Technologies Gds Inc **(HQ)**	8734	C	949 419-1000	22953
Mission Hills Mortgage Corp **(HQ)**	6162	C	714 972-3832	15216
Mission Ldscp Companies Inc	0781	C	800 545-9963	269
Mitsubishi Chemical Crbn Fbr	2891	C	800 929-5471	5187
Mjp Empire Inc **(PA)**	1721	C	714 564-7900	1190
Mobilenet Services Inc **(PA)**	8711	C	949 951-4444	22616
Mobilityware LLC **(PA)**	7371	D	949 788-9900	17662
Modaan Inc **(PA)**	2051	F	949 786-0223	2021
Momentum Textiles LLC **(PA)**	5131	E	949 833-8886	14310
Monarch Healthcare A Medical **(HQ)**	8011	B	949 923-3200	19988
Monroe Magnus LLC **(PA)**	5072	F	714 771-2630	13812
Montage Hotels & Resorts LLC **(PA)**	7011	A	949 715-5002	16572
Montrose Envmtl Group Inc **(PA)**	8748	B	949 988-3500	23475
Montrose Msrmnts Analytics LLC **(HQ)**	8748	E	949 988-3500	23476
Montrose Water and Sustainabil	8748	D	949 988-3500	23477
Mophie Inc **(DH)**	3663	C	888 866-7443	9295
Morinaga America Inc **(HQ)**	2064	E	949 732-1155	2098
Morris & Willner Partners	8742	D	949 705-0682	23276
Morse Micro Inc	3674	D	949 501-7080	9547
Moxie Pest Ctrl Orange Cnty LP	7342	E	951 272-4000	17203
Mp Biomedicals LLC **(HQ)**	3826	E	949 833-2500	10803
Mscsoftware Corporation **(HQ)**	7372	C	714 540-8900	17923
Mtc Financial Inc	6733	E	949 252-8300	16191
Mtc Financial Inc	8741	D	949 252-8300	23069
Multi-Fineline Electronix Inc **(HQ)**	3672	A	949 453-6800	9430
Murtaugh Myer Nlson Trglia LLP	8111	D	949 794-4000	21640
Mve + Partners Inc **(PA)**	8712	D	949 809-3388	22734
My Kids Dentist **(PA)**	8021	D	909 854-1437	20190
N H Research Incorporated	3825	D	949 474-3900	10766
N2 Acquisition Company Inc	6719	D	714 942-3563	16105
N2w Engineering Inc	8748	D	714 716-1711	23479
National Financial Svcs LLC	6211	A	949 476-0157	15302
National Fuel Cell RES Ctr	3536	F	949 824-1509	7699
National Medical Products Inc	3089	F	949 768-1147	5723
Navajo Investments Inc **(PA)**	4522	D	949 863-9200	12337
Navigators Management Co Inc	8741	D	949 255-4860	23071
Nellix Inc	3841	E	650 213-8700	11029
Neomend Inc	3841	D	949 783-3300	11030
Netlist Inc **(PA)**	3674	D	949 435-0025	9548
Network Capital Funding Corp **(PA)**	6162	B	949 442-0060	15220
Netwrix Corporation **(HQ)**	7372	D	888 638-9749	17932
Neudesic LLC **(PA)**	7371	C	949 754-4500	17670
Neuintel LLC **(PA)**	7371	D	949 625-6117	17671
Neuroptics Inc	3841	E	949 250-9792	11031
Neurostructures Inc	3842	F	800 352-6103	11128
Neurovasc Technologies Inc	3841	F	949 258-9946	11032
New Century Mortgage Corp	6162	A	949 440-7030	15221
New First Fincl Resources LLC	6311	C	949 223-2160	15365
New Generation Wellness Inc **(PA)**	2834	C	949 863-0340	4859
New Vista Behavioral Hlth LLC	8052	D	949 284-0095	20538
Newport Corporation **(HQ)**	3821	A	949 863-3144	10660
Newport Energy	1382	E	408 230-7545	460
Newport Meat Southern Cal Inc	5147	C	949 399-4200	14600
Nexgenix Inc **(PA)**	7371	B	714 665-6240	17674
Nextgen Healthcare Info System **(HQ)**	7371	D	949 255-2600	17675
Ngd Systems Inc	3572	E	949 870-9148	8210
Nihon Kohden America Inc **(HQ)**	5047	C	949 580-1555	13505
Nikken Global Inc **(HQ)**	5087	C	949 789-2000	14041
Nikken International Inc **(PA)**	5199	C	949 789-2000	14956
Nimbus Data Inc	7379	E	650 276-4500	18203
Nitto Avecia Pharma Svcs Inc **(DH)**	2834	C	949 951-4425	4862
Nnn Realty Investors LLC	6799	B	714 667-8252	16279
Noevir Holding America Inc **(DH)**	5122	E	949 660-1111	14271
Norman Industrial Mtls Inc	5051	E	949 250-3343	13581
North Amercn Science Assoc Inc	8734	D	949 951-3110	22956
Nossaman LLP	8111	D	949 833-7800	21647
Novare Nat Settlement Svc LLC	6021	E	714 352-4088	15005
NRLL LLC	6799	B	949 768-7777	16281
Nrp Holding Co Inc **(PA)**	6719	C	949 583-1000	16106
Ntrust Infotech Inc	7372	D	562 207-1600	17936
Numecent Inc	7372	E	949 833-2800	17937
Numerical Ctrl Cmpt Sciences **(PA)**	7371	F	949 852-3664	17681
Nutrawise Health & Beauty Corp **(PA)**	2834	D	949 900-2400	4863
Nxt Biomedical LLC	3845	F	201 658-6455	11231
Ocmbc Inc	6162	C	714 479-0999	15222
Ocpc Inc	2752	D	949 475-1900	4381
Offiserve Inc	5044	D	714 547-9500	13365
Old An Inc	3999	F	949 263-1400	11721

Mergent email: customerrelations@mergent.com
1376
2022 Southern California Business Directory and Buyers Guide
(P-0000) Products & Services Section entry number
(PA)=Parent Co (HQ)=Headquarters (DH)=Div Headquarters

	SIC	EMP	PHONE	ENTRY #
Omni Optical Products Inc **(PA)**	3829	E	714 634-5700	10900
Omnitron Systems Tech Inc	5065	D	949 250-6510	13760
On Target Solutions LLC **(PA)**	4899	D	949 543-3200	12788
Oncocyte Corporation **(PA)**	2835	E	949 409-7600	4925
Operation Technology Inc **(PA)**	7371	D	949 462-0100	17684
Optima Technology Corporation	3577	B	949 253-5768	8289
Optumrx Inc **(DH)**	6324	B	714 825-3600	15446
Oracle Corp	8999	A	650 506-7000	23538
Orange Bakery Inc	6512	D	949 454-1247	15686
Orange Bakery Inc **(HQ)**	2051	C	949 863-1377	2028
Orange Circle Studio Corp	2759	D	949 727-0800	4548
Orange County Homecare LLC **(PA)**	8082	D	949 390-7308	21195
Orange County Produce LLC	0171	D	949 451-0880	32
Orange Logic LLC **(PA)**	3571	D	949 396-2233	8169
Orangepeople LLC	8999	D	949 535-1308	23539
Orchard Holdings Group Inc	6531	D	949 502-8300	15936
Ortiz Enterprises Incorporated **(PA)**	1611	D	949 753-1414	904
Owl Education and Training Inc	8331	B	949 797-2000	21964
Pace Punches Inc	3544	D	949 428-2750	7820
Pacific City Bank	6029	D	714 263-1800	15049
Pacific Dental Services LLC **(PA)**	8021	B	714 845-8500	20192
Pacific Handy Cutter Inc **(DH)**	3423	E	714 662-1033	6488
Pacific Pharma Inc	5122	A	714 246-4600	14275
Pacific Premier Bancorp Inc **(PA)**	6022	D	949 864-8000	15036
Pacific Premier Bank **(HQ)**	6022	D	714 431-4000	15037
Pacific Symphony	7929	D	714 755-5788	19373
Pacific Valuation	6531	E	949 271-6377	15941
Pacific World Corporation **(PA)**	2844	D	949 598-2400	5055
Paciolan LLC **(DH)**	7372	C	866 722-4652	17949
Palmieri Tyler Wner Wlhelm Wld	8111	D	949 851-9400	21651
Pan American Bank Fsb	6035	B	949 224-1917	15052
Panattoni Development Co Inc **(PA)**	6552	D	916 381-1561	16067
Pankl Holdings Inc **(DH)**	3714	D	949 567-9000	10112
Panoramic Software Corporation	7372	F	877 558-8526	17951
Parker-Hannifin Corporation	3724	C	949 833-3000	10222
Parker-Hannifin Corporation	3594	C	949 833-3000	8445
Passco Companies LLC **(PA)**	6531	D	949 442-1000	15946
Passy-Muir Inc **(PA)**	3842	E	949 833-8255	11133
Pathway Capital Management LP **(PA)**	8741	D	949 622-1000	23087
Patric Communications Inc **(PA)**	1731	D	619 579-2898	1292
Patron Solutions LLC	7372	C	949 823-1700	17954
Payne & Fears LLP **(PA)**	8111	D	949 851-1101	21657
PCC Rollmet Inc	3339	D	949 221-5333	6286
Peace Kim Dentistry Inc **(PA)**	8021	D	949 679-8762	20193
Peoples Chice HM Ln Scrties Co **(PA)**	6162	D	949 494-6167	15225
Performio Usa Inc **(PA)**	7371	D	833 817-7084	17689
Personal Touch Clg & Maint Inc **(PA)**	7349	D	949 727-4135	17274
Phantom Access Systems LLC	3699	F	949 753-1280	9898
Phiaro Incorporated	3999	E	949 727-1261	11735
Philip Morris USA Inc	2111	D	949 453-3500	2550
Philips Med Systems Clvland In	5047	D	949 699-2300	13511
Phx Investment Properties LLC	7389	E	949 474-7368	18633
Plasto Tech International Inc	3089	E	949 458-1880	5760
Plugg ME LNc	7372	E	949 705-4472	17959
PM Realty Group LP	6512	D	949 390-5500	15690
Pool Water Products **(PA)**	5091	F	949 756-1666	14085
Ppst Inc **(PA)**	3679	E	800 421-1921	9765
Precept Inc **(DH)**	6411	D	949 955-1430	15615
Premier Office Centers LLC **(PA)**	7389	E	949 253-4616	18639
Prestige International USA Inc **(HQ)**	6411	D	949 870-1640	15616
Primecare Quality HM Care Inc	1521	D	949 681-3515	634
Princeton Technology Inc	3577	E	949 851-7776	8292
Printery Inc	2752	F	949 757-1930	4396
Printronix LLC **(PA)**	3577	D	714 368-2300	8293
Printronix Holding Corp	3577	E	714 368-2300	8294
Prism Software Corporation	7372	E	949 855-3100	17961
Pro Corporation	7361	C	949 660-9544	17448
Pro-Dex Inc **(PA)**	3841	C	949 769-3200	11047
Pro-Mart Industries Inc **(PA)**	2392	E	949 428-7700	3115
Producers Inc	7359	D	714 850-1008	17368
Professnal Rprgraphic Svcs Inc	2759	E	949 748-5400	4560
Providence Industries LLC	2326	D	562 420-9091	2787
Providence St Joseph Health	8011	A	949 430-3963	20029
Providence St Joseph Health	8082	A	949 430-3960	21205
Prudential Overall Supply **(PA)**	7218	D	949 250-4855	16885
Qlogic LLC **(DH)**	3674	C	949 389-6000	9562
Qmerit Electrification LLC **(PA)**	8748	C	888 272-0090	23498
Qpe Inc	2754	F	949 263-0381	4467
Qsi 2011 Inc **(PA)**	7372	F	949 855-6885	17966
Quadion LLC	6282	A	714 546-0994	15341
Qualontime Corporation	3599	F	714 523-4751	8753
Quanmax Usa Inc	5045	D	949 272-2930	13430
Quest Group **(PA)**	5099	D	949 585-0111	14176
Quest Intl Monitor Svc Inc **(PA)**	7378	D	949 581-9900	18150
Quilting House	2392	F	949 476-7090	3116
Race Technologies LLC	3714	F	714 438-1118	10120
Racer Media & Marketing Inc	2721	F	949 417-6700	4103
Railpros Inc **(PA)**	8711	C	714 734-8765	22644
Rainbow Magnetics Incorporated	2752	F	714 540-4777	4414
Raise 3d Inc	5045	F	888 963-9028	13431
Raise 3d Technologies Inc	3577	E	949 482-2040	8295
Rally Holdings LLC	5013	A	817 919-6833	13083
Rami Designs Inc	3446	F	949 588-8288	6976
Rand Technology LLC **(PA)**	5065	D	949 255-5700	13767
Randstad Professionals Us LLC	7361	D	781 213-1500	17452
Ranscapes Inc	7349	E	866 883-9297	17280
Razzor Technologies Inc	7372	F	949 202-5846	17970

	SIC	EMP	PHONE	ENTRY #
Reagent World Inc	5049	F	909 947-7779	13537
Rebound Therapeutics Corp	3841	E	949 305-8111	11049
Regis Contractors LP	1522	B	949 253-0455	666
Related/Normont Dev Co LLC	6552	D	949 660-7272	16070
Renovo Solutions LLC	8741	B	714 599-7969	23099
Research Way Ll LLC	2834	F	608 830-6300	4881
Resources Connection Inc **(PA)**	8742	A	714 430-6400	23309
Resources Connection LLC **(HQ)**	7361	D	714 430-6400	17460
Result Group Inc	7373	F	480 777-7130	18062
Reverse Medical Corporation	3841	D	949 215-0660	11050
Reyes Coca-Cola Bottling LLC **(PA)**	2086	B	213 744-8616	2284
Ricoh Electronics Inc	3579	E	714 259-1220	8319
Rightsourcing Inc **(HQ)**	7363	D	800 660-9544	17513
Rms/Endlgix Sdways Merger Corp	3841	E	949 595-7200	11051
Robert Kinsella Inc	5141	D	949 453-9533	14487
Rockefeller Group Dev Corp	6552	C	949 468-1800	16071
Rogerson Aircraft Corporation **(PA)**	3812	D	949 660-0666	10641
Roland Dga Corporation **(HQ)**	5045	C	949 727-2100	13434
Rose Chem Intl - USA Corp	2834	E	678 510-8864	4887
Rose International Inc	8748	C	636 812-4000	23504
Rrds Inc **(PA)**	3827	F	949 482-6200	10858
Rushmore Loan MGT Svcs LLC **(PA)**	6162	A	949 727-4798	15230
Rutan & Tucker LLP **(PA)**	8111	C	714 641-5100	21671
S E O P Inc	8742	C	949 682-7906	23314
Sabra Health Care Ltd Partnr **(HQ)**	6726	D	949 255-7100	16162
Safety Systems Hawaii	3993	E	808 847-4017	11591
Saga Kapital Group Inc	8741	D	714 294-4132	23103
Sage Associates Inc **(PA)**	8711	D	949 724-9600	22650
Sage Software Holdings Inc **(HQ)**	7372	B	866 530-7243	17975
San Jquin Hlls Trnsp Crrdor AG **(PA)**	1611	D	949 754-3400	912
Sanan Inc	8748	E	949 679-9200	23506
Sand Canyon Corporation **(HQ)**	6163	D	949 727-9425	15251
Sander Langston LP	1542	C	949 863-9200	820
Sans Wine & Spirits Co	2084	F	714 423-3883	2221
Santa Catalina Island Company **(PA)**	4725	C	310 510-2000	12410
Savala Equipment Company Inc **(PA)**	7353	D	909 552-1859	17319
SBE Contracting	1731	E	714 544-5066	1313
SBE Electrical Contracting Inc	1731	C	714 544-5066	1314
Schoolsfirst Federal Credit Un	6061	D	800 462-8328	15081
SDC Technologies Inc **(HQ)**	2851	E	714 939-8300	5111
Sdi LLC	5065	F	949 583-1001	13773
Sdi LLC	3599	E	949 351-1866	8791
Sea Breeze Financial Svcs Inc	6162	C	949 223-9700	15231
Seagra Technology Inc **(PA)**	3577	E	949 419-6796	8300
Seal Science Inc **(DH)**	3053	D	949 253-3130	5351
Second Hrvest Fd Bnk Ornge CNT	8322	D	949 653-2900	21887
Secure Channels Inc **(PA)**	7371	F	949 208-7525	17707
Secureauth Corporation **(PA)**	7371	D	949 777-6959	17708
Sega of America Inc	3999	D	415 806-0169	11750
Sega of America Inc **(DH)**	3999	E	949 788-0455	11751
Sekai Electronics Inc **(PA)**	3663	E	949 783-5740	9316
Sema Inc **(PA)**	8721	C	949 830-1400	22812
Senju Fire Protection Corp	3569	F	949 333-1281	8138
Sentinel Monitoring Corp **(HQ)**	7382	D	949 453-1550	18398
Servis One Inc	6163	D	888 738-5873	15253
Seven Resorts Inc **(PA)**	7011	D	949 588-7100	16702
Sfn Group Inc	7363	A	949 727-8500	17516
Shady Canyon Golf Club Inc	7997	C	949 856-7000	19612
Shimano North Amer Holdg Inc **(HQ)**	5091	C	949 951-5003	14087
Shoffeitt Pipeline Inc	1623	D	949 581-1600	970
Shook Hardy & Bacon LLP	8111	C	949 475-1500	21677
Shye West Inc **(PA)**	3993	E	949 486-4598	11594
Signature Control Systems	3523	D	949 580-3640	7619
Signature Rsrces Insur Fncl Sv	6411	D	949 930-2400	15628
Silverado Energy Company	4911	D	949 752-5588	12825
Silverado Senior Living Inc **(PA)**	8051	D	949 240-7200	20466
Silverado Senior Living Inc	8051	D	858 869-0538	20468
Silverado Senior Living Inc	8051	D	949 240-7744	20469
Silverado Snior Lving Hldngs	8361	A	949 240-7200	22153
Sk Chemicals America Inc	2821	F	949 336-8088	4717
Skyworks Solutions Inc **(PA)**	3674	A	949 231-3000	9576
Slalom LLC	8748	C	949 450-1100	23510
Smart Energy Systems Inc **(PA)**	7371	C	909 703-9609	17715
Smart Systems Technologies **(PA)**	7382	D	949 367-9375	18401
Smartlabs Inc	3822	D	800 762-7846	10668
SMC Networks Inc **(HQ)**	5045	D	949 679-8029	13438
Smile Brands Group Inc **(PA)**	8741	D	714 668-1300	23109
Snowmass Apparel Inc **(PA)**	5137	E	949 788-0617	14417
Solarflare Communications Inc **(PA)**	3571	D	949 581-6830	8175
Solvere Inc	4813	E	949 707-0035	12669
Sonnet Technologies Inc	3699	E	949 587-3500	9915
South Coast Baking LLC **(PA)**	2052	D	949 851-9654	2072
Southern Cal Prmnnte Med Group	8011	C	949 262-5780	20075
Southern California Edison Co	4911	C	949 587-5416	12847
Southern Implants Inc	8741	C	949 273-8505	23115
Southern Sierra Energy Company	4911	C	949 752-5588	12861
Southwest Dealer Services Inc **(PA)**	7389	C	949 707-4200	18673
Specialty Interior Mfg Inc	5013	E	714 296-8618	13095
Specialty Rock Inc	1442	F	909 334-2265	574
Specialty Surgical Centers	8011	E	949 341-3499	20095
Specific Media LLC **(DH)**	7311	D	949 861-8888	17056
Spectrum Cnstr Group Inc	1541	D	949 299-1400	718
Spectrum Hotel Group LLC	7011	D	949 471-8888	16723
Spectrum Information Svcs LLC **(PA)**	7331	D	949 752-7070	17141
Spectrum Scientific Inc	3827	E	949 260-9900	10861
Spigen Inc	5162	D	949 502-5121	14765
Spireon Inc **(PA)**	7371	C	800 557-1449	17721

Employment Codes: A=Over 500 employees, B=251-500, C=101-250, D=51-100, E=20-50 F=10-19
2022 Southern California Business Directory and Buyers Guide
© Mergent Inc. 1-800-342-5647
1377

	SIC	EMP	PHONE	ENTRY #
Sport Chalet LLC	7999	D	949 476-9555	19673
Squar Mlner Ptrson Mrnda Wllms **(PA)**	8721	C	949 222-2999	22815
St John Knits Inc **(DH)**	2339	A	949 225-8857	2997
St John Knits Intl Inc **(HQ)**	2339	C	949 863-1171	2998
St Joseph Hospital of Orange	8062	C	714 568-5500	20963
Staco Systems Inc **(HQ)**	3613	D	949 297-8700	8906
Stantec Architecture Inc	8712	C	949 923-6000	22743
Stantec Consulting Svcs Inc	8712	C	949 923-6000	22745
Startel Corporation **(PA)**	7371	D	949 863-8700	17723
Stason Pharmaceuticals Inc **(PA)**	2834	E	949 380-0752	4897
Steadfast Income Reit Inc **(HQ)**	6798	C	949 852-0700	16244
Steadfast Management Co Inc **(PA)**	6531	B	949 748-3000	16012
Stec Inc **(HQ)**	3572	B	415 222-9996	8219
Stm Networks Inc	3663	D	949 273-6800	9319
Str Worldwide Inc	5136	A	949 276-5990	14352
Stracon Inc	3699	F	949 851-2288	9917
Stratacare Llc	7371	C	949 743-1200	17726
Strategy Companion Corp	7372	D	714 460-8398	17989
Strawberry Farms Golf Club LLC	7992	C	949 551-2560	19510
Streamline Avionics Inc	3612	E	949 861-8151	8885
Stretto Inc **(PA)**	8111	D	949 222-1212	21682
STS Instruments Inc	3825	E	580 223-4773	10772
Stussy Inc	5136	D	949 474-9255	14353
Sullivncrtsmnroe Insur Svcs LL **(PA)**	8742	C	800 427-3253	23336
Sun Country Marine Inc	7699	D	909 390-6600	19071
Sun Ten Laboratories Inc	2834	E	949 587-1238	4900
Sun Ten Labs Liquidation Co	5149	E	949 587-0509	14739
Suncore Inc	3674	E	949 450-0054	9586
Sunscape Eyewear Inc	5099	D	949 553-0590	14184
Sunsports LP	3131	E	949 273-6202	5875
Suntsu Electronics Inc	3679	E	949 783-7300	9788
Sunwest Bank **(DH)**	6022	E	714 730-4441	15044
Super Color Digital LLC **(PA)**	2759	E	949 622-0010	4577
Super73 Inc **(PA)**	3751	E	949 313-6340	10502
Support Technologies Inc	7372	F	949 442-2957	17991
Sutter Securities Incorporated	6211	D	415 352-6300	15308
Syneron Inc **(DH)**	3845	C	866 259-6661	11239
Synoptek Inc **(PA)**	7379	D	949 241-8600	18224
Syntiant Corp	3674	D	949 774-4887	9588
Syntiro Healthcare Services **(PA)**	8741	D	949 923-3438	23120
Taco Bell Corp **(HQ)**	6794	A	949 863-4500	16219
Takagi-Ao Smith T W H Co LLC	3639	F	949 770-7171	9016
Talon Therapeutics Inc	2834	D	949 788-6700	4902
Tanaka Farms	5149	D	949 653-2100	14743
Tanz Publishing Inc **(PA)**	2741	E	949 231-2290	4211
Target Technology Company LLC	3695	E	949 788-0909	9840
Taylor & Assoc Architects Inc **(PA)**	8712	D	949 574-1325	22748
Taylor Graphics Inc	2759	E	949 752-5200	4580
Taylor Morrison California LLC	6552	D	949 341-1200	16075
Tca Architects Inc **(PA)**	8712	D	949 862-0270	22749
Tcg Software Services Inc	7371	B	714 665-6200	17731
Tct Mobile Inc	8741	D	949 892-2990	23121
Team Post-Op Inc	5047	C	949 253-5500	13524
Tekia Inc	3851	E	949 699-1300	11265
Teletrac Inc **(HQ)**	4899	B	714 897-0877	12790
Teletrac Navman US Ltd **(HQ)**	3812	E	866 527-9896	10645
Tempo Lighting Inc	3646	E	949 442-1601	9106
Temporary Staffing Union	8631	A	714 728-5186	22302
Ten-X Finance Inc	6531	C	949 465-8523	16015
Teridian Semiconductor Corp **(DH)**	3674	D	714 508-8800	9589
Teridian Smicdtr Holdings Corp **(DH)**	3674	D	714 508-8800	9590
Terran Orbital Corporation **(PA)**	3761	E	212 496-2300	10522
Tetra Tech Inc	8711	D	949 263-0846	22668
Tetra Tech Ec Inc	3826	D	949 809-5000	10818
Teva Parenteral Medicines Inc	2834	A	949 455-4700	4904
Thaihot Investment Co US Ltd	8071	A	949 242-5300	21099
Thales Avionics Inc	3728	E	949 381-3033	10428
Thales Avionics Inc	3728	E	949 790-2500	10429
Thermaprint Corp	3861	E	949 583-0800	11295
Thomas Gallaway Corporation **(PA)**	7371	D	949 716-9500	17734
Timevalue Software	7372	E	949 727-1800	17997
Tivoli LLC	3641	E	714 957-6101	9024
Tnhc Realty and Cnstr Inc **(PA)**	1521	C	949 382-7800	644
Tomorrows Look Inc	2261	D	949 596-8400	2661
Toshiba Amer Elctrnic Cmpnnts **(DH)**	3651	B	949 462-7700	9203
Toshiba Amer Info Systems Inc	3571	D	949 300-9435	8178
Toshiba Amer Info Systems Inc	3571	C	949 583-3000	8179
Toshiba Education Center	8732	C	949 583-3000	22898
Tp-Link USA Corporation **(DH)**	5045	C	626 333-0234	13447
Trace3 LLC **(HQ)**	8742	D	949 333-2300	23350
Traffic Control & Safety Corp **(PA)**	5084	D	949 553-8272	13954
Trantronics Inc	3672	E	949 553-1234	9461
Travel America Inc **(HQ)**	6515	E	949 474-0404	15757
TRC Solutions Inc **(HQ)**	8748	C	949 753-0101	23519
Tri Pointe Contractors LP **(HQ)**	1531	D	949 478-8600	682
Tri Pointe Homes Inc	1522	C	714 389-5933	670
Tri Pointe Homes Inc **(HQ)**	1522	C	949 438-1400	671
Tricom Research Inc	3663	D	949 250-6024	9323
Trimark Raygal LLC	5046	C	949 474-1000	13467
Trinamix Inc **(PA)**	8742	B	408 507-3583	23353
Trivascular Inc **(DH)**	3841	C	707 543-8800	11069
Trivascular Technologies Inc **(HQ)**	3841	D	707 543-8800	11070
Trivista Business Group Inc **(PA)**	8742	C	949 218-4830	23354
Tropitone Furniture Co Inc **(HQ)**	2514	B	949 595-2010	3536
Troutman Pepper Hmlton Snders L	8111	D	949 622-2700	21689
Truabutment Inc	3843	D	714 956-1488	11199
True Air Mechanical Inc	1711	C	888 316-0642	1158
Truesdail Laboratories Inc	8731	E	714 730-6239	22869
Turner Techtronics Inc	7378	C	949 724-1339	18152
Turtle Rock Preschool Inc	8351	D	949 754-1685	22068
Tuttle-Click Ford Inc	7538	C	949 855-1704	18881
TW Security Corp **(DH)**	5045	C	949 932-1000	13450
Tyvak Nn-Satellite Systems Inc	3761	D	949 753-1020	10523
U-Nav Microelectronics Corp	7379	D	949 453-2727	18230
Ubiquity Broadcasting Corp **(HQ)**	7389	E	949 489-7600	18697
Ultimate Ears Consumer LLC	3842	A	949 502-8340	11148
United Agribusiness League **(PA)**	8611	E	800 223-4590	22262
United Scope LLC **(HQ)**	3827	E	949 333-0001	10864
Universal Card Inc	7389	B	949 861-4000	18708
Universal Care Inc **(PA)**	8093	B	562 424-6200	21361
University California Irvine	8731	D	949 824-2819	22870
University California Irvine	8099	C	949 824-2662	21494
University California Irvine	8062	C	949 824-7725	20992
Uoc USA Inc	3841	F	949 328-3366	11072
Uprite Construction Corp	1541	D	949 877-8877	725
Upstanding LLC	7372	C	949 788-9900	18004
Urovant Sciences Inc **(HQ)**	2834	E	949 226-6029	4907
USA Vision Systems Inc **(HQ)**	3699	E	949 583-1519	9926
Usoc Medical	7699	D	949 243-9109	19081
Vanomation Inc	3565	E	877 228-2992	8080
Vantari Medical LLC	3829	F	949 783-5300	10920
Variable Image Printing	2752	F	949 296-1444	4449
Vegatek Corporation	7371	D	949 502-0090	17750
Velocitel Rf Inc	8711	C	949 809-4999	22691
Velocity Tech Solutions Inc	7374	D	949 417-0260	18114
Vendor Surveillance Corp	8742	C	949 833-2111	23359
Veritxt/Clfornia Reporting LLC	7338	E	714 432-1711	17195
Verizon Connect Telo Inc **(DH)**	7374	C	949 389-5500	18116
Verizon Wireless **(PA)**	4812	C	949 286-7000	12620
Vetco Hospitals Inc **(HQ)**	0742	D	858 483-4115	207
Viant Technology LLC **(HQ)**	7311	E	949 861-8888	17068
Victory Foam Inc **(PA)**	5199	D	949 474-0690	14983
Viento Funding II LLC	3621	F	609 524-4500	8935
Viking Products Inc	3545	E	949 379-5100	7877
Vinci Brands LLC	3571	C	949 838-5111	8181
Vinculums Services LLC	8748	C	949 783-3552	23523
Vision 33 Inc **(PA)**	7379	C	949 420-3300	18235
Vision Quest Industries Inc **(PA)**	3842	D	949 261-6382	11151
Vision Solutions Inc **(PA)**	7371	D	949 253-6500	17754
Vizio Inc **(PA)**	3651	C	855 833-3221	9207
Vizio Holding Corp	3651	A	949 428-2525	9208
Vogue Enterprise Inc	5023	F	949 833-9787	13197
Voice Assist Inc	3679	F	949 655-6400	9801
Voit Development Manager Inc	6552	D	949 851-5110	16078
Voit Real Estate Services LLC	6552	D	949 851-5100	16079
Vortex Industries Inc **(PA)**	1751	E	714 434-3000	1462
Vpm Management Inc	8741	C	949 863-1500	23136
Vti Instruments Corporation **(HQ)**	3699	E	949 955-1894	9927
Wade & Lowe A Prof Corp	8111	D	949 753-1000	21692
Wahlco Inc	3599	C	714 979-7300	8843
Wamco Inc **(PA)**	5063	F	714 545-5560	13677
Ware Malcomb **(PA)**	8712	C	949 660-9128	22750
Warmington Homes	1531	C	949 679-3100	685
Waste MGT Collectn Recycl Inc	4953	D	949 451-2600	13000
Waterhealth International Inc	3589	D	949 716-5790	8423
Wavefunction Inc	7371	F	949 955-2120	17757
West Coast Consulting LLC	7372	C	949 250-4102	18009
Western Growers Association **(PA)**	8611	C	949 863-1000	22263
Western Medical Management LLC	8741	E	949 260-6575	23138
Western National Contractors	8741	D	949 862-6200	23139
Western National Group LP	6531	D	949 862-6200	16032
Western National Prpts LLC **(PA)**	1522	C	949 862-6200	674
Western National Securities **(PA)**	6531	C	949 862-6200	16033
Western Telematic Inc	3577	E	949 586-9950	8311
Westside Resources Inc	3843	E	800 944-3939	11203
Whiting-Turner Contracting Co	1542	C	949 863-0800	850
Wm Technology Inc	7372	B	844 933-3627	18010
Woodbridge Village Association	8641	D	949 736-1800	22378
Workway Inc	7361	C	949 553-8700	17480
Worley Field Services Inc	1629	D	949 224-7585	1010
Wynne Systems Inc **(DH)**	7371	D	949 224-6300	17762
Wytcote Inc	7373	F	877 472-5587	18075
Xcelerium Inc	3674	F	949 244-3668	9606
Xidas Inc	3679	F	949 930-0147	9804
Xlsoft Corporation	7372	F	949 453-2781	18012
Xponential Fitness Inc **(HQ)**	7991	B	949 346-3000	19474
Yogurtland Franchising Inc **(PA)**	6794	D	949 265-8000	16225
Young & Rubicam LLC	7311	B	949 754-2000	17072
Young & Rubicam LLC	7311	C	949 754-2100	17073
Young & Rubicam LLC	8742	B	949 224-6300	23370
Zadara Storage Inc	3572	D	949 251-0360	8223
Zbs Law LLP	8111	D	714 848-7920	21704
Zippy Usa Inc	5063	D	949 366-9525	13679
Zo Skin Health Inc **(DH)**	2844	D	949 988-7524	5086
Zymo Research Corporation **(PA)**	8731	D	949 679-1190	22872

IRWINDALE, CA - Los Angeles County

	SIC	EMP	PHONE	ENTRY #
A & M Engineering Inc	3599	D	626 813-2020	8454
Agritec International Ltd	5099	E	626 812-7200	14145
Alpha Printing & Graphics Inc	2752	E	626 851-9800	4225
Altium Packaging	3089	D	626 856-2100	5556
American Capacitor Corporation	3675	E	626 814-4444	9609
AP Express LLC **(PA)**	4731	D	562 236-2250	12422
Arminak & Associates LLC	5199	D	626 358-4804	14912
Arrow Engineering	3599	E	626 960-2806	8503

Mergent email: customerrelations@mergent.com
1378

2022 Southern California Business Directory and Buyers Guide

(P-0000) Products & Services Section entry number
(PA)=Parent Co (HQ)=Headquarters (DH)=Div Headquarters

	SIC	EMP	PHONE	ENTRY #
Best Overnite Express Inc **(PA)**	4213	D	626 256-6340	12014
Bimeda Inc	2834	E	626 815-1680	4798
Breeders Choice Pet Foods LLC	5149	E	626 334-9301	14676
Bsst LLC	3714	C	626 593-4500	10023
Cal Springs LLC	2759	D	562 943-5599	4491
Calibre International LLC **(PA)**	8743	C	626 969-4660	23379
Califrnia Cstm Frits Flvors In **(PA)**	2087	E	626 736-4130	2313
Chem Arrow Corp	2992	E	626 358-2255	5290
Church & Larsen Inc	1742	C	626 303-8741	1371
Clark - Pacific Corporation	3272	E	626 962-8751	6022
Cni Mfg Inc	3599	E	626 962-6646	8558
Davis Wire Corporation **(HQ)**	3315	C	626 969-7651	6222
Decore-Ative Spc NC LLC	2431	C	626 960-7731	3244
Eggleston Youth Centers Inc **(PA)**	8322	D	626 480-8107	21778
Fine Ptch Elctrnic Assmbly LLC	3672	E	626 337-2800	9405
Foley OK Electric Inc	1731	D	818 962-8555	1257
Geary Pacific Corporation	5074	E	626 513-0273	13828
Go2zero Strategies LLC	2611	F	626 840-1850	3743
Halcyon Microelectronics Inc	3674	E	626 814-4688	9512
Hillside Wines & Spirits LLC	2084	F	424 268-5168	2193
Huy Fong Foods Inc	2033	E	626 286-8328	1864
J&R Taylor Brothers Assoc Inc	2047	D	626 334-9301	1958
Johnson & Johnson	3842	B	909 839-8650	11119
Kifuki USA Co Inc **(HQ)**	2015	D	626 334-8090	1761
Km Printing Production Inc	2752	F	626 821-0008	4350
Kong Veterinary Products	3841	F	626 633-0077	11004
Mariposa Landscapes Inc **(PA)**	0782	C	626 960-0196	324
Miller Brewing Co	2082	F	626 353-1604	2150
Million Corporation	2759	D	626 969-1888	4545
Mountain Gear Corporation	5136	C	626 851-2488	14342
Neovia Logistics Dist LP	4731	C	626 359-4500	12488
Pacific Panel Products Corp	2499	E	626 851-0444	3449
Pertronix Inc	3694	E	909 599-5955	9828
Pierre Landscape Inc	0781	C	626 587-2121	275
Q & B Foods Inc **(DH)**	2035	D	626 334-8090	1893
Ready Pac Foods Inc **(HQ)**	2099	A	626 856-8686	2515
Schamas Mfg Coinc	3531	F	626 334-6870	7649
Seaboard Envelope Co Inc	2677	E	626 960-4559	3911
Sierra Alloys Company	3463	D	626 969-6711	7106
Sinecera Inc	7389	D	626 962-1087	18668
Southern California Edison Co	4911	C	626 543-8081	12828
Southern California Edison Co	4911	C	626 815-7296	12842
Southern California Edison Co	4911	C	626 633-3070	12848
Southern California Edison Co	4911	C	626 814-4212	12851
Southern California Edison Co	4911	C	626 812-7380	12856
Spragues Rock and Sand Company **(PA)**	3273	E	626 445-2125	6116
Superior Communications Inc **(PA)**	5065	C	877 522-4727	13777
Tandex Test Labs Inc	8734	E	626 962-7166	22959
United Site Services Cal Inc **(PA)**	7359	E	626 462-9110	17381
Universal Dynamics Inc	1382	E	626 480-0035	472
Universal Metal Plating **(PA)**	7532	F	626 969-7931	18806
US Toyo Fan Corporation **(HQ)**	3564	D	626 338-1111	8059
Valley Lght Ctr For Scial Advn	8331	C	626 337-6200	21970

IVANHOE, CA - Tulare County

	SIC	EMP	PHONE	ENTRY #
Family Healthcare Network	8011	C	559 798-1877	19819
Klink Citrus Association	0723	C	559 798-1881	179

JOSHUA TREE, CA - San Bernardino County

	SIC	EMP	PHONE	ENTRY #
Joshua Tree Memorial Park	6553	E	760 366-9210	16086
Morongo Bsin Amblance Assn Inc	4119	D	760 366-8474	11882

JURUPA VALLEY, CA - Riverside County

	SIC	EMP	PHONE	ENTRY #
A and G Inc **(HQ)**	2329	A	714 765-0400	2795
Act Fulfillment Inc **(PA)**	4225	C	909 930-9083	12182
Activeapparel Inc **(PA)**	2329	F	951 361-0060	2796
Advanced Innvtive Rcvery Tech	2515	E	949 273-8100	3540
Aluminum Die Casting Co Inc	3363	D	951 681-3900	6363
Brothers Machine & Tool Inc	3542	E	951 361-9454	7756
Brothers Machine & Tool Inc **(PA)**	3542	F	951 361-2909	7757
C P S Express **(HQ)**	4212	D	951 685-1041	11959
Calpaco Papers Inc **(PA)**	2679	C	323 767-2800	3924
Calstrip Industries Inc **(PA)**	3316	E	323 726-1345	6242
Calstrip Steel Corporation **(HQ)**	3398	D	323 838-2097	6435
Charles Komar & Sons Inc	2341	B	951 934-1377	3014
Complete Food Service Inc	5149	D	951 685-8490	14683
Costco Wholesale Corporation	4225	B	951 361-3606	12190
Cryoworks Inc	3498	D	951 360-0920	7533
Damco USA Inc	4412	C	951 360-4940	12273
Del Real LLC **(PA)**	2038	C	951 681-0395	1924
Deluxe Auto Carriers Inc	4212	D	909 746-0900	11965
Enhance America Inc	3993	E	951 361-3000	11551
Galassos Bakery **(PA)**	5149	C	951 360-1211	14688
Hartmark Cab Design & Mfg Inc	1799	E	909 591-9153	1664
Highland Plastics Inc	3089	C	951 360-9587	5663
Hino Motors Mfg USA Inc	5013	D	951 727-0286	13064
Hyponex Corporation	2873	C	909 597-2811	5156
Ideal Products Inc	2541	E	951 727-8600	3651
Imperial Western Products Inc	5159	D	951 727-8950	14751
International Vitamin Corp	2834	C	951 361-1120	4831
Johnson Safety Inc	5099	F	909 796-3385	14165
Kovatch Mobile Equipment Corp	3711	E	951 685-1224	9956
Langlois Company	2045	E	951 360-3900	1952
Le Vecke Corporation **(PA)**	5181	D	951 681-8600	14830
Levecke LLC	2084	E	951 681-8600	2203
Lowes Home Centers LLC	5031	C	951 256-9034	13268
March Products Inc	3999	D	909 622-4800	11711
Metal Container Corporation	3411	C	951 360-4500	6466
Nestle Usa Inc	2038	D	951 360-7200	1933
Olivet International Inc **(PA)**	5099	D	951 681-8888	14172
Optimum Con Fundations USA Inc	1771	D	877 212-7994	1544
P R P Multisource Inc	3565	E	951 681-6100	8075
Pacific Award Metals Inc	5033	D	909 390-9880	13326
Pacific Award Metals Inc	3444	E	360 694-9530	6888
Paradigm Label Inc	2759	F	951 372-9212	4554
Pavement Coatings Co **(PA)**	1611	C	714 826-3011	906
Pavement Recycling Systems Inc **(PA)**	5093	C	951 682-1091	14119
Philips North America LLC	3645	C	909 574-1800	9070
Plastic Innovations Inc	3083	F	951 361-0251	5456
Propak Logistics Inc	4789	D	951 934-7160	12582
Pura Naturals Inc	2515	E	949 273-8100	3556
Puri Tech Inc	3589	E	951 360-8380	8406
Racing Plus Inc	3842	E	951 360-5906	11137
Right Angle Solutions Inc	8748	E	951 934-3081	23500
Robinson Engineering Corp	3547	F	951 361-8000	7887
Southwest Material Hdlg Inc **(PA)**	7389	C	951 727-0477	18675
Spartak Enterprises Inc	2517	F	951 360-0610	3562
Superior Filtration Pdts LLC	3564	F	951 681-1700	8055
Time and Alarm Systems **(PA)**	1731	D	951 685-1761	1329
Toll Global Fwdg Scs USA Inc	4731	D	951 360-8310	12538
Total Trnsp Logistics Inc	4213	D	951 360-9521	12083
Triways Inc	4213	D	951 361-4840	12085
Unitek Technology Inc	3571	F	909 930-5700	8180
Vista Pacifica Enterprises Inc **(PA)**	8051	C	951 682-4833	20501
Young Electric Sign Company	3993	E	909 923-7668	11616

KEENE, CA - Kern County

	SIC	EMP	PHONE	ENTRY #
United Farm Workers America **(PA)**	8631	C	661 822-5571	22303

KETTLEMAN CITY, CA - Kings County

	SIC	EMP	PHONE	ENTRY #
Chemical Waste Management Inc	4953	D	559 386-9711	12938
Keenan Farms Inc	0173	D	559 945-1400	56

LA CANADA, CA - Los Angeles County

	SIC	EMP	PHONE	ENTRY #
Child Educational Center	8351	D	818 354-3418	21999
Crescenta-Canada YMCA **(PA)**	8641	C	818 790-0123	22334
Descanso Gardens Guild Inc	8399	D	818 952-4408	22179
Dilbeck Inc **(PA)**	6531	D	818 790-6774	15838
La Canada Flintridge Cntry CLB	7997	D	818 790-0611	19574
La Canada Unified School Dst	4173	D	818 952-8320	11944
Majestic Garlic Inc	2035	F	951 677-0555	1891
Navigage Foundation **(PA)**	8051	D	818 790-2522	20423
Pta CA Cngress of Parnts Palm	8641	D	818 952-8360	22358

LA CANADA FLINTRIDGE, CA - Los Angeles County

	SIC	EMP	PHONE	ENTRY #
Allen Lund Company LLC **(HQ)**	4731	D	818 790-8412	12419
Allen Lund Corporation **(PA)**	4731	E	818 790-8412	12420
Bis Computer Solutions Inc **(PA)**	7371	E	818 248-4282	17565
Cal Tech Emplyees Fderal Cr Un **(PA)**	6061	D	818 952-4444	15060
Holmes Body Shop-Alhambra Inc **(PA)**	7532	D	626 795-6447	18793
Lucare Corporation	3861	F	818 583-7731	11282

LA CRESCENTA, CA - Los Angeles County

	SIC	EMP	PHONE	ENTRY #
Accurate Screen Processing	2396	F	818 957-3965	3167
Balita Media Inc	2711	F	818 552-4503	3952
Brains Out Media Inc	7372	F	818 296-1036	17807
Century 21 Crest	6531	D	818 248-9100	15805
EAM Enterprises Inc **(PA)**	6531	D	818 248-9100	15844
Hamo Constraction	1389	E	818 415-3334	505
Jeremys Electric	2051	F	818 249-5656	2010
Modular Communications Systems	3663	E	818 764-1333	9294
Neardata Inc	8742	D	818 249-2469	23283
Outlook Amusements Inc	7379	C	818 433-3800	18208
Pro Media Merchants	2752	F	818 957-7114	4407

LA HABRA, CA - Orange County

	SIC	EMP	PHONE	ENTRY #
B&W Custom Restaurant Eqp Inc	3589	E	714 578-0332	8367
Ckd Industries Inc	3469	F	714 871-5600	7136
CVS Health Corporation	4225	D	714 578-4601	12195
Haircutters	7241	D	562 690-2217	16921
Ironwood Fabrication Inc	3462	F	714 576-7320	7088
J C Ford Company **(HQ)**	3556	D	714 871-7361	7940
Jcr Aircraft Deburring LLC	3471	D	714 870-4427	7273
JKB Corporation	1771	E	562 905-3477	1533
JWdangelo Company Inc	5087	E	562 690-1000	14039
Lemyn LLC	2844	F	714 617-2410	5043
Life Care Centers America Inc	8051	C	562 690-0852	20391
Los Angeles Salad Intl Inc	2035	E	626 322-9000	1890
Lowes Home Centers LLC	5031	C	562 690-5122	13242
Mmp Sheet Metal Inc	3444	E	562 691-1055	6878
Murphy-Rodgers Incorporated	5084	F	714 525-2952	13921
Orbo Corporation	2531	E	562 806-6171	3629
Pacific Archtectural Mllwk Inc **(PA)**	2431	D	562 905-3200	3279
Peerless Maintenance Svc Inc	7349	B	714 871-3380	17272
Plastic Tops Inc	2542	F	714 738-8128	3691
Precision Landscape & Turf	0781	E	714 525-2318	277
Shepard Bros Inc **(PA)**	3589	C	562 697-1366	8414
Shepard-Thomason Company	3714	D	714 773-5539	10133
Shinsuke Clifford Yamamoto Inc	0782	D	714 992-5783	342
Southwest Inspection and Tstg	7389	D	562 941-2990	18674
Stop-Look Sign Co Intl Inc	3993	F	562 690-7576	11606
Triview Glass Industries LLC	3231	D	626 363-7980	5970
Uvw Inc	3089	F	714 482-2914	5854
VIP Rubber Company Inc **(PA)**	3069	C	562 905-3456	5422

LA HABRA HEIGHTS, CA - Orange County

	SIC	EMP	PHONE	ENTRY #
Graphic Design Services Inc	7336	E	562 282-8000	17176

GEOGRAPHIC

Employment Codes: A=Over 500 employees, B=251-500, C=101-250, D=51-100, E=20-50 F=10-19

2022 Southern California Business Directory and Buyers Guide

© Mergent Inc. 1-800-342-5647

1379

	SIC	EMP	PHONE	ENTRY #
Hacienda Golf Club	7997	D	562 694-1081	19566

LA MIRADA, CA - Los Angeles County

	SIC	EMP	PHONE	ENTRY #
365 Printing Inc	2752	F	714 752-6990	4220
Amerdale Industries Inc	5023	D	714 521-3800	13157
American Power Solutions Inc	3648	E	714 626-0300	9123
B S A Partners	7011	D	714 523-2800	16334
Beemak Plastics LLC	3089	D	800 421-4393	5577
Bigge Group	1799	C	714 523-4092	1640
Bravo Tech Inc	4812	E	714 230-8333	12596
Calwax LLC **(DH)**	5169	E	626 969-4334	14774
Captek Softgel Intl Inc	2834	C	657 325-0412	4805
Cha La Mirada LLC	7011	C	714 739-8500	16376
CHG Security Inc	7381	E	562 284-6260	18262
Crothall Services Group	7699	A	714 562-9275	19032
Domo Company LLC **(PA)**	7372	E	626 407-0015	17840
E T Horn Company **(PA)**	5169	D	714 523-8050	14779
Estes Express Lines	4213	D	714 994-3770	12037
Far East Broadcasting Co Inc	4832	D	562 947-4651	12691
Gallagher Rental Inc	3648	E	714 690-1559	9134
Gemsa Enterprises LLC	2079	E	714 521-1736	2130
General Grinding & Mfg Co LLC	3593	E	562 921-7033	8438
Golden Kraft Inc	2679	B	562 926-8888	3930
Groupex Financial Corporation **(DH)**	6282	B	714 690-8321	15329
Hager Mfg Inc	3728	E	714 522-8870	10342
Headwaters Construction Inc	3241	E	714 523-1530	5976
Healthpointe Medical Group Inc **(PA)**	8011	D	714 956-2663	19837
IL Fornaio (america) LLC	5149	C	714 752-7052	14695
Iqair North America Inc	3564	E	877 715-4247	8048
Jdh Pacific Inc **(PA)**	3321	E	562 926-8088	6259
JM Huber Micropowders Inc	2819	E	714 994-7855	4660
Jmg Machine Inc	3599	E	714 522-6221	8643
Kam Sang Company Inc	7011	D	714 523-2800	16519
Life Care Centers America Inc	8051	C	562 947-8691	20392
Life Care Centers America Inc	8051	C	562 943-7156	20396
Lindblade Metalworks Inc	3441	E	714 670-7172	6629
Living Spaces Furniture LLC **(PA)**	5021	C	714 523-2000	13141
Makita USA Inc **(HQ)**	5072	C	714 522-8088	13811
MEI Rigging & Crating LLC	3559	D	714 712-5888	7989
Mejico Express Inc **(PA)**	4513	C	714 690-8300	12330
Mirada Hills Rehabilitation	8059	D	562 947-8691	20613
Oceania Inc	3081	E	562 926-8886	5437
Orange Courier Inc	7389	B	714 384-3600	18622
Outlook Resources Inc	2395	D	714 522-2452	3162
Philips Rs North America LLC	3842	F	562 483-6805	11135
Physical Distribution Svc Inc **(PA)**	4225	D	323 881-0886	12231
Presentation Products Inc **(PA)**	7373	D	714 367-2900	18058
Prime Value Logistic Inc	4731	E	213 218-3917	12511
Productsgo LLC	4731	E	714 242-4299	12513
RDM Industries	5162	F	714 690-0380	14761
Regal-Piedmont Plastics LLC	5162	E	562 404-4014	14762
Reliance Steel & Aluminum Co	5051	C	714 736-4800	13590
Shasta Beverages Inc	2086	D	714 523-2280	2299
Solid State Devices Inc	3674	C	562 404-4474	9578
Southern Cal Spcialty Care Inc **(DH)**	8062	D	562 944-1900	20949
Stainless Stl Fabricators Inc	5084	D	714 739-9904	13943
Straight Talk Inc	8322	D	562 943-0195	21899
Superior Storage Tank Inc	3443	F	714 226-1914	6757
Tiffany Dale Inc **(PA)**	5023	D	714 739-2700	13189
Tomarco Contractor Spc Inc **(PA)**	5072	D	714 523-1771	13819
Tradesmen International LLC	8741	D	949 588-3280	23125
Tropical Asphalt LLC **(PA)**	2952	F	714 739-1408	5286
US Foods Inc	5141	C	714 670-3500	14517
V Twest Inc	2541	F	714 521-2167	3670
Wesanco Inc	3728	E	714 739-4989	10443
Woobo Distribution	2082	F	714 522-5505	2162

LA PALMA, CA - Orange County

	SIC	EMP	PHONE	ENTRY #
Applecare Medical MGT LLC	8741	C	714 443-4507	22978
Arcadia Contractors Inc	2521	D	714 562-8200	3578
Atlantic Richfield Company **(DH)**	1321	A	800 333-3991	418
CJ Foods Inc **(HQ)**	2099	E	714 367-7200	2409
Commercial Crrers Insur Agcy I	6411	C	562 404-4900	15552
Isec Incorporated	1751	D	714 761-5151	1441
Isec Incorporated	1751	D	714 761-5151	1443
Kaiser Foundation Hospitals	8011	C	714 562-3420	19923
Kaiser Foundation Hospitals	8011	C	714 562-3420	19935
Keebler Company	2052	D	714 228-1555	2067
Lapco West LLC	3714	E	562 348-4850	10089
Norman International Inc	5023	D	562 946-0420	13181
Precision Cutting Tools Inc	3545	E	562 921-7898	7863
Prestige Stations Inc **(DH)**	7549	C	714 670-5145	18941
Ranir LLC	3843	E	866 373-7374	11192
Slade Gorton & Co Inc	5146	D	714 676-4200	14584
Svf Flow Controls Inc	5084	E	562 802-2255	13947
Tech Knowledge Associates LLC	7699	D	714 735-3810	19076
Travelers Club Luggage Inc	5099	D	714 523-8808	14185
Uns Electric Inc	5063	E	714 690-3660	13671

LA PUENTE, CA - Los Angeles County

	SIC	EMP	PHONE	ENTRY #
Alert Insulation Company Inc	1742	D	626 961-9113	1361
Aperto Property Management Inc	6513	C	626 965-1961	15718
Arrow Disposal Services Inc	4953	E	626 336-2255	12928
Athens Disposal Company Inc **(PA)**	4953	B	626 336-3636	12929
Bomark Inc	2893	E	626 968-1666	5201
Cacique Inc	5143	C	626 961-3399	14536
Cad Works Inc	3599	E	626 336-5491	8538
Cal Lift Inc	5084	D	562 566-1400	13893
Cortez Pallets Service Inc **(PA)**	2448	F	626 961-9891	3385
Cott Technologies Inc	3498	F	626 961-3399	7532
County of Los Angeles	8011	D	626 968-3711	19766
County of Los Angeles	3531	F	626 968-3312	7640
Crown Pallet Company Inc	2448	F	626 937-6565	3386
Eemus Manufacturing Corp	3479	F	626 443-8841	7361
Enki Health and RES Systems	8011	D	626 961-8971	19807
Genesis Tc Inc	2512	F	626 968-4455	3503
Herbal Science Intl Inc	2833	F	626 333-9998	4748
Kaiser Foundation Hospitals	8092	C	626 931-3580	21251
LA Signal	1731	F	909 599-2201	1274
Ley Grand Foods Corporation	2051	E	626 336-2244	2015
Mymichelle Company LLC **(HQ)**	2331	B	626 934-4166	2862
Pacific Coast Pallets Inc	2448	F	626 937-6565	3401
Plaza De La Raza Child Dev Svc **(PA)**	8351	D	562 776-1301	22048
Powell Works Inc	5084	B	909 861-6699	13928
San Gabriel Vly Training Ctr **(PA)**	8331	D	626 330-3185	21966
Shift Packaging LLC	2841	F	206 412-4253	4947
Smart & Final Stores Inc	5141	C	626 330-2495	14494
WEI-Chuan USA Inc	5142	E	323 838-0088	14532
Yang-Ming International Corp	7373	E	626 956-0100	18077

LA QUINTA, CA - Riverside County

	SIC	EMP	PHONE	ENTRY #
Adams Learning Center	8351	E	760 777-4260	21980
Cartwright Termite & Pest Ctrl	7342	E	760 771-6091	17200
Chapman Golf Development LLC	7997	D	760 564-8723	19554
Desert Regional Med Ctr Inc	8062	D	760 771-6158	20745
Hideaway	7041	C	760 777-7400	16833
Hideaway Club	7997	A	760 777-7400	19567
Imperial Irrigation District	4939	E	760 398-5811	12877
La Quinta Country Club	7997	D	760 564-4151	19576
LLC Marsh Perkins	2389	F	760 880-4558	3077
Lowes Home Centers LLC	5031	C	760 771-5566	13228
Lqr Property LLC	7011	B	760 564-4111	16547
Madison Club Owners Assn	7992	C	760 777-9320	19498
Mountain View Country Club Inc	7997	D	760 771-4311	19590
Msr Desert Resort LP	7011	A	760 564-5730	16574
Palms Golf Club Inc	7992	D	760 771-2606	19503
Red Rock Pallet Company	4731	E	530 852-7744	12518
Silver Rock Resort Golf Club	7992	D	760 777-8884	19509
Tradition Golf Club Associates	7997	D	760 564-3355	19624
Trilogy Golf At La Quinta	7992	C	760 771-0707	19511
TS Enterprises Inc	2791	E	760 360-5991	4627

LA VERNE, CA - Los Angeles County

	SIC	EMP	PHONE	ENTRY #
Aero Classics Inc	3559	E	909 596-1330	7959
Aero-Clssics Heat Trnsf Pdts I	3443	F	909 596-1330	6724
Alquest Technologies Inc	7378	D	909 592-8708	18142
Automobile Club Southern Cal	8699	D	909 392-1444	22435
Beonca Machine Inc	3599	F	909 392-9991	8525
Brethren Hillcrest Homes	8361	C	909 593-4917	22086
David and Margaret Home Inc	8361	C	909 596-5921	22099
DPI Labs Inc	3728	E	909 392-5777	10312
Durston Manufacturing Company	3423	F	909 593-1506	6477
Farbotech Color Inc	2893	F	909 596-9330	5202
Fortress Inc	2521	E	909 593-3600	3584
Gainey Ceramics Inc	3269	E	909 596-4464	6003
Gilead Sciences Inc	2834	D	650 522-2771	4824
Haaker Equipment Company **(PA)**	5012	D	909 598-2706	13027
Haynes Family Programs Inc	8361	C	909 593-2581	22111
Inseat Solutions LLC	3634	E	562 447-1780	9006
Jet Delivery Inc **(PA)**	4215	D	800 716-7177	12139
Juicy Whip Inc	3556	E	909 392-7500	7941
Layton Printing & Mailing	2752	F	909 592-4419	4354
Massachusetts Electric Company	8741	D	909 962-6001	23059
Metropolitan Water District	4941	B	909 593-7474	12907
Micro Analog Inc	3674	C	909 392-8277	9538
Mitsubishi Elc Pwr Pdts Inc	3613	E	909 447-8410	8900
Mohawk Western Plastics Inc	2673	E	909 593-7547	3887
Novipax Inc	5113	D	909 392-1750	14216
P F Plastics Inc	2519	F	909 392-4488	3570
Pacific Oil Cooler Service In	4581	E	909 593-8400	12365
Plastifab Inc	3083	E	909 596-1927	5459
RES-Care Inc	8052	D	909 596-5360	20542
S & S Bindery Inc	2789	E	909 596-2213	4621
Serco Mold Inc **(PA)**	3089	E	626 331-0517	5817
Sunbelt USA Inc **(PA)**	5099	F	909 593-0500	14183
Synergetic Tech Group Inc	3728	E	909 305-4711	10426
TEC Color Craft **(PA)**	2752	E	909 392-9000	4434
Tofasco of America Inc **(PA)**	8741	D	909 392-8282	23124
Wayfinder Family Services	8361	E	909 305-1948	22167
Wayfinder Family Services	8361	E	909 305-1948	22168
Z Manufacturing Inc	3499	E	909 593-2191	7578
Zimmer Intermed Inc	3842	F	909 392-0882	11156

LADERA RANCH, CA - Orange County

	SIC	EMP	PHONE	ENTRY #
Bau Furniture Mfg Inc **(PA)**	2511	E	949 643-2729	3464
Ksu Corporation	3441	F	951 409-7055	6627
Smartstop Self Storage **(DH)**	4225	D	949 429-6600	12243
Smartstop Self Storage Inc **(HQ)**	4225	D	949 429-6600	12244
Sst IV 8020 Las Vgas Blvd S LL	4225	D	949 429-6600	12247

LAGUNA BEACH, CA - Orange County

	SIC	EMP	PHONE	ENTRY #
Adventist Health System/West	8062	D	949 499-7175	20644
AJ Sons Inc	2038	F	949 497-1741	1913
American Historic Inns Inc	2741	F	949 499-8070	4149
Atlantis Computing Inc	7372	E	650 917-9471	17791
C & B Delivery Services	4225	D	909 623-4708	12186

Mergent email: customerrelations@mergent.com
1380
2022 Southern California Business Directory and Buyers Guide
(P-0000) Products & Services Section entry number
(PA)=Parent Co (HQ)=Headquarters (DH)=Div Headquarters

GEOGRAPHIC SECTION LAKE FOREST, CA

	SIC	EMP	PHONE	ENTRY #
Data Processing Design Inc	7371	F	714 695-1000	17590
Durham School Services L P	4151	C	949 376-0376	11925
Ear Charms Inc	3911	E	949 494-4147	11314
Esolar Inc **(DH)**	1629	D	818 303-9500	996
Exploremypc	7336	E	877 497-1650	17174
Festival of Arts Laguna Beach	7999	D	949 494-1145	19649
Firebrand Media LLC	2752	E	949 715-4100	4294
Home Express Delivery Svc LLC	4731	A	949 715-9844	12470
JC Resorts LLC	8741	B	949 376-2779	23041
Laguna Bch Golf Bnglow Vlg LLC	0291	E	949 499-2271	143
Laguna Playhouse **(PA)**	7922	C	949 497-2787	19321
Montage Hotels & Resorts LLC	8741	A	949 715-6000	23067
Myotek Industries Incorporated **(PA)**	3694	D	949 502-3776	9826
National Film Laboratories	7819	D	323 466-0281	19241
Ophthonix Inc	3851	E	760 842-5600	11259
Pacific Housing Management **(PA)**	6531	D	714 508-1777	15938
Pacific Quartz Inc	3827	E	714 546-8133	10853
RA Industries LLC	3599	E	714 557-2322	8756
Sanctus LLC	8741	C	248 594-2396	23104
Sole Source Technology LLC	3577	F	949 500-3371	8303
Spencer Recovery Centers Inc **(PA)**	8093	D	949 376-3705	21344
Symrise Inc	2087	E	949 276-4600	2337
University California Irvine	8099	C	949 939-7106	21493
USA Express Tire and Service	7538	D	949 494-7111	18883
Vacation Bay Hotel Prpts Inc	7011	C	949 494-8566	16767
Victoria Skimboards	3949	F	949 494-0059	11456

LAGUNA HILLS, CA - Orange County

	SIC	EMP	PHONE	ENTRY #
Adco Products Inc	3679	E	937 339-6267	9671
Allure Medical Staffing Inc	8099	D	888 310-1020	21374
Altec Products Inc **(PA)**	7389	D	949 727-1248	18441
American Capital Group Inc	6159	D	949 271-5800	15160
Automobile Club Southern Cal	8699	D	949 951-1400	22432
Autotechbizcom Inc	3559	F	949 245-7033	7962
Bel Esprit Builders Inc	1542	E	949 709-3500	742
Bingo Publishers Incorporated	2741	F	949 581-5410	4155
Blytheco Inc **(PA)**	7379	E	949 583-9500	18166
California Psychcare Inc	8748	E	833 227-3454	23424
Cecal Enterprises Inc	1791	E	949 380-7100	1569
Charles C Manger III MD Inc	8011	D	949 951-4641	19744
Chavers Gasket Corporation	3053	E	949 472-8118	5332
Cirrus Health II LP	8011	C	949 855-0562	19750
Cmt Sheet Metal	3443	F	949 679-9868	6735
Cynergy Prof Systems LLC	5065	E	800 776-7978	13713
Dan Luna Inc	2431	F	949 859-3631	3240
Djh Enterprises	3663	E	714 424-6500	9267
Ecliptek Inc	3679	F	714 433-1200	9703
Five Star Plastering Inc	1742	D	949 683-5091	1375
Fossil Energy Research Corp	7389	F	949 859-4466	18519
Fox Enterprises LLC **(HQ)**	3679	E	239 693-0099	9713
Garrett Precision Inc	3599	F	949 855-9710	8600
Gate Three Healthcare LLC	8051	C	949 770-3348	20354
Gregory W Peterson DDS **(PA)**	8021	D	626 354-4223	20180
Groundwork Open Source Inc	7375	D	415 992-4500	18123
Hardrock Tile & Marble Inc	1741	D	714 282-1766	1345
Harvest Small Business Fin LLC	6162	D	949 446-8683	15201
Jamboree Realty Corp **(PA)**	6531	C	949 380-0300	15895
Laguna Hills Hotel Dev Ventr	7011	D	949 586-5000	16532
Magic Software Enterprises Inc	7372	E	949 250-1718	17910
Metal Improvement Company LLC	3398	E	949 855-8010	6446
Nms Data Inc	8748	E	949 472-2700	23482
Nvision Laser Eye Centers Inc	8011	D	949 951-1457	20006
Orange Coast Wns Med Group Inc	8742	D	949 829-5500	23290
Peltek Holdings Inc	3479	E	949 855-8010	7396
Pension Group Inc	6411	D	949 768-4015	15611
Pico Instruments LLC	3674	F	949 910-6448	9558
Plastic and Metal Center Inc	3089	E	949 770-0610	5749
Productive Playhouse Inc	7389	B	323 250-3445	18642
Professional Cmnty MGT Cal Inc	6531	C	949 597-4200	15959
Questsoft Corporation	7371	E	949 837-9506	17694
Raintree Business Products Inc	2752	E	949 859-0801	4415
Rakworx Inc	7378	C	949 215-1362	18151
Retina Associates Orange Cnty **(PA)**	8011	D	949 707-5125	20042
Saddleback Memorial Med Ctr **(HQ)**	8062	A	949 837-4500	20926
Saddleback Stair & Millwork	2431	F	949 460-0384	3287
Sonendo Inc **(PA)**	3843	C	949 766-3636	11196
South Cnty Orthpd Spclsts A ME	8011	D	949 586-3200	20068
South Coast Eye Care Centers	8011	D	949 588-2020	20069
South Ornge Cnty Srgcal Med Gr	8011	D	949 457-7900	20071
Starrett Kinemetric Engrg Inc	3545	E	949 348-1213	7871
Starz Inc	5047	F	877 595-6789	13521
Taylor Morse Ltd	7334	E	949 707-5031	17155
Valley Insurance Service Inc	6411	B	949 707-4080	15643
Varsity Contractors Inc	7349	C	949 586-8283	17300

LAGUNA NIGUEL, CA - Orange County

	SIC	EMP	PHONE	ENTRY #
Aegis Senior Communities LLC	8361	D	949 496-8080	22078
Alcon Vision LLC	3841	C	949 753-6218	10927
Aot Electronics Inc	3577	F	949 600-6335	8235
Ardensel & Co Intl Inc	2024	F	949 365-6943	1809
Bitfone Corporation **(PA)**	7371	E	949 234-7000	17566
Burke Display Systems Inc	2542	F	949 248-0091	3677
California Title Company **(PA)**	6541	D	949 582-8709	16037
Career Engagement Group LLC	7371	D	212 235-1470	17574
Childrens Choice Inc	8351	D	949 495-5162	22001
Diversified Waterscapes Inc	8742	F	949 582-5414	23207
Ener-Core Power Inc **(HQ)**	3511	F	949 428-3300	7582
First Team RE - Orange Cnty	6531	C	949 240-7979	15863
Focus 360 Inc	7371	D	949 234-0008	17616
Fuel50 Inc	7371	D	833 844-1103	17621
Life Time Fitness Inc	8099	C	949 238-2700	21450
Merrill Lynch Prce Fnner Smith	6211	D	949 456-8082	15283
Mission Internal Med Group Inc	8011	D	949 364-3605	19982
Morgan Stnley Smith Barney LLC	6022	C	800 490-5412	15034
Moulton Nguel Wtr Dst Pub Fclt **(PA)**	4941	D	949 831-2500	12908
Murrey International Inc	3949	F	310 532-6091	11438
Neways Inc	3679	E	949 264-1542	9756
Pacific Monarch Resorts Inc	7011	D	949 228-1396	16610
Qpc Fiber Optic LLC	3357	E	949 361-8855	6356
Redworks Industries LLC	2499	E	949 334-7081	3453
San Diego Daily Transcript	2621	D	619 232-4381	3769
Spearman Clubs Inc **(PA)**	7999	E	949 496-2070	19671
Sugar Spice Evrything Nice Inc **(PA)**	8351	D	949 307-8674	22062
Trump Card LLC **(HQ)**	4212	D	949 360-7340	12002
Urban Armor Gear LLC **(HQ)**	3089	E	949 329-0500	5851

LAGUNA WOODS, CA - Orange County

	SIC	EMP	PHONE	ENTRY #
Laguna Woods Village	6531	A	949 597-4267	15906
Professional Cmnty MGT Cal Inc	6531	C	949 206-0580	15958
Salameh & Mahmood DDS Inc **(PA)**	8021	D	949 830-6510	20197

LAKE ARROWHEAD, CA - San Bernardino County

	SIC	EMP	PHONE	ENTRY #
Gildan USA Inc	2252	E	909 485-1475	2620
Hi-Desert Publishing Company	2711	E	909 336-3555	3987
Lake Arrwhead Rsort Oprtor Inc **(HQ)**	7011	C	909 336-1511	16533
Mountains Community Hosp Fndtn	8062	C	909 336-3651	20868
Rim of World Unified Schl Dst	4151	D	909 336-0330	11936

LAKE ELSINORE, CA - Riverside County

	SIC	EMP	PHONE	ENTRY #
AAA Restoration Inc	1799	E	951 471-5828	1632
Aerofoam Industries Inc	2531	D	951 245-4429	3618
Afakori Inc	3441	E	949 859-4277	6583
Albertsons LLC	2052	C	951 245-4461	2055
American Compaction Eqp Inc	3531	E	949 661-2921	7634
AWI Management Corporation	8741	C	951 674-8200	22982
Boozak Inc	3444	E	951 245-6045	6797
Carli Suspension Inc	7539	D	951 403-6570	18894
Chief Trnsp & Engrg Contrs Inc	1611	D	951 258-6607	872
Edje-Enterprises	1761	D	951 245-7070	1484
Elsinore Vly Municpl Wtr Dst **(PA)**	4941	D	951 674-3146	12891
Elsinore Vly Municpl Wtr Dst	4952	D	951 245-0276	12924
Empire Pre-Cast Inc	3272	E	951 609-1590	6031
Gbc Concrete Masnry Cnstr Inc	1741	C	951 245-2355	1344
Hakes Sash & Door Inc	1751	C	951 674-2414	1439
Hilz Cable Assemblies Inc	3829	F	951 245-0499	10888
Lake Elsinore Hotel & Casino	7999	C	951 674-3101	19653
Lowes Home Centers LLC	5031	C	951 253-6000	13260
Mercury Metal Die & Ltr Co Inc **(PA)**	3479	F	951 674-8717	7387
Modern Building Inc	1541	E	951 297-3311	709
Mold Vision Inc	3544	F	951 245-8020	7816
Near-Cal Corp	1542	E	951 245-5400	795
Pacific Aggregates Inc	3273	D	951 245-2460	6104
Pacific Clay Products Inc	5032	C	661 857-1401	13310
Perfection Glass Inc	1793	E	951 674-0240	1587
Pro Structural Inc	1741	D	951 526-2010	1351
Quality Foam Packaging Inc	3086	E	951 245-4429	5518
Rancho Ready Mix	3273	D	951 674-0488	6106
Sci Inc	1771	D	951 245-7511	1549
Sigma Faction Inc	8741	E	951 416-0961	23108
Stull Industries Inc	3714	E	951 248-9789	10136
United Wireless Inc **(DH)**	4812	D	951 471-5999	12615
Vertical Doors Inc	2591	E	951 273-1069	3717
Vista Community Clinic	8011	D	951 245-2735	20157
West Coast Ltg & Enrgy Inc	1731	D	951 296-0680	1337

LAKE FOREST, CA - Orange County

	SIC	EMP	PHONE	ENTRY #
ABC Custom Wood Shutters Inc	2431	E	949 595-0300	3227
AC&a Enterprises LLC **(HQ)**	3724	C	949 716-3511	10209
Advanced Innvtive Rcvery Tech **(PA)**	2515	F	949 273-8100	3539
Advanced Protection Inds LLC	7382	D	800 662-1711	18364
Alcon Vision LLC	8734	B	949 505-6890	22928
American Deburring Inc	3599	E	949 457-9790	8495
Aminco International USA Inc	3911	D	949 457-3261	11310
Anabolic Laboratories Inc	2834	E	949 863-0340	4785
Approved Networks LLC **(PA)**	3299	D	800 590-9535	6177
Apria Healthcare Group LLC **(HQ)**	8082	B	949 639-2000	21135
Apria Healthcare LLC **(DH)**	7352	B	949 639-2000	17302
Arb Inc **(HQ)**	1623	C	949 598-9242	933
Associated Electrics Inc	3944	E	949 544-7500	11366
Aveva Software LLC **(DH)**	7373	B	949 727-3200	18019
Avidex Industries LLC	7379	D	949 428-6333	18162
Beech Street Corporation **(DH)**	8741	B	949 672-1000	22984
Berry-Perussi Inc	3469	E	949 461-7000	7127
Betria Interactive LLC	4581	E	949 273-0920	12344
Bikeexchange Inc	7379	F	949 344-2616	18165
Biolase Inc **(PA)**	3843	C	949 361-1200	11163
Cac Inc	3679	E	949 587-3328	9686
Cameo Technologies Inc	3572	E	949 672-7000	8190
Camisasca Automotive Mfg Inc	3469	E	949 452-0195	7134
Camisasca Automotive Mfg Inc **(PA)**	3469	E	949 452-0195	7135
Campbell Engineering Inc	3545	E	949 859-3306	7848
Captivate Brands Usa Inc	3631	F	949 229-8927	8987
Cbr Electric Inc	1731	C	949 455-0331	1231
Cloudradiant Corp **(PA)**	5199	E	408 256-1527	14921
Cod USA Inc	2531	E	949 381-7367	3620
Commercial Indus Design Co Inc	5045	D	949 273-6199	13382

GEOGRAPHIC

Employment Codes: A=Over 500 employees, B=251-500, C=101-250, D=51-100, E=20-50 F=10-19
2022 Southern California Business Directory and Buyers Guide
© Mergent Inc. 1-800-342-5647
1381

	SIC	EMP	PHONE	ENTRY #
Crumbl Cookies	2052	D	949 519-0791	2061
Del Taco Restaurants Inc **(PA)**	6794	C	949 462-9300	16204
Drcollins Inc	3843	E	888 583-6048	11171
Dss Networks Inc	3577	F	949 981-3473	8251
Dynacast LLC	3364	C	949 707-1211	6379
Ellison Educational Eqp Inc **(PA)**	3554	D	949 598-8822	7914
Environmental Resolutions Inc	8748	B	949 457-8950	23438
Environments For Learning Inc **(PA)**	8351	D	949 855-5630	22012
Equimine Inc	7372	F	877 437-8464	17848
Experea Healthcare LLC	5047	D	949 716-3071	13486
Fanuc America Corporation	3559	D	949 595-2700	7974
Fieldcentrix Inc	7372	F	949 784-5000	17856
Focus Industries Inc	3646	D	949 830-1350	9085
Freedom Village Healthcare Ctr	8051	C	949 472-4733	20346
Ganahl Lumber Company	5031	D	949 830-3600	13211
General Monitors Inc **(DH)**	3669	C	949 581-4464	9343
Gigamem LLC	3572	F	949 461-9999	8199
Golden West Custom WD Shutters	5099	E	949 951-0600	14160
Greenshine New Energy LLC	3648	D	949 609-9636	9135
Hardy & Harper Inc	1611	E	714 444-1851	886
Heinaman Contract Glazing Inc **(PA)**	1799	E	949 587-0266	1665
Herbalife Manufacturing LLC	2087	D	949 457-0951	2329
Higher Ground Education Inc **(PA)**	8748	B	949 836-9401	23449
Hongfa America Inc	3625	E	714 669-2888	8955
I Source Technical Svcs Inc **(PA)**	3679	F	949 453-1500	9723
I/Omagic Corporation **(PA)**	3572	E	949 707-4800	8203
IMC Networks Corp **(PA)**	3575	D	949 465-3000	8225
Insight Hlth Svcs Hldings Corp **(PA)**	8071	C	949 282-6000	21072
Insulectro **(PA)**	5065	D	949 587-3200	13730
Itek Services Inc	7379	D	949 770-4835	18194
JB Brananne Inc	3089	E	949 215-7704	5680
Juniper Rock Corporation	1423	E	949 500-1797	564
La Strada Contracting Co	1522	F	949 680-4237	661
Lake Frest No II Mstr Hmwners	8641	D	949 586-0860	22344
Laminating Company of America	3672	E	949 587-3300	9421
Lauree LLC	7389	D	949 446-9900	18573
Life Care Centers America Inc	8051	D	949 380-9380	20395
Metronome Software LLC	7372	E	949 273-5190	17915
Mike Rovner Construction Inc	8741	C	949 458-1562	23065
Mission Pools of Escondido	1799	C	949 588-0100	1675
Monobind Sales Inc **(PA)**	3841	E	949 951-2665	11026
Nakase Brothers Wholesale Nurs	5193	C	949 855-4388	14890
Natures Image Inc	0781	D	949 680-4400	271
Nelson Moving & Storage Inc	4214	E	949 582-0380	12116
Oceania International LLC	3356	E	949 407-8904	6336
Panasonic Avionics Corporation **(DH)**	8711	B	949 672-2000	22630
Parsons Government Svcs Inc **(HQ)**	8711	D	949 768-8161	22632
Performance Building Services	7349	C	949 364-4364	17273
Premier Magnetics Inc	3677	E	949 452-0511	9638
Price Pfister Inc **(DH)**	3432	A	949 672-4000	6565
Pssc Labs	3572	F	949 380-7288	8212
Pura Naturals Inc **(HQ)**	2844	F	949 273-8100	5065
Qf Liquidation Inc **(PA)**	3714	C	949 930-3400	10118
Quantum Technologies Inc	1311	F	949 399-4500	409
Rapid Conn Inc	5051	E	949 951-3722	13587
Se-Gl Products Inc	3444	E	951 737-8320	6907
Semi-Kinetics Inc	3672	D	949 830-7364	9453
Semiq Incorporated	3674	F	949 273-4373	9573
Share Our Selves Corporation	8099	D	949 609-8199	21479
Shmaze Industries Inc	3479	E	949 583-1448	7410
Soaptronic LLC	2842	E	949 465-8955	4978
Sole Technology Inc **(PA)**	3149	C	949 460-2020	5887
Spectrum Brands Inc	3692	A	949 672-4003	9818
Staar Surgical Company **(PA)**	3851	B	626 303-7902	11263
Stanford Materials Corporation	2816	F	949 380-7362	4647
Streamline Finishes Inc	1542	D	949 600-8964	833
Sun Pac Storage Containers Inc	2448	F	949 458-2347	3410
T/Q Systems Inc	3599	E	949 455-0478	8810
Tenex Health Inc	3841	D	949 454-7500	11063
Topac USA Inc **(DH)**	5044	A	949 462-6000	13366
Toshiba Amer Bus Solutions Inc **(DH)**	5044	B	949 462-6000	13367
Toughbuilt Industries Inc **(PA)**	3423	F	949 528-3100	6491
TP Heritg Inn Lk Forest LLC	7011	E	949 461-0470	16756
Tri-Star Laminates Inc	3672	E	949 587-3200	9462
United Industries Group Inc	8711	E	949 759-3200	22682
Universal Printing Svcs Inc	2752	F	951 788-1500	4446
US Critical LLC **(PA)**	3572	D	949 916-9326	8222
US Real Estate Services Inc	6531	D	949 598-9920	16026
Vadnais Trenchless Svcs Inc	1623	C	858 550-1460	981
Vintage Design LLC **(HQ)**	1752	D	949 900-5400	1470
W B Starr Inc	0782	D	949 770-8835	351
Welcome Skateboards Inc	3949	F	949 305-9200	11457
Westamerica Communications Inc	8999	D	949 340-8942	23543
Wide Open Industries LLC	3711	E	949 635-2292	9973
Wonderware Corporation **(DH)**	7372	B	949 727-3200	18011
Xpo Logistics Freight Inc	4213	D	949 581-9030	12099
Young Engineers Inc	3429	D	949 581-9411	6545

LAKE ISABELLA, CA - Kern County

	SIC	EMP	PHONE	ENTRY #
Kern Valley Hosp Foundation **(PA)**	8051	B	760 379-2681	20385
Wick Communications Co	2711	E	760 379-3667	4045

LAKE VIEW TERRACE, CA - Los Angeles County

	SIC	EMP	PHONE	ENTRY #
Phoenix Houses Los Angeles Inc	8361	D	818 686-3000	22145

LAKEWOOD, CA - Los Angeles County

	SIC	EMP	PHONE	ENTRY #
Admiral Hospice Care Inc	8052	D	562 429-1500	20519
American Building Jantr Inc **(PA)**	0752	D	562 986-4474	211
Berro Management	6531	D	562 432-3444	15788
County of Los Angeles	7992	D	562 429-9711	19480
Eve Hair Inc **(PA)**	5199	E	562 377-1020	14928
Glacial Garden Inc **(PA)**	7999	D	714 502-9029	19651
Lakewood Regional Med Ctr Inc	8062	A	562 531-2550	20832
Long Bch - Lkwood Orthpd Med G	8011	D	562 633-3787	19964
Long Beach Seafoods Co	2092	E	562 432-7300	2346
Magma Products LLC	3631	D	562 627-0500	8992
Nationwide Theatres Corp	7933	A	562 421-8448	19404
Precision Netwrk Solutions LLC	7389	D	562 318-4242	18638
R and I Holdings Inc	6719	E	562 483-0577	16109
Sprint Intl Cmmunications Corp	4812	C	562 408-6978	12614
Tarzana Treatment Centers Inc	8093	D	562 428-4111	21349
Tenet Healthsystem Medical Inc	8011	D	562 531-2550	20104
TFC Manufacturing Inc	3444	D	562 426-9559	6930

LAMONT, CA - Kern County

	SIC	EMP	PHONE	ENTRY #
Grimmway Enterprises Inc	5148	C	661 845-3758	14637
Maxco Supply Inc	5113	D	559 646-6700	14212

LANCASTER, CA - Los Angeles County

	SIC	EMP	PHONE	ENTRY #
A V Poles and Lighting Inc	3646	E	661 945-2731	9076
Advanced Clutch Technology Inc	3714	E	661 940-7555	10007
Aerotech News and Review Inc **(PA)**	2721	E	661 945-5634	4050
Aerotech Precision Machining	3599	F	661 802-7185	8481
Antelope Valley Hospital Inc	8011	D	661 726-6180	19712
Antelope Valley Hospital Inc **(PA)**	8062	A	661 949-5000	20678
Antelope Valley Hospital Inc	8062	C	661 949-5936	20679
Antelope Valley Hospital Inc	8062	C	661 949-5000	20680
Antelope Valley Hospital Inc	8062	C	661 726-6050	20681
Antelope Valley Hospital Inc	8062	C	661 949-5938	20682
Antelope Valley Newspapers Inc	2711	E	661 940-1000	3945
Antelope Valley Surgery Ctr LP	8011	E	661 947-4600	19713
Antelope Vly Dom Vlnce Council **(PA)**	8322	C	661 949-1916	21713
Antelope Vly Retirement HM Inc	8051	C	661 949-5584	20245
Antelope Vly Retirement HM Inc	8059	C	661 948-7501	20551
Antelope Vly Retirement HM Inc	8059	C	661 949-5524	20552
Antelope Vly Schl Trnsp Agcy	4151	C	661 952-3106	11917
Arrow Transit Mix	3273	E	661 945-7600	6069
Automobile Club Southern Cal	8699	D	661 948-7361	22421
BDR Industries Inc **(PA)**	4841	D	661 940-8554	12751
C D R Enterprises Inc	1742	D	661 940-0344	1368
California Dairy Distributors **(PA)**	5143	D	661 948-0829	14539
Christian Bethel School	8351	D	661 943-2224	22004
County of Los Angeles	8111	C	661 974-7700	21538
County of Los Angeles	8093	D	661 524-2005	21294
Deluxe Corporation	2782	B	661 942-1144	4609
Desert Haven Enterprises Inc	0782	A	661 948-3402	300
Directv Group Holdings LLC	4841	C	661 632-5562	12759
Do It Right Products LLC **(PA)**	3272	E	661 722-9664	6027
Excel Contractors Inc	1521	D	661 942-6944	604
Go Get Em Inc	7382	D	702 985 5637	18381
Griff Industries Inc	3089	F	661 728-0111	5657
H W Hunter Inc **(PA)**	7538	D	661 948-8411	18838
Hartwig Realty Inc **(PA)**	6531	D	661 948-8424	15880
Harvest Farms Inc	2038	D	661 945-3636	1929
Hemme Hay & Feed Inc	5191	D	661 942-7880	14861
High Dsert Med Corp A Med Grou **(PA)**	8011	C	661 945-5984	19844
Iheartcommunications Inc	4832	D	661 942-1268	12693
J & R Machine Works	3599	E	661 945-8826	8633
Johnson Ford **(PA)**	7538	C	888 483-0454	18844
Kaiser Foundation Hospitals	8099	C	661 729-7250	21446
Kaiser Foundation Hospitals	8062	A	661 726-2500	20804
Kaiser Foundation Hospitals	8062	A	661 949-5000	20810
Kaiser Foundation Hospitals	8011	C	661 951-0070	19905
Keolis Transit America Inc	4111	D	661 341-3910	11814
Lancaster Cmnty Svcs Fndtion I	7538	C	661 723-6230	18851
Lancaster Crdlgy Med Group Inc **(PA)**	8011	D	661 726-3058	19956
Lantz Security Systems Inc **(PA)**	7381	D	661 949-3565	18294
Loandepotcom LLC	6162	A	661 202-1700	15211
Lowes Home Centers LLC	5031	C	661 341-9000	13255
McWhirter Steel Inc	3441	D	661 951-8998	6634
Merrill Lynch Prce Fnner Smith	6211	D	661 802-0764	15279
Mission Linen Supply	7213	D	661 948-5052	16855
Morton Grinding Inc	3965	C	661 298-0895	11499
National Band Saw Company	3556	F	661 294-9552	7946
National Metal Stampings Inc	3469	D	661 945-1157	7168
Nibbelink Masonry Cnstr Corp	1741	D	661 948-7859	1350
Opsec Specialized Protection	7381	D	661 942-3999	18304
Pacific Seismic Products Inc	3491	E	661 942-4499	7451
Pavement Recycling Systems Inc	2951	D	661 948-5599	5276
PCI Care Venture I	8051	D	661 949-2177	20438
Plastic Mart Inc	2821	F	310 268-1404	4709
Precision Welding Inc	3441	E	661 729-3436	6652
Prints 4 Life	2752	E	661 942-2233	4404
Quality Behavior Solutions Inc	8093	D	818 991-7722	21332
Radford Cabinets Inc	2511	D	661 729-8931	3486
Radnet Management I Inc	8011	C	661 945-5855	20036
Robert F Chapman Inc	3444	D	661 940-9482	6903
SA Recycling LLC	4953	D	661 723-1383	12975
Santa Barbara Trnsp Corp	4151	C	661 510-0566	11937
Sarah Elizabeth Treusdell	8093	E	661 949-0131	21338
SE Acqstion Lncaster Cal Inc **(DH)**	7261	D	661 942-1139	16929
Sierra Primary Care Medical **(PA)**	8011	D	661 945-9411	20065
Simulations Plus Inc **(PA)**	7373	D	661 723-7723	18065
Spiral Technology Inc	8711	D	661 723-3148	22658
Sprint Communications Co LP	4812	C	661 951-8927	12613
Sygma Network Inc	5141	C	661 723-0405	14511

(P-0000) Products & Services Section entry number
(PA)=Parent Co (HQ)=Headquarters (DH)=Div Headquarters

	SIC	EMP	PHONE	ENTRY #
Tarzana Treatment Centers Inc	8093	D	661 726-2630	21351
United Parcel Service Inc	4215	C	800 828-8264	12158
US Carenet Services LLC	8082	C	661 945-7350	21227
V Troth Inc	6531	D	661 948-4646	16027

LAWNDALE, CA - Los Angeles County

	SIC	EMP	PHONE	ENTRY #
Automotive Aftermarket Inc	5013	D	310 793-0046	13045
Curry Company LLC	3545	E	310 643-8400	7852
Knr Devco	7011	D	310 676-1111	16528
Los Angles Cnty Mtro Trnsp Aut	4111	A	310 643-3804	11816
McCarthy Framing Cnstr Inc	1542	D	310 219-3038	791
Rockwell Enterprises Inc	5199	E	626 796-1511	14972
Ultimate Maintenance Svcs Inc	7349	E	310 542-1474	17295
Vellios Machine Shop Inc	3599	E	310 643-8540	8838
Westwood Building Materials Co	3273	E	310 643-9158	6128

LEBEC, CA - Kern County

	SIC	EMP	PHONE	ENTRY #
Six Continents Hotels Inc	7011	C	661 343-3316	16713
Technicolor Usa Inc	3651	A	661 496-1309	9199
Tejon Ranch Co **(PA)**	0173	C	661 248-3000	58

LEMOORE, CA - Kings County

	SIC	EMP	PHONE	ENTRY #
Adventist Hlth Systm/West Corp	8062	D	559 924-7711	20660
Agusa	2099	E	559 924-4785	2386
City of Lemoore	4953	E	559 924-6744	12939
Gar Bennett LLC	1711	E	559 582-9336	1073
Kay and Associates Inc	3721	E	559 410-0917	10193
Leprino Foods Company	2022	B	559 924-7722	1777
Leprino Foods Company	2022	C	559 924-7939	1778
Olam Tomato Processors Inc	2033	E	559 447-1390	1872
Tachi Palace Casino Resort	7011	A	559 924-7751	16751
Wood Bros Inc	1629	D	559 924-7715	1009

LINDSAY, CA - Tulare County

	SIC	EMP	PHONE	ENTRY #
Arts Custom Cabinets Inc	2511	E	559 562-2766	3461
California Silver-Agriculture	0851	E	559 562-3795	371
Califrnia Citrus Producers Inc	2037	D	559 562-5169	1895
Doug Deleo Welding Inc	7692	F	559 562-3700	18976
Harvest Container Company	2653	E	559 562-1394	3810
Lo Bue Bros Inc	0723	C	559 562-6367	181
Pallet Depot Inc	2448	D	916 645-0490	3402
Randy Nix Cstm Wldg & Mfg Inc	7692	E	559 562-1958	18994
Suntreat Pkg Shipg A Ltd Prtnr	4783	C	559 562-4991	12558

LITTLE LAKE, CA - Inyo County

	SIC	EMP	PHONE	ENTRY #
Cgp Holdings LLC	4961	D	760 764-1300	13009
Coso Operating Company LLC	4911	D	760 764-1300	12798

LITTLEROCK, CA - Los Angeles County

	SIC	EMP	PHONE	ENTRY #
Hi-Grade Materials Co	3273	D	661 533-3100	6094

LOMA LINDA, CA - San Bernardino County

	SIC	EMP	PHONE	ENTRY #
ABI Document Support Svcs LLC	7389	D	909 793-0613	18429
Bakell LLC	1541	D	800 292-2137	689
Chancellor Hlth Care Cal I Inc **(PA)**	8059	D	909 796-0235	20570
Dvele Inc	2451	E	909 796-2561	3420
Dvele Omega Corporation	2451	D	909 796-2561	3421
Heritage Health Care Inc	8051	C	909 796-0216	20374
J & L Daycare	8361	D	909 796-2656	22118
J Riley Distillery Inc	2085	F	909 792-0510	2243
Linda Loma Univ Hlth Care **(HQ)**	8062	A	909 558-2806	20833
Linda Loma Univ Hlth Care **(PA)**	8011	A	909 558-4729	19961
Loma Linda University Med Ctr	8062	D	909 558-2100	20836
Loma Linda University Med Ctr **(DH)**	8062	A	909 558-4000	20837
Loma Linda University Med Ctr	8062	D	909 558-8244	20838
Loma Linda University Med Ctr	8062	D	909 558-4385	20840
Loma Linda University Med Ctr	8062	D	909 558-4216	20841
Loma Linda University Med Ctr	8062	D	909 796-0167	20842
Loma Lnda Univ Fmly Med Group	8011	D	909 558-6600	19963
Mountain View Child Care Inc **(PA)**	8062	B	909 796-6915	20867
South Coast Childrens Soc Inc	8322	C	909 478-3377	21891
Veterans Health Administration	8011	C	909 825-7084	20149

LOMITA, CA - Los Angeles County

	SIC	EMP	PHONE	ENTRY #
Kaiser Foundation Hospitals	8011	C	310 325-6542	19869
Kaiser Foundation Hospitals	8011	C	310 325-6542	19906
Kaiser Foundation Hospitals	8093	C	424 251-7000	21316
Lomita Verde Inc	8059	D	310 325-1970	20600
Robinson Textiles Inc	2311	F	310 527-8110	2748
Torrance Amateur Rdo Assn Inc	8699	E	310 245-0989	22465

LOMPOC, CA - Santa Barbara County

	SIC	EMP	PHONE	ENTRY #
Analex Corporation	8711	C	805 605-3898	22488
Authority of Housing **(PA)**	6531	D	805 736-3423	15778
Automobile Club Southern Cal	8699	D	805 735-2731	22439
Babcock Enterprises Inc	0172	E	805 736-1455	42
Channel Islnds Yung MNS Chrstn	8641	D	805 736-3483	22326
Citiznship Immigration Svcs US	8111	D	805 588-7002	21531
Crestwood Behavioral Hlth Inc	8051	D	805 308-8720	20307
Ghc of Lompoc LLC	8093	D	805 735-4010	21306
Hilliard Bruce Vineyards LLC **(PA)**	2084	F	805 736-5366	2192
Horizon Well Logging Inc	1389	E	805 733-0972	509
Imerys Minerals California Inc	1481	A	805 736-1221	582
Imerys Minerals California Inc **(DH)**	1499	D	805 736-1221	587
Kustom Kanopies Inc	1541	E	801 399-3400	707
Lompoc Valley Medical Center	8062	C	805 735-9229	20843
Lompoc Valley Medical Center **(PA)**	8062	B	805 737-3300	20844
Lompoc Valley Medical Center	8062	C	805 736-3466	20845
Melville Winery LLC	2084	F	805 735-7030	2207
Orbital Sciences LLC	3812	B	805 734-5400	10632
Santa Barbara Farms LLC **(PA)**	0161	C	805 736-9776	19
Serco Services Inc	7371	C	805 736-3584	17710
Stolpman Vineyards LLC	2084	E	805 736-5000	2223
United Paradyne Corporation	8741	D	805 734-4734	23133
Valiant Technical Services Inc	3731	D	757 628-9500	10455
Valley Med Group Lompoc Inc	8062	D	805 736-1253	20999
Windsor Capital Group Inc	7011	D	805 735-8311	16790

LONE PINE, CA - Inyo County

	SIC	EMP	PHONE	ENTRY #
Frontier Motel Inc	7011	D	760 876-5571	16450
Southern Inyo Healthcare Dst	8062	C	760 876-5501	20950

LONG BEACH, CA - Los Angeles County

	SIC	EMP	PHONE	ENTRY #
A & A Aerospace Inc	3728	F	562 901-6803	10229
A & A Aerospace Inc	3728	F	562 901-6803	10230
A Cdg Boeing Company	3728	E	562 608-2000	10231
A W Chang Corporation **(PA)**	5131	E	310 764-2000	14300
A-Throne Co Inc	7359	D	562 981-1197	17324
Ace Parking Management Inc	7521	D	562 437-6700	18762
Acme Headlining Co	3714	D	562 432-0281	10003
Acom Solutions Inc **(PA)**	7371	E	562 424-7899	17537
Advanced Medical MGT Inc	8741	D	562 766-2000	22967
Advertising Consultants Inc **(PA)**	7319	E	310 233-2750	17093
Advocacy For Rspect Chice - Lo **(PA)**	8331	D	562 597-7716	21936
Aero-Mechanical Engrg Inc	3599	F	323 682-0961	8476
AES Alamitos LLC	4911	D	562 493-7891	12795
Agilon Health Management Inc	8099	A	562 256-3800	21371
Air Rutter International LLC	4522	E	855 359-2576	12334
Air Source Industries	2813	E	562 426-4017	4638
Aircraft Hardware West	5088	E	562 961-9324	14049
Alamitos-Belmont Rehab Inc	8051	C	562 434-8421	20241
ALI Roofg Mtls Long Bch Inc	5033	D	562 595-7377	13324
Altamed Health Services Corp	8099	D	562 595-8040	21381
American Corporate SEC Inc **(PA)**	7381	B	562 216-7440	18242
American Development Corp **(PA)**	6531	D	562 989-3730	15768
American Plant Services Inc **(PA)**	3312	E	562 630-1773	6187
American Textile Maint Co	7213	D	562 438-7656	16841
American Textile Maint Co	7213	D	562 438-1126	16842
American Textile Maint Co	7218	C	562 424-1607	16882
American Trnsp Systems	4142	E	562 531-8000	11908
APR Engineering Inc	3731	E	562 983-3800	10451
Apriso Corporation	7371	C	562 951-8000	17552
Aquarium of Pacific **(PA)**	8422	C	562 590-3100	22237
Argus Management Company LLC	8744	B	562 299-5200	23391
Arias Industries Inc	3714	E	310 532-9737	10018
Assocted Stdnts Cal State Univ	8641	D	562 985-4994	22311
Atlantic Mem Healthcare Assoc **(PA)**	8051	D	562 424-8101	20250
Automobile Club Southern Cal	8699	D	562 425-8350	22442
Aviation Repair Solutions Inc	4581	F	562 437-2825	12343
B & B Pipe and Tool Co **(PA)**	1389	E	562 424-0704	477
Bandag Licensing Corporation	3069	D	562 531-3880	5366
Beach Front Property MGT Inc **(PA)**	6531	D	562 981-7777	15784
Belmont Athletic Club	7997	D	562 438-3816	19543
Belmont Brewing Company Inc	2082	E	562 433-3891	2138
Berns Bros Inc	3599	F	562 437-0471	8527
Beta Operating Company LLC	1311	D	562 628-1526	391
Bethany Baptist School	8351	D	562 985-0714	21988
Big Studio Inc	2261	F	562 989-2444	2656
Bill Williams Welding Co	7692	D	562 432-5421	18970
Blyth/Wndsor Cntry Pk Hlthcare	8052	D	310 385-1090	20524
Boeing Company	3721	A	562 496-1000	10177
Boeing Company	3721	A	562 593-5511	10178
Bragg Investment Company Inc **(PA)**	7353	B	562 984-2400	17306
Bret Boylan Property Mgt	8741	E	562 437-7886	22992
Brightside Scientific Inc	3821	F	626 453-6436	10653
Brittany House LLC	8361	C	562 421-4717	22087
Brittney House	8082	D	562 421-4717	21144
Bryant Rubber Corp **(PA)**	3053	E	310 530-2530	5328
Cabe Brothers	7538	D	562 595-7411	18815
California Broadcast Ctr LLC	4841	C	310 233-2425	12752
California Plastic Cntrs Inc	3089	F	562 423-3900	5595
California State Univ Long Bch	8721	C	562 985-1764	22766
California Traffic Control	7389	D	562 595-7575	18465
Canzone and Company	3993	F	714 537-8175	11532
Capital Engineering LLC	8711	B	562 612-1302	22511
Careonsite Inc **(PA)**	8011	E	562 437-0831	19738
Cargomatic Inc	4731	D	866 513-2343	12428
Carrierx LLC **(PA)**	7371	D	562 437-1411	17575
Carroll Klly Trtter Frnzen A L **(PA)**	8111	D	562 432-5855	21527
Casey Company **(PA)**	5172	C	562 436-9685	14801
Catalina Channel Express Inc	4491	D	562 435-8686	12286
Cavanaugh Machine Works Inc	3599	E	562 437-1126	8544
CE Allencompany Inc	1629	E	562 989-6100	993
Century 21 Landmark Properties	6531	E	562 422-0911	15807
Child Lane **(PA)**	8351	C	562 427-8834	22000
Childnet Youth & Fmly Svcs Inc **(PA)**	8322	C	562 498-5500	21742
Childrens Clnic Srving Chldren	8011	B	562 264-4638	19746
China Mfg Solutions USA LLC **(PA)**	3632	D	562 537-8788	8997
Choura Venue Services	7299	D	562 426-0555	16947
Citibank FSB	6021	C	562 999-3453	14996
City of Long Beach	4581	D	562 570-2600	12347
Clean Hrbors Es Indus Svcs Inc	1799	E	562 436-0636	1647
Cloudstaff LLC **(PA)**	7361	B	888 551-5339	17407
Cmac Construction Company	1623	D	562 435-5611	943
Coastal Alliance Holdings Inc	6531	C	562 370-1000	15817
Coastal Closeouts Inc	7389	D	323 589-7900	18482
Coastal Cmnty Senior Care LLC	8082	C	562 596-4884	21150
Commercial Protective Svcs Inc	7381	A	310 515-5290	18263

GEOGRAPHIC

	SIC	EMP	PHONE	ENTRY #
Community Hospital Long Beach	8062	A	562 494-0600	20728
Compulink Management Ctr Inc **(PA)**	7371	C	562 988-1688	17582
Conservation Corps Long Beach	8331	C	562 986-1249	21946
Continental Graphics Corp	2752	D	714 827-1752	4260
Continental Graphics Corp **(HQ)**	7336	C	714 503-4200	17167
Continental Graphics Corp	8711	D	714 503-4200	22517
Control Switches Intl Inc	3625	E	562 498-7331	8946
Corridor Recycling Inc	4953	D	310 835-3849	12942
Cosco Agencies Los Angeles Inc **(DH)**	4731	D	213 689-6700	12440
County of Los Angeles	8011	D	562 599-9200	19775
Courtyard By Marriott	7011	D	562 435-8511	16391
Covanta Long Bch Rnwble Enrgy	4953	C	562 436-0636	12943
Covenant Care California LLC	8051	D	562 427-7493	20297
Coverance Insur Solutions Inc **(PA)**	6411	D	231 218-6100	15557
CPS Security Solutions Inc **(PA)**	7381	A	310 818-1030	18267
Crane Co	3492	C	562 426-2531	7455
Crestec Usa Inc	2752	E	310 327-9000	4269
Crown Equipment Corporation	3537	D	310 952-6600	7707
Cushman & Wakefield Cal Inc	6531	A	562 276-1400	15832
Custom Fibreglass Mfg Co	3792	C	562 432-5454	10539
Cw Industries	3441	E	562 432-5421	6612
Cw Industries Inc **(PA)**	7692	E	562 432-5421	18973
Davita Medical Management LLC	8099	D	562 432-5661	21412
Davita Medical Management LLC	8011	D	562 304-2100	19784
Davita Medical Management LLC	8011	D	562 420-1338	19785
Davita Medical Management LLC	8099	D	562 429-2473	21418
Davita Medical Management LLC	8011	D	562 988-7000	19786
Davita Medical Management LLC	8011	D	562 426-3333	19790
Daylight Transport LLC **(PA)**	4213	D	310 507-8200	12029
Demler Armstrong & Rowland LLP	8111	E	562 597-0029	21546
Denso Pdts & Svcs Americas Inc **(DH)**	5013	B	310 834-6352	13054
Design Science Inc	7371	E	562 432-2920	17594
Designory Inc **(HQ)**	7336	C	562 624-0200	17171
Dick Howells Hole Drlg Svc Inc	1381	E	562 633-9898	426
Dignity Health	8062	B	805 988-2868	20750
DK Valve & Supply Inc	7699	E	562 529-8400	19033
Duthie Electric Service Corp	7629	E	562 790-1772	18954
Dynamite Sign Group Inc	3993	E	562 595-7725	11544
E4site Inc **(PA)**	7371	F	714 242-5700	17605
Easy Care Mso LLC	8099	C	562 676-9600	21421
Ecamsecure	7382	D	888 246-0556	18372
Eco Services Operations Corp	2819	D	310 885-6719	4657
Edge Systems LLC	4225	E	562 391-2052	12201
Edge Systems LLC **(PA)**	3841	C	800 603-4996	10975
Edgewater Convalescent Hosp	8051	D	562 434-0974	20317
Elements Behavioral Health Inc **(PA)**	8093	C	562 741-6470	21303
Elite Craftsman **(PA)**	7349	C	562 989-3511	17240
Engineering Materials Co Inc	3965	F	562 436-0063	11496
Envent Corporation **(PA)**	8748	D	562 997-9465	23437
Epson Accessories Inc	5045	D	562 981-3840	13394
Erp Integrated Solutions LLC	7371	D	562 425-7800	17610
Everson Spice Company Inc	2099	E	562 595-4785	2430
Evolectric Incorporated	3429	F	714 260-7022	6516
Eye Physcans Long Bch A Med Gr	8011	D	562 421-2757	19809
F-J-E Inc	2541	E	562 437-7466	3646
Family Plg Assoc Med Group **(PA)**	8011	D	213 738-7283	19820
Farm Street Designs Inc	5182	E	562 985-0026	14841
Farmers Merchants Bnk Long Bch **(HQ)**	6022	C	562 437-0011	15022
Federal Express Corporation	4513	C	800 463-3339	12328
Federal Express Corporation	4513	C	562 522-4014	12329
Ferguson Co	3585	F	562 428-3300	8340
Ferraco Inc **(HQ)**	3842	E	562 988-2414	11104
Fine Quality Metal Finshg Inc	3471	F	562 983-7425	7259
First Bank and Trust	6021	D	562 595-8775	15000
First Team RE - Orange Cnty	6531	C	562 346-5088	15862
First Transit Inc	4111	D	310 515-8270	11808
Flynn Signs and Graphics Inc	3993	E	562 498-6655	11555
Foasberg Laundry and Clrs Inc **(PA)**	7213	D	562 426-7345	16852
Ford Wlker Haggerty Behar LLP **(PA)**	8111	D	562 983-2500	21557
Forty-Niner Shops Inc	7021	A	562 985-5093	16811
Foss Maritime Co Inc	4412	D	562 435-0171	12274
Foundation Property MGT Inc **(HQ)**	8742	E	562 257-5100	23221
Free Conferencing Corporation	4813	C	562 437-1411	12636
Frontier Engrg & Mfg Tech Inc	3599	E	562 606-2655	8594
Fulwider and Patton LLP	8111	D	310 824-5555	21561
Fundamental Tech Intl Inc	3823	E	562 595-0661	10695
G B Remanufacturing Inc	3089	D	562 272-7333	5648
Gambol Industries Inc	3732	E	562 901-2470	10464
Gazette Newspapers Inc	2711	E	562 433-2000	3982
Geodis Wilson Usa Inc	4731	B	310 507-6300	12462
George Oliveri Hair Design **(PA)**	7231	D	562 421-4744	16904
German Knife Inc	3541	F	310 900-1081	7732
Get	3589	F	562 989-5400	8383
Gh Group Inc	6719	C	562 264-5078	16101
Ginza Collection Design Inc	2335	E	562 531-1116	2885
Gladstones Inc	2091	F	562 432-8588	2341
Goodwill Srving The Pple Sther **(PA)**	7389	D	562 435-3411	18532
Greater Alarm Company Inc **(DH)**	7382	D	949 474-0555	18382
GTM Management Company Inc	1629	E	562 988-0449	998
Gulf Streams	3721	E	562 420-1818	10188
Gulfstream Aerospace Corp GA	3721	A	562 420-1818	10191
H Roberts Construction	3448	D	562 590-4825	6997
Hanjin Shipping Co Ltd	4499	A	201 291-4600	12299
Hapag-Lloyd (america) LLC	4731	D	562 435-0771	12469
Harbor Diesel and Eqp Inc	5084	D	562 591-5665	13903
Harding Containers Intl Inc	2448	E	310 549-7272	3391
Healthcare Services Group Inc	8999	A	562 494-7939	23535

	SIC	EMP	PHONE	ENTRY #
Healthsmart Pacific Inc **(PA)**	8062	A	562 595-1911	20783
Healthsmart Pacific Inc	8011	B	562 595-1911	19838
HEI Long Beach LLC	7011	C	562 983-3400	16470
Helloworld Travel Svcs USA Inc	4724	D	310 535-1000	12385
Herzog Contracting Corp	1629	C	562 595-7414	999
HFS Concepts 4 Inc	8712	E	562 424-1720	22720
Holland Construction	1521	D	562 285-5300	612
Hornblower Yachts LLC	4724	D	562 901-3420	12387
Howard CDM	1521	E	562 427-4124	613
Hufcor California Inc **(HQ)**	2542	D	562 634-3116	3685
Human Touch LLC	5021	D	562 426-8700	13138
Hutchison Corporation	1742	E	310 763-7991	1378
Hyatt Corporation	7011	B	562 432-0161	16498
Ignify Inc **(DH)**	7373	E	562 219-2000	18037
Ilwu Federal Credit Union	6061	D	310 834-6411	15069
Indel Engineering Inc	3732	E	562 594-0995	10466
Industrial Medical Support Inc	8099	A	877 878-9185	21442
Intercommunity Care Centers	8051	C	562 427-8915	20380
International Trnsp Svc LLC **(PA)**	4491	C	562 435-7781	12288
Intertrend Communications Inc	7311	D	562 733-1888	17024
Interval House	8322	C	562 594-4555	21819
Intervest Property MGT Inc	6513	E	562 634-5672	15728
Intex Recreation Corp **(PA)**	5091	B	310 549-5400	14081
Iqa Solutions Inc	8711	D	562 420-1000	22581
Ixys Long Beach Inc **(DH)**	3674	E	562 296-6584	9526
Jacobs Civil Inc	8711	C	310 847-2500	22583
Jacobson Plastics Inc	3089	D	562 433-4911	5678
Jbi LLC **(PA)**	2599	C	310 886-8034	3733
Jetblue Airways Inc	4512	C	562 394-4397	12307
Jewish Community Ctr Long Bch	8322	C	562 426-7601	21820
Jewish Fmly Chld Svc Long Bch-	8322	E	562 426-7601	21826
Jf Fixtures & Design LLC	7389	F	562 437-7456	18559
Jfe Shoji America Holdings Inc **(DH)**	5051	D	562 637-3500	13572
Joy Processed Foods Inc	2099	F	562 435-1106	2456
Jvckenwood USA Corporation **(HQ)**	5065	C	310 639-9000	13738
Kbr Inc	3624	E	562 436-9281	8938
Keesal Young Logan A Prof Corp **(PA)**	8111	D	562 436-2000	21597
Kirkhill Rubber Company	3069	D	562 803-1117	5387
Knorr-Bremse Evac LLC	3999	E	410 875-0900	11702
Kuster Co Oil Well Services	1381	E	562 595-0661	432
L A Cstm AP & Promotions Inc **(PA)**	2329	D	562 595-1770	2818
La Rutan	3999	F	310 940-7956	11704
Lb Beadels LLC	2064	F	562 726-1700	2091
Ld Products Inc	2621	C	888 321-2552	3760
Life Steps Foundation Inc	8322	D	562 436-0751	21840
Linde Gas & Equipment Inc	2813	E	310 816-9397	4640
Logomart Corporation	2759	F	714 458-3181	4540
Long Bch Hose Coupling Co Inc	5085	F	562 901-2970	13997
Long Bch Museum Art Foundation	8412	D	562 439-2119	22224
Long Bch Rscue Mssion Fndation	8322	D	562 423-2500	21842
Long Beach Care Center Inc	8051	C	562 426-3141	20403
Long Beach Cmnty Action Partnr	8399	D	562 216-4600	22196
Long Beach Day Nursery	8351	D	562 421-1488	22030
Long Beach Medical Center	8062	B	562 933-7701	20846
Long Beach Medical Center **(HQ)**	8062	A	562 933-2000	20847
Long Beach Medical Center	8062	B	562 933-0085	20848
Long Beach Memorial Med Ctr	8062	B	562 933-0432	20849
Long Beach Public Trnsp Co **(PA)**	4111	A	562 599-8571	11815
Long Beach Unified School Dst	4151	D	562 426-6176	11935
Long Beach Unified School Dst	6531	C	562 426-5571	15913
Long Beach Yacht Club	7997	D	562 598-9401	19580
Longwood Management Corp	8059	D	562 432-5751	20607
Lowes Home Centers LLC	5031	C	562 496-8120	13219
Lowes Home Centers LLC	5031	C	562 421-9996	13244
Lubeco Inc	2992	E	562 602-1791	5297
M O Dion & Sons Inc **(PA)**	5172	D	562 432-3946	14805
Macro-Pro Inc **(PA)**	7389	C	562 595-0900	18584
Macs Lift Gate Inc **(PA)**	3999	E	562 529-3465	11710
Malibu Ceramic Works	3259	F	310 455-2485	5989
Mangan Inc **(PA)**	8711	D	310 835-8080	22603
Manson Construction Co	1629	D	562 983-2340	1001
Marisa Foods LLC	2013	F	562 437-7775	1740
Marlora Investments LLC	8051	D	562 494-3311	20414
Martin Bauer Inc	2087	F	310 639-2100	2332
Maruhide Marine Products Inc	5146	D	562 435-6509	14573
Matrix Environmental Inc	1799	D	562 236-2704	1673
Matrix Industries Inc	1799	B	562 236-2700	1674
Medasend Biomedical Inc **(PA)**	8099	C	800 200-3581	21453
Medway Plastics Corporation	3089	C	562 630-1175	5707
Memor Ortho Surgic Group A M	8011	D	562 424-6666	19976
Memorial Healthtec Labratories **(DH)**	8062	E	562 933-0777	20859
Memorial Hlth Svcs - Univ Cal **(PA)**	8062	A	562 933-2000	20860
Mercedes-Benz RE	8731	E	310 547-6086	22851
Mercury Security Products LLC	3699	F	562 986-9105	9893
Merritt Hospitality LLC	7011	C	562 983-3400	16564
Metal Preparations	3471	E	213 628-5176	7281
Metra Electronics Corporation	3714	E	562 470-6601	10102
Mida Industries Inc	7349	C	562 616-1020	17264
Mike Cims Inc	2512	E	562 428-8390	3511
Mikron Products Inc	3061	E	909 545-8600	5359
Mitsubishi Cement Corporation	3241	B	562 495-0600	5980
Mkr Medical Supply Inc	5047	C	310 830-3980	13501
MNX Global Logistics Corp **(HQ)**	4731	D	310 981-0918	12484
Molina Healthcare Inc	8099	D	888 562-5442	21456
Molina Healthcare Inc **(PA)**	8011	A	562 435-3666	19984
Molina Healthcare Inc	8099	D	562 435-3666	21457
Molina Healthcare California	8011	C	800 526-8196	19985

Mergent email: customerrelations@mergent.com
1384
2022 Southern California Business Directory and Buyers Guide
(P-0000) Products & Services Section entry number
(PA)=Parent Co (HQ)=Headquarters (DH)=Div Headquarters

	SIC	EMP	PHONE	ENTRY #
Molina Healthcare New York Inc.	8011	C	888 562-5442	19986
Molina Hlthcare Cal Prtner Pla	6321	A	562 435-3666	15382
Molina Information Systems LLC **(HQ)**	7375	A	916 561-8540	18129
Molina Pathways LLC	8011	B	562 491-5773	19987
Motion Theory Inc	7336	C	310 396-9433	17180
Museum of Latin American Art	8412	E	562 437-1689	22228
Nalco Company LLC	2899	D	310 900-5400	5235
National Emblem Inc **(PA)**	2395	C	310 515-5055	3161
National Gypsum Mfg Office	3275	F	562 435-4465	6129
NC Dynamics Incorporated	3599	C	562 634-7392	8714
NC Dynamics LLC	3599	C	562 634-7392	8715
Neill Aircraft Co	3728	B	562 432-7981	10387
Neurosmith LLC	3944	E	562 296-1100	11386
New Alliance Insurance Brokers	6411	E	424 205-6700	15602
Nexjet Corporation	3721	F	562 395-3030	10196
Noble Investment Group LLC	7011	C	562 436-3000	16583
Noble/Utah Long Beach LLC	7011	C	562 436-3000	16584
Nuspace Inc **(HQ)**	3599	E	562 497-3200	8722
Oakwood Corporate Housing Inc **(PA)**	7021	B	877 902-0832	16812
Oakwood Worldwide LLC **(DH)**	8741	C	877 902-0832	23077
Obagi Cosmeceuticals LLC **(PA)**	2834	C	800 636-7546	4864
Ocean Blue Envmtl Svcs Inc **(PA)**	4212	D	562 624-4120	11985
Olympix Fitness LLC	7991	D	562 366-4600	19464
Omp Inc **(HQ)**	5122	C	562 628-1007	14274
Onewest Bank NA	6035	D	562 433-0971	15051
Onyx Global Hr LLC **(PA)**	8742	D	866 715-4806	23288
OPEN America Inc	7349	C	562 428-9210	17267
Oshyn Inc	7371	D	213 483-1770	17687
Overland Pacific & Cutler LLC **(PA)**	7389	D	800 400-7356	18624
Pacific Energy Resources Ltd **(PA)**	1311	F	562 628-1526	408
Pacific Maritime Freight Inc	4492	D	562 590-8188	12296
Pacific Occptnal Medicine Svcs	8062	E	562 997-2290	20879
Pacific Palms Healthcare LLC **(PA)**	8051	C	562 433-6791	20431
Pacific Shores Med Group Inc **(HQ)**	8011	D	562 590-0345	20017
Palmcrest Grand Care Ctr Inc	8051	D	562 595-4551	20432
Palp Inc	1611	C	562 599-5841	905
Panel Products Inc	3812	E	310 830-3331	10634
Password Enterprise Inc	3369	E	562 988-8889	6421
Pbf Energy Western Region LLC **(DH)**	2911	C	973 455-7500	5257
Pbi-Birkenwald Market Eqp Inc **(PA)**	5046	E	562 595-4785	13465
Pdf Print Communications Inc **(PA)**	2752	D	562 426-6978	4388
Perona Langer Beck A Prof Corp	8111	D	562 426-6155	21659
Piedmont Airlines Inc	4512	C	562 421-1806	12312
Pioneer Medical Group Inc	8062	D	562 597-4181	20895
Plasidyne Engineering & Mfg	3089	E	562 531-0510	5747
Plastic Fabrication Tech LLC	3089	F	773 509-1700	5752
Plastic Sales Southern Inc	5162	E	714 375-7900	14760
Polar Tankers Inc **(DH)**	4424	D	562 388-1400	12278
Port of Long Beach	4491	C	562 283-7000	12290
Posca Brothers Dental Lab Inc	8072	D	562 427-1811	21112
Pponext West Inc	8099	B	888 446-6098	21472
Primus Pipe and Tube Inc **(DH)**	3317	E	562 808-8000	6251
Prindle Decker & Amaro LLP **(PA)**	8111	D	562 436-3946	21664
Product Data Intgrtion Tech In **(PA)**	7373	D	562 495-6500	18059
Psav Holdings LLC **(PA)**	7359	B	562 366-0138	17369
Queen Beach Printers Inc	2752	E	562 436-8201	4413
Queensbay Hotel LLC	7011	D	562 481-3910	16646
Quest Dgnstics Clncal Labs Inc	8071	D	562 424-3039	21091
R & B Realty Group LP	6531	A	310 478-1021	15962
RAD Onc Inc	8011	D	562 492-6695	20033
Radiology Support Devices Inc	3841	E	310 518-0527	11048
Rance King Properties Inc **(PA)**	6513	C	562 240-1000	15746
Rastaclat LLC	3911	E	424 287-0902	11328
Rdc-S111 Inc **(PA)**	8712	C	562 628-8000	22739
Recon Refractory & Cnstr Inc	8711	E	562 988-7981	22645
Redbarn Pet Products Inc **(PA)**	5199	C	562 495-7315	14971
Rehabilitation Assoc Med Group	8011	D	562 424-8111	20040
Relativity Space Inc	3764	B	424 393-4309	10529
Retirement Housing Foundation **(PA)**	6531	D	562 257-5100	15975
Rmd Group Inc	8742	B	562 866-9288	23310
RMS Foundation Inc	7011	A	562 435-3511	16668
Roadex America Inc	4225	D	310 878-9800	12239
Rocket Lab Usa Inc	3761	A	714 465-5737	10516
Rsg/Aames Security Inc	3669	E	562 529-5100	9351
Rubbercraft Corp Cal Ltd **(DH)**	3061	C	562 354-2800	5361
Ruffin Hotel Corp of Cal	7011	B	562 425-5210	16677
Runa Hr Holdings Inc	7371	D	562 883-3546	17704
Safe Place For Youth Inc	8322	D	310 902-2283	21879
Safe Refuge	8093	D	562 987-5722	21335
Sanders Composites Inc **(DH)**	3728	E	562 354-2800	10412
Sanders Inds Holdings Inc **(HQ)**	2821	F	562 354-2920	4715
Sansani Cleaning Solutions LLC	3589	F	310 630-9033	8410
Sas Safety Corporation	3842	D	562 427-2775	11139
Save Queen LLC	7011	D	562 435-3511	16695
Scan Group **(PA)**	6324	B	562 308-2733	15451
Schneider Elc Buildings LLC	3699	C	310 900-2385	9910
Seachrome Corporation	3431	C	310 427-8010	6549
Sears Home Imprv Pdts Inc	1521	C	562 485-4904	637
Senior Care **(PA)**	6324	A	562 989-5100	15452
Senior Care Action Ntwrk Fndti	6324	D	562 492-9878	15453
Sephora Co LLC **(PA)**	2844	F	760 798-7654	5067
Sfpp LP	4613	D	323 636-4447	12376
Shield Security Inc	7381	B	562 283-1100	18335
Shimadzu Precision Instrs Inc **(DH)**	5088	D	562 420-6226	14064
Sj Controls Inc	3823	E	562 494-1400	10724
Smart & Final Stores Inc	5141	C	562 438-0450	14496
Smg Holdings LLC	6512	D	562 499-7611	15698
Snapshot Hair & Extensions LLC	3999	F	877 783-5658	11758
Solvay USA Inc	2819	F	310 669-5300	4670
Southern Cal Inst For RES Edca	8733	D	562 826-8139	22921
Southern California Edison Co	4911	C	562 529-7301	12849
Southern California Edison Co	4911	C	562 491-3803	12854
Special Dispatch Cal Inc **(PA)**	4214	D	714 521-8200	12119
Speed-O-Pin International	2591	F	562 433-4911	3716
SPEP Acquisition Corp **(PA)**	3429	D	310 608-0693	6538
Spinlaunch Inc	8742	D	650 516-7746	23331
Sportsmen Steel Safe Fabg Co **(PA)**	3499	E	562 984-0244	7571
St Mary Medical Center **(DH)**	8062	A	562 491-9000	20967
St Marys Medical Center	8742	A	562 491-9230	23334
Stearns Park	2531	F	562 570-1685	3632
Sterile Proc Svcs Amer LLC **(PA)**	7389	D	562 428-5858	18679
Su Casa Ending Dom Violence	8322	D	562 421-6537	21900
Superior Electrical Advg Inc **(PA)**	3993	D	562 495-3808	11608
Syncis Insurance Solutions Inc **(PA)**	6411	C	424 233-1764	15632
Ta Chen International Inc **(HQ)**	5051	C	562 808-8000	13599
Tabc Inc **(DH)**	3714	A	562 984-3305	10139
Talco Plastics Inc	3089	D	562 630-1224	5834
Talent & Acquisition LLC	7371	C	213 742-1972	17729
Tarzana Treatment Centers Inc	8093	D	562 218-1868	21350
Tatung Company America Inc **(HQ)**	3663	D	310 637-2105	9321
Telecare Corporation	8093	C	562 630-8672	21353
Tell Steel Inc	5051	D	562 435-4826	13600
Termo Company	1382	E	562 595-7401	470
Tesoro Refining & Mktg Co LLC	2911	D	562 728-2215	5261
Texollini Inc	2297	C	310 537-3400	2710
Three Star Rfrgn Engrg Inc	3585	E	310 327-9090	8350
Tonnage Industrial LLC	5085	E	800 893-9681	14026
Traffic Management Inc **(PA)**	7389	C	562 595-4278	18693
Transcendent Security Services	7381	E	562 850-3313	18346
Transltnal Plmnary Immnlogy RE	8011	D	562 490-9900	20111
Tristar Industrial LLC	5085	D	562 634-6425	14028
Tristar Insurance Group Inc **(PA)**	6331	A	562 495-6600	15486
Twining Inc **(PA)**	8734	C	562 426-3355	22960
Undercurrent Educational	2323	D	800 430-1183	2766
Union Pacific Railroad Company	4011	B	562 490-7000	11799
United El Segundo Inc **(PA)**	6531	D	310 323-3992	16025
Urban Commons Queensway LLC	7011	A	562 499-1611	16763
Urban Commons Queensway LLC **(PA)**	7011	D	562 499-1750	16764
URS Group Inc	8711	D	562 420-2933	22686
V A Desert PCF Federal Cr Un	6061	D	562 498-1250	15097
Valmont Coatings Inc	3479	F	310 549-2200	7424
Vanguard Lgistics Svcs USA Inc **(HQ)**	4731	D	310 847-3000	12550
Ventura Transfer Company **(PA)**	4213	D	310 549-1660	12090
Viacare Inc **(PA)**	8059	D	562 591-1411	20638
Villa Serena Healthcare Center	8051	D	562 437-2797	20498
Vinotemp International Corp	2519	E	310 886-3332	3573
Virgin Orbit LLC **(PA)**	3761	A	562 384-4400	10526
Virginia Cntry CLB of Long Bch	7997	C	562 427-0924	19626
W A Rasic Cnstr Co Inc **(PA)**	1623	B	562 928-6111	984
Walter Timmons Enterprises Inc	7538	D	562 595-4601	18887
Warren E&P Inc	1382	D	214 393-9688	473
Western Integrated Mtls Inc **(PA)**	2431	E	562 634-2823	3297
Western Tube & Conduit Corp **(HQ)**	3644	C	310 537-6300	9055
Winchells Franchising LLC	2051	E	562 437-8463	2052
Windes Inc **(PA)**	8721	D	562 435-1191	22820
Windsor Anaheim Healthcare	8051	E	562 422-9219	20510
Womenshelter of Long Beach	8641	E	562 437-7233	22377
World Trade Ctr Ht Assoc Ltd	7011	D	562 983-3400	16804
Worldwide Corporate Housing LP	7021	C	972 392-4747	16814
Worldwide Corporate Housing LP **(HQ)**	7021	A	562 473-7371	16815
Wyatt Precision Machine Inc	3451	E	562 634-0524	7051
Xerox Education Services LLC **(DH)**	5044	D	310 830-9847	13370
Yhb Long Beach LLC	7011	D	562 597-4401	16809
Young Mens Christian Associat	8641	D	562 624-2376	22384
Zwift Inc **(PA)**	7372	B	855 469-9438	18015

LOS ALAMITOS, CA - Orange County

	SIC	EMP	PHONE	ENTRY #
Absolute Sign Inc	3993	F	562 592-5838	11520
Advantage Plumbing Group Inc	1711	D	714 898-6020	1017
Alliance Spacesystems LLC	3624	C	714 226-1400	8936
Arrowhead Products Corporation	3728	A	714 828-7770	10279
Bar Bakers LLC	5149	D	562 719-0300	14675
Barrys Security Services Inc	7381	C	562 493-7007	18255
Bearing Inspection Inc **(DH)**	5085	C	714 484-9373	13974
Bloomfield Bakers	2052	A	626 610-2253	2059
Blue Sphere Inc	2311	E	714 953-7555	2743
Carol Electric Company Inc	1731	D	562 431-1870	1230
College Park Realty Inc **(PA)**	6531	D	562 594-6753	15823
Compass Transportation Inc	4789	D	310 834-4530	12566
Davita Medical Management LLC	8011	D	714 252-1135	19783
Dc-001 Inc	3812	F	833 526-5332	10581
Dwi Enterprises	3651	E	714 842-2236	9173
Epson America Inc **(DH)**	3577	A	800 463-7766	8255
Epson Electronics America Inc **(DH)**	3674	E	408 922-0200	9504
Flowline Inc	3829	E	562 598-3015	10884
Friedas Inc	5148	D	714 826-6100	14631
Ganahl Lumber Company	5031	D	562 346-2100	13210
Golf Design Inc	3949	F	714 899-4040	11421
Grating Pacific Inc **(PA)**	3441	E	562 598-4314	6620
Institute of Elec Elec Engners	8611	D	714 821-8380	22249
Katella Properties	8051	C	562 596-5561	20384
Kdc Inc **(HQ)**	1731	B	714 828-7000	1271
Lab Clean Inc	2842	E	714 689-0063	4967
Los Alamitos Medical Ctr Inc **(HQ)**	8062	A	714 826-6400	20852
Metcalfe Security Inc	1731	D	213 605-2785	1282

	SIC	EMP	PHONE	ENTRY #
Military California Department	8744	B	562 795-2065	23395
Millie and Severson Inc	1541	D	562 493-3611	708
Pcn3 Inc	1542	E	562 493-4124	805
Plh Products Inc	2452	B	714 739-6622	3429
Severson Group Incorporated **(PA)**	1542	D	562 493-3611	824
Southland Credit Union **(PA)**	6061	D	562 862-6831	15090
Spacesystems Holdings LLC	3624	F	714 226-1400	8939
Spinelli Graphic Inc	2759	F	562 431-3232	4576
Spintek Filtration Inc	3569	F	714 236-9190	8139
Sure Forming Systems Inc	1771	E	562 598-6348	1554
Tenet Healthsystem Medical Inc	8011	D	805 546-7698	20106
Thermo Power Industries	1742	E	562 799-0087	1406
Trend Offset Printing Svcs Inc	2752	B	562 598-2446	4440
Trojan Professional Svcs Inc	7375	D	714 816-7169	18134
Utbbb Inc	2052	D	562 594-4411	2076
Vanguard Space Tech Inc	8711	C	858 587-4210	22689
Verlo Industries Inc	2542	F	714 236-2191	3701

LOS ANGELES, CA - Los Angeles County

	SIC	EMP	PHONE	ENTRY #
180la LLC	7311	C	310 382-1400	16988
1integer LLC	7371	E	424 320-2977	17533
3bd Holdings Inc **(PA)**	7372	E	323 524-0541	17769
3dna Corp **(PA)**	7371	D	213 394-4623	17534
3l Capital I LP **(PA)**	6726	D	310 801-3789	16152
417 Stockton St LLC	7011	D	323 327-9656	16309
5 Design Inc	8712	D	323 308-3558	22705
550 Flower St Operations LLC	7011	C	213 892-8080	16310
5525 E Pacific Coast Hwy Inc	6798	D	323 669-9090	16226
5800 Sunset Productions Inc	2711	F	323 460-3987	3942
6417 Selma Hotel LLC	7011	C	323 844-6417	16311
656 Los Angeles Street LLC	8742	E	949 900-6160	23145
6th Street Partners LLC	2599	F	213 377-5277	3720
75s Corp	5093	E	323 234-7708	14106
88rising Inc	7812	E	626 372-7387	19088
8th Street Enterprise Inc	5145	D	213 622-9287	14552
901 West Olympic Blvd Ltd Prtn	7011	C	347 992-5707	16312
A & A Jewelry Tools Findings	3999	F	213 627-8004	11621
A & M Sculptured Metals LLC	3444	E	323 263-2221	6770
A & S Metal Recycling Inc **(PA)**	4212	D	213 623-9443	11947
A A Cater Truck Mfg Co Inc	2514	E	323 233-2343	3523
A Buchalter Professional Corp **(PA)**	8111	C	213 891-0700	21499
A Community of Friends	6513	D	213 480-0809	15716
A Filml Inc	7819	D	213 977-8600	19216
A M I/Coast Magnetics Inc	3677	E	323 936-6188	9618
A M S Partnership **(PA)**	6552	D	310 312-6698	16045
A S G Corporation	3999	F	213 748-6361	11622
A-1 Estrn-Home-Made Pickle Inc	2035	F	323 223-1141	1885
AAA Electric Motor Sales & Svc **(PA)**	5063	F	213 749-2367	13607
AAA Flag & Banner Mfg Co Inc **(PA)**	2399	C	310 836-3200	3187
Aakaa Inc **(PA)**	2339	F	213 221-7086	2909
ABB Enterprise Software Inc	3674	E	213 743-4819	9471
Abilities Recovery Center Inc	8093	D	310 488-1122	21269
Able Sheet Metal Inc **(PA)**	3444	E	323 269-2181	6773
Abode Communities LLC	6531	C	213 629-2702	15763
Abraxis Bioscience LLC **(DH)**	2834	C	800 564-0216	4774
Abraxis Health Inc **(PA)**	8099	D	310 883-1300	21369
Absolute Twing - Hllnbeck Div	7549	E	323 225-9294	18919
Absolute Usa Inc	3651	E	213 744-0044	9154
Accepted Co	2741	F	310 815-9553	4147
Access Finance Inc	7389	E	310 826-4000	18431
Accor Corp	7011	C	310 278-5444	16313
Accurate Courier Services Inc	4212	D	310 481-3937	11952
Accurate Plating Company	3471	E	323 268-8567	7196
Accurate Staging Mfg Inc **(PA)**	3999	F	310 324-1040	11624
Ace Attrney Svc Inc A Cal Corp **(PA)**	7389	D	213 623-3979	18433
Ace Beverage Co	5181	C	323 266-6238	14817
Ace Holdings Inc	3911	F	213 972-2100	11305
Ace Parking Management Inc	7521	D	310 575-3192	18756
Ace Parking Management Inc	7521	D	310 645-6025	18759
Aci International **(PA)**	5139	D	310 889-3400	14428
Action Home Health Care Inc	8082	E	310 659-9930	21127
Active Window Products	3442	D	323 245-5185	6687
Acuant Inc **(HQ)**	7372	C	213 867-2621	17775
AD Receivables Corp **(PA)**	1711	D	323 296-8787	1016
Adams Comm & Engrg Tech Inc	7379	C	301 861-5000	18156
Adcolony Inc	7371	D	650 625-1262	17538
Addaday Inc	3949	F	805 300-3331	11397
Added Value LLC **(HQ)**	8732	C	323 254-4326	22873
Adexa Inc **(PA)**	7372	E	310 642-2100	17778
Adfa Incorporated	3479	E	213 627-8004	7336
Adir Restaurants Corp **(PA)**	6794	B	213 201-2990	16200
Advance Paper Box Company	2653	C	323 750-2550	3782
Advanced Digital Services Inc **(PA)**	7812	D	323 962-8585	19091
Advantage Produce Inc	5148	E	213 627-2777	14611
Adventist Hlth Systm/West Corp	8062	D	323 646-2858	20652
Advexure LLC	3728	F	920 917-9566	10242
Aecom E&C Holdings Inc **(DH)**	8711	D	213 593-8000	22480
Aecom Global II LLC **(HQ)**	8711	D	213 593-8100	22481
Aecom Global II LLC	8748	C	213 996-2200	23402
Aecom MGT Svcs Globl Corp **(HQ)**	8712	B	213 593-8000	22706
Aecom Services Inc **(HQ)**	8712	C	213 593-8000	22707
Aecom Technical Services Inc **(HQ)**	8748	D	213 593-8000	23403
Aecom Usa Inc	8748	C	213 330-7200	23404
Aecom Usa Inc	8748	C	213 593-8000	23405
AEG Management Lacc LLC	8741	C	213 741-1151	22968
AEG Presents LLC **(DH)**	7922	C	323 930-5700	19301
Aercap Global Aviation Trust **(HQ)**	7359	C	310 788-1999	17325
Aercap US Global Aviation LLC **(HQ)**	3721	D	310 788-1999	10175

	SIC	EMP	PHONE	ENTRY #
Aero Precision Engineering	3444	E	310 642-9747	6776
Aero Shade Co Inc **(PA)**	2591	E	323 938-2314	3704
Aerospace Welding Inc	7692	F	310 914-0324	18966
Aerotransporte De Carge Union	4512	B	310 649-0069	12300
Aeroturbine LLC **(DH)**	7359	C	305 406-3090	17326
AES Heavy Equipment Rental Inc	7359	D	213 892-9720	17327
Afc Trading & Wholesale Inc	5141	E	323 223-7738	14451
Aftershock La Studios Inc	7371	D	650 450-9660	17544
Agencycom LLC	7372	B	415 817-3800	17779
Agron Inc	2353	D	310 473-7223	3023
Ahr Signs Incorporated	3993	F	323 255-1102	11521
Al Foods Corporation	5147	E	323 222-0827	14590
Aids Project Los Angeles **(PA)**	8322	D	213 201-1600	21708
Aiminsight Solutions Inc	7379	F	310 313-0047	18158
Air Lease Corporation **(PA)**	7359	C	310 553-0555	17331
Aircoat Inc	3479	E	310 527-2258	7339
Ajit Healthcare Inc	8741	D	213 484-0510	22969
Akerman LLP	8111	D	213 688-9500	21500
Al Asher & Sons Inc	7353	E	800 896-2480	17304
Alan Gordon Enterprises Inc	7819	E	323 466-3561	19218
Alan Lem & Co Inc	3231	E	310 538-4282	5945
Albion Knitting Mills Inc	2339	F	213 624-7740	2914
Alco Plating Corp **(PA)**	3471	E	213 749-7561	7202
Alcoholism Center For Women	8322	E	213 381-8500	21710
Alcott Ctr For Mntal Hlth Svcs	8093	C	310 785-2121	21271
Alex Velvet Inc	3911	F	323 255-6900	11307
Alger-Triton Inc	3645	E	310 229-9500	9056
All3media America LLC **(DH)**	7812	D	424 732-6600	19092
Allagash Industries Inc	3999	F	212 246-5757	11628
Allaquaria LLC	5199	D	310 645-1107	14909
Allbright Group La LLC	8699	E	310 402-3570	22395
Allen Media LLC **(HQ)**	7929	C	310 277-3500	19342
Allen Mtkins Leck Gmble Mllory **(PA)**	8111	C	213 622-5555	21502
Allhealth	3571	F	213 538-0762	8147
Alliance For Housing & Healing **(PA)**	8052	D	323 344-4835	20520
Alliance Ground Intl LLC	4581	C	310 646-2446	12339
Allied Pressroom Products Inc	3952	F	323 266-6250	11466
Allzone Management Svcs Inc	8741	B	213 291-8879	22972
Alna Envelope Company Inc	2754	F	323 235-3161	4465
Alpha Polishing Corporation **(PA)**	3471	D	323 263-7593	7208
Alpha Productions Incorporated	3444	F	310 559-1364	6780
Alpha Source Inc	8731	D	424 270-9600	22822
Alston & Bird LLP	8111	D	213 576-1000	21503
Alta Healthcare System LLC **(HQ)**	8062	C	323 267-0477	20670
Alta Hospitals System LLC **(HQ)**	8062	E	310 943-4500	20672
Alta Verdugo Consulting Inc	8052	D	323 257-5715	20521
Altamed Health Services Corp	8011	C	323 980-4466	19697
Altamed Health Services Corp	8011	C	323 276-0267	19700
Altamed Health Services Corp	8011	C	323 374-6848	19702
Altamed Health Services Corp	8099	D	323 307-0400	21378
Altamed Health Services Corp	8099	D	323 890-8767	21379
Altamed Health Services Corp	8011	C	323 728-0411	19703
Altamed Health Services Corp	8011	C	323 269-0421	19704
Altegra Health	8742	D	310 776-4001	23152
Altmans Products LLC **(HQ)**	3431	E	310 559-4093	6546
Altoon Partners LLP **(PA)**	8712	D	213 225-1900	22708
Altour International Inc **(PA)**	4724	D	310 571-6000	12379
Altour International Inc	4724	D	310 571-6000	12380
Altra Inc **(PA)**	2869	D	310 348-7244	5125
Alvarez Mrsal Bus Cnslting LLC	8742	C	310 975-2600	23153
Alzheimers Greater Los Angeles	8322	D	323 938-3379	21711
Amada Enterprises Inc	8051	C	323 757-1881	20242
Amanecer Cmnty Counseling Svc	8093	D	213 481-7464	21273
Amass Brands Inc	2833	E	619 204-2560	4737
Amays Bakery & Noodle Co Inc **(PA)**	2052	D	213 626-2713	2056
Amberwood Convalescent Hosp	8059	D	323 254-3407	20550
Ambiance USA Inc	2339	E	213 765-9600	2915
Ambiance USA Inc	2339	E	323 587-0007	2916
Ambiance USA Inc **(PA)**	2339	D	323 587-0007	2917
America Wood Finishes Inc	2851	E	323 232-8256	5087
American Airlines Inc	4512	C	213 935-6045	12303
American AP Dyg & Finshg Inc	2231	E	310 644-4001	2610
American Apparel Retail Inc **(DH)**	2211	D	213 483-0226	2557
American Contrs Indemnity Co **(DH)**	6351	C	213 330-1309	15494
American Eye Institute	8011	D	310 652-1396	19707
American Fruits & Flavors LLC	2087	E	323 264-7791	2308
American Funds Distrs Inc **(DH)**	6722	C	213 486-9200	16122
American Furniture Systems Inc	2522	E	626 457-9900	3604
American Marble & Granite Co **(PA)**	3281	F	323 268-7979	6133
American Marble & Onyx Coinc	3281	E	323 776-0900	6134
American Mutual Fund	6722	C	213 436-9200	16123
American Quilting Company Inc	2395	E	323 233-2500	3150
American Realty Advisors	6798	D	818 545-1152	16230
American Red Cross Los Angles **(PA)**	8322	C	310 445-9900	21712
American Soc Cinematographers	8621	F	323 969-4333	22265
American Soc Cmpsers Athors Pb	2741	E	323 883-1000	4150
American Spring Inc	3493	F	310 324-2181	7461
American System Publications	2741	E	323 259-1867	4151
American Tax Solutions	8721	E	323 306-7032	22759
American Textile Maint Co	7213	D	213 749-4433	16840
American Textile Maint Co	7213	D	323 735-1661	16844
American Trading Intl Inc	5145	D	310 445-2000	14556
American Zabin Intl Inc	2759	E	213 746-3770	4479
Americantours Intl LLC **(HQ)**	4724	C	310 341-9953	12383
Americas Gold Inc	3911	E	213 688-4904	11309
Ames Rubber Mfg Co Inc	3069	E	818 240-9313	5365
AMG Employee Management Inc	3873	F	323 254-7448	11300

Mergent email: customerrelations@mergent.com
1386
2022 Southern California Business Directory and Buyers Guide
(P-0000) Products & Services Section entry number
(PA)=Parent Co (HQ)=Headquarters (DH)=Div Headquarters

	SIC	EMP	PHONE	ENTRY #
Amgreen Solar & Electric Inc.	1711	E	213 388-5647	1026
Amgreen Solutions Inc	8742	E	213 388-5647	23155
AMpm Maintenance Corporation	2299	E	424 230-1300	2720
AMS - Exotic LLC	5148	D	213 612-5888	14614
Amtex California Inc	2391	E	323 859-2200	3091
Andaz West Hollywood	7011	D	323 656-1234	16325
Andersen Tax LLC	7291	D	213 593-2300	16935
Anderson Kayne Capital	6282	B	800 231-7414	15316
Anderson Kayne Inv MGT Inc **(PA)**	8742	D	310 556-2721	23156
Anderson McPharlin Conners LLP **(PA)**	8111	D	213 688-0080	21505
Andrews International Inc	7381	C	310 575-4844	18250
Angeles Clinic & RES Inst Inc	8011	D	310 582-7900	19711
Angeles Park Communities Ltd	6531	C	310 277-4900	15769
Angell & Giroux Inc	2522	D	323 269-8596	3605
Angels Garments	2329	F	213 748-0581	2799
Angelus Aluminum Foundry Co	3365	E	323 268-0145	6386
Angelus Sheet Metal Mfg Inc	3444	F	323 221-4191	6785
Angelus Shtmtl & Plbg Sup Inc	5074	F	323 221-4191	13822
Angelus Western Ppr Fibers Inc	5093	D	213 623-9221	14109
Animal Specialty Group	0742	D	818 244-7977	197
Ankura Consulting Group LLC	8748	C	213 223-2109	23414
Anodizing Industries Inc	3471	E	323 227-4916	7212
Anschutz Entrmt Group Inc **(HQ)**	7929	D	213 763-7700	19343
Anschutz Film Group	1742	A	310 887-1000	1365
Anschutz Film Group LLC **(HQ)**	3861	E	310 887-1000	11267
AON/Albert G Ruben Insur Svcs **(DH)**	6411	D	310 234-6800	15533
Apla Health & Wellness	8011	D	213 201-1600	19714
App Wholesale LLC	5149	B	323 980-8315	14669
App Winddown LLC **(HQ)**	2389	F	213 488-0226	3066
Apparel News Group	2721	E	213 327-1002	4052
Appetize Technologies Inc	7372	C	877 559-4225	17785
Apponboard	3652	F	707 933-7729	9211
Aptan Corp	2211	E	213 748-5271	2558
Aputure Imaging Industries	3229	F	626 295-6133	5930
Aquahydrate Inc	2086	D	310 559-5058	2255
Aramark Facility Services LLC	7349	C	213 740-8968	17215
Ararat Home Los Angeles Inc	8059	C	323 256-8012	20554
Arclight Cinema Company	7832	C	323 464-1465	19271
Ares Investments Holdings LLC **(HQ)**	6799	D	310 201-4100	16247
Ares Management Corporation **(PA)**	6722	B	310 201-4100	16124
Ares Management LLC **(HQ)**	6722	D	310 201-4100	16125
Argonaut	2711	E	310 822-1629	3946
Aries 33 LLC	2329	E	310 355-8330	2801
Armand Hmmer Mseum of Art Cltr	8412	C	310 443-7000	22216
Arnies Supply Service Ltd **(PA)**	2448	E	323 263-1696	3381
Aroma Spa & Sports LLC	7999	D	213 387-2111	19635
Arrowhead Brass & Plumbing LLC	1711	D	323 221-9137	1030
Arroyo Vsta Fmly Hlth Fndation	8011	D	323 224-2188	19716
Arthrtis Fundation PCF Reg Inc	8641	E	323 954-5760	22310
Arthur Dogswell LLC **(PA)**	2047	E	888 559-8833	1955
Artist Silva Management LLC **(PA)**	8741	C	323 856-8222	22979
Artwear Inc	5136	E	310 217-1393	14327
Arup North America Limited	8711	B	310 578-4182	22495
Arya Group Inc	1521	E	310 446-7000	593
Arya Ice Cream Distrg Co Inc	5143	D	323 234-2994	14535
Asbestos Instant Response Inc	1799	D	323 733-0508	1637
Ascot Hotel LP	7011	C	310 476-6411	16329
Asian PCF Hlth Care Ventr Inc **(PA)**	8399	C	323 644-3880	22170
Asian Rehabilitation Svc Inc	8331	C	213 680-3790	21941
Associated Entrmt Releasing **(PA)**	7812	E	323 556-5600	19097
Associated Students UCLA **(PA)**	8399	B	310 794-8836	22171
Associated Students UCLA	8399	C	310 794-0242	22172
Associated Students UCLA	8011	C	310 825-9451	19717
Associated Students UCLA	7336	C	310 206-8282	17160
Associated Students UCLA	2711	C	310 825-2787	3950
Assocted Ldscp Dsplay Group In	7389	D	714 558-6100	18450
Assoluto Inc	2339	F	213 748-1116	2919
Astourian Jewelry Mfg Inc	3911	F	213 683-0436	11312
Astrochef LLC	2038	D	213 627-9860	1916
AT&T Corp	4812	D	310 659-7600	12593
Ata-Boy	3999	F	323 644-0117	11634
Atelier Ace LLC	7336	E	503 546-6836	17161
Atelier Luxury Group LLC	2396	E	310 751-2444	3168
Athicon	8711	E	213 454-0662	22497
Atlas Spring Mfgcorp	3495	E	310 532-6200	7482
Attn Inc	7313	C	323 413-2878	17078
Audience Inc	2741	F	323 413-2370	4153
Authority Tax Services LLC	7389	D	213 486-5135	18452
Authorized Cellular Service	7629	D	310 466-4144	18952
Automatic Leasing Inc **(PA)**	5064	B	213 746-4117	13681
Automation Printing Co **(PA)**	2791	E	213 488-1230	4623
Automobile Club Southern Cal **(PA)**	6411	C	213 741-3686	15540
Autry Museum of American West	8412	C	323 667-2000	22217
Avalon Apparel LLC **(PA)**	2335	C	323 581-3511	2878
Avanzato Technology Corp	3559	E	312 509-0506	7963
Avery Group Inc	7349	B	310 217-1070	17217
Avis Roto Die Co	3544	E	323 255-7070	7779
Avison Yung - Southern Cal Ltd **(DH)**	6531	D	424 265-9200	15781
Aviva Family & Childrens Svcs **(PA)**	8322	D	323 876-0550	21719
Awesome Office Inc	5145	D	310 845-7733	14557
Ax II Inc	2241	F	310 292-6523	2615
Axaio Industries LLC	4813	E	323 504-1074	12627
Axminster Medical Group Inc **(PA)**	8011	D	310 670-3255	19718
Azitex Trading Corp	2259	D	213 745-7072	2651
Azteca Jeans Inc	2339	E	323 758-7721	2920
B & C Plating Co	3471	F	323 263-6757	7220
Baby Guess Inc	2369	D	213 765-3100	3039

	SIC	EMP	PHONE	ENTRY #
Babyfirst Americas LLC	7371	D	310 442-9853	17561
Bae Systems Controls Inc	3511	F	323 642-5000	7579
Baker & Hostetler LLP	8111	D	310 820-8800	21507
Baker & McKenzie LLP	8111	C	310 201-4728	21509
Bakers Kneaded LLC	2051	E	213 321-9952	1981
Ballard Spahr LLP	8111	D	424 204-4400	21510
Balmoral Funds LLC **(PA)**	6282	A	310 473-3065	15317
Bamko LLC **(HQ)**	8742	D	310 470-5859	23166
Banamex USA Bancorp **(DH)**	6712	C	310 203-3440	16091
Banc California National Assn	6021	E	310 286-0710	14991
Bandel Mfg Inc	3469	E	818 246-7493	7126
Bank of Hope **(HQ)**	6021	C	213 639-1700	14993
Bank of New York Trust of Cal **(HQ)**	6091	C	213 630-6327	15118
Banzai	5092	F	310 231-7292	14093
Barber-Webb Company Inc **(PA)**	3089	E	541 488-4821	5575
Barfresh Corporation Inc	2086	F	303 502-5233	2257
Barlow Group **(PA)**	8069	C	213 250-4200	21032
Barlow Respiratory Hospital **(PA)**	8069	C	213 250-4200	21033
Barnes & Thornburg LLP	8111	C	310 284-3880	21511
Barry Avenue Plating Co Inc	3471	D	310 478-0078	7221
Barrys Bootcamp Holdings LLC	5091	B	270 535-5005	14074
Barrys Bootcamp LLC **(PA)**	7991	B	323 452-0037	19438
Basic Industries Intl Inc	3443	C	951 226-1500	6729
Baxalta Incorporated	2834	B	818 240-5600	4793
Bb Co Inc	2339	E	213 550-1158	2922
Bdo Capital Advisors LLC	6282	C	310 557-0300	15318
Be Bop Clothing	2339	B	323 846-0121	2923
Beauty Tent Inc	3999	E	323 717-7131	11637
Bebe Studio Inc	2339	C	213 362-2323	2924
Becker Interiors Ltd	5023	F	323 469-1938	13159
Bee Darlin Inc **(PA)**	2335	D	213 749-2116	2880
Behringer Harvard Wilshire Blv	7011	D	310 475-8711	16341
Beitler & Associates Inc **(PA)**	6531	E	310 820-2955	15785
Bel Air Inv Advisors LLC **(DH)**	6282	D	310 229-1500	15319
Bel Air Presbyterian Church	8351	D	818 788-4200	21986
Bel-Air Country Club	7997	C	310 472-9563	19541
Bellrock Media Inc **(PA)**	7371	E	310 315-2727	17562
Benevolence Industries Inc	8322	E	310 800-7963	21723
Bep (lp) I LLC	1311	F	213 225-5900	387
Berg Lacquer Co **(PA)**	5198	D	323 261-8114	14905
Berkeley Hall Schl Foundation	8351	D	310 476-6421	21987
Best Box Company Inc	2653	E	323 589-6088	3786
Best-Way Marble & Tile Co Inc	3281	E	323 266-6794	6135
Bet Tzedek	8111	D	323 939-0506	21516
Beverly Hills Luxury Hotel LLC	7011	B	310 274-9999	16348
Beverly Sunstone Hills LLC	7011	D	310 228-4100	16350
Beverly West Health Care Inc	8051	D	323 938-2451	20254
Bgk Equities Inc **(HQ)**	6531	D	505 982-2184	15790
BH Centro Internacional LLC	6512	D	310 820-8888	15661
Big Chill	2024	F	310 441-0643	1810
Big3 Basketball LLC	7941	D	213 417-2013	19411
Biomat Usa Inc **(DH)**	8099	E	323 225-2221	21390
Bird Mrlla Bxer Wlpert Nssim	8111	D	310 201-2100	21517
Bitmax LLC **(PA)**	3669	E	323 978-7878	9334
Bizz Inc **(PA)**	5137	D	323 235-5450	14365
Blackstone Consulting Inc **(PA)**	8742	B	310 826-4389	23172
Blavity Inc	2741	E	818 669-9162	4156
Blc Residential Care Inc	8322	D	310 722-7541	21725
Blend Inc	6162	D	650 550-4810	15176
Blind Childrens Center Inc	8399	D	323 664-2153	22174
Bliss World LLC	7991	D	323 500-0921	19439
Bls Lmsine Svc Los Angeles Inc	4119	B	323 644-7166	11855
BLT & Associates Inc	7336	C	323 860-4000	17162
Blue Planet International Inc	5137	E	323 526-9999	14366
Blx Group LLC	6282	D	213 612-2400	15320
Blx Group LLC **(PA)**	8742	D	213 612-2200	23173
Bny Mellon National Assn	8748	D	310 551-7600	23419
Boaventure Brewing Co	2082	E	213 236-0802	2139
Bon Appetit Management Co	8741	C	310 440-6052	22989
Bon Appetit Management Co	8741	C	310 440-6209	22991
Bonne Brdges Mller Okefe Nchol **(PA)**	8111	D	213 480-1900	21520
Bonnie Brae Cnvlscent Hosp Inc **(PA)**	8059	D	213 483-8144	20563
Bot Travel & Staffing	7361	D	323 272-4911	17398
Braille Institute America Inc **(PA)**	8322	C	323 663-1111	21726
Breathe La Lhc LLC	8099	E	212 989-9332	21393
Breathe La Lhc LLC	8099	D	800 929-5904	21394
Breitbart News Network LLC	7313	D	424 371-0585	17080
Breitburn Energy Holdings LLC	1382	F	213 225-5900	442
Breitburn GP LLC	1311	F	213 225-5900	394
Brent-Wood Products Inc	2499	E	800 400-7335	3441
Brentwood Bmdical RES Inst Inc	8733	C	310 312-1554	22900
Brentwood Country Club	7997	C	310 451-8011	19550
Bright Foods LLC	2068	F	708 263-7771	2110
Brisam Lax (de) LLC	7011	D	310 649-5151	16355
Brite Plating Co Inc	3471	F	323 263-7593	7227
Broadreach Capitl Partners LLC	6799	A	310 691-5760	16249
Bromwell Company **(PA)**	3263	E	800 683-2626	5995
Bronze-Way Plating Corporation **(PA)**	3471	E	323 266-6933	7228
Browning Apartments	6513	E	213 252-8847	15720
Brud Inc	2741	F	310 806-2283	4159
Bruin Biometrics LLC	3841	F	310 268-9494	10954
Brush Research Mfg Co	3991	C	323 261-2193	11508
Bu Ru LLC	2339	F	424 316-2878	2926
Buena Ventura Care Center Inc **(PA)**	8051	D	323 268-0106	20266
Bungalow 16 Entertainment LLC	5094	E	310 226-7870	14126
Bunkerhill Indus Group Inc	2326	F	323 227-4222	2776
Burke Williams & Sorensen LLP **(PA)**	8111	D	213 236-0600	21524

GEOGRAPHIC

Employment Codes: A=Over 500 employees, B=251-500, C=101-250, D=51-100, E=20-50 F=10-19

2022 Southern California Business Directory and Buyers Guide

© Mergent Inc. 1-800-342-5647

1387

	SIC	EMP	PHONE	ENTRY #
Burlington Convalescent Hosp **(PA)**	8051	D	213 381-5585	20267
Burlington Convalescent Hosp	8051	C	323 295-7737	20268
Burning Torch Inc	2339	E	323 733-7700	2927
Burton Way Hotels LLC	7011	D	310 273-2222	16357
Burton Way Htels Ltd A Cal Ltd **(PA)**	7011	E	310 552-6623	16358
Burton-Way House Ltd A CA	7011	C	310 273-2222	16360
Busa Servicing Inc **(DH)**	6022	C	310 203-3400	15014
BV General Inc	8059	C	323 651-0043	20567
Bwr An Oglvy Pub Rltons Wrldw **(DH)**	8743	E	310 550-7776	23377
Byd Energy LLC	3694	E	661 949-2918	9821
Byd Motors LLC **(HQ)**	3714	E	213 748-3980	10026
Byer California	2253	D	323 780-7615	2627
C & F Foods Inc	2099	B	626 723-1000	2401
C M G Inc	2339	E	323 780-8250	2928
C&C Jewelry Mfg Inc	5094	D	213 623-6800	14127
C-Air International Inc	4731	D	310 695-3400	12426
C-Quest Inc	2331	E	323 980-1400	2839
Ca Inc	7373	D	310 670-6500	18021
Caa Sports LLC **(HQ)**	7941	D	424 288-2000	19412
Cabinet Master & Son Inc **(PA)**	2434	F	323 727-9717	3309
Caer Inc	2032	E	415 879-9864	1846
Cake Collection LLC	5149	E	310 479-7783	14678
Cal Quake Construction Inc	1389	E	323 931-2969	485
Cal Southern Assn Governments **(PA)**	8748	C	213 236-1800	23422
Cal State La Univ Aux Svcs Inc	8741	A	323 343-2531	22996
Calhoun & Poxon Company Inc	3613	F	323 225-2328	8889
Caliber Holdings Corporation	7532	D	323 913-4000	18785
Califia Farms LLC **(PA)**	5143	E	213 694-4667	14537
California Assn Realtors Inc **(PA)**	8611	C	213 739-8200	22243
California Childrens Academy	8351	C	323 263-3846	21993
California Club	8641	C	213 622-1391	22322
California Cmnty Foundation **(PA)**	6732	D	213 413-4130	16165
California Community News LLC **(HQ)**	2711	B	626 388-1017	3955
California Cryobank LLC **(PA)**	8099	D	310 496-5691	21395
California Dynamics Corp **(PA)**	3829	E	323 223-3882	10875
California Endowment **(PA)**	8399	D	213 928-8800	22175
California Fair Plan Assn	6411	D	213 487-0111	15546
California Metal Processing Co	3471	E	323 753-2247	7235
California Pav Grading Co Inc	1611	D	323 372-5920	869
California Rain Company Inc	5137	D	213 623-6061	14367
Califrnia Cstume Cllctions Inc **(PA)**	2389	B	323 262-8383	3068
Califrnia Hosp Med Ctr Fndtion	8062	A	213 748-2411	20691
Califrnia Realtors Mrtg Netwrk	8611	D	213 739-8200	22244
Califrnia Rhblitation Inst LLC	8062	D	424 363-1003	20692
Califrnia Scnce Ctr Foundation	8412	B	213 744-2545	22218
Calimex Deli	2051	E	323 261-7271	1988
Call To Action Partners Llc	6799	C	310 996-7200	16251
Callisonrtkl Inc	8712	C	213 627-7373	22712
Calrad Electronics Inc	5065	E	323 465-2131	13707
Camden Center Inc	8093	C	844 422-6336	21281
Camp Smidgemore Inc **(DH)**	2339	E	323 634-0333	2929
Candleberry Properties LP	7011	E	323 852-7000	16366
Canton Food Co Inc	5141	C	213 688-7707	14458
Canvas Worldwide LLC	7313	C	424 303-4300	17081
Canyon Partners Incorporated **(HQ)**	6211	D	310 272-1000	15263
Cap-Mpt **(PA)**	6351	C	213 473-8600	15495
Capital Brands LLC **(DH)**	5149	E	310 996-7200	14679
Capital Brands Dist LLC **(PA)**	3634	D	310 996-7200	9001
Capital Drywall LP	1742	C	909 599-6818	1369
Capital Group Companies Inc **(PA)**	6282	A	213 486-9200	15321
Capital Guardian Trust Company **(HQ)**	6733	D	213 486-9200	16174
Capital Kingz LLC	6531	E	888 470-4114	15796
Capital Research and MGT Co **(HQ)**	6282	B	213 486-9200	15322
Capnet Financial Services Inc **(PA)**	6159	D	877 980-0558	15161
Capsa Solutions LLC	3572	E	800 437-6633	8191
Cara Communications Corp	7812	E	310 442-5600	19107
Cardigan Road Productions	3679	F	310 289-1442	9688
Cardinal Glass Industries Inc	3231	E	323 319-0070	5947
Career Group Inc **(PA)**	7361	A	310 277-8188	17403
Carpenters Southwest ADM Corp **(PA)**	7011	D	213 386-8590	16367
Caruso MGT Ltd A Cal Ltd Prtnr **(PA)**	6531	D	323 900-8100	15798
Cast Partner	3369	F	323 876-9000	6412
Catame Inc **(PA)**	3965	E	213 749-2610	11495
Cathay Bank **(HQ)**	6022	C	626 279-3698	15015
Cathay General Bancorp **(PA)**	6022	D	213 625-4700	15016
Catholic Chrties Los Angles In **(PA)**	8733	C	213 251-3400	22903
Causeforce Inc **(PA)**	7389	D	323 654-9255	18472
Causeway Capital MGT LLC	6722	C	310 231-6100	16127
CB Richard Ellis Strgc Prtners	6512	D	213 683-4200	15662
Cbj LP	2721	E	323 549-5225	4055
Cbre Inc **(HQ)**	6531	C	213 613-3333	15800
Cbre Consulting Inc	8742	D	213 613-3750	23183
Cbre Global Investors Inc **(DH)**	6531	C	213 683-4200	15801
Cbre Globl Value Investors LLC **(DH)**	6531	C	213 683-4200	15802
Cbre Holdings LLC **(HQ)**	6531	D	213 613-3333	15803
Cbre Services Inc	8742	D	213 613-3333	23185
CBS Studios Inc **(DH)**	7812	B	323 634-3519	19108
Cdr Graphics Inc **(PA)**	2752	E	310 474-7600	4248
Cds California LLC	3861	F	818 766-5000	11269
Cdsnet LLC	8748	A	310 981-9500	23427
Cedars-Sinai Medical Center	8062	B	310 824-3664	20694
Cedars-Sinai Medical Center	8062	B	310 423-6451	20697
Cedars-Sinai Medical Center	8062	B	310 423-8965	20698
Cedars-Sinai Medical Center	8011	C	310 423-3849	19740
Cedars-Sinai Medical Center	8062	B	310 423-3277	20704
Cedars-Sinai Medical Center	8062	B	310 423-9520	20705
Cedars-Sinai Medical Center	8011	C	323 866-8483	19741
Cellco Partnership	4812	D	323 662-0009	12602
Cemcoat Inc	3471	E	323 733-0125	7237
Center For Crgiver Advancement	8631	E	866 888-8213	22288
Center Thtre Group Los Angeles **(PA)**	7922	C	213 972-7344	19306
Centerfield Media Holdings LLC **(PA)**	8742	B	310 341-4420	23186
Centric Brands Inc	2211	E	323 837-3700	2563
Century Properties Owners Assn	6531	E	310 272-8580	15811
Certified Aviation Svcs LLC	4581	D	310 338-1224	12346
Certified Enameling Inc **(PA)**	3479	D	323 264-4403	7352
Certified Frnsic Ln Adtors LLC **(PA)**	8721	C	310 432-6304	22769
Cha Health Systems Inc **(PA)**	8011	A	213 487-3211	19743
Cha Hollywood Medical Ctr LP **(HQ)**	8062	A	213 413-3000	20714
Champion-Arrowhead LLC	3432	E	323 221-9137	6556
Chan Family Partnership LP	8741	D	626 322-7132	23000
Channel 9 Australia Inc **(DH)**	4833	D	323 461-3853	12711
Charles Dunn RE Svcs Inc **(PA)**	6531	D	213 270-6200	15812
Charles Gemeiner Cabinets	2431	F	323 299-8696	3238
Chase Care Center Inc	8059	D	323 935-8490	20571
Chef Bobo Brand Inc **(PA)**	8351	D	800 977-8912	21996
Chicago Title Company **(DH)**	6361	D	213 488-4375	15497
Childrens Bureau Southern Cal **(PA)**	8322	C	213 342-0100	21743
Childrens Health Center	8011	D	310 825-0867	19747
Childrens Hosp Los Angles Med **(PA)**	8062	D	323 361-2336	20718
Childrens Hospital Los Angeles **(PA)**	8069	A	323 660-2450	21038
Childrens Hospital Los Angeles	8062	B	323 361-2751	20719
Childrens Inst Los Angeles	8322	A	213 383-2765	21745
Childrens Inst Los Angeles **(PA)**	8733	C	213 385-5100	22906
Childrens Institute Inc **(PA)**	8322	C	213 385-5100	21746
China Airlines Ltd	4512	D	310 484-18[illegible]8	12304
China Airlines Ltd **(HQ)**	4512	B	310 646-4233	12305
China Pacific Inc	1542	F	323 222-9530	753
Chinatown Service Center **(PA)**	8331	C	213 808-1701	21945
Chinese Laundry Inc	5139	E	310 945-3299	14433
Chol Enterprises Inc	3728	E	310 516-1328	10300
Choon Inc **(PA)**	2335	E	213 225-2500	2882
Christine Alexander Inc	2395	E	213 488-1[illegible]14	3152
Christmas Bonus Fund of The Pl	6733	D	213 385-6[illegible]61	16175
Chromal Plating Company	3471	E	323 222-0119	7239
Chrome Hearts LLC **(PA)**	2386	E	323 957-7544	3054
Chrome River Technology	7372	E	888 781-0088	17816
Churchill Management Corp	6282	E	877 937-7110	15324
Cim Group LP **(PA)**	7011	C	323 860-4900	16381
Cinnabar	7336	C	818 842-8190	17163
Cinnabar California Inc	7336	D	818 842-8190	17164
Citrix Systems Inc	7372	F	800 424-8749	17817
City Bean Inc	5149	F	323 734-0828	14681
City National Bank **(DH)**	6021	B	310 888-6000	14998
City of Los Angeles	0752	C	213 473-7511	212
City Paper Box Co	2653	F	323 231-5990	3793
City Wide Aquatics **(PA)**	7999	D	323 906-7953	19640
Civic Center News Inc	2711	F	213 481-1448	3963
CJ America Inc **(HQ)**	5149	D	213 427-5566	14682
CJ Foods USA Inc	2096	C	213 427-5566	2361
Ckcc Inc	2396	E	213 629-0939	3170
Clairmont Camera Inc **(PA)**	7359	D	818 761-4440	17337
Clark & Trevithick A Prof Corp	8111	D	213 629-5700	21532
Classic Couriers Inc **(PA)**	4215	D	323 461-3741	12125
Classical Silk Inc **(PA)**	7336	D	213 488-0909	17165
Clear Group Inc	7011	D	603 325-5600	16384
Clearview Capital LLC	6799	A	310 806-9555	16254
Cliftonlarsonallen LLP	8721	D	310 273-2501	22773
Clinic Inc	8011	D	323 730-1920	19751
Clinica Msr Oscar A Romero **(PA)**	8011	D	213 989-7700	19752
Clinics On Demand Inc	8082	D	310 709-7355	21149
Closet Factory Inc **(PA)**	1799	D	310 516-7000	1648
Clothing Illustrated Inc **(PA)**	2339	E	213 403-9950	2934
Club Assist North America Inc **(DH)**	5013	D	213 388-4333	13053
CMH Records Inc	3652	E	323 663-8098	9212
Coalition Technologies LLC	7371	E	310 905-8268	17579
Coast Heat Treating Co	3398	F	323 263-6944	6436
Coast Produce Company **(PA)**	5148	C	213 955-4900	14618
Coating Specialties Inc	3728	F	310 639-6900	10301
Coda Automotive Inc	3714	E	310 820-3611	10032
Cohen Asset Management Inc **(PA)**	8741	D	310 860-0598	23005
Collab Inc	7311	D	310 991-0062	16999
Colon Manufacturing Inc **(PA)**	2331	F	213 749-6149	2840
Colormax Industries Inc **(PA)**	2211	E	213 748-6600	2564
Commercial Coating Company Inc	1611	D	323 256-1331	874
Commercial Property Management **(PA)**	6531	D	213 739-2000	15824
Commercial Shtmtl Works Inc	3441	E	213 748-7321	6603
Commodity Forwarders Inc **(DH)**	4731	C	310 348-8855	12438
Commodity Sales Co	2015	C	323 980-5463	1756
Community College Foundation	8322	E	213 427-6910	21754
Community Partners **(PA)**	8399	C	213 346-3200	22178
Community Redevelopment Agency **(PA)**	8748	C	213 977-1600	23430
Comprehensive Cmnty Hlth Ctr	8011	E	323 344-4144	19761
Concord Document Services Inc **(PA)**	7334	D	213 745-3175	17146
Concorde-New Horizons Corp	7812	D	310 820-6733	19110
Concurrent Holdings LLC	3629	A	310 473-3065	8974
Confido LLC	8082	A	310 361-8558	21155
Consensus Cloud Solutions Inc	7372	B	323 860-9200	17826
Consolidated Svc Distrs Inc	5145	D	908 687-5800	14561
Coopertive Amrcn Physcians Inc **(PA)**	8621	D	213 473-8600	22268
Corbis Images LLC **(PA)**	7221	F	323 602-5700	16893
Cordoba Corporation	7373	D	213 895-0224	18026
Core Medical Group Inc	8099	D	310 967-1884	21401
Coresite LLC	6798	D	213 327-1231	16232

Mergent email: customerrelations@mergent.com
1388

2022 Southern California Business
Directory and Buyers Guide

(P-0000) Products & Services Section entry number
(PA)=Parent Co (HQ)=Headquarters (DH)=Div Headquarters

Company	SIC	EMP	PHONE	ENTRY #
Cornerstone Research Inc	8732	D	213 553-2500	22877
Corridor Capital LLC (PA)	6799	C	310 442-7000	16256
Cougar Biotechnology Inc	2834	D	310 943-8040	4811
Country Villa Nursing Ctr Inc	8051	D	213 484-9730	20293
Country Villa Service Corp	8741	C	310 574-3733	23008
Country Villa Terrace (PA)	8059	D	323 653-3980	20574
County of Los Angeles	8099	D	213 739-2360	21402
County of Los Angeles	7375	D	213 974-0515	18119
County of Los Angeles	8069	D	213 974-7284	21042
County of Los Angeles	8062	C	310 668-4545	20738
County of Los Angeles	8093	D	323 897-6187	21291
County of Los Angeles	8011	D	213 744-3919	19765
County of Los Angeles	8011	D	323 226-3373	19767
County of Los Angeles	8721	A	323 267-2136	22775
County of Los Angeles	8093	D	323 769-7800	21292
County of Los Angeles	8069	D	323 226-3468	21043
County of Los Angeles	8099	D	213 351-7800	21407
County of Los Angeles	7371	A	562 940-4324	17585
County of Los Angeles	8062	C	323 226-6021	20739
County of Los Angeles	8011	D	323 730-3507	19770
County of Los Angeles	8011	D	323 226-7131	19774
County of Los Angeles	8062	C	213 473-6100	20740
County of Los Angeles	4789	C	213 974-4561	12568
Courtyard By Marriott/Lax	7011	A	310 981-2350	16392
Covenant House California	8361	C	323 461-3131	22097
Coway Usa Inc	3564	E	213 486-1600	8045
Cox Castle & Nicholson LLP (PA)	8111	A	310 284-2200	21542
CP Auto Products Inc	3471	E	323 266-3850	7244
CP Opco LLC	7359	D	209 524-1966	17339
CP Opco LLC	7359	D	310 966-4900	17340
CR & A Custom Apparel Inc	2759	E	213 749-4440	4506
Crave Foods Inc	2099	E	562 900-7272	2413
Create Music Group Inc	7389	D	310 623-0696	18495
Creative Artsts Agcy Hldngs LL (PA)	7922	A	424 288-2000	19308
Creative Channel Services LLC (HQ)	8742	A	310 482-6500	23199
Creative Circle LLC (DH)	7361	D	323 930-2333	17408
Creative Intelligence Inc	7389	F	323 936-9009	17168
Credible Labs Inc	5045	E	650 866-5861	13384
Crellin Machine Company	3451	E	323 225-8101	7034
Crenshaw Chrstn Ctr Ch Los Ang (PA)	7812	B	323 758-3777	19113
Crenshaw YMCA	8641	C	323 290-9113	22333
Cresa Partners Los Angeles Inc	6531	E	310 207-1700	15827
Crescent Capital Bdc Inc (PA)	6799	C	310 235-5971	16257
Crescent Capital Group LP (HQ)	6282	C	310 235-5900	15325
Crestline Hotels & Resorts Inc (HQ)	7011	C	213 629-1200	16399
Crew Knitwear LLC (PA)	2339	C	323 526-3888	2935
Crown Energy Services Inc	7349	A	213 765-7800	17235
Crucial Power Products	3679	E	323 721-5017	9697
Crystal Stairs Inc (PA)	8322	B	323 299-8998	21765
Ctbla Inc	3713	D	323 276-1933	9980
CTS Cement Manufacturing Corp	2891	F	310 472-4004	5180
Cuddly Toys	3942	F	323 980-0572	11359
Cuevas Mattress Inc	2515	F	310 631-8382	3545
Culinary Services America Inc	7363	E	323 965-7582	17489
Culver West Health Center LLC	8059	E	310 390-9506	20576
Cumming Management Group Inc	8711	D	951 216-6443	22520
Currency Capital LLC	7389	E	310 571-9600	18498
Cushman & Wakefield Cal Inc	6531	A	310 556-1805	15831
Custom Hotel LLC	7011	A	310 645-0400	16403
Custom Lithograph	2752	F	323 778-7751	4270
Custom Upholstered Furn Inc	2512	F	323 731-3033	3500
Cv & Da Holdings Inc (PA)	7532	D	213 261-4161	18786
Cvr Nitrogen LP (HQ)	2873	D	310 571-9800	5154
Cyber Medical Imaging Inc	3843	E	888 937-9729	11165
Cybercopy Inc (PA)	7334	E	310 736-1001	17148
Cyberdefender Corporation	7371	E	323 449-0774	17588
Cybrex Consulting Inc	7372	E	513 999-2109	17831
Czv Inc	3711	E	424 603-1450	9942
D Hauptman Co Inc	3949	F	323 734-2507	11411
Daily Doses LLC (PA)	2711	E	858 220-0076	3968
Daily Journal Corporation (PA)	2711	C	213 229-5300	3969
Daily Sports Seoul Usa Inc	2711	F	213 487-9331	3970
Dailylook Inc	7389	D	888 888-6645	18499
Damo Textile Inc	5137	E	213 741-1323	14369
Daniel J Edelman Inc	7313	D	323 857-9100	17083
Danning Gill Damnd Kollitz LLP	8111	D	310 277-0077	21543
Daqri (HQ)	7371	D	213 375-8830	17589
Darfield Industries Inc (PA)	3354	F	818 247-8350	6306
Davalan Sales Inc	5148	C	213 623-2500	14620
David H Fell & Co Inc (PA)	3341	C	323 722-9992	6291
David Haid	2599	E	323 752-8096	3724
Davis Wright Tremaine LLP	8111	D	213 633-6800	21544
Daviselen Advertising Inc (PA)	7311	D	213 688-7000	17004
Daz Systems LLC	7371	B	310 640-1300	17591
Dbv Inc (PA)	2834	E	323 857-5577	4813
Dcx-Chol Enterprises Inc (PA)	3671	D	310 516-1692	9360
Dcx-Chol Enterprises Inc	3671	F	310 516-1692	9361
Dcx-Chol Enterprises Inc	3671	F	310 516-1692	9362
Dcx-Chol Enterprises Inc	3671	E	310 525-1205	9363
Dda Holdings Inc	2339	D	213 624-5200	2938
De Castro W Chdrow Mndler Glck	8111	D	310 478-2541	21545
Decron Properties Corp (PA)	6531	D	323 556-6600	15835
Decurion Corporation (PA)	7832	D	310 659-9432	19272
Defined Cntrbtion Tr Fund For	6733	D	213 385-6161	16176
Delgado Brothers LLC	2499	E	323 233-9793	3442
Delivery Zone LLC	2099	F	323 780-0888	2419
Deloitte & Touche LLP	8721	A	213 688-0800	22776
Deloitte & Touche LLP	8721	C	213 688-0800	22777
Delta Floral Distributors Inc	5193	C	323 751-8116	14882
Dentons US LLP	8111	D	213 623-9300	21547
Dependable Highway Express Inc (PA)	4213	B	323 526-2200	12032
Design Collection Inc	5131	D	323 277-9200	14303
Designer Imports Intl Inc	5021	E	323 753-5448	13133
Desmond Mail Delivery Service	4212	D	323 262-1085	11966
Destinationrx Inc (DH)	7371	D	800 379-9060	17595
Deutsch La Inc	7311	C	310 862-3000	17006
Deutsche Bank National Tr Co (DH)	6111	D	310 788-6200	15133
Dfusion Software Inc	7371	E	323 617-5577	17596
Dg2 Worldwide Group LLC	7311	E	310 809-0899	17007
Diagnostic Health Corporation	8742	C	310 665-7180	23206
Dial Industries Inc	3089	D	323 263-6878	5626
Digital Domain 30 Inc (PA)	7812	B	310 314-2800	19116
Digital Media Management Inc	8741	D	323 378-6505	23017
Digital Printing Systems Inc (PA)	2752	D	626 815-1888	4276
Dinasty Security Services	7381	E	310 507-7848	18270
Direct Partners Inc (HQ)	7311	D	310 482-4200	17009
Directors Guild America Inc (PA)	7819	C	310 289-2000	19228
Disability Rights California	8111	D	213 213-8000	21549
Discovery Communications Inc (PA)	4899	C	310 975-5906	12784
Diversfied Mrcury Cmmnctons LL	7319	D	508 598-3569	17095
Divine Pasta Company	2099	F	818 559-7440	2425
Dlr Group Inc (HQ)	8712	C	213 800-9400	22713
Dng Fashion	3999	F	917 747-3158	11660
Docupace Technologies LLC	7371	C	310 445-7722	17600
Dolores Canning Co Inc	2032	E	323 263-9155	1849
Dominguez Firm Inc	8111	D	213 388-7788	21550
Dominion Corporation	6162	D	310 477-3041	15187
Don Alderson Associates Inc	2519	E	310 837-5141	3566
Donald T Sterling Corporation	7011	E	310 275-5575	16416
Dosa Inc	2339	E	213 627-3672	2942
Doubleline Capital LP	7389	C	213 633-8200	18505
Doval Industries Inc	3429	D	323 226-0335	6515
Dr Harold Katz LLC	2844	F	323 993-8320	5014
Drew Child Dev Corp Inc (PA)	8322	C	323 249-2950	21773
Drinks Holdings Inc (PA)	5182	C	310 441-8400	14840
Drissi Advertising Inc (PA)	7319	E	323 466-4700	17096
Dti Services Inc (PA)	7379	D	213 670-1100	18174
Duff & Phelps LLC	8742	D	213 270-2300	23209
Durkan Patterned Carpets Inc	2273	D	310 838-2898	2689
Dynamation Research Inc	3728	F	909 864-2310	10320
Dynamic Denim Corporation	2211	F	323 232-2524	2568
Dynamic Dezign	7336	E	562 735-3060	17172
Dynamics Orthtics Prsthtics In	3842	E	213 383-9212	11095
E & C Fashion Inc	7389	B	323 262-0099	18508
E & S Paper Co	5113	C	310 538-8700	14208
E & S Ring Management Corp	6531	D	310 337-5444	15842
E H Summit Inc (PA)	7011	D	310 476-6571	16423
E-Times Corporation Ltd	7375	D	213 452-6720	18121
Ea Mobile Inc	4812	C	310 754-7125	12607
Earth Technology Corp USA	4953	C	213 593-8000	12946
East Los Angles Rmrkble Ctzens	8322	D	323 223-3079	21774
East West Tea Company LLC	2043	C	310 275-9891	1948
Eaton Aerospace LLC	5063	B	818 409-0200	13623
EC Group Inc (PA)	5021	D	310 815-2700	13134
Eclipse Berry Farms LLC	0171	D	310 207-7879	26
Economic Dev Corp Los Angles C	8748	E	213 622-4300	23433
Ecosense Lighting Inc (PA)	5063	D	855 632-6736	13624
Edey Manufacturing Co Inc	3442	E	323 566-6151	6696
Edgemine Inc	5137	C	323 267-8222	14372
Edmund A Gray Co (PA)	3498	C	213 625-0376	7535
Eema Industries Inc	3648	E	323 904-0200	9127
Efaxcom (DH)	3577	D	323 817-3207	8252
Efilm LLC	7812	C	323 463-7041	19121
Egon Zehnder International	8742	B	213 337-1500	23210
Eharmony Inc (HQ)	7299	C	424 258-1199	16954
Eladh LP	8062	B	323 268-5514	20762
Elder Statesman LLC (PA)	5023	F	310 920-4659	13167
Electrical Rebuilders Sls Inc (PA)	3694	D	323 249-7545	9823
Electrolizing	3471	E	213 749-7876	7251
Elevator Equipment Corporation (PA)	5084	D	323 245-0147	13899
Elevator Research & Mfg Co	3534	E	213 746-1914	7677
Elijah Textiles Inc	5023	D	310 666-3443	13168
Elite Intractive Solutions Inc	7382	E	310 740-5426	18374
Ellison Institutional LLC	8734	E	513 403-2628	22941
Embroidertex West Ltd (PA)	2395	F	213 749-4319	3153
Embroidery One Corp	2395	F	213 572-0280	3154
Emerald Trans Los Angeles LLC	4953	E	323 277-2500	12950
Emerik Hotel Corp	7011	C	213 748-1291	16432
Emmis Publishing Corporation	5192	D	323 801-0100	14872
Emp III Inc	6799	D	323 231-4174	16259
Empower Our Youth	6732	D	323 203-5436	16166
Emser International LLC (PA)	5032	D	323 650-2000	13304
Englekirk Institutional Inc	8711	E	323 733-2640	22543
Englekirk Structural Engineers (PA)	8711	E	323 733-6673	22544
Engstrom Lipscomb and Lack A (PA)	8111	D	310 552-3800	22551
Entercom Media Corp	4832	D	323 930-7317	12688
Entertnment Studios Media Inc (PA)	7929	D	310 277-3500	19348
Entertnment Stdios Mtion Pctre	7929	E	310 277-3500	19349
Entravsion Communications Corp	4833	D	323 900-6100	12716
Environmental Science Assoc	8731	D	213 599-4300	22838
Epidaurus	6733	B	213 743-9075	16177
Epstein Becker & Green PC	8111	D	310 556-8861	21552
Eqh Limited Inc	3423	F	310 736-4130	6478
Equator LLC (DH)	7371	C	310 469-9500	17609

	SIC	EMP	PHONE	ENTRY #
Equinox-76th Street Inc	7991	D	310 479-5200	19447
Equinox-76th Street Inc	7991	D	310 552-0420	19450
Ergo Baby Carrier Inc **(HQ)**	3944	F	213 283-2090	11373
Ernst & Young LLP	8721	A	213 977-3200	22781
ESE Electronics Inc	5169	E	213 614-0102	14781
Esi Inc	3674	E	310 670-4974	9505
Essense	8999	A	323 202-4650	23533
Essential Access Health **(PA)**	8399	D	213 386-5614	22183
Ethically Made Goods Inc	2339	F	213 683-1123	2943
Eti Systems	3823	D	310 684-3664	10692
Euro Bello USA	2386	E	213 446-2818	3057
Eva Franco Inc	2337	F	213 746-4776	2902
Everpark Inc	7521	C	310 987-6922	18765
Everspring Chemical Inc	2899	F	310 707-1600	5219
Everytable Pbc **(PA)**	0722	D	917 319-6156	155
Evgo Services LLC	7549	C	310 954-2900	18924
Evocative Inc	7372	D	888 365-2656	17852
Evolve Media Holdings LLC **(PA)**	7311	C	310 449-1890	17012
Evoq Properties Inc	6531	D	213 988-8890	15847
Exactuals LLC	7372	F	310 689-7491	17854
Excel Picture Frames Inc	7699	E	323 231-0244	19037
Exceptional Chld Foundation	8331	C	213 748-3556	21951
Express Group Inc **(PA)**	4215	D	310 474-5999	12128
EZ Lube LLC	7549	D	323 930-9389	18925
EZ Lube LLC	7549	D	310 479-4704	18928
FAA Beverly Hills Inc	7538	D	323 801-1430	18826
Fabritex Inc	2221	F	213 747-1417	2598
Facter Direct Ltd	7389	B	323 634-1999	18517
Factory One Studio Inc	2211	D	323 752-1670	2570
Falck Mobile Health Corp	4119	D	323 720-1578	11865
Falcon Waterfree Tech LLC **(HQ)**	3069	E	310 209-7250	5376
Fame Assistance Corporation	8748	D	323 373-7720	23441
Family Industries LLC	3999	F	619 306-1035	11667
Farsi Jewelry Mfg Co Inc	3911	F	213 624-0043	11316
Fast Pay Partners LLC **(HQ)**	8721	D	310 651-9200	22783
Faze Clan Inc	7999	D	818 538-5204	19647
Fcti Inc **(PA)**	6099	D	310 405-0022	15128
Federal Express Corporation	4513	D	800 463-3339	12326
Federal Home Loan Mrtg Corp	6162	C	213 337-4200	15190
Federal Rsrve Bnk San Frncisco	6011	A	213 683-2300	14988
Fei Enterprises Inc	1731	E	323 937-0856	1253
Felbro Inc	2542	C	323 263-8686	3682
Felbro Food Products Inc	2087	E	323 936-5266	2323
Felix Chevrolet LP **(PA)**	7538	C	213 748-6141	18827
Fender Digital LLC **(DH)**	7371	D	323 462-2198	17614
Fetish Group Inc **(PA)**	2329	E	323 587-7873	2808
Fiesta Fashion Co Inc **(PA)**	5137	E	213 748-5775	14375
Film Payroll Services Inc **(PA)**	8721	D	310 440-9600	22784
Fineman West and Co LLP	8721	D	213 688-9898	22785
Fire Protection Group Amer Inc	8711	E	323 732-4200	22548
Firefighters First Credit Un **(PA)**	6061	C	323 254-1700	15065
First 5 La	8322	D	213 482-9487	21789
First Capitol Consulting Inc	8742	D	213 382-1115	23217
First Choice Bank	6022	D	213 617-0082	15023
First City Credit Union **(PA)**	6061	E	213 482-3477	15066
First Entertainment Credit Un **(PA)**	6061	D	323 851-3673	15067
First Fire Systems Inc **(PA)**	1731	D	310 559-0900	1254
First Legal Network	3825	E	213 250-1111	10753
First Legal Support Svcs LLC **(PA)**	8111	D	213 250-1111	21554
First Republic Bank	6022	D	213 239-8883	15025
First Republic Bank	6029	D	310 712-1888	15047
Firstservice Residential	8741	D	213 213-0886	23026
Fish House Partners One LLC	6799	D	323 460-4170	16262
Five Star Transportation Inc	4729	E	310 348-0820	12414
Flap Happy Inc	2369	F	310 453-3527	3040
Flash Code Solutions LLC	7372	F	800 633-7467	17857
Flaunt Magazine	2721	F	323 836-1044	4070
Flexogenix Group Inc **(PA)**	8062	D	213 622-6010	20770
Flight Centre Usa Inc	4724	D	310 458-3310	12384
Flint Energy Services Inc	8711	D	213 593-8000	22549
Flo-Mac Inc	3498	E	323 583-8751	7538
Fluor Fltron Blfour Btty Drgdo	4789	D	949 420-5000	12571
Focus Line LLC	3648	F	818 517-5171	9133
Focus On All Child Thrpies Inc	8059	D	310 475-9620	20582
Fonco Creative Services	7812	E	415 254-5460	19124
Food & Bev Innovations LLC	3556	F	888 491-3772	7931
Food-O-Mex Corporation	2099	F	323 225-1737	2434
Foothill Group Inc **(HQ)**	6021	C	310 453-7300	15001
For Cali Productions LLC **(DH)**	7819	C	323 956-9508	19233
For Cali Productions LLC	7819	D	323 956-9500	19234
Forme Life Retail LLC	5091	E	703 577-9585	14078
Formsolver Inc	2499	F	323 664-7888	3443
Fortiss LLC	7999	D	323 415-4900	19650
Fortuna Enterprises LP	7011	B	310 410-4000	16446
Fortune Swimwear LLC **(HQ)**	2253	E	310 733-2130	2633
Foster Planing Mill Co	2499	F	323 759-9156	3444
Four Points By Sheraton	7011	D	310 645-4600	16447
Fox Inc **(DH)**	4833	A	310 369-1000	12720
Fox Animation Studios Inc	7812	C	323 857-8800	19125
Fox Baseball Holdings Inc	7941	A	323 224-1500	19416
Fox Broadcasting Company LLC **(HQ)**	4833	C	310 369-1000	12721
Fox Hills Auto Inc **(PA)**	7538	C	310 649-3673	18831
Fox Intrntonal Channels US Inc **(DH)**	4833	D	310 369-8759	12722
Fox Net Inc	7812	A	310 369-1000	19126
Fox Networks Group Inc **(DH)**	4833	C	310 369-1000	12723
Fox Rent A Car Inc **(HQ)**	7514	E	310 342-5155	18741
Fox Sports Inc **(DH)**	4833	C	310 369-1000	12724
Fox Sports Productions Inc	4833	D	310 369-1000	12725
Fox Television Stations Inc **(HQ)**	4833	B	310 584-2000	12726
Fragrant Jewels LLC	3999	E	888 443-5049	11672
Frandzel Share Robins Bloom Lc	8111	D	323 852-1000	21559
Fred Leeds Properties	6531	D	310 826-2466	15871
Freedom Wood Finishing Inc	2269	F	213 534-6620	2671
Freeman Freeman & Smiley **(PA)**	8111	D	310 398-6100	21560
Freestyle Filmworks LLC	3861	F	818 660-2888	11276
Frisco Baking Company Inc	2051	C	323 225-6111	2002
Frm-Usa LLC	3497	F	323 469-9006	7525
Front Line MGT Group Inc	8741	D	310 209-3100	23028
Frontiers Media LLC	2741	E	323 930-3220	4173
Fti Consulting Inc	8711	D	213 689-1200	22558
Fuel Cycle Inc **(PA)**	7371	D	323 556-5400	17620
Fulghum Fibres Inc **(HQ)**	2421	F	706 651-1000	3210
Funny or Die Inc	7379	E	650 461-3929	18179
Futuredontics Inc **(HQ)**	8021	C	310 215-6400	20178
Fx Networks LLC	4841	C	310 369-1000	12768
Fyeo Apparel Inc	8099	E	213 278-0435	21429
G Kagan and Sons Inc **(PA)**	2211	E	323 583-1400	2572
G&A Apparel Group	2396	E	323 234-1746	3173
Gaju Market Corporation	5199	C	213 382-9444	14929
Gali Corporation	3728	E	310 477-1224	10333
Gannett Stllite Info Ntwrk LLC	2711	E	310 846-5870	3979
Gans Ink and Supply Co Inc **(PA)**	2893	E	323 264-2200	5203
Ganz USA LLC	5199	D	323 629-9871	14930
Garda CL West Inc **(DH)**	7381	B	213 383-3611	18278
Garden Crest Cnvlscent Hosp In	8051	D	323 663-8281	20349
Garden Grove Advanced Imaging	8011	C	310 445-2800	19827
Gardena Textile Inc	2253	F	310 327-5060	2635
Gateways Hosp Mental Hlth Ctr	8062	D	323 644-2026	20775
Gateways Hosp Mental Hlth Ctr **(PA)**	8063	C	323 644-2000	21019
Gaze USA Inc	2339	E	213 622-0022	2945
Gaze USA Inc	2335	F	213 622-0022	2884
Geartech Services Inc	3599	F	323 309-7861	8602
Gebe Electronic Services Inc	3479	F	323 731-2439	7367
Gehr Hospitality LLC **(HQ)**	6211	D	323 728-5558	15264
Gehry Partners LLP	8712	C	310 482-3000	22715
Gelfand Rennert & Feldman LLP **(PA)**	7389	C	310 553-1707	18525
Gem Box of West	2653	E	213 748-4875	3806
Gemini GEL Llc	2796	E	323 651-0513	4631
General Carbon Company	2819	E	323 588-9291	4659
General Fire Control	3827	F	323 260-7015	10835
Genesis Healthcare LLC	8059	C	323 461-9961	20590
Genter Capital LLC **(PA)**	6282	D	310 477-6543	15328
George Industries	3471	B	323 264-6660	7262
Giant Steps Trning Prgrams Inc	8331	D	323 733-6401	21953
Gibbs Giden Locher	8111	D	310 552-3400	21563
Gibson Dunn & Crutcher LLP **(PA)**	8111	B	213 229-7000	21564
Gilbert Klly Crwley Jnnett LLP **(PA)**	8111	D	213 615-7000	21565
Gils Distributing Service	7319	C	213 627-0539	17098
Gino Corporation	2321	E	323 234-7979	2756
Gipson Hffman Pncone A Prof Co	8111	D	310 556-4660	21567
Girardi Keese **(PA)**	8111	D	213 977-0211	21568
Girl Scuts Greater Los Angeles **(PA)**	8641	C	626 677-2265	22339
Giroux Glass Inc **(PA)**	1793	C	213 747-7406	1586
Giumarra Bros Fruit Co Inc **(PA)**	5148	D	213 627-2900	14633
Giving Keys Inc	3911	E	213 935-8791	11317
Glaser Weil Fink Jacobs **(PA)**	8111	C	310 553-3000	21569
Global Reach 18 Inc **(PA)**	6726	D	310 203 5850	16154
Global Sales Inc	2844	E	310 474-7700	5025
Global Wide Media Inc **(PA)**	7311	D	805 267-7000	17016
Globe Tire & Motorsports Corp	5014	D	310 836-0804	13116
Godigital Media Group LLC	4899	D	310 853-7940	12785
Gold Parent LP	6211	A	310 954-0444	15266
Golden International	6799	A	213 628-1388	16263
Golden State Mutl Lf Insur Co **(PA)**	6311	D	713 526-4361	15360
Goldman Sachs & Co LLC	6211	C	310 407-5700	15267
Golf Apparel Brands Inc	2339	E	310 327-5188	2946
Good American LLC **(PA)**	2339	E	213 357-5100	2947
Good Samaritan Hospital Aux	8011	C	213 977-2121	19833
Good Worldwide LLC	2741	E	323 206-6495	4176
Goodwill Inds Southern Cal **(PA)**	8331	A	323 223-1211	21956
Gordon Edlstein Krpack Grant F	8111	E	213 739-7000	21570
Gores Radio Holdings LLC	3699	D	310 209-3010	9871
Gores URS Holdings Corp **(PA)**	4213	A	310 209-3010	12048
Gourmet Coffee Warehouse Inc **(PA)**	2095	E	323 871-8930	2354
Grace Communications Inc **(PA)**	2711	E	213 628-4384	3983
Graceful Snscnce Adult Day HLT	8322	F	310 538-5808	21794
Grapefruit Blvd Invstments Inc	2833	F	310 575-1175	4747
Graphic Film Group LLC **(PA)**	2721	F	310 887-6330	4071
Greater Los Angeles Zoo Assn	8399	D	323 644-4200	22184
Greater Los Angles Area Cncil **(PA)**	8641	D	213 413-4400	22340
Greater Los Angles Vtrans RES	6732	D	310 312-1554	16167
Green Equity Investors IV LP **(PA)**	6799	A	310 954-0444	16264
Green Farms California LLC **(PA)**	5148	C	213 747-4411	14635
Green Hasson & Janks LLP	8721	C	310 873-1600	22786
Green Worldwide Shipping LLC	4731	D	310 988-1550	12465
Greenberg Glsker Flds Clman Mc	8111	C	310 553-3610	21571
Greenberg Traurig LLP	8111	D	310 586-7708	21572
Greenscreen	0781	E	310 837-0526	260
Greenspire LLC	8742	E	310 477-7686	23229
Greenwood Hall Inc	8741	C	310 905-8300	23032
Greneker Furniture	2541	F	323 263-9000	3648
Grenfield Consulting	1382	E	310 286-0200	454
Grey Studio Inc	2211	F	323 780-8111	2573
Grifols Biologicals LLC **(DH)**	2836	B	323 225-2221	4935

Mergent email: customerrelations@mergent.com
1390

2022 Southern California Business
Directory and Buyers Guide

(P-0000) Products & Services Section entry number
(PA)=Parent Co (HQ)=Headquarters (DH)=Div Headquarters

GEOGRAPHIC SECTION LOS ANGELES, CA

	SIC	EMP	PHONE	ENTRY #
Grifols Diagnstc Solutions Inc **(HQ)**	8071	A	323 225-2221	21069
Grifols Shared Svcs N Amer Inc **(HQ)**	5122	A	323 225-2221	14246
Grover Products Co	3714	D	323 263-9981	10069
Gruen Associates Inc	8712	D	323 937-4270	22718
Gsa Des Plaines LLC	6799	D	310 557-5100	16266
Guardian Life Insur Co of Amer	6311	D	213 624-2002	15362
Guess Inc **(PA)**	2341	A	213 765-3100	3015
Gursey Schneider & Co LLC **(PA)**	8721	C	310 552-0960	22787
Guru Knits Inc	2331	D	323 235-9424	2845
Gva Enterprises Inc **(PA)**	8051	D	213 484-0510	20369
Gvs Italy	5051	D	424 382-4343	13567
Gypsy 05 Inc	2339	E	323 265-2700	2948
H2 Wellness Incorporated	7372	E	310 362-1888	17878
Haight Brown & Bonesteel LLP **(PA)**	8111	D	213 542-8000	21575
Hamburger Home	1521	D	213 637-5000	609
Hamburger Home **(PA)**	8361	D	323 876-0550	22106
Hamrock Inc	3315	C	562 944-0255	6226
Hana Commercial Finance Inc	6153	D	213 240-1234	15153
Hana Financial Inc **(PA)**	7359	D	213 240-1234	17351
Hanil Development Inc	6553	E	213 387-0111	16084
Hanin Federal Credit Union **(PA)**	6061	E	213 368-9000	15068
Hanmi Bank **(HQ)**	6022	B	213 382-2200	15029
Hannam Chain USA Inc **(PA)**	5046	C	213 382-2922	13457
Happold Holdings (na) Inc **(DH)**	8711	E	310 945-4800	22565
Hardloop LLC	8741	E	310 892-4284	23037
Harkham Industries Inc **(PA)**	2331	E	323 586-4600	2846
Harris Stockwell **(PA)**	8111	E	310 277-6669	21576
Harrys Auto Body Inc	7532	D	323 933-4600	18791
Harvest Sensations LLC	5148	E	305 591-8173	14638
Hatchbeauty Agency LLC **(PA)**	8742	E	310 396-7070	23232
Hatchbeauty Products LLC **(PA)**	5122	D	310 396-7070	14249
Hathaway-Sycmres Child Fmly Svc	8361	C	323 257-9600	22109
Hazens Investment LLC	7011	B	310 642-1111	16468
Hbc Solutions Holdings LLC	3663	E	321 727-9100	9276
Hd Window Fashions Inc **(DH)**	2591	B	213 749-6333	3710
Helicopter Tech Co Ltd Partnr	3728	E	310 523-2750	10344
Here Films	8748	E	310 806-4288	23448
Hff Securities LP **(PA)**	6211	D	310 407-2100	15269
High Rise Gdies Rest Group Inc **(PA)**	6794	C	310 772-0726	16208
High-End Knitwear Inc	2253	E	323 582-6061	2636
Highland Pk Sklled Nrsing Wlln	8051	D	323 254-6125	20375
Hill Farrer & Burrill	8111	D	213 620-0460	21580
Hillcrest Country Club	7997	C	310 553-8911	19568
Hilton Garden Inn	7011	D	323 876-8600	16475
Himco National Inc	1731	F	323 231-9104	1266
Hirsh Inc	1389	E	213 622-9441	508
Hls Intl Tours NY Inc **(DH)**	4724	D	213 624-0777	12386
Hits Magazine Inc **(PA)**	5192	D	323 946-7600	14874
Hitt Contracting Inc	1542	B	424 326-1042	771
Hntb Corporation	8711	D	213 403-1000	22567
Hob Entertainment, LLC **(DH)**	7929	C	323 769-4600	19354
Hogan Lovells US LLP	8111	D	310 785-4600	21581
Hollywood Cmnty Hosp Med Ctr I	8062	C	323 462-2271	20792
Hollywood Hookah Lounge Inc	3999	F	323 469-4622	11686
Hollywood Medical Center LP	8062	A	213 413-3000	20793
Hollywood Partnership	7011	D	323 463-7171	16489
Hollywood Reporter	2711	E	323 525-2000	3990
Hollywood Rntals Prod Svcs LLC **(PA)**	7819	D	818 407-7800	19237
Hollywood Schoolhouse Inc	8351	E	323 465-1320	22020
Holthouse Carlin Van Trigt LLP **(PA)**	8721	C	310 566-1900	22790
Homeboy Industries **(PA)**	8322	B	323 526-1254	21803
Honest Company Inc **(PA)**	2341	C	310 917-9199	3016
Honey Punch Inc **(PA)**	2339	F	323 800-3812	2951
Honey Science LLC	7371	C	949 795-1695	17632
Hong Kong & Shanghai Banking	6081	D	213 626-2460	15117
Honk Technologies Inc	7374	C	800 979-3162	18094
Hope Bancorp Inc **(PA)**	6021	D	213 639-1700	15002
Horizon Media Inc	7311	B	310 282-0909	17017
Hospital Assn Southern Cal **(PA)**	8399	D	213 347-2002	22189
Hotchkis Wiley Capitl MGT LLC **(PA)**	8741	C	213 430-1000	23038
Hotel Bel-Air	7011	B	310 472-1211	16492
Houlihan Lokey Inc **(PA)**	6282	B	310 788-5200	15330
House Ear Clinic Inc **(PA)**	8011	D	213 483-9930	19846
House of Blues Concerts Inc **(DH)**	7929	C	323 769-4977	19357
Housewares International Inc	3089	E	323 581-3000	5667
HR&a Advisors Inc	8742	D	310 581-0900	23237
Htec Group Inc **(PA)**	7371	A	213 785-7824	17633
Hudson Pacific Properties Inc **(PA)**	6798	C	310 445-5700	16234
Hudson Pacific Properties LP **(HQ)**	6798	B	310 445-5700	16235
Hueston Hennigan LLP	8111	D	213 788-4340	21582
Huf Worldwide LLC	4813	C	323 264-8656	12645
Hulu LLC	4813	D	888 631-4858	12646
Humnit Hotel At Lax LLC	7011	D	424 702-1234	16495
Hungry Heart Media Inc	7812	C	323 951-0010	19133
Huntsman Advanced Materials AM	2821	C	818 265-7221	4695
Hyatt Corporation	7011	B	312 750-1234	16497
Hyatt Regency Century Plaza	7011	A	310 228-1234	16500
Hyde Pk Convalescent Hosp Inc	8051	E	323 753-1354	20377
Hyperloop Technologies Inc **(PA)**	4789	C	213 800-3270	12573
Hyrecar Inc	4119	D	888 688-6769	11875
I C I	3825	F	213 749-3709	10756
I D Property Corporation	6531	C	213 625-0100	15887
I S W Inc	5131	E	323 653-6453	14304
I T I Electro-Optic Corp **(PA)**	3823	E	310 445-8900	10701
I T I Electro-Optic Corp	3823	E	310 312-4526	10702
IaMplus LLC	3629	D	323 210-3852	8976
IaMplus Electronics Inc **(PA)**	7372	E	323 210-3852	17881
Ibi Group A California Partnr	8711	D	213 769-0011	22574
Ibisworld Inc **(DH)**	2741	C	310 496-6871	4181
Ibisworld Inc **(DH)**	8732	D	800 330-3772	22886
Idea Tooling and Engrg Inc	3544	D	310 608-7488	7808
Ideal Program Services Inc	8322	D	323 296-2255	21808
IDS Real Estate Group **(PA)**	6531	D	213 627-9937	15888
If Live LLC **(PA)**	7812	D	323 957-6868	19134
Ignition Creative LLC	7812	D	310 315-6300	19135
Ihg Management (maryland) LLC	7011	E	310 642-7500	16501
Ikonick LLC	2752	E	516 680-7765	4320
Imajean Nation Inc	2211	E	323 980-9000	2575
Imax Corporation **(HQ)**	7832	B	310 255-5559	19280
Imhoff & Associates PC	8111	D	310 691-2200	21584
Immortals LLC	7941	D	310 554-8267	19417
Imperial Capital Group LLC **(PA)**	6799	D	310 246-3700	16269
Imperial Capital LLC **(PA)**	6211	D	310 246-3700	15270
Imperial Parking Inds Inc **(PA)**	7521	D	323 651-5588	18766
Improv Tvs Inc **(PA)**	8111	E	323 937-5030	21585
Indie Source	2326	E	424 200-2027	2782
Industrial Glass Products Inc	3231	F	323 526-7125	5957
Infinity Broadcasting Corp Cal	4832	D	323 936-5784	12694
Infokorea Inc	2721	E	213 487-1580	4074
Ink & Color Inc	2752	E	310 280-6060	4329
Insignia/Esg Ht Partners Inc **(DH)**	6512	B	310 765-2600	15673
Institute For Applied Behavior **(PA)**	8049	C	310 649-0499	20219
Institute For Mltcltral Cnslin **(PA)**	8748	D	213 381-1239	23453
Intercare Therapy Inc	8049	C	323 866-1880	20222
Intercoastal Property Svcs LLC **(PA)**	6531	C	310 277-0057	15891
Interfaceflor LLC	2273	D	213 741-2139	2691
International Coffee & Tea LLC **(HQ)**	6794	D	310 237-2326	16209
International Creative Mgt Inc **(HQ)**	7922	C	310 550-4000	19316
International Creative MGT Inc	7922	E	310 550-4000	19317
International Inst Los Angeles **(PA)**	8322	D	323 224-3800	21817
International Lease Fin Corp **(DH)**	7359	A	310 788-1999	17356
International Marine Pdts Inc **(HQ)**	5146	E	213 893-6123	14571
International Medical Corps **(PA)**	8322	D	310 826-7800	21818
Internet Corp For Assgned Nmes **(PA)**	7373	C	310 823-9358	18039
Interntnal Ch of Frsqare Gospl **(PA)**	6512	D	213 989-4234	15674
Interntnal Crtive MGT Prtners **(PA)**	8742	D	310 550-4000	23244
Interntnal Fndtion For Krea Un	8399	B	213 550-2182	22190
Interntonal Metallurgical Svcs	3398	F	310 645-7300	6441
Interstate Steel Center Co	3355	E	323 583-0855	6327
Intrepid Inv Bankers LLC	6799	B	310 478-9000	16270
Investors Business Daily Inc **(HQ)**	2711	C	310 448-6000	3997
Investors Capital MGT Group	8741	B	310 553-5175	23040
Invisble Prtection Systems Inc	7372	E	213 254-0463	17891
Ipayment Inc	7389	D	213 387-1353	18554
Irell & Manella LLP **(PA)**	8111	B	310 277-1010	21586
Iris LLC	8734	E	424 331-5441	22950
Irp Lax Hotel LLC	7011	C	310 645-4600	16508
IV Inc	7371	D	310 658-7374	17646
Ivie McNeill Wyatt A Prof Law	8111	E	213 489-0028	21588
Iw Group **(PA)**	7311	D	213 262-6978	17025
J Alexander Investments Inc **(PA)**	6726	E	213 687-8400	16156
J C Entertainment Ltg Svcs Inc	7922	D	818 252-7481	19318
J C Trimming Company Inc	2335	D	323 235-4458	2887
J H Synder Co LLC	6531	D	323 857-5546	15894
J Hellman Frozen Foods Inc **(PA)**	2037	E	213 243-9105	1901
J K Star Corp	2329	D	310 538-0185	2814
J M Carden Sprinkler Co Inc	1711	D	323 258-8300	1085
J P B Jewelry Box Co **(PA)**	2541	F	323 225-0500	3653
J P H Consulting Inc **(PA)**	8051	E	323 934-5660	20381
J P H Consulting Inc	8051	D	323 934-5660	20382
J W Mrrott Los Angles L A Live	7011	C	213 765-8600	16509
J&C Apparel	2325	E	323 490-8260	2770
J-M Manufacturing Company Inc **(PA)**	3491	C	800 621-4404	7447
J2 Cloud Services LLC **(HQ)**	4822	D	323 860-9200	12682
Jack Engle & Co **(PA)**	5093	D	323 589-8111	14117
Jack Nadel Inc **(PA)**	8742	D	310 815-2600	23247
Jackoway Tyreman Wertheimer Au	8111	D	310 553-0305	21589
Jaltrans Inc **(HQ)**	4522	C	310 215-7471	12335
James Stewart	2834	E	323 778-1687	4834
Jan-Al Innerprizes Inc	3161	E	323 260-7212	5894
Janel Glass Company Inc	3231	E	323 661-8621	5960
Jarrow Formulas Inc **(PA)**	5122	D	310 204-6936	14252
Jason Markk Inc **(PA)**	2842	E	213 687-7060	4965
Jay-Cee Blouse Co Inc	2335	F	213 622-0116	2888
Jd/Cmc Inc	2339	E	818 767-2260	2958
Jeffer Mngels Btlr Mtchell LLP **(PA)**	8111	C	310 203-8080	21591
Jet Fleet International Corp	7299	E	310 440-3820	16960
Jet Plastics **(PA)**	3089	E	323 268-6706	5683
Jetro Holdings LLC	5046	C	213 516-0301	13462
Jewelers Security Products **(PA)**	5085	F	323 231-0600	13994
Jewish Cmnty Fndn of **(PA)**	8641	C	323 761-8700	22342
Jewish Family Svc Los Angeles	8322	D	323 937-5900	21822
Jewish Family Svc Los Angeles **(PA)**	8621	E	323 761-8800	22271
Jewish Family Svc Los Angeles	8322	D	323 937-5900	21824
Jewish Family Svc Los Angeles	8322	D	323 935-5303	21825
Jewish Vocational Services **(PA)**	8331	E	323 761-8888	21957
JH Snyder Company	6552	E	323 857-5546	16053
Jhp Produce Inc	5148	D	213 627-1093	14640
Jim Henson Company Inc **(PA)**	7812	D	323 856-6680	19138
Jodi Kristopher LLC **(PA)**	2335	C	323 890-8000	2889
John A Martin & Associates Inc	8711	D	213 483-6490	22590
John Hancock Life Insur Co USA **(DH)**	6411	A	213 689-0813	15585
John Stewart Company	6531	E	213 787-2700	15897
Johnny Was LLC **(PA)**	5137	C	323 582-1005	14386

GEOGRAPHIC

	SIC	EMP	PHONE	ENTRY #
Johnson Fain Inc	8712	D	323 224-6000	22724
Jonathan Club **(PA)**	8641	C	213 624-0881	22343
Jonathan Louis International	2514	D	323 770-3330	3530
Jones Iron Works	3446	F	323 386-2368	6968
Jong S Yoon Dmd Inc **(PA)**	8021	D	213 383-0010	20184
Joong-Ang Daily News Cal Inc **(DH)**	2711	C	213 368-2500	3998
Joong-Ang Daily News Cal Inc	8072	D	213 487-2355	21108
Jpl Management LLC	8741	D	310 844-3662	23043
Jsl Foods Inc **(PA)**	2099	C	323 223-2484	2457
JT Design Studio Inc **(PA)**	2339	E	213 891-1500	2960
Judy O Productions Inc	2731	E	323 938-8513	4132
Juicy Couture Inc	2221	C	888 824-8826	2600
Jukin Media Inc **(DH)**	7922	C	323 932-0960	19319
Jules and Associates Inc	7359	D	213 362-5600	17359
Julio Gonzalez	8748	D	310 310-4055	23459
Juntee of California Inc	2331	E	213 742-0246	2849
Justice Design Group LLC **(PA)**	5063	E	213 437-0102	13639
Jwc Studio Inc **(PA)**	2335	E	323 231-8222	2890
Jwmcc Limited Partnership	7011	D	310 277-1234	16517
K Too	2331	E	213 747-7766	2850
K-Swiss Inc **(HQ)**	3021	B	323 675-2700	5309
Kaa Design Group Inc	8712	D	310 821-1400	22725
Kaiser Foundation Hospitals	8062	D	323 783-4011	20805
Kaiser Foundation Hospitals	8699	D	213 351-3550	22454
Kaiser Foundation Hospitals	8093	C	213 217-4514	21315
Kaiser Foundation Hospitals	8011	C	323 783-7695	19867
Kaiser Foundation Hospitals	8011	C	323 783-8191	19870
Kaiser Foundation Hospitals	8062	A	323 783-4011	20807
Kaiser Foundation Hospitals	8011	C	323 857-2000	19874
Kaiser Foundation Hospitals	8011	C	323 857-2000	19881
Kaiser Foundation Hospitals	6324	C	800 954-8000	15407
Kaiser Foundation Hospitals	6324	C	800 954-8000	15412
Kaiser Foundation Hospitals	8011	C	310 915-5000	19926
Kaiser Foundation Hospitals	6733	D	323 881-5516	16181
Kaiser Foundation Hospitals	6324	C	323 783-8568	15413
Kaiser Foundation Hospitals	8011	C	323 783-7955	19931
Kaiser Foundation Hospitals	8011	C	323 783-8306	19940
Kaiser Foundation Hospitals	8093	C	323 298-3300	21317
Kaiser Foundation Hospitals	8063	B	213 580-7200	21020
Kal Krshnan Cnsulting Svcs Inc	8711	D	213 488-0900	22595
Kalpana LLC	7011	C	213 624-0000	16518
Kalypsys Inc	2834	E	858 552-0674	4837
Kamiran Inc	2331	F	213 746-9161	2851
Kathryn M Ireland Inc **(PA)**	2211	C	323 965-9888	2578
Katten Muchin Rosenman LLP	8111	D	310 788-4498	21595
Katten Muchin Rosenman LLP	8111	D	310 788-4400	21596
Katz Millennium Sls & Mktg Inc	3663	C	323 966-5066	9281
Kaufman and Broad Limited	1531	C	310 231-4000	677
Kava Holdings Inc **(DH)**	7011	C	310 472-1211	16521
Kayne Andrson Rdnick Inv MGT L	6722	D	310 229-9260	16131
KB Home **(PA)**	1531	D	310 231-4000	678
KB Home Grater Los Angeles Inc **(HQ)**	1521	D	310 231-4000	618
Kc Exclusive Inc **(PA)**	5137	D	213 749-0088	14389
KCS West Inc	1541	D	323 269-0020	705
Keck Hospital of Usc	8062	B	800 872-2273	20822
Kedren Community Hlth Ctr Inc	8322	C	323 524-0634	21830
Kedren Community Hlth Ctr Inc **(PA)**	8063	B	323 233-0425	21022
Keiro Nursing Home	8062	C	323 276-5700	20823
Keiro Services	8741	B	213 873-5700	23045
Kenneth Brdwick Intr Dsgns Inc	7389	D	310 274-9999	18562
Keolis Transit America Inc **(DH)**	4119	E	310 981-9500	11876
Kerlan-Jobe Orthopedic Clinic **(PA)**	8011	D	310 665-7200	19949
Kesmor Associates	3911	E	213 629-2300	11319
Kilroy Realty LP **(PA)**	6531	C	310 481-8400	15902
Kilroy Realty Corporation **(PA)**	6798	C	310 481-8400	16238
Kim Bonjun Inc **(PA)**	3993	E	213 385-1258	11565
Kim Chong	7389	E	323 581-4700	18563
Kimco Staffing Services Inc	7361	A	310 622-1616	17432
Kimpton Hotel & Rest Group LLC	7011	C	323 852-6000	16523
King Hlmes Pterno Soriano LLP	8111	E	310 282-8989	21598
Kingswood Capital MGT LP	6726	C	424 744-8238	16157
Kingz & Kompany LLC	6531	E	888 274-8882	15903
Kintetsu Enterprises	8741	D	213 687-2000	23046
Kintetsu Enterprises Co Amer	7011	E	213 617-2000	16525
Klk Forte Industry Inc **(PA)**	2339	E	323 415-9181	2963
Knit Generation Group Inc	2211	E	213 221-5081	2579
Kobi Katz Inc	3911	F	213 689-9505	11320
Komarov Enterprises Inc	2337	D	213 244-7000	2905
Kor Realty Group LLC **(PA)**	6531	D	323 930-3700	15904
Kora Us LLC **(PA)**	7231	D	424 744-8903	16907
Koram Insurance Center Inc	6411	D	323 660-1000	15587
Korean Air Lines Co Ltd	4512	C	310 646-4866	12308
Korean Airlines Co Ltd	4512	C	310 410-2000	12309
Korean Airlines Co Ltd	4512	D	213 484-1900	12310
Korean Hlth Edcatn Info RES CT **(PA)**	8322	D	213 427-4000	21833
Korean Television Enterprises	4833	D	213 382-6700	12730
Korn Ferry **(PA)**	7361	C	310 552-1834	17435
Kpff Inc	8711	C	310 665-1536	22597
Krissy Op Shins USA Inc	2329	F	213 747-2591	2817
Kritech Corporation **(PA)**	3679	F	310 538-9940	9739
Kwdz Manufacturing LLC **(PA)**	2361	D	323 526-3526	3032
Kxp Carrier Services LLC	4215	C	424 320-5300	12140
Kymsta Corp	2339	F	213 380-8118	2965
L & T Meat Co	5147	D	323 262-2815	14595
L A Air Inc	4512	C	310 215-8245	12311
L A Sani-Felt Co	2299	F	323 233-5278	2727
L and R Auto Parks Inc	7521	C	213 784-3018	18767

	SIC	EMP	PHONE	ENTRY #
L Y A Group Inc	2339	E	213 683-1123	2966
La 1000 Santa Fe LLC	8741	C	213 205-1000	23047
La Aloe LLC	2037	E	888 968-2563	1904
La Asccion Ncnal Pro Prsnas My	8322	D	213 202-5900	21834
La Barca Tortilleria Inc	2099	E	323 268-1744	2462
LA Cabinet & Millwork Inc	2541	E	323 227-5000	3656
La Cienega Associates	6531	D	310 854-0071	15905
La Clippers LLC	7941	D	213 742-7500	19419
La Fortaleza Inc	2099	D	323 261-1211	2465
LA Gem and Jewelry Design **(PA)**	3911	D	213 488-1290	11321
La Gloria Foods Corp **(PA)**	2099	D	323 262-0410	2466
La Gloria Foods Corp	2099	E	323 263-6755	2467
La Indiana Tamales Inc	2032	F	323 262-4682	1853
La La Land Production & Design	3111	E	323 406-9223	5870
La Linen Inc	2392	E	213 745-4004	3105
La Live Properties LLC	7922	E	213 763-7700	19320
La Mamba LLC	2331	E	323 526-3526	2854
La Opinion LP **(HQ)**	2711	D	213 891-9191	4000
La Opinion LP	2711	B	213 896-2222	4001
La Princesita Tortilleria Inc **(PA)**	2099	F	323 267-0673	2468
LA Printing & Graphics Inc	2752	E	310 527-4526	4352
LA Sports Properties Inc	7941	C	213 742-7500	19420
La Times	2711	E	213 237-2279	4002
La6721 LLC	3993	F	323 484-4070	11566
Laaco Ltd **(PA)**	6519	C	213 622-1254	15760
Labeltex Mills Inc **(PA)**	3965	C	323 582-0228	11498
Lac & Usc Medical Center	8011	C	323 409-2345	19955
Lacba Counsel For Justice	8322	D	951 489-2919	21836
Lamonicas Pizza Dough Intl Inc **(PA)**	5142	D	310 208-5535	14527
Lamp Inc	8361	C	213 488-9559	22122
Landmark Imaging LLC	8011	D	310 914-7336	19957
Landslide Technologies Inc **(DH)**	7371	C	412 489-1705	17651
Language Weaver Inc	7371	D	310 437-7300	17652
Larry Spun Products Inc	3469	E	323 881-6300	7160
Lasercare Technologies Inc **(PA)**	3955	E	310 202-4200	11479
Lasr Inc	7334	C	877 591-9979	17151
Latham & Watkins LLP **(PA)**	8111	A	213 485-1234	21604
Latitudes Intl Fragrance Inc	5199	D	866 639-3999	14946
Lauras French Baking Co Inc	2051	F	323 585-5144	2013
Lava Heat Italia	3567	F	310 559-1700	8094
Lavash Corporation of America	2051	E	323 663-5249	2014
Lawa Inc	4581	D	424 646-7770	12360
Lawrys Restaurants II Inc	7299	C	323 664-0228	16962
Lax Hotel Ventures LLC	7011	E	310 645-4600	16537
Lax-C Inc	5141	E	323 343-9000	14474
Le Val of California Inc	7389	E	323 221-9116	18574
Lear Capital Inc	6211	D	310 571-0190	15273
Leatherupcom **(PA)**	2329	F	213 763-6185	2819
Lee Thomas Inc **(PA)**	2339	E	310 532-7560	2968
Leet Technology Inc	3714	F	877 238-4492	10090
Legal Support Network LLC	7389	D	213 975-9850	18575
Legend3d Inc	7812	D	858 793-4420	19140
LEK Consulting LLC	8742	E	310 209-9800	23260
Lenlyn Ltd Which Will Do Bus I **(HQ)**	6099	D	310 417-3432	15129
Lets Go Apparel Inc **(PA)**	2389	E	213 863-1767	3076
Level Four Business MGT LLC	8748	E	310 914-1600	23467
Levity Entertainment Group LLC	8742	E	310 417-4861	23261
Lewis Brsbois Bsgard Smith LLP **(PA)**	8111	A	213 250-1800	21610
Lexicon Marketing (usa) Inc **(PA)**	5049	B	323 782-8282	13534
Lf Sportswear Inc **(PA)**	2331	E	310 437-4100	2855
Lieberman RES Worldwide LLC **(PA)**	8732	C	310 553-0550	22892
Lifetime Entrmt Svcs LLC	4833	B	310 556-7500	12733
Lighthouse Healthcare Ctr LLC	8051	D	323 564-4461	20400
Limnexus LLP **(PA)**	8111	D	213 955-9500	21614
Lindsey & Sons	7389	D	657 306-5369	18578
Linea Solutions Inc	8742	D	310 443-4191	23263
Linen Salvage Et Cie LLC	2269	E	323 904-3100	2674
Liner LLP	8111	C	310 500-3500	21615
Linquest Corporation **(PA)**	8711	C	323 924-1600	22601
Lito Childrens Wear Inc	2311	F	323 260-4692	2745
Livhome Inc **(PA)**	8082	A	800 807-5854	21186
LLP Moss Adams	8721	C	310 477-0450	22803
Lmb Mortgage Services Inc **(HQ)**	6162	C	310 343-6800	15209
Local Inttive Hlth Auth For Lo **(PA)**	6324	A	213 694-1250	15443
Lockton Companies LLC- Pacifi **(HQ)**	6411	B	213 689-0500	15589
Loeb & Loeb LLP **(PA)**	8111	C	310 282-2000	21616
Longwood Management Corp	8059	D	323 735-5146	20601
Longwood Management Corp	8059	D	323 737-7778	20603
Longwood Management Corp	8059	D	213 382-8461	20604
Longwood Management Corp	8051	C	323 933-1560	20408
Los Angeles Apparel Inc	2389	B	323 745-4986	3078
Los Angeles Athletic Club Inc	7991	C	213 625-2211	19457
Los Angeles Bus Jurnl Assoc	2721	E	323 549-5225	4083
Los Angeles Capital MGT LLC **(PA)**	6722	D	310 479-9998	16132
Los Angeles Cardiology Assoc **(HQ)**	8011	D	213 977-0419	19965
Los Angeles Cnty Mseum of Art	8412	D	323 857-6000	22225
Los Angeles Conven and Exh	6512	B	213 741-1151	15676
Los Angeles Country Club	7997	C	310 276-6104	19581
Los Angeles County Bar Assn **(PA)**	8621	D	213 627-2727	22272
Los Angeles Dept Wtr & Pwr	4941	B	323 256-8079	12901
Los Angeles Dept Wtr & Pwr **(HQ)**	4941	A	213 367-1320	12904
Los Angeles Dept Wtr & Pwr	4911	D	213 367-4211	12808
Los Angeles Dept Wtr & Pwr	4941	B	213 367-5706	12905
Los Angeles Dodgers LLC	7941	A	323 224-1507	19421
Los Angeles Education Partnr	8399	D	213 622-5237	22197
Los Angeles Free Clinic	8011	C	323 653-1990	19966
Los Angeles Free Clinic **(PA)**	8011	D	323 653-8622	19967

Mergent email: customerrelations@mergent.com
1392

2022 Southern California Business
Directory and Buyers Guide

(P-0000) Products & Services Section entry number
(PA)=Parent Co (HQ)=Headquarters (DH)=Div Headquarters

	SIC	EMP	PHONE	ENTRY #
Los Angeles Homeless Svcs Auth	8322	A	213 683-3333	21843
Los Angeles Lgbt Center **(PA)**	8399	C	323 993-7618	22198
Los Angeles Mem Coliseum Comm	8699	B	213 747-7111	22455
Los Angeles Mills Inc	2211	F	213 622-8031	2580
Los Angeles Mission Inc **(PA)**	8361	D	213 629-1227	22126
Los Angeles Organizing	7997	E	310 407-0539	19582
Los Angeles Orphans Home Soc **(HQ)**	8361	C	323 463-2119	22127
Los Angeles Philharmonic Assn **(PA)**	7929	C	213 972-7300	19364
Los Angeles Philharmonic Assn	7929	A	323 850-2060	19365
Los Angeles Poultry Co Inc	2015	D	323 232-1619	1762
Los Angeles Produce Distrs LLC **(HQ)**	5148	E	562 448-5555	14643
Los Angeles Rams LLC	8741	D	310 277-4700	23054
Los Angeles Rubber Company **(PA)**	5085	D	323 263-4131	13999
Los Angeles Sentinel Inc	2711	D	323 299-3800	4004
Los Angeles Unified School Dst	8741	D	323 549-2018	23055
Los Angeles Unified School Dst	8748	D	323 265-1898	23469
Los Angeles World Airports **(PA)**	4581	B	310 646-7911	12361
Los Angles Area Chmber Cmmerce	8611	D	213 580-7500	22251
Los Angles Chmber Orchstra Soc	7929	D	213 622-7001	19366
Los Angles Cnty Dvlpmntal Svcs	8099	C	213 383-1300	21451
Los Angles Cnty Employees Assn	8631	D	213 368-8660	22293
Los Angles Cnty Mseum Ntral Hs **(PA)**	8399	C	213 763-3466	22199
Los Angles Cnty Mtro Trnsp Aut	4111	A	213 922-5887	11818
Los Angles Cnty Mtro Trnsp Aut	4111	A	213 922-6301	11819
Los Angles Cnty Mtro Trnsp Aut	4111	A	213 922-6203	11820
Los Angles Cnty Mtro Trnsp Aut	4111	A	213 922-6202	11821
Los Angles Cnty Mtro Trnsp Aut **(PA)**	4111	A	323 466-3876	11822
Los Angles Cnty Mtro Trnsp Aut	4111	A	213 922-6207	11823
Los Angles Cnty Mtro Trnsp Aut	4111	A	213 533-1506	11825
Los Angles Cnty Mtro Trnsp Aut	4111	A	213 922-5012	11826
Los Angles Cnty Mtro Trnsp Aut	4111	A	213 244-6783	11828
Los Angles Cnty Mtro Trnsp Aut	4111	A	213 626-4455	11829
Los Angles Free Clnic Hllywood	8011	D	323 653-8622	19968
Los Angles Fund For Pub Edcatn **(PA)**	8399	D	310 912-3444	22200
Los Angles Sction Nat Cncil JW **(PA)**	8322	E	323 651-2930	21845
Los Angles Tmes Cmmnctions LLC	2711	E	213 237-7987	4006
Los Angles Trism Convention Bd **(PA)**	7389	E	213 624-7300	18582
Los Angles Universal Preschool	8351	C	213 416-1200	22031
Lotus Communications Corp **(PA)**	4832	D	323 512-2225	12701
Lounge Spa Inc	7991	D	310 745-1646	19458
Lovemarks Inc	2331	E	213 514-5888	2856
Low Voltage Architecture Inc	3699	F	310 573-7588	9890
Lowe Enterprises Inc **(PA)**	7011	C	310 820-6661	16546
Lowe Enterprises Inc	6552	D	310 820-6661	16057
Lowe Enterprises Inv MGT **(HQ)**	6726	D	310 820-6661	16158
Lowe Enterprises RE Group	6552	B	310 820-6661	16058
Lowe Enterprises Rlty Svcs Inc **(HQ)**	8741	B	310 820-6661	23056
LPC Commercial Services Inc	6552	C	213 362-9080	16059
Lrw Investments LLC	7521	D	310 337-1944	18768
Lucas Design International Inc **(PA)**	5094	D	213 387-4444	14132
Lucky Strike Entertainment Inc	7933	C	213 542-4880	19399
Lucky Strike Entertainment LLC	7933	C	818 933-3752	19400
Lumenton Inc	3648	F	323 904-0202	9139
Lumina Healthcare LLC **(PA)**	8082	D	888 958-6462	21188
Luna Imaging Inc	7372	E	323 908-1400	17907
Lupitas Bakery Inc **(PA)**	2051	F	323 752-2391	2017
Lusive Decor	8748	D	323 227-9207	23472
Lynberg & Watkins A Prof Corp **(PA)**	8111	E	213 624-8700	21619
Lz Management Group LLC **(PA)**	8741	D	213 383-4800	23057
M & S Acquisition Corporation **(PA)**	6531	C	213 385-1515	15918
M Arthur Gensler Jr Assoc Inc	8712	C	213 927-3600	22730
Machine Building Spc Inc	3556	E	323 666-8289	7943
Madisn/Grham Clor Graphics Inc	2752	B	323 261-7171	4363
Mafab Inc **(PA)**	6719	D	714 893-0551	16104
Magic Castles Inc	7997	D	323 851-3313	19584
Magic Ram Inc	3577	F	213 380-5555	8278
Magma Consulting Group LLC	7379	D	415 315-9364	18200
Magnite Inc **(PA)**	7311	C	310 207-0272	17031
Magnolia Eductl RES Foundation **(PA)**	8399	C	714 892-5066	22202
Major Fulfillment LLC	2752	F	310 204-1874	4366
Malbon Golf LLC	3949	E	323 433-4028	11435
Malibu Leather Inc	3172	C	310 985-0707	5910
Manchster Mnor Cnvlescent Hosp	8051	D	323 753-1789	20412
Mandalay Spt Action Entrmt LLC **(PA)**	7941	D	323 549-4300	19423
Manning Kass Ellrod Rmrez Trst **(PA)**	8111	C	213 624-6900	21622
Manufacturers Bank **(DH)**	6022	C	213 489-6200	15031
Margus Automotive Elc Exch	3714	F	323 232-5281	10098
Marmol Rdzner An Archtctral Co	8712	D	310 826-6222	22731
Marriott International Inc	7011	A	310 641-5700	16556
Marriott International Inc	7011	C	213 284-3862	16559
Marsh Risk & Insurance Svcs	6411	A	213 624-5555	15592
Martin AC Partners Inc	8712	C	213 683-1900	22732
Martin Associates Group Inc **(PA)**	8711	D	213 483-6490	22604
Martin Lther King Jr-Los Angle	8099	C	424 338-8000	21452
Martin Sports Inc **(PA)**	3949	F	509 529-2554	11436
Matchmaster Dyg & Finshg Inc	2269	F	323 233-4281	2675
Matchmaster Dyg & Finshg Inc **(PA)**	2269	C	323 232-2061	2676
Matchmaster Dyg & Finshg Inc	2257	D	323 232-2061	2646
Matrix Aviation Services Inc	4729	C	310 337-3037	12416
Matteo LLC	2392	E	213 617-2813	3107
Matthews Manufacturing Inc	3444	F	323 980-4373	6871
Maxim Healthcare Services Inc	8082	C	866 465-5678	21190
Mayesh Wholesale Florist Inc **(PA)**	5193	E	310 342-0980	14887
McGuirewoods LLP	8111	E	310 315-8200	21623
McGuirewoods LLP	8111	E	213 627-2268	21624
McKenna Boiler Works Inc	7699	E	323 221-1171	19050
McKool Smith Hennigan	8111	D	213 694-1200	21625

	SIC	EMP	PHONE	ENTRY #
Mdc Interior Solutions LLC	2389	E	800 621-4006	3079
Meat Packers Butchers Sup Inc	3556	F	323 268-8514	7944
Med-Life Ambulance Services	4119	D	818 242-1785	11878
Mededge Inc	3841	F	310 745-2290	11014
Media Gobbler Inc	7372	E	323 203-3222	17914
Media Temple Inc	4813	C	877 578-4000	12653
Mediabrands Worldwide Inc	7311	B	323 370-8000	17033
Medical Management Cons Inc **(PA)**	7363	E	310 659-3835	17505
Medsco Fabrication & Dist Inc	3441	D	323 263-0511	6635
Mellano & Co **(PA)**	5193	D	213 622-0796	14888
Memco Holdings Inc	6531	C	310 277-0057	15924
Men Tking Over Rfrming Soc Inc	8322	D	323 338-6633	21849
Merchant of Tennis Inc	7389	A	310 855-1946	18592
Mercury General Corporation **(PA)**	6331	A	323 937-1060	15470
Mercury Insurance Company **(HQ)**	6331	C	323 937-1060	15474
Mercury Insurance Services LLC	6331	A	323 937-1060	15476
Mercury Plastics Inc	3081	D	323 264-2400	5433
Merelex Corporation	2819	E	310 208-0551	4662
Meridan Sport Club LLC **(PA)**	7991	D	818 698-2900	19460
Merle Norman Cosmetics Inc **(PA)**	2844	B	310 641-3000	5047
Merlot Film Productions Inc	7812	C	323 575-2906	19148
Merrill Corporation Inc	2759	E	310 552-5288	4544
Merrill Lynch Prce Fnner Smith	6211	D	310 407-3900	15290
Metropolis Hotel MGT LLC	7011	C	213 683-4855	16567
Metropolitan W Asset MGT LLC **(HQ)**	6211	D	213 244-0000	15296
Meundies Inc	2254	E	888 552-6775	2645
Mexican Amrcn Oprtnty Fndation	8351	D	323 264-4333	22034
Mf Inc	2331	C	213 627-2498	2858
MGT Industries Inc **(PA)**	2339	D	310 516-5900	2973
Michael Levine Inc **(PA)**	5131	D	213 622-6259	14309
Micro Surface Engr Inc **(PA)**	3399	E	323 582-7348	6460
Micross Holdings Inc	3674	D	215 997-3200	9545
Mid Rckland Imging Prtners Inc **(HQ)**	8071	E	310 445-2800	21078
Mid-Cities Association Inc **(PA)**	8331	D	310 537-4510	21961
Midnight Mission **(PA)**	8641	D	213 624-9258	22348
Midthrust Imports Inc	2259	E	213 749-6651	2653
Midway Rent A Car Inc	7514	D	310 330-4600	18744
Midway Rent A Car Inc	7514	D	424 293-4855	18745
Midway Rent A Car Inc	7514	D	310 445-4355	18746
Mighty Soy Inc	3556	F	323 266-6969	7945
Milbank Tweed Hdley McCloy LLP	8111	C	424 386-4000	21629
Mimi Chica **(PA)**	2339	F	323 264-9278	2974
Minal Inc **(PA)**	8011	D	323 957-8787	19979
Mindshow	7372	E	213 531-0277	17917
Miniluxe Inc	7231	D	424 442-1630	16908
Miramax LLC	7812	C	310 409-4321	19152
Miramax Film Ny LLC **(HQ)**	7812	D	310 409-4321	19153
Miss Kim Inc	2335	F	213 741-0888	2893
Mission Beverage Co **(HQ)**	5181	C	323 266-6238	14831
Mission Service Inc	7538	A	323 266-2593	18856
Misyd Corp **(PA)**	2361	D	213 742-1800	3035
Mitchell Silberberg Knupp LLP **(PA)**	8111	B	310 312-2000	21630
Mitratech Holdings Inc	7372	C	323 964-0000	17919
Mixmor Inc	3531	F	323 664-1941	7646
Mjw Inc	3561	D	323 778-8900	8017
Mk Tool and Abrasive Inc	3291	F	562 776-8818	6156
Mnm Corporation **(PA)**	2721	E	213 627-3737	4086
Moaddel Law Firm APC	8111	E	323 999-5099	21631
Mobile Messenger Americas Inc **(PA)**	7389	C	310 957-3300	18600
Mobile Net Posa Inc	7372	F	213 863-0351	17920
Mocean LLC	7374	C	310 481-0808	18102
Mod2 Inc	7372	E	213 747-8424	17921
Model Lyfe	2721	F	224 325-5933	4087
Moelis & Company LLC	6733	D	310 443-2300	16190
Momentfeed Inc	8742	D	310 853-3336	23275
Monarch Landscape Holdings LLC **(PA)**	0782	D	213 816-1750	326
Monopole Inc	2851	E	818 500-8585	5103
Monrow Inc	2331	E	213 741-6007	2859
Monte Nido Holdings LLC	8049	D	310 472-3728	20227
Monterey Canyon LLC **(PA)**	2339	D	213 741-0209	2975
Morgan Services Inc	7213	D	213 485-9666	16867
Morgans Hotel Group MGT LLC	7011	C	323 650-8999	16573
Morgner Technology Management	8741	D	323 900-0030	23068
Morris Polich & Purdy LLP **(PA)**	8111	D	213 891-9100	21633
Morrison & Foerster LLP	8111	C	213 892-5200	21634
Mortgage Capital Partners Inc **(PA)**	6162	D	310 295-2900	15217
Mother Plucker Feather Co Inc	3999	F	213 637-0411	11717
Mothership Technologies Inc	7371	D	310 905-8677	17665
Motion Picture Licensing Corp **(PA)**	7389	D	800 462-8855	18604
Motolease Funding LLC	6159	D	310 601-4779	15165
Motorola Solutions Inc	3663	C	954 723-4730	9298
Mpower Holding Corporation **(HQ)**	4813	A	866 699-8242	12656
Ms Bubbles Inc **(PA)**	5137	D	323 544-0300	14403
Mscp V CC Parent LLC **(HQ)**	7361	D	323 634-0156	17439
Mscsoftware Corporation **(PA)**	7372	C	323 258-9111	17924
MSP Group Inc	2211	E	310 660-0022	2581
MTI Film LLC	7371	F	323 465-6487	17666
Mtroiz International	5065	E	661 998-8013	13753
Mufg Americas Leasing Corp **(DH)**	7359	D	213 488-3700	17364
Mufg Union Bank Foundation	6021	A	213 236-5000	15003
Muir-Chase Plumbing Co Inc	1711	D	818 500-1940	1104
Mulholland SEC & Patrol Inc	7381	B	818 755-0202	18298
Mulroses Usa Inc	0181	D	213 489-1761	86
Munger Tolles & Olson LLP	8111	C	213 683-9100	21636
Munger Tolles Olson Foundation **(PA)**	8111	B	213 683-9100	21637
Murchison & Cumming LLP **(PA)**	8111	D	213 623-7400	21638
Museum Associates	8412	B	323 857-6172	22226

Employment Codes: A=Over 500 employees, B=251-500, C=101-250, D=51-100, E=20-50 F=10-19

2022 Southern California Business Directory and Buyers Guide

1393

	SIC	EMP	PHONE	ENTRY #
Museum of Contemporary Art **(PA)**	8412	C	213 626-6222	22227
Musick Peeler & Garrett LLP **(PA)**	8111	C	213 629-7600	21641
Mutual Trading Co Inc	5199	D	213 229-9393	14954
Mv Medical Management	8742	D	323 257-7637	23278
MXF Designs Inc	2331	D	323 266-1451	2861
My Favorite Company Inc **(PA)**	2064	F	310 659-3611	2099
Myevaluationscom Inc	7371	E	646 422-0554	17667
Myst Therapeutics Inc	8731	D	415 516-8450	22852
Naftex Westside Partners Limit	1311	D	310 277-9004	407
Naked Princess Worldwide LLC **(PA)**	2844	F	310 271-1199	5049
Nasty Gal Inc **(HQ)**	5139	E	213 542-3436	14442
Natals Inc	2834	E	310 866-8145	4856
National Genetics Institute	8734	C	310 996-6610	22955
National Promotions & Advg Inc	7311	E	310 558-8555	17038
National Research Group Inc	8732	B	323 817-2000	22894
Nationwide Jewelry Mfrs Inc	3911	F	213 489-1215	11325
Nationwide Legal LLC **(PA)**	8111	C	213 249-9999	21643
Nationwide Theatres Corp **(HQ)**	7833	D	310 657-8420	19296
Natural History Museum of Los	8412	B	213 763-3442	22229
Naver Band Inc	7372	F	323 847-1750	17926
Nelson Name Plate Company **(DH)**	3479	C	323 663-3971	7390
Ner Precious Metals Inc	5094	D	310 367-3179	14136
Netflix Wrldwide Prdctions LLC **(DH)**	7819	A	310 734-2900	19242
Netmarble Us Inc	2741	D	213 222-7712	4190
Nettwerk Music Group LLC **(DH)**	7389	E	323 301-4200	18611
Network Automation Inc	7372	E	213 738-1700	17931
Network Management Group Inc **(PA)**	8741	C	323 263-2632	23073
New Directions Inc **(PA)**	8322	D	310 914-4045	21854
New Dream Network LLC	4813	D	323 375-3842	12658
New Economics For Women **(PA)**	8322	D	213 483-2060	21855
New Figueroa Hotel Inc	7011	D	213 627-8971	16579
New Green Day LLC	2611	E	323 566-7603	3744
New Regency Productions Inc **(PA)**	7812	D	310 369-8300	19156
New Vista Health Services	8059	C	310 477-5501	20616
Newbook International Inc	8748	D	310 855-3773	23481
Nexstar Digital LLC	7311	D	310 971-9300	17039
Next Auto Tech Center	2221	E	323 483-6767	2601
Nexus Healthcare Solutions Inc	8099	E	310 448-2693	21461
Nexxen Apparel Inc **(PA)**	2339	F	323 267-9900	2976
Nhn Global Inc **(PA)**	5137	D	424 672-1177	14406
Nick Alexander Imports	7549	C	800 800-6425	18939
Nielsen Audio Inc	8732	D	310 824-5906	22895
Ninja Jump Inc	3944	D	323 255-5418	11387
Nix Hospitals System LLC **(HQ)**	8062	C	210 271-1800	20869
Nksfb LLC	7371	E	310 277-4657	17677
Nms Properties Inc	6531	D	310 656-2700	15932
Noarus Investments Inc	7538	D	310 649-2440	18858
Nogales Investors LLC	6799	D	310 276-7439	16280
Nogales Investors MGT LLC **(PA)**	6722	C	310 276-7439	16134
Norchem Corporation **(PA)**	3559	D	323 221-0221	7992
Normandie Country Bakery Inc **(PA)**	2051	F	323 939-5528	2024
Northern Trust Company	6021	E	310 282-3800	15004
Northrop Grumman Systems Corp	3812	B	310 556-4911	10609
Nossaman LLP **(PA)**	8111	D	213 612-7800	21645
Nossaman LLP	8111	D	760 918-0500	21646
Not Only Jeans Inc	2211	E	213 765-9725	2582
Notellage Corporation	8059	D	323 257-8151	20618
Novasignal Corp	3841	F	818 317-4999	11037
Nowcom LLC	7379	C	323 746-6888	18204
Nrea-TRC 711 LLC	7011	C	213 488-3500	16586
Nri Usa LLC **(PA)**	4731	D	323 345-6456	12494
Nuevo Amnecer Latino Chld Svcs **(PA)**	8322	D	323 720-9951	21858
Nuorder Inc **(PA)**	7372	F	310 954-1313	17938
Oak Paper Products Co Inc **(PA)**	5113	C	323 268-0507	14217
Oak View Group LLC **(PA)**	7999	C	310 209-3164	19658
Oaks Diagnostics Inc **(PA)**	8011	D	310 855-0035	20008
Oaktree Capital Group LLC **(HQ)**	6722	D	213 830-6300	16135
Oaktree Capital Management LP **(PA)**	6282	C	213 830-6300	15334
Oaktree Cpitl Group Hldings LP **(PA)**	6722	A	213 830-6300	16136
Oaktree Holdings Inc	6722	A	213 830-6300	16137
Oaktree Intl Holdings LLC **(DH)**	6282	D	213 830-6300	15335
Oaktree Real Estate Opprtnties **(DH)**	6722	D	213 830-6300	16138
Oaktree Real Estate Opprtnties	6722	B	213 830-6300	16139
Oaktree Strategic Income LLC	6722	A	213 830-6300	16140
Oasis Hcp 2 LLC **(PA)**	8051	C	323 987-5954	20426
Oasis West Realty LLC **(PA)**	6726	B	310 274-8066	16159
Oberman Tivoli & Pickert Inc	7373	C	310 440-9600	18056
Oblong Industries Inc **(HQ)**	7371	C	213 683-8863	17682
Ocean Group Inc **(PA)**	5146	D	213 622-3677	14575
Ocm Pe Holdings LP	3679	A	213 830-6213	9758
Ocm Real Estate Opprtnties Fun	6722	B	213 830-6300	16141
Ocs America Inc **(DH)**	7389	E	310 417-0650	18618
Ods Technologies LP **(DH)**	4833	C	310 242-9400	12736
Offenhauser Sales Corp	3714	F	323 225-1307	10111
Offline Inc **(PA)**	2342	E	213 742-9001	3022
Old Country Millwork Inc	3547	E	323 234-2940	7886
Old Pueblo Ranch Inc	2099	E	800 367-7522	2498
Old Spc Inc	3471	E	310 533-0748	7289
Olympia Convalescent Hospital	8059	C	213 487-3000	20619
Olympia Health Care LLC	8062	A	323 938-3161	20874
Omar Leather Co	3199	F	323 227-5220	5914
Omega/Cinema Props Inc	7819	D	323 466-8201	19243
OMelveny & Myers LLP **(PA)**	8111	A	213 430-6000	21648
On-Line Power Incorporated **(PA)**	3612	E	323 721-5017	8880
ONeil Capital Management Inc	2754	C	310 448-6400	4466
ONeil Digital Solutions LLC	7389	C	310 448-6407	18619
Onelegacy **(PA)**	8099	D	213 625-0665	21468

	SIC	EMP	PHONE	ENTRY #
Onni Properties LLC	8741	C	213 568-0278	23078
Ophir Rf Inc	3663	E	310 306-5556	9304
Orange Coast Kommunications	2721	B	949 862-1133	4090
Orbita Corp **(PA)**	2381	F	213 746-4783	3050
Organztion Amrcn Kdaly Edctors	8699	E	310 441-3555	22458
Origen Food Inc **(PA)**	2099	E	800 420-4927	2501
Orlando Wilshire Investments	7011	C	323 658-6600	16598
Orthopaedic Hospital **(PA)**	8062	C	213 742-1000	20877
Otis Elevator Company	5084	E	323 342-4500	13925
Otts Asia Moorer Devon	6799	C	323 603-6959	16282
Outfront Media LLC	7312	E	323 222-7171	17076
Output Inc	7372	F	310 795-6099	17948
Ovation LLC	4833	D	310 430-7575	12737
Overseenet **(PA)**	7311	C	213 408-0080	17042
Oxford Palace Hotel	7011	D	213 382-7756	16604
Oxigen Beverages (usa) Inc	2086	F	424 284-2177	2275
P Kay Metal Inc **(PA)**	3356	E	323 585-5058	6337
P8ge Consulting Inc	8748	E	310 666-2301	23489
Pabst Brewing Company LLC **(PA)**	2082	C	310 470-0962	2152
Pac Fill Inc	2026	E	818 409-0117	1838
Pachulski Stang Zehl Jones LLP **(PA)**	8111	D	310 277-6910	21650
Pacific Air Cargo LLC	4731	D	310 645-2173	12498
Pacific Asian Cnsrtium In Empl **(PA)**	8331	C	213 353-3982	21965
Pacific Coast Bach Label Inc	2269	E	213 612-0314	2677
Pacific Coast Elevator Corp	7699	C	323 345-2550	19053
Pacific Coast Ironworks Inc	3441	F	323 585-1320	6646
Pacific Health Corporation	8062	B	714 619-7797	20878
Pacific Indemnity Company	6411	B	213 622-2334	15607
Pacific Manufacturing MGT Inc	2542	D	323 263-9000	3690
Pacific Paper Converting Inc **(PA)**	5199	D	323 888-1330	14960
Pacific Play Tents Inc	2394	E	323 269-0431	3142
Pacific Premier Bank	6022	D	213 626-0085	15038
Pacific Theaters Inc **(PA)**	7832	C	310 657-8420	19285
Pacific Theatres Entrmt Corp **(HQ)**	7832	D	310 659-9432	19286
Pacific Trellis Fruit LLC **(PA)**	5148	C	323 859-9600	14646
Packard Realty Inc	7011	C	310 649-5151	16615
Pacwest Security Services	7381	C	213 413-3500	18308
Pai Gp Inc	3231	D	323 549-5355	5967
Paint-Chem Inc	2851	F	213 747-7725	5106
Palisades Group LLC	6211	D	424 280-7560	15304
Pallet Masters Inc	2448	D	323 758-1713	3403
Pamc Ltd **(PA)**	8062	A	213 624-8411	20884
Papercutters Inc	2671	E	323 888-1330	3856
Para Sempre Inc	8742	D	310 444-0555	23293
Paracelsus Los Angeles Comm	8062	C	323 267-0477	20885
Paradigm Talent Agency LLC	7922	D	310 288-8000	19326
Paragon Language Services Inc **(PA)**	7389	F	323 966-4655	18628
Paragon Textiles Inc	5137	D	310 323-7500	14409
Paramount Licensing Inc	6794	E	323 956-5634	16215
Paramount Pictures Corporation **(DH)**	7812	A	323 956-5000	19159
Paramunt Contrs Developers Inc	6531	E	323 464-7050	15944
Parker Milliken Clark OHar	8111	D	818 784-8087	21653
Parker Stanbury LLP **(PA)**	8111	D	619 528-1259	21654
Parking Concepts Inc	7521	C	310 208-1611	18772
Parking Concepts Inc	7521	C	213 746-5764	18773
Parking Concepts Inc	7521	C	213 623-2661	18775
Parking Network Inc	1799	C	213 613-1500	1680
Parts Out Inc **(PA)**	3694	F	626 560-1540	9827
Pathways La **(PA)**	8322	E	213 427-2700	21865
Patriot Communications LLC **(PA)**	8748	D	888 833-4711	23492
Paul Hastings LLP **(PA)**	8111	A	213 683-6000	21656
Payden & Rygel **(PA)**	6282	C	213 625-1900	15339
Payrollcentric Inc	7372	E	310 258-9703	17955
Pbf & E LLC	2087	E	213 427-0340	2335
Pcs Property Managment LLC	6531	C	310 231-1000	15948
Peach Inc	4215	C	323 654-2333	12145
Pediatric & Family Medical Ctr	8011	C	213 342-3325	20020
Peep Inc	2339	F	213 748-5500	2981
Pegasus Squire Inc	7379	D	866 208-6837	18210
Peking Noodle Co Inc	2098	E	323 223-0897	2381
Penske Business Media LLC **(HQ)**	2721	D	310 321-5000	4096
Pentrate Metal Processing	3471	E	323 269-2121	7293
People Assisting Homeless	8322	C	323 644-2216	21866
Peoples Sausage Company	2013	F	213 627-8633	1744
Perfection Machine and Tl Work	3599	E	213 749-5095	8738
Performing Arts Ctr Los Angles	7922	C	213 972-7512	19327
Perimetrics LLC	3269	F	310 826-4905	6005
Petco Animal Sups Stores Inc	5199	F	323 852-1370	14964
Pexs International Inc	7379	C	626 365-6706	18211
Phenomenon Mktg & Entrmt LLC **(PA)**	8742	D	323 648-4000	23296
Philmont Management Inc	1542	D	213 380-0159	808
Phoenix Aerial Systems Inc	3829	F	323 577-3366	10903
Phoenix Engineering Co Inc	7363	D	310 532-1134	17507
Phoenix Textile Inc	7389	D	213 239-9640	18632
Phyllis Morris Originals	5021	E	310 289-4800	13148
Pico Cleaner Inc **(PA)**	7216	D	310 274-2431	16876
Pierre Mitri **(PA)**	2339	F	213 747-1838	2983
Piet Retief Inc	2339	E	323 732-8312	2984
Pih Health Good Samaritan Hosp **(HQ)**	8062	A	213 977-2121	20890
Pioneer Diecasters Inc	3363	F	323 245-6561	6370
Pircher Nichols & Meeks **(PA)**	8111	D	310 201-0132	21660
Pixi Inc	5122	D	310 670-7767	14279
Planetizen Inc	2741	E	877 260-7526	4194
Planned Parenthood Los Angeles **(PA)**	8093	D	213 284-3200	21325
Plant Ranch LLC	2099	F	818 384-9727	2509
Plastique Unique Inc	3089	E	310 839-3968	5759
Plastopan Industries Inc **(PA)**	2655	E	323 231-2225	3838

Mergent email: customerrelations@mergent.com
1394
2022 Southern California Business
Directory and Buyers Guide
(P-0000) Products & Services Section entry number
(PA)=Parent Co (HQ)=Headquarters (DH)=Div Headquarters

Company	SIC	EMP	PHONE	ENTRY #
Plastpro 2000 Inc (PA)	3089	C	310 693-8600	5762
Platinum Disc LLC	5099	D	608 784-6620	14174
Platinum Roofing Inc	1761	D	408 280-5028	1502
Playa Proper Jv LLC	7011	D	310 645-0400	16634
Playboy Enterprises Inc	2721	A	310 424-1800	4097
Playboy Enterprises Inc (HQ)	2721	B	310 424-1800	4098
Playboy Enterprises Intl	2741	C	310 424-1800	4195
Playhouse Dental (PA)	8021	D	323 269-5437	20195
Plaza De La Raza Child Develop	8351	C	323 224-1788	22049
PLD Enterprises Inc	5146	D	213 626-4444	14578
Plush Home Inc	2511	F	323 852-1912	3485
Pluto Inc (DH)	7812	D	323 746-0500	19165
Pmk-Bnc Inc (PA)	8743	D	310 854-0455	23384
Pmk-Bnc Inc	8743	E	310 854-4800	23385
Poetry Corporation (PA)	2337	E	213 765-8957	2906
Point360 (PA)	7819	C	818 565-1400	19245
Pollstar LLC	2721	D	559 271-7900	4099
Polsinelli PC	8111	C	310 556-1801	21661
Polyalloys Injected Metals Inc	3532	D	310 715-9800	7661
Polycarbin (PA)	2821	D	203 615-3797	4710
Polytex Manufacturing Inc (PA)	2284	F	323 726-0140	2704
Pomwonderful LLC (DH)	5149	C	310 966-5800	14720
Post Group Inc (PA)	7819	C	323 462-2300	19246
Pouring With Heart LLC	2084	F	213 817-5321	2214
Power Fasteners Inc	3452	A	323 232-4362	7072
Powerfull Systems Inc	1731	E	310 836-9333	1300
Powersource Talent LLC	8742	C	424 835-0878	23298
Practice Management Info Corp (PA)	2731	F	323 954-0224	4135
Prats/Coffee Inc	1542	D	323 780-4022	812
Precise Air Systems Inc	1711	D	818 646-9757	1122
Preciseq Inc	7379	D	310 709-6094	18215
Precision Steel Products Inc	3444	E	310 523-2002	6894
Pressure Profile Systems Inc	3823	F	310 641-8100	10710
Prime Administration LLC	6798	A	323 549-7155	16240
Princess Cruise Lines Ltd	5137	A	213 745-0314	14411
Private Brand Mdsg Corp	2335	E	213 749-0191	2895
Private Suite Lax LLC	4111	D	310 907-9950	11835
Pro-Wash Inc	7215	C	323 756-6000	16873
Professional Produce	5148	D	323 277-1550	14649
Professional Security Cons (PA)	7381	C	310 207-7729	18312
Project Social T LLC	2331	E	323 266-4500	2864
Proland Property Managment LLC (PA)	6531	D	213 738-8175	15960
Promises Promises Inc	2335	E	213 749-7725	2896
Promo Shop Inc (PA)	8742	D	310 821-1780	23301
Prompt Delivery Inc	7389	E	858 549-8000	18645
Prosearch Strategies LLC	8732	C	877 447-7291	22896
Prospect Enterprises Inc (PA)	5146	C	213 599-5700	14579
Prospect Medical Holdings Inc (PA)	8011	B	310 943-4500	20028
Proto Homes LLC	3792	E	310 271-7544	10546
Prototypes Centers For Innov	8322	C	213 542-3838	21874
Providence Rest Partners LLC	6799	C	323 460-4170	16285
Prudential Lighting Corp (PA)	3646	C	213 477-1694	9100
PS Arts	8748	E	310 586-1017	23497
PSM Industries Inc (PA)	3499	D	888 663-8256	7568
Psomas (PA)	8713	C	213 223-1400	22755
Ptm Images LLC	2599	F	310 881-8053	3737
Public Communications Svcs Inc	4813	C	310 231-1000	12665
Public Counsel	8111	D	213 385-2977	21666
Pulse One Care LLC	8322	E	310 657-9300	21875
Puma Biotechnology Inc (PA)	2834	B	424 248-6500	4876
Pureform Global Inc	2869	F	310 666-4869	5145
Pw Eagle Inc	3084	B	800 621-4404	5470
Q&A7 LLC	2339	F	323 364-4250	2987
Qology Direct LLC	7389	C	310 341-4420	18646
Qre Operating LLC	1382	D	213 225-5900	462
Quake City Casuals Inc	5136	C	213 746-0540	14346
Quality Produced LLC (PA)	2037	E	310 592-8834	1908
Quantum Bhvioral Solutions Inc (PA)	8049	D	626 531-6999	20229
Queenscare Health Centers	8011	D	323 780-4510	20031
Queenscare Health Centers	8011	D	323 644-6180	20032
Quick Systems Inc	1711	E	702 335-3574	1125
Quigly-Simpson Heppelwhite Inc	7311	C	310 996-5800	17047
Quinn Emnuel Urqhart Sllvan LL (PA)	8111	B	213 443-3000	21667
Quintile Wealth Management LLC	8742	E	310 806-4000	23304
R & R Electric	1731	E	310 785-0288	1304
R W Zant Co (PA)	5147	D	323 980-5457	14602
Radisson Hotel At Usc	7011	C	213 748-4141	16650
Radix Textile Inc	5131	E	323 234-1667	14316
Radlax Gateway Hotel LLC	7011	A	310 670-9000	16652
Radleys	7812	E	310 765-2223	19169
Radnet Inc (PA)	8071	B	310 445-2800	21093
Radnet Mnaged Imaging Svcs Inc (HQ)	8011	C	310 445-2800	20037
Rafu Shimpo	2711	E	213 629-2231	4025
Rainbow Sublymation Inc	2759	E	213 489-5001	4563
Raleigh Enterprises Inc (PA)	7011	C	310 899-8900	16654
Raleigh Sunset Marquis Ho	7011	D	310 358-3759	16655
Ram Off Road Accessories Inc	3714	E	323 266-3850	10123
Rapp Worldwide California Inc (PA)	7311	C	310 563-7200	17048
Rapp Worldwide Inc	7311	D	310 563-7200	17049
Ravlich Enterprises LLC	3471	F	213 221-6081	7303
Raw Juicery Inc	2037	F	213 221-6081	1909
Rbabs Investments 1 LLC	6531	E	818 577-7171	15966
Rbb Architects Inc (PA)	8712	D	310 479-1473	22738
Ready Industries Inc	7352	F	213 749-2041	4416
Reason Foundation	7389	C	310 391-2245	18649
Red Brick Corporation	2752	F	323 549-9444	4417
Red Hawk Fire & SEC CA Inc (DH)	1731	D	818 683-1500	1307
Reed Smith LLP	8111	C	213 457-8000	21668
Rehababilities Inc	7361	C	310 473-4448	17459
Rehabltion Cntre of Bvrly Hlls	8051	F	323 782-1500	20443
Relational Center	7372	F	323 935-1807	17973
Reliance Steel & Aluminum Co (PA)	5051	C	213 687-7700	13588
Relocity Inc	8741	C	323 207-9160	23098
Remington Hotel Corporation	7011	D	310 553-6561	16659
Renaissance Hotel Operating Co	7011	D	310 337-2800	16660
Rentech Inc (PA)	2999	B	310 571-9800	5301
Rentech Ntrgn Pasadena Spa LLC	2873	E	310 571-9805	5160
Resecurity LLC	5045	E	888 223-8276	13433
Resource Management Group Inc (PA)	4731	D	858 677-0884	12519
Reunify LLC	7299	D	310 893-1736	16975
Revolt Media and Tv LLC	4833	C	323 645-3000	12739
Rexford Industrial Realty Inc (PA)	6798	C	310 966-1680	16243
Rey-Crest Roofg Waterproofing	1799	D	323 257-9329	1686
Reyes Coca-Cola Bottling LLC	2086	D	213 744-8659	2295
Rfl Global Inc	7372	F	323 235-2580	17974
Rhapsody Clothing Inc	2339	D	213 614-8887	2989
Richards Watson & Gershon PC (PA)	8111	C	213 626-8484	21669
Riot Games Inc (DH)	7371	A	310 207-1444	17699
Rnc Capital Management LLC	6282	D	310 477-6543	15344
Rnovate Inc	3568	F	213 489-1617	8109
Robert Consl Englekirk Strctrl (PA)	8711	D	323 733-6673	22647
Rock-It Cargo USA LLC	4731	D	310 410-0935	12520
Rockport ADM Svcs LLC	8051	D	323 223-3441	20451
Rockport ADM Svcs LLC (PA)	8741	C	323 330-6500	23102
Rockwest Technology Group Inc	3089	F	323 256-8700	5795
Rodeo Realty Inc	6531	C	310 873-0100	15980
Rogers & Cowan Inc (HQ)	8743	C	310 854-8100	23386
Rogers Poultry Co	5144	D	800 585-0802	14550
Roland Corporation US (HQ)	5099	C	323 890-3700	14178
Roman Upholstery Mfg Inc	2512	F	310 479-3252	3515
Romar Group Inc (PA)	2321	D	213 621-4403	2760
Romex Textiles Inc (PA)	5131	E	213 749-9090	14317
Ron Teeguarden Enterprises Inc (PA)	2833	E	323 556-8188	4762
Roosevelt Hotel LLC	7011	C	323 466-7000	16670
Ropers Majeski A Prof Corp	8111	E	213 312-2000	21670
Rosano Partners	6531	E	213 802-0300	15990
Roscoe Moss Manufacturing Co (PA)	3317	D	323 261-4185	6252
Rose Genuine Inc	2361	F	213 747-4120	3036
Rosemont Realty LLC (PA)	6531	C	505 992-5100	15991
Rosendin Holdings Inc (PA)	1731	A	213 891-9619	1312
Roy E Hanson Jr Mfg (PA)	3443	D	213 747-7514	6750
Rp Realty Partners LLC	6512	E	310 207-6990	15694
Rpd Hotels 18 LLC (PA)	7011	A	213 746-1531	16674
Rpsz Construction LLC	3949	E	314 677-5831	11444
Rrt Enterprises LP (PA)	8051	B	310 397-2372	20454
Rrt Enterprises LP	8051	B	323 653-1521	20455
Ruben & Leon Inc	3993	F	310 486-6648	11588
Ruben & Leon Inc	7629	E	323 937-4445	18955
Ruby Creek Resources Inc	8742	E	212 671-0404	23313
Rucci Inc	3999	E	323 778-9000	11745
Ruchel Enterprises	6513	C	213 389-6900	15747
Runway Inc	7819	C	310 636-2000	19247
Rustic Canyon Group LLC	6799	D	310 998-8000	16290
Rutherford Co Inc (PA)	1742	D	323 666-5284	1399
Ruzannas Decor	7389	E	323 472-0505	18659
Rvshilfy LLC	5015	C	313 329-0146	13124
S Studio Inc	2337	F	213 388-7400	2907
S W K Properties LLC (PA)	7011	D	213 383-9204	16681
S&B Development Group LLC	2221	E	213 446-2818	2603
Saatchi & Saatchi N Amer LLC	7311	C	310 437-2500	17054
Saban Brands LLC (HQ)	8742	D	310 557-5230	23315
Saban Capital Group Inc (PA)	6799	C	310 557-5100	16292
Sac International Steel Inc (PA)	5051	C	323 232-2467	13593
Saehan Bank (PA)	6022	E	213 368-7700	15042
Sag-Aftra Foundation	8631	C	323 549-6708	22295
Saharan Motor Hotel Inc	7011	D	323 874-6700	16683
Sakura Noodle Inc	2098	F	213 623-2396	2382
Samaritan Imaging Center	8071	A	213 977-2140	21095
San Antonio Winery Inc (PA)	2084	C	323 223-1401	2220
Sanitek Products Inc	2842	C	323 245-6781	4977
Santa Ana Clnica Mdica Gen Med	8011	E	323 221-1111	20054
Santa Mnica Wlshire Imging LLC	8011	E	323 549-3055	20057
Santa Monica Bay Physicians He (PA)	8011	E	310 417-5900	20059
Santa Monica City of	3589	E	310 826-6712	8411
Santee Systems Services II LL	7991	E	323 445-0044	19467
Say It With A Sock LLC	2252	F	800 208-0879	2622
Sbb Roofing Inc (PA)	1761	C	323 254-2888	1505
SBE Entertainment Group LLC (HQ)	7011	D	323 655-8000	16696
SBE Hotel Group LLC (PA)	7011	D	323 655-8000	16697
Sbnw LLC (PA)	3171	C	213 234-5122	5903
Scottel Voice & Data Inc	7629	C	310 737-7300	18956
Scottex Inc	2399	E	310 516-1411	3200
Scv Facilities Services Inc	7349	D	310 803-4588	17282
SDI Media USA Inc (HQ)	7812	D	310 388-8800	19176
Sea Dwelling Creatures Inc	5199	D	310 676-9697	14974
Sea Pac Engineering Inc	1542	D	213 487-6130	822
Sea Snack Foods Inc (PA)	5146	E	213 622-2204	14582
Sea Win Inc	5146	E	213 688-2899	14583
Season Produce Co Inc	5148	B	213 689-0008	14652
Seattle Arprt Hospitality LLC	7011	D	310 476-6411	16700
Second Generation Inc	2339	D	213 743-8700	2992
Second Spectrum Inc	7371	D	213 995-6860	17706
Securitech Security Svcs Inc	7381	C	213 387-5050	18325
Security 20/20 Inc	8748	F	310 475-7780	23507

	SIC	EMP	PHONE	ENTRY #
Security Textile Corporation	2396	E	213 747-2673	3181
Sedas Printing Inc	2752	E	323 469-1034	4420
Seek Capital LLC	8742	D	855 978-6106	23319
Seiu Local 2015	8631	C	213 985-0384	22296
Seiu Local 721	8631	C	213 368-8660	22297
Seiu United Service Workers W **(PA)**	8631	D	213 284-7705	22298
Self-Realization Fellowship Ch **(PA)**	2741	E	323 225-2471	4203
Semore Inc	2325	F	213 746-4122	2774
Senior Keiro Health Care	8361	D	323 263-9651	22152
Sentinel Peak Rsources Cal LLC	1382	D	323 298-2200	468
Seollem Corporation	2326	F	323 265-3266	2789
Serv-Rite Meat Company Inc	2011	D	323 227-1911	1719
Sexual Recovery Institute Inc	8322	B	310 360-0130	21888
Seyfarth Shaw LLP	8111	C	213 270-9600	21674
Seyfarth Shaw LLP	8111	C	310 277-7200	21675
Shadow Animation LLC	7812	E	323 466-7771	19177
Shadowmachine LLC **(PA)**	7812	D	323 466-7388	19178
Shane Hunter LLC	2389	E	415 627-7730	3085
Shani Darden Skincare Inc	2844	E	310 745-3150	5069
Shapiro-Gilman-Shandler Co **(HQ)**	5148	D	213 593-1200	14654
Shawmut Woodworking & Sup Inc	1542	C	323 602-1000	825
Shell New Energies US LLC **(HQ)**	7371	E	888 751-8560	17712
Sheppard Mllin Rchter Hmpton L **(PA)**	8111	B	213 620-1780	21676
Sheraton LLC	7011	D	310 642-1111	16705
Shields For Families **(PA)**	8069	D	323 242-5000	21049
Shilpark Paint Corporation **(PA)**	5198	E	323 732-7093	14906
Shire-NPS Pharmaceuticals Inc	2834	A	818 241-3700	4893
Shivay Hospitality Inc	7011	D	323 702-7103	16708
Shuttle Smart Inc	4111	C	310 338-9466	11840
Sia Engineering (usa) Inc	8711	D	310 693-7108	22654
Siemens Hlthcare Dgnostics Inc	3841	D	310 645-8200	11058
Silq Technologies Corporation	3567	F	310 806-9202	8098
Silverado Senior Living Inc	8051	D	323 984-7313	20475
Silvestri Studio Inc **(PA)**	3999	D	323 277-4420	11756
Silvus Technologies Inc **(PA)**	3663	D	310 479-3333	9318
Sinai Temple	7261	C	323 469-6000	16930
Sinai Temple **(PA)**	7261	B	310 474-1518	16931
Singerlewak LLP **(PA)**	8721	C	310 477-3924	22813
Singularity 6 Corporation **(PA)**	7372	F	310 963-1655	17983
Sissell Bros	3272	E	323 261-0106	6056
Sisters of Nzareth Los Angeles	8361	D	310 839-2361	22154
Sitrick Brincko Group LLC	8742	D	310 788-2850	23324
Skadden Arps Slate Meagher & F	8111	C	213 687-5000	21678
Skillz Inc **(PA)**	7371	B	415 762-0511	17713
Skin Health Experts LLC	7991	D	323 655-7546	19468
Skirball Cultural Center	8412	C	310 440-4500	22236
Sky Jeans Inc	2211	E	323 778-2065	2587
Sky Zone LLC **(HQ)**	7929	C	310 734-0300	19378
Skyline Hlthcare Wllness Ctr L	8051	D	323 665-1185	20476
Skypower Holdings LLC	1711	C	323 860-4900	1139
Skyview Capital LLC	6153	D	310 273-6000	15159
Sleepow Ltd	2211	E	646 688-0808	2588
Sls Hotel At Beverly Hills	7011	D	310 247-0400	16715
SM 10000 Property LLC	6552	D	305 374-5700	16074
Smart & Final Stores Inc	5141	C	323 549-9586	14489
Smartest Edu Inc	7372	F	833 463-6761	17985
Smith-Emery Company **(PA)**	8742	C	213 745-5312	23327
Smoothie Inc	2037	F	310 598-7113	1910
SMS Transportation Svcs Inc	4111	C	213 489-5367	11841
Smwd Inc **(PA)**	4833	D	323 904-4680	12742
Snack It Forward LLC	2096	E	310 242-5517	2366
Society of St Vncent De Paul C **(PA)**	8699	D	323 226-9645	22462
Sodexo Management Inc	8742	B	310 646-3738	23329
Sofa U Love LLC **(PA)**	2512	E	323 464-3397	3517
Sola Impact Fund II LP	6531	E	323 306-4648	16000
Sola Impact Fund II LP	6531	E	323 306-4648	16001
Sola Impact Fund II LP	6531	E	323 306-4648	16002
Sola Impact Fund II LP	6531	E	323 306-4648	16003
Sola Impact Fund II LP	6531	E	323 306-4648	16004
Sola Impact Fund II LP	6531	E	323 306-4648	16005
Sola Rentals Inc	7359	E	323 306-4648	17373
Solace Cst LLC **(HQ)**	3443	D	310 919-5401	6753
Solheim Lutheran Home	8361	C	323 257-7518	22155
Solver Inc	5045	E	310 691-5300	13440
Sonesta Los Angles Arprt Lax L	7011	C	310 642-7500	16719
Songs Music Publishing LLC	2741	F	323 939-3511	4205
Sonicsensory Inc **(PA)**	3021	F	213 336-3747	5317
Sonora Bakery Inc	2051	E	323 269-2253	2035
SOS Security Incorporated	7381	D	310 392-9600	18337
Soundboks Inc	7359	F	310 774-0480	17374
Source It USA Inc	7373	E	714 318-4428	18069
South Bay Senior Services Inc	8082	D	310 338-8558	21213
South Baylo University	8093	C	213 999-0297	21341
South Central Family Hlth Ctr	8011	D	323 908-4200	20067
South China Sheet Metal Inc	1711	E	323 225-1522	1144
South Cntl Los Angles Rgnal CT **(PA)**	8399	C	213 744-7000	22210
Southern Cal Halthcare Sys Inc **(HQ)**	8062	C	310 943-4500	20944
Southern Cal Hsing Rights Ctr	8322	D	213 387-8400	21893
Southern Cal Pipe Trades ADM **(PA)**	6733	D	213 385-6161	16197
Southern Cal Prmnnte Med Group	8011	C	323 857-2000	20078
Southern Cal Prmnnte Med Group	8011	C	323 783-5455	20080
Southern Cal Prmnnte Med Group	8011	C	323 783-4893	20081
Southern Cal Prmnnte Med Group	6324	C	323 564-7911	15459
Southern Cal Rgional Rail Auth **(PA)**	4111	C	213 452-0200	11843
Southern California Gas Co **(DH)**	4924	A	213 244-1200	12866
Southern California Gas Tower	4924	A	213 244-1200	12868
Southern Management Corp	7349	C	213 312-2268	17288

	SIC	EMP	PHONE	ENTRY #
Southland Home Fabrics Inc	2395	F	310 475-1637	3164
Southwest Airlines Co	4512	D	310 665-5700	12317
Southwest Crpnters Trning Fund	8631	D	213 386-8590	22299
Southwest Plating Co Inc	3471	F	323 753-3781	7312
Southwest Rgnal Cncil Crpnters **(PA)**	8631	E	213 385-1457	22300
Sovereign Arts Met Finshg LLC	3471	F	714 742-9944	7313
Spacestor Inc	2521	F	310 410-0220	3600
Spanish Brdcstg Sys of Cal	4832	D	310 203-0900	12706
Special Needs Network	8069	E	323 291-7100	21054
Special Service For Groups Inc **(PA)**	8331	D	213 368-1888	21968
Special Service For Groups Inc	8399	C	213 553-1800	22213
Specialty Surface Grinding Inc	3599	E	310 538-4352	8801
Spectrum MGT Holdg Co LLC	4841	D	323 657-0899	12777
Sprint Communications Co LP	5065	C	310 216-9093	13775
Sprintray Inc	8742	C	800 914-8004	23332
Spus7 125 Cambridgepark LP	6531	D	213 683-4200	16007
Spus7 150 Cambridgepark LP	6531	C	213 683-4200	16008
Srht Property Holding LLC	6531	C	213 683-0522	16009
SSC Apparel Inc	2339	F	213 748-5511	2996
St Annes Maternity Home	8361	C	213 381-2931	22156
St Brnbas Snior Ctr Los Angle	8322	D	213 388-4444	21894
St Jhns Well Child Fmly Ctr I **(PA)**	8021	D	323 541-1600	20200
St Timothy School	8351	D	310 474-1811	22060
St Vncent Snior Ctzen Ntrtn P **(PA)**	8621	D	213 484-7775	22280
Stadco **(PA)**	3545	C	323 227-8888	7870
Stainless Industrial Companies	3544	D	310 575-9400	7832
Standard Homeopathic Company **(PA)**	2834	D	310 768-0700	4896
Standard-Southern Corporation	4222	D	213 624-1831	12177
Standard-Southern Corporation	4222	C	213 624-1831	12178
Standard-Southern Corporation	4222	C	213 624-1831	12179
Standardvision LLC	3993	E	323 222-3630	11605
Stanley M Scher Inc **(PA)**	5013	D	213 746-1922	13097
Stantec Architecture Inc	7389	C	213 955-9775	18677
Stardust Diamond Corp	3915	E	213 239-9999	11339
Starlion Inc	2321	E	323 233-8823	2761
Start Pace Head	8351	D	213 989-3222	22061
State Bar of California	8621	D	213 765-1520	22281
Steinberg Hart **(PA)**	8712	D	408 295-5446	22746
Stepstone Inc	3272	E	310 327-7474	6060
Steriltek Inc	7389	D	213 977-2298	18680
Sterling Westwood Inc	7216	D	310 287-2431	16878
Stevens Pond APT Propty Ownr **(PA)**	6513	D	310 268-8344	15750
Stic-Adhesive Products Co Inc	2891	C	323 268-2956	5197
Stillhouse LLC	2085	E	323 498-1111	2246
Stjohn God Rtirement Care Ctr	8051	C	323 731-0641	20480
Stk	3999	F	310 659-3535	11763
Stockbridge/Sbe Holdings LLC	7011	A	323 655-8000	16732
Stone Canyon Inds Holdings LLC **(PA)**	8742	E	424 316-2061	23335
Stone Canyon Industries LLC **(PA)**	3089	E	310 570-4869	5830
Stonecalibre LLC **(PA)**	6799	D	310 774-0014	16293
Stony Apparel Corp **(PA)**	2339	D	323 981-9080	2999
Stroock & Stroock & Lavan LLP	8111	C	310 556-5800	21683
Strouk Group LLC	5147	D	323 939-7792	14607
Studio Systems Inc **(PA)**	2741	E	323 634-3400	4208
Stutman Trster Glatt Prof Corp	8111	D	310 228-5600	21684
Stv Architects Inc	8712	C	213 482-9444	22747
Subchondral Solutions Inc	3842	F	888 410-5622	11142
Success Healthcare 1 LLC **(PA)**	8082	A	213 989-6100	21219
Sugar Lips Inc	2211	F	213 742-9001	2591
Sugarsync Inc	7372	E	650 571-5105	17990
Sulmeyerkupetz A Prof Corp **(PA)**	8111	D	213 617-5221	21685
Sun Valley Products Inc	3354	E	818 247-8350	6318
Sun Valley Products Inc **(HQ)**	3354	E	818 247-8350	6319
SunAmerica Inc **(HQ)**	6091	A	310 772-6000	15120
SunAmerica Investments Inc **(DH)**	8741	D	310 772-6000	23118
SunAmerica Investments Inc	6722	C	310 772-6000	16145
Sunset Tower Hotel LLC	7011	D	323 654-7100	16740
Sunstone Hotel Properties Inc	7011	C	310 228-4100	16741
Super Center Concepts Inc	2051	C	323 241-6789	2038
Superior Nut Co Inc	5145	F	323 223-2431	14566
Surco Products Inc	3446	F	310 323-2520	6980
Surgeon Worldwide Inc	3144	E	707 501-7962	5883
Svi Lax LLC	7011	D	310 281-0300	16745
Sweatheory LLC	7991	D	310 956-2307	19469
Sweatheory Wellness LLC	8099	D	310 844-3662	21487
Swift Media Entertainment Inc	7389	D	310 308-3694	18682
Swissport Cargo Services LP	4581	C	310 910-9541	12370
Swissport Usa Inc	4581	D	310 345-1986	12371
Swissport Usa Inc	4581	D	310 910-9560	12372
Swisstex California Inc **(PA)**	7389	D	310 516-6800	18683
Sydell Hotels LLC	7011	C	213 381-7411	16748
System1 LLC **(PA)**	8742	C	310 256-4882	23338
Systems Experience Inc	8748	D	310 215-9000	23514
Systems Wire & Cable Limited	3496	F	310 532-7870	7516
T Points Inc	7219	E	323 846-9176	16892
T2c Inc	2331	F	213 741-5232	2867
Taad Group Inc **(HQ)**	2331	F	213 545-0009	2868
Tae Gwang Inc	3993	F	323 233-2882	11609
Talyarps Corporation	2851	E	310 559-2335	5115
Tampico Spice Co Incorporated	2099	E	323 235-3154	2532
Tandem Care Plg A Pub Bneft Co	8082	D	310 281-0028	21220
Target Media Partners Oper LLC	2711	F	323 930-3123	4035
Targeted Medical Pharma Inc **(PA)**	2834	E	310 474-9809	4903
Taschen America LLC **(PA)**	2731	F	323 463-4441	4138
Taseon Inc	3825	F	408 240-7800	10773
Tasker Metal Products	3714	F	213 765-5400	10140
Tax Credit Co LLC **(PA)**	7291	D	323 927-0752	16940

GEOGRAPHIC SECTION

LOS ANGELES, CA

	SIC	EMP	PHONE	ENTRY #
Tbwa Chiat/Day Inc	7389	B	310 305-5000	18685
TCI Supply Inc	7349	E	213 745-7756	17289
Tcj Manufacturing LLC	2339	E	213 488-8400	3000
Tcw Absolute Return Credit LLC	6722	D	213 244-0000	16146
Tcw Group Inc **(PA)**	6282	B	213 244-0000	15350
Tdg Operations LLC	2273	E	323 724-9000	2698
Techncolor Crative Svcs USA Inc **(DH)**	7819	B	818 260-3800	19248
Techture Inc	2741	E	323 347-6209	4214
Teksun Inc	3089	F	310 479-0794	5836
Teledyne Technologies Inc	3679	B	310 822-8229	9795
Temple Israel of Hollywood **(PA)**	7261	D	323 876-8330	16932
Temple Pk Cnvalescent Hosp Inc	8059	D	213 380-2035	20631
Tender Home Healthcare Inc	8082	D	323 466-2345	21221
Tenenblatt Corporation	2257	D	323 232-2061	2648
Tenet Health Systems Norris	8062	B	323 865-3000	20971
Tessie Clvland Cmnty Svcs Corp	8322	D	323 586-7333	21901
Textiles & Son LLC **(PA)**	2299	E	323 965-9888	2739
Thc - Orange County Inc	8062	C	310 642-0325	20976
The Microfilm Company of Cal	2731	F	310 354-2610	4139
The Orthopedic Institute of	8011	A	213 977-2010	20109
The Teecor Group Inc	1799	D	213 632-2350	1695
The/Studio	7389	F	877 647-6447	18688
Theatredreams La/Chi L P	7922	E	323 308-6363	19334
Thebrain Technologies LP	7372	F	310 751-5000	17994
Thewrap	2711	F	424 273-4787	4037
Thinkwell Group Inc **(PA)**	7922	D	818 333-3444	19335
Tianello Inc	2331	C	323 231-0599	2872
Ticketmster New Vntres Hldngs **(HQ)**	7999	A	800 653-8000	19676
Tidings	2711	E	213 637-7360	4038
Tikun Olam Adelanto LLC	2833	F	833 468-4586	4766
Tinco Sheet Metal Inc	1761	C	323 263-0511	1507
Tk and Company Watches	3911	F	213 545-1971	11331
TMC Ice Protection Systems LLC **(PA)**	3812	E	951 677-6934	10647
Tokyopop Inc	2731	D	323 920-5967	4140
Tomasini Inc	2221	F	323 231-2349	2606
Topa Insurance Company **(HQ)**	6411	D	310 201-0451	15636
Topa Property Group Inc **(HQ)**	6512	C	310 203-9199	15703
Topson Downs California Inc	2337	C	310 558-0300	2908
Tortilleria La California Inc	2099	F	323 221-8940	2540
Tortilleria San Marcos	2099	F	323 263-0208	2542
Tosco - Tool Specialty Company	3545	E	323 232-3561	7874
Toska Inc	2339	F	213 746-0088	3004
Total Cmmnicator Solutions Inc	7372	D	619 277-1488	17999
Touch ME Fashion Inc **(PA)**	2339	E	323 234-9200	3005
Trailer Park Inc	7311	D	310 845-8400	17062
Trailer Park Inc	7311	D	310 845-3000	17063
Trailer Park Inc **(PA)**	7311	D	310 845-3000	17064
Transmrica Rtirement Svcs Corp **(PA)**	6311	C	866 498-4557	15370
Transom Capital Group LLC **(PA)**	6799	D	424 293-2818	16297
Transplant Connect Inc	7372	E	310 392-1400	18000
Travel Store **(PA)**	4724	D	310 575-5540	12401
Treivush Industries	2339	D	213 745-7774	3006
Triage Entertainment LLC	7812	D	310 417-4800	19187
Tribe Media Corp	2711	E	213 368-1661	4039
Tribridge Holdings LLC	7371	B	813 287-8887	17744
Tripadvisor LLC	7011	D	323 464-5181	16758
Triyar Sv LLC **(PA)**	6531	B	310 234-2888	16019
Tropi-Con Foods Inc	3499	F	949 472-2200	7573
Tropical Preserving Co Inc	2033	E	213 748-5108	1878
Troygould PC	8111	D	310 553-4441	21690
Truck Underwriters Association **(DH)**	8621	A	323 932-3200	22284
Truconnect Communications Inc **(PA)**	4813	C	512 919-2641	12675
Truex Inc	4899	E	310 657-9900	12792
Tu Vets Printing	2752	E	323 723-4569	4441
Tua Fashion Inc **(PA)**	2211	F	213 422-2384	2592
Tubular Specialties Mfg Inc	3261	D	310 515-4801	5993
Tumbleweed Eductl Entps Inc	7999	C	310 444-3232	19678
Tutoring Expert Services LLC	7372	F	424 297-8318	18002
Twelve Signs Inc	2721	F	310 553-8000	4109
Twenteth Cntury Fox HM Entrmt **(DH)**	7812	A	310 369-1000	19189
Twenteth Cntury Fox Intl TV In **(DH)**	4833	D	310 369-1000	12748
Twentieth Cntury Fox Film Corp **(DH)**	7812	D	310 369-1000	19190
Twentieth Cntury Fox Film Corp	7812	D	310 369-2582	19191
Twentieth Cntury Fox Intl Corp **(DH)**	7822	A	310 969-5300	19263
Twentieth Cntury Fox Japan Inc	7336	A	310 369-4636	17192
Twentieth Television Inc	4833	D	310 584-2000	12749
Twenty Mile Productions LLC	7929	C	412 251-0767	19381
U C L A Conference & Catering	7299	D	310 825-5305	16982
U S Trust Company NA	6282	B	213 861-5000	15352
Ubtech Robotics Corp	3549	E	213 261-7153	7906
Ucla Copy Services	7334	E	310 794-6371	17156
Ucla Foundation	6732	B	310 794-3193	16170
Ucla Health	8062	D	310 825-9111	20985
Ucla Health System Auxiliary	8082	B	310 267-4327	21225
Ultra Built Kitchens Inc	2434	E	323 232-3362	3344
Umeya Inc	2052	E	213 626-8341	2075
Umgee USA Inc	2331	F	323 526-9138	2873
Umina Brothers Inc **(PA)**	5148	D	213 622-9206	14659
Un Deux Trois Inc **(PA)**	2369	E	323 588-1067	3046
UNI Hosiery Co Inc **(PA)**	5136	C	213 228-0100	14357
Uniserve Facilities Svcs Corp	7349	B	310 440-6747	17297
United Amrcn Indian Invlvment **(PA)**	8093	C	213 202-3970	21360
United Artists Pictures Inc **(DH)**	7812	C	310 449-3000	19192
United Artists Productions Inc	7822	C	310 449-3000	19264
United Artists Television Corp	7822	C	310 449-3000	19265
United Convalescent Facilities	8059	D	626 629-6950	20634
United Fabrics Intl Inc	5131	D	213 749-8200	14323
United Food and Commercial **(PA)**	8631	D	213 487-7070	22305
United Ind Taxi Drivers **(PA)**	4121	D	323 462-1088	11902
United Medical Imaging Inc **(PA)**	8011	D	310 943-8400	20118
United Parcel Service Inc	4215	C	310 474-0019	12157
United Parcel Service Inc	4512	D	310 670-5849	12319
United Parcel Service Inc	4215	C	323 729-6762	12166
United States Bakery	2051	E	323 232-6124	2039
United States Fire Insur Co	6411	D	213 797-3100	15641
United Teachers-Los Angeles	8631	D	213 487-5560	22306
United Way Inc **(PA)**	8399	D	213 808-6220	22214
Unity Courier Service Inc **(PA)**	4215	C	323 255-9800	12170
Universal Cushion Company Inc **(PA)**	2392	E	323 887-8000	3122
Universal Dyeing and Prtg Inc	2262	E	213 746-0818	2666
Universal Surface Techlgy Inc	2841	E	310 352-6969	4948
University Cal Los Angeles	8733	C	310 825-7852	22923
University Cal Los Angeles	8062	A	310 825-9111	20988
University Credit Union	6061	C	310 477-6628	15095
University Southern California	8062	A	323 442-8500	20993
Upper Crust Enterprises Inc	2099	D	213 625-0038	2545
Urban Insight Inc	7373	F	213 792-2000	18073
URS Group Inc	8711	D	213 996-2200	22684
URS Group Inc	8711	D	213 996-2200	22685
US Hosiery Inc	2252	F	213 742-0101	2625
US International Media LLC **(PA)**	7311	C	310 482-6700	17067
US Telepacific Corp **(HQ)**	4813	E	877 487-8722	12676
Usc Care Medical Group Inc **(PA)**	8062	C	323 442-5100	20994
Usc Crdiothoracic Surgeons Inc	8011	D	323 442-5849	20128
Usc Credit Union	6061	D	213 821-7100	15096
Usc Emergency Medicine Assoc	8011	D	323 226-6667	20129
Usc Keck School of Medicine **(HQ)**	8062	C	323 442-2830	20995
Usc Surgeons Incorporated	8011	D	323 442-5910	20130
Uscb Inc **(PA)**	7322	C	213 985-2111	17118
Used Cardboard Boxes Inc	5113	D	323 724-2500	14230
V & M Plating Co	3471	F	310 532-5633	7328
Vagrant Records Inc	2782	F	323 302-0100	4615
Vagthols Rsdntial Care Ctr Inc	8361	C	323 464-6067	22161
Vahe Enterprises Inc	3713	D	323 235-6657	10000
Val-Pro Inc	5148	D	213 689-0844	14661
Valet Parking Svc A Cal Partnr **(PA)**	7521	A	323 465-5873	18781
Valmas Inc	2335	F	323 677-2211	2899
Vancrest Construction Corp	1542	E	323 256-0011	846
Vaughn Weedman Inc **(PA)**	0782	C	425 481-0919	348
Vayan Marketing Group LLC	8742	E	310 943-4990	23358
VCA Animal Hospitals Inc **(DH)**	0742	C	310 571-6500	205
VCA Inc **(DH)**	5047	A	310 571-6500	13528
VCA Prfessional Animal Lab Inc	0742	D	310 571-6500	206
Veatch Carlson Grogan & Nelson	8111	E	213 381-2861	21691
Venator Americas LLC	2816	D	323 269-7311	4648
Vendor Direct Solutions LLC **(PA)**	7371	C	213 362-5622	17751
Verifi Inc	8742	D	323 655-5789	23360
Verizon Digital Media Svcs Inc **(HQ)**	7379	B	310 396-7400	18234
Verizon Media Inc **(HQ)**	4812	A	310 907-3016	12617
Vermont Fuel Inc	2841	F	818 339-6623	4949
Versa Products Inc **(PA)**	2522	C	310 353-7100	3617
Vescio Enterprises Inc **(PA)**	5084	D	323 263-7225	13960
Veteran Enterprise Inc	2211	F	323 937-2233	2593
Veterans Health Administration	8011	C	310 478-3711	20142
Veterans Health Administration	8011	C	213 253-2677	20153
Veternary Ctrs of Amrica-Texas **(DH)**	0742	D	310 571-6500	208
Via Care Cmnty Hlth Ctr Inc	8011	D	323 268-9191	20155
Viacom Networks	7812	D	310 752-8000	19196
Vibiana Events LLC	7299	D	213 626-1507	16985
Vicar Operating Inc **(DH)**	0742	B	310 571-6500	209
Victor Wire & Cable Corp	3357	F	310 842-9933	6358
Victor Wire and Cable LLC	3357	F	310 842-9933	6359
Videoamp Inc **(PA)**	7372	D	949 294-0351	18005
Vigilant Drone Defense Inc	3499	E	424 275-8282	7576
Villa Toscana Properties LLC	6531	D	213 223-2261	16029
Village Rdshow Entrmt Group US **(PA)**	7812	E	310 385-4300	19197
Village Road Show Pictures USA	7812	D	310 385-4300	19199
Virgil M Stutzman Inc	3471	F	323 732-9146	7330
Virtis-Us LLC **(PA)**	7382	F	855 796-1457	18404
Vision Envelope & Prtg Co Inc **(PA)**	2677	E	310 324-7062	3912
Vision Produce Acquisition LLC	5148	E	213 622-4435	14664
Vision To Learn	8699	E	800 485-9196	22469
Visionary Vr Inc	7372	F	323 868-7443	18006
Vista Del Mar Child Fmly Svcs **(PA)**	8361	B	310 836-1223	22165
Vital Research LLC	8733	D	323 951-1670	22924
Vivid Digital	7371	D	818 908-0481	17755
Vivid Entertainment LLC	7812	E	323 845-4557	19200
Vmg Partners LLC	6282	D	310 775-8603	15354
Volt Industries	3999	F	323 982-0815	11791
Volume Services Inc	7999	C	323 644-6038	19680
Volunteers of Amer Los Angeles	8322	D	213 749-0362	21910
Volunteers of Amer Los Angeles	8322	D	323 780-3770	21913
Volunteers of Amer Los Angeles	8322	D	213 627-8002	21920
Vxi Global Solutions LLC **(PA)**	7389	A	213 739-4720	18721
W A Benjamin Electric Co	3613	E	213 749-7731	8907
W Cellars Inc	2082	F	714 655-2025	2161
W Los Angeles	7011	B	310 208-8765	16774
W&J Business Ventures LLC	7011	C	310 645-7700	16775
Walker & Dunlop Inc	6162	D	301 215-5500	15233
Walker Foods Inc	2033	D	323 268-5191	1880
Walking Company Holdings Inc **(PA)**	5136	C	805 963-8727	14359
Wanu Water Inc	2086	F	310 401-1733	2303
Wardlow 2 LP **(PA)**	7699	D	562 432-8066	19083
Warner Bros Records Inc **(DH)**	7389	B	818 846-9090	18722

GEOGRAPHIC

Employment Codes: A=Over 500 employees, B=251-500, C=101-250, D=51-100, E=20-50 F=10-19

2022 Southern California Business Directory and Buyers Guide

© Mergent Inc. 1-800-342-5647

1397

	SIC	EMP	PHONE	ENTRY #
Warner/Chappell Music Inc **(DH)**	2741	C	310 441-8600	4218
Warren Distributing Inc **(PA)**	5013	D	562 789-3360	13107
Warren Drye Kelley	8111	E	310 712-6100	21694
Washington Garment Dyeing **(PA)**	2262	E	213 747-1111	2667
Washington Grment Dyg Fnshg In	2261	E	213 747-1111	2662
Wasserman Media Group LLC **(PA)**	8742	C	310 407-0200	23363
Watercraft Mix Inc	3273	E	310 884-9755	6126
Waterfront Design Group LLC	2329	E	213 746-5800	2831
Waterprfing Rofg Solutions Inc	1799	D	310 571-0892	1699
Watertalent LLC	8748	E	424 832-7217	23527
Watts Health Foundation Inc	8069	D	323 750-5284	21057
Watts Healthcare Corporation	8011	C	323 241-1780	20158
Watts Healthcare Corporation **(PA)**	8011	C	323 564-4331	20159
Watts Labor Community Action	8322	C	323 563-5639	21923
Wave Community Newspapers Inc **(PA)**	2711	E	323 290-3000	4043
Wave Plastic Surgery Ctr Inc **(PA)**	8062	D	213 383-4800	21006
Wb Music Corp **(DH)**	2741	C	310 441-8600	4219
We Five-R Corporation	3471	E	323 263-6757	7331
Webcor Construction LP	1542	A	213 239-2800	848
Webtoon Entertainment Inc **(PA)**	7929	D	323 297-3410	19385
Wedbush Securities Inc **(HQ)**	6211	B	213 688-8000	15310
Weingart Center Association	8322	C	213 622-6359	21925
Weitz & Luxenberg PC	8111	D	310 247-0921	21696
Welkin Welkin Capitl Group LLC **(PA)**	6799	D	323 312-3200	16301
Wellmade Inc	8742	D	213 221-1123	23364
Wellman & Company	2821	F	310 980-4918	4728
Wellnest Emtonal Hlth Wellness **(PA)**	8322	C	323 373-2400	21926
Wells Fargo Bank Ltd	6021	D	213 253-6227	15008
Wesley Allen Inc **(PA)**	2514	C	323 231-4275	3538
Wessco Intl Ltd A Cal Ltd Prtn **(PA)**	2393	E	310 477-4272	3131
West Angeles Ch God In Chrst	6512	C	323 731-2567	15707
West Cast Hndcrfted Albums Inc	2782	E	626 253-0335	4616
West Coast Ambulance Corp	4119	D	310 435-1862	11897
West Coast Trimmings Corp **(PA)**	2241	F	323 587-0701	2619
West Side Rehab Corporation	6512	C	323 231-4174	15708
Western Bagel Baking Corp	2051	E	310 479-4823	2051
Western Die & Printing Corp	2759	F	323 665-0474	4594
Western Motor Works Inc	3553	F	310 382-6896	7913
Western Supreme Inc	2015	C	213 627-3861	1764
Westfield LLC **(DH)**	6512	B	813 926-4600	15709
Westfield America Inc **(HQ)**	6512	C	310 478-4456	15710
Westfield America Ltd Partnr	6512	B	310 277-3898	15711
Westlake Health Care Center	8051	B	805 494-1233	20507
Westlake Services LLC **(HQ)**	6159	C	323 692-8800	15168
Westpoint Marketing Intl Inc	7389	D	323 233-0233	18724
Westside Jewish Cmnty Ctr Inc **(PA)**	8399	C	323 938-2531	22215
Westwood Healthcare Center LP	8051	D	310 826-0821	20509
Whb Corporation	7011	A	213 624-1011	16787
White Mem Cmnty Hlth Ctr A Cal	8011	D	323 987-1222	20164
White Mem Pediatrics Med Group	8062	D	323 987-1200	21009
White Memorial Med Group Inc **(PA)**	8011	D	323 987-1300	20165
White Memorial Medical Center	8011	A	323 260-5739	20166
White Memorial Medical Center **(HQ)**	8062	A	323 268-5000	21010
Wiemar Distributors Inc	5148	D	213 747-7036	14667
William Oneil & Co Inc **(PA)**	6211	C	310 448-6800	15312
Wilshire Boulevard Temple	6553	C	323 261-6135	16090
Wilshire Country Club	7997	D	323 934-6050	19628
Wilshire Kingsley Inc	6512	D	213 382-6677	15713
Winc Inc	2084	C	855 282-5829	2239
Windsor Grdns Cnvlscent Hosp I	8051	D	323 937-5466	20515
Winter & Bain Mfg Inc **(PA)**	3534	F	213 749-3568	7682
Wire Technology Corporation	3357	E	310 635-6935	6360
Wise Living Inc	2519	E	323 541-0410	3574
Within Unlimited Inc	7384	E	310 664-1400	18422
Wolf Rfkin Shpiro Schlman Rbk **(PA)**	8111	D	310 445-8817	21697
Womble Bond Dickinson (us) LLP	8111	C	310 207-3800	21699
Wonderful Agency	7311	A	310 966-8600	17070
Wonderful Almond Cooperative	2068	E	310 966-5800	2117
Wonderful Company LLC	0723	B	661 720-2609	195
Wonderful Pstchios Almonds LLC **(HQ)**	2068	E	310 966-4650	2118
Wood Smith Henning Berman LLP **(PA)**	8111	E	310 481-7600	21700
Woodland Bedrooms Inc	2511	F	562 408-1558	3492
Workmens Auto Insurance Co	6331	D	213 742-8700	15491
Works Entertainment LLC	7929	E	310 623-7436	19386
World Acceptance Group Corp **(PA)**	7375	D	800 388-1266	18136
Worldlink LLC **(PA)**	7389	D	323 866-5900	18730
Worldwide Holdings Inc **(PA)**	6411	D	213 236-4500	15652
Worldwide Security Assoc Inc **(HQ)**	7381	B	310 743-3000	18361
Worldwide Specialties Inc	2099	C	323 587-2200	2548
Wrap News Inc	7383	E	424 248-0612	18408
Writers Guild America West Inc	8631	C	323 951-4000	22307
X1 Discovery Inc	7371	E	877 999-1347	17763
Xbiz	2721	F	310 820-0228	4114
Xcast Labs Inc **(PA)**	7371	C	310 861-4700	17764
Xcvi LLC **(PA)**	2211	C	213 749-2661	2594
Xos Inc	3694	C	818 316-1890	9832
Xos Fleet Inc	3711	E	818 316-1890	9974
Xpo Logistics Freight Inc	4213	D	213 744-0664	12100
Yamasa Enterprises	2091	E	213 626-2211	2343
Yamazaki California Inc	2051	F	213 624-2773	2054
Yee Yuen Laundry and Clrs Inc	7213	D	323 734-7205	16870
Yeshivath Torath Emeth Academy **(PA)**	8351	C	323 549-3170	22074
Yf Art Holdings Gp LLC	6719	A	678 441-1400	16118
YMi Jeanswear Inc **(PA)**	2335	F	323 581-7700	2901
YMi Jeanswear Inc	2339	D	213 746-6681	3010
Yobs Technologies Inc	7812	E	213 713-3825	19213
Yocup Company	2656	F	310 884-9888	3844
Young & Rubicam LLC	7311	C	213 930-5000	17074
Young Knitting Mills	2253	E	323 980-8677	2644
Young MNS Chrstn Assn Mtro Los **(PA)**	8641	D	213 380-6448	22386
Young Sung (usa) Inc	2399	F	213 427-2580	3202
Young Wns Chrstn Assn Grter Lo	8641	D	323 295-4280	22391
Young Wns Chrstn Assn Grter Lo	8641	D	323 295-4288	22392
Youngs Market Company LLC	5182	D	213 629-3929	14849
Youth To People Inc	2844	E	309 648-5500	5085
Yucaipa Companies LLC **(PA)**	8748	C	310 789-7200	23529
Yue Feng Inc	8322	D	310 253-9795	21933
Yukevich / Cvanaugh A Law Corp **(PA)**	8111	D	213 362-7777	21703
Yummy Foods LLC	4212	D	323 965-0600	12009
Z B P Inc	2679	F	323 266-3363	3940
Zabin Industries Inc **(PA)**	5131	D	213 749-1215	14324
Zastrow Construction Inc	1522	D	323 478-1956	675
Zeco Systems Inc	5171	D	888 751-8560	14798
Zefr Inc	7371	C	310 392-3555	17766
Zelouf West Ltd **(PA)**	2221	E	213 417-1346	2608
Zia Aamir	3441	E	714 337-7861	6685
Ziffren B B F G-L S&C Fnd	8111	C	310 552-3388	21705
Zimmer Gnsul Frsca Archtcts LL	8712	C	213 617-1901	22753
Zina Sterling Silver Inc	5094	F	310 286-2206	14143
Zynx Health Incorporated **(DH)**	7371	E	310 954-1950	17768

LOS OLIVOS, CA - Santa Barbara County

	SIC	EMP	PHONE	ENTRY #
Beckmen Vineyards	0172	E	805 688-8664	43
Cushman Winery Corporation	5182	E	805 688-9339	14839
Firestone Vineyard LP	2084	D	805 688-3940	2184
Pagliei Collection Inc	3961	F	805 693-9101	11489

LOS OSOS, CA - San Luis Obispo County

	SIC	EMP	PHONE	ENTRY #
Los Osos Community Svcs Dst	8399	E	805 528-9370	22201
Rantec Power Systems Inc **(HQ)**	5065	D	805 596-6000	13768

LOST HILLS, CA - Kern County

	SIC	EMP	PHONE	ENTRY #
Roll Properties Intl Inc	6799	C	661 797-6500	16289
Wonderful Orchards LLC	0173	C	661 797-6400	60

LUCERNE VALLEY, CA - San Bernardino County

	SIC	EMP	PHONE	ENTRY #
Casa Clina Hosp Ctrs For Hlthc	8322	C	760 248-6245	21730
Mitsubishi Cement Corporation	3241	C	760 248-7373	5979
Omya Inc	2819	D	760 248-5200	4664
Specialty Minerals Inc	2819	C	760 248-5300	4672

LYNWOOD, CA - Los Angeles County

	SIC	EMP	PHONE	ENTRY #
Aaron Corporation	2339	C	323 235-5959	2910
Ace Machine Shop Inc	3599	D	310 608-2277	8464
Altamed Health Services Corp	8011	C	310 632-0415	19696
Amerasia Furn Cmpnnts Mfg Impr	2512	E	310 638-0570	3495
Bleeker Brothers Inc1	3444	F	310 639-4367	6796
California Steel Products Inc	3449	F	310 603-5645	7016
Comfort Bedding Mfg Inc	2392	F	310 667-7720	3099
Country Villa Service Corp	8051	C	310 537-2500	20296
Ermm Corporation	3715	F	310 635-0524	10166
First Finish Inc	2211	E	310 631-6717	2571
Golden Mattress Co Inc	2515	D	323 887-1888	3549
Gomen Furniture Mfg Inc	2512	E	310 635-4894	3504
Hgc Holdings Inc	2064	F	323 567-2226	2087
Jwch Institute Inc	8322	C	310 223-1035	21829
Kaiser Foundation Hospitals	8011	C	310 604-5700	19907
Kayo of California **(PA)**	2337	E	323 233-6107	2903
Legacy Frames	5065	D	310 537-4210	13741
Lynwood Unified School Dst	8351	D	310 631-7308	22032
Marlinda Management Inc **(PA)**	8059	C	310 631-6122	20610
Midas Express Los Angeles Inc	4225	C	310 609-0366	12222
Next Day Frame Inc	2519	D	310 886-0851	3568
P & L Development LLC	2834	E	323 567-2482	4867
Pacific Ltg & Standards Co	3646	E	310 603-9344	9098
Processes By Martin Inc	3479	E	310 637-1855	7402
Roger R Caruso Enterprises Inc	2448	E	714 773-6006	3406
Shields For Families	8069	D	310 603-1050	21050
South Cntl Hlth Rhbltion Prgr	8093	D	310 667-4070	21342
Southern CA Hlth & Rhbltn Prg	8011	C	310 631-8004	20072
Southern Cal Prmnnte Med Group	8011	C	310 604-5700	20077
St Francis Medical Center **(DH)**	8062	D	310 900-8900	20958
Therm-O-Namel Inc	3479	E	310 631-7866	7419
Tjs Metal Manufacturing Inc	3446	E	310 604-1545	6983
Triumph Processing Inc	3471	C	323 563-1338	7324
Verity Health System Cal Inc	8062	D	310 900-2000	21003
Via Trading Corporation	5199	D	877 202-3616	14982
Woodville Inc	2511	F	323 636-0223	3493
Xpo Stacktrain LLC	4731	C	310 661-4000	12552

LYTLE CREEK, CA - San Bernardino County

	SIC	EMP	PHONE	ENTRY #
Burlingame Industries Inc	7033	D	909 887-7038	16830
Inland Pacific Coatings Inc	3479	E	909 822-0594	7374

MALIBU, CA - Los Angeles County

	SIC	EMP	PHONE	ENTRY #
Avalon By Sea AC LLC	8361	E	310 457-9111	22082
County of Los Angeles	3531	F	310 456-8014	7641
Curtco Media Group	2721	E	310 589-7700	4061
Curtco Robb Media LLC **(PA)**	2721	E	310 589-7700	4062
Dun & Brdstreet Emrging Bsnsse **(DH)**	7389	C	310 456-8271	18507
Fitness Ridge Malibu LLC	7011	D	818 874-1300	16444
Grasshopper House Partners LLC	8093	C	310 589-2880	21307
Hrl Laboratories LLC	8732	A	310 317-5000	22885
Kor Shots Inc	2037	E	805 351-0700	1903
Lucent Diamonds Inc	3915	E	424 777-2390	11337
Malibu Conference Center Inc	6512	B	818 889-6440	15677

Mergent email: customerrelations@mergent.com
1398
2022 Southern California Business Directory and Buyers Guide
(P-0000) Products & Services Section entry number
(PA)=Parent Co (HQ)=Headquarters (DH)=Div Headquarters

	SIC	EMP	PHONE	ENTRY #
Malibu Times Inc	2711	E	310 456-5507	4007
Marys Country Kitchen	2053	F	310 456-7845	2079
Nexthealth West Hollywood Inc	8011	F	310 295-2075	19996
Robb Curtco Media LLC	2721	E	310 589-7700	4105
Robb Report Collection	2721	E	310 589-7700	4106
Sobaliving Llc	8099	E	800 595-3803	21481
Toymax International Inc **(HQ)**	3944	D	310 456-7799	11394
Westmed Ambulance Inc	4119	D	310 456-3830	11898

MANHATTAN BEACH, CA - Los Angeles County

	SIC	EMP	PHONE	ENTRY #
1334 Partners LP	7997	D	310 546-5656	19526
Adventureplex	7991	E	310 546-7708	19437
Automobile Club Southern Cal	8699	D	310 376-0521	22416
Comstock Crosser Assoc Dev Inc	6552	E	310 546-5781	16050
De Nora Water Technologies LLC	3589	F	310 618-9700	8378
Ebc Inc **(PA)**	1521	D	310 753-6407	602
Emergent Medical Associates **(PA)**	8011	C	310 379-2134	19806
First Republic Bank	6022	D	424 408-6088	15028
Fisker Group Inc **(HQ)**	3711	D	833 434-7537	9947
Fisker Inc **(PA)**	3711	E	833 434-7537	9948
Fox US Productions 27 Inc	4833	C	310 727-2550	12727
GBS Financial Corp	7389	D	310 937-0073	18524
I Brands LLC	5083	C	424 336-5216	13876
Independant Book Publs Assn	2741	F	310 546-1818	4182
Investlinc Group LLC **(PA)**	7389	D	310 997-0580	18553
Jag Professional Services Inc	8748	C	310 945-5648	23457
Kaiser Foundation Hospitals	8011	C	626 405-2589	19873
Kinecta Federal Credit Union **(PA)**	6061	C	310 643-5400	15071
Pancrtic Cncer Action Ntwrk In **(PA)**	8099	C	310 725-0025	21469
Pipeline Health LLC **(PA)**	8062	B	310 379-2134	20897
Re/Max Bch Cties Rlty Mrquee P	6531	D	310 376-2225	15968
Rnj Printing Corporation	2752	F	310 638-7768	4418
Skechers Collection LLC	3021	E	310 318-3100	5314
Skechers USA Inc	3021	E	310 318-3100	5315
Skechers USA Inc **(PA)**	3149	D	310 318-3100	5886
Skechers USA Inc II **(HQ)**	3021	D	800 746-3411	5316
Solartis LLC	7371	E	310 251-4861	17720
Southwestern Orthpd Med Corp	8011	E	562 803-0600	20094
Stanton Carpet Corp	2273	E	562 945-8711	2696
Sunstone Hotel Properties Inc	7011	C	310 546-7627	16742
The Fifty Five Foundry Inc	7371	E	612 760-5900	17733
Tone It Up Inc	2099	E	310 376-7645	2539
Torrance Mem Physicians Netwrk **(HQ)**	8062	E	310 939-7847	20979
Torrance Memorial Medical Ctr	8062	A	310 939-7847	20983
Trilogy Squaw Spa LLC	7231	E	310 760-0044	16919
Trlg Intermediate Holdings LLC **(PA)**	2369	D	323 266-3072	3045
True Religion Sales LLC **(DH)**	5137	B	323 266-3072	14423
Vita-Ray Productions LLC	3861	F	310 220-8963	11297
Weaver and Tidwell LLP	8712	D	310 382-5380	22751

MARCH ARB, CA - Riverside County

	SIC	EMP	PHONE	ENTRY #
Kaiser Foundation Hospitals	8011	C	951 251-7300	19875
Riverside Sheriffs Association	8631	D	951 653-5152	22294
Russell Sigler Inc	4215	C	951 656-3737	12146

MARICOPA, CA - Kern County

	SIC	EMP	PHONE	ENTRY #
Aera Energy Services Company	1381	E	661 665-3200	423
Bc Tree Service Inc	0783	E	805 649-6875	353
Calmat Co	1422	E	661 858-2673	563

MARINA DEL REY, CA - Los Angeles County

	SIC	EMP	PHONE	ENTRY #
3rd Street Billiard Club Inc	7999	D	310 434-1000	19630
4medica Inc **(PA)**	7374	D	310 695-3300	18078
Ace Iron Inc	3446	E	510 324-3300	6947
Apotheka Systems Inc	7372	E	844 777-4455	17784
Armata Pharmaceuticals Inc **(PA)**	2836	E	310 665-2928	4930
Bouqs Company	5193	D	888 320-2687	14877
Calatlantic Group Inc	1521	D	310 821-9843	597
Cfhs Holdings Inc	8062	B	310 823-8911	20710
Cfhs Holdings Inc	8062	B	310 448-7800	20711
Cfhs Holdings Inc **(HQ)**	8062	A	310 823-8911	20712
Chatham Mdr LLC	7011	E	310 301-2000	16379
Del Rey Yacht Club	7997	D	310 823-4664	19557
Deluxe Nms Inc	7822	C	310 760-8500	19258
Diagnstic Intrvntnal Srgcal CT	8011	D	310 574-0400	19799
Dollar Shave Club Inc **(HQ)**	3541	B	310 975-8528	7728
Dr Squatch Inc	2844	E	704 989-9024	5015
E & S Ring Management Corp	6531	D	310 821-4916	15841
Eti Partners IV LLC	3672	E	949 273-4990	9401
Excavo LLC	2426	F	310 823-7670	3218
Executive Network Entps Inc **(PA)**	4119	D	310 447-2759	11864
EZ Lube LLC	7549	D	310 821-2517	18926
Fastxchange Inc	7373	E	310 827-2445	18030
Gebbs Software Intl Inc	7379	D	201 227-0088	18182
Gelsons Markets	2051	D	310 306-3192	2003
Guidance Solutions Inc	7375	E	310 754-4000	18124
Hornblower Yachts LLC	4724	D	310 301-9900	12388
Hornblower Yachts LLC	4489	D	310 301-6000	12282
Liquidate Direct LLC	7373	E	800 750-7617	18045
Marina City Club LP A Cali	6513	C	310 822-0611	15739
Modern Parking Inc	7521	B	310 821-1081	18769
Regents of Uc	8011	D	310 827-3700	20039
Safetypark Corporation **(PA)**	7521	C	310 899-0490	18779
Samvco	3634	F	310 980-5680	9011
Sewer Rodding Equipment Co **(PA)**	3589	E	310 301-9009	8412
Socialcom Inc	8742	D	310 289-4477	23328
Sony Dadc US Inc	3695	F	310 760-8500	9839
Springcoin Inc	7372	D	847 322-6349	17988
Survios Inc	7373	E	310 736-1503	18070
Telecom Lease Advisors LLC **(DH)**	8742	E	877 418-5238	23343
Telesign Holdings Inc **(DH)**	7372	E	310 740-9700	17993
Trendshift LLC	7371	D	866 644-8877	17742
Twin Coast Metrology Inc **(PA)**	3827	F	310 709-2308	10863
USA Travel Services LLC	8699	A	207 899-8803	22466
Venture Aviator	7371	E	212 913-9746	17752
Wynden Stark LLC **(HQ)**	7361	C	424 271-4156	17481

MAYWOOD, CA - Los Angeles County

	SIC	EMP	PHONE	ENTRY #
Cook Induction Heating Co Inc	3398	E	323 560-1327	6438
Gemini Film & Bag Inc **(PA)**	3089	E	323 582-0901	5650
Heritage Leather Company Inc	3111	E	323 983-0420	5869
Kitchen Cuts LLC	2013	D	323 560-7415	1736
Precision Iron Works	3441	F	562 220-2303	6650
R G Canning Enterprises Inc	7389	C	323 560-7469	18647
Regal Machine & Engrg Inc	3599	E	323 773-7462	8762
SJ Distributors Inc	5142	D	888 988-2328	14531
Sonora Face Co	2435	E	323 560-8188	3354
Tapia Enterprises Inc **(PA)**	5141	D	323 560-7415	14515

MC FARLAND, CA - Kern County

	SIC	EMP	PHONE	ENTRY #
A G Hacienda Incorporated	4212	B	661 792-2418	11949
Amaretto Orchards LLC	3999	E	661 399-9697	11629
Aptco LLC **(PA)**	2821	D	661 792-2107	4678
Central Valley Almond Assn	0723	D	661 792-2171	162
Etchegaray Farms LLC	0214	E	661 393-0920	129
Jakov Dulcich and Sons LLC	0191	C	661 792-6360	112

MC KITTRICK, CA - Kern County

	SIC	EMP	PHONE	ENTRY #
Aera Energy LLC	1311	D	661 334-3100	385
Aera Energy Services Company	1381	E	661 665-4400	422
California Resources Prod Corp	1311	E	661 869-8000	397
Wonderful Orchards LLC	0173	C	661 797-2509	61

MECCA, CA - Riverside County

	SIC	EMP	PHONE	ENTRY #
Kent Seatech LLC	0921	E	760 396-2301	373
Kerry Inc	2023	E	760 396-2116	1798
Richard Bagdasarian Inc	0172	D	760 396-2168	53
Western Environmental Inc	3822	E	760 396-0222	10671

MENIFEE, CA - Riverside County

	SIC	EMP	PHONE	ENTRY #
Channell Commercial Corp **(PA)**	3661	D	951 719-2600	9230
City of Menifee	8741	D	951 672-6777	23003
Datatronics Romoland Inc	3612	D	951 928-7700	8867
Lowes Home Centers LLC	5031	C	951 723-1930	13224
Summit Equipment Rentals LLC	7359	D	951 246-3313	17377

MENTONE, CA - San Bernardino County

	SIC	EMP	PHONE	ENTRY #
Bausman and Company Inc **(PA)**	2521	C	909 947-0139	3579
Bps Tactical Inc	2321	F	909 794-2435	2755
Braswlls Mdterranean Grdns Inc	8051	D	909 794-1189	20257
Bristol Omega Inc	2541	E	909 794-6862	3640
Dropship Vendor Group LLC	2511	E	424 391-6943	3469
International Paving Svcs Inc	1611	D	909 794-2101	888
Marwell Corporation	3613	F	909 794-4192	8899
Power Pt Inc **(PA)**	3537	F	951 490-4149	7716

MIDWAY CITY, CA - Orange County

	SIC	EMP	PHONE	ENTRY #
Lin Consulting LLC	3792	E	714 650-8595	10543

MIRA LOMA, CA - Riverside County

	SIC	EMP	PHONE	ENTRY #
General Electric Company	3646	E	951 360-2400	9086
Prevost Car (us) Inc	5013	E	951 360-2550	13080

MISSION HILLS, CA - Los Angeles County

	SIC	EMP	PHONE	ENTRY #
Ararat Home Los Angeles Inc	8059	C	818 837-1800	20553
Ecola Services Inc	7342	D	818 920-7301	17202
El Nido Family Centers **(PA)**	8322	C	818 830-3646	21779
Electric Gate Store Inc	3699	C	818 361-6872	9867
Facey Medical Foundation **(PA)**	8011	C	818 365-9531	19810
Facey Medical Foundation	8099	C	818 837-5677	21424
Facey Medical Foundation	8011	C	818 365-9531	19812
Facey Medical Group PC **(HQ)**	8011	C	818 365-9531	19813
Greater Valley Medical Group **(PA)**	8093	D	818 838-4500	21308
Hemodialysis Inc	8092	C	818 365-6961	21247
Jade Inc	1742	D	818 365-7137	1382
Kaiser Foundation Hospitals	6324	C	888 778-5000	15410
National Business Group Inc **(PA)**	7353	D	818 221-6000	17312
National Cnstr Rentals Inc **(HQ)**	7359	D	818 221-6000	17365
National Insurance Crime Bur	6411	D	818 895-2867	15600
Providence Health & Svcs - Ore	8062	C	818 365-8051	20914
Providence Holy Cross Medical **(PA)**	8062	A	818 365-8051	20916
Scripla LLC	7372	F	818 925-1460	17978
Valterra Products LLC **(PA)**	3494	E	818 898-1671	7478

MISSION VIEJO, CA - Orange County

	SIC	EMP	PHONE	ENTRY #
Advanced Mp Technology LLC **(DH)**	5065	C	800 492-3113	13698
Allergy & Asthma Assoc Cal	8011	D	949 364-2900	19691
American Justice Solutions Inc	8748	D	949 369-6210	23413
Auxilary of Mssion Hosp Mssion	8062	A	949 364-1400	20684
Bailey Industries Inc	3728	F	949 461-0807	10287
Black Dot Wireless LLC	4812	D	949 502-3800	12595
Bridgestone Living LLC	8051	D	949 487-9500	20264
Camden Development Inc	6531	C	949 427-4674	15795
Catholic Family Life Insurance	6311	E	949 472-2284	15358
Coldwell Banker Residential **(DH)**	6531	D	949 837-5700	15819
Coldwell Bnkr Rsdntial Rfrral **(DH)**	6531	B	949 367-1800	15821
Community Merch Solutions LLC	3578	E	877 956-9258	8313
Community Orthpd Med Group Prt	8011	D	949 348-4000	19760

GEOGRAPHIC

Employment Codes: A=Over 500 employees, B=251-500, C=101-250, D=51-100, E=20-50 F=10-19
2022 Southern California Business Directory and Buyers Guide
© Mergent Inc. 1-800-342-5647
1399

	SIC	EMP	PHONE	ENTRY #
Cumming Management Group Inc	8741	D	949 900-0440	23010
Dawson & Dawson Staffing Inc **(PA)**	7361	D	949 421-3966	17410
Dimar Enterprises Inc	7349	C	949 492-1100	17238
Disruptive Visions LLC	8748	D	949 502-3800	23432
Edwards Theatres Circuit Inc	7832	C	949 582-4078	19274
Foundstone Inc	7372	E	949 297-5600	17861
Franchise Services Inc **(PA)**	2752	E	949 348-5400	4299
Golda & I Chocolatiers Inc	5149	D	949 660-9581	14691
Good Shepherd Lutheran Hm of W **(PA)**	8361	C	559 791-2000	22104
Gregg Hammork Enterprizes Inc	1311	E	949 586-7902	404
Immedate Clinic Healthcare Inc **(HQ)**	8082	E	949 487-9500	21173
James Hardie Building Pdts Inc	3241	D	949 348-1800	5977
James Hardie Trading Co Inc	2952	C	949 582-2378	5283
Jedco Inc	3812	E	949 699-2974	10593
Jewish HM For The Aging Ornge	8361	C	949 364-9685	22120
Lake Mission Viejo Association	8641	D	949 770-1313	22345
Leader Hospitality LP	7011	D	949 582-7100	16539
Madison Creek Partners LLC **(PA)**	8051	D	949 449-2500	20411
Mimg Medical Management LLC	8741	D	949 282-1600	23066
Mission Ambltory Srgcenter Ltd	8062	D	949 364-2201	20863
Mission Hosp Regional Med Ctr **(PA)**	8062	A	949 364-1400	20864
Mission Internal Med Group Inc	8011	D	949 364-3570	19981
Mission Viejo Country Club	7997	C	949 582-1550	19588
North American Client Svcs Inc **(PA)**	8741	C	949 240-2423	23075
Northern Pionr Healthcare Inc **(HQ)**	8099	E	949 487-9500	21465
Oracle Corporation	7372	B	626 315-7513	17945
Paydarfar Industries Inc	5045	D	949 481-3267	13424
Pendragon North Amer Auto Inc	7539	D	949 365-8750	18902
Pennant Healthcare Inc **(HQ)**	8051	C	949 487-9500	20440
Postal Instant Press Inc **(HQ)**	2752	E	949 348-5000	4392
Prestige Auto Collision Inc	7532	D	949 470-6031	18799
Prosthtic Orthtic Group Ornge	3842	F	949 242-2237	11136
Prototype Industries Inc **(PA)**	2741	E	949 680-4890	4199
Prx International Corp **(PA)**	3679	D	714 624-0789	9768
Rock Canyon Healthcare Inc	8082	C	719 404-1000	21209
Saddlback Vly Srgcal Med Group	8011	C	949 364-1007	20046
Sir Speedy Inc **(HQ)**	2752	E	949 348-5000	4424
Sizzler USA Restaurants Inc **(HQ)**	6794	C	949 273-4497	16217
Smart & Final Stores Inc	5141	C	949 581-1212	14498
South Cnty Lxus At Mssion Vejo	7549	C	949 347-3400	18943
Southern Cal Prmnnte Med Group	8099	C	949 376-8619	21482
Sovereign Healthcare Oc LLC **(PA)**	8062	D	949 706-9900	20954
St Vincent De Paul Vlg Inc	8699	C	619 233-8500	22464
Technicon Design Corporation	7389	D	949 218-1300	18686
Total Vision LLC	8042	C	949 652-7242	20207
Vocational Visions	8331	C	949 837-7280	21973
W G Holt Inc	3674	D	949 859-8800	9604
Wakunaga of America Co Ltd **(HQ)**	2834	D	949 855-2776	4911
Wild Creek Healthcare Inc **(DH)**	8099	E	775 359-3161	21498
Zensho USA Corporation	8742	A	760 585-8455	23372

MOJAVE, CA - Kern County

	SIC	EMP	PHONE	ENTRY #
Alpha Dyno Nobel	2892	F	661 824-1356	5200
Calportland Company	3241	C	661 824-2401	5974
Commodity Resource Envmtl Inc	3339	E	661 824-2416	6285
Galactic Co LLC **(DH)**	3761	B	661 824-6600	10514
Golden Queen Mining Co LLC	1041	C	661 824-4300	374
Interorbital Systems	3365	F	661 965-0771	6397
Masten Space Systems Inc	3761	E	661 824-3423	10515
PPG Industries Inc	2851	E	661 824-4532	5108
PRC - Desoto International Inc	2891	C	661 824-4532	5192
Ridgetop Energy LLC	4911	E	661 822-2400	12823
Scaled Composites LLC	3721	B	661 824-4541	10202
Trical Inc	2879	E	661 824-2494	5175
United Parcel Service Inc	4215	C	661 824-9391	12156

MONROVIA, CA - Los Angeles County

	SIC	EMP	PHONE	ENTRY #
360 Support Services	8741	D	866 360-6468	22964
3M Unitek Corporation	3843	B	626 445-7960	11158
Adams and Barnes Inc	6531	D	626 358-1858	15764
Alakor Healthcare LLC	8062	C	626 408-9800	20668
Amada Weld Tech Inc **(DH)**	3548	D	626 303-5676	7888
Amatel Inc **(PA)**	8748	D	323 801-0199	23411
Arch Bay Holdings LLC	6719	D	949 679-2400	16094
Aremac Associates Inc	3599	E	626 303-8795	8501
Arrowhead Press Inc	2752	E	626 358-1168	4231
B & H Signs Inc	3993	F	626 359-6643	11525
Belco Packaging Systems Inc	3565	E	626 357-9566	8063
Burnett & Son Meat Co Inc	2011	D	626 357-2165	1706
Cacique Foods LLC **(PA)**	2022	C	626 961-3399	1768
California Business Bureau Inc **(PA)**	8721	C	626 303-1515	22765
Califrnia Nwspapers Ltd Partnr **(DH)**	2711	B	626 962-8811	3956
Chromologic LLC	3841	E	626 381-9974	10962
Clary Corporation	3679	E	626 359-4486	9693
Consilio LLC	8111	C	626 921-1600	21536
Core Monrovia LLC	7011	C	626 357-5211	16389
Ctour Holiday LLC	7999	B	323 261-8811	19641
Decco US Post-Harvest Inc **(HQ)**	2879	E	800 221-0925	5169
Decore-Ative Spc NC LLC **(PA)**	2431	A	626 254-9191	3243
Doubltree By Hlton Ht Monrovia	7011	C	626 357-1900	16418
Ducommun Aerostructures Inc	3728	E	626 358-3211	10314
Duracold Refrigeration Mfg LLC	3448	E	626 358-1710	6992
Ecotech Services Inc	0781	E	626 335-1500	255
Eurofins Eaton Analytical LLC **(DH)**	8734	D	626 386-1100	22944
Executive Auto Reconditioning	7542	E	626 416-3322	18914
Financial Tech Sltons Intl Inc	8742	C	818 241-9571	23215
Foote Axle & Forge LLC	3714	E	323 268-4151	10059
Garden View Inc	0781	E	626 303-4043	258
Global Compliance Inc	2741	E	626 303-6855	4174
H C Olsen Cnstr Co Inc	1541	D	626 359-8900	701
Hale Corporation	1521	D	626 358-4523	608
Harbor Seal Incorporated	3053	F	626 305-5754	5340
Headwinds	3751	F	626 359-8044	10491
Hoya Holdings Inc	3827	D	626 739-5200	10838
Jam Fire Protection Inc **(PA)**	7382	D	626 256-4400	18388
Kentmaster Mfg Co Inc **(PA)**	5084	E	626 359-8888	13910
Kruse and Son Inc	2013	E	626 358-4536	1738
Leekilpatrick Management Inc	8742	D	818 500-9631	23259
Linear Industries Ltd **(PA)**	5085	D	626 303-1130	13995
Micro/Sys Inc	3571	E	818 244-4600	8167
Mulgrew Arcft Components Inc	3728	D	626 256-1375	10385
Naked Juice Co Glendora Inc	2033	B	626 873-2600	1868
Ondax Inc	3827	F	626 357-9600	10850
Parade Designs Inc	5094	F	213 627-4019	14137
Parasoft Corporation **(PA)**	5045	E	626 256-3680	13423
Peck Road Gravel Pit	1442	F	626 574-7570	573
Production Lapping Company	3599	E	626 359-0611	8745
Production Lapping Company	3599	F	626 359-0611	8746
Radcal Corporation	3829	E	626 357-7921	10906
Rayco Burial Products Inc	3444	E	626 357-1996	6900
Renew Health Group LLC	8742	E	310 625-2838	23308
Roncelli Plastics Inc	2821	D	800 250-6516	4713
Sage Hospitality Resources LLC	7011	C	626 357-5211	16682
Shore Western Manufacturing	3826	E	626 357-3251	10811
Southern California Edison Co	4911	C	626 303-8480	12829
St Baldricks Foundation Inc **(PA)**	8621	D	626 792-8247	22279
Transpacific Financial Inc **(PA)**	8742	D	626 447-7838	23351
Trap	7389	D	626 572-5610	18695
Vinyl Technology Inc	2671	C	626 443-5257	3862
Vioski Inc	2512	F	626 359-4571	3521
Vivopools Inc	7389	D	818 952-2121	18717
Vivopools LLC	7389	D	888 702-8486	18718
Wbt Group LLC	3999	E	323 735-1201	11793
Webasto Charging Systems Inc **(DH)**	5013	D	626 415-4000	13108
World Class Distribution Inc	4225	D	909 574-4140	12261
World Vision International **(HQ)**	8699	C	626 303-8811	22471
Xencor Inc	2834	C	626 305-5900	4914

MONTCLAIR, CA - San Bernardino County

	SIC	EMP	PHONE	ENTRY #
A Plus Senior Care Inc	8322	E	909 989-2563	21706
Acapulco Restaurants Inc	3585	D	909 621-3955	8324
Amazing Steel Company	3441	E	909 590-0393	6585
American Nail Plate Ltg Inc	3645	D	909 982-1807	9057
Aragon Construction Inc	1542	D	909 621-2200	737
Arcadia Cabinetry LLC	2434	F	909 550-0074	3305
Archipelago Lighting Inc	5063	D	909 627-5333	13614
California Offset Printers Inc	2752	D	818 291-1100	4246
Cls Landscape Management Inc	0783	B	909 628-3005	355
Cnc Industries Inc	3599	F	909 445-0300	8557
Cosmo Products LLC	3634	E	888 784-3108	9002
Cpd Industries	3086	E	909 465-5596	5495
Cramer Painting Inc	1721	E	909 397-5770	1174
E & R Glass Contractors Inc	3231	E	909 624-1763	5952
E M S Trading Inc	5139	E	909 581-7800	14435
Elements Food Group Inc	2052	D	909 983-2011	2063
Expo Power Systems Inc	5063	E	800 505-9884	13628
Falcon Abrasive Mfg Inc	3291	E	909 598-3078	6152
Fittings That Fit Inc	3496	F	909 248-2808	7501
Foundation For Dance Education	7911	D	909 482-1590	19298
Giant Inland Empire Rv Ctr Inc **(PA)**	7538	C	909 981-0444	18833
Hampton Tdder Tchncal Svcs Inc	8734	F	909 628-1256	22946
Indie Ridge Inc	3559	F	323 207-9181	7981
Industrial Wood Products Inc	2448	F	909 625-1247	3396
Ingredients By Nature LLC	2099	E	909 230-6200	2452
John L Conley Inc	3448	D	909 627-0981	6999
Kaiser Foundation Hospitals	8093	C	909 399-3700	21314
Kaiser Foundation Hospitals	8011	C	909 427-5521	19928
Martinez Steel Inc	1791	D	909 946-0686	1575
McDaniel Inc	3324	F	909 591-8353	6269
Medicrest of California 1	8051	D	909 626-1294	20416
Mitchell Fabrication	3441	E	909 590-0393	6640
Montclair Bronze Inc **(PA)**	3366	E	909 986-2664	6409
National Ewp Inc	1081	F	909 931-4014	377
Oconca Shipping (lax) Inc	4731	E	909 625-5555	12497
Omnitrans Inc	4111	D	909 379-7100	11831
Oparc **(PA)**	8331	E	909 982-4090	21963
Pacific Duct Inc	3444	E	909 635-1335	6889
Prime Healthcare Services-Mont	8062	A	909 625-5411	20903
Prime Hlthcare Srvcs-Mntclair	8062	D	909 625-5411	20905
Prime Hlthcare Srvcs-Mntclair **(DH)**	8062	B	909 625-5411	20906
St George Auto Center Inc **(PA)**	7539	D	909 341-1189	18906
Thomas Burt	2752	F	626 301-9065	4438
United Methodist Federal Cr Un **(PA)**	6061	C	909 946-4096	15094
US Skillserve Inc	8051	A	909 621-4751	20493
West-Tech Mechanical Inc	1711	F	909 635-1170	1161
Westside Accessories Inc **(PA)**	2387	E	626 858-5452	3063

MONTEBELLO, CA - Los Angeles County

	SIC	EMP	PHONE	ENTRY #
2253 Apparel LLC **(PA)**	5136	D	323 837-9800	14325
Academy Awning Inc	2395	E	800 422-9646	3149
All Access Apparel Inc **(PA)**	2361	C	323 889-4300	3027
Altura Management Services LLC	8741	B	323 768-2898	22973
Amplifier Technologies Inc	3663	E	323 278-0001	9252
Arevalo Tortilleria Inc **(PA)**	2099	D	323 888-1711	2391
Atlas Survival Shelters LLC	2514	E	323 727-7084	3526
Automobile Club Southern Cal	8699	D	323 725-6545	22420

	SIC	EMP	PHONE	ENTRY #
Beacon Concrete Inc	3273	E	323 889-7775	6073
Beverly Community Hosp Assn **(PA)**	8062	A	323 726-1222	20687
Big Tree Furniture & Inds Inc **(PA)**	2511	E	310 894-7500	3465
Bimbo Bakeries Usa Inc	2051	F	323 720-6099	1985
Bltee LLC	2331	E	213 802-1736	2837
Bread Los Angeles	2052	F	323 201-3953	2060
Cee Baileys Aircraft Plastics	3751	F	323 721-4900	10486
Conroy & Knowlton Inc	3089	E	323 665-5288	5611
Costco Wholesale Corporation	5014	C	323 890-1904	13114
Craig Manufacturing Company **(PA)**	3714	D	323 726-7355	10036
Cummins Pacific LLC	5084	F	323 728-8111	13897
Davita Medical Management LLC	8011	D	323 720-1144	19788
Delamo Manufacturing Inc	3089	D	323 936-3566	5621
Desser Holding Company LLC **(HQ)**	6719	E	323 721-4900	16098
Desser Tire & Rubber Co LLC	5088	E	323 837-1497	14055
Dow-Elco Inc	3612	E	323 723-1288	8868
Eastwestproto Inc	4119	C	888 535-5728	11861
Epsilon Electronics Inc **(PA)**	5064	D	323 722-3333	13685
Fast Deer Bus Chrtr Incrprtion	4142	D	323 201-8988	11911
Fcs Medical Corporation	8011	D	323 728-3955	19822
H & L Tooth Company **(PA)**	3531	D	323 721-5146	7644
Holiday Tree Farms Inc	0811	C	323 276-1900	368
Howmet Aerospace Inc	3353	C	323 728-3901	6299
Industrial Cont Svcs - CA LLC **(DH)**	5085	C	323 724-8507	13992
Ingalls Conveyors Inc	3535	E	323 837-9900	7691
Katzkin Leather Inc **(PA)**	5199	C	323 725-1243	14943
Komar Alliance LLC **(PA)**	5131	D	323 890-3000	14305
La Bottleworks Inc	2086	E	323 724-4076	2270
LA Envelope Incorporated	2677	E	323 838-9300	3910
Leidos Government Services Inc	7379	C	323 721-6979	18198
Mexican Amrcn Oprtnty Fndation **(PA)**	8322	D	323 890-9600	21850
Mission Linen Supply	7213	D	323 888-8971	16863
Monarch Litho Inc **(PA)**	2752	E	323 727-0300	4377
Montebello Plastics LLC	3081	E	323 728-6814	5434
Niitakaya Usa Inc **(PA)**	5149	E	323 720-5050	14714
Northeast Newspapers Inc	2711	E	213 727-1117	4017
Orora Packaging Solutions	5113	C	323 832-2000	14222
PCI Industries Inc	3999	E	323 889-6770	11731
Performance Forge Inc	3462	E	323 722-3460	7094
Ppp LLC	3089	F	323 832-9627	5769
Quiet Cannon Montebello Inc	7299	D	323 724-4500	16974
Reyes Coca-Cola Bottling LLC	2086	D	323 278-2600	2293
Royal Paper Box Co California **(PA)**	5199	C	323 728-7041	14973
Shyft Group Inc	3711	E	323 276-1933	9966
Source Freight System LLC **(PA)**	4731	D	323 887-3884	12527
Source Logistics Center Corp	4731	D	323 887-3884	12528
Spartan Motors Gtb LLC	3713	F	323 276-1933	9997
Star Scrap Metal Company Inc	4953	D	562 921-5045	12983
Style Knits Inc	2253	F	323 890-9080	2642
Theta Digital Corporation	3651	E	818 572-4300	9202
Thistle Roller Co Inc	3555	E	323 685-5322	7926
Troy Sheet Metal Works Inc **(PA)**	3465	D	323 720-4100	7115
Truck Club Publishing Inc	2731	F	323 726-8620	4142
Turner Fiberfill Inc	2824	E	323 724-7957	4736
Universal Metal Plating	3471	F	626 969-7932	7327
Unix Packaging LLC	2086	C	213 627-5050	2302
US Polymers Inc **(PA)**	3089	D	323 728-3023	5852
Vft Inc	2392	E	323 728-2280	3123
Wilbur Curtis Co Inc	6719	B	800 421-6150	16115
Wilbur Curtis Co Inc	3589	C	323 837-2300	8427
Wilbur Curtis Co Inc	3589	B	323 837-2300	8428
Worldwide Aeros Corp	3721	D	818 344-3999	10207
Worldwide Intgrted Rsurces Inc	5087	D	323 838-8938	14047
Yonekyu USA Inc	2013	D	323 581-4194	1755

MONTEREY PARK, CA - Los Angeles County

	SIC	EMP	PHONE	ENTRY #
Aero Powder Coating Inc	3479	E	323 264-6405	7338
Ahmc Garfield Medical Ctr LP	8051	C	626 573-2222	20239
Alltech Industries Inc	1731	E	323 450-2168	1212
American Reprographics Co LLC	7334	D	626 289-5021	17144
Architectural Woodworking Co	2541	D	626 570-4125	3638
Asia Food Inc	2011	E	626 284-1328	1705
Care 1st Health Plan **(PA)**	8099	C	323 889-6638	21397
Carmichael International Svc **(HQ)**	4731	D	213 353-0800	12429
Chen Dvid MD Dgnstc Med Group	8011	D	626 288-8029	19745
Childrens Law Center Cal **(PA)**	8111	C	323 980-8700	21529
DHm International Corp	2339	F	323 263-3888	2940
Direct Wheel Inc	3714	F	909 390-2824	10046
F & A Federal Credit Union	6061	D	213 268-1226	15062
Franco American Corporation	3292	F	323 268-2345	6163
Garfield Imaging Center Inc	8011	C	626 572-0912	19828
Graphic Color Systems Inc	2752	D	323 283-3000	4306
Guard-Systems Inc	7381	A	323 881-6715	18281
Inertech Supply Inc	3053	D	626 282-2000	5343
Innovations Building Svcs LLC	7349	D	323 787-6068	17251
International Daily News Inc **(PA)**	2711	E	323 265-1317	3996
JC Foodservice Inc **(PA)**	5046	D	626 299-3800	13461
L C Miller Company	3567	E	323 268-3611	8093
La Colonial Tortilla Pdts Inc	2099	C	626 289-3647	2464
Lightcross Inc	3679	F	626 236-4500	9741
Lincoln Plaza Hotel Inc	7011	D	626 571-8818	16542
Los Angeles Dependency Lawyers	8111	D	323 859-5546	21617
Los Olivos Packaging Inc **(PA)**	2033	C	323 261-2218	1866
Mako Inc	2241	F	323 262-2168	2617
Merchants Building Maint Co **(PA)**	7349	A	323 881-6701	17261
Merchants Building Maint Co	7349	C	323 881-8902	17263
Monterey Park Hospital	8062	C	626 570-9000	20865
Monterey Pk Convalescent Hosp	8059	D	626 280-0280	20614
Nannocare Inc	3999	F	818 823-7594	11718
Ntt Data Inc	7373	D	213 228-2500	18055
Oakcroft Associates Inc **(PA)**	5082	E	323 261-5122	13865
Optic Arts Holdings Inc	3646	E	213 250-6069	9097
Pacific Culinary Group Inc	2099	E	626 284-1328	2505
Rigoli Enterprises Inc	3699	F	626 573-0242	9907
Ross Name Plate Company	3993	E	323 725-6812	11587
Rothenberger USA LLC	3541	F	323 268-1381	7743
Sadie & Sage LLC **(PA)**	2331	F	213 234-2188	2865
Sencha Naturals Inc	2064	F	213 353-9908	2105
Southern California Gas Co	4924	C	213 244-1200	12867
State Compensation Insur Fund	6331	D	323 266-5000	15485
Sweety Novelty Inc	2024	F	310 533-6010	1824
Tck USA Corporation	2891	F	323 269-2969	5198
Union Technology Corp	5065	E	323 266-6871	13784
United Parcel Service Inc	7389	D	626 280-8012	18703
Wah Hung Group Inc **(PA)**	3714	E	626 571-8700	10154
Wah Hung Group Inc	3714	E	626 571-8700	10155
West-Bag Inc	3089	E	323 264-0750	5862
Win Fat Food LLC	2015	F	323 261-1869	1765
World Journal La LLC **(HQ)**	2711	C	323 268-4982	4046

MONTROSE, CA - Los Angeles County

	SIC	EMP	PHONE	ENTRY #
Automobile Club Southern Cal	8699	D	818 249-3971	22419
Gloves In A Bottle Inc	5122	E	818 248-9980	14245
Northrop Grumman Systems Corp	3812	C	818 249-5252	10621
Paradis	2024	F	818 248-1004	1821
Vitachrome Graphics Group Inc	2759	E	818 957-0900	4589

MOORPARK, CA - Ventura County

	SIC	EMP	PHONE	ENTRY #
Adventist Health System/West	8062	D	805 955-7000	20648
AG Machining Inc	3441	D	805 531-9555	6584
American Board Assembly Inc	3672	C	805 523-0274	9377
Benchmark Elec Mfg Sltons Mrpa	3672	A	805 532-2800	9385
Cardservice International Inc **(DH)**	7389	B	805 648-1425	18470
Cimatron Gibbs LLC	7371	D	805 523-0004	17577
Citrus North Venture LLC	7011	D	256 428-2000	16383
Conversion Technology Co Inc **(PA)**	3952	E	805 378-0033	11468
Corporate Graphics & Printing	2752	F	805 529-5333	4264
Ensign-Bickford Arospc Def Co	3812	E	805 292-4000	10587
Erp Power LLC **(PA)**	3825	F	805 517-1300	10751
G T Water Products Inc	3432	F	805 529-2900	6561
Global Uxe Inc	3999	E	805 583-4600	11678
Globaluxe Inc	3999	E	805 583-4600	11679
Golden State Prvders A Med Cor **(PA)**	8099	D	805 523-8250	21430
Gooch and Housego Cal LLC	3827	D	805 529-3324	10837
Husky Injction Mlding Systems	3089	D	805 523-9593	5668
Inkjetmadnesscom Inc	2893	F	805 583-7755	5208
Insparation Inc	2844	E	805 553-0820	5033
Koros USA Inc	3841	E	805 529-0825	11006
Kretek International Inc **(DH)**	5194	D	805 531-8888	14903
Laritech Inc	3672	C	805 529-5000	9422
Lifetech Resources LLC	5122	D	805 944-1199	14256
Longs Drug Stores Cal Inc	7384	D	805 530-0283	18410
Marine Holding US Corp	6799	A	805 529-2000	16275
Mc Cully Mac M Corporation	3621	E	805 529-0661	8923
Moller Retail Inc	1389	F	805 299-8200	519
Mpo Videotronics Inc **(PA)**	3861	D	805 499-8513	11286
Muranaka Farm	0191	C	805 529-0201	115
Nea Electronics Inc	3678	E	805 292-4010	9662
Ned L Webster Concrete Cnstr	1771	D	805 529-4900	1543
Pacific Rim Realty Group	6531	E	805 553-9562	15940
Pennymac Mortgage Inv Tr **(PA)**	6162	A	818 224-7442	15224
Penta Financial Inc	3671	E	818 882-3872	9366
Pentair Water Pool and Spa Inc	3589	E	805 553-5003	8403
Picnic Time Inc	5199	E	805 529-7400	14966
Pindler & Pindler Inc **(PA)**	5131	D	805 531-9090	14315
Pom Medical LLC	5047	D	805 306-2105	13512
SCI-Tech Glassblowing Inc	3229	F	805 523-9790	5941
Semiconductor Equipment Corp	3674	F	805 529-2293	9571
Sercomp LLC **(PA)**	3955	D	805 299-0020	11482
Sterisyn Inc	2834	E	805 991-9694	4898
Testequity LLC **(PA)**	7629	C	805 498-9933	18959
Topaz Systems Inc **(PA)**	3577	E	805 520-8282	8305
Ultron Systems Inc	3674	F	805 529-1485	9596
Wave Precision Inc	3827	F	805 529-3324	10865
Wayne J Sand & Gravel Inc	1442	E	805 529-1323	575
Xp Systems Corporation **(HQ)**	7373	C	805 532-9100	18076

MORENO VALLEY, CA - Riverside County

	SIC	EMP	PHONE	ENTRY #
Acapulco Restaurants Inc	7299	D	951 653-8809	16942
Access Info Holdings LLC	4226	C	909 459-1417	12265
Accuturn Corporation	3812	E	951 656-6621	10558
Akh Company Inc	5014	D	951 924-5356	13111
Alta Finish & Stair Inc	1751	D	951 496-0117	1426
Amro Fabricating Corporation	3728	E	951 842-6140	10269
Bcd Industries Corp	3999	F	760 927-8988	11636
Bms Investments LLC	2834	F	714 376-2535	4801
Bowlero Corp	7933	D	951 924-6008	19389
Butler America Holdings Inc	7361	C	951 563-0020	17399
California Supertrucks Inc	3713	E	951 656-2903	9978
Capstone Logistics LLC	4789	A	770 414-1929	12565
Cardinal Glass Industries Inc	3211	E	951 485-9007	5916
Cimc Reefer Trailer Inc **(PA)**	3537	C	951 218-1414	7706
Community Health Systems Inc	8011	C	951 571-2300	19757
Envirnmntal Mlding Cncepts LLC	3069	F	951 214-6596	5375
Family Service Association	8322	D	951 653-8109	21784
Hsb Holdings Inc	3011	E	951 214-6590	5302

GEOGRAPHIC

Employment Codes: A=Over 500 employees, B=251-500, C=101-250, D=51-100, E=20-50 F=10-19
2022 Southern California Business Directory and Buyers Guide
© Mergent Inc. 1-800-342-5647
1401

	SIC	EMP	PHONE	ENTRY #
Kaiser Foundation Hospitals	6733	D	951 601-6174	16182
Kaiser Foundation Hospitals	8011	C	951 243-0811	19945
Lowes Home Centers LLC	5031	C	951 656-1859	13240
Masonite Entry Door Corp	2431	F	951 243-2261	3265
Modular Metal Fabricators Inc	3444	C	951 242-3154	6880
National Construction & Maint	1542	E	909 888-7042	794
Pacific Kiln Insulations Inc	3567	E	951 697-4422	8096
Painted Rhino Inc	3088	E	951 656-5524	5535
Plasma Biolife Services L P	5122	E	951 497-4407	14280
RES-Care Inc	8052	D	951 653-1311	20541
Schoolsfirst Federal Credit Un	6061	D	800 462-8328	15083
Schurman Fine Papers	2771	C	951 653-1934	4605
Think Together	8351	A	951 571-9944	22067
United Material Handling Inc	5084	D	951 657-4900	13955
Waste MGT Collectn Recycl Inc	4953	D	951 242-0421	12997
Waste MGT Collectn Recycl Inc	4953	D	909 242-0421	13001

MORRO BAY, CA - San Luis Obispo County

	SIC	EMP	PHONE	ENTRY #
Compass Health Inc	8051	C	805 772-7372	20287
Mills ASAP Reprographics (PA)	2678	E	805 772-2019	3915
Mission Linen Supply	7213	D	805 772-4451	16856
Smile Housing Corporation	8093	D	805 772-6066	21339

MOUNTAIN PASS, CA - San Bernardino County

	SIC	EMP	PHONE	ENTRY #
Chevron Mining Inc	1221	C	760 856-7625	380
Mp Mine Operations LLC	1481	C	702 277-0848	583

MURRIETA, CA - Riverside County

	SIC	EMP	PHONE	ENTRY #
Abttc Inc (DH)	8361	D	951 837-2400	22076
Automobile Club Southern Cal	8699	E	951 304-3077	22397
B P John Recycle Inc	2421	F	951 696-1144	3208
Bear Creek Golf Club Inc	7997	D	951 677-8621	19539
Bigfogg Inc (PA)	3585	E	951 587-2460	8330
Bop Inc	2752	F	909 598-5776	4238
Bowlero Corp	7933	D	951 698-2202	19394
Busy Bee LLC	7342	C	951 404-9900	17199
California Trusframe LLC (HQ)	2439	A	951 350-4880	3358
CMS Circuit Solutions Inc	3672	E	951 698-4452	9392
Comfort Keepers (PA)	8082	C	951 696-2710	21151
Comprehensive Autism Ctr Inc (PA)	8049	D	951 813-4034	20213
Copan Diagnostics Inc	5122	C	951 696-6957	14237
Crown Surgery Med Group Inc (PA)	8011	D	951 973-7290	19778
Cryogenic Industries Inc	3634	D	951 677-2060	9003
Cumming - LLC	8741	D	951 252-8555	23009
Cumming Corporation	8742	D	951 200-7860	23202
Cumming Management Group Inc	8741	D	415 748-3095	23011
Denso Pdts & Svcs Americas Inc	3714	C	951 698-3379	10044
Elite Cabinetry Inc	2599	F	951 698-5050	3726
Express Systems & Engrg Inc	3089	F	951 461-1500	5642
Faith Quality Auto Body Inc	7532	D	951 698-8215	18789
Gamecloud Studios Inc	7372	E	951 677-2345	17863
Glare Technology Usa Inc	7389	C	909 437-6999	18527
Glassplax	3231	F	951 677-4800	5954
Global Link Sourcing Inc	2671	D	951 698-1977	3854
Iautomation Inc	8742	F	951 304-2222	23239
Ikhana Group LLC	3728	C	951 600-0009	10350
Inland Metal Trading Inc	3444	E	833 396-0740	6853
International Immunology Corp	2835	E	951 677-5629	4923
Jpi Development Group Inc	1711	D	951 973-7680	1087
Kingman Industries Inc	2841	E	951 698-1812	4943
Legacy Tile and Stone Inc	1743	E	951 296-1096	1419
Lobue Laser & Eye Medical Ctrs (PA)	8011	D	951 696-1135	19962
Lowes Home Centers LLC	5031	C	951 461-8916	13237
McHael G Fortansce Physcl Thra	8049	D	626 446-7027	20226
Medical Extrusion Tech Inc (PA)	3089	E	951 698-4346	5706
Medical Lab Svcs Med Group Inc	8071	D	951 834-9020	21077
Miles Construction Group Inc	1521	E	951 260-2504	624
Monique Suraci	7991	D	951 677-8111	19461
Muhlhauser Enterprises Inc (PA)	3441	E	909 877-2792	6643
Muhlhauser Steel Inc	3441	E	909 877-2792	6644
My Kids Dentist	8021	B	951 600-1062	20189
National Bus Invstigations Inc	7389	D	951 677-3500	18608
National Mentor Holdings Inc	8361	C	951 677-1453	22135
Nittobo America Inc	2836	C	951 677-5629	4937
No Prssure Prssure Wshg Svcs L	2842	E	951 477-1988	4973
Nuphoton Technologies Inc	3699	F	951 696-8366	9895
Oak Grove Inst Foundation Inc (PA)	8011	B	951 677-5599	20007
Old Prospectors Assn Amer LLC	2721	E	951 699-4749	4088
Pacific Coast Cheer Inc (PA)	7999	E	951 894-7438	19659
Ptac Rail Ranch Elem School	8641	D	951 696-1404	22360
Rancho Physical Therapy Inc (PA)	8049	C	951 696-9353	20231
Rancon Real Estate Corporation	6531	E	951 677-1800	15965
RCP Block & Brick Inc	5032	D	951 677-1489	13313
SI Inc	1751	E	951 304-9444	1455
Skywest Airlines Inc	4512	D	951 600-9181	12315
Southwest Healthcare Sys Aux	8062	A	800 404-6627	20952
Southwest Healthcare Sys Aux (HQ)	8062	B	951 696-6000	20953
Sunland Scaffold	1799	D	951 595-9402	1691
T & D Services Inc	1381	F	951 304-1190	438
Temecula Valley Drywall Inc	1742	D	951 600-1742	1405
Tesoro Refining & Mktg Co LLC	5172	D	951 461-1063	14809
TMC Ice Protection Systems LLC	3812	E	951 677-6934	10648
Twin Power Usa LLC	1731	E	714 609-6014	1333
United Medical Doctors	8011	D	951 566-5229	20117
Utah Pacific Construction Co	1623	D	951 677-9876	980
Vmc International LLC	3843	D	760 723-1498	11202
Vortex Whirlpool Systems Inc	3088	F	951 940-4556	5538
Wall To Wall Builders Inc	1522	E	909 246-7003	672

	SIC	EMP	PHONE	ENTRY #
Waterstone LLC	5074	C	951 304-0520	13838
Wilson Cycles Sports Corp	3751	E	951 894-5545	10510
Yellow Magic Incorporated	7372	F	951 506-4005	18014

NEEDLES, CA - San Bernardino County

	SIC	EMP	PHONE	ENTRY #
Community Hlthcare Partner Inc	8011	D	760 326-4531	19759
Havasu Landing Casino (PA)	7011	D	760 858-5380	16465
Pacific Gas and Electric Co	4911	C	760 326-2615	12820
Tri State Truss Corporation	2439	E	760 326-3868	3371

NEW CUYAMA, CA - Santa Barbara County

	SIC	EMP	PHONE	ENTRY #
E & B Ntral Resources MGT Corp	1382	F	661 766-250?	448

NEWBERRY SPRINGS, CA - San Bernardino County

	SIC	EMP	PHONE	ENTRY #
Fundamntal Chrstn Endavors Inc	7032	D	760 257-3503	16820

NEWBURY PARK, CA - Ventura County

	SIC	EMP	PHONE	ENTRY #
Amgen Manufacturing Limited	3999	D	787 656-2000	11630
Area Hsing Auth of The Cnty Vn (PA)	6531	E	805 480-9991	15771
Bnk Petroleum (us) Inc	1382	E	805 484-36-3	441
Carefree Communities Inc	6515	C	805 498-2612	15756
CHE Precision Inc	3599	E	805 499-8835	8551
Compulink Business Systems Inc (PA)	7372	C	805 446-2050	17824
Condor Pacific Industries Inc (PA)	3812	C	818 889-2150	10577
Conejo Pacific Technologies	1541	D	805 498-5315	695
Corwin Press Inc (HQ)	2731	C	805 499-9734	4124
CPI Malibu Division	3663	D	805 383-1329	9265
Designworks/Usa Inc (HQ)	8711	D	805 499-9590	22529
Diamond Ground Products Inc	3548	E	805 498-3837	7890
Eca Medical Instruments (DH)	3841	E	805 376-2509	10974
Fc Management Services	3559	E	805 499-0050	7975
Follmer Development Inc	2813	E	805 498-4531	4639
H J S Graphics	2752	F	818 782-5490	4308
Hawaiian Hotels & Resorts Inc	7011	C	805 480-0052	16467
Hmm Construction Inc	1521	D	805 377-1402	611
I C U Security Inc	7382	D	805 498-9620	18385
Isec Incorporated	1751	D	805 375-6957	1442
Isolutecom Inc (PA)	7372	E	805 498-6259	17895
JBW Precision Inc	3444	E	805 499-1973	6856
JW Molding Inc	3544	F	805 499-2682	7809
Longs Drug Stores Cal Inc	7384	C	805 498-4006	18411
Ltd Tech Inc	3549	F	805 480-1886	7905
Mary Hlth SCK Cnvlscnt &NRsng	8051	D	805 498-3644	20415
McKesson Medical-Surgical Inc	5122	D	805 375-8800	14262
Multilayer Prototypes Inc	3672	F	805 498-9390	9431
Odcombe Press (nashville)	2752	E	615 793-5414	4382
Online Media Technologies Ltd	7372	F	209 279-5320	17942
Onyx Pharmaceuticals Inc	2834	A	650 266-0000	4865
Perillo Industries Inc	5065	E	805 498-9838	13762
Qorvo California Inc	3679	C	805 480-5050	9769
R-F Circuits and Assembly Inc	3672	F	805 439-7788	9445
Raise Praise Inc	3931	F	805 498-1747	11349
Scientific Surface Inds Inc	2541	F	805 499-5100	3663
Specialty Concepts Inc	3625	E	818 998-5238	8963
Tom Anderson Guitarworks	3931	F	805 498-1747	11354
Transparent Devices Inc	3577	E	805 499-5000	8307
Trend Design Inc	7336	F	805 498-0457	17191
United Parcel Service Inc	4215	C	805 375-1832	12165
Weldlogic Inc	7692	D	805 375-1670	19002
WV Communications Inc	3663	E	805 376-1820	9328
Xirrus Inc	3823	D	805 262-1600	10733

NEWHALL, CA - Los Angeles County

	SIC	EMP	PHONE	ENTRY #
Berry Petroleum Company LLC	1311	F	661 255-6066	388
Calex Engineering Inc	1794	D	661 254-1866	1592
Green Thumb International Inc	5193	C	661 259-1071	14884
Hollenbeck Palms	8361	C	323 263-6195	22114
Vons Companies Inc	2051	D	661 259-9214	2048

NEWPORT BEACH, CA - Orange County

	SIC	EMP	PHONE	ENTRY #
10632 Bolsa Avenue LP	6513	D	949 673-1221	15715
3650 Industry Avenue LLC	3559	F	949 509-5000	7957
A & A Ready Mixed Concrete Inc (PA)	3273	E	949 253-2800	6065
A Shoc Beverage LLC	2048	E	949 490-1612	1962
Able Software Inc	7372	F	949 274-8321	17772
Acacia Technologies Inc (HQ)	6794	D	949 480-8300	16199
Ace Parking Management Inc	7521	D	949 724-0963	18761
Adaptive Digital Systems Inc	3663	E	949 955-3116	9249
Akua Behavioral Health Inc (PA)	8069	C	949 777-2283	21030
Alliance Oncology LLC (DH)	8011	D	949 242-5345	19692
Alliant Insurance Services Inc (PA)	8748	C	949 756-0271	23409
Allianz Asset MGT Amer LLC (DH)	6722	D	949 219-2200	16119
Allianz Globl Invstors Cpitl L	6722	D	949 219-2200	16120
American Vanguard Corporation (PA)	2879	D	949 260-1200	5165
Amvac Chemical Corporation (HQ)	2879	E	323 264-3910	5166
Anacapa Marine Services (PA)	3732	F	805 985-1818	10458
Andersonpenna Partners Inc (HQ)	8742	E	949 428-1500	23157
Anza Management Company (PA)	6531	C	949 645-1422	15770
Associated Ready Mix Con Inc (PA)	3273	E	949 253-2800	6071
Ault Global Holdings Inc (PA)	3679	E	949 444-5464	9678
Automobile Club Southern Cal	8699	D	949 476-8880	22418
Avenida Partners LLC (PA)	8742	E	949 734-7810	23163
Balboa Bay Club Inc (HQ)	7997	B	949 645-5000	19536
Basin Marine Inc	3732	E	949 673-0360	10459
Bassenian/Lagoni Architects	8712	C	949 553-9100	22711
Beacon Healthcare Services	8093	D	949 650-9750	21276
Beauty Barrage LLC	7231	C	949 771-3399	16661
Ben Bennett Inc (PA)	8059	C	949 209-9712	20560
Big Canyon Country Club	7997	C	949 644-5404	19545

2022 Southern California Business
Directory and Buyers Guide
(P-0000) Products & Services Section entry number
(PA)=Parent Co (HQ)=Headquarters (DH)=Div Headquarters

GEOGRAPHIC SECTION NEWPORT BEACH, CA

	SIC	EMP	PHONE	ENTRY #
Birch Street Systems LLC	7374	D	949 567-7100	18081
Bkf Engineers/Ags	8711	D	949 526-8400	22501
BKM Diablo 227 LLC	6531	D	602 688-6409	15791
Blaze Solutions Inc	7371	D	415 964-5689	17567
Bleeker Manufacturing Inc	3999	E	800 421-1107	11639
Bluestone Medical Inc	3841	F	949 338-3723	10951
Bluewave Technologies	1731	E	949 500-4652	1222
Bny Mellon National Assn	6022	C	877 420-6377	15013
Bremer Whyte Brown Omeara LLP **(PA)**	8111	E	949 221-1000	21523
Buchanan Street Partners LP	6531	D	949 721-1414	15793
C B Coast Newport Properties	6531	A	949 644-1600	15794
C&H Hydraulics Inc	3728	E	949 646-6230	10290
Call & Jensen APC	8111	E	949 717-3000	21526
Calor Apparel Group Intl Corp	2341	E	949 548-9095	3013
Carecar Inc	4119	E	949 287-8349	11857
Cbre Globl Value Investors LLC	8742	D	949 725-8500	23184
CDM Company Inc	3999	E	949 644-2820	11651
Center Line Wheel Corporation	3714	E	562 921-9637	10029
Centurion Security Svcs Inc **(PA)**	7381	D	949 474-0444	18261
Childrens Hospital Orange Cnty	8351	D	949 631-2062	22002
Churm Publishing Inc **(PA)**	2711	E	714 796-7000	3961
Citivest Inc	6531	D	949 474-0440	15815
Clean Energy	4924	A	949 437-1000	12865
Clean Energy Fuels Corp **(PA)**	4932	C	949 437-1000	12874
Closingmark Fincl Group LLC **(DH)**	6162	D	949 833-3600	15183
Coldwell Bnkr Rsdntial Rfrral	6531	A	949 673-8700	15822
Comac America Corporation	3721	F	760 616-9614	10184
Commonwealth Land Title Insur	6361	C	800 432-0706	15499
Concept Technology Inc **(PA)**	8711	B	949 854-7047	22515
Conexant Systems Worldwide Inc	3674	E	949 483-4600	9494
Conversionpoint Holdings Inc	7372	D	888 706-6764	17827
Convoy Technologies LLC	3651	F	949 680-9400	9167
Core Realty Holdings LLC **(PA)**	6798	D	949 863-1031	16231
Core Realty Holdings MGT Inc	6531	D	949 863-1031	15825
Crm Co LLC **(PA)**	3061	E	949 263-9100	5356
Crossport Mocean	2311	F	949 646-1701	2744
DJ John Park MD Inc **(PA)**	8062	D	714 326-7715	20756
Eddie VS Wildfish Newport Bch **(PA)**	8741	D	949 720-9925	23019
Edwards Theatres Circuit Inc **(DH)**	7832	C	949 640-4600	19276
Ekran System Inc	7372	E	424 242-8838	17843
Electronic Commerce LLC	6159	D	800 770-5520	15163
Elevated Resources Inc	7374	C	949 419-6632	18084
Emery Financial Inc **(PA)**	6163	D	949 219-0640	15241
Entrepreneurial Capital Corp	6512	C	949 809-3900	15666
Everest Sonoma Management LLC	7011	D	213 272-0088	16439
Evolus Inc **(PA)**	2834	C	949 284-4555	4818
Excelsior Capital Partners LLC **(PA)**	6531	C	949 566-8110	15849
Experience 1 Inc **(DH)**	6361	D	949 475-3752	15502
Ferruzzo & Ferruzzo LLP	8111	D	949 608-6900	21553
Festival Fun Parks LLC	7999	C	954 921-1411	19648
First Team RE - Orange Cnty	6531	C	949 759-5747	15859
FMC Financial Group **(PA)**	6411	D	949 225-9369	15571
Greystar Management Svcs LP	6531	B	949 705-0010	15877
Grit Management LLC	7991	D	949 220-7765	19451
Gst Inc	3572	D	949 510-1142	8201
Harbor Health Systems LLC	8099	D	949 273-7020	21433
Hard Candy LLC	5122	E	949 515-3923	14248
Hixson Metal Finishing	3471	C	800 900-9798	7268
Hmr Building Systems LLC	2421	D	951 749-4700	3211
Hmwc Cpas & Business Advisors	8721	D	714 505-9000	22789
Hoag Family Cancer Institute **(PA)**	8062	D	949 722-6237	20788
Hoag Hospital Foundation **(HQ)**	8062	E	949 764-7217	20789
Hoag Memorial Hospital Presbt **(PA)**	8062	A	949 764-4624	20790
Hornblower Yachts LLC	4724	D	949 650-2412	12389
Houalla Enterprises Ltd	1542	D	949 515-4350	773
Hyatt Corporation	7011	B	949 729-1234	16499
IL Colore Inc **(PA)**	1742	D	949 975-1325	1379
Innovent Inc **(PA)**	2621	F	949 387-7725	3756
International Bay Clubs LLC **(PA)**	7997	C	949 645-5000	19570
Interstate-Rim MGT Co LLC	7011	C	949 783-2500	16507
Irell & Manella LLP	8111	C	949 760-0991	21587
Iron Press Incorporated	2741	F	714 426-8088	4184
Irvine Eastgate Office II LLC	6798	A	949 720-2000	16237
Isles Ranch Partners **(PA)**	0291	D	949 383-2354	142
Jacksam Corporation	3565	E	800 605-3580	8072
Jaguar Energy LLC **(PA)**	1389	E	949 706-7060	511
James R Gldwell Dntl Crmics In **(PA)**	8072	A	949 440-2600	21107
Jeffrey Rome & Associates	8712	D	949 760-3929	22723
John Hancock Life Insur Co USA	6311	A	949 254-1440	15363
Johnny Was **(PA)**	5137	E	949 219-0557	14385
JS Held LLC	8721	D	949 390-7647	22795
Kadenwood LLC	2833	D	949 287-6703	4751
Kadenwood Per & Pet Care LLC	2023	E	949 287-6789	1797
Kelly Pneumatics Inc	3699	E	800 704-7552	9881
La Habra Villa	8361	D	714 529-1697	22121
Labmed Partners	8742	E	949 242-9925	23255
Landsea Homes Corporation **(HQ)**	1531	D	949 345-8080	679
Landsea Homes US Corporation **(DH)**	6552	D	949 345-8080	16056
Lebata Inc	3273	E	949 253-2800	6098
Lee & Assoc Rlty Group Nwport	6531	E	949 724-1000	15911
Lennar Partners of Los Angeles **(PA)**	7389	D	949 885-8500	18576
Lewis Barricade Inc	2951	D	661 363-0912	5274
Lil O Blossom Inc	2676	F	949 675-3885	3905
Macom Technology Solutions Inc	3663	F	310 320-6160	9288
Makar Properties LLC **(PA)**	6552	A	949 255-1100	16060
Mbit Wireless Inc **(PA)**	4812	E	949 205-4559	12609
McCarthy Bldg Companies Inc	1542	B	949 851-8383	786

	SIC	EMP	PHONE	ENTRY #
McCarthy Bldg Companies Inc	1542	D	949 851-8383	787
Mediterraneotaste Inc **(PA)**	2032	E	714 395-6755	1854
Merrill Lynch Prce Fnner Smith	6211	D	949 467-3760	15281
Mesa Management Inc	6531	D	949 851-0995	15925
Message Broadcast LLC	7389	E	949 428-3111	18597
Metrostudy Inc	8742	C	714 619-7800	23271
Meyers Research LLC **(PA)**	8732	C	714 619-7800	22893
Mf Services Company LLC **(HQ)**	8742	D	949 474-5800	23272
Mfi Inc	3999	F	949 887-8691	11714
Micha-Rettenmaier Partnership	8011	D	714 280-1645	19977
Mig Capital LLC **(PA)**	6282	C	949 474-5800	15333
Mig Management Services LLC	8741	D	949 474-5800	23064
Mindspeed Technologies LLC **(HQ)**	3674	A	949 579-3000	9546
Mmxviii Holdings Inc	3993	E	800 672-3974	11574
Mobilitie Services LLC	4813	B	877 999-7070	12655
Monex Deposit A Cal Ltd Partnr	6722	D	949 752-1400	16133
Mulechain Inc	4212	D	888 456-8881	11982
National Therapeutic Svcs Inc **(PA)**	8093	D	866 311-0003	21322
Newmeyer & Dillion LLP **(PA)**	8111	C	949 854-7000	21644
Newport Beach Country Club Inc	7997	D	949 644-9550	19592
Newport Beach Surgery Ctr LLC	8011	C	949 631-0988	19993
Newport Center Medical Group	8011	D	949 644-3555	19994
Newport Diagnostic Center Inc **(PA)**	8011	D	949 760-3025	19995
Newport Fab LLC	3674	D	949 435-8000	9549
Nguyen Minh	5045	F	949 646-2584	13420
No World Borders **(PA)**	8748	D	949 718-4427	23483
Nuzuna Corporation	7991	D	949 432-4824	19462
Olen Commercial Realty Corp	6512	B	949 644-6536	15683
Olen Residential Realty Corp **(HQ)**	1522	D	949 644-6536	664
One LLP **(PA)**	8111	D	949 502-2870	21649
Optek Group Inc	3845	F	949 629-2558	11232
Osf International Inc	7011	D	949 675-8654	16599
Pacific Altrntive Asset MGT LL **(HQ)**	6282	D	949 261-4900	15336
Pacific Asset Holding LLC	6311	C	949 219-3011	15366
Pacific Bay Properties **(PA)**	1521	E	949 440-7200	627
Pacific Club **(PA)**	7997	D	949 955-1123	19597
Pacific Communities Bldr Inc **(PA)**	1521	D	949 660-8988	628
Pacific Hotel Management Inc	7011	C	949 608-1091	16608
Pacific Hsptlist Assoc A Med C	8611	D	949 610-7245	22254
Pacific Investment MGT Co LLC **(DH)**	6722	C	949 720-6000	16143
Pacific Life & Annuity Company	6311	A	949 219-3011	15367
Pacific Life Fund Advisors LLC	8741	A	949 260-9000	23083
Pacific Life Fund Advisors LLC **(DH)**	6282	D	800 800-7646	15338
Pacific Life Global Funding	6153	D	949 219-3011	15157
Pacific Monarch Resorts Inc **(PA)**	6531	D	949 609-2400	15939
Pacific Select Distributors	6211	D	949 219-3011	15303
Palace Entertainment Inc **(DH)**	7999	E	949 261-0404	19660
Park Newport Ltd **(PA)**	6513	D	949 644-1900	15743
Peninsula Publishing Inc	2721	E	949 631-1307	4095
Pimco Global Advisors LLC **(DH)**	6722	D	949 219-2200	16144
Pimco Mortgage Income Tr Inc	6733	B	949 720-6000	16193
Platescan Inc	3469	F	949 851-1600	7174
PM Realty Group LP	6531	D	949 553-8246	15953
Pressed Juicery Inc	5149	F	949 650-0661	14725
Pressed Juicery Inc	5149	F	949 715-7006	14726
Prosum Inc	7374	D	949 732-1122	18105
Pyramid Peak Corporation	6799	D	949 769-8600	16286
R Mc Closkey Insurance Agency	6411	C	949 223-8100	15620
Real Estate Digital LLC	7371	C	800 234-2139	17696
Redart Corporation	2531	F	714 774-9444	3631
Research Affiliates Capital LP	6282	D	949 325-8700	15342
Research Affiliates MGT LLC	6282	D	949 325-8700	15343
Riverside Research Institute	8733	D	949 631-0107	22918
RMR Financial LLC **(DH)**	6163	D	408 355-2000	15250
Roth Capital Partners LLC **(PA)**	6211	D	800 678-9147	15305
Rsdg International Inc	2361	F	626 256-4190	3037
RSI Construction Inc	1522	D	949 720-1116	668
RSI Insurance Brokers Inc **(DH)**	6411	E	714 546-6616	15623
Sagepoint Financial Inc	6282	B	949 756-1462	15345
Sageview Advisory Group LLC **(PA)**	6282	D	949 955-1395	15347
Saritasa LLC **(PA)**	7374	D	949 200-6839	18108
Sdmv Hotel Partners LP	6512	D	949 516-0088	15695
Sleepy Giant Entertainment Inc	7371	C	949 464-7986	17714
Sleepy Giant Entertainment Inc	7929	D	714 460-4113	19379
Smart Circle International LLC **(PA)**	8742	D	949 587-9207	23326
Sober Living By Sea Inc **(HQ)**	8093	D	949 673-6696	21340
Staffrehab	8093	A	888 835-0894	21345
Steadfast Coml MGT Co Inc **(HQ)**	6531	D	949 852-0700	16011
Sterling Motors Ltd	7515	D	949 645-5900	18754
Stradling Ycca Crlson Ruth A P **(PA)**	8111	C	949 725-4000	21681
Strategic Medical Ventures LLC **(PA)**	3844	F	949 355-5212	11210
Succetti Group Inc	8748	E	949 335-2292	23512
Sun Life Cnada US Holdings Inc	6282	C	949 930-1570	15349
Surterre Properties Inc **(PA)**	6531	C	949 717-7100	16013
T-Force Inc **(PA)**	8748	D	949 208-1527	23515
Tad Group LLC	7382	C	949 476-3601	18403
Ticketsocket Inc	7371	E	917 283-0436	17735
Title365 Company **(DH)**	6541	B	877 365-9365	16043
Toni & Guy Hairdressing **(PA)**	7231	E	949 721-1666	16918
Tower Semicdtr Newport Bch Inc **(DH)**	3674	A	949 435-8000	9593
Trg Insurance Services	6411	D	949 474-1550	15638
Tribeworx LLC	7372	D	800 949-3432	18001
Triton Chandelier Inc	3646	F	714 957-9600	9107
True Investments LLC **(PA)**	6799	E	949 258-9720	16298
Twenty4seven Hotels Corp	8741	B	949 734-6400	23130
U Gym LLC **(PA)**	7991	D	714 668-0911	19471
Uka LLC	7011	D	949 610-8000	16761

GEOGRAPHIC

Employment Codes: A=Over 500 employees, B=251-500, C=101-250, D=51-100, E=20-50 F=10-19
2022 Southern California Business Directory and Buyers Guide
© Mergent Inc. 1-800-342-5647
1403

	SIC	EMP	PHONE	ENTRY #
United Cpitl Fncl Advisers LLC	6282	D	949 999-8500	15353
United Panam Financial Corp **(PA)**	7538	B	949 224-1226	18882
Unitek Learning Inc **(PA)**	7379	D	510 249-1060	18232
Urban Decal LLC **(HQ)**	2844	E	949 574-9712	5078
US Hardship Group LLC	7299	E	877 777-0174	16984
US Lines LLC **(DH)**	4731	D	714 751-3333	12549
Valley Insurance Service Inc **(HQ)**	6411	D	626 966-3664	15642
Vintage Senior Management Inc **(PA)**	6513	A	949 719-4080	15752
Voltedge LLC	3571	F	949 877-8900	8184
Walden Structures Inc	2452	B	909 389-9100	3430
West Dermatology Med MGT Inc	8011	C	909 793-3000	20161
William Hzmlhlch Archtects Inc	8712	D	949 250-0607	22752
William Lyon Homes **(HQ)**	1521	B	949 833-3600	651
William Lyon Homes Inc **(DH)**	1521	D	949 833-3600	652
Windjmmer Capitl Investors LLC	6799	D	949 706-9989	16303
Windjmmer Cpitl Invstors III L	6799	A	949 706-9989	16304
Wj Newport LLC	7011	C	949 476-2001	16802
Wright Finlay & Zak LLP	8111	D	949 477-5050	21702
Ymarketing LLC	8742	D	714 545-2550	23369
Your Practice Online LLC **(PA)**	8742	D	877 388-8569	23371

NEWPORT COAST, CA - Orange County

	SIC	EMP	PHONE	ENTRY #
Concert Golf Partners LLC	7992	A	949 715-0602	19478
Hji Group Corporation **(PA)**	8748	D	714 557-8800	23450
Resort At Pelican Hill LLC	7011	C	949 467-6800	16662

NIPOMO, CA - San Luis Obispo County

	SIC	EMP	PHONE	ENTRY #
Community Hlth Ctrs of Cntl CA **(PA)**	8011	C	805 929-3211	19758
Condition Monitoring Svcs Inc	3826	E	888 359-3277	10790
Jj Fisher Construction Inc	1611	D	805 723-5220	893
L J T Flowers Inc **(PA)**	5191	C	877 929-2476	14863
LR Baggs Corporation	3931	E	805 929-3545	11346
Malcolm Demille Inc	3911	F	805 929-4353	11324
Pre Con Industries Inc	1751	E	805 481-7305	1449
Santa Maria Tire Inc **(PA)**	7534	D	805 347-4793	18810
Statewide Safety & Signs Inc **(HQ)**	7359	E	805 929-5070	17376
Statewide Safety and Signs I	3669	B	714 468-1919	9355
Troesh Readymix Inc	3273	E	805 928-3764	6124
Whites Hvac Services Inc	3585	F	805 801-0167	8358
William James Cellars **(PA)**	2084	E	805 478-9412	2237

NORCO, CA - Riverside County

	SIC	EMP	PHONE	ENTRY #
A Plus Custom Metal Supply Inc	1761	F	951 736-7900	1472
Anna Corporation	1721	E	951 736-6037	1167
Avid Idntification Systems Inc **(PA)**	3674	D	951 371-7505	9486
Better Nutritionals LLC **(PA)**	2023	A	310 356-9019	1783
Bonanza Plumbing Inc **(PA)**	1711	D	951 360-8262	1034
Bowlero Corp	7933	D	951 734-8410	19391
Cal West Underground Inc	1629	D	951 371-6775	991
Cal-West Nurseries Inc	0782	C	951 270-0667	294
City of Norco	8748	D	951 270-5617	23429
Clima-Tech Inc	7623	D	909 613-5513	18945
Epic Sheet Metal Inc	3444	F	714 679-5917	6826
Flavor Factory Inc	2087	F	951 273-9877	2324
Guy Yocom Construction Inc **(PA)**	1771	A	951 284-3456	1527
Industrial Process Eqp Inc	3567	F	714 447-0171	8091
International E-Z Up Inc **(PA)**	2394	D	800 457-4233	3141
Jfp Painting	1721	D	951 736-6037	1185
JIT Corporation	5065	D	805 238-5000	13736
Kraftwerks Prfmce Group LLC	3714	F	951 808-9888	10088
Legal Vision Group LLC	2752	E	310 945-5550	4356
North Orange Coast Pntg Inc	1721	D	951 279-2694	1191
Paragon Building Products Inc **(PA)**	3272	E	951 549-1155	6048
Pro Tech Thermal Services	3398	E	951 272-5808	6451
Royal West Drywall Inc	1742	D	951 271-4600	1398
RPM Grinding Co Inc	3599	F	951 273-0602	8780
S R Machining Inc	3599	E	951 520-9486	8784
S R Machining-Properties LLC	3599	C	951 520-9486	8785
Sierra Woodworking Inc	2431	F	949 493-4528	3288
Spearmint Rhino Cmpnies Wrldwi	8741	D	951 371-3788	23116
Sr Plastics Company LLC **(PA)**	3089	D	951 520-9486	5826
W B Powell Inc	2431	D	951 270-0095	3296

NORTH HILLS, CA - Los Angeles County

	SIC	EMP	PHONE	ENTRY #
Alpha Aviation Components Inc **(PA)**	3599	E	818 894-8801	8492
Galpin Motors Inc **(PA)**	7538	B	818 787-3800	18832
Imperial Toy LLC **(PA)**	3944	C	818 536-6500	11376
Living Colors Inc	1721	D	818 893-5068	1188
Modern Outdoor Designs LLC	7389	F	818 785-0171	18602
Morris Enterprises Inc	3089	F	818 894-9103	5721
New Hrzns Srving Indvdals With **(PA)**	2052	D	818 894-9301	2069
P C A Electronics Inc	5065	E	818 892-0761	13761
Penny Lane Centers **(PA)**	8399	B	818 892-3423	22207
Prn Ambulance LLC	4119	B	818 810-3600	11887
Schrillo Company LLC	3452	E	818 894-8241	7074
Veterans Health Administration	8011	C	818 895-9344	20141
Veterans Health Administration	8011	C	818 891-7711	20147
Veterans Health Administration	8011	C	818 895-9449	20150
Walker & Zanger LLC **(HQ)**	5032	D	818 280-8300	13319

NORTH HOLLYWOOD, CA - Los Angeles County

	SIC	EMP	PHONE	ENTRY #
51 Minds Entertainment LLC	7929	D	818 643-8200	19341
6480 Corporation	2759	F	818 765-9670	4472
A T Parker Inc **(PA)**	3699	E	818 755-1700	9845
ABC Sun Control LLC	2394	F	818 982-6989	3134
Advanced Cable Technologies	1623	E	818 262-6484	932
Advanced Semiconductor Inc	3674	D	818 982-1200	9475
Airdraulics Inc	7539	E	818 982-1400	18889
Akh Company Inc	7539	C	818 691-1978	18890
Alco Tech Inc	3469	E	818 503-9209	7121
Allan Aircraft Supply Co LLC	3494	E	818 765-4992	7469
Almore Dye House Inc	2269	E	818 506-5444	2668
Alpena Sausage Inc	2013	F	818 505-9482	1726
Americh Corporation **(PA)**	3842	C	818 982-1711	11086
Anmar Precision Components Inc	3728	E	818 764-0901	10271
Applica Inc	3663	F	818 565-0011	9254
Apu Inc	5013	D	818 508-7211	13042
Armenco Catrg Trck Mfg Co Inc	3713	E	818 768-0400	9976
Armored Group Inc	2441	E	818 767-3030	3375
Arriaga Usa Inc	1411	D	818 764-1777	561
Arriaga Usa Inc **(PA)**	1743	D	818 982-9559	1411
Artcrafters Cabinets	2434	E	818 752-8960	3306
Arte De Mexico Inc	3646	D	818 753-4510	9078
Artisan House Inc	3499	E	818 767-7475	7549
Asi Semiconductor Inc	3674	E	818 982-1200	9484
Aspect Ratio Inc **(HQ)**	7819	D	323 467-2121	19219
Astro Chrome and Polsg Corp	3471	E	818 781-1463	7218
Ave Jewelry Inc	3911	E	213 488-0097	11313
Avibank Mfg Inc **(DH)**	3728	C	818 392-2100	10284
Babylon Security Services Inc	7381	D	818 766-8122	18253
Backstage Equipment Inc	3449	F	818 504-6026	7015
Basaw Manufacturing Inc **(PA)**	2441	E	818 765-6650	3376
Bento Box Entertainment LLC	7812	B	818 333-7700	19100
Buster and Punch Inc	5023	E	818 392-3827	13163
Cal-June Inc **(PA)**	3429	D	323 877-4164	6509
Capco/Psa	3089	E	818 762-4276	5599
Cats USA Inc	7342	D	818 506-1000	17201
Century National Properties **(PA)**	7011	D	818 760-0880	16374
Century Theatres Inc	7833	C	818 508-1943	19295
Century West BMW	7538	D	818 432-5800	18817
Chapmn/Lnard Stdio Eqp Cnada I **(PA)**	7819	C	323 877-5309	19222
Circulating Air Inc **(PA)**	1711	D	818 764-0530	1045
City Moving Inc	4214	C	888 794-3808	12110
Concorde Career Colleges Inc	8621	D	818 766-3151	22267
Consejosano Inc	7389	D	855 735-6726	18488
Core Bts Inc	7373	C	818 766-2400	18027
Corporate Impressions La Inc	2759	E	818 761-9295	4502
Cosmo - Pharm Inc	2833	F	818 764-0246	4741
Cri-Help Inc **(PA)**	8361	D	818 985-8323	22098
Criterion Labs Inc	8734	D	818 506-8332	22937
Criterion Supply Inc	2273	F	562 222-2382	2687
Davenport International Corp	3651	F	818 765-6400	9170
David S Boyer MD Inc	8011	D	818 754-2090	19780
Dennis Bolton Enterprises Inc	2752	E	818 982-1800	4275
Dowell Aluminum Foundry Inc	3365	E	323 877-9645	6392
Dubnoff Ctr For Child Devl & **(PA)**	8093	D	818 755-4950	21301
E B Bradley Co	5072	E	800 553-3030	13806
Electronic Hardware Limited **(PA)**	5065	E	818 982-6100	13716
Emergency Technologies Inc	7382	D	818 765-4421	18375
Encore Cases Inc	3161	E	818 768-8803	5890
Enviro-Intercept Inc	3585	F	818 982-6063	8338
ESP Computer Services Inc **(PA)**	7374	D	818 487-4500	18088
EZ Lube LLC	7549	D	818 761-5696	18929
Fastener Technology Corp	5085	C	818 764-6467	13983
Fayes Foods Inc	2099	E	818 508-8392	2432
Financial Group Inc	6411	C	818 308-8527	15568
Fluids Manufacturing Inc	5159	C	818 264-4657	14750
G & H Precision Inc	3599	F	818 982-3873	8597
G-2 Graphic Service Inc	2759	D	818 623-3100	4517
General Motors LLC	7532	D	818 752-6619	18790
General Wax Co Inc **(PA)**	3999	D	818 765-5800	11676
Glen Park Retirement Hotel	8052	D	818 769-6626	20530
Gold/Gold/Gold Inc	5094	E	323 845-9746	14131
Graphic Visions Inc	2752	E	818 845-8393	4307
Groundwork Coffee Roasters LLC	2095	C	818 506-6020	2355
Harman Press Inc	2752	E	818 432-0570	4311
Hillsdale Group LP	8059	C	818 623-2170	20595
Hope Plastic Co Inc	3089	E	818 769-5560	5666
Hughes Price & Sharp Inc	2711	F	865 675-6278	3993
Inpatient Consultants Fla Inc **(DH)**	8011	C	888 447-2362	19853
Interact Theatre Co	7922	E	818 765-8732	19315
IPC Healthcare Inc **(DH)**	8011	A	888 447-2362	19856
Irdeto Usa Inc **(DH)**	7375	B	818 508-2333	18125
Jack C Drees Grinding Co Inc	3599	F	818 764-8301	8637
Jackson Shrub Supply Inc	7819	D	818 982-0100	19239
Jam Design Inc	3961	F	818 505-1680	11485
JC Majestic Real Estate LLC	6531	E	800 398-6879	15896
JC Party Rentals Inc	7359	D	818 765-4819	17358
Jessica Cosmetics Intl Inc	5122	D	818 759-1050	14253
Jewish Family Svc Los Angeles	8322	D	818 984-0276	21823
Johnson doc Enterprises	3089	E	818 764-1543	5685
K & G Latirovian Inc **(PA)**	3714	E	818 319-2862	10083
Kaiser Foundation Hospitals	8011	C	888 778-5000	19908
Kaiser Foundation Hospitals	6324	C	818 503-7082	15435
KG Constrctons Sltions USA Inc **(PA)**	1521	D	800 295-9109	620
King Express Inc	2051	F	818 503-2772	2012
Klune Industries Inc **(DH)**	3728	B	818 503-8100	10363
KOA Electronics Distribution **(PA)**	5065	D	818 255-6666	13740
Kobis Windows & Doors Mfg Inc	2434	E	818 764-6400	3324
Landscape Support Services	0782	D	818 475-0680	322
Los Angeles Unified School Dst	8641	D	818 763-6497	22346
Lyonsgate Realty Inc	6531	E	561 961-4934	15917
M Gaw Inc	1799	D	818 503-7997	1672
Mar Engineering Company	3599	E	818 765-4805	8676
Marcus Hotels Inc	7011	C	818 980-8000	16555
Mave Enterprises Inc	2064	E	818 767-4533	2096

Mergent email: customerrelations@mergent.com
1404

2022 Southern California Business
Directory and Buyers Guide

(P-0000) Products & Services Section entry number
(PA)=Parent Co (HQ)=Headquarters (DH)=Div Headquarters

	SIC	EMP	PHONE	ENTRY #
Meco-Nag Corporation	3144	F	818 764-2020	5881
Meggitt North Hollywood Inc **(HQ)**	3728	C	818 765-8160	10379
Messenger Express **(PA)**	4215	C	213 614-0475	12142
Metal Improvement Company LLC	3398	D	818 983-1952	6445
Midway Rent A Car Inc	7515	D	818 985-9770	18752
Mikado Hotels Inc	7011	E	818 763-9141	16569
Mission Linen Supply	7213	D	818 764-0720	16861
Modern-Aire Ventilating Inc	3444	E	818 765-9870	6879
Morigon Technologies LLC	5047	E	818 764-8880	13502
Mtd Kitchen Inc	2431	D	818 764-2254	3272
Neto Express LLC	4213	D	818 625-5615	12068
Ngp Motors Inc	7539	C	818 980-9800	18900
North Highland Company LLC	8742	C	818 509-5100	23285
Northeast Valley Health Corp	8011	D	818 765-8656	20001
O P I Products Inc **(HQ)**	5087	B	818 759-8688	14042
Onnik Shoe Company Inc	3144	F	818 506-5353	5882
Orion Ornamental Iron Inc	3429	E	818 752-0688	6531
Pacific Wire Products Inc	3496	E	818 755-6400	7506
PCL Construction Services Inc	1542	C	818 509-7816	803
Pdu Lad Corporation **(PA)**	3479	D	626 442-7711	7394
Perkins	3548	E	818 764-9293	7894
Perpetual Motion Group Inc	3441	F	818 982-4300	6648
Pie Town Productions Inc	7812	D	818 255-9300	19163
Pierce Brothers **(DH)**	7261	D	818 763-9121	16925
Pilgrim Operations LLC	5043	B	818 478-4500	13348
Pnk Enterprises Inc	3499	E	818 765-3770	7567
Power Generation Entps Inc	5084	C	818 484-8550	13929
Precision Engineering Inds Inc	3679	F	818 767-8590	9766
Reel Efx Inc	3999	E	818 762-1710	11741
Rhi Inc **(PA)**	7538	C	818 508-3800	18867
Rio Vista Development Co Inc **(PA)**	7011	C	818 980-8000	16663
Rodax Distributors	7812	D	818 765-6400	19172
S & K Theatrical Drap Inc	2391	F	818 503-0596	3093
Sada Systems Inc	7379	C	818 766-2400	18219
SCI Western Region Inc	7261	D	818 286-0640	16928
Sealing Corporation	3053	F	818 765-7327	5352
Six Eleven Limited Inc	3281	F	818 764-5810	6145
Southern California Golf Assn **(PA)**	8611	D	818 980-3630	22259
Specialty Coatings & Chem Inc	2851	E	818 983-0055	5114
Starcom Worldwide Inc	7311	C	818 753-7200	17057
Stark Services	7374	D	818 985-2003	18112
Steve Leshner Clear Systems	3089	F	818 764-9223	5829
Stone Image Inc	3281	F	561 547-1177	6147
Sunland Woodworks	2426	F	818 982-3110	3225
Sunrun Installation Svcs Inc	8748	C	818 255-5462	23513
Target Mdia Prtners Intrctive **(HQ)**	2759	F	323 930-3123	4579
Tennessee Hospitalists Inc	8062	D	888 447-2362	20975
Toner Supply USA Inc	5045	E	818 504-6540	13446
Trapdoor Ensemble	7922	E	310 951-4836	19337
United Aeronautical Corp	5088	E	818 764-2102	14069
Universal Studios Company LLC **(DH)**	7812	B	818 777-1000	19195
Utility Refrigerator	3585	E	818 764-6200	8354
Valley Community Healthcare	8011	B	818 763-8836	20131
Valley Vsta Nrsing Trnstnal CA	8051	C	818 763-6275	20495
Valley Wholesale Supply Corp **(PA)**	5023	D	818 769-5656	13195
Vector Electronics & Tech Inc	3672	E	818 985-8208	9466
Village Family Services **(PA)**	8093	D	818 755-8786	21366
Volunteers of Amer Los Angeles	8322	D	818 769-3617	21918
Volunteers of Amer Los Angeles	8322	D	818 506-0597	21919
Wes Go Inc	2759	E	818 504-1200	4592
West Coast Custom Sheet Metal	3444	E	818 252-7500	6941
Western Costume Co **(HQ)**	7299	E	818 760-0900	16987
Wilshire Precision Pdts Inc	3599	E	818 765-4571	8855
Woods Maintenance Services Inc	1799	C	818 764-2515	1704
Young MNS Chrstn Assn Mtro Los	8351	E	818 763-5126	22075

NORTH PALM SPRINGS, CA - Riverside County

	SIC	EMP	PHONE	ENTRY #
E & S Prcsion Shtmetal Mfg Inc	3444	E	760 329-1607	6823
Technique Designs Inc	2541	F	760 904-6223	3668

NORTH TUSTIN, CA - Orange County

	SIC	EMP	PHONE	ENTRY #
Parking Veterans LLC	7299	E	714 699-3541	16971

NORTHRIDGE, CA - Los Angeles County

	SIC	EMP	PHONE	ENTRY #
Afr Apparel International Inc	2341	D	818 773-5000	3012
Alliant Tchsystems Oprtons LLC	3812	B	818 887-8195	10563
Alliant Tchsystems Oprtons LLC	3812	E	818 887-8195	10564
Arete Associates **(PA)**	3812	C	818 885-2200	10568
Artistry In Motion Inc	2679	E	818 994-7388	3923
Assisted Home Recovery Inc **(PA)**	7361	C	818 894-8117	17391
ATI Solutions Inc **(PA)**	3669	F	818 772-7900	9332
Automobile Club Southern Cal	8699	D	818 993-1616	22413
Bellis Steel Company Inc **(PA)**	1791	E	818 886-5601	1568
Burns Environmental Services	2842	E	818 446-9869	4958
Chemat Technology Inc	3821	E	818 727-9786	10655
Child and Family Guidance Ctr **(PA)**	8093	C	818 739-5140	21287
Choosing Independence Inc	8741	D	818 257-0323	23002
Color Design Laboratory Inc **(PA)**	8734	D	818 341-5100	22935
Contemporary Services Corp **(PA)**	7381	A	818 885-5150	18265
DC Partners Inc **(PA)**	3365	E	714 558-9444	6391
Dignity Health	8062	E	818 993-4054	20751
Dignity Health	8062	A	818 885-8500	20752
Dukes Research and Mfg Inc	3728	E	818 998-9811	10319
Eddies Perfume & Cosmtc Co Inc	2844	F	818 341-1717	5018
Emanuel Morez Inc	2511	F	818 780-2787	3470
Family Hospice Ltd	8052	C	818 571-2870	20529
Freshlunches Inc	8322	E	818 885-1718	21791
Gst Industries Inc	3728	E	818 350-1900	10341
Harman Professional Inc **(DH)**	3651	B	818 893-8411	9177
Harman-Kardon Incorporated	5064	B	818 841-4600	13687
Hemacare Corporation **(HQ)**	8099	D	877 310-0717	21436
Ikano Communications Inc **(PA)**	7374	D	801 924-0900	18096
Infinity Aerospace Inc **(PA)**	3728	E	818 998-9811	10352
Institute For Applied Behavior	8049	D	818 341-1933	20218
Instrument Bearing Factory USA	3452	E	818 989-5052	7068
Instrumentation Tech Systems	3577	E	818 886-2034	8268
Kindeva Drug Delivery LP	2834	B	818 341-1300	4840
Lakeside Medical Associates **(PA)**	8741	C	818 637-2000	23048
Lakeside Systems Inc	8741	A	866 654-3471	23049
Lloyd Design Corporation	3714	D	818 768-6001	10092
Lowes Home Centers LLC	5031	C	818 477-9022	13262
Maroney Company	3599	F	818 882-2722	8677
Medtronic Minimed Inc **(DH)**	3841	A	800 646-4633	11019
Mikuni American Corporation **(HQ)**	5013	D	310 676-0522	13073
Ndi **(PA)**	6411	D	818 368-5650	15601
Northridge Emergency Med Group	8062	D	818 700-5603	20872
Northridge Hosp Foundation Aux	8062	D	818 885-5341	20873
Northrop Grmman Innvtion Syste	3812	D	818 887-8100	10605
Northrop Grumman Systems Corp	3812	C	818 887-8110	10616
Northwest Excavating Inc	7353	D	818 349-5861	17315
Pinnacle Estate Properties **(PA)**	6531	C	818 993-4707	15949
Porter Valley Country Club	7997	C	818 360-1071	19600
Quality Speaks LLC **(PA)**	4813	C	818 264-4400	12666
Rashman Corporation	5047	D	818 993-3030	13516
Regal Medical Group Inc **(PA)**	8621	C	818 654-3400	22277
Remax Olson & Associates Inc	6531	D	818 366-3300	15974
Robert H Oliva Inc	3599	E	818 700-1035	8771
Rodeo Realty Inc	6531	D	818 349-9997	15985
Rodeo Realty Inc	6531	D	805 582-8700	15986
Ross Baker Towing Inc	7549	C	818 886-7411	18942
Rotating Prcsion McHanisms Inc	3663	E	818 349-9774	9313
S & S Numerical Control Inc	3599	E	818 341-4141	8782
San Fernando Valley Auto LLC	7538	C	818 832-1600	18870
San Frnndo Vly Intrfith Cncil	8322	D	818 885-5220	21884
Sfv LLC	8082	E	818 839-8881	21211
Sheet Metal Prototype Inc	3444	E	818 772-2715	6908
Skinfood Usa Inc	5122	D	818 998-1142	14289
Smart & Final Stores Inc	5141	C	818 368-6409	14495
Teutonic Holdings LLC **(PA)**	4813	D	818 264-4400	12674
The Community Medical Group of **(PA)**	8011	D	818 707-9603	20108
Thermometrics Corporation **(PA)**	3823	E	818 886-3755	10729
Tiffany Homecare Inc **(PA)**	8082	B	818 886-1602	21223
Tri - Star Win Coverings Inc	5023	E	818 718-3188	13190
Unique Image Inc	2752	F	818 727-7785	4445
Unitech Deco Inc	2759	F	818 700-1373	4586
United Crbral Plsy/Spstic Chld	8052	D	818 727-1067	20544
Universal Ctrl Solutions Corp	3625	F	818 898-3380	8965
Verde Cosmetic Labs LLC	2844	F	818 284-4080	5081
Village At Northridge	8361	C	818 514-4497	22163
What Kids Want Inc	3944	F	818 775-0375	11395
World Private Security Inc	7381	C	818 894-1800	18360

NORWALK, CA - Los Angeles County

	SIC	EMP	PHONE	ENTRY #
Advanced Sealing **(DH)**	3053	D	562 802-7782	5327
Aerospace Tool Grinding	3541	E	562 802-3339	7720
Aerotec Alloys Inc	3363	E	562 809-1378	6361
Aquirecorps Norwalk Auto Auctn	5012	C	562 864-7464	13019
ARC Plastics Inc	3089	E	562 802-3299	5565
Argo Spring Mfg Co Inc	3493	D	800 252-2740	7462
Bestway International Group	3479	F	562 921-7100	7349
Cabinets 2000 LLC	2434	C	562 868-0909	3310
Cargill Meat Solutions Corp	2011	B	562 345-5240	1707
Cellco Partnership	4812	D	562 244-8814	12603
Cnc Worldwide Inc **(PA)**	4731	D	310 670-7121	12437
Coast Plz Dctors Hosp A Cal Lt **(HQ)**	8062	B	562 868-3751	20725
Cph Hospital Management LLC	8062	A	562 838-3751	20742
Dianas Mexican Food Pdts Inc **(PA)**	2099	E	562 926-5802	2422
El Clasificado **(PA)**	2711	D	323 837-4095	3975
Elena Villa Healthcare Center	8059	D	562 868-0591	20578
Eriks North America Inc	3053	D	562 802-7782	5336
Front Prch Cmmnties Svcs - Cas	8059	C	562 868-9761	20589
Golden Specialty Foods LLC	2099	E	562 802-2537	2445
I & I Deburring Inc	3541	F	562 802-0058	7733
Joes Sweeping Inc	4953	D	562 929-4344	12954
Jwch Institute Inc	8733	C	562 281-0306	22912
Kaiser Foundation Hospitals	8011	C	562 807-6100	19909
Keystone Ford Inc **(PA)**	7514	C	562 868-0825	18743
Life Care Centers America Inc	8051	C	562 921-6624	20398
Lowes Home Centers LLC	5031	C	562 926-0826	13229
Master Research & Mfg Inc	3728	D	562 483-8789	10374
McDowell Craig Off Systems Inc	2522	D	562 921-4441	3614
Megabrand Kitchen & Bath Inc	5031	E	562 229-0088	13277
New Cntury Mtals Southeast Inc	3356	A	562 356-6804	6335
Norwalk Meadows Nursing Ctr LP	8051	C	562 864-2541	20425
Paradise Printing Inc	2752	E	714 228-9628	4386
Pedestal Capital II LLC	6799	D	562 863-5555	16283
Polley Inc **(PA)**	3569	F	562 868-9861	8137
Tecno Industrial Engrg Inc	3599	E	562 623-4517	8815
Telecare Act 7	8093	D	562 929-6688	21352
Tvb (usa) Inc **(DH)**	4833	E	562 345-9871	12746
West Central Produce Inc	5148	B	213 629-3600	14666

NUEVO, CA - Riverside County

	SIC	EMP	PHONE	ENTRY #
Oldcastle Infrastructure Inc	3444	E	951 928-8713	6883

GEOGRAPHIC

Employment Codes: A=Over 500 employees, B=251-500, C=101-250, D=51-100, E=20-50 F=10-19

2022 Southern California Business Directory and Buyers Guide

1405

OAK HILLS, CA - San Bernardino County

Company	SIC	EMP	PHONE	ENTRY #
Double Eagle Trnsp Corp	4213	C	760 956-3770	12035
Pathways I Sober Living Inc **(PA)**	8322	D	626 373-6006	21864

OAK PARK, CA - Ventura County

Company	SIC	EMP	PHONE	ENTRY #
Foldimate Inc	3634	E	805 876-4418	9005
TLC Sportswear Inc	5137	F	805 375-2494	14422

OAK VIEW, CA - Ventura County

Company	SIC	EMP	PHONE	ENTRY #
Willis Machine Inc	3599	E	805 604-4500	8853

OCEANO, CA - San Luis Obispo County

Company	SIC	EMP	PHONE	ENTRY #
United Parcel Service Inc	7389	D	805 474-9134	18700

OJAI, CA - Ventura County

Company	SIC	EMP	PHONE	ENTRY #
Community Memorial Health Sys	8062	C	805 646-1401	20731
Dmz Studio Inc **(PA)**	2731	F	805 640-9240	4127
Financial Group Inc	8741	C	805 646-7974	23025
Help Unlmted Personnel Svc Inc	8082	A	805 962-4646	21169
Krishnamurti Foundation Amer **(PA)**	6732	E	805 646-2726	16169
Monica Ros School	8351	D	805 646-8184	22035
Ojai Valley Athletic Club	7997	D	805 646-7213	19596
Ojai Valley Inn Golf Course	7011	D	805 646-2420	16592
Ojai Vly Fmly Medicine Group	8011	D	805 646-7246	20009
Ovis LLC	7011	A	805 646-5511	16603
Rock Blue	8621	D	703 314-0208	22278
Troop Real Estate Inc	6531	D	805 640-1440	16024

ONTARIO, CA - San Bernardino County

Company	SIC	EMP	PHONE	ENTRY #
10-8 Retrofit Inc	7538	F	909 986-5551	18812
A Lot To Say Inc	2399	E	877 366-8448	3186
A-1 Delivery Co	4212	D	909 444-1220	11951
AAA Stamping Inc	3469	F	909 947-4151	7118
Aamp of America	3699	E	805 338-6800	9847
Aaren Laboratories LLC	3827	F	909 906-5400	10821
Aaren Scientific Inc **(DH)**	3827	C	909 937-1033	10822
Abba Roller LLC **(DH)**	3069	F	909 947-1244	5363
Able Industrial Products Inc **(PA)**	3053	E	909 930-1585	5326
Accentcare Home Hlth Yuma Inc	8082	B	909 605-7000	21125
Ace Calendering Entps Inc **(PA)**	3069	F	909 937-1901	5364
ACI Construction Company Inc	8711	E	909 391-4477	22474
Action Embroidery Corp **(PA)**	2399	C	909 983-1359	3188
Adesa International LLC	2032	E	909 321-8240	1844
Adminsure Inc	6411	C	909 718-1200	15526
Advanced Color Graphics	2752	D	909 930-1500	4223
Advanced Pattern & Mold Inc	3334	F	909 930-3444	6280
Advanced Refreshment LLC **(HQ)**	2086	C	425 746-8100	2248
Aerospace and Coml Tooling Inc	3599	F	909 930-5780	8480
Affordable Plas & Packg Inc	2821	F	909 972-1944	4676
Air Control Systems Inc	1711	E	909 786-4230	1020
Ajinomoto Foods North Amer Inc	2038	C	909 477-4700	1914
Ajinomoto Foods North Amer Inc **(DH)**	2038	D	909 477-4700	1915
Akra Plastic Products Inc	3089	E	909 930-1999	5551
Alger Precision Machining LLC	3451	C	909 986-4591	7029
Alta Advanced Technologies Inc	2836	E	909 983-2973	4928
Alum-Alloy Co Inc	3463	E	909 986-0410	7102
Alumin-Art Plating Co Inc	3471	F	909 983-1866	7209
Alumistar Inc	3365	E	562 633-6673	6385
Am-Tek Engineering Inc	3599	F	909 673-1633	8494
AMD International Tech LLC	3444	E	909 985-8300	6781
American Bolt & Screw Mfg Corp **(PA)**	5085	D	909 390-0522	13971
American Business Bank	6022	D	909 919-2040	15009
American Fleet & Ret Graphics	3993	E	909 937-7570	11522
American Premier Corp	3949	E	909 923-7070	11401
AMF Pharma LLC	2834	F	909 930-9599	4781
Amrep Inc **(DH)**	2842	C	909 923-0430	4952
Amrep Manufacturing Co LLC	3559	B	877 468-9278	7961
Androp Packaging Inc	2653	E	909 605-8842	3783
Apollo Wood Recovery Inc	2499	F	909 371-9510	3437
Armorcast Products Company Inc	3089	E	909 390-1365	5567
Arrow Truck Bodies & Eqp Inc	3713	F	909 947-3991	9977
Artesia Sawdust Products Inc	2421	E	909 947-5983	3207
Ashtel Studios Inc	3844	E	909 434-0911	11205
Aspire Bakeries LLC	5149	C	909 472-3500	14670
Astro Display Company Inc	3993	E	909 605-2875	11524
Atchesons Express Inc	4212	E	714 808-9199	11957
Atd Corporation	5014	C	909 481-6210	13112
Athanor Group Inc	3451	F	909 467-1205	7032
Auburn Tile Inc	3272	E	909 984-2841	6018
Automotive Tstg & Dev Svcs Inc **(PA)**	7549	C	909 390-1100	18922
Aveta Health Solution Inc	8742	A	909 605-8000	23164
B Stephen Cooperage Inc	3412	F	909 591-2929	6471
B&D Litho California Inc	2752	F	909 390-0903	4235
Baby Trend Inc **(HQ)**	5137	D	909 773-0018	14363
Balda C Brewer Inc **(DH)**	3089	C	714 630-6810	5574
Barzillai Manufacturing Co Inc	3444	F	909 947-4200	6792
Beauty 21 Cosmetics Inc	5122	C	909 945-2220	14234
Bee Wire & Cable Inc	3357	E	909 923-5800	6342
Behavoral Autism Therapies LLC **(PA)**	8322	C	909 483-5000	21722
Bericap LLC	3089	D	905 634-2248	5579
Best Quality Furniture Mfg Inc	5021	F	909 230-6440	13128
Bhk Inc	3641	F	909 983-2973	9018
Bio-Med Services Inc	8062	D	909 235-4400	20689
Bionime USA Corporation	5047	E	909 781-6969	13480
Black & Decker Corporation	3546	F	909 390-5548	7880
Blumenthal Distributing Inc **(PA)**	5021	C	909 930-2000	13129
Bmci Inc	3549	E	951 361-8000	7900
Bock Machine Company Inc	3599	F	909 947-7250	8530
Bomatic Inc	3089	D	909 947-3900	5583
Bomel Construction Co Inc	1542	D	909 923-3319	746
BP Industries Incorporated	5023	D	909 481-0227	13160
Broker Solutions Inc	8742	D	909 458-0718	23178
C C Graber Co	0179	E	909 983-1761	68
CA Station Management Inc	1623	C	909 245-6251	940
Cal Precision Inc	3599	F	951 273-9901	8539
Calico Brands Inc	5199	E	909 930-5000	14918
Calidad Inc	3365	E	909 947-3937	6388
California Die Casting Inc	3364	E	909 947-9947	6375
California Exotic Novlt LLC	3999	D	909 606-1950	11647
California Mfg Cabinetry Inc	2541	F	909 930-3632	3641
California Physicians Service	6324	D	909 974-5201	15391
California Quality Plas Inc	3089	E	909 930-5667	5596
California Silica Products LLC **(PA)**	2819	E	760 885-5358	4653
Califrnia Nwspapers Ltd Partnr	2711	C	909 987-6397	3957
Cardenas Markets LLC	2038	C	909 947-4824	1919
Cardenas Markets LLC	2038	C	909 923-7426	1920
Care Stffing Professionals Inc	8082	D	909 906-2060	21146
Carl Zeiss Meditec Prod LLC	3827	D	877 644-4657	10828
Case World Co	3172	F	626 330-1000	5906
Castillo Maritess	2394	F	949 216-0468	3136
Celestica Aerospace Tech Corp	3672	C	512 310-7540	9387
Cemex Construction Mtls Inc **(DH)**	5032	E	909 974-5500	13297
Cemex USA Inc	3273	F	909 974-5500	6084
Century American Aluminum Inc	3354	E	909 390-2384	6305
Chenbro Micom (usa) Inc	3572	E	909 937-0100	8194
CHi Doors Holdings Inc	1751	C	909 605-1508	1429
Chino-Pacific Warehouse Corp **(PA)**	4225	D	909 545-8100	12189
Chromcraft Rvngton Douglas Ind **(PA)**	2512	E	909 930-9391	3497
Circle Green Inc	2869	F	909 930-0200	5131
Citistaff Solutions Inc **(PA)**	7361	C	310 763-1636	17406
Citizens Business Bank **(HQ)**	6022	C	909 980-4030	15017
Citrus Motors Ontario Inc **(PA)**	7538	C	909 390-0930	18818
Classic Containers Inc	3085	B	909 930-3610	5474
Coast Plastics Inc **(PA)**	5162	F	626 812-9174	14754
Coca-Cola Company	2087	D	909 975-5200	2315
Comcast Corporation	4841	D	909 890-0886	12753
Commander Packaging West Inc	2653	E	714 921-9350	3795
Communication Tech Svcs LLC	1731	B	508 382-2700	1235
Compart Engineering Inc **(DH)**	5065	D	909 947-6688	13710
Compatico Inc	2541	E	616 940-1772	3644
Compumeric Engineering Inc	3444	E	909 605-7666	6810
Concord Foods Inc **(PA)**	5141	D	909 975-2000	14461
Crown Paper Converting Inc	2621	E	909 923-5226	3749
CTA Fixtures Inc	2542	D	909 390-6744	3680
CU Direct Corporation **(PA)**	7371	C	909 481-2300	17587
Cushman & Wakefield Cal Inc	6531	A	909 980-3781	15830
Customized Dist Svcs Inc	8742	D	909 947-0084	23203
Cvb Financial Corp **(PA)**	6022	D	909 980-4030	15018
Daaze Inc	3444	F	626 442-4961	6815
Damao Luggage Intl Inc	5099	A	909 923-6531	14151
Danco Anodizing Inc	3471	C	909 923-0562	7246
DB Building Fasteners Inc **(PA)**	3449	F	909 581-6740	7019
Dee Engineering Inc	3714	E	909 947-5616	10042
Defoe Furniture For Kids Inc	2531	F	909 947-4459	3622
Delta Tech Industries LLC	3647	E	909 673-1900	9114
Dennis Foland Inc **(PA)**	5099	D	909 930-9900	14152
Dependable Highway Express Inc	4213	D	909 923-0065	12030
DH Caster International Inc	5072	F	909 930-6400	13803
Diagnostic Solutions Intl LLC	3728	F	909 930-3600	10310
Discopylabs	3652	F	909 390-3800	9214
Distribution Alternatives Inc	4225	D	909 673-1000	12199
Diversity Bus Solutions Inc	7361	C	909 395-0243	17413
Dlt Growers Inc	0181	E	909 947-8198	75
Dnick24 Academy	7389	E	310 904-4545	18503
Dominos Pizza LLC	4226	C	909 390-1990	12266
Dorel Home Furnishings Inc	2511	C	909 390-5705	3467
Dorel Juvenile Group Inc	3089	E	909 390-5705	5630
Dpi Specialty Foods West Inc **(DH)**	5141	A	909 975-1019	14465
Dspm Inc	3677	E	714 970-2304	9628
DSV Solutions LLC	4731	C	909 390-4563	12449
Dt Ontrio Ht Prtners Lssee LLC	7011	B	909 937-0900	16420
Duncan Bolt Co	3452	F	909 581-6740	7063
Duralum Products Inc	3355	F	951 736-4500	6326
Eagle Products - Plast Indust	3089	F	909 465-1548	5632
Eagle Signs Inc	3993	F	909 923-3034	11545
Ecko Products Group LLC	2653	E	909 628-5678	3799
Eclipse Prtg & Graphics LLC	2752	E	909 390-2452	4287
Edelmann Usa Inc **(DH)**	3993	F	323 669-5700	11546
Edison Opto USA Corporation	3674	F	909 284-9710	9500
Egr Incorporated **(DH)**	3714	C	909 923-7075	10052
Elegance Upholstery Inc	2599	F	562 698-2584	3725
Emission Methods Inc	3829	E	909 605-6800	10881
Empire Sheet Metal Inc	3444	E	909 923-2927	6825
Employee Owned PCF Cast Pdts I	3365	F	562 633-6673	6394
Emser Tile LLC	1743	D	909 974-1600	1416
Encore Image Inc	3993	E	909 986-4632	11549
Encorr Sheets LLC	2679	D	626 523-4661	3928
Envirokinetics Inc **(PA)**	3559	F	909 621-7599	7972
Eubanks Engineering Co **(PA)**	3549	E	909 483-2456	7901
Eugenios Sheet Metal Inc	3444	E	909 923-2002	6830
Everest Group Usa Inc	2299	E	909 923-1818	2725
Excel Industries Inc	3469	E	909 947-4867	7145
Ez-Flo International Inc **(PA)**	5074	E	909 947-5256	13826
F & D Flores Enterprises Inc	3829	E	909 975-4853	10882
F R T International Inc	4731	D	909 390-4892	12457

Mergent email: customerrelations@mergent.com
1406

2022 Southern California Business
Directory and Buyers Guide

(P-0000) Products & Services Section entry number
(PA)=Parent Co (HQ)=Headquarters (DH)=Div Headquarters

	SIC	EMP	PHONE	ENTRY #
Facility Shield Intl Inc	5063	E	909 923-1800	13629
Federal Express Corporation	4513	E	909 390-3237	12327
Fgs-Wi LLC	2752	E	909 467-8300	4293
Five Star Gourmet Foods Inc	2038	A	909 390-0032	1927
Flow Dynamics Inc	3312	F	909 930-5522	6201
Forbes Industries Div	2599	C	909 923-4559	3729
Fortune Avenue Foods Inc	5141	D	909 930-5989	14468
Foundry Service & Supplies Inc	3299	E	909 284-5000	6180
Four Seasons Surgery Centers	8011	F	909 933-6576	19824
Franklin Renfro	3496	F	909 984-5500	7502
Fuji Natural Foods Inc **(HQ)**	2099	D	909 947-1008	2440
Fullmer Construction	1541	C	909 947-9467	699
Future Commodities Intl Inc	3565	E	909 987-4258	8069
Gardner Trucking Inc **(HQ)**	4213	B	909 563-5606	12047
Geo Labels Inc	2759	F	909 923-6832	4519
George Verhoeven Grain Inc **(PA)**	2048	F	909 605-1531	1965
Glenco Manufacturing Company	3451	E	909 984-3348	7036
Globalux Lighting LLC	3645	F	909 591-7506	9064
Gold Crest Industries Inc	2393	E	909 930-9069	3127
Gold Star Foods Inc **(HQ)**	2099	C	909 843-9600	2444
Gonzalez Kitchen Supplies Inc **(PA)**	3469	F	909 460-0581	7148
Gregg Electric Inc	1731	C	909 983-1794	1260
Greif Bros Corp	2655	E	909 941-4570	3837
Grove Lumber & Bldg Sups Inc **(PA)**	5031	C	909 947-0277	13212
Guard-Systems Inc	7381	A	909 947-5400	18280
Gund Company Inc	3644	F	909 890-9300	9050
Gyl Decauwer LLP	8721	D	909 948-9990	22788
H Fam Engineering Inc	3599	F	909 930-5678	8613
Haldex Brake Products Corp	3714	F	909 974-1200	10070
Halex Corporation **(HQ)**	3423	E	909 629-6219	6482
Halsteel Inc **(DH)**	3315	C	909 937-1001	6225
Hchd	3711	F	909 923-8889	9953
Heat Transfer Pdts Group LLC	5075	C	909 786-3669	13845
Hera Technologies LLC	3599	E	951 751-6191	8615
Herman Engineering & Mfg Inc	3089	F	909 483-1631	5660
HHS Communications Inc	1731	D	909 230-5170	1264
HHS Construction LLC **(HQ)**	1542	C	909 393-3322	770
Hl Perfrmnce Elc Vhcl Systems	3621	E	909 923-1973	8916
HMC Group **(HQ)**	8712	C	909 989-9979	22721
HMC Group	8712	D	909 980-8058	22722
Hongray USA Medical Pdts Inc	3842	E	909 590-1611	11112
Hub Group Trucking Inc	4212	C	951 693-9813	11977
Iapmo Research and Testing Inc **(HQ)**	8611	D	909 472-4100	22248
IDB Holdings Inc **(DH)**	2022	F	909 390-5624	1774
Idx Los Angeles LLC	2542	C	909 212-8333	3686
Imp International Inc **(PA)**	2833	E	909 321-1000	4749
In-Roads Creative Programs	8322	D	909 947-9142	21810
Inca Plastics Molding Co Inc	3089	E	909 923-3235	5672
Index Fasteners Inc **(PA)**	5085	E	909 923-5002	13991
Induspac California Inc	2821	F	909 390-4422	4697
Ink Fx Corporation	2759	E	909 673-1950	4528
Inland Chrstn HM Fundation Inc	8051	C	909 395-9322	20379
Inland Empire Chapter-Assn of	8699	D	512 478-9000	22453
Inland Empire Drv Line Svc Inc **(PA)**	3714	F	909 390-3030	10080
Inland Powder Coating Corp	3479	C	909 947-1122	7375
Inland Signs Inc	3993	F	909 923-0006	11562
Inline Plastics Inc	3089	E	909 923-1033	5674
Innovel Solutions Inc	4731	A	909 605-1446	12472
Inqbrands Inc	7379	D	909 390-7788	18188
Interntnal Assn Plbg Mech Offc **(PA)**	8611	B	909 472-4100	22250
Invapharm Inc	6221	E	909 757-1818	15315
Ivars Display **(PA)**	2541	C	909 923-2761	3652
Jack Jones Trucking Inc	4213	D	909 456-2500	12055
Jamac Steel Inc	3441	E	909 983-7592	6624
James Jones Company	3491	A	909 418-2558	7448
Jcm Engineering Corp	5088	D	909 923-3730	14059
Jeep Chrysler of Ontario	7538	D	909 390-9898	18843
Jeeva Corp	1731	D	909 238-4073	1269
Jns Industries Inc	3599	F	909 923-8334	8644
K & Z Cabinet Co Inc	2434	D	909 947-3567	3321
Kaiser Foundation Hospitals	8011	C	909 724-5000	19910
Kaiser Foundation Hospitals	6324	C	888 750-0036	15419
Kaiser Foundation Hospitals	6324	C	866 205-3595	15420
Kapstone Ontario	2653	F	909 390-0619	3815
KAR Construction Inc	1521	D	909 988-5054	617
Kf Ontario Healthcare LLC	8059	E	909 984-6713	20599
Kik Pool Additives Inc	2899	C	909 390-9912	5225
Kimco Staffing Services Inc	7361	A	909 390-9881	17433
Kindred Healthcare LLC	8062	C	909 391-0333	20826
Kitchen Equipment Mfg Co Inc	3469	E	909 923-3153	7157
Kls Doors LLC **(PA)**	2431	E	909 605-6468	3259
Korden Inc	2522	D	909 988-8979	3613
Kushwood Chair Inc	2521	E	909 930-2100	3589
La Installs Corporation **(PA)**	4789	E	909 923-7076	12577
Landstar Global Logistics Inc	4213	D	909 266-0096	12059
Lanpar Inc	2511	F	541 484-1962	3475
Larry Mthvin Installations Inc **(HQ)**	3231	C	909 563-1700	5961
Las Vegas / LA Express Inc **(PA)**	4213	C	909 972-3100	12060
Lassonde Pappas and Co Inc	2099	E	909 923-4041	2472
Lee & Assoc Comm Real Est Svcs	6531	E	909 989-7771	15910
Leggett & Platt Incorporated	2515	D	909 937-1010	3552
Levco Fab Inc	3498	E	909 465-0840	7540
Liberty Hardware Mfg Corp	5072	D	909 605-2300	13810
Lighting Resources LLC	4953	D	909 923-7252	12955
Logans Candies	2064	F	909 984-5410	2093
Lowes Home Centers LLC	5031	C	909 969-9053	13263
Lynwood Pattern Service Inc	3365	E	310 631-2225	6398

	SIC	EMP	PHONE	ENTRY #
Mag Instrument Inc **(PA)**	3648	A	909 947-1006	9140
Main Street Fibers Inc	4953	D	909 986-6310	12957
Maney Aircraft Inc	3728	E	909 390-2500	10371
Mark Christopher Chevrolet Inc **(PA)**	3714	C	909 321-5860	10099
Marlee Manufacturing Inc	3841	E	909 390-3222	11012
Martinez Steel Corporation	1791	C	909 946-0686	1574
Maury Microwave Inc	5065	C	909 987-4715	13750
Maximum Quality Metal Pdts Inc	3441	E	909 902-5018	6632
McIntyre Company **(PA)**	1791	D	909 962-6322	1576
McKesson Mdcl-Srgcal Mdmart In	5122	D	800 755-2090	14261
McLane Foodservice Dist Inc	5147	D	909 912-3700	14597
McLane Foodservice Dist Inc	4226	D	252 955-9547	12270
Meadow Decor Inc	2519	F	909 923-2558	3567
Medegen LLC **(DH)**	3089	E	909 390-9080	5705
Medrano Raymundo	2284	F	909 947-5507	2703
Melmarc Products Inc	2395	C	714 549-2170	3159
Menzies Aviation (texas) Inc	4581	D	909 937-3998	12362
Merchant of Tennis Inc	7389	A	909 923-3388	18593
Merrill Lynch Prce Fnner Smith	6211	D	909 476-5100	15286
Metal Engineering Inc	3444	E	626 334-1819	6875
Metals USA Building Pdts LP	3355	C	800 325-1305	6329
Michael Baker Intl Inc	8711	D	909 974-4900	22610
Mills Corporation	6512	D	909 484-8300	15678
Minsley Inc	2099	E	909 458-1100	2486
Mission Plastics Inc	3089	C	909 947-7287	5713
Moldings Plus Inc	2431	E	909 947-3310	3270
Myers Power Products Inc **(PA)**	3613	C	909 923-1800	8901
Nac Mfg Inc	2873	F	909 472-3033	5158
NAFTA Distributors	5141	D	800 956-2382	14480
Namm California **(PA)**	8742	D	909 605-8058	23279
Nationwide Trans Inc **(PA)**	4731	D	909 355-3211	12487
Neftaly Imports LLC	7389	B	909 329-1276	18610
Neovia Logistics Dist LP	4225	D	909 657-4900	12226
Net Shapes Inc	3324	C	909 947-3231	6271
New Flyer of America Inc	3711	E	909 456-3566	9960
New Greenscreen Incorporated	2542	E	800 767-9378	3689
New-Indy Containerboard LLC **(DH)**	2621	D	909 296-3400	3763
New-Indy Ontario LLC	2621	C	909 390-1055	3764
Nexus California Inc	3081	E	909 937-1000	5436
Niagara Bottling Intl LLC	2086	F	909 230-5000	2273
Norcal Pottery Products Inc	5023	C	909 390-3745	13180
North American Composites Co	2821	E	909 605-8977	4704
North American Med MGT Cal Inc **(DH)**	8741	D	909 605-8000	23076
One Stop Label Corporation	2759	E	909 230-9380	4547
Ontario Automotive LLC	5012	C	909 974-3800	13034
Ontario Convention Center Corp	7389	C	909 937-3000	18620
Ontario Hospitality Properties	7011	D	909 946-9600	16597
Ontario Refrigeration Svc Inc **(PA)**	1711	D	909 984-2771	1111
Optec Displays Inc	3993	D	626 369-7188	11579
Oregon PCF Bldg Pdts Maple Inc	5031	C	909 627-4043	13280
Osram Sylvania Inc	4225	C	909 923-3003	12227
Otto Instrument Service Inc **(PA)**	3728	E	909 930-5800	10389
Otto International Inc **(PA)**	5136	E	909 937-1998	14344
Pacer Technology **(HQ)**	2891	C	909 987-0550	5188
Pacific Accent Incorporated	3634	F	909 563-1600	9010
Pacific Metals Group LLC	5051	E	909 218-8889	13583
Pacific Rebar Inc	5051	D	909 984-7199	13584
Pacific Urethanes LLC	2392	C	909 390-8400	3113
Pacwest Security Services	7381	C	909 948-0279	18307
Panob Corp	3089	E	909 947-8008	5736
Paramount Panels Inc **(PA)**	3089	E	909 947-8008	5738
Parco LLC **(HQ)**	3053	C	909 947-2200	5347
Park Landscape Maintenance	0782	E	909 605-8878	331
Passport Foods (svc) LLC	2099	C	909 627-7312	2508
Pbb Inc	5072	E	909 923-6250	13813
Perera Cnstr & Design Inc	1081	E	909 484-6350	378
Performance Aluminum Products	3363	E	909 391-4131	6369
Philips Tool & Die Inc	3544	E	909 947-8712	7823
Phoenix Arms	3484	E	909 937-6900	7429
Physician Support Systems Inc **(DH)**	8721	B	717 653-5340	22808
Plasthec Molding Inc	3089	E	909 947-4267	5748
Plastic Engineering Tech LLC	3089	E	909 390-1323	5751
Plastics Research Corporation	3083	D	909 391-9050	5458
Pmr Precision Mfg & Rbr Co Inc	3069	E	909 605-7525	5399
PNC Proactive Nthrn Cont LLC	2653	E	909 390-5624	3825
Polytech Color & Compounding	3089	F	909 923-7008	5767
Pope Mortgage & Associates Inc	6163	D	909 466-5380	15249
Popla International Inc	2045	E	909 923-6899	1953
Posey Products LLC **(HQ)**	5047	C	626 443-3143	13514
PRC Composites LLC **(PA)**	3089	D	909 391-2006	5770
Precise Media Services Inc	3652	E	909 481-3305	9223
Prime Halthcare Foundation Inc **(PA)**	8062	D	909 235-4400	20900
Prime Hlthcare Svcs - Pmpa LLC **(DH)**	8062	B	909 235-4400	20908
Prime Hlthcare Svcs - St John **(DH)**	8062	E	913 680-6000	20911
Prime Hospitality LLC **(PA)**	7011	C	909 212-8000	16640
Primebore Drctonal Boring Corp	1381	F	909 821-4643	437
Proactive Packg & Display LLC **(DH)**	5199	D	909 390-5624	14969
Proform Inc	8071	D	707 752-9010	21089
Q1 Test Inc	3728	E	909 390-9718	10398
Quality Control Plating Inc	3471	E	909 605-0206	7301
Quill LLC	4225	D	909 390-0600	12237
Qycell Corporation	3086	E	909 390-6644	5519
R & B Wholesale Distrs Inc **(PA)**	5064	D	909 230-5400	13692
R & I Industries Inc	3441	E	909 923-7747	6655
Rack Installations Svcs Inc	2542	E	909 261-2243	3692
Rama Food Manufacture Corp **(PA)**	2099	E	909 923-5305	2514
Ramona Auto Services Inc	7538	D	909 986-1785	18864

GEOGRAPHIC

Employment Codes: A=Over 500 employees, B=251-500, C=101-250, D=51-100, E=20-50 F=10-19

2022 Southern California Business Directory and Buyers Guide
© Mergent Inc. 1-800-342-5647
1407

	SIC	EMP	PHONE	ENTRY #
RDM Electric Co Inc **(PA)**	1731	D	909 591-0990	1306
Redlands Employment Services	7361	C	951 688-0083	17457
Redline Prcision Machining Inc	3599	F	909 483-1273	8761
Regal Beloit America Inc	5063	F	909 591-9561	13664
Regards Enterprises Inc	2493	F	909 983-0655	3434
Response Envelope Inc **(PA)**	2759	C	909 923-5855	4566
Reyrich Plastics Inc	3089	E	909 484-8444	5794
Rfc Wire Forms Inc	3496	D	909 467-0559	7512
Robert Moreno Insurance Svcs	6411	C	714 578-3318	15622
Rosen Electronics LLC	5099	D	951 898-9808	14180
Rss Inc **(PA)**	1761	D	909 321-5958	1504
Ruby Industrial Tech LLC	5085	E	909 390-7919	14015
Russell Sigler Inc	1711	D	909 390-7838	1132
Ruuhwa Dann and Associates Inc **(PA)**	4953	D	909 467-4800	12972
Rynoclad Technologies Inc	1793	C	951 264-3441	1588
Safariland LLC	3842	B	909 923-7300	11138
Safran Cabin Materials LLC	3728	E	909 947-4115	10410
Sapa Extrusions Inc	3354	C	909 947-7682	6317
Schrader-Bridgeport Intl Inc	7699	C	909 930-2475	19064
Scripto-Tokai Corporation **(DH)**	3999	D	909 930-5000	11749
Sears Roebuck and Co	7699	C	909 390-4210	19066
Security Metal Products Corp **(DH)**	3442	F	310 641-6690	6719
Sentran L L C **(PA)**	3829	F	888 545-8988	10910
Shii LLC	6531	E	909 354-8000	15998
Shred-Tech Usa LLC	3537	F	909 923-2783	7717
Sigmanet Inc **(HQ)**	5045	C	909 230-7500	13437
Sign Industries Inc	3993	E	909 930-0303	11597
Smg Food and Beverage LLC **(PA)**	7389	D	909 937-3000	18669
Solar Link International Inc	5085	C	909 605-7789	14019
Sotec USA LLC	3532	E	909 525-5861	7662
Soup Bases Loaded Inc	2099	E	909 230-6890	2527
Southland Container Corp	2653	B	909 937-9781	3828
Southwest Concrete Products	3272	D	909 983-9789	6057
Specialized Dairy Service Inc	3523	E	909 923-3420	7620
Specialty Coating Systems Inc	3479	D	909 390-8818	7412
Sprayline Enterprises Inc	3479	F	909 627-8411	7414
SS Heritage Inn Ontario LLC	7011	D	909 937-5000	16728
Star Shield Solutions LLC	3089	D	866 662-4477	5828
Stell Industries Inc	3448	E	951 369-8777	7008
Strada Wheels Inc	3312	F	626 336-1634	6214
Summit Machine LLC	3599	C	909 923-2744	8803
Sun Badge Co	3999	E	909 930-1444	11764
Superior Mold Co	3089	E	909 947-7028	5833
Supreme Machine Products Inc	3599	F	909 974-0349	8806
Surveillance Systems Group Inc	7381	F	877 687-3939	18343
Tactical Command Inds Inc **(DH)**	3669	E	925 219-1097	9356
Target Corporation	4225	C	909 937-5500	12251
Taylor Print Vsual Imprssons I	5112	E	909 357-0661	14199
Taylored Services LLC **(DH)**	4225	D	909 510-4800	12252
Taylored Services Holdings LLC **(HQ)**	4225	D	909 510-4800	12253
Taylored Svcs Parent Co Inc **(PA)**	4731	D	909 510-4800	12536
Tc Cosmotronic Inc	3672	E	949 660-0740	9458
TCI Engineering Inc	3711	D	909 984-1773	9967
Tech Electronic Systems Inc	3679	E	909 986-4395	9790
Teklink Security Inc	3699	F	909 230-6668	9922
Test-Rite Products Corp **(DH)**	5023	D	909 605-9899	13188
Texas Home Health America LP **(PA)**	8082	D	972 201-3800	21222
Thermodyne International Ltd	3089	C	909 923-9945	5837
Tiancheng Intl Inc USA	2834	F	909 947-5577	4905
Tokai Intl Holdings Inc **(PA)**	6719	E	909 930-5000	16114
Tower Industries Inc	3599	C	909 947-2723	8823
Tower Mechanical Products Inc	3812	C	714 947-2723	10649
Tracy Industries Inc	3519	C	562 692-9034	7600
Transcontinental Ontario Inc	2671	E	909 390-8866	3860
Triumph Equipment Inc	3728	F	909 947-5983	10437
Tropicale Foods Inc	2024	E	909 635-0390	1826
Turbine Repair Services LLC **(PA)**	3511	D	909 947-2256	7589
Txd International Usa Inc	2711	F	909 947-6568	4040
Uline Inc	5199	D	909 605-7090	14980
Ultimate Print Source Inc	2752	E	909 947-5292	4443
Ultra Chem Labs Corp	2842	F	909 605-1640	4981
Ultra Solutions LLC	5047	E	909 628-1778	13527
Uncks Unique Plastics Inc	3089	F	909 983-5181	5849
Unifirst Corporation	7218	C	909 390-8670	16886
United Parcel Service Inc	4215	C	909 974-7212	12155
United Parcel Service Inc	7389	D	909 974-7250	18702
United Parcel Service Inc	4513	D	909 974-7190	12333
United Parcel Service Inc	4512	D	909 906-5700	12320
United Parcel Service Inc	4512	D	909 605-7740	12324
United Parcel Service Inc	4215	C	909 974-7000	12167
Universal Wire Inc	3496	F	626 285-2288	7520
Upland Fab Inc	3089	E	909 933-9185	5850
Upm Raflatac Inc	2672	E	909 390-4657	3877
US Duty Gear Inc	3199	F	909 391-8800	5915
USA Sales Inc	2111	E	909 390-9606	2553
Uspar Enterprises Inc	3645	F	909 591-7506	9072
Valley Couriers Inc	4212	D	909 605-2999	12007
Ventura Foods LLC	2079	D	714 257-3700	2132
Ventura Foods LLC	2021	E	323 262-9157	1766
Vertex Coatings Inc	1721	D	909 923-5795	1200
Virgin Atlantic Airways Ltd	4581	D	888 747-7474	12373
Vishay Techno Components LLC	3625	C	909 923-3313	8966
Vishay Thin Film LLC	3674	F	909 923-3313	9600
Vishay Transducers Ltd	3674	E	626 363-7500	9601
Visionary Sleep LLC	2515	D	909 605-2010	3561
Vitco Distributors Inc	5141	D	909 355-1300	14520
Vivotein LLC	2048	F	918 344-8742	1977
Voyager Learning Company	2741	F	909 923-3120	4217
Vsmpo Tirus US	3356	E	909 230-9020	6340
Vsmpo-Tirus US Inc	3356	E	909 230-9020	6341
Wagner Die Supply Inc **(PA)**	3544	E	909 947-3044	7843
Walker Corporation	3469	E	909 390-4300	7191
Walker Spring & Stamping Corp	3469	C	909 390-4300	7192
Wallner Expac Inc **(PA)**	3549	D	909 481-8800	7907
Wangs Alliance Corporation	3645	E	909 230-9401	9074
Watercrest Inc	3443	E	909 390-3944	6766
Watsons Profiling Corp	3599	F	909 923-5500	8846
West Coast Chain Mfg Co	3699	E	909 923-7800	9928
West Coast Corporation	3699	E	909 923-7800	9929
West End Yung MNS Christn Assn	8641	C	909 477-2780	22375
Western States Wholesale Inc **(PA)**	3271	D	909 947-0028	6013
Whiting Door Mfg Corp	7699	D	909 877-0120	19085
Wieland Metal Services W LLC **(DH)**	5051	D	714 692-1000	13606
Workforce Enterprises Wfe Inc	7361	E	909 718-8915	17479
Wti Distribution Inc	4225	D	909 597-8410	12264
Xorail Inc	8711	C	904 443-0083	22704
Yinlun Tdi LLC **(HQ)**	3714	C	909 390-3944	10162
York Employment Services Inc	7361	D	909 581-0181	17482
Zapp Packaging Inc	2631	D	909 930-1500	3778

ORANGE, CA - Orange County

	SIC	EMP	PHONE	ENTRY #
101 Apparel Inc	2321	F	714 454-8988	2754
32 North Brewing Co LLC **(PA)**	2082	F	619 363-2622	2136
5h Sheet Metal Fabrication Inc	3444	F	714 633-7544	6769
Access Dental Plan **(PA)**	8021	D	916 922-5000	20168
Advanced Ceramic Technology	3599	F	714 538-2524	8469
Aecom Usa Inc	8748	C	714 567-2501	23406
Aegean Stoneworks Inc	7389	D	800 762-9089	18435
Air Tube Transfer Systems Inc	3535	E	714 363-0700	7683
Alan Smith Pool Plastering Inc	1742	D	714 628-9494	1360
Alignment Health Plan	6324	D	323 728-7232	15386
Alignment Healthcare Inc	6324	A	844 310-2247	15387
Alignment Healthcare USA LLC **(PA)**	8099	D	844 310-2247	21373
All Diameter Grinding Inc	3599	E	714 744-1200	8486
Allen Mold Inc	3089	F	714 538-6517	5552
Allied Mdular Bldg Systems Inc **(PA)**	3448	E	714 516-1188	6986
American Contractors Inc	1711	D	714 282-5700	1024
American Intgrted Rsources Inc	8741	D	714 921-4100	22974
American PCF Prtrs College Inc	2752	E	949 250-3212	4227
Anaheim Ca LLC	7011	D	714 634-4500	16320
Anchored Prints Inc	2752	E	714 929-9317	4230
Anillo Industries Inc **(PA)**	3452	E	714 637-7000	7055
Ao Science + Technology	8712	C	714 639-9360	22710
APM Manufacturing **(HQ)**	3728	C	714 453-0100	10272
Aquarian Coatings Corp	3471	F	714 632-0230	7214
Arbormed Inc **(PA)**	8099	C	714 689-1500	21386
Arden Engineering Inc	3728	C	714 998-6410	10277
Arden Engineering Holdings Inc **(HQ)**	3728	D	714 998-6410	10278
Arz Tech Inc	3089	F	714 642-9954	5570
Ashunya Inc	7371	D	714 385-1900	17554
Autobahn Construction Inc	3531	F	714 769-7025	7635
Avantec Manufacturing Inc	3672	E	714 532-6197	9384
Bapko Metal Inc	1791	D	714 639-9380	1567
Barnett Customer Management	8741	E	714 747-7908	22983
Bc Rentals LLC **(HQ)**	5084	D	714 974-1190	13889
Bc2 Environmental LLC	8748	D	714 744-2990	23417
Beach Paving Inc	1771	E	714 978-2414	1516
Beks Acquisition Inc	1781	E	714 744-2990	1559
Bernel Inc	1711	C	714 778-6070	1033
Bishop Inc **(PA)**	1761	D	714 628-1208	1474
Boyle Engineering Corporation	8711	D	714 543-5274	22502
Braden Court LLC	3069	F	714 288-3936	5367
Breast Care Center of Orange **(PA)**	8011	D	714 541-0101	19724
Burlington Engineering Inc	3471	F	714 921-4045	7230
Cabinet Factory Outlet	2434	F	714 635-9080	3308
Cadillac Plating Inc	3471	E	714 639-0342	7232
Cal/Pac Pntngs Ctngs Acqstion	1721	D	714 628-1514	1172
Calderon Drywall Contrs Inc **(PA)**	1799	D	714 900-1863	1644
California Concrete Rdymx Inc **(PA)**	3273	E	714 401-4382	6075
California Dept of Pub Hlth	8051	D	714 567-2906	20270
California Gasket and Rbr Corp **(PA)**	3069	E	310 323-4250	5369
Califrnia Anlytical Instrs Inc	3823	D	714 974-5560	10682
Cashcall Inc	6141	A	949 752-4600	15141
CDK Global Inc	6282	D	714 426-4800	15323
Cdsrvs LLC	7699	D	714 912-8353	19030
Cellco Partnership	4812	D	951 205-4170	12601
CF&b Manufacturing Inc	2673	E	714 744-8361	3880
Chapman Global Medical Center	8062	B	714 633-0011	20715
Chapman House Inc	8069	C	714 288-6100	21036
Childrens Healthcare Cal	8011	B	714 997-3000	19748
Childrens Healthcare Cal **(PA)**	8069	A	714 997-3000	21037
Childrens Hospital Orange Cnty **(PA)**	8062	A	714 997-3000	20720
Childrens Hospital Orange Cnty	8062	C	949 365-2416	20721
Choic Admini Insur Servi	6411	B	714 542-4200	15550
Cirtech Inc	7389	E	714 921-0860	18480
City Orange Police Assn Inc	8611	C	714 457-5340	22247
Cleatech LLC	3821	E	714 754-6668	10656
Cleveland Wrecking Company **(DH)**	1795	D	626 967-4287	1611
Cmf Inc	1761	D	714 637-2409	1479
Coastal Component Inds Inc	3679	E	714 635-6677	9694
Coastal Enterprises	2821	E	714 771-4969	4683
Coatings By Sandberg Inc	3479	F	714 538-0888	7353
Coil Winding Specialist Inc	3677	F	714 279-9010	9625
Coilwscom Inc	5153	E	714 279-9010	14749
Commercial Metal Forming Inc	3443	D	714 532-6321	6736

Mergent email: customerrelations@mergent.com
1408
2022 Southern California Business Directory and Buyers Guide
(P-0000) Products & Services Section entry number
(PA)=Parent Co (HQ)=Headquarters (DH)=Div Headquarters

	SIC	EMP	PHONE	ENTRY #
Comppartners Inc	8082	E	949 253-3111	21154
Computrzed Vhcl Rgstration Inc **(HQ)**	7373	E	800 386-1746	18024
Conexis Bnfits Admnstrators LP **(HQ)**	6411	C	714 835-5006	15553
Continuous Coating Corp **(PA)**	3471	D	714 637-4642	7243
County Whl Elc Co Los Angeles	5063	D	714 633-3801	13621
Cruz Modular Inc **(PA)**	4214	D	714 283-2890	12111
Cytec Engineered Materials Inc	2899	C	714 630-9400	5216
Data Aire Inc **(HQ)**	3585	C	800 347-2473	8336
Dental Imaging Tech Corp	8021	A	714 516-7868	20174
Dilco Industrial Inc	3552	F	714 998-5266	7908
Don Miguel Mexican Foods Inc **(HQ)**	2038	E	714 385-4500	1925
Ducommun Aerostructures Inc	3724	C	714 637-4401	10214
Dunham Metal Processing Co	3471	E	714 532-5551	7248
Eagle Graphics Inc **(PA)**	2752	F	714 978-2200	4285
Edgewood Press Inc	2752	F	714 516-2455	4289
Elite Nursing Services Inc	7361	D	714 919-7898	17416
Emercon Construction Inc **(PA)**	1521	E	714 630-9615	603
Emergncy Mdcine Spclist Ornge	7363	C	714 543-8911	17491
Emeritus Corporation	8051	C	714 639-3590	20322
Enterprise Rnt—car Los Angles **(DH)**	7514	D	657 221-4400	18739
Everfocus Electronics Corp **(HQ)**	5065	E	626 844-8888	13721
Fabricated Components Corp	3672	C	714 974-8590	9404
Fabtex Inc	2221	C	714 538-0877	2599
Facility Makers Inc	3444	E	714 544-1702	6838
Fahetas LLC	7371	D	949 280-1983	17613
Fisher Printing Inc **(PA)**	2752	C	714 998-9200	4295
Fletcher Coating Co	3479	E	714 637-4763	7365
Frick Paper Company	5113	C	323 726-8200	14209
Friedl Axle Corporation	3714	E	714 944-5749	10061
Fur Accents LLC	2371	F	714 403-5286	3048
G A Systems Inc	3589	E	714 848-7529	8382
G P Manufacturing Inc	3599	F	714 974-0288	8598
General Coatings Corporation	1721	D	858 587-1277	1181
General Underground	1711	C	714 632-8646	1075
Ggg Demolition Inc **(PA)**	1542	D	714 699-9350	766
Great Atlantic News LLC	5192	C	770 863-9000	14873
H&S Energy LLC **(HQ)**	7389	B	714 761-5426	18536
Hand Piece Parts and Products	3843	E	714 997-4331	11175
Harpers Pharmacy Inc	2834	C	877 778-3773	4829
Harvest Landscape Entps Inc **(PA)**	0781	C	714 693-8100	261
Healthcompare Insur Svcs Inc **(DH)**	6411	D	714 542-4200	15579
Hightower Metal Products	3544	D	714 637-7000	7806
Hightower Plating & Mfg Co	3471	E	714 637-9110	7267
His Industries Inc	3565	E	949 383-4308	8071
Hit Portfolio II Trs LLC	7011	D	714 938-1111	16482
Hoke Outdoor Advertising Inc	3993	F	714 637-3610	11560
Holmes & Narver Inc **(HQ)**	8711	C	714 567-2400	22570
Horizon Personnel Services **(PA)**	7361	C	714 912-7500	17427
Hyperion Motors LLC	3594	E	714 363-5858	8444
Icon Screening Inc	2759	F	714 630-4266	4525
Independent Forge Company	3462	E	714 997-7337	7087
Inductors Inc	5065	E	949 623-2460	13729
Infinite Technologies LLC	7371	C	786 408-7995	17639
Integrated Marketing Group LLC	2211	F	714 771-2401	2576
Intellipower Inc	5065	D	714 921-1580	13731
Interior Electric Incorporated	1731	D	714 771-9098	1268
Invision Networking LLC	7371	C	949 309-3441	17642
Irvine APT Communities LP	6513	C	714 937-8900	15730
ISI Detention Contg Group Inc	3599	D	714 288-1770	8630
J J Foil Company Inc	2675	E	714 998-9920	3898
Jeneric/Pentron Incorporated **(HQ)**	3843	C	203 265-7397	11178
Jezowski & Markel Contrs Inc	1771	C	714 978-2222	1532
John Bishop Design Inc	3993	E	714 744-2300	11563
John Jory Corporation **(PA)**	1742	B	714 279-7901	1383
Jtb Supply Company Inc	3669	D	714 639-9558	9345
K & D Graphics	2675	E	714 639-8900	3899
K & S Air Conditioning Inc	1711	C	714 685-0077	1088
Kaiser Foundation Hospitals	6324	C	888 988-2800	15438
Kerr Corporation **(DH)**	3843	C	714 516-7400	11179
King Plastics Inc	3089	D	714 997-7540	5690
Kisco Senior Living LLC	6513	D	714 997-5355	15738
Kondaur Capital Corporation **(PA)**	6799	C	714 352-2038	16272
Kretus Inc	2851	F	714 694-2061	5099
Lcptracker Inc	7372	E	714 669-0052	17904
Leaf Commercial Capital Inc	8742	E	866 219-7924	23258
Leonard Chaidez Inc	0783	D	714 279-8173	358
Liberty Debt Relief LLC	7299	D	800 756-8447	16963
Lochaber Cornwall Inc	3567	F	714 935-0302	8095
Lonestar Sierra LLC	5085	C	866 575-5680	13996
Lres Corporation **(PA)**	6531	D	714 520-5737	15915
Lucky Strike Entertainment LLC	7933	C	248 374-3420	19403
M & R Engineering Co	3451	F	714 991-8480	7038
M S International Inc **(PA)**	5032	B	714 685-7500	13307
Madden Corporation	4212	D	714 922-1670	11980
Main Street Specialty Surgery	8062	D	714 704-1900	20855
Maintech Incorporated	7371	C	714 921-8000	17656
Marbil Industries Inc	3826	E	714 974-4032	10801
Mark 1 Mortgage Corporation **(PA)**	6163	E	714 752-5700	15246
Marne Construction Inc	1771	D	714 935-0995	1538
Martin Integrated Systems	1742	D	714 998-9100	1386
Mattern Sausages Inc	2011	F	714 628-9630	1715
MB Coatings Inc	7389	D	714 625-2118	18589
McCarthy Bldg Companies Inc	1542	D	949 851-8383	788
Medcor Group Inc	8721	D	714 221-8511	22805
Medical Spc Managers Inc	8742	C	714 571-5000	23270
Megamex Foods LLC **(PA)**	5141	D	714 385-4500	14477
Merlex Stucco Inc	3299	F	877 547-8822	6182
Mesa Safe Company Inc	3499	E	714 202-8000	7565
Metal Art of California Inc **(PA)**	3993	D	714 532-7100	11573
Meyer Coatings Inc	1721	E	714 467-4600	1189
Miller Environmental Inc	1795	C	714 385-0099	1617
Mony Life Insurance Company	6411	D	714 939-6669	15597
Newport Flavors & Fragrances	2087	E	714 771-2200	2334
Nexinfo Solutions Inc	5045	E	714 368-1452	13419
Niedwick Corporation	3599	E	714 771-9999	8719
North American Title Co Inc	6361	C	714 550-6400	15510
Oakmont of Orange LLC	8361	E	714 880-8624	22139
Omega Insurance Services	6411	E	714 973-0311	15604
Omega Products Corp	3299	E	714 935-0900	6183
Opal Service Inc **(PA)**	3299	E	714 935-0900	6184
Orange City Mills Ltd Partnr	6512	D	317 636-1600	15687
Orange Cnty Cncil Boy Scuts AM **(PA)**	8641	D	714 546-4990	22353
Orange Cnty Hlth Auth A Pub AG	8621	B	714 246-8500	22273
Orange County Plating Coinc	3471	F	714 532-4610	7292
Orange County Trnsp Auth **(PA)**	4111	B	714 636-7433	11833
Orange County Trnsp Auth	4111	A	714 999-1726	11834
Orange Hlthcare Wllness Cntre	8051	C	714 633-3568	20428
Orange Woodworks Inc	2431	E	714 997-2600	3278
Ormco Corporation **(HQ)**	3843	D	714 516-7400	11185
Owning Corporation	6531	B	949 269-3300	15937
P & D Consultants Inc **(HQ)**	8711	E	714 835-4447	22626
P H S Management Group **(PA)**	8742	E	714 547-7551	23291
Pacifico Bindery Inc	2789	F	714 744-1510	4619
Padilla Construction Company	1742	C	714 685-8500	1393
Pamona Valley Medical Group **(PA)**	8011	D	909 932-1045	20018
Patio & Door Outlet Inc **(PA)**	2519	E	714 974-9900	3571
Pavilion Surgery Center LLC	8011	D	714 744-8850	20019
Pentron Clinical Tech LLC	8071	D	203 265-7397	21083
Phg Engineering Services LLC	8711	D	714 283-8288	22637
Positive Concepts Inc **(PA)**	2679	E	714 685-5800	3933
Precast Innovations Inc	3272	E	714 921-4060	6050
Presentation Folder Inc	2675	E	714 289-7000	3900
Printing Division Inc	2752	F	714 685-0111	4398
Pro Detention Inc	3315	D	714 881-3680	6231
Project Access Inc **(PA)**	8322	D	949 253-6200	21873
Prospect Medical Systems Inc **(HQ)**	8741	C	714 667-8156	23093
Prototype & Short-Run Svcs Inc	3469	E	714 449-9661	7178
Providence Speech Hearing Ctr	8093	E	714 639-4990	21330
Q4 Services LLC	3669	F	949 421-7856	9349
Quality Aluminum Forge LLC	3463	C	714 639-8191	7105
Quoc Viet Foods	5149	E	714 283-3131	14728
Quotit Corporation	7373	C	714 564-5000	18061
R & B Plastics Inc	3089	F	714 229-8419	5785
Radiation Protection & Spc Inc	3444	F	714 771-7702	6898
Ralis Services Corp	8742	C	844 347-2547	23305
Raymond Group **(PA)**	8741	D	714 771-7670	23096
Realselect Inc	6531	C	661 803-5188	15970
Red Pointe Roofing LP **(PA)**	1761	D	714 685-0010	1503
Redline Detection LLC **(PA)**	3829	E	714 579-6961	10907
Remanfctured Converter MBL LLC	3568	F	714 744-8988	8107
Reyes Coca-Cola Bottling LLC	2086	D	714 974-1901	2294
Rgis LLC	7389	C	714 938-0663	18652
Richardson Group	1542	D	714 997-3970	816
Rick Hamm Construction Inc	1611	D	714 532-0815	909
Rika Corporation	1791	D	949 830-9050	1581
Rio	8093	C	714 633-7400	21334
RJ Noble Company **(PA)**	1611	C	714 637-1550	910
Rlh Industries Inc	3661	E	714 532-1672	9241
Roth Staffing Companies LP **(PA)**	7363	D	714 939-8600	17514
Roto Dynamics Inc	3089	E	714 685-0183	5801
SA Recycling LLC **(PA)**	4953	C	714 632-2000	12974
SA Serving Lines Inc	3444	E	714 848-7529	6906
Sanders & Wohrman Corporation	1721	C	714 919-0446	1198
Scribemd LLC	8011	D	714 543-8911	20062
SE Industries Inc	2434	F	714 744-3200	3336
Securtas Crtcal Infrstrcture S	7381	B	310 817-2177	18329
Selman Chevrolet Company	7515	C	714 633-3521	18753
Sequoia Consultants Inc **(PA)**	8711	D	714 974-6316	22653
Sfpp LP **(DH)**	4613	C	714 560-4400	12377
Sherman Oaks Hspice Care Group	8052	E	714 733-1333	20543
SKB Corporation **(PA)**	3089	B	714 637-1252	5820
Solari Enterprises Inc	6512	C	714 282-2520	15699
Southern California Edison Co	4911	C	714 283-8568	12859
Southern Counties Oil Co **(PA)**	5171	D	714 744-7140	14797
Specialized Pdts & Design Inc	2869	F	714 289-1428	5147
Sport Kites Inc	3721	F	714 998-6359	10204
St Joseph Hospital	8062	E	714 744-8601	20959
St Joseph Hospital of Orange	8062	C	714 771-8222	20960
St Joseph Hospital of Orange	8062	C	714 771-8006	20961
St Joseph Hospital of Orange **(DH)**	8062	A	714 633-9111	20962
St Joseph Hospital of Orange	8062	C	714 771-8037	20964
Standard Insurance Company	6311	D	714 634-8200	15369
Statek Corporation **(HQ)**	3679	C	714 639-7810	9786
States Drawer Box Spc LLC	5031	D	714 744-4247	13289
Stoneriver Inc	7371	D	714 705-8227	17725
Sun Mar Management Services	8059	D	714 385-1006	20629
Surgicare La Veta Ltd A Cal Lt	8011	D	714 744-0900	20101
Sybron Dental Specialties Inc **(HQ)**	3843	C	714 516-7400	11197
Systems Integrated LLC	3829	E	714 998-0900	10914
Tandem Design Inc	3999	E	714 978-7272	11772
Tavistock Restaurants LLC	2082	C	714 939-8686	2156
Technical Screen Printing Inc	2759	F	714 541-8590	4582
Telacu Construction MGT Inc	8741	E	714 541-2390	23123
Thermal-Vac Technology Inc	3398	E	714 997-2601	6455

GEOGRAPHIC

	SIC	EMP	PHONE	ENTRY #
Tiller Constructors Partnr Inc	1542	D	714 771-5600	840
Total Health Environment LLC	5047	E	714 637-1010	13526
Total Telco Specialists Inc	7629	D	805 541-2232	18960
Toyota of Orange Inc	5012	C	714 639-6750	13038
Transportation Chrtr Svcs Inc	4142	E	714 396-0346	11916
Tri Precision Sheetmetal Inc	3444	E	714 632-8838	6934
Tri-Tech Precision Inc	3728	F	714 970-1363	10434
Trisar Inc	2759	F	714 972-2626	4585
Ulti-Mate Connector Inc	3678	C	714 637-7099	9666
University California Irvine	8011	C	714 456-6966	20121
University California Irvine	8011	A	714 456-6170	20122
University California Irvine	8062	A	714 456-6011	20989
University California Irvine	8062	B	714 456-5558	20990
University California Irvine	8011	C	714 456-7890	20126
University California Irvine	8721	D	714 456-6655	22818
URS Resources LLC **(DH)**	8711	E	626 331-0359	22687
US Sensor Corp	3674	D	714 639-1000	9598
Van Dorpe Chou Associates Inc	8711	E	714 978-9780	22688
Varco De Mexico Holdings Inc	7359	D	714 978-1900	17382
VCA Code Group	8711	E	714 363-4700	22690
Villa Ford Inc	7532	C	714 637-8222	18807
Villa Park Landscape **(PA)**	0781	D	714 538-3788	288
Village Nurseries Whl LLC **(PA)**	5193	E	714 279-3100	14898
Vintique Inc	3714	E	714 634-1932	10153
Volt Consulting Group Ltd	7361	C	800 654-2624	17477
Volt Information Sciences Inc **(PA)**	7363	E	714 921-8800	17522
Volt Management Corp	7363	B	800 654-2624	17525
Volt Management Corp **(HQ)**	7363	E	800 654-2624	17529
Vpls Inc	4813	E	213 406-9000	12679
W Corporation	8748	D	714 532-8800	23525
Walswrth Frnklin Bevins McCall **(PA)**	8111	D	714 634-2522	21693
We Do Graphics Inc	2752	E	714 997-7390	4453
Webb Massey Co Inc	2517	E	714 639-6012	3563
West American Rubber Co LLC **(PA)**	3069	C	714 532-3355	5424
West American Rubber Co LLC	3069	C	714 532-3355	5425
West Coast Firestopping Inc	1799	D	714 935-1104	1702
Western Dental Services Inc **(HQ)**	8021	B	714 480-3000	20204
Western Lighting Inds Inc	5063	E	626 969-6820	13678
Western Pacific Distrg LLC	5032	C	714 974-6837	13321
Western Prtg & Graphics LLC **(PA)**	2752	E	714 532-3946	4457
William Getz Corp	3949	F	714 516-2050	11461
Wood Space Industries Inc	4226	F	714 996-4552	12272
Wsp USA Inc	8711	D	714 973-4880	22701
Xpo Logistics Freight Inc	4213	D	714 282-7717	12097
Zettler Components Inc **(PA)**	5065	C	949 831-5000	13788

ORCUTT, CA - Santa Barbara County

	SIC	EMP	PHONE	ENTRY #
Den-Mat Corporation **(DH)**	2844	B	805 922-8491	5010
Spiess Construction Co Inc	1623	D	805 937-5859	973

OROSI, CA - Tulare County

	SIC	EMP	PHONE	ENTRY #
Adventist Hlth Systm/West Corp	8062	D	559 528-6966	20655

OXNARD, CA - Ventura County

	SIC	EMP	PHONE	ENTRY #
24hr Homecare LLC	8082	D	805 988-2205	21121
ACC Precision Inc	3599	F	805 278-9801	8462
Acme Cryogenics Inc	3559	E	805 981-4500	7958
Advanced Structural Tech Inc	3462	C	805 204-9133	7081
AG Rx **(PA)**	5191	D	805 487-0696	14852
Agrifrost LLC	0171	E	805 485-2519	23
Alliance Chemical & Envmtl	3471	F	805 385-3330	7207
Alpha Products Inc	3678	E	805 981-8666	9647
Aluminum Precision Pdts Inc	5051	C	805 488-4401	13545
American Tooth Industries	5047	D	805 487-9868	13474
Amiad USA Inc	3589	E	805 988-3323	8362
Applied Powdercoat Inc	3479	E	805 981-1991	7345
Arizona Channel Isla	7999	D	480 788-0755	19634
Associated Ready Mix Con Inc	1611	C	805 485-4155	859
Associates First Capital Corp	6141	C	805 487-9825	15139
Ava Enterprises Inc	5064	E	805 988-0192	13682
B & S Plastics Inc	3089	A	805 981-0262	5572
Basic Business Forms Inc	2759	E	805 278-4551	4484
Becker Automotive Designs Inc	3711	E	805 487-5227	9937
Beckman Industries	3965	F	805 375-3003	11494
Blois Construction Inc	1623	C	805 485-0011	937
Boskovich Farms Inc **(PA)**	0723	C	805 487-2299	161
Boskovich Fresh Cut LLC	5148	C	805 487-2299	14615
Boss International LLC **(PA)**	3651	D	805 988-0192	9166
Boyd and Associates	7381	D	805 988-8298	18257
Boys Grls Clubs Grter Oxnard P **(PA)**	8641	D	805 815-4959	22319
Cabrillo Crdolgy Med Group Inc	8011	D	805 983-0922	19730
California Resources Prod Corp	1311	D	805 483-8017	396
California Woodworking Inc	2434	E	805 982-9090	3312
Castle Peak Resources LLC	8051	E	805 535-2000	20276
Casualway Usa LLC	2514	D	805 660-7408	3527
Catalytic Solutions Inc **(HQ)**	3822	D	805 486-4649	10663
Cdti Advanced Materials Inc **(PA)**	2819	E	805 639-9458	4656
Channel Islnds Vgtble Frms Inc **(PA)**	0182	D	805 984-1910	99
Chaparral Construction Corp	1611	D	805 647-8606	870
Child Dev Rsrces of Vntura CNT **(PA)**	8322	C	805 485-7878	21739
City of Oxnard **(PA)**	8742	C	805 385-7803	23191
Clamshell Structures Inc	3448	F	805 988-1340	6990
Cloudburst Inc	3564	F	805 986-4125	8044
Coalition For Family Harmony	8322	D	805 983-6014	21748
Coastal Cnting Indus Scale Inc	3545	E	805 487-0403	7849
Comedy Club Oxnard LLC	7997	D	805 535-5400	19556
Complyright Dist Svcs Inc	2761	E	805 981-0992	4599
Component Equipment Coinc	3678	E	805 988-8004	9649
Cool-Pak LLC	3089	D	805 981-2434	5613
Cosmetic Specialties Intl LLC	3089	C	805 487-6698	5615
County of Ventura	4581	D	805 388-4274	12354
Courtyard Oxnard	7011	D	805 988-3600	16396
Covenant Care California LLC	8051	D	805 488-3696	20298
D C H California Motors Inc	7538	D	805 988-7900	18820
Dakota Drilling & Concrete Inc	1771	E	818 833-4654	1521
DBC Printing Incorporated	2752	F	805 988-8855	4273
Dcor LLC **(PA)**	1382	C	805 535-2000	445
Deardorff-Jackson Co	5148	E	805 487-7801	14621
Delnorte Rgnal Rcycl Trnsf Stn **(PA)**	4953	D	805 278-8200	12944
Dieners Electric Inc	1731	D	805 988-1515	1243
Dignity Health	8062	A	805 988-2500	20754
Dignity Health Med Foundation	8062	D	805 981-6101	20755
Diversified Minerals Inc	3273	E	805 247-1069	6090
Djont/Jpm Hsptlity Lsg Spe LLC	7011	D	805 984-2500	16411
Durham School Services L P	4151	C	805 483-6076	11923
E Vasquez Distributors Inc	2448	E	805 487-8458	3388
Eagle Dominion Energy Corp	1382	F	805 272-9557	451
Elite Metal Finishing LLC **(PA)**	3471	D	805 983-4320	7257
Elite Metal Finishing LLC	3471	E	805 983-4320	7258
Ergonom Corporation **(PA)**	2599	D	805 981-9978	3727
Ergonom Corporation	2599	D	805 981-9978	3728
Esco Technologies Inc	3669	E	805 604-3875	9340
Etchandy Farms LLC	0171	D	805 983-4700	27
Ets Express LLC **(DH)**	3479	E	805 278-7771	7363
Fame Systems Inc	7349	E	805 485-0808	17242
Family Circle Inc	8322	D	805 385-4180	21783
Fr-Industries Inc **(DH)**	5099	E	817 645-4366	14157
Frank Stubbs Co Inc	3842	E	805 278-4300	11106
Fresh Innovations LLC	2097	E	805 483-2265	2370
Fresh Venture Farms LLC	0161	D	805 754-4449	14
Gibbs International Inc **(PA)**	7538	D	805 485-0551	18834
Gills Onions LLC	5148	D	805 240-1983	14632
Glenwood Corporation	8051	D	805 983-0305	20360
Gmh Inc	7623	E	805 485-1410	18947
Granatelli Motor Sports Inc	3714	E	805 486-6644	10068
Grolink Plant Company Inc **(PA)**	5193	C	805 984-7958	14886
H G Group Inc	7291	B	805 486-6463	16937
Harris Water Conditioning Inc	7389	D	805 656-4411	18538
Harwil Precision Products	3679	E	805 988-6800	9721
HE Julien & Associates Inc	0782	E	805 488-8342	309
Hel Mar Mfg LLC **(PA)**	3999	E	805 278-9099	11683
High Tide and Green Grass Inc	7992	E	805 981-8722	19495
Hnh Motorsports	3714	F	805 487-0505	10075
Illah Sports Inc A Corporation	3949	E	805 240-7790	11429
Inclusive Edcatn Cmnty Prtnr I	8351	B	805 985-4808	22024
Industrial Tools Inc	3559	E	805 483-1111	7983
Infratab	2836	F	805 986-8880	4936
J Harris Indus Wtr Trtmnt Inc **(PA)**	5074	D	805 656-4411	13831
Jsl Technologies Inc	8711	B	805 985-7700	22591
Kaiser Foundation Hospitals	8011	C	888 515-3500	19911
Kaiser Foundation Hospitals	8011	C	805 988-6300	19913
Kak Industry LLC	3484	E	805 981-4734	7428
Kevita Inc **(HQ)**	2086	D	805 200-2250	2269
Kim Laube & Company Inc	2844	E	805 240-1300	5039
Labaya Beachcomber LP	7532	E	805 278-6688	18794
Las Islas Family Med Group PC	8011	D	805 385-8662	19959
Las Posas Berry Farms LLC	0171	D	805 483-1000	31
Lawyers Title Insurance Corp	6361	C	805 484-2701	15508
Little Castle Furniture Co Inc	2512	E	805 278-4646	3507
Marathon Land Inc	0181	C	805 488-3585	84
Masters In Metal Inc	3263	E	805 988-1992	5996
Maxim Healthcare Services Inc	7363	D	805 278-4593	17500
McConnells Fine Ice Creams LLC	5143	E	805 963-8813	14544
McK Enterprises Inc	2099	D	805 483-5292	2484
Mercury Systems Inc	3672	C	805 388-1345	9428
Merrill Lynch Prce Fnner Smith	6211	D	800 964-5182	15282
Mgr Design International Inc	3999	C	805 981-6400	11715
Millworks Etc Inc	3442	E	805 499-3400	6710
Milwood Healthcare Inc	6512	D	626 274-4345	15679
Mission Linen Supply	7213	D	805 485-6794	16858
Mixtec/Ndgena Cmnty Orgnzing P	8322	D	805 483-1166	21851
N S C Channel Islands Inc	8011	B	805 485-1908	19990
National Graphics LLC	2752	E	805 644-9212	4378
New-Indy Oxnard LLC	2621	C	805 986-3881	3765
Northrop Grumman Systems Corp	3812	C	805 684-6641	10612
Northrop Grumman Systems Corp	3812	C	805 278-2074	10613
Noushig Inc	2051	E	805 983-2903	2025
NRG California South LP	4911	D	805 984-5241	12809
Nu Venture Diving Co	3563	E	805 815-4044	8036
Olde Thompson LLC	2899	C	805 983-0388	5236
Oxnard Lemon Company	2037	E	805 483-1173	1906
Oxnard Prcsion Fabrication Inc	3444	E	805 985-0447	6885
Pacific Beverage Co	5181	D	805 278-5600	14833
Pacific Building Maint Inc **(PA)**	7349	D	805 642-0214	17270
Pacific Coast Produce Inc	5148	E	805 240-3385	14645
Pacific Labor Services Inc	7021	E	805 488-4625	16813
PC Vaughan Mfg Corp	3569	C	805 278-2555	8134
Peak Operator II LLC	1382	F	805 436-2555	461
Pegasus Transit Inc	4141	D	805 988-1540	11907
Pinegrove Industries Inc	2752	E	805 485-3700	4391
Players West Amusements Inc **(PA)**	7993	C	805 983-1400	19513
Primal Nutrition LLC	5122	E	310 317-4414	14283
Procter & Gamble Paper Pdts Co	2676	A	805 485-8871	3907
Produce Available Inc **(PA)**	5148	D	805 483-5292	14648
Pti Technologies Inc **(DH)**	3728	C	805 604-3700	10397

Mergent email: customerrelations@mergent.com
1410
2022 Southern California Business Directory and Buyers Guide
(P-0000) Products & Services Section entry number
(PA)=Parent Co (HQ)=Headquarters (DH)=Div Headquarters

Company	SIC	EMP	PHONE	ENTRY #
Pyramid Flowers Inc	0181	C	805 382-8070	93
Quinn Company	5082	D	805 485-2171	13869
Rakar Incorporated	3089	E	805 487-2721	5786
Ramco Enterprises LP	0723	A	805 486-9328	183
Rapid Product Solutions Inc	3599	E	805 485-7234	8759
Raypak Inc **(DH)**	3433	B	805 278-5300	6574
Regal Kitchens LLC	2434	F	786 953-6578	3332
Reiter Affl Companies LLC **(PA)**	0171	C	805 483-1000	34
Reiter Berry Farms Inc **(PA)**	0171	C	805 483-1000	35
Rescue Mission Alliance **(PA)**	8699	D	805 487-1234	22460
Rincon Iron Inc	3446	F	805 455-2904	6977
River Ridge Farms Inc	0181	D	805 647-6880	95
Royal Wine Corporation	2084	E	805 983-1560	2218
San Miguel Produce Inc	0161	B	805 488-0981	18
Santa Barbara Design Studio **(PA)**	3269	D	805 966-3883	6006
Santa Rosa Berry Farms LLC	0171	B	805 981-3060	37
Saticoy Lemon Association	8611	C	805 654-6543	22257
Scarborough Farms Inc	0191	C	805 483-9113	118
Scosche Industries Inc	3651	C	805 486-4450	9194
Scully Sportswear Inc	2386	D	805 483-6339	3060
Seminis Inc **(DH)**	8731	B	805 485-7317	22863
Seminis Vegetable Seeds Inc **(DH)**	5191	A	855 733-3834	14869
Sound Storm Laboratories LLC	3651	F	805 983-8008	9197
South American Imaging Inc	3621	F	805 824-4036	8931
Spatz Corporation	2844	C	805 487-2122	5071
Stainless Process Systems Inc	3441	F	805 483-7100	6665
State Compensation Insur Fund	6321	D	888 782-8338	15384
Steelworks Etc Inc	3442	F	805 487-3000	6720
Sunrise Growers Inc	2099	C	612 619-9545	2530
Sunshine Floral LLC	5193	D	805 982-8822	14896
Superior Fruit LLC	0171	C	805 485-2519	38
Synectic Solutions Inc **(PA)**	7379	D	805 483-4800	18223
Sysco Ventura Inc	5141	B	805 205-7000	14514
Systems Application & Tech Inc	8711	D	805 487-7373	22664
T & M Machining	3599	E	805 983-6716	8808
T M Mian & Associates Inc	7011	D	805 983-8600	16750
Tanimura Antle Fresh Foods Inc	4225	C	805 483-2358	12250
Tbyci LLC	3732	F	805 985-6800	10472
Toro Enterprises Inc	1611	D	805 483-4515	923
Tradewind Seafood Inc	5146	E	805 483-8555	14586
Trans Fx Inc	3999	F	805 485-6110	11782
Troop Real Estate Inc	6531	D	805 487-2892	16020
V3 Printing Corporation	2752	D	805 981-2600	4447
Venco Western Inc **(PA)**	0782	C	805 981-2400	349
Ventura County Lemon Coops	5148	D	805 385-3345	14663
Ventura Printing Inc **(PA)**	2759	D	805 981-2600	4588
Veterans Health Administration	8011	B	805 983-6384	20145
Victoria Nursery Inc **(PA)**	5193	D	805 985-0855	14897
Vista Ford Inc	7538	D	805 983-6511	18885
Vogue Sign Inc	3993	E	805 487-7222	11615
Volt Management Corp	7363	D	805 485-0506	17531
Vortech Engineering Inc	3564	E	805 247-0226	8061
West Coast Welding & Cnstr	7692	F	805 604-1222	19003
West Coast Wldg & Piping Inc	7692	D	805 246-5841	19004
Western Saw Manufacturers Inc	3425	E	805 981-0999	6493
Western Sierra Landscapes Inc	0781	E	805 983-0070	289
Wiggins Lift Co Inc	5084	E	805 485-7821	13965
Windsor Capital Group Inc	7011	D	805 988-0627	16789
Workrite Uniform Company Inc **(DH)**	7218	B	805 483-0175	16887
Xpo Logistics Freight Inc	4213	D	805 485-6466	12098

PACIFIC PALISADES, CA - Los Angeles County

Company	SIC	EMP	PHONE	ENTRY #
Atria Senior Living Inc	8361	D	310 573-9545	22081
Bel-Air Bay Club Ltd	7997	C	310 230-4700	19540
Berkshire Hathaway Home Servic	8322	C	310 230-3700	21724
Chilicon Power LLC **(PA)**	3825	E	310 800-1396	10746
Get Heal Inc	7363	D	310 528-4957	17493
Lighthouse Capital Funding	6799	E	310 230-8335	16274
Lighthouse Property MGT Inc **(PA)**	8741	D	210 340-7072	23052
Luxe Homecare Inc **(PA)**	8082	D	310 454-5500	21189
Many LLC	7311	D	310 399-1515	17032
Noka LLC	3411	F	214 455-3888	6467
Optimis Services Inc	7372	F	310 230-2780	17943
Optimiscorp	7372	E	310 230-2780	17944
Pipeliner Crm	7372	F	424 280-6445	17957
Pipelinersales Corporation **(PA)**	7372	E	888 843-6699	17958
Rok Drinks LLC	2085	E	323 654-2740	2244
Santa Monica Bay Physcians	8011	D	310 459-2363	20058
Unconditional Love Inc	5137	D	888 860-6888	14425

PACOIMA, CA - Los Angeles County

Company	SIC	EMP	PHONE	ENTRY #
American Etching & Mfg	3479	E	323 875-3910	7341
American Fruits & Flavors LLC **(HQ)**	2087	C	818 899-9574	2306
American Fruits & Flavors LLC	2087	E	818 899-9574	2307
American Range Corporation	3444	C	818 897-0808	6784
Anwright Corporation	3451	E	818 896-2465	7031
APT Metal Fabricators Inc	3469	E	818 896-7478	7124
Burbank Plating Service Corp	3471	F	818 899-1157	7229
Cabrac Inc	3469	E	818 834-0177	7133
California Signs Inc	3993	E	818 899-1888	11531
Chimney Products Inc	7349	F	818 272-2011	17226
Color-TEC Indus Finshg Inc	3479	F	818 897-2669	7354
Cosmetic Enterprises Ltd	2844	F	818 896-5355	5003
County of Los Angeles	4581	C	818 896-5271	12351
County of Los Angeles	4581	C	818 890-5777	12352
County of Los Angeles	8011	D	818 896-1903	19772
CPI Luxury Group	5094	D	818 249-9888	14128
D & M Steel Inc	3441	E	818 896-2070	6613
Dw and Bb Consulting Inc	3769	D	818 896-9899	10532
Eben-Ezer Chld Day Care Ctr **(PA)**	8351	D	818 897-5427	22010
F &L Machine Inc	3599	F	818 899-6738	8585
Flamemaster Corporation	2899	E	818 890-1401	5221
Global Emergency Road Svc LLC	4119	E	818 518-1166	11870
Golden West Security	7381	C	818 897-5965	18279
Gonzalez Management Co Inc	8741	D	818 485-0596	23031
Gscm Ventures Inc	2844	E	818 303-2600	5028
Hanmar LLC **(PA)**	3469	D	818 890-2802	7149
Harters Surfaces	3083	F	818 899-9917	5449
Hathawy-Sycmres Child Fmly Svc	8322	C	626 395-7100	21796
Hillview Mental Health Ctr Inc	8093	D	818 896-1161	21312
Hope of Valley Rescue Mission	8322	D	818 392-0020	21804
Hrk Pet Food Products Inc	2048	E	818 897-2521	1968
Imagemover Inc	2752	F	818 485-8840	4324
JKL Components Corporation	3647	E	818 896-0019	9116
Ketab Corporation	2741	E	310 477-7477	4186
Kitch Engineering Inc	3599	E	818 897-7133	8656
LA Hardwood Flooring Inc **(PA)**	2426	F	818 361-0099	3220
Looney Bins Inc **(HQ)**	4953	D	818 485-8200	12956
Lowes Home Centers LLC	5031	C	818 686-4300	13223
M & R Plating Corporation	3471	F	818 896-2700	7278
Mayoni Enterprises	3444	D	818 896-0026	6872
Moc Products Company Inc **(PA)**	2899	D	818 794-3500	5234
Molding Corporation America	3089	E	818 890-7877	5717
Northeast Valley Health Corp	8011	D	818 896-0531	20002
Nu-Hope Laboratories Inc	3841	E	818 899-7711	11038
Orora North America	5113	E	818 896-3449	14219
Petra-1 LP	2844	F	866 334-3702	5058
Phillips Plywood Co Inc	5031	D	818 897-7736	13281
Pyramid Powder Coating Inc	3479	F	818 768-5898	7404
RMR Products Inc **(PA)**	3272	E	818 890-0896	6055
Scenic Route Inc	1799	E	818 896-6006	1689
Sdi Industries Inc **(PA)**	3535	C	818 890-6002	7694
Sunland Aerospace Fasteners	3452	E	818 485-8929	7077
Surge Globl Bkries Hldings LLC **(PA)**	5149	C	818 896-0525	14740
Swiss Cabinet	2434	F	818 571-9917	3339
Trico Sports Inc	3751	E	818 899-7705	10506
Twin Peak Industries Inc	3949	E	800 259-5906	11454
Ultramet	3471	D	818 899-0236	7326
Volunteers of Amer Los Angeles	8322	D	818 834-9097	21911
Volunteers of Amer Los Angeles	8322	D	818 834-8957	21921
Westcoast Grinding Corporation	3599	F	818 890-1841	8849
Western States Packaging Inc	2673	E	818 686-6045	3893
Wetzel & Sons Mvg & Stor Inc	4214	D	818 890-0992	12122
Xpo Logistics Freight Inc	4213	D	818 890-2095	12096

PALM DESERT, CA - Riverside County

Company	SIC	EMP	PHONE	ENTRY #
Advanced Realtime Systems Inc	7371	F	760 636-0444	17539
Ashford Trs Seven LLC **(PA)**	7011	C	760 776-4150	16330
Associated Desert Shoppers Inc **(DH)**	2741	D	760 346-1729	4152
Bighorn Golf Club Charities	7997	C	760 773-2468	19546
Breeze Air Conditioning LLC	1711	D	760 346-0855	1036
Claro Pool Services Inc	7389	D	760 341-3377	18481
Coachlla Vly Wtr Dst Pub Fclti **(PA)**	4941	C	760 398-2651	12883
Coachlla Vly Wtr Dst Pub Fclti	4941	C	760 398-2651	12884
Cora Constructors Inc	8711	E	760 674-3201	22519
Cove Electric Inc	1731	D	760 568-9924	1237
Daniels Inc **(PA)**	2741	E	801 621-3355	4166
Dave Williams Plbg & Elec Inc	1711	C	760 296-1397	1053
Desert Falls Country Club Inc	7997	D	760 340-5646	19558
Desert Resort Management	6531	D	760 831-0172	15836
Desert Willow Golf Resort Inc	7992	C	760 346-0015	19484
Desertarc	8322	B	760 346-1611	21768
Destination Residences LLC	7011	C	760 346-4647	16405
Dutt Hospitality Group Inc	7011	D	760 340-1001	16422
Entravsion Communications Corp	4833	D	760 836-0466	12717
Equipment De Sport Usa Inc	2395	F	760 772-5544	3155
F M Tarbell Co	6531	E	760 346-7405	15852
Farley Paving Stone Co Inc	3272	D	760 773-3960	6032
Firstservice Residential	8741	D	760 834-2480	23027
Friends of Cultural Center Inc	7922	D	760 346-6505	19310
Gary Cardiff Enterprises Inc	4119	D	760 568-1403	11869
Golfsmith Intl Holdings	5091	E	760 202-1023	14079
Host Hotels & Resorts LP	7011	D	760 341-2211	16491
Jewel Date Company Inc	2064	E	760 399-4474	2090
Kaiser Foundation Hospitals	8011	C	800 777-1256	19912
Kaiser Foundation Hospitals	8011	A	866 984-7483	19914
Kaiser Foundation Hospitals	8011	C	760 360-1475	19942
Kaiser Foundation Hospitals	6324	C	303 404-4700	15436
Karbz Inc	3714	E	760 567-9953	10084
Lakes Country Club Assn Inc **(PA)**	7997	B	760 568-4321	19577
Lexani Wheel Corporation	3714	D	951 368-7526	10091
Lf Visuals Inc	2299	F	760 345-5571	2729
Living Desert	8422	C	760 346-5694	22238
Marriott Rsrts Hspitality Corp	7011	B	760 779-1200	16560
Marriotts Shadow Ridge	7011	C	760 674-2600	16561
Michael Baker Intl Inc	8711	D	760 346-7481	22611
Morgan Stnley Smith Barney LLC	6022	C	760 568-3500	15033
Mountain Vista Golf Course At	7999	D	760 200-2200	19656
Palm Desert Greens Association	8641	D	760 346-8005	22354
Palm Desert Hospitality LLC	7011	D	760 568-1600	16616
Palm Desert Resorter Assn	8641	D	760 345-1954	22355
Pd Group	3993	E	760 674-3028	11581
Pearpoint Inc	3663	E	760 343-7350	9309
Platinum Landscape Inc	0781	C	760 200-3673	276
Plumbing Products Company Inc	3432	F	760 343-3306	6563
Premier Residential Svcs LLC	7299	D	760 773-4081	16973

GEOGRAPHIC

	SIC	EMP	PHONE	ENTRY #
Priority Lighting Inc	3648	F	800 709-1119	9145
Production Associates Inc **(PA)**	7812	D	310 598-7200	19167
Quarry At La Quinta Inc **(PA)**	7992	D	760 777-1100	19504
Rai Care Ctrs Sthern Cal II LL	8092	D	760 346-7588	21262
Renova Energy Corp	1711	E	760 568-3413	1129
Resort Parking Services Inc	7521	C	760 328-4041	18778
Sun City Palm Dsert Cmnty Assn **(PA)**	8641	D	760 200-2100	22370
Temalpakh Inc	1542	D	760 770-5778	839
United Brothers Concrete Inc	1771	C	760 346-1013	1556
Universal Services America LP	7381	A	760 200-2865	18353
Veterans Health Administration	8011	C	760 341-5570	20146
Wanda Matranga	2752	F	760 773-4701	4452
Watermark Rtrment Cmmnties Inc	8051	C	760 346-5420	20503
Webb Del California Corp **(DH)**	6552	B	760 772-5300	16081
West Coast Turf **(PA)**	0181	E	760 340-7300	97

PALM SPRINGS, CA - Riverside County

	SIC	EMP	PHONE	ENTRY #
Ace Direct	7331	E	760 969-5500	17128
Ace Hotel & Swim Club	7011	D	760 325-9900	16314
Adams Trade Press LP **(PA)**	2721	E	760 318-7000	4048
Agre Dcp Palm Sprng Tenant LLC **(PA)**	7011	C	760 327-8311	16315
Agua Caliente Development Auth	6531	D	760 699-6800	15765
Agua Clnte Band Chilla Indians **(PA)**	8699	A	760 699-6800	22394
American Medical Response Inc	4119	C	760 883-5000	11851
Angel View Inc	8361	D	760 322-2440	22080
Automobile Club Southern Cal	8699	D	760 320-1121	22415
Bbva USA	6035	C	760 325-2021	15050
Best Signs Inc **(PA)**	7389	E	760 320-3042	18460
BMW of Palm Springs	2426	F	760 324-7071	3215
Califrnia Nrsing Rhblttion Ctr	8051	D	760 325-2937	20271
Cardinal Health Inc	5047	D	951 360-2199	13483
Carefusion 207 Inc	3841	B	760 778-7200	10958
Colony Palms Hotel LLC	7011	D	760 969-1800	16386
Desert Aids Project **(PA)**	8322	D	760 323-2118	21767
Desert Air Conditioning Inc	1761	E	760 323-3383	1482
Desert Heart Physicians Inc	8011	D	760 325-1203	19794
Desert Medical Group Inc **(PA)**	8011	C	760 320-8814	19795
Desert Publications Inc **(PA)**	2721	E	760 325-2333	4065
Desert Radiology Medical Group	8011	D	760 778-5900	19797
Desert Regional Med Ctr Inc **(HQ)**	8062	A	760 323-6511	20746
Desert Regional Med Ctr Inc	8062	D	760 416-4613	20747
Desert Sun Publishing Co **(DH)**	2711	C	760 322-8889	3972
Desert Water Agency Fing Corp	4941	D	760 323-4971	12887
Diamond Resorts LLC	7011	D	760 866-1800	16406
Door Service Company	3315	F	760 320-0788	6223
Ensign Palm I LLC	8051	D	760 323-2638	20332
First Student Inc	4151	C	760 320-4659	11929
HHC Trs Portsmouth LLC	7011	D	760 322-6000	16473
Hilton Resort Palm Springs	7011	C	760 320-6868	16478
Ingleside Investors Spe LLC	7011	D	760 325-0046	16504
Iqd Frequency Products Inc	3679	E	408 250-1435	9731
Jack Parker Corp	7011	D	760 770-5000	16510
Joe Blasco Enterprises Inc	3999	E	323 467-4949	11696
Just Off Melrose Inc	2052	E	714 533-4566	2066
Kaiser Foundation Hospitals	6324	C	866 370-1942	15427
Ken Hoffmann Inc	3471	E	760 325-6012	7275
Kings Garden LLC	8742	C	760 275-4969	23252
Kittridge Hotels & Resorts LLC	7011	D	760 325-9676	16526
Loandepotcom LLC	6162	A	760 797-6000	15212
Longs Drug Stores Cal LLC	7384	C	760 327-1374	18418
Lowes Home Centers LLC	5031	C	760 866-1901	13234
Matches Inc	2824	B	760 899-1919	4734
Mission Linen Supply	7213	D	760 778-5288	16864
Mizell Senior Center Inc	8322	D	760 323-5689	21852
Mount San Jcnto Winter Pk Auth	7999	D	760 325-1449	19655
Oasis Rehabilitation Center **(HQ)**	8099	E	760 863-8638	21467
Palm Mountain Resort & Spa	7011	D	760 325-1301	16617
Palm Springs Art Museum Inc	8412	D	760 322-4800	22231
Palm Springs Disposal Services	4953	D	760 327-1351	12963
Palm Springs Life	2721	F	760 325-2333	4093
Palm Springs Rental Agency Inc	7011	E	760 320-7451	16618
Palm Sprng Pwr Basbal CLB Inc	7941	D	760 778-4487	19427
Parker Palm Springs LLC	7011	D	760 770-5000	16622
R P S Resort Corp	7011	C	760 327-8311	16649
Rbd Hotel Palm Springs LLC	7011	D	760 322-9000	16656
Remington Hotel Corporation	7011	D	760 322-6000	16658
Riverside County Off Educatn	8748	C	760 320-8266	23502
Riviera Reincarnate LLC	7011	D	760 327-8311	16667
Robray Hotel Partnership LLP	7011	D	760 325-4372	16669
S S W Mechanical Cnstr Inc	1711	C	760 327-1481	1133
Smoke Tree Inc	7011	D	760 327-1221	16716
Spa Resort Casino **(PA)**	7011	A	888 999-1995	16721
Spa Resort Casino	7011	C	760 883-1034	16722
United Parcel Service Inc	4215	C	760 325-1762	12149
Vacation Palm Springs RE Inc	6531	C	760 778-7832	16028
Viasys Respiratory Care Inc	3841	F	714 283-2228	11076
Walters Family Partnership	7011	C	760 320-6868	16777
Western Pacific Roofing Corp	1761	C	661 273-1336	1510
Windsor Crt Asssted Living LLC	8051	E	760 327-8351	20513
Worldmark Club	7011	D	760 416-4428	16805
Xy Corp Inc	3542	F	760 323-0333	7770

PALMDALE, CA - Los Angeles County

	SIC	EMP	PHONE	ENTRY #
Aero Bending Company	3444	D	661 948-2363	6775
Antelope Vly Cntry CLB Imprv	7997	C	661 947-3142	19533
Antelope Vly Rcycl Dspsal Fclt	4953	D	661 945-5944	12925
Azachorok Contract Svcs LLC	3444	F	661 951-6566	6790
Bowlero Corp	7933	D	661 274-2878	19392
Chapman University	8742	D	661 267-2001	23187
Child Care Resource Center Inc	8322	C	661 723-3246	21738
Csi Electrical Contractors Inc	1731	B	661 723-0869	1239
David C Han DDS A Prof Corp **(PA)**	8021	D	661 254-1924	20172
Delta Scientific Corporation **(PA)**	7382	C	661 575-1100	18370
Garrison Family Med Group Inc	8011	D	661 947-7100	19829
Golden Empire Mortgage Inc	6162	B	661 949-3388	15198
Kaiser Foundation Hospitals	6733	D	661 533-7500	16184
Kennedy Engineered Pdts Inc	3714	E	661 272-1147	10085
Lockheed Martin Corporation	3812	A	661 572-7428	10598
Lowes Home Centers LLC	5031	C	661 267-9888	13245
Lowes Home Centers LLC	5031	C	661 533-9900	13258
Lusk Quality Machine Products	3599	E	661 272-0630	8669
Murcal Inc	5063	E	661 272-4700	13651
Northrop Grumman Systems Corp	3721	B	661 272-7000	10197
Northrop Grumman Systems Corp	3812	C	661 540-0446	10623
Palmdale Heat Treating Inc	3398	F	661 274-8604	6449
Palmdale Resort Inc	7011	D	661 947-8055	16619
Palmdale Water District	4941	D	661 947-4111	12913
People Creating Success Inc	8322	D	661 225-9700	21869
Rancho Vista Development Co	7992	D	661 272-9082	19505
Smart & Final Stores Inc	5141	C	661 722-6210	14502
Sun Valley Ltg Standards Inc	3646	D	661 233-2000	9104
Tarzana Treatment Centers Inc	8093	D	818 654-3815	21347
Teletronics Technology Corp	3812	E	661 273-7033	10646
Thi Holdings (delaware) Inc	6411	B	661 266-7423	15634
Ultramar Inc	2911	E	661 944-2496	5265
Universal Pain MGT Med Corp **(PA)**	8011	D	661 267-6876	20120
US Pole Company Inc **(PA)**	3646	D	800 877-6537	9108
Vision Engrg Met Stamping Inc	3646	D	661 575-0933	9109
Waste Management Cal Inc	4953	C	661 947-7197	12994
Western Edge Inc	3479	F	661 947-3900	7425
Wilcompute	3825	F	818 674-0506	10775
Xi Enterprise Inc	7991	D	661 266-3200	19473

PALOS VERDES ESTATES, CA - Los Angeles County

	SIC	EMP	PHONE	ENTRY #
Grosvenor Inv MGT US Inc	6411	D	310 265-0297	15575
Malaga Financial Corporation **(PA)**	6036	D	310 375-9000	15055
Palos Verdes Golf Club	7997	D	310 375-2759	19598
QED Software LLC	7372	E	310 214-3118	17965
Sqa Services Inc	8742	B	800 333-6180	23333

PALOS VERDES PENINSU, CA - Los Angeles County

	SIC	EMP	PHONE	ENTRY #
County of Los Angeles	8062	C	310 222-2401	20737

PANORAMA CITY, CA - Los Angeles County

	SIC	EMP	PHONE	ENTRY #
American Protection Group Inc **(PA)**	7381	C	818 279-2433	18246
Creative Technology Group Inc **(DH)**	7359	D	818 779-2400	17343
Crestview Landscape Inc	0781	D	818 962-7771	252
D X Communications Inc	3663	E	323 256-3000	9266
Deanco Healthcare LLC	8062	A	818 787-2222	20743
Ensign Group Inc	8051	D	818 893-6385	20329
Import Collection **(PA)**	5199	D	818 782-3060	14939
Kaiser Foundation Hospitals	8011	C	818 375-4023	19866
Kaiser Foundation Hospitals	8011	C	818 375-3475	19871
Kaiser Foundation Hospitals	8011	C	818 375-2369	19880
Kaiser Foundation Hospitals	8011	C	818 375-2000	19882
Kaiser Foundation Hospitals	6324	C	818 375-2028	15411
La Sierra Records Inc	5099	E	818 830-1919	14167
Leigh Jerry California Inc **(PA)**	5137	B	818 909-6200	14391
Northeast Valley Health Corp	8011	D	818 988-6335	20003
Puretek Corporation	2834	C	818 361-3949	4877
Raspadoxpress	2741	E	813 892-6969	4201
Southern Cal Prmnnte Med Group	6324	C	800 272-3500	15454
Superior Awning Inc	2394	E	818 780-7200	3146
Transit Care Inc	3211	F	818 267-3002	5924

PARAMOUNT, CA - Los Angeles County

	SIC	EMP	PHONE	ENTRY #
Advanced Industrial Svcs Inc	1721	D	562 940-8305	1165
Aerocraft Heat Treating Co Inc	3398	D	562 674-2400	6427
Amrex-Zetron Inc	3699	E	310 527-6868	9855
Amsco US Inc	3679	E	562 630-0333	9674
Anaplex Corporation	3471	E	714 522-4481	7211
Apollo Metal Spinning Co Inc	3465	F	562 634-5141	7111
Ariza Cheese Co Inc	2022	E	562 630-4144	1767
ARS Enterprises **(PA)**	3842	F	562 946-3505	11089
Asphalt Management Inc	1771	F	562 630-6811	1512
Avantus Aerospace Inc	3429	E	562 633-6626	6502
Aylesva Inc	5139	C	562 688-0592	14430
Bison Engineering Company Inc	3599	F	562 408-1525	8528
Blue Circle Corp	3452	F	562 531-2711	7057
Braun Linen Service **(PA)**	7213	C	909 623-2678	16847
C & J Metal Products Inc	3444	E	562 634-3101	6799
C S Dash Cover Inc	2396	F	562 790-8300	3169
California Air Conveying Corp	1796	F	562 531-4570	1622
California Screw Products Corp	3429	D	562 633-6626	6510
Calmet Inc **(PA)**	4953	C	323 721-8120	12935
Calmet Services Inc	4953	D	562 259-1239	12936
Cfr Rinkens LLC **(PA)**	4731	D	310 639-7725	12434
Cnet Express	4212	C	949 357-5475	11963
Commercial Grinding Co Inc	7389	D	562 531-9970	18485
Cosmo Textiles Inc	2258	D	562 220-1177	2649
Custom Glass Fabricators Inc	3069	F	562 529-2300	5371
Danrich Welding Co Inc	3444	E	562 634-4811	6816
Demaria Electric Inc	7694	E	310 549-4980	19008
Denmac Industries Inc	3479	E	562 634-2714	7357
Die Shop	3544	F	562 630-4400	7796
Dlc Laboratories Inc	2834	F	562 602-2184	4816

Mergent email: customerrelations@mergent.com
1412
2022 Southern California Business Directory and Buyers Guide
(P-0000) Products & Services Section entry number
(PA)=Parent Co (HQ)=Headquarters (DH)=Div Headquarters

	SIC	EMP	PHONE	ENTRY #
Don Brandel Plumbing Inc	1711	E	562 408-0400	1056
Drees Wood Products Inc	2431	E	562 633-7337	3246
Drees Wood Products Inc **(PA)**	2434	E	562 633-7337	3317
Drillmec Inc **(DH)**	1382	E	281 885-0777	447
Durham School Services L P	4151	C	562 408-1206	11920
Ener-Tech Metals Inc	3325	D	562 529-5034	6276
Extrude Hone Deburring Svc Inc	3599	E	562 531-2976	8584
Fenico Precision Castings Inc	3369	D	562 634-5000	6416
George Jue Mfg Co Inc	3546	D	562 634-8181	7881
Golden State Engineering Inc	3549	C	562 634-3125	7902
Graphic Trends Incorporated	2759	E	562 531-2339	4522
Grupo Deco California Corp **(HQ)**	7261	D	562 634-8990	16923
Hoffman Plastic Compounds Inc	2821	D	323 636-3346	4694
ICI Architectural Millwork Inc	2431	F	323 759-4993	3256
Jayone Foods Inc	2099	E	562 633-7400	2454
Jeffrey Fabrication LLC	3444	E	562 634-3101	6857
Jimenes Food Inc	2099	E	562 602-2505	2455
Kindred Healthcare LLC	8062	C	562 531-3110	20829
Kum Kang Trading USAinC	2844	E	562 531-6111	5040
Ld Steel Inc	3446	F	213 632-8073	6972
LMC Enterprises **(PA)**	2842	D	562 602-2116	4968
M & J Seafood Company Inc	5146	D	562 529-2786	14572
Marukan Vinegar U S A Inc **(HQ)**	2099	E	562 630-6060	2480
Mattco Forge Inc **(HQ)**	3462	E	562 634-8635	7091
MB Herzog Electric Inc	1731	C	562 531-2002	1280
Mediland Corporation	3211	D	562 630-9696	5920
Millbrook Kitchens Inc	2434	F	310 684-3366	3326
Modern Dev Co A Ltd Partnr	7389	D	949 646-6400	18601
Mr T Transport	1389	F	562 602-5536	520
Mv Transportation Inc	4111	D	562 259-9911	11830
New Century Industries Inc	3714	E	562 634-9551	10108
Panacea Inc	8731	D	562 860-2869	22858
Paramount Dairy Inc	2026	C	562 361-1800	1839
Paramount Extrusions Company **(PA)**	3354	E	562 634-3291	6314
Paramount Grinding Service	3599	E	562 630-6940	8731
Paramount Laminates Inc **(PA)**	3083	D	562 531-7580	5454
Paramount Petroleum Corp **(DH)**	2911	C	562 531-2060	5256
Piedras Machine Corporation	3599	F	562 602-1500	8740
Pioneer Trading Inc	5149	E	562 531-3842	14718
Popsalot LLC	2096	E	213 761-0156	2364
Premier Mailing Inc	7331	E	562 408-2134	17137
Premium Plastics Machine Inc	3089	E	562 633-7723	5774
Press Forge Company	3462	D	562 531-4962	7096
R & S Manufacturing & Sup Inc	2851	F	909 622-5881	5110
R & S Processing Co Inc	3069	D	562 531-0738	5405
Ramp Engineering Inc	3599	E	562 531-8030	8758
Reliable Energy Management Inc	1711	D	562 984-5511	1128
Robert W Wiesmantel	3599	F	562 634-0442	8772
Sandee Plastic Extrusions	3089	E	323 979-4020	5810
Schulz Leather Company Inc	2394	F	562 633-1081	3145
Sibyl Shepard Inc	2392	E	562 531-8612	3119
Su Mano Inc	3111	E	562 529-8835	5872
Supertec Machinery Inc	3541	F	562 220-1675	7748
Tattooed Chef Inc **(PA)**	2099	D	562 602-0822	2534
Top Line Mfg Inc	3429	E	562 633-0605	6541
Total-Western Inc **(HQ)**	1389	C	562 220-1450	551
TP Solar Inc	3567	F	562 808-2171	8100
Trepanning Specialities Inc	3599	E	562 633-8110	8824
Triage Partners LLC	7379	D	562 634-0058	18228
Valence Surface Tech LLC	3441	F	562 531-7666	6679
Vast Enterprises	2992	F	562 633-3224	5299
Vaughans Industrial Repair Inc	5084	E	562 633-2660	13959
Vi-Star Gear Co Inc	3462	E	323 774-3750	7101
Wagner Plate Works West Inc **(PA)**	3443	E	562 531-6050	6765
Weber Metals Inc	3463	B	562 602-0260	7109
Williamson Granados	2335	F	424 296-5494	2900
Z-Tronix Inc	3679	E	562 808-0800	9806

PASADENA, CA - Los Angeles County

	SIC	EMP	PHONE	ENTRY #
A N Tool & Die	3544	F	626 795-3238	7772
Access Pacific Inc	1542	E	626 792-0616	729
Accredited Nursing Services	8051	C	626 573-1234	20238
Advanced Mtls Joining Corp **(PA)**	3728	E	626 449-2696	10241
Algos Inc A Medical Corp **(PA)**	8093	D	626 696-1400	21272
American General Design	8712	E	626 304-0800	22709
American Multi-Cinema Inc	7832	E	626 585-8900	19269
American Multimedia TV USA	4833	D	626 466-1038	12710
American Reliance Inc	3571	E	626 443-6818	8148
Ameriko Inc **(PA)**	8744	C	626 795-7988	23389
Annandale Golf Club	7997	C	626 796-6125	19532
Arroyo Holdings Inc **(PA)**	3444	E	626 765-9340	6787
Arroyo Seco Medical Group **(PA)**	8011	D	626 795-7556	19715
Art & Logic Inc	7373	D	818 500-1933	18018
Arts Elegance Inc	3911	E	626 793-4794	11311
Atk Space Systems LLC	8731	D	626 351-0205	22826
Auritec Pharmaceuticals Inc	2834	F	424 272-9501	4789
Aurora Las Encinas LLC	8063	C	626 795-9901	21014
Automobile Club Southern Cal	8699	D	626 795-0601	22417
Avery Dennison Corporation	2672	C	626 304-2000	3865
Avicena LLC **(PA)**	8731	D	626 344-9665	22828
Ayzenberg Group Inc	7311	D	626 584-4070	16993
B Jacqueline and Assoc Inc	7371	D	626 844-1400	17560
Biocatalytics Inc	8731	D	626 585-9797	22830
Blaze Pizza LLC **(PA)**	6794	D	626 584-5880	16202
Blue Chip Stamps Inc	5051	A	626 585-6700	13549
Bluebeam Inc **(PA)**	7371	C	626 788-4100	17569
Boswell Properties Inc	0722	A	626 583-3000	150
Brazil Minerals Inc	1499	F	213 590-2500	584
Brighton Convalescent Center	8059	D	626 798-9124	20565
C & D Precision Components Inc	3599	D	626 799-7109	8536
C W Driver Incorporated **(PA)**	1542	D	626 351-8800	748
Cachet Financial Services	8721	D	626 578-9400	22764
California Credits Group LLC	7389	E	626 584-9800	18464
California Institute Tech	8733	A	818 354-9154	22901
Califrnia Clnic Plstic Surgery **(PA)**	8011	D	626 817-0818	19733
Calimmune Inc	2834	F	310 806-6240	4802
Camellia Gardens Care Ctr	8051	D	626 798-6777	20274
Carnegie Institution Wash	8733	D	626 577-1122	22902
Casecentral Inc **(DH)**	7389	D	415 989-2300	18471
Charles Pnkow Bldrs Ltd A Cal **(PA)**	1542	E	626 304-1190	752
CIT Bank NA **(HQ)**	6021	D	626 859-5400	14995
City of Pasadena	7992	D	626 543-4708	19477
Cloud Creations Inc	7379	D	800 951-7651	18169
Collins Cllins Muir Stwart LLP	8111	E	626 243-1100	21533
Community Hlth Alance Pasadena **(PA)**	8062	D	626 398-6300	20726
Connectall LLC	7373	E	800 913-7457	18025
Coronal Energy LLC **(PA)**	8742	D	855 267-6625	23197
Coronal Lost Hills LLC **(PA)**	1711	D	855 267-6625	1049
County of Los Angeles	8099	D	626 229-3825	21406
Cpo Commerce LLC	5072	D	626 585-3600	13802
De Novo Software LLC	7372	E	213 814-1240	17836
Die Cast Model Madness	3544	F	626 791-0364	7795
Dowling Advisory Group	8742	D	626 319-1369	23208
Dpr Construction A Gen Partnr	1542	C	626 463-1265	761
Driver Spg LLC	7389	E	855 300-4774	18506
DVeal Corporation	8399	C	626 296-8900	22181
Dy-Dee Service Pasadena Inc	7219	D	626 792-6183	16889
E Z Data Inc **(HQ)**	7371	D	626 585-3505	17604
East West Bancorp Inc **(PA)**	6022	B	626 768-6000	15019
East West Bank **(HQ)**	6022	B	626 768-6000	15020
Electric Power Group LLC	8742	E	626 685-2015	23211
Electric Svc & Sup Co Pasadena	1731	D	626 795-8641	1246
Employee Benefits Security ADM	6371	D	626 229-1000	15515
Environmental Science Assoc	8731	D	626 204-6170	22837
Everbridge Inc **(PA)**	7372	C	818 230-9700	17851
Evolution Design Lab Inc	3144	E	626 960-8388	5879
Evolution Robotics Inc	7372	D	626 993-3300	17853
Exchangrght Nlp 3 Mstr Lssee L **(PA)**	6799	D	855 317-4448	16260
Exeter Packers Inc	0174	D	626 993-6245	62
Finance America Mortgage LLC	6162	D	215 591-0222	15194
First Quadrant LP **(PA)**	6722	D	626 795-8220	16129
Floor Covering Soft	7372	E	626 683-9188	17858
Foremay Inc **(PA)**	7371	E	408 228-3468	17617
Foundtion For Erly Chldhood Ed **(PA)**	8322	C	626 572-5107	21790
Gem Transitional Care Center	8051	E	626 737-0560	20355
Gemalto Cogent Inc **(DH)**	7373	B	626 325-9600	18033
Gemdale USA Corporation **(HQ)**	6531	D	626 381-9709	15872
George L Throop Co	3272	E	626 796-0285	6035
Gfn North America Corp **(HQ)**	7359	E	626 584-9722	17350
Gmto Corporation	3827	D	626 204-0500	10836
Golden Cross Care Inc	8051	D	626 791-1948	20361
Gooden Center	8069	D	626 356-0078	21046
Grandcare Health Services LLC **(PA)**	8082	C	866 554-2447	21168
Green Dot Corporation **(PA)**	6141	A	626 765-2000	15143
Greensoft Technology Inc	7374	C	323 254-5961	18092
Guardian Life Insur Co of Amer	6311	D	626 792-1935	15361
Guidance Software Inc **(HQ)**	7372	C	626 229-9191	17874
Guidance Software Inc	7372	E	626 229-9199	17875
H M H Emergency Medical Group	7363	D	626 397-5106	17494
Hadsell Strmer Keny Rchrdson R	8111	D	626 585-9600	21574
Hair Perfect International	7231	D	626 304-9286	16905
Hamilton Metalcraft Inc	3444	E	626 795-4811	6850
Hathawy-Sycmres Child Fmly Svc **(PA)**	8361	D	626 395-7100	22110
Hemodialysis Inc	3841	E	626 792-0548	10987
Hertz Claim Management Corp	7514	D	626 296-4760	18742
Hillsides	8361	B	323 254-2274	22113
Honeybee Robotics Ltd	3569	E	510 207-4555	8125
House of Printing Inc	2752	E	626 793-7034	4317
Hunt Ortmann Palffy Nieves	8111	E	626 440-5200	21583
Huntington Ambltry Surg Ctr	8011	E	626 229-8999	19847
Huntington Care LLC	8082	C	877 405-6990	21172
Huntington Med Res Institutes	8733	D	626 397-5804	22909
Huntington Medical Foundation	8011	D	626 795-4210	19848
Huntington Medical Foundation	8062	C	626 792-3141	20796
Huntington Reprodctve Ctr Inc **(PA)**	8011	E	626 204-9699	19850
Idealab **(HQ)**	6726	D	626 356-3654	16155
Idealab Holdings LLC **(PA)**	6799	A	626 585-6900	16268
Innovate Labs LLC	7372	F	917 753-2673	17888
Inteliglas Corporation	3211	E	626 722-8881	5919
Intellectyx Inc	7372	D	720 256-7540	17889
Inter-Con Investigators Inc	7381	D	626 535-2200	18289
Inter-Con Security Systems Inc **(PA)**	7382	A	626 535-2200	18387
Interntional Un Oper Engineers	8631	E	626 792-2519	22291
Invitation Homes Inc	6512	D	805 372-2900	15675
Ironwrker Emplyees Beneft Corp	6733	D	626 792-7337	16179
Jacobs Atcs Fema A Joint Ventr	8711	D	571 218-1115	22582
Jacobs Engineering Company	8711	A	626 449-2171	22584
Jacobs Engineering Group Inc	8711	D	626 578-3500	22585
Jacobs Engineering Inc **(HQ)**	8711	A	626 578-3500	22586
Jacobs International Ltd Inc	8711	B	626 578-3500	22587
Jrw Research & Consulting Inc	8748	E	877 579-1031	23458
Jurlique Hlistic Skin Care Inc **(PA)**	7991	E	914 998-8800	19452
Kaiser Foundation Hospitals	6324	E	626 405-5000	15406
Kaiser Foundation Hospitals	8011	C	626 440-5639	19937
Kaiser Foundation Hospitals	8062	B	626 440-5659	20815

GEOGRAPHIC

Employment Codes: A=Over 500 employees, B=251-500, C=101-250, D=51-100, E=20-50 F=10-19

2022 Southern California Business Directory and Buyers Guide

1413

	SIC	EMP	PHONE	ENTRY #
Kaiser Prmnnte Schl Anesthesia	8011	D	626 564-3016	19948
Kbkg Inc	8721	D	626 449-4225	22796
Kids Klub Care Centers Inc **(PA)**	8351	D	626 795-2501	22026
Kidspace A Prticipatory Museum	8412	D	626 449-9144	22223
Kinemetrics Inc **(DH)**	8711	D	626 795-2220	22596
Kristie L Lin MD Inc **(PA)**	8011	D	626 272-4408	19953
Krost **(PA)**	8721	C	626 449-4225	22799
L A Steel Craft Products **(PA)**	3949	E	626 798-7401	11432
La Asccion Ncnal Pro Prsnas My **(PA)**	8322	A	626 564-1988	21835
Land Design Consultants Inc	8748	D	626 578-7000	23463
Langham Hotels Pacific Corp	7011	D	617 451-1900	16535
Laquer Urban Clfford Hodge LLP	8111	D	626 449-1882	21603
Law School Financial Inc	6111	C	626 243-1800	15134
Legacy Healthcare Center LLC	8099	D	626 798-0558	21449
Licher Direct Mail Inc	2752	E	626 795-3333	4359
Lida Childrens Wear Inc	2361	E	626 967-8868	3034
Lifesource Water Systems Inc **(PA)**	3589	E	626 792-9996	8392
Los Angles Cnty Emplyees Rtrme **(PA)**	6371	C	626 564-6000	15516
Lotus Clinical Research LLC	8071	D	626 381-9830	21075
Madison Radiology Med Group	8011	D	626 793-8189	19970
Materia Inc **(PA)**	2819	C	626 584-8400	4661
Max Leon Inc **(PA)**	2339	D	626 797-6886	2972
Maxar Space Robotics LLC **(DH)**	8711	E	626 296-1373	22606
Maxar Space Robotics LLC	8711	D	626 296-1373	22607
Merrill Lynch Prce Fnner Smith	6211	D	800 637-7455	15292
Mhh Holdings Inc	5149	C	626 744-9370	14708
Monte Vista Grove Homes	8361	D	626 796-6135	22133
Mothers Club Family Lrng Ctr	8322	D	626 792-2687	21853
Multicultural Rdo Brdcstg Inc	4832	D	626 844-8882	12702
Myricom Inc	3571	E	626 821-5555	8168
Ngork Dental Corporation **(PA)**	8021	D	714 200-4095	20191
Normandy Refinishers Inc	3471	E	626 792-9202	7288
Norton Smon Mseum Art At Psden	8412	D	626 449-6840	22230
Openx Technologies Inc **(DH)**	7311	B	855 673-6948	17041
Operating Engineers Funds Inc **(PA)**	6733	C	866 400-5200	16192
Orbits Lightwave Inc	3229	E	626 513-7400	5938
Original Whistle Stop Inc	3944	E	626 796-7791	11388
Owen Group Limited Partnership **(HQ)**	8741	D	800 600-6936	23081
Pacific Huntington Hotel Corp	7011	A	626 568-3900	16609
Pacifica Services Inc	8711	D	626 405-0131	22629
Pak Group LLC	2052	E	626 316-6555	2071
Park Marino Convalescent Ctr	8059	C	626 463-4105	20622
Parsons Constructors Inc	8741	A	626 440-2000	23086
Parsons Engrg Science Inc **(DH)**	8711	B	626 440-2000	22631
Parsons Gvrnment Svcs Intl Inc	1542	C	626 440-6000	801
Parsons Project Services Inc	1541	D	626 440-4000	713
Parsons Services Company	8711	A	626 440-2000	22633
Parsons Wtr Infrastructure Inc	8711	D	626 440-7000	22634
Pasadena Center Operating Co	7389	C	626 795-9311	18630
Pasadena Hospital Assn Ltd **(PA)**	8051	A	626 397-5000	20435
Pasadena Hospital Assn Ltd	8051	B	626 397-3322	20436
Pasadena Hotel Dev Ventr LP	7011	D	626 449-4000	16623
Pasadena Humane Society	8699	D	626 792-7151	22459
Pasadena Madows Nursing Ctr LP	8051	D	626 796-1103	20437
Pasadena Newspapers Inc **(PA)**	2711	C	626 578-6300	4022
Pasadena Senior Center	8322	D	626 795-4331	21863
Pasadena Service Federal Cr Un	6061	D	626 351-9651	15078
Pasadena Unified School Dst	7349	D	626 798-9171	17271
Pasta Piccinini Inc	5149	D	626 798-0841	14715
Patagonia Inc	2389	F	626 795-0319	3081
Phoenix Technologies Ltd **(HQ)**	7372	E	408 570-1000	17956
Polytechnic School	8351	B	626 792-2147	22052
Povac Investments Inc	1542	E	626 405-0400	811
Prima Royale Enterprises Ltd	5139	E	626 960-8388	14445
Principles Inc **(PA)**	8093	D	323 681-2575	21329
Ptsi Managed Services Inc	8711	D	626 440-3118	22640
Ratespecial Interactive LLC **(PA)**	7311	D	626 376-4702	17050
Red Gate Software Inc	7372	E	626 993-3949	17972
Regency Park Senior Living Inc	8361	D	626 396-4911	22149
Regency Park Senior Living Inc	6531	C	626 578-0460	15972
Rockley Photonics Inc **(HQ)**	3674	C	626 304-9960	9566
Rogerson Kratos	3812	C	626 449-3090	10642
Rose Bowl Aquatics Center	7997	D	626 564-0330	19605
Rosemary Childrens Services **(PA)**	8361	C	626 844-3033	22150
Roughan Associates At Linc	8748	E	626 351-0991	23505
Rt Pasad Hotel Partners LP	7011	D	626 403-7600	16675
Sabal Capital Partners LLC	6799	D	949 255-1007	16291
Sabrin Corporation	3728	F	626 792-3813	10406
Saiful/Bquet Cnslting Strl Eng **(PA)**	8711	D	626 304-2616	22651
Saladish Inc	2099	F	626 304-3100	2521
Schaumbond Group Inc **(PA)**	6726	B	626 215-4998	16163
Schmidt Industries Inc	3999	F	323 344-6400	11747
Scratch Financial Inc	7389	D	855 727-2395	18663
Shadecraft Inc	3535	E	818 502-0700	7695
Shriners Hspitals For Children	8069	C	213 388-3151	21052
Slch Inc **(PA)**	8051	E	626 798-0558	20477
Smith Brothers Restaurant Inc	8741	D	626 577-2400	23111
Snapcomms Inc	7371	D	805 715-0300	17717
Solariant Capital LLC	6719	C	626 544-0279	16112
Southern Cal Ibw-Neca ADM Corp **(PA)**	6371	D	323 221-5861	15521
Southern Cal Prmnnte Med Group **(HQ)**	6324	D	626 405-5704	15458
Southland Publishing Inc **(PA)**	2711	F	626 584-1500	4031
Stantec Architecture Inc	8712	D	626 796-9141	22744
Stantec Consulting Svcs Inc	8711	D	626 796-9141	22660
Stinson Commercial Trnsp	4212	D	626 807-6265	11997
Symes Cadillac Inc	7538	D	626 689-4386	18877
Tetra Tech Inc **(PA)**	8711	C	626 351-4664	22667
Tetra Tech Executive Svcs Inc	7361	C	626 470-2400	17475
Tetra Tech Holding LLC **(HQ)**	8711	B	626 351-4664	22670
Tetra Tech International Inc **(HQ)**	8711	C	626 351-4664	22671
Tetra Tech Nus Inc	8711	C	412 921-7090	22672
Ticor Title Insurance Company **(DH)**	6361	D	616 302-3121	15512
Tm Claims Service Inc	6411	D	626 568-7800	15635
Torres Construction Corp **(PA)**	1541	D	323 257-7460	722
Tpusa - Fhcs Inc **(DH)**	7376	B	213 873-5100	18139
Tricom Service Corp **(PA)**	7349	E	888 415-6911	17292
Tridant Solutions Inc	8742	D	310 292-7382	23352
Turbo Coil Inc	3585	E	626 644-6254	8352
Two Palms Nursing Center Inc **(PA)**	8059	E	626 798-8991	20632
Two Palms Nursing Center Inc	8059	C	626 796-1103	20633
Typecraft Inc	2752	E	626 795-8093	4442
Unified Valet Parking Inc	7521	D	818 822-5807	18780
United Agencies Inc **(PA)**	6411	D	818 952-8818	15639
United Couriers Inc **(DH)**	4512	C	213 383-3611	12318
Valley Hunt Club	8641	D	626 793-7134	22374
Vincent Hayley Enterprises	8062	D	626 398-8132	21004
Vons Companies Inc	2051	D	626 798-7603	2044
Wescom Central Credit Union **(PA)**	6062	B	888 493-7266	15116
Western Asset Core Plus Bond P	6722	C	626 844-9400	16148
Western Asset Management Co **(DH)**	6722	E	626 844-9265	16149
Western Asset Management Co	6722	E	626 844-9400	16150
Western Asset Mrtg Capitl Corp	6798	A	626 844-9400	16245
Yes To Inc	2844	E	626 365-1976	5084
Zoominfo Technologies LLC	7375	C	360 783-6924	18137

PASO ROBLES, CA - San Luis Obispo County

	SIC	EMP	PHONE	ENTRY #
Acme Vial & Glass Co	3221	E	805 239-2666	5926
Advance Adapters Inc	3714	E	805 238-7000	10005
Advance Adapters LLC	3714	E	805 238-7000	10006
Advanced Keyboard Tech Inc	3571	F	805 237-2055	8146
AMC Machining Inc	3449	E	805 238-5452	7014
Applied Technologies Assoc Inc **(HQ)**	3829	C	805 239-9100	10869
Arbiter Systems Incorporated **(PA)**	3825	E	805 237-3831	10742
Ayres - Paso Robles LP	7011	C	714 850-0409	16332
Black Oaks Inc	7011	D	805 238-2392	16354
Boneso Brothers Cnstr Inc	1711	D	805 227-4450	1035
Calcareous Vineyard LLC	2084	F	805 239-0289	2170
Calipaso Winery LLC	2084	F	805 226-9296	2171
Cornucopia Tool & Plastics Inc	3089	E	805 238-7660	5614
Ctek Inc	4899	E	310 241-2973	12782
Eagle Med Pckg Strlization Inc	7389	E	805 238-7401	18509
Eos Estate Winery	2084	E	805 239-2562	2182
Firestone Walker Inc **(PA)**	2082	B	805 225-5911	2144
Halter Properties LLC	2084	E	805 226-9455	2189
Halter Winery LLC	2084	E	805 226-9455	2190
Hogue Inc	7699	D	805 239-1440	19041
Hope Family Wines **(PA)**	2084	E	805 238-4112	2194
Iqms LLC **(HQ)**	7372	C	805 227-1122	17894
J & L Vineyards	0172	D	559 268-1627	48
J Lohr Winery Corporation	2084	E	805 239-8900	2196
James Tobin Cellars Inc	2084	E	805 239-2204	2198
JIT Manufacturing Inc	3841	E	805 238-5000	10998
Joslyn Sunbank Company LLC	3678	B	805 238-2840	9659
Justin Vineyards & Winery LLC **(DH)**	2084	E	805 238-6932	2199
Lakeshirts LLC	2395	E	805 239-1290	3157
Lowes Home Centers LLC	5031	C	805 602-9051	13225
Lvp Cy Paso Robles LLC	7011	E	805 239-9700	16548
Marsh Consulting Group	7389	D	239 433-5500	18587
Maxgen Energy Services LLC **(DH)**	4932	D	714 908-5266	12875
McGuire Grinding Inc	3599	F	805 238-9000	8683
McHem Inc **(PA)**	5169	D	541 913-7892	14787
Melissa Trinidad	2844	E	805 536-0954	5046
Mge Underground Inc	1794	D	805 238-3510	1601
Midnight Cellars Inc	2084	F	805 239-8904	2208
Minatronic Inc	3679	F	805 239-8864	9751
Navajo Concrete Inc	3273	F	805 238-0955	6103
News Media Inc	2711	F	805 237-6060	4014
Niner Wine Estates LLC	2084	E	805 239-2233	2210
Oxigenesis Inc	2086	F	805 549-0275	2276
Paso Robles Inn LLC	7011	D	805 238-2660	16624
Paso Robles Tank Inc **(HQ)**	3312	D	805 227-1641	6208
Pearce Services LLC **(HQ)**	8748	E	805 467-2528	23493
Pic Manufacturing Inc	3555	F	805 238-5451	7924
Pro Document Solutions Inc **(PA)**	2752	E	805 238-6680	4406
Rabbit Ridge Wine Sales Inc **(PA)**	2084	F	661 877-7525	2215
Ravine Waterpark LLC	7996	C	805 237-8500	19523
Rbz Vineyards LLC	2084	E	805 542-0133	2216
Smart & Final Stores Inc	5141	C	805 237-0323	14497
Souriau Usa Inc **(DH)**	3643	E	805 238-2840	9046
Summerwood Winery & Inn Inc	7011	E	805 227-1365	16735
Sylvester Winery Inc	2084	F	805 227-4000	2225
Tablas Creek Vineyard LLC	2084	F	805 237-1231	2226
Tooth and Nail Winery	2084	F	805 369-6100	2231
Treana Winery LLC	2084	E	805 237-2932	2232
Trelleborg Sealing Solutions	3841	D	805 239-4284	11068
Volt Management Corp	7363	D	805 237-0882	17523
Wine Wrangler Inc	2084	F	805 238-5700	2240
Worldwind Services LLC	1731	A	661 822-4877	1339

PATTON, CA - San Bernardino County

	SIC	EMP	PHONE	ENTRY #
State Hospitals Cal Dept	8063	B	909 425-7000	21028

PEARBLOSSOM, CA - Los Angeles County

	SIC	EMP	PHONE	ENTRY #
Vulcan Construction Mtls LLC	3273	F	661 810-2285	6125

Mergent email: customerrelations@mergent.com
1414
2022 Southern California Business
Directory and Buyers Guide
(P-0000) Products & Services Section entry number
(PA)=Parent Co (HQ)=Headquarters (DH)=Div Headquarters

PERRIS, CA - Riverside County

	SIC	EMP	PHONE	ENTRY #
AAA Pallet Recycling & Mfg Inc	2448	E	951 681-7748	3380
Accu-Blend Corporation	2911	F	626 334-7744	5247
Alpha Corporation of Tennessee	2821	C	951 657-5161	4677
American Coffee Urn Mfg Co Inc	3444	F	951 943-1495	6783
Aoc LLC	2295	D	951 657-5161	2705
Avalon Shutters Inc	2431	C	909 937-4900	3233
Axxis Corporation	3599	E	951 436-9921	8510
Big Lgue Dreams Consulting LLC	7941	D	619 846-8855	19409
California Composite Cont Corp	2655	F	951 940-9343	3833
California Truss Company **(PA)**	2439	C	951 657-7491	3359
Coreslab Structures La Inc	3272	C	951 943-9119	6025
Craftech Metal Forming Inc	3441	E	951 940-6444	6608
Dropzone Waterpark	7999	C	951 210-1600	19644
Eastern Municipal Water Dst **(PA)**	4941	B	951 928-3777	12889
Eastern Municipal Water Dst	4941	C	951 657-7469	12890
Eci Water Ski Products Inc	3949	E	951 940-9999	11414
Eldorado Stone LLC	5032	A	951 601-3838	13303
Genesis Supreme Rv Inc **(PA)**	3799	E	951 337-0254	10551
Global Plastics Inc	5093	C	951 657-5466	14115
Goldstar Asphalt Products Inc	2951	E	951 940-1610	5272
Green Products Packaging Corp	2655	F	951 940-9343	3836
Grfco Inc	1623	D	951 657-8887	950
HB Parkco Construction Inc **(PA)**	1771	B	714 567-4752	1528
Herca Telecomm Services Inc	5082	D	951 940-5941	13861
Iherb LLC **(PA)**	5122	A	951 616-3600	14251
Inland Truss Inc **(PA)**	2439	D	951 300-1758	3366
Integrity Rebar Placers	1791	C	951 696-6843	1571
J & R Concrete Products Inc	3272	E	951 943-5855	6036
Jeff Carpenter Inc	1794	D	951 657-5115	1599
Kindred Healthcare LLC	8062	C	951 436-3535	20827
Mamco Inc **(PA)**	1611	C	951 776-9300	899
National Retail Trnsp Inc	4213	D	951 243-6110	12066
Navigator Yachts and Pdts Inc	3732	E	951 657-2117	10469
Npg Inc **(PA)**	2951	D	951 940-0200	5275
Pacific Coachworks Inc	3792	C	951 686-7294	10545
Pacific Hydrotech Corporation	8711	C	951 943-8803	22628
Pacific Restoration Group Inc	0781	E	951 940-6069	274
Parkco Building Company	1542	D	714 444-1441	800
Perris Valley AVI Svcs Inc	7363	D	951 657-3904	17506
Perris Valley Cmnty Hosp LLC **(PA)**	8062	C	951 436-5000	20887
Pw Eagle Inc	3084	B	951 657-7400	5471
R-Cold Inc	3585	D	951 436-5476	8346
Silver Creek Industries LLC	1542	C	951 943-5393	828
Soco Group Inc	5172	D	951 657-2350	14807
Spaulding Equipment Company **(PA)**	3532	E	951 943-4531	7663
Star Milling Co	2048	C	951 657-3143	1975
Stearns Product Dev Corp **(PA)**	3569	D	951 657-0379	8140
Stretch Forming Corporation	3444	D	951 443-0911	6921
Stronghold Engineering Inc **(PA)**	1542	D	951 684-9303	834
Timmons Wood Products Inc	2499	E	951 940-4700	3456
Village Nurseries Whl LLC	5193	B	951 657-3940	14899
Walters Wholesale Electric Co	5063	F	951 943-7708	13675
West Coast Yamaha Inc	3568	E	951 943-2061	8110
White House Sanitation Inc	7699	D	951 943-1550	19084

PICO RIVERA, CA - Los Angeles County

	SIC	EMP	PHONE	ENTRY #
Altamed Health Services Corp	8099	D	562 949-8717	21380
Aoclsc Inc	2992	C	813 248-1988	5287
Arnaco Industrial Coatings	3479	E	562 222-1022	7346
Aurora World Inc	5092	C	562 205-1222	14092
Axxion USA Inc	3086	F	213 622-3717	5491
Bakemark USA LLC **(PA)**	2045	A	562 949-1054	1950
Bay Cities Container Corp **(PA)**	2653	C	562 948-3751	3785
Bms Healthcare Inc	8099	C	562 942-7019	21392
C&O Manufacturing Company Inc	3444	D	562 692-7525	6800
CD Container Inc	2653	D	562 948-1910	3792
Chalmers Corporation	1541	D	562 948-4850	692
Coastal Container Inc	2653	E	562 801-4595	3794
Coastwide Tag & Label Co Inc	2759	E	323 721-1501	4498
Cordovan & Grey Ltd	2325	E	562 699-8300	2768
Delta T Thermal Solutions	3567	F	800 928-5828	8087
Endpak Packaging Inc	2674	D	562 801-0281	3896
Fedex Office & Print Svcs Inc	4215	D	562 942-1953	12134
Feit Electric Company Inc **(PA)**	3645	C	562 463-2852	9063
GPde Slva Spces Incrporation **(PA)**	2099	E	562 407-2643	2447
Heath Consultants Incorporated	8748	C	562 942-0315	23447
Herb Thyme Farm Inc	0139	D	603 542-3690	8
Jkv Inc	2653	E	562 948-3000	3814
Kater-Crafts Incorporated	2789	E	562 692-0665	4618
Krikorian Premiere Theatre LLC	7832	D	562 205-3456	19282
Lombard Enterprises Inc	2752	E	562 692-7070	4362
Lowes Home Centers LLC	5031	C	562 942-9909	13239
Manhole Adjusting Inc	1611	E	323 725-1387	900
Metal Tite Products **(PA)**	3442	D	562 695-0645	6709
Mixed Nuts Inc	2068	E	323 587-6887	2113
Mobile Money Inc **(HQ)**	6099	D	562 948-3916	15130
Montebello Orthpd Med Group	8011	D	562 654-6899	19989
Noble Rents Inc	7353	D	855 767-4424	17314
P-W Western Inc	3443	D	562 463-9055	6744
P-W Wiring Systems LLC	3678	F	562 463-9055	9663
Pacific Cast Fther Cushion LLC **(HQ)**	2392	C	562 801-9995	3111
Pacific Logistics Corp **(PA)**	4731	C	562 478-4700	12499
Palace Textile Inc	3552	D	323 587-7756	7911
Pattern Knitting Mills Inc	2253	E	310 801-1126	2640
Porta - Kan Sanitation Inc **(PA)**	4953	C	562 463-8282	12966
Precision Deburring Services	3541	E	562 944-4497	7739
Procases Inc	2441	F	323 585-4447	3379
Reeve Store Equipment Company **(PA)**	2542	D	562 949-2535	3694
Rivera Sanitarium Inc	8051	D	562 949-2591	20447
Riviera Nursing & Conva	8051	C	562 806-2576	20450
Ros Electrical Sup Eqp Co LLC	5063	E	562 695-9000	13666
Sectran Security Incorporated **(PA)**	7381	C	562 948-1446	18321
Sharpdots LLC	3577	F	626 599-9696	8302
Showroom Interiors LLC	7359	C	323 348-1551	17372
Spiral Ppr Tube & Core Co Inc	2655	E	562 801-9705	3840
Suez Wts Services Usa Inc	3589	D	562 942-2200	8420
Three Sons Inc	5147	D	562 801-4100	14608
Tube Bending LLC	3498	F	562 692-5829	7546
Unisource Solutions Inc **(PA)**	5021	C	562 654-3500	13153
United Pacific Waste	4953	D	562 699-7600	12986
W P Keith Co Inc	3567	E	562 948-3636	8101
Whittier Fertilizer Company	2873	D	562 699-3461	5162

PIRU, CA - Ventura County

	SIC	EMP	PHONE	ENTRY #
La Verne Nursery Inc	0181	D	805 521-0111	82
Tesoro Refining & Mktg Co LLC	5172	D	805 521-0615	14811

PISMO BEACH, CA - San Luis Obispo County

	SIC	EMP	PHONE	ENTRY #
Cliffs Resort LLC	7299	E	805 773-5000	16949
Pacific Gas and Electric Co	4911	C	805 546-5267	12819
Pismo Beach Ht Investments LLC	7011	E	805 773-1011	16632
Pismo Coast Village Inc	7011	D	805 773-1811	16633
Seacrest Oceanfront Hotel	7011	D	805 773-4608	16699
Tic Hotels Inc	7011	D	805 773-4671	16754

PIXLEY, CA - Tulare County

	SIC	EMP	PHONE	ENTRY #
California Dairies Inc	5143	C	559 752-5200	14538
Correa Pallet Inc **(PA)**	2448	E	559 757-1790	3384
CT Commodities Inc	6221	D	559 757-3996	15314
Gfp Ethanol LLC	2869	E	559 757-3850	5137
Robert D Vandereyk	0241	D	559 909-3195	136

PLACENTIA, CA - Orange County

	SIC	EMP	PHONE	ENTRY #
Adaptive Engrg Fabrication Inc	8711	F	714 854-1300	22476
Alta Vista Country Club LLC	7997	D	714 524-1591	19529
Altinex Inc	3663	E	714 990-0877	9251
Alva Manufacturing Inc	3728	E	714 237-0925	10267
Anderson Bat Company LLC	3949	D	714 524-7500	11402
Arlon Graphics LLC	3081	C	714 985-6300	5426
Atlas Match LLC	3999	D	714 993-3328	11635
Auger Industries Inc	3599	F	714 577-9350	8506
Bejac Corporation **(PA)**	5084	D	714 528-6224	13890
Bestest International	3823	E	714 974-8837	10680
Bioplate Inc	3841	E	310 815-2100	10948
Bioseal	3841	E	714 528-4695	10949
Caldigit Inc	3572	F	714 572-6668	8189
Cinton Inc	2672	E	714 961-8808	3868
City Service Contracting Inc **(PA)**	1611	D	714 632-6610	873
Coast Aerospace Mfg Inc	3544	E	714 893-8066	7789
Crd Mfg Inc	3429	E	714 871-3300	6513
Customline Professional	7336	B	714 996-1333	17169
Detectors Incorporated	3669	F	714 982-5350	9338
Eclectic Printing & Design LLC	2759	F	714 528-8040	4512
Eisel Enterprises Inc	3272	E	714 993-1706	6029
Elljay Acoustics Inc	1742	D	714 961-1173	1374
Excello Circuits Inc	3672	E	714 993-0560	9402
Facility Solutions Group Inc	5063	D	714 993-3966	13630
GD Heil Inc	1795	C	714 687-9100	1614
Gerard Roof Products LLC **(DH)**	3444	D	714 529-0407	6844
Hai Advnced Mtl Spcialists Inc	3479	F	714 414-0575	7371
Hardy Window Company **(PA)**	5031	C	714 996-1807	13213
Hartwell Corporation **(DH)**	3429	C	714 993-4200	6520
High Five Inc	2752	F	714 847-2200	4316
Industrial Metal Finishing Inc	3471	E	714 628-8808	7269
Interface Rehab Inc	8049	A	714 646-8300	20223
J B Tool Inc	3599	F	714 993-7173	8636
Kaiser Foundation Hospitals	6324	C	714 572-5700	15437
Kipe Molds Inc	3544	F	714 572-9576	7811
L & M Machining Corporation	3678	D	714 414-0923	9660
Label Specialties Inc	2759	E	714 961-8074	4531
Las Colinas	3589	F	714 528-8100	8391
Linda Yorba Water District **(PA)**	4941	D	714 701-3000	12900
Microplex Inc	3674	F	714 630-8220	9540
Moehair Usa Inc	2844	F	888 663-7032	5048
Nalco Wtr Prtrtment Sltons LLC	3589	E	714 792-0708	8400
Nelson Case Corporation	2441	F	714 528-2215	3378
Orange Vise Company LLC	3545	F	714 482-3952	7860
P5 Graphics and Displays Inc	7336	E	714 808-1645	17182
Packers Food Products Inc	2037	E	913 262-6200	1907
Pittman Products Intl Inc	3089	F	562 926-6660	5746
Power Pros Racg Exhust Systems	3714	F	714 777-3278	10114
Quikturn Prof Scrnprinting Inc	2759	F	800 784-5419	4562
Richfield Engineering Inc	3443	E	714 524-3741	6749
Roll Along Vans Inc	3714	E	714 528-9600	10128
Roman Cthlic Diocese of Orange	7389	C	714 528-1794	18655
Rotech Engineering Inc	3679	E	714 632-0532	9775
Sapphire Chandelier LLC	3646	D	714 879-3660	9102
Sapphire Clean Rooms LLC **(PA)**	5049	C	714 316-5036	13540
Sapphire Manufacturing Inc	3446	E	714 401-3117	6979
SGF Produce Holding Corp	5148	F	714 630-6292	14653
Southern Cal Tchnical Arts Inc	3599	E	714 524-2626	8798
Spyder Manufacturing Inc	3524	F	714 528-8010	7631
Tct Circuit Supply Inc	5085	D	714 644-9700	14022
Tenet Healthsystem Medical Inc	8069	D	714 993-2000	21055

Employment Codes: A=Over 500 employees, B=251-500, C=101-250, D=51-100, E=20-50 F=10-19
2022 Southern California Business Directory and Buyers Guide
© Mergent Inc. 1-800-342-5647
1415

	SIC	EMP	PHONE	ENTRY #
United Service Tech Inc.	7699	D	714 224-1406	19079
US Computers Inc	3577	F	714 528-0514	8309
Vanderveer Industrial Plas LLC	3089	E	714 579-7700	5857
Vita-Herb Nutriceuticals Inc	2834	E	714 632-3726	4909
West Coast Metal Stamping Inc	3469	E	714 792-0322	7194
Worksite Labs Inc	8734	D	657 444-9146	22962

PLAYA DEL REY, CA - Los Angeles County

	SIC	EMP	PHONE	ENTRY #
Automate Parking Inc	7521	D	310 674-3396	18764
Chipton-Ross Inc	3721	D	310 414-7800	10182
Los Angeles Dept Wtr & Pwr	4939	B	310 524-8500	12878
Parking Concepts Inc	7521	C	310 322-5008	18776
Sheer Design Inc **(PA)**	2844	E	310 306-2121	5070

PLAYA VISTA, CA - Los Angeles County

	SIC	EMP	PHONE	ENTRY #
72andsunny Midco LLC	7311	A	310 215-9009	16989
AF Technology LLC	7371	E	310 361-5710	17543
Avongard Products USA Ltd	7819	E	310 319-2300	19220
Belkin Inc	3651	C	800 223-5546	9163
Belkin International Inc **(DH)**	3577	B	310 751-5100	8238
Chownow Inc	7372	D	888 707-2469	17815
Cpl Holdings LLC	6719	C	310 348-6800	16097
Foxnext Games LLC **(PA)**	7371	C	424 222-5889	17619
Fullscreen Inc **(DH)**	7311	C	310 202-3333	17013
Gehry Technologies Inc **(HQ)**	7371	D	310 862-1200	17624
Lee Burkhart Liu Inc	8712	D	310 829-2249	22728
Linksys LLC	5065	C	310 751-5100	13743
Linksys Usa Inc	5065	D	310 751-5100	13745
Lmb Opco LLC	6163	B	310 348-6800	15245
Ordermark Inc	7374	D	833 673-3762	18103
Phelps Group	7311	E	310 752-4400	17045
Pop Media Networks LLC **(DH)**	7929	C	323 856-4000	19374
Ryot Corp	7336	D	323 356-1787	17186
Tcg Capital Management LP	6799	C	310 633-2900	16295

PLS VRDS PNSL, CA - Los Angeles County

	SIC	EMP	PHONE	ENTRY #
Converging Systems Inc	3577	F	310 544-2628	8246
Episcopal Communities & Servic	8051	D	310 544-2204	20336
Palos Vrdes Fmly Immdate Med C	8062	E	310 541-7911	20883
Rolling Hills Vineyard Inc	2084	E	310 541-5098	2217

POMONA, CA - Los Angeles County

	SIC	EMP	PHONE	ENTRY #
A/C Folding Gates Inc	3446	F	909 629-3026	6946
Able Iron Works	3441	E	909 397-5300	6578
Acratech Inc	3599	F	909 392-7522	8466
Adame Insurance Services Inc	8721	E	909 620-7098	22758
Aetco Inc	2499	F	909 593-2521	3435
Air Cleaning Systems Inc	3564	F	909 620-7114	8040
Akash Management LLC	8742	A	805 672-2889	23149
Alere San Diego Inc	2835	F	909 482-0840	4917
Als Group Inc	5072	E	909 622-7555	13793
America Metal Mfg Resources	3724	E	909 620-4500	10212
American Rotary Broom Co Inc	3991	E	909 629-9117	11507
Analytical Industries Inc	3823	E	909 392-6900	10676
Atr Technologies Incorporated	3446	F	909 399-9724	6951
Aw Industries Inc	2511	F	909 629-1500	3463
Bell Technologies Inc	5045	F	909 598-1006	13379
Bestway Recycling Company Inc **(PA)**	4953	D	323 588-8157	12931
Bio Cybernetics International	3842	F	909 447-7050	11090
Boom Industrial Inc	3559	D	909 495-3555	7967
Bragel International Inc	2342	E	909 598-8808	3020
Braun Linen Service	7211	E	909 623-2678	16836
Bright Glow Candle Company Inc **(PA)**	3999	E	909 469-4733	11640
Ca-WA Corp	3069	F	909 868-0630	5368
Cal Poly Pomona Foundation Inc	8351	A	909 869-2284	21992
California Acrylic Inds Inc **(HQ)**	3999	B	909 623-8781	11646
California Plastix Inc	2673	E	909 629-8288	3879
Camlever Inc	3531	E	909 629-9669	7637
Cape Robbin Inc	5139	E	626 810-8080	14431
Casa Clina Cmprhnsive Otptent	8093	D	909 596-7733	21282
Casa Colina Inc **(PA)**	8322	A	909 596-7733	21731
Casa Colina Hospital and Cente **(HQ)**	8062	B	909 596-7733	20693
Casa Herrera Inc **(PA)**	3556	C	909 392-3930	7930
Centrescapes Inc	0782	D	909 392-3303	296
CFI Holdings Corp	3324	D	909 595-2252	6265
Commercial Door Company Inc	1751	D	714 529-2179	1431
Continental Agency Inc **(PA)**	4731	D	909 595-8884	12439
Cooltec Refrigeration Corp	3585	E	909 865-2229	8334
Copp Industrial Mfg Inc	3444	E	909 593-7448	6812
County of Los Angeles	7992	D	909 231-0549	19481
Covenant Transport Inc	4213	A	909 469-0130	12026
Da-Ly Glass Corp	3231	E	323 589-5461	5951
De Larshe Cabinetry LLC	2431	E	909 627-2757	3242
Dedicated Fleet Systems Inc **(PA)**	4212	D	909 590-8209	11964
Delphi Control Systems Inc	3823	F	909 593-8099	10689
Desiccare Inc	3295	E	909 444-8272	6166
DOT Blue Safes Corporation	3499	E	909 445-8888	7554
Dow Hydraulic Systems Inc	3599	D	909 596-6602	8574
Eastman Music Company **(PA)**	5099	D	909 868-1777	14154
Electrocube Inc **(PA)**	3679	D	909 595-1821	9707
Elite Stone & Cabinet Inc	2434	F	909 629-6988	3318
Equipment Design & Mfg Inc	3444	D	909 594-2229	6827
Especial T Hvac Shtmtl Fttngs	5075	E	909 869-9150	13842
Essential Pharmaceutical Corp	2834	E	909 623-4565	4817
Fairplex Child Development Ctr	8351	D	909 623-3899	22013
Fairplex Enterprises Inc	7999	D	909 623-3111	19646
FDS Manufacturing Company **(PA)**	2679	D	909 591-1733	3929
Federated Diversified Sls Inc	2671	D	909 591-1733	3853
Ferguson Fire Fabrication Inc **(DH)**	5074	D	909 517-3085	13827
First Baptist Church Pomona **(PA)**	8351	D	909 629-5277	22016
Frank S Smith Masonry Inc	1741	D	909 468-0525	1343
Furniture Trnsp Systems Inc	4731	C	909 869-1200	12459
G Powell Electric	7694	E	909 865-2291	19012
Gemini Aluminum Corporation	3354	E	909 595-7403	6308
Global Rental Co Inc	7353	C	909 469-5160	17309
Golden Grove Trading Inc	2759	F	909 718-8000	4521
Gonzalez Feliciano	2431	F	909 236-1372	3252
Gould & Bass Company Inc	3825	E	909 623-6793	10755
Henkels & McCoy Inc	1623	B	909 517-3011	952
Holland & Herring Mfg Inc	3599	E	909 469-4700	8621
Hospitalist Corp Inland Empire	8062	D	909 398-1550	20795
Howard Roofing Company Inc	1761	D	909 622-5598	1488
Image Distribution Services	2752	F	909 599-7680	4321
In House Custom Decals	2759	F	909 613-1403	4527
Inca Pallets Supply Inc	2448	E	909 622-1414	3395
Industrial Design Products Inc	3537	E	909 468-0693	7710
Injen Technology Company Ltd	5075	E	909 839-0706	13847
Inland Envelope Company	2677	D	909 622-2016	3909
Inland Valley Partners LLC	8049	C	909 623-7100	20217
Inter Valley Health Plan Inc	6324	D	909 623-6333	15400
Inter Valley Pool Supply Inc	5091	D	626 969-5657	14080
Interntonal Super Sensors Corp	3829	F	909 590-5054	10891
J&E Private Security Corp	7381	D	909 594-1111	18290
JES Disc Grinding Inc	3479	F	909 596-3823	7378
K-Max Health Products Corp	2834	E	909 455-0158	4836
K-Max Health Products Internat	2023	F	909 455-0158	1796
Kc Pharmaceuticals Inc **(PA)**	2834	D	909 598-9499	4839
Kelly & Thome	3599	F	909 623-2559	8653
Kittrich Corporation **(PA)**	2591	C	714 736-1000	3712
Kkw Trucking Inc **(PA)**	4225	C	909 869-1200	12215
KP Concrete & Steel Inc	1771	F	909 461-4163	1536
L & H Mold & Engineering Inc **(PA)**	3089	E	909 930-1547	5694
Landmark Medical Services Inc	8063	D	909 593-2585	21024
Latara Enterprise Inc **(PA)**	8071	C	909 623-9301	21074
Lereta LLC **(PA)**	6211	B	626 543-1765	15274
Lexmar Distribution Inc	4213	E	909 620-7001	12061
Lippert Components Mfg Inc	3231	E	909 628-5557	5962
Lock-Ridge Tool Company Inc	3469	D	909 865-8309	7161
Los Angeles County Fair Assn **(PA)**	7999	D	909 623-3111	19654
Los Pericos Food Products LLC	2099	E	909 623-5625	2476
Luxor Industries International	2431	E	909 469-4757	3264
M & M Service	3444	F	909 802-2050	6865
Maxim Healthcare Services Inc	7363	D	626 962-6453	17504
McPrint Corp	2752	F	714 632-9966	4369
Med-Pharmex Inc	2834	C	909 593-7875	4852
Merchants Building Maint Co	7349	D	909 622-8260	17262
Mesa Associates Inc	8711	C	909 979-6609	22609
Mil-Spec Magnetics Inc	3677	E	909 598-8116	9635
Mission Series Inc	5122	E	714 736-1000	14264
Mitchell Processing LLC	3069	E	909 519-5759	5392
Murcor Inc	6531	C	909 623-4001	15930
Natural Envmtl Protection Co	2821	E	909 620-8028	4702
Numatech West (kmp) LLC	2653	D	909 706-3627	3822
NW Packaging LLC **(PA)**	5199	D	909 706-3627	14958
Ormco Corporation	3843	B	714 516-7400	11183
Pacific Wtrprfing Rstrtion Inc	2899	E	909 444-3052	5237
Performance Engineered Pdts	3089	E	909 594-7487	5742
Performnce Engineered Pdts Inc	3089	D	909 594-7487	5743
PHD Marketing Inc	5199	D	909 620-1000	14965
Phenix Enterprises Inc **(PA)**	3713	E	909 469-0411	9994
Pomona Community Health Center	8621	D	909 630-7927	22276
Pomona Quality Foam LLC	3086	D	909 628-7844	5517
Pomona Valley Hospital Med Ctr **(PA)**	8062	A	909 865-9500	20898
Precision Pwdred Met Parts Inc	3399	E	909 595-5656	6461
Premiere Medical Group	8011	D	909 469-9498	20025
Progressive Converting Inc	2679	F	909 392-2201	3935
Qnap Inc	8731	D	909 598-6933	22859
Quality Container Corp	2671	F	909 482-1850	3857
Quinn Company	3523	F	838 987-8466	7616
R & S Automation Inc	3442	E	800 962-3111	6714
R & S Mfg Southern Cal Inc	3442	F	909 596-2090	6715
Radian Audio Engineering Inc	3663	E	714 288-8900	9311
Ramcast Ornamental Sup Co Inc	5051	E	909 469-4767	13586
Rbf Group International	2521	F	626 333-5700	3598
RD Metal Polishing Inc	3471	F	909 594-8393	7305
Real Plating Inc	3471	E	909 623-2304	7306
Regal Cultured Marble Inc	3281	F	909 802-2388	6142
ROC-Aire Corp	3599	E	909 784-3385	8774
Ronford Products Inc	3089	E	909 622-7446	5798
Roofline Supply SRS Dist	5033	D	909 623-8191	13328
Royal Cabinets Inc	2434	A	909 629-8565	3333
Royal Industries Inc	2434	C	909 629-8565	3334
Rwp Transfer Inc	5099	E	909 868-6882	14181
San Gbrl/Pmona Vlleys Dvlpmnta	8322	B	909 620-7722	21885
Silpak Inc **(PA)**	2821	F	909 625-0056	4716
Sky One Inc	3262	F	909 622-3333	5994
Southern Cal Rgional Rail Auth	4111	C	213 808-7043	11842
Southern Cal Trck Bdies Sls In	3713	F	909 469-1132	9996
Southern California Edison Co	4911	C	909 274-1925	12838
Southern California Edison Co	4911	C	909 469-0251	12843
Specialty Car Wash System	3589	F	909 869-6300	8416
Spectra Company	1741	C	909 599-0760	1353
Spiniello Companies	1623	C	909 629-1000	974
Stainless Fixtures Inc	2599	E	909 622-1615	3740
Starwood Htls & Rsrts Wrldwde	7011	C	909 622-2220	16731

Mergent email: customerrelations@mergent.com
1416
2022 Southern California Business Directory and Buyers Guide
(P-0000) Products & Services Section entry number
(PA)=Parent Co (HQ)=Headquarters (DH)=Div Headquarters

	SIC	EMP	PHONE	ENTRY #
Structural Composites Inds LLC **(HQ)**	3443	C	909 594-7777	6756
Superior Duct Fabrication Inc	3444	C	909 620-8565	6922
T & T Box Company Inc	2657	E	909 465-0848	3846
t McGee Electric Inc	1731	D	909 591-6461	1326
Travelers Choice Travelware	3161	D	909 529-7688	5898
Traxx Corporation	3999	D	909 623-8032	11783
Tree Island Wire (usa) Inc	3315	C	909 595-6617	6238
Tri-City Mental Health Auth **(PA)**	8093	D	909 623-6131	21356
Tri-J Metal Heat Treating Co **(PA)**	3398	F	909 622-9999	6456
Trussworks International Inc	3441	D	714 630-2772	6674
Ultimate Removal Inc	1521	C	909 524-0800	646
Urocare Products Inc	3069	F	909 621-6013	5417
Valley Metal Treating Inc	3398	E	909 623-6316	6457
Valley Tool and Machine Co Inc	3599	E	909 595-2205	8836
Vefo Inc	3086	E	909 598-3856	5527
W Why W Enterprises Inc	4214	D	626 969-4292	12121
Weiser Iron Inc	3441	E	909 429-4600	6682
Westcoast Brush Mfg Inc	3991	E	909 627-7170	11515
Western Converting Spc Inc	2759	E	909 392-4578	4593
Western Univ Hlth Sciences	8011	D	909 865-2565	20162
Whitefield Medical Lab Inc **(PA)**	8071	E	909 625-2114	21102
Woodmill Seating Inc	2431	F	909 622-1615	3301
World Trend Inc **(PA)**	3991	F	909 620-9945	11516
Yamamoto of Orient Inc **(HQ)**	6512	C	909 594-7356	15714
Yawitz Inc	3645	E	909 865-5599	9075
Yf Manufacture Inc	3269	F	626 768-0029	6007
Yoshimasa Display Case Inc	2541	E	213 637-9999	3672

PORT HUENEME, CA - Ventura County

	SIC	EMP	PHONE	ENTRY #
Advantedge Technology Inc	8711	D	805 488-0405	22478
Brusco Tug & Barge Inc	4492	C	805 986-1600	12295
Global Auto Proc Svcs Inc **(PA)**	7549	D	805 382-9601	18934
N S Haas Inc	2521	F	805 874-1155	3590
Pac Foundries Inc	3369	C	805 488-6451	6419
Pac Foundries Inc	3366	C	805 986-1308	6410
Windsor Capital Group Inc	7011	D	805 986-5353	16799

PORTER RANCH, CA - Los Angeles County

	SIC	EMP	PHONE	ENTRY #
American Technical Svcs Inc	8711	D	951 372-9664	22485
Beverly Bay Inc **(PA)**	2399	F	818 852-2408	3191
Broker Solutions Inc	6153	D	818 235-0640	15151
Cyberpolicy Inc	6411	C	877 626-9991	15559
Design Todays Inc **(PA)**	2339	E	213 745-3091	2939
Infogen Labs Inc	7379	D	818 825-5024	18186
Leather In Chicago	5199	F	818 349-3456	14947

PORTERVILLE, CA - Tulare County

	SIC	EMP	PHONE	ENTRY #
Bank of Sierra **(HQ)**	6022	C	559 782-4300	15011
Best Western Porterville Inn	7011	D	559 781-7411	16344
Developmental Svcs Cal Dept	8051	A	559 782-2222	20313
Distributors Processing Inc	2087	F	559 781-0297	2320
E M Tharp Inc **(PA)**	5012	D	559 782-5800	13024
Eagle Mountain Casino	7011	C	559 788-6220	16424
Endurequest Corporation	3089	E	559 783-9220	5640
Exeter Packers Inc	0723	C	559 784-8820	168
Family Healthcare Network	8011	C	559 781-7242	19815
Fern Oaks Frms A Cal Gen Prtnr	0241	E	559 684-8220	132
Foster Farms LLC	0252	E	559 793-5501	139
Foster Poultry Farms	2015	B	559 793-5501	1757
Fruit Growers Supply Company	2653	E	559 783-6383	3803
Lowes Home Centers LLC	5031	C	559 306-5000	13271
Moyles Centl Vly Hlth Care Inc	8051	D	559 782-1509	20421
Noticiero Semanal Advertising	2711	F	559 784-5000	4018
Porterville Concrete Pipe Inc	3272	E	559 784-6187	6049
Porterville Dialysis Center	8092	B	559 781-5551	21259
Sierra View Dst Hosp Leag Inc **(PA)**	8011	A	559 784-1110	20066
Tdg Operations LLC	2281	D	559 781-4116	2702
Tharp Truck Rental Inc **(PA)**	7699	C	559 782-5800	19078
Tule River Economic Dev	8748	D	559 781-4271	23520
Tule River Indian Hlth Ctr Inc	8093	D	559 784-2316	21358
Valley Careidence Opco LLC	8051	D	559 784-8371	20494
Wescordon Incorporated **(PA)**	8051	D	559 784-8371	20504

RANCHO CUCAMONGA, CA - San Bernardino County

	SIC	EMP	PHONE	ENTRY #
Adrianas Insurance LLC	6411	D	909 291-4040	15527
Adrianas Insurance Svcs Inc **(PA)**	6411	C	909 291-4040	15528
Advantage Adhesives Inc	2891	E	909 204-4990	5177
Agent Franchise LLC	6321	C	949 930-5025	15374
Air Components Inc	3728	E	909 980-8224	10258
Alcoa Fastening Systems	3965	D	909 483-2333	11493
All Spec Welding Solutions	7692	F	909 794-4828	18969
All Star Precision	3599	E	909 944-8373	8487
Allmark Inc **(PA)**	6531	D	909 989-7556	15767
Aloft Ontario-Rancho Cucamonga	7011	D	909 484-2018	16317
American De Rosa Lamparts LLC	1541	D	800 777-4440	687
AMP Display Inc **(PA)**	8711	E	909 980-1310	22487
Amphastar Pharmaceuticals Inc **(PA)**	2834	C	909 980-9484	4783
Aquamar Inc	2091	C	909 481-4700	2340
Arga Controls Inc	3823	F	626 799-3314	10677
Arrowhead Central Credit Union **(PA)**	6061	B	866 212-4333	15059
Artic Mechanical Inc **(PA)**	1711	D	909 980-2539	1031
Atlas Testing Laboratories Inc	8734	E	909 373-4130	22930
Automobile Club Southern Cal	8699	D	909 477-8600	22396
Automobile Club Southern Cal	6411	D	909 980-0233	15544
Bas Engineering Inc	8711	F	909 484-2575	22498
Bernell Hydraulics Inc **(PA)**	3594	E	909 899-1751	8442
Bowlero Corp	7933	D	909 945-9392	19393
Bradshaw International Inc **(HQ)**	5023	B	909 476-3884	13161
Branlyn Prominence Inc **(PA)**	8082	D	909 476-9030	21141
Brownwood Furniture Inc	2511	C	909 945-5613	3466
Bunzl Retail Services LLC	5113	D	909 476-2457	14205
Butler America Holdings Inc	7361	C	909 417-3660	17401
Butler Home Products LLC	3991	C	909 476-3884	11509
California Box II	2653	E	909 944-9202	3791
Cargill Meat Solutions Corp	2011	B	909 476-3120	1708
Case Paper Company	5113	F	626 358-8450	14207
CDM Constructors Inc	8711	D	909 579-3500	22513
Celestica LLC	8711	B	909 201-3995	22514
Cerenzia Foods Inc	5141	D	909 989-4000	14459
Charter Mgmt LLC	8741	D	909 644-4965	23001
Chick Publications Inc	2731	E	909 987-0771	4123
Ciuti International Inc	2079	F	909 484-1414	2129
CMC Steel Us LLC	3449	F	909 646-7827	7018
Collection Technology Inc	7322	D	800 743-4284	17107
Continental Graphics Corp	2752	D	909 758-9800	4261
Creu LLC	3089	E	909 483-4888	5618
Criticalpoint Capital LLC	2822	D	909 987-9533	4731
Crossroads Eqp Lease & Fin LLC	5046	D	909 291-6400	13455
CU Cooperative Systems Inc **(PA)**	6062	B	909 948-2500	15110
Cucamonga Valley Water Dst	4941	D	909 987-2591	12886
David L Manwarren Corp	1542	E	909 989-5883	758
Davidson Optronics Inc	3829	E	626 962-5181	10877
Directcnnect Lgal Slutions Inc	8111	E	888 685-7771	21548
Distribution Alternatives Inc	4225	D	909 746-5600	12200
Diverse Optics Inc	3089	E	909 593-9330	5627
Doubleco Incorporated	3452	D	909 481-0799	7062
Dow Chemical Co Foundation	2821	C	909 476-4127	4687
Durham School Services L P	4151	C	909 899-1809	11922
Eagle Labs LLC	3841	D	909 481-0011	10973
Eide Bailly LLP	8721	B	909 466-4410	22779
Electro Switch Corp	3613	E	909 581-0855	8896
Electro Switch Corp	3679	E	909 581-0855	9704
ES Kluft & Company Inc **(PA)**	2515	C	909 373-4211	3548
Everidge Inc	3585	D	909 605-6419	8339
Evolution Fresh Inc	5148	C	800 794-9986	14626
Executive Safe and SEC Corp	3499	E	909 947-7020	7557
Falken Tire Holdings Inc	5014	D	800 723-2553	13115
Fan Fave Inc	3993	E	909 975-4999	11554
Faust Printing Inc	2752	F	909 980-1577	4291
Firstsrvice Rsidential Cal Inc **(DH)**	6531	D	909 981-4131	15868
Firth Rixson Inc	3462	E	909 483-2200	7085
Fluorescent Supply Co Inc	3646	E	909 948-8878	9084
Formosa Meat Company Inc	2013	E	909 987-0470	1732
Fox Transportation Inc **(PA)**	8748	D	909 291-4646	23442
Frito-Lay North America Inc	5145	B	909 941-6214	14562
Frozen Bean Inc	2087	E	855 837-6936	2327
Gcn Supply LLC	3448	E	909 643-4603	6996
General Coatings Corporation	1721	D	909 204-4150	1180
General Micro Systems Inc **(PA)**	5045	D	909 980-4863	13401
Gentex Corporation	8731	D	909 481-7667	22841
Global Aerostructures	3728	F	909 987-4888	10339
Golden Island Jerky Co Inc **(DH)**	2013	E	844 362-3222	1733
Good-West Rubber Corp **(PA)**	3069	C	909 987-1774	5378
Goodwest Rubber Linings Inc	3069	E	888 499-0085	5379
Graham Packaging Co Europe LLC	3085	C	909 989-5367	5475
Greenpower Motor Company Inc	3711	E	909 308-0960	9952
Grove Diagnstc Imaging Ctr Inc	8011	A	909 982-8638	19835
Grove Diagnstc Imaging Ctr Inc **(DH)**	8011	E	909 982-8638	19836
H & A Transmissions Inc	7537	E	909 941-9020	18811
Handels Homemade Ice Cream	5149	E	909 989-7065	14693
Honeyville Inc	4221	D	909 980-9500	12171
Honeyville Grain Inc	2041	E	909 243-1050	1944
Horrigan Enterprises Inc	8322	C	909 481-9663	21805
Ifco Systems Us LLC	2448	D	909 484-4332	3394
In-Roads Creative Programs	8322	D	909 989-9944	21809
Infinity Svc Group Inc A Cal C	1711	D	909 466-6237	1084
Inland Empire Health Plan **(PA)**	6321	A	909 890-2000	15380
Innovative Displayworks Inc	5046	E	909 447-8254	13459
Innovative Technologies Group	3089	F	909 476-2555	5675
Intra Aerospace LLC	3599	E	909 476-0343	8628
Isec Incorporated	1522	D	714 761-5151	659
J B Hunt Transport Inc	4213	C	909 466-5361	12054
J Filippi Vintage Co **(PA)**	2084	F	909 899-5755	2195
J T Walker Industries Inc	3442	E	909 481-1909	6702
James Magna Ltd	7539	F	909 391-2025	18899
JCPM Inc	3599	E	909 484-9040	8641
Jet Cutting Solutions Inc	3599	E	909 948-2424	8642
Jones/Covey Group Incorporated	1799	D	888 972-7581	1669
Kaiser Foundation Hospitals	8011	C	562 658-3441	19883
Kaiser Foundation Hospitals	8011	C	888 750-0036	19885
Kaiser Foundation Hospitals	8011	C	909 988-0379	19925
Kathleen Brugger	7692	E	909 226-1372	18988
Kindred Litho Incorporated	2752	E	909 944-4015	4349
Kitchen Post Inc	2434	F	909 948-6768	3323
Knd Development 55 LLC	8062	D	909 581-6400	20831
La Rocque Better Roofs Inc	1761	D	909 476-2699	1494
Laird Construction Co Inc	1611	D	909 989-5595	896
Lanic Engineering Inc **(PA)**	3728	E	877 763-0411	10365
Ledesma & Meyer Cnstr Co Inc	1542	D	909 297-1100	782
Lee Maxton Inc	2752	F	909 483-0688	4355
Little People Pre-School	8351	D	909 989-2804	22028
Lowes Home Centers LLC	5031	C	909 476-9697	13220
Lur Inc	3446	F	909 623-4999	6974
M & G Jewelers Inc	3911	D	909 989-2929	11323
M-5 Steel Mfg Inc **(PA)**	3444	E	323 263-9383	6866

GEOGRAPHIC

Employment Codes: A=Over 500 employees, B=251-500, C=101-250, D=51-100, E=20-50 F=10-19
2022 Southern California Business Directory and Buyers Guide
© Mergent Inc. 1-800-342-5647
1417

	SIC	EMP	PHONE	ENTRY #
Machinehome Inc	5021	E	858 336-9471	13143
Marino Enterprises Inc	3728	E	909 476-0343	10372
Master Builders LLC	2899	A	909 987-1758	5230
McGuire Talent Inc	7922	D	909 527-7006	19324
McLane Foodservice Dist Inc	5147	D	909 484-6100	14599
Merchants Landscape Services	0781	C	909 981-1022	267
Mercury United Electronics Inc	3679	F	909 466-0427	9748
Metal Coaters California Inc	3479	D	909 987-4681	7388
Milky Mama LLC	2051	F	877 886-4559	2019
Mindrum Precision Inc	3824	E	909 989-1728	10739
Mizkan America Inc	2099	D	909 484-8743	2487
Modular Office Solutions Inc	2522	E	909 476-4200	3615
Monte Vista Child Care Ctr Inc **(PA)**	8351	D	909 544-0040	22036
Msblous LLC	4225	D	909 929-9689	12225
National Cmnty Renaissance Cal **(PA)**	6552	D	909 483-2444	16063
National Cmnty Rnssnce Dev Cor **(PA)**	7041	D	909 483-2444	16834
National Community Renaissance **(PA)**	6552	D	909 483-2444	16064
Nationwide Guard Services Inc	7381	B	909 608-1112	18301
Network Intgrtion Partners Inc	7373	D	909 919-2800	18051
New Legend Inc	4213	B	855 210-2300	12069
New World Medical Incorporated	3841	F	909 466-4304	11033
Newco Distributors Inc	5191	D	909 291-2240	14865
Newtex Industries Inc	3999	D	323 277-0900	11720
Nongshim America Inc **(HQ)**	5141	C	909 481-3698	14482
Norm Tessier Cabinets Inc	2434	F	909 987-8955	3328
Novatime Technology Inc **(HQ)**	7361	D	909 895-8100	17440
NRG California South LP	4911	D	909 899-7241	12810
OEM Parts Network Inc	3511	F	909 944-8030	7588
Pac-Rancho Inc **(DH)**	3324	C	909 987-4721	6273
Pacific Pprbd Converting LLC **(PA)**	2679	E	909 476-6466	3932
Packline USA LLC	3089	F	909 392-8000	5735
Pamco Machine Works Inc	3599	E	909 941-7260	8730
Paradigm Packaging East LLC	3089	E	909 985-2750	5737
Paramount Machine Co Inc	3599	E	909 484-3600	8732
Paramunt Plstic Fbricators Inc	3089	E	909 987-4757	5739
Penwal Industries Inc	1542	D	909 466-1555	806
Perimeter Solutions LP	2819	E	909 983-0772	4666
Phil Inter Pharma Usa Inc **(PA)**	2834	F	909 982-3670	4873
Pitbull Gym Incorporated	3089	F	909 980-7960	5745
Plaxicon Holding Corporation	3085	A	909 944-6868	5479
Pneudraulics Inc	3812	B	909 980-5366	10635
Precision Aerospace Corp	3728	D	909 945-9604	10394
Precision Pipeline LLC	1623	B	909 229-6858	966
Pres-Tek Plastics Inc **(PA)**	3089	D	909 360-1600	5776
Prestige Mold Incorporated	3544	D	909 980-6600	7827
Prime Converting Corporation	2679	E	909 476-9500	3934
Priority One Med Trnspt Inc **(PA)**	4119	D	909 948-4400	11886
Professnal Elec Cnstr Svcs Inc	1731	C	909 373-4100	1302
Proulx Manufacturing Inc	3089	E	909 980-0662	5784
Pyramid Mold & Tool	3544	E	909 476-2555	7829
Qst Ingredients and Packg Inc	2099	F	909 989-4343	2512
R M A Group **(PA)**	8711	D	909 980-6096	22643
Rachas Inc	7991	E	626 671-2440	19465
Rafco-Brickform LLC **(PA)**	3545	D	909 484-3399	7866
Rancho Ccamonga Cmnty Hosp LLC	8062	D	909 581-6400	20921
Rancho Pacific Electric Inc	1731	E	909 476-1022	1305
Rancho Technology Inc	3577	F	909 987-3966	8296
Real Vision Foods LLC	2038	E	253 228-5050	1936
Red Hill Country Club	7997	D	909 982-1358	19602
Reyes Coca-Cola Bottling LLC	2086	D	909 980-3121	2290
Robot-Gxg Inc	3651	E	660 324-0030	9189
Rwc Enterprises Inc	8711	E	909 373-4100	22648
Safeland Industrial Supply Inc **(PA)**	3315	E	909 786-1967	6233
Schellinger Spring Inc	3493	E	909 373-0799	7467
Searing Industries Inc	3312	C	909 948-3030	6211
Sheraton LLC	7011	D	909 204-6100	16706
Siemens Rail Automation Corp	3669	D	909 532-5405	9352
Signworld America Inc **(PA)**	3993	D	844 900-7446	11603
Smith International Inc	1389	C	909 906-7900	546
Socco Plastic Coating Company	3479	E	909 987-4753	7411
South Bay International Inc	2515	E	909 718-5000	3560
Spectrasensors Inc	3826	E	909 980-4238	10812
Spectrasensors Inc **(HQ)**	3826	E	909 948-4102	10813
Starco Group Inc **(PA)**	7389	D	909 989-9898	18678
Steelscape LLC	3479	E	909 987-4711	7416
Sumitomo Rubber North Amer Inc **(HQ)**	5014	C	909 466-1116	13120
Sunn America Inc	7359	E	909 944-5756	17378
Superior Elec Mech & Plbg Inc	1731	B	909 357-9400	1322
Superior Tank Co Inc **(PA)**	3443	E	909 912-0580	6758
T E B Inc	3599	F	909 941-8100	8809
Tamco **(HQ)**	3312	B	909 899-0660	6215
Tri-Tech Metals Inc	5051	F	909 948-1401	13603
TRL Systems Incorporated	1731	D	909 390-8392	1331
Tutor Time Learning Ctrs LLC	8351	C	866 930-7975	22070
Union Bank of California **(PA)**	6021	D	909 350-7176	15007
Universal Technical Inst Inc	7389	D	909 484-1929	18712
Usl Parallel Products Cal	2869	E	909 980-1200	5151
Vanguard Tool & Mfg Co Inc	3469	E	909 980-9392	7188
Vehicle Accessory Center LLC	5013	D	909 987-8237	13105
Vocational Imprv Program Inc **(PA)**	8331	D	909 483-5924	21972
Volant Cool Air Intakes Inc	3089	E	909 476-7225	5859
Walco Inc	3559	F	909 483-3333	8001
Waters Edge Wineries Inc	2084	F	909 468-9463	2234
WE Oneil Construction Co Cal	1542	D	909 466-5300	847
Wessex Industries Inc	3498	E	562 944-5760	7547
Wipex Corp **(PA)**	3714	D	909 714-4623	10159
Yuneec USA Inc	5065	D	855 284-8888	13787
Zodiac Aerospace	3728	F	909 652-9700	10448

RANCHO DOMINGUEZ, CA - Los Angeles County

	SIC	EMP	PHONE	ENTRY #
Adf Incorporated	3446	E	310 669-9700	6948
Advanced Fresh Cncpts Frnchise	2092	E	310 604-3200	2344
Advanced Fresh Concepts Corp **(PA)**	6794	D	310 604-3630	16201
Afc Distribution Corp	5141	C	310 604-3630	14450
Allied High Tech Products Inc	5085	D	310 635-2466	13970
Bodycote Thermal Proc Inc	3398	E	310 604-8000	6431
Buff and Shine Mfg Inc	3291	E	310 886-511[illegible]	6151
Caplugs	3089	F	310 537-2300	5600
Carol Anderson Inc **(PA)**	2335	E	310 638-3333	2881
CDS Moving Equipment Inc **(PA)**	5084	D	310 631-1100	13896
Ceratizit Los Angeles LLC	3541	D	310 464-8050	7723
Enlink Geoenergy Services Inc	3585	E	424 242-1200	8337
Fairway Import-Export Inc	3949	E	262 788-73[illegible]3	11415
Giovanni Cosmetics Inc	2844	D	310 952-9960	5023
Global Agri-Trade	2076	E	562 320-8550	2121
Grand General Accessories LLC	3612	E	310 631-2539	8873
Heavy Load Transfer LLC	4212	D	310 816-0260	11973
Iap West Inc	5013	D	310 667-9720	13065
KT Engineering Corporation	3599	F	310 537-3818	8657
Kw International Inc	4731	D	310 747-1380	12476
Kw International Inc	4226	D	213 703-6914	12269
Laclede Inc	3843	E	310 605-4280	11181
Mariak Industries Inc	5023	B	310 661-4400	13177
Mars Food Us LLC **(HQ)**	2099	B	310 933-0670	2478
Mover Services Inc	1799	E	310 868-5143	1676
Neway Packaging Corp **(PA)**	5113	D	602 454-9000	14214
Nippon Ex Nec Lgstics Amer Inc	4212	D	310 604-6100	11984
Parker-Hannifin Corporation	3677	C	310 608-5600	9636
Premium Trnsp Svcs Inc **(PA)**	4225	C	310 816-0260	12234
Protective Industries Inc	3089	D	310 537-2300	5783
R R Donnelley & Sons Company	7331	E	310 784-8485	17139
S L Fusco Inc **(PA)**	3541	E	310 868-1010	7745
Samsung Electronics Amer Inc	5064	D	310 537-7000	13694
Santa Monica Seafood Company **(PA)**	2092	D	310 886-7900	2349
Seeds of Change Inc	5191	C	310 764-7700	14868
Shercon Inc	3069	D	800 228-3218	5411
Southwestern Industries Inc **(PA)**	3541	D	310 608-4422	7747
Spectrum Lifesciences LLC **(HQ)**	2833	F	310 885-4600	4764
Standard Wire & Cable Co **(PA)**	3357	E	310 609-1811	6357
Tda Magnetics LLC	3499	F	424 213-1585	7572
Team Manufacturing Inc	3469	E	310 639-0251	7185
Union Sup Comsy Solutions Inc	5141	C	785 357-5005	14516
Unis LLC	4225	D	310 747-7388	12255
United Bakery Equipment Co Inc **(PA)**	3565	D	310 635-8121	8079
Visionaire Lighting LLC	3646	D	310 512-6480	9110
Westcoast Warehousing LLC	4225	E	310 537-9958	12260
Western Sheld Acquisitions LLC **(PA)**	2754	F	310 527-6212	4469

RANCHO MIRAGE, CA - Riverside County

	SIC	EMP	PHONE	ENTRY #
Agua Clnte Band Chilla Indians	7011	A	760 321-2000	16316
Ameritac Inc **(PA)**	8744	D	925 989-2942	23390
Annenberg Fndtion Tr At Snnyln **(PA)**	6733	C	760 202-2222	16172
Betty Ford Center **(HQ)**	8093	C	760 773-4100	21279
Blx Group Inc	0181	D	760 776-6622	73
Country Villa Rancho	8322	C	760 340-0053	21758
Desert Crdlgy Cons Med Group I	8011	D	760 346-0642	19793
Desert Orthpd Ctr A Med Group **(PA)**	8011	D	760 568-2684	19796
Eisenhower Medical Center **(PA)**	8062	A	760 340-3911	20760
Kathy Ireland Worldwide LLC	2331	E	310 557-2700	2852
Mission Hills Country Club Inc	7997	C	760 324-9400	19587
Mission Hills Senior Living	8361	D	760 770-7737	22132
Morningside Community Assn	8641	D	760 328-3323	22351
Omni Hotels Corporation	7011	D	760 568-2727	16596
Palm Valley School	8748	D	760 328-0861	23490
Richman Management Corporation	7381	B	760 832-8520	18316
Ritz-Carlton Hotel Company LLC	7011	B	760 321-8282	16666
Springs Club Inc	7997	D	760 328-0254	19618
Sunrise Cntry CLB Rncho Mrage	7997	D	760 328-6549	19620
Thunderbird Country Club	7997	D	760 328-2161	19622

RANCHO PALOS VERDES, CA - Los Angeles County

	SIC	EMP	PHONE	ENTRY #
CAW Cowie Inc **(PA)**	7389	E	212 396-9007	18473
Ki-P C USA Jeans Inc	2325	D	310 234-8185	2771
Long Point Development LLC	7011	A	310 265-2800	16545
Normandie Club LP	7999	D	310 352-3486	19657
Pie Rise Ltd	2051	E	310 832-4559	2029
Powerstorm Holdings Inc	3691	F	424 327-2991	9813
Trico Leasing Company LLC	5085	E	877 259-9997	14027
Western Summit Mfg Corp	3081	E	626 333-3333	5442

RANCHO SANTA MARGARI, CA - Orange County

	SIC	EMP	PHONE	ENTRY #
Allstar Microelectronics Inc	3572	F	949 546-0888	8187
Century 21 Superstars **(PA)**	6531	D	949 888-1950	15810
Foundation 9 Entertainment Inc **(PA)**	7372	C	949 698-1500	17859
Glas Werk Inc	3229	E	949 766-1296	5935
Group Rossignol Usa Inc	8711	D	949 452-9050	22563
Jct Company LLC	1711	E	949 589-2021	1086
Jipc Management Inc	8741	A	949 916-2000	23042
Lowes Home Centers LLC	5031	C	949 589-5005	13221
Lubrizol Corporation	2899	F	949 212-1863	5228
Murano Group	7381	D	949 409-1079	18299
Southern California Bancorp	6022	D	949 766-3015	15043

RCHO STA MARG, CA - Orange County

	SIC	EMP	PHONE	ENTRY #
Apollo Technologies Inc	2899	E	949 888-0573	5211
Applied Manufacturing LLC	3841	A	949 713-8000	10935

Mergent email: customerrelations@mergent.com
1418

2022 Southern California Business
Directory and Buyers Guide

(P-0000) Products & Services Section entry number
(PA)=Parent Co (HQ)=Headquarters (DH)=Div Headquarters

	SIC	EMP	PHONE	ENTRY #
Applied Medical Corporation **(PA)**	3841	A	949 713-8000	10936
Applied Medical Dist Corp	3841	A	949 713-8000	10937
Applied Medical Resources	3841	E	949 459-1042	10938
Applied Medical Resources Corp **(HQ)**	3841	A	949 713-8000	10939
Art For Kids Inc	2499	E	949 459-2800	3438
Ats Tool Inc	3544	D	949 888-1744	7778
Ats Workholding Llc	3545	D	800 321-1833	7846
C C I	3491	E	910 616-7426	7439
Capital Invstmnts Vntures Corp **(PA)**	8621	C	949 858-0647	22266
Chapmn-Wlters Intrcoastal Corp	3949	F	949 448-9940	11409
Control Components Inc **(DH)**	3491	B	949 858-1877	7441
Desco Manufacturing Company **(PA)**	3599	F	949 858-7400	8571
Ep Holdings Inc	3572	E	949 713-4600	8198
Fakouri Electrical Engrg Inc	7378	D	949 888-2400	18145
Finance Express LLC **(HQ)**	7373	D	949 635-5892	18031
Form Grind Corporation	3599	E	949 858-7000	8591
Fortron/Source Corporation **(PA)**	3612	D	949 766-9240	8871
Grandis Metals Intl Corp	3356	F	949 459-2621	6332
Grandma Lucys LLC	2047	F	949 206-8547	1957
Hackney Electric Inc **(PA)**	1731	D	949 264-4000	1261
IMI CCI	8711	E	949 858-1877	22575
Impact LLC	3679	E	714 546-6000	9725
Inform Decisions Inc	7372	F	949 709-5838	17885
Kisco Senior Living LLC	6513	D	949 888-2250	15737
Laser Spectrum Inc	3699	E	949 726-2978	9885
Light Composite Corporation	3429	E	949 858-8820	6524
M-Industrial Enterprises	3599	E	949 413-7513	8671
Mc Products Inc	2899	E	949 888-7100	5232
Mission Viejo Pateadores Inc	7941	E	949 350-5590	19424
Multicoat Products Inc	2851	F	949 888-7100	5105
National Tour Intgrted Rsrces	8742	E	949 215-6330	23280
Nucourse Distribution Inc	5065	D	866 655-4366	13758
Padi Americas Inc	8621	C	949 858-7234	22275
Palomar Products Inc	3669	D	949 858-8836	9347
Park Landscape Maintenance **(PA)**	0782	B	949 546-8300	330
Park West Companies Inc **(PA)**	0782	B	949 546-8300	332
Park West Rescom Inc	0782	D	949 546-8300	334
Phyto Tech Corp **(PA)**	2834	E	949 635-1990	4874
Point Conception Inc	2339	E	949 589-6890	2985
Q-Mark Manufacturing Inc	3823	F	949 457-1913	10713
R C Products Corp	3429	E	949 858-8820	6533
Racepak LLC	3714	E	949 709-5555	10121
Racepak LLC	3711	E	888 429-4709	9963
Renaissnce Frnch Dors Sash Inc **(PA)**	2431	C	714 578-0090	3286
Roman Cthlic Diocese of Orange	2721	C	949 766-6000	4107
RPM Products Inc **(PA)**	3053	E	949 888-8543	5350
Santa Margarita Water District **(PA)**	4941	D	949 459-6400	12920
Sarco Inc	5065	E	949 888-5548	13772
Savice Inc	8641	D	949 888-2444	22367
South Coast Stairs Inc	2431	E	949 858-1685	3291
Standard Cable Usa Inc	3496	F	949 888-0842	7514
Style Craft Marketing Inc	7336	E	949 709-2000	17190
Sweegen Inc	2869	F	949 635-1984	5150
Swiss-Micron Inc	3451	D	949 589-0430	7045
Tracy & Ryder Landscape Inc	0782	D	949 858-7017	345
US Alliance Group Inc	7389	E	949 888-8580	18713
Virtium LLC	5045	D	949 888-2444	13451
Wyland International LLC **(PA)**	5199	E	949 643-7070	14987

REDLANDS, CA - San Bernardino County

	SIC	EMP	PHONE	ENTRY #
ABI Attorneys Service Inc **(PA)**	7334	D	909 793-0613	17143
Ach Mechanical Contractors Inc	1711	D	909 307-2850	1014
Advanced Ambltory Srgery Ctr L	8011	E	909 557-1700	19684
Akh Company Inc	7539	D	909 748-5016	18891
American Cinemas Group Inc **(PA)**	7832	C	760 597-5777	19268
Ash Holdings LLC	8051	D	909 793-2600	20247
Ashley Furniture Inds LLC	4225	B	909 825-4900	12185
Ashley Furniture Inds LLC	5021	B	800 240-3440	13126
Automobile Club Southern Cal	8699	D	909 793-3357	22409
AZ Gems Inc **(PA)**	5149	F	909 206-3384	14672
Beaver Medical Clinic Inc **(PA)**	8011	C	909 793-3311	19721
Bon Appetit Management Co	8742	C	909 748-8970	23174
Bradco Industrial Corporation	0851	F	888 272-3261	370
Braswlls Mdterranean Grdns Inc	8051	D	909 793-0433	20258
Buckeye Check Cashing Inc	6099	D	909 792-8816	15123
C C I Redlands Inc	3751	E	909 307-6500	10485
California Prtg Solutions Inc	2752	E	909 307-2032	4247
Califrnia Nwspapers Ltd Partnr	2711	C	909 793-3221	3958
Caseworx Inc	2521	E	909 799-8550	3580
Cemex USA Inc	3273	C	909 798-1144	6083
City of Redlands **(PA)**	8741	D	909 798-7531	23004
CJ Logistics America LLC	4213	C	909 363-4354	12022
Clorox Manufacturing Company	2842	D	909 307-2756	4961
Coast To Coast Mfg LLC	3089	F	909 798-5024	5609
Continental Datalabel Inc	2679	F	909 307-3600	3925
Daryls Pet Shop	3999	F	909 793-1788	11654
David Ollis Landscape Dev Inc	0782	E	909 307-1911	298
Dick Dewese Chevrolet Inc	7538	C	909 793-2681	18824
Enerpath Services Inc	1731	D	909 335-1699	1248
Epic Management LP **(PA)**	8741	D	909 799-1818	23021
Esri International LLC	5045	E	909 793-2853	13395
Express Container Inc	2653	E	909 798-3857	3801
Faith Electric LLC	1731	C	909 767-2682	1252
Flex Trim Industries Inc **(PA)**	3442	D	909 748-6578	6700
Garner Holt Productions Inc	3571	E	909 799-3030	8155
Haralambos Beverage Co	5181	B	562 347-4300	14826
Hospice Redland Community Hosp	8082	D	909 335-5643	21170
Hulsey Contracting Inc	5082	E	951 549-3665	13862
Humangood Norcal	8059	D	909 793-1233	20597
Hydro Tek Systems Inc	5087	D	909 799-9222	14038
Ifit Inc	3949	A	909 335-2888	11428
Inland Hlth Orgnztion of Sther **(DH)**	8062	E	909 335-7171	20797
Interntional Un Oper Engineers	8631	A	909 307-8700	22292
Jonbec Care Incorporated **(PA)**	8052	D	909 798-4003	20533
Kaiser Foundation Hospitals	8011	C	888 750-0036	19876
Ken Grody Redlands LLC	7538	D	909 793-3211	18847
Kyocera Medical Tech Inc	3842	E	909 557-2360	11121
Larry Jacinto Construction Inc	1611	D	909 794-2151	897
Larry Jacinto Farming Inc	0762	D	909 794-2276	224
Lean Supply Solutions Amer Inc **(PA)**	4225	D	844 310-5252	12218
Lois Lauer Realty **(PA)**	6531	C	909 748-7000	15912
Loma Linda University Med Ctr	8062	D	909 558-4000	20835
Loma Linda University Med Ctr	8062	D	909 558-9275	20839
Loran Inc	3612	E	405 340-0660	8877
Lowes Home Centers LLC	5031	C	909 307-8883	13254
M Block & Sons Inc	4225	C	909 335-6684	12221
Medline Industries Inc	5047	E	909 799-8983	13499
Mountain Top Comm Svcs LLC	8748	E	909 798-4400	23478
Mountain West Financial Inc **(PA)**	6162	B	909 793-1500	15219
New Image Commercial Flrg Inc	3996	F	909 796-3400	11620
Option One Home Med Eqp Inc	7352	D	909 478-5413	17303
P & R Paper Supply Co Inc **(HQ)**	5113	C	909 389-1807	14223
Performance Team Frt Sys Inc	4731	C	424 358-6943	12507
Performance Team LLC	4731	C	801 301-1732	12508
Plastics Plus Technology Inc	3089	E	909 747-0555	5757
Plum Healthcare Group LLC	7389	D	909 793-2609	18636
Plumbing Systems West Inc	1711	D	909 794-3823	1120
Precision Hermetic Tech Inc	3679	D	909 381-6011	9767
Prime-Line Products LLC **(DH)**	5072	B	909 887-8118	13816
Pro-Craft Construction Inc	1711	C	909 790-5222	1123
Redlands Cmnty Hosp Foundation	8059	C	909 793-1382	20624
Redlands Community Hospital **(PA)**	8062	D	909 335-5500	20922
Redlands Country Club	7997	D	909 793-2661	19603
Redlands Employment Services **(PA)**	7361	B	909 792-3413	17458
Redlands Fmly Prctice Med Grou	8011	D	909 793-3208	20038
Redlands Foothill Groves	0723	E	909 793-2164	184
Redlands Ford Inc	7532	D	909 793-3211	18802
Rettig Machine Inc	7692	E	909 793-7811	18995
RHS Corp	8741	A	909 335-5500	23100
Silverscreen Healthcare Inc	8059	C	909 793-1382	20627
Soren McAdam Christianson LLP	8721	D	909 798-2222	22814
Spectra Premium (usa) Corp	5013	D	951 653-0640	13096
Stone Age Equipment Inc **(PA)**	5139	E	909 798-4222	14446
Summit Fire Protection	1711	D	909 793-0676	1149
Teledyne Technologies Inc	3691	D	909 793-3131	9814
Venturedyne Ltd	3564	D	909 793-2788	8060
YMCA of East Valley **(PA)**	8641	C	909 798-9622	22380

REDONDO BEACH, CA - Los Angeles County

	SIC	EMP	PHONE	ENTRY #
Aamcom LLC	4813	E	310 318-8100	12622
Advanced Arm Dynamics **(PA)**	3842	E	310 372-3050	11080
Afrix Telecom LLC	4813	D	323 359-8683	12623
Alcast Mfg Inc	3364	E	310 542-3581	6373
Amwins Access Insur Svcs LLC **(HQ)**	6411	D	310 683-0469	15531
B Dazzle Inc	3944	F	310 374-3000	11367
Beach Cities Health District	8399	C	310 374-3426	22173
Bicara Ltd	5147	B	310 316-6222	14591
Catalina Events Inc	8743	E	310 925-6986	23380
Davita Medical Management LLC	8011	D	310 316-0811	19787
Distillery Tech Inc	7371	C	310 776-6234	17599
Dsd Trucking Inc **(PA)**	4581	D	310 338-3395	12356
Fire Safe Systems Inc	1711	D	310 542-0585	1067
Jariet Technologies Inc	3812	E	310 698-1001	10592
Jones Bold Security Inc	7381	D	323 800-2542	18291
K & P Janitorial Services	7349	D	310 540-8878	17255
Leight Sales Co Inc	5072	D	310 223-1000	13809
Main Street Management LLC **(PA)**	6531	D	310 640-3100	15919
Mapcargo Global Logistics **(PA)**	4731	D	310 297-8300	12482
Mulligan Limited **(PA)**	7996	D	714 484-6799	19521
NBC Consulting Inc	8742	D	310 798-5000	23281
Northrop Grumman Intl Inc	3812	E	310 812-4321	10607
Northrop Grumman Systems Corp	3663	C	310 812-5149	9303
Northrop Grumman Systems Corp	8748	C	855 737-8364	23485
Northrop Grumman Systems Corp	3812	C	310 812-4321	10624
Northrop Grumman Systems Corp	3721	B	310 812-1089	10198
Northrop Grumman Systems Corp	3721	B	310 812-4321	10199
Nurturing Tots Inc	8351	D	818 996-1602	22043
Nzg Specialties Inc **(PA)**	5141	D	310 216-7575	14483
Online Land Planning LLC	8748	E	310 594-7782	23487
Portofino Hotel Partners LP	7011	C	310 379-8481	16636
Quantimetrix Corporation	2835	D	310 536-0006	4926
Redondo Beach Brewing Co Inc	2082	E	310 316-8477	2154
Ricardo Ramos	1731	E	310 785-0288	1309
Scat Enterprises Inc	5013	D	310 370-5501	13087
Sierra Monolithics Inc **(HQ)**	8748	D	310 698-1000	23508
Silverado Senior Living Inc	8051	D	424 257-6418	20465
Smart & Final Stores Inc	5141	C	323 497-8528	14499
Stevens Global Logistics Inc **(PA)**	4731	D	310 216-5645	12532
Thorock Metals Inc	3341	E	310 537-1597	6296
Wedgewood Inc **(PA)**	6799	B	310 640-3070	16300
Westwind Engineering Inc	8711	C	310 831-3454	22695
Westwind Engineering Inc	8711	D	310 831-3454	22696

RESEDA, CA - Los Angeles County

	SIC	EMP	PHONE	ENTRY #
Advanced Bioservices LLC **(PA)**	8741	D	818 342-0100	22966
Chase Group Llc	8742	B	818 708-3533	23188

Employment Codes: A=Over 500 employees, B=251-500, C=101-250, D=51-100, E=20-50 F=10-19

2022 Southern California Business Directory and Buyers Guide

© Mergent Inc. 1-800-342-5647

1419

	SIC	EMP	PHONE	ENTRY #
Child Development Institute	8322	D	818 888-4559	21740
Fabulous & Company LLC	7231	E	818 261-7242	16903
L & A Care Corporation **(PA)**	8082	D	323 938-1155	21182
Longwood Management Corp	8062	C	818 881-7414	20851
Los Angles Jewish HM For Aging **(PA)**	8051	B	818 774-3000	20409
Los Angles Jewish HM For Aging	8051	B	818 774-3000	20410
Moore Foundations Inc	8641	E	818 698-4737	22350
Northridge Diagnostic Center	8011	C	818 773-6500	20005
Platinum Boss Intl Intllgnce L	7381	D	818 416-5216	18310
Platinum Boss Intl Prtction Sv	7381	E	818 416-5216	18311
Rj Airwash LLC **(PA)**	3732	E	818 342-8800	10471
Valley Management Associates **(PA)**	6371	D	818 881-6801	15522

RIALTO, CA - San Bernardino County

	SIC	EMP	PHONE	ENTRY #
ABF Prints Inc	2759	E	909 875-7163	4476
Alta Vista Credit Union	6062	D	909 809-3838	15105
American Building Supply Inc	5031	D	909 879-8700	13199
Arnett Construction Inc	1794	E	909 421-7960	1591
B & B Plastics Inc	2821	E	909 829-3606	4679
B & B Plastics Recyclers Inc **(PA)**	5093	C	909 829-3606	14111
Biscomerica Corp	2052	B	909 877-5997	2058
Burlingame Industries Inc **(PA)**	7033	D	909 355-7000	16829
Burlingame Industries Inc	3299	D	909 355-7000	6178
Calcraft Corporation	3441	F	909 879-2900	6597
Caremark Rx Inc	8011	D	909 822-1164	19735
Columbia Steel Inc	3441	D	909 874-8840	6602
Distribution Alternatives Inc	5122	C	909 770-8900	14242
Eagle Roofing Products Fla LLC	3259	D	909 822-6000	5988
H Wayne Lewis Inc	3449	E	909 874-2213	7021
Hazmat Tsdf Inc **(PA)**	4953	D	909 873-4141	12953
Kti Incorporated	3272	D	909 434-1888	6038
Lane Winpak Inc **(HQ)**	5199	D	909 386-1762	14945
Martinez and Turek Inc	3599	C	909 820-6800	8679
Meerkat Inc	3599	F	909 877-0093	8687
Menasha Packaging Company LLC	2653	F	909 442-0668	3820
Mike Dyell Machine Shop Inc **(PA)**	3599	F	909 350-4101	8694
Molina Healthcare Inc	8099	D	909 546-7116	21455
Nelson Adams Inc	2531	F	909 256-8938	3627
Precision Aerial Services Inc	7549	F	909 484-8259	18940
Radial South LP	4225	B	610 491-7000	12238
Rialto Unified School District	8741	D	909 820-7864	23101
Robert Clapper Cnstr Svcs Inc	1542	D	909 829-3688	817
Sierra Lathing Company Inc	1742	C	909 421-0211	1401
So-Cal Strl Stl Fbrication Inc	1791	E	909 877-1299	1583
Spray Enclosure Tech Inc	3444	E	909 419-7011	6917
State Pipe & Supply Inc	3312	E	909 356-5670	6213
State Pipe & Supply Inc **(DH)**	5051	D	909 877-9999	13596
Techniform International Corp	3599	C	909 877-6886	8814
Thompson Pipe Group Inc	2679	E	909 822-0200	3939

RICHGROVE, CA - Tulare County

	SIC	EMP	PHONE	ENTRY #
Castle Rock Farming and Trnspt	0722	D	661 721-1058	152
Famous Vineyards LLC	5148	D	661 392-5000	14628
Sun Pacific Marketing Coop Inc	5148	B	559 784-6845	14656
Vincent B Zaninovich Sons Inc	0172	A	661 720-9031	55

RIDGECREST, CA - Kern County

	SIC	EMP	PHONE	ENTRY #
Adelman Broadcasting Inc	4832	D	760 371-1700	12686
Albertsons LLC	2051	C	760 446-2544	1979
Altaone Federal Credit Union **(PA)**	6061	C	760 371-7000	15056
American Ready Mix Inc	3273	F	760 446-4556	6068
DCS Corporation	8711	D	760 384-5600	22526
Desert Area Resources Training **(PA)**	7349	D	760 375-9787	17237
Desert Area Resources Training	8399	D	760 375-8494	22180
Directv Group Holdings LLC	4841	C	760 375-8300	12757
Kern Community College Dst	8351	D	760 384-6100	22025
Mpb Furniture Corporation	2512	E	760 375-4800	3512
Navair WD	8711	D	760 939-1970	22622
New Directions Tech Inc **(PA)**	7373	D	760 384-2444	18052
Orbital Sciences LLC	3812	B	818 887-8345	10631
Ridgecrest Healthcare Inc **(PA)**	8051	C	323 344-0601	20446
Ridgecrest Regional Hospital **(PA)**	8062	B	760 446-3551	20923
Sierra Group Inc	4581	F	760 377-1000	12369
Sierra View Inc	2711	E	760 371-4301	4027
Southern California Edison Co	4911	C	760 375-1821	12857
Southern Sierra Medical Center	8062	D	760 446-6404	20951
United Parcel Service Inc	4215	C	760 375-7861	12151

RIVERSIDE, CA - Riverside County

	SIC	EMP	PHONE	ENTRY #
20/20 Mobile Corp **(PA)**	4812	D	951 354-8100	12588
20/20 Plumbing & Heating Inc **(PA)**	1711	C	951 396-2020	1011
220 Laboratories LLC **(HQ)**	2844	C	951 683-2912	4986
313 Acquisition LLC	7382	A	801 234-6374	18363
48forty Solutions	7372	F	951 682-3095	17771
A-Check America Inc **(PA)**	7323	C	951 750-1501	17119
A-G Sod Farms Inc	0181	D	951 687-7581	72
Aatech	3589	F	909 854-3200	8360
Accurate Metal Products Inc	3441	F	951 360-3594	6580
Acro-Spec Grinding Co Inc	3599	F	951 736-1199	8467
Acura Spa Systems Inc	3594	F	951 684-6667	8441
Adex Medical Inc	3842	F	951 653-9122	11079
Adkison Engineers Inc	8711	D	951 688-0241	22477
Advanced Engrg Mlding Tech Inc	3089	E	888 264-0392	5547
Adventist Media Center Inc **(PA)**	7922	C	805 955-7777	19300
Air Force Village West Inc	8051	B	951 697-2000	20240
Airgas Specialty Products Inc	5169	D	951 353-2390	14771
Albert A Webb Associates **(PA)**	8711	C	951 686-1070	22482
Albertsons LLC	2051	C	951 656-6603	1978
Alectro Inc	3612	F	909 590-9521	8862
Aleph Group Inc	3711	E	951 213-4815	9933
Aleph Group Inc	3841	F	951 213-4815	10929
Alin Party Supply Co	7389	E	951 682-7441	18439
Allied Steel Co Inc	1791	D	951 241-7000	1564
Alpha Materials Inc	3273	E	951 788-5150	6067
Alstom Signaling Operation LLC	4789	C	951 343-9699	12562
Alta Vista Healthcare and Well	8011	C	951 688-8200	19694
Altium Holdings LLC	3089	B	951 340-9390	5555
Altura Credit Union **(PA)**	6062	D	888 883-722[illegible]	15106
Aluminum Technology Inc	2591	F	909 946-369[illegible]	3706
AMA Plastics **(PA)**	3089	C	951 734-5600	5560
American Asphalt South Inc	1611	D	909 427-8275	857
American Bottling Company	2086	F	951 341-7500	2249
American Med Rspnse Amblnce Sv **(DH)**	4119	A	303 495-12[illegible]7	11849
American Med Rspnse Inland Emp **(DH)**	4119	D	951 782-5200	11850
American Quality Tools Inc	3545	E	951 280-4700	7845
American Textile Maint Co	7213	D	951 684-4940	16843
Artech Industries Inc	3679	E	951 276-3331	9675
Arthur J Gallagher & Co	6411	D	800 217-9800	15537
Arturo Campos	3471	F	951 300-2[illegible]11	7216
Astro Seal Inc	3679	E	951 787-6670	9676
Atco Rubber Products Inc	3443	E	951 788-4345	6727
Automax Styling Inc	3714	E	951 530-1376	10019
Automobile Club Southern Cal	8699	D	951 684-4250	22426
Avendren Building Systems Inc	1542	F	909 806-0938	740
B & B Nurseries Inc	5193	C	951 352-8383	14876
Ba Holdings Inc **(DH)**	3443	E	951 684-5110	6728
Babcock Laboratories Inc	8734	D	951 653-3351	22932
Barrys Security Services Inc **(PA)**	7381	C	951 789-7575	18254
Bedrock Company	1771	D	951 273-1931	1517
Bell Bros Steel Inc	3441	E	951 784-0903	6588
Ben Clymers Body Sp Perris Inc	3711	F	800 338-5872	9938
Bens Asphalt & Maint Co Inc	1611	D	951 248-1103	863
Best Best & Krieger LLP **(PA)**	8111	C	951 686-1450	21514
Better Bar Manufacturing LLC	2023	E	951 525-3111	1782
Black Egle Pllet Logistics Inc **(PA)**	5031	E	951 332-6315	13204
Blazing Industrial Steel Inc	3441	E	951 360-8340	6590
Boise Cascade Company	5031	C	951 343-3000	13205
Bottling Group LLC	2086	D	951 697-3200	2260
Bourns Inc **(PA)**	3677	C	951 781-5500	9622
Bourns APL Corp **(HQ)**	3677	D	951 781-5500	9623
Brenner-Fiedler & Assoc Inc **(PA)**	3829	E	562 404-2721	10873
Bright Expectations Inc	8082	E	951 360-2070	21143
Brightview Landscape Svcs Inc	0781	C	951 684-2730	239
Brightview Landscape Svcs Inc	0781	C	714 939-6600	245
Brimad Enterprises Inc	7312	E	951 354-8187	17075
Broker Solutions Inc	7389	D	951 637-2300	18462
California Interfill Inc	2844	F	951 351-2619	4998
Canine Caviar Pet Foods Inc	2048	E	714 223-1800	1963
Canine Caviar Pet Foods De Inc	2047	F	714 223-1800	1956
Canyon Crest Country Club Inc	7997	D	951 274-7900	19552
Captive-Aire Systems Inc	3444	E	951 231-5102	6806
Career Dev Inst For Excptnal I	6552	E	951 337-3678	16047
Carolyn E Wylie Ctr For Chldre	8322	D	951 683-5193	21729
Champion Electric Inc	1731	D	951 276-9619	1232
Cibaria International Inc	5149	E	951 823-8490	14680
City of Riverside	3589	E	951 351-6140	8372
Clarkwestern Dietrich Building	3444	F	951 360-3500	6808
Coachworks Holdings Inc	3711	F	951 684-9585	9940
Cody Cylinder Service LLC	3599	E	951 786-3650	8560
Codysales Inc	3561	F	951 786-3650	8007
Commander Boats	3732	F	951 273-0100	10461
Complete Coach Works **(HQ)**	7549	B	951 682-2557	18923
Corona - Cllege Hts Ornge Lmon	0723	B	951 359-6451	163
Corporate Alnce Strategies Inc	7382	C	877 777-7487	18369
County of Riverside	8111	C	951 955-6000	21540
County of Riverside	8322	D	951 955-5659	21760
County of Riverside Department **(PA)**	8699	D	951 358-5000	22450
Craftsman Lath and Plaster Inc	1751	B	951 685-9922	1432
CRC Health Group Inc	8093	D	951 784-8010	21296
Crest Steel Corporation	5051	D	310 830-2651	13561
Criterion Automation Inc	3317	F	951 683-2400	6247
Criterion Supply Inc	2273	F	562 222-2382	2686
Cummings Resources LLC	3993	E	951 248-1130	11540
CV Wndows Dors Riverside Inc	3231	F	951 784-8766	5950
D G A Machine Shop Inc	3599	F	951 354-2113	8566
D L B Pallets **(PA)**	2448	F	951 360-9896	3387
D Mills Grnding Machining Inc	3599	C	951 697-6847	8567
Daart Engineering Company Inc	1711	D	909 888-8696	1052
David A Campbell Corporation	7538	C	951 785-4444	18822
Dillon Companies Inc	2051	C	951 352-8353	1995
Dixieline Lumber Company LLC	2439	A	951 224-8491	3360
Dlr Group Inc	8712	D	951 682-0470	22714
Doctors Hospital Riverside LLC **(PA)**	8062	E	951 354-7404	20757
DOE & Ingalls Cal Oper LLC	3826	E	951 801-7175	10791
Doka USA Ltd	3444	F	951 509-0023	6821
Dura Coat Products Inc **(PA)**	3479	D	951 341-6500	7359
Edge Plastics Inc **(PA)**	3089	E	951 786-4750	5635
Ejay Filtration Inc	3496	E	951 683-0805	7500
Eldorado National Cal Inc **(HQ)**	3711	B	951 727-9300	9944
Elias Elliott Lampasi Fehn **(PA)**	8021	D	951 689-5031	20176
Elisid Magazine	2721	E	619 990-9999	4068
Elite Electric	1731	D	951 681-5811	1247
Empire Med Transportations LLC	4731	D	951 530-8420	12453
Empirecare Health Assoc Inc	8621	D	951 686-8202	22269
Erlanger Distribution Ctr Inc	4225	E	951 784-5147	12202

Mergent email: customerrelations@mergent.com
1420

2022 Southern California Business
Directory and Buyers Guide

(P-0000) Products & Services Section entry number
(PA)=Parent Co (HQ)=Headquarters (DH)=Div Headquarters

	SIC	EMP	PHONE	ENTRY #
Esco Industries Inc	3462	F	951 782-2130	7084
Etairos Consulting	7379	E	844 219-7027	18176
Evans Walker Enterprises	3714	E	951 784-7223	10055
Everpac	5082	C	951 774-3274	13858
Fairprice Enterprises Inc	3281	D	951 684-8578	6138
Fencecorp Inc **(HQ)**	1799	C	951 686-3170	1656
Fenceworks Inc **(PA)**	1799	C	951 788-5620	1657
Fleetwood Homes California Inc **(DH)**	2451	B	951 351-2494	3422
Fleetwood Homes of Florida **(DH)**	2451	B	909 261-4274	3423
Fleetwood Motor Homes-Califinc **(DH)**	3716	B	951 354-3000	10173
Fleetwood Motor Homes-Califinc	7699	C	951 274-2000	19038
Fleetwood Travel Trlrs Ind Inc **(DH)**	3792	D	951 354-3000	10540
Fleetwood Travel Trlrs of MD **(DH)**	3792	D	951 351-3500	10541
Foot In Motion Inc	3842	F	312 752-0990	11105
Fpc Graphics Inc	2752	E	951 686-0232	4298
FS Commercial Landscape Inc **(PA)**	0781	D	951 360-7070	257
FSA Arlanza Child Dev Ctr **(PA)**	8351	D	951 352-2810	22018
Fusion Sign & Design Inc **(PA)**	3993	C	877 477-8777	11557
Future Tech Metals Inc	3599	E	951 781-4801	8596
G C Pallets Inc	2448	E	909 357-8515	3389
Ghossain & Truelock Entps Inc	7349	E	951 781-9345	17246
Gless Ranch Inc **(PA)**	0762	E	951 780-8458	222
Golden Star Technology Inc	7378	E	951 778-8930	18146
Good Trading Co	7389	E	951 688-2495	18531
Grech Motors LLC **(PA)**	7694	E	951 688-8347	19013
Growest Inc **(PA)**	2084	F	951 638-1000	2188
Gtt International Inc	5023	E	951 788-8729	13173
Hal Hays Construction Inc **(PA)**	1541	C	951 788-0703	702
Hamblins Bdy Pnt Frame Sp Inc	7538	D	951 689-8440	18841
Harbor Pipe and Steel Inc	5051	C	951 369-3990	13568
Hci Inc **(HQ)**	1623	B	951 520-4200	951
Health Tech Prof Pdts Inc	0742	F	800 424-7536	199
Heider Inspection Group	8734	A	909 673-0292	22947
Henry C Cox II and John L West	7992	D	951 360-2090	19491
Heritage Container Inc	2653	D	951 360-1900	3811
Herman Weissker Inc **(HQ)**	1623	B	951 826-8800	953
Hi-Rel Plastics & Molding Corp	3089	E	951 354-0258	5661
High Performance Logistics LLC	4212	D	702 300-4880	11975
Historic Mission Inn Corp	7011	B	951 784-0300	16481
Hunsaker & Assoc Irvine Inc	8711	D	951 352-7200	22571
Hy-Tech Tile Inc	1752	C	951 788-0550	1467
Hydraforce Incorporated	3561	F	951 689-3987	8015
Icsn Inc **(PA)**	3449	F	951 687-2305	7022
Imperial Pipe Services LLC	3317	E	951 682-3307	6249
IMS Products Inc	3751	F	951 653-7720	10493
Inland Empire Foods Inc **(PA)**	2034	E	951 682-8222	1883
Innovative Emergency Equipment	7699	E	951 222-2270	19044
Innovtive Dsign Shtmtl Pdts In	3444	F	951 222-2270	6854
Insurance Inc Southern Cal	6411	D	951 300-9333	15584
Interdent Service Corporation	8021	C	951 682-1720	20182
Interntnal Communications Corp	7373	E	951 934-0531	18040
Irrometer Company Inc	3829	F	951 682-9505	10892
J D Diffenbaugh Inc	1542	D	951 351-6865	774
J Ginger Masonry LP **(PA)**	1741	B	951 688-5050	1347
J M V B Inc	1721	D	714 288-9797	1184
Jaffa Precision Engrg Inc	3599	F	951 278-8797	8639
James McMinn Inc	1611	E	909 514-1231	891
Jimenez Mexican Foods Inc	2032	E	951 351-0102	1851
Jlg Industries Inc	3531	C	951 358-1915	7645
Joa Corporation **(PA)**	3842	F	951 785-4411	11118
Johnson Machinery Co **(PA)**	5082	C	951 686-4560	13863
Jurupa Community Services Dst	4941	D	951 685-7073	12896
Jurupa Unified School District	7538	D	951 222-7756	18845
K & N Engineering Inc **(PA)**	3751	A	951 826-4000	10495
Kaiser Foundation Hospitals	8011	C	951 353-3790	19878
Kaiser Foundation Hospitals	8011	C	951 248-4000	19915
Kaiser Foundation Hospitals	8011	C	866 984-7483	19916
Kaiser Foundation Hospitals	8049	C	951 353-4670	20225
Kaiser Foundation Hospitals	8011	C	951 352-0292	19934
Kaiser Foundation Hospitals	8011	C	951 353-2000	19944
Kana Pipeline Inc	1623	D	714 986-1400	959
Kawneer Company Inc	3442	D	951 410-4779	6704
Keystone NPS LLC	8399	C	951 785-0504	22195
Kimco Staffing Services Inc	7361	A	951 686-3800	17434
Knollwood Psychtric Hosp Chem	8063	D	951 275-8400	21023
L & L Louvers Inc	3442	E	951 735-9300	6705
L T Seroge Inc	3699	F	951 354-7141	9884
Landcare USA LLC	0782	D	951 320-1522	316
Liberty Landscaping Inc **(PA)**	0782	C	951 683-2999	323
Lineage Logistics Holdings LLC	4789	C	951 369-0230	12578
Lowes Home Centers LLC	5031	C	951 509-5500	13227
Lozano Plumbing Services Inc	1711	C	951 683-4840	1096
LSI Products Inc	3714	F	951 343-9270	10094
Luxfer Inc **(DH)**	3728	D	951 684-5110	10370
Luxfer Inc	3354	E	951 684-5110	6311
Luxfer Inc	3463	E	951 351-4100	7104
M & M Plumbing Inc	1711	D	951 354-5388	1099
Mackie International Inc **(PA)**	2024	E	951 346-0530	1820
Magnolia Rhblttion Nursing Ctr	8059	C	951 688-4321	20609
Magnotek Manufacturing Inc	3677	E	951 653-8461	9632
Mainstreet Communications Inc **(PA)**	7334	F	951 682-2005	17152
Majestic Print Inc	2752	F	951 509-2539	4365
Malcolm Smith Motorcycles Inc	7213	D	951 687-1300	16854
McLane Foodservice Inc	5141	C	951 867-3555	14476
Mdi East Inc **(HQ)**	3089	D	951 509-6918	5704
Mega Machinery Inc	3559	E	951 300-9300	7988
Merchants Metals LLC	3315	E	951 686-1888	6229

	SIC	EMP	PHONE	ENTRY #
Metal Container Corporation	3411	C	951 354-0444	6465
Metric Machining **(PA)**	3599	E	909 947-9222	8693
Metropolitan News Company	2711	E	951 369-5890	4010
Mfi Recovery Center **(PA)**	8093	D	951 683-6596	21319
MGB Construction Inc	1521	C	951 342-0303	623
Micromold Inc	3089	F	951 684-7130	5710
Millers Fab & Weld Corp	3441	E	951 359-3100	6639
Mitchell Rubber Products LLC **(PA)**	3069	C	951 681-5655	5393
Morgan Stnley Smith Barney LLC	6211	D	951 682-1181	15300
Mortan Industries Inc	3069	F	951 682-2215	5395
MSM Industries Inc	8711	E	951 735-0834	22618
MSRS INC	2821	C	310 952-9000	4701
Mt Rubidouxidence Opco LLC	8051	C	951 681-2200	20422
Muth Machine Works	8742	D	951 685-1521	23277
National Paving Company Inc	1611	D	951 369-1332	903
Neal Trucking Inc	4212	D	951 685-5048	11983
Nevada Window Supply Inc	2431	E	951 300-0100	3273
New Power Inc	1711	D	800 980-9825	1107
Newbasis LLC	3272	C	951 787-0600	6040
Newbasis West LLC	3272	C	951 787-0600	6041
Newman Bros California Inc **(PA)**	2431	F	951 782-0102	3274
Novo Distribution LLC	5031	C	951 742-5273	13279
Nsa Holdings Inc	3089	F	951 686-1400	5732
ODonnell Manufacturing Inc	3599	E	562 944-9671	8724
Officeworks Inc	7361	D	951 784-2534	17441
Oldcast Precast **(DH)**	3272	E	951 788-9720	6044
Oldcastle Infrastructure Inc	3272	E	951 788-9720	6045
Onrad Inc	8011	D	800 848-5876	20012
Operation Safe House Inc **(PA)**	8322	D	951 358-4418	21859
Orangetree Convalescent Hosp	8062	C	951 785-6060	20876
OSI Industries LLC	3999	D	951 684-4500	11724
Owen Trailers Inc	3715	E	951 361-4557	10167
Pacific Consolidated Inds LLC	3569	D	951 479-0860	8133
Pacific Monarch Resorts Inc	7011	D	951 342-7970	16611
Pacific Strucframe LLC	1761	D	951 405-8536	1499
Paradise Garden Center Inc	5083	F	951 789-0386	13877
Parex Usa Inc **(DH)**	3299	E	714 778-2266	6185
Parex Usa Inc	3299	E	951 653-3549	6186
Parkview Cmnty Hosp Med Ctr	8062	A	951 354-7404	20886
PCI Holding Company Inc **(PA)**	3569	F	951 479-0860	8135
Pearson Ford Co **(PA)**	7539	C	877 743-0421	18901
Peggs Company Inc **(PA)**	7699	D	253 584-9548	19056
Perry Coast Construction Inc	1542	C	951 774-0677	807
Phenix Technology Corporation	3569	E	951 272-4938	8136
Pierco Incorporated	3999	F	909 251-7100	11736
Pinnacle Rvrside Hspitality LP	7011	C	951 784-8000	16631
Pinnpack Packaging LLC **(DH)**	3089	D	805 385-4100	5744
Plascor Inc	3085	C	951 328-1010	5478
Plastic Technologies Inc	3089	E	951 360-6055	5755
Plasticbagsonsalecom Inc	5113	F	951 710-1340	14226
Polaris Sales Inc	3441	F	951 343-9270	6649
Poly-Fiber Inc **(PA)**	2851	F	951 684-4280	5107
Polymer Logistics Inc	3089	D	951 567-2900	5765
Populus Financial Group Inc	6099	C	951 509-3506	15131
Ppc Enterprises Inc	1711	C	951 354-5402	1121
Precise Distribution Inc	4225	E	951 367-1037	12233
Precision Molded Products Inc	3089	E	951 354-0779	5773
Precision Technology and Mfg	3451	E	951 788-0252	7041
Premier Fuel Distributors Inc	2869	C	760 423-3610	5143
Premier Signs Service Inc	1731	F	951 204-7693	1301
Press-Enterprise Company **(PA)**	2711	A	951 684-1200	4024
Prism Aerospace	3444	E	951 582-2850	6895
Professional Cabinet Solutions	2434	A	909 614-2900	3330
Professional Cabinet Solutions	2434	C	909 614-2900	3331
Professnal Cmmnctons Netwrk LP **(PA)**	7389	E	951 275-9149	18643
Progressive Products Inc	2299	F	951 784-9930	2736
Provident Fincl Holdings Inc **(PA)**	6022	D	951 686-6060	15040
Provident Savings Bank **(HQ)**	6022	C	951 782-6177	15041
Qg Printing Corp	2721	F	951 571-2500	4101
Qg Printing II LLC	2752	C	951 571-2500	4412
Quality Shutters Inc	2431	E	951 683-4939	3285
R & D Nova Inc	3845	F	951 781-7332	11236
Raceway Ford Inc	7538	C	951 571-9300	18863
Rain Mstr Irrgtion Systems Inc	3823	E	805 527-4498	10717
Realty One Group Inc	6531	D	951 565-8105	15971
Recell Usa Inc	2111	F	951 353-1600	2551
Recycler Core Company Inc	4953	D	951 276-1687	12970
Regional Connector Constrs	1521	E	951 368-6400	635
Reisner Enterprises Inc	3599	F	951 786-9478	8764
Rgis LLC	7389	D	951 369-7131	18653
Rhf Plymouth Tower	8051	D	951 248-0456	20445
Riverside Care Inc	8051	C	951 683-7111	20448
Riverside Cmnty Hlth Systems **(DH)**	8062	A	951 788-3000	20924
Riverside Cnty Flood Ctrl Wtr	8999	C	951 955-1200	23541
Riverside Equities LLC	8051	C	951 688-2222	20449
Riverside Lamination Corp	2891	F	951 682-0100	5195
Riverside Machine Works Inc	3599	F	951 685-7416	8770
Riverside Medical Clinic Inc **(PA)**	8011	B	951 683-6370	20044
Riverside Scrap Ir & Met Corp **(PA)**	5093	E	951 686-2120	14121
Riverside Tent and Awng Co Inc	2393	F	951 683-1925	3130
Riverside Transit Agency **(PA)**	4111	B	951 565-5000	11836
Riverside Univ Hlth Sys Fndtio **(PA)**	8062	A	951 358-5000	20925
Robert Half International Inc	7361	D	951 779-9081	17461
Robert P Von Zabern	3841	F	951 734-7215	11052
Roberts & Associates Inc	8082	D	951 727-4357	21208
Rolenn Manufacturing Inc **(PA)**	3089	E	951 682-1185	5796
Roll-A-Shade Inc **(PA)**	2591	E	951 245-5077	3714

	SIC	EMP	PHONE	ENTRY #
Roy E Whitehead Inc	1751	D	951 682-1490	1454
Royal Interpack North Amer Inc	3089	E	951 787-6925	5805
Rubidoux Community Svcs Dst	8611	D	951 684-7580	22255
Ruiz Mexican Foods Inc **(PA)**	2099	C	909 947-7811	2520
Samuel Son & Co (usa) Inc	3354	E	951 781-7800	6316
San Joaquin Window Inc	3442	C	909 946-3697	6718
Santa Ana Watershed Prj Auth	4941	D	951 354-4220	12917
Secure Transportation Company	4119	D	951 737-7300	11889
ServiceMaster By Best Pros Inc	7349	D	951 515-9051	17283
Sharp Industries LLC	3999	F	951 323-3677	11755
Sheet Metal Specialists LLC	3444	E	951 351-6828	6910
Silverado Framing & Cnstr	1521	D	951 352-1100	641
Simpson Strong-Tie Company Inc	2439	C	714 871-8373	3367
Skanska USA Cvil W Cal Dst Inc **(DH)**	1611	A	951 684-5360	916
Skanska USA Cvil W Rcky Mtn Ds **(DH)**	1629	D	970 565-8000	1004
Smart Choice Investments Inc **(PA)**	7361	D	310 944-6985	17466
SMS Fabrications Inc	3444	E	951 351-6828	6913
Snapware Corporation	3089	C	951 361-3100	5823
Social Services Cal Dept	8322	D	951 782-4200	21889
Solcius LLC	1711	D	951 772-0030	1143
South Coast Health Wellness	8051	E	951 686-9001	20478
Southern Cal Prmnnte Med Group	6324	C	866 984-7483	15455
Southwest Site Services Inc	7359	D	866 892-8451	17375
Sphere Alliance Inc	2821	E	951 352-2400	4720
Stainless Fixtures Inc	2599	F	909 622-1615	3739
Standard Textile Co Inc	7389	D	800 999-0400	18676
State Compensation Insur Fund	6331	D	888 782-8338	15484
Steel Unlimited Inc	5051	D	909 873-1222	13597
Sun Mar Management Services	8051	C	951 687-3842	20483
Superform USA Incorporated	3463	E	951 351-4100	7107
Superior Metal Fabricators Inc	3444	E	951 360-2474	6923
Swift Beef Company	2013	C	951 571-2237	1753
Sysco Riverside Inc	5141	B	951 601-5300	14513
T A Rivard Inc	1623	D	951 360-8596	977
T M Cobb Company **(PA)**	2431	E	951 248-2400	3293
T M P Services Inc **(PA)**	3448	E	951 213-3900	7009
Taylors Appliance	7699	E	951 683-6365	19074
Team Air Inc **(PA)**	3585	E	909 823-1957	8349
Team Group LLC	8741	D	951 688-8593	23122
Teaman Ramirez & Smith Inc	8721	D	951 274-9500	22817
Thirkettle Corporation **(PA)**	5084	D	951 637-1400	13948
Thompson & Colegate LLP	8111	E	951 682-5550	21688
Tolco Incorporated	3448	F	951 656-3111	7010
Tom Harris Inc	2099	F	951 352-5700	2538
Tom Leonard Investment Co Inc	3999	E	951 351-7778	11780
Top Priority Couriers Inc **(PA)**	4215	D	951 781-1000	12147
Toyota of Riverside Inc	7538	C	951 687-1622	18880
Trademark Cosmetics Inc	2844	E	951 683-2631	5074
Trademark Plastics Inc	3559	C	909 941-8810	7997
Triple H Food Processors LLC	2099	D	951 352-5700	2543
Tropical Functional Labs LLC	2023	F	951 688-2619	1806
Trutouch Technologies Inc	3829	F	909 703-5963	10918
Tube One Industries Inc	3317	F	951 300-2998	6254
Ufp Riverside LLC	5085	E	951 826-3000	14030
Unique Carpets Ltd	5023	D	951 352-8125	13193
United Carports LLC	3448	F	800 757-6742	7011
Universal Trailers Inc	3799	E	951 784-0543	10556
URS Group Inc	8711	D	951 571-2220	22683
US Door and Fence LLC	2411	E	951 300-0010	3203
US Precision Sheet Metal Inc	3444	D	951 276-2611	6937
US Rubber Roller Company Inc	3069	F	951 682-2221	5419
Van Daele Development Corp	1531	C	951 354-6800	683
Veterinary Service Inc	5047	E	951 328-4900	13529
Villa Convalescent Hosp Inc	8051	D	951 689-5788	20497
Virginia Park LLC	2099	F	816 592-0776	2546
Vitas Healthcare Corp Cal **(DH)**	8082	E	305 374-4143	21231
Volt Management Corp	7363	D	951 789-8133	17530
Waterman Convalescent Hosp Inc	8069	D	951 681-2200	21056
Webcam Inc	3714	F	951 369-5144	10157
West Cast Fire Integration Inc	7382	D	909 824-7980	18405
West Coast Drywall & Co Inc	1742	B	951 778-3592	1409
West Coast Interiors Inc	1721	A	951 778-3592	1201
West Coast Unlimited	3711	E	951 352-1234	9972
West States Skanska Inc	1623	C	970 565-4903	986
Westcoe Realtors Inc	6531	D	951 784-2500	16031
Western Case Incorporated	3089	D	951 214-6380	5863
Western Hydrostatics Inc **(PA)**	3594	E	951 784-2133	8447
Willow Springs LLC	8011	D	951 789-4405	20167
Windsor Capital Group Inc	7011	D	951 276-1200	16801
Windsor Cypress Grdns Hlthcare	8059	A	951 688-3643	20642
Yardney Water MGT Systems Inc **(PA)**	3589	E	951 656-6716	8429
Your Way Fumigation Inc	7342	D	951 699-9116	17207
Youth Enterprise Inc	8093	E	310 902-9266	21368
Z-Best Concrete Inc	1771	D	951 774-1870	1558
Zenith Manufacturing Inc	3728	E	818 767-2106	10447
Ziehm Instrumentarium	3844	E	407 615-8560	11212

RLLNG HLS EST, CA - Los Angeles County

	SIC	EMP	PHONE	ENTRY #
Artists Studio Gallery **(PA)**	7999	D	310 265-2592	19636
Chandlers Plos Vrdes Sand Grav	1442	F	310 784-2900	569
Dincloud Inc	7372	D	310 929-1101	17838
Ecw Technology Inc	3564	F	310 373-0082	8046
Equinox-76th Street Inc	7991	D	310 697-1016	19449
Graphic Prints Inc	2396	E	310 870-1239	3174
Jack Kramer Club	7997	E	310 326-4404	19571
Longs Drug Stores Cal LLC	7384	C	310 377-6728	18417
Maniaci Group Inc	6411	D	310 541-4824	15590
National Media Inc **(HQ)**	2711	E	310 377-6877	4011
Nht Global Inc	5122	D	972 241-6525	14270
Seatech Consulting Group Inc	7379	E	310 356-6828	18221
Sheervision Inc **(PA)**	3841	F	310 265-8918	11057

ROLLING HILLS, CA - Los Angeles County

	SIC	EMP	PHONE	ENTRY #
California Digital Inc **(PA)**	3577	D	310 217-0500	8242
Trams Inc **(DH)**	7373	D	310 641-8726	18071

ROMOLAND, CA - Riverside County

	SIC	EMP	PHONE	ENTRY #
Orco Block & Hardscape	3271	E	951 928-3619	6012
Southern California Edison Co	4911	C	800 336-2822	12834

ROSEMEAD, CA - Los Angeles County

	SIC	EMP	PHONE	ENTRY #
Bhc Alhambra Hospital Inc	8062	D	626 286-1191	20688
Bhc Alhambra Hospital Inc	8099	B	626 286-1191	21388
Bright Care Home Health Inc **(PA)**	8082	D	626 285-9698	21142
BT Baking	2051	F	213 880-9828	1986
C & R Extrusions	3081	F	626 642-0244	5428
Chinese Overseas Mktg Svc Corp **(PA)**	2741	D	626 280-8538	4162
County of Los Angeles	7992	D	626 280-8225	19479
Doubletree Hotel	7011	D	323 722-8800	16417
Durham School Services L P	4151	C	626 573-3769	11924
Edison International **(PA)**	4911	A	626 302-2222	12803
Edison Mission Energy **(DH)**	4911	B	626 302-5778	12804
Edison Mssion Midwest Holdings	4911	A	626 302-2222	12805
Ensign Group Inc	8051	D	626 607-2400	20331
Hartford Great Health Corp **(PA)**	7011	D	626 321-1915	16464
HCC Industries Leasing Inc **(HQ)**	3823	F	626 443-8933	10699
Hermetic Seal Corporation **(DH)**	3679	C	626 443-8931	9722
Holiday Inn Express	7011	D	323 726-1111	16488
Irish Communication Company **(DH)**	1623	D	626 288-6170	956
Irish Construction **(HQ)**	1623	C	626 288-8530	957
J F McCaughin Co	3952	F	626 573-3000	11469
Ldvc Inc	2064	F	626 448 4611	2092
Longwood Management Corp	8051	C	626 280 2293	20406
Longwood Management Corp	8051	C	626 280-4820	20407
Lonix Pharmaceutical Inc	2023	F	626 287-4700	1799
M Argeso & Co Inc	2911	F	626 573-3000	5254
Maryvale	8361	D	626 280-6510	22129
Panda Systems Inc	6794	C	626 799-9898	16213
Prographics Inc	2752	E	626 287-0417	4409
Southern California Edison Co **(HQ)**	4911	A	626 302-1212	12827
Southern California Edison Co	4911	C	626 302-5101	12832
Southern California Edison Co	4911	C	626 302-1212	12837
Southern States Realty	6531	A	626 302-1212	16006
Thai Print USA LLC **(PA)**	2752	F	626 872-6600	4436
Tur-Bo Jet Products Co Inc	3677	D	626 285-1294	9645
Whittier Narrow Golf Course	7999	C	626 288-1044	19681

ROWLAND HEIGHTS, CA - Los Angeles County

	SIC	EMP	PHONE	ENTRY #
Angeles Contractor Inc **(PA)**	1541	D	714 523-1021	688
Diack 1 Inc	3355	E	626 961-2491	6325
Emanate Health	8011	C	626 912-5282	19805
Flora Beauty Inc	5087	D	213 374-0448	14036
Hanson Distributing Company	5099	D	626 839-4026	14163
Istarusa Group	3571	E	888 989-1189	8163
Quality Painting Co	3479	F	626 964-2529	7405
Suzhou South	3578	B	626 322-0101	8317

RUNNING SPRINGS, CA - San Bernardino County

	SIC	EMP	PHONE	ENTRY #
Showtime Custom Coach Inc	7532	E	909 867-7025	18804
Snow Valley Mtn Resort LLC	7032	D	909 867-2751	16827

SAN BERNARDINO, CA - San Bernardino County

	SIC	EMP	PHONE	ENTRY #
Adams and Brooks Inc	2064	D	213 392-8700	2081
Ahtineb Nvels Photos By Design	7335	F	442 327-9234	17157
American Wire Inc	3496	F	909 884-9990	7494
Anco International Inc	3494	E	909 887-2521	7470
Anitas Mexican Foods Corp **(PA)**	2096	B	909 884-8706	2359
Ardent Mills LLC	2041	F	909 887-3407	1943
Arrowhead Country Club Golf Sp	7997	D	909 882-1735	19534
Aviation & Defense Inc	4581	C	909 382-3487	12341
Barrett Business Services Inc	7361	A	909 890-3633	17395
Bio-Medics Inc	8099	C	909 883-9501	21389
Blackcoffee Fabricators Inc	3993	F	909 974-4499	11527
Blood Bnk San Brnrdino Rvrside **(HQ)**	8099	C	909 885-6503	21391
Boyd Dental Corporation **(PA)**	8021	D	909 384-1111	20170
Braswlls Mdterranean Grdns Inc	8051	D	909 793-0433	20259
Brickley Construction Co Inc	1799	E	909 888-2010	1643
Budget Electrical Contrs Inc	1731	C	909 381-2646	1225
C-Pak Industries Inc	3089	E	909 880-6017	5591
Caesar Hardware Intl Ltd	3429	E	800 306-3829	6508
Caldesso LLC	3567	D	909 888-2882	8085
California Steel Services Inc	5051	E	909 796-2222	13554
Carbide Saw and Tool Inc	7699	F	909 884-9956	19028
Care Tech Inc	8051	E	909 882-2965	20275
Caremark Rx Inc	8011	D	909 887-7951	19734
Caston Inc	1742	D	909 381-1619	1370
Childhelp Inc	8322	D	909 335-1164	21741
CJ Logistics America LLC	4731	C	540 377-2302	12436
CMC Rebar West	5051	D	909 713-1130	13558
Community Action Prtnship Sb C	8399	D	909 723-1500	22177
Community Hosp San Bernardino **(DH)**	8062	B	909 887-6333	20727
Container Options	3089	F	909 478-0045	5612
Copier Source Inc	5044	C	909 890-4040	13354
Davidsons AC & Htg Inc	1711	E	909 885-2703	1054
Dean Distributors Inc	2099	E	323 587-8147	2418
Del Rosa Villa Inc	8051	D	909 885-3261	20310
Dish Network Corporation	4841	D	909 381-4767	12764

Mergent email: customerrelations@mergent.com
1422

2022 Southern California Business
Directory and Buyers Guide

(P-0000) Products & Services Section entry number
(PA)=Parent Co (HQ)=Headquarters (DH)=Div Headquarters

	SIC	EMP	PHONE	ENTRY #
Far West Inc	8051	D	909 884-4781	20343
Farmdale Creamery Inc	2026	D	909 888-4938	1834
Fiore Stone Inc	3272	E	909 424-0221	6033
First Hotels International Inc	7011	D	909 884-9364	16443
First Student Inc	4151	C	909 383-1640	11928
Fischer Inc	1711	D	909 881-2910	1069
Gate City Beverage Distrs **(PA)**	5181	B	909 799-0281	14825
Geologic Associates Inc	8999	D	909 383-8728	23534
Global Environmental Pdts Inc	3711	D	909 713-1600	9950
Gresham Savage Nolan & Tilden **(PA)**	8111	E	619 794-0050	21573
Ground Hog Inc	3531	E	909 478-5700	7643
Gunderson Rail Services LLC	4789	D	909 478-0541	12572
H and H Drug Stores Inc	5047	D	909 890-9700	13493
HAM Brokerage	4731	D	909 659-5392	12466
Harbill Inc	5012	D	909 883-8833	13028
Hayden Products LLC	3443	D	951 736-2600	6742
Hernandez Kroone and Assoc Inc	8711	D	909 884-3222	22566
Holliday Rock Trucking Inc	3273	D	888 273-2200	6095
Hospitality Sleep Systems Inc	2515	F	909 387-9779	3550
Hub Construction Spc Inc **(DH)**	7359	E	909 889-0161	17355
Inland Bhavioral Hlth Svcs Inc **(PA)**	8099	D	909 881-6146	21443
Inland Cnties Regional Ctr Inc **(PA)**	8322	A	909 890-3000	21815
Inland Empire 66ers Bsbal CLB	7941	C	909 888-9922	19418
Inland Empire Cmnty Newspapers	2711	F	909 381-9898	3994
Innocor West LLC	3069	B	909 307-3737	5383
Innovative Metal Inds Inc	3449	D	909 796-6200	7023
Institute For Bhvoral Hlth Inc	8099	B	909 289-1041	21444
Iron Workers Local 433	6733	E	909 884-5500	16178
Jenco Productions Inc **(PA)**	7389	C	909 381-9453	18558
Job Options Incorporated	7219	A	909 890-4612	16891
Jon Steel Erectors Inc	7692	E	909 799-0005	18986
Kaiser Foundation Hospitals	8011	C	866 205-3595	19939
Kaiser Foundation Hospitals	8011	C	888 750-0036	19943
Kav America Ag Inc	2095	F	855 528-8721	2356
Kindred Healthcare LLC	8082	D	909 890-1226	21181
Kmb Foods Inc **(PA)**	2013	E	626 447-0545	1737
Kohls Corporation	4225	B	909 382-4300	12216
L & L Nursery Supply Inc **(DH)**	5191	C	909 591-0461	14862
Laymon Candy Co Inc	5145	E	909 825-4408	14564
Legend Pump & Well Service Inc	1381	E	909 384-1000	433
Lewis Brsbois Bsgard Smith LLP	8111	D	909 387-1130	21611
Loma Linda University Med Ctr	8051	D	909 824-6904	20402
Longs Drug Stores Cal Inc	7384	D	909 886-4984	18412
Longs Drug Stores Cal LLC	7384	C	909 884-5364	18419
Lucky Farms Inc	0161	D	909 799-6688	17
M & L Pharmaceuticals Inc	2834	E	909 890-0078	4848
Macroair Technologies Inc **(PA)**	3564	E	909 890-2270	8050
Magnum Abrasives Inc	3291	E	909 890-1100	6154
Marna Health Services Inc	8059	D	909 882-2965	20611
Mars Petcare Us Inc	2047	E	909 887-8131	1959
Matich Corporation **(PA)**	1611	D	909 382-7400	901
Maxim Healthcare Services Inc	7363	D	951 684-4148	17502
Maxim Healthcare Services Inc	8082	C	760 243-3377	21191
Medina Concrete Construction	1771	E	909 474-9640	1540
Mentor Mdia USA Sup Chain MGT	8741	D	909 930-0800	23062
Meridian Rail Acquisition	4789	C	909 478-0541	12579
Michael P Byko DDS A Prof Corp **(PA)**	8021	D	909 888-7817	20188
Millers American Honey Inc	2099	E	909 825-1722	2485
Mkkr Inc	3545	E	909 890-5994	7858
Nagles Veal Inc	2011	E	909 383-7075	1716
National Orange Show **(PA)**	7389	C	909 888-6788	18609
Nitro 2 Go Inc	2833	F	909 864-4886	4754
Nlms Elite Construction Co	1521	F	626 205-8417	626
Northrop Grumman Systems Corp	3812	C	703 713-4096	10627
Ocelot Engineering Inc	5013	C	800 841-2960	13076
Optivus Proton Therapy Inc	3829	D	909 799-8300	10901
Original Mowbrays Tree Svc Inc **(PA)**	0783	C	909 383-7009	359
Paramount Windows & Doors	2431	F	909 888-4688	3280
Park West Enterprises Inc	2077	E	909 383-8341	2127
Pepsico	2086	F	562 818-9429	2279
Plasma Biolife Services L P	8099	E	909 863-3025	21471
Plott Management Co	8051	D	909 883-0288	20441
Preschool Services Department **(PA)**	8351	D	909 383-2000	22053
Quiel Bros Elc Sign Svc Co Inc	3993	E	909 885-4476	11584
R&R Machine Products Inc	3451	F	909 885-7500	7043
Refresco Beverages US Inc	2086	E	909 915-1400	2282
Refresco Beverages US Inc	2086	E	909 915-1430	2283
Rerubber LLC	4953	F	909 786-2811	12971
Rescom Overhead Doors Inc	1751	F	909 799-8555	1453
Rezek Equipment	8711	E	909 885-6221	22646
Robert Ballard Rehab Hospital **(HQ)**	8049	C	909 473-1200	20232
S B H Hotel Corporation	7011	A	909 889-0133	16678
S&E Gourmet Cuts Inc	5145	C	909 370-0155	14565
Sac Health System **(PA)**	8021	D	909 382-7100	20196
Safety Security Patrol LLC	7381	D	909 888-7778	18320
Sample Tile and Stone Inc	3281	E	951 776-8562	6144
San Bernardino California City **(PA)**	8111	B	909 384-7272	21672
San Bernardino Care Company	8059	C	909 884-4781	20625
San Bernardino Hilton **(HQ)**	7011	C	909 889-0133	16687
San Brnrdino Cmnty College Dst	4832	C	909 384-4444	12705
San Brnrdino Cmnty College Dst	2759	E	909 888-6511	4570
San Brnrdino Cnty Prbtion Offc	8322	B	909 887-2544	21882
San Brnrdno Cnty Ret Med Tr	8611	D	909 387-6053	22256
Sb Waterman Holdings Inc **(PA)**	8011	C	909 883-8611	20061
Scdrg Inc	7311	D	818 874-0830	17055
Schoolsfirst Federal Credit Un	6061	D	800 462-8328	15082
Semco	3829	E	909 799-9666	10908
Shorett Printing Inc **(PA)**	2759	E	714 545-4689	4573
Soffietti Co	5072	D	909 907-2277	13818
Sprint Communications Co LP	4813	C	909 382-6030	12672
St Bernardine Med Ctr Aux Inc	8062	C	909 881-4320	20956
St Bernardine Medical Center	8062	B	909 883-8711	20957
Stavatti Industries Ltd	1041	E	651 238-5369	376
Sun Company San Bernardino Cal **(PA)**	2711	B	909 889-9666	4032
Sunbrdge Shndin Hlls Rhbltion	8051	D	909 881-3896	20484
Systems Technology Inc	3565	D	909 799-9950	8078
Ten Days Manufacturing	5085	C	888 222-1575	14023
Think Together	8351	A	909 723-1400	22065
Tree Island Wire (usa) Inc	3496	D	909 899-1673	7519
Trinity Office Furniture Inc	2521	F	909 888-5551	3602
United Cabinet Company Inc	2434	E	909 796-3015	3345
United Medical Management Inc	8059	C	909 886-5291	20636
United Parcel Service Inc	4512	D	800 742-5877	12321
Veronicas Auto Insur Svcs Inc **(PA)**	6411	D	909 723-1910	15646
Victor Cmnty Support Svcs Inc	8093	C	909 890-5930	21365
Vna Hspice Plltive Care Sthern **(PA)**	8082	C	909 624-3574	21232
W B Walton Enterprises Inc	3663	E	951 683-0930	9326
Waterman Convalescent Hosp Inc **(PA)**	8051	C	909 882-1215	20502
Wcs Distributing Inc	5084	E	909 888-2015	13962
Web Educational Services Inc	7372	F	866 719-2159	18007
Willdan Engineering	8711	D	909 386-0200	22697
Woodman Realty Inc	6531	C	909 425-5324	16034
World Class Distribution Inc	4225	D	909 574-4140	12262
YMCA of East Valley	8641	D	909 881-9622	22382

SAN CLEMENTE, CA - Orange County

	SIC	EMP	PHONE	ENTRY #
Automobile Club Southern Cal	8699	D	949 489-5572	22429
Azimuth Electronics Inc	3825	F	949 492-6481	10744
Bella Collina San Clemente	7997	D	949 498-6604	19542
Bemus Landscape Inc	1629	B	714 557-7910	988
Brad Rambo & Associates Inc **(PA)**	5136	D	949 366-9911	14328
Bunker Corp **(PA)**	3714	D	949 361-3935	10024
Capistrano Labs Inc	3841	E	949 492-0390	10956
Cellco Partnership	4812	D	949 488-9990	12604
Clean Wave Management Inc	3721	F	949 488-2922	10183
Clean Wave Management Inc	3562	E	949 361-5356	8027
Coast Valley Moving & Stor Inc	4213	D	949 361-7500	12023
Code-In-Motion LLC	3569	F	949 361-2633	8118
Composite Manufacturing Inc	3841	E	949 361-7580	10966
Custom Ingredients Inc **(PA)**	2087	E	949 276-7994	2318
Dana Innovations	3651	D	949 492-7777	9169
Dealersocket Inc **(PA)**	7371	D	949 900-0300	17592
Dose Medical Corporation	3841	F	949 367-9600	10972
Dragon Alliance Inc	3851	D	760 931-4900	11249
Dual Diagnosis Trtmnt Ctr Inc **(PA)**	8093	B	949 276-5553	21300
Electric Visual Evolution LLC **(PA)**	3851	E	949 940-9125	11250
Elevate Inc	7372	F	949 276-5428	17845
Elotek Systems Inc **(PA)**	5045	E	949 366-4404	13390
Epica Medical Innovations LLC	3841	E	949 238-6323	10981
Evolution Hospitality LLC **(HQ)**	8741	A	949 325-1350	23024
Flow Sports Inc	3949	E	949 361-5260	11417
Four Star Distribution	3021	D	949 369-4420	5308
Frear Consulting Inc	8711	D	307 237-6060	22556
Futurestitch Inc	2253	F	760 707-2003	2634
GCI Construction Inc	1611	E	714 957-0233	880
Glaukos Corporation **(PA)**	3841	C	949 367-9600	10985
Golf Investment LLC **(PA)**	7997	D	949 498-6604	19565
Heritage Golf Group LLC	7992	C	949 369-6226	19492
Hot Shoppe Designs Inc	2329	F	949 487-2828	2812
Icu Medical Inc **(PA)**	3841	A	949 366-2183	10991
Icu Medical Sales Inc **(HQ)**	3841	D	949 366-2183	10992
International Rubber Pdts Inc **(DH)**	3069	D	909 947-1244	5384
Joan Baker Designs Inc	5199	E	949 498-1983	14941
Julius Steve Construction Inc	1541	E	949 369-7820	704
Kelcourt Plastics Inc **(DH)**	3089	D	949 361-0774	5688
Kui Co Inc	2621	E	949 369-7949	3759
Leaf Communications Inc	8748	D	949 388-0192	23465
Left Coast Brewing Company	2082	F	949 218-3961	2149
Life Time Inc	7991	C	949 492-1515	19456
Lowes Home Centers LLC	5031	C	949 369-4644	13226
Luxre Realty Inc	6531	D	949 498-3702	15916
Matsushita International Corp **(PA)**	6799	D	949 498-1000	16277
Merge Mobile Inc	7371	E	949 234-6248	17660
Model Match Inc	7372	F	949 525-9405	17922
Mvm Products LLC	3861	F	949 366-1470	11287
Nation Surfboard Mfg Inc	3949	F	949 370-6607	11439
Netsource Technology Inc	5065	F	949 713-0800	13755
Pacific Medical Group Inc	5047	D	949 493-1030	13507
Plastics Development Corp	3089	E	949 492-0217	5756
R & R Industries Inc	2389	E	800 234-5611	3082
R T C Group	2721	E	949 226-2000	4102
Reshape Weightloss Inc **(HQ)**	3845	E	949 429-6680	11237
Reynard Corporation	3827	E	949 366-8866	10857
Rip Curl Inc **(DH)**	3949	D	714 422-3600	11442
Roberto Martinez Inc	3911	F	800 257-6462	11329
Rosen & Rosen Industries Inc	3949	D	949 361-9238	11443
Rox Medical Inc **(PA)**	3841	F	949 276-8968	11053
Sambazon Inc **(PA)**	5148	D	877 726-2296	14651
San Clemente Villas By Sea Inc	8361	D	949 489-3400	22151
San Diego Gas & Electric Co	4931	D	949 361-8090	12873
Sensory Neurostimulation Inc	2834	F	949 492-0550	4892
Snowpure LLC	3589	E	949 240-2188	8415
Sonance	5064	D	949 492-7777	13695
Songs Dcmmssning Solutions LLC	2819	F	801 649-2223	4671
Stance Inc **(PA)**	5137	C	949 391-9030	14418

GEOGRAPHIC

	SIC	EMP	PHONE	ENTRY #
Streuter Technologies	5051	E	949 369-7676	13598
Verrix LLC	3841	F	949 668-1234	11073
Western Outdoors Publications **(PA)**	2711	E	949 366-0030	4044
Won & Jay Inc	7992	E	949 369-6226	19512
Xlr8 Services Inc	8711	E	949 498-9578	22703

SAN DIMAS, CA - Los Angeles County

	SIC	EMP	PHONE	ENTRY #
Aircraft Stamping Company Inc	3444	F	323 283-1239	6777
Am-PM Printing Inc	2752	F	909 599-0811	4226
American States Water Company **(PA)**	4941	A	909 394-3600	12879
Associations of United Nurses **(PA)**	8631	D	909 599-8622	22287
Automatic Data Processing Inc	7374	C	800 225-5237	18080
Bolide Technology Group Inc	7382	D	909 305-8889	18367
Brault	8721	C	626 447-0296	22762
Buddhist Tzu CHI Foundation **(PA)**	8641	D	909 447-7799	22321
Christian Community Credit Un **(PA)**	6062	D	626 915-7551	15108
Cosmobeauti Labs & Mfg Inc	2844	F	909 971-9832	5006
Curative-Korva LLC	8071	D	424 645-7575	21066
Custom Cooler Inc **(HQ)**	5078	D	909 592-1111	13852
Ego Inc	8721	C	626 447-0296	22778
Elba Jewelry Inc	3911	F	909 394-5803	11315
Emeritus Corporation	8051	C	909 394-0304	20320
Emily Grene Corp	8748	E	855 463-6459	23436
Gilead Palo Alto Inc	2834	E	909 394-4000	4823
Gms Elevator Services Inc	3534	E	909 599-3904	7679
Golden State Water Company **(HQ)**	4941	C	909 394-3600	12892
Hagen-Renaker Inc **(PA)**	3269	D	909 599-2341	6004
Hamilton Sundstrand Corp	3826	C	909 593-5300	10796
Hamilton Sundstrand Spc Systms	3829	D	909 288-5300	10887
Han Rigid Plastics Corp USA	3086	F	909 394-5832	5510
Kaiser Foundation Hospitals	8062	A	909 394-2530	20808
Kap Manufacturing Inc	3599	E	909 599-2525	8650
L Barrios and Associates Inc	0782	E	909 592-5893	314
LAC Motor Enterprises Inc	4212	D	626 329-1411	11979
Legal Solutions Holdings Inc	8111	C	800 244-3495	21608
Lowes Home Centers LLC	5031	C	909 305-2960	13241
Magco Drilling Inc	1781	C	626 969-1000	1562
Magor Mold LLC	3544	D	909 592-3663	7815
McKinley Childrens Center Inc **(PA)**	8361	C	909 599-1227	22130
Med-Legal LLC **(PA)**	8111	C	626 653-5160	21626
Medic-1 Ambulance Service Inc	4119	D	909 592-8840	11879
New Spirit Naturals Inc **(PA)**	8011	E	909 592-4445	19992
Norac Additives LLC	5169	D	909 321-5952	14788
Om Food Sejal Enterprises Inc	8742	D	626 712-3138	23287
Onquest Heaters Inc **(HQ)**	8711	C	909 451-0499	22624
Organic Milling Inc	2043	D	800 638-8686	1949
Organic Milling Corporation **(PA)**	2099	C	909 599-0961	2499
Organic Milling Corporation	2099	E	909 305-0185	2500
Pacific Systems Interiors Inc	1742	C	310 436-6820	1392
Pacific W Space Cmmnctions Inc	1623	D	909 592-4321	964
Pertronix Inc **(PA)**	3822	E	909 599-5955	10667
Prime Health Care	8351	B	909 394-2727	22055
Prime Hlthcare Svcs - San Dmas	8062	B	909 599-6811	20909
Qtc Management Inc **(DH)**	8099	D	800 260-1515	21473
Qtc Mdcal Group Inc A Med Corp	8099	A	800 260-1515	21474
Raging Waters Group Inc	7996	A	909 802-2200	19522
Recom Group	5065	E	909 599-1370	13771
San Dimas Golf Inc	7997	C	909 599-8486	19606
San Dimas Retirement Center **(PA)**	6513	D	909 599-8441	15748
Second Image National LLC **(PA)**	7334	C	800 229-7477	17154
Sharp Profiles LLC	3423	F	760 246-9446	6489
Sigtronics Corporation	3669	E	909 305-9399	9354
Smart & Final Stores Inc	5141	C	909 592-2190	14490
Southern Cal Prmnnte Med Group	6324	C	909 394-2505	15460
Southern California Edison Co	4911	C	909 592-3757	12852
Spectrum Instruments Inc	3825	F	909 971-9710	10771
Sypris Data Systems Inc **(HQ)**	3572	E	909 962-9400	8221
Thorpe Technologies Inc **(DH)**	8711	E	562 903-8230	22674
Thunderbird Industries Inc	3544	F	909 394-1633	7837
Tile King	5032	F	909 599-7300	13315
Transdev North America Inc	4013	D	909 394-2307	11800
Vertex Diamond Tool Co Inc	3545	E	909 599-1129	7876
Walton Construction Inc	1522	D	909 267-7777	673
Wavestream Corporation **(HQ)**	3679	C	909 599-9080	9802
Wellpoint Inc	6311	C	805 375-1605	15372
Western PCF Stor Solutions Inc **(PA)**	2542	D	909 451-0303	3703
Westin Automotive Products Inc **(PA)**	2396	E	626 960-6762	3184
Young Engineering & Mfg Inc **(PA)**	3823	E	909 394-3225	10734

SAN FERNANDO, CA - Los Angeles County

	SIC	EMP	PHONE	ENTRY #
A Thread Ahead Inc	7389	E	818 837-1984	18427
Abex Display Systems Inc **(PA)**	2653	C	800 537-0231	3781
Ahi Investment Inc **(DH)**	5199	E	818 979-0030	14908
Airo Industries Company	2531	E	818 838-1008	3619
All American Asphalt	1611	D	818 361-6141	855
All State Association Inc	8611	C	877 425-2558	22242
American Bottling Company	2086	F	818 898-1471	2251
Araca Merchandise LP	2759	D	818 743-5400	4480
Art Bronze Inc	3366	E	818 897-2222	6405
Arturo Gonzalez	3672	E	818 837-7221	9381
B & B Doors and Windows Inc	3442	F	818 837-8480	6692
Bellows Mfg & RES Inc	3441	E	818 838-1333	6589
Bernards Builders Inc	1522	B	818 898-1521	655
Bernards Inc	8741	D	818 898-1521	22986
Bestway Sandwiches Inc **(PA)**	2051	C	818 361-1800	1984
Blue Cross Beauty Products Inc	2844	F	818 896-8681	4993
Brightview Landscape Dev Inc	1711	D	818 838-4700	1037
C A Schroeder Inc **(PA)**	3296	E	818 365-9561	6169
Cacho Landscape Maint Co Inc	0782	E	818 365-0773	293
California Flex Corporation **(PA)**	3089	D	818 361-1169	5594
Canady Manufacturing Co Inc	3599	F	818 365-9181	8540
Carrillos Tortilleria Inc **(PA)**	2099	F	818 365-1636	2405
Child Care Resource Center Inc	8351	C	818 837-0097	21997
Cockram Construction Inc **(HQ)**	8742	C	818 650-0999	23192
County of Los Angeles	8011	D	818 837-6969	19764
Cousins Foods LLC	2035	E	818 767-3842	1886
De La Mare Engineering Inc	7819	E	818 365-9203	19224
Dg-Displays LLC	3993	E	877 358-5975	11541
Don Whittemore Corp	2024	F	818 994-0111	1815
First Student Inc	4151	C	818 896-0333	11933
Frazier Aviation Inc	3728	E	818 898-1998	10332
Fresh & Ready Foods LLC **(PA)**	2099	D	818 837-7600	2437
Frontier California Inc	4813	B	818 365-0542	12639
General Production Services	3599	E	818 365-4211	8604
Haimetal Duct Inc	3444	E	818 768-2315	6848
Industrial Stitchtech Inc	7389	C	818 361-6319	18548
J L Shepherd and Assoc Inc	3829	E	818 898-2361	10893
J Miller Co Inc	3053	E	818 837-0[illegible]81	5344
Jme Inc **(PA)**	5063	D	201 896-8600	13638
Karoun Dairies Inc **(PA)**	2022	E	818 767-7000	1775
Kraft/Tech Inc	3751	F	818 837-3520	10496
Lehman Foods Inc	2099	E	818 837-7500	2474
Metromedia Technologies Inc	3577	E	818 552-6500	8281
Mr Tortilla Inc	2099	E	818 307-7414	2491
Newco International Inc	2511	F	818 834-7100	3481
Northeast Valley Health Corp	8011	D	818 361-8464	19997
Northeast Valley Health Corp **(PA)**	8322	D	818 898-1388	21857
Northeast Valley Health Corp	8011	D	818 365-3086	19999
Omnical Inc	3842	F	818 837-7531	11130
One Step Gps LLC	3812	E	818 659-2031	10629
Puretek Corporation **(PA)**	2834	E	818 361 3316	4878
Ricon Corp **(HQ)**	3999	C	818 267-3000	11744
San Fernando City of Inc	8322	D	818 898-7340	21883
Santana Formal Accessories Inc	2311	F	818 898-3677	2750
Scenario Cockram USA Inc **(DH)**	1799	C	818 650-0999	1687
Signature Tech Group Inc	3679	F	818 890-7611	9781
Skaug Truck Body Works	3713	F	818 365-9123	9995
Spira Manufacturing Corp	3053	E	818 764-8222	5354
TL Shield & Associates Inc	3534	E	818 509-8228	7681
Triumph Precision Products	3451	E	818 897-4700	7047
Tyan Inc	7381	D	818 785-5831	18347
Universal Mail Delivery Svc **(PA)**	4212	D	818 365-3144	12006
V and L Back Hoe Service Inc	3531	F	818 898-1997	7657
W Machine Works Inc	3599	E	818 890-8049	8842
Winchells Franchising LLC	2051	E	818 361-9017	2053
Wyndham Collection LLC	2434	E	888 522-8476	3349

SAN GABRIEL, CA - Los Angeles County

	SIC	EMP	PHONE	ENTRY #
Ahmc Healthcare Inc	8099	A	626 248-3452	21372
Ahmc Healthcare Inc **(PA)**	8062	C	626 943-7526	20665
American Prcision Grinding Mch	3599	F	626 357-6610	8497
Asia-Pacific California Inc	2711	E	626 281-8500	3948
Asian Youth Center	8322	D	626 309-0622	21717
Bestonlinecabinets	2434	E	626 589-6827	3307
BF Suma Pharmaceuticals Inc	2834	F	626 285-8366	4797
Black Drop Coffee Inc	2095	F	323 742-5666	2352
Cal Southern Services	7213	D	626 281-5942	16850
Chick N Skin LLC	2096	F	626 759-2925	2360
Chineseinvestorscom Inc **(PA)**	7389	D	626 589-2468	18478
Clairbourn School	8351	D	626 286-3108	22005
Classic Tees Inc	2339	F	626 607-0255	2933
Country Villa Service Corp	8059	C	626 285-2165	20573
Facey Medical Foundation	8099	C	626 576-0800	21426
Finch Tree Surgery Inc	0783	D	626 287-9838	356
Hsiao & Montano Inc	3161	E	626 588-2528	5893
IGS Molding LLC	3089	F	562 801-3522	5671
Informtion Rfrral Fdrtion of L	7299	D	626 350-1841	16959
Landwin Hospitality LLC	7011	D	626 270-2700	16534
Life Care Centers America Inc	8051	C	626 289-5365	20393
Life Care Centers America Inc	8051	C	626 289-8889	20394
Longwood Management Corp	8059	D	626 289-3763	20606
Lotus Orient Corp **(PA)**	2335	E	626 285-5796	2892
Marples Gears Inc	3566	E	626 570-1744	8082
Media King Inc	3699	E	626 288-4558	9891
Mueller Gages Company	3545	E	626 287-2911	7859
Normans Nursery Inc **(PA)**	5193	E	626 285-9795	14891
Park Cleaners Inc **(PA)**	7213	D	626 281-5942	16868
R C L Lodging Systems Inc	7011	D	561 833-3000	16648
San Gabriel Country Club	7997	D	626 287-9671	19607
San Gabriel Valley Medical Ctr	8062	A	626 289-5454	20929
San Gbriel Ambltory Srgery Ctr	8011	B	626 300-5300	20051
San Yi US Investment Co Inc	7011	E	626 607-2006	16689
Taotao Manufacturer Inc	3999	F	626 688-9880	11774

SAN JACINTO, CA - Riverside County

	SIC	EMP	PHONE	ENTRY #
Agri-Empire	5148	C	951 654-7311	14612
Amark Industries Inc **(PA)**	3567	E	951 654-7351	8083
CM Machine Inc	3599	F	951 654-6019	8556
Edelbrock Holdings Inc	3714	C	951 654-6677	10051
J Talley Corporation **(PA)**	3446	D	951 654-2123	6964
MTI De Baja Inc	3812	E	951 654-2333	10603
Rama Corporation	3567	E	951 654-7351	8097
Soboba Band Luiseno Indians	7389	A	951 665-1000	18671
Toms Backhoe Services Inc	3531	F	951 634-4075	7653
Valley Wide Recreation Pk Dst **(PA)**	7999	D	951 654-1505	19679
Wallace Wood Products	2541	F	951 654-9311	3671

Mergent email: customerrelations@mergent.com
1424

2022 Southern California Business
Directory and Buyers Guide

(P-0000) Products & Services Section entry number
(PA)=Parent Co (HQ)=Headquarters (DH)=Div Headquarters

SAN JUAN CAPISTRANO, CA - Orange County

	SIC	EMP	PHONE	ENTRY #
117 Global LLC **(PA)**	7389	F	949 570-1552	18423
3gen Inc	3841	F	949 481-6384	10922
Best Wstn Capistrano Inn LLC	7011	D	949 493-5661	16347
Bijou Healthcare Inc	8051	D	949 487-9500	20255
Brightview Landscape Svcs Inc	0781	C	714 546-7843	241
Celera Corporation **(HQ)**	8733	B	510 749-4200	22904
Congaree Health Holdings LLC	8051	D	949 487-9500	20290
Diamond Peo LLC	7361	C	714 728-5186	17412
Diamond Vly Hlth Holdings LLC	8051	D	949 487-9500	20314
Digital Rdlgic Imging Assoc In	8011	D	949 499-1311	19801
Emerald Holding Inc **(PA)**	7389	C	949 226-5700	18512
Emerald X LLC **(HQ)**	7389	C	949 226-5700	18513
Endura Healthcare Inc	8051	D	949 487-9500	20326
Ensign Services Inc	8051	D	949 487-9500	20333
Ensign Southland LLC	8051	B	949 487-9500	20334
Flagstone Healthcare South LLC	8051	D	949 487-9500	20345
Fluidmaster Inc **(PA)**	3089	C	949 728-2000	5647
Freedom Properties-Hemet LLC	6512	C	949 489-0430	15668
Fresenius Med Care San Juan CP	8092	D	949 240-0221	21242
Grand Avenue Hlth Holdings LLC	8051	D	949 487-9500	20366
Huntington Bch Cnvlscent Hosp	8051	D	949 487-9500	20376
Infospan	8742	A	949 260-9990	23243
Ip Access International	7379	E	949 655-1000	18192
Kaiser Foundation Hospitals	6324	C	888 988-2800	15431
Kingdom Entities LLC **(PA)**	8748	D	949 325-9240	23461
Las Glondrinas Mexican Fd Pdts **(PA)**	2099	F	949 240-3440	2471
Marbella Country Club	7997	C	949 248-3700	19585
Marriott International Inc	7011	D	949 503-5700	16558
Medusind Solutions Inc **(PA)**	7389	A	949 240-8895	18590
Merit Logistics LLC	4789	A	949 481-0685	12580
Mission Volkswagen Inc	7538	D	949 493-4511	18857
Nichols Inst Reference Labs **(DH)**	8071	A	949 728-4000	21079
Ospreydata Inc	3826	F	619 971-4662	10804
Pioneer Sands LLC	1446	E	949 728-0171	578
Quest Diagnostics Nichols Inst **(HQ)**	3826	A	949 728-4000	10808
Rancho Mission Viejo LLC	6531	D	949 240-3363	15964
S K Pharmaceuticals Inc	2834	F	949 235-5265	4889
San Juan Golf Inc	7992	D	949 493-1167	19506
Seychelle Envmtl Tech Inc	3589	F	949 234-1999	8413
Silverado Senior Living Inc	8051	D	949 988-0921	20472
Solag Incorporated	4953	B	949 728-1206	12981
Southern Cal Prmnnte Med Group	8011	C	949 234-2139	20087
Summit Trail Hlth Holdings LLC	8051	D	949 487-9500	20481
Sunrise Senior Living LLC	8051	D	949 248-8855	20486
Sunshine Behavioral Health LLC **(PA)**	8093	D	949 835-4375	21346
Surrounding Elements LLC	2514	E	949 582-9000	3534
Teacherzone Inc	7372	F	855 970-9663	17992
Treasure Hls Hlth Hldings LLC	8051	D	949 487-9500	20489

SAN LUIS OBISPO, CA - San Luis Obispo County

	SIC	EMP	PHONE	ENTRY #
3i Infotech Inc	7371	F	805 544-8327	17535
Aee Solar Inc **(DH)**	5063	E	800 777-6609	13610
Air-Vol Block Inc	3271	E	805 543-1314	6008
Alfred Domaine	2084	F	805 541-9463	2165
All About Produce Inc	5148	C	805 543-9000	14613
American Incorporated	1711	B	805 597-6545	1025
American West Worldwide Ex Inc **(PA)**	4214	D	800 788-4534	12106
Amk Foodservices Inc	5141	C	805 544-7600	14454
Apple Farm Collections-Slo Inc **(PA)**	7011	B	805 544-2040	16327
Ashley & Vance Engineering Inc	8711	D	805 545-0010	22496
Associated Students Inc **(PA)**	8322	D	805 756-1281	21718
Automobile Club Southern Cal	8699	D	805 543-6454	22402
Bayshore Healthcare Inc	8051	C	805 544-5100	20252
Boeing Company	4581	F	805 606-6340	12345
Booth Mitchel & Strange LLP	8111	D	805 400-0703	21521
Cannon Corporation **(PA)**	8713	D	805 544-7407	22754
Cattaneo Bros Inc	2013	E	805 543-7188	1730
Central Cast Pthlogy Cons Inc **(DH)**	8071	D	805 541-6033	21062
Chamisal Vineyards LLC	2084	F	866 808-9463	2177
Cloud Company **(PA)**	3569	E	805 549-8093	8117
Cold Canyon Land Fill Inc	4953	E	805 549-8332	12941
Community Action Partnership	8322	D	805 541-4122	21750
Community Action Prtnr San Lui **(PA)**	8351	D	805 544-4355	22006
Community Action Prtnr San Lui	8351	C	805 541-2272	22007
Community Action Prtnr San Lui	8093	C	805 544-2478	21288
Compass Health Inc	8051	C	805 543-0210	20286
Cottage Health	8062	D	805 541-9113	20732
County of San Luis Obispo	8062	C	805 781-4753	20741
Courtside Cellars LLC **(PA)**	2084	E	805 782-0500	2180
Crystal Engineering Corp	3823	E	805 595-5477	10688
David B Anderson	2752	E	805 489-0661	4272
Dozuki	7372	E	805 464-0573	17841
Entegris Gp Inc	3569	C	805 541-9299	8121
Family Care Network Inc **(PA)**	8351	D	805 503-6240	22014
First Transit Inc	4111	C	805 544-2730	11810
French Hospital Medical Center **(DH)**	8062	B	805 543-5353	20773
Fziomed Inc **(PA)**	3841	E	805 546-0610	10984
Gentiva Health Services Inc	8082	D	805 549-0801	21165
Gla Agricultural Elec Inc	3829	E	805 541-3758	10885
Goodwill Central Coast	8322	C	805 544-0542	21793
Guaranteed Rate Inc	6162	C	805 550-6933	15200
Harvest Management Sub LLC	6513	A	805 543-0187	15725
Hj Construction Inc	1623	E	805 534-1617	954
Imdex Technology Usa LLC	3829	E	805 540-2017	10889
ITW Global Tire Repair Inc	3011	D	805 489-0490	5303
James A Quaglino Inc	1761	D	805 543-0560	1490
Jennings Aeronautics LLC	3812	E	805 544-0932	10594
Kairos Manufacturing Inc	3999	F	805 544-2216	11700
Kindred Healthcare LLC	8051	C	805 544-4472	20386
King Ventures	6552	C	805 544-4444	16054
Ksby Communications LLC	4833	D	805 541-6666	12732
Life Steps Foundation Inc	8322	D	805 549-0150	21841
Lockheed Martin Unmanned	7373	D	805 503-4340	18046
Lumina Alliance	8322	D	805 781-6400	21846
M G A Investment Co Inc	2741	F	805 543-9050	4188
Madonna Inn Inc	7991	C	805 543-3000	19459
Meathead Movers Inc **(PA)**	4213	D	805 544-6328	12064
Merrill Lynch Prce Fnner Smith	6211	D	805 596-2222	15295
Mid Coast Suppliers Inc	5039	F	805 543-0871	13336
Mindbody Inc **(PA)**	7374	C	877 755-4279	18101
Mission Country Disposal	4953	D	805 543-0875	12960
Morris Grritano Insur Agcy Inc	6411	D	805 543-6887	15599
Mutt Couture Inc **(PA)**	2323	E	805 469-6888	2765
Myogenix Incorporated	2834	E	800 950-0348	4854
Nesbitt Prtners San Luis Obspo	7011	D	805 549-0800	16578
Next Intent Inc	3599	E	805 781-6755	8717
Northern Holdings	1795	D	805 785-0194	1618
Oddworld Inhabitants Inc	7372	F	805 503-3000	17940
Ottano Inc	2082	E	805 547-2088	2151
Pacific Gas and Electric Co	4911	C	805 545-4562	12816
Parable Group Inc **(PA)**	6794	D	805 543-2644	16214
Phase 2 Cellars LLC	2084	E	805 782-0300	2212
Pipsticks Inc	2678	E	805 439-1692	3917
Postalio Inc	8742	F	408 616-9284	23297
Promega Biosciences LLC	2833	D	805 544-8524	4761
Protective Wther Strctures Inc	1541	F	805 547-8797	715
Prpco	2752	E	805 543-6844	4410
Q S San Luis Obispo LP	7011	D	805 541-5001	16645
Quality Rubber Sourcing Inc	2822	F	805 544-7770	4733
R H Strasbaugh **(PA)**	3541	D	805 541-6424	7741
Rec Solar Commercial Corp	1711	C	844 732-7652	1127
Revasum Inc	3674	C	805 541-6424	9564
Rincon Consultants Inc	8748	C	805 547-0900	23501
Royal Oak Motor Hotel	7011	D	805 544-4410	16673
Rrm Design Group **(PA)**	8712	D	805 439-0442	22741
San Luis Ambulance Service Inc	4119	C	805 543-2626	11888
San Luis Dgnstc Ctr A Cal Ltd	8011	D	805 542-9700	20052
San Luis Obispo County YMCA	8641	D	805 544-7225	22364
San Luis Obispo Golf Cntry CLB	7997	C	805 543-3400	19608
San Luis Obspo Rgnal Trnst Aut	4111	D	805 781-4465	11838
Sauer Brands Inc	2099	D	805 597-8900	2522
Sesloc Federal Credit Union **(PA)**	6061	D	805 543-1816	15088
Sierra Vista Hospital Inc **(HQ)**	8062	A	805 546-7600	20939
Slo New Times Inc	2711	E	805 546-8208	4030
Snapnrack Inc	3429	F	877 732-2860	6536
South County Sanitary Svc Inc	4953	D	805 489-4246	12982
Specialty Construction Inc	1731	D	805 543-1706	1317
SRI International	8733	C	805 542-9330	22922
State Bar of California	8621	D	805 544-7551	22282
Stellar Exploration Inc	3761	E	805 459-1425	10520
Straight Down Enterprises **(PA)**	2329	E	805 543-3086	2826
Sun Delivery LLC	4212	E	336 472-5000	11998
Sunrun Installation Svcs Inc **(HQ)**	1711	D	415 580-6900	1151
Sycamore Mineral Spring Resort	7011	D	805 595-7302	16747
Taco Works Inc	2096	E	805 541-1556	2367
Thoma Electric Inc	1731	D	805 543-3850	1328
Transitions - Mental Hlth Assn **(PA)**	8093	D	805 540-6500	21355
Tri-Cnties Assn For Dvlpmntlly	8322	C	805 543-2833	21905
Trust Automation Inc	8711	D	805 544-0761	22679
Ultra-Stereo Labs Inc	3699	E	805 549-0161	9924
United Crbral Plsy Assn San Lu	4119	D	805 543-2039	11895
United Parcel Service Inc	4215	C	801 973-3400	12161
USA Staffing Inc	7363	D	805 269-2677	17520
Veterans Health Administration	8011	C	805 543-1233	20143
Village Pacific MGT Group Inc	8051	D	805 543-2350	20499
Village Pacific MGT Group Inc **(PA)**	8051	D	805 543-2300	20500
Whitefox Defense Tech Inc	3364	E	805 225-4506	6381
Ws Packaging-Blake Printery	2752	E	805 543-6844	4461
Xpo Logistics Freight Inc	4213	D	805 541-4581	12094

SAN MARINO, CA - Los Angeles County

	SIC	EMP	PHONE	ENTRY #
Advanced Plastics Corporation	3089	F	626 286-7163	5548
Feihe International Inc **(PA)**	2023	A	626 757-8885	1791
Huntingtn Lbrary Art Collctns	8412	B	626 405-2100	22222
Southern California Lrng Corp	8351	E	818 639-9692	22058

SAN MIGUEL, CA - San Luis Obispo County

	SIC	EMP	PHONE	ENTRY #
Courtside Cellars LLC	2084	F	805 467-2882	2179

SAN PEDRO, CA - Los Angeles County

	SIC	EMP	PHONE	ENTRY #
Advent Resources Inc	7371	D	310 241-1500	17542
APM Terminals Pacific LLC	4731	B	310 221-4000	12424
APM Terminals Pacific LLC **(DH)**	4491	C	704 571-2768	12285
Boys Grls Clubs of Los Angles **(PA)**	8641	D	310 833-1322	22320
Bridges At Sn Pdro Pnnsla Hspt	8093	D	310 514-5359	21280
Brouwerij West	2082	F	908 391-2599	2140
Catalina Channel Express Inc **(HQ)**	4489	C	310 519-7971	12280
Catalina Channel Express Inc	4489	D	310 510-1212	12281
City of Los Angeles	8721	A	310 732-3734	22771
Cleantek Electric Inc	1731	E	424 400-3315	1233
Crowley Marine Services Inc	4731	B	310 732-6500	12441
Everport Terminal Services Inc **(PA)**	4491	D	310 221-0220	12287
Fenix Marine Services Ltd **(HQ)**	7359	E	310 548-8877	17348
Florence Macaroni Company	2098	F	310 548-5942	2375

GEOGRAPHIC

	SIC	EMP	PHONE	ENTRY #
Fred Browns Recovery Svcs Inc	7389	D	310 519-8723	18520
Harbor Community Clinic	8093	D	310 547-0202	21310
Healthview Inc **(PA)**	8361	C	310 547-3341	22112
Isabel Garreton Inc **(PA)**	5137	C	310 833-7768	14383
Jankovich Company **(PA)**	5171	D	310 547-3305	14796
Larson Al Boat Shop	3731	D	310 514-4100	10452
Little Ssters of The Poor Los	8051	D	310 548-0625	20401
Meristar San Pedro Hilton LLC	7011	C	310 514-3344	16563
Party Time Ice	2097	F	310 833-0187	2373
Patrol Black Knight Inc	7381	D	213 985-6499	18309
Performance Team LLC	4225	D	310 241-4100	12230
Polar Tankers Inc	4424	C	310 519-8260	12277
Port of Los Angeles	4491	D	310 732-3508	12291
Providence Health & Services S	8062	D	310 832-3311	20913
San Pedro Convalescent HM Inc	8051	D	310 832-6431	20457
San Pedro Fish Market LLC	5146	D	323 775-2921	14581
San Pedro Ownership Inc	7011	D	310 514-3344	16688
Seaborn Canvas	2399	E	310 519-1208	3201
Seacrest Convalescent Hosp Inc	8051	D	310 833-3526	20461
So Cal Ship Services	4489	D	310 519-8411	12284
Space Exploration Tech Corp	3761	E	714 330-8668	10517
Spf Capital Real Estate LLC	7011	D	310 519-8200	16724
Toll Global Fwdg Scs USA Inc	4731	D	732 750-9000	12539
Tri-Marine Fish Company LLC	5146	D	310 547-1144	14587
Victory Oil Company	1311	D	310 519-9500	415
Vopak Terminal Long Beach Inc	5039	D	310 521-7969	13338
Yusen Terminals LLC **(DH)**	4491	D	310 548-8000	12294

SAN SIMEON, CA - San Luis Obispo County

	SIC	EMP	PHONE	ENTRY #
Cavalier Inn Incorporated	7011	D	805 927-6444	16371
Cavalier Inn Inc	7011	D	805 927-4688	16372

SANTA ANA, CA - Orange County

	SIC	EMP	PHONE	ENTRY #
2100 Freedom Inc **(HQ)**	2711	D	714 796-7000	3941
2100 Trust LLC **(PA)**	6733	C	877 469-7344	16171
9edge Inc	7371	E	657 229-3343	17536
A Good Sign & Graphics Co	3993	F	714 444-4466	11518
A Plus Label Inc	2679	E	714 229-9811	3921
A-Z Mfg Inc	3599	E	714 444-4446	8458
AAA Imaging & Supplies Inc	5043	E	714 431-0570	13340
Aardvark Clay & Supplies Inc **(PA)**	3952	E	714 541-4157	11465
Abtech Incorporated	2542	D	714 550-9961	3673
Accelerated Memory Prod Inc	3674	E	714 460-9800	9472
Accent Industries Inc **(PA)**	3442	E	714 708-1389	6686
Accurate Circuit Engrg Inc	3672	D	714 546-2162	9371
Accurate Prfmce Machining Inc	3599	E	714 434-7811	8463
Acd LLC **(DH)**	3443	C	949 261-7533	6723
Ackley Metal Products Inc	3599	E	714 979-7431	8465
Acme United Corporation	2621	E	714 557-2001	3746
Acp Noxtat Inc	2821	E	714 547-5477	4675
Acrontos Manufacturing Inc	3469	E	714 850-9133	7119
Active Plating Inc	3471	E	714 547-0356	7197
Adapt Automation Inc	3549	E	714 662-4454	7898
ADM Works LLC	3365	E	714 245-0536	6382
Advanced Clnroom McRclean Corp	7349	C	714 751-1152	17212
Advantage Manufacturing Inc	5063	E	714 505-1166	13609
AEC Group Inc	3714	F	714 444-1395	10010
Aerospace Driven Tech Inc	3728	F	949 553-1606	10249
Aftco Mfg Co Inc	3949	D	877 489-4278	11398
AGA Precision Systems Inc	3599	E	714 540-3163	8482
Agility Fuel Systems LLC **(DH)**	3714	C	949 236-5520	10011
Aicco Inc **(HQ)**	6141	D	714 481-3215	15136
Airborne Systems N Amer CA Inc	2399	C	714 662-1400	3190
Alan B Whitson Company Inc	8742	A	949 955-1200	23150
Alco Engrg & Tooling Corp	3599	E	714 556-6060	8484
Alco Manufacturing Inc	3544	F	714 549-5007	7774
Alignmed Inc	3842	F	866 987-5433	11084
All American Racers Inc	3751	C	714 557-2116	10480
All Seasons Framing Corp	1751	E	714 634-2324	1425
Allied Electronic Services Inc	3672	E	714 245-2500	9374
Almatron Electronics Inc	3672	E	714 557-6000	9375
Altamed Health Services Corp	8099	D	714 919-0280	21375
Altium Packaging LLC	3089	F	714 241-6640	5558
Altium Packaging LP	3086	C	714 241-6640	5487
Aluminum Precision Pdts Inc **(PA)**	5051	A	714 546-8125	13544
Ambrit Engineering Corporation	3544	D	714 557-1074	7775
America West Airlines Inc	4512	D	949 852-5471	12302
American Cooling Tower Inc **(PA)**	7699	F	714 898-2436	19022
American Pneumatic Tools Inc	3542	F	562 204-1555	7754
AMO Usa Inc	3841	C	714 247-8200	10932
Amwins Connect Insur Svcs LLC	6399	D	714 460-5153	15523
Anello Corporation	3841	E	714 546-0561	10933
Anochem Coatings	3479	F	949 322-3280	7343
Anodyne Inc	3471	E	714 549-3321	7213
Anser Advisory LLC **(PA)**	8742	D	310 351-8907	23158
AP Parpro Inc **(PA)**	7389	C	714 545-8886	18448
Applied Circuit Solutions Inc	3672	F	949 754-1545	9379
Architectural Coatings Inc	1721	E	714 701-1360	1168
Argent Management LLC **(PA)**	6531	B	949 777-4000	15772
Argent Management LLC	6531	D	949 777-4070	15773
Arlon LLC	3089	C	714 540-2811	5566
Artisan Nameplate Awards Corp	2759	E	714 556-6222	4481
Ascent Aerospace	3812	E	586 726-0500	10570
Aspire Bakeries LLC	5149	D	949 261-7400	14671
Atlas Carpet Mills Inc	2273	C	323 724-7930	2682
Atr Sales Inc	3568	E	714 432-8411	8103
Automation West Inc	3599	E	714 556-7381	8507
Axiom Materials Inc	2891	E	949 623-4400	5178
B and Z Printing Inc	2752	E	714 892-2000	4234
B J Bindery Inc	2789	D	714 835-7342	4617
Bambeck Systems Inc **(PA)**	3823	F	949 250-3100	10679
Banc California National Assn **(HQ)**	6021	D	877 770-2262	14990
Banc of California Inc **(PA)**	6021	C	855 361-2262	14992
Behr Holdings Corporation **(HQ)**	2851	D	714 545-7101	5088
Behr Process Corporation **(DH)**	2851	A	714 545-7101	5089
Behr Process Sales Company	8743	E	714 545-7101	23374
Behr Sales Inc **(HQ)**	2851	B	714 545-7101	5090
Bel-Air Machining Co	3599	F	714 953-6615	8522
Bend-Tek Inc	3444	D	714 210-8966	6795
Bens Asphalt Inc	7349	E	714 540-1700	17218
Best Limousines & Trnsp Inc **(PA)**	4119	D	714 375-9128	11854
Beyondgreen Btech Inc DBA Bynd	2759	F	800 983-7221	4485
Bird B Gone LLC **(PA)**	3082	F	949 472-3122	5444
Black Knight Infoserv LLC	7374	C	904 854-5100	18082
Blackburn Alton Invstments LLC	2759	E	714 731-2000	4486
Blind Childrens Lrng Ctr Inc	8351	D	714 573-8838	21990
Blower-Dempsay Corporation **(PA)**	5199	C	714 481-3800	14914
Blower-Dempsay Corporation	2653	E	714 547-9266	3787
BP Communications Inc **(PA)**	4813	C	626 912-0600	12628
Braille Signs Inc	3993	E	949 797-1570	11529
Brandrep LLC	8742	E	800 405-7119	23176
Brandywine Communications	5065	D	714 755-1050	13703
Brasstech Inc **(HQ)**	3432	B	949 417-5207	6553
Brethren Inc	5099	E	714 836-4800	14147
Brightview Landscape Svcs Inc	0781	C	714 546-7843	244
Brixen & Sons Inc	2759	E	714 566-1444	4488
Brothers Intl Desserts **(PA)**	2024	C	949 655-0080	1811
Bsnap LLC	6162	D	657 269-4410	15179
Buk Optics Inc	3827	E	714 384-9620	10827
C & H Letterpress Inc	2752	F	714 438-1350	4242
Cable Devices Incorporated **(HQ)**	3577	C	714 554-4370	8241
Cal Pac Sheet Metal Inc	3444	E	714 979-2733	6801
Cal Trends Accessories LLC	2399	E	714 708-5115	3192
California Composites MGT Inc	3728	E	714 258-0405	10294
Calmont Engrg & Elec Corp **(PA)**	3357	E	714 549-0336	6346
Calvary Church Santa Ana Inc	8351	C	714 973-4800	21994
Captive Ocean Reef Entps Inc **(PA)**	3569	D	714 543-4100	8113
Cascade Optical Coating Inc	3827	F	714 543-9777	10829
CD Alexander LLC	3577	E	949 250-3306	8244
CD Video Manufacturing Inc	3695	D	714 265-0770	9834
Celmol Inc	5199	D	714 259-1000	14919
Cemtek Environmental Inc	8748	E	714 437-7100	23428
Centent Company	3571	F	714 979-6491	8151
Certified Trnsp Svcs Inc	4142	D	714 835-8676	11909
Chamson Management Inc	7011	D	714 751-2400	16377
Chapman Engineering Corp	3599	E	714 542-1942	8550
Charles W Bowers Museum Corp	8412	D	714 567-3600	22219
Chen & Huang Partners LP	7011	D	714 557-8700	16380
Chroma Systems	7217	D	714 557-8480	16879
Ciasons Industrial Inc	3053	E	714 259-0838	5333
Cintas Sales Corporation	7213	D	714 957-2852	16851
Clear-Ad Inc	3089	E	877 899-1002	5607
Codan US Corporation	3089	C	714 430-1300	5610
Cole Instrument Corp	3621	D	714 556-3100	8911
Collectors Universe Inc **(PA)**	7699	B	949 567-1234	19031
Color Science Inc	2865	E	714 434-1033	5121
Columbia Screw Products Inc	3451	E	714 549-1171	7033
Community Patrol	7381	D	657 247-4744	18264
Community Seniorserv Inc	8082	D	714 558-1216	21152
Concept Technology Inc	8711	D	949 851-6550	22516
Connelly Machine Works	3599	E	714 558-6855	8562
Continental Currency Svcs Inc **(HQ)**	6099	E	714 569-0300	15124
Continental Currency Svcs Inc **(PA)**	6099	D	714 569-0300	15125
Contour Engineering Inc	3728	F	562 630-0250	10303
Contractors Flrg Svc Cal Inc	5023	C	714 556-6100	13166
Corbin-Hill Inc	2051	F	714 966-6695	1993
Council of Orange County of St **(PA)**	8331	D	949 653-2900	21948
County of Orange	2759	E	714 567-7444	4505
County of Orange	8651	E	714 567-7422	22393
County of Orange	8111	D	714 796-8200	21539
County of Orange	8052	D	714 834-6021	20528
Covenant Care California LLC	8051	D	714 554-9700	20302
Cowboy Direct Response	3993	E	714 824-3780	11538
CP Opco LLC	7359	D	714 540-6111	17342
CPC Fabrication Inc	3444	E	714 549-2426	6814
CRC Health Corporate	8093	A	714 542-3581	21295
Crown Building Maintenance Co	7349	B	714 434-9494	17234
Crown Facility Solutions	7349	E	657 266-0821	17236
Cult/Cvlt LLC	3751	F	714 435-2858	10487
Custom Hardware Mfg Inc	3429	E	714 547-7440	6514
D F Stauffer Biscuit Co Inc	2052	E	714 546-6855	2062
DAd Investments	2099	E	714 751-8500	2416
Dadee Manufacturing LLC	3713	E	602 276-4390	9981
Dana Creath Designs Ltd	3648	E	714 662-0111	9126
Danchuk Manufacturing Inc	3714	D	714 540-4363	10041
Data Solder Inc	3643	F	714 429-9866	9031
Data Trace Info Svcs LLC **(HQ)**	8999	D	714 250-6700	23531
Davco Enterprises Inc	2891	F	714 432-0600	5182
Davita Medical Management LLC	8099	D	714 835-8501	21415
Davita Medical Management LLC	8099	D	714 964-6229	21419
Debtmerica LLC	7299	D	714 389-4200	16953
Dekra-Lite Industries Inc	7389	D	714 436-0705	18502
Deltronic Corporation	3827	D	714 545-5800	10832
Deschner Corporation	3569	E	714 557-1261	8120
Deutsche Bank National Tr Co	6091	D	714 247-6054	15119

Mergent email: customerrelations@mergent.com
1426

2022 Southern California Business
Directory and Buyers Guide

(P-0000) Products & Services Section entry number
(PA)=Parent Co (HQ)=Headquarters (DH)=Div Headquarters

	SIC	EMP	PHONE	ENTRY #
Dgwb Inc	7311	D	714 881-2300	17008
Dhs Consulting LLC	8741	C	714 276-1135	23016
Diamond Baseball Company Inc	3949	E	800 366-2999	11412
Diamond Gloves	3842	E	714 667-0506	11094
Discovery Scnce Ctr Ornge Cnty	8412	C	866 552-2823	22220
Dish Network Corporation	4841	D	714 424-0503	12766
Diversified Packaging Inc	3086	F	714 850-9316	5497
Dm Software Inc	7372	E	714 953-2653	17839
Documotion Research Inc	2752	F	714 662-3800	4279
Domino Realty Management Co	6513	D	714 556-0466	15723
DOT Corp **(PA)**	2752	E	714 708-5800	4281
DOT Corp	2752	E	714 708-5960	4282
Ducommun Incorporated **(PA)**	3728	B	657 335-3665	10317
Duplo USA Corporation **(PA)**	5044	D	949 752-8222	13356
Durham School Services L P	4173	C	714 542-8989	11942
Dynamic Fabrication Inc	3728	E	714 662-2440	10321
Dynasty Electronic Company LLC	3672	D	714 550-1197	9399
Easyflex Inc	3312	E	888 577-8999	6199
Ecoolthing Corp	3499	E	714 368-4791	7555
Edison Mission Oper & Maint **(DH)**	4931	C	626 302-5151	12870
El Indio Tortilleria	2099	F	714 542-3114	2429
Electrode Technologies Inc	3471	E	714 549-3771	7250
Elite Slides Inc	2426	D	310 537-4210	3217
Embee Performance LLC	5169	E	714 540-1354	14780
Embee Processing LLC	8711	B	714 546-9842	22542
Empire Building Services Inc	7349	D	714 836-7700	17241
Energent Corporation	3511	F	949 885-0365	7583
Energent Corporation	3511	F	949 885-0365	7584
Envelopments Inc	2621	E	714 569-3300	3752
Executive Personnel Services	7361	B	714 310-9506	17424
Experian Corporation	7323	C	714 830-7000	17122
Express Chipping	2741	F	562 789-8058	4171
Express Manufacturing Inc **(PA)**	3679	B	714 979-2228	9710
F M Tarbell Co **(HQ)**	6531	C	714 972-0988	15851
Fabrica International Inc	2273	C	949 261-7181	2690
Fairview Mtm Pharma Inc	2834	F	714 881-0012	4820
Falcon Automotive Inc	2399	F	714 569-1085	3196
Family Asssment Cnsling Edcat	8322	D	714 447-9024	21782
Financial Statement Svcs Inc **(PA)**	7331	C	714 436-3326	17132
First Amercn Specialty Insur **(HQ)**	6331	C	949 474-7500	15467
First American Financial Corp **(PA)**	6361	A	714 250-3000	15503
First American Mortgage Svcs	6361	B	714 250-4210	15504
First American Title Company	6541	A	714 250-3109	16040
First American Title Insur Co **(HQ)**	6361	D	800 854-3643	15505
First American Trust Company **(HQ)**	6282	D	714 560-7856	15326
First Amrcn Mrtg Solutions LLC	8742	D	714 250-3046	23216
First Amrcn Mrtg Solutions LLC **(HQ)**	6163	C	800 333-4510	15242
First Amrcn Prprty Insur Cslty	6411	D	949 474-7500	15570
First Student Inc	4151	C	714 850-7578	11931
Fishel Company	1623	C	714 668-9268	948
Fit-Line Inc	3089	E	714 549-9091	5646
Flame Broiler Inc **(PA)**	6794	C	714 549-2870	16207
Flexible Manufacturing LLC	3678	D	714 259-7996	9654
Fntech	3648	E	714 429-7833	9132
Foodbeast Inc	2741	F	949 344-2634	4172
Foster Printing Company Inc	2752	D	714 731-2000	4296
Foundation Building Mtls Inc **(HQ)**	5031	A	714 380-3127	13208
Freedom Newspapers Inc	2711	F	714 796-7000	3978
Fresh Grill LLC	7389	C	714 444-2126	18522
Freudenberg-Nok General Partnr	3053	C	714 834-0602	5337
Frontera Solutions Inc	3624	F	714 368-1631	8937
Fujifilm Irvine Scientific Inc **(DH)**	2836	E	949 261-7800	4934
Funny-Bunny Inc **(PA)**	2329	D	714 957-1114	2810
G W Maintenance Inc **(PA)**	5085	D	714 541-2211	13984
Gamboa Service Inc	7349	D	714 966-5325	17244
Gardner Systems Inc	3821	F	714 668-9018	10658
Garrison Manufacturing Inc	3714	E	714 549-4880	10065
Gary Siposs Inc	2672	F	714 557-3830	3871
GBF Enterprises Inc	3599	E	714 979-7131	8601
Gemini Industries Inc	3341	D	949 250-4011	6293
Gemtech Inds Good Earth Mfg	3479	E	714 848-2517	7368
Gerald Michael Ltd	5136	E	562 921-9611	14334
Gibralter Convalescent Hosp **(PA)**	8059	D	714 550-5380	20592
GKN Aerospace Camarillo Inc	3444	F	805 383-6684	6845
Goglanian Bakeries Inc **(HQ)**	5149	B	714 338-1145	14690
Gold Coast Baking Company Inc **(PA)**	2051	C	714 545-2253	2005
Goodwill Inds Orange Cnty Cal	8331	C	714 754-7808	21954
Gps Associates Inc	2842	E	949 408-3162	4962
Gps Painting Wallcovering Inc	1721	C	714 730-8904	1182
Greenkraft Inc	3711	F	714 545-7777	9951
Guardsmark LLC **(DH)**	7381	D	714 619-9700	18284
Guys Patio Inc	7641	E	844 968-7485	18963
H & H Agency Inc **(PA)**	6411	C	949 260-8840	15576
Hannah Industries Inc	3589	F	714 939-7873	8385
Hart King A Professional Corp	8111	D	714 432-8700	21577
Harveys Industries Inc	5137	D	714 277-4700	14379
Headmaster Inc **(PA)**	2353	E	714 556-5244	3026
Health Resources Corp	8062	B	714 754-5454	20782
Heart Rate Inc	3949	E	714 850-9716	11424
Helfer Enterprises	3599	E	714 557-2733	8614
Helica Biosystems Inc	2835	F	714 578-7830	4921
Heritage Paper Co **(HQ)**	2653	D	714 540-9737	3812
High End Seating Solutions LLC	3751	E	714 259-0177	10492
High Tech Coatings Inc	3479	F	714 547-2122	7373
Hill Marine Products LLC	3599	F	714 855-2986	8618
Hirsch Electronics LLC	5065	D	949 250-8888	13726
Hitt Companies	3069	E	714 979-1405	5381

	SIC	EMP	PHONE	ENTRY #
Hntb Corporation	8711	D	714 460-1600	22568
Hntb Gerwick Water Solutions	8711	C	714 460-1600	22569
Honav Usa Inc	3651	F	858 634-0617	9179
Hood Manufacturing Inc	3089	D	714 979-7681	5664
Hook It Up	2111	F	714 600-0100	2549
Hpv Technologies Inc	3651	F	949 476-7000	9180
Iaccess Technologies Inc **(PA)**	8748	D	714 922-9158	23451
ICC Collision Centers 6 Inc	3711	F	888 894-4079	9954
IJ Research Inc	3679	E	714 546-8522	9724
Image Apparel For Business Inc	2326	E	714 541-5247	2780
Impco Technologies Inc **(HQ)**	3714	C	714 656-1200	10079
Industrial Cpu Syste	3571	F	714 957-2815	8159
Industrial Cpu Systems Intl	3571	F	714 957-2815	8160
Industrial Printers California	2796	F	714 545-8484	4632
Industrial Relations Cal Dept	8322	D	714 558-4121	21814
Infinite Optics Inc	3827	E	714 557-2299	10841
Insultech LLC **(PA)**	2899	D	714 384-0506	5224
Integral Aerospace LLC	3728	C	949 250-3123	10354
Integrated Communications Inc	2752	E	310 851-8066	4338
Intellitime Systems Corp	7371	D	714 444-3020	17641
Intergro Rehab Service	8049	D	714 901-4200	20224
International Disc Mfr Inc	3652	F	714 210-1780	9222
Irvine Technology Corporation	8748	C	714 445-2624	23455
Itc Sftware Slutions Group LLC **(PA)**	7372	B	877 248-2774	17896
Iteris Inc **(PA)**	3669	B	949 270-9400	9344
J R V Products Inc	3679	E	714 259-9772	9733
JB Plastics Inc	3089	E	714 541-8500	5681
JD Processing Inc	3471	E	714 972-8161	7274
Jdr Engineering Cons Inc **(PA)**	3089	C	714 751-7084	5682
Jhc Investment Inc	7011	D	714 751-2400	16513
Jmac Lending Inc	6162	D	949 390-2688	15205
John Henry Foundation	8322	D	714 554-8906	21827
John M Frank Construction Inc	1542	D	714 210-3600	776
Johnson Jhnson Srgcal Vsion In **(HQ)**	3845	B	714 247-8200	11225
Johnson Precision Products Inc	3599	F	714 824-6971	8646
Jwc Environmental Inc	3589	D	714 662-5829	8390
Jwc Environmental Inc **(DH)**	5084	E	949 833-3888	13908
K Wave 1079	4832	D	714 918-6207	12696
K-P Engineering Corp	3599	E	714 545-7045	8648
K-V Engineering Inc	3541	D	714 229-9977	7735
Kaga (usa) Inc	3469	E	714 540-2697	7155
Kaiser Foundation Hospitals	8011	C	714 223-2606	19917
Kaiser Foundation Hospitals	8011	C	714 830-6500	19924
Kaiser Foundation Hospitals	6324	C	888 988-2800	15422
Kaiser Foundation Hospitals	6324	C	714 967-4700	15439
Kenlor Industries Inc	3841	F	714 647-0770	11003
Kilgore Machine Company Inc	3599	E	714 540-3659	8654
Kindred Healthcare LLC	8062	C	714 564-7800	20828
Kingspan Light & Air LLC	1761	C	714 540-8950	1492
Kirby Industries Inc	1743	F	714 437-0789	1418
Kl Electronics Inc	3672	E	714 751-5611	9420
Kulicke Sffa Wedge Bonding Inc	3699	C	949 660-0440	9882
Kvc Group LLC	8742	D	855 438-0377	23254
Kya Services LLC	1752	E	714 659-6476	1468
L&T Staffing Inc **(PA)**	7361	B	714 558-1821	17436
La Boxing Franchise Corp	7991	C	714 668-0911	19454
Labarge/Stc Inc	3674	A	281 207-1400	9529
Laguna Cookie Company Inc	2052	D	714 546-6855	2068
Land Concern Ltd	0781	D	949 250-4822	264
Land Forms Lanscape Cnstr Inc	1711	E	949 582-0877	1092
Landcare USA LLC	0781	C	949 559-7771	265
Landmark Services Inc	7349	D	714 547-6308	17256
Larry Mthvin Installations Inc	5039	D	714 547-8021	13332
Leader Electronics (na) Inc	3661	E	714 435-0505	9236
Lenox Financial Mortgage Corp	6162	B	949 428-5100	15208
Leonard Craft Co LLC	3911	D	714 549-0678	11322
Level 23 Fab	3441	E	714 979-2323	6628
Limpus Prints Inc	2759	F	714 545-5078	4538
Liquid Graphics Inc	2329	C	949 486-3588	2820
Little Firefighter Corporation	3491	F	714 834-0410	7449
Lotus Hygiene Systems Inc	3261	E	714 259-8805	5992
M & W Machine Corporation	3599	E	714 541-2652	8670
Macro-Z-Technology Company **(PA)**	1611	D	714 564-1130	898
Magnetic Design Labs Inc	3679	F	714 558-3355	9744
Main Electric Supply Co LLC **(PA)**	5063	D	949 833-3052	13644
Maranatha Sheet Metal Inc	1761	D	714 602-7764	1496
Mark Optics Inc	3827	E	714 545-6684	10846
Markland Industries Inc **(PA)**	3751	C	714 245-2850	10498
Markzware	7372	E	949 756-5100	17911
Marlin Designs LLC	2512	C	949 637-7257	3509
Marway Power Systems Inc **(PA)**	3577	E	714 917-6200	8280
Mask Technology Inc	3679	E	714 557-3383	9746
Matrix USA Inc	3672	E	714 825-0404	9425
Maul Mfg Inc **(PA)**	3599	E	714 641-0727	8680
Maxtrol Corporation	3672	E	714 245-0506	9426
McCarthy Bldg Companies Inc	1542	D	949 851-8383	790
McGuff Pharmaceuticals Inc	2834	E	714 918-7277	4850
Medical Network Inc	8741	D	949 863-0022	23060
Medtronic 3f Therapeutics Inc	3845	C	949 399-1675	11230
Medtronic Ats Medical Inc	3841	D	949 380-9333	11018
Mega Plus Pcb Incorporated	3672	F	714 550-0265	9427
Meggitt North Hollywood Inc	3728	E	818 691-6258	10378
Mekong Printing Inc	2752	E	714 558-9595	4370
Melmet Steven J Law Ofc	8111	D	949 263-1000	21627
Memory Experts Intl USA Inc **(HQ)**	3572	E	714 258-3000	8208
Merchants Building Maint Co	7349	D	714 973-9272	17260
Mercy House Living Centers	8611	C	714 836-7188	22253

GEOGRAPHIC

Employment Codes: A=Over 500 employees, B=251-500, C=101-250, D=51-100, E=20-50 F=10-19

2022 Southern California Business Directory and Buyers Guide

© Mergent Inc. 1-800-342-5647

1427

	SIC	EMP	PHONE	ENTRY #
Metal Cast Inc	3325	E	714 285-9792	6277
Metro Digital Printing Inc	2752	E	714 545-8400	4372
Mission Ldscp Companies Inc	0781	C	714 545-9962	268
Modified Plastics Inc **(PA)**	3089	E	714 546-4667	5715
Moms Orange County	8082	E	714 972-2610	21192
Monarch Prcision Deburring Inc	3541	F	714 258-0342	7737
Moore Law Group A Prof Corp	8111	D	714 431-2000	21632
Moorefield Construction Inc **(PA)**	1542	D	714 972-0700	793
Morrison Landscape	0781	E	714 571-0455	270
Mpl Enterprises Inc	0782	D	714 545-1717	327
MRS Foods Incorporated **(PA)**	2099	E	714 554-2791	2492
Mtn Government Services Inc **(DH)**	3448	F	954 538-4000	7005
Murrays Hardware	3442	F	714 543-4023	6711
Mx Electronics Mfg Inc **(HQ)**	3357	D	714 258-0200	6353
Nazca Solutions Inc	7372	E	612 279-6100	17927
Nekter Juice Bar Inc **(PA)**	6794	D	949 660-0071	16212
Newport Laminates Inc	3089	E	714 545-8335	5726
Newport Plastic Inc	3089	E	714 549-1955	5727
Newport Plastics LLC **(PA)**	3089	E	800 854-8402	5728
Nieves Landscape Inc	0781	C	714 835-7332	272
Nis America Inc	7372	E	714 540-1199	17934
Nkmax America Inc	8071	D	949 396-6830	21080
Nnn Realty Advisors Inc	6531	B	714 667-8252	15933
Norotos Inc	3599	C	714 662-3113	8720
NRG Power Inc	1731	D	714 424-6484	1287
Nutrade Inc	2211	F	949 477-2300	2583
Oc 405 Partners Joint Venture	1622	D	858 251-2200	930
Oc Metals Inc	3444	E	714 668-0783	6882
Odyssey Healthcare Inc	8051	D	714 245-7420	20427
OEM Materials & Supplies Inc	2621	E	714 564-9600	3766
Ohno America Inc	2273	E	770 773-3820	2694
Olive Crest **(PA)**	8361	B	714 543-5437	22140
Omniprint Inc	3577	E	949 833-0080	8288
One Stop Parts Source LLC **(DH)**	5013	D	949 955-2600	13077
Optima Tax Relief LLC	7291	C	714 361-4636	16939
Optosigma Corporation	3827	E	949 851-5881	10852
Orange Cnty Emplyees Rtrment S	6722	D	714 558-6200	16142
Orange Coast Title Company **(PA)**	7389	D	714 558-2836	18621
Orange County Head Start Inc **(PA)**	8351	D	714 241-8920	22045
Orange County Health Care Agcy	8621	D	714 568-5683	22274
Orange County Internet Xchange	4813	D	714 450-7109	12661
Orange County Label Co Inc	2759	F	714 437-1010	4549
Orange County Royale Convlscnt **(PA)**	8059	B	714 546-6450	20620
Orange Countys Credit Union **(PA)**	6061	C	714 755-5900	15076
Orange Mtal Spnning Stmping In	3469	E	714 754-0770	7170
Orangewood Foundation	8322	D	714 619-0200	21862
Orchid MPS	3841	D	714 549-9203	11040
Overair Inc	3721	E	949 503-7503	10200
Pacifcare Hlth Plan Admnstrtor **(DH)**	6324	B	714 825-5200	15447
Pacific Aerospace Machine Inc	3599	E	714 534-1444	8728
Pacific Computer Products Inc	3955	E	714 549-7535	11480
Pacific Label Inc	2759	E	714 237-1276	4552
Pacific Rim Contractors Inc	1742	D	714 641-7380	1391
Pacific Rim Mech Contrs Inc	1711	C	714 285-2600	1114
Pacific Stone Design Inc	3272	E	714 836-5757	6047
Parking Concepts Inc	7521	C	714 543-5725	18771
Parpro Technologies Inc	3672	C	714 545-8886	9437
Partners Capital Group Inc **(PA)**	7389	D	949 916-3900	18629
Pds Tech Inc	7361	C	214 647-9600	17443
Pelican Rope Works	2298	F	714 545-0116	2717
Phoenix House Orange County	8361	C	714 953-9373	22144
Pioneer Circuits Inc	3672	B	714 641-3132	9439
Pioneer Packing Inc **(PA)**	5113	E	714 540-9751	14225
Pipe Restoration Inc	1711	E	714 564-7600	1117
Pipeline Group LLC	8741	C	949 296-8375	23088
Pipeline Restoration Plbg Inc	1711	E	949 510-2281	1118
Polaris E-Commerce Inc	3561	E	714 907-0582	8020
Pollution Ctrl Specialists Inc	3564	F	949 474-0137	8052
Post Modern Edit LLC **(PA)**	7812	D	949 608-8700	19166
Power Circuits Inc	3672	C	714 327-3000	9440
Pps Parking Inc	7299	A	949 223-8707	16972
Precious Metals Plating Co Inc	3471	F	714 546-6271	7296
Precision Circuits West Inc	3672	F	714 435-9670	9441
Precision Copy **(PA)**	7334	F	949 833-1213	17153
Prime Forming & Cnstr Sups Inc	3272	E	714 547-6710	6052
Prime Tech Cabinets Inc	1751	C	949 757-4900	1451
Priority Ctr Ending The Gnrtna	8322	D	714 543-4333	21872
Promedia Companies	2721	E	714 444-2426	4100
Property Insight LLC	6541	A	877 747-2537	16041
Prospect Medical Group Inc **(HQ)**	8741	B	714 796-5900	23092
Prototype Express LLC	3699	F	714 751-3533	9902
Q S H Properties Inc	7011	C	714 957-9200	16644
Q-Flex Inc	3672	D	714 664-0101	9443
QED Inc	3823	E	714 546-6010	10714
R & B Wire Products Inc	3496	E	714 549-3355	7509
R A F LP **(PA)**	7261	D	714 633-1442	16926
Rbc Transport Dynamics Corp	5085	C	203 267-7001	14013
Reed Thomas Company Inc	1794	D	714 558-7691	1603
Regal Technology Partners Inc	5045	D	714 835-1162	13432
Regional Ctr Orange Cnty Inc **(PA)**	8322	B	714 796-5100	21877
Reimagine Network **(PA)**	8093	C	714 633-7400	21333
Ricaurte Precision Inc	3599	E	714 667-0632	8767
Rice Drywall Inc	1742	D	714 543-5400	1396
Ricoh Electronics Inc	3861	C	714 566-6079	11291
Robinson Pharma Inc	2834	E	714 241-0235	4882
Robinson Pharma Inc	2834	E	714 241-0235	4883
Robinson Pharma Inc	2834	E	714 241-0235	4884
Robinson Pharma Inc **(PA)**	2834	B	714 241-0235	4885
Robinson Pharma Inc	2834	E	714 241-0235	4886
Royal Family Kids Camps Inc	7032	C	714 438-2494	16826
Royal Manufacturing Inds Inc	3444	F	714 668-9199	6904
RPM Transportation Inc **(DH)**	4213	C	714 388-3500	12075
Rubberite Corp **(PA)**	3069	F	714 546-6464	5407
S & S Precision Mfg Inc	3599	E	714 754-6664	8783
S W K Properties LLC	7011	C	714 481-6300	16680
Saf-T-Co Supply	3644	E	714 547-9975	9053
Sanie Manufacturing Company	3446	F	714 751-7700	6978
Santa Ana Country Club	7997	D	714 556-3000	19609
Santa Ana Radiology Center	8011	D	714 835-6055	20055
Santos Precision Inc	3599	E	714 957-0299	8787
Satellite Management Co **(PA)**	6531	C	714 558-24[illegible]1	15994
Schoolsfirst Federal Credit Un **(PA)**	6061	B	714 258-4000	15085
Scottish American Insurance **(PA)**	6411	D	714 550-5050	15625
Secure Comm Systems Inc **(HQ)**	3663	C	714 547-1174	9315
Semiconductor Components Inc	3674	F	714 547-6059	9570
Senga Engineering Inc	3599	E	714 549-8011	8792
Serve People Inc	8699	D	714 352-2911	22461
Service First Contractors	1542	E	714 573-2200	823
Sev-Cal Tool Inc	3545	F	714 549-3347	7868
Shield Security Inc **(DH)**	7381	B	714 210-1501	18333
Sigmatronix Inc	3651	F	714 436-1618	9195
Sign Specialists Corporation	3993	E	714 641-0064	11599
Silicon Tech Inc	3572	B	949 476-1130	8218
Silverwood Landscape Cnstr Inc	0782	E	714 427-6134	343
Skeffington Enterprises Inc	6719	D	714 540-1700	16111
Skyco Shading Systems Inc	2431	E	714 708-3038	3289
Skyco Skylights Inc	3211	E	949 629-4090	5922
Smart & Final Stores Inc	5141	C	714 549-2362	14493
SMI Architectural Millwork Inc	2431	E	714 567-0112	3290
Smithco Plastics Inc **(PA)**	3089	F	714 545-9107	5822
Smiths Action Plastic Inc **(PA)**	3088	F	714 836-4141	5536
Smiths Intrcnnect Americas Inc	3679	B	714 371-1100	9784
Smt Electronics Mfg Inc	3674	E	714 751-8894	9577
South Coast Circuits Inc	3672	D	714 966-2108	9456
South Coast Global Med Ctr Inc	8011	D	714 953-3582	20070
Southern Cal Prmnnte Med Group	8011	C	714 967-4760	20088
Southern Cal Spcialty Care Inc	8062	C	714 564-7800	20947
Southern California Edison Co	4911	C	714 973-5481	12839
Southern California Plas Inc	2821	D	714 751-7084	4718
Southland Integrated Svcs Inc **(PA)**	8399	D	714 558-6009	22211
Southwest Airlines Co	4512	D	949 252-5200	12316
Southwest Landscape Inc	0781	D	714 545-1084	282
Spec Formliners Inc	3272	E	714 429-9500	6058
Specialty Equipment Co	3713	F	714 258-1622	9999
Spektrum Manufacturing Inc	2326	F	949 702-2807	2790
Spill Magic Inc	2621	E	714 557-2001	3771
SPS Technologies LLC	3965	B	714 545-9311	11501
SPS Technologies LLC	3965	B	714 371-1925	11502
SS Metal Fabricators	3441	F	949 631-4272	6664
St Joseph Heritg Med Group LLC **(PA)**	8011	C	714 633-1011	20096
State Compensation Insur Fund	6331	D	714 565-5000	15480
State Compensation Insur Fund	6331	D	714 565-7000	15482
Stec International Holding Inc	3572	C	949 476-1180	8220
Sterling Plumbing Inc	1711	D	714 641-5480	1148
Strata Forest Products Inc **(PA)**	2421	E	714 751-0800	3213
Stremicks Heritage Foods LLC **(HQ)**	2026	B	714 775-5000	1840
Success Strategies Inst Inc	8331	D	949 721-6808	21969
Sukut Construction LLC	1623	D	714 540-5351	976
Sukut Construction Inc	1794	C	714 540-5351	1607
Sun & Sun Industries Inc	3646	D	714 210-5141	9103
Sundown Liquidating Corp **(PA)**	3211	C	714 540-8950	5923
Sunflower Gardens Inc	8051	D	714 641-0959	20485
Supreme Abrasives	3291	E	949 250-8644	6158
Sureco Hlth Lf Insur Agcy Inc	6411	D	949 333-0263	15631
Syagen Technology LLC	3826	D	714 258-4400	10815
Symbolic Displays Inc	3728	D	714 258-2811	10425
Systems Paving Inc **(PA)**	1611	D	949 263-8301	921
T L C Transportation Staffing **(HQ)**	7361	D	714 541-5415	17470
Taber Company Inc	2431	D	714 543-7100	3294
Tactical Micro Inc **(DH)**	3699	E	714 547-1174	9921
Tailgate Printing Inc	2752	D	714 966-3035	4431
Tait Environmental Svcs Inc **(PA)**	1799	D	714 560-8200	1692
Talimar Systems Inc	2531	E	714 557-4884	3633
Tammy Taylor Nails Inc	2821	E	949 250-9287	4722
Tarbell Financial Corporation **(PA)**	6163	D	714 972-0988	15256
Tay Ho Food Corporation	2032	F	714 973-2286	1857
Taylor Communications Inc	2761	F	714 664-8865	4602
Technology Resource Center Inc **(PA)**	7379	D	714 542-1004	18226
Tecta America Southern Cal Inc	1761	D	714 973-6233	1506
Ted Rieck Enterprises Inc	3444	F	714 542-4763	6928
Tenet Healthsystem Medical Inc	8062	C	714 966-8191	20972
Tenet Healthsystem Medical Inc	8011	D	714 524-4820	20105
Tfn Architectural Signage Inc **(PA)**	3993	E	714 556-0990	11611
Thi Inc	3841	D	714 444-4643	11065
Tivoli Industries Inc	3648	E	714 957-6101	9151
TMC Fluid Systems Inc	3564	F	714 553-0944	8057
Tmx Engineering LLC	8711	D	714 641-5884	22676
Tmx Engineering and Mfg Corp	3599	D	714 641-5884	8820
Tobin Steel Company Inc	3441	D	714 541-2268	6671
Today Pvc Bending Inc	3644	F	714 953-5707	9054
Tomi Engineering Inc	3599	D	714 556-1474	8821
Toms Truck Center Inc	5012	C	714 835-1978	13037
Town Cntry Mnor of Chrstn Mssn	8051	C	714 547-7581	20488
Trans-Pak Incorporated	7389	C	310 618-6937	18694

	SIC	EMP	PHONE	ENTRY #
Transit Air Cargo Inc	4731	C	714 571-0393	12543
Triple DOT Corp	3085	E	714 241-0888	5481
TSC Precision Machining Inc	3599	F	714 542-3182	8828
Ttm Printed Circuit Group Inc **(HQ)**	3672	A	714 327-3000	9463
Ttm Technologies Inc **(PA)**	3672	B	714 327-3000	9464
Tustin Memorial Academy	8641	D	714 730-7546	22372
Twed-Dells Inc	3231	E	714 754-6900	5971
Ullman Sails Inc **(PA)**	2394	F	714 432-1860	3147
Ultra TEC Manufacturing Inc	3559	F	714 542-0608	7998
Umbrla Inc	3523	D	888 909-5564	7623
Undersea Systems Intl Inc	3699	D	714 754-7848	9925
Unit Industries Inc **(PA)**	3678	F	714 871-4161	9667
United Crbral Plsy Assn Ornge	8322	B	949 333-6400	21907
United Syatt America Corp **(PA)**	5013	C	714 568-1938	13103
Universal Protection Gp LLC **(PA)**	7381	C	714 619-9700	18350
Universal Protection Svc LP **(HQ)**	7381	A	714 619-9700	18351
Universal Prtction SEC Systems **(DH)**	7381	E	714 288-2227	18352
Universal Punch Corp	3542	D	714 556-4488	7767
Universal Services America LP	7349	A	714 923-3700	17298
Universal Services America LP **(DH)**	7381	D	866 877-1965	18354
University California Irvine	8011	C	714 480-2443	20123
Unrivaled Brands Inc **(PA)**	3523	E	888 909-5564	7624
US Core Pins Inc	3599	F	714 540-2846	8833
US Rigging Supply Corp	3496	E	714 545-7444	7521
US Saws Inc **(PA)**	3531	F	860 668-2402	7656
Utility Systems Scnce Sftwr In **(PA)**	7371	D	714 542-1004	17749
Vantage Custom Classics Inc	5136	E	714 755-1133	14358
Veterans Affairs US Dept	8011	D	714 568-9802	20140
Visiting Nrse Assn of Inland C **(PA)**	8082	A	951 413-1200	21228
Visiting Nrse Assn Orange Cnty **(PA)**	8082	D	949 263-4700	21229
Vitabest Nutrition Inc	2834	B	714 368-1181	4910
Volunteers of Amer Los Angeles	8322	D	714 426-9834	21917
Waste MGT Collectn Recycl Inc	7353	D	714 637-3010	17320
Waymakers **(PA)**	8322	D	714 492-1010	21924
West Coast Aviation Svcs LLC **(PA)**	8742	E	949 852-8340	23365
West Lake Food Corporation	2011	D	714 973-2286	1725
Western Medical Center Aux **(HQ)**	8062	C	714 835-3555	21008
Westminster Press Inc	2752	E	714 210-2881	4458
Westridge Laboratories Inc	2844	E	714 259-9400	5082
White Cap Construction Supply	5082	A	949 794-5300	13874
Whole Health Pharmacy	5122	E	949 305-0788	14299
Wilkins Design and Mfg Inc	3441	E	714 564-3351	6684
Windsor Capital Group Inc	7011	D	714 241-3800	16800
Wm Vandergeest Ldscp Care Inc	0782	D	714 545-8432	352
Wolf Firm A Law Corporation	8111	D	949 720-9200	21698
Word For Today	2731	D	714 825-9673	4145
Wyvern Technologies	3679	E	714 966-0710	9803
Xs Scuba Inc **(PA)**	3949	E	714 424-0434	11463
Yokohama Corp North America **(HQ)**	3011	C	540 389-5426	5307
Zerotruck	3711	F	714 675-7117	9975

SANTA BARBARA, CA - Santa Barbara County

	SIC	EMP	PHONE	ENTRY #
1260 Bb Property LLC	7011	B	805 969-2261	16305
Adding Technology Inc **(PA)**	7372	F	805 252-6971	17777
Advanced Scntific Concepts Inc	8732	D	805 966-3331	22874
African Women Rising	8641	C	415 278-1784	22309
Alexs Tile Works Inc	1743	E	805 967-5308	1410
Alta Properties Inc	3699	B	805 683-1431	9853
Alta Properties Inc	3825	C	805 683-2575	10741
Alta Properties Inc	3699	B	805 690-5382	9854
Alta Properties Inc	3264	C	805 967-0171	5997
Alta Properties Inc **(PA)**	3264	C	805 967-0171	5998
American Indian Health & Svcs	8099	E	805 681-7356	21383
Ampersand Publishing LLC **(PA)**	2711	E	805 564-5200	3944
Anasys Instruments Corp **(PA)**	3826	F	805 730-3310	10780
Anchore Inc	7371	E	805 456-8981	17547
Anesthsia Med Group Snta Brbar	8011	D	805 682-7751	19710
Aqueos Corporation **(PA)**	3533	D	805 364-0570	7666
Architctral Mllwk Snta Barbara	2431	E	805 965-7011	3231
Automobile Club Southern Cal	8699	D	805 682-5811	22400
Axia Technologies Inc	7372	E	855 376-2942	17792
Axia Technologies Inc	7372	E	855 376-2942	17793
Axxcelera Brdband Wireless Inc **(DH)**	4812	D	805 968-9621	12594
B&B Hardware Inc	3452	F	805 683-6700	7056
Bankers Mrtg Rlty Advsors Snta	8361	E	805 682-9345	22084
Bartlett Pringle & Wolf LLP	8721	E	805 963-7811	22760
Beach Mtl Prtners A Cal Ltd PR	7011	D	800 755-0222	16340
Benefit Software Incorporated	7372	F	805 679-6200	17795
Birnam Wood Golf Club **(PA)**	7997	C	805 969-2223	19547
Brandnew Industries Inc	3953	F	805 964-8251	11471
Brightview Golf Maint Inc	0781	C	805 968-6400	236
Butler America LLC **(HQ)**	8711	A	805 880-1965	22506
Butler America Holdings Inc **(PA)**	7361	C	805 880-1978	17400
Butler International Inc **(PA)**	7361	C	805 882-2200	17402
Butler Service Group Inc **(HQ)**	7363	D	201 891-5312	17487
Caesar and Seider Insur Svcs **(PA)**	6411	D	805 682-2571	15545
California Convalescent Hosp	8051	D	805 682-1355	20269
Canndescent	2834	F	877 778-9587	4803
Carpe Data **(PA)**	8742	D	877 342-2773	23182
Channel Islnds Yung MNS Chrstn	8641	D	805 963-8775	22325
Channel Islnds Yung MNS Chrstn	8641	D	805 687-7727	22328
Channel Islnds Yung MNS Chrstn	8641	D	805 969-3288	22329
Chicago Title Insurance Co **(HQ)**	6361	C	805 565-6900	15498
Child Abuse Lstening Mediation	8322	E	805 965-2376	21736
Cicileo Landscapes Inc	0781	E	805 967-3939	251
Cityfreighter Inc **(PA)**	3714	E	805 455-1440	10031
Clearpathgps LLC	3678	E	805 979-3442	9648
Cliff View Terrace Inc	8361	D	805 682-7443	22093
Commission Junction LLC **(DH)**	7371	D	805 730-8000	17581
Company of Motion LLC	3861	F	805 963-1996	11272
Compass Health Inc	8051	C	805 687-6651	20285
Computational Sensors Corp	3812	E	805 962-1175	10576
Continntal Advnced Ldar Sltons	3714	D	805 318-2072	10035
Cook Hammond and Kell Inc	7389	F	805 682-8900	18492
Cottage Rehabilitation Hosp	8062	E	805 569-8999	20735
Covenant Care California LLC	8051	D	805 964-4871	20300
Covenant Rtirement Communities	8051	D	805 687-0701	20304
Curvature LLC **(DH)**	5045	B	800 230-6638	13385
Dailymedia Inc **(PA)**	2711	F	541 821-5207	3971
Dennis Allen Associates **(PA)**	1521	D	805 884-8777	600
Duncan Carter Corporation **(PA)**	3931	D	805 964-9749	11341
Dupont Displays Inc	8731	C	805 562-5400	22835
Efaxcom	3577	E	805 692-0064	8253
Eim Corporation	7371	E	805 963-2935	17606
El Capitan Canyon LLC	7033	D	805 685-3887	16832
El Encanto Inc	7011	D	805 845-5800	16431
Emcare Inc	7361	D	805 564-5097	17417
Employbridge LLC **(HQ)**	7361	C	805 882-2200	17418
Encina Pepper Tree Joint Ventr **(PA)**	7011	D	805 687-5511	16433
Encina Pepper Tree Joint Ventr	7011	D	805 682-7277	16434
Esperer Holdings Inc **(PA)**	3341	F	805 880-4220	6292
Esperer Webstores LLC	2023	F	805 880-1900	1790
Evans Hardy & Young Inc	7311	E	805 963-5841	17011
Family Svc Agcy Snta Brbara CN	8322	D	805 965-1001	21787
Fastclick Inc	7319	B	805 689-9839	17097
Fess Prker-Red Lion Gen Partnr	7011	C	805 564-4333	16442
Foley Bezek Behle & Curtis LLP	8111	D	805 962-9495	21556
Foodtools Consolidated Inc **(PA)**	3556	E	805 962-8383	7932
Frank Schipper Construction Co	1542	E	805 963-4359	763
Freedom Photonics LLC	3699	E	805 967-4900	9869
Front Prch Cmmnties Svcs - Cas	8059	C	805 687-0793	20587
Girls Rock Sb	8699	D	805 861-8128	22451
Goleta Valley Cottage Hosp Aux	8062	B	805 681-6468	20779
Granite Construction Company	1611	C	805 964-9951	882
Graphiq LLC	2741	C	805 335-2433	4177
Green Hills Software LLC **(HQ)**	7372	C	805 965-6044	17872
H D G Associates	7011	B	805 963-0744	16460
Hg Insights Inc	7389	D	805 880-1100	18542
Hillside House	8052	D	805 687-0788	20531
Impact Radius Inc **(HQ)**	8742	D	805 324-6021	23241
Indaba Group Inc **(HQ)**	7372	E	805 964-3313	17883
Inform Solution Incorporated	7372	F	805 879-6000	17886
Integrity Security Svcs LLC **(DH)**	3699	F	805 965-6044	9873
International Tranducer Corp	3825	C	805 683-2575	10759
Interstate Hotels Resorts Inc	7011	D	805 966-2285	16506
Invenios LLC	3231	D	805 962-3333	5959
Invoca Inc	7371	D	855 977-3154	17643
Ircamera LLC	3827	E	805 965-9650	10842
Jacor Communications Company	4832	D	805 879-8300	12695
Jeannines Bkg Co Santa Barbara **(PA)**	2051	F	805 966-1717	2009
JM Roofing Company Inc	1761	D	805 966-3696	1491
John Kenney Construction Inc	1771	D	805 884-1579	1534
Jordanos Inc **(PA)**	5181	C	805 964-0611	14829
Kate Farms Inc	2099	C	805 845-2446	2458
Kollmorgen Corporation	3621	D	805 696-1236	8920
La Cumbre Country Club	7997	D	805 687-2421	19575
Lafond Vineyard Inc	2084	F	805 962-9303	2201
Laguna Blanca School **(PA)**	8748	D	805 687-2461	23462
Landmark Global Inc **(HQ)**	4731	D	805 679-5029	12478
Landmark Global Inc	8748	D	805 720-5874	23464
Logicmonitor Inc **(PA)**	7375	A	805 394-8632	18128
Marborg Industries **(PA)**	4953	C	805 963-1852	12958
Medeia Inc	3841	F	800 433-4609	11015
Mentor Worldwide LLC	5047	B	805 681-6000	13500
Mercer Global Securities LLC	6282	D	805 565-1681	15332
Merrill Lynch Prce Fnner Smith	7389	C	805 695-7028	18596
Merrill Lynch Prce Fnner Smith	6211	D	805 963-0333	15287
Mission Linen Supply	7213	D	805 963-0414	16860
Mission Linen Supply	7213	D	805 962-7687	16862
MNS Engineers Inc **(PA)**	8711	D	805 692-6921	22615
Montecito Country Club Inc	7997	D	805 969-0800	19589
Montecito Retirement Assn	8051	B	805 969-8011	20419
Morgan Stnley Smith Barney LLC	6211	D	805 565-4447	15299
Morgan Stnley Smith Barney LLC	6211	D	805 963-3381	15301
Motion Engineering Inc **(HQ)**	3577	D	805 696-1200	8282
Mountain View Montessori Schl **(PA)**	8351	D	805 453-3197	22039
Mullen & Henzell LLP	8111	E	805 966-1501	21635
Music Academy of West	7929	D	805 969-4726	19371
Nasif Hicks Harris & Co LLP	8721	D	805 966-1521	22806
Nevins/Adams Properties Inc **(PA)**	6512	C	805 963-2884	15682
Nhr Newco Holdings LLC **(DH)**	5045	C	805 964-9975	13421
Nobbe Orthopedics Inc	3842	C	805 687-7508	11129
Occam Networks Inc **(HQ)**	3661	C	805 692-2900	9238
Ola805 LLC **(PA)**	2844	F	805 258-7680	5051
Olaplex Holdings Inc **(PA)**	2844	F	310 691-0776	5052
Olaplex Intermediate Inc **(HQ)**	5122	E	805 452-8110	14272
Olaplex Intermediate II Inc **(DH)**	5122	E	805 452-8110	14273
Omtek Inc	3674	E	805 687-9629	9551
One Call Plumber Santa Barbara	1711	D	805 364-6337	1110
Ontraport Inc	8741	C	805 568-1424	23079
Oxford Instrs Asylum RES Inc **(HQ)**	3826	D	805 696-6466	10805
P J Milligan Company LLC **(PA)**	2511	F	805 963-4038	3484
Pacific Building Maint Inc	7349	D	805 969-5221	17269
Pacific Coast Bus Times Inc	2711	F	805 560-6950	4021
Pacific Diagnostic Labs LLC **(PA)**	8071	C	805 879-8100	21081

GEOGRAPHIC

	SIC	EMP	PHONE	ENTRY #
Pacific Operators Inc	1381	E	805 899-3144	435
Palette Life Sciences Inc	2833	E	805 869-7020	4759
Parsons Group Inc **(PA)**	6513	D	805 564-3341	15744
Partner Concepts Inc	2721	D	805 745-7199	4094
Penelope Holdings Corp **(DH)**	5122	E	805 452-8110	14277
Penelope Intermediate Corp **(DH)**	5122	E	805 452-8110	14278
Pensinmark Rtirement Group LLC	8742	D	805 456-6260	23295
Pentland USA Inc **(DH)**	5139	E	516 365-1333	14444
People Creating Success Inc	8322	D	805 692-5290	21870
Photothermal Spectroscopy Corp	3826	F	805 730-3310	10807
Pitts & Bachmann Realtors Inc	6531	D	805 969-5005	15951
Pitts & Bachmann Realtors Inc	6531	D	805 963-1391	15952
Planned Prnthood Cal Cntl Cast **(PA)**	8093	D	805 963-2445	21326
Pressed Juicery Inc	5149	F	805 966-0099	14724
Price Postel and Parma LLP	8111	D	805 962-0011	21663
Productplan LLC	7372	E	805 618-2975	17962
Qad Inc **(PA)**	7372	A	805 566-6000	17963
Raoul Textiles Inc	2759	F	805 965-1694	4565
Remedy Intlligent Staffing LLC **(DH)**	7363	D	805 882-2200	17511
Renauds Bakery and Bistro Inc **(PA)**	2051	D	805 569-2400	2032
Rightscale Inc	7371	C	805 500-4164	17698
Rincon Technology Inc **(PA)**	5049	E	805 684-8100	13539
Ritz-Carlton Hotel Company LLC	7011	A	805 968-0100	16665
Ronald L Wolfe & Assoc Inc	6531	E	805 964-6770	15989
S B Hotel Partners	7011	D	805 963-9757	16679
Sansum Clinic **(PA)**	8011	D	805 681-7700	20053
Santa Barbara City of	4725	D	805 962-6464	12409
Santa Barbara Coffee & Tea Inc	2095	D	805 898-3700	2358
Santa Barbara Control Systems	3823	F	805 683-8833	10721
Santa Barbara Cottage	8062	D	805 879-8900	20933
Santa Barbara Independent Inc	2711	E	805 965-5205	4026
Santa Barbara Metro Trnst Dst **(PA)**	4111	C	805 963-3364	11839
Santa Barbara Museum of Art **(PA)**	8412	D	805 963-4364	22234
Santa Barbara San Luis Obispo	6321	C	800 421-2560	15383
Santa Barbara Surgical Ctr Inc	8011	D	805 569-3226	20056
Santa Brbara Cmnty College Dst	7231	B	805 683-4191	16917
Santa Brbara Cttage Hosp Fndti **(HQ)**	8062	A	805 682-7111	20934
Santa Brbara Mseum Ntral Hstor	8412	D	805 682-4711	22235
Santa Brbara Zlgcal Foundation	8422	C	805 962-1673	22241
Sears Roebuck and Co	7699	C	805 569-6700	19067
Select Temporaries LLC **(DH)**	7361	D	805 882-2200	17464
Sheryl Lowe Designs LLC	7389	E	805 969-1742	18665
Sientra Inc **(PA)**	3842	C	805 562-3500	11141
Sikama International Inc	3548	F	805 962-1000	7895
Simpson House Inn Inc	7011	D	805 963-7067	16712
Smith Broadcasting Group Inc **(PA)**	8741	C	805 965-0400	23110
Smith Broadcasting Group Inc	4833	B	805 882-3933	12741
Solid Oak Software Inc **(PA)**	5045	E	805 568-5415	13439
Sonos Inc **(PA)**	3651	D	805 965-3001	9196
Specialty Team Plastering Inc	1742	C	805 966-3858	1402
St Vincents Institution	8322	D	805 683-6381	21897
Steven Handelman Studios **(PA)**	3322	E	805 884-9070	6262
Summit Vntres Santa Barbara LP	8011	D	805 898-2797	20099
Sutter Health	8062	C	805 966-1600	20970
Tecolote Research Inc	8742	D	805 964-6963	23341
Tecolote Research Inc	8742	D	805 964-6963	23342
Tempest Telecom Solutions LLC **(PA)**	8748	D	805 879-4800	23516
The Valley Club of Montecito	7997	E	805 969-2215	19621
Toad & Co International Inc **(PA)**	2339	E	805 957-1474	3003
Topa Topa Brewing	2082	F	805 324-4150	2158
Towbes Group Inc **(PA)**	6552	D	805 962-2121	16077
Town & Cntry Event Rentals Inc	7359	B	805 770-5729	17380
Trackr Inc	7371	D	855 981-1690	17740
Tri-Cnties Assn For Dvlpmntlly **(PA)**	8322	D	805 962-7881	21904
United Paradyne Corporation	8741	D	805 734-2359	23132
United Seal Coating Slurryseal	1542	F	805 563-4922	844
University Business Ctr Assoc	6512	D	601 354-3555	15706
US Data Management LLC **(PA)**	7379	D	888 231-0816	18233
Vet National Inc	5063	E	805 692-8487	13673
Veterans Health Administration	8011	C	805 683-1491	20148
Visiting Nurse & Hospice Care **(PA)**	8082	C	805 965-5555	21230
Volkswagen of Van Nuys Inc	7538	D	323 873-3311	18886
Volt Management Corp	7363	D	805 560-8658	17528
West Bay Company LLC	2084	E	805 969-5803	2235
Westmont College	7371	B	805 565-6000	17760
Yardi Systems Inc **(PA)**	7371	B	951 203-6951	17765
Zyris Inc	3843	E	805 560-9888	11204

SANTA CLARITA, CA - Los Angeles County

	SIC	EMP	PHONE	ENTRY #
3d/International Inc	2842	C	661 250-2020	4951
Aircraft Hinge Inc	3728	E	661 257-3434	10260
American Health Services LLC	8011	D	661 254-6630	19708
Applied Companies	8711	E	661 257-0090	22490
Applied Polytech Systems Inc	2452	E	818 504-9261	3428
Aq Lighting Group Texas Inc	5063	E	818 534-5300	13613
B&B Manufacturing Co **(PA)**	3599	C	661 257-2161	8515
B&D Investment Partners Inc **(PA)**	2842	E	661 255-0955	4956
Broadspire Inc	4813	D	213 785-8043	12629
C Sanders Emblems LP	5199	F	800 336-7467	14917
California Millworks Corp	2431	E	661 294-2345	3236
California Resources Corp **(PA)**	1311	C	888 848-4754	395
California Resources Prod Corp **(HQ)**	1311	C	661 869-8000	398
Califrnia Rsrces Elk Hills LLC	1382	B	661 412-0000	443
Canon Recruiting Group LLC	7363	B	661 252-7400	17488
Certified Thermoplastics Inc	3089	E	661 222-3006	5605
Child & Family Center	8322	C	661 259-9439	21735
Coast Air Supply Co Inc	3643	F	310 472-5612	9027
Community Therapies LLC	8049	E	661 945-7878	20212
Cottrell Paul Enterprises LLC **(PA)**	7381	C	661 212-2357	18266
CRC Services LLC	1382	F	888 848-4754	444
Curtiss-Wrght Cntrls Elctrnic	8711	C	661 257-4430	22522
Curtiss-Wrght Cntrls Elctrnic **(DH)**	8711	C	661 702-1494	22523
Custom Suppression Inc	3677	F	818 718-1040	9627
Daisy Publishing Company Inc	2721	D	661 295-1910	4064
Delphic Enterprises Inc	0742	D	661 254-2000	198
Durable Coating Inc	3479	F	805 299-8850	7360
Elk Hills Power LLC	1382	E	888 848-4754	452
Emerald Landscape Services Inc	0782	D	714 844-2200	303
Facey Medical Foundation	8099	C	661 250-5225	21425
Facey Medical Foundation	8011	C	661 513-2100	19811
Frametent Inc	2394	E	661 290-3375	3139
Friendly Vly Recrtl Assn Inc	8641	E	661 252-3223	22338
Gothic Landscaping Inc **(PA)**	0782	C	661 678-1400	307
Grand-Way Fabri-Graphic Inc	3479	F	818 206-8560	7369
H2w Technologies Inc	3625	F	661 291-1620	8954
Henry Mayo Nwhall Mem Hlth Fnd	8062	D	661 253-8000	20786
Iwerks Entertainment Inc	3699	D	661 678-1800	9876
John Chapman Inc	7389	E	661 212-5053	18560
Jt Resources	7361	C	661 367-6827	17431
Kaiser Foundation Hospitals	8011	C	888 778-5000	19918
Kaiser Foundation Hospitals	8011	C	661 222-2323	19941
Lamsco West Inc	3089	D	661 295-8620	5695
Lansair Corporation	3599	E	661 294-9503	8661
Leatt Corporation **(PA)**	3949	E	661 287-9258	11433
Living Way Industries Inc	2752	F	661 298-3200	4361
Longs Drug Stores Cal Inc	7384	D	661 254-3766	18414
Los Angeles Residential Comm F	8361	D	661 296-8536	22128
Lowes Home Centers LLC	5031	C	661 297-1400	13233
Lowes Home Centers LLC	5031	C	661 678-4430	13273
Madn Aircraft Hinge	3721	E	661 257-3430	10195
Magic Plastics Inc **(PA)**	3089	D	800 369-0303	5702
Marathon Industries Inc	5012	C	661 286-1520	13033
Metalpro Industries Inc	3444	E	661 294-0764	6877
Morgan Products Inc	3599	E	661 257-3022	8710
Mountasia Family Fun Center	7996	D	661 253-4386	19520
Mountasia of Santa Clarita	7299	D	661 253-4386	16967
Old English Mil Woodworks Inc **(PA)**	2431	E	661 294-9171	3277
Packaging Systems Inc	2891	E	661 253-5700	5189
Parrot Communications Intl Inc	2741	E	818 567-4700	4193
Paul Mitchell John Systems **(PA)**	5122	D	800 793-8790	14276
Petersen-Dean Inc	1761	D	661 254-3322	1501
Presidental Services Inc **(PA)**	7323	C	661 259-8987	17126
Princess Cruise Lines Ltd	4724	A	661 753-2197	12397
Princess Cruise Lines Ltd **(HQ)**	4481	A	661 753-0000	12279
Princess Cruise Lines Ltd	4725	A	661 753-0000	12408
RE/Max of Valencia Inc **(PA)**	6531	C	661 255-2650	15969
Santa Clarita Concrete	1771	E	661 252-2012	1548
Santa Clarita Valley Wtr Agcy	4941	C	661 259-2737	12918
Santa Clrita Hlth Care Assn In **(PA)**	8741	D	661 253-8000	23105
Santa Clrita Vly Cmmttee On AG	8322	D	661 259-9444	21886
Santa Clrita Vly Wtr Agcy Fing	4941	C	661 259-2737	12919
Shadow Holdings LLC **(HQ)**	2844	B	661 252-3807	5068
Sheldon Mechanical Corporation	1711	D	661 286-1361	1138
Signal	2711	D	661 259-1234	4028
Southern Cal Prmnnte Med Group	8062	A	661 290-3100	20945
Southern Cal Prmnnte Med Group	8011	C	661 222-2150	20091
Tesco Products	3541	E	661 257-0153	7749
Tri-Signal Integration Inc **(PA)**	1731	D	818 566-8558	1330
True Warrior LLC	2389	E	661 237-6588	3087
Universal Wood Moulding Inc **(PA)**	5023	E	661 362-6262	13194
Val Pak Products	3069	F	661 252-0115	5420
Valencia Hotel Ltd Partnership	7011	D	661 253-2400	16769
Valley Precision Metal Product	3444	E	661 607-0100	6938
Valtron Technologies Inc	7378	D	805 257-0333	18153
Wcc Inc	1799	F	661 251-3865	1701
White Cap Supply Group Inc	5039	A	661 294-7737	13339
Whitmor Plstic Wire Cable Corp **(PA)**	3496	E	661 257-2400	7522
Woodward Hrt Inc **(HQ)**	3625	A	661 294-6000	8967

SANTA FE SPRINGS, CA - Los Angeles County

	SIC	EMP	PHONE	ENTRY #
A-W Engineering Company Inc	3469	E	562 945-1041	7117
ABC Imaging of Washington	2759	F	562 375-7280	4475
Access Business Group LLC	5169	C	808 422-9482	14767
Accuride International Inc **(PA)**	3429	E	562 903-0200	6494
Ace Commercial Inc	2752	E	562 946-6664	4222
Advanced Grund Systems Engrg L **(HQ)**	3724	E	562 906-9300	10211
Aero Chip Inc	3599	E	562 404-6300	8470
Aero Chip Intgrted Systems Inc	3812	F	310 329-8600	10559
Age Incorporated	3613	E	562 483-7300	8888
Akiwa Technology Inc	3572	F	562 407-2782	8186
Al Fakhory Trading LLC **(PA)**	5023	F	323 728-8840	13155
Alegacy Fdsrvice Pdts Group In	2599	D	562 320-3100	3721
All Power Manufacturing Co	3728	E	562 802-2640	10266
All-City Management Svcs Inc **(PA)**	8748	A	310 202-8284	23408
All-Star Lettering Inc	2759	E	562 404-5995	4478
Allblack Co Inc	3471	E	562 946-2955	7206
Allen United Inc	3089	F	562 944-5650	5553
Altro Usa Inc	3996	D	562 944-8292	11618
Amity Washer & Stamping Co	3469	F	562 941-1259	7123
Apffels Coffee Inc	2095	D	562 309-0400	2351
Argus Contracting LLC **(DH)**	1742	D	562 422-7370	1366
Artiva USA Inc	3645	E	562 298-8968	9059
Associated Plating Company	3471	E	562 946-5525	7217
Atlantic Representations Inc	2514	E	562 903-9550	3525
B & B Refractories Inc	3255	E	562 946-4535	5987
B & E Convalescent Center Inc **(PA)**	8059	D	562 923-9449	20557

Mergent email: customerrelations@mergent.com
1430

2022 Southern California Business
Directory and Buyers Guide

(P-0000) Products & Services Section entry number
(PA)=Parent Co (HQ)=Headquarters (DH)=Div Headquarters

GEOGRAPHIC SECTION SANTA FE SPRINGS, CA

	SIC	EMP	PHONE	ENTRY #
B & G Millworks	2431	F	562 944-4599	3234
Barr Engineering Inc	1711	D	562 944-1722	1032
Bdc Epoxy Systems Inc	2821	E	562 944-6177	4680
Bekins Moving Solutions Inc **(PA)**	4214	D	562 356-9460	12107
Bergsen Inc	5051	E	562 236-9787	13548
Best Roll-Up Door Inc	3442	E	562 802-2233	6693
Blue Ribbon Cont & Display Inc	2653	F	562 944-1217	3788
Bodycote W Cast Anlytcal Svc I	3398	E	562 948-2225	6433
Bolero Inds Inc A Cal Corp	3089	E	562 693-3000	5581
Bravo Sports **(HQ)**	3949	D	562 484-5100	11406
Brenntag Pacific Inc **(DH)**	5169	C	562 903-9626	14773
Brown-Pacific Inc	3312	E	562 921-3471	6189
Brunton Enterprises Inc	3441	C	562 945-0013	6593
Bumble Bee Plastics Inc	3089	F	562 903-0833	5586
C & C Die Engraving	3599	E	562 944-3399	8535
C B Sheets Inc	2653	E	562 921-1223	3790
Cableco	2298	E	562 942-8076	2712
Cadnchev Inc	5015	D	562 944-6422	13123
Cal-Tron Plating Inc	3471	E	562 945-1181	7234
California Lab Sciences LLC	8734	B	562 758-6900	22934
California Metal & Supply Inc	3443	F	800 707-6061	6732
California Reamer Company Inc	3545	F	562 946-6377	7847
Calmex Fireplace Eqp Mfg Inc	3429	E	716 645-2901	6511
Camper Packaging LLC	2023	F	562 239-6167	1788
Cascade Pump Company	3561	D	562 946-1414	8005
Catalina Carpet Mills Inc **(PA)**	2273	D	562 926-5811	2684
Cds Cold	8748	E	562 777-9969	23426
Chapman Designs Inc	2421	E	562 698-4600	3209
Chus Packaging Supplies Inc	5199	E	562 944-6411	14920
Cji Process Systems Inc	3443	D	562 777-0614	6734
CMC Rebar West	1541	C	714 692-7082	694
Coast Aluminum Inc **(PA)**	5051	C	562 946-6061	13559
Coast Iron & Steel Co	1791	E	562 946-4421	1570
Coated Fabrics Company **(HQ)**	5162	F	562 298-1300	14755
Collicutt Energy Services Inc	3432	E	562 944-4413	6558
Composites One LLC	5162	F	562 906-0173	14756
Compulocks Brands Inc	3699	F	562 201-2913	9862
Continental Heat Treating Inc	3398	D	562 944-8808	6437
Contract Transportation Sys Co	2851	E	562 696-3262	5094
Conveyor Service & Electric	3535	E	562 777-1221	7689
Coop Engineering Inc	3599	E	562 944-0171	8563
Cosasco Inc	3823	D	562 949-0123	10687
Creative Essences Inc	2087	E	310 638-9277	2317
Crescent Healthcare Inc	8082	D	562 347-2800	21157
Crescent Healthcare Inc **(DH)**	8082	C	714 520-6300	21158
Crescent Healthcare Inc	8082	D	562 347-2900	21159
Crossing Guard Company	7381	C	310 202-8284	18268
Crown Fence Co	1799	D	562 864-5177	1652
Crystal Lighting Corp	3646	F	562 944-0223	9081
Csi Electrical Contractors Inc **(HQ)**	1731	C	562 946-0700	1240
Custom Steel Fabrication Inc	3441	F	562 907-2777	6611
Danne Montague-King Co **(PA)**	5122	E	562 944-0230	14239
Day Star Industries	2431	F	562 926-8800	3241
Deca International Corp	3812	E	714 367-5900	10582
Detoronics Corp	3678	E	626 579-7130	9653
Die Craft Stamping Inc	3494	F	562 944-2395	7472
Distinctive Inds Texas Inc	2386	E	323 889-5766	3055
Distinctive Inds Texas Inc	2386	E	512 491-3500	3056
Distinctive Industries	2396	B	800 421-9777	3172
Diversified Logistic Svcs Inc	4783	E	562 941-3600	12557
Dorco Electronics Inc	2655	F	562 623-1133	3835
Dunstan Enterprises Inc	3599	F	562 630-6292	8575
Dunweizer Machine Inc	3443	F	562 698-7787	6741
Duro Roller Company Inc	3069	F	562 944-8856	5373
Duro-Flex Rubber Products Inc	3069	E	562 946-5533	5374
Dynamic Worldwide West Inc **(PA)**	4731	C	562 407-1000	12451
E & L Electric	7694	F	562 903-9272	19009
E-Liq Cube Inc **(PA)**	3999	F	562 537-9454	11662
Eagleware Manufacturing Co Inc	3469	E	562 320-3100	7143
Ecology Recycling Services LLC **(PA)**	4953	C	562 921-9975	12947
Ecowise Inc	2821	E	626 759-3997	4688
Egge Machine Company Inc **(PA)**	5013	E	562 945-3419	13057
El Monte Rents Inc **(HQ)**	7519	C	562 404-9300	18755
Elastpro Silicone Sheeting LLC	2869	F	562 348-2348	5134
Electric Sales Unlimited	5063	E	562 463-8300	13625
Electromatic	3471	F	562 623-9993	7253
Electronic Chrome Grinding Inc	3471	E	562 946-6671	7255
Elite Mfg Corp	2522	C	888 354-8356	3607
Endotec Inc	3842	E	714 681-6306	11101
Ethosenergy Field Services LLC **(DH)**	1389	E	310 639-3523	500
Eurton Electric Company Inc	7694	E	562 946-4477	19011
Excel Garden Products **(HQ)**	5191	B	562 567-2000	14858
Excel Sheet Metal Inc **(PA)**	3444	D	562 944-0701	6832
Field Foundation	1389	F	562 921-3567	501
Final Finish Inc	2262	F	562 777-7774	2663
Flexline Inc	2796	E	562 921-4141	4630
FN Logistics Llc	4214	D	213 625-5900	12112
Food Technology and Design LLC	2064	E	562 944-7821	2086
Foremost Spring Company Inc	3495	F	562 923-0791	7486
FPec Corporation A Cal Corp **(PA)**	3556	F	562 802-3727	7934
Freestyle Sales Co Ltd Partnr	5043	D	323 660-3460	13345
Fry Reglet Corporation **(PA)**	3354	D	800 237-9773	6307
Fuji Food Products Inc **(PA)**	2099	D	562 404-2590	2439
Fujitec America Inc	8741	D	310 464-8270	23029
Funai Corporation Inc **(HQ)**	3651	E	201 806-7635	9176
Gabriel Container **(PA)**	2653	C	562 699-1051	3805
Galaxy Brazing Co Inc	7692	E	562 946-9039	18978
Gale/Triangle Inc **(PA)**	4212	D	562 741-1300	11967
Galleher LLC **(PA)**	5023	C	562 944-8885	13170
Gasket Manufacturing Co	3053	E	310 217-5600	5339
Gasket Manufacturing Engrg Inc	3469	F	310 217-5600	7146
Gatehouse Msi LLC	1751	E	562 623-3000	1437
General Coatings Manufact	3999	F	562 802-8834	11675
General Lgstics Systems US Inc	4212	C	562 577-6037	11969
Georgia-Pacific LLC	5113	B	562 861-6226	14210
Global Trade Alliance Inc	5013	C	562 944-6422	13060
Golden Supreme Inc	3999	E	562 903-1063	11680
Golden West Machine Inc	3599	E	562 903-1111	8607
Gorlitz Sewer & Drain Inc	3589	E	562 944-3060	8384
GP Merger Sub Inc	3231	D	562 946-7722	5956
Grayd-A Prcsion Met Fbricators	3444	E	562 944-8951	6846
Great Amrcn Logistics Dist Inc	4214	D	800 381-4527	12113
Griffith Company	1611	D	562 929-1128	885
Gundrill Tech Inc	3599	F	562 946-9355	8612
Haringa Inc **(PA)**	7389	D	800 499-9991	18537
Harris L Woods Elec Contr	1731	D	562 945-8751	1262
Heraeus Prcous Mtls N Amer LLC **(DH)**	3341	C	562 921-7464	6294
Holbrook Construction Inc	1542	D	714 523-1150	772
Hydraulic Pneumatic Inc	3593	F	562 926-1122	8439
I-Coat Company LLC	3827	E	562 941-9989	10839
Industrial Manufacturing Inc	3433	F	562 941-5888	6571
Industrial Sprockets Gears Inc	3568	E	323 233-7221	8105
Ink Spot Inc	2752	E	626 338-4500	4330
Ink Spot Digital Printing LLC **(PA)**	2752	E	562 777-1666	4331
Inkovation Inc	2752	E	800 465-4174	4332
Integrated Office Tech LLC **(PA)**	5044	D	562 236-9200	13358
J & H Drilling Co Inc	1381	F	714 994-0402	431
J & J Processing Inc	2087	E	562 926-2333	2330
J & S Machine	3599	E	562 945-6419	8635
J R C Industries Inc	2621	E	562 698-0171	3757
Janus Et Cie **(PA)**	5021	C	310 601-2958	13139
Jarrow Industries Inc	2834	C	562 906-1919	4835
JC Hanscom Inc	2435	E	562 789-9955	3351
Johnson Controls	7382	C	562 405-3817	18389
JR Machine Company Inc	3599	E	562 903-9477	8647
K Metal Products Inc	3496	C	562 693-5425	7503
K S Designs Inc	3993	E	562 929-3973	11564
Kbl Group International Ltd	5137	E	562 699-9995	14388
Kelly Paper Company **(HQ)**	5111	E	909 859-8200	14187
Kelly Spicers Inc **(HQ)**	5111	C	562 698-1199	14188
Kemp Bros Construction Inc	1541	E	562 236-5000	706
Key Air Cnditioning Contrs Inc	1711	D	562 941-2233	1090
Kiewit Infrastructure West Co	1611	C	562 946-1816	895
Kik-Socal Inc	2842	A	562 946-6427	4966
Kingseal Corporation	3089	F	562 944-3100	5691
Kingsolver Inc	3991	F	562 945-7590	11512
Kloeckner Metals Corporation	5051	D	562 906-2020	13575
KS Engineering Inc	3728	F	562 483-7788	10364
L M Scofield Company **(DH)**	2899	E	323 720-3000	5226
LA Specialty Produce Co **(PA)**	5148	B	562 741-2200	14641
LA Supply Company LLC	2869	F	714 735-9053	5141
Lakin Tire West Incorporated **(PA)**	5014	C	562 802-2752	13118
Landcare USA LLC	0782	D	714 936-9512	317
Larsen Supply Co **(PA)**	5074	D	562 698-0731	13833
Leed Electric Inc	1731	C	562 270-9500	1275
Liberty Vegetable Oil Company	2079	E	562 921-3567	2131
Life Paint Company **(PA)**	2851	E	562 944-6391	5101
Lmw Enterprises LLC	3585	F	562 944-1969	8344
Longbar Grinding Inc	3599	F	562 921-1983	8665
Los Angeles Sleeve Co Inc	3714	E	562 945-7578	10093
Louis Levin & Son Inc	3599	E	562 802-8066	8666
Lowers Wldg & Fabrication Inc	3599	F	562 946-4521	8667
M E D Inc	3714	D	562 921-0464	10096
Machine Precision Components	3599	F	562 404-0500	8672
Martin E-Z Stick Labels	2759	F	562 906-1577	4542
Maruichi American Corporation	3317	D	562 903-8600	6250
Masonry Concepts Inc	1741	D	562 802-3700	1349
Master Powder Coating Inc	2851	E	562 863-4135	5102
Material Handling Supply Inc **(HQ)**	5084	D	562 921-7715	13914
Matt Construction Corporation **(PA)**	8742	C	562 903-2277	23269
Maxon Industries Inc	3714	D	562 464-0099	10100
Maxon Lift Corporation	5084	C	562 464-0099	13915
MCI Foods Inc	2099	C	562 977-4000	2483
McMaster-Carr Supply Company	5085	B	562 692-5911	14000
Medlin Ramps	3542	E	877 463-3546	7760
Menasha Packaging Company LLC	2653	D	562 698-3705	3819
Menke Marking Devices Inc	5084	E	562 921-1380	13917
Mias Fashion Mfg Co Inc	5137	B	562 906-1060	14400
Mid-West Fabricating Co	3714	E	562 698-9615	10103
Millennia Stainless Inc	5085	D	562 946-3545	14002
Morgan Gallacher Inc	2842	E	562 695-1232	4972
Morrison Concrete Inc	1771	E	562 802-1450	1542
Motorsport Aftrmrket Group Inc **(PA)**	3714	F	917 838-4002	10107
Multi-Link International Corp	3086	E	562 941-5380	5514
Nakamura-Beeman Inc	2521	E	562 696-1400	3591
Nashua Corporation	2621	D	323 583-8828	3762
ND Industries Inc	5085	D	562 926-3321	14007
Nelson & Associates Inc	5063	D	562 921-4423	13652
Nelson Sports Inc	3149	E	562 944-8081	5884
New Glaspro Inc	3231	E	800 776-2368	5964
Nhk Laboratories Inc **(PA)**	2834	D	562 903-5835	4861
Nikko Enterprise Corporation	2092	E	562 941-6080	2347
Ninos Latino Unidos FSA	8361	D	562 801-5454	22137
Northstar Contg Group Inc	1795	D	714 639-7600	1619

GEOGRAPHIC

Employment Codes: A=Over 500 employees, B=251-500, C=101-250, D=51-100, E=20-50 F=10-19
2022 Southern California Business Directory and Buyers Guide
© Mergent Inc. 1-800-342-5647
1431

	SIC	EMP	PHONE	ENTRY #
Office Chairs Inc	2521	D	562 802-0464	3595
Oil Well Service Company **(PA)**	1389	C	562 612-0600	529
Omega Precision	3599	E	562 946-2491	8726
Orange Cnty Name Plate Co Inc	3993	D	714 522-7693	11580
Orbo Manufacturing Inc	2396	E	562 222-4535	3179
Otafuku Foods Inc	2099	E	562 404-4700	2502
P P Mfg Co Inc	3469	E	562 921-3640	7171
Pacific Coast Bolt Corporation	5085	E	562 944-9549	14010
Pacific Steam Equipment Inc	3443	E	562 906-9292	6745
Pct-Gw Carbide Tools Usa Inc	2819	F	562 921-7898	4665
Pedavena Mould and Die Co Inc	3599	E	310 327-2814	8736
Peoples Care Inc	8351	C	562 320-0174	22047
Performance Team Frt Sys Inc	4225	D	562 741-1300	12229
Phibro-Tech Inc	2819	E	562 698-8036	4667
Philatron International **(PA)**	3699	C	562 802-0452	9899
Pioneer Custom Elec Pdts Corp	3612	D	562 944-0626	8882
Plastiject LLC	3089	F	562 926-6705	5758
Plustek Technology Inc	3577	F	714 670-7713	8291
Precision Tube Bending	3728	D	562 921-6723	10395
Pro-Tech Design & Mfg Inc	7389	D	562 207-1680	18641
Pronto Drilling Inc **(PA)**	3599	E	562 777-0900	8747
Pscmb Repairs Inc	3599	E	626 448-7778	8749
PSI Management Team Inc	1629	D	562 236-3860	1002
Ptm & W Industries Inc	3083	E	562 946-4511	5460
Qspac Industries Inc **(PA)**	2891	D	562 407-3868	5193
Quality Vessel Engineering Inc	3443	F	562 696-2100	6748
R & R Ductwork LLC	3444	F	562 944-9660	6897
R D Rubber Technology Corp	3061	E	562 941-4800	5360
Rack Depot Inc	5084	E	562 777-9809	13933
Ralco Holdings Inc **(DH)**	5013	A	949 440-5500	13082
Raymond Handling Solutions Inc **(DH)**	5084	C	562 944-8067	13935
Rbc Lubron Bearing Systems Inc **(HQ)**	3339	F	714 841-3007	6287
Rebar Engineering Inc	1791	C	562 946-2461	1579
Rebas Inc	5084	C	562 941-4155	13936
Reinhold Industries Inc **(DH)**	3089	C	562 944-3281	5791
Reliance Steel & Aluminum Co	5051	D	562 695-0467	13589
Reliance Steel & Aluminum Co	5051	D	562 944-3322	13592
Rentokil North America Inc	5191	D	562 802-2238	14867
Rev Co Spring Mfanufacturing	3495	F	562 949-1958	7491
Revco Industries Inc **(PA)**	5085	E	562 777-1588	14014
RGA Electric Inc	1731	D	562 941-6380	1308
Riviera Finance of Texas Inc	6153	D	562 777-1300	15158
Rogers Corporation	3069	D	562 404-8942	5406
Rohrback Cosasco Systems Inc **(DH)**	3823	D	562 949-0123	10719
Romeros Food Products Inc **(PA)**	2099	D	562 802-1858	2519
Ross Bindery Inc	2789	C	562 623-4565	4620
Royal Flex Circuits Inc	3672	E	562 404-0626	9450
Royal Paper Corp **(PA)**	5113	D	562 903-9030	14227
Rtm Products Inc	3312	E	562 926-2400	6210
S E Pipe Line Construction Co	1623	D	562 868-9771	968
Saint Nine America Inc	3949	E	562 921-5300	11445
Santa Fe Enterprises Inc	3544	E	562 692-7596	7830
Santa Fe Extruders Inc	3089	E	562 921-8991	5813
Santa Fe Footwear Corporation	3149	F	562 941-9689	5885
Savage Services Corporation	4212	D	562 400-2044	11992
Scorpio Enterprises	1711	D	562 946-9464	1134
Seal Methods Inc **(PA)**	2672	D	562 944-0291	3874
Sequel Contractors Inc	1611	E	562 802-7227	914
Serrano Industries Inc	3599	E	562 777-8180	8793
Shimada Enterprises Inc	3648	E	562 802-8811	9146
Shoring Engineers	1799	D	562 944-9331	1690
Sika Corporation	2899	F	562 941-0231	5242
Silenx Corporation	3823	F	562 941-4200	10723
Simply Display	3993	F	888 767-0676	11604
Sisneros Inc	2522	E	562 777-9797	3616
Sleepcomp West LLC	3086	E	562 946-3222	5521
SMI Ca Inc	3599	E	562 926-9407	8796
Soleffect	2591	F	323 275-9945	3715
Source Code LLC	3571	E	562 903-1500	8176
Southern California Edison Co	4911	C	562 903-3191	12853
Southland Polymers Inc	2821	E	562 921-0444	4719
Spearman Aerospace Inc	8711	E	714 523-4751	22656
Spec Tool Company	3728	E	323 723-9533	10422
Specialized Elevator Svcs LLC **(PA)**	5084	D	562 407-1200	13941
Specialty Paper Mills Inc	2621	C	562 692-8737	3770
Standridge Granite Corporation	3281	E	562 946-6334	6146
Star Die Casting Inc	3429	D	562 698-0627	6539
Steiner & Mateer Inc	2431	F	562 464-9082	3292
Sulzer Pump Services (us) Inc	3561	E	562 903-1000	8024
Superior Food Machinery Inc	3556	E	562 949-0396	7953
Superior Printing Inc	2759	D	888 590-7998	4578
Superprint Lithographics Inc	2752	F	562 698-8001	4429
Swann Communications USA Inc	5065	D	562 777-2551	13778
Sygma Inc	3545	E	562 906-8880	7873
T & S Die Cutting	3544	F	562 802-1731	7835
T & W Converters Inc	5113	F	818 241-1707	14229
T-1 Lighting Inc	3646	F	626 234-2328	9105
TA Industries Inc **(HQ)**	5074	D	562 466-1000	13837
Talley Inc **(PA)**	5065	C	562 906-8000	13779
Tape and Label Converters Inc	2672	E	562 945-3486	3876
Tdi Signs	3993	E	562 436-5188	11610
Teac America Inc **(HQ)**	5045	E	323 726-0303	13445
Tfcf Inc	2261	F	562 469-3444	2660
Think Together	7991	B	562 236-3835	19470
Thrifty Oil Co **(PA)**	6512	E	562 921-3581	15702
Timken Gears & Services Inc	3462	F	310 605-2600	7099
Titan Medical Enterprises Inc	2834	F	562 903-7236	4906
Tj Giant Llc	2759	F	562 906-1060	4584
Tmx Aerospace	5051	C	562 215-4410	13601
Total Import Solutions Inc	5013	F	562 691-6818	13099
Toyota Industries N Amer Inc	5084	E	562 941-4155	13953
Trail Lines Inc	4212	D	562 758-6980	12000
Tri-Star Dyeing & Finshg Inc	2231	D	562 483-0123	2614
Tri-West Ltd **(PA)**	5023	C	562 692-9166	13191
Triangle Tool & Die Corp	3599	F	562 944-2117	8825
Trident Plating Inc	3471	E	562 906-2556	7323
Trojan Battery Company **(HQ)**	3692	B	562 236-3000	9819
Trojan Battery Holdings LLC **(DH)**	3691	D	800 423-6569	9815
Troyer Contracting Company Inc	1799	D	562 944-6452	1696
Tru-Form Industries Inc **(PA)**	3469	D	562 802-2041	7186
True Design Inc	2434	F	562 699-2001	3343
Turbine Eng Cmpnents Tech Corp	3463	C	562 908-0200	7108
Twist Tite Mfg Inc	3452	E	562 229-0990	7079
Ugm Citatah Inc **(PA)**	5032	C	562 921-9549	13316
United Surface Solutions LLC	3559	E	562 693-0202	7999
United Technologies Corp	3728	D	562 944-6244	10440
Universal Asphalt Co Inc	1611	E	562 941-0201	925
Universal Label Printers	2759	E	562 944-0234	4587
Universal Saw Company Inc	7699	F	562 921-8832	19080
US Armor Corporation	3842	E	562 207-4240	11149
US Motor Works LLC **(PA)**	3714	C	562 404-0488	10151
V&H Performance LLC	3751	D	562 921-7461	10508
Valtra Inc **(PA)**	5084	E	562 949-8525	13958
Valverde Construction Inc	1623	D	562 906-1326	982
Van King & Storage Inc	4213	D	562 921-0555	12089
Vantage Associates Inc	3728	E	562 968-1400	10441
Vantage Associates Inc	3088	E	800 995-8322	5537
Vantage Associates Inc **(PA)**	3769	E	619 477-6940	10537
Vantage Associates Inc	3089	D	562 968-1400	5858
Vantage Point Products Corp **(PA)**	3651	D	562 946-1718	9206
Vault Pro	3499	F	800 299-5929	7574
Vescio Threading Co	3599	D	562 802-1868	8840
Vomela Specialty Company	2752	E	562 944-3853	4450
Votaw Precision Technologies	3812	C	562 944-0661	10652
Weber Distribution LLC **(PA)**	4222	B	855 469-3237	12180
Wells Struthers Corporation	3443	E	814 726-1000	6767
West Coast Machining Inc	3599	F	562 229-1087	8848
Western Allied Corporation	1711	E	562 944-6341	1162
Western Corrugated Design Inc	2653	E	562 695-9295	3831
Western Exterminator Company	7342	D	562 802-2238	17206
Western Screw Products Inc	3451	E	562 698-5793	7050
Westmont Industries LLC **(PA)**	3536	E	562 944-6137	7700
Westpac Labs Inc **(PA)**	8071	B	562 906-5227	21101
Westpac Labs Inc	8734	B	562 906-5227	22961
Westrux International Inc **(PA)**	7513	D	562 404-1020	18738
Whittier Mailing Products Inc **(PA)**	3579	E	562 464-3000	8320
Wieland Metal Services LLC	5051	D	562 968-2100	13605
Willick Engineering Co Inc	3844	F	562 946-4242	11211
Wismettac Asian Foods Inc **(HQ)**	5141	C	562 802-1900	14522
Woojin Is America Inc	3743	F	626 386-0101	10479
Xpo Logistics Freight Inc	4213	D	562 946-8331	12103
Zenith Screw Products Inc	3451	E	562 941-0281	7052
Zumar Industries Inc	3993	D	562 941-4633	11617

SANTA MARGARITA, CA - San Luis Obispo County

	SIC	EMP	PHONE	ENTRY #
Pacific Beverage Co	5181	D	805 438-5766	14834

SANTA MARIA, CA - Santa Barbara County

	SIC	EMP	PHONE	ENTRY #
ADS Construction Inc	1742	D	805 310-6788	1359
AG Laboratory Consulting	3826	F	805 739-5333	10778
Alan Johnson Prfmce Engrg Inc	3711	E	805 922-1202	9932
Alltec Integrated Mfg Inc	3089	E	805 595-3500	5554
American Bottling Company	2086	F	805 928-1001	2252
Aramark Healthcare Support	8099	C	805 739-3000	21385
Arrow Screw Products Inc	3599	E	805 928-2269	8504
Atlas Copco Mafi-Trench Co LLC **(DH)**	3564	C	805 352-0112	8041
Automobile Club Southern Cal	8699	D	805 922-5731	22430
Blackjack Frms De La Csta Cntl	0191	C	805 347-1333	101
Boca Mesa Incorporated	8748	D	805 934-9470	23420
Cal Coast Acidizing Co	1389	D	805 934-2411	484
California Department Trnsp	1611	D	805 922-1987	866
Central Coast Distributing LLC	5181	D	805 922-2108	14823
Central Coast Wine Warehouse **(PA)**	2084	E	805 928-9210	2175
Certified Frt Logistics Inc **(PA)**	4213	C	800 592-5906	12021
CJJ Farming Inc	0171	E	805 739-1723	24
Coast Rock Products Inc	5032	E	805 925-2505	13299
Coasthills Credit Union **(PA)**	6062	D	805 733-7600	15109
Country Oaks Care Center Inc	8051	D	805 922-6657	20292
Curation Foods Inc **(HQ)**	2099	D	800 454-1355	2415
Darensberries LLC	0171	C	805 937-8000	25
Diani Building Corp **(PA)**	1542	D	805 925-9533	760
Dignity Health	8062	B	805 739-3000	20749
Edwards Theatres Circuit Inc	7832	C	805 347-1164	19279
Engel & Gray Inc	1389	E	805 925-2771	497
Estes Express Lines	4213	D	805 922-8206	12041
Express Messenger Systems Inc	4215	D	800 488-2829	12130
First Transit	4111	D	805 925-5254	11807
Flood Ranch Company	2084	E	805 937-3616	2185
Foothill Packing Inc	5141	B	805 925-7900	14467
Foxen Vineyard Inc	2084	E	805 937-4251	2186
Fresh Venture Foods LLC	3556	C	805 928-3374	7935
Freshway Farms LLC	0171	C	805 349-7170	28
Frontier California Inc	4813	B	805 925-0000	12638
Gavial Engineering & Mfg Inc	3672	E	805 614-0060	9409
Gavial Holdings Inc **(PA)**	3679	F	805 614-0060	9715

	SIC	EMP	PHONE	ENTRY #
Genesis Healthcare LLC	8051	C	805 922-3558	20357
Glad-A-Way Gardens Inc	0181	C	805 938-0569	77
Gold Coast Farms Inc	0161	D	805 928-2727	16
Good Samaritan Shelter	8322	D	805 346-8185	21792
Greka Inc	1241	F	805 347-8700	382
Greka Integrated Inc **(PA)**	1382	C	805 347-8700	453
Hardy Diagnostics **(PA)**	5047	B	805 346-2766	13494
Impo International LLC	3144	E	805 922-7753	5880
Innovative Produce Inc	0191	E	805 349-2714	111
Insight Management Corporation **(PA)**	3652	E	866 787-3588	9221
J and D Stl Fbrication Repr LP	7692	F	805 928-9674	18983
J&G Berry Farms LLC	0171	C	831 750-9408	29
Jackson Family Wines Inc	2084	E	805 938-7300	2197
L & G Farming Co Inc	0171	E	805 928-1559	30
Life Steps Foundation Inc	8322	D	805 349-9810	21838
Life Steps Foundation Inc	8322	D	805 474-8431	21839
Los Dos Valles Harvstg & Pkg	0722	C	805 739-1688	156
Marian Community Clinic	8062	C	805 739-3867	20856
Matthew Warren Inc	3493	E	805 928-3851	7465
Melfred Borzall Inc	3541	E	805 614-4344	7736
Microwave Applications Group	8711	E	805 928-5711	22614
Mid-State Concrete Pdts Inc	3272	E	805 928-2855	6039
Mission Linen Supply	7213	D	805 922-3579	16865
New Hope Harvesting LLC	0722	D	805 478-4469	157
Nicksons Machine Shop Inc	3599	E	805 925-2525	8718
North American Fire Hose Corp	3052	D	805 922-7076	5321
Northrop Grumman Systems Corp	3812	C	805 315-5728	10620
Nursecore Management Svcs LLC	8361	B	805 938-7660	22138
Oilfield Envmtl Compliance Inc **(PA)**	8734	D	805 922-4772	22957
Okonite Company Inc	3357	D	805 922-6682	6354
Old Time Farming Inc **(PA)**	0191	C	805 349-3886	116
Osr Enterprises Inc	7372	E	805 925-1831	17947
Pacific Beverage Co	5181	D	805 922-7901	14832
PC Mechanical Inc	1389	E	805 925-2888	537
Peoples Self-Help Housing Corp	8748	D	805 349-9341	23494
Pictsweet Company	2038	B	805 928-4414	1935
Plantel Nurseries Inc	5193	D	805 349-8952	14894
Plantel Nurseries Inc **(PA)**	0181	E	805 349-8952	91
Plantel Nurseries Inc	0181	C	805 934-4300	92
Pre Con Industries Inc **(PA)**	1751	D	805 345-3147	1450
Preferred Pump Inc	3561	F	805 922-8510	8021
Primus Group Inc **(PA)**	8742	E	805 922-0055	23299
Prince Lionheart Inc **(PA)**	3089	E	805 922-2250	5778
Princeton Case-West Inc	3089	E	805 928-8840	5779
Quinn Company	5082	D	805 925-8611	13870
Quintron Systems Inc **(PA)**	3661	E	805 928-4343	9240
Radisson Hotel Santa Maria	7011	D	805 928-8000	16651
Ramco Enterprises LP	7361	A	805 922-9888	17451
Rancho Laguna Farms LLC	0191	D	805 925-7805	117
Red Blossom Sales Inc	0171	A	805 349-9404	33
Red Dog Management Inc **(PA)**	8741	C	805 925-1414	23097
Reyes Coca-Cola Bottling LLC	2086	D	805 925-2629	2289
Reyes Coca-Cola Bottling LLC	2086	D	805 614-3702	2291
Riverbench LLC **(PA)**	0172	E	805 937-8340	54
Rlv Tuned Exhaust Products Inc	3714	E	805 925-5461	10127
Safran Seats Santa Maria LLC	3728	A	805 922-5995	10411
Santa Barbara Trnsp Corp	4151	C	805 928-0402	11940
Santa Maria Enrgy Holdings LLC	1382	E	805 938-3320	464
Santa Maria Hotel Corp	7011	D	805 928-6000	16690
Santa Maria Public Airport Dst	4581	D	805 922-1726	12368
Santa Mria Vly Yung MNS Chrstn	8641	C	805 937-8521	22366
Signs of Success Inc	3993	E	805 925-7545	11602
Skylstad-Schoelen Co Inc	7349	D	805 349-0503	17285
Smith McHncl-Lctrical-Plumbing	1541	C	805 621-5000	717
Smith Packing Inc **(PA)**	0722	C	805 348-1818	159
Speeds Oil Tool Service Inc	4212	D	805 925-1369	11995
Sturgeon Son Grading & Pav Inc	8711	C	805 938-0618	22662
Teixeira Farms Desert Inc	0161	D	805 928-3801	20
Tognazzini Beverage Service	2086	E	805 928-1144	2301
Tri-Counties Association F	8621	D	805 922-4640	22283
Truteam of California Inc	1742	D	805 345-3239	1408
United Parcel Service Inc	4215	C	805 922-7851	12163
Valley Garbage Rubbish Co Inc	4953	C	805 614-1131	12988
Veterans Health Administration	8011	C	805 354-6000	20144
Vtc Enterprises **(PA)**	8331	B	805 928-5000	21974
Wasco Sales and Marketing Inc	3643	E	805 739-2747	9049
Work Inc	8322	C	805 739-0451	21931

SANTA MONICA, CA - Los Angeles County

	SIC	EMP	PHONE	ENTRY #
Abacus Wealth Partners LLC **(PA)**	8742	D	707 829-6190	23146
Ace Parking Management Inc	7521	D	310 393-9863	18758
Activision Blizzard Inc **(PA)**	7372	B	310 255-2000	17773
Adconion Media Inc **(PA)**	7311	C	310 382-5521	16990
Advanstar Communications Inc	7389	F	310 857-7500	18434
Aft Corporation	2796	F	310 576-1007	4628
American Retirement Corp	8051	C	310 399-3227	20243
Antinos Management America Inc **(PA)**	8741	D	310 453-8506	22976
Apex Machine Works Inc	8711	D	310 393-5987	22489
Apogee Electronics Corporation	3651	E	310 584-9394	9159
Archipelago Inc	2844	C	213 743-9200	4989
Artisan Entertainment Inc	7812	A	310 449-9200	19096
Atlantic Aviation Holding Corp	4581	D	310 396-6770	12340
Automobile Club Southern Cal	8699	D	310 453-1909	22436
Automotive Lease Guide Alg Inc	2741	B	424 258-8026	4154
Bad Robot Productions Inc	7822	D	310 664-3456	19256
Barclays USA Inc	6029	D	310 829-9539	15046
Basis Worldwide	7311	E	424 261-2354	16994
Beach Club	7997	D	310 395-3254	19538
Beachbody LLC **(HQ)**	7313	B	310 883-9000	17079
Beauty Counter LLC	7231	D	310 828-0111	16898
Berkeley E Convalescent Hosp	8059	C	310 829-5377	20561
Berri Pro Inc	2087	F	781 929-8288	2309
Bird Rides Inc	7371	D	866 205-2442	17563
Bird Rides Inc **(PA)**	7371	B	866 205-2442	17564
Bourget Bros Building Mtls Inc **(PA)**	5085	E	310 450-6556	13976
Boxunion Santa Monica LLC **(PA)**	7991	D	310 882-5508	19440
Boys Grls CLB Snta Monica Inc	8641	D	310 361-8500	22316
By The Blue Sea LLC	7011	B	310 458-0030	16362
C Publishing LLC	2741	E	310 393-3800	4160
C R W Distributors Inc	2013	F	310 463-4577	1729
C W Hotels Ltd	7011	C	310 395-9700	16363
California Semiconductor Tech	8711	C	310 579-2939	22509
Callfire Inc	7371	D	213 221-2289	17573
Cantaloupe Holdings LLC	8059	D	310 451-9706	20568
Capital Oversight Inc **(PA)**	8748	D	310 453-8000	23425
Captive-Aire Systems Inc	3444	E	310 876-8505	6805
Carr Corporation **(PA)**	3844	E	310 587-1113	11207
Casa De Hermandad **(PA)**	3949	E	310 477-8272	11408
Casestack LLC **(HQ)**	4225	D	310 473-8885	12188
CBS Television Distribution	8741	D	310 264-3300	22999
Charles Ting	7011	C	310 828-5517	16378
Clare Matrix **(PA)**	8069	D	310 314-6200	21039
Clearlake Capital Group LP **(PA)**	6722	B	310 400-8800	16128
Clearlake Capital Partners	7372	A	310 400-8800	17818
Coast Flagstone Co	3281	D	310 829-4010	6137
Coastal Health Care Inc	8051	D	310 828-5596	20283
Colony Capital LLC **(PA)**	6799	A	310 282-8820	16255
Connexity Inc **(HQ)**	4813	C	310 571-1235	12632
Converse Inc	5139	D	310 451-0314	14434
Cornerstone Ondemand Inc **(PA)**	7372	A	310 752-0200	17828
Cornerstone Ondmand Globl Oprt **(HQ)**	8331	B	310 752-0200	21947
Counter Brands LLC **(PA)**	5122	D	888 988-9108	14238
Cypress Creek Holdings LLC	4911	D	310 581-6299	12799
Cypress Creek Renewables LLC **(PA)**	4911	C	310 581-6299	12800
Debmar/Mercury LLC	7812	E	310 393-6000	19115
Dext Company of Maryland **(DH)**	2048	E	310 458-1574	1964
Djont/Jpm Hsptlity Lsg Spe LLC	7011	D	310 451-0676	16412
Douglas Emmett Builders	6798	D	310 255-7800	16233
Dsj Printing Inc	2752	F	310 828-8051	4284
Dtrs Santa Monica LLC	7011	B	310 458-6700	16421
Edmunds Holding Company **(PA)**	7375	A	310 309-6300	18122
Edmundscom Inc **(HQ)**	7313	A	310 309-6300	17084
Edward Thomas Hospitality Corp	7011	B	310 458-0030	16427
Emak Worldwide Inc **(PA)**	7311	D	310 633-9311	17010
Entitlement LLC	7929	E	224 336-2669	19350
Entravsion Communications Corp **(PA)**	4833	B	310 447-3870	12718
Epochcom LLC	7374	C	310 664-5700	18087
Eps Corporate Holdings Inc **(DH)**	3498	C	310 204-7238	7536
Et Whitehall Seascape LLC	7011	C	310 581-5533	16437
Executive Network Entps Inc	4119	A	310 457-8822	11863
Express Pipe & Supply Co LLC **(DH)**	3498	D	310 204-7238	7537
Extreme Group Holdings LLC	3652	E	310 899-3200	9217
Figs Inc	2326	C	424 300-8330	2778
Flyr Inc	7374	D	415 841-3597	18090
Ford of Santa Monica Inc	5012	D	310 451-1588	13026
Game Show Network Music LLC **(DH)**	4841	B	310 255-6800	12769
Gc Technology LLC **(PA)**	3663	F	310 633-5095	9275
Genius Products Inc	5099	C	310 453-1222	14158
Georgian Hotel	7011	D	310 395-9945	16454
Gilchrist & Rutter Prof Corp	8111	E	310 393-4000	21566
Glamour Industries Co	5087	D	213 687-8600	14037
Golden State Health Ctrs Inc	8059	C	310 451-9706	20594
Goodrx Inc **(PA)**	7372	F	855 268-2822	17868
Goodrx Holdings Inc **(PA)**	7374	C	855 268-2822	18091
Grow Brains System Inc	3944	E	310 428-6445	11374
Growing Place	8351	D	310 399-7769	22019
Guggenheim Prtners Inv MGT LLC	6722	D	310 576-1270	16130
Gumbiner Savett Inc	6512	D	310 828-9798	15671
Gumgum Sports Inc	7372	E	310 400-0396	17876
Guthy-Renker LLC	5099	D	310 581-6250	14161
Hallmark Labs LLC	2741	C	424 210-3600	4179
Hawke Media Ventures LLC	8742	D	310 451-7295	23233
Hct Packaging Inc **(PA)**	7389	C	310 260-7680	18539
Hirsch Bedner Associates **(PA)**	7389	C	310 829-9087	18543
Hirsch/Bedner Intl Inc **(PA)**	7389	D	310 829-9087	18544
Home Box Office Inc	4841	D	310 382-3000	12771
Hulu LLC **(HQ)**	4813	A	310 571-4700	12647
Image Square Inc	2752	E	310 586-2333	4323
Innovtive Artsts Tlent Ltrary **(PA)**	7922	D	310 656-0400	19314
Inspire Energy Holdings LLC	4911	D	866 403-2620	12807
International Processing Corp **(DH)**	2048	E	310 458-1574	1970
Irvine APT Communities LP	6513	C	310 255-1221	15731
Jakks Pacific Inc **(PA)**	3944	B	424 268-9444	11380
Jerry Bruckheimer Inc	7812	D	310 664-6260	19137
Johnny Was	5137	F	310 656-0600	14384
Jonathan Club	7997	D	310 393-9245	19572
Jones Brothers Cnstr Corp **(PA)**	1542	D	310 470-1885	777
K-Micro Inc	5045	D	310 442-3200	13411
Kargo Global Inc	7313	C	212 979-9000	17087
Kcrw Foundation Inc	8399	D	310 450-5183	22191
Kingcom(us) LLC **(HQ)**	7372	E	424 744-5697	17900
Kite Pharma Inc **(HQ)**	8731	C	310 824-9999	22846
Lanza Research International	2844	F	310 393-5227	5041
Leaf Group Ltd **(PA)**	7374	B	310 656-6253	18097
Lightcrest LLC	7373	E	888 320-8495	18044

GEOGRAPHIC

	SIC	EMP	PHONE	ENTRY #
Lincoln Iron Works	3312	E	310 684-2543	6204
Lions Gate Entertainment Inc **(HQ)**	7812	D	310 449-9200	19143
Lions Gate Films Inc	7812	C	310 449-9200	19144
Lionsgate Productions Inc	7822	A	310 255-3937	19260
Los Angeles Intl Ch Chrst	7371	C	213 351-2300	17655
Luma Pictures Inc	7812	C	310 888-8738	19146
M&C Hotel Interests Inc	7011	C	310 399-9344	16549
Macerich Company **(PA)**	6798	D	310 394-6000	16239
Magna-Pole Products Inc **(PA)**	2542	F	310 453-3806	3688
Mammoth Media Inc	2711	D	832 315-0833	4008
Maui Toys	3949	F	330 747-4333	11437
Medicl Imgng Ctr of Southrn CA	8011	D	310 829-9788	19974
Mens Apparel Guild In Cal Inc	8611	C	310 857-7500	22252
Mercury Insurance Company	6331	B	310 451-4943	15472
Merrill Lynch Prce Fnner Smith	6211	D	310 477-3400	15284
Method Studios LLC	7812	D	310 434-6500	19149
Mgid Inc **(PA)**	8742	D	424 322-8059	23273
Milken Family Foundation	8641	C	310 570-4800	22349
Milken Institute	8733	E	310 570-4600	22914
MJW Investments **(PA)**	6512	D	310 395-3430	15680
Morley Construction Company **(HQ)**	1771	D	310 399-1600	1541
Mygnar Inc **(PA)**	3577	F	626 676-5415	8285
Newlon Rouge LLC	2711	F	310 458-7737	4013
Ocean Avenue LLC	7011	B	310 576-7777	16590
Ocean Park Community Center	8748	D	310 828-6717	23486
Omega Leads Inc	3679	E	310 394-6786	9759
Ontrak Inc **(PA)**	8063	A	310 444-4300	21025
Opiant Pharmaceuticals Inc	2834	F	310 598-5410	4866
Ovation R&G LLC **(PA)**	3663	D	310 430-7575	9307
Pacific Income Advisers Inc **(PA)**	6282	E	310 393-1424	15337
Palisades Media Group Inc **(PA)**	7311	D	310 564-5400	17043
Paradigm Communications Corp	4813	E	310 395-5757	12663
Patientpop Inc	7372	D	844 487-8399	17953
People Concern	8322	C	310 883-1222	21867
People Concern	8322	C	310 450-0650	21868
Perr & Knight Inc **(PA)**	6411	D	310 230-9339	15612
Phonesuit Inc	3663	E	310 774-0282	9310
Platinum Clg Indianapolis LLC	7349	B	310 584-8000	17275
Postaer Rubin and Associates **(PA)**	7311	B	310 394-4000	17046
Pranalytica Inc	3841	F	310 458-3345	11046
Prata Inc	7372	E	512 823-1002	17960
Printing Palace Inc **(PA)**	2752	F	310 451-5151	4401
Providence St Johns Hlth Ctr	8062	B	310 829-6562	20917
Provident Financial Management	8741	D	310 282-0477	23094
Provivi Inc **(PA)**	2869	E	310 828-2307	5144
Radiabeam Technologies LLC **(PA)**	5049	F	310 822-5845	13536
Railstech Inc	7372	E	267 315-2998	17969
Reconserve Inc **(HQ)**	2048	E	310 458-1574	1974
Red Bull Distribution Co Inc **(HQ)**	5149	C	916 515-3501	14730
Red Bull Media Hse N Amer Inc **(HQ)**	5149	C	310 393-4647	14731
Red Bull Media Hse N Amer Inc	2086	D	310 393-4647	2281
Red Interactive Agency LLC **(PA)**	7311	D	310 399-4242	17052
Regents of The University Cal	8099	D	310 267-9308	21475
Richard Cantrell **(PA)**	5137	D	310 399-5511	14413
Ridge Wallet LLC	3172	F	818 636-2832	5911
Ring LLC **(HQ)**	3612	B	800 656-1918	8883
Rock Paper Scissors LLC	7812	E	310 586-0600	19171
Roscoe Real Estate Ltd Partnr	7011	C	310 260-7500	16672
S F Broadcasting of Wisconsin	4833	C	310 586-2410	12740
Saint Jhns Hlth Ctr Foundation	8011	C	310 315-6111	20047
Saint Jhns Hlth Ctr Foundation	8062	D	310 829-8970	20927
Saint Johns Cancer Institute	8733	D	310 449-5253	22919
Salesforcecom Inc	7372	E	310 752-7000	17976
San Antnio Behavioral Hlth LLC **(PA)**	8099	D	310 566-0640	21477
Santa Monica City of	4131	D	310 451-5444	11904
Santa Monica Amusements LLC	7996	B	310 451-9641	19524
Santa Monica Days Inn	7011	D	310 829-6333	16691
Santa Monica Family YMCA	8641	D	310 451-7387	22365
Santa Monica Hotel Owner LLC	7011	C	310 395-3332	16692
Santa Monica Orthopedic **(PA)**	8011	D	310 315-2018	20060
Santa Monica Pet Med Ctr Inc	0742	D	310 393-8218	202
Santa Monica Plastics Llc	3089	F	310 403-2849	5814
Santa Monica Propeller Svc Inc	3728	F	310 390-6233	10413
Santa Monica Proper Jv LLC	7011	C	310 620-9990	16693
Scribble Press Inc	2741	E	212 288-2928	4202
SE Software Inc	7372	F	888 504-9876	17979
Second Street Corporation	7011	C	310 394-5454	16701
Sgi Logistics	4212	E	310 513-5339	11993
Shapco Inc **(PA)**	5051	F	310 264-1666	13595
Snap Inc **(PA)**	7371	A	310 399-3339	17716
Society6 LLC	7374	D	310 394-6400	18110
Solarreserve Inc	4911	D	310 315-2200	12826
Solarreserve LLC **(PA)**	3433	F	310 315-2200	6576
Sonar Entertainment Inc **(PA)**	7822	B	424 230-7140	19261
Spilo Worldwide Inc	5087	D	213 687-8600	14044
Step Up On Second Street Inc **(PA)**	8082	D	310 394-6889	21218
Stephen B Meisel MD A Med Corp **(HQ)**	8011	D	310 828-8843	20098
Storquest Self Storage **(HQ)**	4225	D	310 451-2130	12249
Subtractive Inc **(PA)**	4833	D	310 664-0540	12743
Swvl LLC	2741	F	424 248-3677	4210
Taslimi Construction Co Inc	1542	D	310 447-3000	836
Tbwa Worldwide Inc	7311	C	310 305-4400	17060
Tennenbaum Capitl Partners LLC **(HQ)**	6799	D	310 566-1000	16296
Tennis Channel Inc **(HQ)**	7922	D	310 392-1920	19333
Thatgamecompany Inc	7993	E	310 453-4906	19514
Tomitribe Corporation	7371	E	310 526-7676	17738
Tonopah Solar Energy LLC	1711	D	310 315-2200	1156
Total Beauty Media Inc **(HQ)**	2721	F	310 295-9593	4108
Trey Arch LLC	5045	D	310 581-4700	13449
Truecar Inc **(PA)**	7371	E	800 200-2000	17746
TV Guide Entrmt Group LLC	5064	B	310 360-1441	13696
Ubm Canon LLC **(DH)**	2721	C	310 445-4200	4110
Ucla Healthcare	8062	D	310 319-4560	20986
Umg Commercial Services Inc **(DH)**	2741	D	310 235-4700	4215
Universal Mus Investments Inc **(HQ)**	7389	D	888 583-7176	18710
Universal Music Group Inc **(PA)**	7389	D	310 865-4000	18711
Universal Music Publishing Inc	2741	D	310 235-4700	4216
Vault Prep Inc	3272	E	310 971-9091	6064
Verizon Services Corp	4812	B	310 315-1100	12618
Volkswagen Santa Monica Inc **(PA)**	7532	C	310 829-1888	18808
Watt Communities	7389	D	310 314-2430	18723
Watt Companies Inc **(PA)**	6531	C	310 314-2430	16030
Watt Properties Inc **(PA)**	6552	D	310 314-2430	16080
Wells Fargo Capital Fin LLC **(DH)**	6159	D	310 453-7300	15167
William Warren Properties Inc	6513	D	310 454-1500	15753
Wilshire Advisors LLC **(PA)**	8742	C	310 451-3051	23367
Windsor Capital Group Inc	7011	D	310 566-1100	16791
Windsor Capital Group Inc	7011	D	310 566-1100	16792
Windsor Capital Group Inc	7011	D	209 577-3825	16793
Windsor Capital Group Inc	7011	D	209 577-3825	16794
Windsor Capital Group Inc	7011	D	310 566-1100	16797
Windsor Capital Group Inc	7011	D	310 566-1100	16798
Wtp America LLC **(HQ)**	8748	D	310 356-4336	23528
Yoga Works Inc **(DH)**	7991	E	310 664-6470	19475
Ziprecruiter Inc	8742	A	877 252-1062	23373
Zooey Apparel Inc	2339	E	310 315-2880	3011

SANTA PAULA, CA - Ventura County

	SIC	EMP	PHONE	ENTRY #
Abrisa Industrial Glass Inc **(HQ)**	3827	D	805 525-4902	10823
Abrisa Technologies	3827	E	805 525-4902	10824
Associates Insectary	7342	D	805 933-1301	17197
Aurora Casting & Engrg Inc	5051	D	805 933-2761	13546
Automotive Racing Products Inc	3429	E	805 525-1497	6501
Bendpak Inc **(PA)**	3559	C	805 933-9970	7965
Calavo Growers Inc **(PA)**	2099	A	805 525-1245	2403
Calavo Growers Inc	4783	D	805 525-5511	12555
Calpipe Industries LLC	3312	E	562 803-4388	6194
Carbon California Company LLC	1311	F	805 933-1901	399
Coastal Harvesting Inc	0761	B	805 525-6250	214
Fowlie Enterprises Inc	2052	E	805 583-2800	2064
Limoneira Company **(PA)**	0723	B	805 525-5541	180
Oil Well Service Company	1389	D	805 525-2103	531
Qma Inc	3599	F	805 529-5395	8751
Rico Farm Labor Inc	0762	E	805 525-4523	227
Santa Paula Memorial Hospital	8062	D	805 933-9131	20935
Saticoy Lemon Association **(PA)**	0723	D	805 654-6500	185
Thompco Inc	5082	E	805 933-8048	13872
Troop Real Estate Inc	6531	D	805 921-0030	16023
Turtle Storage Ltd	2542	E	805 933-3688	3699
Ventura County Medical Center	8011	C	805 933-8600	20135
Ventura Rgional Sanitation Dst	4953	D	805 525-8217	12990
Weber Orthopedic LP **(PA)**	3842	D	800 221-5465	11153
Westlake Engrg Roto Form	3089	E	805 525-8800	5864
World Upholstery & Trim Inc	2396	F	805 921-0100	3185

SANTA YNEZ, CA - Santa Barbara County

	SIC	EMP	PHONE	ENTRY #
Bridlewood Winery LLC	2084	E	805 688-9000	2168
Channel Islnds Yung MNS Chrstn	8641	D	805 686-2037	22331
Chumash Casino Resort **(HQ)**	7999	C	805 686-0855	19639
Gainey Vineyard	2084	E	805 688-0558	2187
John S Carter Inc	1799	F	805 962-5889	1668
Valley Oaks Industries	2521	F	805 688-2754	3603

SEAL BEACH, CA - Orange County

	SIC	EMP	PHONE	ENTRY #
Cosmodyne LLC	3559	E	562 795-5990	7968
Country Villa Service Corp	8322	D	562 598-2477	21759
Dendreon Pharmaceuticals Inc	2834	F	562 253-3931	4814
Dendreon Pharmaceuticals LLC **(HQ)**	2834	E	562 252-7500	4815
Diversfied Tchncal Systems Inc **(HQ)**	3825	E	562 493-0158	10748
First Team RE - Orange Cnty	6531	C	562 596-9911	15858
Fisheries Resource Vlntr Corps	8742	C	562 596-9261	23218
Golden Rain Foundation	8011	C	562 493-9581	19832
Hellman Properties LLC	1311	E	562 431-6022	406
Irish Interiors Holdings Inc	3728	E	949 559-0930	10358
Limbach Company LP	1711	C	714 653-7000	1094
Madaluxe Group LLC **(PA)**	5137	E	562 296-1055	14397
Magensa LLC	3578	F	562 546-6689	8315
Magtek Inc **(PA)**	3577	C	562 546-6400	8279
Merrill Lynch Prce Fnner Smith	6211	D	562 493-1300	15293
Olson Company LLC **(PA)**	6552	D	562 596-4770	16065
Olson Urban Housing LLC	6552	D	562 596-4770	16066
Original Parts Group Inc **(PA)**	3465	D	562 594-1000	7112
Premier Healthcare Svcs LLC **(DH)**	7361	C	626 204-7930	17446
Samedan Oil Corporation	1382	D	661 319-5038	463
Sisters of St Joseph Orange	8062	A	562 430-4638	20942
Tenet Healthsystem Medical Inc	8011	D	562 493-9581	20107
Turner John McDonald MD	8011	D	562 799-7071	20114
Tyr Sport Inc	5137	D	562 430-1380	14424
Wells Fargo Clearing Svcs LLC	6211	E	562 594-1220	15311

SEPULVEDA, CA - Los Angeles County

	SIC	EMP	PHONE	ENTRY #
Moore Industries - Europe Inc **(HQ)**	3823	F	818 894-7111	10708

SEQ NATL PK, CA - Tulare County

	SIC	EMP	PHONE	ENTRY #
DNC Prks Rsorts At Sequoia Inc	7011	D	559 565-4070	16414

	SIC	EMP	PHONE	ENTRY #
SHAFTER, CA - Kern County				
Bps Supply Group **(PA)**	5051	D	661 589-9141	13552
Central California Power	7538	E	661 589-2870	18816
Cummings Vacuum Service Inc	1389	D	661 746-1786	493
Delmart Farms Inc	0172	D	661 746-2148	45
Elk Corporation of Texas	3272	C	661 391-3900	6030
Farm Pump & Irrigation Co Inc **(PA)**	5084	E	661 589-6901	13901
Forterra Pipe & Precast LLC	3444	E	661 746-3527	6840
Frank Russell Inc	3599	F	661 324-5575	8593
Garlic Company	0139	C	661 393-4212	6
Grimmway Enterprises Inc	0723	C	661 393-3320	172
Grimmway Enterprises Inc	0191	C	661 399-0844	108
M-I LLC	1389	E	661 321-5400	515
Nikkel Iron Works Corporation	3523	F	661 746-4904	7614
Oil Well Service Company	1389	D	661 746-4809	530
Ponder Environmental Svcs Inc	8744	E	661 589-7771	23396
Richland Chevrolet Co Corp	7539	D	661 746-4981	18903
Standard Industries Inc	5033	D	661 387-1110	13329
Tryad Service Corporation	1389	E	661 391-1524	554
Trymax	3498	F	661 391-1572	7545
U S Weatherford L P	1382	E	661 746-3415	471
Varner Family Ltd Partnership **(PA)**	6733	E	661 399-1163	16198
Wonderful Company LLC	0723	B	661 399-4456	196
Wonderful Orchards LLC **(HQ)**	0173	C	661 399-4456	59
SHANDON, CA - San Luis Obispo County				
Pacific Tank & Cnstr Inc	3443	E	805 237-2929	6746
SHELL BEACH, CA - San Luis Obispo County				
Dolphin Bay Ht & Residence Inc	7011	D	805 773-4300	16415
La Bonne Vie Inc	7991	D	805 773-5003	19453
SHERMAN OAKS, CA - Los Angeles County				
American Med O & P Clinic Inc	3842	E	818 281-5747	11085
American Naturals Company LLC	2099	E	323 201-6891	2389
American Printing & Design Ltd	2752	F	310 287-0460	4228
Ameritrans Express Inc	4731	F	818 201-0524	12421
Ansira Partners Inc	7389	C	818 461-6100	18446
Arclight Cinema Company	7832	D	818 501-0753	19270
Behavioral Learning Center Inc	8322	F	661 254-7086	21721
Ben Group Inc	7372	F	310 342-1500	17794
Branded Entrmt Netwrk Inc **(PA)**	7335	C	310 342-1500	17158
Burbank Partners LLC	7011	D	818 263-8704	16356
Center Automotive Inc	5012	C	818 907-9995	13023
Chambers & Chambers Inc	2084	F	818 995-6961	2176
Coastal Tile Inc	1743	D	818 988-6134	1414
Comfort Care Hospice Inc	8069	D	818 501-3129	21040
Creditors Adjustment Bur Inc	7322	D	818 990-4800	17109
Dynamic Home Care Service Inc **(PA)**	8082	D	818 981-4446	21161
E Z Buy E Z Sell Recycler Corp **(DH)**	2711	C	310 886-7808	3973
Eas Sensorsense Inc	2759	E	818 763-9186	4511
Encompass Dgtal Mdia Group Inc **(PA)**	4833	C	323 344-4500	12715
Envion LLC	3564	D	818 217-2500	8047
Forest Hlls Invstors Mmber LLC **(HQ)**	6531	E	818 808-0600	15870
Golden State Health Ctrs Inc **(PA)**	8051	D	818 385-3200	20363
Grabit Interactive Inc	7313	E	844 472-2488	17086
Gym Consulting Inc	8742	D	818 907-6966	23231
Health Advocates **(PA)**	8111	D	818 995-9500	21578
Help Group West **(PA)**	8093	C	818 781-0360	21311
Homebridge Financial Svcs Inc	6163	A	818 981-0606	15244
Ideal Products LLC	7299	E	818 217-2574	16958
IMT Capital LLC **(PA)**	6798	C	818 784-4700	16236
Investors MGT Tr RE Group Inc **(PA)**	6513	E	818 784-4700	15729
Jesta Digital Entrmt Inc **(HQ)**	7372	C	323 648-4200	17898
Lucky Strike Entertainment Inc **(PA)**	3949	E	818 933-3752	11434
Lucky Strike Entertainment LLC	7933	C	248 374-3420	19401
Lucky Strike Entertainment LLC	7933	D	818 933-0872	19402
Mega Appraisers Inc	7389	A	818 246-7370	18591
Miller Automotive Group Inc **(HQ)**	7538	B	818 787-8400	18855
Monterey Bay Beverage Co Inc	2033	D	818 784-4885	1867
Moss & Company Inc **(PA)**	6531	C	310 453-0911	15927
Mpc Productions LLC	7929	C	310 418-8115	19370
Neurobrands LLC	5149	C	310 393-6444	14713
Nexcare Collaborative **(PA)**	8322	E	818 907-0322	21856
Nile Ai Inc	7372	E	818 689-9107	17933
Premiere Radio Network Inc **(DH)**	7922	C	818 377-5300	19329
Prime Hlthcare Svcs - Shrman O	8062	B	818 981-7111	20910
Psychic Eye Book Shops Inc **(PA)**	7999	D	818 906-8263	19661
Reel Security California Inc	7381	D	818 928-4737	18315
Refinery Av LLC	7336	E	818 843-0004	17185
Rentspree Inc	7371	E	323 515-7757	17697
Rodeo Realty Inc	6531	D	818 986-7300	15979
Rogue Games Inc	7371	F	650 483-8008	17701
Royal Specialty Undwrt Inc	6331	C	818 922-6700	15479
Serviz Inc	7299	D	818 381-4826	16976
Sherman Oaks Health System	8062	D	818 981-7111	20938
Snappays Mobile Inc	7371	F	310 869-6942	17718
Star of Ca LLC	8099	D	818 986-7827	21484
Tharpe & Howell **(PA)**	8111	D	818 205-9955	21687
Tot Squad Services LLC	8322	F	310 895-9983	21903
Village At Sherman Oaks LLC	8361	C	818 994-7900	22164
Vubiquity Holdings Inc **(DH)**	4841	C	818 526-5000	12780
Waldberg Inc	7313	D	818 843-0004	17092
Watt Construction Company **(PA)**	6515	D	818 905-6601	15758
White Zuckerman Warsavsky Luna **(PA)**	8721	D	818 981-4226	22819
Working With Autism Inc	8093	D	818 501-4240	21367
Zalemark Holding Company Inc	3911	F	888 682-6885	11333

	SIC	EMP	PHONE	ENTRY #
SHERWOOD FOREST, CA - Los Angeles County				
Slade Industrial Landscape Inc	0781	D	818 885-1916	281
SIERRA MADRE, CA - Los Angeles County				
Greg Ian Islands Inc	2541	E	626 355-0019	3647
Rt Rogers Brewing Co LLC	2082	F	818 371-0838	2155
SIGNAL HILL, CA - Los Angeles County				
2h Construction Inc	1542	D	562 424-5567	728
AC Pumping Unit Repair Inc	1389	F	562 492-1300	474
Accountble Hlth Cre IPA A Prof	8099	C	562 435-3333	21370
Adaptive Tech Group Inc	3651	E	562 424-1100	9156
Allied Refrigeration Inc **(PA)**	5075	D	562 595-5301	13840
Ancon Marine LLC	4212	E	562 326-5900	11955
Applied Business Software Inc	7372	E	562 426-2188	17787
Asphalt Fabric and Engrg Inc	3949	D	562 997-4129	11403
Black Gold Pump & Supply Inc	1389	F	323 298-0077	481
Bristol Hospice Foundation Cal	8052	C	562 494-7687	20525
C C H S Inc	8741	E	562 424-5188	22995
CJ Precision Industries Inc	3599	E	562 426-3708	8554
Dawson Enterprises **(PA)**	3533	E	562 424-8564	7667
Edco Disposal Corporation **(PA)**	4953	C	619 287-7555	12949
Evolife Scientific Llc	2833	E	888 750-0310	4745
Fenderscape Inc	0781	C	562 988-2228	256
First American Team Realty Inc **(PA)**	6531	C	562 427-7765	15856
Flex-Mate Inc	3423	F	562 426-7169	6479
Gem Mobile Treatment Svcs Inc **(HQ)**	3822	C	562 595-7075	10666
Goldsmith Construction Co Inc	1771	E	562 595-5975	1525
Gregg Drilling LLC	1781	C	562 427-6899	1560
Gregg Drilling & Testing Inc **(PA)**	1799	C	562 427-6899	1663
Harper & Two Inc **(PA)**	3679	F	562 424-3030	9720
Lovco Construction Inc	1794	C	562 595-1601	1600
Nsv International Corp	5013	C	562 438-3836	13075
Opex Communications Inc	4813	C	562 968-5420	12660
P T Industries Inc	3444	F	562 961-3431	6886
Porter Boiler Service Inc	7699	E	562 426-2528	19057
Professional Parking **(DH)**	7521	C	714 722-0242	18777
R D Mathis Company	3313	E	562 426-7049	6219
RAD-Image Med Group Inc A Cal	8011	D	562 912-2500	20034
Relax Medical Systems Inc	3999	F	800 405-7677	11742
Reldom Corporation	3699	E	562 498-3346	9906
Rode Microphones LLC	3651	C	310 328-7456	9191
Ship & Shore Environmental Inc	5084	E	562 997-0233	13938
Signal Health Police Dept	8641	E	562 989-7200	22368
Signal Hill Petroleum Inc	1382	E	562 595-6440	469
Southwest Products Corporation	3519	E	360 887-7400	7598
Tiger Cased Hole Services Inc	1389	E	562 426-4044	549
United States Logistics Group	3715	E	562 989-9555	10169
Viking Office Products Inc **(DH)**	5112	B	562 490-1000	14200
Vollmer-Gray Engrg Labs Inc	8711	E	562 427-8435	22693
Xcom Wireless Inc	3663	F	562 981-0077	9329
SIMI VALLEY, CA - Ventura County				
Acclaimed Trucking Corp **(PA)**	3537	F	805 577-7611	7701
Advanced Metal Mfg Inc	3444	E	805 322-4161	6774
Advanced Spectral Tech Inc	3827	E	805 527-7657	10825
Alta California Med Group Inc	8011	D	805 578-9622	19693
American GNC Corporation	8711	E	805 582-0582	22484
American Vision Windows Inc	7699	C	805 582-1833	19023
Andwin Corporation **(PA)**	5113	D	818 999-2828	14203
Anjana Software Solutions Inc	7371	D	805 583-0121	17548
Arxis Technology Inc	7372	E	805 306-7890	17790
Aveox Inc	3629	D	805 915-0200	8971
B & M Contractors Inc	1771	E	805 581-5480	1513
B & R Mold Inc	3544	E	805 526-8665	7781
Bemco Inc **(PA)**	3826	E	805 583-4970	10785
Bestitcom Inc **(PA)**	7379	C	602 667-5613	18163
Boys Grls CLB Mrpark Simi Vly **(PA)**	8641	E	805 527-4437	22315
Cal State Site Services	3315	E	800 499-5757	6220
Calabasas Tms Center	3312	E	805 261-0824	6190
Calmation Incorporated	5084	E	805 520-2515	13895
Catalina Yachts Inc **(PA)**	3732	E	818 884-7700	10460
CFS Tax Software	7372	E	805 522-1157	17814
Chase Group Llc	8732	B	805 522-9155	22876
Circuit Express Inc	3672	E	805 581-2323	9390
Coast To Coast Cmpt Pdts Inc	7373	C	805 244-9500	18023
Cobalt Construction Company	1522	D	805 577-6222	657
Computer Metal Products Corp	3444	C	805 520-6966	6811
Computerized Mgt Svcs Inc	8721	E	805 522-5940	22774
Creative Dgtal Systems Intgrti	7371	F	805 364-0555	17586
Currie Acquisitions LLC	3751	E	805 522-0500	10488
Datametrics Corporation	3577	E	805 577-9710	8249
Delt Industries Inc	3369	F	805 579-0213	6414
Dpa Labs Inc	3674	E	805 581-9200	9498
Dutton Home Services LLC	1711	E	702 625-9104	1057
Edgeworth Integration LLC	7382	D	805 915-0211	18373
Embedded Systems Inc	3625	D	805 624-6030	8951
Emlinq LLC	3672	C	805 409-4807	9400
Enderle Fuel Injection	3714	E	805 526-3838	10053
Entech Instruments Inc	3826	D	805 527-5939	10793
Fiberoptic Systems Inc	3357	E	805 579-6600	6349
First & La Realty Corp **(PA)**	6531	D	805 581-0021	15854
Ford of Simi Valley Inc	7538	D	805 583-0333	18829
Freedom Designs Inc	3842	E	805 582-0077	11107
Frontier Electronics Corp	3677	F	805 522-9998	9630
GI Industries	4953	D	805 522-2150	12952
Golden Five LLC	7371	E	323 489-8001	17628
Good Shepherd Lutheran HM of W	8361	D	805 526-2482	22105

GEOGRAPHIC

	SIC	EMP	PHONE	ENTRY #
Holiday Inn Express	7011	C	805 584-6006	16487
Howmet Globl Fstning Systems I **(HQ)**	5085	C	805 426-2270	13988
Innotec Group Inc	3629	F	616 772-5959	8977
Interscan Corporation	3824	E	805 823-8301	10738
Jaxx Manufacturing Inc	3679	E	805 526-4979	9735
Kaiser Foundation Hospitals	8011	C	805 582-0100	19862
Kaiser Foundation Hospitals	6324	C	888 515-3500	15430
Key Material Handling Inc	3537	F	805 520-6007	7714
Kidney Center Ventura Inc	8092	D	805 433-7777	21252
L3 Technologies Inc	3663	D	805 584-1717	9285
Landcare USA LLC	0782	D	805 520-9394	315
Lca Promotions Inc	2759	E	818 773-9170	4536
Longs Drug Stores Cal Inc	7384	E	805 581-1504	18415
Lowes Home Centers LLC	5031	C	805 426-2780	13261
Lumber City Corp	0181	D	805 522-0533	83
M Wave Design Corporation	5065	F	805 499-8825	13749
Mabel Baas Inc	3479	E	805 520-8075	7385
Meggitt Safety Systems Inc	3728	D	805 584-4100	10380
Meggitt Safety Systems Inc **(HQ)**	3699	C	805 584-4100	9892
Meggitt Safety Systems Inc	3728	C	805 584-4100	10381
Meggitt-Usa Inc **(HQ)**	3728	B	805 526-5700	10382
Meggitt-Usa Services Inc	3728	F	805 526-5700	10383
Milgard Manufacturing LLC	3231	C	805 581-6325	5963
Millworks By Design Inc	2431	E	818 597-1326	3269
Milodon Incorporated	3714	E	805 577-5950	10104
Newman and Sons Inc **(PA)**	3272	E	805 522-1646	6042
Nubity Inc **(PA)**	7371	E	213 408-4675	17680
Pacific Scientific Company **(DH)**	3812	E	805 526-5700	10633
Parks Optical	3827	F	805 522-6722	10854
Pars Publishing Corp	2752	F	818 280-0540	4387
Pharmaceutic Litho Label Inc	2834	D	805 285-5162	4872
Pharmatech Manufacturing Inc	2023	E	805 404-7169	1804
Pico Rents Inc	7359	D	310 275-9431	17367
Piezo-Metrics Inc **(PA)**	3674	E	805 522-4676	9559
Poly-Tainer Inc **(PA)**	3085	C	805 526-3424	5480
Posada Royale Hotel & Suites	7011	D	805 584-6300	16638
Posh Peanut Inc **(PA)**	5137	D	805 335-1960	14410
Puroflux Corporation	3677	F	805 579-0216	9639
PW Gillibrand Co Inc **(PA)**	1446	D	805 526-2195	579
Rajysan Incorporated **(PA)**	5084	E	661 775-4920	13934
Recycled Aggregate Mtls Co Inc **(PA)**	2951	F	805 522-1646	5277
Replacement Parts Inds Inc	3843	E	818 882-8611	11194
Ricoh Prtg Systems Amer Inc **(HQ)**	3577	B	805 578-4000	8298
Ronald Rgan Prsdntial Fndtion	8412	D	805 522-2977	22233
Rsa Engineered Products LLC	3728	D	805 584-4150	10405
Rugged Info Tech Eqp Corp **(PA)**	3577	E	805 577-9710	8299
Scientific Cutting Tools Inc	3545	E	805 584-9495	7867
Scope City **(PA)**	3827	E	805 522-6646	10859
Sea/Sue Inc **(HQ)**	4953	C	805 526-1919	12978
Senso-Metrics Inc	3829	F	805 527-3640	10909
Sensoscientific Inc	3823	F	800 279-3101	10722
Setarehshenas Dental Corp	8021	C	805 583-5700	20199
Sheetmetal Engineering	3444	E	805 306-0390	6911
Shopper Inc	5046	B	805 527-6700	13466
Sierra Aerospace LLC	3724	F	805 526-8669	10225
Sierra Vista Family Medical	8099	D	805 582-4000	21480
Simi Vly Hosp & Hlth Care Svcs	8062	C	805 955-6000	20940
Simi Vly Hosp & Hlth Care Svcs **(HQ)**	8062	A	805 955-6000	20941
Simi West Inc	7011	C	760 346-5502	16711
Siteserver Inc	8748	E	805 579-7831	23509
Smart & Final Stores Inc	5141	C	805 520-6035	14507
Special Devices Incorporated	3714	A	805 387-1000	10135
Specialized Ldscp MGT Svcs Inc	0781	D	805 520-7590	283
Specialty Fabrications Inc	3444	E	805 579-9730	6916
Specialty Merchandise Corp **(PA)**	5199	E	805 578-5500	14976
Spragues Rock and Sand Company	3273	F	805 522-7010	6117
Stearns Corporation	2844	E	805 582-2710	5072
Stellar Industries	3999	E	818 472-5432	11762
Sub-Zero Excavating Inc	1794	D	805 522-5043	1606
Suttles Plumbing & Mech Corp	1711	D	818 718-9779	1153
Swinks Creations Inc **(PA)**	0781	D	805 522-0412	285
Troop Real Estate Inc **(PA)**	6531	D	805 581-3200	16022
Udash Corporation **(PA)**	3812	F	805 526-5222	10651
United Parcel Service Inc	7389	D	866 553-1069	18706
Usedmac Inc	3575	F	866 769-4777	8230
Vans Manufacturing Inc	3599	F	805 522-6267	8837
Ventura Technology Group	3674	E	805 581-0800	9599
Vibra Finish Co **(PA)**	3291	E	805 578-0033	6160
Vintage Senior Housing LLC	6513	B	805 583-3500	15751
Waste Management Cal Inc	4953	C	805 522-7023	12995
Whittaker Corporation	3728	E	805 526-5700	10444
Wsm Investments LLC	6794	C	818 332-4600	16224
X Weapon Security	8999	D	818 818-9950	23545
Xmultiple Technologies **(PA)**	3571	E	805 579-1100	8185
Young MNS Chrstn Assn Sthast V	8641	E	805 520-6775	22388
Young MNS Chrstn Assn Sthast V	8641	E	805 527-5730	22389
Young MNS Chrstn Assn Sthast V	7999	D	805 583-5338	19683

SKYFOREST, CA - San Bernardino County

	SIC	EMP	PHONE	ENTRY #
Spsv Entertainment LLC	7929	D	909 744-9373	19380

SOLVANG, CA - Santa Barbara County

	SIC	EMP	PHONE	ENTRY #
Alisal Properties **(PA)**	7032	C	805 688-6411	16816
Ballard Inn Inc	7011	D	805 688-7770	16339
Buttonwood Farm Winery Inc	2084	F	805 688-3032	2169
Cottage Health	8062	D	805 688-6432	20733
Lucas & Lewellen Vineyards Inc **(PA)**	5182	E	805 686-9336	14844
MWH Americas Inc	8711	D	805 683-2409	22619
Santa Ynez Vly Cttage Hosp Inc	8062	D	805 688-6431	20937

SOMIS, CA - Ventura County

	SIC	EMP	PHONE	ENTRY #
Dudes Brewing Company	2082	E	424 271-2915	2142
Humphrey Gcpzzi Vtrnary Group	0742	D	805 386-4291	200
Saticoy Country Club	7997	D	805 647-1153	19610
Venegas Farming LLC	0761	E	805 529-5038	219

SOUTH EL MONTE, CA - Los Angeles County

	SIC	EMP	PHONE	ENTRY #
A-1 Building & Fence Mtls Inc	1799	E	562 693-4853	1630
Abacus Powder Coating	3479	E	626 443-7556	7335
Ahmc Healthcare Inc	8062	A	626 579-7777	20666
Al-Mag Heat Treat	3398	F	626 442-8570	6428
American Wrecking Inc	1795	D	626 350-8303	1609
Amro Fabricating Corporation **(PA)**	3728	C	626 579-2200	10270
Anas Iron Supply Inc	1791	F	626 401-0483	1565
Antaeus Fashions Group Inc	2329	E	626 452-0797	2800
Asia Plastics Inc	2673	E	626 448-8100	3878
Bali Construction Inc	1623	D	626 442-8003	936
Bci Inc	3599	E	626 579-4234	8519
Big Tree Sales Inc	5092	F	626 672-0048	14095
Botanas Mexico Inc	2099	F	626 279-1512	2399
Brands Republic Inc	3634	E	302 401-1195	9000
Brass Unique Inc	3441	E	626 444-8977	6592
C W Cole & Company Inc	3646	E	626 443-2473	9080
Cala Action Inc	2211	E	213 272-9759	2561
California Med Response Inc	4119	D	562 968-1818	11856
California Ribbon Carbn Co Inc	3955	D	323 724-9100	11475
California Snack Foods Inc	2064	E	626 444-4508	2082
Dealsaday Inc	3572	F	626 964-4266	8197
Design Shapes In Steel Inc	3312	E	626 579-2032	6198
Dynomill Inc	3599	F	626 454-1805	8577
Electronic Auto Systems Inc	3651	F	626 280-3855	9174
Fabricast Inc **(PA)**	3679	E	626 443-3247	9711
Fresh Air Environmental Svcs	1799	D	323 913 1965	1659
Gama Contracting Services Inc	5082	C	626 442-7200	13859
Golden Color Printing Inc	2752	E	626 455-0850	4303
Grover Smith Mfg Corp	3561	E	323 724-3444	8013
Heeger Inc	3621	F	323 728-5108	8915
Henrys Metal Polishing Inc	3471	F	323 263-9701	7266
Hoefner Corporation	3599	E	626 443-3258	8620
Hog Inc	7336	F	626 279-5275	17178
Interntnal Mdction Systems Ltd	2833	F	626 459-5586	4750
Interntnal Mdction Systems Ltd	2834	A	626 442-6757	4833
Island Powder Coating	3479	E	626 279-2460	7377
J & L Cstm Plstic Extrsons Inc	3089	E	626 442-0711	5677
Kureiji Inc	2331	F	626 788-2657	2853
Leader Industries Inc	4119	C	626 575-0880	11877
Lee Pharmaceuticals	2844	D	626 442-3141	5042
Lincoln Trning Ctr Rhblttion W	8331	D	626 442-0621	21959
Lux Solutions LLC **(PA)**	7929	D	770 591-0463	19367
Manufacturers Service Inc	5084	E	323 283-1013	13913
Master Enterprises Inc	3444	E	626 442-1821	6868
Melkes Machine Inc	3599	E	626 448-5062	8688
Mikelson Machine Shop Inc	3599	E	626 448-3920	8696
Mywi Fabricators Inc	3441	F	626 279-6994	6645
Out of Shell LLC	2099	C	626 401-1923	2503
Pearson Engineering Corp	3479	F	626 442-7436	7395
Plastic Dress-Up Company	3089	D	626 442-7711	5750
Promotonal Design Concepts Inc	3069	D	626 579-4454	5401
Proto Space Engineering Inc	3599	E	626 442-8273	8748
R & R Rubber Molding Inc	3069	E	626 575-8105	5403
Robert P Martin Company	3315	F	323 686-2220	6232
Roselm Industries Inc	3663	E	626 442-6840	9312
S & H Machine Inc	3492	E	626 448-5062	7459
Scodan Systems Inc	3462	F	626 444-1020	7098
Sense Fashion Corporation	2331	F	626 454-3381	2866
Sierra Landscape Development	0781	E	626 447-5260	280
Smith Bros Strl Stl Pdts Inc	3312	F	626 350-1872	6212
Studio9d8 Inc	2253	E	626 350-0832	2641
Ted Levine Drum Co **(PA)**	7699	D	626 579-1084	19077
Thienes Apparel Inc	2253	E	626 575-2818	2643
Tri Service Co Inc	2899	E	626 442-3270	5244
Tri-Fitting Mfg Company	3728	F	626 442-2000	10433
Vacco Industries **(DH)**	3494	C	626 443-7121	7477
Vclad Laminates Inc	3083	E	626 442-2100	5464
Walton Motors & Controls Inc	5063	F	626 442-4610	13676
Wbp Associates Inc	2542	F	626 575-0747	3702

SOUTH GATE, CA - Los Angeles County

	SIC	EMP	PHONE	ENTRY #
5 Star Job Source	7361	D	562 788-7391	17386
Accurate Steel Treating Inc	3398	E	562 927-6528	6425
AG Adriano Goldschmied Inc **(PA)**	2325	D	323 357-1111	2767
Altamed Health Services Corp	8099	D	323 562-6700	21377
Anadite Cal Restoration Tr	3471	C	562 861-2205	7210
Arcadia Inc	3442	E	310 665-0490	6691
Armstrong Flooring Inc	3996	D	323 562-7258	11619
Artsons Manufacturing Company	3312	E	323 773-3469	6188
Astro Aluminum Treating Co	3398	D	562 923-4344	6430
Bell Foundry Co **(PA)**	3949	D	323 564-5701	11405
Buddy Bar Casting LLC	3365	C	562 861-9664	6387
C&C Metal Form & Tooling Inc	3469	F	562 861-9554	7132
Caretex Inc	2865	F	323 567-5074	5120
Century 21 A Better Svc Rlty	6531	D	562 806-1000	15804
Cimc Intermodal Equipment LLC **(DH)**	3715	D	562 904-8600	10165
County of Los Angeles	8099	D	562 861-0316	21408
Custom Leathercraft Mfg LLC **(DH)**	3199	E	323 752-2221	5912
Demenno/Kerdoon Holdings **(DH)**	2992	D	562 231-1550	5293

Mergent email: customerrelations@mergent.com
1436
2022 Southern California Business Directory and Buyers Guide
(P-0000) Products & Services Section entry number
(PA)=Parent Co (HQ)=Headquarters (DH)=Div Headquarters

	SIC	EMP	PHONE	ENTRY #
Dickson Testing Co Inc **(DH)**	8734	D	562 862-8378	22938
Eppink of California Inc	1751	E	562 633-1275	1435
Far West Inc	8051	D	323 564-7761	20342
Firma Plastic Co Inc	5093	B	323 567-7767	14114
Frameless Hardware Company LLC	3429	E	888 295-4531	6517
General Veneer Mfg Co	2435	E	323 564-2661	3350
Glasswerks La Inc **(HQ)**	3231	B	888 789-7810	5955
Graham Lee Associates Inc	2521	F	323 581-8203	3587
Granitize Products Inc	2842	D	562 923-5438	4963
Gwla Acquisition Corp **(PA)**	3211	C	323 789-7800	5918
Harbor Furniture Mfg Inc **(PA)**	2512	E	323 636-1201	3506
Herbert Malarkey Roofing Co	1761	D	562 806-8000	1487
Hughes Bros Aircrafters Inc	3544	E	323 773-4541	7807
Ibitta Enterprises Inc	5141	F	323 588-6300	14472
Interior Rmoval Specialist Inc	1795	C	323 357-6900	1616
Janin	2339	C	323 564-0995	2954
Kimoa Broadcast TV Netwrk	7389	F	213 364-9558	18564
Koos Manufacturing Inc	7389	A	323 249-1000	18567
La Mexicana LLC	2038	E	323 277-3660	1931
Lg Battery	3694	F	323 569-3116	9825
Liberty Container Company	2653	C	323 564-4211	3817
Lunday-Thagard Company **(HQ)**	2999	C	562 928-7000	5300
Lunday-Thagard Company	2952	B	562 928-6990	5284
M D H Burner & Boiler Co Inc	3564	F	562 630-2875	8049
Marquez Marquez Inc	2096	E	562 408-0960	2363
Mercury Engineering Corp	3599	E	562 861-7816	8689
Meribear Productions Inc	7389	D	310 204-5353	18594
Metal Supply LLC	3441	D	562 634-9940	6637
MSI Structural Steel LLC	3441	E	562 473-0066	6642
Nextrade Inc **(PA)**	2299	E	562 944-9950	2732
Pabco Clay Products LLC	5032	D	323 568-1860	13309
Pan Pacific Petroleum Co Inc **(PA)**	4213	D	562 928-0100	12071
Pcs Mobile Solutions LLC	4813	D	323 567-2490	12664
Pluckys Dump Rental LLC	3443	E	323 540-3510	6747
Polymasters Industries Inc	3089	F	213 564-7824	5764
Precision Forging Dies Inc	3544	E	562 861-1878	7826
Privilege International Inc	5021	D	323 585-0777	13150
Productivity California Inc	3089	C	562 923-3100	5782
Pws Inc **(PA)**	5087	D	323 721-8832	14043
Reliable Building Products Inc	3441	E	323 566-5000	6659
Restor-Tech Cnstr Cnslting Inc **(PA)**	8748	D	323 249-2277	23499
Riverton Steel Construction	1791	F	323 564-1881	1582
Samuel J Piazza & Son Inc **(PA)**	4214	D	323 357-1999	12117
Simons Brick Corporation	3297	E	951 279-1000	6174
Suregrip International Co	3949	D	562 923-0724	11450
Sws Panel and Truss Inc	3999	F	323 923-4900	11769
Techni-Cast Corp	3369	D	562 923-4585	6423
Tu-K Industries Inc	2844	E	562 927-3365	5075
Van Brunt Foundry Inc	3365	F	323 569-2832	6402
Win Soon Inc	2026	E	323 564-5070	1841
World Oil Corp	1311	B	562 928-0100	417
World Oil Marketing Company **(PA)**	2951	E	562 928-0100	5278
Xrp Inc **(PA)**	3714	F	562 861-4765	10161

SOUTH PASADENA, CA - Los Angeles County

	SIC	EMP	PHONE	ENTRY #
Cccc Growth Fund LLC	6799	D	626 441-8770	16252
Drivenbi LLC	7371	D	626 795-2088	17603
Ellens Silk Screening Inc	7336	E	626 441-4415	17173
Malibu Design Group	5137	E	323 271-1700	14398
No Holidays Corporation	1522	E	310 848-7351	663
Preco Aircraft Motors Inc	3694	F	626 799-3549	9829
Stargate Films Inc **(PA)**	7812	D	626 403-8403	19185
Stratus Real Estate Inc	6163	D	626 441-5549	15254
Total Education Solutions Inc **(PA)**	8748	E	323 341-5580	23517

SPRINGVILLE, CA - Tulare County

	SIC	EMP	PHONE	ENTRY #
Theodore B Martin	7692	E	559 360-2559	19000

STANTON, CA - Orange County

	SIC	EMP	PHONE	ENTRY #
All Metals Proc San Diego Inc	3471	C	714 828-8238	7204
All Mtals Proc Orange Cnty LLC	3471	C	714 828-8238	7205
Art Gautreau Inc	1542	E	714 934-8066	739
Blaga Precision Inc	3599	E	714 891-9509	8529
Blake Sign Company Inc	3993	E	714 891-5682	11528
Boudraux Prcsion McHining Corp	3599	E	714 894-4523	8531
California Friends Homes	8361	B	714 530-9100	22088
Cameron Welding Supply **(PA)**	7692	E	714 530-9353	18971
CJ Enterprises	3544	F	714 898-8558	7788
Continental Signs Inc	3993	F	714 894-2011	11536
Custom Pipe & Fabrication Inc **(HQ)**	3498	D	800 553-3058	7534
Denver D Darling Inc	1541	D	714 761-8299	696
Design Form Inc	3443	E	714 952-3700	6740
Fang Inc	8011	D	714 898-7785	19821
Field Time Target Training LLC	3483	E	714 677-2841	7427
Great Scott Tree Service Inc **(PA)**	0783	C	714 826-1750	357
Haulaway Storage Cntrs Inc	4225	B	800 826-9040	12213
Johnson & Turner Painting Co	1721	E	714 828-8282	1186
Manti - Machine Co Inc	3599	F	714 902-1465	8675
Muth Development Co Inc	3271	F	714 527-2239	6010
Muth Machine Works **(HQ)**	3599	E	714 527-2239	8712
Newport Industrial Glass Inc	3231	E	714 484-7500	5965
Newport Optical Industries **(PA)**	3827	E	714 484-8100	10849
Oc Fleet Service Inc	3731	F	714 460-8069	10454
Orco Block & Hardscape **(PA)**	3271	D	714 527-2239	6011
Paramount Home Care Inc	8082	D	714 994-1250	21198
Precision Fastener Tooling Inc	3542	E	714 898-8558	7764
Pure-Chem Products Company Inc	2899	E	714 995-4141	5239
RDfabricators Inc	3444	F	714 634-2078	6901

	SIC	EMP	PHONE	ENTRY #
Schaffer Laboratories Inc	3083	F	714 202-1594	5462
Signs and Services Company	3993	E	714 761-8200	11601
Stecher Enterprises Inc	3495	F	714 484-6900	7492
United Contractors Inc	1731	D	714 828-6275	1335
USS Cal Builders Inc	1542	C	714 828-4882	845
West Coast Manufacturing Inc	3469	E	714 897-4221	7193
White Bottle Inc	3089	E	949 788-1998	5865

STEVENSON RANCH, CA - Los Angeles County

	SIC	EMP	PHONE	ENTRY #
Century Bankcard Services	7389	D	818 700-3100	18475
Sport Chalet LLC	5091	D	661 253-3883	14088
UNI Healthcare Inc	8099	E	661 222-9984	21491
Vons Companies Inc	2051	D	661 254-3570	2043

STRATFORD, CA - Kings County

	SIC	EMP	PHONE	ENTRY #
Crisp Warehouse Inc	0723	E	559 947-9221	164
Stone Land Company **(PA)**	0131	D	559 947-3185	4

STRATHMORE, CA - Tulare County

	SIC	EMP	PHONE	ENTRY #
Cellu-Con Inc	2879	E	559 568-0190	5167
Michael D Wilson Inc	3499	E	559 568-1115	7566

STUDIO CITY, CA - Los Angeles County

	SIC	EMP	PHONE	ENTRY #
American Private Duty Inc	8082	D	818 386-6358	21133
Art Drctors Gild Itse Lcal 876	8631	D	818 762-9995	22286
Coding School	8641	D	424 339-3977	22332
Commercial Prgrm Systems Inc **(PA)**	7379	C	818 308-8560	18170
Crown Media Holdings Inc **(HQ)**	4841	C	888 390-7474	12754
Crown Media United States LLC **(DH)**	4833	D	818 755-2400	12712
Edgebrook Productions Inc	7819	D	818 766-6789	19231
Empire Enterprises Inc **(PA)**	5021	F	818 784-8918	13135
Farbod Parvinjah DMD Inc **(PA)**	8021	D	805 583-5589	20177
Fear of God LLC **(PA)**	2329	E	213 235-7985	2807
First Republic Bank	6022	D	818 752-4777	15027
Fort Hill Construction **(PA)**	1521	D	323 656-7425	605
High Technology Video Inc	7812	D	323 969-8822	19131
JBs Private Label Inc	2253	E	818 762-3736	2638
Longwood Management Corp	8059	D	818 980-8200	20605
Motion Pcture Indust Pnsion Hl	6371	C	818 769-0007	15517
Radford Studio Center Inc	7922	B	818 655-5000	19330
Rodeo Realty Inc	6531	D	818 308-8273	15982
Sportsmens Lodge Hotel LLC	7011	D	818 769-4700	16725
Sportsmens Lodge Restaurant	7299	D	818 755-5000	16979
US Arcades LLC **(PA)**	7993	D	818 888-8738	19515

SUN CITY, CA - Riverside County

	SIC	EMP	PHONE	ENTRY #
Bbva USA	6021	C	951 672-4829	14994
Family Service Association	8322	D	951 672-9673	21785
Innovative Power Inc	3612	F	951 928-7700	8874
Menifee Union School District **(PA)**	8741	D	951 672-1851	23061
North County Sand and Grav Inc	1442	F	951 928-2881	572
Physicians For Healthy Hospita	8062	B	951 679-8888	20888
Sunny Rose Glen LLC	8361	D	951 679-3355	22157
United Parcel Service Inc	4513	D	951 928-5221	12332

SUN VALLEY, CA - Los Angeles County

	SIC	EMP	PHONE	ENTRY #
Aadlen Bros Auto Wrecking Inc **(PA)**	5093	D	323 875-1400	14107
Abbott Technologies Inc	3612	E	818 504-0644	8861
Accu-Grinding Inc	3545	F	818 768-4497	7844
Accurate Engineering Inc	3672	E	818 768-3919	9372
Acrylic Distribution Corp	2519	E	818 767-8448	3564
Alcorn Fence Company **(PA)**	1799	D	818 983-0650	1633
Alert Plating Company	3471	E	818 771-9304	7203
American Grip Inc	3648	E	818 768-8922	9122
American Plastic Products Inc	3544	D	818 504-1073	7776
Angelus Block Co Inc **(PA)**	3271	E	714 637-8594	6009
Araco Enterprises LLC	4953	B	818 767-0675	12926
Art Mold Die Casting Inc	3544	E	818 767-6464	7777
ASC Group Inc	3674	A	818 896-1101	9483
Associated Ready Mix Con Inc	3273	E	818 504-3100	6070
AVX Filters Corporation	3569	D	818 767-6770	8112
Beacon Roofing Supply Inc	5085	D	818 768-4661	13972
Ble Inc	1381	E	818 504-9577	424
Builders Fence Company Inc **(PA)**	5031	E	818 768-5500	13206
C A Buchen Corp	3441	E	818 767-5408	6594
Ca937 Afjrotc	3999	D	818 394-3600	11645
Capital Ready Mix Inc	3273	E	818 771-1122	6076
Carlson Arts LLC	3449	F	818 767-1500	7017
Cdeq Inc	3229	F	818 767-5143	5933
Ceramic Tile Art Inc	1743	D	818 767-9088	1412
Classic Bath Designs Inc	2434	E	818 767-1144	3315
Clear Water Corporation Inc	3589	F	818 765-8293	8374
Colorfx Inc	2752	E	818 767-7671	4259
Columbia Showcase & Cab Co Inc	2541	C	818 765-9710	3643
Coronado Manufacturing Inc	3728	E	818 768-5010	10304
Cosmetic Group Usa Inc	2844	C	818 767-2889	5004
Cosrich Group Inc	2844	E	818 686-2500	5007
CSC Auto Salv Dismantling Inc	4731	D	818 532-4624	12442
De Leon Entps Elec Spclist Inc	3672	E	818 252-6690	9397
Desert Block Co Inc	2951	E	661 824-2624	5271
Dillon Aircraft Deburring Inc	3471	F	818 768-0801	7247
Dip Braze Inc	7692	E	818 768-1555	18975
E-Z Mix Inc **(PA)**	2674	E	818 768-0568	3895
Earl Hays Press	2759	F	818 765-0700	4510
El Capitan Environmental Svcs	8748	D	818 768-9222	23435
Emergent Group Inc **(DH)**	3842	D	818 394-2800	11100
Estes Express Lines	4213	D	818 504-4155	12040
Excelity	3369	E	818 767-1000	6415
Express Messenger Systems Inc	4215	D	818 504-9043	12131

GEOGRAPHIC

	SIC	EMP	PHONE	ENTRY #
Firstmed Ambulance Svcs Inc	4119	D	818 982-8333	11868
Florence International Co Inc	3471	E	818 767-9650	7260
Foodology LLC	2099	D	818 252-1888	2435
Forgiato Inc	3714	E	747 271-7151	10060
Four Seasons Hummus Inc	2099	F	305 409-0449	2436
Gedney Foods Company	2035	C	952 448-2612	1887
Gemcon Inc	1731	E	818 767-0892	1259
General Steel Fabricators Inc	3441	E	818 897-1300	6618
Gibbel Bros Inc	3273	E	323 875-1367	6092
Glenoaks Food Inc	2015	E	818 768-9091	1759
Hawker Pacific Aerospace	7699	B	818 765-6201	19040
Hollywood Film Company	3861	E	818 683-1130	11279
Home Deco Corp (PA)	5031	D	818 669-5287	13216
Industrial Battery Engrg Inc	3691	E	818 767-7067	9811
Insua Graphics Incorporated	2752	E	818 767-7007	4337
Jack J Engel Manufacturing Inc	3699	E	818 767-6220	9877
JMI Steel Inc	3446	E	818 768-3955	6967
JP Motorsports Inc	4789	D	818 381-8313	12575
Kenwalt Die Casting Corp	3363	E	818 768-5800	6365
Kitcor Corporation	3469	E	323 875-2820	7158
Kleen Maid Inc	2392	F	323 581-3000	3104
Kvr Investment Group Inc	3559	D	818 896-1102	7987
L A Propoint Inc	3499	E	818 767-6800	7562
LA Gauge Co Inc	3599	E	818 767-7193	8659
LA Hydro-Jet Rooter Svc Inc	7699	D	818 768-4225	19047
Leon Krous Drilling Inc	1381	D	818 833-4654	434
Los Angeles Dept Wtr & Pwr	4941	B	213 367-1342	12902
Los Angles Cnty Mtro Trnsp Aut	4111	A	213 922-6215	11824
M & A Plastics Inc	3089	C	818 768-0479	5701
Magic Jump Inc	7359	E	818 847-1313	17361
Monty Ventsam Inc	2431	F	818 768-6424	3271
Mountain View Child Care Inc	8351	C	818 252-5863	22037
NDT Metal Finishing Inc	3471	F	818 807-1381	7286
Norman Industrial Mtls Inc (PA)	5051	C	818 729-3333	13580
Northeast Valley Health Corp	8099	C	818 432-4400	21464
Nupla LLC	3423	C	818 768-6800	6487
Over & Over Ready Mix Inc	3272	C	818 983-1588	6046
Pacesetter Fabrics LLC (HQ)	2299	F	213 741-9999	2734
Pacific Pavingstone Inc	1771	C	818 244-4000	1545
Pacific Sky Supply Inc	3728	C	818 768-3700	10391
Pacifica of Valley Corporation	8062	A	818 767-3310	20880
Pacobond Inc	2674	E	818 768-5002	3897
Paint Specialists Inc	3479	F	818 771-0552	7393
Peen-Rite Inc	3398	F	818 767-3676	6450
Pena Grading & Demolition Inc	1611	E	818 768-5202	907
Penguin Pumps Incorporated	3561	E	818 504-2391	8018
Pincraft Inc	3961	E	818 248-0077	11490
Pine Grove Hospital Corp	8063	C	818 348-0500	21026
Plumbingandfire Inc	5074	E	818 764-9800	13835
Pmc Inc (HQ)	3728	A	818 896-1101	10393
PMC Capital Partners LLC	6799	A	818 896-1101	16284
PMC Global Inc (PA)	3086	B	818 896-1101	5515
PMC Leaders In Chemicals Inc (HQ)	3086	C	818 896-1101	5516
Precision Arcft Machining Inc	3599	E	818 768-5900	8741
Precision Tile Co	3272	F	818 767-7673	6051
Prime Plating Aerospace Inc	3471	E	818 768-9100	7299
R L Anodizing	3471	E	818 252-3804	7302
Rawlings Mechanical Corp (PA)	1711	D	323 875-2040	1126
Redwood Scientific Tech Inc	2834	E	310 693-5401	4880
Refrigeration Hdwr Sup Corp	5078	C	818 768-3636	13856
REM Optical Company Inc	5049	C	818 504-3950	13538
Rico Corporation (HQ)	3931	C	818 394-2700	11351
Rico Holdings Inc	3931	F	818 394-2700	11352
Rose Brand Wipers Inc	7922	D	818 505-6290	19331
Scenic Express Inc	1799	C	323 254-4351	1688
Schecter Guitar Research Inc	3931	E	818 767-1029	11353
Schmidt Industries Inc	3471	D	818 768-9100	7311
Schneiders Manufacturing Inc	3599	E	818 771-0082	8789
Senna Tree Company LLC	0783	E	818 957-5755	361
Serra Community Med Clinic Inc	8011	C	818 768-3000	20063
Smg Stone Company Inc	1741	C	818 767-0000	1352
Spa De Soleil	5122	E	818 504-3200	14291
Spartan Truck Company Inc	3713	E	818 899-1111	9998
Specialty International Inc	3469	E	818 768-8810	7183
Sscor Inc	3841	F	818 504-4054	11060
Sterndahl Enterprises Inc	1721	E	818 834-8199	1199
Sugar Foods Corporation	7389	C	818 768-7900	18681
Sundial Industries Inc	3479	E	818 767-4477	7417
Sundial Powder Coatings Inc	3479	E	818 767-4477	7418
Superior Plating Inc	3471	E	818 252-1088	7320
Svd Inc	5143	D	818 504-1775	14546
Tecfar Manufacturing Inc	3599	F	818 767-0677	8812
Technical Heaters Inc	3052	F	818 361-7185	5323
Tee -N -Jay Manufacturing Inc	3444	E	818 504-2961	6929
Travis-American Group LLC	2431	F	714 248-1200	3295
USA Waste of California Inc	4953	D	818 252-3112	12987
Verona Quartz Inc	5032	F	818 962-3668	13318
Walker Design Inc	3731	E	818 252-7788	10456
Waste Management Cal Inc (HQ)	4953	C	877 836-6526	12993
Waste Management Recycling	4212	C	818 767-6180	12008
Wet (PA)	7389	C	818 769-6200	18725
Youngs Iron Works Inc	1791	F	818 768-3877	1585

SUNLAND, CA - Los Angeles County

	SIC	EMP	PHONE	ENTRY #
Arcadia Convalescent Hosp Inc	8051	D	818 352-4438	20246
Brightview Tree Company	0811	D	818 951-5500	366
Engineered Products By Lee Ltd	3599	F	818 352-3322	8582
Independent Studio Svcs LLC	7922	D	818 951-5600	19313

	SIC	EMP	PHONE	ENTRY #
New Vista Health Services	8059	C	818 352-1421	20617
P R N Convalescent Hospital	8051	D	818 352-3158	20430
Patriot Brokerage Inc	4731	C	910 227-4142	12504
Sculptor Body Molding (PA)	3089	E	818 761-3767	5816
Shadow Hlls Cnvlscent Hosp Inc	8051	D	818 352-4438	20464
Tierra Del Sol Foundation (PA)	8361	D	818 352-1419	22159
Valley Village	8052	C	818 446-0366	20545

SYLMAR, CA - Los Angeles County

	SIC	EMP	PHONE	ENTRY #
A A Gonzalez Inc	1742	D	818 367-2242	1358
Acufast Aircraft Products Inc	3728	E	818 365-7077	10238
Advanced Bionics LLC (HQ)	3842	B	661 362-1400	11081
Advanced Mnlythic Ceramics Inc	5065	D	818 364-9800	13697
All Nuts and Snacks Inc	5145	F	818 367-5902	14554
Allied Company Holdings Inc (PA)	5181	B	818 493-6400	14819
American Nuts Imprt-Export Inc	5145	E	818 364-8855	14555
Ansett Arcft Spares & Svcs Inc (PA)	5088	C	818 364-1100	14052
Anthony Inc (DH)	3585	A	818 365-9451	8328
Astoria Convalescent Hospital	8051	C	818 367-5681	20248
Atlas Foam Products	3086	F	818 837-3626	5490
Becho Inc	1611	D	818 362-8591	862
Beverly Hills Teddy Bear Co (PA)	5092	E	661 257-0750	14094
C & G Plastics	3089	E	818 837-3773	5587
C & S Plastics	3089	F	818 896-2189	5589
Carroll Fulmer Logistics Corp	4731	B	626 423-0550	12430
Childrens Hunger Fund (PA)	8322	D	818 979-7100	21744
Clear Image Printing Inc	2752	E	818 547-4684	4254
Cowan Precision Grinding Inc	7389	D	818 361-2512	18493
Deiny Automotive Inc	3711	F	818 362-5865	9943
Desert Mechanical Inc	1711	A	702 873-7333	1055
Deveraux Specialties LLC (PA)	5122	F	818 837-3700	14241
Dg Engineering Corp (PA)	3812	E	818 364-9024	10583
E E Black Limited (HQ)	1629	A	671 646-4861	994
Eagle Access Ctrl Systems Inc	3625	C	818 837-7900	8949
Fierrito Metal Stamping	3599	F	818 362-6136	8588
Fisk Electric Company	1731	C	818 884-1166	1255
Fontal Controls Inc	3599	E	818 833-1127	8590
G W Murphy Cnstr Co Inc	1542	C	818 362-8391	764
Gibraltar Plastic Pdts Corp	3089	E	818 365-9318	5652
GL Ventura Inc	3281	E	818 890-1886	6139
Goldak Inc	3812	E	818 240-2666	10590
International Academy of Fin (PA)	2869	E	818 361-7724	5139
ISU Petasys Corp	3672	D	818 833-5800	9416
JW Manufacturing Inc	3452	E	805 498-4594	7069
Kay & James Inc	3599	D	818 958-0357	8651
Laser Operations LLC	3674	E	818 956-0000	9530
Leather Pro Inc	3172	E	818 833-8822	5909
Llamas Plastics Inc	3728	C	818 352-0371	10368
Mason Electric Co	3728	B	818 361-3366	10373
Matthews Studio Equipment Inc	3861	E	818 843-6715	11283
Mb2 Raceway Inc (PA)	7948	D	818 364-8000	19432
Modern Candle Co Inc	5199	D	323 441-0104	14953
MS Aerospace Inc	3452	B	818 833-9095	7070
Oak Springs Nursery Inc	4971	D	818 367-5832	13013
Olive View-Ucla Medical Center (PA)	8011	A	818 364-1555	20010
Orange Bang Inc	2086	D	818 333-1000	2274
Pacesetter Inc	3845	C	818 493-2715	11233
Pacesetter Inc (DH)	3845	A	818 362-6822	11234
Pearson Dental Supplies Inc (PA)	5047	C	818 362-2600	13509
Precise Iron Doors Inc	3442	C	818 338-6269	6712
Professional Finishing Systems	3469	F	818 365-8888	7176
Qpc Lasers Inc	3674	F	818 986-0000	9563
Quallion LLC	3692	C	818 833-2000	9817
Quinn Company	5082	D	818 767-7171	13867
Raspadoxpress	7999	D	818 367-9800	19665
Reyes Coca-Cola Bottling LLC	5149	E	818 362-4307	14732
RWS Research & Development Inc	3494	F	818 364-6766	7476
Schindler Elevator Corporation	7699	C	818 336-3000	19063
Seaman Products of California	3728	F	818 768-4881	10414
Second Sight Medical Pdts Inc	3841	C	818 833-5000	11055
Sierracin Corporation (HQ)	2851	A	818 741-1656	5112
Sierracin/Sylmar Corporation	3089	A	818 362-6711	5819
Sigue Corporation (PA)	7389	D	818 837-5939	18666
Southwest Rgnal Cncil Crpnters	8631	C	818 364-9303	22301
Spears Manufacturing Co (PA)	5083	C	818 364-1611	13879
Spectrolab Inc	3674	B	818 365-4611	9581
Superior Gunite (HQ)	1771	C	818 896-9199	1553
TMW Corporation (PA)	3728	C	818 362-5665	10432
Tutor Perini Corporation (PA)	1542	C	818 362-8391	842
Tutor-Saliba Corporation (HQ)	1542	D	818 362-8391	843
United Crbral Plsy/Spstic Chld	8059	D	818 364-5911	20635
Valley Metal Supply Inc	5033	F	818 837-6566	13330
Valley-Todeco Inc (DH)	3452	D	800 992-4444	7080
Volunteers of Amer Los Angeles	8322	D	818 367-8841	21912
Wayne Tool & Die Co	3312	F	818 364-1611	6217
Wildlife Waystation	8699	E	818 899-5201	22470
Williams Mfg Aero Machining	3494	F	818 898-2272	7479
Winning Performance Pdts Inc	7389	C	818 367-1041	18728

TAFT, CA - Kern County

	SIC	EMP	PHONE	ENTRY #
Adventist Health System/West	8062	D	661 763-5131	20647
Berry Petroleum Company LLC	1311	F	661 769-8820	389
Cellco Partnership	4812	D	661 765-5397	12600
General Production Svc Cal Inc	1623	C	661 765-5330	949
Jerry Melton & Sons Cnstr	1389	D	661 765-5546	512
Mashburn Trnsp Svcs Inc	4213	C	661 765-2012	12063
Modivcare Inc	8093	A	661 765-7025	21321
Taft Production Company	1241	D	661 765-7194	384

GEOGRAPHIC SECTION TEMPLE CITY, CA

	SIC	EMP	PHONE	ENTRY #
TRC Operating Company Inc	1311	F	661 763-0081	411
Watkins Construction Co Inc	1623	D	661 763-5395	985
West Side Dst Hosp Foundation	8062	D	805 763-4211	21007
West Side Recreation & Pk Dst	7991	E	661 763-4246	19472

TARZANA, CA - Los Angeles County

	SIC	EMP	PHONE	ENTRY #
Accelon Inc	7361	E	925 216-5735	17387
Airey Enterprises LLC	5088	C	818 530-3362	14050
Akm Fire Inc	3569	F	818 343-8208	8111
AMI-Hti Trzana Encino Jint Vnt	8062	C	818 881-0800	20673
Amisub of California Inc **(DH)**	8062	A	818 881-0800	20674
Attorney Recovery Systems Inc **(PA)**	7322	D	818 774-1420	17104
Avantgarde Senior Living	8361	C	818 881-0055	22083
Braemar Country Club Inc	7997	C	323 873-6880	19549
Cellco Partnership	4812	D	818 344-3366	12597
Cgm Inc	3915	E	818 609-7088	11335
El Caballero Country Club	7997	C	818 654-3000	19561
Extensions Plus Inc	5087	E	818 881-5611	14035
Guardnow Inc	7381	E	877 482-7366	18282
Hoffman Magnetics Inc	3695	E	818 717-5095	9836
Institute For Applied Behavior	8049	D	818 881-1933	20220
JMJ Enterprises Inc	7299	C	818 343-5151	16961
Little Scholars Montessori	8351	E	818 343-1794	22029
Providence Tarzana Medical Ctr	8062	A	818 881-0800	20918
Repipe1 Restoration Inc	1389	E	626 252-0778	542
San Frnndo Vly Urlgcal Med Gro	8011	D	818 996-4242	20050
Shapp International Trdg Inc	5031	C	818 348-3000	13287
Sinanian Development Inc	1542	D	818 996-9666	831
Tarzana Treatment Centers Inc **(PA)**	8093	C	818 996-1051	21348
Temple Jdea of W San Frnndo Vl	8351	D	818 758-3800	22064
Ultimatte Corporation	3663	E	818 993-8007	9324
Universal Merchandise Inc	2311	F	818 344-2044	2752
Wasserman Comden & Casselman **(PA)**	8111	D	323 872-0995	21695

TEHACHAPI, CA - Kern County

	SIC	EMP	PHONE	ENTRY #
Adaptive Aerospace Corporation	3728	E	661 300-0616	10240
Adventist Health Med Tehachapi **(PA)**	8062	C	661 750-4848	20643
Bear Valley Springs Assn	8641	C	661 821-5537	22312
Chemtool Incorporated	2992	C	661 823-7190	5291
GE Wind Energy LLC **(HQ)**	3511	B	661 822-6835	7585
GE Wind Energy LLC	3511	D	661 823-6423	7586
Henway Inc	3965	F	661 822-6873	11497
Keller Classics Inc **(PA)**	2337	E	805 524-1322	2904
Lehigh Cement West Inc	3241	C	661 822-4445	5978
LLC Woodward West	7032	C	661 822-7900	16824
Pjbs Holdings Inc **(PA)**	4953	D	661 822-5273	12965
Selecta Products Inc **(PA)**	5063	D	661 823-7050	13667
Sierra Technical Services Inc	3324	F	661 823-1092	6274
Tehachapi News Inc **(PA)**	2711	F	661 822-6828	4036
World Wind Electrical Svcs Inc	1731	A	661 822-4877	1338

TEMECULA, CA - Riverside County

	SIC	EMP	PHONE	ENTRY #
3-D Precision Machine Inc	3724	E	951 296-5449	10208
Aard Industries Inc	3495	E	951 296-0844	7480
Abbott Vascular Inc	2834	B	951 941-2400	4773
Absolute EDM	3599	F	951 694-5601	8461
Advantage Chemical LLC	5169	E	951 225-4631	14770
Ameresco Solar LLC	8711	D	888 967-6527	22483
Apex Conveyor Corp	3535	E	951 304-7808	7685
Apex Conveyor Systems Inc	3535	F	951 304-7808	7686
Applied Statistics & MGT Inc	7372	E	951 699-4600	17788
Aquamor LLC	3589	D	951 541-9517	8364
Artificial Grass Liquidators	3999	E	951 677-3377	11633
ASPE Inc	2759	F	951 296-2595	4483
Axeon Water Technologies	3589	D	760 723-5417	8366
Bbk Performance Inc	5013	D	951 296-1771	13048
Bear State Water Heating LLC	3822	F	951 269-3753	10662
Bel Vino LLC	2084	F	951 676-6414	2167
Bomatic Inc **(HQ)**	3089	E	909 947-3900	5582
Brightwater Medical Inc	3841	F	951 290-3410	10953
Cal Mutual Inc	6162	D	888 700-4650	15180
Callaway Vineyard & Winery	2084	D	951 676-4001	2172
Canadas Finest Foods Inc	2037	D	951 296-1040	1896
Commonwealth Land Title Insur	6361	C	951 296-6289	15501
Cumming Management Group Inc	8711	D	951 252-8555	22521
Danza Del Sol Winery Inc	2084	E	951 302-6363	2181
DCH Acura of Temecula	7539	D	877 847-9532	18896
Deans Certified Welding Inc	7692	F	951 676-0242	18974
Designer Sash and Door Sys Inc	3089	E	951 657-4179	5625
Douglas Technologies Group Inc **(PA)**	3714	E	760 758-5560	10048
Dynamic Designs Inc	2844	F	951 302-1344	5016
Eco Farms Avocados Inc **(PA)**	5148	D	951 694-3013	14623
Eco Farms Sales Inc **(PA)**	5148	E	951 694-3013	14624
Eco Farms Trdg Operations LLC	5148	D	951 676-4047	14625
Edwards Theatres Circuit Inc	7832	C	951 296-0144	19277
Electro-Support Systems Corp	3679	D	951 676-2751	9705
Empower Software Tech LLC	7372	F	951 672-6257	17846
Falkner Winery Inc	2084	D	951 676-6741	2183
Fff Enterprises Inc **(PA)**	5122	B	951 296-2500	14243
Freedom Forever LLC	1711	C	888 557-6431	1070
Freedom Solar Services	1711	C	888 557-6431	1071
Garmon Corporation	3999	C	951 296-6308	11674
Gifting Group LLC	5199	D	951 296-0310	14931
Gospel Recordings	3652	F	951 719-1650	9219
Hines Growers Inc	0181	B	800 554-4065	79
Identity Intlligence Group LLC	7382	C	626 522-7993	18386
Infineon Tech Americas Corp	3577	A	951 375-6008	8265
Inland Empire Media Group Inc	2721	E	951 682-3026	4075
Inland Erosion Ctrl Svcs Inc	1794	D	951 301-8334	1598
Inners Tasks LLC	3571	E	951 225-9696	8161
Irriscape Construction Inc	0782	D	951 694-6936	311
Jeb Holdings Corp	3357	E	951 296-9900	6352
Jwc Carbide Inc	3541	F	714 540-8870	7734
Kaiser Foundation Hospitals	6324	C	866 984-7483	15409
Kamm Industries Inc	2396	E	800 317-6253	3177
Kaydan Logistics LLC	4789	D	951 961-9000	12576
Leonard Roofing Inc	1761	C	951 506-3811	1495
Leonesse Cellars LLC	2084	E	951 302-7601	2202
Lewis Brsbois Bsgard Smith LLP	8111	D	951 252-6150	21609
Lifeworks (us) Ltd	8742	D	888 577-3784	23262
Long Machine Inc	3599	E	951 296-0194	8664
Lost Dutchmans Minings Assn **(DH)**	1041	E	951 699-4749	375
Louidar LLC	2084	E	951 676-5047	2204
Lowes Home Centers LLC	5031	C	951 296-1618	13246
MAC Products Inc	3312	E	951 296-3077	6205
Maurice Carrie Winery	2084	F	951 676-1711	2206
Maxim Healthcare Services Inc	7363	D	951 694-0100	17501
Mc Laughlin Engrg & Min Inc **(PA)**	1611	D	951 699-7957	902
McMillin Communities Inc	7992	C	951 506-3303	19499
Medley Communications Inc **(PA)**	1731	C	951 245-5200	1281
Michael Baker Intl Inc	8711	D	951 676-8042	22612
Mikes Precision Welding Inc	7692	F	951 676-4744	18990
Milgard Manufacturing LLC	3089	C	480 763-6000	5711
Molding Intl & Engrg Inc	3089	E	951 296-5010	5718
Monte De Oro Winery	2084	F	951 491-6551	2209
Neighborhood Healthcare	8099	D	951 225-6400	21459
Nimbus Water Systems	3589	F	951 984-2800	8401
Normont Hydraulic Sls Svc Inc	5084	F	951 676-2155	13923
North County Times	2711	E	951 676-4315	4016
Opti-Forms Inc	3471	D	951 296-1300	7291
Opto 22	3679	C	951 695-3000	9762
Oreq Corporation	8741	D	951 296-5076	23080
Pacific Barcode Inc	3555	E	951 587-8717	7922
Paradigm 360 Inc	6411	E	951 638-9917	15610
Partners In Leadership LLC **(HQ)**	8742	D	951 694-5596	23294
Paulson Manufacturing Corp	3842	D	951 676-2451	11134
Pechanga Development Corp	7011	A	951 695-4655	16626
Pechanga Resorts Incorporated	7011	D	888 732-4264	16627
Peed Equipment Company	7353	E	951 657-0900	17317
Pgc Construction Inc	1521	E	760 549-4121	633
Polycraft Inc	2759	E	951 296-0860	4556
Ponte Winery	2084	F	951 694-8855	2213
Qc Manufacturing Inc	3564	D	951 325-6340	8053
Quality Control Solutions Inc	3829	E	951 676-1616	10905
Raintree Systems Inc	7371	C	951 252-9400	17695
Rancho California Water Dst **(PA)**	4941	C	951 296-6900	12914
Rancho Ford Inc	7532	C	951 699-1302	18801
Renzoni Vineyards Inc	0172	E	951 302-8466	52
Responsible Med Solutions Corp	8011	E	951 308-0024	20041
Richman Management Corporation	7381	B	909 296-6189	18317
Robinson Printing Inc	2759	E	951 296-0300	4569
Scotts Temecula Operations LLC **(DH)**	3524	C	951 719-1700	7630
Sft Realty Galway Downs LLC	6531	D	951 232-1880	15996
Sierra Pacific Farms Inc **(PA)**	0762	D	951 699-9980	228
Smokeless Selects LLC **(PA)**	2111	F	619 564-8250	2552
Solar Spectrum LLC	1711	B	844 777-6527	1142
Solex Contracting Inc	1623	C	951 308-1706	971
Sonus Group LLC	3714	F	888 316-5351	10134
South Coast Piering Inc	1542	D	800 922-2488	832
South Coast Winery Inc	2084	E	951 587-9463	2222
Southern California Tele Co **(PA)**	4813	D	951 693-1880	12670
Southwest Traders Incorporated **(PA)**	5141	C	951 699-7800	14510
Spenco Machine & Manufacturing	3599	F	951 699-5566	8802
Sprint Communications Co LP	7375	C	951 303-8501	18131
Starwood Hospitality LLC	7011	D	951 699-4477	16729
Stuart Cellars LLC	2084	F	951 676-6414	2224
Sunstone Components Group Inc **(HQ)**	3469	D	951 296-5010	7184
Talentscale Inc	3721	D	760 458-7633	10205
Temecula Hhg Hotel Dev LP	7011	C	951 331-3622	16752
Temecula Precison Fabrication	3599	F	951 699-4066	8816
Temecula Quality Plating Inc	3471	E	951 296-9875	7322
Temecula T-Shirt Printers Inc	2759	F	951 296-0184	4583
Temecula Valley Unified School	4151	D	951 695-7110	11941
Temecula Valley Winery MGT LLC	2084	D	951 699-8896	2228
Temecula Vly Unified Schl Dst	8641	D	951 302-5140	22371
Thompson Magnetics Inc	3679	E	951 676-0243	9796
Thornton Winery	2084	D	951 699-0099	2230
Top Heavy Clothing Company Inc **(PA)**	2321	D	951 442-8839	2763
Transducer Techniques LLC	3829	E	951 719-3965	10917
TST Molding LLC	3089	E	951 296-6200	5845
Usmilk Nutrition Inc	2082	F	951 888-2228	2160
Vesta Solutions Inc **(HQ)**	3661	B	951 719-2100	9244
Villlage News Inc	2711	E	760 451-3488	4042
W Plastics Inc	3081	E	800 442-9727	5441
Wedgewood Hspitality Group Inc	7299	E	951 491-8110	16986
West Coast Surfaces Inc	1752	E	951 699-0600	1471
Westview Services Inc	8331	D	951 699-0047	21976
Wiens Cellars LLC	2084	E	951 694-9892	2236
Wilson Creek Wnery Vnyards Inc	2084	C	951 699-9463	2238
Windsor Capital Group Inc	7011	D	951 676-5656	16796
Wsr Publishing Inc **(PA)**	2721	F	951 676-4914	4113
Zebrasci Inc **(PA)**	3559	F	800 217-3032	8002

TEMPLE CITY, CA - Los Angeles County

	SIC	EMP	PHONE	ENTRY #
California Flexrake Corp	3423	E	626 443-4026	6474
D D Wire Co Inc **(PA)**	3441	E	626 442-0459	6614

GEOGRAPHIC

	SIC	EMP	PHONE	ENTRY #
Davita Medical Management LLC	8011	D	626 309-7600	19782
Huang Qi	2335	F	626 442-6808	2886
Jantek Electronics Inc	3699	E	626 350-4198	9878
Jon Davler Inc	2844	C	626 941-6558	5036
Santa Anita Cnvlscent Hosp Rtr	8051	C	626 579-0310	20459
Sears Home Imprv Pdts Inc	1521	C	626 988-9134	638
Taotao Manufacturer Inc (PA)	3999	E	626 688-9880	11773

TEMPLETON, CA - San Luis Obispo County

	SIC	EMP	PHONE	ENTRY #
California Department Trnsp	1611	D	805 434-1812	867
Castoro Cellars (PA)	2084	F	805 467-2002	2174
Christian Atascadero Home	8051	C	805 466-0281	20281
Compass Health Inc	8051	C	805 434-3035	20284
Grants Custom Cabinets	1521	C	805 466-9680	607
Mesa Vineyard Management Inc (PA)	0762	D	805 434-4100	225
Pacific Gas and Electric Co	4911	C	805 434-4418	12822
Plasvacc USA Inc	3841	C	805 434-0321	11045
Templeton Community Svc Dst	4941	D	805 434-4900	12921
Templeton Surgery Center LLC	8011	B	805 434-3550	20103
Turley Wine Cellars	2084	C	805 434-1030	2233
Twin Cities Community Hosp Inc	8011	B	805 434-3500	20115

TERRA BELLA, CA - Tulare County

	SIC	EMP	PHONE	ENTRY #
Setton Pstchio Terra Bella Inc (HQ)	5149	D	559 535-6050	14735
Sierra Forest Products	5031	C	559 535-4893	13288
Tuff Stuff Products	2821	B	559 535-5778	4725
Weldcraft Industries Inc	3523	F	559 784-4322	7627

THERMAL, CA - Riverside County

	SIC	EMP	PHONE	ENTRY #
Interntnal Pvment Slutions Inc	1611	E	909 794-2101	889
James Fedor Masonry Inc	1741	D	760 772-3036	1348
Mojave Gold LLC	5149	F	760 397-0408	14709
North Shore Greenhouses Inc	0182	C	760 397-0400	100
Oasis Date Garden Inc	2099	C	760 399-5665	2497
Red Earth Casino	7011	C	760 395-1200	16657
Spates Fabricators Inc	2439	C	760 397-4122	3368
Torres-Mrtnez Dsert Chlla Inda	7011	D	760 395-1200	16755
West Coast Aggregate Supply	1442	F	760 342-7598	576

THOUSAND OAKS, CA - Ventura County

	SIC	EMP	PHONE	ENTRY #
2006 Sage Publications	2731	F	805 499-0721	4117
A P R Inc	7363	C	805 379-3400	17483
Amgen Inc	2836	A	805 447-1000	4929
Amgen USA Inc (HQ)	2834	C	805 447-1000	4782
August Hat Company Inc (PA)	2353	E	805 983-4651	3024
Automobile Club Southern Cal	8699	D	805 497-0911	22403
Baxalta US Inc	3841	C	805 498-8664	10943
BEI North America LLC (DH)	3829	C	805 716-0642	10872
Calleguas Municipal Water Dict	4941	D	805 526-9323	12881
Carros Sensors Systems Co LLC (DH)	3829	C	805 968-0782	10876
Castlewood Treatment Ctr LLC (PA)	8093	D	805 273-5217	21283
Coach Inc	3171	C	805 496-9933	5900
Custom Sensors & Tech Inc (HQ)	3679	A	805 716-0322	9699
Easton Baseball / Softball Inc	5091	F	800 632-7866	14076
Easton Diamond Sports LLC	5091	D	800 632-7866	14077
Evergreen Alliance Golf Ltd LP	7992	C	805 495-6421	19487
Floyd Skeren & Kelly LLP (PA)	8111	D	818 206-9222	21555
G3 Group La Inc (PA)	1542	D	323 848-4186	765
Gemmm Corp (PA)	6531	C	805 496-0555	15873
Gold Store Inc	3911	F	805 495-5464	11318
Instacure Healing Products	2834	E	818 222-9600	4830
Kaiser Foundation Hospitals	8011	C	888 515-3500	19919
Kaiser Foundation Hospitals	8011	C	888 515-3500	19920
Kaiser Foundation Hospitals	6324	C	888 515-3500	15429
Kamsut Incorporated	2844	E	805 495-7479	5037
Kavlico Corporation (DH)	3679	A	805 523-2000	9738
Kevin Persons Inc	0781	C	805 371-8746	263
Longs Drug Stores Cal LLC	7384	C	805 493-1502	18416
Los Robles Bank	6022	D	805 373-6763	15030
Los Robles Regional Med Ctr	8062	B	805 494-0880	20853
Los Robles Regional Med Ctr (DH)	8062	A	805 497-2727	20854
Management Trust Assn Inc	6733	D	805 496-5514	16187
Meisei Tools LLC	3423	F	805 497-2626	6486
Midnight Manufacturing LLC	2833	E	714 833-6130	4753
Miramed Global Services Inc	8748	C	805 277-1017	23474
Natren Inc	2099	D	805 371-4737	2493
Nexsan Corporation (HQ)	4899	D	408 724-9809	12787
Oak Ridge Landworks	0782	D	805 630-8377	328
Oltmans Construction Co	1541	B	805 495-9553	711
Ormond Beach LP	6512	D	805 496-4948	15688
Penney Opco LLC	7231	D	805 497-6811	16912
Prevounce Health LLC	3999	F	800 618-7738	11738
Quantum World Technologies Inc	7361	B	805 834-0532	17450
Red Pocket Inc	4813	D	888 993-3888	12667
Rolling Oaks Radiology Inc	8011	D	805 778-1513	20045
Sensata Technologies Inc	3577	D	805 716-0322	8301
Sherwood Country Club	7997	C	805 496-3036	19613
Smiths Interconnect Inc	3679	E	805 267-0100	9783
Southern California Edison Co	4911	C	818 999-1880	12841
Staff Assistance Inc (PA)	8082	E	818 894-7879	21217
Staff Assistance Inc	7361	B	805 371-9980	17468
Star of Ca LLC	8099	D	805 379-1401	21483
Takeda Pharmaceuticals	2834	F	805 375-6700	4901
Teledyne Redlake Masd LLC (DH)	3826	E	805 373-4545	10817
Teledyne Scentific Imaging LLC (HQ)	8731	C	805 373-4545	22868
Teledyne Technologies Inc (PA)	3679	D	805 373-4545	9794
Thousand Oaks Surgical Hosp LP	8062	D	805 777-7750	20977
Ventu Park LLC	7011	D	805 716-4200	16770
Vorwerk LLC	3469	D	805 413-0800	7190
Wash Depot Auto Centers LP	7542	D	805 379-4900	18918
Young MNS Chrstn Assn Ssthast V	8641	E	805 523-7613	22390

THOUSAND PALMS, CA - Riverside County

	SIC	EMP	PHONE	ENTRY #
A R Electronics Inc	3679	E	760 343-1200	9669
Gulf- California Broadcast Co	4833	D	760 773-0342	12728
Jacobsson Engrg Cnstr Inc	1611	D	760 345-8700	890
Kincaid Industries Inc	1711	C	760 343-5457	1091
Koolfog Inc (PA)	3585	F	760 321-9203	8343
Microcool	3823	F	760 322-1111	10707
Pro-Tech Mats Industries Inc	3069	C	760 343-36E7	5400
Readylink Inc	7361	C	760 343-7000	17454
Readylink Healthcare	7361	C	760 343-7000	17455
San Val Corp (PA)	0781	B	760 346-3999	278
Sunline Transit Agency (PA)	4111	C	760 343-3456	11845
Superior Ready Mix Concrete LP	3273	D	760 343-3418	6123
Therapeutic Industries Inc	3841	F	760 343-2502	11064
Vorwaller & Brooks Inc	1521	D	760 262-6300	648

THREE RIVERS, CA - Tulare County

	SIC	EMP	PHONE	ENTRY #
Innovative Structural GL Inc	3231	D	559 561-7000	5958
Roman Catholic Bishp of Fresno	7032	D	559 561-4499	16825
Sequoia Parks Conservancy	2731	E	559 565-3759	4137

TIPTON, CA - Tulare County

	SIC	EMP	PHONE	ENTRY #
Agnaldos Welding Inc	7692	F	559 752-4254	18968
Bosman Dairy LLC	0241	C	559 752-7018	131

TOLUCA LAKE, CA - Los Angeles County

	SIC	EMP	PHONE	ENTRY #
Gmm Inc	2741	F	818 752-3200	4175
James B Branch Inc (PA)	4212	A	818 765-3521	11978
Shafton Inc	2389	F	818 985-5025	3084
Tre Venezie Inc	7299	D	818 985 4669	16981

TORRANCE, CA - Los Angeles County

	SIC	EMP	PHONE	ENTRY #
21515 Hawthorne Owner LLC	8641	D	310 406-3730	22308
24hr Homecare LLC	8082	D	310 375-5353	21122
A L S Industries Inc	5092	D	310 532-9262	14090
A-Aztec Rents & Sells Inc (PA)	2394	C	310 347-3010	3133
Ace Clearwater Enterprises Inc (PA)	3728	C	310 323-2140	10234
ACS Communications Inc	1731	D	310 767-2145	1209
Act 1 Group Inc (PA)	7361	D	310 750-3400	17388
Advanced Corporate Svcs Inc	8748	E	310 937-6848	23401
Advanced Orthpdic Slutions Inc	3842	E	310 533-9966	11083
Aegis Ambulance Service Inc (PA)	4119	C	626 685-9410	11847
Aero-Electric Connector Inc (PA)	3643	B	310 618-3737	9025
Aeroliant Manufacturing Inc	3599	E	310 257-1903	8479
Aeroworx Inc	7699	E	310 831-0300	19021
AES NDT	3829	E	310 947-6755	10867
Air Products and Chemicals Inc	2911	F	310 212-2800	5248
Aisin World Corp of America	3714	C	310 326-8681	10013
All Access Stging Prdctons Inc (PA)	3648	D	310 784-2464	9121
Allied Digital Services LLC (HQ)	7376	C	310 431-2375	18138
Allied Protection Services Inc	7381	C	310 330-8314	18241
Alliedsignal Arospc Svc Corp (HQ)	3369	D	310 323-9500	6411
Alpine Electronics America Inc (HQ)	5064	C	310 326-8000	13680
Alpine Village	6512	C	310 327-4384	15658
Alpinestars USA	2331	D	310 891-0222	2835
Als Group Usa Corp	8734	D	310 214-0043	22929
Ambulnz Co LLC	6719	C	877 311-5555	16092
Ambulnz Health LLC (PA)	7375	A	877 311-5555	18118
AME-Gyu Co Ltd	6719	A	310 214-9572	16093
American Business Bank	6022	D	310 808-1200	15010
American Honda Finance Corp (DH)	6141	C	310 972-2239	15137
American Honda Motor Co Inc (HQ)	5012	C	310 783-2000	13018
American Honda Motor Co Inc	3732	F	800 382-2238	10457
American Ultraviolet West Inc	3535	C	310 784-2930	7684
Ana Trading Corp USA (DH)	5084	C	310 542-2500	13887
Antcom Corporation	3663	E	310 782-1076	9253
Anton Paar Usa Inc	6512	E	310 775-2196	15659
Arkema Inc	2812	E	310 214-5327	4634
Asiana Cuisine Enterprises Inc	2099	A	310 327-2223	2393
Automobile Club Southern Cal	8699	C	310 325-3111	22404
Bachem Americas Inc (DH)	2836	C	310 784-4440	4931
Bachem Bioscience Inc	2836	E	310 784-7322	4932
Bankcard Services (PA)	7389	C	213 365-1122	18456
Bay Citis Surgery Centre L P	8011	D	310 784-2710	19719
Bayco Financial Corporation (PA)	6531	D	310 378-8181	15783
Benevolence Health Center (PA)	8099	E	323 732-0100	21387
Beranek LLC	3599	E	310 328-9094	8526
Bethebeast Inc	7372	E	424 206-1081	17796
Binex Line Corp (PA)	4513	C	310 416-8600	12325
Bioscreen Testing Services Inc (PA)	8731	E	310 214-0043	22831
Bnl Technologies Inc	3572	C	310 320-7272	8188
BQE Software Inc	7372	C	310 602-4020	17805
Breville Usa Inc	5023	E	310 755-3000	13162
Bright Event Rentals LLC (PA)	7359	C	310 202-0011	17335
Broadata Communications Inc	3357	D	310 530-1416	6344
Cable Aml Inc (PA)	3663	F	310 222-5599	9259
Calcon Steel Construction Inc	3441	C	310 768-8094	6596
Caleb Technology Corporation	3691	F	310 257-4780	9808
California Mfg Tech Consulting	8711	D	310 263-3060	22508
Camfil Farr Inc	3564	F	973 616-7300	8042
Canoo Inc (PA)	3714	C	424 271-2144	10028
Capable Transport Inc	4731	C	310 697-0198	12427
Carley (PA)	3229	E	310 325-8474	5932
Catalina Pacific Concrete	3273	C	310 532-4600	6077
Cedars-Sinai Medical Center	8062	B	310 967-1900	20706

Company	SIC	EMP	PHONE	ENTRY #
Celestron Acquisition LLC	3827	D	310 328-9560	10830
Celestron International	3827	E	310 328-9560	10831
Century 21 Exclusive Realtors	6531	C	310 373-5252	15806
Century Parts Inc	3599	F	310 328-0281	8547
Cerritos Reference Labs Inc		D	562 865-3609	21063
Ceva Logistics LLC	4731	B	310 223-6500	12432
Ceva Logistics US Inc	4731	B	310 972-5500	12433
Choura Events	7359	D	310 320-6200	17336
City of Torrance	4581	D	310 784-7950	12348
Classic Litho & Design Inc	2752	E	310 224-5200	4253
Coast/Dvnced Chip Mgnetics Inc	3677	F	310 370-8188	9624
Cohen Brown MGT Group Inc (PA)	8742	E	310 966-1001	23193
Common Area Maint Svcs Inc (PA)	7349	D	310 390-3552	17231
Compex Legal Services Inc (PA)	8111	C	310 782-1801	21535
Conesys Inc	5065	D	310 618-3737	13711
Continental Dntl Ceramics Inc	8072	E	310 618-8821	21104
Convaid Products LLC	5047	D	310 618-0111	13484
County of Los Angeles	8011	D	310 354-2300	19763
Courtcall LLC (PA)	8111	D	310 342-0888	21541
Courtyard Management Corp	7011	D	310 533-8000	16394
Creative Pathways Inc	3548	E	310 530-1965	7889
Credit Card Services Inc (PA)	7389	D	213 365-1122	18497
Ctc Group Inc (DH)	7011	D	310 540-0500	16402
Daicel America Holdings Inc	8741	B	480 798-6737	23014
Dasco Engineering Corp	3728	C	310 326-2277	10308
Data Linkage Software Inc	7372	F	310 781-3056	17833
Davita Medical Management LLC	8099	D	310 783-5567	21417
Dcw Services LLC	8742	D	310 324-3147	23205
Del AMO Construction	1542	D	310 378-6203	759
Del AMO Grdns Cnvlscent Hosp S	8051	D	310 378-4233	20308
Del AMO Hospital Inc	8093	B	310 530-1151	21297
Delta Computer Consulting	7379	D	310 541-9440	18172
Diamond K2	3425	E	310 539-6116	6492
Diamotec Inc	3545	F	310 539-4994	7853
Dicaperl Corporation (DH)	1499	D	610 667-6640	585
Digestive Care Consultants	8011	D	310 375-1246	19800
Divergent Technologies Inc	8711	D	310 339-1186	22532
Docmagic Inc	7389	C	800 649-1362	18504
Donovan Engineering Corp	3714	F	310 320-3772	10047
Doug Mockett & Company Inc	2511	E	310 318-2491	3468
Dream Home Care Inc	8361	D	562 595-9021	22100
Dreamgear LLC	3944	E	310 222-5522	11371
Edelbrock Holdings Inc	3714	C	310 781-2290	10050
Elers Medical Usa Inc	5047	A	858 336-4900	13485
Ely Co Inc	3599	E	310 539-5831	8580
Emax Laboratories Inc	8734	E	310 618-8889	22942
Emp Connectors Inc	3643	E	310 533-6799	9035
Encore Image Group Inc (PA)	3993	D	310 534-7500	11550
Escape Communications Inc	3663	F	310 997-1300	9272
Excelpro Inc (PA)	2022	E	323 415-8544	1771
Expeditors Intl Wash Inc	4731	B	310 343-6200	12455
Express Imaging Services Inc	4226	D	888 846-8804	12267
EZ Lube LLC	7538	D	310 791-8480	18825
Ezcaretech Usa Inc	4226	B	424 558-3191	18515
FCkingston Co	3491	E	310 326-8287	7444
Fh & Hf-Torrance I LLC	8051	C	310 320-4130	20344
Field Manufacturing Corp (PA)	2542	E	310 781-9292	3683
Fischer Cstm Cmmunications Inc (PA)	3825	D	310 303-3300	10754
Fns Inc (PA)	4731	D	661 615-2300	12458
Forrester Eastland Corporation	3999	E	310 784-2464	11670
Forte Biosciences Inc (PA)	2834	E	310 618-6994	4821
French Tradition (PA)	2511	F	310 719-9971	3472
Friction Materials LLC	8711	C	248 362-3600	22557
Fun Properties Inc (PA)	3423	C	310 787-4500	6480
G F Cole Corporation (PA)	3053	E	310 320-0601	5338
Gable House Inc	7933	D	310 378-2265	19398
Garrett Transportation I Inc (HQ)	3724	C	973 455-2000	10215
Gc Aero Inc	3433	F	310 539-7600	6570
Genequity Mortgage Inc	6211	D	310 540-1550	15265
General Forming Corporation	3444	E	310 326-0624	6843
General Motors LLC	3711	A	313 556-5000	9949
Genesis Healthcare LLC	8051	C	310 370-3594	20356
George P Johnson Company	3993	E	310 965-4300	11558
Geri-Care Inc	8051	D	310 320-0961	20359
Geri-Care II Inc	8059	C	310 328-0812	20591
Gizmac Accessories LLC	3577	F	310 320-5563	8258
Gky Dental Arts Inc (PA)	8072	D	310 214-8007	21106
Global Comm Semiconductors LLC (HQ)	3674	D	310 530-7274	9510
Goeppner Industries Inc	3599	E	310 784-2800	8606
Good Sports Plus Ltd	7371	B	310 671-4400	17629
Goodridge Usa Inc (DH)	5013	D	310 533-1924	13061
Hall Associates Racg Pdts Inc	3799	F	310 326-4111	10552
Harbor Building Services	7349	D	310 320-2966	17248
Harbor Dvlpmntal Dsblties Fndt	8399	C	310 540-1711	22187
Harbor-Ucla Med Foundation Inc	8092	D	310 533-0413	21245
Harbor-Ucla Med Foundation Inc (PA)	8741	D	310 222-5015	23036
Health-Ade LLC (HQ)	2033	F	844 337-6368	1862
Hewitt Industries Los Angeles	3823	E	714 891-9300	10700
Hi-Shear Corporation (DH)	3452	A	310 784-4025	7066
Honeywell International Inc	3724	A	310 323-9500	10216
Howmet Aerospace Inc	3334	B	212 836-2674	6281
Howmet Globl Fstning Systems I	5085	D	310 784-0700	13987
Hua Xing Pcba Limited	3672	E	310 626-7575	9413
Hung Management Inc	8351	D	310 533-4830	22021
Hunt Enterprises Inc	6531	C	310 325-1496	15886
I C Class Components Corp (PA)	5065	D	310 539-5500	13728
Image Solutions Apparel Inc	2326	D	310 464-8991	2781
Imperial Cfs Inc	4226	E	310 768-8188	12268
Indizen Optical Tech Amer LLC	7371	D	310 783-1533	17638
Industrial Dynamics Co Ltd (PA)	3559	C	310 325-5633	7982
Industrial Gasket and Sup Co	3053	E	310 530-1771	5342
Industrial Parts Depot (HQ)	5084	D	310 320-1900	13906
Inmoment Research LLC	4725	D	310 783-4300	12406
Intellisense Systems Inc	3812	C	310 320-1827	10591
J Tech Inc	3643	F	310 533-6700	9039
J-T E C H	3678	D	310 533-6700	9658
Jci Jones Chemicals Inc	2812	F	310 523-1629	4636
Jessie Lord Bakery LLC	5149	E	310 533-6010	14697
John J Ohara MD A Medical Corp	8011	D	310 316-7095	19857
Jos Candies LLC	5145	F	800 770-1946	14563
Jr286 Inc (PA)	3949	F	877 464-5301	11431
Jtb Americas Ltd (HQ)	4724	C	310 406-3121	12391
Just For Fun Inc	2321	E	310 320-1327	2758
Kace Entertainment Inc (PA)	7929	D	310 372-2222	19360
Kaiser Foundation Hospitals	6324	C	800 780-1230	15428
Kakuichi America Inc	3084	D	310 539-1590	5468
KB Delta Inc	3469	E	310 530-1539	7156
Keenan & Associates (HQ)	6411	B	310 212-3344	15586
Keller Engineering Inc	3599	F	310 326-6291	8652
Kepner Plas Fabricators Inc	3089	E	310 325-3162	5689
Kintetsu Enterprises Co Amer (HQ)	7011	C	310 782-9300	16524
Kopykake Enterprises Inc (PA)	3469	F	310 373-8906	7159
Kubota Industrial Equipment	5046	D	817 756-1171	13464
L3 Technologies Inc	3663	B	650 591-8411	9283
La Ejuice LLC (PA)	5194	E	310 257-1198	14904
Laserod Technologies LLC	3699	E	310 328-5869	9887
Ledtronics Inc	3674	F	310 534-1505	9531
Lenntek Corporation	3663	E	310 534-2738	9286
Lg Nanoh2o Inc	2899	E	424 218-4000	5227
Libra Cable Technologies Inc	3679	F	310 618-8182	9740
Lisi Aerospace	3841	E	310 326-8110	11010
Lisi Aerospace North Amer Inc	3324	A	310 326-8110	6268
Little Company Mary Hospital	8062	A	310 540-7676	20834
Loma Scientific International	3663	F	310 328-9655	9287
Long Beach Golden Sails Inc	7011	C	562 596-1631	16544
Los Angeles Waves Netball Club	8699	E	310 346-7211	22456
Lowes Home Centers LLC	5031	C	310 787-1469	13247
Lowes Home Centers LLC	5031	C	310 602-2090	13265
Luminit LLC	3827	E	310 320-1066	10845
Lyncole Grunding Solutions LLC	3643	E	310 214-4000	9041
Lynn Products Inc	3577	A	310 530-5966	8277
Madrona Carwash Inc (PA)	7542	E	310 373-9736	18915
Magnetic Component Engrg Inc (PA)	3499	E	310 784-3100	7563
Magnetron Power Inventions Inc	1382	E	310 462-6970	457
Mahmood Izadi Inc	3569	F	310 320-0463	8129
Manhattan Confectioners Inc	2064	F	310 257-0260	2095
Marcea Inc	2339	F	213 746-5191	2970
Martin Chevrolet	7538	D	323 772-6494	18854
Mediacentric Integration Inc	7379	D	310 325-7900	18201
Medical Chemical Corporation	2899	E	310 787-6800	5233
Medicool Inc	3841	F	310 782-2200	11017
Mercury Air Cargo Inc (HQ)	4581	C	310 258-6100	12363
Messer LLC	2813	F	310 533-8394	4643
Metro Truck Body Incorporated	3713	E	310 532-5570	9993
Microcosm Inc	3764	D	310 219-2700	10527
Micronova Manufacturing Inc	2392	E	310 784-6990	3108
Midnight Sun Enterprises Inc	8748	D	310 532-2427	23473
Mighty Enterprises Inc	5084	D	310 516-7478	13919
Mishima Foods USA Inc (PA)	5141	D	310 787-1533	14479
Mk Diamond Products Inc (PA)	3546	C	310 539-5221	7882
Momentum Management LLC	3069	F	310 329-2599	5394
Moog Inc	3625	B	310 533-1178	8961
Moog Inc	3812	B	310 533-1178	10602
Morinaga Nutritional Foods Inc	2099	F	310 787-0200	2490
Motorcar Parts of America Inc (PA)	3714	A	310 212-7910	10106
Msr Hotels & Resorts Inc	7011	B	310 543-4566	16575
Mycom North America Inc (PA)	5078	E	310 328-1362	13854
Naturalife Eco Vite Labs	2023	D	310 370-1563	1802
Navcom Technology Inc (HQ)	3663	D	310 381-2000	9300
Nc4 Soltra LLC	7372	F	408 489-5579	17928
Nearfield Systems Inc	3825	D	310 525-7000	10767
Neoteryx LLC	8731	E	310 787-8747	22854
New Albertsons Inc	7384	C	310 540-6824	18420
New Generation Engrg Cnstr Inc	5032	E	424 329-3950	13308
Nippon Express USA Inc	4731	E	310 532-6300	12490
Nippon Express USA Inc	4731	E	310 527-4237	12492
Nissin Intl Trnspt USA Inc (HQ)	4731	E	310 222-8500	12493
Nothing To Wear Inc (PA)	2331	E	310 328-0408	2863
Obatake Inc	3911	F	310 782-2730	11327
Ocean Duke Corporation	5146	E	310 326-3198	14574
One Touch Solutions Inc	3555	F	310 320-6868	7921
Onshore Technologies Inc	3679	E	310 533-4888	9761
Opto-Knowledge Systems Inc	8731	E	310 756-0520	22857
Optodyne Incorporation	3663	E	310 635-5481	9306
Organic Inc	7379	D	310 543-4600	18206
Oriental Motor USA Corporation (DH)	5063	D	310 715-3300	13656
Orthalliance Inc	8399	A	310 792-1300	22206
Pacific Echo Inc	5085	E	310 539-1822	14011
Pacific South Bay Dialysis LLC (HQ)	8092	E	310 371-4244	21257
Pacific Wave Systems Inc	3663	F	714 893-0152	9308
Panalpina Inc	4731	D	310 819-4060	12502
Partner Assessment Corporation (PA)	8711	C	800 419-4923	22635
Pasco Corporation of America	2038	E	503 289-6500	1934
Pediatric Therapy Network	8093	F	310 328-0276	21324

	SIC	EMP	PHONE	ENTRY #
Pelican Biopharma LLC	2834	E	310 326-4700	4869
Pelican Products Inc **(PA)**	3648	B	310 326-4700	9143
Peninsula Laboratories LLC	2834	F	310 539-4171	4870
Pentel of America Ltd **(HQ)**	5112	C	310 320-3831	14196
Performance Health Med Group **(PA)**	8099	E	310 540-9699	21470
Performance Team Frt Sys Inc	4731	C	562 345-2200	12506
Pevelers Custom Interiors Inc	1521	F	310 214-5049	632
Pharmaco Inc	8082	D	310 328-3897	21202
Phenomenex Inc **(HQ)**	3826	C	310 212-0555	10806
Phiten Usa Inc **(HQ)**	7231	E	310 225-4300	16915
Photo Sciences Incorporated **(PA)**	3577	E	310 634-1500	8290
Physicians Choice HM Hlth Inc	8082	E	310 793-1616	21203
Pieper and Associates Inc	8743	D	310 515-5600	23383
Pioneer North America Inc **(DH)**	5064	F	310 952-2000	13691
Pioneer Theatres Inc	7389	C	310 532-8183	18634
Plasma Technology Incorporated **(PA)**	3479	D	310 320-3373	7400
Platinum Empire Group Inc	7363	C	310 821-5888	17508
Pmp Products Inc	3161	F	310 549-5122	5895
Polypeptide Laboratories Inc **(DH)**	8071	D	310 782-3569	21086
Precision Fiberglass Products	3644	F	310 539-7470	9052
Pressed Juicery Inc	5149	F	310 214-2144	14722
Prestone Products Corporation	2899	E	424 271-4836	5238
Prime One Inc	7361	C	310 378-1944	17447
Proactive Risk Management Inc	8741	D	213 840-8856	23090
Probe Racing Components Inc	3592	E	310 784-2977	8434
Proprietary Controls Systems	3829	E	310 303-3600	10904
Providence Health System	6733	C	310 370-5895	16196
Providence Health System	8082	C	310 370-5895	21204
PSC Industrial Outsourcing LP	7699	C	310 325-1600	19058
Pulse Instruments	3825	E	310 515-5330	10768
Qpi Holdings Inc **(HQ)**	3728	D	310 539-2855	10399
Quality Forming LLC	3728	D	310 539-2855	10400
Quinstar Technology Inc	5065	D	310 320-1111	13766
Ralph E Ames Machine Works	3599	E	310 328-8523	8757
Rapiscan Systems Inc **(HQ)**	3844	A	310 978-1457	11209
Redman Equipment & Mfg Co	7699	E	310 329-1134	19060
Reinhardt Brothers MBL & Tile	1743	F	310 325-0174	1422
Reliable Circuits Mfg Inc	3672	F	310 373-2174	9447
Resource Collection Inc	7349	D	310 219-3272	17281
Retail Print Media Inc	2759	E	424 488-6950	4567
Roberts Research Laboratory	3489	F	310 320-7310	7434
Robinson Helicopter Co Inc	3728	A	310 539-0508	10402
Rock-Ola Manufacturing Corp	3651	D	310 328-1306	9190
Ryans Express Trnsp Svcs Inc **(PA)**	4142	D	310 219-2960	11915
Sagepoint Financial Inc	6282	D	310 792-0801	15346
Sakura Finetek USA Inc **(HQ)**	5047	C	310 972-7800	13517
Salson Logistics Inc	4731	D	973 986-0200	12521
Sanko Electronics America Inc **(HQ)**	3714	F	310 618-1677	10131
Sanrio Inc **(HQ)**	5092	D	650 952-2880	14101
Santec Inc	3432	E	310 542-0063	6566
Sanyo Denki America Inc **(HQ)**	5045	D	310 783-5400	13435
Sea Electric LLC	3621	E	424 376-3660	8929
Securitas SEC Svcs USA Inc	7381	C	310 787-0747	18323
Shaver Specialty Co Inc	3556	E	310 370-6941	7952
Shimadzu Precision Instrs Inc	5047	D	310 217-8855	13519
Shine Food Inc **(PA)**	2032	E	310 329-3829	1855
Shine Food Inc	2038	D	310 533-6010	1939
Showerdoordirect LLC	3444	E	310 327-8060	6912
Simplehuman LLC **(PA)**	5023	D	310 436-2250	13185
Sirena Incorporated	2759	F	866 548-5353	4574
Sonic Industries Inc	8711	C	310 532-8382	22655
Southbay European Inc	7539	D	310 939-7300	18905
Southern California Ice Co	2097	F	310 325-1040	2374
Southwest Ppline Trnchless Cor **(PA)**	7699	D	310 329-8717	19069
Special Service For Groups Inc	8399	C	310 323-6887	22212
Star Link Company Inc	7336	F	310 787-8299	17189
Stellant Systems Inc **(HQ)**	3671	D	310 517-6000	9368
Stewart Filmscreen Corp **(PA)**	3861	C	310 326-1422	11292
Storm Industries Inc **(PA)**	3523	D	310 534-5232	7622
Storm Manufacturing Group Inc	3491	D	310 326-8287	7452
Struers Inc	5047	E	310 320-6288	13522
Student Sports LLC	2273	F	310 791-1142	2697
Sun Chlorella USA Corp	5149	D	310 891-0600	14738
Sunrider Eastern Europe Inc **(PA)**	5122	C	310 781-3808	14293
Supershuttle Orange County Inc	4111	B	310 222-5500	11846
Sure Power Inc	3679	F	310 542-8561	9789
Sweis Inc **(PA)**	5087	D	310 375-0558	14045
System Technical Support Corp	3625	E	310 845-9400	8964
Takane USA Inc **(HQ)**	3873	C	310 212-1411	11304
Takuyo Corporation	2711	F	310 782-6927	4034
Tcw Trends Inc	2339	E	310 533-5177	3001
Technical Devices Company	3548	E	310 618-8437	7896
Technology Training Corp **(PA)**	7389	F	310 320-8110	18687
Teledyne Defense Elec LLC	3679	C	310 823-5491	9792
Textile Unlimited Corporation **(PA)**	2321	B	310 263-7400	2762
Thg Brands Inc	2099	E	844 694-8327	2537
Topper Manufacturing Corp	3589	F	310 375-5000	8422
Topwin Corporation **(PA)**	5136	D	310 325-2255	14356
Torrance Care Center West Inc	8051	C	310 370-4561	20487
Torrance Health Assn Inc **(PA)**	8062	A	310 325-9110	20978
Torrance Memorial Medical Ctr	8062	A	310 784-6316	20980
Torrance Memorial Medical Ctr	8062	A	310 784-3740	20981
Torrance Memorial Medical Ctr **(HQ)**	8062	A	310 325-9110	20982
Torrance Refining Company LLC	2911	A	310 212-2800	5262
Torrance Steel Window Co Inc	3442	E	310 328-9181	6722
Torrence Trading Inc	3944	E	310 649-1188	11393
Total Management Svcs Amer Inc	7361	E	310 328-0867	17476
Totex Manufacturing Inc	3089	D	310 326-2028	5841
Tower Energy Group **(PA)**	5172	C	310 538-8000	14815
Toyota Logistics Services Inc **(DH)**	3711	C	310 468-4000	9970
Tre Milano LLC	3999	F	310 260-8888	11784
Trendnet Inc **(PA)**	5045	D	310 961-5500	13448
Unico Logistics Usa Inc	4119	E	310 835-5656	11894
Unified Inv Programs Inc **(PA)**	8099	E	310 782-1878	21492
Unify Financial Federal Cr Un **(PA)**	6061	D	310 536-5000	15093
United Parcel Service Inc	4215	C	800 742-5877	12150
United Srgcal Prtners Intl Inc	8011	D	310 325-4555	20119
United States Gypsum Company	3275	D	908 232-8900	6131
Universal Screw Products	3451	F	310 371-1170	7048
US Hybrid Corporation **(HQ)**	3714	E	310 212-1200	10150
US Pharmatech Inc	2834	F	310 219-6003	4908
US Security Associates Inc	7381	B	714 352-0773	18356
V Todays Inc	7011	C	310 781-9100	16766
Vector Resources Inc **(PA)**	1731	B	310 436-1000	1336
Verengo Inc **(DH)**	1796	A	310 803-9053	1628
Virco Inc **(HQ)**	5021	C	310 533-0474	13154
Virco Mfg Corporation **(PA)**	2531	A	310 533-0474	3635
Volt Management Corp	7363	D	310 316-8523	17524
Walker Advertising LLC	7311	E	310 519-4050	17069
Weckerle Cosmetics Usa Inc	5122	E	310 328-7000	14297
William Bounds Ltd	3556	E	310 375-0505	7956
Winther Technologies Inc **(PA)**	3548	E	310 618-8437	7897
Xld Group LLC	7011	D	310 316-3636	16808
Younger Mfg Co **(PA)**	3851	B	310 783-1533	11266
Z C & R Coating For Optics Inc	3827	E	310 381-3060	10866

TRABUCO CANYON, CA - Orange County

	SIC	EMP	PHONE	ENTRY #
AAA Global Consulting LLC **(PA)**	8748	D	949 201-5204	23400
Coto De Caza Golf Club Inc	7941	C	949 766-7886	19414
Td Industries	3999	E	949 939-3685	11775
Techvalve Industries LLC	3999	F	714 264-7950	11777
Total Recon Solutions Inc	8742	D	949 584-8417	23349

TRAVER, CA - Tulare County

	SIC	EMP	PHONE	ENTRY #
Foster Poultry Farms	5191	C	559 457-6509	14859
Maf Industries Inc **(HQ)**	3565	D	559 897-2905	8074

TRONA, CA - San Bernardino County

	SIC	EMP	PHONE	ENTRY #
Searles Valley Minerals Inc	1479	E	760 372-2259	580
Searles Valley Minerals Inc	1479	E	760 672-2053	581
Trona Railway Company	4011	A	760 372-2312	11798

TUJUNGA, CA - Los Angeles County

	SIC	EMP	PHONE	ENTRY #
Crescenta-Canada YMCA	8641	C	818 352-3255	22335
David Kopf Instruments	3841	E	818 352-3274	10967
F J & J Corporation	7819	F	505 452-1700	19232
Volunteers of Amer Los Angeles	8322	D	818 352-5974	21916
Vons Companies Inc	2051	D	818 353-4917	2046

TULARE, CA - Tulare County

	SIC	EMP	PHONE	ENTRY #
Adventist Health Tulare	8062	B	559 688-0821	20650
Altura Centers For Health	8011	D	559 686-9097	19705
Amdal In-Home Care Inc **(PA)**	8082	E	559 686-6611	21132
American Data Vault Inc	3272	F	559 686-2838	6015
Dan Freitas Electric	1731	D	559 686-9572	1241
Dowdys Sales and Services Inc	3523	F	559 688-6973	7610
Fisher Manufacturing Co **(PA)**	3432	E	559 685-5200	6560
Golden Valley Dairy Products	2022	C	559 687-1188	1772
High Sierra Truss Company Inc	2439	F	559 688-6611	3364
Kings County Truck Lines **(HQ)**	4213	C	559 686-2857	12056
Kloeckner Metals Corporation	5051	D	559 688-7980	13576
Land OLakes Inc	2022	D	559 687-8287	1776
Linder Equipment Co	7699	E	559 685-5000	19048
Lowes Home Centers LLC	5031	C	559 366-5000	13264
Morris Levin and Son	1711	C	559 686-8665	1103
Moyles Centl Vly Hlth Care Inc **(PA)**	8051	C	559 688-0288	20420
Moyles Health Care Inc	8059	A	559 686-1601	20615
Mt View Farming Inc	0172	D	559 688-2906	50
Nielsens Creamery **(PA)**	0241	E	559 686-4744	135
Porterville Sheltered Workshop	5047	D	559 684-9168	13513
Russell Kc & Son	3523	F	559 686-3236	7618
Saputo Cheese USA Inc	2022	B	559 687-8411	1780
Southern California Edison Co	4911	C	559 625-7126	12840
Stainless Works Inc	7692	F	559 688-4310	18998
Sundale Fndtion For Stdnts Cmn	8351	C	559 688-3419	22063
Tulare Local Health Care Dst	8062	A	559 685-3462	20984
Tulare Nrsing Rhblttion Hosp I	8051	D	559 686-8581	20491
Turnupseed Electric Service	1731	D	559 686-1541	1332
Utility Vault Co	3272	E	559 688-6686	6063
Whitten Machine	3599	F	559 686-3428	8851

TUPMAN, CA - Kern County

	SIC	EMP	PHONE	ENTRY #
Midstream Energy Partners USA	1231	E	661 765-4087	381

TUSTIN, CA - Orange County

	SIC	EMP	PHONE	ENTRY #
A P R Consulting Inc	7379	B	714 544-3696	18154
ABM Elctrcal Ltg Solutions Inc **(DH)**	7349	E	866 226-2838	17209
Add-On Computer Peripheral Inc	3577	C	949 546-8200	8232
Adel Park LLC	3531	F	213 321-2030	7633
Alene Le DDS MS Inc **(PA)**	8021	D	626 332-6291	20169
Alldigital Holdings Inc	7372	F	949 250-7340	17780
Alliance Funding Group **(PA)**	8741	D	800 978-8817	22971
Allied Lube Inc	7538	D	949 651-8814	18813
Alta Hospitals System LLC	8062	A	714 619-7700	20671
Anajet LLC	3555	E	714 662-3200	7916
Ansar Gallery Inc	5141	C	949 220-0000	14455

Mergent email: customerrelations@mergent.com
1442

2022 Southern California Business
Directory and Buyers Guide

(P-0000) Products & Services Section entry number
(PA)=Parent Co (HQ)=Headquarters (DH)=Div Headquarters

	SIC	EMP	PHONE	ENTRY #
Arq LLC **(PA)**	8711	D	888 384-0971	22494
Autocrib Inc	7389	C	714 274-0400	18453
Avid Bioservices Inc **(PA)**	2834	C	714 508-6000	4791
B2 Services Llc	7361	D	714 363-3481	17393
Baf Industries **(PA)**	2842	E	714 258-8055	4957
Bar None Inc	2085	F	714 259-8450	2241
Behavior One Atism Sltions LLC	8093	D	657 294-5113	21277
Bergelectric Corp	1731	D	949 250-7005	1221
Bernhardt and Bernhardt Inc	3541	E	714 544-0708	7722
Bio-Reigns Inc	3999	E	949 922-2032	11638
Bjb Enterprises Inc	2821	E	714 734-8450	4681
Brandywine Communications **(PA)**	5065	F	714 755-1050	13704
Braxton Caribbean Mfg Co Inc	3469	D	714 508-3570	7130
Briggs Electric Inc **(PA)**	1731	D	714 544-2500	1224
Broker Solutions Inc **(PA)**	8742	A	800 450-2010	23179
Butier Engineering Inc	8741	D	714 832-7222	22994
Caliber Bodyworks Texas Inc	7532	D	714 665-3905	18784
Canon Medical Systems USA Inc **(DH)**	5047	B	714 730-5000	13482
CM Brewing Technologies LLC	3589	F	888 391-9990	8375
Coastal Intl Holdings LLC	7389	C	714 635-1200	18483
Colbi Technologies Inc	2741	E	714 505-9544	4163
Compass Water Solutions Inc **(PA)**	3589	E	949 222-5777	8377
Constellation Homebuilder **(HQ)**	7379	E	714 768-6100	18171
Corner Products Company	5065	D	949 231-5000	13712
Country House	2064	E	714 505-8988	2083
Crestmont Capital LLC	6799	C	949 537-3882	16258
Crown Golf Properties LP	8742	D	714 730-1611	23200
Custom Quilting Inc	2392	E	714 731-7271	3101
Dawn Food Products Inc	2051	C	714 258-1223	1994
Definitive Media Corp **(PA)**	7372	E	714 305-5900	17837
Design West Technologies Inc	3089	D	714 731-0201	5624
Diamond Goldenwest Corporation **(PA)**	5094	C	714 542-9000	14130
Dickeys Barbecue Rest Inc	2033	E	714 602-3874	1861
Distribution Electrnics Vlued	3699	E	714 368-1717	9864
Diversified Printers Inc	2741	D	714 994-3400	4167
Durabag Company Inc	2673	D	714 259-8811	3883
Earthwise Packaging Inc	3643	F	714 602-2169	9033
Expert Assembly Services Inc	3672	E	714 258-8880	9403
First Team RE - Orange Cnty	6531	C	714 544-5456	15864
Foundation Inc	7372	E	310 294-8955	17860
GL Woodworking Inc	2499	D	949 515-2192	3445
Hall Research Technologies LLC **(PA)**	3577	F	714 641-6607	8260
Hayhoe Construction Corp	1542	D	714 508-2400	769
Hazmat Chemical Storage Inc **(PA)**	3448	F	714 480-1290	6998
Health South Tustin Rehab Hosp	8322	C	714 832-9200	21799
Henrys Adio Vsual Slutions Inc	3651	E	714 258-7238	9178
I L S West Inc	8721	E	714 505-7530	22792
Ifiber Optix Inc	3229	E	714 665-9796	5936
Ii-VI Aerospace & Defense Inc	3827	D	714 247-7100	10840
Impressions Vanity Company **(PA)**	5063	D	844 881-0790	13636
Innovative Diversfd Tech Inc	3572	E	949 455-1701	8205
Integrium LLC **(PA)**	8731	C	714 541-5591	22843
Intepro America LP **(PA)**	3825	E	714 953-2686	10758
Irvine APT Communities LP	6513	C	714 505-7181	15735
Jl Design Enterprises Inc	2321	D	714 479-0240	2757
Jmp Electronics Inc	3672	E	714 730-2086	9418
Kaiser Foundation Hospitals	8062	A	951 353-4000	20802
Kaiser Foundation Hospitals	8082	B	714 734-4500	21177
Kaiser Foundation Hospitals	8011	C	888 988-2800	19921
Kaiser Foundation Hospitals	8011	C	310 325-5111	19938
Kingdomway Usa LLC	2834	F	714 832-9700	4841
Landscape Communications Inc	2721	E	714 979-5276	4079
Laser Image Plus	7379	E	714 556-5277	18197
LGarde Inc	3572	E	714 259-0771	8206
Logomark Inc	5199	C	714 675-6100	14948
Lowes Home Centers LLC	5031	C	714 913-2663	13269
Lsf9 Cypress LP **(PA)**	5039	A	714 380-3127	13333
Lsf9 Cypress Parent LLC **(DH)**	5039	A	714 380-3127	13334
Lsf9 Cypress Parent 2 LLC	5039	A	714 380-3127	13335
Lund Motion Products Inc	3714	E	949 221-0023	10095
M & S Trading Inc	5136	D	714 241-7190	14341
Management Trust Assn Inc **(PA)**	6733	D	714 285-2626	16189
Maverick Hospitality Inc	7011	D	714 730-7717	16562
Mec-CCC S All N One	1389	E	909 529-0013	517
Medium Large LLC	7812	F	424 271-9411	19147
Meganutra Inc	2023	F	949 835-2591	1800
Meridian Graphics Inc	2752	D	949 833-3500	4371
Motionloft Inc	3826	E	415 580-7671	10802
Mt Supply Inc **(DH)**	5085	C	800 938-6658	14006
MTI Technology Corporation **(PA)**	3572	C	949 251-1101	8209
Nissan of Tustin	6159	C	714 669-8282	15166
Oak Tree Furniture Inc	2511	F	562 944-0754	3483
Orange Cnty Rescue Mission Inc **(PA)**	8322	D	714 247-4300	21861
Orange County Direct Mail Inc	7331	E	714 444-4412	17135
Pan American Properties Inc	6512	E	714 505-5544	15689
Pl Variables Inc	3669	F	949 415-9411	9348
Pieology Franchise LLC	6794	D	949 774-2380	16216
Pramira Inc	7379	C	800 678-1169	18214
Precision Offset Inc	2752	D	949 752-1714	4393
Pressed Juicery Inc	2033	F	714 258-7266	1873
Priority Posting and Pubg Inc	2741	F	714 338-2568	4197
Pts Advance	7361	C	949 268-4000	17449
Pvp Advanced Eo Systems Inc	3827	E	714 508-2740	10856
Q Railing USA Inc	2431	F	714 259-1372	3284
R Ranch Market	0291	D	714 573-1182	145
Raj Manufacturing LLC	2339	E	714 838-3110	2988
Raj Manufacturing Inc **(PA)**	6531	F	714 838-3110	15963
Rampone Industries LLC	3496	E	949 581-8701	7510
Rjn Investigations Inc	7381	D	951 686-7638	18318
Roman Cthlic Diocese of Orange	8351	C	714 544-1533	22057
Ronco Plastics Inc	3089	E	714 259-1385	5797
Rtr Bakery Inc	5149	E	714 415-2233	14734
Salvation Army	8322	D	714 832-7100	21881
Schick Moving & Storage Co **(PA)**	4214	D	714 731-5500	12118
Schoolsfirst Federal Credit Un	6061	D	480 777-5995	15087
Southern Cal Prmnnte Med Group	6324	C	714 734-4500	15457
Staar Surgical Company	3851	F	626 303-7902	11264
Sterling Collision LLC **(PA)**	7532	D	714 259-1111	18805
Stuart-Dean Co Inc	3471	F	714 544-4460	7317
Sunny America & Global Autotec	3714	E	714 544-0400	10137
Superior Sod I LP	0181	C	909 923-5068	96
Syspro Impact Software Inc	5045	C	714 437-1000	13444
Systems Printing Inc	2791	F	714 832-4677	4626
Texas Instruments Incorporated	3674	C	714 731-7110	9591
Thermeon Corporation **(PA)**	7372	F	714 731-9191	17995
Tk Elevator Corporation	5084	D	714 423-6340	13949
Toan D Nguyen DDS Inc **(PA)**	8021	D	562 926-3354	20201
Trellborg Sling Sltions US Inc **(DH)**	3841	C	714 415-0280	11067
Tricon American Homes LLC	1521	C	844 874-2661	645
Trinity Brdcstg Netwrk Inc	4833	C	714 665-3619	12744
Trinity Christian Center of SA **(PA)**	4833	C	714 665-3619	12745
Urban Futures Inc	8748	D	714 283-9334	23521
US Best Repair Service Inc	1521	C	888 750-2378	647
US Facility Solutions LLC **(PA)**	8744	D	888 904-7900	23397
US Print & Toner Inc	3955	E	619 562-6995	11483
Werner Systems Inc	3355	E	714 838-4444	6330
Wood Gutmann Bogart Insur Brkg	6411	D	714 505-7000	15651
Woodbridge Glass Inc	1793	C	714 838-4444	1590
Worldstage Inc **(PA)**	8741	D	714 508-1858	23142
Xp Power LLC	5065	D	714 597-7100	13786
Yebo Group Inc	2652	E	949 502-3317	3780
Youngs Market Company LLC **(HQ)**	5182	B	800 317-6150	14848

TWENTYNINE PALMS, CA - San Bernardino County

	SIC	EMP	PHONE	ENTRY #
29 Palms Inn	7011	D	760 367-3505	16308
Mark Clemons	4213	C	760 361-1531	12062
Navy United States Department	8099	D	760 830-2124	21458

UNIVERSAL CITY, CA - Los Angeles County

	SIC	EMP	PHONE	ENTRY #
Creative Park Productions LLC	7812	B	818 622-3702	19112
Hilton Los Angles Universal Cy	7011	C	818 506-2500	16477
Hilton Universal Hotel	7011	D	818 506-2500	16479
Lh Universal Operating LLC	7011	B	818 980-1212	16541
NBC Subsidiary (knbc-Tv) LLC	4833	C	818 684-5746	12734
NBC Universal Studios Inc **(HQ)**	7812	D	818 777-5000	19155
Shen Zhen New World II LLC	7011	D	818 980-1212	16704
Sprint Communications Co LP	4813	C	818 755-7100	12671
Sun Hill Properties Inc **(HQ)**	7011	C	818 506-2500	16738
Universal Cble Productions LLC	7929	D	818 777-0351	19383
Universal Cy Stdios Prdctons L **(DH)**	7812	A	818 777-1000	19193
Universal Mus Group Dist Corp	7389	D	818 508-9550	18709
Universal Pctres HM Entrmt LLC **(DH)**	7812	A	818 777-1000	19194
Universal Stdios Licensing LLC	6794	C	818 695-1273	16221

UPLAND, CA - San Bernardino County

	SIC	EMP	PHONE	ENTRY #
10 Gauge Sheet Metal Inc	3444	F	909 208-4525	6768
Allied Prof Nursing Care Inc	8082	D	909 949-1066	21131
Analytik Jena US LLC **(DH)**	3826	D	909 946-3197	10779
Applied Instrument Tech Inc	3826	E	909 204-3700	10781
B & L Consulting LLC	8748	D	682 238-6994	23416
Bms Parent Inc **(PA)**	8721	D	909 981-2341	22761
Bni Enterprises Inc	8743	A	909 305-1818	23375
Bowlero Corp	7933	D	909 946-7006	19390
C P Construction Co Inc	1623	E	909 981-1091	939
California Ldscp & Design Inc	0782	C	909 949-1601	295
California Ramp Works Inc	3448	F	909 949-1601	6989
California Skateparks	0781	C	909 949-1601	250
Camstar International Inc	5072	D	909 931-2540	13798
CCL Label (delaware) Inc	2759	C	909 608-2260	4492
Charles Meisner Inc	3544	E	909 946-8216	7786
Claremont Inst For The Study O **(PA)**	2759	F	909 981-2200	4495
Coast Cutters Co	3312	F	626 444-2965	6197
Diamond Ridge Corporation	6531	C	909 949-0605	15837
Dimic Steel Tech Inc	3444	E	909 946-6767	6820
Easter Seals Southern Cal Inc	8322	D	909 981-4668	21775
Edco Die Inc	3544	E	909 985-4417	7798
Employnet Inc	7361	C	909 458-0961	17419
Exhaust Center Inc	3444	F	951 685-8602	6833
EZ Lube LLC	7549	D	909 920-0476	18927
Families Chice HM Care Svcs In	8322	D	909 303-9377	21780
Firstsight Vision Services Inc **(DH)**	8042	E	909 920-5008	20205
Gar Enterprises	3679	E	909 985-4575	9714
Garhauer Marine Corporation	3429	E	909 985-9993	6519
Garrett J Gentry Gen Engrg Inc	8711	D	909 693-3391	22560
Hamilton Brwart Insur Agcy LLC	6411	D	909 920-3250	15577
Helens Place Inc	2752	E	909 981-5715	4314
Holliday Trucking Inc **(PA)**	3273	D	909 982-1553	6096
Inland Empire Therapy Provider **(PA)**	8049	D	909 985-7905	20216
Inland Valley News Inc	2711	F	909 949-3099	3995
Innovativetek Inc	3699	F	909 981-3401	9872
Judith Von Hopf Inc	2541	E	909 481-1884	3654
La Bath Vanity Inc **(PA)**	2434	F	909 303-3323	3325
Largo Concrete Inc	1771	B	909 981-7844	1537
Lewis Companies **(PA)**	1531	C	909 985-0971	681
Lewis Development Co **(PA)**	1542	C	909 946-7506	783

GEOGRAPHIC

Employment Codes: A=Over 500 employees, B=251-500, C=101-250, D=51-100, E=20-50 F=10-19

2022 Southern California Business Directory and Buyers Guide

© Mergent Inc. 1-800-342-5647

1443

	SIC	EMP	PHONE	ENTRY #
Lexxiom Inc	8741	B	909 581-7313	23051
Lowes Home Centers LLC	5031	C	909 982-4795	13232
Mladen Buntich Cnstr Co Inc	1623	D	909 920-9977	963
Montclair Wood Corporation	2426	F	909 985-0302	3222
Motobell USA Inc	3663	F	909 608-2830	9297
Mountain View Chevrolet Inc	7532	D	909 985-2866	18796
Paat & Kimmel Development Inc	1542	D	909 315-8074	798
Pacific Surveys LLC	1389	F	909 949-0850	534
Park Place Ford LLC	7532	D	909 946-5555	18797
Plum Creek Timberlands LP	2421	C	909 949-2255	3212
Reach Out West End	8399	D	909 982-8641	22209
San Antnio Ambltory Srgcal Ctr	8011	D	909 579-1500	20048
San Antonio Regional Hospital **(PA)**	8062	A	909 985-2811	20928
Sapphire Softech Solutions LLC	7379	D	888 357-5222	18220
Scheu Manufacturing Co **(PA)**	3433	F	909 982-8933	6575
Sela Healthcare Inc **(PA)**	8051	C	909 985-1981	20462
Shield Security Inc	7381	B	909 920-1173	18336
Sign Development Inc	3993	F	909 920-5535	11595
Sport Pins International Inc	3961	F	909 985-4549	11491
St Marks Episcopal Church	8351	D	909 920-5565	22059
Upland Community Care Inc	8051	C	909 985-1903	20492
V C A Central Animal Hospital	0742	D	909 981-2855	203
Vci Construction LLC **(HQ)**	1623	D	909 946-0905	983
Victoria Place Community Assn	8699	D	909 981-4131	22468
Walton Electric Corporation	3669	C	909 981-5051	9359
Welch Management Corporation	7231	D	909 981-4302	16920
Western Inn Upland Co Inc	7011	D	909 949-4800	16784

VALENCIA, CA - Los Angeles County

	SIC	EMP	PHONE	ENTRY #
A & M Electronics Inc	3672	E	661 257-3680	9369
AAA Elctrcal Cmmunications Inc **(PA)**	1731	C	800 892-4784	1207
Academy Swim Club	7997	D	661 702-8585	19527
Access Networks Inc **(PA)**	7379	D	310 453-1800	18155
Acousticfab LLC **(DH)**	3492	D	661 257-2242	7453
Adept Fasteners Inc **(PA)**	5072	C	661 257-6600	13789
Advanced Bionics LLC	3845	E	310 819-4004	11213
Advanced Bionics Corporation **(HQ)**	3842	A	661 362-1400	11082
Advantage Media Services Inc	4225	D	661 705-7588	12183
Advantage Media Services Inc **(PA)**	4783	C	661 775-0611	12554
Aero Engrg & Mfg Co Cal LLC	3728	E	661 295-0875	10243
Aero Sense Inc	3728	F	661 257-1608	10245
Aerospace Dynamics Intl Inc **(DH)**	3728	B	661 257-3535	10250
Aerospace Service & Controls	3728	F	818 833-0088	10254
Aftermarket Services	3728	F	610 251-1000	10256
Air Flow Research Heads Inc	3714	E	661 257-8124	10012
Air Frame Mfg & Supply Co Inc	5088	E	661 257-7728	14048
Allied International LLC **(PA)**	5072	E	818 364-2333	13791
American Med & Hosp Sup Co Inc	5047	E	661 294-1213	13472
Apogee Manufacturing	3599	F	661 467-0440	8498
Applied Companies RE LLC	6512	E	661 257-0090	15660
Aquafine Corporation **(HQ)**	3589	D	661 257-4770	8363
ASC Process Systems Inc	3567	C	818 833-0088	8084
ASC Process Systems Internati	3443	F	818 833-0088	6725
At Battery Company Inc	5063	E	661 775-2020	13615
Atk Audiotek	1731	D	661 705-3700	1217
Automobile Club Southern Cal	8699	D	661 259-6222	22431
Avantus Aerospace Inc **(DH)**	3728	C	661 295-8620	10282
Avibank Mfg Inc	3429	D	661 257-2329	6503
Avion Tl Mfg Machining Ctr Inc	3599	F	661 257-2915	8509
Avita Medical Americas LLC	5047	D	661 367-9170	13478
Bayless Engineering Inc	3599	C	661 257-3373	8518
Bbk Specialties Inc	3261	F	661 255-2857	5991
Bertelsmann Inc	2731	A	661 702-2700	4121
Bioness Inc	3845	C	661 362-4850	11216
Bloomers Metal Stampings Inc	3469	E	661 257-2955	7129
Bluemark Inc	5199	C	323 230-0770	14915
Boston Scientific Corporation	3841	E	800 678-2575	10952
Boston Scntfic Nrmdlation Corp **(HQ)**	3842	B	661 949-4310	11092
C A Rasmussen Inc **(PA)**	1629	E	661 367-9040	990
California Strl Concepts Inc	1542	E	661 257-6903	750
Canyon Engineering Pdts Inc	3728	D	661 294-0084	10296
Canyon Plastics Inc	3089	D	800 350-6325	5598
Capax Technologies Inc	3629	E	661 257-7666	8972
CC Wellness LLC **(PA)**	5122	D	661 714-0841	14236
CF Valencia Arcis LLC	7997	D	661 254-4401	19553
Cicoil LLC	5065	D	661 295-1295	13709
Circle W Enterprises Inc	3496	E	661 257-2400	7497
Classic Wire Cut Company Inc	3599	C	661 257-0558	8555
Cornerstone Display Group Inc	3993	E	661 705-1700	11537
Cosmic Plastics Inc **(PA)**	2821	E	661 257-3274	4684
Creatons Grdn Ntral Fd Mkts In	2833	F	661 877-4280	4742
Crissair Inc	3594	C	661 367-3300	8443
Curran Engineering Company Inc	3446	E	800 643-6353	6958
Curtiss-Wrght Cntrls Intgrted **(DH)**	8711	D	661 257-4430	22524
Curtiss-Wright Flow Control	3491	C	626 851-3100	7442
Cypress Manufacturing LLC	3089	F	818 477-2777	5619
D C Shower Doors Inc	4213	C	661 257-1177	12028
Del West Engineering Inc **(PA)**	3714	C	661 295-5700	10043
Delta Printing Solutions Inc	2752	C	661 257-0584	4274
Dharma Ventures Group Inc **(PA)**	6719	B	661 294-4200	16099
Eckert Zegler Isotope Pdts Inc **(HQ)**	3829	E	661 309-1010	10879
Efs West	8711	E	661 705-8200	22538
Electrofilm Mfg Co LLC	3492	D	661 257-2242	7456
Engeo Incorporated	8999	C	661 257-4004	23532
Exclusive Powder Coatings Inc	3479	E	661 294-9812	7364
Falcon Aerospace Holdings LLC	5088	A	661 775-7200	14056
Fasthouse Inc	3949	F	661 775-5963	11416
Fdsi Logistics LLC	8742	D	818 971-3300	23214
Fidelity Security Services Inc	7381	D	661 295-5007	18274
Finance America Mortgage LLC	6162	D	661 775-6253	15193
Flight Line Products LLC	1799	D	661 775-8366	1658
Foilflex Products Inc	2759	F	661 702-0775	4515
Forrest Machining Llc	3728	C	661 257-0231	10331
Fpk Security Inc	7381	B	661 702-9091	18275
Fruit Growers Supply Company **(PA)**	2653	E	888 997-4855	3802
Galaxy Die and Engineering Inc	3366	E	661 775-9301	6408
Geologics Corporation	8748	B	661 259-5767	23445
Global Aerospace Tech Corp	3728	E	818 407-5600	10338
Global Building Services Inc **(PA)**	7349	A	800 675-6643	17247
Gothic Landscaping Inc	0781	D	661 257-5085	259
Grace To You **(PA)**	4832	D	661 295-5777	12692
Green Convergence **(PA)**	5074	D	661 294-9495	13829
Gruber Systems Inc	3544	E	661 257-0464	7805
H2scan Corporation	3829	E	661 775-9575	10886
Hardcore Racing Components LLC	3944	F	661 294-5032	11375
Hemisphere Design & Mfg LLC	2541	F	661 294-9500	3649
Henry Mayo Newhall Mem Hosp	8011	D	661 253-8[illegible]12	19840
Henry Mayo Newhall Mem Hosp **(PA)**	8062	A	661 253-8000	20785
Henry Mayo Nwhall Mem Hlth Fnd	8062	A	661 253-8000	20787
Heritage Golf Group LLC	7992	C	661 254-4401	19493
Hrd Aero Systems Inc **(PA)**	7699	C	661 295-0670	19042
Hydro Systems Inc **(PA)**	3431	D	661 775-0686	6547
Hypercel Corporation	5065	D	661 310-1000	13727
Ibg Holdings Inc	2844	E	661 702-8680	5031
Image 2000 Inc **(PA)**	7699	E	818 781-2200	19043
Indu-Electric North Amer Inc **(PA)**	3568	E	310 578-2144	8104
Industrial Tube Company LLC	3492	D	661 295-4000	7458
Input/Output Technology Inc	3577	E	661 257-1000	8267
ITT Aerospace Controls LLC	3728	B	661 295-4000	10360
JT Wimsatt Contg Co Inc **(PA)**	1771	B	661 775-8090	1535
King Henrys Inc	2096	E	818 536-3692	2362
Klm Laboratories Inc	5047	D	661 295-2600	13498
Krg Technologies Inc	7371	B	661 257-9967	17650
L3 Technologies Inc	3812	C	818 833-2500	10596
LA Turbine **(HQ)**	3511	D	661 294-8290	7587
Landscape Development Inc **(PA)**	0782	B	661 295-1970	321
Lavi Industries **(PA)**	3446	D	877 275-5284	6971
Legacy Commercial Holdings Inc	2511	E	818 767-6626	3476
Leggett & Platt Incorporated	2541	E	661 775-8500	3657
Leiner Health Products Inc	2834	D	661 775-1422	4845
Leonards Molded Products Inc	3069	E	661 253-2227	5388
Lief Organics LLC **(PA)**	2834	E	661 775-2500	4846
Lightway Industries	3646	E	661 257-0286	9095
Lockwood Industries LLC **(PA)**	3674	C	661 702-6999	9532
Luran Inc	3599	E	661 257-6303	8668
M W Sausse & Co Inc **(PA)**	3625	D	661 257-3311	8959
Magic Acquisition Corp	7538	B	661 332-4700	18852
Master & Sons Inc	7349	D	661 299-9090	17259
Mastey De Paris Inc	2844	E	661 257-4814	5045
Maxim Healthcare Services Inc	7363	D	661 964-6350	17498
Mechanix Wear LLC **(PA)**	2381	C	800 222-4296	3049
Medianews Group Inc	2711	C	661 257-5200	4009
Medical Brkthrugh Mssage Chirs	3999	E	408 677-7702	11712
Mercury Insurance Company	6331	B	661 291-6470	15475
Mye Technologies Inc	3699	E	661 964-0217	9894
N Qiagen Amercn Holdings Inc **(HQ)**	5122	C	800 426-8157	14266
Nasmyth Tmf Inc	3471	D	818 954-9504	7285
Neasi-Weber International LLC **(PA)**	7371	E	818 895-6900	17668
Neotech Products LLC	5047	D	661 775-7466	13504
Neurosurgical Associates **(PA)**	8011	D	661 799-2542	19991
Next Point Bearing Group LLC	3562	E	818 988-1880	8029
Nextclientcom Inc	2741	F	661 222-7755	4192
Nite-Lite Signs Inc	1799	E	818 341-0987	1678
Northeast Valley Health Corp	8011	D	661 287-1551	19998
Novacap LLC	5065	B	661 295-5920	13757
Oakridge Landscape Inc **(PA)**	0721	C	661 295-7228	148
Orange Health Solutions Inc	7371	D	661 310-9333	17686
Pacific Lock Company **(PA)**	3429	E	661 294-3707	6532
Pacific Metal Stampings Inc	3469	E	661 257-7656	7172
Packaging Dist Assembly Group	2631	F	661 607-0600	3776
Penn Engineering Components	5072	E	818 503-1511	13815
Performance Machine Tech Inc	3599	E	661 294-8617	8739
Pharma Alliance Group Inc	2834	F	661 294-7955	4871
Plasma Coating Tech Inc	3479	F	661 670-8810	7399
PRC - Desoto International Inc **(HQ)**	2891	B	661 678-4209	5191
Precision Dynamics Corporation **(HQ)**	2672	C	818 897-1111	3873
Princess Cruises and Tours Inc **(HQ)**	4724	D	206 336-6000	12398
Princeton Tool Inc	3724	F	661 257-1380	10223
Professional Skin Care Inc **(PA)**	2844	E	661 257-7771	5063
Pyramid Enterprises Inc **(PA)**	7999	D	661 702-1420	19662
Qmp Inc	3589	E	661 294-6860	8407
Quadriga USA Enterprises Inc	2679	F	888 669-9994	3937
Quest Dgnstics Clncal Labs Inc	8071	D	661 964-6582	21090
Regent Aerospace Corporation **(PA)**	1799	C	661 257-3000	1684
Remo Inc **(PA)**	3931	B	661 294-5600	11350
Ronan Engineering Company **(PA)**	3823	D	661 702-1344	10720
SA Kitsinian Inc	5094	F	818 988-9961	14138
Sage Staffing Consultants Inc **(PA)**	7363	C	661 254-4026	17515
Salvador Ramirez	3724	F	661 702-1813	10224
Santa Clarita Plastic Molding	3089	E	661 294-2257	5812
Schrey & Sons Mold Co Inc	3544	E	661 294-2260	7831
Scicon Technologies Corp **(PA)**	8711	E	661 295-8630	22652
Scorpion Design LLC	8742	A	661 702-0100	23317
Semiconductor Process Eqp Corp	3674	E	661 257-0934	9572
SGB Enterprises Inc	3575	E	661 294-8306	8228

Mergent email: customerrelations@mergent.com
1444

2022 Southern California Business
Directory and Buyers Guide

(P-0000) Products & Services Section entry number
(PA)=Parent Co (HQ)=Headquarters (DH)=Div Headquarters

	SIC	EMP	PHONE	ENTRY #
Sgl Technic LLC **(DH)**	3295	D	661 257-0500	6168
Shield-Denver Health Care Ctr **(HQ)**	5047	C	661 294-4200	13518
Skm Industries Inc	3469	F	661 294-8373	7182
Softub Inc **(PA)**	3999	D	858 602-1920	11759
Southern California Edison Co	8741	C	661 607-0207	23114
Specialty Laboratories Inc **(DH)**	8071	A	661 799-6543	21096
Specialty Motors Inc	3621	F	800 232-2612	8932
Spencer Aerospace Mfg LLC	3492	D	805 452-3536	7460
Standard Lumber Company Inc **(HQ)**	2448	E	559 651-2037	3409
Star Nail Products Inc	5122	D	661 257-3376	14292
Stoll Metalcraft Inc	3444	C	661 295-0401	6920
Stratasys Direct Inc **(DH)**	3089	C	661 295-4400	5832
Stratoflight **(DH)**	3728	D	949 622-0700	10423
Summer Systems Inc	1542	D	661 257-4419	835
Summit Electric & Data Inc	3699	F	661 775-9901	9918
Sunco Lighting Inc	5063	E	844 334-9938	13669
Sunkist Growers Inc **(PA)**	5148	C	661 290-8900	14658
Sunstar Spa Covers Inc **(HQ)**	3999	E	858 602-1950	11767
Sunvair Inc **(HQ)**	3599	D	661 294-3777	8805
Sunvair Aerospace Group Inc **(PA)**	7699	D	661 294-3777	19072
Sunvair Overhaul Inc	3728	E	661 257-6123	10424
Synergy Microsystems Inc **(DH)**	3571	D	858 452-0020	8177
Ta Aerospace Co **(DH)**	3069	C	661 775-1100	5414
Ta Aerospace Co	2821	C	661 702-0448	4721
Talladium Inc **(PA)**	3843	E	661 295-0900	11198
Tape Specialty Inc	5065	E	661 702-9030	13780
Tara Enterprises Inc	2434	F	661 510-2206	3340
Teague Custom Marine Inc	7699	E	661 295-7000	19075
Technical Manufacturing W LLC	3999	E	661 295-7226	11776
Technical Trouble Shooting Inc	3599	F	661 257-1202	8813
Technifex Products LLC	3291	E	661 294-3800	6159
Timemed Labeling Systems Inc **(DH)**	3069	D	818 897-1111	5415
Transparent Products Inc	3575	E	661 294-9787	8229
Tri Tek Electronics Inc	3679	E	661 295-0020	9798
Triumph Acttion Systems - Vlnc	3728	C	661 702-7537	10436
True Position Technologies LLC	3599	D	661 294-0030	8826
Ultraviolet Devices Inc	5075	D	661 295-8140	13850
Universal Hosiery Inc	2252	D	661 702-8444	2624
Urm Technologies Inc	8741	E	661 705-0500	23134
US Healthworks Inc **(DH)**	8011	D	661 678-2300	20127
US Horizon Manufacturing Inc	3211	E	661 775-1675	5925
Utak Laboratories Inc	2869	E	661 294-3935	5152
V M P Inc	3451	F	661 294-9934	7049
Valencia Pipe Company	3084	D	661 257-3923	5472
Valencia Plastics Inc	3089	F	661 257-0066	5855
Vertiflex Inc	3841	E	442 325-5900	11074
Virgil Walker Inc	3441	F	661 797-4101	6680
Virgil Walker Inc	3675	E	661 294-9142	9615
Vitek Indus Video Pdts Inc	3861	E	661 294-8043	11298
Volunteers of Amer Los Angeles	8322	D	661 290-2829	21915
Wayforward Technologies Inc	7371	E	661 286-2769	17758
Wesco Aircraft Hardware Corp	5088	B	661 775-7200	14071
Weslar Inc	1751	D	661 702-1362	1463
Whi Solutions Inc	5045	C	661 257-2120	13452
Whitmor Plstic Wire Cable Corp	3496	E	661 257-2400	7523
Winning Team Inc	2395	F	661 295-1428	3165

VALLEY VILLAGE, CA - Los Angeles County

	SIC	EMP	PHONE	ENTRY #
Adat ARI El	8351	C	818 766-4992	21981
Afm & Sg-Ftra Intllctual Prprt	7389	D	818 255-7980	18437
Cannalogic	3999	F	619 458-0775	11648
Douglas Steel Supply Inc **(PA)**	5051	D	323 587-7676	13564
FBproductions Inc	2752	F	818 773-9337	4292
Healthy Medical Solutions Inc	8099	D	818 974-1980	21435
Midrange Software Inc	7372	F	818 762-8539	17916

VAN NUYS, CA - Los Angeles County

	SIC	EMP	PHONE	ENTRY #
1370 Realty Corp	6531	E	818 817-0092	15762
412280 Inc **(DH)**	5139	D	209 545-1111	14427
911 Restoration Entps Inc **(PA)**	1799	C	818 373-4880	1629
Advance Overhead Door Inc	3442	E	818 781-5590	6688
Advanced Circuits Inc	3672	F	818 345-1993	9373
Advanced Mobility Inc	3999	F	818 780-1788	11627
Aero-Nasch Aviation Inc	3728	F	818 786-5480	10247
Aeroshear Aviation Svcs Inc **(PA)**	3728	E	818 779-1650	10248
AG Air Conditioning & Htg Inc	1711	E	818 988-5388	1019
Air Lease Corp **(PA)**	7359	D	818 387-8924	17330
Airespring Inc	4813	D	818 786-8990	12624
Alfred Music Group Inc **(PA)**	2731	C	818 891-5999	4119
All American Cabinetry Inc	2541	E	818 376-0500	3636
All Valley Washer Service Inc	7215	D	818 787-1100	16871
Allison-Kaufman Co	3911	E	818 373-5100	11308
Alta Hllywood Cmnty Hosp Van N	8063	A	818 787-1511	21012
Alyn Industries Inc	3679	D	818 988-7696	9672
Ambay Circuits Inc	3672	E	818 786-8241	9376
American Prof Ambulance Corp	4119	D	818 996-2200	11852
Anatex Enterprises Inc	5092	E	818 908-1888	14091
Apprentice Jrnymen Trning Tr F	8331	C	310 604-0892	21938
Apu Inc **(PA)**	5013	D	661 948-2880	13041
Archwood Mfg Group Inc	1411	F	818 781-7673	560
Aspire Bakeries LLC	2052	D	818 904-8230	2057
Auto Gallery **(PA)**	7539	D	818 884-4411	18893
Auto-Chlor System Wash Inc	2842	F	818 376-0940	4954
Avid Technology Inc	3861	C	818 779-7860	11268
Bijan Rad Inc	3559	F	818 902-1606	7966
Brica Inc **(HQ)**	5199	D	818 893-5000	14916
Broadstreet Solar Inc	1711	E	818 206-1464	1039
Broadway AC Htg & Shtmtl	3444	E	818 781-1477	6798
Burtree Inc	3599	E	818 786-4276	8534
C & L Graphics Inc	2752	F	818 785-8310	4243
Caine & Weiner Company Inc **(PA)**	7322	D	818 226-6000	17105
Capstone Green Energy Corp **(PA)**	3511	C	818 734-5300	7580
CCS Los Angeles Janitorial LLC **(HQ)**	7349	E	818 455-4551	17223
CDM Corp	2844	F	818 787-4002	4999
Century-National Insurance Co **(DH)**	6311	B	818 760-0880	15359
Certemy Inc	7372	F	866 907-4088	17812
Challenge Graphics Inc	2752	E	818 892-0123	4250
Chef Merito Inc **(PA)**	2099	D	818 787-0100	2407
Cicon Engineering Inc **(PA)**	3679	C	818 909-6060	9692
Cinema Secrets Inc	2389	D	818 846-0579	3070
City Tile & Stone Tile Inc	1743	D	818 994-0100	1413
Clay Lacy Aviation Inc **(PA)**	4581	B	818 989-2900	12349
Color Fx Inc	2759	F	877 763-7671	4500
Consolidated Fabricators Corp **(PA)**	3443	C	818 901-1005	6738
Consumer Safety Analytics LLC	8734	D	818 922-2416	22936
Contex Inc	3851	F	818 788-5836	11247
Csa Silicon Valley LLC	8071	D	818 922-2416	21065
D&A Metal Fabrication Inc	3441	F	818 780-8231	6615
Dal-Tile Corporation	5032	F	818 780-1301	13301
Data Lights Rigging LLC	3613	E	818 786-0536	8894
Delta D V H Circuits Inc	3672	F	818 786-8241	9398
Dewitt Stern Group Inc	6411	C	818 933-2700	15560
Dfs Flooring Inc **(PA)**	1752	D	818 374-5200	1466
Digital Room Holdings Inc **(PA)**	2759	C	310 575-4440	4507
Dolce Dolci LLC	2024	F	818 343-8400	1814
E & S International Entps Inc **(PA)**	5064	C	818 887-0700	13684
E Alko Inc	3955	E	818 587-9700	11476
EDN Aviation Inc	7699	E	818 988-8826	19035
Edwards Sheet Metal Supply Inc	3444	E	818 785-8600	6824
Energy Enterprises USA Inc **(PA)**	1711	D	424 339-0005	1062
Enterprises Industries Inc	3469	C	818 989-6103	7144
Espana Metal Craft Inc	3444	F	818 988-4988	6829
Far East Landscape & Maint Inc	0782	D	800 887-3227	305
Felix Tool & Engineering	3544	F	830 947-4601	7801
Flannigans Merchandising Inc	2759	F	818 785-7428	4514
Foothill Child Dev Svcs Inc	8351	D	818 353-3772	22017
Fusefx LLC	7819	B	818 237-5052	19236
Ganz USA LLC	8742	D	818 901-0077	23223
George M Rajacich MD PC	8011	E	818 787-2020	19830
Gold Metropolitan Media **(PA)**	2399	E	818 348-1913	3198
Goodnight Industries Inc	3999	F	818 988-2801	11681
Great Western Packaging LLC	2759	D	818 464-3800	4523
Greater Valley Medical Group	8093	C	818 781-7097	21309
Grht Inc	5199	D	323 873-6393	14933
Gulfstream Aerospace Corp GA	3721	E	805 236-5755	10190
H & H Nail Products Inc	5122	F	818 902-9995	14247
Haemo-Stat Inc **(DH)**	8092	D	818 908-0371	21244
Hamburger Home	8361	D	818 980-3200	22107
Happy Cells Inc	2086	F	818 528-5080	2268
Hollywood Software Inc	7372	E	818 205-2121	17879
I and E Cabinets Inc	2434	E	818 933-6480	3320
Icon Media Direct Inc **(PA)**	7311	D	818 995-6400	17018
Industrial Elctrnic Engners In	3577	D	818 787-0311	8264
Industrial Media Inc	7819	C	310 777-1940	19238
International Prtg & Typsg Inc	2752	F	818 787-6804	4340
Interviewing Service Amer LLC **(PA)**	8732	C	818 989-1044	22888
Investment Enterprises Inc **(PA)**	2759	E	818 464-3800	4530
Jet Edge International LLC **(PA)**	4581	D	818 442-0096	12359
Jet/Brella Inc	3724	E	818 786-5480	10219
Jewish Family Service of	8322	D	818 988-7682	21821
Katzirs Floor & HM Design Inc **(PA)**	5023	E	818 988-9663	13175
Kay Automotive Distrs Inc **(PA)**	5013	E	818 781-6850	13070
Keolis Transit America Inc	4111	C	818 616-5254	11813
Keyes Motors Inc **(PA)**	7538	D	818 782-0122	18848
Keylex Inc **(PA)**	7538	D	818 379-4000	18849
Kimball Nelson Inc	3999	F	310 636-0081	11701
L A Party Rents Inc	7359	D	818 989-4300	17360
L3harris Technologies Inc	3812	B	818 901-2523	10597
Lees Maintenance Service Inc	7349	B	818 988-6644	17257
Linea Pelle Inc **(PA)**	3111	F	310 231-9950	5871
Los Angeles Police Credit Un **(PA)**	6062	D	818 787-6520	15114
Louroe Electronics Inc	7382	E	818 994-6498	18394
M P M Building Services Inc	2842	E	818 708-9676	4970
Medresponse **(PA)**	4119	C	818 442-9222	11880
Microfabrica Inc	3679	E	888 964-2763	9749
Microlease Inc **(DH)**	7359	D	866 520-0200	17363
Modern Studio Equipment Inc	3861	F	818 764-8574	11284
Momentous Insurance Brkg Inc	6411	D	818 933-2700	15596
Monarch Art & Frame Inc	7699	E	818 373-6180	19051
Mp Aero LLC	1799	D	818 901-9828	1677
Munchkin Inc **(PA)**	3085	C	800 344-2229	5476
Nafees Memon	7381	D	818 997-1666	18300
Napoleon Perdis Cosmetics Inc	5122	D	323 817-3611	14267
National Commercial Services	7322	D	818 701-4400	17115
Neiman/Hoeller Inc	3993	D	818 781-8600	11577
Neopacific Holdings Inc	3089	E	818 786-2900	5724
Niknejad Inc	2752	E	310 477-0407	4380
Northeast Valley Health Corp	8011	D	818 778-6240	20000
Onegeneration **(PA)**	8351	D	818 708-6625	22044
Optical Zonu Corporation	3661	F	818 780-9701	9239
Orly International Inc **(PA)**	2844	D	818 994-1001	5054
Parkwood Landscape Maint Inc	0782	D	818 988-9677	335
Photo Fabricators Inc	3672	D	818 781-1010	9438
Postcard Press Inc **(PA)**	2759	E	855 898-9870	4557
Power Brands Consulting LLC	2082	E	818 989-9646	2153

GEOGRAPHIC

Employment Codes: A=Over 500 employees, B=251-500, C=101-250, D=51-100, E=20-50 F=10-19
2022 Southern California Business Directory and Buyers Guide
© Mergent Inc. 1-800-342-5647
1445

	SIC	EMP	PHONE	ENTRY #
Precision Glass Bevelling Inc	3229	F	818 989-2727	5940
Pride Collision Centers Inc **(HQ)**	7532	D	818 909-0660	18800
Primex Clinical Labs Inc **(PA)**	8071	D	818 779-0496	21087
Printcom Inc	2752	F	818 891-8282	4395
Printrunner LLC	2752	E	888 296-5760	4403
Prolabs Factory Inc	2844	E	818 646-3677	5064
Prudential Insur Co of Amer	6411	D	818 901-0028	15619
Rbg Holdings Corp **(PA)**	3949	A	818 782-6445	11441
Repairtech International Inc	4581	E	818 989-2681	12366
Riggins Engineering Inc	3599	E	818 782-7010	8768
Rof LLC	2326	E	818 933-4000	2788
Rothlisberger Mfg A Cal Corp	3599	F	818 786-9462	8777
RPC Legacy Inc	3429	F	818 787-9000	6534
S G D Enterprises	0782	E	323 658-1047	340
San Frnndo Vly Cmnty Mntal HLT **(PA)**	8093	D	818 901-4830	21337
Search Associates Inc	7361	D	818 988-5600	17463
SGB Better Baking Co LLC	2051	D	818 787-9992	2033
SGB Bubbles Baking Co LLC	2051	D	818 786-1700	2034
Shelcore Inc **(PA)**	3944	E	818 883-2400	11390
Showbiz Enterprises Inc **(PA)**	7359	E	818 989-5005	17371
Sistone Inc	2541	F	818 988-9918	3665
SMA Builders Inc	1521	E	818 994-8306	642
Southern Cal Orthpd Inst LP **(PA)**	8011	C	818 901-6600	20074
Southland Rgonal Assn Realtors **(PA)**	8611	D	818 786-2110	22260
Spec Engineering Co Inc	3599	E	818 780-3045	8800
Superior Inds Intl Hldings LLC **(HQ)**	3714	C	818 781-4973	10138
Sylmark Inc **(PA)**	8741	D	818 217-2000	23119
Synchronized Technologies Inc	3577	F	213 368-3760	8304
Tek Enterprises Inc	3679	F	818 785-5971	9791
Thompson Gundrilling Inc	3321	E	323 873-4045	6260
Town & Cntry Event Rentals Inc **(PA)**	7359	B	818 908-4211	17379
United Audio Video Group Inc	3695	E	818 980-6700	9842
United Parcel Service Inc	4215	C	404 828-6000	12159
Valley Clark Plbg & Htg Co Inc **(PA)**	1711	E	818 782-1047	1160
Valley Presbyterian Hospital	8062	A	818 782-6600	21000
Van Nuys Care Center Inc	8059	D	818 343-0700	20637
Vanowen Medical Associates	8011	D	818 778-1920	20133
Velocity Arospc - Edn AVI Inc	8711	F	818 988-8826	22692
Western Bagel Baking Corp **(PA)**	2051	C	818 786-5847	2049
Weststar Cinemas Inc	7832	C	818 779-0323	19290
Wsw Corp **(PA)**	3714	E	818 989-5008	10160
Zodiak Services America	3728	E	310 884-7200	10450

VANDENBERG AFB, CA - Santa Barbara County

	SIC	EMP	PHONE	ENTRY #
Henry Call Inc	8744	C	805 734-2762	23392
Indyne Inc	8744	C	805 606-7225	23393
Securtas Crtcal Infrstrcture S	7381	B	805 685-1100	18330
Sumaria Systems Inc	8711	D	805 606-4973	22663
United Launch Alliance LLC	3761	C	303 269-5876	10524

VENICE, CA - Los Angeles County

	SIC	EMP	PHONE	ENTRY #
Alpargatas Usa Inc	3144	E	646 277-7171	5878
Enervee Corporation	7374	D	650 996-7048	18086
Flat Planet Inc	3559	E	310 392-0683	7976
Flex Company **(PA)**	3069	E	424 209-2711	5377
Frankies Bikinis LLC	2369	E	323 354-4133	3041
Gamemine LLC	7372	E	310 310-3105	17864
Intrinsik Envmtl Sciences Inc	8748	D	310 392-6462	23454
Los Angles Cnty Mtro Trnsp Aut	4111	A	310 392-8636	11827
Mad Dogg Athletics Inc **(PA)**	5137	D	310 823-7008	14396
Outrigger Hotels Hawaii	7011	D	310 301-2000	16601
Parking Concepts Inc	7521	C	310 821-1081	18774
Saje Natural Wellness USA Inc **(HQ)**	8099	D	310 317-0421	21476
St Joseph Center	8322	D	310 396-6468	21895
Swartz Glass Company Inc **(PA)**	1793	F	310 392-0001	1589
Syng Inc	3651	D	770 354-0915	9198
T3 Micro Inc **(PA)**	3999	F	310 452-2888	11770
Trg Inc	6531	D	310 396-6750	16018
Venice Fmly Clinic Foundation **(PA)**	8011	C	310 664-7703	20134
Wetransfer Corporation	7371	D	626 626-5565	17761
Windward Yacht & Repair Inc	3732	F	310 823-4581	10476

VENTURA, CA - Ventura County

	SIC	EMP	PHONE	ENTRY #
A M Ortega Construction Inc	1521	D	951 360-1352	589
Aegis Senior Communities LLC	8082	C	805 650-1114	21128
Aera Energy LLC	5172	D	661 427-9717	14799
Agi Holding Corp **(HQ)**	7997	A	805 667-4100	19528
Ais Construction Company	1542	D	805 928-9467	730
ALI Roofg Mtls Long Bch Inc	5033	D	805 656-6319	13323
American Landscape MGT Inc	0782	D	805 647-5077	290
Aquastar Pool Products Inc	3561	E	877 768-2717	8003
Aqueos Corporation	3533	D	805 676-4330	7665
Art Glass Etc Inc	2431	E	805 644-4494	3232
Assa Abloy ACC Door Cntrls Gro	3429	D	805 642-2600	6499
Automobile Club Southern Cal	8699	D	805 644-7171	22405
Automotive Racing Products Inc **(PA)**	3429	D	805 339-2200	6500
Barnett Tool & Engineering	3751	D	805 642-9435	10482
Bell Powder Coating Inc	3479	F	805 658-2233	7348
Bentley-Simonson Inc	1311	E	805 650-2794	386
Beverly Health Care Corp **(PA)**	8741	E	805 642-1736	22987
Blue Ocean Marine LLC **(PA)**	4499	E	805 658-2628	12297
Blue Ribbon Draperies Inc	2391	E	805 983-4848	3092
Boyd and Associates **(PA)**	7381	C	818 752-1888	18258
Brierwood Terrace Ventura Inc **(HQ)**	8059	D	805 642-4101	20564
Brightview Landscape Svcs Inc	0781	C	805 642-9300	246
Brokaw Nursery LLC	0181	D	805 647-2262	74
Brothers of Industry Inc	3999	F	805 628-3545	11641
Btc Laboratories Inc	8734	D	805 656-6074	22933
Buenaventura Medical Group **(PA)**	8011	C	805 477-6000	19727
Buenaventura Medical Group	8011	D	805 477-6220	19728
C & R Molds Inc	3089	E	805 658-7098	5588
C D Lyon Construction Inc **(PA)**	8711	D	805 653-0173	22507
Califrnia Frnsic Med Group Inc	8099	D	805 654-3343	21396
Canon Solutions America Inc	5044	E	844 443-4636	13352
Carter Fire Protection Inc	5087	E	805 648-5906	14033
Catholic Chrties Snta Clara CN	8322	D	805 643-4694	21734
Century Theatres Inc	7833	C	805 641-6555	19294
Channel Islnds Opt-Mchncal Eng	3599	F	805 644-2153	8549
Channel Islnds Yung MNS Chrstn	8641	D	805 484-0423	22330
Chapala Iron & Manufacturing	3312	E	805 654-9803	6196
CJ Seto Support Services LLC **(PA)**	7379	D	805 644-12[illegible]4	18168
Coastal Connections	3661	E	805 644-5051	9231
Coastal View Halthcare Ctr LLC	8059	D	805 642-4101	20572
Cold Steel Inc **(PA)**	3421	F	805 650-8431	6472
Community Mem Hosp San Bnvntur	8062	D	805 652-5072	20729
Community Memorial Health Sys **(PA)**	8062	A	805 652-5011	20730
Connect Systems Inc	3663	E	805 642-7184	9264
Coorstek Inc	3545	D	805 644-5583	7850
County of Ventura	8322	C	805 654-2561	21762
Cummins Pacific LLC	3519	F	805 644-7281	7594
Dairy Farmers America Inc	2026	C	805 653-0042	1833
Del Mar Seafoods Inc	5146	C	805 850-0421	14569
Dna Health Institute Llc	2869	F	805 654-9363	5132
Douglas Maxim Inc	5032	E	805 648-7761	13302
Dow-Key Microwave Corporation	3625	C	805 650-0260	8948
E J Harrison & Sons Inc	4953	C	805 647-1414	12945
E&S Financial Group Inc	6163	D	805 644-1621	15240
Edwards Assoc Cmmnications Inc **(PA)**	2672	C	805 658-2626	3870
Evergreen Alliance Golf Ltd LP	7992	D	805 650-1794	19488
Exam Room Supply LLC	3845	F	805 298-3631	11222
Fabricmate Systems Inc	2221	E	805 642-7470	2597
Fcp Inc	3448	F	805 684-1117	6994
Fermented Sciences Inc	2082	E	818 427-8442	2143
Flir Eoc LLC	3826	E	805 642-4645	10795
Floral Gift HM Decor Intl Inc	0181	E	818 849-8832	76
Flying Embers Brewing Co	5182	D	781 856-3648	14842
Fnc Medical Corporation	2844	E	805 644-7576	5021
Fpl LLC	7011	D	805 643-6144	16449
Freshrealm LLC **(PA)**	2099	F	800 264-1297	2438
G W Surfaces **(PA)**	1799	D	805 642-5004	1660
Giddyup Group Inc	7311	D	800 828-2785	17014
Goldenwood Truss Corporation	2439	D	805 659-2520	3361
Gregory Consulting Inc **(PA)**	7538	C	805 642-0111	18836
Hailwood Inc	6512	F	805 487-4981	15672
Hammerhead Industries Inc	3089	E	805 658-9922	5659
Hampton Fitness Products Ltd	3949	F	805 339-9733	11423
Hearts Delight	2339	E	805 648-7123	2949
Hennis Enterprises Inc	2821	E	805 477-0257	4693
High Tech Pet Products	3999	D	805 644-1797	11684
HK Canning Inc **(PA)**	2033	E	805 652-1392	1863
HMcompany	3599	E	805 650-2651	8619
Implantech Associates Inc	3842	E	805 289-1665	11114
Instrument Control Services	1389	E	805 642-1999	510
Interact Pmti Inc **(DH)**	8711	D	805 658-5600	22579
Island Packers Corporation	4489	D	805 642-1393	12283
Itech Smart Home Inc	3699	F	805 673-8414	9875
Jh Biotech Inc **(PA)**	2875	E	805 650-8933	5164
Juengermann Inc	3493	E	805 644-7165	7464
Kaiser Foundation Hospitals	6324	C	888 515-3500	15421
Kirby Oldsmobile	7538	D	805 644-2241	18850
Kkzz 1590	4832	E	805 289-1400	12697
Lamps Plus Inc	3646	F	805 642-9007	9092
Livingston Mem Vna Hlth Corp	8741	B	805 642-0239	23053
Lowes Home Centers LLC	5031	C	805 675-8800	13249
Lynch Ready Mix Concrete Co	3273	F	805 647-2817	6099
Magnuson Products LLC	3714	E	805 642-8833	10097
Main Electric Supply Co LLC	5063	E	805 654-8600	13646
Matson Company	3479	F	805 643-7166	7386
Meditech Health Services Inc **(PA)**	8099	B	800 538-0900	21454
Mini-Flex Corporation	3599	F	805 644-1474	8700
Nabors Well Services Co	1389	D	805 648-2731	522
Naso Industries Corporation	3672	E	805 650-1231	9433
Nexa3d Inc	3577	E	805 465-9001	8286
Nxt Factory Inc **(PA)**	3021	F	805 340-2340	5311
Nyd Livet Technologies Inc	3479	F	805 643-7166	7392
Offshore Crane & Service Co **(PA)**	7353	D	805 648-3348	17316
Oil Country Manufacturing Inc	3533	C	805 643-1200	7674
Oilfield Electric Company	1731	D	805 648-3131	1289
Ojai Ambulance Inc	4119	C	805 653-9111	11883
Oly-Remington Ventura LLC	7011	D	805 643-6000	16595
Omnisil	3674	E	805 644-2514	9550
Ost Trucks and Cranes Inc	7389	D	805 643-9963	18623
P K Engineering & Mfg Co Inc	3841	F	805 628-9556	11041
Parts Authority LLC	5013	C	805 676-3410	13078
Penta Laboratories LLC	3671	F	818 882-3872	9367
Peter Brasseler Holdings LLC	3841	D	805 658-2643	11042
Peter Brasseler Holdings LLC	5047	D	805 650-5209	13510
Pier Pont Hotel LP	7011	E	805 643-6144	16629
Pierpont Inn Inc	7011	D	805 643-0245	16630
Plowboy Landscapes Inc	0782	D	805 643-4966	337
Real Good Food Company LLC	5149	C	818 299-4179	14729
Registration Ctrl Systems Inc **(PA)**	7389	D	805 654-0171	18650
Reyes Coca-Cola Bottling LLC	2086	D	805 644-2211	2287
Rgc Services Inc **(PA)**	6531	C	805 644-1242	15976
Richard Yarbrough	1389	E	805 643-1021	543

GEOGRAPHIC SECTION VERNON, CA

	SIC	EMP	PHONE	ENTRY #
Robert M Hadley Company Inc	3677	D	805 658-7286	9642
Sam Hill & Sons Inc	1623	E	805 620-0828	969
Santa Monica Millworks	2434	E	805 643-0010	3335
Saticoy Lemon Association	0174	D	805 654-6500	65
Sessa Manufacturing & Welding	3469	E	805 644-2284	7181
Sigma Services Inc **(PA)**	1542	D	805 642-8377	827
SL Power Electronics Corp **(DH)**	5065	D	800 235-5929	13774
Smart & Final Stores Inc	5141	C	805 647-4276	14504
Southern Cal Disc Tire Co Inc	7538	C	805 639-0166	18874
SRS Protection Inc	7381	C	805 744-7122	18341
Star of Ca LLC **(HQ)**	8099	C	805 644-7827	21485
State Ready Mix Inc **(PA)**	3273	E	805 647-2817	6119
Strand Products Inc **(PA)**	3845	E	800 343-7985	11238
Streamline Dsign Slkscreen Inc **(PA)**	2329	D	805 884-1025	2827
Sun Power Source **(PA)**	3648	F	805 644-2520	9148
Sunrun Installation Svcs Inc	1711	B	805 658-1236	1152
Swiss Productions Inc	3083	E	805 654-8525	5463
Taft Electric Company **(PA)**	1731	B	805 642-0121	1327
The Sloan Company Inc **(PA)**	5063	C	805 676-3200	13670
Tidwell Excav Acquisition Inc	1794	D	805 647-4707	1608
TMJ Solutions Inc	3841	D	805 650-3391	11066
Total Structures Inc	3648	E	805 676-3322	9152
Trade Desk Inc **(PA)**	7371	A	805 585-3434	17741
Triad Properties	6512	D	805 648-5008	15704
United Parcel Service Inc	4215	C	805 642-6784	12168
Venoco Inc	1311	E	805 644-1400	414
Ventura Coastal LLC **(PA)**	2037	D	805 653-7000	1912
Ventura County Credit Union **(PA)**	6061	D	805 477-4000	15103
Ventura County Medical Center	8049	D	805 652-6729	20235
Ventura County Medical Center **(PA)**	8011	C	805 652-6000	20136
Ventura County Medical Center	8011	C	805 652-6201	20137
Ventura Feed and Pet Sups Inc	3999	E	805 648-5035	11789
Ventura Harbor Boatyard Inc	3732	E	805 654-1433	10474
Ventura Hsptality Partners LLC	7011	C	805 648-2100	16771
Ventura Hydrulic Mch Works Inc	3599	E	805 656-1760	8839
Ventura Medical Management LLC	8741	B	805 477-6220	23135
Victoria Care Center	8051	D	805 642-1736	20496
Vista Steel Co Inc	1629	E	805 653-1189	1007
Vitalant	8099	D	805 654-1603	21496
W L Rubottom Co	2434	D	805 648-6943	3346
Waveline Creative LLC	2759	E	805 469-1549	4591
Weatherford International LLC	1389	F	805 643-1279	559
Webtez Inc	3799	F	805 856-6585	10557
West Coast Arborists Inc	0783	C	805 671-5092	363
Weststar Cinemas Inc	7832	C	805 658-6544	19292
Wilco Building Corporation	2431	F	805 765-4188	3299
Willdan Engineering	8711	D	805 653-6597	22699
Window Products Management Inc	2431	F	805 677-6800	3300
Wireless Technology Inc	3651	E	805 339-9696	9210
Wm J Matson Company	3479	F	805 684-9410	7426

VERNON, CA - Los Angeles County

	SIC	EMP	PHONE	ENTRY #
A A A Packing and Shipping Inc	4212	E	626 310-7787	11948
A Rudin Inc **(PA)**	2512	D	323 589-5547	3494
A&A Global Imports LLC	3089	E	888 315-2453	5541
Advanced Chemical Technology	2819	E	800 527-9607	4649
Ajax Forge Company **(PA)**	3462	F	323 582-6307	7082
Alberts Organics Inc	5141	D	323 587-6367	14452
All-American Mfg Co	3432	F	323 581-6293	6551
Amcor Industries Inc	3714	E	323 585-2852	10016
American Bottling Company	2086	F	323 268-7779	2253
American Consumer Products LLC	2899	E	323 289-6610	5210
American Cover Design 26 Inc	2273	F	323 582-8666	2681
American Elc Components Inc	7629	E	323 771-4888	18951
AMP Plus Inc	3647	D	323 231-2600	9113
Anaya Brothers Cutting LLC	2389	D	323 582-5758	3065
Anns Trading Company Inc	5199	E	323 585-4702	14911
Aoclsc Inc	2992	E	562 776-4000	5288
Arcadia Inc **(PA)**	3355	C	323 269-7300	6324
AS Match Dyeing Co Inc	2261	C	323 277-0470	2655
Atlas Galvanizing LLC	3479	E	323 587-6247	7347
Atra International Traders Inc	2671	F	562 864-3885	3849
Atv Inc **(PA)**	7538	D	562 977-8565	18814
B Boston & Associates Inc **(PA)**	5137	C	323 264-3915	14362
Bailey 44 LLC	2331	E	213 228-1930	2836
Baker Commodities Inc **(PA)**	2077	C	323 268-2801	2122
Baker Commodities Inc	2077	E	323 318-8260	2124
Baker Coupling Company Inc	3498	E	323 583-3444	7529
Bakery Depot Inc	2051	F	323 261-8388	1982
Bar-S Foods Co	2013	D	323 589-3600	1727
Barksdale Inc **(DH)**	3829	C	323 583-6243	10871
Bcbg Max Azria Group LLC	5137	D	323 589-2224	14364
Belagio Enterprises Inc	2211	E	323 731-6934	2559
Bender Ccp Inc **(PA)**	3599	D	707 745-9970	8523
Berney-Karp Inc	3269	D	323 260-7122	6001
Blue Blush Clothing Inc **(PA)**	2339	F	323 923-2895	2925
Bobco Metals LLC	5051	D	213 748-5171	13550
Bodycote Usa Inc	3398	A	323 264-0111	6432
Brentwood Appliances Inc	3639	E	323 266-4600	9013
C R Laurence Co Inc **(HQ)**	3714	B	323 588-1281	10027
Cadogan Tate Fine Art Lgstics **(PA)**	4214	D	562 206-0191	12108
California Combining Corp	2295	E	323 589-5727	2706
California Restaurant Sup Co	5141	E	213 581-5100	14457
Camino Real Foods Inc **(PA)**	2099	C	323 585-6599	2404
Certified Steel Treating Corp	3471	E	323 583-8711	7238
Charman Manufacturing Inc	3317	F	213 489-7000	6245
Cherokee Chemical Co Inc **(PA)**	5169	E	323 265-1112	14777
Chua & Sons Co Inc	2241	E	323 588-8044	2616
City Fibers Inc **(PA)**	5093	D	323 583-1013	14113
Classic Concepts Inc **(PA)**	5023	F	323 266-8993	13165
Classic Slipcover Inc	2392	F	323 583-0804	3098
Clougherty Packing LLC **(DH)**	2011	B	323 583-4621	1710
Clw Foods LLC	2099	F	323 432-4600	2411
Colorfast Dye & Print Hse Inc	2752	F	323 581-1656	4258
Comak Trading Inc A Cal Corp	5137	D	323 261-3404	14368
Command Packaging LLC **(HQ)**	5199	C	323 980-0918	14922
Complete Clothing Company **(PA)**	2335	E	323 277-1470	2883
Complete Garment Inc	2253	E	323 846-3731	2628
Completely Fresh Foods Inc	5149	C	323 722-9136	14684
Conquer Nation Inc	2389	C	310 562-8000	3071
Continental Vitamin Co Inc	2834	D	323 581-0176	4810
Cottyon Inc	2211	E	323 589-1563	2565
Crestone LLC	2361	F	323 588-8857	3031
Crown Carton Company Inc	2653	E	323 582-3053	3798
Crown Poly Inc	2673	F	323 583-4570	3881
Culinary Brands Inc **(PA)**	2038	C	626 289-3000	1923
Culinary International LLC **(PA)**	2099	C	626 289-3000	2414
D & D Services Inc	2077	E	323 261-4176	2126
D D Office Products Inc	2621	F	323 582-3400	3750
D I F Group Inc	8741	E	323 231-8800	23012
David Grment Ctng Fsing Svc In	2339	E	323 216-1574	2937
Demenno/Kerdoon Holdings	2992	F	323 268-3387	5292
Desert Shades Inc	3999	F	323 731-5000	11657
Directline Motor Express Inc	4213	B	213 266-2670	12034
Dm Collective Inc	2253	F	323 923-2400	2630
Donald O Smith Company	5072	F	323 685-5011	13804
Double Zero Inc **(PA)**	5137	E	323 846-1400	14371
Dunn-Edwards Corporation **(HQ)**	2851	C	888 337-2468	5095
E B Bradley Co **(PA)**	5072	E	323 585-9917	13805
East Shore Garment Company LLC	2211	E	323 923-4454	2569
Eastland Corporation	5147	E	323 261-5388	14593
Edris Plastics Mfg Inc	3089	E	323 581-7000	5636
Engineered Application LLC	3479	F	323 585-2894	7362
Evergreen Industries Inc	3821	D	323 583-1331	10657
F Gavina & Sons Inc	2095	B	323 582-0671	2353
F I O Imports Inc	2099	C	323 263-5100	2431
Fama Holdings LLC	7219	F	323 581-5888	16890
Fantasy Activewear Inc **(PA)**	2253	C	213 705-4111	2631
Fantasy Dyeing & Finishing Inc	2253	E	323 983-9988	2632
Fedex Freight Corporation	4213	C	323 269-9800	12044
Final Touch Apparel Inc	5137	F	323 484-9621	14376
Fishermans Pride Prcessors Inc	2092	B	323 232-1980	2345
Flowserve Corporation	3561	B	323 584-1890	8010
Fresh Packing Corporation	2032	E	213 612-0136	1850
G & G Quality Case Co Inc	3161	D	323 233-2482	5891
Generational Properties Inc	4225	B	323 583-3163	12209
Geo Plastics	3089	E	323 277-8106	5651
Global Truss America LLC	3354	D	323 415-6225	6309
Golden West Food Group Inc **(PA)**	2011	E	888 807-3663	1713
Golden West Trading Inc	5147	C	323 581-3663	14594
Goldman Global Greenfield Inc	3089	F	323 589-3444	5655
Good Fellas Industries Inc	1799	D	323 924-9495	1662
Gourmet Specialties Inc	5148	D	323 587-1734	14634
Great American Packaging	2673	E	323 582-2247	3884
Gts Living Foods LLC	2086	A	323 581-7787	2267
H & N Foods International Inc **(HQ)**	5146	C	323 586-9300	14570
Hannibal Industries Inc **(HQ)**	3317	C	323 513-1200	6248
Hannibal Material Handling Inc	2542	C	323 587-4060	3684
Hawthorne Distribution Ctr Inc	4215	E	213 431-6101	12137
Hawthorne Distribution Inc	3842	F	323 238-7738	11110
Heather By Bordeaux Inc	2339	E	213 622-0555	2950
Hollywood Lamp & Shade Co	3641	E	323 585-3999	9020
Incremento Inc **(PA)**	5137	D	213 624-7777	14382
Indiev Inc	5012	D	323 703-5720	13030
Isabelle Handbags Inc	3171	E	323 277-9888	5901
J & H Production	2396	E	323 261-6600	3176
J & J Snack Foods Corp Cal **(HQ)**	2052	C	323 581-0171	2065
J H Textiles Inc	2299	E	323 585-4124	2726
Jaya Apparel Group LLC	2339	E	714 904-9051	2955
Jaya Apparel Group LLC	2339	E	323 584-3500	2956
Jaya Apparel Group LLC **(PA)**	2339	D	323 584-3500	2957
Jejomi Designs Inc	2386	F	323 584-4211	3058
Jml Textile Inc	2211	E	323 584-2323	2577
Joes Plastics Inc	2821	E	323 771-8433	4699
Jordana Cosmetics LLC	5122	D	310 730-4400	14254
Just For Wraps Inc **(PA)**	2339	C	213 239-0503	2961
K & M Packing Co Inc	2011	E	323 585-5318	1714
Kafco Sales Company	5084	E	323 588-7141	13909
Kaiser Foundation Hospitals	2434	D	323 264-4310	3322
Karen Kane Stores Inc **(PA)**	5137	C	323 588-0000	14387
Kaslen Textiles LLC	2295	F	323 588-7700	2709
Katana Racing Inc **(PA)**	5013	C	562 340-6252	13068
Kelly Toys Holdings LLC	6719	D	323 923-1300	16103
Kennedy Name Plate Co	3479	E	323 585-0121	7379
Kim & Cami Productions Inc	2339	E	323 584-1300	2962
Kng Brnds Inc DBA Pstola DBA D	7389	E	323 588-6903	18566
Koral Industries LLC **(PA)**	2339	D	323 585-5343	2964
Koral LLC	2329	E	323 391-1060	2816
L A S A M Inc	2361	F	323 586-8717	3033
LA Brands LLC	5136	E	323 234-5070	14339
La Spec Industries Inc	3646	F	323 588-8746	9091
Lamonicas Pizza Dough Intl	5142	E	323 263-0644	14526
LAT LLC	2339	E	323 233-3017	2967
Lenovati Inc **(PA)**	5137	E	323 307-9878	14392
Lifoam Industries LLC	3081	D	323 587-1934	5432

GEOGRAPHIC

Employment Codes: A=Over 500 employees, B=251-500, C=101-250, D=51-100, E=20-50 F=10-19
2022 Southern California Business Directory and Buyers Guide
© Mergent Inc. 1-800-342-5647
1447

	SIC	EMP	PHONE	ENTRY #
Lima Trading LLC	5021	E	323 588-7434	13140
Littlejohn-Reuland Corporation	1731	E	323 587-5255	1276
Logistar LLC	5021	D	323 274-9651	13142
Los Angeles Junction Rlwy Co	4011	D	323 277-2004	11796
Los Angeles Regional Food Bank	8322	C	323 234-3030	21844
Love Tree Fashion Inc	5137	E	213 747-3755	14394
Luppen Holdings Inc **(PA)**	3469	E	323 581-8121	7162
Lymi Inc **(PA)**	5137	D	855 756-0560	14395
Mahar Manufacturing Corp **(PA)**	3942	E	323 581-9988	11361
Makabi 26 Inc	3089	F	323 588-7666	5703
Marspring Corporation **(PA)**	2273	E	323 589-5637	2692
Marspring Corporation	2515	E	800 522-5252	3553
Marspring Corporation	2515	E	310 484-6849	3554
Martys Cutting Inc	7389	D	323 582-5758	18588
Mexapparel Inc **(PA)**	2326	E	323 364-8600	2785
Mjck Corporation	2253	F	888 992-8437	2639
Mochi Ice Cream Company LLC **(PA)**	2051	E	323 587-5504	2020
Mola Inc	5137	C	323 582-0088	14402
Moonstar Mfg Inc	2331	F	323 581-1656	2860
Morgan Fabrics Corporation **(PA)**	5131	D	323 583-9981	14311
Nanka Seimen Co	2098	F	323 585-9967	2378
National Corset Supply House **(PA)**	2341	D	323 261-0265	3018
Natures Produce	5148	C	323 235-4343	14644
New Chef Fashion Inc	2311	D	323 581-0300	2746
New Pride Corporation	5137	D	323 584-6608	14404
Norman Fox & Co	5169	E	323 973-4900	14789
Norman Paper and Foam Co Inc	2673	E	323 582-7132	3888
Norton Packaging Inc	3089	E	323 588-6167	5731
Nuconic Packaging LLC	3089	E	323 588-9033	5733
Nux Group Inc	2211	F	323 780-4700	2584
Nydj Apparel LLC	5137	C	323 581-9040	14407
O & K Inc **(PA)**	5137	C	323 846-5700	14408
Oak Manufacturing Company Inc	3581	E	323 581-8087	8323
Ocean Queen 87 Inc	5146	E	323 585-1200	14576
Otimo Inc	2321	E	323 233-8894	2759
Overhill Farms Inc **(DH)**	2099	C	323 582-9977	2504
P M Rehrig Inc **(HQ)**	3089	C	323 262-5145	5734
P&Y T-Shrts Silk Screening Inc	3552	E	323 585-4604	7910
Pabco Building Products LLC	3275	D	323 581-6113	6130
Pacific American Fish Co Inc **(PA)**	5146	C	323 319-1551	14577
Pactiv Packaging Inc **(DH)**	5199	A	323 513-9000	14962
Palisades Ranch Inc	5141	B	323 581-6161	14485
Papa Cantellas Incorporated	2013	D	323 584-7272	1743
Paper Surce Converting Mfg Inc	2621	E	323 583-3800	3768
Paradigm Industries Inc	7389	D	310 965-1900	18627
Patterson Kincaid LLC	2339	D	323 584-3559	2980
Peerless Materials Company	2842	E	323 266-0313	4976
Peter K Inc **(PA)**	2339	C	323 585-5343	2982
Pjy Inc	2211	E	323 583-7737	2585
Pontrelli & Larricchia Ltd	5147	E	323 583-6690	14601
Preferred Frzr Svcs - Lbf LLC	4222	D	323 263-8811	12176
Princess Paper Inc	2676	E	323 588-4777	3906
Proportion Foods LLC	2099	E	515 735-9800	2510
Punch Press Products Inc	3544	D	323 581-7151	7828
Putnam Accessory Group Inc	2339	E	323 306-1330	2986
Quantum Four Labs LLC	2834	F	213 217-9777	4879
R A Reed Electric Company **(PA)**	7694	E	323 587-2284	19015
R B R Meat Company Inc	2011	D	323 973-4868	1718
R Planet Earth LLC	4953	C	213 320-0601	12968
Rancho Foods Inc	5147	D	323 585-0503	14603
Randall Hv Foods LLC	5147	C	323 261-6565	14604
Rcrv Inc **(PA)**	5137	E	323 235-7300	14412
RE Bilt Metalizing Co	3599	F	323 277-8200	8760
Rebecca International Inc	2395	E	323 973-2602	3163
Red Chamber Co **(PA)**	5146	B	323 234-9000	14580
Rehrig Pacific Holdings Inc **(PA)**	3089	B	323 262-5145	5790
Reliance Steel & Aluminum Co	5051	C	323 583-6111	13591
Republic Furniture Mfg Inc	2512	E	323 235-2144	3514
Reynaldos Mexican Food Co LLC **(PA)**	2099	C	562 803-3188	2517
Rezex Corporation	2269	E	213 622-2015	2679
Rggd Inc **(PA)**	5099	D	323 581-6617	14177
Rite-Way Meat Packers Inc	5147	D	323 826-2144	14605
RJ Acquisition Corp **(PA)**	2759	C	323 318-1107	4568
RJ Singer International Inc	3161	E	323 735-1717	5896
Rmi Utility Services Inc	8742	D	323 589-9498	23311
Rmla Inc	2369	F	213 749-4333	3044
Rogers Poultry Co **(PA)**	5144	D	323 585-0802	14549
Romeo Power Inc **(PA)**	3714	E	833 467-2237	10129
Romeo Systems Inc	3699	C	323 675-2180	9909
Rose & Shore Inc	7389	B	323 826-2144	18657
Roshan Trading Inc	5131	E	213 622-9904	14318
Rotax Incorporated	2339	E	323 589-5999	2990
Royal Trim	2396	F	323 583-2121	3180
Rplanet Erth Los Angles Hldngs	3089	D	833 775-2638	5806
Runway Liquidation LLC **(HQ)**	5137	A	323 589-2224	14414
S S Schaffer Co Inc	3541	F	323 560-1430	7746
Saia Motor Freight Line LLC	4213	D	323 277-2880	12078
Saitex (usa) LLC	2211	F	323 391-6116	2586
Same Swim LLC	5137	D	323 582-2588	14415
Samtex Fabrics Inc	4731	E	213 742-0200	12522
Sandberg Furniture Mfg Co Inc **(PA)**	2511	C	323 582-0711	3488
Sas Textiles Inc	2259	D	323 277-5555	2654
Selectra Industries Corp	2341	D	323 581-8500	3019
Seven Licensing Company LLC	5137	D	323 881-0308	14416
Sewing Collection Inc	3053	D	323 264-2223	5353
Shara-Tex Inc	2257	E	323 587-7200	2647
Shason Inc **(PA)**	5131	D	323 269-6666	14319
Shims Bargain Inc **(PA)**	5199	D	323 881-0099	14975
SJ&I Bias Binding & Tex Co Inc	2396	E	213 747-5271	3183
Sklar Bov Solutions Inc	3499	E	323 266-7111	7570
Sll Inc	2339	F	323 581-9040	2993
Smart Foods LLC	2046	E	818 660-2238	1954
Soex West Usa LLC **(PA)**	5136	B	323 264-8300	14350
Sol-Pak Thermoforming Inc	5162	E	323 582-3333	14764
Soofer Co Inc	5149	D	323 234-6666	14737
Spirit Clothing Company	2339	E	213 784-0251	2995
Square H Brands Inc	2013	C	323 267-4600	1752
Starco Enterprises Inc **(PA)**	3559	D	323 266-7111	7995
Stone Harbor Inc	2299	F	323 277-2777	2738
Stratus Group Duo LLC	2086	E	323 581-3663	2300
Streets Ahead Inc	2387	E	323 277-0860	3062
Sunrise Brands LLC **(PA)**	5137	E	323 780-8250	14419
Sunrise Food Service Inc	0241	D	323 264-8364	138
Superior Electric Mtr Svc Inc	7694	F	323 583-1040	19017
Superior Lithographics Inc	2752	D	323 263-8400	4428
Sweetener Products Inc	5149	D	323 234-2200	14741
T & T Foods Inc	2032	E	323 588-2158	1856
Tagtime Usa Inc	2679	B	323 587-1555	3938
Tajima USA Dissolving Corp	3446	D	323 588-1281	6981
Tama Trading Company	5149	D	213 748-8262	14742
Tapatio Foods LLC	2033	F	323 587-8933	1877
Team Fashion	2331	F	323 589-3388	2869
Team USA **(PA)**	3711	F	323 826-9888	9968
Tempted Apparel Corp	2339	E	323 859-2480	3002
Teva Foods Inc	2099	E	323 267-8110	2536
The Ligature Inc **(HQ)**	2752	E	323 585-6000	4437
The Timing Inc **(PA)**	5137	E	323 589-5577	14421
Three Plus One Inc	2331	F	213 623-3070	2871
Tom York Enterprises Inc	3089	D	323 581-6194	5840
True Wrld Fods Los Angeles LLC	5146	D	323 846-3300	14589
Two Lads Inc **(PA)**	3965	E	323 584-0064	11503
Unirex Corp	3674	E	323 589-4000	9597
United Food Group LLC	2011	F	323 588-5286	1721
United Parcel Service Inc	4513	D	323 260-3957	12331
UPD INC	3942	D	323 588-8811	11365
US Radiator Corporation **(PA)**	3714	E	323 826-0965	10152
V & L Produce Inc	5148	C	323 589-3125	14660
Vernon Central Warehouse Inc	4214	C	323 234-2200	12120
Vest Inc	3317	D	800 421-6370	6255
Vie De France Yamazaki Inc	2051	A	323 582-1241	2042
Viva Holdings LLC **(PA)**	2678	F	818 243-1363	3919
Vxb & Orfwid Inc	2339	E	213 222-0030	3008
W & W Concept Inc	2339	D	323 233-9202	3009
W5 Concepts Inc	2331	E	323 231-2415	2875
Wayne Provision Co Inc **(PA)**	5147	D	323 277-5888	14609
West Coast Distribution Inc **(PA)**	4225	D	323 588-6508	12259
West Pico Distributors LLC	5141	D	323 586-9050	14521
West Pico Foods Inc	5142	C	323 586-9050	14534
Westaire Engineering Inc	3585	F	323 587-3347	8357
Western Abrasives Inc	3291	F	323 588-1245	6161
Westgate Mfg Inc	3699	D	877 805-2252	9930
World Variety Produce Inc	5148	B	800 588-0151	14668
Yen-Nhai Inc	2512	E	323 584-1315	3522
Zk Enterprises Inc	2329	E	213 622-7012	2833

VICTORVILLE, CA - San Bernardino County

	SIC	EMP	PHONE	ENTRY #
American Prtctive Svcs Invstgt	7381	C	626 705-8600	18247
Automobile Club Southern Cal	8699	D	760 245-6666	22433
Branlyn Prominence Inc	8082	C	760 843-5655	21140
Coldwell Banker Home Source	6531	D	760 684-8100	15818
Comav LLC **(PA)**	5088	C	760 523-5100	14054
Comav Technical Services LLC	4581	C	760 530-2400	12350
County of San Bernardino	8322	D	760 843-5100	21761
Desert Valley Hospital Inc **(DH)**	8062	C	760 241-8000	20748
Desert Valley Med Group Inc **(PA)**	8011	B	760 241-8000	19798
Devoll Rubber Mfg Group Inc	3069	F	760 246-0142	5372
E & T Foods Inc	0291	B	760 343-7730	141
Elite Diagnostic Imaging LLC	8011	D	760 962-9866	19804
Excel Scientific LLC	5049	E	760 246-4545	13533
Fairway Realty Inc **(PA)**	6531	D	760 245-3471	15853
Family Assistance Program	8322	D	760 843-0701	21781
Gatehouse Media LLC	2711	E	760 241-7744	3981
General Electric Company	3721	E	760 530-5200	10186
Goodman Manufacturing Co LP	3585	B	760 955-7770	8341
Graco Childrens Products Inc	2514	C	770 418-7200	3528
Hartwick & Hand Inc **(PA)**	4212	D	760 245-1666	11972
Heritage Medical Group	8099	C	760 956-1286	21437
Integration Innovation Inc	8731	E	256 513-5179	22842
Jamboor Medical Corporation	8092	D	760 241-8063	21250
Kaiser Foundation Hospitals	6324	C	888 750-0036	15408
Kindred Healthcare LLC	8082	D	760 241-7044	21179
Knolls Convalescent Hosp Inc **(PA)**	8051	C	760 245-5361	20388
Knolls West Enterprise	8051	C	760 245-0107	20389
L & S Investment Co Inc	7011	D	760 245-3461	16531
Landforce Corporation	4213	C	760 843-7839	12058
Lowes Home Centers LLC	5031	C	760 949-9565	13222
Mars Petcare Us Inc	2047	E	760 261-7900	1960
Mojave Copy & Printing Inc	2752	F	760 241-7898	4375
Nu-Way SEC Invstgtive Svcs Inc	7381	D	760 243-7577	18303
Paradise Manufacturing Co Inc	2394	E	909 477-3460	3143
Peoples Care Inc	8082	C	760 962-1900	21201
Premier Food Services Inc	5141	B	760 843-8000	14486
Reyes Coca-Cola Bottling LLC	2086	D	760 241-2653	2296
Robertsons Ready Mix Ltd	5032	C	702 798-0568	13314
Southern California Edison Co	4911	C	760 951-3172	12855

Mergent email: customerrelations@mergent.com
1448
2022 Southern California Business
Directory and Buyers Guide
(P-0000) Products & Services Section entry number
(PA)=Parent Co (HQ)=Headquarters (DH)=Div Headquarters

	SIC	EMP	PHONE	ENTRY #
Speedway Usa Inc	7948	E	760 245-6211	19435
Spring Valley Post Acute LLC	8051	C	760 245-6477	20479
Sunland Ford Inc	7538	D	760 241-7751	18876
Tryvision	8322	E	760 780-0408	21906
TT Trucking Services LLC	4212	D	323 790-3408	12003
Vahi Toyota Inc **(PA)**	7538	C	760 241-6484	18884
Valley Bulk Inc	4213	D	760 843-0574	12088
Victor Cmnty Support Svcs Inc	8093	C	760 987-8225	21363
Victor Cmnty Support Svcs Inc	8093	C	760 245-4695	21364
Victorvlle Trsure Holdings LLC	7011	D	760 245-6565	16772

VIEW PARK, CA - Los Angeles County

	SIC	EMP	PHONE	ENTRY #
Hathaway-Sycmres Child Fmly Svc	8322	C	323 733-0322	21797
Outdoor Recreation Group **(PA)**	2393	E	323 226-0830	3129

VILLA PARK, CA - Orange County

	SIC	EMP	PHONE	ENTRY #
Tropical Plaza Nursery Inc	0782	D	714 998-4100	346

VISALIA, CA - Tulare County

	SIC	EMP	PHONE	ENTRY #
A-C Electric Company	1731	D	559 732-4733	1206
Able Industries Inc	8331	D	559 651-8150	21935
ABM Janitorial Services Inc	7349	D	559 651-1612	17210
AFP Advanced Food Products LLC	2032	E	559 627-2070	1845
AFP Advanced Food Products LLC	2026	C	559 651-1737	1829
Allen Development Partners LLC **(PA)**	6552	D	559 732-5425	16046
American Incorporated **(PA)**	1542	B	559 651-1776	733
Anchor-41 Construction LLC	1542	F	559 740-7776	734
Arthur J Gallagher & Co	6411	D	559 733-1181	15536
Automobile Club Southern Cal	8699	D	559 732-8045	22440
Bluescope Buildings N Amer Inc	3448	C	559 651-5300	6988
Bowie Enterprises	7542	D	559 732-2988	18907
Brecks Electric Motors Inc	7694	F	559 651-1475	19007
Bushnell Industries Inc	2842	E	559 651-9039	4959
C J Ritchie Farms	0131	D	559 625-1114	1
California Dairies Inc **(PA)**	2026	D	559 625-2200	1832
CCS Industries Inc	3999	F	559 786-8489	11650
Central Vly Regional Ctr Inc	8093	C	559 738-2200	21285
City of Visalia	4111	C	559 713-4100	11804
Cleaning For King Inc	7349	C	559 733-3856	17227
CM Construction Services Inc **(PA)**	1542	E	559 735-9556	757
Culinary Staffing of America **(PA)**	7363	D	559 741-1314	17490
David Oppenheimer and Co I LLC	5141	D	559 636-7700	14463
Delta Nrsing Rhbltion Hosp In	8051	E	559 625-4003	20312
Diamond Crystal Brands Inc	2099	E	559 651-7782	2421
Diamond Perforated Metals Inc	3469	D	559 651-1889	7142
Diocese Fresno Education Corp	8322	D	559 734-1572	21770
Ed Tucker Distributor Inc	5013	E	800 347-1010	13056
Edeniq Inc **(PA)**	2869	D	559 302-1777	5133
Equitable Hotels	7011	D	559 738-1700	16435
Erdle Perforating Co Inc	1389	F	559 651-1889	499
Family Healthcare Network	8011	C	559 734-1939	19814
Family Healthcare Network	8011	C	559 741-4500	19816
Family Healthcare Network	8011	C	559 737-4700	19817
Family Services Tulare County	8322	D	559 732-1970	21786
Far West Inc	8051	D	559 627-1241	20341
Far West Inc	8059	D	559 733-0901	20580
Financial Credit Network Inc **(PA)**	7322	D	559 733-7550	17112
Food Machinery Sales Inc	3565	D	559 651-2339	8068
Foremost Fresh Direct LLC **(PA)**	5148	E	559 735-3100	14629
General Lgstics Systems US Inc	4215	C	559 651-1850	12136
Graphic Packaging Intl LLC	5199	C	559 651-3535	14932
Grosvenor Visalia Associates	7011	E	559 651-5000	16458
Guardian Fire Service Inc	1711	E	559 651-0919	1078
Guardian Safety and Supply LLC	5199	D	559 651-0919	14934
Hampton Inn **(PA)**	7011	D	559 732-3900	16461
Hanson Distributing Company	5013	D	559 802-1198	13063
Hellwig Products Company Inc	3714	E	559 734-7451	10073
Hr Mobile Services Inc	8742	D	559 625-2322	23236
Hydrite Chemical Co	5169	D	559 651-3450	14784
J A Contracting Inc	0761	B	559 733-4865	216
Jordan - Link & Company **(PA)**	6531	D	559 733-9696	15898
Kaweah Container Inc **(HQ)**	2653	D	559 651-7846	3816
Kaweah Delta Health Care	8099	D	559 624-2854	21448
Kaweah Delta Health Care Dst	8062	C	559 624-4800	20819
Kaweah Delta Health Care Dst **(PA)**	8062	A	559 624-2000	20820
Kaweah Dlta Hlth Care Dst Gild	8021	D	559 624-3300	21021
Kaweah Dlta Hlth Care Dst Gild	8062	C	559 624-2000	20821
Kawneer Company Inc	3446	C	559 651-4000	6970
Key Medical Group Inc	8399	D	559 734-0388	22193
L E Cooke Co	0181	C	559 732-9146	81
Lowes Home Centers LLC	5031	C	559 624-4300	13248
Lowes Home Centers LLC	5031	C	559 802-9055	13270
Magnetech Industrial Svcs Inc	7694	E	559 651-0606	19014
Mineral King Rdlgcal Med Group	8011	D	559 734-9244	19980
Mission Linen Supply	7211	D	559 625-5423	16837
Mission Linen Supply	7213	D	559 291-7181	16866
Mitchell Buckman Inc **(PA)**	6411	D	559 733-1181	15595
Morgan Kleppe and Nash LLC	6411	D	559 732-3436	15598
Neighborhood Mennonite	7372	E	559 732-9107	17929
Orange Belt Stages **(PA)**	4142	D	559 733-4408	11913
Pace International LLC	2842	F	559 651-4877	4974
Pacific Southwest Cont LLC	2653	E	559 651-5500	3824
Packers Manufacturing Inc	3556	F	559 732-4886	7948
PCI Care Venture I	8051	D	559 735-0828	20439
Penney Opco LLC	7231	D	559 732-4171	16910
Perfection Pet Foods LLC **(DH)**	2047	E	559 302-4880	1961
Polymerpak LLC	3089	C	559 651-1965	5766
Powers Holdings Inc	3679	F	559 651-2222	9764
Premier Trailer Mfg Inc	3799	F	559 651-2212	10554
Printxcel - Visalia	2752	F	559 636-6290	4405
Pro-Youth	8641	B	559 374-2030	22357
Pta California Congress of Par	8641	E	559 622-3195	22359
Quad Knopf Inc **(PA)**	8711	E	559 733-0440	22641
Quail Park Retirement Vlg LLC	8052	D	559 624-3500	20539
R & L Brosamer Inc	1542	B	559 739-8215	813
R Lang Company	3442	D	559 651-0701	6717
Robert Quintero Labor Contg	7361	E	559 732-6954	17462
Santa Barbara Trnsp Corp	4151	C	559 738-5780	11938
Screw Conveyor Pacific Corp	3535	C	559 651-2131	7693
Self Help Enterprises **(PA)**	6531	D	559 651-1000	15995
Sequoia Beverage Company LP	5181	C	559 651-2444	14835
Shyam Bhaskar MD Inc **(PA)**	8011	D	559 635-7100	20064
Sorma USA LLC	2673	B	559 651-1269	3890
Spraying Devices Inc	3523	F	559 734-5555	7621
Stainless Technologies LLC	7692	F	559 651-0460	18997
Tempo Plastic Co	3086	F	559 651-7711	5524
Ti Inc	2873	F	559 972-1475	5161
Tim Hofer Inc	7349	C	559 732-6676	17290
Toor Farming LLC	0191	D	559 500-1331	122
Trical Inc	2879	E	559 651-0736	5173
Veterinary Service Inc	5047	E	559 651-1633	13530
Visalia Country Club	7997	D	559 734-3733	19627
Visalia Ctr 4 Amblty Med Srgr	3842	F	559 740-4094	11150
Visalia Electric Motor Sp Inc	7694	E	559 651-0606	19018
Visalia Medical Clinic Inc **(PA)**	8011	B	559 733-5222	20156
Visalia Pallet LLC	2448	E	559 627-4829	3411
Voltage Multipliers Inc **(PA)**	3674	C	559 651-1402	9603
Welcome Group Management LLC	7011	D	310 378-6666	16782
Westgate Gardens Care Ctr Inc	8051	D	559 733-0901	20506

WALNUT, CA - Los Angeles County

	SIC	EMP	PHONE	ENTRY #
1perfectchoice	2599	F	909 594-8855	3719
Acosolar Inc	1711	F	626 575-8822	1015
Adaptive Inc **(PA)**	7372	E	631 760-6577	17776
Adesso Inc	5045	C	909 839-2929	13371
Aero Pacific Corporation	3728	D	714 961-9200	10244
Ahg Inc	7291	B	703 596-0111	16933
All Strong Industry (usa) Inc **(PA)**	2591	E	909 598-6494	3705
Amergence Technology Inc	3559	E	909 859-8400	7960
Armored Transport Inc **(DH)**	7381	E	909 468-2229	18252
B & S Food Products	5141	F	323 263-6728	14456
Biomechanical Services Inc	3842	E	714 990-5932	11091
Bulk Transportation **(PA)**	4213	D	909 594-2855	12018
C M Automotive Systems Inc **(PA)**	3563	E	909 869-7912	8032
Cal Southern Packg Eqp Inc	5084	F	909 598-3198	13894
Cast Parts Inc **(DH)**	3324	C	909 595-2252	6263
Century 21 Masters **(PA)**	6531	D	909 595-6697	15809
Charades LLC **(PA)**	2389	C	626 435-0077	3069
Clarion Construction Inc	1542	E	909 598-4060	754
Crush Master Grinding Corp	3599	E	909 595-2249	8565
CSB Industries Corp	3366	F	626 964-4058	6406
Diamond Collection LLC	2389	E	626 435-0077	3074
Diana Did-It Designs Inc	2389	E	970 226-5062	3075
Disc Replicator Inc	3652	F	909 385-0118	9213
East Lion Corporation	5139	E	626 912-1818	14436
Edro Engineering Inc **(DH)**	3544	D	909 594-5751	7799
Edro Specialty Steels Inc	3544	F	800 368-3376	7800
Emeritus Corporation	8051	C	909 595-5030	20324
Excellence Opto Inc **(PA)**	3647	E	909 468-0550	9115
Extra Express (cerritos) Inc	4731	E	714 985-6000	12456
Fairway Injection Molds Inc	3089	D	909 595-2201	5644
Gemtek Technology Inc	5045	F	909 444-9288	13400
Golden Applexx Co Inc	2759	E	909 594-9788	4520
Gs Promo Inc **(PA)**	3499	E	626 223-4755	7558
Guesty Inc	7011	C	415 244-0277	16459
Hardware Imports Inc	3713	F	909 595-6201	9989
Harrison Beverage Inc	2024	F	626 757-1159	1818
Hiti Digital America Inc	3861	E	909 594-0099	11278
Holden Industrial Inc	3577	E	909 919-5505	8261
Hupa International Inc	3949	E	909 598-9876	11425
I3 Enterprise Inc	3714	F	626 272-9538	10077
Identigraphix Inc	7336	E	909 468-4741	17179
In Win Development USA Inc	3572	E	909 348-0588	8204
Infinity Watch Corporation	3993	E	626 289-9878	11561
Jakks Pacific Inc	3944	E	909 594-7771	11379
King Audio Inc	5064	F	626 968-8827	13688
Kleverness Incorporated	7372	F	213 559-2480	17901
KS Electronics Inc	3674	E	909 869-8826	9527
Lights of America Inc	3645	A	909 444-2000	9066
Lina Gale (usa) Inc	5122	D	909 595-8898	14257
Longstar Healthpro Inc	5149	F	909 468-9215	14705
Los Angles Ryal Vsta Golf Crse	7997	D	909 595-7441	19583
Loungefly LLC	3961	E	818 718-5600	11487
M & R Joint Venture Electrical	1731	D	909 598-7700	1277
Madaco Safety Products Inc	5099	F	909 614-1756	14168
Markwins Beauty Brands Inc **(PA)**	5122	C	909 595-8898	14259
Mjc America Ltd **(PA)**	3634	E	888 876-5387	9009
New Origins Accessories Inc **(PA)**	3961	F	909 869-7559	11488
Ninas Mexican Foods Inc	2099	E	909 468-5888	2496
Niron Inc	3544	E	909 598-1526	7818
Nu-Health Products Co	2833	E	909 869-0666	4755
Oncehub Inc	7372	F	650 206-5585	17941
Patina Freight Inc	4225	D	909 444-1025	12228
Physicans Formula Holdings Inc **(HQ)**	2844	D	626 334-3395	5059
Racing Power Company	3714	E	909 468-3690	10122
Resident Home LLC **(PA)**	5021	C	888 863-2827	13151

GEOGRAPHIC

Employment Codes: A=Over 500 employees, B=251-500, C=101-250, D=51-100, E=20-50 F=10-19
2022 Southern California Business Directory and Buyers Guide

1449

	SIC	EMP	PHONE	ENTRY #
Ronsin Photocopy Inc **(PA)**	7389	D	909 594-5995	18656
Sea Shield Marine Products	3363	E	909 594-2507	6371
Servers Direct LLC	5045	D	800 576-7931	13436
Settlers Jerky Inc	2013	E	909 444-3999	1751
Shea Hmes Ltd Prtnr A Cal Ltd **(HQ)**	1521	E	909 594-9500	640
Shea Homes Vantis LLC	1522	D	909 594-9500	669
Shea La Quinta LLC	6512	D	909 594-9500	15696
Shogun Labs Inc **(PA)**	8734	D	206 679-1302	22958
Soderberg Manufacturing Co Inc	3647	D	909 595-1291	9118
Southcoast Cabinet Inc **(PA)**	2434	E	909 594-3089	3337
Straight Forwarding Inc	4731	D	909 594-3400	12533
SW Fixtures Inc	2541	F	909 595-2506	3667
Swc Group Inc	2656	F	888 982-1628	3843
Sysco Los Angeles Inc	5141	A	909 595-9595	14512
Total Resources Intl Inc **(PA)**	3842	D	909 594-1220	11145
Tree Island Wire (usa) Inc **(DH)**	3315	C	909 594-7511	6236
Tri-Net Technology Inc	3577	D	909 598-8818	8308
Tul Inc	3429	F	909 444-0577	6542
Unicom Electric Inc	3669	F	626 964-7873	9358
Unis LLC **(PA)**	4731	C	909 839-2600	12548
United Riggers & Erectors Inc **(PA)**	1796	D	909 978-0400	1627
Universal Mercantile Exch Inc	3993	F	909 839-0556	11613
V Manufacturing Logistics Inc	2844	E	909 869-6200	5079
Walnut Valley Water District	4941	D	909 595-7554	12922
Western Hardware Company	3429	E	909 595-6201	6544
Winit America Inc	3577	F	626 606-0308	8312

WASCO, CA - Kern County

	SIC	EMP	PHONE	ENTRY #
Adventist Health System/West	8062	D	661 869-6700	20645
Ag-Weld Inc	7692	E	661 758-3061	18967
Bethlehem Construction Inc	1541	D	661 758-1001	690
Carter Pump & Machine Inc	3599	E	661 393-8620	8542
Certis USA LLC	2879	E	661 758-8471	5168
Community Support Options Inc	8322	C	661 758-5331	21755
Heritage Equipment Company	5046	D	661 587-2250	13458
Primex Farms LLC **(PA)**	2068	E	661 758-7790	2115
Rockview Farms Inc	0241	D	661 792-3583	137
South Valley Almond Co LLC	5159	C	661 391-9000	14752
Sunnygem LLC	2033	B	661 758-0491	1876
Supreme Almonds California Inc	0173	D	661 746-6475	57

WEST COVINA, CA - Los Angeles County

	SIC	EMP	PHONE	ENTRY #
Allen/Clark Cadillac	7549	D	626 966-7441	18920
Assisted Home Recovery Inc	8082	D	626 915-5595	21136
Baatz Enterprises Inc	3711	F	323 660-4866	9936
Big Lgue Dreams Consulting LLC	7941	D	626 839-1100	19410
BKK Corporation **(PA)**	4953	D	626 965-0911	12932
Bowlero Corp	7933	D	626 960-3636	19388
Citrus Vly Hlth Partners Inc	8062	A	626 962-4011	20723
Clara Bldwin Stcker HM For Wme	8051	E	626 962-7151	20282
Doctors Hospital W Covina Inc	8062	C	626 338-8481	20758
East Valley Cmnty Hlth Ctr Inc **(PA)**	8093	D	626 919-3402	21302
Emanate Health Medical Center **(PA)**	8062	A	626 962-4011	20764
Emanate Health Medical Center	8062	A	626 963-8411	20766
Harris & Ruth Painting Contg **(PA)**	1721	D	626 960-4004	1183
Hassen Development Corporation	1522	D	626 967-7374	658
Iheartraves LLC	2331	F	626 628-6482	2847
Impact Realty Inc **(PA)**	6531	C	626 331-4868	15889
Interspace Battery Inc **(PA)**	3356	E	626 813-1234	6333
Kaiser Foundation Hospitals	6324	C	866 319-4269	15414
Kaiser Foundation Hospitals	6324	C	626 856-3045	15425
Lfp Ecommerce LLC	7389	D	314 428-5069	18577
Macdonald Carbide Co	3544	E	626 960-4034	7814
Matrix Group International Inc	1521	D	626 960-6205	622
Ola Nation LLC	2335	E	310 256-0638	2894
Paul Calvo and Company	6531	E	626 814-8000	15947
Penney Opco LLC	7231	D	626 960-3711	16913
Penske Motor Group LLC	7513	B	626 859-1200	18735
Pmb Motorcars LLC **(HQ)**	7538	D	626 859-1200	18861
Portos Bakery West Covina Inc	5149	B	626 214-3490	14721
Positive Behavior Steps Corp	8093	D	626 940-5180	21327
Queen of Valley Hospital	8062	D	626 962-4011	20919
RM Galicia Inc	7322	C	626 813-6200	17116
RSI Leasing LLC	7359	D	626 966-6129	17370
Saint Jseph Communications Inc **(PA)**	7812	E	626 331-3549	19174
Sears Home Imprv Pdts Inc	1521	C	626 671-1892	636
South Hills Country Club	7997	D	626 339-1231	19615
Southern Cal Prmnnte Med Group	6324	C	626 960-4844	15456
Southern Cal Spcialty Care Inc	8062	C	626 339-5451	20948
Specilty Hosp San Gbriel Vly M	8062	D	626 339-5451	20955
Surgical Center of West Covina	8011	D	626 960-6623	20100
Turn Around Communications Inc	1623	C	626 443-2400	979
Universal Bank **(PA)**	6035	D	626 854-2818	15054
Up Packaging Enterprise	2631	F	626 715-2838	3777
Volt Management Corp	7363	D	626 931-1437	17526
Volunteers of Amer Los Angeles	8322	D	626 337-9878	21914
West Covina Foster Family Agcy	6411	D	626 814-9085	15648
West Covina Medical Clinic Inc **(PA)**	8011	C	626 960-8614	20160
Westview Services Inc	8331	D	626 962-0956	21975
Wicoro Inc **(HQ)**	8059	E	626 962-4489	20641

WEST HILLS, CA - Los Angeles County

	SIC	EMP	PHONE	ENTRY #
C B Richard Ellis Inc **(DH)**	6799	C	818 737-1200	16250
Davita Medical Management LLC	8099	D	818 226-3666	21416
Dlh Davinci LLC	8072	D	818 703-5100	21105
Electro Rent Corporation **(HQ)**	7359	C	818 787-2100	17347
Fiserv Inc	7374	D	818 226-4400	18089
Holman Family Counseling Inc **(PA)**	8049	D	818 704-1444	20215
Hvantage Technologies Inc	7371	D	818 661-6301	17634
Insite Digestive Health Care	8011	D	818 346-9911	19854
Jj Acquisitions LLC	3069	E	818 772-0100	5385
Leisure Care LLC	8052	B	818 713-0900	20535
Lowes Home Centers LLC	5031	C	818 610-1960	13231
Mamba Logistics Inc	4212	D	661 234-8050	11981
Old Candle LLC **(PA)**	3999	E	818 436-2776	11722
One Lambda Inc **(HQ)**	8731	B	747 494-1000	22856
Pharmavite LLC **(DH)**	2833	B	818 221-6200	4760
Source Photonics Usa Inc **(PA)**	3674	C	818 773-9044	9579
Unilab Corporation **(HQ)**	8071	B	818 737-6000	21100
West Valley Christian Church	8351	D	818 884-4710	22073

WEST HOLLYWOOD, CA - Los Angeles County

	SIC	EMP	PHONE	ENTRY #
21seeds Inc	2084	F	310 415-8605	2163
603 N La Cienega Boulevard LLC	7389	D	310 855-9955	18425
9200 Data Devices Corporation	6411	E	310 494-1794	15525
Alpha Soft Support LLC	7371	D	857 219-5505	17545
Atlas Entertainment Inc	7812	E	310 786-4900	19099
Auto Club Enterprises	6321	C	310 914-8500	15378
Automobile Club Southern Cal	8699	D	323 525-0018	22445
Boulevard Labs Inc	7371	D	323 310-2093	17571
Carlyle Group Inc **(PA)**	6531	B	310 550-8656	15797
Cedars-Sinai Medical Center	8062	B	310 855-7711	20695
Cedars-Sinai Medical Center	8011	D	800 233-2771	19739
Cedars-Sinai Medical Center	8062	B	310 423-5468	20696
Cedars-Sinai Medical Center	8062	B	310 423-5811	20699
Cedars-Sinai Medical Center	8062	B	310 423-5117	20700
Cedars-Sinai Medical Center	8062	B	310 423-9310	20701
Cedars-Sinai Medical Center	8062	B	310 423-8730	20708
Cedars-Snai Imging Med Group A	8062	D	310 423-8000	20709
Chase-Durer Ltd **(PA)**	3873	F	310 550-7280	11301
Citysearch **(HQ)**	7313	D	310 360-4555	17082
Clique Brands Inc **(PA)**	2721	E	310 623-6916	4059
Cosmo International Corp	2844	D	310 271-1100	5005
Cpe Hr Inc	8742	D	310 270-9800	23198
Cygal Art Deco Inc	2521	F	424 288-4011	3582
Dailey & Associates	7311	D	323 490-3847	17002
Dranse Technology Inc	3663	F	323 908-8554	9269
Essex Property Trust Inc	6513	E	323 461-9346	15724
Fountainhead Industries	3999	E	310 248-2444	11671
Grade A Sign LLC	3993	E	310 652-9700	11559
Harpo Inc	7922	D	312 633-1000	19312
Harpo Productions Inc	7812	C	312 633-1000	19130
Haworth Inc	2522	F	310 854-7633	3612
Hob Entertainment LLC	7929	D	323 848-5100	19353
Jennifer Meyer Inc **(PA)**	3961	E	310 446-0057	11486
Le Montrose Hotel	7011	D	310 855-1115	16538
Liveuniverse Inc	7313	D	310 492-2200	17088
Manske Dental Corporation **(PA)**	8021	D	424 354-9336	20187
Mondrian Holdings LLC	7011	B	323 848-6004	16570
Mortgage Guy Inc **(PA)**	6162	D	310 625-8809	15218
Muzik Inc **(PA)**	3679	E	646 345-6500	9754
Neonroots LLC	7371	C	310 907-9210	17669
NVE Inc **(PA)**	8742	D	323 512-8400	23286
Ols Hotels & Resorts LLC	7011	A	310 855-1115	16593
One Events Inc	7299	D	310 498-5471	16969
Operam Inc	8742	D	855 673-7261	23289
Outrigger Hotels Hawaii	7011	D	323 491-9015	16602
Own LLC	4841	C	323 602-5500	12775
Paul Ferrante Inc	3999	E	310 854-4412	11730
People Media Inc	2711	F	800 600-7111	4023
Phyllis Morris Originals **(PA)**	5021	F	310 289-6868	13147
Pro Tour Memorabilia LLC	2499	E	424 303-7200	3451
Rose K Tarlow Antiques Ltd **(PA)**	5099	D	323 651-2202	14179
Rsg Group USA Inc	6719	A	214 574-4653	16110
S&F Management Company LLC **(PA)**	8051	A	310 385-1090	20456
Service Benefits LLC	8742	D	312 576-2247	23320
Silver Cinemas Acquisition Co **(HQ)**	7832	D	310 473-5701	19289
Snf Management	8741	D	310 385-1090	23112
SOS Beauty Inc	5122	F	424 285-1405	14290
Ssi/Advanced Post Services LLC	7812	D	323 969-9333	19184
Suissa Miller Advertising LLC	7311	D	310 392-9666	17059
Sunset Plaza Hotel	7011	D	323 656-8090	16739
Thiel Capital LLC **(PA)**	8742	E	323 990-2030	23346
Ticketmaster Entertainment LLC	7999	A	800 653-8000	19675
Valadon Hotel LLC	7011	D	310 854-1114	16768
White Rabbit Partners Inc	8361	C	310 975 1450	22169
Windsor Grdns Cnvlscent Hosp I	8051	D	888 234 4442	20514
Wpa Worldwide Production Agcy **(PA)**	7812	D	310 659 9965	19212

WESTLAKE VILLAGE, CA - Ventura County

	SIC	EMP	PHONE	ENTRY #
14 Cannons Brewing Company Inc	2082	F	818 652-6971	2135
A-A Mortgage Opportunities LP **(PA)**	6162	B	888 469-0810	15169
Alston & Bird LLP	8111	D	202 239-3673	21504
Amerihome Inc	6162	A	888 469-0810	15171
Amerihome Mortgage Company LLC	6211	A	888 469-0810	15262
Anchor Loans LP	6162	C	310 395-0010	15172
AP Global Inc	5065	D	818 707-3167	13701
Applied Natural Gas Fuels Inc	2869	F	818 450-3659	5126
Arcutis Biotherapeutics Inc	2834	D	805 418-5006	4787
B Riley Retail Solutions LLC	7389	D	818 884-3737	18455
Baltic Ltvian Unvrsal Elec LLC	3651	E	818 879-5200	9161
Bana Home Loan Servicing	6021	A	213 345-7975	14989
Bankcard USA Merchant Srvc	7389	D	818 597-7000	18457
Blue Microphones LLC	3651	F	818 879-5200	9165
Boys Grls Clubs Grter Cnejo Vl **(PA)**	8641	D	818 706-0905	22318
Burton-Way House Ltd A CA	7011	C	805 214-8075	16359

	SIC	EMP	PHONE	ENTRY #
C&W Facility Services Inc	7349	C	805 267-7123	17221
Cadillac Motor Div Area	3711	C	805 373-9575	9939
Caldera Medical Inc	3841	D	818 879-6555	10955
California Coml Inv Group Inc	8748	E	805 495-8400	23423
Carros Americas Inc	3679	C	805 267-7176	9689
Cash Convenience Inds LLC	7699	F	805 381-0806	19029
Cforia Software Inc	7372	E	818 871-9687	17813
Coastal Rdtion Onclogy Med Gro	8011	D	805 494-4483	19756
Comprhnsive Indus Dsblity MGT	8099	D	866 301-6568	21399
Conico Coro Inc **(HQ)**	7542	D	805 373-1880	18910
Conico Roro Inc **(HQ)**	7542	E	818 716-1238	18911
Country Floral Supply Inc **(PA)**	5193	D	805 520-8026	14881
Dennis M McCoy & Sons Inc	1611	D	818 874-3872	875
Digital Insight Corporation	7375	D	818 879-1010	18120
Dilbeck Inc	6531	E	805 379-1880	15839
Dole Citrus	5148	C	818 879-6600	14622
Dole Food Company Inc **(HQ)**	0179	A	818 874-4000	69
Dole Holding Company LLC	0179	A	818 879-6600	70
Dole Packaged Foods LLC **(HQ)**	2037	A	805 601-5500	1898
Earth Print Inc	2752	F	818 879-6050	4286
Elite Airways LLC **(PA)**	4729	C	805 496-3334	12413
Ember Technologies Inc	3089	E	520 400-9337	5639
Equinox-76th Street Inc	7991	D	805 367-3925	19446
Eta Compute Inc	3825	E	805 379-5121	10752
Fidelity Nat Title Insur Co NY	6541	A	805 370-1400	16039
Four Seasons Westlake	7011	D	818 575-3000	16448
Frontier California Inc	5065	B	805 372-6000	13723
Frontier California Inc	4813	B	805 372-6000	12642
Gamebreaker Inc **(PA)**	3949	E	818 224-7424	11418
Hanover Builders Inc	1521	E	818 706-2279	610
Hec Inc	5065	B	818 879-7414	13725
Hydrodex LLC	3589	E	800 218-8813	8386
Implant Direct Sybron Mfg LLC	3843	C	818 444-3300	11177
Inphi International Pte Ltd	3674	E	805 719-2300	9518
Interntional Photo Plates Corp	3471	E	805 496-5031	7270
Ipayment Inc **(DH)**	7389	C	212 802-7200	18555
Ipayment Holdings Inc **(HQ)**	7389	E	310 436-5294	18556
Jafra Cosmetics Intl Inc **(HQ)**	2844	C	805 449-3000	5034
JD Power	8732	B	805 418-8000	22891
Jri Inc	5065	E	818 706-2424	13737
K-Swiss Sales Corp	3021	D	818 706-5100	5310
Kramer-Wilson Company Inc **(PA)**	6331	C	818 760-0880	15468
Kythera Biopharmaceuticals Inc **(HQ)**	2834	C	818 587-4500	4842
Lantz Security Systems Inc	7381	C	805 496-5775	18293
Los Robles Regional Med Ctr	8011	C	805 370-4531	19969
Lumber City Corp	5031	D	805 497-2753	13276
Mamolos Cntntl Bailey Bakeries	5149	C	805 496-0045	14706
Mannkind Corporation **(PA)**	2834	C	818 661-5000	4849
McBain Systems A Cal Ltd Prtnr	5049	E	805 581-6800	13535
Mediaplex Inc **(DH)**	7311	D	818 575-4500	17034
Merrill Lynch Prce Fnner Smith	6211	D	805 381-2600	15294
Microfinancial Incorporated	7359	C	805 367-8900	17362
Mws Precision Wire Inds Inc	5051	D	818 991-8553	13578
Network Television Time Inc **(PA)**	2741	E	877 468-8899	4191
North Ranch Country Club	7997	C	818 889-3531	19594
Omics Group Inc	2721	B	650 268-9744	4089
Opolo Vineyards Inc	2084	D	805 238-9593	2211
Pacific Compensation Corp **(DH)**	6411	D	602 631-2300	15605
Pacific Compensation Insur Co	6411	C	818 575-8500	15606
Paymentmax Processing Inc	3578	F	805 557-1692	8316
Pennymac Financial Svcs Inc **(PA)**	6162	B	818 224-7442	15223
Pleasant Holidays LLC **(HQ)**	4724	B	818 991-3390	12396
Pmt Crdit Risk Trnsf Tr 2015-2	6733	D	818 224-7442	16194
Pnmac Gmsr Issuer Trust	6733	A	818 746-2271	16195
Pnmac Holdings Inc **(HQ)**	6162	B	818 224-7442	15227
R & R Services Corporation	3069	E	818 889-2562	5404
Radiance Lightworks Inc	3641	F	818 879-1516	9023
Rantec Microwave Systems Inc **(PA)**	3812	D	818 223-5000	10636
Registry Mntring Insur Svcs In	6531	D	800 400-4924	15973
Residual Income Opprtnties Inc	2911	F	818 991-1999	5259
Rodeo Realty Inc	6531	D	805 494-0449	15983
Sdg Enterprises	1711	D	805 777-7978	1135
Search123	4813	D	818 575-4600	12668
Securitas SEC Svcs USA Inc	7381	B	818 706-6800	18322
Securitas SEC Svcs USA Inc	7381	C	818 706-6800	18324
Security Paving Company Inc **(PA)**	1611	D	818 362-9200	913
Select Home Care	8082	D	805 777-3855	21210
Silverado Senior Living Inc	8051	D	805 230-2626	20470
Sky Court USA Inc	7011	B	805 497-9991	16714
Skyguard LLC	3699	E	703 262-0500	9914
Smart & Final Stores Inc	5141	C	818 889-8253	14503
Smith Bros Inc **(PA)**	1751	D	805 449-2841	1457
Southern California Edison Co	4911	C	805 496-3406	12836
Sunbritetv LLC **(DH)**	3663	E	805 214-7250	9320
Swvp Westlake LLC	7011	C	805 557-1234	16746
Testan Law A Professional Corp **(PA)**	8111	E	805 604-1816	21686
Thousand Oaks Prtg & Spc Inc	7389	C	818 706-8330	18689
Toller Enterprises Inc **(PA)**	3732	E	805 374-9455	10473
Troop Real Estate Inc	6531	D	805 402-3028	16021
Truog-Ryding Company Inc	8742	D	805 371-9222	23355
United Online Inc **(HQ)**	7299	D	818 287-3000	16983
United Parcel Service Inc	7389	D	818 735-0945	18704
Velocity Commercial Capitl LLC	6163	E	818 532-3700	15258
Velocity Financial LLC **(PA)**	6163	D	818 532-3700	15259
Ventura Aerospace Inc	3728	F	818 540-3130	10442
Vitavet Labs Inc	3999	E	818 865-2600	11790
Warner Pacific Insur Svcs Inc **(PA)**	6411	C	408 298-4049	15647
Westlake Properties Inc	7011	C	818 889-0230	16785
Weststar Cinemas Inc	7832	C	805 379-8966	19291
Wfg Lenders Services LLC **(HQ)**	6541	D	503 387-3636	16044
Whitman Ptrson Capitl Partners **(PA)**	7011	D	818 483-1060	16788
Xenel International USA **(HQ)**	6719	F	805 496-2227	16117
Xplain Corporation	2721	E	805 494-9797	4115
Young Realtors	6531	D	805 497-0947	16036

WESTMINSTER, CA - Orange County

	SIC	EMP	PHONE	ENTRY #
360 Health Plan Inc	8741	C	800 446-8888	22963
Abrazar Inc	8322	D	714 893-3581	21707
All-In Prdctons Csino Rntals L	7359	D	866 875-8628	17332
Biolargo Inc **(PA)**	2819	F	949 643-9540	4650
Cgr/Thompson Industries Inc	3612	D	714 678-4200	8865
Charmshin Group Inc **(PA)**	5039	F	949 331-0301	13331
Co D L Pham MD	8011	E	714 531-2091	19755
Dang Tha	2531	F	714 898-0989	3621
Dolstra Automatic Products	3599	F	714 894-2062	8573
Eichleay Inc	8711	C	562 256-8600	22539
Einstein Noah Rest Group Inc	2022	C	714 847-4609	1770
Elite Sign Services Inc	3993	F	714 373-0220	11547
Emerald Acquisition LLC	1611	D	714 891-8752	877
Extended Care Hosp Westminster	8051	C	714 891-2769	20340
Fab Four Corp	3714	F	714 901-5300	10057
Honda World Westminster	7539	C	714 890-8900	18898
Inlog Inc	4731	D	949 212-3867	12471
KLA Corporation	3825	F	714 893-2474	10763
Lbs Financial Credit Union **(PA)**	6111	C	562 598-9007	15135
Lexor Inc	3999	D	714 444-4144	11708
National Fail Safe Inc	1731	E	562 493-5447	1285
Neighborhood Steel LLC **(HQ)**	5051	E	714 236-8700	13579
New CAM Commerce Solutions LLC	7371	D	714 338-0200	17673
New Technology Plastics Inc	2821	E	562 941-6034	4703
Nguoi Viet Vtnamese People Inc **(PA)**	2711	E	714 892-9414	4015
Serendipity Hearing Inc **(PA)**	8049	D	562 922-1718	20233
Snowbounders Ski Club	7997	D	714 892-4897	19614
Southern California Edison Co	4911	C	714 934-0838	12831
Southern California Edison Co	4911	C	714 895-0420	12846
Southern California Edison Co	4911	C	714 895-0163	12850
Southern California Edison Co	4911	C	714 895-0119	12858
Stanley Healthcare Center	8059	D	714 893-0026	20628
TBS Contracting Inc	1611	D	714 894-2206	922
Thompson Family Farms LLC	0191	E	714 848-7536	120
Thompson Industries Ltd	3728	D	310 679-9193	10430
Tru-Form Plastics Inc	3089	E	310 327-9444	5844
University California Irvine	8062	B	714 775-3066	20991
Van Mart Inc **(PA)**	3713	F	949 698-2447	10001
West Coast Timber Corp	2411	F	714 893-4374	3206
Western Illuminated Plas Inc	3646	E	714 895-3067	9111
Westview Services Inc	8331	D	714 418-2090	21979

WHITEWATER, CA - Riverside County

	SIC	EMP	PHONE	ENTRY #
Whitewater Rock & Sup Co Inc	5032	E	760 325-2747	13322

WHITTIER, CA - Los Angeles County

	SIC	EMP	PHONE	ENTRY #
A & A Fabrication & Polsg Corp	3441	F	562 696-0441	6577
A F E Industries Inc **(PA)**	2759	F	562 944-6889	4473
AC Products Inc	2891	E	714 630-7311	5176
Aguilar Williams Inc	3471	F	562 693-2736	7201
Ahmc Whittier Hosp Med Ctr LP	8062	A	562 945-3561	20667
Angel Lift Inc	3537	F	310 871-6115	7704
Asian Rehabilitation Svc Inc **(PA)**	8331	D	562 632-1141	21940
Automobile Club Southern Cal	8699	D	562 698-3721	22425
Avca Fixture System Inc	2542	F	562 693-3214	3676
Barlow Respiratory Hospital	8069	E	562 698-0811	21034
Bright Health Physicians **(PA)**	8011	C	562 947-8478	19725
Bruce Iversen	2448	F	310 537-4168	3382
California Department Trnsp	1611	D	562 692-0823	865
Cameron Technologies Us LLC	3823	E	562 222-8440	10683
Champion Chemical Co Cal Inc	5169	E	562 945-1456	14775
Chip-Makers Tooling Supply Inc	3544	F	562 698-5840	7787
Coastal Tag & Label Inc	2759	D	562 946-4318	4497
Comfort Industries Inc	2231	E	562 692-8288	2611
Complete Landscape Care Inc	0782	D	562 946-4441	297
Compu Aire Inc	3585	C	562 945-8971	8333
Consteel Industrial Inc	3441	E	562 806-4575	6605
County of Los Angeles	4151	D	562 945-2581	11918
County Snttion Dst No 2 Los An **(PA)**	4959	A	562 699-7411	13006
Credit Union Southern Cal **(PA)**	6061	C	562 698-8326	15061
Cryostar USA LLC	3561	D	562 903-1290	8008
Denco of Texas Inc **(HQ)**	8741	C	562 777-2249	23015
Ensign Group Inc	8051	D	562 947-7817	20330
Ensign Whittier East LLC	8051	C	562 947-7817	20335
Eontork Power Inc	8711	E	888 959-1311	22545
Epmar Corporation	2851	E	562 946-8781	5097
Equipment Depot Inc	5084	C	562 949-1000	13900
Freedom Painting Inc	1721	E	562 696-0785	1179
Friendly Hlls Cntry CLB Fndtio	7997	C	562 698-0331	19563
General Transistor Corporation **(PA)**	5065	E	310 578-7344	13724
George Coriaty	2752	E	562 698-7513	4302
Georgia Pacific Holdings Inc	2676	A	626 926-1474	3904
Gourmet India Food Company LLC	5149	D	562 698-9763	14692
Gulfstream Aerospace Corp GA	3721	A	562 907-9300	10189
Harris Organs Inc	3931	E	562 693-3442	11344
Hedman Manufacturing **(PA)**	3714	E	562 204-1031	10072
Helpline Youth Counseling Inc **(PA)**	8322	E	562 273-0722	21802
Inclusion Services LLC	8322	C	562 945-2000	21812
Industry Color Printing Inc	2752	F	626 961-2403	4328

GEOGRAPHIC

Employment Codes: A=Over 500 employees, B=251-500, C=101-250, D=51-100, E=20-50 F=10-19

2022 Southern California Business Directory and Buyers Guide

© Mergent Inc. 1-800-342-5647

1451

	SIC	EMP	PHONE	ENTRY #
Interhealth Services Inc **(HQ)**	8082	C	562 698-0811	21176
JC Window Fashions Inc	2591	E	909 364-8888	3711
Kaiser Foundation Hospitals	6324	C	866 340-5974	15417
Longwood Management Corp	8062	C	562 693-5240	20850
Loren Industries	3993	E	562 699-1122	11568
Main Electric Supply Co LLC	5063	E	323 753-5131	13645
Medlin and Son Engrg Svc Inc	3599	E	562 464-5889	8686
Mercedes Diaz Homes Inc	8361	D	562 945-4576	22131
Messer LLC	2813	F	562 903-1290	4642
Miller Castings Inc **(PA)**	3324	B	562 695-0461	6270
Oltmans Construction Co **(PA)**	1541	D	562 948-4242	710
Oltmans Investment Company LLC	6512	D	562 948-4242	15684
Orchard - Post Acute Care Ctr	8051	C	562 693-7701	20429
Pacific Die Services Inc	3544	E	562 907-4463	7821
Pih Health Inc **(PA)**	8062	A	562 698-0811	20889
Pih Health Whittier Hospital **(PA)**	8062	A	562 698-0811	20893
Plaza De La Raza Child Develop	8351	D	562 695-1070	22050
Plymouth Congregational Church	8351	D	562 692-1228	22051
Presbyterian Health Physicians	8062	B	562 464-4717	20899
Pronto Janitorial Services Inc	7349	D	562 273-5997	17278
Quaker City Plating	3471	C	562 945-3721	7300
Quest Dgnstics Clncal Labs Inc	8071	D	562 945-7771	21092
R & R Fabrications Inc	3441	E	562 693-0500	6656
Rahn Industries Incorporated **(PA)**	3585	D	562 908-0680	8347
Rasmussen Iron Works Inc	3433	D	562 696-8718	6573
Rio Hondo Education Consortium	8322	D	562 945-0150	21878
Rose Hills Company **(DH)**	6553	A	562 699-0921	16088
Rose Hills Holdings Corp **(HQ)**	6553	B	562 699-0921	16089
Rose Hills Mortuary Inc	7261	D	562 699-0921	16927
Russ Bassett Corp	2511	C	562 945-2445	3487
Sanittion Dstrcts Los Angles C	4953	A	562 908-4288	12977
Santa Fe Rubber Products Inc	3069	E	562 693-2776	5409
Sas Entertainment Partners Inc	7929	E	213 400-1901	19377
Smart & Final Stores Inc	5141	C	562 907-7037	14505
Southern Cal Univ Hlth Scences	8049	E	562 947-8755	20234
Sprint Communications Co LP	4812	C	562 943-8907	12611
Structural Concrete Group Inc	1771	E	818 923-0984	1552
Swiss Park Banquet Center	3634	F	562 699-1525	9012
Tops Slt Inc	2675	C	562 968-2000	3901
Trans-Dapt California Inc	3714	E	562 921-0404	10142
Triangle Services Inc	7349	D	562 696-0712	17291
Tube-Tainer Inc	2655	E	562 945-3711	3841
Tunnelworks Services Inc **(PA)**	8742	D	562 201-4036	23356
United Memorial Products Inc	3272	E	562 699-3578	6062
US Donuts & Yogurt	2051	E	562 695-8867	2040
Whittier Hospital Med Ctr Inc	8062	C	562 945-3561	21011
Whittier Union High Schl Dist	8322	C	562 693-8826	21929

WILDOMAR, CA - Riverside County

	SIC	EMP	PHONE	ENTRY #
Barns and Buildings Inc	3448	F	951 678-4571	6987
Classic Installs Inc	1796	D	951 678-9906	1623
Diverscape Inc	0782	D	951 245-1686	301
Fcp Inc **(PA)**	3448	D	951 678-4571	6993
General Lgstics Systems US Inc	4212	C	951 677-3972	11968
Inland Vly Rgional Med Ctr Inc	8062	B	951 677-1111	20798
Kaiser Foundation Hospitals	8062	A	951 353-2000	20811
KB Home Grater Los Angeles Inc	1521	C	951 691-5300	619
Mobile Video Systems Inc **(PA)**	3663	F	888 721-5777	9293
Sprint Communications Co LP	4812	C	951 461-9786	12612
Sunpro Solar Inc	1711	D	951 678-7733	1150

WILMINGTON, CA - Los Angeles County

	SIC	EMP	PHONE	ENTRY #
Acx Intermodal Inc	5191	C	310 241-6229	14851
Advanced Cleanup Tech Inc	8744	B	310 763-1423	23388
Air Liquide Electronics US LP	2813	A	310 549-7079	4637
American Soccer Company Inc **(PA)**	2329	B	310 830-6161	2797
Anderson Hay & Grain Co Inc	5191	D	509 925-9818	14853
Assocted Wire Rope Rigging Inc	2298	E	310 448-5444	2711
California Carbon Company Inc	2819	E	562 436-1962	4652
California Sulphur Company	2819	E	562 437-0768	4655
Cooper & Brain Inc	1311	E	310 834-4411	402
Coordnted Wire Rope Rgging Inc **(HQ)**	2298	E	310 834-8535	2713
County of Los Angeles	7992	D	310 549-4953	19482
County of Los Angeles	8011	D	310 518-8800	19771
D-1280-X Inc	2911	F	310 835-6909	5250
Estes Express Lines	4213	D	310 549-7306	12042
Fast Lane Transportation Inc **(PA)**	4213	D	562 435-3000	12043
Harbor Area Gang Altrntves Prg	8399	D	310 519-7233	22186
Harbor Industrial Services	7353	D	310 522-1193	17310
Icpk Corporation	5141	D	310 830-8020	14473
Juanitas Foods	2032	C	310 834-5339	1852
Konoike-Pacific California Inc **(HQ)**	4222	D	310 518-1000	12174
Los Angeles Refining Co	2911	F	310 522-6000	5253
Marine Technical Services Inc	7389	D	310 549-8030	18586
Pacific Fibre & Rope Co Inc	2298	F	310 834-4567	2716
Pacific Green Trucking Inc	3743	F	310 830-4528	10478
Paramount Forge Inc	3462	E	323 775-6803	7093
Pasha Stevedoring Terminals LP	4491	E	310 233-2006	12289
Pasha Stevedoring Terminals LP	4424	D	415 927-6353	12276
Potential Industries Inc **(PA)**	4953	C	310 807-4466	12967
Royal Adhesives & Sealants LLC	2899	E	310 830-9904	5241
Ryo Rio Tinto Minerals	1081	F	310 522-5322	379
San Pedro Sign Company	3993	E	310 549-4661	11593
South Bay Ctr For Counseling	8322	D	310 414-2090	21890
Stratus Real Estate Inc	6163	D	310 549-7028	15255
Tesoro Refining & Mktg Co LLC	5172	D	877 837-6762	14810
Trapac LLC **(HQ)**	4491	E	380 830-2000	12293
Ultramar Inc	1389	E	310 834-7254	556
Valero Ref Company-California	2911	A	562 491-6754	5266
Volunteers of Amer Los Angeles	8322	D	310 830-3404	21922
West Coast Aerospace Inc **(PA)**	3965	D	310 518-3167	11505
Wilmington Machine Inc	3599	E	310 518-3213	8854
Wilmington Woodworks Inc	2448	E	310 834-1015	3412

WINCHESTER, CA - Riverside County

	SIC	EMP	PHONE	ENTRY #
Bill & Daves Ldscp Maint Inc	0781	E	951 943-6455	235
Help Hospitalized Veterans **(PA)**	8322	D	951 926-4500	21801
Skywest Airlines Inc	4512	D	951 926-9511	12314

WINNETKA, CA - Los Angeles County

	SIC	EMP	PHONE	ENTRY #
Life Media Inc	2721	E	800 201-9440	4080
Valley Village **(PA)**	8322	D	818 587-9450	21908
World Class Cheerleading Inc	3949	E	877 923-2645	11462

WINTERHAVEN, CA - Imperial County

	SIC	EMP	PHONE	ENTRY #
Imperial Irrigation District	4971	E	760 572-0392	13012
Quechan Indian Tribe	7999	D	760 572-2413	19663

WOODLAKE, CA - Tulare County

	SIC	EMP	PHONE	ENTRY #
Agri-Link Plastics Inc	3089	E	559 564-2889	5549
Country Plastics Inc	3089	F	559 597-2556	5616
US Tower Corp	3441	D	559 564-6000	6676
US Tower Corp **(PA)**	3441	E	785 524-9956	6677

WOODLAND HILLS, CA - Los Angeles County

	SIC	EMP	PHONE	ENTRY #
21st Century Lf & Hlth Co Inc **(PA)**	6321	C	818 887-4436	15373
21st Century Life Insurance Co **(DH)**	6411	A	877 310-5687	15524
Adcom Interactive Media Inc	7379	D	800 296-7104	18157
Advanstar Communications Inc	2721	F	818 593-5000	4049
Aetna Dental of California	6311	C	860 273-5577	15356
Alliant Asset MGT Co LLC **(PA)**	6531	D	818 668-2805	15766
Alliant Tchsystems Oprtons LLC	3812	E	818 887-8185	10562
Allied Industries Inc **(PA)**	8748	C	800 605-5323	23410
Altour International Inc	4724	D	818 464-9200	12378
American Plastic Card Co	3089	F	818 784-4224	5562
Amwins Insurance Brkg Cal LLC **(HQ)**	6411	D	818 772-1774	15532
Apex Communications Inc **(DH)**	7372	F	818 379-3400	17783
Armani Trade LLC	8748	E	310 849-0067	23415
Asana Integrated Medical Group	8322	D	888 212 7545	21716
Associated Foreign Exch Inc **(HQ)**	6099	D	888 307-2339	15121
Assocted Fgn Exch Holdings Inc **(PA)**	6099	D	818 386-2702	15122
Automobile Club Southern Cal	8699	D	818 883-2660	22423
Beating Wall Street Inc **(PA)**	8742	C	818 332-9696	23170
Benefitvision Inc	8331	D	818 348-3100	21943
Blackline Inc **(PA)**	7372	B	818 223-9008	17798
Blackline Systems Inc **(HQ)**	7372	D	877 777-7750	17799
Blh Construction Company	1522	C	818 905-3837	656
Blue Cross of California **(DH)**	6324	D	805 557-6050	15388
Boething Treeland Farms Inc **(PA)**	0811	D	818 883-1222	365
Boething Treeland Nursery Co	4213	D	818 883-1222	12016
California Physicians Service	6324	D	818 598-8000	15392
Cbj LP	2721	E	818 676-1750	4054
Center For Atism Rlted Dsrders **(PA)**	8049	C	818 345-2345	20211
Cirrus Asset Management Inc **(PA)**	6531	B	818 222-4840	15814
Citrin Cooperman & Company LLP	8721	E	818 783-0570	22770
Citrusbyte LLC	7371	E	888 969-2983	17578
Consumer Attrney Mktg Group LL **(PA)**	7311	D	800 200-2264	17001
Corptax LLC	7371	D	818 316-2400	17584
Digital Communications Network **(PA)**	4812	D	818 227-3333	12605
Divinity Recovery	8322	E	866 757-0474	21772
Dunn & Berger Inc	8082	B	818 986-1234	21160
Environmental Construction Inc	1542	D	818 449-8920	762
Etrade 24 Inc	2299	E	818 712-0574	2724
Ev Ray Inc	5023	E	818 346-5381	13169
Excellent In-Home Care Inc	8082	D	818 755-4900	21164
EZ Lube LLC	7549	D	818 610-8866	18930
Farmers Group Inc **(HQ)**	6411	A	323 932-3200	15564
Farmers Group Inc	6411	A	805 583-7400	15565
Farmers Insurance Exchange **(DH)**	6411	A	888 327-6335	15566
Film Roman Llc	7812	C	818 748-4000	19123
Fire Insurance Exchange **(PA)**	6411	A	323 932-3200	15569
Future Health Company	5137	E	424 244-2221	14377
Goetzman Group Inc **(PA)**	8742	D	818 595-1112	23226
Graham Webb International Inc **(DH)**	2844	D	760 918-3600	5027
Greystar Management Svcs LP	6531	B	818 596-2180	15876
Grosslight Insurance Inc	6411	D	310 473-9611	15574
Guarachi Wine Partners Inc	5182	D	818 225-5100	14843
Health Net LLC **(HQ)**	6324	C	818 676-6000	15397
Health Net LLC	6324	C	818 676-5000	15399
HEI Hospitality LLC	7011	C	818 887-4800	16469
Hertz Investment Group LLC **(PA)**	6531	C	310 584-8000	15881
Hillside Capital Inc	3663	C	650 367-2011	9277
Hilton Woodland Hills & Towers	7011	C	818 595-1000	16480
Home Depot USA Inc	7359	C	818 716-9141	17353
ICON Line Inc	3999	F	818 709-4266	11689
IDS Inc	4724	D	866 297-5757	12390
Image Entertainment Inc **(DH)**	7822	D	818 407-9100	19259
Infinite Home Health Inc	8082	D	818 888-7772	21175
Information Forecast Inc	8742	E	818 888-4445	23242
Input 1 LLC	6153	C	818 340-0030	15154
Inter/Media Time Buying Corp **(PA)**	7311	E	818 995-1455	17022
Interlink Securities Corp	6211	D	818 992-6700	15271
Invotech Systems Inc	7372	F	818 461-9800	17892
Jmg Investments Inc	6799	D	818 519-0670	16271
Joseph C Sansone Company **(PA)**	8111	D	818 226-3400	21593
Kaiser Foundation Hospitals	8062	A	818 719-2000	20801
Kaiser Foundation Hospitals	8011	C	818 719-2000	19865

Mergent email: customerrelations@mergent.com
1452

2022 Southern California Business
Directory and Buyers Guide

(P-0000) Products & Services Section entry number
(PA)=Parent Co (HQ)=Headquarters (DH)=Div Headquarters

	SIC	EMP	PHONE	ENTRY #
Kaiser Foundation Hospitals	8062	A	818 592-3100	20814
Kaiser Foundation Hospitals	6324	C	888 515-3500	15418
Kellogg Andlson Accntancy Corp **(PA)**	8721	D	818 971-5100	22797
Kern Organization Inc	7311	D	818 703-8775	17026
King Nutronics Corporation	3823	E	818 887-5460	10705
La Parent Magazine **(PA)**	2721	F	818 264-2222	4078
Law Offices Berglund & Johnson **(PA)**	8111	D	951 276-4783	21606
Legacy Epoch LLC **(HQ)**	2048	D	844 673-7305	1971
Lewis Marenstein Wicke Sherwin	8111	D	818 703-6000	21612
Lifecare Assurance Company	6321	C	818 887-4436	15381
LLP Moss Adams	8721	D	818 577-1822	22802
Los Angeles Daily News Pubg Co	2711	D	818 713-3883	4003
Los Angeles Unified School Dst	8331	A	818 346-3540	21960
Lumio Inc	3674	F	586 861-2408	9533
Lynx Phtnic Ntworks A Del Corp	3661	E	818 802-0244	9237
Maggz Adult Buddy Care LLC	8741	E	818 396-3338	23058
Managed Dental Care	6324	C	818 598-6599	15444
Markel Corp	6411	B	818 595-0600	15591
Mediscan Diagnostic Svcs LLC	7361	D	818 758-4224	17438
Medpoint Management	8011	E	818 702-0100	19975
Memeged Tevuot Shemesh **(PA)**	1711	D	866 575-1211	1101
Merrill Lynch Prce Fnner Smith	6211	D	818 340-9500	15277
Mid-Century Insurance Company **(DH)**	6331	C	323 932-7116	15477
Mindspark Inc	7371	D	310 396-9292	17661
Morgan Stnley Smith Barney LLC	6211	D	818 715-1800	15297
Motion Picture and TV Fund **(PA)**	8062	A	818 876-1777	20866
Mventix Inc **(PA)**	7389	B	818 337-3747	18607
National Diversified Sales Inc **(HQ)**	3089	C	559 562-9888	5722
Netapp Inc	7373	D	818 227-5025	18050
Network Telephone Services Inc **(PA)**	7389	D	800 742-5687	18612
Neversoft Entertainment Inc	7371	E	818 610-4100	17672
Northrop Grumman Intl Trdg Inc	3812	B	818 715-3607	10608
Northrop Grumman Systems Corp	3812	A	818 715-4040	10610
Northrop Grumman Systems Corp	8731	D	818 676-1321	22855
Northrop Grumman Systems Corp	7373	C	818 715-4854	18053
Northrop Grumman Systems Corp	3812	C	818 715-2597	10614
Omnikron Systems Inc	7379	D	818 591-7890	18205
OSI Digital Inc **(PA)**	7379	E	818 992-2700	18207
Pacific Lodge Youth Svcs Inc	8361	C	818 347-1577	22141
Pacific Protection Svcs Inc **(PA)**	7381	A	818 313-9369	18306
Panavision Inc **(PA)**	7359	C	818 316-1000	17366
Panavision International LP **(HQ)**	3861	B	818 316-1080	11288
Physicians Choice LLC	8721	D	818 340-9988	22809
Pinnacle Contracting Corp	1542	E	818 888-6548	809
Pro-Tek Consulting **(PA)**	7379	C	805 807-5571	18216
Prober & Raphael A Law Corp	8111	D	818 227-0100	21665
Propertyplus Insur Agcy Inc	6411	E	818 432-2640	15617
Qbi LLC **(PA)**	8721	D	818 594-4900	22810
Quantum-Dynamics Co	3823	F	818 719-0142	10715
Ramkade Insurance Services	6411	A	818 444-1340	15621
Reachlocal Inc **(DH)**	7311	A	818 274-0260	17051
Real Software Systems LLC **(PA)**	7372	E	818 313-8000	17971
Remarkable Industries Inc **(PA)**	3999	E	800 579-4380	11743
Reseda Dodge Sales Inc	7538	D	805 581-9090	18866
Rodeo Realty Inc	6531	D	818 999-2030	15988
Salem Polymer Industries	3999	F	818 331-9475	11746
Scherzer International Corp **(PA)**	7389	D	818 227-2770	18662
Senju Usa Inc	2834	D	818 719-7190	4891
Sierra Pacific Constrs Inc	1542	D	747 888-5000	826
Silgan Containers Corporation **(DH)**	3411	D	818 710-3700	6468
Silgan Containers LLC **(HQ)**	3411	D	818 710-3700	6469
Silgan Containers Mfg Corp **(DH)**	3411	B	818 710-3700	6470
Solar Energy LLC	1711	D	818 449-5816	1141
Southern Cal Prmnnte Med Group	8011	D	818 592-3038	20090
Sun-Mate Corp	3944	F	818 700-0572	11392
Superior Galleries Inc **(HQ)**	5094	E	818 444-8699	14140
Tag-It Pacific Inc	2269	D	818 444-4100	2680
Talon International Inc **(PA)**	5131	C	818 444-4100	14322
TI Limited LLC **(PA)**	7372	E	323 877-5991	17996
Tinyinklingcom LLC	3069	E	877 777-6287	5416
Truck Underwriters Association	6311	A	323 932-3200	15371
United Online Advg Netwrk Inc	7311	D	818 287-3000	17066
United Ribbon Company Inc	5044	D	818 716-1515	13369
Valley Business Printers Inc	2752	D	818 362-7716	4448
Verity Medical Foundation **(PA)**	8011	A	408 278-3000	20139
Viking River Cruises Inc **(HQ)**	4724	A	818 227-1234	12403
Way Out West Inc	2326	E	310 769-6937	2792
Weider Health and Fitness	2087	B	818 884-6800	2339
Weider Leasing Inc	2721	D	818 884-6800	4111
Western Bagel Baking Corp	2051	F	818 887-5451	2050
Wham-O Inc	5092	D	818 963-4200	14105
Wildflour Bakery & Cafe LLC	5149	D	818 575-7280	14748
Willits Perpetual LLC	7389	D	818 668-6800	18726
Windsor Insurance Assoc Inc	6411	E	818 710-9890	15650
Wise & Healthy Aging	8322	D	818 876-1402	21930
WM Klorman Construction Corp	1542	D	818 591-5969	851
Zenith Insurance Company **(DH)**	6331	B	818 713-1000	15492
Zenith National Insurance Corp **(HQ)**	6331	D	818 713-1000	15493
Znat Insurance Company	6411	C	818 713-1000	15654

WRIGHTWOOD, CA - San Bernardino County

	SIC	EMP	PHONE	ENTRY #
MHRP Resort Inc	7011	D	760 249-5808	16568
Mountain High Resort Assoc LLC	6531	D	760 249-5808	15928

YORBA LINDA, CA - Orange County

	SIC	EMP	PHONE	ENTRY #
Alpha Omega Swiss Inc	3451	F	714 692-8009	7030
Ambreen Enterprises Inc	8748	D	909 620-1339	23412
American HX Auto Trade Inc	3711	D	909 484-1010	9934
Aseptic Technology LLC	2033	C	714 694-0168	1858
B&K Precision Corporation **(PA)**	3825	E	714 921-9095	10745
Beckers Fabrication Inc	2672	E	714 692-1600	3867
Black Gold Golf Club	7992	E	714 961-0060	19476
Bnsf Railway Company	4011	D	714 348-5810	11794
Boyd Corporation **(PA)**	3441	C	714 533-2375	6591
C4 Litho LLC	2752	D	714 259-1073	4244
Caduceus Physcans Med Group A	8011	D	714 646-8000	19731
Cal Select Builders Inc	1542	D	714 694-0203	749
Carefusion 202 Inc **(DH)**	3841	C	800 231-2466	10957
Dan Copp Crushing Corp	1442	F	714 777-6400	570
Digital Label Solutions LLC	2679	E	714 982-5000	3927
Eastern Star Homes California **(PA)**	8322	D	714 986-2380	21777
Engineering Jk Aerospace & Def	3728	E	714 499-9092	10323
Enterprise Security Inc **(PA)**	7382	D	714 630-9100	18376
Euroline Steel Windows	3442	E	877 590-2741	6698
First Team RE - Orange Cnty	6531	D	714 223-2143	15857
Food Management Associates Inc	8742	E	714 694-2828	23219
Fpg Oc Inc	2087	E	714 692-2950	2326
Gramic Enterprises Inc	2082	F	714 329-8627	2146
Hulk Construction	1795	D	714 701-9458	1615
IMG **(PA)**	7389	E	714 974-1700	18546
Implant Direct Sybron Intl LLC **(HQ)**	3843	F	818 444-3000	11176
Inflight Warning Systems Inc	3728	E	714 993-9394	10353
Infrared Dynamics Inc	3433	E	714 572-4050	6572
Interbase Corporation **(PA)**	7379	D	714 701-3600	18190
Jondo Ltd **(PA)**	3861	D	714 279-2300	11280
Loritz & Associates Inc	3089	E	714 694-0200	5700
Luce Communications LLC	2899	D	657 600-6812	5229
Maxxess Systems Inc **(PA)**	7372	E	714 772-1000	17912
Mc2 Sabtech Holdings Inc	3571	E	714 221-5000	8165
Nasco Gourmet Foods Inc	2033	D	714 279-2100	1869
Nasser Company Inc **(PA)**	5141	C	714 279-2100	14481
Nobel Biocare Usa LLC	8072	B	714 282-4800	21111
Nobel Biocare USA LLC	3843	F	714 282-4800	11182
Omni Optical Products Inc	7699	E	714 692-1400	19052
Pacifictech Molded Pdts Inc	3069	E	714 279-9928	5397
Pdma Ventures Inc	3843	E	714 777-8770	11189
Precision Fluorescent West Inc **(DH)**	5063	D	352 692-5900	13662
Progressive Marketing Pdts Inc	3448	D	714 888-1700	7007
Rgbx Inc	8351	D	714 524-1350	22056
Richard Nixon Foundation	8412	D	714 701-6832	22232
Sabred International Packg Inc	3086	D	714 996-2800	5520
Sesa Inc **(PA)**	7336	E	714 779-9700	17187
Sid-Mar Inc	2752	D	213 626-8121	4423
Specialteam Medical Svc Inc	3841	F	714 694-0348	11059
Specialty Motions Inc	3562	E	951 735-8722	8031
Srd Engineering Inc	1623	D	714 630-2480	975
St Jude Heritage Medical Group	8011	A	714 528-4211	20097
Tom Ponton Industries Inc	8742	F	714 998-9073	23348
Trigon Electronics Inc	3699	D	714 633-7442	9923
Viasys Respiratory Care Inc	3841	D	714 283-2228	11077
Vident	5047	D	714 221-6700	13531
Zet-Tek Precision Machining **(PA)**	3599	F	714 777-8770	8859

YUCAIPA, CA - San Bernardino County

	SIC	EMP	PHONE	ENTRY #
B B G Management Group **(PA)**	5145	E	909 797-9581	14558
Braswlls Mdterranean Grdns Inc	8051	D	909 797-1314	20260
Braswlls Mdterranean Grdns Inc	8051	D	909 795-2421	20261
Braswlls Mdterranean Grdns Inc	8051	D	909 795-2476	20262
Braswlls Mdterranean Grdns Inc	8051	C	909 795-2421	20272
Calimesa Operations LLC	8051	C	909 790-2273	20278
Cedar Operations LLC	8051	D	909 795-2421	20278
Google Fiber Inc **(DH)**	4813	D	650 253-0000	12643
Google International LLC **(DH)**	4813	A	650 253-0000	12644
Hi-Desert Publishing Company	2711	D	909 795-8145	3986
Inter-Continental Hotels Corp **(DH)**	7011	B	770 604-5000	16505
M C C Equipment Rentals Inc	1623	D	909 795-9300	962
Merrimans Incorporated	3441	C	909 795-5301	6636
Sorenson Engineering Inc **(PA)**	3451	C	909 795-2434	7044
Technical Resource Industries **(PA)**	3643	E	909 446-1109	9048
Winegardner Masonry Inc	1741	E	909 795-9711	1357
Yucaipa Valley Water District **(PA)**	4941	D	909 797-5117	12923

YUCCA VALLEY, CA - San Bernardino County

	SIC	EMP	PHONE	ENTRY #
Catalyst Development Corp	7372	E	760 228-9653	17810
Crown Contracting Inc	1521	E	760 203-4613	599
Hi-Desert Publishing Company **(HQ)**	2711	D	760 365-3315	3988
Ie Horticulture & Cultivation	2879	F	909 295-1446	5171
R3 Performance Products Inc	3714	F	760 909-0846	10119
United Parcel Service Inc	4215	C	760 365-3158	12164

Employment Codes: A=Over 500 employees, B=251-500,
C=101-250, D=51-100, E=20-50 F=10-19

2022 Southern California Business
Directory and Buyers Guide

© Mergent Inc. 1-800-342-5647

1453

GEOGRAPHIC